The
Englishman's Hebrew Concordance
of the Old Testament

THE
ENGLISHMAN'S HEBREW CONCORDANCE OF THE OLD TESTAMENT

Coded with the numbering system from *Strong's Exhaustive Concordance of the Bible*

George V. Wigram

THE ENGLISHMAN'S HEBREW CONCORDANCE OF
THE OLD TESTAMENT

George V. Wigram

Coded to Strong's Numbering System

Hendrickson Publishers, Inc.
P. O. Box 3473
Peabody, Massachusetts 01961-3473

ISBN 1-56563-208-7

Reprinted from the third edition originally published by Samuel Bagster and Sons, London, 1874, with *Strong's* numbering added by Hendrickson Publishers.

Fourth Printing — April 2001

Printed in the United States of America

PUBLISHER'S PREFACE TO THE NEW EDITION.

THE *Englishman's Hebrew Concordance of the Old Testament* originally appeared in 1843, the result of decades of labor by numerous Hebrew scholars. Since its appearance, this unique concordance has aided generations of English-speaking Bible students to better understand the Old Testament. *Englishman's Hebrew* gives the reader with no knowledge of Hebrew unprecedented insight into the Hebrew words used by the Old Testament writers. For those who do know Hebrew, *Englishman's Hebrew* serves as a handy reference for a quick scan of a given Hebrew word's occurrences in the Old Testament.

The present volume is based upon the third, corrected, edition of 1874, with the addition of the numbering system from *Strong's Exhaustive Concordance*. This numbering makes the work invaluable in Bible study for those who do not know Hebrew. An example of the kind of word study possible follows below. Numerous additional corrections of errors and misprintings found in this third edition have also been made. The Hebrew and English indexes have been retained at the back of the volume, as has the table of variations of chapters and verses in the English and Hebrew Bibles. In addition, a new index of out-of-sequence *Strong's* numbers allows the reader to quickly and easily locate any word by its *Strong's* number.

A translation, by its nature, is always an interpretation, and the English Bible is no exception. Since no English word carries exactly the same meaning as any one Hebrew word, serious Bible students need to look at the range of occurrences of given Hebrew words, in their biblical contexts, to understand the meaning of the original Hebrew.

For example, the English reader of the song of Moses and Miriam in Exodus 15 (KJV) might want to find out what exactly is meant by the "mercy" with which the Lord led the Israelites in verse 13. The search begins in *Strong's Exhaustive Concordance*. *Strong's* gives the number 2617 to the Hebrew word translated as "mercy" in Exodus 15:13. A quick glance over the *Strong's* entry for "mercy" reveals that there are many different Hebrew words translated into English as "mercy." But with the *Englishman's Hebrew* the non-Hebrew reader can learn more about the specific Hebrew word assigned the number 2617. The *Strong's* number is the key that unlocks the wealth of information contained in *Englishman's Hebrew.*

The *Strong's* numbers listed throughout *Englishman's Hebrew* are in sequence (see below for more on occurrences of out-of-sequence numbers), and so the number 2617 is found on page 448 of *Englishman's Hebrew*, next to the Hebrew word חֶסֶד. What follows are all occurrences of the word *ḥeseḏ* in context, with their biblical references—a visual representation of the frequency of *ḥeseḏ*. The English word or phrase translating the particular Hebrew word is italicized. This arrangement enables the reader to see easily, in context, the various ways a specific Hebrew word has been rendered.

As becomes quickly evident from scanning this entry, the important concept of *ḥeseḏ* in the Old Testament is translated variously by the KJV as mercy, kindness, goodness, and lovingkindness. A more thorough word study continues when the reader consults the contexts of the different verses that contain the word *ḥeseḏ*. There is no substitute for looking at all occurrences of such a word. If time is a factor, however, to get a general idea of the word's usage it is better to look at sample occurrences throughout the different books of the Old Testament, than, say, to look simply at all of the occurrences in Genesis. Asking simple questions of the text—such as noting who is using the word and to whom the word *ḥeseḏ* refers, or what the larger context is (such as the song of thanksgiving in Exodus or the context of covenant in Deuteronomy 7), reveal vital information. The fruit that such a study bears includes deeper insight into the rich meaning of this theologically significant word, which cannot be simply translated by a single English word or phrase. This study also reveals more about the very character of God.

To take a slightly different tack, it is also possible for the reader to use the English and Hebrew index at the back of the volume to find, for example, the different Hebrew words translated by the KJV as "mercy" and the pages on which those words occur in *Englishman's Hebrew.* This index is yet another useful tool for unearthing the rich meaning of the biblical language.

Although the *Strong's* numbers, having been assigned alphabetically, follow by and large the sequence of entries in *Englishman's Hebrew*, occasionally there are missing and out-of-sequence numbers. The omission of a *Strong's* number indicates either that the number has been assigned to a proper name (proper names are not included in *Englishman's Hebrew*), or, in rare instances, that *Englishman's Hebrew* does not treat that particular form. Out-of-sequence numbers, which occur occasionally due to spelling variations and *Strong's* lack of distinction between שׂ (sin) and שׁ (shin) are all listed in a special index at the back of this volume in order of the *Strong's* numbers with their corresponding page number(s) in *Englishman's Hebrew.*

INTRODUCTION.

1st. The Object and Plan. THE chief object proposed by this work is a very simple one. In the present state of lexicography, it seemed, in a peculiar way, desirable to lead each student to deduce his "meaning and definition of words" (so far as possible), *from the use made of them by the Holy Ghost.* That those acquainted with English will by this book, at once, find both the extent to which this *can be* done placed before them, and the difficulties of so doing greatly diminished, is not too much to assume; and if so, the chief end proposed will have been attained. It is also confidently believed, that those who have used the similar Concordance for the Greek New Testament, will anticipate that other and important advantages are likely to result.

To explain very briefly the plan adopted, the work is divided into three parts: Part I. contains, in alphabetical succession, all the Appellatives in the Hebrew and Chaldee Bible. Immediately after each Hebrew or Chaldee word, follows the series of *passages* in which it occurs; with the quotations in the language of the authorised English translation, and in its order of books. *Italic* letters mark the word or words in English which correspond to the Hebrew or Chaldee word. The citations are sufficiently full, to enable any one moderately acquainted with the English Old Testament to recall the context.

Part II. Is an Index shewing, under each Hebrew and Chaldee word, the variations of the English translation.

Part III. Is an Index, to enable the English reader to turn any English word into that which corresponds to it in Hebrew.

Then follow a few Indexes of inferior importance.

Before proceeding further, however, I must distinctly state as to this publication, that I am not the originator of its plan, the executor of it, or even the reviser; but simply its proprietor.

The credit of applying to the English language the principle on which Trom and Kircher formed their works for the Hebrew and Greek, appears *in some sort* to be due to Taylor. His Preface, indeed, shews that he considered the Hebræo-Anglic character of his concordance to be *one* of its recommendations. To any one, however, who knows that work, I need not say, that this *is not*, in any way, an imitation of it; while, at the same time, all that is valuable in Taylor for an Englishman, is found to much greater advantage in this.

2d, Origin. The plan here adopted originated from, and was drawn up by Mr. Wm. Burgh,* a clergyman, of Dublin, about the year 1830.

The rough copy in manuscript likewise was executed under his direction, without any remuneration for his time or superintendence, but at my expense as regards those employed by him in the manual labour; the MS. being considered his property, so long as he might proceed in it without delay. Other occupation, however, arising to him when the rough copy was finished, it was made over to me (in 1832), whose connection with it up to that point was thus *only* of a pecuniary nature.

The method pursued in making the rough draft, was much the same as that described in "The Englishman's Greek Concordance." But the subdivisions in Taylor's work, of the references *according to the forms of the words* in Hebrew, necessitated, of course, a re-arrangement of all the references according to the order of the books and chapters in the Bible; which was not needful in the use of Schmid's work for the New Testament; moreover, the citation in Schmid commonly of three Greek words, and in Taylor of only one Hebrew word, increased the difficulty of preparing this work for the Old Testament, greatly beyond that of making the other for the New Testament.

As the value of a work like this must depend very much upon the quantity of patient labour bestowed upon it, I would state, that no time, labour, or expense have been spared in bringing it to perfection. The rough MS. was finished more than ten years since, and much of the interval has been occupied in different kinds of revision.

* To his instruction I owe *all* the knowledge of Hebrew I may possess: I would here, especially, include whatever is of real value in my Chart Grammars of the Hebrew. Having studied Hebrew under Mr. Burgh, all his thoughts, principles, and ideas, as to the grammar of that language, of course passed through my mind. The charts were the result of an attempt made, some time after having so learned Hebrew, to give a digest of part of Professor Lee's Hebrew Grammar.

3d, First Attempts at Revision. If my reader's patience will permit, I will endeavour to lead him through these labours. And, first, the following quotation from a Prospectus (issued June 1836), will at once explain the difficulties to be contended with, and present an interesting scale as to the value of other more ancient Concordances.

Extract from a Prospectus, dated June, 1836.

"The whole of this has TWICE been verified with Vanderhooght's Hebrew Bible. The process pursued was this:—The MS. was read through, and each word in the various places referred to in it, found in the Bible, and there crossed out. The first of these comparisons was instituted in the Autumn of 1833, and finished in the Spring of 1834, a red chalk pencil being used to cancel the passages in the Bible. On account of the indistinctness arising from the chalk, and for other reasons, this comparison was deemed insufficient. A second similar revision therefore commenced in June, 1834; and a fresh Bible having been prepared for the purpose, interleaved with tissue paper, red ink was substituted for the chalk, and the indistinctness avoided. By these means, as no words were marked in the Bible but those found in the manuscript, of course the words not marked with red ink in the Bible, when the whole comparison was ended, were ALL the words which had been omitted in the manuscript. Each quotation also has been carefully compared with a Hebrew and English Bible. IT IS NOT FEARED, THEREFORE, if a comparison be instituted between the present and any former Concordance, but that this will be found, both as to the correctness and the number of the references, by far the most perfect. And in order to insure this,—at once to prevent the omission of any quotations found in any former Concordance, and to ascertain how many new references have been given,—arrangements have been made to compare each sheet with the works of Buxtorf, of Marius de Calasio, as edited by W. Romaine, and of Taylor.

"The aid of all these very valuable books, as also of Trom, Conrad Kircher, Noldius on the Particles, and many other of the best printed, as well as living, authorities, has been largely used; and but for the assistance ministered by them (but especially by Buxtorf and Noldius), the present work would have failed of much of that accuracy which has been attained.

"That the present edition will be found 'complete' or 'faultless,' is not suggested: but that it will be found, as to matter far *more full* and accurate, as to arrangement more simple and perspicuous, and as to price more accessible than any former work of a similar nature, is confidently believed, to say nothing of superior portability, type, paper, &c.

"P.S. The *first* sheet of the present work was originally set up by the printer in a larger type, and somewhat different form, so as to contain about one-eighth less matter than at present. The result of its comparison with the other Concordances, was the following report of *omissions*, &c.

In Buxtorf, Printed in 1632.

ותאבד 2 Ki. 11: 1.
אבה 1 Ch. 11:19.
ואבי Gen. 11:29.
— Josh. 24: 2.
אבי 2 Ki. 5:13.
— 1 Ch. 8:29.
— 2 Ch. 10:14., 16: 3.
אביו Gen. 9:22., 28: 8.
— Deu. 21:19.
— 1 Ki. 22:51.
— 2 Ch. 33:23., 34: 3.
אביה Nu. 30: 5.
— Jud. 19: 3.
אבות 2 Ch. 25: 4.
האבות 1 Ch. 9:34.
— Ezr. 10:16.
אבותינו — 35.
ואבותינו Jer. 3:25.
כאבותיכם 2 Ch. 30: 7.
אבותיו 21: 1., 26:23.
אבותם Exod. 6:14.
אבותיהם 2 Ch. 13:18.
אבוך Dan. 5:11.
אבנים Deu. 10: 3.
— 2 Sa. 18:17.
ואבן Gen. 2:12.
— 1 Ki. 10:10.

Within the space of eight pages and two columns, besides mistakes regarding the respective *books*, 4;—*chapters*, 17;—*verses*, 92;—*quotations*, 5;—in all 118.

I find also that in א there are 380 omissions, and 1100 errata.

In Marius by Romaine, 1747.

אבד 2 Ki. 21: 3.
יאבד Eccl. 9:18.
יאבדו Jer. 10:11.
אבה 1 Ch. 11:18.
אביו Gen. 9:22., 28: 8.
— Deu. 21:19.
אבותינו Nu. 36: 4.
אביהם — 6.
אבותינו — 7, 8.
אביה — —
אביהי — 12.
אבי 1 Ch. 8:29.
האבות 9:34.
אבותיהם 2 Ch. 13:18.
אבותיו 21: 1., 26:23.
אביו 33:23., 34: 3.
ואבותינו Jer. 3:25.
ואב Eze. 18:20.
אבנים Deu. 10: 3.
— 2 Sa. 18:17.
ואבן Gen. 2:12.
— 1 Ki. 10:10.
— Dan. 6:17(18).

Within the space of fifteen pages, besides a few mistakes in books, chapters, verses, quotations;—in all under twenty.

Rabbi Nathan's work, second edition, Basil, 1581, has fewer mistakes though more omissions than Buxtorf's. In Kircher, I found one, and in Trom about four references not found elsewhere.

In this work ב has 145 omissions.

In Taylor, Printed in 1754.

ותאבד 2 Ki. 11: 1.
אבי 1 Ch. 4:21 *bis leg.*
— 8:29.
אבי 2 Ki. 5:13.
— 2 Ch. 16: 3.
אביו Gen. 9:22.
— Deu. 21:19.
— 27:16.
— 1 Ki. 22:50(51).
— 2 Ch. 33:23.
— 34: 3.
אביה Jud. 19: 3.
לאביו Gen. 27:31.
האבות 1 Ch. 9:34.
— Ezr. 10:16.
אבתיו 2 Ki. 14:20.
אבתם Ex. 6:14.
אבותיהם 2 Ch. 13:18.
— 30: 7.
אבוך Dan. 5:11 *ter leg.*
ואבן Gen. 2:12.
— Pro. 11: 1.
האבן Gen. 28:18.
אבנים Deu. 10: 3.
— 2 Sa. 18:17.

Taylor, in his preface, says, "I have added all the words I could find that *Buxtorf* hath omitted, which amount to 121;" (he certainly added many more, but) OBSERVE, our *first* sheet alone, less than *one* eightieth part of the whole work, adds 25 more.

In this work ב has 250 omissions.

"The preparation of this work for the press has been the labour of many. To Dr. Bialloblotzky, especially, I am indebted more largely than I can here state, as also to his assistant, Mr. Davidson."

4th, Further Revision needful.

But all this labour was abortive, and further delay occurred: for that no superstructure, reared upon or formed out of such materials as had been found ready to our hands, could be made to approach to the measure of accuracy desired, became apparent soon after the publication of the prospectus out of which the above is quoted.

The only prospect of success seemed to be in commencing *de novo*, and forming something which would be in itself a perfect STANDARD of comparison. From this period, indeed, I date the commencement of *the revision* of the work: and we have reason to believe, that if instead of merely making A STANDARD OF COMPARISON, we had also re-written the manuscript from that standard, much trouble and delay would have been saved us. For the rough copy (originally made upon the basis of Taylor's Concordance by those who were employed under Mr. Burgh, and who were wholly incompetent to the task of executing his plan), had come into my hand so replete with inaccuracies, that the corrections, and attempts at corrections, had made any proper revision of it difficult. To re-write the MS., however, did not occur to us till a later period, or else much trouble might have been spared. The formation of such a standard of comparison was, however, undertaken and carried through by the kind aid of many; among the rest, of S. P. Tregelles, on whom the responsibility of the correction of the MS. now also devolved; of B. Davidson, a converted Hebrew (already mentioned); and of W. Chalk, with whom the correction of the press has chiefly rested, &c. &c. &c.; as also, Mr. G. W. Pieritz, Mr. A. Levi, and Mr. N. Davis, afterwards connected with the London Society for Promoting Christianity among the Jews. I cannot explain this portion of our toil more simply, than by reprinting an—

"ACCOUNT OF THE HEBRAIST'S VADE MECUM;"
OR, STANDARD OF COMPARISON.

5th, Formation of a Standard of comparison. "THE supposed inaccuracies, and known omissions in existing Hebrew Concordances, first suggested, 28th October 1836, the idea of the present attempt. In revising the second sheet of the Englishman's Hebrew Concordance, it alone was found to contain 300 citations not in the works of Rabbi Nathan, Buxtorf, Marius, Taylor, Trom, or Kircher. Confessedly, then, none of these works were complete; perhaps, also, none had been made directly from the Hebrew Language, and if so, then none of them could justly be looked upon as 'A Standard.' Complete Hebrew Concordance, presenting a complete balance as to the extent of its contents with that of the Hebrew Bible, there was none. Could such a thing be produced? The plan on which the attempt has been made is a very simple one, namely, that on which catalogues to libraries are usually formed. The thought to be carried into execution, was to 'distribute' (as the printer would say) the Hebrew Bible from Genesis to 2nd Chronicles, the last book according to the Hebrew order, placing each word as it recurs, with those like it which had occurred in the preceding parts of the Bible. In order to effect this,—

"I. The first step taken was to make *a census* of the words in the Bible, so as to be able to say how many words each respective verse in each chapter and book throughout the whole Bible contained. This was easily accomplished,—the number of words in each verse being counted in a copy of Athias's Bible by one person, and this checked by a second, who counted in Vanderhooght's Bible.

Specimen of the Report.

Genesis, Chap. 1 verse 1,	contains	words	7
2,	,,	,,	14
3,	,,	,,	6
4,	,,	,,	12 &c., &c.

II. According to this *census*, *tables* were prepared for each word in each verse, on pages containing 3 columns in width and 27 lines in depth.

"The directions to the writers were these:—

"Write the name of the book, and the figures representing chapter and verse, as often as the census says there are words in the verse.

Specimen of the Tables.

Gen. 1 : 1.
Gen. 1 : 1.
Gen. 1 : 1.
Gen. 1 : 1. } 7 times, because Gen. 1 : 1. has 7 words (*see above.*)
Gen. 1 : 1.
Gen. 1 : 1.
Gen. 1 : 1.

"Thus labels were prepared for each word in each verse in the Bible, of such a nature, as that if the Hebrew word were firmly appended to it, its place in the Bible would be manifest.

"III. Two copies of Vanderhooght's Bible were taken, and by tracing a carmine line through the alternate pages of the two, there was left but one clean Bible.

"IV. Each page was then pared to the edge of the letterpress on every side except the left; each line with its accents and points was divided with scissors from that above and that below it, from right to left, yet not cut off, but allowed to adhere to the white edge which remained on the left side, so that all the lines of each page were bound together in one.

"V. A *paster* having run his brush down the left side of a column in the *Table* (described above, see II.), tore off a line of letterpress, and observing to keep that side uppermost which had no carmine line drawn through the words, separated each word from that which followed, with scissors, into the paste. Each word had then to be laid straight and pressed.

"N.B. As a *sooph passuk* (׃) ends each verse in the Bible, if the report and the table were correct, the last label of each verse would have *sooph passuk*:—this was a check to the *paster*.

"VI. The whole was then read carefully with the Bible, to see that nothing was lost;—thus: first one person held the MS., and a second read aloud from the Hebrew Bible, tapping on the table when he came to a word beginning, in the simple form of it, with א, which the other marked + in the MS.; and then the MS. was carefully read again, to be sure that all the alephs were marked and were correct as to accents, &c., &c.

"VII. The alephs were then cut out with a penknife, divided into appellatives and proper names,—the former sorted, first according to the roots whence derived, then into separate words and forms,—and then pasted.

"For sorting the roots and words we had the use of 1100 lozenge boxes, and used trays for the forms.

"VIII. The *pasted books* of aleph were read, and the contents of each article carefully compared with Buxtorf and with Taylor,—the leading forms compared with Taylor, and again with Buxtorf.

"The order of books, of chapters, and of verses, in each article, severally and separately examined by one person; the words in each article read verbatim by one person, and letter by letter by a second, to prevent there being in any article more than one form.

"IX. A copy of Vanderhooght interleaved was then taken, and each word in the pasted books found in this, the accents compared, and then a line drawn in the Bible over the word, and it ticked in the pasted book. The Bible thus marked was then compared and examined by another, which had been twice carefully revised by competent persons.

"[There was a two-fold object in thus proceeding as to א:—first, it brought the whole work again and again under inspection; and, secondly, enabled us to proceed in the use of aleph in a much shorter space of time than we could, had we waited till the whole Bible was distributed.]

"X. Having thus disposed of aleph, each page in the tables was read down by the *marker*, who placed the initial letter of the simple form after each word, except where it happened to stand without any prefix; and *p. n.* was in addition added to each proper name.

"XI. A box rising from 8 inches depth in the front, to 14 inches depth at the back was provided; it contained 24 departments, each in area about 4 inches. These were labelled with the letters of the alphabet according to their supposed frequency, the less frequent being placed in the less accessible, and the more frequent in the more accessible parts:—21 letters, one place for proper names, and one for שׂ (usually considered in the alphabet under שׁ), left us but one for waste scraps.

"The *tables* were pared and the columns separated: and then the *distributer* proceeded, a column in the left hand and scissors in the right, to distribute. He read as he proceeded, and snipped into its department each labelled word according to the letter after it (see X.), except when his judgment differed from that of the *marker*; in which case Buxtorf and Gesenius were immediately resorted to.

"XII. When the whole was thus distributed, the contents of each department of the box were examined, and all the labels which had not upon them the same letter as marked the department under examination, were set aside for the second judgment of the *distributer*, and then put by the *sorter* into bags.

"XIII. The proper names were distributed, and in like manner looked through.

"XIV. The *marker* then distributed the respective letters into roots, which of course brought under his eye the corrections of his former work by the *distributer*.

"XV. Each word was divided into simple forms, and pasted according to dictionary matter made by the *distributer*, and for the most part agreed to by the *marker*.

"XVI. The order of books, of chapters, and of verses, of each article in the pasted books was then severally and separately examined, and the words read verbatim by one and literatim by a second person (see VII.)

"XVII. Every citation in the pasted books was found in the interleaved Vanderhooght, and the words there marked and the pasted books ticked.

"N.B. In marking this interleaved Vanderhooght, different marks and various coloured inks were used for the different letters. In examining this Bible when the whole was thus verified, it was found that most of the words in it which had no mark over them, were not ticked in the pasted books. I think I may say that not six words out of 400,000 were missing in the pasted books.

"XVIII. The whole contents of the pasted books were then compared with Buxtorf's Hebrew Concordance, to see that our dictionary arrangement had not wandered altogether from the old school, &c., and then all the forms with Fürst's new and valuable edition of that work.

"XIX. And, lastly, it has been twice compared with the Englishman's Hebrew Concordance.

"With reference to the printed specimen on the opposite page, it may be well to notice that the dictionary matter is added *only and solely* for the sake of convenience and comfort to the reader, that he may have a sea neither of Hebrew nor of figures before him, but at least some words which he knows. It was thought to put as dictionary matter, just the translation, of the versions in the respective languages, of the first citation of each word: but upon the whole it is perhaps better as it is. It is new:—in some respects a compilation from Gesenius' Thesaurus, and אוצר לשון הקדש, referred to above as the new and valuable edition of Buxtorf, corrected by Fürst, which has been lately published by TAUCHNITZ, *Leipsic*.* It will not be found bad, considering how concise it is: yet we set no value or store upon it, introducing it chiefly for convenience.

"*Note*.—The Hebrew type is a new fount, cut expressly for this work by Alexander Wilson and Sons."

* Excellent and well corrected as this work is, the Vade Mecum discovered no fewer than *seven corrigenda*, and at least *ten omissions*, in the course of its first *eight* pages.

[SPECIMEN OF HEBRAIST'S VADE MECUM.]

Ch. כְּרָא

k'rāh, to be grieved.

ITHP'EL.

Pret. 3 f. אֶתְכְּרִיַּת
Dan. 7:15

כִּרְבֵּל

kir-bēhl', to be clothed.

Part. pass. מְכֻרְבָּל
1 Ch. 15:27

Ch. f. כַּרְבְּלָא

kar-b'lāh', marg. a turban.

Pl. suff. וְכַרְבְּלָתְהוֹן
Dan. 3:21

כָּרָה I.

kāh-rāh', to dig, etc.

KAL.

Pret. 3 m.
Ps. 7:16—2 Ch. 16:14

2 m. כָּרִיתָ
Ps. 40:7

1 c. כָּרִיתִי
Gen. 50:5

Pl. 3 m. כָּרוּ
Jer. 18:20, 22—Ps. 22:17 & 57:7 & 119:85

suff. כָּרוּהָ
Nu. 21:18

Fut. 3 m. יִכְרֶה
Ex. 21:33

Pl. 3 m. וַיִּכְרוּ
Gen. 26:25

2 m. וְתִכְרוּ
Job 6:27

Part. כֹּרֶה
Pro. 16:27 & 26:27

NIPHAL.

Fut. 3 m. יִכָּרֶה
Ps. 94:13

—— II.

KAL.

Fut. וַיִּכְרֶה
2 Ki. 6:23

1 c. suff. וָאֶכְּרֶהָ
Hos. 3:2

Pl. 3 m. יִכְרוּ
Job 40:30

תִּכְרוּ
Deu. 2:6

Note.—Ps. 22:17, some M.S. read כָּארוּ or כָּרוּ—V. H. כַּאֲרִי

---

f. כֵּרָה

kēh-rāh', a provision.

Pl. c. כְּרֹת
Zep. 2:6

כֵּרָה
2 Ki. 6:23

---

m. כְּרוּב

k'roov, a cherub.

Ex. 25:19 & 37:8—2 Sa. 22:11—Eze. 28:14, 16 & 41:18—Ps. 18:11

הַכְּרוּב
1 Ki. 6:24, 24, 25, 26, 26, 27—Eze. 9:3 & 10:4, 7, 9, 9, 14—2 Ch. 3:11, 12, 12

וּכְרוּב
Ex. 25:19 & 37:8

לִכְרוּב
Eze. 41:18

לַכְּרוּב
Eze. 10:2 & 41:18

Pl. כְּרוּבִים
1 Ki. 6:23, 29, 32, 35 & 7:36—Eze. 10:20 & 41:18, 25—Ps. 99:1—2 Ch. 3:7, 10, 14

כְּרֻבִים
Ex. 25:18 & 26:1, 31 & 36:8, 35 & 37:7

הַכְּרוּבִים
1 Ki. 6:27, 28, 32 & 8:6, 7—Eze. 10:5, 9, 15, 16, 16, 18, 19 & 11:22 & 41:20—1 Ch. 28:18—2 Ch. 3:11, 13 & 5:7, 8, 8

הַכְּרֻבִים
Gen. 3:24—Ex. 25:19, 20, 20, 22 & 37:8, 9, 9—Nu. 7:89—1 Sa. 4:4—2 Sa. 6:2—1 Ki. 6:25, 27 & 8:7—2 Ki. 19:15—Isa. 37:16—Eze. 10:1, 7—Ps. 80:2—1 Ch. 13:6

וְהַכְּרֻבִים
Eze. 10:3

וּכְרוּבִים
1 Ki. 7:29

לַכְּרוּבִים
Eze. 10:7

לַכְּרֻבִים
Eze. 10:2, 6, 8

Ch. m. כָּרוֹז

kāh-rōhz', a herald.

emph. וְכָרוֹזָא
Dan. 3:4

Ch. כְּרַז

k'raz, to proclaim.

APHEL.

Pret. pl. 3 m. וְהַכְרִזוּ
Dan. 5:29

---

m. pl. כָּרִי

kāh-ree', captains.

הַכָּרִי
2 Sa. 20:23 (c'th)—2 Ki. 11:19

לַכָּרִי
2 Ki. 11:4

---

f. כְּרִיתוּת

k'ree-thooth', divorcement, marg. cutting off.

Isa. 50:1

כְּרִיתֻת
Deu. 24:1, 3

Pl. suff. כְּרִיתֻתֶיהָ
Jer. 3:8

---

m. כַּרְכֹּב

kar-kōhv', a compass.

Ex. 27:5

suff. כַּרְכֻּבּוֹ
Ex. 38:4

---

m. כַּרְכֹּם

kar-kōhm', saffron.

וְכַרְכֹּם
Cant. 4:14

---

f. pl. כִּרְכָּרוֹת

kir-kāh-rōhth', swift beasts.

וּבַכִּרְכָּרוֹת
Isa. 66:20

---

com. כֶּרֶם

keh'-rem, a vineyard.

Ex. 22:4—Deu. 20:6 & 28:30—Jud. 15:5—1 Ki. 21:1, 2, 6, 7, 15, 16—Isa. 5:1, 7, 10 & 27:2—Pro. 24:30—Cant. 8:11

בְּכֶרֶם
Deu. 23:25—1 Ki. 21:18

וּבְכֶרֶם
Nu. 20:17 & 21:22

הַכֶּרֶם
Isa. 3:14—Cant. 8:11

וְכֶרֶם
Jer. 35:7, 9—Job 24:6

כָּרֶם
Gen. 9:20—Mic. 1:6—Pro. 31:16

בְּכָרֶם
Isa. 1:8

הַכָּרֶם
Deu. 22:9—Neh. 3:14

וָכָרֶם
Nu. 16:14

suff. כַּרְמִי
1 Ki. 21:6—Isa. 5:3—Jer. 12:10—Cant. 1:6 & 8:12

לְכַרְמִי
Isa. 5:4, 5

כַּרְמְךָ
Lev. 19:10—Deu. 22:9 & 24:21—1 Ki. 21:2, 6

וְכַרְמְךָ
Lev. 19:10 & 25:4

לְכַרְמֶךָ
Ex. 23:11

כַּרְמֶךָ
Lev. 25:3

כַּרְמוֹ
Ex. 22:4

לְכַרְמוֹ
Isa. 5:1

Pl. כְּרָמִים
Deu. 6:11 & 28:39—Jos. 24:13—2 Ki. 19:29—Isa. 37:30 & 65:21—Jer. 31:5 & 39:10—Eze. 28:26—Am. 5:17 & 9:14—Zep. 1:13—Ps. 107:37—Job 24:18—Cant. 2:15—Ecc. 2:4—Neh. 9:25

בַּכְּרָמִים
Jud. 21:20

וּבַכְּרָמִים
Isa. 16:10

שֶׁבַּכְּרָמִים
1 Ch. 27:27

הַכְּרָמִים
Nu. 22:24—Jud. 21:21—Cant. 1:6—1 Ch. 27:27

וּכְרָמִים
1 Sa. 22:7—2 Ki. 5:26 & 18:32—Isa. 36:17—Jer. 32:15

לַכְּרָמִים
Cant. 7:13

const. כַּרְמֵי
Jud. 14:5—Am. 5:11

בְּכַרְמֵי
Cant. 1:14

כְּרָמֶיהָ
Hos. 2:17

וּכְרָמֵינוּ
Cant. 2:15—Neh. 5:3, 4, 5

כַּרְמֵיכֶם
1 Sa. 8:14

וְכַרְמֵיכֶם
1 Sa. 8:15—Am. 4:9

כַּרְמֵיהֶם
Jud. 9:27—Neh. 5:11

---

m. pl. כֹּרֵם

kōh-rēhm', a vinedresser.

Pl. כֹּרְמִים
Joel 1:11

וְכֹרְמִים
2 Ch. 26:10

לְכֹרְמִים
2 Ki. 25:12—Jer. 52:16

suff. וְכֹרְמֵיכֶם
Isa. 61:5

---

m. כַּרְמִיל

kar-meel', crimson.

וּבַכַּרְמִיל
2 Ch. 2:13

וְכַרְמִיל
2 Ch. 2:6 & 3:14

---

m. כַּרְמֶל

kar-mel', the full ear, (of grain); fruit, etc., etc.

Lev. 2:14

בַּכַּרְמֶל
Isa. 32:16

הַכַּרְמֶל
Isa. 16:10—Jer. 2:7 & 4:26

(k'ri) וְהַכַּרְמֶל
Isa. 32:15

וְכַרְמֶל
Lev. 23:14—2 Ki. 4:42—Isa. 32:15 (c'th)

לַכַּרְמֶל
Isa. 32:15

מִכַּרְמֶל
Jer. 48:33

כַּרְמִלּוֹ
Isa. 37:24

וְכַרְמִלּוֹ
Isa. 10:18

Ch. m. כָּרְסֵא

kor-sēh', a throne.

Dan. 5:20

suff. כָּרְסְיֵהּ
Dan. 7:9

Pl. כָּרְסָוָן
Dan. 7:9

כִּרְסֵם

keer-sēhm', to lay waste.

Fut. 3 m. יְכַרְסְמֶנָּה
Ps. 80:14

Having thus briefly explained the object and plan of this Concordance; the method of forming both the MS. and its standard of comparison, I proceed to give a more detailed account of its revision for the press, and correction while passing through it, with a few explanatory remarks upon some of the minutiæ, which may as well be noticed to the reader as left for his observation to discover.

Account of the Revision of the Manuscript.

6th, Actual Revision previous to Printing.

1st. With the Hebrew and English Bible.—Each line of the MS. was read with an interleaved Hebrew and English Bible; in doing this, attention was to be paid to three questions. First, Is that part of the verse cited which really corresponds to the Hebrew word? For in the Prophets and those Scriptures which are written in parallel members, the danger is frequent of citing in English a part of the sentence nearly coinciding in sense with the Hebrew word, but which actually is the translation of the parallel member. Second, Is the English citation so full as to comprehend all that which really translates the Hebrew word, and have such words been selected as best exhibit the sense and connection? Third, As to the words underlined, is there neither more nor less underlined than what exactly answers to the Hebrew word?

2nd. With the English Bible.—After this examination of every line with the Hebrew and English, another individual examined the MS. with an English Bible. The object herein was to correct the spelling, and verify the references, stops, &c. During this revision, memoranda were kept of every particular which appeared doubtful to the reviser.

3rd. To avoid omissions, and revise the general arrangement,—

The whole of the citations were then carefully examined with the pasted books (which form the copy of the Hebraist's Vade Mecum). This was done by two persons, one holding the MS., the other, the pasted books. A check was thus obtained upon the accuracy of the MS. in three particulars. First, As to the insertion of all the occurrences of each word. Second, as to the arrangement and division of the verbs. And, third, As to the correspondence of the English citations underlined with the Hebrew words: fully to secure this last object, the underlined portions of the English were read aloud by one reviser to the other, who held the pasted books before him. Memoranda were kept with respect to any of the above particulars, in which it was judged that the MS. needed correction.

4th. Use made of the Memoranda.—They were put into the hands of the reviser, who had read the MS. with the Hebrew and English texts:

and if he coincided in judgment with those who had made the suggestions, the MS. was at once corrected. In case of difference of opinion, the point was examined afresh with the Hebraist who had conducted the comparison of the MS. with the pasted books.

7th, Revision while at Press. Thus prepared we ventured to go to press; but in order to insure as much accuracy as possible, great and unusual care has been bestowed in CORRECTION WHILE PASSING THROUGH THE PRESS.

After being carefully read at the printing office, each page was—

1st. Compared by one person with the MS. His directions were to read from the MS. to the letter-press, ticking in the latter each line as he saw that it contained the matter in the MS. which his left hand traced down,—especial care being taken as to the italics.

2nd. The same parts were then read from the pasted books of the Vade Mecum into the letter-press, ticking in both the one and the other as he proceeded.

3rd. A comparison then took place between the marks on the letter-press, which were in black, with the marks in the MS., made in red when the MS. was compared with the pasted books, previous to being set up in type.

4th. The whole letter-press was then carefully read with an Oxford Bible (Small Pica Octavo, 1836); the same as that used in the correcting of the Englishman's Greek Concordance.

5th. The order of books, chapters, and verses were then separately examined to avoid needless duplicates—each separately, and the order of the species of the verbs, Kal, Niphal, &c. with their subordinate divisions into tenses ; and lastly, a comparison with the copy for italics alone.

6th. The proof sheets, after being thus corrected by the English reviser, were submitted to another reviser, thoroughly acquainted with Hebrew, who, *first,* read them *through,* marking and correcting whatever appeared necessary; *second,* he compared the headings, &c., with the pasted books, taking notice of whatever queries the first reviser had made; *third,* he read through the italics separately, making frequent reference both to a Hebrew and English Bible, and to the pasted books.

7th. After the stereotype plates were cast, the italics had another revision, in order, if possible, to allow nothing to pass which differed from the principles and arrangement of the work. More labour should have been bestowed, if anything had suggested itself as possible to have added accuracy.

8th, Concluding Remarks as to details of Plan. I conclude with the notice of a few *details* which the reader will need to retain in mind :—

As to headings and order.—The Hebrew and Chaldee will be found under one alphabet; but observe, when any variation in the mode of spelling words exists, we have taken either the form *fullest in letters,* or (when such forms were evidently irregular), *the one most frequently occurring.* When the word does not occur in Scripture in the form given in the heading, the pronunciation is included within brackets, see p. 8 [*ēhr*], and p. 9 [*ăvad*], &c. A pronunciation is added, that those who know nothing of Hebrew may be able to affix *a* name to the words. The system of pronunciation* adopted requires little explanation: the simple English letters have been used so far as their sounds express those of the original. The gutturals are thus represented, ח by *g̔ḥ*; כ by *c̔ḥ*; ע by $\overset{n}{g}$.

The following Tables exhibit the system pursued with regard to the vowels.

ָ	*āh*	ַ *a* combined with a consonant, or *ah*.
ֵ	*ēh*	ֶ *e* ,, ,, ,, or *eh*.
ִי ִ	*ee*	ִ *i* ,, ,, ,,
ֹ, וֹ	*ōh*	ָ *o* ,, ,, ,, or *oh*.
וּ	*oo*	ֻ *oo* ,, ,, ,,

The imperfect vowels are similarly expressed, and distinguished by a short mark, thus

ֲ *ă* followed by a consonant.
ֱ *ĕ* ,, ,, ,,
ֳ *ŏ* ,, ,, ,,

Sh'va, when *moveable,* is represented by an apostrophe being inserted between two letters.

* Hebrew is frequently represented in English by the *Italian* vowel sounds, which differ in some respects from those we have adopted : the *h* which follows some of them here is added simply to avoid mispronunciation.

The syllabification is according to the rules of Hebrew orthography; each *complete* syllable being separated by a hyphen (-). The English reader must be told, that in Hebrew an imperfect vowel (ֲ, ֱ, ֳ) never constitutes a syllable. The accented syllable of the Hebrew is also marked in the pronunciation.

In the verbs, it has been deemed expedient to make—1st, divisions according to the seven more common species, Kal, Niphal, &c. At the commencement of each such species, a double asterisk is used (*KAL.—*Preterite**; see p. 8, *āh-vad'*; the more rare forms, as Hothpael, &c., being pointed out, as they occur); and, 2ndly, subdivisions of each of these heads into Preterite, Future, &c.

When the Hebrew and English differ as to verse and chapter, the latter is placed first, and the former immediately after, in parentheses—thus אָבַד Numbers 17: 12(27) is found to be verse 12 in the English, but verse 27 in the Hebrew.

The word (or words) by which, in the citations from the English version, the Hebrew word is translated appears in *italics*. In preparing the MS. for this, whatever was *combined with* the word itself, whether prefix or suffix, was underlined as well as the word itself; so that the English reader might see *at once* the circumstances of the Hebrew word. In the verbs this has a peculiar importance, because of the influence which the copulative ו exercises in the change of the tenses. Had this been neglected, the English reader would often have been surprised at the use of Futures for Preterites, and *vice versa*. When the personal pronouns were *implied* in the verb, and not expressed by separate words, they were put in *italics*. When the copulative ו prefixed to the Hebrew word is combined in translation with a negative (such as *nor* or *neither*), the combined negative was put in *italics;* not as indicating that such a negative is implied in the Hebrew word with its prefix, but as shewing the combination of the copulative with the Hebrew word. This is often important, especially (as has just been remarked) in the case of verbs.

When two or more passages occur in immediate succession, or within the same chapter, which read exactly alike both in Hebrew and in the English translation, the quotation is only given once after the references.

The marginal renderings of the English version have been carefully inserted, and also occasionally a *literal* rendering.

As to the particles a few words must be said.

The separable particles which form in Hebrew so extensive a class of words, could scarcely, as it is obvious, be inserted in such a Concordance. To say the truth, their occurrences had never been gathered together previously to the making of the Hebraist's Vade Mecum. That they might not, however, be neglected, the following plan was adopted. When the occurrences of any particle did not exceed *twenty*, the whole were inserted in the same manner as other words. When the occurrences were above twenty in number, a selection was made of a few passages, which might serve as specimens of the varied use of the particle; in which cases, "&c., &c." will be found at the end of the series. For this purpose, the *whole* series of each particle was examined with the Hebrew and English Bible, the translation of the word being written down through the whole series of places in which they occurred. Sufficient specimens were chosen of every variety of meaning or of translation, which were written out and adopted into the MS. When a particle had any peculiar combinations with other words, selections were in the same manner made from them. When the particle is omitted in the translation, its place is pointed out by parenthesis marks placed thus)(; the same mark is used with the same purpose, occasionally, with regard to other words.

As every one that knows Taylor and his Concordance, must be aware how its headings are tinged and tainted with his peculiar views, I would only say, *passingly,* that there being no headings or explanations in this work (nothing but the Hebrew and Chaldee words followed by citations from the English Bible), there is no room for any such taint here; and therefore the reader need not be anxious to know the sentiments and thoughts of any of the many who have been employed in it.

The only cautionary remark I would add is this, that without faith, and the Spirit's aid (never withheld from the humble and prayerful Christian), AND A PATIENT EXAMINATION OF THE CONTEXTS, no one can profit aright from this Concordance.

To mete out to each labourer his measure of praise, I know not how: but having thus publicly (as also constantly in private), mentioned whose is the *αρχιτεκτονικη φρονησις* of the plan; and being assured, moreover, that for the last ten years *he* has been known to upwards of a hundred of the clergy of the Establishment in England and Ireland, as the author; and having referred to the arduous labour, indefatigable patience, accuracy, learning and talent of *the many* who have laboured at it through the last eight years, under my direction, I sign my name to this preface, confessing that, with the excellences of the work I desire to claim little connection, beyond that which has resulted from money having passed through my hands for the prosecution of it.

And now may God, even the Father of the Lord Jesus Christ, vouchsafe His Holy Spirit's blessing hereon.

GEORGE V. WIGRAM.

London, September 22nd, 1843.

THE ENGLISHMAN'S
HEBREW AND CHALDEE CONCORDANCE.

א *ah'-leph.*

The first letter of the Alphabet.

---

1 **אָב** *āhv*, m.

Gen. 2:24. leave *his father* and his mother,
4:20. *the father of* such as dwell in
21. *the father of* all such as handle
9:18. *the father of* Canaan.
22. Ham, *the father of* Canaan, saw the nakedness of *his father*,
23. nakedness of *their father;*
— saw not *their father*'s nakedness.
10:21. Shem also, *the father of* all
11:28. Haran died before *his father*
29. *the father of* Milcah, *and the father of*
12. 1. and from *thy father*'s house,
15:15. shalt go to *thy fathers* in peace;
17: 4. *a father of* many nations.
5. *a father of* many nations have I made thee.
19:31. *Our father* (is) old,
32. let us make *our father* drink wine,
—, 34. preserve seed *of our father*.
33, 35. made *their father* drink wine
— lay with *her father;*
34. yesternight with *my father:*
36. with child *by their father*.
37. *the father of* the Moabites
38. *the father of* the children of Ammon
20:12. she (is) the daughter of *my father*,
13. to wander from *my father*'s house,
22: 7. Abraham *his father*, and said, *My father:*
21. Kemuel *the father of* Aram,
24: 7. took me from *my father*'s house,
23. room (in) *thy father*'s house
38. go unto *my father*'s house,
40. of my kindred, and of *my father*'s house:
26: 3. sware unto Abraham *thy father;*
15. which *his father*'s servants had digged
—, 18. days of Abraham *his father*,
18. *his father* had called them.
24. God of Abraham *thy father:*
27: 6. Behold, I heard *thy father* speak
9. savoury meat *for thy father*,
10. bring (it) *to thy father*,
12. *My father* peradventure will feel me,
14. such as *his father* loved.
18. came unto *his father*, and said, *My father:*
19. Jacob said unto *his father*,
22. went near unto Isaac *his father;*
26. *his father* Isaac said unto him,
30. from the presence of Isaac *his father*,
31. brought it *unto his father*, and said *unto his father*, Let *my father* arise,
32. And Isaac *his father* said unto him,
34. when Esau heard the words of *his father*,
— and said *unto his father*, Bless me, (even) me also. *O my father*.
38. Esau said unto *his father*, Hast thou but one blessing, *my father?* bless me, (even) me also, *O my father*.
39. And Isaac *his father* answered
41. wherewith *his father* blessed him:
— The days of mourning for *my father*

Gen28: 2. the house of Bethuel thy mother's *father;*
7. Jacob obeyed *his father* and his mother,
8. pleased not Isaac *his father;*
13. I (am) the Lord God of Abraham *thy father*,
21. I come again to *my father*'s house
29: 9. Rachel came with *her father's* sheep:
12. told Rachel that he (was) *her father*'s bro.,
— she ran and told *her father*.
31: 1. all that (was) *our father's;* and of (that) which (was) *our father's* hath he gotten
3. Return unto the land of *thy fathers*,
5. I see *your father*'s countenance,
— but the God of *my father*
6. I have served *your father*.
7. *And your father* hath deceived me,
9. taken away the cattle of *your father*,
14. inheritance for us in *our father*'s house?
16. which God hath taken *from our father*,
18. for to go to Isaac *his father*
19. stolen the images that (were) *her father's*.
29. God of *your father* spake unto me
30. longedst after *thy father*'s house,
35. And she said to *her father*,
42. Except the God of *my father*,
53. the God of *their father*, judge betwixt us.
— by the fear of *his father* Isaac.
32: 9(10). O God of *my father* Abraham, and God of *my father* Isaac.
33:19. the children of Hamor, Shechem's *father*,
34: 4. Shechem spake unto *his father*
6. Hamor *the father of* Shechem
11. Shechem said unto *her father*
13. Shechem and Hamor *his father*
19. than all the house of *his father*.
35:18. *but his father* called him Benjamin.
22. with Bilhah *his father*'s concubine:
27. Jacob came unto Isaac *his father*
36: 9, 43. Esau *the father of* the Edomites
24. wilderness, as he fed the asses of Zibeon *his father*.
37: 1. the land wherein *his father* was a stranger,
2. sons of Zilpah, *his father*'s wives:
— brought unto *his father* (lit. *their father*)
4. saw that *their father* loved him
10. And he told (it) to *his father*,
— and *his father* rebuked him,
11. *but his father* observed the saying.
12. went to feed *their father*'s flock
22. deliver him to *his father* again.
32. they brought (it) to *their father;*
35. Thus *his father* wept for him.
38:11. Remain a widow at *thy father*'s house.
— Tamar went and dwelt in *her f.*'s house.
41:51. and all *my father*'s house.
42:13. the youngest (is) this day with *our father*,
29. they came unto Jacob *their father*
32. twelve brethren, sons of *our father;*
— the youngest (is) this day with *our father*
35. they *and their father* saw the bundles
36. *their father* said unto them,
37. Reuben spake unto *his father*,
43: 2. *their father* said unto them, Go again,
7. (Is) *your father* yet alive?
8. Judah said unto Israel *his father*,
11. *their father* Israel said unto them,

Gen 43:23. the God of *your father*,
27. and said, (Is) *your father* well,
28. Thy servant *our father* (is) in good health,
44:17. get you up in peace unto *your father*.
19. Have ye *a father*, or a brother?
20. We have *a father*, an old man,
— *and his father* loveth him.
22. The lad cannot leave *his father:* for (if) he should leave *his father*,
24. came up unto thy servant *my father*,
25. And *our father* said,
27. And thy servant *my father* said
30. come to thy servant *my father*,
31. the gray hairs of thy servant *our father*
32. became surety for the lad unto *my father*,
— I shall bear the blame *to my father*
34. shall I go up to *my father*,
— the evil that shall come on *my father*.
45: 3. I (am) Joseph; doth *my father* yet live?
8. hath made me *a father* to Pharaoh,
9. Haste ye, and go up to *my father*,
13. tell *my father* of all my glory in Egypt,
— bring down *my father* hither.
18. take *your father* and your housholds,
19. and bring *your father*, and come.
23. *And to his father* he sent aft. this (manner);
— meat *for his father* by the way.
25. unto Jacob *their father*,
27. the spirit of Jacob *their father* revived:
46: 1. unto the God of *his father* Isaac.
3. I (am) God, the God of *thy father:*
5. carried Jacob *their father*,
29. went up to meet Israel *his father*,
31. and unto *his father*'s house,
— My brethren, and *my father*'s house,
34. both we, (and) also *our fathers:*
47: 1. told Pharaoh, and said, *My father*
3. we, (and) also *our fathers*.
5. *Thy father* and thy brethren are come
6. make *thy father* and brethren to dwell;
7. Joseph brought in Jacob *his father*,
9. the years of the life of *my fathers*
11. Joseph placed *his father*
12. Joseph nourished *his father*, and his brethren, and all *his father*'s houshold,
30. I will lie with *my fathers*,
48: 1. Behold, *thy father* (is) sick:
9. Joseph said unto *his father*,
15. before whom *my fathers* Abraham and
16. the name of *my fathers* Abraham and
17. Joseph saw that *his father* laid
— he held up *his father*'s hand,
18. said unto *his father*, Not so, *my father:*
19. And *his father* refused,
21. unto the land of *your fathers*.
49: 2. hearken unto Israel *your father*.
4. wentest up to *thy father*'s bed;
8. *thy father*'s children shall bow down
25. (Even) by the God of *thy father*,
26. blessings of *thy father* have prevailed
28. *their father* spake unto them,
29. bury me with *my fathers*
50: 1. fell upon *his father*'s face,
2. to embalm *his father:*
5. *My father* made me swear,
— and bury *my father*,
6. Go up, and bury *thy father*,
7. Joseph went up to bury *his father:*
8. his brethren, and *his father*'s house.
10. a mourning *for his father* seven days.
14. went up with him to bury *his father*, after he had buried *his father*.
15. saw that *their father* was dead,
16. *Thy father* did command before
17. the servants of the God of *thy father*.
22. he, and *his father*'s house:
Ex. 2:16. to water *their father*'s flock.
18. when they came to Reuel *their father*,
3: 6. I (am) the God of *thy father*,
13. The God of *your fathers* hath sent me
15, 16. The Lord God of *your fathers*,
4: 5. the Lord God of *their fathers*,
6:14. These(be)the heads of *their fathers*'houses:
25. the heads of *the fathers of* the Levites
10: 6. *thy fathers, nor thy fathers' fs.* have seen,
12: 3. according to the house of (their) *fathers*,
13: 5. which he sware *unto thy fathers*

Ex. 13:11. sware unto thee *and to thy fathers*.
15: 2. *my father*'s God, and I will exalt him.
18: 4. for the God of *my father*,
20: 5. visiting the iniquity of *the fathers*
12. Honour *thy father* and thy mother:
21:15. he that smiteth *his father*,
17. And he that curseth *his father*,
22:17(16). If *her father* utterly refuse to
34: 7. visiting the iniquity of *the fathers*
40:15. as thou didst anoint *their father*,
Lev. 16:32. in the priest's office in *his father*'s
18: 7. The nakedness of *thy father*,
8. The nakedness of *thy father*'s wife
— it (is) *thy father*'s nakedness.
9. the daughter of *thy father*,
11. nakedness of *thy father*'s wife's daughter begotten of *thy father*,
12. the nakedness of *thy father*'s sister: she (is) *thy father*'s near kinswoman.
14. the nakedness of *thy father*'s brother,
19: 3. fear every man his mother, *and his father*
20: 9. every one that curseth *his father*
— he hath cursed *his father*
11. the man that lieth with *his father*'s wife hath uncovered *his father*'s nakedness:
17. take his sister, *his father*'s daughter,
19. nor of *thy father*'s sister:
21: 2. for his mother, *and for his father*,
9. she profaneth *her father*:
11. nor defile himself *for his father*,
22:13. is returned unto *her father*'s house, as in her youth, she shall eat of *her father*'s meat.
25:41. unto the possession of *his fathers*
26:39. the iniquities of *their fathers*
40. and the iniquity of *their fathers*,
Nu. 1: 2. families, by the house of *their fathers*,
4. head of the house of *his fathers*.
16. princes of the tribes of *their fathers*,
18, 20, 22, 24, 26, 28, 30, 32, 34, 36, 38, 40, 42, 45. by the house of *their fathers*,
44. each one was for the house of *his fathers*.
47. after the tribe of *their fathers*
2: 2. with the ensign of *their fathers*' house:
32. by the house of *their fathers:*
34. according to the house of *their fathers*.
3: 4. in the sight of Aaron *their father*.
15. after the house of *their fathers*,
20. according to the house of *their fathers*.
24. chief of the house of *the father*
30. *the father* of the families of the Kohathites
35. *the father* of the families of Merari
4: 2, 29, 38, 40, 42. by the house of *their fathers*,
22. throughout the houses of *their fathers*,
34, 46. after the house of *their fathers*,
6: 7. not make himself unclean *for his father*,
7: 2. heads of the house of *their fathers*,
11:12. land which thou swarest *unto their fathers*?
12:14. *If her father* had but spit in her face,
13: 2. every tribe of *their fathers*
14:18. visiting the iniquity of *the fathers* upon
23. which I sware *unto their fathers*,
17: 2(17). according to the house of (their) *fathers*, of all their princes according to the house of *their fathers*
3(18). the head of the house of *their fathers*.
6(21). according to *their fathers*' houses,
18: 1. thy sons and *thy father*'s house
2. the tribe of *thy father*,
20:15. *our fathers* went down into Egypt,
— the Egyptians vexed us, *and our fathers:*
25:14. prince of a *chief* house(marg. house of *a f.*)
15. a *chief* house in Midian. (lit. house of *a f.*)
26: 2. throughout *their fathers*' house,
55. names of the tribes of *their fathers*
27: 3. *Our father* died in the wilderness,
4. the name of *our father* be done away
— among the brethren of *our father*.
7. among *their father*'s brethren;
— inheritance of *their father* to pass unto
10. his inheritance unto *his father*'s brethren.
11. if *his father have* no brethren,
30: 3(4). (being) in *her father*'s house
4(5). And *her father* hear her vow,
—(-). *her father* shall hold his peace
5(6). if *her father* disallow her
—(-). because *her father* disallowed her.
16(17). between *the father* and his daughter

Nu. 30:16(17). in her youth in *her father*'s house.
31:26. chief *fathers of* the congregation;
32: 8. Thus did *your fathers*,
14. ye are risen up in *your fathers'* stead,
28. *the* chief *fathers of* the tribes
33:54. according to the tribes of *your fathers*
34:14, 14. according to the house of *their fathers*,
36: 1. chief *fathers* of the families of
— chief *fathers* of the children of Israel:
3. the inheritance of *our fathers*,
4. the inheritance of the tribe of *our fathers*.
6. the tribe of *their father* shall they marry.
7. inheritance of the tribe of *his fathers*.
8. the family of the tribe of *her father*,
— the inheritance of *his fathers*.
12. the tribe of the family of *their father*.
Deu. 1: 8. which the Lord sware *unto your fathers*,
11. The Lord God of *your fathers*
21. the Lord God of *thy fathers*
35. which I sware to give *unto your fathers*,
4: 1. which the Lord God of *your fathers*
31. nor forget the covenant of *thy fathers*
37. because he loved *thy fathers*,
5: 3. covenant with *our fathers*,
9. visiting the iniquity of *the fathers*
16. Honour *thy father* and thy mother,
6: 3. as the Lord God of *thy fathers*
10. which he sware *unto thy fathers*,
18. which the Lord sware *unto thy fathers*,
23. which he sware *unto our fathers*.
7: 8. which he had sworn *unto your fathers*,
12, 13. which he sware *unto thy fathers*:
8: 1. which the Lord sware *unto your fathers*.
3. neither did *thy fathers* know;
16. which *thy fathers* knew not,
18. which he sware *unto thy fathers*,
9: 5. which the Lord sware *unto thy fathers*,
10:11. which I sware *unto their fathers*
15. the Lord had a delight *in thy fathers*
22. *Thy fathers* went down into Egypt
11: 9, 21. the Lord sware *unto your fathers*
12: 1. the land, which the Lord God of *thy fathers*
13: 6(7). hast not known, thou, *nor thy fathers*;
17(18). as he hath sworn *unto thy fathers*;
18: 8. which cometh of the sale of his *patrimony*.
(marg. his sales by *the fathers*)
19: 8. as he hath sworn *unto thy fathers*,
— he promised to give *unto thy fathers*;
21:13. and bewail *her father* and her mother
18. not obey the voice of *his father*,
19. shall *his father* and his mother lay hold on
22:15. Then shall *the father of* the damsel,
16. And the damsel'*s father* shall say
19. give (them) *unto the father of* the damsel,
21. the damsel to the door of *her father*'s house,
— to play the whore in *her father*'s house;
29. shall give *unto the* damsel'*s father*
30. (23:1). shall not take *his father*'s wife, nor
discover *his father*'s skirt.
24:16. *The fathers* shall not be put to death
— children be put to death for *the fathers*:
26: 3. which the Lord sware *unto our fathers*
5. A Syrian ready to perish (was) *my father*,
7. Lord God of *our fathers*,
15. as thou swarest *unto our fathers*,
27: 3. the Lord God of *thy fathers*
16. that setteth light by *his father*
20. Cursed (be) he that lieth with *his father*'s
— he uncovereth *his father*'s skirt.
22. with his sister, the daughter of *his father*,
28:11. sware *unto thy fathers* to give thee.
36, 64. thou *nor thy fathers* have known;
29.13(12). as he hath sworn *unto thy fathers*,
25(24). covenant of the Lord God of *their fs.*,
30: 5. the land which *thy fathers* possessed,
— multiply thee *above thy fathers*.
9. as he rejoiced over *thy fathers*:
20. the Lord sware *unto thy fathers*,
31: 7. the Lord hath sworn *unto their fathers*
16. thou shalt sleep with *thy fathers*;
20. the land which I sware *unto their fathers*,
32: 6. (is) not he *thy father* (that) hath bought
7. ask *thy father*, and he will shew thee;
17. whom *your fathers* feared not.
33: 9. Who said *unto his father* and to his mother,
Jos. 1: 6. sware *unto their fathers* to give them.
2:12. shew kindness unto *my father*'s house,

Jos. 2:13. (that) ye will save alive *my father*,
18. thou shalt bring *thy father*, and
— all *thy father*'s houshold, home
4:21. shall ask *their fathers* in time to come,
5: 6. land, which the Lord sware *unto their fs.*
6.23. brought out Rahab, and *her father*,
25. Rahab the harlot alive, and *her father*'s hd.,
14: 1. the heads of *the fathers of* the tribes
15:13. the city of Arba *the father of* Anak,
18. to ask of *her father* a field:
17: 1. Manasseh, *the father of* Gilead:
4. among the brethren of *their father*.
18: 3. which the Lord God of *your fathers*
19:47. after the name of Dan *their father*.
51. the heads of *the fathers* of the tribes
21: 1. the heads of *the fathers of* the Levites
— unto the heads of *the fathers of*
11. the city of Arba *the father of* Anak,
43(41). he sware to give *unto their fathers*;
44(42). all that he sware *unto their fathers*:
22:14. each *chief* house (marg. house of the *f.*)
— head of the house of *their fathers*
28. which *our fathers* made,
24: 2. *Your fathers* dwelt on the other side of the
— Terah, *the father of* Abraham, *and the father of* Nachor:
3. I took *your father* Abraham from the other
6. brought *your fathers* out of Egypt:
— the Egyptians pursued after *your fathers*
14, 15. the gods which *your fathers* served
17. *our fathers* out of the land of Egypt,
32. of Hamor *the father of* Shechem
Jud. 1:14. she moved him to ask of *her father* a field:
2: 1. which I sware *unto your fathers*;
10. were gathered unto *their fathers*:
12. forsook the Lord God of *their fathers*,
17. which *their fathers* walked in,
19. corrupted (themselves) *more than their fs.*
20. which I commanded *their fathers*,
22. as *their fathers* did keep (it), or not.
3: 4. which he commanded *their fathers*
6:11. that (pertained) unto Joash *the Abi*-ezrite:
13. which *our fathers* told us of,
15. I (am) the least in *my father*'s house.
24. it (is) yet in Ophrah of *the Abi*-ezrites.
25. Take *thy father's* young bullock, (lit. which
(is) *to thy father*)
— the altar of Baal that *thy father hath*, (lit.
which (is) *to thy father*)
27. because he feared *his father*'s houshold,
8:32. Joash *his father*, in Ophrah of *the Abi*-ezrites.
9: 1. the house of his mother's *father*,
5. he went unto *his father*'s house
17. For *my father* fought for you,
18. risen up against *my father*'s house
28. Hamor *the father of* Shechem:
56. which he did *unto his father*,
11: 2. shalt not inherit in *our father*'s house;
7. expel me out of *my father*'s house?
36. she said unto him, *My father*,
37. And she said unto *her father*,
39. she returned unto *her father*,
14: 2. told *his father* and his mother,
3. *his father* and his mother said unto him,
— Samson said unto *his father*,
4. *But his father* and his mother knew not
5. went Samson down, *and his father* and his
6. he told not *his father* or his mother
9. came to *his father* and mother,
10. So *his father* went down
15. burn thee and *thy father*'s house
16. I have not told (it) *my father*
19. he went up to *his father*'s house.
15: 1. *her father* would not suffer him to go in.
2. And *her father* said, I verily thought
6. burnt her and *her father* with fire.
16:31. his brethren and all the house of *his father*
— the burying-place of Manoah *his father*.
17:10. be unto me *a father* and a priest,
18:19. be to us *a father* and a priest:
29. after the name of Dan *their father*,
19: 2. away from him unto *her father*'s house
3. she brought him into *her father*'s house:
and when *the father of* the damsel saw
4. *the* damsel'*s father*, retained him;
5. and *the* damsel'*s father* said
6. *the* damsel'*s father* had said unto the man,

Jud. 19: 8. and *the* damsel's *father* said, Comfort
9. his father-in-law, *the* damsel's *father*,
21:22. when *their fathers* or their brethren
Ruth 2:11. thou hast left *thy father* and thy mother,
4:17. *the father of* Jesse, *the father of* David.
1 Sa. 2:25. unto the voice of *their father*,
27. appear unto the house of *thy father*,
28. did I give unto the house of *thy father*
30. and the house of *thy father*,
31. the arm of *thy father*'s house,
9: 3. the asses of Kish Saul's *father*
5. lest *my father* leave (caring) for the asses,
20. and on all *thy father*'s house?
10: 2. *thy father* hath left the care of the asses,
12. But who (is) *their father?*
12: 6. that brought *your fathers* up
7 did to you and to *your fathers*.
8. and *your fathers* cried unto the Lord,
— brought forth *your fathers* out of Egypt,
15. *as* (it was) *against your fathers*.
14: 1. *But* he told not *his father*.
27. Jonathan heard not when *his f.* charged
28. *Thy father* straitly charged
29. *My father* hath troubled the land:
51. Kish (was) *the father of* Saul; and Ner *the father of* Abner (was) the son of *Abiel*.
17:15. to feed *his father*'s sheep
25. make *his father*'s house free in Israel.
34. Thy servant kept *his father*'s sheep,
18. 2. go no more home to *his father*'s house.
18. (or) *my father*'s family in Israel,
19: 2. Saul *my father* seeketh to kill thee:
3. stand beside *my father* in the field
— I will commune with *my father* of thee;
4. spake good of David unto Saul *his father*,
20: 1. what (is) my sin before *thy father*,
2. behold, *my father* will do nothing
— why should *my father* hide this
3. *Thy father* certainly knoweth
6. If *thy father* at all miss me,
8. why shouldest thou bring me to *thy father?*
9. determined by *my father*
10. (if) *thy father* answer thee roughly?
12. when I have sounded *my father*
13. if it please *my father* (to do) thee evil,
— as he hath been with *my father*.
32. Jonathan answered Saul *his father*,
33. it was determined of *his father* to slay
34. because *his father* had done him shame.
22: 1. his brethren and all *his father*'s house
3. Let *my father* and my mother,
11. the son of Ahitub, and all *his father*'s house,
15. the house of *my father:*
16. thou, and all *thy father*'s house.
22. all the persons of *thy father*'s house.
23:17. the hand of Saul *my father*
— that also Saul *my father* knoweth.
24:11 (12). *Moreover, my father*, see,
21 (22). destroy my name out of *my father*'s h.
2 Sa. 2:32. in the sepulchre of *his father*,
3: 7. gone in unto *my father*'s concubine?
8. unto the house of Saul *thy father*,
29. and on all *his father*'s house;
6:21. which chose me *before thy father*,
7:12. thou shalt sleep with *thy fathers*,
14. I will be his *father*, (lit. *for a father* to him,)
9: 7. for Jonathan *thy father*'s sake,
— all the land of Saul *thy father;*
10: 2. as *his father* shewed kindness unto me.
— by the hand of his servants for *his father*.
3. that David doth honour *thy father*,
13: 5. when *thy father* cometh to see thee,
14: 9. the iniquity (be) on me, and on *my father*'s
15:34. (as) I (have been) *thy father*'s servant
16: 3. restore me the kingdom of *my father*.
19. I have served in *thy father*'s presence,
21. Go in unto *thy father*'s concubines,
— thou art abhorred of *thy father:*
22. unto *his father*'s concubines
17: 8. thou knowest *thy father* and his men,
— *and thy father* (is) a man of war,
10. *thy father* (is) a mighty man,
23. in the sepulchre of *his father*.
19:28 (29). all (of) *my father*'s house
37 (38). (be buried) by the grave of *my father*
21:14. the sepulchre of Kish *his father:*
24:17. and against *my father*'s house.

1 K. 1: 6. *his father* had not displeased him
21. the king shall sleep with *his fathers*,
2:10. David slept with *his fathers*,
12. the throne of David *his father;*
24. the throne of David *my father*,
26. ark of the Lord God before David *my f.*,
— in all wherein *my father* was afflicted.
31. and from the house of *my father*.
32. *my father* David not knowing (thereof),
44. that thou didst to David *my father:*
3: 3. the statutes of David *his father:*
6. unto thy servant David *my father* great m.,
7. king instead of David *my father:*
14. as *thy father* David did walk,
5: 1 (15). king in the room of *his father:*
3 (17). Thou knowest how that David *my f.*
5 (19). the Lord spake unto David *my father*,
6:12. which I spake unto David *thy father:*
7:14. *and his father* (was) a man of Tyre,
51. the things which David *his father*
8: 1. the chief of *the fathers*
15. spake with his mouth unto David *my father*,
17. in the heart of David *my father*
18. the Lord said unto David *my father*,
20. in the room of David *my father*,
21. which he made with *our fathers*,
24. hast kept with thy servant David *my father*
25. keep with thy servant David *my father*
26. unto thy servant David *my father*.
34, 48. which thou gavest *unto their fathers*
40. land which thou gavest *unto our fathers*.
53. broughtest *our fathers* out of Egypt,
57. as he was with *our fathers:*
58. which he commanded *our fathers*.
9: 4. as David *thy father* walked,
5. as I promised to David *thy father*,
9. who brought forth *their fathers*
11: 4. as (was) the heart of David *his father*.
6, 33. as (did) David *his father*.
12. I will not do it for David *thy father*'s sake: (but) I will
17. Edomites of *his father*'s servants
21. David slept with *his fathers*,
27. the city of David *his father*.
43. Solomon slept with *his fathers*, and was buried in the city of David *his father:*
12: 4. *Thy father* made our yoke grievous:
— the grievous service of *thy father*,
6. that stood before Solomon *his father*
9. Make the yoke which *thy father* did put
10. *Thy father* made our yoke heavy,
— shall be thicker than *my father*'s loins.
11. whereas *my father* did lade you
— *my father* hath chastised you with whips,
14. *My father* made your yoke heavy,
— *my father* (also) chastised you
13:11. they told also *to their father*.
12. *their father* said unto them,
22. unto the sepulchre of *thy fathers*.
14:15. which he gave *to their fathers*,
20. he slept with *his fathers*,
22. above all that *their fathers* had done.
31. Rehoboam slept with *his fathers*, and was buried with *his fathers*
15: 3. walked in all the sins of *his father*,
— as the heart of David *his father*.
8. Abijam slept with *his fathers;*
11. as (did) David *his father*.
12. all the idols that *his fathers* had made.
15. the things which *his father* had dedicated,
19. between *my father* and *thy father:*
24. Asa slept with *his fathers*, and was buried with *his fs.* in the city of David *his f.*
26. walked in the way of *his father*,
16: 6. Baasha slept with *his fathers*,
28. Omri slept with *his fathers*,
18:18. but thou, and *thy father*'s house,
19: 4. I (am) not better *than my fathers*.
20. kiss *my father* and my mother,
20:34. The cities, which *my father* took from *thy f.*
— as *my father* made in Samaria.
21: 3. the inheritance of *my fathers*
4. thee the inheritance of *my fathers*.
22:40. Ahab slept with *his fathers;*
43. the ways of Asa *his father;*
46 (47). remained in the days of *his father*

1K. 22:50(51). Jehoshaphat slept with *his fathers*, and was buried with *his fathers* in the city of David *his father:*
52(53). walked in the way of *his father*,
53(54). according to all that *his father* had
2K. 2:12. he cried, *My father, my father*, the chariot of Israel,
3: 2. but not *like his father*,
— the image of Baal that *his father* had made.
13. get thee to the prophets of *thy father*,
4:18. he went out to *his father*
19. he said unto *his father*, My head, my head.
5:13. *My father*, (if) the prophet had bid
6:21. *My father*, shall I smite (them)?
8:24. Joram slept with *his fathers*, and was buried with *his fathers*
9.25. rode together after Ahab *his father*,
28. in his sepulchre with *his fathers*
10: 3. set (him) on *his father*'s throne,
35. Jehu slept with *his fathers*:
12:18(19). *his fathers*, kings of Judah,
21(22). buried him with *his fathers*
13: 9. Jehoahaz slept with *his fathers;*
13. Joash slept with *his fathers;*
14. said, *O my father, my father*,
25. hand of Jehoahaz *his father* by war.
14: 3. yet not like David *his father:*
— all things as Joash *his father* did.
5. which had slain the king *his father*.
6. *The fathers* shall not be put to death
— be put to death for *the fathers;*
16. Jehoash slept with *his fathers*,
20. buried at Jerusalem with *his fathers*,
21. king instead of *his father* Amaziah.
22. the king slept with *his fathers*.
29. Jeroboam slept with *his fathers*,
15: 3. according to all that *his father* Amaziah
7. Azariah slept with *his fathers;* and they buried him with *his fathers*
9. as *his fathers* had done;
22. Menahem slept with *his fathers;*
34. all that *his father* Uzziah had done.
38. Jotham slept with *his fathers*, and was buried with *his fathers* in the city of David *his father:*
16: 2. like David *his father*.
20. Ahaz slept with *his fathers*, and was buried with *his fathers*
17:13. I commanded *your fathers*,
14. like to the neck of *their fathers*,
15. covenant that he made with *their fathers*,
41. as did *their fathers*, so do they
18: 3. all that David *his father* did.
19:12. which *my fathers* have destroyed;
20: 5. the God of David *thy father*,
17. that which *thy fathers* have laid up
21. Hezekiah slept with *his fathers:*
21: 3. Hezekiah *his father* had destroyed;
8. the land which I gave *their fathers;*
15. since the day *their fathers* came forth
18. Manasseh slept with *his fathers*,
20. as *his father* Manasseh did.
21. all the way that *his father* walked in, and served the idols that *his father* served,
22. the Lord God of *his fathers*,
22: 2. in all the way of David *his father*,
13. *our fathers* have not hearkened
20. I will gather thee unto *thy fathers*,
23:30. made him king in *his father*'s stead.
32, 37 according to all that *his fathers* had done.
34. in the room of Josiah *his father*,
24: 6. Jehoiakim slept with *his fathers:*
9. according to all that *his father* had done.
1Ch. 2:17. *and the father of* Amasa (was) Jether
21, 23. Machir *the father of* Gilead,
24. Ashur *the father of* Tekoa.
42. which (was) *the father of* Ziph; and the sons of Mareshah *the father of* Hebron.
44. Shema begat Raham, *the father of*
45. Maon (was) *the father of* Beth-zur.
49. Shaaph *the father of* Madmannah, Sheva *the father of* Machbenah, *and the father of*
50, 52. Shobal *the father of* Kirjathjearim,
51. Salma *the father of* Bethlehem, Hareph *the father of* Bethgader.
55. *the father of* the house of Rechab.
4: 3. these (were of) *the father of* Etam;
1Ch. 4: 4. Penuel *the father of* Gedor, and Ezer *the father of* Hushah.
— Ephratah, *the father of* Bethlehem,
5. Ashur *the father of* Tekoa
11. Mehir, which (was) *the father of* Eshton.
12. Tehinnah *the father of* Ir-nahash.
14. Joab, *the father of* the valley of Charashim,
17. Ishbah *the father of* Eshtemoa.
18. Jered *the father of* Gedor, and Heber *the father of* Socho, and Jekuthiel *the father of*
19. Naham, *the father of* Keilah
21. Er *the father of* Lecah, and Laadah *the father of* Mareshah,
38. the house of *their fathers* increased
5: 1. forasmuch as he defiled *his father*'s bed,
13. of the house of *their fathers*
15. chief of the house of *their fathers*.
24. the heads of the house of *their fathers*,
— (and) heads of the house of *their fathers*.
25. the God of *their fathers*,
6:19(4). of the Levites *according to their fathers*.
7: 2. heads of *their fathers'* house,
4. after the house of *their fathers*,
7. heads of the house of (their) *fathers*,
9. heads of the house of *their fathers*,
11. by the heads of *their fathers*,
14. Machir *the father of* Gilead:
22. Ephraim *their father* mourned
31. Malchiel, who (is) *the father of* Birzavith.
40. heads of (their) *father*'s house,
8: 6. these are the heads of *the fathers*
10. These (were) his sons, heads of the *fathers*.
13. who (were) heads of *the fathers* of
28. These (were) heads of *the fathers*,
29. at Gibeon dwelt *the father of* Gibeon
9: 9. chief of *the fathers* in the house of *their fs*.
13. heads of the house of *their fathers*,
19. of the house of *his father*,
— *and their fathers*, (being) over the host
33. chief of *the fathers* of the Levites,
34. These chief *fathers* of the Levites (were)
35. in Gibeon dwelt *the father of* Gibeon,
12:17. the God of *our fathers* look (thereon),
28. of *his father*'s house twenty and two capts.
30. throughout the house of *their fathers*.
15:12. chief of *the fathers* of the Levites:
17:11. thou must go (to be) with *thy fathers*,
13. I will be his *father*, and he shall be
19: 2. because *his father* shewed kindness to me.
— to comfort him concerning *his father*.
3. that David doth honour *thy father*,
21:17. be on me, and on *my father*'s house;
22:10. I (will be) his *father;*
23: 9. the chief of *the fathers* of Laadan.
11. according to (their) *father*'s house.
24. after the house of *their fathers;* (even) the chief of *the fathers*,
24: 2. Nadab and Abihu died before *their father*,
4. of the house of (their) *fathers*,
— according to the house of *their fathers*.
6. (before) the chief of *the fathers* of the pr.
— one *principal* housh. (marg. house of *the f.*)
19. under Aaron *their father*,
30. after the house of *their fathers*.
31. and the chief of *the fathers* of the priests and Levites, even *the* principal *fathers*
25: 3, 6. under the hands of *their father*
26: 6. that ruled throughout the house of *their father:*
10. yet *his father* made him the chief;
13. according to the house of *their fathers*,
21. of the Gershonite Laadan, chief *fathers*,
26. David the king, and *the* chief *fathers*,
31. according to the generations *of* his *fathers*
32. two thousand and seven hundred chief *fs.*,
27: 1. *the* chief *fathers* and captains of thousands
28: 4. chose me before all the house of *my father*
— house of Judah, the house of *my father;* and among the sons of *my father* he liked me
6. (to be) my son, and I will be his *father*.
9. know thou the God of *thy father*,
29: 6. Then the chief of *the fathers*
10. Lord God of Israel *our father*,
15. sojourners, as (were) all *our fathers'*
18. of Abraham, Isaac, & of Israel, *our fathers*
20. the Lord God of *their fathers*,
23. as king instead of David *his father*

2Ch. 1: 2. in all Israel, the chief of *the fathers.*
8. shewed great mercy unto David *my father*,
9. thy promise unto David *my father* be
2: 3(2). As thou didst deal with David *my f.*,
7(6). whom David *my father* did provide.
13(12). of Huram *my father*'s,
14(13). *and his father* (was) a man of Tyre,
—(—). men of my lord David *thy father.*
17(16). David *his father* had numbered them;
3: 1. (the Lord) appeared unto David *his father*,
4:16. all their instruments, did Huram *his father*
5: 1. the things that David *his father* had
2. the chief of *the fathers* of the children of Israel,
6: 4. with his mouth to *my father* David,
7. in the heart of David *my father*
8. the Lord said to David *my father*,
10. in the room of David *my father*,
15. with thy servant David *my father*
16. keep with thy servant David *my father*
25. thou gavest to them *and to their fathers.*
31. the land which thou gavest *unto our fathers.*
38. which thou gavest *unto their fathers*,
7:17. as David *thy father* walked,
18. covenanted with David *thy father*,
22. forsook the Lord God of *their fathers*,
8:14. the order of David *his father*,
9:31. Solomon slept with *his fathers*, and he was buried in the city of David *his father:*
10: 4. *Thy father* made our yoke grievous:
— the grievous servitude of *thy father*,
6. stood before Solomon *his father*
9. the yoke that *thy father* did put
10. *Thy father* made our yoke heavy,
— shall be thicker than *my father*'s loins.
11. whereas *my father* put a heavy yoke
—, 14. *my father* chastised you with whips,
14. *My father* made your yoke heavy,
11:16. unto the Lord God of *their fathers.*
12:16. Rehoboam slept with *his fathers*,
13:12. the Lord God of *your fathers;*
18. they relied upon the L. God of *their fs.*
14: 1. (13:23). Abijah slept with *his fathers*,
4(3). to seek the Lord God of *their fathers*,
15:12. to seek the Lord God of *their fathers*
18. the things that *his father* had dedicated,
16: 3. between *my father* and *thy father:*
13. Asa slept with *his fathers*,
17: 2. which Asa *his father* had taken.
3. in the first ways of *his father* David,
4. sought to the (Lord) God of *his father*,
14. according to the house of *their fathers:*
19: 4. unto the Lord God of *their fathers.*
8. the chief of *the fathers* of Israel,
20: 6. O Lord God of *our fathers*,
32. walked in the way of Asa *his father*,
33. hearts unto the God of *their fathers.*
21: 1. Jehoshaphat slept with *his fathers*, and was buried with *his fathers*
3. *their father* gave them great gifts
4. the kingdom of *his father*,
10. had forsaken the Lord God of *his fathers.*
12. the Lord God of David *thy father*,
— in the ways of Jehoshaphat *thy father*,
13. thy brethren of *thy father*'s house,
19. like the burning of *his fathers.*
22: 4. after the death of *his father*
23: 2. the chief of *the fathers* of Israel,
24:18. the house of the Lord God of *their fathers*,
22. Jehoiada *his father* had done
24. forsaken the Lord God of *their fathers.*
25: 3. that had killed the king *his father.*
4. *The fathers* shall not die for the children, neither shall the children die for *the fs.*,
5. according to the houses of (their) *fathers*,
28. buried him with *his fathers*
26: 1. in the room of *his father* Amaziah.
2. after that the king slept with *his fathers.*
4. according to all that *his father* Amaziah
12. number of the chief of *the fathers*
23. Uzziah slept with *his fathers*, and they buried him with *his fathers*
27. 2. according to all that *his father* Uzziah did:
9. Jotham slept with *his fathers*,
28: 1. like David *his father:*
6. had forsaken the Lord God of *their fathers.*
9. because the Lord God of *your fathers*

2Ch.28:25. to anger the Lord God of *his fathers.*
27. Ahaz slept with *his fathers*,
29: 2. according to all that David *his father*
5. the Lord God of *your fathers*,
6. For *our fathers* have trespassed,
9. lo, *our fathers* have fallen
30: 7. be not ye *like your fathers*,
— against the Lord God of *their fathers*,
8. be ye not stiffnecked, *as your fathers*
19. the Lord God of *his fathers*,
22. confession to the Lord God of *their fathers.*
31:17. the priests by the house of *their fathers.*
32:13. what I *and my fathers* have done
14. that *my fathers* utterly destroyed,
15. out of the hand of *my fathers:*
33. Hezekiah slept with *his fathers*,
33: 3. Hezekiah *his father* had broken down,
8. the land wh. I have appointed *for your fs.;*
12. before the God of *his fathers*,
20. Manasseh slept with *his fathers*,
22. as did Manasseh *his father:*
— images wh. Manasseh *his father* had made,
23. as Manasseh *his f.* had humbled himself;
34: 2. walked in the ways of David *his father*,
3. began to seek after the God of David *his f.:*
21. *our fathers* have not kept the word
28. I will gather thee to *thy fathers*,
32. covenant of God, the God of *their fathers.*
33. following the Lord, the God of *their fathers.*
35: 4. by the houses of *your fathers*,
5. the families of *the fathers* of your brethren
— the families of the Levites. (lit. house of *a father* of the Levites)
12. divisions of the families (lit. house of *fs.*)
24. the sepulchres of *his fathers.*
36: 1. made him king in *his father*'s stead
15. the Lord God of *their fathers* sent to them
Ezr. 1: 5. Then rose up the chief of *the fathers*
2:59. they could not shew *their fathers*' house,
68. (some) of the chief of *the fathers*,
3:12. chief of *the fathers*, (who were) ancient
4: 2. Zerubbabel, and to the chief of *the fathers*,
3. the rest of the chief of *the fathers* of Israel,
7:27. Blessed (be) the Lord God of *our fathers*,
8: 1. These (are) now the chief of *their fathers*,
28. unto the Lord God of *your fathers.*
29. chief of *the fathers* of Israel,
9: 7. Since the days of *our fathers* (have) we
10:11. confession unto the L. God of *your fathers*,
16. the priest, (with) certain chief of *the fathers*, after the house of *their fathers*,
Neh. 1: 6. both I and *my father*'s house have sinned.
2: 3. the place of *my fathers*' sepulchres,
5. unto the city of *my fathers*' sepulchres,
7:61. but they could not shew *their fathers*'
70. the chief of *the fathers* gave unto the
71. the chief of *the fathers* gave to the treas.
8:13. were gathered together the chief of *the fs.*
9: 2. and the iniquities of *their fathers.*
9. didst see the affliction of *our fathers*
16. they *and our fathers* dealt proudly,
23. which thou hadst promised *to their fathers*,
32. *and on our fathers*, and on all thy people,
34. *nor our fathers*, kept thy law,
36. the land that thou gavest *unto our fathers*
10:34(35). after the houses of *our fathers*,
11:13. And his brethren, chief of *the fathers*,
12:12. priests, the chief of *the fathers:*
22. (were) recorded chief of *the fathers:*
23. the chief of *the fathers*,
13:18. Did not *your fathers* thus,
Est. 2: 7. for she had neither *father* nor mother;
— when *her father* and mother were dead,
4:14. thou and *thy father*'s house shall be
Job. 8: 8. prepare thyself to the search of *their fs.:*
15:10. much elder *than thy father.*
18. Which wise men have told *from their fs.*,
17:14. corruption, Thou (art) *my father:*
29:16. I (was) *a father* to the poor:
30: 1. whose *fathers* I would have disdained
31:18. brought up with me, *as* (with) *a father*,
34:36. *My desire* (is that) Job may be tried (See אָב wish.)
38:28. Hath the rain *a father?*
42:15. *their father* gave them inheritance
Ps. 22: 4(5). *Our fathers* trusted in thee:

Ps. 27:10. When *my father* and my mother forsake
39:12(13). a sojourner, as all *my fathers* (were.)
44: 1(2). O God, *our fathers* have told us,
45:10(11). thine own people, and *thy father's*
16(17). Instead of *thy fathers* shall be thy
49:19(20). shall go to the generation of *his fs.;*
68: 5(6). *A father of* the fatherless,
78: 3. *and our fathers* have told us.
5. which he commanded *our fathers,*
8. might not be *as their fathers,*
12. did he in the sight *of their fathers,*
57. dealt unfaithfully *like their fathers:*
89:26(27). He shall cry unto me, Thou (art) *my f.,*
95. 9. When *your fathers* tempted me,
103:13. Like as *a father* pitieth (his) children,
106: 6. We have sinned with *our fathers,*
7. *Our fathers* understood not thy wonders
109:14. Let the iniquity of *his fathers* be
Pro. 1: 8. My son, hear the instruction of *thy father,*
3:12. *even as a father* the son (in whom) he
4: 1. Hear, ye children, the instruction of *a f.,*
3. I was *my father's* son, tender and
6:20. My son, keep *thy father's* commandment,
10: 1. A wise son maketh *a* glad *father:*
13: 1. A wise son (heareth) his *f.'s* instruction:
15: 5. A fool despiseth *his father's* instruction:
20. A wise son maketh *a* glad *father:*
17: 6. the glory of children (are) *their fathers.*
21. *the father of* a fool hath no joy.
25. A foolish son (is) a grief *to his father,*
19:13. A foolish son (is) the calamity *of his f.:*
14. and riches (are) the inheritance of *fathers:*
26. He that wasteth (his) *father,*
20:20. Whoso curseth *his father* or his mother,
22:28. which *thy fathers* have set.
23:22. Hearken *unto thy father* that begat thee,
24. *The father of* the righteous shall greatly
25. *Thy father* and thy mother shall
27:10. *thy father's* friend, forsake not;
28: 7. of riotous (men) shameth *his father.*
24. Whoso robbeth *his father* or his mother,
29: 3. Whoso loveth wisdom rejoiceth *his father:*
30:11. a generation (that) curseth *their father,*
17. The eye (that) mocketh *at* (his) *father,*
Isa. 3: 6. his brother of the house of *his father,*
7:17. upon thy people, and upon *thy father's*
8: 4. *My father,* and my mother,
9: 6(5). *The* everlasting *Father,* The Prince of
14:21. for the iniquity of *their fathers;*
22:21. he shall be *a father* to the inhabitants
23. a glorious throne to *his father's* house.
24. all the glory of *his father's* house,
37:12. which *my fathers* have destroyed,
38: 5. the God of David *thy father,*
19. *the father* to the children shall
39. 6. (that) which *thy fathers* have laid up
43:27. *Thy* first *father* hath sinned,
45:10. that saith *unto* (his) *father,* What
51: 2. Look unto Abraham *your father,*
58:14. the heritage of Jacob *thy father:*
63:16. Doubtless thou (art) *our father,*
— thou, O Lord, (art) *our father,*
64: 8(7). But now, O Lord, thou (art) *our F.;*
11(10). where *our fathers* praised thee,
65: 7. the iniquities of *your fathers* together,
Jer. 2: 5. What iniquity have *your fathers* found
27. Saying to a stock, Thou (art) *my father;*
3: 4. *My father,* thou (art) the guide of my
18. given for an inheritance unto *your fathers.*
19. Thou shalt call me, *My father;*
24. shame hath devoured the labour of *our fs.*
25. against the Lord our God, we *and our fs.,*
6:21. *the fathers* and the sons together
7: 7. the land that I gave *to your fathers,*
14. which I gave to you *and to your fathers,*
18. *and the fathers* kindle the fire,
22. I spake not unto *your fathers,*
25. Since the day that *your fathers* came
26. they did worse *than their fathers.*
9:14(13). after Baalim, which *their fs.* taught
16(15). whom neither they *nor their fathers*
11: 4. Which I commanded *your fathers*
5. which I have sworn *unto your fathers,*
7. I earnestly protested *unto your fathers*
10. the iniquities of *their forefathers,*
— which I made with *their fathers.*
12: 6. thy brethren, and the house of *thy father,*
Jer. 13:14. *even the fathers* and the sons together,
14:20. (and) the iniquity of *our fathers:*
16: 3. concerning *their fathers* that begat them
7. to drink for *their f.* or for their mother.
11. *your fathers* have forsaken me,
12. ye have done worse *than your fathers;*
13. ye know not, (neither) ye *nor your fathers;*
15. land that I gave *unto their fathers.*
19. Surely *our fathers* have inherited lies,
17:22. as I commanded *your fathers.*
19: 4. neither they *nor their fathers* have known,
20:15. the man who brought tidings to *my father,*
22:11. which reigned instead of Josiah *his father,*
15. did not *thy father* eat and drink,
23:27. as *their fathers* have forgotten my name
39. the city that I gave you *and your fathers,*
24:10. that I gave unto them *and to their fathers.*
25: 5. hath given unto you *and to your fathers*
30: 3. the land that I gave *to their fathers,*
31: 9. for I am *a father* to Israel,
29. *The fathers* have eaten a sour grape,
32. the covenant that I made with *their fathers*
32:18. recompensest the iniquity of *the fathers*
22. which thou didst swear *to their fathers*
34: 5. with the burnings of *thy fathers,*
13. I made a covenant with *your fathers*
14. but *your fathers* hearkened not
35: 6, 8. Jonadab the son of Rechab *our father*
10. all that Jonadab *our father* commanded us.
14. but obey *their father's* commandment:
15. given to you *and to your fathers:*
16. performed the commandment of *their f.,*
18. the commandment of Jonadab *your father,*
44: 3. knew not, (neither) they, ye, *nor your fs.,*
9. forgotten the wickedness of *your fs.,*
10. that I set before you, and before *your fathers.*
17. as we have done, we, *and our fathers,*
21. ye, *and your fathers,* your kings,
47: 3. *the fathers* shall not look back to (their)
50: 7. even the Lord, the hope of *their fathers.*
La. 5: 3. We are orphans and *father*less, (lit. no *f.*)
7. *Our fathers* have sinned, (and are) not;
Eze. 2: 3. they *and their fathers* have transgressed
5:10. Therefore *the fathers* shall eat the sons
— and the sons shall eat *their fathers;*
16: 3. *thy father* (was) an Amorite,
45. *and your father* an Amorite.
18: 2. *The fathers* have eaten sour grapes,
4. all souls are mine; as the soul of *the father,*
14. that seeth all *his father's* sins
17. shall not die for the iniquity of *his father,*
18. (As for) *his father,* because he cruelly
19. bear the iniquity of *the father?*
20. son shall not bear the iniquity of *the father*
neither shall *the father* bear the iniquity
20: 4. to know the abominations of *their fathers.*
18. Walk ye not in the statutes of *your fathers,*
24. their eyes were after *their fathers'* idols.
27. Yet in this *your fathers* have blasphemed
30. Are ye polluted after the manner of *your fs.?*
36. Like as I pleaded with *your fathers* in
42. lifted up mine hand to give it *to your fs.*
22: 7. have they set light by *father* and mother.
10. they discovered (their) *father's* nakedness:
11. hath humbled his sister, *his f.'s* daughter.
36:28. the land that I gave *to your fathers;*
37:25. wherein *your fathers* have dwelt;
44:25. but *for father,* or for mother, or for son,
47:14. lifted up mine hand to give it *unto your fs.:*
Dan. 9: 6. to our kings, our princes, *and our fathers,*
8. to our princes, *and to our fathers,*
16. for the iniquities of *our fathers,*
11:24. which *his fathers* have not done, *nor his fathers' fathers;*
37. Neither shall he regard the God of *his fs.,*
38. a god whom *his fathers* knew not
Hos. 9:10. I saw *your fathers* as the firstripe
Joel 1: 2. or even in the days of *your fathers?*
Am. 2: 4. after the which *their fathers* have walked:
7. a man *and his father* will go in
Mic. 7: 6. For the son dishonoureth *the father,*
20. hast sworn *unto our fathers* from the days
Zec. 1: 2. hath been sore displeased with *your fs.*
4. Be ye not *as your fathers,*
5. *Your fathers,* where (are) they?
6. did they not take hold of *your fathers?*
8:14. when *your fathers* provoked me to wrath

Zec.13: 3. then *his father* and his mother that begat
— and *his father* and his mother
Mal. 1: 6. A son honoureth (his) *father*,
— if then I (be) *a father*,
2:10. Have we not all one *father* ?
— by profaning the covenant of *our fathers* ?
3: 7. Even from the days of *your fathers*
4: 6(3:24). turn the heart of *the fathers* to the
—(-:—). the heart of the children to *their fs.*,

---

1 **אָב** *āhv*, m.

Job 34:36. *My desire* (is that) Job may be tried (marg. *My father*, let Job be tried)

---

2 **אַב** *av*, m. Ch.

Ezr. 4:15. the book of the records of *thy fathers.*
5:12. after that *our fathers* had provoked
Dan. 2:23. O thou God of *my fathers*,
5: 2. the golden and silver vessels which *his f.*
11. and in the days of *thy father*
— the king Nebuchadnezzar *thy father*, the king, (I say), *thy father*,
13. whom the king *my f.* brought out of Jewry?
18. God gave Nebuchadnezzar *thy father*

---

3 **אֵב** [*ēhv*] m.

Job 8:12. Whilst it (is) yet *in his greenness*,
Cant.6:11. to see *the fruits of* the valley,

---

4 **אֵב** [*ēhv*] m. Ch.

Dan.4:12(9), 21(18). *and the fruit thereof* much,
14(11). and scatter *his fruit:*

---

6 **אָבַד** *āh-vad′*.

* KAL.—*Preterite.* *

Ex. 10: 7. knowest thou not yet that Egypt *is destroyed?*
Lev.26:38. *And ye shall perish* among the heathen,
Nu. 17:12(27). Behold, we die, *we perish*, *we* all *p.*
21:29. *thou art undone*, O people of Chemosh:
30. Heshbon *is perished* even unto Dibon,
Deu11:17. *and* (lest) *ye perish* quickly from off the
Jos.23:16. *and ye shall perish* quickly from off the
2 K. 9: 8. *For the* whole house of Ahab *shall perish* :
Est. 4:16. and if *I perish*, *I perish.*
Job 4: 7. who (ever) *perished*, being innocent?
11:20. they *shall not escape* (lit. flight *perished* from them; marg. *shall perish*),
18:17. His remembrance *shall perish*
30: 2. in whom old age *was perished?*
Ps. 9: 6(7). their memorial *is perished* with them.
10:16. the heathen *are perished* out of his land.
41: 5(6). When shall he die, *and* his name *perish?*
119:92. I *should* then *have perished* in mine afflict.
142: 4(5). refuge *failed* me; (marg. *perished* from)
146: 4. in that very day his thoughts *perish.*
Pro.11: 7. the hope of unjust (men) *perisheth.*
Ecc. 5:14(13). *But* those riches *perish* by evil travail:
9: 6. their envy, *is* now *perished;*
Isa. 29:14. *for* the wisdom of their wise (men) *shall perish*,
57: 1. The righteous *perisheth*, and no man
Jer. 6:21. and his friend *shall perish.*
7:28. truth *is perished*, and is cut off
9:12(11). the land *perisheth* (and) is burned up
25:35. *And* the shepherds *shall have no way to flee*, (marg. *and* flight *shall perish* from)
27:10. drive you out, *and ye should perish.*
15. *and* that *ye might perish*,
40:15. *and* the remnant in Judah *perish?*
48: 8. the valley *also shall perish*,
36. riches (that) he hath gotten *are perished.*
46. the people of Chemosh *perisheth:*
49: 7. *is* counsel *perished* from the prudent?
Lam.3:18. my hope *is perished* from the Lord:
Eze.12:22. *and* every vision *faileth?*
Eze.19: 5. her hope *was lost*,
26:17. How *art thou destroyed*,
37:11. Our bones are dried, *and* our hope *is lost:*
Joel 1:11. the harvest of the field *is perished.*
Am. 1: 8. *and* the remnant of the Philistines *shall perish*,
2:14. *Therefore* the flight *shall perish* from
3:15. *and* the houses of ivory *shall perish*,
Jon. 4:10. came up in a night, and *perished* in a night:
Mic. 4: 9. *is* thy counsellor *perished?*
7: 2. The good (man) *is perished* out of the earth:
Zec. 9: 5. *and* the king *shall perish* from Gaza,

KAL.—*Infinitive.*

Deu 4:26. ye shall soon *utterly* perish from off the land
7:20. hide themselves from thee, *be destroyed.*
8:19. that ye shall *surely* perish.
28:20. and until *thou perish* quickly;
22. they shall pursue thee until *thou perish.*
30:18. that ye shall *surely* perish, (and that)
Jos.23:13. until *ye perish* from off this good land
Pro.11:10. *and when* the wicked *perish*, (there is)
28:28. *but when they perish*, the righteous
Obad. 12. of Judah in the day of *their destruction;*

KAL.—*Future.*

Nu. 16:33. *and they perished* from among the congreg.
Deu 4:26. *ye shall* soon utterly *perish* from off the
8:19. that *ye shall* surely *perish.*
20. so *shall ye perish ;*
22: 3. of thy brother's, which *he hath lost*,
30:18. *ye shall* surely *perish*,
Jud. 5:31. So *let* all thine enemies *perish*, O Lord:
1Sa. 9: 3. *And* the asses of Kish Saul's f. *were lost.*
2Sa. 1:27. *and* the weapons of war *perished !*
Est. 4:14. and thy father's house *shall be destroyed:*
Job 3: 3. *Let* the day *perish* wherein I was born,
4: 9. By the blast of God *they perish*,
20. *they perish* for ever without any regarding
6:18. they go to nothing, *and perish.*
8:13. the hypocrite's hope *shall perish:*
20: 7. *he shall perish* for ever
Ps. 1: 6. the way of the ungodly *shall perish.*
2:12. lest he be angry, *and ye perish* (from) the
9: 3(4). they shall fall *and perish* at thy pres.
18(19). the expectation of the poor *shall* (not) *perish*
37:20. But the wicked *shall perish*,
49:10(11). the fool and the brutish person *perish*,
68: 2(3). as wax melteth before the fire, (so) *let* the wicked *perish*
73:27. *they* that are far from thee *shall perish :*
80:16(17). *they perish* at the rebuke of thy
83:17(18). let them be put to shame, *and perish:*
92: 9(10). lo, thine enemies *shall perish ;*
102:26(27). *They shall perish*, but thou shalt endu.:
112:10. the desire of the wicked *shall perish.*
Pro.10:28. the expectation of the wicked *shall perish.*
11: 7. a wicked man dieth, (his) expectation *shall perish:*
19: 9. (he that) speaketh lies *shall perish.*
21:28. A false witness *shall perish:*
Isa. 41:11. *and they* that strive with thee *shall perish.*
60:12. that will not serve thee *shall perish ;*
Jer. 4: 9. the heart of the king *shall perish*,
10:15. time of their visitation *they shall perish.*
18:18. the law *shall* not *perish* from the priest,
51:18. time of their visitation *they shall perish.*
Eze. 7:26. the law *shall perish* from the priest,
Jon. 1: 6. God will think upon us, that *we perish* not.
14. *let us* not *perish* for this man's life,
3: 9. from his fierce anger, that *we perish* not?

KAL.—*Participle.* Poel.

Deu26: 5. A Syrian *ready to perish* (was) my father,
32:28. they (are) a nation *void of* counsel,
1Sa. 9:20. as for thine asses *that were lost*
Job 4:11. The old lion *perisheth* for lack of prey,
29:13. The blessings of *him that was ready to perish*
31:19. If I have seen *any perish* for want of
Ps. 31:12(13). I am like a *broken* vessel. (marg. *that perisheth*)
119:176. I have gone astray like a *lost* sheep;
Pro.31: 6. Give strong drink *unto him that is ready to perish*,
Ecc. 7: 15. there is a just (man) *that perisheth* in his
Isa. 27:13. they shall come *which were ready to perish*

Jer.50: 6. My people hath been *lost* sheep:
Eze.34: 4. neither have ye sought *that which was lost;*
16. I will seek *that which was lost,*

* PIEL.—*Preterite.* *

Nu.33:52. *and destroy* all their pictures,
Deu12: 3. *and destroy* the names of them
2K. 13: 7. the king of Syria *had destroyed them,*
21: 3. Hezekiah his father *had destroyed;*
Ps. 9: 5(6). *thou hast destroyed* the wicked,
Jer.15: 7. *I will destroy* my people,
51:55. spoiled B., *and destroyed* out of her the
Lam 2: 9. *he hath destroyed* and broken her bars:
Eze. 6: 3. *and I will destroy* your high places.

PIEL.—*Infinitive.*

Deu12: 2. Ye shall *utterly* destroy all the places,
Est. 3: 9. let it be written *that they may be destroyed:* (marg. *to destroy them*)
13. to kill, *and to cause to perish,* all Jews,
4: 7. for the Jews, *to destroy them.*
7: 4. to be destroyed, to be slain, *and to perish.*
8: 5. which he wrote *to destroy* the Jews
11. to destroy, to slay, *and to cause to perish,*
9: 6. slew *and destroyed* five hundred men. (lit. *and to destroy*)
12. The Jews have slain *and destroyed*
24. devised against the Jews *to destroy them,*
— to consume them, *and to destroy them;*
Ps.119:95. wicked have waited for me *to destroy me:*
Ecc. 3: 6. A time to get, and a time *to lose;*
Jer. 12:17. I will utterly pluck up *and destroy*
Eze.22:27. to shed blood, (and) *to destroy* souls,

PIEL.—*Future.*

Nu.33:52. and *destroy* all their molten images,
Deu11: 4. *and* (how) the Lord *hath destroyed them*
12: 2. *Ye shall* utterly *destroy* all the places,
2K. 11: 1. *and destroyed* all the seed royal.
19:18. *therefore they have destroyed them.*
Job 12:23. He increaseth the nations, *and destroyeth them:*
Ps. 5: 6(7). *Thou shalt destroy* them that speak lea.:
21:10(11). Their fruit *shalt thou destroy* from the
Pro. 1:32. the prosperity of fools *shall destroy them.*
29: 3. he that keepeth company with harlots *spendeth* (his) substance.
Ecc. 7: 7. *and* a gift *destroyeth* the heart.
9:18. one sinner *destroyeth* much good.
Isa. 26:14. *and made* all their memory *to perish.*
37:19. *therefore they have destroyed them.*
Eze.28:16. *and I will destroy thee,* O covering cherub,
Zep. 2:13. against the north, *and destroy* Assyria;

PIEL.—*Participle.*

Jer. 23: 1. Woe be unto the pastors *that destroy* and

* HIPHIL.—*Preterite.* *

Lev.23:30. the same soul *will I destroy*
Nu.24:19. *and shall destroy* him that remaineth
Deu 7:24. *and thou shalt destroy* their name
9: 3. thou drive them out, *and destroy them*
Job 14:19. *thou destroyest* the hope of man.
Ps.143:12. *and destroy* all them that afflict my soul:
Jer. 25:10. *Moreover I will take* from them the voice (marg. *cause to perish*)
49:38. *and will destroy* from thence the king
Eze.25: 7. *and I will cause thee to perish* out of the
16. *and destroy* the remnant of the sea coast.
30:13. *I will also destroy* the idols,
32:13. *I will destroy also* all the beasts
Obad. 8. *Shall I* not in that day, saith the Lord, *even destroy*
Mic.5:10(9). *and I will destroy* thy chariots:
Zep. 2: 5. O Canaan,... *I will even destroy thee,*

HIPHIL.—*Infinitive.*

Deu 7:10. repayeth them that hate him to their face, *to destroy them:*
28:51. until *he have destroyed* thee.
63. the Lord will rejoice over you *to destroy*
Jos. 7: 7. the hand of the Amorites, *to destroy us?*
2K.10:19. to the intent *that he might destroy* the
24: 2. sent them against Judah *to destroy it,*
Jer. 1:10. to pull down, *and to destroy,*
18: 7. to pull down, *and to destroy* (it);
31:28. to throw down *and to destroy,*

HIPHIL.—*Future.*

Jer. 46: 8. *I will destroy* the city and the inhabitants

HIPHIL.—*Participle.*

Deu 8:20. the nations which the Lord *destroyeth*

אֲבַד [*ăvad*] Ch. 7

* P'AL.—*Future.* *

Jer. 10:11. they *shall perish* from the earth,

* APHEL.—*Infinitive.* *

Dan. 2:12. *to destroy* all the wise (men) of Babylon.
24. *to destroy* the wise (men) of Babylon·
7:26. to consume *and to destroy* (it) unto the

APHEL.—*Future.*

Dan. 2:18. Daniel and his fellows *should* not *perish*
24. *Destroy* not the wise (men) of Babylon:

* HOPHAL.—*Preterite.* *

Dan. 7:11. the beast was slain, *and* his body *destroyed,*

אֹבֵד *ōh-vēhd'*, m. 8

Nu. 24:20. end (shall be) *that he perish* for ever. (marg. even to *destruction*)
24. he also *shall perish* for ever. (*to destruction*)

אֲבַדֹּה *ăvad-dōh'*, f. 10

Pro.27:20. (כתיב) Hell *and destruction* are never full;

אֲבֵדָה *ăvēh-dāh'*, f. 9

Ex. 22: 9(8). for any manner of *lost thing,*
Lev. 6: 3(5:22). have found *that which was lost,*
4(-:23). *the lost thing* which he found,
Deu22: 3. with all *lost thing of* thy brother's,

אֲבַדּוֹן *ăvad-dōhn'*, m. 11

Job 26: 6. and *destruction hath* no covering.
28:22. *Destruction* and death say, We have heard
31:12. it (is) a fire (that) consumeth to *destruction,*
Ps. 88:11(12). (or) thy faithfulness *in destruction?*
Pro.15:11. Hell *and destruction* (are) before the Lord:
27:20. (קרי) Hell *and destruction* are never full;

אַבְדָן *av-dāhn'*, m. 12

Est. 9: 5. slaughter, *and destruction,*

אָבְדַן *ov-dan'*, m. 13

[Const. of אַבְדָן.]

Est. 8: 6. how can I endure to see *the destruction of*

אָבָה *āh-vāh'*. 14

Note.—Except Is. 1:19. and Job 39:9. it is always accompanied by a negation.

* KAL.—*Preterite.* *

Ex. 10:27. *he would* not let them go.
Deu. 1:26. Notwithstanding *ye would* not go up,
2:30. Sihon king of H. *would* not let us pass
10:10. the Lord *would* not destroy thee.
23: 5(6). the Lord thy God *would* not hearken
25: 7. *he will* not perform the duty
Jos.24:10. But *I would* not hearken unto Balaam;
Jud.11:17. the king of Moab: but *he would* not
19:10. the man *would* not tarry that night,
25. the men *would* not hearken to him:
20:13. the children of B. *would* not hearken
1Sa.15: 9. and *would* not utterly destroy them:
22:17. the servants of the king *would* not
26:23. *I would* not stretch forth mine hand

1Sa.31: 4. his armourbearer *would* not;
2Sa. 2:21. Asahel *would* not turn aside
6:10. David *would* not remove the ark
12:17. *he would* not, neither did he eat bread
13:14. *he would* not hearken unto her voice:
16. *he would* not hearken unto her.
25. he pressed him: howbeit *he would* not go,
14:29. *he would* not come to him: and when he sent again the second time, *he would* not
23:16. nevertheless *he would* not drink thereof,
17. therefore *he would* not drink it.
1K. 22:49(50). But Jehoshaphat *would* not.
2K. 8:19. the Lord *would* not destroy Judah
13:23. and *would* not destroy them,
24: 4. which the Lord *would* not pardon.
1Ch 10: 4. his armourbearer *would* not;
11:18. David *would* not drink (of) it, but poured
19. Therefore *he would* not drink it.
19:19. neither *would* the Syrians help
2Ch 21: 7. the Lord *would* not destroy the house of
Ps. 81:11(12). Israel *would* none of me.
Pro. 1:25. and *would* none of my reproof:
30. *They would* none of my counsel:
Isa. 28:12. *they would* not hear.
30: 9. children (that) *will* not hear
15. and *ye would* not.
42:24. *they would* not walk in his ways,
Eze.20: 8. they rebelled against me, and *would* not

KAL.—*Future.*

Gen24: 5. Peradventure the woman *will* not *be willing*
8. if the woman *will* not *be willing*
Lev. 26:21. if ye walk contrary unto me, and *will* not
Deu 13: 8(9). *Thou shalt* not *consent* unto him,
29:20(19). The Lord *will* not spare him,
1K. 20: 8. Hearken not (unto him), nor *consent.*
Job 39: 9. *Will* the unicorn *be willing* to serve thee,
Pro. 1:10. if sinners entice thee, *consent thou* not.
6:35. neither *will he rest content,*
Isa. 1:19. If *ye be willing* and obedient,
Eze. 3: 7. the house of Israel *will* not hearken

KAL.—*Participle.* Poel.

Eze. 3: 7. they *will* not hearken unto me:

---

16 אֶבֶה *ēh-vĕh′*, m.

Job 9:26. They are passed away as the *swift* ships: (marg. Ships "of desire," or "of Ebeh")

---

17 אֲבוֹי *ăvōhy.*

Pro.23:29. Who hath woe? who hath *sorrow?*

---

18 אֵבוּס *ēh-voos′*, m.

Job 39: 9. to serve thee, or abide by *thy crib?*
Pro.14: 4. Where no oxen (are), *the crib* (is) clean:
Isa. 1: 3. the ass his master's *crib:*

---

19 אִבְחַת *iv-ghath′*, f.

[Const. of אִבְחָה.]

Eze.21:15(20). I have set the *point of* the sword (marg. "glittering," or "fear")

---

20 אֲבַטִּחִים *ăvat-tee-gheem′*, m. pl.

Nu. 11: 5. *the melons*, and the leeks,

---

24 אָבִיב *āh-veev′*, m.

Ex. 9:31. the barley (was) *in the ear*,
13: 4. This day came ye out in the month *Abib.*
23:15. in the time appointed of the month *Abib;*
34:18. in the time of the month *Abib:* for in the month *Abib* thou camest out
Lev. 2:14. of thy firstfruits *green ears of corn*
Deu16: 1. Observe the month of *Abib,*
— in the month of *Abib* the Lord thy God
Eze. 3:15. came to them of the captivity at Tel-*abib,*

אֶבְיוֹן *ev-yōhn′*, adj. 34

Ex.23: 6. shalt not wrest the judgment of *thy poor*
11. that *the poor of* thy people may eat:
Deu 15: 4. when there shall be no *poor* among you;
7. If there be among you *a poor man*
— nor shut thine hand from thy *poor* brother:
9. thine eye be evil against thy *poor* brother,
11. *the poor* shall never cease out of the land:
— to thy poor, *and to thy needy*, in thy land.
24:14. not oppress an hired servant (that is) poor *and needy,*
1 Sa. 2: 8. lifteth up *the beggar* from the dunghill,
Est. 9:22. portions one to another, and gifts *to the poor.*
Job 5:15. he saveth *the poor* from the sword,
24: 4. They turn *the needy* out of the way:
14. rising with the light killeth the poor *and needy,*
29:16. I (was) a father *to the poor:*
30:25. was (not) my soul grieved *for the poor?*
31:19. or *any poor* without covering; (lit. no covering *to the poor*)
Ps. 9:18(19). *the needy* shall not alway be
12: 5(6). for the sighing of *the needy.*
35:10. the poor *and the needy* from him that spoi.
37:14. to cast down the poor *and needy,*
40:17(18). But I (am) poor *and needy;*
49: 2(3). low and high, rich *and poor*, together.
69:33(34). the Lord heareth *the poor,*
70: 5(6). But I (am) poor *and needy:*
72: 4. he shall save the children of *the needy,*
12. he shall deliver *the needy* when he crieth;
13. He shall spare the poor *and needy*, and shall save the souls of *the needy.*
74:21. let the poor *and needy* praise thy name.
82: 4. Deliver the poor *and needy:*
86: 1. for I (am) poor *and needy.*
107:41. setteth he *the poor* on high from affliction,
109:16. persecuted the poor *and needy* man,
22. For I (am) poor *and needy,*
31. he shall stand at the right hand of *the poor,*
112: 9. hath dispersed, he hath given *to the poor;*
113: 7. (and) lifteth *the needy* out of the dunghill;
132.15. I will satisfy *her poor* with bread.
140:12(13). will maintain...the right of *the poor.*
Pro.14:31. honoureth him hath mercy on *the poor.*
30:14. *and the needy* from (among) men.
31: 9. plead the cause of the poor *and needy.*
20. she reacheth forth her hands *to the needy.*
Isa. 14:30. *and the needy* shall lie down in safety:
25: 4. a strength *to the needy* in his distress,
29:19. *and the poor among* men shall rejoice in
32: 7. even when *the needy* speaketh right.
41:17. (When) the poor *and needy* seek water,
Jer. 2:34. the blood of the souls of the *poor*
5:28. the right of *the needy* do they not judge.
20:13. he hath delivered the soul of *the poor*
22:16. He judged the cause of the poor *and needy;*
Eze.16:49. neither did she strengthen the hand of the poor *and needy.*
18:12. Hath oppressed the poor *and needy,*
22:29. and have vexed the poor *and needy:*
Am. 2: 6. *and the poor* for a pair of shoes;
4: 1. oppress the poor, which crush *the needy,*
5:12. *and* they turn aside *the poor* in the gate
8: 4. O ye that swallow up *the needy,*
6. *and the needy* for a pair of shoes;

אֲבִיּוֹנָה *ăveey-yōh-nāh′*, f. 14

Ecc.12: 5. and *desire* shall fail:

אַבִּיר *ab-beer′*, adj. 47

Jud. 5:22. pransings of *their* (lit. his) *mighty ones.*
1Sa.21: 7(8). *the chiefest of* the herdmen
Job 24:22. He draweth also *the mighty* with his
34:20. *the mighty* shall be taken away
Ps. 22:12(13). *strong* (bulls) *of* Bashan have beset
50:13. Will I eat the flesh of *bulls*, or drink
68:30(31). the multitude of *the bulls,*
76: 5(6). *The stout*hearted are spoiled,
78:25. Man did eat *angels'* food: (marg. the bread of *the mighty*)

Isa. 10:13. put down the inhab. *like a valiant* (man): (marg: *many people*) see כַּבִּיר.
34: 7. the bullocks with *the bulls;*
46:12. Hearken unto me, *ye stout*hearted,
Jer. 8:16. sound of the neighing of *his strong ones;*
46.15. Why are *thy valiant* (men) swept away?
47: 3. of the hoofs of *his strong* (horses),
50:11. as the heifer at grass, and bellow *as bulls;*
Lam. 1:15. trodden under foot all *my mighty* (men)

46 אֲבִיר *ăveer′*, m.

[Const. of אָבִיר.]

Gen49:24. made strong by the hands of *the mighty* (God) *of* Jacob;
Ps.132: 2. vowed *unto the mighty* (God) *of* Jacob;
5. an habitation *for the mighty* (God) *of*
Isa. 1:24. Lord of hosts, *the mighty* One *of* Israel,
49:26 & 60:16. thy Redeemer, *the mighty* One *of*

55 אָבַךְ [*āh-vach′*].

* HITHPAEL.—*Future.* *

Isa. 9:18(17). *and they shall mount up* (like) the lifting up of smoke.

56 אָבַל *āh-val′*

* KAL.—*Preterite.* *

Isa. 3:26. her gates shall lament *and mourn;*
19: 8. that cast angle into the brooks *shall lament,*
24: 4. The earth *mourneth* (and) fadeth away,
7. The new wine *mourneth,*
33: 9. The earth *mourneth* (and) languisheth:
Jer. 12:11. (being) desolate it *mourneth* unto me;
14: 2. Judah *mourneth,* and the gates
23:10. because of swearing the land *mourneth;*
Hos 10: 5. for the people thereof *shall mourn* over it,
Joel 1: 9. the priests, the Lord's ministers, *mourn.*
10. The field is wasted, the land *mourneth;*
Am. 1: 2. *and* the habitations of the shepherds *shall mourn,*
8: 8. *and* every one *mourn* that dwelleth
9: 5. *and* all that dwell therein *shall mourn:*

KAL.—*Future.*

Job 14:22. his soul within him *shall mourn.*
Jer. 4:28. For this *shall* the earth *mourn,*
12: 4. How long *shall* the land *mourn,*
Hos. 4: 3. Therefore *shall* the land *mourn,*

* HIPHIL.—*Preterite.* *

Eze.31:15. when he went down to the grave *I caused a mourning:*

HIPHIL.—*Future.*

Lam. 2: 8. *therefore he made* the rampart and the wall *to lament;*

* HITHPAEL.—*Preterite.* *

1Sa. 15:35. Samuel *mourned* for Saul:

HITHPAEL.—*Imperative.*

2Sa. 14: 2. *feign thyself to be a mourner,*

HITHPAEL.—*Future.*

Gen37:34. *and mourned* for his son many days.
Ex. 33: 4. heard these evil tidings, *they mourned*
Nu. 14:39. *and* the people *mourned* greatly.
1Sa. 6:19. *and* the people *lamented,* because
2Sa. 13:37. *And* (David) *mourned* for his son every
19: 1(2). the king weepeth *and mourneth*
1Ch. 7:22. *And* Ephraim their father *mourned* many
Neh. 1: 4. I...wept, *and mourned* (certain) days,
8: 9. *mourn* not, nor weep.
Eze. 7:12. the buyer rejoice, nor the seller *mourn:*
27. The king *shall mourn,* and the prince

HITHPAEL.—*Participle.*

1Sa. 16: 1. How long *wilt* thou *mourn* for Saul,
2Sa. 14: 2. *that had* a long time *mourned* for the
2Ch 35:24. all Judah and Jerusalem *mourned* for
Ezr. 10: 6. he *mourned* because of the transgression
Isa. 66:10. all ye *that mourn* for her:

Dan. 10: 2. I Daniel *was mourning* three full weeks.

אָבֵל *ăh-vehl′*, adj. 57

Gen37:35. into the grave unto my son *mourning.*
Est. 6:12. Haman hasted to his house *mourning,*
Job 29:25. as one (that) comforteth *the mourners.*
Ps. 35:14. *as one that mourneth* (*for* his) mother.
Isa. 57:18. comforts unto him *and to his mourners.*
61: 2. to comfort all *that mourn;*
3. To appoint *unto them that mourn in* Zion,
Lam. 1: 4. The ways of Zion *do mourn,*

אָבֵל *āh-vehl′*, f. 58

Jud. 11:33. unto *the plain of* the vineyards, (marg. or, Abel)

NOTE.—In like manner, Jud. 7:22. &c. *Abel-*meholah, might be rendered *the plain of* dancing, &c. &c.

אֲבָל *ăvāhl*, conj. 61

Gen17:19. thy wife shall bear thee a son *indeed;*
42:21. We (are) *verily* guilty concerning our
2Sa. 14: 5. I (am) *indeed* a widow woman,
1 K. 1:43. *Verily* our lord king David hath made
2 K. 4:14. *Verily* she hath no child,
2 Ch. 1: 4. *But* the ark of God had David brought
19: 3. *Nevertheless* there are good things found
33:17. *Nevertheless* the people did sacrifice
Ezr. 10:13. *But* the people (are) many,
Dan 10: 7. *but* a great quaking fell upon them,
21. *But* I will shew thee that which is noted

אֵבֶל *ēh′-vel*, m. 60

Gen27:41. The days of *mourning for* my father
50:10. he made a *mourning for* his father
11. saw *the mourning* in the floor of Atad, they said, This (is) *a grievous mourning*
Deu34: 8. the days of weeping (and) *mourning for*
2 Sa 11:27. And when *the mourning* was past,
14: 2. put on now *mourning* apparel,
19: 2(3). that day was (turned) *into mourning*
Est. 4: 3. (there was) great *mourning* among the
9:22. *and from mourning* into a good day:
Job 30:31. My harp also is (turned) *to mourning,*
Ecc. 7: 2. better to go to the house of *mourning,*
4. of the wise (is) in the house of *mourning;*
Isa. 60:20. the days of *thy mourning* shall be ended.
61: 3. the oil of joy for *mourning,*
Jer. 6:26. make thee *mourning,* (as for) an only son,
16: 7. tear (themselves) for them in *mourning,*
31:13. I will turn *their mourning* into joy,
Lam. 5:15. our dance is turned *into mourning.*
Eze. 24:17. make no *mourning* for the dead,
Am. 5:16. they shall call the husbandman to *mourning,*
8:10. I will turn your feasts *into mourning,*
— I will make it *as the mourning of* an only
Mic. 1: 8. *and mourning* as the owls.

אֻבָל see אוּבָל. See 180

אֶבֶן *eh′-ven*, f. 68

Gen. 2:12. bdellium *and the* onyx *stone.*
11: 3. And they had brick *for stone,*
28:11. he took *of the stones of* that place,
18. *the stone* that he had put (for) his pillows,
22. *And* this *stone,* wh. I have set (for) a pillar,
29: 2. *and a* great *stone* (was) upon the well's m.
3. rolled *the stone* from the well's mouth,
— put *the stone* again upon the well's mouth
8. (till) they roll *the stone* fr. the well's mouth;
10. and rolled *the stone* from the well's mouth,
31:45. Jacob took *a stone,* and set it up (for) a pillar.
46. said unto his brethren, Gather *stones;* and they took *stones,* and made an heap:

Gen 35:14. (even) a pillar of *stone:*
49:24. thence (is) the shepherd, *the stone of* Isr.:
Ex. 7:19. (vessels of) wood, *and in* (vessels of) *stone.*
15: 5. they sank into the bottom as *a stone.*
16. they shall be (as) still *as a stone;*
17:12. they took *a stone*, and put (it) under him,
20:25. if thou wilt make me an altar of *stone*,
21:18. one smite another *with a stone*,
24:12. I will give thee tables of *stone*,
25: 7. Onyx *stones, and stones* to be set in
28: 9. thou shalt take two onyx *stones*,
10. names on one *stone*, and (the other) six names of the rest on *the* other *stone*,
11. the work of an engraver in *stone*,
— shalt thou engrave *the* two *stones*
12. thou shalt put *the* two *stones*
— *stones of* memorial unto the children of Is.:
17. set in it settings of *stones*, (even) four rows of *stones:*
21. *And the stones* shall be with the names
31: 5. And in cutting of *stones*, to set (them),
18. tables of *stone*, written with the finger of
34: 1. Hew thee two tables of *stone*
4. And he hewed two tables of *stone*
— took in his hand the two tables of *stone.*
35: 9. *And* onyx *stones, and stones* to be set for
27. the rulers brought onyx *stones*, and *stones*
33. And in the cutting of *stones*,
39: 6. And they wrought onyx *stones*
7. *stones for* a memorial to the children of Is.;
10. And they set in it four rows of *stones:*
14. *And the stones* (were) according to
Lev. 14:40. take away *the stones* in which the plague
42. they shall take other *stones*, and put (them) in the place of *those stones;*
43. he hath taken away *the stones*,
45. break down the house, *the stones of it*,
19:36. Just balances, just *weights*, (marg. *stones*)
20: 2. stone him *with stones.*
27. they shall stone them *with stones:*
24:23. and stone him with *stones.*
26: 1. *neither* shall ye set up (any) image of *stone*
Nu. 14:10. stone them *with stones.*
15:35. stone him *with stones* without the camp.
36. stoned him *with stones*, and he died;
35:17. if he smite him *with* throwing *a stone*,
23. any *stone*, wherewith a man may die,
Deu 4:13. he wrote them upon two tables of *stone.*
28. the work of men's hands, wood *and stone*,
5:22(19). he wrote them in two tables of *stone*,
8: 9. a land *whose stones* (are) iron,
9: 9. to receive the tables of *stone*,
10. the Lord delivered unto me two tables of *s.*
11. the Lord gave me the two tables of *stone*,
10: 1. Hew thee two tables of *stone*
3. hewed two tables of *stone*
13:10(11). thou shalt stone him *with stones*,
17: 5. and shalt stone them *with stones*,
21:21. shall stone him *with stones*,
22:21. shall stone her *with stones*
24. ye shall stone them *with stones*
25:13. Thou shalt not have in thy bag *divers weights*, (marg. *a stone and a stone*)
15. thou shalt have a perfect and just *weight*,
27: 2. thou shalt set thee up great *stones*,
4. ye shall set up these *stones*,
5. unto the Lord thy God, an altar of *stones:*
6. altar of the Lord thy God of whole *stones:*
8. write upon *the stones* all the words of this
28:36. serve other gods, wood *and stone.*
64. (even) wood *and stone.*
29:17(16). and their idols, wood *and stone*,
Jos. 4: 3. where the priests' feet stood firm, twelve *stones*,
5. take you up every man of you a *stone*
6. What (mean) ye by these *stones?*
7. these *stones* shall be for a memorial
8. took up twelve *stones* out of the midst
9. Joshua set up twelve *stones*
20. those twelve *stones*, which they took
21. What (mean) these *stones?*
7:25. all Israel stoned him with *stones*,
— after they had stoned them *with stones.*
26. raised over him a great heap of *stones*
8:29. raise thereon a great heap of *stones*,
31. an altar of whole *stones*,
32. he wrote there upon *the stones* a copy

Jos. 10:11. the Lord cast down great *stones* from
— more which died *with* hail*stones*
18. Roll great *stones* upon the mouth of the
27. laid great *stones* in the cave's mouth,
15: 6. the border went up to *the stone of* Bohan
18:17. descended to *the stone of* Bohan
24:26. took *a* great *stone*, and set it up there
27. Behold, this *stone* shall be a witness
Jud. 9: 5, 18. threescore and ten persons, upon one *stone:*
20:16. every one could sling *stones* at an hair
1Sa. 6:14. where (there was) *a* great *stone:*
15. put (them) on *the* great *stone:*
7:12. Then Samuel took *a stone*,
— called the name of it *Eben*-ezer,
14:33. roll *a* great *stone* unto me this day.
17:40. chose him five smooth *stones*
49. took thence *a stone*, and slang (it),
— *the stone* sunk into his forehead;
50. with a sling *and with a stone*,
20:19. and shalt remain by *the stone* Ezel.
25:37. he became (*as*) *a stone.*
2Sa. 5:11. carpenters, and *masons:* (marg. hewers of *the stone of* the wall)
12:30. a talent of gold *with the* precious *stones:*
14:26. *after the* king's *weight.*
16: 6. And he cast *stones* at David, (lit. he stoned...*with stones*)
13. threw *stones* at him,
18:17. laid a very great heap of *stones* upon him:
20: 8. When they (were) at *the* great *stone*
1 K. 1: 9. by *the stone of* Zoheleth,
5:17(31). brought great *stones*, costly *stones*, (and) hewed *stones*, to lay the foundation
18(32). they prepared timber *and stones*
6: 7. was built of *stone* made ready
18. all (was) cedar; there was no *stone* seen.
7: 9. All these (were of) costly *stones*,
10. the foundation (was of) costly *stones*, even great *stones*, *stones of* ten cubits, and *stones of* eight
11. And above (were) costly *stones*,
8: 9. save the two tables of *stone*,
10: 2. very much gold, *and* precious *stones:*
10. of spices very great store, *and* preciou *stones:*
11. plenty of almug trees, *and* precious *stones.*
27. made silver (to be) in Jerusalem *as stones*
12:18. all Israel stoned him with *stones*,
15:22. they took away *the stones of* Ramah,
18:31. Elijah took twelve *stones*, according to
32. with *the stones* he built an altar
38. the wood, and *the stones*, and the dust,
21:13. stoned him *with stones*, that he died.
2 K. 3:19. mar every good piece of land *with stones*
25. cast every man *his stone*, and filled it;
— left they *the stones thereof;*
12:12(13). And to masons, and hewers of *stone*, and to buy timber *and* hewed *stone*
16:17. put it upon a pavement of *stones.*
19:18. the work of men's hands, wood *and stone:*
22: 6. to buy timber *and* hewn *stone* to repair
1Ch. 12: 2. hand and the left *in* (hurling) *stones*
20: 2. (there were) precious *stones* in it;
22: 2. he set masons to hew wrought *stones*
14. timber also *and stone* have I prepared;
15. workers of *stone* and timber,
29: 2. onyx *stones*, and (stones) to be set, glistering *stones*, and of divers colours, and all manner of precious *stones, and* marble *stones* in abundance.
8. they with whom (precious) *stones* were
2Ch. 1:15. gold at Jerusalem (as plenteous) *as stones*,
2:14(13). in silver, in brass, in iron, *in stone*,
3: 6. with precious *stones* for beauty:
9: 1. gold in abundance, *and* precious *stones:*
9. of spices great abundance, *and* precious *stones:*
10. brought algum trees *and* precious *stones.*
27. made silver in Jerusalem *as stones*,
10:18. stoned him with *stones*, that he died.
16: 6. they carried away *the stones of* Ramah,
24:21. and stoned him with *stones*
26:14. *and* slings (to cast) *stones.* (marg. *and for stones of* slings)
15. to shoot arrows *and* great *stones*
32:27. treasuries...for gold, *and for* precious *s*

2Ch 34:11. to buy hewn *stone*,
Neh. 4: 2(3:34). will they revive *the stones* out of
3(–:35). break down *their stone* wall.
9:11. as *a stone* into the mighty waters.
Job 5:23. be in league with *the stones of* the field:
6:12. (Is) my strength the strength of *stones?*
8:17. seeth the place of *stones*.
14:19. The waters wear *the stones:*
28: 2. *and* brass (is) molten (out of) *the stone*.
3. *the stones of* darkness, and the shadow of
6. *The stones of it* (are) the place of sapphires:
38: 6. or who laid *the* corner *stone* thereof;
30. The waters are hid *as* (with) *a stone*,
41:24(16). His heart is as firm as *a stone;*
28(20). sling*stones* are turned with him into
Ps. 91:12. lest thou dash thy foot *against a stone*.
102:14(15). thy servants take pleasure in *her ss.*,
118:22. *The stone* (which) the builders refused
Pro. 11: 1. *but a* just *weight* (is) his delight. (marg. *a* perfect *stone*)
16:11. all the *weights of* the bag (marg. *stones*)
17: 8. A gift (is as) *a* precious *stone* in the eyes
20:10. *Divers weights*, (and) divers measures, (marg. *A stone and a stone*)
23. *Divers weights* (are) an abomination (lit. *a stone and a stone*)
24:31. *the stone* wall *thereof* was broken down.
26: 8. As he that bindeth *a stone* in a sling,
27. he that rolleth *a stone*, it will return
27: 3. *A stone* (is) heavy, and the sand weighty;
Ecc. 3: 5. A time to cast away *stones*, and a time to gather *stones* together;
10: 9. Whoso removeth *stones* shall be hurt
Isa. 8:14. *but for a stone* of stumbling
14:19. that go down to *the stones of* the pit;
27: 9. when he maketh all *the stones of* the altar *as* chalk*stones* that are beaten in sunder,
28:16. in Zion for a foundation *a stone*, a tried *stone*,
30:30. scattering, and tempest, *and* hail*stones*.
34:11. *and the stones of* emptiness.
37:19. work of men's hands, wood *and stone:*
54:11. I will lay *thy stones* with fair colours,
12. thy gates of carbuncles (lit. *stones of* a sparkling gem), and all thy borders *of* pleasant *stones*.
60:17. for wood brass, and for *stones* iron:
62:10. gather *out the stones;*
Jer. 2:27. *and to a stone*, Thou hast brought me
3: 9. committed adultery with *stones* and
43: 9. Take great *stones* in thine hand,
10. will set his throne upon these *stones*
51:26. *a stone* for a corner, *nor a stone* for found.;
63. thou shalt bind *a stone* to it,
Lam. 3:53. cast *a stone* upon me.
4: 1. *the stones of* the sanctuary are poured out
Eze. 1:26. as the appearance of *a* sapphire *stone:*
10: 1. there appeared over them *as it were a* sapphire *stone*,
9. of the wheels (was) as the colour of *a* beryl *stone*.
11:19. I will take the *stony* heart out of their flesh, (lit. heart of *stone*)
13:11. ye, O great hail*stones*, shall fall;
13. *and* great hail*stones* in (my) fury
16:40. they shall stone thee *with stones*,
20:32. to serve wood *and stone*.
23:47. the company shall stone them with *stones*,
26:12. *and* they shall lay *thy stones*
27:22. with all precious *stones*, and gold.
28:13. every precious *stone* (was) thy covering,
14. walked up and down in the midst of *the stones of* fire.
16. from the midst of *the stones of* fire.
36:26. I will take away the *stony* heart
38:22. *and* great hail*stones*, fire, and brimstone.
40:42. the four tables (were) of hewn *stone*
Dan 11:38. gold, and silver, *and with* precious *stones*,
Mic. 1: 6. I will pour down *the stones thereof*
6:11. and with the bag of deceitful *weights?*
Hab. 2:11. For *the stone* shall cry out of the wall,
19. *to the* dumb *stone*, Arise,
Hag. 2:15. before *a stone* was laid upon *a stone*
Zec. 3: 9. For behold *the stone* that I have laid
— upon one *stone* (shall be) seven eyes:
4: 7. he shall bring forth *the* head*stone*
10. shall see the plummet in the hand of Zerubbabel (marg. *stone of* tin)
Zec. 5: 4. the timber thereof and *the stones thereof*.
8. he cast *the weight of* lead upon the
9:15. shall devour, and subdue with sling *stones*.
16. (they shall be as) *the stones of* a crown,
12: 3. *a* burdensome *stone* for all people:

אֶבֶן *ĕh'-ven*, f. Ch. 69

Ezr. 5: 8. which is builded with great *stones*,
6: 4. three rows of great *stones*,
Dan. 2:34. Thou sawest till that *a stone*
35. *and the stone* that smote the image
45. thou sawest that *the stone*
5: 4. of iron, of wood, *and* of *stone*.
23. of brass, iron, wood, *and stone*,
6:17(18). And *a stone* was brought,

אַבְנֵט *av-nēht'*, m. 73

Ex. 28: 4. a broidered coat, a mitre, *and a girdle*
39. *and* thou shalt make *the girdle*
40. thou shalt make for them *girdles*,
29: 9. thou shalt gird them with *girdles*,
39:29. *a girdle* (of) fine twined linen,
Lev. 8: 7. girded him *with the girdle*,
13. girded them with *girdles*,
16: 4. *and* shall be girded *with a* linen *girdle*,
Isa. 22:21. *and* strengthen him *with thy girdle*,

אָבְנַיִם *ov-nah'-yim*, f. 70

[Dual, in pause, of אֹבֶן.]

Ex. 1:16. see (them) upon *the stools;* if it (be) a
Jer. 18: 3. behold, he wrought a work on *the wheels*, (marg. *frames*, or, *seats*)

אָבַס [*āh-vas'*]. 75

* KAL.—*Participle*. Päul. *

1 K. 4:23(5:3). fallowdeer, and *fatted* fowl.
Pro. 15:17. than a *stalled* ox and hatred therewith.

אֲבַעְבֻּעֹת *ăvag-boo gōth'*, f. pl. 76

Ex. 9: 9. 10. a boil breaking forth (with) *blains*

אָבָק *āh-vāhk'*, m. 80

Ex. 9: 9. And it shall become *small dust*
Deu 28:24. shall make the rain of thy land *powder*
Isa. 5:24. their blossom shall go up *as dust:*
29: 5. strangers shall be *like* small *dust*,
Eze. 26:10. *their dust* shall cover thee
Nah. 1: 3. the clouds (are) *the dust of* his feet.

אָבַק [*āh-vak'*]. 79

* NIPHAL.—*Infinitive*. *

Gen 32:25(26). *as he wrestled* with him.

NIPHAL.—*Future*.

Gen 32:24(25). *and there wrestled* a man with him

אֲבָקַת *av-kath'*, f. 81

[Const. of אֲבָקָה.]

Cant. 3: 6. with all *powders of* the merchant?

אָבַר [*āh-var'*]. 82

* HIPHIL.—*Future*. *

Job 39:26. *Doth* the hawk *fly* by thy wisdom,

אֵבֶר *ēh'-ver*, m. 83

Ps. 55: 6(7). O that I had *wings* like a dove!

Isa. 40:31. they shall mount up with *wings*
Eze 17: 3. long-*winged*, full of feathers,

---

84 **אֶבְרָה** *ev-rāh'*, f.

Deu 32:11. beareth them on *her wings:*
Job 39:13. or *wings* and feathers unto the ostrich? (marg. *feathers* of the stork)
Ps. 68:13(14). *and her feathers* with yellow gold.
91: 4. He shall cover thee *with his feathers*,

---

86 **אַבְרֵךְ** *av-rēhch'*.

Gen 41:43. cried before him, *Bow the knee:* (marg. or, *Tender father*)

Note.—E. T. takes it for Hiph. אַבְרִיךְ I will cause to bow the knee.

---

92 **אֲגֻדָּה** *ăgud-dāh'*, f.

Ex. 12:22. ye shall take *a bunch of* hyssop,
2Sa. 2:25. after Abner, and became one *troop*,
Isa. 58: 6. to undo the heavy *burdens*, (marg. *bundles of* the yoke)
Am. 9: 6. *and* hath founded *his troop* in the earth; (marg. *bundle*)

---

93 **אֱגוֹז** *ĕgōhz*, m.

Cant. 6:11. I went down into the garden of *nuts*

---

95 **אֲגוֹרַת** *ăgōh-rath'*, f

[Const. of אֲגוֹרָה.]

1Sa. 2:36. crouch to him *for a piece of* silver

---

96 **אֶגְלֵי** *eg-lēy'*, m.

[Pl. const. of אֵגֶל.]

Job 38:28. who hath begotten *the drops of* dew?

98, 99 **אֲגַם** *ăgāhm*, m.

Ex. 7:19. upon their rivers, and upon *their ponds*,
8: 5(1). over the rivers, and over *the ponds*,
Ps. 107:35. the wilderness *into a standing* water, (lit. *to a pool of* water)
114: 8. turned the rock (into) *a standing* water, (lit. id.)
Isa. 14:23. *and pools of* water.
19:10. all that make sluices (and) *ponds for* fish.
35: 7. parched ground shall become *a pool*,
41:18. the wilderness *a pool of* water,
42:15. *and* I will dry up *the pools*.
Jer. 51:32. *the reeds* they have burned with fire,

Note.—Isa. 19:10. "ponds for fish;" so Luther, Diodati & Vulg LXX. οἱ τὸν ζύθον ποιοῦντες λυπηθήσονται, ϗ τὰς ψυχὰς πονέσουσι.—They that make barley wine (*i.e.* beer) shall mourn, and be grieved in soul.—*Lowth*.

---

100 **אַגְמוֹן** *ag-mōhn'*, m.

Job 41: 2(40:26). Canst thou put *an hook* into his nose? (lit. *a rush*)
20(12). as (out) of a seething pot *or caldron*.
Isa. 9:14(13). head and tail, branch *and rush*,
19:15. head or tail, branch *or rush*,
58: 5. bow down his head *as a bulrush*,

See 98 **אַגְמֵי** *ag-mēy'*, adj. afflicted.

Pl. const. See note under אֲגַם.

אַגַּן *ag-gan'*, m. 101

[Const. of אַגָּן.]

Ex. 24: 6. took half of the blood, and put (it) *in basons;*
Cant. 7: 2(3). Thy navel (is like) *a* round *goblet*,
Isa. 22:24. from the vessels of *cups*, even to all

אֲגַפִּים [*ăgap-peem'*], m. pl. 102

Eze 12:14. to help him, and all *his bands;*
17:21. fugitives with all *his bands* shall fall by the
38: 6. Gomer, and all *his bands;*
— the north quarters, and all *his bands:*
9. cover the land, thou, and all *thy bands*,
22. I will rain upon him, and upon *his bands*,
39: 4. fall upon the mountains of Israel, thou, and all *thy bands*,

---

אָגַר [*āh-gar'*] 103

* KAL.—*Preterite.* *

Pro. 6: 8. *gathereth* her food in the harvest.

KAL.—*Future.*

Deu 28:39. nor *gather* (the grapes);

KAL.—*Participle.* Poel.

Pro. 10: 5. *He that gathereth* in summer (is) a wise son:

אִגְּרָא *ig-g'rāh'*, f. Ch. 104

Ezr. 4: 8. and Shimshai the scribe wrote *a letter*
11 & 5:6. the copy of *the letter*

אֶגְרוֹף *eg-rōph'*, m. 106

Ex. 21:18. or *with* (his) *fist*, and he die not,
Isa. 58: 4. to smite *with the fist* of wickedness.

אֲגַרְטְלֵי *ăgar-t'lēy'*, m. 105

[Pl. const.]

Ezr. 1: 9. thirty *chargers of* gold, a thousand *chargers of* silver,

---

אִגֶּרֶת *ig-geh'-reth*, f. 107

2Ch 30: 1. wrote *letters* also to Ephraim and Manasseh,
6. So the posts went *with the letters*
Neh. 2: 7. If it please the king, let *letters* be given
8. *And a letter* unto Asaph the keeper of
9. gave them *the* king's *letters*.
6: 5. *with an* open *letter* in his hand;
17. sent many *letters* unto Tobiah, (marg. multiplied *their letters*)
19. Tobiah sent *letters* to put me in fear.
Est. 9:26. for all the words of this *letter*,
29. to confirm this second *letter of* Purim.

אֵד *ēhd*, m. 108

Gen 2: 6. *But* there went up *a mist* from the earth,
Job 36:27. rain according *to the vapour thereof:*

אָדַב [*āh-dav'*]. 109

* HIPHIL.—*Infinitive.* *

1Sa. 2:33. *and to grieve* thine heart:

אֲדוֹם see **אָדֹם**. See 122

113 אָדוֹן *āh-dōhn'*, m.

N.B. אֲדֹנַי Gen. 19:2. "my lords," and *perhaps* Gen. 19:18. the same, only in pause. See the article אֲדֹנָי.

Gen18:12. *my lord* being old *also?*
19: 2. And he said, Behold now, *my lords,*
18. And Lot said unto them, Oh, not so, *my Lord:* (lit. that is if (ָ) is here in pause for (ַ) *my lords*)
23: 6. Hear us, *my lord:* thou (art) a mighty
11. Nay, *my lord,* hear me:
15. *My lord,* hearken unto me:
24: 9. under the thigh of Abraham *his master,*
10. of the camels of *his master,* and departed; for all the goods of *his master* (were) in
12, 42. O Lord God of *my master* Abraham,
— shew kindness unto *my master* Abraham.
14. hast shewed kindness unto *my master.*
18. And she said, Drink, *my lord:*
27. Blessed (be) the Ld. God of *my master* Abm., who hath not left destitute *my master*
— led me to the house of *my master's* brethren.
35. the Lord hath blessed *my master* greatly;
36. And Sarah *my master's* wife bare a son *to my master* when she
37. And *my master* made me swear,
39. And I said unto *my master,* Peradventure
44. appointed out for *my master's* son.
48. and blessed the Lord God of *my master* Abraham,
— to take *my master's* brother's daughter
49. deal kindly and truly with *my master,*
51. let her be *thy master's* son's wife,
54. Send me away *unto my master.*
56. that I may go *to my master.*
65. the servant (had) said, It (is) *my master:*
31:35. Let it not displease *my lord*
32: 4(5). Thus shall ye speak *unto my lord*
5(6). I have sent to tell *my lord,*
18(19). a present sent *unto my lord* Esau:
33: 8. to find grace in the sight of *my lord.*
13. he said unto him, *My lord* knoweth
14. Let *my lord,* I pray thee, pass over
— until I come unto *my lord* unto Seir.
15. let me find grace in the sight of *my lord.*
39: 2. he was in the house of *his master*
3. And *his master* saw that the Lord
7. that *his master's* wife cast her eyes
8. unto *his master's* wife, Behold, *my master*
16. by her, until *his lord* came home.
19. it came to pass, when *his master* heard
20. And Joseph's *master* took him,
40: 1. had offended *their lord* the king of Egypt.
7. with him in the ward of *his lord's* house,
42:10. they said unto him, Nay, *my lord,*
30. The man (who is) *the lord of* the land,
33. And the man, *the lord of* the country,
43:20. O *sir,* we came indeed down at the first
44: 5. (Is) not this (it) in which *my lord* drinketh,
7. Wherefore saith *my lord* these words?
8. should we steal out of *thy lord's* house
9. we also will be *my lord's* bondmen. (lit. servants *to my lord*)
16. What shall we say *unto my lord?*
— behold, we (are) *my lord's* servants, (lit. servants *to my lord*)
18. said, Oh *my lord,* let thy servant, I pray thee, speak a word in *my lord's* ears,
19. *My lord* asked his servants,
20, 22. And we said unto *my lord,*
24. we told him the words of *my lord.*
33. instead of the lad a bondman *to my lord;*
45: 8. *and lord* of all his house,
9. God hath made me *lord* of all Egypt:
47:18. We will not hide (it) *from my lord,*
— *my lord* also hath our herds
— not ought left in the sight of *my lord,*
25. find grace in the sight of *my lord,*
Ex. 21: 4. If *his master* have given him a wife,
— wife and her children shall be *her master's,*
5. shall plainly say, I love *my master,*
6. Then *his master* shall bring him
— *his master* shall bore his ear through
8. If she please not *her master,*
32. he shall give *unto their master*
Ex. 23:17. all thy males shall appear before *the Lord* God.
32:22. Let not the anger of *my lord* wax hot:
34:23. shall all your menchildren appear before *the Lord* God,
Nu. 11:28. *My lord* Moses, forbid them.
12:11. Aaron said unto Moses, Alas, *my lord,*
32:25. Thy servants will do as *my lord*
27. as *my lord* saith.
36: 2. The Lord commanded *my lord*
— *and my lord* was commanded
Deu10:17. *and Lord of lords,* a great God,
23:15(16). Thou shalt not deliver unto *his master* the servant which is escaped from *his master*
Jos. 3:11, 13. *the Lord of* all the earth
5:14. What saith *my lord* unto his servant?
Jud. 1: 5. they found *Adoni*-bezek
6. But *Adoni*-bezek fled;
7. And *Adoni*-bezek said,
3:25. behold, *their lord* (was) fallen down dead
4:18. said unto him, Turn in, *my lord,*
6:13. Gideon said unto him, Oh *my Lord,*
19:11. the servant said unto *his master,*
12. And *his master* said unto him,
26. the man's house where *her lord* (was),
27. And *her lord* rose up in the morning,
Ru. 2:13. find favour in thy sight, *my lord;*
1Sa. 1:15. Hannah answered and said, No, *my lord,*
26. And she said, Oh *my lord,* (as) thy soul liveth, *my lord,*
16:16. Let *our lord* now command thy servants,
20:38. came to *his master.*
22:12. he answered, Here I (am), *my lord.*
24: 6(7). I should do this thing *unto my master,*
8(9). after Saul, saying, *My lord* the king.
10(11). put forth mine hand *against my lord;*
25:10. break away every man from *his master.*
14. David sent...to salute *our master;*
17. evil is determined against *our master,*
24. at his feet, and said, Upon me, *my lord,*
25. Let not *my lord,* I pray thee,
— saw not the young men of *my lord,*
26. Now therefore, *my lord,* (as) the
— they that seek evil to *my lord,*
27. hath brought *unto my lord,*
— the young men that follow *my lord.*
28. for the Lord will certainly make *my lord*
— because *my lord* fighteth the battles
29. but the soul of *my lord* shall be bound
30. shall have done *to my lord*
31. nor offence of heart *unto my lord,*
— or that *my lord* hath avenged himself:
— shall have dealt well *with my lord,*
41. wash the feet of the servants of *my lord.*
26:15. hast thou not kept *thy lord* the king?
— to destroy the king *thy lord.*
16. because ye have not kept *your master,*
17. (It is) my voice, *my lord,* O king.
18. Wherefore doth *my lord* thus pursue
19. let *my lord* the king hear the words
29: 4. reconcile himself unto *his master?*
8. enemies of *my lord* the king?
10. with *thy master's* servants
30:13. *my master* left me,
15. into the hands of *my master,*
2Sa. 1:10. brought them hither unto *my lord.*
2: 5. have shewed this kindness unto *your lord,*
7. *your master* Saul is dead,
3: 21. gather all Israel unto *my lord* the king,
4: 8. the Lord hath avenged *my lord* the king
9: 9. I have given unto *thy master's* son
10. that *thy master's* son may have food to eat: but Mephibosheth *thy master's* son
11. According to all that *my lord* the king
10: 3. Ammon said unto Hanun *their lord,*
11: 9. with all the servants of *his lord,*
11. abide in tents; *and my lord* Joab, and the servants of *my lord,*
13. with the servants of *his lord,*
12: 8. I gave thee *thy master's* house, and *thy master's* wives
13:32. *Let* not *my lord* suppose (that) they
33. therefore let not *my lord* the king
14: 9. *My lord,* O king, the iniquity
12. (one) word unto *my lord* the king.
15. speak of this thing unto *my lord*

2Sa.14:17. The word of *my lord* the king
— so (is) *my lord* the king
18. Let *my lord* the king now speak.
19. (As) thy soul liveth, *my lord* the king,
— ought that *my lord* the king hath spoken:
20. *and my lord* (is) wise,
22. grace in thy sight, *my lord*, O king,
15:15. whatsoever *my lord* the king shall appoint.
21. (as) *my lord* the king liveth, surely in what place *my lord* the king
16: 3. And where (is) *thy master*'s son?
4. find grace in thy sight, *my lord*,
9. this dead dog curse *my lord* the king?
18:28. their hand *against my lord* the king.
31. Tidings, *my lord* the king:
32. The enemies of *my lord* the king,
19:19(20). Let not *my lord* impute iniquity
—(—). the day that *my lord* the king
20(21). go down to meet *my lord* the king.
26(27). he answered, *My lord*, O king,
27(28). thy servant unto *my lord* the king; *but my lord* the king (is) as an angel
28(29). dead men *before my lord* the king:
30(31). forasmuch as *my lord* the king
35(36). a burden unto *my lord* the king?
37(38). let him go over with *my lord* the king;
20: 6. take thou *thy lord*'s servants,
24: 3. that the eyes of *my lord* the king may see (it): *but* why doth *my lord* the king
21. Wherefore is *my lord* the king
22. Let *my lord* the king take
1K. 1: 2. Let there be sought *for my lord*
— that *my lord* the king may get heat. (lit. heat may be *to my lord*)
11. *and* David *our lord* knoweth (it) not?
13. Didst not thou, *my lord*, O king,
17. And she said unto him, *My lord*,
18. *my lord* the king, thou knowest (it) not:
20. And thou, *my lord*, O king, the eyes
—, 27. sit on the throne of *my lord* the king
21. when *my lord* the king shall sleep
24. Nathan said, *My lord*, O king,
27. Is this thing done by *my lord* the king,
31. Let *my lord* king David live for ever.
33. Take with you the servants of *your lord*,
36. the Lord God of *my lord* the king say so
37. As the Lord hath been with *my lord* the
— the throne of *my lord* king David.
43. Verily *our lord* king David
47. came to bless *our lord* king David,
2:38. as *my lord* the king hath said,
3:17. And the one woman said, O *my lord*,
26. she said, O *my lord*,
11:23. which fled from *his lord* Hadadezer
12:27. turn again unto *their lord*,
16:24. Shemer, *owner of* the hill, Samaria.
18: 7. (Art) thou that *my lord* Elijah?
8, 11, 14. go, tell *thy lord*, Behold, Elijah (is here).
10. whither *my lord* hath not sent
13. Was it not told *my lord* what I did
20: 4. king of Israel answered and said, *My lord*,
9. Tell *my lord* the king,
22:17. These have no *master:* (lit. *lords*)
2K. 2: 3, 5. the Lord will take away *thy master*
16. we pray thee, and seek *thy master:*
19. this city (is) pleasant, as *my lord* seeth:
4:16. And she said, Nay, *my lord*,
28. Did I desire a son of *my lord?*
5: 1. was a great man with *his master*,
3. Would God *my lord* (were) with the
4. And (one) went in, and told *his lord*,
18. when *my master* goeth into the house
20. *my master* hath spared Naaman
22. *My master* hath sent me,
25. stood before *his master*.
6: 5. he cried, and said, Alas, *master!*
12. his servants said, None, *my lord*, O king:
15. Alas, *my master!* how shall we do?
22. eat and drink, and go to *their master*.
23. they went to *their master*.
26. Help, *my lord*, O king.
32. the sound of *his master*'s feet behind him?
8: 5. Gehazi said, *My lord*, O king,
12. Hazael said, Why weepeth *my lord?*
14. came to *his master;*
9: 7. smite the house of Ahab *thy master*,

2 K. 9:11. Jehu came forth to the servants of *his lord:*
31. (Had) Zimri peace, who slew *his master?*
10: 2. seeing *your master*'s sons (are) with you,
3. the best and meetest of *your master*'s sons,
— fight for *your master*'s house.
6. the heads of the men *your master*'s sons,
9. behold, I conspired against *my master*,
18:23. give pledges to *my lord* the king
24. captain of the least of *my master*'s servts.,
27. Hath *my master* sent me to *thy master*,
19: 4. the king of Assyria *his master* hath sent
6. Thus shall ye say to *your master*,
1Ch 12:19. He will fall to *his master* Saul
21: 3. but, *my lord* the king, (are) they not all *my lord's* servants (lit. servants *to my lord*)? why then doth *my lord* require this thing?
23. let *my lord* the king do
2Ch. 2:14(13). cunning men of *my lord* David
15(14). which *my lord* hath spoken of,
13: 6. hath rebelled against *his lord*.
18:16. These have no *master;* (lit. *lords*)
Neh. 3: 5. their necks to the work of *their Lord*.
8:10. for (this) day (is) holy *unto our Lord:*
10:29(30). the commandments of the Lord *our Lord*,
Job 3:19. the servant (is) free *from his master*.
Ps. 8: 1(2), 9(10). O Lord *our Lord*, how excellent
12: 4(5). who (is) *lord* over us?
45:11(12). he (is) *thy Lord;* and worship thou
97: 5. at the presence of *the Lord of* the whole
105:21. He made him *lord* of his house,
110: 1. said *unto my Lord*, Sit thou at my right
114: 7. at the presence of *the Lord*,
123: 2. (look) unto the hand of *their masters*,
135: 5. *and* (that) *our Lord* (is) above all gods.
136: 3. O give thanks *to the Lord of lords:*
147: 5. Great (is) *our Lord*, and of great power.
Pro.25:13. refresheth the soul of *his masters*.
27:18. he that waiteth on *his master* shall
30:10. Accuse not a servant unto *his master*,
Isa. 1:24. Therefore saith *the Lord*,
3: 1. behold, *the Lord*, the Lord of hosts,
10:16. Therefore shall *the Lord*, the Lord of hosts,
33. *the Lord*, the Lord of hosts, shall lop
19: 4. into the hand of *a* cruel *lord;* (lit. *Lords*)
— saith *the Lord*,
22:18. the shame of *thy lord*'s house.
24: 2. with the servant, *so with his master;*
26:13. our God, (other) *lords* beside thee
36: 8. to *my master* the king of Assyria,
9. of the least of *my master*'s servants,
12. Hath *my master* sent me to *thy master* and
37: 4. the king of Assyria *his master*
6. shall ye say unto *your master*,
51:22. Thus saith *thy Lord* the Lord,
Jer. 22:18. (saying), Ah *lord!* or, Ah his glory!
27: 4. them, to say unto *their masters*,
— Thus shall ye say unto *your masters;*
34: 5. they will lament thee (saying), Ah *lord!*
37:20. *O my lord* the king:
38: 9. *My lord* the king,
Dan. 1:10. I fear *my lord* the king,
10:16. *O my lord*, by the vision my sorrows are
17. can the servant of this *my lord* talk with this *my lord?*
19. Let *my lord* speak; for thou hast
12: 8. *O my Lord*, what (shall be) the end
Hos.12:14(15). reproach shall *his Lord* return unto
Am. 4: 1. which say *to their masters*, Bring,
Mic. 4:13. *unto the Lord of* the whole earth.
Zep. 1: 9. which fill *their masters'* houses with
Zec. 1: 9. *O my lord*, what (are) these?
4: 4. What (are) these, *my lord?*
5, 13. And I said, No, *my lord*.
14. that stand by *the Lord of* the whole earth.
6: 4. What (are) these, *my lord?*
5. standing before *the Lord of* all the earth
Mal. 1: 6. and a servant *his master:*
— and if I (be) *a master*, where (is) my fear?
3: 1. *the Lord*, whom ye seek,

אֲדֹנָי see אֲדוֹנָי· See 136

116 **אֱדַיִן** *ĕdah'-yin*, adv. Ch.

Ezr 4: 9. *Then* (wrote) Rehum the chancellor,
23. *Now* when the copy of king Artaxerxes'
24. *Then* ceased the work of the house of God
5: 2. *Then* rose up Zerubbabel the son of
4. *Then* said we unto them after this manner,
5. *and then* they returned answer by letter
9. *Then* asked we those elders,
16. *Then* came the same Sheshbazzar,
— since *that time* even until now
6: 1. *Then* Darius the king made a decree,
13. *Then* Tatnai, governor on this side the
Dan 2:14. *Then* Daniel answered with counsel
15. *Then* Arioch made the thing known to
17. *Then* Daniel went to his house,
19. *Then* was the secret revealed
— *Then* Daniel blessed the God of heaven.
25. *Then* Arioch brought in Daniel before the
35. *Then* was the iron, the clay,
46. *Then* the king Nebuchadnezzar fell
48. *Then* the king made Daniel a great man,
3: 3. *Then* the princes, the governors, and
13. *Then* Nebuchadnezzar in (his) rage
— *Then* they brought these men before the
19. *Then* was Nebuchadnezzar full of fury,
21. *Then* these men were bound in their coats,
24. *Then* Nebuchadnezzar the king was
26. *Then* Nebuchadnezzar came near
— *Then* Shadrach, Meshach, and Abed-nego,
30. *Then* the king promoted Shadrach,
4: 7(4). *Then* came in the magicians,
19(16). *Then* Daniel, whose name (was)
5: 3. *Then* they brought the golden vessels
6. *Then* the king's countenance was changed,
8. *Then* came in all the king's wise (men):
9. *Then* was king Belshazzar greatly troubled,
13. *Then* was Daniel brought in before the
17. *Then* Daniel answered and said
24. *Then* was the part of the hand
29. *Then* commanded Belshazzar,
6: 3(4). *Then* this Daniel was preferred
4(5). *Then* the presidents and princes
5(6). *Then* said these men,
6(7). *Then* these presidents and princes
11(12). *Then* these men assembled,
12(13). *Then* they came near,
13(14). *Then* answered they and said
14(15). *Then* the king, when he heard
15(16). *Then* these men assembled unto
16(17). *Then* the king commanded,
18(19). *Then* the king went to his palace,
19(20). *Then* the king arose very early
21(22). *Then* said Daniel unto the king,
23(24). *Then* was the king exceeding glad
25(26). *Then* king Darius wrote
7: 1. *then* he wrote the dream,
11. I beheld *then* because of the voice
19. *Then* I would know the truth

---

117 **אַדִּיר** *ad-deer'*, adj.

Ex. 15:10. they sank as lead in the *mighty* waters.
Jud. 5:13. have dominion *over the nobles*
25. brought forth butter in a *lordly* dish. (lit. a dish or bowl of *princes*)
1Sa. 4: 8. out of the hand of these *mighty* Gods?
2Ch 23:20. captains of hundreds, and *the nobles*,
Neh 3: 5. *but their nobles* put not their necks to
10:29(30). clave to their brethren, *their nobles*,
Ps. 8: 1(2), 9(10). O Lord our Lord, how *excellent* (is) thy name
16: 3. *and* (to) *the excellent*, in whom (is) all my
76: 4(5). Thou (art) more glorious (and) *excellent*
93: 4. The Lord on high (is) *mightier* than
— *the mighty* waves of the sea.
136:18. And slew *famous* kings
Isa. 10:34. Lebanon shall fall *by a mighty one*. (marg. *mightily*)
33:21. But there the *glorious* Lord .
— neither shall *gallant* ship pass
Jer. 14: 3. *And their nobles* have sent
25:34. *ye principal of* the flock:
35. *the principal of* the flock (lit. *from the principal*)
Jer. 25:36. an howling of *the principal of* the flock,
30:21. *their nobles* shall be of themselves, (lit. and *his nobles* shall be)
Eze. 17:23. bear fruit, and be a *goodly* cedar:
32:18. the daughters of the *famous* nations,
Nah 2: 5(6). He shall recount *his worthies*,
3:18. *thy nobles* shall dwell (marg. *valiant ones*)
Zec. 11: 2. because *the mighty* are spoiled (marg *gallants*)

אָדָם *āh-dāhm'*, m. 120

Gen 1:26. Let us make *man* in our image,
27. So God created *man* in his (own) image,
2: 5. *and* (there was) not *a man* to till the
7. And the Lord God formed *man*
— *man* became a living soul.
8. there he put *the man* whom he had formed.
15. the Lord God took *the man*, (marg. *Adam*)
16. the Lord God commanded *the man*,
18. not good that *the man* should be alone;
19. brought (them) unto *Adam* (marg. *the man*)
— whatsoever *Adam* called every living
20. *Adam* gave names to all cattle,
— *but for Adam* there was not found an help
21. caused a deep sleep to fall upon *Adam*,
22. the Lord God had taken from *man*,
— brought her unto *the man*.
23. *Adam* said, This (is) now bone of my
25. both naked, *the man* and his wife,
3: 8. *Adam* and his wife hid themselves
9. And the Lord God called unto *Adam*,
12. *the man* said, The woman whom thou
17. *And unto Adam* he said,
20. *Adam* called his wife's name Eve;
21. *Unto Adam* also and to his wife did the
22. *the man* is become as one of us,
24. So he drove out *the man*;
4: 1. *And Adam* knew Eve his wife;
25. *Adam* knew his wife again;
5: 1. the book of the generations of *Adam*. In the day that God created *man*,
2. called their name *Adam*,
3. And *Adam* lived
4. And the days of *Adam* after
5. the days that *Adam* lived
6: 1. when *men* began to multiply
2. daughters of *men* that they (were) fair;
3. shall not always strive *with man*,
4. came in unto the daughters of *men*,
5. God saw that the wickedness of *man*
6. it repented the Lord that he had made *man* (lit. *the man*)
7. Lord said, I will destroy *man*
— *both man*, and beast, (marg. *from man* unto beast)
7:21. creepeth upon the earth, and every *man*:
23. *both man*, and cattle, (lit. *from man* unto)
8:21. curse the ground any more for *man*'s sake;
— the imagination of *man*'s heart (is) evil
9: 5. and at the hand of *man*;
— will I require the life of *man*.
6. Whoso sheddeth *man*'s blood, *by man* shall his blood be shed: for in the image of God made he *man*.
11: 5. which the children of *men* builded.
16:12. he will be *a* wild *man*;
Ex. 4:11. Who hath made *man's* mouth? (lit. mouth *to man*)
8:17(13). it became lice *in man*, and in beast;
18(14). were lice *upon man*, and upon beast.
9: 9. breaking forth (with) blains upon *man*,
10. breaking forth (with) blains *upon man*,
19. every *man* and beast which shall be found
22. upon *man*, and upon beast,
25 & 12:12. *both man* and beast; (lit. *from man* unto beast)
13: 2. (both) *of man* and of beast: it is mine
13. and all the firstborn of *man*
15. both the firstborn of *man*,
30:32. Upon *man*'s flesh shall it not be poured,
33:20. there shall no *man* see me, and live.
Lev. 1: 2. If any *man* of you bring an offering
5: 3. touch the uncleanness of *man*,
4. that *a man* shall pronounce with an

Lev. 6:3(5:22). in any of all these that *a man*
7:21. the uncleanness of *man*,
13: 2. When *a man* shall have in the skin
9. When the plague of leprosy is *in a man*,
16:17. there shall be no *man* in the tabernacle
18: 5. which if *a man* do, he shall live in them:
22: 5. or *a man* of whom he may take
24:17. he that killeth any *man*
20. he hath caused a blemish *in a man*,
21. he that killeth *a man* shall be
27:28. devoted thing...(both) *of man* and beast, (lit. *from man* unto beast)
29. which shall be devoted of *men*,
Nu. 3:13. *both man* and beast; (lit. *from man* unto)
5: 6. shall commit any sin that *men* commit,
8:17. (both) *man* and beast: (lit. *in man*)
9: 6, 7. defiled by the dead body of *a man*,
12: 3. above all *the men* which (were)
16:29. the common death of all *men*,
— the visitation of all *men;*
32. *the men* that (appertained) unto
18:15. *of men* or beasts, shall be thine: nevertheless the firstborn of *man* shalt thou
19:11. dead body of any *man*
13. the dead body of any *man*
14. when *a man* dieth in a tent:
16. or a bone of *a man*, or a grave,
23:19. neither the son of *man*, that he
31:11. (both) *of men* and of beasts.
26. (both) *of man* and of beast,
28. of *the persons*, and of the beeves,
30. of *the persons*, of the beeves,
35. thirty and two thousand *persons* (lit. soul of *man*)
40. *the persons* (were) sixteen thousand; (lit. soul of *man*)
46. sixteen thousand *persons;* (lit. soul of *man*)
47. (both) of *man* and of beast,
Deu 4:28. the work of *men*'s hands,
32. the day that God created *man*
5:24(21). God doth talk with *man*, and
8: 3. *man* doth not live by bread
— out of the mouth of the Lord doth *man*
20:19. the tree of the field (is) *man*'s (life) (marg. *O man*, the tree of the field &c.)
32: 8. when he separated the sons of *Adam*,
Jos. 3:16. very far *from* the city *Adam*,
11:14. but every *man* they smote
14:15. (Arba was) *a great man* among
Jud. 16: 7, 11. be as another *man*.
17. be like any (other) *man*.
18: 7,28. had no business with (any) *man*.
1Sa. 15:29. not *a man*, that he should repent.
16: 7. for (the Lord seeth) not as *man* seeth; for *man* looketh on the outward
17:32. Let no *man*'s heart fail
24: 9(10). Wherefore hearest thou *men*'s words,
25:29. Yet *a man* is risen to pursue thee,
26:19. if (they be) the children of *men*,
2Sa. 7:14. stripes of the children of *men:*
19. (is) this the manner of *man*,
23: 3. He that ruleth *over men* (must be)
24:14. let me not fall into the hand of *man*.
1K. 4:31(5:11). For he was wiser than all *men;*
8:38. supplication soever be (made) by any *man*,
39. the hearts of all the children of *men;*
46. no *man* that sinneth not,
13: 2. *men*'s bones shall be burnt upon thee.
2K. 7:10. neither voice of *man*,
19:18. the work of *men*'s hands, wood
23:14. their places with the bones of *men*.
20. burned *men*'s bones upon them,
1Ch. 1: 1. *Adam*, Sheth, Enosh,
5:21. of *men* an hundred thousand. (lit. soul of *man*)
17:17. the estate of *a man* of high degree,
21:13. let me not fall into the hand of *man*.
29: 1. for the palace (is) not *for man*,
2Ch. 6:18. will God in very deed dwell with *men*
29. shall be made of any *man*,
30. knowest the hearts of the children of *men:*
36. no *man* which sinneth not,
19: 6. for ye judge not *for man*,
32:19. work of the hands of *man*.
Neh 2:10. that there was come *a man*
12. neither told I (any) *man*
9:29. which if *a man* do, he shall live

Job 5: 7. Yet *man* is born unto trouble,
7:20. O thou preserver of *men?*
11:12. though *man* be born (like) a wild ass's
14: 1. *Man* (that is) born of a woman
10. yea, *man* giveth up the ghost,
15: 7. thou the first *man* (that) was born?
16:21. as *a man* (pleadeth) for his neighbour! (lit. as a son of *man*)
20: 4. since *man* was placed upon earth,
29. the portion of *a* wicked *man*
21: 4. As for me, (is) my complaint *to man?*
33. every *man* shall draw after
25: 6. the son of *man*, (which is) a worm?
27:13. the portion of *a* wicked *man*
28:28. *unto man* he said,
31:33. If I covered my transgressions *as Adam*, (marg. *after the manner of men*)
32:21. give flattering titles unto *man*.
33:17. That he may withdraw *man*
23. to shew *unto man* his uprightness:
34:11. For the work of *a man* shall he
15. *and man* shall turn again
29. or against *a man* only:
30. the hypocrite reign not, (lit. profane *man*)
35: 8. righteousness (may profit) the son of *man*.
36:25. Every *man* may see it;
28. distil upon *man* abundantly.
37: 7. He sealeth up the hand of every *man;*
38:26. wilderness, wherein (there is) no *man;*
Ps. 8: 4(5). the son of *man*, that thou visitest
11: 4. his eyelids try, the children of *men*.
12: 1(2). fail from among the children of *men*.
8(9). when the vilest *men* are exalted.
14: 2. from heaven upon the children of *men*,
17: 4. Concerning the works of *men*,
21:10(11). seed from among the children of *men*.
22: 6(7). a reproach of *men*, and despised
31:19(20). that trust in thee before the sons of *men!*
32: 2. Blessed (is) *the man*
33:13. he beholdeth all the sons of *men*.
36: 6(7). O Lord, thou preservest *man* and beast.
7(8). therefore the children of *men* put
39: 5(6). verily every *man* at his best state (is) altogether vanity.
11(12). surely every *man* (is) vanity.
45: 2(3). fairer than the children of *men;*
49: 2(3). Both *low* and high, (lit. sons of אָדָם, sons of אִישׁ).
12(13). *Nevertheless man* (being) in honour
20(21). *Man* (that is) in honour, and underst.
53: 2(3). from heaven upon the children of *men*,
56:11(12). I will not be afraid what *man* can do
57: 4(5). that are set on fire, (even) the sons of *men*,
58: 1(2). do ye judge uprightly, O ye sons of *men?*
11(12). So that *a man* shall say,
60:11(13). for vain (is) the help of *man*.
62: 9(10). Surely *men of low degree* (are) vanity, (lit. sons of *Adam*)
64: 9(10). all *men* shall fear, and shall declare
66: 5. doing toward the children of *men*.
68:18(19). thou hast received gifts *for men;* (marg. *in the man*)
73: 5. are they plagued like (other) *men*.
76:10(11). the wrath of *man* shall praise thee:
78:60. the tent (which) he placed *among men;*
80:17(18). upon the son of *man* (whom) thou
82: 7. But ye shall die *like men*,
84: 5(6). Blessed (is) *the man* whose strength
12(13). blessed (is) *the man* that trusteth in
89:47(48). hast thou made all *men* in vain?
90: 3. Return, ye children of *men*.
94:10. he that teacheth *man* knowledge,
11. the Lord knoweth the thoughts of *man*,
104:14. herb for the service of *man:*
23. *Man* goeth forth unto his work
105:14. He suffered no *man* to do them wrong:
107: 8, 15, 21, 31. wonderful works to the children of *men!*
108:12(13). for vain (is) the help of *man*.
115: 4. the work of *men*'s hands.
16. hath he given to the children of *men*.
116:11. I said in my haste, All *men* (are) liars.
118: 6. what can *man* do unto me?

Ps.118: 8. than to put confidence *in man.*
119:134. Deliver me from the oppression of *man:*
124: 2. when *men* rose up against us:
135: 8. both *of man* and beast. (lit. *from man* unto).
15. the work of *men*'s hands
140: 1(2). Deliver me, O Lord, *from the* evil *man:*
144: 3. Lord, what (is) *man*, that thou takest
4. *Man* is like to vanity:
145:12. make known to the sons of *men*
146: 3. (nor) in the son of *man*, in whom
Pro. 3: 4. understanding in the sight of God *and man.*
13. Happy (is) *the man* (that) findeth wisdom, *and the man* (that) getteth underst.
30. Strive not with *a man* without cause,
6:12. *A* naughty *person*, a wicked
8: 4. my voice (is) to the sons of *man:*
31. my delights (were) with the sons of *men.*
34. Blessed (is) *the man* that heareth me,
11: 7. When *a* wicked *man* dieth, (his) expectation
12: 3. *A man* shall not be established by
14. recompence of *a man*'s hands shall be
23. *A* prudent *man* concealeth knowledge:
27. the substance of *a* diligent *man* (is)
15:11. the hearts of the children of *men?*
20. but *a* foolish *man* despiseth his mother.
16: 1. The preparations of the heart *in man.*
9. *A man*'s heart deviseth his way:
17:18. *A man* void of understanding striketh
18:16. *A man*'s gift maketh room for him,
19: 3. The foolishness of *man* perverteth his way:
11. discretion of *a man* deferreth his anger;
22. The desire of *a man* (is) his kindness:
20: 6. Most *men* will proclaim every one his own
24. how can *a man then* understand his own way? (lit. *And a man*, how can he understand, &c.)
25. a snare to *the man* (who) devoureth
27. The spirit of *man* (is) the candle of the
21:16. *The man* that wandereth out of the way
20. but a foolish *man* spendeth it up.
23:28. increaseth the transgressors *among men.*
24: 9. the scorner (is) an abomination *to men.*
12. shall (not) he render *to* (every) *man*
30. by the vineyard of *the man* void of
27:19. so the heart of *man to man.*
20. so the eyes of *man* are never satisfied.
28: 2. *but by a man* of understanding
12. when the wicked rise, *a man* is hidden.
14. Happy (is) *the man* that feareth alway:
17. *A man* that doeth violence to the blood
23. He that rebuketh *a man*
28. When the wicked rise, *men* hide themselves:
29:23. *A man*'s pride shall bring him low:
25. The fear of *man* bringeth a snare:
30: 2. have not the understanding of *a man.*
14. the needy *from* (among) *men.*
Ecc. 1: 3. What profit *hath a man* of all his labour (lit. is *to a man*)
13. hath God given to the sons of *man*
2: 3. see what (was) that good for the sons of *men*,
8. the delights of the sons of *men*,
12. what (can) *the man* (do) that cometh
18. I should leave it *unto the man*
21. For there is *a man* whose labour (is) in
— *yet to a man* that hath not laboured
22. For what *hath man* (lit. is *to man*)
24. nothing better *for a man*,
26. (God) giveth *to a man* that (is) good
3:10. which God hath given to the sons of *men*
11. so that no *man* can find out the work
13. every *man* should eat and drink,
18. concerning the estate of the sons of *men*,
19. that which befalleth the sons of *men*
— so that *a man* hath no preeminence
21. Who knoweth the spirit of *man*
22. that *a man* should rejoice in his own
5:19(18). Every *man* also to whom God hath
6: 1. it (is) common among *men:*
7. All the labour of *man* (is) for his mouth,
10. it is known that it (is) *man:*
11. what (is) *man* the better? (lit. what is better *to a man*)
12. who knoweth what (is) good *for man*
— who can tell *a man* what shall be
7: 2. for that (is) the end of all *men;*

Ecc. 7:14. to the end that *man* should find nothing
20. For (there is) not *a* just *man* upon earth
28. one *man* among a thousand have I found,
29. that God hath made *man* upright;
8: 1. *a man*'s wisdom maketh his face to shine,
6. therefore the misery of *man* (is) great
8. no *man* that hath power over the spirit
9. a time wherein (one) *man* ruleth *over another* (lit. *over man*)
11. therefore the heart of the sons of *men*
15. *a man hath* no better thing under the sun, (lit. is *to a man*)
17. *a man* cannot find out the work
— though *a man* labour to seek (it) out,
9: 1. no *man* knoweth either love or hatred
3. the heart of the sons of *men* is full
12. For *man* also knoweth not his time:
— so (are) the sons of *men* snared
15. *yet* no *man* remembered that same poor
10:14. *a man* cannot tell what shall be;
11: 8. But if *a man* live many years,
12: 5. because *man* goeth to his long home,
13. for this (is) the whole (duty) of *man.*
Isa 2: 9. *the mean man* boweth down, and the great
11. The lofty looks of *man* shall be
17. the loftiness of *man* shall be bowed down,
20. In that day *a man* shall cast his idols
22. Cease ye from *man*,
5:15. *the mean man* shall be brought down,
6:11. and the houses without *man*,
12. the Lord have removed *men* far away,
13:12. *even a man* than the golden wedge of Ophir.
17: 7. At that day shall *a man* look to his Maker,
22: 6. Elam bare the quiver with chariots of *men*
29:19. the poor among *men* shall rejoice
21. That make *a man* an offender
31: 3. Now the Egyptians (are) *men*, and not
8. the sword, not of *a mean man*,
37:19. but the work of *men*'s hands, wood and
38:11. I shall behold *man* no more
43: 4. therefore will I give *men* for thee.
44:11. the workmen, they (are) *of men:*
13. according to the beauty of *a man;*
15. Then shall it be *for a man* to burn:
45:12. made the earth, *and* created *man* upon it.
47: 3. I will not meet (thee as) *a man.*
51:12. the son of *man* (which) shall be made
52:14. his form more than the sons of *men:*
56: 2. the son of *man* (that) layeth hold on it;
58: 5. a day for *a man* to afflict his soul?
Jer. 2: 6. where no *man* dwelt?
4:25. I beheld, and, lo, (there was) no *man*,
7:20. poured out upon this place, upon *man*,
9:22(21). Even the carcasses of *men* shall fall
10:14. Every *man* is brutish in (his) knowledge:
23. I know that the way of *man* (is) not *in* himself: (lit. not *to man* (is) his way)
16:20. Shall *a man* make gods unto himself,
17: 5. Cursed (be) the man that trusteth *in man*,
21: 6. both *man* and beast: they shall die
27: 5. I have made the earth, *the man*
31:27. with the seed of *man*, and with the seed of beast.
30. every *man* that eateth the sour grape,
32:19. upon all the ways of the sons of *men;*
20. in Israel, *and among* (other) *men;*
43. desolate without *man*
33: 5. fill them with the dead bodies of *men*,
10. (shall be) desolate without *man*
— that are desolate, without *man*,
12. which is desolate without *man*
36:29. cause to cease from thence *man*
47: 2. then *the men* shall cry,
49:15. despised *among men.*
18, 33. son of *man* dwell in it.
50: 3. they shall depart, *both man* and beast. (lit. *from man* to beast)
40. neither shall any son of *man* dwell
51:14. Surely I will fill thee with *men*,
17. every *man* is brutish by (his) knowledge;
43. neither doth (any) son of *man* pass
62. *neither man* nor beast,
Lam. 3:36. To subvert *a man* in his cause,
39. Wherefore doth *a* living *man* complain,
Eze. 1: 5. they had the likeness of *a man.*
8. (they had) the hands of *a man*

Eze. 1:10. they four had the face of *a man*,
26. likeness as the appearance of *a man*
2: 1, 3. And he said unto me, Son of *man*,
6. And thou, son of *man*,
8. But thou, son of *man*, hear what I say
3: 1, 3, 4, 10. he said unto me, Son of *man*,
17. Son of *man*, I have made thee a watchman
25. But thou, O son of *man*, behold,
4: 1. Thou also, son of *man*, take thee a tile,
12. with dung that cometh out of *man*,
15. I have given thee cow's dung for *man*'s
16. Moreover he said unto me, Son of *man*,
5: 1. And thou, son of *man*, take thee a sharp
6: 2. Son of *man*, set thy face toward the
7: 2. Also, thou son of *man*, thus saith
8: 5, 8. Then said he unto me, Son of *man*,
6. furthermore unto me, Son of *man*,
12. Son of *man*, hast thou seen what the
15, 17. Hast thou seen (this), O Son of *man?*
10: 8. in the cherubims the form of *a man*'s hand
14. second face (was) the face of *a man*,
21. the likeness of the hands of *a man*,
11: 2. Then said he unto me, Son of *man*.
4. prophesy, O son of *man*.
15. Son of *man*, thy brethren,
12: 2. Son of *man*, thou dwellest in the
3. Therefore, thou son of *man*,
9. Son of *man*, hath not the house of Israel,
18. Son of *man*, eat thy bread with quaking,
22. Son of *man*, what (is) that proverb
27. Son of *man*, behold, (they of) the house
13: 2. Son of *man*, prophesy against the
17. Likewise, thou son of *man*, set thy face
14: 3. Son of *man*, these men have set up
13. Son of *man*, when the land sinneth
13, 17. cut off *man* and beast from it:
19, 21. to cut off from it *man* and beast:
15: 2. Son of *man*, What is the vine tree more
16: 2. Son of *man*, cause Jerusalem to know
17: 2. Son of *man*, put forth a riddle,
19: 3. learned to catch the prey; it devoured *men*.
6. to catch the prey. (and) devoured *men*.
20: 3. Son of *man*, speak
4. Wilt thou judge them, son of *man*,
11, 13, 21. which (if) *a man* do, he shall even
27. Therefore, son of *man*, speak unto the
46(21:2). Son of *man*, set thy face toward the
21: 2(7). Son of *man*, set thy face toward
6(11). Sigh therefore, thou son of *man*,
9(14). Son of *man*, prophesy,
12(17). Cry and howl, son of *man*,
14(19). Thou therefore, son of *man*,
19(24). Also, thou son of *man*, appoint thee
28(33). And thou, son of *man*, prophesy
22: 2. Now, thou son of *man*, wilt thou judge,
18. Son of *man*, the house of Israel
24. Son of *man*, say unto her,
23: 2. Son of *man*, there were two women,
36. Son of *man*, wilt thou judge Aholah
42. of the common sort (were) brought (marg. of the multitude of *men*)
24: 2. Son of *man*, write thee the name of the
16. Son of *man*, behold, I take away
25. Also, thou son of *man*, (shall it) not (be)
25: 2. Son of *man*, set thy face against the
13. will cut off *man* and beast from it;
26: 2. Son of *man*, because that Tyrus,
27: 2. Now, thou son of *man*, take up
13. they traded the persons of *men*
28: 2. Son of *man*, say unto the prince of Tyrus,
— yet thou (art) *a man*, and not God,
9. but thou (shalt be) *a man*, and no God,
12. Son of *man*, take up a lamentation
21. Son of *man*, set thy face against Zidon,
29: 2. Son of *man*, set thy face against Pharaoh
8. cut off *man* and beast out of thee.
11. No foot of *man* shall pass through it,
18. Son of *man*, Nebuchadrezzar
30: 2. Son of *man*, prophesy and say,
21. Son of *man*, I have broken the arm of Pharaoh
31: 2. Son of *man*, speak unto Pharaoh
14. in the midst of the children of *men*,
32: 2. Son of *man*, take up a lamentation
13. neither shall the foot of *man*
18. Son of *man*, wail for the multitude
33: 2. Son of *man*, speak to the children

Eze. 33: 7. So thou, O Son of *man*, I have set thee a
10. Therefore, O thou son of *man*, speak
12. Therefore, thou son of *man*, say unto
24. Son of *man*, they that inhabit
30. Also, thou son of *man*, the children
34: 2. Son of *man*, prophesy against
31. the flock of my pasture, (are) *men*,
35: 2. Son of *man*, set thy face against
36: 1. Also, thou son of *man*, prophesy
10. I will multiply *men* upon you,
11. I will multiply upon you *man* and beast;
12. Yea, I will cause *men* to walk upon you
13. Thou (land) devourest up *men*,
14. Therefore thou shalt devour *men* no more,
17. Son of *man*, when the house of Israel
37. I will increase them with *men* like a flock.
38. waste cities be filled with flocks of *men:*
37: 3. Son of *man*, can these bones live?
9. prophesy, son of *man*, and say to the wind,
11. Then he said unto me, Son of *man*,
16. thou son of *man*, take thee one stick,
38: 2. Son of *man*, set thy face against
14. son of *man*, prophesy and say unto Gog,
20. all *the men* that (are) upon the face
39: 1. thou son of *man*, prophesy against Gog,
15. when (any) seeth a *man*'s bone,
17. thou son of *man*, thus saith the Lord
40: 4. Son of *man*, behold with thine eyes,
41:19. So that the face of *a man* (was) toward
43: 7. And he said unto me, Son of *man*,
10. Thou son of *man*, shew the house
18. Son of *man*, thus saith the Lord God;
44: 5. the Lord said unto me, Son of *man*,
25. they shall come at no dead *person*
47: 6. Son of *man*, hast thou seen this?
Dan. 8:16. And I heard *a man*'s voice
17. Understand, O son of *man:* for at the
10:16. like the similitude of the sons of *men*
18. (one) like the appearance of *a man*,
Hos. 6: 7. But they *like men* (marg. *like Adam*) have
9:12. (that there shall) not (be) *a man* (lit. *from man*)
11: 4. I drew them with cords of *a man*,
13: 2. Let *the men* that sacrifice kiss the calves.
Joel 1:12. joy is withered away from the sons of *men*.
Am. 4:13. declareth *unto man* what (is) his thought,
Jon. 3: 7. Let neither *man* nor beast, herd nor flock,
8. But let *man* and beast be covered with
4:11. more than sixscore thousand *persons*
Mic. 2:12. by reason *of* (the multitude of) *men*.
5: 5(4). shepherds, and eight principal *men*.
7(6). nor waiteth for the sons of *men*.
6: 8. He hath shewed thee, *O man*,
7: 2. (there is) none upright *among men:*
Hab. 1:14. makest *men* as the fishes of the sea,
2: 8, 17. because of *men*'s blood,
Zep. 1: 3. I will consume *man* and beast;
— I will cut off *man* from off the land,
17. I will bring distress *upon men*,
Hag. 1:11. and upon *men*, and upon cattle,
Zec. 2: 4(8). for the multitude of *men* and cattle
8. 10. there was no hire for *man*,
— I set all *men* every one against
9: 1. when the eyes of *man*, as of all the
11: 6. I will deliver *the men* every one into
12: 1. formeth the spirit of *man* within him.
13: 5. for *man* taught me to keep cattle
Mal. 3: 8. Will *a man* rob God?

אָדַם [*āh-dam'*] 119

* KAL.—*Preterite.* *

Lam. 4: 7. *they were* more *ruddy* in body than rubies,

* PUAL.—*Participle.* *

Ex. 25: 5 & 26:14 & 35:7. rams' skins *dyed red*,
35:23. and *red* skins of rams,
36:19. rams' skins *dyed red*
39:34. rams' skins *dyed red*,
Nah. 2: 3(4). The shield of his mighty men (is) *made red*,

* HIPHIL.—*Future.* *

Isa. 1:18. though *they be red* like crimson,

* HITHPAEL.—*Future.* *

Pro. 23:31. Look not thou upon the wine when *it is red*,

122 **אָדֹם** *āh-dōhm′*, adj.

Gen25:30. with that *same red* (pottage); (marg. with that *red*, (with that) *red* (pottage)
Nu. 19: 2. that they bring thee a *red* heifer
2K. 3:22. the water on the other side (as) *red* as
Cant.5:10. My beloved (is) white *and ruddy*
Isa. 63: 2. Wherefore (art thou) *red* in thine apparel,
Zec. 1: 8. a man riding upon a *red* horse,
— behind him (were there) *red* horses,
6: 2. In the first chariot (were) *red* horses;

---

124 **אֹדֶם** *ōh′-dem*, m.

Ex. 28:17. (the first) row (shall be) *a sardius*, (marg. *ruby*)
39:10. (the first) row (was) *a sardius*, (marg. *id.*)
Eze.28:13. *the sardius*, topaz, &c. (marg. *id.*)

---

125 **אֲדַמְדָּם** *ădam-dāhm′*, adj.

Lev.13:19. spot, white, and *somewhat reddish*,
24. *somewhat reddish*, or white,
42. a white *reddish* sore;
43. the rising of the sore (be) white *reddish*
49. greenish or *reddish* in the garment,
14:37. hollow strakes, greenish or *reddish*,

---

127 **אֲדָמָה** *ădāh-māh′*, f.

Gen 1:25. thing that creepeth upon *the earth*
2: 5. (there was) not a man to till *the ground*.
6. watered the whole face of *the ground*.
7. formed man (of) the dust of *the ground*,
9. out of *the ground* made the Lord God to
19. out of *the ground* the Lord God formed
3:17. cursed (is) *the ground* for thy sake;
19. till thou return unto *the ground*;
23. to till *the ground* from whence he was
4: 2. Cain was a tiller of *the ground*.
3. Cain brought of the fruit of *the ground*
10. blood crieth unto me from *the ground*.
11. now (art) thou cursed from *the earth*,
12. When thou tillest *the ground*,
14. this day from the face of *the earth*;
5:29. *the ground* which the Lord hath cursed.
6: 1. began to multiply on the face of *the earth*,
7. created from the face of *the earth*;
20. every creeping thing of *the earth*
7: 4. destroy from off the face of *the earth*.
8. that creepeth upon *the earth*,
23. which was upon the face of *the ground*,
8: 8. from off the face of *the ground*;
13. behold, the face of *the ground* was dry.
21. I will not again curse *the ground*
9: 2. upon all that moveth (upon) *the earth*,
20. Noah began (to be) an husbandman, (lit. a man of *the ground*)
12: 3. in thee shall all families of *the earth*
19:25. that which grew upon *the ground*.
28:14. shall all the families of *the earth*
15. will bring thee again into this *land*;
47:18. but our bodies, *and our lands*:
19. shall we die...both we and *our land*? buy us and *our land* for bread, and we *and our land* will be servants
— *that the land* be not desolate.
20. Joseph bought all *the land of* Egypt
22. Only *the land of* the priests bought he not;
— wherefore they sold not *their lands*.
23. bought you this day and *your land*
— and ye shall sow *the land*.
26. Joseph made it a law over *the land of*
— except *the land of* the priests only,
Ex. 3: 5. whereon thou standest (is) holy *ground*.
8:21(17). also *the ground* whereon they (are).
10: 6. the day that they were upon *the earth*
20:12. that thy days may be long upon *the land*
24. An altar of *earth* thou shalt make
23:19. The first of the firstfruits of *thy land*
32:12. consume them from the face of *the earth*?
33:16. that (are) upon the face of *the earth*.
34:26. The first of the firstfruits of *thy land*
Lev.20:24. Ye shall inherit *their land*,
25. that creepeth on *the ground*,
Nu. 11:12. *the land* which thou swarest
12: 3. which (were) upon the face of *the earth*.
16:30. *the earth* open her mouth, and swallow
31. *the ground* clave asunder
32:11. shall see *the land* which I sware unto
Deu 4:10. days that they shall live upon *the earth*,
18. any thing that creepeth *on the ground*,
40. prolong (thy) days upon *the earth*,
5:16. it may go well with thee, in *the land*
6:15. and destroy thee from off the face of *the earth*.
7: 6. that (are) upon the face of *the earth*.
13. the fruit of *thy land*,
— *the land* which he sware unto thy
11: 9, 21. *the land* which the Lord sware unto
17. *and* that *the land* yield not her fruit;
12: 1. the days that ye live upon *the earth*.
19. as long as thou livest upon *the earth*. (lit. *thy earth*)
14: 2. nations that (are) upon *the earth*.
21: 1. If (one) be found slain *in the land*
23. that *thy land* be not defiled,
25:15. thy days may be lengthened in *the land*
26: 2. the first of all the fruit of *the earth*,
10. brought the firstfruits of *the land*,
15. *the land* which thou hast given us,
28: 4. the fruit of *thy ground*,
11. the fruit of *thy ground*, in *the land* which the Lord sware
18, 33, 42, 51. fruit of *thy land*,
21. consumed thee from off *the land*,
63. ye shall be plucked from off *the land*
29:28(27). the Lord rooted them out of *their land*
30: 9. in the fruit of *thy land*,
18. not prolong (your) days upon *the land*,
20. that thou mayest dwell in *the land*
31:13. as long as ye live in *the land*
20. *the land* which I sware unto their fathers,
32:43. will be merciful unto *his land*,
47. ye shall prolong (your) days in *the land*,
Jos. 23:13. perish from off this good *land*
15. destroyed you from off this good *land*
1Sa. 4:12. *with earth* upon his head.
20:15. every one from the face of *the earth*.
31. as long as the son of Jesse liveth upon *the ground*,
2Sa. 1: 2. *and earth* upon his head
9:10. shall till *the land* for him,
14: 7. name nor remainder upon *the earth*.
15:32. *and earth* upon his head:
17:12. as the dew falleth on *the ground*:
1K. 7:46. in *the* clay *ground* between
8:34. bring them again unto *the land*
40. days that they live in *the land*
9: 7. cut off Israel out of *the land*
13:34. destroy (it) from off the face of *the earth*.
14:15. root up Israel out of this good *land*,
17:14. Lord sendeth rain upon *the earth*.
18: 1. I will send rain upon *the earth*.
2K. 5:17. two mules' burden of *earth*?
17:23. carried away out of *their own land*
21: 8. Israel move any more out of *the land*
25:21. Judah was carried away out of *their land*.
1Ch27:26. for tillage of *the ground*
2Ch 4:17. king cast them, in *the* clay *ground*
6:25. bring them again unto *the land*
31. *the land* which thou gavest
7:20. by the roots out of *my land*
26:10. for he loved *husbandry*. (marg. *ground*)
33: 8. the foot of Israel from out of *the land*
Neh. 9: 1. with sackclothes, *and earth* upon them.
25. took strong cities, *and a* fat *land*,
10:35(36). bring the firstfruits of *our ground*,
37(38). the tithes of *our ground* unto the
Job 5: 6. *neither* doth trouble spring *out of the ground*;
31:38. If *my land* cry against me,
Ps. 49:11(12). they call (their) *lands* after their
83:10(11). they became (as) dung *for the earth*.
104:30. thou renewest the face of *the earth*.
105:35. devoured the fruit of *their ground*.
137: 4. Sing the Lord's song in *a* strange *land*
146: 4. he returneth *to his earth*;
Pro.12:11 & 28:19. He that tilleth *his land* shall
Isa. 1: 7. *your land*, strangers devour it
6:11. *and the land* be utterly desolate,
7:16. *the land* that thou abhorrest

Isa. 14: 1. set them in *their own land:*
2. in *the land of* the Lord for servants
15: 9. upon the remnant of *the land.*
19:17. *the land of* Judah shall be a terror
23:17. the world upon the face of *the earth.*
24:21. the kings of *the earth* upon *the earth.*
28:24. break the clods of *his ground?*
30:23. thou shalt sow *the ground* withal; and bread of the increase of *the earth,*
24. young asses that ear *the ground*
32:13. Upon *the land of* my people
45: 9. the potsherds of *the earth.*
Jer. 7:20. upon the fruit of *the ground;*
8: 2. for dung upon the face of *the earth.*
12:14. I will pluck them out of *their land,*
14: 4. Because *the ground* is chapt,
16: 4. as dung upon the face of *the earth:*
15. I will bring them again into *their land*
23: 8. they shall dwell in *their own land.*
24:10. till they be consumed from off *the land*
25: 5. dwell in *the land* that the Lord hath
26. which (are) upon the face of *the earth:*
33. they shall be dung upon *the ground.*
27:10. to remove you far from *your land;*
11. remain still in *their own land,*
28:16. cast thee from off the face of *the earth:*
35: 7. that ye may live many days in *the land*
15. ye shall dwell in *the land* which I
42:12. cause you to return to *your own land.*
52:27. carried away captive out of *his own land.*
Eze. 7: 2. saith the Lord God *unto the land of* Israel;
11:17. I will give you *the land of* Israel.
12:19. of *the land of* Israel;
22. that proverb (that) ye have in *the land of*
13: 9. enter into *the land of* Israel;
18: 2. proverb concerning *the land of* Israel,
20:38. shall not enter into *the land of* Israel:
42. bring you into *the land of* Israel,
21: 2(7). prophesy against *the land of* Israel,
3(8). say *to the land of* Israel,
25: 3, 6. against *the land of* Israel,
28:25. then shall they dwell in *their land*
33:24. those wastes of *the land of* Israel
34:13. will bring them to *their own land*
27. they shall be safe in *their land,*
36: 6. Prophesy therefore concerning *the land of*
17. Israel dwelt in *their own land,*
24. will bring you into *your own land.*
37:12. bring you into *the land of* Israel.
14. I shall place you in *your own land:*
21. bring them into *their own land:*
38:18. shall come against *the land of* Israel,
19. great shaking in *the land of* Israel;
20. upon *the earth,* and all the men that (are) upon the face of *the earth,*
39:26. when they dwelt safely in *their land,*
28. gathered them unto *their own land,*
Dan 11: 9. shall return into *his own land.*
39. *and* shall divide *the land* for gain.
12: 2. in the dust *of the earth* (lit. *earth of* dust)
Hos. 2:18(20). the creeping things of *the ground:*
Joel 1:10. *the land* mourneth;
2:21. Fear not, *O land;* be glad and rejoice:
Am. 3: 2. known of all the families of *the earth:*
5. shall (one) take up a snare from *the earth,*
5: 2. she is forsaken upon *her land;*
7:11. led away captive out of *their own land.*
17. *and thy land* shall be divided by line; and thou shalt die in *a* polluted *land:* and Israel shall surely go into captivity forth of *his land.*
9: 8. destroy it from off the face of *the earth;*
15. I will plant them upon *their land,*
— be pulled up out of *their land*
Jon. 4: 2. when I was yet in *my country?*
Zep. 1: 2. consume all (things) from off *the land,*
3. I will cut off man from off *the land,*
Hag. 1:11. upon (that) which *the ground* bringeth
Zec. 2:12(16) Judah his portion in *the* holy *land,*
9:16. lifted up as an ensign upon *his land.*
13: 5. I (am) an *husbandman;* (lit. man, a tiller of *the ground*)
Mal. 3:11. shall not destroy the fruits of your *ground;* (lit. *the ground*)

---

132 אַדְמוֹנִי & אַדְמֹנִי *ad-mōh-nee'*, adj.

Gen25:25. the first came out *red,*
1Sa. 16:12. Now he (was) *ruddy,*
17:42. he was (but) a youth, *and ruddy,*

אֶדֶן *eh'-den*, m. 134

Ex. 26:19. forty *sockets of* silver under the twenty boards;
—, 21, 25. two *sockets* under one board
—, —, —. two *sockets* under another board
21. And *their* forty *sockets* (of) silver;
25. *and their sockets* (of) silver, sixteen *sockets;*
32. upon *the* four *sockets of* silver.
37. thou shalt cast five *sockets of* brass
27:10. *and their* twenty *sockets* (shall be of)
11. *and their* twenty *sockets* (of) brass;
12. their pillars ten, *and their sockets* ten.
14, 15. pillars three, *and their sockets* three.
16. pillars (shall be) four, *and their sockets*
17, 18. *and their sockets* (of) brass.
35:11. his pillars, and *his sockets,*
17. his pillars, and *their sockets,*
36:24. forty *sockets of* silver he made
—, 26. two *sockets* under one board
—, —. two *sockets* under another board
26. *their* forty *sockets* of silver;
30. *and their sockets* (were) sixteen *sockets* of silver, under every board two *sockets.* (marg. two *ss.*, two *ss.* under one board.)
36. he cast for them four *sockets of* silver.
38. *but their* five *sockets* (were of) brass.
38:10. *and their* brasen *sockets* twenty;
11. *and their sockets* of brass twenty;
12. their pillars ten, *and their sockets* ten;
14, 15. their pillars three, *and their sockets*
17. *And the sockets* for the pillars (were of)
19. *and their sockets* (of) brass four;
27. *the sockets of* the sanctuary, and *the sockets of* the vail; an hundred *sockets* of the hundred talents, a talent *for a socket.*
30. he made *the sockets to* the door
31. *the sockets of* the court round about, and *the sockets of* the court-gate,
39:33. his pillars, *and his sockets,*
40. his pillars, and *his sockets,*
40:18. fastened *his sockets,*
Nu. 3:36. *and the sockets thereof,* and all the
37. *and their sockets,* and their pins,
4:31. pillars thereof, *and sockets thereof,*
32. *and their sockets,* and their pins,
Job. 38: 6. Whereupon are *the foundations thereof* (marg. *sockets*)
Cant. 5:15. of marble, set upon *sockets of* fine gold:

אֲדֹנָי *ădōh-nāhy'*. 136

The English version sometimes renders it as though it were אֲדֹנִי, my lord. For Gen. 19:18 (which is the only place, besides the following citations, in which the form אֲדֹנָי occurs) see אָדוֹן.

N.B. Jud. 13: 8. it is written אֲדוֹנָי

Gen15: 2. And Abram said, *Lord* God,
8. And he said, *Lord* God,
18: 3. *My Lord,* if now I have found
27, 31. taken upon me to speak unto *the Lord,*
30, 32. Oh let not *the Lord* be angry,
20: 4. he said, *Lord,* wilt thou slay also
Ex. 4:10. Moses said unto the Lord, O *my Lord,*
13. And he said, O *my Lord,*
5:22. Moses returned unto the Lord, and said, *Lord,*
15:17. the Sanctuary, *O Lord,* (which) thy hands
34: 9. I have found grace in thy sight, *O Lord,* let *my lord,* I pray thee, go among us;
Nu. 14:17. let the power of *my lord* be great,
Deu 3:24 & 9:26. *O Lord* God,
Jos. 7: 7. Alas, *O Lord* God,
8. *O Lord,* what shall I say,
Jud. 6:15. Oh *my Lord,* wherewith shall I save Israel?
22. Alas, *O Lord* God,
13: 8. *O my Lord,* let the man of God which
16:28. and said, *O Lord* God,
2Sa. 7:18. Who (am) I, *O Lord* God?
19. a small thing in thy sight, *O Lord* God·
— this the manner of man, *O Lord* God?

2Sa.7 :20. thou, *Lord* God, knowest thy servant.
28. *O Lord* God, thou (art) that God,
29. thou, *O Lord* God, hast spoken
1K. 2:26. the ark of *the Lord* God
3:10. And the speech pleased *the Lord,*
8:53. broughtest our fathers out of Egypt, *O Lord*
22: 6. Go up; for *the Lord* shall deliver (it)
2K. 7: 6. *For the Lord* had made the host
19:23. thou hast reproached *the Lord,*
Ezr. 10: 3. according to the counsel of *my lord,*
Neh 1:11. O *Lord,* I beseech thee,
4:14(8). remember *the Lord,*
Job 28:28. Behold, the fear of *the Lord,*
Ps. 2: 4. *the Lord* shall have them in derision.
16: 2. Thou (art) *my Lord:* my goodness
22:30(31). it shall be accounted *to the Lord*
35:17. *Lord,* how long wilt thou look on?
22. *O Lord,* be not far from me.
23. my God *and my Lord.*
37:13. *the Lord* shall laugh at him;
38: 9(10). *Lord,* all my desire (is) before thee;
15(16). thou wilt hear, *O Lord* my God.
22(23). Make haste to help me, *O Lord*
39: 7(8). *Lord,* what wait I for? my hope (is) in
40:17(18). (yet) *the Lord* thinketh upon me:
44:23(24). Awake, why sleepest thou, *O Lord?*
51:15(17). *O Lord,* open thou my lips;
54: 4(6). *The Lord* (is) with them that uphold
55: 9(10). Destroy, *O Lord,* (and) divide their
57: 9(10). I will praise thee, *O Lord,*
59:11(12). bring them down, *O Lord* our shield.
62:12(13). unto thee, *O Lord,* (belongeth)
66:18. *the Lord* will not hear (me):
68:11(12). *The Lord* gave the word:
17(18). *the Lord* (is) among them, (as in)
19(20). Blessed (be) *the Lord,*
20(21). unto God *the Lord* (belong) the
22(23). *The Lord* said, I will bring again
26(27). *The Lord,* from the fountain of Israel.
32(33). O sing praises unto *the Lord;*
69: 6(7). that wait on thee, *O Lord* God of
71: 5. thou (art) my hope, *O Lord* God:
16. I will go in the strength of *the Lord*
73:20. *O Lord,* when thou awakest,
28. I have put my trust *in the Lord*
77: 2(3). day of my trouble I sought *the Lord:*
7(8). Will *the Lord* cast off for ever?
78:65. Then *the Lord* awaked as one out of sleep,
79:12. have reproached thee, *O Lord.*
86: 3. Be merciful unto me, *O Lord:*
4. unto thee, *O Lord,* do I lift up my soul.
5. For thou, *Lord,* (art) good,
8. (there is) none like unto thee, *O Lord;*
9. come and worship before thee, *O Lord;*
12. I will praise thee, *O Lord* my God,
15. But thou, *O Lord,* (art) a God full of
89:49(50). *Lord,* where (are) thy former
50(51). Remember, *Lord,* the reproach of thy
90: 1. *Lord,* thou hast been our dwellingplace
109:21. do thou for me, O God *the Lord,*
110: 5. *The Lord* at thy right hand
130: 2. *Lord,* hear my voice:
3. *O Lord,* who shall stand?
6. My soul (waiteth) for *the Lord*
140: 7(8). O God *the Lord,* the strength
141: 8. eyes (are) unto thee, O God *the Lord:*
Isa. 3:15. saith *the Lord* God of hosts.
17. Therefore *the Lord* will smite
18. In that day *the Lord* will take
4: 4. When *the Lord* shall have washed
6: 1. saw also *the Lord* sitting upon a throne,
8. Also I heard the voice of *the Lord,*
11. Then said I, *Lord,* how long?
7: 7. Thus saith *the Lord* God,
14. Therefore *the Lord* himself
20. In the same day shall *the Lord*
8: 7. Now therefore, behold, *the Lord*
9: 8(7). *The Lord* sent a word into Jacob,
17(16). *the Lord* shall have no joy
10:12. when *the Lord* hath performed
16. shall the Lord, *the Lord* of hosts
23. *the Lord* God of hosts shall make
24. thus saith *the Lord* God of hosts,
11:11. *the Lord* shall set his hand
21: 6. thus hath *the Lord* said
8. *My Lord,* I stand continually

Isa. 21:16. thus hath *the Lord* said
22: 5. of perplexity *by the Lord* God of
12. did *the Lord* God of hosts call to weeping,
14, 15. saith *the Lord* God of hosts.
25: 8. *the Lord* God will wipe away
28: 2. Behold, *the Lord hath* a mighty
16. thus saith *the Lord* God,
22. I have heard from *the Lord*
29:13. Wherefore *the Lord* said,
30:15. thus saith *the Lord* God,
20. *the Lord* give you the bread of adversity,
37:24. hast thou reproached *the Lord,*
38:16. *O Lord,* by these (things men) live,
40:10. *the Lord* God will come with strong
48:16. *the Lord* God, and his Spirit,
49:14. *and my Lord* hath forgotten me
22. Thus saith *the Lord* God,
50: 4. *The Lord* God hath given me
5. *The Lord* God hath opened mine
7. *For the Lord* God will help me;
9. *the Lord* God will help me;
52: 4. thus saith *the Lord* God,
56: 8. *The Lord* God which gathereth
61: 1. The Spirit of *the Lord* God (is)
11. *the Lord* God will cause righteousness
65:13. thus saith *the Lord* God,
15. *the Lord* God shall slay thee,
Jer. 1: 6. Ah, *Lord* God! behold,
2:19. my fear (is) not in thee, saith *the Lord*
22. is marked before me, saith *the Lord*
4:10. Ah, *Lord* God! surely thou hast
7:20. thus saith *the Lord* God;
14:13 & 32:17. Ah, *Lord* God!
32:25. thou hast said unto me, *O Lord*
44:26. saying, *The Lord* God liveth.
46:10. this (is) the day *of the Lord* God
— *the Lord* God of hosts *hath* a sacrifice
49: 5. saith *the Lord* God of hosts,
50:25. the work *of the Lord* God of hosts
31. (O thou) most proud, saith *the Lord*
Lam. 1:14. *the Lord* hath delivered me into
15. *the Lord* hath trodden under
— *the Lord* hath trodden the virgin,
2: 1. How hath *the Lord* covered the
2. *The Lord* hath swallowed up all
5. *The Lord* was an enemy:
7. *the Lord* hath cast off his altar,
18. Their heart cried unto *the Lord,*
19. before the face of *the Lord:*
20. in the sanctuary of *the Lord?*
3:31. *the Lord* will not cast off for ever:
36. *the Lord* approveth not.
37. *the Lord* commandeth (it) not?
58. *O Lord,* thou hast pleaded
Eze. 2: 4 & 3:11, 27. Thus saith *the Lord* God.
4:14. Ah *Lord* God! behold,
5: 5, 7, 8. Thus saith *the Lord* God,
11. (as) I live, saith *the Lord* God;
6: 3. hear the word of *the Lord* God; Thus saith *the Lord* God to the mountains,
11 & 7:2, 5. Thus saith *the Lord* God;
8: 1. the hand of *the Lord* God fell there
9: 8. Ah, *Lord* God! wilt thou destroy
11: 7, 16, 17. thus saith *the Lord* God;
8, 21. saith *the Lord* God.
13. Ah *Lord* God! wilt thou make a
12:10, 19, 23, 28. Thus saith *the Lord* God;
25, 28. saith *the Lord* God.
13: 3, 8, 13, 18, 20. Thus saith *the Lord* God;
8, 16. saith *the Lord* God.
9. ye shall know that I (am) *the Lord*
14: 4, 6, 21. Thus saith *the Lord* God;
11, 14, 16, 18, 20, 23. saith *the Lord* God.
15: 6. thus saith *the Lord* God;
8. saith *the Lord* God.
16: 3, 36, 59. Thus saith *the Lord* God
8, 14, 19, 23, 30, 43, 48 63. saith *the Lord* God,
17: 3, 9, 19, 22. Thus saith *the Lord* God;
16. saith *the Lord* God,
18: 3, 9, 23, 30, 32. saith *the Lord* God,
25, 29. The way of *the Lord* is not equal.
20: 3, 5, 27, 30, 39, 47 (21:3). Thus saith *the Lord* God,
— 31, 33, 36, 40, 44. saith *the Lord* God.
49(21:5). Ah *Lord* God! they say of me.
21: 7(12), 13(18). saith *the Lord* God,

Eze.21:24(29), 26(31), 28(33) & 22:3. thus saith *the Lord* God;
22:12, 31. saith *the Lord* God.
19, 28. thus saith *the Lord* God;
23:22, 28, 32, 35, 46. thus saith *the Lord* God;
34. saith *the Lord* God.
49. ye shall know that I (am) *the Lord*
24: 3, 6, 9, 21. Thus saith *the Lord* God;
14. saith *the Lord* God.
24. ye shall know that I (am) *the Lord*
25: 3. Hear the word of *the Lord* God; Thus saith *the Lord* God; Because
6, 8, 12, 13, 15, 16. thus saith *the Lord* God,
14. saith *the Lord* God.
26: 3, 7, 15, 19. thus saith *the Lord* God;
5, 14, 21. saith *the Lord* God:
27: 3 & 28:2, 6, 12, 22, 25. Thus saith *the Lord* God;
28:10. saith *the Lord* God.
24. they shall know that I (am) *the Lord*
29: 3, 8, 13, 19. Thus saith *the Lord* God;
16. they shall know that I (am) *the Lord*
20. they wrought for me, saith *the Lord*
30: 2, 10, 13, 22. Thus saith *the Lord* God;
6. fall in it by the sword, saith *the Lord*.
31:10, 15. thus saith *the Lord* God,
18. and all his multitude, saith *the Lord*
32: 3, 11. Thus saith *the Lord* God;
8, 14, 16, 31, 32 & 33:11. saith *the Lord* God.
33:17, 20. the way of *the Lord* is not equal:
25, 27 & 34:2, 10, 11, 17, 20. Thus saith *the Lord* God;
34: 8, 15, 30, 31. saith *the Lord* God,
35: 3, 14. Thus saith *the Lord* God;
6, 11. saith *the Lord* God,
36: 2, 3, 4, 5, 6, 7, 13, 22, 33, 37. Thus saith *the Lord* God,
4. hear the word of *the Lord* God;
14, 15, 23, 32. saith *the Lord* God.
37: 3. I answered, *O Lord* God, thou
5, 9, 12, 19, 21 & 38:3, 10, 14, 17. Thus saith *the Lord* God
38:18, 21. saith *the Lord* God.
39: 1, 17, 25. Thus saith *the Lord* God;
5, 8, 10, 13, 20, 29. saith *the Lord* God.
43:18. thus saith *the Lord* God;
19, 27. saith *the Lord* God,
44: 6, 9. Thus saith *the Lord* God;
12, 15, 27. saith *the Lord* God,
45: 9, 18. Thus saith *the Lord* God;
—, 15. saith *the Lord* God.
46: 1, 16 & 47:13. Thus saith *the Lord* God;
47:23 & 48:29. saith *the Lord* God.
Dan. 1: 2. And *the Lord* gave Jehoiakim
9: 3. I set my face unto *the Lord* God,
4. *O Lord*, the great and dreadful God,
7. *O Lord*, righteousness (belongeth)
8. *O Lord*, to us (belongeth) confusion
9. *To the Lord* our God (belong) mercies
15. And now, *O Lord* our God,
16. *O Lord*, according to all thy righteousness,
17. that is desolate, for *the Lord*'s sake.
19. *O Lord*, hear; *O Lord*, forgive; *O Lord*, hearken and do; defer not,
Am. 1: 8. Philistines shall perish, saith *the Lord*
3: 7. *the Lord* God will do nothing, but
8. *the Lord* God hath spoken, who can
11. thus saith *the Lord* God;
13. testify in the house of Jacob, saith *the Lord*
4: 2. *The Lord* God hath sworn
5. saith *the Lord* God.
5: 3. thus saith *the Lord* God;
16. the Lord, the God of hosts, *the Lord*,
6: 8. *The Lord* God hath sworn by
7: 1, 4. Thus hath *the Lord* God shewed unto
2. *O Lord* God, forgive, I beseech thee:
4. *the Lord* God called to contend by
5. *O Lord* God, cease, I beseech thee:
6. This also shall not be, saith *the Lord*
7. *the Lord* stood upon a wall
8. Then said *the Lord*, Behold,
8: 1. Thus hath *the Lord* God shewed
3, 9, 11. saith *the Lord* God
9: 1. I saw *the Lord* standing upon the altar:
5. *And the Lord* God of hosts (is) he
8. the eyes of *the Lord* God (are) upon
Obad. 1. Thus saith *the Lord* God
Mic. 1: 2. let *the Lord* God be witness against you, *the Lord* from his holy temple.
Hab. 3:19. The Lord *God* (is) my strength,
Zep. 1: 7. Hold thy peace at the presence of *the Lord*
Zec. 9: 4. Behold, *the Lord* will cast her out,
14. *and the Lord* God shall blow the
Mal. 1:14. sacrificeth unto *the Lord* a corrupt

אֹדוֹת see אוֹדֹת See 182

אָדַר [*āh-dar'*] 142

*NIPHAL.—*Participle*.*

Ex. 15: 6. hand,...*is become glorious* in power:
11. who is like thee, *glorious* in holiness,

*HIPHIL.—*Future*.*

Isa. 42:21. the law, *and make* (it) *honourable*.

אֲדָר *ădāhr*, m. 143

Est. 3: 7. (month), that (is), the month *Adar*.
13 & 8:12. which (is) the month *Adar*,
9: 1. that (is), the month *Adar*,
15. fourteenth day also of the month *Adar*,
17. thirteenth day of the month *Adar*;
19:21. fourteenth day of the month *Adar*

אֲדָר *ădāhr*, Ch. 144

Ezr. 6:15. on the third day of the month *Adar*,

אֶדֶר *eh'-der*, m. 145

Mic. 2: 8. ye pull off *the robe* with the garment
Zec.11:13. a *goodly* price that I was prised at of them. (lit. *the magnificence of* the price)

אֲדַרְגָּזְרַיָּא *ădar-gāh-z'rahy-yāh'*, m. Ch. pl. 148

Dan. 3: 2. the king sent to gather...*the judges*,
3. Then the princes,...*the judges*,

אַדְרַזְדָּא *ad-raz-dāh'*, adv. Ch. 149

Ezr. 7:23. let it be *diligently* done

אִדְּרֵי *id-d'rey'*, m. Ch. 147

[Pl. cons. of אִדַּר.]

Dan. 2:35. the chaff of *the* summer *threshing-floors*;

אֲדַרְכֹּנִים *ădar-kōh-neem'*, m. pl. 150

1Ch.29: 7. of gold five thousand talents *and* ten thousand *drams*,
Ezr. 8:27. of gold, *of* a thousand *drams*;

אֶדְרָע *ed-rāhg'*, Ch. 153

i. q. דְּרָע and Heb. זְרוֹעַ.

Ezr. 4:23. and made them to cease *by force* and power. (marg. *by arm*)

אַדֶּרֶת *ad-deh'-reth*, f. 155

Gen25:25. *like* an hairy *garment*;
Jos. 7:21. *a* goodly Babylonish *garment*,

Jos. 7:24. and the silver, and *the garment*,
1K. 19:13. he wrapped his face *in his mantle*,
19. and cast *his mantle* upon him.
2K. 2: 8. Elijah took *his mantle*,
13. He took up also *the mantle of* Elijah
14. he took *the mantle of* Elijah
Eze.17: 8. that it might be a *goodly* vine. (lit. a vine of *magnificence*)
Jon. 3: 6. he laid *his robe* from him,
Zec.11: 3. for *their glory* is spoiled:
13: 4. *a* rough *garment* to deceive:

---

156 אָדַשׁ [*āh-dash'*]

i. q. דּוּשׁ.

* KAL.—*Infinitive.* *

Isa. 28:28. he will not ever *be* threshing it, (lit. in *threshing* he will not ever thresh it)

---

157 אָהַב & אָהֵב *āh-hav'* & *āh-hēhv'*.

* KAL.—*Preterite.* *

Gen22: 2. thine only (son) Isaac, whom *thou lovest*,
27: 4. savoury meat, such as *I love*,
9. savoury meat for thy father, such as *he loveth:*
14. savoury meat, such as his father *loved.*
37: 3. Israel *loved* Joseph
4. saw that their father *loved* him
44:20. and his father *loveth him.*
Ex. 21: 5. say, *I love* my master,
Lev.19:18. *but thou shalt love* thy neighbour
34. *and thou shalt love* him as thyself;
Deu 4:37. because *he loved* thy fathers,
6: 5. *And thou shalt love* the Lord
7:13. *And he will love thee*, and bless thee,
10:19. *Love ye therefore* the stranger:
11: 1. *Therefore thou shalt love* the Lord
15:16. because *he loveth thee*
23: 5(6). Lord thy God *loved thee.*
Jud.14:16. Thou dost but hate me, and *lovest me* not:
16:15. How canst thou say, *I love thee*,
Ruth 4:15. daughter in law, which *loveth thee*,
1Sa. 1: 5. *he loved* Hannah:
18:22. his servants *love thee.*
28. Michal Saul's daughter *loved him.*
20:17. for *he loved him* as he loved his own soul.
2Sa.12:24. the Lord *loved him.*
13:15. wherewith *he had loved her.*
1K. 11: 1. Solomon *loved* many strange women,
Job.19:19. they whom *I loved* are turned
Ps. 11: 7. righteous Lord *loveth* righteousness;
26: 8. Lord *I have loved* the habitation
45: 7(8). *Thou lovest* righteousness,
47: 4(5). excellency of Jacob whom *he loved.*
52: 3(5). *Thou lovest* evil more than good;
4(6). *Thou lovest* all devouring words,
78:68. the mount Zion which *he loved.*
99: 4. The king's strength also *loveth* judgment;
116: 1. *I love* the Lord, because he hath heard
119:47, 48. thy commandments, which *I have loved.*
97. O how *love I* thy law!
113. but thy law *do I love.*
119. therefore *I love* thy testimonies.
127. Therefore *I love* thy commandments
140. therefore thy servant *loveth it.*
159. Consider how *I love* thy precepts:
163. (but) thy law *do I love.*
Pro. 8:36. all they that hate me *love* death.
Ecc. 9: 9. Live joyfully with the wife whom *thou lovest*
Cant.1: 3. therefore *do* the virgins *love thee.*
4. the upright *love thee.*
7. O thou *whom* my soul *loveth*,
3: 1. I sought him *whom* my soul *loveth:*
2. I will seek him *whom* my soul *loveth:*
3. Saw ye him *whom* my soul *loveth?*
4. but I found him *whom* my soul *loveth:*
Isa. 43: 4. *I have loved thee:* therefore will I
48:14. The Lord *hath loved him:*
57: 8. *thou lovedst* their bed
Jer. 2:25. for *I have loved* strangers,
5:31. my people *love* (to have it) so:
8: 2. whom *they have loved*,
Jer. 14:10. Thus *have they loved* to wander,
31: 3. Yea, *I have loved thee* with an
Eze.16:37. all (them) that *thou hast loved.*
Hos. 4:18. her rulers (with) shame *do love*,
9: 1. *thou hast loved* a reward
12: 7(8). *he loveth* to oppress.
Am. 4: 5. for this *liketh you*, O ye children (marg. *ye love*)
Mal. 1: 2. *I have loved* you, saith the Lord. Yet ye say, Wherein *hast thou loved us?*
2:11. holiness of the Lord which *he loved*, (marg. *ought to love*)

KAL.—*Infinitive.*

Deu10:12. to walk in all his ways, *and to love* him,
15. a delight in thy fathers *to love* them,
11:13, 22 & 19:9 & 30:6, 16. *to love* the Lord
30:20. That *thou mayest love* the Lord thy God, (lit. *to love*)
Jos.22: 5. *to love* the Lord your God,
23:11. *that ye love* the Lord your God. (lit. *to love*)
2Sa 19: 6(7). *In that thou lovest* thine enemies, (marg. *by loving*)
1K.11: 2. Solomon clave unto these *in love.* (lit. *to love*)
Ecc. 3: 8. A time *to love*, and a time to hate;
Isa. 56: 6. *and to love* the name of the Lord,
Hos. 9:10. *according as they loved.* (lit. *according to their loving*)

KAL.—*Imperative.*

Ps. 31:23(24). *O love* the Lord, all ye his saints:
Pro. 4: 6. *love her*, and she shall keep thee.
Hos. 3: 1. Go yet, *love* a woman beloved of
Am. 5:15. Hate the evil, *and love* the good,
Zec. 8:19. therefore *love* the truth and peace.

KAL.—*Future.*

Gen24:67. she became his wife; *and he loved her:*
25:28. *And* Isaac *loved* Esau, because
29:18. *And* Jacob *loved* Rachel;
30. *and he loved* also Rachel more than Leah,
32. therefore my husband *will love me.*
34: 3 *and he loved* the damsel, and spake kindly
Jud.16: 4. afterward, *that he loved* a woman in the
1Sa.16:21. *and he loved him* greatly;
18: 1. *and* Jonathan *loved him* as his own soul.
20. *and* Michal Saul's daughter *loved* David.
2Sa.13: 1. *and* Amnon the son of David *loved her.*
1K. 3: 3. *And* Solomon *loved* the Lord,
2Ch.11:21. *And* Rehoboam *loved* Maachah
19: 2. and *love* them that hate the Lord?
Est. 2:17. *And* the king *loved* Esther above all
Ps. 4: 2(3). (how long) *will ye love* vanity,
109:17. *As he loved* cursing,
119:167. *and I love them* exceedingly.
Pro. 1:22. How long...*will ye love* simplicity
3:12. whom the Lord *loveth* he correcteth:
8:17. *I love* them that love me;
9: 8. rebuke a wise man, *and he will love thee.*
15: 9. *he loveth* him that followeth after
12. A scorner *loveth* not one that reproveth
16:13. *they love* him that speaketh right. (lit. *he shall love*)
20:13. *Love* not sleep, lest thou come to poverty;
Hos.11: 1. *then I loved him*, and called my son
14: 4(5). *I will love them* freely:
Zec. 8:17. *love* no false oath:
Mal. 1: 2. *yet I loved* Jacob,

KAL.—*Participle.* Poël.

Gen25:28. but Rebekah *loved* Jacob.
Ex. 20: 6. unto thousands *of them that love me*,
Deu 5:10. unto thousands *of them that love me*
7: 9. mercy *with them that love him*
10:18. and widow, *and loveth* the stranger,
13: 3(4). whether ye *love* the Lord your God
Jud. 5:31. *but* (let) *them that love him* (be) as the sun
1Sa.18:16. But all Israel and Judah *loved* David,
2Sa.13: 4. Amnon said unto him, I *love* Tamar,
19: 6(7). hatest *thy friends.*
1K. 5: 1(15). Hiram was ever *a lover* of David.
2Ch.20: 7. Abraham *thy friend* for ever?
26:10. for he *loved* husbandry.
Neh. 1: 5. mercy *for them that love him*
Est. 5:10. he sent and called for *his friends*,

Est. 5:14. Zeresh his wife and all *his friends*
6:13. told Zeresh his wife and all *his friends*
Ps. 5:11(12). let them also *that love* thy name
11: 5. the wicked *and him that loveth* violence, his soul hateth.
33: 5. *He loveth* righteousness and judgment:
34:12(13). desireth life, (and) *loveth* (many)
37:28. For the Lord *loveth* judgment,
38:11(12). *My lovers* and my friends
40:16(17). let *such as love* thy salvation
69:36(37). *and they that love* his name shall
70: 4(5). let *such as love* thy salvation
87: 2. The Lord *loveth* the gates of Zion
88:18(19). *Lover* and friend hast thou put far
97:10. *Ye that love* the Lord, hate evil:
119:132. usest to do *unto those that love* thy name.
165. Great peace *have they which love* thy law: (lit. *to them that love*)
122: 6. they shall prosper *that love thee.*
145:20. preserveth all them *that love him:*
146: 8. the Lord *loveth* the righteous:
Pro. 8:17. I love *them that love me;*
21. That I may cause *those that love me*
12: 1. Whoso *loveth* instruction *loveth* knowledge:
13:24. *but he that loveth him* chasteneth
14:20. *but* the rich (hath) many *friends.* (marg. many are *the lovers of* the rich)
17:17. A friend *loveth* at all times,
19. *He loveth* transgression *that loveth* strife:
18:21. *and they that love it* shall eat the fruit
24. there is *a friend* (that) sticketh closer than
19: 8. getteth wisdom, *loveth* his own soul:
21:17. *He that loveth* pleasure (shall be) a poor man: *he that loveth* wine and oil shall
22:11. *He that loveth* pureness of heart,
27: 6. Faithful (are) the wounds of *a friend;*
29: 3. Whoso *loveth* wisdom rejoiceth
Ecc. 5:10(9). *He that loveth* silver shall not be satisfied with silver; nor he that *loveth*
Isa. 1:23. every one *loveth* gifts,
41: 8. the seed of Abraham *my friend.*
56:10. lying down, *loving* to slumber.
61: 8. For I the Lord *love* judgment,
66:10. all *ye that love her:*
Jer. 20: 4. terror to thyself, and to all *thy friends:*
6. be buried there, thou, and all *thy friends,*
Lam. 1: 2. among all *her lovers*
Dan. 9: 4. mercy *to them that love him,*
Hos. 3: 1. *and love* flagons of wine.
10:11. *loveth* to tread out (the corn);
Mic. 3: 2. Who hate the good, *and love* the evil;

KAL.—*Participle.* Päul.

Deu 21:15. one *beloved,* and another hated,
— (both) *the beloved* and the hated;
16. not make the son of *the beloved* firstborn
Neh 13:26. *and who* was *beloved* of his God,
Hos. 3: 1. love a woman *beloved of* (her) friend,

* NIPHAL.—*Participle.* *

2Sa. 1:23. Saul and Jonathan (were) *lovely*

* PIEL.—*Participle.* *

Jer. 22:20. for all *thy lovers* are destroyed.
22. *and thy lovers* shall go into captivity:
30:14. All *thy lovers* have forgotten thee;
Lam. 1:19. I called *for my lovers,*
Eze. 16:33. givest thy gifts to all *thy lovers,*
36. thy whoredoms with *thy lovers,*
37. I will gather all *thy lovers,*
23: 5. she doted on *her lovers,*
9. delivered her into the hand of *her lovers,*
22. I will raise up *thy lovers* against
Hos. 2: 5(7). I will go after *my lovers,*
7(9). she shall follow after *her lovers,*
10(12). in the sight of *her lovers,*
12(14). rewards that *my lovers* have given
13(15). she went after *her lovers,*
Zec. 13: 6. wounded (in) the house of *my friends.*

160 **אַהֲבָה** *ah-hăvāh'*, f.

Gen 29:20. *for the love he had* to her. (lit. *in his love*)
Deu. 7: 8. But *because* the Lord *loved* you, (lit. *because of the* Lord's *love to*)
1Sa. 18: 3. *because he loved* him as his own soul.
20:17. *because he loved* him (marg. *by his love* toward him): for he loved him *as he loved* (lit. *the love of*) his own soul.
2Sa. 1:26. *thy love* to me was wonderful, *passing the love of* women.
13:15. greater *than the love* wherewith
1K. 10: 9. *because* the Lord *loved* Israel. (lit. *in* the Lord's *love to*)
2Ch. 2:11(10). *Because* the Lord *hath loved* his people,
9: 8. *because* thy God *loved* Israel,
Ps. 109: 4. For *my love* they are my adversaries:
5. hatred for *my love.*
Pro. 5:19. be thou ravished always *with her love.*
10:12. but *love* covereth all sins.
15:17. Better (is) a dinner of herbs *where love* (is), (lit. *and love* there)
17: 9. covereth a transgression seeketh *love;*
27: 5. Open rebuke (is) better *than* secret *love.*
Ecc. 9: 1. no man knoweth either *love* or hatred
6. Also *their love,* and their hatred,
Cant. 2: 4. his banner over me (was) *love.*
5. I (am) sick of *love.*
7, & 3:5. nor awake (my) *love,* till he please. (lit. *the love*)
3:10. midst thereof being paved (with) *love,*
5: 8. that I (am) sick of *love.*
7: 6(7). how pleasant art thou, *O love,* for
8: 4. nor awake (my) *love,* until he please. (lit. *the love*)
6. for *love* (is) strong as death;
7. Many waters cannot quench *love,*
— all the substance of his house *for love,*
Isa. 63: 9. *in his love* and in his pity he redeemed
Jer. 2: 2. *the love of* thine espousals,
33. trimmest thou thy way to seek *love?*
31: 3. Yea, I have loved thee with *an* everlasting *love;*
Hos. 3: 1. *according to the love of* the Lord
9:15. I will *love them* no more:
11: 4. with bands of *love:*
Mic. 6: 8. *and to love* mercy, (lit. *and love of*)
Zep. 3:17. he will rest *in his love,*

אֲהָבִים *ăhāh-veem'*, m. 158

[Pl. of אַהַב.]

Pro. 5:19. the *loving* hind (lit. hind of *loves*)
Hos. 8: 9. Ephraim hath hired *lovers.* (marg. *loves*)

אֳהָבִים *ŏhāh-veem'*, m. 159

[Pl. of אֹהַב.]

Pro. 7:18. let us solace ourselves *with loves.*

אֲהָהּ *ăhāh*, interj. 162

Jos. 7: 7. Joshua said, *Alas,* O Lord
Jud. 6:22. Gideon said, *Alas,* O Lord God!
11:35. *Alas,* my daughter!
2K. 3:10. the king of Israel said, *Alas!*
6: 5. *Alas,* master! for it was borrowed.
15. *Alas,* my master! how shall we do?
Jer. 1: 6 & 4:10 & 14:13. Then said I, *Ah,* Lord G.!
32:17. *Ah* Lord God! behold thou hast
Eze. 4:14. Then said I, *Ah* Lord God!
9: 8. cried, and said, *Ah* Lord God!
11:13. and said, *Ah* Lord God!
20:49(21:5). Then said I, *Ah* Lord God!
Joel 1:15. *Alas* for the day!

אֱהִי *ĕhee*, adv. 165

Hos. 13:10. *I will be* thy king: (or, *where is* thy king?)
14. O death, *I will be* thy plagues; O grave, *I will be* thy destruction: (or, *where?... where?*)

NOTE.—The English translation renders it as if an apocopated future of הָיָה. The margin of the

modern Bibles (*v.* 10) is, however, correct, for
v. 14: אֱהִי דְבָרֶיךָ מָוֶת אֱהִי קָטָבְךָ שְׁאוֹל
LXX. Ποῦ ἡ δίκη σου, θάνατε; ποῦ τὸ κέντρον σου, ᾅδη; which is thus rendered by the Holy Ghost:—Ποῦ σου, θάνατε, τὸ κέντρον; ποῦ σου, ᾅδη τὸ νῖκος; 1 Cor. 15:55.

---

166 **אָהַל** [*āh-hal'*] prob. i. q. **הָלַל.**

* HIPHIL.—*Future.* *

Job25: 5. Behold even to the moon, and *it shineth* not;

---

167 **אָהַל** [*āh-hal'*]

* KAL.—*Future.* *

Gen13:12. *and pitched* (his) *tent* toward Sodom.
18. *Then* Abram *removed* (his) *tent,*

* PIEL.—*Future.* *

Isa. 13:20. neither *shall* the Arabian *pitch tent*

---

168 **אֹהֶל** *ōh'-hel,* m.

Gen. 4:20. the father of such as dwell in *tents,*
9:21. he was uncovered within *his tent.*
27. shall dwell *in the tents of* Shem;
12: 8. pitched *his tent,*
13: 3. place where *his tent* had been
5. Abram, had flocks, and herds, *and tents.*
18: 1. he sat in *the tent* door
2. to meet them from *the tent* door,
6. Abraham hastened *into the tent*
9. And he said, Behold, *in the tent.*
10. Sarah heard (it) in *the tent* door,
24:67. *into* his mother Sarah's *tent,*
25:27. Jacob (was) a plain man, dwelling in *tents.*
26:25. pitched *his tent* there:
31:25. Jacob had pitched *his tent*
33. Laban went *into* Jacob's *tent, and into* Leah's *tent, and into* the two maid-servants' *tents;* but he found (them) not. Then went he *out of* Leah's *tent,* and entered *into* Rachel's *tent.*
34. Laban searched all *the tent,*
33:19. where he had spread *his tent,*
35:21. spread *his tent* beyond the tower
Ex. 16:16. for (them) which (are) *in his tents.*
18: 7. they came *into the tent.*
26: 7. *to be a covering* upon the tabernacle:
9. the forefront of *the tabernacle.*
11. couple *the tent* together, that it may be one. (marg. *covering*)
12, 13. the curtains of *the tent,*
14. a covering *for the tent* (of) rams' skins
36. hanging for the door of *the tent,*
27:21. *In the tabernacle of* the congregation
28:43. come in unto *the tabernacle of* the
29: 4. bring unto the door of *the tabernacle of*
10. before *the tabernacle of* the congregation:
11, 32, 42. the door of *the tabernacle of* the
30. cometh into *the tabernacle of*
44. I will sanctify *the tabernacle of*
30:16. the service of *the tabernacle of*
18. put it between *the tabernacle of*
20. When they go into *the tabernacle of*
26. shalt anoint *the tabernacle of*
36. before the testimony *in the tabernacle of*
31: 7. *The tabernacle of* the congregation,
— all the furniture of *the tabernacle,*
33: 7. Moses took *the tabernacle,*
— called it *the Tabernacle of* the congreg.
— went out unto *the tabernacle of*
8. when Moses went out unto *the tabernacle,*
— every man (at) *his tent* door,
— until he was gone *into the tabernacle.*
9. as Moses entered *into the tabernacle,*
— stood (at) the door of *the tabernacle,*
10. pillar stand (at) *the tabernacle* door:

Ex. 33:10. worshipped, every man (in) *his tent* door.
11. departed not out of *the tabernacle.*
35:11. The tabernacle, *his tent,* and his covering,
21. the work of *the tabernacle of*
36:14. *for the tent* over the tabernacle:
18. to couple *the tent* together,
19. he made a covering *for the tent*
37. an hanging for *the tabernacle* door
38: 8. assembled at the door of *the tabernacle of*
30. the door of *the tabernacle of* the cong.,
39:32. the tabernacle of *the tent of* the cong.
33. the tabernacle unto Moses, *the tent,*
38. the hanging for *the tabernacle* door,
40. the tabernacle, *for the tent of* the cong.,
40: 2, 6, 29. tabernacle of *the tent of* the congreg.
7. between *the tent of* the congregation
12. the door of *the tabernacle of*
19. spread abroad *the tent* over the tabernacle, and put the covering of *the tent* above
22. he put the table *in the tent of*
24. he put the candlestick *in the tent*
26. he put the golden altar *in the tent*
30. the laver between *the tent of*
32. When they went into *the tent of*
34. Then a cloud covered *the tent of*
35. was not able to enter into *the tent of*
Lev. 1: 1. spake unto him *out of the tabernacle of*
3. at the door of *the tabernacle of*
5. (by) the door of *the tabernacle of* the
3: 2. kill it (at) the door of *the tabernacle of*
8, 13. kill it before *the tabernacle of*
4: 4. unto the door of *the tabernacle of*
5. bring it to *the tabernacle of*
7. which (is) *in the tabernacle of* the cong.;
— which (is at) the door of *the tabernacle of*
14. bring him before *the tabernacle of*
16. bring of the bullock's blood to *the tabernacle of*
18. that (is) *in the tabernacle of*
— which (is at) the door of *the tabernacle of*
6:16(9), 26(19). in the court of *the tabernacle of*
30(23). brought into *the tabernacle of*
8: 3, 4. unto the door of *the tabernacle of*
31. Boil the flesh (at) the door of *the tabernacle of*
33. go out of the door of *the tabernacle of*
35. abide (at) the door of *the tabernacle of*
9: 5. Moses commanded before *the tabernacle of*
23. Aaron went into *the tabernacle of*
10: 7. out from the door of *the tabernacle of*
9. when ye go into *the tabernacle of*
12: 6. unto the door of *the tabernacle of*
14: 8. shall tarry abroad out *of his tent*
11, 23 & 15:14, 29 & 16:7. the door of *the tabernacle of*
16:16. so shall he do *for the tabernacle of*
17. no man *in the tabernacle of*
20. reconciling the holy (place), and *the tabernacle of*
23. Aaron shall come into *the tabernacle of*
33. make an atonement for *the tabernacle of*
17: 4, 5, 6, 9 & 19:21. the door of *the tabernacle of*
24: 3. *in the tabernacle of* the congregation,
Nu. 1: 1. the wilderness of Sinai, *in the tabernacle of*
2: 2. far off about *the tabernacle of*
17. Then *the tabernacle of* the congregation
3: 7. before *the tabernacle of* the
8. all the instruments of *the tabernacle of*
25. *in the tabernacle of* the congregation (shall be) the tabernacle, *and the tent,*
— the door of *the tabernacle of*
38. before *the tabernacle of* the congregation
4: 3. to do the work *in the tabernacle of*
4, 15. the sons of Kohath *in the tabernacle of*
23. to do the work *in the tabernacle of*
25. and *the tabernacle of* the congregation,
— hanging for the door of *the tabernacle of*
28. of the sons of Gershon *in the tabernacle of*
30. to do the work of *the tabernacle of*
31, 33. to all their service *in the tabernacle of*
35, 39, 43. for the work *in the tabernacle of*
37, 41. all that might do service *in the tabernacle of*
47. service of the burden *in the tabernacle of*
6:10, 13, 18. the door of *the tabernacle of*
7: 5. to do the service of *the tabernacle of*
89. when Moses was gone into *the tabernacle of*

Nu. 8: 9. bring the Levites before *the tabernacle of*
15. to do the service of *the tabernacle of*
19. *in the tabernacle of* the congregation,
22. to do their service *in the tabernacle of*
24. to wait upon the service of *the tabernacle of*
26. *in the tabernacle of* the congregation,
9:15. *the tent of* the testimony:
17. was taken up from *the tabernacle,*
10: 3. at the door of *the tabernacle of*
11:10. every man in the door of *his tent:*
16. bring them unto *the tabernacle of*
24. set them round about *the tabernacle.*
26. but went not out *unto the tabernacle:*
12: 4. Come out ye three unto *the tabernacle of*
5. stood (in) the door of *the tabernacle*
10. cloud departed from off *the tabernacle;*
14:10. the Lord appeared *in the tabernacle of*
16:18. stood in the door of *the tabernacle of*
19. unto the door of *the tabernacle of*
26. from *the tents of* these wicked men,
27. stood in the door of *their tents,*
42(17:7). that they looked toward *the tabernacle of*
43(17:8). came before *the tabernacle of*
50(17:15). unto the door of *the tabernacle of*
17: 4(19). lay them up *in the tabernacle of*
7(22). *in the tabernacle of* witness.
8(23). into *the tabernacle of* witness;
18: 2. before *the tabernacle of* witness.
3. the charge of all *the tabernacle:*
4. the charge of *the tabernacle of* the congregation, for all the service of *the tabernacle:*
6, 21, 23. the service of *the tabernacle of* the
22. henceforth come nigh *the tabernacle of*
31. for your service *in the tabernacle of*
19: 4. before *the tabernacle of* the congregation
14. when a man dieth *in a tent:* all that come into *the tent,* and all that (is) *in the tent,*
18. sprinkle (it) upon *the tent,*
20: 6. unto the door of *the tabernacle of*
24: 5. How goodly are *thy tents,* O Jacob,
25: 6, & 27:2. *the tabernacle of* the congregation.
31:54. brought it into *the tabernacle of*
Deu. 1:27. ye murmured *in your tents,*
5:30(27). Get you *into your tents* again.
11: 6. their housholds, and *their tents,*
16: 7. and go *unto thy tents.*
31:14, 14. *in the tabernacle of* the congregation.
15. the Lord appeared *in the tabernacle*
— stood over the door of *the tabernacle.*
33:18. Issachar, *in thy tents.*
Jos. 3:14. people removed *from their tents,*
7:21. in the midst of *my tent,*
22. they ran *unto the tent;* and, behold, (it was) hid *in his tent,*
23. out of the midst of *the tent,*
24. *his tent,* and all that he had:
18: 1. set up *the tabernacle of* the congregation
19:51. at the door of *the tabernacle of*
22: 4. get you *unto your tents,*
6. they went unto *their tents.*
7. Joshua sent them away also unto *their tents,*
8. Return with much riches unto *your tents,*
Jud. 4:11. *his tent* unto the plain of Zaanaim,
17. Sisera fled away on his feet to *the tent of*
18. had turned in unto her *into the tent,*
20. Stand in the door of *the tent,*
21. Heber's wife took a nail of *the tent,*
5:24. blessed shall she be above women *in the tent.*
6: 5. their cattle, *and their tents,*
7: 8. Israel every man *unto his tent,*
13. came unto *a tent,* and smote it that it fell, and overturned it, that *the tent* lay along.
8:11. the way of them that dwelt *in tents,*
19: 9. mayest go *home.* (marg. *to thy tent*)
20: 8. not any (of us) go *to his tent,*
1Sa. 2:22. door of *the tabernacle of* the congregation.
4:10. they fled every man *into his tent:*
13: 2. he sent every man *to his tent.*
17:54. but he put his armour *in his tent.*
2Sa. 6:17. in the midst of *the tabernacle* that David
7: 6. walked *in a tent* and in a tabernacle.
16:22. So they spread Absalom *a tent*
18:17. all Israel fled every one *to his tent.*
2Sa. 19: 8(9). Israel had fled every man *to*
20: 1. every man *to his tents,* O Israel.
22. every man *to his tent.*
1K. 1:39. horn of oil out of *the tabernacle,*
2:28. Joab fled unto *the tabernacle of* the Lord,
29. Joab was fled unto *the tabernacle of* the L.;
30. Benaiah came to *the tabernacle of*
8: 4. *the tabernacle of* the congregation, and all the holy vessels that (were) *in the tabernacle,*
66. went *unto their tents* joyful and glad
12:16. *to your tents,* O Israel:
— So Israel departed *unto their tents.*
2K. 7: 7. left *their tents,* and their horses,
8. they went into one *tent,*
— again, and entered into another *tent,*
10. *and the tents* as they (were).
8:21. and the people fled *into their tents.*
13: 5. Israel dwelt *in their tents,*
14:12. they fled every man *to their tents.*
1Ch. 4:41. smote *their tents,*
5:10. they dwelt *in their tents*
6:32(17). dwelling place of *the tabernacle of*
9:19. keepers of the gates *of the tabernacle:*
21. porter of the door *of the tabernacle of*
23. the house of *the tabernacle,* by wards.
15: 1. pitched for it *a tent.*
16: 1. set it in the midst of *the tent*
17. 5. have gone *from tent* to *tent,*
23:32. keep the charge of *the tabernacle of*
2Ch. 1: 3. there was *the tabernacle of* the
4. he had pitched *a tent* for it
6. which (was) *at the tabernacle of*
13. before *the tabernacle of* the congregation,
5: 5. *the tabernacle of* the congregation, and all the holy vessels that (were) *in the tabernacle,*
7:10. he sent the people away *into their tents,*
10:16. every man *to your tents,* O Israel:
— So all Israel went *to their tents.*
14:15(14). They smote also *the tents of* cattle,
24: 6. *for the tabernacle of* witness?
25:22. they fled every man *to his tent.*
Job. 5:24. *thy tabernacle* (shall be) in peace;
8:22. *and the dwelling place of* the wicked
11:14. let not wickedness dwell *in thy tabernacles.*
12: 6. *The tabernacles* of robbers prosper,
15:34. consume *the tabernacles of* bribery.
18: 6. The light shall be dark *in his tabernacle,*
14. rooted *out of his tabernacle,*
15. It shall dwell *in his tabernacle,*
19:12. encamp round *about my tabernacle.*
20:26. him that is left *in his tabernacle.*
21:28. where (are) *the* dwelling *places of* the wicked? (marg. *the tent of* the tabernacles)
22:23. away iniquity far *from thy tabernacles.*
29: 4. secret of God (was) upon *my tabernacle;*
31:31. If the men of *my tabernacle*
Ps. 15: 1. who shall abide *in thy tabernacle?*
19: 4(5). In them hath he set *a tabernacle* for
27: 5. in the secret of *his tabernacle*
6. will I offer *in his tabernacle* sacrifices
52: 5(7). pluck thee *out of* (thy) *dwelling place*
61: 4(5). I will abide *in thy tabernacle* for ever;
69:25(26). (and) let none dwell *in their tents.*
78:51. strength *in the tabernacles of* Ham:
55. the tribes of Israel to dwell *in their tents.*
60. *the tent* (which) he placed among men;
67. he refused *the tabernacle of* Joseph,
83: 6(7). *The tabernacles of* Edom,
84:10(11). to dwell *in the tents of* wickedness.
91:10. any plague come nigh *thy dwelling.*
106:25. But murmured *in their tents,*
118:15. *in the tabernacles of* the righteous:
120: 5. I dwell in *the tents of* Kedar!
132: 3. *into the tabernacle of* my house,
Pro. 14:11. *but the tabernacle of* the upright shall
Cant. 1: 5. comely...*as the tents of* Kedar,
Isa. 16: 5. *in the tabernacle of* David,
33:20. *a tabernacle* (that) shall not be
38:12. removed from me *as a* shepherd's *tent.*
40:22. spreadeth them out *as a tent* to dwell in,
54: 2. Enlarge the place of *thy tent,*
Jer. 4:20. suddenly are *my tents* spoiled,
6: 3. they shall pitch (their) *tents*
10:20. *My tabernacle* is spoiled,

Jer. 10:20. to stretch forth *my tent* any more,
30:18. bring again the captivity of Jacob's *tents*,
35: 7. all your days ye shall dwell *in tents;*
10. But we have dwelt *in tents*,
37:10. they rise up every man *in his tent*,
49:29. *Their tents* and their flocks
Lam. 2: 4. *in the tabernacle of* the daughter of Zion:
Eze.41: 1. the breadth of *the tabernacle*.
Dan 11:45. he shall plant *the tabernacles of* his palace
Hos. 9: 6. thorns (shall be) *in their tabernacles*.
12: 9(10). yet make thee to dwell *in tabernacles*,
Hab. 3: 7. I saw *the tents of* Cushan
Zec.12: 7. shall save *the tents of* Judah first,
Mal. 2:12. *out of the tabernacles of* Jacob,

---

174 אֲהָלִים *ăhāh-leem'*, m. & אֲהָלוֹת *ăhāh-lōth'*, f. pl.

Nu.24: 6. *as the trees of lign aloes*
Ps. 45: 8(9). garments (smell) of myrrh, *and aloes*,
Pro. 7:17. perfumed my bed with myrrh, *aloes*, and
Cant.4:14. *and aloes*, with all the chief spices:

---

176 אֱו *ĕhv*, perhaps אַו, i.q. אַוָּה desire.

Pro. 31:4. (כתיב) nor for princes strong drink: (perhaps, *desire of* strong drink)—קרי has אֵי.

---

176 אוֹ *ōh*, conj.

Gen24:49. to the right hand, *or* to the left.
50. we cannot speak unto thee bad *or* good.
31:43. *or* unto their children which they have
Ex. 19:13. be stoned, *or* shot through;
21:18. with a stone, *or* with (his) fist,
Lev.13:49. or in the skin, *either* in the warp,
20:17. father's daughter, *or* his mother's daughter,
Jud.11:34. beside her he had neither son *nor* daughter.
&c. &c.

It may be repeated in a sentence; as,

Ex. 21.31. *Whether* he have gored a son, *or* have
Lev. 5: 1. *whether* he hath seen *or* known
13:53. *either* in the warp, *or* in the woof, *or* in anything of skin;
&c. &c.

Observe its meanings in

Gen24:55. (a few) days, *at the least* ten;
Lev.26:41. *if* then their uncircumcised hearts
2Sa.18:13. *Otherwise* I should have wrought
Pro.30:31. A greyhound; an he goat *also;*
Cant.2: 7 & 3.5. by the roes, *and* by the hinds
Eze.21:10(15). should we *then* make mirth?

---

178 אוֹב *ōhv*, m.

Lev.19:31. Regard not *them that have familiar spirits*,
20: 6. turneth after *such as have familiar spirits*,
27. A man also, or woman, that hath *a familiar spirit*, (lit. when *a spirit of divination* shall be in them)
Deu18:11. or a consulter with *familiar spirits*,
1Sa.28: 3. put away *those that had familiar spirits*,
7, 7. a woman that hath *a familiar spirit*,
8. divine unto me *by the familiar spirit*,
9. cut off *those that have familiar spirits*,
2K. 21: 6. dealt with *familiar spirits*
23:24. Moreover the (workers with) *familiar spirits*,
1Ch 10:13. *of* (one that had) *a familiar spirit*,
2Ch 33: 6. dealt with *a familiar spirit*,
Job 32:19. is ready to burst *like* new *bottles*.
Isa. 8:19. Seek unto *them that have familiar spirits*,
19: 3. *to them that have familiar spirits*,
29: 4. *as of one that hath a familiar spirit*,

---

180 אוּבָל or אֻבָל *oo-vāhl'*, m.

Dan. 8: 2. and I was by *the river of* Ulai.
Dan. 8: 3. there stood before *the river* a ram
6. which I had seen standing before *the river*,

אוּד *ood*, m. 181

Isa. 7: 4. two tails of these smoking *firebrands*,
Am. 4:11. ye were *as a firebrand* plucked out
Zec. 3: 2. (is) not this *a brand* plucked out of the

אוֹדֹת *ōh-dōhth'*, f. pl. 182

Gen21:11. in Abraham's sight *because of* his son.
25. reproved Abimelech *because of*
26:32. told him *concerning* the well
Ex. 18: 8. to the Egyptians for Israel'*s sake*,
Nu. 12: 1. against Moses *because of* the Ethiopian
13:24. *because of* the cluster of grapes
Jos.14: 6. *concerning me and thee* (lit. *concerning me*, *concerning thee*)
Jud. 6: 7. cried unto the Lord *because of* the
2Sa.13:16. she said unto him (There is) no *cause:*
Jer. 3: 8. I saw, when for all *the causes* whereby

NOTE.—Always preceded by עַל, except 2 Sam. 13: 16. and here עַל is the reading of 17 MSS. instead of אֶל,

---

אָוָה [*āh-vāh'*.] 183-84

N.B. In Num. 34:10. this verb is used in a peculiar sense.

* PIEL.—*Preterite.* *

Job 23:13. (what) his soul *desireth*, even (that) he
Ps. 132:13. *he hath desired* (it) for his habitation.
14. here will I dwell; for *I have desired it*.
Pro.21:10. The soul of the wicked *desireth* evil:
Isa. 26: 9. With my soul *have I desired thee*
Mic. 7: 1. my soul *desired* the firstripe fruit

PIEL.—*Future.*

Deu12:20. because thy soul *longeth* to eat flesh;
14:26. whatsoever thy soul *lusteth after*,
1Sa. 2:16. take (as much) as thy soul *desireth;*
2Sa. 3:21. reign over all that thine heart *desireth*.
1K. 11:37. reign according to all that thy soul *desireth*,

* HITHPAEL.—*Preterite.* *

Nu. 11: 4. mixt multitude that (was) among them fell a *lusting:* (marg. *lusted* a lust)
34:10. *And ye shall point out* your east border
Pro.21:26. *He coveteth* greedily all the day long:
Jer. 17:16. neither *have I desired* the woeful day;

HITHPAEL.—*Future.*

Deu. 5:21(18). neither *shalt thou covet* thy neighbour's
2Sa.23:15. *And* David *longed*, and said,
1Ch 11:17. *And* David *longed*, and said,
Ps. 45:11(12). *So shall* the king *greatly desire* thy beauty:
106:14. *But lusted* exceedingly in the wilderness (marg. *lusted* a lust)
Pro.23: 3. *Be* not *desirous* of his dainties:
6. neither *desire thou* his dainty meats:
24: 1. neither *desire* to be with them.
Ecc. 6: 2. for his soul of all that *he desireth*,

HITHPAEL.—*Participle.*

Nu. 11:34. they buried the people *that lusted*.
Pro.13: 4. The soul of the sluggard *desireth*,
Am. 5:18. Woe unto *you that desire* the day of

אוֹי *ōhy*, interj. 188

Nu.21:29. *Woe* to thee, Moab!
24:23. *Alas*, who shall live when God doeth this!
1Sa. 4: 7. *Woe* unto us!
8. *Woe* unto us! who shall deliver us
Pro.23:29. Who hath *woe?* who hath sorrow?
Isa. 3: 9. *Woe* unto their soul!

Isa. 3:11. *Woe* unto the wicked!
6: 5. *Woe* (is) me!
24:16. My leanness, my leanness, *woe* unto me!
Jer. 4:13. *Woe* unto us! for we are spoiled.
31. *Woe* (is) me now! for my soul is wearied
6: 4. *Woe* unto us! for the day goeth away,
10:19. *Woe* is me for my hurt!
13:27. *Woe* unto thee, O Jerusalem!
15:10. *Woe* is me, my mother,
45: 3. Thou didst say, *Woe* is me now!
48:46. *Woe* be unto thee, O Moab!
Lam. 5:16. *woe* unto us, that we have sinned!
Eze. 16:23. *woe, woe* unto thee! saith the Lord God;
24: 6, 9. *Woe* to the bloody city,
Hos. 7:13. *Woe* unto them!
9:12. *woe* also to them when I depart from

---

190 **אוֹיָה** *ōh-yāh′*, interj.

Ps. 120: 5. *Woe* is me, that I sojourn in Mesech,

---

191 **אֱוִיל** *ĕveel*, adj.

Job 5: 2. For wrath killeth *the foolish man*,
3. I have seen *the foolish* taking root:
Ps. 107:17. *Fools*, because of their transgression,
Pro. 1: 7. *fools* despise wisdom and instruction.
7:22. as *a fool* to the correction of the stocks;
10: 8, 10. *but a* prating *fool* shall fall.
14. the mouth of *the foolish* (is) near destruct.
21. *but fools* die for want of wisdom.
11:29. *the fool* (shall be) servant to the wise
12:15. The way of *a fool* (is) right in his own
16. *A fool*'s wrath is presently known:
14: 3. In the mouth of *the foolish* (is) a rod of
9. *Fools* make a mock at sin:
15: 5. *A fool* despiseth his father's instruction:
16:22. the instruction of *fools* (is) folly.
17:28. Even *a fool*, when he holdeth his peace,
20: 3. but every *fool* will be meddling.
24: 7. Wisdom (is) too high *for a fool:*
27: 3. but *a fool*'s wrath (is) heavier than
22. Though thou shouldest bray *a fool* in
29: 9. contendeth with a *foolish* man,
Isa. 19:11. Surely the princes of Zoan (are) *fools*,
35: 8. the wayfaring men, *though fools*,
Jer. 4:22. For my people (is) *foolish*,
Hos. 9: 7. the prophet (is) *a fool*,

---

193 **אוּל** [*ool*] m.

2K. 24:15. (כתיב) and *the mighty* of the land,
Ps. 73: 4. *their strength* (is) firm.

---

196 **אֱוִלִי** *ĕvee-lee′*, adj.

Zec. 11:15. the instruments of a *foolish* shepherd.

---

194 **אוּלַי** or **אֻלַי**. *oo-lahy′*,

Gen16: 2. *it may be that* I may obtain children
Ex. 32:30. *Peradventure* I shall make an atonement
Nu. 22:33. *unless* she had turned from me
Jos. 9: 7. *Peradventure* ye dwell among us;
14:12. *if so be* the Lord (will be) with me,
1K. 18: 5. *peradventure* we may find grass
27. (or) *peradventure* he sleepeth,
2K. 19: 4. *It may be* the Lord thy God will hear
Job 1: 5. *It may be* that my sons have sinned,
Hos. 8: 7. *if so be* it yield,
Zep. 2: 3. *it may be* ye shall be hid in the day
&c. &c.

---

197 **אוּלָם** or **אֻלָם** *oo-lāhm′*, m.

N.B. Eze. 40:39, 40. אֵלָם in some copies.

1K. 6: 3. *And the porch* before the temple
7: 6. he made *a porch of* pillars;
— *and the porch* (was) before them:
7. *Then* he made *a porch* for the throne
— (even) *the porch of* judgment:
8. (had) another court within *the porch*,
— *like unto* this *porch*.
12. *and for the porch of* the house.
1K. 7:19. of lily work *in the porch*,
21. *in the porch of* the temple:
1Ch 28:11. the pattern of *the porch*,
2Ch. 3: 4. *And the porch* that (was) in the front
8:12. he had built before *the porch*,
15: 8. before *the porch of* the Lord,
29: 7. shut up the doors of *the porch*,
17. came they *to the porch of* the Lord:
Eze. 8:16. between *the porch* and the altar,
40: 7. by *the porch of* the gate within
8. He measured also *the porch of*
9. Then measured he *the porch of*
— *and the porch of* the gate (was) inward.
15. unto the face of *the porch of* the inner
39. *And in the porch of* the gate
40. which (was) *at the porch of* the gate,
48. brought me to *the porch of* the house, and
measured (each) post of *the porch*,
49. The length of *the porch*
41:15. *and the porches of* the court;
25. upon the face of *the porch* without.
26. on the sides of *the porch*,
44: 3. he shall enter by the way of *the porch of*
46: 2. shall enter by the way of *the porch of*
8. he shall go in by the way of *the porch of*
Joel 2:17. weep between *the porch* and the altar,

אוּלָם *oo-lăhm′*, conj. 199

N.B. Job 17:10. וְאֻלָּם,

Gen28:19. *but* the name of that city
48:19. *but truly* his younger brother
Ex. 9:16. *And in very deed* for this
Nu. 14:21. *But* (as) *truly* (as) I live,
Jud 18:29. *howbeit* the name of the city
1Sa 20: 3. *but truly* (as) the Lord liveth,
25:34. *For in very deed*, (as) the Lord
1K. 20:23. *but* let us fight against them
Job 1:11. *But* put forth thine hand now,
2: 5. *But* put forth thine hand now,
5: 8. (lit. *yea*) I would seek unto God,
11: 5. *But* oh that God would speak,
12: 7. *But* ask now the beasts,
13: 3. *Surely* I would speak to the Almighty,
4. *But* ye (are) forgers of lies,
14:18. *And surely* the mountain falling
17:10. *But as for* you all, do ye return,
33: 1. *Wherefore*, Job, I pray thee,
Mic. 3: 8. *But truly* I am full of power

אִוֶּלֶת *iv-veh′-leth*, f. 200

Ps. 38: 5(6). corrupt because of *my foolishness*.
69: 5(6). O God, thou knowest *my foolishness;*
Pro. 5:23. in the greatness of *his folly* he shall
12:23. proclaimeth *foolishness*.
13:16. but a fool layeth open (his) *folly*.
14: 1. *but the foolish* plucketh it down
8. *but the folly of* fools (is) deceit.
17. (He that is) soon angry dealeth *foolishly:*
(lit. will do *foolishness*)
18. The simple inherit *folly:*
24. *the foolishness of* fools (is) *folly*.
29. hasty of spirit exalteth *folly*.
15: 2. mouth of fools poureth out *foolishness*
14. the mouth of fools feedeth on *foolishness*.
21. *Folly* (is) joy (to him that is) destitute of
16:22. the instruction of fools (is) *folly*.
17:12. rather than a fool *in his folly*.
18:13. matter before he heareth (it), it (is) *folly*
19: 3. *The foolishness of* man perverteth his way:
22:15. *Foolishness* (is) bound in the heart of a
24: 9. The thought of *foolishness* (is) sin:
26: 4. Answer not a fool *according to his folly*,
5. Answer a fool *according to his folly*, lest
11. a fool returneth *to his folly*.
27:22. (yet) will not *his foolishness* depart from

אָוֶן *āh′-ven*, m. 205

Gen35:18. called his name Ben-*oni:*
Nu. 23:21. not beheld *iniquity* in Jacob,
Deu26:14. eaten thereof *in my mourning*,
1Sa 15:23. *and* stubbornness (is as) *iniquity* and
Job 4: 8. they that plow *iniquity*,

Job. 5: 6. *affliction* cometh not forth of the dust,
11:11. he seeth *wickedness* also;
14. If *iniquity* (be) in thine hand,
15:35. and bring forth *vanity*, (marg. *iniquity*)
21:19. God layeth up *his iniquity* for his children. (marg. the punishment of *his iniquity*)
22:15. the old way which *wicked* men
31: 3. (punishment) to the workers of *iniquity?*
34: 8. company with the workers of *iniquity*,
22. where the workers of *iniquity* may hide
36. because of (his) answers for *wicked* men.
36:10. commandeth that they return *from iniquity.*
21. Take heed, regard not *iniquity:*
Ps. 5: 5(6). thou hatest all workers of *iniquity.*
6: 8(9). from me, all ye workers of *iniquity;*
7:14(15). Behold, he travaileth with *iniquity*,
10: 7. under his tongue (is) mischief *and vanity.*
14: 4. all the workers of *iniquity* no knowledge?
28: 3. with the workers of *iniquity*,
36: 3(4). The words of his mouth (are) *iniquity*
4(5). He deviseth *mischief* upon his bed; (marg. *vanity*)
12(13). are the workers of *iniquity* fallen:
41: 6(7). his heart gathereth *iniquity* to itself;
53: 4(5). the workers of *iniquity* no knowledge?
55: 3(4). for they cast *iniquity* upon me,
10(11). *mischief also* and sorrow (are) in
56: 7(8). Shall they escape by *iniquity?*
59: 2(3). Deliver me from the workers of *iniquity*,
5(6). merciful to any *wicked* transgressors.
64: 2(3). insurrection of the workers of *iniquity:*
66:18. If I regard *iniquity* in my heart,
90:10. their strength labour *and sorrow;*
92: 7(8). when all the workers of *iniquity*
9(10). all the workers of *iniquity* shall
94: 4. all the workers of *iniquity* boast
16. against the workers of *iniquity?*
23. shall bring upon them *their own iniquity*,
101: 8. that I may cut off all *wicked* doers
119:133. let not any *iniquity* have dominion
125: 5. forth with the workers of *iniquity:*
141: 4. with men that work *iniquity.*
9. the gins of the workers of *iniquity.*
Pro. 6:12. A naughty person, a *wicked* man,
18. deviseth *wicked* imaginations,
10:29. (shall be) to the workers of *iniquity.*
11: 7. the hope of *unjust* (men) perisheth.
12:21. no *evil* happen to the just:
17: 4. giveth heed to *false* lips;
19:28. the wicked devoureth *iniquity.*
21:15. to the workers of *iniquity.*
22: 8. soweth iniquity shall reap *vanity:*
30:20. I have done no *wickedness.*
Isa. 1:13. *iniquity*, even the solemn (marg. *grief*)
10: 1. them that decree *unrighteous* decrees,
29:20. all that watch for *iniquity* are
31: 2. them that work *iniquity.*
32: 6. his heart will work *iniquity*,
41:29. Behold, they (are) all *vanity;*
55: 7. the *unrighteous* man his thoughts: (marg. man of *iniquity*)
58: 9. and speaking *vanity;*
59: 4. and bring forth *iniquity.*
6. their works (are) works of *iniquity*,
7. their thoughts (are) thoughts of *iniquity;*
66: 3. burneth incense, (as if) he blessed *an idol.*
Jer. 4:14. shall *thy vain* thoughts lodge within thee?
15. publisheth *affliction* from mount Ephraim.
Eze 11: 2. these (are) the men that devise *mischief*,
30:17. The young men of *Aven*
Hos. 4:15. neither go ye up to Beth-*aven* (lit. house of *iniquity*)
5: 8. cry aloud (at) Beth-*aven*,
6: 8. Gilead (is) a city of them that work *iniquity*,
9: 4. as the bread of *mourners;*
10: 5. fear because of the calves of Beth-*aven:*
8. The high places also of *Aven*,
12:11(12). (Is there) *iniquity* (in) Gilead?
Am. 1: 5. off the inhabitant from *the* plain of *Aven*,
5: 5. Beth-el shall come *to nought.*
Mic. 2: 1. Woe to them that devise *iniquity*,
Hab. 1: 3. Why dost thou shew me *iniquity*,
3: 7. I saw the tents of Cushan in *affliction:* (marg. *vanity*)
Zec 10: 2. For the idols have spoken *vanity*,

און *ōhn*, m.

Gen49: 3. the beginning of *my strength*,
Deu21:17. for he (is) the beginning of *his strength;*
Job 18: 7. The steps of *his strength* shall be
12. *His strength* shall be hungerbitten,
20:10. his hands shall restore *their goods.*
40:16. *and his force* (is) in the navel
Ps. 78:51. the chief of (their) *strength*
105:36. the chief of all *their strength.*
Isa. 40:26. by the greatness of (his) *might*,
29. no *might* he increaseth strength.
Hos 12: 3(4). *and by his s.* he had power with God:
8(9). I have found me out *substance:*

אוניות *ŏh-neey-yōhth'*, f. pl. 591

כתיב for אֳנִיּוֹת.

2Ch. 8:18. Huram sent him, by the hand of his servants *ships*,

אוֹפָן *ōh-phan'*, m. 212

Ex. 14:25. took off their chariot *wheels*,
1K. 7:30. every base had four brasen *wheels*,
32. under the borders (were) four *wheels;* and the axletrees of *the wheels* (were joined) to the base; and the height of *a wheel*
33. the work of *the wheels* (was) like the work of *a* chariot *wheel:*
Pro. 20:26. bringeth *the wheel* over them.
25:11. A word *fitly* spoken (marg. spoken upon *his wheels*) [See אָפְנַיִם.]
Isa. 28:27. *neither* is *a* cart *wheel* turned
Eze. 1:15. behold one *wheel* upon the earth
16. The appearance of *the wheels*
— *a wheel* in the middle of *a wheel.*
19. *the wheels* went by them:
—,21. *the wheels* were lifted up.
20. *and the wheels* were lifted up
—,21. creature (was) *in the wheels.*
3:13. the noise of *the wheels* over against them,
10: 6. and stood beside *the wheels.*
9. behold *the* four *wheels* by the cherubims, one *wheel* by one cherub, *and* another *wheel* by another cherub: and the appearance of *the wheels*
10. if *a wheel* had been in the midst of *a wheel.*
12. *and the wheels* (were) full of eyes round about, (even) *the wheels* that they four had. (lit. *their wheels* to &c.)
13. *As for the wheels*,
16. *the wheels* went by them:
— *the* same *wheels* also turned not
19. *the wheels also* (were) beside them,
11:22. *the wheels* beside them;
Nah. 3: 2. of the rattling of *the wheels*, (Heb. *wheel*)

אוּץ [*ootz*,] 213

* KAL.—*Preterite.* *

Jos. 10:13. *hasted* not to go down about a whole day.
17:15. if mount Ephraim *be* too *narrow* for thee.
Jer. 17:16. *I have* not *hastened* from (being) a pastor

KAL.—*Participle.*

Ex. 5:13. the taskmasters *hasted* (them),
Pro. 19: 2. *and he that hasteth* with (his) feet sinneth.
21: 5. of every one (that is) *hasty* only to want.
28:20. *but he that maketh haste* to be rich
29:20. Seest thou a man (that is) *hasty* in his words?

* HIPHIL.—*Future.* *

Gen19:15. *then* the angels *hastened* Lot,
Isa. 22: 4. *labour* not to comfort me,

אוֹצָר *ōh-tzāhr'*, m. 214

Deu28:12. open unto thee *his* good *treasure*,
32:34. sealed up *among my treasures?*
Jos. 6:19. come into *the treasury of* the Lord.

Jos. 6:24. they put into *the treasury of*
1K. 7:51. he put *among the treasures of*
14:26. he took away *the treasures of* the house of the Lord, and *the treasures of* the king's house;
15:18. *in the treasures of* the house of the Lord, and *the treasures of* the king's house,
2K. 12:18(19). found *in the treasures of*
14:14 & 16:8 & 18:15. *and in the treasures of* the king's house,
20:13. all that was found *in his treasures:*
15. there is nothing *among my treasures*
24:13. all *the treasures of* the house of the Lord, *and the treasures of* the king's house,
1Ch. 9:26. *treasuries of* the house of God.
26:20. over *the treasures of* the house of God, *and over the treasures of* the dedicated
22. over *the treasures of* the house of
24. ruler of *the treasures.*
26. over all *the treasures of* the
27:25. over *the* king's *treasures*
— over *the storehouses* in the fields,
27. *for the* wine *cellars*
28. over *the cellars of* oil
28:12. *of the treasuries of* the house of God, *and of the treasuries of* the dedicated
29: 8. *to the treasure of* the house of
2Ch. 5: 1. put he *among the treasures of*
8:15. any matter, *or concerning the treasures.*
11:11. *and store of* victual,
12: 9. took away *the treasures of* the house of the Lord, and *the treasures of* the king's
16: 2. out *of the treasures of* the house
25:24. and *the treasures of* the king's house,
32:27. *and* he made himself *treasuries*
36:18. *and the treasures of* the house of the Lord, *and the treasures of* the king,
Ezr. 2:69. *unto the treasure of* the work
Neh. 7:70. gave *to the treasure* a thousand
71. gave *to the treasure of* the work
10:38(39). into *the treasure* house.
12:44. over the chambers *for the treasures,*
13:12. the oil *unto the treasuries.* (marg. *store houses*)
13. made treasurers over *the treasuries,*
Job 38:22. Hast thou entered into *the treasures of* the snow? *or* hast thou seen *the treasures of* the hail,
Ps. 33: 7. he layeth up the depth *in storehouses.*
135: 7. bringeth the wind *out of his treasuries.*
Pro. 8:21. *and* I will fill *their treasures.*
10: 2. *Treasures of* wickedness profit nothing:
15:16. *than* great *treasure* and trouble
21: 6. The getting of *treasures*
20. (There is) *treasure* to be desired
Isa. 2: 7. (is there any) end *of their treasures;*
30: 6. and *their treasures* upon the
33: 6. the fear of the Lord (is) *his treasure.*
39: 2. all that was found *in his treasures:*
4. there is nothing *among my treasures*
45: 3. I will give thee *the treasures of*
Jer. 10:13. forth the wind *out of his treasures.*
15:13. Thy substance *and thy treasures*
17: 3. all *thy treasures* to the spoil,
20: 5. all *the treasures of* the kings
38:11. house of the king under *the treasury,*
48: 7. in thy works *and in thy treasures,*
49: 4. that trusted *in her treasures,*
50:25. The Lord hath opened *his armoury,*
37. a sword (is) upon *her treasures;*
51:13. abundant in *treasures,* thine end is come,
16. the wind *out of his treasures.*
Eze 28: 4. gold and silver *into thy treasures:*
Dan. 1: 2. into the *treasure*house of his god.
Hos 13:15. he shall spoil *the treasure of*
Joel 1:17. *the garners* are laid desolate,
Mic. 6:10. Are there yet *the treasures of*
Mal. 3:10. all the tithes into *the store*house,

---

215 **אוֹר** *ōhr,*

* KAL.—*Preterite.* *

Gen44: 3. As soon as the morning *was light,*
1Sa.14:29. how mine eyes *have been enlightened,*
29:10. early in the morning, *and have light,*
Pro. 4:18. *that shineth* more and more unto the perfect day. (lit. that goeth on, *and shineth*)

KAL.—*Imperative.*

Isa. 60: 1. Arise, *shine;* for thy light is come, (marg. *be enlightened*)

KAL.—*Future.*

1Sa.14:27. (קרי) *and* his eyes *were enlightened.*

* NIPHAL.—*Infinitive.* *

Job 33:30. *to be enlightened* with the light of the

NIPHAL.—*Future.*

2Sa. 2:32. came to Hebron at *break of day.* (lit. *and it became light* to them)

NIPHAL.—*Participle.*

Ps. 76: 4(5). Thou (art) more *glorious* (and) excellent

* HIPHIL.—*Preterite.* *

Ex. 25:37. *that they may give light* over against it.
Ps. 77:18(19). the lightnings *lightened* the world:
97: 4. His lightnings *enlightened* the world:
Eze 43: 2. the earth *shined* with his glory.

HIPHIL.—*Infinitive.*

Gen. 1:15, 17. *to give light* upon the earth:
Ex. 13:21. pillar of fire, *to give* them *light;*
Ezr. 9: 8. *that* our God *may lighten* our eyes,
Neh. 9:12. *to give* them *light* in the way
19. fire by night, *to shew* them *light,*
Ps.105:39. fire *to give light* in the night.

HIPHIL.—*Imperative.*

Ps. 13: 3(4). *lighten* mine eyes, lest I sleep
31:16(17). *Make* thy face *to shine* upon thy servant:
80: 3(4), 7 (8). *and cause* thy face *to shine;* and 19(20). *cause* thy face *to shine;*
119:135. *Make* thy face *to shine* upon thy servant;
Dan. 9:17. *and cause* thy face *to shine* upon thy sanc.

HIPHIL.—*Future.*

Ex. 14:20. *but it gave light* by night
Nu. 6:25. The Lord *make* his face *shine* upon thee,
8: 2. the seven lamps *shall give light*
Job 41:32(24). *maketh* a path *to shine* after him;
Ps. 18:28(29). For *thou wilt light* my candle:
67: 1(2). *cause* his face *to shine* upon us.
118:27. *which hath shewed* us *light:*
119:130. The entrance of thy words *giveth light;*
139:12. but the night *shineth* as the day.
Ecc. 8: 1. wisdom *maketh* his face *to shine,*
Isa. 60:19. *shall* the moon *give light* unto thee:
Eze 32: 7. the moon *shall* not *give* her light. (lit. *cause* her light *to shine*)
Mal. 1:10. neither *do ye kindle* (fire) on mine altar

HIPHIL.—*Participle.*

Ps. 19: 8(9). *enlightening* the eyes.
Pro.29:13. the Lord *lighteneth* both their eyes.
Isa. 27:11. the women come, (and) *set* them *on fire:*

אוֹר *ōhr,* m. 216

Once f. Job 36:32.

Compare Is. 18:4 with אוֹרָה.

Gen. 1: 3. Let there be *light:* and there was *light.*
4. God saw *the light,* that (it was) good: and God divided *the light* from the darkness.
5. God called *the light* Day,
18. divide *the light* from the darkness:
Ex. 10:23. the children of Israel had *light*
Jud.16: 2. In the morning, *when it is day,* (lit. until *the light of* the morning)
19:26. till it was *light.*
1Sa.14:36. until *the* morning *light,*
25:22. by *the* morning *light*
34. unto Nabal by *the* morning *light*
36. until *the* morning *light,*
2Sa.17:22. by *the* morning *light* there lacked not
23: 4. *And* (he shall be) *as the light of*
2K. 7: 9. if we tarry till *the* morning *light,*
Neh. 8: 3. from *the morning* until midday, (marg. *light*)
Job 3: 9. let it look *for light,* but (have) none;
16. as infants (which) never saw *light.*
20. Wherefore is *light* given to him
12:22. bringeth out *to light* the shadow
25. They grope in the dark without *light,*
17:12. *the light* (is) short because of darkness.
18: 5. *the light of* the wicked shall be put out,

Job 18: 6. *The light* shall be dark in his tabernacle,
18. He shall be driven *from light* into darkness,
22:28. *the light* shall shine upon thy ways.
24:13. those that rebel against *the light;*
14. The murderer rising *with the light*
16. they know not *the light.*
25: 3. upon whom doth not *his light* arise?
26:10. until *the day* and night come to an end. (marg. the end of *light* with darkness)
28:11. bringeth he forth to *light.*
29: 3. *by his light* I walked (through) darkness;
24. *and the light of* my countenance
30:26. when I waited *for light,*
31:26. If I beheld *the sun* when it shined, (marg. **the light**)
33:28. his life shall see *the light.*
30. to be enlightened *with the light of* the living.
36:30. he spreadeth *his light* upon it,
32. With clouds he covereth *the light;*
37: 3. *and his lightning* unto the ends of the earth. (marg. *light*)
11. he scattereth *his bright* cloud: (marg. cloud of *his light*)
15. caused *the light of* his cloud to shine?
21. (men) see not *the* bright *light*
38:15. from the wicked *their light* is withholden,
19. the way (where) *light* dwelleth?
24. By what way is *the light* parted,
41:18(10). By his neesings *a light* doth shine,
Ps. 4: 6(7). *the light of* thy countenance
27: 1. The Lord (is) *my light* and my salvation;
36: 9(10). *in thy light* shall we see *light.*
37: 6. bring forth thy righteousness *as the light,*
38:10(11). *as for the light of* mine eyes,
43: 3. O send out *thy light* and thy truth:
44: 3(4). *the light of* thy countenance,
49:19(20). they shall never see *light.*
56:13(14). walk before God *in the light of* the
78:14. all the night *with a light of* fire.
89:15(16). *in the light of* thy countenance.
97:11. *Light* is sown for the righteous,
104: 2. Who coverest (thyself) with *light*
112: 4. Unto the upright there ariseth *light*
119:105. *and a light* unto my path.
136: 7. To him that made great *lights:*
139:11. even the night shall be *light* about me.
148: 3. praise him, all ye stars of *light.*
Pro. 4:18. the just (is) *as the* shining *light,*
6:23. and the law (is) *light;*
13: 9. *The light of* the righteous rejoiceth:
16:15. *In the light of* the king's countenance
Ecc. 2:13. as far as *light* excelleth darkness.
11: 7. Truly *the light* (is) sweet,
12: 2. While the sun, *or the light,*
Isa. 2: 5. walk *in the light of* the Lord.
5:20. put darkness *for light, and light* for darkness;
30. *and the light* is darkened in the heavens
9: 2(1). have seen *a* great *light:*
—(–) upon them hath *the light* shined.
10:17. *the light of* Israel shall be for a fire,
13:10. shall not give *their light:*
— moon shall not cause *her light* to shine.
18: 4. like a clear heat upon *herbs,* (lit. *light;* marg. after rain)
30:26. Moreover *the light of* the moon shall be *as the light of* the sun, *and the light of* the sun shall be sevenfold, *as the light of* seven days,
42: 6. *for a light of* the Gentiles;
16. I will make darkness *light* before them,
45: 7. I form *the light,* and create darkness:
49: 6. give thee *for a light to* the Gentiles,
51: 4. to rest *for a light of* the people.
58: 8. Then shall *thy light* break forth
10. then shall *thy light* rise in obscurity,
59: 9. we wait *for light,* but behold obscurity;
60: 1. Arise, shine; for *thy light* is come,
3. the Gentiles shall come *to thy light,*
19. The sun shall be no more thy *light*
— unto thee *an* everlasting *light,*
20. shall be thine everlasting *light,*
Jer. 4:23. the heavens, and *they* (had) no *light.* (lit. not *their light*)
13:16. while ye look *for light,*
25:10. *and the light of* the candle.
31:35. which giveth the sun *for a light* by day,
— the stars *for a light* by night,

Lam 3: 2. but not (into) *light.*
Eze.32: 7. the moon shall not give *her light.*
8. All the *bright* lights of heaven (marg. lights of *the light* in heaven)
Hos. 6. 5. thy judgments (are as) *the light*
Am. 5:18. day of the Lord (is) darkness, and not *light.*
20. of the Lord (be) darkness, and not *light?*
8: 8. it shall rise up wholly *as a flood;*
9. I will darken the earth in the *clear* day (lit. day of *light*)
Mic. 2: 1. *when* the morning *is light,*
7: 8. the Lord (shall be) *a light* unto me.
9. he will bring me forth *to the light,*
Hab. 3: 4. (his) brightness was *as the light;*
11. *at the light of* thine arrows they went,
Zep. 3: 5. doth he bring his judgment *to light,*
Zec.14: 6. *the light* shall not be clear, (nor) dark:
7. at evening time it shall be *light.*

אוּר *oor,* m. 217, 224

The pl. Is. 24:15, is אֻרִים, elsewhere it is אוּרִים.

Ex. 28:30. put in the breastplate of judgment *the Urim*
Lev. 8: 8. he put in the breastplate *the Urim*
Nu. 27:21. after the judgment of *Urim*
Deu 33: 8. thy Thummim *and thy Urim* (be) with
1 Sa.28: 6. neither by dreams, nor *by Urim,*
Ezr. 2:63. till there stood up a priest *with Urim*
Neh. 7:65. till there stood (up) a priest *with Urim*
Isa. 24:15. glorify ye the Ld. *in the fires,* (marg. *valleys*)
31: 9. the Lord, whose *fire* (is) in Zion,
44:16. I have seen *the fire:*
47:14. (nor) *fire* to sit before it.
50:11. walk *in the light of* your fire,
Eze. 5: 2. Thou shalt burn *with fire* a third part

אוֹרָה *ōh-rāh',* f. 219

Pl. אֹרֹת herbs;—compare אוֹר Is. 18:4.

2K. 4:39. went out into the field to gather *herbs,*
Est. 8:16. The Jews had *light,* and gladness,
Ps.139:12. the darkness and *the light* (are) both *alike* (lit. as darkness *as light*)
Isa. 26:19. thy dew (is as) the dew of *herbs,*

אֻוֵרוֹת *ăvēh-rōth',* f. pl. for אֻרְווֹת 220

2Ch32:28. and *cotes* for flocks. (lit. and flocks *for stalls*)

אַוַּת *av-vath',* f. 185

[Const. of אַוָּה.]

Deu12:15,20,21. whatsoever thy soul *lusteth after,* (lit. in all *the desire of* thy soul)
18: 6. come with all *the desire of* his mind
1 Sa 23:20. according to all *the desire of* thy soul
Jer. 2:24. snuffeth up the wind *at* her *pleasure;* (marg. *the desire of* her heart)
Hos.10:10. (It is) *in my desire* that I should chastise

אוֹת *ōhth,* c. 226

Gen 1:14. let them be *for signs,* and for seasons,
4:15. the Lord set *a mark* upon Cain,
9:12,17. This (is) *the token of* the covenant
13. it shall be *for a token of* a covenant
17:11. it shall be *a token of* the covenant
Ex. 3:12. this (shall be) *a token* unto thee,
4: 8. *the* first *sign,* that they will believe the voice of *the* latter *sign.*
9. will not believe also these two *signs,*
17. wherewith thou shalt do *signs.*
28. all *the signs* which he had commanded
30. did *the signs* in the sight of the people.
7: 3. multiply *my signs* and my wonders
8:23(19). to morrow shall this *sign* be.
10: 1. I might shew these *my signs* before him:

Ex. 10: 2. *my signs* which I have done
12:13. blood shall be to you *for a token*
13: 9. *for a sign* unto thee upon thine hand,
16. shall be *for a token* upon thine hand,
31:13. for it (is) *a sign* between me and you
17. *a sign* between me and the children of Is.
Nu. 2: 2. *with the ensign of* their father's house.
14:11. all *the signs* which I have shewed
22. *my miracles*, which I did in Egypt
16:38 (17:3). they shall be *a sign*
17:10 (25). kept *for a token* against the rebels;
Deu. 4:34. *by signs*, and by wonders,
6: 8. bind them *for a sign* upon thine hand,
22. the Lord shewed *signs* and wonders,
7:19 *and the signs*, and the wonders, and the
11: 3. *his miracles*, and his acts, which he did
18. bind them *for a sign* upon your hand,
13: 1 (2). giveth thee *a sign* or a wonder,
2 (3). *the sign* or the wonder come to pass,
26: 8. *and with signs*, and with wonders:
28:46. they shall be upon thee *for a sign*
29: 3 (2). *the signs*, and those great miracles:
34:11. In all *the signs* and the wonders,
Jos. 2:12. give me *a true token:*
4: 6. That this may be *a sign* among you,
24:17. which did those great *signs* in our sight,
Jud. 6:17. shew me *a sign* that thou talkest with me.
1 Sa. 2:34. this (shall be) *a sign* unto thee.
10: 7. when these *signs* are come unto thee,
9. all those *signs* came to pass that day.
14:10. this (shall be) *a sign* unto us.
2K. 19:29. And this (shall be) *a sign* unto thee,
20: 8. What (shall be) *the sign* that the Lord
9. This *sign* shalt thou have of the Lord,
Neh. 9:10. shewedst *signs* and wonders upon Pharaoh,
Job 21:29. *and* do ye not know *their tokens*,
Ps. 65: 8 (9). uttermost parts are afraid *at thy tokens:*
74: 4. they set up *their ensigns* (for) *signs*.
9. We see not *our signs:*
78:43. How he had wrought *his signs* in Egypt,
86:17. Shew me *a token* for good;
105:27. They shewed *his signs* among them, (marg. words of *his signs*)
135: 9. sent *tokens* and wonders into the midst of
Isa. 7:11. Ask thee *a sign* of the Lord thy God;
14. the Lord himself shall give you *a sign;*
8:18. *for signs* and for wonders in Israel
19:20. it shall be *for a sign* and for a witness
20: 3. *a sign* and wonder upon Egypt
37:30 & 38:7. this (shall be) *a sign* unto thee,
38:22. What (is) *the sign* that I shall go
44:25. frustrateth *the tokens of* the liars,
55:13. *for an* everlasting *sign*
66:19. I will set *a sign* among them,
Jer. 10: 2. *and* be not dismayed *at the signs of* heaven;
32:20. Which hast set *signs* and wonders
21. out of the land of Egypt *with signs*,
44:29. this (shall be) *a sign* unto you,
Eze. 4: 3. This (shall be) *a sign* to the house of Is.
14: 8. will make him *a sign* and a proverb,
20:12. my sabbaths, to be *a sign* between me and
20. they shall be *a sign* between me and you,

---

225 **אוֹת [*ōhth*].**

∗ NIPHAL.—*Future.* ∗

Gen34:15. But in this *will we consent*
22. Only herein *will* the men *consent*
23. only *let us consent* unto them,
2K. 12: 8 (9). *And* the priests *consented* to receive

---

227 **אָז *āhz*, adv.**

Gen12: 6. the Canaanite (was) *then* in the land.
Ex. 15:15. *Then* the dukes of Edom shall be amazed;
Jos. 22:31. *now* ye have delivered the children (marg. *then*)
1K. 9:11. *that then* king Solomon gave Hiram
2K. 5: 3. *for* he would recover him of his leprosy.
1Ch. 20: 4. *at which time* Sibbechai the Hushathite
Job 9:31. *Yet* shalt thou plunge me in the ditch,
Ecc. 2:15. why was I *then* more wise?
&c. &c.

With prefix מֵאָז.

Gen39: 5. *from the time* (that) he had made
Ex. 4:10. neither heretofore, nor *since*
Jos. 14:10. *even since* the Lord spake this word
Ruth 2: 7. *even from* the morning until now,
2Sa. 15:34. thy father's servant *hitherto*,
Ps. 76: 7 (8). thy sight *when once* thou art angry
93: 2. Thy throne (is) established *of old:*
Isa. 16:13. concerning Moab *since that time*.
44: 8. have not I told thee *from that time*,
48: 3. the former things *from the beginning;*
5. I have even *from the beginning* declared
&c. &c.

It is supposed to be understood in

Ps. 39: 3 (4). (*then*) spake I with my tongue,
Jer. 28: 9. (*then*) shall the prophet be known,
51:53. (*yet*) from me shall spoilers come
&c. &c. &c.

אֲזָא & אֲזָה [*ăzāh*] Ch. 228

∗ P'AL.—*Infinitive.* ∗

Dan. 3:19. commanded *that they should heat* the furnace one seven times more than *it* was wont *to be heated*.

P'AL.—*Participle Passive.*

Dan. 3:22. and the furnace exceeding *hot*,

אֲזַד [*ăzad*] Ch. 230

∗ P'AL.—*Preterite.* ∗

Dan. 2: 5. The thing *is gone* from me:
8. ye see the thing *is gone* from me.

אֵזוֹב *ēh-zōhv'*, m. 231

Ex. 12:22. ye shall take a bunch of *hyssop*,
Lev. 14: 4, 49. cedar wood, and scarlet, *and hyssop*.
6. cedar wood, and the scarlet, and *the hyssop*,
51. take the cedar wood, and *the hyssop*, and
52. with the cedar wood, and *with the hyssop*,
Nu. 19: 6. take cedar wood, *and hyssop*,
18. a clean person shall take *hyssop*,
1 K. 4:33 (5:13). *the hyssop* that springeth out of the
Ps. 51: 7 (9). Purge me *with hyssop*,

אֵזוֹר *ēh-zōhr'*, m. 232

2 K. 1: 8. *and* girt *with a girdle of* leather
Job 12:18. girdeth their loins with *a girdle*.
Isa. 5:27. shall *the girdle of* their loins be loosed,
11: 5. righteousness shall be *the girdle of* his loins, and faithfulness *the girdle of* his reins.
Jer. 13: 1. Go and get thee *a* linen *girdle*,
2. So I got *a girdle*
4. Take *the girdle* that thou hast got,
6. take *the girdle* from thence,
7. took *the girdle* from the place
— behold, *the girdle* was marred,
10. shall even be *as this girdle*,
11. as *the girdle* cleaveth to the loins
Eze. 23:15. with *girdles* upon their loins,

אֲזַי *ăzahy*, adv. 233

Ps. 124: 3. *Then* they had swallowed us up
4. *Then* the waters had overwhelmed us,
5. *Then* the proud waters had gone over

אַזְכָּרָה *az-kāh-rāh'*, f. 234

Lev. 2: 2, 16. the priest shall burn *the memorial of it*,
9. the meat offering *a memorial thereof*,
5:12. *a memorial thereof*, and burn (it)
6:15 (8) *the memorial of it*, unto the Lord.
24: 7. it may be on the bread *for a memorial*,
Nu. 5:26. *the memorial thereof*, and burn

235 **אָזַל** *āh-zal'.*

* KAL.—*Preterite.* *

Deu 32:36. he seeth that (their) power *is gone,*
1 Sa. 9: 7. the bread *is spent* in our vessels, (marg. *gone out* of)
Job 14:11. (As) the waters *fail* from the sea,

KAL.—*Future.*

Jer. 2:36. Why *gaddest thou about* so much

KAL.—*Participle.*

Pro. 20:14. *but when he is gone* his way,

* PUAL.—*Participle.* *

Eze. 27:19. and Javan *going to and fro*

---

236 **אֲזַל** *ăzal,* Ch.

* P'AL.—*Preterite.* *

Ezr. 4:23. *they went up* in haste to Jerusalem
5: 8. *we went* into the province of Judea,
Dan. 2:17. Then Daniel *went* to his house,
24. *he went* and said thus
6:18(19). Then the king *went* to his palace,
19(20). and *went* in haste unto the den of

P'AL.—*Imperative.*

Ezr. 5:15. *go,* carry them into the temple

---

237 **אָזֶל** *āh'-zel.*

In pause for אֵזֶל.

1 Sa. 20:19. shalt remain by the stone *Ezel.* (marg. *that sheweth the way*)

238-39 **אָזַן** [*āh-zan'*].

* PIEL.—*Preterite.* *

Ecc. 12: 9. *yea, he gave good heed,* and sought out,

* HIPHIL.—*Preterite.* *

Ex. 15:26. *and wilt give ear* to his commandments,
Deu. 1:45. nor *give ear* unto you.
2 Ch 24:19. but they would not *give ear.*
Neh. 9:30. yet would they not *give ear:*
Ps. 77: 1(2). *and he gave ear* unto me.
Isa. 64: 4(3). nor *perceived by the ear,*

HIPHIL.—*Imperative.*

Gen. 4:23. *hearken unto* my speech:
Nu. 23:18. *hearken* unto me, thou son of Zippor:
Deu 32: 1. *Give ear,* O ye heavens, and I will speak;
Jud. 5: 3. *give ear,* O ye princes;
Job 33: 1. *hearken* to all my words.
34: 2. *give ear* unto me, ye that have knowledge.
16. *hearken* to the voice of my words.
37:14. *Hearken* unto this, O Job:
Ps. 5: 1(2) *Give ear* to my words, O Lord,
17: 1. *give ear* unto my prayer,
39:12(13). *give ear* unto my cry;
49: 1(2). *give ear,* all (ye) inhabitants
54: 2(4). *give ear* to the words of my mouth.
55: 1(2). *Give ear* to my prayer, O God;
78: 1. *Give ear,* O my people, (to) my law:
80: 1(2). *Give ear,* O Shepherd of Israel,
84: 8(9). *give ear,* O God of Jacob.
86: 6. *Give ear,* O Lord, unto my prayer;
140: 6(7). *hear* the voice of my supplications,
141: 1. *give ear* unto my voice, when I cry
143: 1. *give ear* to my supplications:
Isa. 1: 2. Hear, O heavens, *and give ear,* O earth:
10. *give ear* unto the law of our God,
8: 9. *and give ear,* all ye of far countries:
28:23. *Give ye ear,* and hear my voice;
32: 9. *give ear unto* my speech.
51: 4. *give ear* unto me, O my nation:
Jer. 13:15. Hear ye, *and give ear;* be not proud:
Hos. 5: 1. *give ye ear,* O house of the king;
Joel 1: 2. Hear this, ye old men, *and give ear,*

HIPHIL.—*Future.*

Job 9:16. *he had hearkened* unto my voice.
32:11. *I gave ear* to your reasons,
Ps. 135:17. They have ears, but *they hear* not;
Isa. 42:23. Who among you *will give ear* to this?

HIPHIL.—*Participle.*

Pro. 17:4. a liar *giveth ear* to a naughty tongue.

אָזֵן [*āh'-zēhn*] m. 240

Deu 23:13(14). shalt have a paddle upon thy *weapon;*

אֹזֶן *ōh'-zen,* m. 241

Gen 20: 8. told all these things *in their ears:*
23:10. *in the audience* (lit. *in the ears*) *of* the children of Heth,
13. *in the audience of* the people
16. named *in the audience of* the sons of Heth,
35: 4. earrings which (were) *in their ears;*
44:18. speak a word *in* my lord's *ears,*
50: 4. speak, I pray you, *in the ears of* Pharaoh,
Ex. 10: 2. thou mayest tell *in the ears of* thy son, and
11: 2. Speak now *in the ears of* the people,
17:14. rehearse (it) *in the ears of* Joshua:
21: 6. his master shall bore *his ear* through
24: 7. read *in the audience of* the people:
29:20. upon the tip of *the* right *ear of* Aaron, and upon the tip of *the* right *ear of* his sons,
32: 2. which (are) *in the ears of* your wives,
3. the golden earrings which (were) *in their ears,*
Lev. 8:23. upon the tip of Aaron's right *ear,*
24. upon the tip of *their* right *ear,*
14:14, 17, 25, 28. upon the tip of *the* right *ear of*
Nu. 11: 1. it displeased the Lord: (marg. it was evil *in the ears of* the Lord)
18. ye have wept *in the ears of* the Lord,
14:28. as ye have spoken *in mine ears,*
Deu. 5: 1. I speak *in your ears* this day,
15:17. *through his ear* unto the door,
29: 4(3). eyes to see, *and ears* to hear, unto this
31:11. before all Israel *in their hearing.*
28. I may speak these words *in their ears,*
30. Moses spake *in the ears of*
32:44. this song *in the ears of* the people,
Jos. 20: 4. declare his cause *in the ears of* the elders
Jud. 7: 3. proclaim *in the ears of* the people,
9: 2, 3. *in the ears of* all the men of Shechem,
17: 2. spakest of also *in mine ears,*
Ruth 4: 4. I thought to advertise thee, (marg. I said I will reveal (in) *thine ear*)
1 Sa. 3:11. both *the ears* of every one that heareth
8:21. rehearsed them *in the ears of* the Lord.
9:15. told Samuel in his *ear* (marg. revealed *the ear of* Samuel)
11: 4. the tidings *in the ears of* the people:
15:14. this bleating of the sheep *in mine ears,*
18:23. those words *in the ears of* David.
20: 2. but that he will shew it me: (marg. uncover *mine ear*)
12. and shew it thee; (lit. uncover *thy ear*)
13. then I will shew it thee, (marg. uncover *thine ear*)
22: 8. *sheweth me* that my son (marg. uncovereth *mine ear*)
— *sheweth unto me* that my son (lit. uncovereth *mine ear*)
17. did not shew it to me. (lit. uncover *mine ear*)
25:24. speak *in thine audience,* (marg. *ears*)
2 Sa. 3:19. Abner also spake *in the ears of* Benjamin:
— speak *in the ears of* David
7:22. all that we have heard *with our ears.*
27. hast revealed to thy servant, (marg. hast opened *the ear of*)
18:12. *in our hearing* the king charged thee
22: 7. my cry (did enter) *into his ears.*
45. as soon as they hear, (lit. at the hearing of *the ear*)
2 K. 18:26. *in the ears of* the people that (are) on the
19:16. Lord, bow down *thine ear,*
28. is come up *into mine ears,*
21:12. both *his ears* shall tingle.
23: 2. read *in their ears* all the words of the book
1 Ch. 17:20. all that we have heard *with our ears.*
25. O my God, hast told thy servant (marg. hast revealed *the ear of* thy servant)

1Ch.28: 8. *and in the audience of* our God,
2Ch. 6:40. *and* (let) *thine ears* (be) attent unto the
7:15. *and mine ears* attent unto the prayer
34:30. read *in their ears* all the words of the book
Neh. 1: 6. Let *thine ear* now be attentive,
11. let now *thine ear* be attentive to the prayer
8: 3. *and the ears of* all the people
13: 1. *in the audience of* the people ; (marg. *ears*)
Job 4:12. *mine ear* received a little thereof.
12:11. Doth not *the ear* try words?
13: 1. *mine ear* hath heard and understood it.
17. my declaration *with your ears.*
15:21. A dreadful sound (is) *in his ears:*
28:22. heard the fame thereof *with our ears.*
29:11. When *the ear* heard (me),
33: 8. thou hast spoken *in mine hearing,* (marg. *ears*)
16. Then he openeth *the ears of* men,
34: 3. For *the ear* trieth words,
36:10. He openeth also *their ear* to discipline,
15. openeth *their ears* in oppression.
42: 5. by the hearing of *the ear:*
Ps. 10:17. thou wilt cause *thine ear* to hear:
17: 6. incline *thine ear* unto me,
18: 6(7). came before him, (even) *into his ears.*
44(45). As soon as they hear of me, (marg. At the hearing of *the ear*)
31: 2(3). Bow down *thine ear* to me ;
34:15(16). *and his ears* (are open) unto their cry.
40: 6(7). mine *ears* hast thou opened:
44:1(2). We have heard *with our ears,*
45:10(11). consider, and incline *thine ear;*
49: 4(5). I will incline *mine ear* to a parable:
58: 4(5). the deaf adder (that) stoppeth *her ear;*
71: 2. incline *thine ear* unto me,
78: 1. incline *your ears* to the words of my mouth.
86: 1. Bow down *thine ear,* O Lord,
88: 2(3). incline *thine ear* unto my cry;
92:11(12). *mine ears* shall hear (my desire)
94: 9. He that planted *the ear,* shall he
102: 2(3). incline *thine ear* unto me:
115: 6. They have *ears,* but they hear not:
116: 2. he hath inclined *his ear* unto me,
130: 2. let *thine ears* be attentive to the voice of
135:17. They have *ears,* but they hear not;
Pro. 2: 2. incline *thine ear* unto wisdom,
4:20. incline *thine ear* unto my sayings.
5: 1. bow *thine ear* to my understanding:
13. nor inclined *mine ear* to them
15:31. *The ear* that heareth the reproof of life
18:15. *and the ear of* the wise seeketh knowledge.
20:12. The hearing *ear,* and the seeing eye,
21:13. Whoso stoppeth *his ears* at the cry of the
22:17. Bow down *thine ear,* and hear
23: 9. Speak not *in the ears of* a fool:
12. *and thine ears* to the words of knowledge.
25.12. a wise reprover upon *an* obedient *ear.*
26:17. one that taketh a dog *by the ears.*
28: 9. He that turneth away *his ear*
Ecc. 1: 8. nor *the ear* filled with hearing.
Isa. 5: 9. *In mine ears* (said) the Lord of hosts,
6:10. *and* make *their ears* heavy,
— *and* hear *with their ears,*
11: 3. reprove after the hearing of *his ears.*
22:14. it was revealed *in mine ears*
30:21. *And thine ears* shall hear a word
32: 3. *and the ears of* them that hear shall hearken.
33.15. stoppeth *his ears* from hearing of blood,
35: 5. *and the ears of* the deaf shall be unstopped.
36:11. *in the ears of* the people
37:17. Incline *thine ear,* O Lord, and hear;
29. is come up *into mine ears,*
42:20. opening *the ears,* but he heareth not.
43: 8. and the deaf *that* have *ears.*
48: 8. *thine ear* was not opened:
49:20. shall say again *in thine ears,*
50: 4. wakeneth mine *ear* to hear as the learned.
5. The Lord God hath opened mine *ear,*
55: 3. Incline *your ear,* and come unto me:
59: 1. neither *his ear* heavy, that it cannot hear:
Jer. 2: 2. cry *in the ears of* Jerusalem,
5:21. which have *ears,* and hear not:
6:10. *their ear* (is) uncircumcised,
7:24,26. nor inclined *their ear,*
9:20(19). let *your ear* receive the word
11: 8. nor inclined *their ear,*
17:23. neither inclined *their ear,*
Jer. 19: 3. whosoever heareth, *his ears* shall tingle.
25: 4. nor inclined *your ear* to hear.
26:11. as ye have heard *with your ears.*
15. speak all these words *in your ears.*
28: 7. that I speak *in thine ears, and in the ears* of all the people;
29:29. read this letter *in the ears of* Jeremiah
34:14. neither inclined *their ear.*
35:15. ye have not inclined *your ear,*
36: 6. *in the ears of* the people in the Lord's house
— *in the ears of* all Judah
10 *in the ears of* all the people.
13. read the book *in the ears of* the people.
14. thou hast read *in the ears of* the people,
15. read it *in our ears.* So Baruch read (it) *in their ears.*
20. told all the words *in the ears of* the king.
21. Jehudi read it *in the ears of* the king, *and in the ears of* all the princes
44: 5. nor inclined *their ear* to turn
Lam. 3:56. hide not *thine ear* at my breathing,
Eze. 3.10. *and* hear *with thine ears.*
8:18. though they cry *in mine ears*
9: 1. He cried also *in mine ears*
5. to the others he said *in mine hearing,*
10:13. it was cried unto them *in my hearing,*
12: 2. they have *ears* to hear, and hear not.
16:12. earrings in *thine ears,*
23:25. shall take away thy nose *and thine ears;*
24.26. cause (thee) to hear (it) with (thine) *ears?*
40: 4 & 44:5. *and* hear *with thine ears,*
Dan. 9.18. O my God, incline *thine ear,* and hear;
Am. 3:12. or a piece of *an ear;*
Mic. 7:16. *their ears* shall be deaf.
Zec. 7:11. *and* stopped *their ears,*

אֲזִקִּים [*ăzik-keem'*] m. pl. 246

i. q. זִקִּים.

Jer. 40: 1. being bound *in chains* among all (marg. *manicles*)
4. I loose thee this day from *the chains*

אָזַר [*āh-zar'*]. 247

* KAL.—*Preterite.* *

1Sa. 2: 4. they that stumbled *are girded* with strength.

KAL.—*Imperative.*

Job 38: 3. *Gird up* now thy loins like a man;
40: 7. *Gird up* thy loins now like a man.

KAL.—*Future.*

Job 30:18. *it bindeth me about* as the collar
Jer. 1:17. therefore *gird up* thy loins,

KAL.—*Participle.* Päul.

2 K. 1: 8. *girt* with a girdle of leather

* NIPHAL.—*Participle.* *

Ps. 65: 6(7). (being) *girded* with power:

* PIEL.—*Future.* *

2Sa.22:40. *For thou hast girded me with* strength
Ps. 18:39(40). *For thou hast girded me with* strength
30:11(12). *and girded me with* gladness;
Isa. 45: 5. *I girded thee,* though thou hast not

PIEL.—*Participle.*

Ps. 18:32(33). God *that girdeth me* with strength.
Isa. 50:11. *that compass* (yourselves) *about* with sparks.

* HITHPAEL.—*Preterite.* *

Ps. 93: 1. (wherewith) *he hath girded himself:*

HITHPAEL.—*Imperative.*

Isa. 8: 9, 9. *gird yourselves,* and ye shall be broken in pieces;

אֶזְרוֹעַ *ez-rōh'-ăgn*, f. 248

i. q. זְרוֹעַ.

Job 31:22. *and mine arm* be broken
Jer. 32:21. *and with a* stretched out *arm,*

249 **אֶזְרָח** *ez-rāhgh'*, m.

Ex. 12:19. a stranger, *or born* in the land.
48. be *as one that is born* in the land:
49. One law shall be *to him that is homeborn*,
Lev. 16:29. (whether it be) *one of your own country*,
17:15. *one of your own country*,
18:26. *any of your own nation*,
19:34. be unto you *as one born* among you,
23:42. all *that are* Israelites *born*
24:16. *as he that is born in the land*,
22. *as for one of your own country*:
Nu. 9:14. *and for him that was born in*
15:13. All *that are born of the country*
29. *him that is born* among the
30. *born in the land*, or a stranger,
Jos. 8:33. *as he that was born among them*;
Ps. 37.35. *like a* green bay tree, (marg. *a* green *tree that groweth in his own soil*)
Eze. 47:22. shall be unto you *as born in the country*

---

251 **אָח** *āhgh*, m.

אִישׁ...אָחִיו The one.. the other.

Gen 4: 2. And she again bare *his brother* Abel.
8. And Cain talked with Abel *his brother*:
— Cain rose up against Abel *his brother*,
9. Where (is) Abel *thy brother*?
— (Am) I *my brother*'s keeper?
10. the voice of *thy brother*'s blood crieth
11. her mouth to receive *thy brother*'s blood
21. And *his brother*'s name (was) Jubal:
9: 5. at the hand of every man*'s brother*
22. and told *his* two *brethren* without.
25. a servant---shall he be *unto his brethren*.
10:21. *the brother of* Japheth the elder,
25. and *his brother*'s name (was) Joktan.
12: 5. Sarai his wife, and Lot *his brother*'s son,
13: 8. for we (be) *brethren*.
11. separated themselves the one from *the other*.
14:12. And they took Lot, Abram*'s brother*'s son,
13. *brother of* Eshcol, *and brother of* Aner:
14. when Abram heard that *his brother* was
16. also brought again *his brother* Lot,
16.12. in the presence of all *his brethren*.
19: 7. I pray you, *brethren*, do not so wickedly.
20: 5. she herself said, He (is) *my brother*:
13. say of me, He (is) *my brother*
16. Behold, I have given *thy brother*
22:20. born children unto *thy brother* Nahor;
21. Huz his firstborn, and Buz *his brother*,
23. did bear to Nahor, Abraham*'s brother*.
24:15. the wife of Nahor, Abraham*'s brother*,
27. led me to the house of my master*'s brethren*.
29. Rebekah had *a brother*,
48. to take my master*'s brother*'s daughter
53. he gave also *to her brother*
55. *her brother* and her mother said,
25:18. died in the presence of all *his brethren*
26. after that came *his brother* out,
26:31. sware one *to another*:
27: 6. thy father speak unto Esau *thy brother*,
11. Esau *my brother* (is) a hairy man,
23. as *his brother* Esau's hands:
29. be lord *over thy brethren*,
30. Esau *his brother* came in from his hunting.
35. *Thy brother* came with subtilty,
37. all *his brethren* have I given to him
40. shalt serve *thy brother*;
41. then will I slay *my brother* Jacob.
42. Behold, *thy brother* Esau,
43. flee thou to Laban *my brother*
44. until *thy brother*'s fury turn away;
45. Until *thy brother*'s anger turn away
28: 2. the daughters of Laban thy mother*'s brother*.
5. Bethuel the Syrian, *the brother of* Rebekah,
29: 4. *My brethren*, whence (be) ye?
10. the daughter of Laban his mother*'s brother*, and the sheep of Laban his mother*'s brother*,
— the flock of Laban, his mother*'s brother*.
12. Rachel that he (was) her father*'s brother*,
Gen 29:15. Because thou (art) *my brother*,
31:23. he took *his brethren* with him,
25. Laban with *his brethren* pitched
32. before *our brethren* discern thou what
37. set (it) here before *my brethren and thy brethren*,
46. Jacob said *unto his brethren*,
54. called *his brethren* to eat bread:
32: 3(4). messengers before him to Esau *his brother*
6(7). We came to *thy brother* Esau,
11(12). from the hand of *my brother*,
13(14). a present for Esau *his brother*;
17(18). When Esau *my brother* meeteth thee,
33: 3. until he came near to *his brother*.
9. Esau said, I have enough, *my brother*;
34:11. said unto her father and unto *her brethren*,
25. Simeon and Levi, Dinah*'s brethren*,
35: 1. thou fleddest from the face of Esau *thy brother*.
7. when he fled from the face of *his brother*.
36: 6. from the face of *his brother* Jacob.
37: 2. feeding the flock with *his brethren*;
4. *his brethren* saw that their father loved him more than all *his brethren*,
5. dreamed a dream, and he told (it) *his brethren*:
8. *his brethren* said to him,
9. another dream, and told it *his brethren*,
10. told (it) to his father, and to *his brethren*:
— Shall I and thy mother *and thy brethren*
11. *his brethren* envied him;
12. *his brethren* went to feed their
13. Do not *thy brethren* feed (the flock)
14. whether it be well with *thy brethren*,
16. he said, I seek *my brethren*:
17. Joseph went after *his brethren*,
19. they said one to *another*,
23. Joseph was come unto *his brethren*,
26. Judah said unto *his brethren*, What profit (is it) if we slay *our brother*,
27. for he (is) *our brother* (and) our flesh. And *his brethren* were content.
30. he returned unto *his brethren*,
38: 1. Judah went down from *his brethren*,
8. Go in unto *thy brother*'s wife, and marry her, and raise up seed *to thy brother*.
9. he went in unto *his brother*'s wife,
— lest that he should give seed *to his brother*.
11. peradventure he die also, *as his brethren*
29. behold, *his brother* came out:
30. afterward came out *his brother*,
42: 3. Joseph*'s* ten *brethren* went down
4. But Benjamin, Joseph*'s brother*, Jacob sent not with *his brethren*;
6. Joseph*'s brethren* came,
7. Joseph saw *his brethren*,
8. Joseph knew *his brethren*,
13. Thy servants (are) twelve *brethren*,
15. except *your* youngest *brother* come hither.
16. let him fetch *your brother*,
19. let one of *your brethren* be bound
20. bring *your* youngest *brother* unto me;
21. they said one to *another*, We (are) verily guilty concerning *our brother*,
28. he said unto *his brethren*,
— saying one to *another*,
32. We (be) twelve *brethren*,
33. leave one of *your brethren* (here) with me,
34. bring *your* youngest *brother* unto me:
— I deliver you *your brother*,
38. for *his brother* is dead,
43: 3,5. except *your brother* (be) with you.
4. If thou wilt send *our brother* with us,
6. whether ye had yet *a brother*?
7. have ye (another) *brother*?
— Bring *your brother* down?
13. Take also *your brother*,
14. that he may send away *your* other *brother*,
29. saw *his brother* Benjamin,
— (Is) this *your* younger *brother*,
30. his bowels did yern upon *his brother*:
44:14. Judah *and his brethren* came to Joseph's h.
19. Have ye a father, or *a brother*?
20. *and his brother* is dead,
23. Except *your* youngest *brother* come
26. if *our* youngest *brother* be with us,

Gen44:26. *except our* youngest *brother* (be) with us.
33. let the lad go up with *his brethren.*
45: 1. Joseph made himself known unto *his brethren.*
3, 4. Joseph said unto *his brethren,*
— *his brethren* could not answer him;
4. he said, I (am) Joseph *your brother,*
12. the eyes of *my brother* Benjamin,
14. he fell upon *his brother* Benjamin's neck,
15. Moreover he kissed all *his brethren,*
— after that *his brethren* talked with him.
16. Joseph's *brethren* are come:
17. Say unto *thy brethren,*
24. So he sent *his brethren* away,
46:31. Joseph said unto *his brethren,*
— *My brethren,* and my father's house,
47: 1. My father *and my brethren,* and their flocks,
2. he took some of *his brethren,*
3. Pharaoh said unto *his brethren,*
5. Thy father *and thy brethren* are come
6. thy father and *brethren* to dwell;
11. Joseph placed his father and *his brethren,*
12. Joseph nourished his father, and *his brethren,*
48: 6. name of *their brethren* in their inheritance.
19. *his* younger *brother* shall be greater than he,
22. I have given to thee one portion above *thy brethren,*
49: 5. Simeon and Levi (are) *brethren;*
8. Judah, thou (art he) whom *thy brethren*
26. him that was separate from *his brethren.*
50: 8. all the house of Joseph, *and his brethren,*
14. returned into Egypt, he, *and his brethren,*
15. when Joseph's *brethren* saw that their
17. the trespass of *thy brethren,*
18. *his brethren* also went and fell down
24. Joseph said unto *his brethren,*
Ex. 1: 6. And Joseph died, and all *his brethren,*
2:11. that he went out unto *his brethren,*
— an Egyptian smiting an Hebrew, one *of his brethren.*
4:14. (Is) not Aaron the Levite *thy brother?*
18. return unto *my brethren*
7: 1. Aaron *thy brother* shall be thy prophet.
2. Aaron *thy brother* shall speak unto Pharaoh,
10:23. They saw not one *another,*
16:15. they said one to *another,*
25:20. their faces (shall look) one to *another;*
28: 1. take thou unto thee Aaron *thy brother,*
2, 4. holy garments for Aaron *thy brother*
41. put them upon Aaron *thy brother,*
32:27. slay every man *his brother,*
29. upon his son, *and upon his brother;*
37: 9. with their faces one to *another;*
Lev. 7:10. one (as much) *as another.*
10: 4. carry *your brethren* from before the
6. *but* let *your brethren,* the whole house of Is.,
16: 2. Speak unto Aaron *thy brother,*
18:14. the nakedness of thy father's *brother,*
16. the nakedness of *thy brother*'s wife: it (is) *thy brother*'s nakedness.
19:17. Thou shalt not hate *thy brother*
20:21. if a man shall take *his brother*'s wife,
— he hath uncovered *his brother*'s nakedness;
21: 2. for his daughter, *and for his brother,*
10. the high priest *among his brethren,*
25:14. ye shall not oppress one *another:*
25, 35. If *thy brother* be waxen poor,
— redeem that which *his brother* sold.
36. that *thy brother* may live with thee.
39. if *thy brother* (that dwelleth) by thee
46. *but over your brethren* the children of Israel, ye shall not rule one *over another*
47. *thy brother* (that dwelleth) by him
48. one *of his brethren* may redeem him:
26:37. they shall fall one *upon another,*
Nu. 6: 7. *for his brother,* or for his sister,
8:26. But shall minister with *their brethren*
14: 4. they said one to *another,*
16. 10. all *thy brethren* the sons of Levi with thee:
18: 2. *thy brethren* also of the tribe of Levi,
6. I have taken *your brethren* the Levites
20. 3. when *our brethren* died before the Lord!
8. thou, and Aaron *thy brother,*
14. Thus saith *thy brother* Israel,
25: 6. brought unto *his brethren*
27: 4. possession among *the brethren of* our father.

Nu. 27: 7. inheritance among their father's *brethren,*
9. ye shall give his inheritance *unto his brethren.*
10. if he have no *brethren,* then ye shall give his inheritance *unto* his father's *brethren.*
11. if his father have no *brethren,*
13. as Aaron *thy brother* was gathered.
32: 6. Shall *your brethren* go to war,
36: 2. Zelophehad *our brother* unto his daughters
Deu. 1:16. Hear (the causes) between *your brethren,*
— between (every) man and *his brother,*
28. *our brethren* have discouraged our heart,
2: 4. pass through the coast of *your brethren*
8. when we passed by from *our brethren*
3:18. pass over armed before *your brethren*
20. the Lord have given rest *unto your brethren,*
10: 9. no part nor inheritance with *his brethren;*
13: 6(7). If *thy brother,* the son of thy mother,
15: 2. of his neighbour, or of *his brother;*
3. (that) which is thine with *thy brother*
7. a poor man of one of *thy brethren*
— shut thine hand *from thy* poor *brother:*
9. eye be evil *against thy* poor *brother,*
11. open thine hand wide *unto thy brother,*
12. if *thy brother,* an Hebrew man,
17:15. from among *thy brethren* shalt thou set
— which (is) not *thy brother.*
20. That his heart be not lifted up *above his brethren,*
18: 2. no inheritance among *their brethren:*
7. as all *his brethren* the Levites
15. a Prophet from the midst of thee, *of thy brethren,*
18. a Prophet from among *their brethren,*
19:18. hath testified falsely *against his brother;*
19. to have done *unto his brother:*
20: 8. lest *his brethren*'s heart faint
22: 1. Thou shalt not see *thy brother*'s ox
— bring them again *unto thy brother.*
2. if *thy brother* (be) not nigh unto
— until *thy brother* seek after it,
3. with all lost thing of *thy brother*'s,
4. Thou shalt not see *thy brother*'s ass
23: 7(8). for he (is) *thy brother:*
19(20). lend upon usury *to thy brother;*
20(21). *but unto thy brother* thou shalt not lend
24: 7. any *of his brethren* of the children of
14. (whether he be) *of thy brethren,*
25: 3. *thy brother* should seem vile unto thee.
5. If *brethren* dwell together,
6. shall succeed in the name of *his brother*
7. refuseth to raise up *unto his brother*
9. will not build up *his brother*'s house.
11. men strive together one *with another,*
28:54. his eye shall be evil *toward his brother,*
32:50. as Aaron *thy brother* died
33: 9. neither did he acknowledge *his brethren,*
16. (that was) separated from *his brethren.*
24. let him be acceptable to *his brethren,*
Jos. 1:14. ye shall pass before *your brethren*
15. Until the Lord have given *your brethren*
2:13. my father, and my mother, and *my brethren,*
18. and *thy brethren,* and all thy father's
6:23. her father, and her mother, and *her brethren,*
14. 8. *Nevertheless my brethren* that went up
15:17. son of Kenaz, *the brother of* Caleb,
17: 4. an inheritance among *our brethren.*
— among *the brethren of* their father.
22: 3. Ye have not left *your brethren*
4. God hath given rest *unto your brethren,*
7. gave Joshua among *their brethren*
8. spoil of your enemies with *your brethren.*
Jud. 1: 3. Judah said unto Simeon *his brother,*
13. son of Kenaz, Caleb's younger *brother,*
17. Judah went with Simeon *his brother,*
3: 9. son of Kenaz, Caleb's younger *brother.*
8:19. They (were) *my brethren,*
9: 1. to Shechem unto his mother's *brethren,*
3. his mother's *brethren* spake of him
— for they said, He (is) *our brother.*
5. slew *his brethren* the sons of Jerubbaal,
18. because he (is) *your brother;*
21. for fear of Abimelech *his brother.*
24. upon Abimelech *their brother,*
— aided him in the killing of *his brethren.*
26. son of Ebed came *with his brethren,*

Jud. 9:31. son of Ebed *and his brethren*
41. Zebul thrust out Gaal and *his brethren*,
56. in slaying *his* seventy *brethren:*
11: 3. Jephthah fled from *his brethren*,
14: 3. among the daughters of *thy brethren*,
16:31. Then *his brethren* and all the house
18: 8. they came unto *their brethren*
—*their brethren* said unto them,
14. said unto *their brethren*,
19.23. said unto them, Nay, *my brethren*,
20:13. hearken to the voice of *their brethren*
23, 28. the children of Benjamin *my brother?*
21: 6. repented them for Benjamin *their brother*,
22. *their brethren* come unto us to complain,
Ruth 4: 3. which (was) *our brother* Elimelech's:
10. not cut off from among *his brethren*,
1Sa. 14: 3. Ahiah, the son of Ahitub, I-chabod's *bro.*,
16:13. anointed him in the midst of *his brethren:*
17:17. Take now *for thy brethren*
—run to the camp *to thy brethren;*
18. look how *thy brethren* fare,
22. came and saluted *his brethren.*
28. Eliab *his* eldest *brother* heard
20:29. *my brother*, he hath commanded me
— let me get away, I pray thee, and see *my brethren.*
22: 1. when *his brethren* and all his father's house
26: 6. Abishai the son of Zeruiah, *brother to* Joab,
30:23. Ye shall not do so, *my brethren*,
2Sa. 1:26. I am distressed for thee, *my brother*
2:22. I hold up my face to Joab *thy brother?*
26. return from following *their brethren?*
27. every one from following *his brother.*
3: 8. to *his brethren*, and to his friends,
27. for the blood of Asahel *his brother.*
30. Joab and Abishai *his brother* slew Abner, because he had slain *their brother*
4: 6. Rechab and Baanah *his brother*
9. David answered Rechab and Baanah *his brother*,
10:10. into the hand of Abishai *his brother*,
13: 3. Jonadab, the son of Shimeah David's *bro.:*
4. I love Tamar, *my brother* Absalom's sister.
7. Go now to *thy brother* Amnon's house,
8. Tamar went to *her brother* Amnon's
10. into the chamber to Amnon *her brother.*
12. she answered him, Nay, *my brother*,
20. Absalom *her brother* said unto her, Hath Amnon *thy brother* been with thee?
—peace, my sister: he (is) *thy brother;*
—desolate in *her brother* Absalom's house.
26. let *my brother* Amnon go with us.
32. the son of Shimeah David's *brother*,
14: 7. Deliver him that smote *his brother*,
—for the life of *his brother* whom he slew;
15:20. take back *thy brethren:*
18: 2. the son of Zeruiah, Joab's *brother*,
19:12(13). Ye (are) *my brethren*, ye (are) my
41(42). Why have *our brethren* the men of
20: 9. (Art) thou in health, *my brother?*
10. Joab and Abishai *his brother* pursued after
21:21. *the brother of* David slew him.
23:18. Abishai, *the brother of* Joab,
24. Asahel *the brother of* Joab
1K. 1: 9. called all *his brethren* the king's sons,
10. Solomon *his brother*, he called not.
2: 7. I fled because of Absalom *thy brother.*
15. is turned about, and is become *my brother's:*
21. given to Adonijah *thy brother* to wife.
22. for he (is) *mine* elder *brother;*
9:13. which thou hast given me, *my brother?*
12:24. nor fight against *your brethren*
13:30. mourned over him, (saying), Alas, *my brother!*
20:32. (Is) he yet alive? he (is) *my brother.*
33. *Thy brother* Ben-hadad.
2 K. 7: 6. they said one to *another*,
9: 2. make him arise up from among *his brethren*,
10:13. Jehu met with *the brethren of*
—We (are) *the brethren of* Ahaziah;
23: 9. unleavened bread among *their brethren.*
1Ch. 1.19. *his brother's* name (was) Joktan.
2:32. the sons of Jada *the brother of* Shammai;
42. sons of Caleb *the brother of* Jerahmeel
4: 9. Jabez was more honourable *than his brethren:*
11. Chelub *the brother of* Shuah
1Ch 4:27. *but his brethren had* not many children,
5: 2. Judah prevailed *above his brethren*,
7. *And his brethren* by their families,
13. *And their brethren* of the house of
6:39(24). *And his brother* Asaph,
44(29). And *their brethren* the sons of Merari
48(33). *Their brethren also* the Levites
7: 5. *And their brethren* among all the families
16. the name of *his brother* (was) Sheresh;
22. *his brethren* came to comfort him.
35. the sons of *his brother* Helem;
8:32. dwelt with *their brethren* in Jerusalem, over against them. (lit. *their brethren*)
39. the sons of Eshek *his brother*
9: 6. sons of Zerah; Jeuel, *and their brethren*,
9. *And their brethren*, according to their
13. *And their brethren*, heads of the house of
17. Ahiman, *and their brethren:*
19. the son of Korah, *and his brethren*,
25. *And their brethren*, (which were) in
32. *their brethren*, of the sons of the Kohathites,
38. And they also dwelt with *their brethren* at Jerusalem, over against *their brethren.*
11:20. Abishai *the brother of* Joab,
26. Asahel *the brother of* Joab,
38. Joel *the brother of* Nathan,
45. Joha *his brother*, the Tizite,
12: 2. (even) *of* Saul's *brethren* of Benjamin.
29. children of Benjamin, *the kindred of* Saul, (marg. *brethren*)
32. *their brethren* (were) at their commandm.
39. for *their brethren* had prepared for them.
13: 2. let us send abroad unto *our brethren*
15: 5. *and his brethren* an hundred and twenty: (marg. *kinsmen*)
6. *and his brethren* two hundred and twenty:
7. *and his brethren* an hundred and thirty:
8. *and his brethren* two hundred:
9. *and his brethren* fourscore:
10. *and his brethren* an hundred and twelve.
12. (both) ye *and your brethren*,
16. to appoint *their brethren* (to be) the singers
17. Heman the son of Joel; and of *his brethren*,
— of the sons of Merari *their brethren*,
18. with them *their brethren*
16. 7. into the hand of Asaph *and his brethren.*
37. Asaph *and his brethren*, to minister
38. Obed-edom *with their brethren*,
39. Zadok the priest, *and his brethren*
19:11. the hand of Abishai *his brother*,
15. fled before Abishai *his brother*,
20: 5. Jair slew Lahmi *the brother of* Goliath
7. son of Shimea David's *brother*
23:22. *their brethren* the sons of Kish (marg. *kinsmen*)
32. the charge of the sons of Aaron *their brethren*,
24:25. *The brother of* Michah (was) Isshiah:
31. cast lots over against *their brethren*
—over against *their* younger *brethren.*
25: 7. *their brethren* that were instructed
9. *with his brethren* and sons
10, 11, 12, 13, 14, 15, 16, 17, 18, 19, 20, 21, 22, 23, 24, 25, 26, 27, 28, 29, 30, 31. his sons, *and his brethren*, (were) twelve:
26: 7. *whose brethren* (were) strong men,
8. they and their sons *and their brethren*,
9. Meshelemiah had sons *and brethren*,
11. all the sons *and brethren* of Hosah
12. (having) wards one against *another*, (lit. opposite *their brethren*)
22. Zetham, and Joel *his brother*,
25. *And his brethren* by Eliezer;
26. Shelomith *and his brethren*
28. under the hand of Shelomith, *and* of *his brethren.*
30. Hashabiah *and his brethren*,
32. *And his brethren*, men of valour,
27: 7. Asahel *the brother of* Joab,
18. Elihu, (one) *of the brethren of* David:
28: 2. Hear me, *my brethren*, and my people.
2Ch. 5:12. with their sons *and their brethren*,
11: 4. nor fight against *your brethren:*
22. (to be) ruler *among his brethren:*
19:10. shall come to you *of your brethren*
—upon *your brethren:*
21: 2. he had *brethren* the sons of Jehoshaphat,

2Ch 21: 4. all *his brethren* with the sword,
13. slain *thy brethren* of thy father's house,
22: 8. the sons of the *brethren of* Ahaziah,
28: 8. carried away captive *of their brethren*
11. which ye have taken captive *of your brethren:*
15. city of palm trees, to *their brethren:*
29:15. they gathered *their brethren,*
34. *their brethren* the Levites did help
30: 7. *and like your brethren,* which trespassed
9. *your brethren* and your children
31:12. Shimei *his brother* (was) the next.
13. Cononiah and Shimei *his brother,*
15. to give *to their brethren* by courses,
35: 5. the families of the fathers *of your brethren*
6. prepare *your brethren,*
9. Shemaiah and Nethaneel, *his brethren,*
15. for *their brethren* the Levites prepared for
36: 4. Eliakim *his brother* king over Judah
—Necho took Jehoahaz *his brother,*
10. Zedekiah *his brother* king over Judah
Ezr. 3: 2. *and his brethren* the priests, and Zerubbabel the son of Shealtiel, *and his brethren,*
8. *their brethren* the priests and the Levites,
9. Jeshua (with) his sons *and his brethren,*
—their sons *and their brethren* the Levites.
6:20. *and for their brethren* the priests,
8:17. to *his brethren* the Nethinims,
18. with his sons *and his brethren,*
19. *his brethren* and their sons,
24. ten *of their brethren* with them,
10:18. son of Jozadak, *and his brethren;*
Neh 1: 2. That Hanani, one *of my brethren,*
3: 1. *with his brethren* the priests,
18. After him repaired *their brethren,*
4: 2(3:34). he spake before *his brethren*
14(8). fight for *your brethren,*
19(13). one far *from another.*
23(17). So neither I, *nor my brethren,*
5: 1. against *their brethren* the Jews.
5. our flesh (is) as the flesh of *our brethren,*
7. usury, every one *of his brother.*
8. have redeemed *our brethren* the Jews,
—will ye even sell *your brethren?*
10. I likewise, (and) *my brethren,*
14. I *and my brethren* have not eaten
7: 2. That I gave *my brother* Hanani,
10:10(11). *And their brethren,* Shebaniah,
29(30). They clave to *their brethren,*
11:12. *And their brethren* that did the work
13. *And his brethren,* chief of the fathers,
14. *And their brethren,* mighty men
17. Bakbukiah the second *among his brethren,*
19. *and their brethren* that kept the gates,
12: 7. *and of their brethren* in the days of
8. over the thanksgiving, he *and his brethren.*
9. Bakbukiah and Unni, *their brethren,* (were)
24. *with their brethren* over against them,
36. *And his brethren,* Shemaiah,
13:13. to distribute *unto their brethren.*
Est. 10: 3. accepted of the multitude of *his brethren,*
Job. 1:13,18. drinking wine in *their* eldest *brother's*
6:15. *My brethren* have dealt deceitfully
19:13. He hath put *my brethren* far from me,
22: 6. thou hast taken a pledge from *thy brother*
30:29. I am *a brother* to dragons,
41:17(9). They are joined one *to another,*
42:11. Then came there unto him all *his brethren,*
15. gave them inheritance among *their brethren.*
Ps. 22:22(23). I will declare thy name *unto my brethren:*
35:14. *as* though (he had been) my friend (or) *brother:*
49: 7(8). can by any means redeem his *brother,*
50:20. Thou sittest (and) speakest *against thy brother;*
69: 8(9). become a stranger *unto my brethren,*
122: 8. For *my brethren* and companions' sakes,
133: 1. for *brethren* to dwell together in unity!
Pro. 6:19. he that soweth discord among *brethren.*
17: 2. part of the inheritance among *the brethren.*
17. *and a brother* is born for adversity.
18: 9. *brother* to him that is a great waster.
19. *A brother* offended (is harder to be won)
24. a friend (that) sticketh closer *than a brother.*
Pro. 19: 7. All *the brethren of* the poor do hate him:
27:10. neither go into *thy brother's* house in the day of thy calamity: (for) better (is) a neighbour (that is) near *than a brother* far off.
Ecc. 4: 8. neither child *nor brother:*
Cant. 8: 1. O that thou (wert) *as* my *brother,*
Isa. 3: 6. When a man shall take hold *of his brother*
9:19(18). no man shall spare *his brother.*
19: 2. fight every one *against his brother,*
41: 6. *and* (every one) said *to his brother,*
66: 5. *Your brethren* that hated you,
20. they shall bring all *your brethren*
Jer. 7:15. I have cast out all *your brethren,*
9: 4(3). trust ye not in any *brother:* for every *brother* will utterly supplant,
12: 6. For even *thy brethren,* and the house of
13:14. I will dash them one against *another,* (marg. a man against *his brother*)
22:18. Ah *my brother!* or, Ah sister!
23:35. every one to *his brother,*
25:26. far and near, one with *another,*
29:16. *your brethren* that are not gone forth
31:34. every man *his brother,*
34: 9. (to wit), of a Jew *his brother.*
14. let ye go every man *his brother*
17. proclaiming liberty, every one *to his brother,*
35: 3. son of Habaziniah, and *his brethren,*
41: 8. slew them not among *their brethren.*
49:10. *and his brethren,* and his neighbours,
Eze. 4:17. be astonied one *with another,*
11:15. Son of man, *thy brethren,* (even) *thy brethren,* the men of thy kindred,
18:10. doeth *the like* to (any) one of these (marg. to his *brother* besides)
18. spoiled his *brother* by violence,
24:23. mourn one toward *another.*
33:30. every one to *his brother,*
38:21. every man's sword shall be *against his brother.*
44:25. for son, or for daughter, *for brother,*
47:14. inherit it, one *as well as another;*
Hos. 2: 1(3). Say ye *unto your brethren,*
12: 3(4). He took *his brother* by the heel
13:15. Though he be fruitful among (his) *brethren,*
Joel 2: 8. Neither shall one thrust *another;*
Am. 1: 9. remembered not the *brotherly* covenant: (marg. covenant of *brethren*)
11. because he did pursue *his brother*
Obad. 10. For (thy) violence against *thy brother* Jacob
12. have looked on the day of *thy brother*
Mic. 5: 3(2). the remnant of *his brethren*
7: 2. they hunt every man *his brother*
Hag. 2:22. every one by the sword of *his brother.*
Zec. 7: 9. compassions every man to *his brother:*
10. against *his brother* in your heart.
Mal. 1: 2. (Was) not Esau Jacob's *brother?*
2:10. treacherously every man *against his brother,*

אָח *āhgh*, interj. 253

Eze. 6:11. *Alas* for all the evil abominations
21:15(20). *ah!* (it is) made bright,

אָח *āhgh*, f. prob. 254

Jer. 36:22. (a fire) on *the hearth* burning
23. the fire that (was) on *the hearth,*
— in the fire that (was) on *the hearth.*

אַח [*agh*] Ch. m. 252

Ezr. 7:18. whatsoever shall seem good to thee, and to *thy brethren,* to do

---

אָחַד [*āh-ghad'*]. 258

*HITHPAEL.—*Imperative.**

Eze. 21:16(21). *Go thee one way or other,* (either) on

259 **אֶחָד** *eh-'ghāhd'*, adj.

Gen. 1: 5. and the morning were the *first* day.
9. be gathered together unto *one* place,
2:11. The name of *the first* (is) Pison :
21. and he took *one* of his ribs,
24. and they shall be *one* flesh.
3:22. Behold, the man is become *as one* of us,
4:19. the name of *the one* (was) Adah,
8: 5. *on the first* (day) of the month,
13. *in the* six hundredth and *first* year, in the first (month), *the first* (day) of the month,
10:25. the name of *one* (was) Peleg ;
11: 1. the whole earth was of *one* language, and of *one* speech.
6. Behold, the people (is) *one*, and they have all *one* language ;
19: 9. *This one* (fellow) came in to sojourn,
21:15. she cast the child under *one of* the shrubs.
22: 2. upon *one of* the mountains which I will
26.10. *one of* the people might lightly have lien
27:38. Hast thou but *one* blessing, my father?
44. tarry with him *a few* days,
45. deprived also of you both in *one* day?
29:20. they seemed unto him (but) *a few* days,
32: 8 (9). If Esau come to *the one* company,
22 (23). and his eleven sons, (lit. *one*-ten)
33:13. if men should overdrive them *one* day,
34:16. and we will become *one* people.
22. to be *one* people, if every male
37: 9. the moon and the eleven (lit. *and one*-ten)
20. let us slay him, and cast him *into some* pit,
40: 5. each man his dream in *one* night,
41: 5. seven ears of corn came up upon *one* stalk,
11. And we dreamed a dream in *one* night,
22. behold, seven ears came up in *one* stalk,
25. The dream of Pharaoh (is) *one:*
26. the dream (is) *one*.
42:11. We (are) all *one* man's sons ;
13. the sons of *one* man in the land of
— this day with our father, *and one* (is) not.
16. Send *one* of you, and let him fetch
19. let *one* of your brethren be bound
27. And as *one* of them opened his sack
32. brethren, sons of our father ; *one* (is) not,
33. leave *one* of your brethren (here) with me,
44:28. And *the one* went out from me,
48:22. I have given to thee *one* portion above
49:16. Dan shall judge his people, *as one of* the
Ex. 1:15. the name of *the one* (was) Shiphrah,
8:31 (27). there remained not *one*.
9: 6. cattle of the children of Israel died not *one*.
7. there was not *one* of the cattle of the
10:19. there remained not *one* locust
11: 1. will I bring *one* plague (more)
12:18. until *the one* and twentieth day of the
46. In *one* house shall it be eaten ;
49. *One* law shall be to him that is
14:28. remained not so much as *one* of them.
16:22. two omers *for one* (man) :
33. Moses said unto Aaron, Take *a* pot,
17:12. *the one* on the one side, and *the other* on
18: 3. the name of *the one* (was) Gershom ;
4. And the name of *the other* (was) Eliezer ;
23:29. drive them out from before thee in *one*
24: 3. the people answered with *one* voice,
25:12. two rings (shall be) in *the one* side of it,
19. And make *one* cherub on the one end, and *the other* cherub on the other end:
32. branches of the candlestick out of *the one*
33. a flower in *one* branch ; and three bowls made like almonds in *the other* branch,
36. all of it (shall be) *one* beaten work
26: 2, 8. The length of *one* curtain (shall be)
—, —. the breadth of *one* curtain four cubits:
— the curtains shall have *one* measure.
4. blue upon the edge of *the one* curtain
5. shalt thou make in *the one* curtain,
6. and it shall be *one* tabernacle.
8. and the eleven curtains (shall be all) of *one* measure.
10. fifty loops on the edge of *the one*'
11. couple the tent together, that it may be *one*.
16. a cubit and a half (shall be) the breadth of *one* board.
17. Two tenons (shall there be) in *one* board,

Ex. 26:19, 21, 25. two sockets under *one* board
—, —, —. and two sockets under *another* board
24. above the head of it unto *one* ring:
26. for the boards of *the one* side
27: 9. an hundred cubits long for *one* side·
28:10. Six of their names on *one* stone,
17. (this shall be) *the first* row.
29: 1. Take *one* young bullock,
3. thou shalt put them into *one* basket,
15. Thou shalt also take *one* ram ;
23. And *one* loaf of bread, and *one* cake of oiled bread, and *one* wafer
39. *The one* lamb thou shalt offer in the
40. And with *the one* lamb a tenth deal of flour
30:10. upon the horns of it *once* in
— *once* in the year shall he make atonement
33: 5. up into the midst of thee in *a* moment,
36: 9. of *one* curtain (was) twenty and eight cubits, and the breadth of *one* curtain four cubits: the curtains (were) all of *one* size.
10. curtains *one* unto *another:* and (the other) five curtains he coupled *one* unto *another*.
11. loops of blue on the edge of *one* curtain
12. Fifty loops made he in *one* curtain,
— the loops held *one* (curtain) to *another*.
13. the curtains *one* unto *another* with the taches: so it became *one* tabernacle.
15. The length of *one* curtain (was) thirty cubits, and four cubits (was) the breadth of *one* curtain: the eleven curtains (were) of *one* size.
18. the tent together, that it might be *one*.
21. and the breadth of *a* board one cubit and
22. *One* board had two tenons, equally distant *one* from *another:*
24, 26. two sockets under *one* board
—, —. and two sockets under *another* board
29. together at the head thereof, to *one*
30. under *every* board two sockets.
31. the boards of the *one* side of the tabernacle,
37: 3. two rings upon *the one* side of it,
8. *One* cherub on the end on this side, and *another* cherub on the (other) end
18. branches of the candlestick out of *the one*
19. after the fashion of almonds in *one* branch,
— made like almonds in *another* branch,
22. all of it (was) *one* beaten work
39:10. this (was) the *first* row.
40: 2. On the *first* day of the first month
17. *on the first* (day) of the month,
Lev. 4: 2. shall do *against any* of them:
13. they have done (somewhat against) *any*
22. through ignorance (against) *any*
27. if *any* one of the common people sin (marg. *any* soul)
— while he doeth (somewhat against) *any*
5: 4, 5. he shall be guilty *in one* of these.
7. *one* for a sin offering, *and the other* for a
13. he hath sinned *in one of* these,
17. a soul sin, and commit *any* of these
6: 3, (5:22). *any* of all these that a man doeth,
7, (—:26). shall be forgiven him for *any thing*
7: 7. (there is) *one* law for them:
14. he shall offer *one* out of the whole oblation
8:26. he took *one* unleavened cake, and *a* cake of oiled bread, and *one* wafer,
12: 8. the *one* for the burnt offering, *and the other* for a sin offering:
13: 2. the priest, or unto *one* of his sons
14: 5. that *one* of the birds be killed
10. *one* ewe lamb of the first year
— and *one* log of oil.
12. And the priest shall take *one* he lamb,
21. shall take *one* lamb (for) a trespass
— and *one* tenth deal of fine flour
22. the *one* shall be a sin offering, *and the other* a burnt offering.
30. he shall offer *the one* of the turtledoves,
31. *the one* (for) a sin offering, and *the other*
50. he shall kill *the one* of the birds
15:15. *the one* (for) a sin offering, *and the other* (for) a burnt offering ;
30. *the one* (for) a sin offering, and *the other*
16: 5. *one* ram for a burnt offering.
8. *one* lot for the Lord, and *the other* lot for

Lev 16:34. for all their sins *once* a year.
22:28. shall not kill it and her young both in *one*
23:18. *one* young bullock, and two rams:
19. ye shall sacrifice *one* kid of the goats
24. In the seventh month, *in the first* (day)
24: 5. two tenth deals shall be in *one* cake.
22. Ye shall have *one* manner of law,
25:48. *one* of his brethren may redeem him:
26.26. ten women shall bake your bread in *one*
Nu. 1: 1, 18. *on the first* (day) of the second month,
41. tribe of Asher, (were) 40 & *one* th. & 500.
44. each *one* was for the house of his fathers.
2:16. the camp of R. (were) 100 th. & 50 & *one*
28. that were numbered of them, (were) 40 & *one* th. & 500.
6:11. *the one* for a sin offering, *and the other* for
14. *one* he lamb of the first year
— *one* ewe lamb of the first year
— *one* ram without blemish
19. and *one* unleavened cake out of the basket, and *one* unleavened wafer,
7: 3. and *for each one* an ox:
11. *each* prince on his day, (lit. *one* prince in a day, *one* prince in a day)
13, 19, 25, 31, 37, 49, 55, 61, 67, 73, 79. *one* silver charger,......*one* silver bowl
14. *One* spoon of ten (shekels) of gold,
15, 21, 27, 33, 39, 45, 51, 57, 63, 69, 75, 81. *One* young bullock, *one* ram, *one* lamb
16, 22, 28, 34, 40, 46, 52, 58, 64, 70, 76, 82. *One* kid of the goats
20. *One* spoon of gold of ten (shekels),
26, 32, 38, 44, 50, 56, 62, 68, 74, 80. *One* golden spoon of ten (shekels),
43. *one* silver charger......*a* silver bowl
85. *Each* charger of silver (weighing) an hundred and thirty (shekels), *each* bowl seventy:
8:12. the *one* (for) a sin offering, and *the other*
9:14. ye shall have *one* ordinance,
10: 4. if they blow (but) *with one* (trumpet),
11:19. Ye shall not eat *one* day,
26. the name of *the one* (was) Eldad,
13: 2. of every tribe of their fathers shall ye send *a man*, (lit. *one* man, *one* man for a tribe)
23. a branch with *one* cluster of grapes,
14:15. kill (all) this people as *one* man,
15: 5. burnt offering or sacrifice, for *one* lamb.
11. Thus shall it be done for *one* bullock, or for *one* ram,
12. so shall ye do *to every one*
15. *One* ordinance (shall be both) for you
16. *One* law and *one* manner shall be for you,
24. *one* young bullock for a burnt offering,
— and *one* kid of the goats for a sin offering.
27. if *any* soul sin through ignorance,
29. Ye shall have *one* law for him that
16:15. I have not taken *one* ass from them, neither have I hurt *one* of them.
22. shall *one* man sin, and wilt thou be wroth
17: 3(18). *one* rod (shall be) for the head of
6(21). every one of their princes gave him a rod *apiece*, for each prince *one*, (marg. a rod for *one* prince, a rod for *one* prince)
28: 4. *The one* lamb shalt thou offer in the
7. fourth (part) of an hin for *the one* lamb:
11, 19. two young bullocks, and *one* ram,
12. for *one* bullock;
— for *one* ram;
13. unto *one* lamb;
15. *one* kid of the goats for a sin offering
21. shalt thou offer for *every* lamb,
22. *one* goat (for) a sin offering,
27. two young bullocks, *one* ram,
28. three tenth deals unto *one* bullock, two tenth deals unto *one* ram,
29. A several tenth deal unto *one* lamb,
30. *one* kid of the goats, to make an atonement
29: 1. in the seventh month, *on the first* (day) of
2, 8. *one* young bullock, *one* ram,
4. *one* tenth deal for *one* lamb,
5. *one* kid of the goats (for) a sin offering,
9. two tenth deals to *one* ram,
10. A several tenth deal for *one* lamb,
11, 16, 19, 25. *One* kid of the goats (for) a sin

Nu. 29:14. three tenth deals unto *every* bullock
— two tenth deals to *each* ram
15. a several tenth deal to *each* lamb
22, 28, 31, 34, 38. *one* goat (for) a sin offering;
36. *one* bullock, *one* ram,
31:28. *one* soul of five hundred,
30. thou shalt take *one* portion of fifty,
34. threescore and *one* thousand asses,
39. Lord's tribute (was) threescore and *one*.
47. Moses took *one* portion of fifty,
33:38. *in the first* (day) of the fifth month.
34:18. ye shall take *one* prince of every tribe, (lit. *one* prince, *one* prince)
35:30. *one* witness shall not testify against any
36: 3. be married *to any* of the sons of the (other)
8. shall be wife *unto one* of the family of
Deu. 1: 2. *eleven* days' (journey) from (lit. *one*-ten)
3. *on the first* (day) of the month,
23. I took twelve men of you, *one* of a tribe:
4:42. that fleeing unto *one* of these cities
6: 4. The Lord our God (is) *one* Lord:
12:14. the Lord shall choose *in one of* thy tribes,
13:12(13). If thou shalt hear (say) *in one of* thy
15: 7. a poor man *of one of* thy brethren *within any of* thy gates
16: 5. not sacrifice the passover *within any of*
17. 2. among you, *within any of* thy gates
6. at the mouth of *one* witness he shall not
18: 6. if a Levite come *from any of* thy gates
19: 5. he shall flee unto *one of* those cities,
11. and fleeth into *one of* these cities:
15. *One* witness shall not rise up
21:15. two wives, *one* beloved, *and another* hated,
23:16(17). which he shall choose *in one of* thy
24: 5. he shall be free at home *one* year,
25: 5. If brethren dwell together, and *one* of
11. the wife of *the one* draweth near
28: 7. they shall come out against thee *one* way,
25. shalt go out *one* way against them,
55. will not give *to any* of them of the flesh
32:30. How should *one* chase a thousand,
Jos. 3:12. out of *every* tribe *a* man. (lit. *one* man, *one* man for a tribe)
13. and they shall stand upon *an* heap.
16. stood (and) rose up upon *an* heap
4: 2, 4. out of every tribe *a* man, (lit. *one* man, *one* man for a tribe)
5. take you up every man of you *a* stone
6: 3. go round about the city *once*. (lit. *one* time)
11. compassed the city, going about (it) *once*: (lit. *one* time)
14. the second day they compassed the city *once*, (lit. *one* time)
7:21. I saw among the spoils *a* goodly B. garment, and two hundred shekels of silver, and *a* wedge of gold
9: 2. with Joshua and with Israel, with *one*
10: 2. a great city, *as one of* the royal cities,
42. did Joshua take at *one* time,
12: 9, 10, 11, 12, 13, 14, 15, 16, 17, 18, 19, 20, 21, 22, 23. The king of ... *one*; the king of ... *one*;
24. The king of Tirzah, *one*: all the kings thirty *and one*.
15:51. eleven cities with their (lit. *one*-ten)
17:14. thou given me (but) *one* lot and *one* portion
17. thou shalt not have *one* lot (only):
20: 4. he that doth flee unto *one* of those cities
22:14. of each chief house *a* prince (lit. *one* prince, *one* prince for a chief house)
20. that man perished not *alone* (lit. and he *one* man perisheth not)
23:10. *One* man of you shall chase a thousand:
14. not *one* thing hath failed of all
— not *one* thing hath failed thereof.
Jud. 4:16. there was not *a* man left. (marg. unto *one*)
6:16. shalt smite the Midianites as *one* man.
8:18. each *one* resembled the children of a king.
9: 2. or that *one* reign over you?
5, 18. threescore and ten persons, upon *one*
37. *another* company come along (lit. *one* head)
53. *a certain* woman cast a piece of a
13: 2. *a certain* man (lit. *one* man) of Zorah,
15: 4. put *a* firebrand in the midst
16: 7, 11. I be weak, and be *as another* man. (marg. as *one*)

Jud. 16:28. that I may be *at once* avenged of the
29. of *the one* with his right hand, *and* of *the other* with his left.
17: 5. and consecrated *one* of his sons,
11. was unto him *as one* of his sons.
18:19. a priest unto the house of *one* man,
19:13. let us draw near *to one of* these places
20: 1. congregation was gathered together as *one*
8. all the people arose as *one* man,
11. knit together as *one* man.
31. *one* goeth up to the house of God, *and the other* to Gibeah in the field,
21: 3. that there should be to day *one* tribe
6. There is *one* tribe cut off from Israel
8. What *one* (is there) of the tribes of Israel
Ruth 1: 4. the name of *the one* (was) Orpah,
2:13. though I be not *like unto one of* thine
1 Sa. 1: 1. there was *a certain* man
2. the name of *the one* (was) Hannah,
5. unto Hannah he gave *a* worthy portion;
24. three bullocks, and *one* ephah of flour,
2:34. in *one* day they shall die both of them.
36. I pray thee, into *one of* the priest's offices,
6: 4. for *one* plague (was) on you all,
7. Now therefore make *a* new cart,
12. the highway, (lit. in *one* path)
17. for Ashdod *one*, for Gaza *one*, for Askelon *one*, for Gath *one*, for Ekron *one*;
7: 9. And Samuel took *a* sucking lamb,
12. Then Samuel took *a* stone,
9: 3. Take now *one* of the servants
15. told Samuel in his ear *a* day before
10: 3. *one* carrying three kids, *and another* carrying three loaves of bread, *and another* carrying a bottle of wine:
11: 7. came out with *one* consent (marg. *as one* man)
13:17. *one* company turned unto the way (that)
18. And *another* company turned the way (to) Beth-horon: and *another* company
14: 4. the name of *the one* (was) Bozez, and the name of *the other* Seneh,
5. The forefront of *the one* (was) situate
— *and the other* southward
40. Be ye on *one* side, and I and Jonathan my son will be on *the other*
16:18. Then answered *one* of the servants,
20. a bottle of wine, and *a* kid,
17:36. uncircumcised Philistine shall be *as one*
22:20. *one* of the sons of Ahimelech
24:14 (15). after a dead dog, after *a* flea.
25:14. *one* of the young men told Abigail,
26: 8. with the spear even to the earth at once, (lit. *one* time)
15. there came *one of* the people in to destroy
20. is come out to seek *a* flea,
22. let *one* of the young men come over
27: 1. I shall now perish *one* day
5. give me a place *in some* town
2Sa. 1:15. And David called *one* of the young men,
2: 1. Shall I go up *into any of* the cities
18. Asahel (was as) light of foot *as a* wild roe. (marg. *as one of* the roes)
21. lay thee hold on *one* of the young men,
25. and became *one* troop, and stood on the top of *an* hill.
3:13. *one* thing I require of thee,
4: 2. the name of *the one* (was) Baanah,
6:19. to every one *a* cake of bread, and *a* good piece (of flesh), and *a* flagon (of wine).
20. as *one of* the vain fellows shamelessly
7: 7. spake I a word with *any of* the tribes of
23. what *one* nation in the earth (is) like
9:11. at my table, *as one* of the king's sons.
12: 1. There were two men in *one* city; *the one* rich, *and the other* poor.
3. had nothing, save *one* little ewe lamb,
13:13. thou shalt be *as one of* the fools
30. all the king's sons, and there is not *one* of
14: 6. but *the one* smote *the other*,
27. *one* daughter, whose name (was) Tamar:
15: 2. Thy servant (is) *of one of* the tribes of
17: 9. he is hid now *in some* pit, or *in some* (other)
12. So shall we come upon him *in some* place
— there shall not be left so much as *one*.
22. there lacked not *one* of them that was not
18:10. *a certain* man saw (it), and told Joab,
2Sa. 18:11. given thee ten (shekels) of silver, and *a*
19:14 (15). even as (the heart of) *one* man;
23: 8. eight hundred, whom he slew at *one* time.
24:12. three (things); choose thee *one* of them,
1 K. 2:16. now I ask *one* petition of thee,
20. I desire *one* small petition of thee;
3:17. And the *one* woman said, O my lord, I and this woman dwell in *one* house;
25. Divide the living child in two, and give half *to the one*, and half *to the other*.
4: 7. *each man* his month in a year
19. *the only* officer which (was) in the land.
22 (5:2). Solomon's provision for *one* day
6:24. five cubits (was) *the one* wing of the
25. the cherubims (were) of *one* measure and *one* size.
26. height of *the one* cherub (was) ten cubits,
27. the wing of *the one* touched
34. two leaves of *the one* door (were) folding,
38. in the eleventh year, (lit. *one*-tenth)
7:15. eighteen cubits high *apiece*: (lit. 18 cubits was the height of *one* pillar)
16. the height of *the one* chapiter (was) five
17. seven for *the one* chapiter,
18. round about upon *the one* network,
27. four cubits (was) the length of *one* base,
30. And *every* base had four brasen wheels,
32. the height of *a* wheel (was) a cubit and
34. undersetters to the four corners of *one*
37. all of them had *one* casting, *one* measure, (and) *one* size.
38. *one* laver contained forty baths: (and) *every* laver was four cubits: (and) upon every *one* of the ten bases *one* laver.
42. two rows of pomegranates for *one* netw.,
44. *one* sea, and twelve oxen under the sea;
8:56. there hath not failed *one* word of all
10:14. that came to Solomon in *one* year
16. (shekels) of gold went to *one* target.
17. pound of gold went to *one* shield:
22. *once* in three years came the navy
11:13. will give *one* tribe to thy son
32. he shall have *one* tribe for my servant
36. unto his son will I give *one* tribe,
12:29. he set *the one* in Beth-el, and *the other* put
30. the people went (to worship) before *the one*,
13:11. there dwelt *an* old prophet in Beth-el;
14:21. Rehoboam (was) forty *and one* years old
15:10. forty *and one* years reigned he in Jerusa.
16:23. In the thirty *and first* year of Asa
18: 6. Ahab went *one* way by himself, and Obadiah went *another* way by himself.
23. let them choose *one* bullock for themselves,
— and I will dress *the other* bullock,
25. Choose you *one* bullock for yourselves,
19: 2. thy life as the life of *one* of them
4. came and sat down under *a* juniper tree:
5. as he lay and slept under *a* juniper tree,
20:13. there came *a* prophet unto Ahab
29. an hundred thousand footmen in *one* day.
35. *a certain* man of the sons of the prophets
22: 8. (There is) yet *one* man, Micaiah the son of
9. Then the king of Israel called *an* officer,
13. with *one* mouth: let thy word, I pray thee, be like the word of *one* of them,
2 K. 2:16. cast him *upon some* mountain, (marg. *one of* the mountains) or *into some* valley.
3:11. *one* of the king of Israel's servants
4: 1. there cried *a certain* woman of
22. *one* of the young men, *and one* of the asses,
35. walked in the house to and fro; (lit. *once* hither, *and once* thither)
39. And *one* went out into the field
6: 2. and take thence every man *a* beam,
3. And *one* said, Be content, I pray thee,
5. But as *one* was felling a beam,
10. saved himself there, not *once* nor twice.
12. And *one* of his servants said,
7: 8. they went into *one* tent, and did eat and
13. And *one* of his servants answered and said,
8: 6. unto her *a certain* officer,
26. he reigned *one* year in Jerusalem.
9: 1. Elisha the prophet called *one* of the children
29. the eleventh year of (lit. *one*-tenth)
12: 9 (10). Jehoiada the priest took *a* chest,
14:23. (and reigned) forty *and one* years.
15:20. of *each* man fifty shekels of silver,

2 K.17:27. Carry thither *one* of the priests,
28. *one* of the priests whom they had
18:24. thou turn away the face of *one* captain *of*
22: 1. he reigned thirty *and one* years in
23:36. *and* he reigned eleven years (lit. *and one*-ten)
24:18. Zedekiah (was) twenty *and one* years old
— *and* he reigned eleven years (lit. *and one*-ten)
25:16. *one* sea, and the bases which Solomon (marg. *the one* sea)
17. The height of *the one* pillar (was) eighteen
19. out of the city he took *an* officer
1Ch. 1:19. the name of *the one* (was) Peleg;
11:11. three hundred slain (by him) at *one* time.
12:14. *one* of the least (was) over an hundred,
38. the rest also of Israel (were) of *one* heart
17: 6. spake I a word to *any of* the judges of
21. what *one* nation in the earth (is) like
21:10. three (things): choose thee *one* of them,
23:11. therefore they were in *one* reckoning,
24: 6. *one* principal houshold being taken
17. The *one* and twentieth to Jachin,
25:28. The *one* and twentieth to Hothir,
27: 1. of *every* course (were) twenty and four
29: 1. my son, whom *alone* God hath chosen,
2 Ch. 3:11. *one* wing (of the one cherub was) five
12. And (one) wing of the *other* cherub
17. *one* on the right hand, *and the other* on the
4:13. two rows of pomegranates on *each* wreath,
15. *One* sea, and twelve oxen under it.
5:13. as the trumpeters and singers (were) *as one*, to make *one* sound to be heard
9:13. that came to Solomon in *one* year
15. (shekels) of beaten gold went to *one* targ.
16. (shekels) of gold went to *one* shield.
21. every three years *once* came the ships
12:13. Rehoboam (was) *one* and forty years old
16:13. and died in the *one* and fortieth year
18: 7. (There is) yet *one* man, by whom we may
8. the king of Israel called for *one* (of his)
12. with *one* assent; let thy word therefore, I pray thee, be *like one* of theirs,
22: 2. he reigned *one* year in Jerusalem.
24: 8. at the king's commandment they made *a* chest,
28: 6. an hundred and twenty thousand in *one*
29:17. they began *on the first* (day) of the first
30:12. hand of God was to give them *one* heart
32:12. Ye shall worship before *one* altar,
34: 1. in Jerusalem *one* and thirty years.
36: 5. *and* he reigned eleven years (lit. *and one*-ten)
11. Zedekiah (was) *one* and twenty years
— *and* reigned eleven (lit. *and one*-ten)
22. the *first* year of Cyrus king of Persia,
Ezra 1: 1. the *first* year of Cyrus king of Persia,
2:26. Gaba, six hundred twenty *and one*.
64. The whole congregation *together* (lit. *as one*)
3: 1. gathered themselves together as *one* man
6. From the *first* day of the seventh month
9. the sons of Judah, *together*, (marg. *as one*)
6:20. the Levites were purified *together*,
7: 9. *upon the first* (day) of the first month
— *and on the first* (day) of the fifth
10:13. (is this) a work of *one* day or two:
16. in the *first* day of the tenth
17. by the *first* day of the first month.
Neh. 1: 2. Hanani, *one* of my brethren,
4:17 (11). *with one of* his hands wrought in the work, *and* with *the other* (hand) held a weapon.
5:18. prepared (for me) daily (lit. *one* day) (was) *one* ox
7:30. Gaba, six hundred twenty *and one*.
37. and Ono, seven hundred twenty *and one*.
66. The whole congregation *together*
8. 1. gathered themselves together as *one* man
2. upon the *first* day of the seventh month.
11: 1. cast lots, to bring *one* of ten to dwell
Est. 3: 8. There is *a certain* people
13. in *one* day,
4:11. (there is) *one* law of his to put (him) to
7: 9. Harbonah, *one* of the chamberlains,
8:12. Upon *one* day in all the provinces
Job 2:10. Thou speakest as *one of* the foolish women
Job 9: 3. he cannot answer him *one* of a thousand.
22. This (is) *one* (thing), therefore I said (it),
14: 4. clean (thing) out of an unclean? not *one*.
23:13. he (is) *in one* (mind), and who can turn
31:15. did not *one* fashion us in the womb?
33:14. For God speaketh *once*,
23. an interpreter, *one* among a thousand,
40: 5. *Once* have I spoken; but I will not
41:16 (8). *One* is so near *to another*,
42:11. every man also gave him *a* piece of money, and every one *an* earring of gold.
14. And he called the name of *the first*,
Ps. 14: 3. none that doeth good, no, not *one*.
27: 4. *One* (thing) have I desired of the Lord,
34:20 (21). He keepeth all his bones: not *one* of
53: 3 (4). none that doeth good, no, not *one*.
62:11 (12). God hath spoken *once*;
82: 7. like men, *and* fall *like one* of the princes.
89:35 (36). *Once* have I sworn by my holiness
106:11. there was not *one* of them left.
139:16. (as yet there was) none (lit. not *one*)
Pro. 1:14. thy lot among us; let us all have *one*
28:18. shall fall *at once*.
Ecc. 2:14. *one* event happeneth to them all.
3:19. even *one* thing befalleth them:
— yea, they have all *one* breath;
20. All go unto *one* place;
4: 8. There is *one* (alone), and (there is) not a
9. Two (are) better than *one*;
10. *the one* will lift up his fellow: but woe to him (that is) *alone*
11. *but* how can *one* be warm (alone)?
12. if *one* prevail against him,
6: 6. do not all go to *one* place?
7:27. (counting) *one by one*, to find out the (marg. *one* thing *after another*)
28. *one* man among a thousand have I
9: 2. (there is) *one* event to the righteous,
3. (there is) *one* event unto all:
18. but *one* sinner destroyeth much good.
11: 6. whether they both (shall be) *alike* good.
12:11. are given from *one* shepherd.
Cant. 4: 9. hast ravished my heart *with one* of thine eyes, *with one* chain of thy neck.
6: 9. My dove, my undefiled is (but) *one*; she (is) the (only) *one* of her mother,
Isa. 4: 1. seven women shall take hold of *one* man,
5:10. ten acres of vineyard shall yield *one* bath,
6: 2. *each one had* six wings; (lit. *to one*)
6. Then flew *one* of the seraphims unto me,
9:14 (13). branch and rush, in *one* day.
10:17. his thorns and his briers in *one* day;
19:18. *one* shall be called, The city of destruction.
23:15. according to the days of *one* king:
27:12. ye shall be gathered *one by one*, O ye
30:17. *One* thousand (shall flee) at the rebuke of *one*;
34:16. no *one* of these shall fail,
36: 9. turn away the face of *one* captain of
47: 9. shall come to thee in a moment in *one* day,
51: 2. I called him *alone*, and blessed him,
65:25. The wolf and the lamb shall feed *together*,
66: 8. Shall the earth be made to bring forth in *one* day? (or) shall a nation be born at once? (lit. *one* time)
17. themselves in the gardens behind *one* (tree)
Jer. 3:14. I will take you *one* of a city,
10: 8. *But* they are *altogether* brutish and foolish: (marg. *in one*, or, *at once*)
24: 2. *One* basket (had) very good figs,
— and *the other* basket (had) very naughty
32:39. will give them *one* heart, and *one* way,
35: 2. house of the Lord, into *one* of the
51:60. Jeremiah wrote in *a* book
52: 1. Zedekiah (was) *one* and twenty years old
— *and* he reigned eleven (lit. *and one*-ten)
20. *one* sea, and twelve brasen bulls
21. the height of *one* pillar (was) eighteen
22. the height of *one* chapiter (was) five
25. He took also out of the city *an* eunuch,
Eze. 1: 6. *every one had* four faces, and *every one had* four wings.
15. behold *one* wheel upon the earth
16. and they four had *one* likeness:
4: 9. and put them in *one* vessel,
7: 5. An evil, an *only* evil, behold, is come.
8: 7. I looked, behold *a* hole in the wall.

Eze. 8: 8. had digged in the wall, behold *a* door.
9: 2. *one* man among them (was) clothed with
10: 9. *one* wheel by *one* cherub, and *another* wheel by *another* cherub:
10. they four had *one* likeness,
14. And *every one had* four faces: *the first* face (was) the face of a cherub,
21. *Every one had* four faces apiece, and *every one* four wings;
11:19. And I will give them *one* heart,
16: 5. None eye pitied thee, to do *any* of these
17: 7. There was also *another* great eagle
18:10. (that) doeth the like *to* (any) *one* of these
19: 3. And she brought up *one* of her whelps:
5. she took *another* of her whelps,
21:19 (24). twain shall come forth out of *one*
23: 2. two women, the daughters of *one* mother:
13. they (took) both *one* way,
26: 1 & 29:17. *in the first* (day) of the month,
30:20. in the eleventh year, (lit. *in the one*-tenth)
31: 1. in the eleventh year, (lit. *in the one*-tenth)
— & 32:1. *in the first* (day) of the month,
33: 2. if the people of the land take *a* man
24. Abraham was *one*, and he inherited
30. and speak one to *another*,
34:23. I will set up *one* shepherd over them,
37:16. son of man, take thee *one* stick,
— then take *another* stick,
17. join them *one* to *another* into *one* stick; and they shall become *one*
19. and make them *one* stick, and they shall be *one* in mine hand.
22. And I will make them *one* nation
— *one* king shall be king to them all:
24. and they all shall have *one* shepherd:
40: 5. the breadth of the building, *one* reed; and the height, *one* reed.
6. (which was) *one* reed broad; and the *other* threshold (of the gate, which was) *one* reed
7. (every) little chamber (was) *one* reed long, and *one* reed broad;
— by the porch of the gate within (was) *one* reed.
8. the porch of the gate within, *one* reed.
10. they three (were) of *one* measure: and the posts had *one* measure
12. before the little chambers (was) *one* cubit (on this side), and the space (was) *one*
26, 49. *one* on this side, *and another* on that
42. of *a* cubit and an half long, and *a* cubit and an half broad, and *one* cubit high:
43. And within (were) hooks, *an* hand broad,
44. *one* at the side of the east gate
41:11. *one* door toward the north, and *another*
24. two (leaves) for the *one* door,
42: 4. a way of *one* cubit;
43:13. thereof round about (shall be) *a* span:
14. and the breadth *one* cubit;
45: 7. (shall be) over against *one* of the portions,
11. The ephah and the bath shall be of *one*
15. *one* lamb out of the flock,
18. *in the first* (day) of the month,
46:17. his inheritance *to one* of his servants,
22. these four corners (were) of *one* measure.
48: 1. *a* (portion for) Dan. (lit. Dan *one*)
2. *a* (portion for) Asher.
3. *a* (portion for) Naphtali.
4. *a* (portion for) Manasseh.
5. *a* (portion for) Ephraim.
6. *a* (portion for) Reuben.
7. *a* (portion for) Judah.
8. (in) length *as one of* the (other) parts,
23. Benjamin (shall have) *a* (portion). (marg. *one*)
24. Simeon (shall have) *a* (portion).
25. Issachar *a* (portion).
26. Zebulun *a* (portion).
27. Gad *a* (portion).
31. *one* gate of Reuben, *one* gate of Judah, *one* gate of Levi.
32. *one* gate of Joseph, *one* gate of Benjamin, *one* gate of Dan.
33. *one* gate of Simeon, *one* gate of Issachar, *one* gate of Zebulun.
34. *one* gate of Gad, *one* gate of Asher, *one* gate of Naphtali.

Dan. 1:21. continued (even) unto the *first* year of
8: 3. there stood before the river *a* ram
— *but one* (was) higher than the other,
9. out of *one* of them came forth *a* little
13. I heard *one* saint speaking, and *another*
9: 1. In the *first* year of Darius
2. In the *first* year of his reign
27. the covenant with many for *one* week:
10: 5. behold *a certain* man (marg. *one* man)
13. withstood me *one and* twenty days: but, lo, Michael, *one of* the chief princes, came (marg. *the first*)
21. none (lit. not *one*) that holdeth with me
11: 1. Also I in the *first* year of Darius
20. within *few* days he shall be destroyed,
27. they shall speak lies at *one* table;
12: 5. *one* on this side of the bank of the river, *and the other* on that side
Hos. 1:11 (2:2). and appoint themselves *one* head,
Am. 4: 7. I caused it to rain upon *one* city, and caused it not to rain upon *another* city: *one* piece was rained upon,
8. three cities wandered unto *one* city,
6: 9. if there remain ten men in *one* house,
Obad. 11. thou (wast) *as one* of them.
Jon. 3: 4. *a* day's journey,
Zep. 3: 9. to serve him with *one* consent.
Hag. 1: 1. in the *first* day of the month,
2: 1. in the *one and* twentieth (day)
6. Yet *once*, it (is) a little while,
Zec. 3: 9. upon *one* stone (shall be) seven eyes:
— remove the iniquity of that land in *one*
4: 3. *one* upon the right (side) of the bowl, *and the other* upon the left
5: 7. this (is) *a* woman that sitteth in the
8:21. inhabitants of *one* (city) shall go to *another*,
11: 7. *the one* I called Beauty, *and the other* I called Bands;
8. Three shepherds also I cut off in *one*
14: 7. it shall be *one* day which shall be known
9. in that day shall there be *one* Lord, and his name *one*.
Mal. 2:10. Have we not all *one* father? hath not *one* God created us?
15. And did not he make *one?*
— And wherefore *one?*

אָחוּ *āh'-ghoo*, m. 260

Gen41. 2, 18. they fed *in a meadow*.
Job. 8:11. can *the flag* grow without water?

אַחְוָה [*agh-vāh'*] f. 262

Job 13:17. *and my declaration* with your ears.

אַחֲוָה *ah-ghăvāh'*, f. 264

Zec.11:14. break *the brotherhood* between Judah and

אַחֲוָיַת *ah-ghăvāh-yath'*, Ch. 263

[Const. of אַחֲוָיָה]

Dan 5:12. *and shewing* of hard sentences,

אָחוֹר *āh-ghōr'*, m. 268

Gen49:17. so that his rider shall fall *backward*.
Ex. 26:12. over *the backside of* the tabernacle.
33:23. thou shalt see *my back parts:*
2Sa. 1:22. the bow of Jonathan turned not *back*,
10: 9. battle was against him before *and behind*,
1 K. 7:25. all *their hinder parts* (were) inward.
1Ch.19:10. was set against him before *and behind*,
2Ch. 4: 4. all *their hinder parts* (were) inward.
13:14. the battle (was) before *and behind:*
Job 23: 8. *and backward*, but I cannot perceive
Ps. 9: 3 (4). When mine enemies are turned *back*
35: 4. let them be turned *back* and brought

Ps. 40:14 (15). let them be driven *backward*
44:10 (11). Thou makest us to turn *back*
18 (19). Our heart is not turned *back*,
56: 9 (10). then shall mine enemies turn *back:*
70: 2 (3). let them be turned *backward*,
78:66. his enemies *in the hinder part:*
114: 3. The sea saw (it), and fled: Jordan was driven *back*.
5. Jordan, (that) thou wast driven *back?*
129: 5. Let them all be confounded and turned *back*
139: 5. hast beset me *behind* and before,
Pro. 29:11. a wise (man) keepeth it in *till afterwards*.
Isa. 1: 4. they are gone away *backward*.
9:12 (11). The Syrians before, and the Philistines *behind;*
28:13. that they might go, and fall *backward*,
41:23. Shew the things that are to come *hereaft.*,
42:17. They shall be turned *back*,
23. hear *for the time to come?* (marg. *for the after* (time)
44:25. that turneth wise (men) *backward*,
50: 5. rebellious, neither turned away *back*.
59:14. judgment is turned away *backward*.
Jer. 7:24. went *backward*, and not forward.
15: 6. thou art gone *backward:*
38:22. they are turned away *back*.
46: 5. dismayed (and) turned away *back?*
Lam. 1: 8. she sigheth, and turneth *backward*.
13. he hath turned me *back:*
2: 3. hath drawn *back* his right hand
Eze. 2:10. it (was) written within *and without:*
8:16. with *their backs* toward the temple

---

269 אָחוֹת *āh-ghōth'*, f.

אֲחֹתָהּ···אִשָּׁה, one...another.

Gen. 4:22. *and the sister of* Tubal-cain (was)
12:13. Say, I pray thee, thou (art) *my sister:*
19. Why saidst thou, She (is) *my sister?*
20: 2. said of Sarah his wife, She (is) *my sister:*
5. Said he not unto me, She (is) *my sister?*
12. yet indeed (she is) *my sister;*
24:30. bracelets upon *his sister*'s hands, and when he heard the words of Rebekah *his sister*,
59. they sent away Rebekah *their sister*,
60. said unto her, Thou (art) *our sister*,
25:20. *the sister to* Laban the Syrian.
26: 7. he said, She (is) *my sister:*
9. how saidst thou, She (is) *my sister?*
28: 9. *the sister of* Nebajoth, to be his wife.
29:13. heard the tidings of Jacob *his sister*'s son,
30: 1. Rachel envied *her sister;*
8. have I wrestled with *my sister*,
34:13. he had defiled Dinah *their sister:*
14. *our sister* to one that is uncircumcised;
27. because they had defiled *their sister*.
31. Should he deal with *our sister* as with
36: 3. Ishmael's daughter, *sister of* Nebajoth.
22. *and* Lotan's *sister* (was) Timna.
46:17. Isui, and Beriah, and Serah *their sister:*
Ex. 2: 4. *his sister* stood afar off,
7. Then said *his sister* to Pharaoh's daughter,
6:23. *sister of* Naashon, to wife;
15:20. the prophetess, *the sister of* Aaron,
26: 3. coupled together one to *another;*
— five curtains (shall be) coupled one to *another*.
5. that the loops may take hold one of *another*.
6. couple the curtains *together*
17. set in order one against *another:*
Lev. 18: 9. The nakedness of *thy sister*,
11. begotten of thy father, she (is) *thy sister*,
12. the nakedness of thy father's *sister:*
13. the nakedness of thy mother's *sister:*
18. shalt thou take a wife to *her sister*,
20: 17. if a man shall take *his sister*,
— hath uncovered *his sister*'s nakedness;
19. the nakedness of thy mother's *sister*, nor of thy father's *sister:*
21: 3. *And for his sister* a virgin,
Nu. 6: 7. for his brother, *or for his sister*,
25:18. daughter of a prince of Midian, *their sister*,
Nu. 26:59. Miriam *their sister*.
Deu 27:22. Cursed (be) he that lieth with *his sister*,
Josh. 2:13. my brethren, and *my sisters*,
Jud. 15: 2. (is) not *her* younger *sister* fairer
2Sa. 13: 1. Absalom the son of David had *a* fair *sister*
2. that he fell sick for *his sister* Tamar;
4. I love Tamar, my brother Absalom's *sister*
5. let *my sister* Tamar come, and give
6. let Tamar *my sister* come, and make me
11. Come lie with me, *my sister*.
20. but hold now thy peace, *my sister:*
22. because he had forced *his sister* Tamar.
32. from the day that he forced *his sister*
17:25. *sister to* Zeruiah Joab's mother.
1 K. 11:19. gave him to wife *the sister of* his own wife, *the sister of* Tahpenes the queen.
20. *the sister of* Tahpenes bare him
2 K. 11: 2. *sister of* Ahaziah, took Joash
1 Ch. 1:39. *and* Timna (was) Lotan's *sister*.
2:16. *Whose sisters* (were) Zeruiah, and Abigail.
3: 9. Tamar *their sister*.
19. Shelomith *their sister:*
4: 3. the name of *their sister* (was) Hazelelponi:
19. Hodiah *the sister of* Naham,
7:15. *whose sister*'s name (was) Maachah;
18. *And his sister* Hammoleketh
30. Beriah, and Serah *their sister*.
32. Hotham, and Shua *their sister*.
2 Ch 22:11. for she was *the sister of* Ahaziah,
Job. 1: 4. sent and called for *their* three *sisters*
17:14. (Thou art) my mother, *and my sister*.
42:11. all his brethren, and all *his sisters*,
Pro. 7: 4. Say unto wisdom, Thou (art) *my sister;*
Cant. 4: 9. Thou hast ravished my heart, *my sister*,
10. How fair is thy love, *my sister*,
12. A garden inclosed (is) *my sister*,
5: 1. I am come into my garden, *my sister*,
2. Open to me, *my sister*,
8: 8. We have *a little sister*,
— what shall we do *for our sister*
Jer. 3: 7. *her* treacherous *sister* Judah saw (it).
8. *her* treacherous *sister* Judah feared not,
10. *her* treacherous *sister* Judah hath not
22:18. Ah my brother! or, Ah *sister!*
Eze. 1: 9. Their wings (were) joined one to *another;*
23. the one toward *the other:*
3:13. living creatures that touched one *another*,
16:45. *and* thou (art) *the sister of thy sisters*,
46. *And thine* elder *sister* (is) Samaria,
— *and thy* younger *sister*, that dwelleth
48. Sodom *thy sister* hath not done,
49. was the iniquity of *thy sister* Sodom,
51. hast justified *thy sisters* in all
52. Thou also, which hast judged *thy sisters*,
— in that thou hast justified *thy sisters*.
55. *When thy sisters*, Sodom and her daughters,
56. *thy sister* Sodom was not mentioned
61. when thou shalt receive *thy sisters*,
22:11. another in thee hath humbled *his sister*,
23: 4. Aholah the elder, and Aholibah *her sister:*
11. when *her sister* Aholibah saw (this),
— more than *her sister* in (her) whoredoms.
18. like as my mind was alienated from *her sister*.
31. Thou hast walked in the way of *thy sister;*
32. Thou shalt drink of *thy sister*'s cup
33. with the cup of *thy sister* Samaria.
44:25. *for sister* that hath had no husband,
Hos. 2. 1 (3). *and to your sisters*, Ruhamah.

אָחַז *āh-ghaz'*. 270

NOTE.—1 Ch. 24:6. וְאָחֻז אָחֻז; 7 MSS. read וְאֶחָד אָחֻז.

* KAL.—*Preterite*. *

Ex. 15:14. sorrow *shall take hold* on the inhabitants (lit. *has taken hold*)
2 Sa. 1: 9. for anguish *is come upon me*, (marg. my coat of mail, &c. *hindereth me*)
1 K. 1:51. *he hath caught hold* on the horns
Job. 16:12. *he hath also taken* (me) by my neck,
18:20. they that went before were affrighted. (marg. *laid hold on* horror)
21: 6. *and* trembling *taketh hold* on my flesh.

Job 23:11. My foot *hath held* his steps,
Ps. 48: 6 (7). Fear *took hold upon them* there,
73:23. *thou hast holden* (me) by my right hand.
77: 4 (5). *Thou holdest* mine eyes waking:
119:53. Horror *hath taken hold upon me*
Cant. 3. 4. *I held him*, and would not let him go,
Isa. 21: 3. pangs *have taken hold upon me*,
33:14. fearfulness *hath surprised* the hypocrites.
Jer. 49:24. anguish and sorrows *have taken her*,

KAL.—*Infinitive.*

1 K. 6: 6. should not *be fastened* in the walls
1Ch13: 9. put forth his hand *to hold* the ark;
Job.38.13. *That it might take hold* of the ends of the
Ps. 56: [title] (1). *when* the Philistines *took* him
Eccl. 2. 3. *and to lay hold* on folly,

KAL.—*Imperative.*

Ex. 4: 4. *and take it* by the tail.
Ruth3:15. the vail that (thou hast) upon thee, *and hold* it.
2Sa. 2:21. *and lay* thee *hold* on one of the young
Neh. 7: 3. let them shut the doors, *and bar* (them):
Cant.2:15. *Take* us the foxes, the little foxes,

KAL.—*Future.*

Ex. 15:15. trembling *shall take hold upon them*;
Deu.32:41. *and* mine hand *take hold* on judgment;
Jud. 1: 6. pursued after him, *and caught* him,
12: 6. *Then they took* him, and slew him
16: 3. *and took* the doors of the gate
21. *But* the Philistines *took him*,
20: 6. *And I took* my concubine,
Ruth 3:15. *And when she held* it,
2Sa. 4:10. *I took hold* of him, and slew (lit. *and I* &c.)
6: 6. *and took hold* of it; for the oxen
20. 9. *And* Joab *took* Amasa by the beard
1 K. 6:10. *and they rested* on the house with timber
Job.17: 9. The righteous *also shall hold on* his way,
18: 9. The gin *shall take* (him) by the heel,
30:16. days of affliction *have taken hold upon me.*
Ps.137: 9. Happy (shall he be), *that taketh* and
139:10. *and* thy right hand *shall hold me.*
Eccl. 7:18. (It is) good that *thou shouldest take hold* of
Cant.7. 8 (9). *I will take hold* of the boughs thereof.
Isai. 5:29. *and lay hold* of the prey,
13: 8. pangs and sorrows *shall take hold of them*;
Jer. 13:21. *shall* not sorrows *take thee*,

KAL.—*Participle.* Poel.

Gen25:26. his hand *took hold* on Esau's heel;
2Ch.25: 5. *that could handle* spear and shield.

KAL.—*Participle.* Päul.

Nu. 31:30. thou shalt take one *portion* of fifty,
47. Moses took one *portion* of fifty,
1Ch.24: 6. principal houshold *being taken* for Eleazar *and* (one) *taken* for Ithamar. (lit. *and taken, taken* for Ithamar)
Est. 1 : 6. *fastened* with cords of fine linen
Eccl. 9:12. birds *that are caught* in the snare;
Cant. 3: 8. *They* all *hold* swords, (being) expert in
Eze.41: 6. that they might *have hold*, (marg. *be holden*) but they had not *hold* in the

* NIPHAL.—*Preterite.* *

Nu. 32:30. *they shall have possessions* among you
Jos.22: 9. whereof *they were possessed*,

NIPHAL.—*Imperative.*

Gen34:10. *and get you possessions* therein.
Jos. 22:19. *and take possession* among us:

NIPHAL.—*Future.*

Gen47:27. *and they had possessions* therein,

NIPHAL.—*Participle.*

Gen22:13. a ram *caught* in a thicket by his horns:
Eccl. 9:12. the fishes *that are taken* in an evil net,

* PIEL.—*Participle.* *

Job. 26: 9. *He holdeth back* the face of his throne,

* HOPHAL.—*Participle.* *

2 Ch. 9:18. (which were) *fastened* to the throne,

---

272 אֲחֻזָּה *ăghuz-zāh'*, f.

Gen17: 8. *for an* everlasting *possession*;
23: 4. *a possession of* a buryingplace
Gen23: 9, 20. *for a possession of* a buryingplace
36:43. in the land of *their possession*:
47.11. them *a possession* in the land of Egypt.
48: 4. (for) *an* everlasting *possession.*
49:30 & 50:13. *for a possession of* a buryingp.
Lev.14:34. which I give to you *for a possession*,
— in a house of the land of *your possession*;
25:10. return every man unto *his possession*,
13. return every man unto *his possession.*
24. in all the land of *your possession*
25. hath sold away (some) *of his possession*,
27. that he may return *unto his possession.*
28. he shall return *unto his possession.*
32. the houses of the cities of *their possession*,
33. the city of *his possession*,
— *their possession* among the children of
34. for it (is) their perpetual *possession.*
41. unto *the possession of* his fathers shall he
45. they shall be your *possession.* (lit. to you *for a possession*)
46. to inherit (them for) *a possession*,
27:16. unto the Lord (some part) of a field of *his possession*,
21. *the possession thereof* shall be the priest's.
22. which (is) not of the fields of *his possession*;
24. whom *the possession of* the land
28. the field of *his possession*,
Nu. 27: 4. Give unto us (therefore) *a possession*
7. shalt surely give them *a possession of*
32: 5. be given unto thy servants *for a possession*,
22. this land shall be your *possession*
29. give them the land of Gilead *for a possession*:
32. that *the possession of* our inheritance
35: 2. the inheritance of *their possession*
8. *of the possession of* the children of Israel
28. return into the land of *his possession.*
Deu32:49. unto the children of Israel *for a possession*:
Jos. 21:12. Caleb the son of Jephunneh *for his possession.*
41 (39). *the possession of* the children of
22: 4. unto the land of *your possession*,
9. to the land of *their possession*,
19. if the land of *your possession*
— the land of *the possession of* the Lord,
1 Ch. 7:28. *And their possessions* and habitations
9: 2. that (dwelt) *in their possessions*
2Ch11:14. Levites left their suburbs *and their possession*,
31: 1. every man *to his possession*,
Neh11: 3. every one *in his possession*
Ps. 2: 8. *and* the uttermost parts of the earth (for) *thy possession.*
Eze.44:28. *and* ye shall give them no *possession* in Israel: I (am) *their possession.*
45: 5. *for a possession for* twenty chambers.
6. *And* ye shall appoint *the possession of*
7. *and of the possession of* the city,
— before *the possession of* the city,
8. In the land shall be his *possession*
46:16. it (shall be) *their possession* by inheritance.
18. to thrust them *out of their possession*;
— sons inheritance *out of his own possession*: that my people be not scattered every man *from his possession.*
48:20. with *the possession of* the city.
21. *and of the possession of* the city,
22. *Moreover from the possession of* the Levites, *and from the possession of* the city,

---

אֲחִידָן *ăghee-dāhn'*, Ch. 280

[Pl. of אֲחִידָה]

Dan 5:12. and shewing of *hard sentences*,

אֹחִים *ōh-gheem'*, m. 255

[Pl. of אֹחַ]

Is. 13:21 their houses shall be full of *doleful creatures*; (marg. Ochim)

305 אֲחַלֵי ah-ghălēy', & אַחֲלַי ah-ghălay', interj.

2 Ki.5: 3. *Would God* my lord
Ps.119: 5. *O that* my ways were directed

306 אַחְלָמָה ăgh-lāh-māh', f.

Ex.28:19 & 39:12. the third row a ligure, an agate, *and an amethyst.*

307 אַחְמְתָא ăgh-m'thāh', Ch.

Ezra 6: 2. And there was found *at Achmetha*, (marg. *Ecbatana*, or, *in a coffer*)

309 אָחַר [āh-ghar'].

* KAL.—*Future.* *

Gen32:4 (5). *and stayed there* until now:
2Sa. 20:5. (קרי) *but he tarried longer* than the set time

* PIEL.—*Preterite.* *

Gen34:19. the young man *deferred* not to do the
Jud. 5:28. why *tarry* the wheels of his chariots?

PIEL.—*Future.*

Gen24:56. he said unto them, *Hinder* me not,
Ex. 22.29 (28). *Thou shalt* not *delay* (to offer) the
Deu. 7:10. *he will* not *be slack* to him that hateth
23:21 (22). *thou shalt* not *slack* to pay it:
Ps. 40:17 (18). *make* no *tarrying*, O my God.
70: 5 (6). O Lord, *make* no *tarrying*.
Ecc. 5: 4 (3). *defer* not to pay it;
Isa. 46:13. my salvation *shall* not *tarry*:
Dan 9:19. *defer* not, for thine own sake,
Hab. 2: 3. it will surely come, *it will* not *tarry*.

PIEL.—*Participle.*

Ps.127: 2. vain for you to rise up early, *to* sit up *late*,
Pro.23:30. *They that tarry long* at the wine;
Isa. 5:11. *that continue* until night,

310 אַחַר ah-ghar', m.

Gen.5: 4. *after* he had begotten Seth
7. *after* he begat Enos
10. *after* he begat Cainan
13. *after* he begat Mahalaleel
16. *after* he begat Jared
19. *after* he begat Enoch eight hundred
22. *after* he begat Methuselah
26. *after* he begat Lamech
30. *after* he begat Noah
6: 4. also *after* that, when the sons of God
9: 9. with your seed *after you*;
28. Noah lived *after* the flood three hundred
10: 1. unto them were sons born *after* the flood.
18. *and afterward* were the families of the
32. divided in the earth *after* the flood.
11:10. begat Arphaxad two years *after* the flood:
11. Shem lived *after* he begat Arphaxad
13. Arphaxad lived *after* he begat Salah
15. Salah lived *after* he begat Eber
17. Eber lived *after* he begat Peleg
19. Peleg lived *after* he begat Reu
21. Reu lived *after* he begat Serug
23. Serug lived *after* he begat Nahor
25. Nahor lived *after* he begat Terah
13:14. *after that* Lot was separated from him,
14:17. *after* his return from the slaughter
15: 1. *After* these things the word of the Lord
14. *and after*ward shall they come out
16:13. I also here looked *after* him that seeth me?
17: 7. between me and thee and thy seed *after thee*
— a God unto thee, and to thy seed *after thee*.
8. to thy seed *after thee*,
9. thy seed *after thee* in their generations.
10. between me and you and thy seed *after thee*;
Gen17.19. with his seed *after him*.
18: 5. *after that* ye shall pass on:
10. the tent door, which (was) *behind him*.
12. *After* I am waxed old shall I have
19. his children and his houshold *after him*,
19: 6. shut the door *after him*,
17. look not *behind thee*,
26. his wife looked back *from behind him*,
22: 1. it came to pass *after* these things
13. *behind* (him) a ram caught in a thicket
20. it came to pass *after* these things,
23:19. *And after* this, Abraham buried Sarah
24: 5. will not be willing to follow me (lit. go *after me*)
8. not be willing to follow thee, (lit. go *after thee*)
36. son to my master *when* she was old:
39. the woman will not follow me. (lit. go *after me*)
55. *after that* she shall go.
61. the camels, and followed the man: (lit. went *after*)
67. Isaac was comforted *after* his mother's
25:11. it came to pass *after* the death of
26. *And after* that came his brother out,
26:18. had stopped them *after* the death of
30:21. *And afterwards* she bare a daughter,
31:23. pursued *after him* seven days' journey;
36. thou hast so hotly pursued *after me*?
32:18 (19). behold, also he (is) *behind us*
19 (20). all that followed the droves, (lit. going *after*)
20 (21). Behold, thy servant Jacob (is) *behind us*.
—(—) *and afterward* I will see his face;
33: 7. *and after* came Joseph near
35: 5. they did not pursue *after* the sons of
12. to thy seed *after thee* will I give the land.
37:17. Joseph went *after* his brethren,
38:30. *And afterward* came out his brother,
39: 7 & 40:1. it came to pass *after* these things,
41: 3, 19. seven other kine came up *after them*
6, 23. with the east wind sprung up *after them*.
27. that came up *after them* (are) seven years;
30. there shall arise *after them* seven years
31. by reason of that famine *following*; (lit. *after* that)
39. *Forasmuch* as God hath shewed thee
44: 4. Up, follow *after* the men;
45:15. *and after* that his brethren talked with
46:30. *since* I have seen thy face,
48: 1. it came to pass *after* these things,
4. will give this land to thy seed *after thee*
6. which thou begettest *after them*,
50:14. *after* he had buried his father.
Ex. 3: 1. led the flock *to the backside* of the desert,
20. *and after* that he will let you go.
5: 1. *And afterward* Moses and Aaron went in,
7:25. *after* that the Lord had smitten the river.
10:14. *neither after them* shall be such.
11: 1. *after*wards he will let you go hence:
5. the maidservant that (is) *behind* the mill;
8. *and after* that I will go out.
14: 4. that he shall follow *after them*;
8. he pursued *after* the children of Israel:
9. But the Egyptians pursued *after them*,
10. the Egyptians marched *after them*;
17. they shall follow them: (lit. come *after them*)
19. removed and went *behind them*;
— stood *behind them*:
23. went in *after them* to the midst of the sea,
28. that came into the sea *after them*;
15:20. all the women went out *after her*
18: 2. *after* he had sent her back,
23: 2. Thou shalt not follow a multitude to (do) evil; (lit. be *after*)
— to decline *after* many to wrest
28:43. his seed *after him*.
29:29. Aaron shall be his sons' *after him*,
33: 8. looked *after* Moses, until he was gone
34:15. they go a whoring *after* their gods,
16. go a whoring *after* their gods, and make thy sons go a whoring *after* their gods.
32. *And after*ward all the children of Israel
Lev.13: 7. *after* that he hath been seen

Lev.13:35. in the skin *after* his cleansing;
55. *after that* it is washed:
56. somewhat dark *after* the washing
14: 8. *and after that* he shall come into
19. *and afterward* he shall kill the burnt off.:
36. *and afterward* the priest shall go in to see
43. *after that* he hath taken away the stones, *and after* he hath scraped the house, *and after* it is plaistered;
48. *after* the house was plaistered:
15:28. *and after that* she shall be clean.
16: 1. *after* the death of the two sons of Aaron,
26. *and after*ward come into the camp.
28. *and after*ward he shall come into the
17: 7. *after* whom they have gone a whoring. (lit. that...*after them*)
20: 5. all that go a whoring *after him*, to commit whoredom *with* Molech,
6. to go a whoring *after them*,
22: 7. *and* shall *afterward* eat of the holy things;
25:15. number of years *after* the jubile
46. inheritance for your children *after you*,
48. *After that* he is sold he may be redeemed
26:33. will draw out a sword *after you:*
27:18. if he sanctify his field *after* the jubile,
Nu. 3:23. pitch *behind* the tabernacle westward.
4:15. *after* that, the sons of Kohath shall come
5:26. *and afterward* shall cause the woman
6:19. *after* (the hair of) his separation is
20. *and after that* the Nazarite may drink
7:88. *after* that it was anointed.
8:15. *And after* that shall the Levites go in
22. *And after* that went the Levites in
9:17. *then after* that the children of Israel
12:14. *and after that* let her be received in
16. *And afterward* the people removed
14:24. hath followed me fully, (lit fulfilled *after me*)
43. ye are turned *away from* the Lord,
15:39. seek not *after* your own heart *and* (lit. *and after*) your own eyes, *after which*
16:25. the elders of Israel followed him. (lit. went *after him*)
19: 7. *and afterward* he shall come into the
25: 8. he went *after* the man of Israel
13. he shall have it, and his seed *after him*,
26: 1 (25:19). it came to pass *after* the plague,
30:15 (16). make them void *after that* he hath
31: 2. *afterward* shalt thou be gathered
24. *and afterward* ye shall come into the
32:11. they have not wholly followed me: (marg. fulfilled *after me*)
12. for they have wholly followed the Lord. (lit. fulfilled *after*, &c.)
15. if ye turn away *from after him*,
22. *then afterward* ye shall return,
35:28. *after* the death of the high priest
Deu. 1: 4. *After* he had slain Sihon the king
8. to their seed *after them*.
36. because he hath wholly followed the Lord. (marg. fulfilled (to go) *after*)
4: 3. the men that *followed* Baal-peor, (lit. went *after*)
37. therefore he chose their seed *after them*,
40. with thy children *after thee*,
6:14. Ye shall not go *after* other gods,
7: 4. turn away thy son *from following me*,
8:19. and walk *after* other gods,
10:15. he chose their seed *after them*,
11: 4. as they pursued *after you*,
28. to go *after* other gods, which ye have
30. *by* the way where the sun goeth down,
12:25, 28. with thy children *after thee*,
30. be not snared by following them, (marg. *after them*) *after that* they be destroyed
13: 2 (3). Let us go *after* other gods,
4 (5). Ye shall walk *after* the Lord your
19: 6. of the blood pursue the slayer, (lit. pursue *after* the &c.)
21:13. *and after* that thou shalt go in unto her,
23:14 (15). turn away *from thee*.
24: 4. *after that* she is defiled;
20. thou shalt not go over the boughs *again:* (marg. bough (it) *after thee*)
21. thou shalt not glean (it) *afterward:* (marg. *after thee*)
25:18. all (that were) feeble *behind thee*,

Deu28:14. to go *after* other gods to serve them.
29:22 (21). that shall rise up *after you*,
31:16. go a whoring *after* the gods of the
27. how much more *after* my death?
29. I know that *after* my death ye will
Jos. 1: 1. Now *after* the death of Moses
2: 5. pursue *after them* quickly;
7. the men pursued *after them*
— *as soon* as they which pursued *after them*
16. *and afterward* may ye go your way,
3: 3. remove from your place, and go *after it*.
6: 8. the Lord followed them. (lit. going *after them*)
9, 13. the rereward came *after* the ark,
7: 8. when Israel turneth their backs (lit. *after* that)
8: 2. lay thee an ambush for the city *behind it*.
4. *behind* the city: go not very far
6. For they will come out *after us*
14. ambush against him *behind* the city.
16. were called together to pursue *after them:* and they pursued *after* Joshua,
17. that went not out *after* Israel: and they left the city open, and pursued *after*
20. when the men of Ai looked *behind them*,
34. *And after*ward he read all the words
9:16. *after* they had made a league with them,
10:14. was no day like that before it *or after it*,
19. stay ye not, (but) pursue *after* your
26. *after*ward Joshua smote them, and slew
14: 8. I wholly followed the Lord my God. (lit. fulfilled *after*)
9. thou hast wholly followed the Lord my God. (lit. fulfilled *after*)
14. he wholly followed the Lord God of Israel. (lit. *after*)
20: 5. avenger of blood pursue *after him*,
22:16, 18, 29. this day *from following* the Lord,
23. an altar to turn *from following* the Lord,
27. our generations *after us*,
23: 1. it came to pass a long time *after*
24: 5. *and afterward* I brought you out.
6. the Egyptians pursued *after* your fathers
20. consume you, *after* that he hath done
29. it came to pass *after* these things,
31. all the days of the elders that overlived Joshua, (marg. prolonged their days *after* Joshua)
Jud. 1: 1. Now *after* the death of Joshua
6. fled; and they pursued *after him*,
9. *And afterward* the children of Judah
2: 7. all the days of the elders that outlived Joshua, (marg. prolonged days *after*)
10. arose another generation *after them*,
12. followed other gods, (lit. went *after*)
17. they went a whoring *after* other gods,
19. in following other gods to serve them, (lit. going *after*)
3:22. the haft also went in *after* the blade;
28. he said unto them, Follow *after me:*
— they went down *after him*,
31. *And after him* was Shamgar
4:14. ten thousand men *after him*.
16. Barak pursued *after* the chariots, *and after* the host,
5:14. *after thee*, Benjamin, among thy people;
6:34. Abi-ezer was gathered *after him*.
35. who also was gathered *after him:*
7:11. *and afterward* shall thine hands
23. pursued *after* the Midianites.
8: 5. I am pursuing *after* Zebah and Zalmunna,
12. he pursued *after them*, and took the two
27. went thither a whoring *after it:*
33. went a whoring *after* Baalim,
9: 3. their hearts inclined *to follow* Abimelech; (marg. *after*)
4. persons, which followed him. (lit. went *after*)
49. followed Abimelech, (lit. went *after*)
10: 1. *after* Abimelech there arose
3. *after him* arose Jair,
11:36. *forasmuch* as the Lord hath taken
12: 8. *after him* Ibzan of Beth-lehem
11. *after him* Elon, a Zebulonite,
13. *after him* Abdon the son of Hillel,
13:11. Manoah arose, and went *after* his wife,
15: 7. *and after that* I will cease.

Jud.16: 4. it came to pass *after*ward,
18:12. behold, (it is) *behind* Kirjath-jearim.
19: 3. her husband arose, and went *after her*
5. *and afterward* go your way.
23. *seeing* that this man is come into
20:40. the Benjamites looked *behind them*,
45. pursued hard *after them* unto Gidom,
Ruth 1:15. return thou *after* thy sister in law.
16. to return *from following after thee:*
2: 2. glean ears of corn *after* (him)
3. gleaned in the field *after* the reapers:
7. let me glean and gather *after* the reapers
9. they do reap, and go thou *after them:*
11. *since* the death of thine husband:
3:10. thou followedst not young men, (lit. to go *after*)
4: 4. I (am) *after thee*. And he said, I will
1Sa. 1: 9. *after* they had eaten in Shiloh, *and after*
5: 9. *after* they had carried it about,
6: 7. bring their calves home *from them:*
12. the lords of the Philistines went *after them*
7: 2. house of Israel lamented *after* the Lord.
8: 3. but turned aside *after* lucre,
9:13. *after*wards they eat that be bidden.
10: 5. *After* that thou shalt come to the hill
11: 5. Saul came *after* the herd out of the field;
7. Whosoever cometh not forth *after* Saul *and after* Samuel,
12:14. continue following the Lord your God: (marg. be *after*)
20. turn not aside *from following* the Lord,
21. for (then should ye go) *after* vain
13: 4. were called together *after* Saul to Gilgal.
7. all the people *followed him* trembling. (marg. trembled *after him*)
14:12. Come up *after me:*
13. his armourbearer *after him:*
— his armourbearer slew *after him.*
22. they also followed hard *after them*
36. Let us go down *after* the Philistines
37. Shall I go down *after* the Philistines?
46. went up *from following* the Philistines:
15:11. for he is turned back *from following me*,
31. So Samuel turned again *after* Saul;
17:13. followed Saul to the (lit. went *after*)
14. the three eldest followed (lit. went *after*)
35. I went out *after him*,
53. returned from chasing *after* the
20:37, 38. Jonathan cried *after* the lad,
21: 9 (10). wrapped in a cloth *behind* the ephod:
22:20. Abiathar, escaped, and fled *after* David.
23:25. he pursued *after* David in the wilderness
28. Saul returned from pursuing *after* David,
24: 1 (2). returned *from following* the Philistines, (marg. *after*)
5 (6). it came to pass *after*ward,
8 (9). David also arose *after*ward, and went out of the cave, and cried *after* Saul,
— when Saul looked *behind him*,
14 (15). *After* whom is the king of Israel come out? *after* whom dost thou pursue? *after* a dead dog, *after* a flea.
21 (22). not cut off my seed *after me*,
25:13. there went up *after* David
19. behold, I come *after you*.
42. and she went *after* the messengers of
26: 3. Saul came *after him* into the wilderness.
18. my lord thus pursue *after* his servant?
30: 8. Shall I pursue *after* this troop?
21. that they could not follow (lit. go *after*)
2Sa. 1: 1. Now it came to pass *after* the death of
7. when he looked *behind him*,
10. he could not live *after that* he was fallen:
2: 1. it came to pass *after* this,
10. of Judah followed David. (lit. were *after*)
19. Asahel pursued *after* Abner;
— right hand nor to the left *from following*
20. Then Abner looked *behind him*,
21. not turn aside from *following of him.*
22. Turn thee aside *from following me:*
23. Abner *with the hinder end of* the spear
— the spear came out *behind him;*
24. Joab also and Abishai pursued *after*
25. gathered themselves together *after* Abner,
26. return *from following* their brethren?
27. every one *from following* his brother.

2Sa. 2:28. pursued *after* Israel no more,
30. Joab returned *from following* Abner.
3:16. weeping *behind her* to Bahurim.
26. he sent messengers *after* Abner,
28. *after*ward when David heard (it),
31. followed the bier. (lit. went *after*)
5:13. *after* he was come from Hebron:
23. fetch a compass *behind them*,
7: 8. *from following* the sheep, (marg. *from after*)
12. I will set up thy seed *after thee*,
8: 1. *after* this it came to pass,
10: 1. it came to pass *after* this,
11: 8. followed him (marg. went out *after him*)
15. retire ye *from* (lit. *from after*) *him*, that he
13: 1. it came to pass *after* this,
17. bolt the door *after her*.
18. bolted the door *after her*.
34. by the way of the hill side *behind him.*
15: 1. it came to pass *after* this,
13. the men of Israel are *after* Absalom.
17. 1. I will arise and pursue *after* David
9. the people that *follow* Absalom.
21. it came to pass, *after* they were departed,
18:16. returned from pursuing *after* Israel:
22. let me, I pray thee, also run *after* Cushi.
19:30 (31). *forasmuch* as my lord the king is
20: 2. every man of Israel went up *from after* David, (and) *followed* Sheba the son of
6. pursue *after him*, lest he get him fenced
7. there went out *after him* Joab's men,
—, 13. pursue *after* Sheba the son of Bichri.
10. pursued *after* Sheba the son of Bichri.
11. he that (is) for David, (let him go) *after*
13. all the people went on *after* Joab,
14. gathered together, and went also *after him.*
21: 1. three years, year *after* year;
14. *after* that God was intreated for the land
18. it came to pass *after* this,
23: 9. *And after him* (was) Eleazar the son
10. the people returned *after him* only
11. *And after him* (was) Shammah
24:10. David's heart smote him *after* that
1 K. 1: 6. (his mother) bare him *after* Absalom.
7. they *following* Adonijah helped (him). (marg. helped *after* Adonijah)
13, 17, 30. Solomon thy son shall reign *after me*,
14. I also will come in *after thee*,
20, 27. throne of my lord the king *after him.*
24. Adonijah shall reign *after me*,
35. Then ye shall come up *after him*,
40. all the people came up *after him*,
2:28. for Joab had turned *after* Adonijah, though he turned not *after* Absalom.
3:12. *neither after thee* shall any arise like unto thee. (lit. *and after thee* shall not)
9: 6. turn *from following me*, ye or your
21. Their children that were left *after them*
10:19. the top of the throne (was) round *behind:* (marg. *on the hinder part thereof*)
11: 2. turn away your heart *after* their gods:
4. turned away his heart *after* other gods:
5. Solomon went *after* Ashtoreth
— and *after* Milcom the abomination
6. went not fully *after* the Lord,
10. that he should not go *after* other gods:
12:20. none *that followed* the house of David,
13:14. went *after* the man of God,
23. it came to pass, *after* he had eaten bread, *and after* he had drunk,
31. it came to pass, *after* he had buried him,
33. *After* this thing Jeroboam returned not
14: 8. who *followed me* with all his heart, (lit. went *after me*)
9. hast cast me *behind* thy back:
10. take away *the remnant of* the house
15: 4. to set up his son *after him*,
16: 3. I will take away *the posterity of* Baasha, *and the posterity of* his house;
21. of the people followed Tibni (lit. was *after*)
— half *followed* Omri.
22. the people that *followed* Omri prevailed against the people that *followed* Tibni
17:17. it came to pass *after* these things,
18:18. thou hast followed (lit. walked *after*) Baalim.

1 K. 18:21. if the Lord (be) God, follow him (lit. go *after him*): but if Baal, (then) follow him. (lit. go *after him*)
19:11. *and after* the wind an earthquake;
12. *And after* the earthquake a fire;
— *and after* the fire a still small voice.
20. he left the oxen, and ran *after* Elijah,
— I will *follow thee*. (lit. come *after thee*)
21. he returned *back from him*,
— Then he arose, and went *after* Elijah,
20:15. *and after them* he numbered all
19. the army which *followed them*.
21: 1. it came to pass *after* these things,
21. will take away *thy posterity*,
26. he did very abominably in following idols, (lit. going *after*)
22:33. they turned back *from pursuing him*.
2 K. 1: 1. against Israel *after* the death of Ahab.
2:24. he turned *back*, and looked on them,
4:30. he arose, and followed her. (lit. went *after her*)
5:20. (as) the Lord liveth, I will run *after him*.
21. So Gehazi followed *after* Naaman. And when Naaman saw (him) running *after him*,
6:19. follow me, (marg. come ye *after me*)
24. it came to pass *after* this,
32. sound of his master's feet *behind him?*
7:14. the king sent *after* the host of the Syrians,
15. they went *after them* unto Jordan:
9:18, 19. turn thee *behind me*.
25. I and thou rode together *after* Ahab
27. Jehu followed *after him*,
10:29. Jehu departed not *from after them*,
11: 6. a third part at the gate *behind* the guard:
15. that followeth her (lit. goeth *after her*)
13: 2. followed the sins of Jeroboam (marg. walked *after*)
14:17. Joash king of Judah lived *after* the
19. they sent *after him* to Lachish,
22. *after that* the king slept with
17:15. they followed vanity, (lit. went *after*)
— *and* went *after* the heathen
21. drave Israel *from following* the Lord,
18: 5. *so that after him* was none like
6. departed not *from following him*, (marg. *from after him*)
19:21. Jerusalem hath shaken her head *at thee*.
23: 3. to walk *after* the Lord,
25. *neither after him* arose there (any)
25: 5. the Chaldees pursued *after* the king,
1 Ch. 2:21. *And afterward* Hezron went in to the
24. *And after that* Hezron was dead
5:25. went a whoring *after* the gods
10: 2. the Philistines followed hard *after* Saul, *and after* his sons;
11:12. *And after him* (was) Eleazar
14:14. God said unto him, Go not up *after them*;
17: 7. from *following* the sheep, (marg. *after*)
11. I will raise up thy seed *after thee*,
18: 1. Now *after* this it came to pass,
19: 1. Now it came to pass *after* this,
20: 4. it came to pass *after* this,
27: 7. Zebadiah his son *after him*:
34. *And after* Ahithophel (was) Jehoiada
28: 8. inheritance for your children *after you*
2 Ch. 1:12. *neither* shall there any *after thee* have the like. (lit. *and after thee* shall not)
2:17 (16). *after* the numbering wherewith
8: 8. who were left *after them* in the land,
11:16. *And after them* out of all the tribes
20. *And after her* he took Maachah
13:13. an ambushment to come *about behind them*:
— the ambushment (was) *behind them*.
19. Abijah pursued *after* Jeroboam,
18:32. turned back again *from pursuing him*. (marg. *from after him*)
20: 1. It came to pass *after* this also,
35. *And after* this did Jehoshaphat
21:18. *And after* all this the Lord
22: 4. *after* the death of his father
23:14. whoso followeth *her*, (lit. goeth *after her*)
24: 4. it came to pass *after* this,
17. *Now after* the death of Jehoiada
25:14. Now it came to pass, *after that* Amaziah

2 Ch 25:25. lived *after* the death of Joash
27. did turn away *from following* the Lord
— they sent to Lachish *after him*,
26: 2. *after* that the king slept with
17. Azariah the priest went in *after him*,
32: 1. *After* these things, and the establishment
9. *After* this did Sennacherib king
23. in the sight of all nations *from thence*forth.
33:14. *Now after* this he built a wall
34:31. to walk *after* the Lord,
33. departed not *from following* the Lord, (marg. *from after*)
35:14. *And afterward* they made ready
20. *After* all this, when Josiah had
Ezr. 3: 5. *And after*ward (offered) the continual
7: 1. *Now after* these things,
9:10. what shall we say *after* this?
13. *And after* all that is come upon us
Neh. 3:16. *After him* repaired Nehemiah
17. *After him* repaired the Levites,
18. *After him* repaired their brethren,
20. *After him* Baruch the son of Zabbai
21. *After him* repaired Meremoth
22. *And after him* repaired the priests,
23. *After him* repaired Benjamin
— *After him* repaired Azariah
24. *After him* repaired Binnui
25. *After him* Pedaiah the son of Parosh.
27. *After them* the Tekoites repaired (lit. *after him*)
29. *After them* repaired Zadok (lit. *after him*)
— *After him* repaired *also* Shemaiah
30. *After him* repaired Hananiah
— *After him* repaired Meshullam
31. *After him* repaired Malchiah
4:13 (7). the lower places *behind* the wall,
16 (10). the rulers (were) *behind* all the
23 (17). nor the men of the guard which *followed me*,
5:15. *beside* forty shekels of silver;
9:26. cast thy law *behind* their backs,
11: 8. *And after him* Gabbai, Sallai,
12:32. *after them* went Hoshaiah,
38. went over against (them), and I *after them*,
13:19. not be opened till *after* the sabbath:
Esth. 2: 1. *After* these things, when the wrath
3: 1. *After* these things did king Ahasuerus
Job. 3: 1. *After* this opened Job his mouth,
18: 2. *and afterwards* we will speak.
19:26. *And* (though) *after* my skin (worms)
21: 3. *and after* that I have spoken, mock on.
21. in his house *after him*,
33. *and* every man shall draw *after him*,
29:22. *After* my words they spake not again;
31: 7. *and* mine heart walked *after* mine eyes,
34:27. Because they turned back *from him*, (marg. *from after him*)
37: 4. *After it* a voice roareth:
39: 8. *and* he searcheth *after* every green thing.
10. or will he harrow the vallies *after thee?*
41:32 (24). He maketh a path to shine *after him*;
42: 7. *after* the Lord had spoken these words
16. *After* this lived Job an hundred and
Ps. 45:14 (15). the virgins her companions *that follow her*
49:13 (14). *yet their posterity* approve their
17 (18). his glory shall not descend *after him*.
50:17. castest my words *behind thee*.
63: 8 (9). My soul followeth hard *after thee*:
68:25 (26). players on instruments (followed) *after*;
73:24. *and afterward* receive me (to) glory.
78:71. *From following* the ewes great (marg. *From after*)
94:15. *and* all the upright in heart shall follow it. (marg. (shall be) *after it*)
Pro. 7:22. He goeth *after her* straightway,
20: 7. his children (are) blessed *after him*.
17. *but afterwards* his mouth shall be
25. *and after* vows to make enquiry.
24:27. *afterwards* build thine house.
28:23. He that rebuketh a man *afterwards*
Eccl. 2:12. the man (do) that cometh *after* the king?
18. unto the man that shall be *after me*.
3:22. bring him to see what shall be *after him?*
6:12. who can tell a man what shall be *after him*
7:14. that man should find nothing *after him*.

Eccl. 9: 3. *and after that* (they go) to the dead.
10:14. what shall be *after him,*
12: 2. nor the clouds return *after* the rain:
Cant. 1: 4. Draw me, we will run *after thee:*
2: 9. he standeth *behind* our wall,
Isai. 1:26. *after*ward thou shalt be called,
30:21. shall hear a word *behind thee,*
37:22. Jerusalem hath shaken her head *at thee.*
38:17. thou hast cast all my sins *behind*
43:10. no God formed, *neither* shall there be *after me.*
45:14. they shall come *after thee;*
57: 8. *Behind* the doors *also* and the posts
59:13. departing *away from* our God,
65: 2. *after* their own thoughts;
66:17. *behind* one (tree) in the midst, (marg. one *after* another)
Jer. 2: 2. when thou wentest *after me*
5. have walked *after* vanity,
8. *and* walked *after* (things that) do not
23. I have not gone *after* Baalim?
25. *and after them* will I go.
3: 7. *after* she had done all these (things),
17. *after* the imagination of their evil heart.
19. *and* shalt not turn away *from me.* (marg. *from after me*)
7: 6. *neither* walk *after* other gods to your
9. walk *after* other gods whom ye know
8: 2. *after whom* they have walked,
9:14 (13). have walked *after* the imagination of their own heart, *and after* Baalim,
16 (15). I will send a sword *after them,*
22 (21). as the handful *after* the harvestman,
11:10. they went *after* other gods
12: 6. have called a multitude *after thee:*
15. *after that* I have plucked them out
13:10. walk *after* other gods, to serve them,
27. when (shall it) once be? (marg. *after* when yet?)
16:11. have walked *after* other gods,
12. *after* the imagination of his evil heart,
16. *and after* will I send for many
17:16. from (being) a pastor *to follow thee:* (marg. *after thee*)
18:12. we will walk *after* our own devices,
21: 7. *And after*ward, saith the Lord,
24: 1. *after that* Nebuchadrezzar king of
25: 6. go not *after* other gods to serve them,
26. of Sheshach shall drink *after them.*
28:12. *after that* Hananiah the prophet
29: 2. *After that* Jeconiah the king,
18. I will *persecute them* with the sword, (lit. pursue *after them*)
31:19. *after that* I was turned, I repented; *and after* that I was instructed,
33. *After* those days, saith the Lord.
32:16. *when* I had delivered the evidence
18. into the bosom of their children *after them:*
39. of their children *after them:*
40. I will not turn away *from them,* (marg. *from after them*)
34: 8. *after that* the king Zedekiah
11. *after*ward they turned,
35:15. go not *after* other gods to serve them,
36:27. *after that* the king had burned
39: 5. the Chaldeans' army pursued *after them,*
40: 1. *after that* Nebuzar-adan the captain
41:16. *after* (that) he had slain Gedaliah
42:16. shall follow close *after you*
46:26. *and after*ward it shall be inhabited,
48: 2. the sword shall pursue thee. (marg. go *after thee*)
49: 6. *And after*ward I will bring again
37. I will send the sword *after them,*
50:21. waste and utterly destroy *after them,*
51:46. *and after that* in (another) year
52: 8. the Chaldeans pursued *after* the king,
Eze. 3:12. I heard *behind me* a voice of a great
5: 2, 12. I will draw out a sword *after them.*
6: 9. which go a whoring *after* their idols:
9: 5. Go ye *after him* through the city,
10:11. they *followed it;* (lit. went *after it*)
12:14. I will draw out the sword *after them.*
13: 3. that follow their own spirit, (marg. walk *after*)
14: 7. which separateth himself *from me,*
Eze. 14:11. Israel may go no more astray *from me*
16:23. it came to pass *after* all thy wickedness,
34. *whereas* none *followeth thee*
20:16. for their heart went *after* their idols.
24. *and* their eyes were *after* their fathers
30. *after* their abominations?
39. *and hereafter* (also), if ye will not
23:30. thou hast gone a whoring *after* the
35. and cast me *behind* thy back,
29:16. when they shall look *after them:*
33:31. their heart goeth *after* their covetousness.
40: 1. fourteenth year *after* that the city was
41:15. the separate place which (was) *behind it,*
44:10. astray away from me *after* their idols;
26. *And after* he is cleansed,
46:12. *after* his going forth (one) shall
Dan. 8: 1. *after* that which appeared unto me
9:26. *And after* threescore and two weeks
Hos. 1: 2. (departing) *from* the Lord.
2: 5 (7). I will go *after* my lovers,
13 (15). she went *after* her lovers,
3: 5. *Afterward* shall the children of Israel
5: 8. *after* thee, O Benjamin.
11. walked *after* the commandment.
11:10. They shall walk *after* the Lord:
Joel 2: 2. *neither* shall be any more *after it,*
3. *and behind them* a flame burneth:
— and *behind them* a desolate wilderness;
14. leave a blessing *behind him;*
28 (3:1). come to pass *after*ward,
Am. 2: 4. *after* the which their fathers have (lit. which---*after them*)
7: 1. latter growth *after* the king's mowings.
15. took me *as I followed* the flock, (marg. *from behind*)
Zep. 1: 6. them that are turned *back from*
Zec. 1: 8. *and behind him* (were there) red
2: 8 (12). *After* the glory hath he sent me
6: 6. the white go forth *after them;*
7:14. Thus the land was desolate *after them,*

אַחֵר *ah-ghēhr′*, adj. 312

Gen. 4:25. appointed me *another* seed instead
8:10, 12. he stayed yet *other* seven days;
17:21. at this set time in the *next* year.
26:21. And they digged *another* well,
22. and digged *another* well;
29:19. I should give her to *another* man:
27. serve with me yet seven *other* years.
30. with him yet seven *other* years.
30:24. Lord shall add to me *another* son.
37: 9. he dreamed yet *another* dream,
41: 3, 19. seven *other* kine came up after them
43:14. he may send away your *other* brother,
22. *other* money have we brought down
Ex. 20: 3. Thou shalt have no *other* gods before me.
21:10. If he take him *another* (wife);
22: 5 (4). shall feed in *another man*'s field;
23:13. make no mention of the name of *other*
34:14. thou shalt worship no *other* god:
Lev. 6:11 (4). put on *other* garments,
14:42. they shall take *other* stones,
— and he shall take *other* morter,
27:20. if he have sold the field to *another* man,
Nu. 14:24. because he had *another* spirit
23:13. with me unto *another* place,
27. I will bring thee unto *another* place;
36: 9. remove from (one) tribe to *another*
Deu. 5: 7. Thou shalt have none *other* gods before
6:14. Ye shall not go after *other* gods,
7: 4. that they may serve *other* gods:
8:19. walk after *other* gods, and serve them,
11:16. ye turn aside, and serve *other* gods,
28. to go after *other* gods, which ye have not
13: 2 (3). saying, Let us go after *other* gods,
6 (7), 13 (14). Let us go and serve *other*
17: 3. hath gone and served *other* gods,
18:20. that shall speak in the name of *other* gods,
20: 5. in the battle, and *another* man dedicate it.
6. in the battle, and *another* man eat of it.
7. in the battle, and *another* man take her.
24: 2. she may go and be *another* man's (wife).
28:14. to go after *other* gods to serve them.
30. *another* man shall lie with her:
32. (shall be) given unto *another* people,

Deu28:36. there shalt thou serve *other* gods,
64. and there thou shalt serve *other* gods,
29:26 (25). they went and served *other* gods.
28 (27). cast them into *another* land,
30:17. worship *other* gods, and serve them;
31:18. in that they are turned unto *other* gods.
20. then will they turn unto *other* gods,
Jos. 23:16. have gone and served *other* gods,
24: 2. and they served *other* gods.
16. forsake the Lord, to serve *other* gods;
Jud. 2:10. there arose *another* generation
12. and followed *other* gods,
17. they went a whoring after *other* gods,
19. in following *other* gods to serve them,
10:13. ye have forsaken me, and served *other*
11: 2. for thou (art) the son of a *strange* woman.
Ruth 2: 8. Go not to glean in *another* field,
22. they meet thee not in any *other* field.
1Sa. 8: 8. served *other* gods, so do they also
10: 6. shalt be turned into *another* man.
9. God gave him *another* heart:
17:30. he turned from him toward *another*,
19:21. he sent *other* messengers,
21: 9 (10). for (there is) no *other* save that here.
26:19. saying, Go, serve *other* gods.
28: 8. disguised himself, and put on *other*
2Sa. 13:16. greater *than the other* that thou didst
18:20. thou shalt bear tidings *another* day:
26. the watchman saw *another* man
1 K. 3:22. *the other* woman said, Nay;
7: 8. (had) *another* court within the porch,
9: 6. but go and serve *other* gods,
9. have taken hold upon *other* gods,
11: 4. turned away his heart after *other* gods:
10. that he should not go after *other* gods:
13:10. So he went *another* way,
14: 9. thou hast gone and made thee *other* gods,
20:37. Then he found *another* man, and said,
2 K. 1:11. he sent unto him *another* captain
5:17. burnt offering nor sacrifice unto *other*
6:29. I said unto her on *the next* day, (marg. *other*)
7: 8. entered into *another* tent,
17: 7. had feared *other* gods,
35, 37. Ye shall not fear *other* gods,
38. neither shall ye fear *other* gods.
22:17. burned incense unto *other* gods,
1 Ch. 2:26. Jerahmeel had also *another* wife,
16:20. from (one) kingdom to *another* people;
23:17. Eliezer had none *other* sons;
2Ch. 3:11, 12. to the wing of *the other* cherub.
— *the other* wing (was likewise) five
12. the *other* wing (was) five cubits
7:19. shall go and serve *other* gods,
22. laid hold on *other* gods,
28:25. to burn incense unto *other* gods,
30:23. took counsel to keep *other* seven days:
32: 5. *another* wall without,
34:25. have burned incense unto *other* gods,
Ezr. 1:10. *other* vessels a thousand.
2:31. The children of the *other* Elam,
Neh. 5: 5. *other men have* our lands and vineyards. (lit. are *to other men*)
7:33. The men of the *other* Nebo,
34. The children of the *other* Elam,
Est. 4:14. arise to the Jews from *another* place;
Job. 8:19. out of the earth shall *others* grow.
31: 8. let me sow, *and* let *another* eat;
10. let my wife grind *unto another,* and let *others* bow down upon her.
34:24. set *others* in their stead.
Ps. 16: 4. multiplied (that) hasten (after) *another*
49:10 (11). leave their wealth *to others*.
105:13. from (one) kingdom to *another* people;
109: 8. let *another* take his office.
13. in the generation *following*
Pro. 5: 9. Lest thou give thine honour *unto others*,
25: 9. discover not a secret to *another:*
Eccl. 7:22. thou thyself likewise hast cursed *others*.
Isa. 28:11. with stammering lips and *another* tongue
42: 8. my glory will I not give *to another*,
48:11. I will not give my glory *unto another*.
65:15. call his servants by *another* name:
22. not build, *and another* inhabit; they shall not plant, *and another* eat:
Jer. 1:16. have burned incense unto *other* gods,
3: 1. become *another* man's,
Jer. 6:12. their houses shall be turned *unto others*,
7: 6. neither walk after *other* gods to your hurt:
9. walk after *other* gods whom ye know not;
18. pour out drink offerings unto *other* gods,
8:10. will I give their wives *unto others*,
11:10. they went after *other* gods to serve
13:10. walk after *other* gods, to serve them,
16:11. have walked after *other* gods,
13. there shall ye serve *other* gods
18: 4. so he made it again *another* vessel,
19: 4. burned incense in it unto *other* gods,
13. poured out drink offerings unto *other*
22: 9. worshipped *other* gods, and served them.
26. into *another* country, where ye were not
25: 6. go not after *other* gods to serve them,
32:29. poured out drink offerings unto *other*
35:15. go not after *other* gods to serve them,
36:28. Take thee again *another* roll,
32. Then took Jeremiah *another* roll,
44: 3. to serve *other* gods, whom they knew not,
5. burn no incense unto *other* gods.
8. burning incense unto *other* gods
15. had burned incense unto *other* gods,
Eze. 12: 3. remove from thy place to *another* place
40:40. the *other* side, which (was) at the porch
41:24. two leaves *for the other* (door).
42:14. shall put on *other* garments,
44:19. they shall put on *other* garments;
Dan 11: 4. *even for others* beside those.
12: 5. there stood *other* two,
Hos. 3: 1. who look to *other* gods,
Joel 1: 3. their children *another* generation.
Zec. 2: 3 (7). *another* angel went out to meet him,

אַחֲרוֹן *ah-ghărōhn'*, adj. 314

Gen 33: 2. Leah and her children *after*, and Rachel and Joseph *hindermost*.
Ex. 4: 8. will believe the voice of the *latter* sign.
Nu. 2:31. go *hindmost* with their standards.
Deu. 11:24. even unto the *uttermost* sea
13: 9 (10). *afterwards* the hand of all the people.
17: 7. *afterward* the hands of all the people.
24: 3. (if) *the latter* husband hate her,
— or if *the latter* husband die,
29:22 (21). So that the generation *to come*
34: 2. all the land of Judah, unto *the utmost* sea,
Ruth 3:10. hast shewed more kindness in *the latter end*,
1Sa. 29: 2. passed on *in the rereward* with Achish,
2Sa. 2:26. it will be bitterness *in the latter* end?
19:11 (12). Why are ye *the last* to bring the
12 (13). are ye *the last* to bring back the
23: 1. Now these (be) *the last* words of David
1 K. 17:13. *after* make for thee and for thy son.
1Ch. 23:27. For by *the last* words of David
29:29. acts of David the king, first *and last*,
2 Ch. 9:29. rest of the acts of Solomon, first *and last*,
12:15. Now the acts of Rehoboan, first *and last*,
16:11. the acts of Asa, first *and last*.
20:34. the acts of Jehoshaphat, first *and last*,
25:26. the acts of Amaziah, first *and last*,
26:22. rest of the acts of Uzziah, first *and last*,
28:26. rest of his aets and of all his ways, first *and last*,
35:27. his deeds, first *and last*,
Ezr. 8:13. *the last* sons of Adonikam,
Neh. 8:18. from the first day unto *the last* day,
Job. 18:20. *they that come after* (*him*) shall be
19:25 *and* (that) he shall stand *at the latter*
Ps. 48:13 (14). may tell (it) to the generation *following*.
78: 4 shewing to the generation *to come*
6. That the generation *to come* might know
102:18 (19). be written for the generation *to come*
Pro. 31:25. she shall rejoice in time *to come*.
Eccl. 1:11. remembrance of (things) that are to *come* with (those) that shall come *after*,
4:16. *they* also *that come after* shall not rejoice
Isa. 9: 1 (8:23). *and afterward* did more grievously
30: 8. may be for the time *to come* (marg. the *latter* day.)
41: 4. I the Lord, the first, and with *the last;*
44: 6 I (am) the first, and I (am) *the last;*
48.12. I (am) he; I (am) the first, I also (am) *the last*.
Jer. 50:17. and *last* this Nebuchadrezzar

Dan. 8: 3. the other, and the higher came up *last.*
11:29. it shall not be as the former, *or as the latter.*
Joel 2:20. his hinder part toward *the utmost* sea,
Hag. 2: 9. The glory of this *latter* house
Zec. 14: 8. half of them toward the *hinder* sea:

---

311 **אַחֲרֵי** *ah-ghărēy'*, Ch. prep.

Dan. 2:29. what should come to pass here*after:*
45. what shall come to pass here*after:* (marg. *after* this)
7:24. and another shall rise *after them;*

---

317 **אָחֳרִי** *oh-ghŏree'*, Ch. adj.

Dan. 2:39. shall arise *another* kingdom inferior to thee, and *another* third kingdom
7: 5. And behold *another* beast,
6. I beheld, and lo *another,*
8. among them *another* little horn,
20. *and* (*of*) *the other* which came up,

---

318 **אָחֳרֵין** *oh-ghŏrĕhn'*, Ch adv. at last.

[Preceded by עַד]·

Dan. 4: 8 (5). But at *the last* Daniel came in

---

319 **אַחֲרִית** *ah-ghăreeth'*, f.

Gen 49: 1. which shall befall you *in the last* days. (lit. *end of* the days)
Nu. 23:10. let *my last end* be like his!
24:14. shall do to thy people *in the latter* days.
20. *but his latter end* (shall be) that he perish
Deu. 4:30. (even) *in the latter* days,
8:16. to do thee good *at thy latter end;*
11:12. even unto *the end of* the year.
31:29. evil will befall you *in the latter* days;
32:20. I will see what *their end* (shall be):
29. (that) they would consider *their latter end!*
Job. 8: 7. *yet thy latter end* should greatly increase.
42:12. So the Lord blessed *the latter end of* Job
Ps. 37:37. for *the end* of (that) man (is) peace.
38. *the end of* the wicked shall be cut off.
73:17. (then) understood I *their end.*
109:13. Let *his posterity* be cut off;
139: 9. dwell *in the uttermost* parts of the sea;
Pro. 5: 4. *But her end* is bitter as wormwood,
11. And thou mourn *at the last,* (lit. *at thy last*)
14:12. *but the end thereof* (are) the ways of death.
13. *and the end of* that mirth is heaviness.
16:25. *but the end thereof* (are) the ways of death.
19:20. that thou mayest be wise *in thy latter end.*
20:21. *but the end thereof* shall not be blessed.
23:18. For surely there is *an end;*
32. *At the last* it biteth like a serpent,
24:14. then there shall be *a reward,*
20. there shall be no *reward* to the evil (man);
25: 8. what to do *in the end thereof,*
29:21. him become (his) son *at the length.*
Eccl. 7: 8. Better (is) *the end of* a thing
10.13. *and the end of* his talk (is) mischievous
Isa. 2: 2. it shall come to pass *in the last* days,
41:22. know *the latter end of them;*
46:10. Declaring *the end* from the beginning,
47: 7. didst remember *the latter end of it.*
Jer. 5:31. will ye do *in the end thereof?*
12: 4. He shall not see *our last end.*
17:11. *and at his end* shall be a fool.
23:20. *in the latter* days ye shall consider it
29:11. to give you an expected *end.*
30:24. *in the latter* days ye shall consider it.
31:17. there is hope *in thine end,*
48:47. the captivity of Moab *in the latter* days,
49:39. But it shall come to pass *in the latter* days,
50:12. *the hindermost of* the nations
Lam. 1: 9. she remembereth not *her last end;*
Eze. 23:25. *and thy remnant* shall fall by the sword:
— *and thy residue* shall be devoured by the fire.
38: 8. *in the latter* years thou shalt come into
Eze. 38:16. it shall be *in the latter* days,
Dan. 8:19. what shall be *in the last end of* the
23. *And in the latter time of* their kingdom,
10:14. what shall befall thy people *in the latter*
11: 4. and not *to his posterity,* nor according
12: 8. what (shall be) *the end of* these (things)?
Hos. 3: 5. fear the Lord and his goodness *in the latter* days.
Am. 4: 2. *and your posterity* with fishhooks.
8:10. *and the end thereof* as a bitter day.
9: 1. *and* I will slay *the last of them* with the
Mic. 4: 1. *in the last* days it shall come to pass,

אַחֲרִית *ah-ghăreeth'*, Ch. f. 320

Dan. 2:28. what shall be *in the latter* days.

אָחֳרָן *oh-ghŏrāhn'*, Ch. adj. 321

Dan. 2:11. *and* there is none *other* that can shew it
44. shall not be left to *other* people,
3:29. because there is no *other* God
5:17. give thy rewards *to another;*
7:24. *and another* shall rise after them;

אָחֳרֵן see **אָחֳרֵין**· See 318

אֲחֹרַנִּית *ăghōh-ran-neeth'*, adv. 322

Gen. 9:23. both their shoulders, and went *backward,*
— their faces (were) *backward,*
1 Sa. 4:18. he fell from off the seat *backward*
1 K. 18:37. hast turned their heart *back again.*
2 K. 20:10. shadow return *backward* ten degrees.
11. brought the shadow ten degrees *backward,*
Isa. 38: 8. sun dial of Ahaz, ten degrees *backward.*

אֲחַשְׁדַּרְפְּנַיָּא *ăghash-dar-p'nay-yāh'* 324
Ch. m. pl. emph.

Dan. 3: 2. the king sent to gather together *the princes,*
3. Then *the princes,* the governors,
27. And *the princes,* governors,
6: 1 (2). an hundred and twenty *princes,*
2 (3). that *the princes* might give accounts
3 (4). above the presidents *and princes,*
4 (5). Then the presidents *and princes*
6 (7). Then these presidents *and princes*
7 (8). the governors, *and the princes,*

אֲחַשְׁדַּרְפְּנִים *ăghash-dar-p'neem'*, 323
m. pl.

Ezr. 8:36. *unto the* king's *lieutenants,*
Est. 3:12. unto *the* king's *lieutenants,*
8: 9. and to *the lieutenants,*
9: 3. *and the lieutenants,*

אֲחַשְׁתְּרָנִים *ăghash-t'rāh-neem'*, m.pl. 327

Est. 8:10. *camels,* (and) young dromedaries:
14. rode upon mules (and) *camels* went out,

אַט *at*, adv. 328

[לְ is prefixed, except in 1 Kings.]

2Sa. 18: 5. (Deal) *gently* for my sake
1 K. 21:27. lay in sackcloth, and went *softly.*
Job 15:11. is there any *secret* thing with thee?
Isa. 8: 6. the waters of Shiloah that go *softly,*

אָטָד *āh-tāhd'*, m. 329

Gen 50:10. they came to the threshingfloor of *Atad,*

Gen50:11. saw the mourning in the floor of *Atad*,
Jud. 9:14. Then said all the trees unto *the bramble*, (marg. *thistle*)
15. *the bramble* said unto the trees,
— let fire come out of *the bramble*,
Ps. 58: 9 (10). Before your pots can feel *the thorns.*

---

330 **אֵטוּן** *ēh-toon'*, m.

Pro. 7:16. with carved (works), with *fine linen of*

---

328 **אִטִּי** *it-tee'*, adv.

[With לְ prefixed.]

Gen33:14. I will lead on *softly*,

---

328 **אִטִּים** *it-teem'*, m. pl.

Isa. 19: 3. seek to the idols, and to *the charmers*,

---

331 **אָטַם** [*āh-tam'*].

* KAL.—*Participle.* *

1 K. 6: 4. he made windows of *narrow* lights. (marg. broad (within), and) *narrow* (without): or, skewed (and) *closed*)
Pro.17:28. *he that shutteth* his lips (is esteemed)
21:13. *Whoso stoppeth* his ears at the cry
Isa. 33:15. *that stoppeth* his ears from hearing
Eze.40:16. *narrow* windows to the little chambers, (marg. *closed*)
41:16. The door posts, and the *narrow* windows,
26. *narrow* windows and palm trees

* HIPHIL.—*Future.* *

Ps. 58: 4 (5). like the deaf adder (that) *stoppeth*

---

332 **אָטַר** [*āh-tar'*].

* KAL.—*Future.* *

Ps. 69:15 (16). *let* not the pit *shut* her mouth upon me.

---

334 **אִטֵּר** *it-tēhr'*, adj.

Jud. 3:15. a Benjamite, a man lefthanded: (marg. *shut of* his right hand)
20:16. seven hundred chosen men lefthanded; (lit. *shut of* his right hand)

---

335 **אֵי** *ēh*, adv.

Gen 4: 9. *Where* (is) Abel thy brother?
Pro.31: 4. (קרי) nor for princes strong drink: (lit. (to be) *where* is strong drink)
&c. &c.

With suff. אַיֶּכָּה.

Gen 3: 9. *Where* (art) *thou?*

אַיּוֹ

Job 20: 7. *Where* (is) *he?* &c. &c.

אַיָּם

Isa. 19:12. *Where* (are) *they?*
Nah. 3:17. is not known *where they* (are).

Observe its meaning in

Jer. 5: 7. *How* shall I pardon thee for this?

It is used in combination; with זֶה

1 Sa. 9:18. *where* the seer's house (is).
1 K. 13:12. *What* way went he?
22:24. *Which way* went the Spirit of the Lord
2Ch.18:23. *Which* way went the Spirit of the Lord
Job 38:24. *By what* way is the light parted,
Ecc.11: 6. thou knowest not *whether* shall prosper, &c. &c.

with מִזֶּה

Gen16: 8. *whence* camest thou?
2Sa.15: 2. *Of what* city (art) thou?
Job 2: 2. *From whence* comest thou?
&c. &c.

See also אֵיזֶה, אֵיךְ, אֵיכָה, אֵיכֹה, אֵיפֹה, &c.

אִי *ee*, m. 336, 339

Gen10: 5. By these were *the isles of* the Gentiles
Est.10: 1. *and* (upon) *the isles of* the sea.
Job 22:30. He shall deliver *the island of* the innocent
Ps. 72:10. The kings of Tarshish *and* of *the isles*
97: 1. let the multitude of *isles* be glad
Isa. 11:11. *and from the islands of* the sea.
20: 6. inhabitant of this *isle* shall (marg. *country*)
23: 2. Be still, ye inhabitants of *the isle*;
6. howl, ye inhabitants of *the isle.*
24:15. the Lord God of Israel *in the isles of* the
40:15. he taketh up *the isles* as a very little
41: 1. Keep silence before me, *O islands;*
5. *The isles* saw (it), and feared;
42: 4. *the isles* shall wait for his law.
10. *the isles*, and the inhabitants thereof.
12. declare his praise *in the islands.*
15. I will make the rivers *islands*,
49: 1. Listen, *O isles*, unto me;
51: 5. *the isles* shall wait upon me,
59:18. *to the islands* he will repay recompence.
60: 9. Surely *the isles* shall wait for me,
66:19. Tubal, and Javan, (to) *the isles* afar off,
Jer. 2:10. pass over *the isles of* Chittim,
25:22. *the isles* which (are) beyond the sea, (marg. *region* by the sea side)
31:10. declare (it) *in the isles* afar off,
47: 4. the remnant of *the country of* Caphtor. (marg. *isle*)
50:39. with the wild beasts of *the islands*
Eze.26:15. Shall not *the isles* shake at the sound
18. Now shall *the isles* tremble
— *the isles* that (are) in the sea
27: 3. a merchant of the people for many *isles*,
6. (brought) *out of the isles of* Chittim.
7. blue and purple *from the isles of* Elishah
15. many *isles* (were) the merchandise
35. All the inhabitants of *the isles*
39: 6. them that dwell carelessly in *the isles:*
Dan 11:18. turn his face *unto the isles*,
Zeph 2:11. (even) all *the isles of* the heathen.

אִי *ee*, interj. 337

Ecc.10:16. *Woe* to thee, O land, when thy king

With suff. אִילוֹ.

Ecc. 4:10. *but woe to him* (that is) alone

אָיַב [*āh-yav'*]. 340-41

* KAL.—*Preterite.* *

Ex. 23:22. *then I will be an enemy* unto thine enemies,

Participle. Poël.

Gen22:17. shall possess the gate of *his enemies;*
49: 8. (shall be) in the neck of *thine enemies;*
Ex. 15: 6. hath dashed in pieces *the enemy.*
9. *The enemy* said, I will pursue,
23: 4. If thou meet *thine enemy's* ox or
22. I will be an enemy unto *thine enemies*,
27. I will make all *thine enemies* turn their
Lev.26: 7. ye shall chase *your enemies*,
8. *your enemies* shall fall before you
16. for *your enemies* shall eat it.
17. ye shall be slain before *your enemies:*
25. delivered into the hand of *the enemy.*
32. *your enemies* which dwell therein
34. ye (be) in *your enemies'* land;
36. in the lands of *their enemies;*
37. no power to stand before *your enemies.*
38. the land of *your enemies* shall eat you up.
39. their iniquity in *your enemies'* lands;
41. them into the land of *their enemies;*
44. when they be in the land of *their enemies*,
Nu. 10: 9. ye shall be saved *from your enemies.*
35. let *thine enemies* be scattered;

Nu. 14:42. that ye be not smitten before *your enemies.*
23:11. I took thee to curse *mine enemies,*
24:10. I called thee to curse *mine enemies,*
18. Seir also shall be a possession for *his enemies ;*
32:21. he hath driven out *his enemies*
35:23. that he die, and (was) not his *enemy,*
Deu. 1:42. lest ye be smitten before *your enemies.*
6:19. To cast out all *thine enemies* from before
12:10. he giveth you rest from all *your enemies*
20: 1. out to battle against *thine enemies,*
3. this day unto battle against *your enemies :*
4. to fight for you against *your enemies,*
14. thou shalt eat the spoil of *thine enemies,*
21:10. goest forth to war against *thine enemies,*
23: 9 (10). goeth forth against *thine enemies,*
14 (15). to give up *thine enemies* before thee;
25:19. given thee rest from all *thine enemies*
28: 7. The Lord shall cause *thine enemies*
25. thee to be smitten before *thine enemies :*
31. sheep (shall be) given *unto thine enemies,*
48. Therefore shalt thou serve *thine enemies*
53. wherewith *thine enemies* shall distress thee:
55. wherewith *thine enemies* shall distress
57. wherewith *thine enemy* shall distress
68. ye shall be sold *unto your enemies*
30: 7. put all these curses upon *thine enemies,*
32:27. I feared the wrath of *the enemy,*
31. *even our enemies* themselves (being) judges.
42. beginning of revenges upon *the enemy.*
33:27. he shall thrust out *the enemy*
29. *thine enemies* shall be found liars
Jos. 7: 8. turneth their backs before *their enemies !*
12. Israel could not stand before *their enemies,* (but) turned (their) backs before *their enemies,*
13. thou canst not stand before *thine enemies,*
10:13. avenged themselves upon *their enemies.*
19. pursue after *your enemies,*
25. thus shall the Lord do to all *your enemies*
21:44 (42). stood not a man of all *their enemies*
— (—) delivered all *their enemies* into their
22: 8. divide the spoil of *your enemies*
23: 1. rest unto Israel from all *their enemies*
Jud. 2:14. them into the hands of *their enemies*
— any longer stand before *their enemies.*
18. out of the hand of *their enemies*
3:28. the Lord hath delivered *your enemies*
5:31. So let all *thine enemies* perish,
8:34. out of the hands of all *their enemies*
11:36. taken vengeance for thee *of thine enemies,*
16:23. hath delivered Samson *our enemy*
24. hath delivered into our hands *our enemy,*
1 Sa. 2: 1. my mouth is enlarged over *mine enemies;*
4: 3. save us out of the hand of *our enemies.*
12:10. deliver us out of the hand of *our enemies,*
11. out of the hand of *your enemies*
14:24. I may be avenged *on mine enemies.*
30. the spoil of *their enemies*
47. fought against all *his enemies*
18:25. to be avenged *of* the king's *enemies.*
29. Saul became David's *enemy* continually.
19:17. sent away *mine enemy,*
20:15. the Lord hath cut off *the enemies of*
16. require (it) at the hand of David's *enemies.*
24: 4 (5). I will deliver *thine enemy* into thine
19 (20). For if a man find *his enemy,*
25:22. more also do God *unto the enemies of*
26. now let *thine enemies,* and they that seek
29. the souls of *thine enemies,*
26: 8. God hath delivered *thine enemy*
29: 8. I may not go fight *against the enemies of*
30:26. the spoil of *the enemies of* the Lord;
2 Sa. 3:18. out of the hand of all *their enemies.*
4: 8. Ish-bosheth the son of Saul *thine enemy,*
5:20. hath broken forth upon *mine enemies*
7: 1. rest round about from all *his enemies;*
9. have cut off all *thine enemies*
11. caused thee to rest from all *thine enemies.*
12:14. given great occasion to *the enemies of*
18:19. the Lord hath avenged him of *his enemies.*
32. *The enemies of* my lord the king,
19: 9 (10). out of the hand of *our enemies,*
22: 1. out of the hand of all *his enemies,*
4. so shall I be saved *from mine enemies.*
18. delivered me *from my* strong *enemy,*
38. I have pursued *mine enemies,*

2Sa. 22:41. *also* given me the necks of *mine enemies,*
49. bringeth me forth *from mine enemies:*
1 K. 3:11. nor hast asked the life of *thine enemies ;*
8:33. Israel be smitten down before *the enemy,*
37. if *their enemy* besiege them in the land
44. go out to battle against *their enemy,*
46. deliver them to *the enemy,*
— captives unto the land of *the enemy,*
48. in the land of *their enemies,*
21:20. Hast thou found me, *O mine enemy?*
2 K. 17:39. you out of the hand of all *your enemies.*
21:14. deliver them into the hand of *their enemies;*
— a prey and a spoil to all *their enemies ;*
1Ch. 14:11. God hath broken in upon *mine enemies*
17: 8. have cut off all *thine enemies*
10. I will subdue all *thine enemies.*
21:12. while that the sword of *thine enemies*
22: 9. I will give him rest from all *his enemies*
2Ch. 6:24. be put to the worse before *the enemy,*
28. if *their enemies* besiege them
34. go out to war against *their enemies*
36. deliver them over before (their) *enemies,*
20:27. had made them to rejoice *over their enemies.*
29. the Lord fought against *the enemies of*
25: 8. God shall make thee fall before *the enemy :*
26:13. to help the king against *the enemy.*
Ezra 8:22. help us *against the enemy* in the way:
31. delivered us from the hand of *the enemy,*
Neh. 4:15 (9). when *our enemies* heard that
5: 9. reproach of the heathen *our enemies?*
6: 1. Geshem the Arabian, and the rest of *our enemies,*
16. that when all *our enemies* heard
9:28. them in the hand of *their enemies*
Est. 7: 6. The adversary *and enemy*
8:13. to avenge themselves *on their enemies.*
9: 1. the day that *the enemies of* the Jews
5. Thus the Jews smote all *their enemies*
16. had rest *from their enemies,*
22. the Jews rested *from their enemies,*
Job 13:24. holdest me *for* thine *enemy?*
27: 7. Let *mine enemy* be as the wicked,
33:10. he counteth me *for* his *enemy,*
Ps. 3: 7 (8). thou hast smitten all *mine enemies*
6:10 (11). Let all *mine enemies* be ashamed
7: 5 (6). Let *the enemy* persecute my soul,
8: 2 (3). that thou mightest still *the enemy*
9: 3 (4). When *mine enemies* are turned
6 (7). *O thou enemy,* destructions are come
13: 2 (3) how long shall *mine enemy* be exalted
4 (5). Lest *mine enemy* say,
17: 9. *my* deadly *enemies,* (who) compass me
18: [title] (1). from the hand of all *his enemies,*
3 (4). so shall I be saved from *mine enemies.*
17 (18). delivered me *from my* strong *enemy,*
37 (38). I have pursued *mine enemies,*
40 (41). *also* given me the necks of *mine enemies ;*
48 (49). He delivereth me *from mine enemies :*
21: 8 (9). shall find out all *thine enemies :*
25: 2. let not *mine enemies* triumph over
19. Consider *mine enemies ;*
27: 2. wicked, (even) mine enemies *and my foes,*
6. mine head be lifted up above *mine enemies,*
30: 1 (2). hast not made *my foes* to rejoice
31: 8 (9). into the hand of *the enemy :*
15 (16). me from the hand of *mine enemies,*
35:19. Let not them that are *mine enemies*
37:20. *and the enemies of* the Lord (shall be) as
38:19 (20). *But mine enemies* (are) lively,
41: 2 (3). him unto the will of *his enemies.*
5 (6). *Mine enemies* speak evil of me,
11 (12). *mine enemy* doth not triumph
42: 9 (10), 43:2. because of the oppression of *the enemy?*
44:16 (17). by reason of *the enemy* and avenger.
45: 5 (6). in the heart of the king's *enemies ;*
54: 7 (9). *and* mine eye hath seen (his desire) *upon mine enemies.*
55: 3 (4). Because of the voice of *the enemy*
12 (13). For (it was) not *an enemy* (that)
56: 9 (10). then shall *mine enemies* turn back:
59: 1 (2). Deliver me *from mine enemies,*
61: 3 (4). a strong tower from *the enemy.*
64: 1 (2). preserve my life from fear of *the enemy.*
66: 3. shall *thine enemies* submit

Ps. 68: 1(2). let *his enemies* be scattered:
21(22). God shall wound the head of *his enemies*,
23(24). dipped in the blood *of* (thine) *enemies*,
69: 4(5). (being) *mine enemies* wrongfully,
18(19). deliver me because of *mine enemies*.
71:10. For *mine enemies* speak against me;
72: 9. *and his enemies* shall lick the dust.
74: 3. all (that) *the enemy* hath done
10. shall *the enemy* blaspheme thy name
18. *the enemy* hath reproached,
78:53. but the sea overwhelmed *their enemies*.
80: 6(7). *our enemies* laugh among themselves.
81:14(15). I should soon have subdued *their enemies*,
83: 2(3). For, lo, *thine enemies* make a tumult:
89:10(11). thou hast scattered *thine enemies*
22(23). *The enemy* shall not exact upon him;
42(43). thou hast made all *his enemies* to
51(52). Wherewith *thine enemies* have
92: 9(10). For, lo, *thine enemies*, O Lord, for, lo, *thine enemies* shall perish;
102: 8(9). *Mine enemies* reproach me all the day;
106:10. redeemed them from the hand of *the enemy*.
42. *Their enemies* also oppressed them,
110: 1. until I make *thine enemies* thy footstool.
2. rule thou in the midst of *thine enemies*.
119:98. hast made me wiser *than mine enemies*:
127: 5. but they shall speak with *the enemies*
132:18. *His enemies* will I clothe with shame:
138: 7. against the wrath of *mine enemies*,
139:22. I count them mine *enemies*.
143: 3. For *the enemy* hath persecuted my soul;
9. Deliver me, O Lord, *from mine enemies*:
12. of thy mercy cut off *mine enemies*,
Pro.16: 7. he maketh even *his enemies* to be at peace
24:17. Rejoice not when *thine enemy* falleth,
Isa. 1:24. avenge me *of mine enemies*:
9:11(10). join *his enemies* together;
42:13. he shall prevail against *his enemies*.
59:18. recompence *to his enemies*;
62: 8. give thy corn (to be) meat *for thine enemies*;
63:10. therefore he was turned *to be* their *enemy*,
66: 6. the Lord that rendereth recompence *to his enemies*.
14. (his) indignation toward *his enemies*.
Jer. 6:25. for the sword *of the enemy*
12: 7. into the hand of *her enemies*.
15: 9. I deliver to the sword before *their enemies*,
11. I will cause *the enemy* to entreat thee
14. I will make (thee) to pass with *thine enemies*
17: 4. I will cause thee to serve *thine enemies*
18:17. as with an east wind before *the enemy*;
19: 7. to fall by the sword before *their enemies*,
9. straitness, wherewith *their enemies*,
20: 4. shall fall by the sword of *their enemies*,
5. I give into the hand of *their enemies*,
21: 7. into the hand of *their enemies*,
30:14. with the wound of *an enemy*,
31:16. come again from the land of *the enemy*.
34:20. give them into the hand of *their enemies*,
21. I give into the hand of *their enemies*,
44:30. king of Egypt into the hand of *his enemies*,
— Nebuchadrezzar king of Babylon, *his ene.*,
49:37. Elam to be dismayed before *their enemies*,
Lam. 1: 2. they are become her *enemies*.
5. *her enemies* prosper;
9. for *the enemy* hath magnified (himself).
16. because *the enemy* prevailed.
21. all *mine enemies* have heard
2: 3. his right hand from before *the enemy*,
4. He hath bent his bow *like an enemy*:
5. The Lord was *as an enemy*:
7. given up into the hand of *the enemy*
16. All *thine enemies* have opened their mouth
17. he hath caused (thine) *enemy* to rejoice
22. hath *mine enemy* consumed.
3:46. All *our enemies* have opened their mouths
52. *Mine enemies* chased me sore,
4:12. *and the enemy* should have entered
Eze.36: 2. Because *the enemy* hath said
39:27. gathered them out of *their enemies'* lands,
Hos. 8: 3. *the enemy* shall pursue him.
Am. 9: 4. they go into captivity before *their enemies*,
Mic. 2: 8. my people is risen up *as an enemy*:
4:10. redeem thee from the hand of *thine enemies*.
5: 9(8). all *thine enemies* shall be cut off.
7: 6. a man's *enemies* (are) the men of his own
8. Rejoice not against me, *O mine enemy*:
10. Then (she that is) *mine enemy* shall see
Nah. 1: 2. he reserveth (wrath) *for his enemies*.
8. *and* darkness shall pursue *his enemies*.
3:11. seek strength *because of the enemy*.
13. shall be set wide open *unto thine enemies*:
Zep. 3:15. he hath cast out *thine enemy*:

אֵיבָה *ēh-vāh'*, f. 342

Gen. 3:15. *And* I will put *enmity* between thee
Nu. 35:21. Or *in enmity* smite him with his hand.
22. he thrust him suddenly without *enmity*,
Eze.25:15. to destroy (it) for the old *hatred*;
35: 5. thou hast had a perpetual *hatred*,

אֵיד *ēhd*, m. 343

Deu 32:35. the day of *their calamity* (is) at hand,
2Sa.22:19. prevented me in the day of *my calamity*:
Job 18:12. *and destruction* (shall be) ready at his
21:17. (how oft) cometh *their destruction* upon
30. the wicked is reserved to the day of *destruction*?
30:12. against me the ways of *their destruction*.
31: 3. (Is) not *destruction* to the wicked?
23. *destruction* (from) God (was) a terror to
Ps. 18:18 (19). in the day of *my calamity*:
Pro. 1:26. I also will laugh *at your calamity*;
27. *and your destruction* cometh as a
6:15. Therefore shall *his calamity* come
17: 5. he that is glad *at calamities* shall not
24:22. For *their calamity* shall rise suddenly;
27:10. brother's house in the day of *thy calamity*:
Jer. 18:17. in the day of *their calamity*.
46:21. because the day of *their calamity* was
48:16. *The calamity of* Moab (is) near
49: 8. I will bring *the calamity of* Esau
32. I will bring *their calamity* from all
Eze.35: 5. the sword in the time of *their calamity*,
Obad. 13,13,13. in the day of *their calamity*;

אַיָּה *ahy-yāh'*, f. 344

Lev. 11:14. *the kite* after his kind;
Deu.14:13. the glede, and *the kite*,
Job. 28: 7. which *the vulture's* eye hath not seen:

אַיֵּה *ahy-yēh'*, adv. 346

Gen18: 9. *Where* (is) Sarah thy wife?
Jer.37:19. *Where* (are) now your prophets
&c. &c.

אִיִּים *eey-yim'*, m. 338

Isa. 13:22. *the wild beasts of the islands* shall cry (marg. Iim)
34:14. *the wild beasts of the island*, (marg. Ijim)
Jer. 50:39. with *the wild beasts of the islands*

אֵיזֶה *ēh-zeh'*. 335

Job 38: 19, 24. i. q. אֵי זֶה

אֵיךְ *ēh'ch*, adv. 349

Gen44:34. For *how* shall I go up to my father,
Jud.16:15. *How* canst thou say, I love thee,
2Ch 10: 6. saying *What* counsel give ye (me) to return
&c. &c.

אֵיכָה *ēh-chāh'*, adv. 349

Deu 1:12. *How* can I myself alone bear
7:17. *how* can I dispossess them?

But observe its meaning, in

Cant.1: 7. Tell me,...*where* thou feedest, *where* thou makest (thy flock) to rest &c. &c.

---

351 **אֵיכֹה for אֵיכוֹ (קרי)** *ēh-chōh'*, adv.

2 K. 6:13. Go and spy *where* he (is),

---

349 **אֵיכָכָה** *ēh-chāh-chāh*, adv.

מלעיל in Cant. מלרע in Est.

Est. 8: 6. For *how* can I endure to see
— *or how* can I endure to see
Cant.5: 3. *how* shall I put it on?
— *how* shall I defile them?

---

354 **אַיָּל** *ahy-yāhl'*, com.

Deu12:15. *and as of the hart.*
22. as the roebuck and *the hart* is eaten,
14: 5. *The hart*, and the roebuck,
15:22. as the roebuck, *and as the hart.*
1 K. 4:23 (5:3). an hundred sheep, beside *harts.* (lit. beside *of the hart*)
Ps. 42: 1 (2). *As the hart* panteth after the water
Cant.2: 9, 17. a young *hart:* (lit. the fawn of *harts*)
8:14. or to a young *hart* upon the mountains
Isa. 35: 6. Then shall the lame (man) leap *as an hart*,
Lam. 1: 6. her princes are become *like harts*

---

352 **אַיִל** *ah'-yil*, m.

In Ezekiel it occurs in const. and pl. without (י).

Gen15: 9. *and a ram* of three years old,
22:13. behind (him) *a ram* caught
— Abraham went and took *the ram*,
31:38. *and the rams of* thy flock
32:14 (15). two hundred ewes, *and* twenty *rams*,
Ex. 25: 5. And *rams'* skins dyed red,
26:14. covering for the tent (of) *rams'* skins
29: 1. *and* two *rams* without
3. with the bullock and *the* two *rams*.
15. Thou shalt also take one *ram;*
— put their hands upon the head of *the ram.*
16. thou shalt slay *the ram*,
17. thou shalt cut *the ram* in pieces,
18. burn *the* whole *ram* upon the altar:
19. thou shalt take *the* other *ram;*
— put their hands upon the head of *the ram.*
20. Then shalt thou kill *the ram*,
22. Also thou shalt take of *the ram*
— for it (is) *a ram of* consecration:
26. the breast *of the ram of* Aaron's
27. *of the ram of* the consecration,
31. thou shalt take *the ram of* the consecration,
32. shall eat the flesh of *the ram*,
35: 7. And *rams'* skins dyed red,
23. and red skins of *rams*,
36:19. covering for the tent (of) *rams'* skins
39:34. the covering of *rams'* skins dyed red,
Lev. 5:15, 18. *a ram* without blemish
16. *with the ram of* the trespass offering,
6: 6 (5:25). *a ram* without blemish
8: 2. bullock for the sin offering, and two *rams*,
18. brought *the ram for* the burnt offering:
— hands upon the head of *the ram.*
20. he cut *the ram* into pieces;
21. Moses burnt *the* whole *ram*
22. he brought *the* other *ram*, *the ram of* consecration: and Aaron and his sons laid their hands upon the head of *the ram.*
29. *of the ram of* consecration
9: 2. *and a ram* for a burnt offering,
4. *and a ram* for peace offerings,
18. slew also the bullock and *the ram*
19. the fat of the bullock and of *the ram*,
16: 3. *and a ram* for a burnt offering.
5. *and* one *ram* for a burnt offering.
19:21. *a ram for* a trespass offering.
22. *with the ram of* the trespass offering
23:18. one young bullock, *and* two *rams:*
Nu. 5: 8. beside *the ram of* the atonement,
6:14. *and* one *ram* without blemish
17. offer *the ram* (for) a sacrifice
19. take the sodden shoulder of *the ram*,
7:15, 21, 27, 33, 39, 45, 51, 57, 63, 69, 75, 81. One young bullock, one *ram*,
17, 23, 29, 35, 41, 47, 53, 59, 65, 71, 77, 83 peace offerings, two oxen, five *rams*,
87. twelve bullocks, *the rams* twelve,
88. four bullocks, *the rams* sixty,
15: 6. Or *for a ram*, thou shalt prepare
11. or *for* one *ram*, or for a lamb,
23: 1. prepare me here seven oxen and seven *rams.*
2, 4. (every) altar a bullock *and a ram.*
14, 30. offered a bullock *and a ram* on (every)
29. seven bullocks and seven *rams.*
28:11. two young bullocks, *and* one *ram*,
12. mingled with oil, *for* one *ram;*
14. the third (part) of an hin *unto a ram*,
19. two young bullocks, *and* one *ram*,
20. two tenth deals *for a ram;*
27. two young bullocks, one *ram*,
28. two tenth deals *unto* one *ram*,
29: 2, 8. one young bullock, one *ram*,
3. two tenth deals *for a ram*,
9. two tenth deals *to one ram*,
13, 17. young bullocks, two *rams*,
14. two tenth deals *to* each *ram* of *the* two *rams*,
18, 21, 24, 27, 30, 33. for the bullocks, *for the rams*,
20. eleven bullocks, two *rams*,
23. ten bullocks, two *rams*,
26. nine bullocks, two *rams*,
29. eight bullocks, two *rams*,
32. seven bullocks, two *rams*,
36. one bullock, one *ram*,
37. for the bullock, *for the ram*,
Deu32:14. *and rams* of the breed of Bashan,
1Sa.15:22. to hearken than the fat of *rams.*
1 K. 6:31. *the lintel* (and) side posts
2 K. 3: 4. an hundred thousand *rams*,
1Ch.15:26. offered seven bullocks and seven *rams.*
29:21. a thousand bullocks, a thousand *rams*,
2Ch.13: 9. a young bullock *and* seven *rams*,
17:11. seven thousand and seven hundred *rams*,
29:21. seven bullocks, *and* seven *rams*,
22. when they had killed *the rams*,
32. an hundred *rams*, (and) two hundred
Ezr. 8:35. ninety and six *rams*,
10:19. (they offered) *a ram of* the flock
Job 42: 8. seven bullocks and seven *rams*,
Ps. 66:15. with the incense of *rams;*
114: 4. The mountains skipped *like rams*,
6. Ye mountains, (that) ye skipped *like rams;*
Isa. 1:11. I am full of the burnt offerings of *rams*,
34: 6. the fat of the kidneys of *rams:*
60: 7. *the rams of* Nebaioth
Jer. 51:40. *like rams* with he goats.
Eze.27:21. occupied with thee in lambs, *and rams*,
34:17. *between the rams* and the he goats.
39:18. of *rams*, of lambs, and of goats,
40: 9. *and the posts thereof*, two cubits;
10. *the posts had* one measure (lit. one measure *to the posts*)
14. He made also *posts* of threescore cubits, even unto *the post of* the court round
16. to *their posts* within the gate
— upon (each) *post* (were) palm trees.
21, 29, 33. *and the posts thereof* and the arches
24. he measured *the posts thereof*
26. upon *the posts thereof.*
31, 34. palm trees (were) upon *the posts thereof:*
36. *the posts thereof*, and the arches
37. *And the posts thereof* (were) toward
— palm trees (were) upon *the posts thereof*,
38. (were) *by the posts* of the gates,
48. and measured (each) *post* of the porch,
49. (there were) pillars by *the posts*,
41: 1. measured *the posts*,
3. measured *the post of* the door,
43:23, 25. *and a ram* out of the flock
45:23. seven bullocks and seven *rams*
24. an ephah *for a ram*,
46. 4. *and a ram* without blemish.
5, 7. an ephah *for a ram*,

Eze.46: 6. six lambs, *and a ram:*
11. an ephah *to a ram,*
Dan. 8: 3. there stood before the river *a ram*
4. I saw *the ram* pushing westward,
6. he came to *the ram* that had two horns,
7. I saw him come close unto *the ram,*
— smote *the ram,*
— there was no power *in the ram*
— none that could deliver *the ram*
20. *The ram* which thou sawest
Mic. 6: 7. be pleased with thousands of *rams,*

352 אֵילֵי *ēh-lēh*, m. pl.

[Const. of אֵילִים.]

Ez. 31 : 14. it is without (י) אֵל

Ex. 15:15. *the mighty men of* Moab,
2 K.24:15. (קרי) *the mighty of* the land,
Job.41:25 (17). he raiseth up himself, *the mighty* are
Isa. 1:29. they shall be ashamed *of the oaks*
61: 3. that they might be called *trees of*
Eze.17:13. he hath also taken *the mighty of* the land:
31:14. neither *their trees* stand up in their

353 אֱיָל *ĕyāhl*, m.

Ps. 88: 4 (5). I am as a man (that hath) no *strength:*

355 אַיָּלָה *ahy-yāh-lāh'*, f.

Gen49:21. Naphtali (is) *a hind* let loose:
2Sa.22:34. He maketh my feet *like hinds'* (feet):
Job.39: 1. canst thou mark when *the hinds* do
Ps. 18:33 (34). He maketh my feet *like hinds'* (feet),
29: 9. of the Lord maketh *the hinds* to calve,
Cant.2: 7. & 3:5. *by the hinds of* the field,
Hab. 3:19. he will make my feet *like hinds'*

360 אֱיָלוּת *ĕhyāh-looth'*, f.

Ps. 22:19 (20). *O my strength,* haste thee to help me.

361 אֵלַמִּים & אֵילַמִּים [*ēh-lam-meem'*]

[all are קרי] m. pl.

See also אֵלַמּוֹת.

Eze.40:21. the posts thereof *and the arches thereof*
22. their windows, *and their arches,*
—, 26, 33. *and the arches thereof*
24, 29. *and the arches thereof* according
25, 29, 33. *and in the arches thereof* round about,
31, 34. *And the arches thereof* (were) toward
36. *and the arches thereof,* and the windows

363 אִילָן *ee-lāhn'*, Ch. m.

Dan. 4:10 (7). I saw, and behold *a tree*
11 (8). *The tree* grew, and was strong,
14 (11). Hew down *the tree,*
20 (17). *The tree* that thou sawest,
23 (20). Hew *the tree* down, and destroy it;
26 (23). to leave the stump of *the tree*

365 אַיֶּלֶת *ahy-yeh'-leth*, f.

Ps. 22: [title] (1). chief Musician upon *Aijeleth*
Pro. 5:19. (Let her be as) the loving *hind*
Jer. 14: 5. the *hind* also calved in the field,

366 אָיֹם *āh-yōhm'*, adj.

Cant.6: 4, 10. *terrible* as (an army) with banners.
Hab. 1: 7. They (are) *terrible* and dreadful:

367 אֵימָה *ēh-māh'*, f.

Gen15:12. *an horror* of great darkness fell
Ex. 15:16. *Fear* and dread shall fall upon them;
23:27. I will send *my fear* before thee,
Deu32.25. The sword without, and *terror* within,
Jos. 2: 9. that *your terror* is fallen upon us,
Ezr. 3: 3. *fear* (was) upon them
Job 9:34. *and* let not *his fear* terrify me:
13:21. *and* let not *thy dread* make me afraid.
20:25. *terrors* (are) upon him.
33: 7. *my terror* shall not make thee afraid,
39:20. of his nostrils (is) *terrible.* (marg. *terror*)
41:14 (6). his teeth (are) *terrible* round about.
Ps. 55: 4 (5). *and the terrors of* death are fallen
88:15 (16). I suffer *thy terrors* I am distracted.
Pro.20: 2. *The fear of* a king (is) as the roaring
Isa. 33:18. Thine heart shall meditate *terror.*
Jer. 50:38. *and* they are mad *upon* (their) *idols.*

אַיִן *ah'-yin*, part. used adverbially. 369

Properly a subst.

Gen 2: 5. and (there was) *not* a man to till
30: 1. or *else* (lit. and if *not*) I die.
41:49. for (it was) *without* number.
44:26. *except* our youngest brother (be) with us.
45: 6. (there shall) *neither* (be) earing nor harvest.
Jud.14: 3. (Is there) *never a* woman among the
1Sa.10:14. saw that (they were) *no where,* we came
1K. 18:26. (there was) *no* voice, *nor any* that answered.
20:40. was busy here and there, he *was gone.*
1Ch.22: 4. in abundance: (lit. *without* number)
2Ch.20:25. more than (lit. *till not*) they could carry
21:18. an *incurable* disease.
Job 5: 9. great things and *unsearchable;*
8:22. place of the wicked shall come *to nought.*
9:10. Which doeth great things *past* finding out;
Ps. 38:10 (11). it also is *gone from* me.
73: 2. my steps had *well nigh* slipped.
Ecc. 3:14. *nothing* can be put to it, *nor any thing*
Isa. 40:16. to burn, *nor* the beasts thereof
44:12. *and* his strength *faileth:*
45:21. a Saviour; (there is) *none* beside me.
Jer. 7:32. *till* there be *no* place.
46:23. and (are) *innumerable.*
Lam. 5: 3. orphans *and* father*less,*
7. have sinned, *and* (are) *not;*
Eze.28:19. and *never* (shalt) thou (be) any more.
Nah. 3: 9. and (it was) *infinite;*
&c. &c.

מֵאַיִן of the same form as the next word occurs twice.

Isa. 41:24. Behold ye, (are) *of nothing,*
Jer.30: 7. that *none* (is) like it:

אַיִן *ah'-yin*, adv. 370

Only found with prefix מֵאַיִן, signifying, *whence.*

Gen29: 4. My brethren, *whence* (be) ye?
42: 7. *Whence* come ye?
Nu. 11:13. *Whence* should I have flesh
Jos. 2: 4. I wist not *whence* they (were):
9: 8. *and from whence* come ye?
Jud.17: 9. *Whence* comest thou?
19:17. *and whence* comest thou?
2 K. 5:25. *Whence* (comest thou), Gehazi?
6:27. *whence* shall I help thee?
20:14. *and from whence* came they unto thee?
Job 1: 7. *Whence* comest thou?
28:12. But *where* shall wisdom be found?
20. *Whence* then cometh wisdom?
Ps.121: 1. *from whence* cometh my help.
Isa. 39: 3. *and from whence* came they unto thee?
Jon. 1: 8. *and whence* comest thou?
Nah 3: 7. *whence* shall I seek comforters for thee?

אִין *een*, adv. 371

1Sa.21: 8 (9). *And* is there *not* here under thine

אֵיפָה *ēh-phāh'*, f. 374

Also written אֵפָה.

Ex. 16:36. the tenth (part) of *an ephah.*

Lev. 5:11 & 6:20 (13). the tenth part of *an ephah*
19:36. just weights, *a* just *ephah*,
Nu. 5:15. the tenth (part) of *an ephah*
28: 5. a tenth (part) of *an ephah*
Deu25:14. have in thine house *divers measures*, (marg *an ephah and an ephah*)
15. a perfect and just *measure*
Jud. 6:19. cakes of *an ephah of* flour:
Ruth 2:17. *about an ephah* of barley.
1Sa. 1:24. *and* one *ephah* of flour,
17:17. *an ephah of* this parched (corn),
Pro. 20:10. *divers measures*, (marg. *an ephah and an ephah*)
Isa. 5:10. an homer shall yield *an ephah*.
Eze. 45:10. *and a* just *ephah*,
11. *The ephah* and the bath
— *the ephah* the tenth part of an homer:
13. the sixth part of *an ephah*
— give the sixth part of *an ephah*
24. *an ephah* for a bullock, *and an ephah* for a ram, and an hin of oil *for an ephah*.
46: 5. (shall be) *an ephah* for a ram,
— 7, 11. an hin of oil *to an ephah*.
7. *an ephah* for a bullock, *and an ephah* for a
11. *an ephah* to a bullock, *and an ephah* to a
14. the sixth part of *an ephah*,
Am. 8: 5. making *the ephah* small,
Mic. 6:10. *and the* scant *measure* (that is)
Zec. 5: 6. This (is) *an ephah* that goeth forth.
7. sitteth in the midst of *the ephah*.
8. into the midst of *the ephah*;
9. they lifted up *the ephah*
10. Whither do these bear *the ephah*?

---

375 **אֵיפֹה** *ēhy-phōh'*, adv.

Gen37:16. tell me, I pray thee, *where* they feed
Jud. 8:18. *What manner of* men (were they) whom
Ruth 2:19. said unto her, *Where* hast thou gleaned
1Sa. 19:22. and said, *Where* (are) Samuel and David?
2Sa. 9: 4. the king said unto him, *Where* (is) he?
Job. 4: 7. *or where* were the righteous cut off?
38: 4. *Where* wast thou when I laid the
Isa. 49:21. I was left alone; these, *where* (had) they
Jer. 3: 2. and see *where* thou hast not been
36:19. and let no man know *where* ye be.

---

376 **אִישׁ** *eesh*, m.

אָחִיו, or אִישׁ....רֵעֵהוּ, the one....the other.
אִישׁ....אִישׁ, every one.

In 2 Sa. 14:19, and perhaps Mic. 6:10, it is without (י) אִשׁ.

Gen. 2:23. she was taken *out of Man*.
24. Therefore shall *a man* leave
3: 6. gave also *unto her husband*
16. desire (shall be) to *thy husband*,
4: 1. I have gotten *a man* from the Lord.
23. I have slain *a man* to my wounding,
6: 9. Noah was *a* just *man*
7: 2, 2. *the male* and his female:
9: 5. at the hand of *every man's* brother
20. an husband*man*, (lit. *a man* of the earth)
10: 5. *every one* after his tongue,
11: 3. they said *one* to another, (marg. *a man* said to his neighbour)
7. understand *one* another's speech.
13:11. *the one* from the other.
16. if *a man* can number the dust
15:10. *each* piece one against another:
16: 3. to *her husband* Abram to be his wife.
19: 8. which have not known *man*;
9. pressed sore *upon the man*,
31. *and* (there is) not *a man* in the earth
20: 7. restore *the man* (his) wife;
23: 6. none of us shall (lit. *a man* shall not)
24:16. *neither* had *any man* known her:
21. *And the man* wondering at her
22. that *the man* took a golden
26. *the man* bowed down his head,
29. ran out unto *the man*,
30. Thus spake *the man* unto me; that he came unto *the man*

Gen24:32. *the man* came into the house:
58. Wilt thou go with this *man*?
61. and followed *the man*:
65. What *man* (is) this that walketh
25:27. Esau was a cunning hunter (lit. *a man* understanding hunting), *a man of* the field; and Jacob (was) *a* plain *man*,
26:11. He that toucheth this *man*
13. *the man* waxed great,
31. sware *one* to another:
27:11. my brother (is) *a* hairy *man*, and I (am) *a* smooth *man*:
29:19. I should give her *to* another *man*:
32. *my husband* will love me.
34. *my husband* be joined unto me,
30:15. that thou hast taken *my husband*?
18. given my maiden *to my husband*:
20. *my husband* dwell with me,
43. *the man* increased exceedingly,
31:49. absent *one* from another.
50. no *man* (is) with us;
32: 6(7). four hundred *men* with him.
24(25). there wrestled *a man* with him
33: 1. with him four hundred *men*.
34:14. *to one* that is uncircumcised;
25. took *each man* his sword,
37:15. *a* certain *man* found him,
— *the man* asked him,
17. *the man* said,
19. And they said *one* to another,
38: 1. turned in to *a certain* Adullamite,
2. daughter of *a certain* Canaanite,
25. *By the man*, whose these (are),
39: 1. an Egyptian, (lit. *a man* an Egyptian)
2. he was *a* prosperous *man*;
11. none of the men (lit. not *a man*)
14. an Hebrew (lit. a *man* a Hebrew)
40: 5. *each man* his dream
— *each man* according to the
41:11. *each man* according to the interpretation
12. *each man* according to his dream
33. *a man* discreet and wise,
38. *a man* in whom the Spirit of God (is)?
44. no *man* lift up his hand
42:11. We (are) all one *man's* sons;
13. the sons of one *man*
21. they said *one* to another,
25. *every man's* money into his sack,
28. saying *one* to another,
30. *The man*, (who is) the lord
33. *the man*, the lord of the country,
35. behold, every *man's* bundle of money
43: 3. *The man* did solemnly protest
5. *the man* said unto us,
6. to tell *the man* whether ye had
7. *The man* asked us straitly
11. carry down *the man* a present,
13. go again unto *the man*:
14. give you mercy before *the man*,
17. *the man* did as Joseph bade; and *the man*
19. *the steward* of Joseph's house, (lit. *the man* over)
21. (every) *man's* money (was) in the mouth of his sack,
24. *the man* brought the men into
33. marvelled *one* at another.
44: 1. put every *man's* money in his sack's
11. took down every *man* his sack to the ground, and opened every *man* his sack.
13. and laded every *man* his ass,
15. wot ye not that such *a man*
17. *the man* in whose hand
26. may not see *the man's* face,
45: 1. Cause *every man* to go out
— there stood no *man* with him,
22. he gave *each man* changes
47:20. sold *every man* his field,
49: 6. in their anger they slew *a man*,
28. *every one* according to his blessing
Ex. 1: 1. *every man* and his houshold
2: 1. *a man* of the house of Levi,
11. Egyptian (lit. *a man* an Egyptian) smiting an Hebrew, (lit. *a man* an Hebrew)
12. saw that (there was) no *man*,
14. thee a prince (marg. *a man* a prince) and a judge
19. An Egyptian (lit. *a man* an Egyptian)

Ex. 2:20. ye have left *the man?*
21. dwell with *the man:*
4:10. I (am) not eloquent, (marg. *a man of* words)
7:12. cast down *every man* his rod,
10:23. They saw not *one* another, neither rose *any*
11: 2. let every *man* borrow
3. *the man* Moses (was) very great
7. *against man* or beast:
12: 3. take to them *every man* a lamb,
4. *every man* according to his eating
22. *none* of you shall (lit. no *man*)
44. But every *man*'s servant
15: 3. The Lord (is) *a man of* war:
16:15. they said *one* to another,
16. Gather of it *every man*
— take ye *every man* for (them)
18. gathered *every man* according
19. Let no *man* leave of it
21. *every man* according to his eating:
29. *every man* in his place, let no *man* go out
18: 7. they asked *each* other
16. *one* and another, (marg. *a man* and his fellow)
19:13. whether (it be) beast or *man*,
21: 7. if *a man* sell his daughter
12. He that smiteth *a man*,
14. if *a man* come presumptuously
16. he that stealeth *a man*,
18. *one* smite another with a stone,
20. if *a man* smite his servant,
26. if *a man* smite the eye
28. If an ox gore *a man*
29. he hath killed *a man*
33. if *a man* shall open a pit, or if *a man*
35. if one *man*'s ox hurt
22: 1 (21:37). If *a man* shall steal an ox,
5 (4). If *a man* shall cause a field
7 (6). If *a man* shall deliver unto his
— (-). and it be stolen out of *the man*'s
10 (9). If *a man* deliver unto his neighbour
14 (13). if *a man* borrow (ought) of his
16 (15). if *a man* entice a maid
25: 2. of *every man* that giveth it
20. their faces (shall look) *one* to another;
28:21. *every one* with his name
30:12. give *every man* a ransom
33. Whosoever (lit. *a man* who) compoundeth
38. Whosoever (lit. *a man* who) shall make like unto that,
32: 1, 23. *the man* that brought us up
27. Put *every man* his sword
— slay *every man* his brother, *and every man* his companion, *and every man* his
28. about three thousand *men*.
29. *every man* upon his son,
33: 4. no *man* did put on him
8. *every man* (at) his tent door,
10. *every man* (in) his tent door.
11. as *a man* speaketh unto his friend.
34: 3. *And* no *man* shall come up with thee, neither let *any man* be seen
24. neither shall *any man* desire thy land,
35:21. every *one* whose heart stirred
22. and every *man* that offered
23. every *man*, with whom was
29. every *man* and woman,
36: 1, 2. every wise hearted *man*,
4. came *every man* (lit. *a man a man*)
6. neither *man* nor woman
37: 9. with their faces *one* to another;
39:14. *every one* with his name,
Lev. 7: 8. *any man*'s burnt offering,
10. *one* (as much) as another.
10: 1. took *either of them* his censer,
13:29. *If a man* or woman have
38. *If a man also* or a woman
40. *And the man* whose hair is fallen
44. He is *a* leprous *man*,
14:11. shall present *the man*
15: 2. When *any man* hath (lit. *a man a man*)
5. *And whosoever* toucheth his bed
16. *And if any man*'s seed of copulation
18. with whom *man* shall lie
24. if *any man* lie with her
33. *and of him* that lieth with her

Lev. 16:21. by the hand of *a* fit *man*
17: 3. *What man soever* (there be) of the house of Israel, (lit. *a man a man*)
4. be imputed *unto that man*;
— 9, that *man* shall be cut off
8. *Whatsoever man* (there be) (lit. *a man a man*)
10. *And whatsoever man* (lit. *and a man, a man*)
13. *whatsoever man* (there be) of the children
18: 6. None of you shall (lit. *a man, a man* shall not)
19: 3. fear *every man* his mother,
11. neither lie *one* to another.
20. *And whosoever* lieth carnally
— betrothed *to an husband*,
20: 2. *Whosoever* (he be) (lit. *a man, a man*)
3. I will set my face *against that man*.
4. hide their eyes from *the man*,
5. set my face *against that man*,
9. *every one* that curseth (lit. *a man a man*)
10. *And the man* that committeth adultery with (another) *man*'s wife,
11. *And the man* that lieth with
12. *And* if *a man* lie with his daughter
13. If *a man* also lie
14. *And* if *a man* take a wife
15. *And* if *a man* lie with a beast,
17. *And* if *a man* shall take his sister,
18, 20. *And* if *a man* shall lie with
21. *And* if *a man* shall take his brother's
27. *A man also* or woman
21: 3. had no *husband*; (lit. was not *unto a man*)
7. a woman put away *from her husband:*
9. the daughter of *any* priest,
17. *Whosoever* (he be) of thy seed
18. For whatsoever *man* (he be)
— *a* blind *man*, or a lame,
19. Or *a man* that is brokenfooted,
21. No *man* that hath a blemish
22: 3. *Whosoever* (he be) of all your
4. *What man soever* of the seed of Aaron (is) a leper, (lit. *a man, a man*)
— or *a man* whose seed goeth
5. Or whos*oever* toucheth
12. (married) unto a stranger, (marg. *a man* a stranger)
14. *And if a man* eat (of) the holy thing
18. *Whatsoever* (he be) (lit. *a man, a man*)
21. *And whosoever* offereth a sacrifice
24:10. father (was) an Egyptian, (lit. an Egyptian *man*)
— *and a man* of Israel strove
15. *Whosoever* curseth his God (lit. *a man, a man*)
17. *And he* that killeth any man
19. *And if a man* cause a blemish
25:10. ye shall return *every man* unto his *man* session, *and* ye shall return *every man*
13. ye shall return *every man*
14. ye shall not oppress *one* another:
17. not therefore oppress *one* another;
26. *And if the man* have none to redeem it.
27. restore the overplus *unto the man*
29. *And if a man* sell a dwelling house
46. shall not rule *one* over another
26:37. they shall fall *one* upon another,
27: 2. When *a man* shall make
14. *And* when *a man* shall sanctify
16. if *a man* shall sanctify
20. sold the field *to* another *man*,
26. no *man* shall sanctify it;
28. that *a man* shall devote
31. if *a man* will at all redeem
Nu. 1: 4. *a man* of every tribe (lit. *a man, a man* for a tribe); *every one* head of
44. princes of Israel, (being) twelve **men**: *each* one was for the house
52. *every man* by his own camp, *and every man* by his own standard,
2: 2. *Every man* of the children of Israel
17. *every man* in his place
34. *every one* after their families,
4:19. appoint them *every one* (lit. *a man, a man*
49. *every one* according (lit. *a man, a man*)
5: 6. When *a man* or woman shall
8. if *the man have* no kinsman

Nu. 5:10. *And every man*'s hallowed things
— whatsoever *any man* giveth
12. If *any man*'s wife (lit. *a man, a man*)
13. And *a man* lie with her carnally, and it be hid from the eyes of *her husband*,
15. Then shall *the man* bring
19. If no *man* have lain with thee,
— 20. (another) instead of *thy husband*,
20. some *man* have lain with thee beside *thine husband:*
27. have done trespass *against her husband*,
29. instead of *her husband*,
30. Or when the spirit of jealousy cometh (lit. or of *a man*, when, &c.)
31. Then shall *the man* be guiltless
6: 2. When either *man* or woman
7: 5. to *every man* according to his service.
9:10. If *any man* (lit. *a man, a man*)
13. *But the man* that (is) clean,
— that *man* shall bear his sin.
11:10. *every man* in the door of his tent:
16. Gather unto me seventy *men*
24. gathered the seventy *men*
25 unto the seventy elders: (lit. *men* the elders)
12: 3. *Now the man* Moses
13: 2. of every tribe...shall ye send a *man*, (lit. one *man* one *man* for a tribe)
14: 4. they said *one* to another,
15. this people *as* one *man*,
15:32. *a man* that gathered sticks
35. *The man* shall be surely put to death:
16: 7. *the man* whom the Lord doth choose,
17. take *every man* his censer,
— before the Lord *every man* his censer,
— *each* (of you) his censer.
18. they took *every man* his censer,
22. shall one *man* sin,
35. two hundred and fifty *men*
40 (17:5). no stranger, (lit. *a man* a stranger)
17: 2 (17). write thou *every man*'s name
5 (20). *the man*'s rod, whom I shall
9 (24). took *every man* his rod.
19: 9. *a man* (that is) clean
18. *a* clean *person* shall take hyssop,
20. *But the man* that shall
21: 9. serpent had bitten *any man*,
23:19. God (is) not *a man*,
25: 5. Slay ye *every one* his men
6. *one* of the children of Israel
8. he went after *the man* of Israel
— *the man of* Israel, and the woman
14. the name of the *Israelite* (lit. *man of* Israel)
26:10. two hundred and fifty *men:*
54. to *every one* shall his inheritance
64. there was not *a man*
65. there was not left *a man* of them,
27: 8. If *a man* die,
16. set *a man* over the congregation,
18. *a man* in whom (is) the spirit,
30: 2 (3). If *a man* vow a vow
6 (7). if she had at all *an husband*,
7 (8). *her husband* heard (it),
8 (9). But if *her husband* disallowed
10 (11). vowed in *her husband*'s house,
11 (12). *her husband* heard (it),
12 (13). But if *her husband* hath
— (—). *her husband* hath made them
13 (14). *her husband* may establish it, *or her husband* may make it void.
14 (15). But if *her husband* altogether hold
16 (17). between *a man* and his wife,
31:17. that hath known *man*
49. there lacketh not one *man* of us.
50. what *every man* hath gotten,
53. *every man* for himself.
32:18. *every man* his inheritance.
35: 8. *every one* shall give of his cities
36: 7. *every one* of the children of Israel
8. may enjoy *every man* the inheritance
9. but *every one* of the tribes
Deu 1:16. between (every) *man* and his brother,
17. be afraid of the face of *man;*
23. one of a tribe: (lit. one *man*)
31. as *a man* doth bear his son,
35. there shall not *one* of these men

Deu. 1:41. girded on *every man* his weapons
3:11. after the cubit of *a man*.
20. return *every man* unto his possession,
4: 3. *the men* that followed Baal-peor,
7:24. there shall no *man* be able
8: 5. as *a man* chasteneth his son.
11:25. There shall no *man* be able
12: 8. *every man* whatsoever (is) right
16:17. *Every man* (shall give)
17: 2. *man* or woman, that hath
5. bring forth that *man*
— that *man* or that woman,
12. *And the man* that will do presumptuously,
— even that *man* shall die:
15. not set a stranger (lit. *a man* a stranger)
18:19. whosoever will not hearken
19:11. if *any man* hate his neighbour,
15. *against a man* for any iniquity,
16. rise up *against any man*
20: 5. What *man* (is there) that hath
— *and* another *man* dedicate it.
6. what *man* (is he) that hath
— die in the battle, *and* another *man* eat of it.
7. what *man* (is there) that
— *and* another *man* take her.
8. What *man* (is there that is) fearful
21:15. If *a man have* two wives,
18. If *a man have* a stubborn
22. if *a man* have committed a sin
22:13. If *any man* take a wife,
16. daughter *unto* this *man* to wife,
18. shall take *that man* and chastise him;
22. If *a man* be found lying
— *the man* that lay with the
23. betrothed *unto an husband*, and *a man* find her in the city,
24. *the man*, because he hath humbled
25. if *a man* find a betrothed damsel
— and *the man* force her,
— then *the man* only that lay with her
26. for as when *a man* riseth
28. If *a man* find a damsel
29. Then *the man* that lay with her
30 (23:1). *A man* shall not take his
23:10 (11). *any man*, that is not clean
24: 1, 5. When *a man* hath taken
2. and be another *man's* (wife).
3. (if) *the* latter *husband* hate her,
— or if *the* latter *husband* die,
7. If *a man* be found stealing
11. *and the man* to whom thou dost lend
12. And if *the man* (be) poor,
16. *every man* shall be put
25: 5. shall not marry without unto a stranger (lit. *to a man* a stranger)
7. if *the man* like not to take
9. be done *unto that man*
11. men strive together *one* with another,
— for to deliver *her husband*
27:14. say unto all *the men of* Israel
15. Cursed (be) *the man* that maketh
28:30. *and* another *man* shall lie with her:
54. *the man* (that is) tender among you,
56. *toward the husband of* her bosom,
29:10 (9). (with) all *the men of* Israel,
18 (17). should be among you *man*,
20 (19). smoke *against* that *man*,
32:25. with *the man of* gray hairs.
33: 1. *the man of* God blessed the children
8. *with* thy holy *one*, (lit. *to the man of* thy saints)
34: 6. but no *man* knoweth of his
Josh. 1: 5. There shall not *any man* be able
18. Whosoever (he be) that doth rebel (lit. every *man* who &c.)
2:11. courage *in any man*, because
3:12. take you twelve *men*
— out of every tribe a *man*. (lit. one *man*, one *man* for a tribe)
4:2, 4. out of every tribe a *man*, (lit. one *man*, one *man* for a tribe)
4. Joshua called *the* twelve *men*,
5. take you up *every man* of you
5:13. stood *a man* over against him
6: 5, 20. *every man* straight before him.
21. *both man* and woman, (lit. *from man*)

Josh. 6:26. Cursed (be) *the man* before the
7: 3. about two or three thousand *men* (marg. about two thousand *men*, (or), about three thousand *men*)
4. about three thousand *men:*
5. about thirty and six *men:*
8: 3. Joshua chose out thirty thousand mighty *men*
12. he took about five thousand *men*,
17. there was not *a man* left
25. both *of men* and women, (lit. *from man*)
9: 6. and to *the men of* Israel,
7. *the men of* Israel said unto the Hivites,
10: 8. there shall not *a man* of them
14. hearkened unto the voice of *a man:*
21. *against any of* the children of Israel.
24. called for all *the men of* Israel,
14: 6. Moses *the man of* God
17: 1. because he was *a man of* war,
21:44(42). there stood not *a man*
22:14. *and each one* (was) an head
20. that *man* perished not alone
23: 9. no *man* hath been able to stand
10. One *man* of you shall chase
24:28. *every man* unto his inheritance.
Jud. 1: 4. slew of them in Bezek ten thousand *men*.
24. the spies saw *a man* come
25. let go *the man* and all his family.
26. *the man* went into the land
2: 6. *every man* unto his inheritance
21. drive out *any* from before them
3:15. a Benjamite, *a man* lefthanded:
17. Eglon (was) *a* very fat *man*.
28. suffered not *a man* to pass
29. about ten thousand *men*,
— all *men of* valour; and there escaped not *a man*.
31. six hundred *men* with an ox goad:
4: 6. take with thee ten thousand *men*
10. with ten thousand *men* at his feet:
14. ten thousand *men* after him.
20. *when any man* doth come
— Is there *any man* here?
22. I will shew thee *the man*
6: 8. Lord sent a prophet (marg. *a man*, a prophet)
16. the Midianites *as* one *man*.
29. they said *one* to another,
7: 6. were three hundred *men:*
7. By *the* three hundred *men*
— *every man* unto his place.
8. all (the rest of) Israel (lit. every *man of*) *every man* unto his tent, and retained those three hundred *men:*
13. (there was) *a man* that told
14. Gideon the son of Joash, *a man*
16. divided *the* three hundred *men*
19. Gideon, and the hundred *men*
21. stood *every man* in his place
22. *every man*'s sword against his fellow,
23. *the men of* Israel gathered
24. *the men of* Ephraim gathered
8: 1. *the men of* Ephraim said
4. *the* three hundred *men*
10. thousand *men* that drew (marg. *every one* drawing) sword.
14. threescore and seventeen *men*.
21. for *as the man* (is, so is) his strength.
22. Then *the men of* Israel
24. give me *every man* the earrings
25. cast therein *every man* the earrings
9: 2. threescore and ten *persons*, reign over you, or that one reign over you? (lit. one *man*)
5, 18. threescore and ten *persons*, upon one
49. cut down *every man* his bough,
— about a thousand *men* and women.
55. when *the men of* Israel saw
— departed *every man* unto his place.
10: 1. *a man of* Issachar;
18. princes of Gilead said *one* to another, What *man* (is he) that will
11:39. and she knew no *man*.
12: 1. *the men of* Ephraim gathered
2. I and my people were at great strife (lit. *a man of* strife was I and my people)
13: 2. there was *a* certain *man* of Zorah,
Jud. 13:6. came and told *her husband*, saying, *A man of* God came unto me,
8. *the man of* God which thou didst send
9. Manoah *her husband* (was) not
10. shewed *her husband*,
— *the man* hath appeared
11. came to *the man*,
— (Art) thou *the man* that spakest
14:15. Entice *thy husband*,
19. slew thirty *men* of them,
15:10. And *the men of* Judah said,
11. three thousand *men* of Judah went
15. slew *a* thousand *men* therewith.
16. have I slain *a* thousand *men*.
16: 5. *every one* of us eleven hundred
19. she called *for a man*,
27. about three thousand *men*
17: 1. there was *a man* of mount Ephraim,
5. *And the man* Micah had an house
6. *every man* did (that which was)
8. *the man* departed out
11. content to dwell with *the man;*
18:11. six hundred *men*
16. *the* six hundred *men* appointed
17. *the* six hundred *men* (that were)
19. priest unto the house of one *man*,
19: 1. that there was *a certain* Levite
3. And *her husband* arose,
6. damsel's father had said unto *the man*,
7, 9. when *the man* rose up to depart,
10. *the man* would not tarry
15. no *man* that took them into his house
16. there came an old *man*
— which (was) *also* of mount Ephraim; (lit. *and the man*, &c.)
17. he saw *a* wayfaring *man*
—, 20. and *the* old *man* said,
18. no *man* that receiveth me
22. spake to the master (lit. *the man*, the master)
— Bring forth *the man* that came
23. *the man*, the master of the house,
— seeing that this *man* is come
24. *but unto* this *man* do not so vile
25. so *the man* took his concubine,
26. at the door of *the man*'s house
28. Then *the man* took her
20: 1. was gathered together *as* one *man*,
2. four hundred thousand foot*men*
4. the Levite, (marg. *the man* the Levite) *the husband of* the woman
8. people arose *as* one *man*, saying, We will not *any* (of us) go to his tent, neither will we *any* (of us) turn
11. *the men of* Israel were gathered against the city, knit together *as* one *man*.
15. twenty and six thousand *men*
—, 16. seven hundred chosen *men*.
17. *And the men of* Israel,
— four hundred thousand *men* that drew sword: all these (were) *men of* war.
20. *the men of* Israel went out
— *the men of* Israel put themselves
21. twenty and two thousand *men*.
22. *the men of* Israel encouraged
25, 44. eighteen thousand *men;*
31. about thirty *men of* Israel.
33. all *the men of* Israel rose up
34. ten thousand chosen *men*
35. and five thousand and an hundred *men:*
36. *the men of* Israel gave place
38. *between the men of* Israel
39. when *the men of* Israel retired
— kill of *the men of* Israel about thirty *persons:*
41. *when the men of* Israel turned again, *the men of* Benjamin were amazed:
42. before *the men of* Israel
45. highways five thousand *men;*
— slew two thousand *men*
46 twenty and five thousand *men*
47. But six hundred *men* turned and fled
48. *And the men of* Israel turned
21: 1. *Now the men of* Israel had sworn
— There shall not *any* of us give
8. there came none (lit. no *man*)
9. (there were) none (lit. no *man*)

Jud 21:10. sent thither twelve thousand *men*
12. that had known no *man*
21. catch you *every man* his wife
22. *each man* his wife in the war:
24. *every man* to his tribe
— *every man* to his inheritance.
25. *every man* did (that which was)
Ruth 1: 1. *a* certain *man of* Beth-lehem-judah
2. name of *the man* (was) Elimelech,
3. Elimelech Naomi's husband
5. of her two sons *and her husband.*
9. in the house of *her husband.*
12. I am too old to have *an husband.*
— I should have *an husband*
13. for them from having *husbands?*
2: 1. a kinsman *of her husband's, a* mighty *man*
11. since the death of *thine husband:*
19. *The man*'s name with whom
20. *The man* (is) near of kin unto us,
3: 3. thyself known *unto the man,*
8. that *the man* was afraid,
14. before *one* could know another.
16. all that *the man* had done
18. for *the man* will not be in rest,
4: 7. *a man* plucked off his shoe,
1Sa. 1: 1. Now there was *a* certain *man*
3. this *man* went up out of his city
8. Then said Elkanah *her husband* to her,
21. And *the man* Elkanah, and all his house,
22. for she said *unto her husband,*
23. And Elkanah *her husband* said unto her,
2: 9. by strength shall no *man* prevail.
13. when *any man* offered sacrifice,
15. said *to the man* that sacrificed,
16. (if) *any man* said unto him,
19. when she came up with *her husband*
25. If *one man* sin *against another,*
— but if *a man* sin against the Lord,
27. there came *a man of* God
33. *And the man* of thine,
4: 2. about four thousand *men.*
10. fled *every man* into his tent:
12. there ran *a man of* Benjamin
13. *when the man* came into the city,
14. *And the man* came in hastily,
16. *the man* said unto Eli,
18. for he was *an* old *man,*
19, 21. father in law *and her husband*
6.19. fifty thousand and threescore and ten *men:* (lit. 70 *men* 50,000 *men*)
8:22. Go ye *every man* unto his city.
9: 1. Now there was *a man* of Benjamin,
— the son of Aphiah, a Benjamite, (lit. the son of *a man* of Jemini,)
2. of Israel *a* goodlier *person* than he:
6. in this city *a man* of God, *and* (he is) an honourable *man;*
7. what shall we bring *the man?*
— to bring *to the man of* God:
8. I give *to the man of* God,
9. when *a man* went to enquire
10. where *the man of* God (was).
16. I will send thee *a man*
17. Behold *the man* whom I spake to thee of!
22. about thirty *persons.*
10: 6. shalt be turned *into* another *man.*
11. people said *one* to another, (marg. *a man* to his neighbour)
12. *one* of the same place answered
22. if *the man* should yet come
25. *every man* to his house.
11: 7. out *with* one *consent.* (marg. *as* one *man*)
8. *and the men of* Judah thirty thousand.
9. Thus shall ye say *unto the men of*
13. There shall not *a man* be put
12: 4. taken ought of *any man*'s hand.
13: 2. *every man* to his tent.
6. *When the men of* Israel saw
14. *a man* after his own heart,
15. about six hundred *men.*
20. to sharpen *every man* his share,
14: 2. about six hundred *men;*
14. was about twenty *men,*
20. *every man*'s sword
22. Likewise all *the men of* Israel
24. *And the men of* Israel were distressed

1Sa. 14.24, 28. Cursed (be) *the man* that eateth
28. Then answered *one* of the
34. Bring me hither *every man* his ox, *and every man* his sheep,
— brought *every man* his ox
36. let us not leave *a man*
52. when Saul saw any strong *man,*
15: 3. slay *both man* and woman,
4. ten thousand *men of* Judah.
16:16. seek out *a man,*
17. Provide me now *a man*
18. *and a man of* war,
— *and a* comely *person,*
17: 2. Saul *and the men of* Israel were gathered
4. went out *a champion* (lit. *a* middle *man*)
8. choose you *a man* for you,
10. give me *a man,*
12. David (was) the son of that Ephrathite (lit. *a man* that Ephrathite)
— *and the man* went among
19. all *the men of* Israel,
23. came up *the champion,* (lit. *a* middle *man*)
24. And all *the men of* Israel, when they saw *the man,*
25. And *the men of* Israel said, Have ye seen this *man*
— *the man* who killeth him,
26. What shall be done *to the man*
27. So shall it be done *to the man*
33. *a man of* war from his youth.
41. *and the man* that bare the shield
18:23. I (am) *a* poor *man,*
27. of the Philistines two hundred *men*
20:15. *every one* from the face of the earth.
41. they kissed *one* another, and wept *one* with another,
21: 1(2). and no *man* with thee?
2(3). Let no *man* know any thing
7(8). Now *a* certain *man* of the servants
14(15). ye see *the man* is mad:
22: 2. every *one* (that was) in distress, and every *one* that (was) in debt, and every *one* (that was) discontented,
— about four hundred *men.*
18. fourscore and five *persons*
19. *both men* and women,
23:13. six hundred, (lit. 600 *men*)
24: 2(3). three thousand chosen *men*
19(20). if *a man* find his enemy,
25: 2. *And* (there was) *a man* in Maon,
— *and the man* (was) very great,
3. the name of *the man* (was) Nabal;
— *but the man* (was) churlish and evil in his
10. *every man* from his master.
13. Gird ye on *every man* his sword. And they girded on *every man* his sword;
— about four hundred *men;*
19. *But* she told not *her husband*
25. regard this *man* of Belial,
26: 2. having three thousand chosen *men*
15. (Art) not thou *a* (valiant) *man?*
23. The Lord render *to every man*
27: 2. with *the* six hundred *men*
3. *every man* with his houshold,
9. left neither *man* nor woman
11. And David saved neither *man*
28:14. *An* old *man* cometh up;
29: 4. Make *this fellow* return,
30: 2. they slew not *any,*
6. *every man* for his sons
9. *men* that (were) with him,
10. four hundred *men:* for two hundred (lit. *men*)
11. found an Egyptian (lit. *a man* an Egyptian)
13. to an Amalekite; (lit. to *a man* an Amalekite)
17. there escaped not *a man*
— save four hundred young *men,*
22. all the wicked *men*
— save to *every man* his wife
31:12. All *the* valiant *men* arose,
2Sa. 1: 2. *a man* came out of the camp
13. son of a stranger, (lit. *a man* a stranger)
2: 3. *every man* with his houshold:
16. they caught *every one* his
27. *every one* from following his brother.

2Sa. 2:30. of David's servants nineteen *men*
31. three hundred and threescore *men*
3:15. took her from (her) *husband,*
16. *her husband* went with her
4:11. have slain *a* righteous *person*
6:19. as well to the women *as men, to every one* a cake of bread,
— departed *every one* to his house.
8: 4. twenty thousand foot*men:*
5. two and twenty thousand *men.*
10. for Hadadezer had wars with (lit. was *a man* of wars with)
9: 3. (Is) there not yet *any* of the
10: 6. twenty thousand footmen, and of king Maacah a thousand *men, and of Ish*-tob 12,000 (lit. 12,000 *men*)
8. of Rehob, *and Ish*-tob,
11:26. that Uriah *her husband*
12: 4. a traveller *unto the* rich *man,*
— took the poor *man*'s lamb, and dressed it *for the man* that
5. was greatly kindled *against the man ;*
— *the man* that hath done this
7. Thou (art) *the man.*
13: 3. Jonadab (was) *a* very subtil *man.*
9. Have out all *men* from me. And they went out *every man*
29. *every man* gat him up
14: 5. *mine husband* is dead.
7. shall not leave *to my husband*
16. out of the hand of *the man*
19. none (lit. no *man*) can turn to the right
25. none (lit. no *man*) to be so much praised
15: 1. fifty *men* to run before him.
2. *any man* that had a controversy
4. *every man* which hath any suit
5. when *any man* came nigh
11. with Absalom went two hundred *men*
13. The hearts of *the men of* Israel
18. six hundred *men*
30. covered *every man* his head,
16: 5. thence came out *a man*
7. thou bloody *man, and* thou *man of* Belial:
8. because thou (art) *a* bloody *man.*
15. *the men of* Israel, came to Jerusalem,
18. all *the men of* Israel,
23. (קרי) as if *a man* had enquired
17: 1. choose out twelve thousand *men.*
3. *the man* whom thou seekest
8. thy father (is) *a man of* war,
14. Absalom and all *the men of* Israel
18. came to *a man*'s house
24. he and all *the men of* Israel
25. which Amasa (was) *a man*'s son,
18:10. *a* certain *man* saw (it),
11. Joab said *unto the man*
12. *the man* said unto Joab,
17. Israel fled *every one* to his tent.
20. bear tidings (marg. *be a man of* tidings)
24. and behold *a man* running alone.
26. saw another *man* running:
— Behold, (another) *man* running alone.
27. He (is) *a* good *man,*
19: 7(8). there will not tarry *one* (lit. *a man*)
8(9). *every man* to his tent.
14(15). the heart of all *the men of* Judah, even *as* (the heart of) one *man ;*
16(17). came down with *the men*
17(18). (there were) *a* thousand *men*
22(23). shall there *any man* be
32(33). for he (was) *a* very great *man.*
41(42). all *the men of* Israel came
—(—). Why have our brethren *the men of*
42(43). *the men of* Judah answered *the men of* Israel,
43(44). *the men of* Israel answered *the men of* Judah,
—(—). the words of *the men of* Judah were fiercer than the words of *the men of* Is.
20: 1. there happened to be there *a man*
— Bichri, a Benjamite: (lit. *a man* of Jemini)
— *every man* to his tents,
2. *every man of* Israel went up
— *but the men of* Judah clave
4. Assemble me *the men of* Judah
11. *And one* of Joab's men stood

2Sa 20:12. when *the man* saw
13. all *the people* went on
21. *a man* of mount Ephraim,
22. *every man* to his tent.
21: 4. shalt thou kill *any man*
5. *The man* that consumed us,
20. where was *a man of* (great) stature.
22:49. delivered me *from the* violent *man.*
23: 7. *But the man* (that) shall touch them
9. *the men of* Israel were gone away:
20. the son of *a* valiant *man,*
21. he slew an Egyptian, (lit. *a man* an Egyptian) (קרי) a goodly *man:*
24: 9. eight hundred thousand valiant *men*
— *and the men of* Judah (were) five hundred thousand *men.*
15. seventy thousand *men.*
1 K. 1: 5. fifty *men* to run before him.
42. for thou (art) *a* valiant *man,*
49. went every *man* his way.
2: 2. shew thyself *a man ;*
4. *a man* on the throne of Israel.
9. thou (art) *a* wise *man,*
26. (art) *worthy of* death: (marg. *a man of* death)
3:13. there shall not be *any* among the kings
4:25(5:5). *every man* under his vine
27(5:7). *every man* in his month;
28(5:8). (the officers) were, *every man* according to his charge.
5: 6(20). (there is) not among us *any*
13(27). the levy was thirty thousand *men.*
7:14. his father (was) *a man of* Tyre,
30. at the side of *every* addition.
36. the proportion of *every one,*
8: 2. all *the men of* Israel
25. There shall not fail thee *a man*
31. If *any man* trespass against
38. which shall know *every man*
39. give *to every man* according
9: 5. There shall not fail thee *a man*
10:25. brought *every man* his present,
11:28. *And the man* Jeroboam
12:22. Shemaiah *the man of* God,
24. return *every man* to his
13: 1. there came *a man of* God
4. the saying of *the man of* God,
5. which *the man of* God had
6, 7. unto *the man of* God,
— *the man of* God besought the Lord
8. *the man of* God said
11. *the man of* God had done
12. what way *the man of* God
14. went after *the man of* God,
— (Art) thou *the man of* God
21. he cried unto *the man of* God
26. It (is) *the man of* God,
29. the carcase of *the man of* God,
31. wherein *the man of* God (is) buried;
17:18. O thou *man of* God?
24. thou (art) *a man of* God,
18: 4. hid them by fifty (lit. *men*) in a cave,
13. hid an hundred *men* of the Lord's prophets by fifty (lit. fifty *men*) in a cave,
22. four hundred and fifty *men.*
40. let not *one* of them escape. (lit. *a man*)
44. like *a man*'s hand.
20:20. they slew *every one his man:*
24. *every man* out of his place,
28. there came *a man of* God,
30. twenty and seven thousand of the *men*
35. *And a* certain *man* of the sons
— *the man* refused to smite him.
37. Then he found another *man,*
— *the man* smote him,
39. *a man* turned aside, and brought *a man* unto me, and said, Keep this *man:*
42. let go out of (thy) hand *a man*
22: 6. about four hundred *men,*
8. (There is) yet one *man,*
10. sat *each* on his throne,
17. let them return *every man*
34. *And a* (certain) *man* drew a bow
36. *Every man* to his city, *and every man* to
2 K. 1: 6. There came *a man* up
7. What manner of *man* (was he)
8. (He was) *an* hairy *man.*

2 K. 1: 9. Thou *man of* God,
10. If I (be) *a man of* God,
11. *O man of* God, thus hath
12. If I (be) *a man of* God,
13. *O man of* God, I pray
2: 7. fifty *men* of the sons of the
17. They sent therefore fifty *men*;
3. 23. they have smitten *one* another:
25. cast *every man* his stone,
26. took with him seven hundred *men*
4: 1. Thy servant *my husband* is dead;
7. she came and told *the man of* God.
9. she said unto *her husband*,
— this (is) *an* holy *man of* God,
14. *and her husband* is old.
16. Nay, my lord, (thou) *man of* God,
21. on the bed of *the man of* God,
22. she called unto *her husband*,
— that I may run to *the man of*
25. came unto *the man of* God
— when *the man of* God saw her
26. (is it) well *with thy husband?*
27. when she came to *the man of*
— *the man of* God said,
29. if thou meet *any man*,
— if *any* salute thee,
40. *O* (thou) *man of* God,
42. *And* there came *a man* from Baal-shalisha, and brought *the man of* God bread
43. set this before an hundred *men?*
5: 1. was *a* great *man* with his master,
— he was *also a* mighty *man*
7. unto me to recover *a man*
8, 20. Elisha *the man of* God
14. according to the saying of *the man of*
15. he returned to *the man of* God,
26. when *the man* turned
6: 2. take thence *every man*
6. *the man of* God said,
9. *the man of* God sent
10. which *the man of* God
15. the servant of *the man of* God
19. I will bring you to *the man*
32. sent *a man* from before him:
7: 2. answered *the man of* God,
3, 9. they said *one* to another,
5, 10. (there was) no *man* there.
6. they said *one* to another,
17. as *the man of* God had said,
18. as *the man of* God had spoken
19. answered *the man of* God,
8: 2. did after the saying of *the man of* God:
4. Gehazi the servant of *the man of* God,
7. *The man of* God is come hither.
8. and go, meet *the man of* God,
11. and *the man of* God wept.
9: 11. Ye know *the man*,
13. took *every man* his garment,
21. *each* in his chariot,
10: 5. make *any* king: (lit. cause *a man* to reign)
6. (being) seventy *persons*,
7. slew seventy *persons*,
14. two and forty *men*; neither left he *any*
19. let none be wanting: (lit. let *a man* not)
21. there was not *a man* left
24. appointed fourscore *men*
— (If) *any* of the men
25. let none come forth. (lit. let *a man* not)
11: 8, 11. *every man* with his weapons
9. they took *every man*
12: 4(5). money of *every one* that passeth
—(–). that cometh into any *man's* heart
5(6). *every man* of his acquaintance:
9(10) as *one* cometh
13: 19. *the man of* God was wroth
21. as they were burying *a man*,
— they cast *the man* into the sepulchre of Elisha: and when *the man* was let down,
14: 6. but *every man* shall be
12. fled *every man* to their tents.
15: 20. *of* each *man* fifty shekels
25. with him fifty *men* of the Gileadites:
18: 21. on which if *a man* lean,
31. *every man* of his own vine, *and every one* of his fig tree, and drink ye *every one*
33. Hath *any* of the gods
22: 15. Tell *the man* that sent you

2K. 23: 2. all the *men of* Judah
8. which (were) on *a man's* left hand
10. that no *man* might make
16. which *the man of* God proclaimed,
17. the sepulchre of *the man of* God,
18. let no *man* move his bones.
35. *every one* according
25: 19. threescore *men of* the people
1Ch. 10: 1. *the men of* Israel fled
7. all *the men of* Israel
12. arose, all *the* valiant *men*,
11: 22. the son of *a* valiant *man*
23. slew an Egyptian (lit. a *man* an Egyptian), *a man of* (great) stature,
16: 3. dealt to *every one of* Israel, both *man* and woman, *to every one* a loaf
21. He suffered no *man* to do them wrong.
43. *every man* to his house:
18: 4. twenty thousand foot*men*:
5. two and twenty thousand *men*.
10. Hadarezer had war (marg. was *the man of* wars)
19: 18. forty thousand foot*men*,
20: 6. where was *a man of* (great) stature,
21: 5. an hundred thousand *men*
— ten thousand *men*
14. seventy thousand *men*.
22: 9. who shall be *a man of* rest;
23: 14. Moses *the man of* God,
26: 8. able *men* for strength
27: 32. *a* wise *man*, and a scribe:
28: 3. thou (hast been) *a man of* war,
2Ch. 2: 2(1). threescore and ten thousand *men*
—(–). fourscore thousand (lit. 80 000 *men*)
7(6). Send me now therefore *a man*
13(12). now I have sent *a* cunning *man*,
14(13). his father (was) *a man of* Tyre,
5: 3. all *the men of* Israel assembled
6: 5. neither chose I any *man*
16. shall not fail thee *a man*
22. If *a man* sin against his
29. *every one* shall know his own
30. render *unto every man* according
7: 18. shall not fail thee *a man*
8: 14. David *the man of* God commanded.
9: 24. brought *every man* his present,
10: 16. *every man* to your tents,
11: 2. to Shemaiah *the man of* God,
4. return *every man* to his house:
13: 3. four hundred thousand chosen *men*:
— eight hundred thousand chosen *men*,
15. the *men of* Judah gave a shout: and as *the men of* Judah shouted,
17. five hundred thousand chosen *men*.
15: 13. *whether man* or woman. (lit. *from man* unto woman)
18: 5. four hundred *men*,
7. (There is) yet one *man*,
9. sat *either of them* on his throne,
16. *every man* to his house
33. *And a* (certain) *man* drew a bow
20: 23. *every one* helped to destroy
27. they returned, every *man*
23: 7. *every man* with his weapons
8. took *every man* his men
10. *every man* having his weapon (lit. *and every man* his weapon)
25: 4. but *every man* shall die for his own sin.
7. *But* there came *a man of* God to him,
9. Amaziah said *to the man of* God,
— *the man of* God answered,
22. *every man* to his tent.
30: 16. Moses *the man of* God:
31: 1. *every man* to his possession,
2. *every man* according
34: 23. Tell ye *the man* that sent you
30. all *the men of* Judah,
Ezr. 2: 1. *every one* unto his city;
3: 1. *as* one *man* to Jerusalem.
2. law of Moses *the man of* God.
8: 18. brought us *a man of* understanding,
Neh. 1: 11. mercy in the sight of this *man*.
3: 28. *every one* over against his house.
4: 15(9). *every one* unto his work.
18(12). *every one* had his sword
19(13). *one* far from another.
22(16). Let *every one* with his servant

Neh. 4:23(17). *every one* put them off
5. 7. *every one* of his brother.
13. *every man* from his house,
17. an hundred and fifty (lit. 150 *men*)
6:11. Should such *a man* as I flee?
7: 2. for he (was) *a* faithful *man*,
3. *every one* in his watch, *and every one*
6. *every one* unto his city;
8: 1. *as* one *man* into the street
2. *both of men* and women, (lit. *from man*)
16. *every one* upon the roof
11: 3. *every one* in his possession
20. *every one* in his inheritance.
12:24, 36. of David *the man of* God,
13:10. *every one* to his field.
30. *every one* in his business;
Est. 1: 8. *every man*'s pleasure. (lit. of *man and man*)
22. that every *man* should bear rule
2: 5. *a certain* Jew, (lit. *a man*, a Jew)
— of Kish, a Benjamite; (lit. *a man* of Jemini)
4:11. whether *man* or woman,
6: 6. What shall be done *unto the man*
7. *the man* whom the king delighteth
9. delivered to the hand of *one*
— they may array *the man*
— 11. Thus shall it be done *to the man*
7: 6. The adversary (marg. The *man* adversary)
9: 2. *and* no *man* could withstand them;
4. *this man* Mordecai waxed
6, 12. destroyed five hundred *men*.
15. slew three hundred *men*
19, 22. sending portions *one* to another.
Job 1: 1. There was *a man* in the land
— and that *man* was perfect
3. so that this *man* was the greatest
4. *every one* his day;
8 & 2:3. a perfect and an upright *man*,
2: 4. all that *a man hath*
11. they came *every one* from his own place;
12. they rent *every one* his mantle,
9:32. For (he is) not *a man*, as
11: 2. should *a man* full of talk
12. *For* vain *man* would be wise,
12:10. breath of all *man*kind. (marg. flesh of *man*)
14. he shutteth up *a man*,
14:12. *So man* lieth down,
15:16. abominable and filthy (is) *man*,
22: 8. *But* (as for) the mighty *man*,
31:35. mine adversary had written a book. (lit. *the man of* my quarrel)
32:13. God thrusteth him down, not *man*.
21. accept any *man*'s person,
34:11. and cause *every man*
21. eyes (are) upon the ways of *man*,
23. he will not lay upon *man*
35: 8. Thy wickedness (may hurt) *a man*
37:20. if *a man* speak,
38:26. on the earth, (where) no *man* (is);
41:17(9). They are joined *one* to another,
42:11. *every man* also gave him a piece of money, *and every one* an earring
Ps. 1: 1. Blessed (is) *the man*
4: 2(3). O ye sons of *men*,
5: 6(7). the bloody and deceitful *man*.
12: 2(3). They speak vanity *every one*
18:48(49). delivered me *from the* violent *man*.
22: 6(7). I (am) a worm, and no *man*;
25:12. What *man* (is) he that feareth
31:20(21). from the pride of *man*:
34:12(13). What *man* (is he that) desireth
37: 7. *because of the man* who bringeth
37. for the end *of* (that) *man* (is) peace.
38:14(15). Thus I was *as a man* that heareth
39: 6(7). *every man* walketh in a vain shew:
11(12). dost correct *man* for iniquity,
41: 9(10). mine own familiar *friend*, (marg. *the man* of my peace)
43: 1. *from the* deceitful and unjust *man*.
49: 2(3). both low and *high*, (sons of אָדָם, sons of אִישׁ)
7(8). None (of them) can (lit. *a man* not)
16(17). afraid when *one* (lit. *a man*)
62: 3(4) imagine mischief against *a man*?
9(10). men of *high degree* (lit. sons of *man*)
12(13). *to every man* according
64: 6(7). (thought) of *every one* (of them),

Ps. 78:25. *Man* did eat (marg. *Every one* did eat)
80:17 (18). upon *the man of* thy right hand,
87: 5. *This and that man* was born (lit. *a man and a man*)
90: [title] (1). A Prayer of Moses *the man of* God.
92: 6(7). *A* brutish *man* knoweth not;
105:17. He sent *a man* before them,
109:16. the poor and needy *man*,
112: 1. Blessed (is) *the man* (that) feareth
5. *A* good *man* sheweth favour,
140: 1(2), 4(5). me *from the* violent *man*;
11(12). Let not an evil speaker be established (marg. *a man of* tongue)
— (—). evil shall hunt the violent *man* (marg. a wicked *man of* violence)
141: 4. with *men* that work iniquity:
147:10. pleasure in the legs of *a man*.
Pro. 2:12. *from the man* that speaketh froward
3:31. Envy thou not the oppressor, (marg. *a man of* violence)
5:21. For the ways of *man* (are) before
6:11. thy want *as an* armed *man*.
12. *a* wicked *man*, walketh with a
26. the adulteress (marg. woman of *a man*, or, *a man*'s wife) will hunt for
27. Can *a man* take fire in his bosom,
28. Can *one* go upon hot coals, (lit. a *man*)
7:19. For *the goodman* (is) not
8: 4. Unto you, *O men*, I call;
10:23. but *a man of* understanding *hath* wisdom.
11:12. *but a man of* understanding
17. *The* merciful *man* doeth good
12: 2. *but* a *man of* wicked devices
8. *A man* shall be commended
14. *A man* shall be satisfied
25. Heaviness in the heart of *man*
13: 2. *A man* shall eat good by the fruit
8. The ransom of *a man*'s life
14: 7. Go from the presence *of a* foolish *man*,
12. which seemeth right unto *a man*,
14. *a* good *man* (shall be satisfied)
17. *and a man of* wicked devices is hated.
15:18. *A* wrathful *man* stirreth up strife:
21. *but a man of* understanding
23. *A man hath* joy by the answer
16: 2. All the ways of *a man* (are) clean
7. When *a man*'s ways please the Lord,
14. *but a* wise *man* will pacify it.
25. that seemeth right unto *a man*,
27. *An* ungodly *man* diggeth up
28. *A* froward *man* soweth strife:
29. *A* violent *man* enticeth his
17:12. robbed of her whelps meet *a man*,
27. *a man of* understanding
18: 4. The words of *a man*'s mouth
12. the heart of *man* is haughty,
14. The spirit of *a man* will sustain
20. *A man*'s belly shall be satisfied
24. *A man* (that hath) friends
19: 6. a friend *to him* that giveth gifts. (marg. *a man of* gifts)
21. many devices in *a man*'s heart;
22. a poor man (is) better *than a* liar. (lit. *than a man of* lies)
20: 3. an honour *for a man* to cease from strife:
5. the heart of *man* (is like) deep water; *but a man of* understanding
6. *every one* his own goodness: *but a* faithful *man* who can find?
17. Bread of deceit (is) sweet *to a man*;
21: 2. Every way of *a man* (is) right in
8. The way of *man* (is) froward
17. pleasure (shall be) *a* poor *man*.
28. *but the man* that heareth
29. *A* wicked *man* hardeneth
22: 7. the borrower (is) servant *to the* lender (marg. *to the man* that lendeth)
24. with *a* furious *man* thou shalt not go:
29. Seest thou *a man* diligent
24: 5. *yea, a man of* knowledge increaseth
29. I will render *to the man* according
30. the field of the slothful, (lit. slothful *man*
34. thy want *as an* armed *man*.
25:14. *Whoso* boasteth himself
18. *A man* that beareth false witness
28. *He* that (hath) no rule
26:12. Seest thou *a man* wise in his
19. *the man* (that) deceiveth his

Pro. 26:21. *so* (is) *a* contentious *man* to kindle
27: 8. so (is) *a man* that wandereth from
17. *so a man* sharpeneth the countenance
21. *so* (is) *a man* to his praise.
28:11. *The* rich *man* (is) wise in his own
20. *A* faithful *man* shall abound
22. *He* that hasteth to be rich
24. companion of a destroyer. (marg. **a** *man* destroying)
29: 1. *He*, that being often reproved (marg. *A man* of reproofs)
3. *Whoso* loveth wisdom
4. *but he* that receiveth gifts (marg. *a man of* oblations)
6. In the transgression of *an* evil *man*
9. (If) *a* wise *man* contendeth with *a* foolish *man*,
13. The poor *and the* deceitful *man*
20. Seest thou *a man* (that is) hasty
22. *An* angry *man* stirreth up strife,
26. but (every) *man's* judgment
27. *An* unjust *man* (is) an abomination
30: 2. I (am) more brutish *than* (any) *man*,
Ecc. 1: 8. *man* cannot utter (it):
4: 4. for this *a man* is envied
6: 2. *A man* to whom God hath given
— a stranger (lit. *a* strange *man*) eateth it:
3. If *a man* beget an hundred (children),
7: 5. *than for a man* to hear the song
9:15. found in it *a* poor wise *man*,
— that same poor *man*.
Cant. 3: 8. every *man* (hath) his sword upon his
8: 7. if *a man* would give all the substance
11. *every one* for the fruit thereof
Isa. 2: 9. *the great man* humbleth himself:
3: 2. The mighty man, *and the man of* war,
5. *every one, by another, and every one* by
6. *a man* shall take hold of his brother
4: 1. shall take hold *of* one *man*,
5: 3. *and men of* Judah, judge,
7. *and the men of* Judah his pleasant plant:
15. *the mighty man* shall be humbled,
6: 5. I (am) *a man of* unclean lips,
7:21. *a man* shall nourish a young cow,
9:19(18). no *man* shall spare his brother.
20(19). eat *every man* the flesh of his own
13: 8. shall be amazed *one* at another; (marg. *every man* at his neighbour)
14. *every man* turn to his own people, *and* flee *every one* into his own land.
14:16. *the man* that made the earth to tremble,
18. *every one* in his own house.
19: 2. *every one* against his brother, *and every one*
21: 9. here cometh a chariot of *men*,
31: 7. *every man* shall cast away
8. not of *a mighty man;*
32: 2. *a man* shall be as an hiding place
36: 6. whereon if *a man* lean,
16. eat ye *every one* of his vine, *and every one* of his fig tree, and drink ye *every one*
18. Hath *any* of the gods of the nations
40:13. his counsellor (marg. *and man of* his counsel)
26. not *one* faileth.
41: 6. helped *every one* his neighbour;
28. I beheld, and (there was) no *man;*
42:13. jealousy *like a man of* war:
44:13. maketh it after the figure of *a man*,
46:11. *the man* that executeth my counsel
47:15. they shall wander *every one*
50: 2. when I came, (was there) no *man?*
52:14. was so marred *more than any man*,
53: 3. rejected of *men; a man of* sorrows,
6. we have turned *every one* to his own
55: 7. *and the* unrighteous *man* his thoughts:
56:11. *every one* for his gain,
57: 1. no *man* layeth (it) to heart:
59:16. he saw that (there was) no *man*,
63: 3. (there was) none with me: (lit. not *a man*)
66: 3. (is as if) he slew *a man;*
13. *As one* whom his mother comforteth,
Jer. 1:15. shall set *every one* his throne
2: 6. a land that no *man* passed through,
3: 1. If *a man* put away his wife, and she go from him, and become another *man's*,
4: 3. thus saith the Lord *to the men of* Judah
4. ye *men of* Judah

Jer. 4:29. not *a man* dwell therein.
5: 1. if ye can find *a man*,
8. *every one* neighed after his
6: 3. they shall feed *every one*
11. for even *the husband* with the wife
23. set in array *as men* for war
7: 5. between *a man* and his neighbour;
8: 6. no *man* repented him
9: 4(3). Take ye heed *every one*
5(4). *And* they will deceive *every one*
10(9). that *none* can pass (lit. without a *man*)
12(11). Who (is) *the* wise *man*,
10:23. (it is) not in *man* that walketh
11: 2. speak unto *the men of* Judah,
3. Cursed (be) *the man* that obeyeth not
8. but walked *every one* in the
9. is found *among the men*
12:11. because no *man* layeth (it) to heart.
15. *every man* to his heritage, *and every man* to
13:11. cleaveth to the loins of *a man*,
14. I will dash them *one* against another, (marg. *a man* against his brother)
14: 9. Why shouldest thou be *as a man*
15:10. thou hast borne me *a man of* strife *and a man of* contention to the whole earth
16:12. *every one* after the imagination
17:10. to give *every man* according
25. their princes, *the men of* Judah,
18:11. speak to *the men of* Judah,
— return ye now *every one* from his
12. *and* we will *every one* do the
19: 9. *and* they shall eat *every one* the flesh
20:15. Cursed (be) *the man*
16. let that *man* be as the cities
22: 7. *every one* with his weapons:
8. say *every man* to his neighhour,
28. this *man* Coniah a despised broken idol?
30. Write ye this *man* childless,
— no *man* of his seed shall prosper,
23: 9. I am *like a* drunken *man*,
14. none doth return (lit. not *a man*)
24. Can *any* hide himself
27. they tell *every man* to his neighbour,
30. *every one* from his neighbour.
34. punish that *man* and his house.
35. ye say *every one* to his neighbour, *and every one* to his brother,
36. *every man's* word shall be his burden;
25: 5. Turn ye again now *every one*
26. *one* with another,
26: 3. turn *every man* from his evil way,
11. This *man* (is) worthy to die;
16. This *man* (is) not worthy to die.
20. was also *a man* that prophesied
29:26. for *every man* (that is) mad,
32. he shall not have *a man*
31:30. *every one* shall die for his own
34. teach no more *every man* his neighbour, *and every man* his brother,
32:19. to give *every one* according to his ways,
32. *and the men of* Judah,
33:17. David shall never want *a man*
18. *a man* before me to offer
34: 9. That *every man* should let his manservant, *and every man* his maidservant,
— none should serve (lit. not *a man*)
10. that *every one* should let his manservant, *and every one* his maidservant, go free,
14. let ye go *every man* his brother
15. *every man* to his neighbour;
16. *every man* his servant, *and every man* his
17. *every one* to his brother, and *every man* to
35: 4. the son of Igdaliah, *a man* of God,
13. tell *the men of* Judah
15. Return ye now *every man* from his evil
19. shall not want *a man* to stand
36: 3. return *every man* from his evil way;
7. return *every one* from his evil way:
16. were afraid both *one* and other,
19. *and* let no *man* know where
31. and upon *the men of* Judah, all the evil
37:10. rise up *every man* in his tent,
38: 4. let this *man* be put to death:
— this *man* seeketh not the welfare
7. *one of* the eunuchs which was
24. Let no *man* know of these words,
40:15. *and* no *man* shall know (it):

Jer. 41: 4. *and* no *man* knew (it),
5. from Samaria, (even) fourscore *men*,
44: 7. from you *man* and woman,
26. in the mouth of any *man*
27. all *the men of* Judah that (are)
46: 16. *one* fell upon another:
49: 5. ye shall be driven out *every man*
18. no *man* shall abide there,
33. there shall no *man* abide there,
50: 16. shall turn *every one* to his people, *and* they shall flee *every one*
40. (so) shall no *man* abide there,
42. *like a man* to the battle,
51: 6. deliver *every man* his soul:
9. go *every one* into his own country:
22. *man* and woman;
43. a land wherein no *man* dwelleth,
45. deliver ye *every man* his soul
52: 25. threescore *men* of the people
Lam. 3: 33. nor grieve the children of *men*.
Eze. 1: 9. went *every one* straight forward.
11. (wings) *of every one* (were) joined *one to another*,
12. *And* they went *every one* straight forward:
23. *every one had* two, which covered on this side, *and every one had* two,
3: 26. shalt not be to them a reprover: (lit. *for a man* reproving)
4: 17. be astonied *one* with another,
7: 13. neither (lit. *and* not) shall *any*
16. *every one* for his iniquity.
8: 11. stood before them seventy *men*
— *with every man* his censer,
12. *every man* in the chambers of his
16. about five and twenty *men*,
9: 1. *even every man* (with) his destroying
2. *and every man* a slaughter weapon
— *and* one *man* among them (was)
3. he called to *the man* clothed
6. but come not near any *man*
11. *the man* clothed with linen,
10: 2. he spake unto *the man*
3. when *the man* went in;
6. commanded *the man* clothed
22. they went *every one* straight forward.
11: 1. five and twenty *men*;
14: 4. *Every man* of the house of (lit. *man, man*)
7. *every one* of the house of (lit. *man, man*)
8. I will set my face *against* that *man*,
16: 32. strangers instead of *her husband!*
45. that lotheth *her husband*
18: 5. *But* if *a man* be just,
7. *And* hath not oppressed *any*,
8. true judgment between *man and man*,
16. *Neither* hath oppressed *any*,
30. *every one* according to his ways,
20: 7. Cast ye away *every man*
8. they did not *every man* cast
39. Go ye, serve ye *every one* his idols,
22: 6. *every one* were in thee
11. *And one* hath committed abomination (marg. *every one*)
— *and another* hath lewdly defiled (marg. *every one*)
— *and another* in thee hath humbled
30. I sought for *a man* among them,
24: 23. mourn *one* toward another.
32: 10. *every man* for his own life,
33: 2. take *a man* of their coasts,
20. I will judge you *every one*
26. *and* ye defile *every one* his
30. *every one* to his brother,
38: 21. *every man*'s sword shall be against
39: 20. and with all *men of* war,
40: 3. behold, (there was) *a man*,
4. *the man* said unto me,
5. in *the man*'s hand a measuring reed
43: 6. *and the man* stood by me.
44: 2. *and* no *man* shall enter in
25. that hath had no *husband*, (lit. that hath not been *to a man*)
45: 20. *for every one* that erreth,
46: 16. give a gift *unto any* of his sons,
18. *every man* from his possession.
47: 3. *the man* that had the line
14. *one* as well as another:
Dan. 9: 7. *to the men of* Judah,
21. *even the man* Gabriel,
Dan 10: 5. *a* certain *man* clothed in linen,
11. O Daniel, *a man* greatly beloved,
19. *O man* greatly beloved,
12: 6. said *to the man* clothed in linen,
7. I heard *the man* clothed in linen,
Hos. 2: 2(4). my wife, neither (am) I *her husband*:
7(9). will go and return to *my* first *husband*;
10(12). *and* none shall deliver her (lit. *and* not *a man*)
16(18). shalt call me *Ishi* (i. e. *my husband*);
3: 3. thou shalt not be *for* (another) *man*:
4: 4. Yet let no *man* strive, nor reprove *another*.
6: 9. as troops of robbers wait for *a man*,
9: 7. (is) a fool, the spiritual *man* (is) mad,
11: 9. for I (am) God, and not *man*;
Joel 2: 7. *and* they shall march *every one* on his
8. *Neither* shall *one* thrust another;
Am. 2: 7. *and a man* and his father will go
5: 19. As if *a man* did flee from a lion,
Obad. 9. *every one* of the mount of Esau
Jon. 1: 5. cried *every man* unto his god,
7. they said *every one* to his fellow,
14. not perish for this *man*'s life,
3: 8. let them turn *every one*
Mic. 2: 2. *even a man* and his heritage.
11. If *a man* walking in the spirit
4: 4. sit *every man* under his vine
5. *every one* in the name of his god,
5: 7(6). that tarrieth not *for man*,
6: 10. (marg.) is there yet unto *every man* an
7: 2. they hunt *every man* his brother
6. *a man*'s enemies (are) the
Zep. 2: 11. *every one* from his place,
3: 6. so that there is no *man*,
Hag. 1: 9. ye run *every man* unto his own
2: 12. If *one* bear holy flesh
22. *every one* by the sword of his
Zec. 1: 8. *a man* riding upon a red horse,
10. *the man* that stood among
21(2:4). so that no *man* did lift up
2: 1(5). *a man* with a measuring line
3: 10. call *every man* his neighbour
4: 1. *as a man* that is wakened
6: 12. *the man* whose name (is) The BRANCH;
7: 9. *every man* to his brother:
10. let none of you imagine (lit. *a man* not)
8: 4. *and every man* with his staff
10. *every one* against his neighbour.
16. Speak ye *every man* the truth
17. *And* let none of you imagine evil (lit. *and a man*—not)
23. *him that is* a Jew, (lit. a Jewish *man*)
10: 1. *to every one* grass in the field.
11: 6. *every one* into his neighbour's hand,
13: 3. when *any* shall yet prophesy,
4. *every one* of his vision,
5. I (am) an husband*man*;
14: 13. *every one* on the hand of his neighbour,
Mal. 2: 10. why do we deal treacherously *every man*
12. The Lord will cut off *the man*
3: 16. spake often *one* to another:
17. as *a man* spareth his own son

אִישׁ [*eesh*]. 377

* HITHPALEL.—*Imperative.* *

Isa. 46: 8. *and shew yourselves men*:

אִישׁוֹן *ee-shōhn'*, m. 380

Deu 32: 10. kept him *as the apple of* his eye.
Ps. 17: 8. Keep me *as the apple* of the eye, (lit. *as the apple*, the daughter of, &c.)
Pro. 7: 2. my law *as the apple of* thine eye.
9. *in the black* and dark night:
20: 20. (קרי) be put out *in obscure* darkness.

אִיתוֹן *ee-thōhn'*, m. See 2978

Eze. 40: 15. (קרי) the gate of *the entrance*

אִיתַי *ee-thahy'*, part. Ch. 383

Ezr. 4: 16. thou *shalt have* no portion on this side (lit. *there shall be* to thee)

Ezr. 5:17. whether *it be* (so), that a decree
Dan. 2:10. *There is* not a man upon the earth
11. *there is* none other that can shew it
— whose dwelling *is* not with flesh.
26. *Art thou* able to make known
28. *there is* a God in heaven that
30. wisdom that I *have* (lit. *is* in me)
3:12. *There are* certain Jews
14. *do* not *ye* serve my gods,
15. Now if *ye be* ready that at what
17. our God whom we serve *is* able
18. *we will not* serve thy gods,
25. and they *have* no hurt; (marg. *there is* no hurt in them)
29. *there is* no other God that can
4:35(32). and none *can* stay his hand,
5:11. *There is* a man in thy kingdom,

---

386 **אֵיתָן & אֵתָן** *ēh-thāhn'*, m.

Gen49:24. But his bow abode *in strength*,
Exo.14:27. the sea returned *to his strength*
Nu. 24:21. *Strong* is thy dwellingplace,
Deu21: 4. the heifer unto a *rough* valley,
1 K. 8: 2. at the feast in the month *Ethanim*,
Job. 12:19. *and* overthroweth *the mighty*.
33.19. multitude of his bones with *strong* (pain):
Psa.74:15. driedst up *mighty* rivers. (marg. rivers of *strength*)
Pro.13:15. the way of transgressors (is) *hard*.
Jer. 5:15. it (is) a *mighty* nation,
49:19. against the habitation of *the strong*:
50:44. unto the habitation of *the strong*:
Am. 5:24. righteousness as a *mighty* stream.
Mic. 6: 2. *and* ye *strong* foundations of the earth:

---

389 **אַךְ** *ăcḥ*, part.

Gen. 7:23. the earth: and Noah *only* remained
9: 4. *But* flesh with the life thereof, (which is)
18:32. and I will speak *yet but* this once:
26: 9. Behold, *of a surety* she (is) thy wife:
27:30. and Jacob was *yet* scarce gone out from
29:14. *Surely* thou (art) my bone and my flesh.
Ex. 12:15. *even* the first day ye shall put away leaven
16. in them, *save* (that) which every man
21:21. *Notwithstanding*, if he continue a day
31:13. *Verily* my sabbaths ye shall keep:
Lev.11: 4. *Nevertheless* these shall ye not eat
23:27. *Also* on the tenth (day) of this seventh
Jud. 7:19. *and* they had *but* newly set the watch:
1 Sa.8: 9. hearken unto their voice: *howbeit* yet
21: 4(5). have kept themselves *at least* from
Ps. 37: 8. fret not thyself *in any wise* to do evil.
Jer. 10:19. but I said, *Truly* this (is) a grief,
Lam. 2:16. *certainly* this (is) the day that we looked
&c. &c. &c.

It occurs three times וְאַךְ:—

Gen. 9: 5. *And surely* your blood of your lives will I
Nu. 22:20. *but yet* the word which I shall say unto
Jos. 22:19. *Notwithstanding*, if the land of your

And once כִּי אַךְ:—

2 K. 5: 7. leprosy? *wherefore* consider, I pray you,

---

391 **אַכְזָב** *ăcḥ-zāhv'*, adj.

Jer. 15:18. wilt thou be altogether unto me as *a liar*,
Mic. 1:14. *a lie* to the kings of Israel.

---

393 **אַכְזָר** *ăcḥ-zāhr'*, adj.

Deu32:33. the *cruel* venom of asps.
Job 30:21. Thou art become *cruel*
41:10(2). None (is so) *fierce* that dare
Lam 4: 3. daughter of my people (is become) *cruel*,

---

394 **אַכְזָרִי** *ăcḥ-zāh-ree'*, adj.

Pro. 5: 9. and thy years *unto the cruel*:
11:17. (he that is) *cruel* troubleth his own flesh.
Pro.12:10. mercies of the wicked (are) *cruel*.
17:11. a *cruel* messenger shall be sent
Isa. 13: 9. the day of the Lord cometh, *cruel*
Jer. 6:23. they (are) *cruel*, and have no mercy;
30:14. the chastisement of *a cruel one*,
50:42. they (are) *cruel*, and will not shew mercy.

אַכְזְרִיּוּת *ăcḥ-z'reey-yooth,'* f. 395

Pro.27: 4. Wrath (is) *cruel*, (marg. *cruelty*)

אֲכִילָה *ăchee-lāh'*, f. 396

1K. 19: 8. and went in the strength of that *meat*

אָכַל *āh-chāl'*. 398

* KAL.—*Preterite.* *

Gen 3:11. *Hast thou eaten* of the tree,
18. *and thou shalt eat* the herb of the field;
22. take also of the tree of life, *and eat*,
14:24. that which the young men *have eaten*,
27:10. *that he may eat*, and that he may
31:38. the rams of thy flock *have I* not *eaten*.
40. in the day the drought *consumed me*,
37:20, 33. evil beast *hath devoured him:*
40:19. *and* the birds *shall eat* thy flesh
47:22. *and did eat* their portion which
Ex. 10: 5. *and they shall eat* the residue
— *and shall eat* every tree which groweth
12: 8. *And they shall eat* the flesh
11. *and ye shall eat* it in haste:
16:35. the children of Israel *did eat* manna
— *they did eat* manna, until
23:11. *that* the poor of thy people *may eat:*
29:32. *And* Aaron and his sons *shall eat*
33. *And they shall eat* those things
34:15. *and thou eat* of his sacrifice;
28. *he did* neither *eat* bread,
Lev. 7:21. *and eat* of the flesh of the sacrifice
10:13. *And ye shall eat* it in the holy place,
17. Wherefore *have ye* not *eaten*
19. *and* (if) *I had eaten* the sin offering
24: 9. *and they shall eat* it in the holy place:
25:19. *and ye shall eat* your fill,
22. *and eat* (yet) of old fruit
26: 5. *and ye shall eat* your bread
10. *And ye shall eat* old store,
16. *for* your enemies *shall eat it.*
26. *and ye shall eat*, and not be satisfied.
29. *And ye shall eat* the flesh of your sons,
38. *and* the land of your enemies *shall eat* you
Nu.11:18. *and ye shall eat* flesh:
— give you flesh, *and ye shall eat.*
21. *that they may eat* a whole month.
18:31. *And ye shall eat* it in every place,
21:28. *it hath consumed* Ar of Moab,
Deu 2: 6. for money, *that ye may eat;*
28. meat for money, *that I may eat;*
6:11. *when thou shalt have eaten*
7:16. *And thou shalt consume* all the people
8:10. *When thou hast eaten* and art full,
9: 9. *I* neither *did eat* bread
18. *I did* neither *eat* bread, nor drink
11:15. *that thou mayest eat* and be full.
12: 7. *And* there *ye shall eat*
15. thou mayest kill *and eat* flesh
21. *and thou shalt eat* in thy gates
14:21. in thy gates, *that he may eat it;*
23. *And thou shalt eat* before the Lord
26. *and thou shalt eat* there before the Lord
29. *and shall eat* and be satisfied;
16: 7. And thou shalt roast *and eat* (it)
20:14. *and thou shalt eat* the spoil
23:24(25). *then thou mayest eat* grapes
26:12. *that they may eat* within thy gates,
14. *I have* not *eaten* thereof
27: 7. *and shalt eat* there, and rejoice
28:51. *And he shall eat* the fruit
53. *And thou shalt eat* the fruit
29: 6(5). *Ye have* not *eaten* bread,
31:20. *and they shall have eaten*
Ruth 2:14. *and eat* of the bread,

1Sa. 9:19. *for ye shall eat* with me to day,
14:30. if haply the people *had eaten* freely
34. slay (them) here, *and eat;*
20:34. *did eat* no meat the second day
28:20 & 30:12. for *he had eaten* no bread
2Sa. 9:10. *that* thy master's son may have food *to eat* (lit. *and he may eat it*)
13: 5. that I may see (it), *and eat* (it)
18: 8. than the sword *devoured.*
19:42(43). *have we eaten* at all of the king's
1K. 13:28. the lion *had* not *eaten* the carcase,
17:12. *that we may eat it,* and die.
21: 4. and *would eat* no bread.
2K. 23: 9. *but they did eat* of the unleavened bread
25:29. *and he did eat* bread continually before
2Ch 30:18. yet *did they eat* the passover
Ezra 9:12. *and eat* the good of the land,
10: 6. *he did eat* no bread,
Neh. 5:14. *have* not *eaten* the bread
Job 13:28. as a garment that is moth *eaten.* (lit. the moth *hath eaten it*)
15:34. and fire *shall consume* the tabernacles
21:25. never *eateth* with pleasure.
22:20. the remnant of them the fire *consumeth.*
31:17. the fatherless *hath* not *eaten* thereof;
39. If *I have eaten* the fruits thereof
Ps. 14: 4. eat up my people (as) *they eat* bread,
22:29(30). upon earth *shall eat* and worship
53: 4(5). (as) *they eat* bread:
69: 9(10). of thine house *hath eaten me up;*
78:25. Man *did eat* angels' food:
63. The fire *consumed* their young men;
79: 7. For *they have devoured* Jacob,
102: 9(10). For *I have eaten* ashes like bread,
Pro. 23: 8. The morsel (which) *thou hast eaten* shalt
30:20. *she eateth,* and wipeth her mouth,
Cant 5: 1. *I have eaten* my honeycomb
Isa. 10:17. and it shall burn *and devour*
24: 6. *hath* the curse *devoured* the earth,
65:21. *and eat* the fruit of them.
Jer. 2:30. your own sword *hath devoured*
3:24. shame *hath devoured* the labour
5:14. *and it shall devour them.*
17. *And they shall eat up* thine harvest,
10:25. for *they have eaten up* Jacob, *and devoured him,*
17:27. *and it shall devour* the palaces
21:14. *and it shall devour* all things
22:15. *did* not thy father *eat* and drink,
31:29. The fathers *have eaten* a sour grape,
46:10. *and* the sword *shall devour,*
14. for the sword *shall devour*
49:27. *and it shall consume* the palaces
50: 7. All that found them *have devoured them:*
17. king of Assyria *hath devoured him;*
32. *and it shall devour* all round
51:34. the king of Babylon *hath devoured me,*
52:33. *and he did* continually *eat* bread
Lam 2: 3. (which) *devoureth* round about.
Eze. 4:14. *have* I not *eaten* of that
16. *and they shall eat* bread by weight,
15: 4. the fire *devoureth* both the ends
5. when the fire *hath devoured it,*
16:13. *thou didst eat* fine flour,
18: 6. *hath* not *eaten* upon the mountains,
11. *hath eaten* upon the mountains,
15. *hath* not *eaten* upon the mountains,
19: 3. to catch the prey; *it devoured* men.
6. to catch the prey, (and) *devoured* men.
12. the fire *consumed them.*
14. (which) *hath devoured* her fruit,
20:47(21:3). *and it shall devour* every green
22: 9. in thee *they eat* upon the mountains:
25. *they have devoured* souls;
28:18. *it shall devour thee,*
39:17. *that ye may eat* flesh,
19. *And ye shall eat* fat till ye
Dan 10: 3. *I ate* no pleasant bread,
Hos. 2:12(14). *and* the beasts of the field *shall eat them.*
4:10. *For they shall eat,* and not have
7: 7. *and have devoured* their judges;
9. Strangers *have devoured* his strength,
8:14. *and it shall devour* the palaces
10:13. *ye have eaten* the fruit of lies:
11: 6. *and devour* (them),
Joel 1: 4. *hath* the locust *eaten;*
— *hath* the cankerworm *eaten;*
— *hath* the caterpiller *eaten.*
19, 20. the fire *hath devoured* the pastures
2: 3. A fire *devoureth* before them:
25. that the locust *hath eaten,*
26. *And ye shall eat* in plenty,
Am. 1: 4, 12. *which shall devour* the palaces of
7, 10. which *shall devour* the palaces
14. *and it shall devour* the palaces thereof,
2: 2, 5. *and it shall devour* the palaces of
5: 6. in the house of Joseph, *and devour* (it),
7: 4. *and did eat up* a part.
9:14. *and eat* the fruit of them.
Obad. 18. *and devour them;*
Mic. 3: 3. also *eat* the flesh of my people,
Nah. 3:13. the fire *shall devour* thy bars.
Zec. 9:15. *and they shall devour,* and subdue
12: 6. *and they shall devour* all the people

KAL.—*Infinitive.*

Gen. 2:16. every tree of the garden thou mayest *freely* eat: (marg. *eating* thou shalt eat)
17. the day that *thou eatest* thereof
3: 5. in the day *ye eat* thereof,
11. thee that thou *shouldest* not *eat?*
24:33. set (meat) before him *to eat:*
28:20. will give me bread *to eat,*
31:15. hath *quite* devoured also our money. (lit. hath eaten even *by eating*)
54. called his brethren *to eat*
37:25. they sat down *to eat* bread:
43: 2. *when they had eaten* up the corn
32. might not *eat* bread with the
47:24. *and for food* for your little ones.
Ex. 16: 3. *when we did eat* bread to the full;
8. in the evening flesh *to eat,*
18:12. *to eat* bread with Moses' father in law
32: 6. the people sat down *to eat*
Lev. 7:24. *but* ye shall *in no wise* eat of it. (lit. *but eating* ye shall not eat)
10:18. ye should *indeed* have eaten it
22:16. *when they eat* their holy things:
25: 7. the increase thereof be *meat.* (lit. *to eat*)
Nu. 15:19. *when ye eat* of the bread of the land,
26:10. *what time* the fire *devoured*
Deu 12:17. Thou mayest not *eat* within thy gates
20. thy soul longeth *to eat* flesh;
23. be sure that thou *eat* not the blood:
31:17. shall be *devoured,* (lit. be *for devouring*
Jos. 5:12. *after they had eaten* of the old corn
Jud. 14: 9. went on *eating,* and came to his father
Ruth 3: 3. until he shall have done *eating*
1 Sa. 1: 9. rose up after *they had eaten*
2:36. *that I may eat* a piece of bread.
9:13. he go up to the high place *to eat:*
14:30. if haply the people had eaten *freely*
33. *in that they eat* with the blood.
34. sin not against the Lord *in eating*
20: 5. to sit with the king *at meat:*
24. the king sat him down *to eat* meat.
2 Sa. 11:11. *to eat* and to drink,
13: 9. but he refused *to eat.*
11. brought (them) unto him *to eat,*
16: 2. for the young men *to eat;*
17:29. *to eat:* for they said, The people
18: 8. the wood devoured more (marg. multiplied *to devour*)
19:42(43). have we eaten *at all* of the king's
1K. 1:41. as they had made an end of *eating.*
13:23. it came to pass, after *he had eaten*
18:42. Ahab went up *to eat* and to drink.
2 K. 4: 8. she constrained him *to eat*
— he turned in thither *to eat* bread.
40. they poured out for the men *to eat.*
— *as they were eating* of the pottage,
— they could not *eat* (thereof).
43. *They shall eat,* and shall leave
18:27. *that they may eat* their own dung,
19:29. *Ye shall eat* this year
2 Ch. 7:13. I command the locusts *to devour* the land,
31:10. we have had enough *to eat,*
Neh. 8:12. the people went their way *to eat,*
9:36. *to eat* the fruit thereof
Job 1: 4. *to eat* and to drink with them.
34: 3. the mouth tasteth *meat.*
Ps. 27: 2. came upon me *to eat* up my flesh,

Ps. 59:15(16). wander up and down *for meat*, (marg. *to eat*)
78:24. down manna upon them *to eat*,
102: 4(5). so that I forget *to eat* my bread.
Pro. 25:27. not good *to eat* much honey:
30:14. *to devour* the poor
Ecc. 5:18(17). comely (for one) *to eat* and to drink,
19(18). hath given him power *to eat*
6: 2. God giveth him not power *to eat*
8:15. than *to eat*, and to drink,
Isa. 5:24. *as* the fire *devoureth* the stubble,
21: 5. watch in the watchtower, *eat*, drink:
22:13. *eating* flesh, and drinking wine: *let us eat*
23:18. *to eat* sufficiently, and for durable clothing.
36:12. *that they may eat* their own dung,
37:30. *Ye shall eat* (this) year
56: 9. ye beasts of the field, come *to devour*,
Jer. 2: 7. *to eat* the fruit thereof
15: 3. *to devour* and destroy.
16: 8. to sit with them *to eat*
Eze. 16:20. thou sacrificed unto them *to be devoured*, (marg. *to devour*)
33:27. will I give to the beasts *to be devoured*, (marg. *to devour him*)
44: 3. he shall sit in it *to eat* bread
Joel 2:26. ye shall eat *in plenty*,
Am. 7: 2. when they had made an end of *eating*
Mic. 7: 1. (there is) no cluster *to eat*:
Hab. 1: 8. eagle (that) hasteth to *eat*.
3:14. as *to devour* the poor secretly.
Hag. 1: 6. *ye eat*, but ye have not enough;

KAL.—*Imperative.*

Gen27:19. sit *and eat* of my venison,
45:18. *and ye shall eat* the fat of the land.
Ex. 16:25. Moses said, *Eat that* to day;
Lev. 10:12. *and eat it* without leaven
1Sa. 9:24. set (it) before thee, (and) *eat*:
28:22. *and eat*, that thou mayest have strength,
1K. 13:15. Come home with me, *and eat*
18:41. Get thee up, *eat* and drink;
19: 5, 7. Arise (and) *eat*.
21: 7. arise, (and) *eat* bread,
2K. 18:31. *eat ye* every man of his own vine,
19:29. *and eat* the fruits thereof.
Neh. 8:10. *eat* the fat, and drink the sweet,
Pro. 23: 7. *Eat* and drink, saith he to thee;
24:13. My son, *eat* thou honey,
25:16. *eat* so much as is sufficient
Ecc. 9: 7. *eat* thy bread with joy,
Cant. 5: 1. *eat*, O friends; drink, yea,
Isa. 36:16. *and eat* ye every one of his vine,
37:30. *and eat* the fruit thereof.
55: 1. come ye, buy, *and eat*;
2. *and eat ye* (that which is) good,
Jer. 7:21. your sacrifices, *and eat* flesh.
29: 5. *and eat* the fruit of them;
28. plant gardens, *and eat* the fruit
Eze. 2: 8. open thy mouth, *and eat* that
3: 1. Son of man, *eat* that thou findest; *eat* this roll, and go speak
Am. 7:12. *and* there *eat* bread, and prophesy there:

KAL.—*Future.*

Gen. 2:16. *thou mayest* freely *eat*: (marg. eating *thou shalt eat*)
17. *thou shalt* not *eat* of it:
3: 1. *Ye shall* not *eat* of every tree
2. *We may eat* of the fruit
3. God hath said, *Ye shall* not *eat* of it,
6. *and did eat*, and gave also unto her husband with her; *and he did eat*.
12. of the tree, *and I did eat*.
13. beguiled me, *and I did eat*.
14. dust *shalt thou eat* all the days
17. *and hast eaten* of the tree, of which I commanded thee, saying, *Thou shalt* not *eat*
— in sorrow *shalt thou eat* (of) *it*
19. In the sweat of thy face *shalt thou eat*
9: 4. *shall ye* not *eat*.
18: 8. under the tree, *and they did eat*.
19: 3. unleavened bread, *and they did eat*.
24:33. but he said, *I will* not *eat*,
54. *And they did eat* and drink,
25:34. *and he did eat* and drink,
26:30. made them a feast, *and they did eat*
27: 4. bring (it) to me, *that I may eat*;
7. savoury meat, *that I may eat*,
Gen27:25. *and I will eat* of my son's venison,
— near to him, *and he did eat*:
31. *and eat* of his son's venison,
33. *and I have eaten* of all before thou
31:15. *and hath* quite *devoured* also our money.
46. *and they did eat* there upon the heap.
54. *and they did eat* bread,
32:32(33). the children of Israel *eat* not
41: 4, 20. *And* the...kine *did eat up*
43:16. (these) men *shall dine* with me (marg. *eat*)
25. they heard that *they should eat*
49:27. in the morning *he shall devour*
Ex. 2:20. call him, *that he may eat* bread.
10:12. *and eat* every herb of the land,
15. *and they did eat* every herb
12: 7. wherein *they shall eat* it.
8. with bitter (herbs) *they shall eat it*.
9. *Eat* not of it raw, nor sodden at all
11. And thus shall ye *eat* it;
15. Seven days *shall ye eat* unleavened
18. *ye shall eat* unleavened bread,
20. *Ye shall eat* nothing leavened;
— *shall ye eat* unleavened bread.
43. There *shall* no stranger *eat* thereof:
44. then *shall he eat* thereof.
45. an hired servant *shall* not *eat* thereof.
48. no uncircumcised person *shall eat* thereof.
13: 6. Seven days *thou shalt eat*
15: 7. *consumed them* as stubble.
16:12. At even *ye shall eat* flesh,
22:31(30). neither *shall ye eat* (any) flesh
23:11. the beasts of the field *shall eat*.
15. *thou shalt eat* unleavened bread
24:11. they saw God, *and did eat* and drink.
29:33. but a stranger *shall* not *eat* (thereof),
34:18. Seven days *thou shalt eat*
Lev. 3:17. that *ye eat* neither fat nor blood.
6:10(3). which the fire *hath consumed*
16(9). *shall* Aaron and his sons *eat*:
—(–) the congregation *they shall eat it*.
18(11). the children of Aaron *shall eat of it*
26(19). that offereth it for sin *shall eat it*:
29(22). the priests *shall eat* thereof:
7: 6. the priests *shall eat thereof*:
19. all that be clean *shall eat* thereof.
20. But the soul that *eateth* (of) the flesh
23. *Ye shall eat* no manner of fat,
24. but *ye shall* in no wise *eat of it*.
26. *ye shall eat* no manner of blood,
27. Whatsoever soul (it be) that *eateth*
8:31. and there *eat* it with the bread
— Aaron and his sons *shall eat it*.
9:24. *and consumed* upon the altar
10: 2. *and devoured* them, and they died
14. breast and heave shoulder *shall ye eat*
18. *ye should* indeed *have eaten* it
11: 2. which *ye shall eat* among all the beasts
3. among the beasts, that *shall ye eat*.
4. these *shall ye* not *eat*
8. Of their flesh *shall ye* not *eat*,
9. These *shall ye eat* of all that
— and in the rivers, them *shall ye eat*.
11. *ye shall* not *eat* of their flesh,
21. Yet these *may ye eat*
22. these of them *ye may eat*;
42. *them ye shall* not *eat*;
17:10. that *eateth* any manner of blood;
12. No soul of you *shall eat* blood, neither *shall* any stranger...among you *eat* blood.
14. *Ye shall eat* the blood of no
15. every soul that *eateth* that
19:25. in the fifth year *shall ye eat*
26. *Ye shall* not *eat* (any thing)
21:22. *He shall eat* the bread of his God,
22: 4. *he shall* not *eat* of the holy things,
6. *shall* not *eat* of the holy things,
7. *shall* afterward *eat* of the holy things;
8. *he shall* not *eat* to defile himself
10. There shall no stranger *eat*
— shall not *eat* (of) the holy thing.
11. *he shall eat* of it,
— *they shall eat* of his meat.
12. *she may* not *eat* of an offering
13. *she shall eat* of her father's meat: but there *shall* no stranger *eat* thereof.
14. if a man *eat* (of) the holy thing

Lev.23: 6. seven days *ye must eat* unleavened
14. And *ye shall eat* neither bread,
25:12. *ye shall eat* the increase thereof
20. What *shall we eat* the seventh year?
22. *ye shall eat* (of) the old (store).
26:29. the flesh of your daughters *shall ye eat.*
Nu. 6: 3. nor *eat* moist grapes,
4. shall he *eat* nothing
9:11. *eat it* with unleavened bread
11: 1. *and consumed* (them that were)
5. We remember the fish, which *we did eat*
13. Give us flesh, *that we may eat.*
19. *Ye shall* not *eat* one day,
16:35. *and consumed* the two hundred
18:10. In the most holy (place) *shalt thou eat it;* every male *shall eat it:*
11. in thy house *shall eat* of it.
13. clean in thine house *shall eat* (of) it.
23:24. until he *eat* (of) the prey,
24: 8. *he shall eat up* the nations
25: 2. *and* the people *did eat,*
Deu.4:28. nor hear, nor *eat,* nor smell.
5:25 (22). this great fire *will consume us:*
8: 9. A land wherein *thou shalt eat* bread
12. Lest (when) *thou hast eaten*
12:15. the unclean and the clean *may eat thereof,*
16. Only *ye shall* not *eat* the blood;
18. But thou must *eat them* before
20. thou shalt say, *I will eat*
— *thou mayest eat* flesh,
22. *so thou shalt eat them:* the unclean and the clean *shall eat* (of) *them*
23. *thou mayest* not *eat* the life
24, 25. *Thou shalt* not *eat it;*
27. and *thou shalt eat* the flesh.
14: 3. *Thou shalt* not *eat* any
4. These (are) the beasts which *ye shall eat:*
6. among the beasts, that *ye shall eat.*
7. these *ye shall* not *eat*
8. *ye shall* not *eat* of their flesh,
9. These *ye shall eat* of all
— that have fins and scales *shall ye eat:*
10. not fins and scales *ye may* not *eat;*
11. (Of) all clean birds *ye shall eat.*
12. (are they) of which *ye shall* not *eat:*
20. (But of) all clean fowls *ye may eat.*
21. *Ye shall* not *eat* (of) any thing that
15:20. *Thou shalt eat it* before the Lord
22. *Thou shalt eat it* within thy gates:
23. *thou shalt* not *eat* the blood
16: 3. *Thou shalt eat* no leavened bread with it; seven days *shalt thou eat*
8. Six days *thou shalt eat*
18: 1. *they shall eat* the offerings of the Lord
8. *They shall have* like portions *to eat,*
20:19. for *thou mayest eat* of them,
28:31. and *thou shalt* not *eat* thereof:
33. *shall* a nation which thou knowest not *eat* up;
39. for the worms *shall eat them.*
55. his children whom he *shall eat:*
57. *she shall eat them* for want
32:13. *that he might eat* the increase of the fields;
22. *and shall consume* the earth (marg. *hath consumed*)
38. *did eat* the fat of their sacrifices,
42. my sword *shall devour* flesh;
Jos. 5:11. *And they did eat* of the old corn
12. *but they did eat* of the fruit
Jud. 6:21. *and consumed* the flesh
9:15. *and devour* the cedars of Lebanon.
20. *and devour* the men of Shechem,
— *and devour* Abimelech.
27. *and did eat* and drink,
13: 4. and *eat* not any unclean (thing):
7. neither *eat* any unclean (thing):
14. *She may* not *eat* of any (thing) that
— nor *eat* any unclean (thing):
16. *I will* not *eat* of thy bread·
14: 9. he gave them, *and they did eat:*
19: 4. *so they did eat* and drink,
6. they sat down, *and did eat*
8. *and they did eat* both of them.
21. *and did eat* and drink.
Ruth.2:14. *and she did eat,* and was sufficed,
3: 7. *when* Boaz *had eaten* and drunk,
1 Sa.1: 7. therefore she wept, and *did* not *eat.*

1 Sa.1: 8. and why *eatest thou* not?
18. the woman went her way, *and did eat,*
9:13. *will* not *eat* until he come,
— afterwards *they eat* that be bidden.
24. *So* Saul *did eat* with Samuel
14:24, 28. Cursed (be) the man that *eateth*
32. *and* the people *did eat* (them)
28:23. he refused, and said, *I will* not *eat.*
25. before his servants; *and they did eat.*
30:11. gave him bread, *and he did eat;*
12. *and when he had eaten,*
2 Sa.2:26. *Shall* the sword *devour* for ever?
9: 7. *thou shalt eat* bread at my table
10. Mephibosheth thy master's son *shall eat*
11:13. *And...he did eat* and drink
25. the sword *devoureth* one as well as
12: 3. *it did eat* of his own meat,
20. they set bread before him, *and he did eat*
21. thou didst rise *and eat* bread.
19:35(36). taste what *I eat* or what I drink?
22: 9. fire out of his mouth *devoured:*
1K.13: 8, 16. neither *will I eat* bread
9. *Eat* no bread, nor drink water,
17. *Thou shalt eat* no bread
18. *that he may eat* bread and drink water.
19. *and did eat* bread in his house,
22. *and hast eaten* bread and drunk water
— *Eat* no bread, and drink no water;
14:11 & 16:4. in the city *shall* the dogs *eat;*
— & —:- *shall* the fowls of the air *eat:*
17:15. *and* she, and he, and her house, *did eat*
18:38. *and consumed* the burnt sacrifice,
19: 6. *And he did eat* and drink,
8. he arose, *and did eat* and drink,
21. gave unto the people, *and they did eat.*
21:23. The dogs *shall eat* Jezebel
24. Ahab in the city the dogs *shall eat;*
— *shall* the fowls of the air *eat.*
2K. 1:10, 12. *and consume* thee and thy fifty.
—, — *and consumed* him and his fifty.
14. *and burnt up* the two captains
4:41. for the people, *that they may eat.*
42. Give unto the people, *that they may eat.*
43. Give the people, *that they may eat:*
44. before them, *and they did eat,*
6:22. *that they may eat* and drink,
23. *when they had eaten* and drunk,
28. *that we may eat him* to day, and *we will eat*
29. we boiled my son, *and did eat him:*
— Give thy son, *that we may eat him:*
7: 2, 19. but *shalt* not *eat* thereof.
8. *and did eat* and drink,
9:10. the dogs *shall eat* Jezebel
34. *he did eat* and drink,
36. portion of Jezreel *shall* dogs *eat*
1Ch.29:22. *And did eat* and drink before the Lord
2Ch. 7: 1. *and consumed* the burnt offering
30:22. *and they did eat* throughout
Ezra 2:63. *should* not *eat* of the most holy things,
6:21. to seek the Lord God of Israel, *did eat,*
Neh. 5: 2. *that we may eat,* and live.
7:65. *should* not *eat* of the most holy things,
9:25. *so they did eat,* and were filled,
Est. 4:16. neither *eat* nor drink three days,
Job 1:16. sheep, and the servants, *and consumed them;*
5: 5. the hungry *eateth up,*
18:13. *It shall devour* the strength
— *shall devour* his strength.
31: 8. *let* another *eat;*
12. a fire (that) *consumeth* to destruction,
17. *Or have eaten* my morsel
40:15. *he eateth* grass as an ox.
42:11. *and did eat* bread with him
Ps. 18: 8(9). fire out of his mouth *devoured:*
21: 9(10). *and* the fire *shall devour them.*
22:26(27). The meek *shall eat* and be satisfied:
50: 3. a fire *shall devour* before him,
13. *Will I eat* the flesh of bulls,
78:29. *So they did eat,* and were well filled:
45. flies among them, *which devoured them;*
105:35. *And did eat up* all the herbs in their land, *and devoured* the fruit of their
106:28. *and ate* the sacrifices of the dead.
128: 2. *thou shalt eat* the labour of thine
Pro. 1:31. *Therefore shall they eat* of the fruit of
13: 2. A man *shall eat* good by the
18:21. they that love it *shall eat* the fruit

Pro.27:18. the fig tree *shall eat* the fruit
30:17. *and* the young eagles *shall eat it.*
31:27. and *eateth* not the bread of
Ecc. 2:24. *that he should eat* and drink,
25. For who *can eat*, or who else
3:13. *that* every man *should eat* and drink,
5:12(11). whether *he eat* little or much:
17(16). All his days also *he eateth*
6: 2. but a stranger *eateth it:*
10:16. thy princes *eat* in the morning!
17. thy princes *eat* in due season,
Cant.4:16. *and eat* his pleasant fruits.
Isa. 1:19. *ye shall eat* the good of the land:
3:10. for *they shall eat* the fruit
4: 1. *We will eat* our own bread,
5:17. the fat ones *shall* strangers *eat.*
7:15. Butter and honey *shall he eat,*
22. *he shall eat* butter: for butter and honey *shall* every one *eat*
9:12(11). *and they shall devour* Israel
18(17). *it shall devour* the briers and thorns,
20(19). *and he shall eat* on the left
—(—). *they shall eat* every man
11: 7. the lion *shall eat* straw like the ox.
26:11. thine enemies *shall devour them.*
30:24. *shall eat* clean provender,
31: 8. not of a mean man, *shall devour him:*
33:11. your breath, (as) fire, *shall devour you.*
44:16. with part thereof *he eateth*
19. I have roasted flesh, and *eaten* (it):
50: 9. the moth *shall eat them up.*
51: 8. For the moth *shall eat them up*
— the worm *shall eat them* like wool:
61: 6. *ye shall eat* the riches of the Gentiles,
62: 9. have gathered it *shall eat it,*
65:13. Behold, my servants *shall eat,*
22. they shall not plant, and another *eat:*
25. the lion *shall eat* straw like the bullock:
Jer. 5:17. (which) thy sons and thy daughters *should eat: they shall eat up* thy flocks and thine herds: *they shall eat up* thy
8:16. *and have devoured* the land,
15:16. were found, *and I did eat them;*
19: 9. *they shall eat* every one
41: 1. *and* there *they did eat* bread together
48:45. *and shall devour* the corner of Moab,
Lam. 2:20. *Shall* the women *eat* their fruit,
4:11. *and it hath devoured* the foundations
Eze. 3: 3. *Then did I eat* (it);
4: 9. three hundred and ninety days *shalt thou eat thereof.*
10. thy meat which *thou shalt eat*
— from time to time *shalt thou eat it.*
12. *thou shalt eat it* (as) barley cakes,
13. Even thus *shall* the children of Israel *eat*
5:10. Therefore the fathers *shall eat* the sons
— the sons *shall eat* their fathers;
7:15. and pestilence *shall devour him.*
12:18. *eat* thy bread with quaking,
19. *They shall eat* their bread with
15: 7. and (another) fire *shall devour them;*
18: 2. The fathers *have eaten* sour grapes,
24:17. and *eat* not the bread of men.
22. nor *eat* the bread of men.
25: 4. *they shall eat* thy fruit,
33:25. *Ye eat* with the blood,
34: 3. *Ye eat* the fat, and ye clothe
28. *shall* the beast of the land *devour them;*
36:14. *thou shalt devour* men no more,
39:18. *Ye shall eat* the flesh of the mighty,
42: 5. were higher than these, (marg. *did eat* of these)
13. *shall eat* the most holy things:
44:29. *They shall eat* the meat offering,
31. The priests *shall* not *eat*
Dan 1:12. pulse *to eat*, (marg. *that we may eat*)
Hos. 4: 8. *They eat up* the sin of my people,
5: 7. now *shall* a month *devour them*
8:13. of mine offerings, and *eat* (it);
9: 3. *they shall eat* unclean (things)
13: 8. *and* there *will I devour them* like a lion:
Am. 4: 9. the palmerworm *devoured*
7: 4. *and it devoured* the great deep,
Mic. 6:14. *Thou shalt eat*, but not be satisfied;
Nah 2:13(14). the sword *shall devour* thy
3:15. There *shall* the fire *devour thee;*
— *it shall eat thee* up
Zec. 7: 6. when *ye did eat*, and when ye
Zec.11: 1. *that* the fire *may devour* thy cedars.
9. *let* the rest *eat* every one the flesh
16. *he shall eat* the flesh of the fat,

KAL.—*Participle.* Poel.

Gen 39: 6. save the bread which he *did eat.*
40:17. the birds *did eat* them
43:32. the Egyptians, *which did eat*
Ex. 12:15. whosoever *eateth* leavened bread
19. whosoever *eateth* that
24:17. like *devouring* fire on the top
Lev. 7:18. the soul *that eateth* of it shall bear
25. For whosoever *eateth* the fat
— even the soul *that eateth* (it) shall
11:40. *And he that eateth* of the carcase
14:47. *and he that eateth* in the house
17:10. against that soul *that eateth* blood,
14. whosoever *eateth it* shall be cut off.
19: 8. *Therefore* (every one) *that eateth it*
Nu. 13:32. *eateth up* the inhabitants thereof;
Deu. 4:24. the Lord thy God (is) a *consuming* fire,
9: 3. (as) a *consuming* fire he shall destroy
Jos. 24:13. which ye planted not *do* ye *eat.*
Jud.14:14. *Out of the eater* came forth meat,
1Sa.30:16. *eating* and drinking, and dancing,
2Sa. 9:11. *he shall eat* at my table,
13. for he *did eat* continually at the
19:28(29). *among them that did eat* at thine own
1K. 1:25. *they eat* and drink before him,
2: 7. *of those that eat* at thy table:
4:20. *eating* and drinking, and making merry.
18:19. *which eat* at Jezebel's table.
21: 5. that thou *eatest* no bread?
1Ch 12:39. *eating* and drinking:
Job 1:13,18. *eating* and drinking wine
Ps. 14: 4. *who eat up* my people
41: 9(10). *which did eat of* my bread,
53: 4(5). *who eat up* my people
106:20. the similitude of an ox *that eateth* grass.
127: 2. *to eat* the bread of sorrows:
Pro.13:25. The righteous *eateth* to the
Ecc. 4: 5. *and eateth* his own flesh.
5:11(10). they are increased *that eat them:*
Isa. 1: 7. strangers *devour* it in your presence,
29: 6. and the flame of *devouring* fire.
8. dreameth, and, behold, *he eateth;*
30:27. his tongue as a *devouring* fire:
30 (with) the flame of a *devouring* fire,
33:14. shall dwell with the *devouring* fire?
55:10. and bread *to the eater:*
59: 5. *he that eateth* of their eggs dieth,
65: 4. *which eat* swine's flesh,
66:17. *eating* swine's flesh,
Jer. 2: 3. all *that devour him* shall offend;
12:12. the sword of the Lord *shall devour*
30:16. Therefore all *they that devour thee*
31:30. every man *that eateth* the sour grape,
Lam. 4: 5. *They that did feed* delicately
Eze.36:13. Thou (land) *devourest up* men,
Dan. 1:13. *that eat* of the portion of the king's meat:
15. *which did eat* the portion of the king's
11:26. *Yea, they that feed* of the portion of his
Hos. 9: 4. all *that eat thereof*
Joel 2: 5. fire *that devoureth* the stubble,
Am. 6: 4. *and eat* the lambs out of the flock,
Nah. 3:12. fall into the mouth of *the eater.*
Zec. 7: 6. *did* not ye *eat*
Mal. 3:11. I will rebuke *the devourer*

* NIPHAL.—*Preterite.* *

Ex. 22: 6(5). or the field, *be consumed*

NIPHAL.—*Infinitive.*

Lev. 7:18. his peace offerings be eaten *at all*
19: 7. if it be eaten *at all* on the third day, (lit. *being eaten* be eaten)

NIPHAL.—*Future.*

Gen 6:21. unto thee of all food that *is eaten,*
Ex. 12:16. which every man *must eat,*
46. In one house shall it *be eaten;*
13: 3. *shall* no leavened bread *be eaten.*
7. Unleavened bread *shall be eaten*
21:28. his flesh *shall* not *be eaten;*
29:34. *it shall* not *be eaten,*
Lev. 6:16(9). unleavened bread shall *it be eaten*
23(16). *it shall* not *be eaten.*
26(19). in the holy place *shall it be eaten,*
30(23). no sin offering...*shall be eaten:*

Lev. 7: 6. *it shall be eaten* in the holy place:
15. *shall be eaten* the same day
16. *it shall be eaten* the same day
— the remainder of it *shall be eaten:*
18. his peace offerings *be eaten* at all
19. any unclean (thing) *shall* not *be eaten;*
11:13. *they shall* not *be eaten,*
34. Of all meat which *may be eaten,*
41. *it shall* not *be eaten.*
47. the beast that *may* not *be eaten.*
17:13. fowl that *may be eaten;*
19: 6. *It shall be eaten* the same day
7. if *it be eaten* at all on the
23. *it shall* not *be eaten* of.
22:30. same day it shall *be eaten*
Nu. 12:12. the flesh *is* half *consumed*
28:17. *shall* unleavened bread *be eaten.*
Deu12:22. the roebuck and the hart *is eaten,*
14:19. *they shall* not *be eaten.*
Job 6: 6. *Can* that which is unsavoury *be eaten*
Jer. 24: 2. which *could* not *be eaten,*
3. that cannot *be eaten,*
8. which *can*not *be eaten,*
29:17. that *cannot be eaten,*
30:16. they that devour thee *shall be devoured;*
Eze.23:25. thy residue shall *be devoured*
45:21. unleavened bread *shall be eaten.*
Zep. 1.18. *shall be devoured* by the fire
3: 8. *shall be devoured* with the fire
Zec. 9: 4. she *shall be devoured* with fire.

NIPHAL—*Participle.*

Lev.11:47. the beast *that may be eaten*

* PIEL.—*Future.* *

Job 20:26. a fire not blown *shall consume him;*

* PUAL.—*Preterite.* *

Neh 2: 3. the gates thereof *are consumed* with fire?
13. the gates thereof *were consumed* with fire.
Nah 1:10. *they shall be devoured* as stubble

PUAL.—*Future.*

Isa. 1:20. *ye shall be devoured* with the sword:

PUAL.—*Participle.*

Ex. 3: 2. the bush (*was*) not *consumed.*

* HIPHIL.—*Preterite.* *

Ex. 16:32. where*with I have fed* you
Ps. 80: 5(6). *Thou feedest them with* the bread
Isa. 49:26. *And I will feed* them that oppress thee *with*
58:14. *and feed thee with* the heritage of Jacob
Jer. 19: 9. *And I will cause them to eat*
Eze.16:19. (wherewith) *I fed thee,*

HIPHIL.—*Infinitive.*

Eze.21:28(33). *to consume* because of the glittering:

HIPHIL.—*Imperative.*

1K. 22:27. *and feed him with* bread of affliction
2Ch 18:26. *and feed him with* bread
Pro.25:21. *give him* bread *to eat;*

HIPHIL.—*Future.*

Nu. 11: 4, 18. Who *shall give us* flesh *to eat?*
Deu 8: 3. *and fed thee with* manna,
2Ch 28:15. *and gave them to eat* and to drink,
Ps. 81:16(17). *He should have fed them also* (lit. *fed him*)
Eze. 3: 2. *and he caused me to eat* that roll.
3. *cause* thy belly *to eat,*
Hos.11: 4. *I laid meat* unto them.

HIPHIL.—*Participle.*

Deu 8:16. *Who fed thee* in the wilderness *with* manna,
Jer. 9:15(14). *I will feed them,* (even) this people, *with*
23:15. I will *feed* them *with* wormwood,

---

399 אֲכַל *ăc̣hal,* Ch.

* P'AL.—*Preterite.* *

Dan 3: 8. *and accused* the Jews. (lit. *and ate* their pieces of the Jews)
6:24(25). those men which *had accused* Daniel,

P'AL.—*Imperative.*

Dan 7: 5. Arise, *devour* much flesh.

P'AL.—*Future.*

Dan 4:33(30). *did eat* grass as oxen,
7:23. *and shall devour* the whole earth,

P'AL.—*Participle.*

Dan 7: 7. *it devoured* and brake in pieces,
19. (which) *devoured,* brake in pieces,

אֹכֶל *ōh'-c̣hel,* m. 400

Gen14:11. all *their victuals,* and went
41:35. let them gather all *the food*
— let them keep *food* in the cities.
36. *that food* shall be for store
48. he gathered up all *the food*
— laid up *the food* in the cities: *the food of*
42: 7. From the land of Canaan to buy *food,*
10. but to buy *food* are thy servants come.
43: 2. Go again, buy us *a* little *food.*
4. we will go down and buy thee *food:*
20. at the first time to buy *food:*
22. in our hands to buy *food:*
44: 1. Fill the men's sacks (with) *food,*
25. Go again, (and) buy us *a* little *food.*
47:24. seed of the field, *and for your food,*
Ex. 12: 4 & 16:16, 18. every man according to *his eating*
16:21. every man according to *his eating:*
Lev.11:34. Of all *meat* which may be eaten,
25:37. nor lend him *thy victuals* for
Deu 2: 6. Ye shall buy *meat* of them
28. Thou shalt sell me *meat*
23:19(20). usury of money, usury of *victuals,*
Ruth 2:14. At *meal*time come thou hither,
Job 9:26. as the eagle (that) hasteth to *the prey.*
12:11. the mouth taste his *meat?*
20:21. There shall none *of his meat* be left;
36:31. he giveth *meat* in abundance.
38:41. they wander for lack of *meat.*
39:29. thence she seeketh *the prey,*
Ps. 78:18. by asking *meat* for their lust.
30. while *their meat* (was) yet
104:21. seek *their meat* from God.
27. give (them) *their meat* in due season.
107:18. abhorreth all manner of *meat;*
145:15. thou givest them *their meat*
Pro.13:23. Much *food* (is in) the tillage
Lam 1:11. given their pleasant things *for meat*
19. while they sought their *meat*
Joel 1:16. Is not *the meat* cut off
Hab 3:17. the fields shall yield no *meat;*
Mal. 1:12. *his meat,* (is) contemptible.

אָכְלָה *oc̣h-lāh',* f. 402

Gen 1:29. to you it shall be *for meat.*
30. every green herb *for meat:*
6:21. and it shall be *for food* for thee,
9: 3. shall be *meat* for you;
Ex. 16:15. the Lord hath given you *to eat.*
Lev.11:39. of which ye *may eat,* (lit. which is to you *for food*)
25: 6. the sabbath of the land shall be *meat*
Jer. 12: 9. all the beasts of the field, come *to devour.*
Eze.15: 4. it is cast into the fire *for fuel;*
6. I have given to the fire *for fuel,*
21:32(37). Thou shalt be *for fuel*
23:37. to pass for them through (the fire), *to devour*
29: 5. I have given thee *for meat*
34: 5. became *meat* to all the beasts
8. my flock became *meat* to every beast
10. that they may not be *meat*
35:12. they are given us *to consume.*
39: 4. the beasts of the field *to be devoured.* (marg. *to devour*)

אָכֵן *āh-c̣hēhn',* part. 403

Gen28:16. *Surely* the Lord is in this place;
Ex. 2:14. *Surely* this thing is known.
1Sa.15:32. *Surely* the bitterness of death is past.
1K. 11: 2. *surely* they will turn away
Job.32: 8. *But* (there is) a spirit in man:
Ps. 31:22(23). *nevertheless* thou heardest the voice

Ps. 66:19. (But) *verily* God hath heard (me);
82: 7. *But* ye shall die like men,
Isa. 40: 7. *surely* the people (is) grass.
45:15. *Verily* thou (art) a God
49: 4. *surely* my judgment (is) with the Lord,
53: 4. *Surely* he hath borne our griefs,
Jer. 3:20. *Surely* (as) a wife treacherously
23. *Truly* in vain (is salvation hoped for)
— *truly* in the Lord our God
4:10. *surely* thou hast greatly deceived
8: 8. Lo, *certainly* in vain made he (it);
Zep. 3: 7. *but* they rose early, (and) corrupted all

---

404 אָכַף *āh-chaph'.*

* KAL.—*Preterite.* *

Pro.16:26. for his mouth *craveth* it of him. (marg. *boweth* unto him)

---

405 אֶכֶף [*eh'-cheph*] m.

Job 33: 7. *neither* shall *my hand* be heavy

---

406 אִכָּר *ik-kāhr'*, m.

2Ch.26:10. *husbandmen* (also), and vine dressers
Isa. 61: 5. of the alien (shall be) *your plowmen*
Jer. 14: 4. *the plowmen* were ashamed,
31:24. cities thereof together, *husbandmen*,
51:23. will I break in pieces *the husbandman*
Joel 1:11. Be ye ashamed, *O ye husbandmen;*
Am. 5:16. they shall call *the husbandman*

---

408 אַל *al*, adv.

Gen 13: 8. Let there be *no* strife, I pray thee
19: 8. only unto these men do *nothing;*
Ex. 34: 3. *neither* let any man be seen throughout all the mount; *neither* let the flocks
Jos. 22:19. against the Lord, *nor* rebel against us,
Jud.19:23. and said unto them, *Nay*, my brethren,
1Sa.27:10. Whither have ye made a road to day? (marg. Did you *not* make a road, &c.)
2 K. 9:15. let *none* go forth (nor) escape out
Ps. 57 & 58 & 59 & 75: [title] (1). To the chief Musician, *Al*-taschith (lit. destroy *not*),
Pro.17:12. *rather than* a fool (lit. and *not*)
Dan. 9:19. defer *not*, for thine own sake, O my God: &c. &c.

Once לְאַל

Job 24:25. make my speech *nothing worth* (lit. *of nought*)?

With לְעֹלָם.

Psa. 31: 1 (2). let me *never* be ashamed: deliver me
71: 1. let me *never* be put to confusion.

---

409 אַל *al*, adv. Ch.

Dan. 2:24. Destroy *not* the wise (men) of Babylon:
4:19 (16). *not* the dream, or the interpretation
5:10. let *not* thy thoughts trouble thee, *nor* let thy countenance be changed:

---

410 אֵל *ēhl*, m.

Compare with אֵילִי.

Gen 14:18. he (was) the priest *of the* most high *God.*
19. Blessed (be) Abram *of the* most high *God,*
20. blessed be *the* most high *God,*
22. unto the Lord, *the* most high *God,*
16:13. Thou *God* seest me.
17: 1. I (am) *the* Almighty *God;*
21:33. *the* everlasting *God.*
28: 3. *And God* Almighty bless thee,
31:13. I (am) *the God of* Beth-el,
29. It is *in the power of* my hand
33:20. called it *El*-elohe-Israel. (marg. *God* the God of Israel)
35: 1. make there an altar *unto God,*
3. I will make there an altar *unto God,*
7. called the place *El*-beth-*el:* (marg. *God* of Beth-*el*)
11. God said unto him, I (am) *God*
43:14. *And God* Almighty give you mercy
46: 3. I (am) *God*, the God of thy father:
48: 3. *God* Almighty appeared unto me
49:25. (Even) *by the God of* thy father,
Ex. 6: 3. *by* (the name of) *God* Almighty,
15: 2. become my salvation: he (is) *my God,*
11. Who (is) like unto thee, O Lord, *among the gods?* (marg. *mighty ones*)
20: 5. a jealous *God*, visiting the iniquity
34: 6. The Lord *God*, merciful and gracious,
14. For thou shalt worship no other *god:*
— name (is) Jealous, (is) *a* jealous *God:*
Nu. 12:13. Heal her now, *O God*, I beseech thee.
16:22. fell upon their faces, and said, *O God,*
23: 8. How shall I curse, whom *God* hath not
19. *God* (is) not a man, that he should lie;
22. *God* brought them out of Egypt;
23. What hath *God* wrought!
24: 4, 16. which heard the words of *God,*
8. *God* brought him forth out of Egypt;
23. who shall live when *God* doeth this!
Deu. 3:24. what *God* (is there) in heaven or in
4:24. a consuming fire, (even) *a* jealous *God.*
31. the Lord thy God (is) a merciful *God;*
5: 9. I the Lord thy God (am) *a* jealous *God,*
6:15. the Lord thy God (is) *a* jealous *God*
7: 9. he (is) God, *the* faithful *God,*
21. *a* mighty *God* and terrible.
10:17. *a* great *God*, a mighty, and a terrible,
28:32. (there shall be) no *might* in thine hand.
32: 4. *a God of* truth and without iniquity,
12. (there was) no strange *god* with him.
18. hast forgotten *God* that formed thee.
21. to jealousy with (that which is) not *God;*
33:26. none *like unto the God of* Jeshurun,
Jos. 3:10. know that *the* living *God* (is) among
22:22. Lord *God of* gods, the Lord *God of* gods,
24:19. he (is) *a* jealous *God;*
Jud. 9:46. the house of the *god* Berith.
1Sa. 2: 3. the Lord (is) *a God of* knowledge,
2Sa.22:31. (As for) *God*, his way (is) perfect;
32. For who (is) *God*, save the Lord?
33. *God* (is) my strength (and) power:
48. It (is) *God* that avengeth me,
23: 5. Although my house (be) not so with *God;*
Neh. 1: 5. *the* great and terrible *God,*
5: 5. neither (is it) *in* our *power* (lit. *in the power of* our hand)
9:31. thou (art) *a* gracious and merciful *God.*
32. *the* terrible *God*, who keepest covenant
Job. 5: 8. I would seek unto *God,*
8: 3. Doth *God* pervert judgment?
5. If thou wouldest seek unto *God* betimes,
13. So (are) the paths of all that forget *God;*
20. *God* will not cast away a perfect (man),
9: 2. how should man be just with *God?*
12: 6. they that provoke *God* are secure;
13: 3. I desire to reason with *God.*
7. Will ye speak wickedly *for God?*
8. will ye contend *for God?*
15: 4. restrainest prayer before *God.*
11. (Are) the consolations of *God* small
13. That thou turnest thy spirit against *God,*
25. he stretcheth out his hand against *God,*
16:11. *God* hath delivered me to the ungodly,
18:21. the place (of him that) knoweth not *God.*
19:22. Why do ye persecute me as *God,*
20:15. *God* shall cast them out of his belly.
29. appointed unto him *by God.*
21:14. Therefore they say *unto God,*
22. Shall (any) teach *God* knowledge?
22: 2. Can a man be profitable *unto God,*
13. thou sayest, How doth *God* know?
17. Which said *unto God,*
23:16. *For God* maketh my heart soft,
25: 4. can man be justified with *God?*
27: 2 (As) *God* liveth, (who) hath taken
9. Will *God* hear his cry
11. I will teach you by the hand of *God:*
13. the portion of a wicked man with *God,*
31:14. What then shall I do when *God* riseth up?
23. destruction (from) *God* (was) a terror to
28. I should have denied *the God* (that is)

Job 32:13. *God* thrusteth him down, not man.
33: 4. The Spirit of *God* hath made me,
6. (am) according to thy wish *in God's stead:*
14. For *God* speaketh once, yea twice,
29. worketh *God* oftentimes with man.
34: 5. *and God* hath taken away my judgment.
10. far be it *from God,*
12. surely *God* will not do wickedly,
23. should enter into judgment with *God.*
31. it is meet to be said unto *God,*
37. multiplieth his words *against God.*
35: 2. My righteousness (is) more *than God's?*
13. Surely *God* will not hear vanity,
36: 5. *God* (is) mighty, and despiseth not (any):
22. Behold, *God* exalteth by his power:
26. *God* (is) great, and we know (him) not,
37: 5. *God* thundereth marvellously with his
10. By the breath of *God* frost is given:
14. consider the wondrous works of *God.*
38:41. when his young ones cry unto *God,*
40: 9. Hast thou an arm *like God?*
19. He (is) the chief of the ways of *God:*
Ps. 5: 4(5). (art) not *a God* that hath pleasure in
7:11(12). *and God* is angry (with the wicked)
10:11. said in his heart, *God* hath forgotten:
12. *O God,* lift up thine hand:
16: 1. Preserve me, O *God:*
17: 6. for thou wilt hear me, O *God:*
18: 2(3). *my God,* my strength, in whom I will
30(31). (As for) *God,* his way (is) perfect:
32(33). (It is) *God* that girdeth me with
47(48). (It is) *God* that avengeth me,
19: 1(2). The heavens declare the glory of *God;*
22: 1(2). *My God, my God,* why hast thou
10(11). thou (art) *my God* from my mother's
29: 1. Give unto the Lord, O ye *mighty,* (marg. sons of *the mighty*)
3. the *God of* glory thundereth:
31: 5(6). thou hast redeemed me, O Lord *God of*
36: 6(7). like the *great* mountains; (marg. mountains of *God*)
42: 2(3). *for the* living *God:*
8(9). my prayer *unto the God of* my life.
9(10). I will say *unto God* my rock,
43: 4. unto *God* my exceeding joy:
44:20(21). stretched out our hands *to a* strange *god;*
50: 1. The *mighty* God, (even) the Lord,
52: 1(3). the goodness of *God*
5(7). *God* shall likewise destroy thee
55:19(20). *God* shall hear, and afflict them,
57: 2(3). *unto God* that performeth
63: 1(2). thou (art) *my God;*
68:19(20). (even) *the God of* our salvation.
20(21). (He that is) our *God* (is) *the God of*
24(25). (even) the goings of *my God,*
35(36). *the God of* Israel (is) he that giveth
73:11. they say, How doth *God* know?
17. I went into the sanctuary of *God;*
74: 8. burned up all the synagogues of *God*
77: 9(10). Hath *God* forgotten to be gracious?
13(14). who (is so) great *a God*
14(15). Thou (art) *the God* that doest
78: 7. and not forget the works of *God,*
8. whose spirit was not stedfast with *God.*
18. they tempted *God* in their heart
19. Can *God* furnish a table in the
34. returned and enquired early after *God.*
35. *and the* high *God* their redeemer.
41. Yea, they turned back and tempted *God,*
80:10(11). the boughs thereof (were like) the *goodly* cedars. (marg. cedars of *God*)
81: 9(10). There shall no strange *god* be in thee; neither shalt thou worship any strange *god.*
82: 1. God standeth in the congregation of *the mighty* (lit. of *God*);
83: 1(2). be not still, *O God.*
84: 2(3). my flesh crieth out for *the* living *God.*
85: 8(9). I will hear what *God* the Lord
86:15. (art) *a God* full of compassion,
89: 6(7). (who) among the sons of *the mighty*
7(8). *God* is greatly to be feared
26(27). Thou (art) my father, *my God,*
90: 2. from everlasting to everlasting, thou (art) *God.*

Ps. 94: 1. *O* Lord *God,* to whom vengeance belongeth; *O God,* to whom vengeance
95: 3. For the Lord (is) *a* great *God,*
99: 8. thou wast *a God* that forgavest them,
102:24(25). *O my God,* take me not away
104:21. seek their meat *from God.*
106:14. tempted *God* in the desert.
21. They forgat *God* their saviour,
107:11. they rebelled against the words of *God,*
118:27. *God* (is) the Lord, which hath shewed us
28. (art) *my God,* and I will praise thee:
136:26. O give thanks *unto the God of* heaven:
139:17. are thy thoughts unto me, *O God!*
23. Search me, *O God,* and know my heart:
140: 6(7). said unto the Lord, Thou (art) *my God:*
146: 5. Happy (is he) *that* (hath) *the God of*
149: 6. high (praises) of *God* (be) in their
150: 1. Praise *God* in his sanctuary:
Pro. 3:27. *in the power of* thine hand to do (it).
Isa. 5:16. *and God* that is holy
7:14. call his name Immanu*el.* (lit. *God* with us)
8: 8. fill the breadth of thy land, O Immanu*el.*
10. it shall not stand: for *God* (is) with us.
9: 6(5). The mighty *God,* The everlasting
10:21. remnant of Jacob, unto *the* mighty *God.*
12: 2. Behold, *God* (is) my salvation;
14:13. exalt my throne above the stars of *God:*
31: 3. the Egyptians (are) men, and not *God;*
40:18. To whom then will ye liken *God?*
42: 5. Thus saith *God* the Lord, he that created
43:10. before me there was no *God* formed,
12. witnesses, saith the Lord, that I (am) *God.*
44.10. Who hath formed *a god,*
15. maketh *a god,* and worshippeth (it);
17. the residue thereof he maketh *a god,*
— Deliver me; for thou (art) *my god.*
45:14. Surely *God* (is) in thee;
15. Verily thou (art) *a God*
20. pray unto *a god* (that) cannot save.
21. *a* just *God* and a Saviour;
22. I (am) *God,* and (there is) none else.
46: 6. he maketh it *a god:*
9. for I (am) *God,* and (there is) none else;
57: 5. Enflaming yourselves *with idols* (marg. *among the oaks*)
Jer. 32:18. the Great, *the* Mighty *God,*
48:13. Israel was ashamed of Beth-*el* their
51:56. for the Lord *God of* recompences
Lam. 3:41. our heart with (our) hands unto *God*
Eze. 10: 5. as the voice of *the* Almighty *God*
28: 2. thou hast said, I (am) *a God,*
— thou (art) a man, and not *God,*
9. thou (shalt be) a man, and no *God,*
31:11. into the hand of *the mighty one of* the
32:21. *The strong among* the mighty shall speak
Dan. 9: 4. *the* great and dreadful *God,*
11:36. magnify himself above every *god,* and shall speak marvellous things against *the God* of *gods,*
Hos. 1:10(2:1) (Ye are) the sons of *the* living *God.*
11: 9. for I (am) *God,* and not man;
12 (12:1) but Judah yet ruleth with *God,*
Jon. 4: 2. I knew that thou (art) *a* gracious *God,*
Mic. 2: 1. because it is *in the power of* their hand.
7:18. Who (is) *a God* like unto thee,
Nah. 1: 2. *God* (is) jealous, and the Lord (marg. The Lord (is) a jealous *God*)
Zec. 7: 2. sent unto the house of *God*
Mal. 1: 9. beseech *God* that he will be gracious
2:10. hath not one *God* created us?
11. married the daughter of *a* strange *god.*

אֵל ēhl, pron. pl. 411

Gen19: 8. only unto *these* men do nothing;
25. And he overthrew *those* cities,
26: 3. I will give all *these* countries,
4. give unto thy seed all *these* countries;
Lev.18:27. For all *these* abominations
Deu. 4:42. fleeing unto one of *these* cities
7:22. put out *those* nations before thee
19:11. fleeth into one of *these* cities:
1Ch.20: 8. *These* were born unto the giant

412 אֵל *ēhl*, pron. pl. Ch.

Ezr. 5:15. (קרי) said unto him, Take *these* vessels,

413 אֶל *el*, prep.

Gen. 1: 9. be gathered together *unto* one place,
4: 8. And Cain talked *with* Abel his brother:
— Cain rose up *against* Abel his brother,
6: 6. and it grieved him *at* his heart.
18. and thou shalt come *into* the ark,
8:21. and the Lord said *in* his heart,
12:15. saw her, and commended her *before*
14: 7. they returned, and came *to* En-mishpat,
20: 2. said *of* Sarah his wife, She (is) my sister:
22:12. Lay not thine hand *upon* the lad,
24:11. to kneel down without the city *by* a well
30:40. faces of the flocks *toward* the ringstraked,
47:18. my lord also *hath* our herds of cattle;
Ex. 8:25(21). Pharaoh called *for* Moses and for
19:20. upon mount Sinai, *on* the top
29:12. the blood *beside* the bottom of the altar.
36:22. two tenons, equally distant one *from*
Lev. 4:12. clean place, *where* the ashes are poured
20: 6. the soul that turneth *after* such as have
26:25. gathered together *within* your cities,
Nu. 25: 8. and the woman *through* her belly
Jos. 8:33. half of them *over* against mount Gerizim,
13:22. slay with the sword *among* them that were
15:13. *according to* the commandment of the
1Sa. 3:12. which I have spoken *concerning* his house:
4:19. when she heard the tidings *that* the ark
21. *because* the ark of God was taken,
2Sa. 2:23. the spear smote him *under* the fifth (rib),
3:27. Joab took him aside in the gate
14:30. Joab's field is *near* mine, and he hath
2K. 11: 7. of the house of the Lord *about* the king.
2Ch34:26. And *as for* the king of Judah,
Job. 5: 5. and taketh it even *out of* the thorns,
Jer. 22:11. For thus saith the Lord *touching* Shallum
36:16. *both* one *and* other, and said unto Baruch,
40: 4. *whither* it seemeth good and convenient
Eze. 21:12(17). terrors *by reason of* the sword shall
44: 7. covenant *because of* all your abominations.
&c. &c.

417 אֶלְגָּבִישׁ *el-gāh-veesh'*, m.

Eze. 13:11. O *great hail*stones, shall fall;
13. and *great hail*stones in (my) fury
38:22. and *great hail*stones, fire,

418 אַלְגּוּמִּים *al-goom-meem'*, m. pl.

See also אַלְמֻגִּים.

2Ch. 2: 8(7). *and algum* trees, out of Lebanon:
9:10. *algum* trees and precious stones.
11. the king made (of) *the algum* trees

421 אָלָה [*āh-lāh'*]

* KAL.—*Imperative*. *

Joel. 1: 8. *Lament* like a virgin girded with

422 אָלָה [*āh-lāh'*.]

* KAL.—*Preterite*. *

Jud. 17: 2. about which thou *cursedst*,

KAL.—*Infinitive*.

Hos. 4: 2. *By swearing*, and lying, and killing,
10: 4. *swearing* falsely in making a covenant:

* HIPHIL.—*Infinitive*. *

1 K. 8:31. laid upon him *to cause him to swear*,
2 Ch. 6:22. laid upon him *to make him swear*,

HIPHIL.—*Future*.

1Sa. 14:24. for Saul *had adjured* the people,

אָלָה *āh-lāh'*, f. 423

Gen 24:41. be clear *from* (this) *my oath*,
— thou shalt be clear *from my oath*.
26:28. Let there be now *an oath* betwixt us,
Lev. 5: 1. hear the voice of *swearing*,
Nu. 5:21. the woman with an oath of *cursing*,
— The Lord make thee *a curse*
23. the priest shall write these *curses*
27. shall be *a curse* among her people.
Deu 29:12(11). *and into his oath*, which the Lord
14(13). I make this covenant and this *oath*;
19(18). he heareth the words of this *curse*,
20(19). all *the curses* that are written
21(20). according to all *the curses*
30: 7. put all these *curses* upon thine enemies,
1 K. 8:31. *an oath* be laid upon him
— *the oath* come before thine altar
2Ch. 6:22. *an oath* be laid upon him
— *the oath* come before thine altar
34:24. all *the curses* that are written
Neh 10:29(30). entered *into a curse*,
Job. 31:30. by wishing *a curse* to his soul.
Ps. 10: 7. His mouth is full of *cursing*
59:12(13). *and for cursing* and lying
Pro. 29:24. he heareth *cursing*,
Isa. 24: 6. Therefore hath *the curse* devoured
Jer. 23:10. because of *swearing* the land mourneth; (marg. *cursing*)
29:18. *to be a curse*, and an astonishment, (marg. *for a curse*)
42:18. ye shall be *an execration*,
44:12. they shall be *an execration*,
Eze. 16:59. which hast despised *the oath*
17:13. hath taken *an oath* of him:
16. whose *oath* he despised,
18. Seeing he despised *the oath*
19. *mine oath* that he hath despised,
Dan. 9:11. therefore *the curse* is poured upon us,
Zec. 5: 3. This (is) *the curse* that goeth forth

אַלָּה *al-lāh'*, f. 427

Jos. 24:26. set it up there under *an oak*,

אֵלָה *ēh-lāh'*, f. 424

Gen 35: 4. Jacob hid them under *the oak*
Jud. 6:11. sat under *an oak* which (was)
19. out unto him under *the oak*,
1Sa. 17: 2. pitched by the valley of *Elah*,
19 (were) in the valley of *Elah*,
21: 9(10). thou slewest in the valley of *Elah*,
2Sa. 18: 9. under the thick boughs of *a* great *oak*, and his head caught hold *of the oak*,
10. I saw Absalom hanged *in an oak*.
14. alive in the midst of *the oak*.
1K. 13:14. found him sitting under *an oak*:
1Ch. 10:12. buried their bones under *the oak*
Isa. 1:30. shall be *as an oak* whose leaf fadeth,
6:13. *as a teil tree*, and as an oak,
Eze. 6:13. under every thick *oak*,
Hos. 4:13. under oaks and poplars *and elms*, (lit. *and terebinth*)

אֱלָהּ *ĕlāh'*, m. Ch. 426

Ezr. 4:24. the work of the house of *God*
5: 1. in the name of *the God of*
2. and began to build the house of *God*
— with them (were) the prophets of *God*
5. But the eye of *their God* was upon
8. to the house of *the* great *God*,
11. are the servants of *the God of* heaven
12. our fathers had provoked *the God of*
13. to build this house of *God*.
14. gold and silver of the house of *God*,
15. let the house of *God* be builded
16. laid the foundation of the house of *God*
17. to build this house of *God* at Jerusalem,
6: 3. (concerning) the house of *God*
5. vessels of the house of *God*,
— and place (them) in the house of *God*.

Ezr. 6: 7. Let the work of this house of *God* alone;
— build this house of *God*
8. for the building of this house of *God:*
9. burnt offerings *of the God of* heaven,
10. sweet savours *unto the God of* heaven,
12. *And the God* that hath caused his name
— to destroy this house of *God*
14. commandment of *the God of* Israel,
16. dedication of this house of *God* with joy,
17. at the dedication of this house of *God*
18. for the service of *God,*
7:12, 21. scribe of the law of *the God of* heaven,
14. according to the law of *thy God*
15. freely offered *unto the God of* Israel,
16. willingly for the house of *their God*
17. the altar of the house of *your God*
18. that do after the will of *your God.*
19. the service of the house of *thy God,* (those) deliver thou before *the God of* Jerusalem.
20. needful for the house of *thy God,*
23. commanded by *the God of* heaven,
— for the house of *the God of* heaven:
24. ministers of this house of *God,*
25. after the wisdom of *thy God,*
— such as know the laws of *thy God;*
26. will not do the law of *thy God,*
Jer. 10:11. *The gods* that have not made the
Dan. 2:11. except *the gods,* whose dwelling
18. desire mercies of *the God of* heaven
19. Daniel blessed *the God of* heaven.
20. Blessed be the name of *God*
23. O thou *God of* my fathers,
28. there is *a God* in heaven that revealeth
37. *the God of* heaven hath given thee
44. shall *the God of* heaven set up a kingdom,
45. *the* great *God* hath made known
47. *your God* (is) *a God of gods,*
3:12. they serve not *thy gods,* nor worship
14. do not ye serve *my gods,* nor worship
15. who (is) that *God* that shall deliver you
17. *our God* whom we serve is able
18. that we will not serve *thy gods,*
25. is like the Son of *God.*
26. ye servants of *the* most high *God,*
28. Blessed (be) *the God* of Shadrach,
— worship any *god,* except *their own God.*
29. against *the God* of Shadrach, (lit. against *their God*)
— there is no other *God* that can
4: 2(3:32). and wonders that *the* high *God*
8(5). according to the name of *my god,* and in whom (is) the spirit of *the* holy *gods:*
9(6), 18(15). the spirit of *the* holy *gods* (is)
5: 3. of the temple of the house of *God*
4. and praised *the gods of* gold,
11. in whom (is) the spirit of *the* holy *gods;*
— like the wisdom of *the gods,*
14. that the spirit of *the gods* (is) in thee,
18. *the* most high *God* gave Nebuchadnezzar
21. till he knew that *the* most high *God* ruled
23. *and* thou hast praised *the gods of* silver,
— *and the God* in whose hand thy breath (is),
26. *God* hath numbered thy kingdom,
6: 5(6). concerning the law of *his God.*
7(8). shall ask a petition of *any God*
10(11). gave thanks before *his God,*
11(12). making supplication before *his God.*
12(13). that shall ask (a petition) of any *God*
16(17), 20(21). *Thy God* whom thou servest
20(21). servant of *the* living *God,*
22(23). *My God* hath sent his angel,
23(24). because he believed *in his God.*
26(27). and fear before *the God* of Daniel: for he (is) *the* living *God,*

---

428 אֵלֶּה *ēhl'-leh*, pron. pl.

Gen 2: 4. *These* (are) the generations of the
33: 5. and said, Who (are) *those* with thee?
44: 6. he spake unto them *these same* words.
Ex. 38:21. *This* is the sum of the tabernacle,
Lev. 18:24. yourselves in any of *these* things:
Nu. 10:28. *Thus* (were) the journeyings of the
Deu 5: 3. (even) us, *who* (are) all of us here
22: 5. for all that do *so* (are) abomination
25:16. For all that do *such* things, (and) all
Jos. 8:22. *some* on this side, and *some* on that
1Sa. 17:23. according to *the same* words:
1 K. 20:29. they pitched *one* over against *the other*
1Ch 23: 4. Of *which,* twenty and four thousand
24: 5. divided by lot, *one sort* with *another;*
Ezr. 2:65. of *whom* (there were) seven thousand
Isa. 28: 7. But *they* also have erred through wine,
Eze. 4: 6. when thou hast accomplished *them,*
9: 5. to the *others* he said in mine hearing,
&c. &c.

אֵלֶּה *ēhl'-leh*, pron. Ch. 429

Jer. 10:11. and from under *these* heavens.

אֱלָהּ see אֱלוֹהַּ. See 433

אֱלֹהִים *ĕlōh-heem'*, m. pl. 430

Gen 1: 1. *God* created the heaven and the earth.
2. Spirit of *God* moved upon the face of
3. *God* said, Let there be light:
4. And *God* saw the light, that (it was) good: and *God* divided the light
5. *God* called the light Day,
6. And *God* said, Let there be a firmament
7. *God* made the firmament,
8. And *God* called the firmament Heaven.
9. *God* said, Let the waters under
10. And *God* called the dry (land) Earth;
— 12, 18, 21, 25. and *God* saw that (it was)
11. *God* said, Let the earth bring forth
14. And *God* said, Let there be lights
16. *God* made two great lights;
17. And *God* set them in the firmament
20. *God* said, Let the waters bring forth
21. And *God* created great whales,
22. *God* blessed them, saying,
24. And *God* said, Let the earth bring forth
25. *God* made the beast of the earth
26. And *God* said, Let us make man
27. So *God* created man in his (own) image, in the image of *God* created he him;
28. *God* blessed them, and *God* said unto
29. And *God* said, Behold, I have given
31. *God* saw every thing that he
2: 2. on the seventh day *God* ended
3. *God* blessed the seventh day,
— which *God* created and made.
4. the Lord *God* made the earth
5. for the Lord *God* had not caused
7. And the Lord *God* formed man
8. the Lord *God* planted a garden
9. the Lord *God* to grow every tree
15. the Lord *God* took the man,
16. the Lord *God* commanded the man,
18. And the Lord *God* said,
19. the Lord *God* formed every beast
21. And the Lord *God* caused a deep sleep
22. the Lord *God* had taken from man,
3: 1. which the Lord *God* had made.
— *God* said, Ye shall not eat of
3. *God* hath said, Ye shall not eat of
5. For *God* doth know
— ye shall be *as gods,*
8. heard the voice of the Lord *God*
— from the presence of the Lord *God*
9. the Lord *God* called unto Adam,
13. *God* said unto the woman,
14. the Lord *God* said unto the serpent,
21. the Lord *God* make coats of skins,
22. the Lord *God* said, Behold, the man
23. Therefore the Lord *God* sent
4:25. *God,* (said she), hath appointed me
5: 1. In the day that *God* created man, in the likeness of *God* made
22, 24. Enoch walked with *God*
24. for *God* took him.
6: 2. the sons of *God* saw the
4. when the sons of *God* came in
9. Noah walked with *God.*
11. also was corrupt before *God,*
12. *God* looked upon the earth,
13. *God* said unto Noah,

Gen 6:22. according to all that *God* commanded
7: 9. as *God* had commanded Noah.
16. as *God* had commanded him:
8: 1. *God* remembered Noah,
— *God* made a wind to pass over
15. *God* spake unto Noah,
9: 1. *God* blessed Noah and his sons,
6. in the image of *God* made he man.
8. *God* spake unto Noah,
12. *God* said, This (is) the token
16. between *God* and every living creature
17. *God* said unto Noah,
26. Blessed (be) the Lord *God of* Shem;
27. *God* shall enlarge Japheth,
17: 3. *God* talked with him,
7. to be *a God* unto thee, and to thy seed
8. I will be their *God*.
9, 15. *God* said unto Abraham,
18. Abraham said unto *God*,
19. *God* said, Sarah thy wife
22. *God* went up from Abraham.
23. as *God* had said unto him.
19:29. when *God* destroyed the cities of the plain, that *God* remembered
20: 3. *God* came to Abimelech
6. *God* said unto him in a dream,
11. the fear of *God* (is) not in this place;
13. *God* caused me to wander
17. So Abraham prayed unto *God*: and *God*
21: 2. time of which *God* had spoken to him.
4. as *God* had commanded him.
6. *God* hath made me to laugh,
12. And *God* said unto Abraham,
17. *God* heard the voice of the lad; and the angel of *God* called to Hagar...fear not; for *God* hath heard the voice of the lad
19. *God* opened her eyes,
20. *God* was with the lad;
22. *God* (is) with thee in all
23. swear unto me here *by God*
22: 1. *that God* did tempt Abraham,
3. the place of which *God* had told him.
8. *God* will provide himself a lamb
9. the place which *God* had told him
12. I know that thou fearest *God*,
23: 6. a *mighty* prince (marg. a prince of *God*)
24: 3. swear by the Lord, the *God of* heaven, *and the God of* the earth,
7. The Lord *God of* heaven,
12, 42. O Lord *God of* my master Abraham,
27, 48. the Lord *God of* my master
25:11. that *God* blessed his son Isaac;
26:24. I (am) the *God of* Abraham
27:20. the Lord *thy God* brought (it) to me.
28. *God* give thee of the dew of heaven,
28: 4. which *God* gave unto Abraham.
12. the angels of *God* ascending
13. said, I (am) the Lord *God of* Abraham thy father, *and the God of* Isaac:
17. this (is) none other but the house of *God*,
20. If *God* will be with me,
21. then shall the Lord be my *God*:
22. shall be *God*'s house:
30: 2. he said, (Am) I in *God*'s stead,
6. Rachel said, *God* hath judged me,
8. With *great* wrestlings (marg. wrestlings of *God*)
17. *God* hearkened unto Leah,
18. *God* hath given me my hire,
20. *God* hath endued me
22. *God* remembered Rachel, and *God*
23. *God* hath taken away my reproach:
31: 5. *but the God of* my father hath been
7. *God* suffered him not to hurt me.
9. Thus *God* hath taken away
11. the angel of *God* spake
16. all the riches which *God* hath
— whatsoever *God* hath said
24. *God* came to Laban the Syrian
29. *but the God of* your father spake
30. hast thou stolen *my gods*?
32. With whomsoever thou findest *thy gods*,
42. Except *the God of* my father, *the God of*
— *God* hath seen mine affliction
50. *God* (is) witness betwixt me and thee.
53. *The God of* Abraham, *and the God of* Nahor, *the God of* their father,

Gen32: 1(2). the angels of *God* met him.
2(3). he said, This (is) *God*'s host:
9(10). *O God of* my father Abraham, *and God of* my father Isaac,
28(29). a prince hast thou power with *God*
30(31). I have seen *God* face to face,
33: 5. The children which *God* hath
10. as though I had seen the face of *God*,
11. *God* hath dealt graciously with me,
20. called it El-*elohe*-Israel. (marg. God, *the God of* Israel)
35: 1. *God* said unto Jacob, Arise,
2. Put away *the* strange *gods*
4. they gave unto Jacob all *the* strange *gods*
5. the terror of *God* was upon the cities
7. there *God* appeared unto him,
9. *God* appeared unto Jacob again
10, 11. *God* said unto him,
13. *God* went up from him
15. the place where *God* spake with him,
39: 9. great wickedness, and sin *against God*?
40: 8. interpretations (belong) *to God*?
41:16. *God* shall give Pharaoh an answer
25. *God* hath shewed Pharaoh what he
28. What *God* (is) about to do
32. the thing (is) established by *God*, *and God* will shortly bring it to pass.
38. a man in whom the Spirit of *God* (is)?
39. *God* hath shewed thee all this,
51. the firstborn Manasseh: For *God*,
52. *God* hath caused me to be fruitful
42:18. This do, and live; (for) I fear *God*:
28. What (is) this (that) *God* hath done
43:23. *your God, and the God of* your father,
29. *God* be gracious unto thee,
44:16. *God* hath found out the iniquity
45: 5. *God* did send me before you
7. *God* sent me before you
8. not you (that) sent me hither, but *God*:
9. *God* hath made me lord of all Egypt:
46: 1. *unto the God of* his father Isaac.
2. *God* spake unto Israel
3. I (am) God, *the God of* thy father:
48: 9. whom *God* hath given me
11. *God* hath shewed me also
15. *God*, before whom my fathers
— *God* which fed me all my life
20. *God* make thee as Ephraim
21. but *God* shall be with you,
50:17. the servants of *the God of* thy father.
19. for (am) I in the place of *God*?
20. *God* meant it unto good,
24. *and God* will surely visit you,
25. *God* will surely visit you,
Ex. 1:17. But the midwives feared *God*,
20. *God* dealt well with the midwives:
21. because the midwives feared *God*,
2:23. their cry came up unto *God*
24. *God* heard their groaning, and *God*
25. *God* looked upon the children of Israel, and *God* had respect unto (them).
3: 1. came to the mountain of *God*,
4. *God* called unto him
6. I (am) *the God of* thy father, *the God of* Abraham, *the God of* Isaac, *and the God of* Jacob.
— for he was afraid to look upon *God*.
11, 13. Moses said unto *God*,
12. ye shall serve *God* upon this mountain.
13. *The God of* your fathers hath sent me
14. *God* said unto Moses,
15. *God* said moreover unto Moses,
— The Lord *God of* your fathers, *the God of* Abraham, *the God of* Isaac, *and the God of* Jacob,
16. The Lord *God of* your fathers, *the God of*
18. The Lord *God of* the Hebrews
— sacrifice to the Lord *our God*.
4: 5. the Lord *God of* their fathers, *the God of* Abraham, *the God of* Isaac, *and the God of* Jacob, hath appeared
16. thou shalt be to him *instead of God*.
20. Moses took the rod of *God* in his hand.
27. met him in the mount of *God*,
5: 1. Thus saith the Lord *God of* Israel,
3. *The God of* the Hebrews hath met
— sacrifice unto the Lord *our God*;

Ex. 5: 8. Let us go (and) sacrifice *to our God.*
6: 2. *God* spake unto Moses,
7. be to you *a God:* and ye shall know that I (am) the Lord *your God,*
7: 1. I have made thee *a god* to Pharaoh:
16. The Lord *God of* the Hebrews
8: 10(6). none like unto the Lord *our God.*
19(15). This (is) the finger of *God:*
25(21). sacrifice *to your God* in the land.
26(22). the Egyptians to the Lord *our God:*
27(23). sacrifice to the Lord *our God,*
28(24). sacrifice to the Lord *your God*
9: 1, 13. Thus saith the Lord *God of* the
28. *mighty* thunderings (marg. voices of *God*)
30. ye will not yet fear the Lord *God.*
10: 3. Thus saith the Lord *God of* the Hebrews,
7. that they may serve the Lord *their God:*
8. serve the Lord *your God:*
16. I have sinned against the Lord *your God,*
17. intreat the Lord *your God,*
25. sacrifice unto the Lord *our God.*
26. to serve the Lord *our God;*
12: 12. all *the gods of* Egypt (marg. *princes*)
13: 17. *God* led them not (through) the way
— *God* said, Lest peradventure
18. But *God* led the people about,
19. *God* will surely visit you;
14: 19. the angel of *God,* which went
15: 2. my father's *God,* and I will exalt him.
26. to the voice of the Lord *thy God,*
16: 12. know that I (am) the Lord *your God.*
17: 9. with the rod of *God* in mine hand.
18: 1. heard of all that *God* had done
4. for *the God of* my father,
5. he encamped at the mount of *God:*
11. the Lord (is) greater than all *gods:*
12. burnt offering and sacrifices *for God:*
— with Moses' father in law before *God.*
15. come unto me to enquire of *God:*
16. make (them) know the statutes of *God,*
19. *God* shall be with thee: Be thou for the people to *God*-ward, that thou mayest bring the causes unto *God:*
21. able men, such as fear *God,*
23. do this thing, and *God* command
19: 3. Moses went up unto *God,*
17. out of the camp to meet with *God;*
19. *and God* answered him by a voice.
20: 1. *God* spake all these words,
2. I (am) the Lord *thy God,*
3. Thou shalt have no other *gods* before me.
5. I the Lord *thy God*
7. the name of the Lord *thy God*
10. the sabbath of the Lord *thy God:*
12. which the Lord *thy God* giveth thee.
19. but let not *God* speak with us,
20. *God* is come to prove you,
21. the thick darkness where *God* (was).
23. not make with me *gods of* silver, *neither* shall ye make unto you *gods of* gold.
21: 6. shall bring him unto *the judges;*
13. *but God* deliver (him) into his hand;
22: 8(7). shall be brought unto *the judges,*
9(8). both parties shall come before *the judges;* (and) whom *the judges* shall
20(19). He that sacrificeth *unto* (any) *god,*
28(27). Thou shalt not revile *the gods,* (marg. *judges*)
23: 13. mention of the name of other *gods,*
19. into the house of the Lord *thy God.*
24. Thou shalt not bow down *to their gods,*
25. ye shall serve the Lord *your God,*
32. with them, *nor* with *their gods.*
33. for if thou serve *their gods,*
24: 10. they saw *the God of* Israel:
11. they saw *God,* and did eat and drink.
13. Moses went up into the mount of *God.*
29: 45. and will be their *God.*
46. know that I (am) the Lord *their God,*
— I (am) the Lord *their God.*
31: 3. filled him with the spirit of *God,*
18. written with the finger of *God.*
32: 1, 23. make us *gods,* which shall go before
4, 8. These (be) *thy gods,* O Israel,
11. Moses besought the Lord *his God,*
16. the tables (were) the work of *God,* and the writing (was) the writing of *God,*

Ex. 32: 27. Thus saith the Lord *God of* Israel,
31. have made them *gods of* gold.
34: 15. they go a whoring after *their gods,* and do sacrifice *unto their gods,*
16. go a whoring after *their gods,* and make thy sons go a whoring after *their gods.*
17. Thou shalt make thee no molten *gods.*
23. the Lord God, *the God of* Israel.
24. appear before the Lord *thy God*
26. bring unto the house of the Lord *thy God.*
35: 31. he hath filled him with the spirit of *God,*
Lev. 2: 13. the salt of the covenant of *thy God*
4: 22. the commandments of the Lord *his God*
11: 44. For I (am) the Lord *your God:*
45. out of the land of Egypt, to be your *God:*
18: 2, 4, 30. I (am) the Lord *your God.*
21. shalt thou profane the name of *thy God:*
19: 2. I the Lord *your God* (am) holy.
3, 4, 10, 25, 31, 34, 36. the Lord *your God.*
4. *nor* make to yourselves molten *gods:*
12. shalt thou profane the name of *thy God:*
14. but shalt fear *thy God:*
32. fear *thy God:* I (am) the Lord.
20: 7, 24. I (am) the Lord *your God.*
21: 6. They shall be holy *unto their God,* and not profane the name of *their God:*
— the bread of *their God,*
7. for he (is) holy *unto his God.*
8. for he offereth the bread of *thy God:*
12. the sanctuary of *his God;* for the crown of the anointing oil of *his God*
17. approach to offer the bread of *his God.*
21. nigh to offer the bread of *his God.*
22. He shall eat the bread of *his God,*
22: 25. shall ye offer the bread of *your God*
33. the land of Egypt, to be your *God:*
23: 14. have brought an offering unto *your God:*
22, 43. I (am) the Lord *your God.*
28. for you before the Lord *your God.*
40. rejoice before the Lord *your God*
24: 15. Whosoever curseth *his God* shall
22. for I (am) the Lord *your God.*
25. 17. but thou shalt fear *thy God:* for I (am) the Lord *your God.*
36. but fear *thy God;*
38, 55. I (am) the Lord *your God,*
— (and) to be your *God.*
43. but shalt fear *thy God.*
26: 1, 13. I (am) the Lord *your God.*
12. walk among you, and will be your *God,*
44. for I (am) the Lord *their God.*
45. that I might be their *God:*
Nu. 6. 7. consecration of *his God* (is) upon his
10: 9. be remembered before the Lord *your God,*
10. for a memorial before *your God:* I (am) the Lord *your God.*
15: 40. be holy *unto your God.*
41. the Lord *your God,* which brought you out of the land of Egypt, to be your *God:* I (am) the Lord *your God.*
16: 9. *the God of* Israel hath separated
22. *the God of* the spirits of all flesh,
21: 5. the people spake *against God,*
22: 9, 20. *God* came unto Balaam,
10. Balaam said unto *God,*
12. *God* said unto Balaam,
18. beyond the word of the Lord *my God,*
22. *God*'s anger was kindled
38. word that *God* putteth in my mouth,
23: 4. And *God* met Balaam:
21. the Lord *his God* (is) with him,
27. peradventure it will please *God*
24: 2. the spirit of *God* came upon him.
25: 2. unto the sacrifices of *their gods:*
— and bowed down *to their gods.*
13. because he was zealous *for his God,*
27: 16. *the God of* the spirits of all flesh,
33: 4. *upon their gods also* the Lord executed
Deu. 1: 6. The Lord *our God* spake unto us
10. The Lord *your God* hath multiplied
11. The Lord *God of* your fathers
17. for the judgment (is) *God's:*
19. as the Lord *our God* commanded us;
20. the Lord *our God* doth give
21. the Lord *thy God* hath set the land
— Lord *God of* thy fathers hath said
25. which the Lord *our God* doth give us.

Deu. 1:26. the commandment of the Lord *your God:*
30. The Lord *your God*
31. the Lord *thy God* bare thee,
32. ye did not believe the Lord *your God,*
41. all that the Lord *our God* commanded
2: 7. the Lord *thy God* hath blessed thee
— the Lord *thy God* (hath been) with thee;
29. which the Lord *our God* giveth us.
30. the Lord *thy God* hardened his spirit,
33. the Lord *our God* delivered him
36. the Lord *our God* delivered all unto us:
37. whatsoever the Lord *our God* forbad us.
3: 3. So the Lord *our God* delivered
18. The Lord *your God* hath given you
20. which the Lord *your God* hath given them
21. that the Lord *your God* hath done
22. Lord *your God* he shall fight for you.
4: 1. which the Lord *God of* your fathers
2. the commandments of the Lord *your God*
3. the Lord *thy God* hath destroyed them
4. did cleave unto the Lord *your God*
5. as the Lord *my God* commanded
7. who (hath) *God* (so) nigh unto them, as the Lord *our God* (is) in all
10. stoodest before the Lord *thy God* in Horeb,
19. which the Lord *thy God* hath divided
21,40. which the Lord *thy God* giveth thee
23. the covenant of the Lord *your God,*
— which the Lord *thy God* hath forbidden thee.
24. Lord *thy God* (is) a consuming fire,
25. in the sight of the Lord *thy God,*
28. there ye shall serve *gods,*
29. thou shalt seek the Lord *thy God,*
30. if thou turn to the Lord *thy God,*
31. For the Lord *thy God*
32. since the day that *God* created man
33. Did (ever) people hear the voice of *God*
34. Or hath *God* assayed to go
— all that the Lord *your God* did
35. know that the Lord he (is) *God;*
39. Lord he (is) *God* in heaven above,
5: 2. The Lord *our God* made a covenant
6. I (am) the Lord *thy God,*
7. Thou shalt have none other *gods*
9. for I the Lord *thy God*
11. name of the Lord *thy God* in vain:
12,16. as the Lord *thy God* hath commanded
14. the sabbath of the Lord *thy God:*
15. the Lord *thy God* brought thee out
— the Lord *thy God* commanded thee
16. which the Lord *thy God* giveth thee.
24(21). the Lord *our God* hath shewed us
—(—). that *God* doth talk with man,
25(22). hear the voice of the Lord *our God*
26(23). hath heard the voice of *the* living *God*
27(24). hear all that the Lord *our God*
— all that the Lord *our God* shall speak
32(29),33(30) Lord *your God* hath commanded
6: 1. which the Lord *your God* commanded
2. thou mightest fear the Lord *thy God,*
3. the Lord *God of* thy fathers hath promised
4. The Lord *our God* (is) one Lord:
5. thou shalt love the Lord *thy God*
10. when the Lord *thy God* shall have
13. Thou shalt fear the Lord *thy God,*
14. Ye shall not go after other *gods, of the gods of* the people which (are) round
15. For the Lord *thy God* (is) a jealous
— lest the anger of the Lord *thy God*
16. Ye shall not tempt the Lord *your God,*
17. the commandments of the Lord *your God,*
20. the Lord *our God* hath commanded you?
24. to fear the Lord *our God,*
25. commandments before the Lord *our God,*
7: 1. When the Lord *thy God* shall bring thee
2,23. Lord *thy God* shall deliver them
4. that they may serve other *gods:*
6. an holy people unto the Lord *thy God:* the Lord *thy God* hath chosen thee
9. Know therefore that the Lord *thy God,* he (is) *God,*
12. that the Lord *thy God* shall keep
16. which the Lord *thy God* shall deliver thee;
— neither shalt thou serve *their gods;*
18. the Lord *thy God* did unto Pharaoh,
19. whereby the Lord *thy God* brought thee out: so shall the Lord *thy God* do

Deu. 7:20. the Lord *thy God* will send the hornet
21. for the Lord *thy God* (is) among you,
22. the Lord *thy God* will put out those
25. The graven images of *their gods*
— an abomination to the Lord *thy God.*
8: 2. the way which the Lord *thy God* led
5. the Lord *thy God* chasteneth thee.
6. the commandments of the Lord *thy God,*
7. the Lord *thy God* bringeth thee
10. thou shalt bless the Lord *thy God*
11. thou forget not the Lord *thy God,*
14. and thou forget the Lord *thy God,*
18. thou shalt remember the Lord *thy God:*
19. at all forget the Lord *thy God,* and walk after other *gods,*
20. the voice of the Lord *your God.*
9: 3. the Lord *thy God* (is) he
4. after that the Lord *thy God*
5. the Lord *thy God* doth drive them out
6. the Lord *thy God* giveth thee not
7. how thou provokedst the Lord *thy God*
10. written with the finger of *God;*
16. sinned against the Lord *your God,*
23. the commandment of the Lord *your God,*
10: 9. as the Lord *thy God* promised him.
12. what doth the Lord *thy God* require of thee, but to fear the Lord *thy God,*
— to serve the Lord *thy God*
14. the heaven of heavens (is) the Lord's *thy God,*
17. For the Lord *your God* (is) *God of gods,* and Lord of lords,
20. Thou shalt fear the Lord *thy God;*
21. He (is) thy praise, and he (is) *thy God,*
22. the Lord *thy God* hath made thee
11: 1. thou shalt love the Lord *thy God,*
2. the chastisement of the Lord *your God,*
12. the Lord *thy God* careth for: the eyes of the Lord *thy God* (are)
13,22. to love the Lord *your God,*
16. serve other *gods,* and worship them;
25. the Lord *your God* shall lay the fear
27,28. the commandments of the Lord *your God.*
28. to go after other *gods,*
29. when the Lord *thy God* hath brought
31. which the Lord *your God* giveth
12: 1. which the Lord *God of* thy fathers
2. shall possess served *their gods,*
3. the graven images of *their gods,*
4. not do so unto the Lord *your God.*
5. the place which the Lord *your God*
7. ye shall eat before the Lord *your God,*
— the Lord *thy God* hath blessed thee.
9. Lord *your God* giveth (lit. *thy God*)
10. which the Lord *your God* giveth
11. the Lord *your God* shall choose
12. rejoice before the Lord *your God,*
15. the blessing of the Lord *thy God*
18. eat them before the Lord *thy God* in the place which the Lord *thy God*
— rejoice before the Lord *thy God*
20. When the Lord *thy God* shall
21. which the Lord *thy God* hath chosen
27. upon the altar of the Lord *thy God:*
— out upon the altar of the Lord *thy God,*
28. in the sight of the Lord *thy God.*
29. the Lord *thy God* shall cut off
30. enquire not *after their gods,* saying, How did these nations serve *their gods?*
31. Thou shalt not do so unto the Lord *thy God:*
— have they done *unto their gods;*
— they have burnt in the fire *to their gods.*
13: 2(3). Let us go after other *gods,*
3(4). the Lord *your God* proveth you, to know whether ye love the Lord *your God*
4(5). walk after the Lord *your God,*
5(6). to turn (you) away from the Lord *your God,*
—(—). the way which the Lord *thy God*
6(7),13(14). Let us go and serve other *gods,*
7(8). *of the gods of* the people which
10(11). thee away from the Lord *thy God,*
12(13). which the Lord *thy God* hath given
16(17). every whit, for the Lord *thy God* ·
18(19). to the voice of the Lord *thy God,*
—(—). right in the eyes of the Lord *thy God.*

Deu 14: 1. Ye (are) the children of the Lord *your God:*
2, 21. an holy people unto the Lord *thy God,*
23. shalt eat before the Lord *thy God,*
— learn to fear the Lord *thy God*
24, 25. which the Lord *thy God* shall choose
— when the Lord *thy God* hath blessed thee:
26. shalt eat there before the Lord *thy God,*
29. that the Lord *thy God* may bless thee
15: 4, 7. which the Lord *thy God* giveth thee
5. hearken unto the voice of the Lord *thy God,*
6. the Lord *thy God* blesseth thee,
10, 18. the Lord *thy God* shall bless thee
14. the Lord *thy God* hath blessed thee
15. the Lord *thy God* redeemed thee:
19. sanctify unto the Lord *thy God:*
20. eat (it) before the Lord *thy God*
21. sacrifice it unto the Lord *thy God.*
16: 1, 2. passover unto the Lord *thy God:*
— the Lord *thy God* brought thee
5, 18, 20. which the Lord *thy God* giveth thee:
6, 7. which the Lord *thy God* shall choose
8. solemn assembly to the Lord *thy God:*
10. feast of weeks unto the Lord *thy God*
— according as the Lord *thy God* hath blessed
11. rejoice before the Lord *thy God,*
— which the Lord *thy God* hath chosen
15. solemn feast unto the Lord *thy God*
— the Lord *thy God* shall bless thee
16. appear before the Lord *thy God*
17. the blessing of the Lord *thy God*
21. unto the altar of the Lord *thy God,*
22. which the Lord *thy God* hateth.
17: 1. sacrifice unto the Lord *thy God*
— an abomination unto the Lord *thy God.*
2. which the Lord *thy God* giveth
— in the sight of the Lord *thy God,*
3. hath gone and served other *gods,*
8, 15. the Lord *thy God* shall choose;
12. there before the Lord *thy God,*
14. land which the Lord *thy God* giveth thee,
19. learn to fear the Lord *his God,*
18: 5. Lord *thy God* hath chosen him
7. in the name of the Lord *his God,*
9. the Lord *thy God* giveth thee,
12. the Lord *thy God* doth drive them
13. perfect with the Lord *thy God.*
14. the Lord *thy God* hath not suffered
15. The Lord *thy God* will raise up
16. thou desiredst of the Lord *thy God*
— again the voice of the Lord *my God,*
20. speak in the name of other *gods,*
19: 1. When the Lord *thy God* hath cut off the nations, whose land the Lord *thy God* giveth
2, 10. thy land, which the Lord *thy God* giveth thee
3. which the Lord *thy God* giveth thee
8. if the Lord *thy God* enlarge
9. to love the Lord *thy God,*
14. the land that the Lord *thy God* giveth
20: 1. the Lord *thy God* (is) with thee,
4. the Lord *your God* (is) he that goeth
13. when the Lord *thy God* hath delivered
14. which the Lord *thy God* hath given
16. which the Lord *thy God* doth give
17. as the Lord *thy God* hath
18. they have done *unto their gods;* so should ye sin against the Lord *your God.*
21: 1, 23. which the Lord *thy God* giveth
5. them the Lord *thy God* hath chosen
10. the Lord *thy God* hath delivered
23. he that is hanged (is) accursed of *God;*
22: 5. abomination unto the Lord *thy God.*
23: 5(6). Nevertheless the Lord *thy God*
—(—). the Lord *thy God* turned the curse
—(—). because the Lord *thy God* loved thee.
14(15). For the Lord *thy God* walketh
18(19). the house of the Lord *thy God*
—(—). abomination unto the Lord *thy God.*
20(21). that the Lord *thy God* may bless thee
21(22). a vow unto the Lord *thy God,*
—(—). the Lord *thy God* will surely require it
23(24). hast vowed unto the Lord *thy God,*
24: 4. which the Lord *thy God* giveth
9. Remember what the Lord *thy God* did
13. before the Lord *thy God.*
18. the Lord *thy God* redeemed thee

Deu 24: 19. that the Lord *thy God* may bless thee
25: 15, 19. the land which the Lord *thy God* giveth
16. an abomination unto the Lord *thy God.*
18. he feared not *God.*
19. the Lord *thy God* hath given thee
26: 1. the land which the Lord *thy God* giveth
2. that the Lord *thy God* giveth thee,
— the Lord *thy God* shall choose
3. this day unto the Lord *thy God,*
4. before the altar of the Lord *thy God.*
5, 13. say before the Lord *thy God,*
7. the Lord *God of* our fathers,
10. set it before the Lord *thy God,* and worship before the Lord *thy God:*
11. which the Lord *thy God* hath given
14. to the voice of the Lord *my God,*
16. the Lord *thy God* hath commanded thee
17. the Lord this day to be thy *God,*
19. an holy people unto the Lord *thy God,*
27: 2, 3. which the Lord *thy God* giveth thee,
3. as the Lord *God of* thy fathers
5. build an altar unto the Lord *thy God,*
6. build the altar of the Lord *thy God*
— thereon unto the Lord *thy God:*
7. rejoice before the Lord *thy God.*
9. become the people of the Lord *thy God.*
10. obey the voice of the Lord *thy God,*
28: 1, 2, 15, 45. unto the voice of the Lord *thy God,*
— the Lord *thy God* will set thee on high
8. which the Lord *thy God* giveth
9, 13. commandments of the Lord *thy God,*
14. to go after other *gods* to serve them.
36. there shalt thou serve other *gods,*
47. servedst not the Lord *thy God*
52, 53. which the Lord *thy God* hath given
58. and fearful name, The Lord *Thy God;*
62. obey the voice of the Lord *thy God.*
64. there thou shalt serve other *gods,*
29: 6(5). I (am) the Lord *your God.*
10(9). all of you before the Lord *your God;*
12(11). covenant with the Lord *thy God,*
—(—). which the Lord *thy God* maketh
13(12). he may be unto thee *a God,*
15(14). this day before the Lord *our God,*
18(17). away this day from the Lord *our God,* to go (and) serve *the gods of* these nations;
25(24). covenant of the Lord *God of* their fathers,
26(25). they went and served other *gods,*
—(—). *gods* whom they knew not,
29(28). secret (things belong) unto the Lord *our God:*
30: 1. whither the Lord *thy God* hath driven thee,
2. return unto the Lord *thy God,*
3. the Lord *thy God* will turn thy
— whither the Lord *thy God* hath scattered
4. will the Lord *thy God* gather thee,
5. the Lord *thy God* will bring thee
6. the Lord *thy God* will circumcise
—, 16. to love the Lord *thy God*
7. the Lord *thy God* will put all
9. the Lord *thy God* will make
10. unto the voice of the Lord *thy God,*
— if thou turn unto the Lord *thy God*
16. the Lord *thy God* shall bless thee
17. worship other *gods,* and serve them;
20. thou mayest love the Lord *thy God,*
31: 3. The Lord *thy God,* he will go
6. Lord *thy God,* he (it is) that doth go
11. to appear before the Lord *thy God*
12. fear the Lord *your God,*
13. learn to fear the Lord *your God,*
16. go a whoring after *the gods of*
17. because *our God* (is) not among us?
18. they are turned unto other *gods.*
20. then will they turn unto other *gods,*
26. the covenant of the Lord *your God,*
32: 3. ascribe ye greatness *unto our God.*
17. to *gods* whom they knew not,
37. he shall say, Where (are) *their gods,*
39. and (there is) no *god* with me:
33: 1. Moses the man of *God*
27. *The* eternal *God* (is thy) refuge,
Jos. 1: 9. for the Lord *thy God* (is) with thee
11, 15. which the Lord *your God* giveth
13. The Lord *your God* hath given you
17. the Lord *thy God* be with thee,

Jos. 2:11. for the Lord *your God*, he (is) *God* in
3: 3. the covenant of the Lord *your God*,
9. hear the words of the Lord *your God*.
4: 5. before the ark of the Lord *your God*
23. the Lord *your God* dried up the waters
— Lord *your God* did to the Red sea,
24. fear the Lord *your God* for ever.
7:13. thus saith the Lord *God of* Israel,
19. glory to the Lord *God of* Israel,
20. sinned against the Lord *God of* Israel,
8: 7. the Lord *your God* will deliver it
30. unto the Lord *God of* Israel
9: 9. the name of the Lord *thy God:*
18. sworn unto them by the Lord *God of*
19. sworn unto them by the Lord *God of*
23. for the house of *my God*.
24. how that the Lord *thy God*
10:19. the Lord *your God* hath delivered
40. as the Lord *God of* Israel commanded.
42. Lord *God of* Israel fought for Israel.
13:14. sacrifices of the Lord *God of* Israel
33. the Lord *God of* Israel (was) their
14: 6. Moses the man of *God*
8. I wholly followed the Lord *my God*.
9. wholly followed the Lord *my God*.
14. wholly followed the Lord *God of*
18: 3. which the Lord *God of* your fathers
6. for you here before the Lord *our God*.
22: 3. the commandment of the Lord *your God*.
4. now the Lord *your God* hath given
5. to love the Lord *your God*,
16. committed *against the God of* Israel,
19. the altar of the Lord *our God*.
22. The Lord God of *gods*, the Lord God of *gods*,
24. to do with the Lord *God of* Israel?
29. beside the altar of the Lord *our God*
33. the children of Israel blessed *God*,
34. between us that the Lord (is) *God*.
23: 3. all that the Lord *your God* hath done
— the Lord *your God* (is) he
5. the Lord *your God*, he shall expel
— as the Lord *your God* hath promised
7. make mention of the name of *their gods*,
8. cleave unto the Lord *your God*,
10. the Lord *your God*, he (it is) that
11. that ye love the Lord *your God*.
13. the Lord *your God* will no more
—, 15. which the Lord *your God* hath given
14. which the Lord *your God* spake
15. which the Lord *your God* promised
16. the covenant of the Lord *your God*,
— have gone and served other *gods*,
24: 1. they presented themselves before *God*.
2. Thus saith the Lord *God of* Israel,
— and they served other *gods*.
14. put away *the gods* which your
15. *the gods* which your fathers served
— or *the gods of* the Amorites,
16. forsake the Lord, to serve other *gods;*
17. For the Lord *our God*,
18. serve the Lord; for he (is) *our God*.
19. for he (is) *an* holy *God;*
20. and serve strange *gods*,
23. the strange *gods* which (are) among
— heart unto the Lord *God of* Israel.
24. The Lord *our God* will we serve,
26. in the book of the law of *God*,
27. lest ye deny *your God*.
Jud. 1: 7. so *God* hath requited me.
2: 3. *and their gods* shall be a snare
12. forsook the Lord *God of* their fathers,
— followed other *gods*, *of the gods of* the
17. they went a whoring after other *gods*,
19. in following other *gods* to serve them,
3: 6. and served *their gods*.
7. forgat the Lord *their God*,
20. a message from *God* unto thee.
4: 6. Hath not the Lord *God of* Israel
23. So *God* subdued on that day Jabin
5: 3. I will sing (praise) to the Lord *God of*
5. before the Lord *God of* Israel.
8. They chose new *gods;*
6: 8. Thus saith the Lord *God of* Israel,
10. I (am) the Lord *your God;* fear not the *gods of* the Amorites,
20. the angel of *God* said unto him,
26. build an altar unto the Lord *thy God*

Jud. 6:31. if he (be) *a god*, let him plead
36, 39. Gideon said unto *God*,
40. *God* did so that night:
7:14. his hand hath *God* delivered Midian,
8: 3. *God* hath delivered into your hands
33. made Baalberith their *god*.
34. Israel remembered not the Lord *their God*,
9: 7. that *God* may hearken unto you.
9. wherewith by me they honour *God*
13. which cheereth *God* and man,
23. Then *God* sent an evil spirit
27. went into the house of *their god*,
56. *God* rendered the wickedness
57. did *God* render upon their heads:
10: 6. *the gods of* Syria, & *the gods of* Zidon, & *the gods of* Moab, & *the gods of* the children of Ammon, & *the gods of* the
10. because we have forsaken *our God*,
13. served other *gods:*
14. cry unto *the gods* which ye have
16. they put away *the* strange *gods*
11:21. the Lord *God of* Israel delivered
23. So now the Lord *God of* Israel
24. Chemosh *thy god* giveth thee
— the Lord *our God* shall drive out
13: 5. a Nazarite unto *God* from the womb:
6. A man of *God* came unto me,
— the countenance of an angel of *God*,
7. a Nazarite to *God* from the womb
8. let the man of *God* which thou
9. *God* hearkened to the voice of Manoah; and the angel of *God* came again
22. because we have seen *God*.
15:19. *God* clave an hollow place
16:17. a Nazarite unto *God* from my
23. a great sacrifice unto Dagon *their god*,
— *Our god* hath delivered Samson
24. praised *their god:* for they said, *Our god*
28. only this once, *O God*,
17: 5. the man Micah had an house of *gods*,
18: 5. Ask counsel, we pray thee, *of God*,
10. *God* hath given it into your
24. Ye have taken away *my gods*
31. all the time that the house of *God*
20: 2. in the assembly of the people of *God*,
18. and asked counsel *of God*,
27. the ark of the covenant of *God*
21: 2. abode there till even before *God*,
3. And said, O Lord *God of* Israel,
Ru. 1:15. unto her people, and unto *her gods:*
16. *and thy God my God:*
2:12. of the Lord *God of* Israel,
1Sa. 1:17. *and the God of* Israel grant (thee) thy
2: 2. neither (is there) any rock *like our God*.
25. *the judge* shall judge him:
27. there came a man of *God* unto Eli,
30. Wherefore the Lord *God of* Israel
3: 3. ere the lamp of *God* went out
— where the ark of *God* (was),
17. *God* do so to thee, and more also,
4: 4. with the ark of the covenant of *God*.
7. *God* is come into the camp.
8. out of the hand of these mighty *Gods?* these (are) *the Gods* that smote
11. the ark of *God* was taken;
13. his heart trembled for the ark of *God*.
17, 22. the ark of *God* is taken.
18. he made mention of the ark of *God*,
19, 21. the ark of *God* was taken,
5: 1, 2. the Philistines took the ark of *God*,
7. ark of *the God of* Israel shall not
— upon Dagon *our god*.
8. with the ark of *the God of* Israel?
— Let the ark of *the God of* Israel
— carried the ark of *the God of* Israel
10. they sent the ark of *God*
— as the ark of *God* came to Ekron,
— brought about the ark of *the God of*
11. Send away the ark of *the God of*
— the hand of *God* was very heavy there.
6: 3. away the ark of *the God of* Israel,
5. ye shall give glory *unto the God of*
— and from off *your gods*,
20. to stand before this holy Lord *God?*
7: 3. put away *the* strange *gods*
8. to cry unto the Lord *our God*
8: 8. forsaken me, and served other *gods*,

1Sa. 9: 6. in this city a man of *God*,
7. to bring to the man of *God:*
8. will I give to the man of *God*,
9. when a man went to enquire of *God*,
10. the city where the man of *God*
27. that I may shew thee the word of *God*.
10: 3. meet thee three men going up to *God*
5. thou shalt come to the hill of *God*,
7. for *God* (is) with thee.
9. *God* gave him another heart:
10. the Spirit of *God* came upon him,
18. Thus saith the Lord *God of* Israel,
19. ye have this day rejected *your God*,
26. whose hearts *God* had touched.
11: 6. the Spirit of *God* came upon Saul
12: 9. when they forgat the Lord *their God*,
12. the Lord *your God* (was) your king.
14. continue following the Lord *your God:*
19. thy servants unto the Lord *thy God*,
13: 13. the commandment of the Lord *thy God*,
14: 15. a *very great* trembling. (marg. a trembling of *God*)
18. Bring hither the ark of *God*. For the ark of *God* was at that time
36. Let us draw near hither unto *God*
37. Saul asked counsel *of God*,
41. Saul said unto the Lord *God of*
44. *God* do so and more also:
45. he hath wrought with *God*
15: 15, 21. sacrifice unto the Lord *thy God;*
30. that I may worship the Lord *thy God*.
16: 15. an evil spirit from *God* troubleth thee.
16. when the evil spirit from *God*
23. spirit from *God* was upon Saul,
17: 26. defy the armies of *the* living *God?*
36. defied the armies of *the* living *God*.
43. the Philistine cursed David *by his gods*.
45. *the God of* the armies of Israel,
46. know that there is *a God* in Israel.
18: 10. the evil spirit from *God* came
19: 20. the Spirit of *God* was upon the messengers
23. the Spirit of *God* was upon him
20: 12. O Lord *God of* Israel,
22: 3. till I know what *God* will do
13. hast enquired *of God* for him,
15. begin to enquire *of God* for him?
23: 7. *God* hath delivered him
10. Then said David, O Lord *God of*
11. O Lord *God of* Israel, I beseech thee,
14. *God* delivered him not into his hand.
16. strengthened his hand *in God*.
25: 22. do *God* unto the enemies of David,
29. with the Lord *thy God;*
32. Blessed (be) the Lord *God of* Israel,
34. the Lord *God of* Israel liveth,
26: 8. *God* hath delivered thine enemy
19. saying, Go, serve other *gods*.
28: 13. I saw *gods* ascending out of the earth.
15. *and God* is departed from me,
29: 9. as an angel of *God:*
30: 6. encouraged himself in the Lord *his God*.
15. Swear unto me *by God*,
2Sa. 2: 27. Joab said, (As) *God* liveth,
3: 9. So do *God* to Abner, and more also,
35. So do *God* to me, and more also,
5: 10. the Lord *God of* hosts (was) with him.
6: 2. bring up from thence the ark of *God*,
3. they set the ark of *God* upon
4. accompanying the ark of *God:*
6. put forth (his hand) to the ark of *God*,
7. *God* smote him there for (his) error; and there he died by the ark of *God*.
12. because of the ark of *God*.
— brought up the ark of *God*
7: 2. but the ark of *God* dwelleth
22. Wherefore thou art great, O Lord *God:*
— neither (is there any) *God* beside thee,
23. whom *God* went to redeem
— the nations *and their gods?*
24. thou, Lord, art become their *God*.
25. O Lord *God*, the word that thou
26. The Lord of hosts (is) *the God*
27. thou, O Lord of hosts, *God of* Israel,
28. thou (art) that *God*,
9: 3. may shew the kindness of *God*
10: 12. for the cities of *our God:*
12: 7. Thus saith the Lord *God of*

2Sa. 12: 16. David therefore besought *God*
14: 11. remember the Lord *thy God*,
13. a thing against the people of *God?*
14. neither doth *God* respect (any) person:
16. out of the inheritance of *God*.
17. for as an angel of *God*,
— therefore the Lord *thy God* will be
20. to the wisdom of an angel of *God*,
15. 24. bearing the ark of the covenant of *God* and they set down the ark of *God;*
25. Carry back the ark of *God*
29. carried the ark of *God* again
32. where he worshipped *God*,
16: 23. had enquired at the oracle of *God*:
18: 28. Blessed (be) the Lord *thy God*,
19: 13(14). *God* do so to me, and more also,
27(28). the king (is) as an angel of *God:*
21: 14. *God* was intreated for the land.
22: 3. *The God of* my rock;
7. and cried to *my God:*
22. not wickedly departed *from my God*.
30. *by my God* have I leaped over a wall.
32. who (is) a rock, save *our God?*
47. *the God of* the rock of my salvation.
23: 1. the anointed of *the God of* Jacob,
3. *The God of* Israel said,
— ruling in the fear of *God*.
24: 3. Now the Lord *thy God* add
23. The Lord *thy God* accept thee.
24. unto the Lord *my God*
1K. 1: 17. thou swarest by the Lord *thy God*
30. I sware unto thee by the Lord *God of*
36. the Lord *God of* my lord the king
47. *God* make the name of Solomon
48. Blessed (be) the Lord *God of* Israel,
2: 3. keep the charge of the Lord *thy God*,
23. *God* do so to me, and more also,
3: 5. *God* said, Ask what I shall give
7. O Lord *my God*, thou hast made
11. And *God* said unto him,
28. they saw that the wisdom of *God*
4: 29(5:9). *God* gave Solomon wisdom
5: 3(17). the name of the Lord *his God*
4(18). the Lord *my God* hath given
5(19). unto the name of the Lord *my God*,
8: 15. Blessed (be) the Lord *God of* Israel,
17, 20. for the name of the Lord *God of*
23. he said, Lord *God of* Israel, (there is) no *God* like thee,
25. Lord *God of* Israel,
26. O *God of* Israel, let thy word,
27. will *God* indeed dwell on the earth?
28. to his supplication, O Lord *my God*,
57. The Lord *our God* be with us,
59. be nigh unto the Lord *our God*
60. may know that the Lord (is) *God*.
61. be perfect with the Lord *our God*,
65. before the Lord *our God*,
9: 6. serve other *gods*, and worship them:
9. Because they forsook the Lord *their God*,
— have taken hold *upon* other *gods*,
10: 9. Blessed be the Lord *thy God*,
24. which *God* had put in his heart.
11: 2. turn away your heart after *their gods:*
4. heart after other *gods:* and his heart was not perfect with the Lord *his God*,
5, 33. Ashtoreth *the goddess of* the Zidonians,
8. and sacrificed *unto their gods*.
9. turned from the Lord *God of* Israel,
10. that he should not go after other *gods:*
23. *God* stirred him up (another) adversary,
31. thus saith the Lord, *the God of* Israel,
33. Chemosh *the god of* the Moabites, and Milcom *the god of* the children of
12: 22. But the word of *God* came unto Shemaiah the man of *God*,
28. *thy gods*, O Israel, which brought thee up
13: 1. there came a man of *God*
4. heard the saying of the man of *God*,
5. which the man of *God* had given
6. said unto the man of *God*, Intreat now the face of the Lord *thy God*,
— And the man of *God* besought the Lord,
7. the king said unto the man of *God*,
8. the man of *God* said unto the king,
11. works that the man of *God* had
12. what way the man of *God* went,

1K. 13:14. went after the man of *God*,
— the man of *God* that camest from
21. he cried unto the man of *God*
— which the Lord *thy God* commanded
26. he said, It (is) the man of *God*,
29. the carcase of the man of *God*,
31. wherein the man of *God* (is) buried;
14: 7. Thus saith the Lord *God of* Israel,
9. gone and made thee other *gods*,
13. toward the Lord *God of* Israel
15: 3. was not perfect with the Lord *his God*,
4. for David's sake did the Lord *his God*
30. he provoked the Lord *God of*
16:13. in provoking the Lord *God of* Israel
26, 33. to provoke the Lord *God of* Israel
17: 1. the Lord *God of* Israel liveth,
12. the Lord *thy God* liveth,
14. thus saith the Lord *God of* Israel,
18. to do with thee, O thou man of *God?*
20. unto the Lord, and said, O Lord *my God*,
21. said, O Lord *my God*, I pray thee,
24. I know that thou (art) a man of *God*,
18:10. the Lord *thy God* liveth,
21. if the Lord (be) *God*, follow him:
24. call ye on the name of *your gods*,
— *the God* that answereth by fire, let him be *God*.
25. call on the name of *your gods*,
27. Cry aloud: for he (is) *a god;*
36. Lord *God of* Abraham, Isaac, &c.
— known this day that thou (art) *God*
37. may know that thou (art) the Lord *God*,
39. they said, The Lord, he (is) *the God;* the Lord, he (is) *the God*.
19: 2. So let *the gods* do (to me), and more
8. unto Horeb the mount of *God*.
10, 14. very jealous for the Lord *God of* hosts:
20:10. *The gods* do so unto me, and more also,
23. *Their gods* (are) *gods of* the hills;
28. there came a man of *God*,
— The Lord (is) *God of* the hills, but he (is) not *God of* the vallies,
21:10. Thou didst blaspheme *God*
13. Naboth did blaspheme *God*
22:53(54). provoked to anger the Lord *God of*
2K. 1: 2. enquire of Baal-zebub *the god of*
3. not *a God* in Israel, (that) ye go to enquire of Baal-zebub *the god of* Ekron?
6. not *a God* in Israel, (that) thou sendest to enquire of Baal-zebub *the god of*
9. he spake unto him, Thou man of *God*,
10. If I (be) a man of *God*,
11, 13. said unto him, O man of *God*,
12. If I (be) a man of *God*,
— the fire of *God* came down from heaven,
16. Baal-zebub the *god of* Ekron, (is it) not because (there is) no *God* in Israel
2:14. Where (is) the Lord *God of* Elijah?
4: 7. she came and told the man of *God*.
9. that this (is) an holy man of *God*,
16. Nay, my lord, (thou) man of *God*,
21. on the bed of the man of *God*,
22. that I may run to the man of *God*,
25. came unto the man of *God*
— when the man of *God* saw her
27. she came to the man of *God*
— the man of *God* said,
40. O (thou) man of *God*,
42. brought the man of *God* bread
5: 7. *God*, to kill and to make alive,
8. Elisha the man of *God* had heard
11. call on the name of the Lord *his God*,
14. to the saying of the man of *God:*
15. he returned to the man of *God*,
— I know that (there is) no *God*
17. nor sacrifice *unto* other *gods*,
20. the servant of Elisha the man of *God*,
6: 6. the man of *God* said,
9. the man of *God* sent
10. the place which the man of *God*
15. the servant of the man of *God*
31. *God* do so and more also to me,
7: 2, 19. answered the man of *God*,
17. as the man of *God* had said,
18. as the man of *God* had spoken
8: 2. after the saying of the man of *God:*
4. the servant of the man of *God*,

2K. 8: 7. The man of *God* is come hither.
8. meet the man of *God*,
11. the man of *God* wept.
9: 6. Thus saith the Lord *God of* Israel,
10:31. the law of the Lord *God of* Israel
13:19. the man of *God* was wroth
14:25. to the word of the Lord *God of*
16: 2. in the sight of the Lord *his God*,
17: 7. sinned against the Lord *their God*,
— and had feared other *gods*,
9. against the Lord *their God*,
14. did not believe in the Lord *their God*.
16, 19. commandments of the Lord *their God*,
26, 26, 27. the manner of *the God of* the land.
29. every nation made *gods of their own*,
31. *the gods of* Sepharvaim.
33. served *their own gods*,
35, 37. Ye shall not fear other *gods*,
38. neither shall ye fear other *gods*.
39. the Lord *your God* ye shall fear;
18: 5. He trusted in the Lord *God of* Israel.
12. the voice of the Lord *their God*,
22. We trust in the Lord *our God:*
33. Hath any of *the gods of* the nations
34. Where (are) *the gods of* Hamath, and of Arpad? where (are) *the gods of*
35. among all *the gods of* the countries,
19: 4. It may be the Lord *thy God*
— sent to reproach *the* living *God;*
— the words which the Lord *thy God*
10. Let not *thy God* in whom
12. Have *the gods of* the nations
15. O Lord *God of* Israel,
— thou art *the God*, (even) thou alone,
16. sent him to reproach *the* living *God*.
18. have cast *their gods* into the fire: for they (were) no *gods*,
19. Now therefore, O Lord *our God*,
— thou (art) the Lord *God*, (even) thou
20. Thus saith the Lord *God of* Israel.
37. in the house of Nisroch *his god*,
20: 5. *the God of* David thy father,
21:12. thus saith the Lord *God of* Israel,
22. he forsook the Lord *God of* his fathers,
22:15, 18. Thus saith the Lord *God of* Israel,
17. have burned incense *unto* other *gods*,
23:16. which the man of *God* proclaimed,
17. the sepulchre of the man of *God*,
21. the passover unto the Lord *your God*,
1Ch. 4:10. Jabez called *on the God of* Israel.
— *God* granted him that
5:20. they cried *to God* in the battle,
22. because the war (was) *of God*.
25 *against the God of* their fathers, and went a whoring after *the gods of* the people of the land, whom *God* destroyed
26. *the God of* Israel stirred up
6:48(33). the tabernacle of the house of *God*.
49(34). the servant of *God* had commanded.
9:11. the ruler of the house of *God;*
13. the service of the house of *God*.
26. treasuries of the house of *God*.
27. lodged round about the house of *God*,
10:10. in the house of *their gods*,
11: 2. the Lord *thy God* said unto thee,
19. *My God* forbid it me,
12:17. *the God of* our fathers look
18. for *thy God* helpeth thee.
22. a great host, like the host of *God*.
13: 2. (that it be) of the Lord *our God*,
3. bring again the ark of *our God*
5. bring the ark of *God* from Kirjath-jearim.
6. bring up thence the ark of *God*
7. they carried the ark of *God*
8. David and all Israel played before *God*
10. there he died before *God*.
12. David was afraid of *God*
— How shall I bring the ark of *God*
14. the ark of *God* remained with
14:10. David enquired *of God*,
11. *God* hath broken in upon
12. And when they had left *their gods* there,
14. David enquired again *of God;* and *God* said unto him,
15. *God* is gone forth before thee
16. therefore did as *God* commanded
15: 1. prepared a lace for the ark of *God*,

1Ch.15. 2. None ought to carry the ark of *God*
— chosen to carry the ark of *God*,
12, 14. the ark of the Lord *God of* Israel
13. the Lord *our God* made a breach
15. the Levites bare the ark of *God*
24. the trumpets before the ark of *God:*
26. when *God* helped the Levites
16: 1. So they brought the ark of *God*,
— peace offerings before *God*.
4. praise the Lord *God of* Israel:
6. before the ark of the covenant of *God*.
14. He (is) the Lord *our God;*
25. (is) to be feared above all *gods*.
26. For all *the gods of* the people
35. Save us, O *God of* our salvation,
36. Blessed (be) the Lord *God*
42. with musical instruments of *God*.
17: 2. for *God* (is) with thee.
3. the word of *God* came to Nathan,
16. Who (am) I, O Lord *God*,
17. a small thing in thine eyes, *O God;*
— a man of high degree, O Lord *God*.
20. neither (is there any) *God* beside
21. whom *God* went to redeem
22 thou, Lord, becamest their *God*.
24. The Lord of hosts (is) *the God of* Israel,
(even) *a God* to Israel:
25. For thou, O *my God*, hast told
26. now, Lord, thou art *God*,
19:13. for the cities of *our God:*
21: 7. *God* was displeased with this
8, 17. David said unto *God*,
15. *God* sent an angel unto Jerusalem
17. I pray thee, O Lord *my God*,
30. not go before it to enquire of *God:*
22: 1. This (is) the house of the Lord *God*,
2. wrought stones to build the house of *God*.
6. for the Lord *God of* Israel.
7. unto the name of the Lord *my God:*
11. the house of the Lord *thy God*,
12. keep the law of the Lord *thy God*.
18. (Is) not the Lord *your God*
19. to seek the Lord *your God;*
— the sanctuary of the Lord *God*,
— the holy vessels of *God*,
23:14. Moses the man of *God*,
25. The Lord *God of* Israel hath
28. the service of the house of *God;*
24: 5. governors (of the house) of *God*,
19. as the Lord *God of* Israel had
25: 5. the king's seer in the words of *God*,
— *God* gave to Heman
6. for the service of the house of *God*,
26: 5. for *God* blessed him.
20. over the treasures of the house of *God*,
32. for every matter pertaining to *God*,
28: 2. for the footstool of *our God*,
3. *But God* said unto me,
4. Howbeit the Lord *God of* Israel
8. in the audience of *our God*,
— commandments of the Lord *yourGod:*
9. know thou *the God of* thy father,
12. the treasuries of the house of *God*,
20. nor be dismayed, for the Lord *God*, (even)
my God, (will be) with thee;
21. for all the service of the house of *God*:
29: 1. whom alone *God* hath chosen,
— but for the Lord *God*.
2. my might for the house of *my God*
3. my affection to the house of *my God*,
— have given to the house of *my God*,
7. for the service of the house of *God*
10. Blessed (be) thou, Lord *God of* Israel
13. Now therefore, *our God*,
16. O Lord *our God*, all this store
17. I know also, *my God*,
18. O Lord *God of* Abraham,
20. Now bless the Lord *your God*.
— the Lord *God of* their fathers,
2Ch. 1: 1. the Lord *his God* (was) with him,
3. of the congregation of *God*,
4. the ark of *God* had David brought
7. In that night did *God* appear
8. Solomon said *unto God*,
9. O Lord *God*, let thy promise
11. *God* said to Solomon,
2: 4(3). to the name of the Lord *my God*,

2 Ch. 2: 4(3). the solemn feasts of the Lord *our God*.
5(4). which I build (is) great: for great (is)
our God above all *gods*.
12(11). Blessed (be) the Lord *God of* Israel,
3: 3. for the building of the house of *God*.
4:11. for king Solomon for the house of *God;*
19. vessels that (were for) the house of *God*,
5: 1. the treasures of the house of *God*.
14. the Lord had filled the house of *God*.
6: 4. Blessed (be) the Lord *God of* Israel,
7, 10. the name of the Lord *God of* Israel.
14. *God of* Israel, (there is) no *God* like thee
16, 17. O Lord *God of* Israel,
18. But will *God* in very deed
19. to his supplication, O Lord *my God*,
40. Now, *my God*, let, I beseech thee,
41. therefore arise, O Lord *God*,
— let thy priests, O Lord *God*,
42. O Lord *God*, turn not away
7: 5. the people dedicated the house of *God*.
19. shall go and serve other *gods*,
22. Because they forsook the Lord *God of*
— laid hold *on* other *gods*,
8:14. David the man of *God* commanded.
9: 8. Blessed be the Lord *thy God*,
— for the Lord *thy God:* because *thy God*
23. that *God* had put in his heart.
10:15. for the cause was of *God*,
11: 2. to Shemaiah the man of *God*,
16. to seek the Lord *God of* Israel
— unto the Lord *God of* their fathers.
13: 5. to know that the Lord *God of* Israel
8. which Jeroboam made you *for gods*.
9. be a priest of (them that are) no *gods*.
10. But as for us, the Lord (is) *our God*,
11. keep the charge of the Lord *our God;*
12. *God himself* (is) with us
— fight ye not against the Lord *God of*
15. it came to pass, *that God* smote
16. *God* delivered them into their hand.
18. they relied upon the Lord *God of*
14: 2(1). in the eyes of the Lord *his God:*
4(3). to seek the Lord *God of* their fathers,
7(6). we have sought the Lord *our God*,
11(10). Asa cried unto the Lord *his God*,
—(—). help us, O Lord *our God;*
—(—). O Lord, thou (art) *our God;*
15: 1. the Spirit of *God* came upon
3. Israel (hath been) without *the* true *God*,
4. did turn unto the Lord *God of*
6. *God* did vex them with all
9. that the Lord *his God* (was) with him.
12. a covenant to seek the Lord *God of*
13. would not seek the Lord *God of*
18. he brought into the house of *God*
16: 7. not relied on the Lord *thy God*,
17: 4. sought *to the* (Lord) *God of* his father,
18: 5. *God* will deliver (it) into the king's
13. even what *my God* saith,
31. *God* moved them (to depart) from
19: 3. hast prepared thine heart to seek *God*.
4. unto the Lord *God of* their fathers.
7. no iniquity with the Lord *our God*,
20: 6. O Lord *God of* our fathers, (art) not thou
God in heaven?
7. (Art) not thou *our God*,
12. *O our God*, wilt thou not judge
15. the battle (is) not your's, but *God's*.
19. to praise the Lord *God of* Israel
20. Believe in the Lord *your God*,
29. the fear of *God* was on all the
30. for *his God* gave him rest round about.
33. *unto the God of* their fathers.
21:10. forsaken the Lord *God of* his fathers.
12. Thus saith the Lord *God of* David
22: 7. *And* the destruction of Ahaziah was *of God*
12. hid in the house of *God* six years:
23: 3. with the king in the house of *God*.
9. which (were) in the house of *God*.
24: 5. repair the house of *your God*
7. had broken up the house of *God;*
9. Moses the servant of *God*
13. set the house of *God* in his state,
16. both toward *God*, and toward his house.
18. the Lord *God of* their fathers,
20. the Spirit of *God* came upon
— Thus saith *God*, Why transgress ye

2Ch24:24. forsaken the Lord *God of* their fathers.
27. the repairing of the house of *God*,
25: 7. there came a man of *God* to him,
8. *God* shall make thee fall before the enemy: for *God* hath power to help,
9. Amaziah said to the man of *God*,
— the man of *God* answered,
14. he brought *the gods of* the children of Seir, and set them up (to be) his *gods*,
15. sought after *the gods of* the people,
16. I know that *God* hath determined
20. would not hear; for it (came) *of God*,
— they sought after *the gods of* Edom.
24. found in the house of *God*
26: 5. he sought *God* in the days of
— understanding in the visions of *God*:
— *God* made him to prosper.
7. *God* helped him against the
16. transgressed against the Lord *his God*,
18. for thine honour from the Lord *God*.
27: 6. his ways before the Lord *his God*.
28: 5. the Lord *his God* delivered him
6. they had forsaken the Lord *God of*
9. because the Lord *God of* your fathers
10. sins against the Lord *your God*?
23. he sacrificed *unto the gods of*
— *the gods of* the kings of Syria help
24, 24. the vessels of the house of *God*,
25. to burn incense *unto* other *gods*, and provoked to anger the Lord *God of*
29: 5. sanctify the house of the Lord *God of* your fathers
6. evil in the eyes of the Lord *our God*,
7. *unto the God of* Israel.
10. a covenant with the Lord *God of*
36. that *God* had prepared the people:
30: 1, 5. passover unto the Lord *God of* Israel.
6. turn again unto the Lord *God of*
7. trespassed against the Lord *God of*
8. serve the Lord *your God*,
9. for the Lord *your God* (is) gracious
12. the hand of *God* was to give them
16. the law of Moses the man of *God*:
19. prepareth his heart to seek *God*, the Lord *God of* his fathers,
22. confession to the Lord *God of*
31: 6. consecrated unto the Lord *their God*,
13. the ruler of the house of *God*.
14. over the freewill offerings of *God*,
20. before the Lord *his God*.
21. in the service of the house of *God*,
— the commandments, to seek *his God*,
32: 8. but with us (is) the Lord *our God*
11. The Lord *our God* shall deliver
13. were *the gods of* the nations
14. Who (was there) among all *the gods of*
— that *your God* should be able
15. how much less shall *your God*
16. spake yet (more) against the Lord *God*,
17. to rail on the Lord *God of* Israel,
— *As the gods of* the nations
— so shall not *the God of* Hezekiah
19. they spake against *the God of* Jerusalem, as against *the gods of*
21. was come into the house of *his god*,
29. for *God* had given him
31. *God* left him, to try him,
33: 7. in the house of *God*, of which *God* had
12. he besought the Lord *his God*,
— before the *God of* his fathers,
13. Manasseh knew that the Lord he (was) *God*.
15. he took away *the* strange *gods*,
16. to serve the Lord *God of* Israel.
17. unto the Lord *their God* only.
18. his prayer unto *his God*,
— in the name of the Lord *God of*
34: 3. began to seek *after the God of*
8. repair the house of the Lord *his God*.
9. brought into the house of *God*,
23, 26. Thus saith the Lord *God of* Israel,
25. have burned incense *unto* other *gods*,
27. didst humble thyself before *God*,
32. according to the covenant of *God*
—, 33. *the God of* their fathers.
33. to serve the Lord *their God*.
35: 3. serve now the Lord *your God*,

2Ch.35: 8. rulers of the house of *God*,
21. *for God* commanded me to make haste: forbear thee *from* (meddling with) *God*,
22. from the mouth of *God*,
36: 5, 12. evil in the sight of the Lord *his God*
13. who had made him swear *by God*:
— from turning unto the Lord *God of*
15. the Lord *God of* their fathers
16. they mocked the messengers of *God*,
18. all the vessels of the house of *God*,
19. they burnt the house of *God*,
23. hath the Lord *God of* heaven given me;
— The Lord *his God* (be) with him,
Ezr. 1: 2. The Lord *God of* heaven hath given
3. *his God* be with him,
— build the house of the Lord *God of* Israel, he (is) *the God*,
4. freewill offering for the house of *God*
5. all (them) whose spirit *God* had
7. had put them in the house of *his gods*;
2:68. offered freely for the house of *God*
3: 2. builded the altar of *the God of*
— in the law of Moses the man of *God*.
8. their coming unto the house of *God*
9. the workmen in the house of *God*:
4: 1. the temple unto the Lord *God of*
2. for we seek *your God*,
3. to build an house *unto our God*;
— will build unto the Lord *God of*
6:21. to seek the Lord *God of* Israel,
22. the work of the house of *God*, *the God of*
7: 6. the Lord *God of* Israel had given:
— to the hand of the Lord *his God*
9. according to the good hand of *his God*
27. Blessed (be) the Lord *God of*
28. as the hand of the Lord *my God*
8:17. ministers for the house of *our God*,
18. by the good hand of *our God*
21. afflict ourselves before *our God*,
22. The hand of *our God* (is) upon all
23. besought *our God* for this:
25. the offering of the house of *our God*,
28. unto the Lord *God of* your fathers.
30. unto the house of *our God*.
31. the hand of *our God* was upon us,
33. weighed in the house of *our God*
35. burnt offerings *unto the God of*
36. and the house of *God*.
9: 4. at the words of *the God of* Israel,
5. my hands unto the Lord *my God*,
6. O *my God*, I am ashamed and blush to lift up my face to thee, *my God*:
8. been (shewed) from the Lord *our God*,
— that *our God* may lighten our eyes,
9. yet *our God* hath not forsaken us
— to set up the house of *our God*,
10. *our God*, what shall we say
13. seeing that thou *our God*
15. O Lord *God of* Israel,
10: 1, 6. before the house of *God*,
2. We have trespassed *against our God*,
3. make a covenant *with our God*
— the commandment of *our God*;
9. in the street of the house of *God*,
11. make confession unto the Lord *God of*
14. until the fierce wrath of *our God*
Neh. 1: 4. prayed before *the God of* heaven,
5. I beseech thee, O Lord *God of* heaven,
2: 4. I prayed to *the God of* heaven.
8. according to the good hand of *my God*
12. what *my God* had put in my heart
18. I told them of the hand of *my God*
20. *The God of* heaven, he will prosper us;
4: 4(3:36). *O our God*; for we are despised:
9(3). we made our prayer unto *our God*,
15(9). *God* had brought their counsel
20(14). *our God* shall fight for us.
5: 9. walk in the fear of *our God*
13. So *God* shake out every man
15. because of the fear of *God*.
19. Think upon me, *my God*, for good,
6:10. meet together in the house of *God*,
12. I perceived that *God* had not sent him
14. *My God*, think thou upon Tobiah
16. this work was wrought of *our God*.
7: 2. a faithful man, and feared *God* above
5. *my God* put into mine heart

Neh. 8: 6. Ezra blessed the Lord, *the* great *God.*
8. read in the book in the law of *God*
9. holy unto the Lord *your God;*
16. in the courts of the house of *God,*
18. he read in the book of the law of *God.*
9: 3. the book of the law of the Lord *their God*
— worshipped the Lord *their God.*
4. a loud voice unto the Lord *their God.*
5. bless the Lord *your God* for ever
7. Thou (art) the Lord *the God,*
18. This (is) *thy God* that brought thee up
32. *our God,* the great, the mighty,
10:28(29). of the lands unto the law of *God,*
29(30). to walk in *God's* law, which was given by Moses the servant of *God,*
32(33). the service of the house of *our God;*
33(34). all the work of the house of *our God.*
34(35). bring (it) into the house of *our God,*
—(—). upon the altar of the Lord *our God,*
36(37). the house of *our God,* unto the priests that minister in the house of *our God:*
37(38). the chambers of the house of *our God;*
38(39). the tithes unto the house of *our God,*
39(40). will not forsake the house of *our God.*
11:11. the ruler of the house of *God.*
16. outward business of the house of *God.*
22. over the business of the house of *God.*
12:24. commandment of David the man of *God,*
36. instruments of David the man of *God,*
40. thanks in the house of *God,*
43. *God* had made them rejoice
45. the porters kept the ward of *their God,*
46. praise and thanksgiving *unto God.*
13: 1. into the congregation of *God* for ever;
2. howbeit *our God* turned the curse
4. the chamber of the house of *our God,*
7. in the courts of the house of *God.*
9. the vessels of the house of *God,*
11. Why is the house of *God* forsaken?
14, 22, 31. Remember me, *O my God,*
— I have done for the house of *my God,*
18. did not *our God* bring all this
25. made them swear *by God,*
26. who was beloved *of his God,* and *God* made him king over all
27. to transgress *against our God*
29. Remember them, *O my God,*
Job 1: 1. one that feared *God,*
5. cursed *God* in their hearts.
6. when the sons of *God* came
8. one that feareth *God,*
9. Doth Job fear *God* for nought?
16. The fire of *God* is fallen from heaven,
22. nor charged *God* foolishly.
2: 1. a day when the sons of *God* came
3. one that feareth *God,*
9. retain thine integrity? curse *God,* and die.
10. we receive good at the hand of *God,*
5: 8. and unto *God* would I commit
20:29. the portion of a wicked man *from God,*
28:23. *God* understandeth the way
32: 2. justified himself *rather than God.*
34: 9. he should delight himself with *God.*
38: 7. all the sons of *God* shouted
Ps. 3: 2(3). no help for him *in God.*
7(8). Arise, O Lord; save me, *O my God:*
4: 1(2). *O God of* my righteousness:
5: 2(3). my King, *and my God:* for unto thee
10(11). Destroy thou them, *O God;*
7: 1(2). O Lord *my God,* in thee do I put
3(4). O Lord *my God,* if I have done
9(10). the righteous *God* trieth the hearts
10(11). My defence (is) of *God,*
11(12). *God* judgeth the righteous,
8: 5(6). made him a little lower *than the angels,*
9:17(18). all the nations that forget *God.*
10: 4. *God* (is) not in all his thoughts.
13. doth the wicked contemn *God?*
13: 3(4). (and) hear me, O Lord *my God:*
14: 1. said in his heart, (There is) no *God.*
2. did understand, (and) seek *God.*
5. *God* (is) in the generation of the
18: 6(7). cried unto *my God:*
21(22). not wickedly departed *from my God.*
28(29). the Lord *my God* will enlighten
29(30). *and by my God* have I leaped over
31(32). who (is) a rock save *our God?*

Ps. 18:46(47). let *the God of* my salvation be
20: 1(2). name of *the God of* Jacob
5(6). in the name of *our God* we will
7(8). the name of the Lord *our God.*
22: 2(3). *O my God,* I cry in the daytime,
24: 5. righteousness *from the God of* his
25: 2. *O my God,* I trust in thee:
5. for thou (art) *the God of* my salvation;
22. Redeem Israel, *O God,* out of all
27: 9. neither forsake me, *O God of* my salvation.
30: 2(3). O Lord *my God,* I cried unto thee,
12(13). O Lord *my God,* I will give thanks
31:14(15). I said, Thou (art) *my God.*
33:12. Blessed (is) the nation *whose God*
35:23. unto my cause, *my God* and my Lord.
24. Judge me, O Lord *my God,*
36: 1(2). no fear of *God* before his eyes.
7(8). excellent (is) thy lovingkindness, *O God!*
37:31. The law of *his God*
38:15(16). thou wilt hear, O Lord *my God.*
21(22). *O my God,* be not far from me.
40: 3(4). praise *unto our God:*
5(6). Many, O Lord *my God,*
8(9). I delight to do thy will, *O my God:*
17(18). make no tarrying, *O my God.*
41:13(14). Blessed (be) the Lord *God of* Israel
42: 1(2). so panteth my soul after thee, *O God.*
2(3). My soul thirsteth *for God,*
—(-). I come and appear before *God?*
3(4). say unto me, Where (is) *thy God?*
4(5). with them to the house of *God,*
5(6), 11(12). hope thou *in God:*
6(7). *O my God,* my soul is cast down
10(11). daily unto me, Where (is) *thy God?*
11(12). of my countenance, *and my God.*
43: 1. Judge me, *O God,* and plead my cause
2. thou (art) *the God of* my strength:
4. will I go unto the altar of *God,*
— upon the harp will I praise thee, *O God my God.*
5. hope *in God:* for I shall yet praise
— of my countenance, *and my God.*
44: 1(2). We have heard with our ears, *O God,*
4(5). Thou art my King, *O God:*
8(9). *In God* we boast all the day
20(21). forgotten the name of *our God,*
21(22). Shall not *God* search this out?
45: 2(3). therefore *God* hath blessed thee
6(7). Thy throne, *O God,* (is) for ever
7(8). hatest wickedness: therefore *God, thy God,* hath anointed thee
46: 1(2). *God* (is) our refuge and strength,
4(5). shall make glad the city of *God,*
5(6). *God* (is) in the midst of her; she shall not be moved: *God* shall help her,
7(8), 11(12). *the God of* Jacob (is) our refuge.
10(11). know that I (am) *God:*
47: 1(2). shout *unto God* with the voice
5(6). *God* is gone up with a shout,
6(7). Sing praises to *God,* sing praises:
7(8). *God* (is) the King of all the earth:
8(9). *God* reigneth over the heathen: *God* sitteth upon the throne
9(10). the people of *the God of* Abraham: for the shields of the earth (belong) *unto God:*
48: 1(2), 8(9). in the city of *our God,*
3(4). *God* is known in her palaces
8(9). *God* will establish it for ever.
9(10). thy lovingkindness, *O God,*
10(11). According to thy name, *O God,*
14(15). For this *God* (is) *our God*
49: 7(8). nor give *to God* a ransom for him:
15(16). But *God* will redeem my soul
50: 1. The mighty *God,* (even) the Lord,
2. perfection of beauty, *God* hath shined.
3. *Our God* shall come,
6. for *God* (is) judge himself.
7. I (am) *God,* (even) *thy God.*
14. Offer *unto God* thanksgiving;
16. But unto the wicked *God* saith,
23. will I shew the salvation of *God.*
51: 1(3). Have mercy upon me, *O God,*
10(12). Create in me a clean heart, *O God;*
14(16). Deliver me from bloodguiltiness, *O God,* thou *God of* my salvation:
17(19). The sacrifices of *God* (are) a broken

Ps. 51:17(19). a contrite heart, *O God*, thou wilt not despise.
52: 7(9). man (that) made not *God* his strength;
8(10). olive tree in the house of *God:* I trust in the mercy of *God* for ever
53: 1(2). said in his heart, (There is) no *God*.
2(3). *God* looked down from heaven
—(-). did understand, that did seek *God*.
4(5). they have not called upon *God*.
5(6). for *God* hath scattered the bones
—(-). because *God* hath despised them.
6(7). When *God* bringeth back the captivity
54: 1(3). Save me, *O God*, by thy name,
2(4). Hear my prayer, *O God;*
3(5). they have not set *God* before them.
4(6). Behold, *God* (is) mine helper:
55: 1(2). Give ear to my prayer, *O God;*
14(15). walked unto the house of *God*
16(17). As for me, I will call upon *God;*
19(20). therefore they fear not *God*.
23(24). But thou, *O God*, shalt bring
56: 1(2). Be merciful unto me, *O God:*
4(5). *In God* I will praise his word, *in God* I have put my trust;
7(8). cast down the people, *O God*.
9(10). this I know; for *God* (is) for me.
10(11). *In God* will I praise (his) word:
11(12). *In God* have I put my trust:
12(13). Thy vows (are) upon me, *O God:*
13(14). that I may walk before *God*
57: 1(2). Be merciful unto me, *O God*,
2(3). I will cry *unto God* most high;
3(4). *God* shall send forth his mercy
5(6), 11(12). Be thou exalted, *O God*, above
7(8). My heart is fixed, *O God*,
58: 6(7). Break their teeth, *O God*,
11(12). verily he is *a God* that judgeth
59: 1(2). from mine enemies, *O my God:*
5(6). Thou therefore, O Lord *God of* hosts, *the God of* Israel,
9(10), 17(18). for *God* (is) my defence.
10(11). *The God of* my mercy shall prevent me: *God* shall let me see
13(14). let them know that *God* ruleth
17(18). *the God of* my mercy.
60: 1(3). *O God*, thou hast cast us off,
6(8). *God* hath spoken in his holiness;
10(12). (Wilt) not thou, *O God*,
—(—). *O God*, (which) didst not go out
12(14). *Through God* we shall do valiantly:
61: 1(2). Hear my cry, *O God;*
5(6). For thou, *O God*, hast heard
7(8). He shall abide before *God* for ever:
62: 1(2). Truly my soul waiteth upon *God:*
5(6) My soul, wait thou only *upon God;*
7(8). In *God* (is) my salvation
—(-). my refuge, (is) *in God*.
8(9). *God* (is) a refuge for us.
11(12). *God* hath spoken once;
—(—). that power (belongeth) *unto God*.
63: 1(2). *O God*, thou (art) my God;
11(12). But the king shall rejoice *in God;*
64: 1(2). Hear my voice, *O God*, in my prayer:
7(8). But *God* shall shoot at them
9(10). shall declare the work of *God;*
65: 1(2). Praise waiteth for thee, *O God*,
5(6). wilt thou answer us, *O God of* our
9(10). enrichest it with the river of *God*,
66: 1. Make a joyful noise *unto God*,
3. Say *unto God*, How terrible (art thou)
5. Come and see the works of *God:*
8. O bless *our God*, ye people,
10. For thou, *O God*, hast proved us:
16. hear, all ye that fear *God*,
19. verily *God* hath heard (me);
20. Blessed (be) *God*, which hath
67: 1(2). *God* be merciful unto us,
3(4), 5(6). people praise thee, *O God;*
6(7). *God*, (even) *our own God*, shall bless
7(8). *God* shall bless us; and all the
68: 1(2). Let *God* arise, let his enemies be
2(3). wicked perish at the presence of *God*.
3(4). let them rejoice before *God:*
4(5). Sing *unto God*, sing praises
5(6). *God* in his holy habitation.
6(7). *God* setteth the solitary in families:
7(8). *O God*, when thou wentest forth

Ps. 68: 8(9). dropped at the presence of *God:* (even) Sinai itself (was moved) at the presence of *God*, *the God of* Israel.
9(10). Thou, *O God*, didst send a plentiful
10(11). thou, *O God*, hast prepared
15(16). The hill of *God* (is as) the hill of
16(17). the hill (which) *God* desireth
17(18). The chariots of *God* (are)
18(19). that the Lord *God* might dwell
21(22). *God* shall wound the head of his
24(25). They have seen thy goings, *O God;*
26(27). Bless ye *God* in the congregations,
28(29). *Thy God* hath commanded thy strength: strengthen, *O God*, that
31(32). soon stretch out her hands *unto God*.
32(33). Sing *unto God*, ye kingdoms
34(35). Ascribe ye strength *unto God:*
35(36). *O God*, (thou art) terrible
—(—). Blessed (be) *God*.
69: 1(2). Save me, *O God;* for the waters
3(4). fail while I wait *for my God*.
5(6). *O God*, thou knowest my foolishness;
6(7). for my sake, *O God of* Israel.
13(14). *O God*, in the multitude of
29(30). *O God*, set me up on high.
30(31). I will praise the name of *God*
32(33). your heart shall live that seek *God*.
35(36). For *God* will save Zion,
70: 1(2). (Make haste), *O God*, to deliver
4(5). say continually, Let *God* be magnified.
5(6). make haste unto me, *O God:*
71: 4. Deliver me, *O my God*, out of the hand
11. Saying, *God* hath forsaken him:
12. *O God*, be not far from me: *O my God*,
17. *O God*, thou hast taught me
18. *O God*, forsake me not;
19. Thy righteousness also, *O God*,
— *O God*, who (is) like unto thee!
22. (even) thy truth, *O my God:*
72: 1. Give the king thy judgments, *O God*,
18. Blessed (be) the Lord *God*, *the God of*
73: 1. Truly *God* (is) good to Israel,
26. *God* (is) the strength of my heart,
28. good for me to draw near to *God:*
74: 1. *O God*, why hast thou cast (us) off
10. *O God*, how long shall the adversary
12. *For God* (is) my King of old,
22. Arise, *O God*, plead thine own cause:
75: 1(2). Unto thee, *O God*, do we give thanks
7(8). But *God* (is) the judge:
9(10). I will sing praises *to the God of*
76: 1(2). In Judah (is) *God* known:
6(7). At thy rebuke, *O God of* Jacob,
9(10). When *God* arose to judgment,
11(12). pay unto the Lord *your God:*
77: 1(2). *God* with my voice, (even) unto *God*
3(4). I remembered *God*, and was troubled:
13(14). way, *O God*, (is) in the sanctuary: who (is so) great a God *as* (our) *God!*
16(17). The waters saw thee, *O God*,
78: 7. they might set their hope *in God*,
10. They kept not the covenant of *God*,
19. Yea, they spake *against God;*
22. Because they believed not *in God*,
31. The wrath of *God* came upon them,
35. they remembered that *God*
56. and provoked the most high *God*,
59. When *God* heard (this), he was wroth,
79: 1. *O God*, the heathen are come
9. Help us, *O God of* our salvation,
10. the heathen say, Where (is) *their God?*
80: 3(4). Turn us again, *O God*,
4(5). O Lord *God* of hosts, how long
7(8). Turn us again, *O God* of hosts,
14(15). Return, we beseech thee, *O God* of
19(20). Turn us again, O Lord *God* of hosts,
81: 1(2). Sing aloud *unto God* our strength: make a joyful noise *unto the God of*
4(5). a law *of the God of* Jacob.
10(11). I (am) the Lord *thy God*,
82: 1. *God* standeth in the congregation of the mighty; he judgeth among *the gods*.
6. I have said, Ye (are) *gods;*
8. Arise, *O God*, judge the earth:
83: 1(2). Keep not thou silence, *O God:*
12(13). the houses of *God* in possession.
13(14). *O my God*, make them like a wheel,

Ps. 84. 3(4). Lord of hosts, my King, *and my God.*
7(8). in Zion appeareth before *God.*
8(9). O Lord *God* of hosts, hear my prayer: give ear, *O God of* Jacob.
9(10). Behold, *O God* our shield,
10(11). doorkeeper in the house of *my God,*
11(12). For the Lord *God* (is) a sun
85: 4(5). Turn us, *O God of* our salvation,
86: 2. O thou *my God,* save thy servant
8. *Among the gods* (there is) none
10. thou (art) *God* alone.
12. I will praise thee, O Lord *my God,*
14. *O God,* the proud are risen
87: 3. are spoken of thee, O city of *God.*
88: 1(2). O Lord *God of* my salvation,
89: 8(9). O Lord *God of* hosts,
90: [title](1). Prayer of Moses the man of *God.*
17. the beauty of the Lord *our God*
91: 2. *my God;* in him will I trust.
92: 13(14). flourish in the courts of *our God.*
94: 7. neither shall *the God of* Jacob
22. *and my God* (is) the rock of
23. the Lord *our God* shall cut them off.
95: 3. a great King above all *gods.*
7. For he (is) *our God;*
96: 4. he (is) to be feared above all *gods.*
5. For all *the gods of* the nations
97. 7. worship him, all (ye) *gods.*
9. thou art exalted far above all *gods.*
98: 3. have seen the salvation of *our God.*
99: 5. Exalt ye the Lord *our God,*
8. Thou answeredst them, O Lord *our God:*
9. Exalt the Lord *our God,*
— for the Lord *our God* (is) holy.
100: 3. Know ye that the Lord he (is) *God:*
104: 1. O Lord *my God,* thou art very great;
33. I will sing praise *to my God* while
105: 7. He (is) the Lord *our God:*
106: 47. Save us, O Lord *our God,*
48. Blessed (be) the Lord *God of* Israel
108: 1(2). *O God,* my heart is fixed;
5(6). Be thou exalted, *O God,* above
7(8). *God* hath spoken in his holiness;
11(12). *O God,* (who) hast cast us off? and wilt not thou, *O God,* go forth with
13(14). *Through God* we shall do valiantly:
109: 1. Hold not thy peace, *O God of*
26. Help me, O Lord *my God:*
113: 5. Who (is) like unto the Lord *our God,*
115: 2. Where (is) now *their God?*
3. *But our God* (is) in the heavens:
116: 5. *yea, our God* (is) merciful.
118: 28. *my God,* I will exalt thee.
119: 115. keep the commandments of *my God.*
122: 9. the house of the Lord *our God*
123: 2. our eyes (wait) upon the Lord *our God,*
135: 2. in the courts of the house of *our God,*
5. and (that) our Lord (is) above all *Gods.*
136: 2. O give thanks *unto the God of gods:*
138: 1. before *the gods* will I sing praise
143: 10. for thou (art) *my God:*
144: 9. a new song unto thee, *O God:*
15. *whose God* (is) the Lord.
145: 1. I will extol thee, *my God,*
146: 2. I will sing praises *unto my God*
5. whose hope (is) in the Lord *his God:*
10. *thy God,* O Zion, unto all generations.
147: 1. good to sing praises unto *our God;*
7. sing praise upon the harp *unto our God:*
12. praise *thy God,* O Zion.
Pro. 2: 5. and find the knowledge of *God.*
17. forgetteth the covenant of *her God.*
3: 4. in the sight of *God* and man.
25: 2. the glory of *God* to conceal a thing:
30: 9. take the name of *my God*
Ecc. 1: 13. this sore travail hath *God* given
2: 24. that it (was) from the hand of *God.*
26. good before *God.*
3: 10. *God* hath given to the sons of men
11. the work that *God* maketh
13. all his labour, it (is) the gift of *God.*
14. whatsoever *God* doeth, it shall be
— *and God* doeth (it), that (men) should fear
15. *and God* requireth that which is past.
17. *God* shall judge the righteous
18. that *God* might manifest them,
5: 1(4:17). when thou goest to the house of *God,*
Ecc. 5: 2(1). utter (any) thing before *God:* for *God*
4(3). When thou vowest a vow *unto God,*
6(5). wherefore should *God* be angry
7(6). but fear thou *God.*
18(17). which *God* giveth him:
19(18). to whom *God* hath given riches
—(—). this (is) the gift of *God.*
20(19). *God* answereth (him) in the joy of
6: 2. A man to whom *God* hath given riches,
— yet *God* giveth him not power
7: 13. Consider the work of *God:*
14. *God* also hath set the one over
18. he that feareth *God* shall come
26. whoso pleaseth *God* shall escape
29. that *God* hath made man
8: 2. in regard of the oath of *God.*
12. be well with them that fear *God,*
13. because he feareth not before *God.*
15. which *God* giveth him under
17. I beheld all the work of *God,*
9: 1. their works, (are) in the hand of *God:*
7. for *God* now accepteth thy works.
11: 5. knowest not the works of *God*
9. *God* will bring thee into judgment.
12. 7. shall return unto *God* who gave it.
13. Fear *God,* and keep his commandments
14. For *God* shall bring every work
Isa. 1: 10. give ear unto the law of *our God,*
2: 3. to the house of *the God of* Jacob;
7: 11. Ask thee a sign of the Lord *thy God;*
13. but will ye weary *my God* also?
8. 19. not a people seek unto *their God?*
21. curse their king *and their God,*
13. 19. shall be as when *God* overthrew
17. 6. saith the Lord *God of* Israel.
10. thou hast forgotten *the God of* thy
21. 9. all the graven images of *her gods*
10. the Lord of hosts, *the God of* Israel,
17. for the Lord *God of* Israel hath
24: 15. the name of the Lord *God of* Israel
25: 1. O Lord, thou (art) *my God;*
9. in that day, Lo, this (is) *our God;*
26: 13. O Lord *our God,* (other) lords
28: 26. For *his God* doth instruct him
29: 23. shall fear *the God of* Israel.
30: 18. for the Lord (is) *a God of* judgment:
35: 2. the excellency of *our God.*
4. *your God* will come (with) vengeance, (even) *God* (with) a recompence;
36: 7. We trust in the Lord *our God:*
18. Hath any of *the gods of* the nations
19. Where (are) *the gods of* Hamath and Arphad? where (are) *the gods of*
20. among all *the gods of* these lands,
37: 4. It may be the Lord *thy God*
— hath sent to reproach *the* living *God,*
— which the Lord *thy God* hath heard:
10. Let not *thy God,* in whom thou
12. Have *the gods of* the nations
16. O Lord of hosts, *God of* Israel,
— thou (art) *the God,* (even) thou
17. hath sent to reproach *the* living *God.*
19. have cast *their gods* into the fire: for they (were) no *gods,*
20. Now therefore, O Lord *our God,*
21. Thus saith the Lord *God of* Israel,
38. in the house of Nisroch *his god,*
38. 5. *the God of* David thy father,
40: 1. comfort ye my people, saith *your God.*
3. in the desert a highway *for our God.*
8. but the word of *our God* shall
9. the cities of Judah, Behold *your God!*
27. *and* my judgment is passed over *from my God?*
28. *the* everlasting *God,*
41: 10. be not dismayed; for I (am) *thy God:*
13. I the Lord *thy God* will hold
17. (I) *the God of* Israel will not
23. that we may know that ye (are) *gods:*
42: 17. the molten images, Ye (are) *our gods.*
43: 3. For I (am) the Lord *thy God,*
44: 6. beside me (there is) no *God.*
45: 3. by thy name, (am) *the God of* Israel.
5. (there is) no *God* beside me:
14. (there is) no *God.*
15. *O God of* Israel, the Saviour.
18. *God* himself that formed the earth

Isa. 45:21. and (there is) no *God* else beside
46: 9. (I am) *God*, and (there is) none like me,
48: 1. *and* make mention *of the God of* Israel,
2. stay themselves upon *the God of* Israel;
17. I (am) the Lord *thy God*
49: 4. my work with *my God.*
5. *and my God* shall be my strength.
50:10. and stay *upon his God.*
51:15. But I (am) the Lord *thy God,*
20. the rebuke of *thy God.*
22. *and thy God* (that) pleadeth the cause
52: 7. that saith unto Zion, *Thy God* reigneth!
10. shall see the salvation of *our God.*
12. *the God of* Israel (will be) your
53: 4. smitten of *God*, and afflicted.
54: 5. *The God of* the whole earth
6. thou wast refused, saith *thy God.*
55: 5. because of the Lord *thy God,*
7. to *our God*, for he will abundantly
57:21. no peace, saith *my God*, to the wicked.
58: 2. the ordinance of *their God:*
— take delight in approaching to *God.*
59: 2. separated between you and *your God,*
13. departing away from *our God,*
60: 9. unto the name of the Lord *thy God,*
19. *and thy God* thy glory.
61: 2. the day of vengeance *of our God;*
6. call you the Ministers of *our God:*
10. my soul shall be joyful *in my God:*
62: 3. a royal diadem in the hand of *thy God.*
5. shall *thy God* rejoice over thee.
64: 4(3). neither hath the eye seen, *O God,*
65:16. shall bless himself *in the God of* truth;
— shall swear *by the God of* truth;
66: 9. and shut (the womb)? saith *thy God.*
Jer. 1:16. have burned incense *unto* other *gods,*
2:11. (their) *gods*, which (are) yet no *gods?*
17, 19. thou hast forsaken the Lord *thy God,*
28. But where (are) *thy gods*
— the number of thy cities are *thy gods,*
3:13. transgressed against the Lord *thy God,*
21. have forgotten the Lord *their God.*
22. for thou (art) the Lord *our God.*
23. *our God* (is) the salvation of Israel.
25. sinned against the Lord *our God,*
— obeyed the voice of the Lord *our God.*
5: 4, 5. the judgment of *their God.*
7. sworn by (them that are) no *gods:*
14. thus saith the Lord *God of* hosts,
19. Wherefore doeth the Lord *our God* all
— served strange *gods* in your land,
24. Let us now fear the Lord *our God,*
7: 3, 21. saith the Lord of hosts, *the God of*
6. walk after other *gods* to your hurt:
9. after other *gods* whom ye know not;
18. drink offerings *unto* other *gods,*
23. my voice, and I will be your *God,*
28. not the voice of the Lord *their God,*
8:14. for the Lord *our God* hath put us
9:15(14). the Lord of hosts, *the God of* Israel;
10:10. the Lord (is) the true *God*, he (is) the living *God*, and an everlasting king:
11: 3. Thus saith the Lord *God of* Israel;
4. my people, and I will be your *God:*
10. went after other *gods* to serve them:
12. go, and cry unto *the gods*
13. the number of thy cities were *thy gods,*
13:10. walk after other *gods,*
12. Thus saith the Lord *God of* Israel,
16. Give glory to the Lord *your God,*
14:22. (art) not thou he, O Lord *our God?*
15:16. by thy name, O Lord *God of* hosts.
16: 9. the Lord of hosts, *the God of* Israel;
10. committed against the Lord *our God?*
11. have walked after other *gods,*
13. there shall ye serve other *gods*
20. Shall a man make *gods* unto himself, and they (are) no *gods?*
19: 3, 15. the Lord of hosts, *the God of* Israel;
4. have burned incense in it *unto* other *gods,*
13. drink offerings *unto* other *gods.*
21: 4. Thus saith the Lord *God of* Israel;
22: 9. forsaken the covenant of the Lord *their God*, and worshipped other *gods,*
23: 2. thus saith the Lord *God of* Israel
23. (Am) I *a God* at hand, saith the Lord, and not *a God* afar off?

Jer. 23:36. perverted the words of *the* living *God*, of the Lord of hosts *our God.*
24: 5. Thus saith the Lord, *the God of*
7. and I will be their *God:*
25: 6. go not after other *gods*
15. thus saith the Lord *God of* Israel
27. the Lord of hosts, *the God of* Israel;
26:13. obey the voice of the Lord *your God;*
16. in the name of the Lord *our God.*
27: 4, 21. the Lord of hosts, *the God of* Israel;
28: 2, 14 & 29:4, 8, 21, 25. the Lord of hosts, *the God of* Israel,
30: 2. Thus speaketh the Lord *God of* Israel,
9. they shall serve the Lord *their God,*
22. my people, and I will be your *God.*
31: 1. will I be *the God* of all the families
6. go up to Zion unto the Lord *our God.*
18. for thou (art) the Lord *my God.*
23. the Lord of hosts, *the God of* Israel;
33. and will be their *God*, and they shall be
32:14, 15. the Lord of hosts, *the God of* Israel;
27. I (am) the Lord, *the God of* all flesh:
29. poured out drink offerings *unto* other *gods,*
36. thus saith the Lord, *the God of* Israel,
38. my people, and I will be their *God:*
33: 4 & 34:2, 13. thus saith the Lord, *the God of*
35: 4. the son of Igdaliah, a man of *God,*
13, 18, 19. the Lord of hosts, *the God of* Israel;
15. go not after other *gods* to serve
17. thus saith the Lord *God of* hosts, *the God of* Israel;
37: 3. Pray now unto the Lord *our God* for us.
7. Thus saith the Lord, *the God of* Israel;
38:17. Thus saith the Lord, *the God of* hosts, *the God of* Israel;
39:16. the Lord of hosts, *the God of* Israel;
40: 2. The Lord *thy God* hath pronounced this
42. 2. pray for us unto the Lord *thy God,*
3. That the Lord *thy God* may shew us
4. I will pray unto the Lord *your God*
5. the Lord *thy God* shall send thee
6, 6. the voice of the Lord *our God,*
9. Thus saith the Lord, *the God of* Israel,
13. obey the voice of the Lord *your God,*
15, 18. the Lord of hosts, *the God of* Israel;
20. ye sent me unto the Lord *your God*, saying, Pray for us unto the Lord *our God;* and according unto all that the Lord *our God*
21. obeyed the voice of the Lord *your God,*
43: 1. all the words of the Lord *their God*, for which the Lord *their God* had sent him
2. the Lord *our God* hath not sent thee
10. the Lord of hosts, *the God of* Israel;
12. in the houses of *the gods of* Egypt;
13. the houses of *the gods of* the Egyptians
44: 2, 11, 25. saith the Lord of hosts, *the God of*
3. to serve other *gods,*
5. to burn no incense *unto* other *gods.*
7. thus saith the Lord, *the God of* hosts, *the God of* Israel;
8. burning incense *unto* other *gods*
15. had burned incense *unto* other *gods,*
45: 2. Thus saith the Lord, *the God of* Israel,
46:25. The Lord of hosts, *the God of* Israel,
— Pharaoh, and Egypt, with *their gods,*
48: 1. the Lord of hosts, *the God of* Israel;
35. him that burneth incense *to his gods.*
50: 4. shall go, and seek the Lord *their God.*
18. the Lord of hosts, *the God of* Israel:
28. the vengeance of the Lord *our God,*
40. *God* overthrew Sodom and Gomorrah
51: 5. nor Judah *of his God,*
10. in Zion the work of the Lord *our God.*
33. the Lord of hosts, *the God of* Israel;
Eze. 1: 1. opened, and I saw visions of *God.*
8: 3. brought me in the visions of *God*
4. glory of *the God of* Israel (was) there,
9: 3. glory of *the God of* Israel was gone
10:19. glory of *the God of* Israel (was) over
20. I saw under *the God of* Israel
11:20. my people, and I will be their *God.*
22. the glory of *the God of* Israel
24. in a vision by the Spirit of *God*
14:11. I may be their *God,*
20: 5, 7, 19, 20. I (am) the Lord *your God;*
28:2. I sit (in) the seat of *God,*

Eze. 28: 2. set thine heart as the heart of *God:*
6. thine heart as the heart of *God;*
9. before him that slayeth thee, I (am) *God?*
13. hast been in Eden the garden of *God;*
14. upon the holy mountain of *God;*
16. as profane out of the mountain of *God:*
26. know that I (am) the Lord *their God.*
31: 8. The cedars in the garden of *God*
— nor any tree in the garden of *God*
9. that (were) in the garden of *God,*
34:24. I the Lord will be their *God,*
30. they know that I the Lord *their God*
31. I (am) *your God,* saith the Lord
36:28. I will be your *God.*
37:23, 27. I will be their *God.*
39:22, 28. I (am) the Lord *their God*
40: 2. In the visions of *God* brought he me
43: 2. the glory of *the God of* Israel
44: 2. because the Lord, *the God of* Israel,
Dan. 1: 2. the vessels of the house of *God:*
— to the house of *his god;*
— into the treasure house of *his god.*
9. *God* had brought Daniel into favour
17. *God* gave them knowledge and skill
9: 3. I set my face unto the Lord *God,*
4. I prayed unto the Lord *my God,*
9. To the Lord *our God* (belong) mercies
10. obeyed the voice of the Lord *our God.*
11. law of Moses the servant of *God,*
13. prayer before the Lord *our God,*
14. the Lord *our God* (is) righteous
15. now, O Lord *our God,*
17. Now therefore, *O our God,*
18. *O my God,* incline thine ear,
19. for thine own sake, *O my God:*
20. my supplication before the Lord *my God* for the holy mountain of *my God;*
10:12. to chasten thyself before *thy God,*
11: 8. carry captives into Egypt *their gods,*
32. do know *their God* shall be strong,
37. Neither shall he regard *the God of*
Hos. 1: 7. will save them by the Lord *their God,*
2:23(25). they shall say, (Thou art) *my God.*
3: 1. who look to other *gods,*
5. seek the Lord *their God,*
4: 1. nor knowledge of *God* in the land.
6. thou hast forgotten the law of *thy God,*
12. gone a whoring from under *their God.*
5: 4. doings to turn unto *their God:*
6: 6. the knowledge of *God* more than
7:10. return to the Lord *their God,*
8: 2. Israel shall cry unto me, *My God,*
6. therefore it (is) not *God:*
9: 1. hast gone a whoring from *thy God,*
8. of Ephraim (was) with *my God:*
— hatred in the house of *his God.*
17. *My God* will cast them away,
12: 3(4). he had power with *God:*
5(6). Even the Lord *God of* hosts;
6(7). Therefore turn thou *to thy God:*
—(–). wait on *thy God* continually.
9(10). I (that am) the Lord *thy God*
13: 4. Yet I (am) the Lord *thy God*
— *and* thou shalt know no *god* but me:
16(14:1). she hath rebelled *against her God:*
14: 1(2). return unto the Lord *thy God;*
3(4). work of our hands, (Ye are) *our gods:*
Joel 1:13. ye ministers of *my God:*
— from the house of *your God.*
14. the house of the Lord *your God,*
16. gladness from the house of *our God?*
2:13. turn unto the Lord *your God:*
14. drink offering unto the Lord *your God?*
17. among the people, Where (is) *their God?*
23. rejoice in the Lord *your God:*
26. praise the name of the Lord *your God,*
27 & 3:17(4:17). I (am) the Lord *your God,*
Am. 2: 8. the condemned (in) the house of *their god.*
3:13. *the God of* hosts,
4:11. as *God* overthrew Sodom
12. prepare to meet *thy God,* O Israel.
13. *The God of* hosts, (is) his name.
5:14. *the God of* hosts, shall be with you,
15. the Lord *God of* hosts will be gracious
16. Therefore the Lord, *the God of* hosts,
26. the star of *your god,*
27. whose name (is) *The God of* hosts.
Am. 6: 8. saith the Lord *the God of* hosts,
14. saith the Lord *the God of* hosts;
8:14. and say, *Thy god,* O Dan, liveth;
9:15. given them, saith the Lord *thy God.*
Jon. 1: 5. cried every man unto *his god,*
6. call upon *thy God,* if so be that *God* will
9. I fear the Lord, *the God of* heaven,
2: 1(2). Jonah prayed unto the Lord *his God*
6(7). from corruption, O Lord *my God.*
3: 3. was *an exceeding* great city (marg. *of God*)
5. the people of Nineveh believed *God,*
8. cry mightily unto *God:*
9. Who can tell (if) *God* will turn
10. *God* saw their works,
— *God* repented of the evil, that he
4: 6. the Lord *God* prepared a gourd,
7. But *God* prepared a worm
8. *God* prepared a vehement east wind;
9. *God* said to Jonah,
Mic. 3: 7. for (there is) no answer of *God.*
4: 2. to the house of *the God of* Jacob;
5. the name of *his god,* and we will walk in the name of the Lord *our God*
5: 4(3). the name of the Lord *his God;*
6: 6. bow myself *before the* high *God?*
8. to walk humbly with *thy God?*
7: 7. I will wait *for the God of* my salvation: *my God* will hear me.
10. Where is the Lord *thy God?*
17. shall be afraid of the Lord *our God,*
Nah. 1:14. out of the house of *thy gods*
Hab. 1:12. from everlasting, O Lord *my God,*
3:18. joy *in the God of* my salvation.
Zep. 2: 7. Lord *their God* shall visit them,
9. the Lord of hosts, *the God of* Israel,
11. will famish all *the gods of* the earth;
3: 2. she drew not near to *her God.*
17. The Lord *thy God* in the midst
Hag. 1:12. obeyed the voice of the Lord *their God,*
— as the Lord *their God* had sent
14. the house of the Lord of hosts, *their God,*
Zec. 6:15. obey the voice of the Lord *your God.*
8: 8. I will be their *God,*
23. we have heard (that) *God* (is) with you.
9: 7. even he, (shall be) *for our God,*
16. the Lord *their God* shall save them
10: 6. I (am) the Lord *their God,*
11: 4. Thus saith the Lord *my God;*
12: 5. in the Lord of hosts *their God.*
8. the house of David (shall be) *as God,*
13: 9. The Lord (is) *my God.*
14: 5. the Lord *my God* shall come,
Mal. 2:15. That he might seek a *godly* seed. (marg. seed of *God*)
16. For the Lord, *the God of* Israel,
17. Where (is) *the God of* judgment?
3: 8. Will a man rob *God?*
14. It (is) vain to serve *God:*
15. tempt *God* are even delivered.
18. between him that serveth *God*

אֱלוּ *ăloo*, Ch. 431

Dan. 2:31. *and behold* a great image.
4:10(7). *and behold* a tree in the midst
13(10). *and, behold,* a watcher
7: 8. *and, behold,* there came up
— *and, behold,* in this horn

אִלּוּ *il-loo'.* 432

Est. 7: 4. *But if* we had been sold for
Ecc. 6: 6. *Yea, though* he live a thousand years

אֱלוֹהַּ *ĕlōh'ăh*, m. 433

[For pl. see אֱלֹהִים.]

Deu 32:15. he forsook *God* (which) made him,
17. They sacrificed unto devils, not, to *God;*
2Ch 32:15. for no *god* of any nation or kingdom
Neh. 9:17. thou (art) *a God* ready to pardon,
Job 3: 4. let not *God* regard it

Job 3:23. whom *God* hath hedged in?
4: 9. By the blast of *God* they perish,
17. man be more just *than God?*
5:17. the man whom *God* correcteth:
6: 4. the terrors of *God* do set themselves
8. that *God* would grant (me) the
9. Even that it would please *God*
9:13. *God* will not withdraw his anger,
10: 2. I will say unto *God*,
11: 5. But oh that *God* would speak,
6. Know therefore that *God* exacteth
7. Canst thou by searching find out *God?*
12: 4. who calleth *upon God*,
6. into whose hand *God* bringeth
15: 8. Hast thou heard the secret of *God?*
16:20. mine eye poureth out (tears) unto *God*.
21. might plead for a man with *God*,
19: 6. Know now that *God* hath
21. the hand of *God* hath touched me.
26. yet in my flesh shall I see *God:*
21. 9. neither (is) the rod of *God* upon them.
19. *God* layeth up his iniquity
22:12. (Is) not *God* in the height of heaven?
26. shalt lift up thy face unto *God*.
24:12. *yet God* layeth not folly
27: 3. the spirit of *God* (is) in my
8. when *God* taketh away his soul?
10. will he always call upon *God?*
29: 2. the days (when) *God* preserved me;
4. the secret of *God* (was) upon my
31: 2. what portion of *God* (is there) from
6. that *God* may know mine integrity.
33:12. that *God* is greater than man.
26. He shall pray unto *God*,
35:10. Where (is) *God* my maker,
36: 2. (I have) yet to speak *on God's behalf.*
37:15. Dost thou know when *God*
22. with *God* (is) terrible majesty.
39:17. *God* hath deprived her of wisdom,
40: 2. he that reproveth *God*,
Ps. 18:31(32). For who (is) *God* save the Lord?
50:22. ye that forget *God*,
114: 7. at the presence of *the God of* Jacob;
139:19. thou wilt slay the wicked, *O God:*
Pro.30: 5. Every word of *God* (is) pure:
Isa.44: 8. Is there *a God* beside me?
Dan11:37. nor regard any *god:*
38. honour *the God* of forces: *and a god*
39. the most strong holds with *a* strange *god*,
Hab. 1:11. this his power *unto his god*.
3: 3. *God* came from Teman,

---

435 ## אֱלוּל *ĕlool*, m.

Neh. 6:15. twenty and fifth(day)of (the month) *Elul*,

---

437 ## אַלּוֹן *al-lōhn'*, m.

Gen35: 8. buried beneath Beth-el under *an oak:* and the name of it was called *Allon-bachuth*. (marg. *The oak of* weeping)
Isa. 2:13. upon all *the oaks of* Bashan,
6:13. as a teil tree, *and as an oak*,
44:14. taketh the cypress *and the oak*,
Eze.27: 6. *the oaks* of Bashan have they
Hos. 4:13. upon the hills, under *oaks*
Am. 2: 9. he (was) strong *as the oaks;*
Zec.11: 2. howl, *O ye oaks of* Bashan;

---

436 ## אֵלוֹן *ēh'-lōhn*, m.

i. q. אֵלָה.

Gen12: 6. unto *the plain of* Moreh.
13:18. came and dwelt *in the plain of* Mamre, (marg. *plains*)
14:13. he dwelt *in the plain of* Mamre
18: 1. unto him *in the plains of* Mamre:
Deu11:30. beside *the plains of* Moreh?
Jud. 4:11. pitched his tent unto *the plain of*
9: 6. made Abimelech king, by *the plain of* (marg. *oak*)
37. by *the plain of* Meonenim.
1Sa.10: 3. thou shalt come to *the plain of* Tabor,

אַלּוּף & אַלֻּף *al-looph'*, m. 441

Gen36:15. These (were) *dukes of* the sons
— *duke* Teman, *duke* Omar, *duke* Zepho, *duke* Kenaz,
16. *Duke* Korah, *duke* Gatam, (and) *duke* Amalek: these (are) *the dukes* (that came) *of* Eliphaz
17. *duke* Nahath, *duke* Zerah, *duke* Shammah, *duke* Mizzah: these (are) *the dukes* (that came) *of* Reuel
18. *duke* Jeush, *duke* Jaalam, *duke* Korah: these (were) *the dukes* (that came) *of*
19. these (are) *their dukes*.
21. these (are) *the dukes of* the Horites,
29. These (are) *the dukes* (that came) *of* the Horites; *duke* Lotan, *duke* Shobal, *duke* Zibeon, *duke* Anah,
30. *Duke* Dishon, *duke* Ezer, *duke* Dishan: these (are) *the dukes* (that came) *of* Hori, *among their dukes* in the land of
40. these (are) the names of *the dukes* (that came) *of* Esau,
— *duke* Timnah, *duke* Alvah, *duke* Jetheth,
41. *Duke* Aholibamah, *duke* Elah, *duke* Pinon,
42. *Duke* Kenaz, *duke* Teman, *duke* Mibzar,
43. *Duke* Magdiel, *duke* Iram: these (be) *the dukes of* Edom,
Ex. 15:15. *the dukes of* Edom shall be amazed;
1Ch. 1:51. *the dukes of* Edom were; *duke* Timnah, *duke* Aliah, *duke* Jetheth,
52. *Duke* Aholibamah, *duke* Elah, *duke* Pinon,
53. *Duke* Kenaz, *duke* Teman, *duke* Mibzar,
54. *Duke* Magdiel, *duke* Iram. These (are) *the dukes of* Edom.
Ps. 55:13(14). *my guide*, and mine acquaintance.
144:14. *our oxen* (may be) strong to labour;
Pro. 2:17. Which forsaketh *the guide of* her youth,
16:28. a whisperer separateth *chief friends*.
17: 9. a matter separateth (very) *friends*.
Jer. 3: 4. thou (art) *the guide of* my youth?
11:19. I (was) like a lamb (or) *an ox*
13:21. hast taught them (to be) *captains*,
Mic. 7: 5. put ye not confidence *in a guide*.
Zec. 9: 7. he shall be *as a governor*
12: 5. *the governors of* Judah shall say
6. will I make *the governors of* Judah

אָלַח [*āh-lagh'*] 444

* NIPHAL.—*Preterite.* *

Ps. 14: 3. *they are* (all) together *become filthy:* (marg. *stinking*)
53: 3(4). they are altogether *become filthy;*

NIPHAL.—*Participle.*

Job 15:16. much more abominable *and filthy* (is)

אַלְיָה *al-yāh'*, f. 451

Ex. 29:22. of the ram the fat *and the rump*,
Lev. 3: 9. the fat thereof, (and) *the* whole *rump*,
7: 3. all the fat thereof; *the rump*, and
8:25. he took the fat, and *the rump*,
9:19. of the bullock and of the ram, *the rump*,

אֱלִיל *ĕleel*, m. 434, 457

Job 13:4 is without (י).

Lev.19: 4. Turn ye not unto *idols*,
26: 1. Ye shall make you no *idols*
1Ch.16:26. the gods of the people (are) *idols:*
Job 13: 4. ye (are) all physicians of *no value*.
Ps. 96: 5. all the gods of the nations (are) *idols:*
97: 7. that boast themselves *of idols:*
Isa. 2: 8. Their land also is full of *idols;*
18. *And the idols* he shall utterly abolish.
20. a man shall cast his *idols of* silver, and his *idols of* gold,
10:10. hath found the kingdoms of *the idols*, (lit. *idol*)
11. done unto Samaria *and her idols*,
19: 1. *the idols of* Egypt shall be moved

Isa. 19: 3. and they shall seek to *the idols*,
31: 7. every man shall cast away his *idols of* silver, *and* his *idols of* gold,
Jer. 14:14. divination, *and a thing of nought*,
Eze. 30:13. I will cause (their) *images* to cease
Hab. 2:18. to make dumb *idols?*
Zec. 11:17. Woe to *the idol* shepherd

---

459 אִלֵּין *il-lēhn'*, pron. pl. Ch.

In ch. 6:6(7). it is אִלֵּן.

Dan. 2:40. and as iron that breaketh all *these*,
44. and consume all *these* kingdoms,
6: 2(3). that *the* princes might give accounts
6(7). Then *these* presidents
7:17. *These* great beasts, which are four,

---

479 אִלֵּךְ *il-lēch*, Ch.

Ezr. 4:21. cause *these* men to cease,
5: 9. Then asked we *those* elders,
6: 8. shall do to the elders of *these* Jews
— expences be given unto *these* men,
Dan. 3:12. *these* men, O king, have not regarded
13. Then they brought *these* men
21. Then *these* men were bound
22. the flame of the fire slew *those* men
23. And *these* three men,
27. saw *these* men, upon whose bodies
6: 5(6). Then said *these* men,
11(12), 15(16). Then *these* men assembled,
24(25). and they brought *those* men

See 457 אֱלִל see אֱלִיל·

---

480 אַלְלַי *al-le-lahy'*, interj.

Job 10:15. If I be wicked, *woe* unto me;
Mic. 7: 1. *Woe* is me! for I am as when

---

481 אָלַם *āh-lam'*.

* NIPHAL.—*Preterite.* *

Ps. 39: 2(3). *I was dumb* with silence,
9(10). *I was dumb*, I opened not my
Isa. 53: 7. as a sheep before her shearers *is dumb*,
Eze. 3:26. *that thou shalt be dumb*, and shalt not be
33:22. *I was* no more *dumb*.
Dan 10:15. toward the ground, *and I became dumb*.

NIPHAL.—*Future.*

Ps. 31:18(19). *Let* the lying lips *be put to silence;*
Eze. 24:27. thou shalt speak, and *be* no more *dumb:*

* PIEL.—*Participle.* *

Gen 37: 7. For, behold, we (were) *binding*

---

482 אֵלֶם *ēh'-lem*, m.

Ps. 56: [title] (1) upon Jonath-*elem*-rechokim, (lit. dove of *silence* (among) strangers)
58: 1(2). Do ye indeed speak righteousness, *O congregation?*

---

483 אִלֵּם *il-lēhm'*, adj.

Ex. 4:11. or who maketh *the dumb*,
Ps. 38:13(14). *and* (I was) *as a dumb man*
Pro. 31: 8. Open thy mouth *for the dumb*
Isa. 35: 6. the tongue of *the dumb* sing:
56:10. they (are) all *dumb* dogs,
Hab. 2:18. to make *dumb* idols?

See 197 אֻלָם see אוּלָם·

אַלְמֻגִּים *al-moog-geem'*, m. pl. 484

See also אַלְגּוּמִּים.

1 K. 10:11. great plenty of *almug trees*,
12. the king made of *the almug trees* pillars,
— there came no such *almug trees*,

אֲלֻמָּה [*ălum-māh'*] f. 485

Gen 37: 7. we (were) binding *sheaves* in the field, and, lo, *my sheaf* arose, and also stood upright; and, behold, *your sheaves* stood round about, and made obeisance *to my sheaf*.
Ps. 126: 6. bringing *his sheaves* (with him).

אֵלַמּוֹת *ēh-lam-mōth'*, f. pl. 361

See also אֵילַמִּים.

Eze 40:16. likewise *to the arches:*
30. *And the arches* round about

אַלְמָן *al-māhn'*, adj. 488

Jer. 51: 5. For Israel (hath) not (been) *forsaken*,

אַלְמֹן *al-mōhn'*, m. 489

Isa. 47: 9. the loss of children, *and widowhood:*

אַלְמָנָה *al-māh-nāh'*, f. 490

Gen 38:11. Remain *a widow* at thy father's house,
Ex. 22:22(21). Ye shall not afflict any *widow*,
24(23). your wives shall be *widows*,
Lev. 21:14. *A widow*, or a divorced woman,
22:13. if the priest's daughter be *a widow*,
Nu. 30: 9(10). But every vow of *a widow*,
Deu 10:18. of the fatherless *and widow*,
14:29 & 16:11, 14. the stranger, and the fatherless, *and the widow*,
24:17. nor take *the widow*'s raiment to pledge:
19, 20, 21. for the stranger, for the fatherless, *and for the widow:*
26:12. the stranger, the fatherless, *and the widow*,
13. to the fatherless, *and to the widow*,
27:19. the stranger, fatherless, *and widow*.
2 Sa. 14: 5. I (am) indeed *a widow* woman,
1 K. 7:14. He (was) *a widow*'s son of the tribe
11:26. whose mother's name (was) Zeruah, *a widow*
17: 9. I have commanded *a widow* woman
10. *the widow* woman (was) there
20. brought evil upon *the widow*
Job 22: 9. Thou hast sent *widows* away
24: 3. they take *the widow*'s ox
21. *and* doeth not good to *the widow*.
27:15. *and his widows* shall not weep.
29:13. I caused *the widow*'s heart to sing
31:16. caused the eyes of *the widow* to fail;
Ps. 68: 5(6). a judge of the *widows*,
78:64. *and their widows* made no lamentation.
94: 6. They slay *the widow* and the stranger,
109: 9. his wife *a widow*.
146: 9. he relieveth the fatherless *and widow:*
Pro. 15:25. establish the border of *the widow*.
Isa. 1:17. plead for *the widow*.
23. neither doth the cause of *the widow*
9:17(16). mercy on their fatherless and *widows:*
10: 2. that *widows* may be their prey,
47: 8. I shall not sit (as) *a widow*,
Jer. 7: 6. the fatherless, *and the widow*,
15: 8. *Their widows* are increased to me
18:21. bereaved of their children, *and* (be) *widows;*
22: 3. the fatherless, *nor the widow*,
49:11. *and* let *thy widows* trust in me.
Lam. 1: 1. is she become *as a widow!*
5: 3. our mothers (are) *as widows*.
Eze 22: 7. they vexed the fatherless *and the widow*.
25. they have made *her* many *widows*

Eze.44:22. Neither (lit. *and*...not) shall they take for their wives *a widow*,
— *or a widow* that had a priest before. (lit. *or a widow* who shall be *a widow* from a priest)
Zec. 7:10. *And* oppress not *the widow*,
Mal. 3: 5. *the widow*, and the fatherless,

---

490 **אַלְמְנוֹת** *al-m'nōth'*, f. pl.

[Const. of אַלְמָנוֹת.]

Isa. 13:22. shall cry *in their desolate houses*, (marg. *palaces*)
Eze 19: 7. he knew *their desolate palaces*, (marg. *their widows*)

---

491 **אַלְמְנוּת** *al-m'nooth'*, f.

[Const. of אַלְמָנוּת.]

Gen 38:14. she put *her widow*'s garments off
19. put on the garments of *her widowhood*.
2 Sa.20: 3. living in *widowhood*.
Isa. 54: 4. the reproach of *thy widowhood*

---

492 **אַלְמֹנִי** *al-mōh-nee'*, m.

Always joined to פְּלֹנִי.

Ruth 4: 1. Ho, such *a one!* turn aside,
1Sa.21: 2(3). to such *and such* a place.
2 K. 6: 8. In such *and such* a place

See 459 **אֵלֶן** see **אֵלִין**.

---

502 **אָלַף** [*āh-laph'*]

* KAL.—*Future.* *

Pro.22:25. Lest *thou learn* his ways,

* PIEL.—*Future.* *

Job 15: 5. thy mouth *uttereth* thine iniquity, (marg. *teacheth*)
33:33. *and I shall teach thee* wisdom.

PIEL.—*Participle.*

Job 35:11. *Who teacheth us* more than the beasts

---

503 **אָלַף** [*āh-laph'*]

* HIPHIL.—*Participle.* *

Ps. 144:13. our sheep *may bring forth thousands*

504-05 **אֶלֶף** *eh'-leph*, m.

Gen20:16. thy brother *a thousand* (pieces) *of* silver.
24:60. thou (the mother) *of thousands of* millions,
Ex. 12:37. about 600 *thousand* on foot
18:21. (to be) rulers of *thousands*, (and) rulers
25. rulers of *thousands*, rulers of
20: 6. shewing mercy *unto thousands*
32:28. the people that day about three *thousand*
34: 7. Keeping mercy *for thousands*,
38:25. *and a thousand* 775 shekels,
26. *thousand* and three *thousand* and 550
28. of *the thousand* 775 (shekels) he made
29. *and two thousand* and 400 shekels.
Nu. 1:16. heads of *thousands in* Israel.
21. of Reuben, (were) 46 *thousand* and 500.
23. of Simeon, (were) 59 *thousand* and 300.
25. of Gad, (were) 45 *thousand* 650.
27. of Judah, (were) 74 *thousand* and 600.
29. of Issachar, (were) 54 *thousand* and 400.
31. of Zebulun, (were) 57 *thousand* and 400.
33. of Ephraim, (were) 40 *thousand* and 500.
35. of Manasseh, (were) 32 *thousand* and 200.
37. of Benjamin, (were) 35 *thousand* and 400.
39. of Dan, (were) 62 *thousand* and 700.
41. of Asher, (were) 41 *thousand* and 500.
Nu. 1:43. of Naphtali, (were) 53 *thousand* and 400.
46. they that were numbered were 600 *thousand* and three *thousand* and 550.
2: 4. numbered of them, (were) 74 *thousand*
6. numbered thereof, (were) 54 *thousand*
8. numbered thereof, (were) 57 *thousand*
9. of Judah (were) 100 *thousand* and 80 *thousand* and six *thousand* and 400,
11. numbered thereof, (were) 46 *thousand*
13. numbered of them, (were) 59 *thousand*
15. numbered of them, (were) 45 *thousand*
16. Reuben (were) 100 *thousand* and 51 *thousand*
19. numbered of them, (were) 40 *thousand*
21. numbered of them, (were) 32 *thousand*
23. numbered of them, (were) 35 *thousand*
24. of Ephraim (were) 100 *thousand* and eight *thousand* and 100,
26. numbered of them, (were) 62 *thousand*
28. numbered of them, (were) 41 *thousand*
30. numbered of them, (were) 53 *thousand*
31. Dan (were) 100 *thousand*, and 57 *thousand*
32. their hosts (were) 600 *thousand* and three *thousand* and 550.
3:22. numbered of them (were) seven *thousand*
28. old and upward, (were) eight *thousand*
34. old and upward, (were) six *thousand* and
39. old and upward, (were) 22 *thousand*.
43. numbered of them, were 22 *thousand*
50. the money; *a thousand* 365 (shekels),
4:36. by their families were *two thousand* 750.
40. of their fathers, were *two thousand* and
44. families, were three *thousand* and 200.
48. numbered of them, were eight *thousand*
7:85. silver vessels (weighed) *two thousand* and
10: 4. (which are) heads of *the thousands of*
36. unto the many *thousands of* Israel.
11:21. six hundred *thousand* footmen;
16:49(17:14). in the plague were 14 *thousand*
25: 9. died in the plague were 24 *thousand*.
26: 7. numbered of them were 43 *thousand* and
14. the Simeonites, 22 *thousand* and 200.
18. numbered of them, 40 *thousand* and 500.
22. numbered of them, 76 *thousand* and 500.
25. numbered of them, 64 *thousand* and 300.
27. numbered of them, 60 *thousand* and 500.
34. numbered of them, 52 *thousand* and 700.
37. numbered of them, 32 *thousand* and 500.
41. numbered of them (were) 45 *thousand* and
43. numbered of them, (were) 64 *thousand*
47. of them; (who were) 53 *thousand* and
50. of them (were) 45 *thousand* and 400.
51. of Israel, 600 *thousand and a thousand*
62. numbered of them were 23 *thousand*,
31: 4. Of every tribe *a thousand*, (marg. *A thousand* of a tribe, *a thousand* of a tribe)
5. *out of the thousands of* Israel, *a thousand* of (every) tribe, 12 *thousand* armed for
6. to the war, *a thousand* of (every) tribe,
14. the captains over *thousands*, and captains
32. had caught, was 600 *thousand* and 70 *thousand* and five *thousand* sheep,
33. And 72 *thousand* beeves,
34. And 61 *thousand* asses,
35. And 32 *thousand* persons in all,
36. *thousand* and 37 *thousand* (lit. 30 *thousand* and 7 *thousands*) and 500
38. And the beeves (were) 36 *thousand*;
39. And the asses (were) 30 *thousand* and
40. And the persons (were) 16 *thousand*;
43. (unto) the congregation was 300 *thousand* and 30 *thousand* (and) seven *thousand*
44. And 36 *thousand* beeves,
45. And 30 *thousand* asses and 500,
46. And 16 *thousand* persons;
48. the officers which (were) *over thousands of* the host, the captains of *thousands*,
52. the captains of *thousands*, and of the captains of hundreds, was 16 *thousand* 750
54. the gold of the captains of *thousands*
35: 4. outward *a thousand* cubits round about.
5. the east side *two thousand* cubits, and on the south side *two thousand* cubits, and on the west side *two thousand* cubits, and on the north side *two thousand*
Deu. 1:11. make you *a thousand* times so many
15. heads over you, captains over *thousands*,

Deu. 5:10. shewing mercy *unto thousands*
7: 9. his commandments *to a thousand*
13 & 28:4, 18, 51. the increase of *thy kine*,
32:30. How should one chase *a thousand*,
33:17. they (are) *the thousands of* Manasseh.
Jos. 3: 4. about *two thousand* cubits by measure:
4:13. About 40 *thousand* prepared for war
7: 3. but let *about two* or three *thousand* men (marg. about *two thousand* men, or, about three *thousand*)
4. of the people about three *thousand* men:
8: 3. Joshua chose out 30 *thousand* mighty
12. he took about five *thousand* men,
25. 12 *thousand*, (even) all the men of Ai.
18:28. Zelah, *Eleph*, and Jebusi,
22:14. *among the thousands of* Israel.
21, 30. heads of *the thousands of* Israel,
23:10. man of you shall chase *a thousand:*
Jud. 1: 4. of them in Bezek ten *thousand* men.
3:29. of Moab at that time about ten *thousand*
4: 6. and take with thee ten *thousand* men
10. he went up with ten *thousand* men
14. from mount Tabor, and ten *thousand*
5: 8. or spear seen among forty *thousand*
6:15. *my family* (is) poor in Manasseh, (marg. *my thousand*)
7: 3. of the people twenty and two *thousand;* and there remained ten *thousand*.
8:10. hosts with them, about fifteen *thousand*
— an hundred and twenty *thousand* men
26. *a thousand* and seven hundred (shekels)
9:49. *about a thousand* men and women.
12: 6. of the Ephraimites forty and two *thousand*.
15:11. Then three *thousand* men of Judah
15. slew *a thousand* men therewith.
16. have I slain *a thousand* men.
16: 5. eleven hundred (pieces) of silver. (lit. *a thousand* and a hundred)
27. about three *thousand* men and women,
17: 2, 3. The eleven hundred (shekels) (lit. *a thousand* and a hundred)
20: 2. four hundred *thousand* footmen
10. and an hundred *of a thousand, and a thousand* out of ten thousand,
15. out of the cities 26 *thousand* men
17. were numbered 400 *thousand* men that
21. of the Israelites that day 22 *thousand*
25. of the children of Israel again 18 *thousand*
34. against Gibeah 10 *thousand* chosen men
35. of the Benjamites that day 25 *thousand*
44. there fell of Benjamin 18 *thousand* men;
45. in the highways five *thousand* men;
— unto Gidom, and slew *two thousand* men
46. that day of Benjamin were 25 *thousand*
21:10. thither 12 *thousand* men of the valiantest,
1Sa. 4: 2. in the field about four *thousand* men.
10. there fell of Israel 30 *thousand* footmen.
6:19. smote of the people 50 *thousand* and 70
8:12. will appoint him captains over *thousands*,
10:19. by your tribes, *and by your thousands*.
11: 8. the children of Israel were 300 *thousand*, and the men of Judah 30 *thousand*.
13: 2. Saul chose him three *thousand* (men) of Israel; (whereof) *two thousand* were
— *and a thousand* were with Jonathan
5. to fight with Israel, 30 *thousand* chariots, and six *thousand* horsemen,
15: 4. numbered them in Telaim, 200 *thousand* footmen, and 10 *thousand* men of Judah.
17: 5. weight of the coat (was) five *thousand*
18. unto the captain of (their) *thousand*,
18: 7. Saul hath slain *his thousands*,
8. to me they have ascribed (but) *thousands:*
13. made him his captain over *a thousand;*
21:11(12). Saul hath slain *his thousands*,
22: 7. (and) make you all captains of *thousands*,
23:23. throughout all *the thousands of* Judah.
24: 2(3). Saul took three *thousand* chosen men
25: 2. had three *thousand* sheep, *and a thousand*
26: 2. having three *thousand* chosen men
29: 2. by hundreds, *and by thousands:*
5. Saul slew *his thousands*,
2Sa. 6: 1. (the) chosen (men) of Israel, 30 *thousand*.
8: 4. took from him *a thousand* (chariots),
— and 20 *thousand* footmen:
5. David slew of the Syrians 22 *thousand*
13. valley of salt, (being) 18 *thousand* (men).

2Sa. 10: 6. and the Syrians of Zoba, 20 *thousand* footmen, and of king Maacah *a thousand* men, and of Ish-tob 12 *thousand* men.
18. of the Syrians, and 40 *thousand* horsemen,
17: 1. Let me now choose out 12 *thousand* men,
18: 1. and set captains of *thousands* and captains
3. (thou art) worth 10 *thousand* of us:
4. came out by hundreds *and by thousands*.
7. a great slaughter that day of 20 *thousand*
12. I should receive *a thousand* (shekels) of
19:17(18). *And* (there were) *a thousand* men of
24: 9. and there were in Israel 800 *thousand*
— the men of Judah (were) 500 *thousand*
15. from Dan even to Beer-sheba 70 *thousand*
1 K. 3: 4. *a thousand* burnt offerings did Solomon
4:26(5:6). had 40 *thousand* stalls of horses for his chariots, and 12 *thousand* horsemen.
32(5:12). spake three *thousand* proverbs: and his songs were *a thousand and* five.
5:11(25). Solomon gave Hiram 20 *thousand*
13(27). and the levy was 30 *thousand* men.
14(28). 10 *thousand* a month by courses:
15(29). And Solomon had 70 *thousand* that bare burdens, and 80 *thousand* hewers in
16(30). three *thousand* and 300, which ruled
7:26. of lilies: it contained *two thousand* baths.
8:63. offered unto the Lord, 22 *thousand* oxen, and 120 *thousand* sheep.
10:26. and he had *a thousand* and 400 chariots, and 12 *thousand* horsemen,
12:21. 180 *thousand* chosen men, which were
19:18. Yet I have left (me) 7 *thousand* in Israel,
20:15. the children of Israel, (being) 7 *thousand*.
29. Israel slew of the Syrians 100 *thousand*
30. and (there) a wall fell upon 27 *thousand*
2 K. 3: 4. 100 *thousand* lambs, and 100 *thousand* rams,
5: 5. and six *thousand* (pieces) of gold,
13: 7. ten chariots, and 10 *thousand* footmen;
14: 7. in the valley of salt 10 *thousand*,
15:19. gave Pul *a thousand* talents of silver,
18:23. and I will deliver thee *two thousand* horses,
19:35. in the camp of the Assyrians 185 *thousand:*
24:14. men of valour, (even) 10 *thousand*
16. seven *thousand*, and craftsmen and smiths *a thousand*,
1Ch 5:18. *thousand* 760, that went out to the war.
21. of their camels 50 *thousand*, and of sheep 250 *thousand*, and of asses *two thousand*, and of men 100 *thousand*.
7: 2. in the days of David 22 *thousand* and 600.
4. bands of soldiers for war, 36 *thousand*
5. in all by their genealogies 87 *thousand*.
7. by their genealogies 22 *thousand* and 34
9. mighty men of valour, (was) 20 *thousand*
11. men of valour, (were) 17 *thousand* and
40. the war (and) to battle (was) 26 *thousand*
9:13. *a thousand* and 760; very able men for the
12:14. and the greatest *over a thousand*.
20. captains of *the thousands* that (were) of
24. shield and spear (were) 6 *thousand* and
25. valour for the war, 7 *thousand* and 100.
26. children of Levi 4 *thousand* and 600.
27. Aaronites, and with him (were) 3 *thousand*
29. the kindred of Saul, 3 *thousand:*
30. children of Ephraim 20 *thousand* and 800,
31. the half tribe of Manasseh 18 *thousand*,
33. *thousand*, which could keep rank:
34. of Naphtali *a thousand* captains, and with them with shield and spear 37 *thousand*.
35. The Danites expert in war 28 *thousand*
36. to battle, expert in war, 40 *thousand*.
37. of war for the battle, 120 *thousand*.
13: 1. consulted with the captains of *thousands*
15:25. and the captains over *thousands*, went to
16:15. (which) he commanded *to a thousand*
18: 4. David took from him *a thousand* chariots, and 7 *thousand* horsemen, and 20 *thousand*
5. David slew of the Syrians 22 *thousand* men.
12. Edomites in the valley of salt 18 *thousand*.
19: 6. of Ammon sent *a thousand* talents of
7. So they hired 32 *thousand* chariots,
18. slew of the Syrians 7 *thousand* (men which fought in) chariots, and 40 *thousand*
21: 5. all (they of) Israel were *a thousand thousand* and 100 *thousand* men that drew sword: and Judah (was) 470 *thousand*
14. and there fell of Israel 70 *thousand* men.

1Ch 22:14. *thousand* talents of gold, and *a thousand thousand* talents of silver;
23: 3. their polls, man by man, was 38 *thousand*.
4. *thousand* (were) to set forward the work of the house of the Lord; and 6 *thousand*
5. *thousand* (were) porters; and 4 *thousand*
26:26. the captains over *thousands* and hundreds,
30. brethren, men of valour, *a thousand* and
32. men of valour, (were) *two thousand* and
27: 1. the chief fathers and captains of *thousands*
— of every course (were) 24 *thousand*.
2, 5, 7, 8, 9, 10, 11, 12, 13, 14, 15. and in his course (were) 24 *thousand*.
4. in his course likewise (were) 24 *thousand*.
28: 1. and the captains over *the thousands*,
29: 4. *thousand* talents of gold, of the gold of Ophir, and 7 *thousand* talents of
6. and the captains of *thousands*
7. *thousand* talents and 10 thousand drams, and of silver 10 *thousand* talents, and of brass, 18 *thousand* talents, and 100 *thousand* talents of iron.
21. (even) *a thousand* bullocks, *a thousand* rams, (and) *a thousand* lambs,
2Ch 1: 2. to the captains of *thousands* and of
6. and offered *a thousand* burnt offerings
14. and he had *a thousand* and 400 chariots, and 12 *thousand* horsemen,
2: 2(1). *thousand* men to bear burdens, and 80 *thousand* to hew in the mountain, and 3 *thousand* and 600 to oversee them.
10(9). *thousand* measures of beaten wheat, and 20 *thousand* measures of barley, and 20 *thousand* baths of wine, and 20 *thousand* baths of oil.
17(16). found 150 *thousand*, and 3 *thousand* and
18(17). *thousand* of them (to be) bearers of burdens, and 80 *thousand* (to be) hewers in the mountain, and 3 *thousand* and 600
4: 5. (and) it received and held 3 *thousand* baths.
7: 5. of 22 *thousand* oxen, and 120 *thousand*
9:25. had 4 *thousand* stalls for horses and chariots, and 12 *thousand* horsemen;
11: 1. 180 *thousand* chosen (men), which were
12: 3. *With* 1200 (lit. *a thousand* and 200) chariots, and 60 *thousand* horsemen:
13: 3. of war, (even) 400 *thousand* chosen men:
— with 800 *thousand* chosen men, (being)
17. slain of Israel 500 *thousand* chosen men.
14: 8(7). out of Judah 300 *thousand*; and out of Benjamin, that bare shields and drew bows, 280 *thousand*:
9(8). with an host of *a thousand thousand*,
15:11. oxen and 7 *thousand* sheep.
17:11. *thousand* and 700 rams, and 7 *thousand*
14. Of Judah, the captains of *thousands*;
— mighty men of valour 300 *thousand*.
15. the captain, and with him 280 *thousand*.
16. 200 *thousand* mighty men of valour.
17. men with bow and shield 200 *thousand*.
18. 180 *thousand* ready prepared for the war.
25: 5. made them captains over *thousands*,
— and found them 300 *thousand* choice (men),
6. He hired also 100 *thousand* mighty men
11. smote of the children of Seir 10 *thousand*.
12. And (other) 10 *thousand* (left) alive
13. three *thousand* of them, and took much
26:12. men of valour (were) *two thousand* and
13. an army, 300 *thousand*, and 7 *thousand* and
27: 5. ten *thousand* measures of wheat, and 10 *thousand*
28: 6. slew in Judah 120 *thousand* in one day,
8. captive of their brethren 200 *thousand*,
29:33. six hundred oxen, and 3 *thousand* sheep.
30:24. *a thousand* bullocks and 7 *thousand* sheep;
— *a thousand* bullocks and 10 *thousand*
35: 7. of 30 *thousand*, and 3 *thousand* bullocks:
8. passover offerings *two thousand* and 600
9. for passover offerings 5 *thousand* (small)
Ezr. 1: 9. *a thousand* chargers of silver,
10. (and) other vessels *a thousand*.
11. of gold and of silver (were) 5 *thousand*
2: 3. The children of Parosh, *two thousand* and 172
6. of Jeshua (and) Joab, *two thousand*
7. The children of Elam, *a thousand* 254.
12. The children of Azgad, *a thousand* 222.
Ezr. 2:14. The children of Bigvai, *two thousand* 56.
31. children of the other Elam, *a thousand* 254.
35. The children of Senaah, 3 *thousand* 630.
37. The children of Immer, *a thousand* 52.
38. The children of Pashur, *a thousand* 247.
39. The children of Harim, *a thousand* 17.
64. together (was) forty *two thousand* 360,
65. of whom (there were) 7 *thousand* 337:
67. (their) asses, 6 *thousand* 720.
69. treasure of the work 60 *and one thousand* drams of gold, and 5 *thousand* pound of
8:27. basons of gold, of *a thousand* drams;
Neh 3.13. *and a thousand* cubits on the wall unto
7: 8. The children of Parosh, *two thousand* 172.
11. of Jeshua and Joab, *two thousand* 818.
12. The children of Elam, *a thousand* 254.
17. The children of Azgad, *two thousand* 322.
19. The children of Bigvai, *two thousand* 67.
34. children of the other Elam, *a thousand* 254.
38. The children of Senaah, 3 *thousand* 930.
40. The children of Immer, *a thousand* 52.
41. The children of Pashur, *a thousand* 247.
42. the children of Harim, *a thousand* 17.
66. together (was) forty *two thousand* 360,
67. of whom (there were) 7 *thousand* 337:
69. six *thousand* 720 asses.
70. Tirshatha gave to the treasure *a thousand*
71. and *two thousand* and 200 pound of silver.
72. and *two thousand* pound of silver,
Est. 3: 9. I will pay 10 *thousand* talents of silver
9:16. and slew of their foes 75 *thousand*,
Job 1: 3. was 7 *thousand* sheep, and 3 *thousand*
9: 3. cannot answer him one of *a thousand*.
33:23. one among *a thousand*,
42:12. *thousand* sheep, and 6 *thousand* camels, *and a thousand* yoke of oxen, *and a thousand* she asses.
Ps. 8: 7(8). All sheep *and oxen*,
50:10. the cattle upon *a thousand* hills.
60: [title] (2). in the valley of salt 12 *thousand*.
68:17(18). (are) 20 thousand, (even) *thousands of*
84:10(11). thy courts (is) better *than a thousand*.
90: 4. For *a thousand* years in thy sight
91: 7. *A thousand* shall fall at thy side,
105: 8. he commanded *to a thousand* generations.
119:72. better unto me *than thousands of* gold
Pro. 14: 4. Where no *oxen* (are), the crib (is) clean:
Ecc. 6: 6. though he live *a thousand* years
7:28. one man *among a thousand*
Cant. 4: 4. whereon there hang *a thousand* bucklers,
8:11. the fruit thereof was to bring *a thousand*
12. thou, O Solomon, (must have) *a thousand*,
Isa. 7:23. were *a thousand* vines *at a thousand*
30:17. *thousand* (shall flee) at the rebuke of one;
24. *The oxen likewise* and the young asses
36: 8. and I will give thee *two thousand* horses,
37:36. the camp of the Assyrians 185 *thousand*:
60:22. A little one shall become *a thousand*,
Jer. 32:18. shewest lovingkindness *unto thousands*,
52:28. in the seventh year, 3 *thousand* Jews
30. all the persons (were) 4 *thousand* and
Eze. 45: 1. the length of 25 *thousand* (reeds), and the breadth (shall be) 10 *thousand*.
3. *thousand*, and the breadth of 10 *thousand*:
5. *thousand* of length, and the 10 *thousand*
6. city 5 *thousand* broad, and 25 *thousand*
47: 3. he measured *a thousand* cubits,
4, 4. Again he measured *a thousand*,
5. Afterward he measured *a thousand*;
48: 8. offer of 25 *thousand* (reeds in) breadth,
9. *thousand* in length, and of 10 *thousand*
10. toward the north 25 *thousand* (in length), and toward the west 10 *thousand* in breadth, and toward the east 10 *thousand* in breadth, and toward the south 25 *thousand* in length;
13. *thousand* in length, and 10 *thousand* in breadth: all the length (shall be) 25 *thousand*, and the breadth 10 *thousand*.
15. the 5 *thousand*, that are left in the breadth over against the 25 *thousand*,
16. the north side 4 *thousand* and 500, and the south side 4 *thousand* and 500, and on the east side 4 *thousand* and 500, and the west side 4 *thousand* and 500.
18. ten *thousand* eastward, and 10 *thousand*
20. (shall be) 25 *thousand* by 25 *thousand*:

Eze.48:21. over against the 25 *thousand* of the oblation
— and westward over against the 25 *thousand*
30, 33. four *thousand* and 500 measures.
32. at the east side 4 *thousand* and 500:
34. At the west side 4 *thousand* and 500,
35. (It was) round about 18 *thousand*
Dan. 8:14. unto me, Unto *two thousand* and 300 days;
12:11. (there shall be) *a thousand* 290 days.
12. and cometh to *the thousand* 335 days.
Am. 5: 3. The city that went out (by) *a thousand*
Mic. 5: 2(1). thou be little *among the thousands of*
6: 7. Will the Lord be pleased *with thousands of*

---

506 אֶלֶף *eh'-leph* & אֲלַף *ălaph*, Ch. m.

Dan 5: 1. a great feast to *a thousand* of his lords, and drank wine before the *thousand*.
7:10. *thousand thousands* ministered

---

509 אָלַץ [*āh-latz'*].

* PIEL.—*Future.* *

Jud.16:16. with her words, *and urged him*,

---

510 אַלְקוּם *al-koom'*.

Pro.30:31. against whom (there is) *no rising up*.

---

517 אֵם *ēhm*, f.

Gen 2:24. a man leave his father and *his mother*,
3:20. she was *the mother of* all living.
20:12. but not the daughter of *my mother*;
21:21. *his mother* took him a wife
24:28. told (them of) *her mother*'s house these
53. *and to her mother* precious things.
55. her brother *and her mother* said,
67. into *his mother* Sarah's tent,
— Isaac was comforted after *his mother*'s
27:11. Jacob said to Rebekah *his mother*,
13. And *his mother* said unto him,
14. brought (them) *to his mother*: and *his mother* made savoury meat,
29. let *thy mother*'s sons bow down
28: 2. the house of Bethuel *thy mother*'s father;
— Laban *thy mother*'s brother.
5. Jacob's and Esau's *mother*.
7. obeyed his father and *his mother*,
29:10. the daughter of Laban *his mother*'s brother, and the sheep of Laban *his mother*'s
— the flock of Laban *his mother*'s brother.
30:14. brought them unto *his mother* Leah.
32:11(12). *the mother* with the children.
37:10. Shall I *and thy mother* and thy brethren
43:29. Benjamin, *his mother*'s son,
44:20. he alone is left *of his mother*,
Ex. 2: 8. called the child's *mother*.
20:12. Honour thy father and *thy mother*:
21:15. smiteth his father, *or his mother*,
17. curseth his father, *or his mother*,
22:30(29). seven days it shall be with *his dam*;
23:19 & 34:26. seethe a kid in *his mother*'s milk.
Lev.18: 7. or the nakedness of *thy mother*,
— she (is) *thy mother*;
9. or daughter of *thy mother*,
13. the nakedness of *thy mother*'s sister: for she (is) *thy mother*'s near kinswoman.
19: 3. Ye shall fear every man *his mother*,
20: 9. curseth his father or *his mother*
— cursed his father *or his mother*;
14. if a man take a wife and *her mother*,
17. or *his mother*'s daughter,
19. the nakedness of *thy mother*'s sister,
21: 2. *for his mother*, and for his father,
11. for his father, *or for his mother*;
22:27. shall be seven days under *the dam*;
24:11. *his mother*'s name (was) Shelomith,
Nu. 6: 7. for his father, *or for his mother*,
12:12. cometh out of *his mother*'s womb.
Deu 5:16. Honour thy father and *thy mother*,
13: 6(7). the son of *thy mother*,
Deu14:21. not seethe a kid in *his mother*'s milk.
21:13. bewail her father and *her mother*
18. or the voice of *his mother*,
19. *and his mother* lay hold on him,
22: 6. *and the dam* sitting upon the young,
— shalt not take *the dam* with the young:
7. thou shalt in any wise let *the dam* go,
15. of the damsel, *and her mother*,
27:16. setteth light by his father *or his mother*.
22. or the daughter of *his mother*.
33: 9. unto his father *and to his mother*,
Jos. 2:13. save alive my father, and *my mother*,
18. bring thy father, and *thy mother*,
6:23. her father, and *her mother*,
Jud. 5: 7. I arose *a mother* in Israel.
28. *The mother of* Sisera looked out
8:19. the sons of *my mother*:
9: 1. unto *his mother*'s brethren,
— the house of *his mother*'s father,
3. *his mother*'s brethren spake
14: 2. told his father *and his mother*,
3. Then his father *and his mother*
4. But his father *and his mother*
5. his father *and his mother*,
6. told not his father *or his mother*
9. his father and *mother* (lit. and *his mother*)
16. not told (it) my father *nor my mother*,
16:17. from *my mother*'s womb:
17: 2. he said *unto his mother*,
— And *his mother* said, Blessed
3. eleven hundred (shekels) of silver *to his mother*, *his mother* said, I had wholly
4. he restored the money *unto his mother*; and *his mother* took two hundred
Ruth 1: 8. return each to *her mother*'s house:
2:11. hast left thy father *and thy mother*,
1Sa. 2:19. *his mother* made him a little coat,
15:33. so shall *thy mother* be childless,
20:30. the confusion of *thy mother*'s nakedness?
22: 3. Let my father *and my mother*,
2Sa.17:25. sister to Zeruiah Joab's *mother*.
19:37(38). grave of my father *and* of *my mother*.
20:19. destroy a city *and a mother*
1 K. 1:11 & 2:13. Bath-sheba the *mother of* Solomon,
2:19. to be set *for* the king's *mother*;
20. *my mother*: for I will not say thee nay.
22. said *unto his mother*,
3:27. she (is) *the mother thereof*.
11:26. *whose mother*'s name (was) Zeruah,
14:21, 31. *his mother*'s name (was) Naamah,
15: 2, 10. *his mother*'s name (was) Maachah,
13. also Maachah *his mother*, even her he
17:23. delivered him *unto his mother*:
19:20. kiss my father *and my mother*,
22:42. *his mother*'s name (was) Azubah
52(53). in the way of *his mother*,
2 K. 3: 2. not like his father, *and like his mother*:
13. to the prophets of *thy mother*.
4:19. Carry him to *his mother*.
20. brought him to *his mother*,
30. *the mother of* the child said,
8:26. *his mother*'s name (was) Athaliah,
9:22. so long as the whoredoms of *thy mother*
11: 1. Athaliah *the mother of* Ahaziah
12: 1(2). *his mother*'s name (was) Zibiah
14: 2. *his mother*'s name (was) Jehoaddan
15: 2. *his mother*'s name (was) Jecholiah
33. *his mother*'s name (was) Jerusha,
18: 2. *His mother*'s name also (was) Abi,
21: 1. *his mother*'s name (was) Hephzibah.
19. *his mother*'s name (was) Meshullemeth,
22: 1. *his mother*'s name (was) Jedidah,
23:31. *his mother*'s name (was) Hamutal,
36. *his mother*'s name (was) Zebudah,
24: 8. *his mother*'s name (was) Nehushta,
12. *and his mother*, and his servants,
15. and the king's *mother*,
18. *his mother*'s name (was) Hamutal,
1Ch. 2:26. she (was) *the mother of* Onam.
4: 9. *and his mother* called his name Jabez,
2Ch12:13. *his mother*'s name (was) Naamah
13: 2. *His mother*'s name also (was) Michaiah
15:16. *the mother of* Asa the king,
20:31. *his mother*'s name (was) Azubah
22: 2. *His mother*'s name also (was) Athaliah
3. for *his mother* was his counsellor
10. Athaliah *the mother of* Ahaziah

2Ch 24: 1. *His mother*'s name also (was) Zibiah
25: 1. *his mother*'s name (was) Jehoaddan
26: 3. *His mother*'s name also (was) Jecoliah
27: 1. *His mother*'s name also (was) Jerushah,
29: 1. *his mother*'s name (was) Abijah,
Est. 2: 7. she had neither father *nor mother*,
— when her father *and mother* were dead,
Job 1:21. Naked came I out of *my mother*'s
17:14. to the worm, (Thou art) *my mother*,
31:18. from *my mother*'s womb ;
Ps. 22: 9(10). upon *my mother*'s breasts.
10(11). my God from *my mother*'s belly.
27:10. my father *and my mother* forsake me,
35:14. one that mourneth (for his) *mother*.
50:20. slanderest *thine own mother*'s son.
51: 5(7). in sin did *my mother* conceive
69: 8(9). an alien unto *my mother*'s children.
71: 6. took me out of *my mother*'s bowels:
109:14. let not the sin of *his mother* be blotted out.
113: 9. a joyful *mother of* children.
131: 2. a child that is weaned of *his mother:*
139:13. hast covered me in *my mother*'s womb.
Pro. 1: 8. forsake not the law of *thy mother:*
4: 3. in the sight of *my mother*.
6:20. forsake not the law of *thy mother:*
10: 1. the heaviness of *his mother*.
15:20. a foolish man despiseth *his mother*.
19:26. chaseth away (his) *mother*,
20:20. curseth his father *or his mother*,
23:22. despise not *thy mother* when
25. Thy father *and thy mother* shall be glad,
28:24. robbeth his father *or his mother*,
29:15. bringeth *his mother* to shame.
30:11. doth not bless *their mother*.
17. despiseth to obey (his) *mother*,
31: 1. the prophecy that *his mother* taught him.
Ecc. 5:15(14). came forth of *his mother*'s womb,
Cant 1: 6. *my mother*'s children were angry
3: 4. brought him into *my mother*'s house,
11. wherewith *his mother* crowned him
6: 9. she (is) the (only) one *of her mother*,
8: 1. sucked the breasts of *my mother!*
2. bring thee into *my mother*'s house,
5. there *thy mother* brought thee forth:
Isa. 8: 4. to cry, My father, *and my mother*,
49: 1. from the bowels of *my mother*
50: 1. the bill of *your mother*'s divorcement,
— is *your mother* put away.
66:13. one whom *his mother* comforteth,
Jer. 15: 8. *the mother of* the young men
10. Woe is me, *my mother*,
16: 3. concerning *their mothers* that bare them,
7. for their father or for *their mother*.
20:14. the day wherein *my mother*
17. that *my mother* might have been my grave,
22:26. and *thy mother* that bare thee,
50:12. *Your mother* shall be sore confounded ;
52: 1. *his mother*'s name (was) Hamutal
Lam. 2:12. They say *to their mothers*,
— poured out into *their mothers*' bosom.
5: 3. *our mothers* (are) as widows.
Eze. 16: 3. *and thy mother* an Hittite.
44. *As* (is) *the mother*, (so is) her daughter.
45. Thou (art) *thy mother*'s daughter, that
— *your mother* (was) an Hittite,
19: 2. What (is) *thy mother?*
10. *Thy mother* (is) like a vine
21:21(26). stood at *the parting of* the way, (marg. at *the mother of* the way)
22: 7. they set light by father *and mother:*
23: 2. the daughters of one *mother:*
44:25. but for father, *or for mother*,
Hos. 2: 2(4). Plead *with your mother*,
5(7) For *their mother* hath played
4: 5. I will destroy *thy mother*.
10:14. *the mother* was dashed in pieces
Mic. 7: 6. the daughter riseth up *against her mother*,
Zec. 13: 3. then his father *and his mother*
— his father *and his mother*

---

518 **אִם** *eem*, part.

Gen 4: 7. *If* thou doest well, shalt thou not
14:23. *That* I will *not* (take) from a thread
— *and* that I will *not* take any thing
24:21. made his journey prosperous *or* not.
Gen 38: 9. *when* he went in unto his brother's
Ex. 19:13. *whether* (it be) beast *or* man, it shall
Nu. 14:23. *Surely* they shall *not* see the land
30. *Doubtless* ye shall *not* come into
32:11. *Surely none* of the men that came up
Jud. 13:16. *Though* thou detain me, I will not eat
1Sa. 17:55. soul liveth, O king, I *cannot* tell.
19: 6. the Lord liveth, he shall *not* be slain.
20:14. shalt not only *while* yet I live
24:21(22). *that* thou wilt *not* cut off my seed
28:10. *there shall no* punishment happen
30:15. that thou wilt *neither* kill me, *nor*
2Sa. 17:13. *Moreover, if* he be gotten into a
1Ch 4:10. *Oh that* thou wouldest bless me indeed,
21:12. *Either* three years' famine; or three months
2Ch 33: 8. so that (lit. *if* only) they will take
Job 14: 5. *Seeing* his days (are) determined,
22:20. *Whereas* our substance is not cut down,
Isa. 62: 8. *Surely* I will *no more* give thy corn
Jer. 23:38. But *since* ye say, The burden of
Eze. 14:20. they shall deliver *neither* son *nor* daughter;
35: 6. *sith* thou hast not hated blood,
Joel 1: 2. in your days, *or* even in the days
&c. &c.

Observe the meaning of כִּי־אִם.

Gen 32:26(27). let thee go, *except* thou bless me.
39: 6. *save* the bread which he did eat.
Ex. 22:23(22). afflict them in any wise, *and* they cry
Lev. 22: 6. eat of the holy things, *unless* he wash
Nu. 24:22. *Nevertheless* the Kenite shall be wasted,
Jud. 15: 7. *yet* will I be avenged of you,
Ru. 3:18. be in rest, *until* he have finished
1Sa. 21: 5(6). *Of a truth* women (have been) kept
2K. 9:35. no *more* of her *than* the scull,
2Ch 2: 6(5). *save only* to burn sacrifice before him
Ecc. 5:11(10). *saving* the beholding (of them)
&c. &c.

Notice the meaning of אִם־לֹא.

Gen 24:38. *But* thou shalt go unto my father's house,
43: 9. *if* I bring him *not* unto thee,
Nu. 14:35. I will *surely* do it unto all this
Jer. 15:11. *Verily* it shall be well with thy remnant; *verily* I will cause the enemy
&c. &c.

אָמָה *āh-māh'*, f. 519

Gen 20:17. his wife, *and his maidservants ;*
21:10. Cast out this *bondwoman* and her son: for the son of this *bondwoman*
12. because of *thy bondwoman ;*
13. also of the son of *the bondwoman*
30: 3. Behold *my maid* Bilhah,
31:33. into the two *maidservants'* tents ;
Ex. 2: 5. she sent *her maid* to fetch it.
20:10. thy manservant, *nor thy maidservant*,
17. *nor his maidservant*, nor his ox,
21: 7. his daughter *to be a maidservant*,
20. smite his servant, or *his maid*,
26. or the eye of *his maid*,
27. or *his maidservant*'s tooth;
32. a manservant or a *maidservant ;*
23:12. the son of *thy handmaid*,
Lev. 25: 6. for thy servant, *and for thy maid*,
44. bondmen, *and thy bondmaids*,
— ye buy bondmen *and bondmaids*.
Deu 5:14. thy manservant, *nor thy maidservant*,
— *and thy maidservant* may rest as well
21(18). *or his maidservant*, his ox,
12:12. menservants, *and your maidservants*,
18. thy manservant, *and thy maidservant*,
15:17. also *unto thy maidservant*
16:11, 14. thy manservant, *and thy maidservant*,
Jud. 9:18. the son of *his maidservant*,
19:19. also for me, *and for thy handmaid*,
Ru. 3: 9. I (am) Ruth *thine handmaid:* spread therefore thy skirt over *thine handmaid;*
1Sa. 1:11. the affliction of *thine handmaid*, and remember me, and not forget *thine handmaid*, but wilt give *unto thine handmaid*
16. Count not *thine handmaid* for
25:24. let *thine handmaid*, I pray thee, speak in thine audience, and hear the words of *thine handmaid*.

1 Sa. 25:25. but I *thine handmaid* saw not
28. forgive the trespass of *thine handmaid:*
31. then remember *thine handmaid.*
41. (let) *thine handmaid* (be) a servant
2 Sa. 6:20. eyes of *the handmaids of* his servants,
22. of *the maidservants* which thou hast spoken of. (marg. *of the handmaids* of my servants)
14:15. perform the request of *his handmaid.*
16. to deliver *his handmaid* out of the hand
20:17. Hear the words of *thine handmaid.*
1 K. 1:13. O king, swear *unto thine handmaid,*
17. swarest by the Lord thy God *unto thine handmaid,*
3:20. *while thine handmaid* slept,
Ezr. 2:65. Beside their servants *and their maids,*
Neh 7:67. their manservants *and their maidservants,*
Job 19:15. *and my maids,* count me for a stranger:
31:13. *or of my maidservant,*
Ps. 86:16. save the son of *thine handmaid.*
116:16. the son of *thine handmaid:*
Nah 2: 7(8). *and her maids* shall lead

---

520 אַמָּה *am-māh'*, f.

Gen. 6:15. the ark (shall be) three hundred *cubits,* the breadth of it fifty *cubits,* and the height of it thirty *cubits.*
16. in *a cubit* shalt thou finish it
7:20. Fifteen *cubits* upward did the
Ex. 25:10. *two cubits* and a half (shall be) the length thereof, *and a cubit* and a half the breadth thereof, *and a cubit* and a half the height
17. *two cubits* and a half (shall be) the length thereof, *and a cubit* and a half the breadth
23. *two cubits* (shall be) the length thereof, *and a cubit* the breadth thereof, *and a cubit* and a half the height
26: 2. eight and twenty *cubits,*
—, 8. the breadth of one curtain four *cubits:*
8. thirty *cubits,* (lit. *in cubit*)
13. *And a cubit* on the one side, *and a cubit* on the other side
16. Ten *cubits* (shall be) the length of a board, *and a cubit* and a half (lit. and the half of *a cubit*)
27: 1. five *cubits* long, and five *cubits* broad;
— height thereof (shall be) three *cubits.*
9, 18. an hundred *cubits* (lit. *in cubit*)
12. hangings of fifty *cubits:*
13. eastward (shall be) fifty *cubits.*
14. side (of the gate shall be) fifteen *cubits:*
16. an hanging of twenty *cubits,*
18. height five *cubits* (of) fine twined linen,
30: 2. *A cubit* (shall be) the length thereof, *and a cubit* the breadth thereof;
— *and two cubits* (shall be) the height
36: 9. twenty and eight *cubits,* and the breadth of one curtain four *cubits:* (lit. *in cubit*)
15. curtain (was) thirty *cubits* (lit. *in cubit*), and four *cubits* (was) the breadth
21. ten *cubits,* and the breadth of a board *one cubit* and a half. (lit. and half *a cubit*)
37: 1. *two cubits* and a half (was) the length of it, *and a cubit* and a half the breadth of it, *and a cubit* and a half the height
6. *two cubits* and a half (was) the length thereof, *and one cubit* and a half the
10. *two cubits* (was) the length thereof, *and a cubit* the breadth thereof, *and a cubit* and a half the height
25. the length of it (was) *a cubit, and* the breadth of it *a cubit;*
— *and two cubits* (was) the height
38: 1. five *cubits* (was) the length thereof, and five *cubits*
- - three *cubits* the height
9. fine twined linen, an hundred *cubits:* (lit. *in cubit*)
11. (the hangings were) an hundred *cubits,* (lit. *in cubit*)
12. hangings of fifty *cubits,* (lit. *in cubit*)
13. east side eastward fifty *cubits.*
14. one side (of the gate were) fifteen *cubits;*
15. hangings of fifteen *cubits;*

Ex. 38:18. twenty *cubits* (was) the length,
— the breadth (was) five *cubits,*
Nu. 11:31. *and as it were two cubits*
35: 4. a thousand *cubits* round about.
5. *cubits,* and on the south side two thousand *cubits,* and on the west side two thousand *cubits,* and on the north side two thousand *cubits;* (lit. *in cubit*)
Deu. 3:11. *cubits* (was) the length thereof, and four *cubits*
— *after the cubit* of a man.
Jos. 3: 4. about two thousand *cubits*
1 Sa. 17: 4. whose height (was) six *cubits* and a span.
1 K. 6: 2. length thereof (was) threescore *cubits,*
— the height thereof thirty *cubits.*
3. twenty *cubits* (was) the length thereof,
— ten *cubits* (was) the breadth
6. five *cubits* broad, and the middle (was) six *cubits* broad, and the third (was) seven *cubits* (lit. *in cubit*)
10. against all the house, five *cubits* high:
16. he built twenty *cubits* on the
17. the temple before it, was forty *cubits* (lit. *in cubit*)
20. twenty *cubits* in length, and twenty *cubits* in breadth, and twenty *cubits* in the height
23. olive tree, (each) ten *cubits*
24. five *cubits* (was) the one wing of the cherub, and five *cubits* the other wing
— of the other (were) ten *cubits.*
25. the other cherub (was) ten *cubits:* (lit. *in cubit*)
26. the one cherub (was) ten *cubits,*
7: 2. an hundred *cubits,* and the breadth thereof fifty *cubits,* and the height thereof thirty *cubits,*
6. the length thereof (was) fifty *cubits,* and the breadth thereof thirty *cubits:*
10. ten *cubits,* and stones of eight *cubits.*
15. of eighteen *cubits* high apiece:
— a line of twelve *cubits*
16. one chapiter (was) five *cubits,* and the height of the other chapiter (was) five *cubits:*
19. lily work in the porch, four *cubits.*
23. ten *cubits* from the one brim to the other:
— his height (was) five *cubits:* and a line of thirty *cubits* (lit. *in cubit*) did compass it
24. compassing it, ten *in a cubit,*
27. four *cubits* (was) the length of one base, and four *cubits* the breadth thereof, and three *cubits* (lit. *in cubit*)
31. within the chapiter and above (was) *a cubit:* (lit. *in cubit*)
— the work of the base, *a cubit* and an half: (lit. a half *a cubit*)
32. the height of a wheel (was) a *cubit* and half *a cubit.*
35. a round compass of half *a cubit*
38. every laver was four *cubits:* (lit. *in cubit*)
2 K. 14:13. unto the corner gate, four hundred *cubits.*
25:17. one pillar (was) eighteen *cubits,*
— The height of the chapiter three *cubits;*
1 Ch 11:23. of (great) stature, five *cubits* (lit. *in cubit*) high;
2 Ch 3: 3. The length by *cubits* after the first measure (was) threescore *cubits,* and the breadth twenty *cubits.*
4, 8. breadth of the house, twenty *cubits,*
8. and the breadth thereof twenty *cubits:*
11. the cherubims (were) twenty *cubits* long: one wing (of the one cherub was) five *cubits,*
— the other wing (was likewise) five *cubits,*
12. the other cherub (was) five *cubits,*
— the other wing (was) five *cubits*
13. spread themselves forth twenty *cubits:*
15. pillars of thirty and five *cubits*
— each of them (was) five *cubits.*
4: 1. twenty *cubits* the length thereof, and twenty *cubits* the breadth thereof, and ten *cubits* the height thereof.
2. a molten sea *of* ten *cubits* from brim to brim, round in compass, and five *cubits* the height thereof; and a line *of* thirty *cubits* (lit. *in cubit*)

2Ch. 4: 3. ten *in a cubit*, compassing the sea round
6: 13. a brasen scaffold, of five *cubits* long, and five *cubits* broad, *and* three *cubits* high,
25: 23. to the corner gate, four hundred *cubits*.
Neh. 3: 13. a thousand *cubits* on the wall
Est. 5: 14. be made of fifty *cubits* high,
7: 9. also, the gallows fifty *cubits* high,
Isa. 6: 4. *the posts* of the door moved
Jer. 51: 13. *the measure of* thy covetousness.
52: 21. one pillar (was) eighteen *cubits*;
— a fillet of twelve *cubits* did compass it;
22. one chapiter (was) five *cubits*,
Eze. 40: 5. of six *cubits* (long) *by the cubit*
7. the little chambers (were) five *cubits*;
9. the porch of the gate, eight *cubits*; and the posts thereof, two *cubits*;
11. the entry of the gate, ten *cubits*; (and) the length of the gate, thirteen *cubits*.
12. one *cubit* (on this side), *and* the space (was) one *cubit*
— six *cubits* on this side, and six *cubits* on
13. breadth (was) five and twenty *cubits*,
14. made also posts of threescore *cubits*,
15. the inner gate (were) fifty *cubits*.
19. an hundred *cubits* eastward
21. *cubits*, and the breadth five and twenty *cubits*. (lit. *in cubit*)
23. from gate to gate an hundred *cubits*.
25, 36. the length (was) fifty *cubits*, and the breadth five and twenty *cubits*.
27. toward the south an hundred *cubits*.
29. fifty *cubits* long, and five and twenty *cubits* broad.
30. five and twenty *cubits* long, and five *cubits*
33. *cubits* long, and five and twenty *cubits*
42. *a cubit* and an half long, and *a cubit* and an half broad, and one *cubit* high:
47. an hundred *cubits* long, and an hundred *cubits* broad,
48. five *cubits* on this side, and five *cubits* on
— three *cubits* on this side, and three *cubits*
49. of the porch (was) twenty *cubits*, and the breadth eleven *cubits*;
41: 1. six *cubits* broad on the one side, and six *cubits* broad on the other
2. the door (was) ten *cubits*; and the sides of the door (were) five *cubits* on the one side, and five *cubits* on the other side:
— and he measured the length thereof, forty *cubits*: and the breadth, twenty *cubits*.
3. two *cubits*, and the door, six *cubits*; and the breadth of the door, seven *cubits*.
4. the length thereof, twenty *cubits*; and the breadth, twenty *cubits*,
5. the wall of the house, six *cubits*;
— of (every) side chamber, four *cubits*,
8. a full reed of six great *cubits*.
9. without, (was) five *cubits*:
10. the wideness of twenty *cubits*
11. five *cubits* round about.
12. seventy *cubits* broad;
— five *cubits* thick round about,
— the length thereof ninety *cubits*.
13, 13. an hundred *cubits* long;
14. toward the east, an hundred *cubits*.
15. the other side, an hundred *cubits*,
22. three *cubits* high, and the length thereof two *cubits*;
42: 2. the length of an hundred *cubits*
— the breadth (was) fifty *cubits*.
4. a walk of ten *cubits* breadth inward, a way of one *cubit*;
7. the length thereof (was) fifty *cubits*.
8. in the utter court (was) fifty *cubits*:
— the temple (were) an hundred *cubits*.
16. five hundred reeds, (כתיב five *cubits* of reeds)
43: 13. altar after *the cubits*: The *cubit* (is) *a cubit* and an hand breadth; even the bottom (shall be) *a cubit*, *and* the breadth *a cubit*,
14. two *cubits*, and the breadth one *cubit*;
— four *cubits*, and the breadth (one) *cubit*.
15. the altar (shall be) four *cubits*;
17. about it (shall be) half *a cubit*; and the bottom thereof (shall be) *a cubit* about;
45: 2. fifty *cubits* round about for the suburbs

Eze. 47: 3. he measured a thousand *cubits*, (lit. *in cubit*)
Zec. 5: 2. the length thereof (is) twenty *cubits*, and the breadth thereof ten *cubits*. (lit. *in cubit*)

אַמָּה see אֵימָה. See 367

אֻמָּה *oom-māh'*, f. Ch. 524

Ezr. 4: 10. And the rest of the *nations*
Dan 3: 4. O people, *nations*, and languages,
7. all the people, *the nations*, and
29. That every people, *nation*, and language,
4: 1(3:31) & 5: 19 & 6: 25(26) & 7: 14. all people, *nations*, and languages,

---

אָמוֹן *āh-mōhn'*, 525

Pro. 8: 30. *one brought up* (with him):

אָמוֹן *āh-mōhn'*, m. 527

Jer. 46: 25. I will punish the *multitude* of No, (marg. *Amon*, or *nourisher*)
52: 15. the rest of *the multitude*.
Nah. 3: 8. Art thou better than *populous* No,

אֵמוּן *ēh-moon'*, m. 529

Deu 32: 20. children in whom (is) no *faith*.
Pro. 13: 17. *a faithful* ambassador (is) health.
14: 5. *A faithful* witness will not lie:
20: 6. *a faithful* man who can find?
Isa. 26: 2. which keepeth *the truth* may enter in (marg. *truths*)

אֱמוּנָה *ĕmoo-nah'*, *also* אֱמֻנָה, f. 530

Ex. 17: 12. his hands were *steady* until
Deu 32: 4. a God of *truth* and without iniquity,
1 Sa. 26: 23. his righteousness and *his faithfulness*:
2K. 12: 15(16). for they dealt *faithfully*.
22: 7. because they dealt *faithfully*.
1 Ch 9: 22. did ordain *in their set office*. (marg. *trust*)
26. were *in* (their) *set office*, (marg. *trust*)
31. had *the set office* over the things (marg. *trust*)
2 Ch 19: 9. *faithfully*, and with a perfect heart.
31: 12. the dedicated (things) *faithfully*:
15. *in* (their) *set office*, to give (marg. *trust*)
18. *in their set office* they sanctified (marg. *trust*)
34: 12. the men did the work *faithfully*:
Ps. 33: 4. all his works (are done) *in truth*.
36: 5(6). *thy faithfulness* (reacheth) unto the
37: 3. *verily* thou shalt (marg. *in truth*, or *stableness*)
40: 10(11). I have declared *thy faithfulness*
88: 11(12). *thy faithfulness* in destruction?
89: 1(2). will I make known *thy faithfulness*
2(3). *thy faithfulness* shalt thou establish
5(6). *thy faithfulness* also in the congregation
8(9). *or to thy faithfulness* round about
24(25). *But my faithfulness* and my mercy
33(34). nor suffer *my faithfulness* to fail.
49(50). swarest unto David *in thy truth*?
92: 2(3). *and thy faithfulness* every night,
96: 13. and the people *with his truth*.
98: 3. his mercy *and his truth*
100: 5. *his truth* (endureth) to all generations.
119: 30. I have chosen the way of *truth*:
75. *and* (that) thou in *faithfulness* hast
86. All thy commandments (are) *faithful*:
90. *Thy faithfulness* (is) unto all
138. righteous *and* very *faithful*.
143: 1. *in thy faithfulness* answer me,
Pro. 12: 17. speaketh *truth* sheweth forth
22. but they that deal *truly* (are) his delight.

Pro.28:20. *A faithful* man (lit. a man of *faithfulnesses*)
Isa. 11: 5. *and faithfulness* the girdle of his reins.
25: 1. of old (are) *faithfulness* (and) truth.
33: 6. shall be *the stability* of thy times,
59: 4. nor (any) pleadeth *for truth:*
Jer. 5: 1. that seeketh *the truth;*
3. O Lord, (are) not thine eyes *upon the truth?*
7:28. *truth* is perished, and is cut off
9: 3(2). *for the truth* upon the earth;
Lam 3:23. great (is) *thy faithfulness.*
Hos. 2:20(22). betroth thee unto me *in faithfulness:*
Hab. 2: 4. but the just shall live *by his faithful.*

523 אֻמּוֹת & אֻמִּים *oom-mōth'*, & *oom-meem'*, pl. f. & pl. m.

Gen25:16. twelve princes *according to their nations.*
Nu. 25:15. he (was) head over *a people,*
Ps. 117: 1. praise him, all *ye people.*

520 אַמִּין *am-meen'*, pl. f. Ch.

Ezr. 6: 3. threescore *cubits,* (and) the breadth thereof threescore *cubits;*
Dan. 3: 1. image of gold, whose height (was) threescore *cubits,* (and) the breadth thereof six *cubits:*

533 אַמִּיץ & אַמִּץ *am-meetz'*, adj.

2Sa.15:12. and the conspiracy was *strong;*
Job 9: 4. wise in heart, *and mighty* in strength:
19. If (I speak) of strength, lo, (he is) *strong:*
Isa. 28: 2. the Lord hath a mighty *and strong one,*
40:26. *for that* (he is) *strong* in power;
Am. 2:16. *And* (he that is) courageous (marg. *strong of* his heart)

534 אָמִיר *āh-meer'*, m.

Isa. 17: 6. the top of the uppermost *bough,*
9. forsaken bough *and an* uppermost *branch,*

535 אָמַל [*āh-mal'*]

* KAL.—*Participle.* Päul. *

Eze.16:30. How *weak* is thine heart, saith the Lord

* PULAL.—*Preterite.* *

1Sa. 2: 5. that hath many children *is waxed feeble.*
Isa. 16: 8. For the fields of Heshbon *languish,*
19: 8. spread nets upon the waters *shall languish.*
24: 4. world *languisheth* (and) fadeth away, the haughty people of the earth *do languish.*
7. new wine mourneth, the vine *languisheth,*
33: 9. The earth mourneth (and) *languisheth:*
Jer. 14: 2. the gates thereof *languish;*
15: 9. She that hath borne seven *languisheth:*
Lam 2: 8. they *languished* together.
Hos. 4: 3. *and* every one that dwelleth therein *shall languish,*
Joel 1:10. wine is dried up, the oil *languisheth.*
12. the fig tree *languisheth;*
Nah 1: 4. Bashan *languisheth,* and Carmel, and the flower of Lebanon *languisheth.*

537 אֲמֵלָל [*ămēh-lāhl'*], adj.

Neh. 4: 2(3:34). What do these *feeble* Jews?

536 אֻמְלַל *oom-lal'*, adj.

Ps. 6: 2(3). for I (am) *weak:* O Lord, heal me;

539 אָמַן [*āh-man'*],

* KAL.—*Participle.* Poël. *

Nu. 11:12. as *a nursing father* beareth the
Ru. 4:16. became *nurse* unto it.
2Sa. 4: 4. *his nurse* took him up,
2K. 10: 1. *them that brought up* Ahab's (marg *nourishers*)
5. *and the bringers up.*
Est. 2: 7. he brought up Hadassah (lit. was *bringing up;* marg. nourished)
Isa. 49:23. kings shall be *thy nursing fathers,* (marg. *nourishers*)

KAL.—*Participle.* Päul.

2Sa.20:19. peaceable (and) *faithful in* Israel:
Ps. 12: 1(2). for *the faithful* fail from among
31:23(24). the Lord preserveth *the faithful,*
Lam 4: 5. *brought up* in scarlet

* NIPHAL.—*Preterite.* *

2Sa. 7:16. *and* thy kingdom *shall be established*
Ps. 78: 8. whose spirit *was* not *stedfast* with God.
37. neither *were they stedfast* in his covenant.
93: 5. Thy testimonies *are* very *sure:*
Pro.11:13. he that *is* of a *faithful* spirit
Jer. 15:18. waters (that) *fail?* (marg. *be* not *sure?*)

NIPHAL.—*Future.*

Gen42:20. *so shall* your words *be verified,*
1 K. 8:26. *let* thy word, I pray thee, *be verified,*
1Ch.17:23. *let* the thing...*be established* for ever,
24. *Let it even be established,* that thy name
2Ch. 1: 9. *let* thy promise...*be established:*
6:17. God of Israel, *let* thy word *be verified,*
20:20. *so shall ye be established;* believe
Isa. 7: 9. *ye shall* not *be established.* (marg. (it is) because *ye are* not *stable*)
60: 4. daughters *shall be nursed* at (thy) side.

NIPHAL.—*Participle.*

Nu. 12: 7. who (is) *faithful* in all mine house.
Deu 7: 9. he (is) God, the *faithful* God,
28:59. great plagues, *and of long continuance,* and sore sicknesses, *and of long continuance.*
1Sa. 2:35. I will raise me up a *faithful* priest,
— I will build him a *sure* house:
3:20. knew that Samuel (was) *established* (to be) (marg. *faithful*)
22:14. who (is so) *faithful* among all
25:28. certainly make my lord a *sure* house;
1K. 11:38. and build thee a *sure* house,
Neh 9: 8. And foundest his heart *faithful* before
13:13. for they were counted *faithful,*
Job 12:20. the speech *of the trusty,* (marg. *faithful*)
Ps. 19: 7(8). the testimony of the Lord (is) *sure,*
89:28(29). my covenant *shall stand fast*
37(38). a *faithful* witness in heaven.
101: 6. *upon the faithful of* the land,
111: 7. all his commandments (are) *sure.*
Pro.25:13. a *faithful* messenger to them
27: 6. *Faithful* (are) the wounds of a
Isa. 1:21. How is the *faithful* city become
26. the *faithful* city.
8: 2. I took unto me *faithful* witnesses
22:23. fasten him (as) a nail in a *sure* place;
25. fastened in the *sure* place be removed,
33:16. his waters (shall be) *sure.*
49: 7. because of the Lord that is *faithful,*
55: 3. the *sure* mercies of David.
Jer. 42: 5. true *and faithful* witness between us,
Hos. 5: 9. made known *that which shall surely be.*
11:12(12:1). and is *faithful* with the saints.

* HIPHIL.—*Preterite.* *

Gen15: 6. *And he believed* in the Lord;
45:26. for *he believed* them not.
Ex. 4: 8. *that they will believe* the voice
Nu. 20:12. Because *ye believed* me not,
Deu 9:23. and *ye believed* him not,
Jud.11:20. But Sihon *trusted* not Israel
1K. 10: 7. Howbeit *I believed* not the words,
2K. 17:14. that *did* not *believe* in the Lord
2Ch. 9: 6. Howbeit *I believed* not their words,
Ps. 27:13. unless *I had believed* to see
78:22. Because *they believed* not in God,
32. *believed* not for his wondrous works.
106:24. *they believed* not his word:
116:10. *I believed,* therefore have I spoken:
119:66. *I have believed* thy commandments.
Isa.53: 1. Who *hath believed* our report?
Jer.40:14. the son of Ahikam *believed* them not.
Lam 4:12. of the world, would not *have believed*

HIPHIL.—*Imperative.*

2Ch 20:20. *Believe* in the Lord your God,
— *believe* his prophets,

HIPHIL.—*Future.*

Ex. 4: 1. *they will* not *believe* me,
5. That *they may believe* that
8. if *they will* not *believe* thee,
9. if *they will* not *believe* also these
31. *And* the people *believed:* and when they
14:31. *and believed* the Lord, and his servant
19: 9. and *believe* thee for ever.
Nu. 14:11. long will it be ere *they believe* me,
Deu28:66. *shalt have* none *assurance* of thy life:
1Sa. 27:12. *And* Achish *believed* David,
2Ch 32:15. you on this manner, neither yet *believe*
Job 4:18. *he put* no *trust* in his servants;
9:16. *would I* not *believe* that he had hearkened
15:15. *he putteth* no *trust* in his saints;
22. *He believeth* not that he shall
31. *Let* not *him* that is deceived *trust*
24:22. no (man) *is sure* of life.
29:24. I laughed on them, *they believed* (it) not;
39:12. *Wilt thou believe* him,
24. neither *believeth he* that (it is) the sound
Ps. 106:12. *Then believed* they his words;
Pro. 14:15. The simple *believeth* every word:
26:25. When he speaketh fair, *believe* him not:
Isa. 7: 9. If *ye will* not *believe*, (marg. *do ye* not *believe*)
43:10. that ye may know *and believe* me,
Jer. 12: 6. *believe* them not, though they speak
Jon. 3: 5. *So* the people of Nineveh *believed*
Mic. 7: 5. *Trust ye* not in a friend,
Hab. 1: 5. *ye will* not *believe*,

HIPHIL.—*Participle.*

Deu 1:32. *ye did* not *believe* the Lord
Isa. 28:16. *he that believeth* shall not make haste.

---

541 **אָמַן** [*āh-man'*].

*HIPHIL.—*Future.**

Isa. 30:21. when *ye turn to the right*

---

540 **אֲמַן** [*ăman*], Ch.

* APHEL.—*Preterite.* *

Dan. 6:23(24). because *he believed* in his God.

APHEL.—*Participle.*

Dan: 2:45. the interpretation thereof *sure.*
6: 4(5). forasmuch as he (was) *faithful*,

---

542 **אָמָּן** *āh-māhn'*, m.

Cant 7: 1(2). the hands of *a cunning workman.*

---

543 **אָמֵן** *āh-mēhn'*.

Nu. 5:22. And the woman shall say, *Amen, amen.*
Deu27:15. the people shall answer and say, *Amen.*
16, 17, 18, 19, 20, 21, 22, 23, 24, 25, 26. all the people shall say, *Amen.*
1 K. 1:36. answered the king, and said, *Amen:*
1Ch 16:36. And all the people said, *Amen,*
Neh. 5:13. all the congregation said, *Amen,*
8: 6. the people answered, *Amen, Amen,*
Ps. 41:13(14). to everlasting. *Amen, and Amen.*
72:19. filled (with) his glory; *Amen, and Amen:*
89:52(53). for evermore. *Amen, and Amen.*
106:48. *Amen.* Praise ye the Lord.
Isa. 65:16. bless himself in the God of *truth;*
— shall swear by the God of *truth;*
Jer. 11: 5. and said, *So be it*, O Lord. (marg. *Amen*)
28: 6. the prophet Jeremiah said, *Amen:*

---

544 **אֹמֶן** *ōh'-men*,

Isa. 25: 1. faithfulness (and) *truth.*

אֵמוּן see **אֵמֻן** See 529

אֱמוּנָה see **אֱמֻנָה** See 530

אֲמָנָה *ămāh-nāh'*, f. 548-49

2 K. 5:12. (Are) not *Abana* (קרי & marg. *Amana*)
Neh. 9:38(10:1). because of all this we make a *sure*
11:23. *that a certain portion* should be (marg. to *a sure ordinance*)
Cant. 4: 8. look from the top of *Amana*,

אָמְנָה *om-nāh'*, part. 546

Gen20:12. yet *indeed* (she is) my sister;
Jos. 7:20. *Indeed* I have sinned against

אָמְנָה *om-nah'* f. 545

Est. 2:20. as *when* she was *brought up*

אֹמְנוֹת *ōh-m'noth*, f. pl. 547

2K. 18:16. *The pillars* which Hezekiah king of Judah

אָמְנָם *om-nāhm'*, part. 551

Ruth 3:12. *it is true* that I (am thy) near kinsman:
2K. 19:17. *Of a truth*, Lord, the kings of Assyria
Job 9: 2. I know (it is) so *of a truth:*
12: 2. *No doubt* but ye (are) the people,
19: 4. be it *indeed* (that) I have erred,
5. If *indeed* ye will magnify
34:12. *surely* God will not do wickedly,
36: 4. *truly* my words (shall) not (be) false:
Isa. 37:18. *Of a truth*, Lord, the kings of Assyria

אֻמְנָם *oom-nahm'*, part. 552

Gen18:13. Shall I *of a surety* bear a child,
Nu. 22:37. am I not able *indeed* to promote
1 K. 8:27. will God *indeed* dwell on the earth?
2 Ch. 6:18. But will God *in very deed* dwell
Ps. 58: 1(2). Do ye *indeed* speak righteousness,

אָמַץ [*āh-matz'*]. 553

* KAL.—*Preterite.* *

2 Sa22:18. for *they were* too *strong* for me.
Ps. 18:17(18). for *they were* too *strong* for me.
142: 6(7). for *they are stronger* than I.

KAL.—*Imperative.*

Deu31: 6. Be strong, *and of a good courage,*
7, 23. Be strong, *and of a good courage:*
Jos. 1: 6. Be strong, *and of a good courage:*
7. be thou strong, *and* very *courageous,*
9, 18. Be strong, *and of a good courage;*
10:25. be strong, *and of good courage:*
1Ch 22:13 & 28:20. be strong, *and of good courage;*
2Ch 32: 7. Be strong *and courageous*, be not afraid

KAL.—*Future.*

Gen25:23. *shall be stronger* than (the other)
2Ch 13:18. *and* the children of Judah *prevailed,*

* PIEL.—*Preterite.* *

Deu 2:30. *and made* his heart *obstinate,*
Ps. 80:15(16). *thou madest strong* for thyself.
17(18). *thou madest strong* for thyself.
Isa. 41:10. *I will strengthen thee;*

PIEL.—*Infinitive.*

Pro. 8.28. *When he established* the clouds

PIEL.—*Imperative.*

Deu. 3:28. encourage him, *and strengthen him:*
Isa. 35: 3. *confirm* the feeble knees.
Nah. 2: 1(2). *fortify* (thy) power mightily.

PIEL.—*Future.*

Deu 15: 7. *thou shalt* not *harden* thine heart,
2Ch.11:17. *and made* Rehoboam...*strong,*
24:13. in his state, *and strengthened it.*
36:13. *and hardened* his heart from
Job 4: 4. *thou hast strengthened* the feeble
16: 5. *I would strengthen you* with
Ps. 89:21(22). mine arm also *shall strengthen him.*
Pro.31:17. *and strengtheneth* her arms.
Isa. 44:14. *which he strengtheneth* for himself (marg. *taketh courage*)
Am. 2:14. *shall* not *strengthen* his force,

PIEL.—*Participle.*

Pro.24: 5. man of knowledge *increaseth* strength. (marg. *strengtheneth* might)

* HIPHIL.—*Future.* *

Ps. 27:14. *and he shall strengthen* thine heart:
31:24(25). *and he shall strengthen* your heart,

* HITHPAEL.—*Preterite.* *

1 K.12:18. *made speed* to get (marg. *strengthened himself*)
2Ch 10:18. *made speed* to get him (marg. *strengthened himself*)

HITHPAEL.—*Future.*

2Ch 13: 7. *and have strengthened themselves*

HITHPAEL.—*Participle.*

Ru. 1:18. *she was stedfastly minded* (marg. *strengthened herself*)

See 533 אַמִּיץ see אַמִּיץ

---

555 אֹמֶץ *ōh'-metz,* m.

Job 17: 9. shall be stronger and *stronger.* (marg. shall add *strength*)

---

556 אַמְצָה *am-tzāh',* f.

Zec 12: 5. my *strength* in the Lord of hosts

---

554 אֲמֻצִּים, *ămootz-tzeem'.*

Zec. 6: 3. fourth chariot grisled and *bay* horses. (marg. *strong*)
7. *And the bay* went forth, (lit. *the strong*)

---

559 אָמַר, *āh-mar',*

* KAL.—*Preterite.* *

Gen. 3: 1. Yea, *hath* God *said,* Ye shall not eat
3. God *hath said,* Ye shall not eat
16. Unto the woman *he said,*
17. And unto Adam *he said,* Because
12:12. *that they shall say,* This (is) his wife:
19. Why *saidst thou,* She (is) my sister?
13:14. the Lord *said* unto Abram,
16:13. for *she said,* Have I also here
18:17. the Lord *said,* Shall I hide from
20: 5. *Said* he not unto me, She (is) my sister? and she, even *she* herself *said,*
11. Because *I thought,* Surely the fear of God
16. And unto Sarah *he said,*
21: 1. the Lord visited Sarah as he *had said,*
16. for *she said,* Let me not see the
22: 3. the place of which God *had told* him.
9. which God *had told* him of;
24:14. *and she shall say,* Drink,
43. *and I say* to her, Give me,
44. *And she say* to me, Both drink
26: 9. and how *saidst thou,* She (is) my sister?
— Because *I said,* Lest I die for her.
27: 6. Rebekah *spake* unto Jacob
29:32. for *she said,* Surely the Lord
31:16. whatsoever God *hath said* unto thee,
29. the God of your father *spake* unto me
31. for *I said,* Peradventure thou wouldest
49. for *he said,* The Lord watch
32: 4(5). Thy servant Jacob *saith* thus,
12(13). thou *saidst,* I will surely do thee good,
Gen32:18(19). *Then thou shalt say,* (They be) thy
20(21). *And say ye* moreover, Behold,
—(—) *he said,* I will appease him
37:20. *and we will say,* Some evil beast
38:11. for *he said,* Lest peradventure
22. also the men of the place *said,*
41:54. according as Joseph *had said:*
42: 4. for *he said,* Lest peradventure
22. *Spake I* not unto you,
43: 5. for the man *said* unto us,
17. the man did as Joseph *bade;*
27. the old man of whom *ye spake?*
29. of whom *ye spake* unto me?
44: 4. Joseph *said* unto his steward,
— overtake them, *say* (lit. *and say*) unto
45: 9. *and say* unto him, Thus *saith* thy son
46:33. *and shall say,* What (is) your occupation?
34. *That ye shall say,* Thy servants' trade
Ex. 2:22. *he said,* I have been a stranger
3:13. *and shall say* unto them,
— *and they shall say* to me,
16. *and say* unto them, The Lord God
18. *and ye shall say* unto him,
4:22. *thou shalt say* unto Pharaoh, Thus *saith*
26. So he let him go: then *she said,*
5: 1. Thus *saith* the Lord God of Israel,
10. saying, Thus *saith* Pharaoh, I will
6:26. to whom the Lord *said,*
7: 9. *then thou shalt say* unto Aaron,
16. *And thou shalt say* unto him,
17. Thus *saith* the Lord,
8: 1(7:26), 20(16). *and say* unto him, Thus *saith* the Lord,
9: 1. Thus *saith* the Lord God
13. *and say* unto him, Thus *saith* the Lord
10: 3 & 11:4. Thus *saith* the Lord
12:27. *That ye shall say,* It (is) the sacrifice
33. *they said,* We (be) all dead
13:14. *that thou shalt say* unto him,
17. for God *said,* Lest peradventure
14: 3. *For* Pharaoh *will say* of the
15: 9. The enemy *said,* I will pursue,
17:10. Joshua did as Moses *had said*
18: 3. for *he said,* I have been an alien
24. did all that *he had said.*
23:13. in all (things) that *I have said*
24: 1. And *he said* unto Moses,
14. *he said* unto the elders,
32:13. this land that *I have spoken* of
27. Thus *saith* the Lord God
33:12. Yet thou *hast said,* I know thee
Lev. 1: 2. Israel, *and say* unto them,
15: 2. Israel, *and say* unto them,
17. 2. *and say* unto them;
12. *I said* unto the children of Israel,
18: 2 & 19:2 & 21:1 & 22:18 & 23:2, 10 & 25:2 & 27:2. *and say* unto them,
Nu. 5:12. *and say* unto them,
19. *and say* unto the woman,
21. *and* the priest *shall say* unto the woman,
22. *And* the woman *shall say,*
6: 2. Israel, *and say* unto them,
8: 2. Aaron, *and say* unto him,
10:29. the place of which the Lord *said,*
11:21. thou *hast said,* I will give
13:31. the men that went up with him *said,*
14:14. *And they will tell* (it) to the
15. *then* the nations...*will speak,*
31. which *ye said* should be a prey,
40. which the Lord *hath promised:*
15: 2, 18. *and say* unto them,
38. *and bid* them that they make
16:34. fled at the cry of them: for *they said,*
18:24. therefore *I have said* unto them,
26. the Levites, *and say* unto them,
30. *Therefore thou shalt say* unto them,
20:14. Thus *saith* thy brother Israel,
21:16. the well whereof the Lord *spake* unto
22:16. Thus *saith* Balak the son of Zippor,
23:19. *hath he said,* and shall he not
30. Balak did as Balaam *had said,*
24:11. *I thought* to promote thee
26:65. For the Lord *had said* of them,
28: 2. children of Israel, *and say* unto them,
3. *And thou shalt say* unto them,
33:51 & 34:2 & 35:10. *and say* unto them,
Deu. 1:39. which *ye said* should be a prey,

Deu 4: 6. *and say*, Surely this great nation
6:21. *Then thou shalt say* unto thy son,
8:17. *And thou say* in thine heart,
9:25. the Lord *had said* he would destroy
10: 1. the Lord *said* unto me,
12:20. *and thou shalt say*, I will eat flesh,
17:14. *and shalt say*, I will set a king
16. as the Lord *hath said* unto you,
20: 3. *And shall say* unto them,
8. the people, *and they shall say*,
21: 7. they shall answer *and say*,
20. *And they shall say* unto the elders
22:14. *and say*, I took this woman,
16. *And* the damsel's father *shall say*
25: 7. *and say*, My husband's brother
8. *and say*, I like not to take her;
9. and shall answer *and say*,
26: 3. *and say* unto him, I profess
5. *and say* before the Lord thy God,
13. *Then thou shalt say* before the Lord
27:14. *and say* unto all the men of Israel
15. the people shall answer *and say*, Amen.
16, 17, 18, 19, 20, 21, 22, 23, 24, 25, 26. *And* all the people *shall say*, Amen.
28:68. by the way whereof *I spake* unto thee,
29:22(21). *So that*...shall *say*, when they see
24(23). *Even* all nations *shall say*,
25(24). *Then* men *shall say*, Because they
31: 2. also the Lord *hath said* unto me,
17. *so that they will say* in that day,
32:26. *I said*, I would scatter them
37. *And he shall say*, Where (are)
40. *and say*, I live for ever.
33: 8. And of Levi *he said*,
12. (And) of Benjamin *he said*,
13. And of Joseph *he said*,
18. And of Zebulun *he said*,
20. And of Gad *he said*,
22. And of Dan *he said*,
23. And of Naphtali *he said*,
24. And of Asher *he said*,
Jos. 1:12. *spake* Joshua, saying,
4: 7. *Then ye shall answer* them,
5: 2. At that time the Lord *said*
6:22. Joshua *had said* unto the two
7:13. sanctify the people, *and say*,
— thus *saith* the Lord God of Israel,
9:11. meet them, *and say* unto them,
11: 9. unto them as the Lord *bade* him:
22:16. Thus *saith* the whole congregation
28. *that we may say* (again), Behold
33. *did* not *intend* to go up against
24: 2. Thus *saith* the Lord God of Israel,
Jud. 2: 3. Wherefore *I* also *said*, I will not
4:20. *and say*, Is there any man here? *that thou shalt say*, No.
5:23. *said* the angel of the Lord,
6: 8. Thus *saith* the Lord God of Israel,
7:18. *and say*, (The sword) of the Lord,
9: 3. for *they said*, He (is) our brother.
11:15. Thus *saith* Jephthah, Israel took not away
12: 4. because *they said*, Ye Gileadites
13:13. Of all that *I said* unto the woman
15: 2. And her father said, *I* verily *thought*
16:24. for *they said*, Our god hath
17: 2. *spakest* of also in mine ears,
19:30. *that* all that saw (it) *said*,
20:32. the children of Israel *said*,
39. for *they said*, Surely they are smitten
21:22. *that we will say* unto them, Be favourable
Ru. 1:12. If *I should say*, I have hope,
2:21. He *said* unto me also,
3:17. for *he said* to me, Go not empty
4: 4. I *thought* to advertise thee, (marg. I *said*)
1Sa. 1:22. *she said* unto her husband,
2:15. *and said* to the man that sacrificed,
16. *then he would answer* him,
20. *and said*, The Lord give thee seed
27. said unto him, Thus *saith* the Lord,
30. *I said* indeed (that) thy house,
36. *and shall say*, Put me, I pray thee,
3: 9. *that thou shalt say*, Speak,
4: 7. for *they said*, God is come
5: 7. *they said*, The ark of the God
8: 6. when *they said*, Give us a king
9: 5. Saul *said* to his servant
9. thus he *spake*, Come, and let us go

1Sa. 9:17. the man whom *I spake* to thee of!
23. of which *I said* unto thee,
27. Samuel *said* to Saul,
10: 2. *and they will say* unto thee,
15. what Samuel *said* unto you.
16. whereof Samuel *spake*, he told him not.
18. Thus *saith* the Lord God
27. the children of Belial *said*,
12: 1. in all that *ye said* unto me,
13:19. for the Philistines *said*,
14:34. *and say* unto them, Bring
15: 2. Thus *saith* the Lord of hosts,
16: 2. *and say*, I am come to sacrifice
17:55. *he said* unto Abner, the captain
18:17. For Saul *said*, Let not mine hand
19:17. Michal answered Saul, He *said* unto me,
20: 6. *then say*, David earnestly asked
26. for *he thought*, Something hath befallen
23:22. *it is told* me (that) he dealeth
24: 4(5). the day of which the Lord *said* unto
10(11). *and* (some) *bade* (me) kill thee:
25: 6. *And* thus *shall ye say* to him
21. Now David *had said*, Surely
35. and *said* unto her, Go up in peace
29: 9. the princes of the Philistines *have said*,
30: 6. the people *spake* of stoning him,
2Sa. 3:18. for the Lord *hath spoken* of David, saying,
6:22. which *thou hast spoken* of,
7: 5. *and tell* my servant David, Thus *saith* the
8. Thus *saith* the Lord of hosts,
11:20. the king's wrath arise, *and he say* unto
21. *then say thou*, Thy servant Uriah
12: 7. Thus *saith* the Lord God
11. Thus *saith* the Lord,
18. for *they said*, Behold, while the child
22. for *I said*, Who can tell
13: 5. father cometh to see thee, *say* unto him,
28. *when I say* unto you,
15:10. *then ye shall say*, Absalom reigneth
34. *and say* unto Absalom,
16: 3. *he said*, To day shall the
7. And *thus said* Shimei when he cursed,
10. the Lord *hath said* unto him, Curse
11. the Lord *hath bidden* him.
17: 9. whosoever heareth it *will say*,
29. *they said*, The people (is) hungry,
18:18. for *he said*, I have no son
19. Then *said* Ahimaaz the son
33(19:1). as he went, thus *he said*, O my son
19:26(27). for thy servant *said*, I will saddle
29(30). *I have said*, Thou and Ziba
23: 3. The God of Israel *said*,
24:12. *saith* the Lord, I offer
1K. 1:13. *and say* unto him,
24. My lord, O king, *hast* thou *said*,
34. *and say*, God save king Solomon.
48. also thus *said* the king,
2:26. unto Abiathar the priest *said* the king,
30. Thus *saith* the king,
8:12. Then *spake* Solomon, The Lord *said*
29. the place of which *thou hast said*,
9: 8. *and they shall say*, Why hath the Lord
9. *And they shall answer*, Because
11: 2. the Lord *said* unto the children
18. *appointed* him victuals, and gave him
31. thus *saith* the Lord, the God of Israel,
12.24. Thus *saith* the Lord,
13: 2. O altar, altar, thus *saith* the Lord;
21. Thus *saith* the Lord, Forasmuch
14. 5. the Lord *said* unto Ahijah,
7. Thus *saith* the Lord God of Israel,
17:14. For thus *saith* the Lord God
18:10. *and when they said*, (He is) not (there);
20. 2(3). Thus *saith* Ben-hadad,
5. Thus *speaketh* Ben-hadad,
13, 14, 42. Thus *saith* the Lord,
23. servants of the king of Syria *said*
28. *saith* the Lord, Because the Syrians *have said*,
32. Thy servant Ben-hadad *saith*,
35. man of the sons of the prophets *said*
21:19, 19. Thus *saith* the Lord,
22:11. Thus *saith* the Lord, With these
18. *Did I* not *tell* thee that he
27. *And say*, Thus *saith* the king,
32. that *they said*, Surely it (is) the
49(50). Then *said* Ahaziah the son

2K. 1: 4, 6, 16. thus *saith* the Lord,
11. thus *hath* the king *said*,
2: 9. that Elijah *said* unto Elisha,
18. *Did I* not *say* unto you, Go not?
21. *saith* the Lord, I have healed these
3. 16. *saith* the Lord, Make this valley
17. For thus *saith* the Lord,
4: 24. except *I bid* thee.
28. *did I* not *say*, Do not deceive
43. for thus *saith* the Lord,
5: 11. *I thought* (marg. *said*, or *said* with myself), He will surely come out
13. when he *saith* to thee, Wash,
6: 10. which the man of God *told* him
28. This woman *said* unto me,
32. *he said* to the elders,
7: 1. Thus *saith* the Lord,
4. If *we say*, we will enter
8: 14. What *said* Elisha to thee?
— *He told* me (that) thou shouldest surely
19. as *he promised* him to give
9: 3. on his head, *and say*, Thus *saith* the Lord,
6. *saith* the Lord God of Israel,
12. *spake* he to me, saying, Thus *saith* the
18, 19. Thus *saith* the king, (Is it) peace?
11: 15. priest *had said*, Let her not be slain
17: 12. idols, whereof the Lord *had said*
18: 19. Thus *saith* the great king,
20. *Thou sayest* (marg. *talkest*), but (they are but) vain words,
25. The Lord *said* to me, Go up
29. *saith* the king, Let not Hezekiah
31. for thus *saith* the king of Assyria,
19: 3. unto him, Thus *saith* Hezekiah,
6, 20, 32. Thus *saith* the Lord,
20: 1. *saith* the Lord, Set thine house
5. *and tell* Hezekiah the captain of my people, Thus *saith* the Lord,
14. What *said* these men? and from whence
17. nothing shall be left, *saith* the Lord.
21: 4, 7. of which the Lord *said*,
12. thus *saith* the Lord God
22: 15, 16, 18. Thus *saith* the Lord
23: 27. *I said*, My name shall be there.
1Ch 15: 2. Then David *said*, None ought
17: 4. *and tell* David my servant, Thus *saith* the
7. Thus *saith* the Lord of hosts,
21: 10, 11. Thus *saith* the Lord,
17. I (that) *commanded* the people
18. angel of the Lord *commanded* Gad
23: 25. David *said*, The Lord God of
27: 23. the Lord *had said* he would increase
28: 3. But God *said* unto me,
2Ch. 2: 15(14). which my lord *hath spoken of*,
6: 1. *said* Solomon, The Lord *hath said*
20. whereof *thou hast said* that thou wouldest
7: 21. *so that he shall say*, Why hath
22. *And it shall be answered*,
8: 11. for *he said*, My wife shall not
11: 4 & 12: 5 & 18: 10. Thus *saith* the Lord,
18: 17. *Did I* not *tell* thee
26. *And say*, Thus *saith* the king,
31. that *they said*, It (is) the king
20: 15. Thus *saith* the Lord unto you,
21: 7. as *he promised* to give a light
12. Thus *saith* the Lord God
22: 9. Because, *said* they, he (is) the son of
23: 14. For the priest *said*, Slay her not in
24: 20. said unto them, Thus *saith* God,
22. *he said*, The Lord look upon
25: 19. *Thou sayest*, Lo, thou hast
26: 23. for *they said*, He (is) a leper:
29: 24. the king *commanded* (that) the burnt
32: 10. Thus *saith* Sennacherib
33: 4. whereof the Lord *had said*,
7. of which God *had said* to
34: 23, 26. Thus *saith* the Lord God of Israel,
24. *saith* the Lord, Behold,
35: 21. God *commanded* me to make haste:
36: 23. *saith* Cyrus king of Persia,
Ezr. 1: 2. Thus *saith* Cyrus king of Persia,
8: 22. because *we had spoken* unto the king,
Neh. 2: 18. that he *had spoken* unto me.
4: 22(16). at the same time *said I*
9: 23. which *thou hadst promised* to their fathers,
Est. 1: 10. *he commanded* Mehuman,
17. king Ahasuerus *commanded*

Est. 4: 7. that Haman *had promised* to pay
9: 25. the king, *he commanded* by letters
Job 1: 5. Job *said*, It may be that my sons
3: 3. the night (in which) *it was said*,
6: 22. *Did I say*, Bring unto me?
7: 4. *I say*, When shall I arise,
13. When *I say*, My bed shall comfort me,
9: 22. (is) one (thing), therefore *I said*
22: 13. *And thou sayest*, How doth God know?
28: 14. depth *saith*, It (is) not in me: and the sea *saith*,
22: Destruction and death *say*, We have
31: 24. or *have said* to the fine gold,
31. the men of my tabernacle *said* not,
32: 7. *I said*, Days should speak, and
10. *I said*, Hearken to me;
33: 8. Surely *thou hast spoken* in mine
34: 5. For Job *hath said*, I am righteous:
9. For *he hath said*, It profiteth a man
35: 2. this to be right, (that) *thou saidst*,
10. But none *saith*, Where (is) God
36: 23. who *can say*, Thou hast wrought
37: 20. if a man *speak*, surely he shall be
Ps. 2: 7. the Lord *hath said* unto me,
10: 6, 11, 13. He *hath said* in his heart,
12: 4(5). Who *have said*, With our tongue
14: 1. fool *hath said* in his heart,
16: 2. *thou hast said* unto the Lord,
27: 8. my heart *said* unto thee,
30: 6(7). in my prosperity *I said*,
31: 14(15). *I said*, Thou (art) my God.
22(23). For *I said* in my haste,
32: 5. *I said*, I will confess my transgressions
33: 9. For *he spake*, and it was (done);
35: 21. *said*, Aha, aha, our eye hath
38: 16(17). For *I said*, (Hear me), lest
39: 1(2). *I said*, I will take heed to
40: 7(8). Then *said I*, Lo, I come:
10(11). *I have declared* thy faithfulness
41: 4(5). *I said*, Lord, be merciful
50: 16. But unto the wicked God *saith*,
53: 1(2). fool *hath said* in his heart,
64: 5(6). *they say*, Who shall see them?
68: 22(23). The Lord *said*, I will bring
71: 10. For mine enemies *speak* against
73: 11. *And they say*, How doth God
15. If *I say*, I will speak thus;
74: 8. *They said* in their hearts,
75: 4(5). *I said* unto the fools, Deal not
78: 19. *they said*, Can God furnish a table
82: 6. *I have said*, Ye (are) gods;
83: 4(5). have *said*, Come, and let us
12(13). Who *said*, Let us take to ourselves
89: 2(3). *I have said*, Mercy shall be built
94: 18. When *I said*, My foot slippeth;
105: 31. *He spake*, and there came divers sorts of
34. *He spake*, and the locusts came,
106: 34. concerning whom the Lord *commanded*
48. *and let* all the people *say*, Amen.
116: 11. *I said* in my haste, All men
119: 57. *I have said* that I would keep
129: 8. Neither do they which go by *say*,
140: 6(7). *I said* unto the Lord,
142: 5(6). *I said*, Thou (art) my refuge
Pro. 5: 12. *And say*, How have I hated instruction,
9: 4. that wanteth understanding, *she saith* to
16. *and* (as for) him that wanteth understanding, *she saith*
22: 13 & 26: 13. The slothful (man) *saith*,
26: 19. *and saith*, Am not I in sport?
30: 9. *and say*, Who (is) the Lord?
15. four (things) *say* not, (It is) enough:
16. the fire (that) *saith* not, (It is) enough.
20. *and saith*, I have done no wickedness.
Ecc. 1: 2. Vanity of vanities, *saith* the Preacher,
2: 1. I *said* in mine heart, Go to now,
2. *I said* of laughter, (It is) mad:
15. *Then said* I in my heart,
3: 17, 18. I *said* in mine heart,
6: 3. *I say*, (that) an untimely birth
7: 23. *I said*, I will be wise;
27. this have I found, *saith* the preacher,
8: 14. *I said* that this also (is) vanity.
9: 16. *Then said* I, Wisdom (is) better
10: 3. *and he saith* to every one
12: 8. Vanity of vanities, *saith* the preacher;
Cant. 2: 10. My beloved spake, *and said* unto me

Cant.7: 8(9). *I said*, I will go up to the palm
Isa. 2: 3. many people shall go *and say*,
6: 3. *and said*, Holy, holy, holy, (is) the
9. Go, *and tell* this people, Hear ye indeed,
7: 4. *And say* unto him, Take heed,
7. Thus *saith* the Lord God,
8: 11. For the Lord *spake* thus to me
10: 13. For he *saith*, By the strength
24. Therefore thus *saith* the Lord
12: 1. *And* in that day *thou shalt say*,
4. *And* in that day *shall ye say*,
14: 4. *and say*, How hath the oppressor
13. thou *hast said* in thine heart,
18: 4. For so the Lord *said* unto me,
20: 6. *And* the inhabitant of this isle *shall say*
21: 6. thus *hath* the Lord *said* unto me,
12. The watchman *said*, The morning
16. For thus hath the Lord *said*
22: 4. Therefore *said I*, Look away from
14. till ye die, *saith* the Lord God of hosts.
15. Thus *saith* the Lord God of hosts,
23: 4. for the sea *hath spoken*,
25: 9. *And it shall be said* in that day,
28: 12. To whom *he said*, This (is) the rest
15. Because *ye have said*, We have made
16. thus *saith* the Lord God, Behold,
29: 11. *And he saith*, I cannot; for it (is) sealed:
12. *and he saith*, I am not learned.
16. or *shall* the thing framed *say* of him
22. Therefore thus *saith* the Lord, who
30: 10. Which *say* to the seers, See not;
12. thus *saith* the Holy One of Israel,
15. For thus *saith* the Lord God,
31: 4. thus *hath* the Lord *spoken* unto me,
36: 4. Thus *saith* the great king,
5. *I say*, (sayest thou), but
10. the Lord *said* unto me, Go up
14. Thus *saith* the king, Let not Hezekiah
16. for thus *saith* the king of Assyria,
37: 3. Thus *saith* Hezekiah, This day
6. Thus *saith* the Lord, Be not afraid
21. Thus *saith* the Lord God of Israel,
33. *saith* the Lord concerning the king of
38: 1. *saith* the Lord, Set thine house in order.
5. Go, *and say* to Hezekiah, Thus *saith* the
10. I *said* in the cutting off of my days,
11. *I said*, I shall not see the Lord,
15. *he hath both spoken* unto me,
39: 3. What *said* these men? and from whence
6. nothing shall be left, *saith* the Lord.
40: 6. *And he said*, What shall I cry?
42: 5. Thus *saith* God the Lord,
43: 1, 14, 16, & 44: 2, 6, 24 & 45: 1, 11, 14. thus *saith* the Lord
45: 13. *saith* the Lord of hosts.
18. For thus *saith* the Lord that created
19. *I said* not unto the seed of Jacob,
24. Surely, *shall* (one) *say*, in the Lord (marg. *he shall say*)
47: 10. *thou hast said*, None seeth me.
48: 17. Thus *saith* the Lord, thy
22. no peace, *saith* the Lord,
49: 4. Then I *said*, I have laboured
5. And now, *saith* the Lord that formed me
7, 8, 25. Thus *saith* the Lord,
21. *Then shalt thou say* in thine heart,
22. Thus *saith* the Lord God,
50: 1. Thus *saith* the Lord, Where (is) the bill of
51: 22. Thus *saith* thy Lord the Lord, and thy
23. which *have said* to thy soul, Bow down,
52: 3. thus *saith* the Lord, Ye have sold yourselves
4. thus *saith* the Lord God, My people went
54: 1. of the married wife, *saith* the Lord.
6. when thou wast refused, *saith* thy God.
8. *saith* the Lord thy Redeemer.
10. *saith* the Lord that hath mercy on thee.
56: 1. Thus *saith* the Lord, Keep ye judgment,
4. For thus *saith* the Lord unto the
57: 10. *saidst thou* not, There is no hope:
14. *And shall say*, Cast ye up,
15. For thus *saith* the high and lofty One
19. *saith* the Lord; and I will heal him.
21. no peace, *saith* my God, to the
59: 21. my covenant with them, *saith* the Lord;
— of thy seed's seed, *saith* the Lord,
65: 1. *I said*, Behold me, behold me,
7. iniquities of your fathers together, *saith*

Isa. 65: 8. Thus *saith* the Lord, As the new wine
— *and* (one) *saith*, Destroy it not;
13. thus *saith* the Lord God, Behold,
25. in all my holy mountain, *saith* the Lord.
66: 1. Thus *saith* the Lord, The heaven
5. that cast you out for my name's sake, *said*,
9. and shut (the womb)? *saith* thy God.
12. For thus *saith* the Lord, Behold,
20. holy mountain Jerusalem, *saith* the Lord,
21. for Levites, *saith* the Lord.
23. worship before me, *saith* the Lord.
Jer. 2: 2. Thus *saith* the Lord; I remember thee,
5. Thus *saith* the Lord, What iniquity
6. Neither *said they*, Where (is) the Lord
8. The priests *said* not, Where (is) the Lord?
31. wherefore *say* my people, We are lords;
3: 12. *and say*, Return, thou backsliding Israel,
19. But I *said*, How shall I put thee
4: 3. For thus *saith* the Lord to the men of
27. thus *hath* the Lord *said*,
5: 4. Therefore I *said*, Surely these
14. thus *saith* the Lord God of hosts,
19. *then shalt thou answer* them,
24. Neither *say they* in their heart,
6: 6. thus hath the Lord of hosts *said*,
9. Thus *saith* the Lord of hosts,
15. they shall be cast down, *saith* the Lord.
16. Thus *saith* the Lord, Stand ye
21. Therefore thus *saith* the Lord,
22. Thus *saith* the Lord, Behold, a people
7: 2. *and say*, Hear the word of the Lord,
3, 21. Thus *saith* the Lord of hosts,
10. *and say*, We are delivered to do
20. Therefore thus *saith* the Lord God;
28. *But thou shalt say* unto them, This
8: 4. *Moreover thou shalt say* unto them, Thus *saith* the Lord;
12. they shall be cast down, *saith* the Lord.
9: 7(6), 15(14), 17(16). thus *saith* the Lord of
23(22). *saith* the Lord, Let not the wise
10: 2. *saith* the Lord, Learn not the way
18. thus *saith* the Lord, Behold, I will sling
19. but I *said*, Truly this (is) a grief,
11: 3. *And say* thou unto them, Thus *saith* the Lord God of Israel;
11. Therefore thus *saith* the Lord, Behold,
21. *saith* the Lord of the men of Anathoth,
22. thus *saith* the Lord of hosts, Behold,
12: 4. because *they said*, He shall not see
14. Thus *saith* the Lord against
13: 1. Thus *saith* the Lord unto me,
9. Thus *saith* the Lord, After this manner
12. *Therefore thou shalt speak* unto them this word; Thus *saith* the Lord
— *and they shall say* unto thee,
13. *Then shalt thou say* unto them, Thus *saith* the Lord,
14: 10. Thus *saith* the Lord unto this people,
15. Therefore thus *saith* the Lord concerning
17. *Therefore thou shalt say* this word unto
15: 2. *then thou shalt tell* them, Thus *saith* the
11. The Lord *said*, Verily it shall be well
19. Therefore thus *saith* the Lord,
16: 3. For thus *saith* the Lord concerning
5. For thus *saith* the Lord, Enter not
9. thus *saith* the Lord of hosts,
10. *and they shall say* unto thee,
11. *Then shalt thou say* unto them,
17: 5. Thus *saith* the Lord; Cursed (be) the man
19. Thus *said* the Lord unto me; Go
20. *And say* unto them, Hear ye
21. Thus *saith* the Lord; Take heed
18: 10. wherewith *I said* I would benefit them.
11. Thus *saith* the Lord; Behold, I frame evil
12. *And they said*, There is no hope:
13. Therefore thus *saith* the Lord; Ask
19: 1. Thus *saith* the Lord, Go and get
3. *And say*, Hear ye the word of the Lord,
— Thus *saith* the Lord of hosts, the God
11. *And shalt say* unto them, Thus *saith*
15. Thus *saith* the Lord of hosts, the God
20: 4. For thus *saith* the Lord, Behold,
9. *Then I said*, I will not make mention
21: 4. Thus *saith* the Lord God of Israel;
8. *saith* the Lord; Behold, I set before you
12. thus *saith* the Lord; Execute judgment
22: 1. Thus *saith* the Lord; Go down

Jer. 22: 2. *And say*, Hear the word of the Lord,
3. Thus *saith* the Lord; Execute ye
6. For thus *saith* the Lord unto the king's
8. *and they shall say* every man
9. *Then they shall answer*, Because
11. For thus *saith* the Lord touching
18. thus *saith* the Lord concerning
21. *thou saidst*, I will not hear.
30. *saith* the Lord, Write ye
23: 2. Therefore thus *saith* the Lord God
15. Therefore thus *saith* the Lord of hosts
16. Thus *saith* the Lord of hosts,
17. and *they say* unto every one
25. I have heard what the prophets *said*,
33. *thou shalt then say* unto them, What
38. therefore thus *saith* the Lord; Because
24: 5. *saith* the Lord, the God of Israel;
8. surely thus *saith* the Lord,
25: 8, 27, 28, 32. thus *saith* the Lord of hosts;
15. thus *saith* the Lord God of Israel
27. *Therefore thou shalt say* unto them,
28. *then shalt thou say* unto them,
30. *and say* unto them, The Lord shall roar
26: 2. Thus *saith* the Lord; Stand
4. *And thou shalt say* unto them, Thus *saith* the Lord;
18. Thus *saith* the Lord of hosts;
27: 2. Thus *saith* the Lord to me;
4, 19, 21. Thus *saith* the Lord of hosts,
16. *saith* the Lord; Hearken not
28: 1. *spake* unto me in the house
2. Thus *speaketh* the Lord of hosts,
11. Thus *saith* the Lord; Even so
13. Go *and tell* Hananiah, saying, Thus *saith*
14. thus *saith* the Lord of hosts, the God of
16. Therefore thus *saith* the Lord;
29: 4, 8, 17, 21. Thus *saith* the Lord of hosts,
10. For thus *saith* the Lord, That after
15. Because *ye have said*, The Lord hath
16. that thus *saith* the Lord of the king
25. Thus *speaketh* the Lord of hosts,
31. *saith* the Lord concerning Shemaiah
32. thus *saith* the Lord; Behold, I will
30: 2. Thus *speaketh* the Lord God of
3. my people Israel and J., *saith* the Lord:
5, 12, 18 & 31:2, 7, 15, 16, 23, 35, 37 & 32:3, 14, 15. thus *saith* the Lord;
32:25. And thou *hast said* unto me,
28. Therefore thus *saith* the Lord;
36. thus *saith* the Lord,
42. For thus *saith* the Lord;
33: 2. Thus *saith* the Lord the maker
4. For thus *saith* the Lord,
10. Thus *saith* the Lord; Again
11. as at the first, *saith* the Lord.
12. Thus *saith* the Lord of hosts;
13. that telleth (them), *saith* the Lord.
17. For thus *saith* the Lord; David shall never
20. *saith* the Lord; If ye can break
25. *saith* the Lord; If my covenant (be) not
34: 2. *saith* the Lord, the God of Israel; Go *and speak* to Zedekiah king of Judah, *and tell* him, Thus *saith* the Lord;
4. Thus *saith* the Lord of thee,
13. Thus *saith* the Lord, the God of
17. Therefore thus *saith* the Lord; Ye have
35:13. Thus *saith* the Lord of hosts,
— Go *and tell* the men of Judah
17. *saith* the Lord God of hosts, the God
18. Jeremiah *said* unto the house of the Rechabites, Thus *saith* the Lord of
19. *saith* the Lord of hosts, the God of Israel;
36:29. *saith* the Lord; Thou hast burned
30. Therefore thus *saith* the Lord of
37: 7, 9 & 38:2, 3, 17. Thus *saith* the Lord,
38:25. *and say* unto thee, Declare
26. *Then thou shalt say* unto them,
39:16. Go *and speak* to Ebed-melech
—Thus *saith* the Lord of hosts,
40:15. *spake* to Gedaliah in Mizpah
42: 5. Then they *said* to Jeremiah,
9, 15, 18. Thus *saith* the Lord,
43:10. *And say* unto them, Thus *saith* the Lord
44: 2, 7, 11, 25, 30. Thus *saith* the Lord
26. *saith* the Lord, that my name
45: 2. Thus *saith* the Lord, the God of
3. *Thou didst say*, Woe is me

Jer. 45: 4. The Lord *saith* thus; Behold,
46:25. the God of Israel, *saith*;
47: 2. Thus *saith* the Lord;
48: 1. Against Moab thus *saith* the Lord
8. be destroyed, as the Lord *hath spoken*.
40. For thus *saith* the Lord; Behold,
49: 1. thus *saith* the Lord; Hath Israel
2. that were his heirs, *saith* the Lord.
7. thus *saith* the Lord of hosts;
12. thus *saith* the Lord; Behold, they
18. *saith* the Lord, no man shall abide there,
28. thus *saith* the Lord; Arise ye,
35. Thus *saith* the Lord of hosts; Behold.
50: 7. their adversaries *said*, We offend not,
18. Therefore thus *saith* the Lord
33. Thus *saith* the Lord of hosts;
51: 1. Thus *saith* the Lord; Behold,
33. thus *saith* the Lord of hosts,
36. Therefore thus *saith* the Lord;
58. Thus *saith* the Lord of hosts;
62. *Then shalt thou say*, O Lord,
64. *And thou shalt say*, Thus shall Babylon
Lam. 2:16. *they say*, We have swallowed
3:24. The Lord (is) my portion, *saith* my soul;
37. Who (is) he (that) *saith*,
54. *I said*, I am cut off.
57. I called upon thee: *thou saidst*, Fear not.
4:15. *they said* among the heathen,
20. of whom *we said*, Under his
Eze. 2: 4. *and thou shalt say* unto them, Thus *saith*
3:11. *and tell* them, Thus *saith* the Lord God;
27. *and thou shalt say* unto them, Thus *saith*
5: 5. Thus *saith* the Lord God;
7, 8. thus *saith* the Lord God;
6: 3. *And say*, Ye mountains of Israel,
— 11 & 7:2, 5. Thus *saith* the Lord God
9: 5. to the others *he said*
9. *they say*, The Lord hath forsaken
11: 5. *saith* the Lord; Thus *have ye said*,
7. Therefore thus *saith* the Lord God;
15. the inhabitants of Jerusalem *have said*,
16, 17. Thus *saith* the Lord God;
12: 9. *said* unto thee, What doest thou?
10, 23, 28. Thus *saith* the Lord God;
19. *And say* unto the people of the land, Thus *saith*
13: 2. *and say* thou unto them that
3, 8, 13. Thus *saith* the Lord God;
7. and *have ye* not *spoken* a lying
18. *And say*, Thus *saith* the Lord God;
20. Wherefore thus *saith* the Lord
14: 4. *and say* unto them, Thus *saith* the Lord
6. Thus *saith* the Lord God; Repent,
17. *and say*, Sword, go through
21. *saith* the Lord God; How much more
15: 6. thus *saith* the Lord God;
16: 3. *And say*, Thus *saith* the Lord God
36, 59. Thus *saith* the Lord God;
17: 3. *And say*, Thus *saith* the Lord God;
9, 19, 22. Thus *saith* the Lord God;
18:19. *Yet say ye*, Why? doth not the son bear
25. *Yet ye say*, The way of the Lord
29. *Yet saith* the house of Israel,
19: 2. *And say*, What (is) thy mother?
20: 3, 5, 27. *and say* unto them, Thus *saith*
30, 39, 47(21:3). Thus *saith* the Lord God;
47(21:3). *say* to the forest of the south,
21: 3(8). *And say* to the land of Israel, Thus *saith*
7(12). *that thou shalt answer*, For the tidings;
9(14). prophesy, *and say*, Thus *saith* the
24(29), 26(31). thus *saith* the Lord God;
28(33). prophesy *and say*, Thus *saith* the
—(—). *even say* thou, The sword,
22: 3. *Then say thou*, Thus *saith* the Lord God;
19, 28 & 23:22, 28, 32, 35, 46. thus *saith* the Lord God;
24: 3. *and say* unto them, Thus *saith* the Lord
6. Wherefore thus *saith* the Lord
9. Therefore thus *saith* the Lord
21. Thus *saith* the Lord God;
25: 3. *And say* unto the Ammonites,
3, 6, 8, 12, 13, 15, 16. Thus *saith* the Lord
26: 2. Tyrus *hath said* against Jerusalem,
3, 7, 15, 19. thus *saith* the Lord God;
17. *and say* to thee, How art thou destroyed,
27: 3. *And say* unto Tyrus,
— *saith* the Lord God; O Tyrus, thou *hast said*,

Eze.28: 2, 6, 25. Thus *saith* the Lord God;
12. *and say* unto him, Thus *saith* the Lord
22. *And say,* Thus *saith* the Lord God;
29: 3. Speak, *and say,* Thus *saith* the Lord God;
— which *hath said,* My river (is) mine own,
8, 19. Therefore thus *saith* the Lord God;
9. because *he hath said,* The river (is) mine,
13. Yet thus *saith* the Lord
30: 2. prophesy *and say,* Thus *saith* the Lord
6. Thus *saith* the Lord;
10, 13, 22 & 31:10, 15. Thus *saith* the Lord
32: 2. *and say* unto him, Thou art like
3, 11. Thus *saith* the Lord God;
33: 2. *and say* unto them, When I bring
10. Thus *ye speak,* saying,
17. *Yet* the children of thy people *say,* The
20. *Yet ye say,* The way of the Lord
25, 27. Thus *saith* the Lord God;
34: 2. *and say* unto them, Thus *saith* the Lord
10, 11, 17, 20. Thus *saith* the Lord God;
35: 3. *And say* unto it, Thus *saith* the Lord God;
12. which *thou hast spoken* against
14. Thus *saith* the Lord God;
36: 1. *and say,* Ye mountains of Israel,
2. *saith* the Lord God; Because the enemy *hath said*
3. *and say,* Thus *saith* the Lord God;
4, 5, 6, 7, 13, 22, 33, 37. Thus *saith* the Lord
6. *and say* unto the mountains,
35. *And they shall say,* This land
37. 4. *and say* unto them, O ye dry bones,
5, 19, 21. Thus *saith* the Lord God
9. *and say* to the wind, Thus *saith* the Lord
12. *and say* unto them, Thus *saith* the Lord
38: 3. *And say,* Thus *saith* the Lord God;
10, 17. Thus *saith* the Lord God;
11. *And thou shalt say,* I will go up
14. *and say* unto Gog, Thus *saith* the Lord
39: 1. *and say,* Thus *saith* the Lord God;
17, 25 & 43:18. thus *saith* the Lord God;
44: 6. *And thou shalt say* to the rebellious,
— 9 & 45:9, 18 & 46:1, 16 & 47:13. Thus *saith* the Lord God;
Dan. 1:18. the king *had said* he should bring
Hos. 2: 5(7). *she said,* I will go after my lovers,
7(9). *then shall she say,* I will go
12(14). whereof *she hath said,* These (are)
23(25). *and I will say* to
10: 8. *and they shall say* to the mountains,
13:10. thy judges of whom *thou saidst,*
Joel 2:32(3:5). as the Lord *hath said,*
Am. 1: 3, 6, 9, 11, 13. *saith* the Lord; For three
5. into captivity unto Kir, *saith* the Lord.
8. shall perish, *saith* the Lord
15. he and his princes together, *saith* the
2: 1, 4, 6. *saith* the Lord, For three
3. the princes thereof with him, *saith* the
3:11. thus *saith* the Lord God; An adversary
12. *saith* the Lord; As the shepherd
5: 3. For thus *saith* the Lord God; The city
4. For thus *saith* the Lord unto the house
14. as *ye have spoken.*
16. the Lord, *saith* thus; Wailing
17. I will pass through thee, *saith* the Lord.
27 captivity beyond Damascus, *saith* the
6:10. *and shall say* unto him that (is)
— *and he shall say,* No. *Then shall he say,*
7: 3. It shall not be, *saith* the Lord.
6. shall not be, *saith* the Lord God.
11. For thus Amos *saith,*
17. Therefore thus *saith* the Lord;
8:14. *and say,* Thy god, O Dan,
9:15. *saith* the Lord thy God.
Obad. 1. *saith* the Lord God concerning
Jon. 2: 4(5). Then *I said,* I am cast out
Mic. 2: 3. thus *saith* the Lord; Behold,
4. *say,* We be utterly spoiled:
3: 5. Thus *saith* the Lord concerning
4: 2. *and say,* Come, and let us go
Nah. 1:12. Thus *saith* the Lord; Though (they be)
3: 7. *and say,* Nineveh is laid waste:
Zep. 3: 7. *I said,* Surely thou wilt fear
20. before your eyes, *saith* the Lord.
Hag. 1: 2. Thus *speaketh* the Lord of hosts, saying, This people *say,*
5, 7. thus *saith* the Lord of hosts; Consider
8 I will be glorified, *saith* the Lord.
Hag. 2: 6. For thus *saith* the Lord of hosts;
7. house with glory, *saith* the Lord of hosts.
9. of the former, *saith* the Lord of hosts:
11. *saith* the Lord of hosts; Ask now
Zec. 1: 3. *Therefore say thou* unto them, Thus *saith*
— I will turn unto you, *saith* the Lord
4, 14, 17. Thus *saith* the Lord of hosts;
16. Therefore thus *saith* the Lord;
2: 8(12). *saith* the Lord of hosts; After the
3: 7. *saith* the Lord of hosts; If thou wilt
4: 6. but by my spirit, *saith* the Lord
6:12. *And speak* unto him, saying, Thus *speaketh*
7: 9. Thus *speaketh* the Lord of hosts,
13. *saith* the Lord of hosts:
8: 2, 4, 6, 7, 9, 14, 19, 20, 23. Thus *saith* the Lord
3. Thus *saith* the Lord; I am returned
14. provoked me to wrath, *saith* the Lord of
11: 4. Thus *saith* the Lord my God;
12: 5. *And* the governors of Judah *shall say*
13: 3. *shall say* unto him, Thou shalt not live;
5. *But he shall say,* I (am) no prophet,
6. *And* (one) *shall say* unto him, What
— *Then he shall answer,* (Those) with which
9. *I will say,* It (is) my people:
Mal. 1: 2. I have loved you, *saith* the Lord. *Yet ye say,* Wherein hast thou loved
4. thus *saith* the Lord of hosts,
6. *saith* the Lord of hosts unto you,
— *And ye say,* Wherein have we despised
7. *and ye say,* Wherein have we polluted
8, 9, 10, 11, 13, 14. *saith* the Lord of hosts.
13. *Ye said also,* Behold, what a weariness
— accept this of your hand? *saith* the Lord.
2: 2, 4, 8, 16. *saith* the Lord of hosts,
14. *Yet ye say,* Wherefore? Because
16. the God of Israel, *saith* that he hateth
17. *Yet ye say,* Wherein have we wearied
3: 1, 5, 7, 10, 11, 12, 17. *saith* the Lord of hosts.
7. *But ye said,* Wherein shall we return?
8. *But ye say,* Wherein have we robbed
13. against me, *saith* the Lord. *Yet ye say,*
14. *Ye have said,* It (is) vain to serve God:
4: 1(3:19). burn them up, *saith* the Lord of
3(-:21). I shall do (this), *saith* the Lord of

KAL.—*Infinitive.*

Gen. 1:22. God blessed them, *saying,* Be fruitful,
2:16. *saying,* Of every tree of the garden
3:17. *saying,* Thou shalt not eat of it.
5:29. *saying,* This (same) shall comfort us
8:15. God spake unto Noah, *saying,*
9: 8. to his sons with him, *saying,*
15: 1. *saying,* Fear not, Abram.
4. *saying,* This shall not be
18. made a covenant with Abram, *saying,*
17: 3. God talked with him, *saying,*
18:12. Sarah laughed within herself, *saying,*
13. Wherefore did Sarah laugh, *saying,*
15. Sarah denied, *saying,* I laughed not;
19:15. *saying,* Arise, take thy wife,
21:22. spake unto Abraham, *saying,*
22:20. it was told Abraham, *saying,*
23: 3. spake unto the sons of Heth, *saying,*
5. answered Abraham, *saying*
8. he communed with them, *saying,*
10. at the gate of his city, *saying,*
13. *saying,* But if thou (wilt give)
14. Ephron answered Abraham, *saying*
24: 7. that sware unto me, *saying,*
30. the words of Rebekah his sister, *saying,*
37. my master made me swear, *saying,*
26: 7. for he feared *to say,* (She is) my wife;
11. *saying,* He that toucheth this man
20. *saying,* The water (is) ours:
27: 6. spake unto Jacob her son, *saying,*
— speak unto Esau thy brother, *saying,*
28: 6. he gave him a charge, *saying,*
20. Jacob vowed a vow, *saying,*
30:24. *and said,* The Lord shall add
31: 1. heard the words of Laban's sons, *saying,*
29. spake unto me yesternight, *saying,*
32: 4(5). he commanded them, *saying,*
6(7). messengers returned to Jacob, *saying,*
17(18). commanded the foremost, *saying,*
—(—). asketh thee, *saying,* Whose (art)
19(20). *saying,* On this manner shall ye speak
34: 4. *saying,* Get me this damsel to wife.

Gen34: 8. *saying*, The soul of my son
20. with the men of their city, *saying*,
37:15. the man asked him, *saying*,
38:13. it was told Tamar, *saying*,
21. *saying*, Where (is) the harlot,
24. that it was told Judah, *saying*,
25. *saying*, By the man, whose
28. *saying*, This came out first.
39:12. *saying*, Lie with me:
14. spake unto them, *saying*,
17. *saying*, The Hebrew servant,
19. which she spake unto him, *saying*,
40: 7. *saying*, Wherefore look ye (so) sadly
41: 9. *saying*, I do remember my faults
15. I have heard *say* of thee,
16. Joseph answered Pharaoh, *saying*,
42:14. I spake unto you, *saying*,
22. them, *saying*, Spake I not unto you, *saying*,
28. *saying* one to another,
29. told him all that befell unto them; *saying*,
37. Reuben spake unto his father, *saying*,
43: 3. Judah spake unto him, *saying*,
— *saying*, Ye shall not see my face,
7. *saying*, (Is) your father yet alive?
44: 1. *saying*, Fill the men's sacks
19. My lord asked his servants, *saying*,
32. *saying*, If I bring him not
45:16. *saying*, Joseph's brethren are come:
26. told him, *saying*, Joseph (is) yet
47: 5. spake unto Joseph, *saying*,
15. *and said*, Give us bread:
48:20. he blessed them that day, *saying*, In thee shall Israel bless, *saying*,
50: 4. spake unto the house of Pharaoh, *saying*,
— in the ears of Pharaoh, *saying*,
5. My father made me swear, *saying*,
16. unto Joseph, *saying*, Thy father did command before he died, *saying*,
25. *saying*, God will surely visit you,
Ex. 1: 22. Pharaoh charged all his people, *saying*,
3:16. appeared unto me, *saying*,
5: 6. and their officers, *saying*,
8. *saying*, Let us go (and) sacrifice
10. *saying*, Thus saith Pharaoh,
13. the taskmasters hasted (them), *saying*,
14. were beaten, (and) *demanded*,
15. cried unto Pharaoh, *saying*,
19. in evil (case), *after it was said*,
6:10, 29. the Lord spake unto Moses, *saying*,
12. Moses spake before the Lord, *saying*,
7: 8. unto Moses and unto Aaron, *saying*,
9. Pharaoh shall speak unto you, *saying*,
16. *saying*, Let my people go,
9: 5. appointed a set time, *saying*,
11: 8. bow down themselves unto me, *saying*,
12: 1. Aaron in the land of Egypt, *saying*,
3. *saying*, In the tenth (day) of this month
13: 1. the Lord spake unto Moses, *saying*,
8. shew thy son in that day, *saying*,
14. in time to come, *saying*, What (is) this?
19. *saying*, God will surely visit you;
14: 1. the Lord spake unto Moses, *saying*,
12. that we did tell thee in Egypt, *saying*,
15: 1. unto the Lord, and spake, *saying*,
24. *saying*, What shall we drink?
16:11. the Lord spake unto Moses, *saying*,
12. speak unto them, *saying*,
17: 4. Moses cried unto the Lord, *saying*,
7. *saying*, Is the Lord among us, or not?
19: 3. *saying*, Thus shalt thou say to the
12. *saying*, Take heed to yourselves,
23. for thou chargedst us, *saying*,
20: 1. God spake all these words, *saying*,
21: 5. if the servant shall *plainly* say, I (marg. *saying* shall say)
25: 1 & 30:11, 17, 22. the Lord spake unto Moses, *saying*,
30:31. speak unto the children of Israel, *saying*,
31: 1. the Lord spake unto Moses, *saying*,
12. the Lord spake unto Moses, *saying*,
13. unto the children of Israel, *saying*,
32:12. should the Egyptians speak, *and say*,
33: 1. *saying*, Unto thy seed will I give it:
35: 4. of the children of Israel, *saying*,
— which the Lord commanded, *saying*,
36: 5. And they spake unto Moses, *saying*,
6. *saying*, Let neither man nor woman

Ex. 40: 1. the Lord spake unto Moses, *saying*,
Lev. 1: 1. tabernacle of the congregation, *saying*,
4: 1. the Lord spake unto Moses, *saying*,
2. Speak unto the children of Israel, *saying*,
5:14 & 6:1 (5:20), 8(1), 19(12), 24(17). the Lord spake unto Moses, *saying*,
6: 9(2). Command Aaron and his sons, *saying*,
25(18). and to his sons, *saying*,
7:22, 28. the Lord spake unto Moses, *saying*,
23. *saying*, Ye shall eat no manner of fat,
29. unto the children of Israel, *saying*,
8: 1. the Lord spake unto Moses, *saying*,
31. as I commanded, *saying*, Aaron
9: 3. *saying*, Take ye a kid of the goats
10: 3. This (is it) that the Lord spake, *saying*,
8. the Lord spake unto Aaron, *saying*,
16. of Aaron (which were) left (alive), *saying*,
11: 1. and to Aaron, *saying* unto them,
2. unto the children of Israel, *saying*,
12: 1. the Lord spake unto Moses, *saying*,
2. unto the children of Israel, *saying*,
13: 1. spake unto Moses and Aaron, *saying*,
14: 1. the Lord spake unto Moses, *saying*,
33. unto Moses and unto Aaron, *saying*,
35. shall come and tell the priest, *saying*,
15: 1. unto Moses and to Aaron, *saying*,
17: 1. the Lord spake unto Moses, *saying*,
2. the Lord hath commanded, *saying*,
18: 1 & 19:1 & 20:1 & 21:16. the Lord spake unto Moses, *saying*,
21:17. Speak unto Aaron, *saying*,
22: 1, 17, 26. the Lord spake unto Moses, *saying*,
23: 1, 9, 23, 26, 33. the Lord spake unto Moses, *saying*,
24, 34. unto the children of Israel, *saying*,
24: 1, 13. the Lord spake unto Moses, *saying*,
15. unto the children of Israel, *saying*,
25: 1. unto Moses in mount Sinai, *saying*,
27: 1. the Lord spake unto Moses, *saying*,
Nu. 1: 1. come out of the land of Egypt, *saying*,
48. had spoken unto Moses, *saying*,
2: 1. unto Moses and unto Aaron, *saying*,
3: 5, 11, 44. the Lord spake unto Moses, *saying*,
14. in the wilderness of Sinai, *saying*,
4: 1, 17. unto Moses and unto Aaron, *saying*,
21 & 5:1, 5, 11 & 6:1, 22. the Lord spake unto Moses, *saying*,
6:23. unto Aaron and unto his sons, *saying*,
— the children of Israel, *saying* unto them,
7: 4 & 8:1, 5, 23. the Lord spake unto Moses, *saying*,
9: 1. come out of the land of Egypt, *saying*,
9. the Lord spake unto Moses, *saying*,
10. unto the children of Israel, *saying*,
10: 1. the Lord spake unto Moses, *saying*,
11:13. *saying*, Give us flesh, that we may eat.
18. *saying*, Who shall give us flesh to eat?
20. have wept before him, *saying*,
12:13. *saying*, Heal her now, O God,
13: 1. the Lord spake unto Moses, *saying*,
32. *saying*, The land, through which
14: 7. *saying*, The land, which we passed
15. heard the fame of thee will speak, *saying*,
17. according as thou hast spoken, *saying*,
26. unto Moses and unto Aaron, *saying*,
40. the top of the mountain, *saying*,
15: 1, 17. the Lord spake unto Moses, *saying*,
37. the Lord spake unto Moses, *saying*,
16: 5. *saying*, Even to morrow the Lord
20. unto Moses and unto Aaron, *saying*,
23, 36, 44(17:1, 9). the Lord spake unto Moses, *saying*,
24. Speak unto the congregation, *saying*,
26. he spake unto the congregation, *saying*,
41(17:6). *saying*, Ye have killed the people
17: 1(16). the Lord spake unto Moses, *saying*,
12(27). *saying*, Behold, we die, we perish,
18:25. the Lord spake unto Moses, *saying*,
19: 1. unto Moses and unto Aaron, *saying*,
2. *saying*, Speak unto the children of
20: 3. *saying*, Would God that we had
7. the Lord spake unto Moses, *saying*,
23. the coast of the land of Edom, *saying*,
21:21. Sihon king of the Amorites, *saying*,
22: 5. *saying*, Behold, there is a people
23:26. *saying*, All that the Lord speaketh,
24:12. which thou sentest unto me, *saying*,

Nu. 25:10, 16. the Lord spake unto Moses, *saying*,
26: 1. the son of Aaron the priest, *saying*,
3. by Jordan (near) Jericho, *saying*,
52. the Lord spake unto Moses, *saying*,
27: 2. tabernacle of the congregation, *saying*,
6. the Lord spake unto Moses, *saying*,
8. *saying*, If a man die,
15. Moses spake unto the Lord, *saying*,
28: 1. the Lord spake unto Moses, *saying*,
30: 1(2). concerning the children of Israel, *saying*,
31: 1. the Lord spake unto Moses, *saying*,
3. Moses spake unto the people, *saying*,
25. the Lord spake unto Moses, *saying*,
32: 2. the princes of the congregation, *saying*,
10. and he sware, *saying*,
25. spake unto Moses, *saying*,
31. *saying*, As the Lord hath said
33:50. by Jordan (near) Jericho, *saying*,
34: 1, 16. the Lord spake unto Moses, *saying*,
13. commanded the children of Israel, *saying*,
35: 1. by Jordan (near) Jericho, *saying*,
9. the Lord spake unto Moses, *saying*,
36: 5. according to the word of the Lord, *saying*,
6. the daughters of Zelophehad, *saying*,
Deu 1: 5. began Moses to declare this law, *saying*,
6. *saying*, Ye have dwelt long enough
9. I spake unto you at that time, *saying*,
16. your judges at that time, *saying*,
28. discouraged our heart, *saying*,
34. was wroth, and sware, *saying*,
37. *saying*, Thou also shalt not go
2: 2. the Lord spake unto me, *saying*,
4. command thou the people, *saying*,
17. the Lord spake unto me, *saying*,
26. with words of peace, *saying*,
3:18. I commanded you at that time, *saying*,
21. I commanded Joshua at that time, *saying*,
23. the Lord at that time, *saying*,
4:10. *when* the Lord *said* unto me,
5: 5. went not up into the mount; *saying*,
6:20. asketh thee in time to come, *saying*,
9: 4. cast them out from before thee, *saying*,
13. *saying*, I have seen this people,
23. *saying*, Go up and possess the land
12:30. *saying*, How did these nations serve
13: 2(3). *saying*, Let us go after other gods,
6(7). entice thee secretly, *saying*,
12(13). given thee to dwell there, *saying*,
13(14). the inhabitants of their city, *sayin*
15: 9. in thy wicked heart, *saying*,
11. therefore I command thee, *saying*,
18:16. *saying*, Let me not hear again
19: 7. Wherefore I command thee, *saying*,
20: 5. shall speak unto the people, *saying*,
22:17. *saying*, I found not thy daughter
27: 1. commanded the people, *saying*,
9. spake unto all Israel, *saying*,
11. charged the people the same day, *saying*,
29:19(18). he bless himself in his heart, *saying*,
30:12. *that thou shouldest say*, Who shall go
13. *that thou shouldest say*, Who shall go
31:10. Moses commanded them, *saying*,
25. the covenant of the Lord, *saying*,
32:48. unto Moses that selfsame day, *saying*,
34: 4. *saying*, I will give it unto thy seed:
Jos. 1: 1. unto Joshua...Moses' minister, *saying*,
10. the officers of the people, *saying*,
11. command the people, *saying*,
12. spake Joshua, *saying*,
13. of the Lord commanded you, *saying*,
16. they answered Joshua, *saying*,
2: 1. *saying*, Go view the land,
2. told the king of Jericho, *saying*,
3. *saying*, Bring forth the men
3: 3. they commanded the people, *saying*,
6. *saying*, Take up the ark of the covenant,
8. *saying*, When ye are come
4: 1, 15. the Lord spake unto Joshua, *saying*,
3. command ye them, *saying*,
6. *saying*, What (mean) ye by these
17. *saying*, Come ye up out of Jordan.
21. spake unto the children of Israel, *saying*,
— *saying*, What (mean) these stones?
22. *saying*, Israel came over this
6: 8. *when* Joshua *had spoken*
10. *saying*, Ye shall not shout,

Jos. 6:10. until the day *I bid* you shout;
26. *saying*, Cursed (be) the man
7: 2. *saying*, Go up and view the country.
8: 4. he commanded them, *saying*,
9:11. spake to us, *saying*, Take victuals
22. them, *saying*, Wherefore have ye beguiled us, *saying*,
10: 3. unto Debir king of Eglon, *saying*,
6. *saying*, Slack not thy hand
17. *saying*, The five kings are found
14: 9. Moses sware on that day, *saying*,
17: 4. *saying*, The Lord commanded
14. *saying*, Why hast thou given me
17. *saying*, Thou (art) a great people,
18: 8. *saying*, Go and walk through the land,
20: 1. spake unto Joshua, *saying*,
2. Speak to the children of Israel, *saying*,
21: 2. in the land of Canaan, *saying*,
22: 8. he spake unto them, *saying*,
11. the children of Israel heard *say*,
15. they spake with them, *saying*,
24. *saying*, In time to come
— might speak unto our children, *saying*,
Jud. 1: 1. asked the Lord, *saying*,
5: 1. on that day, *saying*,
6:13. our fathers told us of, *saying*,
32. *saying*, Let Baal plead against him,
7: 2. *saying*, Mine own hand hath
3. proclaim in the ears of the people, *saying*,
24. *saying*, Come down against the Midianites,
8: 9. also unto the men of Penuel, *saying*,
15. ye did upbraid me, *saying*,
9: 1. house of his mother's father, *saying*,
31. *saying*, Behold, Gaal the son of Ebed
10:10. Israel cried unto the Lord, *saying*,
11:12. *saying*, What hast thou to do
17. unto the king of Edom, *saying*,
13: 6. *saying*, A man of God came
15: 2. I *verily* thought that thou hadst
13. they spake unto him, *saying*,
16: 2. *saying*, Samson is come hither.
— *saying*, In the morning, when it
18. *saying*, Come up this once,
19:22. *saying*, Bring forth the man
20: 8. the people arose as one man, *saying*,
12. the tribe of Benjamin, *saying*,
23. *saying*, Shall I go up again
28. *saying*, Shall I yet again go out
21: 1. *saying*, There shall not any
5. *saying*, He shall surely be put to death.
10. and commanded them, *saying*,
18. of Israel have sworn, *saying*,
20. *saying*, Go and lie in wait in the
Ru. 2:15. commanded his young men, *saying*,
4: 4. *saying*, Buy (it) before the inhabitants.
17. *saying*, There is a son born to Naomi;
1Sa. 2:30. I said *indeed*(lit. *saying*) (that) thy house,
4:21. named the child I-chabod, *saying*,
5:10. that the Ekronites cried out, *saying*,
6: 2. *saying*, What shall we do
21. *saying*, The Philistines have
7: 3. unto all the house of Israel, *saying*,
9:15. a day before Saul came, *saying*,
24. *since I said*, I have invited the people.
26. Saul to the top of the house, *saying*,
10: 2. *saying*, What shall I do for my son?
11: 7. *saying*, Whosoever cometh not forth
13: 3. *saying*, Let the Hebrews hear.
4. And all Israel heard *say*
14:24. had adjured the people, *saying*,
28. *saying*, Cursed (be) the man
33. Then they told Saul, *saying*,
15:10. word of the Lord unto Samuel, *saying*,
12. it was told Samuel, *saying*,
16:22. Saul sent to Jesse, *saying*,
17:26. *saying*, What shall be done
27. *saying*, So shall it be done
18:22. *and say*, Behold, the king
24. *saying*, On this manner spake David.
19: 2. Jonathan told David, *saying*,
11. *saying*, If thou save not thy life
15. *saying*, Bring him up to me
19. it was told Saul, *saying*,
20:21. If I *expressly* say unto the lad,
42. in the name of the Lord, *saying*,
21:11(12). *saying*, Saul hath slain his
23: 1. Then they told David, *saying*,

1Sa. 23: 2. David enquired of the Lord, *saying*,
19. *saying*, Doth not David hide
27. *saying*, Haste thee, and come;
24: 1(2). *saying*, Behold, David (is) in the
8(9). cried after Saul, *saying*,
9(10). hearest thou men's words, *saying*,
25:14. told Abigail, Nabal's wife, *saying*,
40. they spake unto her, *saying*,
26: 1. *saying*, Doth not David hide
6. *saying*, Who will go down
14. *saying*, Answerest thou not,
19. *saying*, Go, serve other gods.
27:11. *saying*, Lest they should tell on us, *saying*,
12. Achish believed David, *saying*,
28:10. *saying*, (As) the Lord liveth,
12. the woman spake to Saul, *saying*,
29: 5. *saying*, Saul slew his thousands,
30: 8. enquired at the Lord, *saying*,
26. *saying*, Behold a present for you
2Sa. 1:16. *saying*, I have slain the Lord's
2: 1. enquired of the Lord, *saying*,
4. they told David, *saying*,
22. Abner *said* again to Asahel,
3:12. on his behalf, *saying*, Whose (is) the land? *saying*
13. *that is* (marg. *saying*), Thou shalt not see
14. to Ish-bosheth Saul's son, *saying*,
17. with the elders of Israel, *saying*,
18. the Lord hath spoken of David, *saying*,
23. *saying*, Abner the son of Ner
35. David sware, *saying*, So do God to me,
4:10. When one told me, *saying*,
5. 1. *saying*, Behold, we (are) thy bone
6. which spake unto David, *saying*,
— *thinking* (marg. *saying*), David cannot
19. David enquired of the Lord, *saying*,
6:12. it was told king David, *saying*,
7: 4. of the Lord came unto Nathan, *saying*,
7. to feed my people Israel, *saying*,
26. thy name be magnified for ever, *saying*,
27. *saying*, I will build thee an house:
11:10. when they had told David, *saying*,
15. he wrote in the letter, *saying*,
19. charged the messenger, *saying*,
13: 7. David sent home to Tamar, *saying*,
28. commanded his servants, *saying*,
30. tidings came to David, *saying*,
33. *to think* that all the king's sons
14:32. I sent unto thee, *saying*,
— *to say*, Wherefore am I come
15: 8. *saying*, If the Lord shall bring
10. all the tribes of Israel, *saying*,
13. *saying*, The hearts of the men of
31. And (one) told David, *saying*,
17: 6. Absalom spake unto him, *saying*,
16. quickly, and tell David, *saying*,
18: 5. *saying*, (Deal) gently for my sake with
12. Abishai and Ittai, *saying*,
19: 2(3). for the people heard *say*
8(9). they told unto all the people, *saying*,
9(10). *saying*, The king saved us
11(12). *saying*, Speak unto the elders of Judah, *saying*,
20:18. Then she spake, *saying*,
— *saying*, They shall surely ask
21:17. *saying*, Thou shalt go no more
24: 1. *to say*, Go, number Israel
11. prophet Gad, David's seer, *saying*,
1K. 1: 5. *saying*, I will be king:
6. displeased him at any time *in saying*,
11. the mother of Solomon, *saying*,
13. swear unto thine handmaid, *saying*,
23. they told the king, *saying*,
30. by the Lord God of Israel, *saying*,
47. bless our lord king David, *saying*,
51. it was told Solomon, *saying*,
— *saying*, Let king Solomon swear
2: 1. charged Solomon his son, *saying*,
4. *saying*, If thy children take heed
— there shall not fail thee *said he*
8. I sware to him by the Lord, *saying*,
23. *saying*, God do so to me, and more
29. *saying*, Go, fall upon him.
30. *saying*, Thus said Joab,
39. they told Shimei, *saying*,
42. protested unto thee, *saying*,
5: 2(16). Solomon sent to Hiram, *saying*,

1K. 5: 5(19). spake unto David my father, *saying*,
8(22). Hiram sent to Solomon, *saying*,
6:11. of the Lord came to Solomon, *saying*,
8:15. hath with his hand fulfilled (it), *saying*,
25. that thou promisedst him, *saying*,
47. *saying*, We have sinned, and have done
55. of Israel with a loud voice, *saying*,
9: 5. to David thy father, *saying*,
12: 3. spake unto Rehoboam, *saying*,
6. *and said*, How do ye advise
7. they spake unto him, *saying*,
9. who have spoken to me, *saying*,
10. *saying*, Thus shalt thou speak
— that spake unto thee, *saying*,
12. *saying*, Come to me again
14. *saying*, My father made your yoke
16. the people answered the king, *saying*,
22. unto Shemaiah the man of God, *saying*,
23. to the remnant of the people, *saying*,
13: 3. he gave a sign the same day, *saying*,
4. put forth his hand from the altar, *saying*,
9. by the word of the Lord, *saying*,
18. *saying*, Bring him back with thee
21. *saying*, Thus saith the Lord,
27. he spake to his sons, *saying*,
31. he spake to his sons, *saying*,
15:18. that dwelt at Damascus, *saying*,
16: 1. Hanani against Baasha, *saying*,
16. people (that were) encamped heard *say*,
17: 2, 8. of the Lord came unto him, *saying*,
18: 1. *saying*, Go, shew thyself unto Ahab;
26. *saying*, O Baal, hear us.
31. *saying*, Israel shall be thy name:
19: 2. *saying*, So let the gods do (to me),
20: 5. Thus speaketh Ben-hadad, *saying*, Although I have sent unto thee, *saying*,
17. they told him, *saying*,
21: 2. *saying*, Give me thy vineyard,
9. wrote in the letters, *saying*,
10. to bear witness against him, *saying*,
13. in the presence of the people, *saying*,
14. they sent to Jezebel, *saying*,
17, 28. came to Elijah the Tishbite, *saying*,
19, 19. *saying*, Thus saith the Lord,
23. of Jezebel also spake the Lord, *saying*
22:12. *saying*, Go up to Ramoth-gilead,
13. Micaiah spake unto him, *saying*,
31. *saying*, Fight neither with small
36. *saying*, Every man to his city,
2K. 3: 7. Jehoshaphat the king of Judah, *saying*
4: 1. of the prophets unto Elisha, *saying*,
31. *saying*, The child is not awaked.
5: 4. (one) went in, and told his lord, *saying*,
6. letter to the king of Israel, *saying*,
8. he sent to the king, *saying*,
10. *saying*, Go and wash in Jordan
22. My master hath sent me, *saying*,
6: 8. took counsel with his servants, *saying*,
9. sent unto the king of Israel, *saying*,
13. *saying*, Behold, (he is) in Dothan.
26. *saying*, Help, my lord, O king.
7:10. *saying*, We came to the camp
12. *saying*, When they come out
14. the Syrians, *saying*, Go and see.
18. had spoken to the king, *saying*,
8: 1. *saying*, Arise, and go thou
4. *saying*, Tell me, I pray thee,
6. *saying*, Restore all that (was) hers,
7. it was told him, *saying*,
8, 9. *saying*, Shall I recover of this disease?
9:12. *saying*, Thus saith the Lord,
18, 20. the watchman told, *saying*,
36. by his servant Elijah the Tishbite, *saying*,
10: 1. brought up Ahab's (children), *saying*,
5. sent to Jehu, *saying*, We (are)
6. *saying*, If ye (be) mine,
8. told him, *saying*, They have
11: 5. he commanded them, *saying*,
14: 6. wherein the Lord commanded, *saying*,
8. *saying*, Come, let us look one another
9. sent to Amaziah king of Judah, *saying*,
— *saying*, Give thy daughter to
15:12. *saying*, Thy sons shall sit on
16: 7. *saying*, I (am) thy servant and thy son:
15. commanded Urijah the priest, *saying*,
17:13. *saying*, Turn ye from your evil ways.
26. they spake to the king of Assyria, *saying*,

2 K.17.27. the king of Assyria commanded, *saying*,
35. *saying*, Ye shall not fear other gods,
18:14. to Lachish, *saying*, I have offended;
30. make you trust in the Lord, *saying*,
32. *saying*, The Lord will deliver us.
36. *saying*, Answer him not.
19: 9. And when he heard *say* of Tirhakah
— messengers again unto Hezekiah, *saying*,
10. *saying*, Let not thy God
— *saying*, Jerusalem shall not be
20. *saying*, Thus saith the Lord
20: 2. prayed unto the Lord, *saying*,
4. the Lord came to him, *saying*,
21.10. by his servants the prophets, *saying*,
22: 3. to the house of the Lord, *saying*,
10. the scribe shewed the king, *saying*,
12. Asahiah a servant of the king's, *saying*,
23:21. commanded all the people, *saying*,
1Ch. 4: 9. *saying*, Because I bare him with
10. called on the God of Israel, *saying*,
11: 1. *saying*, Behold, we (are) thy bone
12:19. *saying*, He will fall to his master
13:12. *saying*, How shall I bring the ark
14:10. David enquired of God, *saying*,
16:18. *Saying*, Unto thee will I give
17: 3. the word of God came to Nathan, *saying*,
6. commanded to feed my people, *saying*,
24. *saying*, The Lord of hosts
21: 9. spake unto Gad, David's seer, *saying*,
10. Go and tell David, *saying*,
18. commanded Gad *to say* to David,
22: 8. the word of the Lord came to me, *saying*,
2Ch. 2: 3(2). sent to Huram the king of Tyre, *saying*,
6: 4. with his mouth to my father David, *saying*,
16. *saying*, There shall not fail thee a man
37. *saying*, We have sinned, we have done amiss,
7:18. *saying*, There shall not fail thee
10: 3. came and spake to Rehoboam, *saying*,
6. *saying*, What counsel give ye (me)
7. they spake unto him, *saying*,
9. which have spoken to me, *saying*,
10. *saying*, Thus shalt thou answer
— that spake unto thee, *saying*,
12. as the king bade, *saying*,
14. *saying*, My father made your yoke
16. the people answered the king, *saying*,
11: 2. to Shemaiah the man of God, *saying*,
3. Israel in Judah and Benjamin, *saying*,
12: 7. *saying*, They have humbled themselves;
16: 2. that dwelt at Damascus, *saying*,
18:11. *saying*, Go up to Ramoth-gilead,
12. to call Micaiah spake to him, *saying*,
30. chariots that (were) with him, *saying*,
19: 9. he charged them, *saying*,
20: 2. some that told Jehoshaphat, *saying*,
8. a sanctuary therein for thy name, *saying*,
37. *saying*, Because thou hast joined
21:12. *saying*, Thus saith the Lord God
25: 4. where the Lord commanded, *saying*,
7. *saying*, O king, let not the army
17. *saying*, Come, let us see one another
18. to Amaziah king of Judah, *saying*,
— *saying*, Give thy daughter to
30: 6. *saying*, Ye children of Israel,
18. Hezekiah prayed for them, *saying*,
32: 4. *saying*, Why should the kings of
6. spake comfortably to them, *saying*,
9. all Judah that (were) at Jerusalem, *saying*,
11. *saying*, The Lord our God shall deliver
12. *saying*, Ye shall worship before one altar,
17. *and to speak* against him, *saying*,
34:16. *saying*, All that was committed
18. *saying*, Hilkiah the priest hath given me
20. Asaiah a servant of the king's, *saying*,
35:21. *saying*, What have I to do with thee,
36:22. and (put it) also in writing, *saying*,
Ezra 1: 1. (put it) also in writing, *saying*,
8:22. we had spoken unto the king, *saying*,
9: 1. *saying*, The people of Israel,
11. by thy servants the prophets, *saying*,
Neh. 1: 8. *saying*, (If) ye transgress, I will
6: 2. *saying*, Come, let us meet together
3. *saying*, I (am) doing a great work,
7. *saying*, (There is) a king in Judah:
8. Then I sent unto him, *saying*,
9. they all made us afraid, *saying*,
8:11. *saying*, Hold your peace,
Neh 8:15. *saying*, Go forth unto the mount,
Est. 1:17. they shall despise their husbands...*when it shall be reported*, The king
3: 4. *when they spake* daily unto him,
6: 4. *to speak* unto the king to hang
Job 9:27. If *I say*, I will forget my complaint,
24:15. *saying*, No eye shall see me:
34:18. (Is it fit) *to say* to a king,
Ps. 42: 3(4). *while they* continually *say* unto me.
10(11). *while they say* daily unto me,
71:11. *Saying*, God hath forsaken him:
105:11. *Saying*, Unto thee will I give
119:82. *saying*, When wilt thou comfort me?
Pro.25: 7. *that it be said* unto thee, Come up
Ecc. 1:16. *saying*, Lo, I am come to great estate,
Isa. 3: 7. In that day shall he swear, *saying*,
4: 1. *saying*, We will eat our own bread,
7: 2. it was told the house of David, *saying*,
5. taken evil counsel against thee, *saying*,
10. Lord spake again unto Ahaz, *saying*,
8: 5. Lord spake also unto me again, *saying*,
11. walk in the way of this people, *saying*,
9: 9(8). *that say* in the pride and stoutness
14:24. *saying*, Surely as I have thought,
16:14. now the Lord hath spoken, *saying*,
19:25. *saying*, Blessed (be) Egypt my people,
20: 2. by Isaiah the son of Amoz, *saying*,
23: 4. *saying*, I travail not, nor bring forth
29:11, 12. *saying*, Read this, I pray thee:
30:21. *saying*, This (is) the way, walk ye in it,
36:15. *saying*, The Lord will surely deliver
18. *saying*, The Lord will deliver us.
21. the king's commandment was, *saying*,
37: 9. he heard *say* concerning Tirhakah
— he sent messengers to Hezekiah, *saying*,
10. Hezekiah king of Judah, *saying*,
— *saying*, Jerusalem shall not be
15. Hezekiah prayed unto the Lord, *saying*,
21. *saying*, Thus saith the Lord
38: 4. the word of the Lord to Isaiah, *saying*,
44:19. nor understanding *to say*, I have burned part
28. *even saying* to Jerusalem, Thou shalt be built;
49: 9. *That thou mayest say* to the prisoners,
51:16. *and say* unto Zion, Thou (art) my people.
56: 3. speak, *saying*, The Lord hath utterly
Jer. 1: 4, 11. word of the Lord came unto me, *saying*,
13. came unto me the second time, *saying*,
2: 1. the word of the Lord came to me, *saying*,
2. *saying*, Thus saith the Lord;
35. because *thou sayest*, I have not sinned.
3: 1. *They say* (marg. *Saying*), If a man put away
4:10. *saying*, Ye shall have peace;
5:20. publish it in Judah, *saying*,
6:14. *saying*, Peace, peace; when (there is) no
7: 1. to Jeremiah from the Lord, *saying*,
4. *saying*, The temple of the Lord,
23. *saying*, Obey my voice, and I
8: 6. his wickedness, *saying*, What have I done?
11. *saying*, Peace, peace; when (there)
11: 1. to Jeremiah from the Lord, *saying*,
4, 7. *saying*, Obey my voice.
6. *saying*, Hear ye the words
21. *saying*, Prophesy not in the name
13: 3. came unto me the second time, *saying*,
8. of the Lord came unto me, *saying*,
16: 1. came also unto me, *saying*,
18: 1. to Jeremiah from the Lord, *saying*,
5. the word of the Lord came to me, *saying*,
11. *saying*, Thus saith the Lord;
20:15. *saying*, A man child is born
21: 1. Maaseiah the priest, *saying*,
23:17. They say *still* (lit. *saying*) unto them
25. lies in my name, *saying*, I have dreamed,
33. or a priest, shall ask thee, *saying*,
38. Because *ye say* this word, The burden of the Lord, and I have sent unto you, *saying*,
24: 4. the word of the Lord came unto me, *saying*,
25: 2. to all the inhabitants of Jerusalem, *saying*,
5. *They said*, Turn ye again now
26: 1. came this word from the Lord, *saying*,
8. took him, *saying*, Thou shalt surely die.
9. *saying*, This house shall be like
11. *saying*, This man (is) worthy to die;
12. *saying*, The Lord sent me to prophesy
17. all the assembly of the people, *saying*,

Jer. 26:18. *saying*, Thus saith the Lord
27: 1. unto Jeremiah from the Lord, *saying*,
4. them *to say* (marg. *saying*) unto their masters,
9. which speak unto you, *saying*,
12. according to all these words, *saying*,
14. that speak unto you, *saying*,
16. to all this people, *saying*,
— that prophesy unto you, *saying*,
28: 1. of the priests and of all the people, *saying*,
2. *saying*, I have broken the yoke of
11. in the presence of all the people, *saying*,
12. neck of the prophet Jeremiah, *saying*,
13. Go and tell Hananiah, *saying*,
29: 3. Nebuchadnezzar king of Babylon *saying*,
22. which (are) in Babylon, *saying*,
24. Shemaiah the Nehelamite, *saying*,
25. *saying*, Because thou hast sent
— and to all the priests, *saying*,
28. *saying*, This (captivity is) long:
30. of the Lord unto Jeremiah, *saying*,
31. *saying*, Thus saith the Lord
30: 1. Jeremiah from the Lord, *saying*,
2. *saying*, Write thee all the words
31:34. every man his brother, *saying*,
32: 3. *saying*, Wherefore dost thou prophesy, *and say*,
6. The word of the Lord came unto me, *saying*,
7. shall come unto thee, *saying*,
13. I charged Baruch before them, *saying*,
16. I prayed unto the Lord, *saying*,
26. of the Lord unto Jeremiah, *saying*,
33: 1. in the court of the prison, *saying*,
19. of the Lord came unto Jeremiah, *saying*,
23. of the Lord came to Jeremiah, *saying*,
24. what this people have spoken, *saying*,
34: 1. against all the cities thereof, *saying*,
12. to Jeremiah from the Lord, *saying*,
13. out of the house of bondmen, *saying*,
35: 1. the son of Josiah king of Judah, *saying*,
6. our father commanded us, *saying*,
12. word of the Lord unto Jeremiah, *saying*,
15. *saying*, Return ye now every man
36: 1. unto Jeremiah from the Lord, *saying*,
5. *saying*, I (am) shut up;
14. *saying*, Take in thine hand
17. they asked Baruch, *saying*,
27. at the mouth of Jeremiah, *saying*,
29. Thou hast burned this roll, *saying*, Why hast thou written therein, *saying*,
37: 3. to the prophet Jeremiah, *saying*,
6. unto the prophet Jeremiah, *saying*,
9. Deceive not yourselves, *saying*,
13. *saying*, Thou fallest away
19. which prophesied unto you, *saying*,
38: 1. had spoken unto all the people, *saying*,
8. spake to the king, *saying*,
10. *saying*, Take from hence thirty men
16. sware secretly unto Jeremiah, *saying*,
39:11. the captain of the guard, *saying*,
15. in the court of the prison, *saying*,
16. *saying*, Thus saith the Lord
40: 9. sware unto them and to their men, *saying*,
15. *saying*, Let me go, I pray thee,
42:14. *Saying*, No; but we will go
20. *saying*, Pray for us unto the Lord
43: 2. *to say*, Go not into Egypt to sojourn
8. unto Jeremiah in Tahpanhes, *saying*,
44: 1. in the country of Pathros, *saying*,
4. *saying*, Oh, do not this abominable
15. answered Jeremiah, *saying*,
20. which had given him (that) answer, *saying*,
25. the God of Israel, *saying*;
— fulfilled with your hand, *saying*,
45: 1. son of Josiah king of Judah, *saying*,
49:34. Zedekiah king of Judah, *saying*,
Eze 3:16. of the Lord came unto me, *saying*,
18. *When I say* unto the wicked,
6: 1 & 7:1. of the Lord came unto me, *saying*,
9: 1. with a loud voice, *saying*,
11. *saying*, I have done as thou hast
10: 6. *saying*, Take fire from between
11:14. word of the Lord came unto me, *saying*,
12: 1. also came unto me, *saying*,
8. the word of the Lord unto me, *saying*,
17, 26. the word of the Lord came to me, *saying*,
21. word of the Lord came unto me, *saying*,
Eze 12:22. *saying*, The days are prolonged,
13: 1. word of the Lord came unto me, *saying*,
10. *saying*, Peace; and (there was) no
14: 2. word of the Lord came unto me, *saying*,
12. of the Lord came again to me, *saying*,
15: 1 & 16:1. of the Lord came unto me, *saying*,
16:44. *saying*, As (is) the mother,
17: 1, 11. word of the Lord came unto me, *saying*,
18: 1. came unto me again, *saying*,
2. concerning the land of Israel, *saying*,
20: 2. the word of the Lord unto me, *saying*,
5. *saying*, I (am) the Lord your God;
45(21:1)&21:1(6), 8(13). word of the Lord came unto me, *saying*,
21:18(23). came unto me again, *saying*,
22: 1, 17, 23. Lord came unto me, *saying*,
23: 1. came again unto me, *saying*,
24: 1. of the Lord came unto me, *saying*,
15. of the Lord came unto me, *saying*,
20. of the Lord came unto me, *saying*,
25: 1. came again unto me, *saying*,
3. Because *thou saidst*, Aha,
8. Because that Moab and Seir *do say*,
26: 1. the Lord came unto me, *saying*,
27: 1&28:1. the Lord came again unto me, *saying*,
28: 9. Wilt thou *yet* say (lit. *in saying* wilt thou say)
11, 20. of the Lord came unto me, *saying*,
29: 1, 17. word of the Lord came unto me, *saying*,
30: 1. came again unto me, *saying*,
20 & 31:1 & 32: 1, 17. the word of the Lord came unto me, *saying*,
33: 1, 23. word of the Lord came unto me, *saying*,
8. *When I say* unto the wicked,
10. ye speak, *saying*, If our transgressions
13. *When I shall say* to the righteous,
14. *Again, when I say* unto the wicked,
21. *saying*, The city is smitten.
24. *saying*, Abraham was one, and he inherited
30. every one to his brother, *saying*,
34:1 & 35 1. of the Lord came unto me, *saying*,
35:10. Because *thou hast said*,
12. *saying*, They are laid desolate,
36:16. word of the Lord came unto me, *saying*,
20. *when they said* to them, These
37:15. came again unto me, *saying*,
18. *saying*, Wilt thou not shew us
38: 1. word of the Lord came unto me, *saying*,
Am. 2:12. commanded the prophets, *saying*,
3: 1. brought up from the land of Egypt, *saying*,
7:10. sent to Jeroboam king of Israel, *saying*,
8: 5. *Saying*, When will the new moon
Jon. 1: 1. Jonah the son of Amittai, *saying*,
3: 1. unto Jonah the second time, *saying*,
7. *saying*, Let neither man nor beast,
Mic. 3:11. *and say* (marg. *saying*), (Is) not the Lord
Hag. 1: 1. son of Josedech, the high priest, *saying*,
2. speaketh the Lord of hosts, *saying*,
3. by Haggai the prophet, *saying*,
13. *saying*, I (am) with you, saith the Lord.
2: 1. by the prophet Haggai, *saying*,
2. to the residue of the people, *saying*,
10. by Haggai the prophet, *saying*,
11. the priests (concerning) the law, *saying*,
20. four and twentieth (day) of the month, *saying*,
21. *saying*, I will shake the heavens
Zec. 1: 1, 7. the son of Iddo the prophet, *saying*,
4. the former prophets have cried, *saying*,
14. Cry thou, *saying*, Thus saith the Lord
17. Cry yet, *saying*, Thus saith the Lord
21(2:4). spake, *saying*, These (are) the horns
2: 4(8). speak to this young man, *saying*,
3: 4. *saying*, Take away the filthy garments
6. protested unto Joshua, *saying*,
4: 4. *saying*, What (are) these, my lord?
6. he answered and spake unto me, *saying*,
— *saying*, Not by might, nor by power,
8. word of the Lord came unto me, *saying*,
13. he answered me *and said*,
6: 8. and spake unto me, *saying*,
9. word of the Lord came unto me, *saying*,
12. *saying*, Thus speaketh the Lord of hosts, *saying*,
7: 3. *to speak* unto the priests
— to the prophets, *saying*,
4. word of the Lord of hosts unto me, *saying*,

Zec. 7: 5. *saying*, When ye fasted and mourned
8. of the Lord came unto Zechariah, *saying*,
9. speaketh the Lord of hosts, *saying*,
8: 1. of the Lord of hosts came (to me), *saying*,
18. of the Lord of hosts came unto me, *saying*,
21. of one (city) shall go to another, *saying*,
23. *saying*, We will go with you:
Mal. 1: 7. *In that ye say*, The table of the Lord
12. have profaned it, *in that ye say*,
2:17. *When ye say*, Every one that doeth

KAL.—*Imperative.*

Gen12:13. *Say*, I pray thee, thou (art) my sister.
20:13. *say* of me, He (is) my brother.
45:17. *Say* unto thy brethren, This do ye;
Ex. 6: 6. *say* unto the children of Israel,
7:19. *Say* unto Aaron, Take thy rod,
8: 5(1). *Say* unto Aaron, Stretch forth
16(12). *Say* unto Aaron, Stretch out
16: 9. *Say* unto all the congregation
33: 5. *Say* unto the children of Israel, Ye
Lev.21: 1. *Speak* unto the priests the sons
22: 3. *Say* unto them, Whosoever (he be)
Nu. 14:28. *Say* unto them, (As truly as) I live,
16:37(17:2). *Speak* unto Eleazar the son
25:12. Wherefore *say*, Behold, I give
Deu 1:42. *Say* unto them, Go not up,
5:30(27). Go *say* to them, Get you into
Jud.12: 6. *Say* now Shibboleth: and he said
1Sa. 9:27. *Bid* the servant pass on
2Sa.20:16. *say*, I pray you, unto Joab,
1K. 2:17. he said, *Speak*, I pray thee,
12:23. *Speak* unto Rehoboam, the son of
14: 7. Go, *tell* Jeroboam, Thus saith
18: 8, 11, 14. go, *tell* thy lord, Behold, Elijah
44. Go up, *say* unto Ahab, Prepare
20: 9. *Tell* my lord the king,
2K. 4:13. *Say* now unto her, Behold, thou hast been
26. *and say* unto her, (Is it) well
8:10: Go, *say* unto him, Thou mayest
18:19. *Speak* ye now to Hezekiah,
22:15. *Tell* the man that sent you
1Ch 16:35. *And say ye*, Save us, O God
2Ch 11: 3. *Speak* unto Rehoboam the son of
34:23. *Tell ye* the man that sent you
Est. 5:14. *speak thou* unto the king
Ps. 4: 4(5). *commune* with your own heart
35: 3. *say* unto my soul, I (am) thy salvation.
66: 3. *Say* unto God, How terrible
96:10. *Say* among the heathen (that) the Lord
Pro. 7: 4. *Say* unto wisdom, Thou (art) my sister;
Isa. 3:10. *Say ye* to the righteous, that (it)
35: 4. *Say* to them (that are) of a fearful
36: 4. *Say ye* now to Hezekiah,
40: 9. *say* unto the cities of Judah,
48:20. *say ye*, The Lord hath redeemed
62:11. *Say ye* to the daughter of Zion,
Jer. 4: 5. *and say*, Blow ye the trumpet
— *and say*, Assemble yourselves, and let us
13:18. *Say* unto the king and to the queen,
18:11. *speak* to the men of Judah,
31: 7. *and say*, O Lord, save thy people,
10. *and say*, He that scattered Israel
46:14. *say ye*, Stand fast, and prepare
48:17. *say*, How is the strong staff broken,
19. *say*, What is done?
50: 2. *say*, Babylon is taken, Bel is confounded,
Eze. 6:11. *and say*, Alas for all the evil
11: 5. *Speak;* Thus saith the Lord;
16, 17. Therefore *say*, Thus saith the Lord
12:10. *Say* thou unto them, Thus saith
11. *Say*, I (am) your sign: like as
23. *Tell* them therefore, Thus saith
28. Therefore *say* unto them,
13:11. *Say* unto them which daub
14: 6. *say* unto the house of Israel,
17: 9. *Say* thou, Thus saith the Lord
12. *Say* now to the rebellious house,
— *tell* (them), Behold, the king
20:30. *say* unto the house of Israel,
21: 9(14). *Say*, A sword, a sword is sharpened,
22:24. *say* unto her, Thou (art) the land
24:21. *Speak* unto the house of Israel,
28: 2. *say* unto the prince of Tyrus,
31: 2. *speak* unto Pharaoh king of
33:10. *speak* unto the house of
11. *Say* unto them, (As) I live,
Eze.33:12. *say* unto the children of thy people,
25. Wherefore *say* unto them,
36:22. *say* unto the house of
39:17. *Speak* unto every feathered fowl,
Hos. 2: 1(3). *Say ye* unto your brethren,
14: 2(3). *say* unto him, Take away
Am. 3: 9. *and say*, Assemble yourselves
Hag. 2: 2. *Speak* now to Zerubbabel
21. *Speak* to Zerubbabel, governor
Zec. 7: 5. *Speak* unto all the people

KAL.—*Future.*

Gen 1: 3, 6, 9, 11, 14, 20, 24, 26, 29. *And* God *said*,
28. *and* God *said* unto them,
2:18. *And* the Lord God *said*,
23. *And* Adam *said*, This (is) now bone
3: 1. *And he said* unto the woman,
2, 13. *And* the woman *said*
4. *And* the serpent *said* unto the woman,
9. unto Adam, *and said* unto him,
10. *And he said*, I heard thy voice
11. *And he said*, Who told thee
12. *And* the man *said*, The woman
13, 14, 22. *And* the Lord God *said*
4: 1. *and said*, I have gotten a man
6. *And* the Lord *said* unto Cain,
8. *And* Cain *talked* with Abel
9. *And* the Lord *said* unto Cain,
— *And he said*, I know not:
10. *And he said*, What hast thou done?
13. *And* Cain *said* unto the Lord,
15. *And* the Lord *said* unto him,
23. *And* Lamech *said* unto his wives,
6: 3. *And* the Lord *said*, My spirit
7. *And* the Lord *said*, I will destroy
13. *And* God *said* unto Noah,
7: 1. *And* the Lord *said* unto Noah,
8:21. *and* the Lord *said* in his heart,
9: 1. *And said* unto them, Be fruitful,
8. *And* God *spake* unto Noah,
12. *And* God *said*, This (is) the token
17. *And* God *said* unto Noah,
25. *And he said*, Cursed (be) Canaan;
26. *And he said*, Blessed (be) the
11: 3. *And they said* one to another,
4. *And they said*, Go to, let us
6. *And* the Lord *said*, Behold,
12: 1. *Now* the Lord *had said*
7. *and said*, Unto thy seed will I give
11. *that he said* unto Sarai his wife,
18. Pharaoh called Abram, *and said*,
13: 8. *And* Abram *said* unto Lot,
14:19. he blessed him, *and said*,
21. *And* the king of Sodom *said*
22. *And* Abram *said* to the king
23. lest *thou shouldest say*, I have made
15: 2. *And* Abram *said*, Lord God,
3. *And* Abram *said*, Behold,
5. *and said*, Look now toward heaven,
— *and he said* unto him, So shall thy seed
7. *And he said* unto him, I (am) the Lord
8. *And he said*, Lord God,
9. *And he said* unto him, Take
13. *And he said* unto Abram, Know
16: 2. *And* Sarai *said* unto Abram, Behold
5. *And* Sarai *said* unto Abram, My wrong
6. *But* Abram *said* unto Sarai,
8. *And he said*, Hagar, Sarai's maid,
— *And she said*, I flee from
9, 10, 11. *And* the angel of the Lord *said*
17: 1. *and said* unto him, I (am)
9, 15. *And* God *said* unto Abraham,
17. laughed, *and said* in his heart,
18. *And* Abraham *said* unto God,
19. *And* God *said*, Sarah thy wife
18: 3. *And said*, My Lord, if now
5. *And they said*, So do, as thou
6. into the tent unto Sarah, *and said*,
9. *And they said* unto him, Where
— *And he said*, Behold, in the
10. *And he said*, I will certainly
13. *And* the Lord *said* unto Abraham,
15. *And he said*, Nay; but thou didst laugh.
20. *And* the Lord *said*, Because the cry
23. Abraham drew near, *and said*,
26. *And* the Lord *said*, If I find
27. Abraham answered *and said*,

Gen18:28. *And he said*, If I find there
29. *and said*, Peradventure there shall be
—, 30. *And he said*, I will not do
30. *And he said* (unto him), Oh let not
31. *And he said*, Behold now,
—, 32. *And he said*, I will not destroy
32. *And he said*, Oh let not the Lord
19: 2. *And he said*, Behold now, my lords,
— *And they said*, Nay; but we
5. called unto Lot, *and said* unto him,
7. *And said*, I pray you, brethren,
9. *And they said*, Stand back. *And they said*
12. *And* the men *said* unto Lot,
14. *and said*, Up, get you out of this
17. *that he said*, Escape for thy life;
18. *And* Lot *said* unto them,
21. *And he said* unto him,
31. *And* the firstborn *said* unto the younger,
34. *that* the firstborn *said* unto the younger,
20: 2. *And* Abraham *said* of Sarah his wife,
3. in a dream by night, *and said* to him,
4. *and he said*, Lord, wilt thou
6. *And* God *said* unto him
9. *and said* unto him, What hast thou done
10. *And* Abimelech *said* unto Abraham,
11. *And* Abraham *said*, Because
13. *that I said* unto her, This (is) thy
15. *And* Abimelech *said*, Behold,
21: 6. *And* Sarah *said*, God hath
7. *And she said*, Who would have said
10. *Wherefore she said* unto Abraham,
12. *And* God *said* unto Abraham,
— in all that Sarah *hath said* unto thee,
17. *and said* unto her, What aileth thee,
22. *that* Abimelech...*spake* unto Abraham
24. *And* Abraham *said*, I will swear.
26. *And* Abimelech *said*, I wot not
29. *And* Abimelech *said* unto Abraham,
30. *And he said*, For (these) seven ewe lambs
22: 1. *and said* unto him, Abraham: *And he said*,
Behold,
2. *And he said*, Take now thy son,
— mountains which *I will tell* thee *of*.
5. *And* Abraham *said* unto his young men,
7. *And* Isaac *spake* unto Abraham his father,
and said, My father: *and he said*, Here
(am) I, my son. *And he said*,
8. *And* Abraham *said*, My son,
11. *and said*, Abraham, Abraham: *and he said*,
12. *And he said*, Lay not thine hand
16. *And said*, By myself have I sworn,
24: 2. *And* Abraham *said* unto his eldest
5. *And* the servant *said* unto him,
6. *And* Abraham *said* unto him,
12. *And he said*, O Lord God
14. that the damsel to whom *I shall say*,
17. the servant ran to meet her, *and said*,
18. *And she said*, Drink, my lord:
19. *she said*, I will draw (water)
23. *And said*, Whose daughter (art)
24. *And she said* unto him,
25. *She said moreover* unto him,
27. *And he said*, Blessed (be) the Lord
31. *And he said*, Come in,
33. *but he said*, I will not eat,
— *And he said*, Speak on.
34. *And he said*, I (am) Abraham's servant.
39. *And I said* unto my master,
40. *and he said* unto me, The Lord,
42. *and said*, O Lord God of my master
45. *and I said* unto her, Let me drink,
46. *and said*, Drink, and I will give
47. *and said*, Whose daughter (art) thou?
And she said,
50. Laban and Bethuel answered *and said*,
54. *and he said*, Send me away
55. *And* her brother and her mother *said*,
56. *And he said* unto them, Hinder me not,
57. *And they said*, We will call the damsel,
58. *and said* unto her, Wilt thou go
— *And she said*, I will go.
60. *and said* unto her, Thou (art) our sister
65. *For she* (had) *said* unto the servant,
— *And* the servant (had) *said*.
25:22. *and she said*, If (it be) so, why
23. *And* the Lord *said* unto her,
30. *And* Esau *said* to Jacob,

Gen25:31. *And* Jacob *said*, Sell me this day
32. *And* Esau *said*, Behold, I (am) at
33. *And* Jacob *said*, Swear to me
26: 2. the Lord appeared unto him, *and said*,
— the land which *I shall tell* thee of:
7. *and he said*, She (is) my sister:
9. Abimelech called Isaac, *and said*,
— *And* Isaac *said* unto him,
10. *And* Abimelech *said*, What (is) this
16. *And* Abimelech *said* unto Isaac,
22. *and he said*, For now the Lord
24. *and said*, I (am) the God of Abraham
27. *And* Isaac *said* unto them,
28. *And they said*, We saw certainly
— *and we said*, Let there be now an oath
32. *and said* unto him, We have found
27: 1. *and said* unto him, My son: *and he said*
2. *And he said*, Behold now, I am old,
11. *And* Jacob *said* to Rebekah
13. *And* his mother *said* unto him,
18. he came unto his father, *and said*, My
father: *and he said*, Here (am) I;
19. *And* Jacob *said* unto his father,
20. *And* Isaac *said* unto his son,
— *And he said*, Because the Lord
21. *And* Isaac *said* unto Jacob,
22. *and said*, The voice (is) Jacob's voice,
24. *And he said*, (Art) thou my very son
Esau? *And he said*, I (am).
25. *And he said*, Bring (it) near
26. *And* his father Isaac *said* unto him,
27. *and said*, See, the smell of my son
31, 34. *and said* unto his father,
32. *And* Isaac his father *said* unto him,
— *And he said*, I (am) thy son,
33. Isaac trembled very exceedingly, *and said*,
35. *And he said*, Thy brother came
36. *And he said*, Is not he rightly named
— *And he said*, Hast thou not reserved
37. Isaac answered *and said* unto Esau,
38. *And* Esau *said* unto his father,
39. his father answered *and said*
41. *and* Esau *said* in his heart,
42. *and said* unto him, Behold,
46. *And* Rebekah *said* to Isaac,
28: 1. charged him, *and said* unto him,
13. *and said*, I (am) the Lord God
16. *and he said*, Surely the Lord is in this
17. he was afraid, *and said*,
29: 4. *And* Jacob *said* unto them,
— *And they said*, Of Haran (are) we.
5. *And he said* unto them, Know ye
— *And they said*, We know (him).
6. *And he said* unto them, (Is) he well? *And
they said*, (He is) well:
7. *And he said*, Lo, (it is) yet high day,
8. *And they said*, We cannot, until
14. *And* Laban *said* to him,
15. *And* Laban *said* unto Jacob,
18. Jacob loved Rachel; *and said*,
19. *And* Laban *said*, (It is) better
21. *And* Jacob *said* unto Laban,
25. *and he said* to Laban, What (is) this
26. *And* Laban *said*, It must not
33, 34. and bare a son; *and said*,
35. *she said*, Now will I praise the Lord:
30: 1. *and said* unto Jacob, Give me children,
2. *and he said*, (Am) I in God's stead,
3. *And she said*, Behold my maid
6. *And* Rachel *said*, God hath judged
8. *And* Rachel *said*, With great wrestlings
11. *And* Leah *said*, A troop cometh:
13. *And* Leah *said*, Happy am I,
14. *Then* Rachel *said* to Leah,
15. *And she said* unto her,
— *And* Rachel *said*, Therefore he shall
16. *and said*, Thou must come in
18. *And* Leah *said*, God hath given
20. *And* Leah *said*, God hath endued
23. *and said*, God hath taken away
25. *that* Jacob *said* unto Laban, Send me
27. *And* Laban *said* unto him, I pray
28. *And he said*, Appoint me thy wages,
29. *And he said* unto him, Thou knowest
31. *And he said*, What shall I give thee? *And*
Jacob *said*, Thou shalt not give me
34. *And* Laban *said*, Behold, I would it might

Gen31: 3. *And* the Lord *said* unto Jacob,
5. *And said* unto them, I see
8. If *he said* thus, The speckled shall
— if *he said* thus, The ringstraked
11. *And* the angel of God *spake* unto me
— Jacob: *And I said*, Here (am) I.
12. *And he said*, Lift up now thine eyes,
14. answered *and said* unto him,
24. *and said* unto him, Take heed that
26. *And* Laban *said* to Jacob,
31, 36. Jacob answered *and said* to Laban,
35. *And she said* to her father,
43. Laban answered *and said* unto Jacob,
46. *And* Jacob *said* unto his brethren,
48. *And* Laban *said*, This heap (is) a witness
51. *And* Laban *said* to Jacob, Behold this
32: 2(3). *And* when Jacob saw them, *he said*,
4(5). Thus *shall ye speak* unto my lord
8(9). *And said*, If Esau come to the one
9(10). *And* Jacob *said*, O God of my father
16(17). *and said* unto his servants,
26(27). *And he said*, Let me go, for the day breaketh. *And he said*, I will not
27(28). *And he said* unto him, What (is) thy name? *And he said*, Jacob.
28(29). *And he said*, Thy name shall be called
29(30). Jacob asked (him), *and said*,
—(—). *And he said*, Wherefore (is) it
33: 5. *and said*, Who (are) those with thee? *And he said*,
8. *And he said*, What (meanest) thou
— *And he said*, (These are) to find grace
9. *And* Esau *said*, I have enough,
10. *And* Jacob *said*, Nay, I pray thee,
12. *And he said*, Let us take our journey,
13. *And he said* unto him, My lord knoweth
15. *And* Esau *said*, Let me now leave
— *And he said*, What needeth it?
34: 4. *And* Shechem *spake* unto his father
11. *And* Shechem *said* unto her father
— what *ye shall say* unto me
12. according as *ye shall say* unto me:
14. *And they said* unto them,
30. *And* Jacob *said* to Simeon and Levi,
31. *And they said*, Should he deal
35: 1. *And* God *said* unto Jacob,
2. *Then* Jacob *said* unto his houshold,
10. *And* God *said* unto him, Thy name
11. *And* God *said* unto him, I (am) God
17. *that* the midwife *said* unto her
37: 6. *And he said* unto them, Hear,
8. *And* his brethren *said* to him,
9. *and said*, Behold, I have dreamed
10. *and said* unto him, What (is) this dream
13. *And* Israel *said* unto Joseph,
— *And he said* to him, Here (am I).
14. *And he said* to him, Go,
16. *And he said*, I seek my brethren:
17. *And* the man *said*, They are departed
19. *And they said* one to another,
21. *and said*, Let us not kill him.
22. *And* Reuben *said* unto them,
26. *And* Judah *said* unto his brethren,
30. *and said*, The child (is) not;
32. *and said*, This have we found:
33. he knew it, *and said*, (It is) my
35. *and he said*, For I will go down
38: 8. *And* Judah *said* unto Onan,
11. *Then said* Judah to Tamar
16. *and said*, Go to, I pray thee,
— *And she said*, What wilt thou
17. *And he said*, I will send (thee) a kid
— *And she said*, Wilt thou give (me)
18. *And he said*, What pledge shall I give thee? *And she said*, Thy signet, and
21. *And they said*, There was no harlot
22. *and said*, I cannot find her;
23. *And* Judah *said*, Let her take (it) to her,
24. *And* Judah *said*, Bring her forth,
25. *and she said*, Discern, I pray thee,
26. Judah acknowledged (them), *and said*,
29. *and she said*, How hast thou broken
39. 7. *and she said*, Lie with me.
8. *and said* unto his master's wife,
14. *and spake* unto them, saying,
40: 8. *And they said* unto him, We have dreamed
— *And* Joseph *said* unto them,

Gen40: 9. *and said* to him, In my dream,
12. *And* Joseph *said* unto him,
16. (lit. *and*) *he said* unto Joseph, I also
18. Joseph answered *and said*, This (is) the
41: 15, 39, 41, 44. *And* Pharaoh *said* unto Joseph,
24. *and I told* (this) unto the magicians;
25. *And* Joseph *said* unto Pharaoh,
38. *And* Pharaoh *said* unto his servants,
55. *and* Pharaoh *said* unto all the Egyptians,
— what *he saith* to you, do.
42: 1. *Now*...Jacob *said* unto his sons,
2. *And he said*, Behold, I have heard
7. *and he said* unto them, Whence come ye? *And they said*, From the land
9. *and said* unto them, Ye (are) spies;
10. *And they said* unto him, Nay,
12. *And he said* unto them, Nay,
13. *And they said*, Thy servants (are) twelve
14, 18. *And* Joseph *said* unto them,
21. *And they said* one to another,
28. *And he said* unto his brethren,
31. *And we said* unto him, We (are) true
33. *And* the man, the lord of the country, *said*
36. *And* Jacob their father *said* unto them,
37. *And* Reuben *spake* unto his father,
38. *And he said*, My son shall not
43: 2. (lit. *and*) their father *said* unto them, Go
3. *And* Judah *spake* unto him,
6. *And* Israel *said*, Wherefore dealt
7. *And they said*, The man asked
— certainly know that *he would say*,
8. *And* Judah *said* unto Israel his father,
11. *And* their father Israel *said* unto them,
16. *And...he said* to the ruler of his house,
18. *and they said*, Because of the money
20. *And said*, O sir, we came indeed
23. *And he said*, Peace (be) to you,
27. *and said*, (Is) your father well,
28. *And they answered*, Thy servant
29. *and said* (Is) this your younger
— *And he said*, God be gracious
31. *and said*, Set on bread.
44: 7. *And they said* unto him, Wherefore
10. *And he said*, Now also
15. *And* Joseph *said* unto them,
16. *And* Judah *said*, What *shall we say* unto
17. *And he said*, God forbid that I should
18. *and said*, Oh my lord,
20, 22. *And we said* unto my lord,
21, 23. *And thou saidst* unto thy servants,
25. *And* our father *said*, Go again,
26. *And we said*, We cannot go
27. *And* thy servant my father *said* unto us,
28. *and I said*, Surely he is torn
45: 3, 4. *And* Joseph *said* unto his brethren,
4. *And he said*, I (am) Joseph your brother,
17. *And* Pharaoh *said* unto Joseph,
24. *and he said* unto them,
28. *And* Israel *said*, (It is) enough;
46: 2. *And* God *spake* unto Israel in
— *and said*, Jacob, Jacob. *And he said*,
3. *And he said*, I (am) God, the God of
30. *And* Israel *said* unto Joseph,
31. *And* Joseph *said* unto his brethren,
— go up, and shew Pharaoh, *and say*
47: 1. *and said*, My father and my brethren,
3. *And* Pharaoh *said* unto his brethren,
— *And they said* unto Pharaoh,
4. *They said moreover* unto Pharaoh,
5. *And* Pharaoh *spake* unto Joseph,
8. *And* Pharaoh *said* unto Jacob,
9. *And* Jacob *said* unto Pharaoh,
16. *And* Joseph *said*, Give your cattle;
18. *and said* unto him, We will not hide
23. *Then* Joseph *said* unto the people,
25. *And they said*, Thou hast saved
29. *and said* unto him, If now I have found
30. *And he said*, I will do as thou
31. *And he said*, Swear unto me.
48: 1. *that* (one) *told* Joseph, Behold,
2. And (one) told Jacob, *and said*,
3. *And* Jacob *said* unto Joseph,
4. *And said* unto me, Behold,
8. *and said*, Who (are) these?
9, 18. *And* Joseph *said* unto his father,
— *And he said*, Bring them,
11, 21. *And* Israel *said* unto Joseph,

Gen48:15. he blessed Joseph, *and said,*
19. his father refused, *and said,*
49: 1. *and said,* Gather yourselves together,
29. he charged them, *and said*
50: 6. *And* Pharaoh *said,* Go up, and bury
11. *And...they said,* This (is) a grievous
15. *And...they said,* Joseph will peradventure
17. So *shall ye say* unto Joseph,
18. *and they said,* Behold, we (be) thy
19. *And* Joseph *said* unto them, Fear not:
24. *And* Joseph *said* unto his brethren,
Ex. 1: 9. *And he said* unto his people,
15. *And* the king of Egypt *spake*
16. *And he said,* When ye do the
18. *and said* unto them, Why
19. *And* the midwives *said* unto Pharaoh,
2: 6. *and said,* This (is one) of the Hebrews'
7. *Then said* his sister to Pharaoh's
8. *And* Pharaoh's daughter *said* to her,
9. *And* Pharaoh's daughter *said* unto her,
10. she called his name Moses: *and she said,*
13. *and he said* to him that did the wrong,
14. *And he said,* Who made thee
— And Moses feared, *and said,*
18. *And...*they came to Reuel their father, *he said,*
19. *And they said,* An Egyptian
20. *And he said* unto his daughters,
3: 3. *And* Moses *said,* I will now turn aside,
4. *and said,* Moses, Moses. *And he said,*
5. *And he said,* Draw not nigh
6. *Moreover he said,* I (am) the God
7. *And* the Lord *said,* I have surely seen
11, 13. *And* Moses *said* unto God,
12. *And he said,* Certainly I will be
13. what *shall I say* unto them?
14. *And* God *said* unto Moses,
— *and he said,* Thus *shalt thou say* unto
15. God *said moreover* unto Moses, Thus *shalt thou say* unto
17. *And I have said,* I will bring
4: 1. Moses answered *and said,*
— *they will say,* The Lord hath not
2. *And* the Lord *said* unto him,
— in thine hand? *And he said,* A rod.
3. *And he said,* Cast it on the ground.
4, 19, 21. *And* the Lord *said* unto Moses,
6. *And* the Lord *said* furthermore unto him,
7. *And he said,* Put thine hand
10. *And* Moses *said* unto the Lord,
11. *And* the Lord *said* unto him,
13. *And he said,* O my Lord, send,
14. *and he said,* (Is) not Aaron the Levite
18. *and said* unto him, Let me go,
— *And* Jethro *said* to Moses, Go in peace.
23. *And I say* unto thee,
25. cast (it) at his feet, *and said,*
27. *And* the Lord *said* to Aaron,
5: 1. went in, *and told* Pharaoh,
2. *And* Pharaoh *said,* Who (is) the Lord,
3. *And they said,* The God of the
4. *And* the king of Egypt *said* unto them,
5. *And* Pharaoh *said,* Behold, the people
10. *and they spake* to the people,
17. *But he said,* Ye (are) idle,
21. *And they said* unto them,
22. Moses returned unto the Lord, *and said,*
6: 1. *Then* the Lord *said* unto Moses,
2. *and said* unto him, I (am) the Lord:
30. *And* Moses *said* before the Lord,
7: 1, 14. *And* the Lord *said* unto Moses,
8, 19. *And* the Lord *spake* unto Moses
8: 1(7:26), 5(1). *And* the Lord *spake* unto
8(4). *and said,* Intreat the Lord,
9(5). *And* Moses *said* unto Pharaoh,
10(6). *And he said,* To morrow. *And he said,*
16(12), 20(16). *And* the Lord *said* unto Moses,
19(15). *Then* the magicians *said*
25(21). *and said,* Go ye, sacrifice to your God
26(22). *And* Moses *said,* It is not
27(23). as *he shall command* us.
28(24). *And* Pharaoh *said,* I will let you go,
29(25). *And* Moses *said,* Behold, I go
9: 1. *Then* the Lord *said* unto Moses,
8, 13, 22. *And* the Lord *said* unto Moses
27. *and said* unto them, I have sinned
29. *And* Moses *said* unto him,

Ex. 10: 1, 12, 21. *And* the Lord *said* unto Moses.
3. unto Pharaoh, *and said* unto him,
7. *And* Pharaoh's servants *said* unto
8, 10. *and he said* unto them,
9. *And* Moses *said,* We will go
16. *and he said,* I have sinned
24. *and said,* Go ye, serve the Lord;
25. *And* Moses *said,* Thou must give
28. *And* Pharaoh *said* unto him,
29. *And* Moses *said,* Thou hast spoken
11: 1, 9. *And* the Lord *said* unto Moses,
4. *And* Moses *said,* Thus saith the Lord,
12: 1. *And* the Lord *spake* unto Moses
21. *and said* unto them, Draw out
26. when your children *shall say*
31. *and said,* Rise up, (and) get you forth
43. *And* the Lord *said* unto Moses
13: 3. *And* Moses *said* unto the people,
14: 5. *and they said,* Why have we
11. *And they said* unto Moses,
13. *And* Moses *said* unto the people,
15, 26. *And* the Lord *said* unto Moses,
25. *so that* the Egyptians *said,*
15: 1. *and spake,* saying, I will sing
26. *And said,* If thou wilt diligently
16: 3. *And* the children of Israel *said*
4. *Then said* the Lord unto Moses,
6. *And* Moses and Aaron *said* unto all
8. *And* Moses *said,* (This shall be),
9. *And* Moses *spake* unto Aaron,
15. *they said* one to another, It (is) manna:
— *And* Moses *said* unto them,
19. *And* Moses *said,* Let no man leave
23. *And he said* unto them,
25. *And* Moses *said,* Eat that
28. *And* the Lord *said* unto Moses,
32. *And* Moses *said,* This (is) the thing
33. *And* Moses *said* unto Aaron,
17: 2. *and said,* Give us water that we may drink. *And* Moses *said* unto them,
3. murmured against Moses, *and said,*
5, 14. *And* the Lord *said* unto Moses,
9. *And* Moses *said* unto Joshua,
16. *For he said,* Because the Lord
18: 6. *And he said* unto Moses,
10. *And* Jethro *said,* Blessed (be) the Lord,
14. *he said,* What (is) this thing that thou doest
15. *And* Moses *said* unto his father in law,
17. *And* Moses' father in law *said*
19: 3. Thus *shalt thou say* to the house
8. *and said,* All that the Lord hath spoken
9, 10, 21. *And* the Lord *said* unto
15. *And he said* unto the people,
23. *And* Moses *said* unto the Lord,
24. *And* the Lord *said* unto him,
25. unto the people, *and spake* unto them.
20: 19. *And they said* unto Moses, Speak thou
20. *And* Moses *said* unto the people,
22. *And* the Lord *said* unto Moses, Thus *thou shalt say* unto the
21. 5. if the servant *shall* plainly *say,*
22: 9(8). which (another) *challengeth* to be his,
24: 3. answered with one voice, *and said,*
7. *and they said,* All that the Lord
8. sprinkled (it) on the people, *and said,*
12 & 30:34. *And* the Lord *said* unto Moses,
31: 12. *And* the Lord *spake* unto Moses,
32: 1. *and said* unto him, Up, make us gods,
2. *And* Aaron *said* unto them, Break off
4. *and they said,* These (be) thy gods,
5. *and said,* To morrow (is) a feast
8. *and said,* These (be) thy gods,
9, 33. *And* the Lord *said* unto Moses,
11. besought the Lord his God, *and said.*
12. should the Egyptians *speak,* and say,
17. as they shouted, *he said* unto Moses,
18. *And he said,* (It is) not the voice
21. *And* Moses *said* unto Aaron,
22. *And* Aaron *said,* Let not the anger of
23. *For they said* unto me, Make us
24. *And I said* unto them, Whosoever
26. stood in the gate of the camp, *and said,*
27. *And he said* unto them,
29. *For* Moses *had said,* Consecrate
30. *that* Moses *said* unto the people,
31. returned unto the Lord, *and said,*
33: 5. *For* the Lord *had said* unto Moses,

Ex. 33:12. *And* Moses *said* unto the Lord,
14. *And he said*, My presence shall go
15. *And he said* unto him, If thy presence
17. *And* the Lord *said* unto Moses,
18. *And he said*, I beseech thee, shew me
19. *And he said*, I will make all my
20. *And he said*, Thou canst not see
21. *And* the Lord *said*, Behold,
34: 1, 27. *And* the Lord *said* unto Moses,
9. *And he said*, If now I have found
10. *And he said*, Behold, I make a covenant:
35: 1. *and said* unto them, These (are) the words
4. *And* Moses *spake* unto all the congregation
30. *And* Moses *said* unto the children of
36: 5. *And they spake* unto Moses,
Lev. 8: 5. *And* Moses *said* unto the congregation,
31. *And* Moses *said* unto Aaron
9: 2. *And he said* unto Aaron, Take thee
6. *And* Moses *said*, This (is) the thing
7. *And* Moses *said* unto Aaron,
10: 3. *Then* Moses *said* unto Aaron,
4. *and said* unto them, Come near,
6. *And* Moses *said* unto Aaron,
16: 2. *And* the Lord *said* unto Moses,
17: 8. And *thou shalt say* unto them,
14. *therefore I said* unto the children of Israel,
20: 2. *thou shalt say* to the children of Israel,
24. *But I have said* unto you, Ye shall
21: 1. *And* the Lord *said* unto Moses,
25:20. And if *ye shall say*, What shall we eat
Nu. 3:40. *And* the Lord *said* unto Moses,
7: 4. *And* the Lord *spake* unto Moses,
11. *And* the Lord *said* unto Moses,
9: 7. *And* those men *said* unto him,
8. *And* Moses *said* unto them, Stand still,
10:29. *And* Moses *said* unto Hobab,
30. *And he said* unto him, I will not go;
31. *And he said*, Leave us not,
35. *that* Moses *said*, Rise up, Lord,
36. *And* when it rested, *he said*, Return,
11: 4. *and said*, Who shall give us flesh to
11. *And* Moses *said* unto the Lord,
12. that *thou shouldest say* unto me,
16, 23. *And* the Lord *said* unto Moses,
18. *say thou* unto the people,
21. *And* Moses *said*, The people,
27. told Moses, *and said*, Eldad and
28. answered *and said*, My lord Moses, forbid
29. *And* Moses *said* unto him,
12: 2. *And they said*, Hath the Lord
4. *And* the Lord *spake* suddenly
6. *And he said*, Hear now my words:
11. *And* Aaron *said* unto Moses, Alas,
14. *And* the Lord *said* unto Moses,
13:17. *and said* unto them, Get you up
27. *and said*, We came unto the land
30. *and said*, Let us go up at once,
14: 2. *and* the whole congregation *said* unto them,
4. *And they said* one to another, Let us make
7. *And they spake* unto all the company
10. *But* all the congregation *bade* stone
11. *And* the Lord *said* unto Moses, How long
13. *And* Moses *said* unto the Lord,
20. *And* the Lord *said*, I have pardoned
41. *And* Moses *said*, Wherefore now do ye
15:35. *And* the Lord *said* unto Moses,
37. *And* the Lord *spake* unto Moses,
16: 3. *and said* unto them, (Ye take) too much
8, 16. *And* Moses *said* unto Korah,
12. *which said*, We will not come up:
15. *and said* unto the Lord, Respect not
22. they fell upon their faces, *and said*,
28. *And* Moses *said*, Hereby ye shall know
46(17:11). *And* Moses *said* unto Aaron,
17:10(25). *And* the Lord *said* unto Moses, Bring
12(27). *And* the children of Israel *spake* unto Moses,
18: 1. *And* the Lord *said* unto Aaron,
20. *And* the Lord *spake* unto Aaron,
20: 3. the people chode with Moses, *and spake*,
10. *and he said* unto them, Hear now,
12, 23. *And* the Lord *spake* unto Moses
18. *And* Edom *said* unto him,
19. *And* the children of Israel *said* unto him,
20. *And he said*, Thou shalt not go
21: 2. vowed a vow unto the Lord, *and said*,
Nu. 21: 7. the people came to Moses, *and said*,
8, 34. *And* the Lord *said* unto Moses,
27. they that speak in proverbs *say*,
22: 4. *And* Moab *said* unto the elders of Midian,
8. *And he said* unto them, Lodge
9. And God came unto Balaam, *and said*,
10. *And* Balaam *said* unto God,
12. *And* God *said* unto Balaam,
13. *and said* unto the princes of Balak,
14. they went unto Balak, *and said*,
16. they came to Balaam, *and said*
17. I will do whatsoever *thou sayest*
18. Balaam answered *and said*
20. unto Balaam at night, *and said* unto him,
28. *and she said* unto Balaam,
29. *And* Balaam *said* unto the ass,
30. *And* the ass *said* unto Balaam,
— to do so unto thee? *And he said*, Nay.
32. *And* the angel of the Lord *said* unto
34. *And* Balaam *said* unto the angel
35. *And* the angel of the Lord *said* unto
37. *And* Balak *said* unto Balaam,
38. *And* Balaam *said* unto Balak,
23: 1, 3, 29. *And* Balaam *said* unto Balak,
4. *and he said* unto him, I have prepared
5. *and said*, Return unto Balak,
7, 18. he took up his parable, *and said*,
11, 25. *And* Balak *said* unto Balaam,
12. And he answered *and said*,
13. *And* Balak *said* unto him, Come,
15. *And he said* unto Balak, Stand
16. *and said*, Go again unto Balak,
17. *And* Balak *said* unto him, What hath
26. But Balaam answered *and said*
27. *And* Balak *said* unto Balaam, Come,
24: 3, 15, 20, 21, 23. took up his parable, *and said*,
10. *and* Balak *said* unto Balaam, I called thee
12. *And* Balaam *said* unto Balak, Spake I
25: 4. *And* the Lord *said* unto Moses,
5. *And* Moses *said* unto the judges
26: 1. *that* the Lord *spake* unto Moses
27: 6. *And* the Lord *spake* unto Moses,
12, 18. *And* the Lord *said* unto Moses,
29:40(30:1). *And* Moses *told* the children of
31:15. *And* Moses *said* unto them, Have ye saved
21. *And* Eleazar the priest *said* unto the
25. *And* the Lord *spake* unto Moses,
49. *And they said* unto Moses, Thy servants
32: 2. came *and spake* unto Moses,
5. *Wherefore, said they*, if we have
6. *And* Moses *said* unto the children of Gad
16. they came near unto him, *and said*,
20. *And* Moses *said* unto them, If ye
25. *And*...children of Reuben *spake* unto Moses,
29. *And* Moses *said* unto them, If the children
36: 2. *And they said*, The Lord commanded
Deu 1: 9. *And I spake* unto you at that time,
14. ye answered me, *and said*,
20. *And I said* unto you, Ye are come
22. unto me every one of you, *and said*,
25. *and said*, (It is) a good land
27. ye murmured in your tents, *and said*,
29. *Then I said* unto you, Dread not,
41. *and said* unto me, We have sinned
42. *And* the Lord *said* unto me,
2: 2. *And* the Lord *spake* unto me,
9, 31 & 3:2, 26. *And* the Lord *said* unto me,
5: 1. *and said* unto them, Hear, O Israel,
24(21). *And ye said*, Behold, the Lord
27(24). all that the Lord our God *shall say:*
28(25). *and* the Lord *said* unto me, I have
7:17. If *thou shalt say* in thine heart,
9: 4. *Speak* not *thou* in thine heart,
12. *And* the Lord *said* unto me, Arise,
13. *Furthermore* the Lord *spake*
26. I prayed therefore unto the Lord, *and said*,
28. whence thou broughtest us out *say*,
10:11. *And* the Lord *said* unto me,
15:16. it shall be, if *he say* unto thee,
17:11. the judgment which *they shall tell* thee,
18:17. *And* the Lord *said* unto me,
21. if *thou say* in thine heart,
28:67. In the morning *thou shalt say*,
— at even *thou shalt say*,
29: 2(1). *and said* unto them, Ye have seen
31: 2. *And he said* unto them, I (am)
7. *and said* unto him in the sight of

Deu31:14, 16. *And* the Lord *said* unto Moses,
23. the son of Nun a charge, *and said,*
32: 7. thy elders, *and they will tell* thee.
20. *And he said,* I will hide my face
27. lest *they should say,* Our hand
46. *And he said* unto them, Set your hearts
33: 2. *And he said,* The Lord came from Sinai,
7. *and he said,* Hear, Lord, the voice
27. *and shall say,* Destroy (them).
34: 4. *And* the Lord *said* unto him, This
Jos. 1: 1. *that* the Lord *spake* unto Joshua
2: 4. *and said* thus, There came men
9 *And she said* unto the men,
14. *And* the men *answered* her, Our life
16. *And she said* unto them, Get you
17. *And* the men *said* unto her,
21. *And she said,* According unto your words,
24. *And they said* unto Joshua, Truly
3: 5. *And* Joshua *said* unto the people,
6. *And* Joshua *spake* unto the priests,
7. *And* the Lord *said* unto Joshua,
9. *And* Joshua *said* unto the children of
10. *And* Joshua *said,* Hereby ye shall know
4: 1. over Jordan, *that* the Lord *spake* unto
5. *And* Joshua *said* unto them, Pass
15. *And* the Lord *spake* unto Joshua,
21. *And* he *spake* unto the children of
5: 9. *And* the Lord *said* unto Joshua, This day
13. *and said* unto him, (Art) thou for us,
14. *And he said,* Nay; but (as) captain
— did worship, *and said* unto him,
15. *And* the captain of the Lord's host *said*
6: 2. *And* the Lord *said* unto Joshua,
6. *and said* unto them, Take up the ark
7. *And he said* unto the people, Pass on,
16. *when*...Joshua *said* unto the people, Shout;
7: 2. *and spake* unto them, saying, Go up
3. returned to Joshua, *and said*
7. *And* Joshua *said,* Alas, O Lord God,
8. O Lord, what *shall I say,*
10. *And* the Lord *said* unto Joshua,
19. *And* Joshua *said* unto Achan,
20. Achan answered Joshua, *and said,*
25. *And* Joshua *said,* Why hast thou troubled
8: 1, 18. *And* the Lord *said* unto Joshua,
6. for *they will say,* They flee
9: 6. *and said* unto him, and to the men of
7. *And* the men of Israel *said* unto the
8. *And they said* unto Joshua, We (are) thy servants. *And* Joshua *said*
9. *And they said* unto him, From
11. *Wherefore* our elders...*spake* to us,
19. *But* all the princes *said* unto all
21. *And* the princes *said* unto them,
24. they answered Joshua, *and said,*
10: 8. *And* the Lord *said* unto Joshua,
12. *and he said* in the sight of Israel, Sun,
18. *And* Joshua *said,* Roll great stones
22. *Then said* Joshua, Open the mouth
24. *and said* unto the captains
25. *And* Joshua *said* unto them, Fear not,
11: 6. *And* the Lord *said* unto Joshua,
13: 1. *and* the Lord *said* unto him, Thou
14: 6. *and* Caleb the son of Jephunneh...*said*
15:16. *and* Caleb *said,* He that smiteth
18. *and* Caleb *said* unto her, What wouldest
19. *Who answered,* Give me a blessing;
17:15. *And* Joshua *answered* them, If thou
16. *And* the children of Joseph *said,*
17. *And* Joshua *spake* unto the house of
18: 3. *And* Joshua *said* unto the children of
22: 2. *And said* unto them, Ye have kept
8. *And he spake* unto them, saying, Return
24. your children *might speak* unto our
26. *Therefore we said,* Let us now prepare
27. that your children *may* not *say* to our
28. *Therefore said we,* that it shall be, *when they should* (so) *say*
31. *And* Phinehas the son of Eleazar the priest *said*
23: 2. *and said* unto them, I am old
24: 2, 27. *And* Joshua *said* unto all the people,
16. And the people answered *and said,*
19, 22. *And* Joshua *said* unto the people,
21, 24. *And* the people *said* unto Joshua,
22. *And they said,* (We are) witnesses.
Jud 1: 2. *And* the Lord *said,* Judah shall go

Jud. 1: 3. *And* Judah *said* unto Simeon
7. *And* Adoni-bezek *said,* Threescore
12. *And* Caleb *said,* He that smiteth
14. *and* Caleb *said* unto her, What wilt thou?
15. *And she said* unto him, Give me
24. *and they said* unto him, Shew us,
2: 1. *and said,* I made you to go up
— *and I said,* I will never break
20. was hot against Israel; *and he said,*
3:19. *and said,* I have a secret errand unto thee, O king: *who said,*
20. *And* Ehud *said,* I have a message
24. *and*...*they said,* Surely he covereth
28. *And he said* unto them,
4: 6. *and said* unto him, Hath not the Lord
8. *And* Barak *said* unto her,
9. *And she said,* I will surely go
14. *And* Deborah *said* unto Barak,
18. *and said* unto him, Turn in,
19. *And he said* unto her, Give me
20. *Again he said* unto her, Stand in
22. *and said* unto him, Come,
6: 8. unto the children of Israel, *which said*
10. *And I said* unto you, I (am)
12. *And said* unto him, The Lord (is) with
13. *And* Gideon *said* unto him,
14. *and said,* Go in this thy might,
15. *And he said* unto him, Oh my Lord,
16. *And* the Lord *said* unto him, Surely
17. *And he said* unto him, If now
18. *And he said,* I will tarry
20. *And* the angel of God *said* unto him,
22. *and*...Gideon *said,* Alas, O Lord God!
23. *And* the Lord *said* unto him,
25. *that* the Lord *said* unto him, Take
29. *And they said* one to another,
— *and*...*they said,* Gideon the son of Joash
30. *Then* the men of the city *said* unto Joash,
31. *And* Joash *said* unto all that stood
36, 39. *And* Gideon *said* unto God,
7: 2, 4, 5, 7. *And* the Lord *said* unto Gideon,
4. of whom *I say* unto thee, This shall go
— of whomsoever *I say* unto thee, This shall
9. *that* the Lord *said* unto him, Arise,
13. *and said,* Behold, I dreamed
14. his fellow answered *and said,*
15. *and said,* Arise; for the Lord
17. *And he said* unto them, Look on me
8: 1. *And* the men of Ephraim *said*
2. *And he said* unto them,
5. *And he said* unto the men of
6. *And* the princes of Succoth *said,*
7. *And* Gideon *said,* Therefore when
9. *And he spake* also unto the men
15. *and said,* Behold, Zebah and Zalmunna,
18. *Then said* he unto Zebah
— *And they answered,* As thou (art),
19. *And he said,* They (were) my brethren,
20. *And he said* unto Jether his firstborn,
21. *Then* Zebah and Zalmunna *said,*
22. *Then* the men of Israel *said*
23, 24. *And* Gideon *said* unto them,
25. *And they answered,* We will
9: 7. *and said* unto them, Hearken
8. *and they said* unto the olive tree,
9. *But* the olive tree *said* unto them,
10. *And* the trees *said* to the fig tree,
11. *But* the fig tree *said* unto them,
12. *Then said* the trees unto the vine,
13. *And* the vine *said* unto them,
14. *Then said* all the trees
15. *And* the bramble *said* unto the trees,
28. *And* Gaal the son of Ebed *said,*
29. *And he said* to Abimelech,
36. *and*...*he said* to Zebul, Behold,
— *And* Zebul *said* unto him,
37. Gaal spake again and *said,*
38. *Then said* Zebul unto him,
— wherewith *thou saidst,* Who (is)
48. *and said* unto the people
54. *and said* unto him, Draw thy sword,
— that men *say* not of me, A woman
10:11. *And* the Lord *said* unto the children
15. *And* the children of Israel *said*
18. *And* the people (and) princes of Gilead *said*
11: 2. *and said* unto him, Thou shalt not

Jud. 11: 6. *And they said* unto Jephthah,
7. *And* Jephthah *said* unto the elders
8, 10. *And* the elders of Gilead *said*
9. *And* Jephthah *said* unto the elders
13. *And* the king...of Ammon *answered*
15. *And said* unto him, Thus saith
19. *and* Israel *said* unto him, Let us pass
30. *and said*, If thou shalt without fail
35. *and said*, Alas, my daughter!
36. *And she said* unto him,
37. *And she said* unto her father,
38. *And he said*, Go. And he sent her
12: 1. *and said* unto Jephthah,
2. *And* Jephthah *said* unto them,
5. Ephraimites which were escaped *said*,
— *that said* unto him, (Art) thou an Ephraimite? *If he said*,
6. *Then said they* unto him,
— *and he said* Sibboleth:
13: 3. appeared unto the woman, *and said* unto
6. came *and told* her husband,
7. *But he said* unto me, Behold,
8. intreated the Lord, *and said*, O my Lord,
10. *and said* unto him, Behold,
11. *and said* unto him, (Art) thou the man
— *And he said*, I (am).
12. *And* Manoah *said*, Now let thy words
13, 16. *And* the angel of the Lord *said*
15, 17. *And* Manoah *said* unto the angel
18. *And* the angel of the Lord *said* unto him,
22. *And* Manoah *said* unto his wife,
23. *But* his wife *said* unto him,
14: 2. *and said*, I have seen a woman
3. *Then* his father and his mother *said*
— *And* Samson *said* unto his father,
12. *And* Samson *said* unto them,
13. *And they said* unto him, Put forth
14. *And he said* unto them, Out of
15. *that they said* unto Samson's wife
16. wept before him, *and said*,
— *And he said* unto her, Behold,
18. *And* the men of the city *said* unto him
— *And he said* unto them, If ye had not
15: 1. *and he said*, I will go in
2. *And* her father *said*, I verily
3. *And* Samson *said* concerning them,
6. *Then* the Philistines *said*, Who
— *And they answered*, Samson,
7, 12. *And* Samson *said* unto them,
10. *And* the men of Judah *said*,
— *And they answered*, To bind Samson
11. *and said* to Samson, Knowest thou not
— *And he said* unto them, As they did
12. *And they said* unto him, We are come
13. *And they spake* unto him,
16. *And* Samson *said*, With the jawbone
18. called on the Lord, *and said*,
16: 5. *and said* unto her, Entice him,
6. *And* Delilah *said* to Samson,
7. *And* Samson *said* unto her, If they bind
9. *And she said* unto him,
10, 13. *And* Delilah *said* unto Samson,
11. *And he said* unto her, If they bind
12, 14. *and said* unto him, The Philistines
13. *And he said* unto her, If thou weavest
15. *And* she *said* unto him, How *canst thou say*,
17. told her all his heart, *and said* unto her,
20. *And she said*, The Philistines
— his sleep, *and said*, I will go out
23. *for they said*, Our god hath
25. *that they said*, Call for Samson,
26. *And* Samson *said* unto the lad
28. *and said*, O Lord God, remember
30. *And* Samson *said*, Let me die
17: 2. *And he said* unto his mother,
— *And* his mother *said*, Blessed
3. *And*...his mother *said*, I had wholly
9, 10. *And* Micah *said* unto him,
— *And he said* unto him,
13. *Then said* Micah, Now know
18: 2. *and they said* unto them, Go,
3. *and said* unto him, Who brought
4. *And he said* unto them, Thus
5. *And they said* unto him, Ask
6. *And* the priest *said* unto them, Go
8. *and* their brethren *said* unto them,
9. *And they said*, Arise, that we

Jud. 18: 14. *and said* unto their brethren,
18. *Then said* the priest unto them,
19. *And they said* unto him. Hold
23. *and said* unto Micah, What aileth
24. *And he said*, Ye have taken away
— what (is) this (that) *ye say*
25. *And* the children of Dan *said*
19: 5, 8. *and* the damsel's father *said*
6. *for* the damsel's father *had said*
9. *And*...the damsel's father, *said* unto him,
11. *and* the servant *said* unto his master,
12. *And* his master *said* unto him,
13. *And he said* unto his servant,
17. *and* the old man *said*, Whither
18. *And he said* unto him, We (are) passing
20. *And* the old man *said*, Peace
22. *and spake* to the master of the house,
23. *and said* unto them, Nay,
28. *And he said* unto her, Up,
20: 3. *Then said* the children of Israel,
4. answered *and said*, I came
18. asked counsel of God, *and said*,
– *And* the Lord *said*, Judah
23, 28. *And* the Lord *said*, Go up
32. *And* the children of Benjamin *said*,
21: 3. *And said*, O Lord God of Israel,
5. *And* the children of Israel *said*,
6. *and said*, There is one tribe cut off
8. *And they said*, What one
16. *Then* the elders of the congregation *said*,
17. *And they said*, (There must be)
19. *Then they said*, Behold,
Ru. 1: 8. *And* Naomi *said* unto her two daughters
10. *And they said* unto her, Surely
11. *And* Naomi *said*, Turn again,
15. *And she said*, Behold, thy sister in law
16. *And* Ruth *said*, Intreat me not
19. *and they said*, (Is) this Naomi?
20. *And she said* unto them, Call
2: 2, 21. *And* Ruth the Moabitess *said*
— *And she said* unto her, Go, my daughter.
4. *and said* unto the reapers,
— *And they answered* him, The Lord
5. *Then said* Boaz unto his servant
6. answered *and said*, It (is) the Moabitish
7. *And she said*, I pray you, let me
8. *Then said* Boaz unto Ruth,
10. *and said* unto him, Why have I
11. Boaz answered *and said* unto her,
13. *Then she said*, Let me find
14. *And* Boaz *said* unto her, At
19. *And* her mother in law *said*
— *and said*, The man's name
20. *And* Naomi *said* unto her daughter in law
— *And* Naomi *said* unto her,
22. *And* Naomi *said* unto Ruth
3: 1. *Then* Naomi her mother in law *said*
5. *And she said* unto her, All that *thou sayest*
9. *And he said*, Who (art) thou? *And she answered*,
10. *And he said*, Blessed (be) thou
11. do to thee all that *thou requirest:*
14. *And he said*, Let it not be known
15. *Also he said*, Bring the vail
16. *And*...*she said*, Who (art) thou,
17. *And she said*, These six
18. *Then said she*, Sit still,
4: 1. unto whom *he said*, Ho,
2. *and said*, Sit ye down here.
3. *And he said* unto the kinsman,
4. *And he said*, I will redeem (it).
5. *Then said* Boaz, What day thou buyest
6. *And* the kinsman *said*, I cannot
8. *Therefore* the kinsman *said*
9. *And* Boaz *said* unto the elders,
11. *And* all the people...*said*, (We are)
14. *And* the women *said* unto Naomi,
1Sa. 1: 8. *Then said* Elkanah her husband
11. she vowed a vow, *and said*,
14. *And* Eli *said* unto her,
15. Hannah answered *and said*,
17. Then Eli answered *and said*,
18. *And she said*, Let thine handmaid
23. *And* Elkanah her husband *said*
26. *And she said*, Oh my lord,
2: 1. Hannah prayed, *and said*,
16. *And* (if) any man *said* unto him,

1 Sa. 2:23. *And he said* unto them,
27. unto Eli, *and said* unto him,
3: 4. *and he answered,* Here (am) I.
5. he ran unto Eli, *and said,*
— *And he said,* I called not;
6, 8. went to Eli, *and said,* Here (am) I;
— *And he answered,* I called not,
9. *Therefore* Eli *said* unto Samuel,
10. *Then* Samuel *answered,* Speak;
11. *And* the Lord *said* to Samuel,
16. *and said,* Samuel, my son. *And he answered,*
17. *And he said,* What (is) the thing
18. *And he said,* It (is) the Lord:
4: 3. *And*...the elders of Israel *said,*
6. *And*...*they said,* What (meaneth) the
7. *And they said,* Woe unto us!
14. *And*...*he said,* What (meaneth) the noise
16. *And* the man *said* unto Eli,
— *And he said,* What is there done,
17. the messenger answered *and said,*
22. *And she said,* The glory is departed
5: 8. *and said,* What shall we do with the
— *And they answered,* Let the ark
11. *and said,* Send away the ark
6: 3. *And they said,* If ye send away
4. *Then said they,* What (shall be)
— *They* (lit. *and They*) *answered,* Five golden
20. *And* the men of Beth-shemesh *said,*
7: 3. *And* Samuel *spake* unto all
5. *And* Samuel *said,* Gather all Israel
6. *and said* there, We have sinned
8. *And* the children of Israel *said*
12. *saying,* Hitherto hath the Lord
8: 5. *And said* unto him, Behold, thou
7. *And* the Lord *said* unto Samuel,
— in all that *they say* unto thee:
10. *And* Samuel *told* all the words
11. *And he said,* This will be the
19. *and they said,* Nay; but we will have
22. *And* the Lord *said* to Samuel,
— *And* Samuel *said* unto the men
9: 3. *And* Kish *said* to Saul his son,
6. *And he said* unto him, Behold
7, 10. *Then said* Saul to his servant,
8. the servant answered Saul again, *and said,*
11. *and said* unto them, Is the seer
12. they answered them, *and said,* He is;
18. *and said,* Tell me, I pray thee,
19. Samuel answered Saul, *and said,*
21. Saul answered *and said,*
23. *And* Samuel *said* unto the cook,
24. *And* (Samuel) *said,* Behold that which is
10: 1. *and said,* (Is it) not because the Lord
11. *then* the people *said* one to another,
12. of the same place answered *and said,*
14. *And* Saul's uncle *said* unto him
— *And he said,* To seek the asses:
15. *And* Saul's uncle *said,* Tell me,
16. *And* Saul *said* unto his uncle,
18. *And said* unto the children of Israel,
19. *and ye have said* unto him,
22. *And* the Lord *answered,* Behold,
24. *And* Samuel *said* to all the people,
— all the people shouted, *and said,*
11: 1. *and* all the men of Jabesh *said* unto
2. *And* Nahash the Ammonite *answered*
3. *And* the elders of Jabesh *said* unto him,
5. *and* Saul *said,* What (aileth) the people
9. *And they said* unto the messengers that came, Thus *shall ye say* unto the men
10. *Therefore* the men of Jabesh *said,*
12. *And* the people *said* unto Samuel,
13. *And* Saul *said,* There shall not a man
14. *Then said* Samuel to the people,
12: 1. *And* Samuel *said* unto all Israel,
4. *And they said,* Thou hast not
5. *And he said* unto them, The Lord (is)
— *And they answered,* (He is) witness.
6, 20. *And* Samuel *said* unto the people,
10. *and said,* We have sinned,
12. *And*...*ye said* unto me, Nay;
19. *And* all the people *said* unto Samuel,
13: 9. *And* Saul *said,* Bring hither a burnt
11. *And* Samuel *said,* What hast thou done? *And* Saul *said,* Because I saw that
12. *Therefore said I,* The Philistines

1 Sa13:13. *And* Samuel *said* to Saul,
14: 1. *that* Jonathan the son of Saul *said*
6. *And* Jonathan *said* to the young
7. *And* his armourbearer *said* unto him,
8. *Then said* Jonathan, Behold, we
9. If *they say* thus unto us, Tarry
10. if *they say* thus, Come up unto us;
11. *and* the Philistines *said,* Behold,
12. *and said,* Come up to us,
— *And* Jonathan *said* unto his armourbearer,
17. *Then said* Saul unto the people
18. *And* Saul *said* unto Ahiah,
19. *and* Saul *said* unto the priest,
28. answered one of the people, *and said,*
29. *Then said* Jonathan, My father
33. *And he said,* Ye have transgressed:
34. *And* Saul *said,* Disperse yourselves
36. *And* Saul *said,* Let us go down
— *And they said,* Do whatsoever seemeth
— *Then said* the priest, Let us
38. *And* Saul *said,* Draw ye near
40. *Then said he* unto all Israel,
— *And* the people *said* unto Saul,
41. *Therefore* Saul *said* unto the Lord
42. *And* Saul *said,* Cast (lots) between
43. *Then* Saul *said* to Jonathan,
— *and said,* I did but taste a little
44. *And* Saul *answered,* God do so
45. *And* the people *said* unto Saul,
15: 1. Samuel *also said* unto Saul,
6. *And* Saul *said* unto the Kenites,
13. *and* Saul *said* unto him,
14. *And* Samuel *said,* What (meaneth)
15. *And* Saul *said,* They have brought
16. *Then* Samuel *said* unto Saul,
— *And he said* unto him, Say on.
17. *And* Samuel *said,* When thou (wast)
18. sent thee on a journey, *and said,*
20, 24. *And* Saul *said* unto Samuel,
22. *And* Samuel *said,* Hath the Lord
26. *And* Samuel *said* unto Saul, I will not
28. *And* Samuel *said* unto him,
30. *Then he said,* I have sinned:
32. *Then said* Samuel, Bring ye
— *And* Agag *said,* Surely the bitterness
33. *And* Samuel *said,* As thy sword
16: 1. *And* the Lord *said* unto Samuel,
2. *And* Samuel *said,* How can I go?
— *And* the Lord *said,* Take
3. whom *I name* unto thee.
4. *and said,* Comest thou peaceably?
5. *And he said,* Peaceably: I am come
6. *and said,* Surely the Lord's anointed
7. *But* the Lord *said* unto Samuel,
8, 9. *And he said,* Neither hath the Lord
10, 11, 11. *And* Samuel *said* unto Jesse,
11. *And he said,* There remaineth yet the
12. *And* the Lord *said,* Arise, anoint him:
15. *And* Saul's servants *said* unto him,
16. *Let* our lord now *command*
17. *And* Saul *said* unto his servants,
18. answered one of the servants, *and said,*
19. *and said,* Send me David thy son,
17: 8. *and said* unto them, Why are ye come
10. *And* the Philistine *said,* I defy the
17. *And* Jesse *said* unto David his son,
25. *And* the men of Israel *said,*
26. *And* David *spake* to the men
27. *And* the people *answered* him
28. *and he said,* Why camest thou
29. *And* David *said,* What have I now done?
30. toward another, *and spake* after the same
32. *And* David *said* to Saul,
33. *And* Saul *said* to David,
34, 39. *And* David *said* unto Saul,
37. David *said moreover,* The Lord
— *And* Saul *said* unto David,
43. *And* the Philistine *said* unto David,
44. *And* the Philistine *said* to David,
45. *Then said* David to the Philistine,
55. *And* Abner *said,* (As) thy soul liveth,
56. *And* the king *said,* Enquire thou
58. *And* Saul *said* to him, Whose son
— *And* David *answered,* (I am) the son
18: 7. *and said,* Saul hath slain
8. displeased him; *and he said,*
11. *for he said,* I will smite David

1Sa.18:17. *And* Saul *said* to David, Behold
18. *And* David *said* unto Saul,
21. *And* Saul *said*, I will give him
— *Wherefore* Saul *said* to David,
23. *And* David *said*, Seemeth it to you
25. *And* Saul *said*, Thus *shall ye say* to David,
19: 4. *and said* unto him, Let not the king
14. *And*...to take David, *she said*, He (is) sick.
17. *And* Saul *said* unto Michal, Why
— *And* Michal *answered* Saul,
22. he asked *and said*, Where (are) Samuel
— *And* (one) *said*, Behold, (they be)
24. Wherefore *they say*, (Is) Saul also
20: 1. came *and said* before Jonathan,
2. *And he said* unto him, God forbid;
3. David sware moreover, *and said*,
— *and he saith*, Let not Jonathan know
4. *Then said* Jonathan unto David, Whatsoever thy soul *desireth*, (marg. *speaketh*, or, *thinketh*)
5. *And* David *said* unto Jonathan,
7. If *he say* thus, (It is) well;
9. *And* Jonathan *said*, Far be it from thee:
10. *Then said* David to Jonathan,
11, 12. *And* Jonathan *said* unto David,
18. *Then* Jonathan *said* to David,
21. If *I* expressly *say* unto the lad,
22. if *I say* thus unto the young man,
27. *and* Saul *said* unto Jonathan his son,
29. *And he said*, Let me go,
30. *and he said* unto him, Thou son
32. answered Saul his father, *and said*
36. *And he said* unto his lad, Run,
37. Jonathan cried after the lad, *and said*,
40. *and said* unto him, Go, carry
42. *And* Jonathan *said* to David, Go
21: 1(2). *and said* unto him, Why (art) thou
2(3), 8(9). *And* David *said* unto Ahimelech
—(–). *and hath said* unto me, Let no man
4(5). the priest answered David, *and said*,
5(6). David answered the priest, *and said*
9(10). *And* the priest *said*, The sword of
—(—). *And* David *said*, (There is) none
11(12). *And* the servants of Achish *said*
14(15). *Then said* Achish unto his
22. 3. *and he said* unto the king
5. *And* the prophet Gad *said* unto David,
7. *Then* Saul *said* unto his servants
9. *and said*, I saw the son of Jesse
12. *And* Saul *said*, Hear now,
— *And he answered*, Here I (am),
13. *And* Saul *said* unto him,
14. answered the king, *and said*,
16. *And* the king *said*, Thou shalt
17. *And* the king *said* unto the footmen
18. *And* the king *said* to Doeg,
22. *And* David *said* unto Abiathar,
23: 2. *And* the Lord *said* unto David,
3. *And* David's men *said* unto him,
4. the Lord answered him *and said*,
7. *And* Saul *said*, God hath delivered
9. *and he said* to Abiathar the priest,
10. *Then said* David, O Lord God
11. *And* the Lord *said*, He will come down.
12. *Then said* David, Will the men
— *And* the Lord *said*, They will
17. *And he said* unto him, Fear not:
21. *And* Saul *said*, Blessed (be) ye of the
24. 4(5). *And* the men of David *said*
6(7). *And he said* unto his men,
9(10). *And* David *said* to Saul, Wherefore
10(11). *and I said*, I will not put forth
13(14). As *saith* the proverb of the ancients,
16(17). *that* Saul *said*, (Is) this thy voice,
17(18). *And he said* to David, Thou (art)
25: 5. *and* David *said* unto the young men,
10. *and said*, Who (is) David?
13. *And* David *said* unto his men,
19. *And she said* unto her servants,
24 And fell at his feet, *and said*,
32. *And* David *said* to Abigail,
39. *And*...*he said*, Blessed (be) the Lord,
41. on (her) face to the earth, *and said*,
26: 6. *and said* to Ahimelech the Hittite,
— *And* Abishai *said*, I will go down
8. *Then said* Abishai to David,
9. *And* David *said* to Abishai,

1Sa.26.10. David *said furthermore*, (As) the Lord
14. Then Abner answered *and said*,
15. *And* David *said* to Abner, (Art) not thou
17. *and said*, (Is) this thy voice,
— *And* David *said*, (It is) my voice,
18. *And he said*, Wherefore doth
21. *Then said* Saul, I have sinned:
22. David answered *and said*, Behold
25. *Then* Saul *said* to David, Blessed
27: 1. *And* David *said* in his heart,
5. *And* David *said* unto Achish,
10. *And* Achish *said*, Whither have ye
— *And* David *said*, Against the south
28: 1. *And* Achish *said* unto David,
2. *And* David *said* to Achish, Surely
— *And* Achish *said* to David, Therefore
7. *Then said* Saul unto his servants,
— *And* his servants *said* to him, Behold,
8. *and he said*, I pray thee, divine unto me
— whom *I shall name* unto thee.
9. *And* the woman *said* unto him,
11. *Then said* the woman, Whom
— *And he said*, Bring me up Samuel.
12. *and* the woman *spake* to Saul,
13. *And* the king *said* unto her,
— *And* the woman *said* unto Saul, I saw
14. *And he said* unto her, What form
— *And she said*, An old man cometh up;
15. *And* Samuel *said* to Saul,
— *And* Saul *answered*, I am sore
16. *Then said* Samuel, Wherefore
21. *and said* unto him, Behold,
23. But he refused, *and said*, I will not eat.
29: 3. *Then said* the princes of the Philistines,
— *And* Achish *said* unto the princes
4. *and* the princes of the Philistines *said*
6. Achish called David, *and said* unto him,
8. *And* David *said* unto Achish,
9. Achish answered *and said* to David,
30: 7. *And* David *said* to Abiathar
8. *And he answered* him, Pursue:
13. *And* David *said* unto him,
— *And he said*, I (am) a young man of
15. *And* David *said* to him,
— *And he said*, Swear unto me
20. *and said*, This (is) David's spoil.
22. *and said*, Because they went not
23. *Then said* David, Ye shall not
31: 4. *Then said* Saul unto his armourbearer,
2Sa. 1: 3. *And* David *said* unto him, From whence
— *And he said* unto him, Out of the camp
4, 14. *And* David *said* unto him, How
— *And he answered*, That the people
5, 13. *And* David *said* unto the young man
6. *And* the young man that told him *said*,
7. *And I answered*, Here (am) I.
8. *And he said* unto me, Who (art) thou? *And I answered* him, I (am) an Amalekite.
9. *He said* unto me *again*, Stand,
13. *And he answered*, I (am) the son
15. *and said*, Go near, (and) fall upon
16. *And* David *said* unto him, Thy blood
18. *Also he bade* them teach
2: 1. *And* the Lord *said* unto him, Go up. *And* David *said*,
— *And he said*, Unto Hebron.
5. *and said* unto them, Blessed (be) ye
14. *And* Abner *said* to Joab, Let the
— *And* Joab *said*, Let them arise.
20. *and said*, (Art) thou Asahel? *And he answered*,
21. *And* Abner *said* to him, Turn
26. Abner called to Joab, *and said*,
— how long shall it be then, ere *thou bid*
27. *And* Joab *said*, (As) God liveth,
3: 7. *And* (Ish-bosheth) *said* to Abner,
8. *and said*, (Am) I a dog's head,
13. *And he said*, Well; I will make
16. *Then said* Abner unto him, Go, return.
21. *And* Abner *said* unto David, I
24. *and said*, What hast thou done?
28. *And*...*he said*, I and my kingdom (are)
31. *And* David *said* to Joab,
33. *and said*, Died Abner as a fool
38. *And* the king *said* unto his servants,
4: 8. *and said* to the king, Behold the head
9. *and said* unto them, (As) the Lord liveth,

2Sa. 5: 1. to David unto Hebron, *and spake*,
2. *and* the Lord *said* to thee, Thou
6. *which spake* unto David,
8. *And* David *said* on that day,
— Wherefore *they said*, The blind
19. *And* the Lord *said* unto David, Go up:
20. David smote them there, *and said*,
23. *And* when David enquired of the Lord, *he said*,
6: 9. *and said*, How shall the ark of the Lord
20. *and said*, How glorious was the king
21. *And* David *said* unto Michal,
7: 2. *That* the king *said* unto Nathan
3. *And* Nathan *said* to the king,
8. therefore so *shalt thou say*
18. *and he said*, Who (am) I, O Lord God?
9: 1. *And* David *said*, Is there yet any
2. *And* when they had called him...the king *said*
— *And he said*, Thy servant (is he).
3. *And* the king *said*, (Is) there not
—, 4. *And* Ziba *said* unto the king,
4. *And* the king *said* unto him, Where (is)
6. *And* David *said*, Mephibosheth. *And he answered*,
7. *And* David *said* unto him, Fear not:
8. he bowed himself, *and said*,
9. *and said* unto him, I have given
11. *Then said* Ziba unto the king,
10: 2. *Then said* David, I will shew
3. *And...said* unto Hanun their lord,
5. *and* the king *said*, Tarry at Jericho
11. *And he said*, If the Syrians be
11: 3. *And* (one) *said*, (Is) not this Bath-sheba,
5. *and said*, I (am) with child.
8. *And* David *said* to Uriah, Go down
10. *And* when they had told David,...David *said*
11. *And* Uriah *said* unto David, The ark,
12. *And* David *said* to Uriah, Tarry
23. *And* the messenger *said* unto David,
25. *Then* David *said* unto the messenger, Thus *shalt thou say* unto Joab,
12: 1. *and said* unto him, There were
5. *and he said* to Nathan, (As)
7. *And* Nathan *said* to David, Thou
13. *And* David *said* unto Nathan,
— *And* Nathan *said* unto David,
18. if *we tell* him that the child
19. *therefore* David *said* unto his servants,
— *And they said*, He is dead.
21. *Then said* his servants unto him,
22. *And he said*, While the child
27. *and said*, I have fought against
13: 4. *And he said* unto him, Why
— *And* Amnon *said* unto him,
5. *And* Jonadab *said* unto him,
6. *and* when the king was come...Amnon *said*
9. *And* Amnon *said*, Have out all men
10. *And* Amnon *said* unto Tamar, Bring
11. *and said* unto her, Come lie
12. *And she answered* him, Nay,
15. *And* Amnon *said* unto her, Arise,
16. *And she said* unto him, (There is) no
17. *and said*, Put now this (woman) out
20. *And* Absalom her brother *said* unto
24. *and said*, Behold now, thy servant
25. *And* the king *said* to Absalom, Nay
26. *Then said* Absalom, If not,
— *And* the king *said* unto him, Why
32. *and said*, *Let* not my lord *suppose*
35. *And* Jonadab *said* unto the king,
14: 2. *and said* unto her, I pray thee, feign
4. And *when* the woman of Tekoah *spake*
— did obeisance, *and said*, Help, O king.
5. *And* the king *said* unto her, What
— *And she answered*, I (am) indeed
7. *and they said*, Deliver him that smote
8. *And* the king *said* unto the woman, Go
9. *And* the woman of Tekoah *said* unto
10. *And* the king *said*, Whosoever saith
11. *Then said she*, I pray thee, let the
— *And he said*, (As) the Lord liveth,
12. *Then* the woman *said*, Let thine handmaid,
— *And he said*, Say on.
13. *And* the woman *said*, Wherefore then
15. *and* thy handmaid *said*, I will now
17. *Then* thine handmaid *said*, The word of

2Sa. 14: 18. Then the king answered *and said* unto
— *And* the woman *said*, Let my lord
19. *And* the king *said*, (Is not) the hand
— the woman answered *and said*,
21. *And* the king *said* unto Joab, Behold
22. *and* Joab *said*, To day thy servant
24. *And* the king *said*, Let him turn to
30. *Therefore he said* unto his servants,
31. *and said* unto him, Wherefore
32. *And* Absalom *answered* Joab, Behold,
15: 2. *and said*, Of what city (art) thou? *And he said*,
3. *And* Absalom *said* unto him, See,
4. Absalom *said moreover*, Oh that
7. *that* Absalom *said* unto the king, I pray
9. *And* the king *said* unto him, Go
14. *And* David *said* unto all his servants
15. *And* the king's servants *said* unto the
19. *Then said* the king to Ittai the Gittite,
21. Ittai answered the king, *and said*,
22. *And* David *said* to Ittai, Go
25. *And* the king *said* unto Zadok, Carry
26. But if *he* thus *say*, I have no delight
27. The king *said also* unto Zadok the priest,
31. *And* David *said*, O Lord, I pray thee,
33. Unto whom David *said* (lit. *also*), If thou
16: 2. *And* the king *said* unto Ziba, What
— *And* Ziba *said*, The asses (be) for
3. *And* the king *said*, And where (is) thy
— *And* Ziba *said* unto the king, Behold,
4. *Then said* the king to Ziba, Behold,
— *And* Ziba *said*, I humbly beseech thee
9. *Then said* Abishai the son of Zeruiah
10. *And* the king *said*, What have I to do
— Who *shall* then *say*, Wherefore hast
11. *And* David *said* to Abishai, and to all
16. *that* Hushai *said* unto Absalom,
17. *And* Absalom *said* to Hushai, (Is) this
18. *And* Hushai *said* unto Absalom, Nay;
20. *Then said* Absalom to Ahithophel,
21. *And* Ahithophel *said* unto Absalom,
17: 1. *Moreover* Ahithophel *said* unto
5. *Then said* Absalom, Call now Hushai
6. *And* when Hushai was come...Absalom *spake*
7. *And* Hushai *said* unto Absalom, The
8. *For*, *said* Hushai, thou knowest thy
14. *And* Absalom and all the men of Israel *said*,
15. *Then said* Hushai unto Zadok
20. *And* when Absalom's servants...*they said*,
— *And* the woman *said* unto them,
21. *and said* unto David, Arise,
18: 2. *And* the king *said* unto the people,
3. *But* the people *answered*, Thou
4. *And* the king *said* unto them, What
10. *and said*, Behold, I saw Absalom
11. *And* Joab *said* unto the man that told
12. *And* the man *said* unto Joab.
14. *Then said* Joab, I may not tarry
20. *And* Joab *said* unto him, Thou shalt
21. *Then said* Joab to Cushi, Go tell
22. *Then said* Ahimaaz the son of Zadok
— *And* Joab *said*, Wherefore wilt thou
23. *And he said* unto him, Run.
25. *And* the king *said*, If he (be) alone,
26. *and said*, Behold (another) man running
— *And* the king *said*, He also bringeth
27. *And* the watchman *said*, Me thinketh
— *And* the king *said*, He (is) a good man,
28. *and said* unto the king, All is well.
— *and said*, Blessed (be) the Lord
29. *And* the king *said*, Is the young man
— *And* Ahimaaz *answered*, When
30. *And* the king *said* (unto him), Turn
31. *and* Cushi *said*, Tidings, my lord
32. *And* the king *said* unto Cushi,
— *And* Cushi *answered*, The enemies
19: 5(6). into the house to the king, *and said*,
13(14). And *say ye* to Amasa, (Art) thou not
19(20). *And said* unto the king, Let not my
21(22). son of Zeruiah answered *and said*,
22(23). *And* David *said*, What have I to do
23(24). *Therefore* the king *said* unto Shimei,
25(26). *that* the king *said* unto him,
26(27). *And he answered*, My lord, O king
29(30). *And* the king *said* unto him, Why
30(31). *And* Mephibosheth *said* unto the king,

2Sa.19:33(34). *And* the king *said* unto Barzillai,
34(35). *And* Barzillai *said* unto the king,
38(39). *And* the king *answered*, Chimham
41(42). *and said* unto the king, Why
43(44). *and said*, We have ten parts in the
20: 1. *and said*, We have no part in David,
4. *Then said* the king to Amasa, Assemble
6. *And* David *said* to Abishai, Now shall
9. *And* Joab *said* to Amasa, (Art) thou
11. *and said*, He that favoureth Joab,
17. *And* when he was come...the woman *said*,
— *And he answered*, I (am he). *Then she said*
— *And he answered*, I do hear.
18. *Then she spake*, saying, They were
20. *and said*, Far be it,
21. *And* the woman *said* unto Joab, Behold,
21: 1. *And* the Lord *answered*, (It is) for Saul,
2. called the Gibeonites, *and said* unto them;
3. *Wherefore* David *said* unto the Gibeonites,
4. *And* the Gibeonites *said* unto him,
— *And he said*, What ye shall say,
5. *And they answered* the king, The man
6. *And* the king *said*, I will give (them).
16. *thought* (lit. *and thought*) to have slain
22: 2. *And he said*, The Lord (is) my rock,
23:15. David longed, *and said*, Oh that
17. *And he said*, Be it far from me,
24: 2. *For* the king *said* to Joab
3. *And* Joab *said* unto the king,
10. *And* David *said* unto the Lord, I have
13. *and said* unto him, Shall seven years
14. *And* David *said* unto Gad, I am
16. *and said* to the angel that destroyed
17. *And* David *spake* unto the Lord
— *and said*, Lo, I have sinned,
18. *and said* unto him, Go up, rear
21. *And* Araunah *said*, Wherefore is
— *And* David *said*, To buy the threshingfloor
22. *And* Araunah *said* unto David, Let
23. *And* Araunah *said* unto the king,
24. *And* the king *said* unto Araunah, Nay;
1K. 1: 2. *Wherefore* his servants *said* unto him,
11. *Wherefore* Nathan *spake* unto Bath-sheba
16. *And* the king *said*, What wouldest thou?
17. *And she said* unto him, My lord,
24. *And* Nathan *said*, My lord, O king,
25. *and say*, God save king Adonijah.
28. king David answered *and said*,
29. the king sware, *and said*,
31. *and said*, Let my lord king David live
32. *And* king David *said*, Call me Zadok
33. The king *also said* unto them,
36. *and said*, Amen: the Lord God of my lord the king *say* so (too).
39. *and* all the people *said*, God save
41. *And...he said*, Wherefore (is this) noise
42. *and* Adonijah *said* unto him, Come in;
43. Jonathan answered *and said*
52. *And* Solomon *said*, If he will shew
53. *and* Solomon *said* unto him, Go to
2:13. *And she said*, Comest thou peaceably? *And he said*, Peaceably.
14. *He said moreover*, I have
— *And she said*, Say on.
15. *And he said*, Thou knowest that
16. *And she said* unto him, Say on.
17. *And he said*, Speak, I pray thee,
18. *And* Bath-sheba *said*, Well; I will
20. *Then she said*, I desire one small
— *And* the king *said* unto her, Ask
21. *And she said*, Let Abishag
22. answered *and said* unto his mother,
30. *and said* unto him, Thus saith
— *And he said*, Nay; but I will die
31. *And* the king *said* unto him,
36. *and said* unto him, Build thee
38. *And* Shimei *said* unto the king,
42. *and said* unto him, Did I not make
— *and thou saidst* unto me, The word
44. The king *said moreover* to Shimei,
3: 5. *and* God *said*, Ask what I shall give
6. *And* Solomon *said*, Thou hast shewed
11. *And* God *said* unto him, Because thou
17. *And* the one woman *said*, O my lord,
22. *And* the other woman *said*, Nay;
23. *Then said* the king, The one
24. *And* the king *said*, Bring me a sword.

1K. 3:25. *And* the king *said*, Divide the living child
26. *Then spake* the woman whose the living
— *and she said*, O my lord, give her
27. Then the king answered *and said*, Give
5: 6(20). all that *thou shalt appoint:* (marg. *say*)
7(21). *and said*, Blessed (be) the Lord
8:15. *And he said*, Blessed (be) the Lord God
18. *And* the Lord *said* unto David
23. *And he said*, Lord God of Israel,
9: 3. *And* the Lord *said* unto him, I have
13. *And he said*, What cities (are) these
10: 6. *And she said* to the king, It was a true
11:11. *Wherefore* the Lord *said* unto Solomon,
21. *And* when Hadad heard...Hadad *said*
22. *Then* Pharaoh *said* unto him, But what
— *And he answered*, Nothing:
31. *And he said* to Jeroboam, Take thee
12: 5. *And he said* unto them, Depart
9. *And he said* unto them, What counsel
10. Thus *shalt thou speak* unto this
26. *And* Jeroboam *said* in his heart, Now
28. *and said* unto them, It is too much
13: 2. *and said*, O altar, altar,
6. the king answered *and said* unto the man
8. *And* the man of God *said* unto the king,
13. *And he said* unto his sons, Saddle
14. *and he said* unto him, (Art) thou
— *And he said*, I (am).
15. *Then he said* unto him, Come
16. *And he said*, I may not return
18. *He* (lit. *and He*) *said* unto him, I (am) a
26. *And* when the prophet...heard (thereof), *he said*,
31. *that he spake* to his sons,
14: 2. *And* Jeroboam *said* to his wife, Arise,
6. *that he said*, Come in, thou wife of
17: 1. *And* Elijah the Tishbite,...*said*
10. *and said*, Fetch me, I pray thee,
11. he called to her, *and said*, Bring me,
12. *And she said*, (As) the Lord thy God
13. *And* Elijah *said* unto her, Fear not;
18. *And she said* unto Elijah, What have
19. *And he said* unto her,
20, 21. *and said*, O Lord my God,
23. *and* Elijah *said*, See, thy son liveth.
24. *And* the woman *said* to Elijah, Now
18: 5. *And* Ahab *said* unto Obadiah, Go
7. *and said*, (Art) thou that my lord
8. *And he answered* him, I (am):
9. *And* he *said*, What have I sinned,
15. *And* Elijah *said*, (As) the Lord of hosts
17. *that* Ahab *said* unto him, (Art) thou
18. *And he answered*, I have not troubled
21. *and said*, How long halt ye between
22. *Then said* Elijah unto the people,
24. all the people answered *and said*,
25. *And* Elijah *said* unto the prophets
27. Elijah mocked them, *and said*, Cry
30. *And* Elijah *said* unto all the people,
33(34). *and said*, Fill four barrels with water,
34. *And he said*, Do (it) the second time.
— *And he said*, Do (it) the third time.
36. *and said*, Lord God of Abraham,
39. *and they said*, The Lord, he (is) the God;
40. *And* Elijah *said* unto them, Take
41. *And* Elijah *said* unto Ahab, Get thee
43. *And said* to his servant, Go up
— *and said*, (There is) nothing. *And he said*, Go again seven times.
44. *that he said*, Behold, there ariseth
— *And he said*, Go up, say unto Ahab,
19: 4. *and said*, It is enough; now, O Lord,
5. *and said* unto him, Arise (and) eat.
7. *and said*, Arise (and) eat;
9. *and he said* unto him, What doest
10, 14. *And he said*, I have been very jealous
11. *And he said*, Go forth, and stand
13. *and said*, What doest thou here, Elijah?
15. *And* the Lord *said* unto him, Go,
20. *and said*, Let me, I pray thee, kiss
— *And he said* unto him, Go back
20: 2(3). *and said* unto him, Thus saith
4, 11. the king of Israel answered *and said*,
5. *and said*, Thus speaketh Ben-hadad,
7. *and said*, Mark, I pray you, and see how
8. *And* all the elders...*said* unto him,
9. *Wherefore he said* unto the messengers

1K. 20: 10. *and said*, The gods do so unto me,
12. *that he said* unto his servants, Set
13. unto Ahab king of Israel, *saying*,
14. *And* Ahab *said*, By whom? *And he said*,
— *Then he said*, Who shall order the battle? *And he answered*,
18. *And he said*, Whether they be come
22. *and said* unto him, Go, strengthen
28. *and spake* unto the king of Israel, *and said*,
31. *And* his servants *said* unto him,
32. *and said*, Thy servant Ben-hadad
— *And he said*, (Is) he yet alive?
33. *and they said*, Thy brother Ben-hadad. *Then he said*,
34. *And* (Ben-hadad) *said* unto him,
36. *Then said he* unto him, Because thou
37. *and said*, Smite me, I pray thee.
39. *and he said*, Thy servant went out
— *and said*, Keep this man:
40. *And* the king of Israel *said* unto him,
42. *And he said* unto him, Thus saith
21: 3. *And* Naboth *said* to Ahab, the Lord
4. *for he had said*, I will not give
6. *and said* unto him, Give me
— *and he answered*, I will not give thee
7. *And* Jezebel his wife *said* unto him,
15. *that* Jezebel *said* to Ahab, Arise, take
20. *And* Ahab *said* to Elijah, Hast thou
— *And he answered*, I have found
22: 3, 8, 18, 30. *And* the king of Israel *said* unto
4. *And* he *said* unto Jehoshaphat, of
— *And* Jehoshaphat *said* to the king of
5. *And* Jehoshaphat *said* unto the king
6. *and said* unto them, Shall I go
— *And they said*, Go up;
7. *And* Jehoshaphat *said*, (Is there) not
8. *And* Jehoshaphat *said*, *Let* not the king *say* so.
9. *and said*, Hasten (hither) Micaiah
11. *and he said*, Thus saith the Lord,
14. *And* Micaiah *said*, (As) the Lord liveth, what the Lord *saith* unto me,
15. *And* the king *said* unto him,
— *And he answered* him, Go,
16. *And* the king *said* unto him, How
17. *And he said*, I saw all Israel scattered
— *and* the Lord *said*, These have no master:
19. *And he said*, Hear thou therefore
20. *And* the Lord *said*, Who shall persuade
— *And* one *said* on this manner,
21. *and said*, I will persuade him.
22(21). *And* the Lord *said* unto him, Wherewith? *And he said*, I will go forth,
— *And he said*, Thou shalt persuade
24. *and said*, Which way went the Spirit
25. *And* Micaiah *said*, Behold, thou
26. *And* the king of Israel *said*, Take
28. *And* Micaiah *said*, If thou return
— *And he said*, Hearken, O people,
34. *wherefore he said* unto the driver
2K. 1: 2. *and said* unto them, Go,
5. *he said* unto them, Why are ye
6. *And they said* unto him, There came
— *and said* unto us, Go,
8. *And they answered* him,
— *And he said*, It (is) Elijah
2: 2. *And* Elijah *said* unto Elisha, Tarry
— *And* Elisha *said* (unto him, As) the Lord
3, 5. *and said* unto him, Knowest thou
— *And he said*, Yea, I know (it);
4. *And* Elijah *said* unto him, Elisha, tarry
— *And he said*, (As) the Lord liveth,
5. *And he answered*, Yea, I know
6. *And* Elijah *said* unto him, Tarry,
— *And he said*, (As) the Lord liveth,
9. *And* Elisha *said*, I pray thee, let
10. *And he said*, Thou hast asked a hard
14. smote the waters, *and said*,
15. *And...they said*, The spirit of Elijah
16. *And they said* unto him, Behold
— *And he said*, Ye shall not send.
17. *And*...till he was ashamed, *he said*,
18. *And...he said* unto them, Did I not say
19. *And* the men of the city *said* unto
20. *And he said*, Bring me a new cruse,
21. *and said*, Thus saith the Lord,
23. *and said* unto him, Go up,

2K. 3: 7. *And he said*, I will go up:
8. *And he said*, Which way shall we go up? *And he answered*,
10. *And* the king of Israel *said*, Alas!
11. *But* Jehoshaphat *said*, (Is there) not
— of Israel's servants answered *and said*,
12. *And* Jehoshaphat *said*, The word
13. *And* Elisha *said* unto the king of
— *And* the king of Israel *said* unto him,
14. *And* Elisha *said*, (As) the Lord
16. *And he said*, Thus saith the Lord,
23. *And they said*, This (is) blood:
4: 2. *And* Elisha *said* unto her, What shall
— *And she said*, Thine handmaid
3. *Then he said*, Go, borrow thee vessels
6. *that she said* unto her son, Bring
— *And he said* unto her, (There is) not
7. *And he said*, Go, sell the oil,
9. *And she said* unto her husband, Behold
12. *And he said* to Gehazi his servant,
13. *And he said* unto him, Say now
— *And she answered*, I dwell among
14. *And he said*, What then (is) to be done for her? *And* Gehazi *answered*, Verily
15. *And he said*, Call her.
16. *And he said*, About this season,
— *And she said*, Nay, my lord,
19. *And he said* unto his father, My head,
— *And he said* to a lad, Carry him
22. *and said*, Send me, I pray thee,
23. *And he said*, Wherefore wilt thou go
— *And she said*, (It shall be) well.
24. *and said* to her servant, Drive, and
25. *that he said* to Gehazi his servant,
26. *And she answered*, (It is) well.
27. *And* the man of God *said*, Let her alone;
28. *Then she said*, Did I desire a son
29. *Then he said* to Gehazi, Gird up
30. *And* the mother of the child *said*,
36. he called Gehazi, *and said*,
— *And* when she was come in unto him, *he said*,
38. *and he said* unto his servant, Set on
40. *and said*, O (thou) man of God,
41. *But he said*, Then bring meal.
— *and he said*, Pour out for the people,
42. *And he said*, Give unto the people,
43. *And* his servitor *said*, What,
— *He said again*, Give the people,
5: 3. *And she said* unto her mistress,
5. *And* the king of Syria *said*, Go to,
7. *and said*, (Am) I God, to kill and to
11. went away, *and said*, Behold, I thought,
13. spake unto him, *and said*,
15. stood before him: *and he said*, Behold,
16. *But he said*, (As) the Lord liveth,
17. *And* Naaman *said*, Shall there not
19. *And he said* unto him, Go in peace.
20. *But* Gehazi, the servant of Elisha...*said*,
21. *and said*, (Is) all well?
22. *And he said*, All (is) well.
23. *And* Naaman *said*, Be content,
25. *And* Elisha *said* unto him, Whence
— *And he said*, Thy servant went no whither.
26. *And he said* unto him, Went not
6: 1. *And* the sons of the prophets *said*
2. *And he answered*, Go ye.
3. *And* one *said*, Be content, I pray
— *And he answered*, I will go.
5. he cried, *and said*, Alas, master!
6. *And* the man of God *said*, Where fell
7. *Therefore said he*, Take (it) up
11. *and said* unto them, Will ye not shew
12. *And* one of his servants *said*, None,
13. *And he said*, Go and spy where he (is),
15. *And* his servant *said* unto him, Alas,
16. *And he answered*, Fear not:
17. Elisha prayed, *and said*,
18. *and said*, Smite this people,
19. *And* Elisha *said* unto them, This
20. *that* Elisha *said*, Lord, open the eyes
21. *And* the king of Israel *said* unto Elisha,
22. *And he answered*, Thou shalt not
27. *And he said*, If the Lord do not help
28. *And* the king *said* unto her,
— *And she answered*, This woman
29. *and I said* unto her on the next day,

2 K. 6:31. *Then he said*, God do so and more
33. came down unto him: *and he said*,
7: 1. *Then* Elisha *said*, Hear ye the
2. answered the man of God, *and said*,
— *And he said*, Behold, thou shalt see
3. *and they said* one to another, Why
6. *and they said* one to another, Lo,
9. *Then they said* one to another, We do
12. *and said* unto his servants, I will now
13. one of his servants answered *and said*,
19. answered the man of God, *and said*,
— *And he said*, Behold, thou shalt see
8: 5. *And* Gehazi *said*, My lord, O king,
8. *And* the king *said* unto Hazael, Take
9. *and said*, Thy son Ben-hadad
10. *And* Elisha *said* unto him, Go,
12. *And* Hazael *said*, Why weepeth my lord? *And he answered*, Because
13. *And* Hazael *said*, But what, (is) thy
— *And* Elisha *answered*, The Lord
14. came to his master; *who said* to him,
— *And he answered*, He told me
9: 1. *and said* unto him, Gird up
5. *and he said*, I have an errand to thee,
— *And* Jehu *said*, Unto which of all us? *And he said*, To thee, O captain.
6. *and said* unto him, Thus saith the Lord
11. *and* (one) *said* unto him, (Is) all well?
— *And he said* unto them, Ye know
12. *And they said*, (It is) false;
— *And he said*, Thus and thus spake
13. blew with trumpets, *saying*,
15. *And* Jehu *said*, If it be your minds,
17. *and said*, I see a company. *And* Joram *said*, Take an horseman,
— *and let him say*, (Is it) peace?
18, 19. *and said*, Thus saith the king,
— *And* Jehu *said*, What hast thou to do
19. *And* Jehu *answered*, What hast
21. *And* Joram *said*, Make ready.
22. *that he said*, (Is it) peace, Jehu? *And he answered*, What peace,
23. *and said* to Ahaziah, (There is) treachery,
25. *Then said* (Jehu) to Bidkar
27. *and said*, Smite him also in the chariot.
31. *And...she said*, (Had) Zimri peace,
32. *and said*, Who (is) on my side?
33. *And he said*, Throw her down.
34. *and said*, Go, see now this cursed
36. *And he said*, This (is) the word of the
37. *they shall* not *say*, This (is) Jezebel.
10: 4. *and said*, Behold, two kings stood not
5. will do all that *thou shalt bid* us;
8. *And he said*, Lay ye them in two heaps
9. *and said* to all the people, Ye (be)
13. *and said*, Who (are) ye? *And they answered*,
14. *And he said*, Take them alive.
15. *and said* to him, Is thine heart right,
— *And* Jehonadab *answered*, It is.
16. *And he said*, Come with me,
18. *and said* unto them, Ahab
20. *And* Jehu *said*, Proclaim a solemn
22. *And he said* unto him that (was) over
23. *and said* unto the worshippers of Baal,
24. *and said*, (If) any of the men whom I
25. *that* Jehu *said* to the guard
30. *And* the Lord *said* unto Jehu,
11:12. *and said*, God save the king.
15. *and said* unto them, Have her forth
12: 4(5). *And* Jehoash *said* to the priests,
7(8). *and said* unto them, Why repair ye
13:14. *and said*, O my father, my father,
15. *And* Elisha *said* unto him, Take bow
16. *And he said* to the king of Israel,
17. *And he said*, Open the window eastward.
— *Then* Elisha *said*, Shoot.
— *And he said*, The arrow of the Lord's
18. *And he said*, Take the arrows.
— *And he said* unto the king of Israel,
19. *and said*, Thou shouldest have smitten
17:26. *Wherefore they spake* to the king of
18:19. *And* Rab-shakeh *said* unto them,
22. But if *ye say* unto me, We trust in
— *and hath said* to Judah and Jerusalem,
26. *Then said* Eliakim the son
27. *But* Rab-shakeh *said* unto them,

2 K. 18:28. *saying*, Hear the word of the great king,
19: 3. *And they said* unto him,
6. *And* Isaiah *said* unto them, Thus *shall ye say* to your master,
10. Thus *shall ye speak* to Hezekiah
15. *and said*, O Lord God of Israel,
23. *and hast said*, With the multitude
20: 1. *and said* unto him, Thus saith
7. *And* Isaiah *said*, Take a lump of figs.
8. *And* Hezekiah *said* unto Isaiah,
9. *And* Isaiah *said*, This sign shalt thou
10. *And* Hezekiah *answered*, It is
14. *and said* unto him, What said
— *And* Hezekiah *said*, They are come
15. *And he said*, What have they seen
— *And* Hezekiah *answered*, All (the things)
16. *And* Isaiah *said* unto Hezekiah,
19. *Then said* Hezekiah unto Isaiah,
— *And he said*, (Is it) not (good), if
22: 8. *And* Hilkiah the high priest *said*
9. *and said*, Thy servants have gathered
15. *And she said* unto them,
18. thus *shall ye say* to him,
23:17. *Then he said*, What title (is) that
— *And* the men of the city *told* him,
18. *And he said*, Let him alone; let no
27. *And* the Lord *said*, I will remove
25:24. *and said* unto them, Fear not
1Ch. 10: 4. *Then said* Saul to his armourbearer,
11: 2. *and* the Lord thy God *said* unto thee,
5. *And* the inhabitants of Jebus *said*
6. *And* David *said*, Whosoever smiteth
17. David longed, *and said*,
19. *And said*, My God forbid it me,
12:17. answered *and said* unto them,
13: 2. *And* David *said* unto all the congregation
4. *And* all the congregation *said* that
14:10. *And* the Lord *said* unto him, Go up;
11. *Then* David *said*, God hath broken
12. *And*...David *gave a commandment*, and they
14. *and* God *said* unto him, Go not up
15:12. *And said* unto them, Ye (are) the
16. *And* David *spake* to the chief
16:31. *and let* (men) *say* among the nations,
36. *And* all the people *said*, Amen,
17: 1. *that* David *said* to Nathan
2. *Then* Nathan *said* unto David,
7. therefore thus *shalt thou say* unto my
16. *and said*, Who (am) I, O Lord God,
19. 2. *And* David *said*, I will shew kindness
3. *But* the princes of the children of Ammon *said*
5. *And* the king *said*, Tarry at Jericho
12. *And he said*, If the Syrians be too strong
21: 2. *And* David *said* to Joab and to
3. *And* Joab *answered*, The Lord
8. *And* David *said* unto God, I have
11. to David, *and said* unto him
13. *And* David *said* unto Gad, I am
15. *and said* to the angel that destroyed,
17. *And* David *said* unto God, (Is it)
22. *Then* David *said* to Ornan, Grant
23. *And* Ornan *said* unto David, Take (it) to
24. *And* king David *said* to Ornan, Nay;
27. *And* the Lord *commanded* the angel;
22: 1. *Then* David *said*, This (is) the house
2. *And* David *commanded* to gather
5. *And* David *said*, Solomon my son (is)
7. *And* David *said* to Solomon, My son,
28. 2. *and said*, Hear me, my brethren,
6. *And he said* unto me, Solomon
20. *And* David *said* to Solomon his son,
29: 1. *Furthermore* David the king *said* unto all
10. *and* David *said*, Blessed (be) thou, Lord
20. *And* David *said* to all the congregation,
2Ch. 1: 2. *Then* Solomon *spake* unto all Israel,
7. *and said* unto him, Ask what
8. *And* Solomon *said* unto God, Thou hast
11. *And* God *said* to Solomon, Because
2: 1(1:18). *And* Solomon *determined* to build
11(10). *Then* Huram the king of Tyre *answered*
12(11). Huram *said moreover*, Blessed (be) the
6: 4. *And he said*, Blessed (be) the Lord
8. *But* the Lord *said* to David
14. *And said*, O Lord God of Israel,
7:12. *and said* unto him, I have heard

2Ch. 9: 5. *And she said* to the king,
10: 5. *And he said* unto them, Come again
9. *And he said* unto them, What advice
10. Thus *shalt thou answer* the people
— thus *shalt thou say* unto them,
12: 5. *and said* unto them, Thus saith
6. *and they said*, The Lord (is) righteous.
13: 4. *and said*, Hear me, thou Jeroboam,
14: 4(3). *And commanded* Judah to seek
7(6). *Therefore he said* unto Judah,
11(10). *and said*, Lord, (it is) nothing with
15: 2. *and said* unto him, Hear ye me,
16: 7. *and said* unto him, Because
18: 3. *And* Ahab king of Israel *said* unto
— *And he answered* him, I (am)
4. *And* Jehoshaphat *said* unto the king
5. *and said* unto them, shall we go
— *And they said*, Go up;
6. *But* Jehoshaphat *said*, (Is there) not
7, 29. *And* the king of Israel *said* unto
— *And* Jehoshaphat *said*, *Let* not the king *say* so.
8. *and said*, Fetch quickly Micaiah
10. *and said*, Thus saith the Lord,
13. *And* Micaiah *said*, (As) the Lord liveth, even what my God *saith*,
14. *and* when he was come...the king *said*
— *And he said*, Go ye up, and prosper,
15. *And* the king *said* to him,
16. *Then he said*, I did see all Israel
— *and* the Lord *said*, These have no master;
17. *And* the king of Israel *said* to Jehoshaphat,
18. *Again he said*, Therefore hear the
19. *And* the Lord *said*, Who shall entice
— *And* one *spake* saying after
20. *and said*, I will entice him. *And* the Lord *said* unto him, Wherewith?
21. *And he said*, I will go out, and be
— *And* (the Lord) *said*, Thou shalt entice
23. *and said*, Which way went the Spirit
24. *And* Micaiah *said*, Behold, thou
25. *Then* the king of Israel *said*, Take
27. *And* Micaiah *said*, If thou certainly
— *And he said*, Hearken, all ye people.
33. *therefore he said* to his chariot man,
19: 2. *and said* to king Jehoshaphat,
6. *And said* to the judges, Take heed
20: 6. *And said*, O Lord God of our fathers,
15. *And he said*, Hearken ye, all
20. Jehoshaphat stood *and said*, Hear me,
23: 3. *And he said* unto them, Behold,
11. *and said*, God save the king.
13. Athaliah rent her clothes, *and said*,
14. *and said* unto them, Have her forth
24: 5. *and said* to them, Go out
6. *and said* unto him, Why hast
8. *And at the* king's *commandment* they made (lit. *and* the king *said* and they made)
20. *and said* unto them, Thus saith God,
25: 9. *And* Amaziah *said* to the man of God,
— *And* the man of God *answered*,
15. *which said* unto him, Why hast thou
16. *that* (the king) *said* unto him,
— Then the prophet forbare, *and said*,
26: 18. *and said* unto him, (It appertaineth) not
28: 9. *and said* unto them, Behold,
13. *And said* unto them, Ye shall not
23. *and he said*, Because the gods
29: 5. *And said* unto them, Hear me,
18. *and said*, We have cleansed all
21. *And he commanded* the priests
27. *And* Hezekiah *commanded* to offer
30. *Moreover* Hezekiah the king...*commanded*
31. Then Hezekiah answered *and said*,
31: 4. *Moreover* he *commanded* the people
10. *And* Azariah...*answered* him, *and said*,
11. *Then* Hezekiah *commanded* to prepare
32: 1. *and thought* to win them for himself.
12. *and commanded* Judah and Jerusalem,
24. *and he spake* unto him, and he gave
33: 16. *and commanded* Judah to serve
34: 15. Hilkiah answered *and said*
23. *And she answered* them, Thus
26. so *shall ye say* unto him, Thus
35: 3. *And said* unto the Levites
23. *and* the king *said* to his servants,
25. *and* all the singing men...*spake*

Ezr. 2: 63. *And* the Tirshatha *said* unto them,
4: 2. *and said* unto them, Let us build
3. *But* Zerubbabel,...*said* unto them,
8: 28. *And I said* unto them, Ye (are) holy
9: 6. *And said*, O my God, I am ashamed
10. O our God, what *shall we say* after this?
10: 2. answered *and said* unto Ezra,
10. *and said* unto them, Ye have transgressed,
12. the congregation answered *and said*
Neh. 1: 3. *And they said* unto me, The remnant
5. *And said*, I beseech thee, O Lord
2: 2. *Wherefore* the king *said* unto me,
3. *And said* unto the king, Let the king
4. *Then* the king *said* unto me,
5. *And I said* unto the king, If it
6. *And* the king *said* unto me,
7. *Moreover I said* unto the king,
17. *Then said I* unto them, Ye see
18. *And they said*, Let us rise up and build.
19. *and said*, What (is) this thing that ye do?
20. *and said* unto them, The God of
4: 2(3:34). *And he spake* before his brethren
—(–:—). *and said*, What do these feeble
3(3:35). *and he said*, Even that which they
10(4). *And* Judah *said*, The strength of the
11(5). *And* our adversaries *said*,
12(6). it came to pass, *that...they said* unto
14(8). *and said* unto the nobles, and to the
19(13). *And I said* unto the nobles,
5: 7. *and said* unto them, Ye exact
8. *And I said* unto them, We
9. *Also I said*, It (is) not good that ye do:
12. *Then said they*, We will restore (them),
13. Also I shook my lap, *and said*,
— *And* all the congregation *said*, Amen,
6: 10. *and he said*, Let us meet together
11. *And I said*, Should such a man
7: 3. *And I said* unto them, Let not
65. *And* the Tirshatha *said* unto them,
8: 1. *and they spake* unto Ezra the scribe
9. *And* Nehemiah,...*said* unto all the people,
10. *Then he said* unto them, Go
9: 5. *Then* the Levites, Jeshua, and...*said*,
15. *and promisedst* them that they should
18. *and said*, This (is) thy God that brought
13: 9. *Then I commanded*, and they
11. *and said*, Why is the house of God
17. *and said* unto them, What evil
19. it came to pass, *that...I commanded* that the gates should be shut, *and charged*
21. *and said* unto them, Why lodge ye
22. *And I commanded* the Levites
Est. 1: 13. *Then* the king *said* to the wise men,
16. *And* Memucan *answered* before the
18. *shall* the ladies of Persia and Media *say*
2: 2. *Then said* the king's servants
13. whatsoever *she desired* was given
15. the keeper of the women, *appointed*.
22. *and* Esther *certified* the king
3: 3. *Then...said* unto Mordecai, Why
8. *And* Haman *said* unto king Ahasuerus,
11. *And* the king *said* unto Haman,
4: 10. *Again* Esther *spake* unto Hatach,
13. *Then* Mordecai *commanded* to answer
15. *Then* Esther *bade* (them) return
5: 3. *Then said* the king unto her, What
4. *And* Esther *answered*, If (it seem) good
5. *Then* the king *said*, Cause Haman
6. *And* the king *said* unto Esther
7. Then answered Esther, *and said*,
12. Haman *said moreover*, Yea,
14. *Then said* Zeresh his wife and
6: 1. *and he commanded* to bring the book
3. *And* the king *said*, What honour
— *Then said* the king's servants
4. *And* the king *said*, Who (is) in
5. *And* the king's servants *said* unto him.
— *And* the king *said*, Let him come in,
6. *And* the king *said* unto him,
— *Now* Haman *thought* in his heart,
7. *And* Haman *answered* the king,
10. *Then* the king *said* to Haman,
13. *Then said* his wise men and Zeresh
7: 2. *And* the king *said* again unto Esther
3. Esther the queen answered *and said*,
5. *Then* the king Ahasuerus *answered and said*

Est. 7: 6. *And* Esther *said*, The adversary
8. *Then said* the king, Will he
9. *And* Harbonah, one of the chamberlains, *said*
— *Then* the king *said*, Hang him thereon.
8: 5. *And said*, If it please the king,
7. *Then* the king Ahasuerus *said*
9:12. *And* the king *said* unto Esther
13. *Then said* Esther, If it please
14. *And* the king *commanded* it so
Job 1: 7, 8, 12. *And* the Lord *said* unto Satan,
—, 9. Satan answered the Lord, *and said*,
14. *and said*, The oxen were plowing,
16. *and said*, The fire of God is fallen
17, 18. there came also another, *and said*,
21. *And said*, Naked came I out
2: 2, 3, 6. *And* the Lord *said* unto Satan,
—, 4. Satan answered the Lord, *and said*,
9. *Then said* his wife unto him,
10. *But he said* unto her, Thou
3: 2. And Job spake, *and said*,
4: 1. the Temanite answered *and said*,
6: 1. But Job answered *and said*,
8: 1. answered Bildad the Shuhite, *and said*,
10. Shall not they teach thee, (and) *tell* thee,
9: 1. Then Job answered *and said*,
12. who *will say* unto him, What doest
10: 2. *I will say* unto God, Do not condemn
11: 1. Zophar the Naamathite, *and said*,
4. *For thou hast said*, My doctrine
12: 1. And Job answered *and said*,
15: 1. Eliphaz the Temanite, *and said*,
16: 1. Then Job answered *and said*,
18: 1. answered Bildad the Shuhite, *and said*,
19: 1. Then Job answered *and said*,
28. But *ye should say*, Why persecute
20: 1. Zophar the Naamathite, *and said*,
7. they which have seen him *shall say*,
21: 1. But Job answered *and said*,
14. *Therefore they say* unto God,
28. For *ye say*, Where (is) the house
22: 1. the Temanite answered *and said*,
29. *then thou shalt say*, (There is) lifting up;
23: 1. Then Job answered *and said*,
5. understand what *he would say* unto me.
25: 1. Bildad the Shuhite, *and said*,
26: 1. But Job answered *and said*,
27: 1. Job continued his parable, *and said*,
28:28. *And* unto man he *said*, Behold,
29: 1. Job continued his parable, *and said*,
18. *Then I said*, I shall die
32: 6. of Barachel the Buzite answered *and said*,
13. Lest *ye should say*, We have found
33:24. he is gracious unto him, *and saith*,
27. *and* (if any) *say*, I have sinned,
34: 1. Elihu answered *and said*,
34. *Let* men of understanding *tell* me,
35: 1. Elihu spake moreover, *and said*,
3. For *thou saidst*, What advantage
14. Although *thou sayest* thou shalt
36: 1. Elihu also proceeded, *and said*,
10. *and commandeth* that they return
37: 6. For *he saith* to the snow,
19. Teach us what *we shall say* unto him;
38: 1. out of the whirlwind, *and said*,
11. *And said*, Hitherto shalt thou
35. *and say* unto thee, Here we (are)?
39:25. *He saith* among the trumpets,
40: 1. the Lord answered Job, *and said*,
3. Job answered the Lord, *and said*,
6. unto Job out of the whirlwind, *and said*,
42: 1. Job answered the Lord, *and said*,
7. the Lord *said* to Eliphaz
Ps. 11: 1. how *say ye* to my soul, Flee
12: 5(6). now will I arise, *saith* the Lord;
13: 4(5). Lest mine enemy *say*, I have
18: [title](2). the hand of Saul: *And he said*,
35:10. All my bones *shall say*, Lord,
25. *Let them* not *say* in their hearts,
— *let them* not *say*, We have swallowed
27. *yea, let them say* continually,
40:16(17). *let* such as love thy salvation *say*
41: 5(6). Mine enemies *speak* evil of me,
42: 9(10). *I will say* unto God my rock,
50:12. hungry, *I would* not *tell* thee:
52: [title](2). came and told Saul, *and said* unto
54: [title](2). when the Ziphims came *and said*

Ps. 55: 6(7). *And I said*, Oh that I had wings
58:11(12). *So* that a man *shall say*,
70: 4(5). *let* such as love thy salvation *say*
77:10(11). *And I said*, This (is) my infirmity:
79:10. Wherefore *should* the heathen *say*,
89:19(20). to thy holy one, *and saidst*, I have
90: 3. *and sayest*, Return, ye children of men.
91: 2. *I will say* of the Lord, (He is) my
94: 7. *Yet they say*, The Lord shall not see,
95:10. *and said*, It (is) a people that do err
102:24(25). *I said*, O my God, take me not
106:23. *Therefore he said* that he would
107: 2. *Let* the redeemed of the Lord *say*
25. *For he commandeth*, and raiseth
115: 2. Wherefore *should* the heathen *say*,
118: 2. *Let* Israel now *say*, that his mercy
3. *Let* the house of Aaron now *say*,
4. *Let them* now that fear the Lord *say*,
124: 1. was on our side, now *may* Israel *say*;
126: 2. *then said they* among the heathen,
129: 1. from my youth, *may* Israel now *say*:
139:11. *If I say*, Surely the darkness shall cover
20. *they speak against thee* wickedly,
145: 6. And (men) *shall speak* of the might
11. *They shall speak* of the glory
Pro. 1:11. *they say*, Come with us, let us lay wait
21. in the city *she uttereth* her words,
3:28. *Say* not unto thy neighbour, Go,
4: 4. He taught me also, *and said* unto me,
7:13. (*and*) with an impudent face *said*
20: 9. Who *can say*, I have made my
14. (it is) naught, *saith* the buyer:
22. *Say* not *thou*, I will recompense
23: 7. Eat and drink, *saith he* to thee;
24:12. *If thou sayest*, Behold, we knew
29. *Say* not, I will do so to him as he hath
Ecc. 1:10. *whereof it may be said*, See, this (is) new?
5: 6(5). neither *say thou* before the angel,
7:10. *Say* not *thou*, What is (the cause) that the
8: 4. who *may say* unto him, What doest
17. though a wise (man) *think* to know (it),
12: 1. when *thou shalt say*, I have no pleasure
Isa. 1:11. your sacrifices unto me? *saith* the Lord:
18. reason together, *saith* the Lord:
3:16. *Moreover* the Lord *saith*, Because
6: 5. *Then said I*, Woe (is) me!
7. *and said*, Lo, this hath touched
8. *Then said I*, Here (am) I; send me.
9. *And he said*, Go, and tell this people,
11. *Then said I*, Lord, how long? *And he answered*, Until the cities
7. 3. *Then said* the Lord unto Isaiah,
12. *But* Ahaz *said*, I will not ask,
13. *And he said*, Hear ye now, O house of
8: 1. *Moreover* the Lord *said* unto me,
3. *Then said* the Lord to me, Call
12. *Say ye* not, A confederacy, to all (them to) whom this people *shall say*,
19. when *they shall say* unto you, Seek
20. if *they speak* not according to this
10: 8. For *he saith*, (Are) not my princes
14:10. All they shall speak *and say* unto
19:11. how *say ye* unto Pharaoh, I (am) the son
20: 3. *And* the Lord *said*, Like as my servant
21: 9. And he answered *and said*,
23:12. *And he said*, Thou shalt no more
24:16. *But I said*, My leanness,
29:13. *Wherefore* the Lord *said*, Forasmuch
15. *and they say*, Who seeth us?
16. for *shall* the work *say* of him that
30:16. *But ye said*, No; for we will flee
22. *thou shalt say* unto it, Get thee hence.
33:10. Now will I rise, *saith* the Lord;
24. And the inhabitant *shall* not *say*, I am
36: 4. *And* Rabshakeh *said* unto them,
7. But if *thou say* to me, We trust
— *and said* to Judah and to Jerusalem,
11. *Then said* Eliakim and Shebna
12. *But* Rabshakeh *said*, Hath
13. *and said*, Hear ye the words of the
37: 3. *And they said* unto him, Thus saith
6. *And* Isaiah *said* unto them, Thus *shall ye say*
10. Thus *shall ye speak* to Hezekiah king of
24. *and hast said*, By the multitude of
38: 1. *and said* unto him, Thus saith
3. *And said*, Remember now, O Lord,

Isa. 38.21. *For* Isaiah *had said*, Let them take
22. Hezekiah *also had said*, What
39: 3. *and said* unto him, What said
— *And* Hezekiah *said*, They are come from
4. *Then said he*, What have they seen
— *And* Hezekiah *answered*, All that
5. *Then said* Isaiah to Hezekiah,
8. *Then said* Hezekiah to Isaiah,
— *He said moreover*, For there shall be
40: 1. comfort ye my people, *saith* your God.
25. or shall I be equal? *saith* the Holy
27. *Why sayest thou*, O Jacob, and speakest
41: 6. and (every one) *said* to his brother,
9. *and said* unto thee, Thou (art) my
21. Produce your cause, *saith* the Lord;
— strong (reasons), *saith* the King of Jacob.
26. *that we may say*, (He is) righteous?
43: 6. *I will say* to the north, Give up;
9. let them hear, *and say*, (It is) truth.
44: 5. One *shall say*, I (am) the Lord's;
16. *and saith*, Aha, I am warm,
17. *and saith*, Deliver me; for thou (art)
20. deliver his soul, nor *say*,
45: 9. *Shall* the clay *say* to him
47: 7. *And thou saidst*, I shall be
10. *and thou hast said* in thine heart,
48: 5. lest *thou shouldest say*, Mine idol
7. lest *thou shouldest say*, Behold, I
49: 3. *And said* unto me, Thou (art) my servant,
6. *And he said*, It is a light thing
14. *But* Zion *said*, The Lord hath forsaken
20. *shall say* again in thine ears,
56: 3. Neither *let* the son of the stranger...*speak*,
saying, The Lord,
— neither *let* the eunuch *say*, Behold,
58: 9. *and he shall say*, Here I (am).
63: 8. *For he said*, Surely they (are) my
66: 9. not cause to bring forth? *saith* the Lord:
Jer. 1: 6. *Then said I*, Ah, Lord God!
7. *But* the Lord *said* unto me, *Say* not,
9. *And* the Lord *said* unto me, Behold,
11. *And I said*, I see a rod of an almond tree.
12. *Then said* the Lord unto me, Thou
13. *And I said*, I see a seething pot;
14. *Then* the Lord *said* unto me, Out
2:20. *and thou saidst*, I will not transgress;
23. How *canst thou say*, I am not polluted,
25. *but thou saidst*, There is no hope:
27. time of their trouble *they will say*,
35. *Yet thou sayest*, Because I am
3: 6. The Lord *said also* unto me
7. *And I said* after she had done all
11. *And* the Lord *said* unto me, The
16. *they shall say* no more, The ark of the
19. *and I said*, Thou shalt call me, My father;
4:10. *Then said I*, Ah, Lord God!
5. 2. though *they say*, The Lord liveth;
12. belied the Lord, *and said*, (It is) not
19. shall come to pass, when *ye shall say*,
6:16. *But they said*, We will not walk
17. *But they said*, We will not hearken.
8: 8. How *do ye say*, We (are) wise,
9:13(12). *And* the Lord *saith*, Because
11: 5. Then answered I, *and said*, So be it,
6. *Then* the Lord *said* unto me, Proclaim
9. *And* the Lord *said* unto me,
13: 6. *that* the Lord *said* unto me, Arise,
21. What *wilt thou say* when he shall
22. if *thou say* in thine heart, Wherefore
14:11. *Then said* the Lord unto me,
13. *Then said I*, Ah, Lord God!
14. *Then* the Lord *said* unto me,
15: 1. *Then said* the Lord unto me,
2. if *they say* unto thee, Whither
16:19. *and shall say*, Surely our fathers have
18:18. *Then said they*, Come, and let us devise
19:14. *and said* to all the people,
20: 3. *Then said* Jeremiah unto him,
21: 3. *Then said* Jeremiah unto them, Thus *shall*
ye say to Zedekiah:
8. unto this people *thou shalt say*,
23: 7. that *they shall* no more *say*, The Lord
34. the people, that *shall say*, The burden
35. Thus *shall ye say* every one to his
37. Thus *shalt thou say* to the prophet,
38. But since *ye say*, The burden of
-- *Ye shall* not *say*, The burden of the

Jer. 24: 3. *Then said* the Lord unto me, What
— *And I said*, Figs; the good figs, very
26:11. *Then spake* the priests and the
12. *Then spake* Jeremiah unto all the princes
16. *Then said* the princes and all the
17. *and spake* to all the assembly of the
18. *and spake* to all the people of Judah,
27: 4. Thus *shall ye say* unto your masters;
28: 5. *Then* the prophet Jeremiah *said*
6. *Even* the prophet Jeremiah *said*,
11. *And* Hananiah *spake* in the presence
15. *Then said* the prophet Jeremiah
29:24. *shalt thou* also *speak* to Shemaiah
31:23. As yet *they shall use* this speech
29. In those days *they shall say* no more,
32: 6. *And* Jeremiah *said*, The word of the
8. *and said* unto me, Buy my field,
35: 5. *and I said* unto them, Drink ye wine.
6. *But they said*, We will drink no wine:
11. *that we said*, Come, and let us go to
36:15. *And they said* unto him, Sit down
16. *and said* unto Baruch, We will surely
18. *Then* Baruch *answered* them,
19. *Then said* the princes unto Baruch,
29. *thou shalt say* to Jehoiakim
37: 7. Thus *shall ye say* to the king of Judah,
14. *Then said* Jeremiah, (It is) false;
17. *and said*, Is there (any) word from the Lord
And Jeremiah *said*, There is: *for, said he*,
18. *Moreover* Jeremiah *said* unto king
38: 4. Therefore the princes *said* unto
5. *Then* Zedekiah the king *said*, Behold,
12. *And* Ebed-melech the Ethiopian *said*
14. *and* the king *said* unto Jeremiah,
15. *Then* Jeremiah *said* unto Zedekiah,
17. *Then said* Jeremiah unto Zedekiah,
19. *And* Zedekiah the king *said* unto
20. *But* Jeremiah *said*, They shall not
24. *Then said* Zedekiah unto Jeremiah,
40: 2. took Jeremiah, *and said* unto him,
14. *And said* unto him, Dost thou
16: *But* Gedaliah the son of Ahikam *said*
41: 6. *he said* unto them, Come to Gedaliah
8. *that said* unto Ishmael, Slay us not:
42: 2. *And said* unto Jeremiah the prophet,
4. *Then* Jeremiah the prophet *said*
9. *And said* unto them, Thus saith
20. all that the Lord our God *shall say*,
43: 2. *Then spake* Azariah the son of
44:20. *Then* Jeremiah *said* unto all the people,
24. *Moreover* Jeremiah *said* unto all
45: 4. Thus *shalt thou say* unto him,
46: 8. *and he saith*, I will go up, (and)
16. *and they said*, Arise, and let us go
48:14. How *say ye*, We (are) mighty
51:35. *shall* the inhabitant of Zion *say*;
— of Chaldea, *shall* Jerusalem *say*.
61. *And* Jeremiah *said* to Seraiah,
Lam. 2:12. *They say* to their mothers, Where
15. the city *that* (men) *call* The perfection
3:18. *And I said*, My strength and my hope
Eze. 2: 1, 3. *And he said* unto me, Son of man,
3: 1, 10. *Moreover he said* unto me, Son of man
3, 4. *And he said* unto me, Son of man,
22. *and he said* unto me, Arise, go forth
24. spake with me, *and said* unto me, Go,
4:13. *And* the Lord *said*, Even thus shall
14. *Then said I*, Ah Lord God!
15. *Then he said* unto me, Lo, I have
16. *Moreover he said* unto me, Son of man,
8: 5, 8. *Then said he* unto me, Son of man,
6. *He said furthermore* unto me,
9. *And he said* unto me, Go in,
12. *Then said he* unto me, Son of man,
13. *He said also* unto me, Turn thee
15. *Then said he* unto me, Hast thou
17. *Then he said* unto me, Hast thou seen
9: 4. *And* the Lord *said* unto him, Go
7. *And he said* unto them, Defile
8. cried, *and said*, Ah Lord God!
9. *Then said he* unto me,
10: 2. *And he spake* unto the man clothed with
linen, *and said*, Go in between
11: 2. *Then said* he unto me, Son of man,
5. upon me, *and said* unto me, Speak;
13. *and said*, Ah Lord God! wilt thou make
13:15. *and will say* unto you, The wall (is) no

Eze.16: 6. in thine own blood, *I said* unto thee
— *yea, I said* unto thee (when thou wast) in
20: 7. *Then said I* unto them, Cast ye away
8. *then I said*, I will pour out my fury
13, 21. *then I said*, I would pour out my fury
18. *But I said* unto their children in the
29. *Then I said* unto them, What (is) the
49(21:5). *Then said I*, Ah Lord God!
21: 7(12). when they *say* unto thee, Wherefore
23:36. The Lord *said moreover* unto me;
43. *Then said I* unto (her that was) old
24:19. *And* the people *said* unto me, Wilt
20. *Then I answered* them, The word
28: 2. *and thou hast said*, I (am) a God, I sit
9. *Wilt thou* yet *say* before him that slayeth
33:27. *Say thou* thus unto them, Thus saith
37: 3. *And he said* unto me, Son of man,
— *And I answered*, O Lord God, thou
4. *Again he said* unto me, Prophesy
9. *Then said* he unto me, Prophesy
11. *Then he said* unto me, Son of man, these
18. of thy people *shall speak* unto thee,
38:13. *shall say* unto thee, Art thou come to
41: 4. *and he said* unto me, This (is) the most
42:13. *Then said he* unto me, The north
43: 7, 18. *And he said* unto me, Son of man,
44: 2. *Then said* the Lord unto me; This gate
5. *And* the Lord *said* unto me, Son of
46:20. *Then said he* unto me, This (is) the
24. *Then said he* unto me, These (are) the
47: 6. *And he said* unto me, Son of man,
8. *Then said he* unto me, These waters
Dan 1: 3. *And* the king *spake* unto Ashpenaz
10. *And* the prince of the eunuchs *said*
11. *Then said* Daniel to Melzar,
2: 2. *Then* the king *commanded* to call
3. *And* the king *said* unto them, I have
8:13. *and* another saint *said* unto that certain
14. *And he said* unto me, Unto
16. which called, *and said*, Gabriel,
17. *but he said* unto me, Understand,
19. *And he said*, Behold, I will make thee
9: 4. *and said*, O Lord, the great and dreadful
22. *and said*, O Daniel, I am now come
10:11. *And he said* unto me, O Daniel,
12. *Then said he* unto me, Fear not, Daniel:
16. *and said* unto him that stood before me,
19. *And said*, O man greatly beloved,
— strengthened, *and said*, Let my lord speak;
20. *Then said he*, Knowest thou wherefore
12: 6. *And* (one) *said* to the man clothed in
8. *then said I*, O my Lord, what
9. *And he said*, Go thy way, Daniel:
Hos. 1: 2. *And* the Lord *said* to Hosea, Go, take
4. *And* the Lord *said* unto him, Call
6. *And* (God) *said* unto him, Call her name
9. *Then said* (God), Call his name Lo-ammi:
2:23(25). and *they shall say*, (Thou art) my
3: 1. *Then said* the Lord unto me, Go yet,
3. *And I said* unto her, Thou shalt abide
7: 2. *they consider* not in their hearts
10: 3. For now *they shall say*, We have no king,
12: 8(9). *And* Ephraim *said*, Yet I am become
14: 3(4). neither *will we say* any more to the
Joel 2:17. *and let them say*, Spare thy people,
— wherefore *should they say* among the
19. will answer *and say* unto his people,
3:10(4:10). *let* the weak *say*, I (am) strong.
Am. 1: 2. *And he said*, The Lord will roar
5:16. *they shall say* in all the highways,
7: 2. *then I said*, O Lord God, forgive,
5. *Then said I*, O Lord God, cease,
8. *And* the Lord *said* unto me,
— *And I said*, A plumbline. *Then said* the
12. *Also* Amaziah *said* unto Amos,
14. *and said* to Amaziah, I (was) no
15. *and* the Lord *said* unto me, Go, prophesy
8: 2. *And he said*, Amos, what seest thou? *And I said*,
— *Then said* the Lord unto me, The end
9: 1. *and he said*, Smite the lintel of
Jon. 1: 6. *and said* unto him, What meanest thou,
7. *And they said* every one to his fellow,
8. *Then said they* unto him, Tell us,
9. And *he said* unto them, I (am) an
10. the men exceedingly afraid, *and said*
11. *Then said they* unto him, What shall
Jon. 1:12. *And he said* unto them, Take me up,
14. *and said*, We beseech thee, O Lord,
2: 2(3). *And said*, I cried by reason of mine
10(11). *And* the Lord *spake* unto the fish,
3: 4. he cried, *and said*, Yet forty days,
7. *and published* through Nineveh (marg. *said*)
4: 2. *and said*, I pray thee, O Lord, (was) not
4. *Then said* the Lord, Doest thou well
8. *and said*, (It is) better for me to die
9. *And* God *said* to Jonah, Doest thou well
— *And he said*, I do well to be angry,
10. *Then said* the Lord,
Mic. 3: 1. *And I said*, Hear, I pray you, O heads
Hab. 2: 2. the Lord answered me, *and said*, Write
6. a taunting proverb against him, *and say*,
Hag. 1:13. *Then spake* Haggai the Lord's messenger
2:12. the priests answered *and said*, No.
13. *Then said* Haggai, If (one that is) unclean
— the priests answered *and said*, It shall be
14. *Then* answered Haggai, *and said*,
Zec. 1: 6. they returned *and said*, Like as the Lord
9. *Then said I*, O my lord, what (are) these? *And* the angel that talked with me *said*
10. *and said*, These (are they) whom the
11. *and said*, We have walked to and fro
12. the angel of the Lord answered *and said*,
14. *said* unto me, Cry thou, saying, Thus
19(2:2). *And I said* unto the angel that talked
—(-:-). *And he answered* me, These (are)
21(2:4). *Then said I*, What come these to do? *And he spake*,
2: 2(6). *Then said I*, Whither goest thou? *And he said*
4(8). *And said* unto him, Run, speak to
3: 2. *And* the Lord *said* unto Satan, The Lord
4. he answered *and spake* unto those
— *And* unto him he *said*, Behold, I have
5. *And I said*, Let them set a fair mitre
4: 2. *And said* unto me, What seest thou? *And I said*,
4. So I answered *and spake* to the angel
5. answered *and said* unto me, Knowest thou not what these be? *And I said*, No, my lord.
6. Then he answered *and spake* unto me,
11. Then answered I, *and said* unto him,
12. I answered again, *and said* unto him,
13. *And he answered* me and said,
— what these (be)? *And I said*, No, my
14. *Then said he*, These (are) the two
5: 2. *And he said* unto me, What seest thou? *And I answered*, I see
3. *Then said he* unto me, This (is) the curse
5. *and said* unto me, Lift up now thine
6. *And I said*, What (is) it? *And he said*,
— *He said moreover*, This (is) their
8. *And he said*, This (is) wickedness.
10. *Then said I* to the angel that talked
11. *And he said* unto me, To build
6: 4. Then I answered *and said* unto
5. the angel answered *and said* unto me,
7. *and he said*, Get you hence, walk to
11: 5. that sell them *say*, Blessed (be) the Lord;
9. *Then said I*, I will not feed you:
12. *And I said* unto them,
13. *And* the Lord *said* unto me, Cast it
15. *And* the Lord *said* unto me, Take
13: 9. and *they shall say*, The Lord (is) my
Mal. 1: 4. Whereas Edom *saith*, We are
5. *ye shall say*, The Lord will be magnified

KAL.—*Participle*. Poël.

Gen32: 9(10). the Lord *which saidst* unto me,
37:17. for I heard *them say*,
Ex. 2:14. *intendest* thou to kill me,
5:16. *they say* to us, Make brick:
17. therefore ye *say*, Let us go
33:12. See, thou *sayest* unto me,
Deu33: 9. *Who said* unto his father
1Sa.11:12. Who (is) *he that said*,
2Sa.21: 4. What ye *shall say*, (that) will I do
1K. 3:22. And this *said*, No; but the dead
23. The one *saith*, This (is) my son
— and the other *saith*, Nay;
26. slay it. But the other *said*,
5: 5(19). I *purpose* to build an house (marg. *say*)

1K. 18:11,14. now thou *sayest*, Go, tell thy lord,
22:20. and another *said* on that manner.
2Ch 13: 8. now ye *think* to withstand
18:19. one spake *saying* after this manner, and another *saying* after that manner.
20:21. *and to say*, Praise the Lord;
28:10. now ye *purpose* to keep
13. ye *intend* to add (more) to our sins
Neh. 5: 2. For there were *that said*,
3. also there were *that said*,
4. There were also *that said*,
12. so will we do as thou *sayest*.
6: 6. among the heathen, and Gashmu *saith*
8. are no such things done as thou *sayest*,
19. *they reported* his good deeds before me,
Job 9: 7. *Which commandeth* the sun,
22:17. *Which said* unto God, Depart
Ps. 3: 2(3). *which say* of my soul,
4: 6(7). (There be) many *that say*,
29: 9. *doth* every one *speak* of (his) glory.
40:15(16). *that say* unto me, Aha, aha.
45: 1(2). I *speak* of the things
70: 3(4). a reward of their shame *that say*,
122: 1. I was glad *when they said*
137: 7. *who said*, Rase (it), rase (it),
Pro. 24:24. *He that saith* unto the wicked,
28:24. his father or his mother, *and saith*,
Isa. 5:19. *That say*, Let him make speed,
20. *that call* evil good, (marg. *say* concerning)
6: 8. I heard the voice of the Lord, *saying*,
40: 6. The voice *said*, Cry.
41: 7. *saying*, It (is) ready for the sodering:
13. *saying* unto thee, Fear not;
42:17. *that say* to the molten images,
22. for a spoil, and none *saith*, Restore.
44:26. *that saith* to Jerusalem,
27. *That saith* to the deep,
28. *That saith* of Cyrus, (He is) my
45:10. Woe unto him *that saith*
46:10. *saying*, My counsel shall stand,
47: 8. *that sayest* in thine heart,
52: 7. *that saith* unto Zion,
65: 5. *Which say*, Stand by thyself,
Jer. 2:27. *Saying* to a stock, Thou (art) my
14:13. the prophets *say* unto them,
15. I sent them not, yet *they say*,
17:15. Behold, *they say* unto me,
21:13. *which say*, Who shall come
22:14. *That saith*, I will build
23:17. *They say* still unto them
27: 9. *which speak* unto you, saying,
14. *that speak* unto you, saying
32:36. concerning this city, whereof ye *say*,
43. whereof ye *say*, (It is) desolate
33:10. which ye *say* (shall be) desolate
11. the voice of *them that shall say*,
38:22. *shall say*, Thy friends have set
42:13. But if ye *say*, We will not
43: 2. the proud men, *saying* unto Jeremiah,
44:26. *saying*, The Lord God liveth.
Eze. 8:12. for *they say*, The Lord seeth us not;
11: 3. *Which say*, (It is) not near;
12:27. the house of Israel *say*,
13: 6. *saying*, The Lord saith: and the Lord
7. *whereas ye say*, The Lord
20:32. that ye *say*, We will be as the heathen,
49(21:5). they *say* of me, Doth he not
22:28. *saying*, Thus saith the Lord God,
33:24. *speak*, saying, Abraham was one,
36:13. Because *they say* unto you,
37:11. *they say*, Our bones are dried,
Hos 13: 2. they *say* of them, Let the men
Am. 4: 1. *which say* to their masters, Bring,
6:13. *which say*, Have we not taken
7:16. Thou *sayest*, Prophesy not against
9:10. *which say*, The evil shall not overtake
Oba. 3. *that saith* in his heart, Who shall bring
Mic. 4:11. *that say*, Let her be defiled,
6: 1. Hear ye now what the Lord *saith*;
7:10. *which said* unto me, Where is
Hab 2:19. Woe unto him *that saith* to the wood,
Zep. 1:12. *that say* in their heart, The Lord
2:15. *that said* in her heart, I (am),

KAL.—*Participle.* Paül.

Mic. 2: 7. O (thou that art) *named* the house of

* NIPHAL.—*Preterite.* *

Dan 8:26. which *was told* (is) true:

NIPHAL.—*Infinitive.*

Job 34:31. Surely it is meet *to be said* unto God,

NIPHAL.—*Future.*

Gen10: 9. wherefore *it is said*, Even as Nimrod
22:14. as *it is said* (to) this day, In the mount
32:28(29). Thy name *shall be called* no more
Nu. 21:14. Wherefore *it is said* in the book of
23:23. *it shall be said* of Jacob and of Israel,
Jos. 2: 2. *And it was told* the king of Jericho,
Ps. 87: 5. And of Zion *it shall be said*, This
Isa. 4: 3. *shall be called* holy, (even) every one
19:18. one *shall be called*, The city of destruction
32: 5. nor the churl *said* (to be) bountiful.
61: 6. (men) *shall call* you the Ministers of our God: (lit. *it shall be said* to you)
62: 4. Thou *shalt* no more *be termed* Forsaken; neither *shall* thy land any more *be termed*
Jer. 4:11. At that time *shall it be said*
7:32. *it shall* no more *be called* Tophet,
16:14. *it shall* no more *be said*, The Lord
Eze. 13:12. *shall it* not *be said* unto you, Where (is)
Hos 1:10(2:1). where *it was said* unto them, Ye (are) not my people, (there) *it shall be said*
Zep. 3:16. In that day *it shall be said* to

* HIPHIL.—*Preterite.* *

Deu 26:17. *Thou hast avouched* the Lord
18. the Lord *hath avouched thee*

* HITHPAEL.—*Future.* *

Ps. 94: 4. workers of iniquity *boast themselves?*

אֲמַר *ămar*, Ch. 560

* P'AL.—*Preterite.* *

Ezr. 5: 4. Then *said we* unto them after this
9. (and) *said* unto them thus, Who
15. *And said* unto him, Take these
Dan 2:12. *and commanded* to destroy all the wise
24,25. and *said* thus unto him;
46. *commanded* that they should offer
3:13. in (his) rage and fury *commanded*
20. And *he commanded* the most mighty
4: 8(5). and before him *I told* the dream,
26(23). whereas *they commanded*
5: 2. *commanded* to bring the golden
10. the queen spake *and said*,
29. Then *commanded* Belshazzar,
6:16(17). Then the king *commanded*,
23(24). and *commanded* that they should take
24(25). *And* the king *commanded*,
7: 1. (and) *told* the sum of the matters.
16. *So he told* me, and made me know
23. Thus *he said*, The fourth beast

P'AL.—*Infinitive.*

Ezr. 5:11. they returned us answer, *saying*,
Dan 2: 9. and corrupt words *to speak* before me,

P'AL.—*Imperative.*

Dan 2: 4. *tell* thy servants the dream, and we
9. therefore *tell* me the dream,
4: 9(6). *tell* me the visions of my dream
18(15). *declare* the interpretation

P'AL.—*Future.*

Jer. 10:11. Thus *shall ye say* unto them,
Dan 2: 7. *Let* the king *tell* his servants the dream,
36. and *we will tell* the interpretation
3:29. which *speak* any thing amiss
4:35(32). *or say* unto him, What doest

P'AL.—*Participle.*

Ezr. 5: 3. and *said* thus unto them, Who hath
Dan 2: 5,8,26. The king answered *and said*
7. They answered again *and said*,
10. answered before the king, *and said*,
15. He answered *and said* to Arioch
20. Daniel answered *and said*, Blessed
27. answered in the presence of the king, *and said*,
47. The king answered unto Daniel, *and said*,

Dan. 3: 4. To you *it is commanded*, O people, (marg *they command*)
9. They spake *and said* to the king
14. Nebuchadnezzar spake *and said*
16. answered *and said* to the king,
19. he spake, *and commanded* that they should
24. rose up in haste, (and) spake, *and said*
— They answered *and said* unto the king,
25. He answered *and said*, Lo, I see four
26. (and) spake, *and said*, Shadrach,
28. Nebuchadnezzar spake, *and said*,
4: 7(4). and *I told* the dream before them;
14(11). He cried aloud, and *said* thus,
19(16), 30(27). The king spake, *and said*,
—(—). Belteshazzar answered *and said*,
23(20). *and saying*, Hew the tree down,
31(28). Nebuchadnezzar, to thee it is *spoken*, (lit. to thee (they are) *speaking*)
5: 7. the king spake, *and said* to the wise (men)
13. the king spake *and said* unto Daniel,
17. Daniel answered *and said* before the king,
6: 5(6). Then *said* these men,
6(7). to the king, and *said* thus unto him,
12(13). Then they came near, *and spake*
—(—). The king answered *and said*,
13(14). Then answered they *and said* before
15(16). *and said* unto the king,
16(17). the king spake *and said* unto Daniel,
20(21). the king spake *and said* to Daniel,
7: 2. Daniel spake *and said*, I saw in my
5. and *they said* thus unto it, Arise,

---

561 אֵמֶר [*ēh'-mer*] m.

Gen49:21. let loose: he giveth goodly *words*,
Nu. 24: 4, 16. which heard *the words of* God,
Deu32: 1. hear, O earth, *the words of* my mouth.
Jos. 24:27. it hath heard all *the words of* the Lord
Jud. 5:29. she returned *answer* to herself, (marg. *her words*)
Job 6:10. not concealed *the words of* the Holy One.
25. How forcible are right *words!*
26. *the speeches of* one that is desperate,
8: 2. (how long shall) *the words of* thy mouth
20:29. the heritage *appointed unto him* by God. (marg. *of his decree*)
22:22. lay up *his words* in thine heart.
23:12. I have esteemed *the words of* his mouth
32:12. that answered *his words:*
14. neither (lit. *and* not) will I answer him *with your speeches.*
33: 3. *My words* (shall be of) the uprightness
34:37. multiplieth *his words* against God.
Ps. 5: 1(2). Give ear to *my words*, O Lord,
19:14(15). Let *the words of* my mouth, and
54: 2(4). give ear *to the words of* my mouth.
78: 1. incline your ears *to the words of* my
107:11. rebelled against *the words of* God,
138: 4. when they hear *the words of* thy mouth.
141: 6. they shall hear *my words*;
Pro. 1: 2. to perceive *the words of* understanding;
21. in the city she uttereth *her words*,
2: 1. if thou wilt receive *my words*,
16. stranger (which) flattereth with *her words*;
4: 5. neither decline *from the words of*
10. O my son, and receive *my sayings*;
20. incline thine ear *unto my sayings.*
5: 7. depart not *from the words of* my
6: 2. Thou art snared *with the words of* thy mouth, thou art taken *with the words of*
7: 1. My son, keep *my words*,
5. (which) flattereth with *her words.*
24. attend *to the words of* my mouth.
8: 8. All *the words of* my mouth (are) in
15:26. (words) of the pure (are) pleasant *words.*
16:24. Pleasant *words* (are as) an honeycomb,
17:27. hath knowledge spareth *his words:*
19: 7. he pursueth (them with) *words*,
27. to err *from the words of* knowledge.
22:21. the certainty of *the words of* truth;
— that thou mightest answer the *words* of
23:12. thine ears *to the words of* knowledge.
Isa. 32: 7. to destroy the poor with lying *words*,
41:26. none that heareth *your words.*
Hos. 6: 5. I have slain them *by the words of*

אֹמֶר *ōh'-mer*, m. 562

Job 22:28. Thou shalt also decree *a thing*,
Ps. 19: 2(3). Day unto day uttereth *speech*,
3(4). (There is) no *speech* nor language, (where)
68:11(12). The Lord gave *the word:* great
77: 8(9). doth (his) *promise* fail for evermore?
Hab. 3: 9. the oaths of the tribes, (even thy) *word.*

אֶמְרָה [*em-rāh'*] f. 565

Lam. 2:17. he hath fulfilled *his word*

אִמְרָה [*im-rāh'*] f. 565

Gen. 4:23. of Lamech, hearken unto *my speech:*
Deu32: 2. *my speech* shall distil as the dew,
33: 9. they have observed *thy word*,
2Sa 22:31. *the word of* the Lord (is) tried:
Ps. 12: 6(7). *The words of* the Lord (are) pure *words*:
17: 6. (hear) *my speech.*
18:30(31). *the word of* the Lord is tried:
105:19. *the word of* the Lord tried him.
119:11. *Thy word* have I hid in mine heart,
38. Stablish *thy word* unto thy servant,
41. salvation, *according to thy word.*
50. for *thy word* hath quickened me.
58. merciful unto me *according to thy word.*
67. but now have I kept *thy word.*
76. *according to thy word* unto thy servant.
82. Mine eyes fail *for thy word*,
103. How sweet are *thy words* unto my
116. Uphold me *according unto thy word*,
123. *and for the word of* thy righteousness.
133. Order my steps *in thy word:*
140. *Thy word* (is) very pure: therefore
148. that I might meditate *in thy word.*
154. quicken me *according to thy word.*
158. because they kept not *thy word.*
162. I rejoice at *thy word*, as one
170. deliver me *according to thy word.*
172. My tongue shall speak of *thy word.*
138: 2. thou hast magnified *thy word* above
147:15. sendeth forth *his commandment*
Pro 30: 5. Every *word of* God (is) pure:
Isa. 5:24. despised *the word of* the Holy One
28:23. hearken, and hear *my speech.*
29: 4. *thy speech* shall be low out of
— *thy speech* shall whisper out
32: 9. give ear unto *my speech.*

אִמְּרִין *im-m'reen'*, Ch. pl 563

Ezr. 6: 9. both young bullocks, and rams, *and lambs*,
17. four hundred *lambs;*
7:17. *lambs*, with their meat offerings

אֶמֶשׁ *eh'-mesh*, adv. 570

Gen19:34. I lay *yesternight* with my father:
31:29. of your father spake unto me *yesternight*,
42. rebuked (thee) *yesternight.*
2K. 9:26. I have seen *yesterday* the blood of
Job 30: 3. *in former time* desolate and waste. (marg, *yesternight*)

אֱמֶת *ĕmeth*, f. 571

Gen24:27. of his mercy *and his truth:*
48. led me in the *right* way
49. deal kindly *and truly* with my master,
32:10(11). and of all *the truth*, which thou hast
42:16. *whether* (there be any) *truth* in you:
47:29. deal kindly *and truly* with me;
Ex. 18:21. such as fear God, men of *truth*,
34: 6. abundant in goodness *and truth*,
Deu13:14(15). behold, (if it be) *truth*,
17: 4. behold, (it be) *true*, (lit. *truth*)
22:20. But if this thing be *true*, (lit. *truth*)

Jos. 2:12. give me a *true* token: (lit. of *truth*)
14. deal kindly *and truly* with thee.
24:14. serve him in sincerity *and in truth:*
Jud. 9:15. If *in truth* ye anoint me king
16. if ye have done *truly*
19. If ye then have dealt *truly*
1Sa 12:24. serve him *in truth* with all
2Sa. 2: 6. shew kindness *and truth* unto you:
7:28. thy words be *true*, (lit. *truth*)
15:20. mercy *and truth* (be) with thee.
1K. 2: 4. to walk before me *in truth*
3: 6. he walked before thee *in truth*,
10: 6. It was a *true* report (lit. *truth*)
17:24. of the Lord in thy mouth (is) *truth*.
22:16. nothing but (that which is) *true*
2K. 20: 3. I have walked before thee *in truth*
19. if peace *and truth* be in my days?
2Ch. 9: 5. (It was) a *true* report which I heard
15: 3. without the *true* God, (lit. of *truth*)
18:15. say nothing but *the truth*
31:20. (that which was) good and right *and truth*
32: 1. After these things, *and the establishment*
Neh. 7: 2. he (was) a *faithful* man, (lit. a man of *truth*)
9:13. and *true* laws, (marg. of *truth*)
33. thou hast done *right*, but we have done
Est. 9:30. words of peace *and truth*,
Ps. 15: 2. speaketh *the truth* in his heart.
19: 9(10). *true* (and) righteous (marg. *truth*)
25: 5. Lead me *in thy truth*,
10. mercy *and truth* unto such
26: 3. I have walked *in thy truth*.
30: 9(10). shall it declare *thy truth?*
31: 5(6). O Lord God of *truth*.
40:10(11). *and thy truth* from the great
11(12). *and thy truth* continually preserve
43: 3. O send out thy light *and thy truth:*
45: 4(5). because of *truth* and meekness
51: 6(8). thou desirest *truth* in the inward parts:
54: 5(7). cut them off *in thy truth*.
57: 3(4). send forth his mercy *and his truth*.
10(11). and *thy truth* unto the clouds.
61: 7(8). O prepare mercy *and truth*,
69:13(14). *in the truth of* thy salvation.
71:22. with the psaltery, (even) *thy truth*,
85:10(11). Mercy *and truth* are met together.
11(12). *Truth* shall spring out of the earth;
86:11. I will walk *in thy truth:*
15. plenteous in mercy *and truth*.
89:14(15). mercy *and truth* shall go before
91: 4. *his truth* (shall be thy) shield
108: 4(5). *and thy truth* (reacheth) unto the
111: 7. The works of his hands (are) *verity*
8. done *in truth* and uprightness.
115: 1. for thy mercy, (and) for *thy truth*'s sake.
117: 2. *and the truth of* the Lord (endureth) for
119:43. take not the word of *truth*
142. thy law (is) *the truth*.
151. all thy commandments (are) *truth*.
160. Thy word (is) *true* (lit. *truth*)
132:11. The Lord hath sworn (in) *truth*
138: 2. thy lovingkindness and for *thy truth:*
145:18. to all that call upon him *in truth*.
146: 6. which keepeth *truth* for ever:
Pro. 3: 3. Let not mercy *and truth* forsake
8: 7. For my mouth shall speak *truth;*
11:18. a *sure* reward. (lit. reward of *truth*)
12:19. The lip of *truth* shall be established
14:22. mercy *and truth* (shall be) to them
25. A *true* witness delivereth souls:
16: 6. By mercy *and truth* iniquity is
20:28. Mercy *and truth* preserve the king:
22:21. the certainty of the words of *truth;* that thou mightest answer the words of *truth*
23:23. Buy *the truth*, and sell (it) not;
29:14. The king that *faithfully* judgeth
Ecc. 12:10. upright, (even) words of *truth*.
Isa. 10:20. the Lord, the Holy One of Israel, *in truth*.
16: 5. and he shall sit upon it *in truth*
38: 3. how I have walked before thee *in truth*
18. into the pit cannot hope for *thy truth*.
19. shall make known *thy truth*.
39: 8. For there shall be peace *and truth*
42: 3. bring forth judgment *unto truth*.
43: 9. let them hear, and say, (It is) *truth*.
Isa. 48: 1. of the God of Israel, (but) not *in truth*,
59:14. for *truth* is fallen in the street,
15. Yea, *truth* faileth;
61: 8. and I will direct their work *in truth*,
Jer. 2:21. wholly a *right* seed: (lit. seed of *truth*)
4: 2. The Lord liveth, *in truth*, in judgment,
9: 5(4). *and* will not speak *the truth:*
10:10. the Lord (is) the *true* God, (marg. of *truth*)
14:13. *assured* peace (marg. peace of *truth*)
23:28. let him speak my word *faithfully*.
26:15. for *of a truth* the Lord hath sent
28: 9. the Lord hath *truly* sent him.
32:41. *assuredly* (marg. *in truth*, or, *stability*) with my
33: 6. the abundance of peace *and truth*.
42: 5. The Lord be a *true* (lit. of *truth*)
Eze. 18: 8. executed *true* judgment (lit. of *truth*)
9. kept my judgments, to deal *truly;*
Dan. 8:12. cast down *the truth* to the ground;
26. which was told (is) *true:* (lit. *truth*)
9:13. and understand *thy truth*.
10: 1. *and* the thing (was) *true*,
21. which is noted in the scripture of *truth:*
11: 2. now will I shew thee *the truth*.
Hos. 4: 1. because (there is) no *truth*,
Mic. 7:20. Thou wilt perform *the truth*
Zec. 7: 9. Execute *true* judgment, (lit. of *truth*)
8: 3. shall be called a city of *truth;*
8. *in truth* and in righteousness.
16. Speak ye every man *the truth*
— execute the judgment of *truth*
19. *therefore* love *the truth* and peace.
Mal. 2: 6. The law of *truth* was in his mouth,

אַמְתַּחַת *am-tah'-ghath*, f. 572

Gen 42:27. it (was) in *his sack*'s mouth.
28. and, lo, (it is) even *in my sack:*
43:12. in the mouth of *your sacks*,
18. the money that was returned *in our sacks*
21. that we opened *our sacks*,
— in the mouth of *his sack*,
22. who put our money *in our sacks*.
23. hath given you treasure *in your sacks:*
44: 1. Fill the men's *sacks* (with) food,
— put every man's money in *his sack*'s
2. *the sack*'s mouth of the youngest,
8. which we found in *our sacks*' mouths,
11. every man *his sack* to the ground, and opened every man *his sack*.
12. the cup was found *in* Benjamin's *sack*.

אֵמְתָנִי *em-thāh'-nee*, adj. Ch. 574

Dan. 7: 7. a fourth beast, dreadful *and terrible*,

אָן *āhn*, adv. 575

1Sa. 10:14. and to his servant, *Whither* went ye?
Job 8: 2. *How* long wilt thou speak these (things)?

It is found with ה parag. אָנָה.

Gen 37:30. (is) not; and I, *whither* shall I go?
2K. 6: 6. the man of God said, *Where* fell it?
Eze. 21:16(21). the left, *whithersoever* thy face (is) set.
&c. &c.

The same word, perhaps, is found also pointed אֵנָה.

1K. 2.36. and go not forth thence any whither. (lit. *hither* and thither)
42. and walkest abroad any whither, (lit. *hither* and thither)
2K. 5:25. Thy servant went no whither. (lit. *id.*)

אַן see אוֹן· See 204

אֲנָא & אֲנָה *ănāh*, pron. Ch. 576

אֲנָא occurs only, Ez. 6 : 12 & Dan. 2 : 8.

Ezr. 6:12. *I* Darius have made a decree:

Ezr. 7:21. *I* Artaxerxes the king,
Dan. 2: 8. *I* know of certainty that ye
23. *I* thank thee, and praise thee,
30. *But as for me*, this secret is not
3:25. Lo, *I* see four men loose,
4: 4(1). *I* Nebuchadnezzar was at rest
7(4). and *I* told the dream before them;
9(6). *I* know that the spirit of the holy gods
18(15). This dream *I* king Nebuchadnezzar
30(27). great Babylon, that *I* have built for
34(31). at the end of the days *I* Nebuchad.
37(34). Now *I* Nebuchadnezzar praise
5:16. *And I* have heard of thee, that thou
7:15. *I* Daniel was grieved in my spirit
28. *As for me* Daniel, my cogitations

---

577 אָנָּא & אָנָּה *āhn'-nāh*, interj.

Gen50:17. Forgive, *I pray thee* now,
Ex. 32:31. *Oh*, this people have sinned
2K. 20: 3. *I beseech thee*, O Lord,
Neh. 1: 5. *I beseech thee*, O Lord God
11. O Lord, *I beseech thee*,
Ps. 116: 4. *I beseech thee*, deliver my soul.
16. *O* Lord, truly I (am) thy servant;
118:25. Save now, *I beseech thee*, O Lord: O Lord, *I beseech thee*, send now
Isa. 38: 3. Remember now, O Lord, *I beseech thee*,
Dan. 9: 4. *O* Lord, the great and dreadful God,
Jon. 1:14. *We beseech thee*, O Lord,
4: 2. and said, *I pray thee*, O Lord,

---

578 אָנָה [*āh-nāh'*]

* KAL.—*Preterite.* *

Isa. 3:26. *And* her gates *shall lament*
19: 8. The fishers *also shall mourn*,

---

579 אָנָה [*āh-nāh'*]

* PIEL.—*Preterite.* *

Ex. 21:13. but God *deliver* (him) into his hand;

* PUAL.—*Future.* *

Ps. 91:10. There *shall* no evil *befall* thee,
Pro. 12:21. There *shall* no evil *happen* to the just:

* HITHPAEL.—*Participle.* *

2K. 5: 7. see how *he seeketh a quarrel*

See 575 אָנָה see אָן

See 577 אָנָּה see אָנָּא

See 576 אֲנָה see אֲנָא

See 575 אָנֶה see אָן

---

580 אָנוּ *ănoo*, pron.

כתיב once.

Jer. 42: 6. to whom *we* send thee;

---

581 אִנּוּן *in-noon'*, m. & אִנִּין *in-neen'*, f. Ch. pron. pl.

Ezr. 5: 4. What *are* (lit. *they*) the names of the men
Dan. 2:44. And in the days of *these* kings
Dan. 6:24(25). *them*, their children, and their wives;
7:17. These great beasts, which *are* (lit. *they*) four,

אֱנוֹשׁ *ĕnōhsh*, m. 582

Gen. 6: 4. which (were) of old, *men of* renown.
12:20. commanded (his) *men* concerning
13: 8. we (be) brethren. (marg. *men* brethren)
13. *But the men of* Sodom
14. 24. *the men* which went with me,
17:23. every male *among the men of* Abraham's
27. all *the men of* his house,
18: 2. three *men* stood by him:
16. *the men* rose up from thence,
22. And *the men* turned their faces
19: 4. *But* before they lay down, *the men of* the city, (even) *the men of* Sodom,
5. Where (are) *the men* which came
8. only *unto* these *men* do nothing;
10. But *the men* put forth their hand,
11. they smote *the men* that (were) at
12. *the men* said unto Lot,
16. *the men* laid hold upon his hand,
20: 8. *the men* were sore afraid.
24:13. the daughters of *the men of* the city
32. *the men*'s feet that (were) with him.
54. he *and the men* that (were) with him,
59. Abraham's servant, and *his men*.
26: 7. And *the men of* the place
— lest, (said he), *the men of* the place should
29:22. all *the men of* the place,
32:28(29). thou power with God and with *men*,
34: 7. *the men* were grieved,
20. communed with *the men of* their city,
21. These *men* (are) peaceable
22. Only herein will *the men* consent
37:28. passed by Midianites (lit. *men* Midianites)
38:21. Then he asked *the men of* that place,
22. also *the men of* the place
39:11. none *of the men of* the house there
14. she called *unto the men of* her house,
43:15. *the men* took that present,
16. Bring (these) *men* home,
— for (these) *men* shall dine with me
17, 24. brought *the men* into Joseph's house.
18. *the men* were afraid,
33. *the men* marvelled one at another.
44: 1. Fill *the men*'s sacks (with) food,
3. *the men* were sent away, they and their
4. follow after *the men*;
46:32. *And the men* (are) shepherds, for *their trade* hath been to feed cattle; (marg. they are *men of* cattle)
34. Thy servants' trade hath been about cattle (lit. have been *men of* cattle)
47: 2. some of his brethren, (even) five *men*,
6. if thou knowest (any) *men of* activity
Ex. 2:13. two *men* of the Hebrews strove
4:19. all *the men* are dead which sought
5: 9. more work be laid upon *the men*,
10: 7. let *the men* go, that they may serve
16:20. but *some of them* left of it (lit. *men*)
17: 9. said unto Joshua, Choose us out *men*,
18:21. able *men*, such as fear God, *men of*
25. Moses chose able *men* out of all
21:18. if *men* strive together,
22. If *men* strive, and hurt a woman
22:31(30). *And* ye shall be holy *men* unto me:
35:22. they came, both *men* and women,
Lev. 18:27. have *the men of* the land
Nu. 1: 5. these (are) the names of *the men*
17. Moses and Aaron took these *men*
9: 6. there were *certain men*,
7. those *men* said unto him,
11:26. there remained two (of the) *men*
13: 2. Send thou *men*, that they may
3. all those *men* (were) heads
16. These (are) the names of the *men*
31. *But the men* that went up
32. in it (are) *men of* a great stature.
14:22. all *those men* which have seen
36. *And the men*, which Moses sent
37. Even *those men* that did bring up
38. *the men* that went to search
16: 2. *with certain* of the children of Israel,
— famous in the congregation, *men of*

Nu. 16:14. put out the eyes of these *men?*
26. from the tents of these wicked *men,*
30. these *men* have provoked the Lord.
22: 9. What *men* (are) these with thee?
20. If *the men* come to call thee,
35. said unto Balaam, Go with *the men:*
25: 5. Slay ye every one *his men*
31: 3. Arm *some* (lit. *men*) of yourselves
21. the priest said unto *the men of* war
28. the *men of* war which went out
42. Moses divided from *the men* that
49. have taken the sum of *the men of* war
53. *the men of* war had taken spoil,
32:11. Surely none of *the men*
14. an increase of sinful *men,*
34:17. These (are) the names of *the men*
19. the names of *the men* (are) these:
Deu 1:13. Take you wise *men,* and understanding,
15. the chief of your tribes, wise *men,*
22. We will send *men* before us,
23. I took twelve *men* of you,
35. there shall not one *of* these *men*
2:14. all the generation of *the men of* war
16. when all *the men of* war
13:13(14). (Certain) *men,* the children of Belial,
19:17. Then both *the men,* between whom
21:21. all *the men of* his city
22:21. *the men of* her city shall stone her
25: 1. If there be a controversy between *men,*
11. When *men* strive together
31:12. *men,* and women, and children,
32:26. to cease *from among men:*
Jos. 2: 1. sent out of Shittim two *men*
2. there came *men* in hither
3. Bring forth *the men* that are
4. the woman took the two *men,*
— There came *men* unto me,
5. *that the men* went out: whither *the men*
7. *And the men* pursued after them
9. she said unto *the men,* I know
14. *the men* answered her, Our life
17. *the men* said unto her, We (will be)
23. So *the* two *men* returned, and descended
4: 2. Take you twelve *men* out of the people,
5: 4. *the men of* war, died in the wilderness
6. the people (that were) *men of* war,
6: 3. compass the city, all (ye) *men of* war,
22. Joshua had said unto *the* two *men*
7: 2. Joshua sent *men* from Jericho to Ai,
— *the men* went up and viewed Ai.
4. and they fled before *the men of* Ai.
5. *the men of* Ai smote of them
8:14. *the men of* the city went out
20. when *the men of* Ai looked
21. slew *the men of* Ai.
25. all *the men of* Ai.
9:14. *the men* took of their victuals,
10: 2. all *the men thereof* (were) mighty.
6. *the men of* Gibeon sent unto
18. set *men* by it for to keep them:
24. the captains of *the men of* war
18: 4. Give out from among you three *men*
8 *the men* arose, and went away:
9. *the men* went and passed through
Jud. 6:27. Gideon took ten *men* of his servants,
— *the men of* the city,
28. when *the men of* the city arose
30. Then *the men of* the city said
8: 5. he said *unto the men of* Succoth,
8. *the men of* Penuel answered him as *the men of* Succoth had answered
9. he spake also *unto the men of* Penuel,
14. a young man *of the men of* Succoth,
15. he came unto *the men of* Succoth,
— that we should give bread *unto thy men*
16. with them he taught *the men of* Succoth.
17. slew *the men of* the city.
18. What manner of *men* (were they)
9: 4. Abimelech hired vain and light *persons,*
9. they honour God *and man,*
13. which cheereth God *and man,*
28. serve *the men of* Hamor
36. the mountains *as* (if they were) *men.*
49. so that all *the men of* the tower
51. thither fled all *the men* and women,
57. all the evil of *the men of* Shechem
11: 3. there were gathered vain *men*

Jud. 12: 4. gathered together all *the men of* Gilead,
— *the men of* Gilead smote Ephraim,
5. that *the men of* Gilead said
14:18. *the men of* the city said unto him
16:27. the house was full of *men* and women;
18: 2. five *men* from their coasts, *men of* valour,
7. Then *the* five *men* departed,
14. Then answered *the* five *men*
17. *the* five *men* that went to spy
22. *the men* that (were) in the houses
25. lest angry *fellows* run upon thee,
19:16. *but the men of* the place (were) Benjamites.
22. *the men of* the city, *certain* sons of Belial, (lit. *men of* the sons, &c.)
25. But *the men* would not hearken
20:10. we will take ten *men* of an hundred
12. the tribes of Israel sent *men*
13. Now therefore deliver (us) *the men,*
44, 46. all these (were) *men of* valour.
Ru. 1:11. that they may be your *husbands?*
4: 2. he took ten *men* of the elders
1Sa. 1:11. unto thine handmaid a *man* child, (marg. seed of *men*)
2:17. for *men* abhorred the offering of the
26. both with the Lord, and also with *men.*
33. die *in the flower of their age.* (marg. *men*)
4: 9. Be strong, and quit yourselves *like men,*
— quit yourselves *like men,* and fight.
5: 7. when *the men of* Ashdod saw
9. he smote *the men of* the city,
12. *And the men* that died not were smitten
6:10. *the men* did so; and took two milch kine,
15. *and the men of* Beth-shemesh offered
19. he smote *the men of* Beth-shemesh,
20. *the men of* Beth-shemesh said,
7: 1. *the men of* Kirjath-jearim came,
11. *the men of* Israel went out of Mizpeh,
8:22. Samuel said unto *the men of* Israel,
10: 2. then thou shalt find two *men*
3. there shall meet thee three *men*
11: 1. all *the men of* Jabesh said
5. the tidings of *the men of* Jabesh.
9. came and shewed (it) *to the men of* Jabesh;
10. Therefore *the men of* Jabesh said,
12. bring *the men,* that we may put them
15. Saul and all *the men of* Israel
14: 8. we will pass over unto (these) *men,*
12. *the men of* the garrison answered
17:12. the man went *among men* (for) an old
26. David spake to *the men* that stood
28. when he spake unto *the men;*
52. *the men of* Israel and of Judah arose,
18: 5. Saul set him over *the men of* war,
27. went, he *and his men,* and slew
22: 6. discovered, *and the men* that (were) with
23: 3. David's *men* said unto him,
5. David *and his men* went to Keilah,
8. to besiege David and *his men.*
12. deliver me and *my men* into the hand
13. Then David *and his men,* (which were)
24. David *and his men* (were) in the wilderness
25. Saul also *and his men* went
26. David and *his men* on that side of
— *and his men* compassed David *and his men*
24: 2(3). to seek David *and his men*
3(4). David *and his men* remained
4(5). *the men of* David said unto him,
6(7). he said *unto his men,* The Lord forbid
7(8). So David stayed *his servants* with
22(23). David *and his men* gat them up
25:11. give (it) *unto men,* whom I know not
13. David said *unto his men,*
15. *But the men* (were) very good unto us,
20. David *and his men* came down against
27: 3. with Achish at Gath, he *and his men,*
8. David *and his men* went up, and invaded
28: 1. with me to battle, thou *and thy men.*
8. he went, and two *men* with him,
29: 2. David *and his men* passed on
4. with the heads of these *men?*
11. So David *and his men* rose up
30: 1. when David *and his men* were come
3. So David *and his men* came
21. David came to *the* two hundred *men,*
22. *of those* that went with David, (marg. *men*)
31. David himself *and his men* were wont
31: 1. *the men of* Israel fled from before

1Sa.31: 3. the archers hit him; (marg. shooters, *men* with bows)
6. and all *his men*, that same day
7. when *the men of* Israel that (were)
— saw that *the men of* Israel fled,
2Sa. 1:11. likewise all *the men* that (were) with
2: 3. *And his men* that (were) with him
4. *the men of* Judah came,
— *the men of* Jabesh-gilead (were they)
5. messengers unto *the men of* Jabesh-gilead,
17. Abner was beaten, *and the men of* Israel,
29. Abner *and his men* walked
31. smitten of Benjamin, *and of* Abner's *men*,
32. Joab *and his men* went all night,
3:20. to Hebron, and twenty *men* with him. And David made Abner *and the men*
39. *and* these *men* the sons of Zeruiah
4: 2. Saul's son had two *men*
11. when wicked *men* have slain a righteous
5: 6. the king *and his men* went to Jerusalem
21. David *and his men* burned them.
7:14. will chasten him with the rod of *men*,
10: 5. because *the men* were greatly ashamed:
11:16. where he knew that valiant *men*
17. *the men of* the city went out, and
23. Surely *the men* prevailed against us,
12: 1. There were two *men* in one city;
15: 6. Absalom stole the hearts of *the men of*
22. the Gittite passed over, and all *his men*,
16:13. as David *and his men* went by the way,
17: 8. thou knowest thy father *and his men*, that
12. all *the men* that (are) with him
18:28. which hath delivered up *the men*
19:28(29). my father's house were but dead *men*
41(42). David's *men* with him, over Jordan?
20: 7. there went out after him Joab's *men*,
21: 6. Let seven *men* of his sons be delivered
17. Then *the men of* David sware unto him,
23:17. blood of *the men* that went in jeopardy
1K. 1: 9. all *the men of* Judah the king's servants:
2:32. fell upon two *men* more righteous
9:22. but they (were) *men of* war,
27. ship*men* that had knowledge
10: 8. Happy (are) *thy men*,
15. *of the* merchant*men*, and of the traffick
11:17. he *and certain* Edomites (lit. *and men* Edomites)
18. took *men* with them out of Paran,
24. he gathered *men* unto him,
13:25. *men* passed by, and saw the carcase
20:17. There are *men* come out of Samaria.
33. *Now the men* did diligently
21:10. set two *men*, sons of Belial,
11. *the men of* his city, (even) the elders
13. there came in two *men*, children of Belial,
— *the men of* Belial witnessed
2K. 2:16. with thy servants fifty strong *men*;
19. *the men of* the city said
4:40. So they poured out *for the men*
5:24. he let *the men* go, and they departed.
7: 3. there were four leprous *men*
10: 6. the heads of *the men* your master's sons,
24. (If) any of *the men* whom I have
11: 9. they took every man *his men*
12:15(16). they reckoned not with *the men*,
17:30. *And the men of* Babylon made Succoth-benoth, *and the men of* Cuth made Nergal, *and the men of* Hamath made Ashima,
18:27. to *the men* which sit on the wall,
20:14. What said these *men?* and from whence
23:17. *the men of* the city told him,
24:16. all *the men of* might,
25: 4. all *the men of* war (fled) by night
19. set over *the men of* war, and five *men*
23. they *and* their *men*, heard that the king
— a Maachathite, they *and their men*.
24. *and to their men*, and said unto them,
25. of the seed royal, came, and ten *men*
1Ch. 4:12. These (are) *the men of* Rechah.
22. *and the men of* Chozeba,
42. of the sons of Simeon, five hundred *men*,
5:18. *men* able to bear buckler and sword,
24. mighty *men* of valour, famous *men*,
7:21. whom *the men of* Gath
40. battle (was) twenty and six thousand *men*.
8:40. were mighty *men* of valour,
9: 9. All these *men* (were) chief

1Ch.11:19. shall I drink the blood of these *men*
12: 8. *men of* war (fit) for the battle,
30. famous (marg. *men of* names) throughout the house
38. All these *men of* war, that could keep
19: 5. told David how *the men* were served.
— for *the men* were greatly ashamed.
25: 1. the number of the work*men* according to
2Ch. 2:17(16). Solomon numbered all the *strangers* (marg. *the men* the strangers)
8: 9. but they (were) *men of* war,
9: 7. Happy (are) *thy men*,
14. Beside (that which) chap*men* and
13: 7. there are gathered unto him vain *men*,
14:11(10). let not *man* (marg. *mortal man*) prevail against thee.
17:13. *and the men of* war,
23: 8. and took every man *his men* that were
24:24. came with a small company of *men*,
28:12. Then *certain* of the heads of (lit. *men*)
15. And *the men* which were expressed by
30:11. Nevertheless *divers* of Asher (lit. *men*)
31:19. *the men* that were expressed by name,
34:12. *And the men* did the work faithfully:
Ezr. 1: 4. let *the men of* his place help him
2: 2. The number of *the men of* the people
22. *The men of* Netophah,
23. *The men of* Anathoth,
27. *The men of* Michmas,
28. *The men of* Beth-el and Ai,
10: 1. Israel a very great congregation of *men*
9. all *the men of* Judah and Benjamin
16. *certain* chief of the fathers, (lit. *men*)
17. they made an end with all *the men*
Neh. 1: 2. he *and* (certain) *men* of Judah;
2:12. in the night, I *and* some few *men*
3: 2. unto him builded *the men of* Jericho.
7. *the men of* Gibeon, and of Mizpah,
22. repaired the priests, *the men of* the plain.
4:23(17). *nor the men of* the guard which
7: 7. of *the men of* the people of Israel
26. *The men of* Beth-lehem and Netophah,
27. *The men of* Anathoth,
28. *The men of* Beth-azmaveth,
29. *The men of* Kirjath-jearim,
30. *The men of* Ramah and Gaba,
31. *The men of* Michmas,
32. *The men of* Beth-el and Ai,
33. *The men of* the other Nebo,
8: 3. before *the men* and the women,
11: 2. people blessed all *the men*, that willingly
6. four hundred threescore and eight valiant *men*.
12:44. at that time were *some* appointed
13:25. smote *certain* of them, (lit. *men*)
Job 4:13. when deep sleep falleth on *men*,
17. Shall *mortal man* be more just
5:17. happy (is) *the man* whom God
7: 1. an appointed time *to man* upon earth?
17. What (is) *man*, that thou shouldest
9: 2. but how should *man* be just with God?
10: 4. or seest thou as *man* seeth?
5. (Are) thy days as the days of *man?*
13: 9. as one man mocketh *another*, (lit. as the mocking *at a man*)
14:19. thou destroyest the hope of *man*.
15:14. What (is) *man*, that he should be clean?
25: 4. How then can *man* be justified
6. How much less *man*, (that is) a worm?
28: 4. they are gone away *from men*.
13. *Man* knoweth not the price thereof;
32: 1. So these three *men* ceased to answer
5. in the mouth of (these) three *men*,
8. But (there is) a spirit *in man:*
33:12. that God is greater *than man*.
15. when deep sleep falleth upon *men*,
16. Then he openeth the ears of *men*,
26. he will render *unto man* his righteousness.
27. He looketh upon *men*,
34: 8. walketh with wicked *men*.
10. ye *men of* understanding:
34. Let *men of* understanding tell me,
36. because of (his) answers *for* wicked *men*.
36:24. his work, which *men* behold.
25. *man* may behold (it) afar off.
37: 7. that all *men* may know his work.
24. *Men* do therefore fear him:
Ps. 8: 4(5). What is *man*, that thou art mindful

Ps. 9:19(20). Arise, O Lord; let not *man* prevail:
20(21). know themselves (to be but) *men.*
10:18. that *the man* of the earth may no more
26: 9. nor my life with bloody *men:*
55:13(14). But (it was) thou, a *man* mine equal,
23(24). and deceitful *men* shall not live out
56: 1(2). for *man* would swallow me up;
59: 2(3). *and* save me *from* bloody *men.*
66:12. Thou hast caused *men* to ride over
73: 5. They (are) not in trouble (as other) *men;*
76: 5(6). none of *the men of* might have found
90: 3. Thou turnest *man* to destruction;
103:15. (As for) *man,* his days (are) as grass:
104:15. wine (that) maketh glad the heart of *man,*
— bread (which) strengtheneth *man*'s heart.
119:24. my counsellors.(marg. *men of* my counsel)
139:19. depart from me *therefore,* ye bloody *men.*
144: 3. the son of *man,* that thou makest account
Pro.24: 1. Be not thou envious *against* evil *men,*
25: 1. which *the men of* Hezekiah king of Judah
28: 5. Evil *men* understand not judgment:
29: 8. Scornful *men* bring a city into a snare:
10. *The* blood*thirsty* (marg. *Men of* blood) hate
Ecc. 9:14. a little city, *and* few *men* within it;
12: 3. *the* strong *men* shall bow themselves,
Isa. 2:11. haughtiness of *men* shall be bowed down,
17. the haughtiness of *men* shall be made low:
5:22. *and men of* strength to mingle strong
7:13. a small thing for you to weary *men,*
8: 1. write in it with a *man*'s pen
13: 7. every *man*'s heart shall melt:
12. I will make *a man* more precious than
24: 6. are burned, and few *men* left.
28:14. ye scornful *men,* that rule this people
29:13. taught by the precept of *men:*
33: 8. he regardeth no *man.*
36:12. to *the men* that sit upon the wall,
39: 3. What said these *men?* and from whence
41:11. *they that* strive with thee (marg. *the men of* thy strife) shall perish.
12. *them that* contended with thee: (marg. *men of* thy contention) *they that* war against thee (marg. *the men of* thy war)
45:14. *men of* stature, shall come over unto thee,
51: 7. fear ye not the reproach of *men,*
12. shouldest be afraid *of a man* (that) shall
56: 2. Blessed (is) *the man* (that) doeth
57: 1. *and* merciful *men* (are) taken away,
66:24. look upon the carcases of *the men*
Jer. 5:26. they set a trap, they catch *men.*
11:21. saith the Lord of *the men of* Anathoth,
23. I will bring evil upon *the men of* Anathoth,
18:21. *and* let *their men* be put to death;
19:10. in the sight of *the men* that go
20:10. All my familiars watched for my halting, (marg. Every *man* of my peace)
26:17. rose up *certain* (lit. *men*) of the elders
22. Jehoiakim the king sent *men* into Egypt,
— *and* (certain) *men* with him into Egypt.
29: 6. give your daughters *to husbands,*
34:18. I will give *the men* that have transgressed
37:10. there remained(but) wounded *men* among
38: 4. weakeneth the hands of *the men of* war
9. these *men* have done evil in all that
10. Take from hence thirty *men* with thee,
11. So Ebed-melech took *the men* with him,
16. I give thee into the hand of these *men*
22. Thy friends (marg. *Men of* thy peace) have set thee on,
39: 4. saw them, and all *the men of* war,
17. be given into the hand of *the men*
40: 7. they *and their men,* heard that the king
— committed unto him *men,* and women,
8. they *and their men.*
9. sware unto them *and to their men,*
41: 1. even ten *men* with him,
2. *and the* ten *men* that were with him,
3. that were found there, (and) *the men of*
5. That there came *certain* from Shechem,
7. he, *and the men* that (were) with him.
8. But ten *men* were found among them
9. cast all the dead bodies of *the men.*
12. Then they took all *the men,* and went
15. escaped from Johanan with eight *men,*
16. mighty *men of* war, and the women, and
Jer. 42:17. So shall it be with all *the men* that set
43: 2. the son of Kareah, and all *the* proud *men,*
9. in the sight of *the men* of Judah;
44:15. Then all *the men* which knew that
19. unto her, without *our men?* (marg. *husbands*)
48:14. mighty *and* strong *men* for the war?
31. shall mourn for *the men of* Kir-heres.
36. sound like pipes for *the men of* Kir-heres:
49:26. all *the men of* war shall be cut off
50:30. all her *men of* war shall be cut off
51:32. *and the men of* war are affrighted.
52: 7. *the men of* war fled, and went forth
25. charge of *the men of* war; and seven *men*
Eze. 9: 2. six *men* came from the way of the
4. set a mark upon the foreheads of *the men*
6. Then they began *at the* ancient *men*
11: 2. these (are) *the men* that devise mischief,
15. thy brethren, *the men of* thy kindred,
12:16. I will leave a few *men of* them
14: 1. Then came *certain* of the elders
3. these *men* have set up their idols in
14. these three *men,* Noah, Daniel, and Job,
16. (Though) these three *men* (were) in it,
18. Though these three *men* (were) in it,
16:45. which lothed *their husbands* and their
20: 1. *certain* of the elders of Israel
21:31(36). into the hand of brutish *men,*
22: 9. In thee are *men* that carry tales
23:14. she saw *men* pourtrayed upon the wall,
40. that ye have sent *for men* to come from
42. with *the men* of the common sort (were)
45. *And the* righteous *men,* they shall judge
24:17. eat not the bread of *men.*
22. nor eat the bread of *men.*
27:10. were in thine army, thy *men of* war:
27. all thy *men of* war, that (are) in thee,
39:14. *And* they shall sever out *men of* continual
Dan10: 7. *for the men* that were with me saw
Joel 2: 7. shall climb the wall *like men of* war;
3: 9(4:9). let all *the men of* war draw near;
Am. 6: 9. if there remain ten *men* in one house,
Obad. 7. All *the men of* thy confederacy have
— *the men that* were at peace with thee
Jon. 1:10. Then were *the men* exceedingly afraid,
— For *the men* knew that he fled from
13. Nevertheless *the men* rowed hard
16. Then *the men* feared the Lord exceedingly,
3: 5. So *the people of* Nineveh believed God,
Mic. 7: 6. enemies (are) *the men of* his own house.
Nah. 2: 3(4). *the* valiant *men* (are) in scarlet:
Zep. 1:12. punish *the men* that are settled on
3: 4. prophets (are) light (and) treacherous *persons:*
Zec. 3: 8. for they (are) *men* wondered at:
7: 2. *and their men,* to pray before the Lord,
8:23. that ten *men* shall take hold

אָנַח [*āh-nagh'.*] 584

*** NIPHAL.—*Preterite.* ***

Isa. 24: 7. all the merryhearted *do sigh.*
Lam. 1: 8. she *sigheth,* and turneth backward.

NIPHAL.—*Imperative.*

Eze.21: 6(11). *Sigh* therefore, thou son of man,

NIPHAL.—*Future.*

Ex. 2:23. *and* the children of Israel *sighed* by reason
Pro.29: 2. wicked beareth rule, the people *mourn.*
Eze.21: 6(11). with bitterness *sigh* before their eyes.

NIPHAL.—*Participle.*

Lam. 1: 4. her priests *sigh,* her virgins are afflicted,
11. All her people *sigh,* they seek bread;
21. They have heard that I *sigh:*
Eze. 9: 4. of the men *that sigh* and that cry for all
21: 7(12). they say unto thee, Wherefore *sighest*
Joel 1:18. How do the beasts *groan!*

אֲנָחָה *ănāh-ghāh',* f. 585

Job. 3:24. *my sighing* cometh before I eat,
23: 2. my stroke is heavier than *my groaning.*

Ps. 6: 6(7). I am weary *with my groaning;*
31:10(11). spent with grief, and my years *with sighing:*
38: 9(10). *and my groaning* is not hid from thee.
102: 5(6). By reason of the voice of *my groaning*
Isa. 21: 2. *the sighing thereof* have I made to cease.
35:10. sorrow *and sighing* shall flee away.
51:11. sorrow *and mourning* shall flee away.
Jer. 45: 3. I fainted *in my sighing*, and I find no rest.
Lam. 1:22. *my sighs* (are) many, and my heart (is)

---

586 **אֲנַחְנָא & (Ezr. 4:16) אֲנַחְנָה** *ănag̣h'-nāh*, Ch. pron. pl.

Ezr. 4:16. *We* certify the king that, if this city
5:11. *We* are the servants of the God
Dan. 3:16. *we* (are) not careful to answer
17. our God whom *we* serve is able

---

587 **אֲנַחְנוּ** *ănag̣h'-noo*, pron. pl. c.

Gen 19:13. For *we* will destroy this place,
Nu. 32:17. *But* we *ourselves* will go ready armed
Deu 5: 3. but with us, (even) *us*, who
2Ch 20:12. *neither* know *we* what to do:
Neh 4:23(17). none *of us* put off our clothes,
Jer. 26:19. *Thus* might *we* procure great evil
&c. &c.

---

589 **אֲנִי** *ănee*, pron. c.

Gen 6:17. *And*, behold, *I*, even I, do bring a flood
9:12. the token of the covenant which *I* make
17: 4. *As for me*, behold, my covenant
18:13. bear a child, *which* (lit. *and I*) am old?
Ex. 6:12. hear me, *who* (lit. *and I*) (am) of
1Sa. 25:24. Upon me, my lord, (upon) *me*
2Sa. 11:11. shall *I then* go into mine house,
18: 2. surely go forth with you *myself* also.
19:43(44). Israel answered...*we* have also
Ps. 73:28. *But* (lit. *But I*) (it is) good for me
Pro. 23:15. my heart shall rejoice, even *mine*.
Isa. 66: 9. Shall *I* bring to the birth, and not
Jer. 1:18. *For*, behold, *I* have made thee this day
&c. &c.

---

590 **אֳנִי** *ŏnee*, c.

1K. 9:26. *And* king Solomon made *a navy of ships*
27. Hiram sent *in the navy* his servants,
10:11. *the navy* also of Hiram, that brought
22. *a navy of* Tharshish with *the navy of* Hiram: once in three years came *the navy*
Isa. 33:21. wherein shall go no *galley* with oars,

---

592 **אֲנִיָּה** *ăneey-yāh'*, f.

Isa. 29: 2. there shall be heaviness *and sorrow:*
Lam. 2: 5. of Judah mourning *and lamentation.*

---

591 **אֳנִיָּה** *ŏneey-yāh'*, f.

Gen 49:13. he (shall be) for an haven of *ships;*
Deu 28:68. bring thee into Egypt again *with ships*,
Jud. 5:17. why did Dan remain *in ships?*
1K. 9:27. *ship*men (lit. men of *ships*) that had
22:48(49). Jehoshaphat made *ships of* Tharshish
—(—). for thus *the ships* were broken at Ezion-geber.
49(50). go with thy servants *in the ships.*
2Ch. 8:18. (קרי) by the hands of his servants *ships*,
9:21. *the* king's *ships* went to Tarshish
— came *the ships of* Tarshish
20:36. to make *ships* to go to Tarshish: and they made the *ships* in Ezion-gaber.
37. *the ships* were broken,
Job 9:26. passed away as *the* swift *ships:*
Ps. 48: 7(8). Thou breakest *the ships of* Tarshish
104:26. There go *the ships:* (there is) that
107:23. that go down to the sea *in ships*,
Pro. 30:19. of *a ship* in the midst of the sea;
31:14. She is *like the* merchants' *ships;*
Isa. 2:16. upon all *the ships of* Tarshish,
23: 1, 14. Howl, ye *ships of* Tarshish;
43:14. the Chaldeans, whose cry (is) *in the ships.*
60: 9. *and* the *ships* of Tarshish first, to bring
Eze. 27: 9. *the ships of* the sea with their mariners
25. *The ships of* Tarshish did sing of
29. shall come down *from their ships*,
Dan 11:40. with horsemen, *and with* many *ships;*
Jon. 1: 3. he found *a ship* going to Tarshish:
4. *so that the ship* was like to be broken.
5. the wares that (were) *in the ship*

אֲנָךְ *ănāhcḥ*, m. 594

Am. 7: 7. by *a plumbline*, with *a plumbline* in his
8. seest thou? And I said, *A plumbline.*
— I will set *a plumbline* in the midst of

אָנֹכִי *āh-nōh-cḥee'*, pron. c. 595

Gen 3:10. because *I* (was) naked;
18:27. *which* (lit. *and I*) (am but) dust and ashes:
1Sa. 12:23. Moreover *as for me*, God forbid that
&c. &c.

אָנַן [*āh-nan'.*] 596

* HITHPAEL.—*Future.* *

Lam. 3:39. Wherefore *doth* a living man *complain*, (marg. *murmur*)

HITHPAEL.—*Participle.*

Nu. 11: 1. And (when) the people *complained*, (marg. were *as* it were *complainers*)

אָנַס [*āh-nas'.*] 597

KAL.—*Participle.* Poël.

Est. 1: 8. none *did compel:* for so the king

אֲנַס [*ănas.*] Ch. 598

P'AL.—*Participle.*

Dan 4: 9(6). and no secret *troubleth* thee,

אָנַף [*āh-naph'.*] 599

* KAL.—*Preterite.* *

1K. 8:46. *and thou be angry* with them,
2Ch. 6:36. *and thou be angry* with them,
Ps. 60: 1(3). *thou hast been displeased;* O turn
Isa. 12: 1. though *thou wast angry* with me, thine

KAL.—*Future.*

Ezr. 9:14. *wouldest* not *thou be angry* with us till
Ps. 2:12. Kiss the Son, lest *he be angry*,
79: 5. *wilt thou be angry* for ever? shall
85: 5(6). *Wilt thou be angry* with us for ever?

* HITHPAEL.—*Preterite.* *

Deu 1:37. Also the Lord *was angry* with
4:21. the Lord *was angry* with me
9:20. the Lord *was* very *angry* with Aaron,

HITHPAEL.—*Future.*

Deu 9: 8. *so that* the Lord *was angry*
1K. 11: 9. *And* the Lord *was angry* with Solomon,
2K. 17:18. *Therefore* the Lord *was* very *angry*

אֲנָפָה *ănāh-phāh'*, f, 601

Lev. 11:19. *the heron* after her kind,
Deu 14:18. *and the heron* after her kind,

אַנְפִּין *an-peen'*, Ch. 600

[pl. of אַנַף.]

Dan. 2:46. Nebuchadnezzar fell upon *his face*,
3:19. the form of *his visage* was changed

602 אָנַק [*āh-nak'.*]

* KAL.—*Infinitive.* *
Eze.26:15. *when* the wounded *cry*, when the slaughter

KAL.—*Future.*
Jer. 51:52. all her land the wounded *shall groan.*

* NIPHAL.—*Infinitive.* *
Eze.24:17. Forbear *to cry*, make no mourning

NIPHAL.—*Participle.*
Eze. 9: 4. *and that cry* for all the abominations

603-04 אֲנָקָה *ănāh-kāh'*, f.

Lev.11:30. *And the ferret*, and the chameleon,
Ps. 12: 5(6). *for the sighing of* the needy,
79:11. Let *the sighing of* the prisoner come
102:20(21). To hear *the groaning of* the prisoner;
Mal. 2:13. with weeping, *and* with *crying out*,

605 אָנַשׁ [*āh-nash'.*]

* KAL.—*Participle.* Päul. *
Job 34: 6. my wound (is) *incurable* without
Isa. 17:11. in the day of grief and of *desperate* sorrow.
Jer. 15:18. my wound *incurable*, (which) refuseth
17: 9. above all (things), *and desperately wicked:*
16. neither have I desired the *woeful* day;
30:12. Thy bruise (is) *incurable*, (and) thy
15. thy sorrow (is) *incurable* for the
Mic. 1: 9. For her wound (is) *incurable*; (marg. (she is) *grievously sick of* her wounds)

* NIPHAL.—*Future.* *
2Sa.12:15. unto David, *and it was very sick.*

606 אֱנָשׁ *ĕnāhsh*, Ch.

Dan. 2:10. it is אֱנָשׁ.

Ezr. 4:11. Thy servants *the men* on this side the
6:11. that whosoever shall alter (lit. every *man* who)
Dan 2:10. There is not *a man* upon the earth
38. wheresoever the children of *men* dwell,
43. mingle themselves with the seed of *men:*
3:10. that every *man* that shall hear the sound
4:16(13). Let his heart be changed from *man*'s,
17(14), 25(22), 32(29). ruleth in the kingdom of *men*,
—(—) setteth up over it the basest of *men.*
25(22). That they shall drive thee from *men*,
32(29). they shall drive thee from *men*,
33(30). and he was driven from *men*,
5: 5. came forth fingers of a *man*'s hand,
7. Whosoever (lit. every *man* who) shall read this writing,
21. he was driven from the sons of *men;*
— God ruled in the kingdom of *men*,
6: 7(8). a petition of any God or *man*
12(13). that every *man* that shall ask (a petition) of any God or *man* within thirty
7: 4. made stand upon the feet *as a man*, and *a man*'s heart was given to it.
8. eyes like the eyes of *man*,
13. behold, (one) like the Son of *man* came

See 582 אֲנָשִׁים see אֱנוֹשׁ.

607 אַנְתְּ *ant*, pron. Ch.

Ezr. 7:25. *And thou*, Ezra, after the wisdom
Dan 2:29. *As for thee*, O king, thy thoughts
31. *Thou*, O king, sawest, and behold
37. *Thou*, O king, (art) a king of kings:
38. *Thou* (art) this head of gold.
3:10. *Thou*, O king, hast made a decree,
4:18(15). *Now thou*, O Belteshazzar, declare
—(—). *but thou* (art) able; for the spirit
22(19). *It* (is) *thou*, O king, that art
5:13. (Art) *thou* that Daniel, which (art)
18. *O thou* king, the most high God gave
Dan 5:22. *And thou* his son, O Belshazzar,
23. *and thou*, and thy lords, thy wives,
6:16(17), 20(21). Thy God whom *thou* servest

אַנְתּוּן *an-toon'*, Ch. pron. pl. 608

Dan 2: 8. of certainty that *ye* would gain the time,

אָסוּךְ *āh-sooch'*, m. 610

2K. 4: 2. any thing in the house, save *a pot of* oil.

אָסוֹן *āh-sōhn'*, m. 611

Gen42: 4. Lest peradventure *mischief* befall
38. if *mischief* befall him by the way
44:29. this also from me, and *mischief* befall him
Ex. 21:22. and yet no *mischief* follow: he shall
23. if (any) *mischief* follow, then

אֵסוּר *ēh-soor'*, m. 612

Jud.15:14. and *his bands* loosed from off his hands.
Ecc. 7:26. her hands (as) *bands:*
Jer. 37:15. put him in prison (lit. house of *binding*)

אֱסוּר *ĕsoor*, m. Ch. 613

Ezr. 7:26. confiscation of goods, *or to imprisonment.*
Dan 4:15(12), 23(20). *even with a band of* iron and

אָסִיף & אָסִף *āh-seeph'*, m. 614

Ex. 23:16 & 34:22. the feast of *ingathering*,

אָסִיר *āh-seer'*, m. 615

Gen39:20. where the king'*s prisoners* (were)
22. all *the prisoners* that (were)
Job 3:18. *the prisoners* rest together;
Ps. 68: 6(7). he bringeth out *those which are bound*
69:33(34). despiseth not *his prisoners.*
79:11. Let the sighing of *the prisoner*
102:20(21). To hear the groaning of *the prisoner;*
107:10. *bound in* affliction and iron;
Isa. 14:17. opened not the house of *his prisoners?*
Lam.3:34. under his feet all *the prisoners of* the earth,
Zec. 9:11. I have sent forth *thy prisoners*
12. ye *prisoners of* hope:

אַסִּיר *as-seer'*, m. 616

Isa. 10: 4. bow down under *the prisoners*,
24:22. *prisoners* are gathered in the pit,
42: 7. to bring out *the prisoners*

אֲסָמִים [*ăsāh-meem'*,] m. pl. 618

Deu28: 8. upon thee *in thy storehouses*, (marg. *barns*)
Pro. 3:10. So shall *thy barns* be filled

אָסַף *āh-saph'.* 622

* KAL.—*Preterite.* *
Gen 6:21. *and thou shalt gather* (it) to thee;
30:23. God *hath taken away* my reproach:
Ex. 3:16. Go, *and gather* the elders of Israel
23:10. *and shalt gather* in the fruits thereof:
Lev.25: 3. *and gather* in the fruit thereof;
Nu. 11:32. he that gathered least *gathered* ten
19: 9. *And* a man (that is) clean *shall gather*
Deu 11:14. *that thou mayest gather in* thy corn,
22: 2. *then thou shalt bring it* unto thine own
Josh20: 4. *they shall take* him into the city
Jud.18:25. *and thou lose* thy life, with the lives
Ru. 2: 7. let me glean *and gather* after the
2K. 5: 6. *that thou mayest recover him* of his leprosy.
11. over the place, *and recover* the leper.
22: 4. *have gathered* of the people:

2Ch 34: 9. *had gathered* of the hand of Manasseh
Ps. 85: 3(4). *Thou hast taken away* all thy wrath:
Pro.30: 4. who *hath gathered* the wind in his fists?
Isa. 10:14. (that are) left, *have I gathered* all the
11:12. *and shall assemble* the outcasts of Israel,
Jer. 16: 5. for *I have taken away* my peace from
21: 4. *and I will assemble* them into the
Eze.11:17. *and assemble* you out of the countries
Dan 11:10. *and shall assemble* a multitude of
Joel 2:10 & 3:15(4:15). and the stars *shall withdraw*
Zeph 3:18. *I will gather* (them that are) sorrowful
Zec.14: 2. *For I will gather* all nations against

KAL.—*Infinitive.*

Ex. 23:16. *when thou hast gathered in* thy labours
Lev. 23:39. *when ye have gathered in* the fruit of
Deu 16:13. *after that thou hast gathered in* thy corn
2K. 5: 7. *to recover* a man of his leprosy?
Ecc. 2:26. *to gather* and to heap up, that he
Isa. 10:14. *and as one gathereth* eggs (that are) left,
17: 5. *as when* the harvestman *gathereth* the corn,
Jer. 8:13. I will *surely* consume them, (marg. *In gathering* I will, &c.)
Mic. 2:12. I will *surely* assemble, (lit. *assembling* I will assemble)
Zeph 1: 2. I will *utterly* consume (marg. *By taking away* I will make an end)
3: 8. *to gather* the nations, that I may

KAL.—*Imperative.*

Nu. 11:16. *Gather* unto me seventy men of the
21:16. *Gather* the people *together*, and I will give
1 Sa.14:19. unto the priest, *Withdraw* thine hand.
2Sa.12:28. *gather* the rest of the people *together*,
Ps. 50: 5. *Gather* my saints *together* unto me;
Isa. 4: 1. *to take* (marg. *take thou*) *away* our
Jer. 10:17. *Gather* up thy wares out of the land,
12: 9. *assemble* all the beasts of the field,
40:10. ye, *gather* ye wine, and summer fruits,
Eze.24: 4. *Gather* the pieces thereof into it,
Joel 1:14. *gather* the elders (and) all the inhabitants
2:16. *Gather* the people, sanctify the congregation, assemble the elders, *gather* the

KAL.—*Future.*

Gen 29:22. *And* Laban *gathered* together all
42:17. *And he put* them *all together* (marg. *gathered*)
49:33. *And* when...*he gathered up* his feet
Ex. 4:29. *and gathered together* all the elders of
Lev. 25:20. shall not sow, nor *gather in* our increase:
Nu. 11:24. *and gathered* the seventy men of the
32. *and they gathered* the quails:
21:23. *but* Sihon *gathered* all his people *together*,
Deu 28:38. *shalt gather* (but) little *in*;
Jos. 2:18. *thou shalt bring* thy father, (marg. *gather*)
24: 1. *And* Joshua *gathered* all the tribes
Jud. 3:13. *And he gathered* unto him the children
11:20. *but* Sihon *gathered* all his people *together*,
1 Sa. 5: 8. They sent therefore *and gathered* all
11. they sent *and gathered together* all
14:52. *and* when Saul saw...*he took him* unto him.
15: 6. lest *I destroy you* with them:
17: 1. *Now* the Philistines *gathered* together
2Sa. 6: 1. *Again*, David *gathered together* all
10:17. *And* when it was told David, *he gathered* all Israel *together*,
11:27. David sent *and fetched her* to his house,
12:29. *And* David *gathered* all the people *together*,
21:13. *and they gathered* the bones of them
1K. 10:26. *And* Solomon *gathered together* chariots
2K 5: 3. *he would recover* (marg. *gather in*) him of
23: 1. *and they gathered* unto him all
1Ch 15: 4. *And* David *assembled* the children of
19:17. *and he gathered* all Israel, and passed over
23: 2. *And he gathered together* all the princes
2Ch 1:14. *And* Solomon *gathered* chariots
24:11. *and gathered* money in abundance.
28:24. *And* Ahaz *gathered together* the vessels
29: 4. *and gathered them together* into
15. *And they gathered* their brethren,
20. *and gathered* the rulers of the city,
34:29. the king sent *and gathered together*
Job 34:14. *he gather* unto himself his spirit
39:12. thy seed, and *gather* (it into) thy barn?
Ps. 26: 9. *Gather* not (marg. *Take* not *away*) my
27:10. Lord *will take me up*. (marg. *gather me*)
Ps. 104:29. *thou takest away* their breath,
Isa. 58: 8. the Lord *shall be thy rereward.* (marg, *gather thee up*)
Jer. 40:12. *and gathered* wine and summer fruits
Mic. 2:12. *I will* surely *assemble*, O Jacob,
4: 6. *will I assemble* her that halteth,
Hab 1: 9. *and they shall gather* the captivity
15. *and gather them* in their drag:
2: 5. *but gathereth* unto him all nations,

KAL.—*Participle.* Poël.

Nu. 19:10. *he that gathereth* the ashes of
2K. 22:20. I *will gather thee* unto thy fathers,
2Ch 34:28. I *will gather thee* to thy fathers,
Ps. 39: 6(7). and knoweth not who *shall gather them*

KAL.—*Participle.* Päul.

Eze.34:29. no more *consumed with* hunger (marg. *taken away*)

* NIPHAL.—*Preterite.* *

Gen 29: 3. *And* thither *were* all the flocks *gathered*:
34:30. *and...they shall gather themselves together*
Lev. 26:25. *and when ye are gathered together*
Nu. 27:13. *thou also shalt be gathered* unto thy people, as Aaron thy brother *was gathered*.
Jud. 2:10. *were gathered* unto their fathers:
6:33. *were gathered* together, and went over,
16:23. the Philistines *gathered them together*
1Sa. 13: 5. the Philistines *gathered themselves together*
17: 2. the men of Israel *were gathered together*,
2Sa. 23: 9. *were* there *gathered together* to battle,
2K. 22:20. *and thou shalt be gathered* into thy grave
1Ch 11:13. the Philistines *were gathered together*
19: 7. of Ammon *gathered themselves together*
2Ch 12: 5. that *were gathered together*
30: 3. had the people *gathered themselves together*
34:28. *and thou shalt be gathered* to thy grave
Neh 8:13. on the second day *were gathered together*
9: 1. the children of Israel *were assembled*
Ps. 35:15. *and gathered themselves together*: (yea), the abjects *gathered themselves together*
47: 9(10). the people *are gathered together*,
Pro 27:25. *and* herbs of the mountains *are gathered*.
Isa. 16:10. *And* gladness *is taken away*,
57: 1. the righteous *is taken away* from the evil
Jer. 48:33. *And* joy and gladness *is taken*
Mic. 4:11. many nations *are gathered*
Zec.12: 3. *though* all the people of the earth *be gathered together*

NIPHAL.—*Infinitive.*

Gen 29: 7. cattle *should be gathered together*:
Nu. 12:15. till Miriam *was brought in*
2Sa.17:11. be *generally* gathered (lit. *in gathering* be gathered)

NIPHAL.—*Imperative.*

Gen 49: 1. *Gather yourselves together*, that I
Deu 32:50. *and be gathered* unto thy people;
Jer. 4: 5. and say, *Assemble yourselves*, and let us
8:14. do we sit still? *assemble yourselves*,
47: 6. *put up thyself* into thy (marg. *gather*)
Eze.39:17. *gather yourselves* on every side
Am. 3: 9. *Assemble yourselves* upon the

NIPHAL.—*Future.*

Gen 25: 8. *and was gathered* to his people.
17. *and was gathered* unto his people.
29: 8. all the flocks *be gathered together*,
35:29 & 49:33. *and was gathered* unto his people.
Ex. 9:19. *shall* not *be brought*
32:26. *And...gathered themselves together* unto him.
Nu. 11:22. *shall* all the fish of the sea *be gathered together*
30. *And* Moses *gat him* into the camp,
12:14. *let her be received in* (again).
20:24, 26. Aaron *shall be gathered*
31: 2. afterward *shalt thou be gathered*
Deu 32:50. *and was gathered* unto his people:
Jos. 10: 5. *Therefore...gathered themselves together*, and
Jud. 9: 6. *And* all the men of Shechem *gathered together*,
10:17. *And* the children of Israel *assembled themselves together*,
20:11. *So* all the men of Israel *were gathered*
14. *But* the children of Benjamin *gathered themselves*

1Sa.17: 1. *and were gathered together* at Shochoh,
2Sa.10:15. *And* when the Syrians saw...*they gathered themselves*
14:14. which cannot *be gathered up again;*
17:11. *be* generally *gathered* unto thee,
13. if *he be gotten* into a city,
23:11. *And* the Philistines were *gathered together*
2Ch 30:13. *And there assembled* at Jerusalem
Ezr. 3: 1. the people *gathered themselves together*
9: 4. Then *were assembled* unto me
Neh 8: 1. *And* all the people *gathered themselves together*
12:28. *And* the sons of the singers *gathered themselves together,*
Job 27:19. but *he shall* not *be gathered:*
Ps.104:22. *they gather themselves together,*
Isa. 43: 9. *and let* the people *be assembled:*
49: 5. Though Israel *be* not *gathered,* (marg. That Israel *may be gathered* to him, &c.)
60:20. *shall* thy moon *withdraw itself:*
Jer. 8: 2. *they shall* not *be gathered,*
25:33. shall not be lamented, neither *gathered,*
Eze.29: 5. *thou shalt* not *be brought together,*
Hos. 4: 3. of the sea also *shall be taken away.*

NIPHAL.—*Participle.*

Gen49:29. I *am to be gathered* unto my
1Sa.13:11. the Philistines *gathered themselves together*
Isa. 13: 4. kingdoms of nations *gathered together:*
57: 1. merciful men (are) *taken away,*

* PIEL.—*Participle.* *

Nu. 10:25. *the rereward* of all the camps
Jos. 6: 9. *and the rereward* (marg. *gathering* (host))
13. *but the rereward* came after
Jud.19:15. *that took* them *into* his house
18. *that receiveth* (marg. *gathereth*) me to
Isa. 52:12. *and* the God of Israel (will be) *your rereward.* (marg. *gather you up*)
62: 9. But *they that have gathered it*
Jer. 9:22(21). none *shall gather* (them).

* PUAL.—*Preterite.* *

Isa. 24:22. *And they shall be gathered* together,
33: 4. *And* your spoil *shall be gathered*
Hos.10:10. *and* the people *shall be gathered*
Zec.14:14. *and* the wealth...*shall be gathered together,*

PUAL.—*Participle.*

Eze.38:12. upon the people (that are) *gathered*

HITHPAEL.—*Infinitive.*

Deu33: 5. *when*...the tribes of Israel *were gathered together.*

---

625 **אֹסֶף** *ōh'-seph*, m.

Isa. 32:10. *the gathering* shall not come.
33: 4. *the gathering of* the caterpiller:
Mic. 7: 1. *as when they have gathered* the summer fruits, (marg. *the gatherings of* summer)

---

626 **אֲסֵפָה** *ăsēh-phāh'*, f.

Isa. 24:22. they shall be gathered *together,* (lit. *a gathering*)

---

627 **אֲסֻפּוֹת** *ăsoop-pōth'*, f. pl.

Ecc.12:11. fastened (by) the masters of *assemblies,*

---

624 **אֲסֻפִּים** *ăsoop-peem'*, m. pl.

1Ch 26:15. the house of *Asuppim.* (marg. *gatherings*)
17. *and toward Asuppim* two (and) two.
Neh 12:25. *at the thresholds of* the gates. (marg. *treasuries,* or, *assemblies*)

---

628 **אֲסַפְסֻף** *ăsaph-sooph'*, m.

Nu. 11: 4. *And the mixt multitude* that (was) among

אָסְפַּרְנָא *os-par'-nāh*, adv. Ch. 629

Ezr. 5: 8. and this work goeth *fast* on,
6: 8. *forthwith* expences be given unto these
12. let it be done *with speed.*
13. the king had sent, so they did *speedily.*
7:17. That thou mayest buy *speedily* with this
21. of you, it be done *speedily,*
26. let judgment be executed *speedily*

אָסַר [*āh-sar'.*] 631

* KAL.—*Preterite.* *

Nu. 30: 3(4). *and bind* (herself) by a bond,
4(5), 4(5), 5(6). wherewith *she hath bound*
6(7), 7(8), 8(9), 11(12). wherewith *she bound* her soul;
9(10). wherewith they *have bound* their souls,
10(11). or *bound* her soul by a bond
Jud.16: 5. *that we may bind him* to afflict him:
1Sa. 6: 7. *and tie* the kine to the cart,
Job 36:13. they cry not when *he bindeth them*
Eze. 3:25. *and shall bind thee* with them,

KAL.—*Infinitive.*

Nu. 30: 2(3). swear an oath *to bind* his soul
Jud.15:10. *To bind* Samson are we come
12. We are come down *to bind thee,*
13. will bind thee *fast,* (lit. *in binding* bind)
16:11. If they bind me *fast* with new ropes
Ps.105:22. *To bind* his princes at his pleasure;
149: 8. *To bind* their kings with chains,
Hos.10:10. *when they shall bind themselves* (marg. I *shall bind them,*)

KAL.—*Imperative.*

1K. 18:44. unto Ahab, *Prepare* (marg. *Tie,* or, *Bind*)
2K. 9:21. And Joram said, *Make ready.* (marg. *Bind*)
Ps.118:27. *bind* the sacrifice with cords,
Jer. 46: 4. *Harness* the horses; and get up,

KAL.—*Future.*

Gen42:24. *and bound* him before their eyes.
46:29. *And* Joseph *made ready* his chariot,
Ex. 14: 6. *And he made ready* his chariot,
Jud.15:13. but *we will bind thee* fast,
— *And they bound him* with two new cords,
16: 7. If *they bind me* with seven green
8. *and she bound him* with them.
11. If *they bind me* fast with new ropes
12. *and bound him* therewith,
21. *and bound him* with fetters
1Sa. 6:10. *and tied them* to the cart,
1K. 20:14. Who *shall order* the battle? (marg. *bind,* or, *tie*)
2K. 9:21. *And* his chariot *was made ready.*
17: 4. *and bound him* in prison.
23:33. *And* Pharaoh-nechoh *put him in bands*
25: 7. *and bound him* with fetters
2Ch 13: 3. *And* Abijah *set* the battle *in array* (marg. *bound together*)
33:11. *and bound him* with fetters,
36: 6. *and bound him* in fetters,
Job 12:18. *and girdeth* their loins
Jer. 39: 7. *and bound him* with chains,
52:11. *and* the king of Babylon *bound him*

KAL.—*Participle.* Poël.

Gen49:11. *Binding* his foal unto the vine,

KAL—*Participle.* Päul.

Gen39:20. the king's prisoners (were) *bound:*
40: 3. the place where Joseph (was) *bound.*
5. which (were) *bound* in the prison.
Jud.16:21. the *prison* house. (lit. house of *prisoners*)
25. called for Samson out of the *prison* house;
2Sa. 3:34. Thy hands (were) not *bound,*
2K. 7:10. horses *tied,* and asses *tied,* and the tents
Neh 4:18(12). every one had his sword *girded*
Job 36: 8. if (they be) *bound* in fetters,
Ps.146: 7. The Lord looseth *the prisoners:*
Ecc. 4:14. out of prison (lit. house of *prisoners*) he
Cant.7: 5(6). the king (is) *held* (marg. *bound*) in the
Isa. 49: 9. That thou mayest say *to the prisoners,*
61: 1. *and*...the prison *to* (them that are) *bound;*

Jer. 40: 1. *being bound* in chains

* NIPHAL.—*Imperative.* *

Gen42:16. *ye shall be kept* in prison, (marg. *bound*)

NIPHAL.—*Future.*

Gen42:19. *let* one of your brethren *be bound*
Jud. 16. 6, 10, 13. wherewith *thou mightest be bound*

* PUAL.—*Preterite.* *

Isa. 22: 3. they *are bound* by the archers: all that are found in thee *are bound*

---

632 **אֱסָר** *ĕsāhr* & **אִסָּר** *is-sāhr'*, m.

Nu. 30: 2(3). to bind his soul with *a bond;*
3(4). bind (herself) by *a bond,*
4(5). *and her bond* wherewith
—(–). every *bond* wherewith she hath
5(6). *or of her bonds* wherewith she
7(8). *and her bonds* wherewith she bound
10(11). bound her soul by *a bond*
11(12). every *bond* wherewith she bound
12(13). or concerning *the bond* of her soul,
13(14). every *binding* oath to afflict
14(15). or all *her bonds,*

---

633 **אֱסָר** *ĕsāhr*, m. Ch.

Dan 6: 7(8). make *a* firm *decree,* (marg. *interdict*)
8(9). O king, establish *the decree,*
9(10). signed the writing *and the decree.*
12(13). concerning *the* king's *decree;* Hast thou not signed *a decree,*
13(14). nor *the decree* that thou
15(16). That no *decree* nor statute

---

636 **אָע** *āhg*, m. Ch.

Ezr. 5: 8. *and timber* is laid in the walls,
6: 4. and a row of new *timber:*
11. let *timber* be pulled down
Dan 5: 4. of brass, of iron, of *wood,* and of stone.
23. of brass, iron, *wood,* and stone,

---

638 **אַף** *aph*, conj. Ch.

Ezr. 5:10. We asked their names *also,*
14. *And* the vessels *also* of gold and silver
6: 5. *And also* let the golden and silver
Dan 6:22(23). *and also* before thee, O king,

---

637 **אַף** *aph*. part.

Gen40:16. unto Joseph, I *also* (was) in my dream,
Lev.26:28. and I, *even* I, will chastise you
44. *And yet* for all that, when they be
Nu. 16:14. *Moreover* thou hast not brought us
Deu33: 3. *Yea,* he loved the people;
20. the arm *with* the crown of the head.
1Sa. 2: 7. he bringeth low, *and* lifteth up.
1Ch. 8:32. And these *also* dwelt with their brethren
2Ch.12: 5. and *therefore* have I *also* left you in
Job 4:19. *How much less* (in) them that dwell
Ps. 44: 9(10). *But* thou hast cast off, and put
&c. &c.

It is frequently followed by **כִּי**.

Gen 3: 1. the woman, *Yea,* hath God said,
1Sa.14:30. *How much more,* if haply the people
1K. 8:27. *how much less* this house that I
2K. 5:13. *how much rather then,* when he saith
Job 35:14. *Although* thou sayest thou shalt not see
Eze.23:40. *And furthermore,* that ye have *sent*
&c. &c.

---

639 **אַף** *aph*, m.

Gen 2: 7. breathed *into his nostrils*
3:19. In the sweat of *thy face* shalt
7:22. *in whose nostrils* (was) the breath of
19: 1. with his *face* toward the ground;
24:47. earring upon *her face,* (lit. *her nose*)
27:45. Until thy brother's *anger* turn away
Gen30: 2. Jacob's *anger* was kindled
39:19. that *his wrath* was kindled.
42: 6. (with) their *faces* to the earth.
44:18. let not *thine anger* burn
48:12. bowed himself *with his face* to the
49: 6. *in their anger* they slew a man,
7. Cursed (be) *their anger,*
Ex. 4:14. *the anger of* the Lord was kindled
11: 8. went out from Pharaoh in *a* great *anger,*
15: 8. with the blast of *thy nostrils*
22:24(23). *my wrath* shall wax hot,
32:10. that *my wrath* may wax hot
11. why doth *thy wrath* wax hot
12. Turn from thy fierce *wrath,*
19. Moses' *anger* waxed hot,
22. Let not *the anger of* my lord
34: 6. gracious, long*suffering,*
Nu. 11: 1. *his anger* was kindled;
10. *the anger of* the Lord was kindled
20. until it come *out at your nostrils,*
33. *the wrath of* the Lord was kindled
12: 9. *the anger of* the Lord was kindled
14:18. The Lord (is) long*suffering,*
22:22. God's *anger* was kindled
27. Balaam's *anger* was kindled,
31. fell flat *on his face.*
24:10. Balak's *anger* was kindled
25: 3. *the anger of* the Lord was kindled
4. that *the* fierce *anger of* the Lord
32:10, 13. *the* Lord's *anger* was kindled
14. augment yet *the* fierce *anger of* the Lord
Deu 6:15. lest *the anger of* the Lord
7: 4. so will *the anger of* the Lord
9:19. I was afraid of *the anger*
11:17. *the* Lord's *wrath* be kindled
13:17(18). turn from the fierceness of *his anger,*
29:20(19). but then *the anger of* the Lord
23(22). which the Lord overthrew *in his anger,*
24(23). the heat of this great *anger?*
27(26). *the anger of* the Lord was kindled
28(27). rooted them out of their land *in anger,*
31:17. Then *my anger* shall be kindled
32:22. For a fire is kindled *in mine anger,*
33:10. shall put incense *before thee,* (marg. *at thy nose*)
Jos. 7: 1. *the anger of* the Lord was kindled
26. turned from the fierceness of *his anger.*
23:16. then shall *the anger of* the Lord be
Jud. 2:14, 20, & 3:8. *the anger of* the Lord was hot
6:39. Let not *thine anger* be hot
9:30. *his anger* was kindled.
10: 7. *the anger of* the Lord was hot
14:19. *his anger* was kindled.
1Sa. 1: 5. But unto Hannah he gave *a worthy* portion; (marg. *double* lit. one portion of *two faces*)
11: 6. *his anger* was kindled greatly.
17:28. Eliab's *anger* was kindled
20:30. Saul's *anger* was kindled
34. arose from the table in fierce *anger,*
41. fell *on his face* to the ground,
24: 8(9). David stooped with his *face*
25:23. fell *before* David on her face,
41. bowed herself on (her) *face* to the earth,
28:14. stooped with (his) *face* to the ground,
18. nor executedst *his* fierce *wrath*
2Sa. 6: 7. the *anger of* the Lord was kindled
12: 5. David's *anger* was greatly
14: 4. she fell on *her face* to the ground,
33. bowed himself on *his face*
18:28. *upon his face* before the king,
22: 9. went up a smoke *out of his nostrils,*
16. at the blast of the breath of *his nostrils.* (lit. *anger*)
24: 1. again *the anger of* the Lord was kindled
20. before the king on *his face* upon the
1K. 1:23. with *his face* to the ground.
31. bowed with (her) *face* to the earth,
2K. 13: 3. And *the anger of* the Lord was kindled
19:28. I will put my hook *in thy nose,*
23:26. from the fierceness of *his* great *wrath,* wherewith *his anger* was kindled
24:20. through *the anger of* the Lord
1Ch.13:10. *the anger of* the Lord was kindled
21:21. with (his) *face* to the ground.
2Ch. 7: 3. with their *faces* to the ground
12:12. *the wrath of* the Lord turned
20:18. with (his) *face* to the ground:

2Ch.25:10. wherefore *their anger* was greatly
— they returned home in great *anger*.
15. *the anger of* the Lord was kindled
28:11. for *the* fierce *wrath of* the Lord
13. (there is) fierce *wrath* against Israel.
29:10. that *his* fierce *wrath* may turn away
30: 8. that the fierceness of *his wrath*
Ezr. 8:22. his power *and his wrath* (is) against all
10:14. *the* fierce *wrath of* our God for this matter
Neh 8: 6. with (their) *faces* to the ground.
9:17. merciful, slow to *anger*,
Job 4: 9. by the breath of *his nostrils*
9: 5. overturneth them *in his anger*.
13. God will not withdraw *his anger*,
14:13. keep me secret, until *thy wrath* be past,
16: 9. He teareth (me) in *his wrath*,
18: 4. He teareth himself *in his anger:*
19:11. He hath also kindled *his wrath*
20:23. cast the fury of *his wrath* upon him,
28. shall flow away in the day of *his wrath*.
21:17. distributeth sorrows *in his anger*.
27: 3. the spirit of God (is) *in my nostrils;*
32: 2. Then was kindled *the wrath of*
— against Job was *his wrath* kindled,
3. against his three friends was *his wrath*
5. then *his wrath* was kindled.
35:15. he hath visited in *his anger;*
36:13. hypocrites in heart heap up *wrath:*
40:11. Cast abroad the rage of *thy wrath:*
24. (his) *nose* pierceth through snares.
41: 2(40:26). Canst thou put an hook *into his nose?*
42: 7. *My wrath* is kindled against thee,
Ps. 2: 5. speak unto them *in his wrath*,
12. when *his wrath* is kindled
6: 1(2). rebuke me not *in thine anger*,
7: 6(7). Arise, O Lord, *in thine anger*,
10: 4. through the pride of *his countenance*,
18: 8(9). went up a smoke *out of his nostrils*,
15(16). the blast of the breath of *thy nostrils*.
21: 9(10). shall swallow them up *in his wrath*,
27: 9. put not thy servant away *in anger:*
30: 5(6). *his anger* (endureth but) a moment;
37: 8. Cease *from anger*, and forsake wrath:
55: 3(4). *and in wrath* they hate me.
56: 7(8). *in* (thine) *anger* cast down the people,
69: 24(25). let *thy* wrathful *anger* take hold
74: 1. doth *thine anger* smoke against
76. 7(8). when once *thou art angry?* (lit. in the time of *thy anger?*)
77: 9(10). hath he *in anger* shut up
78:21. *anger* also came up against Israel;
31. *The* (lit. *And the*) *wrath of* God came
38. turned he *his anger* away,
49. cast upon them the fierceness of *his anger*,
50. He made a way *to his anger;*
85: 3(4). from the fierceness of *thine anger*.
5(6). wilt thou draw out *thine anger*
86:15. gracious, long*suffering*,
90: 7. we are consumed *by thine anger*,
11. Who knoweth the power of *thine anger?*
95:11. Unto whom I sware *in my wrath*
103: 8. gracious, slow to *anger*,
106:40. Therefore was *the wrath of* the
110: 5. in the day of *his wrath*.
115: 6. *noses* have they, but they smell not:
124: 3. when *their wrath* was kindled
138: 7. against *the wrath of* mine enemies,
145: 8. slow to *anger*, and of great mercy.
Pro.11:22. a jewel of gold *in* a swine's *snout*,
14:17. (He that is) soon *angry* dealeth foolishly:
29. (He that is) slow to *wrath* (is) of great
15: 1. grievous words stir up *anger*.
18. (he that is) slow to *anger* appeaseth strife.
16:32. (He that is) slow to *anger* (is) better than
19:11. discretion of a man deferreth *his anger;*
21:14. A gift in secret pacifieth *anger:*
22:24. Make no friendship with an *angry* man;
24:18. he turn away *his wrath*
25:15. By long *forbearing* is a prince persuaded,
27: 4. *anger* (is) outrageous;
29: 8. but wise (men) turn away *wrath*.
22. An *angry* man stirreth up strife,
30:33. the wringing of *the nose* bringeth forth blood: so the forcing of *wrath*
Cant.7: 4(5). *thy nose* (is) as the tower of Lebanon
8(9). the smell of *thy nose* like apples;

Isa. 2:22. whose breath (is) *in his nostrils:*
3:21. The rings, and *nose* jewels,
5:25. Therefore is *the anger of* the Lord
— For all this *his anger* is not
7: 4. for the fierce *anger of* Rezin with Syria,
9:12(11), 17(16), 21(20) & 10:4. For all this *his anger* is not
10: 5. O Assyrian, the rod of *mine anger*,
25. *and mine anger* in their destruction.
12: 1. *thine anger* is turned away,
13: 3. called my mighty ones *for mine anger*,
9. both with wrath and fierce *anger*,
13. in the day of *his* fierce *anger*.
14: 6. he that ruled the nations *in anger*,
30:27. burning (with) *his anger*,
30. with the indignation of (his) *anger*,
37:29. I put my hook *in thy nose*,
42:25. poured upon him the fury of *his anger*,
48: 9. will I defer *mine anger*,
49:23. with (their) *face* toward the earth,
63: 3. for I will tread them *in mine anger*,
6. tread down the people *in mine anger*,
65: 5. These (are) a smoke *in my nose*, a fire
66:15. to render *his anger* with fury,
Jer. 2:35. surely *his anger* shall turn
4: 8. for *the* fierce *anger of* the Lord
26. by *his* fierce *anger*.
7:20. *mine anger* and my fury shall be
10:24. not *in thine anger*, lest
12:13. because of *the* fierce *anger of*
15:14. for a fire is kindled *in mine anger*,
15. in thy longsuffering: (lit. the length of *thine anger*)
17: 4. have kindled a fire *in mine anger*,
18:23. with them in the time of *thine anger*.
21: 5. *even in anger*, and in fury,
23:20. *The anger of* the Lord shall
25:37. because of *the* fierce *anger of*
38. because of *his* fierce *anger*.
30:24. *The* fierce *anger of* the Lord
32:31. to me (as) a provocation of *mine anger*
37. I have driven them *in mine anger*,
33: 5. whom I have slain *in mine anger*
36: 7. for great (is) *the anger* and the fury
42:18. As *mine anger* and my fury hath been
44: 6. *and mine anger* was poured forth,
49:37. evil upon them, (even) *my* fierce *anger*,
51:45. from *the* fierce *anger of* the Lord.
52: 3. through *the anger of* the Lord
Lam. 1:12. in the day of *his* fierce *anger*.
2: 1. with a cloud *in his anger*,
— his footstool in the day of *his anger!*
3. He hath cut off in (his) fierce *anger*
6. the indignation of *his anger*
21. slain (them) in the day of *thine anger;*
22. in the day of the Lord's *anger*
3:43. Thou hast covered *with anger*,
66. Persecute and destroy them *in anger*
4:11. he hath poured out *his* fierce *anger*,
20. The breath of *our nostrils*, the anointed
Eze. 5:13. Thus shall *mine anger* be accomplished,
15. *in anger* and in fury
7: 3. I will send *mine anger* upon thee,
8. accomplish *mine anger* upon thee:
8:17. they put the branch to *their nose*.
13:13. an overflowing shower *in mine anger*,
16:12. a jewel on *thy forehead*, [or *nose*]
20: 8, 21. to accomplish *my anger*
22:20. so will I gather (you) *in mine anger*
23:25. they shall take away *thy nose*
25:14. in Edom *according to mine anger*
35:11. I will even do *according to thine anger*,
38:18. my fury shall come up *in my face*.
43: 8. I have consumed them *in mine anger*.
Dan. 9:16. let *thine anger* and thy fury
11:20. destroyed, neither *in anger*, nor in battle.
Hos. 8: 5. *mine anger* is kindled against them:
11: 9. execute the fierceness of *mine anger*,
13:11. I gave thee a king *in mine anger*,
14: 4(5). for *mine anger* is turned away
Joel 2:13. slow to *anger*, and of great kindness,
Am. 1:11. *his anger* did tear perpetually,
4:10. to come up *unto your nostrils:*
Jon. 3: 9. turn away from *his* fierce *anger*,
4: 2. slow to *anger*, and of great kindness,
Mic. 5:15(14). I will execute vengeance *in anger*
7:18. he retaineth not *his anger*

Nah. 1: 3. The Lord (is) slow to *anger*, and great
6. abide in the fierceness of *his anger?*
Hab. 3: 8. *thine anger* against the rivers?
12. thou didst thresh the heathen *in anger*.
Zep. 2: 2. before *the* fierce *anger of* the Lord
— before the day of *the* Lord's *anger* come
3. hid in the day of *the* Lord's *anger*.
3: 8. (even) all *my* fierce *anger:*
Zec.10: 3. *Mine anger* was kindled

640 אָפַד [*āh-phad'*].

* KAL.—*Preterite.* *

Ex. 29: 5. *and gird* him with the curious

KAL.—*Future.*

Lev. 8: 7. *and bound* (it) unto him

See 646 אֵפֹד see אֵפוֹד.

642 אֲפֻדָּה [*ăphood-dāh'*] f.

Ex. 28: 8. the curious girdle of *the ephod*,
39: 5. the curious girdle of *his ephod*,
Isa. 30:22. *the ornament of* thy molten images

643 אַפֶּדֶן [*ap-peh'-den*] m.

Dan11:45. plant the tabernacles of *his palace*

644 אָפָה *āh-phāh'*.

* KAL.—*Preterite.* *

Gen19: 3. *did bake* unleavened bread,
Lev.24: 5. *and bake* twelve cakes thereof:
26:26. ten women *shall bake* your bread
Isa. 44:15. he kindleth (it), *and baketh* bread;
19. *I have baked* bread upon the coals

KAL.—*Imperative.*

Ex. 16:23. *bake* (that) which ye will bake

KAL.—*Future.*

Ex. 12:39. *And they baked* unleavened cakes
16:23. bake (that) which *ye will bake*
1Sa.28:24. *and did bake* unleavened bread *thereof:*
Eze.46:20. where *they shall bake* the meat offering;

KAL.—*Participle.* Pöel.

Gen40: 1. *and* (his) *baker* had offended
2. against the chief of *the bakers*.
5. *and the baker* of the king of Egypt,
16. When *the* chief *baker* saw that
17. all manner of *bake*meats (marg. meat, ...the work of a *baker*, or, *cook*)
20. of *the* chief *baker* among
22. But he hanged *the* chief *baker:*
41:10. (both) me and *the* chief *baker:*
1Sa. 8:13. and (to be) cooks, and (to be) *bakers*.
Jer. 37:21. a piece of bread out of *the bakers'* street,
Hos. 7: 4. as an oven heated *by the baker*,
6. *their baker* sleepeth all the night;

* NIPHAL.—*Future.* *

Lev. 6:17(10). *It shall* not *be baken* with leaven.
7: 9. all the meat offering that *is baken*
23:17. *they shall be baken* with leaven;

645 אֵפוֹ & אֵפוֹא *ēh-phōh'*, part.

Gen27:33. Who? *where* (is) he that hath taken venison,
37. what shall I do *now* unto thee, my son?
43:11. If (it must be) so *now*, do this;
Ex. 33:16. wherein shall it be known *here*
Ju. 9:38. Where (is) *now* thy mouth,
2K. 10:10. Know *now* that there shall fall
Job 9:24. if not, *where*, (and) who (is) he?
17:15. where (is) *now* my hope?
19: 6. Know *now* that God hath overthrown me,
Job 19:23. Oh that my words were *now* written!
24:25. And if (it be) not (so) *now*, who will
Pro. 6: 3. Do this *now*, my son, and deliver
Isa. 19:12. *where* (are) thy wise (men)?
22: 1. What aileth thee *now*,
Hos.13:10. *where* (is any other) that may save

אֵפוֹד & אֵפֹד *ēh-phōhd'*, m. 646

Ex. 25: 7. stones to be set *in the ephod*,
28: 4. a breastplate, *and an ephod*,
6. they shall make *the ephod*
12. upon the shoulders of *the ephod*
15. after the work of *the ephod*
25. on the shoulderpieces of *the ephod*
26. which (is) in the side of *the ephod*
27. on the two sides of *the ephod*
— the curious girdle of *the ephod*.
28. unto the rings of *the ephod*
— above the curious girdle of *the ephod*,
— be not loosed from *the ephod*.
31. make the robe of *the ephod*
29: 5. the robe of *the ephod*, and *the ephod*, and
— with the curious girdle of *the ephod:*
35: 9, 27. *for the ephod*, and for the breastplate.
39: 2. he made *the ephod* (of) gold,
7. put them on the shoulders of *the ephod*,
8. like the work of *the ephod;*
18. the shoulderpieces of *the ephod*,
19. which (was) on the side of *the ephod*
20. put them on the two sides of *the ephod*
— 21. the curious girdle of *the ephod*.
21. unto the rings of *the ephod*
— might not be loosed from *the ephod;*
22. he made the robe of *the ephod*
Lev. 8: 7. put *the ephod* upon him,
— with the curious girdle of *the ephod*,
Jud. 8:27. Gideon made *an ephod* thereof,
17: 5. made *an ephod*, and teraphim,
18:14. there is in these houses *an ephod*,
17. took the graven image, and *the ephod*,
18. fetched the carved image, *the ephod*, and
20. he took *the ephod*, and the teraphim,
1Sa. 2:18. girded with a linen *ephod*.
28. to wear *an ephod* before me?
14: 3. priest in Shiloh, wearing *an ephod*.
21: 9(10). wrapped in a cloth behind *the ephod:*
22:18. that did wear a linen *ephod*.
23: 6. came down (with) *an ephod*
9. Bring hither *the ephod*.
30: 7. bring me hither *the ephod*. And Abiathar brought thither *the ephod*
2Sa. 6:14. David (was) girded with a linen *ephod*.
1Ch.15:27. David also (had) upon him *an ephod of*
Hos. 3: 4. without *an ephod*, and (without) teraphim:

אֲפִילֹת *ăphee-lōhth'*, adj. pl. 648

Ex. 9:32. for they (were) *not grown up*. (marg. *hidden*, or, *dark*)

אָפִיק [*āh-pheek'*] m. 650

2Sa.22:16. *the channels of* the sea appeared.
Job 6:15. *as the stream of* brooks
12:21. weakeneth the strength of *the mighty*.
40:18. His bones (are as) *strong pieces of*
41:15(7). *scales* (are his) pride, (marg. *strong pieces of* shields)
Ps. 18:15(16). Then the *channels of* waters
42: 1(2). panteth after the water *brooks*,
126: 4. *as the streams* in the south.
Cant.5:12. doves by *the rivers of* waters,
Isa. 8: 7. he shall come up over all *his channels*,
Eze. 6: 3. *to the rivers*, and to the vallies;
31:12. broken by all *the rivers of* the land;
32: 6. *and the rivers* shall be full
34:13. the mountains of Israel *by the rivers*,
35: 8. and in all *thy rivers*,
36: 4, 6. *to the rivers*, and to the valleys, (marg. *bottoms*, or, *dales*)
Joel 1:20. for *the rivers of* waters
3:18(4:18). and all *the rivers of* Judah

651 **אָפֵל** *āh-phēhl′*, adj.

Am. 5:20. *even very dark*, and no brightness

652 **אֹפֶל** *ōh′-phel*, m.

Job 3: 6. let *darkness* seize upon it;
10:22. A land of darkness, as *darkness*
— and (where) the light (is) as *darkness*.
23:17. (neither) hath he covered *the darkness*
28: 3. the stones of *darkness*,
30:26. for light, there came *darkness*.
Ps. 11: 2. that they may *privily* shoot (marg. in *darkness*)
91: 6. the pestilence (that) walketh *in darkness*;
Isa. 29:18. *and* the eyes of the blind shall see *out of obscurity*,

653 **אֲפֵלָה** *ăphēh-lāh′*, f.

Ex. 10:22. there was a *thick* darkness
Deu28:29. as the blind gropeth *in darkness*,
Pro. 4:19. The way of the wicked (is) *as darkness*:
7: 9. in the black *and dark* night:
Isa. 8:22. *and* (they shall be) driven to *darkness*.
58:10. *and thy darkness* (be) as the noon day:
59: 9. we walk *in darkness*.
Jer. 23:12. as slippery (ways) *in the darkness*:
Joel 2: 2. A day of darkness *and* of *gloominess*,
Zep. 1:15. a day of darkness *and gloominess*,

655 **אָפְנִים** [*oph-neem′*] m.

Pro. 25:11. A word *fitly* spoken (is like) (marg. spoken upon *his wheels*)

656 **אָפֵס** *āh-phēhs′*.

* KAL.—*Preterite.* *

Gen47:15. for the money *faileth*.
16. give you for your cattle, if money *fail*.
Ps. 77: 8(9). *Is* his mercy *clean gone* for ever?
Isa. 16: 4. the extortioner *is at an end*,
29:20. the terrible one *is brought to nought*,

657 **אֶפֶס** *eh′-phes*, m.

With the conj. כִּי it is used as an adverb.

Nu. 13:28. *Nevertheless* the people (be) strong
22:35. *but only* the word that I shall
23:13. thou shalt see *but* the utmost part
Deu15: 4. *Save* when there shall be no poor
32:36. *and* (there is) *none* shut up, or left.
33:17. to *the ends of* the earth:
Jud. 4: 9. *notwithstanding* the journey
1Sa. 2:10. the Lord shall judge *the ends of*
2Sa. 9: 3. (Is) *there not* yet any of the house
12:14. *Howbeit*, because by this deed
2K. 14:26. *for* (there was) *not any* shut up, *nor any* left,
Job 7: 6. are spent *without* hope.
Ps. 2: 8. *the uttermost parts of* the earth
22:27(28). All *the ends of* the world
59:13(14). *unto the ends of* the earth.
67: 7(8). all *the ends of* the earth shall fear him.
72: 8. unto *the ends of* the earth.
98: 3. all *the ends of* the earth have
Pro. 14:28. *but in the want* of people
26:20. *Where no* wood is,
30: 4. established all *the ends of* the earth?
Isa. 5: 8. till (there be) *no* place,
34:12. all her princes shall be *nothing*.
40:17. counted to him *less than nothing*,
41:12. and *as a thing of nought*.
29. their works (are) *nothing*:
45: 6. that (there is) *none beside* me.
14. and (there is) none else, (there is) *no* God.
22. saved, all *the ends of* the earth:
Isa. 46: 9. *and* (there is) *none* like me,
52: 4. oppressed them *without cause*.
10. all *the ends of* the earth shall see
54:15. together, (but) *not* by me:
Jer. 16:19. *from the ends of* the earth,
Eze.47: 3. the waters (were) to *the ancles*.
Dan 8:25. *but* he shall be broken *without* hand.
Am. 6:10. and he shall say, *No*.
9: 8. *saving* that I will not utterly
Mic. 5: 4(3). unto *the ends of* the earth.
Zec. 9:10. to *the ends of* the earth.

אַפְסִי *aph-see′* part. 657

Isa. 47: 8, 10. I (am), *and none* else *beside me*;
Zep. 2:15. *and* (there is) *none beside me*:

אֶפַע [*eh′-phag̃*], m. 659

Isa. 41:24. your work *of nought*: (marg. (worse) *than of a viper*)

אֶפְעֶה *eph-g̃eh′*, m. 660

Job 20:16. *the viper*'s tongue shall slay him.
Isa. 30: 6. *the viper* and fiery flying serpent,
59: 5. is crushed breaketh out into *a viper*.

אָפַף [*āh-phaph′*]. 661

* KAL.—*Preterite.* *

2Sa. 22: 5. the waves of death *compassed me*,
Ps. 18: 4(5). The sorrows of death *compassed me*,
40:12(13). innumerable evils *have compassed*
116: 3. The sorrows of death *compassed me*,
Jon. 2: 5(6). The waters *compassed me*

אָפַק [*āh-phak′*]. 662

* HITHPAEL.—*Preterite.* *

Isa. 63:15. toward me? *are they restrained?*

HITHPAEL.—*Infinitive.*

Gen45: 1. Joseph could not *refrain himself*

HITHPAEL.—*Future.*

Gen 43:31. *and refrained himself*, and said,
1Sa. 13:12. *I forced myself therefore*, and offered
Est. 5:10. *Nevertheless* Haman *refrained himself*:
Isa. 42:14. I have been still, (and) *refrained myself*:
64:12(11). *Wilt thou refrain thyself* for these

אֵפֶר *ēh′-pher*, m. 665

Gen18:27. which (am but) dust *and ashes*:
Nu. 19: 9. *the ashes of* the heifer,
10. he that gathereth *the ashes of*
2Sa. 13:19. Tamar put *ashes* on her head,
Est. 4: 1. put on sackcloth *with ashes*,
3. many lay in sackcloth *and ashes*.
Job 2: 8. he sat down among *the ashes*.
13:12. Your remembrances (are) like unto *ashes*,
30:19. I am become like dust *and ashes*.
42: 6. repent in dust *and ashes*.
Ps. 102: 9(10). For I have eaten *ashes* like bread,
147:16. he scattereth the hoarfrost *like ashes*.
Isa. 44:20. He feedeth on *ashes*:
58: 5. to spread sackcloth *and ashes*
61: 3. to give unto them beauty for *ashes*,
Jer. 6:26. wallow thyself *in ashes*:
Lam. 3:16. he hath covered me *with ashes*.
Eze. 27:30. wallow themselves *in the ashes*:
28:18. I will bring thee *to ashes*
Dan. 9: 3. with fasting, and sackcloth, *and ashes*:
Jon. 3: 6. and sat in *ashes*.
Mal. 4: 3(3:21). for they shall be *ashes*

666 **אֵפֶר** *ăphēhr*, m.

1K. 20:38. disguised himself *with ashes* upon his face.
41. took *the ashes* away from his face;

667 **אֶפְרֹחִים** *eph-rōḥ-ḡheem'*, m.
[pl. of אֶפְרֹחַ].

Deu22: 6. (whether they be) *young ones*, or eggs, and the dam sitting upon *the young*,
Job 39:30. *Her young ones also* suck up blood:
Ps. 84: 3(4). where she may lay *her young*,

668 **אַפִּרְיוֹן** *ap-pir-yōhn'*, m.

Cant.3: 9. King Solomon made himself *a chariot* (marg. *bed*)

674 **אַפְּתֹם** *ap-p'thōhm'*, Ch.

Ezr. 4:13. *and* (so) thou shalt endamage *the revenue* of the kings. (marg. *strength*)

676 **אֶצְבַּע** *etz-baḡ'*, f.

Ex. 8:19(15). This (is) *the finger of* God:
29:12. the horns of the altar *with thy finger*,
31:18. written *with the finger of* God.
Lev. 4: 6, 17. the priest shall dip *his finger* in
25. blood of the sin offering *with his finger*,
30. take of the blood thereof *with his finger*,
34. blood of the sin offering *with his finger*,
8:15. of the altar round about *with his finger*,
9: 9. he dipped *his finger* in the blood,
14:16. the priest shall dip *his* right *finger*
— sprinkle of the oil *with his finger*
27. the priest shall sprinkle *with his* right *finger*
16:14. and sprinkle (it) *with his finger*
— of the blood *with his finger* seven times.
19. blood upon it *with his finger* seven times,
Nu. 19: 4. shall take of her blood *with his finger*,
Deu 9:10. written *with the finger of* God;
2Sa.21:20. that had on every hand six *fingers*, *and* on every foot six *toes*, (lit. and the *fingers* of his hands and the *fingers* of his feet, six and six)
1Ch.20: 6. *whose fingers and toes* (were) four and twenty, six (on each hand), and six (on each foot): (lit. *and his fingers* (were) twenty-four, six and six)
Ps. 8: 3(4). the work of *thy fingers*,
144: 1. teacheth my hands to war, (and) *my fingers* to fight:
Pro. 6:13. he teacheth *with his fingers*;
7: 3. Bind them upon *thy fingers*,
Cant.5: 5. *and my fingers* (with) sweet smelling
Isa. 2: 8. that which *their own fingers* have made:
17: 8. (that) which *his fingers* have made,
58: 9. the putting forth of *the finger*,
59: 3. *and your fingers* with iniquity;
Jer. 52:21. the thickness thereof (was) four *fingers*:

677 **אֶצְבְּעָן** *etz-b'ḡāhn'*, f. pl. Ch.

Dan 2:41. thou sawest the feet *and toes*,
42. *And* (as) *the toes of* the feet
5: 5. In the same hour came forth *fingers*

679 **אַצִּיל** [*atz-tzeel'*].

Jer. 38:12. rotten rags under thine arm*holes*
Eze.13:18. sew pillows to all arm*holes*, (marg. *elbows*)
41: 8. a full reed of six *great* cubits.

אֲצִילִים [*ătzeé-leem'*], m. pl. 678

Ex. 24:11. upon *the nobles of* the children
Isa. 41: 9. *and* called thee *from the chief men thereof*,

אָצַל [*āh-tzal'*]. 680

* KAL.—*Preterite.* *

Gen27:36. *Hast thou* not *reserved* a blessing
Nu. 11:17. *and I will take* of the spirit
Ecc. 2:10. *I kept* not from them,

* NIPHAL.—*Preterite.* *

Eze.42: 6. *was straitened* more than the

* HIPHIL.—*Future.* *

Nu. 11:25. *and took* of the spirit that (was) upon him,

אֵצֶל *ēh'-tzel.* 681

Gen39:10. to lie *by her*, (or) to be with her.
15, 18. he left his garment *with me*,
16. she laid up his garment *by her*,
41: 3. stood *by* the (other) kine
Lev. 1:16. cast it *beside* the altar
6:10(3). he shall put them *beside* the altar.
10:12. eat it without leaven *beside* the altar:
Deu11:30. *beside* the plains of Moreh?
16:21. any trees *near unto* the altar
Jud.19:14. (when they were) *by* Gibeah,
1Sa. 5: 2. set it *by* Dagon.
17:30. he turned *from him* toward
20:19. shalt remain *by* the stone Ezel.
41. out of (a place) *toward* the south,
1K. 1: 9. which (is) *by* En-rogel,
2:29. behold, (he is) *by* the altar.
3:20. took my son *from beside me*,
4:12. which (is) *by* Zartanah
10:19. two lions stood *beside* the stays.
13:24. the ass stood *by it*, the lion also stood *by*
25. the lion standing *by* the carcase:
28. *and* the lion standing *by* the carcase:
31. lay my bones *beside* his bones:
20:36. as he was departed *from him*,
21: 1. *hard by* the palace of Ahab
2. because it (is) near *unto* my house:
2K. 12: 9(10). set it *beside* the altar,
2Ch 9:18. two lions standing *by* the stays:
28:15. *to* their brethren: then they returned
Neh 2: 6. the queen also sitting *by him*,
3:23. the son of Ananiah *by* his house.
4: 3(3:35). Tobiah the Ammonite (was) *by him*,
12(6). the Jews which dwelt *by them*
18(12). sounded the trumpet (was) *by me*.
8: 4. *beside him* stood Mattithiah,
Pro. 7: 8. through the street *near* her corner;
12. *and* lieth in wait *at* every
8:30. Then I was *by him*,
Isa. 19:19. a pillar *at* the border thereof
Jer. 35: 4. which (was) *by* the chamber
41:17. which is *by* Beth-lehem,
Eze. 1:15. *by* the living creatures,
19. the wheels went *by them*:
9: 2. stood *beside* the brasen altar.
10: 6. stood *beside* the wheels.
9. four wheels *by* the cherubims, one wheel *by* one cherub, and another wheel *by*
16. the wheels went *by them*:
— turned not *from beside them*.
33:30. against thee *by* the walls
39:15. he set up a sign *by it*,
40: 7. *by* the porch of the gate
43: 6. the man stood *by me*.
8. their post *by* my posts,
Dan 8: 7. I saw him come close *unto* the ram,
17. So he came *near* where I stood:
10:13. I remained there *with* the king's
Am. 2: 8. laid to pledge *by* every altar,

אֶצְעָדָה *etz-ḡāh-dāh'*, f. 685

Nu. 31:50. of gold, *chains*, and bracelets,
2Sa. 1:10. *and the bracelet* that (was) on his arm,

686 **אָצַר** [*āh-tzar'*],

* KAL.—*Preterite.* *

2K. 20:17. thy fathers *have laid up in store*
Isa. 39: 6. thy fathers *have laid up in store*

KAL.—*Future.*

Neh 13:13. *And I made treasurers* over

KAL.—*Participle.* Pöel.

Am. 3:10. *who store up* violence

* NIPHAL.—*Future.* *

Isa. 23:18. *it shall* not *be treasured*

---

688 **אֶקְדָּח** *ek-dāgh'*, m.

Isa. 54:12. and thy gates of *carbuncles*, (lit. stones of *carbuncles*)

---

689 **אַקּוֹ** *ak-kōh*, m.

Deu 14: 5. fallow deer, *and the wild goat*,

---

691 **אֶרְאֵל** [*er-ēhl'*], m.

Isa. 33: 7. *their valiant ones* (marg. *messengers*) shall

---

693 **אָרַב** *āh-rav'*.

* KAL.—*Preterite.* *

Deu 19:11. *and lie in wait* for him,
Jud. 21:20. Go *and lie in wait* in the vineyards;
Job 31: 9. *I have laid wait* at my
Ps. 59: 3(4). *they lie in wait* for my soul:
Lam 4:19. *they laid wait* for us

KAL.—*Infinitive.*

Pro. 12: 6. *to lie in wait* for blood:
Hos. 7: 6. *whiles they lie in wait:*

KAL.—*Imperative.*

Jud. 9:32. *and lie in wait* in the field:

KAL.—*Future.*

Jud. 9:34. *and they laid wait* against
43. *and laid wait* in the field,
16: 2. *and laid wait* for him
Ps. 10: 9. *He lieth in wait* secretly as a lion in his den: *he lieth in wait* to catch
Pro. 1:11. *let us lay wait* for blood,
18. *they lay wait* for their (own) blood;
7:12. *lieth in wait* at every corner.
23:28. *She* also *lieth in wait*
24:15. *Lay* not *wait*, O wicked (man),
Mic. 7: 2. *they* all *lie in wait* for blood;

KAL.—*Participle.* Pöel.

Jos. 8: 2. lay thee *an ambush* for the city
4. ye *shall lie in wait*
7. ye shall rise up *from the ambush*,
12. set them *to lie in ambush*
14. *liers in ambush* against him
19. *And the ambush* arose quickly
21. saw that *the ambush* had taken
Jud. 16: 9. *Now* (there were) *men lying in wait*,
12. *And* (there were) *liers in wait*
20:29. Israel set *liers in wait*
33. *and the liers in wait of* Israel
36. they trusted unto *the liers in wait*
37. *And the liers in wait* hasted, and rushed upon Gibeah; and *the liers in wait* drew
38. and *the liers in wait*,
1Sa. 22: 8, 13. *to lie in wait*, as at this day?
Ezr. 8:31. *and of such as lay in wait*
Jer. 51:12. prepare *the ambushes:* (marg. *liers in wait*)
Lam 3:10. He (was) unto me (as) a bear *lying in wait*,

* PIEL.—*Participle.* *

Jud. 9:25. set *liers in wait* for him
2Ch 20:22. the Lord set *ambushments*,

* HIPHIL.—*Future.* *

1Sa. 15: 5. and *laid wait* in the valley. (marg. *fought* as if derived from ריב)

אֶרֶב [*eh'-rev*], m. 695

Job 37: 8. Then the beasts go *into dens*,
38:40. abide in the covert *to lie in wait?*

אֹרֶב [*ōh'-rev*], m. 696

Jer. 9: 8(7). in heart he layeth *his wait.*

אַרְבֶּה *ar-beh'*, m. 697

Ex. 10: 4. will I bring *the locusts* into thy
12. the land of Egypt *for the locusts*,
13. the east wind brought *the locusts.*
14. *the locusts* went up over
— there were no such *locusts*
19. which took away *the locusts*,
— there remained not one *locust*
Lev. 11:22. *the locust* after his kind,
Deu 28:38. for *the locust* shall consume it.
Jud. 6: 5. they came as *grasshoppers*
7:12. lay along in the valley *like grasshoppers*
1K. 8:37. blasting, mildew, *locust*,
2Ch 6:28. blasting, or mildew, *locusts*,
Job 39:20. make him afraid *as a grasshopper?*
Ps. 78:46. their labour *unto the locust.*
105:34. He spake, and *the locusts* came,
109:23. up and down *as the locust.*
Pro 30:27. *The locusts* have no king,
Jer. 46:23. they are more *than the grasshoppers*,
Joel 1: 4. hath *the locust* eaten; and that which *the locust* hath left
2:25. that *the locust* hath eaten,
Nah. 3:15. make thyself many *as the locusts.*
17. Thy crowned (are) *as the locusts*,

אֲרֻבָּה *ăroob-bāh'*, f. 699

Gen 7:11. *and the windows* (marg. *floodgates*) *of*
8: 2. *and the windows of* heaven were stopped,
2K. 7: 2. (if) the Lord would make *windows* in
19. the Lord should make *windows*
Ecc. 12: 3. those that look *out of the windows*
Isa. 24:18. for *the windows* from on high
60: 8. as the doves to *their windows?*
Hos. 13: 3. as the smoke *out of the chimney.*
Mal. 3:10. open you *the windows of* heaven,

אָרְבוֹת *or-bōhth'*, f. 698

Isa. 25:11. with *the spoils of* their hands.

אַרְבַּע *ar-bag'*, f. 702

אַרְבָּעָה *ar-bāh-gāh'*, m.

Gen. 2:10. and became *into four* heads.
11:13. after he begat Salah *four* hundred *and*
15. after he begat Eber *four* hundred *and*
16. Eber lived *four* and thirty years,
17. after he begat Peleg *four* hundred *and*
14: 5. *And in* the *four*teenth year came
9. *four* kings with five.
15:13. they shall afflict them *four* hundred
23:15, 16. *four* hundred shekels of silver;
31:41. I served thee *four*teen years
32: 6(7). *and four* hundred men with him.
33: 1. and with him *four* hundred men.
46:22. all the souls (were) *four*teen.
47:24. *and four* parts shall be your own,
Ex. 12: 6. the *four*teenth day of the same month:
18. *on the four*teenth day of the month
40, 41. *four* hundred *and* thirty years.
22: 1(21:37). *four* sheep for a sheep.
25:12. thou shalt cast *four* rings

Ex. 25:12. put (them) in the *four* corners
26. thou shalt make for it *four* rings of gold, and put the rings in the *four* corners that (are) *on* the *four* feet
34. *four* bowls made like unto almonds,
26: 2, 8. the breadth of one curtain *four* cubits:
32. *four* pillars of shittim (wood)
— upon *the four* sockets of silver.
27: 2. the *four* corners thereof:
4. shalt thou make *four* brasen rings in the *four* corners thereof.
16. their pillars (shall be) *four*, and their sockets *four*.
28:17. *four* rows of stones:
36: 9. the breadth of one curtain *four* cubits:
15. *four* cubits (was) the breadth
36. *four* pillars (of) shittim (wood),
— *four* sockets of silver.
37: 3, 13. he cast for it *four* rings of gold,
— (to be set) by the *four* corners
13. put the rings upon the *four* corners that (were) *in* the *four* feet
20. *four* bowls made like almonds,
38: 2. made the horns thereof on the *four*
5. he cast *four* rings *for the four* ends
19. their pillars (were) *four*, and their sockets (of) brass *four*;
29. two thousand *and four* hundred shekels.
39:10. *four* rows of stones:
Lev. 11:20. All fowls that creep, going upon (all) *four*,
21. creeping thing that goeth upon (all) *four*,
23. flying creeping things, which have *four*
27. all manner of beasts that go on (all) *four*,
42. whatsoever goeth upon (all) *four*,
23: 5. *In* the *four*teenth (day) of the first
Nu. 1:27. threescore and *four*teen thousand and six
29. fifty and *four* thousand *and four* hundred.
31. fifty and seven thousand *and four*
37. thirty and five thousand *and four* hundred.
43. fifty and three thousand *and four*
2: 4. threescore and *four*teen thousand and 600.
6. fifty and *four* thousand *and four* hundred.
8. fifty and seven thousand *and four*
9. 186 thousand *and four* hundred,
16. 151 thousand *and four* hundred and fifty,
23. thirty and five thousand *and four*
30. fifty and three thousand *and four*
7: 7. Two wagons and *four* oxen
8. *four* wagons and eight oxen
85. two thousand *and four* hundred (shekels),
88. twenty *and four* bullocks,
9: 3. *In* the *four*teenth day of this month,
5. *on* the *four*teenth day of the first month
11. The *four*teenth day of the second month
16:49(17:14). *four*teen thousand and seven
25: 9. twenty and *four* thousand.
26:25. threescore and *four* thousand and 300.
43. threescore and *four* thousand *and four*
47. fifty and three thousand *and four* hundred.
50. forty and five thousand *and four*
28:16. *in* the *four*teenth day of the first
29:13. *four*teen lambs of the first year;
15. each lamb *of the four*teen lambs:
17, 20, 23, 26, 29, 32. *four*teen lambs of the
Deu. 3:11. *and four* cubits the breadth
22:12. the *four* quarters of thy vesture,
Jos. 5:10. kept the passover *on the four*teenth day
15:36 & 18:28. *four*teen cities with their villages:
19: 7. *four* cities and their villages:
21:18, 22, 24, 29, 31, 35, 39 (37). *four* cities.
Jud. 9:34. wait against Shechem in *four* companies.
11:40. to lament the daughter of J. ...*four* days
19: 2. and was there *four* whole months.
20: 2. *four* hundred thousand footmen
17. *four* hundred thousand men
47. abode in the rock Rimmon *four* months.
21:12. *four* hundred young virgins,
1Sa. 4: 2. in the field *about four* thousand men.
22: 2. with him *about four* hundred men.
25:13. after David *about four* hundred men;
27: 7. a full year *and four* months.
30:10. David pursued, he *and four* hundred
17. *four* hundred young men,
2Sa. 21:20. *four and* twenty in number;
22. These *four* were born to the giant in
1K. 6: 1. in the *four* hundred *and* eightieth year
7: 2. *four* rows of cedar pillars,

1K. 7:19. the chapiters...*four* cubits.
27. *four* cubits (was) the length of one base, *and four* cubits the breadth thereof,
30. *And* every base had *four* brasen wheels,
— *and* the *four* corners thereof had
32. *And* under the borders (were) *four* wheels;
34. *And* (there were) *four* undersetters to the *four* corners of one base:
38. every laver was *four* cubits:
42. *four* hundred pomegranates
8:65. seven days and seven days, (even) *four*teen days.
9:28. gold, *four* hundred and twenty talents,
10:26. a thousand *and four* hundred chariots,
15:33. twenty *and four* years.
18:19. the prophets of Baal *four* hundred and fifty, and the prophets of the groves *four* hundred,
22. Baal's prophets (are) *four* hundred and
33(34). Fill *four* barrels with water,
22: 6. *about four* hundred men,
41. in the *fourth* year of Ahab
2K. 7: 3. *And* there were *four* leprous men
14:13. unto the corner gate, *four* hundred cubits.
18:13. *Now in* the *four*teenth year of king
1Ch. 3: 5. Shimea, and Shobab, and Nathan, and Solomon, *four*,
5:18. *four and* forty thousand 760,
7: 1. Tola, and Puah, Jashub, and Shimrom, *four*.
7. twenty and two thousand and thirty *and four*.
9:24. *In four* quarters were the porters,
26. the *four* chief porters,
12:26. *four* thousand and six hundred.
20: 6. whose fingers and toes (were) *four and*
21: 5. *four* hundred threescore and ten thousand men
20. *and* his *four* sons with him hid themselves.
23: 4. twenty *and four* thousand (were) to set
5. *Moreover four* thousand (were) porters; *and four* thousand praised the Lord with the instruments
10. These *four* (were) the sons of Shimei.
12. Amram, Izhar, Hebron, and Uzziel, *four*.
24:13. the *four*teenth to Jeshebeab,
18. the *four* and twentieth to Maaziah.
25: 5. God gave to Heman *four*teen sons
21. *The four*teenth *to* Mattithiah,
31. The *four* and twentieth to Romamti-ezer,
26:17. northward *four* a day, southward *four* a
18. *four* at the causeway,
27: 1, 2, 4, 5, 7, 8, 9, 10, 11, 12, 13, 14, 15. twenty *and four* thousand.
2Ch. 1:14. a thousand *and four* hundred chariots,
3: 2. in the *fourth* year of his reign.
4:13. *four* hundred pomegranates
8:18. *four* hundred and fifty talents
9:25. Solomon had *four* thousand stalls
13: 3. *four* hundred thousand chosen men:
21. Abijah...married *four*teen wives,
18: 5. of prophets *four* hundred men,
25:23. to the corner gate, *four* hundred cubits.
30:15. killed the passover *on* the *four*teenth
35: 1. *on* the *four*teenth (day) of the first
Ezr. 1:10. silver basons...*four* hundred and ten,
11. and of silver (were) five thousand *and four* hundred.
2: 7. of Elam, 1250 *and four*.
15. children of Adin, *four* hundred fifty *and four*.
31. of the other Elam, 1250 *and four*.
40. children of Hodaviah, seventy *and four*.
64. forty and two thousand (lit. *four* ten thousands, &c.)
67. Their camels, *four* hundred thirty and
6:19. kept the passover upon the *four*teenth
Neh. 6: 4. they sent unto me *four* times
7:12. of Elam, 1250 *and four*.
23. of Bezai, three hundred twenty *and four*.
34. of the other Elam, 1250 *and four*.
43. the children of Hodevah, seventy *and four*.
66. congregation together (was) forty and two thousand (lit. *four* ten thousands, &c.)
69. camels, *four* hundred thirty and five:
9: 1. in the twenty *and fourth* day

Neh 11: 6. *four* hundred threescore and eight valiant men.
18. in the holy city (were) 280 *and four.*
Est. 9:15. on the *four*teenth day also of the month
17. *on* the *four*teenth day of the same
18. *and on* the *four*teenth thereof;
19, 21. the *four*teenth day of the month
Job 1:19. smote the *four* corners of the house,
42:12. he had *four*teen thousand sheep,
16. and his sons' sons, (even) *four*
Pro.30:15. *four* (things) say not, (It is) enough:
18. *yea, four* which I know not:
21. *four* (which) it cannot bear:
24. *four* (things which are) little
29. *yea, four* are comely in going:
Isa. 11:12. *from* the *four* corners of the earth.
17: 6. *four* (or) five in the outmost
36: 1. *in* the *four*teenth year of king Hezekiah,
Jer. 15: 3. I will appoint over them *four* kinds,
36:23. when Jehudi had read three *or four* leaves,
49:36. I bring the *four* winds *from* the *four*
52:21. the thickness thereof (was) *four* fingers:
30. the persons (were) *four* thousand and 600.
Eze. 1: 5. the likeness of *four* living creatures.
6. *And* every one had *four* faces, *and* every one had *four* wings.
8. *four* sides; and *they four had* their faces
10. *they four had* the face of a man,
— *they four had* the face of an ox
— *they four* also *had* the face of an eagle.
15. *with* his *four* faces.
16. *they four had* one likeness:
17. they went upon their *four* sides:
18. full of eyes round *about them four.*
7: 2. the *four* corners of the land.
10: 9. the *four* wheels by the cherubims,
10. *they four had* one likeness,
11. they went upon their *four* sides;
12. the wheels that *they four had.*
14. *And* every one had *four* faces:
21. Every one had *four* faces apiece (lit. *four, four* faces to one), *and* every one *four* wings;
14:21. when I send my *four* sore judgments
37: 9. Come *from* the *four* winds, O breath,
40: 1. *in* the *four*teenth year
41. *Four* tables (were) on this side, *and four* tables on that side,
42. *And* the *four* tables (were) of hewn
41: 5. the breadth of (every) side chamber, *four*
42:20. He measured it *by* the *four* sides:
43:14. to the greater settle (shall be) *four*
15. the altar (shall be) *four* cubits; and from the altar and upward (shall be) *four*
16. square in the *four* squares thereof.
17. the settle (shall be) *four*teen (cubits) long and *four*teen broad *in* the *four* squares thereof;
20. on the *four* horns of it, and on the *four*
45:19. upon the *four* corners of the settle
21. *in* the *four*teenth day of the month,
46:21. the *four* corners of the court;
22. *In* the *four* corners of the court
— *these four* corners (were) *of* one measure.
23. round about *them four,*
48:16, 16, 16, 16, 30, 32, 33, 34. side *four* thousand *and* five hundred,
Dan. 1:17. *these four* children,
8: 8. came up *four* notable ones *toward* the *four* winds
22. whereas *four* stood up for it, *four* kingdoms shall stand up
10: 4. in the *four and* twentieth day
11: 4. *toward* the *four* winds of heaven;
Am. 1: 3, 6, 9, 11, 13 & 2:1, 4, 6. For three transgressions...and for *four,*
Hag. 1:15. In the *four and* twentieth day
2:10, 20. the *four and* twentieth (day) of the
18. from the *four* and twentieth day
Zec. 1: 7. Upon the *four and* twentieth day
18(2:1). saw, and behold *four* horns.
20(2:3). the Lord shewed me *four* carpenters,
2: 6(10). *as* the *four* winds of the heaven,
6: 1. there came *four* chariots
5. the *four* spirits of the heavens,
7: 1. in the *fourth* year of king Darius,
in the fourth (day) of the ninth

אַרְבַּע *ar-bag̃*, f. 703

אַרְבְּעָה *ar-bāh-g̃āh'*, m. Ch.

Ezr. 6:17. *four* hundred lambs;
Dan. 3:25. Lo, I see *four* men loose, walking
7: 2. the *four* winds of the heaven strove
3. *And four* great beasts came up from
6. upon the back of it *four* wings of a fowl; the beast had *also four* heads;
17. great beasts, which are *four,* (are) *four* kings,

אַרְבָּעִים *ar-bāh-g̃eem'.* 705

Gen 5:13. Cainan lived...eight hundred and *forty*
7: 4, 12. *forty* days *and forty* nights;
17. the flood was *forty* days upon
8: 6. at the end of *forty* days,
18:28. If I find there *forty* and five,
29. there shall be *forty* found there.
— I will not do (it) for *forty*'s sake.
25:20. Isaac was *forty* years old
26:34. Esau was *forty* years old
32:15(16). *forty* kine, and ten bulls,
47:28. of J. was an hundred *forty and* seven
50: 3. *forty* days were fulfilled
Ex. 16:35. did eat manna *forty* years,
24:18. in the mount *forty* days *and forty* nights.
26:19. thou shalt make *forty* sockets
21. *And* their *forty* sockets (of) silver;
34:28. there with the L. *forty* days *and forty*
36:24. *And forty* sockets of silver
26. *And* their *forty* sockets of silver;
Lev.25: 8. be unto thee *forty and* nine years.
Nu. 1:21. *forty and* six thousand and five hundred.
25. *forty and* five thousand six hundred and
33. *forty* thousand and five hundred.
41. *forty* and one thousand and five hundred.
2:11. (were) *forty and* six thousand and 500.
15. *forty and* five thousand and 650.
19. *forty* thousand and five hundred.
28. *forty and* one thousand and five hundred.
13:25. searching of the land after *forty* days.
14:33. wander in the wilderness *forty* years,
34. searched the land, (even) *forty* days,
— bear your iniquities, (even) *forty* years,
26: 7. numbered of them were *forty and* three thousand and 730.
18. *forty* thousand and five hundred.
41. *forty and* five thousand and six hundred.
50. *forty and* five thousand and four hundred.
32:13. wander in the wilderness *forty* years,
33:38. and died there, in *the fortieth* year
35: 6. ye shall add *forty* and two cities.
7. (shall be) *forty* and eight cities:
Deu. 1: 3. *in* the *fortieth* year,
2: 7. these *forty* years the Lord thy God
8: 2. led thee these *forty* years in the wilderness,
4. neither did thy foot swell, these *forty*
9: 9, 11, 18. *forty* days *and forty* nights,
25. *forty* days and *forty* nights, as I fell
10:10. *forty* days *and forty* nights; and the Lord
25: 3. *Forty* stripes he may give him,
29: 5(4). I have led you *forty* years
Jos. 4:13. *About forty* thousand prepared for war
5: 6. walked *forty* years in the wilderness,
14: 7. *Forty* years old (was) I
10. these *forty* and five years,
21:41(39). *forty* and eight cities
Jud. 3:11. the land had rest *forty* years.
5: 8. *among forty* thousand in Israel?
31. the land had rest *forty* years.
8:28. the country was in quietness *forty* years
12: 6. of the Ephraimites *forty* and two thousand.
14. *forty* sons and thirty nephews,
13: 1. into the hand of the Philistines *forty* years.
1Sa. 4:18. judged Israel *forty* years.
17:16. and presented himself *forty* days.
2Sa. 2:10. Ish-bosheth Saul's son (was) *forty* years
5: 4. he reigned *forty* years.
10:18. *and forty* thousand horsemen,
15: 7. it came to pass after *forty* years,
1K. 2:11. that David reigned over Israel (were) *forty* years:

1K. 4:26(5:6). Solomon had *forty* thousand stalls
6:17. *And* the house,...was *forty* cubits (long).
7: 3. that (lay) on *forty* five pillars,
38. one laver contained *forty* baths:
11:42. over all Israel (was) *forty* years.
14:21. Rehoboam (was) *forty* and one years old
15:10. *And forty* and one years reigned he in
19: 8. went in the strength of that meat *forty* days *and forty* nights
2K. 2:24. tare *forty* and two children
8: 9. good thing of Damascus, *forty* camels'
10:14. two and *forty* men;
12: 1(2). *and forty* years reigned he in Jerusalem.
14:23. (reigned) *forty* and one years.
1Ch. 5:18. four and *forty* thousand 760,
12:36. expert in war, *forty* thousand.
19:18. *and forty* thousand footmen,
26:31. In the *fortieth* year of the reign of David
29:27. the time that he reigned over Israel (was) *forty* years;
2Ch. 9:30. in Jerusalem over all Israel *forty* years.
12:13. Rehoboam (was) one and *forty* years old
16:13. Asa...died in the one and *fortieth* year
22: 2. *Forty* and two years old (was) Ahaziah
24: 1. *and* he reigned *forty* years in Jerusalem.
Ezr. 2: 8. of Zattu, nine hundred *forty* and five.
10. of Bani, six hundred *forty* and two.
24. The children of Azmaveth, *forty* and two.
25. seven hundred *and forty* and three.
34. of Jericho, three hundred *forty* and five.
38. of Pashur, a thousand two hundred *forty* and seven.
66. their mules, two hundred *forty* and five;
Neh. 5:15. *forty* shekels of silver;
7:13. of Zattu, eight hundred *forty* and five.
15. of Binnui, six hundred *forty* and eight.
28. The men of Beth-azmaveth, *forty* and
29. The men of K., ...seven hundred *forty*
36. of Jericho, three hundred *forty* and five.
41. of Pashur, 1200 *forty* and seven.
44. of Asaph, an hundred *forty* and eight.
62. the children of N., six hundred *forty* and
67. they had 200 *forty* and five singing men
68. their mules, two hundred *forty* and five:
9:21. *Yea, forty* years didst thou sustain them
11:13. of the fathers, two hundred *forty* and two:
Job 42:16. lived Job an hundred *and forty* years,
Ps. 95:10. *Forty* years long was I grieved
Jer. 52:30. seven hundred *forty* and five persons:
Eze. 4: 6. iniquity of the house of Judah *forty* days:
29:11. neither shall it be inhabited *forty* years.
12. shall be desolate *forty* years:
13. At the end of *forty* years
41: 2. the length thereof, *forty* cubits:
46:22. courts joined of *forty* (cubits) long
Am. 2:10. led you *forty* years
5:25. offerings in the wilderness *forty* years,
Jon. 3: 4. Yet *forty* days, and Nineveh shall be

---

706 **אַרְבַּעְתַּיִם** *ar-bag'-tah'-yim'.*

2Sa.12: 6. he shall restore the lamb *fourfold,*

---

707 **אָרַג** [*āh-rag'*].

* KAL.—*Future.* *

Jud.16:13. If *thou weavest* the seven locks
Isa. 59: 5. and *weave* the spider's web:

KAL.—*Participle.* Pöel.

Ex. 28:32. it shall have a binding of *woven* work (lit. work of *the weaver*)
35:35. in fine linen, *and of the weaver,*
39:22. the robe of the ephod (of) *woven* work, (lit. work of *the weaver*),
27. (of) *woven* work for Aaron,
1Sa.17: 7. his spear (was) like a *weaver*'s beam;
2Sa.21:19. the son of Jaare-*oregim,*
— whose spear (was) like a *weaver*'s beam.
2K. 23: 7. where the women *wove* hangings
1Ch.11:23. a spear like a *weaver*'s beam;
1Ch.20: 5. spear staff (was) like a *weaver*'s beam.
Isa. 19: 9. *and they that weave* networks,
38:12. I have cut off *like a weaver* my life:

אֶרֶג *eh'-reg,* m. 708

Jud.16:14. went away with the pin of *the beam,*
Job 7: 6. swifter than *a weaver's shuttle,*

אַרְגְּוָן *ar-g'vāhn',* m. 710

2Ch. 2:7(6). in iron, *and in purple,*

אַרְגְּוָנָא *ar-g'vāh-nāh,* Ch. m. emph. 711

Dan 5: 7. shall be clothed with *scarlet,* (marg. or, *purple*)
16. thou shalt be clothed with *scarlet,*
29. they clothed Daniel with *scarlet,*

אַרְגָּז *ar-gāhz',* m. 712

1Sa. 6: 8. *in a coffer* by the side thereof;
11. *the coffer* with the mice of gold
15. *the coffer* that (was) with it,

אַרְגָּמָן *ar-gāh-māhn',* m. 713

Ex. 25: 4 & 26:1, 31, 36 & 27:16. blue, *and purple,* and scarlet,
28: 5. blue, and *purple,* and scarlet,
6, 15, 33. blue, *and* (of) *purple,*
8 & 35:6. blue, *and purple,* and scarlet,
35:25. of blue, and of *purple,* (and) of scarlet,
35. in blue, *and in purple,*
36: 8, 35, 37 & 38:18. blue, *and purple,* and scarlet:
38:23. *and in purple,* and in scarlet,
39: 1. the blue, *and purple,* and scarlet,
2. blue, *and purple,* and scarlet,
3. in the blue, and in *the purple,*
5, 8, 24, 29. blue, *and purple,* and scarlet,
Nu. 4:13. spread a *purple* cloth thereon:
Jud. 8:26. and *purple* raiment
2Ch. 2:14(13). in timber, *in purple,*
3:14. blue, *and purple,* and crimson,
Est. 1: 6 & 8:15. fine linen *and purple*
Pro.31:22. her clothing (is) silk *and purple.*
Cant 3:10. the covering of it (of) *purple,*
7: 5(6). the hair of thine head *like purple;*
Jer. 10: 9. blue *and purple* (is) their clothing:
Eze.27: 7. blue *and purple* from the isles (marg. purple *and scarlet*)
16. *purple,* and broidered work,

אָרָה [*āh-rāh'*], 717

* KAL.—*Preterite.* *

Ps. 80:12(13). *so* that all they which pass by the way *do pluck her?*
Cant5: 1. *I have gathered* my myrrh

אֲרוּ *ăroo,* interj. Ch. 718

Dan 7: 2. *and, behold,* the four winds of the heaven
5. *And behold* another beast,
6. *and lo* another, like a leopard,
7. *and behold* a fourth beast,
13. *and, behold,* (one) like the Son of man

אֲרֻכָה & אֲרוּכָה *ăroo-chāh',* f. 724

2Ch.24:13. the work was *perfected* (marg. the *healing* went up upon the work)
Neh. 4: 7(1). the walls of Jerusalem were *made up,* (lit. *healing* went up to the walls)
Isa. 58: 8. *and thine health* shall spring

Jer. 8:22. why then is not *the health of* the
30:17. For I will restore *health* unto thee,
33: 6. I will bring it *health* and cure,

---

727 **אָרוֹן & אָרֹן** *āh-rōhn'*, c.

Gen50:26. he was put *in a coffin* in Egypt.
Ex. 25:10. they shall make *an ark* (of) shittim wood:
14. into the rings by the sides of *the ark*, that *the ark* may be borne
15. shall be in the rings of *the ark:*
16. thou shalt put into *the ark*
21. the mercy seat above upon *the ark;* and in *the ark* thou shalt put
22. which (are) upon *the ark of* the
26:33. within the vail *the ark of* the
34. upon *the ark of* the testimony
30: 6. that (is) by *the ark of* the testimony,
26. therewith, and *the ark of* the testimony,
31: 7. *the ark* of the testimony,
35:12. *The ark*, and the staves thereof,
37: 1. Bezaleel made *the ark*
5. the sides of *the ark*, to bear *the ark.*
39:35. *The ark of* the testimony, and the
40: 3. thou shalt put therein *the ark of* the testimony, and cover *the ark* with the vail.
5. before *the ark of* the testimony,
20. put the testimony into *the ark*, and set the staves on *the ark*, and put the mercy seat above upon *the ark:*
21. he brought *the ark* into the tabernacle,
— covered *the ark of* the testimony;
Lev.16: 2. which (is) upon *the ark;*
Nu. 3:31. their charge (shall be) *the ark*,
4: 5. cover *the ark of* testimony with it:
7:89. the mercy seat that (was) upon *the ark of*
10:33. *and the ark of* the covenant
35. when *the ark* set forward,
14:44. *nevertheless the ark of* the covenant
Deu10: 1. make thee *an ark of* wood.
2. thou shalt put them *in the ark.*
3. made *an ark* (*of*) shittim wood,
5. put the tables *in the ark*
8. to bear *the ark of* the covenant
31: 9. which bare *the ark of* the covenant
25. which bare *the ark of* the covenant
26. the side of *the ark of* the covenant
Jos. 3: 3. When ye see *the ark of* the covenant
6. Take up *the ark of* the covenant,
— they took up *the ark of* the covenant,
8. that bear *the ark of* the covenant,
11. Behold, *the ark of* the covenant
13. that bear *the ark of* the Lord,
14. the priests bearing *the ark*
15. as they that bare *the ark*
— 17. the priests that bare *the ark*
4: 5. Pass over before *the ark of*
7. before *the ark of* the covenant
9. which bare *the ark of* the covenant
10. the priests which bare *the ark*
11. that *the ark of* the Lord passed over,
16. the priests that bear *the ark of*
18. when the priests that bare *the ark of*
6: 4. seven priests shall bear before *the ark*
6. Take up *the ark of* the covenant,
— 7, 13. before *the ark of* the Lord.
8. *and the ark of* the covenant
9. the rereward came after *the ark*,
11. *the ark of* the Lord compassed the city,
12. the priests took up *the ark of*
13. but the rereward came after *the ark of*
7: 6. before *the ark of* the Lord
8:33. stood on this side *the ark*
— which bare *the ark of* the covenant
Ju. 20:27. *the ark of* the covenant of God
1Sa. 3: 3. where *the ark of* God (was),
4: 3. Let us fetch *the ark of* the
4. bring from thence *the ark of*
— there with *the ark of* the covenant
5. when *the ark of* the covenant
6. that *the ark of* the Lord was come
11. *And the ark of* God was taken;
13. his heart trembled for *the ark of*
17. *and the ark of* God is taken.
18. he made mention of *the ark of*

1Sa. 4:19. that *the ark of* God was taken,
21. because *the ark of* God was taken,
22. for *the ark of* God is taken.
5: 1. the Philistines took *the ark of* God,
2. When the Philistines took *the ark of*
3, 4. before *the ark of* the Lord.
7, 8, 8. *The ark of* the God of Israel
8. What shall we do *with the ark of*
10. Therefore they sent *the ark of*
— as *the ark of* God came to Ekron,
— They have brought about *the ark of*
11. Send away *the ark of* the God of
6: 1. *the ark of* the Lord was in the country
2. What shall we do *to the ark of*
3. If ye send away *the ark of*
8. take *the ark of* the Lord,
11. they laid *the ark of* the Lord
13. saw *the ark*, and rejoiced to see
15. the Levites took down *the ark of*
18. whereon they set down *the ark of*
19. because they had looked *into the ark of*
21. Philistines have brought again the *ark of*
7: 1. fetched up *the ark of* the Lord,
— Eleazar his son to keep *the ark of*
2. while *the ark* abode in Kirjath-jearim,
14:18. Bring hither *the ark of* God. For *the ark of* God was at that time
2Sa. 6: 2. bring up from thence *the ark of* God,
3. they set *the ark of* God upon a new cart,
4. accompanying *the ark of* God: and Ahio went before *the ark.*
6. put forth (his hand) to *the ark of* God,
7. there he died by *the ark of* God.
9. How shall *the ark of* the Lord
10. David would not remove *the ark of*
11. *the ark of* the Lord continued
12. because of *the ark of* God. So David went and brought up *the ark of*
13. when they that bare *the ark of*
15. brought up *the ark of* the Lord
16. as *the ark of* the Lord came
17. they brought in *the ark of* the Lord,
7: 2. *but the ark of* God dwelleth within
11:11. *The ark*, and Israel, and Judah,
15:24. *the ark of* the covenant of God: and they set down *the ark of* God;
25. Carry back *the ark of* God
29. carried *the ark of* God again
1K. 2:26. because thou barest *the ark of*
3:15. stood before *the ark of* the covenant
6:19. set there *the ark of* the covenant
8: 1. bring up *the ark of* the covenant
3. the priests took up *the ark.*
4. they brought up *the ark of* the Lord,
5. with him before *the ark*,
6. the priests brought in *the ark of*
7. *the ark*, and the cherubims covered *the ark*
9. nothing *in the ark* save the two tables
21. I have set there a place *for the ark*,
2K. 12: 9(10). Jehoiada the priest took a *chest*,
10(11). much money *in the chest*,
1Ch. 6:31(16). after that *the ark* had rest.
13: 3. let us bring again *the ark of*
5. bring *the ark of* God from Kirjath-jearim.
6. to bring up thence *the ark of* God
7. they carried *the ark of* God
9. put forth his hand to hold *the ark;*
10. because he put his hand to *the ark:*
12. How shall I bring *the ark of*
13. David brought not *the ark*
14. *the ark of* God remained
15: 1. prepared a place *for the ark of* God,
2. None ought to carry *the ark of* God
— the Lord chosen to carry *the ark of*
3, 14. to bring up *the ark of* the Lord
12. may bring up *the ark of* the Lord
15. the Levites bare *the ark of* God
23, 24. doorkeepers *for the ark.*
24. with the trumpets before *the ark of*
25. bring up *the ark of* the covenant
26. helped the Levites that bare *the ark of*
27. the Levites that bare *the ark*,
28. Thus all Israel brought up *the ark of*
29. *the ark of* the covenant of the Lord
16: 1. they brought *the ark of* God,
4. Levites to minister before *the ark of*
6. 37. before *the ark of* the covenant

1Ch.16:37. to minister before *the ark* continually,
17: 1. *but the ark of* the covenant of the Lord
22:19. to bring *the ark of* the covenant
28: 2. an house of rest *for the ark of*
18. covered *the ark of* the covenant
2Ch. 1: 4. But *the ark of* God had David
5: 2. to bring up *the ark of* the covenant
4. the Levites took up *the ark.*
5. they brought up *the ark,*
6. assembled unto him before *the ark,*
7. the priests brought in *the ark of*
8. *the ark,* and the cherubims covered *the ark*
9. were seen from *the ark*
10. nothing *in the ark* save the two tables
6:11. in it have I put *the ark,*
41. *and the ark of* thy strength:
8:11. whereunto *the ark of* the Lord hath
24: 8. they made a *chest,* and set it without
10. cast *into the chest,*
11. *the chest* was brought unto the king's office
— came and emptied *the chest,*
35: 3. Put *the* holy *ark* in the house
Ps.132: 8. thou, *and the ark of* thy strength.
Jer. 3:16. *The ark of* the covenant of the Lord:

---

723 אֻרוֹת *oo-rāh-vōhth′*, & אֻרְיוֹת [*oo-rāh-yōhth′*], f. pl.

1K. 4:26(5:6). had forty thousand *stalls of* horses
2Ch. 9:25. had four thousand *stalls for* horses
32:28. *and stalls* for all manner of beasts,

---

730 אֶרֶז *eh′-rez*, m.

Lev.14: 4, 49. *cedar* wood, and scarlet, and hyssop:
6. *the cedar* wood, and the scarlet,
51. he shall take *the cedar* wood,
52. with *the cedar* wood,
Nu. 19: 6. the priest shall take *cedar* wood,
24: 6. *as cedar trees* beside the waters.
Jud. 9:15. devour *the cedars of* Lebanon.
2Sa. 5:11. *cedar* trees, and carpenters,
7: 2. I dwell in an house of *cedar,*
7. build ye not me an house of *cedar?*
1K. 4:33(5:13). from *the cedar tree* that (is) in Lebanon
5: 6(20). that they hew me *cedar trees*
8(22). concerning timber of *cedar,*
10(24). Hiram gave Solomon *cedar* trees
6: 9. with beams and boards *of cedar.*
10. on the house with timber of *cedar.*
15. within with boards of *cedar,*
16. the walls with boards of *cedar:*
18. *And the cedar* of the house
— all (was) *cedar;* there was no stone
20. covered the altar (which was of) *cedar.*
36. a row of *cedar* beams.
7: 2. upon four rows of *cedar* pillars, with *cedar* beams upon the pillars.
3. covered *with cedar* above
7. covered *with cedar* from one side
11. hewed stones, *and cedars.*
12. a row of *cedar* beams,
9:11. furnished Solomon with *cedar* trees
10:27. *cedars* made he (to be) as
2K. 14: 9. sent to *the cedar* that (was) in Lebanon,
19:23. cut down *the* tall *cedar trees thereof,*
1Ch.14: 1. timber of *cedars,* with masons
17: 1. I dwell in an house of *cedars,*
6. have ye not built me an house of *cedars?*
22: 4. Also *cedar* trees in abundance:
— brought much *cedar* wood to David.
2Ch. 1:15. *cedar trees* made he as
2: 3(2). didst send him *cedars* to build
8(7). Send me also *cedar* trees,
9:27. *cedar trees* made he as the
25:18. sent to *the cedar* that (was) in Lebanon,
Ezr. 3: 7. to bring *cedar* trees from Lebanon
Job 40:17. He moveth his tail like *a cedar:*
Ps. 29: 5. the Lord breaketh *the cedars;* yea, the Lord breaketh *the cedars of*
80:10(11). (were like) *the* goodly *cedars.*
92:12(13). he shall grow *like a cedar*
Ps. 104:16. *the cedars of* Lebanon,
148: 9. fruitful trees, and all *cedars:*
Cant.1:17. The beams of our house (are) *cedar,*
5:15. excellent *as the cedars.*
8: 9. inclose her with boards of *cedar.*
Isa. 2:13. upon all *the cedars of* Lebanon,
9:10(9). *but* we will change (them into) *cedars.*
14: 8. *the cedars of* Lebanon,
37:24. cut down *the* tall *cedars thereof,*
41:19. plant in the wilderness *the cedar,*
44:14. He heweth him down *cedars,*
Jer. 22: 7. shall cut down *thy* choice *cedars,*
14. cieled *with cedar,* and painted
15. thou closest (thyself) *in cedar?*
23. that makest thy nest *in the cedars,*
Eze.17: 3. took the highest branch of *the cedar:*
22. the highest branch of *the* high *cedar,*
23. be *a* goodly *cedar:*
27: 5. they have taken *cedars* from
31: 3. the Assyrian (was) *a cedar*
8. *The cedars* in the garden of God
Am. 2: 9. like the height of *the cedars,*
Zec.11: 1. that the fire may devour *thy cedars.*
2. for *the cedar* is fallen;

אַרְזָה *ar-zāh′*, f. 731

Zep. 2:14. he shall uncover *the cedar work.*

אֲרֻזִים *ăroo-zeem′*, adj. 729

Eze.27:24. bound with cords, *and made of cedar,*

אָרַח *āh-ragh′*, 732

✱ KAL.—*Preterite.* ✱

Job 34: 8. *Which goeth* in company

KAL.—*Participle.* Poël.

Gen37:25. *a company of* Ishmeelites came
Jud.19:17. he saw a *wayfaring* man
2Sa.12: 4. to dress *for the wayfaring man*
Isa. 21:13. *O ye travelling companies of* Dedanim.
Jer. 9: 2(1). a lodging place of *wayfaring men;*
14: 8. *and as a wayfaring man*

אֹרַח *ōh′-ragh*, com. 734

Gen18:11. after *the manner of* women.
49:17. an adder in *the path,*
Jud. 5: 6. *the highways* were unoccupied, and the travellers walked through by*ways.*
Job 6:18. *The paths of* their way are turned
19. *The troops of* Tema looked,
8:13. *the paths of* all that forget God;
13:27. lookest narrowly unto all *my paths;*
16:22. *then* I shall go *the way* (whence)
19: 8. He hath fenced up *my way*
22:15. Hast thou marked *the* old *way*
30:12. *the ways of* their destruction.
31:32. I opened my doors *to the traveller.* (marg. *way*)
33:11. he marketh all *my paths.*
34:11. *and* cause every man to find *according to* (his) *ways.*
Ps. 8: 8(9). passeth through *the paths of* the seas.
16:11. Thou wilt shew me *the path of* life:
17: 4. *the paths of* the destroyer.
19: 5(6). as a strong man to run *a race.*
25: 4. teach me *thy paths.*
10. All *the paths of* the Lord (are) mercy
27:11. lead me *in a* plain *path,*
44:18(19). have our steps declined from *thy way;*
119: 9. shall a young man cleanse *his way?*
15. have respect unto *thy ways.*
101. refrained my feet from every evil *way,*
104. therefore I hate every false *way.*

Ps 119:128. I hate every false *way*.
139: 3. Thou compassest *my path*
142: 3(4). *In the way* wherein I walked
Pro. 1:19. *the ways of* every one that is greedy
2: 8. He keepeth *the paths of* judgment,
13. Who leave *the paths of* uprightness,
15. *Whose ways* (are) crooked, (lit. who *their ways*)
19. neither take they hold of *the paths of*
20. *and* keep *the paths of* the righteous.
3: 6. he shall direct *thy paths*.
4:14. Enter not into the *path of* the
18. *But the path of* the just
5: 6. Lest thou shouldest ponder *the path of*
8:20. I lead *in the way of* righteousness,
9:15. passengers who go right on *their ways:*
10:17. He (is in) *the way of* life
12:28. *In the way of* righteousness
15:10. unto him that forsaketh *the way:*
19. *but the way of* the righteous (is) made plain.
24. *The way of* life (is) above
17:23. to pervert *the ways of* judgment.
22:25. Lest thou learn *his ways*,
Isa. 2: 3. we will walk *in his paths :*
3:12. destroy the way of *thy paths*.
26: 7. *The way of* the just (is) uprightness:
8. *in the way of* thy judgments,
30:11. Get you out of *the way*,
33: 8. the *way*faring man ceaseth: (lit. passer of *the way*)
40:14. taught him *in the path of*
41: 3. by *the way* (that) he had not gone
Joel 2: 7. they shall not break *their ranks:*
Mic. 4: 2. we will walk *in his paths :*

---

735 אֳרְחָא [*or-ghah'*], f. Ch.

Dan 4:37(34). *and his ways* judgment:
5:23. and whose (are) all *thy ways*,

---

736 אֹרְחָה see אֹרַח

---

737 אֲרֻחָה *ăroo-ghah'*, f.

2K. 25:30. *And his allowance* (was) *a* continual *allowance*
Pro.15:17. Better (is) *a dinner of* herbs
Jer. 40: 5. captain of the guard gave him *victuals*
52:34. *And* (for) *his diet*, there was a continual *diet* given

---

738 אֲרִי & אַרְיֵה *ăree & ar-yeh'*, m.

Gen49: 9. Judah (is) a *lion*'s whelp:
— he couched *as a lion*,
Nu. 23:24. *and* lift up himself *as a young lion :*
24: 9. he lay down *as a lion*,
Deu33:22. Dan (is) *a lion*'s whelp:
Jud.14: 5. a young *lion* roared against him. (lit. whelp of *lions*)
8. to see the carcase of *the lion :*
— honey in the carcase of *the lion*.
9. honey out of the carcase of *the lion*.
18. what (is) stronger *than a lion?*
1Sa.17:34. there came *a lion*, and a bear,
36. Thy servant slew both *the lion*
37. out of the paw of *the lion*,
2Sa. 1:23. they were stronger *than lions*.
17:10. whose heart (is) as the heart of *a lion*,
23:20. he went down also and slew *a lion*
1K. 7:29. (were) between the ledges (were) *lions*,
— beneath *the lions* and oxen
36. he graved cherubims, *lions*,
10:19. two *lions* stood beside the stays.
20. twelve *lions* stood there
13:24. *a lion* met him by the way,
— *the lion also* stood by the carcase.
25. *the lion* standing by the carcase:
26. delivered him *unto the lion*,
1K. 13:28. *and the lion* standing by the carcase: *the lion* had not eaten the carcase,
20:36. *a lion* shall slay thee.
— *a lion* found him, and slew him.
2K. 17:25. the Lord sent *lions* among them,
26. he hath sent *lions* among them,
1Ch 11:22. slew *a lion* in a pit in a snowy day.
12: 8. whose faces (were like) the faces of *lions*,
2Ch 9.18. two *lions* standing by the stays:
19. twelve *lions* stood there
Job 4:10. The roaring of *the lion*,
Ps. 7: 2(3). Lest he tear my soul *like a lion*,
10: 9. lieth in wait secretly *as a lion*
17:12. Like *as a lion* (that) is greedy
22:13(14). ravening and *a* roaring *lion*.
16(17). *they pierced* (lit. *like a lion*) my hands
21(22). Save me from *the lion*'s mouth:
Pro.22:13. (There is) *a lion* without,
26:13. *a lion* (is) in the streets.
28:15. *a* roaring *lion*, and a ranging bear;
Ecc. 9: 4. a living dog is better than *a* dead *lion*.
Cant.4: 8. from *the lions*' dens,
Isa. 11: 7. *and the lion* shall eat straw
15: 9. *lions* upon him that escapeth
21: 8. he cried, *A lion* (marg. *as a lion*) *:* My lord,
31: 4. Like as *the lion* and the
35: 9. No *lion* shall be there,
38:13. *as a lion*, so will he break
65:25. *and the lion* shall eat straw
Jer. 2:30. *like a* destroying *lion*.
4: 7. *The lion* is come up from his
5: 6. *a lion* out of the forest shall slay them,
12: 8. Mine heritage is unto me *as a lion*
49:19 & 50:44. he shall come up *like a lion*
50:17. *the lions* have driven (him) away:
51:38. they shall yell as *lions*' whelps.
Lam. 3:10. (as) *a lion* in secret places.
Eze. 1:10. the face of *a lion*, on the right side:
10:14. the third the face of *a lion*,
19: 2. she lay down among *lions*,
6. went up and down among *the lions*,
22:25. *like a* roaring *lion*
Hos.11:10. he shall roar *like a lion :*
Joel 1: 6. whose teeth (are) the teeth of *a lion*,
Am. 3: 4. Will *a lion* roar in the forest,
8. *The lion* hath roared,
12. out of the mouth of *the lion*
5:19. if a man did flee from *a lion*,
Mic. 5: 8(7). in the midst of many people *as a lion*
Nah 2:11(12). Where (is) the dwelling of *the lions*,
—(—). where *the lion*, (even) the old lion, walked, (and) *the lion*'s whelp, and none
12(13). *The lion* did tear in pieces
Zep 3: 3. princes within her (are) roaring *lions;*

אֲרִאֵל אֲרִיאֵל & אֲרִאֵל *ăree-ehl'*, m. 739-41

2Sa.23:20. he slew two *lionlike men of* Moab: (marg. *lions of God*)
1Ch 11:22. he slew two *lionlike men of*
Isa. 29: 1. Woe to *Ariel*, to *Ariel*, (marg. *lion of God*)
2. Yet I will distress *Ariel*,
— it shall be unto me *as Ariel*.
7. all the nations that fight against *Ariel*,
Eze.43:15. *and from the altar* and upward (marg. *lion of God*)
16. *And the altar* (shall be) twelve (cubits)

אַרְיֵה *ar-yeh*, m. Ch. 744

Dan 6: 7(8), 12(13). be cast into the den of *lions*.
16(17). and cast (him) into the den of *lions*.
19(20). went in haste unto the den of *lions*.
20(21). able to deliver thee from *the lions ?*
22(23). and hath shut the *lions*' mouths,
24(25). they cast (them) into the den of *lions*,
—(—). and the *lions* had the mastery of them,
27(28). Daniel from the power of *the lions*.
7: 4. The first (was) *like a lion*,

אַרְיֵה see אֲרִי See 738

See 723 אֲרָוֹת see אֲרָיוֹת

748 אָרַךְ [*āh-rach'*]

* KAL.—*Preterite.* *

Gen26: 8. when he *had been* there a *long* time, (lit. days *were prolonged* to him)

KAL.—*Future.*

Eze.12:22. The days *are prolonged,*
31: 5. *and* his branches *became long*

* HIPHIL.—*Preterite.* *

Deu 5:33(30). *and* (that) *ye may prolong* (your) days
22: 7. *and* (that) *thou mayest prolong*
Jos.24:31. that overlived (marg. *prolonged* their days after)
Jud. 2: 7. that outlived (marg. *prolonged* days after)
1K. 3:14. *then I will lengthen* thy days.
Ps.129: 3. *they made long* their furrows.
Pro.19:11. discretion of a man *deferreth*

HIPHIL.—*Infinitive.*

Nu. 9:19. *And when* the cloud *tarried long* (marg. *prolonged*)
22. *that* the cloud *tarried*

HIPHIL.—*Imperative.*

Isa. 54: 2. spare not, *lengthen* thy cords,

HIPHIL.—*Future.*

Ex. 20:12. that thy days *may be long*
Deu 4:26. *ye shall* not *prolong* (your) days
40. that *thou mayest prolong* (thy) days
5:16 & 6:2. that thy days *may be prolonged,*
11: 9. that *ye may prolong* (your) days
17:20. that *he may prolong* (his) days
25:15. that thy days *may be lengthened*
30:18. *ye shall* not *prolong* (your) days
32:47. *ye shall prolong* (your) days
1K. 8: 8. *And they drew out* the staves,
2Ch 5: 9. *And they drew out* the staves
Job 6:11. that *I should prolong* my life?
Pro.28: 2. the state (thereof) *shall be prolonged.*
16. hateth covetousness *shall prolong* (his)
Ecc. 8:13. neither shall *he prolong* (his) days,
Isa. 48: 9. *will I defer* mine anger,
53:10. *he shall prolong* (his) days,
57: 4. a wide mouth, (and) *draw out* the tongue?

HIPHIL.—*Participle.*

Ecc. 7:15. a wicked (man) *that prolongeth*
8:12. *and* his (days) *be prolonged,*

749 אֲרַךְ [*ărach*] Ch.

P'AL.—*Part.*

Ezr. 4:14. it was not *meet* for us to see the king's

750 אֶרֶךְ *ēh'-rech*, adj.

Ex. 34: 6. merciful and gracious, *long*suffering,
Nu. 14:18. The Lord (is) *long*suffering,
Neh 9:17. *slow to* anger, and of great kindness,
Ps. 86:15. *long*suffering, and plenteous in mercy
103: 8. *slow to* anger, and plenteous in mercy.
145: 8. *slow to* anger, and of great mercy.
Pro.14:29. *slow to* wrath (is) of great understanding:
15:18. *but* (he that is) *slow to* anger
16:32. (He that is) *slow to* anger
Ecc. 7: 8. *the patient* in spirit (is) better
Jer. 15:15. take me not away *in* thy *long*suffering:
Eze.17: 3. *long*winged, full of feathers,
Joel. 2:13. *slow to* anger, and of great kindness,
Jon. 4: 2. *slow to* anger, and of great kindness,
Nah 1: 3. The Lord (is) *slow to* anger,

753 אֹרֶךְ *ōh'-rech*, m.

Gen 6:15. *The length of* the ark (shall be)
13:17. through the land *in the length of it*
Ex. 25:10. and a half (shall be) *the length thereof,*
17. and a half (shall be) *the length thereof,*
23. two cubits (shall be) *the length thereof,*
26: 2, 8. *The length of* one curtain
13. which remaineth *in the length of* the
16. Ten cubits (shall be) *the length of* a board,
27: 1. an altar (of) shittim wood, five cubits *long,*
9. of an hundred cubits *long*
11. for the north side *in length* (there shall be) hangings of an hundred (cubits) *long,*
18. *The length of* the court
28:16. a span (shall be) *the length thereof,*
30: 2. A cubit (shall be) *the length thereof,*
36: 9, 15. *The length of* one curtain
21. *The length of* a board (was) ten cubits,
37: 1. and a half (was) *the length of it,*
6. and a half (was) *the length thereof,*
10. two cubits (was) *the length thereof,*
25. *the length of it* (was) a cubit,
38: 1. five cubits (was) *the length thereof,*
18. twenty cubits (was) *the length,*
39: 9. a span (was) *the length thereof,*
Deu 3:11. nine cubits (was) *the length thereof,*
30:20. *and the length of* thy days:
Jud. 3:16. which had two edges, *of* a cubit *length;*
1K. 6: 2. *the length thereof* (was) threescore cubits,
3. twenty cubits (was) *the length thereof,*
20. the forepart (was) twenty cubits in *length,*
7: 2. *the length thereof* (was) an hundred cubits,
6. *the length thereof* (was) fifty cubits,
27. four cubits (was) *the length of* one base,
2Ch 3: 3. *The length* by cubits after the first
4. *the length* (of it was) according
8. *the length whereof* (was) according
11. (were) twenty cubits *long:* (lit. *their length*)
15. thirty and five cubits *high,* (marg. *long.*)
4: 1. of brass, twenty cubits *the length thereof,*
6:13. brasen scaffold, *of* five cubits *long,* (marg. *the length thereof*)
Job 12:12. *and in length of* days understanding.
Ps. 21: 4(5). *length of* days for ever and ever.
23: 6. I will dwell in the house of the Lord for ever. (marg. *to length of* days)
91:16. With *long* (marg. *length of* days) life will
93: 5. holiness becometh thine house, O Lord, for ever. (marg. *to length of days*)
Pro. 3: 2. *length of* days, and long life,
16. *Length of* days (is) in her right hand;
25:15. *By long* forbearing is a prince persuaded,
Lam. 5:20. forsake us *so long* time? (marg. *for length of* days)
Eze.31: 7. *in the length of* his branches:
40: 7. (every) little chamber (was) one reed *long,*
11. *the length of* the gate,
18. over against *the length of* the gates
20. he measured *the length thereof,*
21. *the length thereof* (was) fifty cubits,
25. *the length* (was) fifty cubits,
29. (was) fifty cubits *long,*
30. five and twenty cubits *long,*
33. (it was) fifty cubits *long,*
36. *the length* (was) fifty cubits,
42. of a cubit and an half *long,*
47. an hundred cubits *long,*
49. *The length of* the porch
41: 2. measured *the length thereof,* forty
4. he measured *the length thereof,* twenty
12. *and the length thereof* ninety cubits.
13, 13. an hundred cubits *long;*
15. he measured *the length of* the building
22. *and the length thereof* two cubits;
— *and the length thereof,* and the walls
42: 2. *the length of* an hundred cubits
7. *the length thereof* (was) fifty cubits.
8. *the length of* the chambers
11. *as long as they,* (and) as broad as they:
20. five hundred (reeds) long,
43:16. the altar (shall be) twelve (cubits) *long,*
17. the settle (shall be) fourteen (cubits) *long*
45: 1. *the length* (shall be) *the length of*
3. *the length of* five and twenty thousand,
5. five and twenty thousand of *length,*
6. *and* five and twenty thousand *long,*
7. *and the length* (shall be) over against one
46:22. courts joined of forty (cubits) *long*
48: 8. *and* (in) *length* as one of the (other) parts,
9, 10. five and twenty thousand *in length*

Eze.48:13. (shall have) five and twenty thousand *in length,*
— all *the length* (shall be) five and twenty thousand,
18. the residue *in length*
Zec. 2: 2(6). what (is) *the length thereof.*
5: 2. *the length thereof* (is) twenty cubits,

754 ## אַרְכָא *ar-kāh'*, f. Ch.

Dan. 4:27(24). it may be *a lengthening of* thy tranquillity. (marg. *an healing of* thine error)

752 ## אֲרֻכָּה *ărook-kah'*, f. adj.

2Sa. 3: 1. Now there was *long* war
Job 11: 9. The measure thereof (is) *long*er than the earth,
Jer. 29:28. This (captivity is) *long:* build ye houses,

754 ## אַרְכָה *ar-chāh'*, f. Ch.

Dan. 7:12. *yet* their lives were *prolonged* (marg. *a prolonging* in life was given them)

See 724 ## אֲרֻכָה see אֲרוּכָה

755 ## אַרְכֻבָּה *ar-koo-vāh'*, f. Ch.

Dan. 5: 6. *and his knees* smote one against another.

759 ## אַרְמוֹן *ar-mōhn'*, m.

With fem. pl. וֹת.

1K. 16:18. he went into *the palace of* the king's
2K. 15:25. *in the palace of* the king's house,
2Ch.36:19. burnt all *the palaces thereof*
Ps. 48: 3(4). God is known *in her palaces*
13(14). consider *her palaces;*
122: 7. prosperity *within thy palaces.*
Pro.18:19. like the bars of *a castle.*
Isa. 23:13. they raised up *the palaces thereof;*
25: 2. *a palace of* strangers to be no city;
32:14. Because *the palaces* shall be forsaken;
34:13. thorns shall come up in *her palaces,*
Jer. 6: 5. let us destroy *her palaces.*
9:21(20) is entered *into our palaces,*
17:27. shall devour *the palaces of* Jerusalem,
30:18. *and the palace* shall remain
49:27. shall consume *the palaces of* Ben-hadad.
Lam. 2: 5. he hath swallowed up all *her palaces:*
7. of the enemy the walls of *her palaces;*
Hos. 8:14. it shall devour *the palaces thereof.*
Am. 1: 4. shall devour *the palaces* of Ben-hadad.
7, 10, 14. shall devour *the palaces thereof:*
12. which shall devour *the palaces of* Bozrah.
2: 2. it shall devour *the palaces of* Kirioth:
5. shall devour *the palaces of* Jerusalem.
3: 9. Publish in *the palaces* at Ashdod, and in *the palaces* in the land of Egypt,
10. robbery *in their palaces.*
11. *thy palaces* shall be spoiled.
6: 8. *and* hate *his palaces:*
Mic. 5: 5(4). when he shall tread *in our palaces,*

766 ## אֹרֶן *ōh'-ren*, m.

Isa. 44:14. he planteth *an ash*, and the rain doth

768 ## אַרְנֶבֶת *ar-neh'-veth*, f.

Lev.11: 6. *the hare*, because he cheweth the cud,
Deu14: 7. the camel, and *the hare*, and the coney:

אַרְקָא *ar-găh'* (כְּתִיב) Ch 772

אֲרַע *ărağ*, f. Ch.

Ezr. 5:11. servants of the God of heaven *and earth.*
Jer. 10:11. they shall perish *from the earth,*
Dan. 2:35. and filled *the* whole *earth.*
39. which shall bear rule over all *the earth.*
— shall arise another kingdom *inferior*
4: 1(3:31). and languages, that dwell in all *the earth;*
10(7). a tree in the midst of *the earth,*
11(8). thereof to the end of all *the earth:*
15(12). the stump of his roots *in the earth,*
—(—). the beasts in the grass of *the earth:*
20(17). and the sight thereof to all *the earth;*
22(19). thy dominion to the end of *the earth.*
23(20). of the roots thereof *in the earth,*
35(32). And all the inhabitants of *the earth*
—(—) and (among) the inhabitants of *the earth.*
6:25(26). and languages, that dwell in all *the earth;*
27(28). signs and wonders in heaven *and in earth,*
7: 4. and it was lifted up from *the earth,*
17. shall arise out of *the earth.*
23. shall be the fourth kingdom *upon earth,*
— and shall devour *the* whole *earth,*

אַרְעִית *ar-ğeeth'*, f. Ch. 773

Dan. 6:24(25). ever they came *at the bottom* of the den.

אֶרֶץ *eh'-retz*, com. 776

Gen. 1: 1. created the heaven and *the earth.*
2. *And the earth* was without form
10. God called the dry (land) *Earth;*
11. Let *the earth* bring forth grass,
— seed (is) in itself, upon *the earth:*
12. *the earth* brought forth grass,
15, 17. to give light upon *the earth:*
20. fowl (that) may fly above *the earth*
22. let fowl multiply *in the earth.*
24. Let *the earth* bring forth the living
— beast of *the earth* after his kind:
25. God made the beast of *the earth*
26. over all *the earth,* and over every creeping thing that creepeth upon *the earth.*
28. multiply, and replenish *the earth,*
— living thing that moveth upon *the earth.*
29. which (is) upon the face of all *the earth,*
30. to every beast of *the earth,*
— every thing that creepeth upon *the earth,*
2: 1. Thus the heavens *and the earth*
4. of the heavens *and of the earth*
— the Lord God made *the earth*
5. before it was *in the earth,*
— caused it to rain upon *the earth,*
6. there went up a mist from *the earth,*
11. compasseth *the* whole *land of* Havilah,
12. the gold of that *land* (is) good:
13. compasseth *the* whole *land of* Ethiopia.
4:12. a vagabond shalt thou be *in the earth.*
14. a fugitive and a vagabond *in the earth;*
16. dwelt *in the land of* Nod,
6: 4. There were giants *in the earth*
5. wickedness of man (was) great *in the earth,*
6. that he had made man *on the earth,*
11. *The earth* also was corrupt before God, and *the earth* was filled with violence.
12. God looked upon *the earth,*
— had corrupted his way upon *the earth.*
13. *the earth* is filled with violence
— I will destroy them with *the earth.*
17. a flood of waters upon *the earth,*
— every thing that (is) *in the earth*
7: 3. alive upon the face of all *the earth.*
4. will cause it to rain upon *the earth*
6. the flood of waters was upon *the earth.*
10. waters of the flood were upon *the earth.*
12. the rain was upon *the earth*

Gen 7: 14. that creepeth upon *the earth*
17. the flood was forty days upon *the earth;*
— it was lift up above *the earth.*
18. were increased greatly upon *the earth;*
19. prevailed exceedingly upon *the earth;*
21. all flesh died that moved upon *the earth.*
— that creepeth upon *the earth,*
23. they were destroyed from *the earth:*
24. the waters prevailed upon *the earth*
8: 1. God made a wind to pass over *the earth,*
3. the waters returned from off *the earth*
7. were dried up from off *the earth.*
9. on the face of *the* whole *earth:*
11. were abated from off *the earth.*
13. were dried up from off *the earth:*
14. day of the month, was *the earth* dried.
17. creepeth upon *the earth;* that they may breed abundantly *in the earth,* and be fruitful, and multiply upon *the earth.*
19. whatsoever creepeth upon *the earth,*
22. While *the earth* remaineth,
9: 1. multiply, and replenish *the earth.*
2. be upon every beast of *the earth,*
7. bring forth abundantly *in the earth,*
10. every beast of *the earth* with you;
— to every beast of *the earth.*
11. a flood to destroy *the earth.*
13. between me and *the earth.*
14. when I bring a cloud over *the earth,*
16, 17. all flesh that (is) upon *the earth.*
19. was *the* whole *earth* overspread.
10: 5. divided *in their lands;*
8. to be a mighty one *in the earth.*
10. *in the land of* Shinar.
11. Out of that *land* went forth Asshur,
20. after their tongues, *in their countries,*
25. in his days was *the earth* divided;
31. after their tongues, *in their lands,*
32. were the nations divided *in the earth*
11: 1. *the* whole *earth* was of one language,
2. they found a plain *in the land of*
4. upon the face of *the* whole *earth.*
8, 9. upon the face of all *the earth:*
9. confound the language of all *the earth:*
28. *in the land of* his nativity,
31. to go *into the land of* Canaan;
12: 1. Get thee *out of thy country,*
— unto *a land* that I will shew thee:
5. to go *into the land of* Canaan; and *into the land of* Canaan they came.
6. Abram passed *through the land*
— the Canaanite (was) then *in the land.*
7. Unto thy seed will I give *this land.*
10. there was a famine *in the land:*
— the famine (was) grievous *in the land.*
13: 6. *the land* was not able to bear
7. Perizzite dwelled then *in the land.*
9. (Is) not *the* whole *land* before thee?
10. *like the land of* Egypt,
12. Abram dwelled *in the land of* Canaan,
15. all *the land* which thou seest, to thee
16. thy seed as the dust of *the earth:*
— can number the dust of *the earth,*
17. Arise, walk *through the land*
14: 19, 22. possessor of heaven *and earth:*
15: 7. to give thee this *land* to inherit
13. seed shall be a stranger *in a land*
18. Unto thy seed have I given this *land,*
16: 3. had dwelt ten years *in the land of*
17: 8. *the land wherein* thou art a stranger, all *the land of* Canaan,
18: 2. bowed himself *toward the ground,*
18. all the nations of *the earth* shall be
25. Shall not the Judge of all *the earth*
19: 1. with his face *toward the ground;*
23. The sun was risen upon *the earth*
28. toward all *the land of* the plain,
— the smoke of *the country* went up
31. not a man *in the earth* to come
— after the manner of all *the earth:*
20: 1. *toward the* south *country,* and dwelled
15. *my land* (is) before thee: dwell where
21: 21. took him a wife *out of the land of* Egypt.
23. to *the land* wherein thou hast sojourned.
32. returned into *the land of* the Philistines.
34. *in the* Philistines' *land* many days.
22: 2. get thee into *the land of* Moriah;

Gen 22: 18. all the nations of *the earth* be blessed;
23: 2, 19. Hebron *in the land of* Canaan:
7. bowed himself to the people of *the land*
12. before the people of *the land.*
13. the audience of the people of *the land,*
15. *the land* (is worth) four hundred
24: 3. of heaven, and the God of *the earth,*
4. But thou shalt go unto *my country,*
5. to follow me unto this *land:*
— unto *the land* from whence thou camest?
7. *and from the land of* my kindred,
— Unto thy seed will I give this *land;*
37. the Canaanites, *in whose land* I dwell:
52. the Lord, (bowing himself) *to the earth.*
62. for he dwelt *in the* south *country.*
25: 6. eastward, unto *the* east *country.*
26: 1. there was a famine *in the land,*
2. dwell *in the land* which I shall
3. Sojourn *in this land,* and I will
— I will give all these *countries,*
4. give unto thy seed all these *countries;*
— all the nations of *the earth* be blessed;
12. Then Isaac sowed *in* that *land,*
22. we shall be fruitful *in the land.*
27: 28. the fatness of *the earth,* and plenty
39. shall be the fatness of *the earth,*
46. of the daughters of *the land,*
28: 4. *the land wherein* thou art a stranger,
12. behold a ladder set up *on the earth,*
13. *the land* whereon thou liest, to thee
14. shall be as the dust of *the earth,*
29: 1. came *into the land of* the people
30: 25. mine own place, *and to my country.*
31: 3. Return unto *the land of* thy fathers,
13. get thee out from this *land,* and return unto *the land of* thy kindred.
18. his father *in the land of* Canaan.
32: 3(4). *unto the land of* Seir, the country of
9(10). Return *unto thy country,* and to thy
33: 3. bowed himself *to the ground* seven
18. which (is) *in the land of* Canaan,
34: 1. to see the daughters of *the land.*
2. Hivite, prince of *the country,*
10. *and the land* shall be before you;
21. let them dwell *in the land,* and trade therein; *for the land,*
30. among the inhabitants of *the land,*
35: 6. which (is) *in the land of* Canaan,
12. *the land* which I gave Abraham
— after thee will I give *the land.*
16. there was but *a* little *way* (marg. a little piece of *ground*)
22. when Israel dwelt *in* that *land,*
36: 5. born unto him *in the land of* Canaan.
6. he had got *in the land of* Canaan; and went into *the country* from the face
7. *the land wherein* they were strangers
16. of Eliphaz *in the land of* Edom;
17. of Reuel *in the land of* Edom;
20. of Seir the Horite, who inhabited *the land;*
21. children of Seir *in the land of* Edom.
30. their dukes *in the land of* Seir.
31. that reigned *in the land of* Edom,
34. Husham *of the land of* Temani
43. *in the land of* their possession:
37: 1. Jacob dwelt *in the land wherein* his father was a stranger, *in the land of*
10. bow down ourselves to thee *to the earth?*
38: 9. he spilled (it) *on the ground,*
40: 15. *out of the land of* the Hebrews:
41: 19, 44. in all *the land of* Egypt
29, 46. throughout all *the land of* Egypt:
30. shall be forgotten *in the land of* Egypt and the famine shall consume *the land;*
31. plenty shall not be known *in the land*
33. set him over *the land of* Egypt.
34. appoint officers over *the land,* and take up the fifth part of *the land of* Egypt
36. food shall be for store *to the land*
— *in the land of* Egypt; that *the land*
41, 43. over all *the land of* Egypt.
45. went out over (all) *the land of* Egypt.
47. *the earth* brought forth by handfuls.
48. which were *in the land of* Egypt,
52. be fruitful *in the land of* my affliction.
53. plenteousness, that was *in the land of* Egypt,

Gen41:54. the dearth was in all *lands;* but in all *the land of* Egypt
55. when all *the land of* Egypt was famished,
56. over all the face of *the earth:*
— famine waxed sore *in the land of* Egypt.
57. And all *countries* came into Egypt
— the famine was (so) sore in all *lands.*
42: 5. the famine was *in the land of* Canaan.
6. Joseph (was) the governor over *the land,*
— sold to all the people of *the land :*
— before him (with) their faces *to the earth.*
7. *From the land of* Canaan to buy food.
9. to see the nakedness of *the land*
12. but to see the nakedness of *the land*
13. sons of one man *in the land of*
29. their father *unto the land of* Canaan,
30. The man, (who is) the lord of *the land,*
— took us for spies of *the country.*
32. with our father *in the land of* Canaan.
33. the man, the lord of *the country,*
34. ye shall traffick in *the land.*
43: 1. the famine (was) sore *in the land.*
11. take of the best fruits in *the land*
26. bowed themselves to him *to the earth.*
44: 8. unto thee *out of the land of* Canaan:
11. every man his sack *to the ground,*
14. they fell before him *on the ground.*
45: 6. years (hath) the famine (been) in *the land:*
7. to preserve you a posterity *in the earth,*
8. throughout all *the land of* Egypt.
10. thou shalt dwell *in the land of* Goshen,
17. get you *unto the land of* Canaan;
18. the good of *the land of* Egypt, and ye shall eat the fat of *the land.*
19. wagons *out of the land of* Egypt
20. for the good of all *the land of* Egypt
25. came into *the land of* Canaan
26. governor over all *the land of* Egypt.
46: 6. they had gotten *in the land of* Canaan,
12. Er and Onan died *in the land of* Canaan.
20. unto Joseph *in the land of* Egypt
28. they came *into the land of* Goshen.
31. which (were) *in the land of* Canaan,
34. ye may dwell *in the land of* Goshen;
47: 1. come *out of the land of* Canaan; and, behold, they (are) *in the land of* Goshen.
4. For to sojourn *in the land* are we
— famine (is) sore *in the land of* Canaan:
— let thy servants dwell *in the land of*
6. *The land of* Egypt (is) before thee; in the best of *the land* make thy father
— *in the land of* Goshen let them dwell:
11. possession *in the land of* Egypt, in the best of *the land, in the land of* Rameses,
13. (there was) no bread in all *the land;*
— *the land of* Egypt *and* (all) *the land of*
14. money that was found *in the land* of Egypt, *and in the land of* Canaan,
15. money failed *in the land of* Egypt, *and in the land of* Canaan,
20. so *the land* became Pharaoh's.
27. Israel dwelt *in the land of* Egypt, *in the country of* Goshen;
28. Jacob lived *in the land of* Egypt
48: 3. at Luz *in the land of* Canaan,
4. will give this *land* to thy seed
5. born unto thee *in the land of* Egypt
7. Rachel died by me *in the land of*
— when yet (there was) but *a little way*
12. bowed himself with his face *to the earth.*
16. a multitude in the midst of *the earth.*
21. you again unto *the land of* your fathers.
49:15. and *the land* that (it was) pleasant;
30. Mamre, *in the land of* Canaan,
50: 5. I have digged for me *in the land of*
7. all the elders of *the land of* Egypt,
8. they left *in the land of* Goshen.
11. when the inhabitants of *the land,*
13. carried him *into the land of* Canaan,
24. out of this *land* unto *the land* which
Ex. 1: 7. *the land* was filled with them.
10. get them up out of *the land.*
2:15. dwelt *in the land of* Midian:
22. have been a stranger *in a* strange *land.*
3: 8. to bring them up out of that *land* unto a good *land* and a large,

Ex. 3:8, 17. unto *a land* flowing with milk
17. unto *the land of* the Canaanites,
4: 3. And he said, Cast it *on the ground.* And he cast it *on the ground,*
20. he returned *to the land of* Egypt:
5: 5. the people of *the land* now (are) many,
12. throughout all *the land of* Egypt
6: 1. shall he drive them *out of his land.*
4. to give them *the land of* Canaan, *the land of* their pilgrimage,
8. I will bring you in unto *the land,*
11. children of Israel go *out of his land.*
13. Israel *out of the land of* Egypt.
26. children of Israel *from the land of* Egypt
28. unto Moses *in the land of* Egypt,
7: 2. the children of Israel *out of his land.*
3. my wonders *in the land of* Egypt.
4. *out of the land of* Egypt by great
19, 21. throughout all *the land of* Egypt,
8: 5(1). frogs to come up upon *the land of*
6(2). came up, and covered *the land of*
7(3). brought up frogs upon *the land of*
14(10). upon heaps: and *the land* stank.
16(12). dust of *the land,* that it may become lice throughout all *the land of*
17(13). smote the dust of *the earth,*
—(—). all the dust of *the land* became lice throughout all *the land of* Egypt.
22(18). sever in that day *the land of* Goshen,
—(—). I (am) the Lord in the midst of *the earth.*
24(20). into all *the land of* Egypt: *the land*
25(21). sacrifice to your God *in the land.*
9: 5. the Lord shall do this thing *in the land.*
9. small dust in all *the land of* Egypt,
— upon beast, throughout all *the land of*
14. none like me in all *the earth.*
15. thou shalt be cut off from *the earth.*
16. may be declared throughout all *the earth.*
22. be hail in all *the land of* Egypt,
— of the field, *throughout the land of* Egypt.
23. the fire ran along *upon the ground;*
— rained hail upon *the land of* Egypt.
24. none like it in all *the land of*
25. smote throughout all *the land of* Egypt
26. Only *in the land of* Goshen,
29. how that *the earth* (is) the Lord's.
33. rain was not poured *upon the earth.*
10: 5. they shall cover the face of *the earth,* that one cannot be able to see *the earth:*
12. over *the land of* Egypt for the locusts, that they may come up upon *the land of* Egypt, and eat every herb of *the land,*
13. his rod over *the land of* Egypt,
— brought an east wind *upon the land*
14. locusts went up over all *the land of*
15. covered the face of *the* whole *earth,* so that *the land* was darkened; and they did eat every herb of *the land,*
— through all *the land of* Egypt.
21. be darkness over *the land of* Egypt,
22. thick darkness in all *the land of* Egypt
11: 3. Moses (was) very great *in the land of*
5. all the firstborn *in the land of* Egypt
6. throughout all *the land of* Egypt,
9. may be multiplied *in the land of* Egypt.
10. the children of Israel go *out of his land.*
12: 1. Moses and Aaron *in the land of* Egypt,
12. I will pass *through the land of* Egypt
—, 29. the firstborn *in the land of* Egypt,
13. when I smite *the land of* Egypt.
17. your armies *out of the land of* Egypt:
19. be a stranger, or born in *the land.*
25. when ye be come to *the land* which
33. send them out of *the land* in haste;
41. went out *from the land of* Egypt.
42. bringing them out *from the land of* Egypt:
48. as one that is born in *the land:*
51. of Israel out *of the land of* Egypt
13: 5, 11. shall bring thee into *the land of* the
— *a land* flowing with milk and honey,
15. the firstborn *in the land of* Egypt,
17. the way of *the land of* the Philistines,
18. harnessed *out of the land of* Egypt.
14: 3. They (are) entangled *in the land,*
15:12. *the earth* swallowed them.
16: 1. after their departing *out of the land of*

Ex. 16: 3. hand of the Lord *in the land of* Egypt,
6. brought you *out from the land of* Egypt:
14. small as the hoarfrost on *the ground.*
32. brought you forth *from the land of* Egypt.
35. until they came to *a land* inhabited;
— the borders of *the land of* Canaan.
18: 3. been an alien *in a* strange *land:*
27. he went his way into *his own land.*
19: 1. gone forth *out of the land of* Egypt,
5. for all *the earth* (is) mine:
20: 2. brought thee *out of the land of* Egypt,
4. or that (is) *in the earth* beneath, or that (is) in the water under *the earth:*
11. six days the Lord made heaven and *earth,*
22:21(20) & 23:9. strangers *in the land of* Egypt.
23:10. six years thou shalt sow *thy land,*
26. nor be barren, *in thy land:*
29. lest *the land* become desolate,
30. be increased, and inherit *the land.*
31. deliver the inhabitants of *the land*
33. They shall not dwell *in thy land,*
29:46. brought them forth *out of the land of*
31:17. the Lord made heaven and *earth,*
32: 1, 23. brought us up *out of the land of*
4, 8. brought thee up *out of the land of*
7. which thou broughtest *out of the land of*
11. hast brought forth *out of the land of*
13. all this *land* that I have spoken of
33: 1. *out of the land of* Egypt, unto *the land*
3. *a land* flowing with milk and honey:
34: 8. bowed his head *toward the earth,*
10. as have not been done in all *the earth,*
12, 15. with the inhabitants of *the land*
24. neither shall any man desire *thy land,*
Lev. 4:27. if any one of the *common* people (marg. people of *the land*)
11: 2. the beasts that (are) on *the earth.*
21. to leap withal upon *the earth;*
29, 42. that creep upon *the earth;*
41. that creepeth upon *the earth*
44. thing that creepeth upon *the earth.*
45. bringeth you up *out of the land of* Egypt,
46. that creepeth upon *the earth:*
14:34. ye be come into *the land of* Canaan,
— in a house of *the land of* your possession;
16:22. iniquities unto *a land* not inhabited:
18: 3. the doings of *the land of* Egypt,
— the doings of *the land of* Canaan,
25, 27. *the land* is defiled:
— *the land* itself vomiteth out
27. abominations have the men of *the land*
28. That *the land* spue not you out
19: 9. when ye reap the harvest of *your land,*
23. when ye shall come into *the land,*
29. lest *the land* fall to whoredom, and *the land* become full of wickedness.
33. sojourn with thee *in your land,*
34. ye were strangers *in the land of* Egypt:
36. brought you *out of the land of*
20: 2. the people of *the land* shall stone him
4. if the people of *the land* do any
22. *the land,* whither I bring you to dwell
24. *a land* that floweth with milk and honey:
22:24. *neither* (lit. *and* not) shall ye make (any offering thereof) *in your land.*
33. That brought you *out of the land of*
23:10. When ye be come into *the land* which
22. when ye reap the harvest of *your land,*
39. gathered in the fruit of *the land,*
43. I brought them *out of the land of*
25: 2. When ye come into *the land* which I give you, then shall *the land* keep
4. be a sabbath of rest *unto the land,*
5. a year of rest *unto the land.*
6. the sabbath of *the land* shall be meat
7. and for the beast that (are) *in thy land,*
9. throughout all *your land.*
10. liberty *throughout* (all) *the land* unto all
18. ye shall dwell in *the land*
19. *the land* shall yield her fruit,
23. *The land* shall not be sold for ever: for *the land* (is) mine;
24. in all *the land of* your possession ye shall grant a redemption *for the land.*
31. counted as the fields of *the country:*
38. brought you forth *out of the land of* Egypt, to give you *the land of* Canaan,

Lev.25:42, 55. brought forth *out of the land of* Egypt:
45. which they begat *in your land:*
26: 1. image of stone *in your land,*
4. *the land* shall yield her increase,
5. dwell *in your land* safely.
6. I will give peace *in the land,*
— evil beasts out of *the land,* neither shall the sword go *through your land.*
13. you forth *out of the land of* Egypt,
19. heaven as iron, and *your earth* as brass:
20. *your land* shall not yield her increase, neither shall the trees of *the land*
32. I will bring *the land* into desolation:
33. *your land* shall be desolate,
34. Then shall *the land* enjoy her sabbaths,
— ye (be) *in* your enemies' *land;* (even) then shall *the land* rest, and enjoy
36. *in the lands of* their enemies;
38. *the land of* your enemies shall eat
39. *in* your enemies' *lands;*
41. brought them *into the land of* their
42. *and* I will remember *the land.*
43. *The land also* shall be left of them,
44. when they be *in the land of* their
45. brought forth *out of the land of* Egypt
27:24. to whom the possession of *the land* (did belong).
30. all the tithe of *the land,* (whether) of the seed of *the land,*
Nu. 1: 1. they were come *out of the land of* Egypt,
3:13. smote all the firstborn *in the land of*
8:17. smote every firstborn *in the land of*
9: 1. after they were come *out of the land of*
14. for him that was born in *the land.*
10: 9. if ye go to war *in your land*
30. I will depart to *mine own land,*
11:31. upon the face of *the earth.*
13: 2. that they may search *the land of* Canaan,
16. which Moses sent to spy out *the land.*
17. them to spy out *the land of* Canaan,
18. see *the land,* what it (is);
19. what *the land* (is) that they dwell
20. what *the land* (is), whether it (be)
— bring of the fruit of *the land.*
21. they went up, and searched *the land*
25. returned from searching of *the land*
26. shewed them the fruit of *the land.*
27. We came unto *the land* whither thou
28. people (be) strong that dwell *in the land,*
29. Amalekites dwell *in the land of*
32. brought up an evil report of *the land*
— *The land,* through which we have gone
— *a land* that eateth up the inhabitants
14: 2. that we had died *in the land of*
3. the Lord brought us unto this *land,*
6. of them that searched *the land,*
7. *The land,* which we passed through to search it, (is) *an* exceeding good *land.*
8. then he will bring us into this *land,*
— *a land* which floweth with milk
9. neither fear ye the people of *the land;*
14. to the inhabitants of this *land:*
16. bring this people into *the land*
21. all *the earth* shall be filled
23. they shall not see *the land*
24. him will I bring into *the land*
30. ye shall not come into *the land,*
31. they shall know *the land*
34. in which ye searched *the land,*
36. which Moses sent to search *the land,*
— by bringing up a slander upon *the land,*
37. bring up the evil report upon *the land,*
38. the men that went to search *the land.*
15: 2. When ye be come into *the land of*
18. When ye come into *the land*
19. when ye eat of the bread of *the land,*
41. which brought you *out of the land of*
16:13. hast brought us up *out of a land*
14. hast not brought us into *a land*
32. *the earth* opened her mouth,
33. *the earth* closed upon them:
34. Lest *the earth* swallow us up
18:13. first ripe *in the* (lit. *in their*) *land,*
20. have no inheritance *in their land,*
20:12. bring this congregation into *the land*
17. us pass, I pray thee, *through thy country:*
23. by the coast of *the land of* Edom,

Nu. 20:24. he shall not enter into *the land*
21: 4. to compass *the land of* Edom:
22. Let me pass *through thy land:*
24. possessed *his land* from Arnon
26. taken all *his land* out of his hand,
31. Thus Israel dwelt *in the land of*
34. all his people, and *his land;*
35. they possessed *his land.*
22: 5. the river of *the land of* the children
— they cover the face of *the earth,*
6. I may drive them out of *the land:*
11. which covereth the face of *the earth:*
13. Get you into *your land:*
26: 4. went forth *out of the land of* Egypt.
10. *the earth* opened her mouth,
19. Er and Onan died *in the land of*
53. Unto these *the land* shall be
55. *the land* shall be divided by lot:
27:12. see *the land* which I have given
32: 1. *the land of* Jazer, and *the land of* Gilead,
4. *the country* which the Lord smote
— *a land for* cattle,
5. let this *land* be given unto thy servants
7. from going over into *the land*
8. from Kadesh-barnea to see *the land.*
9. and saw *the land,* they discouraged
— should not go into *the land*
17. because of the inhabitants of *the land.*
22. *the land* be subdued before the Lord:
— this *land* shall be your possession
29. *the land* shall be subdued before you; then ye shall give them *the land of* Gilead
30. possessions among you *in the land of*
32. before the Lord into *the land of* Canaan,
33. *the land,* with the cities thereof
— the cities of *the country* round about.
33: 1. which went forth *out of the land of*
37. in the edge of *the land of* Edom.
38. Israel were come *out of the land of*
40. in the south *in the land of* Canaan,
51. over Jordan into *the land of* Canaan;
52. inhabitants of *the land* from before you,
53. dispossess (the inhabitants of) *the land,*
— I have given you *the land*
54. ye shall divide *the land*
55. drive out the inhabitants of *the land*
— shall vex you in *the land*
34: 2. When ye come into *the land of* Canaan; this (is) *the land* that shall fall
— (even) *the land of* Canaan
12. this shall be your *land*
13. This (is) *the land* which ye shall inherit
17. which shall divide *the land*
18. to divide *the land* by inheritance.
29. children of Israel *in the land of* Canaan.
35:10. over Jordan *into the land of* Canaan;
14. shall ye give *in the land of* Canaan,
28. the slayer shall return into *the land of*
32. should come again to dwell *in the land,*
33. not pollute *the land* wherein ye (are) : for blood it defileth *the land: and the land* cannot
34. Defile not therefore *the land*
36: 2. to give *the land* for an inheritance
Deu. 1: 5. *in the land of* Moab, began Moses
7. to *the land of* the Canaanites,
8. I have set *the land* before you: go in and possess *the land*
21. thy God hath set *the land* before thee:
22. they shall search us out *the land,*
25. they took of the fruit of *the land*
— *a* good *land* which the Lord our God
27. brought us forth *out of the land of*
35. see that good *land,* which I sware
36. to him will I give *the land*
2: 5. I will not give you *of their land,*
9. I will not give thee *of their land*
12. did *unto the land of* his possession,
19. I will not give thee *of the land of*
20. also was accounted *a land of* giants:
24. the Amorite, king of Heshbon, and *his land:*
27. Let me pass *through thy land:*
29. into *the land* which the Lord
31. to give Sihon and *his land*
— that thou mayest inherit *his land.*
37. unto *the land of* the children of Ammon

Deu. 3: 2. all his people, and *his land,*
8. *the land* that (was) on this side
12. this *land,* (which) we possessed
13. which was called *the land of* giants.
18. hath given you this *land*
20. they also possess *the land*
24. what God (is there) in heaven *or in earth,*
25. go over, and see *the* good *land*
28. he shall cause them to inherit *the land*
4: 1. go in and possess *the land*
5. that ye should do so in *the land*
14. that ye might do them *in the land*
17. of any beast that (is) *on the earth,*
18. the waters beneath *the earth:*
21. go in unto that good *land,*
22. But I must die *in* this *land,*
— possess that good *land.*
25. ye shall have remained long *in the land,*
26. I call heaven and *earth* to witness
— utterly perish from off *the land*
32. God created man upon *the earth,*
36. upon *earth* he shewed
38. to give thee *their land* (for) an inheritance,
39. upon the *earth* beneath:
43. *in the* plain *country,*
46. *in the land of* Sihon king of the
47. possessed *his land,* and *the land of* Og
5: 6. brought thee *out of the land of* Egypt,
8. or that (is) *in the earth* beneath, or that (is) in the waters beneath *the earth:*
15. a servant *in the land of* Egypt,
31(28). *in the land* which I give them
33(30). may prolong (your) days *in the land*
6: 1. *in the land* whither ye go to possess
3. in *the land* that floweth with milk
10. brought thee into *the land* which he sware
12. *out of the land of* Egypt,
18. go in and possess *the* good *land*
23. to give us *the land* which he sware
7: 1. shall bring thee into *the land*
8: 1. go in and possess *the land*
7. into a good *land, a land of* brooks
8. *A land of* wheat and barley,
— *a land of* oil olive, and honey;
9. *A land* wherein thou shalt eat bread
— *a land* whose stones (are) iron,
10. *the* good *land* which he hath given thee.
14. thee forth *out of the land of* Egypt,
9: 4. brought me in to possess this *land:*
5. dost thou go to possess *their land.*
6. giveth thee not this good *land* to possess
7. didst depart *out of the land of* Egypt,
23. Go up and possess *the land*
28. Lest *the land* whence thou broughtest us
— to bring them into *the land*
10: 7. *a land of* rivers of waters.
11. go in and possess *the land,*
14. *the earth* (also), with all that therein (is).
19. ye were strangers *in the land of* Egypt.
11: 3. king of Egypt, and unto all *his land;*
6. *the earth* opened her mouth,
8. go in and possess *the land,*
9. *a land* that floweth with milk
10. For *the land,* whither thou goest
— (is) not *as the land of* Egypt,
11. *But the land,* whither ye go
— *a land of* hills and valleys,
12. *A land* which the Lord thy God
14. rain of *your land* in his due season,
17. quickly from off *the* good *land*
21. as the days of heaven upon *the earth.*
25. dread of you upon all *the land* that
29. unto *the land* whither thou goest
30. *in the land of* the Canaanites,
31. to go in to possess *the land*
12: 1. ye shall observe to do *in the land,*
10. dwell *in the land* which
16. ye shall pour it upon *the earth*
24. thou shalt pour it upon *the earth*
29. dwellest *in their land;*
13: 5(6). brought you out *of the land of* Egypt,
7(8). from the (one) end of *the earth* even unto the (other) end of *the earth;*
10(11). which brought thee out *of the land of*
15: 4. shall greatly bless thee *in the land*
7. within any of thy gates *in thy land*
11. the poor shall never cease out of *the land:*

Deu 15:11. thy poor, and to thy needy, *in thy land.*
15. wast a bondman *in the land of* Egypt,
23. pour it upon *the ground* as water.
16: 3. *out of the land of* Egypt in haste:
— thou camest forth *out of the land of* Egypt
20. inherit *the land* which the Lord thy God
17. 14. When thou art come unto *the land*
18: 9. When thou art come into *the land*
19: 1. *whose land* the Lord thy God giveth thee,
2. cities for thee in the midst of *thy land,*
3. divide the coasts of *thy land,*
8. give thee all *the land* which he
10. innocent blood be not shed in *thy land,*
14. which thou shalt inherit *in the land*
20: 1. brought thee up *out of the land of* Egypt.
22: 6. in any tree, or on *the ground,*
23: 7(8) thou wast a stranger in *his land.*
20(21). in *the land* whither thou goest
24: 4. thou shalt not cause *the land* to sin,
14. strangers that (are) *in thy land*
22. a bondman *in the land of* Egypt:
25:19. *in the land* which the Lord thy God
26: 1. thou (art) come in unto *the land*
2. shalt bring *of thy land* that the Lord
3. that I am come unto *the country*
9. hath given us this *land,*
—, 15. *a land* that floweth with milk and
27. 2. shall pass over Jordan unto *the land*
3. that thou mayest go in unto *the land*
— *a land* that floweth with milk and honey;
28: 1. above all nations of *the earth:*
8. he shall bless thee *in the land*
10. all people of *the earth* shall see
12. unto *thy land* in his season,
23. *and the earth* that (is) under thee
24. the rain of *thy land* powder and dust:
25. into all the kingdoms of *the earth.*
26. unto the beasts of *the earth,*
49. from the end of *the earth,*
52, 52. throughout all *thy land:*
56. the sole of her foot upon *the ground*
64. from the one end of *the earth* even unto the other; (lit. from the end of *the earth* and unto the end of *the earth*)
29: 1(28:69). of Israel *in the land of* Moab,
2(1). before your eyes *in the land of* Egypt
—(–). unto all *his land;*
8(7). we took *their land,*
16(15). how we have dwelt *in the land of* E.;
22(21). shall come *from a* far *land,* shall say, when they see the plagues of that *land,*
23(22). the whole *land thereof* (is) brimstone,
24(23). done thus *unto* this *land?*
25(24). them forth *out of the land of* Egypt:
27(26). was kindled *against this land,*
28(27). and cast them into another *land,*
30: 5. will bring thee into *the land*
16. God shall bless thee *in the land*
19. I call heaven and *earth* to record
31: 4. *and unto the land of them,* whom
7. must go with this people unto *the land*
16. the gods of the strangers of *the land,*
21. before I have brought them into *the land*
23. into *the land* which I sware unto them:
28. call heaven and *earth* to record
32: 1. hear, O *earth,* the words of my mouth.
10. He found him *in a* desert *land,*
13. ride on the high places of *the earth,*
22. shall consume *the earth*
49. which (is) *in the land of* Moab,
— behold *the land of* Canaan,
52. shalt see *the land* before (thee);
— unto *the land* which I give
33:13. Blessed of the Lord (be) *his land,*
16. And for the precious things of *the earth*
17. to the ends of *the earth:*
28. *a land of* corn and wine;
34: 1. the Lord shewed him all *the land* of
2. *the land of* Ephraim, and Manasseh, and all the *land of* Judah,
4. This (is) *the land* which I sware
5. died there *in the land of* Moab,
6. in a valley *in the land of* Moab,
11. sent him to do *in the land of* Egypt
— all his servants, and to all *his land,*
Jos 1: 2. unto *the land* which I do give
4. all *the land of* the Hittites,

Jos. 1: 6. divide for an inheritance *the land,*
11. to go in to possess *the land,*
13. and hath given you this *land.*
14. shall remain *in the land* which Moses
15. they also have possessed *the land*
— ye shall return *unto the land of*
2: 1. Go view *the land,* even Jericho.
2. children of Israel to search out *the country*
3. be come to search out all *the country.*
9. the Lord hath given you *the land,*
— all the inhabitants of *the land* faint
11. in heaven above, and in *earth* beneath.
14. when the Lord hath given us *the land,*
18. we come *into the land,* thou shalt bind
24. into our hands all *the land;* for even all the inhabitants of *the country*
3:11, 13. the Lord of all *the earth*
4:24. That all the people of *the earth*
5: 6. that he would not shew them *the land,*
— *a land* that floweth with milk and honey.
11. eat of the old corn of *the land*
12. eaten of the old corn of *the land;*
— did eat of the fruit of *the land of*
14. fell on his face *to the earth,*
6:22. men that had spied out *the country,*
27. throughout all *the country.*
7: 2. Go up and view *the country.*
6. fell *to the earth* upon his face
9. all the inhabitants of *the land* shall hear
— cut off our name from *the earth:*
21. they (are) hid *in the earth*
8: 1. and his city, and *his land:*
9: 6. We be come *from a* far *country:*
9. *From a* very far *country* thy servants
11. and all the inhabitants of *our country*
24. to give you all *the land,* and to destroy all the inhabitants of *the land*
10:40. Joshua smote all *the country* of the hills,
41. and all *the country of* Goshen,
42. all these kings and *their land*
11: 3. *in the land of* Mizpeh.
16. Joshua took all that *land,*
— all *the land of* Goshen,
22. none of the Anakims left *in the land of*
23. Joshua took *the* whole *land,*
— *And the land* rested from war.
12: 1. these (are) the kings of *the land,*
— possessed *their land* on the other
7. these (are) the kings of *the country*
13: 1. *and* there remaineth yet very much *land*
2. This (is) *the land* that yet remaineth:
4. all *the land of* the Canaanites,
5. *And the land of* the Giblites,
7. divide this *land* for an inheritance
21. dukes of Sihon, dwelling in *the country.*
25. half *the land of* the children of Ammon,
14: 1. inherited *in the land of* Canaan,
4. no part unto the Levites *in the land,*
5. they divided *the land.*
7. from Kadesh-barnea to espy out *the land;*
9. *the land* whereon thy feet have trodden
15. *And the land* had rest from war.
15:19. thou hast given me *a* south *land;*
17: 5. beside *the land of* Gilead
6. *and* the rest of Manasseh's sons had *the land of* Gilead.
8. Manasseh had *the land of*
12. the Canaanites would dwell *in* that *land.*
15. *in the land of* the Perizzites
16. that dwell *in the land of* the valley
18: 1. *And the land* was subdued before them.
3. slack to go to possess *the land,*
4. rise, and go *through the land,*
6. Ye shall therefore describe *the land*
8. that went to describe *the land,* saying, Go and walk *through the land,*
9. went and passed *through the land,*
10. there Joshua divided *the land*
19:49. dividing *the land* for inheritance
51. made an end of dividing *the country.*
21: 2. *in the land of* Canaan,
43(41). gave unto Israel all *the land* which
22: 4. unto *the land of* your possession,
9. *in the land of* Canaan, to go unto *the country of* Gilead, to *the land of*
10. that (are) *in the land of* Canaan,
11. over against *the land of* Canaan,

Jos. 22:13. into *the land of* Gilead, Phinehas
15. unto *the land of* Gilead, and they
19. if *the land of* your possession (be) unclean, (then) pass ye over unto *the land of*
32. *out of the land of* Gilead, unto *the land of*
33. to destroy *the land* wherein
23: 5. ye shall possess *their land,*
14. I (am) going the way of all *the earth:*
16. perish quickly from off *the* good *land*
24: 3. led him throughout all *the land of*
8. brought you into *the land of* the Amorites,
— that ye might possess *their land;*
13. *a land* for which ye did not labour,
15. *in whose land* ye dwell:
17. *out of the land of* Egypt,
18. which dwelt in *the land:*
Jud. 1: 2. I have delivered *the land* into his hand.
15. thou hast given me *a* south *land;*
26. the man went into *the land of*
27. the Canaanites would dwell *in* that *land.*
32, 33. the inhabitants of *the land:*
2: 1. have brought you unto *the land*
2. with the inhabitants of this *land;*
6. his inheritance to possess *the land.*
12. brought them out *of the land of* Egypt,
3:11. *the land* had rest forty years.
25. fallen down dead on *the earth.*
30. *the land* had rest fourscore years.
4:21. fastened it *into the ground:*
5: 4. *the earth* trembled, and the heavens
31. And *the land* had rest forty years.
6: 4. destroyed the increase of *the earth,*
5. they entered *into the land*
9. gave you *their land;*
10. *in whose land* ye dwell:
37. dry upon all *the earth*
39. upon all *the ground* let there be dew.
40. there was dew on all *the ground.*
8:28. *the country* was in quietness forty
9:37. people down by the middle of *the land,*
10: 4. which (are) *in the land of* Gilead.
8. *in the land of* the Amorites,
11: 3. dwelt *in the land of* Tob:
5. fetch Jephthah *out of the land of* Tob:
12. come against me to fight *in my land?*
13. Israel took away *my land,*
15. Israel took not away *the land of* Moab, *nor the land of* the children of Ammon:
17. I pray thee, pass *through thy land:*
18. compassed *the land of* Edom, and *the land of* Moab, and came by the east side *of the land of* Moab,
19. *through thy land* into my place.
21. Israel possessed all *the land of* the Amorites, the inhabitants of that *country.*
12:12. in Aijalon *in the country of* Zebulun.
15. in Pirathon *in the land of* Ephraim,
13:20. fell on their faces *to the ground.*
16:24. the destroyer of *our country,*
18: 2. to spy out *the land,*
— Go, search *the land:*
7. no magistrate *in the land,*
9. for we have seen *the land,*
— to enter to possess *the land.*
10. a people secure, *and to a* large *land:*
— any thing that (is) *in the earth.*
14. men that went to spy out *the country*
17. men that went to spy out *the land*
30. day of the captivity of *the land.*
19:30. came up *out of the land of* Egypt
20: 1. to Beer-sheba, *with the land of* Gilead,
21, 25. destroyed down *to the ground*
21:12. Shiloh, which (is) *in the land of* Canaan.
21. go to *the land of* Benjamin.
Ru. 1: 1. there was a famine *in the land.*
7. to return unto *the land of* Judah.
2:10. bowed herself *to the ground,*
11. *and the land of* thy nativity, and art
1Sa. 2: 8. the pillars of *the earth* (are) the Lord's,
10. shall judge the ends of *the earth;*
3:19. none of his words fall *to the ground.*
4: 5. a great shout, so that *the earth* rang
5: 3. fallen upon his face *to the earth*
4. fallen upon his face *to the ground*
6: 5. images of your mice that mar *the land;*
— off your gods, and from off *your land.*

1Sa. 9: 4. passed *through the land of* Shalisha,
— they passed *through the land of* Shalim,
— passed *through the land of* the Benjamites,
5. they were come *to the land of* Zuph,
16. thee a man *out of the land of* Benjamin,
12: 6. fathers up *out of the land of* Egypt.
13: 3. the trumpet throughout all *the land,*
7. over Jordan to *the land of* Gad
17. unto *the land of* Shual.
19. throughout all *the land of* Israel:
14:15. they also trembled, and *the earth* quaked:
25. (they of) *the land* came to a wood;
29. My father hath troubled *the land:*
32. slew (them) *on the ground:*
45. hair of his head fall *to the ground;*
17:46. to the wild beasts of *the earth;* that all *the earth* may know
49. he fell upon his face *to the earth.*
20:41. fell on his face *to the ground,*
21:11(12). David the king of *the land?*
22: 5. get thee into *the land of* Judah.
23:23. if he be *in the land,*
27. the Philistines have invaded *the land.*
24: 8(9). stooped with his face *to the earth,*
25:23. bowed herself to *the ground,*
41. bowed herself on (her) face *to the earth,*
26: 7. his spear stuck *in the ground*
8. the spear *even to the earth* at once,
20. let not my blood fall *to the earth*
27: 1. escape into *the land of* the Philistines;
8. of old the inhabitants of *the land,*
— even unto *the land of* Egypt.
9. David smote *the land,* and left neither
28: 3. and the wizards, *out of the land.*
9. the wizards, out of *the land:*
13. I saw gods ascending out of *the earth.*
14. stooped with (his) face *to the ground,*
20. straightway all along *on the earth,*
23. So he arose *from the earth,*
29:11. return into *the land of* the Philistines.
30:16. spread abroad upon all *the earth,*
— *out of the land of* the Philistines, *and out of the land of* Judah.
31: 9. sent *into the land of* the Philistines
2Sa. 1: 2. he fell *to the earth,* and did obeisance.
2:22. should I smite thee *to the ground?*
3:12. Whose (is) *the land?*
4:11. take you away from *the earth?*
5: 6. Jebusites, the inhabitants of *the land:*
7: 9. the great (men) that (are) *in the earth.*
23. what one nation *in the earth*
— great things and terrible, *for thy land,*
8: 2. casting them down *to the ground;*
10: 2. into *the land of* the children of Ammon.
12:16. lay all night *upon the earth.*
17. to raise him up from *the earth:*
20. Then David arose *from the earth,*
13:31. tare his garments, and lay *on the earth;*
14: 4. she fell on her face *to the ground,*
11. hair of thy son fall *to the earth.*
14. as water spilt *on the ground,*
20. know all (things) that (are) in *the earth.*
22. Joab fell *to the ground*
33. bowed himself on his face *to the ground*
15: 4. that I were made judge *in the land,*
23. all *the country* wept with a loud voice,
17:26. pitched in *the land of* Gilead.
18: 8. scattered over the face of all *the country:*
9. between the heaven and *the earth;*
11. smite him there *to the ground?*
28. he fell down *to the earth*
19: 9(10). he is fled out of *the land*
20:10. shed out his bowels *to the ground,*
21:14. *in the country of* Benjamin
— God was intreated *for the land.*
22: 8. Then *the earth* shook and trembled;
43. as small as the dust of *the earth,*
23: 4. the tender grass (springing) *out of the earth*
24: 6. to *the land of* Tahtim-hodshi;
8. when they had gone through all *the land,*
13. come unto thee *in thy land?*
— three days' pestilence *in thy land?*
20. on his face *upon the ground.*
25. the Lord was intreated *for the land,*
1K. 1:23. the king with his face *to the ground.*
31. bowed with (her) face to *the earth,*

1K. 1:40. so that *the earth* rent with the sound
52. not an hair of him fall *to the earth:*
2: 2. I go the way of all *the earth:*
4:10. and all *the land of* Hepher:
19. the son of Uri (was) *in the country of* Gilead, (in) *the country of* Sihon king
— the only officer which (was) *in the land.*
21(5:1). river unto *the land of* the Philistines,
34(5:14). from all kings of *the earth,*
6: 1. come out *of the land of* Egypt,
8: 9. came out *of the land of* Egypt.
21. he brought them *out of the land of*
23. in heaven above, or on *earth* beneath,
27. will God indeed dwell on *the earth?*
36. give rain upon *thy land,*
37. If there be *in the land* famine,
— if their enemy besiege them *in the land of*
41. cometh *out of a* far *country*
43. that all people of *the earth* may know
46. *the land of* the enemy, far or near;
47. *in the land* whither they were carried
— make supplication unto thee *in the land*
48. *in the land of* their enemies,
— pray unto thee toward *their land,*
53. from among all the people of *the earth,*
60. all the people of *the earth* may know
9: 8. the Lord done thus *unto* this *land,*
9. their fathers *out of the land of* Egypt,
11. Hiram twenty cities *in the land of* Galilee.
13. he called them *the land of* Cabul
18. Tadmor in the wilderness, *in the land,*
19. in all *the land of* his dominion.
21. that were left after them *in the land,*
26. *in the land of* Edom.
10: 6. report that I heard *in mine own land*
13. turned and went *to her own country,*
15. and of the governors of *the country.*
23. exceeded all the kings of *the earth*
24. all *the earth* sought to Solomon,
11:18. appointed him victuals, *and* gave him *land.*
21. that I may go to *mine own country.*
22. thou seekest to go to *thine own country?*
12:28. brought thee up *out of the land of*
14:24. there were also sodomites *in the land:*
15:12. took away the sodomites out of *the land,*
20. with all *the land of* Naphtali.
17: 7. there had been no rain *in the land.*
18: 5. said unto Obadiah, Go *into the land,*
6. they divided *the land* between them
42. cast himself down *upon the earth,*
20: 7. called all the elders of *the land,*
27. but the Syrians filled *the country.*
22:36. and every man to *his own country.*
46(47). he took out of *the land.*
2K. 2:15. themselves *to the ground* before him.
19. *and the ground* barren.
3:20. *the country* was filled with water.
27. and returned *to* (their own) *land.*
4:37. bowed herself *to the ground,*
38. (there was) a dearth *in the land;*
5: 2. away captive *out of the land of* Israel
4. that (is) *of the land of* Israel.
15. no God in all *the earth,*
19. departed from him *a* little *way.* (marg. piece of *ground*)
6:23. came no more *into the land of* Israel.
8: 1. it shall also come upon *the land*
2. sojourned *in the land of* the Philistines
3. *out of the land of* the Philistines:
6. since the day that she left *the land,*
10:10. there shall fall *unto the earth*
33. all *the land of* Gilead,
11: 3. Athaliah did reign over *the land.*
14. all the people of *the land* rejoiced,
18. all the people of *the land* went
19. guard, and all the people of *the land;*
20. all the people of *the land* rejoiced,
13:18. Smite *upon the ground.*
20. Moabites invaded (lit. came *into*) *the land*
15: 5. judging the people of *the land.*
19. king of Assyria came against *the land:*
20. stayed not there *in the land.*
29. all *the land of* Naphtali,
16:15. all the people of *the land,*
17: 5. throughout all *the land,*
7. *out of the land of* Egypt,

2K. 17:26, 26, 27. the manner of the God of *the land*
36. up *out of the land of* Egypt
18:25. Go up against this *land,*
32. away to *a land like your own land, a land of* corn and wine, *a land of* bread and vineyards, *a land of* oil
33. gods of the nations delivered at all *his land*
35. among all the gods of *the countries,* that have delivered *their country*
19: 7. shall return *to his own land;*
— fall by the sword *in his own land.*
11. have done to all *lands,*
15. of all the kingdoms of *the earth;* thou hast made heaven and *earth.*
17. destroyed the nations and *their lands,*
19. that all the kingdoms of *the earth*
37. they escaped into *the land of*
20:14. They are come *from a* far *country,*
21:24. the people of *the land* slew all
— the people of *the land* made Josiah
23:24. that were spied *in the land of* Judah
30. the people of *the land* took
33. Riblah *in the land of* Hamath,
— put *the land* to a tribute
35. but he taxed *the land*
— the gold of the people of *the land,*
24: 7. any more *out of his land:*
14. poorest sort of the people of *the land.*
15. the mighty of *the land,*
25: 3. for the people of *the land.*
12. left of the poor of *the land*
19. mustered the people of *the land,* and threescore men of the people of *the land*
21. Riblah *in the land of* Hamath.
22. that remained *in the land of* Judah,
24. dwell *in the land,* and serve
1Ch. 1:10. he began to be mighty *upon the earth*
19. in his days *the earth* was divided:
43. that reigned *in the land of* Edom
45. *of the land of* the Temanites
2:22. twenty cities *in the land of* Gilead.
4:40. *and the land* (was) wide,
5: 9. multiplied *in the land of* Gilead.
11. *in the land of* Bashan
23. Manasseh dwelt *in the land:*
25. the gods of the people of *the land,*
6:55(40). Hebron *in the land of* Judah,
7:21. (that were) born *in* (that) *land*
10: 9. sent *into the land of* the Philistines
11: 4. the inhabitants of *the land.*
13: 2. left in all *the land of* Israel,
14:17. fame of David went out into all *lands;*
16:14. his judgments (are) in all *the earth.*
18. Unto thee will I give *the land of*
23. Sing unto the Lord, all *the earth;*
30. Fear before him, all *the earth:*
31. let *the earth* rejoice:
33. he cometh to judge *the earth.*
17: 8. the great men that (are) *in the earth.*
21. what one nation *in the earth*
19: 2. servants of David came into *the land of*
3. to spy out *the land?*
20: 1. wasted *the country of*
21:12. even the pestilence, *in the land,*
16. between *the earth* and the heaven,
21. with (his) face *to the ground.*
22: 2. that (were) *in the land of* Israel;
5. throughout all *countries:*
8. shed much blood *upon the earth*
18. given the inhabitants of *the land*
— *the land* is subdued before the Lord,
28: 8. ye may possess this good *land,*
29:11. in the heaven *and in the earth*
15. our days on *the earth* (are) as a
30. all the kingdoms of *the countries.*
2Ch. 1: 9. like the dust of *the earth*
2:12(11). that made heaven and *earth,*
17(16). that (were) *in the land of* Israel,
6: 5. *out of the land of* Egypt
14. *nor in the earth;* which keepest
18. very deed dwell with men on *the earth?*
27. send rain upon *thy land,*
28. If there be dearth *in the land,*
— in the cities *of* their *land;*
32. is come *from a* far *country*
33. that all people *of the earth*

2Ch. 6:36. away captives unto *a land* far off
37. bethink themselves *in the land*
— pray unto thee *in the land of*
38. *in the land of* their captivity,
— pray toward *their land,*
7: 3. with their faces *to the ground*
13. the locusts to devour *the land,*
14. will heal *their land.*
21. the Lord done thus *unto* this *land,*
22. forth *out of the land of* Egypt,
8: 6. throughout all *the land of*
8. who were left after them *in the land,*
17. *in the land of* Edom.
9: 5. which I heard *in mine own land*
11. none such seen before *in the land of*
12. went away *to her own land,*
14. governors of *the country*
22. passed all the kings of *the earth*
23. all the kings of *the earth* sought
26. unto *the land of* the Philistines,
28. and out of all *lands.*
11:23. throughout all *the countries of*
12: 8. the kingdoms of *the countries.*
13: 9. the nations of (other) *lands?*
14: 1(13:23). In his days *the land* was
6(5). for *the land* had rest,
7(6). *the land* (is) yet before us;
15: 5. the inhabitants of *the countries.*
8. out of all *the land of* Judah
16: 9. throughout *the* whole *earth,*
17: 2. set garrisons *in the land of* Judah,
10. all the kingdoms of *the lands*
19: 3. taken away the groves out of *the land,*
5. he set judges *in the land*
20: 7. drive out the inhabitants of this *land*
10. when they came *out of the land of*
18. with (his) face *to the ground:*
24. dead bodies fallen *to the earth,*
29. on all the kingdoms of (those) *countries,*
22:12. Athaliah reigned over *the land.*
23:13, 20, 21. all the people of *the land*
26:21. judging the people of *the land.*
30: 9. they shall come again *into* this *land:*
10. *through the country of* Ephraim
25. strangers that came *out of the land of*
32: 4. ran through the midst of *the land,*
13. unto all the people of (other) *lands?*
— the nations of those *lands* any ways able to deliver *their lands*
17. the nations of (other) *lands*
19. gods of the people of *the earth,*
21. with shame of face *to his own land.*
31. that was (done) *in the land,*
33:25. But the people of *the land*
— the people of *the land* made
34: 7. throughout all *the land of* Israel,
8. when he had purged *the land,*
33. abominations out of all *the countries*
36: 1. the people of *the land* took Jehoahaz
3. condemned *the land*
21. until *the land* had enjoyed her sabbaths:
23. All the kingdoms of *the earth*
Ezr. 1: 2. All the kingdoms of *the earth;*
3: 3. because of the people of those *countries:*
4: 4. Then the people of *the land*
6:21. filthiness of the heathen of *the land,*
9: 1. from the people of *the lands,*
2. with the people of (those) *lands:*
7. of the kings of *the lands,*
11. *The land,* unto which ye go to possess it, is *an* unclean *land* with the filthiness of the people of *the lands,*
12. eat the good of *the land,*
10: 2. strange wives of the people of *the land:*
11. from the people of *the land,*
Neh. 4: 4(3:36). a prey *in the land of* captivity:
5:14. governor *in the land of* Judah,
8: 6. with (their) faces *to the ground.*
9: 6. *the earth,* and all (things) that (are)
8. to give *the land of* the Canaanites,
10. on all the people of *his land:*
15. go in to possess *the land*
22. possessed *the land of* Sihon, and *the land of* the king of Heshbon, and *the land of* Og
23. broughtest them into *the land,*
24. went in and possessed *the land,*

Neh. 9:24. the inhabitants of *the land,*
— the people of *the land,*
30. the hand of the people of *the lands.*
35. in the large *and* fat *land*
36. *and* (for) *the land* that thou gavest
10:28(29). from the people of *the lands*
30(31). daughters unto the people of *the land,*
31(32). the people of *the land* bring ware
Est. 8:17. many of the people of *the land*
10: 1. laid a tribute upon *the land,*
Job 1: 1. There was a man *in the land of* Uz,
7. From going to and fro *in the earth,*
8. none like him *in the earth,*
10. his substance is increased *in the land.*
20. fell down upon *the ground,*
2: 2. From going to and fro *in the earth,*
3. none like him *in the earth,*
13. sat down with him *upon the ground.*
3:14. kings and counsellors of *the earth,*
5:10. Who giveth rain upon *the earth,*
22. be afraid of the beasts of *the earth.*
25. as the grass of *the earth.*
7: 1. appointed time to man upon *earth?*
8: 9. our days upon *earth* (are) a shadow:
9: 6. shaketh *the earth* out of her place,
24. *The earth* is given into the
10:21. to *the land of* darkness
22. *A land of* darkness, as darkness
11: 9. measure thereof (is) longer *than the earth,*
12: 8. Or speak *to the earth,*
15. they overturn *the earth.*
24. the chief of the people of *the earth,*
14: 8. root thereof wax old *in the earth,*
19. grow (out) of the dust of *the earth;*
15:19. Unto whom alone *the earth* was
29. the perfection thereof *upon the earth.*
16:13. poureth out my gall *upon the ground.*
18. *O earth,* cover not thou my blood,
18: 4. shall *the earth* be forsaken
10. snare (is) laid for him *in the ground,*
17. shall perish from *the earth,*
20: 4. since man was placed upon *earth,*
27. *and the earth* shall rise up
22: 8. the mighty man, he had *the earth,*
24: 4. the poor of *the earth*
18. their portion is cursed *in the earth:*
26: 7. hangeth *the earth* upon nothing.
28: 5. (As for) *the earth,* out of it
13. neither is it found *in the land of*
24. he looketh to the ends of *the earth,*
30: 8. they were viler than *the earth.*
34:13. given him a charge *over the earth?*
35:11. more than the beasts of *the earth,*
37: 3. lightning unto the ends of *the earth.*
6. Be thou (on) *the earth;*
12. the face of the world *in the earth.*
13. or *for his land,* or for mercy.
17. when he quieteth *the earth*
38: 4. when I laid the foundations of *the earth?*
13. take hold of the ends of *the earth,*
18. perceived the breadth of *the earth?*
24. scattereth the east wind upon *the earth?*
26. To cause it to rain on *the earth,*
33. set the dominion thereof *in the earth?*
39:14. leaveth her eggs *in the earth,*
24. He swalloweth *the ground*
42:15. in all *the land* were no women
Ps. 2: 2. The kings of *the earth*
8. the uttermost parts of *the earth*
10. ye judges of *the earth.*
7: 5(6). tread down my life *upon the earth,*
8: 1(2), 9(10). thy name in all *the earth!*
10:16. the heathen are perished *out of his land.*
18. that the man of *the earth* may
12: 6(7). silver tried in a furnace *of earth,*
16: 3. to the saints that (are) *in the earth,*
17:11. bowing down *to the earth;*
18: 7(8). Then *the earth* shook
19: 4(5). gone out through all *the earth,*
21:10(11). shalt thou destroy *from the earth,*
22:27(28). All the ends of *the world*
29(30). All (they that be) fat upon *earth*
24: 1. *The earth* (is) the Lord's,
25:13. his seed shall inherit *the earth.*
27:13. *in the land of* the living.
33: 5. *the earth* is full of the goodness
8. Let all *the earth* fear the Lord:

Ps. 33:14. upon all the inhabitants of *the earth.*
34:16(17). remembrance of them *from the earth.*
35:20. (them that are) quiet in *the land.*
37: 3. shalt thou dwell in *the land,*
9. they shall inherit *the earth.*
11. the meek shall inherit *the earth;*
22. shall inherit *the earth;*
29. The righteous shall inherit *the land,*
34. shall exalt thee to inherit *the land:*
41: 2(3). he shall be blessed *upon the earth:*
42: 6(7). *from the land of* Jordan,
44: 3(4). they got not *the land* in possession
25(26). our belly cleaveth *unto the earth.*
45:16(17). make princes in all *the earth.*
46: 2(3). though *the earth* be removed,
6(7). *the earth* melted.
8(9). desolations he hath made *in the earth.*
9(10). to cease unto the end of *the earth;*
10(11). I will be exalted *in the earth.*
47: 2(3). a great King over all *the earth.*
7(8). God (is) the King of all *the earth:*
9(10). for the shields of *the earth*
48: 2(3). the joy of the whole *earth,*
10(11). thy praise unto the ends of *the earth:*
50: 1. called *the earth* from the rising
4. and to *the earth,*
52: 5(7). root thee out *of the land of* the
57: 5(6), 11(12). thy glory (be) above all *the earth.*
58: 2(3). violence of your hands *in the earth.*
11(12). a God that judgeth *in the earth.*
59:13(14). unto the ends of *the earth.*
60: 2(4). Thou hast made *the earth* to tremble;
61: 2(3). From the end of *the earth*
63: 1(2). *in a* dry and thirsty *land,*
9(10). go into the lower parts of *the earth.*
65: 5(6). confidence of all the ends of *the earth,*
9(10). Thou visitest *the earth,*
66: 1. noise unto God, all ye *lands:* (marg. *the earth*)
4. All *the earth* shall worship thee,
67: 2(3). That thy way may be known *upon earth,*
4(5). govern the nations *upon earth.*
6(7). shall *the earth* yield her increase;
7(8). the ends of *the earth* shall fear
68: 8(9). *The earth* shook,
32(33). ye kingdoms of *the earth;*
69:34(35). Let the heaven *and earth* praise him,
71:20. from the depths of *the earth.*
72: 6. as showers (that) water *the earth.*
8. unto the ends of *the earth.*
16. an handful of corn *in the earth*
— flourish like grass of *the earth.*
19. let *the* whole *earth* be filled
73: 9. their tongue walketh *through the earth.*
25. and (there is) none *upon earth*
74: 7. of thy name *to the ground.*
8. the synagogues of God *in the land.*
12. salvation in the midst of *the earth.*
17. hast set all the borders of *the earth:*
20. the dark places of *the earth*
75: 3(4). *The earth* and all the inhabitants
8(9). all the wicked of *the earth*
76: 8(9). *the earth* feared, and was still,
9(10). to save all the meek of *the earth.*
12(13). terrible to the kings of *the earth.*
77:18(19). *the earth* trembled and shook.
78:12. *in the land of* Egypt,
69. *like the earth* which he hath
79: 2. unto the beasts of *the earth.*
80: 9(10). and it filled *the land.*
81: 5(6). he went out through *the land*
10(11). brought thee *out of the land of*
82: 5. all the foundations of *the earth*
8. Arise, O God, judge *the earth:*
83:18(19). the most high over all *the earth.*
85: 1(2). hast been favourable unto *thy land:*
9(10). that glory may dwell *in our land.*
11(12) Truth shall spring *out of the earth;*
12(13). *and our land* shall yield her increase.
88:12(13). thy righteousness *in the land of*
89:11(12). *the earth* also (is) thine:
27(28). higher than the kings of *the earth.*
39(40). (by casting it) *to the ground.*
44(45). cast his throne down *to the ground.*
90: 2. or ever thou hadst formed *the earth*
94: 2. thou judge of *the earth:*

Ps. 95: 4. the deep places of *the earth:*
96: 1. sing unto the Lord, all *the earth.*
9. fear before him, all *the earth.*
11. let *the earth* be glad;
13. he cometh to judge *the earth:*
97: 1. let *the earth* rejoice;
4. *the earth* saw, and trembled.
5. the Lord of *the* whole *earth.*
9. high above all *the earth:*
98: 3. all the ends of *the earth*
4. joyful noise unto the Lord, all *the earth:*
9. he cometh to judge *the earth:*
99: 1. let *the earth* be moved.
100: 1. a joyful noise unto the Lord, all ye *lands* (marg. *the earth*)
101: 6. upon the faithful of *the land,*
8. destroy all the wicked of *the land;*
102:15(16). all the kings of *the earth* thy glory.
19(20). did the Lord behold *the earth;*
25(26). laid the foundation of *the earth:*
103:11. the heaven is high above *the earth,*
104: 5. laid the foundations of *the earth,*
9. turn not again to cover *the earth.*
13. *the earth* is satisfied with the fruit
14. bring forth food out of *the earth;*
24. *the earth* is full of thy riches.
32. He looketh *on the earth,*
35. be consumed out of *the earth,*
105: 7. his judgments (are) in all *the earth.*
11. thee will I give *the land of* Canaan,
16. he called for a famine upon *the land*
23. Jacob sojourned *in the land of*
27. wonders *in the land of* Ham.
30. *Their land* brought forth frogs
32. flaming fire *in their land.*
35. all the herbs *in their land,*
36. all the firstborn *in their land,*
44. gave them *the lands of* the heathen:
106:17. *The earth* opened and swallowed
22. Wondrous works *in the land of*
24. they despised *the* pleasant *land,*
27. to scatter them *in the lands.*
38. *the land* was polluted with
107: 3. *And* gathered them *out of the lands,*
34. A fruitful *land* into barrenness,
35. *and* dry *ground* into watersprings.
108: 5(6). thy glory above all *the earth;*
109:15. the memory of them *from the earth.*
110: 6. wound the heads over many *countries.*
112: 2. His seed shall be mighty *upon earth:*
113: 6. in heaven, *and in the earth!*
114: 7. Tremble, *thou earth,*
115:15. which made heaven *and earth.*
16. *but the earth* hath he given
116: 9. *in the land of* the living.
119:19. I (am) a stranger *in the earth:*
64. *The earth,* O Lord, is full of thy mercy:
87. had almost consumed me *upon earth;*
90. thou hast established *the earth,*
119. away all the wicked of *the earth*
121: 2 & 124:8 & 134:3. made heaven *and earth.*
135: 6. did he in heaven, *and in earth,*
7. to ascend from the ends of *the earth;*
12. gave *their land* (for) an heritage,
136: 6. To him that stretched out *the earth*
21. gave *their land* for an heritage:
138: 4. All the kings of *the earth*
139:15. in the lowest parts of *the earth.*
140:11(12). be established *in the earth:*
141: 7. cleaveth (wood) *upon the earth.*
142: 5(6). *in the land of* the living.
143: 3. smitten my life down *to the ground;*
6. after thee, *as a* thirsty *land.*
10. lead me *into the land of* uprightness.
146: 6. Which made heaven, *and earth,*
147: 6. casteth the wicked down to *the ground.*
8. who prepareth rain *for the earth,*
15. his commandment (upon) *earth:*
148: 7. Praise the Lord from *the earth,*
11. Kings of *the earth,*
— all judges of *the earth:*
13. his glory (is) above *the earth*
Pro. 2:21. the upright shall dwell in *the land,*
22. the wicked shall be cut off *from the earth*
3:19. by wisdom hath founded *the earth;*
8:16. (even) all the judges of *the earth.*
23. or ever *the earth* was.

Pro. 8:26. as yet he had not made *the earth*,
29. appointed the foundations of *the earth:*
31. the habitable part of *his earth;*
10:30. the wicked shall not inhabit *the earth*.
11:31. shall be recompensed *in the earth:*
17:24. in the ends of *the earth*.
21:19. *in the* wilderness, (marg. *in the land of* desert)
25: 3. *and the earth* for depth,
25. so (is) good news *from a* far *country*.
28: 2. For the transgression of *a land*
29: 4. The king by judgment establisheth *the land:*
30: 4. established all the ends of *the earth?*
14. to devour the poor *from off the earth*,
16. *the earth* (that) is not filled
21. For three (things) *the earth* is disquieted,
24. (which are) little upon *the earth*,
31:23. he sitteth among the elders of the *land*.
Ecc. 1: 4. *but the earth* abideth for ever.
3:21. goeth downward *to the earth?*
5: 2(1). and thou upon *earth:*
9(8). the profit of *the earth* is for all:
7:20. not a just man *upon earth*,
8:14, 16. is done upon *the earth;*
10: 7. walking as servants upon *the earth*.
16. Woe to thee, *O land*,
17. Blessed (art) thou, *O land*,
11: 2. what evil shall be upon *the earth*.
3. empty (themselves) upon *the earth:*
12: 7. shall the dust return to *the earth*
Cant. 2:12. The flowers appear *on the earth;*
— the turtle is heard *in our land;*
Isa. 1: 2. Hear, O heavens, and give ear, *O earth:*
7. *Your country* (is) desolate,
19. ye shall eat the good of *the land:*
2: 7. *Their land* also is full of silver
— *their land* is also full of horses,
8. *Their land* also is full of idols;
19, 21. he ariseth to shake terribly *the earth*.
3:26. shall sit *upon the ground*.
4: 2. the fruit of *the earth*
5: 8. placed alone in the midst of *the earth!*
26. from the end of *the earth:*
30. if (one) look *unto the land*,
6: 3. *the* whole *earth* (is) full of his glory.
12. forsaking in the midst of *the land*.
7:18. that (is) *in the land of* Assyria.
22. every one eat that is left in *the land*.
24. because all *the land* shall
8: 8. shall fill the breadth of *thy land*,
9. all ye of far *countries:*
22. they shall look unto *the earth;*
9: 1(8:23). *the land of* Zebulun *and the land of*
2(1). they that dwell *in the land of*
19(18). is *the land* darkened,
10:14. have I gathered all *the earth;*
23. in the midst of all *the land*.
11: 4. for the meek of *the earth:* and he shall smite *the earth*
9. for *the earth* shall be full
12. from the four corners of *the earth*.
16. came up *out of the land of* Egypt.
12: 5. this (is) known in all *the earth*.
13: 5. They come *from a* far *country*,
— to destroy *the* whole *land*.
9. to lay *the land* desolate:
13. and *the earth* shall remove
14. flee every one into *his own land*.
14: 7. The whole *earth* is at rest,
9. all the chief ones of *the earth;*
12. art thou cut down *to the ground*,
16. the man that made *the earth* to tremble,
20. thou hast destroyed *thy land*,
21. nor possess *the land*,
25. break the Assyrian *in my land*,
26. purposed upon *the* whole *earth:*
16: 1. the lamb to the ruler of *the land*
4. are consumed out of *the land*.
18: 1. Woe to *the land* shadowing
2, 7. *whose* (lit. who *his*) *land* the rivers have
3. and dwellers on *the earth*,
6. the beasts of *the earth:* and the fowls
— all the beasts of *the earth* shall winter
19:18. shall five cities *in the land of*
19. in the midst of *the land of* Egypt,
20. Lord of hosts *in the land of* Egypt:

Isa. 19:24. a blessing in the midst of *the land:*
21: 1. *from a* terrible *land*.
9. he hath broken *unto the ground*.
14. The inhabitants of *the land of*
22:18. (like) a ball *into a* large *country:*
23: 1. *from the land of* Chittim it is revealed
8. traffickers (are) the honourable of *the earth?*
9. contempt all the honourable of *the earth*.
10. Pass through *thy land* as a river,
13. *the land of* the Chaldeans;
17. with all the kingdoms of *the world*
24: 1. the Lord maketh *the earth* empty,
3. *The land* shall be utterly emptied,
4. *The earth* mourneth
— people of *the earth* do languish.
5. *The earth also* is defiled
6. hath the curse devoured *the earth*,
— the inhabitants of *the earth*
11. the mirth of *the land* is gone.
13. shall be in the midst of *the land*
16. From the uttermost part of *the earth*
17. O inhabitant of *the earth*.
18. the foundations of *the earth* do shake.
19. *The earth* is utterly broken down, *the earth* is clean dissolved, *the earth* is moved exceedingly.
20. *The earth* shall reel to and fro
25: 8. take away from off all *the earth:*
12. bring *to the ground*,
26: 1. be sung *in the land of* Judah;
5. he layeth it low, (even) to *the ground;*
9. when thy judgments (are) *in the earth*,
10. *in the land of* uprightness
15. far (unto) all the ends of *the earth*.
18. wrought any deliverance in *the earth;*
19. *and the earth* shall cast out the dead.
21. to punish the inhabitants of *the earth*
— *the earth* also shall disclose
27:13. were ready to perish *in the land of* Assyria and the outcasts *in the land of* Egypt,
28: 2. shall cast down *to the earth*
22. determined upon *the* whole *earth*.
29: 4. shalt speak *out of the ground*,
— familiar spirit, *out of the ground*,
30: 6. *into the land of* trouble
32: 2. a great rock *in a* weary *land*.
33: 9. *The earth* mourneth
17. *the land* that is very far off.
34: 1. let *the earth* hear,
6. a great slaughter *in the land of*
7. *their land* shall be soaked
9. and *the land thereof* shall
36:10. against this *land*, to destroy it?
— Go up against this *land*,
17. take you away to *a land like your own land*, *a land of* corn and wine, *a land of* bread
18. delivered *his land* out of the hand
20. among all the gods of these *lands*, that have delivered *their land*
37: 7. return to *his own land;*
— fall by the sword *in his own land*.
11. have done to all *lands*
16, 20. all the kingdoms of *the earth:*
— thou hast made heaven and *earth*.
18. *the nations* (marg. *lands*), and *their countries*,
38. they escaped into *the land of*
38:11. *in the land of* the living:
39: 3. They are come *from a* far *country*
40:12. comprehended the dust of *the earth*
21. from the foundations of *the earth?*
22. sitteth upon the circle of *the earth*,
23. he maketh the judges of *the earth*
24. shall not take root *in the earth:*
28. the Creator of the ends of *the earth*,
41: 5 the ends of *the earth* were afraid,
9. have taken from the ends of *the earth*,
18. *and the* dry *land* springs of water.
42: 4. till he have set judgment *in the earth:*
5. he that spread forth *the earth*,
10. his praise from the end of *the earth*,
43: 6. my daughters from the ends of *the earth;*
44:23. shout, ye lower parts of *the earth:*
24. that spreadeth abroad *the earth*
45: 8. let *the earth* open,
12. I have made *the earth*,

Isa. 45:18. God himself that formed *the earth*
19. secret, in a dark place of *the earth :*
22. all the ends of *the earth:*
46:11. counsel *from a* far *country :*
47: 1. sit *on the ground:*
48:13. laid the foundation of *the earth,*
20. it (even) to the end of *the earth ;*
49: 6. unto the end of *the earth.*
8. to establish *the earth,*
12. these *from the land of* Sinim.
13. Sing, O heavens ; and be joyful, *O earth,*
19. *and the land of* thy destruction,
23. with (their) face toward *the earth,*
51: 6. look upon *the earth* beneath:
— *and the earth* shall wax old
13. laid the foundations of *the earth ;*
16. lay the foundations of *the earth,*
23. thou hast laid thy body *as the ground,*
52:10. all the ends of *the earth* shall see
53: 2. as a root *out of a* dry *ground:*
8. he was cut off *out of the land*
54: 5. The God of *the* whole *earth*
9. no more go over *the earth ;*
55: 9. the heavens are higher *than the earth,*
10. but watereth *the earth,*
57:13. his trust in me shall possess *the land,*
58:14. upon the high places of *the earth,*
60: 2. the darkness shall cover *the earth,*
18. shall no more be heard *in thy land,*
21. they shall inherit *the land* for ever,
61: 7. *in their land* they shall possess
11. *as the earth* bringeth forth
62: 4. neither shall *thy land* any more
— *and thy land* Beulah:
— *and thy land* shall be married.
7. he make Jerusalem a praise *in the earth.*
11. unto the end of *the world,*
63: 6. bring down their strength *to the earth.*
65:16. he who blesseth himself *in the earth*
— he that sweareth *in the earth*
17. create new heavens *and a* new *earth:*
66: 1. *and the earth* (is) my footstool:
8. Shall *the earth* be made to bring
22. the new heavens *and the* new *earth,*
Jer. 1: 1. *in the land of* Benjamin:
14. upon all the inhabitants of *the land.*
18. brazen walls against *the* whole *land,*
— against the people of *the land.*
2: 2. *in a land* (that was) not sown.
6. brought us up *out of the land of*
— *through a land of* deserts and of pits, *through a land of* drought,
— *a land* that no man passed through,
7. brought you into *a* plentiful *country,*
— ye defiled *my land,*
15. they made *his land* waste:
31. *a land of* darkness?
3: 1. shall not that *land* be greatly
2. thou hast polluted *the land*
9. that she defiled *the land,*
16. increased *in the land,*
18. *out of the land of* the north to *the land*
19. give thee *a* pleasant *land,*
4: 5. Blow ye the trumpet *in the land :*
7. to make *thy land* desolate;
16. watchers come *from a* far *country,*
20. for *the* whole *land* is spoiled:
23. I beheld *the earth,*
27. *The* whole *land* shall be desolate;
28. For this shall *the earth* mourn,
5:19. strange gods *in your land,* so shall ye serve strangers *in a land*
30. is committed *in the land ;*
6: 8. *a land* not inhabited.
12. upon the inhabitants of *the land,*
19. Hear, *O earth:* behold I will
20. the sweet cane *from a* far *country?*
22. cometh *from the* north *country,*
— be raised from the sides of *the earth.*
7: 7. *in the land* that I gave
22. brought them out *of the land of*
25. came forth *out of the land of*
33. for the beasts of *the earth;*
34. for *the land* shall be desolate.
8:16. the whole *land* trembled
— and have devoured *the land,*
19. them that dwell *in a* far *country:*

Jer. 9: 3(2). valiant for the truth *upon the earth;*
12(11). for what *the land* perisheth
19(18). because we have forsaken *the land.*
24(23). righteousness, *in the earth:*
10:10. at his wrath *the earth* shall tremble,
12. He hath made *the earth*
13. from the ends of *the earth;*
17. Gather up thy wares *out of the land,*
18. sling out the inhabitants of *the land*
22. commotion *out of the* north *country,*
11: 4. forth *out of the land of* Egypt,
5. to give them *a land* flowing with
7. them up *out of the land of* Egypt,
19. him off *from the land of* the living,
12: 4. How long shall *the land* mourn,
5. *and* (if) *in the land of* peace,
11. *the* whole *land* is made desolate,
12. from the (one) end of *the land* even to the (other) end of *the land:*
15. every man *to his land.*
13:13. fill all the inhabitants of this *land,*
14: 2. they are black *unto the ground;*
4. there was no rain *in the earth,*
8. be as a stranger *in the land,*
15. famine shall not be *in this land;*
18. into *a land* that they know not.
15: 3. the beasts of *the earth,*
4. into all kingdoms of *the earth,*
7. in the gates of *the land;*
10. contention to the whole *earth!*
14. pass with thine enemies *into a land*
16: 3. that begat them *in* this *land;*
4. for the beasts of *the earth.*
6. great and the small shall die *in* this *land:*
13. cast you out of this *land* into *a land*
14. *out of the land of* Egypt;
15. *from the land of* the north, and from all *the lands*
18. they have defiled *my land,*
19. from the ends of *the earth,*
17: 4. to serve thine enemies *in the land*
6. *a* salt *land* and not inhabited.
13. shall be written *in the earth,*
26. *and from the land of* Benjamin,
18:16. To make *their land* desolate,
19: 7. for the beasts of *the earth.*
22:10. no more, nor see his native *country.*
12. shall see this *land* no more.
26. another *country,* where ye were not
27. But to *the land* whereunto they
28. are cast into *a land* which
29. O *earth, earth, earth,* hear the word of
23: 3. my flock out of all *countries*
5. judgment and justice *in the earth.*
7. *out of the land of* Egypt;
8. *out of the* north *country,* and from all *countries* whither I had
10. For *the land* is full of adulterers; for because of swearing *the land*
15. profaneness gone forth into all *the land.*
24. Do not I fill heaven and *earth?*
24: 5. into *the land of* the Chaldeans
6. bring them again to this *land:*
8. that remain *in* this *land,* and them that dwell *in the land of* Egypt:
9. into all the kingdoms of *the earth*
25: 9. bring them against this *land,*
11. *this* whole *land* shall be a
12. and *the land of* the Chaldeans,
13. I will bring upon that *land*
20. the kings of *the land of* Uz, and all the kings of *the land of* the Philistines,
26. and all the kingdoms of *the world,*
29, 30. all the inhabitants of *the earth,*
31. to the ends of *the earth;*
32. from the coasts of *the earth.*
33. from (one) end of *the earth* even unto the (other) end of *the earth:*
38. for *their land* is desolate
26: 6. to all the nations of *the earth.*
17. certain of the elders of *the land,*
20. against this *land*
27: 5. I have made *the earth,* the man and the beast that (are) upon *the ground,*
6. now have I given all these *lands*
7. until the very time of *his land* come
28: 8. both against many *countries,*

Jer. 29:18. to all the kingdoms of *the earth*,
30: 3. cause them to return to *the land*
10. and thy seed *from the land of* their
31: 8. *from the* north *country*, and gather them from the coasts of *the earth*,
16. shall come again *from the land of*
22. created a new thing *in the earth*,
23. use this speech *in the land of* Judah
32. out *of the land of* Egypt;
37. the foundations of *the earth*
32: 8. which (is) *in the country of* Benjamin:
15. be possessed again *in* this *land*.
17. made the heaven and *the earth*
20. wonders *in the land of* Egypt,
21. *out of the land of* Egypt
22. hast given them this *land*,
— *a land* flowing with milk and
37. gather them out of all *countries*.
41. I will plant them *in* this *land*
43. fields shall be bought *in* this *land*,
44. take witnesses *in the land of*
33: 9. before all the nations of *the earth*,
11. to return the captivity of *the land*,
13. *and in the land of* Benjamin, and
15. righteousness *in the land*.
25. ordinances of heaven *and earth;*
34: 1, 17. all the kingdoms of *the earth*
13. *out of the land of* Egypt,
19. all the people of *the land*,
20. to the beasts of *the earth*.
35:11. came up into *the land*,
36:29. certainly come and destroy this *land*,
37: 1. made king *in the land of* Judah
2. nor the people of *the land*,
7. return to Egypt *into their own land*.
12. to go into *the land of* Benjamin,
19. nor against this *land?*
39: 5. *in the land of* Hamath,
10. had nothing, *in the land of* Judah,
40: 4. all *the land* (is) before thee:
6. that were left *in the land*.
7. Ahikam governor *in the land*,
— of the poor of *the land*,
9. dwell *in the land*,
11. that (were) in all *the countries*,
12. came to *the land of* Judah,
41: 2. had made governor *over the land*.
18. made governor *in the land*.
42:10. If ye will still abide *in* this *land*,
13. We will not dwell *in* this *land*,
14. we will go into *the land of* Egypt,
16. overtake you there *in the land of*
43: 4. to dwell *in the land of* Judah.
5. to dwell *in the land of* Judah;
7. they came into *the land of* Egypt:
11. he shall smite *the land of* Egypt,
12. array himself with *the land of* Egypt,
13. that (is) *in the land of* Egypt;
44: 1, 13, 26. dwell *in the land of* Egypt,
— *and in the country of* Pathros,
8. other gods *in the land of* Egypt,
— all the nations of *the earth?*
9. committed *in the land of* Judah,
12. go into *the land of* Egypt
— fall in *the land of* Egypt;
14. which are gone *into the land of* Egypt
— should return *into the land of* Judah,
15. that dwelt *in the land of* Egypt,
21. the people of *the land*,
22. therefore is *your land*
24, 27. that (are) *in the land of* Egypt:
26. in all *the land of* Egypt,
28. shall return out of *the land of* Egypt into *the land of* Judah,
— that are gone *into the land of* Egypt
45: 4. even this whole *land*.
46: 8. will cover *the earth;*
10. hath a sacrifice *in the* north *country*
12. thy cry hath filled *the land:*
13. smite *the land of* Egypt.
16. to *the land of* our nativity,
27. thy seed *from the land of*
47: 2. shall overflow *the land*,
— all the inhabitants of *the land*
48:21. upon the plain *country;*
24. all the cities of *the land of* Moab,
33. *and from the land of* Moab;

Jer. 49:21. *The earth* is moved at the noise
50: 1. against *the land of* the Chaldeans
3. shall make *her land* desolate,
8. *and* go forth *out of the land of*
9. *from the* north *country:*
16. flee every one *to his own land*.
18. the king of Babylon and *his land*,
21. Go up against *the land*
22. A sound of battle (is) *in the land*,
23. *the* whole *earth* cut asunder
25. *in the land of* the Chaldeans.
28. escape *out of the land of* Babylon,
34. that he may give rest to *the land*,
38. for it (is) *the land of* graven images,
41. from the coasts of *the earth*.
45. against *the land of* the Chaldeans:
46. taking of Babylon *the earth* is moved,
51: 2. shall empty *her land:*
4. the slain shall fall *in the land of*
5. though *their land* was filled
7. that made all *the earth* drunken:
9. every one *into his own country:*
15. He hath made *the earth*
16. to ascend from the ends of *the earth:*
25. which destroyest all *the earth:*
27. Set ye up a standard *in the land*,
28. all *the land of* his dominion.
29. *the land* shall tremble
— to make *the land of* Babylon a desolation
41. the praise of *the* whole *earth*
43. *a* dry *land*, and a wilderness, *a land* wherein no man dwelleth,
46. rumour that shall be heard *in the land;*
— violence *in the land*,
47. *her* whole *land* shall be confounded,
48. Then the heaven *and the earth*,
49. the slain of all *the earth*. (marg. *country*)
52. through all *her land*
54. *from the land of* the Chaldeans:
52: 6. for the people of *the land*.
9, 27. *in the land of* Hamath;
16. left (certain) of the poor of *the land*
25. the people of *the land;* and threescore men of the people of *the land*,
Lam. 2: 1. cast down from heaven unto *the earth*
2. brought (them) down *to the ground:*
9. Her gates are sunk *into the ground;*
10. sit *upon the ground*,
— hang down their heads to *the ground*.
11. my liver is poured *upon the earth*,
15. The joy of *the* whole *earth?*
21. and the old lie *on the ground*
3:34. all the prisoners of *the earth*,
4:12. The kings of *the earth*,
21. that dwellest *in the land of* Uz;
Eze. 1: 3. *in the land of* the Chaldeans
15. behold one wheel *upon the earth*
19. creatures were lifted up from *the earth*,
21. those were lifted up from *the earth*,
5: 5. the nations and *countries*
6. more than *the countries*
6: 8. scattered *through the countries*.
14. and make *the land* desolate,
7: 2. come upon the four corners of *the land*.
7. O thou that dwellest in *the land:*
21. to the wicked of *the earth*
23. for *the land* is full of bloody crimes,
27. the hands of the people of *the land*
8: 3. between *the earth* and the heaven,
12. the Lord hath forsaken *the earth*.
17. have filled *the land* with violence,
9: 9. *the land* is full of blood,
— The Lord hath forsaken *the earth*,
10:16. to mount up from *the earth*,
19. mounted up from *the earth*
11:15. unto us is this *land* given
16. scattered them *among the countries*,
— as a little sanctuary *in the countries*
17. assemble you out of *the countries*
12: 6. that thou see not *the ground:*
12. that he see not *the ground*
13. *the land of* the Chaldeans;
15. disperse them *in the countries*.
19. say unto the people of *the land*,
— that *her land* may be desolate
20. *and the land* shall be desolate;
13:14. bring it down to *the ground*,

Eze. 14:13. when *the land* sinneth
15. beasts to pass *through the land,*
16. *but the land* shall be
17. *land,* and say, Sword, go *through the land;*
19. Or (if) I send a pestilence into that *land,*
15: 8. I will make *the land* desolate,
16: 3. thy nativity (is) *of the land of*
29. multiplied thy fornication in *the land of*
17: 4. carried it into *a land of* traffick;
5. took also of the seed of *the land,*
13. taken the mighty of *the land:*
19: 4. with chains unto *the land of* Egypt.
7. and *the land* was desolate,
12. she was cast down *to the ground,*
13. *in a* dry and thirsty *ground.*
20: 5. *in the land of* Egypt,
6. bring them *forth of the land of* Egypt into *a land* that I
— 15. which (is) the glory of all *lands:*
8. in the midst of *the land of* Egypt.
9. bringing them forth *out of the land of*
10. go forth *out of the land of* Egypt,
15. would not bring them into *the land*
23. disperse them *through the countries;*
28. when I had brought them into *the land,*
32. as the families of *the countries,*
34, 41. gather you out of *the countries*
36. the wilderness of *the land of* Egypt,
38. bring them forth *out of the country*
40. all of them *in the land,*
42. into *the country* (for) the which
21:19(24). shall come forth *out of* one *land:*
30(35). *in the land of* thy nativity.
32(37). shall be in the midst of *the land;*
22: 4. a mocking to all *countries.*
15. disperse thee *in the countries,*
24. Thou (art) *the land* that is not
29. The people of *the land* have used
30. in the gap before me for *the land,*
23:15. *the land of* their nativity:
19. played the harlot *in the land of*
27. *from the land of* Egypt:
48. lewdness to cease out of *the land,*
24: 7. she poured it not upon *the ground,*
25: 7. to perish out of *the countries:*
9. the glory of *the country,*
26:11. shall go down *to the ground.*
16. they shall sit upon *the ground,*
20. *in* the low parts of *the earth,*
— set glory *in the land of* the living;
27:17. Judah, *and the land of* Israel,
29. they shall stand upon *the land;*
33. enrich the kings of *the earth*
28:17. I will cast thee to *the ground,*
18. bring thee to ashes upon *the earth*
29: 5. to the beasts of *the field*
9. *the land of* Egypt shall be desolate
10. make *the land of* Egypt utterly waste
12. I will make *the land of* Egypt desolate
— in the midst of *the countries*
— disperse them *through the countries.*
14. to return (into) *the land of* Pathros, into *the land of* their habitation;
19. I will give *the land of* Egypt
20. I have given him *the land of* Egypt
30: 5. men of *the land* that is in league,
7. in the midst of *the countries*
11. be brought to destroy *the land:*
— fill *the land* with the slain.
12. sell *the land* into the hand
— I will make *the land* waste,
13. *of the land of* Egypt: and I will put a fear *in the land of* Egypt.
23. disperse them *through the countries.*
25. shall stretch it out upon *the land of*
26. disperse them *among the countries;*
31:12. by all the rivers of *the land;* and all the people of *the earth*
14. to the nether parts of *the earth,*
16. comforted *in* the nether parts of *the earth.*
18. unto the nether parts of *the earth:*
32: 4. will I leave thee *upon the land,*
— the beasts of *the* whole *earth*
6. *the land* wherein thou swimmest,
8. set darkness upon *thy land,*
9. into *the countries* which thou

Eze. 32:15. I shall make *the land of* Egypt desolate, and *the country* shall be destitute
18. unto the nether parts of *the earth,*
23. which caused terror *in the land of*
24. nether parts of *the earth,* which caused their terror *in the land of*
25. was caused *in the land of* the living,
26. they caused their terror *in the land of*
27. the mighty *in the land of* the living.
32. have caused my terror *in the land of*
33: 2. When I bring the sword upon *a land,* if the people of *the land*
3. seeth the sword come upon *the land,*
24. Abraham was one, and he inherited *the land:* but we (are) many; *the land* is given us
25, 26. *and* shall ye possess *the land?*
28. I will lay *the land* most desolate,
29. when I have laid *the land*
34: 6. upon all the face of *the earth,*
13. gather them from *the countries,*
— inhabited places of *the country.*
25. evil beasts to cease out of *the land:*
27. *and the earth* shall yield her increase,
28. neither shall the beast of *the land*
29. consumed with hunger *in the land,*
35:10. two nations and these two *countries*
14. When *the* whole *earth* rejoiceth,
36: 5. which have appointed *my land*
18. they had shed upon *the land,*
19. dispersed *through the countries:*
20. *and* are gone forth *out of his land.*
24. gather you out of all *countries,*
28. ye shall dwell *in the land*
34. *And* the desolate *land* shall be tilled,
35. This *land* that was desolate
37:22. *in the land* upon the mountains
25. they shall dwell in *the land*
38: 2. *the land of* Magog,
8. thou shalt come into *the land*
9. be like a cloud to cover *the land,*
11. I will go up to *the land of*
12. that dwell in the midst of *the land.*
16. as a cloud to cover *the land;*
— bring thee against *my land,*
20. every wall shall fall *to the ground.*
39:12. that they may cleanse *the land.*
13. all the people of *the land*
14. passing *through the land*
— upon the face of *the earth,*
15. passengers (that) pass *through the land,*
16. Thus shall they cleanse *the land.*
18. the princes of *the earth,*
27. *out of* their enemies' *lands,*
40: 2. brought he me into *the land of* Israel,
41:16. *and* from *the ground* up
20. *From the ground* unto above the door
42: 6. the middlemost *from the ground.*
43: 2. *and the earth* shined with his glory.
14. from the bottom (upon) *the ground*
45: 1. ye shall divide by lot *the land*
— an holy portion of *the land:*
4. The holy (portion) of *the land*
8. *In the land* shall be his possession
— *and* (the rest of) *the land* shall they give
16. All the people of *the land*
22. for all the people of *the land*
46: 3, 9. the people of *the land*
47:13. ye shall inherit *the land*
14. and this *land* shall fall
15. this (shall be) the border of *the land*
18. from *the land of* Israel
21. So shall ye divide this *land*
48:12. (this) oblation of *the land*
14. alienate the firstfruits of *the land:*
29. This (is) *the land* which ye shall
Dan. 1: 2. which he carried into *the land of* Shinar
8: 5. on the face of *the* whole *earth,* and touched not *the ground:*
7. he cast him down *to the ground,*
10. the host and of the stars *to the ground,*
12. it cast down the truth *to the ground;*
18. sleep on my face *toward the ground:*
9: 6. to all the people of *the land.*
7. through all *the countries*
15. forth *out of the land of* Egypt
10: 9, 15. my face *toward the ground.*

Dan 11:16. he shall stand *in the* glorious *land*,
19. toward the fort of *his own land :*
28. Then shall he return into *his land*
— return *to his own land.*
40. he shall enter into *the countries*,
41. enter also *into* the glorious *land*,
42. his hand also *upon the countries: and the land of* Egypt shall not
Hos. 1: 2. for *the land* hath committed
11(2:2). shall come up out of *the land:*
2: 3(5). set her *like a* dry *land*,
15(17). she came up *out of the land of*
18(20). the battle out of *the earth*,
21(23). they shall hear *the earth;*
22(24). *And the earth* shall hear the corn,
23(25). sow her unto me *in the earth ;*
4: 1. the inhabitants of *the land*,
— nor knowledge of God *in the land.*
3. Therefore shall *the land* mourn,
6: 3. former rain unto *the earth.*
7:16. their derision *in the land of*
9: 3. shall not dwell *in the* LORD'*s land ;*
10: 1. according to the goodness *of his land*
11: 5. He shall not return into *the land of*
11. as a dove *out of the land of*
12: 9(10), & 13:4. *from the land of* Egypt
13: 5. *in the land of* great drought.
Joel 1: 2. all ye inhabitants of *the land.*
6. a nation is come up upon *my land*,
14, & 2:1. all the inhabitants of *the land*
2: 3. *the land* (is) as the garden of Eden
10. *The earth* shall quake
18. the LORD be jealous *for his land*,
20. will drive him into *a land* barren
30(3:3). in the heavens *and in the earth*,
3: 2(4:2). the nations, and parted *my land.*
16(4:16). heavens *and the earth* shall shake:
19(4:19). shed innocent blood *in their land.*
Am. 2: 7. pant after the dust of *the earth*
10. I brought you up *from the land of*
— to possess *the land of* the Amorite.
3: 1. I brought up *from the land of*
5. bird fall in a snare upon *the earth*,
9. in the palaces *in the land of* Egypt,
11. even round about *the land;*
14. and fall *to the ground.*
4:13. upon the high places of *the earth*,
5: 7. leave off righteousness *in the earth*,
8. them out upon the face of *the earth:*
7: 2. eating the grass of *the land*,
10. *the land* is not able to bear
12. flee thee away into *the land of* Judah,
8: 4. make the poor of *the land* to fail,
8. Shall not *the land* tremble
9. will darken *the earth* in the clear day:
11. I will send a famine *in the land*,
9: 5. of hosts (is) he that toucheth *the land*,
6. hath founded his troop in *the earth ;*
— them out upon the face of *the earth:*
7. brought up Israel *out of the land of*
9. least grain fall upon *the earth.*
Obad. 3. bring me down to *the ground?*
Jon. 1: 8. what (is) *thy country?*
2: 6(7). *the earth* with her bars
Mic. 1: 2. Hear, all ye people; hearken, *O earth*,
3. the high places of *the earth.*
4:13. the Lord of *the* whole *earth.*
5: 4(3). great unto the ends of *the earth.*
5(4). the Assyrian shall come *into our land:*
6(5). waste *the land of* Assyria with the sword, and *the land of* Nimrod
—(–)he cometh *into our land*,
11(10). will cut off the cities of *thy land*,
6: 2. ye strong foundations of *the earth:*
4. I brought thee up *out of the land of*
7: 2. good (man) is perished out of *the earth:*
13. Notwithstanding *the land* shall be
15. coming *out of the land of* Egypt
17. like worms of *the earth:*
Nah. 1: 5. and *the earth* is burned at his presence,
2:13(14). cut off thy prey *from the earth*,
3:13. the gates of *thy land*
Hab 1: 6. through the breadth of *the land*,
2: 8, 17. the violence of *the land*,
14. For *the earth* shall be filled
20. let all *the earth* keep silence
3: 3. and *the earth* was full of his praise.

Hab. 3: 6. He stood, and measured *the earth:*
7. the curtains of *the land of* Midian
9. Thou didst cleave *the earth*
12. Thou didst march through *the land*
Zeph 1:18. *the* whole *land* shall be devoured
— all them that dwell in *the land.*
2: 3. all ye meek of *the earth*,
5. O Canaan, *the land of* the Philistines,
11. famish all the gods of *the earth ;*
3: 8. all *the earth* shall be devoured
19. praise and fame in every *land*
20. among all people of *the earth*,
Hag. 1:10. *and the earth* is stayed
11. I called for a drought upon *the land*,
2: 4. all ye people of *the land*,
6, 21. will shake the heavens, and *the earth*,
Zec. 1:10. walk to and fro *through the earth.*
11. walked to and fro *through the earth*,
— all *the earth* sitteth still,
21(2:4). over *the land of* Judah
2: 6(10). flee *from the land of* the north,
3: 9. remove the iniquity of that *land*
4:10. run to and fro through *the* whole *earth.*
14. by the Lord of *the* whole *earth.*
5: 3. over the face of *the* whole *earth:*
6. resemblance through all *the earth.*
9. between *the earth* and the heaven.
11. an house *in the land of* Shinar:
6: 5. before the Lord of all *the earth.*
6. go forth into *the* north *country;*
— toward *the* south *country.*
7, 7, 7. to and fro *through the earth:*
8. that go toward *the* north *country* have quieted my spirit *in the* north *country.*
7: 5. Speak unto all the people of *the land*,
14. *Thus the land* was desolate
— they laid *the* pleasant *land*
8: 7. save my people *from the* east *country, and from the* west *country;*
12. *and the ground* shall give her increase,
9: 1. *in the land of* Hadrach,
10. to the ends of *the earth.*
10:10. bring them again also *out of the land of*
— bring them into *the land of* Gilead and
11: 6. pity the inhabitants of *the land*,
— they shall smite *the land*,
16. raise up a shepherd *in the land*,
12. 1. layeth the foundation of *the earth*,
3. though all the people of *the earth*
12. *the land* shall mourn,
13: 2. the idols out of *the land*,
— to pass out of *the land.*
8. in all *the land*, saith the LORD,
14: 9. be king over all *the earth:*
10. All the *land* shall be turned
17. the families of *the earth*
Mal. 3:12. ye shall be *a* delightsome *land*,
4: 6(3:24). smite *the earth* with a curse.

אַרְקָא *ar-kāh'*, f. emph. Ch. 778

Jer. 10:11. have not made the heavens *and the earth*,

אָרַר [*āh-rar'*], 779

*** KAL.—*Preterite.* ***

Mal. 2: 2. *and I will curse* your blessings: yea, *I have cursed them* already,

KAL.—*Infinitive.*

Jud. 5:23. curse ye *bitterly* the inhabitants (lit. *cursing* curse)

KAL.—*Imperative.*

Nu. 22: 6. *curse* me this people;
23: 7. Come, *curse* me Jacob,
Jud. 5:23. *Curse* ye Meroz, said the angel of the LORD, *curse ye* bitterly the inhabitants

KAL.—*Future.*

Gen 12: 3. and *curse* him that curseth thee:
Ex. 22:28(27). nor *curse* the ruler of thy people.
Nu. 22: 6. he whom *thou cursest* is cursed.
12. *thou shalt* not *curse* the people:

KAL.—*Participle.* Pöel.

Gen27:29. cursed (be) *every one that curseth thee,*
Nu. 24: 9. cursed (is) he *that curseth thee.*
Job 3: 8. Let them curse it *that curse* the day,

KAL.—*Participle.* Päul.

Gen 3:14. thou (art) *cursed* above all cattle,
17. *cursed* (is) the ground for thy sake;
4:11. now (art) thou *cursed* from the earth,
9:25. he said, *Cursed* (be) Canaan;
27:29. *cursed* (be) every one that curseth thee,
49: 7. *Cursed* (be) their anger,
Nu. 24: 9. *and cursed* (is) he that curseth thee.
Deu 27:15. *Cursed* (be) the man that maketh
16. *Cursed* (be) he that setteth light
17. *Cursed* (be) he that removeth
18. *Cursed* (be) he that maketh
19. *Cursed* (be) he that perverteth
20, 21, 22, 23. *Cursed* (be) he that lieth with
24. *Cursed* (be) he that smiteth
25. *Cursed* (be) he that taketh
26. *Cursed* (be) he that confirmeth
28:16. *Cursed* (shalt) thou (be) in the city, *and cursed* (shalt) thou (be) in the field.
17. *Cursed* (shall be) thy basket and thy store.
18. *Cursed* (shall be) the fruit of thy body,
19. *Cursed* (shalt) thou (be) when thou comest in, *and cursed* (shalt) thou (be) when
Josh 6:26. *Cursed* (be) the man before the Lord,
9:23. Now therefore ye (are) *cursed,*
Jud. 21:18. *Cursed* (be) he that giveth
1Sa. 14:24, 28. *Cursed* (be) the man that eateth
26:19. *cursed* (be) they before the Lord;
2K. 9:34. see now this *cursed* (woman),
Ps. 119:21. rebuked the proud (that are) *cursed,*
Jer. 11: 3. *Cursed* (be) the man that obeyeth not
17: 5. *Cursed* (be) the man that trusteth
20:14. *Cursed* (be) the day wherein
15. *Cursed* (be) the man who
48:10. *Cursed* (be) he that doeth
— *and cursed* (be) he that keepeth
Mal. 1:14. *But cursed* (be) the deceiver,

* NIPHAL.—*Participle.* *

Mal. 3: 9. Ye (are) *cursed* with a curse:

* PIEL.—*Preterite.* *

Gen 5:29. which the Lord *hath cursed.*

PIEL.—*Participle.*

Nu. 5:18, 19, 24. bitter water *that causeth the curse:*
22, 24, 27. water *that causeth the curse*

* HOPHAL.—*Future.* *

Nu. 22: 6. he whom thou cursest *is cursed.*

---

781 ## אָרַשׂ [*āh-ras'*],

* PIEL.—*Preterite.* *

Deu 20: 7. that *hath betrothed* a wife,
2Sa. 3:14. which *I espoused* to me
Hos. 2:19(21). *And I will betroth thee* unto me for ever; *yea, I will betroth thee* unto me in
20(22). *I will even betroth thee* unto me in

PIEL.—*Future.*

Deu 28:30. *Thou shalt betroth* a wife,

* PUAL.—*Preterite.* *

Ex. 22:16(15). that *is* not *betrothed,*
Deu 22:28. which *is* not *betrothed,*

PUAL.—*Participle.*

Deu 22:23. *be betrothed* unto an husband,
25. But if a man find a *betrothed*
27. the *betrothed* damsel cried,

---

782 ## אֲרֶשֶׁת *ăreh'-sheth,* f.

Ps. 21: 2(3). *and* hast not withholden *the request of*

---

784 ## אֵשׁ *ēhsh,* com.

Gen 15:17. a *burning* lamp that passed between (marg. lamp of *fire*)
Gen 19:24. brimstone *and fire* from the Lord
22: 6. he took *the fire* in his hand,
7. Behold *the fire* and the wood:
Ex. 3: 2. appeared unto him in a flame of *fire*
— the bush burned *with fire,*
9:23. *the fire* ran along upon the ground;
24. *and fire* mingled with the hail,
12: 8. roast with *fire,* and unleavened bread;
9. but roast (with) *fire;* his head with
10. ye shall burn *with fire.*
13:21. by night in a pillar of *fire,*
22. nor the pillar of *fire* by night,
14:24. through the pillar of *fire*
19:18. the Lord descended upon it *in fire:*
22: 6(5). If *fire* break out, and catch in thorns,
24:17. *like* devouring *fire* on the top
29:14. shalt thou burn *with fire*
34. burn the remainder *with fire:*
32:20. burnt (it) *in the fire,*
24. then I cast it *into the fire*
35: 3. Ye shall kindle no *fire*
40:38. *and fire* was on it by night,
Lev. 1: 7. shall put *fire* upon the altar, and lay the wood in order upon *the fire:*
8, 12. the wood that (is) on *the fire*
17. the wood that (is) upon *the fire:*
2:14. green ears of corn dried by the *fire,*
3: 5. the wood that (is) on *the fire:*
4:12. burn him on the wood *with fire:*
6: 9(2). *and the fire of* the altar
10(3). which *the fire* hath consumed
12(5). *And the fire* upon the altar
13(6). *The fire* shall ever be burning
30(23). it shall be burnt *in the fire.*
7:17, 19. shall be burnt *with fire.*
8:17. burnt *with fire* without
32. the bread shall ye burn *with fire.*
9:11. burnt *with fire* without
24. there came *a fire* out
10: 1. put *fire* therein,
— strange *fire* before the Lord,
2. there went out *fire* from the Lord,
13:24. in the skin whereof (there is) a *hot* burning, (marg. burning of *fire*)
52. it shall be burnt *in the fire.*
55. thou shalt burn it *in the fire;*
57. that wherein the plague (is) *with fire.*
16:12. full of burning coals of *fire*
13. put the incense upon *the fire*
27. they shall burn *in the fire*
19: 6. it shall be burnt *in the fire.*
20:14. they shall be burnt *with fire,*
21: 9. she shall be burnt *with fire.*
Nu. 3: 4. they offered strange *fire*
6:18. and put (it) in *the fire*
9:15. as it were the appearance of *fire,*
16. the appearance of *fire* by night.
11: 1. *the fire of* the Lord burnt
2. *the fire* was quenched.
3. because *the fire of* the Lord burnt
14:14. in a pillar of *fire* by night.
16: 7. And put *fire* therein,
18. and put *fire* in them,
35. *And* there came out *a fire*
37(17:2). scatter thou *the fire* yonder;
46(17:11). put *fire* therein from off the
18: 9. (reserved) from *the fire:*
21:28. For there is *a fire* gone out
26:10. what time *the fire* devoured
61. when they offered strange *fire*
31:10. all their goodly castles, *with fire.*
23. Every thing that may abide *the fire,*
— make (it) go *through the fire,*
— all that abideth not *the fire*
Deu. 1:33. *in fire* by night,
4:11. the mountain burned *with fire*
12, 15, 33, 36. out of the midst of *the fire:*
24. Lord thy God (is) a consuming *fire,*
36. he shewed thee *his* great *fire;*
5: 4, 22(19), 24(21), 26(23). out of the midst of *the fire,*
5. ye were afraid by reason of *the fire,*
23(20). the mountain did burn *with fire,*
25(22). for this great *fire* will consume us:
7: 5. burn their graven images *with fire.*
25. shall ye burn *with fire:*
9: 3. (as) *a* consuming *fire* he shall destroy

Deu. 9:10. out of the midst of *the fire*
15. the mount burned *with fire:*
21. burnt it *with fire,*
10: 4. out of the midst of *the fire*
12: 3. burn their groves *with fire;*
31. they have burnt *in the fire*
13:16(17). shalt burn *with fire* the city,
18:10. to pass *through the fire,*
16. neither let me see this great *fire*
32:22. For *a fire* is kindled in mine anger,
33: 2. his right hand (went) a *fiery* law for them. (marg. *a fire of* law)
Jos. 6:24. they burnt the city *with fire,*
7:15. accursed thing shall be burnt *with fire,*
25. burned them *with fire,*
8: 8. ye shall set the city *on fire:*
19. hasted and set the city *on fire.*
11: 6. burn their chariots *with fire.*
9. burnt their chariots *with fire.*
11. he burnt Hazor *with fire.*
Jud. 1: 8. set the city *on fire.*
6:21. there rose up *fire* out of the rock,
9:15. let *fire* come out of the bramble,
20. let *fire* come out from Abimelech,
— let *fire* come out from the men
49. set the hold *on fire*
52. the tower to burn it *with fire.*
12: 1. burn thine house upon thee *with fire.*
14:15. burn thee and thy father's house *with fire:*
15: 5. when he had set the brands on *fire,*
6. burnt her and her father *with fire.*
14. as flax that was burnt *with fire,*
16: 9. when it toucheth *the fire.*
18:27. burnt the city *with fire.*
20:48. they set *on fire* all the cities
1Sa.30: 1. burned it *with fire;*
3. behold, (it was) burned *with fire;*
14. we burned Ziklag *with fire.*
2Sa.14:30. go and set it *on fire.* And Absalom's servants set the field *on fire.*
31. have thy servants set my field *on fire?*
22: 9. *and fire* out of his mouth
13. were coals of *fire* kindled.
23: 7. *and* they shall be utterly burned *with fire*
1K. 9:16. burnt it *with fire,*
16:18. the king's house over him *with fire,*
18:23. *and* put no *fire* (under):
— *and* put no *fire* (under):
24. the God that answereth *by fire,*
25. *but* put no *fire* (under).
38. Then *the fire of* the Lord fell,
19:12. *a fire;* (but) the Lord (was) not *in the fire:* and after *the fire* a still small
2K. 1:10, 12. let *fire* come down from heaven,
— there came down *fire* from heaven,
12. *the fire of* God came down
14. there came *fire* down
2:11. a chariot of *fire,* and horses of *fire,*
6:17. full of horses and chariots of *fire*
8:12. their strong holds wilt thou set *on fire,*
16: 3. made his son to pass *through the fire,*
17:17. their daughters to pass *through the fire,*
31. burnt their children *in fire*
19:18. And have cast their gods *into the fire:*
21: 6. made his son pass *through the fire,*
23:10. to pass *through the fire* to Molech.
11. burned the chariots of the sun *with fire.*
25: 9. great (man's) house burnt he *with fire.*
1Ch.14:12. they were burned *with fire.*
21:26. answered him from heaven *by fire*
2Ch. 7: 1. *Now...the fire* came down
3. Israel saw how *the fire* came down,
28: 3. burnt his children *in the fire,*
33: 6. his children to pass *through the fire*
35:13. they roasted the passover *with fire*
36:19. all the palaces thereof *with fire,*
Neh. 1: 3. the gates thereof are burned *with fire.*
2: 3. gates thereof are consumed *with fire?*
13. gates thereof were consumed *with fire.*
17. the gates thereof are burned *with fire:*
9:12. in the night by a pillar of *fire,*
19. neither the pillar of *fire.*
Job 1:16. *The fire of* God is fallen
15:34. *and fire* shall consume the tabernacles
18: 5. the spark of *his fire* shall not
20:26. *a fire* not blown shall consume him;
22:20. the remnant of them *the fire*
Job 28: 5. it is turned up as it were *fire.*
31:12. For it (is) *a fire* (that) consumeth
41:19(11). sparks of *fire* leap out.
Ps. 11: 6. *fire* and brimstone,
18: 8(9). *and fire* out of his mouth
12(13),13(14). hail (stones) and coals of *fire.*
21: 9(10). shalt make them as *a fiery* oven (lit. oven of *fire*)
—(—). *the fire* shall devour them.
29: 7. divideth the flames of *fire.*
39: 3(4). while I was musing *the fire*
46: 9(10). he burneth the chariot *in the fire.*
50: 3. *a fire* shall devour before him,
66:12. we went *through fire*
68: 2(3). as wax melteth before *the fire,*
74: 7. They have cast *fire into* thy sanctuary, (marg. sent thy sanctuary *into the fire*)
78:14. all the night with a light of *fire.*
21. *so a fire* was kindled
63. *The fire* consumed their young men;
79: 5. shall thy jealousy burn like *fire?*
80:16(17). (It is) burned *with fire,*
83:14(15). *As the fire* burneth a wood.
89:46(47). shall thy wrath burn like *fire?*
97: 3. *A fire* goeth before him,
104: 4. his ministers *a* flaming *fire:*
105:32. flaming *fire* in their land.
39. *and fire* to give light in the night.
106:18. *a fire* was kindled in their company;
118:12. quenched *as the fire of* thorns:
140:10(11). let them be cast *into the fire;*
148: 8. *Fire,* and hail; snow, and vapours;
Pro. 6:27. Can a man take *fire* in his bosom,
16:27. in his lips (there is) *as a* burning *fire.*
26:20. *the fire* goeth out:
21. and wood *to fire;*
30:16. *the fire* (that) saith not,
Cant.8: 6. the coals thereof (are) coals of *fire,*
Isa. 1: 7. your cities (are) burned with *fire:*
4: 5. the shining of *a* flaming *fire*
5:24. *the fire* devoureth (marg. tongue of *fire*)
9: 5(4). burning (and) fuel of *fire.*
18(17). For wickedness burneth *as the fire:*
19(18). shall be as the fuel of *the fire:*
10:16. a burning like the burning of *a fire.*
17. Israel shall be *for a fire,*
26:11. *the fire of* thine enemies shall
29: 6. the flame of devouring *fire.*
30:14. a sherd to take *fire* from the hearth,
27. his tongue *as a* devouring *fire:*
30. the flame of a devouring *fire,*
33. the pile thereof (is) *fire*
33:11. your breath, (as) *fire,* shall devour
12. shall they be burned *in the fire.*
14. shall dwell with the devouring *fire?*
37:19. have cast their gods *into the fire:*
43: 2. when thou walkest through *the fire,*
44:16. He burneth part thereof in *the fire;*
19. I have burned part of it in *the fire;*
47:14. *the fire* shall burn them;
50:11. all ye that kindle *a fire,*
— walk in the light of *your fire,*
54:16. that bloweth the coals *in the fire,*
64: 2(1). *the* melting *fire* burneth, *the fire* causeth the waters to boil,
11(10). is burned up with *fire:*
65: 5. *a fire* that burneth all the day.
66:15. the Lord will come *with fire,*
— his rebuke with flames of *fire.*
16. For *by fire* and by his sword
24. neither (lit. *and* not) shall *their fire* be
Jer. 4: 4. lest my fury come forth *like fire,*
5:14. make my words in thy mouth *fire,*
6:29. the lead is consumed *of the fire;*
7:18. the fathers kindle *the fire,*
31. their sons and their daughters *in the fire;*
11:16. he hath kindled *fire* upon it,
15:14. *a fire* is kindled in mine anger,
17: 4. ye have kindled *a fire* in mine anger,
27. then will I kindle *a fire* in the gates
19: 5. to burn their sons *with fire*
20: 9. *as a* burning *fire* shut up
21:10. he shall burn it *with fire.*
12. lest my fury go out *like fire,*
14. I will kindle *a fire* in the forest
22: 7. cast (them) into *the fire.*
23:29. (Is) not my word like *as a fire?*

Jer. 29:22. the king of Babylon roasted *in the fire;*
32:29. shall come and set *fire* on this city,
34: 2. he shall burn it *with fire:*
22. and burn it *with fire:*
36:23. cast (it) into *the fire*
— the roll was consumed in *the fire*
32. Judah had burned *in the fire:*
37: 8. take it, and burn it *with fire.*
10. burn this city *with fire.*
38:17. this city shall not be burned *with fire;*
18. they shall burn it *with fire,*
23. cause this city to be burned *with fire.*
39: 8. the houses of the people, *with fire,*
43:12. I will kindle *a fire* in the houses
13. shall he burn *with fire.*
48:45. *a fire* shall come forth out of Heshbon,
49: 2. her daughters shall be burned *with fire:*
27. I will kindle *a fire* in the wall
50:32. I will kindle *a fire* in his cities,
51:32. the reeds they have burned *with fire,*
58. her high gates shall be burned *with fire;*
— and the folk in *the fire,*
52:13. burned he *with fire:*
Lam. 1:13. From above hath he sent *fire*
2: 3. against Jacob *like a* flaming *fire,*
4. he poured out his fury *like fire.*
4:11. hath kindled *a fire* in Zion,
Eze. 1: 4. *and a fire* infolding itself,
— out of the midst of *the fire.*
13. (was) like burning coals of *fire,*
— and *the fire* was bright, and out of *the fire*
27. as the appearance of *fire*
— as it were the appearance of *fire,*
5: 4. into the midst of *the fire,* and burn them *in the fire;* (for) thereof shall *a fire*
8: 2. a likeness as the appearance of *fire:*
— even downward, *fire;*
10: 2. fill thine hand with coals of *fire*
6. Take *fire* from between the wheels,
7. *the fire* that (was) between
15: 4. *into the fire* for fuel; *the fire* devoureth
5. when *the fire* hath devoured it,
6. I have given *to the fire* for fuel,
7. shall go out *from* (one) *fire, and* (another) *fire* shall devour
16:41. they shall burn thine houses *with fire,*
19:12. *the fire* consumed them.
14. *fire* is gone out of a rod
20:31. to pass *through the fire,*
47(21:3). I will kindle *a fire* in thee,
21:31(36). against thee *in the fire of* my wrath,
32(37). Thou shalt be for fuel *to the fire;*
22:20. to blow *the fire* upon it,
21. blow upon you *in the fire of* my wrath,
31. consumed them *with the fire of*
23:25. thy residue shall be devoured *by the fire.*
47. burn up their houses *with fire.*
24:10. Heap on wood, kindle *the fire,*
12. her scum (shall be) *in the fire.*
28:14. down in the midst of the stones of *fire.*
16. from the midst of the stones of *fire.*
18. therefore will I bring forth *a fire*
30: 8. when I have set *a fire* in Egypt,
14. will set *fire* in Zoan,
16. I will set *fire* in Egypt:
36: 5. Surely *in the fire of* my jealousy
38:19. *in the fire of* my wrath
22. *fire,* and brimstone.
39: 6. I will send *a fire* on Magog,
9. burn them with *fire* seven years:
10. they shall burn the weapons with *fire:*
Dan 10: 6. his eyes as lamps of *fire,*
Hos. 7: 6. it burneth *as a* flaming *fire.*
8:14. but I will send *a fire* upon his
Joel. 1:19. for *the fire* hath devoured
20. *and the fire* hath devoured
2: 3. *A fire* devoureth before them;
5. like the noise of a flame of *fire*
30(3:3). blood, *and fire,* and pillars of smoke.
Am. 1: 4. I will send *a fire* into the house
7, 10. I will send *a fire* on the wall
12. I will send *a fire* upon Teman,
14. I will kindle *a fire* in the wall
2: 2. I will send *a fire* upon Moab,
5. I will send *a fire* upon Judah,
5: 6. lest he break out *like fire*
7 4. the Lord God called to contend *by fire,*
Obad. 18. the house of Jacob shall be *a fire,*
Mic. 1: 4. as wax before *the fire,*
7. shall be burned *with the fire,*
Nah. 1: 6. his fury is poured out *like fire,*
2: 3(4). *with flaming* (marg. *fiery,* lit. *with fire of*) torches in the day
3:13. *the fire* shall devour thy bars.
15. There shall *the fire* devour thee:
Hab 2:13. people shall labour in the very *fire,*
Zep. 1:18. *but* the whole...devoured *by the fire of*
3: 8. shall be devoured *with the fire*
Zec. 2: 5(9). will be unto her a wall of *fire*
3: 2. a brand plucked *out of the fire?*
9: 4. she shall be devoured *with fire.*
11: 1. that *the fire* may devour
12: 6. like an hearth of *fire* among the wood, and like a torch of *fire* in a sheaf;
13: 9. bring the third part *through the fire,*
Mal. 3: 2. for he (is) *like a* refiner's *fire,*

אִשׁ *eesh.* 786

2 Sa. 14:19. *none can* turn to the right
Mic. 6:10. *Are there* yet the treasures (marg. (Is there) yet unto *every man*)

אֶשָּׁא *esh-shāh',* f. emph. Ch. 785

Dan 7:11. and given to the burning *flame.*

אֶשֶׁד *eh'-shed,* m. 793

Nu. 21:15. *And at the stream of* the brooks

אֲשֵׁדוֹת *ăsheh-dōhth',* f. pl. const. 794, 798
אַשְׁדוֹת *ash-dōhth'.*

Deu 3:17. under *Ashdoth*-pisgah eastward. (marg. *the springs of* Pisgah)
4:49. under *the springs of* Pisgah.
Josh 10:40. *and of the springs,* and all their kings:
12: 3. under *Ashdoth*-pisgah: (marg. *the springs of* Pisgah)
8. *and in the springs,* and in the wilderness,
13:20. Beth-peor, *and Ashdoth*-pisgah, (marg. *springs of* Pisgah)

אֶשָּׁה *esh-shāh',* f. 800

Jer. 6:29. the lead is consumed *of the fire;* (lit. according to כתיב, *of their fire*)

See also under אֵשׁ

אִשֶּׁה *eesh-shĕh',* f. 801

Ex. 29:18, 25, 41. *an offering made by fire* unto the
30:20. to burn *offering made by fire*
Lev. 1: 9, 13, 17 & 2:2, 9. *an offering made by fire,* of
2: 3, 10. *of the offerings of* the Lord *made by fire.*
11. *offering* of the Lord *made by fire.*
16 & 3:3, 9, 14. *an offering made by fire* unto
3: 5. *an offering made by fire,* of a sweet
11. *the offering made by fire* unto the Lord.
16. the food of the *offering made by fire*
4:35 & 5:12. *the offerings made by fire unto* the
6:17(10). portion *of my offerings made by fire;*
18(11). *concerning the offerings of* the Lord *made by fire:*
7: 5, 25. *an offering made by fire* unto the Lord:
30. bring *the offerings of* the Lord *made by fire,*
35. *out of the offerings of* the Lord *made by fire,*
8:21, 28. *an offering made by fire* unto the Lord;
10:12. *of the offerings of* the Lord *made by fire,*
13. *of the sacrifices of* the Lord *made by fire:*
15. with *the offerings made by fire of*
21: 6, 21. *the offerings of* the Lord *made by fire,*
22:22. *nor* make *an offering by fire*
27. for an offering made *by fire*
23: 8, 13, 25, 27, 36, 36, 37. *an offering made by fire*
18. *an offering made by fire,* of sweet
24: 7. *an offering made by fire* unto the Lord.

Lev.24: 9. *of the offerings of* the Lord *made by fire*
Nu. 15: 3. will make *an offering by fire*
10, 13, 14. *an offering made by fire*, of a sweet
25. *a sacrifice made by fire* unto the Lord,
18:17. *an offering made by fire*, for a sweet
28: 2. *for my sacrifices made by fire*,
3. This (is) *the offering made by fire*
6, 13. *a sacrifice made by fire* unto the Lord.
8. *a sacrifice made by fire*, of a sweet
19. ye shall offer *a sacrifice made by fire*
24. the meat of *the sacrifice made by fire*,
29: 6. *a sacrifice made by fire* unto the Lord.
13, 36. *a sacrifice made by fire*, of a sweet
Deu 18: 1. *the offerings of* the Lord *made by fire*,
Josh13:14. *sacrifices of* the Lord God of Israel *made by fire*
1Sa. 2:28. all the *offerings made by fire of* the

---

802 **אִשָּׁה** *eesh-shāh'*, f.

Gen 2:22. made he (lit. built he *into*) *a woman*,
23. she shall be called *Woman*,
24. shall cleave *unto his wife:*
25. both naked, the man *and his wife*,
3: 1. he said unto *the woman*,
2. *the woman* said unto the serpent,
4. the serpent said unto *the woman*,
6. when *the woman* saw that
8. Adam *and his wife* hid themselves
12. *The woman* whom thou gavest
13. the Lord God said *unto the woman*,
— And *the woman* said,
15. enmity between thee and *the woman*,
16. Unto *the woman* he said,
17. hearkened unto the voice of *thy wife*,
20. Adam called *his wife*'s name Eve;
21. Unto Adam also *and to his wife*
4: 1. Adam knew Eve *his wife;*
17. Cain knew *his wife;*
25. Adam knew *his wife* again;
6:18. thy sons, *and thy wife*,
7: 2, 2. the male *and his female:*
7. Noah went in, and his sons, *and his wife*,
13. sons of Noah, *and* Noah'*s wife*,
8:16. thou, *and thy wife*, and thy sons,
18. his sons, *and his wife*,
11:29. the name of Abram'*s wife* (was) Sarai; and the name of Nahor'*s wife*, Milcah,
31. his son Abram'*s wife;*
12: 5. Abram took Sarai *his wife*,
11. he said unto Sarai *his wife*,
— a fair *woman* to look upon:
12. This (is) *his wife:*
14. the Egyptians beheld *the woman*
15. *the woman* was taken into Pharaoh's
17. because of Sarai Abram'*s wife*.
18. not tell me that she (was) *thy wife?*
19. taken her to me *to wife:* now therefore behold *thy wife*, take (her),
20. they sent him away, and *his wife*,
13: 1. out of Egypt, he, *and his wife*,
16: 1. Now Sarai Abram'*s wife*
3. Sarai Abram'*s wife* took Hagar
— her husband Abram to be his *wife*. (lit. *for a wife* to him)
17:15. As for Sarai *thy wife*,
19. Sarah *thy wife* shall bear thee a son
18: 9. Where (is) Sarah *thy wife?*
10. Sarah *thy wife* shall have a son.
19:15. take *thy wife*, and thy two daughters,
16. upon the hand of *his wife*,
26. But *his wife* looked back from behind him, and
20: 2. Abraham said of Sarah *his wife*,
3. *the woman* which thou hast taken;
7. therefore restore the man (his) *wife;*
11. they will slay me for *my wife*'s sake.
12. she became my *wife*.
14. restored him Sarah *his wife*.
17. God healed Abimelech, and *his wife*,
18. because of Sarah Abraham'*s wife*.
21:21. his mother took him *a wife* out
23:19. Abraham buried Sarah *his wife*
24: 3, 37. thou shalt not take *a wife*
4. take *a wife* unto my son Isaac.
Gen24: 5. Peradventure *the woman* will
7. thou shalt take *a wife* unto my son
8. if *the woman* will not be willing
15. *the wife of* Nahor, Abraham's brother,
36. Sarah my master'*s wife* bare a son
38. take *a wife* unto my son.
39. Peradventure *the woman* will not follow
40. thou shalt take *a wife* for my son
44. (let) the same (be) *the woman*
51. let her be thy master's son'*s wife*,
67. and she became his *wife;*
25: 1. Then again Abraham took *a wife*,
10. was Abraham buried, and Sarah *his wife*.
20. he took Rebekah *to wife*,
21. Isaac intreated the Lord for *his wife*,
— Rebekah *his wife* conceived.
26: 7. men of the place asked (him) *of his wife;*
— he feared to say, (She is) *my wife;*
8. Isaac (was) sporting with Rebekah *his wife*.
9. Behold, of a surety she (is) *thy wife:*
10. might lightly have lien with *thy wife*,
11. He that toucheth this man *or his wife*
34. when he took to *wife* Judith
27:46. if Jacob take *a wife* of the daughters
28: 1, 6. Thou shalt not take *a wife*
2. take thee *a wife* from thence
6. to take him *a wife* from thence;
9. the sister of Nebajoth, to be his *wife*.
29:21. said unto Laban, Give (me) *my wife*,
28. gave him Rachel his daughter *to wife*
30: 4. Bilhah her handmaid *to wife:*
9. her maid, and gave her Jacob *to wife*.
34: 4. Get me this damsel *to wife*.
8. I pray you give her him *to wife*.
12. but give me the damsel *to wife*.
36:10. of Adah *the wife of* Esau, Reuel the son of Bashemath *the wife of* Esau.
12. the sons of Adah Esau'*s wife*.
13, 17. the sons of Bashemath Esau'*s wife*.
14. the daughter of Zibeon, Esau'*s wife:*
18. the sons of Aholibamah Esau'*s wife;*
— the daughter of Anah, Esau'*s wife*.
39. *his wife*'s name (was) Mehetabel,
38: 6. Judah took *a wife* for Er his firstborn,
8. Go in unto thy brother'*s wife*,
9. he went in unto his brother'*s wife*,
12. the daughter of Shuah Judah'*s wife*
14. she was not given unto him *to wife*.
20. (his) pledge from *the woman*'s hand:
39: 7. his master'*s wife* cast her eyes
8. said unto his master'*s wife*,
9. because thou (art) *his wife:*
19. his master heard the words of *his wife*,
41:45. he gave him *to wife* Asenath
44:27. Ye know that *my wife* bare me two (sons):
46:19. The sons of Rachel Jacob'*s wife;*
49:31. Abraham and Sarah *his wife;* there they buried Isaac and Rebekah *his wife;*
Ex. 2: 2. *the woman* conceived,
7. Shall I go and call to thee a nurse (lit. nursing *woman*)
9. *the woman* took the child,
3:22. But *every woman* shall borrow
4:20. Moses took *his wife* and his sons,
6:20. Jochebed his father's sister *to wife;*
23. sister of Naashon, *to wife;*
25. (one) of the daughters of Putiel *to wife;*
11: 2. *and every woman* of her neighbour,
18: 2. took Zipporah, Moses' *wife*,
5. came with his sons *and his wife*
6. come unto thee, *and thy wife*,
19:15. come not at (your) *wives*.
20:17. shalt not covet thy neighbour'*s wife*,
21: 3. if he were married (lit. the master of *a wife*), then *his wife* shall go out
4. have given him *a wife*,
— *the wife* and her children
5. I love my master, *my wife*,
22. hurt *a woman* with child,
— according as *the woman*'s husband
28. If an ox gore a man or *a woman*,
29. hath killed a man or *a woman;*
22:16(15). shall surely endow her to be his *wife*.
26: 3. shall be coupled together *one* to another; and (other) five curtains (shall be) coupled *one* to another.

Ex. 26: 5. may take hold *one* of another.
6. couple the curtains *together* (lit. *a woman* to her sister)
17. set in order *one* against another:
35:25. all *the women* that were wise hearted
29. every man *and woman*,
36: 6. Let neither man *nor woman*
Lev. 12: 2. If *a woman* have conceived seed,
13:29. If a man or *woman* have a plague
38. If a man also or *a woman* have
15:18. *The woman also* with whom
19. *And if a woman* have an issue,
25. *And if a woman* have an issue
18: 8. nakedness of thy father's *wife* shalt
11. nakedness of thy father's *wife's*
14. thou shalt not approach to *his wife:*
15. she (is) thy son's *wife ;*
16. the nakedness of thy brother's *wife:*
17. uncover the nakedness of *a woman*
18. *Neither* shalt thou take *a wife* (lit. *and a woman* thou shalt not)
19. thou shalt not approach unto *a woman*
20. carnally with thy neighbour's *wife*,
22. with mankind, as with *woman*kind:
23. neither (lit. *and* not) shall *any woman*
19:20. *a woman*, that (is) a bondmaid,
20:10. adultery with (another) man's *wife*,
— adultery with his neighbour's *wife*,
11. the man that lieth with his father's *wife*
13. as he lieth with *a woman*,
14. if a man take *a wife*
16. *And if a woman* approach unto any beast,
— thou shalt kill *the woman*,
18. if a man shall lie with *a woman*
21. if a man shall take his brother's *wife*,
27. A man also or *woman*
21: 7. They shall not take *a wife*
— *neither* shall they take *a woman*
13. he shall take *a wife* in her virginity.
14. a virgin of his own people *to wife*.
24:10. the son of an Israelitish *woman*,
11. the Israelitish *woman's* son
Nu. 5: 6. When a man or *woman* shall
12. If any man's *wife* go aside,
14, 14. he be jealous of *his wife*,
15. the man bring *his wife*
18. shall set *the woman* before the Lord, and uncover *the woman's* head,
19. say unto *the woman*,
21. the priest shall charge *the woman*
— the priest shall say *unto the woman*,
22. *the woman* shall say, Amen,
24. he shall cause *the woman* to drink
25. jealousy offering out of *the woman's* hand,
26. shall cause *the woman* to drink
27. *the woman* shall be a curse
28. if *the woman* be not defiled,
29. when *a wife* goeth aside (to another)
30. he be jealous over *his wife*, and shall set *the woman* before the Lord,
31. *and* this *woman* shall bear her iniquity.
6: 2. When either man or *woman*
12: 1. because of *the* Ethiopian *woman*
— he had married *an* Ethiopian *woman*.
25: 8. *the woman* through her belly.
15. the name of *the* Midianitish *woman*
26:59. the name of Amram's *wife*
30: 3(4). If *a woman also* vow a vow
16(17). between a man *and his wife*,
31:17. kill every *woman* that hath known man
36: 8. shall be *wife* unto one
Deu 5:21(18). shalt thou desire thy neighbour's *wife*,
13: 6(7). or *the wife of* thy bosom,
17: 2. man or *woman*, that hath wrought
5. bring forth that man or that *woman*,
— (even) that man or that *woman*,
20: 7. (is there) that hath betrothed *a wife*,
21:11. among the captives *a* beautiful *woman*,
— wouldest have her *to* thy *wife ;*
13. she shall be thy *wife*.
22: 5. *The woman* shall not wear
— shall a man put on *a woman's* garment:
13. If any man take *a wife*,
14. I took this *woman*,
16. I gave my daughter unto this man *to wife*,
19, 29. she shall be his *wife ;*

Deu 22:22. be found lying with *a woman*
— (both) the man that lay with *the woman, and the woman:*
24. he hath humbled his neighbour's *wife :*
30(23:1). man shall not take his father's *wife*
24: 1. When a man hath taken *a wife*,
3. took her (to be) his *wife ;*
4. again to be his *wife*,
5. When a man hath taken *a* new *wife*,
— shall cheer up *his wife* which
25: 5. *the wife of* the dead shall not
— take her to him *to wife*,
11. *the wife of* the one draweth near
27:20. he that lieth with his father's *wife ;*
28:30. Thou shalt betroth *a wife*,
54. *and toward the wife of* his bosom,
29:18(17). be among you man, or *woman*,
Jos. 2: 1. came into an harlot's house, (lit. *a woman* an harlot)
4. *the woman* took the two men,
6:21. both man and *woman*,
22. Go into the harlot's house (lit. *the woman* the harlot), and bring out thence *the woman*,
8:25. both of men and *women*,
15:16. will I give Achsah my daughter *to wife*.
17. he gave him Achsah his daughter *to wife*.
Jud. 1:12. will I give Achsah my daughter *to wife*.
13. he gave him Achsah his daughter *to wife*
4: 4. Deborah, a prophetess (lit. *a woman* prophetess), *the wife of* Lapidoth,
9. sell Sisera into the hand of *a woman*.
17. to the tent of Jael *the wife of* Heber
21. Then Jael Heber's *wife*
5:24. Jael *the wife of* Heber the Kenite
9:49. a thousand men *and women*.
53. *a* certain *woman* cast a piece
54. *A woman* slew him.
11: 1. he (was) the son of an harlot: (marg. *a woman* an harlot)
2. Gilead's *wife* bare him sons ; and his *wife's*
— thou (art) the son of *a* strange *woman*.
13: 2. *and his wife* (was) barren,
3. appeared unto *the woman*,
6. Then *the woman* came and told
9. came again unto *the woman*
10. *the woman* made haste, and ran,
11. Manoah arose, and went after *his wife*,
— the man that spakest unto *the woman ?*
13. Of all that I said unto *the woman*
19, 20. Manoah *and his wife* looked on.
21. appear to Manoah and to *his wife*.
22. Manoah said unto *his wife*,
23. But *his wife* said unto him,
24. And *the woman* bare a son,
14: 1. saw *a woman* in Timnath
2. I have seen *a woman* in Timnath
— now therefore get her for me *to wife*.
3. (Is there) never *a woman* among
— thou goest to take *a wife* of the
7. talked *with the woman ;*
10. his father went down unto *the woman :*
15. they said *unto* Samson's *wife*,
16. Samson's *wife* wept before him,
20. Samson's *wife* was (given) to his
15: 1. Samson visited *his wife* with a kid; and he said, I will go in to *my wife*
6. because he had taken *his wife*,
16: 1. Then went Samson to Gaza, and saw there an harlot, (marg. *a woman* an harlot)
4. that he loved *a woman*
27. three thousand men *and women*,
19: 1. who took to him a concubine (marg. *a woman* a concubine, or, *a wife* a con.)
26. Then came *the woman* in
27. *the woman* his concubine
20: 4. the husband of *the woman*
21: 1. give his daughter unto Benjamin *to wife*.
11. every *woman* that hath lain by man.
16. seeing *the women* are destroyed
18. he that giveth *a wife* to Benjamin.
21. catch you every man *his wife*
22. we reserved not to each man *his wife*
Ru. 1: 1. he, *and his wife*, and his two sons.
2. the name of *his wife* Naomi,
5. *the woman* was left of her two sons
8. return *each* to her mother's house:

Ruth 1: 9. *each* (of you) in the house
3: 8. behold, *a woman* lay at his feet.
11. that thou (art) *a* virtuous *woman*.
14. Let it not be known that *a woman*
4: 5. *the wife of* the dead,
10. *the wife of* Mahlon, have I purchased *to be* my *wife*,
11. The Lord make *the woman*
13. she was his *wife:*
1Sa. 1: 4. he gave to Peninnah *his wife*.
15. I (am) *a woman* of a sorrowful spirit:
18. So *the woman* went her way,
19. Elkanah knew Hannah *his wife;*
23. So *the woman* abode,
26. I (am) *the woman* that stood by
2:20. Eli blessed Elkanah and *his wife*,
— The Lord give thee seed of this *woman*
4:19. his daughter in law, Phinehas' *wife*,
14:50. the name of Saul's *wife* (was) Ahinoam,
15: 3. slay both man and *woman*,
18:17. Merab, her will I give thee *to wife:*
19. unto Adriel the Meholathite *to wife*.
27. gave him Michal his daughter *to wife*.
19:11. Michal David's *wife* told him,
21: 4(5). kept themselves at least *from women*.
5(6). Of a truth *women* (have been)
22:19. both men and *women*,
25: 3. the name of *his wife* Abigail: *and* (she was) *a woman* of good understanding,
14. told Abigail, Nabal's *wife*,
37. *his wife* had told him these things,
39. to take her to him *to wife*.
40. to take thee to him *to wife*.
42. messengers of David, and became his *wife*.
44. Michal his daughter, David's *wife*,
27: 3. Abigail the Carmelitess, Nabal's *wife*.
9. left neither man *nor woman*
11. David saved neither man *nor woman*
28: 7,7. *a woman* that hath a familiar spirit,
8. they came to *the woman* by night:
9. *the woman* said unto him,
11. Then said *the woman*,
12. when *the woman* saw Samuel,
— *the woman* spake to Saul,
13. *the woman* said unto Saul,
21. *the woman* came unto Saul,
23. together with *the woman*,
24. *And the woman had* a fat calf
30: 5. Abigail *the wife of* Nabal
22. save to every man *his wife*
2Sa. 2: 2. Abigail Nabal's *wife*
3: 3. Abigail *the wife of* Nabal
5. by Eglah David's *wife*.
8. with a fault concerning *this woman?*
14. Deliver (me) *my wife* Michal,
6:19. as well to *the women*
11: 2. from the roof he saw *a woman*
— *and the woman* (was) very beautiful
3. David sent and enquired *after the woman*.
— *the wife of* Uriah the Hittite?
5. And *the woman* conceived,
11. and to lie with *my wife?*
21. did not *a woman* cast a piece
26. when *the wife of* Uriah heard
27. she became his *wife*,
12: 9. hast taken *his wife* (to be) thy *wife*,
10. hast taken *the wife of* Uriah the Hittite to be thy *wife*.
15. Uriah's *wife* bare unto David,
24. David comforted Bathsheba *his wife*,
14: 2. fetched thence *a* wise *woman*,
— be *as a woman* that had
4. when *the woman* of Tekoah spake
5. I (am) indeed *a* widow *woman*,
8. the king said unto *the woman*,
9. *the woman* of Tekoah said
12. Then *the woman* said, let thine
13. And *the woman* said, Wherefore then
18. answered and said unto *the woman*,
— And *the woman* said,
19. *the woman* answered and said,
27. she was *a woman* of a fair countenance.
17:19. *the woman* took and spread a covering
20. Absalom's servants came to *the woman*
— *the woman* said unto them,
20:16. Then cried *a* wise *woman*
17. *the woman* said, (Art) thou Joab?

2Sa.20:21. *the woman* said unto Joab,
22. Then *the woman* went unto
1Ki. 2:17. give me Abishag the Shunammite *to wife*.
21. be given to Adonijah thy brother *to wife*.
3:17. *the* one *woman* said,
— I *and* this *woman* dwell in one house;
18. that this *woman* was delivered
19. this *woman*'s child died
22. *the* other *woman* said,
26. Then spake *the woman*
4:11. Taphath the daughter of Solomon *to wife:*
15. Basmath the daughter of Solomon *to wife:*
7:14. He (was) a widow's son (marg. son of *a* widow *woman*)
9:16. unto his daughter, Solomon's *wife*.
11:19. to *wife* the sister of *his own wife*,
26. name (was) Zeruah, *a* widow *woman*,
14: 2. Jeroboam said *to his wife*,
— not known to be *the wife of* Jeroboam;
4. Jeroboam's *wife* did so,
5. *the wife of* Jeroboam cometh
6. Come in, thou *wife of* Jeroboam;
17. Jeroboam's *wife* arose,
16:31. he took to *wife* Jezebel
17: 9. I have commanded *a* widow *woman*
10. *the* widow *woman* (was) there
17. (that) the son of *the woman*,
24. *the woman* said to Elijah,
21: 5. But Jezebel *his wife* came
7. Jezebel *his wife* said
25. whom Jezebel *his wife* stirred up.
2Ki. 4: 1. *Now* there cried *a* certain *woman*
8. where (was) *a* great *woman;*
17. *the woman* conceived,
5: 2. she waited on Naaman's *wife*.
6:26. there cried *a woman* unto him,
28. This *woman* said unto me,
30. the king heard the words of *the woman*,
8: 1. Then spake Elisha unto *the woman*,
2. *the woman* arose, and did after
3. that *the woman* returned
5. *the woman*, whose son he had
— My lord, O king, this (is) *the woman*,
6. when the king asked *the woman*,
18. the daughter of Ahab was his *wife:*
14: 9. Give thy daughter to my son *to wife:*
22:14. *the wife of* Shallum the son of Tikvah,
1Ch. 1:50. *his wife*'s name (was) Mehetabel,
2:18. begat (children) of Azubah (his) *wife*,
24. *then* Abiah Hezron's *wife*
26. Jerahmeel had also another *wife*,
29. the name of *the wife of* Abishur
35. to Jarha his servant *to wife;*
3: 3. the sixth, Ithream by Eglah *his wife*.
4:18. *And his wife* Jehudijah bare Jered
19. the sons of (his) *wife* Hodiah
7:15. Machir took to *wife* (the sister) of
16. Maachah *the wife of* Machir
23. when he went in to *his wife*,
8: 9. he begat of Hodesh *his wife*,
29&9:35. *whose wife*'s name (was) Maachah.
16: 3. both man and *woman*,
2Ch. 2:14(13). *a woman* of the daughters of Dan,
8:11. My *wife* shall not dwell
11:18. of Jerimoth the son of David to *wife*,
15:13. whether man or *woman*.
21: 6. he had the daughter of Ahab *to wife:*
22:11. *the wife of* Jehoiada the priest,
25:18. Give thy daughter to my son *to wife:*
34:22. *the wife of* Shallum the son of Tikvath,
Ezr. 2:61. which took *a wife* of the
Neh. 7:63. daughters of Barzillai the Gileadite *to wife*,
8: 2. both of men and *women*,
Est. 4:11. whether man *or woman*.
5:10. called for his friends, and Zeresh *his wife*.
14. Then said Zeresh *his wife*
6:13. Haman told Zeresh *his wife*
— and Zeresh *his wife* unto him,
Job 2: 9. Then said *his wife* unto him,
14: 1. Man (that is) born of *a woman*
15:14. (he which is) born of *a woman*,
19:17. My breath is strange *to my wife*,
25: 4. (that is) born of *a woman?*
31: 9. have been deceived by *a woman*,
10. let *my wife* grind unto another,

Ps. 58: 8(9). (like) the untimely birth of *a woman*,
109: 9. *and his wife* a widow.
128: 3. *Thy wife* (shall be) as a fruitful vine
Pro. 2:16. deliver thee *from the* strange *woman*,
5:18. rejoice *with the wife of* thy youth.
6:24. To keep thee *from the* evil *woman*,
26. by means of *a* whorish *woman*
— *and* the adulteress (marg. *woman of* a man, or, *a* man's *wife*) will hunt for the precious life.
29. he that goeth in to his neighbour's *wife;*
32. whoso committeth adultery with *a woman*
7: 5. keep thee *from the* strange *woman*,
10. there met him *a woman*
9:13. *A* foolish *woman* (is) clamorous:
11:16. *A* gracious *woman* retaineth honour:
22. (so is) *a* fair *woman* which is without
12: 4. *A* virtuous *woman* (is) a crown
18:22. (Whoso) findeth *a wife* findeth
19:13. the contentions of *a wife* (are) a
14. *a* prudent *wife* (is) from the Lord.
21: 9. *than with a* brawling *woman*
19. *than with a* contentious and an angry *woman*.
25:24. *than with a* brawling *woman*
27:15. *and a* contentious *woman* are alike.
30:20. the way of *an* adulterous *woman;*
31:10. Who can find *a* virtuous *woman?*
30. *a woman* (that) feareth the Lord,
Ecc. 7:26. *the woman*, whose heart (is) snares
28. *but a woman* among all
9: 9. Live joyfully with *the wife*
Isa. 34:15. *every one* with her mate.
16. *none* (lit. no *female*) shall want her mate:
45:10. *or to the woman*, What hast thou
49:15. Can *a woman* forget her sucking child,
54: 6. called thee *as a woman* forsaken
— *and a wife of* youth,
Jer. 3: 1. If a man put away *his wife*,
3. thou hadst a whore's forehead, (lit. *a woman* a whore)
20. Surely (as) *a wife* treacherously
5: 8. neighed after his neighbour's *wife*.
6:11. *the wife* shall be taken,
9:20(19). *and every one* her neighbour
13:21. sorrows take thee, as *a woman in* travail?
16: 2. Thou shalt not take thee *a wife*,
44: 7. to cut off from you man *and woman*,
48:41 & 49:22. as the heart of *a woman* in her
51:22. I break in pieces man *and woman;*
Eze. 1: 9. Their wings (were) joined *one* to another; (lit. *a woman* to her sister)
23. *the one* toward the other:
3:13. living creatures that touched *one* another,
16:30. the work of *an* imperious whorish *woman*,
32. (But as) *a wife* that committeth
18: 6, 15. defiled his neighbour's *wife*,
— come near to *a* menstruous *woman*,
11. defiled his neighbour's *wife*,
22:11. abomination with his neighbour's *wife;*
23:44. they go in unto *a woman* that playeth
— Aholah and unto Aholibah, *the* lewd *women*.
24:18. at even *my wife* died;
33:26. ye defile every one his neighbour's *wife:*
Hos. 1: 2. take unto thee *a wife of* whoredoms
2: 2(4). for she (is) not *my wife*, neither (am)
3: 1. love *a woman* beloved of (her) friend,
12:12(13). Israel served *for a wife, and for a wife* he kept (sheep).
Am. 4: 3. *every* (cow at that which is) before her;
7:17. *Thy wife* shall be an harlot in the city,
Zec. 5: 7. this (is) *a woman* that sitteth
11: 9. let the rest eat *every one* the flesh
Mal. 2:14. between thee and *the wife of* thy youth,
— *and the wife of* thy covenant.
15. *and* let none deal treacherously *against the wife of* his youth.

---

380 אֱשׁוּן *ĕshoon*, (קרי)

Pro. 20:20. shall be put out *in obscure* darkness.

See אִישׁוֹן.

אָשְׁיּוֹת *osh-yōhth'*, f. pl. (קרי) (כתיב אֲשׁוּית) 803

Jer. 50:15. *her foundations* are fallen,

אֻשִּׁין *oosh-sheen'*, Ch. m. pl. 787

From אשׁ.

Ezr. 4:12. *and* joined the *foundations*,
5:16. laid the *foundation* of the house of God
6: 3. *and* let *the foundations thereof* be

אֲשֵׁרָה see אֲשֵׁרָה See 842

אֲשִׁישׁ [*āh-sheesh'*,] m. 808

Isa. 16: 7. *for the foundations of* Kir-hareseth

אֲשִׁישָׁה *ăshee-shāh'*, f. 809

2Sa. 6:19. *and a flagon* (of wine).
1Ch 16: 3. *and a flagon* (of wine).
Cant. 2: 5. Stay me *with flagons*,
Hos. 3: 1. love *flagons of* wine.

אֶשֶׁךְ [*eh'-shech*], m. 810

In pause.

Lev. 21:20. or hath his *stones* broken;

אֶשְׁכֹּל & אֶשְׁכּוֹל *esh-kōhl'*, m. 811

Gen 40:10. *the clusters thereof* brought forth
Nu. 13:23. came unto the brook of *Eshcol*,
— a branch *with* one *cluster of* grapes,
24. was called the brook *Eshcol*, because of *the cluster of grapes*
32: 9. went up unto the valley of *Eshcol*,
Deu 1:24. came unto the valley of *Eshcol*,
32:32. their *clusters* (are) bitter:
Cant. 1:14. My beloved (is) unto me (as) *a cluster of*
7: 7(8). thy breasts *to clusters* (of grapes).
8(9). thy breasts shall be *as clusters of*
Isa. 65: 8. new wine is found *in the cluster*,
Mic. 7: 1. no *cluster* to eat:

אֶשְׁכָּר *esh-kāhr'*, m. 814

Ps. 72:10. kings of Sheba and Seba shall offer *gifts*.
Eze. 27:15. they brought *thee* (for) *a present*

אֶשֶׁל *ēh'-shel*, m. 815

Gen 21:33. And (Abraham) planted *a grove* (marg. *tree*)
1Sa. 22: 6. in Gibeah under *a tree* (marg. or, *grove*)
31:13. buried (them) under *a tree*

אָשַׁם *āh-sham'* & אָשֵׁם *āh-shēhm'*, 816

* KAL.—*Preterite*. *

Lev. 4:13. should not be done, *and are guilty;*
22. should not be done, *and is guilty;*
27. ought not to be done, *and be guilty;*
5: 2. he also shall be unclean, *and guilty*.
3, 4. *then he shall be guilty*.
17. he wist (it) not, *yet is he guilty*,
19. *he hath* certainly *trespassed*
6: 4(5:23). he hath sinned, *and is guilty*,
Nu. 5: 6. *and* that person *be guilty;*
7. against whom *he hath trespassed*.
Pro. 30:10. he curse thee, *and thou be found guilty*.

Eze. 22: 4. *Thou art become guilty* in thy blood.
Hab. 1:11. he shall pass over, *and offend*,

KAL.—*Infinitive.*

Lev. 5:19. he hath *certainly* trespassed (lit. *trespassing* he hath trespassed)
Eze. 25:12. hath *greatly* offended, (lit. *offending* hath offended)

KAL.—*Future.*

Lev. 5: 5. when *he shall be guilty* in one
Jud. 21:22. (that) *ye should be guilty.*
2Ch 19:10. even warn them that *they trespass* not
— and *ye shall* not *trespass.*
Ps. 34:21(22). they that hate the righteous *shall be desolate.* (marg. *guilty*)
22(23). that trust in him *shall be desolate.*
Isa. 24: 6. *and they* that dwell therein *are desolate:*
Jer. 2: 3. all that devour him *shall offend;*
50: 7. their adversaries said, *We offend* not,
Eze. 6: 6. may be laid waste *and made desolate,*
25:12. *and hath* greatly *offended,*
Hos. 4:15. *let* not Judah *offend;*
5:15. till *they acknowledge their offence,* (marg. *be guilty*)
10: 2. now *shall they be found faulty:*
13: 1. but *when he offended* in Baal,
16(14:1). Samaria *shall become desolate;*
Zec. 11: 5. *hold themselves* not *guilty:*

* NIPHAL.—*Preterite.* *

Joel 1:18. flocks of sheep *are made desolate.*

* HIPHIL.—*Imperative.* *

Ps. 5:10(11). *Destroy thou them* (marg. *Make them guilty*), O God;

---

817 ## אָשָׁם *āh-shāhm'*, m.

Gen 26:10. have brought *guiltiness* upon us.
Lev. 5: 6. he shall bring *his trespass offering*
7. for *his trespass*, which he hath
15. he shall bring for *his trespass*
—, 18. *for a trespass offering:*
16. the ram of *the trespass offering,*
19. It (is) *a trespass offering:*
6: 6(5:25). he shall bring *his trespass offering*
—(–:—). *for a trespass offering,*
17(10). *and as the trespass offering.*
7: 1. this (is) the law of *the trespass offering:*
2. they kill *the trespass offering:*
5. it (is) *a trespass offering.*
7. *so* (is) *the trespass offering:*
37. *and of the trespass offering,*
14:12. offer him *for a trespass offering,*
13. *the trespass offering:* it (is) most holy:
14, 17, 25, 28. the blood of *the trespass offering,*
21. take one lamb (for) *a trespass offering*
24, 25. the lamb of *the trespass offering,*
19:21. he shall bring *his trespass offering*
— a ram for *a trespass offering.*
22. the ram of *the trespass offering*
Nu. 5: 7. he shall recompense *his trespass*
8. to recompense *the trespass* unto, let *the trespass* be recompensed
6:12. first year *for a trespass offering:*
18: 9. every *trespass offering of their's,*
1Sa. 6: 3. return him *a trespass offering:*
4. What (shall be) *the trespass offering*
8. return him (for) *a trespass offering,*
17. returned (for) *a trespass offering*
2K. 12:16(17). The *trespass* money
Ps. 68:21(22). goeth on still *in his trespasses.*
Pro. 14: 9. Fools make a mock at *sin:*
Isa. 53:10. make his soul *an offering for sin,*
Jer. 51: 5. their land was filled with *sin*
Eze. 40:39 & 42:13 & 44:29. the sin offering *and the trespass offering.*
46:20. shall boil *the trespass offering*

---

818 ## אָשֵׁם *āh-shēhm'*, adj.

Gen 42:21. We (are) verily *guilty* concerning
2Sa. 14:13. speak this thing *as one which is faulty,*
Ezr. 10:19. *and* (being) *guilty,* (they offered)

אַשְׁמָה *ash-māh'*, f. 819

Lev. 4: 3. *according to the sin of* the people;
6: 5(5:24). in the day of *his trespass offering.* (marg. *his trespass*, or, *his being found guilty*)
7(5:26). *in trespassing* therein.
22:16. bear the iniquity of *trespass,*
1Ch 21: 3. he be *a cause of trespass*
2Ch 24:18. Jerusalem *for* this *their trespass.*
28:10. *sins* against the Lord your God?
13. we have *offended* against the Lord (lit. *to the offence of* the Lord is upon us)
— to our sins and to *our trespass:* for our *trespass* is great,
33:23. Amon *trespassed* more and more. (marg. multiplied *trespass*)
Ezr. 9: 6. *and our trespass* (marg. *guiltiness*) is
7. we (been) *in a great trespass*
13. *and for our* great *trespass,*
15. we (are) before thee *in our trespasses:*
10:10. to increase *the trespass of* Israel.
19. of the flock for *their trespass.*
Ps. 69: 5(6). *and my sins* (marg. *guiltiness*) are not
Am. 8:14. that swear *by the sin of* Samaria,

אַשְׁמוּרָה & אַשְׁמֻרָה *ash-moo-rāh'*, f 821

Ex. 14:24. *in the* morning *watch* the Lord looked
Jud. 7:19. the beginning of *the* middle *watch;*
1Sa. 11:11. the host *in the* morning *watch,*
Ps. 63: 6(7). meditate on thee *in the* (night) *watches.*
90: 4. *and* (as) *a watch* in the night.
119:148. Mine eyes prevent *the* (night) *watches,*
Lam. 2:19. the beginning of *the watches*

אַשְׁמַנִּים *ash-man-neem'*, m. pl. 820

Isa. 59:10. *in desolate places* as dead (men).

אַשְׁמֹרֶת see אַשְׁמוּרָה, See 821

אֶשְׁנָב *esh-nāhv'*, m. 822

Jud. 5:28. and cried through *the lattice,*
Pro. 7: 6. I looked through *my casement,*

אַשָּׁף *ash-shāhph'*, Ch. m. 826

Dan 2:10. such things at any magician, *or astrologer,*
27. cannot the wise (men), *the astrologers,*
4: 7(4). came in the magicians, *the astrologers,*
5: 7. cried aloud to bring in *the astrologers,*
11. master of the magicians, *astrologers,*
15. *the astrologers,* have been brought in

אַשְׁפָּה *ash-pāh'*, f. 827

Job 39:23. *The quiver* rattleth against him,
Ps. 127: 5. the man that hath *his quiver*
Isa. 22: 6. Elam bare *the quiver*
49: 2. *in his quiver* hath he hid me;
Jer. 5.16. *Their quiver* (is) as an open sepulchre,
Lam. 3:13. He hath caused the arrows of *his quiver*

אַשְׁפּוֹת *ash-pōhth'*, m. 830

1Sa. 2: 8. (and) lifteth up the beggar *from the dunghill,*
Neh. 2:13. and to *the dung* port,
3:13. the wall unto *the dung* gate.
14. But *the dung* gate repaired
12:31. the wall toward *the dung* gate:
Ps. 113: 7. the needy *out of the dunghill;*
Lam. 4: 5. brought up in scarlet embrace *dunghills.*

825 **אַשָּׁפִים** *ash-shāh-pheem'*, m. pl.

Dan 1:20. *astrologers* that (were) in all his
2: 2. the magicians, *and the astrologers*,

---

829 **אֶשְׁפָּר** *esh-pāhr'*, m.

2Sa. 6:19. *and* a *good piece* (of flesh),
1Ch 16: 3. *and a good piece of flesh*,

---

833 **אָשַׁר** [*āh-shar'*],

* KAL.—*Imperative.* *

Pro. 9: 6. *and go* in the way of understanding.

* PIEL.—*Preterite.* *

Gen 30:13. for the daughters *will call me blessed:*
Mal. 3:12. *And* all nations *shall call* you *blessed:*

PIEL.—*Imperative.*

Pro. 23:19. *and guide* thine heart in the way.
Isa. 1:17. seek judgment, *relieve* (marg. *righten*) the

PIEL.—*Future.*

Job 29:11. ear heard (me), *then it blessed me;*
Ps. 72:17. all nations *shall call him blessed.*
Pro. 4:14. *go* not in the way of evil (men).
31:28. children arise up, *and call her blessed;*
Cant. 6: 9. saw her, *and blessed her;*

PIEL.—*Participle.*

Isa. 3:12. *they which lead thee* (marg. *call thee blessed*)
9:16(15). For *the leaders of* this people (marg. *they that call them blessed*)
Mal. 3:15. now we *call* the proud *happy;*

* PUAL.—*Preterite.* *

Ps. 41: 2(3). (and) *he shall be blessed* upon the earth:

PUAL.—*Participle.*

Pro. 3:18. *happy* (is every one) that retaineth
Isa. 9:16(15). *and* (they that are) *led of them* (marg. *called blessed*)

---

834 **אֲשֶׁר** *ăsher*, part. relative.

Gen 1: 7. the waters *which* (were) under the firmament from the waters *which* (were) above
31. every thing *that* he had made,
2: 8. the man *whom* he had formed.
3:17. the tree, *of which* I commanded thee,
6: 4. *when* the sons of God
11: 7. *that* they may not understand
13:16. *so that* if a man can number
14:24. *that which* the young men have eaten,
17:14. *whose* flesh of his foreskin
18:17. Shall I hide from Abraham *that thing which*
19:21. this city, *for the which* thou hast spoken.
22:14. *as* it is said (to) this day,
24:15. *who* was born to Bethuel,
26:18. the names *by which* his father had called
27:41. the blessing *wherewith* his father blessed
28:15. in all (places) *whither* thou goest,
30:18. my hire, *because* I have given
31:32. With *whomsoever* thou findest thy gods,
49. And Mizpah; *for* he said,
38:10. And *the thing which* he did
42:21. We (are) verily guilty...*in that* we saw
49:28. *every* one according to his blessing
&c. &c.

With prefix, as **בַּאֲשֶׁר**.

Gen 39: 9. *because* thou (art) his wife:
Jud. 5:27. *where* he bowed, there he fell down dead.
1Sa. 23:13. and went *whithersoever* they could go.
2Ki. 8: 1. sojourn *wheresoever* thou canst sojourn:
Ecc. 3: 9. *in that wherein* he laboureth?
7: 2. *for* that (is) the end of all men;
Isa. 47:12. *wherein* thou hast laboured
&c. &c.

as **כַּאֲשֶׁר**.

Gen 7: 9. *as* God had commanded Noah.
12:11. it came to pass, *when* he was come
18:33. *as soon as* he had left
27: 4. savoury meat, *such as* I love,
43:14. *If* I be bereaved
44: 1. *as much as* they can carry,
Nu. 14:17. *according as* thou hast spoken,
Deu 4: 5. *even as* the Lord my God commanded
Jos. 24: 5. *according to that which* I did
Jud. 16:22. to grow again *after* he was shaven.
1Sa. 28:18. *Because* thou obeyedst not
Neh. 6: 3. *whilst* I leave it,
Ecc. 9: 2. All (things come) *alike* to all:
Isa. 11:16. *like as* it was to Israel
24: 2. *so with* the giver of usury to him.
29: 8. *as when* an hungry (man) dreameth,
51:13. *as if* he were ready to destroy?
Zec. 10: 6. they shall be *as though* I had not
&c. &c.

as **לַאֲשֶׁר**.

Gen 27: 8. *according to that which* I command
Ex. 16:16. every man *for* (them) *which* (are) in
Jud. 21: 5. *concerning him that* came not
1Sa. 30:27. *To* (them) *which* (were) in Beth-el,
&c. &c.

as **מֵאֲשֶׁר**.

Ex. 5:11. get you straw *where* ye can find it:
29:27. *of* (that) *which* (is) for Aaron,
Lev. 14:30. young pigeons, *such as* he can get;
Nu. 6:11. *for that* he sinned by the dead,
Jos. 10:11. *than* (they) *whom* the children of Israel
&c. &c.

as **וַאֲשֶׁר**.

Gen 7:23. *and they that* (were) with him in the ark.
Ex. 20: 4. *or that* (is) in the earth beneath, *or that*
&c. &c.

The meaning of **אֲשֶׁר** is often influenced by a preceding word; as,

I. preceded by **כֹּל**.

Gen 19:12. *whatsoever* thou hast in the city,
Jos. 1:16. *whithersoever* thou sendest us,
2:19. *whosoever* shall go out of the doors
Zep. 3: 7. *howsoever* I punished them:
&c. &c.

II. preceded by **לְמַעַן**.

Gen 18:19. For I know him, *that* he will command
Nu. 16:40(17:5). a memorial unto the children of Israel, *that* no stranger,
&c. &c.

III. preceded by **יַעַן**.

Gen 22:16. for *because* thou hast done this thing,
Deu 1:36. *because* he hath wholly followed
1Ki. 8:18. *Whereas* it was in thine heart
&c. &c.

IV. preceded by **עֵקֶב**.

Gen 22:18. *because* thou hast obeyed
2Sa. 12: 6. *because* he did this thing,

V. preceded by **בַּעֲבוּר**.

Gen 27:10. *and that* he may bless thee

VI. preceded by **עַד**.

Gen 27:44. *until* thy brother's fury turn away.
28:15. I will not leave thee, *until* I have done
&c. &c.

VII. preceded by **אֵת**.

Gen 30:29. Thou knowest *how* I have served thee, *and how* thy cattle was with me.
2Sa. 19:35(36). thy servant taste *what* I eat or *what* I

VIII. preceded by **מָה**.

Gen 38:18. *What* pledge shall I give thee?

IX. preceded by **עַל**.

Ex. 16: 5. it shall be twice *as much as* they gather
32:35. plagued the people, *because* they made

X. preceded by מִפְּנֵי.

Ex. 19:18. *because* the Lord descended
Jer. 44:23. *Because* ye have burned incense,

XI. preceded by אִישׁ.

Ex. 30:33. *Whosoever* compoundeth (any) like it,
38. *Whosoever* shall make like

XII. preceded by מִי.

Ex. 32:33. *Whosoever* hath sinned against me,

XIII. preceded by תַּחַת.

Nu. 25:13. he shall have it,...*because* he was zealous
Deu 21:14. *because* thou hast humbled her.
28:62. *whereas* ye were as the stars

XIV. preceded by עַל דְּבַר.

Deu 22:24. the damsel, *because* she cried not,
— the man, *because* he hath humbled

XV. preceded by אַחֲרֵי.

Jud. 11:36. *forasmuch as* the Lord hath taken
2Sa. 19:30(31). *forasmuch as* my lord the king is

XVI. preceded by בְּשֶׁל.

Ecc. 8:17. *because though* a man labour

אֲשֶׁר is sometimes combined with a following word in translation; as

I. שָׁם.

Gen 2:11. the whole land of Havilah, *where* (there is)
Deu 12: 2. the places, *wherein* the nations
1Ki. 18:10. *whither* my lord hath not sent
&c. &c.

II. שָׁמָּה.

Deu 11: 8. the land, *whither* ye go
&c. &c.

III. מִשָּׁם.

Jos. 20: 6. unto the city *from whence* he fled.
&c. &c.

Also, with pronominal suffixes to a following word, it forms the different cases of the relative; as

Gen 1:11. *whose* seed (is) in itself,
44:16. with *whom* the cup is found.
Ex. 35:29. every man and woman, *whose* heart
Nu. 5: 3. in the midst *whereof* I dwell.
Deu 8: 9. a land, *whose* stones (are) iron,
&c. &c.

Followed by אֹתוֹ &c., as

Ex. 6: 5. *whom* the Egyptians keep in bondage;
35:21. every one *whom* his spirit made willing,
Lev. 18: 5. judgments: *which* if a man do,
&c. &c.

אֲשֶׁר is very frequently followed by a preposition with a pronominal suffix, and it is generally combined with it in sense; thus,

Followed by בּוֹ.

Gen 7:15. *wherein* (is) the breath of life.
41:38. a man *in whom* the Spirit of God (is)?

Followed by עָלָיו.

Ex. 3: 5. the place *whereon* thou standest

Followed by לָהֶם.

Ex. 6:26. Aaron and Moses, *to whom* the Lord said,

It is similarly combined with בְּתוֹכוֹ, מִמֶּנּוּ, מֵהֶם, מִפְּנֵיהֶם, &c.—the pronominal suffixes varying.

---

838 אַשֻּׁר *ash-shoor'*, f.

Job 31: 7. If *my step* hath turned
Ps. 17:11. compassed us in *our steps:*

אֲשֻׁר *ăshoor*, f. 838-39

Job 23:11. My foot hath held *his steps,*
Ps. 17: 5. Hold up *my goings* in thy paths,
37:31. none of *his steps* (marg. *goings*) shall slide.
40: 2(3). established *my goings.*
44:18(19). neither have *our steps* (marg. *goings*)
73: 2. *my steps* had well nigh slipped.
Pro. 14:15. looketh well *to his going.*
Eze. 27: 6. *the Ashurites* have made (prob. id. q. תְּאַשּׁוּר)

אֹשֶׁר [*ōh'-sher*], m. 837

Gen 30:13. Leah said, *Happy am I,* (marg. *In my happiness*)

אֲשֵׁרָה & אֲשֵׁירָה *ăshēh-rāh'*, f. 842

Ex. 34:13. their images, and cut down *their groves:*
Deu 7: 5. *and* cut down *their groves,*
12: 3. *and* burn *their groves*
16:21. Thou shalt not plant thee *a grove*
Jud. 3: 7. served Baalim and *the groves.*
6:25. cut down *the grove* that (is) by
26. with the wood of *the grove*
28. *and the grove* was cut down
30. he hath cut down *the grove*
1Ki. 14:15. they have made *their groves,*
23. *and groves,* on every high hill,
15:13. she had made an idol *in a grove;*
16:33. Ahab made *a grove;*
18:19. the prophets of *the groves*
2Ki. 13: 6. there remained *the grove*
17:10. *and groves* in every high hill,
16. and made *a grove,*
18: 4. cut down *the groves,*
21: 3. and made *a grove,* as did Ahab
7. set a graven image of *the grove*
23: 4. for Baal, *and for the grove,*
6. he brought out *the grove*
7. wove hangings *for the grove.*
14. the images, and cut down *the groves,*
15. burned *the grove.*
2Ch 14: 3(2). cut down *the groves:*
15:16. she had made an idol *in a grove:*
17: 6. took away the high places and *groves*
19: 3. thou hast taken away *the groves*
24:18. served *groves* and idols:
31: 1. cut down *the groves,*
33: 3. and made *groves,* and worshipped
19. set up *groves* and graven images,
34: 3,4. *and the groves,* and the carved images,
7. the altars and *the groves,*
Isa. 17: 8. *either the groves,* or the images.
27: 9. *the groves* and images shall not
Jer. 17: 2. their altars *and their groves*
Mic. 5:14(13). I will pluck up *thy groves*

אַשְׁרֵי *ash-rey'*, m. pl. const. 835

Deu 33:29. *Happy* (art) *thou,* O Israel:
1Ki. 10: 8. *Happy* (are) thy men, *happy* (are) these
2Ch 9: 7. *Happy* (are) thy men, *and happy* (are)
Job 5:17. *happy* (is) the man whom God
Ps. 1: 1. *Blessed* (is) the man that
2:12. *Blessed* (are) all they
32: 1. *Blessed* (is he whose) transgression
2. *Blessed* (is) the man unto whom
33:12. *Blessed* (is) the nation whose God
34: 8(9). *blessed* (is) the man (that) trusteth
40: 4(5). *Blessed* (is) that man that maketh
41: 1(2). *Blessed* (is) he that considereth
65: 4(5). *Blessed* (is the man whom) thou
84: 4(5). *Blessed* (are) they that dwell
5(6). *Blessed* (is) the man whose strength
12(13). *blessed* (is) the man that trusteth
89:15(16). *Blessed* (is) the people that know
94:12. *Blessed* (is) the man whom thou
106: 3. *Blessed* (are) they that keep
112: 1. *Blessed* (is) the man (that) feareth
119: 1. *Blessed* (are) the undefiled
2. *Blessed* (are) they that keep

Ps.127: 5. *Happy* (is) the man that hath
128: 1. *Blessed* (is) every one that feareth
2. *happy* (shalt) *thou* (be),
137: 8. *happy* (shall he be), that rewardeth
9. *Happy* (shall he be), that taketh
144:15,15. *Happy* (is that) people,
146: 5. *Happy* (is he) that (hath) the God
Pro. 3:13. *Happy* (is) the man (that) findeth
8:32. *for blessed* (are they that) keep
34. *Blessed* (is) the man that
14:21. hath mercy on the poor, *happy* (is) *he*.
16:20. trusteth in the Lord, *happy* (is) *he*.
20: 7. his children (are) *blessed* after him.
28:14. *Happy* (is) the man that feareth
29:18. he that keepeth the law, *happy* (is) *he*.
Ecc.10:17. *Blessed* (art) *thou*, O land,
Isa. 30:18. *blessed* (are) all they that wait
32:20. *Blessed* (are) *ye* that sow
56: 2. *Blessed* (is) the man (that) doeth
Dan12:12. *Blessed* (is) he that waiteth,

---

846 אֻשַּׁרְנָא *oosh-shar-nāh'*, Ch. m.

Ezr. 5: 3. this house, *and* to make up this *wall?*
9. this house, *and* to make up these *walls?*

See 376 אֲשַׁשׁ see אִישׁ·

See 802 אֵשֶׁת see אִשָּׁה·

---

849 אֶשְׁתַּדּוּר *esh-tad-door'*, Ch. m.

Ezr. 4:15. *and* that they have moved *sedition*
19. and (that) rebellion *and sedition*

---

859 אַתְּ *at*, particle. f. pron.

Gen24:23. Whose daughter (art) *thou?*
60. *Thou* (art) our sister,
39: 9. because *thou* (art) his wife:
&c. &c.

853-54 אֵת *ēhth*, particle.

N.B. The place of אֵת (when nothing is given in the English as its meaning) is marked thus,)(.

Gen 1: 1. In the beginning God created)(the heaven *and*)(the earth.
4. And God saw)(the light,
4: 1. And Adam knew)(Eve his wife; and she conceived, and bare)(Cain, and said, I have gotten a man *from* the Lord.
5:22. Enoch walked *with* God after he begat)(M.
6:13. I will destroy them *with* the earth.
14. rooms shalt thou make *in* the ark,
13: 5. Lot also, which went *with* Abram,
14: 2. (these) made war *with* Bera
4. Twelve years they served)(Chedorlaomer,
19:13. For we will destroy)(this place, because the cry of them is waxen great *before*
37:23. they stript)(Joseph *out of* his coat,
49:25. *and by* the Almighty,
Ex. 39: 3. And they did beat the gold *into* thin
Lev. 5: 7. he shall bring *for* his trespass,
Jud. 1:16. they went and dwelt *among* the people.
1Ki.16:22. prevailed *against* the people
1Ch 2:18. Caleb...begat (children) *of* Azubah (his)
Isa. 1: 4. they have forsaken)(the Lord, they have provoked)(the Holy One
6: 1. I saw also)(the Lord sitting upon a
— his train filled)(the temple.
7:12. neither will I tempt)(the Lord.
19: 4. And)(the Egyptians will I give over
&c. &c. *passim.*

With pronominal suffixes;

I. אֹתָךְ, אֹתְךָ, אֹתִי, אֶתְהֶן, אֶתְהֶם, אֶתְכֶם
אֹתָם, אוֹתְכֶם, אֹתָנוּ, אֹתָהּ, אֹתוֹ, &c.

Gen47:23. I have bought *you* this day
Ex. 18:20. And thou shalt teach *them*
Lev.14:40. cast *them* into an unclean place
Nu. 14:22. have tempted *me* now these
Deu 9:14. I will make of *thee* a nation
Jos. 14:12. if so be the Lord (will be) *with me*,
1Ki.20:25. we will fight *against them* in the plain,
Eze. 3:27. when I speak *with thee*,
Zec. 6: 8. Then cried he *upon me*,
&c. &c.

II. אִתָּנוּ, אִתָּהּ, אִתּוֹ, אִתָּךְ, אִתְּךָ, אִתִּי,
אִתָּם, אִתְּכֶם.

Gen 14:24. the men which went *with me*,
26:24. fear not, for I (am) *with thee*,
34: 6. unto Jacob to commune *with him*.
21. These men (are) peaceable *with us;*
42:16. whether (there be any) truth *in you:*
43:16. Joseph saw Benjamin *with them*,
Lev. 6: 4(5:23). that which was delivered *him* to
Jud.11:27. thou doest *me* wrong to war
&c. &c.

אֵת [*ēhth*] m. 855

1Sa.13:20. his share, and *his coulter*,
21. *and for the coulters*,
Isa. 2: 4. beat their swords *into plowshares*,
Joel 3:10(4:10). Beat *your plowshares* into
Mic. 4: 3. beat their swords *into plowshares*,

אָתָה & אָתָא, *āh-thāh'*. 857

* KAL.—*Preterite.* *

Deu33: 2. *and he came* with ten thousands
Isa. 21:12. The morning *cometh*,
Jer. 3:22. *we come* unto thee;

KAL.—*Imperative.*

Isa. 21:12. enquire ye: return, *come*.
56: 9. All ye beasts of the field, *come*
12. *Come* ye, (say they), I will fetch wine,

KAL.—*Future.*

Deu33:21. *and he came* with the heads
Job 3:25. which I greatly feared *is come upon me*,
16:22. When a few years *are come*,
30:14. *They came* (upon me) as a wide
37:22. Fair weather *cometh* out of
Ps. 68:31(32). Princes *shall come* out of Egypt;
Pro. 1:27. destruction *cometh* as a whirlwind;
Isa. 41: 5. drew near, *and came*.
25. from the north, *and he shall come:*
Mic 4: 8. unto thee *shall it come*,

KAL.—*Participle.* Pöel.

Isa. 41:23. Shew *the things that are to come*
44: 7. *and the things that are coming*,
45:11. Ask me of *things to come*

* HIPHIL.—*Preterite.* *

Isa. 21:14. *brought* water to him that was thirsty. (marg. *bring ye*)

HIPHIL.—*Imperative.*

Jer. 12: 9. beasts of the field, *come* to devour. (marg. *cause them to come*)

אֲתָה & אֲתָא *ăthāh*, Ch. 858

* P'AL.—*Preterite.* *

Ezr. 4:12. *are come* unto Jerusalem,
5: 3. At the same time *came* to them Tatnai,
16. Then *came* the same Sheshbazzar,
Dan 7:22. Until the Ancient of days *came*,

P'AL.—*Infinitive.*

Dan 3: 2. *to come* to the dedication of the image

P'AL.—*Imperative.*

Dan 3:26. come forth, *and come* (hither).

P'AL.—*Participle.*

Dan 7:13. (one) like the Son of man *came* with the

* APHEL.—*Preterite.* *

Dan 5: 3. Then *they brought* the golden vessels

Dan 5:13. my father *brought out* of Jewry?
23. and *they have brought* the vessels
6:16(17). *and they brought* Daniel, and cast (him)
24(25). and *they brought* those men which

APHEL.—*Infinitive.*

Dan 3:13. Nebuchadnezzar in (his) rage and fury commanded *to bring*
5: 2. commanded *to bring* the golden and

* HOPHAL.—*Preterite.* *

Dan 3:13. Then *they brought* these men before the
6:17(18). *And* a stone *was brought*, and laid

---

859 **אַתָּה**, *at-tāh'*, particle. m. pron.

Gen 3:14. *thou* (art) cursed above all cattle,
19. for dust *thou* (art), and unto dust
6:18. thou shalt come into the ark, *thou*, and
&c. &c.

---

860 **אָתוֹן**, *āh-thōhn'*, f.

Gen 12:16. *and she asses*, and camels.
32:15(16). twenty *she asses*,
45:23. ten *she asses* laden with
49:11. *his ass*'s colt unto the choice
Nu. 22:21. and saddled *his ass*,
22. Now he was riding upon *his ass*,
23, 25, 27. *the ass* saw the angel of the Lord
— *the ass* turned aside
— Balaam smote *the ass*,
27. he smote *the ass* with a staff.
28. the Lord opened the mouth of *the ass*,
29. Balaam said *unto the ass*,
30. *the ass* said unto Balaam, (Am) not I *thine ass*,
32. Wherefore hast thou smitten *thine ass*
33. And *the ass* saw me,
Jud. 5:10. that ride on white *asses*,
1Sa. 9: 3. And *the asses* of Kish
— arise, go seek *the asses*.
5. leave (caring) for *the asses*,
20. *And as for* thine *asses* that were lost
10: 2. *The asses* which thou wentest to seek
— hath left the care of *the asses*,
14. To seek *the asses*:
16. He told us plainly that *the asses*
2Ki. 4:22. and one of *the asses*,
24. Then she saddled *an ass*,
1Ch 27:30. and over *the asses*
Job 1: 3. five hundred *she asses*,
14. *and the asses* feeding beside
42:12. a thousand *she asses*.
Zec 9: 9. upon a colt the foal of *an ass*.

---

861 **אַתּוּן** *at-toon'*, Ch. c.

Dan 3: 6, 11, 15. into the midst of *a* burning fiery *furnace*.
17. deliver us from *the* burning fiery *furnace*,
19. heat *the furnace* one seven times more
20. (and) to cast (them) *into the* burning fiery *furnace*.
21, 23. the midst of *the* burning fiery *furnace*.
22. *and the furnace* exceeding hot,
26. to the mouth of *the* burning fiery *furnace*,

---

862 **אַתּוּק** *at-took'*, m.

Eze. 41:15. (כתיב) *and the galleries thereof* on the one side and (marg. *several walks*, or, *walks with pillars*)

See 859 **אַתִּי** *at-ti'* (כתיב for אַתְּ).

---

852 **אָתִין** *āh-theen'*, Ch. m. pl.

Dan. 4: 2(3:32). I thought it good to shew *the signs*
Dan 4: 3(3:33). How great (are) *his signs!*
6:27(28). he worketh *signs* and wonders in

אַתִּיק *at-teek'*, m. 862

Eze. 41:15. *and the galleries thereof* on the one side (marg. *several walks*, or, *walks with pillars*)
16. *and the galleries* round about
42: 3. *gallery* against *gallery*
5. *the galleries* were higher than

אַתֶּם *at-tem'*, particle. m. pl. pron. 859

Gen 29: 4. My brethren, whence (be) *ye?*
42: 9. said unto them, *Ye* (are) spies;
19. If *ye* (be) true (men),
&c. &c.

אֶתְמוֹל & אֶתְמוּל *eth-mōhl'* & *eth-mool'*. 865

1Sa. 4: 7. hath not been such a thing heretofore. (marg. *yesterday*, or the third day)
10:11. when all that knew him beforetime (lit. *from yesterday* the third day)
14:21. with the Philistines before that time, (lit. *as yesterday* the third day)
19: 7. he was in his presence, *as* in times past. (marg. *as yesterday*, third day)
2Sa. 5: 2. Also in time past, (lit. also *yesterday* also the third day)
Ps. 90: 4. in thy sight (are but) as *yester*day (lit. the day of *yesterday*)
Isa. 30:33. Tophet (is) ordained *of old;* (marg. *from yesterday*)
Mic. 2: 8. *Even of late* my people is risen (marg. *yesterday*)

אַתֵּן see **אִיתָן**· See 386

אַתֵּן & אַתֵּנָה *at-tēhn'* & *at-tēh-nāh'*, 859
particles. f. pl. pron.

Gen 31: 6. *And ye* know that with all my power
Eze. 13:11. *and ye*, O great hailstones, shall fall;
20. wherewith *ye* there hunt the souls
34:17. *And* (as for) *you*, O my flock,
31. *And ye* my flock,

אֶתְנָה *eth-nāh'*, f. 866

Hos 2:12(14). These (are) my *rewards* that my

אֶתְנַן & אֶתְנָן *eth-nāhn'* & *eth-nan'*, m. 868

Deu 23:18(19). shalt not bring *the hire of* a whore,
Isa. 23:17. Tyre, and she shall turn *to her hire*,
18. *and her hire* shall be holiness to the Lord:
Eze. 16:31. in that thou scornest *hire;*
34. in that thou givest *a reward, and* no *reward* is given unto thee,
41. thou also shalt give no *hire* any more.
Hos 9: 1. thou hast loved *a reward*
Mic. 1: 7. all *the hires thereof* shall be
— she gathered (it) *of the hire of* an harlot, and they shall return to *the hire* of an harlot.

אֲתַר *ăthar*, Ch. m. 870

Ezr. 5:15. let the house of God be builded in *his place*.
6: 3. *the place* where they offered sacrifices,
5. (every one) *to his place*, and place (them
7. build this house of God in *his place*.
Dan 2:35. that no *place* was found for them:
39. *And after thee* shall arise

Dan 7: 6. *After* this I beheld, and lo another,
7. *After* this I saw in the night visions,

871 אֲתָרִים *ăthăh-reem'*, m. pl.

Nu.21: 1. Israel came by the way of *the spies;*

ב *bēhth*,

The second letter of the Alphabet.

872 בִּאָה *bee-āh'*, f.

Eze. 8: 5. this image of jealousy *in the entry.*

873 בְּאוּשׁ *bee-oosh'*, Ch. adj.

Ezr. 4:12. building the rebellious *and* the *bad* city,

874 בָּאַר [*bāh-ar'*]

* PIEL.—*Infinitive.* *

Deu 1: 5. began Moses *to declare* this law,

PIEL.—*Imperative.*

Deu 27: 8. all the words of this law very *plainly.* (lit. *declare* well)
Hab 2: 2. *and make* (*it*) *plain* upon tables,

875 בְּאֵר *b'ēhr*, f.

Gen14.10. Siddim (was full of) slime*pits;* (lit. *pits pits*)
16:14. *the well* was called *Beer*-lahai-roi;
21:19. she saw *a well of* water;
25. because of *a well of* water,
30. that I have digged this *well.*
24:11. by *a well of* water
20. ran again unto *the well*
26:15. For all *the wells* which his
18. Isaac digged again *the wells of* water,
19. found there *a well of* springing water.
20. called the name of *the well* Esek;
21. they digged another *well,*
22. digged another *well;*
25. Isaac's servants digged *a well.*
32. told him concerning *the well*
29: 2. behold *a well* in the field,
— for out of that *well*
—, 3. upon *the well*'s mouth.
3, 8, 10. from *the well*'s mouth,
Ex. 2:15. he sat down by *a well.*
Nu. 20:17. the water of *the wells:*
21:16. from thence (they went) *to Beer:* that (is) *the well* whereof the Lord spake
17. Spring up, *O well;* sing ye unto it:
18. The princes digged *the well,*
22. the waters of *the well:*
2Sa.17:18. which had *a well* in his court;
19. a covering over *the well*'s mouth,
21. they came up *out of the well,*
Ps. 55:23(24). them down *into the pit of* destruction:
69:15(16). let not *the pit* shut her mouth
Pro. 5:15. waters out of *thine own well.*
23:27. *and* a strange woman (is) *a* narrow *pit.*
Cant.4:15. *a well of* living waters,

877 בֹּאר *bōhr*, m. (i. q. בּוֹר)

Jer. 2:13. hewed them out *cisterns*, broken *cisterns,*

887 בָּאַשׁ *bāh-ash'.*

* KAL.—*Preterite.* *

Ex. 7:18. *and* the river *shall stink;*

KAL.—*Future.*

Ex. 7:21. *and* the river *stank,*
Ex. 8:14(10). *and* the land *stank.*
16:20. it bred worms, *and stank:*
Isa. 50: 2. their fish *stinketh,*

* NIPHAL.—*Preterite.* *

1Sa.13: 4. Israel also *was had in abomination* (marg. *did stink*)
2Sa.10: 6. Ammon saw that *they stank*
16:21. *thou art abhorred* of thy father:

* HIPHIL.—*Preterite.* *

Ex. 5:21. *ye have made* our savour *to be abhorred* (marg. *to stink*)
16:24. and it *did* not *stink,*
1Sa.27:12. *He hath made* his people Israel utterly *to abhor him;* (marg. *to stink*)
Ps. 38: 5(6). My wounds *stink*

HIPHIL.—*Infinitive.*

Gen34:30. troubled me *to make me to stink*
1Sa.27:12. He hath made his people Israel *utterly* to abhor him; (lit. *in making* himself *stink,* he hath made himself stink)

HIPHIL.—*Future.*

Pro.13: 5. a wicked (man) *is loathsome,* and cometh
Ecc.10: 1. *cause* the ointment of the apothecary to send forth *a stinking savour:*

* HITHPAEL.—*Preterite.* *

1Ch19: 6. saw that *they had made themselves odious* (marg. *to stink*)

בְּאֵשׁ *b'ēhsh*, Ch. 888

P'AL.—*Preterite.*

Dan 6:14(15). *was* sore *displeased* with himself,

בְּאשׁ *b'ōhsh*, m. 889

Isa. 34: 3. *their stink* shall come up
Joel 2:20. *his stink* shall come up,
Am. 4:10. made *the stink of* your camps

בָּאְשָׁה *bo-shāh'*, f. 890

Job 31:40. *cockle* instead of (marg. *noisome weeds*)

בְּאֻשִׁים *b'oo-sheem'*, m. pl. 891

Isa. 5: 2. it brought forth *wild grapes.*
4. brought it forth *wild grapes?*

בְּאַתַר see אֲתַר See 870

בָּבָה [*bāh-vāh'*,] f. 892

Zec. 2: 8(12). toucheth *the apple of* his eye.

בָּג *bāhg*, m. (כתיב) 897

Eze.25: 7. will deliver thee *for a spoil* (marg. *meat,* following the כתיב)

בָּגַד *bāh-gad'.* 898

* KAL.—*Preterite.* *

1Sa.14:33. he said, *Ye have transgressed:*
Job 6:15. My brethren *have dealt deceitfully*
Ps. 73:15. *I should offend* (against) the
Isa. 24:16. *have dealt treacherously,*
— *have dealt* very *treacherously.*
33: 1. *they dealt* not *treacherously*
Jer. 3:20. a wife *treacherously departeth*
— *ye dealt treacherously* with me,
5:11. *have dealt* very *treacherously*
12: 6. *they have dealt treacherously*

Lam 1: 2. *have dealt treacherously*
Hos 5: 7. They *have dealt treacherously*
6: 7. *have they dealt treacherously* against me.
Mal 2:11. Judah *hath dealt treacherously*,
14. *thou hast dealt treacherously:*

KAL.—*Infinitive.*

Ex. 21: 8. *seeing he hath dealt deceitfully* with her.
Isa. 33: 1. an end *to deal treacherously*,
48: 8. thou wouldest deal *very* treacherously, (lit. *dealing treacherously* wouldest, &c.)
Jer. 5:11. have dealt *very treacherously* against me,

KAL.—*Future.*

Jud. 9:23. *and* the men of Shechem *dealt treacherously*
Ps. 78:57. *and dealt unfaithfully* like their fathers:
Isa. 33: 1. *they shall deal treacherously* with thee.
48: 8. *wouldest deal* very *treacherously*,
Mal 2:10. why *do we deal treacherously*
15. *let* none *deal treacherously* (marg. *unfaithfully*)
16. *ye deal* not *treacherously.*

KAL.—*Participle.* Poel.

Ps. 25: 3. *which transgress* without cause.
59: 5(6). to any wicked *transgressors.*
119:158. I beheld *the transgressors*,
Pro. 2:22. *and the transgressors* shall be
11: 3. the perverseness of *transgressors*
6. *transgressors* shall be taken
13: 2. the soul of *the transgressors* (shall eat) violence.
15. the way of *transgressors* (is) hard.
21:18. *the transgressor* for the upright.
22:12. the words of *the transgressor.*
23:28. *and* increaseth *the transgressors*
25:19. Confidence in *an unfaithful man*
Isa. 21: 2. *the treacherous dealer dealeth treacherously*,
24:16, 16. *the treacherous dealers* have dealt
33: 1. *and dealest treacherously*,
Jer. 3: 8. yet her *treacherous* sister Judah
11. *more than treacherous* Judah.
9: 2(1). an assembly of *treacherous men.*
12: 1. *that deal* very *treacherously?*
Hab 1:13. upon *them that deal treacherously*,
2: 5. *he transgresseth* (lit. is *transgressing*)

---

899 ## בֶּגֶד *beh'-ged*, m.

Gen 24:53. jewels of gold, *and raiment*,
27:15. Rebekah took goodly *raiment*
27. smelled the smell of *his raiment*,
28:20. *and raiment* to put on,
37:29. he rent *his clothes.*
38:14. she put her widow's *garments*
19. put on *the garments of* her widowhood.
39:12. she caught him *by his garment*,
— he left *his garment* in her hand,
13. saw that he had left *his garment*
15. that he left *his garment*
16. she laid up *his garment* by her,
18. he left *his garment* with me,
41:42. arrayed him in *vestures of* fine linen,
Ex. 28: 2. thou shalt make holy *garments*
3. that they may make Aaron's *garments*
4. these (are) *the garments*
— they shall make holy *garments*
29: 5. thou shalt take *the garments*,
21. and upon *his garments*, and upon his sons, and upon *the garments of* his sons
— he shall be hallowed, *and his garments*, and his sons, *and* his sons' *garments* with
29. *And the* holy *garments*
31:10. *the cloths of* service, and *the* holy *garments* for Aaron the priest, and *the garments of*
35:19. *The cloths of* service, to do
— *the* holy *garments* for Aaron the priest, and *the garments of* his sons,
21. *and for the* holy *garments.*.
39: 1. they made *cloths of* service,
— made *the* holy *garments*
41. *The cloths of* service
— *the* holy *garments* for Aaron the priest, and his sons' *garments*,
40:13. put upon Aaron *the* holy *garments*,

Lev. 6:11(4). he shall put off *his garments*, and put on other *garments*,
27(20). thereof upon any *garment*,
8: 2. *the garments*, and the anointing oil,
30. upon *his garments*, and upon his sons, and upon his sons' *garments*
— Aaron, (and) *his garments*, and his sons, and his sons' *garments* with him.
10: 6. *neither* rend *your clothes;*
11:25, 28, 40, 40. shall wash *his clothes*,
32. any vessel of wood, or *raiment*,
13: 6, 34. he shall wash *his clothes*,
45. *his clothes* shall be rent,
47. *The garment also* that the plague of leprosy is in, (whether it be) *a* woollen *garment*, or *a* linen *garment;*
49. or reddish *in the garment*,
51. be spread *in the garment*,
52. shall therefore burn *that garment*,
53. be not spread *in the garment*,
56. he shall rend it out of *the garment*,
57. if it appear still *in the garment*,
58. *And the garment*, either warp,
59. in *a garment* of woollen or linen,
14: 8. shall wash *his clothes*,
9. he shall wash *his clothes*,
47,47. shall wash *his clothes;*
55. for the leprosy of *a garment*,
15: 5, 6, 7, 10, 21, 22. shall wash *his clothes*,
8, 11, 13, 27. wash *his clothes*, and bathe
17. And every *garment*,
16: 4. these (are) holy *garments;*
23. shall put off *the* linen *garments*,
24. put on *his garments*,
26, 28. shall wash *his clothes*,
32. shall put on *the* linen *clothes*, (even) *the* holy *garments:*
17:15. he shall both wash *his clothes*,
19:19. *neither* shall *a garment*
21:10. is consecrated to put on *the garments*,
— *nor* rend *his clothes;*
Nu. 4: 6. over (it) *a cloth* wholly of blue,
7, 11. they shall spread *a cloth of* blue,
8. upon them *a cloth of* scarlet,
9. they shall take *a cloth* of blue,
12. put (them) in *a cloth of* blue,
13. spread *a* purple *cloth* thereon:
8: 7. let them wash *their clothes*,
21. they washed *their clothes;*
14: 6. that searched the land, rent *their clothes:*
15:38. in the borders of *their garments*
19: 7. Then the priest shall wash *his clothes*,
8. he that burneth her shall wash *his clothes*
10. shall wash *his clothes*, and be
19. and wash *his clothes*,
21. water of separation shall wash *his clothes;*
20:26. strip Aaron of *his garments*,
28. Moses stripped Aaron of *his garments*,
31:20. purify all (your) *raiment*,
24. ye shall wash *your clothes*
Deu 24:17. nor take the widow's *raiment*
Jud. 8:26. *and* purple *raiment*
11:35. that he rent *his clothes*,
14:12,13. thirty change of *garments:*
17:10. and a suit of *apparel*, (marg. an order of *garments*, or, a double *suit*)
1Sa. 19:13. covered (it) *with a cloth.*
24. he stripped off *his clothes*
27: 9. the camels, *and the apparel*,
28: 8. put on other *raiment*,
2Sa. 1: 2. *with his clothes* rent,
11. David took hold *on his clothes*,
3:31. Rend *your clothes*,
13:31. the king arose, and tare *his garments*,
— stood by with their *clothes* rent.
14: 2. put on now mourning *apparel*,
19:24(25). nor washed *his clothes*,
20:12. cast *a cloth* upon him,
1K. 1: 1. they covered him *with clothes*,
21:27. that he rent *his clothes*,
22:10. having put on (their) *robes*,
30. but put thou on *thy robes.*
2K. 2:12. he took hold *of his own clothes*,
4:39. wild gourds *his lap* full,
5: 5. ten changes of *raiment.*
7. that he rent *his clothes*,
8. the king of Israel had rent *his clothes*,

2K. 5: 8. hast thou rent *thy clothes?*
22,23. two changes of *garments.*
26. to receive *garments,*
6:30. that he rent *his clothes;*
7: 8. thence silver, and gold, *and raiment,*
15. all the way (was) full of *garments*
9:13. took every man *his garment,*
11:14. Athaliah rent *her clothes,*
18:37. with (their) *clothes* rent,
19: 1 & 22:11. that he rent *his clothes,*
22:14. keeper of *the wardrobe;* (marg. *garments*)
19. hast rent *thy clothes,*
25:29. changed his prison *garments:*
2Ch 18: 9. clothed in (their) *robes,*
29. but put thou on *thy robes.*
23:13. Athaliah rent *her clothes,*
34:19. that he rent *his clothes.*
22. keeper of *the wardrobe;* (marg. *garments*)
27. didst rend *thy clothes,*
Ezr. 9: 3. I rent *my garment* and my mantle,
5. having rent *my garment*
Neh. 4:23(17). none of us put off *our clothes,*
Est. 4: 1. Mordecai rent *his clothes,*
4. she sent *raiment* to clothe
Job 13:28. *as a garment* that is moth eaten.
22: 6. *and* stripped the naked of their *clothing.*
37:17. How *thy garments* (are) warm,
Ps. 22:18(19). They part *my garments*
45: 8(9). All *thy garments* (smell) of
102:26(27). shall wax old *like a garment;*
109:19. Let it be unto him *as the garment*
Pro. 6:27. *and his clothes* not be burned?
20:16. Take *his garment* that is surety
25:20. he that taketh away *a garment*
27:13. Take *his garment* that is surety
Ecc. 9: 8. Let *thy garments* be always
Isa. 24:16. *yea,* the treacherous dealers have dealt *very* treacherously. (lit. deceived *deceit*)
36:22. to Hezekiah with (their) *clothes* rent,
37: 1. that he rent his *clothes,*
50: 9. they all shall wax old *as a garment;*
51: 6. the earth shall wax old *like a garment,*
8. shall eat them up *like a garment,*
52: 1. put on thy beautiful *garments,*
59: 6. Their webs shall not become *garments,* (lit. *for a garment*)
17. he put on the *garments of*
61:10. clothed me with the *garments of*
63: 1. with dyed *garments* from Bozrah?
2. *and thy garments* like him
3. shall be sprinkled upon *my garments,*
64: 6(5). *and* all our righteousnesses (are) *as* filthy *rags;*
Jer. 12: 1. *very* treacherously? (lit. deceiving *deceit*)
36:24. afraid, nor rent *their garments,*
41: 5. and their *clothes* rent,
43:12. as a shepherd putteth on *his garment;*
52:33. changed his prison *garments:*
Eze. 16:16. *of thy garments* thou didst
18. tookest thy broidered *garments,*
39. strip thee also of *thy clothes,*
18: 7. covered the naked with *a garment;*
16. covered the naked with *a garment,*
23:26. strip thee out of *thy clothes,*
26:16. put off their broidered *garments:*
27:20. *in* precious *clothes* for chariots.
42:14. there they shall lay *their garments*
— shall put on other *garments,*
44:17. shall be clothed with linen *garments;*
19. they shall put off *their garments*
— they shall put on other *garments;*
— the people *with their garments.*
Joel 2:13. and not *your garments,*
Am. 2: 8. lay (themselves) down upon *clothes*
Hag 2:12. flesh in the skirt of *his garment,*
Zec. 3: 3. was clothed with filthy *garments,*
4. Take away *the* filthy *garments*
5. clothed him with *garments.*
14:14. gold, and silver, *and apparel,*

---

900 **בֹּגְדוֹת** *bōh-g'dōhth',* f. pl.

Zep. 3: 4. light (and) *treacherous* persons: (lit. men of *treachery*)

בָּגוֹד *bāh-gōhd',* adj. 901

Jer. 3: 7,10. her *treacherous* sister Judah

בַּד *bad,* m. 905

Ex. 30:34. *of each* shall there be *a like* (weight): [בַּד בְּבַד]

In all other occurrences of בַּד in the singular, it is used with prefixes, as a part. adverbially.

I. לְבַד as,

Ex. 12:37. men, *beside* children.
Est. 4:11. *except* such to whom the king
Ecc. 7:29. Lo, this *only* have I found,
Zec. 12:12. mourn, every family *apart;*
&c. &c.

Also with suffixes, as לְבַדִּי &c.

Nu. 11:14. able to bear all this people *alone,*
Deu 1: 9. not able to bear you *myself alone:*
8: 3. man doth not live by bread *only,*
2Sa. 10: 8. *by themselves* in the field.
&c. &c.

II. מִלְּבַד.

Gen 26: 1. *beside* the first famine
Lev. 9:17. *beside* the burnt-sacrifice
&c. &c.

With suffix מִלְּבַדּוֹ.

Deu 4:35. none else *beside him.*

בַּדִּים pl. of the above.

Ex. 25:13. thou shalt make *staves* (of)
14. thou shalt put *the staves*
15. *The staves* shall be in the rings
27. for places *of the staves*
28. thou shalt make *the staves*
27: 6. thou shalt make *staves* for the altar, *staves* (of) shittim wood,
7. *the staves* shall be put (lit. *its staves*)
— *the staves* shall be upon
30: 4. *for the staves* to bear it
5. thou shalt make *the staves*
35:12. and *the staves thereof,*
13. table, and *his staves,*
15. the incense altar, and *his staves,*
16. *his staves,* and all his vessels,
37: 4. he made *staves* (of) shittim wood,
5. he put *the staves* into the rings
14. the places *for the staves*
15,28. he made *the staves* (of) shittim wood,
27. to be places *for the staves*
38: 5. places *for the staves.*
6. he made *the staves* (of) shittim wood,
7. he put *the staves* into the rings
39:35. *the staves thereof,*
39. *his staves,* and all his vessels,
40:20. set *the staves* on the ark,
Nu. 4: 6. shall put in *the staves thereof.*
8. shall put in *the staves thereof.*
11. shall put to *the staves thereof:*
14. put to *the staves of it.*
1K. 8: 7. *the staves thereof* above.
8. they drew out *the staves,* that the ends of *the staves* were seen
2Ch 5: 8. *the staves thereof* above.
9. they drew out *the staves* (of the ark), that the ends of *the staves* were seen
Job 17:16. They shall go down to *the bars of*
18:13. devour *the strength of* (marg. *bars*)
— death shall devour *his strength.*
Eze. 17: 6. brought forth *branches,*
19:14. is gone out of a rod of *her branches,*
Hos 11: 6. shall consume *his branches,*

בַּד *bad,* m. 907

Job 11: 3. *thy lies* make men hold (marg. *devices*).

Job 41:12(4). I will not conceal *his parts*,
Isa. 16: 6. *his lies* (shall) not (be) so.
44:25. frustrateth the tokens of *the liars*,
Jer. 48:30. *his lies* shall not so effect (it). (marg. *bars*; or, *those on whom he stayeth*)
50:36. A sword (is) upon *the liars*; (marg. *bars*, or, *chief stays*)

906 **בַּד** *bad*, m.

Ex. 28:42. thou shalt make them *linen* breeches
39:28. *linen* breeches (of) fine twined linen,
Lev 6:10(3). put on his *linen* garment, and his *linen*
16: 4. He shall put on the holy *linen* coat, and he shall have the *linen* breeches upon his flesh, and shall be girded with a *linen* girdle, and with the *linen* mitre
23. shall put off the *linen* garments,
32. shall put on the *linen* clothes,
1Sa. 2:18. girded with a *linen* ephod.
22:18. that did wear a *linen* ephod.
2Sa. 6:14. David (was) girded with a *linen* ephod.
1Ch 15:27. also (had) upon him an ephod of *linen*.
Eze. 9: 2. among them (was) clothed with *linen*,
3. called to the man clothed with *linen*,
11. the man clothed with *linen*,
10: 2,6. the man clothed with *linen*,
7. (him that was) clothed with *linen*:
Dan 10: 5. a certain man clothed in *linen*,
12: 6. said to the man clothed in *linen*,
7. I heard the man clothed in *linen*,

908 **בָּדָא** *bāh-dāh'*.

* KAL.—*Preterite*. *

1K. 12:33. in the month which *he had devised*

KAL.—*Participle*. Poel.

Neh 6: 8. but thou *feignest them*

909 **בָּדַד** [*bāh-dad'*].

* KAL.—*Participle*. Poel. *

Ps. 102: 7(8). am as a sparrow *alone*
Isa. 14:31. none (shall be) *alone*
Hos 8: 9. a wild ass *alone* by himself:

910 **בָּדָד** *bāh-dāhd'*, m.

Lev. 13:46. he shall dwell *alone*;
Nu. 23: 9. the people shall dwell *alone*,
Deu 32:12. the Lord *alone* did lead him,
33:28. Israel then shall dwell in safety *alone*:
Nu. 4: 8(9). for thou, Lord, *only* makest me dwell
Isa. 27:10. the defenced city (shall be) *desolate*,
Jer. 15:17. I sat *alone* because of thy hand:
49:31. (which) dwell *alone*.
Lam 1: 1. How doth the city sit *solitary*,
3:28. He sitteth *alone* and keepeth silence,
Mic 7:14. which dwell *solitarily* (in) the wood,

913 **בְּדִיל** *b'deel*, m.

Nu. 31:22. the brass, the iron, *the tin*,
Isa. 1:25. take away all *thy tin*:
Eze. 22:18. all they (are) brass, *and tin*,
20. brass, and iron, and lead, *and tin*,
27:12. with silver, iron, *tin*,
Zec. 4:10. shall see the plummet in the hand (marg. stone of *tin*)

914 **בָּדַל** [*bāh-dal'*],

* NIPHAL.—*Preterite*. *

1Ch 12: 8. *there separated themselves* unto David
Ezr. 9: 1. *have* not *separated themselves*

NIPHAL.—*Imperative*.

Nu. 16:21. *Separate yourselves*
Ezr. 10:11. *and separate yourselves*

NIPHAL.—*Future*.

1Ch 23:13. *and* Aaron *was separated*,
Ezr. 10: 8. and himself *separated*
16. *and* all of them by (their) names, *were separated*,
Neh 9: 2. *And* the seed of Israel *separated themselves*

NIPHAL.—*Participle*.

Ezr. 6:21. all such *as had separated themselves*
Neh 10:28(29). *that had separated themselves*

* HIPHIL.—*Preterite*. *

Ex. 26:33. *and* the vail *shall divide* unto you
Lev. 20:24. which *have separated* you
25. *Ye shall therefore put difference*
— which I *have separated*
Nu. 8:14. *Thus shalt thou separate*
16: 9. the God of Israel *hath separated*
Deu 10: 8. the Lord *separated* the tribe of Levi,
29:21(20). *And* the Lord *shall separate him*
1K. 8:53. For *thou didst separate them*
Eze. 22:26. *they have put* no *difference*

HIPHIL.—*Infinitive*.

Gen 1:14. *to divide* the day from the night:
18. *and to divide* the light
Lev. 10:10. *And that ye may put difference*
11:47. *To make a difference* between
Isa. 56: 3. The Lord hath *utterly separated* me (lit. *separating* hath separated)
Eze. 42:20. *to make a separation*

HIPHIL.—*Future*.

Gen 1: 4. *and* God *divided* the light
7. *and divided* the waters
Lev. 1:17 & 5:8. *shall* not *divide* (it) *asunder*:
20:26. *and have severed* you
Deu 4:41. Then Moses *severed* three cities
19: 2, 7. *Thou shalt separate* three cities for thee
1Ch 25: 1. *Moreover* David...*separated*
2Ch 25:10. *Then* Amaziah *separated them*,
Ezr. 8:24. *Then I separated* twelve
Neh 13: 3. *that they separated* from Israel
Isa. 56: 3. *hath* utterly *separated me*
Eze. 39:14. *they shall sever out* men

HIPHIL.—*Participle*.

Gen 1: 6. let it *divide* the waters
Isa. 59: 2. your iniquities *have separated*

בָּדָל *bāh-dāhl'*, m. 915

Am. 3:12. or *a piece of* an ear;

בְּדֹלַח *b'dōh-lag̣h'*, m. 916

Gen 2:12. there (is) *bdellium* and the onyx stone.
Nu. 11: 7. colour thereof as the colour of *bdellium*.

בָּדַק [*bāh-dak'*]. 918

* KAL.—*Infinitive*. *

2Ch 34:10. *to repair* and amend the house:

בֶּדֶק *beh'-dek*, m. 919

2K. 12: 5(6). let them repair *the breaches of* the house, wheresoever any *breach* shall be
6(7). not repaired *the breaches of* the house.
7(8). repair ye not *the breaches of* the house?
—(–). but deliver it *for the breaches of*
8(9). to repair *the breaches of* the house.
12(13). stone to repair *the breaches of*
22: 5. to repair *the breaches of* the house,
Eze. 27: 9, 27. *thy* calkers: (marg. stoppers of *chinks*)

בְּדַר [*b'dar*], Ch. 921

* PAEL.—*Preterite*. *

Dan 4:14(11). *and scatter* his fruit:

922 **בֹּהוּ** *bōh'-hoo*, m.

Gen 1: 2. without form *and void;*
Isa. 34:11. the stones of *emptiness.*
Jer. 4:23. without form *and void;*

---

923 **בַּהַט** *bah'-hat*, m.

Est. 1: 6. of *red*, and blue, and white, and black, marble. (marg. *porphyre*)

---

924 **בְּהִילוּ** *b'hee-loo'*, Ch. f.

Ezr. 4:23. they went up *in haste* to Jerusalem

---

925 **בָּהִיר** *bāh-heer'*, adj.

Job 37:21. now (men) see not the *bright* light

---

926 **בָּהַל** or **בָּהֵל** [*bāh-hal'* or *bāh-hēhl'*].

* NIPHAL.—*Preterite.* *

Gen45: 3. for *they were troubled* (marg. *terrified*)
Ex. 15:15. of Edom *shall be amazed;*
1Sa.28:21. saw that *he was* sore *troubled,*
2Sa. 4: 1. all the Israelites *were troubled.*
Job 21: 6. when I remember *I am afraid,*
Ps. 6: 2(3). for my bones *are vexed.*
3(4). My soul *is* also sore *vexed:*
48: 5(6). *they were troubled,* (and) hasted away.
90: 7. by thy wrath *are we troubled.*
Isa. 13: 8. *And they shall be afraid:* pangs
21: 3. *I was dismayed* at the seeing
Jer. 51:32. the men of war *are affrighted.*
Eze.26:18. *yea,* the isles that (are) in the sea *shall be troubled*

NIPHAL.—*Future.*

Jud.20:41. the men of Benjamin *were amazed:*
Job 4: 5. toucheth thee, *and thou art troubled.*
23:15. Therefore *am I troubled*
Ps. 6:10(11). be ashamed *and* sore *vexed:*
83:17(18). Let them be confounded *and troubled*
104:29. hidest thy face, *they are troubled:*
Ecc. 8: 3. *Be* not *hasty* to go out
Eze. 7:27. the people of the land *shall be troubled:*

NIPHAL.—*Participle.*

Ps. 30: 7(8). hide thy face, (and) I was *troubled.*
Pro.28:22. He *that hasteth* to be rich
Zep 1:18. make even a *speedy* riddance

* PIEL.—*Infinitive.* *

2Ch 32:18. *and to trouble them;*
35:21. God commanded me *to make haste:*

PIEL.—*Future.*

Est. 2: 9. *and he speedily gave* her
Job 22:10. *and* sudden fear *troubleth thee;*
Ps. 2: 5. *vex them* in his sore (marg. *trouble*)
83:15(16). and *make them afraid*
Ecc. 5: 2(1). *Be* not *rash* with thy mouth,
7: 9. *Be* not *hasty* in thy spirit
Dan 11:44. out of the north *shall trouble him:*

PIEL.—*Participle.*

Ezr. 4: 4. *and troubled* them in building,

* PUAL.—*Participle.* *

Est. 8:14. *being hastened* and pressed
Pro.20:21. inheritance (may be) *gotten hastily*

* HIPHIL.—*Preterite.* *

Job 23:16. the Almighty *troubleth me:*

HIPHIL.—*Future.*

2Ch.26:20. *and they thrust him out* from thence;
Est. 6:14. *and hasted* to bring Haman

---

927 **בְּהַל** [*b'hal*], Ch.

* PUAL.—*Future.* *

Dan 4: 5(2). the visions of my head *troubled me.*
Dan. 4:19(16). and his thoughts *troubled him.*
— (—) the interpretation thereof, *trouble thee*
5: 6. and his thoughts *troubled him,*
10. let not thy thoughts *trouble thee,*
7:15. and the visions of my head *troubled me.*
28. my cogitations much *troubled me,*

* ITHP'AL.—*Infinitive.* *

Dan. 2:25. brought in Daniel before the king *in haste,*
3:24. was astonied, and rose up *in haste,*
6:19(20). *and* went *in haste* unto the den of

ITHP'AL.—*Participle.*

Dan. 5: 9. was king Belshazzar greatly *troubled,*

בֶּהָלָה *beh-hāh-lāh'*, f. 928

Lev.26:16. will even appoint over you *terror,*
Ps. 78:33. their years *in trouble.*
Isa. 65:23. nor bring forth *for trouble;*
Jer. 15: 8. *and terrors* upon the city.

בְּהֵמָה *b'hēh-māh'*, f. 929-30

Gen 1:24. *cattle,* and creeping thing,
25. *cattle* after their kind,
26. *and over the cattle,* and over
2:20. Adam gave names to all *cattle,*
3:14. thou (art) cursed above all *cattle,*
6: 7. both man, and *beast,*
20. *cattle* after their kind,
7: 2. Of every clean *beast*
— of *beasts* that (are) not clean
8. Of clean *beasts,* and of *beasts* that (are) not clean,
14. all *the cattle* after their kind,
21. of fowl, *and of cattle,* and of beast,
23. both man, and *cattle,*
8: 1. all *the cattle* that (was) with him
17. of fowl, *and of cattle,*
20. took of every clean *beast,*
9:10. of the fowl, *of the cattle,*
34:23. every *beast of their's* (be) ours?
36: 6. and all *his beasts,*
47:18. hath our herds of *cattle;*
Ex. 8:17(13). became lice in man, *and in beast;*
18(14). lice upon man, *and upon beast.*
9: 9. blains upon man, and upon *beast,*
10. blains upon man, *and upon beast.*
19. every man *and beast*
22. upon man, and upon *beast,*
25. both man and *beast;*
11: 5. all the firstborn of *beasts.*
7. against man or *beast:*
12:12. both man and *beast;*
29. all the firstborn of *cattle.*
13: 2. of man *and of beast:*
12. that cometh of *a beast*
15. the firstborn of *beast:*
19:13. whether (it be) *beast* or man,
20:10. thy maidservant, *nor thy cattle,*
22:10(9). or an ox, or a sheep, or any *beast,*
19(18). Whosoever lieth with *a beast*
Lev. 1: 2. bring your offering of *the cattle,*
5: 2. or a carcase of unclean *cattle,*
7:21. or (any) unclean *beast,*
25. whosoever eateth the fat of *the beast,*
26. of fowl *or of beast,*
11: 2. all *the beasts* that (are) on
3. cheweth the cud, *among the beasts,*
26. every *beast* which divideth the hoof,
39. any *beast,* of which ye may
46. This (is) the law of *the beasts,*
18:23. Neither shalt thou lie with any *beast*
— shall any woman stand before *a beast*
19:19. Thou shalt not let *thy cattle*
20:15. if a man lie *with a beast,*
— ye shall slay *the beast.*
16. if a woman approach unto any *beast,*
— kill the woman, and *the beast:*
25. between clean *beasts* and unclean,
— your souls abominable *by beast,*
24:18. he that killeth *a beast*
21. he that killeth *a beast,*
25: 7. *And for thy cattle,* and for

Lev.26:22. and destroy *your cattle,*
27: 9. And if (it be) *a beast,*
10. if he shall at all change *beast for beast,*
11. if (it be) any unclean *beast,*
— he shall present *the beast*
26. Only the firstling *of the beasts,*
27. if (it be) *of an* unclean *beast,*
28. of man *and beast,*
Nu. 3:13. both man and *beast:*
41. *the cattle of* the Levites
— firstlings among *the cattle of*
45. *the cattle of* the Levites instead of *their cattle;*
8:17 (both) man *and beast:*
18:15. (whether it be) of men or *beasts,*
— the firstling of unclean *beasts*
31:9. took the spoil of all *their cattle,*
11. of men *and of beasts.*
26. of man *and of beast,*
30. of all manner of *beasts,*
47. of man and of *beast,*
32:26. and all *our cattle,*
35: 3. shall be *for their cattle,*
Deu 2:35. Only *the cattle* we took
3: 7. But all *the cattle,*
4:17. The likeness of any *beast*
5:14. nor any of *thy cattle,*
7:14. among you, *or among your cattle.*
11:15. send grass in thy fields *for thy cattle,*
13:15(16). and *the cattle thereof,*
14: 4. These (are) *the beasts*
6. every *beast* that parteth the hoof,
— cheweth the cud *among the beasts,*
20:14. the little ones, *and the cattle,*
27:21. that lieth with any manner of *beast.*
28: 4. the fruit of *thy cattle,*
11. in the fruit of *thy cattle,*
26. *and unto the beasts of* the earth,
51. he shall eat the fruit of *thy cattle,*
30: 9. in the fruit of *thy cattle,*
32:24. will also send the teeth of *beasts*
Jos. 8: 2. *and the cattle thereof,* shall ye take
27. Only *the cattle* and the spoil
11:14. these cities, *and the cattle,*
21: 2. the suburbs thereof *for our cattle.*
Jud.20:48. the men of (every) city, as *the beast,*
1Sa.17:44. *and to the beasts of* the field.
1K. 4:33(5:13). he spake also of *beasts,*
18: 5. that we lose not *all the beasts.* (marg. *from the beasts*)
2K. 3: 9. *and for the cattle* that followed
17. your cattle, *and your beasts.*
2Ch 32:28. stalls *for all manner of beasts,* (lit. and for every *beast and beast*)
Ezr. 1: 4. with goods, *and with beasts,*
6. with goods, *and with beasts,*
Neh 2:12. *neither* (was there any) *beast* with me, save *the beast* that I rode upon.
14. *for the beast* (that was) under me
9:37. our bodies, *and over our cattle,*
10:36(37). *and of our cattle,*
Job 12: 7. But ask now *the beasts,*
18: 3. are we counted *as beasts,*
35:11. teacheth us *more than the beasts of*
40:15. Behold now *behemoth,*
Ps. 8: 7(8). oxen, yea, and *the beasts of* the field;
36: 6(7). thou preservest man *and beast.*
49:12(13),20(21). is *like the beasts* (that) perish.
50:10. *the cattle* upon a thousand
73:22. I was (as) *a beast* before thee.
104:14. the grass to grow *for the cattle,*
107:38. *and* suffereth not *their cattle*
135: 8. both of man and *beast.*
147: 9. He giveth *to the beast* his food,
148:10. Beasts, and all *cattle;*
Pro.12:10. regardeth the life of *his beast:*
30:30. A lion (which is) strongest *among beasts,*
Ecc. 3:18. see that they themselves are *beasts.*
19. the sons of men befalleth *beasts;*
— hath no preeminence above *a beast:*
21. the spirit of *the beast*
Isa. 18: 6. *and to the beasts of* the earth:
— all *the beasts of* the earth
30: 6. The burden of *the beasts of* the south:
46: 1. *and upon the cattle:*
63:14. *As a beast* goeth down
Jer. 7:20. upon man, and upon *beast,*
Jer. 7:33. *and for the beasts of* the earth;
9:10(9). the fowl of the heavens and *the beast*
12: 4. *the beasts* are consumed,
15: 3. *the beasts of* the earth,
16: 4 & 19:7. *and for the beasts of* the earth.
21: 6. both man and *beast:*
27: 5. *the beast* that (are) upon the ground,
31:27. with the seed of *beast.*
32:43. desolate without man *or beast;*
33:10. without man and without *beast,*
— without inhabitant, and without *beast,*
12. without man and without *beast,*
34:20. *and to the beasts of* the earth.
36:29. to cease from thence man *and beast?*
50: 3. both man and *beast.*
51:62. neither man nor *beast,*
Eze. 8:10. *and* abominable *beasts,*
14:13. will cut off man *and beast*
17. so that I cut off man *and beast*
19,21. to cut off from it man *and beast.*
25:13. will cut off man *and beast*
29: 8. cut off man *and beast*
11. nor foot of *beast*
32:13. destroy also all *the beasts thereof*
— nor the hoofs of *beasts*
36:11. multiply upon you man *and beast;*
44:31. whether it be fowl or *beast.*
Joel 1:18. How do *the beasts* groan!
20. *The beasts of* the field
2:22. *ye beasts of* the field:
Jon. 3: 7. Let neither man *nor beast,*
8. But let man *and beast* be
4:11. *and* (also) much *cattle?*
Mic. 5: 8(7). *among the beasts of* the forest,
Hab. 2:17. the spoil of *beasts,*
Zep. 1: 3. I will consume man *and beast;*
Hag. 1:11. upon men, and upon *cattle,*
Zec. 2: 4(8). multitude of men *and cattle*
8:10. nor any hire for *beast;*
14:15. all *the beasts* that shall be

בֹּהֶן *bōh'-hen,* m. 931

Ex. 29:20. upon *the thumb of* their right hand, and upon *the great toe of* their right foot,
Lev. 8:23. upon *the thumb of* his right hand, and upon *the great toe of* his right foot.
24. upon *the thumbs of* their right hands, and upon *the great toes of* their right feet:
14:14, 17, 25, 28. upon *the thumb of* his right hand, and upon *the great toe of* his right foot:
Jud. 1: 6. cut off his *thumbs* and his great toes. (lit. *thumbs of* his hands and of his feet)
7. having their *thumbs* and their great toes (marg. *the thumbs of* their hands and of their feet)

בֹּהַק *bōh'-hak,* m. 933

Lev.13:39. it (is) a *freckled spot*

בַּהֶרֶת *bah-heh'-reth,* f. 934

Lev.13: 2. a rising, a scab, or *bright spot,*
4. If *the bright spot* (be) white
19. or *a bright spot,* white,
23, 28. if *the bright spot* stay
24. have *a* white *bright spot,*
25. the hair *in the bright spot*
26. no white hair *in the bright spot,*
38. in the skin of their flesh *bright spots,* (even) white *bright spots;*
39. *the bright spots* in the skin
14:56. *and for a bright spot:*

בּוֹא *bōh.* 935

* KAL.—*Preterite.* *

Gen. 6:13. The end of all flesh *is come*
18. *and thou shalt come* into the ark,
7: 9. *There went in* two and two

Gen. 7:13. In the selfsame day *entered* Noah,
16. *went in* male and female
14: 5. in the fourteenth year *came*
15:17. when the sun *went down*,
16: 8. whence *camest thou?*
19: 5. which *came in* to thee
8. for therefore *came they*
9. This one (fellow) *came in* to
23. when Lot *entered* into Zoar.
24: 1. *well stricken* in age: (marg. *gone* into days)
62. Isaac *came* from the way
26:27. Wherefore *come ye* to me,
27:30. Esau his brother *came in*
35. Thy brother *came* with subtilty,
28:11. because the sun *was set;*
29: 9. Rachel *came* with her father's sheep:
30:11. And Leah said, A troop *cometh:*
32: 6(7). *We came* to thy brother Esau,
34: 7. *came* out of the field when they heard
27. The sons of Jacob *came* upon the slain,
37:23. when Joseph *was come*
39:14. *he came in* unto me to lie
17. *came in* unto me to mock me:
41:21. that *they had eaten* them; (lit. *were come* to the inward parts of them)
57. all countries *came* into Egypt
42: 7. Whence *come ye?*
9, 12. nakedness of the land *ye are come.*
10. to buy food *are* thy servants *come.*
21. therefore is this distress *come*
43:21. when *we came* to the inn,
23. I *had* your money. (marg. your money *came* to me)
45:16. Joseph's brethren *are come:*
19. bring your father, *and come.*
46:31. *are come* unto me;
47: 1. *are come* out of the land
4. to sojourn in the land *are we come;*
5. thy brethren *are come* unto thee:
Ex. 1: 1. man and his houshold *came* with Jacob.
3: 9. the cry of the children of Israel *is come*
18. *and thou shalt come,* thou and the
5: 1. Moses and Aaron *went in,*
23. For since *I came* to Pharaoh
8: 3(7:28). *and come* into thine house,
15:19. For the horse of Pharaoh *went in*
19: 1. the same day *came they*
20:20. for God *is come* to prove you,
22:15(14). *it came* for his hire.
Lev. 13:16. *he shall come* unto the priest; (lit. *and he*, &c.)
14:35. *And he* that owneth the house *shall come*
44. *Then* the priest *shall come*
15:14. *and come* before the Lord
16:23. *And* Aaron *shall come* into the tabernacle
22: 7. And *when* the sun *is down,*
25:25. *and if* any of his kin *come*
Nu. 4: 5. *And* when the camp setteth forward, Aaron *shall come,*
5:22. *And* this water that causeth the curse *shall go*
24. *and* the water that causeth the curse *shall enter*
27. *that* the water that causeth the curse *shall enter*
8:22. after that *went* the Levites
13:27. *We came* unto the land
14:24. the land whereinto *he went;*
22:20. If the men *come* to call thee,
38. Lo, *I am come* unto thee:
32:19. because our inheritance *is fallen*
Deu. 1:20. *Ye are come* unto the mountain
4: 1. *and go in* and possess the land
6:18. *and that thou mayest go in*
8: 1 & 11:8. *and go in* and possess the land
12: 5. *and* thither *thou shalt come:*
9. *ye are* not as yet *come*
26. *and go* unto the place
13: 2(3). *And* the sign or the wonder *come to pass,*
14:29. *And* the Levite,...*shall come*, and shall eat
17: 9. *And thou shalt come* unto the priests
18: 6. *and come* with all the desire of his
22:13. *and go in* unto her,
26: 3. *And thou shalt go* unto the priest
— that *I am come* unto the country
28: 2. *And* all these blessings *shall come*
15. *that* all these curses *shall come*

Deu. 28:45. *Moreover* all these curses *shall come*
32:17. to new (gods that) *came newly up,*
33: 2. The Lord *came* from Sinai,
Jos. 2: 2. *there came* men *in* hither
3. which *are entered* into thine house: for *they be come* to search out all
4. *There came* men unto me, but
5:14. of the Lord *am I* now *come.*
9: 6. *We be come* from a far country:
9. thy servants *are come*
13: 1. Joshua was old (and) *stricken* (lit. *gone*)
— (and) *stricken* in years, (lit. *thou art gone*)
20: 6. *and come* unto his own city,
21:45(43). all *came to pass.*
23: 1. *stricken* in age. (marg. *come* into days)
2. I am old (and) *stricken* (lit. *I am gone*)
12. *and go in* unto them,
14. all *are come to pass* unto you,
15. all good things *are come* upon you,
Jud. 3:20. Ehud *came* unto him;
24. his servants *came;* and when they saw
5:19. The kings *came* (and) fought,
23. because *they came* not to the help
6: 5. *and they came* as grasshoppers
19. Gideon *went in,* and made ready
9:37. another company *come*
11: 7. why *are ye come* unto me
12. that *thou art come* against me
18. but *came* not within the border
13: 6. A man of God *came* unto me,
10. that *came* unto me the (other) day.
15:14. when *he came* unto Lehi,
16: 2. Samson *is come* hither.
18:17. *came in* thither,
18. these *went* into Micah's house,
19:16. *there came* an old man
22. the man that *came* into thine house.
23. this man *is come* into mine
20: 4. *I came* into Gibeah
21: 8. *there came* none to the camp
Ru. 1:22. *they came* to Beth-lehem
2:12. under whose wings *thou art come*
3: 4. *and thou shalt go in,* and uncover his feet,
14. a woman *came* into the floor.
1Sa. 2:13. *when* any man offered sacrifice, the priest's servant *came,*
15. the priest's servant *came,*
4: 6. the ark of the Lord *was come*
7. God *is come* into the camp.
9: 5. when they *were come*
12. for *he came* to day to the city;
16. their cry *is come* unto me.
10: 3. *and thou shalt come* to the plain
22. *if* the man *should* yet *come*
11: 5. Saul *came* after the herd
12: 8. When Jacob *was come* into Egypt,
12. Ammon *came* against you,
13: 8. Samuel *came* not to Gilgal;
11. *thou camest* not within
14:25. all (they of) the land *came*
15:12. Saul *came* to Carmel,
16: 2. *I am come* to sacrifice to the Lord.
5. *I am come* to sacrifice unto the Lord:
— *and come* with me to the sacrifice.
17:12. and the man *went* among men
34. *and there came* a lion,
20:19. *and come* to the place where thou
27. Wherefore *cometh* not the son of Jesse
29. Therefore *he cometh* not
22: 5. *and get* thee into the land of Judah.
23: 7. told Saul that David *was come*
27. *there came* a messenger
25: 5. *and go* to Nabal,
8. for *we come* in a good day:
26: 3. he saw that Saul *came* after
4. understood that Saul *was come*
15. for *there came* one of the people
29:10. that *are come* with thee:
2Sa. 2:24. the sun *went down* when *they were come*
3: 7. Wherefore *hast thou gone in*
23. that (was) with him *were come,*
— Abner the son of Ner *came*
25. that *he came* to deceive thee,
4: 6. And they *came* thither
5:18. The Philistines also *came*
23. *and come* upon them
12:16. David fasted, *and went in,*

2Sa.13: 5. and *when* thy father *cometh*
30. that tidings *came* to David, saying,
35. Behold, the king's sons *come*:
36. behold, the king's sons *came*,
14: 3. *And come* to the king,
15. Now therefore that *I am come*
32. Wherefore *am I come* from
15:18. six hundred men which *came*
32. that (when) David *was come*
16: 5. And *when* king David *came*
15. the men of Israel, *came*
16. *was come* unto Absalom,
17:12. *So shall we come* upon him
24. David *came* to Mahanaim.
25. that *went in* to Abigail
19: 7(8). all the evil that *befell* thee from thy
11(12). all Israel *is come* to the king,
15(16). Judah *came* to Gilgal,
20(21). I *am come* the first this day
24(25). until the day *he came*
25(26). when *he was come* to
30(31). as my lord the king *is come*
20: 3. but *went* not in unto them.
8. Amasa *went* before them.
23:19. howbeit *he attained* not
23. *he attained* not to the (first)
24:21. *is* my lord the king *come*
1K. 1: 1. *stricken* in years; (marg. *entered* into days)
22. Nathan the prophet also *came in*.
35. *that he may come* and sit
42. Abiathar the priest *came*:
47. the king's servants *came*
2:28. Then tidings *came* to Joab:
8:31. *and* the oath *come* before
41. *but cometh* out of a far country
42. *when he shall come* and pray
10: 7. I believed not the words, until *I came*,
10. *there came* no more such
12. *there came* no such almug trees,
14. Now the weight of gold that *came*
12: 1. all Israel *were come* to Shechem
13: 1. *there came* a man of God
10. returned not by the way that *he came*
12. which *came* from Judah.
14. that *camest* from Judah?
21. that *came* from Judah,
14: 3. *and go* to him:
17:12. *that I may go in* and dress it
18. *art thou come* unto me
18:12. *and* (so) *when I come* and tell Ahab,
19:15. and *when thou comest*, anoint
2K. 4: 1. the creditor *is come* to take
4. And *when thou art come in*, thou shalt
5:22. even now *there be come* to me
7:10. *We came* to the camp
8: 1. *it shall* also *come* upon the land
7. The man of God *is come* hither.
9: 2. And *when thou comest* thither,
— *and go in*, and make him arise up
11. wherefore *came* this
18. The messenger *came* to them,
20. *He came* even unto them,
31. as Jehu *entered in* at the gate,
10:21. not a man left that *came* not.
15:19. *came* against the land:
29. *came* Tiglath-pileser king of
16: 6. the Syrians *came* to Elath,
18:21. on which if a man lean, *it will go* into
19: 3. for the children *are come*
28. by the way by which *thou camest*.
20:14. *They are come* from a far country,
23:17. which *came* from Judah,
18. that *came* out of Samaria.
25: 1. Nebuchadnezzar king of Babylon *came*,
8. *came* Nebuzar-adan,
25. *came*, and ten men with him,
1Ch. 2:21. afterward Hezron *went in*
11:21. howbeit *he attained* not
25. but *attained* not to the (first)
12:17. If *ye be come* peaceably
23. *came* to David to Hebron,
38. *came* with a perfect heart
14: 9. the Philistines *came*
14. *and come* upon them
15:29. the ark of the covenant of the Lord *came*
16:33. because *he cometh* to judge
19: 3. *are* not his servants *come*

1Ch.19: 9. the kings that *were come*
2Ch. 6:22. *and* the oath *come* before
32. *but is come* from a far country
— *if they come* and pray
8:11. the ark of the Lord *hath come*.
9: 6. I believed not their words, until *I came*,
13. Now the weight of gold that *came*
10: 1. to Shechem *were* all Israel *come*
11:16. *came* to Jerusalem,
12: 3. that *came* with him
5. Then *came* Shemaiah
11. the guard *came* and fetched them,
14:11(10). *we go* against this multitude.
16: 7. Hanani the seer *came* to Asa
20: 1. *came* against Jehoshaphat to battle.
4. *they came* to seek the Lord.
24. Judah *came* toward the watch tower
24:11. *and* the high priest's officer *came*
17. *came* the princes of Judah,
24. *came* with a small company
25: 7. But *there came* a man of God
10. the army that *was come*
27: 2. howbeit *he entered* not
28:17. again the Edomites *had come*
29:17. *came they* to the porch of the Lord.
32: 1. Sennacherib king of Assyria *came*,
2. saw that Sennacherib *was come*,
26. the wrath of the Lord *came* not
Ezr. 2: 2. Which *came* with Zerubbabel:
7: 9. *came he* to Jerusalem,
Neh. 2:10. that *there was come* a man
4:12(6). the Jews which dwelt by them *came*
6:10. *I came* unto the house of Shemaiah
13: 6. *came I* unto the king,
21. *came they* no (more) on the sabbath.
Est. 6: 4. Now Haman *was come*
8: 1. Mordecai *came* before the king;
9:11. *was brought* before the king.
Job 1:14. *there came* a messenger
19. *there came* a great wind
6:20. *they came* thither,
38:16. *Hast thou entered* into
22. *Hast thou entered* into
Ps. 40: 7(8). Then said I, Lo, *I come*:
41: 6(7). if *he come* to see (me),
44:17(18). All this *is come upon us*;
51 [title] (2). after *he had gone in* to
52 [title] (2). David *is come* to the house
66:12. *we went* through fire
69: 1(2). for the waters *are come in* unto
2(3). *I am come* into deep waters,
79: 1. O God, the heathen *are come*
96:13. the Lord: for *he cometh*, for *he cometh* to
98: 9. *he cometh* to judge the earth:
102:13(14). the set time, *is come*.
105:18. he *was laid* in iron: (lit. *came into*)
Pro. 6: 3. when *thou art come* into
11. *So shall* thy poverty *come*
11: 2. (When) pride *cometh*,
18: 3. (then) *cometh* also contempt,
17. *but* his neighbour *cometh*
24:34. *So shall* thy poverty *come*
Ecc. 1: 4. (another) generation *cometh*:
5. *and* the sun *goeth down*,
5:15(14). he return to go *as he came*,
16(15). in all points *as he came*,
6: 4. For *he cometh in* with vanity,
8:10. *who had come* and gone
9:14. *and there came* a great king
11: 8. All *that cometh* (is) vanity.
Cant.5: 1. *I am come* into my garden,
Isa. 2:19. *And they shall go* into the holes
7:17. days that *have* not *come*,
19. *And they shall come*,
10:28. *He is come* to Aiath,
13: 9. the day of the Lord *cometh*,
14:31. for *there shall come* from the north
16:12. *that he shall come* to his sanctuary
19: 1. *and shall come* into Egypt:
23. *and* the Assyrian *shall come* into Egypt,
27:13. *and they shall come* which were ready
30:27. the name of the Lord *cometh*
35:10. *and come* to Zion with songs
36: 6. *if* a man lean, *it will go* into his hand,
37: 3. the children *are come* to the birth,
29. the way by which *thou camest*.
34. By the way that *he came*,

Isa. 39: 3. *They are come* from a far country
42: 9. the former things *are come to pass*,
47: 9. *they shall come* upon thee
11. *Therefore shall* evil *come* upon thee;
49:18. gather themselves together, (and) *come*
50: 2. when *I came*, (was there) no man?
51:11. *and come* with singing
59:20. *And* the Redeemer *shall come* to Zion,
60: 1. Arise, shine; for thy light *is come*,
4. *they come* to thee:
66:18. *and they shall come*, and see
Jer. 1:15. *and they shall come*, and they
4:29. *they shall go* into thickets,
7:10. *And come* and stand
9:21(20). *is entered* into our palaces,
12:12. The spoilers *are come*
14: 3. *they came* to the pits,
18. if *I enter* into the city,
15: 9. her sun *is gone down*
17:25. *Then shall there enter* into the gates
26. *And they shall come* from the cities
22: 4. *then shall there enter in*
25:31. A noise *shall come* (even) to the ends of the earth;
27:18. *go* not to Babylon.
31:12. *Therefore they shall come* and sing
32:24. *they are come* unto the city
29. *And* the Chaldeans,...*shall come* and set
34:10. which *had entered* into the covenant,
36: 6. *Therefore go* thou, and read
37: 4. Now Jeremiah *came in*
16. When Jeremiah *was entered*
38:25. *and they come* unto thee,
39: 1. *came* Nebuchadrezzar king of
40:13. *came* to Gedaliah to Mizpah,
41: 1. *came* unto Gedaliah the son of Ahikam
42:15. *and go* to sojourn there;
43:11. And *when he cometh*,
46:20. destruction *cometh; it cometh* out of the
21. the day of their calamity *was come*
22. *come* against her with axes,
47: 5. Baldness *is come* upon Gaza;
48:21. judgment *is come* upon the plain
49: 9. If grapegatherers *come* to thee,
51:33. *and* the time of her harvest *shall come*.
46. a rumour *shall* both *come*
51. for strangers *are come*
56. Because the spoiler *is come*
52: 4. Nebuchadrezzar king of Babylon *came*,
12. *came* Nebuzar-adan, captain of
Lam. 1:10. *entered* into her sanctuary,
4:18. for our end *is come*.
Eze. 4:14. neither *came there*
7: 2. the end *is come* upon the four
6. An end *is come*, the end *is come*:
7. The morning *is come*
— the time *is come*, the day of trouble
12. The time *is come*,
22. *for* the robbers *shall enter* into it,
25. Destruction *cometh*;
11:16. where *they shall come*.
18. *And they shall come* thither,
12:16. the heathen whither *they come*;
14: 4. *and cometh* to the prophet; I the Lord will answer him that *cometh*
7. *and cometh* to a prophet
17: 3. *came* unto Lebanon,
20: 1. certain of the elders of Israel *came*
21:25(30). whose day *is come*,
29(34). whose day *is come*,
23:24. *And they shall come*
40. lo, *they came*: for whom thou didst wash
44. so *went they in* unto Aholah
24:14. *it shall come to pass*, and I will do (it);
30: 4. *And* the sword *shall come*
33:21. *came* unto me, saying,
36:20. whither *they went*,
21. whither *they went*.
22. whither *ye went*.
38:15. *And thou shalt come* from thy place
39: 8. Behold, *it is come*,
41: 3. *Then went he* inward,
43: 2. the glory of the God of Israel *came*
4. the glory of the Lord *came*
44: 2. *hath entered in* by it,
46: 2. *And* the prince *shall enter*
9. whereby *he came in*,
Eze. 47: 8. *and go* into the sea:
9. these waters *shall come* thither:
Dan 1: 1. *came* Nebuchadnezzar king of
9:13. all this evil *is come* upon us:
23. *I am come* to shew
10: 3. neither *came* flesh nor wine
12. *I am come* for thy words.
13. *came* to help me;
14. *Now I am come* to make
20. wherefore *I come* unto thee?
— the prince of Grecia *shall come*.
11: 9. *So* the king of the south *shall come*
10. *and* (one) *shall* certainly *come*,
21. *but he shall come in* peaceably,
29. *and come* toward the south;
30. *For* the ships of Chittim *shall come*
40. *and he shall enter* into the
41. *He shall enter also* into the glorious land,
45. *yet he shall come* to his end,
Hos. 9: 7. The days of visitation *are come*, the days of recompence *are come*;
10. *they went* to Baal-peor,
Joel 2: 1. for the day of the Lord *cometh*,
Am. 5:19. *or went* into the house,
6: 1. to whom the house of Israel *came!*
8: 2. The end *is come* upon my people
Obad. 5. If thieves *came* to thee,
— if the grapegatherers *came*
11. foreigners *entered into* his gates,
Mic. 1: 9. for *it is come* unto Judah;
3: 6. *and* the sun *shall go down*
4: 8. *even* the first dominion; the kingdom *shall come*
10. *and thou shalt go* (even) to
7: 4. thy visitation *cometh*;
Hag. 2: 7. *and* the desire of all nations *shall come*:
16. when (one) *came* to an heap
— when (one) *came* to the pressfat
Zec. 5: 4. *and it shall enter* into the
6:10. which *are come* from Babylon, *and come* thou the same day, *and go* into the house
8:22. *Yea*, many people and strong nations *shall come*
14: 1. the day of the Lord *cometh*,
5. *and* the Lord my God *shall come*,
18. go not up, and *come* not,
21. *and* all they that sacrifice *shall come*
Mal. 3: 1. behold, *he shall come*, saith the Lord

KAL.—*Infinitive.*

Gen10:19. *as thou comest* to Gerar, unto Gaza; *as thou goest*, unto Sodom,
30. *as thou goest*, unto Sephar
12:11. was come near *to enter into* Egypt,
14. *that, when* Abram *was come*
13:10. *as thou comest* unto Zoar.
15:12. *when* the sun *was going down*,
19:22. do any thing till *thou be come*
31. *to come in* unto us
24:62. Isaac came *from the way of*
25:18. *as thou goest* toward Assyria:
30:38. *when they came* to drink.
31:18. *for to go* to Isaac his father
33:18. *when he came* from
34: 5. until *they were come*.
35: 9. *when he came* out of Padan-aram,
16. a little way *to come* to Ephrath:
37:10. Shall I and thy mother and thy brethren *indeed* come (lit. *coming* shall, &c.)
39:16. until his lord *came* home.
41:54. seven years of dearth began *to come*,
42:15. except your youngest brother *come*
43:25. against Joseph *came* at noon:
44:30. *when I come* to thy servant
48: 5. before *I came* unto thee
7. *when I came* from Padan,
— but a little way *to come*
Ex. 2:18. How (is it that) ye are *come*
10:26. until *we come* thither.
12:23. suffer the destroyer *to come* in
16:35. until *they came* to a land inhabited;
— until *they came* unto the borders
17:12. until *the going down* of the sun.
22:26(25). by that the sun *goeth down*:
28:29, 35. *when he goeth in* unto the holy
30. *when he goeth in* before the Lord:
43. *when they come in* unto the

Ex. 30:20. *When they go* into the tabernacle
33: 8. until *he was gone*
9. *as* Moses *entered* into the tabernacle,
34:34. *But when* Moses *went in*
35. until *he went in* to speak
40:32. When *they went* into the tent
35. Moses was not able *to enter*
Lev.10: 9. *when ye go* into the tabernacle
14:48. if the priest shall come in, (marg. *in coming in*, shall come in)
16:17. *when he goeth in* to make
23. *when he went* into the holy
25:22. until her fruits *come in*
Nu. 7:89. *And when* Moses *was gone*
10:21. tabernacle against *they came*.
13:21. *as* men *come* to Hamath.
15:18. *When ye come* into the land
32: 9. that *they should* not *go*
33:40. heard of *the coming of* the
34: 8. unto *the entrance of* Hamath;
Deu 1:31. until *ye came* into this place.
4:21. that I *should* not *go in*
34. Or hath God assayed *to go*
9: 1. *to go in* to possess nations
7. until *ye came* unto this place,
11: 5. until *ye came* into this place;
31. *to go in* to possess the land
16: 6. *at the going down of* the sun,
20:19. *to employ* (them) in the siege: (marg. *to go* from before thee)
23:11(12). *and when* the sun *is down*,
24:13. *when* the sun *goeth down*,
28: 6. *when thou comest in*, and blessed
19. *when thou comest in*, and cursed
30:18. over Jordan *to go* to possess it.
31: 2. can no more go out *and come in:*
11. *When* all Israel *is come*
Jos. 1:11. *to go in* to possess the land,
3: 8. *When ye are come* to the brink
15. *And as* they that bare the ark *were come*
8:29. *and as soon as* the sun *was down*,
10:13. hasted not *to go down*
19. suffer them not *to enter*
27. at the time of *the going down of*
13: 5. unto *the entering into* Hamath.
14:11. both to go out, *and to come in*.
15:18. *as she came* (unto him),
18: 3. How long (are) ye slack *to go*
23: 7. That *ye come* not among
Jud. 1:14. *when she came* (to him),
3: 3. unto *the entering in of* Hamath.
27. *when he was come*,
5:28. Why is his chariot (so) long *in coming?*
6: 4. till *thou come* unto Gaza,
18. until *I come* unto thee,
9:24. sons of Jerubbaal *might come*,
11:33. even till *thou come* to Minnith,
15: 1. would not suffer him *to go in*.
18: 9. *to enter* to possess the land.
10. *When ye go*, ye shall come
19:15. *to go in* (and) to lodge
20:10. *when they come* to Gibeah
Ru. 1:19. until *they came* to Beth-lehem.
— *when they were come* to Beth-lehem,
1Sa. 4: 5. *when* the ark...of the Lord *came*
5:10. *as* the ark of God *came to*
7:13. they *came* no more (lit. they added no more *to come*)
9: 6. cometh *surely to pass:* (lit. *in coming* shall come)
13. *As soon as ye be come* into the city,
— will not eat until *he come*,
15. a day before Saul *came*,
10: 5. *when thou art come* thither
8. till *I come* to thee,
15: 7. *thou comest* to Shur,
16: 4. *Comest thou* peaceably?
6. *when they were come*, that he
11. sit down till *he come* hither.
17:52. until *thou come* to the valley,
18: 6. it came to pass *as they came*,
19:23. until *he came* to Naioth
20: 9. were determined by my father *to come*
23: 7. *by entering* into a town
10. that Saul seeketh *to come*
25:26. withholden thee *from coming*
33. *from coming* to (shed) blood,
1Sa.27: 8. *as thou goest* to Shur,
29: 6. thy going out *and thy coming in*
— since the day of *thy coming*
30: 1. *when* David and his men *were come*
2Sa. 1: 2. *when he came* to David,
3:13. *when thou comest* to see my face.
35. till the sun *be down*.
4: 4. *when* the tidings *came* of Saul
5:13. after *he was come* from
25. until *thou come* to Gazer.
14:29,29. he would not *come*
15: 2. *came* to the king for judgment, (marg. *to come*)
20. Whereas *thou camest*
28. until *there come* word
17:17. not be seen *to come* into
27. *when* David *was come*
19: 3(4). *gat* them by stealth that day *into* (lit. stole *to enter*)
1K. 2:13. *Comest thou* peaceably?
3: 7. to go out *or come in*.
8:65. *from the entering in of* Hamath
11:17. *to go into* Egypt;
13:16. *nor go in* with thee:
14: 5. *when she cometh in*, that she
12. *when* thy feet *enter* into
28. the king *went* into the house
18:46. to *the entrance* of Jezreel. (marg. till *thou come* to)
22:27. until *I come* in peace.
30. *and enter* into the battle;
36. *about the going down of* the sun,
2K. 4:10. *when he cometh* to us,
5: 6. *when* this letter *is come*
18. *when* my master *goeth*
6:20. *when they were come* into Samaria,
23. *came* no more into the land (lit. they added no more *to come*)
32. *when* the messenger *cometh*,
7: 5. *to go* unto the camp of the Syrians:
6. the Egyptians, *to come* upon us.
9:17. spied the company of Jehu *as he came*,
10: 2. *as soon as* this letter *cometh*
7. *when* the letter *came* to them,
11: 8. as he goeth out *and as he cometh in*.
12: 9(10). on the right side *as* one *cometh*
14:25. *from the entering of* Hamath
16:11. against king Ahaz *came* from Damascus.
18:32. Until *I come* and take you away
19:27. thy going out, *and thy coming in*,
23:11. *at the entering in of* the house
1Ch 5: 9. unto *the entering in of* the wilderness
9:25. *to come* after seven days
12:19. *when he came* with the
31. *to come* and make David king.
13: 5. unto *the entering of* Hemath,
24:19. *to come* into the house
2Ch 7: 2. the priests could not *enter*
8. *from the entering in of* Hamath
12:11. when the king *entered*
13:13. *to come* about behind them:
18:29. *and will go* to the battle;
34. the time of the sun *going down*
20:10. not let Israel in*vade*, *when they came* out
11. *to come* to cast us out
22: 7. *by coming* to Joram: *for when he was come*,
23: 7. with the king *when he cometh in*,
25:14. Amaziah *was come* from the slaughter
26: 8. to *the entering in of* Egypt;
30: 1. *that they should come* to the house
5. *should come* to keep the passover
33:14. *even to the entering in* at the fish gate,
Ezr. 2:68. *when they came* to the house
3: 8. in the second year *of their coming*
Neh 4: 8(2). *to come* (and) to fight
9:15,23. *that they should go in* to possess
Est. 1:12. Vashti refused *to come*
2:12. every maid's turn was come *to go in*
13. was given her *to go* with her
15. was come *to go in* unto the king,
4: 2. for none (might) *enter*
8. *that she should go in* unto the king,
11. *to come in* unto the king
9:25. *But when* (Esther) *came* (marg. *she came*)
Job 2:11. *to come* to mourn with him
14:14. till my change *come*.
Ps. 51:[title] (2). *when* Nathan the prophet *came*

Ps. 52: [title] (2). *when* Doeg the Edomite *came*
54: [title] (2). *when* the Ziphims *came*
71: 3. *I may* continually *resort:*
105:19. Until the time that his word *came:*
121: 8. *and thy coming in* from this time
126: 6. shall *doubtless* come *again* (lit. *in coming* shall come)
Pro. 1:26. I will mock *when* your fear *cometh;*
27. *When* your fear *cometh* as desolation,
— *when* distress and anguish *cometh*
18: 3. *When* the wicked *cometh,*
Isa. 2:21. *To go* into the clefts of the rocks,
13:22. her time (is) near *to come,*
14: 9. to meet (thee) at *thy coming:*
20: 1. In the year *that* Tartan *came*
23: 1. *no entering in:* (lit. *from entering*)
24:10. *that no man may come in.*
30:29. *to come* into the mountain
36:17. Until *I come* and take you away
37:28. *and thy coming in,* and thy rage
56: 1. for my salvation (is) near *to come,*
59:14. equity cannot *enter.*
Jer. 8: 7. observe the time of *their coming;*
17:27. *even entering in* at the gates of Jerusalem
22:23. *when* pangs *come* upon thee,
27: 7. until the very time of his land *come:*
28: 9. *when* the word of the prophet *shall come to pass,*
36: 5. I cannot *go* into the house
29. The king of Babylon shall *certainly* come
40: 4,4. *to come* with me into Babylon,
41: 7. *when they came* into the midst
17. to go *to enter into* Egypt,
42.15. set your faces *to enter into* Egypt,
17. set their faces *to go into* Egypt
18. *when ye shall enter into* Egypt:
22. the place whither ye desire *to go*
44:12. have set their faces *to go into*
46:13. *how* Nebuchadrezzar...*should come*
48:16. The calamity of Moab (is) near *to come,*
51:61. *When thou comest to* Babylon,
Eze. 10: 3. *when* the man *went in;*
16.33. *that they may come* unto thee
21:19(24). *that* the sword of the king of Babylon *may come:*
20(25). *that* the sword *may come*
27(32). until *he come* whose right it is;
22: 3. that her time *may come,*
23:44. *as* they *go in* unto a woman that
24:24. and *when this cometh,* ye shall know
26:10. *when he shall enter* into thy gates,
33.22. afore he that was escaped *came;*
— until *he came* to me
33. *And when* this *cometh to pass,*
36: 8. for they are at hand *to come.*
38:18. the same time *when* Gog *shall come*
42: 9. *as one goeth* into them (marg. *he came*)
12. *as one entereth into them.*
14. *When* the priests *enter therein,*
43: 3. *when I came* to destroy
44:17. *when they enter in* at the gates
21. *when they enter* into the inner
27. in the day *that he goeth*
46: 8. *And when* the prince *shall enter,*
9. *But when* the people of the land *shall come*
10. *when they go in,* shall go in;
47:15. *as men go* to Zedad;
20. till *a man come* over against
48: 1. *as one goeth to* Hamath,
Dan 8:17. *and when he came,* I was afraid,
11:10. and (one) shall *certainly* come,
13. shall *certainly* come after certain
17. He shall also set his face *to enter*
Joel 2:31(3:4). the terrible day of the Lord *come.*
Am. 6:14. *from the entering in of* Hemath
Jon. 1: 3. *to go* with them unto Tarshish
3: 4. Jonah began *to enter* into the city
Hab. 2: 3. it will *surely* come,
Hag. 1: 2. The time *is* not *come,*
Mal. 3: 2. who may abide the day of *his coming?*
4: 5(3:23). before *the coming of* the great

KAL.—*Imperative.*

Gen 7: 1. *Come* thou and all thy house
16: 2. *go in* unto my maid;
19:34. *and go thou in,* (and) lie
24:31. *Come in,* thou blessed of the Lord;
Gen 30: 3. *go in* unto her;
38: 8. *Go in* unto thy brother's wife,
45:17. *get you* unto the land
18. *and come* unto me:
Ex. 6:11. *Go in,* speak unto Pharaoh
8: 1(7:26). *Go* unto Pharaoh,
9: 1 & 10:1. *Go in* unto Pharaoh,
Nu. 21:27. *Come* into Heshbon,
Deu 1: 7. *and go* to the mount
8. *go in* and possess the land
Jos. 6:22. *Go* into the harlot's house,
Jud. 9:15. *come* (and) put your trust
1Sa. 20:21. *then come thou:*
2Sa. 13:11. *Come* lie with me,
14:32. *Come* hither, that I may send
16:21. *Go in* unto thy father's concubines,
1K. 1:13. *and get thee in* unto king David,
42. *Come in;* for thou (art) a valiant man,
13: 7. *Come* home with me,
14: 6. *Come in,* thou wife of Jeroboam;
17:13. *go* (and) do as thou hast said:
20:33. Then he said, *Go ye,* bring him.
2K. 5: 5. Go to, *go,* and I will send
10: 6. *and come* to me to Jezreel by to morrow
25. *Go in,* (and) slay them; let none come
1Ch 16:29. *and come* before him:
2Ch 25: 8. But if thou *wilt go,* do (it), be strong
30: 8. *and enter* into his sanctuary,
Est. 5:14. *then go thou in* merrily
Job 17:10. do ye return, *and come* now:
Ps. 95: 6. *O come,* let us worship
96: 8. *and come* into his courts.
100: 2. *come* before his presence
4. *Enter* into his gates
Cant. 4:16. *and come,* thou south;
Isa. 2:10. *Enter* into the rock,
22:15. Go, *get thee* unto this treasurer,
26:20. Come, my people, *enter thou*
30: 8. *go,* write it before them
45:20. Assemble yourselves *and come;*
47: 5. *and get thee* into darkness,
Jer. 35:11. *Come,* and let us go to Jerusalem
40: 4. *come;* and I will look well unto thee:
41: 6. *come* to Gedaliah the son of
49:14. *and come* against her,
50: 5. *Come,* and let us join ourselves
26. *Come* against her from the
51:10. *come,* and let us declare in Zion
Eze. 3: 4. go, *get thee* unto the house
11. *get thee* to them of the captivity,
24. *Go,* shut thyself within thine house.
8: 9. *Go in,* and behold the wicked
10: 2. *Go in* between the wheels,
33:30. *Come,* I pray you, and hear
37: 9. *Come* from the four winds,
39:17. Assemble yourselves, *and come;*
Joel 1:13. *come,* lie all night in sackcloth,
3:11(4:11). Assemble yourselves, *and come,*
13(-:13). *come,* get you down;
Am. 4: 4. *Come* to Beth-el, and transgress;
Nah. 3:14. *go* into clay, and tread the morter,

KAL.—*Future.*

Gen. 6: 4. when the sons of God *came in* unto
20. *shall come* unto thee,
7: 7. *And* Noah *went in,*
15. *And they went in* unto Noah
8:11. *And* the dove *came in*
11:31. *and they came* unto Haran,
12: 5. *and* into the land of Canaan *they came.*
13:18. *and came* and dwelt in the plain
14: 7. *and came* to En-mishpat,
13. *And there came* one that had escaped,
15:15. thou *shalt go* to thy fathers
16: 4. *And he went in* unto Hagar,
19: 1. *And there came* two angels to Sodom
3. *and entered* into his house;
33. *and* the firstborn *went in,*
20: 3. *But* God *came* to Abimelech
13. every place whither *we shall come,*
22: 9. *And they came* to the place
23: 2. *and* Abraham *came* to mourn for Sarah,
24:30. *that he came* unto the man;
32. *And the man came* into the house:
41. when *thou comest* to my kindred;
42. *And I came* this day
25:29. *and* Esau *came* from the field,

Gen 26:32. *that* Isaac's servants *came*,
27:18. *And he came* unto his father,
33. eaten of all before *thou camest*,
29:21. *that I may go in* unto her.
23. *and he went in* unto her.
30. *And he went in* also unto
30: 4. *and* Jacob *went in* unto her.
16. *And* Jacob *came* out of the field
— Thou *must come in* unto me;
33. when *it shall come* for my hire
38. when the flocks *came* to drink,
31:24. *And* God *came* to Laban
33. *And* Laban *went* into Jacob's
— *and entered* into Rachel's tent.
32: 8(9). And said, If Esau *come* to
11(12). lest *he will come* and smite me,
33:14. until *I come* unto my lord
18. *And* Jacob *came* to Shalem
34:20. *And* Hamor and Shechem his son *came*
25. *and came* upon the city
35: 6. *So* Jacob *came* to Luz,
27. *And* Jacob *came* unto Isaac
37:10. *Shall* I and thy mother and thy brethren indeed *come*
14. *and he came* to Shechem.
38: 2. *and went in* unto her.
16. *let me come in* unto thee;
— that *thou mayest come in* unto me?
18. *and came in* unto her,
39:11. *that* (Joseph) *went* into the house
40: 6. *And* Joseph *came in* unto them
41:14. *and came in* unto Pharaoh.
21. And *when* they *had eaten* them up, (marg. *come* to the inward parts of them)
50. before the years of famine *came*,
42: 5. *And* the sons of Israel *came*
6. *and* Joseph's brethren *came*,
29. *And they came* unto Jacob
43:26. *And when* Joseph *came* home,
30. *and he entered* into (his) chamber,
44:14. *And* Judah and his brethren *came*
45:25. *and came* into the land
46: 1. *and came* to Beer-sheba,
6. *and came* into Egypt,
28. *and they came* into the land of
47: 1. *Then* Joseph *came* and told Pharaoh,
15. the Egyptians *came* unto Joseph,
18. *they came* unto him the second year,
49: 6. *come* not *thou* into their secret;
10. until Shiloh *come*;
50:10. *And they came* to the threshingfloor
Ex. 1:19. ere the midwives *come in*
2:16. *and they came* and drew
17. *And* the shepherds *came*
18. *And when they came* to Reuel
3: 1. *and came* to the mountain of God,
5:15. *Then* the officers of the children of Israel *came*
7:10. *And* Moses and Aaron *went in*
23. Pharaoh turned *and went* into
8:24(20). *and there came* a grievous swarm
10: 3. *And* Moses and Aaron *came in*
12:25. when *ye be come* to the land
14:16. *and* the children of Israel *shall go*
17. *and they shall follow* them: (lit. *and they shall go* after them)
20. *And it came* between the camp
22. *And* the children of Israel *went* into the
23. *and went in* after them
15:23. And *when they came* to Marah,
27. *And they came* to Elim,
16: 1. Israel *came* unto the wilderness
22. *and* all the rulers of the congregation *came*
17: 8. *Then came* Amalek,
18: 5. *And* Jethro, Moses' father in law, *came*
7. *and they came* into the tent.
12. *and* Aaron *came*, and all the elders
15. the people *come* unto me to enquire
23. all this people *shall* also *go*
19: 2. *and were come* (to) the desert
7. *And* Moses *came* and called for the elders
20:24. *I will come* unto thee,
21: 3. If *he came in* by himself,
22: 9(8). the cause of both parties *shall come*
23:27. to whom *thou shalt come*,
24: 3. *And* Moses *came* and told the people
18. *And* Moses *went* into the midst

Ex. 29:30. when *he cometh* into the tabernacle
35:10. every wise hearted among you *shall come*,
21. *And they came*, every one
22. *And they came*, both men and women,
36: 4. *And* all the wise men,...*came*
Lev. 9:23. *And* Moses and Aaron *went*
11:34. on which (such) water *cometh*
12: 4. nor *come* into the sanctuary,
14: 8. after that *he shall come*
34. When *ye be come* into the land
36. before the priest *go* (into it) to see
— the priest *shall go in* to see
48. if the priest *shall come in*,
16: 2. that *he come* not at all times
3. Thus *shall* Aaron *come* into
26. afterward *come* into the camp.
28. afterward *he shall come*
19:23. when *ye shall come* into the land,
21:11. Neither *shall he go in*
23. Only *he shall* not *go in*
23:10. When *ye be come* into the land
25: 2. When *ye come* into the land
Nu. 4:15. *shall come* to bear (it):
19. Aaron and his sons *shall go in*,
20. But *they shall* not *go in* to see
6: 6. *he shall come* at no dead body.
8:15. *shall* the Levites *go in* to do
24. *they shall go in* to wait
10: 9. if *ye go* to war in your land
13:22. *and came* unto Hebron;
23. *And they came* unto the brook
26. they went *and came* to Moses,
14:30. Doubtless *ye shall* not *come*
15: 2. When *ye be come* into the land
16:43(17:8). *And* Moses and Aaron *came*
17: 8(23). *that* on the morrow Moses *went* into the tabernacle
19: 7. afterward *he shall come* into the camp
20: 1. *Then came* the children
6. *And* Moses and Aaron *went*
22. *and came* unto mount Hor.
24. *he shall* not *enter*
21: 7. *Therefore* the people *came*
23. *and he came* to Jahaz,
22: 7. *and they came* unto Balaam,
9,20. *And* God *came* unto Balaam,
14. *and they went* unto Balak,
16. *And they came* to Balaam,
39. *and they came* unto Kirjath-huzoth.
23:17. *And when he came* to him,
25: 8. *And he went* after the man
27:17. which *may go in* before them,
21. at his word *they shall come in*,
31:23. Every thing that *may abide* (lit. *go* into) the fire,
— all that *abideth* not the fire
24. afterward *ye shall come*
32: 2. *came* and spake unto Moses,
6. *Shall* your brethren *go*
33: 9. *and came* unto Elim:
Deu 1:19. *and we came* to Kadesh-barnea.
22. into what cities *we shall come*.
24. *and came* unto the valley of Eshcol,
37. Thou also *shalt* not *go in* thither.
38. *he shall go in* thither:
39. *they shall go in* thither,
10:11. *that they may go in* and possess
17:14. When *thou art come*
18: 6. And if a Levite *come* from any of thy
22. follow not, nor *come to pass*,
19: 5. As when a man *goeth*
21:13. after that *thou shalt go in*
23: 1(2). *shall* not *enter* into the congregation
2(3). A bastard *shall* not *enter*
—(-). *shall he* not *enter* into
3(4). Ammonite or Moabite *shall* not *enter*
—(-). *shall they* not *enter*
8(9). *shall enter* into the congregation
10(11). *he shall* not *come* within
11(12). *he shall come* into the camp
24(25), 25(26). When *thou comest* into
24:10. *thou shalt* not *go* into his house
15. neither *shall* the sun *go down*
25: 5. *shall go in* unto her,
26: 1. when *thou* (art) *come*
27: 3. *thou mayest go in* unto the land
29: 7(6). *And when ye came* unto this

Deu 29:22(21). the stranger that *shall come*
30: 1. all these things *are come*
31: 7. *thou must go* with this people unto
32:44. *And* Moses *came* and spake
52. *thou shalt* not *go* thither
33:16. *let* (the blessing) *come*
Jos. 2: 1. *and came* into an harlot's house,
22. *and came* unto the mountain,
23. *and came* to Joshua the son of Nun,
3: 1. *and came* to Jordan,
6:11. *and they came* into the camp,
19. *they shall come* into the treasury
23. *And* the young men that were spies *went in*,
8:11. *and came* before the city,
19. *and they entered* into the city,
9: 8. from whence *come ye?*
17. *and came* unto their cities
10: 9. Joshua *therefore came* unto them
20. *entered* into fenced cities.
11: 5. *they came* and pitched together
7. *So* Joshua *came*, and all the people
21. *And* at that time *came* Joshua,
18: 4. *and they shall come*
9. *and came* (again) to Joshua
22:10. And *when they came*
15. *And they came* unto the
24: 6. *and ye came* unto the sea;
11. *and came* unto Jericho:
Jud. 3:22. *And* the haft also *went in*
4:20. when any man *doth come*
21. *and went* softly unto him,
22. And *when he came* into her (tent),
6: 5. (כתיב) *and they came* as grasshoppers
— *and they entered* into the land
11. *And there came* an angel
7:13. And *when* Gideon *was come*,
— *and came* unto a tent,
19. *So* Gideon,...*came* unto the outside
8: 4. *And* Gideon *came* to Jordan,
15. *And* he *came* unto the men of Succoth,
9: 5. *And he went* unto his father's house
26. *And* Gaal the son of Ebed *came*
27. *and went* into the house of their god,
46. *they entered* into an hold
52. *And* Abimelech *came* unto
57. *and* upon them *came* the curse
11:16. *and came* to Kadesh;
18. *and came* by the east side
34. *And* Jephthah *came* to Mizpeh
13: 6. *Then* the woman *came*
8. *let* the man of God...*come* again
9. *and* the angel of God *came*
11. *and came* to the man,
12. Now *let* thy words *come to pass*.
17. that when thy sayings *come to pass*
14: 5. *and came* to the vineyards of Timnath:
18. before the sun *went down*,
15: 1. *I will go in* to my wife
16: 1. *and went in* unto her.
17: 8. *and he came* to mount Ephraim
9. Whence *comest thou?*
18: 2. *who when they came to* mount Ephraim,
7. *and came* to Laish,
8. *And they came* unto their brethren
10. *ye shall come* unto a people
13. *and came* unto the house of Micah.
15. *and came* to the house of the young man
20. *and went* in the midst
27. *and came* unto Laish,
19:10. *and came* over against Jebus,
14. *and* the sun *went down*
15. and *when he went in*, he sat him down
17. whence *comest thou?*
26. *Then came* the woman
29. And *when he was come* into
20:26. *and came* unto the house of God,
34. *And there came* against Gibeah
21: 2. *And* the people *came* to the house
22. their brethren *come* unto us
Ru. 1: 2. *And they came* into the
2: 3. she went, *and came*,
7. among the sheaves: *so she came*,
18. *and went* into the city:
3: 7. *he went* to lie down
— *and she came* softly,
15. *and she went* into the city.
16. And *when she came* to her mother in law,

Ru. 3:17. *Go* not empty unto thy mother in law.
4:13. *and when he went in* unto her,
1Sa. 1:19. *and came* to their house to Ramah:
2:27. *And there came* a man of God
34. that *shall come* upon thy two sons,
36. *shall come* (and) crouch to him
3:10. *And* the Lord *came*, and stood,
4: 3. And *when* the people *were come*
— that, *when it cometh* among us,
12. *and came* to Shiloh the same day
13. And *when he came*, lo, Eli
14. And the man *came in* hastily, (lit. and the man hastened, *and he came*)
7: 1. *And* the men of Kirjath-jearim *came*,
8: 4. *and came* to Samuel unto Ramah,
9: 6. all that he saith *cometh*
10: 5. After that *thou shalt come*
7. when these signs *are come*
9. *and* all those signs *came to pass*
10. And *when they came* thither
13. *And* when he had made an end...*he came*
14. *and* when we saw...*we came* to Samuel.
11: 4. *Then came* the messengers
9. *And* the messengers *came* and shewed
11. *and they came* into the midst
14:20. *and they came* to the battle:
26. *And when* the people *were come*
15: 5. *And* Saul *came* to a city of Amalek,
13. *And* Samuel *came* to Saul:
16: 4. *and came* to Beth-lehem.
21. *And* David *came* to Saul,
17:20. *and he came* to the trench,
22. *and came* and saluted his brethren.
18:13. *and came in* before the people.
19:16. And *when* the messengers *were come*
18. *and came* to Samuel
22. *and came* to a great well
20: 1. *and came* and said before Jonathan,
37. And *when* the lad *was come*
38. *and came* to his master.
21: 1(2). *Then came* David to Nob
10(11). *and went* to Achish
15(16). *shall* this (fellow) *come*
22: 5. *and came* into the forest of Hareth.
11. *and they came* all of them
24: 3(4). *And he came* to the sheepcotes
—(–). *and* Saul *went in* to cover his feet:
25: 9. And *when* David's young men *came*,
12. *and came* and told him all those sayings.
34. *and come* to meet me,
36. *And* Abigail *came* to Nabal;
40. And *when* the servants of David *were come*
26: 1. *And* the Ziphites *came* unto Saul
5. *and came* to the place where Saul
7. *So* David and Abishai *came*
10. or his day *shall come* to die;
27: 9. *and came* to Achish.
28: 4. *and came* and pitched in Shunem:
8. *and they came* to the woman
21. *And* the woman *came* unto Saul,
29: 8. that *I may* not *go* fight
30: 3. *So* David and his men *came*
9. *and came* to the brook Besor,
21. *And* David *came* to the two hundred
26. And *when* David *came* to Ziklag,
31: 4. lest these uncircumcised *come*
7. *and* the Philistines *came*
8. *when* the Philistines *came*
12. *and came* to Jabesh,
2Sa. 1: 3. From whence *comest thou?*
2: 4. *And* the men of Judah *came*,
29. *and they came* to Mahanaim.
3:20. *So* Abner *came* to David
24. *Then* Joab *came* to the king,
35. And *when* all the people *came*
4: 5. *and came* about the heat of the day
7. For *when they came* into the house,
5: 1. *Then came* all the tribes of Israel
3. *So* all the elders of Israel *came*
6. *thou shalt* not *come in*
— David cannot *come in* hither. (marg. *shall* not, &c.)
8. *shall* not *come* into the house.
20. *And* David *came* to Baal-perazim,
6: 6. And *when they came* to Nachon's
9. How *shall* the ark of the Lord *come*
7.18. *Then went* king David *in*,

2Sa. 8: 5. And *when* the Syrians of Damascus *came*
9: 6. Now *when* Mephibosheth,...*was come*
10: 2. *And* David's servants *came*
14. *and entered* into the city.
— *and came* to Jerusalem.
16. *and they came* to Helam;
17. *and came* to Helam.
11: 4. *and she came in* unto him,
7. And *when* Uriah *was come*
11. *shall* I then *go* into mine house,
22. *and came* and shewed David
12: 1. *And he came* unto him,
4. *And there came* a traveller unto the
20. *and came* into the house of the Lord,
— *then he came* to his own house;
24. *and went in* unto her,
13: 5. *let* my sister Tamar *come*,
6. *and when* the king *was come*
— *let* Tamar my sister *come*,
24. *And* Absalom *came* to the king,
14:31. *and came* to Absalom
33. *So* Joab *came* to the king,
— *and* when he had called for Absalom, *he came* to the king,
15: 4. suit or cause *might come* unto me,
6. all Israel that *came* to the king
13. *And there came* a messenger
37. *So* Hushai David's friend *came* into
— Absalom *came* into Jerusalem.
16:14. *And* the king,...*came*
22. *and* Absalom *went in* unto his father's
17: 2. *And I will come* upon him
6. *And when* Hushai *was come*
18. *and came* to a man's house
20. *And when* Absalom's servants *came*
18: 9. *and* the mule *went* under the thick
27. and *cometh* with good tidings.
19: 5(6). *And* Joab *came* into the house
8(9). *And* all the people *came*
15(16). returned, *and came* to Jordan.
20: 3. *And* David *came* to his house
14. *and went* also after him.
15. *And* they *came* and besieged him
22. *Then* the woman *went*
23:13. *and came* to David in the harvest time
24: 6. *Then they came* to Gilead,
— *and they came* to Dan-jaan,
7. *And came* to the strong hold
8. *So* when they had gone...*they came* to
13. *So* Gad *came* to David,
— *Shall* seven years of famine *come*
18. *And* Gad *came* that day to David,
1K. 1:14. I also *will come in* after thee,
15. *And* Bath-sheba *went in*
23. And *when he was come in* before
28. *And she came* into the king's presence,
32. *And they came* before the king.
53. *And he came* and bowed himself
2:13. *And* Adonijah the son of Haggith *came*
19. Bath-sheba *therefore went*
30. *And* Benaiah *came* to the tabernacle
3:15. *And he came* to Jerusalem,
16. Then *came there* two women,
4:34(5:14). *And* there *came* of all people
7:14. *And he came* to king Solomon,
8: 3. *And* all the elders of Israel *came*,
9:28. *And they came* to Ophir,
10: 1. *And* when the queen....she *came* to prove
2. *And she came* to Jerusalem
— and *when she was come*
22. once in three years *came* the
11: 2. *Ye shall* not *go in* to them, neither *shall they come in*
18. *and came* to Paran:
— *and they came* to Egypt,
12: 3. *And* Jeroboam and all the congregation of Israel *came*,
12. *So* Jeroboam and all the people *came*
21. *And when* Rehoboam *was come*
13: 8. *I will* not *go in* with thee,
11. *and* his sons *came* and told him
22. thy carcase *shall* not *come*
25. *and they came* and told (it) in the
29. *and* the old prophet *came* to the city,
14: 4. *and came* to the house
13. he only of Jeroboam *shall come* to the
17. arose, and departed, *and came* to Tirzah

1K. 16:10. *And* Zimri *went in* and smote him,
18. *that he went* into the palace
17:10. And *when he came* to the gate
19: 3. *and came* to Beer-sheba,
4. *and came* and sat down under a juniper
9. *And he came* thither unto a cave,
20:30. *and came* into the city,
32. *and came* to the king of Israel,
43. *and came* to Samaria.
21: 4. *And* Ahab *came* into his house
5. *But* Jezebel his wife *came* to him,
13. *And there came in* two men,
22:15. *So he came* to the king.
25. when *thou shalt go* into
30. *and went* into the battle.
37. *and was brought* to Samaria;
2K. 1:13. *and came* and fell on his knees
2: 4. *So they came* to Jericho.
15. *And they came* to meet him,
3:24. *And when they came* to the camp
4: 7. (כתיב) *Then she came* and told the man
11. *that he came* thither,
25. *she* went *and came* unto the man
27. And *when she came* to the man
32. *And when* Elisha *was come*
33. *He went in therefore*, and shut
36. *And when she was come in* unto him,
37. *Then she went in*, and fell
39. *and came* and shred (them) into the pot
5: 4. *And* (one) *went in*,
8. *let him come* now to me,
9. *So* Naaman *came* with his horses
15. *and came*, and stood before him:
24. And *when he came* to the tower,
6: 4. *And when they came* to Jordan,
14. *and they came* by night,
32. ere the messenger *came*
7: 4. *we will enter* into the city,
5. and *when they were come* to the
8. *And when* these lepers *came* to the uttermost part of the camp, *they went* into
— *and entered* into another tent,
9. *that we may go* and tell
10. *So they came* and called
12. *we shall* catch them alive, and *get* into
8: 7. *And* Elisha *came* to Damascus;
9. *and came* and stood before him,
14. *and came* to his master;
9: 5. And *when he came*, behold,
6. *and went* into the house;
19. on horseback, *which came to* them,
30. And *when* Jehu *was come*
34. And *when he was come in*, he did
10: 8. *And there came* a messenger,
12. he arose *and departed*,
17. And *when he came* to Samaria,
21. *and* all the worshippers of Baal *came*.
— *And they came* into the house of Baal;
23. *And* Jehu *went*,
24. *And when they went in* to offer
11: 9. *and came* to Jehoiada the priest.
13. *And* when Athaliah heard...*she came* to the
16. *and she went* by the way
18. *And* all the people of the land *went*
19. *and came* by the way of the gate
13:20. And the bands of the Moabites in*vaded*
14:13. *and came* to Jerusalem,
15:14. *and came* to Samaria,
16:12. And *when* the king *was come*
17:28. *Then* one of the priests...*came*
18:17. *and came* to Jerusalem. *And* when they were come up, *they came* and stood by
37. *Then came* Eliakim
19: 1. *and went* into the house of the
5. *So* the servants of king Hezekiah *came*
23. *and I will enter* into the
32. *He shall* not *come* into this city,
33. By the way that *he came*,
— *shall* not *come* into this city,
20: 1. *And* the prophet Isaiah the son of Amoz *came*
14. *Then came* Isaiah the prophet
— from whence *came they*
22: 9. *And* Shaphan the scribe *came*
23:34. *and he came* to Egypt,
24:10. and the city was besieged. (marg. *and* the city *came* into siege)

2K. 24:11. *And* Nebuchadnezzar king of Babylon *came*
25: 2. And the city was besieged (lit. *and* the city *came* into siege)
23. *there came* to Gedaliah
26. *and came* to Egypt:
1Ch. 4:41. *And* these written by name *came*
7:22. *and* his brethren *came* to comfort him.
23. And *when he went in* to his wife,
10: 4. lest these uncircumcised *come*
7. *and* the Philistines *came* and dwelt
8. *when* the Philistines *came*
11: 3. *Therefore came* all the elders
5. *Thou shalt* not *come* hither.
12:16. *And there came* of the
22. *there came* to David to help
13: 9. And *when they came* unto
17:16. *And* David the king *came* and sat
18: 5. And *when* the Syrians of Damascus *came*
19: 2. *So* the servants of David *came*
7. *who came* and pitched before
— *and came* to battle.
15. *and entered* into the city. *Then* Joab *came* to Jerusalem.
17. *and came* upon them,
20: 1. *and came* and besieged Rabbah.
21: 4. *and came* to Jerusalem.
11. *So* Gad *came* to David,
21. *And* as David *came* to Ornan,
2Ch. 1:10. go out *and come in* before this people:
13. *Then* Solomon *came*
5: 4. *And* all the elders of Israel *came;*
8:18. *and they went* with the servants
9: 1. *she came* to prove Solomon with
— and *when she was come* to Solomon,
21. *came* the ships of Tarshish
10: 3. *So* Jeroboam and all Israel *came*
12. *So* Jeroboam and all the people *came*
11: 1. And *when* Rehoboam *was come*
12: 4. *and came* to Jerusalem.
14: 9(8). *and came* unto Mareshah.
15:12. *And they entered* into a covenant
18:14. And *when he was come* to the king,
24. that day when *thou shalt go*
29. *and they went* to the battle.
19:10. what cause soever *shall come*
20: 2. *Then there came* some that told
9. If, (when) evil *cometh* upon us,
25. And *when* Jehoshaphat and his people *came*
28. *And they came* to Jerusalem
21:12. *And there came* a writing to him
23: 2. *and they came* to Jerusalem.
6. *let* none *come* into the house
— *they shall go in*, for they are holy:
12. *Now* when Athaliah heard...*she came* to
15. and *when she was come* to
17. *Then* all the people *went*
19. any thing *should enter in.*
20. *and they came* through the high gate into
24:23. *and they came* to Judah
25: 7. *let* not the army of Israel *go*
26:16. *and went* into the temple
17. *And* Azariah the priest *went in*
28:20. *And* Tilgath-pilneser king of Assyria *came*
29:15. sanctified themselves, *and came,*
16. *And* the priests *went* into the inner
18. *Then they went in* to Hezekiah
30:11. humbled themselves, *and came* to
27. *and* their prayer *came*
31: 8. And *when* Hezekiah and the princes *came*
32: 1. *and entered* into Judah, and
4. *should* the kings of Assyria *come,*
21. And *when he was come* into the house
34: 9. And *when they came* to Hilkiah
35:22. *and came* to fight in the valley of Megiddo.
Ezr. 7: 8. *And he came* to Jerusalem in the fifth
8:32. *And we came* to Jerusalem,
10: 8. that whosoever *would* not *come*
14. *let* all *them...come* at appointed times,
Neh. 1: 2. *That* Hanani, one of my brethren, *came,*
2: 7. till *I come* into Judah;
8. for the house that *I shall enter*
9. *Then I came* to the governors
11. *So I came* to Jerusalem,
15. *and entered* by the gate

Neh. 4:11(5). till *we come* in the midst
6:11. *would go* into the temple to save his life? *I will* not *go in.*
9:24. *So* the children *went in*
13: 1. *should* not *come* into
7. *And I came* to Jerusalem,
19. *there should* no burden *be brought*
Est. 1:19. That Vashti *come* no more
2:14. *she came in* unto the king no more,
4: 2. *And came* even before the king's
4. *So* Esther's maids and her chamberlains *came*
9. *And* Hatach *came* and told Esther
11. *shall come* unto the king
16. so *will I go in* unto the king,
5: 4, 8. *let* the king and Haman *come*
5. *So* the king and Haman *came*
10. *and when he came* home,
6: 5. And the king said, *Let him come in.*
6. *So* Haman *came in.*
7: 1. *So* the king and Haman *came*
Job 1: 6. a day *when* the sons of God *came*
— *and* Satan *came* also among them.
7. Whence *comest thou?*
2: 1. a day *when* the sons of God *came*
— *and* Satan *came* also among them
2. From whence *comest thou?*
11. *Now* when Job's three friends heard...*they came*
3: 6. *let it* not *come* into the
7. *let* no joyful voice *come* therein.
24. For my sighing *cometh*
25. which I was afraid of *is come*
26. *yet* trouble *came.*
4: 5. But now *it is come* upon thee,
5:21. afraid of destruction when *it cometh.*
26. *Thou shalt come* to (thy) grave
6: 8. Oh that *I might have* my request; (lit. my request *would come*)
9:32. *we should come* together
13:16. an hypocrite *shall* not *come*
15:21. the destroyer *shall come upon him.*
19:12. His troops *come* together,
20:22. the wicked *shall come upon him.*
21:17. *and* (how oft) *cometh* their
22: 4. *will he enter* with thee
21. thereby good *shall come unto thee.*
23: 3. *I might come* (even) to his seat!
27: 9. when trouble *cometh* upon him?
28:20. Whence then *cometh* wisdom?
29:13. that was ready to perish *came*
30:26. then evil *came* (unto me): *and* when I waited for light, *there came* darkness.
37: 8. *Then* the beasts *go* into dens,
9. Out of the south *cometh*
38:11. Hitherto *shalt thou come,*
41:13(5). who *can come* (to him) with
16(8). no air *can come* between them.
42:11. *Then came there* unto him
Ps. 5: 7(8). *I will come* (into) thy house
18: 6(7). my cry *came* before him,
22:31(32). *They shall come,* and shall declare
24: 7, 9. *and* the King of glory *shall come in.*
26: 4. neither *will I go in* with
35: 8. *Let* destruction *come upon him*
36:11(12). *Let* not the foot of pride *come against me,*
37:13. he seeth that his day *is coming.*
15. Their sword *shall enter*
42: 2(3). when *shall I come* and appear
43: 4. *Then will I go* unto the altar
45:15(16). *they shall enter* into the king's palace.
49:19(20). *He shall go* to the generation of his (marg. (The soul) *shall go*)
50: 3. Our God *shall come,*
55: 5(6). trembling *are come* upon me,
63: 9(10). *shall go* into the lower parts
65: 2(3). unto thee *shall* all flesh *come.*
66:13. *I will go* into thy house
69:27(28). *let them* not *come*
71:16. I *will go* in the strength of the Lord
18. to every one (that) *is to come.*
73:17. Until *I went* into the sanctuary
79:11. *Let* the sighing of the prisoner *come*
86: 9. whom thou hast made *shall come*
88: 2(3). *Let* my prayer *come* before thee:
95:11. *they should* not *enter*

Ps.101: 2. O when *wilt thou come*
102: 1(2). *let* my cry *come* unto thee.
105:23. Israel *also came* into Egypt;
31. *and there came* divers sorts of flies,
34. He spake, *and* the locusts *came*,
109:17. *so let it come unto him:*
18. *so let it come* into his bowels
118:19. *I will go* into them,
20. into which the righteous *shall enter*.
119:41. *Let* thy mercies *come also unto me*,
77. *Let* thy tender mercies *come unto me*,
170. *Let* my supplication *come*
121: 1. from whence *cometh* my help.
126: 6. *shall* doubtless *come* again
132: 3. Surely *I will* not *come* into
7. *We will go* into his tabernacles:
143: 2. And *enter* not into judgment
Pro. 2:10. When wisdom *entereth* into
3:25. desolation of the wicked, when *it cometh*.
4:14. *Enter* not into the path
6:15. Therefore *shall* his calamity *come*
7:20. *will come* home at the day appointed.
22. as an ox *goeth* to the slaughter,
10:24. *it shall come upon him:*
11: 2. *then cometh* shame:
8. *and* the wicked *cometh* in his
27. *it shall come unto him.*
18: 6. A fool's lips *enter* into contention,
17. (כתיב) [The קרי reads in preterite, which the English follows; the lit. of כתיב is, his neighbour *shall come*]
22:24. with a furious man *thou shalt* not *go:*
23:10. *enter* not into the fields
24:25. a good blessing *shall come*
26: 2. the curse causeless *shall* not *come*.
27:10. neither *go* into thy brother's house
28:22. that poverty *shall come upon him.*
Ecc. 2:12. *that cometh* after the king?
12: 1. while the evil days *come* not,
Cant.4: 8. *Come* with me from Lebanon,
16. *Let* my beloved *come*
Isa. 1:12. When *ye come* to appear before
23. neither *doth* the cause of the widow *come*
3:14. The Lord *will enter* into judgment
5:19. Holy One of Israel draw nigh *and come*,
26. *they shall come* with speed
7:24. with bows *shall* (men) *come*
25. there *shall* not *come* thither
10: 3. desolation (which) *shall come* from far?
13: 2. *that they may go* into the gates
6. *it shall come* as a destruction
26: 2. which keepeth the truth *may enter in*.
28:15. *it shall* not *come unto us:*
30:13. whose breaking *cometh* suddenly
32:10. the gathering *shall* not *come*.
35: 4. your God *will come* (with) vengeance,
— he *will come* and save you.
36:22. *Then came* Eliakim,
37: 1. *and went* into the house
5. *So* the servants of king Hezekiah *came*
24. *and I will enter* into the height
33. *He shall* not *come* into this city,
34. *shall* not *come* into this city,
38: 1. *And* Isaiah the prophet the son of Amoz *came* unto him,
39: 3. *Then came* Isaiah the prophet
— from whence *came they*
40:10. the Lord God *will come*
41: 3. *he had* not *gone* with his feet.
25. *and he shall come* upon princes
44: 7. and *shall come*,
45:24. to him *shall* (men) *come;*
47: 9. *But* these two (things) *shall come*
11. *and* desolation *shall come*
13. that *shall come* upon thee.
48: 3. suddenly, *and they came to pass.*
5. before *it came to pass*
49:12. these *shall come* from far:
52: 1. *there shall* no more *come* into
57: 2. *He shall enter* into peace: (marg. *go in* peace)
59:19. When the enemy *shall come in* like a flood,
60: 4. thy sons *shall come* from far,
5. the Gentiles *shall come* unto thee.
6. all they from Sheba *shall come:*
13. The glory of Lebanon *shall come*
20. Thy sun *shall* no more *go down;*

Isa. 66: 7. before her pain *came*, she was delivered
15. the Lord *will come* with fire,
23. *shall* all flesh *come* to worship
Jer. 2: 3. evil *shall come* upon them,
7. *but when ye entered,*
31. *we will come* no more unto thee?
3:18. *and they shall come* together
4: 5. *and let us go* into the defenced cities.
12. *shall come* unto me:
5:12. neither *shall* evil *come*
6: 3. their flocks *shall come* unto her;
20. To what purpose *cometh there*
26. the spoiler *shall* suddenly *come*
8:14. *and let us enter* into the
16. *for they are come*, and have
9:17(16). mourning women, *that they may come;*
—(—). cunning (women), *that they may come:*
16: 5. *Enter* not into the house
8. *Thou shalt* not also *go* into the house of feasting,
19. the Gentiles *shall come*
17: 6. shall not see when good *cometh;*
8. shall not see when heat *cometh*,
15. *let it come* now.
19. the kings of Judah *come in*,
19:14. *Then came* Jeremiah
20: 6. *thou shalt come* to Babylon,
21:13. who *shall enter* into our
23:17. No evil *shall come* upon
26:21. *and went* into Egypt;
31: 9. *They shall come* with weeping,
32: 8. *So* Hanameel mine uncle's son *came* to me
23. *And they came in*, and possessed
34: 3. *thou shalt go* to Babylon.
35:11. *and let us go* to Jerusalem
36:14. *and came* unto them.
20. *And they went in* to the king
29. The king of Babylon *shall* certainly *come*
37:19. The king of Babylon *shall* not *come*
38:11. *and went* into the house
27. *Then came* all the princes
39: 3. *And* all the princes of the king of Babylon *came in*,
40: 6. *Then went* Jeremiah
8. *Then they came* to Gedaliah
10. which *will come* unto us:
12. *and came* to the land of Judah,
41: 5. *That there came* certain
42:14. but *we will go* into the land
19. *Go ye* not into Egypt:
43: 2. *Go* not into Egypt
7. *So they came* into the land
— *thus came they* (even) to
46:18. by the sea, (so) *shall he come.*
48: 8. *And* the spoiler *shall come*
49: 4. Who *shall come* unto me?
36. the outcasts of Elam *shall* not *come.*
50: 4. the children of Israel *shall come*, they and
51:48. for the spoilers *shall come*
53. from me *shall* spoilers *come*
60. evil that *should come* upon Babylon,
52: 5. *So* the city *was* besieged (lit. *and* the city *came* into siege)
Lam. 1:10. *they should* not *enter*
22. *Let* all their wickedness *come*
4:12. the enemy *should have entered*
5: 4. our wood *is* sold unto us. (marg. *cometh* for price)
Eze. 2: 2. *And* the spirit *entered*
3:15. *Then I came* to them of the
24. *Then* the spirit *entered*
7:26. Mischief *shall come* upon
8:10. *So I went in* and saw;
9: 2. *and they went in*, and stood
10: 2. *And he went in* in my sight.
6. *then he went in*, and stood
13: 9. neither *shall they enter*
14: 1. *Then came* certain of the
16: 7. *and thou art come* to
8. *and entered* into a covenant with thee,
20:38. *they shall* not *enter* into the land of Israel:
22: 4. *and art come* (even) unto
23:17. *And* the Babylonians *came* to her
39. *then they came* the same day into my
44. *Yet they went in* unto her, as they
24:16. neither *shall* thy tears *run down.* (marg. *go*)
26. *shall come* unto thee,

Eze.32:11. of Babylon *shall come upon thee.*
33: 4, 6. *if* the sword *come,* and take
31. *And they come* unto thee
36:20. *And when they entered*
37:10. *and* the breath *came* into them,
38: 8. *thou shalt come* into the land
9. Thou shalt ascend and *come*
11. *I will go* to them
40: 6. *Then came he* unto the gate
44: 2. no man *shall enter in*
3. *he shall enter* by the way
9. *shall enter* into my sanctuary,
16. They *shall enter* into my sanctuary,
25. *they shall come* at no dead
46: 8. *he shall go in* by the way
10. of them, when they go in, *shall go in;*
47: 9. whithersoever the rivers *shall come,*
— whither the river *cometh.*
Dan 2: 2. *So they came* and stood before the king.
8: 6. *And he came* to the ram
17. *So he came* near where I stood:
11: 6. *shall come* to the king of the
7. *which shall come* with an army, *and shall enter* into the fortress
13. *shall* certainly *come*
15. *So* the king of the north *shall come,*
24. *He shall enter* peaceably
Hos. 4:15. *come* not *ye* unto Gilgal,
6: 3. *and he shall come* unto us
7: 1. and the thief *cometh in,*
9: 4. *shall* not *come* into the house
10:12. till *he come* and rain
11: 9. *I will* not *enter* into the city.
13:13. *shall come* upon him:
15. an east wind *shall come,*
Joel 1:15. from the Almighty *shall it come.*
2: 9. *they shall enter in* at the windows
Am. 5: 5. nor *enter* into Gilgal,
9. so that the spoiled shall *come*
Obad. 13. *Thou shouldest* not *have entered*
Jon. 1: 8. and whence *comest thou?*
2: 7(8). *and* my prayer *came in* unto thee,
Mic. 1:15. *he shall come* unto Adullam
3:11. none evil *can come* upon us.
5: 5(4). when the Assyrian *shall come*
6(5). when *he cometh* into our
7:12. *he shall come* even to thee
Hab. 1: 8. their horsemen *shall come*
9. *They shall come* all for violence:
2: 3. because *it will* surely *come,*
3: 3. God *came* from Teman,
16. rottenness *entered* into my bones,
Zep. 2: 2. of the Lord *come* upon you, before the day of the Lord's anger *come*
Hag. 1:14. *and they came* and did work
Zec. 1:21(2:4). *but* these *are come* to fray
6:15. they (that are) far off *shall come*
8:20. that *there shall come* people,
9: 9. thy King *cometh* unto thee:
Mal. 3: 1. *shall* suddenly *come* to his temple,
4: 6(3:24). lest *I come* and smite the earth

KAL.—*Participle.* Poel.

Gen 7:16. *And they that went in,* went in
18:11. *well stricken* in age;
21. *which is come* unto me;
23:10, 18. all *that went in* at the gate
24:63. the camels (were) *coming.*
29: 6. Rachel his daughter *cometh*
32:13(14). took of that *which came*
33: 1. Esau *came,* and with him four hundred
37:19. this dreamer *cometh.*
25. a company of Ishmeelites *came*
30. whither *shall* I *go?*
38: 9. when *he went in* unto his brother's wife,
41:29. *there come* seven years
35. food of those good years *that come,*
42: 5. among those *that came:*
46: 8. of the children of Israel, *which came*
26. All the souls *that came* with Jacob
27. *which came* into Egypt,
48: 2. thy son Joseph *cometh*
Ex. 1: 1. of Israel, *which came* into Egypt;
3:13. I *come* unto the children of Israel,
14:28. the host of Pharaoh *that came*
18: 6. I thy father in law Jethro *am come*
16. *they come* unto me;

Ex. 19: 9. Lo, I *come* unto thee
34:12. the land whither thou *goest,*
Lev.14:46. *Moreover he that goeth* into the house
Nu. 4: 3. all *that enter* into the host,
23. all *that enter in* to perform
30, 35, 39, 43. every one *that entereth* into the
47. every one *that came* to do
19:14. all *that come* into the tent,
21: 1. heard tell that Israel *came*
22:36. Balak heard that Balaam *was come,*
25: 6. one of the children of Israel *came*
31:14. *which came* from the battle.
21. unto the men of war *which went*
34: 2. When ye *come* into the land
Deu 4: 5. the land whither ye *go* to possess
7: 1. the land whither thou *goest*
9: 5. *dost* thou *go* to possess
11:10. the land, whither thou *goest in*
29. the land whither thou *goest* to
12:29. whither thou *goest* to possess
18: 9. When thou *art come* into the land
23:20(21) & 28:21, 63 & 30:16. whither thou *goest* to possess it.
31:16. whither they *go* (to be) among them,
Jos. 2: 3. Bring forth the men *that are come*
18. we *come* into the land,
6: 1. and none *came in.*
Jud. 7:17. *when* I *come* to the outside
9:31. *be come* to Shechem;
Ru. 2: 4. Boaz *came* from Beth-lehem,
4:11. the woman *that is come* into
1Sa. 2:14. all the Israelites *that came*
31. Behold, the days *come,*
4:13. And when the man *came* into the
16. I (am) *he that came* out of the army,
5: 5. nor any *that come into* Dagon's
6:14. the cart *came* into the field
9:14. when they *were come*
11: 9. the messengers *that came,*
13:10. behold, Samuel *came;*
17:43. that thou *comest* to me
45. Thou *comest* to me with a sword,
— but I *come* to thee
18:16. went out *and came in*
20:41. as soon as the lad *was gone,*
42(21:1). Jonathan *went into* the city.
22: 9. I saw the son of Jesse *coming*
25:19. behold, I *come* after you.
30:23. the company *that came*
2Sa. 1: 2. behold, a man *came* out of the
2:23. as many *as came* to the place
3:22. Joab *came* from (pursuing) a troop,
24. behold, Abner *came* unto thee;
6:16. as the ark of the Lord *came*
11:10. *Camest* thou not from (thy) journey?
12: 4. the wayfaring man *that was come*
— dressed it for the man *that was come*
18:31. And, behold, Cushi *came;*
19:41(42). all the men of Israel *came*
20:12. every one *that came* by him stood
1 K. 14: 5. the wife of Jeroboam *cometh*
6. *as she came in* at the door,
17. (and) *when* she *came* to the threshold
15:17. to go out *or come in* to Asa
2 K. 3:20. behold, *there came* water
4:42. *there came* a man
5:25. But he *went in,* and stood
11: 5. *that enter in* on the sabbath
8. *and he that cometh* within the ranges,
9. *that were to come in* on the sabbath,
15. *and him that followeth* (lit. *goeth* after) her
13:20. invaded the land *at the coming in of* the
20:17. Behold, the days *come,*
1Ch 2:55. the Kenites *that came* of Hemath,
4:38. These *mentioned* (marg. *coming*) by (their)
12: 1. these (are) they *that came* to David
27: 1. *which came in* and went out month by
2Ch 7:11. all *that came* into Solomon's heart
13: 9. so that whosoever *cometh* to consecrate
15: 5. *nor to him that came in,*
16: 1. let none go out *or come in*
20: 2. There *cometh* a great multitude
12. this great company *that cometh*
22. *which were come* against Judah;
22: 1. the band of men *that came*
23: 4. part of you *entering* on the sabbath,
7. *and whosoever* (else) *cometh*

2Ch 23: 8. his men *that were to come in* on the sabbath,
14. and *whoso followeth* her, (lit. *goeth* after)
28: 9. went out before the host *that came*
12. stood up against them *that came*
30:25. all the congregation *that came* out of Israel, and the strangers *that came*
31:16. unto every one *that entereth*
Ezr. 3: 8. all *they that were come*
8:15. to the river *that runneth*
35. *which were come* out of the captivity,
9:11. unto which ye *go* to possess
13. after all *that is come* upon us
Neh 5:17. *beside those that came* unto us
6:10. for *they will come* to slay thee; yea, in the night *will they come*
17. and (the letters) of Tobiah *came* unto them.
7: 7. *Who came* with Zerubbabel,
9:33. in all that *is brought* upon us;
10:29(30). *and entered* into a curse,
13:22. *and* (that) *they should come*
Est. 1:17. but *she came* not.
2:13. Then thus *came* (every) maiden
14. In the evening she *went*,
Job 1:16, 17, 18. there *came* also another,
2:11. all this evil *that was come*
Ps. 118:26. Blessed (be) *he that cometh* in the name
Pro. 2:19. None *that go unto her* return again,
6:29. So *he that goeth in* to his
13:12. but (when) the desire *cometh*,
23:30. *they that go* to seek mixed wine.
Ecc. 1: 4. (another) generation *cometh*:
2:16. in the days *to come*
5: 3(2). a dream *cometh*
Cant. 2: 8. he *cometh* leaping
Isa. 13: 5. *They come* from a far country,
21: 1. *it cometh* from the desert,
9. here *cometh* a chariot of men,
27: 6. He shall cause *them that come*
11. the women *come*, (and) set them on fire:
39: 6. Behold, the days *come*,
41:22. declare us *things for to come*.
62:11. thy salvation *cometh*;
63: 1. Who (is) this *that cometh* from Edom,
4. the year of my redeemed *is come*.
66:18. their thoughts: *it shall come*,
Jer. 4:16. watchers *come* from a far country,
6:22. a people *cometh* from the north
7: 2. *that enter in* at these gates
32 & 9:25(24). behold, the days *come*,
10:22. the noise of the bruit *is come*,
13:20. *them that come* from the north:
16:14. behold, the days *come*, saith the Lord,
17:20. *that enter in* by these gates:
19: 6. behold, the days *come*, saith the Lord,
22: 2. thy people *that enter in*
23: 5, 7. Behold, the days *come*,
26: 2. *which come* to worship
27: 3. *which come to* Jerusalem
28: 4. *that went* into Babylon,
30: 3. For, lo, the days *come*,
31:27, 31, 38. Behold, the days *come*,
32: 7. thine uncle *shall come* unto thee,
33: 5. *They come* to fight with the
14. Behold, the days *come*,
36: 6. *that come out* of their cities.
9. to all the people *that came*
44: 8. whither ye *be gone*
14. *which are gone* into the land
28. *that are gone* into the land
47: 4. Because of the day *that cometh*
48:12 & 49:2. behold, the days *come*,
50:27. for their day *is come*,
31. for thy day *is come*,
41. a people *shall come* from the north,
51:13. thine end *is come*,
47, 52. behold, the days *come*,
Lam 1: 4. none *come to* the solemn feasts:
Eze. 1: 4. a whirlwind *came* out of the north,
7: 5. an only evil, behold, *is come*.
6. behold, *it is come*.
7. the time *is come*,
10. Behold the day, behold, *it is come*:
9: 2. six men *came* from the way
16:16. (the like things) *shall* not *come*,
17:12. the king of Babylon *is come*
20: 3. *Are* ye *come* to enquire of me?
Eze. 20:29. the high place whereunto ye *go*?
21: 7(12). For the tidings; because *it cometh*:
—(—) weak (as) water: behold, *it cometh*,
23:40. sent for men *to come* (marg. *coming*)
30: 9. as in the day of Egypt: for, lo, *it cometh*.
33: 3. when he seeth the sword *come*
6. if the watchman see the sword *come*,
33. lo, *it will come*,
38:13. *Art* thou *come* to take a spoil?
41: 6. *and they entered* into the wall
46: 9. *he that entereth in* by the way
— *and he that entereth* by the way
Dan 8: 5. an he goat *came* from the west
9:26. the prince *that shall come*
11:16. But *he that cometh* against
Am. 4: 2. the days *shall come* upon you,
8:11 & 9:13. Behold, the days *come*,
Jon. 1: 3. he found a ship *going to* Tarshish:
Zec. 1:21(2:4). What *come* these to do?
2:10(14). for, lo, I *come*,
8:10. to him that went out *or came in*
12: 9. nations *that come* against
14:16. *which came* against
Mal 4: 1(3:19). the day *cometh*, that shall burn
—(-:—) the day *that cometh* shall burn

* HIPHIL.—*Preterite*. *

Gen 4: 4. *he* also *brought* of the firstlings
20: 9. *thou hast brought* on me
26:10. *and thou shouldest have brought*
27:10. *And thou shalt bring* (it) to
12. *and I shall bring* a curse
31:39. *I brought* not unto thee;
39:14. *he hath brought in* an Hebrew
17. which *thou hast brought*
43: 2. which *they had brought* out
9. if *I bring him* not unto thee,
46: 7. *brought he* with him into Egypt.
32. *they have brought* their flocks,
Ex. 6: 8. *And I will bring* you
18:19. *that* thou *mayest bring*
23:23. *and bring thee in* unto the Amorites,
25:14. *And thou shalt put* the staves
26:11. *and put* the taches into the loops,
33. *that thou mayest bring in* thither
32:21. that *thou hast brought* so great
35:21. *they brought* the Lord's offering
22. *brought* bracelets, and earrings,
23. badgers' skins, *brought* (them).
24. *brought* the Lord's offering:
— for any work of the service, *brought* (it).
27. the rulers *brought* onyx stones,
29. Israel *brought* a willing offering
36: 3. Israel *had brought* for the work
— they *brought* yet unto him
40: 4. *And thou shalt bring in* the table,
— *and thou shalt bring in* the candlestick,
Lev. 2: 2. *And he shall bring it* to Aaron's sons
8. *And thou shalt bring* the meat offering
4: 4. *And he shall bring* the bullock
5. *and bring* it to the tabernacle
14. *and bring* him before the tabernacle
16. *And* the priest that is anointed *shall bring*
23. *he shall bring* his offering,
28. *then he shall bring* his offering,
5: 6. *And he shall bring* his trespass offering
7, 15. *then he shall bring* for his trespass,
8. *And he shall bring* them unto the priest,
11. *then he* that sinned *shall bring*
12. *Then shall he bring it* to the priest,
18. *And he shall bring* a ram
14:23. *And he shall bring* them
42. take other stones, *and put* (them) *in*
15:29. *and bring* them unto the priest,
16:12. *and bring* (it) within the vail:
15. *and bring* his blood within the vail,
17: 4. *bringeth it* not unto the door
5. *even that they may bring them* unto
19:21. *And he shall bring* his trespass offering
23:10. *then ye shall bring* a sheaf
26:25. *And I will bring* a sword upon you,
36. *I will send* a faintness
41. *and have brought* them into
Nu. 5:15. *Then shall* the man *bring*
— *and he shall bring* her offering
6:12. *and shall bring* a lamb
14: 8. *then he will bring* us

Nu. 14:24. *him will I bring* into the land
31. them *will I bring in*,
15:25. they *shall bring* their offering,
16:14. *thou hast* not *brought us*
20: 4. why *have ye brought* up
32:17. until *we have brought them*
Deu 9: 4. *hath brought me in* to possess
12: 6. *And* thither *ye shall bring*
21:12. *Then thou shalt bring her* home
26:10. *I have brought* the firstfruits
30: 5. *And* the Lord thy God *will bring thee*
Jos. 18: 6. *and bring* (the description) hither (lit. *and bring them*)
Jud. 7:25. and *brought* the heads of Oreb and Zeeb
12: 9. *took in* thirty daughters
18: 3. Who *brought thee* hither?
1Sa. 1:22. *and* (then) *I will bring him*,
10:27. *brought* him no presents.
15:15. Saul said, *They have brought them*
16:17. *and bring* (him) to me.
20: 8. *thou hast brought* thy servant
21:15(16). that *ye have brought* this
25:27. which thine handmaid *hath brought*
35. which *she had brought* him,
2Sa. 3:22. *brought in* a great spoil
7:18. *thou hast brought me* hitherto?
9:10. *and thou shalt bring in* (the fruits),
14:10. *bring him* to me,
1K. 9: 9. the Lord *brought* upon them
10:11. *brought in* from Ophir great plenty
2K. 5:20. that which *he brought:*
9: 2. *and carry* him to an inner chamber;
10: 8. *brought* the heads of the king's sons.
19:25. now *have I brought it to pass*,
1Ch 11:19. their lives *they brought it*.
17:16. *thou hast brought me* hitherto?
22: 4. *brought* much cedar wood
2Ch 7:22. *hath he brought* all this evil
9:10. which *brought* gold from Ophir, *brought* algum trees
12. which *she had brought* unto the
15:11. the spoil (which) *they had brought*,
24:14. *they brought* the rest of the money
28:27. *they brought him* not into the
29:32. which the congregation *brought*,
31: 5. all (things) *brought they in* abundantly.
6. *they* also *brought in* the tithe
36: 7. Nebuchadnezzar also *carried*
18. all (these) *he brought* to Babylon.
Neh 1: 9. *and will bring them* unto the place
3: 5. *put* not their necks to the work
13:12. Then *brought* all Judah the tithe
Est. 5:12. the queen *did let* no man *come in*
Job 12: 6. into whose hand God *bringeth*
42:11. the Lord *had brought* upon him:
Ps. 66:11. *Thou broughtest us* into the net;
78:71. *he brought him* to feed Jacob
Cant. 1: 4. the king *hath brought me*
2: 4. *He brought me* to the banqueting
3: 4. until *I had brought him*
Isa. 14: 2. *and bring them* to their place:
37:26. now *have I brought it to pass*,
43:23. *Thou hast* not *brought* me
48:15. *I have brought him*, and he shall
49:22. *and they shall bring* thy sons
56: 7. *Even them will I bring* to my holy
66:20. *And they shall bring* all your
Jer. 3:14. *and I will bring* you to Zion:
15: 8. *I have brought* upon them
17:21. *nor bring* (it) *in* by the gates
20: 5. *and carry them* to Babylon.
23: 8. *led* the seed of the house of Israel
25: 9. *and will bring them* against this land,
13. *And I will bring* upon that land
32:42. Like as *I have brought* all this
35: 2. *and bring them* into the house
36:31. *and I will bring* upon them,
44: 2. all the evil that *I have brought*
49: 8. *I will bring* the calamity of Esau
36. *And* upon Elam *will I bring*
37. *and I will bring* evil upon them,
Lam. 1:21. *thou wilt bring* the day
3:13. *He hath caused* the arrows of his quiver *to enter*
Eze. 7:24. *Wherefore I will bring* the worst of the heathen,
12:13. *and I will bring* him to Babylon
Eze. 14:22. the evil that *I have brought*
— all that *I have brought* upon it.
17:20. *and I will bring him* to Babylon,
20:35,37. *And I will bring* you
23:22. *and I will bring them* against
27:26. Thy rowers *have brought thee*
34:13. *and will bring them* to their own land,
36:24. *and will bring* you
37:12. *and bring* you into the land of Israel.
21. *and bring* them into their own land:
38:16. *and I will bring thee* against
39: 2. *and will bring thee* upon the mountains
40: 2. In the visions of God *brought he me*
Dan. 1: 2. *brought* the vessels into the treasure house
Joel 3: 5(4:5). *have carried* into your temples
Am. 8: 9. *that I will cause* the sun *to go down*
Hag 1: 8. *and bring* wood, and build the house;
9. and *when ye brought* (it) home,
Zec. 8: 8. *And I will bring* them,
13: 9. *And I will bring* the third part
Mal. 1:13. *and ye brought* (that which)
— *thus ye brought* an offering:

HIPHIL.—*Infinitive.*

Gen 18:19. the Lord *may bring* upon Abraham
27: 5. to hunt (for) venison, (and) *to bring*
Ex. 23:20. *and to bring thee* into the place
35:29. made them willing *to bring*
36: 5. *bring* much more than enough (lit. increase *to bring*)
6. were restrained *from bringing*.
Lev. 23:14. that *ye have brought* an offering
15. the day *that ye brought*
Nu. 14:16. was not able *to bring* this people
20: 5. *to bring* us in unto this evil place?
Deu 4:38. *to bring thee in*, to give thee
6:23. that *he might bring* us in,
9:28. *to bring them* into the land
29:27(26). *to bring* upon it all the curses
1Sa. 9: 7. not a present *to bring* to the man
27:11. *to bring* (tidings) *to* Gath,
2Sa. 3:13. except *thou* first *bring* Michal
17:14. that the Lord *might bring* evil
2K. 12: 4(5). *to bring* into the house of the Lord,
1Ch 13: 5. *to bring* the ark of God
22:19. *to bring* the ark of the covenant
2Ch 24: 6. required of the Levites *to bring in*
9. *to bring in* to the Lord
31:10. Since (the people) began *to bring*
Ezr. 3: 7. *to bring* cedar trees from Lebanon
8:17. *that they should bring* unto us
30. *to bring* (them) to Jerusalem
Neh 8: 1. *to bring* the book of the law
10:34(35). *to bring* (it) into the house of our
35(36). *And to bring* the firstfruits
36(37). *to bring* to the house of our God,
11: 1. *to bring* one of ten to dwell
12:27. *to bring them* to Jerusalem,
Est. 1:11. *To bring* Vashti the queen
17. Vashti the queen *to be brought in* (lit. *to bring* Vashti)
3: 9. *to bring* (it) into the king's treasuries.
6: 1. *to bring* the book of records
14. hasted *to bring* Haman unto
Job 34:28. *So that they cause* the cry of the poor *to come*
Isa. 1:13. *Bring* no more vain oblations; (lit. add not *to bring*)
60: 9. *to bring* thy sons from far,
11. *that* (men) *may bring* unto thee
Jer. 17:18. *bring* upon them the day
24. *to bring in* no burden
39: 7. *to carry* him to Babylon.
41: 5. *to bring* (them) *to* the house
Eze. 20:15. that I would not *bring* them
42. *when I shall bring* you
32: 9. *when I shall bring* thy destruction
38:17. *that I would bring* thee
44: 7. *In that ye have brought* (into my)
Dan 1: 3. *that he should bring* (certain)
18. *he should bring them in*,
9:12. *by bringing* upon us
24. *and to bring in* everlasting
Hag 1: 6. *and bring in* little;

HIPHIL.—*Imperative.*

Gen 27: 4. *and bring* (it) to me,
7. *Bring* me venison,

Gen42:19. *carry* corn for the famine
34. *And bring* your youngest brother
43:16. *Bring* (these) men home,
Ex. 4: 6. *Put* now thine hand into thy
32: 2. *and bring* (them) unto me.
1Sa.20:40. Go, *carry* (them) to the city.
2Sa.13:10. *Bring* the meat into
1Ch 21: 2. *and bring* the number of them
2Ch 29:31. *and bring* sacrifices
Neh. 8:15. *and fetch* olive branches,
Pro.23:12. *Apply* thine heart unto
Isa. 16: 3. *Take* counsel, execute judgment; (marg. *Bring*)
43: 6. *bring* my sons from far,
Jer. 27:12. *Bring* your necks under the
Am. 4: 1. *Bring*, and let us drink.
4. *and bring* your sacrifices
Mal 3:10. *Bring* ye all the tithes

HIPHIL.—*Future.*

Gen 2:19. *and brought* (them) unto Adam
22. *and brought her* unto the man.
4: 3. *that* Cain *brought* of the fruit of the
6:19. two of every (sort) *shalt thou bring*
8: 9. *and pulled* her *in* unto him (marg: *caused* her *to come*)
19:10. *and pulled* Lot into the house
24:67. *And* Isaac *brought her* into his mother Sarah's tent,
27:14. *and brought* (them) to his mother:
25. *and he brought* him wine, and he
31. *and brought* it unto his father,
33. *and brought* (it) me,
29:13. *and brought him* to his house.
23. *and brought* her to him;
30:14. *and brought* them unto his mother
37: 2. *and* Joseph *brought* unto his father
28. *and they brought* Joseph into Egypt.
32. *and they brought* (it) to their father;
42:20. *bring* your youngest brother
37. Slay my two sons, if *I bring him* not
43:17,24. *and* the man *brought* the men
26. *they brought* him the present
44:32. If *I bring him* not unto thee,
47: 7. *And* Joseph *brought in* Jacob
14. *and* Joseph *brought* the money
17. *And they brought* their cattle
Ex. 2:10. *and she brought him* unto
4: 6. *And he put* his hand into his bosom:
11: 1. Yet *will I bring* one plague (more)
13: 5,11. the Lord *shall bring thee* into the land
15:17. *Thou shalt bring them in,*
16: 5. which *they bring in;*
18:22. they *shall bring* unto thee,
26. the hard causes *they brought*
19: 4. *and brought* you unto myself.
22:13(12). *let him bring it* (for) witness,
23:19. *thou shalt bring* into the house
32: 3. *and brought* (them) unto Aaron.
34:26. firstfruits of thy land *thou shalt bring*
35: 5. *let him bring it,* an offering
25. *and brought* that which they had
37: 5 & 38:7. *And he put* the staves
39:33. *And they brought* the tabernacle
40:21. *And he brought* the ark
Lev. 4:32. if *he bring* a lamb for a sin offering, *he shall bring it* a female
6: 6(5:25). *he shall bring* his trespass offering
21(14). *thou shalt bring it in:*
7:29. *shall bring* his oblation
30. His own hands *shall bring*
— *it shall he bring,*
10:15. the wave breast *shall they bring*
12: 6. *she shall bring* a lamb
17: 5. *may bring* their sacrifices,
9. *bringeth it* not unto the door
23:17. *Ye shall bring* out of your
24:11. *And they brought* him unto Moses:
Nu. 6:10. *he shall bring* two turtles,
13. he *shall be brought* (lit. (one) *shall bring* him)
7: 3. *And they brought* their offering
18:13. *they shall bring* unto the Lord,
20:12. therefore *ye shall* not *bring*
27:17. which *may bring them in;*
31:12. *And they brought* the captives,
54. *and brought* it into the tabernacle

Deu 6:10. the Lord thy God *shall have brought thee*
7: 1. *shall bring thee* into the land
26. Neither *shalt thou bring*
11:29. *hath brought thee in* unto the land
12:11. thither *shall ye bring* all
23:18(19). *Thou shalt* not *bring*
26: 2. which *thou shalt bring*
9. *And he hath brought us* into this
31:20. For when *I shall have brought them*
21. before *I have brought them*
23. for *thou shalt bring*
33: 7. *bring him* unto his people:
Jos. 7:23. *and brought them* unto Joshua,
23:15. so *shall* the Lord *bring* upon you
24: 7. *and brought* the sea upon them,
8. *And I brought* you into the land
Jud. 1: 7. *And they brought him* to Jerusalem,
2: 1. *and have brought* you unto the land
19: 3. *and she brought him* into her father's
21. *So he brought him* into his house,
21:12. *and they brought* them
1Sa. 1:24. *and brought him* unto the house
25. *and brought* the child to Eli.
5: 1. *and brought it* from Eben-ezer
2. *they brought* it into the house
7: 1. *and brought* it into the house
9: 7. what *shall we bring* the man?
22. *and brought them* into the
15:20. *and have brought* Agag
16:12. he sent, *and brought* him *in.*
17:18. *carry* these ten cheeses
54. *and brought it* to Jerusalem;
57. *and brought him* before Saul
18:27. *and* David *brought* their foreskins,
19: 7. *And* Jonathan *brought* David
20: 8. why *shouldest thou bring* me
21:14(15). wherefore (then) *have ye brought*
2Sa. 1:10. *and have brought them* hither
4: 8. *And they brought* the head
6:17. *And they brought in* the ark
8: 7. *and brought them* to Jerusalem.
13:10. *and brought* (them) into the chamber
14:23. *and brought* Absalom to Jerusalem.
23:16. *and brought* (it) to David:
1K. 1: 3. *and brought* her to the king.
2:40. *and brought* his servants
3: 1. *and brought her* into the city
24. *And they brought* a sword
4:28(5:8). dromedaries *brought they*
7:51. *And* Solomon *brought in*
8: 6. *And* the priests *brought in*
9:28. talents, *and brought* (it) to king Solomon.
15:15. *And he brought in* the things
20:39. *and brought* a man unto me,
21:29. *I will* not *bring* the evil
— *will I bring* the evil upon his
2K. 4:20. *and brought him* to his mother,
42. *and brought* the man of God
5: 6. *And he brought* the letter to the king
11: 4. *and brought* them to him
17:24. *And* the king of Assyria *brought*
20:20. *and brought* water into the city,
23: 8. *And he brought* all the priests
30. *and brought him* to Jerusalem,
24:16. *even them* the king of Babylon *brought*
25: 7. *and carried him* to Babylon.
1Ch. 4:10. *And* God *granted* him that
5:26. *and brought them* unto Halah,
9:28. *they should bring them in*
10:12. *and brought them* to Jabesh,
11:18. *and brought* (it) to David:
13:12. How *shall I bring* the ark
16: 1. *So they brought* the ark of God,
18: 7. *and brought them to* Jerusalem.
2Ch. 2:16(15). *and we will bring it* to thee
5: 1. *and* Solomon *brought in* (all) the
7. *And* the priests *brought in*
8:18. *and brought* (them) to king Solomon.
15:18. *And he brought into* the house
22: 9. *and brought him* to Jehu:
24:10. *and brought in,* and cast into the
11. at what time the chest *was brought*
25:12. *and brought them* unto the
14. *that he brought* the gods
23. *and brought him to* Jerusalem,
28: 5. *and brought* (them) *to* Damascus.
8. *and brought* the spoil to Samaria.

2Ch 28:13. *Ye shall* not *bring in*
15. *and brought them to* Jericho,
29: 4. *And he brought in* the priests
21. *And they brought* seven bullocks,
31. *And* the congregation *brought in*
30:15. *and brought in* the burnt offerings
31:12. *And brought in* the offerings
33:11. *Wherefore* the Lord *brought* upon them
34:16. *And* Shaphan *carried* the book
36: 4. *and carried him* to Egypt.
10. *and brought him* to Babylon,
Ezr. 8:18. *And...they brought* us a man
Neh 8: 2. *And* Ezra the priest *brought*
16. went forth, *and brought* (them),
9:23. *and broughtest them* into the
10:37(38). *we should bring* the firstfruits
39(40). *shall bring* the offering of the corn,
13:18. *and did* not our God *bring*
Est. 5:10. *and called* for his friends, (marg. *caused to come*)
6: 8. *Let* the royal apparel *be brought* (marg. *Let them bring*, &c.)
Job 14: 3. and *bringest* me into judgment with thee?
Ps. 43: 3. *let them bring me* unto thy holy hill,
78:29. for *he gave* them their own desire;
54. *And he brought them* to the border
90:12. *that we may apply* (marg. *cause to come*) (our) hearts unto wisdom.
105:40. *and he brought* quails,
Pro.21:27. *he bringeth it* with a wicked mind?
31:14. *she bringeth* her food from afar.
Ecc. 3:22. for who *shall bring him*
11: 9. God *will bring thee* into judgment.
12:14. God *shall bring* every work into
Cant.8: 2. I would lead thee, (and) *bring thee*
11. *was to bring* a thousand (pieces) of silver.
Isa. 7:17. The Lord *shall bring* upon thee,
31: 2. *and will bring* evil,
43: 5. *I will bring* thy seed from the east,
46:11. *I will* also *bring it to pass;*
58: 7. that *thou bring* the poor
60:17. For brass *I will bring* gold, and for iron *I will bring* silver,
66: 4. *will bring* their fears upon them;
20. as the children of Israel *bring*
Jer. 2: 7. *And I brought* you into a plentiful
11: 8. *therefore I will bring* upon them
23. for *I will bring* evil upon
13: 1. and *put it* not in water.
18:22. when *thou shalt bring* a troop
23:12. for *I will bring* evil upon them,
24: 1. *and had brought them to* Babylon.
26:23. *and brought him* unto Jehoiakim
27:11. But the nations that *bring*
28: 3. *and carried them to* Babylon:
35: 4. *And I brought* them *into* the house
37:14. *and brought him* to the princes.
40: 3. *Now* the Lord *hath brought*
48:44. for *I will bring* upon it,
49:32. *I will bring* their calamity
52:11. *and carried him* to Babylon,
Lam. 5: 9. *We gat* our bread with (the peril of) our lives (lit. upon our souls *we brought* our bread)
Eze. 5:17. *I will bring* the sword upon thee.
8: 3. *and brought* me in the visions
7. *And he brought* me to the door
14. *Then he brought* me to the door
16. *And he brought* me into
11: 1. *and brought* me unto the east gate
8. *I will bring* a sword upon you,
24. *and brought me* in a vision
14:17. Or (if) *I bring* a sword upon that
17: 4. *and carried it* into a land
12. *and led* them with him
13. *and hath taken* an oath of him: (lit. *and hath brought* him to an oath)
19: 4. *and they brought him* with
9. *and brought him* to the king
— *they brought him* into holds,
20:10. *and brought them* into the wilderness.
28. *when I had brought them* into the land,
33: 2. When *I bring* the sword upon a land,
40: 1. *and brought* me thither.
3. *And he brought* me thither,
17. *Then brought he me* into the
28, 35, 48. *And he brought me* to the
Eze.40:32. *And he brought me* into
41: 1. *Afterward he brought me* to the
42: 1. *and he brought me* into the
43: 5. *and brought me* into the inner court;
44: 4. *Then brought he me* the way
46:19. *After he brought me* through
Dan 1: 2. *which he carried into* the land
18. *then* the prince of the eunuchs *brought them*
9:14. *and brought it* upon us:
11: 8. *shall* also *carry* captives *into* Egypt
Mic. 1:15. Yet *will I bring* an heir unto thee,
Zep 3:20. At that time *will I bring* you
Zec.10:10. *I will bring them* again

HIPHIL.—*Participle.*

Gen 6:17. *do bring* a flood of waters
Ex. 10: 4. to morrow *will* I *bring* the locusts
Lev.18: 3. whither I *bring* you, shall ye
20:22. whither I *bring* you to dwell
Nu. 14: 3. wherefore *hath* the Lord *brought*
15:18. the land whither I *bring* you,
Deu 8: 7. the Lord thy God *bringeth thee*
2Sa. 5: 2. *and broughtest in* Israel:
1K. 10:25. they *brought* every man his present,
14:10. I *will bring* evil upon the house
17: 6. the ravens *brought* him bread
21:21. I *will bring* evil upon thee,
2K. 10:24. any of the men whom I *have brought*
21:12. I (am) *bringing* (such) evil
22:16. I *will bring* evil upon this place,
20. which I *will bring* upon this place.
1Ch 11: 2. *and broughtest in* Israel:
12:40. *brought* bread on asses,
2Ch 9:14. chapmen and merchants *brought*.
— *brought* gold and silver to Solomon.
24. they *brought* every man his present,
17:11. the Philistines *brought*
— the Arabians *brought* him flocks,
32:23. many *brought* gifts
34:24. I *will bring* evil upon this place,
28. the evil that I *will bring* upon this
Neh 10:31(32). the people of the land *bring* ware
13:15. *and bringing in* sheaves,
— *which they brought into* Jerusalem
16. *which brought* fish,
Ps. 74: 5. *according as* he *had lifted* up (lit. *carried* on high)
Jer. 4: 6. for I *will bring* evil from the north,
5:15. I *will bring* a nation upon you
6:19. I *will bring* evil upon this people,
11:11. I *will bring* evil upon them,
17:26. *bringing* burnt offerings,
— *and bringing* sacrifices of praise,
19: 3. I *will bring* evil upon this
15. I *will bring* upon this city
31: 8. I *will bring* them from the north
32:42. so *will* I *bring* upon them all
33:11. of them *that shall bring*
35:17. I *will bring* upon Judah
39:16. I *will bring* my words upon
42:17. the evil that I *will bring*
45: 5. I *will bring* evil upon all flesh,
49: 5. I *will bring* a fear upon thee,
51:64. the evil that I *will bring*
Eze. 6: 3. *will bring* a sword upon you,
26: 7. I *will bring* upon Tyrus
28: 7. I *will bring* strangers upon thee,
29: 8. I *will bring* a sword upon thee,
37: 5. I *will cause* breath *to enter*
42: 9. (כתיב) *the entry* on the east side, (marg. or, *he that brought me*)
Dan 11: 6. *and they that brought her*,
Zec. 3: 8. I *will bring forth* my servant

* HOPHAL.—*Preterite.* *

Gen33:11. my blessing that *is brought*
43:18. *they were brought into* Joseph's house;
Ex. 27: 7. *And* the staves *shall be put*
Lev.10:18. the blood of it *was* not *brought*
13: 2, 9. *then he shall be brought* unto
14: 2. *He shall be brought* unto the priest:
16:27. whose blood *was brought in*
Eze.40: 4. *art thou brought* hither:

HOPHAL.—*Future.*

Lev. 6:30(23). whereof (any) of the blood *is brought*
32. *it must be put* into water,

2K. 12: 4(5). that *is brought into* the house
16(17). *was* not *brought into* the house
Jer. 10: 9. Silver spread into plates *is brought*
27:22. *They shall be carried* to Babylon,

HOPHAL.—*Participle.*

Gen 43:18. at the first time *are* we *brought in;*
2K. 12: 9(10), 13(14). money (that was) *brought into*
22: 4. the silver *which is brought into*
2Ch 34: 9, 14. the money *that was brought into*
Ps. 45:14(15). that follow her *shall be brought*
Eze.23:42. the common sort (were) *brought*
30:11. *shall be brought* to destroy

---

936 בּוּז [*booz*].

∗ KAL.—*Preterite.* ∗

Pro. 1: 7. fools *despise* wisdom and instruction.
Zec 4:10. who *hath despised* the day

KAL.—*Infinitive.*

Cant 8: 7. it would *utterly* be contemned.

KAL.—*Future.*

Pro. 6:30. (Men) *do* not *despise* a thief,
23: 9. *he will despise* the wisdom of thy words.
22. *despise* not thy mother when she is old.
30:17. *and despiseth* to obey (his) mother,
Cant 8: 1. I *should* not *be despised.* (marg. *they should* not *despise* me)
7. it *would* utterly *be contemned.* (lit. contemning *they will contemn* it)

KAL.—*Participle.* Poel.

Pro.11:12. void of wisdom *despiseth* his neighbour:
13:13. *Whoso despiseth* the word
14:21. *He that despiseth* his neighbour

---

937 בּוּז *booz*, m.

Gen 38:23. lest we be *shamed:* (marg. become *a contempt*)
Job 12: 5. a lamp *despised* in the thought of him
21. He poureth *contempt* upon princes,
31:34. *or* did *the contempt of* families
Ps. 31:18(19). *and contemptuously* against the
107:40. He poureth *contempt* upon
119:22. Remove from me reproach *and contempt;*
123: 3. are exceedingly filled with *contempt.*
4. with *the contempt* of the proud.
Pro. 12: 8. a perverse heart shall be *despised.* (lit. shall be *for contempt*)
18: 3. cometh also *contempt,*

---

939 בּוּזָה *boo-zāh'*, f.

Neh 4: 4(3:36). for we are *despised:* (marg. *despite*)

---

943 בּוּךְ [*booch*].

∗ NIPHAL.—*Preterite.* ∗

Joel 1:18. the herds of cattle *are perplexed,*

NIPHAL.—*Participle.*

Ex. 14: 3. They (are) *entangled* in the land,
Est. 3:15. the city Shushan *was perplexed.*

944-45 בּוּל *bool*, m.

1K. 6:38(37). in the month *Bul,*
Job 40:20. the mountains bring him forth *food,*
Isa. 44:19. *to the stock of* a tree? (marg. *that which comes of*)

בּוּן see בִּין.

בּוּס [*boos*]. 947

∗ KAL.—*Future.* ∗

Ps. 44: 5(6). *will we tread* them *under*
60:12(14) & 108:13(14). *shall tread* down our enemies.
Pro.27: 7. The full soul *loatheth* an honeycomb; (marg. *treadeth under foot*)
Isa. 14:25. upon my mountains *tread him under foot.*
63: 6. *And I will tread down* the people

KAL.—*Participle.* Poel.

Zec.10: 5. as mighty (men), *which tread down*

∗ POLEL.—*Preterite.* ∗

Isa. 63:18. *have trodden down* thy sanctuary.
Jer. 12:10. *they have trodden* my portion *under foot,*

∗ HOPHAL.—*Participle.* ∗

Isa. 14:19. as a carcase *trodden under feet.*

∗ HITHPOLEL.—*Participle.* ∗

Eze.16: 6. saw thee *polluted* in thine own blood, (marg. *trodden under foot*)
22. *wast polluted* in thy blood.

בּוּץ *bootz*, m. 948

1Ch 4:21. that wrought *fine linen,*
15:27. clothed with a robe of *fine linen,*
2Ch 2:14(13). *and in fine linen,* and in crimson;
3:14. crimson, *and fine linen,*
5:12. arrayed in *white linen,*
Est. 1: 6. fastened with cords of *fine linen*
8:15. with a garment of *fine linen*
Eze.27:16. *and fine linen,* and coral,

בּוּקָה *boo-kāh'*, f. 950

Nah. 2:10(11). *She is empty,* and void,

בּוֹקֵר *bōh-kēhr'*, m. 951

Am. 7:14. but I (was) *an herdman,*

בּוֹר *bōhr*, m. 953

Gen 37:20. cast him into some *pit,* (lit. one of *the pits*)
22. cast him into this *pit*
24. cast him *into a pit: and the pit* (was)
28. lifted up Joseph out of *the pit,*
29. Reuben returned unto *the pit;* and, behold, Joseph (was) not *in the pit;*
40:15. should put me *into the dungeon.*
41:14. brought him hastily out of *the dungeon:*
Ex. 12:29. the captive that (was) in *the dungeon;* (lit. house of *the pit*)
21:33. open *a pit,* or if a man shall dig *a pit,*
34. The owner of *the pit* shall make
Lev.11:36. Nevertheless a fountain *or pit,*
Deu 6:11. *and wells* digged,
1Sa.13: 6. in high places, *and in pits.*
19:22. came to *a great well*
2Sa. 3:26. brought him again *from the well of*
23:15. the water *of the well of* Beth-lehem,
16. drew water *out of the well of*
20. in the midst of *a pit* in time
2K. 10:14. slew them at *the pit of* the shearing house,
18:31. the waters of *his cistern:* (marg. *pit*)
1Ch 11:17. the water *of the well of* Beth-lehem,
18. drew water *out of the well of* Beth-lehem,
22. slew a lion in *a pit*
2Ch 26:10. digged many *wells:* (marg. *cisterns*)
Neh 9:25. *wells* digged, vineyards, (marg. *cisterns*)
Ps. 7:15(16). He made *a pit,* and digged it,
28: 1. them that go down into *the pit.*
30: 3(4). that I should not go down to *the pit.*
40: 2(3). also *out of an* horrible *pit*
88: 4(5). them that go down into *the pit:*
6(7). Thou hast laid me *in the* lowest *pit,*
143: 7. them that go down into *the pit.*
Pro. 1:12. as those that go down into *the pit:*
5:15. Drink waters *out of thine own cistern,*
28:17. person shall flee to *the pit;*

Ecc.12: 6. or the wheel broken at *the cistern.*
Isa. 14:15. to the sides of *the pit.*
19. that go down to the stones of *the pit;*
24:22. prisoners are gathered in *the pit,* (marg. or, *dungeon*)
36:16. the waters of *his own cistern;*
38:18. they that go down into *the pit*
51: 1. to the hole of *the pit*
Jer. 6: 7. (כתיב) As *a fountain* casteth out
37:16. into *the dungeon,* (lit. house of *the pit*)
38: 6. cast him into *the dungeon*
— *And in the dungeon* (there was) no
7. had put Jeremiah in *the dungeon;*
9. they have cast into *the dungeon;*
10. the prophet out of *the dungeon,*
11. down by cords into *the dungeon*
13. took him up out of *the dungeon.*
41: 7. into the midst of *the pit,*
9. *Now the pit* wherein Ishmael
Lam 3:53. cut off my life *in the dungeon,*
55. *out of the* low *dungeon.*
Eze.26:20. with them that descend into *the pit,*
— with them that go down to *the pit,*
31:14. with them that go down to *the pit.*
16. with them that descend into *the pit:*
32:18. with them that go down into *the pit.*
23. set in the sides of *the pit,*
24, 25, 29, 30. them that go down to *the pit.*
Zec. 9:11. sent forth thy prisoners *out of the pit*

---

952 בּוּר *boor.*

* KAL.—*Infinitive.* *

Ecc. 9: 1. *even to declare* all this,

---

954 בּוֹשׁ *bōhsh.*

* KAL.—*Preterite.* *

Ezr. 8:22. *I was ashamed* to require
9: 6. *I am ashamed* and blush
Job 6:20. *They were confounded*
Ps. 22: 5(6). and *were* not *confounded.*
71:24. for *they are confounded,*
Isa. 19: 9. *Moreover they* that work...*shall be confounded.*
20: 5. they shall be afraid *and ashamed*
24:23. *and* the sun *ashamed,*
37:27. they were dismayed *and confounded:*
45:16. *They shall be ashamed,*
Jer. 2:36. as *thou wast ashamed of* Assyria.
9:19(18). *we are* greatly *confounded,*
12:13. *and they shall be ashamed*
14: 3. *they were ashamed* and confounded,
4. the plowmen *were ashamed,*
15: 9. *she hath been ashamed* and confounded:
20:11. *they shall be* greatly *ashamed;*
31:19. *I was ashamed,* yea, even
48:13. *And* Moab *shall be ashamed* of Chemosh, as the house of Israel *was ashamed*
39. Moab turned the back *with shame!*
49:23. Hamath *is confounded,*
50:12. Your mother *shall be* sore *confounded;*
51:51. *We are confounded,* because
Eze.16:63. That thou mayest remember, *and be confounded,*
Mic. 3: 7. *Then shall* the seers *be ashamed,* and the diviners

KAL.—*Infinitive.*

Jud. 3:25. they tarried till *they were ashamed:*
2K. 2:17. they urged him till *he was ashamed,*
8:11. until *he was ashamed:*
Jer. 6:15 & 8:12. they were not *at all* ashamed, (lit. *in being ashamed* they were not ashamed)

KAL.—*Imperative.*

Isa. 23: 4. *Be thou ashamed,* O Zidon:
Eze.16:52. *be thou confounded* also,
36:32. *be ashamed* and confounded

KAL.—*Future.*

2K. 19:26. they were dismayed *and confounded;*
Job 19: 3. *ye are* not *ashamed*
Ps. 6:10(11). *Let* all mine enemies *be ashamed*
—(—). let them return (and) *be ashamed*
25: 2. I trust in thee: *let me* not *be ashamed,*
3. *let* none that wait on thee *be ashamed: let* them *be ashamed*
20. *let me* not *be ashamed;* for I put
31: 1(2). *let me* never *be ashamed:*
17(18). *Let me* not *be ashamed,*
—(—) *let* the wicked *be ashamed,*
35: 4. *Let them be confounded* and put
26. *Let them be ashamed* and brought
37:19. *They shall* not *be ashamed*
40:14(15). *Let them be ashamed* and confounded
69: 6(7). *Let* not *them* that wait on thee,...*be ashamed*
70: 2(3). *Let them be ashamed*
71: 1. *let me* never *be put to confusion.*
13. *Let them be confounded* (and) consumed
83:17(18). *Let them be confounded* and troubled
86:17. may see (it), *and be ashamed:*
97: 7. *Confounded be* all *they*
109:28. *let them be ashamed;* but let
119: 6. Then *shall I* not *be ashamed,*
46. and *will* not *be ashamed.*
78. *Let* the proud *be ashamed;*
80. that *I be* not *ashamed.*
127: 5. *they shall* not *be ashamed,*
129: 5. *Let them* all *be confounded*
Isa. 1:29. For *they shall be ashamed*
26:11. *and be ashamed for* (their) envy
29:22. Jacob *shall* not now *be ashamed,*
41:11. *shall be ashamed* and confounded:
42:17. *they shall be* greatly *ashamed,*
44: 9. that *they may be ashamed.*
11. all his fellows *shall be ashamed:*
— *they shall be ashamed* together.
45:17. *ye shall* not *be ashamed*
24. *and* all that are incensed against him *shall be ashamed.*
49:23. *they shall* not *be ashamed*
50: 7. that *I shall* not *be ashamed.*
54: 4. for *thou shalt* not *be ashamed:*
65:13. but ye *shall be ashamed:*
66: 5. they *shall be ashamed.*
Jer. 2:36. *thou* also *shalt be ashamed of*
6:15 & 8:12. *they were* not at all *ashamed,*
17:13. all that forsake thee *shall be ashamed,*
18. *Let them be confounded*
— *let* not *me be confounded:*
22:22. surely then *shalt thou be ashamed*
51:47. her whole land *shall be confounded,*
Hos. 4:19. *and they shall be ashamed*
10: 6. *and* Israel *shall be ashamed*
13:15. *and* his spring *shall become dry,*
Joel 2:26,27. my people *shall* never *be ashamed.*
Mic. 7:16. The nations shall see *and be confounded*
Zep. 3:11. In that day *shalt thou* not *be ashamed*
Zec.13: 4. the prophets *shall be ashamed* every one

KAL.—*Part.* Poel.

Eze.32:30. *they are ashamed* of their might;

* PIEL.—*Preterite.* *

Ex. 32: 1. Moses *delayed* to come down
Jud. 5:28. Why *is* his chariot (so) *long*

* HIPHIL.—*Preterite.* *

Ps. 44: 7(8). *hast put* them *to shame*
53: 5(6). *thou hast put* (them) *to shame,*

HIPHIL.—*Future.*

Ps. 14: 6. *Ye have shamed* the counsel
119:31. *put me* not *to shame.*
116. *let me* not *be ashamed*

HIPHIL.—*Part.*

Pro.10: 5. a son *that causeth shame.*
12: 4. but *she that maketh ashamed*
14:35. *him that causeth shame.*
17: 2. over a son *that causeth shame,*
19:26. (is) a son *that causeth shame,*
29:15. *bringeth* his mother *to shame.*

* HITHPOLEL.—*Future.* *

Gen 2:25. and *were* not *ashamed.*

בּוּשָׁה *boo-shāh',* f. 955

Ps. 89:45(46). thou hast covered him with *shame.*

Eze. 7:18. *shame* (shall be) upon all faces,
Obad. 10. *shame* shall cover thee,
Mic. 7:10. *shame* shall cover her

956 **בּוּת [*booth*], Ch.**

* P'AL.—*Preterite.* *

Dan. 6:18(19). *and passed the night* fasting:

957 **בָּז & בַּז *bāhz* & *baz*, m.**

Nu. 14: 3. our children should be *a prey?*
31. which ye said should be *a prey,*
31:32. *the prey* which the men of war
Deu 1:39. which ye said should be *a prey,*
2K. 21:14. they shall become *a prey*
Isa. 8: 1. concerning Maher-shalal-hash-*baz*.(marg. in making speed to the spoil he hasteth *the prey*)
10: 6. and to take *the prey,*
33:23. the lame take *the prey.*
42:22. they are *for a prey,*
Jer. 2:14. why is he *spoiled?* (marg: (become) *a spoil*)
15:13. will I give *to the spoil* without price,
17: 3. all thy treasures *to the spoil,*
30:16. that prey upon thee will I give *for a prey.*
49:32. their camels shall be *a booty,*
Eze. 7:21. into the hands of the strangers for *a prey,*
23:46. to be removed *and spoiled.* (lit. *and for spoil*)
25: 7. will deliver thee *for a spoil* (see בַּג)
26: 5. it shall become *a spoil*
29:19. and take *her prey;*
34: 8. because my flock became *a prey,*
22. they shall no more be *a prey;*
28. they shall no more be *a prey*
36: 4. which became *a prey*
5. to cast it out *for a prey.*
38:12. and to take *a prey;*
13. gathered thy company to take *a prey?*

958 **בָּזָא [*bāh-zāh'*].**

* KAL.—*Preterite.* *

Isa. 18: 2,7. whose land the rivers *have spoiled!* (marg: *despise*)

959 **בָּזָה *bāh-zāh'*.**

* KAL.—*Preterite.* *

Nu. 15:31. Because *he hath despised*
2Sa.12: 9. Wherefore *hast thou despised*
10. because *thou hast despised me,*
2K. 19:21. *hath despised* thee,
Ps. 22:24(25). *he hath* not *despised*
69:33(34). *despiseth* not his prisoners.
102:17(18). not *despise* their prayer.
Isa. 37:22. *hath despised* thee,
Eze.16:59. which *hast despised* the oath
17:16. whose oath *he despised,*
18. *Seeing he despised* the oath
19. mine oath that *he hath despised,*
22: 8. *Thou hast despised* mine holy things,
Mal. 1: 6. Wherein *have we despised* thy name?

KAL.—*Future.*

Gen25:34. *thus* Esau *despised* (his) birthright.
1Sa. 10:27. *And they despised him,* and brought
17:42. *he disdained him:*
2Sa. 6:16. *and she despised* him in her heart.
1Ch 15:29. *and she despised* him in her heart.
Neh 2:19. *and despised* us, and said,
Est. 3: 6. And he thought scorn to lay hands (lit. *and despised* in his eyes)
Ps. 51:17(19). *thou wilt* not *despise.*
73:20. *thou shalt despise* their image.

KAL.—*Participle.* Poel.

1Sa. 2:30. *and they that despise me*
2Ch 36:16. *and despised* his words,
Pro.14: 2. perverse in his ways *despiseth him.*
15:20. a foolish man *despiseth* his mother.
19:16. *he that despiseth* his ways
Mal. 1: 6. *that despise* my name.

KAL.—*Participle.* Paül.

Ps. 22: 6(7). *and despised of* the people.
Ecc. 9:16. the poor man's wisdom (is) *despised,*
Jer. 49:15. *despised* among men.
Obad. 2. thou *art* greatly *despised.*

* NIPHAL.—*Participle.* *

Ps. 15: 4. In whose eyes a vile person *is contemned.*
119:141. I (am) small *and despised:*
Isa. 53: 3. *He is despised* and rejected
— *he was despised,* and we esteemed
Jer. 22:28. this man Coniah a *despised* broken idol?
Dan11:21. shall stand up *a vile person,*
Mal. 1: 7. The table of the Lord (is) *contemptible.*
12. his meat, (is) *contemptible.*
2: 9. have I also made you *contemptible*

* HIPHIL.—*Infinitive.* *

Est. 1:17. *so that they shall despise*

בִּזּוֹה *bāh-zōh'*, adj. 960

Isa. 49: 7. *to him whom* man *despiseth,* (marg. *despised* in soul)

בִּזָּה *biz-zāh'*, f. 961

2Ch 14:14(13). there was exceeding much *spoil*
25:13. three thousand of them, and took much *spoil.*
28:14. *the spoil* before the princes
Ezr. 9: 7. *and to a spoil,* and to confusion
Neh 4: 4(3:36). give them *for a prey*
Est. 9:10. *but on the spoil* laid they
15. *but on the prey* they laid
16. *but* they laid not their hands *on the prey,*
Dan 11:24. he shall scatter among them *the prey,*
33. by captivity, *and by spoil,*

בָּזַז *bāh-zaz'*. 962

* KAL.—*Preterite.* *

Nu. 31: 9. *took the spoil* of all their cattle,
32. which the men of war *had caught,*
53. the men of war *had taken spoil,*
Deu 2:35. *we took for a prey* unto ourselves,
3: 7. *we took for a prey* to ourselves.
Jos. 8:27 & 11:14. *took for a prey* unto themselves,
2Ch 28: 8. *took* also *away* much spoil
Isa. 33:23. the lame *take* the prey.
Jer. 20: 5. *which shall spoil them,* and take
Eze.26:12. *and make a prey* of thy merchandise:
29:19. *and take* her prey; (marg. *and prey* her prey)
39:10. *and rob* those that robbed

KAL.—*Infinitive.*

2Ch.20:25. people came *to take away*
Est. 3:13 & 8:11. the spoil of them *for a prey.*
Isa. 10: 6. *and to take* the prey,
Eze.38:12. *and to take* a prey; (marg. *to prey* the prey)
13. gathered thy company *to take* a prey?

KAL.—*Imperative.*

Nah. 2: 9(10). *Take ye the spoil* of silver, *take the spoil* of gold:

KAL.—*Future.*

Gen34:27. *and spoiled* the city,
29. *and spoiled* even all that
Deu20:14. *shalt thou take* unto thyself; (marg. *spoil*)
Jos. 8: 2. *shall ye take for a prey*
1Sa.14:36. *and spoil* them until the morning
2K. 7:16. *and spoiled* the tents

2 Ch 14:14(13). *and they spoiled* all the cities;
25:13. *and took* much spoil. (lit. *and spoiled* much spoil)
Ps. 109:11. *and let* the strangers *spoil*
Isa. 10: 2. (that) *they may rob* the fatherless!
11:14. *they shall spoil* them of the east
Zep. 2: 9. my people *shall spoil* them,

KAL.—*Participle.* Poel.

2 Ch 20:25. they were three days *in gathering*
Isa. 17:14. the lot *of them that rob us.*
42:24. Israel *to the robbers?*
Jer. 30:16. all *that prey upon thee*
Eze. 39:10. rob those *that robbed them,*

KAL.—*Participle.* Paül.

Isa. 42:22. But this (is) a people *robbed*

* NIPHAL.—*Preterite.* *

Am. 3:11. *and* thy palaces *shall be spoiled.*

NIPHAL.—*Infinitive.*

Isa. 24: 3. *and utterly* spoiled: (lit. *and in being spoiled* shall be, &c)

NIPHAL.—*Future.*

Isa. 24: 3. and utterly *spoiled:*

* PUAL.—*Preterite.* *

Jer. 50:37. *and they shall be robbed.*

---

963 בִּזָּיוֹן *biz-zāh-yōhn'*, m.

Est. 1:18. too much *contempt* and wrath.

---

965 בָּזָק *bāh-zāhk'*, m.

Eze. 1:14. as the appearance of *a flash of lightning.*

---

967 בָּזַר [*bāh-zar'*].

* KAL.—*Future.* *

Dan 11:24. *he shall scatter* among them

* PIEL.—*Preterite.* *

Ps. 68:30(31). *scatter thou* the people (that) delight in war. (marg. *he scattereth*)

---

969 בָּחוֹן *bāh-ghōhn'*, adj.

Jer. 6:27. I have set thee (for) *a tower*

---

969 בַּחוּן [*bāh-ghoon'*], m.

Isa. 23:13. they set up *the towers thereof,*

---

970 בָּחוּר *bāh-ghoor'*, m.

Deu 32:25. destroy both *the young man*
Jud. 14:10. for so used *the young men* to do.
Ru. 3:10. thou followedst not *young men,*
1 Sa. 8:16. *your* goodliest *young men,*
9: 2. *a choice young man*, and a goodly:
2 K. 8:12. *and their young men*
2 Ch 36:17. who slew *their young men*
— no compassion upon *young man*
Ps. 78:31. *and* smote down the *chosen* (men) *of* Israel. (marg. *young*)
63. The fire consumed *their young men;*
148:12. Both *young men*, and maidens;
Pro. 20:29. The glory of *young men*
Ecc. 11: 9. Rejoice, *O young man,*
Isa. 9:17(16). have no joy in *their young men,*
23: 4. neither do I nourish up *young men,*
31: 8. *and his young men* shall be
40:30. *and the young men* shall utterly fall:
42:22. (they are) all of them snared *in holes*, [as from חוּר, but marg. reads, in snaring all *the young men* of them.]
62: 5. For (as) *a young man* marrieth
Jer. 6:11. the assembly of *young men*
9:21(20). *the young men* from the streets.
11:22. *the young men* shall die by the sword;
15: 8. the mother of *the young men*
18:21. *their young men* (be) slain
31:13. *both young men* and old together:
48:15. *his* chosen *young men*
49:26. *her young men* shall fall
50:30. Therefore shall *her young men* fall
51: 3. spare ye not *her young men;*
22. *the young man* and the maid;
Lam. 1:15. to crush *my young men:*
18. *and my young men* are gone
2:21. *and my young men* are fallen
5:13. They took *the young men*
14. *the young men* from their musick.
Eze. 9: 6. Slay utterly old (and) *young,*
23: 6,12,23. all of them desirable *young men,*
30:17. *The young men of* Aven
Joel 2:28(3:1). *your young men* shall see visions:
Am. 2:11. *and of your young men* for Nazarites.
4:10. *your young men* have I slain
8:13. *and young men* faint for thirst.
Zec. 9:17. make *the young men* chearful,

בְּחוּרוֹת [*b'ghoo-rōhth'*], f. pl. 979

Ecc. 11: 9 & 12:1. in the days of *thy youth,*

בַּחִין (כתיב) see בַּחוּן (קרי). 971

בָּחִיר [*bāh-gheer'*], adj. 972

2 Sa. 21: 6. (whom) the Lord *did choose.* (marg. *chosen of* the Lord)
1 Ch. 16:13. ye children of Jacob, *his chosen ones.*
Ps. 89: 3(4). I have made a covenant *with my chosen,*
105: 6. ye children of Jacob *his chosen.*
43. *his chosen* with gladness:
106: 5. That I may see the good of *thy chosen.*
23. had not Moses *his chosen*
Isa. 42: 1. *mine elect*, (in whom) my soul
43:20. give drink to my people, *my chosen.*
45: 4. and Israel *mine elect,*
65: 9. *mine elect* shall inherit it,
15. for a curse *unto my chosen:*
22. *mine elect* shall long enjoy

בָּחַל [*bāh-ghal'*]. 973

* KAL.—*Preterite.* *

Zec. 11: 8. their soul also *abhorred* me.

* PUAL.—*Part.* *

Pro. 20:21. (כתיב) An inheritance (may be) *gotten hastily*

בָּחַן [*bāh-ghan'*]. 974

* KAL.—*Preterite.* *

Job 23:10. *he hath tried me*, I shall
Ps. 17: 3. *Thou hast proved* mine heart;
66:10. *thou*, O God, *hast proved us:*
95: 9. *proved me*, and saw my work.
Jer. 6:27. mayest know *and try* their way.
9: 7(6). I will melt them, *and try them;*
12: 3. *and tried* mine heart
Zec. 13: 9. *and will try them* as gold
Mal. 3:15. yea, (they that) *tempt* God

KAL.—*Infinitive.*

Zec. 13: 9. will try them *as* gold *is tried:*

KAL.—*Imperative.*

Ps. 26: 2. *Examine me*, O Lord,
139:23. *try me*, and know my thoughts:
Mal. 3:10. *and prove me* now herewith,

KAL.—*Future.*

Job 7:18. *try him* every moment?
12:11. *Doth* not the ear *try* words?
34: 3. For the ear *trieth* words,

Ps. 11: 4. his eyelids *try*, the children of men.
5. The Lord *trieth* the righteous:
81: 7(8). *I proved thee* at the waters

KAL.—*Part.* Poel.

1Ch.29:17. that thou *triest* the heart,
Ps. 7: 9(10). *for* the righteous God *trieth*
Pro.17: 3. *but* the Lord *trieth* the hearts.
Jer. 11:20. *that triest* the reins
17:10. (I) *try* the reins,
20:12. *that triest* the righteous,

* NIPHAL.—*Future.* *

Gen42:15. Hereby *ye shall be proved:*
16. *that* your words *may be proved,*
Job 34:36. Job *may be tried* unto the end

* PUAL.—*Preterite.* *

Eze.21:13(18). Because (it is) *a trial,*

---

975 ## בַּחַן *bah'-ghan*, m.

Isa. 32:14. the forts *and towers* (marg. *watchtowers*)

---

976 ## בֹּחַן *bōh'-ghan*, m.

Isa. 28:16. *a tried* stone, a precious (lit. a stone of *trial;* or, of *proof*)

---

977 ## בָּחַר *bāh-ghar'*.

* KAL.—*Preterite.* *

Gen. 6. 2. wives of all which *they chose.*
Deu. 7: 6. the Lord thy God *hath chosen* thee
14: 2. the Lord *hath chosen* thee
18: 5. the Lord thy God *hath chosen* him
21: 5. the Lord thy God *hath chosen*
30:19. *therefore choose* life,
Jos.24:22. that *ye have chosen* you the Lord,
Jud.10:14. the gods which *ye have chosen;*
1Sa. 8:18. which *ye shall have chosen*
10:24. him whom the Lord *hath chosen,*
12:13 the king whom *ye have chosen,*
16: 8, 9. Neither *hath* the Lord *chosen* this.
10. The Lord *hath* not *chosen* these.
2Sa. 6:21. which *chose* me before thy father,
16:18. all the men of Israel, *choose,*
1K. 3: 8. thy people which *thou hast chosen,*
8:16. *I chose* no city out of all
44. which *thou hast chosen,*
48. which *thou hast chosen,*
11:13. Jerusalem's sake which *I have chosen.*
32. the city which *I have chosen*
34. David my servant's sake, whom *I chose,*
36. the city which *I have chosen*
14:21. which the Lord *did choose*
2K. 21: 7. which *I have chosen* out of all
23:27. Jerusalem which *I have chosen,*
1Ch 15: 2. them *hath* the Lord *chosen*
28: 4. *he hath chosen* Judah
6. *I have chosen* him (to be) my son,
10. the Lord *hath chosen* thee
29: 1. whom alone God *hath chosen,*
2Ch 6: 5. *I chose* no city among all
— neither *chose I* any man
34, 38. which *thou hast chosen,*
7:12. *and have chosen* this place
16. For now *have I chosen*
12:13. which the Lord *had chosen*
29:11. the Lord *hath chosen* you to stand before him,
33: 7. which *I have chosen* before all
Neh 1: 9. the place that *I have chosen*
9: 7. who *didst choose* Abram,
Job 36:21. this *hast thou chosen*
Ps. 33:12. the people (whom) *he hath chosen*
78:67. *chose* not the tribe of Ephraim:
84:10(11). *I had rather be* a doorkeeper
105:26. Aaron whom *he had chosen.*
119:30. *I have chosen* the way of truth:
173. for *I have chosen* thy precepts.
132:13. the Lord *hath chosen* Zion;
135: 4. the Lord *hath chosen* Jacob
Pro. 1:29. *did* not *choose* the fear of the Lord:
Isa. 1:29. the gardens that *ye have chosen.*
14: 1. *and will* yet *choose* Israel,
41: 8. Jacob whom *I have chosen,*
9. *I have chosen thee,* and not cast
43:10. my servant whom *I have chosen:*
44: 1. Israel, whom *I have chosen:*
2. Jesurun, whom *I have chosen.*
48:10. *I have chosen thee* in the furnace of affliction.
56: 4. *and choose* (the things) that please
65:12. *did choose* (that) wherein I delighted
66: 3. *they have chosen* their own ways,
4. *and chose* (that) in which
Jer. 33:24. which the Lord *hath chosen,*
Hag. 2:23. for *I have chosen* thee,
Zec. 1:17. *and shall* yet *choose* Jerusalem.
2:12(16). *and shall choose* Jerusalem

KAL.—*Infinitive.*

1Sa. 2:28. *And did* I *choose* him
Isa. 7:15, 16. *and choose* the good.
Eze.20: 5. In the day when *I chose* Israel,

KAL.—*Imperative.*

Ex. 17: 9. *Choose* us *out* men,
Jos. 24:15. *choose* you this day
2Sa.24:12. *choose* thee one of them,
1K. 18:25. *Choose* you one bullock
1Ch 21:10. *choose* thee one of them,

KAL.—*Future.*

Gen13:11. *Then* Lot *chose* him all the plain
Ex. 18:25. *And* Moses *chose* able men
Nu. 16: 5. even (him) whom *he hath chosen*
7. the man whom the Lord *doth choose,*
17: 5(20). the man's rod, whom *I shall choose,*
Deu 4:37. *therefore he chose* their seed
7: 7. *nor choose* you, because
10:15. *and he chose* their seed
12: 5. the Lord your God *shall choose*
11. the Lord your God *shall choose*
14, 26. which the Lord *shall choose*
18. which the Lord thy God *shall choose,*
21. which the Lord thy God *hath chosen*
14:23. the place which *he shall choose*
24. which the Lord thy God *shall choose*
25. the Lord thy God *shall choose:*
15:20 & 16:2. in the place which the Lord *shall choose,*
16: 6. which the Lord thy God *shall choose*
7. which the Lord thy God *shall choose:*
11. the Lord thy God *hath chosen*
15. which the Lord *shall choose:*
16. the place which *he shall choose;*
17: 8. which the Lord thy God *shall choose;*
10. which the Lord *shall choose*
15. whom the Lord thy God *shall choose:*
18: 6. unto the place which the Lord *shall choose;*
23:16(17). in that place which *he shall choose*
26: 2. the place which the Lord thy God *shall choose*
31:11. the place which *he shall choose,*
Jos. 8: 3. *and* Joshua *chose out*
9:27. the place which *he should choose.*
Jud. 5: 8. *They chose* new gods;
1Sa.13: 2. Saul *chose* him three thousand (men)
17:40. *and chose* him five smooth stones
2Sa.10: 9. *he chose* of all the choice (men)
15:15. my lord the king *shall appoint.* (marg. *choose*)
17: 1. *Let me* now *choose out*
19:38(39). whatsoever *thou shalt require* (marg. *choose*)
1K. 8:16. *but I chose* David
18:23. *and let them choose* one
1Ch 19:10. *he chose* out of all the choice
28: 4. *Howbeit* the Lord God of Israel *chose*
5. *he hath chosen* Solomon my son
2Ch 6: 6. *But I have chosen* Jerusalem,
— *and have chosen* David to be over
Job 7:15. *So that* my soul *chooseth*
9:14. shall I answer him, (and) *choose out*
15: 5. *and thou choosest* the tongue
29:25. *I chose out* their way,
34: 4. *Let us choose* to us judgment:
33. or whether *thou choose;*
Ps. 25:12. the way (that) *he shall choose.*

Ps. 47: 4(5). *He shall choose* our inheritance
65: 4(5). Blessed (is the man whom) *thou choosest,*
78:68. *But chose* the tribe of Judah,
70. *He chose* David *also* his servant,
Pro. 3:31. *choose* none of his ways.
Isa. 40:20. he hath no oblation *chooseth* a tree
41:24. an abomination (is he that) *chooseth*
49: 7. *and he shall choose thee.*
58: 5. Is it such a fast *that I have chosen?*
6. (Is) not this the fast *that I have chosen?*
66: 4. *I* also *will choose* their delusions,

KAL.—*Participle.* Poel.

1Sa.20:30. I know that thou *hast chosen*
Zec. 3: 2. the Lord *that hath chosen* Jerusalem

KAL.—*Participle.* Paül.

Ex. 14: 7. he took six hundred *chosen* chariots,
Jud.20:15,16. seven hundred *chosen* men.
34. ten thousand *chosen* men
1Sa.24: 2(3). three thousand *chosen* men
26: 2. three thousand *chosen* men *of* Israel
2Sa. 6: 1. all (the) *chosen* (men) *of* Israel,
10: 9. he chose of all the *choice* (men) *of*
1K. 12:21. fourscore thousand *chosen men,*
1Ch 19:10. all *the choice* of Israel, (marg. *young men*)
2Ch 11: 1. fourscore thousand *chosen* (men),
13: 3. four hundred thousand *chosen* men:
— eight hundred thousand *chosen*
17. five hundred thousand *chosen*
25: 5. three hundred thousand *choice* (men),
Ps. 89:19(20). exalted (one) *chosen* out of the people.
Cant.5:15. *excellent* as the cedars.
Jer. 49:19 & 50:44. who (is) a *chosen* (man),

* NIPHAL.—*Preterite.* *

Jer. 8: 3. *And* death *shall be chosen*

NIPHAL.—*Participle.*

Pro. 8:10. rather than *choice* gold.
19. my revenue than *choice* silver.
10:20. The tongue of the just (is as) *choice* silver:
16:16. *rather to be chosen* than silver?
21: 3. justice and judgment (is) *more acceptable*
22: 1. A (good) name (is) *rather to be chosen*

* PUAL.—*Future.* *

Ecc. 9: 4. (כתיב) For to him that *is joined*

---

979 בְּחֻרִים [*b'ghoo-reem'*]. m. pl.

Nu. 11:28. servant of Moses, (one) *of his young men,*

---

981 בָּטָא & בָּטָה [*bāh-tāh'*].

* KAL.—*Participle.* Poel. *

Pro.12:18. There is *that speaketh* like

* PIEL.—*Infinitive.* *

Lev. 5: 4. *pronouncing* with (his) lips

PIEL.—*Future.*

Lev. 5: 4. *shall pronounce* with an oath,
Ps.106:33. *so that he spake unadvisedly*

---

982 בָּטַח *bāh-tagh'*.

* KAL.—*Preterite.* *

Jud.20:36. because *they trusted* unto the
2K. 18: 5. *He trusted* in the Lord God
19. wherein *thou trustest?*
20. on whom *dost thou trust,*
21. *thou trustest* upon the staff
22. *We trust* in the Lord our God:
1Ch. 5:20. because *they put their trust* in him.
Job 6:20. because *they had hoped;*
11:18. *And thou shalt be secure,*
Ps. 13: 5(6). *I have trusted* in thy mercy;
22: 4(5). Our fathers *trusted* in thee: *they trusted,* and thou didst
5(6). *they trusted* in thee,
25: 2. O my God, *I trust* in thee:
26: 1. *I have trusted* also in the Lord;
28: 7. my heart *trusted* in him,
31: 6(7). but *I trust* in the Lord.
14(15). But *I trusted* in thee,
33:21. *we have trusted* in his holy name.
41: 9(10). in whom *I trusted,*
52: 8(10). *I trust* in the mercy of God
56: 4(5). in God *I have put my trust;*
11(12). In God *have I put my trust:*
78:22. *trusted* not in his salvation:
119:42. for *I trust* in thy word.
143: 8. for in thee *do I trust:*
Pro.31:11. her husband *doth safely trust* in her,
Isa. 36: 4. wherein *thou trustest?*
5. on whom *dost thou trust,*
6. *thou trustest* in the staff
7. *We trust* in the Lord
Jer. 39:18. *thou hast put thy trust* in me,
Eze.33:13. if *he trust* to his own righteousness,
Hos.10:13. *thou didst trust* in thy way,
Hab. 2:18. the maker of his work *trusteth*
Zep. 3: 2. *she trusted* not in the Lord;

KAL.—*Infinitive.*

Ps.118: 8. *than to put confidence* in man.
9. *than to put confidence* in princes.
Isa. 59: 4. *they trust* (lit. *to trust*) in vanity, and speak lies;
Jer. 48: 7. because *thou hast trusted*

KAL.—*Imperative.*

Ps. 4: 5(6). *and put your trust* in the Lord.
37: 3. *Trust* in the Lord,
5. *trust also* in him;
62: 8(9). *Trust* in him at all times;
115: 9. *trust thou* in the Lord:
10,11. *trust* in the Lord:
Pro. 3: 5. *Trust* in the Lord
Isa. 26: 4. *Trust ye* in the Lord for ever:

KAL.—*Future.*

Jud. 9:26. *and* the men of Shechem *put* their *confidence*
2K. 18:24. *and put thy trust* on Egypt
Job 39:11. *Wilt thou trust* him,
40:23. *he trusteth* that he can draw
Ps. 9:10(11). *And* they that know thy name *will put their trust*
40: 3(4). *and shall trust* in the Lord.
44: 6(7). *I will* not *trust* in my bow,
52: 7(9). *but trusted* in the abundance
55:23(24). but *I will trust* in thee.
56: 3(4). *I will trust* in thee.
62:10(11). *Trust* not in oppression,
91: 2. my God; in him *will I trust.*
146: 3. *Put* not *your trust* in
Pro.28: 1. but the righteous *are bold*
Isa. 12: 2. *I will trust,* and not be afraid:
30:12. *and trust* in oppression
31: 1. *and trust* in chariots,
36: 9. *and put thy trust* on Egypt
47:10. *For thou hast trusted*
50:10. *let him trust* in the name
Jer. 7: 4. *Trust ye* not in lying words,
9: 4(3). *trust ye* not in any brother:
13:25. *and trusted* in falsehood.
17: 5. the man that *trusteth* in man,
7. Blessed (is) the man that *trusteth*
49:11. *let* thy widows *trust* in me.
Eze.16:15. *But thou didst trust* in thine own
Mic. 7: 5. *put ye* not *confidence*

KAL.—*Participle.* Poel.

Deu28:52. wherein thou *trustedst,*
Jud.18: 7,27. quiet *and secure;*
10. come unto a people *secure,*
2K. 18:21. all *that trust* on him.
19:10. in whom thou *trustest*
2Ch 32:10. Whereon *do ye trust,*
Ps. 21: 7(8). the king *trusteth* in the Lord,
27: 3. in this (will) I (be) *confident.*
32:10. *but he that trusteth* in the Lord,
49: 6(7). *They that trust* in their wealth,
84:12(13). blessed (is) the man *that trusteth*
86: 2. save thy servant *that trusteth*
115: 8. every one *that trusteth* in them.

Ps.125: 1. *They that trust* in the Lord
135:18. every one *that trusteth* in them.
Pro.11:15. he that hateth suretiship *is sure.*
28. *He that trusteth* in his riches
14:16. rageth, *and is confident.*
16:20. *and whoso trusteth* in the Lord,
28:25. *but he that putteth his trust* in the Lord
26. *He that trusteth* in his own heart
29:25. *but whoso putteth his trust* in the Lord
Isa. 32: 9. ye *careless* daughters;
10. ye be troubled, *ye careless women:*
11. be troubled, *ye careless ones:*
36: 6. all *that trust* in him.
37:10. thy God, in whom thou *trustest,*
42:17. *that trust* in graven images,
Jer. 5:17. thy fenced cities, wherein thou *trustedst,*
7: 8. ye *trust* in lying words,
14. wherein ye *trust,*
12: 5. in the land of peace, (wherein) thou *trustedst,*
46:25. *them that trust* in him:
49: 4. *that trusted* in her treasures,
Am. 6: 1. *and trust* in the mountain

KAL.—*Participle.* Paül.

Ps.112: 7. *trusting* in the Lord.
Isa. 26: 3. because *he trusteth* in thee.

* HIPHIL.—*Preterite.* *

Jer.28:15. *thou makest* this people *to trust*

HIPHIL.—*Future.*

2K. 18:30. Neither *let* Hezekiah *make* you *trust* in the Lord,
Isa. 36:15. Neither *let* Hezekiah *make* you *trust* in the Lord,
Jer. 29:31. *and he caused* you *to trust*

HIPHIL.—*Participle.*

Ps. 22: 9(10). *thou didst make me hope* (marg: *keptest me in safety*)

---

983 בֶּטַח *beh'-tağh*, m.

Gen34:25. came upon the city *boldly,*
Lev.25:18. dwell in the land *in safety.*
19. dwell therein *in safety.*
26: 5. dwell in your land *safely.*
Deu12:10. so that ye dwell *in safety;*
33:12. of the Lord shall dwell *in safety*
28. Israel then shall dwell *in safety*
Jud. 8:11. for the host was *secure.*
18: 7. how they dwelt *careless,*
1Sa.12:11. and ye dwelled *safe.*
1K. 4:25(5:5). Judah and Israel dwelt *safely,* (marg. *confidently*)
Job 11:18. thou shalt take thy rest *in safety.*
24:23. it be given him (to be) *in safety,*
Ps. 4: 8(9). only makest me dwell *in safety.*
16: 9. my flesh also shall rest *in hope.* (marg. dwell *confidently*)
78:53. he led them on *safely,*
Pro. 1:33. unto me shall dwell *safely,*
3:23. shalt thou walk in thy way *safely,*
29. seeing he dwelleth *securely*
10: 9. He that walketh uprightly walketh *surely:*
Isa. 14:30. the needy shall lie down *in safety:*
32:17. quietness *and assurance* for ever.
47: 8. that dwellest *carelessly,*
Jer. 23: 6. Israel shall dwell *safely:*
32:37. I will cause them to dwell *safely:*
33:16. Jerusalem shall dwell *safely:*
49:31. that dwelleth *without care,*
Eze.28:26. they shall dwell *safely* (marg. *with confidence*)
— they shall dwell *with confidence,*
30: 9. to make the *careless* Ethiopians afraid,
34:25. they shall dwell *safely*
27. they shall be *safe* in their land,
28. but they shall dwell *safely,*
38: 8. they shall dwell *safely*
11. that dwell *safely,* (marg. *confidently*)
14. my people of Israel dwelleth *safely,*
39: 6. among them that dwell *carelessly* (marg. *confidently*)
26. when they dwelt *safely*
Hos. 2:18(20). will make them to lie down *safely.*
Mic. 2: 8. them that pass by *securely*
Zep. 2:15. the rejoicing city that dwelt *carelessly,*
Zec.14:11. Jerusalem shall be *safely* inhabited.

בִּטְחָה *bit-ğhāh'.* 985

Isa. 30:15. *and in confidence* shall be your strength:

בִּטָּחוֹן *bit-tāh-ğhōhn'*, m. 986

2K. 18:19. What *confidence* (is) this
Ecc. 9: 4. to all the living there is *hope:*
Isa. 36: 4. What *confidence* (is) this

בַּטֻּחוֹת *bat-too-ğhōhth'*, f. pl. 987

Job 12: 6. *and* they that provoke God *are secure;*

בָּטַל [*bāh-tal'*]. 988

* KAL.—*Preterite.* *

Ecc.12: 3. *and* the grinders *cease* (marg. *fail*)

בְּטֵל [*b'tēhl*], Ch. 989

* P'AL.—*Preterite.* *

Ezr. 4:23. *and made* them *to cease* by force and
24. Then *ceased* the work of the house of God
5: 5. that *they could* not *cause* them *to cease,*

P'AL.—*Infinitive.*

Ezr. 4:21. commandment *to cause* these men *to cease,*
6: 8. expences be given unto these men, *that they be* not *hindered.* (marg. *made to cease*)

P'AL.—*Participle.*

Ezr. 4:24. So it *ceased* unto the second year (lit. was *ceasing*)

בֶּטֶן *beh'-ten*, f. 990

Gen25:23. Two nations (are) *in thy womb,*
24. twins *in her womb.*
30: 2. withheld from thee the fruit of *the womb?*
38:27. twins (were) *in her womb.*
Nu. 5:21. *thy belly* to swell;
22. to make (thy) *belly* to swell,
27. *her belly* shall swell,
Deu 7:13. bless the fruit of *thy womb,*
28: 4. Blessed (shall be) the fruit of *thy body,*
11. in the fruit of *thy body,* (marg. *belly*)
18. Cursed (shall be) the fruit of *thy body,*
53. the fruit of *thine own body,* (marg. *belly*)
30: 9. in the fruit of *thy body,*
Jud. 3:21. thrust it *into his belly:*
22. not draw the dagger out *of his belly;*
13: 5. a Nazarite unto God from *the womb:*
7. a Nazarite to God from *the womb*
16:17. *from* my mother's *womb:*
1K. 7:20. over against *the belly*
Job 1:21. Naked came I out *of* my mother's *womb,*
3:10. not up the doors of *my* (mother's) *womb,*
11. when I came *out of the belly?*
10:19. carried *from the womb* to the grave.
15: 2. fill *his belly* with the east wind?
35. *and their belly* prepareth deceit.
19:17. of *mine own body.* (marg. *my belly*)
20:15. God shall cast them out *of his belly.*
20. shall not feel quietness *in his belly,*
23. he is about to fill *his belly,*
31:15. Did not he that made me *in the womb*
18. *and* I have guided her *from* my mother's *womb;*
32:18. the spirit *within me* (marg. of *my belly*)
19. *my belly* (is) as wine
38:29. *Out of* whose *womb* came
40:16. his force (is) in the navel of *his belly.*
Ps. 17:14. *whose belly* thou fillest
22: 9(10). he that took me out *of the womb:*
10(11). thou (art) my God *from* my mother's *belly.*

Ps. 31: 9(10). my soul *and my belly.*
44:25(26). *our belly* cleaveth unto the earth.
58: 3(4). they go astray *as soon as they be born,* (marg. *from the belly*)
71: 6. been holden up *from the womb:*
127: 3. the fruit of *the womb*
132:11. fruit of *thy body* will I set (marg. *belly*)
139:13. hast covered me *in* my mother's *womb.*
Pro.13:25. *but the belly of* the wicked
18: 8. the innermost parts of *the belly.*
20. A man's *belly* shall be satisfied
20:27,30. the inward parts of *the belly.*
22:18. if thou keep them *within thee;* (marg. *in thy belly*)
26:22. the innermost parts of *the belly.*
31: 2. the son of *my womb?*
Ecc. 5:15(14). he came forth *of* his mother's *womb,*
11: 5. the bones (do grow) *in the womb of* her
Cant.7: 2(3). *thy belly* (is like) an heap
Isa. 13:18. on the fruit of *the womb;*
44: 2,24. formed thee *from the womb,*
46: 3. borne (by me) from *the belly,*
48: 8. called a transgressor *from the womb.*
49: 1. The Lord hath called me *from the womb;*
5. that formed me *from the womb*
15. compassion on the son of *her womb?*
Jer. 1: 5. Before I formed thee *in the belly*
Eze. 3: 3. cause *thy belly* to eat,
Hos 9:11. from the birth, *and from the womb,*
16. the beloved (fruit) of *their womb.*
12: 3(4). by the heel *in the womb,*
Jon. 2: 2(3). *out of the belly of* hell
Mic. 6: 7. the fruit of *my body* (marg. *belly*)
Hab 3:16. *my belly* trembled;

---

992 בָּטְנִים *bot-neem'*, m. pl.

Gen43:11. myrrh, *nuts,* and almonds:

---

994 בִּי *bee*, part. interj.

Gen43:20. *O* sir, we came indeed down
44:18. *Oh* my lord, let thy servant,
Ex. 4:10. *O* my Lord, I (am) not eloquent,
13. *O* my Lord, send, I pray thee,
Nu. 12:11. Aaron said unto Moses, *Alas,*
Jos. 7: 8. *O* Lord, what shall I say,
Jud. 6:13. Gideon said unto him, *Oh* my Lord,
15. *Oh* my Lord, wherewith shall I save
13: 8. *O* my Lord, let the man of God
1Sa. 1:26. *Oh* my lord, (as) thy soul liveth,
1K. 3:17. the one woman said, *O* my lord,
26. *O* my lord, give her the living child,

---

996 בֵּין *bēhn.* part prep.

[Properly constr. of בַּיִן]

Gen15:17. passed *between* those pieces.
31:37. that they may judge *betwixt* us both.
Ex. 12: 6. shall kill it *in* the evening. (marg. *between* the two evenings)
16:12. *At* even ye shall eat
Jud. 5:16. *among* the sheepfolds,
2K. 2:11. and parted them both *asunder;*
2Ch 14:11(10). *whether* with many, or with them
Job 24:11. make oil *within* their walls,
&c. &c.

It is frequently doubled in a sentence, and the second is commonly omitted in translation. The place of the omitted בֵּין is marked)(.

Gen 1: 4. God divided)(the light *from* the darkness. (marg. *between* the light *and between* the darkness)
9:16. covenant *between* God *and*)(every living
32:16(17). a space *betwixt* drove *and*)(drove.
Lev.27:12. *whether it be* good *or*)(bad:
&c. &c.

It occurs with prefixes: as, בְּבֵין (once):—

Isa. 44: 4. they shall spring up (as) *among* the grass,

לְבֵין (once):—

Isa. 59: 2. between you *and*)(your God,

מִבֵּין, as,

Ex. 25:22. *from between* the two cherubims
Nu. 16:37(17:2). take up the censers *out of* the
Ps.104:12. (which) sing *among* the branches.
Jer. 48:45. a flame *from the midst of* Sihon,
Eze.37:21. the children of Israel *from among* the
47:18. shall measure *from* (marg. *from between*) Hauran, *and from* Damascus, *and from* Gilead, *and from* the
&c. &c.

With pronominal suffixes: as,

Gen23:15. what (is) that *betwixt me and thee?*
26:28. *betwixt us and thee,*
&c. &c.

בֵּין is used in the plural בֵּינוֹת.

Eze.10: 2. Go in *between* the wheels,
— coals of fire *from between* the cherubims,
&c. &c.

בֵּין *bēhn*, Ch. prep. 997

Dan 7: 5. three ribs in the mouth of it *between* the
8. there came up *among them* another little

בִּין *been.* 995

* KAL.—*Preterite.* *

Ps.139: 2. *thou understandest* my thought
Dan 9: 2. I Daniel *understood* by books
10: 1. *and he understood* the thing,

KAL.—*Infinitive.*

Pro.23: 1. consider *diligently* what (is) before thee,

KAL.—*Imperative.*

Deu32: 7. *consider* the years of many
Ps. 5: 1(2). *consider* my meditation.
50:22. Now *consider* this,
94: 8. *Understand,* ye brutish among
Dan. 9:23. *therefore understand* the matter,

KAL & HIPHIL.—*Future.*

Deu32:29. *they would consider* their latter end!
1Sa. 3: 8. *And* Eli *perceived* that the Lord
2Sa.12:19. *But* when David saw...David *perceived*
2Ch 11:23. *And he dealt wisely,*
Ezr. 8:15. *and I viewed* the people,
Neh 8: 8. *and caused* (them) *to understand*
13: 7. *and understood* of the evil
Job 6:30. *cannot* my taste *discern* perverse things?
9:11. but *I perceive* him not.
13: 1. ear hath heard *and understood*
14:21. but *he perceiveth* (it) not
15: 9. *understandest thou,* which (is) not
18: 2. *mark,* and afterwards we will speak.
23: 5. *and understand* what he would
8. but *I cannot perceive* him:
32: 8. *giveth them understanding.*
9. neither *do* the aged *understand*
36:29. Also *can* (any) *understand*
38:20. that *thou shouldest know*
42: 3. I uttered that *I understood* not;
Ps. 19:12(13). Who can *understand* (his) errors?
28: 5. *they regard* not the works
49:20(21). and *understandeth* not,
58: 9(10). your pots *can feel* the thorns,
73:17. *understood I* their end.
82: 5. neither *will they understand;*
92: 6(7). neither *doth* a fool *understand*
94: 7. neither *shall* the God of Jacob *regard*
Pro. 2: 5,9. Then *shalt thou understand*
7: 7. *I discerned* among the youths,
14:15. the prudent (man) *looketh well*
19:25. (and) *he will understand* knowledge.
20:24. how can a man then *understand*
21:29. *he directeth* his way. (marg. *considereth.* The text follows the כתיב).
23: 1. *consider* diligently what (is) before thee:
24:12. he that pondereth the heart *consider*

Pro.28: 5. Evil men *understand* not
— *they* that seek the Lord *understand*
29: 7. the wicked *regardeth* not
19. though *he understand* he will not
Isa. 6: 9. but *understand* not;
10. *understand* with their heart,
28: 9. whom *shall he make to understand*
32: 4. the rash *shall understand*
40:14. *and* (who) *instructed him*, (marg. *made him understand*)
43:10. *and understand* that I (am) he:
44:18. have not known nor *understood:*
Jer. 9:12(11). *that may understand* this?
Dan 9:22. *And he informed* (me),
11:30. *and have intelligence* with them
33. the people *shall instruct* many:
37. Neither *shall he regard*
— nor *regard* any god:
12: 8. but *I understood* not:
10. none of the wicked *shall understand;* but the wise *shall understand.*
Hos 4:14. *doth* not *understand*
14: 9(10). *and he shall understand*

KAL.—*Participle.*

Jer. 49: 7. perished *from the prudent?*

* NIPHAL.—*Preterite.* *

Isa. 10:13. for *I am prudent:*

NIPHAL.—*Participle.*

Gen41:33. look out a man *discreet* and wise,
39. none so *discreet* and wise as thou
Deu 1:13. wise men, *and understanding*,
4: 6. wise *and understanding* people.
1Sa.16:18. *and prudent in* matters,
1K. 3:12. a wise *and an understanding* heart;
Pro. 1: 5. *and a man of understanding*
10:13. the lips of *him that hath understanding*
14: 6. easy *unto him that understandeth.*
33. of *him that hath understanding:*
15:14. The heart of *him that hath understanding*
16:21. wise in heart shall be called *prudent:*
17:28. *a man of understanding.*
18:15. The heart of *the prudent*
19:25. reprove *one that hath understanding*,
Ecc. 9:11. nor yet riches *to men of understanding*,
Isa. 3: 3. *and the eloquent* orator. (marg. *skilful of* speech)
5:21. and *prudent* in their own sight!
29:14. the understanding of *their prudent* (men)
Jer. 4:22. they *have* none *understanding:*
Hos14: 9(10). *prudent*, and he shall know them?

* POLEL.—*Future.* *

Deu32:10. *he instructed him*,

* HIPHIL.—*Preterite.* *

Neh 8:12. because *they had understood*
Job 28:23. God *understandeth* the way
Isa. 29:16. *He had* no *understanding?*
40:21. *have ye* not *understood*
Dan 1:17. Daniel *had understanding* (marg. *he made* Daniel *understand*)
Mic. 4:12. *understand they* his counsel.

HIPHIL.—*Infinitive.*

1K. 3: 9. *that I may discern*
11. hast asked for thyself *understanding*
Ps. 32: 9. *have* no *understanding:*
Pro. 1: 2. *to perceive* the words of
6. *To understand* a proverb,
14: 8. *to understand* his way:
Isa. 28:19. (to) *understand* the report. (marg. (when) *he shall make* (you) *to understand*)
56:11. cannot *understand:* (lit. know not *to understand*)
Dan10:12. didst set thine heart *to understand*,
14. come *to make thee understand*

HIPHIL.—*Imperative.*

Job 6:24. *cause* me *to understand*
Ps.119:27. *Make me to understand* the way
34. *Give me understanding*, and I
73. *give me understanding*, that I
125. *give me understanding*, that I
144. *give me understanding*, and I
169. *give me understanding* according
Pro. 8: 5. O ye simple, *understand* wisdom:
Pro. 8: 5. *be ye of an understanding* heart.
Dan 8:16. *make* this (man) *to understand*
17. *Understand*, O son of man:
9:23. the matter, *and consider* the vision.
10:11. *understand* the words

HIPHIL.—*Future.*
See under Kal.

HIPHIL.—*Participle.*

1Ch 15:22. because he (was) *skilful.*
25: 7. all *that were cunning*,
8. *the teacher* as the scholar.
27:32. a *wise* man, and a scribe:
28: 9. and *understandeth* all
2Ch 26: 5. *who had understanding*
34:12. all *that could skill* of
35: 3. *that taught* all Israel,
Ezr. 8:16. *men of understanding.*
Neh 8: 2. all *that* could hear *with understanding*, (marg. *that understood* in hearing)
3. *and those that could understand;*
7. *caused* the people *to understand*
9. the Levites *that taught* the people,
10:28(29). *and having understanding;*
Ps. 33:15. *he considereth* all their works.
119:130. *it giveth understanding unto* the
Pro. 8: 9. plain *to him that understandeth*,
17:10. A reproof entereth more *into a wise man*
24. *him that hath understanding;*
28: 2. by a man *of understanding*
7. Whoso keepeth the law (is) a *wise* son:
11. the poor *that hath understanding*
Isa. 57: 1. none *considering* that the righteous
Dan 1: 4. *and understanding* science,
8: 5. as I was *considering*,
23. *and understanding* dark
27. but none *understood*

* HITHPOLEL.—*Preterite.* *

Job 38:18. *Hast thou perceived* the breadth
Ps. 37:10. *yea, thou shalt diligently consider*
Isa. 1: 3. my people *doth* not *consider.*
52:15. they had not heard *shall they consider.*

HITHPOLEL.—*Imperative.*

Job 37:14. *and consider* the wondrous works
Jer. 2:10. *and consider* diligently,
9:17(16). *Consider ye*, and call for the

HITHPOLEL.—*Future.*

1K. 3:21. *but when I had considered* it
Job 11:11. *will he* not then *consider*
23:15. *when I consider*, I am afraid
26:14. of his power who *can understand?*
30:20. *and thou regardest* me
31: 1. why then *should I think*
32:12. Yea, *I attended* unto you,
Ps.107:43. *even they shall understand*
119:95. *I will consider* thy testimonies.
100. *I understand* more than the
104. Through thy precepts *I get understanding:*
Isa. 14:16. look upon thee, (and) *consider* thee,
43:18. neither *consider* the things of old.
Jer. 23:20. *ye shall consider* it perfectly.
30:24. in the latter days *ye shall consider*

בִּינָה *bee-nāh'*, f. 998

Deu 4: 6. *and your understanding* in the sight
1Ch 12:32. that had *understanding*
22:12. wisdom *and understanding*,
2Ch 2:12(11). prudence *and understanding*,
13(12). endued with *understanding*,
Job 20: 3. the spirit *of my understanding*
28:12, 20. where (is) the place of *understanding?*
28. to depart from evil (is) *understanding.*
34:16. If now (thou hast) *understanding*,
38: 4. declare, if thou hast *understanding.*
36. or who hath given *understanding*
39:17. hath he imparted to her *understanding.*
26. Doth the hawk fly *by thy wisdom*,
Pro. 1: 2. to perceive the words of *understanding;*
2: 3. if thou criest *after knowledge*,
3: 5. lean not unto *thine own understanding.*
4: 1. attend to know *understanding.*

Pro. 4: 5. Get wisdom, get *understanding:*
7. with all thy getting get *understanding.*
7: 4. call *understanding* (thy) kinswoman:
8:14. I (am) *understanding;* I have strength.
9: 6. go in the way of *understanding.*
10. knowledge of the holy (is) *understanding.*
16:16. *understanding* rather to be chosen
23: 4. cease *from thine own wisdom.*
23. and instruction, *and understanding.*
30: 2. have not *the understanding of* a man.
Isa. 11: 2. wisdom *and understanding,*
27:11. a people of no *understanding:*
29:14. *and the understanding of* their prudent
24. shall come to *understanding,*
33:19. (that thou canst) not *understand.* (lit. (of which there is) no *understanding*)
Jer. 23:20. ye shall consider it *perfectly.* (lit. ye shall understand it (with) *understanding*)
Dan 1:20. wisdom (and) *understanding,*
8:15. the vision, and sought for *the meaning,*
9:22. to give thee skill and *understanding.*
10: 1. *and* had *understanding* of the vision.

---

999 בִּינָה *bee-nāh'*, Ch. f.

Dan. 2:21. knowledge to them that know *understanding*

1000 בֵּיצִים *bēh-tzeem'*, f. pl.

Deu22: 6. young ones, or *eggs,*
— or upon *the eggs,*
Job 39:14. Which leaveth *her eggs* in the earth,
Isa. 10:14. as one gathereth *eggs* (that are) left,
59: 5. They hatch cockatrice' *eggs,*
— he that eateth *of their eggs* dieth,

---

953 בַּיִר *bah'-yir*, f.

Jer. 6: 7. As *a fountain* casteth out her waters,

1002 בִּירָה *bee-rāh'*, f.

1Ch 29: 1. for *the palace* (is) not for man,
19. to build *the palace,*
Neh 1: 1. as I was in Shushan *the palace,*
2: 8. beams for the gates of *the palace*
7: 2. the ruler of *the palace,*
Est. 1: 2. which (was) in Shushan *the palace,*
5. present in Shushan *the palace,*
2: 3. the fair young virgins unto Shushan *the palace,*
5. in Shushan *the palace*
8. together unto Shushan *the palace,*
3:15. decree was given in Shushan *the palace.*
8:14. decree was given at Shushan *the palace.*
9: 6. And in Shushan *the palace*
11. that were slain in Shushan *the palace*
12. five hundred men in Shushan *the palace,*
Dan 8: 2. that I (was) at Shushan (in) *the palace,*

1001 בִּירָה *bee-rāh'* Ch. f.

Ezr. 6: 2. *in the palace* that (is) in the province of the Medes,

---

1003 בִּירָנִיּוֹת *bee-rāh-neey-yōth'*, f. pl.

2Ch 17:12. *castles,* and cities of store. (marg. *palaces*)
27: 4. he built *castles* and towers.

1004 בַּיִת *bah'-yith*, m.

Gen 6:14. shall pitch it *within* and without with
7: 1. Come thou and all *thy house* into the ark;
12: 1. *and from* thy father's *house,*
15. was taken into Pharaoh's *house.*
17. plagued Pharaoh and *his house*
14:14. born in *his own house,*
15: 2. the steward of *my house*
3. one born in *my house* is mine
17:12. he that is born in *the house,*
Gen 17:13. He that is born in *thy house,*
23. all that were born in *his house,*
— the men of Abraham's *house;*
27. all the men of *his house,* born in *the house,*
18:19. *his houshold* after him,
19: 2. into your servant's *house,*
3. and entered into *his house;*
4. compassed *the house* round,
10. pulled Lot *into the house*
11. at the door of *the house*
20:13. to wander *from* my father's *house,*
18. the wombs *of the house of*
24: 2. unto his eldest servant of *his house,*
7. took me *from* my father's *house,*
23. is there room (in) thy father's *house*
27. the Lord led me to *the house of*
28. her mother's *house* these things.
31. for I have prepared *the house,*
32. the man came *into the house:*
38. go unto my father's *house,*
40. of my kindred, *and of* my father's *house:*
27:15. which (were) with her *in the house,*
28: 2. *to the house of* Bethuel
17. none other but *the house of* God,
21. come again to my father's *house*
22. set (for) a pillar, shall be God's *house:*
29:13. and brought him to *his house.*
30:30. provide *for mine own house*
31:14. inheritance for us *in* our father's *house?*
30. thou sore longedst *after* thy father's *house,*
37. thou found of all *thy houshold* stuff?
41. have I been twenty years *in thy house;*
33:17. built him *an house,*
34:19. than all *the house of* his father.
26. took Dinah *out of* Shechem's *house,*
29. even all that (was) *in the house.*
30. I shall be destroyed, I *and my house.*
35: 2. Jacob said unto *his houshold,*
36: 6. and all the persons of *his house,*
38:11. Remain a widow at thy father's *house,*
— went and dwelt in her father's *house.*
39: 2. he was *in the house of* his master
4. overseer over *his house,*
5. overseer *in his house,*
— blessed the Egyptian's *house*
— all that he had *in the house,*
8. what (is) with me *in the house,*
9. none greater *in* this *house*
11. that (Joseph) went *into the house*
— none of the men of *the house* there *within.*
14. called unto the men of her *house,*
16. until his lord came *home.*
20. put him into the prison, (lit. *house of* the prison)
— in the prison. (lit. *in the house of* the prison)
21, 22, 23. the keeper of the prison. (lit. *house of,* &c.)
22. the prisoners that (were) in the prison; (lit. *house of,* &c.)
40: 3. in ward in *the house of* the captain of the guard, into the prison, (lit. *house of* the prison)
5. which (were) bound *in the* prison. (lit. *in the house of*)
7. in the ward of his lord's *house,*
14. bring me out of this *house:*
41:10. in the captain of the guard's *house,*
40. Thou shalt be over *my house,*
51. all my toil, and all my father's *house.*
42:19. *in the house of* your prison: go ye, carry corn for the famine of *your houses:*
33. the famine of *your housholds,*
43:16. he said to the ruler of *his house,* Bring (these) men *home,*
17, 24. brought the men *into* Joseph's *house.*
18. they were brought into Joseph's *house;*
19. the steward of Joseph's *house,*
— at the door of *the house,*
26. when Joseph came *home,*
— in their hand *into the house,*
44: 1. commanded the steward of *his house,*
4. Joseph said unto his steward, (lit. to (him) that (was) over *his house*)
8. *out of* thy lord's *house*
14. his brethren came *to* Joseph's *house;*
45: 2. *the house of* Pharaoh heard.
8. to Pharaoh, and lord of all *his house,*

Gen 45:11. lest thou, *and thy houshold,*
16. was heard in Pharaoh's *house,*
18. take your father and *your housholds,*
46:27. all the souls *of the house of* Jacob,
31. unto his brethren, and unto his father's *house,*
— My brethren, *and* my father's *house,*
47:12. and all his father's *houshold,*
14. the money *into* Pharaoh's *house.*
24. and for them *of your housholds,*
50: 4. spake unto *the house of* Pharaoh,
7. the elders of *his house,*
8. all *the house of* Joseph, and his brethren, *and* his father's *house:*
22. dwelt in Egypt, he, *and* his father's *house:*
Ex. 1: 1. every man *and his houshold* came
21. that he made them *houses.*
2: 1. went a man *of the house of* Levi,
3:22. that sojourneth in *her house,*
6:14. heads of their fathers' *houses:*
7:23. Pharaoh turned and went into *his house,*
8: 3(7:28). shall go up and come *into thine house,*
—(-:—). *and into the house of* thy servants,
9(5). to destroy the frogs from thee *and thy houses,*
11(7). *and from thy houses,* and from
13(9). the frogs died out of *the houses,*
21(17). *and into thy houses:* and *the houses of* the Egyptians
24(20). *into the house of* Pharaoh, *and* (into) his servants' *houses,*
9:19. shall not be brought *home,*
20. flee into *the houses:*
10: 6. they shall fill *thy houses, and the houses of* all thy servants, *and the houses of* all the
12: 3. *according to the house of* (their) fathers, a lamb *for an house:*
4. if *the houshold* be too little
— his neighbour next unto *his house*
7. door post of *the houses,*
13. for a token upon *the houses*
15. leaven *out of your houses:*
19. no leaven found *in your houses:*
22. shall go out at the door of *his house*
23. to come in unto *your houses*
27. over *the houses of* the children of
— and delivered *our houses.*
29. that (was) *in the* dungeon; (marg. *house of* the pit)
30. (there was) not *a house*
46. *In* one *house* shall it be eaten;
— the flesh abroad out of *the house;*
13: 3. out *of the house of* bondage;
14. *from the house of* bondage:
16:31. And *the house of* Israel called
19: 3. Thus shalt thou say *to the house of* Jacob,
20: 2. *out of the house of* bondage.
17. shalt not covet thy neighbour's *house,*
22: 7(6). it be stolen *out of the* man's *house;*
8(7). the master of *the house* shall be brought
23:19. shalt bring into *the house of* the Lord
25:11. *within* and without
27. be *for places* of the staves
26:29. *places* for the bars:
33. bring in thither *within* the
28:26. in the side of the ephod *inward.*
30: 4. they shall be *for places*
34:26. thou shalt bring unto *the house*
36:34. *places* for the bars,
37: 2. *within* and without,
14. *the places* for the staves
27. *to be places* for the staves
38: 5. *places* for the staves.
39:19. on the side of the ephod *inward.*
40:38. in the sight of all *the house of* Israel,
Lev.10: 6. *the* whole *house of* Israel, bewail
14:34. the plague of leprosy *in a house of*
35. And he that owneth *the house*
— as it were a plague *in the house:*
36. that they empty *the house,*
— all that (is) *in the house*
— shall go in to see *the house:*
37. in the walls of *the house*
38. the priest shall go out of *the house* to the door of *the house,* and shut up *the house* seven days:

Lev.14:39. spread in the walls of *the house;*
41. cause *the house* to be scraped *within*
42. shall plaister *the house.*
43. break out *in the house,*
— and after he hath scraped *the house,*
44. the plague be spread *in the house,* it (is) a fretting leprosy *in the house:*
45. he shall break down *the house,*
— all the morter of *the house;*
46. he that goeth into *the house*
47. he that lieth *in the house*
— he that eateth *in the house*
48. plague hath not spread *in the house,* after *the house* was plaistered:
— shall pronounce *the house* clean,
49. he shall take to cleanse *the house*
51. sprinkle *the house* seven times:
52. he shall cleanse *the house*
53. make an atonement for *the house:*
55. of a garment, *and of a house,*
16: 2. *within* the vail before the
6, 11. an atonement for himself, and for *his house.*
12. bring (it) *within* the vail:
15. bring his blood *within* the vail,
17. for himself, and for *his houshold,*
17: 3, 8, 10. (there be) *of the house of* Israel,
18: 9. born *at home,* or born abroad,
22:11. and he that is born in *his house:*
13. and is returned unto her father's *house,*
18. Whatsoever (he be) *of the house of*
25:29. if a man sell a dwelling *house*
30. then *the house* that (is) in
31. *But the houses of* the villages
32,33. *the houses of* the cities
33. then *the house* that was sold,
27:14. when a man shall sanctify *his house*
15. that sanctified it will redeem *his house,*
Nu. 1: 2, 18, 20, 22, 24, 26, 28, 30, 32, 34, 36, 38, 40, 42, 45. *by the house of* their fathers,
4. every one head *of the house of*
44. each one was *for the house of* his fathers.
2: 2. with the ensign *of* their fathers' *house:*
32. *by the house of* their fathers:
34. according to *the house of*
3:15. *after the house of* their fathers,
20. *according to the house of* their fathers.
24, 30, 35. the chief of *the house of* the
4: 2, 29, 40, 42. *by the house of* their fathers,
22. *throughout the houses of* their fathers,
34, 46. *and after the house of* their fathers,
38. *and by the house of* their fathers,
7: 2. heads of *the house of* their fathers,
12: 7. who (is) faithful in all *mine house.*
16:32. and *their houses,* and all the men
17: 2(17). *according to the house of* (their) fathers,
-(—). *according to the house of* their fathers
3(18). for the head of *the house of*
6(21). *according to* their fathers' *houses,*
8(23). the rod of Aaron *for the house of* Levi
18: 1. and thy sons *and* thy father's *house*
7. *and within* the vail;
11. every one that is clean *in thy house*
13. every one that is clean *in thine house*
31. in every place, ye *and your housholds:*
20:29. (even) all *the house of* Israel.
22:18&24:13. If Balak would give me *his house* full
25:14. *a* chief *house* among
15. of *a* chief *house* in Midian.
26: 2. *throughout* their fathers' *house,*
30: 3(4). (being) *in* her father's *house* in her youth;
10(11). in her husband's *house,*
16(17). in her youth in her father's *house.*
32:18. return unto *our houses,*
34:14,14. *according to the house of*
Deu 5: 6. *from the house of* bondage.
21(18). covet thy neighbour's *house,*
6: 7. when thou sittest *in thine house,*
9. write them upon the posts of *thy house,*
11. *And houses* full of all good
12. *from the house of* bondage.
22. Pharaoh, and upon all *his houshold,*
7: 8. *out of the house of* bondmen,
26. an abomination into *thine house,*
8:12. *and* hast built goodly *houses,*
14. *from the house of* bondage;

Deu 11: 6. and *their housholds*, and their tents,
19. when thou sittest *in thine house*,
20. upon the door posts of *thine house*,
12: 7. *and your housholds*, wherein the Lord
13: 5(6). *out of the house of* bondage,
10(11). *from the house of* bondage.
14:26. thou, *and thine houshold*,
15:16. loveth thee and *thine house*,
20. shall choose, thou *and thy houshold*.
19: 1. in their cities, *and in their houses;*
20: 5. that hath built *a* new *house*,
— let him go and return *to his house*,
6, 7, 8. go and return *unto his house*,
21:12. bring her home to *thine house;*
13. shall remain *in thine house*,
22: 2. bring it unto *thine own house*,
8. When thou buildest *a* new *house*,
— bring not blood *upon thine house*,
21. the damsel to the door of her father's *house*,
— to play the whore in her father's *house:*
23:18(19). into *the house of* the Lord thy God
24: 1. and send her *out of his house*.
2. when she is departed *out of his house*,
3. and sendeth her *out of his house;*
5. he shall be free *at home* one year,
10. not go into *his house* to fetch his pledge.
25: 9. build up his brother's *house*.
10. *The house of* him that hath
14. Thou shalt not have *in thine house*
26:11. *and unto thine house*,
13. the hallowed things out of (mine) *house*,
28:30. thou shalt build *an house*,
Jos. 2: 1. and came into an harlot's *house*,
3. which are entered *into thine house:*
12. shew kindness unto my father's *house*,
15. for *her house* (was) upon the
18. and all thy father's *houshold, home*
19. shall go out of the doors of *thy house*
— shall be with thee *in the house*,
6:17. all that (are) with her *in the house*,
22. Go into the harlot's *house*,
24. into the treasury of *the house of* the Lord.
25. the harlot alive, and her father's *houshold*,
7:14. shall come *by housholds; and the houshold*
18. brought *his houshold* man by man;
9:12. provision *out of our houses*
23. *for the house of* my God.
17:17. Joshua spake unto *the house of* Joseph,
18: 5. *and the house of* Joseph shall abide
19:27. toward the sunrising to *Beth*-dagon,
— toward the north side of *Beth*-emek,
20: 6. and unto *his own house*,
21:45(43). had spoken unto *the house of* Israel;
22:14. *of* each chief *house* a prince
— head of *the house of* their fathers
24:15. but as for me *and my house*, we will
17. *from the house of* bondage,
Jud. 1:22. *the house of* Joseph, they also went up
23. And the *house of* Joseph sent to descry
35. the hand of *the house of* Joseph prevailed,
4:17. and *the house of* Heber
6: 8. *out of the house of* bondage;
15. and I (am) the least *in* my father's *house*.
27. because he feared his father's *houshold*,
8:27. a snare unto Gideon, *and to his house*.
29. and dwelt *in his own house*.
35. shewed they kindness to *the house of*
9: 1. all the family of *the house of*
4. *out of the house of* Baal-berith,
5. he went unto his father's *house* at Ophrah,
6. all *the house of* Millo,
16. dealt well with Jerubbaal and *his house*,
18. ye are risen up against my father's *house*
19. with Jerubbaal and with *his house*
20. and *the house of* Millo;
— *and from the house of* Millo,
27. went into *the house of* their god,
46. an hold of *the house of* the god Berith.
10: 9. *and against the house of* Ephraim;
11: 2. shalt not inherit *in* our father's *house;*
7. expel me *out of* my father's *house?*
31. cometh forth of the doors of *my house*
34. Jephthah came to Mizpeh unto *his house*,
12: 1. we will burn *thine house*
14:15. lest we burn thee and thy father's *house*
19. and he went up to his father's *house*.
16:21. he did grind *in the* prison *house*.
Jud. 16:25. *out of the* prison *house*,
26. whereupon *the house* standeth,
27. *Now the house* was full
29. upon which *the house* stood,
30. and *the house* fell upon the lords,
31. and all *the house of* his father
17: 4. they were *in the house of* Micah.
5. the man Micah had *an house of* gods,
8. to *the house of* Micah,
12. was *in the house of* Micah.
18: 2. to *the house of* Micah,
3. When they (were) by *the house of*
13. came unto *the house of* Micah.
14. there is *in* these *houses*
15. came to *the house of* the young man the Levite, (even) unto *the house of* Micah,
18. these went into Micah's *house*,
19. to be a priest *unto the house of*
22. *from the house of* Micah, the men that (were) *in the houses* near to Micah's *house*
25. thy life, with the lives of *thy houshold*.
26. he turned and went back unto *his house*.
31. all the time that *the house of* God was in
19: 2. away from him unto her father's *house*
3. brought him into her father's *house:*
15. no man that took them *into* his *house*
18. going to *the house of* the Lord;
— no man that receiveth me *to house*.
21. So he brought him *into his house*,
22. beset *the house* round about,
— spake to the master of *the house*,
— that came into *thine house*,
23. the man, the master of *the house*,
— come into *mine house*,
26. at the door of the man's *house*
27. opened the doors of *the house*,
— the door of *the house*,
29. when he was come into *his house*,
20: 5. beset *the house* round about
8. will we any (of us) turn *into his house*.
Ru. 1: 8. return each *to* her mother's *house:*
9. each (of you) in *the house of*
2: 7. she tarried a little in *the house*.
4:11. come into *thine house* like Rachel and like Leah, which two did build *the house of*
12. And let *thy house* be *like the house of* Pharez,
1Sa. 1: 7. when she went up *to the house of*
19. came to *their house*
21. the man Elkanah, and all *his house*,
24. brought him unto *the house of*
2:11. Elkanah went to Ramah to *his house*.
27. appear unto *the house of* thy father,
— in Egypt *in* Pharaoh's *house?*
28. *unto the house of* thy father
30. *thy house, and the house of* thy father,
31. the arm of thy father's *house*,
— an old man *in thine house*.
32. an old man *in thine house*
33. the increase of *thine house*
35. I will build him *a* sure *house;*
36. every one that is left *in thine house*
3:12. which I have spoken concerning *his house:*
13. that I will judge *his house*
14. I have sworn *unto the house of* Eli, that the iniquity of Eli's *house*
15. opened the doors of *the house of*
5: 2. brought it into *the house of*
5. that come into Dagon's *house*,
6: 7. bring their calves *home*
10. *and* shut up their calves *at home:*
7: 1. brought it into *the house of*
2. all *the house of* Israel
3. Samuel spake unto all *the house of*
17. for there (was) *his house;*
9:18. where the seer's *house* (is)
20. and on all thy father's *house?*
10:25. all the people away, every man *to his house*.
26. Saul also went *home* to Gibeah;
15:34. Saul went up to *his house* to Gibeah
17:25. make his father's *house* free in Israel.
18: 2. no more home to his father's *house*.
10. in the midst of *the house:*
19: 9. as he sat *in his house* with his javelin
11. sent messengers unto David's *house*,
20:15. cut off thy kindness from *my house*
16. made (a covenant) with *the house of*
21:15(16). shall this (fellow) come into *my house?*

1Sa.22: 1. when his brethren and all his father's *house* heard
11. and all his father's *house*,
14. and is honourable *in thine house?*
15. all *the house of* my father:
16. Ahimelech, thou, and all thy father's *house*.
22. all the persons of thy father's *house*.
23:18. and Jonathan went *to his house*.
24:21(22). *out of* my father's *house*.
22(23). And Saul went *home;*
25: 1. and buried him *in his house* at Ramah.
6. both to thee, *and* peace (be) *to thine house*,
17. and against all *his houshold:*
28. make my lord *a* sure *house;*
35. Go up in peace *to thine house;*
36. he held a feast *in his house*,
27: 3. and his men, every man *with his houshold*,
28:24. had a fat calf *in the house;*
31: 9. (in) *the house of* their idols,
10. put his armour *in the house of* Ashtaroth:
2Sa. 1:12. and for *the house of* Israel;
2: 3. bring up, every man *with his houshold:*
4. anointed David king over *the house of* Judah.
7. *the house of* Judah have anointed me
10. But *the house of* Judah followed David.
11. king in Hebron over *the house of* Judah
3: 1. *the house of* Saul and *the house of* David:
— *and the house of* Saul waxed weaker
6. while there was war between *the house of* Saul and *the house of* David, that Abner made himself strong *for the house of*
8. unto *the house of* Saul thy father,
10. *from the house of* Saul,
19. the whole *house of* Benjamin.
29. of Joab, and on all his father's *house;*
— *from the house of* Joab
4: 5. to *the house of* Ish-bosheth,
6. into the midst of *the house*,
7. when they came into *the house*,
11. a righteous person *in his own house*
5: 8. shall not come into *the house*.
9. from Millo *and inward*.
11. they built David *an house*.
6: 3,4. brought it *out of the house of*
5,15. David and all *the house of* Israel
10. into *the house of* Obed-edom
11. continued in *the house of* Obed-edom
— blessed Obed-edom, and all *his houshold*.
12. The Lord hath blessed *the house of*
— the ark of God *from the house of* Obed-edom
19. departed every one *to his house*.
20. returned to bless *his houshold*.
21. and before all *his house*,
7: 1. when the king sat *in his house*,
2. I dwell *in an house of* cedar,
5. Shalt thou build me *an house*
6. I have not dwelt *in* (any) *house*
7. Why build ye not me *an house of* cedar?
11. he will make thee *an house*.
13. He shall build *an house*
16. And *thine house* and thy kingdom
18. and what (is) *my house*,
19. hast spoken also of thy servant's *house*
25. thy servant, and concerning *his house*,
26. *and* let *the house of* thy servant David be
27. I will build thee *an house:*
29. bless *the house of* thy servant,
— let *the house of* thy servant be
9: 1. that is left *of the house of* Saul,
2. *And* (there was) *of the house of* Saul
3. not yet any *of the house of* Saul,
4. he (is) in *the house of* Machir,
5. fetched him *out of the house of* Machir,
9. to Saul and to all *his house*.
12. all that dwelt in *the house of* Ziba
11: 2. walked upon the roof of the king's *house:*
4. she returned unto *her house*.
8. Go down *to thy house*, and wash
— Uriah departed *out of the* king's *house*,
9. slept at the door of the king's *house*
— and went not down to *his house*.
10. Uriah went not down unto *his house*,
— go down unto *thine house?*
11. shall I then go into *mine house*,
13. but went not down to *his house*.
27. David sent and fetched her to *his house*,

2Sa.12: 8. I gave thee thy master's *house*,
— gave thee *the house of* Israel
10. shall never depart *from thine house;*
11. against thee *out of thine own house*,
15. Nathan departed unto *his house*.
17. the elders of *his house* arose,
20. came into *the house of* the Lord, and worshipped: then he came to *his own house;*
13: 7. David sent *home* to Tamar, saying, Go now to thy brother Amnon's *house*,
8. Tamar went to her brother Amnon's *house;*
20. in her brother Absalom's *house*.
14: 8. Go *to thine house*,
9. on me, and on my father's *house:*
24. Let him turn to *his own house*,
— returned to *his own house*,
31. came to Absalom *unto* (his) *house*,
15:16. the king went forth, and all *his houshold*
— concubines, to keep *the house*.
17. tarried *in a place* that was far off.
35. *out of* the king's *house*,
16: 2. The asses (be) *for* the king's *houshold*
3. To day shall *the house of* Israel
5. the family of *the house of* Saul,
8. the blood of *the house of* Saul,
21. he hath left to keep *the house;*
17:18. came to a man's *house*
20. came to the woman *to the house*,
23. and gat him *home* to *his house*, (lit. went to *his house*)
— and put *his houshold* in order, (marg. gave charge concerning *his house*)
19: 5(6). Joab came *into the house*
11(12). to bring the king back to *his house?*
—(—). (even) to *his house*.
17(18). Ziba the servant of *the house of* Saul,
18(19). boat to carry over the king's *houshold*,
20(21). the first this day of all *the house of*
28(29). all (of) my father's *house* were
30(31). in peace unto *his own house*.
41(42). brought the king, and *his houshold*,
20: 3. David came to *his house* at Jerusalem;
— left to keep *the house*, and put them in ward, (marg. *a house of* ward)
21: 1. and for (his) bloody *house*,
4. of Saul, nor of *his house;*
23: 5. Although *my house* (be) not so
24:17. *and against* my father's *house*.
1K. 1:53. Go *to thine house*.
2:24. who hath made me *an house*,
27. spake concerning *the house of*
31. and from *the house of* my father.
33. *and upon his house*, and upon his throne,
34. he was buried *in his own house*
36. Build thee *an house* in Jerusalem,
3: 1. made an end of building *his own house*, and *the house of* the Lord,
2. because there was no *house*
17. I and this woman dwell *in* one *house;*
— with her *in the house*.
18. no stranger with us *in the house*, save we two *in the house*.
4: 6. Ahishar (was) over *the houshold:*
7. victuals for the king and *his houshold:*
5: 3(17). could not build *an house*
5(19). I purpose to build *an house*
—(—). he shall build *an house*
9(23). in giving food for *my houshold*.
11(25). (for) food *to his houshold*,
14(28). two months *at home:*
17(31). to lay the foundation of *the house*.
18(32). and stones to build *the house*.
6: 1. he began to build *the house*
2. *And the house* which king Solomon
3. the temple of *the house*,
— according to the breadth of *the house;*
— the breadth thereof before *the house*.
4. And *for the house* he made
5. against the wall of *the house*
— (against) the walls of *the house*
6. without (in the wall) *of the house*
— be fastened in the walls of *the house*.
7. *And the house*, when it was in
— heard *in the house*,
8. in the right side of *the house:*
9. So he built *the house*, and finished it; and covered *the house*

1K. 6:10. against all *the house*, five cubits high: and they rested on *the house*
12. this *house* which thou art in
14. So Solomon built *the house*,
15. he built the walls of *the house within* with boards of cedar, both the floor of *the house*, and the walls of the ceiling: (and) he covered (them) *on the inside* with wood, and covered the floor of *the house*
16. on the sides of *the house*,
— built (them) for it *within*,
17. *the house*, that (is), the temple
18. the cedar of *the house*
19. the oracle he prepared in *the house*
21. Solomon overlaid *the house*
22. the whole *house* he overlaid with gold, until he had finished all *the house*:
27. the cherubims within *the* inner *house*:
— in the midst of *the house*.
29. he carved all the walls of *the house*
30. the floor of *the house*
37. was the foundation of *the house of*
38. was *the house* finished
7: 1. was building *his own house*
— and he finished all *his house*.
2. He built also *the house of*
8. *And his house* where he dwelt (had) another court *within* the porch,
— Solomon made *also an house*
9. *within* and without, even from the
12. the inner court of *the house of* the Lord,
— for the porch of *the house*.
25. all their hinder parts (were) *inward*.
31. *within* the chapiter and above
39. on the right side of *the house*, and five on the left side of *the house*: and he set the sea on the right side of *the house*
40, 45, 51. for *the house of* the Lord:
48. unto *the house of* the Lord:
50. doors of *the* inner *house*, the most holy (place, and) for the doors of *the house*,
51. the treasures of *the house of* the Lord.
8: 6. into the oracle of *the house*,
10. the cloud filled *the house of* the Lord,
11. of the Lord had filled *the house of*
13. surely built thee *an house to* dwell in,
16. the tribes of Israel to build *an house*,
17. David my father to build *an house*
18. to build *an house* unto my name,
19. thou shalt not build *the house*;
— he shall build *the house*
20. have built *an house*
27. how much less this *house*
29. be open toward this *house*
31. before thine altar *in* this *house*:
33. make supplication unto thee *in* this *house*:
38. spread forth his hands toward this *house*:
42. shall come and pray toward this *house*;
43. this *house*, which I have builded,
44. *and* (toward) *the house* that I have built
48. *and the house* which I have built
63. dedicated *the house of* the Lord.
64. before *the house of* the Lord:
9: 1. had finished the building of *the house of* the Lord, and the king's *house*,
3. I have hallowed this *house*,
7. and this *house*, which I have hallowed
8. *And* at this *house*, (which) is high,
— unto this land, *and to* this *house*?
10. Solomon had built *the* two *houses*, *the house of* the Lord, and *the* king's *house*,
15. *the house of* the Lord, and *his own house*,
24. unto *her house* which
25. So he finished *the house*.
10: 4. *and the house* that he had built,
5. went up unto *the house of* the Lord;
12. pillars *for the house of* the Lord, *and for the* king's *house*,
17. the king put them in *the house of*
21. all the vessels of *the house of*
11:18. which gave him *an house*,
20. weaned in Pharaoh's *house*: and Genubath was in Pharaoh's *houshold*
28. over all the charge of *the house of* Joseph.
38. and build thee *a sure house*,
12:16. now see to *thine own house*,
19. Israel rebelled *against the house of* David

1K. 12:20. none that followed *the house of*
21. he assembled all *the house of*
— to fight against *the house of* Israel,
23. unto all *the house of* Judah and Benjamin,
24. return every man to *his house*;
26. return *to the house of* David:
27. sacrifice *in the house of* the Lord
31. he made *an house of* high places,
13: 2. *unto the house of* David,
7. Come *home* with me,
8. If thou wilt give me half *thine house*,
15. Come *home* with me,
18. Bring him back with thee into *thine house*,
19. and did eat bread *in his house*,
32. against all *the houses of*
34. unto *the house of* Jeroboam,
14: 4. came to *the house of* Ahijah.
8. *from the house of* David,
10. I will bring evil upon *the house of*
— the remnant of *the house of* Jeroboam,
12. get thee *to thine own house*:
13. in *the house of* Jeroboam.
14. who shall cut off *the house of*
17. the threshold of *the door*,
26. the treasures of *the house of* the Lord, and the treasures of the king's *house*;
27. which kept the door of the king's *house*.
28. when the king went into *the house of*
15:15. into *the house of* the Lord,
18. of *the house of* the Lord, and the treasures of the king's *house*,
27. *of the house of* Issachar,
29. he smote all *the house of* Jeroboam;
16: 3. the posterity of *his house*; and will make *thy house like the house of* Jeroboam
7. and against *his house*,
— in being *like the house of* Jeroboam;
9. in *the house of* Arza steward of (his) *house*
11. he slew all *the house of* Baasha:
12. destroy all *the house of*
18. into the palace of the king's *house*, and burnt the king's *house* over him
32. in *the house of* Baal,
17:15. he, *and her house*,
17. the mistress of *the house*,
23. out of the chamber *into the house*,
18: 3. the governor of (his) *house*.
18. but thou, *and* thy father's *house*,
32. *as great as would contain* two measures (lit. *as the house of* two measures)
20: 6. they shall search *thine house*, and *the houses of* thy servants;
31. the kings of *the house of* Israel (are)
43. the king of Israel went to *his house* heavy
21: 2. because it (is) near unto *my house*:
4. Ahab came into *his house* heavy
22. And will make *thine house like the house of* Jeroboam the son of Nebat, *and like the house of* Baasha
29. will I bring the evil upon *his house*.
22:17. let them return every man *to his house*
27. Put this (fellow) in the prison, (lit. *house of* the prison)
39. *and the* ivory *house* which he made,
2K. 4: 2. what hast thou *in the house*?
— hath not any thing *in the house*, save
32. Elisha was come *into the house*,
35. walked *in the house* to and fro;
5: 9. stood at the door of *the house*
18. goeth into *the house of* Rimmon
— I bow myself in *the house of* Rimmon. when I bow down myself in *the house of*
24. bestowed (them) *in the house*:
6:30. (he had) sackcloth *within* upon his flesh.
32. But Elisha sat *in his house*,
7: 9. we may go and tell the king's *houshold*.
11. and they told (it) to the king's *house*
8: 1. go thou *and thine houshold*,
2. she went *with her houshold*,
3. to cry unto the king for *her house*
5. cried to the king for *her house*
18. as did *the house of* Ahab:
27. he walked in the way of *the house of*
— *as* (did) *the house of* Ahab: for he (was) the son in law of *the house of*
9: 6. went *into the house*:
7. thou shalt smite *the house of* Ahab

2K. 9: 8. For the whole *house of* Ahab
9. I will make *the house of* Ahab *like the house of* Jeroboam the son of Nebat, *and like the house of* Baasha
27. he fled by the way of *the* garden *house.*
10: 3. fight for your master's *house.*
5. he that (was) over *the house,*
10. concerning *the house of* Ahab:
11. Jehu slew all that remained *of the house of*
12. as he (was) at *the* shearing *house*
14. slew them at the pit of *the* shearing *house,*
21. they came into *the house of* Baal; and *the house of* Baal was full
23. into *the house of* Baal, and said
25. went to the city of *the house of* Baal.
26. images out of *the house of* Baal,
27. brake down *the house of* Baal,
30. hast done *unto the house of* Ahab
11: 3. he was with her hid in *the house of*
4. brought them to him into *the house of*
— took an oath of them *in the house of* the Lord,
5. watch of the king's *house;*
6. keep the watch of *the house,*
7. even they shall keep the watch of *the house of*
10. that (were) *in the temple of* the Lord.
11. from the right corner of *the temple* to the left corner of *the temple,* (along) by the altar *and the temple.*
13. she came to the people into *the temple of*
15. Have her forth *without* the ranges:
— Let her not be slain in *the house of* the Lord.
16. horses came into the king's *house:*
18. went into *the house of* Baal,
— over *the house of* the Lord.
19. *from the house of* the Lord,
— to the king's *house.*
20. with the sword (beside) the king's *house.*
12: 4(5), 16(17). brought into *the house of* the Lord,
-(-). to bring into *the house of* the Lord,
5(6). repair the breaches of *the house,*
6(7). repaired the breaches of *the house.*
7(8). repair ye not the breaches of *the house?*
-(-). deliver it for the breaches of *the house.*
8(9). to repair the breaches of *the house.*
9(10). as one cometh into *the house of*
-(—), 13(14). brought into *the house of* the Lord.
10(11). found in *the house of* the Lord.
11(12). that had the oversight of *the house of*
—(—). that wrought upon *the house of*
12(13). to repair the breaches of *the house of*
—(—). that was laid out for *the house*
13(14). made for *the house of* the Lord
14(15). repaired therewith *the house of*
18(19). found in the treasures of *the house of* the Lord, *and* in the king's *house,*
20(21). slew Joash in *the house of* Millo, (marg. *Beth*-millo)
13: 6. the sins of *the house of* Jeroboam,
14: 10. and tarry *at home:* (marg. *at thy house*)
14. that were found in *the house of* the Lord, and in the treasures of the king's *house,*
15: 5. dwelt *in a* several *house.* And Jotham the king's son (was) over *the house,*
25. in the palace of the king's *house,*
35. He built the higher gate of *the house of*
16: 8. found *in the house of* the Lord, and in the treasures of the king's *house,*
14. from the forefront of *the house,* from between the altar and *the house of*
18. that they had built *in the house,*
— turned he from *the house of* the Lord
17: 4. and bound him in prison. (lit. *house of* prison)
21. he rent Israel from *the house of* David;
29. put (them) *in the houses of*
32. *in the houses of* the high places.
18: 15. found *in the house of* the Lord, and in the treasures of the king's *house.*
18, 37. which (was) over *the houshold,*
19: 1. went into *the house of* the Lord.
2. which (was) over *the houshold,*
14. Hezekiah went up into *the house of*
30. that is escaped of *the house of* Judah

2K. 19: 37. as he was worshipping in *the house of*
20: 1. Set *thine house* in order; (marg. Give charge *concerning thine house*)
5. go up unto *the house of* the Lord.
8. that I shall go up into *the house of*
13. shewed them all *the house of*
— and (all) *the house of* his armour,
— there was nothing *in his house,*
15. What have they seen *in thine house?*
— *in mine house* have they seen:
17. all that (is) *in thine house,*
21: 4. he built altars *in the house of*
5. in the two courts of *the house of*
7. that he had made *in the house,*
— *In* this *house,* and in Jerusalem,
13. the plummet of *the house of* Ahab:
18. in the garden of *his own house,*
23. slew the king *in his own house.*
22: 3. to *the house of* the Lord,
4. brought into *the house of* the Lord,
5. that have the oversight *of the house of*
— which (is) *in the house of* the Lord, to repair the breaches of *the house,*
6. hewn stone to repair *the house.*
8. found the book of the law *in the house of*
9. that was found *in the house,*
— that have the oversight of *the house of*
23: 2. the king went up into *the house of*
— found *in the house of* the Lord.
6. *from the house of* the Lord,
7. brake down *the houses of* the sodomites, that (were) *by the house of* the Lord, where the women wove *hangings* (marg. *houses*)
11. at the entering in of *the house of*
12. in the two courts of *the house of*
19. all *the houses* also *of* the
24. found in *the house of* the Lord.
27. and *the house* of which I said,
24: 13. all the treasures of *the house of* the Lord, and the treasures of the king's *house,*
25: 9. he burnt *the house of* the Lord, and the king's *house,* and all *the houses of* Jerusalem, and every great (man's) *house* burnt he with fire.
13. that (were) in *the house of* the Lord,
— that (was) *in the house of* the Lord,
16. made *for the house of* the Lord;
27. Jehoiachin king of Judah *out of* prison; (lit. *out of the house of* prison)
1Ch 2: 54. Ataroth, *the house of* Joab,
55. the father of *the house of* Rechab.
4: 21. the families of *the house of* them that wrought fine linen, *of the house of*
38. *and the house of* their fathers
5: 13. *of the house of* their fathers
15. chief *of the house of* their fathers.
24. the heads of *the house of* their fathers,
— heads *of the house of* their fathers.
6: 10(5:36). *in the temple* that Solomon (marg. *house*)
31(16). in *the house of* the Lord,
32(17). until Solomon had built *the house of*
48(33). the tabernacle of *the house of*
7: 2. heads *of* their father's *house,*
4. *after the house of* their fathers,
7. heads of *the house of* (their) fathers
9. heads of *the house of* their fathers,
23. because it went evil *with his house.*
40. heads of (their) fathers' *house,*
9: 9. *in the house of* their fathers.
11. the ruler of *the house of* God;
13. heads *of the house of* their fathers,
— the work of the service of *the house of* God.
19. *of the house of* his father,
23. the gates *of the house of* the Lord, (namely), *the house of* the tabernacle,
26. and treasures of *the house of* God.
27. round about *the house of* God,
10: 6. and all *his house* died together.
10. his armour in *the house of* their gods, and fastened his head in *the temple of*
12: 28. *and* of his father's *house* twenty and two captains.
29. had kept the ward of *the house of* Saul.
30. famous *throughout the house of*
13: 7. *out of the house of* Abinadab:

1 Ch 13:13. carried it aside into *the house of*
14. the ark of God remained with *the family of* Obed-edom *in his house* three months. And the Lord blessed *the house of*
14: 1. to build him *an house.*
15: 1. (David) made him *houses*
25. out of *the house of* Obed-edom
16:43. the people departed every man *to his house:* and David returned to bless *his house.*
17: 1. it came to pass, as David sat *in his house,*
— Lo, I dwell *in an house of* cedars,
4. Thou shalt not build me *an house*
5. For I have not dwelt *in an house*
6. Why have ye not built me *an house of*
10. *that* the Lord will build thee *an house.*
12. He shall build me *an house,*
14. But I will settle him *in mine house*
16. what (is) *mine house,*
17. spoken of thy servant's *house*
23. thy servant and concerning *his house*
24. *and* (let) *the house of* David thy servant
25. that thou wilt build him *an house:*
27. bless *the house of* thy servant,
21:17. be on me, *and on* my father's *house;*
22: 1. This (is) *the house of* the Lord
2. to build *the house of* God.
5. *and the house* (that is) to be builded
6. charged him to build *an house*
7. it was in my mind to build *an house*
8. thou shalt not build *an house*
10. He shall build *an house*
11. build *the house of* the Lord
14. I have prepared *for the house of*
19. *into the house* that is to be
23: 4. to set forward the work of *the house of*
11. *according to* (their) father's *house.*
24. *after the house of* their fathers;
— 28, 32. service of *the house of* the Lord,
28. work of the service of *the house of* God;
24: 4. chief men *of the house of* (their) fathers,
— *according to the house of* their fathers.
6. one principal *houshold* (marg. *house of* the father)
19. to come *into the house of* the Lord,
30. *after the house of* their fathers.
25: 6. song (in) *the house of* the Lord,
— for the service of *the house of*
26: 6. that ruled *throughout the house of*
12. to minister *in the house of* the Lord.
13. *according to the house of* their fathers,
15. to his sons *the house of* Asuppim.
20. Ahijah (was) over the treasures of *the house of*
22. the treasures of *the house of* the Lord.
27. to maintain *the house of* the Lord.
28: 2. in mine heart to build *an house of* rest
3. Thou shalt not build *an house*
4. before all *the house of* my father
— *and of the house of* Judah, *the house of* my father;
6. Solomon thy son, he shall build *my house*
10. hath chosen thee to build *an house*
11. and of *the houses thereof,*
— *and of the place of* the mercy seat,
12. the courts of *the house of* the Lord,
— the treasuries of *the house of* God,
13. the service of *the house of* the Lord, and for all the vessels of service in *the house of* the Lord.
20. for the service of *the house of*
21. all the service of *the house of* God:
29: 2. *for the house of* my God
3. affection *to the house of* my God,
— I have given *to the house of*
— I have prepared *for the* holy *house,*
4. to overlay the walls of *the houses*
7. gave for the service of *the house of* God
8. the treasure of *the house of* the Lord,
16. we have prepared to build thee *an house*
2 Ch 2: 1(1:18). Solomon determined to build *an house*
—(-:—). *and an house* for his kingdom.
3(2). to build him *an house* to dwell
4(3). build *an house* to the
5(4). *And the house* which I build (is) great:
6(5). who is able to build him *an house,*
—(-). that I should build him *an house,*

2 Ch 2: 9(8). *the house* which I am about to build
12(11). that might build *an house* for the Lord, *and an house* for his kingdom.
3: 1. to build *the house of* the Lord
3. instructed for the building of *the house of* God.
4. according to the breadth of *the house,*
5. *the* greater *house* he cieled
6. he garnished *the house* with
7. He overlaid also *the house,*
8. *the* most holy *house,* the length whereof (was) according to the breadth of *the house,*
10. *in the* most holy *house*
11. reaching to the wall of *the house.*
12. reaching to the wall of *the house:*
13. their faces (were) *inward.* (marg: or, *toward the house*)
15. Also he made before *the house*
4: 4. all their hinder parts (were) *inward.*
11. for king Solomon *for the house of* God;
16. to king Solomon *for the house of* the Lord
19. the vessels that (were for) *the house of* God,
22. the entry of *the house,*
— the doors of *the house*
5: 1. made *for the house of* the Lord
— among the treasures of *the house of* God.
7. to the oracle of *the house,*
13. *that* (then) *the house* was filled with a cloud, (even) *the house of* the Lord;
14. glory of the Lord had filled *the house of* God.
6: 2. But I have built *an house of*
5. the tribes of Israel to build *an house*
7. David my father to build *an house*
8. to build *an house* for my name,
9. thou shalt not build *the house;*
— he shall build *the house*
10. have built *the house* for
18. how much less this *house*
20. may be open upon this *house*
22. before thine altar *in* this *house;*
24. before thee *in* this *house;*
29. spread forth his hands in this *house:*
32. if they come and pray in this *house;*
33. may know that this *house*
34. *and the house* which I have built
38. *and toward the house* which I have built
7: 1. the glory of the Lord filled *the house.*
2. could not enter into *the house of* the Lord,
— of the Lord had filled the Lord's *house.*
3. the glory of the Lord upon *the house,*
5. the people dedicated *the house of* God.
7. the court that (was) before *the house of* the Lord:
11. Thus Solomon finished *the house of* the Lord, and the king's *house:* and all that came into Solomon's heart to make *in the house of* the Lord, *and in his own house,*
12. *for an house of* sacrifice.
16. have I chosen and sanctified this *house,*
20. and this *house,* which I have sanctified
21. *And* this *house,* which is high,
— thus unto this land, *and unto* this *house?*
8: 1. Solomon had built *the house of* the Lord and *his own house,*
11. *unto the house* that he had built
— shall not dwell *in the house of*
16. the foundation of *the house of* the Lord,
— (So) *the house of* the Lord was perfected.
9: 3. *and the house* that he had built,
4. by which he went up into *the house of* the Lord;
11. terraces *to the house of* the Lord, *and to* the king's *palace,*
16. the king put them *in the house of*
20. the vessels of *the house of* the forest
10:16. see to *thine own house.*
19. rebelled *against the house of*
11: 1. he gathered of *the house of* Judah
4. return every man *to his house:*
12: 9. the treasures of *the house of* the Lord, and the treasures of the king's *house;*
10. that kept the entrance of *the* king's *house*
11. when the king entered into *the house of*
15:18. he brought into *the house of* God

2Ch 16: 2. of the treasures of *the house of* the Lord *and of* the king's *house*,
10. put him in *a* prison *house;*
17: 14. *according to the house of* their
18: 16. return (therefore) every man *to his house*
26. Put this (fellow) in the prison, (lit. *house of* the prison)
19: 1. the king of Judah returned to *his house*
11. the ruler *of the house of* Judah,
20: 5. *in the house of* the Lord, before the new
9. we stand before this *house*,
— for thy name (is) *in* this *house*,
28. harps and trumpets unto *the house of* the Lord.
21: 6. like as did *the house of* Ahab:
7. would not destroy *the house of* David,
13. the whoredoms of *the house of* Ahab,
— slain thy brethren of thy father's *house*,
17. substance that was found *in* the king's *house*,
22: 3. in the ways of *the house of* Ahab:
4. *like the house of* Ahab:
7. to cut off *the house of* Ahab.
8. upon *the house of* Ahab,
9. So *the house of* Ahaziah *had* no power (lit. power was not *to the house of* Ahaziah)
10. seed royal *of the house of* Judah.
12. was with them hid *in the house of* God
23: 3. with the king *in the house of* God.
5. a third part (shall be) *at* the king's *house;*
— in the courts of *the house of* the Lord.
6. let none come into *the house of* the Lord,
7. cometh into *the house*,
9. which (were) in *the house of* God.
10. from the right side of *the temple* (marg. *house*) to the left side of *the temple*, along by the altar *and the temple*,
12. to the people into *the house of* the Lord:
14. Have her *forth of* (lit. to *the outside*)
— Slay her not in *the house of* the Lord.
15. the horse gate by the king's *house*,
17. went to *the house of* Baal,
18. the offices of *the house of* the Lord
— David had distributed in *the house of* the Lord,
19. at the gates of *the house of* the Lord,
20. *from the house of* the Lord: and they came through the high gate into the king's *house*,
24: 4, 12. to repair *the house of* the Lord.
5. repair *the house of* your God
7. had broken up *the house of* God; and also all the dedicated things of *the house of* the Lord
8. at the gate of *the house of* the Lord.
12. the service of *the house of* the Lord,
— brass to mend *the house of* the Lord.
13. they set *the house of* God in his state,
14. vessels *for the house of* the Lord,
— burnt offerings *in the house of* the Lord
16. toward God, *and* toward *his house*.
18. And they left *the house of* the Lord
21. in the court of *the house of* the Lord.
27. the repairing of *the house of* God,
25: 5. *according to the houses of* (their)
19. abide now *at home;*
24. *in the house of* God with Obed-edom, and the treasures of the king's *house*,
26: 19. before the priests *in the house of* the Lord,
21. dwelt in *a* several *house*, (being) a leper; for he was cut off *from the house of*
— Jotham his son (was) over the king's *house*,
27: 3. the high gate of *the house of* the Lord,
28: 7. the governor of *the house*,
21. took away a portion (out) of *the house of* the Lord, and (out) of *the house of* the king,
24. the vessels of *the house of* God, and cut in pieces the vessels of *the house of* God, and shut up the doors of *the house of the* Lord,
29: 3. opened the doors of *the house of* the Lord,
5. and sanctify *the house of* the Lord God
15. to cleanse *the house of* the Lord.
16. the inner part of *the house of* the Lord,

2Ch 29: 16. the court of *the house of* the Lord.
17. so they sanctified *the house of*
18. We have cleansed all *the house of*
20. went up to *the house of*
25. he set the Levites in *the house of*
31. thank offerings *into the house of* the Lord.
35. the service of *the house of* the Lord
30: 1. they should come *to the house of* the Lord
15. the burnt offerings into *the house of* the Lord.
31: 10. *of the house of* Zadok
— the offerings into *the house of* the Lord,
11. chambers *in the house of* the Lord;
13. Azariah the ruler of *the house of* God.
16. that entereth *into the house of* the Lord,
17. *by the house of* their fathers,
21. began in the service of *the house of* God,
32: 21. he was come into *the house of* his god,
33: 4. he built altars *in the house of* the Lord,
5. in the two courts of *the house of*
7. *in the house of* God, of which God had
— *In* this *house*, and in Jerusalem,
15. *out of the house of* the Lord,
— the mount of *the house of* the Lord,
20. they buried him in *his own house:*
24. slew him *in his own house*.
34: 8. purged the land, *and the house*,
— to repair *the house of* the Lord
9. was brought into *the house of* God,
10. that had the oversight *of the house of*
— the workmen that wrought *in the house of* the Lord, to repair and amend *the house:*
11. to floor *the houses*
14. that was brought into *the house of*
15. found the book of the law *in the house of*
17. the money that was found *in the house of*
30. king went up into *the house of* the Lord,
— that was found in *the house of* the Lord.
35: 2. to the service of *the house of* the Lord,
3. Put the holy ark *in the house*
4. *by the houses of* your fathers,
5. the divisions of *the families of* the fathers (marg. *house*)
— the division of the families (lit. *house of* a father)
8. rulers of *the house of* God,
12. the divisions of the families of (lit. *of a house of* fathers)
20. Josiah had prepared *the temple*, (marg. *house*)
21. but against *the house wherewith*
36: 7. the vessels of *the house of* the Lord
10. goodly vessels of *the house of* the Lord,
14. polluted *the house of* the Lord
17. *in the house of* their sanctuary,
18. all the vessels of *the house of* God,
— the treasures of *the house of* the Lord,
19. And they burnt *the house of* God,
23. to build him *an house*
Ezr. 1: 2. charged me to build him *an house*
3. and build *the house of*
4. freewill offering *for the house of* God
5. to go up to build *the house of*
7. the vessels of *the house of* the Lord,
— had put them *in the house of* his gods:
2: 36. *of the house of* Jeshua,
59. they could not shew their father's *house*,
68. when they came *to the house of* the Lord which (is) at Jerusalem, offered freely *for the house of* God
3: 8. of their coming unto *the house of* God
— the work of *the house of* the Lord.
9. set forward the workmen *in the house of* God:
11. the foundation of *the house of* the Lord
12. that had seen *the* first *house*, when the foundation of this *house*
4: 3. to do with us to build *an house*
6: 22. in the work of *the house of* God,
7: 27. to beautify *the house of* the Lord
8: 17. bring unto us ministers *for the house of*
25. (even) the offering of *the house of*
29. the chambers of *the house of* the Lord.
30. *unto the house of* our God.
33. weighed *in the house of* our God
36. furthered the people, and *the house of* God
9: 9. to set up *the house of* our God,

Ezr.10: 1. himself down before *the house of* God,
6. rose up from before *the house of* God,
9. the people sat in the street of *the house of* God,
16. *after the house of* their fathers,
Neh 1: 6. both I *and* my father's *house* have sinned.
2: 3. *the place of* my fathers' sepulchres,
8. which (appertained) *to the house*,
— *and for the house* that I shall
3:10. even over against *his house*.
16. unto *the house of* the mighty.
20. unto the door of *the house of*
21. from the door of *the house of* Eliashib even to the end of *the house of*
23. and Hashub over against *their house*.
— the son of Ananiah by *his house*.
24. *from the house of* Azariah
25. *from* the king's high *house*,
28. every one over against *his house*.
29. the son of Immer over against *his house*.
31. unto *the place of* the Nethinims,
4:14(8). your wives, *and your houses*.
16(10). behind all *the house of* Judah.
5: 3. our lands, vineyards, *and houses*,
11. their oliveyards, *and their houses*,
13. God shake out every man *from his house*,
6:10. Afterward I came unto *the house of*
— meet together *in the house of* God,
7: 3. every one (to be) over against *his house*.
4. and *the houses* (were) not builded.
39. *of the house of* Jeshua,
61. they could not shew their fathers' *house*,
8:16. and in the courts of *the house of* God,
9·25. possessed *houses* full of all
10.32(33). for the service of *the house of* our God;
33(34). all the work of *the house of* our God.
34(35). to bring (it) *into the house of* our God, *after the houses of* our fathers,
35(36). year by year, *unto the house of* the Lord:
36(37). to bring *to the house of* our God, unto the priests that minister *in the house of* our God:
37(38). to the chambers of *the house of* our God;
38(39). of the tithes *unto the house of* our God, to the chambers, *into the* treasure *house*.
39(40). we will not forsake *the house of* our God.
11:11. the ruler of *the house of* God.
12. that did the work *of the house*
16. the outward business *of the house of* God.
22. over the business of *the house of* God.
12:29. *Also from the house of* Gilgal,
37. above *the house of* David,
40. thanks *in the house of* God,
13: 4. of the chamber of *the house of* our God,
7. in the courts of *the house of* God.
8. I cast forth all the *houshold* stuff
9. again the vessels of *the house of* God,
11. Why is *the house of* God forsaken?
14. that I have done *for the house of*
Est. 1: 8. appointed to all the officers of *his house*,
9. for the women (in) *the* royal *house*
22. should bear rule *in his own house*,
2: 3. to *the house of* the women,
8. brought also unto the king's *house*,
9. given her *out of* the king's *house*:
— of *the house of* the women.
11. before the court of the women's *house*,
13. *of the house of* the women unto the king's *house*.
14. into *the* second *house*
16. Ahasuerus into his *house* royal
4:13. that thou shalt escape in the king's *house*,
14. thou *and* thy father's *house* shall be destroyed:
5: 1. stood in the inner court of the king's *house*, over against the king's *house*: and the king sat upon his royal throne *in the* royal *house*, over against the gate of *the house*.
10. and when he came *home*, (lit. to *his house*)
6: 4. the outward court of the king's *house*,
12. Haman hasted to *his house* mourning,
7: 8. into *the place of* the banquet
— before me *in the house*?
9. standeth *in the house of* Haman.
8: 1. give *the house of* Haman

Est. 8: 2. Esther set Mordecai over *the house of*
7. I have given Esther *the house of*
9: 4. Mordecai (was) great *in* the king's *house*,
Job 1: 4. his sons went and feasted (in their) *houses*,
10. an hedge about him, and about *his house*,
13, 18. *in* their eldest brother's *house*:
19. smote the four corners of *the house*,
3:15. who filled *their houses* with silver:
4:19. that dwell in *houses of* clay,
7:10. He shall return no more *to his house*,
8:14. *and* whose trust (shall be) a spider's *web*. (marg. *house*)
15. He shall lean upon *his house*,
17. seeth *the place of* stones.
15:28. in *houses* which no man
17:13. the grave (is) *mine house*:
19:15. They that dwell *in mine house*,
20:19. violently taken away *an house*
28. The increase of *his house* shall depart,
21: 9. *Their houses* (are) safe from fear,
21. pleasure (hath) he *in his house* after him,
28. Where (is) *the house of* the prince?
22:18. Yet he filled *their houses* with good
24:16. In the dark they dig through *houses*,
27:18. He buildeth *his house* as a moth,
30:23. *and* (to) *the house* appointed
38:20. the paths (to) *the house thereof*?
39: 6. *Whose house* I have made (lit. who, *his house*)
42:11. did eat bread with him *in his house*:
Ps. 5: 7(8). I will come (into) *thy house*
23: 6. I will dwell *in the house of* the
26: 8. I have loved the habitation of *thy house*,
27: 4. I may dwell *in the house of* the Lord
30[title](1). the dedication of *the house*
31: 2(3). *for an house of* defence
36: 8(9). satisfied with the fatness of *thy house*;
42: 4(5). I went with them to *the house of* God,
45:10(11). own people, *and* thy father's *house*;
49:11(12). *their houses* (shall continue) for ever,
16(17). when the glory of *his house* is
50: 9. I will take no bullock out *of thy house*,
52[title](2). David is come to *the house of*
8(10). like a green olive tree *in the house of*
55:14(15). walked *unto the house of* God
59[title](1). they watched *the house* to kill
65: 4(5). satisfied with the goodness of *thy house*,
66:13. I will go into *thy house* with
68: 6(7). God setteth the solitary *in families*:
12(13). she that tarried *at home* divided
69: 9(10). For the zeal of *thine house*
84: 3(4). the sparrow hath found *an house*,
4(5). Blessed (are) they that dwell *in thy house*:
10(11). a doorkeeper *in the house of*
92:13(14). that be planted *in the house of* the
93: 5. holiness becometh *thine house*,
98: 3. his truth *toward the house of* Israel:
101: 2. I will walk within *my house*
7. deceit shall not dwell within *my house*:
104:17. the fir trees (are) *her house*.
105:21. He made him lord *of his house*,
112: 3. Wealth and riches (shall be) *in his house*:
113: 9. the barren woman to keep *house*,
114: 1. *the house of* Jacob from a people
115:10. *O house of* Aaron, trust
12. he will bless *the house of* Israel; he will bless *the house of* Aaron.
116:19. In the courts of *the* Lord's *house*,
118: 3. Let *the house of* Aaron now say,
26. *out of the house of* the Lord.
119:54. *in the house of* my pilgrimage.
122: 1. Let us go into *the house of* the Lord.
5. the thrones *of the house of* David.
9. Because of *the house of* the Lord
127: 1. Except the Lord build *the house*,
128: 3. by the sides of *thine house*:
132: 3. into the tabernacle of *my house*,
134: 1. which by night stand *in the house of* the
135: 2. Ye that stand in *the house of* the Lord, in the courts of *the house of* our God,
19. Bless the Lord, *O house of* Israel: bless the Lord, *O house of* Aaron:
20. Bless the Lord, *O house of* Levi:
Pro. 1:13. we shall fill *our houses* with
2:18. For *her house* inclineth unto death,
3:33. *in the house of* the wicked:

Pro. 5: 8. come not nigh the door of *her house:*
10. thy labours (be) *in the house of* a stranger;
6:31. he shall give all the substance of *his house.*
7: 6. For at the window of *my house*
8. he went the way to *her house,*
11. her feet abide not *in her house:*
19. the goodman (is) not *at home,*
20. will come *home* at the day
27. *Her house* (is) the way to hell,
8: 2. in *the places of* the paths. (lit. *house of*)
9: 1. Wisdom hath builded *her house,*
14. she sitteth at the door of *her house,*
11:29. He that troubleth *his own house*
12: 7. *but the house of* the righteous
14: 1. wise woman buildeth *her house:*
11. *The house of* the wicked shall be
15: 6. In *the house of* the righteous
25. will destroy *the house of* the proud:
27. troubleth *his own house;*
17: 1. *than an house* full of sacrifices
13. evil shall not depart *from his house.*
19:14. *House* and riches (are) the inheritance
21: 9. *in a* wide *house.*
12. considereth *the house of* the
24: 3. Through wisdom is *an house* builded;
27. afterwards build *thine house.*
25:17. *from* thy neighbour's *house;*
24. *and in a* wide *house.*
27:10. *neither* (lit. *and* not) go into thy brother's *house*
27. for the food of *thy houshold,*
30:26. yet make they *their houses*
31:15. giveth meat *to her houshold,*
21. of the snow *for her houshold:* for all *her houshold* (are) clothed
27. looketh well to the ways of *her houshold,*
Ecc. 2: 4. I builded me *houses;*
7. and had servants born in my *house;*
4:14. For out of prison he cometh (lit. *out of the house of* prisoners)
5: 1(4:17). when thou goest to *the house of* God,
7: 2. better to go to *the house of* mourning, than to go to *the house of* feasting:
4. the wise (is) *in the house of* mourning; but the heart of fools (is) *in the house of*
10:18. of the hands *the house* droppeth through.
12: 3. the keepers of *the house* shall
5. man goeth to his long *home,*
Cant. 1:17. The beams of *our house*
2: 4. He brought me to *the* banqueting *house,*
3: 4. brought him into my mother's *house,*
8: 2. bring thee into my mother's *house,*
7. all the substance of *his house*
Isa. 2: 2. the mountain of the Lord's *house*
3. to *the house of* the God of Jacob;
5. *O house of* Jacob, come ye,
6. hast forsaken thy people *the house of*
3: 6. of *the house of* his father,
7. *for in my house* (is) neither bread
14. the poor (is) *in your houses.*
20. the headbands, *and the tablets,* (marg. *and the houses of* the soul)
5: 7. the Lord of hosts (is) *the house of* Israel,
8. them that join *house to house,*
9. Of a truth many *houses* shall
6: 4. *and the house* was filled
11. *and the houses* without man,
7: 2. it was told *the house of* David,
13. *O house of* David;
17. and upon thy father's *house,* days
8:14. to both *the houses of* Israel,
17. *from the house of* Jacob,
10:20. such as are escaped of *the house of* Jacob,
32. the mount of *the daughter of* Zion, (כתיב *house of*)
13:16. *their houses* shall be spoiled,
21. and *their houses* shall be full
14: 1. they shall cleave to *the house of* Jacob.
2. *the house of* Israel shall possess them
17. opened not *the house* of his prisoners? (marg. did not let his prisoners loose *homeward*)
18. every one *in his own house.*
22: 8. of *the house of* the forest.
10. ye have numbered *the houses of* Jerusalem, and *the houses* have ye broken
15. which (is) over *the house,*

Isa. 22:18. (shall be) the shame of thy lord's *house.*
21. *and to the house of* Judah.
22. the key of *the house of* David
23. a glorious throne *to* his father's *house.*
24. all the glory of his father's *house,*
23: 1. laid waste, so that there is *no house,*
24:10. every *house* is shut up,
29:22. concerning *the house of* Jacob,
31: 2. will arise against the *house of*
32:13. upon all *the houses of* joy
36: 3. which was over *the house,*
22. that (was) over *the houshold,*
37: 1. and went into *the house of* the Lord.
2. Eliakim, who (was) over *the houshold,*
14. Hezekiah went up unto *the house of* the
31. escaped of *the house of* Judah
38. worshipping in *the house of*
38: 1. Set *thine house* in order: (marg. Give charge *concerning thy house*)
20. of our life in *the house of* the Lord.
22. that I shall go up to *the house of* the Lord?
39: 2. shewed them *the house of* his
— and all *the house of* his armour,
— there was nothing *in his house,*
4. What have they seen *in thine house?*
— All that (is) *in mine house*
6. all that (is) *in thine house,*
42: 7. *out of the* prison *house.*
22. *and* they are hid *in* prison *houses:*
44:13. that it may remain *in the house.*
46: 3. O *house of* Jacob, and all the remnant of *the house of* Israel,
48: 1. Hear ye this, *O house of* Jacob,
56: 5. them will I give *in mine house*
7. and make them joyful *in* my *house of*
— for *mine house* shall be called *an house of*
58: 1. *and the house of* Jacob their sins.
7. the poor that are cast out to thy *house?*
60: 7. *and* I will glorify *the house of* my
63: 7. great goodness *toward the house of* Israel,
64:11(10). Our holy and our beautiful *house,*
65:21. And they shall build *houses,*
66: 1. where (is) *the house* that ye
20. in a clean vessel into *the house of* the
Jer. 2: 4. *O house of* Jacob, and all the families of *the house of* Israel:
14. (is) he a *home*born (slave)?
26. so is *the house of* Israel ashamed;
3:18. *the house of* Judah shall walk with *the house of* Israel,
20. dealt treacherously with me, *O house of*
5: 7. *and* assembled themselves by troops in the harlots' *houses.*
11. For *the house of* Israel *and the house of*
15. *O house of* Israel, saith the Lord:
20. Declare this *in the house of* Jacob,
27. *their houses* full of deceit:
6:12. *their houses* shall be turned
7: 2. Stand in the gate of the Lord's *house,*
10. stand before me *in* this *house,*
11. Is this *house,* which is called
14. will I do *unto* (this) *house,*
30. *in the house* which is called
9:26(25). *the house of* Israel (are) uncircumcised
10: 1. the Lord speaketh unto you, *O house of*
11:10. *the house of* Israel *and the house of* Judah
15. my beloved to do *in mine house,*
17. the evil of *the house of* Israel *and* of *the house of* Judah,
12: 6. *and the house of* thy father,
7. I have forsaken *mine house,*
14. pluck out *the house of* Judah
13:11. *the* whole *house of* Israel and *the* whole *house of* Judah,
16: 5. Enter not into *the house of* mourning,
8. not *also* go into *the house of* feasting,
17:22. a burden *out of your houses*
26. sacrifices of praise, unto *the house of* the
18: 2. go down to the potter's *house,*
3. Then I went down to the potter's *house,*
6. *O house of* Israel, cannot I do with you
— so (are) ye in mine hand, *O house of* Israel.
22. Let a cry be heard *from their houses,*
19:13. And *the houses of* Jerusalem, *and the houses of* the kings
— because of all *the houses*
14. in the court of the Lord's *house;*

Jer. 20: 1. governor *in the house of* the Lord,
2. which (was) *by the house of* the Lord.
6. all that dwell in *thine house*
21:11. *And touching the house of*
12. *O house of* David, thus saith
22: 1. Go down to *the house of* the king
4. enter in by the gates of this *house*
5. that this *house* shall become
6. unto the king's *house* of Judah;
13. buildeth *his house* by unrighteousness,
14. I will build me *a* wide *house*
23: 8. led the seed of *the house of* Israel
11. *in my house* have I found their
34. I will even punish that man and *his house.*
26: 2. Stand in the court of the Lord's *house,*
— which come to worship in the Lord's *house,*
6. Then will I make this *house*
7. these words *in the house of* the Lord.
9. This *house* shall be like Shiloh,
— against Jeremiah *in the house of* the Lord.
10. they came up *from* the king's *house* unto *the house of* the Lord,
12. to prophesy against this *house*
18. *the house* as the high places
27:16. the vessels of *the* Lord's *house*
18. *in the house of* the Lord, *and* (in) *the house of* the king of Judah,
21. (in) *the house of* the Lord, *and* (in) *the house of* the king of Judah
28: 1. spake unto me *in the house of* the Lord,
3. all the vessels of the Lord's *house,*
5. the people that stood *in the house of* the Lord,
6. bring again the vessels of the Lord's *house,*
29: 5, 28. Build ye *houses,* and dwell
26. officers in *the house of* the Lord,
31:27. I will sow *the house of* Israel and *the house of* Judah
31. covenant with *the house of* Israel, and with *the house of* Judah:
33. I will make with *the house of* Israel;
32: 2. in the king of Judah's *house.*
15. *Houses* and fields and vineyards
29. burn it with *the houses,*
34. abominations *in the house,*
33: 4. concerning *the houses of* this city, and concerning *the houses of* the kings
11. sacrifice of praise into *the house of* the Lord.
14. unto *the house of* Israel and to *the house of* Judah.
17. upon the throne of *the house of* Israel;
34:13. *out of the house of* bondmen,
15. before me *in the house*
35: 2. Go unto *the house of* the Rechabites,
— bring them into *the house of* the Lord,
3. and *the* whole *house of* the Rechabites;
4. brought them into *the house of* the Lord,
5. the sons of *the house of* the Rechabites
7. *Neither* shall ye build *house,* (lit. *and a house* ye shall not build)
9. Nor to build *houses* for us
18. *And* Jeremiah said *unto the house of* the
36: 3. It may be that *the house of* Judah
5. I cannot go into *the house of*
6. in the Lord's *house* upon the fasting day:
8. of the Lord in the Lord's *house.*
10. words of Jeremiah in the *house of* the Lord,
— the new gate of *the* Lord's *house,*
12. he went down into the king's *house,*
22. the king sat in *the* winter-*house*
37: 4. they had not put him into prison. (lit. *house of* the prison)
15. and put him in prison (lit. *house of* binding) in *the house of* Jonathan the scribe: for they had made that the prison. (lit. *house of* the prison)
16. Jeremiah was entered into the dungeon, (lit. *house of* the pit)
17. asked him secretly *in his house,*
18. that ye have put me in prison? (lit. *house of* prison)
20. not to return to *the house of* Jonathan
38: 7. eunuchs which was *in* the king's *house,*
8. went forth *out of* the king's *house,*
11. went into *the house of*
14. the third entry that (is) *in the house of*
17. thou shalt live, *and thine house:*

Jer. 38:22. left *in* the king of Judah's *house*
26. to return to Jonathan's *house,*
39: 8. burned the king's *house,* and *the houses of* the people,
14. that he should carry him *home:*
41: 5. to bring (them) to *the house of* the Lord.
43: 9. at the entry of Pharaoh's *house*
12. I will kindle a fire *in the houses of*
13. break also the images of *Beth*-shemesh, (marg. or, *the house of* the sun)
— and *the houses of* the gods
48:13. as *the house of* Israel was ashamed
51:51. the sanctuaries of the Lord's *house.*
52:11. and put him in prison (lit. *in house of* the wards)
13. burned *the house of* the Lord, and the king's *house;* and all *the houses of* Jerusalem, and all *the houses of* the great
17. *in the house of* the Lord, and the bases, and the brasen sea that (was) *in the house of*
20. Solomon had made *in the house of* the Lord:
31. brought him forth out of prison, (lit. *out of the house of* the prison)
Lam. 1:20. *at home* (there is) as death.
2: 7. made a noise *in the house of* the Lord,
5: 2. *our houses* to aliens.
Eze. 1:27. of fire round about *within* it,
2: 5. for they (are) *a* rebellious *house,*
6. though they (be) *a* rebellious *house.*
8. *like* that rebellious *house:*
3: 1. go speak unto *the house of* Israel.
4. get thee unto *the house of* Israel,
5. (but) to *the house of* Israel;
7. *But the house of* Israel will not hearken
— all *the house of* Israel (are) impudent
9. though they (be) *a* rebellious *house.*
17. a watchman *unto the house of* Israel:
24. shut thyself within *thine house.*
26, 27. for they (are) *a* rebellious *house.*
4: 3. This (shall be) a sign *to the house of* Israel.
4, 5. the iniquity of *the house of* Israel
6. the iniquity of *the house of* Judah
5: 4. fire come forth into all *the house of* Israel.
6:11. abominations of *the house of* Israel!
7:15. pestilence and the famine *within:*
24. they shall possess *their houses:*
8: 1. I sat *in mine house,*
6. great abominations that *the house of*
10. all the idols of *the house of* Israel,
11, 12. the ancients of *the house of* Israel,
14. of the gate of the Lord's *house*
16. the inner court of the Lord's *house,*
17. a light thing *to the house of* Judah
9: 3. to the threshold of *the house.*
6. which (were) before *the house.*
7. Defile *the house,* and fill
9. The iniquity of *the house of* Israel and
10: 3. on the right side *of the house,*
4. over the threshold of *the house;* and *the house* was filled with the cloud,
18. from off the threshold of *the house,*
19. of the east gate of the Lord's *house;*
11: 1. unto the east gate of the Lord's *house,*
3. let us build *houses:*
5. Thus have ye said, *O house of* Israel:
15. and all *the house of* Israel wholly,
12: 2. in the midst of *a* rebellious *house,*
— for they (are) *a* rebellious *house.*
3. though they (be) *a* rebellious *house.*
6. (for) a sign *unto the house of* Israel.
9. *the house of* Israel, *the* rebellious *house,*
10. and all *the house of* Israel
24. divination within *the house of* Israel.
25. *O* rebellious *house,*
27. (they of) *the house of* Israel say,
13: 5. the hedge for *the house of* Israel
9. in the writing of *the house of* Israel,
14: 4. Every man *of the house of* Israel
5. I may take *the house of* Israel
6. say unto *the house of* Israel, Thus saith
7. every one *of the house of* Israel,
11. That *the house of* Israel may go no more
16:41. they shall burn *thine houses*
17: 2. speak a parable unto *the house of* Israel;
12. Say now *to the* rebellious *house,*
18: 6, 15. the idols of *the house of* Israel,

Eze. 18:25. Hear now, *O house of* Israel;
29. Yet saith *the house of* Israel,
— *O house of* Israel, are not my ways
30. I will judge you, *O house of* Israel,
31. for why will ye die, *O house of* Israel?
20: 5. unto the seed of *the house of* Jacob,
13. But *the house of* Israel rebelled
27. speak unto *the house of* Israel, and say
30. Wherefore say unto *the house of* Israel,
31. be enquired of by you, *O house of* Israel?
39. As for you, *O house of* Israel,
40. there shall all *the house of* Israel,
44. your corrupt doings, O ye *house of* Israel,
22:18. *the house of* Israel is to me become
23:39. in the midst of *mine house.*
47. *and* burn up *their houses* with
24: 3. unto *the* rebellious *house,*
21. Speak *unto the house of* Israel,
25: 3. against *the house of* Judah,
8. *the house of* Judah (is) like
12. *against the house of* Judah
26:12. *and* destroy thy pleasant *houses:*
27:14. They of *the house of* Togarmah
28:24. a pricking brier *unto the house of* Israel,
25. When I shall have gathered *the house of*
26. and shall build *houses,*
29: 6. a staff of reed *to the house of* Israel.
16. the confidence *of the house of* Israel,
21. the horn *of the house of* Israel to bud
33: 7. a watchman *unto the house of* Israel;
10. speak unto *the house of* Israel;
11. for why will ye die, *O house of* Israel?
20. *O* ye *house of* Israel, I will judge
30. in the doors of *the houses,*
34:30. *the house of* Israel, (are) my people,
35:15. the inheritance of *the house of* Israel,
36:10. all *the house of* Israel, (even) all of it:
17. when *the house of* Israel dwelt in
21. which *the house of* Israel had profaned
22. say *unto the house of* Israel,
— I do not (this) for your sakes, *O house of*
32. for your own ways, *O house of* Israel.
37. be enquired of *by the house of* Israel,
37:11. these bones are *the* whole *house of* Israel:
16. all *the house of* Israel his companions:
38: 6. *the house of* Togarmah
39:12. shall *the house of* Israel be burying
22. So *the house of* Israel shall know
23. *the house of* Israel went into captivity
25. mercy upon *the* whole *house of* Israel,
29. poured out my spirit upon *the house of*
40: 4. that thou seest *to the house of* Israel.
5. outside *of the house*
7, 8. the porch of the gate *within*
9. and the porch of the gate (was) *inward.*
43. *within* (were) hooks,
45. of the charge of *the house.*
47. the altar (that was) before the *house.*
48. to the porch of *the house,*
41: 5. he measured the wall of *the house,*
— round *about the house*
6. which (was) *of the house*
— had not hold in the wall of *the house.*
7. the winding about of *the house* went still upward round *about the house:* therefore the breadth *of the house*
8. I saw also the height *of the house*
9. which (was) left (was) *the place of* the side chambers that (were) *within.*
10. round *about the house*
13. So he measured *the house,*
14. the breadth of the face of *the house,*
17. even unto *the* inner *house,*
19. all *the house* round about.
26. the side chambers of *the house,*
42:15. an end of measuring *the* inner *house,*
43: 4. of the Lord came into *the house*
5. of the Lord filled *the house.*
6. speaking unto me *out of the house;*
7. shall *the house of* Israel no more defile,
10. shew *the house* to *the house of* Israel,
11. shew them the form of *the house,*
12, 12. This (is) the law of *the house,*
21. the appointed place of *the house,*
44: 4. the north gate before *the house:*
— filled *the house of* the Lord:
5. the ordinances of *the house of* the Lord,

Eze. 44: 5. the entering in of *the house,*
6. to *the house of* Israel, Thus saith the Lord God; *O ye house of* Israel,
7. to pollute it, (even) *my house,*
11. of *the house,* and ministering to *the house:*
12. *the house of* Israel to fall into iniquity;
14. of the charge of *the house,*
17. the inner court, *and within.*
22. of the seed of *the house of* Israel,
30. to rest in *thine house.*
45: 4. it shall be a place *for* their *houses,*
5. the ministers of *the house,*
6. it shall be for *the* whole *house of* Israel.
8. the land shall they give to *the house of*
17. all solemnities of *the house of* Israel:
— reconciliation for *the house of* Israel.
19. upon the posts of *the house,*
20. so shall ye reconcile *the house.*
46:24. These (are) *the places of*
— where the ministers of *the house*
47: 1. unto the door of *the house;*
— under the threshold of *the house* eastward: for the forefront of *the house*
— from the right side of *the house,*
48:21. the sanctuary of *the house*
Dan 1: 2. the vessels of *the house of* God:
— to *the house of* his god;
— into the treasure *house of* his god.
Hos 1: 4. upon *the house of* Jehu,
— the kingdom of *the house of* Israel.
6. have mercy upon *the house of* Israel;
7. have mercy upon *the house of* Judah,
5: 1. hearken, ye *house of* Israel; *and* give ye ear, *O house of* the king;
12. and *to the house of* Judah
14. as a young lion *to the house of*
6:10. an horrible thing *in the house of* Israel:
8: 1. as an eagle against *the house of* the Lord,
9: 4. shall not come into *the house of*
8. *in the house of* his God.
15. I will drive them out *of mine house,*
11:11. I will place them in *their houses,*
12(12:1). and *the house of* Israel with deceit:
Joel 1: 9. is cut off *from the house of*
13. *from the house of* your God.
14. *the house of* the Lord your God,
16. joy and gladness *from the house of*
2: 9. they shall climb up *upon the houses;*
3:18(4:18). shall come forth *of the house of*
Am. 1. 4. send a fire *into the house of*
5. *from the house of* Eden: (marg. or, *from Beth*-eden)
2: 8. (in) *the house of* their god.
3:13. and testify *in the house of* Jacob,
15. I will smite *the* winter *house* with *the* summer *house;* and *the houses of* ivory shall perish, and *the* great *houses* shall
5: 1. (even) a lamentation, *O house of* Israel.
3. shall leave ten, *to the house of* Israel.
4. thus saith the Lord *unto the house of*
6. break out like fire in *the house of* Joseph,
11. ye have built *houses of* hewn stone,
19. or went into *the house,*
25. forty years, *O house of* Israel?
6: 1. to whom *the house of* Israel came!
9. remain ten men *in* one *house,*
10. bring out the bones out of *the house,*
— by the sides of *the house,*
11. he will smite *the* great *house* with breaches, *and the* little *house* with clefts.
14. against you a nation, *O house of* Israel,
7: 9. I will rise against *the house of* Jeroboam
10. in the midst of *the house of* Israel:
13. *and* it (is) the king's *court.* (marg. *and the house of* the kingdom)
16. against *the house of* Isaac.
9: 8. not utterly destroy *the house of* Jacob,
9. I will sift *the house of* Israel
Obad. 17. and *the house of* Jacob shall possess
18. And *the house of* Jacob shall be a fire, *and the house of* Joseph a flame, *and the house of* Esau for stubble,
— remaining *of the house of* Esau;
Mic 1: 5. for the sins of *the house of* Israel.
10. *in the house* of Aphrah
11. the mourning of *Beth*-ezel; (marg. or, *a place* near)

Mic. 1:14. *the houses of* Achzib (shall be) a lie
2: 2. *and houses*, and take (them) away: so they oppress a man *and his house*,
7. (that art) named *the house of* Jacob,
9. *from* their pleasant *houses;*
3: 1. ye princes of *the house of* Israel;
9. ye heads of *the house of* Jacob, and princes of *the house of* Israel,
12. the mountain of *the house*
4: 1. the mountain of *the house of* the Lord
2. to *the house of* the God of Jacob;
6: 4. *and* redeemed thee *out of the house of*
10. *in the house of* the wicked,
16. all the works of *the house of*
7: 6. the men of *his own house*.
Nah. 1:14. *out of the house of* thy gods
Hab. 2: 9. an evil covetousness *to his house*,
10. hast consulted shame *to thy house*
3:13. *out of the house of* the wicked,
Zep. 1: 9. fill their masters' *houses*
13. shall become a booty, *and their houses* a desolation: they shall also build *houses*,
2: 7. the remnant of *the house of* Judah;
— *in the houses of* Ashkelon
Hag. 1: 2. that the Lord's *house* should be built.
4. to dwell *in your* cieled *houses, and* this *house* (lie) waste?
8. and build *the house;*
9. when ye brought (it) *home*,
— Because of *mine house* that (is) waste, and ye run every man *unto his own house*.
14. did work *in the house of* the Lord
2: 3. among you that saw this *house*
7. and I will fill this *house* with glory,
9. The glory of this latter *house*
Zec. 1:16. *my house* shall be built in it,
3: 7. thou shalt also judge *my house*,
4: 9. have laid the foundation of this *house;*
5: 4. it shall enter into *the house of* the thief, and into *the house of* him that sweareth
— and it shall remain in the midst of *his house*,
11. To build it *an house* in the land of Shinar:
6:10. go into *the house of* Josiah
7: 2. When they had sent unto *the house of*
3. the priests which (were) *in the house of* the Lord
8: 9. the foundation of *the house of* the Lord
13. *O house of* Judah, *and house of* Israel;
15. and to *the house of* Judah:
19. shall be *to the house of* Judah
9: 8. I will encamp *about mine house*
10: 3. visited his flock *the house of* Judah,
6. I will strengthen *the house of* Judah, and I will save *the house of* Joseph,
11:13. to the potter in *the house of* the Lord.
12: 4. upon *the house of* Judah,
7. that the glory of *the house of* David
8. *and the house of* David
10. I will pour upon *the house of* David,
12. the family of *the house of* David
— the family of *the house of* Nathan
13. The family of *the house of* Levi apart,
13: 1. a fountain opened *to the house of*
6. I was wounded (in) *the house of* my friends.
14: 2. and *the houses* rifled,
20. the pots *in* the Lord's *house*
21. Canaanite *in the house of* the Lord of hosts.
Mal. 3:10. all the tithes into *the* store*house*, that there may be meat *in mine house*,

---

1005 בַּיִת [*bah'-yith*], Ch. m.

Ezr. 4:24. Then ceased the work of *the house of* God
5: 2. and began to build *the house of* God
3. Who hath commanded you to build this *house*,
8. *to the house of* the great God,
9. Who commanded you to build this *house*,
11. and build *the house* that was builded
12. who destroyed this *house*,
13. Cyrus made a decree to build this *house of* God.
14. of gold and silver of *the house of* God,
Ezr. 5:15. *and* let *the house of* God be builded
16. the foundation of *the house of* God
17. search made *in* the king's treasure *house*,
— to build this *house of* God at Jerusalem,
6: 1. and search was made *in the house of* the rolls,
3. made a decree (concerning) *the house of* God
— Let *the house* be builded,
4. expences be given out of the king's *house:*
5. and silver vessels of *the house of* God,
— and place (them) *in the house of* God.
7. Let the work of this *house of* God alone;
— elders of the Jews build this *house of* God
8. for the building of this *house of* God:
11. let timber be pulled down from *his house*,
— *and* let *his house* be made a dunghill
12. to destroy this *house of* God
15. And this *house* was finished on the third day
16. kept the dedication of this *house of* God
17. at the dedication of this *house of* God
7:16. offering willingly *for the house of* their God
17. offer them upon the altar of *the house of* your God
19. for the service of *the house of* thy God,
20. shall be needful for *the house of* thy God,
— bestow (it) out of the king's treasure *house*.
23. let it be diligently done *for the house of* the God of heaven:
24. Nethinims, or ministers of this *house of* God,
Dan 2: 5. *and your houses* shall be made a dunghill.
17. Daniel went *to his house*, and made
3:29. *and their houses* shall be made a dunghill:
4: 4(1). I Nebuchadnezzar was at rest *in mine house*,
30(27). that I have built *for the house of* the kingdom
5: 3. taken out of the temple of *the house of*
10. and his lords came *into the* banquet *house*.
23. they have brought the vessels of *his house*
6:10(11). he went *into his house;* and his windows

בִּיתָן *bee-thāhn'*, m. 1055

Est. 1: 5. the garden of the king's *palace;*
7: 7. into the *palace* garden:
8. returned out of the *palace* garden

בָּכָא *bāh-chāh'*, m. 1056-57

2Sa. 5:23. over against *the mulberry trees*.
24. in the tops of *the mulberry trees*,
1Ch 14:14. over against *the mulberry trees*.
15. in the tops of *the mulberry trees*,
Ps. 84: 6(7). through the valley of *Baca* (marg: *mulberry trees*)

בָּכָה *bāh-chāh'*. 1058

* KAL.—*Preterite*. *

Gen45:14. Benjamin *wept* upon his neck.
Nu. 11:18. *ye have wept* in the ears of
Deu21:13. *and bewail* her father and her mother
2Sa. 13:36. his servants *wept* very sore.
Ezr. 10: 1. for the people *wept* very sore.
Job 30:25. *Did* not *I weep*
Ps. 137: 1. *we wept*, when we remembered Zion.
Eze. 27:31. *and they shall weep* for thee
Hos. 12: 4(5). *he wept*, and made supplication

KAL.—*Infinitive*.

Gen23: 2. to mourn for Sarah, *and to weep for her*.
43:30. he sought (where) *to weep;*
1Sa. 1:10. prayed unto the Lord, *and* wept *sore*. (lit. *and weeping* she wept)
30: 4. had no more power *to weep*.
2Sa. 3:16. went with her along *weeping*
34. all the people *wept* again over him. (lit. added *to weep*)

2Sa.15:30. they went up, *weeping*
Ps.126: 6. He that goeth forth *and weepeth*,
Ecc. 3: 4. A time *to weep*, and a time to laugh;
Isa. 30:19. thou shalt weep no *more*: (lit. *weeping* thou shalt not weep)
Jer. 22:10. weep *sore* for him that goeth away: (lit. *weeping* weep)
50: 4. going *and weeping*:
Lam.1: 2. She weepeth *sore* in the night, (lit. *in weeping* she weepeth)
Mic. 1:10. weep ye not *at all*: (lit. *weeping* ye shall not weep)

KAL.—*Imperative.*

2Sa. 1:24. Ye daughters of Israel, *weep* over Saul,
Jer.22:10. *weep* sore for him that goeth
Joel 1: 5. Awake, ye drunkards, *and weep*;

KAL.—*Future.*

Gen21:16. lift up her voice, *and wept.*
27:38. Esau lifted up his voice, *and wept.*
29:11. and lifted up his voice, *and wept.*
33: 4. kissed him: *and they wept.*
37:35. *Thus* his father *wept* for him.
42:24. about from them, *and wept*;
43:30. entered into (his) chamber, *and wept* there.
45:14. his brother Benjamin's neck, *and wept*;
15. *and wept* upon them:
46:29. *and wept* on his neck
50: 1. *and wept* upon him,
3. *and* the Egyptians *mourned* (marg. *wept*)
17. *And* Joseph *wept* when they spake
Lev.10: 6. *let* your brethren, the whole house of Israel, *bewail*
Nu. 11: 4. Israel *also wept* again,
13. for *they weep* unto me,
20. *and have wept* before him, saying,
14: 1. *and* the people *wept* that night.
20:29. *And* when all the congregation saw that Aaron was dead, *they mourned*
Deu 1:45. *and wept* before the Lord;
34: 8. *And* the children of Israel *wept*
Jud 2: 4. lifted up their voice, *and wept.*
11:37. *and bewail* my virginity,
38. *and bewailed* her virginity
14:16. *And* Samson's wife *wept* before him,
17. *And she wept* before him
20:23. *and wept* before the Lord
26. came unto the house of God, *and wept*,
21: 2. lifted up their voices, *and wept*
Ru. 1: 9, 14. lifted up their voice, *and wept.*
1Sa. 1: 7. *therefore she wept*, and did not eat.
8. Hannah, why *weepest thou?*
10. prayed unto the Lord, and *wept* sore.
11: 4. lifted up their voices, *and wept.*
5. What (aileth) the people that *they weep?*
20:41. *and wept* one with another,
24:16(17). Saul lifted up his voice, *and wept.*
30: 4. lifted up their voice *and wept*,
2Sa. 1:12. they mourned, *and wept*,
3:32. the king lifted up his voice, *and wept*
— *and* all the people *wept.*
12:21. thou didst fast *and weep*
22. I fasted *and wept*:
13:36. lifted up their voice *and wept*:
18:33(19:1). to the chamber over the gate, *and wept.*
2K. 8:11. *and* the man of God *wept.*
13:14. *and wept* over his face,
20: 3. *And* Hezekiah *wept* sore.
22:19. *and wept* before me;
2Ch34:27. *and weep* before me;
Neh 1: 4. I sat down *and wept*,
8: 9. mourn not, nor *weep.*
Est. 8: 3. *and* besought him *with tears* (marg: *and she wept*, and besought him)
Job 2:12. they lifted up their voice, *and wept*;
27:15. his widows *shall* not *weep.*
31:38. furrows likewise thereof *complain*; (marg. *weep*)
Ps. 69:10(11). *When I wept*, (and chastened)
78:64. their widows *made* no *lamentation.*
Isa. 16: 9. Therefore *I will bewail*
30:19. *thou shalt weep* no more:
33: 7. ambassadors of peace *shall weep*
38: 3. *And* Hezekiah *wept* sore.
Jer. 9: 1(8:23). *that I might weep* day and night
Jer. 13:17. my soul *shall weep* in secret
22:10. *Weep ye* not for the dead,
48:32. *I will weep* for thee with the weeping of Jazer:
Lam.1: 2. *She weepeth* sore in the night,
Eze.24:16. neither shalt thou mourn nor *weep*, (lit. *and thou shalt* not *weep*)
23. ye shall not mourn nor *weep*;
Joel 2:17. *Let* the priests, the ministers of the Lord, *weep*
Mic. 1:10. *weep ye* not at all:
Zec. 7: 3. *Should I weep* in the fifth month,

KAL.—*Participle.* Poel.

Ex. 2: 6. behold, the babe *wept.*
Nu. 11:10. Moses heard the people *weep*
25: 6. who (were) *weeping* (before) the door
Jud 2: 1. came up from Gilgal to *Bochim*,
5. called the name of that place *Bochim*: (marg. *Weepers*)
2Sa.15:23. all the country *wept*
30. *and wept* as he went up, (marg. *and weeping*)
19: 1(2). Behold, the king *weepeth*
2K. 8:12. Why *weepeth* my lord?
Ezr. 3:12. *wept* with a loud voice;
10: 1. *weeping* and casting himself down
Neh 8: 9. For all the people *wept*,
Job 30:31. the voice of them *that weep.*
Jer. 41: 6. *weeping* all along as he went: (marg. in going *and weeping*)
Lam.1:16. For these (things) I *weep*;

* PIEL.—*Participle.* *

Jer. 31:15. Rahel *weeping* for her children
Eze. 8:14. there sat women *weeping*

בֶּכֶה *beh'-cheh*, m. 1059

Ezr.10: 1. for the people wept very *sore.* (marg. a great *weeping*)

בְּכוֹר *b'chōhr*, m. 1060

Gen10:15. Canaan begat Sidon *his firstborn*,
22:21. Huz *his firstborn*,
25:13. *the firstborn of* Ishmael,
27:19. I (am) Esau *thy firstborn*;
32. I (am) thy son, *thy firstborn*
35:23. Reuben, Jacob's *firstborn*,
36:15. *the firstborn* (son) *of* Esau;
38: 6. Judah took a wife for Er *his firstborn*,
7. Er, Judah's *firstborn*,
41:51. called the name of *the firstborn*
43:33. *the firstborn* according to his birthright,
46: 8. Reuben, Jacob's *firstborn.*
48:14. for Manasseh (was) *the firstborn.*
18. for this (is) *the firstborn*;
49: 3. Reuben, thou (art) *my firstborn*,
Ex. 4:22. Israel (is) my son, (even) *my firstborn*:
23. I will slay thy son, (even) *thy firstborn.*
6:14. *the firstborn of* Israel;
11: 5. all *the firstborn* in the land of Egypt shall die, *from the firstborn of* Pharaoh that sitteth upon his throne, even unto *the firstborn of* the maidservant that (is) behind the mill; and all *the firstborn of* beasts.
12:12. will smite all *the firstborn*
29. the Lord smote all *the firstborn* in the land of Egypt, *from the firstborn of* Pharaoh that sat on his throne unto *the firstborn of* the captive that (was) in the dungeon; and all *the firstborn of* cattle.
13: 2. Sanctify unto me all *the firstborn*,
13. all *the firstborn of* man
15. the Lord slew all *the firstborn* in the land of Egypt, *both the firstborn of* man, and *the firstborn of* beast:
— all *the firstborn of* my children
22:29(28), & 34:20. *the firstborn of* thy sons

Lev.27:26. Only *the firstling* of the beasts, (marg. *firstborn*)
Nu. 1:20. Israel's *eldest son*,
3: 2. Nadab *the firstborn*,
12, 41, 45. instead of all *the firstborn*
13. all *the firstborn* (are) mine; (for) on the day that I smote all *the firstborn*
— I hallowed unto me all *the firstborn*
40. Number all *the firstborn of*
41. instead of all *the firstborn*
— instead of all *the firstlings*
42. all the *firstborn* among the
43. all the *firstborn* males
45. instead of all *the firstborn*
46. *of the firstborn of* the children of
50. Of *the firstborn of* the children of
8:16. *the firstborn of* all the children
17. *the firstborn of* the children of
— I smote every *firstborn* in the land
18. the Levites for all *the firstborn*
18:15. nevertheless *the firstborn of* man
— *the firstling of* unclean beasts
17. But *the firstling of* a cow, or *the firstling of* a sheep, or *the firstling of* a goat,
26: 5. Reuben, *the eldest son of* Israel:
33: 4. the Egyptians buried all (their) *firstborn*,
Deu15:19. All the *firstling* males that
— *with the firstling of* thy bullock, nor shear *the firstling of* thy sheep.
21:15. the *firstborn* son be her's
16. (which is indeed) *the firstborn:*
17. the son of the hated (for) *the firstborn*,
25: 6. *the firstborn* which she beareth
33:17. (like) *the firstling of* his bullock,
Jos. 6:26. the foundation thereof *in his firstborn*,
17: 1. he (was) *the firstborn of* Joseph;
— *the firstborn of* Manasseh,
Jud. 8:20. he said unto Jether *his firstborn*,
1Sa. 8: 2. the name of his *firstborn* was Joel;
17:13. Eliab *the firstborn*,
2Sa. 3: 2. *his firstborn* was Amnon,
1K. 16:34. in Abiram *his firstborn*,
2K. 3:27. Then he took his *eldest* son
1Ch 1:13. Canaan begat Zidon *his firstborn*,
29. *The firstborn of* Ishmael,
2: 3. Er, *the firstborn of* Judah,
13. Jesse begat *his firstborn*
25. *the firstborn of* Hezron were, Ram *the firstborn*,
27. *the firstborn of* Jerahmeel
42. Jerahmeel (were), Mesha *his firstborn*,
50. *the firstborn of* Ephratah;
3: 1. *the firstborn* Amnon,
15. *the firstborn* Johanan,
4: 4. *the firstborn of* Ephratah,
5: 1. Reuben *the firstborn of* Israel, for he (was) *the firstborn;*
3. Reuben *the firstborn of* Israel
6:28(13). *the firstborn* Vashni,
8: 1. Benjamin begat Bela *his firstborn*,
30. his *firstborn* son Abdon,
39. Ulam *his firstborn*,
9: 5. Asaiah *the firstborn*,
31. who (was) *the firstborn*
36. his *firstborn* son Abdon,
26: 2. Zechariah *the firstborn*,
4. Shemaiah *the firstborn*,
10. he was not *the firstborn*,
2Ch 21: 3. because he (was) *the firstborn.*
Neh10:36(37). Also *the firstborn of* our sons,
Job 1:13, 18. in their *eldest* brother's house:
18:13. *the firstborn of* death
Ps. 78:51. smote all *the firstborn*
89:27(28). I will make him (my) *firstborn*,
105:36. He smote also all *the firstborn*
135: 8. Who smote *the firstborn of*
136:10. that smote Egypt *in their firstborn:*
Isa. 14:30. *the firstborn of* the poor
Jer. 31: 9. Ephraim (is) *my firstborn.*
Mic. 6: 7. shall I give *my firstborn*
Zec.12:10. is in bitterness for (his) *firstborn.*

1061 בִּכּוּר [*bik-koor'*], m.

Ex. 23:16. *the firstfruits of* thy labours,
23:19. The first of *the firstfruits of*
34:22. *the firstfruits of* wheat harvest,
26. The first of *the firstfruits of*
Lev. 2:14. thy *firstfruits* unto the Lord,
— the meat offering of *thy firstfruits*
23:17. *the firstfruits* unto the Lord.
20. with the bread of *the firstfruits*
Nu. 13:20. the time of the *firstripe* grapes.
18:13. whatsoever is *first ripe* in the land,
28:26. Also in the day of *the firstfruits*,
2K. 4:42. bread of *the firstfruits*,
Neh10:35(36). And to bring *the firstfruits of* our ground, *and the firstfruits of* all fruit
13:31. *and for the firstfruits.*
Isa. 28: 4. *as the hasty fruit* before the summer; (lit. *as her first fruit*)
Eze.44:30. the first of all *the firstfruits of*
Nah. 3:12. fig trees with *the firstripe figs:*

בְּכוֹרָה *b'chōh-rāh'*, f. 1062

Gen 4: 4. he also brought *of the firstlings of* his flock
25:31. Sell me this day *thy birthright.*
32. shall this *birthright* do to me?
33. he sold *his birthright*
34. thus Esau despised (his) *birthright.*
27:36. he took away *my birthright;*
43:33. *according to his birthright*,
Deu 12: 6. *and the firstlings of* your herds
17. *or the firstlings of* thy herds
14:23. *and the firstlings of* thy herds
21:17. the right of *the firstborn*
1Ch 5: 1. *his birthright* was given
— to be reckoned *after the birthright.*
2. *but the birthright* (was) Joseph's:
Neh10:36(37). *the firstlings of* our herds

בִּכּוּרָה *bik-koo-rāh'*, f. 1063

Hos. 9:10. *as the firstripe* in the fig tree
Mic. 7: 1. my soul desired *the firstripe fruit.*

בַּכּוּרָה [*bak-koo-rāh'*], f. 1073

Jer. 24: 2. like the figs (that are) *firstripe:*

בָּכוּת *bāh-chooth'*, f. 439

Gen35: 8. it was called Allon-*bachuth.* (marg. The oak of *weeping*)

בְּכִי *b'chee*, m. 1065

Gen45: 2. And he *wept* aloud: (marg. gave forth his voice *in weeping*)
Deu34: 8. so the days of *weeping*
Jud.21: 2. and wept *sore;* (lit. *a* great *weeping*)
2Sa.13:36. wept very *sore.* (marg. with *a* great *weeping* greatly)
2K. 20: 3. Hezekiah wept *sore.* (marg. with *a* great *weeping*)
Ezr. 3:13. from the noise of *the weeping of*
Est. 4: 3. fasting, *and weeping*, and wailing;
Job 16:16. My face is foul with *weeping*,
28:11. He bindeth the floods *from overflowing* (marg. *weeping*)
Ps. 6: 8(9). hath heard the voice of *my weeping.*
30: 5(6). *weeping* may endure for a night,
102: 9(10). mingled my drink *with weeping*,
Isa. 15: 2. the high places, *to weep:*
3. every one shall howl, *weeping* abundantly. (marg. descending *into weeping*, or, coming down *with weeping*)
5. *with weeping* shall they go
16: 9. I will bewail *with the weeping of*
22: 4. I will *weep* bitterly, (marg. I will be bitter *in weeping*)
12. the Lord God of hosts call *to weeping*,
38: 3. Hezekiah wept *sore.* (marg. with great *weeping*)
65:19. the voice of *weeping* shall be no

Jer. 3:21. *weeping* (and) supplications
9:10(9). take up *a weeping* and wailing,
31: 9. They shall come *with weeping*,
15. lamentation, (and) bitter *weeping;*
16. Refrain thy voice *from weeping*,
48: 5. *continual weeping* shall go up; (lit. *in weeping* shall go up *weeping*)
32. *with the weeping of* Jazer:
Joel 2:12. with fasting, *and with weeping*,
Mal. 2:13. with *weeping*, and with crying

1067 בְּכִירָה *b'chee-rāh'*, adj. f.

Gen19:31, 34. *the firstborn* said unto the younger,
33. *the firstborn* went in,
37. *the firstborn* bare a son,
29:26. to give the younger before *the firstborn.*
1Sa. 14:49. the name of *the firstborn* Merab,

1068 בְּכִית [*b'cheeth*], f.

Gen50: 4. the days of *his mourning* were past,

1069 בָּכַר [*bāh-char'*].

* PIEL.—*Infinitive.* *

Deu21:16. *make* the son of the beloved *firstborn*

PIEL.—*Future.*

Eze.47:12. *it shall bring forth new fruit* (marg. *principal*)

* PUAL.—*Future.* *

Lev.27:26. *should be* the Lord's *firstling*,

* HIPHIL.—*Participle.* *

Jer. 4:31. *as of her that bringeth forth her first child*,

1070, 1072 בֶּכֶר [*beh'-cher*], m. & בִּכְרָה *bich-rāh*, f.

Isa. 60: 6. *the dromedaries of* Midian and Ephah;
Jer. 2:23. *a* swift *dromedary* traversing

1077 בַּל *bal*, part.

Ps. 10:15. seek out his wickedness (till) thou find *none.*
16: 4. of blood will I *not* offer, *nor* take up
32: 9. *lest* they come near unto thee.
Pro. 9:13. (she is) simple, *and* knoweth *nothing.* (lit. *and* knoweth *not* what)
Isa. 14:21. *that* they do *not* rise,
26:10. (yet) will he *not* learn righteousness:
— *and* will *not* behold the majesty
18. we have *not* wrought *any* deliverance in the earth; *neither* have the inhabitants
33:21. wherein shall go *no* galley with oars, &c. &c.

1079 בָּל *bāhl*, Ch. m.

Dan 6:14(15). and set (his) *heart* on Daniel to deliver him:

1080 בְּלָא [*b'lāh*], Ch.

* PAEL.—*Future* *

Dan. 7:25. and *shall wear out* the saints of the most High,

1082 בָּלַג [*bāh-lag'*].

* HIPHIL.—*Future.* *

Job 9:27. *and comfort* (myself):
Job 10:20. *that I may take comfort* a little,
Ps. 39:13(14). *that I may recover strength*, before

HIPHIL.—*Participle.*

Am. 5: 9. *That strengtheneth* the spoiled

בָּלַהּ [*bāh-lah'*]. 1089

* PIEL.—*Participle.* *

Ez. 4: 4. (כתיב) *and troubled* them in building,

בָּלָה [*bāh-lāh'*]. 1086

* KAL.—*Preterite.* *

Deu. 8: 4. Thy raiment *waxed* not *old*
29: 5(4). your clothes *are* not *waxen old* upon you, and thy shoe *is* not *waxen old*
Jos. 9:13. *become old* by reason of the very long
Neh 9:21. their clothes *waxed* not *old*,
Ps. 32: 3. my bones *waxed old* through

KAL.—*Infinitive.*

Gen18:12. After *I am waxed old*

KAL.—*Future.*

Job 13:28. as a rotten thing, *consumeth*,
Ps.102:26(27). all of them *shall wax old*
Isa. 50: 9. they all *shall wax old* as a garment;
51: 6. the earth *shall wax old* like a garment,

* PIEL.—*Preterite.* *

Lam. 3: 4. My flesh and my skin *hath he made old;*

PIEL.—*Infinitive.*

1Ch 17: 9. shall the children of wickedness *waste them*
Ps. 49:14(15) their beauty *shall consume*

PIEL.—*Future.*

Job 21:13. (כתיב) *They spend* their days in wealth,
Isa. 65:22. *shall long enjoy* the work of their hands. (marg. *make them continue long*, or, *wear out*)

בָּלֶה [*bāh-leh'*], adj. 1087

Jos. 9: 4. took *old* sacks upon their asses, and wine bottles, *old*, and rent,
5. *old* shoes and clouted upon their feet, and *old* garments upon them;
Eze.23:43. Then said I *unto* (her that was) *old*

בַּלָּהָה *bal-lāh-hāh'*, f. 1091

Job 18:11. *Terrors* shall make him afraid
14. bring him to the king of *terrors.*
24:17. *the terrors of* the shadow of death.
27:20. *Terrors* take hold on him
30:15. *Terrors* are turned upon me:
Ps. 73:19. are utterly consumed with *terrors.*
Isa. 17:14. behold at eveningtide *trouble;*
Eze.26:21. I will make thee *a terror*, and thou (shalt be) no (more): (marg. *terrors*)
27:36. thou shalt be *a terror*, (marg. *terrors*)
28:19. thou shalt be *a terror*, (marg. *terrors*)

בְּלוֹ *b'lōh*, Ch. m. 1093

Ezr. 4:13. (then) will they not pay toll, *tribute*, and
20. and toll, *tribute*, and custom, was paid
7:24. not be lawful to impose toll, *tribute*, or

בְּלוֹא [*b'lōh*], m. 1094

Jer. 38:11. took thence *old* cast clouts *and old* rotten rags,
12. Put now (these) *old* cast clouts

בְּלִי *b'lee*, part. 1097

Gen31:20. in that he told him *not* that he fled.

Job 8:11. can the flag grow *without* water?
Ps. 63: 1(2). thirsty land, *where no* water *is*; (marg. *without* water)
Isa. 14: 6. is persecuted, (and) *none* hindereth,
&c. &c.

With prefixes בִּבְלִי : as,

Deu 4:42. should kill his neighbour *un*awares,
19: 4. Whoso killeth his neighbour *ig*norantly,
Jos. 20: 5. he smote his neighbour *un*wittingly,
Job 35:16. he multiplieth words *without* knowledge.
&c. &c.

לִבְלִי : as,

Job 38:41. they wander *for lack of* meat.
41:33(25). who is made *without* fear.

מִבְּלִי : as,

Job 4:11. The old lion perisheth *for lack of* prey,
18:15. in his tabernacle, *because* (it is) *none* of his:
Ecc. 3:11. *so that no* man can find out
&c. &c.

It occurs once as a substantive.
Isa. 38:17. from the pit of *corruption:*

1098 בְּלִיל *b'leel*, m.

Job 6: 5. or loweth the ox over *his fodder?*
24: 6. They reap (every one) *his corn* (marg. *mingled corn*, or, *dredge*)
Isa. 30:24. shall eat clean *provender*,

1099 בְּלִימָה *b'lee-māh'*, f.

Job 26: 7. hangeth the earth upon *nothing*.

1100 בְּלִיַּעַל *b'leey-yah'-ngal*, m.

Deu 13:13(14). the children of *Belial*, (marg. *naughty* men)
15: 9. a thought in thy *wicked* heart,
Jud 19:22. certain sons of *Belial*,
20:13. the children of *Belial*,
1Sa. 1:16. for a daughter of *Belial:*
2:12. the sons of Eli (were) sons of *Belial;*
10:27. But the children of *Belial* said,
25:17. for he (is such) a son of *Belial*,
25. regard this man of *Belial*,
30:22. *and* (men) of *Belial*,
2Sa. 16: 7. thou man of *Belial:*
20: 1. be there a man of *Belial*,
22: 5. the floods of *ungodly men* (marg. *Belial*)
23: 6. *But* (the sons) of *Belial*
1K. 21:10. set two men, sons of *Belial*,
13. two men, children of *Belial*,
— the men of *Belial* witnessed
2Ch 13: 7. vain men, the children of *Belial*,
Job 34:18. say to a king, (Thou art) *wicked?*
Ps. 18: 4(5). the floods of *ungodly men* (marg. *Belial*)
41: 8(9). An *evil* disease, (say they), cleaveth fast (marg. A thing of *Belial*)
101: 3. I will set no *wicked* thing before (marg. thing of *Belial*)
Pro. 6:12. A *naughty* person,
16:27. An *ungodly* man diggeth up evil: (marg. A man of *Belial*)
19:28. An *ungodly* witness scorneth (marg. A witness of *Belial*)
Nah. 1:11. a *wicked* counsellor. (marg. counsellor of *Belial*)
15(2:1). *the wicked* shall no more pass

1101 בָּלַל *bāh-lal'*.

* KAL.—*Preterite.* *

Gen 11: 9. because the Lord *did* there *confound*
Ps. 92:10(11). *I shall be anointed* with fresh oil.

KAL.—*Future.*

Gen 11: 7. *and* there *confound* their language,
Jud 19:21. *and gave provender* unto the asses:

KAL.—*Participle.* Paül.

Ex. 29: 2. unleavened *tempered* with oil,
40. a tenth deal of flour *mingled*
Lev. 2: 4. fine flour *mingled* with oil,
5. unleavened, *mingled* with oil.
7:10. meat offering, *mingled* with oil,
12. unleavened cakes *mingled* with oil,
— cakes *mingled* with oil,
9: 4 & 14:10. a meat offering *mingled* with oil:
14:21. deal of fine flour *mingled* with oil
23:13. fine flour *mingled* with oil,
Nu. 6:15. cakes of fine flour *mingled*
7:13, 19, 25, 31, 37, 43, 49, 55, 61, 67, 73, 79 & 8:8. fine flour *mingled* with oil
15: 4. a tenth deal of flour *mingled*
6. two tenth deals of flour *mingled*
9. three tenth deals of flour *mingled*
28: 5. *mingled* with the fourth (part)
9, 12, 12. a meat offering, *mingled* with oil,
13. tenth deal of flour *mingled* with oil
20, 28 & 29:3, 9, 14. flour *mingled* with oil:

* HIPHIL.—*Future.* *

Isa. 64: 6(5). *and we* all *do fade* as a leaf; [perhaps from נָבַל]

* HITHPOEL.—*Future.* *

Hos. 7: 8. he *hath mixed himself* among the people;

בָּלַם [*bāh-lam'*]. 1102

* KAL.—*Infinitive.* *

Ps. 32: 9. whose mouth *must be held in*

בָּלַס [*bāh-las'*]. 1103

* KAL.—*Participle.* Poel. *

Am. 7:14. *and a gatherer of* sycomore fruit:

בָּלַע *bāh-lang'*. 1104

* KAL.—*Preterite.* *

Nu. 16:30. *and swallow* them *up*,
Job 20:15. *He hath swallowed down* riches,
Ps. 124: 3. Then *they had swallowed us up*
Jer. 51:34. *he hath swallowed me up* like a dragon,

KAL.—*Infinitive.*

Job 7:19. till *I swallow down* my spittle?
Jon. 1:17(2:1). a great fish *to swallow up* Jonah.

KAL.—*Future.*

Gen 41: 7. *And* the seven thin ears *devoured*
24. *And* the thin ears *devoured*
Ex. 7:12. *but* Aaron's rod *swallowed up*
15:12. the earth *swallowed them.*
Nu. 16:32. *and swallowed* them *up*,
34. Lest the earth *swallow us up*
26:10. *and swallowed* them *up*
Deu 11: 6. *and swallowed them up*,
Job 20:18. *shall* not *swallow* (it) *down:*
Ps. 69:15(16). neither *let* the deep *swallow me up*,
106:17. *and swallowed up* Dathan,
Pro. 1:12. *Let us swallow them up* alive
Isa. 28: 4. yet in his hand *he eateth it up.* (marg. *swalloweth*)
Hos. 8: 7. the strangers *shall swallow it up.*

* NIPHAL.—*Preterite.* *

Isa. 28: 7. *they are swallowed up* of wine,
Hos. 8: 8. Israel *is swallowed up:*

* PIEL.—*Preterite.* *

Ps. 35:25. *We have swallowed him up.*
Isa. 3:12. *destroy* the way of thy paths. (marg. *swallow up*)

Isa. 25: 7. *And he will destroy* (marg. *swallow up*)
8. *He will swallow up* death
Lam. 2: 2. The Lord *hath swallowed up*
5. *he hath swallowed up* Israel, *he hath swallowed up* all her
16. *We have swallowed* (her) *up:*

PIEL.—*Infinitive.*

Nu. 4:20. *when* the holy things *are covered,*
Job 2: 3. *to destroy him* without cause. (marg. *swallow him up*)
Lam. 2: 8. withdrawn his hand *from destroying:* (marg. *swallowing up*)
Hab 1:13. *when* the wicked *devoureth*

PIEL.—*Imperative.*

Ps. 55: 9(10). *Destroy*, O Lord, (and) divide

PIEL.—*Future.*

2Sa. 20:19. why *wilt thou swallow up*
20. that *I should swallow up*
Job 8:18. If *he destroy him* from his place,
10: 8. round about; *yet thou dost destroy me.*
Ps. 21: 9(10). the Lord *shall swallow them up*
Pro. 19:28. the wicked *devoureth* iniquity.
21:20. a foolish man *spendeth it up.*
Ecc. 10:12. the lips of a fool *will swallow up himself.*
Isa. 19: 3. *I will destroy* the counsel thereof: (marg. *swallow up*)

PIEL.—*Participle.*

Isa. 49:19. *they that swallowed thee up*

* PUAL.—*Future.* *

2Sa. 17:16. lest the king *be swallowed up,*
Job 37:20. surely *he shall be swallowed up.*

PUAL.—*Participle.*

Isa. 9:16(15). led of them (are) *destroyed.* (marg. *swallowed up*)

* HITHPAEL.—*Future.* *

Ps. 107:27. *are at* their wit's *end.* (marg. all their wisdom *is swallowed up*)

1105 בֶּלַע [*beh'-lag̃*], m.

Ps. 52: 4(6). Thou lovest all *devouring* words,
Jer. 51:44. *that which he hath swallowed up:*

1107 בִּלְעֲדֵי *bil-găděh'*, & בַּלְעֲדֵי *bal-găděh'*, part.

Gen 14:24. *Save* only that which the young men
41:16. (It is) *not in me:*
44. *and without thee* shall no man
Nu. 5:20. lain with thee *beside* thine husband:
Jos. 22:19. *beside* the altar of the Lord
2Sa. 22:32. who (is) God, *save* the Lord? and who (is) a rock, *save* our God?
2K. 18:25. Am I now come up *without* the Lord
Job 34:32. I see *not* teach thou me:
Ps. 18:31(32). who (is) God *save* the Lord?
Isa. 36:10. am I now come up *without*
43:11. *beside me* (there is) no saviour.
44: 6. *and beside me* (there is) no God.
8. Is there a God *beside me?*
45: 6. that (there is) none *beside me.*
21. none *beside me.*
Jer. 44:19. *without* our men?

1110 בָּלַק [*bāh-lak'*].

* KAL.—*Participle.* Poel. *

Isa. 24: 1. *and maketh it waste,* and turneth

* PUAL.—*Participle.* *

Nah 2:10(11). She is empty, and void, *and waste:*

1115 בִּלְתִּי *bil-tee'*, part.

Gen 21:26. yet heard I (of it) *but* to day
Gen 43: 3. *except* your brother (be) with you.
Ex. 22:20(19). unto (any) god, *save* unto the Lord
Nu. 11: 6. nothing at all, *beside* this manna,
21:35. until there was *none* left
1Sa. 20:26. he (is) *not* clean;
Job 14:12. till the heavens (be) *no more,*
Isa. 14: 6. with a continual stroke, (marg. a stroke *without* removing)
Dan 11:18. *without* his own reproach he shall cause
Am. 3: 3. Can two walk together, *except* they be agreed?
4. if he have taken *nothing?*
&c. &c.

בִּלְתִּי is twice rendered as with a pronominal suffix of the first person:

Isa. 10: 4. *Without me* they shall bow down
Hos. 13: 4. for (there is) no saviour *beside me.*

It once occurs with a suffix of the second person, בִּלְתֶּךָ:

1Sa. 2: 2. for (there is) none *beside thee:*

It occurs with prefixes: as, לְבִלְתִּי

Gen 3:11. I commanded thee *that* thou shouldest *not* eat?
4:15. *lest* any finding him should kill him.
38: 9. *lest that* he should give
Ex. 8:22(18). *that no* swarms (of flies) shall be there;
29(25). *in not* letting the people go
Lev. 20: 4. *and* kill him *not:*
Jos. 22:25. cease *from* fearing the Lord.
Jud. 2:23. left those nations, *without* driving them out
Ru. 3:10. *inasmuch as* thou followedst *not* young men,
2K. 12: 8(9). to receive *no* (more) money of the people, *neither* to repair
2Ch 16: 1. *to the intent that* he might let *none* go out
Isa. 44:10. (that) is profitable *for nothing?*
Jer. 17:24. to do *no* work therein;
&c. &c.

מִבִּלְתִּי

Nu. 14:16. *Because* the Lord was *not* able
Eze. 16:28. *because* thou wast *un*satiable;

בָּמָה *bāh-māh'*, f. 1116

Lev. 26:30. I will destroy *your high places,*
Nu. 21:28. *the high places of* Arnon.
22:41. into *the high places of* Baal,
33:52. pluck down all *their high places:*
Deu 32:13. He made him ride on *the high places of*
33:29. thou shalt tread upon *their high places.*
Jos. 13:17. *and Bamoth*-baal, (marg. *the high places of,* &c.)
1Sa. 9:12. the people to day *in the high place:*
13. before he go up *to the high place*
14. for to go up to *the high place.*
19. before me unto *the high place;*
25. come down *from the high place*
10: 5. coming down *from the high place*
13. he came to *the high place.*
2Sa. 1:19. slain upon *thy high places:*
25. slain *in thine high places.*
22:34. setteth me upon *my high places.*
1K. 3: 2. the people sacrificed *in high places,*
3. sacrificed and burnt incense *in high places.*
4. for that (was) *the* great *high place:*
11: 7. Solomon build *an high place*
12:31. he made an house of *high places,*
32. the priests of *the high places*
13: 2. offer the priests of *the high places*
32. all the houses of *the high places*
33, 33. priests of *the high places:*
14:23. they also built them *high places,*
15:14. *But the high places* were not removed:
22:43(44). *the high places* were not taken
—(—). burnt incense yet *in the high places.*
2K. 12: 3(4). *the high places* were not taken
—(—). burnt incense *in the high places.*
14: 4. Howbeit *the high places* were not
— burnt incense *on the high places.*

2K. 15: 4, 35. *the high places* were not removed:
— burnt incense still *on the high places.*
35. burned incense still *in the high places.*
16: 4. burnt incense *in the high places,*
17: 9. they built them *high places*
11. they burnt incense in all *the high places,*
29. put (them) in the houses of *the high places*
32. lowest of them priests of *the high places,*
— in the houses of *the high places.*
18: 4. He removed *the high places,*
22. he, *whose high places*
21: 3. he built up again *the high places*
23: 5. to burn incense *in the high places*
8. defiled *the high places*
— brake down *the high places*
9. the priests of *the high places* came
13. *the high places* that (were) before
15. at Beth-el, (and) *the high place*
— both that altar and *the high place*
— burned *the high place,*
19. all the houses also of *the high places*
20. he slew all the priests of *the high places*
1Ch 16:39. *in the high place* that (was) at Gibeon,
21:29. *in the high place* at Gibeon.
2Ch 1: 3, 13. *to the high place* that (was) at Gibeon;
11:15. ordained him priests *for the high places,*
14: 3(2). *and the high places,* and brake down
5(4). *the high places* and the images:
15:17. *But the high places* were not
17: 6. he took away *the high places*
20:33. Howbeit *the high places* were not
21:11. made *high places* in the mountains
28: 4. burnt incense *in the high places,*
25. he made *high places* to burn incense
31: 1. threw down *the high places*
32:12. taken away *his high places*
33: 3. he built again *the high places*
17. the people did sacrifice still *in the high places,*
19. the places wherein he built *high places,*
34: 3. Jerusalem from *the high places,*
Job 9: 8. treadeth upon *the waves of* the sea. (marg. *heights*)
Ps. 18:33(34). setteth me upon *my high places.*
78:58. to anger *with their high places,*
Isa. 14:14. I will ascend above *the heights of*
15: 2. *the high places,* to weep:
16:12. Moab is weary on *the high place,*
36: 7. *whose high places* and whose altars
58:14. to ride upon *the high places of* the earth,
Jer. 7:31. they have built *the high places of*
17: 3. *thy high places* for sin,
19: 5. They have built also *the high places of*
26:18. *as the high places of* a forest.
32:35. they built *the high places of* Baal,
48:35. him that offereth in *the high places,*
Eze. 6: 3. I will destroy *your high places.*
6. *and the high places*
16:16. deckedst thy *high places* with
20:29. What (is) *the high place*
— the name thereof is called *Bamah*
36: 2. *even the* ancient *high places*
43: 7. their kings in *their high places.*
Hos 10: 8. *The high places* also *of* Aven,
Am. 4:13. treadeth upon *the high places of*
7: 9. *the high places of* Isaac shall be
Mic 1: 3. tread upon *the high places of* the
5. what (are) *the high places of* Judah?
3:12. *as the high places of* the forest.
Hab 3:19. to walk upon *mine high places.*

1119 ## בְּמוֹ *b'mōh*, part.

Job 9:30. (כתיב) If I wash myself *with* snow *water,* (following the קרי)
16. 4. shake mine head at you. (lit. shake at you *with* my head)
5. I would strengthen you *with* my mouth,
19:16. I intreated him *with* my mouth.
37: 8. Then the beasts go *into* dens,
Ps. 11: 2. they may privily shoot (marg. *in* darkness)
Isa. 25:10. as straw is trodden down *for* the dunghill
43: 2. when thou walkest *through* the fire,
44:16. He burneth part thereof *in* the fire;
19. I have burned part of it *in* the fire;

בֵּן *bĕhn*, m. 1121

Gen 3:16. in sorrow thou shalt bring forth *children;*
4:17. after the name of *his son,* Enoch.
25. and she bare *a son,*
26. to him also there was born *a son;*
5: 4, 7, 10, 13, 16, 19, 22, 26, 30. begat *sons* and daughters:
28. and begat *a son:*
32. Noah was five hundred years *old:* (lit. was *son of* five hundred)
6: 2. *the sons of* God saw the daughters of
4. when *the sons of* God came in
10. Noah begat three *sons,*
18. *and thy sons,* and thy wife, and *thy sons'* wives
7: 6. And Noah (was) six hundred years *old*
7. *and his sons,* and his wife, and *his sons'*
13. *the sons of* Noah, and Noah's wife, and the three wives of *his sons*
8:16. *and thy sons,* and *thy sons'* wives
18. Noah went forth, *and his sons,* and his wife, and *his sons'* wives
9: 1. God blessed Noah and *his sons,*
8. God spake unto Noah, and to *his sons*
18. And *the sons of* Noah,
19. These (are) *the* three *sons of* Noah:
24. what *his* younger *son* had done
10: 1. generations of *the sons of* Noah,
— unto them were *sons* born
2. *The sons of* Japheth;
3. *And the sons of* Gomer;
4. *And the sons of* Javan;
6. *And the sons of* Ham; Cush,
7. *And the sons of* Cush;
— *and the sons of* Raamah;
20. These (are) *the sons of* Ham,
21. the father of all *the children of* Eber,
22. *The children of* Shem;
23. *And the children of* Aram;
25. unto Eber were born two *sons:*
29. all these (were) *the sons of* Joktan.
31. These (are) *the sons of* Shem,
32. the families of *the sons of* Noah,
11: 5. which *the children of* men builded.
10. Shem (was) an hundred years *old,*
11, 13, 15, 17, 19, 21, 23, 25. begat *sons* and daughters.
31. Terah took Abram *his son,* and Lot *the son of* Haran *his son's son,* and Sarai his daughter in law, *his son* Abram's wife;
12: 4. Abram (was) seventy and five years *old*
5. and Lot his brother's *son,*
14:12. took Lot, Abram's brother's *son,*
15: 2. *and the steward* (lit. *the son of* the possession) of my house
3. *one born* in (lit. *the son of*) my house is
16:11. and shalt bear *a son,*
15. Hagar bare Abram *a son:* and Abram called *his son's* name,
16. Abram (was) fourscore and six years *old,*
17: 1. Abram was ninety years *old* and nine,
12. *And* he that *is* eight days *old* (marg. *a son of* eight days)
— bought with money of any stranger, (lit. *son of* a stranger)
16. give thee *a son* also of her:
17. be born *unto him* that is an hundred years *old?*
19. Sarah thy wife shall bear thee *a son*
23. Abraham took Ishmael *his son,*
24. Abraham (was) ninety years *old*
25. Ishmael *his son* (was) thirteen years *old,*
26. was Abraham circumcised, and Ishmael *his son.*
27. of the stranger, (lit. *son of* a stranger)
18: 7. fetcht a calf (lit. *a son of* the herd) tender
8. *and* the calf (lit. *son of* the herd) which
10. Sarah thy wife shall have *a son.*
14. and Sarah shall have *a son.*
19. that he will command *his children*
19:12. son in law, *and thy sons,* and thy
37. the firstborn bare *a son,*
38. she also bare *a son,* and called his name *Ben*-ammi: the same (is) the father of *the children of*

Gen 21: 2. bare Abraham *a son*
3. Abraham called the name of *his son*
4. Abraham circumcised *his son* Isaac being eight days *old*,
5. Abraham was an hundred years *old*, when *his son* Isaac was born
7. Sarah should have given *children* suck? for I have born (him) *a son*
9. Sarah saw *the son of* Hagar
10. this bondwoman and *her son*: for *the son of* this bondwoman shall not be heir with *my son*,
11. in Abraham's sight because of *his son*.
13. also of *the son of* the bondwoman
22: 2. And he said, Take now *thy son*,
3. young men with him, and Isaac *his son*,
6. laid (it) upon Isaac *his son*;
7. and he said, Here (am) I, *my son*.
8. And Abraham said, *My son*,
9. and bound Isaac *his son*,
10. took the knife to slay *his son*.
12. seeing thou hast not withheld *thy son*,
13. for a burnt offering in the stead of *his son*.
16. and hast not withheld *thy son*,
20. she hath also born *children*
23: 3. spake unto *the sons of* Heth,
5. *the children of* Heth answered
7. *to the children of* Heth.
8. Ephron *the son of* Zohar,
10. Ephron dwelt among *the children of* Heth:
— in the audience of *the children of*
11. in the presence of *the sons of*
16. in the audience of *the sons of* Heth,
18. in the presence of *the children of* Heth,
20. by *the sons of* Heth.
24: 3. thou shalt not take a wife *unto my son*
4, 38. and take a wife *unto my son*
5. must I needs bring *thy son* again
6. Beware thou that thou bring not *my son*
7. thou shalt take a wife *unto my son*
8. only bring not *my son* thither
15. *son of* Milcah, the wife of Nahor,
24. Bethuel *the son of* Milcah,
36. bare *a son* to my master
37. Thou shalt not take a wife *to my son*
40. thou shalt take a wife *for my son* of my
44. *for* my master's *son*.
47. Bethuel, Nahor's *son*,
48. brother's daughter *unto his son*.
51. let her be thy master's *son's* wife,
25: 3. *And the sons of* Dedan
4. *And the sons of* Midian;
— All these (were) *the children of*
6. *But unto the sons of* the concubines,
— and sent them away from Isaac *his son*,
9. And *his sons* Isaac and Ishmael
— the field of Ephron *the son of* Zohar
10. purchased of *the sons of* Heth:
11. that God blessed *his son* Isaac;
12. the generations of Ishmael, Abraham's *son*,
13. the names of *the sons of* Ishmael,
16. These (are) *the sons of* Ishmael,
19. Isaac, Abraham's *son*:
20. Isaac was forty years *old*
22. And *the children* struggled together
26. Isaac (was) threescore years *old*
26:34. Esau was forty years *old*
27: 1. he called Esau *his* eldest *son*, and said unto him, *My son*:
5. heard when Isaac spake to Esau *his son*.
6. Rebekah spake unto Jacob *her son*,
8, 43. *my son*, obey my voice
13. Upon me (be) thy curse, *my son*:
15. took goodly raiment of *her* eldest *son*
— put them upon Jacob *her* younger *son*:
17. into the hand of *her son* Jacob.
18. Here (am) I; who (art) thou, *my son*?
20. Isaac said unto *his son*, How (is it) that thou hast found (it) so quickly, *my son*?
21. that I may feel thee, *my son*, whether thou (be) *my* very *son* Esau
24. (Art) thou *my* very *son* Esau?
25. I will eat of *my son*'s venison,
26. Come near now, and kiss me, *my son*.
27. the smell of *my son* (is) as the smell
29. let thy mother's *sons* bow down
31. arise, and eat of *his son*'s venison,

Gen 27:32. I (am) *thy son*, thy firstborn
37. what shall I do now unto thee, *my son*?
42. words of Esau *her* elder *son* were told
— sent and called Jacob *her* younger *son*,
28: 5. *son of* Bethuel the Syrian,
9. Ishmael Abraham's *son*,
29: 1. the land of *the people of* the east. (marg. *children*)
5. Know ye Laban *the son of* Nahor?
12. that he (was) Rebekah's *son*:
13. the tidings of Jacob his sister's *son*,
32. Leah conceived, and bare *a son*,
33, 34, 35. she conceived again, and bare *a son*;
34. because I have born him three *sons*:
30: 1. Give me *children*, or else I die.
5. and bare Jacob *a son*.
6. hath given me *a son*:
7, 12. bare Jacob *a* second *son*.
10. Leah's maid bare Jacob *a son*.
14. Give me, I pray thee, of *thy son*'s mandrakes.
15. thou take away *my son*'s mandrakes
— to night for *thy son*'s mandrakes.
16. hired thee with *my son*'s mandrakes.
17. bare Jacob *the* fifth *son*.
19. bare Jacob *the* sixth *son*.
20. because I have born him six *sons*:
23. she conceived, and bare *a son*;
24. The Lord shall add to me another *son*.
35. gave (them) into the hand of *his sons*.
31: 1. he heard the words of Laban's *sons*,
16. that (is) ours, *and our children's*:
17. and set *his sons* and his wives upon camels
28. hast not suffered me to kiss *my sons*
43. *and* (these) *children* (are) *my children*,
— or *unto their children* which they have born
55(32:1). and kissed *his sons* and his daughters,
32:11(12). the mother with *the children*.
15(16). Thirty milch camels *with their colts*,
32(33). Therefore *the children of* Israel eat not
33:19. at the hand of *the children of* Hamor,
34: 2. when Shechem *the son of* Hamor
5. *now his sons* were with his cattle
7. *And the sons of* Jacob came out
8. The soul of *my son* Shechem longeth
13. *the sons of* Jacob answered
18. Shechem Hamor's *son*.
20. Hamor and Shechem *his son* came
24. unto Hamor and unto Shechem *his son*
25. that two of *the sons of* Jacob,
26. slew Hamor and Shechem *his son*
27. *The sons of* Jacob came
35: 5. did not pursue after *the sons of*
17. thou shalt have this *son* also.
18. she called his name *Ben*-oni: (marg. *son of* my sorrow)
— his father called him *Ben*jamin. (marg. *son of* the right hand)
22. Now *the sons of* Jacob were twelve:
23. *The sons of* Leah;
24. *The sons of* Rachel;
25. *And the sons of* Bilhah,
26. *And the sons of* Zilpah,
— these (are) *the sons of* Jacob,
29. and *his sons* Esau and Jacob buried him.
36: 5, 19. these (are) *the sons of* Esau,
6. Esau took his wives, and *his sons*,
10. These (are) the names of Esau's *sons*; Eliphaz *the son of* Adah
— Reuel *the son of* Bashemath
11. *the sons of* Eliphaz were Teman,
12. Timna was concubine to Eliphaz Esau's *son*;
—, 16. these (were) *the sons of* Adah
13. these (are) *the sons of* Reuel;
— these were *the sons of* Bashemath
14. these were *the sons of* Aholibamah,
15. dukes of *the sons of* Esau: *the sons of*
17. these (are) *the sons of* Reuel Esau's *son*;
— these (are) *the sons of* Bashemath
18. these (are) *the sons of* Aholibamah
20. These (are) *the sons of* Seir
21. *the children of* Seir
22. *the children of* Lotan
23. *the children of* Shobal
24. these (are) *the children of* Zibeon;

Gen 36:25. *the children of* Anah
26. these (are) *the children of* Dishon;
27. *The children of* Ezer
28. *The children of* Dishan
31. *over the children of* Israel.
32. Bela *the son of* Beor
33. Jobab *the son of* Zerah
35. Hadad *the son of* Bedad,
38, 39. Baal-hanan *the son of* Achbor
37: 2. Joseph, (being) seventeen years *old*,
— the lad (was) with *the sons of* Bilhah, and with *the sons of* Zilpah,
3. loved Joseph more than all *his children*, because he (was) *the son of* his old age:
32. know now whether it (be) *thy son*'s coat
33. and said, (It is) *my son*'s coat;
34. and mourned for *his son* many days.
35. all *his sons* and all his daughters rose
— I will go down into the grave unto *my son*
38: 3. she conceived, and bare *a son;*
4. she conceived again, and bare *a son;*
5. she yet again conceived, and bare *a son;*
11. till Shelah *my son* be grown:
26. I gave her not to Shelah *my son.*
41:46. Joseph (was) thirty years *old*
50. unto Joseph were born two *sons*
42: 1. Jacob said *unto his sons*,
5. *the sons of* Israel came
11. We (are) all one man's *sons;*
13. *the sons of* one man
32. twelve brethren, *sons of* our father;
37. Slay *my* two *sons*, if I bring him not
38. *My son* shall not go down with
43:29. his mother's *son*,
— God be gracious unto thee, *my son.*
45: 9. Thus saith *thy son* Joseph,
10. *and thy children, and thy children's children*,
21. *the children of* Israel did so:
28. Joseph *my son* (is) yet alive:
46: 5. *the sons of* Israel carried Jacob
7. *His sons, and his sons' sons* with him, his daughters, and *his sons'* daughters,
8. the names of *the children of* Israel,
— Jacob *and his sons:*
9. *And the sons of* Reuben;
10. *And the sons of* Simeon;
— Shaul *the son of* a Canaanitish
11. *And the sons of* Levi;
12. *And the sons of* Judah;
— *the sons of* Pharez were Hezron
13. *And the sons of* Issachar;
14. *And the sons of* Zebulun;
15. These (be) *the sons of* Leah,
— all the souls of *his sons* and his daughters
16. *And the sons of* Gad;
17. *And the sons of* Asher;
— *and the sons of* Beriah;
18. These (are) *the sons of* Zilpah,
19. *The sons of* Rachel
21. *And the sons of* Benjamin
22. These (are) *the sons of* Rachel,
23. *And the sons of* Dan;
24. *And the sons of* Naphtali,
25. These (are) *the sons of* Bilhah,
26. besides Jacob's *sons'* wives,
27. *And the sons of* Joseph,
47:29. and he called *his son* Joseph,
48: 1. and he took with him *his* two *sons*,
2. Behold, *thy son* Joseph cometh unto thee:
5. *thy* two *sons*, Ephraim and Manasseh,
8. Israel beheld Joseph's *sons*,
9. They (are) *my sons*,
19. I know (it), *my son*, I know (it):
49: 1. Jacob called unto *his sons*,
2. *ye sons of* Jacob;
8. thy father's *children* shall bow down
9. from the prey, *my son*, thou art gone up:
11. his ass's *colt* unto the choice vine;
22. Joseph (is) *a* fruitful *bough*, (even) *a* fruitful *bough* by a well;
32. from *the children of* Heth.
33. Jacob had made an end of commanding *his sons*,
50:12. *his sons* did unto him according as
13. *his sons* carried him into the land of Canaan,

Gen 50:23. Joseph saw Ephraim's *children of* the third (generation): *the children also of* Machir *the son of* Manasseh
25. Joseph took an oath of *the children of*
26. an hundred and ten years *old:*
Ex. 1: 1. the names of *the children of* Israel,
7. *And the children of* Israel were fruitful,
9. the people of *the children of* Israel
12. because of *the children of* Israel.
13. *the children of* Israel to serve with
16. if it (be) *a son*,
22. Every *son* that is born
2: 2. the woman conceived, and bare *a son:*
10. he became her *son.*
22. she bare (him) *a son*,
23. *the children of* Israel sighed
25. God looked upon *the children of* Israel,
3: 9. the cry of *the children of* Israel
10. my people *the children of* Israel out of Egypt.
11. that I should bring forth *the children of*
13. come unto *the children of* Israel,
14. Thus shalt thou say *unto the children of*
15. Thus shalt thou say unto *the children of*
22. ye shall put (them) upon *your sons*,
4:20. Moses took his wife and *his sons*,
22. Israel (is) *my son*, (even) my firstborn:
23. Let *my son* go, that he may serve
— behold, I will slay *thy son*,
25. and cut off the foreskin of *her son*,
29. the elders of *the children of* Israel:
31. had visited *the children of* Israel,
5:14,15,19. the officers of *the children of* Israel,
6: 5. the groaning of *the children of* Israel,
6. say *unto the children of* Israel,
9. spake so unto *the children of* Israel:
11. that he let *the children of* Israel go
12. *the children of* Israel have not
13. a charge unto *the children of* Israel,
— to bring *the children of* Israel
14. *The sons of* Reuben
15. *And the sons of* Simeon;
— Shaul *the son of* a Canaanitish woman:
16. the names of *the sons of* Levi
17. *The sons of* Gershon;
18. *And the sons of* Kohath;
19. *And the sons of* Merari;
21. *And the sons of* Izhar;
22. *And the sons of* Uzziel;
24. *And the sons of* Korah;
25. Eleazar Aaron's *son*
26. Bring out *the children of* Israel
27. to bring out *the children of* Israel
7: 2. that he send *the children of* Israel
4. my people *the children of* Israel,
5. bring out *the children of* Israel
7. Moses (was) fourscore years *old*, and Aaron fourscore and three years *old*,
9: 4. of all (that is) *the children's of* Israel. (lit. *to the children of*)
6. cattle of *the children of* Israel died not
26. where *the children of* Israel (were),
35. would he let *the children of* Israel
10: 2. that thou mayest tell in the ears of *thy son, and* of *thy son's son*,
9. *with our sons* and with our daughters,
20. let *the children of* Israel go.
23. all *the children of* Israel had light
11: 7. against any of *the children of* Israel
10. would not let *the children of* Israel go
12: 5. *of* the *first* year: (marg. *the son of* a year)
24. an ordinance to thee *and to thy sons*
26. when *your children* shall say
27. over the houses of *the children of*
28. *the children of* Israel went away,
31. both ye and *the children of* Israel;
35. *And the children of* Israel did according
37. *the children of* Israel journeyed
40. the sojourning of *the children of* Israel,
42. to be observed of all *the children of*
43. There shall no stranger eat thereof: (lit. *son of* a stranger)
50. Thus did all *the children of* Israel;
51. the Lord did bring *the children of*
13: 2. *among the children of* Israel,
8. thou shalt shew *thy son* in that day,
13. the firstborn of man *among thy children*

Ex. 13 14. when *thy son* asketh thee in time
15. all the firstborn of *my children*
18. *the children of* Israel went up
19. he had straitly sworn *the children of*
14: 2, 15. Speak unto *the children of* Israel,
3. Pharaoh will say *of the children of* Israel,
8. pursued after *the children of* Israel: *and the children of* Israel went out
10. *the children of* Israel lifted up their eyes,
— *the children of* Israel cried out
16. *the children of* Israel shall go
22. *the children of* Israel went
29. *But the children of* Israel walked
15: 1. Moses *and the children of* Israel
19. *but the children of* Israel went
16: 1,2,9,10. congregation of *the children of*
3. *the children of* Israel said
6. Aaron said unto all *the children of* Israel,
12. the murmurings of *the children of* Israel:
15. when *the children of* Israel saw
17. *the children of* Israel did so,
35. *And the children of* Israel did eat
17: 1. congregation of *the children of* Israel
3. *our children* and our cattle
7. the chiding of *the children of* Israel,
18: 3. And *her* two *sons;*
5. came *with his sons* and his wife
6. *her* two *sons* with her.
19: 1. when *the children of* Israel were gone
3. and tell *the children of* Israel;
6. speak unto *the children of* Israel.
20: 5. the fathers upon *the children*
10. shalt not do any work, thou, *nor thy son,*
22. say unto *the children of* Israel,
21: 4. she have born him *sons*
5. I love my master, my wife, and *my children;*
9. if he have betrothed her *unto his son,*
31. Whether he have gored *a son,*
22:24(23). *and your children* fatherless.
29(28). the firstborn of *thy sons* shalt thou
23:12. and *the son of* thy handmaid,
24: 5. young men of *the children of* Israel,
11. the nobles of *the children of* Israel
17. in the eyes of *the children of* Israel.
25: 2. Speak unto *the children of* Israel,
22. unto *the children of* Israel.
27:20. thou shalt command *the children of*
21. Aaron *and his sons* shall order it
— the behalf of *the children of* Israel.
28: 1. Aaron thy brother, and *his sons* with him, from among *the children of* Israel,
— Eleazar and Ithamar, Aaron's *sons.*
4. for Aaron thy brother, *and his sons,*
9, 11, 21, 29. the names of *the children of*
12. memorial *unto the children of* Israel:
30. the judgment of *the children of* Israel
38. which *the children of* Israel shall hallow
40. *And for* Aaron's *sons*
41. Aaron thy brother, and *his sons* with him;
43. upon Aaron, and upon *his sons,*
29: 1. Take one young bullock, (lit. one steer, *the son of* a bull)
4. Aaron and *his sons* thou shalt bring
8. thou shalt bring *his sons,* and put coats
9. with girdles, Aaron *and his sons,*
— thou shalt consecrate Aaron and *his sons.*
10, 19. and Aaron *and his sons* shall put
15. Aaron *and his sons* shall put
20. upon the tip of the right ear of *his sons,*
21. upon *his sons,* and upon the garments of *his sons* with him: and he shall be hallowed, and his garments, *and his sons,* and *his sons'* garments
24. and in the hands of *his sons;*
27. of (that) which is *for his sons:*
28. it shall be Aaron's *and his sons'* by a statute for ever from *the children of* Israel:
— an heave offering from *the children of* Israel
29. shall be *his sons'* after him, (lit. shall be *unto his sons*)
30. *that son* that is priest (marg. (he) *of his sons*)
32. Aaron *and his sons* shall eat
35. do unto Aaron, *and to his sons,*

Ex. 29:38. two lambs *of* the *first* year (lit. *sons of* a year)
43. I will meet *with the children of* Israel,
44. sanctify also both Aaron and *his sons,*
45. I will dwell among *the children of* Israel,
30:12. the sum of *the children of* Israel
14. *from* twenty years *old*
16. atonement money of *the children of* Israel,
— memorial *unto the children of* Israel
19. Aaron *and his sons* shall wash their hands
30. thou shalt anoint Aaron and *his sons,*
31. speak unto *the children* of Israel,
31: 2. *the son of* Uri, *the son of* Hur,
6. Aholiab, *the son of* Ahisamach,
10. and the garments of *his sons,*
13. Speak thou also unto *the children of*
16. *the children of* Israel shall keep
17. between me and *the children of* Israel
32: 2. of *your sons,* and of your daughters,
20. made *the children of* Israel drink
26. *the sons of* Levi gathered themselves
28. *the children of* Levi did according
29. every man *upon his son,*
33: 5. Say unto *the children of* Israel,
6. *the children of* Israel stripped themselves
11. Joshua, *the son of* Nun,
34: 7. of the fathers upon *the children,* and upon *the children's children,*
16. thou take of their daughters *unto thy sons,*
— and make *thy sons* go a whoring
20. All the firstborn of *thy sons*
30. all *the children of* Israel saw Moses,
32. afterward all *the children of* Israel
34. spake unto *the children of* Israel
35. *the children of* Israel saw the face
35: 1, 4, 20. congregation of *the children of* Israel
19. and the garments of *his sons,* to minister
29. *The children of* Israel brought
30. Moses said unto *the children of*
— Bezaleel *the son of* Uri, *the son of* Hur,
34. Aholiab, *the son of* Ahisamach,
36: 3. which *the children of* Israel had
38:21. *son to* Aaron the priest.
22. Bezaleel *the son of* Uri, *the son of* Hur,
23. Aholiab, *son of* Ahisamach,
26. *from* twenty years *old*
39: 6, 14. the names of *the children of*
7. a memorial *to the children of* Israel;
27. for Aaron, *and for his sons,*
32. *the children of* Israel did according
41. and *his sons'* garments, to minister
42. *the children of* Israel made
40:12. thou shalt bring Aaron and *his sons*
14. thou shalt bring *his sons,*
31. Moses and Aaron *and his sons*
36. *the children of* Israel went
Lev. 1: 2. Speak unto *the children of* Israel,
5. he shall kill the bullock (lit. *son of* the bull)
— Aaron's *sons,* shall bring the blood,
7. *the sons of* Aaron the priest
8. the priests, Aaron's *sons,*
11. Aaron's *sons,* shall sprinkle his blood
14. or of *young* pigeons. (lit. *sons of* the dove)
2: 2. he shall bring it to Aaron's *sons*
3, 10. (shall be) Aaron's *and his sons':*
3: 2. Aaron's *sons* the priests
5. Aaron's *sons* shall burn it
8. Aaron's *sons* shall sprinkle the blood
13. *the sons of* Aaron shall sprinkle
4: 2. Speak unto *the children of* Israel,
3. a *young* bullock without blemish (lit. a steer, *the son of* a bull)
14. shall offer a *young* bullock (lit. *id.*)
5: 7, 11. two *young* pigeons, (lit. *sons of* a dove)
6: 9(2). Command Aaron and *his sons,*
14(7). *the sons of* Aaron shall offer
16(9). shall Aaron *and his sons* eat.
18(11). *among the children of* Aaron
20(13). the offering of Aaron *and of his sons,*
22(15). And the priest *of his sons* that is
25(18). Speak unto Aaron and to *his sons,*
7:10. shall all *the sons of* Aaron have,
23, 29. Speak unto *the children of* Israel,
31. the breast shall be Aaron's *and his sons'.*
33. *among the sons of* Aaron,
34. taken of *the children of* Israel

Lev. 7:34. the priest *and unto his sons* by a statute for ever from among *the children of* Israel.
35. of the anointing of *his sons*,
36. to be given them of *the children of* Israel,
38. that he commanded *the children of* Israel
8: 2. Take Aaron and *his sons* with him,
6. Moses brought Aaron and *his sons*,
13. Moses brought Aaron's *sons*,
14. Aaron *and his sons* laid their hands
18, 22. Aaron *and his sons* laid their hands
24. he brought Aaron's *sons*,
27. and upon *his sons'* hands,
30. upon *his sons*, and upon *his sons'* garments
— and *his sons*, and *his sons'* garments
31. Moses said unto Aaron and to *his sons*,
— Aaron *and his sons* shall eat it.
36. Aaron *and his sons* did all things
9: 1. Moses called Aaron *and his sons*,
2. Take thee a *young* calf (lit. a calf *the son of* a bull)
3. unto *the children of* Israel thou shalt speak,
— a calf and a lamb, (both) *of* the *first* year,
9. *the sons of* Aaron brought the blood
12, 18. Aaron's *sons* presented unto him
10: 1. Nadab and Abihu, *the sons of* Aaron,
4. *the sons of* Uzziel
6. unto Eleazar and unto Ithamar. *his sons*,
9. thou, *nor thy sons* with thee,
11. ye may teach *the children of* Israel
12. unto Eleazar and unto Ithamar, *his sons*
13, 14. thy due, and *thy sons'* due,
14. thou, *and thy sons*, and thy daughters
— peace offerings of *the children of* Israel.
15. it shall be thine, *and thy sons'*
16. Eleazar and Ithamar, *the sons of* Aaron
11: 2 & 12: 2. unto *the children of* Israel, saying,
12: 6. of her purifying are fulfilled, *for a son*,
— a lamb *of* the *first* year (marg. *son of* his year)
— *and a young* pigeon, (lit. *and a son of* a dove)
8. two *young* pigeons; (lit. *sons of* a pigeon)
13: 2. unto one *of his sons* the priests:
14:22. or two *young* pigeons,
30. of the *young* pigeons,
15: 2. Speak unto *the children of* Israel,
14, 29. two *young* pigeons,
31. separate *the children of* Israel
16: 1. after the death of *the* two *sons of* Aaron,
3. with a *young* bullock for a sin offering,
5. the congregation of *the children of* Israel
16, 19. the uncleanness of *the children of* Israel,
21. the iniquities of *the children of* Israel,
34. an atonement for *the children of* Israel
17: 2. Speak unto Aaron, and unto *his sons*, and unto all *the children of* Israel,
5. that *the children of* Israel may bring
12. I said *unto the children of* Israel,
13. whatsoever man (there be) *of the children of*
14. therefore I said *unto the children of*
18: 2. Speak unto *the children of* Israel,
10. of *thy son*'s daughter, or of thy daughter's
15. she (is) *thy son*'s wife;
17. shalt thou take *her son*'s daughter,
19: 2. the congregation of *the children of* Israel,
18. against *the children of* thy people,
20: 2. say to *the children of* Israel, Whosoever (he be) *of the children of* Israel,
17. be cut off in the sight of their people: (lit. *the children of* their people)
21: 1. the priests *the sons of* Aaron,
2. *and for his son*, and for his daughter,
24. unto Aaron, and to *his sons*, and unto all *the children of* Israel.
22: 2. Speak unto Aaron and to *his sons*,
—, 15. the holy things of *the children of*
3. which *the children of* Israel hallow
18. Speak unto Aaron, and to *his sons*, and unto all *the children of* Israel,
25. Neither from a stranger's hand (lit. *son of* a stranger)
28. *her young* both in one day.
32. hallowed among *the children of* Israel:
23: 2, 10, 24, 34. Speak unto *the children of*
12. *of* the *first* year (lit. *son of* his year)

Lev. 23:18. lambs without blemish *of* the *first* year,
— and one *young* bullock, (lit. a steer, *the son of* a bull)
19. two lambs *of* the *first* year for a
43. I made *the children of* Israel to dwell
44. Moses declared unto *the children of*
24: 2. Command *the children of* Israel,
8. (taken) from *the children of* Israel
9. it shall be Aaron's *and his sons'*;
10. *the son of* an Israelitish woman, whose father (was) (lit. and he *the son of*), an Egyptian went out among *the children of* Israel: and this *son of* the Israelitish
11. the Israelitish woman's *son*
15. thou shalt speak unto *the children of* Israel,
23. Moses spake to *the children of* Israel,
— *And the children of* Israel did
25: 2. Speak unto *the children of* Israel,
33. (are) their possession among *the children of*
41, 54. (both) he *and his children* with him,
45. *of the children of* the strangers
46. inheritance *for your children* after you,
— over your brethren *the children of* Israel,
49. or his uncle's *son*,
55. unto me *the children of* Israel (are) servants;
26:29. ye shall eat the flesh of *your sons*,
46. between him and *the children of* Israel
27: 2. Speak unto *the children of* Israel,
3. *from* twenty years *old* even unto sixty years *old*,
5. *from* five years *old* even unto twenty years *old*,
6. *from* a month *old* even unto five years *old*,
7. *from* sixty years *old*
34. for *the children of* Israel in mount Sinai.
Nu. 1: 2, 53. the congregation of *the children of*
3. *From* twenty years *old*
5. Elizur *the son of* Shedeur.
6. Shelumiel *the son of* Zurishaddai.
7. Nahshon *the son of* Amminadab.
8. Nethaneel *the son of* Zuar.
9. Eliab *the son of* Helon.
10. *Of the children of* Joseph: of Ephraim; Elishama *the son of* Ammihud: of Manasseh; Gamaliel *the son of* Pedahzur.
11. Abidan *the son of* Gideoni.
12. Ahiezer *the son of* Ammishaddai.
13. Pagiel *the son of* Ocran.
14. Eliasaph *the son of* Deuel.
15. Ahira *the son of* Enan.
18, 20, 22, 24, 26, 28, 30, 32, 34, 36, 38, 40, 42, 45. *from* twenty years *old*
20. *the children of* Reuben,
22. *Of the children of* Simeon,
24. *Of the children of* Gad,
26. *Of the children of* Judah,
28. *Of the children of* Issachar,
30. *Of the children of* Zebulun,
32. *Of the children of* Joseph, (namely), *of the children of* Ephraim,
34. *Of the children of* Manasseh,
36. *Of the children of* Benjamin,
38. *Of the children of* Dan,
40. *Of the children of* Asher,
42. *Of the children of* Naphtali,
45. that were numbered of *the children of* Israel,
49. the sum of them among *the children of*
52. *the children of* Israel shall pitch their tents,
54. *the children of* Israel did according
2: 2. Every man of *the children of* Israel
3. Nahshon *the son of* Amminadab (shall be) captain *of the children of* Judah.
5. Nethaneel *the son of* Zuar (shall be) captain *of the children of* Issachar.
7. Eliab *the son of* Helon (shall be) captain *of the children of* Zebulun.
10. the captain *of the children of* Reuben (shall be) Elizur *the son of* Shedeur.
12. the captain *of the children of* Simeon (shall be) Shelumiel *the son of* Zurishaddai.
14. the captain *of the sons of* Gad (shall be) Eliasaph *the son of* Reuel.
18. the captain *of the sons of* Ephraim (shall be) Elishama *the son of* Ammihud.
20. the captain *of the children of* Manasseh (shall be) Gamaliel *the son of* Pedahzur.

Nu. 2:22. the captain *of the sons of* Benjamin (shall be) Abidan *the son of* Gideoni.
25. the captain *of the children of* Dan (shall be) Ahiezer *the son of* Ammishaddai.
27. the captain *of the children of* Asher (shall be) Pagiel *the son of* Ocran.
29. the captain *of the children of* Naphtali (shall be) Ahira *the son of* Enan.
32. which were numbered of *the children of* Israel
33. not numbered among *the children of* Israel;
34. *the children of* Israel did according
3: 2, 3. the names of *the sons of* Aaron;
4. *and* they had no *children:*
8. the charge of *the children of* Israel,
9, 48, 51. unto Aaron *and to his sons:*
— given unto him out of *the children of* Israel.
10. shalt appoint Aaron and *his sons,*
12. from among *the children of* Israel
— the matrix *among the children of* Israel:
15. Number *the children of* Levi
—, 22, 28, 34, 39, 40, 43. *from* a month *old*
17. these were *the sons of* Levi
18. the names of *the sons of* Gershon
19. *And the sons of* Kohath
20. *And the sons of* Merari
24. (shall be) Eliasaph *the son of* Lael.
25. the charge of *the sons of* Gershon
29. The families of *the sons of* Kohath
30. (shall be) Elizaphan *the son of* Uzziel.
32. Eleazar *the son of* Aaron the priest
35. of Merari (was) Zuriel *the son of* Abihail:
36. charge of *the sons of* Merari
38. Moses, and Aaron *and his sons,* keeping
— for the charge of *the children of* Israel;
40. of the males *of the children of* Israel
41, 42, 45. the firstborn *among the children of* Israel;
— firstlings among the cattle of *the children of*
46, 50. the firstborn of *the children of* Israel,
4: 2. Take the sum of *the sons of* Kohath from among the *sons of* Levi,
3. *From* thirty years *old* and upward even until fifty years *old,*
4. the service of *the sons of* Kohath
5. Aaron shall come, *and his sons,*
15. when Aaron *and his sons* have made
— after that, *the sons of* Kohath
— the burden of *the sons of* Kohath
16. Eleazar *the son of* Aaron
19. Aaron *and his sons* shall go in, and
22. Take also the sum of *the sons of*
23. *From* thirty years *old* and upward until fifty years *old*
27. At the appointment of Aaron *and his sons* shall be all the service of *the sons of* the Gershonites,
28. the families of *the sons of* Gershon
—, 33. Ithamar *the son of* Aaron
29. As for *the sons of* Merari,
30, 35, 39, 43, 47. *From* thirty years *old* and upward even unto fifty years *old*
33, 42, 45. the families of *the sons of* Merari,
34. numbered *the sons of* the Kohathites
38. numbered of *the sons of* Gershon,
41. the families of *the sons of* Gershon,
5: 2. Command *the children of* Israel,
4. *the children of* Israel did so, and put
— so did *the children of* Israel.
6, 12. Speak unto *the children of* Israel,
9. the holy things of *the children of* Israel,
6: 2. Speak unto *the children of* Israel,
10. two *young* pigeons, (lit. *sons of* a dove)
12, 14. lamb *of* the *first* year
23. Speak unto Aaron and unto *his sons,* saying, On this wise ye shall bless *the children of*
27. put my name upon *the children of*
7: 7. he gave *unto the sons of* Gershon,
8. he gave *unto the sons of* Merari,
— Ithamar *the son of* Aaron
9. *But unto the sons of* Kohath
12, 17. Nahshon *the son of* Amminadab,
15, 21, 27, 33, 39, 45, 51, 57, 63, 69, 75, 81. One *young* bullock (lit. one steer, *son of* a bull), one ram, one lamb *of* the *first* year,

Nu. 7:17, 23, 29, 35, 41, 47, 53, 59, 65, 71, 77, 83. five lambs of the *first* year: (lit. *sons of* a year)
18, 23. Nethaneel *the son of* Zuar,
24, 29. Eliab *the son of* Helon,
— *of the children of* Zebulun,
30, 35. Elizur *the son of* Shedeur,
— *the children of* Reuben,
36, 41. Shelumiel *the son of* Zurishaddai,
— prince *of the children of* Simeon,
42, 47. Eliasaph *the son of* Deuel,
— prince *of the children of* Gad,
48, 53. Elishama *the son of* Ammihud,
— prince *of the children of* Ephraim,
54, 59. Gamaliel *the son of* Pedahzur,
— prince *of the children of* Manasseh:
60, 65. Abidan *the son of* Gideoni,
— prince *of the children of* Benjamin,
66, 71. Ahiezer *the son of* Ammishaddai,
— prince *of the children of* Dan,
72, 77. Pagiel *the son of* Ocran,
— prince *of the children of* Asher
78, 83. Ahira *the son of* Enan,
— prince *of the children of* Naphtali,
87, 88. the lambs *of* the *first* year (lit. *sons of* a year)
8: 6, 14. the Levites from among *the children of* Israel,
8. let them take a *young* bullock (lit. one steer *the son of* a bull)
— another *young* bullock shalt thou take
9. the whole assembly of *the children of* Israel
10. and *the children of* Israel shall put
11. an offering of *the children of* Israel,
13, 22. before Aaron, and before *his sons,*
16. from among *the children of* Israel;
— the firstborn *of* all *the children of* Israel,
17, 18. all the firstborn *of the children of* Israel
19. *and to his sons* from among *the children of* Israel, to do the service of *the children of* Israel in the tabernacle of the congregation, and to make an atonement for *the children of* Israel: that there be no plague *among the children of* Israel, when *the children of* Israel come
20. the congregation of *the children of* Israel,
— so did *the children of* Israel
24. *from* twenty and five years *old*
25. *And from the age of* fifty years
9: 2. *the children of* Israel also keep the passover
4. Moses spake unto *the children of* Israel,
5. Moses, so did *the children of* Israel.
7. season among *the children of* Israel?
10. Speak unto *the children of* Israel,
17. *the children of* Israel journeyed:
— there *the children of* Israel pitched
18. *the children of* Israel journeyed,
19. then *the children of* Israel kept the charge
22. *the children of* Israel abode in their tents,
10: 8. *And the sons of* Aaron,
12. *the children of* Israel took their journeys
14. the camp of *the children of* Judah
— Nahshon *the son of* Amminadab.
15. the tribe of *the children of* Issachar (was) Nethaneel *the son of* Zuar.
16. the tribe of *the children of* Zebulun (was) Eliab *the son of* Helon.
17. and *the sons of* Gershon *and the sons of* Merari
18. Elizur *the son of* Shedeur.
19. the tribe of *the children of* Simeon (was) Shelumiel *the son of* Zurishaddai.
20. the tribe of *the children of* Gad (was) Eliasaph *the son of* Deuel.
22. camp of *the children of* Ephraim
— Elishama *the son of* Ammihud.
23. the tribe of *the children of* Manasseh (was) Gamaliel *the son of* Pedahzur.
24. the tribe of *the children of* Benjamin (was) Abidan *the son of* Gideoni.
25. the camp of *the children of* Dan
— Ahiezer *the son of* Ammishaddai.
26. the tribe of *the children of* Asher (was) Pagiel *the son of* Ocran.
27. the tribe of *the children of* Naphtali (was) Ahira *the son of* Enan.
28. the journeyings of *the children of* Israel

Nu. 10:29. Hobab, *the son of* Raguel
11: 4. and *the children of* Israel also wept
28. Joshua *the son of* Nun,
13: 2. which I give *unto the children of* Israel:
3. heads of *the children of* Israel.
4. Shammua *the son of* Zaccur.
5. Shaphat *the son of* Hori.
6. Caleb *the son of* Jephunneh.
7. Igal *the son of* Joseph.
8, 16. Oshea *the son of* Nun.
9. Palti *the son of* Raphu.
10. Gaddiel *the son of* Sodi.
11. Gaddi *the son of* Susi.
12. Ammiel *the son of* Gemalli.
13. Sethur *the son of* Michael.
14. Nahbi *the son of* Vophsi.
15. Geuel *the son of* Machi.
24. which *the children of* Israel cut down
26. the congregation of *the children of* Israel,
32. had searched unto *the children of* Israel,
33. *the sons of* Anak,
14: 2. *the children of* Israel murmured
5. the congregation of *the children of* Israel.
6, 38. Joshua *the son of* Nun, and Caleb *the son of* Jephunneh,
7. the company of *the children of* Israel,
10. before all *the children of* Israel.
18. of the fathers upon *the children*
27. heard the murmurings of *the children of*
29. *from* twenty years *old* and upward,
30. save Caleb *the son of* Jephunneh, and Joshua *the son of* Nun.
33. *And your children* shall wander in the wilderness
39. sayings unto all *the children of* Israel:
15: 2, 18, 38. Speak unto *the children of* Israel,
8. when thou preparest a bullock (lit. *son of* a bull)
9. bring with a bullock a meat offering (lit. *son of* a bullock)
24. one *young* bullock (lit. one steer *the son of* a bull)
25, 26. the congregation of *the children of*
29. born *among the children of* Israel,
32. while *the children of* Israel were
16: 1. Korah, *the son of* Izhar, *the son of* Kohath, *the son of* Levi, and Dathan and Abiram, *the sons of* Eliab, and On, *the son of* Peleth, *sons of* Reuben,
2. with certain *of the children of* Israel,
7. too much upon you, *ye sons of*
8. Hear, I pray you, *ye sons of* Levi:
10. all thy brethren *the sons of* Levi
12. *the sons of* Eliab:
27. *and their sons*, and their little children.
37(17:2). Speak unto Eleazar *the son of* Aaron
38(17:3). shall be a sign *unto the children of* Israel.
40(17:5). a memorial *unto the children of*
41(17:6). the congregation of *the children of*
17: 2(17). Speak unto *the children of* Israel,
5(20). the murmurings of *the children of*
6(21). Moses spake unto *the children of*
9(24). before the Lord unto all *the children of* Israel:
10(25). *against* the rebels; (marg. *children of* rebellion)
12(27). *the children of* Israel spake unto
18: 1. Thou *and thy sons* and thy father's house
—, 2, 7. thou *and thy sons* with thee
5. no wrath any more upon *the children of*
6. the Levites from among *the children of*
8. hallowed things of *the children of* Israel;
— *and to thy sons*, by an ordinance
9. most holy for thee *and for thy sons*.
11. the wave offerings of *the children of* Israel: I have given them unto thee, *and to thy sons*
16. *from* a month *old*
19. *the children of* Israel offer unto the Lord, have I given thee, *and thy sons*
20. thine inheritance among *the children of*
21. *And*, behold, I have given *the children of* Levi
22. Neither must *the children of* Israel
23. among *the children of* Israel they have
24. the tithes of *the children of* Israel,

Nu. 18:24. Among *the children of* Israel they shall
26. When ye take of *the children of* Israel
28. which ye receive of *the children of* Israel;
32. the holy things of *the children of* Israel,
19: 2. Speak unto *the children of* Israel,
9. the congregation of *the children of* Israel
10. it shall be *unto the children of* Israel,
20: 1. Then came *the children of* Israel,
12. in the eyes of *the children of* Israel,
13. because *the children of* Israel strove
19. *the children of* Israel said unto him,
22. *the children of* Israel, (even) the whole
24. which I have given *unto the children of*
25. Take Aaron and Eleazar *his son*,
26. put them upon Eleazar *his son:*
28. and put them upon Eleazar *his son;*
21: 10. *the children of* Israel set forward,
24. even unto *the children of* Ammon: for the border of *the children of* Ammon (was) strong.
29. he hath given *his sons* that escaped,
35. So they smote him, and *his sons*,
22: 1. And *the children of* Israel set forward,
2, 4, 10, 16. Balak *the son of* Zippor
3. distressed because of *the children of*
5. Balaam *the son of* Beor
— the land of *the children of* his people,
23: 18. thou *son of* Zippor:
19. *neither the son of* man,
24: 3, 15. Balaam *the son of* Beor hath said,
17. destroy all *the children of* Sheth.
25: 6. one *of the children of* Israel came
— the congregation of *the children of* Israel,
7, 11. *the son of* Eleazar, *the son of* Aaron
8. the plague was stayed from *the children of*
11. wrath away from *the children of* Israel,
— I consumed not *the children of* Israel
13. an atonement for *the children of* Israel.
14. Zimri, *the son of* Salu,
26: 1. Eleazar *the son of* Aaron
2. the congregation of *the children of* Israel,
—, 4. *from* twenty years *old* and upward,
4. Moses *and the children of* Israel,
5. *the children of* Reuben;
8. *And the sons of* Pallu;
9. *And the sons of* Eliab;
11. *Notwithstanding the children of* Korah died not.
12. *The sons of* Simeon
15. *The children of* Gad
18. the families of *the children of* Gad
19, 20. *The sons of* Judah
21. *the sons of* Pharez were;
23. *the sons of* Issachar
26. *the sons of* Zebulun
28. *The sons of* Joseph
29. Of *the sons of* Manasseh:
30. These (are) *the sons of* Gilead:
33. *the son of* Hepher had no *sons*,
35. These (are) *the sons of* Ephraim
36. these (are) *the sons of* Shuthelah:
37. the families of *the sons of* Ephraim
— These (are) *the sons of* Joseph
38. *The sons of* Benjamin
40. *the sons of* Bela
41. These (are) *the sons of* Benjamin
42. These (are) *the sons of* Dan
44. *the children of* Asher
45. *Of the sons of* Beriah:
47. the families of *the sons of* Asher
48. *the sons of* Naphtali
51. the numbered of *the children of* Israel,
62. *from* a month *old* and upward:
— not numbered among *the children of*
— given them among *the children of* Israel.
63, 64. numbered *the children of* Israel
65. Caleb *the son of* Jephunneh, and Joshua *the son of* Nun.
27: 1. Zelophehad, *the son of* Hepher, *the son of* Gilead, *the son of* Machir, *the son of* Manasseh, of the families of Manasseh *the son of* Joseph:
3. *and* had no *sons*.
4. because he hath no *son?*
8. thou shalt speak unto *the children of* Israel, saying, If a man die, *and* have no *son*,

Nu. 27:11. *unto the children of* Israel a statute
12. which I have given *unto the children of*
18. Take thee Joshua *the son of* Nun,
20. of *the children of* Israel may be obedient.
21. and all *the children of* Israel with him,
28: 2. Command *the children of* Israel,
3. two lambs *of* the *first* year without spot
9. two lambs *of* the *first* year without spot,
11. two *young* bullocks (lit. steers, *sons of* a bull), and one ram, seven lambs *of* the *first* year
19, 27. two *young* bullocks, and one ram, and seven lambs *of* the *first* year:
29: 2, 8. one *young* bullock, one ram, (and) seven lambs *of* the *first* year
13. thirteen *young* bullocks, two rams,
—, 17, 20, 23, 26, 29, 32. fourteen lambs *of* the *first* year;
17. twelve *young* bullocks,
36. seven lambs *of* the *first* year
40(30:1). Moses told *the children of* Israel
30: 1(2). *concerning the children of* Israel,
31: 2. Avenge *the children of* Israel of
6. Phinehas *the son of* Eleazar
8. Balaam also *the son of* Beor
9. *the children of* Israel took (all)
12. the congregation of *the children of* Israel,
16. Behold, these caused *the children of* (lit. were *to the children of*)
30, 42, 47. of *the children of* Israel's half,
54. a memorial *for the children of* Israel
32: 1. Now *the children of* Reuben *and the children of* Gad *had*
2, 25, 29, 31. *The children of* Gad *and the children of* Reuben
6. Moses said *unto the children of* Gad *and to the children of* Reuben,
7, 9. the heart of *the children of* Israel
11. *from* twenty years *old* and upward,
12. Save Caleb *the son of* Jephunneh the Kenezite, and Joshua *the son of* Nun:
17. ready armed before *the children of*
18. until *the children of* Israel have inherited
28. Joshua *the son of* Nun,
— the tribes *of the children of* Israel:
33. *to the children of* Gad, *and to the children of* Reuben, and unto half the tribe of Manasseh *the son of*
34. *the children of* Gad built Dibon,
37. *And the children of* Reuben
39. *the children of* Machir *the son of* Manasseh
40. unto Machir *the son of* Manasseh;
41. Jair *the son of* Manasseh
33: 1. the journeys of *the children of* Israel,
3. *the children of* Israel went out
5. *the children of* Israel removed
31. pitched *in Bene*-jaakan.
32. they removed *from Bene*-jaakan,
38. after *the children of* Israel were come out
39. Aaron (was) an hundred and twenty and three years *old*
40. heard of the coming of *the children of* Israel.
51. Speak unto *the children of* Israel,
34: 2. Command *the children of* Israel,
13. Moses commanded *the children of* Israel,
14. the tribe of *the children of* Reuben
— the tribe of *the children of* Gad
17. Joshua *the son of* Nun.
19. Caleb *the son of* Jephunneh.
20. the tribe of *the children of* Simeon, Shemuel *the son of* Ammihud.
21. Elidad *the son of* Chislon.
22. the tribe of *the children of* Dan, Bukki *the son of* Jogli.
23. The prince *of the children of* Joseph, for the tribe of *the children of* Manasseh, Hanniel *the son of* Ephod.
24. the tribe of *the children of* Ephraim, Kemuel *the son of* Shiphtan.
25. the tribe of *the children of* Zebulun, Elizaphan *the son of* Parnach.
26. the tribe of *the children of* Issachar, Paltiel *the son of* Azzan.
27. the tribe of *the children of* Asher, Ahihud *the son of* Shelomi.

Nu. 34:28. the tribe of *the children of* Naphtali, Pedahel *the son of* Ammihud.
29. the inheritance unto *the children of* Israel
35: 2. Command *the children of* Israel,
8. the possession of *the children of* Israel:
10. Speak unto *the children of* Israel,
15. a refuge, (both) *for the children of* Israel,
34. dwell among *the children of* Israel.
36: 1. families of *the children of* Gilead, *the son of* Machir, *the son of* Manasseh, of the families of *the sons of* Joseph,
— the chief fathers *of the children of* Israel:
2. an inheritance by lot *to the children of*
3. if they be married to any *of the sons of* the (other) tribes of *the children of* Israel,
4. the jubile *of the children of* Israel
5. Moses commanded *the children of* Israel
— The tribe of *the sons of* Joseph
7. the inheritance *of the children of* Israel
— every one of *the children of* Israel shall
8. any tribe of *the children of* Israel,
— that *the children of* Israel may enjoy
9. the tribes of *the children of* Israel
11. *unto* their father's brothers' *sons:*
12. the families of *the sons of* Manasseh *the son of* Joseph,
13. by the hand of Moses unto *the children of* Israel
Deu 1: 3. Moses spake unto *the children of* Israel,
28. we have seen *the sons of* the Anakims
31. as a man doth bear *his son,*
36. Save Caleb *the son of* Jephunneh;
— *and to his children,* because he hath wholly followed
38. Joshua *the son of* Nun,
39. *and your children,* which in that day
2: 4. your brethren *the children of* Esau,
8. our brethren *the children of* Esau,
9, 19. *unto the children of* Lot
12. *but the children of* Esau succeeded
19. over against *the children of* Ammon,
—, 37. the land of *the children of* Ammon
22. As he did *to the children of* Esau,
29. As *the children of* Esau
33. we smote him, and *his sons,* and all his people.
3:11. Rabbath of *the children of* Ammon?
14. Jair *the son of* Manasseh
16. the border of *the children of* Ammon;
18. your brethren *the children of* Israel, all (that are) *meet* for the war. (lit. *sons of* valour)
4: 9. teach them *thy sons, and thy sons' sons;*
10. they may teach *their children.*
25. When thou shalt beget *children, and children's children,*
40. with thee, *and with thy children* after thee,
44. which Moses set before *the children of*
45. Moses spake unto *the children of* Israel,
46. whom Moses *and the children of* Israel smote,
5: 9. the iniquity of the fathers upon *the children*
14. shalt not do any work, thou, *nor thy son,*
29(26). *and with their children* for ever!
6: 2. thou, *and thy son, and thy son's son,*
7. teach them diligently *unto thy children,*
20. when *thy son* asketh thee in time to come,
21. Then thou shalt say *unto thy son,*
7: 3. thou shalt not give *unto his son,* nor his daughter shalt thou take *unto thy son.*
4. For they will turn away *thy son*
8: 5. as a man chasteneth *his son,*
9: 2. *the children of* the Anakims,
— stand before *the children of* Anak!
10: 6. *And the children of* Israel took their journey from Beeroth of *the children of* Jaakan
— Eleazar *his son* ministered
11: 2. for (I speak) not with *your children*
6. *the sons of* Eliab, *the son of* Reuben:
19. ye shall teach them *your children,*
21. the days of *your children,*
12:12. ye, *and your sons,*
18. thou, *and thy son,* and thy daughter,
25, 28. well with thee, *and with thy children* after thee,
31. *their sons* and their daughters they have

Deu 13: 6(7). *the son of* thy mother, or *thy son,*
13(14). *the children of* Belial,
14: 1. Ye (are) *the children* of the Lord
16:11, 14. thou, *and thy son,* and thy daughter,
17:20. he, *and his children,* in the midst of Israel.
18: 5. him *and his sons* for ever.
10. that maketh *his son* or his daughter to pass
21: 5. the priests *the sons of* Levi
15. and they have born him *children,*
— (if) *the* firstborn *son* be her's
16. when he maketh *his sons* to inherit
— he may not make *the son of* the
— before *the son* of the hated,
17. he shall acknowledge *the son of*
18. have *a* stubborn and rebellious *son,*
20. This *our son* (is) stubborn
22: 6. thou shalt not take the dam with *the young:*
7. let the dam go, and take *the young*
23: 4(5). Balaam *the son of* Beor
8(9). *The children* that are begotten
17(18). a sodomite *of the sons of* Israel.
24: 7. his brethren *of the children of* Israel,
16. be put to death for *the children, neither* shall *the children* be put to death
25: 2. man (be) *worthy to* be beaten, (lit. be a *son of* stripes)
5. *and* have no *child,*
28:32. *Thy sons* and thy daughters (shall be) given
41. Thou shalt beget *sons*
53. the flesh of *thy sons* and of thy daughters,
54. the remnant of *his children* which he
55. the flesh of *his children* whom he shall eat:
56. *and toward her son,* and toward her daughter,
57. *and toward her children* which she shall bear:
29: 1(28:69). make with *the children of* Israel
22(21). generation to come of *your children*
29(28). unto us *and to our children*
30: 2. thee this day, thou *and thy children,*
31: 2. I (am) an hundred and twenty years *old*
9. unto the priests *the sons of* Levi,
13. *And* (that) *their children,* which have not
19. teach it *the children of* Israel:
— a witness for me *against the children of* Israel.
22. and taught it *the children of* Israel.
23. he gave Joshua *the son of* Nun
— thou shalt bring *the children of* Israel
32: 5. their spot (is) not (the spot) of *his children:*
8. when he separated *the sons of* Adam,
— according to the number of *the children of*
14. rams of *the breed of* Bashan,
19. because of the provoking of *his sons,*
20. *children* in whom (is) no faith.
44. Hoshea *the son of* Nun.
46. ye shall command *your children*
49. which I give *unto the children of* Israel
51. among *the children of* Israel
— in the midst of *the children of* Israel.
52. which I give *the children of* Israel.
33: 1. blessed *the children of* Israel before his death.
9. nor knew *his own children:*
24. Asher (be) blessed *with children;*
34: 7. Moses (was) an hundred and twenty years *old*
8. *the children of* Israel wept for Moses
9. Joshua *the son of* Nun was full of the spirit
— *the children of* Israel hearkened unto him,

Jos. 1: 1. spake unto Joshua *the son of* Nun,
2. to them, (even) *to the children of* Israel.
2: 1. Joshua *the son of* Nun sent out
2. men in hither to night *of the children of*
23. came to Joshua *the son of* Nun,
3: 1. he and all *the children of* Israel,
9. Joshua said unto *the children of* Israel,
4: 4. he had prepared *of the children of* Israel,
5, 8. the tribes of *the children of* Israel:
6. when *your children* ask
7. a memorial *unto the children of* Israel
8. *the children of* Israel did so as Joshua
12. And *the children of* Reuben, *and the children of* Gad,
— armed before *the children of* Israel,
21. he spake unto *the children of* Israel, saying, When *your children* shall ask
22. ye shall let *your children* know,
5: 1. from before *the children of* Israel,

Jos. 5. 1. because of *the children of* Israel.
2. circumcise again *the children of* Israel
3. circumcised *the children of* Israel
6. *the children of* Israel walked forty years
7. And *their children,* (whom) he raised
10. *the children of* Israel encamped in Gilgal,
12. neither had *the children of* Israel manna
6: 1. because of *the children of* Israel:
6. Joshua *the son of* Nun
7: 1. *the children of* Israel committed a trespass
—, 18. Achan, *the son of* Carmi, *the son of* Zabdi, *the son of* Zerah,
— was kindled *against the children of* Israel.
12. *the children of* Israel could not stand
19. Joshua said unto Achan, *My son,*
23. unto all *the children of* Israel,
24. took Achan *the son of* Zerah,
— and *his sons,* and his daughters,
8:31. the Lord commanded *the children of* Israel,
32. in the presence of *the children of* Israel.
9:17. *the children of* Israel journeyed,
18. *the children of* Israel smote them
26. out of the hand of *the children of*
10: 4. peace with Joshua and with *the children of*
11. whom *the children of* Israel slew
12. the Amorites before *the children of*
20. *and the children of* Israel had made an end
21. against any *of the children of* Israel.
11:14. *the children of* Israel took for a prey
19. that made peace with *the children of* Israel,
22. Anakims left in the land of *the children of*
12: 1. which *the children of* Israel smote,
2. the border of *the children of* Ammon;
6. *and the children of* Israel smite:
7. Joshua *and the children of* Israel smote
13: 6. will I drive out from before *the children of*
10. the border of *the children of* Ammon;
13. *the children of* Israel expelled not
15. the tribe of *the children of* Reuben
22. Balaam also *the son of* Beor, the soothsayer, did *the children of* Israel slay
23. the border of *the children of* Reuben
— inheritance of *the children of* Reuben
24. *unto the children of* Gad
25. half the land of *the children of*
28. inheritance of *the children of* Gad
29. half tribe of *the children of* Manasseh
31. *unto the children of* Machir *the son of* Manasseh, (even) to the one half of *the children of* Machir
14: 1. which *the children of* Israel inherited
— Joshua *the son of* Nun,
— of the tribes *of the children of* Israel,
4. *the children of* Joseph
5. so *the children of* Israel did,
6. Then *the children of* Judah
—, 13, 14. Caleb *the son of* Jephunneh
7. Forty years *old* (was) I
9. thine inheritance, *and thy children's* for ever,
10. I (am) this day fourscore and five years *old.*
15: 1. the tribe of *the children of* Judah
6. Bohan *the son of* Reuben:
8. by the valley of *the son of* Hinnom
12. the coast of *the children of* Judah
13. Caleb *the son of* Jephunneh he gave a part among *the children of* Judah,
14. *the* three *sons of* Anak,
17. Othniel *the son of* Kenaz,
20, 21. the tribe of *the children of* Judah
63. *the children of* Judah could not
— Jebusites dwell with *the children of* Judah
16: 1. the lot *of the children of* Joseph
4. So *the children of* Joseph,
5. the border of *the children of* Ephraim
8. the tribe of *the children of* Ephraim
9. cities *for the children of* Ephraim
— inheritance of *the children of* Manasseh,
17: 2. the rest *of the children of* Manasseh by their families; for *the children of* Abiezer, *and for the children of* Helek, *and for the children of* Asriel, *and for the children of* Shechem, *and for the children of* Hepher, *and for the children of* Shemida: these (were) *the* male *children of* Manasseh *the son of* Joseph

Jos. 17: 3. Zelophehad, *the son of* Hepher, *the son of* Gilead, *the son of* Machir, *the son of* Manasseh, had no *sons*,
4. Joshua *the son of* Nun,
6. an inheritance among *his sons:* and the rest *of* Manasseh's *sons had* the land
8. *to the children of* Ephraim;
12. Yet *the children of* Manasseh
13. when *the children of* Israel were waxen
14. *the children of* Joseph spake
16. *the children of* Joseph said,
18: 1. *the children of* Israel assembled together
2. there remained *among the children of* Israel
3. Joshua said unto *the children of* Israel,
10. Joshua divided the land *unto the children of*
11, 21. the tribe of *the children of* Benjamin
— between *the children of* Judah and *the children of* Joseph.
14. a city of *the children of* Judah:
16. the valley of *the son of* Hinnom,
17. Bohan *the son of* Reuben,
20, 28. inheritance of *the children of* Benjamin,
19: 1, 8. the tribe of *the children of* Simeon
— inheritance of *the children of*
9. the portion of *the children of* Judah (was) the inheritance of *the children of* Simeon: for the part of *the children of* Judah was too much for them: therefore *the children of* Simeon had
10. came up *for the children of* Zebulun
16. inheritance of *the children of* Zebulun
17. *for the children of* Issachar
23. the tribe of *the children of* Issachar
24, 31. the tribe of *the children of* Asher
32. came out *to the children of* Naphtali, (even) *for the children of* Naphtali
39. the tribe of *the children of* Naphtali
40, 48. the tribe of *the children of* Dan
47. the coast of *the children of* Dan
— *the children of* Dan went up
49. *the children of* Israel gave an inheritance
—, 51. Joshua *the son of* Nun,
— of the tribes of *the children of* Israel,
20: 2. Speak to *the children of* Israel,
9. cities appointed for all *the children of* Israel,
21: 1. Joshua *the son of* Nun,
— of the tribes *of the children of* Israel;
3. *the children of* Israel gave unto the Levites
4. *the children of* Aaron the priest,...had (lit. were *to the children of*)
5. *And* the rest *of the children of* Kohath
6. *And the children of* Gershon
7. *The children of* Merari
8. *the children of* Israel gave by lot
9. the tribe of *the children of* Judah, and out of the tribe of *the children of* Simeon,
10. Which *the children of* Aaron,
— *of the children of* Levi,
12. gave they to Caleb *the son of* Jephunneh
13. *Thus* they gave *to the children of* Aaron
19. the cities of *the children of* Aaron,
20, 26. families of *the children of* Kohath,
— remained *of the children of* Kohath,
27. *And unto the children of* Gershon,
34. families of *the children of* Merari,
40(38). the cities *for the children of* Merari
41(39). the possession of *the children of* Israel
22: 9, 10, 11, 21, 30, 34. *the children of* Reuben *and the children of* Gad
— departed from *the children of* Israel
11. And *the children of* Israel heard say,
— the passage of *the children of* Israel.
12. when *the children of* Israel heard (of it), the whole congregation of *the children of* Israel
13. And *the children of* Israel sent
—, 15, 31. unto *the children of* Reuben, and to *the children of* Gad,
—, 31, 32. Phinehas *the son of* Eleazar the priest,
20. Did not Achan *the son of* Zerah
24. In time to come *your children* might speak *unto our children*,
25. *ye children of* Reuben *and children of* Gad; ye have no part in the Lord: so shall *your children* make *our children* cease from
27. that *your children* may not say *to our children* in time to come,

Jos. 22: 30. *and the children of* Manasseh
31. and to *the children of* Manasseh,
— ye have delivered *the children of* Israel
32. returned from *the children of* Reuben, and from *the children of* Gad,
— to *the children of* Israel,
33. the thing pleased *the children of* Israel; and *the children of* Israel blessed God,
— wherein *the children* of Reuben *and* Gad (lit. *and the children of* Gad)
24: 4. Jacob *and his children* went down
9. Then Balak *the son of* Zippor,
— Balaam *the son of* Beor
29. Joshua *the son of* Nun,
— an hundred and ten years *old.*
32. which *the children of* Israel brought up
— Jacob bought of *the sons of* Hamor
— inheritance *of the children of* Joseph.
33. Eleazar *the son of* Aaron
— (that pertained to) Phinehas *his son*,
Jud. 1: 1. *the children of* Israel asked the Lord,
8. Now *the children of* Judah
9. afterward *the children of* Judah
13. Othniel *the son of* Kenaz,
16. *And the children of* the Kenite,
— with *the children of* Judah
20. expelled thence *the* three *sons of*
21. And *the children of* Benjamin
— dwell with *the children of* Benjamin
34. the Amorites forced *the children of* Dan
2: 4. spake these words unto all *the children of*
6. *the children of* Israel went every man
8. Joshua *the son of* Nun,
— an hundred and ten years *old.*
11. *the children of* Israel did evil
3: 2. the generations of *the children of* Israel
5. *And the children of* Israel dwelt among
6. gave their daughters *to their sons*,
7. *the children of* Israel did evil
8, 14. *the children of* Israel served
9, 15. *the children of* Israel cried unto the Lord,
— a deliverer *to the children of* Israel,
—, 11. Othniel *the son of* Kenaz,
12. *the children of* Israel did evil again
13. gathered unto him *the children of*
15. Ehud *the son of* Gera, a Benjamite, (marg. or, *the son of* Jemini)
— *the children of* Israel sent
27. *the children of* Israel went down
31. Shamgar *the son of* Anath,
4: 1. *the children of* Israel again did evil
3. *the children of* Israel cried unto the Lord:
— oppressed *the children of* Israel.
5. *the children of* Israel came up to her
6, 12. Barak *the son of* Abinoam
— *of the children of* Naphtali *and of the children of* Zebulun?
11. *of the children of* Hobab
23. of Canaan before *the children of* Israel.
24. the hand of *the children of* Israel prospered,
5: 1. Barak *the son of* Abinoam
6. Shamgar *the son of* Anath,
12. thou *son of* Abinoam.
6: 1. *the children of* Israel did evil in the
2. *the children of* Israel made them the dens
3, 33. *and the children of* the east,
6. *the children of* Israel cried unto the Lord.
7. when *the children of* Israel cried
8. sent a prophet unto *the children of* Israel,
11. *his son* Gideon threshed wheat
29. Gideon *the son of* Joash hath done
30. Bring out *thy son*, that he may die:
7: 12. all *the children of* the east
14. Gideon *the son of* Joash,
8: 10. the hosts of *the children of* the east:
13, 32. Gideon *the son of* Joash
18. resembled *the children of* a king.
19. *the sons of* my mother:
22. and *thy son*, and *thy son's son* also:
23. neither shall *my son* rule over you:
28. subdued before *the children of* Israel,
29. Jerubbaal *the son of* Joash
30. Gideon had threescore and ten *sons*
31. she also bare him *a son*,
33. *the children of* Israel turned again,
34. *the children of* Israel remembered
9: 1. Abimelech *the son of* Jerubbaal

Jud. 9: 2, 5. *the sons of* Jerubbaal,
5. the youngest *son of* Jerubbaal
18. and have slain *his sons*, threescore and ten
— Abimelech, *the son of* his maidservant,
24. threescore and ten *sons of* Jerubbaal
26. Gaal *the son of* Ebed came
28. Gaal *the son of* Ebed said,
— (is) not (he) *the son of* Jerubbaal?
30. the words of Gaal *the son of* Ebed,
31. Gaal *the son of* Ebed and his brethren
35. Gaal *the son of* Ebed went
57. Jotham *the son of* Jerubbaal.
10: 1. Tola *the son of* Puah, *the son of* Dodo,
4. he had thirty *sons* that rode
6. *the children of* Israel did evil again
— the gods of *the children of* Ammon,
7. into the hands of *the children of* Ammon.
8. and oppressed *the children of* Israel
— all *the children of* Israel
9. *the children of* Ammon passed over
10. *the children of* Israel cried unto the Lord,
11. Lord said unto *the children of* Israel,
— from *the children of* Ammon,
15. *the children of* Israel said unto the Lord,
17. Then *the children of* Ammon were gathered
— *the children of* Israel assembled themselves
18. fight *against the children of* Ammon?
11: 1. he (was) *the son of* an harlot:
2. Gilead's wife bare him *sons;* and his wife's *sons* grew up,
— thou (art) *the son of* a strange woman.
4. that *the children of* Ammon
5. *the children of* Ammon made war
6. fight *with the children of* Ammon.
8, 9. *against the children of* Ammon,
12, 13, 14, 28, king of *the children of* Ammon,
15. the land of *the children of* Ammon:
25. Balak *the son of* Zippor,
27. between *the children of* Israel and *the children of* Ammon.
29, 30. *the children of* Ammon.
31. *from the children of* Ammon,
32. over unto *the children of* Ammon
33. *the children of* Ammon were subdued before *the children of*
34. he had neither *son* nor daughter.
36. *of the children of* Ammon.
12: 1. to fight *against the children of* Ammon,
2. strife *with the children of* Ammon;
3. against *the children of* Ammon,
9. he had thirty *sons*,
— daughters from abroad *for his sons*.
13, 15. Abdon *the son of* Hillel,
14. he had forty *sons* and thirty *nephews*, (marg. *sons' sons*)
13: 1. *the children of* Israel did evil again
3. thou shalt conceive, and bear *a son*.
5, 7. thou shalt conceive, and bear *a son;*
24. the woman bare *a son*,
14: 16. put forth a riddle *unto the children of*
17. she told the riddle *to the children of*
17: 2. Blessed (be thou) of the Lord, *my son*.
3. unto the Lord from my hand *for my son*,
5. consecrated one *of his sons*,
11. was unto him as one *of his sons*.
18: 2. *the children of* Dan sent
— from their coasts, men of valour, (marg. men *sons of* valour)
16. which (were) *of the children of* Dan,
22. overtook *the children of* Dan.
23. they cried unto *the children of* Dan.
25. *the children of* Dan said
26. *the children of* Dan went their way:
30. *the children of* Dan set up the graven image: and Jonathan, *the son of* Gershom, *the son of* Manasseh, he *and his sons* were priests
19: 12. that (is) not *of the children of* Israel;
16. the men of the place (were) *Benjamites*.
22. certain *sons of* Belial,
30. the day that *the children of* Israel came
20: 1. all *the children of* Israel went out,
3. Now *the children of* Benjamin heard that *the children of* Israel were gone up to Mizpeh. Then said *the children of* Israel,
7. Behold, ye (are) all *children of* Israel;
13. *the children of* Belial,

Jud. 20: 13. But *the children of* Benjamin would
— their brethren *the children of* Israel:
14. But *the children of* Benjamin
— to battle against *the children of* Israel.
15. *the children of* Benjamin were
18. *the children of* Israel arose,
—, 23, 28. against *the children of* Benjamin?
19. *the children of* Israel rose up
21. *the children of* Benjamin came
23. *the children of* Israel went up and wept
24. *the children of* Israel came near against *the children of* Benjamin
25. to the ground *of the children of* Israel
26. *the children of* Israel, and all the people,
27. *the children of* Israel enquired of the Lord,
28. Phinehas, *the son of* Eleazar, *the son of* Aaron,
30. *the children of* Israel went up against *the children of* Benjamin
31. *the children of* Benjamin went out
32. *the children of* Benjamin said,
— *But the children of* Israel said,
35. *the children of* Israel destroyed
36. So *the children of* Benjamin saw
48. upon *the children of* Benjamin,
21: 5. *the children of* Israel said,
6. *the children of* Israel repented them
10. twelve thousand men *of the* valiantest, (lit. *of the children of* valour)
13. to speak to *the children of* Benjamin
18. *the children of* Israel have sworn,
20. commanded *the children of* Benjamin,
23. *the children of* Benjamin did so,
24. *the children of* Israel departed thence
Ru 1: 1. and his wife, and *his* two *sons*.
2. the name of *his* two *sons* Mahlon and
3. she was left, and *her* two *sons*.
11. yet (any more) *sons* in my womb,
12. should also bear *sons;*
4: 13. and she bare *a son*.
15. which is better to thee than seven *sons*,
17. There is *a son* born to Naomi;
1Sa. 1: 1. Elkanah, *the son of* Jeroham, *the son of* Elihu, *the son of* Tohu, *the son of* Zuph,
3. *the* two *sons of* Eli,
4. and to all *her sons* and her daughters,
8. better to thee than ten *sons?*
20. that she bare *a son*,
23. gave *her son* suck
2: 5. she that hath many *children*
12. *Now the sons of* Eli (were) *sons of* Belial;
21. she conceived, and bare three *sons*
22. heard all that *his sons* did
24. Nay, *my sons;* for (it is) no good report
28. offerings made by fire of *the children of* Israel?
29. and honourest *thy sons* above me,
34. that shall come upon *thy* two *sons*,
3: 6. I called not, *my son;* lie down again.
13. because *his sons* made themselves vile,
16. and said, Samuel, *my son*.
4: 4, 11. *the* two *sons of* Eli,
15. Eli was ninety and eight years *old;*
16. What is there done, *my son?*
17. *thy* two *sons* also, Hophni and Phinehas,
20. for thou hast born *a son*.
6: 7. bring *their calves* home from them:
10. and shut up *their calves* at home:
7: 1. sanctified Eleazar *his son* to keep the ark
4. *the children of* Israel did put away
6. Samuel judged *the children of* Israel
7. Philistines heard that *the children of* Israel
— when *the children of* Israel heard (it),
8. *the children of* Israel said to Samuel,
8: 1. he made *his sons* judges over Israel.
2. the name of *his* firstborn (lit. *his son* the firstborn)
3. And *his sons* walked not in his ways,
5. thou art old, *and thy sons* walk not
11. He will take *your sons*,
9: 1. Kish, *the son of* Abiel, *the son of* Zeror, *the son of* Bechorath, *the son of* Aphiah, a *Benjamite*, (marg. or, *the son of* a man of Jemini)
2. And he had *a son*,
— (there was) not *among the children of* Israel
3. Kish said to Saul *his son*,

1Sa. 9:21. (Am) not I a *Benjamite*,
10: 2. What shall I do *for my son?*
11. What (is) this (that) is come *unto the son of*
18. said unto *the children of* Israel,
21. Saul *the son of* Kish was taken:
27. *But the children of* Belial said,
11: 8. *the children of* Israel were three hundred thousand,
12: 2. *and*, behold, *my sons* (are) with you:
12. the king of *the children of* Ammon
13: 1. Saul reigned one year; (marg. *the son of* one year in his reigning)
16. And Saul, and Jonathan *his son*,
22. with Saul and with Jonathan *his son*
14: 1. Jonathan *the son of* Saul
3. Ahiah, *the son of* Ahitub,
— *the son of* Phinehas, *the son of* Eli,
18. at that time *with the children of* Israel.
32. took sheep, and oxen, *and* calves, (lit. *and the sons of* a bull)
39. though it be in Jonathan *my son*,
40. I and Jonathan *my son* will be on
42. Cast (lots) between me and Jonathan *my son.*
47. *and against the children of* Ammon,
49. Now *the sons of* Saul
50. Abner, *the son of* Ner,
51. *the son of* Abiel.
52. or any valiant *man*, (lit. *son of* valour)
15: 6. shewed kindness to all *the children of*
16: 1. provided me a king *among his sons.*
5. he sanctified Jesse and *his sons*,
10. Jesse made seven of *his sons* to pass
18. I have seen *a son* of Jesse
19. Send me David *thy son*, which (is) with
20. sent (them) by David *his son* unto Saul.
17:12. Now David (was) *the son of*
— he had eight *sons:*
13. *the* three eldest *sons of* Jesse went
— the names of *his* three *sons* that went
17. Jesse said unto David *his son*,
53. *the children of* Israel returned
55. whose *son* (is) this youth?
56. Enquire thou whose *son* the
58. Whose *son* (art) thou,
— I (am) *the son of* thy servant
18:17. only be thou valiant for me, (marg. *a son of* valour)
19: 1. Saul spake to Jonathan *his son*,
2(1). But Jonathan Saul's *son*
20:27. Saul said unto Jonathan *his son*, Wherefore cometh not *the son of* Jesse
30. Thou *son of* the perverse rebellious
— thou hast chosen *the son of* Jesse
31. as long as *the son of* Jesse liveth
— for he shall surely die. (marg. (is) *the son of* death)
22: 7. Hear now, ye *Benjamites* (lit. *sons of* Jemini); will *the son of* Jesse give every one
8. *my son* hath made a league with *the son of* Jesse,
— that *my son* hath stirred up
9. I saw *the son of* Jesse coming to Nob, to Ahimelech *the son of* Ahitub.
11. Ahimelech the priest, *the son of* Ahitub,
12. Hear now, thou *son of* Ahitub.
13. thou *and the son of* Jesse,
20. And one of *the sons* of (lit. one *son* of) Ahimelech *the son of* Ahitub,
23: 6. Abiathar *the son of* Ahimelech
16. Jonathan Saul's *son* arose,
24:16(17). (Is) this thy voice, *my son*
25: 8. unto thy servants, *and to thy son* David.
10. who (is) *the son of* Jesse?
17. for he (is such) *a son of* Belial,
44. Phalti *the son of* Laish,
26: 5, 14. Abner *the son of* Ner,
6. Abishai *the son of* Zeruiah,
16. ye (are) *worthy to* die, (marg. *the sons of* death)
17. (Is) this thy voice, *my son* David?
19. but if (they be) *the children of* men,
21. I have sinned: return, *my son* David:
25. Blessed (be) thou, *my son* David:
27: 2. Achish, *the son of* Maoch,

1Sa.28:19. to morrow (shalt) thou *and thy sons* (be) with me:
30: 3. *and their sons*, and their daughters,
6. every man for *his sons* and for his daughters:
7. Abiathar the priest, Ahimelech's *son*,
19. neither *sons* nor daughters,
22. to every man his wife and *his children*,
31: 2. hard upon Saul and upon *his sons;*
— Abinadab, and Melchi-shua, Saul's *sons.*
6. Saul died, and *his* three *sons*,
7. that Saul *and his sons* were dead,
8. found Saul and *his* three *sons*
12. of Saul and the bodies of *his sons*
2Sa. 1: 4. Saul and Jonathan *his son* are dead also.
5. that Saul and Jonathan *his son* be dead?
12. for Saul, and for Jonathan *his son*,
13. I (am) *the son of* a stranger,
17. over Saul and over Jonathan *his son:*
18. bade them teach *the children of* Judah
2: 7. be ye valiant: (marg. *the sons of* valour)
8, 12. Abner *the son of* Ner,
—, 12, 15. Ish-bosheth *the son of* Saul,
10. Ish-bosheth Saul's *son* (was) forty years *old*
13. Joab *the son of* Zeruiah,
18. there were three *sons of* Zeruiah
25. *the children of* Benjamin
3: 2. unto David were *sons* born
3. Absalom *the son of* Maacah
4. Adonijah *the son of* Haggith; and the fifth, Shephatiah *the son of* Abital;
14. Ish-bosheth Saul's *son*,
15. Phaltiel *the son of* Laish.
23, 25, 28, 37. Abner *the son of* Ner
34. as a man falleth before wicked *men*, (marg. *children of* iniquity)
39. these men *the sons of* Zeruiah
4: 1. when Saul's *son* heard that Abner
2. Saul's *son* had two men
— *the sons of* Rimmon a Beerothite, *of the children of* Benjamin:
4. Jonathan, Saul's *son*, had *a son* (that was) lame of (his) feet. He was five years *old*
5, 9. *the sons of* Rimmon the Beerothite,
8. Ish-bosheth *the son of* Saul
5: 4. David (was) thirty years *old*
13. there were yet *sons* and daughters
6: 3. Uzzah and Ahio, *the sons of* Abinadab,
7: 6. I brought up *the children of* Israel out of Egypt,
7. walked with all *the children of* Israel
10. neither shall *the children of* wickedness
14. he shall be my *son*. (lit. to me *for a son*)
— with the stripes of *the children of* men:
8: 3. Hadadezer, *the son of* Rehob,
10. Toi sent Joram *his son* unto king David,
12. *and of the children of* Ammon,
— Hadadezer, *son of* Rehob,
16. Joab *the son of* Zeruiah
— Jehoshaphat *the son of* Ahilud
17. Zadok *the son of* Ahitub, and Ahimelech *the son of* Abiathar,
18. Benaiah *the son of* Jehoiada
— *and* David's *sons* were chief rulers.
9: 3. Jonathan hath yet *a son*,
4, 5. Machir, *the son of* Ammiel,
6. *the son of* Jonathan, *the son of* Saul,
9. I have given *unto* thy master's *son*
10. Thou therefore, *and thy sons*,
— that thy master's *son* may have food
— Mephibosheth thy master's *son*
— Ziba had fifteen *sons* and twenty servants.
11. as one *of* the king's *sons.*
12. Mephibosheth had *a* young *son*,
10: 1. the king of *the children of* Ammon died, and Hanun *his son* reigned
2. Hanun *the son of* Nahash,
— into the land of *the children of* Ammon.
3. the princes of *the children of* Ammon
6. when *the children of* Ammon
— *the children of* Ammon sent and hired
8. *the children of* Ammon came
10. array against *the children of* Ammon.
11. if *the children of* Ammon
14. *when the children of* Ammon saw

2Sa. 10:14. returned from *the children of* Ammon,
19. feared to help *the children of* Ammon
11: 1. destroyed *the children of* Ammon,
21. Abimelech *the son of* Jerubbesheth?
27. and bare him *a son.*
12: 3. with him, and with *his children;*
5. shall *surely* die: (marg. (is) *worthy to* die; lit. (is) *a son of* death)
9. with the sword of *the children of* Ammon.
14. *the child* also (that is) born
24. and she bare *a son,*
26. Rabbah of *the children of* Ammon,
31. the cities of *the children of* Ammon.
13: 1. Absalom *the son of* David
— Amnon *the son of* David loved
3, 32. Jonadab, *the son of* Shimeah
4. Why (art) thou, (being) the king's *son,*
23. Absalom invited all the king's *sons.*
25. Nay, *my son,* let us not all now go,
27. all the king's *sons* go with him.
28. be courageous, and be valiant. (marg. *sons of* valour)
29. Then all the king's *sons* arose,
30. Absalom hath slain all the king's *sons,*
32. all the young men the king's *sons;*
33. that all the king's *sons* are dead:
35, 36. Behold, the king's *sons*
37. went to Talmai, *the son of*
— mourned for *his son* every day.
14: 1. Now Joab *the son of* Zeruiah
6. thy handmaid had two *sons,*
11. to destroy any more, lest they destroy *my son.*
— there shall not one hair of *thy son* fall
16. the man (that would) destroy me and *my son*
27. unto Absalom there were born three *sons,*
15:27. and *your* two *sons* with you, Ahimaaz *thy son,* and Jonathan *the son of*
36. (they have) there with them *their* two *sons,*
16: 3. where (is) thy master's *son?*
5. Shimei, *the son of* Gera:
8. into the hand of Absalom *thy son:*
9. Then said Abishai *the son of* Zeruiah
10. What have I to do with you, *ye sons of*
11. Behold, *my son,* which came forth
— much more now (may this) *Ben*jamite (lit. *son of* Jemini)
19. (should I) not (serve) in the presence of *his son?*
17:10. And he also (that is) valiant, (lit. *the son of* valour)
— *and* (they) which (be) with him (are) valiant *men.*
25. Amasa (was) a man's *son,*
27. that Shobi *the son of* Nahash of Rabbah of *the children of* Ammon, and Machir *the son of* Ammiel
18: 2. Abishai *the son of* Zeruiah,
12. forth mine hand against the king's *son:*
18. I have no *son* to keep my name
19, 22, 27. Ahimaaz *the son of* Zadok,
20. because the king's *son* is dead.
22. Wherefore wilt thou run, *my son,*
33(19:1). O *my son* Absalom, *my son, my son* Absalom! would God I had died for thee, O Absalom, *my son, my son!*
19: 2(3). how the king was grieved for *his son.*
4(5). O *my son* Absalom, O Absalom, *my son, my son!*
5(6). the lives of *thy sons* and of thy daughters,
16(17). Shimei *the son of* Gera, a Benjamite,
17(18). and *his* fifteen *sons* and his twenty
18(19). Shimei *the son of* Gera fell down
21(22). Abishai *the son of* Zeruiah
22(23). What have I to do with you, *ye sons of*
24(25). Mephibosheth *the son of* Saul
32(33). a very aged man, (even) fourscore years *old:*
35(36). I (am) this day fourscore years *old:*
20: 1, 2, 6, 7, 10, 13, 21, 22. Sheba, *the son of* Bichri,
— have we inheritance *in the son of* Jesse:
23. Benaiah *the son of* Jehoiada

2Sa. 20:24. Jehoshaphat *the son of* Ahilud
21: 2. Gibeonites (were) not *of the children of* Israel,
— *and the children of* Israel had sworn unto
— *to the children of* Israel and Judah.
6. Let seven men *of his sons* be delivered
7. Mephibosheth, *the son of* Jonathan *the son of* Saul,
— between David and Jonathan *the son of*
8. the king took *the* two *sons of* Rizpah
— *the* five *sons of* Michal
— Adriel *the son of* Barzillai
12, 13. of Saul and the bones of Jonathan *his son*
14. the bones of Saul and Jonathan *his son*
17. Abishai *the son of* Zeruiah
19. Elhanan *the son of* Jaare-oregim,
21. Jonathan *the son of* Shimeah
22:45. Strangers shall submit themselves (marg. *Sons of* the stranger)
46. Strangers shall fade away, (lit. *Sons of* the stranger)
23: 1. David *the son of* Jesse said,
9. Eleazar *the son of* Dodo the Ahohite, (lit. *the son of* Ahohi)
11. Shammah *the son of* Agee
18. *the son of* Zeruiah,
20, 22. Benaiah *the son of* Jehoiada,
— *the son of* a valiant man,
24. Elhanan *the son of* Dodo
26. Ira *the son of* Ikkesh
29. Heleb *the son of* Baanah,
— Ittai *the son of* Ribai out of Gibeah of *the children of*
32. of *the sons of* Jashen,
33. Ahiam *the son of* Sharar
34. Eliphelet *the son of* Ahasbai, *the son of* the Maachathite, Eliam *the son of* Ahithophel
36. Igal *the son of* Nathan
37. Joab *the son of* Zeruiah,
1 K. 1: 5, 11. Adonijah *the son of* Haggith
7. with Joab *the son of* Zeruiah,
8, 26, 32, 36, 38, 44. Benaiah *the son of* Jehoiada,
9. called all his brethren the king's *sons,*
12. the life of *thy son* Solomon.
13, 17, 30. Assuredly Solomon *thy son* shall
19. called all *the sons of* the king,
21. I *and my son* Solomon shall be counted
25. called all the king's *sons,*
33. cause Solomon *my son* to ride upon
42. Jonathan *the son of* Abiathar
52. If he will shew himself a worthy *man,* (lit. if he shall be *for a son of* valour)
2: 1. he charged Solomon *his son,* saying,
4. If *thy children* take heed to their way,
5. what Joab *the son of* Zeruiah did
— Abner *the son of* Ner, and unto Amasa *the son of* Jether,
7. *But* shew kindness *unto the sons of* Barzillai
8. Shimei *the son of* Gera, a Benjamite
13. Adonijah *the son of* Haggith
22. for Joab *the son of* Zeruiah.
25. by the hand of Benaiah *the son of* Jehoiada;
29. Solomon sent Benaiah *the son of* Jehoiada.
32. Abner *the son of* Ner,
— Amasa *the son of* Jether,
34. Benaiah *the son of* Jehoiada went up,
35. Benaiah *the son of* Jehoiada in his room
39. Achish *son of* Maachah king of
46. commanded Benaiah *the son of* Jehoiada
3: 6. thou hast given him *a son*
19. this woman's *child* died in the night;
20. took *my son* from beside me,
— and laid *her* dead *child* in my bosom.
21. in the morning to give *my child* suck,
— it was not *my son,* which I did bear.
22. the living (is) *my son, and* the dead (is) *thy son.* And this said, No; but the dead (is) *thy son, and* the living (is) *my son.*
23. This (is) *my son* that liveth, *and thy son* (is) the dead: and the other saith, Nay; but *thy son* (is) the dead, *and my son*

1K. 3:26. the woman whose *the* living *child* (lit. *her son*)
— her bowels yearned upon *her son,*
4: 2. Azariah *the son of* Zadok
3. *the sons of* Shisha, scribes; Jehoshaphat *the son of* Ahilud,
4. Benaiah *the son of* Jehoiada
5. Azariah *the son of* Nathan
— Zabud *the son of* Nathan
6. Adoniram *the son of* Abda
8. *The son of* Hur, in mount Ephraim: (marg. *Ben*-hur)
9. *The son of* Dekar, (marg. *Ben*-dekar)
10. *The son of* Hesed, (marg. *Ben*-hesed)
11. *The son of* Abinadab, (marg. *Ben*-abinadab)
12. Baana *the son of* Ahilud;
13. *The son of* Geber, (marg. *Ben*-geber)
— Jair *the son of* Manasseh,
14. Ahinadab *the son of* Iddo
16. Baanah *the son of* Hushai
17. Jehoshaphat *the son of* Paruah,
18. Shimei *the son of* Elah,
19. Geber *the son of* Uri
30(5:10). the wisdom of all *the children of* the east
31(5:11). Chalcol, and Darda, *the sons of* Mahol:
5: 5(19). *Thy son,* whom I will set upon thy throne
7(21). hath given unto David *a* wise *son*
6: 1. after *the children of* Israel were come
13. I will dwell among *the children of* Israel,
7:14. He (was) a widow's *son*
8: 1. chief of the fathers *of the children of* Israel,
9. (a covenant) with *the children of* Israel,
19. but *thy son* that shall come forth
25. so that *thy children* take heed to
39. the hearts of all *the children of* men;
63. the king and all *the children of* Israel
9: 6. ye *or your children,*
20. which (were) not *of the children of* Israel,
21. *Their children* that were left after them in the land, whom *the children of* Israel
22. *But of the children of* Israel did
11: 2. the Lord said unto *the children of*
7. the abomination of *the children of* Ammon.
12. I will rend it out of the hand of *thy son.*
13. (but) will give one tribe *to thy son*
20. of Tahpenes bare him Genubath *his son,*
— among *the sons of* Pharaoh.
23. Rezon *the son of* Eliadah,
26. Jeroboam *the son of* Nebat,
33. Milcom the god of *the children of* Ammon,
35. take the kingdom out of *his son*'s hand,
36. *And unto his son* will I give one tribe,
43. Rehoboam *his son* reigned in his stead.
12: 2, 15. Jeroboam *the son of* Nebat,
16. inheritance *in the son of* Jesse:
17. *But* (as for) *the children of* Israel which dwelt
21, 23. Rehoboam *the son of* Solomon.
24. against your brethren *the children of* Israel:
31. which were not *of the sons of* Levi.
33. ordained a feast *unto the children of* Israel:
13: 2. *a child* shall be born
11. and *his sons* came and told him (lit. *son*)
12. For *his sons* had seen what way
13. And he said unto *his sons,*
27. And he spake to *his sons,*
31. he spake to *his sons,* saying,
14: 1. Abijah *the son of* Jeroboam
5. to ask a thing of thee for *her son;*
20. Nadab *his son* reigned in his stead.
21. Rehoboam *the son of* Solomon
— Rehoboam (was) forty and one years *old*
24. the Lord cast out before *the children of*
31. Abijam *his son* reigned in his stead.
15: 1. Jeroboam *the son of* Nebat
4. to set up *his son* after him, and to establish
8. Asa *his son* reigned in his stead:
18. Ben-hadad, *the son of* Tabrimon, *the son of* Hezion,
24. Jehoshaphat *his son* reigned in his stead.
25. Nadab *the son of* Jeroboam began
27, 33. Baasha *the son of* Ahijah,
16: 1, 7. Jehu *the son of* Hanani

1K. 16: 3, 26, 31. Jeroboam *the son of* Nebat
6. Elah *his son* reigned in his stead.
8. Elah *the son of* Baasha
13. of Baasha, and the sins of Elah *his son,*
21, 22. followed Tibni *the son of* Ginath,
28. Ahab *his son* reigned in his stead.
29. began Ahab *the son of* Omri to reign over Israel: and Ahab *the son of* Omri reigned
30. Ahab *the son of* Omri did evil
34. he spake by Joshua *the son of* Nun.
17:12. I may go in and dress it for me *and my son,*
13. and after make for thee *and for thy son.*
17. *the son of* the woman,
18. remembrance, and to slay *my son?*
19. Give me *thy son.*
20. with whom I sojourn, by slaying *her son?*
23. Elijah said, See, *thy son* liveth.
18:20. Ahab sent unto all *the children of* Israel,
31. the tribes of *the sons of* Jacob,
19:10, 14. *the children of* Israel have forsaken
16. Jehu *the son of* Nimshi
—, 19. Elisha *the son of* Shaphat
20: 3. thy wives also *and thy children,*
5. thy gold, and thy wives, *and thy children;*
7. for my wives, *and for my children,*
15. all *the children of* Israel, (being) seven
27. *And the children of* Israel were numbered,
— *the children of* Israel pitched before them
29. *the children of* Israel slew of the Syrians
35. a certain man *of the sons of* the prophets
21:10. set two men, *sons of* Belial,
13. two men, *children of* Belial,
22. Jeroboam *the son of* Nebat,
— Baasha *the son of* Ahijah,
26. the Lord cast out before *the children of*
29. in *his son*'s days will I bring the evil
22: 8, 9. Micaiah *the son of* Imlah,
11. Zedekiah *the son of* Chenaanah made him
24. Zedekiah *the son of* Chenaanah went near,
26. to Joash the king's *son;*
40. Ahaziah *his son* reigned in his stead.
41. Jehoshaphat *the son of* Asa
42. Jehoshaphat (was) thirty and five years *old*
49(50), 51(52). Ahaziah *the son of* Ahab
50(51). and Jehoram *his son* reigned
52(53). Jeroboam *the son of* Nebat,
2K. 1:17. Jehoram *the son of* Jehoshaphat king of Judah; because he had no *son.*
2: 3. *the sons of* the prophets that (were)
5. *the sons of* the prophets that (were) at
7. fifty men *of the sons of* the prophets
15. when *the sons of* the prophets
16. there be with thy servants fifty strong *men;* (marg. *sons of* strength)
3: 1. Now Jehoram *the son of* Ahab
3. Jeroboam *the son of* Nebat,
11. Here (is) Elisha *the son of* Shaphat,
27. he took *his* eldest *son* that should
4: 1. the wives of *the sons of* the prophets
4. shut the door upon thee and upon *thy sons,*
5. the door upon her and upon *her sons,*
6. that she said unto *her son,*
7. live thou and *thy children* of the rest.
14. Verily she hath no *child,*
16. thou shalt embrace *a son.*
17. the woman conceived, and bare *a son*
28. Did I desire *a son* of my lord?
36. he said, Take up *thy son.*
37. took up *her son,*
38. *and the sons of* the prophets
— *for the sons of* the prophets.
5:22. two young men *of the sons of* the
6: 1. *the sons of* the prophets said unto Elisha,
28. Give *thy son,* that we may eat him to day, and we will eat *my son* to morrow.
29. So we boiled *my son,* and did eat
— Give *thy son,* that we may eat him: and she hath hid *her son.*
31. Elisha *the son of* Shaphat
32. See ye how this *son of* a murderer
8: 1, 5. whose *son* he had restored (lit. who *her son*)
5. and this (is) *her son,*
9. *Thy son* Ben-hadad king of Syria
12. thou wilt do *unto the children of*
16, 25, 28, 29. Joram *the son of* Ahab

2K. 8:16. Jehoram *the son of* Jehoshaphat king of
17. Thirty and two years *old*
19. him alway a light, (and) *to his children.*
24. Ahaziah *his son* reigned in his stead.
25, 29. Ahaziah *the son of* Jehoram
26. Two and twenty years *old*
9: 1. *of the children of* the prophets,
2, 14. Jehu *the son of* Jehoshaphat *the son of* Nimshi,
9. Jeroboam *the son of* Nebat, and like the house of Baasha *the son of* Ahijah:
20. driving of Jehu *the son of* Nimshi;
26. the blood of Naboth, and the blood of *his sons,*
29. Joram *the son of* Ahab
10: 1. Ahab had seventy *sons*
2. seeing your master's *sons*
3. the best and meetest *of* your master's *sons,*
6. the heads of the men your master's *sons,*
— *Now* the king's *sons,*
7. that they took the king's *sons,*
8. have brought the heads of the king's *sons.*
13. to salute *the children of* the king *and the children of* the queen.
15, 23. Jehonadab *the son of* Rechab
29. the sins of Jeroboam *the son of* Nebat,
30. thy *children of* the fourth (generation)
35. Jehoahaz *his son* reigned in his stead.
11: 1. saw that *her son* was dead,
2. took Joash *the son of* Ahaziah, and stole him from among the king's *sons*
4. shewed them the king's *son.*
12. he brought forth the king's *son,*
21(12:1). Seven years *old* (was) Jehoash
12:21(22). Jozachar *the son of* Shimeath, and Jehozabad *the son of* Shomer,
— (—) and Amaziah *his son* reigned
13: 1. Joash *the son of* Ahaziah king of Judah Jehoahaz *the son of* Jehu began
2, 11. the sins of Jeroboam *the son of* Nebat,
3. the hand of Ben-hadad *the son of* Hazael,
5. and *the children of* Israel dwelt in their
9. And Joash *his son* reigned in his stead.
10, 25. Jehoash *the son of* Jehoahaz
24. and Ben-hadad *his son* reigned
25. the hand of Ben-hadad *the son of* Hazael
14: 1. Joash *son of* Jehoahaz
—, 17, 23. Amaziah *the son of* Joash
2. was twenty and five years *old*
6. But *the children of* the murderers
— shall not be put to death for *the children, nor the children* be put to death
8. Jehoash, *the son of* Jehoahaz *son of* Jehu,
9. Give thy daughter *to my son*
13. *the son of* Jehoash *the son of* Ahaziah,
14. and hostages (lit. *sons of* pledges), and returned to Samaria.
16. Jeroboam *his son* reigned in his stead.
17. Jehoash *son of* Jehoahaz
21. Azariah, which (was) sixteen years *old,*
23. Jeroboam *the son of* Joash
24. the sins of Jeroboam *the son of* Nebat,
25. *the son of* Amittai, the prophet,
27. the hand of Jeroboam *the son of*
29. Zachariah *his son* reigned in his stead.
15: 1. began Azariah *son of* Amaziah
2. Sixteen years *old* was he when he began
5. Jotham the king's *son* (was) over
7. Jotham *his son* reigned in his stead.
8. Zachariah *the son of* Jeroboam
9, 18, 24, 28. the sins of Jeroboam *the son of*
10, 13, 14. Shallum *the son of* Jabesh
12. Thy *sons* shall sit on the throne
14, 17. Menahem *the son of* Gadi
22. Pekahiah *his son* reigned in his stead.
23. Pekahiah *the son of* Menahem
25, 27, 30, 32, 37. Pekah *the son of* Remaliah,
— with him fifty men *of the* Gileadites: (lit. *of the children of* the Gileadites)
30. Hoshea *the son of* Elah made a
—, 32. Jotham *the son of* Uzziah.
33. Five and twenty years *old* was he
38. Ahaz *his son* reigned in his stead.
16: 1. Pekah *the son of* Remaliah Ahaz *the son of* Jotham
2. Twenty years *old* (was) Ahaz when
3. made *his son* to pass through the fire,

2K. 16: 3. cast out from before *the children of* Israel.
5. Pekah *son of* Remaliah
7. saying, I (am) thy servant *and thy son:*
20. Hezekiah *his son* reigned in his stead.
17: 1. Hoshea *the son of* Elah
7. that *the children of* Israel had sinned
8. whom the Lord cast out from before *the children of* Israel,
9. *the children of* Israel did secretly
17. they caused *their sons*
21. Jeroboam *the son of* Nebat
22. *the children of* Israel walked in all the sins
24. instead of *the children of* Israel:
31. burnt *their children* in fire
34. commanded *the children of* Jacob,
41. both *their children, and their children's children:*
18: 1, 9. Hoshea *son of* Elah king of Israel,
— Hezekiah *the son of* Ahaz
2. Twenty and five years *old* was he
4. *the children of* Israel did burn incense
18, 26, 37. Eliakim *the son of* Hilkiah,
—, 37. Joah *the son of* Asaph
19: 2. Isaiah the prophet *the son of* Amoz.
3. for *the children* are come
12. *and the children of* Eden
20. Then Isaiah *the son of* Amoz sent
37. Adrammelech and Sharezer *his sons* smote him
— Esarhaddon *his son* reigned in his stead.
20: 1. the prophet Isaiah *the son of* Amoz
12. Berodach-baladan, *the son of* Baladan,
18. *And of thy sons* that shall issue from thee,
21. Manasseh *his son* reigned in his stead.
21: 1. Manasseh (was) twelve years *old*
2, 9. before *the children of* Israel.
6. he made *his son* pass through the fire,
7. the Lord said to David, and to Solomon *his son,*
18. Amon *his son* reigned in his stead.
19. Amon (was) twenty and two years *old*
24. made Josiah *his son* king
26. Josiah *his son* reigned in his stead.
22: 1. Josiah (was) eight years *old* when he
3. Shaphan *the son of* Azaliah, *the son of* Meshullam,
12. Ahikam *the son of* Shaphan, and Achbor *the son of* Michaiah,
14. the wife of Shallum *the son of* Tikvah, *the son of* Harhas,
23: 6. the graves of *the children of* the people.
10. (כתיב) in the valley of *the children of* Hinnom, (קרי *son of*)
— might make *his son* or his daughter
13. the abomination of *the children of*
15. Jeroboam *the son of* Nebat,
30. took Jehoahaz *the son of* Josiah,
31. Jehoahaz (was) twenty and three years *old*
34. made Eliakim *the son of* Josiah king
36. Jehoiakim (was) twenty and five years *old*
24: 2. bands of *the children of* Ammon,
6. Jehoiachin *his son* reigned in his stead.
8. Jehoiachin (was) eighteen years *old*
18. Zedekiah (was) twenty and one years *old*
25: 7. they slew *the sons of* Zedekiah
22. Gedaliah *the son of* Ahikam, *the son of* Shaphan, ruler.
23. Ishmael *the son of* Nethaniah, and Johanan *the son of* Careah, and Seraiah *the son of* Tanhumeth the Netophathite, and Jaazaniah *the son of*
25. Ishmael *the son of* Nethaniah, *the son of* Elishama,
1Ch 1: 5. *The sons of* Japheth;
6. *And the sons of* Gomer;
7. *And the sons of* Javan;
8. *The sons of* Ham;
9. *And the sons of* Cush;
— *And the sons of* Raamah;
17. *The sons of* Shem;
19. unto Eber were born two *sons:*
23. All these (were) *the sons of* Joktan.
28. *The sons of* Abraham;
31. These are *the sons of* Ishmael.
32. *Now the sons of* Keturah,
— *And the sons of* Jokshan; Sheba, and
33. *And the sons of* Midian;

1Ch 1:33. All these (are) *the sons of* Keturah.
34. *The sons of* Isaac; Esau and Israel.
35. *The sons of* Esau;
36. *The sons of* Eliphaz;
37. *The sons of* Reuel;
38. *And the sons of* Seir;
39. *And the sons of* Lotan;
40. *The sons of* Shobal;
— *And the sons of* Zibeon; Aiah, and Anah.
41. *The sons of* Anah; Dishon. *And the sons of* Dishon;
42. *The sons of* Ezer;
— *The sons of* Dishan;
43. king reigned *over the children of* Israel; Bela *the son of* Beor:
44. Jobab *the son of* Zerah
46. Hadad *the son of* Bedad,
49. Baalhanan *the son of* Achbor
2: 1. These (are) *the sons of* Israel;
3. *The sons of* Judah;
4. All *the sons of* Judah (were) five.
5. *The sons of* Pharez;
6. *And the sons of* Zerah;
7. *And the sons of* Carmi;
8. *And the sons of* Ethan;
9. *The sons also* of Hezron,
10. prince of *the children of* Judah;
16. *And the sons of* Zeruiah;
18. Caleb *the son of* Hezron
— *her sons* (are) these; Jesher,
21. when he (was) threescore years *old;*
23. All these (belonged to) *the sons of*
25. *the sons of* Jerahmeel
27. *the sons of* Ram
28. *the sons of* Onam
— *And the sons of* Shammai;
30. *And the sons of* Nadab;
— Seled died without *children.*
31. *And the sons of* Appaim; Ishi. *And the sons of* Ishi; Sheshan. *And the children of* Sheshan;
32. *And the sons of* Jada
— Jether died without *children.*
33. *And the sons of* Jonathan;
— These were *the sons of* Jerahmeel.
34. Now Sheshan had no *sons,*
42. *Now the sons of* Caleb
— *and the sons of* Mareshah the father of
43. *And the sons of* Hebron;
45. *And the son of* Shammai
47. *And the sons of* Jahdai;
50. These were *the sons of* Caleb *the son of* Hur,
52. of Kirjath-jearim had *sons;*
54. *The sons of* Salma;
3: 1. these were *the sons of* David,
2. Absalom *the son of* Maachah
— Adonijah *the son of* Haggith:
9. all *the sons of* David, beside *the sons of* the concubines,
10. *And* Solomon's *son* (was) Rehoboam, Abia *his son,* Asa *his son,* Jehoshaphat *his son,*
11. Joram *his son,* Ahaziah *his son,* Joash *his son,*
12. Amaziah *his son,* Azariah *his son,* Jotham *his son,*
13. Ahaz *his son,* Hezekiah *his son,* Manasseh *his son,*
14. Amon *his son,* Josiah *his son.*
15. *And the sons of* Josiah
16. *And the sons of* Jehoiakim: Jeconiah *his son,* Zedekiah *his son.*
17. *And the sons of* Jeconiah; Assir, Salathiel *his son,*
19. *And the sons of* Pedaiah (were), Zerubbabel, and Shimei: *and the sons of* Zerubbabel;
21. *And the sons of* Hananiah;
— *the sons of* Rephaiah, *the sons of* Arnan, *the sons of* Obadiah, *the sons of* Shechaniah.
22. *And the sons of* Shechaniah;
— *and the sons of* Shemaiah;
23. *And the sons of* Neariah; (lit. *son*)
24. *And the sons of* Elioenai
4: 1. *The sons of* Judah;
2. Reaiah *the son of* Shobal

1Ch 4: 4. These (are) *the sons of* Hur,
6. These (were) *the sons of* Naarah.
7. *And the sons of* Helah
8. Aharhel *the son of* Harum.
13. *And the sons of* Kenaz;
— *and the sons of* Othniel;
15. *And the sons of* Caleb *the son of* Jephunneh;
— *and the sons of* Elah,
16. *And the sons of* Jehaleleel;
17. *And the sons of* Ezra (were),
18. these (are) *the sons of* Bithiah
19. *And the sons of* (his) wife
20. *And the sons of* Shimon (were), Amnon, and Rinnah, *Ben*-hanan, and Tilon. *And the sons of* Ishi (were), Zoheth, and *Ben*-zoheth.
21. *The sons of* Shelah *the son of* Judah
24. *The sons of* Simeon
25. Shallum *his son,* Mibsam *his son,* Mishma *his son.*
26. *And the sons of* Mishma; Hamuel *his son,* Zacchur *his son,* Shimei *his son.*
27. Shimei had sixteen *sons*
— his brethren had not many *children,*
— like to *the children of* Judah.
34. Joshah *the son of* Amaziah,
35. Jehu *the son of* Josibiah, *the son of* Seraiah, *the son of* Asiel,
37. Ziza *the son of* Shiphi, *the son of* Allon, *the son of* Jedaiah, *the son of* Shimri, *the son of* Shemaiah;
42. of *the sons of* Simeon,
— *the sons of* Ishi.
5: 1. *Now the sons of* Reuben
— *unto the sons of* Joseph *the son of* Israel:
3. *The sons,* (I say), *of* Reuben
4. *The sons of* Joel; Shemaiah *his son,* Gog *his son,* Shimei *his son,*
5. Micah *his son,* Reaia *his son,* Baal *his son,*
6. Beerah *his son,* whom Tilgath-pilneser
8. Bela *the son of* Azaz, *the son of* Shema, *the son of* Joel,
11. *And the children of* Gad dwelt over against them,
14. These (are) *the children of* Abihail *the son of* Huri, *the son of* Jaroah, *the son of* Gilead, *the son of* Michael, *the son of* Jeshishai, *the son of* Jahdo, *the son of* Buz;
15. Ahi *the son of* Abdiel, *the son of* Guni,
18. *The sons of* Reuben, and the Gadites, and half the tribe of Manasseh, of valiant *men,* (marg. *sons of* valour)
23. *And the children of* the half tribe of
6: 1(5:27),16(1). *The sons of* Levi;
2(5:28),18(3). And *the sons of* Kohath;
3(5:29). *And the children of* Amram; Aaron, and Moses, and Miriam. *The sons also of* Aaron;
17(2). the names of *the sons of* Gershom;
19(4). *The sons of* Merari;
20(5). Of Gershom; Libni *his son,* Jahath *his son,* Zimmah *his son,*
21(6). Joah *his son,* Iddo *his son,* Zerah *his son,* Jeaterai *his son.*
22(7). *The sons of* Kohath; Amminadab *his son,* Korah *his son,* Assir *his son,*
23(8). Elkanah *his son,* and Ebiasaph *his son,* and Assir *his son,*
24(9). Tahath *his son,* Uriel *his son,* Uzziah *his son,* and Shaul *his son.*
25(10). *And the sons of* Elkanah;
26(11). *the sons of* Elkanah; Zophai *his son,* and Nahath *his son,*
27(12). Eliab *his son,* Jeroham *his son,* Elkanah *his son.*
28(13). *And the sons of* Samuel;
29(14). *The sons of* Merari; Mahli, Libni *his son,* Shimei *his son,* Uzza *his son,*
30(15). Shimei *his son,* Haggiah *his son,* Asaiah *his son.*
33(18). they that waited *with their children. Of the sons of* the Kohathites: Heman a singer, *the son of* Joel, *the son of* Shemuel,
34(19). *The son of* Elkanah, *the son of* Jeroham, *the son of* Eliel, *the son of* Toah,

1Ch. 6:35(20). *The son of* Zuph, *the son of* Elkanah, *the son of* Mahath, *the son of* Amasai,
36(21). *The son of* Elkanah, *the son of* Joel, *the son of* Azariah, *the son of* Zephaniah,
37(22). *The son of* Tahath, *the son of* Assir, *the son of* Ebiasaph, *the son of* Korah,
38(23). *The son of* Izhar, *the son of* Kohath, *the son of* Levi, *the son of* Israel.
39(24). Asaph *the son of* Berachiah, *the son of* Shimea,
40(25). *The son of* Michael, *the son of* Baaseiah, *the son of* Malchiah,
41(26). *The son of* Ethni, *the son of* Zerah, *the son of* Adaiah,
42(27). *The son of* Ethan, *the son of* Zimmah, *the son of* Shimei,
43(28). *The son of* Jahath, *the son of* Gershom, *the son of* Levi.
44(29). *And* their brethren *the sons of* Merari (stood) on the left hand: Ethan *the son of* Kishi, *the son of* Abdi, *the son of* Malluch,
45(30). *The son of* Hashabiah, *the son of* Amaziah, *the son of* Hilkiah,
46(31). *The son of* Amzi, *the son of* Bani, *the son of* Shamer,
47(32). *The son of* Mahli, *the son of* Mushi, *the son of* Merari, *the son of* Levi.
49(34). Aaron *and his sons* offered
50(35). these (are) *the sons of* Aaron; Eleazar *his son*, Phinehas *his son*, Abishua *his son*,
51(36). Bukki *his son*, Uzzi *his son*, Zerahiah *his son*,
52(37). Meraioth *his son*, Amariah *his son*, Ahitub *his son*,
53(38). Zadok *his son*, Ahimaaz *his son*.
54(39). *of the sons of* Aaron,
56(41). to Caleb *the son of* Jephunneh.
57(42). *And to the sons of* Aaron they gave
61(46). *And unto the sons of* Kohath,
62(47). *And to the sons of* Gershom
63(48). *Unto the sons of* Merari
64(49). And *the children of* Israel gave
65(50). the tribe of *the children of* Judah, and out of the tribe of *the children of* Simeon, and out of the tribe of *the children of* Benjamin,
66(51). the families of *the sons of* Kohath
70(55). the remnant *of the sons of* Kohath.
71(56). *Unto the sons of* Gershom
77(62). *Unto* the rest *of the children of*
7: 1. *Now the sons of* Issachar
2. *And the sons of* Tola;
3. *And the sons of* Uzzi; Izrahiah: *and the sons of* Izrahiah;
4. for they had many wives *and sons*.
7. *And the sons of* Bela;
8. *And the sons of* Becher;
— All these (are) *the sons of* Becher.
10. *The sons also of* Jediael; Bilhan: *and the sons of* Bilhan;
11. All these *the sons of* Jediael,
12. and Huppim, *the children of* Ir, (and) Hushim, *the sons of* Aher.
13. *The sons of* Naphtali;
— Shallum, *the sons of* Bilhah.
14. *The sons of* Manasseh;
16. the wife of Machir bare *a son*,
— *and his sons* (were) Ulam and Rakem.
17. *And the sons of* Ulam; Bedan. These (were) *the sons of* Gilead, *the son of* Machir, *the son of* Manasseh.
19. *the sons of* Shemidah
20. *And the sons of* Ephraim; Shuthelah, and Bered *his son*, and Tahath *his son*, and Eladah *his son*, and Tahath *his son*,
21. Zabad *his son*, and Shuthelah *his son*,
23. she conceived, and bare *a son*,
25. Rephah (was) *his son*, also Resheph, and Telah *his son*, and Tahan *his son*,
26. Laadan *his son*, Ammihud *his son*, Elishama *his son*,
27. Non *his son*, Jehoshuah *his son*.
29. by the borders of *the children of* Manasseh,
— *the children of* Joseph *the son of* Israel.
30. *The sons of* Asher;

1Ch. 7:31. *And the sons of* Beriah;
33. *And the sons of* Japhlet;
— These (are) *the children of* Japhlet.
34. *And the sons of* Shamer;
35. *And the sons of* his brother Helem; (lit. *son*)
36. *The sons of* Zophah;
38. *And the sons of* Jether;
39. *And the sons of* Ulla;
40. All these (were) *the children of* Asher,
8: 3. *the sons of* Bela
6. these (are) *the sons of* Ehud:
10. These (were) *his sons*, heads of the fathers.
12. *The sons of* Elpaal; (lit. *and the sons*)
16. *the sons of* Beriah;
18. *the sons of* Elpaal;
21. *the sons of* Shimhi;
25. *the sons of* Shashak;
27. *the sons of* Jeroham.
30. *And his* firstborn *son*
34. *And the son of* Jonathan
35. *And the sons of* Micah
37. Rapha (was) *his son*, Eleasah *his son*, Azel *his son*:
38. Azel had six *sons*,
— All these (were) *the sons of* Azel.
39. *And the sons of* Eshek
40. *the sons of* Ulam
— and had many *sons, and sons' sons*,
— All these (are) *of the sons of* Benjamin.
9: 3. dwelt of *the children of* Judah, and of *the children of* Benjamin, and of *the children of* Ephraim,
4. Uthai *the son of* Ammihud, *the son of* Omri, *the son of* Imri, *the son of* Bani, of *the children of* Pharez *the son of* Judah.
5. Asaiah the firstborn, *and his sons*.
6. of *the sons of* Zerah;
7. of *the sons of* Benjamin; Sallu *the son of* Meshullam, *the son of* Hodaviah, *the son of* Hasenuah,
8. Ibneiah *the son of* Jeroham, and Elah *the son of* Uzzi, *the son of* Michri, and Meshullam *the son of* Shephathiah, *the son of* Reuel, *the son of* Ibnijah;
11. Azariah *the son of* Hilkiah, *the son of* Meshullam, *the son of* Zadok, *the son of* Meraioth, *the son of* Ahitub,
12. Adaiah *the son of* Jeroham, *the son of* Pashur, *the son of* Malchijah, and Maasiai *the son of* Adiel, *the son of* Jahzerah, *the son of* Meshullam, *the son of* Meshillemith, *the son of* Immer;
14. Shemaiah *the son of* Hasshub, *the son of* Azrikam, *the son of* Hashabiah, of *the sons of* Merari;
15. Mattaniah *the son of* Micah, *the son of* Zichri, *the son of* Asaph;
16. Obadiah *the son of* Shemaiah, *the son of* Galal, *the son of* Jeduthun, and Berechiah *the son of* Asa, *the son of* Elkanah,
18. the companies of *the children of* Levi.
19. Shallum *the son of* Kore, *the son of* Ebiasaph, *the son of* Korah,
20. Phinehas *the son of* Eleazar
21. Zechariah *the son of* Meshelemiah
23. So they *and their children*
30. *the sons of* the priests
32. *the sons of* the Kohathites,
36. *And his* firstborn *son*
40. *And the son of* Jonathan
41. *And the sons of* Micah
43. Rephaiah *his son*, Eleasah *his son*, Azel *his son*.
44. Azel had six *sons*,
— these (were) *the sons of* Azel.
10: 2. followed hard after Saul, and after *his sons*;
— and Malchi-shua, *the sons of* Saul.
6. So Saul died, and *his* three *sons*,
7. that Saul *and his sons* were dead,
8. they found Saul and *his sons* fallen
12. the body of Saul, and the bodies of *his sons*,
14. unto David *the son of* Jesse.

1Ch 11: 6. Joab *the son of* Zeruiah went first
11. *an* Hachmonite, (marg. or, *son of* Hachmoni)
12. Eleazar *the son of* Dodo,
22, 24. Benaiah *the son of* Jehoiada,
— *the son of* a valiant man
26. Elhanan *the son of* Dodo
28. Ira *the son of* Ikkesh
30. Heled *the son of* Baanah
31. Ithai *the son of* Ribai of Gibeah, (that pertained) to *the children of*
34. *The sons of* Hashem the Gizonite, Jonathan *the son of* Shage
35. Ahiam *the son of* Sacar the Hararite, Eliphal *the son of* Ur,
37. Naarai *the son of* Ezbai,
38. Mibhar *the son of* Haggeri,
39. Joab *the son of* Zeruiah,
41. Zabad *the son of* Ahlai,
42. Adina *the son of* Shiza
43. Hanan *the son of* Maachah,
44. Shama and Jehiel *the sons of* Hothan
45. Jediael *the son of* Shimri,
46. *the sons of* Elnaam,
12: 1. because of Saul *the son of* Kish:
3. *the sons of* Shemaah
— *the sons of* Azmaveth;
7. *the sons of* Jeroham of Gedor.
14. These (were) *of the sons of* Gad,
16. there came of *the children of* Benjamin
18. on thy side, thou *son of* Jesse:
24. *The children of* Judah
25. Of *the children of* Simeon,
26. Of *the children of* Levi
29. And of *the children of* Benjamin,
30. of *the children of* Ephraim
32. *And of the children of* Issachar,
14: 3. David begat more *sons*
15: 4. David assembled *the children of* Aaron,
5. *Of the sons of* Kohath;
6. *Of the sons of* Merari;
7. *Of the sons of* Gershom;
8. *Of the sons of* Elizaphan;
9. *Of the sons of* Hebron;
10. *Of the sons of* Uzziel;
15. *the children of* the Levites
17. Heman *the son of* Joel; and of his brethren, Asaph *the son of* Berechiah; and of *the sons of* Merari their brethren, Ethan *the son of* Kushaiah;
16: 13. *ye children of* Jacob,
38. also *the son of* Jeduthun
42. *And the sons of* Jeduthun
17: 9. neither shall *the children of* wickedness
11. after thee, which shall be *of thy sons;*
13. he shall be my *son:* (lit. shall be to me *for a son*)
18: 10. He sent Hadoram *his son* to king David,
11. *and from the children of* Ammon,
12. Abishai *the son of* Zeruiah
15. Joab *the son of* Zeruiah
— Jehoshaphat *the son of* Ahilud,
16. Zadok *the son of* Ahitub, and Abimelech *the son of* Abiathar,
17. Benaiah *the son of* Jehoiada
— *and the sons of* David (were) chief
19: 1. the king of *the children of* Ammon died, and *his son* reigned in his stead.
2. Hanun *the son of* Nahash,
— into the land of *the children of* Ammon
3. the princes of *the children of* Ammon
6. when *the children of* Ammon saw
— *and the children of* Ammon sent
7. *And the children of* Ammon gathered
9. *the children of* Ammon came out,
11. array against *the children of* Ammon.
12. if *the children of* Ammon be too strong
15. *when the children of* Ammon saw
19. would the Syrians help *the children of*
20: 1. the country of *the children of* Ammon,
3. the cities of *the children of* Ammon.
5. Elhanan *the son of* Jair
7. Jonathan *the son of* Shimea
21: 20. *his* four *sons* with him hid themselves.
22: 5. Solomon *my son* (is) young and tender,
6. he called for Solomon *his son,*
7. David said to Solomon, *My son,*

1Ch 22: 9. Behold, *a son* shall be born to thee,
10. he shall be my *son,* (lit. shall be to me *for a son*)
11. Now, *my son,* the Lord be with thee;
17. to help Solomon *his son,* (saying),
23: 1. he made Solomon *his son* king
3. *from the age of* thirty years
6. courses *among the sons of* Levi,
8. *The sons of* Laadan;
9, 10. *The sons of* Shimei;
10. *And the sons of* Shimei
11. Beriah had not many *sons;*
12. *The sons of* Kohath;
13. *The sons of* Amram;
— he *and his sons* for ever,
14. Moses the man of God, *his sons* were
15. *The sons of* Moses
16. Of *the sons of* Gershom,
17. *the sons of* Eliezer (were), Rehabiah the chief. And Eliezer had none other *sons; but the sons of* Rehabiah were
18. Of *the sons of* Izhar;
19. Of *the sons of* Hebron;
20. Of *the sons of* Uzziel;
21. *The sons of* Merari; Mahli, and Mushi. *The sons of* Mahli;
22. Eleazar died, and had no *sons,*
— their brethren *the sons of* Kish
23. *The sons of* Mushi;
24. These (were) *the sons of* Levi
— *from the age of* twenty years
27. *the* Levites (lit. *the sons of* Levi) (were) numbered *from* twenty years *old*
28. to wait on *the sons of* Aaron
32. the charge of *the sons of* Aaron
24: 1. *Now* (these are) the divisions *of the sons of* Aaron. *The sons of* Aaron;
2. *and* had no *children:*
3. Zadok of *the sons of* Eleazar, and Ahimelech of *the sons of* Ithamar,
4. more chief men found of *the sons of* Eleazar than of *the sons of* Ithamar;
— *Among the sons of* Eleazar
— *and* eight *among the sons of* Ithamar
5. were *of the sons of* Eleazar, *and of the sons of* Ithamar.
6. Shemaiah *the son of* Nethaneel
— Ahimelech *the son of* Abiathar,
20. *And* the rest *of the sons of* Levi (were these): *Of the sons of* Amram; Shubael: *of the sons of* Shubael;
21. *of the sons of* Rehabiah,
22. *of the sons of* Shelomoth;
23. *And the sons* (of Hebron); Jeriah
24. *the sons of* Uzziel; Michah: *of the sons of* Michah;
25. *of the sons of* Isshiah;
26. *The sons of* Merari
— *the sons of* Jaaziah; *Beno.* [or, *his son*]
27. *The sons of* Merari by Jaaziah; *Beno,* [or, *his son*]
28. Eleazar, who had no *sons.*
29. *the son of* Kish (was) Jerahmeel. (lit. *sons*)
30. *The sons also of* Mushi;
— These (were) *the sons of* the Levites
31. their brethren *the sons of* Aaron
25: 1, 2. *of the sons of* Asaph,
2. *the sons of* Asaph
3. *the sons of* Jeduthun;
4. *the sons of* Heman;
5. All these (were) *the sons* of Heman
— God gave to Heman fourteen *sons*
9. with his brethren *and sons*
10, 11, 12, 13, 14, 15, 16, 17, 18, 19, 20, 21, 22, 23, 24, 25, 26, 27, 28, 29, 30, 31. (he), *his sons,* and his brethren, (were) twelve.
26: 1. Meshelemiah *the son of* Kore, of *the sons of* Asaph.
2. *the sons* of Meshelemiah
4. *the sons* of Obed-edom
6. unto Shemaiah *his son* were *sons* born,
7. *The sons of* Shemaiah;
— whose brethren (were) strong *men,*
8. All these *of the sons of* Obed-edom: they *and their sons*
9. Meshelemiah had *sons* and brethren, strong *men,*

1Ch 26:10. Hosah, of *the children of* Merari, had *sons;* Simri the chief,
11. all *the sons* and brethren of Hosah
14. for Zechariah *his son,* a wise counsellor,
15. *and to his sons* the house of Asuppim.
19. *among the sons of* Kore, *and among the sons of* Merari.
21. *the sons of* Laadan; *the sons of* the
22. *The sons of* Jehieli;
24. Shebuel *the son of* Gershom, *the son of* Moses,
25. Rehabiah *his son,* and Jeshaiah *his son,* and Joram *his son,* and Zichri *his son,* and Shelomith *his son.*
28. Saul *the son of* Kish, and Abner *the son of* Ner, and Joab *the son of* Zeruiah,
29. Chenaniah *and his sons*
30, 32. his brethren, *men of* valour,
27: 1. *Now the children of* Israel after their
2. Jashobeam *the son of* Zabdiel:
3. Of *the children of* Perez
5. Benaiah *the son of* Jehoiada,
6. in his course (was) Ammizabad *his son.*
7. Zebadiah *his son* after him:
9. Ira *the son of* Ikkesh
10, 14. of *the children of* Ephraim:
16. Eliezer *the son of* Zichri: of the Simeonites, Shephatiah *the son of* Maachah:
17. Hashabiah *the son of* Kemuel:
18. Omri *the son of* Michael:
19. Ishmaiah *the son of* Obadiah: of Naphtali, Jerimoth *the son of* Azriel:
20. *Of the children of* Ephraim, Hoshea *the son of* Azaziah:
— Joel *the son of* Pedaiah:
21. Iddo *the son of* Zechariah: of Benjamin, Jaasiel *the son of* Abner:
22. Azareel *the son of* Jeroham.
23. *from* twenty years *old*
24. Joab *the son of* Zeruiah
25. Azmaveth *the son of* Adiel:
— Jehonathan *the son of* Uzziah:
26. Ezri *the son of* Chelub:
29. Shaphat *the son of* Adlai:
32. Jehiel *the son of* Hachmoni (was) with the king's *sons:*
34. Jehoiada *the son of* Benaiah,
28: 1. possession of the king, *and of his sons,*
4. *among the sons of* my father
5. And of all *my sons,* for the Lord hath given me many *sons,* he hath chosen Solomon *my son*
6. he said unto me, Solomon *thy son,*
— I have chosen him (to be) my *son,* (lit. to me *for a son*)
8. an inheritance *for your children*
9. And thou, Solomon *my son,* know
11. David gave to Solomon *his son*
20. David said to Solomon *his son,*
29: 1. Solomon *my son,* whom alone God
19. give unto Solomon *my son* a perfect heart,
22. made Solomon *the son of* David king
24. all *the sons* likewise *of* king David,
26. David *the son of* Jesse reigned over
28. Solomon *his son* reigned in his stead.
2Ch 1: 1. Solomon *the son of* David
5. Bezaleel *the son of* Uri, *the son of* Hur,
2:12(11). hath given to David the king *a* wise *son,*
14(13). *The son of* a woman
5: 2. of the fathers *of the children of* Israel,
10. (a covenant) with *the children of* Israel,
12. *with their sons* and their brethren,
6: 9. but *thy son* which shall come forth
11. that he made with *the children of* Israel.
16. yet so that *thy children* take heed
30. the hearts of *the children of* men:
7: 3. all *the children of* Israel saw how
8: 2. caused *the children of* Israel to dwell
8. of *their children,* who were left
— *the children of* Israel consumed not,
9. of *the children of* Israel did Solomon
9:29. Jeroboam *the son of* Nebat?
31. Rehoboam *his son* reigned in his stead.
10: 2, 15. Jeroboam *the son of* Nebat,
16. inheritance *in the son of* Jesse:
17. But (as for) *the children of* Israel that dwelt

2Ch 10:18. and *the children of* Israel stoned him
11: 3, 17. Rehoboam *the son of* Solomon,
14. Jeroboam *and his sons* had cast them
18. (כתיב) *the daughter of* (קרי בַּת) Jerimoth *the son of* David
— Eliab *the son of* Jesse;
19. Which bare him *children;*
21. begat twenty and eight *sons,*
22. Abijah *the son of* Maachah
23. dispersed of all *his children* throughout
12:13. Rehoboam (was) one and forty years *old*
16. Abijah *his son* reigned in his stead.
13: 5. to him *and to his sons* by a covenant
6. Yet Jeroboam *the son of* Nebat, the servant of Solomon *the son of* David,
7. *the children of* Belial,
— against Rehoboam *the son of* Solomon,
8. in the hand of *the sons of* David;
9, 10. *the sons of* Aaron, and the Levites,
— to consecrate himself with *a young* bullock (lit. a steer *the son of* a bull)
12. *O children of* Israel, fight ye not
16. And *the children of* Israel fled before
18. *the children of* Israel were brought
— *the children of* Judah prevailed,
21. begat twenty and two *sons,*
14: 1(13:23). Asa *his son* reigned in his stead.
15: 1. Azariah *the son of* Oded:
17: 1. Jehoshaphat *his son* reigned in his stead,
16. Amasiah *the son of* Zichri,
18: 7, 8. Micaiah *the son of* Imla.
10, 23. Zedekiah *the son of* Chenaanah
25. to Joash the king's *son;*
19: 2. Jehu *the son of* Hanani
11. Zebadiah *the son of* Ishmael,
20: 1. *the children of* Moab, *and the children of* Ammon,
10, 23. *the children of* Ammon and Moab
13. their wives, *and their children.*
14. Jahaziel *the son of* Zechariah, *the son of* Benaiah, *the son of* Jeiel, *the son of* Mattaniah, a Levite of *the sons of* Asaph,
19. *the children of* the Kohathites, and of *the children of* the Korhites,
22. against *the children of* Ammon,
31. thirty and five years *old*
34. Jehu *the son of* Hanani,
37. Then Eliezer *the son of* Dodavah
21: 1. Jehoram *his son* reigned in his stead.
2, 2. *the sons of* Jehoshaphat,
5. Jehoram (was) thirty and two years *old*
7. to give a light to him *and to his sons*
14. smite thy people, *and thy children,*
17. and *his sons* also,...so that there was never *a son* left him, save Jehoahaz, the youngest of *his sons.*
20. Thirty and two years *old* was he
22: 1. Ahaziah *his* youngest *son*
— Ahaziah *the son of* Jehoram king of Judah reigned.
2. Forty and two years *old* (was) Ahaziah
5. went with Jehoram *the son of* Ahab
6. Azariah *the son of* Jehoram king of Judah went down to see Jehoram *the son of* Ahab
7. against Jehu *the son of* Nimshi,
8. *and the sons of* the brethren
9. he (is) *the son of* Jehoshaphat,
10. saw that *her son* was dead,
11. took Joash *the son of* Ahaziah, and stole him from among the king's *sons*
23: 1. Azariah *the son of* Jeroham, and Ishmael *the son of* Jehohanan, and Azariah *the son of* Obed, and Maaseiah *the son of* Adaiah, and Elishaphat *the son of* Zichri,
3. Behold, the king's *son* shall reign, as the Lord hath said of *the sons of* David.
11. they brought out the king's *son,*
— Jehoiada *and his sons* anointed him,
24: 1. Joash (was) seven years *old* when he began
3. he begat *sons* and daughters.
7. For *the sons* of Athaliah, (lit. for Athaliah *her sons*)
15. an hundred and thirty years *old*
20. Zechariah *the son of* Jehoiada

2Ch 24:22. had done to him, but slew *his son.*
25. for the blood of *the sons of* Jehoiada
26. Zabad *the son of* Shimeath an Ammonitess, and Jehozabad *the son of* Shimrith
27. *Now* (concerning) *his sons,* and the greatness
— Amaziah *his son* reigned in his stead.
25: 1. Amaziah (was) twenty and five years *old*
4. But he slew not *their children,*
— The fathers shall not die for *the children, neither* shall *the children* die
5. *from* twenty years *old* and above,
7. all *the children of* Ephraim.
11. smote of *the children of* Seir
12. did *the children of* Judah carry
13. *But the soldiers of* the army (marg. *the sons of* the band)
14. the gods of *the children of* Seir,
17. Joash, *the son of* Jehoahaz, *the son of* Jehu,
18. Give thy daughter *to my son* to wife:
23. *the son of* Joash, *the son of* Jehoahaz,
24. the hostages also, (lit. *children of* pledges)
25. Amaziah *the son of* Joash
— death of Joash *son of* Jehoahaz
26: 1. Uzziah, who (was) sixteen years *old,*
3. Sixteen years *old* (was) Uzziah when he began
17. (that were) valiant *men:*
18. the priests *the sons of* Aaron,
21. Jotham *his son* (was) over the king's house,
22. Isaiah the prophet, *the son of* Amoz,
23. Jotham *his son* reigned in his stead.
27: 1. Jotham (was) twenty and five years *old*
5. the king of *the Ammonites,* (lit. *children of* Ammon)
— *the children of* Ammon gave
— So much did *the children of*
8. He was five and twenty years *old*
9. Ahaz *his son* reigned in his stead.
28: 1. Ahaz (was) twenty years *old* when he began
3. the valley of *the son of* Hinnom, and burnt *his children* in the fire,
— cast out before *the children of* Israel.
6. Pekah *the son of* Remaliah
— all valiant *men;* (marg. *sons of* valour)
7. slew Maaseiah the king's *son,*
8. *the children of* Israel carried away
— women, *sons,* and daughters,
10. keep under *the children of* Judah
12. *the children of* Ephraim, Azariah *the son of* Johanan, Berechiah *the son of* Meshillemoth, and Jehizkiah *the son of* Shallum, and Amasa *the son of* Hadlai, stood up
27. Hezekiah *his son* reigned in his stead.
29: 1. five and twenty years *old,*
9. *and our sons* and our daughters
11. *My sons,* be not now negligent:
12. Mahath *the son of* Amasai, and Joel *the son of* Azariah, of *the sons of* the Kohathites: and of *the sons of* Merari, Kish *the son of* Abdi, and Azariah *the son of* Jehalelel: and of the Gershonites; Joah *the son of* Zimmah, and Eden *the son of* Joah:
13. *the sons of* Elizaphan; Shimri, and Jeiel: and of *the sons of* Asaph;
14. *the sons of* Heman;
— *the sons of* Jeduthun;
21. commanded the priests *the sons of*
30: 6. Ye *children of* Israel, turn again
9. your brethren *and your children*
21. *the children of* Israel that were present
26. Solomon *the son of* David
31: 1. Then all *the children of* Israel returned,
5. *the children of* Israel brought in
6. *And* (concerning) *the children of* Israel
14. Kore *the son of* Imnah
16. *from* three years *old* and upward,
17. *from* twenty years *old* and upward,
18. their wives, *and their sons,*
19. *Also of the sons of* Aaron
32:20. the prophet Isaiah *the son of* Amoz,
32. Isaiah the prophet, *the son of* Amoz,
33. the sepulchres of *the sons of* David:
— Manasseh *his son* reigned in his stead.

2Ch 33: 1. Manasseh (was) twelve years *old*
2. the Lord had cast out before *the children of*
6. caused *his children* to pass through the fire in the valley of *the son of* Hinnom:
7. to David and to Solomon *his son,*
9. had destroyed before *the children of*
20. Amon *his son* reigned in his stead.
21. Amon (was) two and twenty years *old*
25. made Josiah *his son* king in his stead.
34: 1. Josiah (was) eight years *old*
8. Shaphan *the son of* Azaliah,
— Joah *the son of* Joahaz
12. of *the sons of* Merari; and Zechariah and Meshullam, of *the sons of* the
20. Ahikam *the son of* Shaphan, and Abdon *the son of* Micah,
22. the wife of Shallum *the son of* Tikvath, *the son of* Hasrah,
33. that (pertained) *to the children of* Israel,
35: 3. which Solomon *the son of* David
4. to the writing of Solomon *his son.*
5. your brethren the people, (marg. *sons of* the people)
7. Josiah gave to the people (lit. *to the sons of* the people), of the flock, lambs and kids, (lit. *and sons of* goats)
12. divisions of the families of the people, (lit. *of the sons of* the people)
13. speedily among all the people. (lit. *sons of* the people)
14. because the priests *the sons of* Aaron
— for the priests *the sons of* Aaron.
15. the singers *the sons of* Asaph
17. And *the children of* Israel that
36: 1. took Jehoahaz *the son of* Josiah,
2. Jehoahaz (was) twenty and three years *old*
5. Jehoiakim (was) twenty and five years *old*
8. Jehoiachin *his son* reigned in his stead.
9. Jehoiachin (was) eight years *old*
11. Zedekiah (was) one and twenty years *old*
20. they were servants to him *and his sons*
Ezr. 2: 1. these (are) *the children of* the province
3. *The children of* Parosh,
4. *The children of* Shephatiah,
5. *The children of* Arah,
6. *The children of* Pahath-moab, *of the children of* Jeshua (and) Joab,
7. *The children of* Elam,
8. *The children of* Zattu,
9. *The children of* Zaccai,
10. *The children of* Bani,
11. *The children of* Bebai,
12. *The children of* Azgad,
13. *The children of* Adonikam,
14. *The children of* Bigvai,
15. *The children of* Adin,
16. *The children of* Ater
17. *The children of* Bezai,
18. *The children of* Jorah,
19. *The children of* Hashum,
20. *The children of* Gibbar,
21. *The children of* Beth-lehem,
24. *The children of* Azmaveth,
25. *The children of* Kirjath-arim,
26. *The children of* Ramah
29. *The children of* Nebo,
30. *The children of* Magbish,
31. *The children of* the other Elam,
32. *The children of* Harim,
33. *The children of* Lod,
34. *The children of* Jericho,
35. *The children of* Senaah,
36. The priests: *the children of* Jedaiah,
37. *The children of* Immer,
38. *The children of* Pashur,
39. *The children of* Harim,
40. *the children of* Jeshua and Kadmiel, *of the children of* Hodaviah,
41. The singers: *the children of* Asaph,
42. *The children of* the porters: *the children of* Shallum, *the children of* Ater, *the children of* Talmon, *the children of* Akkub, *the children of* Hatita, *the children of* Shobai,
43. *the children of* Ziha, *the children of* Hasupha, *the children of* Tabbaoth,

Ezr. 2:44. *The children of* Keros, *the children of* Siaha, *the children of* Padon,
45. *The children of* Lebanah, *the children of* Hagabah, *the children of* Akkub,
46. *The children of* Hagab, *the children of* Shalmai, *the children of* Hanan,
47. *The children of* Giddel, *the children of* Gahar, *the children of* Reaiah,
48. *The children of* Rezin, *the children of* Nekoda, *the children of* Gazzam,
49. *The children of* Uzza, *the children of* Paseah, *the children of* Besai,
50. *The children of* Asnah, *the children of* Mehunim, *the children of* Nephusim,
51. *The children of* Bakbuk, *the children of* Hakupha, *the children of* Harhur,
52. *The children of* Bazluth, *the children of* Mehida, *the children of* Harsha,
53. *The children of* Barkos, *the children of* Sisera, *the children of* Thamah,
54. *The children of* Neziah, *the children of*
55. *The children of* Solomon's servants: *the children of* Sotai, *the children of* Sophereth, *the children of* Peruda,
56. *The children of* Jaalah, *the children of* Darkon, *the children of* Giddel,
57. *The children of* Shephatiah, *the children of* Hattil, *the children of* Pochereth of Zebaim, *the children of* Ami.
58. *and the children of* Solomon's servants,
60. *The children of* Delaiah, *the children of* Tobiah, *the children of* Nekoda,
61. *And of the children of* the priests: *the children of* Habaiah, *the children of* Koz, *the children of* Barzillai;
3: 1. *and the children of* Israel (were) in the
2, 8. Jeshua *the son of* Jozadak,
—, 8. Zerubbabel *the son of* Shealtiel,
8. *from* twenty years *old* and upward,
9. Jeshua (with) *his sons* and his brethren, Kadmiel *and his sons, the sons of* Judah,
— *the sons of* Henadad, (with) *their sons* and
10. the Levites *the sons of* Asaph
4: 1. heard that *the children of* the captivity (marg. *sons of* the transportation)
6:19, 20. *the children of* the captivity
21. And *the children of* Israel, which were
7: 1. Ezra *the son of* Seraiah, *the son of* Azariah, *the son of* Hilkiah,
2. *The son of* Shallum, *the son of* Zadok, *the son of* Ahitub,
3. *The son of* Amariah, *the son of* Azariah, *the son of* Meraioth,
4. *The son of* Zerahiah, *the son of* Uzzi, *the son of* Bukki,
5. *The son of* Abishua, *the son of* Phinehas, *the son of* Eleazar, *the son of* Aaron
7. (some) *of the children of* Israel,
8: 2. *Of the sons of* Phinehas; Gershom: *of the sons of* Ithamar; Daniel: *of the sons of* David; Hattush.
3. *Of the sons of* Shechaniah, *of the sons of*
4. *Of the sons of* Pahath-Moab; Elihoenai *the son of* Zerahiah,
5. *Of the sons of* Shechaniah; *the son of* Jahaziel,
6. *Of the sons also of* Adin; Ebed *the son of* Jonathan,
7. *And of the sons of* Elam; Jeshaiah *the son of* Athaliah,
8. *And of the sons of* Shephatiah; Zebadiah *the son of* Michael,
9. *Of the sons of* Joab; Obadiah *the son of* Jehiel,
10. *And of the sons of* Shelomith; *the son of*
11. *And of the sons of* Bebai; Zechariah *the son of* Bebai,
12. *And of the sons of* Azgad; Johanan *the son of* Hakkatan,
13. *And of the* last *sons of* Adonikam,
14. *Of the sons also of* Bigvai;
15. *and* found there none *of the sons of* Levi.
18. *of the sons of* Mahli, *the son of* Levi, *the son of* Israel; and Sherebiah, *with his sons*
19. Jeshaiah *of the sons of* Merari, his brethren *and their sons,*

Ezr. 8:33. Meremoth *the son of* Uriah the priest. and with him (was) Eleazar *the son of* Phinehas; and with them (was) Jozabad *the son of* Jeshua, and Noadiah *the son of*
35. *the children of* those that had been
9: 2. for themselves, *and for their sons:*
12. your daughters *unto their sons,* neither take their daughters *unto your sons,*
— inheritance *to your children* for ever.
10: 2. Shechaniah *the son of* Jehiel, (one) *of the sons of* Elam,
6. Johanan *the son of* Eliashib:
7. unto all *the children of* the captivity,
15. Only Jonathan *the son of* Asahel and Jahaziah *the son of* Tikvah
16. *the children of* the captivity did so.
18. *among the sons of* the priests
— *of the sons of* Jeshua *the son of* Jozadak,
20. *And of the sons of* Immer;
21. *And of the sons of* Harim;
22. *And of the sons of* Pashur;
25. *of the sons of* Parosh;
26. *And of the sons of* Elam;
27. *And of the sons of* Zattu;
28. *Of the sons also of* Bebai;
29. *And of the sons of* Bani;
30. *And of the sons of* Pahath-moab;
31. *And* (of) *the sons of* Harim;
33. *Of the sons of* Hashum;
34. *Of the sons of* Bani;
43. *Of the sons of* Nebo;
44. by whom they had *children.*
Neh 1: 1. Nehemiah *the son of* Hachaliah.
6. for *the children of* Israel thy servants, and confess the sins of *the children of* Israel,
2:10. seek the welfare *of the children of* Israel.
3: 2. builded Zaccur *the son of* Imri.
3. did *the sons of* Hassenaah build,
4, 21. Meremoth *the son of* Urijah, *the son of* Koz.
— Meshullam *the son of* Berechiah, *the son of* Meshezabeel. And next unto them repaired Zadok *the son of* Baana.
6. Jehoiada *the son of* Paseah, and Meshullam *the son of*
8. Uzziel *the son of* Harhaiah,
— Hananiah *the son of* (one of) the
9. Rephaiah *the son of* Hur,
10. Jedaiah *the son of* Harumaph,
— Hattush *the son of* Hashabniah.
11. Malchijah *the son of* Harim, and Hashub *the son of* Pahath-moab,
12. Shallum *the son of* Halohesh,
14. Malchiah *the son of* Rechab,
15. Shallun *the son of* Col-hozeh,
16. Nehemiah *the son of* Azbuk,
17. Rehum *the son of* Bani.
18. Bavai *the son of* Henadad,
19. Ezer *the son of* Jeshua,
20. Baruch *the son of* Zabbai
23. Azariah *the son of* Maaseiah *the son of* Ananiah
24. Binnui *the son of* Henadad
25. Palal *the son of* Uzai,
— Pedaiah *the son of* Parosh.
29. Zadok *the son of* Immer
— Shemaiah *the son of* Shechaniah,
30. Hananiah *the son of* Shelemiah, and Hanun *the* sixth *son of* Zalaph,
— Meshullam *the son of* Berechiah
31. Malchiah the goldsmith's *son*
4:14(8). *your sons,* and your daughters,
5: 2. We, *our sons,* and our daughters,
5. *our children as their children:* and, lo, we bring into bondage *our sons*
6:10. Shemaiah *the son of* Delaiah *the son of* Mehetabeel,
18. Shechaniah *the son of* Arah; and *his son* Johanan had taken the daughter of Meshullam *the son of* Berechiah.
7: 6. These (are) *the children of* the province,
8. *The children of* Parosh,
9. *The children of* Shephatiah,
10. *The children of* Arah,
11. *The children of* Pahath-moab, *of the children of* Jeshua and Joab,
12. *The children of* Elam,

Neh 7:13. *The children of* Zattu,
14. *The children of* Zaccai,
15. *The children of* Binnui,
16. *The children of* Bebai,
17. *The children of* Azgad,
18. *The children of* Adonikam,
19. *The children of* Bigvai,
20. *The children of* Adin,
21. *The children of* Ater
22. *The children of* Hashum,
23. *The children of* Bezai,
24. *The children of* Hariph,
25. *The children of* Gibeon,
34. *The children of* the other Elam,
35,42. *The children of* Harim,
36. *The children of* Jericho,
37. *The children of* Lod,
38. *The children of* Senaah,
39. *the children of* Jedaiah,
40. *The children of* Immer,
41. *The children of* Pashur,
43. *the children of* Jeshua, of Kadmiel, (and) *of the children of* Hodevah,
44. *the children of* Asaph,
45. *the children of* Shallum, *the children of* Ater, *the children of* Talmon, *the children of* Akkub, *the children of* Hatita, *the children of* Shobai,
46. *the children of* Ziha, *the children of* Hashupha, *the children of* Tabbaoth,
47. *The children of* Keros, *the children of* Sia, *the children of* Padon,
48. *The children of* Lebana, *the children of* Hagaba, *the children of* Shalmai,
49. *The children of* Hanan, *the children of* Giddel, *the children of* Gahar,
50. *The children of* Reaiah, *the children of* Rezin, *the children of* Nekoda,
51. *The children of* Gazzam, *the children of* Uzza, *the children of* Phaseah,
52. *The children of* Besai, *the children of* Meunim, *the children of* Nephishesim,
53. *The children of* Bakbuk, *the children of* Hakupha, *the children of* Harhur,
54. *The children of* Bazlith, *the children of* Mehida, *the children of* Harsha,
55. *The children of* Barkos, *the children of* Sisera, *the children of* Tamah,
56. *The children of* Neziah, *the children of*
57. *The children of* Solomon's servants: *the children of* Sotai, *the children of* Sophereth, *the children of* Perida,
58. *The children of* Jaala, *the children of* Darkon, *the children of* Giddel,
59. *The children of* Shephatiah, *the children of* Hattil, *the children of* Pochereth of Zebaim, *the children of* Amon.
60. *and the children of* Solomon's servants,
62. *The children of* Delaiah, *the children of* Tobiah, *the children of* Nekoda,
63. *the children of* Habaiah, *the children of* Koz, *the children of* Barzillai,
73. *the children of* Israel (were) in their
8. 14. *the children of* Israel should dwell in
17. Jeshua *the son of* Nun unto that day had not *the children of* Israel done so.
9: 1. *the children of* Israel were assembled
2. separated themselves from all strangers, (lit. *children of* the stranger; marg. strange *children*)
23. *Their children also* multipliedst thou
24. *the children* went in and possessed the
10: 1 (2). *the son of* Hachaliah, and Zidkijah,
9(10). both Jeshua *the son of* Azaniah, Binnui *of the sons of* Henadad,
28(29). *their sons*, and their daughters,
30(31). take their daughters *for our sons:*
36(37). Also the firstborn *of our sons*,
38(39). the priest *the son of* Aaron
39(40). *the children of* Israel *and the children of* Levi
11: 3. *and the children of* Solomon's servants.
4. *of the children of* Judah, *and of the children of* Benjamin. *Of the children of* Judah; Athaiah *the son of* Uzziah, *the son of* Zechariah, *the son of* Amariah, *the son of* Shephatiah, *the son of* Mahalaleel, *of the children of* Perez;

Neh 11: 5. *the son of* Baruch, *the son of* Col-hozeh, *the son of* Hazaiah, *the son of* Adaiah, *the son of* Joiarib, *the son of* Zechariah, *the son of* Shiloni.
6. All *the sons of* Perez
7. these (are) *the sons of* Benjamin; Sallu *the son of* Meshullam, *the son of* Joed, *the son of* Pedaiah, *the son of* Kolaiah, *the son of* Maaseiah, *the son of* Ithiel, *the son of* Jesaiah.
9. Joel *the son of* Zichri (was) their overseer: and Judah *the son of* Senuah
10. Jedaiah *the son of* Joiarib,
11. Seraiah *the son of* Hilkiah, *the son of* Meshullam, *the son of* Zadok, *the son of* Meraioth, *the son of* Ahitub,
12. *the son of* Jeroham, *the son of* Pelaliah, *the son of* Amzi, *the son of* Zechariah, *the son of* Pashur, *the son of* Malchiah,
13. *the son of* Azareel, *the son of* Ahasai, *the son of* Meshillemoth, *the son of* Immer,
14. *the son of* (one of) the great men.
15. *the son of* Hashub, *the son of* Azrikam, *the son of* Hashabiah, *the son of* Bunni;
17. *the son of* Micha, *the son of* Zabdi, *the son of* Asaph,
— *the son of* Shammua, *the son of* Galal, *the son of* Jeduthun.
22. *the son of* Bani, *the son of* Hashabiah, *the son of* Mattaniah, *the son of* Micha. *Of the sons of* Asaph,
24. Pethahiah *the son of* Meshezabeel, *of the children of* Zerah *the son of* Judah,
25. *of the children of* Judah
31. *The children also of* Benjamin
12: 1. Zerubbabel *the son of* Shealtiel,
23. *The sons of* Levi,
— Johanan *the son of* Eliashib.
24. Jeshua *the son of* Kadmiel,
26. Joiakim *the son of* Jeshua, *the son of* Jozadak,
28. *the sons of* the singers
35. *And* (certain) *of the* priests' *sons* with trumpets; (namely), Zechariah *the son of* Jonathan, *the son of* Shemaiah, *the son of* Mattaniah, *the son of* Michaiah, *the son of* Zaccur, *the son of* Asaph:
45. of David, (and) of Solomon *his son.*
47. *unto the children of* Aaron.
13: 2. they met not *the children of* Israel
13. Hanan *the son of* Zaccur, *the son of* Mattaniah:
16. *unto the children of* Judah,
24. *And their children* spake half in the speech
25. give your daughters *unto their sons*, nor take their daughters *unto your sons*,
28. *And* (one) *of the sons of* Joiada, *the son of* Eliashib
Est. 2: 5. Mordecai, *the son of* Jair, *the son of* Shimei, *the son of* Kish,
3: 1, 10. Haman *the son of* Hammedatha
5: 11. and the multitude of *his children*,
8: 5. Haman *the son of* Hammedatha
10. camels, (and) *young* dromedaries: (lit. *sons of*)
9: 10, 12. *The* ten *sons of* Haman
—, 24. Haman *the son of* Hammedatha,
13. let Haman's ten *sons* be hanged
14. they hanged Haman's ten *sons*.
25. that he and *his sons* should be hanged
Job. 1: 2. seven *sons* and three daughters.
3. greatest of all *the men of* the east. (marg. *sons*)
4. And *his sons* went and feasted
5. It may be that *my sons* have sinned,
6. when *the sons of* God came
13. *when his sons* and his daughters (were)
18. *Thy sons* and thy daughters (were) eating
2: 1. a day when *the sons of* God came
4: 11. *and* the stout lion's *whelps*
5: 4. *His children* are far from safety,
7. *as* the sparks fly upward. (marg. *the sons of* the burning coal)
8: 4. If *thy children* have sinned against him,
14: 21. *His sons* come to honour,
16: 21. as a man (pleadeth) for his neighbour! (lit. *and a son of* man)
17: 5. even the eyes of *his children* shall fail.

Job. 19:17. I intreated *for the children's* (sake)
20:10. *His children* shall seek to please the poor,
21:19. God layeth up his iniquity *for his children:*
25: 6. *and the son of* man, (which is) a worm?
27:14. If *his children* be multiplied,
28: 8. The lion's *whelps* have not trodden it,
30: 8. (They were) *children of* fools, yea, *children of* base men:
32: 2, 6. Elihu *the son of* Barachel
35: 8. *and* thy righteousness (may profit) *the son of* man.
38: 7. all *the sons of* God shouted for joy?
32. canst thou guide Arcturus with *his sons?*
39: 4. *Their young ones* are in good liking,
16. She is hardened against *her young ones,*
41:28(20). The arrow (lit. *the son of* a bow) cannot make him flee:
34(26). a king over all *the children of* pride.
42:13. seven *sons* and three daughters.
16. saw *his sons,* and *his sons' sons,*
Ps. 2: 7. Thou (art) *my Son;* this day
3: [title](1). when he fled from Absalom *his son.*
4: 2(3). *O ye sons of* men, how long
7: [title](1). the words of Cush the *Ben*jamite. (lit. *son of* Jemini)
8: 4(5). *and the son of* man, that thou
9: [title](1). chief Musician upon Muth-*labben,*
11: 4. his eyelids try, *the children of* men.
12: 1(2). *from among the children of* men.
8(9). when the vilest men are exalted. (marg. vilest *of the sons of* men)
14: 2. upon *the children of* men, to see
17:14. they are full of *children,*
18:44(45). the strangers shall submit themselves (lit. *children of* the stranger)
45(46). The strangers shall fade away, (lit. *children of* the stranger)
21:10(11). *from among the children of* men.
29: 1. Give unto the Lord, *O ye* mighty, (marg. *sons of* the mighty)
6. Lebanon and Sirion like a *young* unicorn. (lit. *the son of* the unicorns)
31:19(20). before *the sons of* men!
33:13. beholdeth all *the sons of* men.
34:11(12). Come, *ye children,* hearken unto me:
36: 7(8). *therefore the children of* men
42 & 44 & 45: [title] (1). *for the sons of* Korah.
45: 2(3). fairer *than the children of* men:
16(17). of thy fathers shall be *thy children,*
46 & 47 & 48 & 49: [title](1). *for the sons of* Korah, (marg. or, *of the sons of*)
49: 2(3). Both low and high, (lit. *sons of* אָדָם —*sons of* אִישׁ)
50:20. slanderest thine own mother's *son.*
53: 2(3). upon *the children of* men,
57: 4(5). *the sons of* men, whose teeth (are) spears and arrows,
58: 1(2). *O ye sons of* men?
62: 9(10). Surely *men of* low degree (lit. *sons of* אָדָם) (are) vanity, (and) *men of* high degree (lit. *sons of* אִישׁ) (are) a lie:
66: 5. (in his) doing toward *the children of* men.
69: 8(9). an alien *unto* my mother's *children.*
72: 1. thy righteousness *unto* the king's *son.*
4. he shall save *the children of*
20. The prayers of David *the son of*
73:15. (against) the generation of *thy children.*
77:15(16). *the sons of* Jacob and Joseph.
78: 4. will not hide (them) *from their children,*
5. make them known *to their children:*
6. *the children* (which) should be born;
— declare (them) *to their children:*
9. *The children of* Ephraim,
79:11. *those that are appointed to* die; (marg. *the children of* death)
80:15(16). *the branch* (that) thou madest
17(18). upon *the son of* man
82: 6. *and* all of you (are) *children of* the most high.
83: 8(9). have holpen *the children of* Lot.
84 & 85: [title](1). A Psalm *for the sons of* Korah (marg. or, *of the sons of*)
86: 16. save *the son of* thine handmaid.
87 & 88: [title](1). *for the sons of* Korah. (marg. or, *of the sons of*)

Ps. 89: 6(7). *among the sons of* the mighty
22(23). *nor the son of* wickedness
30(31). If *his children* forsake my law,
47(48). wherefore hast thou made all *men* (lit. *sons of* Adam) in vain?
90: 3. Return, *ye children of* men.
16. thy glory unto *their children.*
102:20(21). *those that are appointed to* death; (marg. *the children of* death)
28(29). *The children of* thy servants
103: 7. his acts *unto the children of* Israel.
13. as a father pitieth (his) *children,*
17. his righteousness *unto children's children,*
105: 6. *ye children of* Jacob his chosen.
106:37. they sacrificed *their sons*
38. the blood of *their sons*
107: 8, 15, 21, 31. wonderful works *to the children of* men!
109: 9. Let *his children* be fatherless,
10. Let *his children* be continually vagabonds,
113: 9. a joyful mother of *children.*
114: 4, 6. little hills *like* lambs. (lit. *like the sons of* sheep)
115:14. you and *your children.*
16. hath he given *to the children of* men.
116:16. *the son of* thine handmaid:
127: 3. *children* (are) an heritage of the Lord:
4. *children of* the youth.
128: 3. *thy children* like olive plants round
6. thou shalt see *thy children's children,*
132:12. If *thy children* will keep my covenant
— *their children* shall also sit
137: 7. *the children of* Edom
144: 3. *the son of* man, that thou makest
7, 11. from the hand of strange *children;*
12. That *our sons* (may be) as plants grown
145:12. To make known *to the sons of* men
146: 3. *in the son of* man, in whom
147: 9. *to the young* ravens which cry.
13. he hath blessed *thy children* within thee.
148:14. (even) *of the children of* Israel, a people
149: 2. let *the children of* Zion be joyful
Pro. 1: 1. Solomon *the son of* David,
8. *My son,* hear the instruction of thy father,
10. *My son,* if sinners entice thee,
15. *My son,* walk not thou in the way
2: 1. *My son,* if thou wilt receive
3: 1. *My son,* forget not my law;
11. *My son,* despise not the chastening
12. even as a father *the son*
21. *My son,* let not them depart
4: 1. Hear, ye *children,* the instruction
3. For I was my father's *son,*
10. Hear, *O my son,* and receive my sayings;
20. *My son,* attend to my words;
5: 1. *My son,* attend unto my wisdom,
7. Hear me now therefore, *O ye children,*
20. And why wilt thou, *my son,* be ravished
6: 1. *My son,* if thou be surety
3. Do this now, *my son,* and deliver
20. *My son,* keep thy father's commandment,
7: 1. *My son,* keep my words,
7. I discerned *among the youths,* (marg. *sons*)
24. unto me now therefore, *O ye children,*
8: 4. my voice (is) to *the sons of* man.
31. my delights (were) with *the sons of*
32. hearken unto me, *O ye children:*
10: 1. *A* wise *son* maketh a glad father: *but a* foolish *son* (is) the heaviness
5. gathereth in summer (is) *a* wise *son:*
— *a son* that causeth shame.
13: 1. *A* wise *son* (heareth) his father's instruction:
22. inheritance to *his children's children:*
24. He that spareth his rod hateth *his son:*
14:26. *and his children* shall have a place
15:11. the hearts of *the children of* men?
20. *A* wise *son* maketh a glad father:
17: 2. shall have rule *over a son*
6. *Children's children* (are) the crown of old men; and the glory of *children*
25. *A* foolish *son* (is) a grief to his father,
19:13. *A* foolish *son* (is) the calamity of
18. Chasten *thy son* while there is hope,
26. *a son* that causeth shame,
27. Cease, *my son,* to hear the instruction
20: 7. *his children* (are) blessed after him.

Pro.23:15. *My son*, if thine heart be wise,
19. Hear thou, *my son*, and be wise,
26. *My son*, give me thine heart,
24:13. *My son*, eat thou honey,
21. *My son*, fear thou the Lord
27:11. *My son*, be wise, and make my heart
28: 7. Whoso keepeth the law (is) *a* wise *son* :
29:17. Correct *thy son*, and he shall give thee rest;
30: 1. The words of Agur *the son of* Jakeh,
4. what (is) *his son*'s name,
17. the *young* eagles shall eat it.
31: 5. the judgment of any of the afflicted. (marg. all *the sons of* affliction)
8. all *such as are appointed to* destruction. (marg. *the sons of* destruction)
28. *Her children* arise up,
Ecc. 1: 1. the Preacher, *the son of* David,
13. hath God given *to the sons of* man
2: 3. that good *for the sons of* men,
7. *and* had *servants born in* my house; (marg. *and sons of* my house)
8. the delights of *the sons of* men,
3:10. God hath given *to the sons of* men
18. concerning the estate of *the sons of* men,
19. befalleth *the sons of* men
21. Who knoweth the spirit of man (marg. of *the sons of* man)
4: 8. he hath neither *child* nor brother:
5:14(13). he begetteth *a son*,
8:11 & 9:3. the heart of *the sons of* men
9:12. so (are) *the sons of* men
10:17. when thy king (is) *the son of* nobles,
12:12. And further, by these, *my son*,
Cant.1: 6. my mother's *children* were angry
2: 3. so (is) my beloved among *the sons*.
Isa. 1: 1. The vision of Isaiah *the son of* Amoz,
2. I have nourished and brought up *children*,
4. *children* that are corrupters:
2: 1. Isaiah *the son of* Amoz
5: 1. hath a vineyard in a very fruitful hill: (marg. the horn of *the son of* oil)
7: 1. Ahaz *the son of* Jotham, *the son of* Uzziah,
— Pekah *the son of* Remaliah,
3. and Shear-jashub *thy son*,
4. *and of the son of* Remaliah.
5. *and the son of* Remaliah,
6. *the son of* Tabeal:
9. the head of Samaria (is) Remaliah'*s son*.
14. and bear *a son*,
8: 2. Zechariah *the son of* Jeberechiah.
3. and bare *a son*.
6. rejoice in Rezin *and* Remaliah'*s son*;
9: 6(5). unto us *a son* is given:
11:14. shall spoil *them of* the east (marg. *the children of* the east)
— *and the children of* Ammon shall obey
13: 1. Isaiah *the son of* Amoz did see.
18. their eye shall not spare *children*.
14:12. O Lucifer, *son of* the morning!
21. Prepare slaughter *for his children*
17: 3. as the glory of *the children of* Israel,
9. because of *the children of* Israel:
19:11. I (am) *the son of* the wise, *the son of* ancient kings?
20: 2. by Isaiah *the son of* Amoz,
21:10. *and the corn of* my floor: (marg. *& the son of*)
17. the mighty men of *the children of* Kedar,
22:20. Eliakim *the son of* Hilkiah:
27:12. one by one, *O ye children of* Israel.
30: 1. Woe to the rebellious *children*,
9. a rebellious people, lying *children*, *children* (that) will not hear
31: 6. *the children of* Israel have deeply revolted.
36: 3. Eliakim, Hilkiah'*s son*,
— and Joah, Asaph'*s son*, the recorder.
22. Then came Eliakim, *the son of* Hilkiah,
— and Joah, *the son of* Asaph, the recorder,
37: 2. Isaiah the prophet *the son of* Amoz.
3. for *the children* are come
12. *and the children of* Eden
21. Then Isaiah *the son of* Amoz
38. Adrammelech and Sharezer *his sons* smote him
— Esar-haddon *his son* reigned in his
38: 1. Isaiah the prophet *the son of* Amoz
19. *to the children* shall make known
Isa. 39: 1. Merodach-baladan, *the son of* Baladan,
7. *And of thy sons* that shall issue from thee,
43: 6. bring *my sons* from far,
45:11. things to come concerning *my sons*,
49:15. compassion on *the son of* her womb?
17. *Thy children* shall make haste;
20. *The children which* thou shalt have,
22. they shall bring *thy sons* in (their) arms,
25. and I will save *thy children*.
51:12. *and of the son of* man (which) shall be
18. none to guide her among all *the sons*
— all *the sons* (that) she hath brought up.
20. *Thy sons* have fainted,
52:14. *more than the sons of* men:
54: 1. more (are) *the children of* the desolate *than the children of* the married
13. all *thy children* (shall be) taught of the Lord; and great (shall be) the peace of *thy children*.
56: 2. *and the son of* man (that) layeth hold
3. Neither let *the son of* the stranger,
5. a name better *than of sons*
6. *Also the sons of* the stranger,
57: 3. *ye sons of* the sorceress,
60: 4. *thy sons* shall come from far,
9. to bring *thy sons* from far,
10. *the sons of* strangers shall build
14. *The sons* also *of* them that afflicted thee
61: 5. *and the sons of* the alien
62: 5. marrieth a virgin, (so) shall *thy sons* marry thee:
8. and *the sons of* the stranger
63: 8. *children* (that) will not lie:
65:20. the child shall die an hundred years *old*; but the sinner (being) an hundred years *old*
66: 8. she brought forth *her children*.
20. as *the children of* Israel bring
Jer. 1: 1. Jeremiah *the son of* Hilkiah,
2. Josiah *the son of* Amon
3. Jehoiakim *the son of* Josiah
— Zedekiah *the son of* Josiah
2: 9. with *your children's children*
16. Also *the children of* Noph
30. In vain have I smitten *your children*;
3:14. Turn, O backsliding *children*,
19. shall I put thee *among the children*,
21. supplications of *the children of* Israel:
22. Return, ye backsliding *children*,
24. *their sons* and their daughters.
4:22. they (are) sottish *children*,
5: 7. *thy children* have forsaken me,
17. *thy sons* and thy daughters should eat:
6: 1. *O ye children of* Benjamin,
21. the fathers *and the sons* together
7:18. *The children* gather wood,
30. *the children of* Judah
31. the valley of *the son of* Hinnom, to burn *their sons* and their daughters
32. nor the valley of *the son of* Hinnom,
9:26(25). and *the children of* Ammon,
10:20. *my children* are gone forth of me,
11:22. *their sons* and their daughters
13:14. the fathers *and the sons* together,
14:16. *nor their sons*, nor their daughters:
15: 4. Manasseh *the son of* Hezekiah
16: 2. neither shalt thou have *sons* or daughters
3. saith the Lord concerning *the sons*
14,15. that brought up *the children of* Israel
17: 2. Whilst *their children* remember their altars
19. the gate of *the children of* the people,
18:21. deliver up *their children* to the famine
19: 2,6. the valley of *the son of* Hinnom,
5. to burn *their sons* with fire
9. to eat the flesh of *their sons*
20: 1. Pashur *the son of* Immer
15. *A* man *child* is born unto thee:
21: 1. Pashur *the son of* Melchiah, and Zephaniah *the son of* Maaseiah
22:11. Shallum *the son of* Josiah
18. Jehoiakim *the son of* Josiah
24. Coniah *the son of* Jehoiakim
23: 7. which brought up *the children of* Israel
24: 1. Jeconiah *the son of* Jehoiakim
25: 1. Jehoiakim *the son of* Josiah
3. Josiah *the son of* Amon king of Judah,
21. and *the children of* Ammon,

Jer. 26: 1. the reign of Jehoiakim *the son of* Josiah
20. Urijah *the son of* Shemaiah
22. Elnathan *the son of* Achbor,
23. the graves of the *common* people. (marg. *sons of* the people)
24. Ahikam *the son of* Shaphan
27: 1. Jehoiakim *the son of* Josiah
3. to the king of *the* Ammon*ites*, (lit. *children of* Ammon)
7. shall serve him, and *his son*, and *his son's son*,
20. Jeconiah *the son of* Jehoiakim
28: 1. Hananiah *the son of* Azur
4. Jeconiah *the son of* Jehoiakim
29: 3. Elasah *the son of* Shaphan, and Gemariah *the son of* Hilkiah,
6. beget *sons* and daughters; and take wives *for your sons*,
— that they may bear *sons*
21. Ahab *the son of* Kolaiah, and of Zedekiah *the son of* Maaseiah,
25. Zephaniah *the son of* Maaseiah
30:20. *Their children* also shall be as
31:12. for *the young of* the flock
15. Rahel weeping for *her children* refused to be comforted for *her children*,
17. that thy *children* shall come again
20. Ephraim my dear *son?*
29. and *the children*'s teeth are set on edge.
32: 7. Hanameel *the son of* Shallum
8. Hanameel mine uncle's *son* came
9. the field of Hanameel my uncle's *son*,
12. Baruch *the son of* Neriah, *the son of* Maaseiah,
16. unto Baruch *the son of* Neriah,
18. into the bosom of *their children*
19. upon all the ways of *the sons of* men:
30. For *the children of* Israel *and the children of* Judah
— for *the children of* Israel have only provoked
32. of *the children of* Israel *and* of *the children of* Judah,
35. the valley of *the son of* Hinnom, to cause *their sons* and their daughters
39. *and of their children* after them:
33:21. should not have *a son* to reign
35: 1. Jehoiakim *the son of* Josiah
3. *the son of* Jeremiah, *the son of* Habaziniah, and his brethren, and all *his sons*,
4. the chamber of *the sons of* Hanan, *the son of* Igdaliah, a man of God,
— Maaseiah *the son of* Shallum,
5. I set before *the sons of* the house
6. for Jonadab *the son of* Rechab
— ye, *nor your sons* for ever:
8. the voice of Jonadab *the son of* Rechab
— *our sons*, nor our daughters;
14. Jonadab *the son of* Rechab, that he commanded *his sons* not to drink
16. Because *the sons of* Jonadab *the son of* Rechab
19. Jonadab *the son of* Rechab shall not
36: 1, 9. Jehoiakim *the son of* Josiah
4, 8. Baruch *the son of* Neriah:
10,12. Gemariah *the son of* Shaphan
11. Michaiah *the son of* Gemariah, *the son of* Shaphan,
12. Delaiah *the son of* Shemaiah, and Elnathan *the son of* Achbor,
— and Zedekiah *the son of* Hananiah,
14. Jehudi *the son of* Nethaniah, *the son of* Shelemiah, *the son of* Cushi,
— Baruch *the son of* Neriah
26. Jerahmeel *the son of* Hammelech, and Seraiah *the son of* Azriel, and Shelemiah *the son of* Abdeel,
32. Baruch the scribe, *the son of* Neriah;
37: 1. Zedekiah *the son of* Josiah reigned instead of Coniah *the son of* Jehoiakim,
3. Jehucal *the son of* Shelemiah, and Zephaniah *the son of* Maaseiah
13. *the son of* Shelemiah, *the son of* Hananiah;
38: 1. Shephatiah *the son of* Mattan, and Gedaliah *the son of* Pashur, and Jucal *the son of* Shelemiah, and Pashur *the son of* Malchiah,
6. Malchiah *the son of* Hammelech,
23. all thy wives and *thy children*

Jer. 39: 6. slew *the sons of* Zedekiah
14 & 40:5, 9. Gedaliah *the son of* Ahikam *the son of* Shaphan,
40: 6, 7. Gedaliah *the son of* Ahikam
8. Ishmael *the son of* Nethaniah, and Johanan and Jonathan *the sons of* Kareah, and Seraiah *the son of* Tanhumeth, *and the sons of* Ephai the Netophathite, and Jezaniah *the son of* a Maachathite,
11. *and among the* Ammon*ites*, (lit. *and among the children of* Ammon)
— Gedaliah *the son of* Ahikam *the son of* Shaphan;
13,15,16. Johanan *the son of* Kareah,
14. Baalis the king of *the* Ammon*ites* (lit. *children of* Ammon)
—,15. Ishmael *the son of* Nethaniah
—,16. Gedaliah *the son of* Ahikam
41: 1. Ishmael *the son of* Nethaniah *the son of* Elishama,
—, 6, 10, 16, 18. Gedaliah *the son of* Ahikam
2, 6, 7, 10, 11, 12, 15, 16, 18. Ishmael *the son of* Nethaniah,
— Gedaliah *the son of* Ahikam *the son of* Shaphan
9. Ishmael *the son of* Nethaniah
10. departed to go over to *the* Ammon*ites*. (lit. *children of* Ammon)
11, 13, 14, 16. Johanan *the son of* Kareah,
15. went to *the* Ammon*ites*. (lit. *children of* Ammon)
42: 1, 8. Johanan *the son of* Kareah,
— and Jezaniah *the son of* Hoshaiah,
43: 2. spake Azariah *the son of* Hoshaiah,
—, 4, 5. Johanan *the son of* Kareah,
3. Baruch *the son of* Neriah
6. Gedaliah *the son of* Ahikam *the son of* Shaphan,
— Baruch *the son of* Neriah.
45: 1. Baruch *the son of* Neriah,
— & 46:2. Jehoiakim *the son of* Josiah king of
47: 3. shall not look back to (their) *children*
48:45. the crown of the head of *the* tumultuous *ones*. (marg. *children of* noise)
46. for *thy sons* are taken captives,
49: 1. *Concerning the* Ammon*ites*, (lit. *to the children of* Ammon)
— Hath Israel no *sons?*
2. heard in Rabbah of *the* Ammon*ites*; (lit. *children of* Ammon)
6. the captivity of *the children of* Ammon,
18. neither shall *a son of* man dwell
28. spoil *the men of* the east.
33. nor (any) *son of* man dwell in it.
50: 4. *the children of* Israel shall come, they *and the children of* Judah
33. *The children of* Israel *and the children of*
40. neither shall any *son of* man dwell
51:43. neither doth (any) *son of* man pass
59. Seraiah *the son of* Neriah, *the son of* Maaseiah,
52: 1. Zedekiah (was) one and twenty years *old*
10. slew *the sons of* Zedekiah before his eyes:
Lam. 1:16. *my children* are desolate, because
3:13. He hath caused *the arrows of* his quiver (marg. *sons*)
33. nor grieve *the children of* men.
4: 2. *The* precious *sons of* Zion,
Eze. 1: 3. Ezekiel the priest, *the son of* Buzi,
2: 1, 3. he said unto me, *Son of* man,
3. I send thee to *the children of* Israel,
4. *For* (they are) impudent *children*
6, 8. thou, *son of* man,
3: 1, 3, 4, 10, 17, 25. *Son of* man,
11. of the captivity, unto *the children of* thy
4: 1, 16. *son of* man,
13. thus shall *the children of* Israel eat
5: 1. And thou, *son of* man,
10. the fathers shall eat *the sons* in the midst of thee, *and the sons* shall eat
6: 2. *Son of* man, set thy face toward
5. the dead carcases of *the children of*
7: 2 & 8:5, 6, 8, 12, 15, 17. *son of* man,
8:11. Jaazaniah *the son of* Shaphan,
11: 1. Jaazaniah *the son of* Azur, and Pelatiah *the son of* Benaiah,
2, 4, 15. *Son of* man,

Eze 11:13. Pelatiah *the son of* Benaiah
12: 2,3,9,18,22,27&13:2,17&14:3,13. *Son of* man,
14:16. they shall deliver neither *sons*
18. deliver neither *sons* nor daughters,
20. shall deliver neither *son* nor daughter;
22. *sons* and daughters:
15: 2&16:2. *Son of* man,
16:20. thou hast taken *thy sons*
21. That thou hast slain *my children*,
26. fornication with *the* Egypt*ians* (lit. *children of* Egypt)
28. hast played the whore also with *the* Assyr*ians*, (lit. *children of* Asshur)
36. and by the blood of *thy children*,
45. her husband *and her children*;
— lothed their husbands *and their children*:
17: 2. *Son of* man, put forth a riddle,
18: 2. *the children*'s teeth are set on edge?
4. also the soul of *the son* is mine:
10. If he beget *a son* (that is) a robber,
14. Now, lo, (if) he beget *a son*,
19. Why? doth not *the son* bear the iniquity of the father? *When the son* hath
20. *The son* shall not bear the iniquity
— the father bear the iniquity of *the son*:
20: 3, 4, 27. *Son of* man,
18. But I said unto *their children*
21. *the children* rebelled against me:
31. ye make *your sons* to pass
46(21:2) & 21:2(7), 6(11), 9(14), 12(17), 14 (19), 19(24), 28(33). *Son of* man,
21:10(15). it contemneth the rod of *my son*,
20(25). come to Rabbath of *the* Ammon*ites*, (lit. *children of* Ammon)
28(33). Thus saith the Lord God concerning *the* Ammon*ites*, (lit. *children of* Ammon)
22: 2, 18, 24 & 23:2. *son of* man,
23: 4. they bare *sons* and daughters.
7. *the* chosen *men of* Assyria,
9. into the hand of *the* Assyr*ians*, (lit. *children of* Asshur)
10. they took *her sons* and her daughters,
12. She doted upon *the* Assyr*ians* (lit. *children of* Asshur)
15. after the manner of *the* Babylon*ians* (lit. *children of* Babylon)
17. *the* Babylon*ians* came to her (marg. *children of* Babel)
23. *The* Babylon*ians*, and all (lit. *children of* Babylon)
— all *the* Assyr*ians* with them: (lit. *children of* Asshur)
25. they shall take *thy sons* and thy daughters;
36. *Son of* man, wilt thou judge
37. have also caused *their sons*,
39. when they had slain *their children*
47. they shall slay *their sons*
24: 2, 16, 25. *Son of* man,
21. *and your sons* and your daughters
25. *their sons* and their daughters,
25: 2. *Son of* man, set thy face against *the* Ammon*ites*, (lit. *children of* Ammon)
3. say *unto the* Ammon*ites*, (lit. *to the children of* Ammon)
4. I will deliver thee *to the men of* the east (marg. *children*)
5. *the* Ammon*ites* a couchingplace (lit. *children of* Ammon)
10. *Unto the men of* the east with *the* Ammon*ites*, (lit. *children of* Ammon)
— that *the* Ammon*ites* may not be
26: 2 & 27:2. *Son of* man,
27:11. *The men of* Arvad
15. *The men of* Dedan
28. 2, 12, 21 & 29:2, 18 & 30:2. *Son of* man,
30: 5. *and the men of* the land (marg. *children*)
21. *Son of* man, I have broken the arm of
31: 2. *Son of* man, speak unto Pharaoh
14. in the midst of *the children of* men,
32: 2. *Son of* man, take up a lamentation
18. *Son of* man, wail for the multitude
33: 2. *Son of* man, speak to *the children of*
7, 10, 12, 24, 30. *son of* man,
12. say unto *the children of* thy people,
17. Yet *the children of* thy people
30. *the children of* thy people still are
34: 2. *Son of* man, prophesy against

Eze 35: 2. *Son of* man, set thy face against mount
5. shed (the blood of) *the children of* Israel
36: 1, 17 & 37:3, 9, 11, 16. *son of* man,
37:16. *and for the children of* Israel his
18. when *the children of* thy people
21. I will take *the children of* Israel
25. they, *and their children, and their children's children*
38: 2, 14 & 39:1, 17 & 40:4. *Son of* man,
40:46. these (are) *the sons of* Zadok *among the sons of* Levi,
43: 7, 10, 18. *Son of* man,
— in the midst of *the children of* Israel
19. a *young* bullock for a sin offering. (lit. one steer *the son of* a bull)
23. thou shalt offer a *young* bullock
25. shall also prepare a *young* bullock,
44: 5. *Son of* man, mark well, and behold
7. ye have brought (into my sanctuary) strangers, (marg. *children of* a stranger)
9. No stranger, uncircumcised in heart, (lit. *son of* a stranger)
— any stranger (lit. *id.*) that (is) among the *children of* Israel.
15. the Levites, *the sons of* Zadok,
— *the children of* Israel went astray
25. *or for son*, or for daughter,
45:18. thou shalt take a *young* bullock
46: 6. a *young* bullock without blemish,
13. of the *first* year (marg. *a son of* his year)
16. a gift unto any *of his sons*, the inheritance thereof shall be *his sons'*;
17. his inheritance shall be *his sons'*
18. he shall give *his sons* inheritance
47: 6. *Son of* man, hast thou seen (this)?
22. which shall beget *children* among you:
— in the country *among the children of*
48:11. sanctified *of the sons of* Zadok;
— when *the children of* Israel went astray,
Dan. 1: 3. (certain) *of the children of* Israel,
6. *of the children of* Judah,
8:17. Understand, *O son of* man:
9: 1. Darius *the son of* Ahasuerus,
10:16. like the similitude of *the sons of* men
11:10. *But his sons* shall be stirred up,
14. also the robbers of thy people (marg. *also the children of* robbers)
41. the chief of *the children of* Ammon.
12: 1. which standeth for *the children of* thy
Hos. 1: 1. Hosea *the son of* Beeri, in the days
— Jeroboam *the son of* Joash, king of Israel.
3. and bare him *a son*.
8. she conceived, and bare *a son*.
10(2:1). the number of *the children of* Israel
—(-:-). (Ye are) *the sons of* the living God.
11(2:2). Then shall *the children of* Judah *and the children of* Israel be gathered
2: 4(6). I will not have mercy upon *her children*; for they (be) *the children of*
3: 1. toward *the children of* Israel,
4. *the children of* Israel shall abide
5. shall *the children of* Israel return,
4: 1. *ye children of* Israel:
6. I will also forget *thy children*.
5: 7. they have begotten strange *children*:
9:12. Though they bring up *their children*,
13. Ephraim shall bring forth *his children*
10: 9. against *the children of* iniquity
14. dashed in pieces upon (her) *children*.
11: 1. called *my son* out of Egypt.
10. *the children* shall tremble
13:13. he (is) *an unwise son*;
— the breaking forth of *children*.
Joel 1: 1. Joel *the son of* Pethuel.
3. Tell ye *your children* of it, *and* (let) *your children* (tell) *their children, and their children* another generation.
12. joy is withered away from *the sons of*
2:23. Be glad *then, ye children of* Zion,
28(3:1). and *your sons* and your daughters
3: 6(4:6). *The children also of* Judah *and the children of* Jerusalem have ye sold *unto the* Grecians, (marg. *unto the sons of* the Grecians)
8(4:8). I will sell *your sons* and your daughters into the hand of *the children of*
16(4:16). the strength *of the children of* Israel.

Joel 3:19(4:19). *the children of* Judah,
Am. 1: 1. Jeroboam *the son of* Joash
13. transgressions of *the children of* Ammon,
2:11. I raised up *of your sons*
— (Is it) not even thus, *O ye children of*
3: 1. spoken against you, *O children of* Israel,
12. so shall *the children of* Israel be taken
4: 5. *O ye children of* Israel,
7:14. neither (was) I a prophet's *son;*
17. *and thy sons* and thy daughters shall fall
9: 7. ye not *as children of* the Ethiopians unto me, *O children of* Israel?
Obad 12. rejoiced *over the children of* Judah
20. this host *of the children of* Israel
Jon. 1: 1. Jonah *the son of* Amittai,
4:10. *which came up in* a night, (marg. *which* was *the son of* the night)
— *and* perished *in* a night: (lit. *and the son of* a night perished)
Mic. 1:16. poll thee for thy delicate *children;*
5: 3(2). return unto *the children of* Israel.
7(6). waiteth *for the sons of* men.
6: 5. Balaam *the son of* Beor answered
6. with calves of a year *old?* (marg. *sons of* a year)
7: 6. *the son* dishonoureth the father,
Zep. 1: 1. Zephaniah *the son of* Cushi, *the son of* Gedaliah, *the son of* Amariah, *the son of* Hizkiah, in the days of Josiah *the son of* Amon, king of Judah.
8. and the king's *children,*
2: 8. the revilings of *the children of* Ammon,
9. *and the children of* Ammon
Hag. 1: 1, 12, 14 & 2:2. Zerubbabel *the son of* Shealtiel,
—, 12, 14 & 2:2. Joshua *the son of* Josedech,
2: 4. O Joshua, *son of* Josedech,
23. my servant, *the son of* Shealtiel,
Zec. 1: 1, 7. Zechariah, *the son of* Berechiah, *the son of* Iddo the prophet,
4:14. These (are) the two anointed *ones,* (marg. *sons of* oil)
6:10. Josiah *the son of* Zephaniah;
11. Joshua *the son of* Josedech,
14. Hen *the son of* Zephaniah,
9: 9. upon a colt *the foal of* an ass.
13. and raised up *thy sons,* O Zion, against *thy sons,*
10: 7. *yea, their children* shall see
9. they shall live with *their children,*
Mal. 1: 6. *A son* honoureth (his) father,
3: 3. he shall purify *the sons of* Levi,
6. *ye sons of* Jacob are not consumed.
17. as a man spareth *his own son*
4: 6(3:24). the heart of the fathers to *the children,* and the heart of *the children* to

---

1123 ## בֵּן [*bēhn*], Ch. m.

Ezr. 6: 9. *both young* bullocks, and rams,
10. pray for the life of the king, *and of his sons.*
16. And *the children of* Israel, the priests,
— and the rest of *the children of* the captivity, (marg. *sons of* the transportation)
7:23. the realm of the king *and his sons?*
Dan 2:25. I have found a man of the captives (marg. *children of* the captivity)
38. wheresoever *the children of* men dwell,
5:13. which (art) of *the children of* the captivity
21. he was driven from *the sons of* men;
6:13(14). That Daniel, which (is) of *the children of* the captivity
24(25). into the den of lions, them, *their children,*

1129 ## בָּנָה *bāh-nāh'.*

✱ KAL.—*Preterite.* ✱

Gen11: 5. the children of men *builded.*
Nu. 32:37. the children of Reuben *built* Heshbon,
38. the cities which *they builded.*
Deu 6:10. which *thou buildedst* not,
20: 5. that *hath built* a new house,
20. *and thou shalt build* bulwarks
27: 5. *And* there *shalt thou build*
Jos. 6:26. *and buildeth* this city Jericho:
22:11. *have built* an altar
24:13. cities which *ye built* not,
Jud. 6:26. *And build* an altar unto the
Ru. 4:11. which two *did build* the house of
1Sa. 2:35. *and I will build* him a sure house
2Sa. 7: 7. Why *build ye* not me an house
1K. 6: 2. the house which king Solomon *built*
7: 1. Solomon *was building* his own house
8:13. *I have* surely *built* thee an house
27. that *I have builded?*
43. which *I have builded,*
44. the house that *I have built*
48. the house which *I have built*
9: 3. which *thou hast built,*
10. Solomon *had built* the two houses,
24. which (Solomon) *had built* for her: then *did he build* Millo.
25. the altar which *he built* unto the
10: 4. and the house that *he had built,*
11:27. Solomon *built* Millo,
38. *and build* thee a sure house, as *I built* for David,
15:22. wherewith Baasha *had builded;*
23. the cities which *he built,*
16:24. the name of the city which *he built,*
32. which *he had built* in Samaria.
34. *did* Hiel the Beth-elite *build* Jericho:
22:39. the ivory house which *he made,* and all the cities that *he built,*
2K. 14:22. *He built* Elath, and restored it
15:35. *He built* the higher gate
16:18. that *they had built* in the house,
21: 4. *And he built* altars in the house
23:13. Solomon the king of Israel *had builded*
1Ch. 6:10(5:36). that Solomon *built* in Jerusalem:
8:12. who *built* Ono, and Lod,
17: 6. Why *have ye* not *built* me
22:11. *and build* the house of the Lord
2Ch. 6: 2. But *I have built* an house
18, 33. this house which *I have built!*
34, 38. the house which *I have built* for thy
8: 1. Solomon *had built* the house
2. Solomon *built* them,
4. which *he built* in Hamath.
11. the house that *he had built* for her:
12. which *he had built* before the
9: 3. the house that *he had built,*
16: 6. wherewith Baasha *was building;*
26: 2. *He built* Eloth,
27: 3. *He built* the high gate
— on the wall of Ophel *he built*
4. *he built* cities in the mountains of Judah, and in the forests *he built* castles
33: 4. *Also he built* altars in the house
14. after this *he built* a wall
15. all the altars that *he had built*
19. the places wherein *he built*
35: 3. the son of David king of Israel *did build;*
Neh 2:18. Let us rise up *and build.*
20. we his servants will arise *and build:*
3: 2. next unto him *builded* the men
— next to them *builded* Zaccur
3. *did* the sons of Hassenaah *build,*
13. *they built it,* and set up the doors
6: 1. heard that *I had builded*
12:29. the singers *had builded* them
Job 27:18. *He buildeth* his house
Ps. 89: 4(5). *and build up* thy throne
102:16(17). the Lord *shall build up* Zion,
Pro. 9: 1. Wisdom *hath builded* her house,
14: 1. Every wise woman *buildeth*
24:27. *and* afterwards *build* thine house.
Ecc. 2: 4. *I builded* me houses;
9:14. *and built* great bulwarks
Isa. 58:12. *And* (they that shall be) of thee *shall build*
60:10. *And* the sons of strangers *shall build up*
61: 4. *And they shall build* the old wastes.
65:21. *And they shall build* houses,
Jer. 7:31. *And they have built* the high places
19: 5. *They have built also* the high places
24: 6. *and I will build them,* and not pull
32:31. the day that *they built* it
33: 7. *and will build them,* as at the first.
42:10. *then will I build* you, and not
45: 4. which *I have built* will I break
Lam. 3: 5. *He hath builded* against me,

Eze. 4: 2. *and build* a fort against it,
16:25. *Thou hast built* thy high place
27: 5. *They have made* (marg. *built*) all thy (ship) boards
28:26. *and shall build* houses,
36:36. that *I* the Lord *build* the
39:15. *then shall he set up* a sign (marg. *build*)
Am. 5:11. *ye have built* houses of hewn stone,
9:11. *and I will build it* as in the
14. *and they shall build* the waste
Zep. 1:13. *they shall also build* houses,
Zec. 6:12. *and he shall build* the temple
15. *and build* in the temple

KAL.—*Infinitive.*

Gen11: 8. they left off *to build* the city.
Jos. 22:16. *in that ye have builded* you
19. *in building* you an altar (lit. *in your building* for you)
23. *That* we *have built* us an altar
26. Let us now prepare *to build*
29. *to build* an altar
1Sa. 14:35. the first altar *that he built* (marg. he began *to build*)
2Sa. 24:21. *to build* an altar unto the Lord,
1K. 3: 1. until he had made an end *of building*
5: 3(17). my father could not *build*
5(19). behold, I purpose *to build*
18(32). timber and stones *to build* the house.
8:13. I have *surely* built thee an house
16. tribes of Israel *to build* an house,
17. David my father *to build* an house
18. *to build* an house unto my name,
9: 1. Solomon had finished *the building*
15. *to build* the house of the Lord,
19. which Solomon desired *to build*
15:21. that he left off *building*
1Ch 6:32(17). until Solomon *had built*
14: 1. *to build* him an house.
17:25. *that thou wilt build* him an
22: 2. *to build* the house of God.
5. *to be builded* for the Lord
6. *to build* an house for the Lord
7. it was in my mind *to build*
28: 2. in mine heart *to build* an
— and had made ready *for the building*.
10. *to build* an house for the sanctuary:
29:16. *to build* thee an house
19. *and to build* the palace,
2Ch 2: 1(1:18). Solomon determined *to build*
3(2). send him cedars *to build*
6(5). But who is able *to build*
3: 1. Solomon began *to build* the house
2. And he began *to build*
3. *for the building of* the house
6: 5. *to build* an house in,
7. David my father *to build* an house
8. *to build* an house for my name,
8: 6. desired *to build* in Jerusalem,
16: 5. that he left off *building*
36:23. *to build* him an house
Ezr. 1: 2. *to build* him an house
5. *to build* the house of the Lord
4: 3. *to build* an house unto our God;
4. troubled them *in building*,
Neh 4:10(4). we are not able *to build* the wall.
Ecc. 3: 3. a time *to build up;*
Jer. 1:10 & 18:9 & 31:28. *to build*, and to plant.
35: 9. Nor *to build* houses for us
Eze. 11: 3. *let us build* houses:
16:31. *In that thou buildest* (marg. *thy daughters*, as from בַּת)
17:17. *and building* forts,
21:22(27). *to build* a fort.
Dan. 9:25. to restore *and to build*
Mic. 7:11. the day that thy walls *are to be built*,
Zec. 5:11. *To build* it an house in the

KAL.—*Imperative.*

Nu. 23: 1, 29. *Build* me here seven altars,
32:24. *Build* you cities for your little ones,
1K. 2:36. *Build* thee an house
1Ch 22:19. *and build ye* the sanctuary
Jer. 29: 5, 28. *Build ye* houses,
Hag 1: 8. *and build* the house;

KAL.—*Future.*

Gen 2:22. *And* the rib,...*made he* a woman, (marg. *builded*)
8:20. *And* Noah *builded* an altar
10:11. *and builded* Nineveh,
11: 4. Go to, *let us build* us a city
12: 7. *and* there *builded he* an altar
8. *and* there *he builded* an altar unto
13:18. *and built* there an altar
22: 9. *and* Abraham *built* an altar there,
26:25. *And* he *builded* an altar there,
33:17. *and built* him an house,
35: 7. *And he built* there an altar,
Ex. 1:11. *And they built* for Pharaoh
17:15. *And* Moses *built* an altar,
20:25. *thou shalt* not *build* it of hewn stone:
24: 4. *and builded* an altar under the hill,
32: 5. *he built* an altar before it;
Nu. 23:14. *and built* seven altars,
32:16. *We will build* sheepfolds
34. *And* the children of Gad *built* Dibon,
Deu 8:12. and *hast built* goodly houses,
22: 8. When *thou buildest* a new house,
25: 9. that *will* not *build up*
27: 6. *Thou shalt build* the altar
28:30. *thou shalt build* an house,
Jos. 8:30. Then Joshua *built* an altar
19:50. *and he built* the city,
22:10. *And* when they came...half tribe of Manasseh *built*
Jud. 1:26. *and built* a city,
6:24. *Then* Gideon *built* an altar
18:28. *And they built* a city,
21: 4. *and built* there an altar,
23. *and repaired* the cities,
1Sa. 7:17. *and* there *he built* an altar unto the Lord.
14:35. *And* Saul *built* an altar unto the Lord:
2Sa. 5: 9. *And* David *built* round about
11. *and they built* David an house.
7: 5. *Shalt* thou *build* me an house
13. He *shall build* an house
27. *I will build* thee an house:
24:25. *And* David *built* there an altar
1K. 5: 5(19). he *shall build* an house
6: 1. *that he began to build* the house (marg. *built*)
5. *And* against the wall of the house *he built*
9. *So he built* the house,
10. *And* (then) *he built* chambers against all
14. *So* Solomon *built* the house,
15. *And he built* the walls of the house
16. *And he built* twenty cubits on
— *he even built* (them) for it
36. *And he built* the inner court
38. *So was he* seven years *in building it.*
7: 2. *He built also* the house of the
8:19. thou *shalt* not *build* the house;
— he *shall build* the house
20. *and have built* an house
9:17. *And* Solomon *built* Gezer,
11: 7. Then *did* Solomon *build*
12:25. *Then* Jeroboam *built* Shechem
— *and built* Penuel.
14:23. *For they* also *built* them high places,
15:17. *and built* Ramah,
22. *and* king Asa *built* with them Geba
16:24. *and built* on the hill,
18:32. *And* with the stones *he built*
2K. 16:11. *And* Urijah the priest *built* an altar
17: 9. *and they built* them high places
21: 3. *For he built up* again the high places
5. *and he built* altars for all the host of
25: 1. *and they built* forts against it
1Ch. 7:24. *who built* Beth-horon
11: 8. *And he built* the city round about,
17: 4. Thou *shalt* not *build* me an house
10. that the Lord *will build* thee an house.
12. He *shall build* me an house,
21:22. *that I may build* an altar
26. *And* David *built* there an altar
22: 8. *thou shalt* not *build* an house
10. He *shall build* an house
28: 3. *Thou shalt* not *build* an house
6. he *shall build* my house
2Ch. 2: 6(5). that *I should build* him an house,
12(11). that *might build* an house
6: 9. thou *shalt* not *build* the house:
— he *shall build* the house
10. *and have built* the house
8: 4. *And he built* Tadmor in the wilderness,
5. *Also he built* Beth-horon the upper,

2Ch.11: 5. *and built* cities for defence
6. *He built even* Beth-lehem,
14: 6(5). *And he built* fenced cities in Judah:
7(6). *Let us build* these cities,
—(-). *So they built* and prospered.
16: 1. *and built* Ramah,
6. *and he built* therewith Geba
17:12. *and he built* in Judah castles,
20: 8. *and have built* thee a sanctuary
26: 6. *and built* cities about Ashdod,
9. *Moreover* Uzziah *built* towers in Jerusalem
10. *Also he built* towers in the desert,
32: 5. *and built up* all the wall
33: 3. *For he built* again the high places
5. *And he built* altars for all the host of
16. *And he repaired* the altar
Ezr. 1: 3. *and build* the house of the
3: 2. *and builded* the altar of the God
4: 2. *Let us build* with you:
3. *we* ourselves together *will build*
Neh. 2: 5. *that I may build it.*
17. *and let us build up* the wall
3: 1. *and they builded* the sheep gate;
14. *he built it,* and set up the doors
15. *he built it,* and covered it,
4: 6(3:38). *So built we* the wall;
Job 20:19. an house which *he builded* not;
Ps. 28: 5. and not *build them up.*
51:18(20). *build thou* the walls of Jerusalem.
69:35(36). save Zion, *and will build* the cities of Judah:
78:69. *And he built* his sanctuary
127: 1. Except the Lord *build* the house,
Cant. 8: 9. *we will build* upon her
Isa. 5: 2. *and built* a tower in the
9:10(9). but *we will build* with
45:13. *he shall build* my city,
65:22. *They shall* not *build,*
66: 1. where (is) the house that *ye build*
Jer. 22:14. *I will build* me a wide house
31: 4. Again *I will build thee,*
32:35. *And they built* the high places
35: 7. Neither *shall ye build* house,
52: 4. *and built* forts against it
Eze.16:24. *thou hast also built* unto thee
Hos. 8:14. *and buildeth* temples;
Zec. 6:13. Even he *shall build* the temple
9: 3. *And* Tyrus *did build* herself
Mal. 1: 4. return *and build* the desolate places;
— They *shall build,* but I will

KAL.—*Part.* Poel.

Gen. 4:17. and he *builded* a city, (lit. he was *building*)
1K. 5:18(32). And Solomon's *builders and* Hiram's *builders*
6:12. which thou art *in building,*
2K. 12:11(12). to the carpenters *and builders,*
22: 6. Unto carpenters, *and builders,*
2Ch. 2: 4(3). I *build* an house
5(4). the house which I *build*
9(8). for the house which I *am about to build*
34:11. to the artificers *and builders*
Ezr. 3:10. when *the builders* laid the foundation
4: 1. the children of the captivity *builded* the temple
Neh. 4: 1(3:33). heard that we *builded*
3(3:35). that which they *build,*
5(3:37). to anger before the *builders.*
17(11). *They which builded* on the wall,
18(12). *For the builders,* every one
—(—). *and* (so) *builded.*
6: 6. for which cause thou *buildest*
Job 3:14. *which built* desolate places
Ps.118:22. The stone (which) *the builders*
127: 1. they labour in vain *that build* (marg. *builders of it* in it)
147: 2. The Lord *doth build up*
Jer. 22:13. Woe unto him *that buildeth*
Eze.13:10. one *built up* a wall,
27: 4. *thy builders* have perfected thy beauty.
Am. 9: 6. *he that buildeth* his stories
Mic. 3:10. *They build up* Zion
Hab. 2:12. Woe to *him that buildeth*

KAL.—*Participle.* Paül.

Jud. 6:28. upon the altar (that was) *built.*
Neh. 7: 4. the houses (were) not *builded.*

Ps.122: 3. Jerusalem *is builded* as a city
Cant.4: 4. *builded* for an armoury,

* NIPHAL.—*Preterite.* *

Nu. 13:22. Hebron *was built* seven years
1K. 3: 2. *there was* no house *built*
6: 7. *was built* of stone made ready
Neh. 7: 1. when the wall *was built,*
Jer. 12:16. *then shall they be built* in the midst
30:18. *and* the city *shall be builded*
31: 4. *and thou shalt be built,* O virgin
38. *that* the city *shall be built*
Eze.36:33. *and* the wastes *shall be builded.*
Dan 9:25. the street *shall be built* again, (marg. return *and be builded*)
Mal. 3:15. they that work wickedness *are set up;* (marg. *built*)

NIPHAL.—*Infinitive.*

1K. 6: 7. *when it was in building,*
— *while it was in building.*
Hag. 1: 2. *that* the Lord's house *should be built.*
Zec. 8: 9. *that* the temple *might be built.*

NIPHAL.—*Future.*

Gen16: 2. it may be that *I may obtain children* by her. (marg. *be builded*)
30: 3. *that* I *may* also *have children* by her. (marg. *be built*)
Nu. 21:27. *let* the city of Sihon *be built*
Deu13:16(17). *it shall* not *be built* again.
Job 12:14. *it cannot be built again:*
22:23. *thou shalt be built up,* thou shalt
Ps. 89: 2(3). Mercy *shall be built up* for ever:
Pro.24: 3. Through wisdom *is* an house *builded;*
Isa. 25: 2. *it shall* never *be built.*
44:26. *Ye shall be built,*
28. *Thou shalt be built;*
Eze.26:14. *thou shalt be built* no more:
36:10. the wastes *shall be builded:*
Zec. 1:16. my house *shall be built*

NIPHAL.—*Participle.*

1Ch 22:19. the house *that is to be built*

בְּנָה & בְּנָא [*b'nāh*], Ch. 1124

* P'AL.—*Preterite.* *

Ezr. 5:11. which a great king of Israel *builded* and
6:14. *And they builded,* and finished (it),
Dan. 4:30(27). that I *have built* for the house of the

P'AL.—*Infinitive.*

Ezr. 5: 2. and began *to build* the house of God
3. Who hath commanded you *to build*
9. Who commanded you *to build* this house,
13. Cyrus made a decree *to build* this house
17. was made of Cyrus the king *to build* this
6: 8. *for the building* of this house of God:

P'AL.—*Future.*

Ezr. 6: 7. and the elders of the Jews *build* this house

P'AL.—*Participle.*

Ezr. 4:12. *building* the rebellious and the bad city,
5: 4. What are the names of the men that *make* (marg. *build*) this building?
11. *and build* the house that was
6:14. And the elders of the Jews *builded,*

P'AL.—*Participle. Pass.*

Ezr. 5:11. *builded* these many years ago,

* ITHP'IL.—*Future.* *

Ezr. 4:13. if this city *be builded,* and the walls
16. if this city *be builded* (again), and the
21. and that this city *be not builded,*
5:15. *let* the house of God *be builded*
6: 3. *Let* the house *be builded,*

ITHP'IL.—*Participle.*

Ezr. 5: 8. which *is builded* with great stones,
16. even until now *hath it been in building,*

1140 **בִּנְיָה [bin-yāh'], f.**

Eze.41:13. *and the building*, with the walls

1143 **בֵּנַיִם bēh-nah'-yim, dual.**

1Sa.17: 4. And there went out a champion (lit. a man of *the two intermediates*)
23. behold, there came up the champion, (lit. a man of *the two intermediates*)

1146 **בִּנְיָן bin-yāhn', m.**

Eze.40: 5. the breadth of *the building*,
41:12. *Now the building* that (was) before
— the wall of *the building*
15. the length of *the building*
42: 1. which (was) before *the building*
5. the middlemost of *the building*.
10. over against *the building*.

1147 **בִּנְיָן [bin-yāhn'], Ch. m.**

Ezr. 5: 4. What are the names of the men that make this *building?*

1149 **בְּנַס b'nas, Ch.**

* P'AL.—*Preterite*. *

Dan. 2:12. the king *was angry* and very furious,

1154 **בֶּסֶר [bĕh'-ser], m.**

Job 15:33. He shall shake off *his unripe grape*

1155 **בֹּסֶר bōh'-sĕhr, m.**

Isa. 18: 5. *and the sour grape* is ripening
Jer.31:29. The fathers have eaten *a sour grape*,
30. every man that eateth *the sour grape*,
Eze.18: 2. The fathers have eaten *sour grapes*,

1157 **בְּעַד b'ⁿgad. part.**

Gen26: 8. looked out *at* a window,
Ex. 32:30. make an atonement *for* your sin.
Jos. 2:15. by a cord *through* the window:
Jud. 3:22. the fat closed *upon* the blade,
1Sa. 1: 6. the Lord had shut *up* her womb.
4:18. *by* the side of the gate,
2Sa.20:21. thrown to thee *over* the wall.
Job 1:10. *and about* his house, *and about* all
Pro. 6:26. For *by means of* a whorish woman &c. &c.

With prefix מִבַּעַד.

Cant.4: 1. thou (hast) doves' eyes *within* thy locks:
3. of a pomegranate *within* thy locks.
6: 7. thy temples *within* thy locks.

It also occurs with pronominal suffixes: as,

Gen20: 7. he shall pray *for thee*,
Ex. 8:28(24). intreat *for me*.
Lev.16: 6. and make an atonement *for himself*,
2K. 4: 5. and shut the door *upon her*
Ps.139:11. the night shall be light *about me*.
Jer. 7:16. neither lift up cry nor prayer *for them*,
21: 2. Enquire, I pray thee, of the Lord *for us*; &c. &c.

1158 **בָּעָה [bāh-ⁿgāh'].**

* KAL.—*Imperative*. *

Isa. 21:12. if ye will enquire, *enquire ye:*

KAL.—*Future*.

Isa. 21:12. if *ye will enquire*, enquire ye:
64: 2(1). the fire *causeth* the waters *to boil*,

* NIPHAL.—*Preterite*. *

Obad 6. *are* his hidden things *sought up!*

NIPHAL.—*Participle*.

Isa. 30:13. *swelling out* in a high wall,

בְּעָה & בְּעָא b'ⁿgāh, Ch. 1156

* P'AL.—*Preterite*. *

Dan. 2:13. *and they sought* Daniel and his fellows
16. Daniel went in, *and desired* of the king
23. made known unto me now what *we desired*
49. Then Daniel *requested* of the king,

P'AL.—*Infinitive*.

Dan. 2:18. *That they would desire* mercies of the God

P'AL.—*Future*.

Dan. 4:36(33). and my lords *sought* unto me;
6: 7(8). whosoever *shall ask* a petition
12(13). every man that *shall ask* (a petition)
7:16. and *asked* him the truth of all this.

P'AL.—*Participle*.

Dan. 6: 4(5). *sought* to find occasion against Daniel
11(12). and found Daniel *praying*
13(14). but *maketh* his petition three times a

בָּעוּ bāh'-ⁿgoo, Ch. f. 1159

Dan. 6: 7(8). whosoever shall ask *a petition*
13(14). but maketh *his petition* three times

בִּעוּתִים [bee-ⁿgoo-theem'], m. pl. 1161

Job 6: 4. *the terrors of* God do set
Ps. 88:16(17). *thy terrors* have cut me off.

בָּעַט [bāh-ⁿgat']. 1163

* KAL.—*Future*. *

Deu32:15. Jeshurun waxed fat, *and kicked:*
1Sa. 2:29. Wherefore *kick ye* at my sacrifice

בְּעִי b'ⁿgee, m. 1164

Job 30:24. stretch out (his) hand to *the grave*, (marg. *heap*)

בְּעִיר [b'ⁿgeer], m. 1165

Gen45:17. lade *your beasts*, and go,
Ex. 22: 5(4). shall put in *his beast*,
Nu.20: 4. that we *and our cattle* should die
8. and *their beasts* drink.
11. drank, *and their beasts* (also).
Ps. 78:48. He gave up *their cattle* also

בָּעַל bāh-ⁿgal'. 1166

* KAL.—*Preterite*. *

Deu21:13. *and be her husband*,
24: 1. taken a wife, *and married her*,
1Ch 4:22. who *had the dominion* in Moab,
Isa. 26:13. beside thee *have had dominion over us:*
Jer. 3:14. for *I am married* unto you:
31:32. although *I was an husband*
Mal 2:11. *and hath married* the daughter

KAL.—*Future*.

Isa. 62: 5. a young man *marrieth* a virgin, (so) *shall* thy sons *marry thee:*

KAL.—*Participle*. Poel.

Isa. 54: 5. For thy Maker (is) *thine husband;*

KAL.—*Participle*. Paül.

Gen20: 3. she (is) a man's *wife*. (marg. *married* to an husband)
Deu22:22. a woman *married* to an husband.
Isa. 54: 1. the children of *the married wife*,
62: 4. and thy land *Beulah:* (marg. *Married*)

* NIPHAL.—*Future.* *

Pro. 30:23. an odious (woman) when *she is married;*
Isa . 62: 4. thy land *shall be married.*

1167 בַּעַל *bah'-ğal,* m.

Gen14:13. these (were) confederate (lit. *masters of* a covenant)
20: 3. for she (is) *a man's* wife.
37:19. Behold, this dreamer cometh. (marg. *master of* dreams)
49:23. The archers (lit. *masters of* arrows) have sorely
Ex. 21: 3. if he were married, (lit. *husband of* a wife)
22. according as the woman's *husband* will lay
28. *but the owner of* the ox (shall be) quit.
29. hath been testified *to his owner,*
— *his owner* also shall be put to death.
34. *The owner of* the pit shall make
— give money unto *the owner of them;*
36. *his owner* hath not kept him in;
22: 8(7). then *the master of* the house
11(10). *the owner of it* shall accept
12(11). restitution *unto the owner thereof.*
14(13). *the owner thereof* (being) not with it,
15(14). if *the owner thereof* (be) with it,
24:14. if any man have any matters to do, (lit. who is *a master of* business)
Lev.21: 4. *a chief man* among his people, (marg. *an husband*)
Nu. 21:28. *the lords of* the high places
Deu15: 2. Every creditor that lendeth (marg. *master of* the lending of his hand)
22:22. a woman married to *an husband,*
24: 4. *Her* former *husband,*
Jos. 24:11. *the men of* Jericho fought against you,
Jud. 9: 2, 3. the ears of all *the men of* Shechem,
6. all *the men of* Shechem gathered
7. Hearken unto me, *ye men of* Shechem,
18. king over *the men of* Shechem,
20. devour *the men of* Shechem,
— come out *from the men of* Shechem,
23. between Abimelech and *the men of* Shechem; and *the men of* Shechem
24. upon *the men of* Shechem,
25. *the men of* Shechem set liers in wait
26. *the men of* Shechem put their confidence
39. went out before *the men of* Shechem,
46, 47. all *the men of* the tower
51. and all *they of* the city,
19:22, 23. *the master of* the house,
20: 5. *the men of* Gibeah rose against me,
1Sa.23:11. Will *the men of* Keilah deliver
12. Will *the men of* Keilah deliver me and
2Sa. 1: 6. and, lo, the chariots and horsemen (lit. *and masters of* the horsemen)
11:26. she mourned for *her husband.*
21:12. from *the men of* Jabesh-gilead,
2K. 1: 8. an hairy man, (lit. a man, *an owner of* hair)
Neh 6:18. many in Judah sworn (lit. *masters of* oath) unto him,
Est. 1:17. they shall despise *their husbands*
20. wives shall give *to their husbands*
Job 31:39. *the owners thereof* to lose their life:
Pro. 1:17. in the sight of any *bird.* (marg. eyes of every thing *that hath* a wing. lit. *owner of* a wing)
19. the life of *the owners thereof.*
3:27. *from them to whom it is due,* (marg. *from the owners thereof*)
12: 4. a crown to *her husband:*
16:22. a wellspring of life *unto him that hath it:*
17: 8. in the eyes of *him that hath it:*
18: 9. brother to him that is *a great* waster.
22:24. Make no friendship with *an angry man;*
23: 2. if thou (be) *a man given to* appetite.
24: 8. shall be called *a* mischievous *person.*
29:22. *and a* furious *man*
31:11. The heart of *her husband*
23. *Her husband* is known in the gates,
28. *her husband* (also), and he praiseth her.
Ecc. 5:11(10). good (is there) *to the owners thereof,*
13(12). riches kept *for the owners thereof*
7:12. giveth life to *them that have it.*
8: 8. deliver *those that are given to it.*
Ecc.10:11. a babbler is no better. (marg. *the master of* the tongue)
20. *and that which hath* wings shall tell (lit. *and the master of* wings)
12:11. fastened (by) *the masters of* assemblies,
Isa. 1: 3. and the ass *his master's* crib:
16: 8. *the lords of* the heathen
41:15. threshing instrument *having* teeth:
50: 8. who (is) mine adversary? (marg. *the master of* my cause)
Jer. 37:13. *a captain of* the ward (was) there,
Dan. 8: 6. he came to the ram *that had* two horns,
20. The ram which thou sawest *having* two horns
Hos. 2:16(18). and shalt call me no more *Baali.* (marg. *My lord*)
Joel 1: 8. for *the husband of* her youth.
Nah. 1: 2. and (is) furious; (marg. *that hath* fury)

בְּעֵל *b'ğehl,* Ch. m. 1169

Ezr. 4: 8. Rehum the chancellor (lit. *master of* counsel)
9. Then (wrote) Rehum the chancellor, (lit. *id.*)
17. an answer unto Rehum the chancellor, (lit. *id.*)

בַּעֲלָה [*bağăh-lāh'*], f. 1172

1Sa.28: 7, 7. a woman *that hath* a familiar spirit, (lit. *mistress of* a familiar spirit)
1K. 17:17. *the mistress of* the house,
Nah. 3: 4. *the mistress of* witchcrafts,

בָּעַר [*bāh-ğar'*]. 1197

* KAL.—*Preterite.* *

Nu. 11: 3. the Lord *burnt* among them.
Jud.15:14. as flax that *was burnt*
2Sa.22: 9. coals *were kindled* by it.
13. before him *were* coals of fire *kindled.*
Est. 1:12. his anger *burned* in him.
Ps. 18: 8(9). coals *were kindled* by it.
Isa. 1:31. *and they shall* both *burn*
9:18(17). For wickedness *burneth* as the fire:
10:17. *and it shall burn* and devour
Jer. 4: 4. *and burn* that none can quench
7:20. *and it shall burn,* and shall not
21:12. *and burn* that none can quench

KAL.—*Future.*

Ex. 3: 3. why the bush *is* not *burnt.*
Nu.11: 1. *and* the fire of the Lord *burnt*
Job 1:16. *and hath burned up* the sheep,
Ps. 2:12. when his wrath *is kindled*
39: 3(4). while I was musing the fire *burned:*
79: 5. *shall* thy jealousy *burn* like fire?
83:14(15). As the fire *burneth* a wood,
89:46(47). *shall* thy wrath *burn* like fire?
106:18. *And* a fire *was kindled*
Isa. 42:25. *and it burned* him,
43: 2. neither *shall* the flame *kindle* upon thee.
62: 1. as a lamp (that) *burneth.*
Jer. 10: 8. But *they are* altogether *brutish*
44: 6. *and was kindled* in the cities
Lam.2: 3. *and he burned* against Jacob

KAL.—*Participle.* Poel.

Ex. 3: 2. the bush *burned* with fire,
Deu 4:11. the mountain *burned* with fire
5:23(20). the mountain *did burn* with fire,
9:15. the mount *burned* with fire:
Ps. 94: 8. *ye brutish* among the people:
Isa. 30:27. *burning* (with) his anger,
33. a stream of brimstone, *doth kindle*
34: 9. shall become *burning* pitch.
Jer.20: 9. was in mine heart as a *burning* fire
Eze. 1:13. like *burning* coals of fire,
21:31(36). into the hand of *brutish* men, (marg. or, *burning*)
Hos. 7: 4. as an oven *heated* by the baker,
6. in the morning it *burneth* as a flaming fire.
Mal. 4: 1 (3:19). *that shall burn* as an oven;

* NIPHAL.—*Preterite.* *

Jer. 10:14. Every man *is brutish*
21. the pastors *are become brutish,*
51:17. Every man *is brutish*

NIPHAL.—*Participle.*

Isa. 19:11. counsel of the wise counsellors of Pharaoh *is become brutish:*

* PIEL.—*Preterite.* *

Ex. 22: 5(4). *and shall feed* in another man's field;
Lev. 6:12(5). *and* the priest *shall burn* wood
Deu 13: 5(6). *So shalt thou put* the evil *away*
17: 7. *So thou shalt put* the evil *away*
12. *and thou shalt put away* the evil
19:13. *but thou shalt put away* (the guilt)
19. *so shalt thou put* the evil *away*
21:21 & 22:21. *so shalt thou put* evil *away*
22:22. *so shalt thou put away* evil
24. *so thou shalt put away* evil from among
24: 7. *and thou shalt put* evil *away* from
26:13. *I have brought away* the hallowed
14. neither *have I taken away*
2Sa. 4:11. *and take* you *away* from the earth?
1K. 14:10. *and will take away* the remnant
21:21. *and will take away* thy posterity,
22:46(47). *he took out* of the land.
2K. 23:24. *did* Josiah *put away,*
2Ch 19: 3. in that *thou hast taken away*
Isa. 3:14. *ye have eaten up* the vineyard; (marg. *burnt*)
50:11. the sparks (that) *ye have kindled.*
Eze.20:48(21:4). I the Lord *have kindled it:*
39: 9. *and shall set on fire*
— *and they shall burn* them

PIEL.—*Infinitive.*

Nu. 24:22. the Kenite shall be *wasted,*
2Ch. 4:20. *that they should burn* after the manner
13:11. *to burn* every evening:
Neh 10:34(35). *to burn* upon the altar
Isa. 4: 4. by the spirit of *burning.*
5: 5. and it shall be *eaten up;*
6:13. and shall be *eaten:*
40:16. Lebanon (is) not sufficient *to burn,*
44:15. shall it be for a man *to burn:*

PIEL.—*Future.*

Ex. 35: 3. *Ye shall kindle* no fire
Deu 21: 9. So *shalt* thou *put away*
Jud.20:13. *and put away* evil from Israel.
1K. 14:10. as a man *taketh away* dung, till it be
Eze.39:10. *they shall burn* the weapons

PIEL.—*Participle.*

Jer. 7:18. the fathers *kindle* the fire,

* PUAL.—*Participle.* *

Jer.36:22. on the hearth *burning* before him.

* HIPHIL.—*Preterite.* *

Nah. 2:13(14). *and I will burn* her chariots

HIPHIL.—*Future.*

Ex. 22: 5(4). *shall cause* a field or vineyard *to be eaten,*
Jud.15: 5. *when he had set* the brands on fire,
— *and burnt up* both the shocks,
2Ch 28: 3. *and burnt* his children in the fire,
Eze. 5: 2. *Thou shalt burn* with fire

HIPHIL.—*Participle.*

Ex. 22: 6(5). *he that kindled* the fire
1K. 16: 3. I *will take away* the posterity

1198 בַּעַר *bah'-gar*, m.

Ps. 49:10(11). the fool *and the brutish person*
73:22. So *foolish* (was) I, and ignorant:
92: 6(7). A *brutish* man knoweth not:
Pro.12: 1. he that hateth reproof (is) *brutish.*
30: 2. Surely I (am) more *brutish*

1200 בְּעֵרָה *b'gēh-rāh'*, f.

Ex. 22: 6(5). he that kindled *the fire*

בָּעַת [*bāh-gath'*]. 1204

* NIPHAL.—*Preterite.* *

1Ch 21:30. for *he was afraid* because of
Est. 7: 6. Then Haman *was afraid*
Dan. 8:17. when he came, *I was afraid,*

* PIEL.—*Preterite.* *

1Sa.16:14. from the Lord *troubled him.* (marg. *terrified*)
Job 18:11. Terrors *shall make him afraid*
Isa. 21: 4. fearfulness *affrighted me:*

PIEL.—*Future.*

2Sa.22: 5. ungodly men *made me afraid;*
Job 3: 5. *let* the blackness of the day *terrify it.*
7:14. and *terrifiest me* through visions:
9:34. *let* not his fear *terrify me:*
13:11. *Shall* not his excellency *make* you *afraid?*
21. *let* not thy dread *make me afraid.*
15:24. anguish *shall make him afraid;*
33: 7. my terror *shall* not *make thee afraid,*
Ps. 18: 4(5). ungodly men *made me afraid.*

PIEL.—*Participle.*

1Sa.16:15. an evil spirit from God *troubleth thee.*

בְּעָתָה *b'gāh-thāh'*, f. 1205

Jer. 8:15. for a time of health, and behold *trouble!*
14:19. the time of healing, and behold *trouble!*

בִּעוּתִים see בִּעֻתִים See 1161

בֹּץ *bōhtz*, m. 1206

Jer. 38:22. thy feet are sunk *in the mire,*

בִּצָּה *bitz-tzāh'*, f. 1207

Job 8:11. Can the rush grow up without *mire?*
40:21. in the covert of the reed, *and fens.*
Eze.47:11. But *the miry places thereof*

בָּצִיר *bāh-tzeer'*, m. 1208, 1210

Lev. 26: 5. shall reach unto *the vintage, and the vintage* shall reach
Jud. 8: 2. better *than the vintage of* Abi-ezer?
Isa. 24:13. when *the vintage* is done.
32:10. for *the vintage* shall fail,
Jer. 48:32. upon *thy vintage.*
Mic. 7: 1. as the grapegleanings of *the vintage:*
Zec 11: 2. for the forest of *the vintage* (marg. or, the *defenced* forest כתיב)

בֶּצֶל [*beh'-tzel*], m. 1211

Nu. 11: 5. the leeks, and *the onions,*

בָּצַע [*bāh-tzag'*]. 1214

* KAL.—*Infinitive.* *

Eze.22:27. *to get* dishonest gain.

KAL.—*Imperative.*

Am. 9: 1. *and cut them* in the head, (marg. *wound*

KAL.—*Future.*

Job 27: 8. though *he hath gained,*
Joel 2: 8. *they shall* not *be wounded.*

KAL.—*Participle.* Poel.

Ps. 10: 3. *and* blesseth *the covetous,*
Pro. 1:19. every one *that is greedy of* gain;
15:27. *He that is greedy of* gain
Jer. 6:13. every one (is) *given to* covetousness;
8:10. unto the greatest *is given to* covetousness,
Hab. 2: 9. Woe to *him that coveteth* (marg. *gaineth*)

* PIEL.—*Preterite.* *

Lam. 2:17. *he hath fulfilled* his word

PIEL.—*Future.*

Job 6: 9. *and cut me off!*
Isa. 10:12. when the Lord *hath performed*
38:12. *he will cut me off* with pining
Eze. 22:12. *and thou hast greedily gained*
Zec. 4: 9. his hands *shall* also *finish it;*

1215 **בֶּצַע** *beh'-tzag*, m.

Gen37:26. What *profit* (is it) if we slay
Ex. 18:21. men of truth, hating *covetousness;*
Jud. 5:19. they took no *gain of* money.
1Sa. 8: 3. but turned aside after *lucre,*
Job 22: 3. or (is it) *gain* (to him),
Ps. 30: 9(10). What *profit* (is there) in my blood,
119:36. not to *covetousness.*
Pro. 1:19. every one that is greedy of *gain;*
15:27. He that is greedy of *gain*
28:16. he that hateth *covetousness*
Isa. 33:15. he that despiseth *the gain of*
56:11. every one for *his gain*
57:17. For the iniquity of *his covetousness*
Jer. 6:13. every one (is) given to *covetousness;*
8:10. is given to *covetousness,*
22:17. but for *thy covetousness,*
51:13. the measure of *thy covetousness.*
Eze. 22:13. smitten mine hand at *thy dishonest gain*
27. to get *dishonest gain.*
33:31. goeth after *their covetousness.*
Mic. 4:13. I will consecrate *their gain*
Hab. 2: 9. *an* evil *covetousness* to his house, (marg. *gain*)
Mal. 3:14. what *profit* (is it) that we have

1216 **בָּצֵק** [*bāh-tzēhk'*].

* KAL.—*Preterite.* *

Deu 8: 4. neither *did* thy foot *swell,*
Neh 9:21. their feet *swelled* not.

1217 **בָּצֵק** *bāh-tzēhk'*, m.

Ex. 12:34. the people took *their dough*
39. baked unleavened cakes of *the dough*
2Sa. 13: 8. And she took *flour,* (marg. or, *paste*)
Jer. 7:18. the women knead (their) *dough,*
Hos 7: 4. after he hath kneaded *the dough,*

1219 **בָּצַר** [*bāh-tzar'*].

* KAL.—*Future.* *

Lev. 25: 5. neither *gather* the grapes
11. nor *gather* (the grapes) in it
Deu 24:21. When *thou gatherest* the grapes
Jud. 9:27. *and gathered* their vineyards,
Ps. 76:12(13). *He shall cut off* the spirit of princes:

KAL.—*Participle.* Poel.

Jer. 6: 9. turn back thine hand *as a grapegatherer*
49: 9. If *grapegatherers* come to thee,
Obad. 5. if *the grapegatherers* came

KAL.—*Participle.* Paül.

Nu. 13:28. and the cities (are) *walled.*
Deu 1:28. *and walled up* to heaven;
3: 5. these cities (were) *fenced* with
9: 1. cities great *and fenced* up to heaven,
28:52. until thy high *and fenced* walls
Jos. 14:12. the cities (were) great (and) *fenced:*
2Sa. 20: 6. lest he get him *fenced* cities,
2K. 18:13. come up against all the *fenced* cities
19:25. shouldest be to lay waste *fenced* cities
2Ch 17: 2. placed forces in all the *fenced* cities
19: 5. throughout all the *fenced* cities
32: 1. encamped against the *fenced* cities,
33:14. in all the *fenced* cities of Judah.
Neh 9:25. they took *strong* cities,
Isa. 2:15. upon every *fenced* wall,
25: 2. a *defenced* city a ruin:
27:10. Yet the *defenced* city
36: 1. against all the *defenced* cities
37:26. to lay waste *defenced* cities
Jer. 15:20. unto this people a *fenced* brasen
33: 3. shew thee great *and mighty things,* (marg. *hidden*)
Eze. 21:20(25). Judah in Jerusalem *the defenced.*
36:35. desolate and ruined cities (are become) *fenced,*
Hos 8:14. Judah hath multiplied *fenced* cities:
Zep 1:16. against the *fenced* cities,
Zec. 11: 2. (כתיב) the forest of *the vintage* [according to the קרי] is come down. (marg. *defenced* forest [following the כתיב])

* NIPHAL.—*Future.* *

Gen 11: 6. nothing *will be restrained*
Job 42: 2. no thought *can be withholden* (marg. *be hindered*)

* PIEL.—*Infinitive.* *

Isa. 22:10. broken down *to fortify* the wall.

PIEL.—*Future.*

Jer. 51:53. though *she should fortify*

בֶּצֶר [*beh'-tzer*], m. 1220

Job 22:24. Then shalt thou lay up *gold*
25. the Almighty shall be *thy defence,*

בְּצַר [*b'tzar*], m. 1222

Job 36:19. not *gold,* nor all the forces of strength.

בָּצְרָה [*botz-rāh'*], f. 1223

Mic 2:12. as the sheep of *Bozrah,* [Gesenius—*of the fold*]

בִּצָּרוֹן *bitz-tzāh-rōhn'*, m. 1225

Zec. 9:12. Turn you *to the strong hold.*

בַּצֹּרֶת *batz-tzōh'-reth*, f. 1226

Jer. 14: 1. concerning *the dearth.* (marg. *dearths,* or, *restraints*)
17: 8. be careful in the year of *drought,* (marg. *restraint*)

בַּקְבּוּק *bak-book'*, m. 1228

1K. 14: 3. *and a cruse of* honey, (marg. *bottle*)
Jer. 19: 1. get a potter's earthen *bottle,*
10. Then shalt thou break *the bottle*

בְּקִיעַ [*b'kee'ăg*], m. 1233

Isa. 22: 9. *the breaches of* the city of David,
Am. 6:11. the little house with *clefts.*

בָּקַע *bāh-kag'*. 1234

* KAL.—*Preterite.* *

Neh 9:11. *thou didst divide* the sea
Ps 74:15. *Thou didst cleave* the fountain
78:13. *He divided* the sea,
Isa. 34:15. make her nest, and lay, *and hatch,*
Eze. 29: 7. *and rend* all their shoulder:

KAL.—*Infinitive.*

2Ch 32: 1. thought *to win them* for himself. (marg. *to break them up*)
Am. 1:13. *they have ripped up* the women with child (marg. or, *divided* the mountains)

KAL.—*Imperative.*

Ex. 14:16. over the sea, *and divide it:*

KAL.—*Future.*

Jud.15:19. *But* God *clave* an hollow place
2Sa.23:16. *And* the three mighty men *brake through*
1Ch 11:18. *And* the three *brake through*
2Ch 21:17. *and brake into it*, and carried
Isa. 48:21. *he clave* the rock *also*,

KAL.—*Participle.* Poel.

Ps.141: 7. when one cutteth *and cleaveth*
Ecc.10: 9. *he that cleaveth* wood
Isa. 63:12. *dividing* the water before them,

* NIPHAL.—*Preterite.* *

Gen 7:11. *were* all the fountains of the great deep *broken up*,
2Ch 25:12. they all *were broken in pieces.*
Job 26: 8. the cloud *is* not *rent* under them.
Pro. 3:20. By his knowledge the depths *are broken up*,
Isa. 35: 6. in the wilderness *shall* waters *break out*,
Zec.14: 4. *and* the mount of Olives *shall cleave*

NIPHAL.—*Infinitive.*

Eze.30:16. No shall be *rent asunder*, (lit. *to be rent*)

NIPHAL.—*Future.*

Ex. 14:21. *and* the waters *were divided.*
Nu. 16:31. *that* the ground *clave asunder*
1K. 1:40. *so that* the earth *rent*
2K. 25: 4. *And* the city *was broken up*,
Job 32:19. *it is ready to burst* like new bottles.
Isa. 58: 8. Then *shall* thy light *break forth*
59: 5. *breaketh out* into a viper.
Jer. 52: 7. *Then* the city *was broken up*,

* PIEL.—*Preterite.* *

2K. 15:16. that were with child *he ripped up.*
Job 28:10. *He cutteth out* rivers
Isa. 59: 5. *They hatch* cockatrice' eggs,
Eze.13:13. *I will even rend* (it) with a stormy wind

PIEL.—*Future.*

Gen 22: 3. *and clave* the wood for the
1Sa. 6:14. *and they clave* the wood
2K. 2:24. *and tare* forty and two children
8:12. and *rip up* their women with child.
Ps. 78:15. *He clave* the rocks in the wilderness,
Eze.13:11. a stormy wind *shall rend* (it).
Hos 13: 8. the wild beast *shall tear them.*
Hab 3: 9. *Thou didst cleave* the earth

* PUAL.—*Future.* *

Hos 13:16(14.1). their women with child *shall be ripped up.*

PUAL.—*Participle.*

Jos. 9: 4. wine bottles, old, *and rent*,
Eze.26:10. a city *wherein is made a breach.*

* HIPHIL.—*Infinitive.* *

2K. 3:26. that drew swords, *to break through*

HIPHIL.—*Future.*

Isa. 7: 6. *let us make a breach therein* for us,

* HOPHAL.—*Preterite.* *

Jer. 39: 2. the city *was broken up.*

* HITHPAEL.—*Preterite.* *

Jos. 9:13. behold, *they be rent:*

HITHPAEL.—*Future.*

Mic 1: 4. the valleys *shall be cleft*,

1235 **בֶּקַע** *beh'-kag*, m.

Gen 24:22. a golden earring of *half a shekel* weight,
Ex. 38:26. *A bekah* for every man,

בִּקְעָא [*bik-gāh'*], Ch. f. 1236

Dan 3: 1. he set it up *in the plain of* Dura,

בִּקְעָה *bik-gāh'*, f. 1237

Gen 11: 2. that they found *a plain*
Deu 8: 7. depths that spring *out of valleys*
11:11. a land of hills *and valleys*,
34: 3. the plain of *the valley of* Jericho,
Jos. 11: 8. unto *the valley of* Mizpeh
17 & 12:7. Baal-gad *in the valley of* Lebanon
2Ch 35:22. came to fight *in the valley of* Megiddo.
Neh 6: 2. *in the plain of* Ono.
Ps. 104: 8. they go down by *the valleys.*
Isa. 40: 4. the rough places *plain:* (marg. *a plain place*)
41:18. in the midst of *the valleys:*
63:14. As a beast goeth down *into the valley*,
Eze. 3:22. go forth into *the plain*, and I will
23. went forth into *the plain:*
8: 4. according to the vision that I saw *in the plain.*
37: 1. in the midst of *the valley*
2. very many in the *open valley;* (marg. *champaign*)
Am. 1: 5. *from the plain of* Aven, (marg. *Bikath*-aven)
Zec. 12:11. *in the valley* of Megiddon.

בָּקַק [*bāh-kak'*]. 1238

* KAL.—*Preterite.* *

Jer. 19: 7. *And I will make void* the counsel
Nah 2: 2(3). the emptiers *have emptied them out*,

KAL.—*Participle.* Poel.

Isa. 24: 1. the Lord *maketh* the earth *empty*,
Hos 10: 1. Israel (is) an *empty* vine, (marg. *emptying*)
Nah 2: 2(3). *the emptiers* have emptied them

* NIPHAL.—*Preterite.* *

Isa. 19: 3. *And* the spirit of Egypt *shall fail* (marg. *be emptied*)

NIPHAL.—*Infinitive.*

Isa. 24: 3. The land shall be *utterly* emptied,

NIPHAL.—*Future.*

Isa. 24: 3. The land *shall be* utterly *emptied*,

* POLEL.—*Future.* *

Jer. 51: 2. *and shall empty* her land:

בָּקַר [*bāh-kar'*]. 1239

* PIEL.—*Preterite.* *

Eze.34:11. search my sheep, *and seek them out.*

PIEL.—*Infinitive.*

2K. 16:15. shall be for me *to enquire*
Ps. 27: 4. *and to enquire* in his temple.
Pro.20:25. after vows *to make enquiry.*

PIEL.—*Future.*

Lev.13:36. the priest *shall* not *seek*
27:33. *He shall* not *search*
Eze.34:12. so *will I seek out* my sheep,

בְּקַר [*b'kar*], Ch. 1240

* PAEL.—*Preterite.* *

Ezr. 4:19. I commanded, *and search hath been made*,
6: 1. *and search was made* in the

PAEL.—*Infinitive.*

Ezr. 7:14. *to enquire* concerning Judah and

PAEL.—*Future.*

Ezr. 4:15. That *search may be made*

* ITHPAEL.—*Future.* *

Ezr. 5:17. *let there be search made* in the king's treasure house,

1241 בָּקָר bāh-kāhr', com.

פַּר בֶּן בָּקָר ¹ בֶּן בָּקָר ²

Gen 12:16. he had sheep, *and oxen,*
13: 5. had flocks, *and herds,*
18: 7. Abraham ran unto *the herd,* and fetcht a ²*calf* tender and good, (lit. son of *a bull*)
8. the ²*calf* (lit. son of *a bull*) which he had
20:14. Abimelech took sheep, *and oxen,*
21:27. Abraham took sheep *and oxen,*
24:35. hath given him flocks, *and herds,*
26:14. possession of *herds,*
32: 7(8). the flocks, and *herds,*
33:13. the flocks *and herds*
34:28. took their sheep, and *their oxen,*
45:10. thy flocks, *and thy herds,*
46:32 & 47:1. their flocks, *and their herds,*
47:17. for the cattle of *the herds,*
50: 8. their flocks, *and their herds,*
Ex. 9: 3. *upon the oxen,* and upon the sheep:
10: 9. *and with our herds* will we go;
24. let your flocks *and your herds*
12:32. take your flocks and *your herds,*
38. flocks, *and herds,*
20:24. thy sheep, and *thine oxen:*
22: 1(21:37). shall restore five *oxen* for an ox,
29: 1. Take one young ¹*bullock,* (lit. one steer son of *a bull*)
34: 3. neither let the flocks *nor herds* feed
Lev. 1: 2. of *the herd,* and of the flock.
3. a burnt sacrifice of *the herd,*
5. he shall kill ²*the bullock* (lit. son of *a bull*)
3: 1. if he offer (it) of *the herd;*
4: 3. a young ¹*bullock* without blemish
14. shall offer a young ¹ *bullock*
9: 2. Take thee a young calf (lit. a calf son of *a bull*)
16: 3. a young ¹ *bullock* for a sin offering,
22:19. *of the beeves,* of the sheep,
21. a freewill offering *in beeves*
23:18. one young ¹ *bullock,*
27:32. concerning the tithe of *the herd,*
Nu. 7: 3. covered wagons, and twelve *oxen;*
6. took the wagons and *the oxen,*
7. Two wagons and four *oxen*
8. four wagons and eight *oxen*
15, 21, 27, 33, 39, 45, 51, 57, 63, 69, 75, 81. One young ¹ *bullock,*
17, 23, 29, 35, 41, 47, 53, 59, 65, 71, 77, 83. two *oxen,* five rams,
87. All the *oxen* for the burnt offering
88. all *the oxen for* the sacrifice
8: 8. take a young ¹ *bullock*
— another young ¹ *bullock* shalt thou take
11:22. the flocks *and the herds*
15: 3. of *the herd,* or of the flock:
8. when thou preparest a ² *bullock*
9. bring with a ² *bullock* a meat offering
24. shall offer one young ¹ *bullock*
22:40. Balak offered *oxen* and sheep,
28:11, 19, 27. two young ¹ *bullocks,*
29: 2, 8. one young *bullock,*
13. thirteen young ¹ *bullocks,*
17. twelve young ¹ *bullocks,*
31:28. and of *the beeves,*
30. of the persons, of *the beeves,*
33. *And* threescore and twelve thousand *beeves,*
38. *And the beeves* (were) thirty and six
44. *And* thirty and six thousand *beeves,*
Deu 8:13. *And* (when) *thy herds* and thy flocks
12: 6. the firstlings of *your herds*
17. or the firstlings of *thy herds*
21. thou shalt kill *of thy herd*
14:23. the firstlings of *thy herds*
26. *for oxen,* or for sheep,
15:19. *of thy herd* and of thy flock
16: 2. of the flock *and the herd,*
21: 3. the elders of that city shall take an heifer, (lit. an heifer of *the herd*)
32:14. Butter of *kine,* and milk of sheep,
Jud. 3:31. six hundred men with an *ox* goad:
1Sa. 11: 5. Saul came after *the herd*
7. he took a yoke of *oxen,*
— so shall it be done *unto his oxen.*
14:32. took sheep, *and oxen,* and ²*calves,* and slew (them) on the ground:
1Sa. 15: 9, 15. the best of the sheep, *and of the oxen,*
14. the lowing of *the oxen*
21. took of the spoil, sheep *and oxen,*
16: 2. Take an heifer with thee, (lit. an heifer of *the herd*)
27: 9. took away the sheep, *and the oxen,*
30:20. took all the flocks *and the herds,*
2Sa. 6: 6. for *the oxen* shook (it).
12: 2. exceeding many flocks *and herds:*
4. *and of his own herd,* to dress
17:29. cheese of *kine,* for David,
24:22. *oxen* for burnt sacrifice,
— and (other) instruments of *the oxen*
24. *the oxen* for fifty shekels
1K. 1: 9. Adonijah slew sheep *and oxen*
4:23(5:3). Ten fat *oxen,* and twenty *oxen* out of the pastures,
7:25. It stood upon twelve *oxen,*
29. lions, *oxen,* and cherubims:
— beneath the lions *and oxen*
44. twelve *oxen* under the sea;
8: 5. sacrificing sheep *and oxen,*
63. two and twenty thousand *oxen,*
19:20. he left *the oxen,* and ran after
21. took a yoke of *oxen,*
— with the instruments of *the oxen,*
2 K. 5:26. vineyards, and sheep, *and oxen,*
16:17. from off *the* brasen *oxen*
1Ch 12:40. on mules, *and on oxen,*
— oil, *and oxen,* and sheep
13: 9. for *the oxen* stumbled.
21:23. I give (thee) *the oxen* (also)
27:29. over *the herds* that fed
— *the herds* (that were) in the vallies
2Ch. 4: 3. the similitude of *oxen,*
— Two rows of *oxen* (were) cast,
4. It stood upon twelve *oxen,*
15. twelve *oxen* under it.
5: 6. sacrificed sheep *and oxen,*
7: 5. twenty and two thousand *oxen,*
13: 9. consecrate himself with a young ¹ *bullock*
15:11. seven hundred *oxen*
18: 2. Ahab killed sheep *and oxen*
29:22. So they killed *the bullocks,*
32. threescore and ten *bullocks,*
33. six hundred *oxen*
31: 6. brought in the tithe of *oxen*
32:29. possessions of flocks *and herds*
35: 7. *and* three thousand *bullocks:*
8. *and* three hundred *oxen.*
9. *and* five hundred *oxen.*
12. so (did they) *with the oxen.*
Neh 10:36(37). the firstlings of *our herds*
Job 1: 3. five hundred yoke of *oxen,*
14. *The oxen* were plowing, and the asses feeding
40:15. he eateth grass *as an ox.*
42:12. a thousand yoke of *oxen,*
Ps. 66:15. I will offer *bullocks* with goats.
Ecc. 2: 7. *great* and small cattle above all (lit. *oxen* and sheep)
Isa. 7:21. a man shall nourish a young *cow,* (lit. an heifer of *the herd*)
11: 7. the lion shall eat straw *like the ox.*
22:13. slaying *oxen,* and killing sheep,
65:10. a place for *the herds* to lie down
25. the lion shall eat straw *like the bullock:*
Jer. 3:24. their flocks and *their herds,*
5:17. shall eat up thy flocks *and thine herds:*
31:12. the young of the flock *and of the herd:*
52:20. *and* twelve brasen *bulls*
Eze. 4:15. I have given thee *cow's* dung
43:19. a young ¹ *bullock* for a sin offering.
23. offer a young ¹ *bullock* without blemish,
25. shall also prepare a young ¹ *bullock,*
45:18. take a young ¹ *bullock* without blemish,
46: 6. a young ¹ *bullock* without blemish,
Hos. 5: 6. *and with their herds* to seek the
Joel 1:18. *the herds* of cattle are perplexed,
Am. 6:12. will (one) plow (there) *with oxen?*
Jon. 3: 7. man nor beast, *herd* nor flock,
Hab. 3:17. no *herd* in the stalls:

בֹּקֶר bōh'-ker, m. 1242

Gen. 1: 5, 8, 13, 19, 23, 31. the evening and *the morning*

Gen19:27. Abraham gat up early *in the morning*
20: 8. Abimelech rose early *in the morning,*
21:14 & 22:3. Abraham rose up early *in the morning,*
24:54. they rose up *in the morning,*
26:31. rose up betimes *in the morning,*
28:18. Jacob rose up early *in the morning,*
29:25. came to pass, that *in the morning,*
31:55(32·1). early *in the morning* Laban rose
40: 6. came in unto them *in the morning,*
41: 8. it came to pass *in the morning*
44: 3. As soon as *the morning* was light,
49:27. *in the morning* he shall devour
Ex. 7:15. Get thee unto Pharaoh *in the morning ;*
8:20(16) & 9:13. Rise up early *in the morning,*
10:13. when it was *morning,*
12:10. nothing of it remain until *the morning ;*
— remaineth of it until *the morning*
22. of his house until *the morning.*
14:24. that in the *morning* watch
27. when *the morning* appeared;
16: 7. *And in the morning,* then ye shall see
8. *in the morning* bread to the full;
12. *and in the morning* ye shall be
13. *and in the morning* the dew
19. Let no man leave of it till *the morning.*
20. left of it until *the morning,*
21. they gathered it *every morning,* (lit. *in the morning in the morning*)
23. to be kept until *the morning.*
24. they laid it up till *the morning,*
18:13. from *the morning* unto the evening.
14. from *morning* unto even?
19:16. on the third day in *the morning,*
23:18. remain until *the morning.*
24: 4. rose up early *in the morning,*
27:21. from evening to *morning*
29:34. remain unto *the morning,*
39. thou shalt offer *in the morning;*
41. the meat offering of *the morning,*
30: 7. sweet incense *every morning :* (lit. *in the morning, in the morning*)
34: 2. be ready *in the morning,* and come up *in the morning*
4. Moses rose up early *in the morning,*
25. the passover be left *unto the morning.*
36: 3. yet unto him free offerings *every morning.* (lit. *in the morning, in the morning*)
Lev. 6: 9(2). all night unto *the morning,*
12(5). shall burn wood on it *every morning,* (lit. *in the morning, in the morning*)
20(13). half of it *in the morning,*
7:15. leave any of it until *the morning.*
9:17. burnt sacrifice of *the morning.*
19:13. all night until *the morning.*
22:30. none of it until *the morrow :*
24: 3. from the evening unto *the morning*
Nu. 9:12. leave none of it unto *the morning,*
15. of fire, until *the morning.*
21. abode from even unto *the morning,* and (that) the cloud was taken up *in the morning,*
14:40. they rose up early *in the morning,*
16: 5. Even *to morrow* the Lord will
22:13, 21. Balaam rose up *in the morning,*
41. it came to pass *on the morrow,*
28: 4. shalt thou offer *in the morning,*
8. as the meat offering of *the morning,*
23. the burnt offering in *the morning,*
Deu16: 4. remain all night *until the morning.*
7. thou shalt turn *in the morning,*
28:67. *In the morning* thou shalt say,
— Would God it were *morning!*
Jos. 3: 1 & 6:12. Joshua rose early *in the morning;*
7:14. *In the morning* therefore ye shall
16, & 8:10. Joshua rose up early *in the morning,*
Jud. 6:28. arose early *in the morning,*
31. put to death whilst (it is yet) *morning:*
9:33. it shall be, (that) *in the morning,*
16: 2. In *the morning,* when it is day,
19: 5. when they arose early *in the morning,*
8. he arose early *in the morning*
25. all the night until *the morning:*
26. in the dawning of *the day,*
27. her lord rose up *in the morning,*
20:19. Israel rose up *in the morning,*

Ruth.2: 7. from *the morning* until now,
3:13. it shall be *in the morning,*
— lie down until *the morning.*
14. lay at his feet until *the morning :*
1Sa. 1:19. they rose up *in the morning*
3:15. Samuel lay until *the morning,*
5: 4. they arose early *on the* morrow *morning,*
9:19. *to morrow* I will let thee go,
11:11. in *the morning* watch,
14:36. spoil them until the *morning* light,
15:12. early to meet Saul *in the morning,*
17:20. rose up early *in the morning,*
19: 2. take heed to thyself *until the morning,*
11. to slay him *in the morning :*
20:35. it came to pass *in the morning,*
25:22, 34. by the *morning* light
36. until the *morning* light.
37. it came to pass *in the morning,*
29:10. rise up early *in the morning*
— be up early *in the morning,*
11. early to depart *in the morning,*
2Sa. 2:27. surely then *in the morning*
11:14. it came to pass *in the morning,*
13: 4. (being) the king's son, lean from *day to day?* (marg. *morning by morning*)
17:22. by the *morning* light
23: 4. as the light of *the morning,*
— *a morning* without clouds;
24:11. David was up *in the morning,*
15. *from the morning* even to the time
1 K. 3:21. when I rose *in the morning*
— when I had considered it *in the morning,*
17: 6. bread and flesh *in the morning,*
18:26. *from morning* even until noon,
2 K. 3:20. it came to pass *in the morning,*
22. they rose up early *in the morning,*
7: 9. if we tarry till the *morning* light,
10: 8. the gate until *the morning.*
9. it came to pass *in the morning,*
16:15. the *morning* burnt offering,
19:35. when they arose early *in the morning,*
1Ch. 9:27. the opening thereof *every morning* (lit. *and to morning to morning*)
16:40. continually *morning* and evening, (marg. *in the morning*)
23:30. to stand *every morning* to (lit. *in the morning, in the morning*)
2Ch. 2: 4(3). the burnt offerings *morning* (lit. *for morning*) and evening,
13:11. *every morning* and every evening (lit. *in the morning, in the morning*)
20:20. they rose early *in the morning,*
31: 3. for *the morning* and evening
Ezr. 3: 3. burnt offerings *morning* (lit. *for morning*) and evening.
Est. 2:14. *and on the morrow* she returned
5:14. *and to morrow* speak thou
Job 1: 5. rose up early *in the morning,*
4:20. destroyed *from morning* to evening:
7:18. shouldest visit him *every morning,* (lit. *to mornings*)
11:17. thou shalt shine forth, thou shalt be *as the morning.*
24:17. For *the morning* (is) to them
38: 7. When the *morning* stars sang
12. Hast thou commanded *the morning*
Ps. 5: 3(4). My voice shalt thou hear *in the morning,* O Lord; *in the morning* will I
30: 5(6). *but* joy (cometh) *in the morning.*
46: 5(6). help her,(and that) right *early.*(marg. when *the morning* appeareth)
49:14(15). over them *in the morning;*
55:17(18). Evening, and *morning,*
59:16(17). sing aloud of thy mercy *in the morning:*
65: 8(9). *the morning* and evening to rejoice.
73:14. chastened *every morning.* (lit. *to the mornings*)
88:13(14). *and in the morning* shall
90: 5. *in the morning* (they are) like
6. *In the morning* it flourisheth,
14. O satisfy us *early* with thy mercy;
92: 2(3). thy lovingkindness *in the morning,*
101: 8. I will *early* destroy all (lit. *to the mornings*)
130: 6, 6. they that watch *for the morning :*
143: 8. thy lovingkindness *in the morning ·*
Pro. 7:18. our fill of love until *the morning :*

Pro.27:14. rising early *in the morning*,
Ecc.10:16. thy princes eat *in the morning!*
11: 6. *In the morning* sow thy seed,
Isa. 5:11. that rise up early *in the morning*,
17:11. *and in the morning* shalt thou make
14. before *the morning* he (is) not.
21:12. *The morning* cometh,
28:19. *morning by morning* shall it pass over, (lit. *in the morning, in the morning*)
33: 2. be thou their arm *every morning*, (lit. *to the mornings*)
37:36. when they arose early *in the morning*,
38:13. I reckoned till *morning*,
50: 4. he wakeneth *morning by morning*, (lit. *in the morning, in the morning*)
Jer. 20:16. and let him hear the cry *in the morning*,
21:12. Execute judgment *in the morning*,
Lam.3:23. (They are) new *every morning:* (lit. *to the mornings*)
Eze.12: 8. And *in the morning* came the
24:18. I spake unto the people *in the morning:*
— I did *in the morning* as I was
33:22. until he came to me *in the morning;*
46:13. prepare it *every morning.* (marg. *morning by morning*)
14. a meat offering for it *every morning*, (lit. *id.*)
15. the meat offering, and the oil, *every morning* (lit. *id.*)
Dan. 8:14. Unto two thousand and three hundred days; (marg. evening *morning*)
26. the vision of the evening *and the morning*
Hos. 6: 4. your goodness (is) as a *morning* cloud,
7: 6. *in the morning* it burneth as a flaming fire.
13: 3. they shall be as the *morning* cloud,
Am. 4: 4. bring your sacrifices *every morning*, (lit. *to the morning*)
5: 8. shadow of death *into the morning*,
Mic. 2: 1. when *the morning* is light,
Zep. 3: 3. gnaw not the bones *till the morrow.*
5. *every morning* doth he bring (marg. *morning by morning*)

1243 בַּקָּרָה [*bak-kāh-rāh'*], f.

Eze.34:12. *As* a shepherd *seeketh out* his (marg. *According to the seeking*)

1244 בִּקֹּרֶת *bik-kōh'-reth*, f.

Lev.19:20. she *shall be scourged;* (marg. there shall be *a scourging*)

1245 בָּקַשׁ [*bāh-kash'*].

* PIEL.—*Preterite.* *

Nu. 16:10. *and seek ye* the priesthood
Deu 4:29. *But if* from thence *thou shalt seek*
13:10(11). because *he hath sought* to thrust thee
1Sa.13:14. the Lord *hath sought* him a man
14: 4. Jonathan *sought* to go over
20:16. *Let* the Lord *even require*
2Sa. 4: 8. which *sought* thy life;
2Ch 15:15. *sought him* with their whole desire;
Ezr. 2:62. These *sought* their register
Neh 5:18. for all this *required* not *I* the
7:64. These *sought* their register
12:27. *they sought* the Levites
Est. 2:15. *she required* nothing
6: 2. who *sought* to lay hand on
Ps. 54: 3(5). oppressors *seek* after my soul:
86:14. *have sought* after my soul;
Pro.14: 6. A scorner *seeketh* wisdom,
Ecc. 7:28. Which yet my soul *seeketh*,
29. *they have sought out* many
12:10. The preacher *sought* to find
Cant.3: 1. By night on my bed *I sought*
—, 2. *I sought him*, but I found him not.
5: 6. *I sought him*, but I could not find him;
Isa. 1:12. who *hath required* this
65: 1. found of (them that) *sought me* not:
Jer. 29:13. *And ye shall seek* me,
Lam.1:19. while *they sought* their meat

Eze. 7:25. *and they shall seek* peace,
26. *then shall they seek* a vision
34: 4. neither *have ye sought*
Dan. 1:20. the king *enquired* of them,
Hos. 2: 7(9). *and she shall seek them*, but shall not
3: 5. *and seek* the Lord their God,
5:15. *and seek* my face:
7:10. nor *seek him* for all this.
Zep. 1: 6. that *have* not *sought* the Lord,

PIEL.—*Infinitive.*

1Sa.10: 2. which thou wentest *to seek* are found:
14. *To seek* the asses:
23:15. Saul was come out *to seek*
25. Saul also and his men went *to seek*
24: 2(3). went *to seek* David
25:29. *and to seek* thy soul:
26: 2. *to seek* David in the wilderness
20. come out *to seek* a flea,
27: 1. *to seek me* any more
4. and he *sought* no more again *for him.*
2Sa. 5:17. the Philistines came up *to seek*
1K. 2:40. to Achish *to seek* his servants:
18:10. my lord hath not sent *to seek thee:*
1Ch 4:39. *to seek* pasture for their flocks.
14: 8. the Philistines went up *to seek*
2Ch 11:16. to *seek* the Lord God of Israel
20: 4. *to ask* (help) of the Lord:
— they came *to seek* the Lord.
Ezr. 8:21. *to seek* of him a right way
Neh 2:10. *to seek* the welfare of the children of
Est. 4: 8. *and to make request* before him
7: 7. Haman stood up *to make request*
Ps. 104:21. *and seek* their meat from God.
Ecc. 3: 6. A time *to get*, and a time to lose; (marg. *seek*)
7:25. *and to seek out* wisdom,
8:17. though a man labour to *seek*
Jer. 2:33. Why trimmest thou thy way *to seek*
Dan. 9: 3. *to seek* by prayer and supplications,
Hos. 5: 6. with their herds *to seek* the Lord;
Am. 8:12. *to seek* the word of the Lord,
Zec. 8:21. *and to seek* the Lord of hosts:
22. shall come *to seek* the Lord

PIEL.—*Imperative.*

1Sa. 9: 3. arise, go *seek* the asses.
28: 7. *Seek* me a woman that hath
1Ch 16:11. *seek* his face continually.
Ps. 27: 8. *Seek ye* my face;
34:14(15). *seek* peace, and pursue it.
105: 4. *seek* his face evermore.
119:176. *seek* thy servant;
Isa. 45:19. *Seek ye me* in vain:
Jer. 5: 1. *and seek* in the broad places
Zep. 2: 3. *Seek ye* the Lord, all ye meek
— *seek* righteousness, *seek* meekness.

PIEL.—*Future.*

Gen31:39. of my hand *didst thou require it*,
37:15. What *seekest thou?*
43: 9. of my hand *shalt thou require him:*
30. *and he sought* (where) to weep;
Ex. 2:15. *he sought* to slay Moses.
4:24. *and sought* to kill him.
Lev.19:31. neither *seek* after wizards,
Jos. 2:22. *and* the pursuers *sought*
22:23. *let* the Lord himself *require*
Jud. 6:29. And when they enquired *and asked*,
Ru. 3: 1. *shall I* not *seek* rest for thee,
1Sa.10:21. and *when they sought him*, he could not
16:16. *to seek out* a man,
19:10. *And* Saul *sought* to smite David
22:23. for he that *seeketh* my life *seeketh* thy life:
23:14. *And* Saul *sought him* every day,
2Sa. 4:11. *shall I* not therefore now *require*
12:16. David *therefore besought* God
17:20. And *when they had sought* and could not find
21: 1. *and* David *enquired* of the Lord. (marg. *sought* the face of)
2. *and* Saul *sought* to slay them
1K. 1: 2. *Let there be sought* for my lord (marg. *Let them seek*)
3. *So they sought* for a fair damsel
11:40. *sought therefore* to kill Jeroboam.
19:10, 14. *and they seek* my life, to take it away.
2K. 2:16. *and seek* thy master:
17. *and they sought* three days,

2K. 6:19. bring you to the man whom *ye seek.*
1Ch 21: 3. *doth* my lord *require* this thing?
2Ch 7:14. *and seek* my face,
15: 4. God of Israel, *and sought him*, he was found
22: 9. *And he sought* Ahaziah:
Ezr. 8:23. *and besought* our God for this:
Neh. 5:12. We will restore (them), and *will require* nothing
Est. 2: 2. *Let there be* fair young virgins *sought*
21. *and sought* to lay hand on
3: 6. *wherefore* Haman *sought* to destroy
Job 10: 6. *thou enquirest* after mine iniquity,
Ps. 4: 2(3). *seek* after leasing?
27: 4. that *will I seek after;*
8. Thy face, Lord, *will I seek.*
37:36. *yea, I sought him*, but he could
63: 9(10). But those (that) *seek* my soul,
83:16(17). *that they may seek* thy name,
122: 9. *I will seek* thy good.
Pro. 2: 4. If *thou seekest her* as silver,
11:27. diligently seeketh good *procureth* favour:
15:14. understanding *seeketh* knowledge:
17:11. An evil (man) *seeketh* only rebellion:
18: 1. *seeketh* (and) intermeddleth
15. the ear of the wise *seeketh* knowledge.
23:35. *I will seek it* yet again.
29:10. but the just *seek* his soul.
Ecc. 3:15. God *requireth* that which is past.
Cant. 3: 2. *I will seek* him whom my soul loveth:
6: 1. *that we may seek him* with thee.
Isa. 40:20. *he seeketh* unto him a cunning
41:12. *Thou shalt seek them*, and shalt not
Jer. 4:30. *they will seek* thy life.
26:21. *And* when Jehoiakim...heard his words, the king *sought*
45: 5. *And seekest* thou great things for thyself? *seek* (them) not:
50: 4. and *seek* the Lord their God.
Eze. 3:18, 20. his blood *will I require*
22:30. *And I sought* for a man
33: 8. his blood *will I require*
34:16. *I will seek* that which was lost,
Dan 1: 8. *therefore he requested* of the prince
8:15. *and sought* for the meaning,
Nah. 3: 7. *shall I seek* comforters for thee?
11. *thou* also *shalt seek* strength
Zec. 6: 7. *and sought* to go that they might
11:16. neither *shall seek* the young
12: 9. *I will seek* to destroy all the nations
Mal. 2: 7. *they should seek* the law

PIEL.—*Participle.*

Gen37:16. I *seek* my brethren:
Ex. 4:19. are dead *which sought* thy life.
10:11. for that ye *did desire.*
33: 7. every one *which sought*
Nu. 35:23. neither *sought* his harm:
Jud. 4:22. the man whom thou *seekest.*
14: 4. that he *sought* an occasion against
18: 1. Danites *sought* them
1Sa. 19: 2. Saul my father *seeketh*
20: 1. he *seeketh* my life?
23:10. Saul *seeketh* to come
24: 9(10). David *seeketh* thy hurt?
25:26. *and they that seek* evil
2Sa. 3:17. Ye *sought* for David
16:11. *seeketh* my life:
17: 3. the man whom thou *seekest*
20:19. thou *seekest* to destroy
1K. 10:24. *sought* to Solomon,
11:22. thou *seekest* to go
20: 7. *seeketh* mischief:
1Ch 16:10. rejoice *that seek* the Lord.
2Ch 9:23. the kings of the earth *sought*
Ezr. 8:22. for good *that seek him*
Neh. 2: 4. what *dost* thou *make request?*
Est. 9: 2. *on such as sought* their hurt:
Ps. 24: 6. *that seek* thy face, O Jacob.
35: 4. *that seek* after my soul:
37:25. nor his seed *begging* bread.
32. *and seeketh* to slay him.
38:12(13). *They* also *that seek after* my life
40:14(15). *that seek after* my soul
16(17). Let all *those that seek thee*
69: 6(7). let not *those that seek thee*
70: 2(3). *that seek after* my soul:
4(5). Let all those *that seek thee*

Ps. 71:13. dishonour *that seek* my hurt.
24. brought unto shame, *that seek* my hurt.
105: 3. rejoice *that seek* the Lord.
Pro. 17: 9. covereth a transgression *seeketh* love;
19. *seeketh* destruction.
21: 6. to and fro of *them that seek* death.
28: 5. *but they that seek* the Lord
29:26. Many *seek* the ruler's favour;
Isa. 41:17. poor and needy *seek* water,
51: 1. ye *that seek* the Lord:
Jer. 2:24. all *they that seek her* will not
5: 1. *that seeketh* the truth;
11:21. *that seek* thy life,
19: 7. the hands of them *that seek*
9. *and they that seek* their lives,
21: 7. the hand of *those that seek* their life:
22:25. the hand of *them that seek* thy life,
34:20, 21. the hand of *them that seek* their life:
38:16. these men *that seek* thy life.
44:30. the hand of *them that seek* his life;
— *and that sought* his life.
46:26. the hand of *those that seek* their lives,
49:37. before *them that seek* their life:
Lam. 1:11. *they seek* bread;
Eze. 34: 6. none did search or *seek*
Mal. 2:15. *That he might seek* a godly seed.
3: 1. the Lord, whom ye *seek*,

* PUAL.—*Future.* *

Est. 2:23. And *when inquisition was made* of the
Jer. 50:20. iniquity of Israel *shall be sought for*,
Eze. 26:21. *though thou be sought for*, yet shalt thou

בַּקָּשָׁה [*bak-kāh-shāh'*], f. 1246

Ezr. 7: 6. granted him all *his request*,
Est. 5: 3, 6. and what (is) *thy request?*
7. My petition *and my request*
8. to perform *my request*,
7: 2. what (is) *thy request?* and it shall be performed,
3. my people *at my request:*
9:12. or what (is) *thy request*

בַּר *bar*, m. 1248

Ps. 2:12. Kiss *the Son*, lest he be angry,
Pro. 31: 2. What, *my son?* and what, *the son of* my womb? and what, *the son of* my vows?

בַּר *bar*, adj. 1249

Job 11: 4. *and* I am *clean* in thine eyes.
Ps. 19: 8(9). the commandment of the Lord (is) *pure*,
24: 4. *and a pure* heart;
73: 1. *to such as are of* a *clean* heart.
Pro. 14: 4. Where no oxen (are), the crib (is) *clean:*
Cant. 6: 9. *the choice* (one) of her that bare her.
10. fair as the moon, *clear* as the sun,

בַּר & בָּר *bar* & *bāhr*, m. 1250

Gen 41:35. lay up *corn* under the hand of
49. Joseph gathered *corn* as the sand
42: 3. went down to buy *corn* in Egypt.
25. to fill their sacks with *corn*,
45:23. ten she asses laden with *corn*
Job 39: 4. they grow up *with corn;*
Ps. 65:13(14). the valleys also are covered over with *corn;*
72:16. There shall be an handful of *corn*
Pro. 11:26. He that withholdeth *corn*,
Jer. 23:28. What (is) the chaff to *the wheat?*
Joel 2:24. the floors shall be full of *wheat*,
Am. 5:11. take from him burdens of *wheat:*
8: 5. that we may set forth *wheat*,
6. sell the refuse of the *wheat?*

בַּר *bar*, Ch. m. 1247

Ezr. 5: 1. Zechariah *the son of* Iddo, prophesied

Ezr. 5: 2. Zerubbabel *the son of* Shealtiel, and Jeshua *the son of* Jozadak, and began
6:14. and Zechariah *the son of* Iddo.
Dan 3:25. the fourth is like *the Son of* God.
5:22. And thou *his son*, O Belshazzar,
31(6:1). (being) *about* threescore and two years *old*. (marg. (he) *as the son of*)
7:13. and, behold, (one) *like the Son of* man

1251 ## בַּר [*bar*], Ch. m.

Dan 2:38. the beasts of *the field* and the fowls
4:12(9). the beasts of *the field* had shadow
15(12), 23(20). the tender grass of *the field;*
21(18). under which the beasts of *the field*
23(20), 25(22), 32(29). with the beasts of *the field,*

1252 ## בֹּר *bōhr*, m.

2Sa. 22:21. *according to the cleanness of* my hands
25. *according to my cleanness* in his
Job 9:30. make my hands *never so* clean; (lit. cleanse my hands *in purity*)
22:30. *by the pureness of* thine hands.
Ps. 18:20(21), 24(25). *according to the cleanness of* my hands
Isa. 1:25. *purely* purge away (marg. *according to pureness*)

1254 ## בָּרָא *bāh-rāh'*.

* KAL.—*Preterite.* *

Gen 1: 1. God *created* the heaven and the earth.
27. in the image of God *created he* him; male and female *created he* them.
2: 3. which God *created* and made.
5: 2. Male and female *created he them;*
6: 7. whom *I have created*
Deu 4:32. since the day that God *created* man
Ps. 89:12(13). thou *hast created them:*
47(48). wherefore *hast thou made* all men
Isa. 4: 5. *And* the Lord *will create*
40:26. who *hath created* these (things),
41:20. the Holy One of Israel *hath created it.*
43: 7. *I have created him* for my glory,
45: 8. I the Lord *have created it.*
12. *created* man upon it:
18. *he created it* not in vain,
54:16. I *have created* the smith
— I *have created* the waster to destroy.
Jer. 31:22. the Lord *hath created* a new thing
Mal. 2:10. hath not one God *created us?*

KAL.—*Infinitive.*

Gen 5: 1. In the day that God *created* man,

KAL.—*Imperative.*

Ps. 51:10(12). *Create* in me a clean heart,

KAL.—*Future.*

Gen 1:21. *And* God *created* great whales,
27. *So* God *created* man
Nu. 16:30. if the Lord *make* a new thing, (marg. *create* a creature)

KAL.—*Participle.* Poel.

Ecc. 12: 1. Remember now *thy Creator*
Isa. 40:28. *the Creator of* the ends of the earth,
42: 5. *he that created* the heavens,
43: 1. thus saith the Lord *that created thee,*
15. *the creator of* Israel, your King.
45: 7. *and create* darkness: I make peace, *and create* evil:
18. *that created* the heavens;
57:19. *I create* the fruit of the lips;
65:17. I *create* new heavens and a new earth:
18. for ever (in that) which I *create:* for, behold, I *create* Jerusalem a rejoicing,
Am. 4:13. *and createth* the wind,

* NIPHAL.—*Preterite.* *

Ex. 34:10. such as *have* not *been done*
Ps. 148: 5. he commanded, *and they were created.*
Isa. 48: 7. *They are created* now,
Eze. 21:30(35). the place where *thou wast created,*

NIPHAL.—*Infinitive.*

Gen 2: 4. *when they were created,* in the day
5: 2. in the day when *they were created.*
Eze. 28:13. in the day that *thou wast created.*
15. from the day that *thou wast created,*

NIPHAL.—*Future.*

Ps. 104:30. sendest forth thy spirit, *they are created*

NIPHAL.—*Participle.*

Ps. 102:18(19). the people which *shall be created*

* PIEL.—*Preterite.* *

Jos. 17:15. *and cut down* for thyself
18. a wood, *and thou shalt cut it down:*

PIEL.—*Infinitive.*

Eze. 23:47. *and dispatch* them with (marg. or, *single* them *out*)

PIEL.—*Imperative.*

Eze. 21:19(24). *choose* thou a place, *choose* (it) at the head of the way

* HIPHIL.—*Infinitive.* *

1Sa. 2:29. *to make yourselves fat* with the chiefest

בַּרְבֻּרִים *bar-boo-reem'*, m. pl. 1257

1K. 4:23(5:3). fallowdeer, *and* fatted *fowl.*

בָּרַד *bāh-rad'*. 1258

* KAL.—*Preterite.* *

Isa. 32:19. *When it shall hail,* coming down

בָּרָד *bāh-rāhd'*, m. 1259

Ex. 9:18. to rain *a* very grievous *hail,*
19. *the hail* shall come down
22. that there may be *hail*
23. the Lord sent thunder *and hail,*
— rained *hail* upon the land
24. So there was *hail,* and fire mingled with *the hail,*
25. *the hail* smote throughout
— *the hail* smote every herb
26. was there no *hail.*
28. no (more) mighty thunderings *and hail;*
29. *neither* shall there be any more *hail;*
33. the thunders *and hail* ceased,
34. saw that the rain *and the hail*
10: 5. remaineth unto you from *the hail,*
12. all that *the hail* hath left.
15. which *the hail* had left:
Jos. 10:11. more which died with *hail*stones
Job 38:22. hast thou seen the treasures of *the hail,*
Ps. 18:12(13), 13(14). *hail* (stones) and coals of fire.
78:47. He destroyed their vines *with hail,*
48. He gave up their cattle also *to the hail,*
105:32. He gave them *hail* for rain,
148: 8. Fire, *and hail;* snow, and vapours;
Isa. 28: 2. as a tempest of *hail*
17. *the hail* shall sweep away
30:30. tempest, and *hail*stones.
Hag 2:17. with mildew *and with hail*

בָּרֹד [*bāh-rōhd'*], adj. 1261

Gen 31:10, 12. ringstraked, speckled, *and grisled.*
Zec. 6: 3. *grisled* and bay horses.
6. *and the grisled* go forth

בָּרָה *bāh-rāh'*. 1262

* KAL.—*Preterite.* *

2Sa. 12:17. neither *did he eat* bread with them.

KAL.—*Imperative.*

1Sa.17: 8. *choose you* a man for you,

KAL.—*Future.*

2Sa.13: 6. *that I may eat* at her hand.
10. *that I may eat* of thine hand.

* PIEL.—*Infinitive.* *

Lam.4:10. they were their *meat* (lit. *for eating* to them)

* HIPHIL.—*Infinitive.* *

2Sa. 3:35. to *cause* David *to eat* meat

HIPHIL.—*Future.*

2Sa.13: 5. come, *and give me* meat, (lit. *cause me to eat* bread)

1264 בְּרוֹמִים *b'rōh-meem'*, m. pl.

Eze.27:24. in chests of *rich apparel*,

1265 בְּרוֹשׁ *b'rōhsh*, m.

2Sa. 6: 5. of (instruments made of) *fir* wood,
1K. 5: 8(22). concerning timber of *fir*.
10(24). gave Solomon cedar trees and *fir* trees
6:15. floor of the house with planks of *fir*.
34. the two doors (were of) *fir* tree:
9:11. with cedar trees and *fir* trees,
2K. 19:23. the choice *fir trees thereof:*
2Ch 2: 8(7). Send me also cedar trees, *fir trees*,
3: 5. the greater house he cieled with *fir* tree,
Ps.104:17. *the fir trees* (are) her house.
Isa. 14: 8. Yea, *the fir trees* rejoice at thee,
37:24. the choice *fir trees thereof:*
41:19. I will set in the desert *the fir tree*,
55:13. shall come up *the fir tree*,
60:13. *the fir tree*, the pine tree,
Eze.27: 5. thy (ship) boards of *fir trees* of Senir:
31: 8. *the fir trees* were not like his
Hos 14: 8(9). I (am) *like a green fir tree.*
Nah 2: 3(4). *and the fir trees* shall be terribly
Zec.11: 2. Howl, *fir tree;* for the cedar is fallen;

1266 בְּרוֹתִים *b'rōh-theem'*, m. pl.

Cant.1:17. our rafters of *fir*.

1267 בָּרוּת [*bāh-rooth'*], f.

Ps. 69:21(22). gave me also gall *for my meat;*

1270 בַּרְזֶל *bar-zel'*, m.

Gen 4:22. every artificer in brass *and iron:*
Lev.26:19. I will make your heaven *as iron*,
Nu. 31:22. the silver, the brass, *the iron*,
35:16. with an instrument of *iron*,
Deu 3:11. his bedstead (was) a bedstead of *iron*,
4:20. brought you forth out of the *iron* furnace,
8: 9. a land whose stones (are) *iron*,
19: 5. *the head* (marg. *iron*) slippeth from the helve,
27: 5. thou shalt not lift up (any) *iron*
28:23. the earth that (is) under thee (shall be) *iron*.
48. he shall put a yoke of *iron* upon
33:25. Thy shoes (shall be) *iron* and brass;
Jos. 6:19. vessels of brass *and iron*,
24. vessels of brass *and of iron*,
8:31. over which no man hath lift up (any) *iron:*
17:16. have chariots of *iron*,
18. though they have *iron* chariots,
22: 8. with gold, and with brass, *and with iron*,
Jud. 1:19. because they had chariots of *iron*.
4: 3, 13. nine hundred chariots of *iron;*
1Sa.17: 7. six hundred shekels of *iron*.
2Sa.12:31. and under harrows of *iron*, and under axes of *iron*,
23: 7. with *iron* and the staff of a spear;
1K. 6: 7. any tool of *iron* heard in the
8:51. the midst of the furnace of *iron:*
22:11. of Chenaanah made him horns of *iron:*
2K. 6: 5. *the ax head* fell into the water:
6. *the iron* did swim.
1Ch 20: 3. with harrows of *iron*,
22: 3. *And* David prepared *iron*
14. of brass *and iron* without weight;
16. the brass, *and the iron*.
29: 2. *the iron for* (things) *of iron*, and wood
7. *and* one hundred thousand talents of *iron*.
2Ch 2: 7(6). in brass, *and in iron*,
14(13). in silver, in brass, *in iron*,
18:10. Chenaanah had made him horns of *iron*,
24:12. also such as wrought *iron*
Job 19:24. they were graven with an *iron* pen
20:24. He shall flee from the *iron* weapon,
28: 2. *Iron* is taken out of the earth,
40:18. his bones (are) like bars of *iron*.
41:27(19). He esteemeth *iron* as straw,
Ps. 2: 9. break them with a rod of *iron;*
105:18. he was laid in *iron:*
107:10. bound in affliction *and iron;*
16. cut the bars of *iron* in sunder.
149: 8. their nobles with fetters of *iron;*
Pro.27:17. *Iron* sharpeneth *iron;*
Ecc.10:10. If *the iron* be blunt,
Isa. 10:34. the thickets of the forest *with iron*,
44:12. The smith with (lit. artificer of *iron*)
45: 2. cut in sunder the bars of *iron:*
48: 4. thy neck (is) as an *iron* sinew,
60:17. for *iron* I will bring silver, and for wood brass, and for stones *iron:*
Jer. 1:18. and an *iron* pillar,
6:28. (they are) brass *and iron;*
11: 4. from the *iron* furnace,
15:12. Shall *iron* break *the* northern *iron*
17: 1. written with a pen of *iron*,
28:13. thou shalt make for them yokes of *iron*.
14. I have put a yoke of *iron* upon
Eze. 4: 3. take thou unto thee an *iron* pan, and set it (for) a wall of *iron*
22:18. tin, *and iron*, and lead,
20. brass, *and iron*, and lead,
27:12. with silver, *iron*, tin, and lead,
19. bright *iron*, cassia, and calamus,
Am. 1: 3. Gilead with threshing instruments of *iron:*
Mic. 4:13. for I will make thine horn *iron*,

בָּרַח *bāh-ragh'*. 1272

* KAL.—*Preterite.* *

Gen31:22. on the third day that Jacob *was fled*.
Ex. 14: 5. the king of Egypt that the people *fled:*
1Sa.19:18. So David *fled*, and escaped,
27: 4. it was told Saul that David *was fled*
2Sa.13:37. Absalom *fled*, and went to Talmai,
38. Absalom *fled*, and went to Geshur,
19: 9(10). now *he is fled* out of the land
1K. 11:23. which *fled* from his lord
12: 2. *he was fled* from the presence of
2Ch 10: 2. *he had fled* from the presence of
Job 9:25. *they flee away*, they see no good.
Isa. 22: 3. *have fled* from far.

KAL.—*Infinitive.*

Gen31:27. Wherefore didst thou *flee away*
35: 1. *when thou fleddest* from
7. *when he fled* from the face of
Ex. 36:33. made the middle bar *to shoot*
1Sa.23: 6. *when* Abiathar the son of Ahimelech *fled*
1K. 2: 7. *when I fled* because of Absalom
Job 27:22. he would *fain* flee out of his hand. (marg. *in fleeing* he would flee)
Ps. 3[title](1). *when he fled* from Absalom
57[title](1). *when he fled* from Saul
Jon. 1: 3. Jonah rose up *to flee* unto Tarshish
4: 2. Therefore I *fled* before unto Tarshish: (lit. I prevented *to flee*)

KAL.—*Imperative.*

Gen27:43. *flee* thou to Laban my brother

Nu. 24:11. Therefore now *flee* thou to
Cant.8:14. *Make haste*, my beloved, (marg. or, *Flee away*)
Isa. 48:20. *flee ye* from the Chaldeans,
Am. 7:12. *flee* thee *away* into the land

KAL.—*Future.*

Gen16: 6. *And* when Sarai dealt hardly with her, *she fled*
31:21. *So he fled* with all that he had;
Ex. 2:15. *But* Moses *fled* from the face of Pharaoh,
Jud. 9:21. Jotham ran away, *and fled*,
11: 3. *Then* Jephthah *fled* from his brethren,
1Sa.19:12. he went, *and fled*, and escaped.
20: 1. *And* David *fled* from Naioth
21:10(11). *and fled* that day for fear of Saul,
22:20. *and fled* after David.
2Sa. 4: 3. *And* the Beerothites *fled*
13:34. *But* Absalom *fled*.
15:14. Arise, *and let us flee;*
1K. 2:39. *that* two of the servants of Shimei *ran away*
11:17. *That* Hadad *fled*, he and certain Edomites
40. Jeroboam arose, *and fled* into Egypt,
Neh 6:11. *Should* such a man as I *flee?*
13:10. *for* the Levites...*were fled* every one
Job 14: 2. *he fleeth also* as a shadow,
20:24. *He shall flee* from the iron weapon,
27:22. *he would* fain *flee* out of his hand.
Ps.139: 7. or whither *shall I flee* from
Jer. 26:21. *and fled*, and went into Egypt;
39: 4. *then they fled*, and went forth
52: 7. all the men of war *fled*,
Dan10: 7. *so that they fled* to hide themselves.
Hos.12:12(13). *And* Jacob *fled* into the country

KAL.—*Part.* Poel.

Gen16: 8. I *flee* from the face of my mistress
31:20. he told him not that he *fled*.
1Sa.22:17. because they knew when he *fled*,
Jer. 4:29. The whole city *shall flee* for the noise
Jon. 1:10. the men knew that he *fled* from the presence

* HIPHIL.—*Preterite.* *

1Ch 8:13. who *drove away* the inhabitants

HIPHIL.—*Future.*

1Ch12:15. *and they put to flight* all (them) of
Neh13:28. *therefore I chased him* from me.
Job 41:28(20). The arrow *cannot make him flee:*
Pro.19:26. *chaseth away* (his) mother,

HIPHIL.—*Participle.*

Ex. 26:28. *shall reach* from end to end.

1274 בְּרִי [*b'ree*], adj.

Eze.34:20. I will judge between *the fat* cattle

1277 בָּרִיא *bāh-ree'*, adj.

Gen41: 2. well favoured kine *and fat*fleshed;
4. the seven well favoured *and fat* kine.
5. upon one stalk, *rank* and good. (marg. *fat*)
7. devoured the seven *rank* and full ears.
18. *fat*fleshed and well favoured;
20. did eat up the first seven *fat* kine:
Jud. 3:17. Eglon (was) a very *fat* man.
1K. 4:23(5:3). Ten *fat* oxen, and twenty oxen
Ps. 73: 4. *but* their strength (is) *firm*. (marg. *fat*)
Eze.34: 3. ye kill *them that are fed:*
Dan. 1:15. appeared fairer *and fatter in*
Hab. 1:16. and their meat *plenteous*. (marg. *fat*, or, *dainty*)
Zec.11:16. he shall eat the flesh of *the fat*,

1278 בְּרִיאָה *b'ree-āh'*, f.

Nu. 16:30. if the Lord make *a new thing*, (marg. create *a creature*)

1279 בִּרְיָה *beer-yāh'*, f.

2Sa. 13: 5. and dress *the meat* in my sight,
7. and dress him *meat*.
10. Bring *the meat* into the chamber,

בָּרִיחַ *bāh-ree'ăgh*, m. 1281

Job 26:13. hath formed the *crooked* serpent.
Isa. 27: 1. leviathan the *piercing* serpent, (marg. *crossing like a bar*)
43:14. brought down all their *nobles*, (marg. *bars*)

בְּרִיחַ *b'ree'ăgh*, m. 1280

Ex. 26:26. thou shalt make *bars* (of)
27, 27. five *bars* for the boards
28. *And the* middle *bar*
29. rings (of) gold (for) places *for the bars:*
— overlay *the bars* with gold.
35:11. *his bars*, his pillars, and his sockets,
36:31. he made *bars of* shittim wood;
32, 32. five *bars* for the boards of
33. he made *the* middle *bar* to shoot
34. rings (of) gold (to be) places *for the bars*, and overlaid *the bars* with gold.
39:33. *his bars*, and his pillars, and his sockets,
40:18. put in *the bars thereof*,
Nu. 3:36 & 4:31. *and the bars thereof*, and the pillars
Deu 3: 5. with high walls, gates, *and bars;*
Jud 16: 3. away with them, *bar* and all,
1Sa.23: 7. that hath gates *and bars*.
1K. 4:13. with walls *and* brasen *bars:*
2Ch 8: 5. with walls, gates, *and bars;*
14: 7(6). walls, and towers, gates, *and bars*,
Neh 3: 3, 6, 13, 14, 15. the locks thereof, *and the bars thereof*.
Job 38:10. set *bars* and doors,
Ps.107:16. *and* cut *the bars of* iron in sunder.
147:13. strengthened *the bars of* thy gates;
Pro.18:19. *like the bars of* a castle
Isa. 15: 5. *his fugitives* (shall flee) unto Zoar, (marg. *to the borders thereof*)
45: 2. *and* cut in sunder *the bars of* iron:
Jer. 49:31. which have neither gates nor *bars*,
51:30. *her bars* are broken.
Lam.2: 9. destroyed and broken *her bars:*
Eze.38:11. having *neither bars* nor gates,
Am. 1: 5. I will break also *the bar of*
Jon. 2: 6(7). the earth with *her bars*
Nah. 3:13. the fire shall devour *thy bars*.

בְּרִית *b'reeth*, f. 1285

Gen.6:18. will I establish *my covenant;*
9: 9. behold, I establish *my covenant*
11. I will establish *my covenant*
12, 17. This (is) the token of *the covenant*
13. shall be for a token of *a covenant*
15. I will remember *my covenant*,
16. *the* everlasting *covenant*
14:13. con*federate* with Abram. (lit. masters of *a covenant*)
15:18. the Lord made *a covenant* with
17: 2. I will make *my covenant*
4. behold, *my covenant* (is) with thee,
7. I will establish *my covenant*
— *for an* everlasting *covenant*,
9. Thou shalt keep *my covenant*
10. This (is) *my covenant*,
11. a token of *the covenant* betwixt
13. and *my covenant* shall be in your flesh *for an* everlasting *covenant*.
14. he hath broken *my covenant*.
19. I will establish *my covenant* with him *for an* everlasting *covenant*,
21. But *my covenant* will I establish
21:27. both of them made *a covenant*.
32. Thus they made *a covenant*
26:28 & 31:44. let us make *a covenant*
Ex. 2:24. God remembered *his covenant*
6: 4. I have also established *my covenant*
5. I have remembered *my covenant*.
19: 5. and keep *my covenant*,
23:32. Thou shalt make no *covenant*
24: 7. he took the book of *the covenant*,

Ex. 24: 8. Behold the blood of *the covenant,*
31:16. *a* perpetual *covenant.*
34:10. Behold, I make *a covenant:*
12, 15. lest thou make *a covenant*
27. of these words I have made *a covenant*
28. the tables the words of *the covenant,*
Lev. 2:13. the salt of *the covenant of* thy God
24: 8. by *an* everlasting *covenant.*
26: 9. establish *my covenant* with you.
15. that ye break *my covenant:*
25. avenge the quarrel of (my) *covenant:*
42. Then will I remember *my covenant* with Jacob, and also *my covenant* with Isaac, and also *my covenant* with Abraham
44. to break *my covenant* with them:
45. remember *the covenant of* their ancestors,
Nu. 10:33 & 14:44. the ark of *the covenant of* the Lord
18:19. it (is) *a covenant of* salt for ever
25:12. I give unto him *my covenant of* peace:
13. *the covenant of* an everlasting
Deu. 4:13. declared unto you *his covenant,*
23. lest ye forget *the covenant of*
31. nor forget *the covenant of* thy fathers
5: 2. The Lord our God made *a covenant*
3. The Lord made not this *covenant*
7: 2. thou shalt make no *covenant*
9. which keepeth *covenant* and mercy
12. God shall keep unto thee *the covenant*
8:18. that he may establish *his covenant*
9: 9, 11. the tables of *the covenant*
15. the two tables of *the covenant*
10: 8. to bear the ark of *the covenant of*
17: 2. in transgressing *his covenant,*
29: 1(28:69). These (are) the words of *the covenant,*
—(—:—). beside *the covenant* which he made
9(8). Keep therefore the words of this *covenant,*
12(11). That thou shouldest enter *into covenant with*
14(13). only do I make this *covenant*
21(20). all the curses of *the covenant*
25(24). have forsaken *the covenant of*
31: 9. which bare the ark of *the covenant of*
16. break *my covenant*
20. provoke me, and break *my covenant.*
25. which bare the ark of *the covenant of*
26. in the side of the ark of *the covenant of*
33: 9. *and* kept *thy covenant.*
Jos. 3: 3. When ye see the ark of *the covenant of*
6. Take up the ark of *the covenant,*
— they took up the ark of *the covenant,*
8. that bear the ark of *the covenant,*
11. Behold, the ark of *the covenant of*
14. bearing the ark of *the covenant*
17. the priests that bare the ark of *the covenant of*
4: 7. the ark of *the covenant of*
9. which bare the ark of *the covenant*
18. that bare the ark of *the covenant of*
6: 6. Take up the ark of *the covenant,*
8. and the ark of *the covenant of*
7:11. also transgressed *my covenant*
15. he hath transgressed *the covenant of*
8:33. which bare the ark of *the covenant of*
9: 6. make ye *a league* with us.
7. how shall we make *a league* with you?
11. now make ye *a league* with us.
15. made *a league* with them,
16. after they had made *a league*
23:16. ye have transgressed *the covenant of*
24:25. So Joshua made *a covenant*
Jud. 2: 1. I will never break *my covenant*
2. ye shall make no *league*
20. transgressed *my covenant*
20:27. for the ark of *the covenant of*
1Sa. 4: 3. Let us fetch the ark of *the covenant of*
4. from thence the ark of *the covenant of*
— with the ark of *the covenant of* God.
5. when the ark of *the covenant of*
11: 1. Make *a covenant* with us,
18: 3. Jonathan and David made *a covenant,*
20: 8. brought thy servant *into a covenant of*
23:18. they two made *a covenant*
2Sa. 3:12. Make *thy league* with me,
13. I will make *a league* with thee:
21. that they may make *a league*

2Sa. 5: 3. king David made *a league*
15:24. bearing the ark of *the covenant of*
23: 5. made with me *an* everlasting *covenant,*
1K. 3:15. before the ark of *the covenant of*
5:12(26). they two made *a league* together.
6:19. the ark of *the covenant of* the Lord.
8: 1. bring up the ark of *the covenant of*
6. brought in the ark of *the covenant of*
21. wherein (is) *the covenant of* the Lord,
23. who keepest *covenant* and mercy
11:11. thou hast not kept *my covenant*
15:19. *a league* between me and thee,
— break *thy league* with Baasha
19:10, 14. have forsaken *thy covenant,*
20:34. send thee away *with this covenant.* So he made *a covenant* with him,
2K. 11: 4. made *a covenant* with them,
17. Jehoiada made *a covenant*
13:23. because of *his covenant*
17:15. and *his covenant* that he made
35. the Lord had made *a covenant,*
38. *And the covenant* that I have
18:12. but transgressed *his covenant,*
23: 2. words of the book of *the covenant*
3. made *a covenant* before the Lord,
— the words of this *covenant*
— And all the people stood *to the covenant*
21. as (it is) written in the book of this *covenant.*
1Ch 11: 3. David made *a covenant*
15:25, 26, 28, 29. the ark of *the covenant of* the Lord
16: 6. before the ark of *the covenant of* God.
15. Be ye mindful always of *his covenant;*
17. to Israel (for) *an* everlasting *covenant,*
37 & 17:1 & 22:19 & 28:2, 18. the ark of *the covenant of* the Lord
2Ch. 5: 2, 7. the ark of *the covenant of* the Lord
6:11. wherein (is) *the covenant of* the Lord,
14. which keepest *covenant,*
13: 5. by *a covenant of* salt?
15:12. entered *into a covenant*
16: 3. *a league* between me and thee,
— break *thy league* with Baasha
21: 7. because of *the covenant* that he
23: 1. *into covenant* with him.
3. the congregation made *a covenant*
16. Jehoiada made *a covenant*
29:10. make *a covenant* with the Lord God
34:30. the book of *the covenant*
31. made *a covenant* before the Lord,
— to perform the words of *the covenant*
32. *according to the covenant of* God,
Ezr. 10: 3. therefore let us make *a covenant*
Neh. 1: 5. that keepeth *covenant* and mercy
9: 8. madest *a covenant* with him
32. who keepest *covenant* and mercy,
13:29. *and the covenant of* the priesthood,
Job 5:23. *thou shalt be in league* with (lit. *thy covenant*)
31: 1. I made *a covenant* with mine eyes;
41: 4(40:28). Will he make *a covenant* with thee?
Ps. 25:10. unto such as keep *his covenant*
14. *and* he will shew them *his covenant.*
44:17(18). have we dealt falsely *in thy covenant.*
50: 5. have made *a covenant with me*
16. shouldest take *my covenant*
55:20(21). he hath broken *his covenant.*
74:20. Have respect *unto the covenant:*
78:10. They kept not *the covenant of* God,
37. neither were they stedfast *in his covenant.*
83: 5(6). they are confederate (lit. they have made *a covenant*)
89: 3(4). I have made *a covenant* with
28(29). *and my covenant* shall stand fast
34(35). *My covenant* will I not break,
39(40). hast made void *the covenant of*
103:18. To such as keep *his covenant,*
105: 8. He hath remembered *his covenant*
10. to Israel (for) *an* everlasting *covenant:*
106:45. he remembered for them *his covenant,*
111: 5. will ever be mindful of *his covenant.*
9. he hath commanded *his covenant*
132:12. If thy children will keep *my covenant*
Pro. 2:17. forgetteth *the covenant of* her God.
Isa. 24: 5. broken the everlasting *covenant.*

Isa. 28.15. We have made *a covenant* with death,
18. *your covenant* with death
33: 8. he hath broken *the covenant*,
42: 6 & 49:8. give thee *for a covenant of* the
54:10. *neither* shall *the covenant of* my peace
55: 3. I will make *an* everlasting *covenant*
56: 4. take hold *of my covenant;*
6. taketh hold *of my covenant;*
59:21. As for me, this (is) *my covenant;*
61: 8. *and* I will make *an* everlasting *covenant*
Jer. 3:16. The ark of *the covenant of* the Lord:
11: 2, 6. Hear ye the words of this *covenant*,
3. that obeyeth not the words of this *covenant*,
8. all the words of this *covenant*,
10. Judah have broken *my covenant*
14:21. break not *thy covenant*
22: 9. Because they have forsaken *the covenant of*
31:31. that I will make *a* new *covenant*
32. Not *according to the covenant*
— which *my covenant* they brake,
33. this (shall be) *the covenant* that I will
32:40. I will make *an* everlasting *covenant*
33:20. If ye can break *my covenant of* the day, and *my covenant of* the night,
21. may also *my covenant* be broken
25. If *my covenant* (be) not
34: 8. had made *a covenant* with all
10. which had entered into *the covenant*,
13. I made *a covenant* with your fathers
15. ye had made *a covenant*
18. that have transgressed *my covenant*,
— performed the words of *the covenant*
50: 5. to the Lord in *a* perpetual *covenant*
Eze.16: 8. entered *into a covenant* with thee,
59. in breaking *the covenant*.
60. I will remember *my covenant*
— establish unto thee *an* everlasting *covenant*.
61. for daughters, but not *by thy covenant*.
62. I will establish *my covenant*
17:13. and made *a covenant* with him,
14. that by keeping of *his covenant*
15. or shall he break *the covenant*,
16. *whose covenant* he brake,
18. by breaking *the covenant*,
19. *and my covenant* that he hath
20:37. into the bond of *the covenant:*
30: 5. the land *that is in league*, (lit. of *the covenant*)
34:25. make with them *a covenant of* peace,
37:26. I will make *a covenant of* peace
— an everlasting *covenant*
44: 7. they have broken *my covenant*
Dan. 9: 4. keeping *the covenant* and mercy
27. he shall confirm *the covenant*
11:22. also the prince of *the covenant*.
28, 30. against *the* holy *covenant;*
30. that forsake *the* holy *covenant*.
32. such as do wickedly against *the covenant*
Hos. 2:18(20). in that day will I make *a covenant*
6: 7. have transgressed *the covenant:*
8: 1. they have transgressed *my covenant*,
10: 4. swearing falsely in making *a covenant:*
12: 1(2). *and* they do make *a covenant*
Am. 1: 9. remembered not *the* brotherly *covenant:*
Obad 7. All the men of *thy confederacy*
Zec. 9:11. by the blood of *thy covenant*
11:10. that I might break *my covenant*
Mal. 2: 4. that *my covenant* might be with
5. *My covenant* was with him
8. corrupted *the covenant of* Levi,
10. by profaning *the covenant of*
14. the wife of *thy covenant*.
3: 1. even the messenger of *the covenant*,

1287 בֹּרִית *bōh-reeth'*, f.

Jer. 2:22. take thee much *sope*,
Mal. 3: 2. *and like* fullers' *sope:*

1288 בָּרַךְ [*bāh-rach'*].

* KAL.—*Infinitive.* *

Jos. 24:10. therefore he blessed you *still:* (lit. *blessing* he blessed you)
1Sa.13:10. *that he might salute him.* (marg. *bless*)

KAL.—*Future.*

2Ch. 6:13. *and kneeled down* upon his knees
Ps. 95: 6. *let us kneel* before the Lord

KAL.—*Participle.* Paül.

Gen. 9:26. *Blessed* (be) the Lord God of Shem;
14:19. *Blessed* (be) Abram of the
20. *And blessed* be the most high God,
24:27. *Blessed* (be) the Lord God
31. Come in, thou *blessed of* the Lord;
26:29. thou (art) now *the blessed of* the Lord.
27:29. *blessed* (be) he that blesseth thee.
33. he shall be *blessed*.
Ex. 18:10. Jethro said, *Blessed* (be) the Lord,
Nu. 22:12. for they (are) *blessed*.
24: 9. *Blessed* (is) he that blesseth thee,
Deu. 7:14. Thou shalt be *blessed* above all
28: 3. *Blessed* (shalt) thou (be) in the city, *and blessed* (shalt) thou (be) in the field.
4. *Blessed* (shall be) the fruit
5. *Blessed* (shall be) thy basket
6. *Blessed* (shalt) thou (be) when
— *and blessed* (shalt) thou (be)
33:20. *Blessed* (be) he that enlargeth
24. Asher (be) *blessed* with children;
Jud.17: 2. *Blessed* (be thou) of the Lord,
Ruth2:19. *blessed* be he that did take
20. *Blessed* (be) he of the Lord, who hath not
3:10. *Blessed* (be) thou of the Lord,
4:14. *Blessed* (be) the Lord,
1Sa.15:13. *Blessed* (be) thou of the Lord:
23:21. *Blessed* (be) ye of the Lord;
25:32. *Blessed* (be) the Lord God
33. *And blessed* (be) thy advice, *and blessed* (be) thou,
39. *Blessed* (be) the Lord, that hath
26:25. *Blessed* (be) thou, my son David:
2Sa. 2: 5. *Blessed* (be) ye of the Lord,
18:28. *Blessed* (be) the Lord thy God,
22:47. *and blessed* (be) my rock;
1 K. 1:48. *Blessed* (be) the Lord God of Israel,
2:45. king Solomon (shall be) *blessed*,
5: 7(21). *Blessed* (be) the Lord this day,
8:15. *Blessed* (be) the Lord God of Israel,
56. *Blessed* (be) the Lord,
10: 9. *Blessed* be the Lord thy God,
1Ch.16:36. *Blessed* (be) the Lord God of Israel
29:10. *Blessed* (be) thou, Lord God of
2Ch. 2:12(11) & 6:4. *Blessed* (be) the Lord God of Israel,
9: 8. *Blessed* be the Lord thy God,
Ezr. 7:27. *Blessed* (be) the Lord God
Ps. 18:46(47). *and blessed* (be) my rock;
28: 6. *Blessed* (be) the Lord, because
31:21(22). *Blessed* (be) the Lord: for he hath
41:13(14). *Blessed* (be) the Lord God
66:20. *Blessed* (be) God, which hath
68:19(20). *Blessed* (be) the Lord,
35(36). unto (his) people. *Blessed* (be) God.
72:18. *Blessed* (be) the Lord God,
19. *And blessed* (be) his glorious
89:52(53). *Blessed* (be) the Lord for evermore.
106:48. *Blessed* (be) the Lord God
115:15. Ye (are) *blessed* of the Lord
118:26. *Blessed* (be) he that cometh
119:12. *Blessed* (art) thou, O Lord:
124: 6. *Blessed* (be) the Lord,
135:21. *Blessed* be the Lord out of Zion,
144: 1. *Blessed* (be) the Lord my strength,
Pro. 5:18. Let thy fountain be *blessed:*
Isa. 19:25. *Blessed* (be) Egypt my people,
65:23. the seed of *the blessed of* the Lord,
Jer. 17: 7. *Blessed* (is) the man that trusteth
20:14. my mother bare me be *blessed*.
Eze. 3:12. *Blessed* (be) the glory of the Lord
Zec. 11: 5. *Blessed* (be) the Lord;

* NIPHAL.—*Preterite.* *

Gen.12: 3. *and* in thee *shall* all families of the earth *be blessed*.
18:18. *and* all the nations of the earth *shall be blessed*
28:14. *and* in thee...*shall* all the families of the earth *be blessed*.

* PIEL.—*Preterite.* *

Gen17:16. *And I will bless* her, and give thee a son also of her: *yea, I will bless her,*
20. Behold, *I have blessed* him,
24: 1. the Lord *had blessed* Abraham
35. the Lord *hath blessed* my master
26:24. I (am) with thee, *and will bless thee,*
27:27. which the Lord *hath blessed:*
41. wherewith his father *blessed him:*
28: 6. Esau saw that Isaac *had blessed*
32:26(27). except *thou bless me.*
49:28. to his blessing *he blessed them.*
Ex. 12:32. be gone; *and bless* me also.
20:11. the Lord *blessed* the sabbath day,
24. *and I will bless thee.*
23:25. *and he shall bless* thy bread,
Nu. 23:11. *thou hast blessed* (them) altogether.
20. *and he hath blessed;* and I cannot
24:10. *thou hast* altogether *blessed*
Deu. 2: 7. the Lord thy God *hath blessed thee*
7:13. will love thee, *and bless thee,*
— *he will also bless* the fruit of
8:10. *then thou shalt bless* the Lord
12: 7. the Lord thy God *hath blessed thee.*
15: 6. the Lord thy God *blesseth thee,*
14. the Lord thy God *hath blessed thee*
18. *and* the Lord thy God *shall bless thee*
24:13. in his own raiment, *and bless thee:*
28: 8. *and he shall bless thee*
30:16. *and* the Lord thy God *shall bless thee*
33: 1. Moses the man of God *blessed*
Jos. 17:14. forasmuch as the Lord *hath blessed me*
1Sa. 2:20. *And* Eli *blessed* Elkanah and his wife,
2Sa. 6:12. The Lord *hath blessed* the house
1K. 21:10. *Thou didst blaspheme* God
13. Naboth *did blaspheme* God
1Ch 17:27. for thou *blessest,* O Lord,
26: 5. for God *blessed him.*
2Ch 20:26. for there *they blessed* the Lord:
31:10. the Lord *hath blessed* his people;
Job 1: 5. *and cursed* God in their hearts.
10. *thou hast blessed* the work of
31:20. If his loins *have* not *blessed me,*
42:12. the Lord *blessed* the latter end of
Ps. 10: 3. and *blesseth* the covetous,
45: 2(3). God *hath blessed thee* for ever.
118:26. *we have blessed you* out of the
129: 8. *we bless* you in the name of the Lord.
147:13. *he hath blessed* thy children
Isa. 19:25. Whom the Lord of hosts *shall bless,* (lit. *shall bless him*)
61: 9. the seed (which) the Lord *hath blessed.*

PIEL.—*Infinitive.*

Gen22:17. That *in blessing* I will bless
27:30. Isaac had made an end *of blessing*
28: 6. and that *as he blessed* him
Nu. 23:11. thou hast blessed (them) *altogether.* (lit. *blessing* thou hast blessed)
20. received (commandment) *to bless:*
25. nor bless them *at all.*
24: 1. it pleased the Lord *to bless* Israel,
10. thou hast *altogether* blessed
Deu10: 8. *and to bless* in his name,
15: 4. the Lord shall *greatly* bless
21: 5. *and to bless* in the name of
27:12. Gerizim *to bless* the people,
28:12. *and to bless* all the work
Jos. 8:33. *that they should bless* the people
1Sa.25:14. *to salute* our master;
2Sa. 6:20. David returned *to bless* his houshold.
8:10. to salute him, *and to bless him,*
1K. 1:47. came *to bless* our lord king David,
1Ch 4:10. Oh that thou wouldest bless me *indeed,*
16:43. David returned *to bless* his house.
17:27. *to bless* the house of thy servant.
18:10. *and to congratulate him,* (marg. *bless*)
23:13. *and to bless* in his name for ever.
Ps.132:15. I will *abundantly* bless her (marg. *surely*)

PIEL.—*Imperative.*

Gen27:34, 38. *Bless me,* (even) me also,
Deu26:15. *and bless* thy people Israel,
33:11. *Bless,* Lord, his substance,
Jud. 5: 2. *Praise ye* the Lord for the
9. *Bless ye* the Lord.
2Sa. 7:29. let it please thee *to bless* (marg. *and bless*)
2Sa.21: 3. *that ye may bless* the inheritance
1Ch 29:20. Now *bless* the Lord your God
Neh 9: 5. *bless* the Lord your God
Job 2: 9. *curse* God, and die.
Ps. 28: 9. *and bless* thine inheritance:
66: 8. *O bless* our God, ye people,
68:26(27). *Bless ye* God in the congregations,
96: 2. Sing unto the Lord, *bless* his name;
100: 4. be thankful unto him, (and) *bless*
103: 1, 2, 22. *Bless* the Lord, O my soul:
20. *Bless* the Lord, ye his angels,
21. *Bless ye* the Lord,
22. *Bless* the Lord, all his works
104: 1. *Bless* the Lord, O my soul.
35. *Bless thou* the Lord, O my soul.
134: 1. *bless ye* the Lord, all (ye) servants
2. *and bless* the Lord.
135:19. *Bless* the Lord, O house of Israel: *bless* the Lord, O house of Aaron:
20. *Bless* the Lord, O house of Levi: ye that fear the Lord, *bless* the Lord.

PIEL.—*Future.*

Gen 1:22, 28. *And* God *blessed* them,
2: 3. *And* God *blessed* the seventh day,
5: 2. created he them; *and blessed* them,
9: 1. *And* God *blessed* Noah and his sons,
12: 2. *and I will bless thee,* and make
3. *And I will bless* them that bless thee,
14:19. *And he blessed him,* and said, Blessed
22:17. in blessing *I will bless thee,*
24:48. *and blessed* the Lord God of my master
60. *And they blessed* Rebekah,
25:11. *that* God *blessed* his son Isaac;
26: 3. *and will bless thee;* for unto thee,
12. *and* the Lord *blessed him.*
27: 4, 25. my soul *may bless thee*
7. *and bless thee* before the Lord
10. and that *he may bless thee*
19, 31. that thy soul *may bless me.*
23. Esau's hands: *so he blessed him.*
27. *and blessed him,* and said,
33. before thou camest, *and have blessed him?*
28: 1. Isaac called Jacob, *and blessed* him,
3. God Almighty *bless* thee,
30:27. *that* the Lord *hath blessed me*
30. *and* the Lord *hath blessed* thee
31:55(32:1). *and blessed* them: and Laban
32:29(30). *And he blessed* him there.
35: 9. out of Padan-aram, *and blessed* him.
39: 5. *that* the Lord *blessed* the Egyptian's house
47: 7, 10. *and* Jacob *blessed* Pharaoh.
48: 3. the land of Canaan, *and blessed* me,
9. unto me, *and I will bless them.*
15. *And he blessed* Joseph,
16. from all evil, *bless* the lads;
20. *And he blessed them* that day, saying, In thee *shall* Israel *bless,*
49:25. the Almighty, *who shall bless thee*
28. spake unto them, *and blessed* them;
Ex. 39:43. *and* Moses *blessed* them.
Lev. 9:22. toward the people, *and blessed them,*
23. came out, *and blessed* the people:
Nu. 6:23. *ye shall bless* the children of Israel,
24. The Lord *bless thee,* and keep thee:
27. and *I will bless them.*
22: 6. he whom *thou blessest* (is) blessed,
23:25. nor *bless them* at all.
Deu 1:11. *and bless* you, as he hath promised
14:24. the Lord thy God *hath blessed thee:*
29. the Lord thy God *may bless thee*
15: 4. the Lord shall greatly *bless thee*
10. the Lord thy God *shall bless thee*
16:10. the Lord thy God *hath blessed thee:*
15. the Lord thy God *shall bless thee*
23:20(21)&24:19. the Lord thy God *may bless thee*
Jos. 14:13. *And* Joshua *blessed him,*
22: 6. *So* Joshua *blessed them,*
7. unto their tents, *then he blessed them,*
33. *and* the children of Israel *blessed* God,
24:10. *therefore he blessed* you still:
Jud.13:24. *and* the Lord *blessed him.*
Ru. 2: 4. The Lord *bless thee.*
1Sa. 9:13. because *he doth bless* the sacrifice;
2Sa. 6:11. *and* the Lord *blessed* Obed-edom,
18. *And* as soon as...*he blessed* the people
13:25. he would not go, *but blessed him.*

2Sa. 14:22. bowed himself, *and thanked* the king:
19:39(40). kissed Barzillai, *and blessed him;*
1K. 8:14, 55. *and blessed* all the congregation
66. *and they blessed* the king, (marg. or, *thanked*)
2K. 4:29. if thou meet any man, *salute him* not; and if any *salute thee*,
10:15. *and he saluted him*, and said (marg. *blessed*)
1Ch 4:10. Oh that *thou wouldest bless me* indeed,
13:14. *And* the Lord *blessed* the house of
16: 2. *he blessed* the people
29:10. *Wherefore* David *blessed* the Lord
20. *And* all the congregation *blessed* the Lord
2Ch 6. 3. *and blessed* the whole congregation
30:27. *and blessed* the people:
31: 8. *they blessed* the Lord,
Neh 8: 6. *And* Ezra *blessed* the Lord,
9: 5. *and blessed be* thy glorious name, (lit. *they shall bless*)
11: 2. *And* the people *blessed* all the men,
Job 1:11 & 2:5. *he will curse thee* to thy face.
Ps. 5:12(13). thou, Lord, *wilt bless* the righteous;
16: 7. *I will bless* the Lord,
26:12. *will I bless* the Lord.
29:11. the Lord *will bless* his people
34: 1(2). *I will bless* the Lord at all times:
49:18(19). while he lived *he blessed* his soul:
62: 4(5). *they bless* with their mouth,
63: 4(5). Thus *will I bless thee* while I live:
65:10(11). *thou blessest* the springing thereof.
67: 1(2). God be merciful unto us, *and bless us;*
6(7). our own God, *shall bless us.*
7(8). God *shall bless us;*
72:15. daily *shall he be praised.* (lit. *shall* (one) *bless him*)
107:38. *He blesseth them also*, so that they
109:28. Let them curse, but *bless* thou:
115:12. *he will bless* (us); *he will bless* the house of Israel; *he will bless* the house of
13. *He will bless* them that fear the Lord,
18. But *we will bless* the Lord
128: 5. The Lord *shall bless thee*
132:15. *I will* abundantly *bless* her provision:
134: 3. *bless thee* out of Zion.
145: 1. *and I will bless* thy name for ever
2. Every day *will I bless thee;*
10. thy saints *shall bless thee.*
21. *and let* all flesh *bless* his holy name
Pro. 3:33. *he blesseth* the habitation of the just.
30:11. *doth* not *bless* their mother.
Isa. 51: 2. I called him alone, *and blessed him*,
Jer. 31:23. The Lord *bless thee*,
Hag 2:19. from this day *will I bless*

PIEL.—*Participle.*

Gen 12: 3. I will bless *them that bless thee*,
27:29. *and* blessed (be) *he that blesseth thee.*
Nu. 24: 9. Blessed (is) *he that blesseth thee*,
Pro. 27:14. *He that blesseth* his friend with a loud
Isa. 66: 3. he that burneth incense, (as if) *he blessed*

* PUAL.—*Future.* *

Jud. 5:24. *Blessed* above women *shall* Jael the wife of Heber the Kenite *be*, *blessed shall she be* above women
2Sa. 7:29. *let* the house of thy servant *be blessed*
Ps. 112: 2. the upright *shall be blessed.*
128: 4. thus *shall* the man *be blessed*
Pro. 20:21. the end thereof *shall* not *be blessed.*
22: 9. a bountiful eye *shall be blessed;*

PUAL.—*Participle.*

Nu. 22: 6. he whom thou blessest (is) *blessed*,
Deu 33:13. *Blessed of* the Lord (be) his land,
1Ch 17:27. *and* (it shall be) *blessed* for ever.
Job 1:21. *blessed* be the name of the Lord.
Ps. 37:22. For (such as be) *blessed of him*
113: 2. *Blessed* be the name of the Lord

* HIPHIL.—*Future.* *

Gen 24:11. *And he made* his camels *to kneel down*

* HITHPAEL.—*Preterite.* *

Gen 22:18 & 26:4. *And* in thy seed *shall* all the nations of the earth *be blessed;*
Deu 29:19(18). *that he bless himself* in his heart,
Jer. 4: 2. *and* the nations *shall bless themselves*

HITHPAEL.—*Future.*

Ps. 72:17. *and* (men) *shall be blessed* in him:
Isa. 65:16. *shall bless himself* in the God of truth;

HITHPAEL.—*Participle.*

Isa. 65:16. That *he who blesseth himself*

בְּרַךְ [*b'rach*], Ch. 1289

* P'AL.—*Participle.* *

Dan 6:10(11). *he kneeled* upon his knees three

P'AL.—*Participle. Passive.*

Dan 3:28. *Blessed* (be) the God of Shadrach,

* PAEL.—*Preterite.* *

Dan 2:19. Daniel *blessed* the God of heaven.
4:34(31). and *I blessed* the most High,

PAEL.—*Participle.*

Dan 2:20. *Blessed* be the name of God

בֶּרֶךְ *beh'-rech*, f. 1290

Gen 30: 3. she shall bear upon *my knees*,
48:12. out from between *his knees*,
50:23. brought up upon Joseph's *knees.*
Deu 28:35. The Lord shall smite thee in *the knees*,
Jud. 7: 5. boweth down upon *his knees*
6. bowed down upon *their knees*
16:19. she made him sleep upon *her knees;*
1K. 8:54. from kneeling on *his knees*
18:42. put his face between *his knees*,
19:18. all *the knees* which have not
2K. 1:13. came and fell on *his knees*
4:20. he sat on *her knees* till noon,
2Ch 6:13. kneeled down upon *his knees*
Ezr. 9: 5. I fell upon *my knees*,
Job 3:12. Why did *the knees* prevent me?
4: 4. *and* thou hast strengthened *the* feeble *knees.*
Ps. 109:24. *My knees* are weak through fasting;
Isa. 35: 3. *and* confirm *the* feeble *knees.*
45:23. unto me every *knee* shall bow,
66:12. be dandled upon (her) *knees.*
Eze. 7:17 & 21:7(12). all *knees* shall be weak (as) water.
47: 4. the waters (were) to *the knees.*
Dan 10:10. which set me upon *my knees*
Nah. 2:10(11). and *the knees* smite together,

בֶּרֶךְ [*beh'-rech*], Ch. f. 1291

Dan 6:10(11). kneeled upon *his knees*

בְּרָכָה *b'rāh-chāh'*, f. 1293

Gen 12: 2. thou shalt be *a blessing:*
27:12. and not *a blessing.*
35. hath taken away *thy blessing.*
36. hath taken away *my blessing.*
— Hast thou not reserved *a blessing*
38. Hast thou but one *blessing*,
41. because of *the blessing*
28: 4. give thee *the blessing of* Abraham,
33:11. Take, I pray thee, *my blessing*
39: 5. and *the blessing of* the Lord
49:25. bless thee with *blessings of* heaven above, *blessings of* the deep that lieth under, *blessings of* the breasts,
26. *The blessings of* thy father have prevailed above *the blessings of* my progenitors
28. every one *according to his blessing*
Ex. 32:29. he may bestow upon you *a blessing*
Lev. 25:21. Then I will command *my blessing*
Deu 11:26. *a blessing* and a curse;
27. *A blessing*, if ye obey
29. thou shalt put *the blessing* upon
12:15 & 16:17. *according to the blessing of* the Lord
23: 5(6). turned the curse *into a blessing*
28: 2. all these *blessings* shall come on
8. The Lord shall command *the blessing*
30: 1. *the blessing* and the curse,
19. life and death, *blessing* and cursing:

Deu33: 1. this (is) *the blessing*, wherewith Moses
23. full with *the blessing of* the Lord:
Jos. 8:34. *the blessings* and cursings,
15:19. Give me *a blessing;*
Jud. 1:15. Give me *a blessing:*
1Sa.25:27. this *blessing* which thine handmaid (marg. *present*)
30:26. *a present* for you of the spoil (marg. *blessing*)
2Sa. 7:29. *and with thy blessing* let the
2K. 5:15. take *a blessing* of thy servant.
18:31. with me by *a present*, (marg. *blessing;* or, *favour*)
2Ch 20:26. in the valley of *Berachah;* (marg. *Blessing*)
— The valley of *Berachah*, unto this day.
Neh 9: 5. exalted above all *blessing* and praise.
13: 2. God turned the curse *into a blessing.*
Job 29:13. *The blessing of* him that was ready
Ps. 3: 8(9). *thy blessing* (is) upon thy people.
21: 3(4). with *the blessings of* goodness:
6(7). thou hast made him *most blessed* for ever: (marg. set him (to be) *blessings*)
24: 5. receive *the blessing* from the Lord,
37:26. his seed (is) *blessed.* (lit. *for a blessing*)
84: 6(7). the rain also filleth *the pools.*
109:17. as he delighted not *in blessing,*
129: 8. *The blessing of* the Lord
133: 3. there the Lord commanded *the blessing,*
Pro.10: 6. *Blessings* (are) upon the head of
7. The memory of the just (is) *blessed:* (lit. *for a blessing*)
22. *The blessing of* the Lord,
11:11. *By the blessing of* the upright
25. The *liberal* soul shall be made fat: (marg. The soul of *blessing*)
26. *but blessing* (shall be) upon the
24:25. *a* good *blessing* shall come
28:20. man shall abound with *blessings:*
Isa. 19:24. *a blessing* in the midst of the land:
36:16. Make (an agreement) with me (by) *a present*, (marg. *blessing*, or, *favour*)
44: 3. *and my blessing* upon thine offspring:
65: 8. for *a blessing* (is) in it:
Eze.34:26. round about my hill *a blessing,*
— there shall be showers of *blessing.*
44:30. that he may cause *the blessing*
Joel 2:14. repent, and leave *a blessing*
Zec. 8:13. ye shall be *a blessing:*
Mal. 2: 2. I will curse your *blessings:*
3:10. pour you out *a blessing,*

1295 בְּרֵכָה *b'reh-chāh'*, f.

2Sa. 2:13. by *the pool of* Gibeon: and they sat down, the one on the one side of *the pool*, and the other on the other side of *the pool.*
4:12. over *the pool* in Hebron.
1K. 22:38. washed the chariot in *the pool of*
2K. 18:17. the conduit of *the* upper *pool,*
20:20. how he made *a pool,*
Neh 2:14. to *the* king's *pool:*
3:15. the wall of *the pool of* Siloah
16. to *the pool* that was made,
Ecc. 2: 6. I made me *pools of* water,
Cant.7: 4(5). thine eyes (like) *the fishpools*
Isa. 7: 3. the conduit of *the* upper *pool*
22: 9. the waters of *the* lower *pool.*
11. for the water of *the* old *pool:*
36: 2. by the conduit of *the* upper *pool*
Nah.2: 8(9). Nineveh (is) of old *like a pool of*

1297 בְּרַם *b'ram*, Ch. adv.

Ezr. 5:13. *But* in the first year of Cyrus
Dan 2:28. *But* there is a God in heaven
4:15(12). *Nevertheless* leave the stump
23(20). *yet* leave the stump
5:17. *yet* I will read the writing

1299 בָּרַק [*bāh-rak'*].

* KAL.—*Imperative.* *

Ps.144: 6. *Cast forth* lightning, and scatter them:

בָּרָק *bāh-rāhk'*, m. 1300

Ex. 19:16. there were thunders *and lightnings,*
Deu32:41. If I whet my *glittering* sword, (lit. *the lightning of* my sword)
2Sa.22:15. *lightning*, and discomfited them.
Job 20:25. *yea, the glittering sword* cometh
38:35. Canst thou send *lightnings,*
Ps. 18:14(15). *and* he shot out *lightnings,*
77:18(19). *the lightnings* lightened the world:
97: 4. *His lightnings* enlightened the world:
135: 7. he maketh *lightnings* for the rain;
144: 6. Cast forth *lightning*, and scatter them:
Jer. 10:13 & 51:16. he maketh *lightnings* with rain,
Eze. 1:13. out of the fire went forth *lightning.*
21:10(15). it is furbished that it may *glitter:* (lit. have *lightning*)
15(20). ah! (it is) made *bright*, (lit. *unto glittering*)
28(33). because of *the glittering:*
Dan 10: 6. as the appearance of *lightning,*
Nah. 2: 4(5). shall run *like the lightnings.*
3: 3. the bright sword *and the glittering* spear: (marg. *and the lightning of* the spear)
Hab. 3:11. at the shining of thy *glittering* spear.
Zec. 9:14. shall go forth *as the lightning:*

בַּרְקָנִים *bar-kāh-neem'*, m. pl. 1303

Jud. 8: 7. thorns of the wilderness and with *briers.*
16. thorns of the wilderness and *briers,*

בָּרֶקֶת *bāh-reh'-keth*, f. 1304

Ex. 28:17 & 39:10. sardius, a topaz, *and a carbuncle:*

בָּרְקַת *bāh-r'kath'*, f. 1304

Eze.28:13. emerald, *and the carbuncle,*

בָּרַר [*bāh-rar'*]. 1305

* KAL.—*Preterite.* *

Eze.20:38. *And I will purge out* from

KAL.—*Infinitive.*

Ecc. 3:18. *that* God *might manifest* them, (marg. or, *that they might clear* God)

KAL.—*Participle.* Paül.

1Ch 7:40. *choice* (and) mighty men of valour,
9:22. *chosen* to be porters in the gates
16:41. the rest *that were chosen,*
Neh 5:18. one ox (and) six *choice* sheep;
Job 33: 3. my lips shall utter knowledge *clearly.*
Isa. 49: 2. made me a *polished* shaft;
Zep. 3: 9. turn to the people a *pure* language,

* NIPHAL.—*Imperative.* *

Isa. 52:11. *be ye clean*, that bear the vessels

NIPHAL.—*Participle.*

2Sa.22:27. With *the pure* thou wilt shew thyself
Ps. 18:26(27). With *the pure* thou wilt shew thyself

* PIEL.—*Infinitive.* *

Dan 11:35. to try them, *and to purge,*

* HIPHIL.—*Infinitive.* *

Jer. 4:11. not to fan, nor *to cleanse,*

HIPHIL.—*Imperative.*

Jer.51:11. *Make bright* the arrows; (marg. *pure*)

* HITHPAEL.—*Future.* *

2Sa.22:27. *thou wilt shew thyself pure;*
Ps. 18:26(27). the pure *thou wilt shew thyself pure;*
Dan 12:10. Many *shall be purified,*

בְּשׂוֹרָה *b'sōh-rāh*, f. 1309

2Sa. 4:10. given him *a reward for his tidings:* (or, lit. which were *the tidings* I gave him.)

2Sa. 18:20. Thou shalt not bear *tidings*
22. thou hast no *tidings* ready?
25. If he (be) alone, (there is) *tidings*
27. cometh with good *tidings.*
2K. 7: 9. this day (is) a day of *good tidings,*

1313 **בָּשָׂם** [*bāh-sāhm'*], m.

Cant. 5: 1. gathered my myrrh with *my spice;*

1314 **בֶּשֶׂם** *beh'-sem*, m.

Ex. 25: 6. *spices* for anointing oil,
30:23. also unto thee principal *spices,*
— of *sweet* cinnamon half so much,
35: 8. *spices* for anointing oil,
1K. 10: 2. with camels that bare *spices,*
10. *and of spices* very great store,
25. garments, and armour, *and spices,*
2K. 20:13. and *the spices*, and the precious ointment,
1Ch 9:29. the frankincense, *and the spices.*
30. made the ointment *of the spices.*
2Ch 9: 1. camels that bare *spices,*
9. *and of spices* great abundance,
24. raiment, harness, *and spices,*
16:14. was filled with *sweet odours*
32:27. precious stones, *and for spices,*
Est. 2:12. six months *with sweet odours,*
Cant. 4:10. thine ointments than all *spices!*
14. with all *the* chief *spices:*
16. *the spices thereof* may flow
8:14. upon the mountains of *spices.*
Isa. 39: 2. the gold, and *the spices,*

1314 **בֹּשֶׂם** *bōh'-sem*, m.

Ex. 30:23. and of *sweet* calamus two hundred and fifty
35:28. *spice*, and oil for the light,
1K. 10:10. no more *such* abundance of *spices*
2Ch 9: 9. neither was there any *such spice*
Cant. 5:13. His cheeks (are) as a bed of *spices,*
6: 2. to the beds of *spices,*
Isa. 3:24. instead of sweet *smell*
Eze. 27:22. in thy fairs with chief of all *spices,*

1319 **בָּשַׂר** [*bāh-sar'*].

* PIEL.—*Preterite.* *

2Sa. 18:20. *but thou shalt bear tidings* another day:
Ps. 40: 9(10). *I have preached* righteousness
Jer. 20:15. who *brought tidings* to my father,

PIEL.—*Infinitive.*

1Sa. 31: 9. *to publish* (it in) the house
1Ch 10: 9. *to carry tidings* unto their idols,
Isa. 61: 1. *to preach good tidings* unto the meek;

PIEL.—*Imperative.*

1Ch 16:23. *shew forth* from day to day
Ps. 96: 2. *shew forth* his salvation

PIEL.—*Future.*

2Sa. 1:20. *publish* (it) not in the streets
18:19. *and bear* the king *tidings,*
20. *thou shalt bear* no *tidings,*
1K. 1:42. and *bringest* good *tidings.*
Isa. 60: 6. *they shall shew forth* the praises

PIEL.—*Participle.*

1Sa. 4:17. *the messenger* answered and said,
2Sa. 4:10. thinking to *have brought good tidings,* (lit. he was *as a bringer of good tidings*
18:26. He also *bringeth tidings.*
Ps. 68:11(12). company of *those that published*
Isa. 40: 9. O Zion, *that bringest good tidings,* (marg. *thou that tellest good tidings to* Zion)
— O Jerusalem, *that bringest good tidings,* (marg. *thou that tellest good tidings to* Jerusalem)
41:27. to Jerusalem *one that bringeth good tidings.*
52: 7. the feet of him *that bringeth good tidings,* that publisheth peace; *that bringeth good tidings of* good
Nah. 1:15(2:1). the feet of him *that bringeth good tidings,*

* HITHPAEL.—*Future.* *

2Sa. 18:31. Cushi came; and Cushi said, *Tidings,* (marg. *Tidings is brought*)

בָּשָׂר *bāh-sāhr'*, m. 1320

Gen 2:21. closed up *the flesh* instead thereof;
23. *and flesh of my flesh:*
24. they shall be one *flesh.*
6: 3. for that he also (is) *flesh:*
12. all *flesh* had corrupted his way
13. The end of all *flesh* is come
17. to destroy all *flesh,*
19. every living thing of all *flesh,*
7:15. two and two of all *flesh,*
16. went in male and female of all *flesh,*
21. all *flesh* died that moved upon
8:17. of all *flesh,* (both) of fowl, and of cattle
9: 4. But *flesh* with the life thereof,
11. neither shall all *flesh* be cut off
15, 16. every living creature of all *flesh;*
— become a flood to destroy all *flesh.*
17. between me and all *flesh*
17:11. ye shall circumcise *the flesh*
13. my covenant shall be *in your flesh*
14. whose *flesh of* his foreskin
23. circumcised *the flesh of* their
24. he was circumcised in *the flesh of*
25. circumcised in *the flesh of* his foreskin.
29:14. Surely thou (art) my bone *and my flesh*
37:27. he (is) our brother (and) *our flesh.*
40:19. the birds shall eat *thy flesh*
41: 2. and fat*flesh*ed; (lit. fat of *flesh*)
3. and lean*flesh*ed; (lit. lean of *flesh*)
4. lean*flesh*ed kine
18. fat*flesh*ed and well favoured;
19. and lean*flesh*ed, such as I never
Ex. 4: 7. turned again *as his* (other) *flesh.*
12: 8. they shall eat *the flesh*
46. carry forth ought of *the flesh*
16: 3. when we sat by the *flesh* pots,
8. give you in the evening *flesh*
12. At even ye shall eat *flesh,*
21:28. *his flesh* shall not be eaten;
22:31(30). neither (lit. *and* not) shall ye eat (any) *flesh*
28:42. linen breeches to cover their nakedness; (marg. *flesh of* their nakedness)
29:14. *the flesh of* the bullock,
31. seethe *his flesh* in the holy place.
32. his sons shall eat *the flesh of*
34. if ought *of the flesh of* the
30:32. Upon man's *flesh* shall it not
Lev. 4:11. and all *his flesh,*
6:10(3). shall he put upon *his flesh,*
27(20). shall touch *the flesh thereof*
7:15. *And the flesh of* the sacrifice
17. But the remainder *of the flesh of*
18. if (any) *of the flesh of* the sacrifice
19. *And the flesh* that toucheth any
— *and* as for *the flesh,* all that be clean shall eat *thereof.* (lit. *the flesh*)
20. But the soul that eateth (of) *the flesh*
21. and eat *of the flesh of* the sacrifice
8:17. the bullock, and his hide, *his flesh,*
31. Boil *the flesh* (at) the door
32. that which remaineth of *the flesh*
9:11. *the flesh* and the hide
11: 8. *Of their flesh* shall ye not eat,
11. ye shall not eat *of their flesh,*
12: 3. in the eighth day *the flesh of*
13: 2. shall have in the skin of *his flesh*
— it be in the skin of *his flesh*
3. the plague in the skin of *the flesh:*
— deeper than the skin of *his flesh,*
4. spot (be) white in the skin of *his flesh,*
10. quick raw *flesh* in the rising;
11. leprosy in the skin of *his flesh,*
13. the leprosy have covered all *his flesh,*
14. But when raw *flesh* appeareth
15. the priest shall see *the* raw *flesh,*
— *the* raw *flesh* (is) unclean:
16. if *the* raw *flesh* turn again,
18. *The flesh also,* in which,
24. Or if there be (any) *flesh,*
38. have in the skin of *their flesh*

Lev.13:39. bright spots in the skin of *their flesh*
43. appeareth in the skin of *the flesh;*
14: 9. also he shall wash *his flesh*
15: 2. hath a running issue *out of his flesh,*
3. whether *his flesh* run with his issue, or *his flesh* be stopped
7. he that toucheth *the flesh of* him
13. bathe *his flesh* in running water,
16. then he shall wash all *his flesh*
19. her issue *in her flesh*
16: 4. the linen breeches upon *his flesh,*
— therefore shall he wash *his flesh*
24. he shall wash *his flesh*
26, 28. bathe *his flesh* in water,
27. *their flesh,* and their dung.
17:11. For the life of *the flesh*
14. For (it is) the life of all *flesh;*
— eat the blood of no manner of *flesh:* for the life of all *flesh*
16. *nor* bathe *his flesh;*
18: 6. to any that is near of *kin* (marg. remainder of *his flesh*)
19:28. make any cuttings *in your flesh*
21: 5. *nor* make any cuttings *in their flesh.*
22: 6. unless he wash *his flesh*
25:49. that is nigh of *kin* unto him (lit. remainder of *his flesh*)
26:29. ye shall eat *the flesh of* your sons, *and the flesh of* your daughters
Nu. 8: 7. let them shave all *their flesh,*
11: 4, 18. Who shall give us *flesh* to eat?
13. Whence should I have *flesh*
— Give us *flesh,* that we may eat.
18. ye shall eat *flesh:*
— the Lord will give you *flesh,*
21. I will give them *flesh,*
33. while *the flesh* (was) yet between
12:12. of whom *the flesh* is half consumed (lit. *his flesh*)
16:22. the God of the spirits of all *flesh,*
18:15. that openeth the matrix in all *flesh,*
18. *And the flesh of them* shall be
19: 5. her skin, and *her flesh,*
7, 8. bathe *his flesh* in water,
27:16. the God of the spirits of all *flesh,*
Deu 5:26(23). For who (is there of) all *flesh,*
12:15. thou mayest kill and eat *flesh*
20. thou shalt say, I will eat *flesh,* because thy soul longeth to eat *flesh;* thou mayest eat *flesh,*
23. mayest not eat the life with *the flesh.*
27. *the flesh* and the blood,
— *and* thou shalt eat *the flesh.*
14: 8. ye shall not eat *of their flesh,*
16: 4. neither shall there (any thing) of *the flesh,*
28:53. *the flesh of* thy sons
55. *of the flesh of* his children
32:42. my sword shall devour *flesh;*
Jud. 6:19. *the flesh* he put in a basket,
20. Take *the flesh* and the
21. touched *the flesh* and the
— consumed *the flesh*
8: 7. then I will tear *your flesh*
9: 2. I (am) your bone *and your flesh.*
1Sa. 2:13. while *the flesh* was in seething,
15. Give *flesh* to roast for the priest; for he will not have sodden *flesh*
17:44. I will give *thy flesh* unto the fowls
2Sa. 5: 1. we (are) thy bone *and thy flesh.*
19:12(13). ye (are) my bones *and my flesh:*
13(14). thou not of my bone, *and* of *my flesh?*
1K. 17: 6. bread *and flesh* in the morning, and bread *and flesh* in the evening;
19:21. boiled their *flesh* with the instruments
21:27. put sackcloth upon *his flesh,*
2K. 4:34. *the flesh of* the child waxed warm.
5:10. and *thy flesh* shall come again
14. and *his flesh* came again *like unto the flesh of* a little child,
6:30. sackcloth within upon *his flesh.*
9:36. shall dogs eat *the flesh of* Jezebel:
1Ch 11: 1. we (are) thy bone *and thy flesh.*
2Ch 32: 8. With him (is) an arm of *flesh;*
Neh 5: 5. Yet now *our flesh* (is) *as the flesh of* our
Job 2: 5. touch his bone and *his flesh,*
4:15. the hair of *my flesh* stood up.
6:12. or (is) *my flesh* of brass?

Job 7: 5. *My flesh* is clothed with worms
10: 4. Hast thou eyes of *flesh?*
11. clothed me with skin *and flesh,*
12:10. the breath of all man*kind.* (marg. *flesh of* man)
13:14. Wherefore do I take *my flesh*
14:22. *But his flesh* upon him shall
19:20. to my skin *and to my flesh,*
22. *and* are not satisfied *with my flesh?*
26. *yet in my flesh* shall I see God:
21: 6. trembling taketh hold on *my flesh.*
31:31. Oh that we had *of his flesh!*
33:21. *His flesh* is consumed away,
25. *His flesh* shall be fresher
34:15. All *flesh* shall perish together,
41:23(15). The flakes of *his flesh* are joined
Ps. 16: 9. *my flesh* also shall rest in hope.
27: 2. came upon me to eat up *my flesh,*
38: 3(4), 7(8). no soundness *in my flesh*
50:13. Will I eat *the flesh of* bulls,
56: 4(5). I will not fear what *flesh* can do
63: 1(2). *my flesh* longeth for thee
65: 2(3). unto thee shall all *flesh* come.
78:39. remembered that they (were but) *flesh;*
79: 2. *the flesh of* thy saints unto the beasts
84: 2(3). my heart *and my flesh* crieth
102: 5(6). bones cleave *to my skin.* (marg. *flesh*)
109:24. *and my flesh* faileth of fatness.
119:120. *My flesh* trembleth for fear of thee;
136:25. Who giveth food to all *flesh:*
145:21. let all *flesh* bless his holy name
Pro. 4:22. health to all *their flesh.*
5:11. when *thy flesh* and thy body
14:30. A sound heart (is) the life of *the flesh:*
23:20. among riotous eaters of *flesh:*
Ecc. 2: 3. to give *myself* unto wine, (marg. draw *my flesh*)
4: 5. and eateth *his own flesh.*
5: 6(5). thy mouth to cause *thy flesh* to sin;
11:10. put away evil *from thy flesh:*
12:12. much study (is) a weariness of *the flesh.*
Isa. 9:20(19). eat every man *the flesh of* his own
10:18. both soul and *body:* marg. (and even to *the flesh*)
17: 4. the fatness of *his flesh*
22:13. eating *flesh,* and drinking wine:
31: 3. their horses *flesh,* and not spirit.
40: 5. all *flesh* shall see (it) together:
6. All *flesh* (is) grass,
44:16. with part thereof he eateth *flesh;*
19. I have roasted *flesh,*
49:26. that oppress thee with *their own flesh;*
— and all *flesh* shall know
58: 7. *and* that thou hide not thyself *from thine own flesh?*
65: 4. which eat swine's *flesh,*
66:16. will the Lord plead with all *flesh:*
17. eating swine's *flesh,*
23. shall all *flesh* come to worship
24. shall be an abhorring unto all *flesh.*
Jer. 7:21. your sacrifices, and eat *flesh.*
11:15. *and the* holy *flesh* is passed from thee?
12:12. no *flesh* shall have peace.
17: 5. maketh *flesh* his arm,
19: 9. to eat *the flesh of* their sons and *the flesh of* their daughters, and they shall eat every one *the flesh of* his friend
25:31. he will plead with all *flesh;*
32:27. the Lord, the God of all *flesh:*
45: 5. I will bring evil upon all *flesh,*
Lam. 3: 4. *My flesh* and my skin
Eze. 4:14. neither came there abominable *flesh*
10:12. And *their* whole *body,* (marg. *flesh*)
11: 3. and we (be) *the flesh.*
7. they (are) *the flesh,*
11. neither shall ye be *the flesh* (lit. *for the flesh*)
19. take the stony heart *out of their flesh,* and will give them an heart of *flesh:*
16:26. Egyptians thy neighbours, great of *flesh;*
20:48(21:4). And all *flesh* shall see that
21: 4(9). out of his sheath against all *flesh*
5(10). That *all flesh* may know that
23:20. whose *flesh* (lit. *their flesh*) (is as) *the flesh of* asses,
24:10. consume *the flesh,*
32: 5. I will lay *thy flesh* upon the

Eze.36:26. the stony heart *out of your flesh*, and I will give you an heart of *flesh*.
37: 6. will bring up *flesh* upon you,
8. the sinews *and the flesh* came up
39:17. that ye may eat *flesh*,
18. Ye shall eat *the flesh of* the
40:43. *the flesh of* the offering.
44: 7. and uncircumcised in *flesh*,
9. nor uncircumcised in *flesh*,
Dan 1:15. appeared fairer and fatter in *flesh*
10: 3. neither (lit. *and* not) came *flesh* nor
Hos 8:13. They sacrifice *flesh* (for) the
Joel 2:28(3:1). I will pour out my spirit upon all *flesh*;
Mic. 3: 3. *and as flesh* within the caldron.
Hag. 2:12. If one bear holy *flesh* in the
Zec. 2:13(17). Be silent, *O* all *flesh*,
11: 9. eat every one *the flesh of* another.
16. *but* he shall eat *the flesh of*
14:12. Their *flesh* shall consume

See 1309 **בְּשׂוֹרָה** see **בְּשֹׂרָה**

1321 **בְּשַׂר** *b'sar*, Ch. m.

Dan. 2:11. whose dwelling is not with *flesh*.
4:12(9). and all *flesh* was fed of it.
7: 5. Arise, devour much *flesh*.

1310 **בָּשַׁל** *bāh-shal'*.

* KAL.—*Preterite*. *

Eze.24: 5. *let them seethe* the bones
Joel 3:13(4:13). for the harvest *is ripe*:

* PIEL.—*Preterite*. *

Ex. 29:31. *and seethe* his flesh
Nu. 11: 8. *and baked* (it) in pans.
Deu16: 7. *And thou shalt roast*
1K. 19:21. and *boiled their* flesh
2Ch 35:13. but the (other) holy (offerings) *sod they*
Lam. 4:10. *have sodden* their own children:
Zec.14:21. *and seethe* therein:

PIEL.—*Infinitive*.

1Sa. 2:13. *while* the flesh *was in seething*,

PIEL.—*Imperative*.

Ex. 16:23. *seethe* that ye will seethe;
Lev. 8:31. *Boil* the flesh (at) the door
2K. 4:38. *and seethe* pottage for the sons

PIEL.—*Future*.

Ex. 16:23. seethe that *ye will seethe;*
23:19 & 34:26. *Thou shalt* not *seethe* a kid
Deu14:21. *Thou shalt* not *seethe* a kid
2Sa.13: 8. *and did bake* the cakes.
2K. 6:29. *So we boiled* my son,
2Ch 35:13. *And they roasted* the passover
Eze 46:20. the priests *shall boil* the trespass offering
24. the ministers of the house *shall boil*

PIEL.—*Participle*.

Eze.46:24. the places of *them that boil*,

* PUAL.—*Preterite*. *

Lev. 6:28(21). if *it be sodden* in a brasen pot,

PUAL.—*Future*.

Lev. 6:28(21). vessel wherein *it is sodden* shall be broken:

PUAL.—*Participle*.

Ex. 12: 9. nor *sodden* at all with water,
1Sa. 2:15. he will not have *sodden* flesh

* HIPHIL.—*Preterite*. *

Gen40:10. *brought forth* ripe grapes:

1311 **בָּשֵׁל** *bāh-shēhl'*, adj.

Ex. 12: 9. *nor* sodden *at all* with water, (lit. *and boiled* sodden)

Nu. 6:19. shall take the *sodden* shoulder

בָּשְׁנָה *bosh-nāh'*, f. 1317

Hos.10: 6. Ephraim shall receive *shame*,

בָּשַׁס [*bāh-shas'*]. 1318

* POEL.—*Infinitive*. *

Am. 5:11. as *your treading* (is) upon the poor,

בֹּשֶׁת *bōh'-sheth*, f. 1322

1Sa.20:30. *to thine own confusion, and unto the confusion of*
2Ch.32:21. So he returned *with shame of* face
Ezr. 9: 7. *and to confusion of* face,
Job 8:22. shall be clothed with *shame;*
Ps. 35:26. let them be clothed with *shame*
40:15(16). for a reward of *their shame*
44:15(16). *and the shame of* my face
69:19(20). my reproach, *and my shame*,
70: 3(4). for a reward of *their shame*
109:29. with *their own confusion*,
132:18. His enemies will I clothe with *shame:*
Isa. 30: 3. Pharaoh be your *shame*,
5. but *a shame*, and also a reproach.
42:17. they shall be *greatly* ashamed, (lit. be ashamed *a shame*)
54: 4. thou shalt forget *the shame of* thy youth.
61: 7. For *your shame* (ye shall have) double
Jer. 2:26. *As* the thief *is ashamed* (lit. *as the shame of* the thief)
3:24. *For shame* hath devoured
25. We lie down *in our shame*,
7:19. to *the confusion of* their own faces?
11:13. set up altars *to* (that) *shameful thing*, (marg. *shame*)
20:18. should be consumed *with shame?*
Dan 9: 7. but unto us *confusion of* faces,
8. to us (belongeth) *confusion of* face,
Hos. 9:10. separated themselves *unto* (that) *shame;*
Mic. 1:11. having thy *shame* naked:
Hab. 2:10. Thou hast consulted *shame*
Zep. 3: 5. the unjust knoweth no *shame*.
19. every land where *they have been put to shame*. (marg. *their shame*)

בַּת *bath*, f. 1323

Gen 5: 4, 7, 10, 13, 16, 19, 22, 26, 30. begat sons *and daughters:*
6: 1. *and daughters* were born unto them,
2. saw *the daughters of* men
4. came in unto *the daughters of* men,
11:11, 13, 15, 17, 19, 21, 23, 25. begat sons *and daughters*.
29. *the daughter of* Haran,
17:17. that is ninety years *old*, bear? (lit. that is *a daughter of* ninety years)
19: 8. I have two *daughters*
12. and thy sons, *and thy daughters*,
14. sons in law, which married *his daughters*,
15. and *thy* two *daughters*,
16. and upon the hand of *his* two *daughters;*
30. in the mountain, and *his* two *daughters*
— he and *his* two *daughters*.
36. Thus were both *the daughters of* Lot
20:12. she (is) *the daughter of* my father, but not *the daughter of* my mother;
24: 3. *of the daughters of* the Canaanites,
13. *and the daughters of* the men of
23, 47. Whose *daughter* (art) thou?
24, 47. *the daughter of* Bethuel
37. *of the daughters of* the Canaanites,
48. my master's brother's *daughter*
25:20. *the daughter of* Bethuel
26:34. Judith *the daughter of* Beeri the Hittite, and Bashemath *the daughter of* Elon
27:46. because of *the daughters of* Heth: if Jacob take a wife *of the daughters of* Heth, such as these (which are) *of the daughters of* the land,

Gen28: 1, 6. take a wife *of the daughters of* Canaan.
2. *of the daughters of* Laban
8. seeing that *the daughters of* Canaan
9. Mahalath *the daughter of* Ishmael
29: 6. Rachel *his daughter* cometh with the sheep.
10. Jacob saw Rachel *the daughter of*
16. Laban had two *daughters :*
18. seven years for Rachel *thy* younger *daughter.*
23. took Leah *his daughter*, and brought her to him ;
24. gave unto *his daughter* Leah Zilpah
28. he gave him Rachel *his daughter* to wife
29. Laban gave to Rachel *his daughter*
30. 13. for *the daughters* will call me blessed:
21. afterwards she bare *a daughter*,
31 : 26. and carried away *my daughters*, as
28. to kiss my sons *and my daughters ?*
31. thou wouldest take by force *thy daughters*
41. for *thy* two *daughters*,
43. (These) *daughters* (are) *my daughters*,
— *and* what can I do this day *unto* these *my daughters*,
50. If thou shalt afflict *my daughters*, or if thou shalt take (other) wives beside *my daughters*,
55(32:1). kissed his sons *and his daughters*
34: 1. Dinah *the daughter of* Leah,
— to see *the daughters of* the land.
3. Dinah *the daughter of* Jacob,
5. that he had defiled Dinah *his daughter* :
7. Israel in lying with Jacob's *daughter ;*
8. Shechem longeth *for your daughter :*
9. give *your daughters* unto us, and take *our daughters* unto you.
16. Then will we give *our daughters*
— we will take *your daughters*
17. then will we take *our daughter*,
19. because he had delight *in* Jacob's *daughter:*
21. let us take *their daughters* to us
— let us give them *our daughters.*
36: 2. wives *of the daughters of* Canaan ; Adah *the daughter of* Elon the Hittite,
—, 14. Aholibamah *the daughter of* Anah *the daughter of* Zibeon
3. Bashemath Ishmael's *daughter*,
6. his wives, and his sons, and *his daughters,*
18, 25. Aholibamah *the daughter of* Anah,
39. *the daughter of* Matred, the *daughter of* Mezahab.
37:35. and all *his daughters* rose up to comfort
38: 2. Judah saw there *a daughter of*
12. *the daughter of* Shuah Judah's wife
41:45, 50. Asenath *the daughter of* Poti-pherah
46: 7. *his daughters, and* his sons' *daughters*,
15. with *his daughter* Dinah: all the souls of his sons *and his daughters* (were) thirty and three.
18. whom Laban gave to Leah *his daughter*,
20. Asenath *the daughter of* Poti-pherah
25. Laban gave unto Rachel *his daughter*,
49:22. *branches* run over the wall: (marg. *daughters*)
Ex. 1:16. but if it (be) *a daughter*,
22. every *daughter* ye shall save alive.
2: 1. took (to wife) *a daughter of* Levi.
5. *the daughter of* Pharaoh came
7. Then said his sister to Pharaoh's *daughter*,
8. Pharaoh's *daughter* said to her,
9. Pharaoh's *daughter* said unto her,
10. brought him *unto* Pharaoh's *daughter*,
16. the priest of Midian had seven *daughters :*
20. And he said unto *his daughters*,
21. he gave Moses Zipporah *his daughter.*
3:22. and upon *your daughters ;*
6:23. Elisheba, *daughter of* Amminadab,
25. took him (one) *of the daughters of* Putiel
10: 9. with our sons *and with our daughters*,
20:10. any work, thou, nor thy son, *nor thy daughter*,
21: 4. born him sons or *daughters ;*
7. if a man sell *his daughter*
9. after the manner of *daughters*
31. or have gored *a daughter*,
32: 2. of your sons, *and of your daughters*,
34:16. take *of their daughters* unto thy sons, and *their daughters* go a whoring

Lev. 10:14. thou, and thy sons, *and thy daughters* with thee:
11:16. And the owl, (lit. *the daughter of* the owl)
12: 6. or *for a daughter*,
14:10. one ewe lamb *of* the *first* year (marg. *daughter of* her year)
18: 9. the *daughter of* thy father, or *daughter of*
10. The nakedness of thy son's *daughter*, or of *thy daughter's daughter*,
11. nakedness of thy father's wife's *daughter*,
17. nakedness of a woman *and her daughter*, neither shalt thou take her son's *daughter*, or *her daughter's daughter*,
19:29. Do not prostitute *thy daughter*,
20:17. take his sister, his father's *daughter*, or his mother's *daughter*,
21: 2. for his son, *and for his daughter*,
9. *And the daughter of* any priest,
22:12. *If* the priest's *daughter*
13. *But* if the priest's *daughter*
24:11. Shelomith, *the daughter of* Dibri,
26:29. the flesh of *your daughters*
Nu. 6:14. one ewe lamb *of* the *first* year (lit. *daughter of* her year)
15:27. bring a she goat *of the first* year
18:11. and to thy sons *and to thy daughters* with thee,
19. thy sons *and thy daughters* with thee,
21:25. in all *the villages thereof.* (marg. *daughters*)
29. *and his daughters*, into captivity unto
32. they took *the villages thereof*,
25: 1. with *the daughters of* Moab.
15. *the daughter of* Zur ;
18. *the daughter of* a prince of Midian,
26:33. had no sons, but *daughters :* and the names of *the daughters of*
46. the name of *the daughter of* Asher
59. Jochebed, *the daughter of* Levi,
27: 1. Then came *the daughters of* Zelophehad,
— these (are) the names of *his daughters ;*
7. *The daughters of* Zelophehad speak right:
8. shall cause his inheritance to pass *unto his daughter.*
9. if he have no *daughter*,
30:16(17). between the father *and his daughter*,
32:42. Kenath, and *the villages thereof*,
36: 2. of Zelophehad our brother *unto his daughters.*
6. *concerning the daughters of* Zelophehad,
8. every *daughter*, that possesseth
10. so did *the daughters of* Zelophehad:
11. *the daughters of* Zelophehad, were
Deu. 5:14. not do any work, thou, nor thy son, *nor thy daughter*,
7: 3. *thy daughter* thou shalt not give unto his son, *nor his daughter* shalt thou take
12:12. your sons, *and your daughters*,
18. thou, and thy son, *and thy daughter*,
31. even their sons and *their daughters*
13: 6(7). of thy mother, or thy son, or *thy daughter*,
14:15. And the owl, (lit. *the daughter of* the owl)
16:11, 14. thou, and thy son, *and thy daughter*,
18:10. his son *or his daughter* to pass through the
22:16. I gave *my daughter* unto this man
17. I found not *thy daughter* a maid ; and yet these (are the tokens of) *my daughter's*
23:17(18). no whore *of the daughters of* Israel,
27:22. *the daughter of* his father, or *the daughter of* his mother.
28:32. Thy sons *and thy daughters* (shall be)
41. Thou shalt beget sons *and daughters*,
53. the flesh of thy sons *and* of *thy daughters*,
56. *and toward her daughter*,
32:19. the provoking of his sons, *and* of *his daughters.*
Jos. 7:24. wedge of gold, and his sons, and *his daughters*,
15:16. will I give Achsah *my daughter* to wife.
17. gave him Achsah *his daughter* to wife.
45. Ekron, *with her towns*
47. Ashdod with *her towns*
— Gaza with *her towns*
17: 3. had no sons, but *daughters :* and these (are) the names of *his daughters*,
6. Because *the daughters of* Manasseh
11, 16. Beth-shean *and her towns*,

Jos. 17:11. Ibleam *and her towns*, and the inhabitants of Dor *and her towns*, and the inhabitants of En-dor *and her towns*, and the inhabitants of Taanach *and her towns*, and the inhabitants of Megiddo *and her towns*,
Jud. 1:12. will I give Achsah *my daughter* to wife.
13. he gave him Achsah *his daughter* to wife.
27. Beth-shean and *her towns*, nor Taanach and *her towns*, nor the inhabitants of Dor and *her towns*, nor the inhabitants of Ibleam and *her towns*, nor the inhabitants of Megiddo and *her towns :*
3: 6. they took *their daughters* to be their wives, and gave *their daughters* to their sons,
11:26. in Heshbon *and her towns*, and in Aroer *and her towns*,
34. *his daughter* came out to meet him
— he had neither son nor *daughter*.
35. Alas, *my daughter !* thou hast brought me
40. *the daughters of* Israel went yearly
— to lament *the daughter of*
12: 9. thirty sons, and thirty *daughters*,
— took in thirty *daughters* from abroad
14: 1, 2. *of the daughters of* the Philistines.
3. *among the daughters of* thy brethren,
19:24. Behold, (here is) *my daughter* a maiden,
21: 1. not any of us give *his daughter* unto Benjamin
7. give them *of our daughters* to wives?
18. give them wives *of our daughters :*
21. if *the daughters of* Shiloh
— *of the daughters of* Shiloh,
Ru. 1:11, 12. Turn again, *my daughters :*
13. nay, *my daughters ;* for it grieveth me
2: 2. she said unto her, Go, *my daughter*.
8. Hearest thou not, *my daughter ?*
22. (It is) good, *my daughter*, that thou go
3: 1. *My daughter*, shall I not seek rest for
10. Blessed (be) thou of the Lord, *my daughter :*
11. And now, *my daughter*, fear not;
16. Who (art) thou, *my daughter ?*
18. said she, Sit still, *my daughter*,
1Sa. 1: 4. to all her sons *and her daughters*,
16. thine handmaid for *a daughter of*
2:21. three sons and two *daughters*.
8:13. *And* he will take *your daughters*
14:49. the names of *his* two *daughters*
50. *the daughter of* Ahimaaz:
17:25. with great riches, and will give him *his daughter*,
18:17. Behold *my* elder *daughter* Merab,
19. Saul's *daughter* should have been
20. Michal Saul's *daughter* loved
27. gave him Michal *his daughter* to wife.
28. Michal Saul's *daughter* loved him.
25:44. But Saul had given Michal *his daughter*,
30: 3. their sons, *and their daughters*,
6. for his sons and for *his daughters :*
19. neither sons *nor daughters*,
2Sa. 1:20. *the daughters of* the Philistines
— *the daughters of* the uncircumcised
24. *Ye daughters of* Israel, weep over Saul,
3: 3. Maacah *the daughter of* Talmai
7. *the daughter of* Aiah:
13. bring Michal Saul's *daughter*,
5:13. there were yet sons *and daughters*
6:16. Michal Saul's *daughter* looked
20, 23. Michal *the daughter of* Saul
11: 3. Bath-sheba, *the daughter of* Eliam,
12: 3. was unto him *as a daughter*.
13:18. such robes were the king's *daughters*
14:27. three sons, *and* one *daughter*,
17:25. Abigail *the daughter of* Nahash,
19: 5(6). lives of thy sons *and of thy daughters*,
21: 8, 10, 11. Rizpah *the daughter of* Aiah,
— Michal *the daughter of* Saul,
1K. 3: 1. took Pharaoh's *daughter*,
4:11. Taphath *the daughter of* Solomon
15. Basmath *the daughter of* Solomon
7: 8. an house *for* Pharaoh's *daughter*,
9:16. given it (for) a present *unto his daughter*,
24. Pharaoh's *daughter* came up
11: 1. together with *the daughter of*
15: 2, 10. Maachah, *the daughter of* Abishalom.
16:31. Jezebel *the daughter of* Ethbaal

1K. 22:42. Azubah *the daughter of* Shilhi.
2K. 8:18. for *the daughter of* Ahab was his wife:
26. *the daughter of* Omri
9:34. for she (is) a king's *daughter*.
11: 2. *the daughter of* king Joram,
14: 9. Give *thy daughter* to my son to wife:
15:33. *the daughter of* Zadok.
17:17. caused their sons and *their daughters*
18: 2. Abi, *the daughter of* Zachariah.
19:21. The virgin *the daughter of* Zion
— *the daughter of* Jerusalem
21:19. *the daughter of* Haruz
22: 1. *the daughter of* Adaiah
23:10. or *his daughter* to pass through the fire
31. *the daughter of* Jeremiah
36. *the daughter of* Pedaiah
24: 8. *the daughter of* Elnathan
18. *the daughter of* Jeremiah
1Ch 1:50. *the daughter of* Matred, *the daughter of*
2: 3. *of the daughter of* Shua
21. went in to *the daughter of* Machir
23. and *the towns thereof*,
34. Sheshan had no sons, but *daughters*.
35. Sheshan gave *his daughter* to Jarha
49. *and the daughter of* Caleb
3: 2. Maachah *the daughter of* Talmai
5. of Bath-shua *the daughter of*
4:18. *the daughter of* Pharaoh,
27. sixteen sons *and* six *daughters ;*
5:16. *and in her towns*,
7:15. Zelophehad had *daughters*.
24. *And his daughter* (was) Sherah, who built
28. Beth-el *and the towns thereof*,
— Gezer, *with the towns thereof:* Shechem also *and the towns thereof*, unto Gaza *and the towns thereof :*
29. Beth-shean *and her towns*, Taanach *and her towns*, Megiddo *and her towns*, Dor *and her towns*.
8:12. and Lod, *with the towns thereof :*
14: 3. begat more sons *and daughters*.
15:29. Michal *the daughter of* Saul
18: 1. took Gath *and her towns*
23:22. had no sons, but *daughters :*
25: 5. fourteen sons *and* three *daughters*.
2Ch 2:14(13). a woman of *the daughters of* Dan,
8:11. brought up *the daughter of* Pharaoh
11:18. Mahalath *the daughter of* Jerimoth
— Abihail *the daughter of* Eliab
20, 21. Maachah *the daughter of* Absalom;
21. and threescore *daughters*.
13: 2. Michaiah *the daughter of* Uriel
19. Beth-el with *the towns thereof*, and Jeshanah with *the towns thereof*, and Ephrain *with the towns* thereof.
21. and sixteen *daughters*.
20:31. Azubah *the daughter of* Shilhi.
21: 6. he had *the daughter of* Ahab
22: 2. Athaliah *the daughter of* Omri.
11. *the daughter of* the king,
— *the daughter of* king Jehoram,
24: 3. begat sons *and daughters*.
25:18. Give *thy daughter* to my son to wife:
27: 1. Jerushah, *the daughter of* Zadok.
28: 8. women, sons, *and daughters*,
18. Shocho *with the villages thereof*, and Timnah with *the villages thereof*, Gimzo also and *the villages thereof :*
29. 1. Abijah, *the daughter of* Zechariah.
9. our sons *and our daughters*
31:18. their sons, *and their daughters*,
Ezr. 2:61. took a wife *of the daughters of*
9: 2. they have taken *of their daughters*
12. give not *your daughters*
— *neither* take *their daughters*
Neh 3:12. of Jerusalem, he *and his daughters*.
4:14(8). your sons, *and your daughters*,
5: 2. We, our sons, *and our daughters*,
5. our sons and *our daughters* to be servants, and (some) *of our daughters* are brought
6:18. had taken *the daughter of* Meshullam
7:63. took (one) *of the daughters of*
10:28(29). their sons, *and their daughters*,
30(31). would not give *our daughters*
—(—). nor take *their daughters*
11:25. *and* (in) *the villages thereof*, and at Dibon, *and* (in) *the villages thereof*,

Neh 11:27. at Beer-sheba, *and* (in) *the villages thereof,*
28. at Mekonah, *and in the villages thereof,*
30. at Azekah, *and* (in) *the villages thereof.*
31. and Beth-el, *and* (in) *their villages,*
13:25. Ye shall not give *your daughters*
— nor take *their daughters*
Est. 2: 7. Esther, his uncle's *daughter:*
— took *for* his own *daughter.*
15. *the daughter of* Abihail
— who had taken her *for* his *daughter,*
9:29. *the daughter of* Abihail,
Job 1: 2. seven sons and three *daughters.*
13. when his sons *and his daughters* (were)
18. Thy sons *and thy daughters* (were) eating
30:29. and a companion to owls. (lit. *to the daughters of* the owl)
42:13. seven sons and three *daughters.*
15. found (so) fair *as the daughters of* Job:
Ps. 9:14(15). in the gates of *the daughter of* Zion:
17: 8. Keep me as the apple of the eye, (lit. as *the daughter of* the eye)
45: 9(10). Kings' *daughters* (were) among
10(11). Hearken, *O daughter,* and consider,
12(13). *And the daughter of* Tyre
13(14). The king's *daughter* (is) all glorious
48:11(12). let *the daughters of* Judah be glad,
97: 8. *the daughters of* Judah rejoiced
106:37. sacrificed their sons and *their daughters*
38. of their sons *and* of *their daughters,*
137: 8. *O daughter of* Babylon,
144:12. *our daughters* (may be) as corner stones,
Pro. 30:15. The horseleach hath two *daughters,*
31:29. Many *daughters* have done virtuously,
Ecc. 12: 4. all *the daughters of* musick
Cant. 1: 5. *O ye daughters of* Jerusalem,
2: 2. so (is) my love among *the daughters.*
7. *O ye daughters of* Jerusalem,
3: 5. I charge you, *O ye daughters of* Jerusalem,
10. *for the daughters of* Jerusalem.
11. Go forth, *O ye daughters of* Zion,
5: 8. I charge you, *O daughters of* Jerusalem,
16. my friend, *O daughters of* Jerusalem.
6: 9. *The daughters* saw her,
7: 1(2). *O prince's daughter!*
4(5). by the gate of *Bath*-rabbim: (lit. *daughter of* many)
8: 4. I charge you, *O daughters of* Jerusalem,
Isa. 1: 8. *the daughter of* Zion
3:16. Because *the daughters of* Zion
17. the head of *the daughters of* Zion,
4: 4. the filth of *the daughters of* Zion,
10:30. Lift up thy voice, *O daughter of* Gallim:
32. the mount of *the daughter of* Zion,
13:21. owls shall dwell there, (marg. *daughters of* the owl)
16: 1. the mount of *the daughter of* Zion.
2. *the daughters of* Moab shall be
22: 4. the spoiling of *the daughter of* my people.
23:10. *O daughter of* Tarshish:
12. oppressed virgin, *daughter of* Zidon:
32: 9. hear my voice, *ye* careless *daughters;*
34:13. a court *for* owls. (marg. *daughters of* the owl; or, ostriches)
37:22. The virgin, *the daughter of* Zion,
— *the daughter of* Jerusalem
43: 6. *and my daughters* from the ends of the earth;
20. the dragons *and* the owls: (marg. *daughters of* the owl)
47: 1. O virgin *daughter of* Babylon,
—, 5. *O daughter of* the Chaldeans:
49:22. *and thy daughters* shall be carried
52: 2. *O* captive *daughter of* Zion.
56: 5. better than of sons *and of daughters:*
60: 4. *and thy daughters* shall be nursed at (thy) side.
62:11. Say ye *to the daughter of* Zion,
Jer. 3:24. their sons and *their daughters.*
4:11. toward *the daughter of* my people,
31. the voice of *the daughter of* Zion,
5:17. (which) thy sons *and thy daughters* should
6: 2. I have likened *the daughter of* Zion
14. the hurt of *the daughter of* my people
23. *O daughter of* Zion.
26. *O daughter of* my people,
7:31. their sons and *their daughters*
8:11. *the daughter of* my people slightly,

Jer. 8:19. the cry of *the daughter of* my people
21. the hurt of *the daughter of* my people
22. the health of *the daughter of* my people
9: 1(8:23). the slain of *the daughter of* my
7(6). for *the daughter of* my people?
20(19). teach *your daughters* wailing,
11:22. *and their daughters* shall die
14:16. their sons, *nor their daughters:*
17. for the virgin *daughter of* my people
16: 2. neither shalt thou have sons *or daughters*
3. concerning *the daughters*
19: 9. the flesh of *their daughters,*
29: 6. beget sons *and daughters;*
— give *your daughters* to husbands, that they may bear sons *and daughters;*
31:22. wilt thou go about, *O thou* backsliding *daughter?*
32:35. *their daughters* to pass through
35: 8. our sons, *nor our daughters;*
41:10. (even) the king's *daughters,*
43: 6. and the king's *daughters,*
46:11. O virgin, *the daughter of* Egypt:
19. O thou *daughter* dwelling in Egypt,
24. *The daughter of* Egypt shall be
48:18. *Thou daughter* that dost inhabit Dibon,
46. taken captives, *and thy daughters* captives.
49: 2. *and her daughters* shall be burned with fire:
3. cry, *ye daughters of* Rabbah,
4. O backsliding *daughter?* that trusted
50:39. the owls shall dwell therein: (lit. *daughters of* the owl)
42. against thee, *O daughter of* Babylon.
51:33. *The daughter of* Babylon
52: 1. *the daughter of* Jeremiah
Lam. 1: 6. from *the daughter of* Zion
15. *the daughter of* Judah,
2: 1. the Lord covered *the daughter of* Zion
2. the strong holds of *the daughter of* Judah;
4. the tabernacle of *the daughter of* Zion:
5. increased *in the daughter of* Judah
8. to destroy the wall of *the daughter of* Zion:
10. The elders of *the daughter of* Zion
11. the destruction of *the daughter of* my people;
13. *O daughter of* Jerusalem?
— O virgin *daughter of* Zion?
15. at *the daughter of* Jerusalem,
18. O wall of *the daughter of* Zion,
— let not *the apple of* thine eye
3:48. the destruction of *the daughter of* my people.
51. because of all *the daughters of*
4: 3. *the daughter of* my people (is become)
6. the iniquity of *the daughter of* my people
10. destruction of *the daughter of* my people.
21, 22. *O daughter of* Edom,
22. *O daughter of* Zion;
Eze. 13:17. against *the daughters of* thy people,
14:16. deliver neither sons nor *daughters;*
18. deliver neither sons *nor daughters,*
20. deliver neither son nor *daughter;*
22. sons *and daughters:*
16:20. thou hast taken thy sons and *thy daughters,*
27. *the daughters of* the Philistines, (marg. *cities*)
44. the mother, (so is) *her daughter.*
45. Thou (art) thy mother's *daughter,*
46. *and her daughters* that dwell at
—, 53, 55. Sodom *and her daughters.*
48. she *nor her daughters,* as thou hast done, thou *and thy daughters.*
49. was in her *and in her daughters,*
53, 55. Samaria *and her daughters,*
55. then thou *and thy daughters* shall return
57. reproach of *the daughters of* Syria,
— *the daughters of* the Philistines,
61. give them unto thee *for daughters,*
22:11. humbled his sister, his father's *daughter.*
23: 2. *the daughters of* one mother:
4. they bare sons *and daughters.*
10. they took her sons *and her daughters,*
25. they shall take thy sons *and thy daughters;*
47. slay their sons *and their daughters,*
24:21. your sons *and your daughters*
25. their sons *and their daughters,*
26: 6. *And her daughters* which (are) in
8. He shall slay with the sword *thy daughters*
27: 6. *the company of* the Ashurites (marg. *daughter*)

Eze.30:18. *and her daughters* shall go into
32:16. *the daughters of* the nations
18. *and the daughters of* the famous
44:25. for son, *or for daughter,*
Dan11: 6. *for* the king's *daughter*
17. *and* he shall give him *the daughter of*
Hos. 1: 3. took Gomer *the daughter of* Diblaim;
6. and bare *a daughter.*
4:13. *your daughters* shall commit
14. I will not punish *your daughters*
Joel 2:28(3:1). your sons *and your daughters*
3: 8(4:8). I will sell your sons and *your daughters*
Am. 7:17. *and thy daughters* shall fall by the sword.
Mic. 1: 8. mourning as the owls. (marg. *as the daughters of* the owl)
13. the sin *to the daughter of* Zion:
4: 8. the strong hold of *the daughter of* Zion,
— shall come *to the daughter of* Jerusalem.
10. *O daughter of* Zion, like a woman
13. Arise and thresh, *O daughter of* Zion:
5: 1(4:14). *O daughter of* troops:
7: 6. *the daughter* riseth up against
Zep. 3:10. *the daughter of* my dispersed,
14. Sing, *O daughter of* Zion;
— *O daughter of* Jerusalem.
Zec. 2: 7(11). dwellest (with) *the daughter of*
10(14). Sing and rejoice, *O daughter of* Zion:
9: 9. Rejoice greatly, *O daughter of* Zion; shout, *O daughter of* Jerusalem:
Mal. 2:11. married *the daughter of* a strange god.

See 1323 & 3284 ## בַּת־יַעֲנָה see under בַּת & יַעֲנָה

1324 ## בַּת *bath*, com.

1K. 7:26. contained two thousand *baths.*
38. one laver contained forty *baths:*
2Ch 2:10(9). twenty thousand *baths* of wine, and twenty thousand *baths* of oil.
4: 5. held three thousand *baths.*
Isa. 5:10. of vineyard shall yield one *bath,*
Eze.45:10. a just ephah, *and a* just *bath.*
11. *and the bath* shall be of one measure, that *the bath* may contain
14. *the bath of* oil, (ye shall offer) the tenth part of *a bath*
— an homer of ten *baths;* for ten *baths* (are)

1325 ## בַּת [*bath*], Ch.

Ezr. 7:22. and to an hundred *baths* of wine, and to an hundred *baths* of oil,

1326 ## בָּתָה *bāh-thāh'*, f.

Isa. 5: 6. I will lay it *waste:*

1330 ## בְּתוּלָה *b'thoo-lāh'*, f.

Gen24:16. very fair to look upon, *a virgin,*
Ex. 22:16(15). if a man entice *a maid*
17(16). according to the dowry of *virgins.*
Lev.21: 3. for his sister *a virgin,*
14. but he shall take *a virgin*
Deu22:19. an evil name upon *a virgin of* Israel:
23. If a damsel (that is) *a virgin*
28. If a man find a damsel (that is) *a virgin,*
32:25. both the young man and *the virgin,*
Jud.19:24. my daughter *a maiden,*
21:12. four hundred young *virgins,*
2Sa.13: 2. for she (was) *a virgin;*
18. the king's daughters (that were) *virgins*
1K. 1: 2. for my lord the king *a young virgin:*
2K. 19:21. *The virgin* the daughter of Zion
2Ch36:17. upon young man *or maiden,*
Est. 2: 2. Let there be fair young *virgins* sought
3. all the fair young *virgins*
17. more than all *the virgins;*
19. when *the virgins* were gathered together
Job 31: 1. should I think upon *a maid?*
Ps. 45:14(15). *the virgins* her companions
78:63. *and their maidens* were not given
148:12. Both young men, *and maidens;*
Isa. 23: 4. bring up *virgins.*
12. *O* thou oppressed *virgin,*
37:22. *The virgin,* the daughter of Zion,
47: 1. *O virgin* daughter of Babylon,
62: 5. For (as) a young man marrieth *a virgin,*
Jer. 2:32. Can *a maid* forget her ornaments,
14:17. *the virgin* daughter of my people
18:13. *the virgin of* Israel hath done a very
31: 4, 21. *O virgin of* Israel:
13. Then shall *the virgin* rejoice
46:11. *O virgin,* the daughter of Egypt:
51:22. the young man *and the maid;*
Lam. 1: 4. *her virgins* are afflicted,
15. hath trodden *the virgin,* the daughter of Judah, (as) in a winepress. (marg. the winepress *of the virgin*)
18. *my virgins* and my young men
2:10. *the virgins of* Jerusalem
13. *O virgin* daughter of Zion?
21. *my virgins* and my young men are fallen
5:11. *the maids* in the cities of Judah.
Eze. 9: 6. *both maids,* and little children,
44:22. but they shall take *maidens*
Joel 1: 8. Lament *like a virgin* girded with
Am. 5: 2. *The virgin of* Israel is fallen;
8:13. In that day shall *the* fair *virgins*
Zec. 9:17. make the young men chearful, and new wine *the maids.*

בְּתוּלִים *b'thoo-leem'*, m. pl. 1331

Lev.21:13. he shall take a wife *in her virginity.*
Deu22:14. when I came to her, I found her not *a maid:* (lit. I found not *virginity* in her)
15. bring forth (the tokens of) the damsel's *virginity*)
17. I found not thy daughter *a maid;* (lit. I found not *virginity* in her)
— these (are the tokens of) my daughter's *virginity.*
20. *virginity* be not found for the damsel:
Jud.11:37. and bewail *my virginity,*
38. and bewailed *her virginity*
Eze.23: 3. bruised the teats of *their virginity.*
8. bruised the breasts of *her virginity,*

בַּתּוֹת *bat-tōhth'*, f. pl. 1327

Isa. 7:19. all of them in the *desolate* valleys, (lit. valleys of *the desolations*)

בָּתַק [*bāh-thak'*]. 1333

✻ PIEL.—*Preterite.* ✻

Eze.16:40. *and thrust thee through* with

בָּתַר *bāh-thar'*. 1334

✻ KAL.—*Preterite.* ✻

Gen15:10. but the birds *divided he* not.

✻ PIEL.—*Future.* ✻

Gen15:10. *and divided* them in the midst,

בְּתַר (Ch.) see אֲתַר See 870

בֶּתֶר [*beh'-ther*], m. 1335

Gen15:10. laid each *piece* one against another: (lit. each *his piece*)
Cant.2:17. the mountains of *Bether.* (marg. *division*)
Jer. 34:18. between *the parts thereof,*
19. between *the parts of* the calf;

ג *gee'-mel.*

The third letter of the Alphabet.

1341 ## גֵּא gēy, adj.

Isa. 16: 6. (he is) very *proud:*

1342 ## גָּאָה gāh-āh'.

* KAL.—*Preterite.* *

Ex. 15: 1, 21. for *he hath triumphed* gloriously:
Eze. 47: 5. for the waters *were risen,*

KAL.—*Infinitive.*

Ex. 15: 1, 21. for he hath triumphed *gloriously:*

KAL.—*Future.*

Job 8: 11. *Can* the rush *grow up* without mire?
10: 16. *For it increaseth.* Thou huntest me

1343 ## גֵּאֶה gēh-eh', adj.

Job 40: 11. behold every one (that is) *proud,*
12. Look on every one (that is) *proud,*
Ps. 94: 2. render a reward to *the proud.*
123: 4. (and) with the contempt of the proud. (see כתיב גֵּאֲיוֹן)
140: 5(6). *The proud* have hid a snare
Pro. 15: 25. destroy the house of *the proud:*
16: 19. to divide the spoil with *the proud.*
Isa. 2: 12. every (one that is) *proud* and lofty,
Jer. 48: 29. he is exceeding *proud*

1344 ## גֵּאָה gēh-āh', f.

Pro. 8: 13. *pride,* and arrogancy, and the evil way,

1346 ## גַּאֲוָה gah-ăvāh', f.

Deu 33: 26. *and in his excellency* on the sky.
29. who (is) the sword of *thy excellency!*
Job 41: 15(7). (His) scales (are his) *pride,*
Ps. 10: 2. The wicked *in* (his) *pride* (marg. *In the pride of* the wicked)
31: 18(19). which speak grievous things *proudly*
23(24). and plentifully rewardeth the *proud*
36: 11(12). Let not the foot of *pride* come
46: 3(4). shake *with the swelling thereof.*
68: 34(35). *his excellency* (is) over Israel,
73: 6. *pride* compasseth them about
Pro. 14: 3. of the foolish (is) a rod of *pride:*
29: 23. man's *pride* shall bring him low:
Isa. 9: 9(8). that say *in the pride*
13: 3. them that rejoice in *my highness.*
11. *and* will lay low *the haughtiness of*
16: 6. *his haughtiness,* and his pride,
25: 11. he shall bring down *their pride*
Jer. 48: 29. his arrogancy, *and his pride,*
Zep. 3: 11. them that rejoice in *thy pride,*

1347 ## גָּאוֹן gāh-ōhn', m.

Ex. 15: 7. the greatness of *thine excellency*
Lev. 26: 19. I will break *the pride of* your
Job 35: 12. because of *the pride of* evil men.
37: 4. with the voice of *his excellency;*
38: 11. here shall thy *proud* waves be stayed? (marg. *the pride of* thy waves)
40: 10. Deck thyself now (with) *majesty*
Ps. 47: 4(5). *the excellency of* Jacob
59: 12(13). even be taken *in their pride:*
Pro. 8: 13. pride, *and arrogancy,* and the evil way,
16: 18. *Pride* (goeth) before destruction,
Isa. 2: 10, 19, 21. and for the glory of *his majesty.*
4: 2. the fruit of the earth (shall be) *excellent* (lit. *for excellency*)
13: 11. I will cause *the arrogancy of*
19. the beauty of the Chaldees' *excellency,*
14: 11. *Thy pomp* is brought down
16: 6. We have heard of *the pride of*
— his haughtiness, *and his pride,*
Isa. 23: 9. to stain *the pride of* all glory,
24: 14. shall sing *for the majesty of* the Lord,
60: 15. I will make thee *an* eternal *excellency,*
Jer. 12: 5. *in the swelling of* Jordan?
13: 9. will I mar *the pride of* Judah, and *the* great *pride of* Jerusalem.
48: 29. We have heard *the pride of* Moab,
— *his arrogancy,* and his pride,
49: 19 & 50: 44. like a lion *from the swelling of*
Eze. 7: 20. he set it *in majesty:*
24. make *the pomp of* the strong to
16: 49. iniquity of thy sister Sodom, *pride,*
56. in the day of *thy pride,* (marg. *prides,* or, *excellencies*)
24: 21. *the excellency of* your strength,
30: 6. *the pride of* her power
18. *the pomp of* her strength
32: 12. they shall spoil *the pomp of*
33: 28. *the pomp of* her strength
Hos. 5: 5. *the pride of* Israel doth testify
7: 10. *the pride of* Israel testifieth
Am. 6: 8. I abhor *the excellency of* Jacob,
8: 7. sworn *by the excellency of* Jacob,
Mic. 5: 4(3). *in the majesty of* the name of
Nah 2: 2(3). turned away *the excellency of* Jacob, *as the excellency of* Israel: (marg. or, *pride...pride*)
Zep. 2: 10. This shall they have for *their pride,*
Zec. 9: 6. I will cut off *the pride of* the Philistines.
10: 11. *the pride of* Assyria shall be
11: 3. for *the pride of* Jordan is spoiled.

גֵּאוּת gēh-ooth', f. 1348

Ps. 17: 10. with their mouth they speak *proudly.* (lit. *with pride*)
89: 9(10). Thou rulest *the raging of* the sea:
93: 1. he is clothed with *majesty;*
Isa. 9: 18(17). *the lifting up of* smoke.
12: 5. he hath done *excellent things:*
26: 10. behold *the majesty of* the Lord.
28: 1. Woe to the crown of *pride,*
3. The crown of *pride,* the drunkards

גַּאֲיוֹן [gah-ăyōhn'], adj. 1349

Ps. 123: 4. (כתיב) with the contempt of *the proud.*

גֵּאָיוֹת see גַּיְא See 1516

גָּאַל gāh-al'. 1350

* KAL.—*Preterite.* *

Ex. 6: 6. *and I will redeem* you
15: 13. the people which *thou hast redeemed:*
Lev. 25: 25. *then shall he redeem* that
Ru. 3: 13. *then will* I *do the part of a kinsman to thee,*
Ps. 74: 2. *thou hast redeemed;* this mount
77: 15(16). with (thine) arm *redeemed*
107: 2. whom *he hath redeemed* (lit. *redeemed them*)
Isa. 43: 1 & 44: 22. for *I have redeemed thee,*
44. 23. the Lord *hath redeemed* Jacob,
48: 20. The Lord *hath redeemed* his servant
52: 9. *he hath redeemed* Jerusalem.
63: 9. in his pity *he redeemed them;*
Jer. 31: 11. *and ransomed him* from the
Lam. 3: 58. *thou hast redeemed* my life.

KAL.—*Infinitive.*

Lev. 27: 13. But if he will *at all* redeem it, (lit. *redeeming* will redeem it)
19. the field will *in any wise* redeem it,
31. if a man will *at all* redeem
Ru. 3: 13. he will not *do the part of a kinsman to thee,*
4: 4. none *to redeem* (it) beside thee;
6. I cannot *redeem* (it) for myself,
— for I cannot *redeem* (it).

KAL.—*Imperative.*

Ru. 4. 4. If thou wilt redeem (it), *redeem* (it):

Ru. 4: 6. *redeem* thou my right
Ps. 69:18(19). *redeem it:* deliver me
119:154. Plead my cause, *and deliver me:*

KAL.—*Future.*

Lev.25:33. if a man *purchase* of the Levites, (marg. or, (one) of the Levites *redeem*)
48. his brethren *may redeem him:*
49. his uncle's son, *may redeem him,*
— of his family *may redeem him;*
27:13. if *he will* at all *redeem it,*
15. *will redeem* his house,
19. *will* in any wise *redeem* it,
20. if *he will* not *redeem* the field,
31. if a man *will* at all *redeem*
Ru. 3:13. if *he will perform unto thee the part of a kinsman,* well; *let him do the kinsman's part:*
4: 4. If *thou wilt redeem* (it), redeem (it): but if *thou wilt* not *redeem* (it),
— *I will redeem* (it).
Job 3: 5. the shadow of death *stain it;* (marg. or, *challenge*)
Ps. 72:14. *He shall redeem* their soul
106:10. *and redeemed them* from
Hos13:14. *I will redeem them* from death:
Mic. 4:10. the Lord *shall redeem thee*

KAL.—*Participle.* Poel.

Gen48:16. *which redeemed* me from all evil,
Lev.25:25. if any of his kin come *to redeem* (lit. the *redeemer thereof,* that is near unto him, shall come)
26. if the man have none *to redeem* (lit. not *a redeemer*)
Nu. 5: 8. if the man have no *kinsman*
35:12. for refuge *from the avenger;*
19. *The revenger of* blood himself
21. *the revenger of* blood shall slay
24. the slayer and *the revenger of* blood
25. the hand of *the revenger of* blood,
27. *the revenger of* blood find
— *the revenger of* blood kill the slayer;
Deu19: 6. Lest *the avenger of* the blood pursue
12. into the hand of *the avenger of*
Jos.20: 3. *from the avenger of* blood.
5. if *the avenger of* blood pursue
9. by the hand of *the avenger of* blood,
Ru. 2:20. *one of our next kinsmen.* (marg. or, *one that hath right to redeem*)
3: 9. for thou (art) *a near kinsman.* (marg. or, *one that hath right to redeem*)
12. it is true that I (am thy) *near kinsman:* howbeit there is *a kinsman* nearer than I.
4: 1. *the kinsman* of whom Boaz spake
3. he said *unto the kinsman,*
6. And *the kinsman* said,
8. *the kinsman* said unto Boaz,
14. left thee this day without *a kinsman,* (marg. *redeemer*)
2Sa.14:11. suffer *the revengers of* blood
1K. 16:11. *neither of his kinsfolks,* (marg. or, *both his kinsmen*)
Job 19:25. I know (that) *my redeemer* liveth,
Ps. 19:14(15). my strength, *and my redeemer.*
78:35. the high God *their redeemer.*
103: 4. *Who redeemeth* thy life from
Pro.23:11. For *their redeemer* (is) mighty;
Isa. 41:14. the Lord, *and thy redeemer,*
43:14. the Lord, *your redeemer,*
44: 6. *and his redeemer* the Lord
24. Thus saith the Lord, *thy redeemer,*
47: 4. *our redeemer,* the Lord of hosts
48:17. Thus saith the Lord, *thy Redeemer,*
49: 7. *the Redeemer of* Israel,
26. thy Saviour *and thy Redeemer,*
54: 5. *and thy Redeemer* the Holy One
8. saith the Lord *thy Redeemer.*
59:20. *the Redeemer* shall come to Zion,
60:16. thy Saviour *and thy Redeemer,*
63:16. our father, *our redeemer;*
Jer. 50:34. *Their Redeemer* (is) strong;

KAL.—*Participle.* Paül.

Ps.107: 2. Let *the redeemed of* the Lord say
Isa. 35: 9. but *the redeemed* shall walk
51:10. a way for *the ransomed* to pass
Isa. 62:12. *The redeemed of* the Lord:
63: 4. the year of *my redeemed* is come.

* NIPHAL.—*Preterite.* *

Lev.25:49. *he may redeem himself.*

NIPHAL.—*Future.*

Lev.25:30. if *it be* not *redeemed*
54. And if *he be* not *redeemed*
27:20. *it shall* not *be redeemed* any more.
27. or if *it be* not *redeemed,*
28. shall be sold or *redeemed:*
33. *it shall* not *be redeemed.*
Isa. 52: 3. *ye shall be redeemed*

גָּאַל [*gāh-al'*]. 1351

* NIPHAL.—*Preterite.* *

Isa. 59: 3. your hands *are defiled* with blood,
Lam.4:14. *they have polluted themselves*

NIPHAL.—*Participle.*

Zep. 3: 1. her that is filthy *and polluted,*

* PIEL.—*Preterite.* *

Mal. 1: 7. Wherein *have we polluted thee?*

* PUAL.—*Future.* *

Ezr. 2:62. *therefore were they, as polluted, put* from the priesthood. (marg. *polluted* from the priesthood)
Neh 7:64. *therefore were they, as polluted, put* from the priesthood.

PUAL.—*Participle.*

Mal. 1: 7. Ye offer *polluted* bread
12. The table of the Lord (is) *polluted;*

* HIPHIL.—*Preterite.* *

Isa. 63: 3. *I will stain* all my raiment.

* HITHPAEL.—*Future.* *

Dan 1: 8. *he would* not *defile himself*
— that *he might* not *defile himself.*

גֹּאֶל [*gōh'-el*]. 1352

Neh 13:29. because *they have defiled* the priesthood, (marg. for *the defilings*)

גְּאֻלָּה *g'ool-lāh',* f. 1353

Lev.25:24. ye shall grant *a redemption*
26. himself be able to *redeem it;* (lit. sufficiency of *redemption thereof*)
29. then he may *redeem it* (lit. *the redemption thereof* shall be to him)
— a full year may he *redeem it.* (lit. *the redemption thereof* shall be to him)
31. they may be *redeemed,* (marg. *redemption* belongeth unto it)
32. may the Levites *redeem*
48. is sold he may be *redeemed* again; (lit. *redemption* belongs unto)
51, 52. *the price of his redemption*
Ru. 4: 6. redeem thou *my right*
7. concerning *redeeming*
Jer. 32: 7. for the right of *redemption* (is) thine
8. *the redemption* (is) thine; buy (it)
Eze.11:15. the men of *thy kindred,*

גַּב *gav,* m. 1354

Lev.14: 9. and his eye*brows,*
1K. 7:33. their axletrees, *and their naves,*
Job 13:12. *your bodies to bodies of* clay.
15:26. upon the thick *bosses of* his
Ps.129: 3. The plowers plowed upon *my back:*
Eze. 1:18. *As for their rings,* they were so
— *and their rings* (were) full (marg. *strakes*)
10:12. *and their backs,* and their hands,
16:24. built unto thee *an eminent place,* (marg. or, *brothel house*)
31. thou buildest *thine eminent place*

Eze. 16:39. throw down *thine eminent place,*
43:13. *the higher place of* the altar.

1355 ## גַּב [*gav*], m. Ch.

Dan 7: 6. which had upon *the back of it*

1356 ## גֵּב *gēhv*, m.

1K. 6: 9. covered the house with *beams* (marg. or, *the vaultbeams*)
2K. 3:16. Make this valley *full of ditches.* (lit. *ditches ditches*)
Isa. 10:31. the inhabitants of *Gebim* [or, *the ditches*]
Jer. 14: 3. they came to the *pits,*

1357 ## גֵּב [*gēhv*], m.

Isa. 33: 4. the running to and fro of *locusts*

1358 ## גֹּב *gōhv*, Ch.

Dan 6: 7(8), 12(13). shall be cast *into the den of* lions.
16(17). and cast (him) *into the den* of
17(18). and laid upon the mouth of *the den;*
19(20). went in haste *unto the den*
20(21). when he came *to the den,*
23(24). should take Daniel up out of *the den.* So Daniel was taken up out of *the den,*
24(25). *and* they cast (them) *into the den of*
—(—). or ever they came at the bottom of *the den.*

1360 ## גֶּבֶא *geh'-veh*, m.

Isa. 30:14. take water (withal) *out of the pit.*
Jer. 14: 3. they came to *the pits,*
Eze. 47:11. *and the marishes thereof*

1361 ## גָּבַהּ *gāh-vah'.*

** KAL.—Preterite. **

2Ch 26:16 & 32:25. his heart *was lifted up*
Job 35: 5. *are higher* than thou.
Ps. 131: 1. my heart *is* not *haughty,*
Isa. 3:16. the daughters of Zion *are haughty,*
52:13. *and be* very *high.*
55: 9. (as) the heavens *are higher* than the earth, so *are* my ways *higher*
Eze. 28: 2. Because thine heart *is lifted up,*
17. Thine heart *was lifted up*
31: 5. Therefore his height *was exalted*
10. Because *thou hast lifted up thyself*

KAL.—*Infinitive.*

Ps. 103:11. *as* the heaven *is high* above (marg. *according to the height of* the heaven)
Zep. 3:11. thou shalt no more *be haughty*

KAL.—*Future.*

1Sa. 10:23. *and* when he stood...*he was higher* than any of the people
2Ch 17: 6. *And* his heart *was lifted up*
Job 36: 7. *and they are exalted.*
Pro. 18:12. the heart of man *is haughty,*
Isa. 5:16. *But* the Lord of hosts *shall be exalted*
Jer. 13:15. give ear; *be* not *proud:*
Eze. 16:50. *And they were haughty,*
19:11. *and* her stature *was exalted*
28: 5. *and* thine heart *is lifted up*
31:14. *exalt themselves* for their height,

** HIPHIL.—Preterite. **

Eze. 17:24. *have exalted* the low tree,

HIPHIL.—*Infinitive.*

Isa. 7:11. or in *the height* above. (lit. *to exalt*)
Eze. 21:26(31). *exalt* (him that is) low,

HIPHIL.—*Future.*

2Ch 33:14. *and raised it up* a very *great height,*
Job 5: 7. as the sparks fly *upward.* (marg. *lift up* to fly)
39:27. *Doth* the eagle *mount up*
Jer. 49:16. *thou shouldest make* thy nest as *high*
Obad. 4. Though *thou exalt* (thyself) as the eagle,

HIPHIL.—*Participle.*

Ps. 113: 5. our God, who dwelleth *on high,* (marg *exalteth* (himself) to dwell)
Pro. 17:19. *he that exalteth* his gate

גָּבָהּ [*gāh-vāh'*], adj. 1362

Ps. 101: 5. *him that hath an high* look (lit. *the high of* eyes)
Pro. 16: 5. Every one (that is) *proud in* heart
Ecc. 7: 8. better *than the proud in* spirit.
Eze. 31: 3. *and* of *an high* stature;

גֹּבַהּ *gōh'-vah*, m. 1363

1Sa. 17: 4. *whose height* (was) six cubits
2Ch 3: 4. *and the height* (was)
32:26. *for the pride of* his heart, (marg. *lifting up*)
Job 11: 8. *as high as* heaven; (marg. the *heights of* heaven)
22:12. God in *the height of* heaven?
40:10. majesty *and excellency;*
Ps. 10: 4. *through the pride of* his countenance,
Pro. 16:18. an *haughty* spirit before a fall.
Jer. 48:29. *his loftiness,* and his arrogancy,
Eze. 1:18. *so high* that they were dreadful;
19:11. she appeared *in her height*
31:10. his heart is lifted up *in his height;*
14. their trees stand up *in their height,*
40:42. *and* one cubit *high:*
41: 8. I saw also *the height* of the house
Am. 2: 9. whose *height* (lit. who *his height*) (was) *like the height of* the cedars,

גַּבְהוּת *gav-hooth'*, f. 1365

Isa. 2:11. The *lofty* looks of man
17. *the loftiness of* man

גָּבֹהַּ & גָּבוֹהַּ *gāh-vōh'ăh*, adj. 1364

Gen 7:19. all the *high* hills,
Deu 3: 5. cities (were) fenced with *high* walls,
28:52. until thy *high* and fenced walls
1Sa. 2: 3. Talk no more *so exceeding proudly;* (lit. *high high*)
9: 2. *higher* than any (lit. *high* before)
16: 7. or on *the height of* his stature;
1K. 14:23. on every *high* hill,
2K. 17:10. groves in every *high* hill,
Est. 5:14. a gallows be made of fifty cubits *high,*
7: 9. the gallows fifty cubits *high,*
Job 41:34(26). He beholdeth all *high* (things):
Ps. 104:18. The *high* hills (are) a refuge
138: 6. *but the proud* he knoweth afar off.
Ecc. 5: 8(7). for (he that is) *higher* than *the highest* (lit. *high* above *the high*)
—(—). *and* (there be) *higher* than they. (lit. *and high* above them)
12: 5. be afraid *of* (that which is) *high,*
Isa. 2:15. upon every *high* tower,
5:15. the eyes of *the lofty* shall be humbled:
10:33. *and the haughty* shall be humbled.
30:25. upon every *high* mountain,
40: 9. get thee up into the *high* mountain;
57: 7. Upon a *lofty* and high mountain
Jer. 2:20. when upon every *high* hill
3: 6. upon every *high* mountain
17: 2. by the green trees upon the *high* hills.
51:58. her *high* gates shall be burned
Eze. 17:22. plant (it) upon an *high* mountain
24. have brought down the *high* tree,
21:26(31). *and* abase (him that is) *high.*
40: 2. upon a very *high* mountain,
41:22. of wood (was) three cubits *high,*
Dan 8: 3. the two horns (were) *high;*
— one (was) *higher* than (lit. *high* before)
— *and the higher* came up last
Zep. 1:16. against the *high* towers.

1366 **גְּבוּל** *g'vool*, m.

Gen10:19. *the border of* the Canaanites
23:17. in all *the borders* (lit. *border thereof*) round
47:21. end of *the borders of* Egypt
Ex. 8: 2(7:27). I will smite all *thy borders*
10: 4. I bring the locusts *into thy coast:*
14, 19. in all *the coasts of* Egypt:
13: 7. with thee in all *thy quarters.*
23:31. I will set *thy bounds* from
34:24. enlarge *thy borders:*
Nu. 20:16. a city in the uttermost of *thy border:*
17. until we have passed *thy borders.*
21. *through his border:* wherefore Israel
23. by *the coast of* the land of Edom,
21:13. that cometh *out of the coasts of* the Amorites: for Arnon (is) *the border of* Moab,
15. lieth *upon the border of* Moab.
22. until we be past *thy borders.*
23. to pass *through his border:*
24. for *the border of* the children of Ammon
22:36. which (is) in *the border of* Arnon, which (is) in *the* utmost *coast.*
33:44. Ije-abarim, *in the border of* Moab.
34: 3. and your south *border* shall be
4. And your *border* shall turn
5. *the border* shall fetch a compass
6. *And* (as for) *the* western *border,* ye shall even have the great sea for *a border:* this shall be your west *border*)
7, 9. this shall be your north *border.*
8. the goings forth of *the border*
9. And *the border* shall go on to
10. ye shall point out your east *border* (lit. *for a border* eastward)
11. And *the coast* shall go down
— *the border* shall descend,
12. *the border* shall go down
35:26. without *the border of* the city of his refuge,
27. find him without *the borders of* the city
Deu 2: 4. to pass *through the coast*
18. *the coast of* Moab,
3:14. unto *the coasts of* Geshuri
16. *and the border* even unto the
— *the border of* the children of
17. *and the coast* (thereof),
11:24. shall *your coast* be.
12:20. God shall enlarge *thy border,*
16: 4. with thee in all *thy coast*
19: 3. divide *the coasts of* thy land,
8. God enlarge *thy coast,*
14. not remove thy neighbour's *landmark,*
27:17. removeth his neighbour's *landmark.*
28:40. throughout all *thy coasts,*
Jos. 1: 4. shall be *your coast.*
12: 2. *the border of* the children of
4. *And the coast of* Og king
5. unto *the border of* the
— *the border of* Sihon king of
13: 3. unto *the borders of* Ekron
4. to *the borders of* the Amorites:
10. unto *the border of* the children
11. *and the border of* the Geshurites
16. their *coast* was from Aroer,
23. *the border of* the children of
— *and the border* (thereof).
25. their *coast* was Jazer,
26. unto *the border* of Debir;
27. Jordan *and* (his) *border,*
30. And *their coast* was from
15: 1. to *the border of* Edom
2. their south *border* was from
4. the goings out of that *coast* were at the sea: this shall be your south *coast.*
5. *And the* east *border* (was) the salt
— *And* (their) *border* in the
6, 6, 8, 8. *the border* went up
7. *the border* went up toward
— *the border* passed toward
9, 9, 11. *the border* was drawn
10. *the border* compassed from Baalah
11. *the border* went out unto the
— the goings out of *the border* were at
12. *And the* west *border* (was) to the great sea, *and the coast* (thereof). This (is) *the coast of* the children of Judah
21. toward *the coast of* Edom

Jos. 15:47. (כתיב) and the *great* sea, (lit. according to כתיב, the sea of *the border*)
— *and the border* (thereof):
16: 2. unto *the borders of* Archi
3. to the *coast of* Japhleti, unto *the coast of*
5. *the border of* the children of Ephraim
— even *the border of* their inheritance
6. *the border* went out toward
— *the border* went about eastward
8. *The border* went out from
17: 7. *the coast of* Manasseh
— *the border* went along
8. Tappuah on *the border of* Manasseh
9. And *the coast* descended
— *the coast of* Manasseh *also*
10. the sea is *his border;*
18: 5. abide in *their coast* on the south,
— Joseph shall abide in *their coasts*
11. and *the coast of* their lot
12. And their *border* on the north
— *the border* went up to the side of
13. *the border* went over
— *the border* descended to
14. *the border* was drawn
15. *the border* went out on
16. *the border* came down to the end
19. *the border* passed along
— the outgoings of *the border*
— this (was) *the* south *coast.*
19:10. *the border of* their inheritance
11. *their border* went up
12. unto *the border of* Chisloth-tabor,
14. *the border* compasseth it
18. *their border* was toward Jezreel,
22. *the coast* reacheth to Tabor,
— the outgoings of *their border*
25. *their border* was Helkath,
29. *the coast* turneth to Ramah,
— *the coast* turneth to Hosah;
33. *their coast* was from Heleph,
34. *the coast* turneth westward
41. *the coast of* their inheritance
46. with *the border* before
47. *the coast of* the children
22:25. *For* the Lord hath made Jordan *a border*
24:30. *in the border of* his inheritance
Jud. 1:18. Gaza with *the coast thereof,* and Askelon with *the coast thereof,* and Ekron with *the coast thereof.*
36. *And the coast of* the Amorites
2: 9. *in the border of* his inheritance
11:18. *within the border of* Moab: for Arnon (was) *the border of* Moab.
20. to pass through *his coast:*
22. they possessed all *the coasts of*
19:29. into all *the coast of* Israel.
1Sa. 5: 6. Ashdod and *the coasts thereof.*
6: 9. by the way of *his own coast*
12. unto *the border of* Beth-shemesh.
7:13. came no more *into the coast of*
14. and *the coasts thereof*
10: 2. *in the border of* Benjamin
11: 3. unto all *the coasts of* Israel:
7. throughout all *the coasts of* Israel
13:18. the way of *the border* that looketh
27: 1. any more in any *coast of* Israel:
2Sa. 21: 5. in any of *the coasts of* Israel,
1K. 1: 3. throughout all *the coasts of* Israel,
4:21(5:1). unto *the border of* Egypt:
2K. 3:21. stood in *the border.*
10:32. smote them in all *the coasts of*
14:25. He restored *the coast of* Israel
15:16. *the coasts thereof* from Tirzah:
18: 8. and *the borders thereof,*
1Ch 4:10. enlarge *my coast,*
6:54(39). their castles *in their coasts,*
66(51). had cities of *their coasts*
21:12. throughout all *the coasts of* Israel.
2Ch 9:26. to *the border of* Egypt.
11:13. resorted to him out of all *their coasts.*
Job 38:20. to *the bound thereof,*
Ps. 78:54. he brought them to *the border of*
104: 9. Thou hast set *a bound*
105:31. lice in all *their coasts.*
33. brake the trees of *their coasts*
147:14. maketh peace (in) *thy borders,*
Pro. 15:25. establish *the border of* the widow.

Pro.22:28. Remove not *the* ancient *landmark*, (marg. or, *bound*)
23:10. Remove not *the* old *landmark;* (marg. or, *bound*)
Isa. 15: 8. about *the borders of* Moab;
19:19. a pillar at *the border thereof*
54:12. all *thy borders* of pleasant stones.
60:18. destruction *within thy borders;*
Jer. 5:22. *the bound* of the sea
15:13. even in all *thy borders.*
17: 3. throughout all *thy borders.*
31:17. come again *to their own border.*
Eze.11:10. judge you in *the border of* Israel;
11. I will judge you in *the border of* Israel:
27: 4. *Thy borders* (are) in the midst
29:10. even unto *the border of* Ethiopia.
40:12. *The space also* before the (marg. *limit*, or, *bound*)
— and *the space* (was) one cubit on
43:12. *the* whole *limit thereof* round
13. *and the border thereof* by the edge
17. *and the border* about
20. upon *the border* round about:
45: 1. holy in all *the borders thereof*
7. *from the* west *border* unto *the* east *border.*
47:13. This (shall be) *the border,*
15. this (shall be) *the border of* the land
16. between *the border of* Damascus and *the border of* Hamath; Hazar-hatticon, which (is) by *the coast of* Hauran.
17. *the border* from the sea shall be Hazar-enan, *the border of* Damascus,
— *and the border of* Hamath.
18. *from the border* unto the east sea.
20. the great sea *from the border,*
48: 1. *the border of* Damascus northward,
2. by *the border of* Dan,
3. by *the border of* Asher,
4. by *the border of* Naphtali,
5. by *the border of* Manasseh,
6. by *the border of* Ephraim,
7. by *the border of* Reuben,
8. by *the border of* Judah,
12. by *the border of* the Levites.
13. against *the border of* the priests
21. toward *the* east *border,*
— toward *the* west *border,*
22: between *the border of* Judah and *the border of* Benjamin,
24. by *the border of* Benjamin,
25. by *the border of* Simeon,
26. by *the border of* Issachar,
27. by *the border of* Zebulun,
28. by *the border of* Gad,
— *the border* shall be even from
Hos 5:10. them that remove *the bound;*
Joel 3: 6(4:6). far from *their border.*
Am. 1:13. that they might enlarge *their border:*
6: 2. or *their border* greater *than your border?*
Obad. 7. brought thee (even) to *the border:*
Mic. 5: 6(5). treadeth *within our borders.*
Zep. 2: 8. against *their border.*
Mal. 1: 4. *The border of* wickedness,
5. from *the border of* Israel. (marg. from *upon the border*)

1367 **גְּבוּלָה** [*g'voo-lāh'*], f.

Nu. 32:33. cities thereof *in the coasts,*
34: 2. of Canaan *with the coasts thereof:*
12. *with the coasts thereof* round about.
Deu32: 8. he set *the bounds of* the people
Jos. 18:20. by *the coasts thereof*
19:49. by *their coasts,*
Job 24: 2. remove *the landmarks;*
Ps. 74:17. Thou hast set all *the borders of*
Isa. 10:13. I have removed *the bounds of*
28:25. the rie in *their place?* (marg. *border?*)

1368 **גִּבּוֹר** *gib-bōhr'*, adj.

Gen 6: 4. the same (became) *mighty men*
10: 8. he began to be *a mighty one*
9. He was a *mighty* hunter
— Nimrod the *mighty* hunter
Deu10:17. *a mighty*, and a terrible,
Jos. 1:14. all *the mighty men of* valour,
6: 2. *the mighty men of* valour.
8: 3. thirty thousand *mighty* men *of*
10: 2. all the men thereof (were) *mighty.*
7. all *the mighty men of* valour.
Jud. 5:13. have dominion *over the mighty.*
23. the help of the Lord *against the mighty.*
6:12. thou *mighty man of* valour.
11: 1. was *a mighty man of* valour,
Ru. 2: 1. a *mighty* man *of* wealth,
1 Sa. 2: 4. The bows of *the mighty men*
9: 1. *a mighty man of* power.
14:52. when Saul saw any *strong* man,
16:18. *and a mighty* valiant *man,*
17:51. saw *their champion* was dead,
2Sa. 1:19, 25, 27. how are *the mighty* fallen!
21. there the shield of *the mighty*
22. from the fat of *the mighty,*
10: 7. all the host of *the mighty men.*
16: 6. all *the mighty men*
17: 8. that they (be) *mighty men,*
10. that thy father (is) *a mighty man,*
20: 7. all *the mighty men:*
22:26. with *the* upright *man*
23: 8. the names of *the mighty men*
9. *the* three *mighty men*
16. *the* three *mighty men* brake
17. did these three *mighty men.*
22. among three *mighty men.*
1 K. 1: 8. *and the mighty men*
10. and *the mighty men,*
11:28. *a mighty man of* valour:
2 K. 5: 1. he was also *a mighty* man *in* valour
15:20. all *the mighty men of* wealth,
24:14. all *the mighty men of* valour,
16. all (that were) *strong*
1Ch. 1:10. he began to be *mighty*
5:24. *mighty* men *of* valour,
7: 2. *valiant men of* might
5. *valiant men of* might, reckoned
7, 11. *mighty men of* valour;
9, 40 & 8:40. *mighty men of* valour,
9:13. *very* able *men* for the work (marg. *mighty men of* valour)
26. the four *chief* porters,
11:10. the chief of *the mighty men*
11. the number of *the mighty men*
12. who (was one) of *the* three *mighties.*
19. These things did these three *mightiest.*
24. a name among *the* three *mighties.*
26. *Also the valiant men of* the
12: 1. they (were) *among the mighty men,*
4. *a mighty man* among the thirty,
8. *men of* might, (lit. *mighty men of* valour)
21, 25. *mighty men of* valour,
28. a young man *mighty of* valour,
30. *mighty men of* valour,
19: 8. all the host of *the mighty men.*
26: 6. they (were) *mighty men of* valour.
31. among them *mighty men of* valour
27: 6. *mighty* (among) the thirty,
28: 1. *and with the mighty men,* and with all *the* valiant *men,*
29:24. *and the mighty men,* and all the sons
2 Ch13: 3. *men of* war,
— *mighty men of* valour.
14: 8(7) & 17:13, 14. *mighty men of* valour.
17:16. *mighty men of* valour.
17. *a mighty man of* valour,
25: 6. *mighty men of* valour
26:12. the fathers *of the mighty men of*
28: 7. *a mighty man of* Ephraim,
32: 3. *and his mighty men* to stop
21. cut off all *the mighty men of*
Ezr. 7:28. before all the king's *mighty* princes.
Neh. 3:16. unto the house of *the mighty.*
9:32. the great, *the mighty*, and the terrible
11:14. *mighty men of* valour,
Job.16:14. he runneth upon me *like a giant.*
Ps. 19: 5(6). rejoiceth *as a strong man*
24: 8. The Lord strong *and mighty*, the Lord *mighty in* battle.
33:16. *a mighty man* is not delivered
45: 3(4). upon (thy) thigh, *O* (most) *mighty,*
52: 1(3). *O mighty man?* the goodness of God
78:65. *like a mighty man* that shouteth

Ps. 89:19(20). laid help upon (one that is) mighty ;
103:20. that excel in strength, (marg. mighty in)
112: 2. His seed shall be mighty upon
120: 4. Sharp arrows of the mighty,
127: 4. in the hand of a mighty man ;
Pro. 16:32. better than the mighty ;
21:22. scaleth the city of the mighty,
30:30. strongest among beasts,
Ecc. 9:11. nor the battle to the strong,
Cant.3: 7. threescore valiant men (are) about it, of the valiant of Israel.
4: 4. all shields of mighty men.
Isa. 3: 2. The mighty man, and the man
5:22. Woe unto (them that are) mighty
9: 6(5) & 10:21. The mighty God,
13: 3. I have also called my mighty ones
21:17. the mighty men of the children of
42:13. go forth as a mighty man,
49:24. Shall the prey be taken from the mighty,
25. the captives of the mighty
Jer. 5:16. they (are) all mighty men.
9:23(22). neither let the mighty man
14: 9. as a mighty man (that) cannot
20:11. with me as a mighty terrible one:
26:21. with all his mighty men,
32:18. the Great, The Mighty God,
46: 5. and their mighty ones are beaten
6. nor the mighty man escape ;
9. let the mighty men come forth ;
12. for the mighty man hath stumbled against the mighty,
48:14. How say ye, We (are) mighty
41. the mighty men's hearts in Moab
49:22. the heart of the mighty men of Edom
50: 9. as of a mighty expert man ;
36. a sword (is) upon her mighty men ;
51:30. The mighty men of Babylon
56. and her mighty men are taken,
57. and her mighty men : and they shall sleep
Eze.32:12. By the swords of the mighty
21. The strong among the mighty
27. they shall not lie with the mighty
— the terror of the mighty
39:18. eat the flesh of the mighty,
20. with mighty men,
Dan 11: 3. a mighty king shall stand
Hos 10:13. the multitude of thy mighty men.
Joel 2: 7. shall run like mighty men ;
3: 9(4:9). wake up the mighty men,
10(4:10). let the weak say, I (am) strong.
11(4:11). cause thy mighty ones to come
Am. 2:14. neither (lit. and not) shall the mighty
16. courageous among the mighty
Obad 9. thy mighty men, O Teman,
Nah. 2: 3(4). The shield of his mighty men
Zep. 1:14. the mighty man shall cry
3:17. in the midst of thee (is) mighty ;
Zec. 9:13. as the sword of a mighty man.
10: 5. they shall be as mighty men,
7. Ephraim shall be like a mighty man,

1369 גְּבוּרָה g'voo-rāh', f.

Ex. 32:18. of (them that) shout for mastery,
Deu. 3:24. and according to thy might ?
Jud. 5:31. when he goeth forth in his might.
8:21. as the man (is, so is) his strength.
1 K. 15:23. and all his might,
16: 5. what he did, and his might,
27. which he did, and his might
22:45(46). and his might that he shewed,
2 K. 10:34. and all his might,
13: 8, 12. all that he did, and his might,
14:15. which he did, and his might,
28. all that he did, and his might,
18:20. counsel and strength for the war.
20:20. and all his might,
1 Ch 29:11. the greatness, and the power,
12. in thine hand (is) power and might ;
30. all his reign and his might,
2 Ch 20: 6. power and might,
Est. 10: 2. his power and of his might,
Job. 12:13. With him (is) wisdom and strength,
26:14. the thunder of his power
39:19. Hast thou given the horse strength ?
41:12(4). nor his power, (lit. the word of powers)
Ps. 20: 6(7). with the saving strength of (marg. by the strength of the salvation of)
21:13(14). we sing and praise thy power.
54: 1(3). and judge me by thy strength.
65: 6(7). girded with power :
66: 7. He ruleth by his power
71:16. I will go in the strength of
18. thy power to every one
80: 2(3). stir up thy strength,
89:13(14). Thou hast a mighty arm: (marg an arm with might)
90:10. if by reason of strength
106: 2. Who can utter the mighty acts of
8. make his mighty power to be
145: 4. and shall declare thy mighty acts.
11. and talk of thy power ;
12. to the sons of men his mighty acts,
147:10. in the strength of the horse:
150: 2. Praise him for his mighty acts :
Pro. 8:14. I (am) understanding ; I have strength.
Ecc. 9:16. Wisdom (is) better than strength :
10:17. for strength, and not for drunkenness !
Isa. 3:25. and thy mighty in the war. (marg. might)
11: 2. the spirit of counsel and might,
28: 6. and for strength to them
30:15. in confidence shall be your strength :
33:13. acknowledge my might.
36: 5. counsel and strength for war:
63:15. where (is) thy zeal and thy strength,
Jer. 9:23(22). mighty (man) glory in his might,
10: 6. thy name (is) great in might.
16:21. mine hand and my might ;
23:10. and their force (is) not right.
49:35. the chief of their might.
51:30. their might hath failed ;
Eze.32:29. with their might are laid
30. they are ashamed of their might ;
Mic. 3: 8. judgment, and of might,
7:16. be confounded at all their might :

גְּבוּרָה [g'voo-rāh'], Ch. f. 1370

Dan. 2:20. wisdom and might are his:
23. who hast given me wisdom and might,

גִּבֵּחַ gib-bēh'ăgh, adj. 1371

Lev. 13:41. he (is) forehead bald :

גַּבַּחַת gab-bah'-ghath, f 1372

Lev. 13:42. or bald forehead,
— or his bald forehead.
43. or in his bald forehead,
55. bare within or without. (marg. bald in the head thereof, or in the forehead thereof)

גְּבִינָה g'vee-nāh', f. 1385

Job 10:10. and curdled me like cheese ?

גָּבִיעַ g'vee'ăg, m. 1375

Gen 44: 2. And put my cup, the silver cup,
12. the cup was found in
16. with whom the cup is found.
17. the man in whose hand the cup
Ex. 25:31. his branches, his bowls,
33, 33. Three bowls made like
34. four bowls made like
37:17. his branch, his bowls,
19. Three bowls made after the
— and three bowls made like almonds
20. in the candlestick (were) four bowls
Jer. 35: 5. of the Rechabites pots full of wine,

גְּבִיר g'veer, m. 1376

Gen 27:29. be lord over thy brethren,
37. I have made him thy lord,

1377 **גְּבִירָה** *g'vee-rāh'*, f.

1K. 11:19. the sister of Tahpenes *the queen.*
15:13. he removed *from* (being) *queen,*
2K. 10:13. the children of *the queen.*
2Ch 15:16. he removed her *from* (being) *queen,*
Jer. 13:18. the king *and to the queen,*
29: 2. the king, *and the queen,*

1378 **גָּבִישׁ** *gāh-veesh'*, m.

Job. 28:18. made of coral, *or* of *pearls :*

1379 **גָּבַל** [*gāh-val'*].

* KAL.—*Preterite.* *

Deu 19:14. they of old time *have set*

KAL.—*Future.*

Jos. 18:20. Jordan *was the border* of it on the east
Zec. 9: 2. Hamath also *shall border* thereby ;

* HIPHIL.—*Preterite.* *

Ex. 19:12. *And thou shalt set bounds unto* the people

HIPHIL.—*Imperative.*

Ex. 19:23. *Set bounds about* the mount,

1383 **גַּבְלוּת** *gav-looth'*, f.

Ex. 28:22 & 39:15. the breastplate chains at *the ends*

1382 **גִּבְלִי** *giv-lee'*, m.

Jos. 13: 5. the land of *the Giblites,*
1K. 5:18(32). and *the stonesquarers :* (marg. or, *Giblites*)

1384 **גִּבֵּן** *gib-bēhn'*, adj.

Lev. 21:20. Or *crookbackt*, or a dwarf,

1386 **גַּבְנֻנִּים** *gav-noon-neem'*, m. pl.

Ps. 68:15(16). an *high* hill (as) the hill of Bashan
16(17). Why leap ye, ye *high* hills ?

1389 **גִּבְעָה** *giv-ⁿgāh'*, f.

Gen 49:26. bound of *the* everlasting *hills :*
Ex. 17: 9. I will stand on the top of *the hill*
10. went up to the top of *the hill.*
Nu. 23: 9. *and from the hills* I behold him:
Deu 12: 2. upon *the hills,*
33:15. precious things of *the* lasting *hills,*
Jos. 5: 3. at *the hill of* the foreskins.
24:33. they buried him *in a hill* (that pertained to) Phinehas
Jud. 7: 1. *by the hill of* Moreh,
1Sa. 7: 1. the house of Abinadab *in the hill,*
10: 5. thou shalt come to *the hill of* God,
10. they came thither *to the hill,*
23:19. *in the hill of* Hachilah,
26: 1. David hide himself *in the hill of*
3. Saul pitched *in the hill of*
2Sa. 2:24. they were come to *the hill of*
25. stood on the top of *an hill.*
6: 3. Abinadab that (was) *in Gibeah :* (marg. or, *the hill*)
4. which (was) *at Gibeah,*
1K. 14:23. on every high *hill,*
2K. 16: 4. and on *the hills*, and under every
17:10. groves in every high *hill,*
2Ch 28: 4. on *the hills*, and under every
Job. 15: 7. wast thou made before *the hills ?*
Ps. 65:12(13). and *the little hills* rejoice
72: 3. *and the little hills*, by righteousness.
114: 4. *the little hills* like lambs.
6. *ye little hills*, like lambs ?
Ps. 148: 9. Mountains, and all *hills ;*
Pro. 8:25. before *the hills* was I brought forth:
Cant. 2: 8. skipping upon *the hills.*
4: 6. to *the hill of* frankincense.
Isa. 2: 2. shall be exalted *above the hills ;*
14. upon all *the hills*
10:32. *the hill of* Jerusalem.
30:17. as an ensign on *an hill.*
25. upon every high *hill,*
31: 4. for *the hill thereof.*
40: 4. every mountain *and hill* shall
12. *and the hills* in a balance ?
41:15. *and* shalt make *the hills*
42:15. make waste mountains *and hills,*
54:10. *and the hills* be removed ;
55:12. the mountains *and the hills*
65: 7. blasphemed me upon *the hills :*
Jer. 2:20. when upon every high *hill*
3:23. *from the hills*, (and from) the
4:24. all *the hills* moved lightly.
13:27. abominations on *the hills*
16:16. and from every *hill,*
17: 2. upon *the* high *hills.*
31:39. upon *the hill* Gareb,
49:16. holdest the height of *the hill :*
50: 6. gone from mountain to *hill,*
Eze. 6: 3. *and to the hills*, to the rivers,
13. upon every high *hill,*
20:28. they saw every high *hill,*
34: 6. upon every high *hill :*
26. the places round about *my hill*
35: 8. in *thy hills*, and in thy valleys,
36: 4, 6. *and to the hills*, to the rivers,
Hos. 4:13. burn incense upon *the hills,*
10: 8. *and to the hills*, Fall on us.
Joel 3:18(4:18). *and the hills* shall flow
Am. 9:13. all *the hills* shall melt.
Mic. 4: 1. shall be exalted *above the hills*
6: 1. let *the hills* hear thy voice.
Nah. 1: 5. *and the hills* melt,
Hab. 3: 6. *the* perpetual *hills* did bow:
Zep. 1:10. a great crashing *from the hills.*

גִּבְעֹל *giv-ⁿgōhl'*, m. 1392

Ex. 9:31. the flax (was) *bolled.*

גָּבַר *gāh-var'*. 1396

* KAL.—*Preterite.* *

Gen 7:19. the waters *prevailed* exceedingly
20. upward *did* the waters *prevail;*
49:26. of thy father *have prevailed*
Ex. 17:11. *that* Israel *prevailed : and* when he let down his hand, Amalek *prevailed.*
2Sa. 1:23. *they were stronger* than lions.
11:23. Surely the men *prevailed*
1Ch 5: 2. Judah *prevailed* above his
Job 21: 7. *are mighty* in power ?
Ps. 65: 3(4). Iniquities *prevail* against me:
103:11. *great is* his mercy toward them
117: 2. his merciful kindness *is great*
Jer. 9: 3(2). *they are* not *valiant* for the truth
Lam. 1:16. because the enemy *prevailed.*

KAL.—*Future.*

Gen 7:18, 24. *And* the waters *prevailed,*
1Sa. 2: 9. by strength *shall* no man *prevail.*

* PIEL.—*Preterite.* *

Zec. 10: 6. *And I will strengthen* the house
12. *And I will strengthen them* in the Lord ;

PIEL.—*Future.*

Ecc. 10:10. then *must he put to more* strength:

* HIPHIL.—*Preterite.* *

Dan 9:27. *And he shall confirm* the covenant

HIPHIL.—*Future.*

Ps. 12: 4(5). With our tongue *will we prevail;*

* HITHPAEL.—*Future.* *

Job 15:25. *strengtheneth himself* against

Job 36. 9. that *they have exceeded.*
Isa. 42:13. *he shall prevail* against his (marg. or, *behave himself mightily*)

1397 **גבר** *geh'-ver*, m.

Ex. 10:11. go now ye (that are) *men,*
12:37. on foot (that were) *men,*
Nu. 24: 3, 15. *the man* whose eyes are open
Deu22: 5. that which pertaineth unto *a man*, neither shall *a man* put on
Jos. 7:14. shall come *man by man.*
17. Zarhites *man by man;*
18. his houshold *man by man;*
Jud. 5:30. to every *man* a damsel
2Sa.23: 1. *the man* (who was) raised up
1Ch23: 3. by their polls, *man by man,*
24: 4. there were more chief *men*
26:12. among *the* chief *men,*
Job 3: 3. There is *a man* child
23. *to a man* whose way is hid,
4:17. shall *a man* be more pure
10: 5. thy years as *man*'s days,
14:10. *But man* dieth, and wasteth
14. If *a man* die, shall he live
16:21. O that one might plead *for a man*
22: 2. Can *a man* be profitable
33:17. hide pride *from man.*
29. God oftentimes with *man,*
34: 7. What *man* (is) like Job,
9. It profiteth *a man* nothing
34. *and* let *a* wise *man* hearken
38: 3. Gird up now thy loins *like a man;*
40: 7. Gird up thy loins now *like a man:*
Ps. 34: 8(9). blessed (is) *the man* (that) trusteth
37:23. The steps of *a* (good) *man*
40: 4(5). Blessed (is) *that man*
52: 7(9). Lo, (this is) *the man* (that) made not
88: 4(5). I am *as a man* (that hath)
89:48(49). What *man* (is he that) liveth,
94:12. Blessed (is) *the man* whom
127: 5. Happy (is) *the man* that hath
128: 4. thus shall *the man* be blessed
Pro. 6:34. jealousy (is) the rage of *a man:*
20:24. *Man*'s goings (are) of the Lord
24: 5. *A* wise *man* (is) strong;
28: 3. *A* poor *man* that oppresseth
21. for a piece of bread (that) *man* will transgress.
29. 5. *A man* that flattereth his neighbour
30: 1. *the man* spake unto Ithiel,
19. the way of *a man* with a maid.
Isa. 22:17. carry thee away with a *mighty* captivity, (marg. the captivity of *a man*)
Jer. 17: 5. Cursed (be) *the man* that trusteth in man,
7. Blessed (is) *the man* that trusteth
22:30. *a man* (that) shall not prosper
23: 9. *and like a man* whom wine
30: 6. every *man* with his hands
31:22. A woman shall compass *a man.*
41:16. *mighty* men of war,
43: 6. *men,* and women, and children,
44:20. to *the men,* and to the women,
Lam. 3: 1. I (am) *the man* (that) hath seen
27. good *for a man* that he bear
35. To turn aside the right of *a man*
39. *a man* for the punishment
Dan 8:15. as the appearance of *a man.*
Joel 2: 8. they shall walk *every one*
Mic. 2: 2. so they oppress *a man*
Hab. 2: 5. *a* proud *man,*
Zec. 13: 7. against *the man* (that is) my fellow,

1399 **גבר** *g'var*, m.

Ps. 18:25(26). with *an* upright *man*

1400 **גבר** *g'var*, Ch. m.

Ezr. 4:21. to cause these *men* to cease,
5: 4. What are the names of *the men*
10. that we might write the names of *the men*
6: 8. expences be given *unto* these *men,*
Dan 2:25. I have found *a man* of the captives
3: 8. at that time *certain* Chaldeans came near,
12. There are *certain* Jews whom thou
— these *men,* O king, have not regarded
13. Then they brought these *men* before the king.
20. *And* he commanded the most mighty *men*
21. these *men* were bound in their coats,
22. the fire slew those *men* that took up Shadrach,
23. *And* these three *men,* Shadrach, Meshach,
24. Did not we cast three *men* bound
25. Lo, I see four *men* loose, walking
27. saw these *men,* upon whose bodies
5:11. There is *a man* in thy kingdom,
6: 5(6). Then said these *men,*
11(12). Then these *men* assembled, and found
15(16). Then these *men* assembled unto the king,
24(25). and they brought those *men*

גבר [*gib-bāhr'*], Ch. m. 1401

Dan 3:20. commanded the most *mighty* men

גברת *g'veh'-reth*, f. 1404

Gen16: 4. *her mistress* was despised
8. from the face of *my mistress*
9. Return to *thy mistress,*
2K. 5: 3. she said unto *her mistress,*
Ps. 123: 2. unto the hand of *her mistress;*
Pro. 30:23. that is heir to *her mistress.*
Isa. 24: 2. as with the maid, *so with her mistress;*
47: 5. *The lady of* kingdoms.
7. I shall be *a lady* for ever.

גג *gāhg*, m. 1406

Ex. 30: 3. with pure gold, *the top thereof,* (marg. *roof*)
37:26. *the top of it,* and the sides thereof
Deu22: 8. make a battlement *for thy roof,*
Jos. 2: 6. brought them up *to the roof of the house,*
— she had laid in order upon *the roof.*
8. came up unto them upon *the roof;*
Jud. 9:51. gat them up to *the top of* the tower.
16:27. upon *the roof* about three thousand
1Sa. 9:25. Saul upon *the top of the house.*
26. Saul to *the top of the house,*
2Sa. 11: 2. walked upon *the roof of* the king's house: and from *the roof* he saw
16:22. a tent upon *the top of the house;*
18:24. the watchman went up to *the roof over* the gate
2K. 19:26. the grass on *the house tops,*
23:12. the altars that (were) on *the top of* the upper
Neh 8:16. every one upon *the roof of his house,*
Ps. 102: 7(8). as a sparrow alone upon *the house top.*
129: 6. as the grass (upon) *the housetops,*
Pro. 21: 9. better to dwell in a corner of *the housetop,*
25:24. to dwell in the corner of *the housetop,*
Isa. 15: 3. on *the tops of their houses,*
22: 1. art wholly gone up *to the housetops?*
37:27. the grass on *the housetops,*
Jer. 19:13. upon whose *roofs* they have burned (lit. which upon *their roofs*)
32:29. upon whose *roofs* they have offered
48:38. upon all *the housetops of* Moab,
Eze. 40:13. *from the roof* of (one) little chamber *to the roof of another:*
Zep. 1: 5. upon *the housetops;*

גד *gāhd*, m. 1407

Ex. 16:31. like *coriander* seed,
Nu. 11: 7. as *coriander* seed.

גד *gad*, m. 1409

Gen30:11. Leah said, *A troop* cometh:
Isa. 65:11. prepare a table *for that troop,* (marg. *Gad*)

1411 גְּדָבְרִין [*g'dāhv-reen'*], Ch. m. pl.

Dan 3: 2, 3. captains, the judges, *the treasurers,*

1413 גָּדַד [*gāh-dad'*].

* KAL.—*Future.* *

Ps. 94:21. *They gather themselves together* against

* HITHPOEL.—*Future.* *

Deu 14: 1. *ye shall* not *cut yourselves,*
1K. 18:28. they cried aloud, *and cut themselves*
Jer. 5: 7. and *assembled themselves by troops*
16: 6. nor *cut themselves,* nor make
47: 5. how long *wilt thou cut thyself?*
Mic. 5: 1(4:14). Now *gather thyself in troops,*

HITHPOEL.—*Participle.*

Jer. 41: 5. *and having cut themselves,*

1414 גְּדַד [*g'dad*], Ch.

* P'AL.—*Imperative.* *

Dan 4:14(11). *Hew down* the tree,
23(20). *Hew* the tree *down,*

1415 גָּדָה [*gāh-dāh'*], f.

Jos. 3:15. overfloweth all *his banks*
4:18. flowed over all *his banks,*
1Ch 12:15. had overflown all *his banks;*
Isa. 8: 7. go over all *his banks:*

1416 גְּדוּד *g'dood*, m.

Gen 49:19. Gad, *a troop* shall overcome
1Sa. 30: 8. Shall I pursue after this *troop?*
15. bring me down to this *company?*
— bring thee down to this *company.*
23. delivered *the company*
2Sa. 3:22. came *from* (pursuing) *a troop,*
4: 2. captains of *bands:*
22:30. I have run through *a troop:*
1K. 11:24. became captain over *a band,*
2K. 5: 2. had gone out *by companies,*
6:23. So *the bands of* Syria
13:20. *And the bands of* the Moabites
21. they spied *a band* (of men);
24: 2. and the Lord sent against him *bands of* the Chaldees, and *bands of* the Syrians, and *bands of* the Moabites, and *bands of* the children of Ammon,
1Ch 7. 4. *bands of* soldiers for war,
12:18. made them captains of *the band.*
21. they helped David against *the band*
2Ch 22: 1. *the band of men* that came
25: 9. I have given to *the army of* Israel? (marg. *band*)
10. *the army* that was come
13. But the soldiers of *the army* (marg. sons of *the band*)
26:11. that went out to war *by bands,*
Job 19:12. *His troops* come together,
25: 3. Is there any number *of his armies?*
29:25. dwelt as a king *in the army,*
Ps. 18:29(30). I have run through *a troop;*
Jer. 18:22. when thou shalt bring *a troop*
Hos. 6: 9. as *troops of robbers* wait
7: 1. *the troop of robbers* spoileth
Mic. 5: 1(4:14). gather thyself in troops, O daughter of *troops:*

1417-18 גְּדוּד *g'dood*, m.

Ps. 65:10(11). thou settlest *the furrows thereof:*
Jer. 48:37. upon all the hands (shall be) *cuttings,*

1419 גָּדוֹל *gāh-dōhl'*, adj.

Gen 1:16. God made two *great* lights; the *greater* light to rule the day,
21. God created *great* whales,
4:13. *greater* than I can bear.
Gen 10:12. the same (is) a *great* city.
21. the brother of Japheth *the elder,*
12: 2. I will make of thee a *great* nation,
17. with *great* plagues
15:12. horror of *great* darkness fell
14. come out with *great* substance.
18. unto the *great* river,
17:20. I will make him a *great* nation.
18:18. become a *great* and mighty nation,
19:11. both small and *great:*
20: 9. on my kingdom a *great* sin?
21: 8. Abraham made a *great* feast
18. I will make him a *great* nation.
27: 1. he called Esau his *eldest* son,
15. raiment of her *eldest* son
33. Isaac trembled *very* exceedingly, (marg. with a *great* trembling)
34. a *great* and exceeding bitter cry,
42. these words of Esau her *elder* son
29: 2. a *great* stone (was) upon
7. Lo, (it is) yet *high* day, (marg. yet the day (is) *great*)
16. the name of *the elder* (was) Leah,
39: 9. none *greater* in this house
— can I do this *great* wickedness,
14. I cried with a *loud* voice: (marg. *great*)
41:29. seven years of *great* plenty
44:12. began *at the eldest,*
45: 7. save your lives by a *great* deliverance.
46: 3. I will there make of thee a *great* nation:
50:10. with a *great* and very sore lamentation:
Ex. 3: 3. see this *great* sight,
6: 6. with *great* judgments:
7: 4. by *great* judgments.
11: 3. the man Moses (was) very *great*
6. there shall be a *great* cry
12:30. there was a *great* cry in Egypt;
14:31. Israel saw that *great* work
15:16. *by the greatness of* thine arm
18:11. the Lord (is) *greater* than all gods:
22. every *great* matter they shall bring
32:10. I will make of thee a *great* nation.
11. of Egypt with *great* power,
21. so *great* a sin upon them?
30. Ye have sinned a *great* sin:
31. this people have sinned a *great* sin,
Lev. 19:15. honour the person of *the mighty:*
21:10. And (he that is) the *high* priest
Nu. 13:28. walled, (and) very *great:*
14:12. make of thee a *greater* nation
22:18. to do less or *more.*
34: 6. have the *great* sea for a border:
7. from the *great* sea
35:25. unto the death of the *high* priest,
28. until the death of the *high* priest: but after the death of the *high* priest
Deu 1: 7. unto the *great* river,
17. the small as well *as the great;*
19. all that *great* and terrible wilderness,
28. The people (is) *greater* and taller
— the cities (are) *great*
2: 7. through this *great* wilderness:
10, 21. a people *great,* and many,
4: 6. Surely this *great* nation
7, 8. what nation (is there so) *great,*
32. as this *great* thing
34. by *great* terrors,
36. he shewed thee his *great* fire;
37. with his *mighty* power
38. *greater* and mightier than thou
5:22(19). with a *great* voice:
25(22). this *great* fire will consume
6:10. to give thee *great* and goodly cities,
22. *great* and sore,
7:19. *The great* temptations
21. a *mighty* God and terrible.
23. destroy them with a *mighty*
8:15. through that *great* and terrible wilderness,
9: 1. nations *greater* and mightier
— cities *great* and fenced up to heaven,
2. A people *great* and tall,
29. by thy *mighty* power
10:17. a *great* God, a mighty,
21. for thee these *great* and terrible
11: 7. have seen all the *great* acts
23. ye shall possess *greater* nations
18:16. let me see this *great* fire

Deu 25:13, 14. *a great* and a small.
26: 5. *great*, mighty, and populous:
8. with *great* terribleness,
27: 2. thou shalt set thee up *great* stones,
28:59. (even) *great* plagues,
29: 3(2). *The great* temptations
—(-). those *great* miracles:
24(23). the heat of this *great* anger?
28(27). and in *great* indignation,
34:12. in all the *great* terror
Jos. 1: 4. even unto the *great* river,
— unto the *great* sea
6: 5. shall shout with a *great* shout;
20. shouted with a *great* shout,
7: 9. what wilt thou do unto thy *great* name?
26. they raised over him a *great* heap
8:29. raise thereon a *great* heap of stones,
9: 1. the *great* sea over against Lebanon,
10: 2. Gibeon (was) a *great* city,
— because it (was) *greater* than
10. slew them with a *great* slaughter
11. the Lord cast down *great* stones
18. Roll *great* stones upon the mouth
20. slaying them with a very *great* slaughter,
27. laid *great* stones in the cave's mouth,
14:12. the cities (were) *great*
15. a *great* man among the Anakims.
15:12. to the *great* sea,
47. and the *great* sea,
17:17. hast *great* power:
20: 6. the death of the *high* priest
22:10. a *great* altar to see to.
23: 4. even unto the *great* sea
9. before you *great* nations
24:17. which did those *great* signs
26. took a *great* stone,
Jud. 2: 7. had seen all the *great* works
5:15. *great* thoughts of heart.
16. *great* searchings of heart.
11:33. with a very *great* slaughter.
15: 8. with a *great* slaughter:
18. hast given this *great* deliverance
16: 5. see wherein his *great* strength
6, 15. wherein thy *great* strength
23. to offer a *great* sacrifice
21: 2. and wept *sore;* (lit. and wept *a great* weeping)
5. For they had made a *great* oath
1Sa. 2:17. was very *great* before the Lord:
4: 5. Israel shouted with a *great* shout,
6. the noise of this *great* shout
10. there was a very *great* slaughter;
17. there hath been also a *great* slaughter
5: 9. with a very *great* destruction:
— both small and *great*,
6: 9. he hath done us this *great* evil:
14. (there was) a *great* stone:
15. put (them) on the *great* stone:
18. even unto the *great* (stone of) Abel,
19. with a *great* slaughter.
7:10. thundered with a *great* thunder
12:16. stand and see this *great* thing,
22. for his *great* name's sake:
14:20. a very *great* discomfiture.
33. roll a *great* stone unto me
45. who hath wrought this *great* salvation
17:13. the three *eldest* sons of Jesse
14. the three *eldest* followed Saul.
25. will enrich him with *great*
28. Eliab his *eldest* brother heard
18:17. my *elder* daughter Merab,
19: 5. wrought a *great* salvation
8. slew them with a *great* slaughter;
22. came to a *great* well
20: 2. do nothing either *great* or small,
22:15. less or *more.* (marg. little or *great*)
23: 5. smote them with a *great* slaughter.
25: 2. the man (was) very *great*,
36. less *or more*,
28:12. she cried with a *loud* voice:
30: 2. either *great* or small,
16. because of all the *great* spoil
19. neither small nor *great*,
2Sa. 3:38. *and a great man* fallen
5:10. David went on, *and* grew *great*,
7: 9. have made thee a *great* name, like unto the name of *the great* (men)
2Sa. 13:15. Amnon hated her exceedingly; (marg. with *great* hatred greatly)
— *greater* than the love wherewith
16. *greater* than the other
36. wept very *sore.* (marg. a *great* weeping)
15:23. the country wept with a *loud* voice,
18: 7. there was there a *great* slaughter
9. the thick boughs of a *great* oak,
17. cast him into a *great* pit
— laid a very *great* heap of stones
29. I saw a *great* tumult,
19: 4(5). the king cried with a *loud* voice,
32(33). for he (was) a very *great* man.
20: 8. they (were) at the *great* stone
23:10, 12. wrought a *great* victory
1K. 1:40. rejoiced with *great* joy,
2:22. for he (is) mine *elder* brother;
3: 4. that (was) the *great* high place:
6. unto thy servant David my father *great* mercy,
— kept for him this *great* kindness,
4:13. threescore *great* cities
5:17(31). they brought *great* stones,
7: 9. toward the *great* court.
10. even *great* stones,
12. the *great* court round about
8:42. they shall hear of thy *great* name,
55. congregation of Israel with a *loud* voice,
65. with him, a *great* congregation,
10:18. the king made a *great* throne of ivory,
18:27. Cry aloud: (marg. with a *great* voice)
28. And they cried aloud, (lit. with a *great* voice)
45. there was a *great* rain.
19:11. a *great* and strong wind rent
20:13. Hast thou seen all this *great*
21. slew the Syrians with a *great* slaughter.
28. deliver all this *great* multitude
22:31. Fight neither with small nor *great*,
2K. 3:27. there was *great* indignation
4: 8. where (was) a *great* woman;
38. Set on the *great* pot,
5: 1. was a *great* man
13. had bid thee (do some) *great* thing,
6:23. he prepared *great* provision
25. there was a *great* famine
7: 6. the noise of a *great* host:
8: 4. all *the great things* that
13. that he should do this *great*
10: 6. with *the great men of* the city,
11. all *his great men*,
19. for I have a *great* sacrifice
12:10(11). scribe and the *high* priest
16:15. Upon the *great* altar
17:21. made them sin a *great* sin.
36. the land of Egypt with *great* power
18:19. Thus saith the *great* king,
28. cried with a *loud* voice
— Hear the word of the *great* king,
20: 3. Hezekiah wept *sore.* (marg. a *great* weeping)
22: 4. Go up to Hilkiah the *high* priest,
8. Hilkiah the *high* priest said
13. for *great* (is) the wrath of the Lord
23: 2. both small and *great:*
4. Hilkiah the *high* priest,
26. the fierceness of his *great* wrath,
25: 9. every *great* (man's) house
26. both small and *great*,
1Ch 11: 9. David waxed greater *and greater:* (lit. went going *and great*)
14. saved (them) by a *great* deliverance.
12:14. *and the greatest* over a thousand.
22. until (it was) a *great* host,
16:25. For *great* (is) the Lord,
17: 8. like the name of *the great men*
22: 8. hast made *great* wars:
25: 8 & 26:13. as well the small *as the great*,
29: 1. the work (is) *great:*
9. the king also rejoiced with *great* joy.
22. on that day with *great* gladness.
2Ch 1: 8. Thou hast shewed *great* mercy
10. thy people, (that is so) *great?*
2: 5(4). the house which I build (is) *great:* for *great* (is) our God
9(8). am about to build (shall be) wonderful *great.* (marg. *great* and wonderful)

2Ch 3: 5. And the *greater* house
4: 9. and the *great* court,
6:32. for thy *great* name's sake,
7: 8. a very *great* congregation,
9:17. the king made a *great* throne
15:13. whether small or *great*,
14. unto the Lord with a *loud* voice,
16:14. they made a very *great* burning
18:30. Fight ye not with small or *great*,
20:19. the Lord God of Israel with a *loud* voice
21:14. with a *great* plague
26:15. shoot arrows and *great* stones
28: 5. carried away a *great* multitude
— who smote him with a *great* slaughter.
30:21. with *great* gladness:
26. there was *great* joy in Jerusalem:
31:15. *as well to the great* as to the small·
32:18. Then they cried with a *loud* voice
34: 9. Hilkiah the *high* priest,
21. for *great* (is) the wrath of the Lord
30. all the people, *great* (lit. *from great* to small) and small:
36:18. *great* and small,
Ezr. 3:11. the people shouted with a *great* shout,
12. wept with a *loud* voice;
13. shouted with a *loud* shout,
9: 7. in a *great* trespass unto this day;
13. for our *great* trespass,
10:12. said with a *loud* voice,
Neh 1: 3. in *great* affliction and reproach:
5. the *great* and terrible God,
10. redeemed by thy *great* power,
2:10. it grieved them exceedingly (lit. with a *great* grief)
3: 1, 20. Eliashib the *high* priest
27. over against the *great* tower
4:14(8). the Lord, (which is) *great* and terrible,
5: 1. there was a *great* cry
7. I set a *great* assembly
6: 3. I (am) doing a *great* work,
7: 4. the city (was) large *and great:*
8: 6. blessed the Lord, the *great* God.
12. to make *great* mirth,
17. there was very *great* gladness.
9: 4. cried with a *loud* voice
18, 26. wrought *great* provocations;
25. in thy *great* goodness.
32. our God, *the great*, the mighty,
37. we (are) in *great* distress.
11:14. the son of (one of) *the great men.* (marg. or, the son of *Haggedolim*)
12:31. appointed two *great* (companies)
43. they offered *great* sacrifices,
— made them rejoice with *great* joy:
13: 5. prepared for him a *great* chamber,
27. to do all this *great* evil,
28. Eliashib the *high* priest,
Est. 1: 5. *both unto great* and small,
20. *both to great* and small.
2:18. the king made a *great* feast
4: 1. with a *loud* and a bitter cry;
3. *great* mourning among the
8:15. with a *great* crown of gold,
9: 4. *great* in the king's house,
— waxed greater *and greater.*
10: 3. *and great* among the Jews,
Job 1: 3. was the *greatest* of all the men
19. there came a *great* wind
3:19. The small *and great* are there;
5: 9 & 9:10. Which doeth *great things*
37: 5. *great things* doeth he,
Ps. 12: 3(4). that speaketh *proud things:*
21: 5(6). His glory (is) *great* in thy salvation:
47: 2(3). a *great* King over all the earth.
48: 1(2). *Great* (is) the Lord,
57:10(11). For thy mercy (is) *great*
71:19. who hast done *great things:*
76: 1(2). his name (is) *great* in Israel.
77:13(14). who (is so) *great* a God as (our) God!
86:10. For thou (art) *great*,
13. *great* (is) thy mercy toward me:
95: 3. the Lord (is) a *great* God, and a *great* King above all gods.
96: 4. For the Lord (is) *great*,
99: 2. The Lord (is) *great* in Zion;
3. praise thy *great* and terrible name;
104:25. this *great* and wide sea,
Ps. 104:25. both small and *great* beasts.
106:21. which had done *great things*
108: 4(5). thy mercy (is) *great* above the heavens:
111: 2. The works of the Lord (are) *great*,
115:13. small and *great.*
131: 1. exercise myself *in great matters*,
135: 5. I know that the Lord (is) *great*,
136: 4. who alone doeth *great* wonders:
7. To him that made *great* lights:
17. To him which smote *great* kings:
138: 5. for *great* (is) the glory of the Lord.
145: 3. *Great* (is) the Lord,
8. slow to anger, *and of great* (lit. *and great of*) mercy.
147: 5. *Great* (is) our Lord,
Pro. 18:16. bringeth him before *great men.*
19:19. *A man of great* (lit. *the great of*) wrath
25: 6. stand not in the place of *great* (men):
27:14. blesseth his friend with a *loud* voice,
Ecc. 9:13. *and* it (seemed) *great* unto me:
14. there came a *great* king
— *great* bulwarks against it:
10: 4. yielding pacifieth *great* offences.
Isa. 5: 9. *great* and fair,
8: 1. Take thee a *great* roll,
9: 2(1). have seen a *great* light:
12: 6. for *great* (is) the Holy One of Israel
27: 1. with his sore *and great* and strong sword
13. the *great* trumpet shall be
29: 6. earthquake, and *great* noise,
34: 6. a *great* slaughter in the land
36: 4. Thus saith the *great* king, the king of Assyria,
13. cried with a *loud* voice
— Hear ye the words of the *great* king,
38: 3. Hezekiah wept *sore*, (marg. with *great* weeping)
54: 7. with *great* mercies will I gather
56:12. *much* more abundant.
Jer. 4: 6. and a *great* destruction.
5: 5. get me unto the *great* men,
6: 1. and *great* destruction.
13. even unto *the greatest of them*
22. a *great* nation shall be raised
8:10. even unto *the greatest*
10: 6. O Lord; thou (art) *great, and* thy name (is) *great*
22. a *great* commotion out of
11:16. with the noise of a *great* tumult
14:17. my people is broken with a *great* breach
16: 6. Both *the great* and the small
10. pronounced all this *great* evil
21: 5. and in *great* wrath.
6. they shall die of a *great* pestilence.
22: 8. done thus unto this *great* city?
25:14. *great* kings shall serve
32. a *great* whirlwind shall be
26:19. procure *great* evil against
27: 5. by my *great* power
7. many nations and *great* kings
28: 8. against *great* kingdoms,
30: 7. Alas! for that day (is) *great*,
31: 8. a *great* company shall return
34. unto *the greatest of them*,
32:17. heaven and the earth by thy *great* power
18. *the Great*, the Mighty God,
19. *Great in* counsel,
21. and with *great* terror;
37. and in *great* wrath;
42. brought all this *great* evil
33: 3. shew thee *great* and mighty things,
36: 7. for *great* (is) the anger
42: 1. from the least even unto *the greatest*,
8. from the least even to *the greatest*,
43: 9. Take *great* stones in thine hand,
44: 7. *great* evil against your souls,
12. from the least even unto *the greatest*,
15. a *great* multitude,
26. I have sworn by my *great* name,
45: 5. seekest thou *great things*
48: 3. spoiling and *great* destruction.
50: 9. an assembly of *great* nations
22. and of *great* destruction.
41. and a *great* nation,
51:54. *great* destruction from the land
55. destroyed out of her the *great* voice;
52:13. all the houses of *the great* (men),

Lam. 2:13. thy breach (is) *great* like the sea:
Eze. 1: 4. out of the north, a *great* cloud,
3:12. behind me a voice of a *great*
13. a noise of a *great* rushing.
8: 6. the *great* abominations
—, 13, 15. thou shalt see *greater* abominations.
18 & 9:1. in mine ears with a *loud* voice,
9: 9. Judah (is) exceeding *great*,
11:13. cried with a *loud* voice,
16:46. thine *elder* sister (is) Samaria,
61. thine *elder* and thy younger:
17: 3. Thus saith the Lord God; A *great* eagle *with great* (lit. *great of*) wings,
7. There was also another *great* eagle *with great* wings and many feathers:
9. even without *great* power
17. Pharaoh with (his) *mighty* army
21:14(19). it (is) the sword of the *great*
23: 4. Aholah *the elder*,
25:17. I will execute *great* vengeance
29: 3. the *great* dragon that lieth
18. to serve a *great* service against
36:23. I will sanctify my *great* name,
37:10. an exceeding *great* army.
38:13. to take a *great* spoil?
15. a *great* company, and a mighty
19. there shall be a *great* shaking
39:17. a *great* sacrifice upon the
43:14. lesser settle (even) to *the greater*
47:10. as the fish of the *great* sea,
15. from the *great* sea,
19. the river to the *great* sea.
20. the *great* sea from the border,
48:28. the river toward the *great* sea.
Dan 8: 8. the *great* horn was broken;
21. the *great* horn that (is) between
9: 4. the *great* and dreadful God,
12. by bringing upon us a *great* evil:
10: 1. the time appointed (was) *long:* (marg. *great*)
4. by the side of the *great* river,
7. a *great* quaking fell upon them,
8. saw this *great* vision,
11: 2. the fourth shall be *far* richer (lit. shall be rich *great* riches above)
13, 25. with a *great* army
25. with a very *great* and mighty army;
28. return into his land with *great* riches;
44. shall go forth with *great* fury
12: 1. the *great* prince which standeth
Hos 1:11(2:2). *great* (shall be) the day
Joel 2:11. of the Lord (is) *great* and very terrible;
25. my *great* army which I sent
31(3:4). the *great* and the terrible day
Am. 6:11. he will smite the *great* house
Jon. 1: 2. Nineveh, that *great* city,
4. the Lord sent out a *great* wind
— there was a *mighty* tempest
10. Then were the men exceedingly afraid, (marg. afraid with *great* fear)
12. this *great* tempest (is) upon you.
16. the men feared the Lord *exceedingly*, (lit. with a *great* fear)
17(2:1). had prepared a *great* fish
3: 2. go unto Nineveh, that *great* city,
3. an exceeding *great* city
5. *from the greatest of them* even to
7. of the king *and his nobles*, (marg. *great men*)
4: 1. displeased Jonah exceedingly, (lit. with a *great* grief)
6. So Jonah was exceeding glad (marg. rejoiced with *great* joy)
11. spare Nineveh, that *great* city,
Mic. 7: 3. *and the great* (man), he uttereth
Nah. 1: 3. *and great in* power,
3:10. all *her great men* were bound in chains.
Zep. 1:10. a *great* crashing from the hills.
14. The *great* day of the Lord
Hag. 1: 1, 12, 14, & 2:2. Joshua the son of Josedech, the *high* priest,
2: 4. Joshua, son of Josedech, the *high* priest;
9. shall be *greater* than of the former,
Zec. 1:14. for Zion with a *great* jealousy.
15. I am *very* sore displeased (lit. with *great* displeasure)
3: 1. shewed me Joshua the *high* priest
Zec. 3: 8. O Joshua the *high* priest,
4: 7. O *great* mountain?
6:11. of Josedech, the *high* priest;
7:12. came a *great* wrath from the Lord
8: 2. for Zion with *great* jealousy, and I was jealous for her with *great* fury.
14: 4. a very *great* valley;
Mal. 1:11, 11. my name (shall be) *great*
14. for I (am) a *great* King,
4: 5(3:23). of the *great* and dreadful day

גְּדוּלָה *g'doo-lāh'*, & גְּדֻלָּה *g'dool-lāh'*, f. 1420

2Sa. 7:21. done all these *great things*,
23. to do for you *great things*
1Ch 17:19. hast thou done all this *greatness*, in making known all (these) *great things.*
21. a name of *greatness* and terribleness,
29:11. Thine, O Lord, (is) *the greatness*,
Est. 1: 4. the honour of *his* excellent *majesty*
6: 3. What honour *and dignity*
10: 2. the *greatness of* Mordecai,
Ps. 71:21. Thou shalt increase *my greatness*,
145: 3. *and his greatness* (is) unsearchable. (marg. *and of his greatness*)
6. and I will declare *thy greatness.*

גִּדּוּף [*gid-dooph'*], m. 1421

Isa. 43:28. Jacob to the curse, and Israel *to reproaches.*
51: 7. *neither* be ye afraid *of their revilings.*
Zep. 2: 8. *and the revilings of* the

גְּדוּפָה *g'doo-phāh'*, f. 1422

Eze. 5:15. shall be a reproach *and a taunt*,

גְּדִי *g'dee*, m. 1423

Gen27: 9. from thence two good *kids of*
16. she put the skins of *the kids of*
38:17. send (thee) *a kid* from the flock. (marg. *a kid of* the goats)
20. Judah sent *the kid* by the hand
23. I sent this *kid*,
Ex. 23:19 & 34:26. Thou shalt not seethe *a kid*
Deu 14:21. Thou shalt not seethe *a kid*
Jud. 6:19. made ready *a kid*, (marg. *a kid of* the goats)
13:15. have made ready *a kid* for thee. (lit. *id.*)
19. So Manoah took *a kid* (lit. *id.*)
14: 6. as he would have rent *a kid*,
15: 1. Samson visited his wife *with a kid;* (lit. *with a kid of* the goats)
1Sa. 10: 3. one carrying three *kids*,
16:20. a bottle of wine, *and a kid*, (lit. *and a kid of* the goats)
Isa. 11: 6. shall lie down with *the kid;*

גִּדְיָה [*gid-yāh'*], f. 1428

1Ch 12:15. (כתיב) when it had overflown all *his banks;*

גְּדִיָּה [*g'deey-yāh'*], f. 1429

Cant. 1: 8. feed *thy kids* beside the

גָּדִישׁ *gāh-deesh'*, m. 1430

Ex. 22: 6(5). so that *the stacks of corn*,
Jud. 15: 5. burnt up *both the shocks*,
Job 5:26. like as *a shock of corn* cometh
21:32. shall remain in *the tomb.* (marg. watch in *the heap*)

1431 ## גָּדַל gāh-dal'

* KAL.—*Preterite.* *

Gen19:13. the cry of them *is waxen great*
26:13. went forward, and grew until *he became* very *great:*
38:14. she saw that Shelah *was grown,*
1Sa.26:24. as thy life *was much set by*
2Sa. 7:22. Wherefore *thou art great,*
1K. 12: 8, 10. *that were grown up* with him,
2Ch10: 8, 10. *that were brought up* with him,
Ezr. 9: 6. our trespass *is grown up*
Job. 2:13. saw that (his) grief *was* very *great.*
31:18. *he was brought up with me,*
Ps. 92: 5(6). how *great are* thy works!
104: 1. *thou art* very *great;*
Ecc. 2: 9. *So I was great,* and increased
Jer. 5:27. *they are become great,* and waxen rich.

KAL.—*Future.*

Gen21: 8. *And* the child *grew,*
20. God was with the lad; *and he grew,*
24:35. *and he is become great:* and he hath
25:27. *And* the boys *grew:*
26:13. *And* the man *waxed great,*
38:11. till Shelah my son *be grown:*
41:40. *will I be greater* than thou.
48:19. *he also shall be great:*
— *shall be greater* than he,
Ex. 2:10. *And* the child *grew,*
11. *when* Moses *was grown,*
Nu. 14:17. *let* the power of my Lord *be great,*
Jud.11: 2. *and* his wife's sons *grew up,*
13:24. *and* the child *grew,*
Ru. 1:13. tarry for them till *they were grown?*
1 Sa. 2:21. *And* the child Samuel *grew*
3:19. *And* Samuel *grew,*
26:24. *let* my life *be much set by*
2Sa. 7:26. *And let* thy name *be magnified*
12: 3. *and it grew up* together
1K. 10:23. *So* king Solomon *exceeded*
2K. 4:18. And *when* the child *was grown,*
1Ch 17:24. *that* thy name *may be magnified*
2Ch 9:22. *And* king Solomon *passed* all
Ps. 35:27. *Let* the Lord *be magnified,*
40:16(17). The Lord *be magnified.*
70: 4(5). *Let* God *be magnified.*
Lam.4: 6. *For* the punishment...*is greater*
Eze.16: 7. hast increased *and waxen great,*
Dan 8: 9. *which waxed* exceeding *great,*
10. *And it waxed great,* (even) to the host
Mic. 5: 4(3). now *shall he be great* unto the
Zec.12: 7. of Jerusalem *do* not *magnify*
11. In that day *shall there be a great*
Mal. 1: 5. The Lord *will be magnified*

* PIEL.—*Preterite.* *

Jos. 4:14. the Lord *magnified* Joshua
Est. 3: 1. *did* king Ahasuerus *promote*
5:11. wherein the king *had promoted him,*
10: 2. whereunto the king *advanced him,* (marg. *made him great*)
Isa. 1: 2. *I have nourished* and brought up
23: 4. neither *do I nourish up* young men,
49:21. who *hath brought up* these?
51:18. the sons (that) *she hath brought up.*
Eze.31: 4. The waters *made him great,* (marg. or, *nourished him*)
Jon. 4:10. neither *madest it grow;*

PIEL.—*Infinitive.*

Nu. 6: 5. shall let the locks of the hair of his head *grow.*
Jos. 3: 7. will I begin *to magnify thee*
1Ch 29:12. in thine hand (it is) *to make great,*
Dan 1: 5. *so nourishing them* three years,

PIEL.—*Imperative.*

Ps. 34: 3(4). *O magnify* the Lord

PIEL.—*Future.*

Gen12: 2. *and make* thy name *great;*
1K. 1:37, 47. *and make* his throne *greater*
1Ch29:25. *And* the Lord *magnified*
2Ch 1: 1. *and magnified him* exceedingly.
Job 7:17. that *thou shouldest magnify him?*
Ps. 69:30(31). *and will magnify him* with
Isa. 44:14. the rain *doth nourish* (it).
Hos 9:12. Though *they bring up*

PIEL.—*Participle.*

2K. 10: 6. *which brought them up.*

* PUAL.—*Participle.* *

Ps.144:12. as plants *grown up* in their youth;

* HIPHIL.—*Preterite.* *

1Sa.12:24. *great* (things) *he hath done*
20:41. until David *exceeded.*
Ps. 38:16(17). *they magnify* (themselves)
41: 9(10). *hath lifted up* (his) heel against (marg. *magnified*)
55:12(13). *did magnify* (himself) against
126: 2. The Lord *hath* done *great things* for them. (marg. *hath magnified* to do)
3. The Lord *hath* done *great things* (lit. *id.*)
138: 2. *thou hast magnified* thy word above
Ecc. 1:16. *I am come to great estate,*
2: 4. *I made* me *great* works;
Isa. 9: 3(2). (and) not *increased* the joy:
28:29. (and) *excellent* in working.
Jer. 48:26. for *he magnified* (himself) against
42. because *he hath magnified*
Lam 1: 9. the enemy *hath magnified*
Dan 8: 4. *and became great.*
8. the he goat *waxed* very *great:*
11. Yea, *he magnified*
Joel 2:20. because *he hath* done *great things.* (marg. *hath magnified* to do)
21. for the Lord *will* do *great things.* (lit. *id.*)

HIPHIL.—*Infinitive.*

1Ch22: 5. for the Lord (must be) exceeding *magnifical,*
Am. 8: 5. *and* the shekel *great,*

HIPHIL.—*Future.*

Gen19:19. *and thou hast magnified* thy mercy,
Job 19: 5. If indeed *ye will magnify*
Isa. 42:21. *he will magnify* the law,
Eze.24: 9. *I will* even *make* the pile for fire *great.*
35:13. *Thus* with your mouth *ye have boasted* (marg. *magnified*)
Dan. 8:25. *he shall magnify* (himself) in his heart,
Obad 12. *shouldest thou have* spoken *proudly* (marg. *shouldest thou have magnified* thy mouth)
Zep. 2: 8, 10. *and magnified* (themselves) against

HIPHIL.—*Participle.*

2Sa.22:51. (כתיב) (He is) *the tower of* salvation
Ps. 18:50(51). *Great* deliverance *giveth he* (lit. *magnifying* salvation)
35:26. *that magnify* (themselves)

* HITHPAEL.—*Preterite.* *

Eze.38:23. *Thus will I magnify myself,*

HITHPAEL.—*Future.*

Isa. 10:15. *shall* the saw *magnify itself*
Dan11:36. *and magnify himself* above every god,
37. *he shall magnify himself* above all.

גָּדֵל gāh-dēhl', adj. 1432

Gen26:13. *and grew* until he became (lit. *and great*)
1Sa. 2:26. And the child Samuel *grew* on, (lit. going *and great*)
2Ch 17:12. And Jehoshaphat waxed *great* (lit. *id.*)
Eze.16:26. thy neighbours, *great of* flesh;

גֹּדֶל gōh'-del, m. 1433

Nu. 14:19. *according unto the greatness of* thy mercy,
Deu 3:24. shew thy servant *thy greatness,*
5:24(21). his glory and *his greatness,*
9:26. redeemed *through thy greatness,*
11: 2. *his greatness,* his mighty hand,
32: 3. ascribe ye *greatness* unto our God.
Ps. 79:11. *according to the greatness of* thy power
150: 2. according to *his* excellent *greatness.*
Isa. 9: 9(8). the pride *and stoutness of* heart.
10:12. I will punish the fruit of the *stout* heart (marg. *greatness of* the heart)
Eze.31: 2. Whom art thou like *in thy greatness?*

Eze.31: 7. Thus was he fair *in his greatness,*
18. in glory *and in greatness*

1434 גְּדִלִים *g'dee-leem'*, m. pl.

Deu22:12. Thou shalt make thee *fringes*
1K. 7:17. *wreaths* of chain work,

1438 גָּדַע *gāh-dag'*.

* KAL.—*Preterite.* *

1Sa. 2:31. *that I will cut off* thine arm,
Lam.2: 3. *He hath cut off* in (his) fierce anger

KAL.—*Future.*

Zec.11:10. *and cut it asunder*, that I
14. *Then I cut asunder* mine other staff,

KAL.—*Participle.* Paül.

Isa. 10:33. high ones of stature (shall be) *hewn down,*
15: 2. baldness, (and) every beard *cut off.*

* NIPHAL.—*Preterite.* *

Jud.21: 6. There *is* one tribe *cut off*
Isa. 14:12. *art thou cut down* to the ground,
22:25. *and be cut down*, and fall;
Jer. 48:25. The horn of Moab *is cut off,*
50:23. How *is* the hammer of the whole earth *cut asunder*
Eze. 6: 6. *and* your images *may be cut down,*
Am. 3:14. *and* the horns of the altar *shall be cut off,*

* PIEL.—*Preterite.* *

2Ch34: 4. above them, *he cut down;*
7. *cut down* all the idols
Ps.107:16. *cut* the bars of iron *in sunder.*

PIEL.—*Future.*

Deu 7: 5. *cut down* their groves,
12: 3. *ye shall hew down* the graven images
2Ch14: 3(2). *and cut down* the groves:
31: 1. *and cut down* the groves,
Ps. 75:10(11). the wicked also *will I cut off;*
Isa. 45: 2. and *cut in sunder* the bars of iron:

* PUAL.—*Preterite.* *

Isa. 9:10(9). the sycomores *are cut down,*

1442 גָּדַף *[gāh-daph']*.

* PIEL.—*Preterite.* *

2K. 19: 6. servants of the king of Assyria *have blasphemed* me.
22. hast thou reproached *and blasphemed?*
Isa. 37: 6. servants of the king of Assyria *have blasphemed* me.
23. hast thou reproached *and blasphemed?*
Eze.20:27. your fathers *have blasphemed* me,

PIEL.—*Participle.*

Nu. 15:30. the same *reproacheth* the Lord;
Ps. 44:16(17). reproacheth *and blasphemeth;*

1443 גָּדַר *gāh-dar'*.

* KAL.—*Preterite.* *

Job 19: 8. *He hath fenced up* my way
Lam.3: 7. *He hath hedged* me about,
9. *He hath inclosed* my ways
Hos. 2: 6(8). *and make* a wall, (marg. *wall* a wall)
Am. 9:11. *and close up* the breaches thereof; (marg. *hedge*, or, *wall*)

KAL.—*Future.*

Eze.13: 5. *neither made up* the hedge (marg. *hedged*)

KAL.—*Participle.* Poel.

2K. 12:12(13). *And to masons*, and hewers of stone,
22: 6. carpenters, and builders, *and masons,*
Isa. 58:12. *The repairer of* the breach,
Eze.22:30. *that should make up* the hedge,

גָּדֵר *gāh-dehr'*, com. 1447

Nu. 22:24. *a wall* (being) on this side, *and a wall* on that side.
Ezr. 9: 9. to give us *a wall* in Judah
Ps. 62: 3(4). *a* tottering *fence.*
80:12(13). broken down *her hedges,*
Ecc.10: 8. whoso breaketh *an hedge,*
Isa. 5: 5. break down *the wall thereof,*
Eze.13: 5. neither made up *the hedge*
22:30. that should make up *the hedge,*
42: 7. *And the wall* that (was) without
Hos. 2: 6(8). and make *a wall*, (lit. *her wall*)
Mic. 7:11. the day that *thy walls* are to be built,

Note.—In Hos. 2:6(8), some copies read גדרה omitting the Mappik, which our English translation has followed; in which case this passage would belong to the next article but one.

גֶּדֶר *geh'-der*, m. 1444

Pro.24:31. *and the* stone *wall* thereof
Eze.42:10. in the thickness of *the wall of*

גְּדֵרָה *g'dēh-rāh'*, f. 1448

Nu. 32:16. We will build sheep*folds*
24. *and folds* for your sheep;
36. fenced cities: *and folds for* sheep.
1Sa.24: 3(4). he came to the sheep*cotes*
1Ch. 4:23. dwelt among plants *and hedges:*
Ps. 89:40(41). hast broken down all *his hedges:*
Jer. 49: 3. run to and fro *by the hedges;*
Eze.42:12. the way directly before *the wall*
Nah. 3:17. which camp *in the hedges*
Zep. 2: 6. *and folds for* flocks.

גֵּה *gēh* 1454

Eze.47:13. *This* (shall be) the border,

Note.—This probably is an erroneous reading for זֶה

גָּהָה *[gāh-hāh']*. 1455

* KAL.—*Future.* *

Hos. 5:13. nor *cure* you of your wound.

גֵּהָה *gēh-hāh'*, f. 1456

Pro.17:22. doeth good (like) *a medicine:*

גָּהַר *[gāh-har']*. 1457

* KAL.—*Future.* *

1K. 18:42. *and he cast himself down* upon the earth,
2K. 4:34. *and he stretched himself* upon
35. *and stretched himself* upon him:

גַּו *[gav]*, m. 1458

1K. 14: 9. hast cast me behind *thy back:*
Neh. 9:26. cast thy law behind *their backs,*
Eze.23:35. cast me behind *thy back,*

גַּו *[gav]*, Ch. m. 1459

Ezr. 4:15. moved sedition *within the same*
5: 7. *wherein* was written thus; (marg. *in the midst whereof*)
6: 2. *and therein* (was) a record thus written:
Dan 3: 6, 11, 15. *into the midst of* a burning fiery
21, 23. *into the midst of* the burning fiery
24. bound *into the midst of* the fire?
25. walking *in the midst of* the fire,
26. came forth of *the midst of* the fire.
4:10(7). behold a tree *in the midst of* the earth,
7:15. in my spirit *in the midst of* (my) body,

1460 גֵּו *gēhv*, m.

Job 30: 5. driven forth from *among* (men),
Pro. 10:13. a rod (is) *for the back of* him
19:29. stripes *for the back of* fools.
26: 3. a rod *for* the fool's *back*.
Isa. 38:17. cast all my sins behind *thy back*.
50: 6. I gave *my back* to the smiters,
51:23. thou hast laid *thy body*

1461 גּוּב [*goov*].

* KAL.—*Participle*. *

2K. 25:12. (כתיב) vinedressers *and husbandmen*.

1462 גּוֹב *gōhv*, m.

Am. 7: 1. he formed *grasshoppers* (marg. or, *green worms*)
Nah. 3:17. *as the great grasshoppers*, (lit. *as the grasshopper of grasshoppers*)

1464 גּוּד [*good*].

* KAL.—*Future*. *

Gen 49:19. a troop *shall overcome him*: but he *shall overcome* at the last.
Hab. 3:16. *will invade them* with his troops. (marg. or, *cut them*)

1465 גֵּוָה *geh-vāh'*, f.

Job 20:25. cometh *out of the body*;

1466 גֵּוָה *geh-vāh*, f.

Job 22:29. (There is) *lifting up*;
33:17. *and* hide *pride* from man.
Jer. 13:17. weep in secret places *for* (your) *pride*:

1467 גֵּוָה *geh-vāh'*, Ch. f.

Dan 4:37(34). and those that walk *in pride*

1468 גּוּז [*gooz*].

* KAL.—*Preterite*. *

Ps. 90:10. for it *is* soon *cut off*,

KAL.—*Future*.

Nu. 11:31. *and brought* quails from the sea,

1469 גּוֹזָל *gōh-zāhl'*, m.

Gen 15: 9. *and a young pigeon*.
Deu 32:11. fluttereth over *her young*,

1471 גּוֹי *gōh'y*.

Gen 10: 5. the isles of *the Gentiles*
— after their families, *in their nations*.
20. their countries, (and) *in their nations*.
31. in their lands, *after their nations*.
32. their generations, *in their nations*:
— *the nations* divided in the earth
12: 2. I will make of thee *a* great *nation*,
14: 1, 9. Tidal king of *nations*;
15:14. And also *that nation*,
17: 4. thou shalt be a father of many *nations*.
5. for a father of many *nations*
6. I will make *nations* of thee,
16. she shall be (a mother) *of nations*;
20. I will make him *a* great *nation*.
18:18. become *a* great and mighty *nation*,
— *the nations of* the earth shall be blessed
20: 4. wilt thou slay also *a* righteous *nation*?
21:13. of the son of the bondwoman will I make *a nation*,
18. I will make him *a* great *nation*.
Gen 22:18. all *the nations of* the earth be blessed;
25:23. Two *nations* (are) in thy womb,
26: 4. shall all *the nations of* the earth be blessed;
35:11. *a nation* and a company of *nations*
46: 3. I will there make of thee *a* great *nation*:
48:19. shall become a multitude of *nations*.
Ex. 9:24. since it became *a nation*.
19: 6. *and an* holy *nation*.
32:10. I will make of thee *a* great *nation*.
33:13. this *nation* (is) thy people.
34:10. nor in any *nation*: (lit. in all the *nations*)
24. I will cast out *the nations*
Lev. 18:24. in all these *the nations* are defiled
28. as it spued out *the nations*
20:23. walk in the manners of *the nation*,
25:44. *the heathen* that are round about
26:33. scatter you *among the heathen*,
38. perish *among the heathen*,
45. in the sight of *the heathen*,
Nu. 14:12. will make of thee *a* greater *nation*
15. then *the nations* which have
23: 9. *and* shall not be reckoned *among the nations*.
24: 8. he shall eat up *the nations*
20. Amalek (was) the first of *the nations*;
Deu 4: 6. Surely this great *nation*
7, 8. what *nation* (is there so) great,
27. few in number *among the heathen*,
34. to go (and) take him *a nation* from the midst of (another) *nation*,
38. To drive out *nations* from before thee
7: 1. hath cast out many *nations*
— seven *nations* greater and mightier than
17. These *nations* (are) more than I;
22. God will put out those *nations*
8:20. *As the nations* which the Lord
9: 1. to go in to possess *nations*
4, 5. the wickedness of these *nations*
14. I will make of thee *a nation*
11:23. drive out all these *nations*
— ye shall possess greater *nations*
12: 2. *the nations* which ye shall possess
29. thy God shall cut off *the nations*
30. How did these *nations* serve
15: 6. thou shalt lend unto many *nations*,
— thou shalt reign *over* many *nations*,
17:14. like as all *the nations*
18: 9. the abominations of those *nations*.
14. For these *nations*, which thou
19: 1. thy God hath cut off *the nations*,
20:15. not of the cities of these *nations*.
26: 5. became there *a nation*,
19. to make thee high above all *nations*
28: 1. on high above all *nations of* the earth:
12. thou shalt lend unto many *nations*,
36. unto *a nation* which neither
49. The Lord shall bring *a nation*
— *a nation* whose tongue
50. *A nation of* fierce countenance,
65. *And among* these *nations*
29:16(15). how we came through *the nations*
18(17). serve the gods of these *nations*;
24(23). Even all *nations* shall say,
30: 1. to mind among all *the nations*,
31: 3. he will destroy these *nations*
32: 8. the Most High divided to *the nations*
21. to anger *with a* foolish *nation*.
28. they (are) *a nation* void of counsel,
43. Rejoice, *O ye nations*,
Jos. 3:17. until all *the people* were passed
4: 1. when all *the people* were clean
5: 6. all *the people* (that were) men of war,
8. had done circumcising all *the people*,
10:13. until *the people* had avenged
23: 3. hath done unto all these *nations*
4. unto you by lot these *nations*
— with all *the nations* that I have
7. That ye come not *among* these *nations*,
9. from before you great *nations*
12. unto the remnant of these *nations*,
13. these *nations* from before you;
Jud. 2:20. this *people* hath transgressed
21. *the nations* which Joshua left
23. Therefore the Lord left those *nations*,
3: 1. Now these (are) *the nations*
4: 2, 13, 16. Harosheth of *the Gentiles*.
1Sa. 8: 5. to judge us like all *the nations*.

1Sa 8:20. may be like all *the nations;*
2Sa. 7:23. what one *nation* in the earth
— *the nations* and their gods?
8:11. that he had dedicated of all *nations*
22:44. kept me (to be) head of *the heathen:*
50. unto thee, O Lord, *among the heathen,*
1K. 4:31(5:11). his fame was in all *nations*
11: 2. Of *the nations* (concerning) which
14:24. all the abominations of *the nations*
18:10. there is no *nation* or kingdom,
— took an oath of the kingdom and *nation,*
2K. 6:18. Smite this *people,*
16: 3. the abominations of *the heathen,*
17: 8. walked in the statutes of *the heathen,*
11. *as* (did) *the heathen* whom
15. went after *the heathen*
26. *The nations* which thou hast
29. Howbeit *every nation* made gods (lit. *a nation, a nation*)
— *every nation* in their cities (lit. *id.*)
33. after the manner of *the nations*
41. So these *nations* feared the Lord,
18:33. Hath any of the gods of *the nations*
19:12. Have the gods of *the nations*
17. have destroyed *the nations*
21: 2. the abominations of *the heathen,*
9. more evil than did *the nations*
1Ch 14:17. the fear of him upon all *nations.*
16:20. they went *from nation* to *nation,*
24. Declare his glory *among the heathen;*
31. say *among the nations,*
35. deliver us from *the heathen,*
17:21. what one *nation* in the earth
— by driving out *nations* from
18:11. brought from all (these) *nations;*
2Ch 15: 6. *nation* was destroyed *of nation,*
20: 6. all the kingdoms of *the heathen?*
28: 3. the abominations of *the heathen*
32:13. were the gods of *the nations of*
14. among all the gods of those *nations*
15. for no god of any *nation*
17. As the gods of *the nations of*
23. in the sight of all *nations*
33: 2. the abominations of *the heathen,*
9. to do worse than *the heathen,*
36:14. all the abominations of *the heathen;*
Ezr. 6:21. from the filthiness of *the heathen of*
Neh 5: 8. which were sold *unto the heathen;*
9. because of the reproach of *the heathen*
17. came unto us from among *the heathen*
6: 6. It is reported *among the heathen,*
16. all *the heathen* that (were) about
13:26. *yet among* many *nations*
Job 12:23. He increaseth *the nations,*
— he enlargeth *the nations,*
34:29. against *a nation,* or against
Ps. 2: 1. Why do *the heathen* rage,
8. I shall give (thee) *the heathen*
9: 5(6). Thou hast rebuked *the heathen,*
15(16). *The heathen* are sunk down
17(18). all *the nations* that forget God.
19(20). let *the heathen* be judged in thy
20(21). *the nations* may know themselves
10:16. *the heathen* are perished out of
18:43(44). hast made me the head of *the heathen:*
49(50). unto thee, O Lord, *among the heathen,*
22:27(28). all the kindreds of *the nations*
28(29). (is) the governor *among the nations.*
33:10. bringeth the counsel of *the heathen*
12. Blessed (is) *the nation*
43: 1. my cause *against an* ungodly *nation:*
44: 2(3). thou didst drive out *the heathen*
11(12). *and* hast scattered us *among the heathen.*
14(15). a byword *among the heathen,*
46: 6(7). *The heathen* raged,
10(11). I will be exalted *among the heathen,*
47: 8(9). God reigneth over *the heathen:*
59: 5(6). awake to visit all *the heathen:*
8(9). have all *the heathen* in derision.
66: 7. his eyes behold *the nations:*
67: 2(3). thy saving health among all *nations.*
72:11. all *nations* shall serve him.
17. all *nations* shall call him blessed.
78:55. He cast out *the heathen*
79: 1. *the heathen* are come into thine
6. Pour out thy wrath upon *the heathen*

Ps. 79:10. Wherefore should *the heathen* say,
— be known *among the heathen*
80: 8(9). thou hast cast out *the heathen,*
82: 8. thou shalt inherit all *nations.*
83: 4(5). cut them off *from* (being) *a nation;*
86: 9. All *nations* whom thou hast made
94:10. He that chastiseth *the heathen,*
96: 3. Declare his glory *among the heathen,*
10. Say *among the heathen*
98: 2. in the sight of *the heathen.*
102:15(16). So *the heathen* shall fear
105:13. they went *from one nation* to *another,* (lit. *from nation* to *nation*)
44. gave them the lands of *the heathen:*
106: 5. rejoice in the gladness of *thy nation,*
27. To overthrow their seed also *among the nations,*
35. were mingled *among the heathen,*
41. into the hand of *the heathen;*
47. gather us from among *the heathen,*
110: 6. shall judge *among the heathen,*
111: 6. give them the heritage of *the heathen.*
113: 4. The Lord (is) high above all *nations,*
115: 2. Wherefore should *the heathen* say,
117: 1. O praise the Lord, all *ye nations:*
118:10. All *nations* compassed me about:
126: 2. then said they *among the heathen,*
135:10. Who smote great *nations,*
15. The idols of *the heathen*
147:20. He hath not dealt so with any *nation:*
149: 7. To execute vengeance *upon the heathen,*
Pro. 14:34. Righteousness exalteth *a nation:*
Isa. 1: 4. Ah sinful *nation,*
2: 2. all *nations* shall flow unto it.
4. he shall judge among *the nations,*
— *nation* shall not lift up sword against *nation,*
5:26. lift up an ensign *to the nations*
9: 1(8:23). in Galilee of *the nations.*
3(2). Thou hast multiplied *the nation,*
10: 6. *against an* hypocritical *nation,*
7. cut off *nations* not a few.
11:10. to it shall *the Gentiles* seek:
12. set up an ensign *for the nations,*
13: 4. noise of the kingdoms of *nations*
14: 6. he that ruled *the nations*
9, 18. all the kings of *the nations.*
12. which didst weaken *the nations!*
26. stretched out upon all *the nations.*
32. then answer the messengers of *the nation.*
16: 8. the lords of *the heathen*
18: 2. to *a nation* scattered and peeled,
—, 7. *a nation* meted out and trodden
23: 3. she is a mart of *nations.*
25: 3. the city of *the* terrible *nations*
7. the vail that is spread over all *nations.*
26: 2. that *the* righteous *nation*
15, 15. Thou hast increased *the nation,*
29: 7, 8. the multitude of all *the nations*
30:28. to sift *the nations*
33: 3. of thyself *the nations* were scattered.
34: 1. Come near, *ye nations,*
2. of the Lord (is) upon all *nations,*
36:18. Hath any of the gods of *the nations*
37:12. Have the gods of *the nations*
40:15. *the nations* (are) as a drop
17. All *nations* before him
41: 2. to his foot, gave *the nations* before him
42: 1. bring forth judgment *to the Gentiles.*
6. for a light of *the Gentiles;*
43: 9. Let all *the nations* be gathered
45: 1. to subdue *nations* before him;
20. ye (that are) escaped of *the nations:*
49: 6. for a light to *the Gentiles,*
7. whom *the nation* abhorreth,
22. lift up mine hand to *the Gentiles,*
52:10. in the eyes of all *the nations;*
15. So shall he sprinkle many *nations;*
54: 3. thy seed shall inherit *the Gentiles,*
55: 5. thou shalt call *a nation*
— *and nations* (that) knew not thee
58: 2. *as a nation* that did righteousness,
60: 3. *the Gentiles* shall come to thy light.
5, 11. the forces of *the Gentiles*
12. For *the nation* and kingdom
— *nations* shall be utterly wasted.
16. suck the milk of *the Gentiles,*
22. a small one *a* strong *nation:*

Isa. 61: 6. shall eat the riches of *the Gentiles*,
9. seed shall be known *among the Gentiles*,
11. before all *the nations*.
62: 2. *the Gentiles* shall see
64. 2(1). *the nations* may tremble
65: 1. unto *a nation* (that) was not
66: 8. shall *a nation* be born
12. the glory of *the Gentiles*
18. that I will gather all *nations*
19. that escape of them unto *the nations*,
— declare my glory *among the Gentiles*.
20. out of all *nations*
Jer. 1: 5. a prophet *unto the nations*.
10. set thee over *the nations*
2:11. Hath *a nation* changed (their) gods,
3:17. all *the nations* shall be gathered
19. heritage of the hosts of *nations?*
4: 2. *the nations* shall bless themselves
7. the destroyer of *the Gentiles* is on his way;
16. Make ye mention *to the nations;*
5: 9, 29. avenged *on* such *a nation* as this?
15. I will bring *a nation* upon you
— it (is) *a* mighty *nation*, it (is) *an* ancient *nation*, *a nation* whose language
6:18. hear, *ye nations*, and know,
22. *and a* great *nation* shall be
7:28. This (is) *a nation* that obeyeth
9: 9(8). avenged *on* such *a nation*
16(15). scatter them also *among the heathen*,
26(25). (these) *nations* (are) uncircumcised,
10: 2. Learn not the way of *the heathen*,
— for *the heathen* are dismayed
7. O King of *nations?* for to thee
— all the wise (men) of *the nations*,
10. *the nations* shall not be able
25. Pour out thy fury upon *the heathen*
12:17. pluck up and destroy *that nation*,
14:22. the vanities of *the Gentiles*
16:19. *the Gentiles* shall come
18: 7, 9. I shall speak concerning *a nation*,
8. If that *nation*, against whom
13. Ask ye now *among the heathen*,
22: 8. many *nations* shall pass by
25: 9. against all these *nations*
11. these *nations* shall serve
12. that *nation*, saith the Lord,
13. against all *the nations*.
14. many *nations* and great kings
15. cause all *the nations*,
17. made all *the nations* to drink,
31. a controversy *with the nations*,
32. evil shall go forth *from nation* to *nation*,
26: 6. to all *the nations of* the earth.
27: 7. all *nations* shall serve him,
— many *nations* and great kings
8. *the nation* and kingdom
— that *nation* will I punish,
11. *But the nations* that bring
13. hath spoken against *the nation*
28:11. from the neck of all *nations*
14. the neck of all these *nations*,
29:14. gather you from all *the nations*,
18. among all *the nations* whither I have
30:11. make a full end of all *nations*
31: 7. shout among the chief of *the nations:*
10. *O ye nations*, and declare
36. Israel also shall cease from being *a nation*
33: 9. before all *the nations of* the earth,
24. that they should be no more *a nation*
36: 2. against all *the nations*,
43: 5. were returned from all *nations*,
44: 8. among all *the nations of* the earth?
46: 1. Jeremiah the prophet against *the Gentiles;*
12. *The nations* have heard
28. a full end of all *the nations*
48: 2. let us cut it off *from* (being) *a nation*.
49:14. is sent *unto the heathen*,
15. small *among the heathen*,
31. up unto *the* wealthy *nation*,
36. there shall be no *nation*
50: 2. Declare ye *among the nations*,
3. there cometh up *a nation*
9. an assembly of great *nations*
12. the hindermost of *the nations*
23. desolation *among the nations!*
41. *and a* great *nation*,
46. the cry is heard *among the nations*.
Jer. 51: 7. *the nations* have drunken of her wine; therefore *the nations* are mad.
20. I break in pieces *the nations*,
27. blow the trumpet *among the nations*, prepare *the nations* against her,
28. Prepare against her *the nations*
41. astonishment *among the nations!*
44. *the nations* shall not flow
Lam. 1: 1. great *among the nations*,
3. dwelleth *among the heathen*,
10. she hath seen (that) *the heathen*
2: 9. princes (are) *among the Gentiles:*
4:15. they said *among the heathen*,
17. we have watched for *a nation*
20. we shall live *among the heathen*.
Eze. 2: 3. to *a* rebellious *nation* (marg. *nations*)
4:13. defiled bread *among the Gentiles*,
5: 5. in the midst of *the nations*
6. wickedness more than *the nations*,
7, 7. *the nations* that (are) round about you,
8. in the sight of *the nations*.
14. reproach *among the nations*
15. *unto the nations* that (are) round
6: 8. escape the sword *among the nations*,
9. remember me *among the nations*
7:24. bring the worst of *the heathen*,
11:12. after the manners of *the heathen*
16. far off *among the heathen*,
12:15. scatter them *among the nations*,
16. abominations *among the heathen*
16:14. went forth *among the heathen*
19: 4. *The nations* also heard of him;
8. *the nations* set against him
20: 9, 14. be polluted before *the heathen*,
22. in the sight of *the heathen*,
23. scatter them *among the heathen*,
32. We will be *as the heathen*,
41. sanctified in you before *the heathen*.
22: 4. a reproach *unto the heathen*,
15. scatter thee *among the heathen*,
16. in the sight of *the heathen*,
23:30. a whoring after *the heathen*,
25: 7. for a spoil *to the heathen;*
8. like unto all *the heathen;*
10. remembered *among the nations*.
26: 3. will cause many *nations* to come
5. become a spoil *to the nations*.
28: 7. the terrible of *the nations:*
25. in the sight of *the heathen*,
29:12. the Egyptians *among the nations*,
15. any more above *the nations:*
— no more rule *over the nations*.
30: 3. it shall be the time of *the heathen*.
11. the terrible of *the nations*,
23, 26. the Egyptians *among the nations*,
31: 6. under his shadow dwelt all great *nations*.
11. the mighty one of *the heathen;*
12. the terrible of *the nations*,
16. I made *the nations* to shake
17. in the midst of *the heathen*.
32: 2. like a young lion of *the nations*,
9. thy destruction *among the nations*,
12. the terrible of *the nations*,
16. the daughters of *the nations*
18. the daughters of *the* famous *nations*,
34:28. be a prey *to the heathen*,
29. neither bear the shame of *the heathen* any more.
35:10. hast said, These two *nations*
36: 3, 4, 5. the residue of *the heathen*,
6. have borne the shame of *the heathen:*
7. Surely *the heathen* that (are)
13. hast bereaved *thy nations;*
14. *neither* bereave *thy nations*
15. hear in thee the shame of *the heathen*
— *neither* shalt thou cause *thy nations*
19. scattered them *among the heathen*,
20. they entered unto *the heathen*,
21. had profaned *among the heathen*,
22. ye have profaned *among the heathen*,
23. was profaned *among the heathen*,
— *the heathen* shall know that
24. take you from among *the heathen*,
30. reproach of famine *among the heathen*.
36. Then *the heathen* that are left
37:21. Israel from among *the heathen*,
22. I will make them one *nation*

Eze.37:22. shall be no more two *nations,*
28. *the heathen* shall know that
38:12. gathered *out of the nations,*
16. that *the heathen* may know
23. in the eyes of many *nations,*
39: 7. *the heathen* shall know that
21. set my glory *among the heathen,* and all *the heathen* shall see
23. *the heathen* shall know
27. in the sight of many *nations;*
28. led into captivity among *the heathen:*
Dan 8:22. shall stand up *out of the nation,*
11:23. strong with *a* small *people.*
12: 1. since there was *a nation*
Hos 8: 8. shall they be *among the Gentiles*
10. have hired *among the nations,*
9:17. be wanderers *among the nations.*
Joel 1: 6. *a nation* is come up upon my
2:17. that *the heathen* should rule
19. a reproach *among the heathen:*
3: 2(4:2). I will also gather all *nations,*
—(-:-). scattered *among the nations,*
8(-:8). to *a people* far off:
9(-:9). Proclaim ye this *among the Gentiles;*
11(-:11). come, all *ye heathen,*
12(-:12). Let *the heathen* be wakened,
—(-:—). all *the heathen* round about.
Am. 6: 1. named chief of *the nations,*
14. raise up against you *a nation,*
9: 9. Israel among all *nations,*
12. of all *the heathen,* which are called
Obad. 1. is sent *among the heathen,*
2. thee small *among the heathen:*
15. the Lord (is) near upon all *the heathen:*
16. shall all *the heathen* drink
Mic. 4: 2. many *nations* shall come,
3. rebuke strong *nations* afar off;
— *nation* shall not lift up a sword against *nation,*
7. cast far off *a* strong *nation:*
11. also many *nations* are gathered
5: 8(7). shall be *among the Gentiles*
15(14). anger and fury upon *the heathen,*
7:16. *The nations* shall see
Nah 3: 4. that selleth *nations*
5. I will shew *the nations* thy nakedness,
Hab 1: 5. Behold ye *among the heathen,*
6. bitter and hasty *nation,*
17. continually to slay *the nations?*
2: 5. gathereth unto him all *nations,*
8. thou hast spoiled many *nations,*
3: 6. drove asunder *the nations;*
12. thou didst thresh *the heathen*
Zep. 2: 1. *O nation* not desired;
5. *the nation of* the Cherethites!
9. the remnant of *my people* shall possess
11. all the isles of *the heathen.*
14. all the beasts of *the nations:*
3: 6. I have cut off *the nations:*
8. determination (is) to gather *the nations,*
Hag 2: 7. I will shake all *nations,* and the desire of all *nations*
14. so (is) this *nation*
22. the kingdoms of *the heathen;*
Zec. 1:15. sore displeased with *the heathen*
21(2:4). them, to cast out the horns of *the Gentiles,*
2: 8(12). he sent me unto *the nations*
11(15). many *nations* shall be joined
7:14. among all *the nations*
8:13. a curse *among the heathen,*
22. many people *and* strong *nations* shall
23. all languages of *the nations,*
9:10. he shall speak peace *unto the heathen:*
12: 3. all *the people of* the earth
9. destroy all *the nations*
14: 2. I will gather all *nations*
3. fight *against* those *nations,*
14. the wealth of all *the heathen*
16. every one that is left of all *the nations*
18. the Lord will smite *the heathen*
19. the punishment of all *nations*
Mal. 1:11. great *among the Gentiles;*
— (shall be) great *among the heathen,*
14. dreadful *among the heathen.*
3: 9. this whole *nation.*
12. all *nations* shall call you blessed:

גְּוִיָּה *g'vee-yāh',* f. 1472

Gen 47:18. but *our bodies,* and our lands:
Jud. 14: 8. and honey *in the carcase of* the lion.
9. honey *out of the carcase of* the lion.
1Sa. 31:10. they fastened *his body*
12. took *the body of* Saul and *the bodies of* his sons
Neh 9:37. they have dominion over *our bodies,*
Ps. 110: 6. fill (the places) with *the dead bodies;*
Eze. 1:11. two covered *their bodies.*
23. covered on that side, *their bodies.*
Dan 10: 6. *His body also* (was) like the beryl,
Nah 3: 3. none end *of* (their) *corpses;* they stumble *upon their corpses:*

גּוֹלָה *gōh-lāh',* f. 1473

2K. 24:15. carried he into *captivity*
16. the king of Babylon brought *captive* to Babylon. (lit. into *captivity*)
1Ch 5:22. dwelt in their steads until *the captivity.*
Ezr. 1:11. bring up with (them of) *the captivity* (marg. *transportation*)
2: 1. *of those which had been carried away*
4: 1. that the children of *the captivity* (marg. sons of *the transportation*)
6:19, 20. the children of *the captivity*
21. were come again *out of captivity,*
8:35. children of *those that had been carried away,*
9: 4. *those that had been carried away;*
10: 6. *them that had been carried away.*
7. all the children of *the captivity,*
8. *those that had been carried away.*
16. the children of *the captivity* did so.
Neh 7: 6. of *those that had been carried away,*
Est. 2: 6. Jerusalem with *the captivity*
Jer. 28: 6. all *that is carried away captive,* from
29: 1. elders *which were carried away captives,*
4. all *that are carried away captives,*
16. gone forth with you *into captivity;*
20. all *ye of the captivity,*
31. Send to all *them of the captivity,*
46:19. furnish thyself to go into *captivity:*
48: 7. Chemosh shall go forth *into captivity*
11. *neither* hath he gone *into captivity:*
49: 3. their king shall go *into captivity,*
Eze. 1: 1. as I (was) among *the captives* (marg. *captivity*)
3:11. get thee to *them of the captivity,*
15. I came to *them of the captivity*
11:24. into Chaldea, to *them of the captivity.*
25. Then I spake unto *them of the captivity*
12: 3. prepare thee stuff for *removing,*
4. as stuff for *removing:*
— as they that go forth into *captivity.*
7. as stuff for *captivity,*
11. *remove* (and) go into captivity. (marg. *by removing* go into captivity)
25: 3. when they went *into captivity;*
Am. 1:15. their king shall go *into captivity,*
Nah 3:10. Yet (was) she *carried away,*
Zec. 6:10. Take of (them of) *the captivity,*
14: 2. of the city shall go forth *into captivity,*

גּוּמָּץ *goom-matz',* m. 1475

Ecc. 10: 8. He that diggeth *a pit* shall fall into it;

גָּוַע *gāh-vag'.* 1478

* KAL.—*Preterite.* *

Nu. 17:12(27). saying, Behold, *we die,*
20: 3. Would God that *we had died*
29. saw that Aaron *was dead,*
Jos. 22:20. that man *perished* not alone
Lam. 1:19. mine elders *gave up the ghost*

KAL.—*Infinitive.*

Nu. 17:13(28). shall we be consumed *with dying?*
20: 3. *when* our brethren *died*

KAL.—*Future.*

Gen 6:17. that (is) in the earth *shall die.*
7:21. *And* all flesh *died*
25: 8. *Then* Abraham *gave up the ghost,*
17. *and he gave up the ghost* and died;
35:29. *And* Isaac *gave up the ghost,*
49:33. *and yielded up the ghost,*
Job 3:11. *did I* (not) *give up the ghost*
10:18. *Oh that I had given up the ghost,*
13:19. *I shall give up the ghost.*
14:10. *yea,* man *giveth up the ghost,*
27: 5. that I should justify you: till *I die*
29:18. *I shall die* in my nest,
34:15. All flesh *shall perish* together,
36:12. *and they shall die* without knowledge.
Ps.104:29. *they die,* and return to their dust.
Zec.13: 8. parts therein shall be cut off (and) *die;*

KAL.—*Participle.* Poel.

Ps. 88:15(16). I (am) afflicted *and ready to die*

1479 גּוּף [*gooph*].

* HIPHIL.—*Future.* *

Neh 7: 3. *let them shut* the doors,

1480 גּוּפָה [*goo-phāh'*].

1Ch 10:12. took away *the body of* Saul, and *the bodies of* his sons,

---

1481 גּוּר *goor.*

* KAL.—*Preterite.* *

Gen21:23. wherein *thou hast sojourned.*
32: 4(5). *I have sojourned* with Laban,
35:27. Abraham and Isaac *sojourned.*
Ex. 6: 4. wherein they *were strangers.*
Jud.17: 7. and *he sojourned* there.
19:16. *he sojourned* in Gibeah:
Ps.105:23. Jacob *sojourned* in the land of Ham.
120: 5. that *I sojourn* in Mesech,
Isa. 11: 6. The wolf *also shall dwell* with
54:15. whosoever *shall gather together*
Eze.47:23. in what tribe the stranger *sojourneth,*

KAL.—*Infinitive.*

Gen12:10. went down into Egypt *to sojourn*
19: 9. This one (fellow) came in *to sojourn,*
47: 4. *For to sojourn* in the land
Jud.17: 8. *to sojourn* where he could find
9. I go *to sojourn* where I may
Ru. 1: 1. went *to sojourn* in the country
Isa. 23: 7. shall carry her afar off *to sojourn.*
52: 4. into Egypt *to sojourn* there;
54:15. they shall *surely* gather together, (lit. *gathering* they shall gather)
Jer. 42:15. and go *to sojourn* there;
17. go into Egypt *to sojourn* there;
22. ye desire to go (and) *to sojourn.*
43: 2. Go not into Egypt *to sojourn*
5. *to dwell* in the land of Judah;
44: 8. whither ye be gone *to dwell,*
12, 28. the land of Egypt *to sojourn*
14. the land of Egypt *to sojourn*
Lam 4:15. They shall no more *sojourn*

KAL.—*Imperative.*

Gen26: 3. *Sojourn* in this land,
2K. 8: 1. *and sojourn* wheresoever thou
Job 19:29. *Be ye afraid* of the sword:
Ps. 22:23(24). *and fear* him, all ye the seed of Israel.

KAL.—*Future.*

Gen20: 1. between Kadesh and Shur, *and sojourned* in Gerar.
21:34. *And* Abraham *sojourned*
Ex. 12:48. when a stranger *shall sojourn*
Lev.17: 8. which *sojourn* among you,
19:33. if a stranger *sojourn* with thee
Nu. 9:14. if a stranger *shall sojourn*
15:14. if a stranger *sojourn* with you,
22: 3. *And* Moab *was* sore *afraid*
Deu 1:17. *ye shall* not *be afraid*
18:22. *thou shalt* not *be afraid* of him.
26: 5. *and sojourned* there
32:27. that *I feared* the wrath of the enemy,
Jud. 5:17. why *did* Dan *remain* in ships?
1Sa.18:15. *he was afraid* of him.
2K. 8: 1. wheresoever *thou canst sojourn:*
2. *and sojourned* in the land of
Job 41:25(17). the mighty *are afraid:*
Ps. 5: 4(5). neither *shall* evil *dwell with thee.*
15: 1. who *shall abide* in thy tabernacle? (marg. *sojourn*)
33: 8. *let* all the inhabitants of the world *stand in awe*
56: 6(7). *They gather themselves together,*
59: 3(4). the mighty *are gathered*
61: 4(5). *I will abide* in thy tabernacle
140: 2(3). continually *are they gathered*
Isa. 16: 4. *Let* mine outcasts *dwell* with
33:14. Who among us *shall dwell* with the devouring fire? who among us *shall dwell*
54:15. they *shall* surely *gather together,*
Jer. 49:18. neither *shall* a son of man *dwell* in it.
33. nor (any) son of man *dwell* in it.
50:40. neither *shall* any son of man *dwell* therein.
Eze.14: 7. the stranger that *sojourneth*
Hos 10: 5. The inhabitants of Samaria *shall fear*

KAL.—*Participle.* Poel.

Ex. 3:22. *and of her that sojourneth in* her house,
12:49. unto the stranger *that sojourneth*
Lev.16:29. or a stranger *that sojourneth*
17:10, 13. the strangers *that sojourn*
12. any stranger *that sojourneth*
18:26. nor any stranger *that sojourneth*
19:34. the stranger *that dwelleth*
20: 2. or of the strangers *that sojourn*
25: 6. stranger *that sojourneth* with thee,
45. *that do sojourn* among you,
Nu. 15:15, 16, 26, 29 & 19:10. the stranger *that sojourneth*
Deu 18: 6. out of all Israel, where he *sojourned,*
Jos. 20: 9. the stranger *that sojourneth*
Jud.19: 1. there was a certain Levite *sojourning*
2Sa. 4: 3. were *sojourners* there until this day.
1Ch 16:19. even a few, *and strangers* in it
2Ch 15: 9. *and the strangers* with them
Ezr. 1: 4. where he *sojourneth,*
Job 19:15. *They that dwell in* mine house.
28: 4. The flood breaketh out from *the inhabitant;*
Ps.105:12. yea, very few, *and strangers* in it.
Isa. 5:17. of the fat ones shall *strangers* eat.
Jer. 35: 7. the land where ye (be) *strangers.*
Eze.47:22. the strangers that *sojourn*

* HITHPOLEL.—*Future.* *

Hos. 7:14. *they assemble themselves* for corn

HITHPOLEL.—*Participle.*

1K. 17:20. evil upon the widow with whom I *sojourn,*

גּוֹר [*gōhr*], com. 1484

Jer. 51:38. they shall yell *as* lions' *whelps.*
Nah 2:12(13). in pieces enough for *his whelps,*

גּוּר *goor,* m. 1482

Gen49: 9. Judah (is) a lion's *whelp:*
Deu33:22. Dan (is) a lion's *whelp:*
Lam 4: 3. give suck to *their young ones:*
Eze.19: 2. she nourished *her whelps*
3. brought up one *of her whelps:*
5. she took another *of her whelps,*
Nah 2:11(12). *the* lion's *whelp,*

1486 גּוֹרָל *gōh-rāhl'*, m.

Lev.16: 8. Aaron shall cast *lots*
— one *lot* for the Lord, *and the* other *lot* for the scapegoat.
9. upon which the Lord's *lot* fell,
10. on which *the lot* fell
Nu. 26:55. the land shall be divided *by lot:*
56. According to *the lot* shall the
33:54. ye shall divide the land *by lot*
— the place where his *lot* falleth ;
34:13. which ye shall inherit *by lot,*
36: 2. the land for an inheritance *by lot*
3. *so* shall it be taken *from the lot*
Jos. 14: 2. *By lot* (was) their inheritance,
15: 1. (This) then was *the lot*
16: 1. *the lot* of the children of Joseph
17: 1. There was also *a lot* for
14. hast thou given me (but) one *lot*
17. thou shalt not have one *lot*
18: 6. that I may cast *lots* for you
8. that I may here cast *lots*
10. Joshua cast *lots* for them
11. *the lot of* the tribe of the children
— the coast of *their lot*
19: 1. *the* second *lot* came forth
10. *the* third *lot* came up
17. *the* fourth *lot* came out
24. *the* fifth *lot* came out
32. *The* sixth *lot* came out
40. *the* seventh *lot* came out
51. divided for an inheritance *by lot*
21: 4. *the lot* came out
— the Levites, had *by lot*
5. the children of Kohath (had) *by lot*
6. the children of Gershon (had) *by lot*
8. the children of Israel gave *by lot*
10. for their's was *the* first *lot.*
20. they had the cities of *their lot*
40(38). were (by) *their lot* twelve cities.
Jud. 1: 3. Come up with me *into my lot,*
— go with thee *into thy lot.*
20: 9. *by lot* against it;
1Ch 6:54(39). for their's was *the lot.*
61(46). Manasseh, *by lot,* ten cities.
63(48). Merari (were given) *by lot,*
65(50). they gave *by lot* out of
24: 5. Thus were they divided *by lot,*
7. Now *the* first *lot* came forth
31. These likewise cast *lots*
25: 8. they cast *lots,* ward against
9. Now *the* first *lot* came
26:13. they cast *lots,* as well the small
14. *the lot* eastward fell to
— they cast *lots;* and *his lot* came out northward.
Neh 10:34(35). *And* we cast *the lots* among
11: 1. the rest of the people also cast *lots,*
Est. 3: 7. they cast Pur, that (is), *the lot,*
9:24. and had cast Pur, that (is), *the lot,*
Ps. 16: 5. thou maintainest *my lot.*
22:18(19). cast *lots* upon my vesture.
125: 3. shall not rest upon *the lot of*
Pro. 1:14. Cast in *thy lot* among us ;
16:33. *The lot* is cast into the lap ;
18:18. *The lot* causeth contentions
Isa. 17:14. *and the lot* of them that rob
34:17. he hath cast *the lot* for them,
57: 6. they, they (are) *thy lot:*
Jer. 13:25. This (is) *thy lot,* the portion
Eze.24: 6. let no *lot* fall upon it.
Dan12:13. stand *in thy lot* at the end of the days.
Joel 3: 3(4:3). they have cast *lots* for my people ;
Obad 11. cast *lots* upon Jerusalem,
Jon. 1: 7. Come, and let us cast *lots,*
— So they cast *lots,* and *the lot* fell upon Jonah.
Mic. 2: 5. cast a cord *by lot*
Nah. 3:10. they cast *lots* for her honourable men,

1487 גּוּשׁ *goosh*, m.

Job 7: 5. *and clods of* dust;

גֵּז *gehz*, m. 1488

Deu18: 4. the first of *the fleece of* thy sheep,
Job 31:20. *and* (if) he were (not) warmed *with the fleece*
Ps. 72: 6. upon *the mown grass:*
Am. 7: 1. after the king's *mowings.*

גִּזְבָּר *giz-bāhr'*, m. 1489

Ezr. 1: 8. Mithredath *the treasurer,*

גִּזְבָּר [*giz-bāhr'*], Ch. m. 1490

Ezr. 7:21. do make a decree to all *the treasurers*

גָּזָה [*gāh-zāh'*]. 1491

* KAL.—*Participle.* Poel. *

Ps. 71: 6. thou art he *that took me* out of my mother's bowels:

גִּזָּה *giz-zāh'*, f. 1492

Jud. 6:37. I will put *a fleece of* wool in the floor ; (and) if the dew be on *the fleece* only,
38. thrust *the fleece* together, and wringed the dew out of *the fleece,*
39. but this once *with the fleece;* let it now be dry only upon *the fleece,*
40. it was dry upon *the fleece*

גָּזַז [*gāh-zaz'*]. 1494

* KAL.—*Infinitive.* *

Gen31:19. Laban went *to shear* his sheep:
38:13. to Timnath *to shear* his sheep.
1Sa.25: 2. he was *shearing* his sheep

KAL.—*Imperative.*

Jer. 7:29. *Cut off* thine hair,
Mic. 1:16. *and poll thee* for thy delicate children ;

KAL.—*Future.*

Deu15:19. nor *shear* the firstling of thy sheep.
Job 1:20. *and shaved* his head,

KAL.—*Participle.* Poel.

Gen38:12. went up unto his sheep*shearers*
1Sa.25: 4. that Nabal *did shear* his sheep.
7. heard that thou hast *shearers:*
11. that I have killed *for my shearers,*
2Sa.13:23. Absalom had *sheepshearers*
24. thy servant hath *sheepshearers;*
Isa. 53: 7. as a sheep before *her shearers*

* NIPHAL.—*Preterite.* *

Nah. 1:12. *shall they be cut down,* (marg. *shorn*)

גָּזִית *gāh-zeeth'*, f. 1496

Ex. 20:25. build it of *hewn stone:*
1K. 5:17(31). costly stones, (and) *hewed* stones,
6:36. with three rows of *hewed stone,*
7: 9. according to the measures of *hewed stones,*
11. after the measures of *hewed stones,*
12. with three rows of *hewed stones,*
1Ch 22: 2. set masons to hew *wrought* stones
Isa. 9:10(9). *but* we will build with *hewn stones:*
Lam.3: 9. inclosed my ways *with hewn stone,*
Eze.40:42. four tables (were) of *hewn stone*
Am. 5:11. ye have built houses of *hewn stone,*

גָּזַל *gāh-zal'*. 1497

* KAL.—*Preterite.* *

Gen21:25. servants *had violently taken away.*

Lev. 6: 4(5:23). that which *he took violently away,*
Jud.21:23. whom *they caught:* and they went
Job 20:19. *he hath violently taken away* an house
24: 2. *they violently take away* flocks,
Ps. 69: 4(5). which *I took* not *away.*
Eze.18:12. *hath spoiled* by violence,
16. neither *hath spoiled* by violence,
18. *spoiled* his brother by violence,
22:29. *and exercised* robbery,
Mic. 2: 2. *and take* (them) *by violence;*

KAL.—*Infinitive.*

Isa. 10: 2. *and to take away* the right

KAL.—*Future.*

Gen 31:31. *thou wouldest take by force*
Lev.19:13. neither *rob* (him):
Jud. 9:25. *and they robbed* all that came
2Sa.23:21. *and plucked* the spear out of
1Ch 11:23. *and plucked* the spear out of
Job 24: 9. *They pluck* the fatherless
19. heat *consume* the snow waters:
Pro.22:22. *Rob* not the poor,
Eze.18: 7. *hath spoiled* none by violence,

KAL.—*Participle.* Poel.

Ps. 35:10. *from him that spoileth him?*
Pro.28:24. *Whoso robbeth* his father
Mic. 3: 2. *who pluck off* their skin

KAL.—*Participle.* Paül.

Deu 28:29. only oppressed *and spoiled*
31. *violently taken away* from
Jer.21:12. deliver (him that is) *spoiled*
22: 3. deliver *the spoiled* out of
Mal. 1:13. and ye brought (that which was) *torn,*

* NIPHAL.—*Preterite.* *

Pro. 4:16. *and* their sleep *is taken away,*

1498 **גָּזֵל** *gāh-zēhl'*, m.

Lev. 6: 2(5:21). *or in a thing taken away by violence,*
Ps. 62:10(11). *and* become not vain *in robbery:*
Isa. 61: 8. I hate *robbery* for burnt offering;
Eze.22:29. and exercised *robbery,*

1499 **גֶּזֶל** *gēh'-zel*, m.

Ecc. 5: 8(7). *and violent perverting of* judgment
Eze.18:18. spoiled his brother *by violence,*

1500 **גְּזֵלָה** *g'zēh-lāh'*, f.

Lev. 6: 4(5:23). *that* which he took violently away, (lit. *the spoil* which he took, &c.)
Isa. 3:14. *the spoil of* the poor
Eze.18: 7. hath spoiled none *by violence,*
12. hath spoiled *by violence,*
16. *neither* hath spoiled *by violence,*
33:15. give again *that he had robbed,*

1501 **גָּזָם** *gāh-zāhm'*, m.

Joel 1: 4. That which *the palmerworm*
2:25. *and the palmerworm,* my great army
Am. 4: 9. *the palmerworm* devoured

1503 **גֶּזַע** *geh'-zag*, m.

Job 14: 8. *the stock thereof* die
Isa. 11: 1. a rod *out of the stem of* Jesse,
40:24. *their stock* shall not take root

1504 **גָּזַר** *gāh-zar'.*

* KAL.—*Preterite.* *

Hab. 3:17. the flock *shall be cut off*

KAL.—*Imperative.*

1K. 3:25. *Divide* the living child in two,
1K. 3:26. Let it be neither mine nor thine, (but) *divide*

KAL.—*Future.*

2K. 6: 4. And when they came to Jordan, *they cut down*
Job 22:28. *Thou shalt also decree* a thing,
Isa. 9:20(19). *And he shall snatch* on the (marg. *cut*)

KAL.—*Participle.* Poel.

Ps.136:13. *To him which divided* the Red sea

* NIPHAL.—*Preterite.* *

2Ch 26:21. for *he was cut off* from the
Est. 2: 1. what *was decreed* against her.
Ps. 88: 5(6). they *are cut off* from
Isa. 53: 8. for *he was cut off* out of the land
Lam.3:54. I said, *I am cut off.*
Eze.37:11. *we are cut off* for our parts.

גְּזַר [*g'zar*], Ch. 1505

* P'AL.—*Participle.* *

Dan 2:27. *the soothsayers,* shew unto the king;
4: 7(4) & 5:7. the Chaldeans, *and the soothsayers:*
5:11. Chaldeans, (and) *soothsayers;*

* ITHP'AL.—*Preterite.* *

Dan 2:34. till that a stone *was cut out* without hands,
45. the stone *was cut out* of the mountain

גֶּזֶר [*geh'-zer*], m. 1506

Gen15:17. that passed between those *pieces.*
Ps.136:13. divided the Red sea *into parts:*

גְּזֵרָה *g'zēh-rāh'*, f. 1509

Lev.16:22. unto a land *not inhabited:* (marg. of *separation*)

גְּזֵרָה [*g'zēh-rāh'*], Ch. f. 1510

Dan 4:17(14). *by the decree of* the watchers,
24(21). *and* this (is) *the decree of* the most High,

גִּזְרָה *giz-rāh'*, f. 1508

Lam.4: 7. *their polishing* (was) of sapphire:
Eze.41:12. before *the separate place*
13. *and the separate place,*
14. *and* of *the separate place*
15. over against *the separate place*
42: 1. over against *the separate place,*
10. over against *the separate place,*
13. before *the separate place,*

גָּחוֹן *gāh-ghōhn'*, m. 1512

Gen 3:14. upon *thy belly* shalt thou go,
Lev.11:42. goeth upon *the belly,*

גַּחֶלֶת *gah-gheh'-leth*, f. 1513

Lev.16:12. a censer full of burning *coals* (lit. *coals of* fire)
2Sa.14: 7. so they shall quench *my coal*
22: 9. *coals* were kindled by it.
13. before him were *coals of* fire
Job 41:21(13). His breath kindleth *coals,*
Ps. 18: 8(9). *coals* were kindled by it.
12(13), 13(14). hail (stones) *and coals of* fire.
120: 4. with *coals of* juniper.
140:10(11). Let *burning coals* fall upon
Pro. 6:28. Can one go upon *hot coals,*
25:22. thou shalt heap *coals of fire*
26:21. coals (are) *to burning coals,*

Isa. 44:19. baked bread upon *the coals thereof;*
47:14. not (be) *a coal* to warm
Eze. 1:13. *like* burning *coals of* fire,
10: 2. fill thine hand with *coals of*
24:11. set it empty upon *the coals thereof,*

1516 **גַּיְא** *gah'y*, com.

Nu. 21:20. from Bamoth (in) *the valley*, that (is) in the country
Deu 3:29. So we abode *in the valley*
4:46. *in the valley* over against
34: 6. he buried him *in a valley*
Jos. 8:11. *now* (there was) *a valley*
15: 8. by *the valley of* the son of Hinnom
— before *the valley of* Hinnom
18:16. *the valley of* the son of Hinnom,
— descended *to the valley of* Hinnom,
19:14. are *in the valley of* Jiphthah-el:
27. *and to the valley of* Jiphthah-el
1Sa. 13:18. looketh to *the valley of* Zeboim
17: 3. *and* (there was) *a valley* between
52. until thou come to *the valley*,
2Sa. 8:13. *in the valley of* salt,
2K. 2:16. or into some *valley*. (lit. one of *the valleys*)
14: 7. He slew of Edom *in the valley of*
23:10. *in the valley of* the children of Hinnom,
1Ch 4:14. the father of *the valley of* Charashim;
39. unto the east side of *the valley*,
18:12. Edomites *in the valley of* salt
2Ch 14:10(9). they set the battle in array in *the valley of*
25:11. went to *the valley of* salt,
26: 9. and at *the valley* gate.
28: 3 & 33:6. *in the valley of* the son of Hinnom,
Neh 2:13, 15. by the gate of *the valley*,
3:13. *The valley* gate repaired Hanun,
11:30. unto *the valley of* Hinnom.
35. Lod, and Ono, *the valley of* craftsmen.
Ps. 23: 4. I walk *through the valley of* the shadow
60[title](2). smote of Edom *in the valley of*
Isa. 22: 1. burden of *the valley of* vision.
5. *in the valley of* vision,
28: 1. on the head of *the* fat *valleys*
4. on the head of *the* fat *valley*,
40: 4. Every *valley* shall be exalted,
Jer. 2:23. see thy way *in the valley*,
7:31. *in the valley* of the son of Hinnom,
32. *nor the valley of* the son of Hinnom, but *the valley of* slaughter:
19: 2. *the valley of* the son of Hinnom,
6. *nor The valley of* the son of Hinnom, but *The valley of* slaughter.
32:35. *in the valley of* the son of Hinnom,
Eze. 6: 3. to the rivers, *and to the valleys;*
7:16. like doves of *the valleys*,
31:12. and in all *the valleys*
32: 5. fill *the valleys* with thy height.
35: 8. in thy hills, *and in thy valleys*,
36: 4, 6. to the rivers, *and to the valleys*,
39:11. *the valley of* the passengers
—, 15. *The valley of* Hamon-gog.
Mic. 1: 6. the stones thereof *into the valley*,
Zec. 14: 4. *a* very great *valley;*
5. ye shall flee (to) *the valley of* the mountains; for *the valley of* the mountains

1517 **גִּיד** *geed*, m.

Gen32:32(33). eat not (of) *the sinew* which
—(—). *in the sinew* that shrank.
Job 10:11. hast fenced me with bones *and sinews*
40:17. *the sinews of* his stones
Isa. 48: 4. *and* thy neck (is) an iron *sinew*,
Eze. 37: 6. I will lay *sinews* upon you,
8. *the sinews* and the flesh

1518 **גִּיחַ** [*gee'ăgh* or **גּוּחַ** [*goo'ăgh*].

* KAL.—*Infinitive.* *

Job 38: 8. *when it brake forth*, (as if) it had issued

KAL.—*Imperative.*

Mic. 4:10. *and labour to bring forth*, O daughter

KAL.—*Future.*

Job 40:23. he trusteth that *he can draw up*
Eze. 32: 2. *and thou camest forth* with thy rivers,

KAL.—*Participle.*

Ps. 22: 9(10). *he that took me out*

* HIPHIL. *Participle.* *

Jud. 20:33. *came forth* out of their places,

גִּיחַ [*gee'ăgh*] or **גּוּחַ** [*goo'ăgh*]. 1519

* APHEL.—*Participle.* *

Dan 7: 2. the four winds of the heaven *strove*

גִּיל [*geel*] or **גּוּל** [*gool*]. 1523

* KAL.—*Preterite.* *

Isa. 65:19. *And I will rejoice* in Jerusalem,

KAL.—*Imperative.*

Ps. 2:11. *and rejoice* with trembling.
32:11. *and rejoice*, ye righteous:
Isa. 49:13. *and be joyful*, O earth;
65:18. But be ye glad *and rejoice*
66:10. *and be glad* with her,
Joel 2:21. Fear not, O land; *be glad* and rejoice:
23. *Be glad* then, ye children of Zion,
Zec. 9: 9. *Rejoice* greatly, O daughter

KAL.—*Future.*

1Ch 16:31. *and let* the earth *rejoice:*
Ps. 9:14(15). *I will rejoice* in thy salvation.
13: 4(5). those that trouble me *rejoice*
5(6). my heart *shall rejoice* in thy salvation
14: 7. Jacob *shall rejoice*,
16: 9. *and* my glory *rejoiceth:*
21: 1(2). how greatly *shall he rejoice!*
31: 7(8). *I will be glad* and rejoice
35: 9. my soul *shall be joyful*
48:11(12). *let* the daughters of Judah *be glad*,
51: 8(10). bones (which) thou hast broken *may rejoice.*
53: 6(7). Jacob *shall rejoice*,
89:16(17). In thy name *shall they rejoice*
96:11. *and let* the earth *be glad;*
97: 1. *let* the earth *rejoice;*
8. *and* the daughters of Judah *rejoiced*
118:24. *we will rejoice* and be glad
149: 2. *let* the children of Zion *be joyful*
Pro. 2:14. *delight* in the frowardness
23:24. of the righteous *shall* greatly *rejoice:*
25. *and* she that bare thee *shall rejoice.*
24:17. *let* not thine heart *be glad*
Cant. 1: 4. *we will be glad* and rejoice
Isa. 9: 3(2). as (men) *rejoice* when they divide
25: 9. *we will be glad* and rejoice
29:19. the poor among men *shall rejoice*
35: 1. *and* the desert *shall rejoice*,
2. *and rejoice* even with joy
41:16. *thou shalt rejoice* in the Lord,
61:10. my soul *shall be joyful* in my God;
Hos. 10: 5. the priests thereof (that) *rejoiced*
Hab. 1:15. they rejoice *and are glad.*
3:18. *I will joy* in the God of my
Zep. 3:17. *he will joy* over thee
Zec. 10: 7. their heart *shall rejoice* in the

גִּיל *geel*, m. 1524

Job 3:22. Which rejoice *exceedingly*, (lit. rejoicing unto *gladness*)
Ps. 43: 4. unto God *my* exceeding *joy:*
45:15(16). With gladness *and rejoicing*
65:12(13). *and* the little hills rejoice (marg. are girded *with joy*)
Pro. 23:24. The father of the righteous shall *greatly* rejoice: (lit. shall rejoice *joy*)
Isa. 16:10. *and joy* out of the plentiful field;
Jer. 48:33. And joy *and gladness*
Dan 1:10. which (are) *of your sort?* (marg. or, *term*, or, *continuance*)
Hos. 9: 1. Rejoice not, O Israel, for *joy*,
Joel 1:16. joy *and gladness* from the house

1525 **גִּילָה** *gee-lāh'*, f.

Isa. 35: 2. rejoice even with *joy*
65:18. I create Jerusalem *a rejoicing*,

1615 **גִּיר** *geer*, m.

Isa. 27: 9. of the altar as *chalk*stones

1528 **גִּיר** [*geer*], Ch. m.

Dan 5: 5. upon *the plaister* of the wall

1616 **גֵּיר** [*gēhr*], m.

2Ch 2:17(16). And Solomon numbered all *the strangers*
(See also גֵּר)

1487 **גִּישׁ** *geesh.*

Job 7: 5. (כתיב)My flesh is clothed with worms *and clods of* dust;

1530 **גַּל** *gal*, m.

Gen31:46. and made *an heap:* and they did eat there upon *the heap.*
47. but Jacob called it *Gal*eed. (marg. the *heap of* witness)
48. This *heap* (is) a witness between
— was the name of it called *Gal*eed;
51. Laban said to Jacob, Behold this *heap*,
52. This *heap* (be) witness,
— I will not pass over this *heap* to thee, and that thou shalt not pass over this *heap*
Jos. 7:26. raised over him *a* great *heap*
8:29. raise thereon *a* great *heap of* stones,
2Sa.18:17. laid *a* very great *heap of* stones
2K. 19:25. fenced cities (into) ruinous *heaps.*
Job 8:17. His roots are wrapped about *the heap*,
15:28. which are ready *to become heaps.*
38:11. here shall *thy* proud *waves* be (marg. the pride of *thy waves*)
Ps. 42: 7(8). all thy waves *and thy billows*
65: 7(8). the noise of the seas, the noise of *their waves*,
89: 9(10). when *the waves thereof* arise,
107:25. which lifteth up *the waves thereof.*
29. so that *the waves thereof* are still.
Cant.4:12. *a spring* shut up,
Isa. 10:30. O daughter of *Gallim:* (lit. *heaps*)
25: 2. hast made of a city *an heap;*
37:26. defenced cities (into) ruinous *heaps.*
48:18. *as the waves of* the sea:
51:15. *whose waves* roared:
Jer. 5:22. though *the waves thereof* toss
9:11(10). I will make Jerusalem *heaps*,
31:35. when *the waves thereof* roar;
51:37. Babylon shall become *heaps*,
42. with the multitude of *the waves thereof.*
55. when *her waves* do roar
Eze.26: 3. the sea causeth *his waves* to come
Hos 12:11(12). their altars (are) *as heaps*
Jon. 2: 3(4). *and thy waves* passed over
Zec.10:11. shall smite *the waves*

1531 **גֹּל** [*gōhl*], m.

Zec. 4: 2. *with a bowl* upon the top (marg. *her bowl*)

1532 **גַּלָּב** [*gal-lāhv'*], m.

Eze. 5: 1. take thee *a barber*'s razor,

1534 **גַּלְגַּל** *gal-gal'*, m.

Ps. 77:18(19). thy thunder (was) *in the heaven:*
83:13(14). make them *like a wheel*,
Ecc.12: 6. or *the wheel* broken at the
Isa. 5:28. *and their wheels* like a whirlwind:
17:13. *and like a rolling thing* (marg. *thistledown*)
Jer. 47: 3. the rumbling of *his wheels*,
Eze.10: 2. Go in between *the wheels*,
6. Take fire from between *the wheels*,
13. cried unto them in my hearing, *O wheel.*
23:24. wagons, *and wheels*,
26:10. noise of the horsemen, *and of the wheels*,

גַּלְגַּל [*gal-gal'*], Ch. m. 1535

Dan 7: 9. (and) *his wheels* (as) burning fire.

גִּלְגָּל *gil-gāhl'*, m. 1536

Isa. 28:28. *the wheel of* his cart,

גֻּלְגֹּלֶת *gool-gōh'-leth*, f. 1538

Ex. 16:16. an omer *for every man*, (marg. *by the poll*, or, *head*)
38:26. A bekah *for every man*, (marg. *a poll*)
Nu. 1: 2. every male *by their polls;*
18. upward, *by their polls.*
20, 22. the names, *by their polls*,
3:47. five shekels apiece *by the poll*,
Jud. 9:53. all to brake *his scull.*
2K. 9:35. no more of her than *the scull*,
1Ch 10:10. fastened *his head* in the temple
23: 3. their number *by their polls*,
24. number of names *by their polls*,

גֶּלֶד [*geh'-led*], m. 1539

Job 16:15. sewed sackcloth upon *my skin*,

גָּלָה *gāh-lāh'.* 1540

* KAL.—*Preterite.* *

1Sa. 4:21,22. The glory *is departed* from Israel:
9:15. the Lord *had told* Samuel (marg. *revealed*)
20:12. send not unto thee, *and shew it* thee; (marg. *uncover* thine ear)
13. *then I will shew* it thee,
22:17. did not *shew* it to me.
2Sa. 7:27. *hast revealed* to thy servant, (marg. *opened* the ear)
1Ch 17:25. For thou, O my God, *hast told* thy servant (marg. *revealed* the ear)
Pro.27:25. The hay *appeareth*,
Isa. 5:13. my people *are gone into captivity*,
24:11. the mirth of the land *is gone.*
Lam.1: 3. Judah *is gone into captivity*
Eze.12: 3. *and thou shalt remove* from thy place
39:23. Israel *went into captivity*
Hos 10: 5. because *it is departed* from it.
Am. 1: 5. *and* the people of Syria *shall go into captivity*
3: 7. but *he revealeth* his secret
Mic. 1:16. for *they are gone into captivity*

KAL.—*Infinitive.*

Jud.18:30. until the day of *the captivity of*
Jer. 1: 3. *the carrying away of* Jerusalem *captive*
Am. 5: 5. Gilgal shall *surely* go into captivity,
7:11. Israel shall *surely* be led away captive
17. Israel shall *surely* go into captivity

KAL.—*Imperative.*

Eze.12: 3. *and remove* by day

KAL.—*Future.*

Ru. 4: 4. And I thought to *advertise* (marg. *I will reveal* (in) thine ear)
1Sa.20: 2. but that *he will shew* it me: (marg. *uncover* mine ear)
2K. 17:23. *So* was Israel *carried away*
25:21. *So* Judah *was carried away*
Job 20:28. The increase of his house *shall depart*,
33:16. Then *he openeth* the ears (marg. *revealeth* or, *uncovereth*)

Job 36:10. *He openeth also* their ear
15. *and openeth* their ears
Jer. 52:27. *Thus* Judah *was carried away captive*
Am. 5: 5. Gilgal *shall* surely *go into captivity*,
6: 7. now *shall they go captive*
7:11. Israel *shall* surely *be led away captive*
17. Israel *shall* surely *go into captivity*

KAL.—*Participle.* Poel.

1Sa.22: 8. none *that sheweth* me (marg. *uncovereth* mine ear)
— *or sheweth* unto me
2Sa.15:19. thou (art) a stranger, and also *an exile.*
2K. 24:14. ten thousand *captives,*
Pro.20:19. a talebearer *revealeth* secrets:
Isa. 49:21. am desolate, *a captive,*
Am. 6: 7. with the first that *go captive,*

KAL.—*Participle.* Paül.

Nu. 24: 4, 16. *but having* his eyes *open:*
Est. 3:14. *was published* unto all people,
8:13. *published* unto all people, (marg. *revealed*)
Jer. 32:11. and that *which was open:*
14. and this evidence *which is open;*

* NIPHAL.—*Preterite.* *

Gen35: 7. there God *appeared* unto him,
1Sa. 2:27. *Did I* plainly *appear*
3:21. the Lord *revealed himself* to Samuel
14: 8. *and we will discover ourselves*
2Sa. 6:20. who *uncovered himself* to day
Job 38:17. *Have* the gates of death *been opened*
Isa. 22:14. *And it was revealed* in mine ears
23: 1. from the land of Chittim *it is revealed* to
38:12. *and is removed* from me
40: 5. *And* the glory of the Lord *shall be revealed,*
53: 1. to whom *is* the arm of the Lord *revealed?*
Jer. 13:22. of thine iniquity *are* thy skirts *discovered,*
Eze.13:14. *so that* the foundation thereof *shall be discovered,*
23.29. *and* the nakedness of thy whoredoms *shall be discovered,*
Dan 10: 1. a thing *was revealed* unto Daniel,
Hos 7: 1. *then* the iniquity of Ephraim *was discovered,*

NIPHAL.—*Infinitive.*

1Sa. 2:27. Did I *plainly* appear (lit. *appearing* did I appear)
2Sa. 6:20. *as* one of the vain fellows *shamelessly* (marg. or, *openly*) *uncovereth himself!*

[כְּהִגָּלוֹת נִגְלוֹת]

Isa. 56: 1. my righteousness *to be revealed.*
Eze.21:24(29). *in that* your transgressions *are discovered,*

NIPHAL.—*Imperative.*

Isa. 49: 9. that (are) in darkness, *Shew yourselves.*

NIPHAL.—*Future.*

Ex. 20:26. that thy nakedness *be* not *discovered*
1Sa. 3: 7. neither *was* the word of the Lord yet *revealed*
14:11. *And* both of them *discovered*
2Sa.22:16. foundations of the world *were discovered,*
Ps. 18:15(16). *and* the foundations of the world *were discovered*
Pro.26:26. wickedness *shall be shewed*
Isa. 47: 3. Thy nakedness *shall be uncovered,*
Eze.16:36. *and* thy nakedness *discovered* through thy
57. thy wickedness *was discovered,*

NIPHAL.—*Participle.*

Deu29:29(28). *but those* (things which are) *revealed*

* PIEL.—*Preterite.* *

Lev.20:11. *hath uncovered* his father's nakedness:
17. *he hath uncovered* his sister's nakedness;
18. *and shall uncover* her nakedness;
— *she hath uncovered* the fountain
20. *he hath uncovered* his uncle's nakedness:
21. *he hath uncovered* his brother's nakedness;
Deu27:20. *he uncovereth* his father's skirt.
Ru. 3: 4. *and uncover* his feet,
Job 41:13(5). Who *can discover* the face of
Ps. 98: 2. his righteousness *hath he openly shewed* (marg. or, *revealed*)
Isa. 26:21. the earth *also shall disclose*
57: 8. for *thou hast discovered*
Jer. 11:20. unto thee *have I revealed* my cause.
20:12. unto thee *have I opened* my cause.
33: 6. *and will reveal* unto them
49:10. *I have uncovered* his secret places,
Lam. 2:14. *they have* not *discovered*
4:22. *he will discover* thy sins. (marg. or, *he will carry* (thee) *captive* for)
Eze.16:37. *and will discover* thy nakedness
22:10. In thee *have they discovered*
23:10. These *discovered* her nakedness:
Nah. 3: 5. *and I will discover* thy skirts

PIEL.—*Infinitive.*

Lev.18: 6. *to uncover* (their) nakedness:
17, 18, 19. *to uncover* her nakedness;

PIEL.—*Imperative.*

Ps.119:18. *Open* thou mine eyes, (marg. *Reveal*)
Isa. 47: 2. *uncover* thy locks, make bare the leg, *uncover* the thigh,

PIEL.—*Future.*

Lev.18: 7. *shalt thou* not *uncover:*
—, 11, 15. *thou shalt* not *uncover* her nakedness.
8. of thy father's wife *shalt thou* not *uncover:*
9, 10. their nakedness *thou shalt* not *uncover.*
12, 13, 14, 15, 16, 17. *Thou shalt* not *uncover* the nakedness
20:19. *thou shalt* not *uncover* the nakedness
Nu. 22:31. *Then* the Lord *opened* the eyes
Deu22:30(23:1). nor *discover* his father's skirt.
Ru. 3: 7. *and uncovered* his feet,
Job 20:27. The heaven *shall reveal*
Pro.25: 9. *discover* not a secret to another:
Isa. 16: 3. *bewray* not him that wandereth.
22: 8. *And he discovered* the covering
Eze.23:18. *So she discovered* her whoredoms, *and discovered* her nakedness:
Hos. 2:10(12). now *will I discover* her lewdness
Mic. 1: 6. *I will discover* the foundations

PIEL.—*Participle.*

Job 12:22. *He discovereth* deep things
Pro.11:13. A talebearer *revealeth* secrets:

* PUAL.—*Preterite.* *

Nah. 2: 7(8). Huzzab *shall be led away captive*, (marg. *discovered*)

PUAL.—*Participle.*

Pro.27: 5. *Open* rebuke (is) better than secret love.

* HIPHIL.—*Preterite.* *

2K. 17:11. whom the Lord *carried away*
26. The nations which *thou hast removed,*
27. whom *ye brought* from thence;
28. whom *they had carried away*
33. whom *they carried away*
24:14. *And he carried away* all Jerusalem,
25:11. *did* Nebuzar-adan the captain of the guard *carry away.*
1Ch 5: 6. Tilgath-Pilneser king of Assyria *carried away*
8: 7. *he removed them,* and begat
Ezr. 2: 1. the king of Babylon *had carried away*
Neh 7: 6. the king of Babylon *had carried away,*
Est. 2: 6. the king of Babylon *had carried away.*
Jer.20; 4. *and he shall carry them captive* into
22:12. *they have led* him *captive,*
29: 1. Nebuchadnezzar *had carried away*
4. whom I *have caused to be carried away*
7. *I have caused* you *to be carried away captives,*
14. *I caused* you *to be carried away captive.*
39: 9 & 52:15, 30. the guard *carried away captive*
52:28. Nebuchadrezzar *carried away captive:*
29. *he carried away captive* from Jerusalem
Am. 5:27. *Therefore will I cause* you *to go into captivity*

Note.—הָגְלָה Jer. 52:29. is omitted in many copies.

HIPHIL.—*Infinitive.*

1Ch 6:15(5:41). *when* the Lord *carried away* Judah

Jer. 24: 1. *had carried away captive* Jeconiah
27:20. *when he carried away captive* Jeconiah
43: 3. *and carry* us *away captives*
Lam.4:22. *carry thee away into captivity:*
Eze.39:28. *which caused* them *to be led into captivity* (marg. *by my causing of*)
Am. 1: 6. because *they carried away captive*

HIPHIL.—*Future.*

2K. 15:29. *and carried them captive* to Assyria.
16: 9. *and carried* (the people of) *it captive*
17: 6. *and carried* Israel *away*
18:11. *And* the king of Assyria *did carry away*
24:15. *And he carried away* Jehoiachin
1Ch 5:26. of Assyria, *and he carried them away,*
8: 6. *and they removed them* to Manahath:
2Ch 36:20. *And* them that had escaped from the sword *carried he away* to Babylon;

* HOPHAL.—*Preterite.* *

1Ch 9: 1. *were carried away* to Babylon
Est. 2: 6. Who *had been carried away*
— the captivity which *had been carried away*
Jer. 13:19. Judah *shall be carried away captive* all of it, *it shall be* wholly *carried away captive.*
40: 7. that *were* not *carried away captive*

HOPHAL.—*Participle.*

Jer. 40: 1. *which were carried away captive*

* HITHPAEL.—*Infinitive.* *

Pro.18: 2. *that* his heart *may discover itself.*

HITHPAEL.—*Future.*

Gen 9:21. *and he was uncovered* within his tent.

1541 גְּלָה [*g'lāh*], Ch.

* P'AL.—*Infinitive.* *

Dan 2:47. seeing thou couldest *reveal* this

P'AL.—*Participle. Active.*

Dan 2:22. He *revealeth* the deep and secret
28. there is a God in heaven *that revealeth*
29. *and he that revealeth* secrets
47. *and a revealer* of secrets,

P'AL.—*Participle. Passive.*

Dan 2:19. Then *was* the secret *revealed*
30. *is* not *revealed* to me for (any) wisdom

* APHEL.—*Preterite.* *

Ezr. 4:10. Asnapper *brought over,* and set in the cities
5:12. and *carried* the people *away* into Babylon.

See 1473 גּוֹלָה see גֹּלָה

1543 גֻּלָּה *gool-lāh'*, f.

Jos. 15:19. give me also *springs of* water. And he gave her *the* upper *springs,* and *the* nether *springs.*
Jud. 1:15. give me also *springs of* water. And Caleb gave her *the* upper *springs* and *the* nether *springs.*
1K. 7:41. *and the* (two) *bowls*
—, 42. to cover *the* two *bowls of*
2Ch 4:12. *and the pommels,*
—, 13. to cover *the* two *pommels of*
Ecc.12: 6. or the golden *bowl* be broken,
Zec. 4: 3. upon the right (side) of *the bowl,*

1544 גִּלּוּלִים *gil-loo-leem'*, m. pl.

Lev.26:30. upon the carcases of *your idols,*
Deu 29:17(16). *their idols,* wood (marg. *dungy gods*)
1K. 15:12. removed all *the idols*
21:26. abominably in following *idols,*
2K. 17:12. For they served *idols,*
21:11. Judah also to sin *with his idols:*
21. served *the idols* that his father
23:24. the images, and *the idols,*
Jer. 50: 2. *her images* are broken in pieces.
Eze. 6: 4. your slain (men) before *your idols.*
5. children of Israel before *their idols;*
6. *your idols* may be broken
9. go a whoring after *their idols:*
13. shall be among *their idols*
— offer sweet savour to all *their idols.*
8:10. *the idols of* the house of Israel,
14: 3. these men have set up *their idols*
4. that setteth up *his idols*
— the multitude of *his idols;*
5. estranged from me *through their idols.*
6. turn (yourselves) from *your idols;*
7. setteth up *his idols* in his heart,
16:36. with all *the idols of* thy abominations,
18: 6, 15. to *the idols of* the house of Israel,
12. hath lifted up his eyes to *the idols,*
20: 7. *and* defile not yourselves *with the idols of* Egypt:
8. did they forsake *the idols of* Egypt:
16. their heart went after *their idols.*
18. *nor* defile yourselves *with their idols:*
24. their eyes were after their fathers' *idols.*
31. yourselves with all *your idols,*
39. serve ye every one *his idols,*
— with your gifts, *and with your idols.*
22: 3. maketh *idols* against herself
4. *and* hast defiled thyself *in thine idols*
23: 7. with all *their idols* she defiled
30. thou art polluted *with their idols.*
37. with *their idols* have they
39. slain their children *to their idols,*
49. bear the sins of *your idols:*
30:13. I will also destroy *the idols,*
33:25. lift up your eyes toward *your idols,*
36:18. upon the land, *and for their idols*
25. from all *your idols,*
37:23. any more *with their idols,*
44:10. from me after *their idols;*
12. ministered unto them before *their idols,*

גְּלוֹם [*g'lōhm*], m. 1545

Eze.27:24. *in* blue *clothes,* and broidered work, (marg. *foldings*)

גָּלוּת *gāh-looth'*, f. 1546

2K. 25:27. thirtieth year *of the captivity of*
Isa. 20: 4. *the* Ethiopians *captives,*
45:13. *and* he shall let go *my captives,*
Jer. 24: 5. *them that are carried away captive of* Judah, (marg. *the captivity*)
28: 4. with all *the captives of* Judah, (marg. *captivity*)
29:22. a curse by all *the captivity of*
40: 1. all *that were carried away captive of*
52:31. thirtieth year *of the captivity of* Jehoiachin
Eze. 1: 2. the fifth year *of* king Jehoiachin's *captivity,*
33:21. the twelfth year *of our captivity,*
40: 1. twentieth year *of our captivity,*
Am. 1: 6. carried away captive *the* whole *captivity,*
9. delivered up *the* whole *captivity*
Obad. 20. *And the captivity of* this host
— *and the captivity of* Jerusalem,

גָּלוּת [*gāh-looth'*], Ch. f. 1547

Ezr. 6:16. the rest of the children of *the captivity,* (marg. sons of *the transportation*)
Dan. 2:25. a man of the captives of Judah, (marg. children of *the captivity*)
5:13. which (art) of the children of *the captivity*
6:13(14). which (is) of the children of *the captivity*

גָּלַח [*gāh-lagh'*]. 1548

* PIEL.—*Preterite.* *

Lev. 14: 8. *and shave off* all his hair,
Nu. 6 9. *then he shall shave* his head
18. *And* the Nazarite *shall shave*

Deu 21:12. *and she shall shave* her head,
2Sa. 14:26. heavy on him, *therefore he polled it:*

PIEL.—*Infinitive.*

2Sa. 14:26. *And when he polled* his head,

PIEL.—*Future.*

Gen41:14. *and he shaved* (himself),
Lev. 13:33. the scall *shall he* not *shave;*
14: 9. *that he shall shave* all his hair
— even all his hair *he shall shave off:*
21: 5. neither *shall they shave off*
Nu. 6: 9. on the seventh day *shall he shave it.*
Jud. 16:19. *and she caused* him *to shave off*
2Sa. 10: 4. *and shaved off* the one half
14:26. at every year's end that *he polled* (it):
1Ch 19: 4. *and shaved them,* and cut off
Isa. 7:20. *shave* with a razor that is hired,
Eze. 44:20. Neither *shall they shave*

* PUAL.—*Preterite.* *

Jud. 16:17. if *I be shaven,* then my strength
22. after *he was shaven.*

PUAL.—*Participle.*

Jer. 41: 5. *having* their beards *shaven,*

* HITHPAEL.—*Preterite.* *

Lev. 13:33. *He shall be shaven,* but the scall

HITHPAEL.—*Infinitive.*

Nu. 6:19. after (the hair of) his separation *is shaven:*

1549 גִּלָּיוֹן *gil-lāh-yōhn',* m.

Isa. 3:23. *The glasses,* and the fine linen,
8: 1. Take thee *a* great *roll,*

1550 גָּלִיל [*gāh-leel'*], adj.

1K. 6:34. leaves of the one door (were) *folding,*
— the other door (were) *folding.*
Est. 1: 6. to silver *rings* and pillars of marble:
Cant. 5:14. His hands (are as) gold *rings*

1552 גְּלִילָה *g'lee-lāh',* f.

Jos. 13: 2. all *the borders of* the Philistines,
22:10. came unto *the borders of* Jordan,
11. in *the borders of* Jordan,
Eze. 47: 8. issue out toward *the* east *country,*
Joel 3: 4(4:4). all *the coasts of* Palestine?

1556 גָּלַל [*gāh-lal'*].

* KAL.—*Preterite.* *

Gen29: 3. *and they rolled* the stone
8. *and* (till) *they roll* the stone
Jos. 5: 9. This day *have I rolled away*

KAL.—*Infinitive.*

Ps. 22: 8(9). *He trusted* on the Lord (marg. *He rolled* himself)

KAL.—*Imperative.*

Jos. 10:18. *Roll* great stones upon the
1Sa. 14:33. *roll* a great stone unto me
Ps. 37: 5. *Commit* thy way unto the Lord; (marg. *Roll*)
119:22. *Remove* from me reproach and contempt;
Pro. 16: 3. *Commit* thy works unto the Lord, (marg. *Roll*)

KAL.—*Participle.* Poel.

Pro. 26:27. *and he that rolleth* a stone,

* NIPHAL.—*Preterite.* *

Isa. 34: 4. *and* the heavens *shall be rolled together*

NIPHAL.—*Future.*

Am. 5:24. *But let* judgment *run down* (marg. *roll*)

* POAL.—*Participle.* *

Isa. 9: 5(4). and garments *rolled* in blood;

* HIPHIL.—*Future.* *

Gen29:10. *and rolled* the stone from

* HITHPOEL.—*Infinitive.* *

Gen43:18. *that he may seek occasion* against us, (marg. *roll himself* upon us)

HITHPOEL.—*Participle.*

2Sa. 20:12. Amasa *wallowed* in blood

* PILPEL.—*Preterite.* *

Jer. 51:25. *and roll thee down* from the rocks,

* HITHPALPEL.—*Preterite.* *

Job 30:14. in the desolation *they rolled themselves*

גָּלָל *gāh-lāhl',* m. 1557

1K. 14:10. as a man taketh away *dung,*

גָּלָל *gāh-lāhl',* m. 1558

Gen12:13. my soul shall live *because of thee.*
30:27. hath blessed me *for thy sake.*
39: 5. Egyptian's house *for* Joseph's *sake;*
Deu. 1:37. angry with me *for your sakes,*
15:10. *because that for* this thing
18:12. *and because of* these abominations
1K. 14:16. *because of* the sins of Jeroboam,
Jer. 11:17. *for* the evil of the house of Israel
15: 4. *because of* Manasseh the son of
Mic. 3:12. shall Zion *for your sake* be plowed

גְּלָל *g'lāhl,* Ch. m. 1560

Ezr. 5: 8. which is builded with *great* stones, (marg. stones of *rolling*)
6: 4. (With) three rows of *great* stones,

גֵּלֶל [*gēh'-lel*], m. 1561

Job 20: 7. for ever *like his own dung:*
Eze. 4:12. thou shalt bake it *with dung*
15. cow's dung for man's *dung,*
Zep. 1:17. and their flesh *as the dung.*

גָּלַם [*gāh-lam'*]. 1563

* KAL.—*Future.* *

2K. 2: 8. *and wrapped* (it) *together,* and smote

גֹּלֶם [*gōh'-lem*], m. 1564

Ps. 139:16. did see *my substance, yet being unperfect;*

גַּלְמוּד *gal-mood',* adj. 1565

Job 3: 7. let that night be *solitary,*
15:34. of hypocrites (shall be) *desolate,*
30: 3. want and famine (they were) *solitary;* (marg. or, *dark as the night*)
Isa. 49:21. *and* am *desolate,* a captive,

גָּלַע [*gāh-lag'*]. 1566

* HITHPAEL.—*Preterite.* *

Pro. 17:14. before *it be meddled with.*

HITHPAEL.—*Future.*

Pro. 18: 1. *intermeddleth* with all wisdom.
20: 3. every fool *will be meddling.*

גָּלַשׁ [*gāh-lash'*]. 1570

* KAL.—*Preterite.* *

Cant. 4: 1 & 6:5. a flock of goats, *that appear* (marg. or, *that eat of*)

גַּם *gam*, part conj.

Gen. 3: 6. and gave *also* unto her husband
20: 5. and she, *even* she herself said,
6. *Yea*, I know that thou didst this
24:25. We have *both* straw *and* provender enough, *and* room to lodge in.
32:19(20). And *so* commanded he the second, *and* the third, *and* all
20(21). And say ye *moreover*, Behold,
44:16. we (are) my lord's servants, *both* we, *and* (he) *also* with whom the cup is found.
Lev.26:24. and will punish you *yet* seven times
44. And yet *for all* that, when they be
Deu12:30. even so will I do *likewise*.
1Sa.12:16. Now *therefore* stand and see
19:24. he stripped off his clothes *also*, and prophesied before Samuel *in like manner*,
2Sa.17:12. there shall not be left *so much as* one.
13. there be not *one* small stone found
1Ch 11: 2. *And moreover* in time past, (marg. *both* yesterday *and* the third day)
2Ch 20:13. stood before the Lord, *with* their little ones,
Neh. 5:15. *yea, even* their servants bare rule
6: 1. *though* at that time I had not set
13:26. *nevertheless even* him did outlandish
Job 2:10. *What?* shall we receive good
12: 3. *But* I have understanding as well as you;
Pro.20:10. both of them (are) *alike* abomination
Ecc. 4:11. *Again*, if two lie together, then they have heat:
9: 1. no man knoweth *either* love *or* hatred (by) all (that is) before them.
Isa. 66: 8. for *as soon* as Zion travailed, she brought forth
Jer. 6:15. *nay*, they were not at all ashamed, *neither* could they blush:
33:26. *Then* will I cast away the seed of Jacob,
51:49. *As* Babylon (hath caused) the slain of Israel to fall, *so* at Babylon shall fall the slain
&c. &c.

It occurs with prefixes וְגַם & הֲגַם; and also the following: שֶׁגַּם.

Ecc. 1:17. I perceived *that* this *also* is vexation
2:15 & 8:14. *that* this *also* (is) vanity.

And (perhaps) בְּשַׁגָּם.

Gen. 6: 3. *for that he also* (is) flesh:

1572 ## גָּמָא [*gāh-māh'*,].

∗ PIEL.—*Future.* ∗

Job 39:24. *He swalloweth* the ground

∗ HIPHIL.—*Imperative.* ∗

Gen24:17. *Let me*, I pray thee, *drink* a little

1573 ## גֹּמֶא *gōh'-meh*, m.

Ex. 2: 3. took for him an ark of *bulrushes*,
Job 8:11. Can *the rush* grow up
Isa. 18: 2. even in vessels of *bulrushes*
35: 7. with reeds *and rushes*.

1574 ## גֹּמֶד *gōh'-med*, m.

Jud. 3:16. of *a cubit* length;

1575 ## גַּמָּדִים *gam-māh-deem'*, m. pl.

Eze.27:11. *and the Gammadims* (lit. probably *warriors*)

1576 ## גְּמוּל *g'mool*, m.

Jud. 9:16. *according to the deserving of* his hands;
2Ch 32:25. *according to the benefit* (done) unto him;
Ps. 28: 4. render to them *their desert*.
94: 2. render *a reward* to the proud.
103: 2. forget not all *his benefits:*
137: 8. as thou hast served us. (marg. *thy deed* which thou didst to us)
Pro.12:14. *and the recompence of* a man's
19:17. *and that which he hath given* (marg. or, *his deed*)
Isa. 3:11. for *the reward of* his hands
35: 4. God (with) *a recompence;*
59:18. *recompence* to his enemies; to the islands he will repay *recompence*.
66: 6. the Lord that rendereth *recompence*
Jer. 51: 6. render unto her *a recompence*.
Lam. 3:64. Render unto them *a recompence*,
Joel 3: 4(4:4) will ye render me *a recompence?*
—(-:-) will I return *your recompence*
7(4:7). will return *your recompence*
Obad. 15. *thy reward* shall return

גְּמוּלָה *g'moo-lāh'*, f. 1578

2Sa.19:36(37). with *such a reward?*
Isa. 59:18. According to (their) *deeds*, (marg. *recompences*)
Jer. 51:56. the Lord God of *recompences*

גָּמַל *gāh-mal'*. 1580

∗ KAL.—*Preterite.* ∗

Gen50:15. which *we did* unto him.
17. for *they did unto thee* evil:
1Sa. 1:24. And when *she had weaned him*,
24:17(18). for thou *hast rewarded me* good, whereas I *have rewarded thee* evil.
Ps. 7: 4(5). If *I have rewarded* evil
13: 6. *he hath dealt bountifully* with me.
103:10. nor *rewarded* us according
116: 7. the Lord *hath dealt bountifully*
137: 8. as thou hast served us. (marg. thy deed *which thou didst* to us)
Pro. 3:30. if *he have done thee* no harm.
31:12. *She will do him* good
Isa. 3: 9. *they have rewarded* evil
63: 7. that the Lord *hath bestowed on us*,
— which *he hath bestowed on them* according

KAL.—*Infinitive.*

1Sa. 1:23. until *thou have weaned* him;
— until *she weaned* him.

KAL.—*Imperative.*

Ps.119:17. *Deal bountifully* with thy

KAL.—*Future.*

Nu. 17: 8(23). *and yielded* almonds.
Deu32: 6. *Do ye* thus *requite* the Lord,
2Sa.19:36(37). should the king *recompense it me*
22:21. The Lord *rewarded me*
1K. 11:20. *whom* Tahpenes *weaned*
Ps. 18:20(21). The Lord *rewarded me* according to
142: 7(8). *thou shalt deal bountifully* with
Hos 1: 8. Now *when she had weaned*

KAL.—*Participle.* Poel.

2Ch 20:11. Behold, (I say, how) *they reward* us,
Pro.11:17. The merciful man *doeth good*
Isa. 18: 5. the sour grape *is ripening*
Joel 3: 4(4:4). and if ye *recompense* me,

KAL.—*Participle.* Paül.

Ps.131: 2. *as a child that is weaned* of his mother: my soul (is) even *as a weaned child*.
Isa. 11: 8. *the weaned child* shall put
28: 9. *weaned* from the milk,

∗ NIPHAL.—*Infinitive.* ∗

Gen21: 8. that Isaac *was weaned*.

NIPHAL.—*Future.*

Gen21: 8. the child grew, *and was weaned:*
1Sa. 1:22. until the child *be weaned,*

1581 גָּמָל *gāh-māhl'*, com.

Gen12:16. she asses, *and camels.*
24:10. the servant took ten *camels of the camels of*
11. he made his *camels* to kneel
14. I will give *thy camels* drink
19. draw (water) *for thy camels* also,
20. drew for all *his camels.*
22. as *the camels* had done drinking,
30. he stood by *the camels* at the well.
31. and room *for the camels.*
32. and he ungirded (his) *camels,*
— provender *for the camels,*
35. *and camels,* and asses.
44. I will also draw *for thy camels:*
46. I will give *thy camels* drink
— and she made *the camels* drink
61. they rode upon *the camels,*
63. behold, *the camels* (were) coming.
64. she lighted off *the camel.*
30:43. menservants, *and camels,*
31:17. set his sons and his wives upon *camels;*
34. put them in *the camel's* furniture,
32: 7(8). *and the camels,* into two bands;
15(16). Thirty milch *camels*
37:25. came from Gilead *with their camels*
Ex. 9: 3. upon the asses, *upon the camels,*
Lev.11: 4. *the camel,* because he cheweth
Deu14: 7. *the camel,* and the hare,
Jud. 6: 5. both they *and their camels*
7:12. *and their camels* (were) without
8:21. that (were) on *their camels'* necks.
26. that (were) about *their camels'* necks.
1Sa.15: 3. ox and sheep, *camel* and ass.
27: 9. the asses, *and the camels,*
30:17. which rode upon *camels,*
1K. 10: 2. with *camels* that bare spices,
2K. 8: 9. of Damascus, forty *camels'* burden,
1Ch 5:21. of *their camels* fifty thousand,
12:40. bread on asses, *and on camels,*
27:30. Over *the camels* also (was) Obil
2Ch 9: 1. *and camels* that bare spices,
14:15(14). carried away sheep *and camels*
Ezr. 2:67. *Their camels,* four hundred
Neh 7:69. *camels,* four hundred thirty
Job 1: 3. three thousand *camels,*
17. fell upon *the camels,*
42:12. six thousand *camels,*
Isa. 21: 7. a chariot of *camels;*
30: 6. upon the bunches of *camels,*
60: 6. The multitude of *camels*
Jer. 49:29. and all their vessels, *and their camels;*
32. *And their camels* shall be a booty,
Eze.25: 5. make Rabbah a stable for *camels,*
Zec.14:15. of the mule, of *the camel,*

1584 גָּמַר *gāh-mar'.*

* KAL.—*Preterite.* *

Ps. 12: 1(2). for the godly man *ceaseth;*
77: 8(9). *doth* (his) promise *fail*

KAL.—*Future.*

Ps. 7: 9(10). *let* the wickedness of the wicked *come to an end;*
138: 8. The Lord *will perfect*

KAL.—*Participle.* Poel.

Ps. 57: 2(3). *that performeth* (all things) for me.

1585 גְּמַר [*g'mar*], Ch.

* P'AL.—*Participle.* Passive. *

Ezr. 7:12. a scribe of the law of the God of heaven, *perfect* (peace), (marg. or, a *perfect* scribe, &c.)

1588 גַּן *gan,* com.

Gen 2: 8. the Lord God planted *a garden*
9. in the midst of *the garden,*
10. out of Eden to water *the garden;*
15. put him into *the garden of*
16 & 3:1. Of every tree of *the garden*
3: 2. the fruit of the trees of *the garden:*
3. which (is) in the midst of *the garden,*
8. the Lord God walking *in the garden*
— amongst the trees of *the garden.*
10. I heard thy voice *in the garden,*
23. sent him forth *from the garden of*
24. at the east *of the garden of* Eden
13:10. *as the garden of* the Lord,
Deu 11:10. *as a garden of* herbs:
1K. 21: 2. that I may have it *for a garden of*
2K. 9:27. he fled by the way of *the garden* house.
21:18. was buried *in the garden of* his
—, 26. *in the garden of* Uzza:
25: 4. which (is) by the king's *garden:*
Neh 3:15. *by* the king's *garden,*
Cant.4:12. *A garden* inclosed (is) my sister,
15. A fountain of *gardens,*
16. blow upon *my garden,*
— come *into his garden,*
5: 1. I am come *into my garden,*
6: 2. is gone down *into his garden,*
— to feed *in the gardens,*
8:13. Thou that dwellest *in the gardens,*
Isa. 51: 3. her desert *like the garden of*
58:11. thou shalt be *like a* watered *garden,*
Jer. 31:12. shall *be as a* watered *garden;*
39: 4. by the way of the king's *garden,*
52: 7. which (was) by the king's *garden;*
Lam.2: 6. *as* (if it were of) *a garden:*
Eze.28:13. Thou hast been in Eden *the garden of*
31: 8. The cedars *in the garden of* God
— nor any tree *in the garden of* God
9. that (were) *in the garden of* God,
36:35. is become *like the garden of* Eden;
Joel 2: 3. the land (is) *as the garden of* Eden

גָּנַב [*gāh-nav'*]. 1589

* KAL.—*Preterite.* *

Gen31:30. wherefore *hast thou stolen*
32. that Rachel *had stolen them.*
Jos. 7:11. and *have* also *stolen,*
2Sa.19:41(42). *have* our brethren the men of Judah *stolen thee away,*
21:12. which *had stolen* them
Job 21:18. *that* the storm *carrieth away.* (marg. *stealeth away*)
27:20. a tempest *stealeth him away*
Pro.30: 9. or lest I be poor, *and steal,*

KAL.—*Infinitive.*

Ex. 22:12(11). if it be stolen from him, (lit. *stealing* it be stolen)
Jer. 7: 9. *Will ye steal,* murder, and commit
Hos 4: 2. killing, *and stealing,*

KAL.—*Future.*

Gen31:19. *and* Rachel *had stolen*
20. *And* Jacob *stole away* unawares
26. *that thou hast stolen away*
27. *and steal away* from me; (marg. *hast stolen* me)
44: 8. how then *should we steal*
Ex. 20:15. *Thou shalt* not *steal.*
22: 1(21:37). If a man *shall steal* an ox,
Lev.19:11. *Ye shall* not *steal,*
Deu 5:19(17). Neither *shalt thou steal.*
2K. 11: 2. *and stole* him from among
2Ch 22:11. *and stole* him from among
Pro. 6:30. if *he steal* to satisfy his soul
Obad. 5. *would they* not *have stolen*

KAL.—*Participle.* Poel.

Ex. 21:16. *And he that stealeth* a man,
Deu24: 7. If a man be found *stealing*
Zec. 5: 3. every one *that stealeth*

KAL.—*Participle.* Paül.

Gen30:33. that shall be counted *stolen*
31:39. (whether) *stolen* by day, *or stolen* by night.
Pro. 9:17. *Stolen* waters are sweet,

* NIPHAL.—*Future.* *

Ex. 22:12(11). if *it be stolen* from him,

* PIEL.—*Future.* *

2Sa.15: 6. *so* Absalom *stole* the hearts

PIEL.—*Participle.*

Jer. 23:30. *that steal* my words

* PUAL.—*Preterite.* *

Gen40:15. For indeed *I was stolen away*
Ex. 22: 7(6). *and it be stolen* out of

PUAL.—*Infinitive.*

Gen40:15. For *indeed* I was stolen away (lit. *being stolen* I was stolen)

PUAL.—*Future.*

Job 4:12. a thing *was secretly brought* (marg. *by stealth*)

* HITHPAEL.—*Future.* *

2Sa.19: 3(4). *And* the people gat them *by stealth*
—(-). being ashamed *steal away*

1590 ## גַּנָּב *gan-nāhv'*, m.

Ex. 22: 2(1). If *a thief* be found breaking
7(6). if *the thief* be found,
8(7). If *the thief* be not found,
Deu24: 7. then that *thief* shall die;
Job 24:14. in the night is *as a thief.*
30: 5. cried after them *as* (after) *a thief;*
Ps. 50:18. When thou sawest *a thief,*
Pro. 6:30. (Men) do not despise *a thief,*
29:24. Whoso is partner with *a thief*
Isa. 1:23. companions of *thieves:*
Jer. 2:26. As *the thief* is ashamed when he
48:27. was he found *among thieves?*
49: 9. if *thieves* by night,
Hos. 7: 1. *and the thief* cometh in,
Joel 2: 9. in at the windows *like a thief.*
Obad. 5. If *thieves* came to thee,
Zec. 5: 4. enter into the house of *the thief,*

1591 ## גְּנֵבָה *g'nēh-vāh*, f.

Ex. 22: 3(2). he shall be sold *for his theft.*
4(3). If *the theft* be certainly found

1593 ## גַּנָּה *gan-nāh'*, f.

Nu. 24: 6. *as gardens* by the river's side,
Job 8:16. his branch shooteth forth in *his garden.*
Ecc. 2: 5. I made me *gardens* and orchards,
Isa. 1:29. *for the gardens* that ye have
30. *and as a garden* that hath no water.
61:11. *and as the garden* causeth the things
65: 3. that sacrificeth *in gardens,*
66:17. in *the gardens* behind one
Jer. 29: 5,28. plant *gardens,* and eat the fruit
Am. 4: 9. when *your gardens* and your vineyards
9:14. they shall also make *gardens,*

1594 ## גִּנָּה [*gin-nāh'*], f.

Est. 1: 5. in the court of *the garden of*
7: 7. into the palace *garden:*
8. returned *out of* the palace *garden*
Cant.6:11. I went down into *the garden of* nuts

1595 ## גְּנָזִים [*g'nāh-zeem'*], m. pl.

Est. 3: 9. bring (it) into the king's *treasuries.*
4: 7. to pay to the king's *treasuries*
Eze.27:24. *and in chests of* rich apparel,

1596 ## גִּנְזִין [*gin-zeen'*], Ch. m. pl.

Ezr. 5:17. search made in the king's *treasure* house,
Ezr. 6: 1. where *the treasures* were laid up
7:20. bestow (it) out of the king's *treasure* house.

גַּנְזַךְ [*gan-zach'*], m. 1597

1Ch 28:11. *and of the treasuries thereof,*

גָּנַן [*gāh-nan'*]. 1598

* KAL.—*Preterite.* *

2K. 19:34. *For I will defend* this city,
20: 6. *and I will defend* this city
Isa. 37:35. *For I will defend* this city
38: 6. *and I will defend* this city.

KAL.—*Infinitive.*

Isa. 31: 5. *defending* also he will deliver

* HIPHIL.—*Future.* *

Isa. 31: 5. so *will* the Lord of hosts *defend*
Zec. 9:15. The Lord of hosts *shall defend*
12: 8. In that day *shall* the Lord *defend*

גָּעָה [*gāh-ngāh'*]. 1600

* KAL.—*Infinitive.* *

1Sa. 6:12. *lowing* as they went,

KAL.—*Future.*

Job 6: 5. *loweth* the ox over his fodder?

גָּעַל [*gāh-ngal'*]. 1602

* KAL.—*Preterite.* *

Lev.26:30. *and* my soul *shall abhor* you.
43. their soul *abhorred* my statutes.
44. neither *will I abhor them,*
Jer. 14:19. *hath* thy soul *lothed* Zion?
Eze.16:45. which *lothed* their husbands

KAL.—*Future.*

Lev.26:11. my soul *shall* not *abhor* you.
15. if your soul *abhor* my judgments,

KAL.—*Participle.* Poel.

Eze.16:45. *that lotheth* her husband

* NIPHAL.—*Preterite.* *

2Sa. 1:21. the mighty *is vilely cast away,*

* HIPHIL.—*Future.* *

Job 21:10. Their bull gendereth, and *faileth* not;

גֹּעַל *gōh'-ngal*, m. 1604

Eze.16: 5. *to the lothing of* thy person,

גָּעַר *gāh-ngar'*. 1605

* KAL.—*Preterite.* *

Ps. 9: 5(6). *Thou hast rebuked* the heathen,
119:21. *Thou hast rebuked* the proud
Isa. 17:13. *but* (God) *shall rebuke* them,
Jer. 29:27. why *hast thou* not *reproved*
Mal. 3:11. *And I will rebuke* the devourer

KAL.—*Infinitive.*

Isa. 54. 9. *nor rebuke* thee.

KAL.—*Imperative.*

Ps. 68:30(31). *Rebuke* the company of spearmen,

KAL.—*Future.*

Gen37:10. *and* his father *rebuked* him,
Ru. 2:16. and *rebuke* her not.
Ps.106: 9. *He rebuked* the Red sea *also,*
Zec. 3: 2. The Lord *rebuke* thee, O Satan; *even* the Lord that hath chosen Jerusalem *rebuke* thee:

KAL.—*Participle.* Poel.

Nah. 1: 4. *He rebuketh* the sea,
Mal. 2: 3. I *will corrupt* your seed, (marg. *reprove*)

1606 **גְּעָרָה** *g'^{n}gāh-rāh'*, f.

2Sa.22:16. *at the rebuking of* the Lord,
Job 26:11. are astonished *at his reproof.*
Ps. 18:15(16). were discovered *at thy rebuke,*
76: 6(7). *At thy rebuke,* O God of Jacob,
80:16(17). *at the rebuke of* thy countenance.
104: 7. At *thy rebuke* they fled;
Pro.13: 1. a scorner heareth not *rebuke.*
8. the poor heareth not *rebuke.*
17:10. *A reproof* entereth more into
Ecc. 7: 5. better to hear *the rebuke of* the wise,
Isa. 30:17. at *the rebuke of* one; at *the rebuke of* five shall ye flee:
50: 2. *at my rebuke* I dry up the sea,
51:20. *the rebuke of* thy God.
66:15. *and his rebuke* with flames

1607 **גָּעַשׁ** [*gāh-^{n}gash'*].

* KAL.—*Future.* *

2Sa.22: 8. (כתיב) *Then* the earth *shook*
Ps. 18: 7(8). *Then* the earth *shook*

* PUAL.—*Future.* *

Job 34:20. the people *shall be troubled*

* HITHPAEL.—*Future.* *

2Sa.22: 8. *Then* the earth *shook*
— heaven moved *and shook,*
Ps. 18: 7(8). the hills moved *and were shaken,*
Jer. 5:22. *and* though the waves thereof *toss themselves,*
46: 7. whose waters *are moved*

* HITHPOEL.—*Preterite.* *

Jer. 25:16. they shall drink, *and be moved,*

HITHPOEL.—*Future.*

Jer. 46: 8. waters *are moved* like the rivers;

1610 **גַּף** [*gaph*], m.

Ex. 21: 3. If he came in *by himself* (marg. *with his body*), he shall go out *by himself:*
4. he shall go out *by himself.*
Pro. 9: 3. upon the highest places (lit. *pinnacles of* the high places)

1611 **גַּף** [*gaph*], Ch. m.

Dan 7: 4. like a lion, *and* had eagle's *wings:* I beheld till *the wings thereof*
6. upon the back of it four *wings* of a fowl;

1612 **גֶּפֶן** *geh'-phen*, m.

Gen40: 9. behold, *a vine* (was) before me;
10. *And in the vine* (were) three
49:11. Binding his foal *unto the vine,*
Nu. 6: 4. that is made *of* the vine *tree,* (marg. *vine of* the wine)
20: 5. or of figs, *or* of *vines,*
Deu. 8: 8. wheat, and barley, *and vines,*
32:32. For *their vine* (is) *of the vine of* Sodom,
Jud. 9:12. Then said the trees *unto the vine,*
13. *the vine* said unto them,
13:14. any (thing) that cometh *of the vine,*
1K. 4:25(5:5). every man under *his vine*
2K. 4:39. found *a* wild *vine,*
18:31. eat ye every man of *his own vine,*
Job 15:33. his unripe grape *as the vine,*
Ps. 78:47. He destroyed *their vines*
80: 8(9). Thou hast brought *a vine* out
14(15). behold, and visit this *vine;*
105:33. He smote *their vines* also
128: 3. Thy wife (shall be) *as a* fruitful *vine*
Cant.2:13. *and the vines* (with) the
6:11. to see whether *the vine* flourished,
Cant.7: 8(9). shall be as clusters of *the vine,*
12(13). see if *the vine* flourish,
Isa. 7:23. where there were a thousand *vines*
16: 8, 9. *the vine of* Sibmah:
24: 7. *the vine* languisheth,
32:12. for *the* fruitful *vine.*
34: 4. as the leaf falleth off *from the vine,*
36:16. eat ye every one of *his vine,*
Jer. 2:21. the degenerate plant of *a* strange *vine*
5:17. they shall eat up *thy vines*
6: 9. the remnant of Israel *as a vine:*
8:13. no grapes *on the vine,*
48:32. *O vine of* Sibmah,
Eze.15: 2. What is *the vine* tree more
6. As *the vine* tree among the
17: 6. became *a* spreading *vine*
— so it became *a vine,*
7. this *vine* did bend her roots
8. that it might be *a* goodly *vine.*
19:10. Thy mother (is) *like a vine*
Hos. 2:12(14). I will destroy *her vines* and her fig
10: 1. Israel (is) *an* empty *vine,*
14: 7(8). grow *as the vine:*
Joel 1: 7. He hath laid *my vine* waste,
12. *The vine* is dried up,
2:22. the fig tree *and the vine*
Mic. 4: 4. sit every man under *his vine*
Hab. 3:17. neither (shall) fruit (be) *in the vines;*
Hag. 2:19. yea, as yet *the vine,*
Zec. 3:10. under *the vine* and under the fig tree.
8:12. *the vine* shall give her fruit,
Mal. 3:11. neither shall your *vine* cast

גֹּפֶר *gōh-pher.* 1613

Gen. 6:14. Make thee an ark of *gopher* wood;

גָּפְרִית *goph-reeth'*, f. 1614

Gen19:24. Sodom and upon Gomorrah *brimstone*
Deu29:23(22). the whole land thereof (is) *brimstone,*
Job 18:15. *brimstone* shall be scattered
Ps. 11: 6. rain snares, fire *and brimstone,*
Isa. 30:33. like a stream of *brimstone,*
34: 9. the dust thereof *into brimstone,*
Eze.38:22. fire, *and brimstone.*

גָּר see **גּוּר** See 1481

גֵּר *gēhr*, m. 1616

Gen15:13. shall be *a stranger* in a land
23: 4. I (am) *a stranger* and a sojourner
Ex. 2:22. I have been *a stranger*
12:19. *whether he be a stranger,* or born
48. when *a stranger* shall sojourn
49. *and unto the stranger* that sojourneth
18: 3. I have been *an alien* in
20:10. *nor thy stranger* that (is)
22:21(20). Thou shalt *neither* vex *a stranger,*
—(—). ye were *strangers* in the land
23: 9. *Also* thou shalt not oppress *a stranger:* for ye know the heart of *a stranger,* seeing ye were *strangers*
12. *and the stranger,* may be refreshed.
Lev.16:29. *or a stranger* that sojourneth
17: 8. or of *the strangers* which sojourn
10, 13. *the strangers* that sojourn
12. *neither* shall any *stranger*
15. of your own country, *or a stranger,*
18:26. *nor* any *stranger* that sojourneth
19:10. for the poor *and stranger:*
33. if *a stranger* sojourn with
34. *the stranger* that dwelleth
— ye were *strangers* in the land of
20: 2. or of *the strangers* that sojourn
22:18. or of *the strangers* in Israel,
23:22. the poor, *and to the stranger:*
24:16. *as well the stranger,* as he that is born
22. *as well for the stranger,* as for one

Lev.25:23. for ye (are) *strangers*
35. *a stranger*, or a sojourner;
47. if *a sojourner* or stranger wax rich
— sell himself *unto the stranger*
— or to the stock of *the stranger's* family:
Nu. 9:14. if *a stranger* shall sojourn
— *both for the stranger*, and for him
15:14. if *a stranger* sojourn with you,
15. *and* also *for the stranger* that sojourneth
— *so* shall *the stranger*
16. *and for the stranger* that sojourneth
26. *and the stranger* that sojourneth
29. *and for the stranger* that sojourneth
30. born in the land, or *a stranger*,
19:10. *and unto the stranger* that sojourneth
35:15. *and for the stranger*, and for the
Deu 1:16. *the stranger* (that is) *with him.*
5:14. *nor thy stranger* that (is) within
10:18. loveth *the stranger*,
19. Love ye therefore *the stranger:* for ye were *strangers* in the
14:21. thou shalt give it *unto the stranger*
29 & 16:11. *and the stranger*, and the fatherless,
16:14. *the stranger*, and the fatherless,
23: 7(8). thou wast *a stranger* in his land.
24:14. or *of thy strangers*
17. the judgment of *the stranger*,
19, 20, 21. it shall be *for the stranger*,
26:11. *and the stranger* that (is)
12. unto the Levite, *the stranger*,
13. *and unto the stranger*,
27:19. the judgment of *the stranger*,
28:43. *The stranger* that (is) within
29:11(10). *and thy stranger* that (is) in thy
31:12. *and thy stranger* that (is) within
Jos. 8:33. *as well the stranger*, as he
35. the little ones, *and the strangers*
20: 9. *and for the stranger* that sojourneth
2Sa. 1:13. I (am) the son of *a stranger*, (lit. a man *a stranger*)
1Ch 22: 2. commanded to gather together *the strangers*
29:15. For we (are) *strangers* before thee,
2Ch 30:25. *and the strangers* that came
Job 31:32. *The stranger* did not lodge
Ps. 39:12(13). for I (am) *a stranger* with thee,
94: 6. the widow *and the stranger*,
119:19. I (am) *a stranger* in the earth:
146: 9. The Lord preserveth *the strangers;*
Isa. 14: 1. and *the strangers* shall be joined
Jer. 7: 6. (If) ye oppress not *the stranger*,
14: 8. be *as a stranger* in the land,
22: 3. *and* do no wrong, do no violence to *the stranger*,
Eze.14: 7. *or of the stranger* that sojourneth
22: 7. dealt by oppression *with the stranger:*
29. they have oppressed *the stranger*
47:22. *and to the strangers* that sojourn
23. in what tribe *the stranger* sojourneth,
Zec. 7:10. nor the fatherless, *the stranger*,
Mal. 3: 5. that turn aside *the stranger*

See 1484 גֵּר see גוֹר

1618 גָּרָב *gāh-rāhv'*, m.

Lev.21:20. or be *scurvy*, or scabbed,
22:22. or having a wen, or *scurvy*,
Deu28:27. *and with the scab*, and with

1620 גַּרְגַּר [*gar-gar'*], m.

Isa. 17: 6. two (or) three *berries* in the top

1621 גַּרְגְּרוֹת [*gar-g'rōhth'*], f. pl.

Pro. 1: 9. chains *about thy neck.*
3: 3. bind them about *thy neck;*
22. grace *to thy neck.*
26: 1. tie them about *thy neck.*

גָּרַד [*gāh-rad'*]. 1623

* HITHPAEL.—*Infinitive.* *

Job 2: 8. a potsherd *to scrape himself*

גָּרָה [*gāh-rāh'*]. 1624

* PIEL.—*Future.* *

Pro.15:18. A wrathful man *stirreth up* strife
28:25. of a proud heart *stirreth up*
29:22. An angry man *stirreth up* strife,

* HITHPAEL.—*Preterite.* *

Jer. 50:24. because thou *hast striven*

HITHPAEL.—*Imperative.*

Deu 2:24. *and contend* with him in battle.

HITHPAEL.—*Future.*

Deu 2: 5. *Meddle* not with them;
9. neither *contend* with them
19. nor *meddle* with them:
2K. 14:10. why *shouldest thou meddle*
2Ch 25:19. why *shouldest thou meddle*
Pro.28: 4. such as keep the law *contend*
Dan 11:10. his sons *shall be stirred up*, (marg. or, *shall war*)
— then shall he return, *and be stirred up*,
25. the king of the south *shall be stirred* up

גֵּרָה *gēh-rāh'*, f. 1625

Lev.11: 3. cheweth *the cud*, among the beasts,
4. of them that chew *the cud*,
—, 5, 6. because he cheweth *the cud*,
7. yet he cheweth not *the cud;*
26. *nor* cheweth *the cud*,
Deu 14: 6. cheweth *the cud*
7. of them that chew *the cud*,
— for they chew *the cud*,
8. yet cheweth not *the cud*,

גֵּרָה *gēh-rāh*, f. 1626

Ex. 30:13. a shekel (is) twenty *gerahs:*
Lev.27:25. twenty *gerahs* shall be the shekel.
Nu. 3:47. the shekel (is) twenty *gerahs:*
18:16. which (is) twenty *gerahs.*
Eze.45:12. the shekel (shall be) twenty *gerahs:*

גָּרוֹן *gāh-rōhn'*, m. 1627

Ps. 5: 9(10). *their throat* (is) an open sepulchre;
69: 3(4). *my throat* is dried:
115: 7. speak they *through their throat.*
149: 6. high (praises) of God (be) *in their mouth*, (marg. *throat*)
Isa. 3:16. walk with stretched forth *necks*
58: 1. Cry *aloud*, spare not, lift up thy voice (marg. *with the throat*)
Jer. 2:25. *and thy throat* from thirst:
Eze.16:11. a chain on *thy neck.*

גֵּרוּת *gēh-rooth'*, f. 1628

Jer. 41:17. dwelt *in the habitation of* Chimham,

גָּרַז [*gāh-raz'*]. 1629

* NIPHAL.—*Preterite.* *

Ps. 31:22(23). *I am cut off* from before

גַּרְזֶן *gar-zen'*, m. 1631

Deu 19: 5. *with the ax* to cut down
20:19. by forcing *an ax* against
1K. 6: 7. neither hammer *nor ax*
Isa. 10:15. Shall *the ax* boast itself

1632 גָּרֹל [*gāh-rōhl'*], adj.

Pro.19:19.(כתיב) *A man of great* wrath shall

1633 גָּרַם [*gāh-ram'*].

* KAL.—*Preterite.* *

Zep. 3: 3. *they gnaw* not *the bones*

* PIEL.—*Future.* *

Nu. 24: 8. *shall break* their bones,
Eze.23:34. *thou shalt break* the sherds

1634 גֶּרֶם *geh'-rem*, m.

Gen49:14. Issachar (is) a *strong* ass couching
2K. 9:13. on *the top of* the stairs,
Job 40:18. *his bones* (are) like bars of iron.
Pro.17:22. a broken spirit drieth *the bones.*
25:15. a soft tongue breaketh *the bone.*

1635 גְּרַם [*geh'-rem*], Ch. m.

Dan 6:24(25). and brake all *their bones* in pieces

1637 גֹּרֶן *gōh'-ren*, m.

Gen50:10. they came to *the threshingfloor of* Atad,
11. the mourning *in the floor of* Atad,
Nu. 15:20. heave offering of *the threshingfloor,*
18:27. the corn of *the threshingfloor,*
30. the increase of *the threshingfloor,*
Deu15:14. *and out of thy floor,*
16:13. thou hast gathered in *thy corn* (marg. *floor*)
Jud. 6:37. put a fleece of wool *in the floor;*
Ru. 3: 2. to night in *the threshingfloor.*
3. get thee down to *the floor:*
6. she went down unto *the floor,*
14. came into *the floor.*
1Sa.23: 1. they rob *the threshingfloors.*
2Sa. 6: 6. came to Nachon's *threshingfloor,*
24:16. of the Lord was by *the threshingplace*
18. *in the threshingfloor of* Araunah
21. To buy *the threshingfloor*
24. David bought *the threshingfloor*
1K. 22:10. *in a void place* in the entrance (marg. *floor*)
2K. 6:27. out of *the barnfloor,*
1Ch 13: 9. *the threshingfloor of* Chidon,
21:15. angel of the Lord stood by *the threshing-floor of*
18, 28. *in the threshingfloor of* Ornan
21. went out of *the threshingfloor,*
22. Grant me the place of (this) *threshingfloor,*
2Ch 3: 1. *in the threshingfloor of* Ornan
18: 9. they sat *in a void place* (marg. or, *floor*)
Job 39:12. *and* gather (it into) *thy barn?*
Isa. 21:10. the corn of *my floor:*
Jer. 51:33. of Babylon (is) *like a threshingfloor,*
Hos. 9: 1. a reward upon every corn*floor.*
2. *The floor* and the winepress
13: 3. with the whirlwind *out of the floor,*
Joel 2:24. *the floors* shall be full of wheat,
Mic. 4:12. as the sheaves *into the floor.*

1638 גָּרַס [*gāh-ras'*].

* KAL.—*Preterite.* *

Ps.119:20. My soul *breaketh* for the

* HIPHIL.—*Future.* *

Lam.3:16. *He hath also broken* my teeth

1639 גָּרַע [*gāh-rag'*].

* KAL.—*Infinitive.* *

Ecc. 3:14. nor *any thing taken* from it:

KAL.—*Future.*

Ex. 5: 8. *ye shall* not *diminish*
Ex. 5:19. *Ye shall* not *minish*
21:10. *shall he* not *diminish.*
Deu 4: 2. neither *shall ye diminish*
12:32(13:1). nor *diminish* from it.
Job 15: 4. *and restrainest* prayer before God.
8. *and dost thou restrain* wisdom
36: 7. *He withdraweth* not his eyes
Jer. 26: 2. *diminish* not a word:
Eze. 5:11. therefore *will I* also *diminish*
16:27. *and have diminished* thine

KAL.—*Participle.* Paül.

Jer. 48:37. every beard *clipped:* (marg. *diminished*)

* NIPHAL.—*Preterite.* *

Lev.27:18. *and it shall be abated* from thy
Nu. 36: 3. *then shall* their inheritance *be taken*

NIPHAL.—*Future.*

Nu. 9: 7. wherefore *are we kept back,*
27: 4. *should* the name of our father *be done away* (marg. *diminished*)
36: 3. so *shall it be taken* from the lot
4. so *shall* their inheritance *be taken away*

NIPHAL.—*Participle.*

Ex. 5:11. of your work *shall be diminished.*

* PIEL.—*Future.* *

Job 36:27. *he maketh small* the drops of

גָּרַף [*gāh-raph'*]. 1640

* KAL.—*Preterite.* *

Jud. 5:21. The river of Kishon *swept them away,*

גָּרַר [*gāh-rar'*]. 1641

* KAL.—*Future.* *

Hab. 1:15. *they catch them* in their net,
Pro.21: 7. of the wicked *shall destroy them;*

* NIPHAL.—*Future.* *

Lev.11: 7. yet *he cheweth* not the cud;

* POAL.—*Participle.* *

1K. 7: 9. *sawed* with saws,

* HITHPOEL.—*Participle.* *

Jer. 30:23. a *continuing* whirlwind: (marg. *cutting*)

גֶּרֶשׂ *geh'-res*, m. 1643

Lev. 2:14. *corn beaten* out of full ears.
16. *of the beaten corn thereof,*

גָּרַשׁ [*gāh-rash'*]. 1644

* KAL.—*Future.* *

Isa. 57:20. whose waters *cast up* mire

KAL.—*Participle.* Poel.

Ex. 34:11. I *drive out* before thee the Amorite,

KAL.—*Participle.* Paül.

Lev.21: 7. *put away* from her husband:
14. A widow, *or a divorced woman,*
22:13. be a widow, *or divorced,*
Nu. 30: 9(10). *and of her that is divorced,*
Eze.44:22. *nor her that is put away:* (marg. *thrust forth*)

* NIPHAL.—*Preterite.* *

Am. 8: 8. *and it shall be cast out* and drowned,
Jon. 2: 4(5). *I am cast out* of thy sight;

NIPHAL.—*Participle.*

Isa. 57:20. the wicked (are) like the *troubled* sea,

* PIEL.—*Preterite.* *

Gen. 4:14. *thou hast driven* me *out*
Ex. 23:28. *which shall drive out* the Hivite,
31. *and thou shalt drive them out* before thee.
33: 2. *and I will drive out* the
Nu. 22:11. to overcome them, *and drive them out.*

1Sa 26:19. for *they have driven me out* this day
Eze.31:11. *I have driven him out* for his wickedness.

PIEL.—*Infinitive.*

Ex. 11: 1. he shall *surely* thrust you out hence altogether. (lit. *thrusting* he shall thrust out)
1Ch 17:21. *by driving out* nations
2Ch 20:11. to come *to cast us out*
Pro.22:10. *Cast out* the scorner,

PIEL.—*Imperative.*

Gen21:10. *Cast out* this bondwoman

PIEL.—*Future.*

Gen. 3:24. *So he drove out* the man;
Ex. 2:17. came *and drove them away:*
6: 1. with a strong hand *shall he drive them out*
10:11. *And* they *were driven out* (lit. *and* (one) *drove* them *out*)
11: 1. *he shall* surely *thrust* you *out*
23:29. *I will* not *drive them out*
30. By little and little *I will drive them out*
Nu. 22: 6. *and* (that) *I may drive them out*
Deu 33:27. *and he shall thrust out* the enemy
Jos. 24:12. *which drave them out* from before
18. *And* the Lord *drave out* from before us
Jud. 2: 3. *I will* not *drive* them *out*
6: 9. *and drave them out* from before
9:41. *and* Zebul *thrust out* Gaal
11: 2. *and they thrust out* Jephthah,
7. Did not ye hate me, *and expel me*
1K. 2:27. *So* Solomon *thrust out* Abiathar
Ps. 34[title](1). *who drove him away*, and he departed.
78:55. *He cast out* the heathen *also*
80: 8(9). *thou hast cast out* the heathen,
Hos. 9:15. *I will drive them out* of mine house,
Mic. 2: 9. of my people *have ye cast out*
Zep. 2: 4. *they shall drive out* Ashdod

* PUAL.—*Preterite.* *

Ex. 12:39. *they were thrust out* of Egypt,

PUAL.—*Future.*

Job 30: 5. *They were driven forth*

1645 **גֶּרֶשׁ** *geh'-resh*, m.

Deu 33:14. *put forth* by the moon,(marg. *thrust forth*)

1646 **גְּרֻשָׁה** [*g'roo-shāh'*], f.

Eze.45: 9. take away *your exactions* (marg. *expulsions*)

1652 **גָּשַׁם** [*gāh-sham'*].

* HIPHIL.—*Participle.* *

Jer. 14:22. of the Gentiles *that can cause rain?*

1653 **גֶּשֶׁם** *geh'-shem*, m.

Gen. 7:12. *the rain* was upon the earth
8: 2. *the rain* from heaven
Lev.26: 4. Then I will give *you rain* (lit. *your rain*)
1K. 17: 7. there had been no *rain*
14. sendeth *rain* upon the earth.
18:41. a sound of abundance of *rain*.
44. that *the rain* stop thee not.
45. there was *a* great *rain*.
2K. 3:17. neither shall ye see *rain;*
Ezr.10: 9. *and for the great rain*. (marg. *showers*)
13. a time of *much rain*, (lit. *rains*)
Job 37: 6. *likewise* to *the* small *rain*, *and* to *the* great *rain*
Ps. 68: 9(10). didst send *a* plentiful *rain*,
105:32. gave *them* hail for *rain*, (marg. *their rain*)
Pro.25:14. clouds and wind without *rain*. (lit. *and* not *rain*)
23. The north wind driveth away *rain:*
Ecc.11: 3. If the clouds be full of *rain*,
12: 2. nor the clouds return after *the rain:*
Cant.2:11. *the rain* is over (and) gone;
Isa. 44:14. *and the rain* doth nourish (it).
55:10. For as *the rain* cometh down,
Jer. 5:24. that giveth *rain*,
14: 4. there was no *rain* in the earth,
Eze. 1:28. that is in the cloud in the day of *rain*,
13:11. there shall be *an* overflowing *shower;*
13. *and* there shall be *an* overflowing *shower*
34:26. I will cause *the shower* to come
— there shall be *showers of* blessing.
38:22. *and* I will rain...*an* overflowing *rain*,
Hos 6: 3. he shall come unto us *as the rain*,
Joel 2:23. to come down for you *the rain*,
Am. 4: 7. also I have withholden *the rain*
Zec.10: 1. and give them showers of *rain*,
14:17. even upon them shall be no *rain*.

גְּשֵׁם [*geh'-shem*], Ch. m. 1655

Dan. 3:27. *upon whose bodies* the fire had no power,
28. and yielded *their bodies*,
4:33(30) & 5:21. *his body* was wet with the dew
7:11. and *his body* destroyed, and given

גֹּשֶׁם [*gōh'-shem*], m. 1656

Eze.22:24. nor *rained upon* in the day

גָּשַׁשׁ [*gāh-shash'*]. 1659

* PIEL.—*Future.* *

Isa. 59:10. *We grope* for the wall like the blind, and *we grope* as if (we had) no eyes:

גַּת *gath*, f. 1660

Jud. 6:11. threshed wheat *by the winepress*,
Neh 13:15. treading *wine presses*
Isa. 63: 2. that treadeth *in the winefat?*
Lam. 1:15. in *a winepress*.
Joel 3:13(4:13). for *the press* is full,

גִּתִּית *git-teeth'*, f. 1665

Ps. 8 & 81 & 84[title](1). the chief Musician upon *Gittith*,

---

ד *dāh'-leth*,

The fourth letter of the Alphabet.

דָּא *dāh*, Ch. pron. 1668

Dan 4:30(27). Is not *this* great Babylon,
5: 6. and his knees smote *one* against *another*.
7: 3. diverse *one* from *another*.
8. in *this* horn (were) eyes like the

דָּאַב [*dāh-av'*]. 1669

* KAL.—*Preterite.* *

Ps. 88: 9(10). Mine eye *mourneth* by reason
Jer. 31:25. replenished every *sorrowful* soul.

KAL.—*Infinitive.*

Jer. 31:12. they shall not *sorrow* any more (lit. add *to sorrow*)

דְּאָבָה *d'āh-vāh'*, f. 1670

Job 41:22(14). *sorrow* is turned into joy

1671 **דְּאָבוֹן** [*d'āh-vōhn'*], m.

Deu28:65. *and sorrow of* mind:

1709 **דָּאג** *dāhg*, m.

Neh13:16. (כתיב) which brought *fish*,

1672 **דָּאַג** *dāh-ag'*.

* KAL.—*Preterite.* *

1Sa. 9: 5. *and take thought* for us.
10: 2. *and sorroweth* for you,
Isa. 57:11. of whom *hast thou been afraid*

KAL.—*Future.*

Ps. 38:18(19). *I will be sorry* for my sin.
Jer. 17: 8. *shall* not *be careful* in the year

KAL.—*Participle.* Poel.

Jer. 38:19. I *am afraid* of the Jews
42:16. whereof ye *were afraid*,

1674 **דְּאָגָה** *d'āh-gāh'*, f.

Jos. 22:24. *for fear* of (this) thing,
Pro. 12:25. *Heaviness* in the heart
Jer. 49:23. *sorrow* on the sea;
Eze. 4:16. bread by weight, *and with care;*
12:18. with trembling *and with carefulness;*
19. eat their bread *with carefulness*,

1675 **דָּאָה** [*dāh-āh'*].

* KAL.—*Future.* *

Deu28:49. as the eagle *flieth;*
Ps. 18:10(11). *yea, he did fly* upon the wings
Jer. 48:40. *he shall fly* as an eagle,
49:22. *and fly* as the eagle,

1676 **דָּאָה** *dāh-āh'*, f.

Lev. 11:14. *the vulture*, and the kite

See 1756 **דּאר** see **דּוֹר**

1677 **דֹּב** & **דּוֹב** *dōhv*, m.

1Sa. 17:34. there came a lion, and *a bear*,
36. slew both the lion and *the bear:*
37. out of the paw of *the bear*,
2Sa. 17: 8. *as a bear* robbed of her whelps
2K. 2:24. there came forth two *she bears*
Pro. 17:12. Let *a bear* robbed of her whelps
28:15. *and a* ranging *bear;*
Isa. 11: 7. the cow *and the bear* shall feed;
59:11. We roar all *like bears*,
Lam. 3:10. He (was) unto me (as) *a bear*
Hos 13: 8. I will meet them *as a bear*
Am. 5:19. *a bear* met him;

1678 **דֹּב** *dōhv*, Ch. m.

Dan. 7: 5. a second, like *to a bear*,

1679 **דֹּבֶא** [*dōh'-veh*], m.

Deu33:25. as thy days, (so shall) *thy strength*

1680 **דָּבַב** [*dāh-vav'*].

* KAL.—*Participle.* Poel. *

Cant. 7: 9(10). *causing* the lips of those that are asleep *to speak.*

דִּבָּה *dib-bāh'*, f. 1681

Gen37: 2. unto his father *their evil report.*
Nu. 13:32. they brought up *an evil report of*
14:36. by bringing up *a slander*
37. bring up *the evil report upon* the land,
Ps. 31:13(14). I have heard *the slander of* many:
Pro. 10:18. he that uttereth *a slander*, (is) a fool.
25:10. *and thine infamy* turn not away.
Jer. 20:10. I heard *the defaming of* many,
Eze. 36: 3. *and* (are) *an infamy of* the people:

דְּבוֹרָה *d'vōh-rāh'*. 1682

Deu. 1:44. chased you, as *bees* do,
Jud. 14: 8. a swarm of *bees* and honey
Ps. 118:12. compassed me about *like bees;*
Isa. 7:18. *and for the bee* that (is) in the land

דְּבַח [*d'vagh*], Ch. 1684

* P'AL.—*Participle.* Active. *

Ezr. 6: 3. the place where *they offered* sacrifices,

דְּבַח [*d'vagh*], Ch. m. 1685

Ezr. 6: 3. where they offered *sacrifices*,

דִּבְיוֹנִים *div-yōh-neem'*, m. pl. 1686

2K. 6:25. fourth part of a cab of *dove's dung*

דְּבִיר *d'veer*, m. 1687

1K. 6: 5. the temple *and of the oracle:*
16. *for the oracle*, (even) for the most holy
19. *And the oracle* he prepared
20. And *the oracle* in the forepart
21. chains of gold before *the oracle;*
22. that (was) *by the oracle*
23. *within the oracle* he made two
31. for the entering of *the oracle*
7:49. before *the oracle*,
8: 6. into *the oracle of* the house,
8. before *the oracle*,
2Ch. 3:16. (as) *in the oracle*,
4:20. before *the oracle*,
5: 7. to *the oracle of* the house,
9. from the ark before *the oracle;*
Ps. 28: 2. my hands toward thy holy *oracle.*

דְּבֵלָה *d'vēh-lāh'*, f. 1690

1Sa. 25:18. two hundred *cakes of figs*,
30:12. they gave him a piece of *a cake of figs*,
2K. 20: 7. Take *a lump of* figs.
1Ch 12:40. meat, meal, *cakes of figs*,
Isa. 38:21. Let them take *a lump of* figs,

דָּבַק *dāh-vak'*, & **דָּבֵק** [*dāh-vēhk'*] 1692

* KAL.—*Preterite.* *

Gen. 2:24. *and shall cleave* unto his wife:
Deu28:60. *and they shall cleave* unto thee.
Jos. 23:12. *and cleave* unto the remnant
Ru. 1:14. but Ruth *clave* unto her.
2Sa. 20: 2. the men of Judah *clave* unto their king,
1K. 11: 2. Solomon *clave* unto these in love.
2K. 3: 3. Nevertheless *he cleaved* unto the
Job 19:20. My bone *cleaveth* to my skin
29:10. their tongue *cleaved* to the roof of
31: 7. *hath cleaved* to mine hands;
41:23(15). his flesh *are joined together:*
Ps. 44:25(26). our belly *cleaveth* unto the earth.
63: 8(9). My soul *followeth hard*
102: 5(6). my bones *cleave* to my skin.
119:25. My soul *cleaveth* unto the dust:
31. *I have stuck* unto thy testimonies:
Lam 4: 4. The tongue of the sucking child *cleaveth*

KAL.—*Infinitive.*

Deu11:22. *and to cleave* unto him ;
30:20. *and that thou mayest cleave* unto him:
Jos. 22: 5. *and to cleave* unto him,

KAL.—*Future.*

Gen19:19. lest some evil *take me,*
34: 3. *And* his soul *clave* unto Dinah
Nu. 36: 7. of Israel *shall keep himself* to the inheritance (marg. *cleave* to)
9. of Israel *shall keep himself to* his own
Deu10:20. to him *shalt thou cleave,*
13: 4(5). and *cleave* unto him.
17(18). *there shall cleave* nought of the
Jos. 23: 8. But *cleave* unto the Lord
Ru. 2: 8. *abide* here *fast* by my maidens:
21. *Thou shalt keep fast* by my
23. *So she kept fast* by the maidens
2Sa. 23:10. *and* his hand *clave* unto the sword:
2K. 5:27. Naaman *shall cleave* unto thee,
18: 6. *For he clave* to the Lord,
Ps. 101: 3. *shall* not *cleave* to me.
137: 6. *let* my tongue *cleave* to the
Jer. 13:11. as the girdle *cleaveth* to the loins of a man,
42:16. *shall follow close* after you there in Egypt; (marg. *cleave*)
Eze. 29: 4. the fish of thy rivers *shall stick*

* PUAL.—*Future.* *

Job 38:38. the clods *cleave fast together?*
41:17(9). *They are joined* one to another,

* HIPHIL.—*Preterite.* *

Jud. 20:42. but the battle *overtook them;*
2Sa. 1: 6. horsemen *followed hard after him.*
Jer. 13:11. so *have I caused to cleave*
Eze. 29: 4. *and I will cause* the fish of thy rivers *to stick*

HIPHIL.—*Future.*

Gen31:23. *and they overtook* him
Deu28:21. *shall make* the pestilence *cleave*
Jud. 18:22. *and overtook* the children of Dan.
20:45. *and pursued hard* after them
1Sa. 14:22. even they *also followed hard*
31: 2. *And* the Philistines *followed hard upon*
1Ch 10: 2. *And* the Philistines *followed hard*
Eze. 3:26. And *I will make* thy tongue *cleave*

* HOPHAL.—*Participle.* *

Ps. 22:15(16). my tongue *cleaveth* to my jaws;

1693 **דְּבַק** [*d'vak*], Ch.

* P'AL.—*Participle.* Active. *

Dan. 2:43. but they *shall* not *cleave* one to another,

1695 **דָּבֵק** *dāh-vēhk'*, adj.

Deu. 4: 4. But ye *that did cleave* unto the Lord
2Ch. 3:12. *joining* to the wing of the other
Pro. 18:24. there is a friend (that) *sticketh closer*

1694 **דֶּבֶק** *deh'-vek*, m.

1K. 22:34. between *the joints* of the harness:
2Ch 18:33. between *the joints* of the harness:
Isa. 41: 7. It (is) ready *for the sodering:* (marg. or, *of the soder,* It (is) good)

1696 **דָּבַר** [*dāh-var'*].

* KAL.—*Infinitive.* *

Ps. 51: 4(6). be justified *when thou speakest,*

KAL.—*Participle.* Poel.

Gen16:13. the Lord *that spake* unto her,
Ex. 6:29. all that I *say* unto thee.
Nu. 27: 7. daughters of Zelophehad *speak* right:
32:27. before the Lord to battle, as my lord *saith.*
Nu. 36: 5. of Joseph *hath said* well.
Deu. 5: 1. I *speak* in your ears this day,
Est. 10: 3. *and speaking* peace to all his seed.
Job 2:13. none *spake* a word unto him:
Ps. 5: 6(7). destroy *them that speak* leasing:
15: 2. *and speaketh* the truth
28: 3. *which speak* peace to their neighbours,
31:18(19). *which speak* grievous things
58: 3(4). as they be born, *speaking* lies.
63:11(12). *them that speak* lies shall be
101: 7. *he that telleth* lies
109:20. *and* of *them that speak* evil
Pro. 16:13. *and* they love *him that speaketh*
Isa. 9:17(16). and every mouth *speaketh* folly.
33:15. *and speaketh* uprightly;
45:19. I the Lord *speak* righteousness,
Jer. 28: 7. that I *speak* in thine ears,
32:42. the good that I *have promised*
38:20. which I *speak* unto thee:
40:16. thou *speakest* falsely of Ishmael.
Dan 10:11. the words that I *speak* unto thee,
Am. 5:10. *and* they abhor *him that speaketh*
Jon. 3: 2. the preaching that I *bid* thee.
Mic. 7: 3. he *uttereth* his mischievous
Zec. 1: 9, 13, 19(2:2). the angel *that talked* with me
14. the angel *that communed* with
2: 3(7) & 4:1, 4, 5 & 5:5, 10 & 6:4. the angel *that talked* with me

KAL.—*Participle.* Paül.

Pro. 25:11. A word fitly *spoken*

* NIPHAL.—*Preterite.* *

Ps. 119:23. Princes also did sit (and) *speak*
Mal. 3:13. What *have we spoken*
16. *spake often* one to another:

NIPHAL.—*Participle.*

Eze. 33:30. *still are talking* against thee

* PIEL.—*Preterite.* *

Gen12: 4. as the Lord *had spoken* unto him;
17:23. as God *had said* unto him.
18: 5. So do, as *thou hast said.*
19. that which he *hath spoken*
19:21. city, for the which *thou hast spoken.*
21: 1. unto Sarah as *he had spoken.*
2. which God *had spoken* to him.
23:16. which *he had named*
24: 7. which *spake* unto me,
30. Thus *spake* the man unto me;
33. until *I have told* mine errand.
51. as the Lord *hath spoken.*
27:19. done according as *thou badest* me:
28:15. which *I have spoken* to thee *of.*
35:13, 14. where *he talked* with him.
15. where God *spake* with him,
39:19. which *she spake* unto him,
41:28. the thing which *I have spoken*
42:14. that *I spake* unto you,
30. *spake* roughly to us,
44: 2. the word that Joseph *had spoken.*
45:15. after that his brethren *talked* with
27. which *he had said* unto them:
49:28. their father *spake* unto them,
Ex. 1:17. the king of Egypt *commanded*
4:15. *And thou shalt speak* unto him,
16. *And he shall be* thy *spokesman* (lit. *and he shall speak* for thee)
30. which the Lord *had spoken*
7:13, 22. as the Lord *had said.*
8:15(11), 19(15). as the Lord *had said.*
9: 1. Go in unto Pharaoh, *and tell* him,
12, 35. as the Lord *had spoken*
10:29. *Thou hast spoken* well,
12:25. according as *he hath promised,*
32. as *ye have said,*
14:12. the word that *we did tell* thee
16:23. which the Lord *hath said,*
19: 8. All that the Lord *hath spoken*
20:22. Ye have seen that *I have talked*
24: 3. which the Lord *hath said*
7. All that the Lord *hath said*
25:22. *and I will commune* with thee
32:14. the evil which *he thought* to do
34. of which *I have spoken* unto thee:
33: 9. *and* (the Lord) *talked* with Moses,

Ex. 33:11. *And* the Lord *spake* unto Moses
17. do this thing also that *thou hast spoken:*
34:32. all that the Lord *had spoken*
34. *and spake* unto the children of
Lev.10: 3. This (is it) that the Lord *spake*,
5. as Moses *had said*.
11. which the Lord *hath spoken*
Nu. 5: 4. as the Lord *spake* unto Moses,
10:29. the Lord *hath spoken* good
11:17. come down *and talk* with thee
12: 2. Hath the Lord indeed *spoken* only by Moses? *hath he* not *spoken* also by us?
14:17. according as *thou hast spoken*,
28. as *ye have spoken* in mine ears,
35. I the Lord *have said*,
15:22. which the Lord *hath spoken*
16:40(17.5). as the Lord *said* to him
47(17:12). Aaron took as Moses *commanded*,
20: 8. *and speak ye* unto the rock
21: 7. *we have spoken* against the Lord,
23: 2. Balak did as Balaam *had spoken;*
17. What *hath* the Lord *spoken?*
19. *or hath he spoken*, and shall he not
26. *Told* not *I* thee, saying,
24:12. *Spake I* not also to thy messengers
27:23. as the Lord *commanded*
32:31. As the Lord *hath said*
Deu. 1: 1. which Moses *spake* unto all Israel
3. Moses *spake* unto the children of
6. The Lord our God *spake*
11. as *he hath promised* you!
14. The thing which *thou hast spoken*
21. the Lord God of thy fathers *hath said*
2: 1. as the Lord *spake* unto me:
4:45. Moses *spake* unto the children
5: 4. The Lord *talked* with you
22(19). the Lord *spake* unto all
28(25). which *they have spoken* unto thee: they have well said all that *they have spoken*.
6: 3. God of thy fathers *hath promised* thee,
7. *and shalt talk* of them
19. as the Lord *hath spoken*.
9: 3. as the Lord *hath said*
10. which the Lord *spake* with you
28. the land which *he promised* them,
10: 4. which the Lord *spake* unto you
9. as the Lord thy God *promised* him.
11:25. as *he hath said* unto you.
12:20. as *he hath promised* thee,
13: 2(3). whereof *he spake* unto thee,
5(6). *he hath spoken* to turn (you) away
15: 6. as *he promised* thee:
18: 2. as *he hath said* unto them.
17. which *they have spoken*.
18. *and he shall speak* unto them
21, 22. which the Lord *hath* not *spoken?* (lit. *spoken it*)
22. the prophet *hath spoken it*
19: 8. all the land which *he promised*
20: 2. *and speak* unto the people,
5. *And* the officers *shall speak*
23:23(24). which *thou hast promised*
25: 8. *and speak* unto him:
26:18. as *he hath promised* thee,
19. as *he hath spoken*.
27: 3. God of thy fathers *hath promised* thee.
29:13(12). as *he hath said* unto thee,
31: 3. as the Lord *hath said*.
Jos. 1: 3. as *I said* unto Moses.
4: 8. as the Lord *spake* unto Joshua,
12. as Moses *spake* unto them:
9:21. as the princes *had promised*
11:23. to all that the Lord *said* unto Moses;
13:14. as *he said* unto them.
33. as *he said* unto them.
14: 6. the thing that the Lord *said* unto Moses
10. as *he said*, these forty and five years, even since the Lord *spake*
12. whereof the Lord *spake*
— as the Lord *said*.
20: 2. whereof *I spake* unto you
4. *and shall declare* his cause
21:45(43). which the Lord *had spoken*
22: 4. as *he promised* them:
30. the children of Manasseh *spake*,
23: 5. as the Lord your God *hath promised* unto you.

Jos. 23:10. as *he hath promised* you.
14. which the Lord your God *spake*
15. the Lord your God *promised* you;
24:27. which *he spake* unto us:
Jud. 1:20. as Moses *said:*
2:15. as the Lord *had said*,
6:27. did as the Lord *had said*
36, 37. by mine hand, as *thou hast said*,
13:11. (Art) thou the man that *spakest*
Ru. 2:13. for that *thou hast spoken*
4: 1. of whom Boaz *spake* came by;
1Sa. 1:16. *have I spoken* hitherto.
3:12. all (things) which *I have spoken*
17. that (the Lord) *hath said*
— that *he said* unto thee.
9:21. wherefore then *speakest thou* so to me?
14:19. while Saul *talked* unto the priest,
15:16. what the Lord *hath said*
16: 4. that which the Lord *spake*,
17:31. which David *spake*,
18:24. On this manner *spake* David.
20:23. which thou and I *have spoken* of,
26. Saul *spake* not any thing that day:
25:30. all the good that *he hath spoken*
28:17. as *he spake* by me:
21. words which *thou spakest* unto me.
2Sa. 2:27. unless *thou hadst spoken*,
7: 7. *spake I* a word with any
17. so *did* Nathan *speak* unto David.
25. the word that *thou hast spoken*
— do as *thou hast said*.
29. thou, O Lord God, *hast spoken* (it):
12:18. was yet alive, *we spake* unto him,
13:22. Absalom *spake* unto his brother
14: 3. *and speak* on this manner
19. that my lord the king *hath spoken:*
17: 6. Ahithophel *hath spoken* after
23: 2. The Spirit of the Lord *spake*
3. the Rock of Israel *spake* to me,
24:12. Go *and say* unto David,
1K. 2: 4. which *he spake* concerning me,
23. if Adonijah *have* not *spoken*
24. as *he promised*,
27. which *he spake* concerning
30. Thus *said* Joab,
31. Do as *he hath said*,
38. as my lord the king *hath said*,
5: 5(19). as the Lord *spake* unto David
12(26). as *he promised* him:
6:12. which *I spake* unto David
8:15. which *spake* with his mouth
20. performed his word that *he spake*,
— as the Lord *promised*,
24, 25. that *thou promisedst* him:
26. which *thou spakest* unto thy servant
53. as *thou spakest* by the hand of
56. according to all that *he promised:*
— which *he promised* by the hand of
9: 5. as *I promised* to David
12: 7. *and speak* good words to them,
9. who *have spoken* to me,
10. this people that *spake* unto thee,
12. as the king *had appointed*,
15. which the Lord *spake* by
13: 3. which the Lord *hath spoken;*
11. the words which *he had spoken*
18. an angel *spake* unto me
22. which (the Lord) *did say* to thee,
26. which *he spake* unto him.
14: 2. which *told* me that
11. for the Lord *hath spoken*
18. *he spake* by the hand of
15:29. which *he spake* by his servant
16:12. which *he spake* against
34. which *he spake* by Joshua
17:16. which *he spake* by Elijah.
21: 4. Naboth the Jezreelite *had spoken* to him:
19, 19. *And thou shalt speak* unto him,
23. of Jezebel also *spake* the Lord,
22:13. gone to call Micaiah *spake* unto him,
— *and speak* (that which is) good.
23. *hath spoken* evil concerning
28. the Lord *hath* not *spoken* by me.
38. word of the Lord which *he spake*.
2K. 1: 3. the angel of the Lord *said* to Elijah
6. *and say* unto him,
9. the king *hath said*, Come down.

2K. 1:17. which Elijah *had spoken.*
2:22. the saying of Elisha which *he spake.*
4:17. that Elisha *had said* unto her,
5: 4. Thus and thus *said* the maid
13. (if) the prophet *had bid* thee (do some) great thing,
7:17. as the man of God *had said,* who *spake* when the king came
8: 1. Then *spake* Elisha unto the woman,
9:36. which *he spake* by his servant
10:10. which the Lord *spake* concerning
— which *he spake* by his servant
17. which *he spake* to Elijah.
14:25. which *he spake* by the hand of
27. the Lord *said* not that he would
15:12. which *he spake* unto Jehu,
17:23. as *he had said* by all
19:21. *hath spoken* concerning him;
20: 9. the thing that he *hath spoken:*
19. which *thou hast spoken.*
22:19. what *I spake* against this place,
24: 2. which *he spake* by his servants the prophets.
13. of the Lord, as the Lord had *said.*
1Ch 17: 6. *spake I* a word to any
15. so *did* Nathan *speak* unto David.
23. the thing that *thou hast spoken*
— do as *thou hast said.*
21:10. Go *and tell* David,
19. which *he spake* in the name
22:11. as *he hath said* of thee.
2Ch 6: 4. which *he spake* with his mouth
10. his word that *he hath spoken:*
— as the Lord *promised,*
15, 16. that which *thou hast promised*
17. which *thou hast spoken*
10: 7. *and speak* good words to them,
9. which *have spoken* to me,
10. that *spake* unto thee,
12. as the king *bade,*
15. which *he spake* by the
18:12. went to call Micaiah *spake*
— *and speak thou* good.
22. *hath spoken* evil against
27. *hath* not the Lord *spoken*
23: 3. as the Lord *hath said* of the sons of David.
32:16. his servants *spake* yet
Neh 6:12. but that *he pronounced*
Est. 6:10. as *thou hast said,*
— of all that *thou hast spoken.*
7: 9. who *had spoken* good for the
Job 33: 2. my tongue *hath spoken*
40: 5. Once have *I spoken;*
42: 7. after the Lord *had spoken*
— for *ye have* not *spoken*
8. in that *ye have* not *spoken* of
9. as the Lord *commanded* them:
Ps. 17:10. *they speak* proudly.
18[title](1). who *spake* unto the Lord
38:12(13). *speak* mischievous things,
39: 3(4). *spake I* with my tongue,
50: 1. the Lord, *hath spoken,*
60: 6(8). God *hath spoken* in his holiness;
62:11(12). God *hath spoken* once;
66:14. *and* my mouth *hath spoken,*
89:19(20). Then *thou spakest* in vision
108: 7(8). God *hath spoken* in his holiness;
109: 2. *they have spoken* against me
144: 8, 11. Whose mouth *speaketh* vanity,
Ecc. 1:16. *I communed* with mine own heart,
2:15. *Then I said* in my heart,
Isa. 1: 2. for the Lord *hath spoken,*
20. the mouth of the Lord *hath spoken*
16:13. *hath spoken* concerning Moab
14. now the Lord *hath spoken,*
20: 2. At the same time *spake* the Lord
21:17. the Lord God of Israel *hath spoken*
22:25. for the Lord *hath spoken* (it).
24: 3. the Lord *hath spoken* this word.
25: 8. for the Lord *hath spoken*
37:22. *hath spoken* concerning him;
38: 7. do this thing that *he hath spoken;*
39: 8. which *thou hast spoken.*
40: 5. the mouth of the Lord *hath spoken*
45:19. *I have* not *spoken* in secret,
46:11. yea, *I have spoken* (it),
48:15. I, (even) I, *have spoken;*
16. *I have* not *spoken* in secret

Isa. 58:14. the mouth of the Lord *hath spoken*
59: 3. your lips *have spoken* lies,
65:12. when *I spake,* ye did not hear;
66: 4. when *I spake,* they did not hear:
Jer. 1:16. *And I will utter* my judgments
17. *and speak* unto them
3: 5. *thou hast spoken* and done
4:28. because *I have spoken*
7:22. For *I spake* not unto your fathers,
27. *thou shalt speak* all these words
9: 8(7). *it speaketh* deceit:
12(11). the mouth of the Lord *hath spoken,*
10: 1. the Lord *speaketh* unto you,
11: 2. *and speak* unto the men of Judah,
17. *hath pronounced* evil against
13:15. for the Lord *hath spoken.*
14:14. neither *spake* unto them:
16:10. the Lord *pronounced* all this
18: 8. whom *I have pronounced,*
19: 5. commanded not, nor *spake*
15. the evil that *I have pronounced*
22: 1. *and speak* there this word,
21. *I spake* unto thee in thy prosperity;
23:17. The Lord *hath said,*
21. *I have* not *spoken* to them,
35, 37. What *hath* the Lord *spoken?*
25: 2. *spake* unto all the people
13. which *I have pronounced*
26: 2. *and speak* unto all the cities of
13. the evil that *he hath pronounced*
16. *he hath spoken* to us in the
19. the evil which *he had pronounced*
27:12. I *spake* also to Zedekiah king of
13. as the Lord *hath spoken*
16. Also *I spake* to the priests
28:16. because *thou hast taught*
29:32. *he hath taught* rebellion
30: 2. all the words that *I have spoken*
4. *spake* concerning Israel
32: 4. *and shall speak* with him
24. what *thou hast spoken* is come
33:14. which *I have promised*
24. what this people *have spoken,*
34: 5. for *I have pronounced* the word,
35: 2. *and speak* unto them,
14. *I have spoken* unto you,
17. all the evil that *I have pronounced*
— because *I have spoken* unto them,
36: 2. all the words that *I have spoken*
— from the day *I spake* unto thee,
4. which *he had spoken*
7. *hath pronounced* against this
31. all the evil that *I have pronounced*
37: 2. which *he spake* by the prophet
38:25. hear that *I have talked* with thee,
— what *thou hast said* unto the king,
— also what the king *said* unto thee:
40: 2. *hath pronounced* this evil
3. done according as *he hath said:*
42:19. *hath said* concerning you,
44:16. the word that *thou hast spoken*
45: 1. Jeremiah the prophet *spake*
46:13. *spake* to Jeremiah the prophet,
50: 1. the Lord *spake* against Babylon
51:12. done that which *he spake*
62. thou *hast spoken* against this
Eze. 2: 2. when *he spake* unto me,
7. *thou shalt speak* my words
3: 4. *and speak* with my words
11. *and speak* unto them,
18. *nor speakest* to warn the wicked
5:13, 15, 17. I the Lord *have spoken*
6:10. *I have* not *said* in vain
13: 7. I *have* not *spoken?*
14: 9. *when he hath spoken* a thing,
17:21, 24. I the Lord *have spoken*
21:17(22). I the Lord *have said*
32(37). for I the Lord *have spoken*
22:14. I the Lord *have spoken*
28. when the Lord *hath* not *spoken.*
23:34. for I *have spoken*
24:14. I the Lord *have spoken*
26: 5. for I *have spoken*
14. for I the Lord *have spoken*
28:10. for I *have spoken*
30:12. I the Lord *have spoken*
33: 8. if *thou dost* not *speak* to warn

Eze.33:30. *and speak* one to another,
34:24. I the Lord *have spoken*
36: 5. *have I spoken* against
6. *I have spoken* in my jealousy
36 & 37:14. I the Lord *have spoken*
38:17. *I have spoken* in old time
19. in the fire of my wrath *have I spoken*,
39: 5. for *I have spoken*
8. the day whereof *I have spoken*.
Dan. 9: 6. which *spake* in thy name
12. which *he spake* against us,
Hos. 2:14(16). *and speak* comfortably unt
7:13. yet *they have spoken* lies
10: 4. *They have spoken* words,
12:10(11). *I have also spoken* by the
Joel 3: 8(4:8). for the Lord *hath spoken*
Am. 3: 1. that the Lord *hath spoken*
8. the Lord God *hath spoken*,
Obad 18. for the Lord *hath spoken*
Jon. 3:10. the evil, that *he had said*
Mic. 4: 4. the mouth of the Lord of hosts *hath spoken*
6:12. the inhabitants thereof *have spoken* lies,
Zec. 9:10. *and he shall speak* peace
10: 2. the idols *have spoken* vanity,
13: 3. for *thou speakest* lies

PIEL.—*Infinitive.*

Gen17:22. he left off *talking* with him,
18:27, 31. *to speak* unto the Lord,
29. he *spake* unto him yet again, (lit. added *to speak*)
33. as soon as he had left *communing*
24:15. before he had done *speaking*,
45. before I had done *speaking*
50. we cannot *speak* unto thee
27: 5. *when* Isaac *spake* to Esau
31:29. *that thou speak not* to Jacob
34: 6. unto Jacob *to commune* with him.
37: 4. could not *speak* peaceably *unto him.*
39:10. *as she spake* to Joseph
50:17. Joseph wept *when they spake*
Ex. 4:10. nor since *thou hast spoken*
14. I know that he can speak *well.* (lit. *speaking* he will speak)
5:23. *to speak* in thy name,
6:28. the day (when) the Lord *spake* unto Moses
7: 7. *when they spake* unto Pharaoh.
12:31. serve the Lord, *as ye have said.*
16:10. *as* Aaron *spake* unto the
19: 9. may hear *when I speak* with thee,
29:42. *to speak* there unto thee.
31:18. he had made an end *of communing*
34:29. *while he talked* with him.
33. Moses had done *speaking* with
34. *to speak* with him,
35. until he went in *to speak*
Nu. 3: 1. the day (that) the Lord *spake* with Moses
7:89. *to speak* with him,
12: 8. then were ye not afraid *to speak*
16:31. had made an end *of speaking*
22:19. what the Lord will *say* unto me more.(lit. will add *to say*)
38. any power at all *to say* any thing?
23:12. Must I not take heed *to speak*
Deu 3:26. *speak* no more unto me (lit. add not *to speak*)
4:15. the day (that) the Lord *spake* unto you
5:28(25). *when ye spake* unto me;
11:19. *speaking* of them when thou sittest
18:20. which shall presume *to speak*
— have not commanded him *to speak*,
20: 8. the officers shall *speak* further (lit. shall add *to speak*)
9. have made an end *of speaking*
32:45. Moses made an end *of speaking*
Jos. 4:10. *to speak* unto the people,
Jud. 2: 4. *when* the angel of the Lord *spake*
8: 3. *when he had said* that.
9:37. And Gaal *spake* again (lit. added *to speak*)
12: 6. frame *to pronounce* (it) right.
15:17. when he had made an end *of speaking*,
19: 3. *to speak* friendly unto her,
Ru. 1:18. then she left *speaking* unto her.
1Sa.17:28. *when he spake* unto the men;
18: 1. had made an end *of speaking*
24:16(17). David had made an end *of speaking*
1Sa.25:17. *that* (a man) *cannot speak*
2Sa. 3:19. *to speak* in the ears of David
27. *to speak* with him quietly,
7:20. what can David *say* more
11:19. When thou hast made an end *of telling*
13:36. had made an end *of speaking*,
14:15. I am come *to speak of* this thing
20:18. They were *wont* to speak (lit. *speaking* they will speak)
1K. 2:19. *to speak* unto him for Adonijah.
22:24. *to speak* unto thee?
2K. 2:11. as they still went on, *and talked*,
4:13. *be spoken* for to the king,
7:18. *as* the man of God *had spoken*
18:27. *to speak* these words?
2Ch 18:23. *to speak* unto thee?
25:16. *as he talked* with him,
Ezr. 8:17. what they should *say* unto Iddo, (lit. words *to say*)
Neh. 9:13. *and spakest* with them
13:24. could not *speak* in the Jews' language,
Job 2:10. *as* one of the foolish women *speaketh.*
11: 5. But oh that God would *speak*,
21: 3. after that *I have spoken*,
Ps. 34:13(14). thy lips *from speaking* guile.
52: 3(5). *rather than to speak* righteousness.
Pro.23:16. *when* thy lips *speak* right
Ecc. 1: 8. man cannot *utter*
3: 7. and a time *to speak;*
Cant.5: 6. my soul failed *when he spake:*
Isa. 7:10. the Lord *spake* again unto
8: 5. *spake* also unto me again, (lit. added *to speak*)
32: 4. shall be ready *to speak*
6. *and to utter* error against
7. *even when* the needy *speaketh*
36:12. *to speak* these words?
58: 9. *and speaking* vanity;
13. *nor speaking* (thine own) words:
59: 4. trust in vanity, *and speak* lies;
13. *speaking* oppression and revolt,
Jer. 1: 6. I cannot *speak:* for I (am) a child.
5:13. *and the word* (is) not in them:
14. Because *ye speak* this word,
7:13. rising up early *and speaking*,
9: 5(4). taught their tongue *to speak* lies,
18:20. *to speak* good for them,
25: 3. rising early *and speaking;*
26: 2. I command thee *to speak* unto them;
8. had made an end *of speaking* all that the Lord had commanded (him) *to speak*
15. *to speak* all these words
31:20. since *I spake* against him, I do earnestly
35:14. rising early *and speaking;*
38: 4. *in speaking* such words
43: 1. had made an end *of speaking*
Eze. 3:27. *But when I speak* with thee,
10: 5. of the Almighty God *when he speaketh.*
13: 8. Because *ye have spoken* vanity,
Dan 8:18. *Now as he was speaking* with me,
10:11. *And when he had spoken* this
15. *And when he had spoken* such
17. can the servant of this my lord *talk*
19. *And when he had spoken* unto me,
Hos. 1: 2. The beginning of *the word of* the Lord
13: 1. *When* Ephraim *spake* trembling,

PIEL.—*Imperative.*

Gen24:33. he said, *Speak on.*
50: 4. *speak*, I pray you,
Ex. 6:11. *speak* unto Pharaoh king of
29. *speak* thou unto Pharaoh
11: 2. *Speak* now in the ears of
12: 3. *Speak ye* unto all the congregation
14: 2, 15. *Speak* unto the children of Israel,
16:12. *speak* unto them, saying,
20:19. *Speak* thou with us,
25: 2. *Speak* unto the children of Israel,
31:13. *Speak* thou also unto the
Lev. 1: 2 & 4:2. *Speak* unto the children of Israel,
6:25(18). *Speak* unto Aaron
7:23, 29. *Speak* unto the children of Israel,
11: 2. *Speak* unto the children of
12: 2. *Speak* unto the children of
15: 2. *Speak* unto the children of
16: 2 & 17:2. *Speak* unto Aaron
18: 2. *Speak* unto the children of

Lev.19: 2. *Speak* unto all the congregation
21:17 & 22:2, 18. *Speak* unto Aaron,
23: 2, 10, 24, 34 & 25:2 & 27:2. *Speak* unto the children of Israel,
Nu. 5: 6, 12 & 6:2. *Speak* unto the children of Israel,
6:23 & 8:2. *Speak* unto Aaron
9:10 & 15:2, 18, 38. *Speak* unto the children of
16:24. *Speak* unto the congregation,
17: 2(17) & 19:2 & 33:51 & 35:10. *Speak* unto the children of
Jos.20: 2. *Speak* to the children of Israel,
Jud. 5:12. awake, awake, *utter* a song:
9: 2. *Speak*, I pray you,
19:30. take advice, *and speak*
20: 3. *Tell* (us), how was this wickedness?
1Sa. 3: 9. *Speak*, Lord; for thy servant heareth.
10. *Speak;* for thy servant heareth.
15:16. he said unto him, *Say on.*
18:22. *Commune* with David secretly,
2Sa.13:13. *speak* unto the king;
14:12. he said, *Say on.*
17: 6. do (after) his saying? if not; *speak* thou.
19: 7(8). *and speak* comfortably unto
11(12). *Speak* unto the elders of Judah,
1K. 2:14. she said, *Say on.*
16. she said unto him, *Say on.*
20:11. *Tell* (him), Let not him
2K. 1: 3. *and say* unto them,
18:26. *Speak*, I pray thee,
Job 33:32. *speak*, for I desire to justify thee.
34:33. *speak* what thou knowest.
Isa. 8:10. *speak* the word, and it shall not
30:10. *speak* unto us smooth things,
36:11. *Speak*, I pray thee,
40: 2. *Speak ye* comfortably to Jerusalem,
Jer. 9:22(21). *Speak*, Thus saith the Lord,
Eze. 3: 1. *speak* unto the house of Israel.
12:23. but *say* unto them,
14: 4. Therefore *speak* unto them,
20: 3. *speak* unto the elders of Israel,
27. *speak* unto the house of Israel,
29: 3. *Speak*, and say, Thus saith the Lord
33: 2. *speak* to the children of thy people,
37:19. *Say* unto them,
21. *And say* unto them,
Zec. 2: 4(8). *speak* to this young man,
8:16. *Speak ye* every man the truth

PIEL.—*Future.*

Gen. 8:15. *And* God *spake* unto Noah,
17: 3. *and* God *talked* with him,
18:30. *and I will speak:* Peradventure
32. *and I will speak* yet but
19:14. *and spake* unto his sons in law,
20: 8. *and told* all these things
23: 3. *and spake* unto the sons of Heth,
8. *And he communed* with them,
13. *he spake* unto Ephron
31:24. Take heed that *thou speak* not
32:19(20). On this manner *shall ye speak*
34: 3. *and spake* kindly unto the damsel.
8. *And* Hamor *communed* with them,
13. *and said*, because he had defiled
20. *and communed* with the men
39:17. *And she spake* unto him
41: 9. *Then spake* the chief butler
17. *And* Pharaoh *said* unto Joseph,
42: 7. *and spake* roughly unto them;
24. *and communed* with them,
43:19. *and they communed* with him
44: 6. *he spake* unto them
7. Wherefore *saith* my lord
16. What *shall we speak*,
18. *let* thy servant, I pray thee, *speak* a word
45:27. *And they told* him all the words
50: 4. *And* when the days...were past, Joseph *spake*
21. *and spake* kindly unto them.
Ex. 4:12. teach thee what *thou shalt say.*
14. I know that *he can speak* well.
30. *And* Aaron *spake* all the words
6: 2. *And* God *spake* unto Moses,
9. *And* Moses *spake* so unto the
10. *And* the Lord *spake* unto Moses,
12. *And* Moses *spake* before the Lord,
13. *And* the Lord *spake* unto Moses and unto
29. *That* the Lord *spake* unto Moses,

Ex. 7: 2. Thou *shalt speak* all that
— Aaron thy brother *shall speak*
9. When Pharaoh *shall speak*
13: 1 & 14:1 & 16:11. *And* the Lord *spake* unto Moses,
19: 6. the words which *thou shalt speak*
19. Moses *spake*, and God answered
20: 1. *And* God *spake* all these words,
19. *let* not God *speak* with us,
23:22. do all that *I speak;*
25: 1. *And* the Lord *spake* unto Moses,
28: 3. thou *shalt speak* unto all
30:11, 17. *And* the Lord *spake* unto Moses,
22. *Moreover* the Lord *spake* unto Moses,
31. *thou shalt speak* unto the
31: 1. *And* the Lord *spake* unto Moses,
32: 7. *And* the Lord *said* unto Moses,
13. *and saidst* unto them,
33: 1. *And* the Lord *said* unto Moses,
11. as a man *speaketh* unto his
34:31. *and* Moses *talked* with them.
40: 1. *And* the Lord *spake* unto Moses,
Lev. 1: 1. *and spake* unto him
4: 1 & 5:14 & 6:1(5:20), 8(1), 19(12), 24(17) & 7:22, 28 & 8:1. *And* the Lord *spake* unto Moses,
9: 3. unto the children of Israel *thou shalt speak*,
10: 8. *And* the Lord *spake* unto Aaron,
12. *And* Moses *spake* unto Aaron,
19. *And* Aaron *said* unto Moses,
11: 1. *And* the Lord *spake* unto Moses and to
12: 1 & 13:1 & 14:1, 33 & 15:1 & 16:1 & 17:1 & 18:1 & 19:1 & 20:1 & 21:16. *And* the Lord *spake* unto Moses,
21:24. *And* Moses *told* (it) unto Aaron,
22: 1, 17, 26 & 23:1, 9, 23, 26, 33. *And* the Lord *spake* unto Moses,
23:44. *And* Moses *declared* unto
24: 1, 13. *And* the Lord *spake* unto Moses,
15. *thou shalt speak* unto the
23. *And* Moses *spake* to the children of
25: 1 & 27:1. *And* the Lord *spake* unto Moses
Nu. 1: 1. *And* the Lord *spake* unto Moses in the
48. *For* the Lord *had spoken*
2 1 & 3:5, 11, 14, 44 & 4:1, 17, 21 & 5:1, 5, 11 & 6:1, 22. *And* the Lord *spake* unto Moses
7:89. *and he spake* unto him.
8: 1, 5, 23 & 9:1. *And* the Lord *spake* unto Moses,
9: 4. *And* Moses *spake* unto the children of
9 & 10:1. *And* the Lord *spake* unto Moses,
11:24. *and told* the people
25. *and spake* unto him,
12: 1. *And* Miriam and Aaron *spake* against
6. *will speak* unto him in a dream.
8. With him *will I speak* mouth to mouth,
13: 1. *And* the Lord *spake* unto Moses,
14:26. *And* the Lord *spake* unto Moses and unto
39. *And* Moses *told* these sayings
15: 1, 17. *And* the Lord *spake* unto Moses,
16: 5. *And he spake* unto Korah
20, 23. *And* the Lord *spake* unto Moses
26. *And he spake* unto the congregation,
36(17:1), 44(17:9) & 17:1(16). *And* the Lord *spake* unto Moses,
17: 6(21). *And* Moses *spake* unto the
18: 8. *And* the Lord *spake* unto Aaron,
25. *And* the Lord *spake* unto Moses,
26. Thus *speak* unto the Levites,
19: 1 & 20:7. *And* the Lord *spake* unto Moses
21: 5. *And* the people *spake* against God,
22: 7. *and spake* unto him
8. as the Lord *shall speak* unto me:
20. the word which *I shall say*
35. only the word that *I shall speak* unto thee, that *thou shalt speak*.
38. putteth in my mouth, that *shall I speak.*
23: 5. thus *thou shalt speak.*
16. Go again unto Balak, and *say* thus.
26. All that the Lord *speaketh*,
24:13. what the Lord *saith*, that *will I speak?*
25:10, 16. *And* the Lord *spake* unto Moses,
26: 3. *And* Moses and Eleazar the priest *spake*
52. *And* the Lord *spake* unto Moses,
27: 8. *thou shalt speak* unto the

Nu. 27:15. *And* Moses *spake* unto the Lord,
28: 1. *And* the Lord *spake* unto Moses,
30: 1(2). *And* Moses *spake* unto the heads of
31: 1. *And* the Lord *spake* unto Moses,
3. *And* Moses *spake* unto the people,
33:50 & 34:1, 16 & 35:1, 9. *And* the Lord *spake* unto Moses
36: 1. *and spake* before Moses,
Deu. 1:43. *So I spake* unto you;
2:17. *That* the Lord *spake* unto me,
4:12. *And* the Lord *spake* unto you
5:24(21). that God *doth talk* with man,
27(24). *speak* thou unto us all that the Lord our God *shall speak*
31(28). *and I will speak* unto thee
18:19. which *he shall speak* in my name,
20. or that *shall speak* in the name
22. When a prophet *speaketh* in the
27: 9. *And* Moses and the priests the Levites *spake*
31: 1. *and spake* these words unto all Israel.
28. that *I may speak* these words
30. *And* Moses *spake* in the ears of
32: 1. Give ear, O ye heavens, *and I will speak;*
44. came *and spake* all the words
48. *And* the Lord *spake* unto Moses
Jos. 9:22. *and he spake* unto them, saying,
10:12. Then *spake* Joshua to the Lord
17:14. *And* the children of Joseph *spake*
20: 1. The Lord *also spake* unto Joshua,
21: 2. *And they spake* unto them
22:15. *and they spake* with them,
21. *and said* unto the heads of the thousands
Jud. 6:39. *and I will speak* but this once:
7:11. hear what *they say;*
8: 8. *and spake* unto them
9: 1. *and communed* with them,
3. *And* his mother's brethren *spake*
11:11. *and* Jephthah *uttered* all his words
14: 7. *and talked* with the woman;
16:10, 13. *and told* me lies:
21:13. *to speak* to the children of Benjamin (lit. *and spake* to, &c.)
1Sa. 2: 3. *Talk* no more so exceeding
4:20. the women that stood by her *said*
8:21. *and he rehearsed them* in the ears
9: 6. all that *he saith* cometh surely
25. *And* when they were come...(Samuel) *communed*
10:25. *Then* Samuel *told* the people
11: 4. *and told* the tidings
17:23. *and spake* according to the
18:23. *And* Saul's servants *spake* those words
19: 1. *And* Saul *spake* to Jonathan
3. I *will commune* with
4. *And* Jonathan *spake* good of David
25: 9. *And* when David's young men came, *they spake*
24. *and let* thine handmaid, I pray thee, *speak*
39. sent *and communed* with Abigail,
40. *they spake* unto her,
2Sa. 3:19. *And* Abner also *spake* in the
7:19. *but thou hast spoken* also
28. *and thou hast promised* this goodness
14:12. *Let* thine handmaid, I pray thee, *speak*
15. *I will* now *speak* unto the king;
18. *Let* my lord the king now *speak.*
19:29(30). Why *speakest thou* any more
20:16. *that I may speak* with thee.
18. *They were* wont *to speak* in old time, (lit. speaking *they will speak*)
22: 1. *And* David *spake* unto the Lord
1K. 2:18. *I will speak* for thee unto the
3:22. *Thus they spake* before the king.
4:32(5:12). *And he spake* three thousand proverbs:
33(5:13). *And he spake* of trees,
—(-:—). *he spake also* of beasts,
8:24. *thou spakest also* with thy mouth,
10: 2. *and* when she was come to Solomon, *she communed*
12: 3. *and spake* unto Rehoboam,
7. *And they spake* unto him,
10. *and* the young men...*spake* unto him, saying,
— thus *shalt thou say* unto them,
14. *And spake* to them after the
1K. 13: 7. *And* the king *said* unto the man of God,
12. *And* their father *said*
25. they came *and told* (it) in the city
27. *And he spake* to his sons,
14: 5. thus and thus *shalt thou say*
21: 2. *And* Ahab *spake* unto Naboth,
5. *and said* unto him, Why is thy spirit so
6. *And he said* unto her, Because *I spake* unto Naboth
22:14. that *will I speak.*
16. that *thou tell* me nothing
2K. 1: 7. *And he said* unto them,
— *and told* you these words?
9. *And he spake* unto him,
10. Elijah answered *and said*
11. And he answered *and said* unto him,
12. Elijah answered *and said*
13. besought him, *and said* unto him,
15. *And* the angel of the Lord *said*
16. *And he said* unto him,
5:13. *and spake* unto him,
6:12. that *thou speakest*
18:26. and *talk* not with us
28. in the Jews' language, *and spake,*
21:10. *And* the Lord *spake* by his servants
22:14. *and they communed* with her.
25: 6. *and they gave* judgment upon him. (marg. *spake* judgment)
28. *And he spake* kindly to him,
1Ch 17:17. *for thou hast* (also) *spoken*
26. *and hast promised* this
21: 9. *And* the Lord *spake* unto Gad,
2Ch 6:15. *and spakest* with thy mouth,
9: 1. *and* when she was come to Solomon, *she communed*
10: 3. came *and spake* to Rehoboam.
7. *And they spake* unto him,
10. *And* the young men...*spake* unto him,
14. *And answered* them after
18:13. that *will I speak.*
15. that *thou say* nothing
22:10. she arose *and destroyed* all
30:22. *And* Hezekiah *spake* comfortably
32: 6. *and spake* comfortably to them,
19. *And they spake* against
33:10. *And* the Lord *spake* to Manasseh,
34:22. *and they spake* to her
Est. 8: 3. And Esther *spake yet* again (lit. And Esther added *and spake*)
Job 2:10. *Thou speakest* as one of the foolish women
7:11. *I will speak* in the anguish of
9:35. (Then) *would I speak,* and not fear
10: 1. *I will speak* in the bitterness
13: 3. Surely *I would speak*
7. *Will ye speak* wickedly for God? and *talk* deceitfully for him?
13. *that* I *may speak,* and let come
22. or *let me speak,* and answer
16: 4. I also *could speak* as ye
6. Though *I speak,* my grief is not
18: 2. afterwards *we will speak.*
19:18. *and they spake* against me.
21: 3. Suffer me that I *may speak;*
27: 4. My lips *shall* not *speak*
32: 7. I said, Days *should speak,*
16. for *they spake* not,
20. *I will speak,* that I may be
33:14. God *speaketh* once, yea twice,
31. and I *will speak.*
34:35. Job *hath spoken* without knowledge,
37:20. Shall it be told him that *I speak?*
41: 3(40:27). *will he speak* soft(words)unto thee?
42: 4. and I *will speak:*
Ps. 2: 5. Then *shall he speak* unto them
12: 2(3). *They speak* vanity every one
—(-). with a double heart *do they speak.*
35:20. For *they speak* not peace:
37:30. his tongue *talketh* of judgment.
40: 5(6). I would declare *and speak*
41: 6(7). *he speaketh* vanity:
—(-). goeth abroad, *he telleth,*
49: 3(4). My mouth *shall speak* of wisdom;
50: 7. my people, *and I will speak;*
20. *speakest* against thy brother;
58: 1(2). *Do ye* indeed *speak* righteousness,
73: 8. *and speak* wickedly (concerning) oppression: *they speak* loftily.

Ps. 75: 5(6). *speak* (not with) a stiff neck.
77: 4(5). I am so troubled that *I cannot speak.*
78:19. *Yea, they spake* against God;
85: 8(9). what God the Lord *will speak:* for *he will speak* peace
94: 4. they utter (and) *speak* hard things?
99: 7. *He spake* unto them in the
115: 5. They have mouths, but *they speak* not:
116:10. therefore *have I spoken:*
119:46. *I will speak* of thy testimonies *also*
120: 7. but when *I speak,*
122: 8. *I will* now *say,* Peace (be) within thee.
127: 5. but *they shall speak* (marg. or, *subdue*)
135:16. but *they speak* not;
145:11. and *talk of* thy power;
21. My mouth *shall speak* the praise
Pro. 8: 6. *I will speak* of excellent things;
18:23. The poor *useth* intreaties; (lit. *speaketh* with intreaties)
21:28. but the man that heareth *speaketh*
23: 9. *Speak* not in the ears of a fool:
33. thine heart *shall utter* perverse
24: 2. their lips *talk of* mischief.
Ecc. 7:21. all words that *are spoken;*
Isa. 28:11. *will he speak* to this people.
29: 4. *shalt speak* out of the ground,
32: 6. the vile person *will speak*
36:11. and *speak* not to us in the
38:15. What *shall I say?*
40:27. *and speakest,* O Israel,
41: 1. then *let them speak:*
Jer. 1: 7. I command thee *thou shalt speak.*
4:12. *will* I *give* sentence against
5: 5. *and will speak* unto them;
15. understandest what *they say.*
6:10. To whom *shall I speak,*
7:13. *and I spake* unto you,
8: 6. *they spake* not aright:
9: 5(4). *will* not *speak* the truth:
8(7). *speaketh* peaceably to his
10: 5. as the palm tree, but *speak* not:
12: 1. *let me talk* with thee
6. though *they speak* fair words
18: 7, 9. *I shall speak* concerning a nation,
19: 2. the words that *I shall tell* thee,
20: 8. For since *I spake,*
9. nor *speak* any more
23:16. *they speak* a vision of their
28. *let him speak* my word
25: 3. *and I have spoken* unto you,
29:23. *and have spoken* lying words
34: 3. *he shall speak* with thee
6. *Then* Jeremiah the prophet *spake*
38: 8. *and spake* to the king,
39: 5. *where he gave* judgment upon him. (marg. *spake* with him judgments)
12. even as *he shall say* unto thee.
44:25. Ye and your wives *have both spoken*
52: 9. *where he gave* judgment upon him.
32. *And spake* kindly unto him,
Eze. 2: 1. *and I will speak* unto thee.
3:10. all my words that *I shall speak*
22. *I will* there *talk* with thee.
24. *and spake* with me,
11:25. *Then I spake* unto them
12:25. For I (am) the Lord: *I will speak,* and the word that *I shall speak*
— *will I say* the word, and will perform
28. the word which *I have spoken*
24:18. *So I spake* unto the people
27. *and thou shalt speak,* and be no more
32:21. The strong among the mighty *shall speak*
40: 4. *And* the man *said* unto me,
45 & 41:22. *And he said* unto me,
Dan 1:19. *And* the king *communed* with
2: 4. *Then spake* the Chaldeans
9:22. *and talked* with me,
10:16. I opened my mouth, *and spake,*
19. *Let* my lord *speak;*
11:27. and *they shall speak* lies
36. *shall speak* marvellous things
Hos 12: 4(5). there *he spake* with us;
Hab. 2: 1. will watch to see what *he will say*
Zep. 3:13. nor *speak* lies;
Zec. 6: 8. Then cried he upon me, *and spake* unto me, saying,
10: 2. and *have told* false dreams;

PIEL.—*Participle.*

Gen 27: 6. I heard thy father *speak*
29: 9. while he yet *spake* with them,
45:12. that (it is) my mouth *that speaketh*
Ex. 6:27. These (are) *they which spake*
Deu. 4:33. hear the voice of God *speaking*
5:26(23). *speaking* out of the midst of the fire,
Jos. 5:14. What *saith* my lord
Jud. 6:17. that thou *talkest* with me.
1Sa. 1:13. she *spake* in her heart;
17:23. as he *talked* with them,
2Sa. 14:10. *Whosoever saith* (ought) unto thee,
1K. 1:14. while thou yet *talkest* there
22. while she yet *talked* with the king,
42. while he yet *spake,*
2K. 6:33. while he yet *talked* with them,
8: 4. the king *talked* with Gehazi
2Ch 33:18. the words of the seers *that spake*
Neh 13:24. their children *spake* half
Est. 1:22. *and that* (it) *should be published* (marg. *one should publish* (it))
6:14. while they (were) yet *talking*
Job 1:16, 17, 18. While he (was) yet *speaking,*
Ps. 12: 3(4). the tongue *that speaketh* proud things:
Pro. 2:12. the man *that speaketh* froward things;
Isa. 19:18. *speak* the language of Canaan,
52: 6. I (am) he *that doth speak:*
63: 1. I *that speak* in righteousness,
65:24. while they *are* yet *speaking,*
Jer. 26: 7. heard Jeremiah *speaking*
38: 1. the words that Jeremiah *had spoken*
43: 2. saying unto Jeremiah, Thou *speakest* falsely:
Eze. 1:28. I heard a voice of *one that spake.*
2: 8. hear what I *say* unto thee;
44: 5. all that *I say* unto thee
Dan 8:13. Then I heard one saint *speaking,*
— that certain (saint) *which spake,*
9:20, 21. whiles I was *speaking,*

* PUAL.—*Future.* *

Cant. 8: 8. *when* she *shall be spoken for?*

PUAL.—*Participle.*

Ps. 87: 3. Glorious things *are spoken* of thee,

* HIPHIL.—*Future.* *

Ps. 18:47(48). *and subdueth* the people unto me.
47: 3(4). *He shall subdue* the people

* HITHPAEL.—*Participle.* *

Nu. 7:89. he heard the voice of *one speaking*
2Sa. 14:13. *for* the king *doth speak*
Eze. 2: 2. I heard *him that spake*
43: 6. I heard (him) *speaking* unto me

דָּבָר *dāh-vāhr',* m. 1697

²דִּבְרֵי הַיָּמִים lit. *words of* the days.

Gen 11: 1. *and* of one *speech.* (marg. *words*)
12:17. *because of* Sarai Abram's wife.
15: 1. After these *things the word of* the Lord came
4. behold, *the word of* the Lord
18:14. Is *any thing* too hard for the Lord?
25. to do *after* this *manner,*
19: 8. only unto these men do nothing; (lit. not *a thing*)
21. accepted thee *concerning* this *thing*
22. I cannot do *any thing* till thou
20: 8. told all these *things*
10. that thou hast done this *thing?*
11. they will slay me for my wife's *sake.*
18. *because* of Sarah Abraham's wife.
21:11. *the thing* was very grievous
26. I wot not who hath done this *thing:*
22: 1. came to pass after these *things*
16. because thou hast done this *thing,*
20. it came to pass after these *things,*
24: 9. sware to him concerning that *matter.*
28. her mother's house these *things.*
30. when he heard *the words of*
33. until I have told *mine errand.*
50. *The thing* proceedeth from the Lord:
52. Abraham's servant heard *their words,*
66. the servant told Isaac all *things*

Gen27:34. when Esau heard *the words of*
42. And *these words of* Esau
29:13. he told Laban all these *things*.
30:31. if thou wilt do this *thing*
34. might be *according to thy word*.
31: 1. he heard *the words of* Laban's
32:19(20). *On* this *manner* shall ye
34:14. We cannot do this *thing*,
18. *their words* pleased Hamor,
19. deferred not to do *the thing*,
37: 8. and for *his words*.
11. his father observed *the saying*.
14. bring me *word* again.
39: 7. came to pass after these *things*,
17. *according to* these *words*,
19. heard *the words of* his wife,
— *After* this *manner* did thy
40: 1. it came to pass after these *things*,
41:28. This (is) *the thing* which I have
32. because *the thing* (is) established
37. *the thing* was good in the eyes of
42:16. that *your words* may be proved,
20. so shall *your words* be verified,
43: 7. to the tenor of these *words* :
18. *Because of* the money that was returned
44: 2. *according to the word* that Joseph had spoken.
6. spake unto them these same *words*.
7. saith my lord these *words* ?
— do *according to* this *thing* :
10. *according unto your words* :
18. speak *a word* in my lord's ears,
24. we told him *the words of* my lord.
45:27. they told him all *the words of* Joseph,
47:30. I will do *as thou hast said*. (lit. *as thy word*)
48: 1. it came to pass after these *things*,
Ex. 1:18. Why have ye done this *thing*,
2:14. Surely *this thing* is known.
15. when Pharaoh heard this *thing*,
4:10. O my Lord, I (am) not eloquent, (marg. a man of *words*)
15. put *words* in his mouth:
28. Moses told Aaron all *the words of*
30. Aaron spake all *the words*
5: 9. let them not regard vain *words*.
11. yet not *ought* of your work
13. Fulfil your works, (your) daily *tasks*, (marg. *a matter of* a day in his day)
19. from your bricks of your daily *task*.
8:10(6). *according to thy word*: that thou
12(8). *because of* the frogs
13(9), 31(27). *according to the word of* Moses;
9: 4. there shall no*thing* die of all (that is) the
5. the Lord shall do this *thing*
6. the Lord did that *thing*
20. He that feared *the word of* the Lord
21. he that regarded not *the word of* the Lord
12:24. ye shall observe this *thing*
35. did *according to the word of* Moses;
14:12. *the word* that we did tell thee
16: 4. gather *a certain rate* every day, (marg. *the portion of* a day in his day)
16, 32. This (is) *the thing* which the Lord
18:11. for *in the thing* wherein they dealt
14. What (is) this *thing* that thou
16. When they have *a matter*,
17. *The thing* that thou doest
18. this *thing* (is) too heavy for thee;
19. bring *the causes* unto God:
22. every great *matter* they shall bring unto thee, but every small *matter*
23. If thou shalt do this *thing*,
26. *the* hard *causes* they brought unto Moses, but every small *matter*
19: 6. These (are) *the words*
7. before their faces all these *words*
8. Moses returned *the words of*
9. Moses told *the words of*
20: 1. God spake all these *words*,
22: 9(8). For all *manner of* trespass,
—(–). *the cause of* both parties
23: 7. Keep thee far *from a* false *matter*;
8. perverteth *the words of* the righteous.
24: 3. told the people all *the words of* the Lord,
— All *the words* which the Lord
4. Moses wrote all *the words of*
8. concerning all these *words*.

Ex. 24:14. if any man have any *matters*
29: 1. *the thing* that thou shalt do
32:28. did *according to the word of* Moses:
33: 4. the people heard these evil *tidings*,
17. I will do this *thing*
34: 1. *the words* that were in the first
27. Write thou these *words*: for after the tenor of these *words*
28. *the words of* the covenant, *the* ten *commandments*.
35: 1. These (are) *the words* which
4. *the thing* which the Lord commanded,
Lev. 4:13. *the thing* be hid from
5: 2. if a soul touch any unclean *thing*,
8: 5. This (is) *the thing* which the
36. So Aaron and his sons did all *things*
9: 6. *the thing* which the Lord commanded
10: 7. did *according to the word of* Moses.
17: 2. This (is) *the thing* which the Lord
23:37. every *thing* upon his day:
Nu. 11:23. whether *my word* shall come to pass
24. told the people *the words of*
12: 6. Hear now *my words*:
13:26. brought back *word*
14:20. pardoned *according to thy word*:
39. Moses told these *sayings*
15:31. he hath despised *the word of*
16:31. speaking all these *words*,
49(17:14). died about *the matter of* Korah.
18: 7. for every *thing of* the altar,
20:19. without (doing) *any thing*
22: 7. spake unto him *the words of*
8. I will bring you *word* again,
20. yet *the word* which I shall say
35. only *the word* that I shall speak
38. *the word* that God putteth
23: 3. *and* whats*oever* he sheweth me
5. put *a word* in Balaam's mouth,
16. put *a word* in his mouth,
25:18. in *the matter of* Peor, and in *the matter of* Cozbi,
— in the day of the plague for Peor's *sake*.
30: 1(2). *the thing* which the Lord hath commanded.
2(3). he shall not break *his word*,
31:16. *through the counsel of* Balaam,
— in *the matter of* Peor,
23. Every *thing* that may abide
32:20. If ye will do this *thing*,
36: 6. *the thing* which the Lord doth
Deu 1: 1. These (be) *the words* which
14. *The thing* which thou hast spoken
17. *and the cause* that is too hard
18. all *the things* which ye should
22. bring us *word* again
23. *the saying* pleased me well:
25. brought us *word* again,
32. *Yet in* this *thing* ye did
34. the Lord heard the voice of *your words*,
2: 7. thou hast lacked no*thing*.
26. with *words of* peace,
3:26. unto me *of* this *matter*.
4: 2. Ye shall not add unto *the word*
9. lest thou forget *the things*
10. I will make them hear *my words*,
12. ye heard the voice of *the words*,
13. to perform, (even) ten *commandments*;
21. angry with me for *your sakes*,
30. all these *things* are come
32. *as* this great *thing*
36. *and* thou heardest *his words*
5: 5. to shew you *the word of* the Lord:
22(19). These *words* the Lord spake
28(25). heard the voice of *your words*,
—(—). have heard the voice of *the words of*
6: 6. these *words*, which I command
9: 5. *the word* which the Lord sware
10. according to all *the words*,
10: 2. *the words* that were in the
4. the ten *commandments*, (marg. *words*)
11:18. lay up these *my words*
12:28. Observe and hear all these *words*
32(13:1). What *thing* soever I command you,
13: 3(4). hearken unto *the words of* that
11(12). shall do no more *any such* wickedness (lit. *according to* this evil *thing*)
14(15). *the thing* certain,

Deu. 15: 2. this (is) *the manner of* the release:
9. that there be not *a thought* (marg. *word*)
10. because that for this *thing*
15. therefore I command thee this *thing*
16:19. pervert *the words of* the righteous. (marg. or, *matters*)
17: 1. wherein is blemish, (or) any evilfavoured*ness:* (lit. *an* evil *thing*)
4. true, (and) *the thing* certain,
5. have committed that wicked *thing*,
8. If there arise *a matter* too hard
— *matters of* controversy
9. they shall shew thee *the sentence of*
10. thou shalt do according to *the sentence*, (lit. the mouth of *the word*)
11. shalt not decline from *the sentence*
19. keep all *the words of* this law
18:18. will put *my words* in his
19. will not hearken unto *my words*
20. to speak *a word* in my name,
21. How shall we know *the word*
22. if *the thing* follow not,
— that (is) *the thing* which the Lord
19: 4. this (is) *the case of* the slayer,
15. shall *the matter* be established.
20. commit no more *any such* evil among you.
22:14. give occasions of *speech*
17. he hath given occasions of *speech*
20. But if this *thing* be true,
24. because she cried not,
— *because* he hath humbled his neighbour's
26. unto the damsel thou shalt do no*thing;*
— even so (is) this *matter:*
23: 4(5). Be*cause* they met you not
9(10). keep thee from every wicked *thing*.
14(15). no unclean *thing* in thee,
19(20). usury of any *thing*
24: 1. he hath found *some* unclean*ness* (lit. nakedness of *a thing*)
5. neither shall he be charged with any *business:* (marg. not any *thing* shall pass upon him)
18, 22. command thee to do this *thing*.
27: 3. upon them all *the words of* this law,
8. upon the stones all *the words of* this law
26. not (all) *the words of* this law
28:14. *the words* which I command thee
58. do all *the words of* this law
29: 1(28:69). These (are) *the words of* the covenant,
9(8). Keep therefore *the words of* this
19(18). when he heareth *the words of*
29(28). do all *the words of* this law.
30: 1. these *things* are come upon thee,
14. *the word* (is) very nigh unto thee,
31: 1. spake these *words* unto all
12. observe to do all *the words of* this law:
24. an end of writing *the words of* this law
28. that I may speak these *words*
30. *the words of* this song,
32:44. spake all *the words of* this song
45. an end of speaking all these *words*
46. all *the words* which I testify
— all *the words of* this law.
47. For it (is) not *a* vain *thing*
— *and through* this *thing*
Jos. 1:13. Remember *the word* which
18. will not hearken unto *thy words*
2:14. if ye utter not this *our business*.
20. if thou utter this *our business*,
21. *According unto your words*, so (be) it.
3: 9. hear *the words of* the Lord
4:10. every *thing* was finished
5: 4. *the cause* why Joshua did
6:10. neither shall (any) *word* proceed
8: 8. *according to the commandment of*
27. *according unto the word of* the Lord
34. he read all *the words of* the law,
35. There was not *a word* of all
9:24. have done this *thing*.
11:15. he left no*thing* undone of all that
14: 6. *the thing* that the Lord said
7. I brought him *word* again
10. since the Lord spake this *word*
20: 4. shall declare *his cause*
21:45(43). There failed not *ought* of any good *thing* which the Lord

Jos. 22:24. done it for fear *of* (this) *thing*,
30. heard *the words* that
32. brought them *word* again.
33. *the thing* pleased the children of
23:14. that not one *thing* hath failed of all the good *things*
— not one *thing* hath failed
15. all good *things* are come upon
— bring upon you all evil *things*,
24:26. Joshua wrote these *words*
29. came to pass after these *things*,
Jud. 2: 4. the angel of the Lord spake these *words*
3:19. I have *a* secret *errand*
20. I have *a message from* God
6:29. Who hath done this *thing?*
— the son of Joash hath done this *thing*.
8: 1. Why hast thou served us *thus*, (marg. What *thing* (is) this thou hast done unto us)
3. when he had said *that*. (lit. this *thing*)
9: 3. men of Shechem all these *words:*
30. heard *the words of* Gaal
11:10. *according to thy words*.
11. Jephthah uttered all *his words*
28. hearkened not unto *the words of*
37. Let this *thing* be done for me:
13:12. Now let *thy words* come to pass.
17. when *thy sayings* come to pass
16:16. pressed him daily *with her words*,
18: 7. to shame in (any) *thing;*
— *and* had no *business* with (any) man.
10. no want of any *thing*
28. they had no *business* with
19:19. no want of any *thing*.
24. do not so vile *a thing*. (marg. *the matter of* this folly)
20: 7. give here your *advice*
9. this (shall be) *the thing*
21:11. this (is) *the thing* that ye shall do,
Ru. 3:18. how *the matter* will fall:
— until he have finished *the thing*
4: 7. for to confirm all *things;*
1 Sa. 1:23. the Lord establish *his word*.
2:23. Why do ye *such things?* (lit. *according to* these *things*) for I hear of *your* evil *dealings*
3: 1. *And the word of* the Lord
7. neither was *the word of* the
11. I will do *a thing* in Israel,
17. What (is) *the thing*
— if thou hide (any) *thing* (marg. *word*) from me of all *the things* that he said
18. told him every *whit*, (marg. all *the things*, or, *words*)
19. did let none of *his words* fall
21. *by the word of* the Lord.
4: 1. *the word of* Samuel came
16. What is *there done*, my son? (marg. *the thing*)
8: 6. *the thing* displeased Samuel,
10. Samuel told all *the words of*
21. Samuel heard all *the words of*
9:10. Then said Saul...Well *said;* (lit. *thy word* is good)
21. wherefore then speakest thou *so* (marg. *according to* this *word*)
27. that I may shew thee *the word of* God.
10: 2. hath left *the care of* the asses, (marg. *business*)
16. But of *the matter of* the kingdom,
11: 4. and told *the tidings* in the ears
5. they told him *the tidings of*
6. when he heard those *tidings*,
12:16. stand and see this great *thing*,
14:12. we will shew you *a thing*.
15: 1. the voice of *the words of* the Lord.
10. Then came *the word of* the Lord
11. performed *my commandments*.
13. I have performed *the commandment of*
23, 26. rejected *the word of* the Lord,
24. the commandment of the Lord, and *thy words:*
16:18. prudent in *matters*, (marg. or, *speech*)
17:11. Saul and all Israel heard those *words of*
23. *according to the* same *words:*
27. answered him *after* this *manner*,
29. (Is there) not *a cause?*

1Sa. 17:30. spake *after the* same *manner* (marg. *word*): and the people answered him (lit. returned *a word*) *after the* former *manner.*
31. when *the words* were heard
18: 8. *the saying* displeased him;
20. *the thing* pleased him.
23. Saul's servants spake those *words*
24. *On* this *manner* spake David. (lit. *according to* these *words*)
26. told David these *words, it* pleased David well (lit. *the thing* was right)
19: 7. Jonathan shewed him all those *things.*
20: 2. will do no*thing* either great or small, (lit. *a* great *thing* or *a* small *thing*)
— hide this *thing* from me?
21. and no *hurt;* (marg. not (any) *thing*)
23. *And* (as touching) *the matter*
39. Jonathan and David knew *the matter.*
21: 2(3). hath commanded me *a business,*
—(–). know any thing of *the business*
8(9). *the* king's *business* required
12(13). David laid up these *words*
22:15. the king impute (any) *thing*
— knew no*thing* of all this, less or more.
24: 6(7). that I should do this *thing*
7(8). stayed his servants with these *words,*
9(10). hearest thou men's *words,*
16(17). an end of speaking these *words*
25: 9. according to all those *words*
12. told him all those *sayings.*
24. hear *the words of* thine handmaid.
36. told him no*thing*, less or more,
37. his wife had told him these *things,*
26:16. This *thing* (is) not good
19. hear *the words of* his servant.
28:10. happen to thee *for* this *thing.*
18. hath the Lord done this *thing*
20. *because of the words of* Samuel:
21. and have hearkened unto *thy words*
30:24. hearken unto you *in* this *matter?*
2Sa. 1: 4. How went *the matter?*
2: 6. because ye have done this *thing.*
3: 8. Abner very wroth for *the words of*
11. could not answer Abner *a word* again,
13. but one *thing* I require
17. *And* Abner had *communication*
7: 4. that *the word of* the Lord came
7. spake I *a word* with any
17. According to all these *words,*
21. For *thy word*'s sake,
25. *the word* that thou hast spoken concerning thy servant,
28. *and thy words* be true,
11:11. I will not do this *thing.*
18. all *the things concerning* the war;
19. an end of telling the *matters of* the war
25. Let not this *thing* displease
27. But *the thing* that David had done
12: 6. because he did this *thing,*
9. despised *the commandment of*
12. I will do this *thing* before all Israel,
14. *by* this *deed* thou hast given
21. What *thing* (is) this that thou
13:20. regard not this *thing.*
21. David heard of all these *things,*
22. *because* he had forced his sister
33. take *the thing* to his heart,
35. *as* thy servant *said,* (marg. *according to the word of* thy servant)
14: 3. speak on this *manner* unto him. So Joab put *the words* in her mouth.
12. speak (one) *word* unto my lord
13. the king doth speak this *thing*
15. come to speak of this *thing*
— perform *the request of* his handmaid.
17. *The word of* my lord the king
18. *the thing* that I shall ask
19. he put all these *words* in the
20. To fetch about this form of *speech* hath thy servant Joab done this *thing:*
21. I have done this *thing:*
22. fulfilled *the request of* his servant.
15: 3. See, *thy matters* (are) good and right;
6. *on* this *manner* did Absalom
11. they knew not any *thing.*
28. until there come *word*

2Sa. 15:35. what *thing* soever thou shalt hear
36. every *thing* that ye can hear.
16:23. enquired *at the oracle of* God: (marg. *word*)
17: 4. *the saying* pleased Absalom
6. hath spoken *after* this *manner:* shall we do (after) *his saying?*
19. *the thing* was not known.
18: 5. gave all the captains charge *concerning* (lit. upon *the affair of*)
13. there is no *matter* hid from the
19:11(12). *seeing the speech of* all Israel
29(30). thou any more of *thy matters?*
42(43). be ye angry for this *matter?*
43(44). that *our advice* should be
—(—). *the words of* the men of Judah were fiercer *than the words of* the
20:17. Hear *the words of* thine handmaid.
21. *The matter* (is) not so:
22: 1. *the words of* this song
23: 1. these (be) *the* last *words of* David.
24: 3. the king delight *in* this *thing?*
4. the king's *word* prevailed
11. *the word of* the Lord came
13. see what *answer*
19. *according to* the *saying* of Gad, went up
1K. 1: 7. And he conferred (marg. *his words* were) with Joab the son
14. and confirm *thy words.*
27. Is this *thing* done by my lord
2: 4. the Lord may continue *his word*
14. I have *somewhat to say* unto thee.
23. have not spoken this *word*
27. that he might fulfil *the word of*
30. Benaiah brought the king *word* again,
38. *The saying* (is) good:
42. *The word* (that) I have heard
3:10. *the speech* pleased the Lord, that Solomon had asked this *thing.*
11. thou hast asked this *thing,*
12. done *according to thy words:*
4:27(5:7). every man in his month: they lacked no*thing.*
5: 7(21). when Hiram heard *the words of*
6:11. *the word of* the Lord came
12. then will I perform *my word*
38. the house finished throughout all *the parts thereof,*
8:20. hath performed *his word*
26. let *thy word,* I pray thee, be verified,
56. there hath not failed one *word* of all *his* good *promise,*
59. let these *my words,*
— at all times, as *the matter* shall require. (marg. *the thing of* a day in his day)
9:15. this (is) *the reason of* the levy
10: 3. told her all *her questions* (marg. *words*): there was not (any) *thing*
6. It was *a* true *report* (marg. *word*)
— mine own land of *thy acts* (marg. *sayings*)
7. Howbeit I believed not *the words,*
25. *a rate* year by year.
11:10. concerning this *thing,*
27. *the cause* that he lifted up
41. the rest of *the acts of* Solomon, (marg. *words*, or, *things*)
— in the book of *the acts of* Solomon?
12: 6. that I may answer (lit. return *word*) this
7. speak good *words* to them,
9. that we may answer (lit. return *word*)
15. that he might perform *his saying,*
16. the people answered (lit. returned *word*)
22. But *the word of* God came
24. for this *thing* is from me. They hearkened therefore to *the word of* the Lord, and returned to depart, *according to the word of* the Lord.
30. this *thing* became a sin:
13: 1. *by the word of* the Lord unto Beth-el:
2. *in the word of* the Lord,
4. king Jeroboam heard *the saying of*
5. given *by the word of* the Lord.
9. charged me *by the word of* the Lord,
11. *the words* which he had spoken
17. For it was *said* (marg. *a word* (was)) to me *by the word of* the Lord,
18. unto me *by the word of* the Lord,

1K. 13:20. that *the word of* the Lord came
26. *according to the word of* the Lord,
32. For *the saying* which he cried *by the word of* the Lord
33. After this *thing* Jeroboam
34. this *thing* became sin
14: 5. cometh to ask *a thing* of thee
13. there is found (some) good *thing*
18. *according to the word of* the Lord,
19. the rest of *the acts of* Jeroboam,
—, 29. written in the book of the chronicles[2]
29. the rest of *the acts of* Rehoboam,
15: 5. *in the matter of* Uriah
7. the rest of *the acts of* Abijam,
—, 23, 31. written in the book of the chronicles[2]
23. rest of all *the acts of* Asa,
29. *according unto the saying of* the Lord,
31. the rest of *the acts of* Nadab,
16: 1. *the word of* the Lord came
5. the rest of *the acts of* Baasha,
—, 14, 20, 27. written in the book of the chronicles[2]
7. came *the word of* the Lord
12, 34. *according to the word of* the Lord,
14. the rest of *the acts of* Elah,
20. the rest of *the acts of* Zimri,
27. the rest of *the acts of* Omri
17: 1. according to *my word.*
2, 8. *the word of* the Lord came
5. did *according unto the word of* the Lord:
13. do *as thou hast said:*
15. *according to the saying of* Elijah:
16. *according to the word of* the Lord,
17. came to pass after these *things,*
24. (and) *that the word of* the Lord
18: 1. *that the word of* the Lord came
21. answered him not *a word.*
24. answered and said, It is well *spoken.* (marg. *The word* (is) good)
31. *the word of* the Lord came,
36. *and* (that) I have done all these *things at thy word.*
19: 9. *the word of* the Lord
20: 4. O king, *according to thy saying,*
9. *but* this *thing* I may not do.
— brought him *word* again.
12. heard this *message,* (marg. *word*)
24. And do this *thing,*
35. *in the word of* the Lord,
21: 1. came to pass after these *things,*
4. displeased because of *the word* which
17, 28. *the word of* the Lord came
27. when Ahab heard those *words,*
22: 5. at *the word of* the Lord
13. *the words of* the prophets
— let *thy word,* I pray thee, be *like the word of* one of them,
19. therefore *the word of* the Lord:
38. *according unto the word of* the Lord
39. the rest of *the acts of* Ahab,
—, 45(46). in the book of the chronicles[2]
45(46). the rest of *the acts of* Jehoshaphat,
2K. 1: 7. told you these *words?*
16. to enquire *of his word?*
17. *according to the word of* the Lord
18. the rest of *the acts of* Ahaziah
— written in the book of the chronicles[2]
2:22. *according to the saying of* Elisha
3:12. *The word of* the Lord
4:41. there was no harm (marg. evil *thing*)
44. *according to the word of* the Lord.
5:13. bid thee (do some) great *thing,*
14. *according to the saying of* the man
18. *In* this *thing* the Lord pardon
— pardon thy servant *in* this *thing.*
6:11. sore troubled for this *thing;*
12. *the words* that thou speakest
18. *according to the word of* Elisha.
30. when the king heard *the words of*
7: 1. Hear ye *the word of* the Lord;
2. might this *thing* be?
16. *according to the word of* the Lord.
19. the Lord should make windows in heaven, might *such a thing* be?
8: 2. did *after the saying of* the man of God:
13. that he should do this great *thing?*
23. the rest of *the acts of* Joram,

2K. 8:23. written in the book of the chronicles[2]
9: 5. I have *an errand* to thee,
26. *according to the word of* the Lord.
36. This (is) *the word of* the Lord,
10:10. nothing *of the word of* the Lord,
17. *according to the saying of* the Lord,
34. the rest of *the acts of* Jehu,
— in the book of the chronicles[2]
11: 5. This (is) *the thing* that ye shall do;
12:19(20). the rest of *the acts of* Joash,
—(—) written in the book of the chronicles[2]
13: 8. the rest of *the acts of* Jehoahaz,
—, 12. written in the book of the chronicles[2]
12. the rest of *the acts of* Joash,
14:15. the rest of *the acts of* Jehoash
—, 18, 28. written in the book of the chronicles[2]
18. the rest of *the acts of* Amaziah,
25. *according to the word of* the
28. the rest of *the acts of* Jeroboam,
15: 6. the rest of *the acts of* Azariah,
—, 11, 15, 21, 26, 31, 36. written in the book of the chronicles[2]
11. the rest of *the acts of* Zachariah,
12. *the word of* the Lord
15. the rest of *the acts of* Shallum,
21. the rest of *the acts of* Menahem,
26. the rest of *the acts of* Pekahiah,
31. the rest of *the acts of* Pekah,
36. the rest of *the acts of* Jotham,
16:19. the rest of *the acts of* Ahaz
— written in the book of the chronicles[2]
17: 9. Israel did secretly (those) *things*
11. wrought wicked *things*
12. Ye shall not do this *thing.*
18:20. but (they are but) vain *words,* (marg. *word of* the lips)
27. to speak these *words?*
28. Hear *the word of* the great king,
36. answered him not *a word:*
37. told him *the words of* Rab-shakeh.
19: 4. It may be the Lord thy God will hear all *the words of* Rab-shakeh,
— reprove *the words* which the Lord
6. Be not afraid of *the words*
16. hear *the words of* Sennacherib,
21. This (is) *the word* that the
20: 4. *that the word of* the Lord came
9. that the Lord will do *the thing*
13. no*thing* in his house,
15. no*thing* among my treasures
16. Hear *the word of* the Lord.
17. no*thing* shall be left,
19. Good (is) *the word of* the Lord
20. the rest of *the acts of* Hezekiah,
— written in the book of the chronicles[2]
21:17. the rest of *the acts of* Manasseh,
—, 25. written in the book of the chronicles[2]
25. the rest of *the acts of* Amon
22: 9. brought the king *word*
11. heard *the words of* the book
13. concerning *the words of* this book
— hearkened unto *the words of* this book,
16. all *the words of* the book
18. *the words* which thou hast heard;
20. brought the king *word* again.
23: 2. all *the words of* the book
3. *the words of* this covenant
16. *according to the word of* the Lord
— who proclaimed these *words.*
17. proclaimed these *things*
24. perform *the words of* the law
28. the rest of *the acts of* Josiah,
— written in the book of the chronicles[2]
24: 2. *according to the word of* the Lord,
5. the rest of *the acts of* Jehoiakim,
— written in the book of the chronicles[2]
25:30. *a* daily *rate* for every day,
1Ch 4:22. *And* (these are) ancient *things.*
10:13. against *the word of* the Lord,
11: 3, 10. *according to the word of* the Lord
13: 4. for *the thing* was right
15:15. *according to the word of* the Lord.
16:15. *the word* (which) he commanded
37. *as* every day's *work* required:
17: 3. that *the word of* God
6. spake I *a word* to any
15. According to all these *words,*

1Ch 17:23. let *the thing* that thou hast
21: 4. *Nevertheless* the king's *word* prevailed
6. the king's *word* was abominable
7. was displeased with this *thing;*
8. because I have done this *thing:*
12. what *word* I shall bring
19. David went up *at the saying of* Gad,
22: 8. *the word of* the Lord came
23:27. *by the* last *words of* David
25: 5. the king's seer *in the words of* God, (marg. or, *matters*)
26:32. every *matter pertaining to* God, *and affairs* (marg. *thing*) *of* the king.
27: 1. in any *matter of* the courses,
24. put in the account of the chronicles[2] (lit. *words of* the days)
28:21. wholly at *thy commandment.*
29:29. *Now the acts of* David the king, first and last, behold, they (are) written in *the book of* Samuel the seer, and in *the book of* Nathan the prophet, and in *the book of* Gad the seer,
2Ch 1: 9. let *thy promise* unto David
6:10. hath performed *his word*
17. let *thy word* be verified, which thou
8:13. *Even after a certain rate* every day,
14. *as the duty of* every day
15. concerning any *matter,*
9: 2. told her all *her questions:* and there was no*thing* hid
5. (It was) *a* true *report* (marg. *word*)
— in mine own land of *thine acts,* (marg. or, *sayings*)
6. I believed not *their words,*
24. *a rate* year by year.
29. the rest of *the acts of* Solomon,
— written in *the book of* Nathan (marg. *words*)
10: 6. to return *answer*
7. speak good *words* to them,
9. we may return *answer*
15. might perform *his word,*
11: 2. *the word of* the Lord came
4. for this *thing* is done of me. And they obeyed *the words of* the Lord,
12: 7. *the word of* the Lord came
12. also in Judah *things* went well.
15. *Now the acts of* Rehoboam,
— *in the book of* Shemaiah (marg. *words*)
13:22. the rest of *the acts of* Abijah, and his ways, *and his sayings,*
15: 8. when Asa heard these *words,*
16:11. behold, *the acts of* Asa,
18: 4. at *the word of* the Lord
12. *the words of* the prophets
— let *thy word* therefore,
18. hear *the word of* the Lord;
19: 3. there are good *things* found in thee,
6. who (is) with you in the judgment. (marg. *in the matter of* judgment)
11. in all *matters of* the Lord;
— for all the king's *matters:*
20:34. the rest of *the acts of* Jehoshaphat.
— *in the book of* Jehu (marg. *words*)
23: 4. *the thing* that ye shall do;
19. unclean in any *thing*
24: 5. see that ye hasten *the matter.*
25:26. the rest of *the acts of* Amaziah,
26:22. the rest of *the acts of* Uzziah,
27: 7. the rest of *the acts of* Jotham,
28:26. Now the rest of *his acts*
29:15. *by the words of* the Lord, (marg. or, *in the business of*)
30. *with the words of* David,
36. *the thing* was (done) suddenly.
30: 4. *the thing* pleased the king
5. So they established *a decree*
12. *by the word of* the Lord.
31: 5. as soon as *the commandment* came abroad,
16. his daily *portion*
32: 1. After these *things,*
8. *the words of* Hezekiah king of Judah.
32. the rest of *the acts of* Hezekiah,
33:18. the rest of *the acts of* Manasseh,
— *and the words of* the seers
— (written) in *the book of* the kings
19. written among *the sayings of* the seers.
34:16. brought the king *word*

2Ch 34:19. the king had heard *the words of* the law,
21. concerning *the words of* the book
— have not kept *the word of*
26. *the words* which thou hast heard;
27. when thou heardest *his words*
28. brought the king *word* again.
30. *the words of* the book
31. to perform *the words of* the covenant
35: 6. *according to the word of* the Lord
22. hearkened not unto *the words of*
26. the rest of *the acts of* Josiah,
27. *And his deeds,* first and last,
36: 8. the rest of *the acts of* Jehoiakim,
16. and despised *his words,*
21. To fulfil *the word of* the Lord
22. that *the word of* the Lord
Ezr. 1: 1. that *the word of* the Lord
3: 4. as *the duty of* every day required; (marg. *the matter of* the day in his day)
7: 1. Now after these *things,*
11. *the words of* the commandments
8:17. I told them *what* they should say (marg. I put *words* in their mouth)
9: 3. when I heard this *thing,*
4. *at the words of* the God of Israel,
10: 4. for (this) *matter* (belongeth) unto
5. do *according to* this *word.*
9. because of (this) *matter,*
12. *As thou hast said,* (lit. *according to thy word*)
13. transgressed *in* this *thing.*
14. until the fierce wrath of our God *for* this *matter* be turned
16. to examine *the matter.*
Neh 1: 1. *The words of* Nehemiah
4. when I heard these *words,*
8. *the word* that thou commandedst
2:18. as also the king's *words*
19. What (is) this *thing* that ye do?
20. Then answered I them, (lit. returned *a word*)
5: 6. when I heard their cry and these *words.*
8. found no*thing* (to answer).
9. It (is) not good *that* ye do:
12, 13. *according to* this *promise.*
13. that performeth not this *promise,*
6: 4. four times *after* this *sort;*
— *after the* same *manner.*
5. *in* like *manner* the fifth time
6, 7. *according to* these *words.*
8. There are no such *things* (lit. not *as* these *things*)
19. *and* uttered *my words* (marg. or, *matters*)
8: 4. had made *for the purpose;*
9. when they heard *the words of* the law.
12. had understood *the words*
13. understand *the words of* the law.
9: 8. hast performed *thy words;*
11:23. *due for* every day.
24. all *matters* concerning the people.
12:23. written in the book of the chronicles[2]
47. every day his *portion:*
13:17. What evil *thing* (is) this
Est. 1:12. *at* the king's *commandment*
13. so (was) the king's *manner*
17. For (this) *deed of* the queen
18. heard of *the deed of* the queen.
19. let there go *a* royal *commandment*
21. And *the saying* pleased the king
— did *according to the word of* Memucan:
2: 1. After these *things,*
4. *the thing* pleased the king;
8. when the king's *commandment*
15. she required no*thing*
22. *the thing* was known
23. inquisition was made of *the matter,*
— written in the book of the chronicles[2]
3: 1. After these *things* did king Ahasuerus
4. to see whether Mordecai's *matters* would
15. *by* the king's *commandment,*
4: 3. the king's *commandment*
9. told Esther *the words of* Mordecai.
12. told to Mordecai Esther's *words.*
5: 5. do as Esther *hath said.* (lit. *the word of*)
8. to morrow *as* the king *hath said.* (lit. *according to the word of* the king)
14. *the thing* pleased Haman;
6: 1. records of the chronicles;[2]

Est. 6: 3. There is no*thing* done for him.
10. let no*thing* fail of all
7: 8. As *the word* went out
8: 5. and *the thing* (seem) right before
14. *by* the king's *commandment.*
17. the king's *commandment* and his
9: 1. when the king's *commandment*
20. Mordecai wrote these *things,*
26. all *the words of* this letter,
30. *words of* peace and truth,
31. *the matters of* the fastings
32. these *matters of* Purim ;
10: 2. written in the book of the chronicles [2]
Job 2:13. none spake *a word*
4: 2. we assay *to commune* with (marg. *a word*)
12. *a thing* was secretly brought
6: 3. *my words* are swallowed up.
9:14. choose out *my words*
11: 2. Should not the multitude of *words*
15: 3. reason *with* unprofitable *talk?*
11. any secret *thing* with thee ?
16: 3. Shall vain *words have* an end ?
19:28. *the matter* is found in me?
26:14. how little *a portion* is heard
29:22. After *my words* they spake not again ;
31:40. *The words of* Job are ended.
32: 4. Elihu had waited till Job *had spoken,* (marg. expected Job *in words*)
11. I waited *for your words ;*
33: 1. hearken to all *my words.*
13. he giveth not account of any of *his matters.*
34:35. *and his words* (were) without
41:12(4). conceal his parts, nor his power, (lit. *and the word of* his power)
42: 7. had spoken these *words*
Ps. 7[title](1). concerning *the words of* Cush (marg. or, *business*)
17: 4. *by the word of* thy lips
18[title](1). *the words of* this song
19: 3(4). no speech nor *language,*
22: 1(2). *the words of* my roaring ?
33: 4. *the word of* the Lord (is) right ;
6. *By the word of* the Lord
35:20. they devise deceitful *matters* against
36: 3(4). *The words of* his mouth
41: 8(9). *An* evil *disease,* (say they), cleaveth fast (marg. *A thing of* Belial)
45: 1(2). is inditing *a* good *matter :*
4(5). *because of* truth and meekness
50:17. castest *my words* behind thee.
52: 4(6). Thou lovest all devouring *words,*
55:21(22). *his words* were softer than oil,
56: 4(5). I will praise *his word,*
5(6). Every day they wrest *my words :*
10(11). In God will I praise (his) *word:* in the Lord will I praise (his) *word.*
59:12(13). *the words of* their lips
64: 3(4). (even) bitter *words :*
5(6). themselves (in) *an* evil *matter :*
65: 3(4). Iniquities prevail against me: (marg. *Words,* or, *Matters of* iniquities)
79: 9. for the glory of thy name: (lit. upon *the matter of* the glory)
101: 3. I will set no wicked *thing*
103:20. do *his commandments,* hearkening unto the voice of *his word.*
105: 8. *the word* (which) he commanded
19. the time that *his word* came:
27. They shewed his signs among them, (marg. *words of* his signs)
28. rebelled not against *his word.*
42. remembered his holy *promise,*
106:12. Then believed they *his words ;*
24. they believed not *his word :*
107:20. He sent *his word,*
109: 3. compassed me about *also with words of*
112: 5. he will guide *his affairs*
119: 9. taking heed (thereto) *according to thy word.*
16. I will not forget *thy word.*
17. I may live, and keep *thy word.*
25. quicken thou me *according to thy word.*
28. strengthen thou me *according unto thy word.*
42. *wherewith* to answer him that reproacheth me (marg. or, answer him that reproacheth me in *a thing*): for I trust *in thy word.*
43. take not *the word of* truth

Ps.119:49. Remember *the word* unto thy
57. that I would keep *thy words.*
65. O Lord, *according unto thy word.*
74. I have hoped *in thy word.*
81, 114. I hope *in thy word.*
89. *thy word* is settled in heaven.
101. that I might keep *thy word.*
105. *Thy word* (is) a lamp unto my feet,
107. O Lord, *according unto thy word.*
130. The entrance of *thy words* giveth
139. mine enemies have forgotten *thy words.*
147. I hoped *in thy word.*
160. *Thy word* (is) true
161. *but* my heart standeth in awe *of thy word.*
169. understanding *according to thy word.*
130: 5. *and in his word* do I hope.
137: 3. carried us away captive required of us a song ; (marg. *the words of* a song)
141: 4. my heart *to* (any) evil *thing,*
145: 5. *and* of thy wondrous *works.* (marg *things* or, *words*)
147:15. *his word* runneth very
18. He sendeth out *his word,*
19. (קרי) He sheweth *his word* unto Jacob, his statutes (marg. *words* כתיב)
148: 8. stormy wind fulfilling *his word:*
Pro. 1: 6. *the words of* the wise,
23. I will make known *my words*
4: 4. Let thine heart retain *my words :*
20. attend *to my words;*
10:19. In the multitude of *words*
11:13. concealeth *the matter.*
12: 6. *The words of* the wicked
25. *but a* good *word* maketh it glad.
13: 5. A righteous (man) hateth lying: (lit. *the word of* falsehood)
13. Whoso despiseth *the word*
14:15. The simple believeth every *word :*
23. *but the talk of* the lips
15: 1. *but* grievous *words* stir up anger.
23. *and a word* (spoken) in due season,
16:20. He that handleth *a matter*
17: 9. he that repeateth *a matter*
18: 4. *The words of* a man's mouth
8. *The words of* a talebearer
13. He that answereth *a matter*
22:12. *the words of* the transgressor. (marg. or, *the matters*)
17. hear *the words of* the wise,
23: 8. lose *thy* sweet *words.*
24:26. that giveth a right *answer.* (marg. answereth right *words*)
25: 2. the glory of God to conceal *a thing :*
— to search out *a matter.*
11. *A word* fitly spoken
26: 6. He that sendeth *a message* by
22. *The words of a* talebearer
27:11. I may answer (lit. return *a word*) him that reproacheth me.
29:12. If a ruler hearken to lies, (lit. *the word of* falsehood)
19. A servant will not be corrected *by words :*
20. hasty *in his words?*
30: 1. *The words of* Agur
6. Add thou not unto *his words,*
8. Remove far from me vanity and lies: (lit. *and the word of* falsehood)
31: 1. *The words of* king Lemuel,
Ecc. 1: 1. *The words of* the Preacher,
8. All *things* (are) full of labour ;
10. Is there (any) *thing*
5: 2(1). to utter (any) *thing* before God: (marg. *word*)
—(-). therefore let *thy words* be few.
3(2). by multitude of *words.*
7(6). *and* many *words* (there are) also
6:11. Seeing there be many *things*
7: 8. Better (is) the end of *a thing*
21. take no heed unto all *words*
8: 1. the interpretation of *a thing?*
3. stand not *in an* evil *thing;*
4. Where *the word of* a king (is),
5. shall feel no evil *thing :*
9:16. *and his words* are not heard.
17. *The words of* wise (men are) heard in quiet
10:12. *The words of* a wise man's mouth
13. The beginning of *the words of* his mouth

Ecc.10:14. A fool also is full of *words*.
20. shall tell *the matter*.
12:10. sought to find out acceptable *words*:
— (even) *words of* truth.
11. *The words of* the wise
13. the conclusion of *the* whole *matter*:
Isa. 1:10. Hear *the word of* the Lord,
2: 1. *The word* that Isaiah the
3. *and the word of* the Lord
8:10. speak *the word*, and it shall not stand:
20. if they speak not *according to this word*,
9: 8(7). The Lord sent *a word*
16:13. *the word* that the Lord hath
24: 3. the Lord hath spoken this *word*.
28:13. But *the word of* the Lord
14. hear *the word of* the Lord,
29:11. *as the words of* a book
18. hear *the words of* the book,
21. an offender *for a word*,
30:12. Because ye despise this *word*,
21. shall hear *a word* behind thee,
31: 2. and will not call back *his words*:
36: 5. but (they are but) vain *words* (marg. *a word of* lips)
12. to speak these *words*?
13. Hear ye *the words of* the great king,
21. answered him not *a word*:
22. told him *the words of* Rabshakeh.
37: 4. hear *the words of* Rabshakeh,
— will reprove *the words* which
6. Be not afraid of *the words*
17. all *the words of* Sennacherib,
22. This (is) *the word* which
38: 4. Then came *the word of* the Lord
7. the Lord will do this *thing*
39: 2. there was no*thing* in his house,
4. there is no*thing* among my treasures
5. Hear *the word of* the Lord
6. no*thing* shall be left,
8. Good (is) *the word of* the Lord
40: 8. *but the word of* our God
41:28. could answer *a word*.
42:16. These *things* will I do
44:26. confirmeth *the word of* his servant,
45:23. *the word* is gone out
50: 4. I should know how to speak *a word*
51:16. I have put *my words* in thy
55:11. So shall *my word* be that goeth
58:13. nor speaking (thine own) *words*:
59:13. uttering from the heart *words of* falsehood.
21. *and my words* which I have put
66: 2. trembleth at *my word*.
5. Hear *the word of* the Lord, ye that tremble at *his word*;
Jer. 1: 1. *The words of* Jeremiah
2. To whom *the word of* the Lord
4. Then *the word of* the Lord came
9. I have put *my words* in thy
11. Moreover *the word of* the Lord
12. I will hasten *my word* to perform
13. *the word of* the Lord came
2: 1. Moreover *the word of* the Lord came
4. Hear ye *the word of* the Lord,
31. see ye *the word of* the Lord.
3:12. Go and proclaim these *words*
5:14. Because ye speak this *word*, behold, I will make *my words*
28. they overpass *the deeds of* the
6:10. *the word of* the Lord is unto
19. have not hearkened unto *my words*,
7: 1. *The word* that came to Jeremiah
2. proclaim there this *word*, and say, Hear *the word of* the Lord,
4. Trust ye not in lying *words*,
8. ye trust in lying *words*,
22. concerning burnt offerings (marg. concerning *the matter of* burnt offerings)
23. But this *thing* commanded I them,
27. speak all these *words* unto them;
8: 9. have rejected *the word of* the Lord;
9:20(19). Yet hear *the word of* the Lord,
—(—). receive *the word of* his mouth,
10: 1. Hear ye *the word* which the Lord
11: 1. *The word* that came to Jeremiah
2, 6. Hear ye *the words of* this covenant,
3. obeyeth not *the words of* this covenant,
6. Proclaim all these *words*

Jer. 11: 8. all *the words of* this covenant,
10. which refused to hear *my words*
13: 2. *according to the word of* the Lord,
3, 8. *the word of* the Lord came
10. which refuse to hear *my words*,
12. speak unto them this *word*;
14: 1. *The word of* the Lord that came
— concerning the dearth. (marg. *words of* the dearths)
17. thou shalt say this *word* unto them;
15:16. *Thy words* were found,
— *thy word* was unto me
16: 1. *The word of* the Lord came also
10. shalt shew this people all these *words*,
17:15. Where (is) *the word of* the Lord?
20. Hear ye *the word of* the Lord,
18: 1. *The word* which came to Jeremiah
2. there I will cause thee to hear *my words*.
5. Then *the word of* the Lord came
18. *nor the word* from the prophet.
— let us not give heed to any of *his words*.
19: 2. proclaim there *the words*
3. Hear ye *the word of* the Lord,
15. that they might not hear *my words*.
20: 1. prophesied these *things*.
8. because *the word of* the Lord
21: 1. *The word* which came unto
11. Hear ye *the word of* the Lord;
22: 1. speak there this *word*,
2. Hear *the word of* the Lord,
4. if ye do this *thing* indeed,
5. if ye will not hear these *words*,
29. hear *the word of* the Lord.
23: 9. because of *the words of* his holiness.
16. Hearken not unto *the words of*
18. hath perceived and heard *his word*? who hath marked *his word*,
22. had caused my people to hear *my words*,
28. he that hath *my word*, let him speak *my word* faithfully.
29. (Is) not *my word* like as a fire?
30. that steal *my words* every one
36. every man's *word* shall be his burden; for ye have perverted *the words of* the living God,
38. Because ye say this *word*,
24: 4. Again *the word of* the Lord came
25: 1. *The word* that came to Jeremiah
3. *the word of* the Lord hath come
8. ye have not heard *my words*,
13. bring upon that land all *my words*
30. against them all these *words*,
26: 1. came this *word* from the Lord,
2. *the words* that I command thee
— diminish not *a word*:
5. hearken to *the words of* my servants
7. heard Jeremiah speaking these *words*
10. princes of Judah heard these *things*,
12. against this city all *the words*
15. to speak all these *words*
20. according to all *the words of* Jeremiah:
21. heard *his words*,
27: 1. came this *word* unto Jeremiah
12. according to all these *words*,
14. hearken not unto *the words of*
16. Hearken not to *the words of*
18. if *the word of* the Lord be
28: 6. the Lord perform *thy words*
7. hear thou now this *word*
9. when *the word of* the prophet
12. *the word of* the Lord came
29: 1. Now these (are) *the words of*
10. perform *my* good *word*
19. have not hearkened to *my words*,
20. Hear ye therefore *the word of*
23. have spoken lying *words*
30. Then came *the word of* the Lord
30: 1. *The word* that came to Jeremiah
2. Write thee all *the words* that I have spoken
4. these (are) *the words* that
31:10. Hear *the word of* the Lord,
23. they shall use this *speech* in the land of
32: 1. *The word* that came to Jeremiah
6. *The word of* the Lord came unto me,
8. *according to the word of* the Lord,
— this (was) *the word of* the Lord.
17. there is no*thing* too hard for thee:

Jer. 32:26. Then came *the word of* the Lord
27. is there any *thing* too hard for me?
33: 1, 19. *the word of* the Lord came
14. I will perform that good *thing*
23. Moreover *the word of* the Lord
34: 1. *The word* which came
4. Yet hear *the word of* the Lord,
5. for I have pronounced *the word*,
6. spake all these *words*
8. *the word* that came unto
12. Therefore *the word of* the Lord
18. performed *the words of* the covenant
35: 1. *The word* which came
12. Then came *the word of* the Lord
13. to hearken to *my words?*
14. *The words of* Jonadab
36: 1. this *word* came unto Jeremiah
2. write therein all *the words*
4, 11. all *the words of* the Lord,
6. *the words of* the Lord in the ears
8. reading in the book *the words of*
10. *the words of* Jeremiah
13. all *the words* that he had heard,
16. they had heard all *the words*,
— tell the king of all these *words*.
17. write all these *words* at his mouth?
18. He pronounced all these *words*
20. told all *the words* in the ears of the king.
24. that heard all these *words*.
27. Then *the word of* the Lord came
— *the words* which Baruch wrote
28. write in it all *the* former *words*
32. all *the words of* the book
— besides unto them many like *words*.
37: 2. hearken unto *the words of* the
6. Then came *the word of* the Lord
17. Is there (any) *word* from the Lord?
38: 1. heard *the words* that Jeremiah
4. in speaking *such words*
5. can do (any) *thing* against you.
14. I will ask thee *a thing;* hide no*thing* from
21. *the word* that the Lord hath shewed me:
24. Let no man know *of* these *words*,
27. according to all these *words*
— *the matter* was not perceived.
39:15. Now *the word of* the Lord came
16. I will bring *my words* upon this
40: 1. *The word* that came to Jeremiah
3. this *thing* is come upon you.
16. Thou shalt not do this *thing:*
42: 3. *the thing* that we may do.
4. *according to your words;*
— whatsoever *thing* the Lord shall
— I will keep no*thing* back
5. even according to all *things*
7. that *the word of* the Lord came
15. hear *the word of* the Lord,
43: 1. all *the words of* the Lord
— (even) all these *words*,
8. Then came *the word of* the Lord
44: 1. *The word* that came to Jeremiah
4. do not this abominable *thing*
16. *the word* that thou hast spoken
17. whatsoever *thing* goeth forth
20. given him (that) *answer*,
24. Hear *the word of* the Lord,
26. hear ye *the word of* the Lord,
28. shall know whose *words*
29. *my words* shall surely stand against
45: 1. *The word* that Jeremiah the
— when he had written these *words*
46: 1. *The word of* the Lord which came
13. *The word* that the Lord spake
47: 1. *The word of* the Lord that came
48:27. for since *thou spakest* of him, (lit. from *thy words*)
49:34. *The word of* the Lord that came
50: 1. *The word* that the Lord spake
51:59. *The word* which Jeremiah
60. (even) all these *words*
61. shalt read all these *words;*
64. Thus far (are) *the words of* Jeremiah.
52:34. every day *a portion* (marg. *the matter of* the day in his day)
Eze. 1: 3. *The word of* the Lord came
2: 6. *neither* be afraid of *their words*,
— be not afraid *of their words*, nor
Eze. 2: 7. thou shalt speak *my words*
3: 4. speak with *my words*
6. *whose words* thou canst not understand. (lit. *their words*)
10. all *my words* that I shall speak
16. that *the word of* the Lord came
17. hear *the word* at my mouth,
6: 1. *the word of* the Lord came
3. hear *the word of* the Lord God;
7: 1. Moreover *the word of* the Lord
9:11. reported *the matter*, (marg. returned *the word*)
11:14. Again *the word of* the Lord came
25. all *the things* that the Lord had shewed
12: 1. *The word of* the Lord also came
8. in the morning came *the word of* the Lord
17, 21, 26. Moreover *the word of* the Lord came
23. *and the effect of* every vision.
25. *the word* that I shall speak
— will I say *the word*,
28. shall none of *my words* be prolonged
— *the word* which I have spoken
13: 1. *the word of* the Lord came
2. Hear ye *the word of* the Lord;
6. they would confirm *the word*.
14: 2. *the word of* the Lord came
9. when he hath spoken *a thing*,
12 & 15:1 & 16:1. *The word of* the Lord came
16:35. hear *the word of* the Lord:
17: 1, 11 & 18:1. *the word of* the Lord came
20: 2. Then came *the word of* the
45(21:1). *the word of* the Lord came
47(21:3). Hear *the word of* the Lord;
21: 1(6), 8(13), 18(23). *the word of* the Lord
22: 1, 17, 23 & 23:1 & 24:1, 15. *the word of* the Lord came
24:20. *The word of* the Lord came unto me,
25: 1. *The word of* the Lord came again unto me,
3. Hear *the word of* the Lord
26: 1. *the word of* the Lord came
27: 1 & 28:1. *The word of* the Lord came again
28:11. Moreover *the word of* the Lord
20. Again *the word of* the Lord
29: 1, 17. *the word of* the Lord came
30: 1. *The word of* the Lord came again
20 & 31:1 & 32:1, 17. *the word of* the Lord came
33: 1, 23. *the word of* the Lord came.
7. thou shalt hear *the word* at my mouth,
30. what is *the word* that cometh
31, 32. they hear *thy words*,
34: 1. And *the word of* the Lord came
7, 9. hear *the word of* the Lord;
35: 1. Moreover *the word of* the Lord
13. have multiplied *your words*
36: 1. hear *the word of* the Lord:
4. hear *the word of* the Lord God;
16. Moreover *the word of* the Lord
37: 4. hear *the word of* the Lord.
15 & 38:1. *The word of* the Lord came
38:10. shall *things* come into thy mind,
Dan. 1: 5. appointed them *a* daily *provision*
14. consented to them *in* this *matter*,
20. in all *matters of* wisdom
9: 2. whereof *the word of* the Lord
12. he hath confirmed *his words*,
23. *the commandment* came forth, (marg. *word*)
— therefore understand *the matter*,
25. going forth of *the commandment*
10: 1. *a thing* was revealed
— *the thing* (was) true,
— he understood *the thing*,
6. the voice of *his words*
9. Yet heard I the voice of *his words:* and when I heard the voice of *his words*,
11. understand *the words* that I speak
— when he had spoken this *word*
12. *thy words* were heard, and I am come *for thy words*.
15. when he had spoken *such words*
12: 4. shut up *the words*,
9. *the words* (are) closed up and sealed
Hos. 1: 1. *The word of* the Lord that came
4: 1. Hear *the word of* the Lord,
10: 4. They have spoken *words*,
14: 2(3). Take with you *words*,

Joel 1: 1. *The word of* the Lord
2:11. that executeth *his word:*
Am. 1: 1. *The words of* Amos,
3: 1. Hear this *word* that the Lord
7. Surely the Lord God will do no*thing,*
4: 1. Hear this *word,* ye kine
5: 1. Hear ye this *word*
6:13. rejoice in *a thing* of nought,
7:10. is not able to bear all *his words.*
16. hear thou *the word of* the Lord:
8:11. hearing *the words of* the Lord:
12. seek *the word of* the Lord,
Jon. 1: 1 & 3:1. *the word of* the Lord came
3: 3. *according to the word of* the Lord.
6. *word* came unto the king
4: 2. this *my saying,* when
Mic. 1: 1. *The word of* the Lord that came
2: 7. do not *my words* do good
4: 2. *and the word of* the Lord
Zep. 1: 1. *The word of* the Lord which came
2: 5. *the word of* the Lord (is) against
Hag. 1: 1. came *the word of* the Lord
3. Then came *the word of* the Lord
12. *the words of* Haggai the prophet,
2: 1, 10. came *the word of* the Lord
5. *the word* that I covenanted
20. again *the word of* the Lord came
Zec. 1: 1, 7. came *the word of* the Lord
6. But *my words* and my statutes,
13. talked with me (with) good *words* (and) comfortable *words.*
4: 6. This (is) *the word of* the Lord
8 & 6:9. *the word of* the Lord came
7: 1. *the word of* the Lord came unto
4. Then came *the word of* the Lord
7. *the words* which the Lord
8. *the word of* the Lord came
12. *the words* which the Lord of hosts
8: 1, 18. *the word of* the Lord of hosts
9. these *words* by the mouth of
16. *the things* that ye shall do;
9: 1. The burden of *the word of* the Lord
11:11. it (was) *the word of* the Lord.
12: 1. *the word of* the Lord for Israel,
Mal. 1: 1. The burden of *the word of* the Lord to
2:17. wearied the Lord *with your words.*
3:13. *Your words* have been stout

1698 **דֶּבֶר** *deh'-ver,* m.

Ex. 5: 3. he fall upon us *with pestilence,*
9: 3. *a* very grievous *murrain.*
15. thy people *with pestilence;*
Lev. 26:25. I will send *the pestilence*
Nu. 14:12. smite them *with the pestilence,*
Deu 28:21. The Lord shall make *the pestilence*
2Sa. 24:13. three days' *pestilence* in thy land?
15. So the Lord sent *a pestilence*
1K. 8:37. if there be *pestilence,*
1Ch 21:12. *even the pestilence,* in the land,
14. So the Lord sent *pestilence*
2Ch. 6:28. if there be *pestilence,*
7:13. or if I send *pestilence* among
20: 9. judgment, *or pestilence,* or famine,
Ps. 78:50. gave their life over *to the pestilence;* (marg. or, beasts *to the murrain*)
91: 3. *from the* noisome *pestilence.*
6. *for the pestilence* (that) walketh
Jer. 14:12. by the famine, *and by the pestilence.*
21: 6. they shall die *of a* great *pestilence.*
7. this city from *the pestilence,*
9. by the famine, *and by the pestilence:*
24:10. *the pestilence,* among them,
27: 8. with the famine, *and with the pestilence,*
13. by the famine, *and by the pestilence,*
28: 8. of evil, *and of pestilence.*
29:17. the famine, and *the pestilence,*
18. the famine, *and with the pestilence,*
32:24. the famine, *and of the pestilence:*
36. by the famine, *and by the pestilence;*
34:17. to the sword, to *the pestilence,*
38: 2 & 42:17, 22 & 44:13. by the famine, *and by the pestilence:*
Eze. 5:12. shall die *with the pestilence,*
5:17. *and pestilence* and blood
6:11. by the famine, *and by the pestilence.*
12. shall die *of the pestilence;*
7:15. *and the pestilence* and the famine
— famine *and pestilence* shall devour
12:16. the famine, *and from the pestilence;*
14:19. Or (if) I send *a pestilence* into that
21. the noisome beast, *and the pestilence,*
28:23. I will send into her *pestilence,*
33:27. shall die *of the pestilence.*
38:22. plead against him *with pestilence*
Hos 13:14. O death, I will be *thy plagues;*
Am. 4:10. I have sent among you *the pestilence*
Hab. 3: 5. Before him went *the pestilence,*

דֹּבֶר [*dōh'-ver*], m. 1699

Isa. 5:17. the lambs feed *after their manner,*
Mic. 2:12. in the midst of *their fold:*

דִּבְרָה [*div-rāh'*], f. 1700

Job 5: 8. unto God would I commit *my cause:*
Ps. 110: 4. after *the order of* Melchizedek.
Ecc. 3:18. concerning *the estate of* the sons of
7:14. to *the end* that man should find
8: 2. in *regard of* the oath of God.

דִּבְרָה [*div-rāh'*], f. Ch. 1701

Dan. 2:30. but for (their) *sakes* that shall make known the interpretation
4:17(14). *to the intent* that the living

דַּבְּרוֹת [*dab-b'rōhth'*], f. pl. 1703

Deu 33: 3. (every one) shall receive *of thy words.*

דֹּבְרוֹת *dōh-v'rōhth',* f. pl. 1702

1K. 5: 9(23). convey them by sea *in floats*

דְּבַשׁ *d'vash,* m. 1706

Gen 43:11. a little balm, and *a* little *honey,*
Ex. 3: 8, 17 & 13:5. a land flowing with milk *and honey;*
16:31. like wafers (made) *with honey.*
33: 3. a land flowing with milk *and honey:*
Lev. 2:11. no leaven, nor any *honey,*
20:24. that floweth with milk *and honey:*
Nu. 13:27 & 14:8 & 16:13, 14. floweth with milk *and honey;*
Deu. 6: 3. the land that floweth with milk *and honey.*
8: 8. a land of oil olive, *and honey;*
11: 9 & 26:9, 15 & 27:3 & 31:20. that floweth with milk *and honey.*
32:13. he made him to suck *honey*
Jos. 5: 6. a land that floweth with milk *and honey.*
Jud. 14: 8. a swarm of bees *and honey*
9. that he had taken *the honey*
18. What (is) sweeter *than honey?*
1Sa. 14:25. there was *honey* upon the ground
26. *the honey* dropped;
27. dipped it in an *honey*comb,
29. because I tasted a little of this *honey.*
43. I did but taste *a* little *honey*
2Sa. 17:29. *And honey,* and butter, and sheep.
1K. 14: 3. a cruse of *honey,*
2K. 18:32. a land of oil olive *and of honey,*
2Ch 31: 5. wine, and oil, *and honey,* (marg. or, *dates*)
Job 20:17. the brooks of *honey* and butter.
Ps. 19:10(11). sweeter also *than honey*
81:16(17). and with *honey* out of the rock

Ps.119:103. *than honey* to my mouth!
Pro.16:24. Pleasant words (are as) an *honey*comb,
24:13. My son, eat thou *honey*,
25:16. Hast thou found *honey?*
27. not good to eat much *honey :*
Cant.4:11. *honey* and milk (are) under thy tongue;
5: 1. eaten my honeycomb with *my honey ;*
Isa. 7:15. Butter *and honey* shall he eat,
22. butter *and honey* shall every one
Jer. 11: 5 & 32:22. a land flowing with milk *and honey*,
41: 8. barley, and of oil, *and of honey*.
Eze. 3: 3. was in my mouth *as honey*
16:13. fine flour, *and honey*, and oil:
19. fine flour, and oil, *and honey*,
20: 6, 15. flowing with milk *and honey*,
27:17. *and honey*, and oil, and balm.

1707 דַּבֶּשֶׁת *dab-beh'-sheth*, f.

Isa. 30: 6. upon *the bunches of* camels,

1709 דָּג *dāhg*, m.

Gen. 9: 2. upon all *the fishes of* the sea;
Nu. 11:22. or shall all *the fish of* the sea
1K. 4:33(5:13). creeping things, and of *fishes*.
2Ch 33:14. the entering in at the *fish* gate,
Neh 3: 3. But the *fish* gate did the
12:39. and above the *fish* gate,
13:16. which brought *fish*,
Job 12: 8. *the fishes of* the sea shall
41: 7(40:31). or his head with *fish* spears?
Ps. 8: 8(9). *and the fish of* the sea,
Ecc. 9:12. *as the fishes* that are taken
Eze.38:20. So that *the fishes of* the sea,
Hos. 4: 3. yea, *the fishes of* the sea also
Jon. 1:17(2:1). the Lord had prepared *a great fish*
—(-:-). Jonah was in the belly of *the fish*
2:10(11). the Lord spake *unto the fish*,
Hab. 1:14. makest men *as the fishes of* the sea,
Zep. 1: 3. *and the fishes of* the sea,
10. the noise of a cry from the *fish* gate,

1710 דָּגָה *dāh-gāh'*, f.

Gen. 1:26, 28. *over the fish of* the sea,
Ex. 7:18. *And the fish* that (is) in the
21. *And the fish* that (was) in the
Nu. 11: 5. We remember *the fish*, which we
Deu. 4:18. the likeness of any *fish*
Ps.105:29. and slew *their fish*.
Isa. 50: 2. *their fish* stinketh,
Eze.29: 4. will cause *the fish of* thy rivers
—, 5. all *the fish of* thy rivers
47: 9. shall be a very great multitude of *fish*,
10. *their fish* shall be according to their kinds, *as the fish* of the great sea,
Jon. 2: 1(2). out of *the fish*'s belly,

1711 דָּגָה [*dāh-gāh'*].

* KAL.—*Future.* *

Gen48:16. *and let them grow* (marg. *as fishes do increase*)

1713 דָּגַל [*dāh-gal'*].

* KAL.—*Future.* *

Ps. 20: 5(6). *we will set up* (our) *banners :*

KAL.—*Participle.* Paül.

Cant.5:10. *the chiefest* among ten thousand. (marg. *a standardbearer*)

* NIPHAL.—*Participle.* *

Cant.6: 4, 10. terrible *as* (an army) *with banners*.

דֶּגֶל *deh'-gel*, m. 1714

Nu. 1:52. every man by *his own standard*,
2: 2. Israel shall pitch by *his own standard*,
3. *the standard of* the camp of Judah
10. *the standard of* the camp of Reuben
17. in his place *by their standards*.
18. *the standard of* the camp of Ephraim
25. *The standard of* the camp of Dan
31. go hindmost *with their standards*.
34. they pitched *by their standards*,
10:14, 22, 25. *the standard of* the camp of the children
18. *the standard of* the camp of Reuben
Cant.2: 4. *and his banner* over me (was) love.

דָּגָן *dāh-gāhn'*, m. 1715

Gen27:28. plenty of *corn* and wine:
37. *and with corn* and wine
Nu. 18:12. of the wine, *and of the wheat*,
27. *as though* (it were) *the corn*
Deu 7:13. *thy corn*, and thy wine,
11:14. thou mayest gather in *thy corn*,
12:17. tithe of *thy corn*, or of thy wine,
14:23. the tithe of *thy corn*, of thy wine,
18: 4. The firstfruit (also) of *thy corn*,
28:51. shall not leave thee (either) *corn*,
33:28. a land of *corn* and wine;
2K. 18:32. a land of *corn* and wine,
2Ch31: 5. in abundance the firstfruits of *corn*,
32:28. for the increase of *corn*,
Neh 5: 2. therefore we take up *corn*
3. that we might buy *corn*,
10. exact of them money *and corn:*
11. *and of the corn*, the wine, and the oil,
10:39(40). bring the offering of *the corn*,
13: 5. the tithes of *the corn*,
12. the tithe of *the corn*
Ps. 4: 7(8). more than in the time (that) *their corn*
65: 9(10). thou preparest *them corn*,
78:24. *and* had given them of *the corn of* heaven.
Isa. 36:17. a land of *corn* and wine,
62: 8. I will no more give *thy corn*
Jer. 31:12. for *wheat*, and for wine,
Lam.2:12. Where (is) *corn* and wine?
Eze.36:29. I will call for *the corn*,
Hos 2: 8(10). I gave her *corn*, and wine,
9(11). take away *my corn*
22(24). the earth shall hear *the corn*,
7:14. assemble themselves for *corn*
9: 1. upon every *corn*floor.
14: 7(8). they shall revive (as) *the corn*,
Joel 1:10. for *the corn* is wasted:
17. for *the corn* is withered.
2:19. I will send you *corn*,
Hag. 1:11. and upon *the corn*,
Zec. 9:17. *corn* shall make the young men

דָּגַר *dāh-gar'*. 1716

* KAL.—*Preterite.* *

Isa. 34:15. *and gather* under her shadow:
Jer. 17:11. the partridge *sitteth* (marg. or, *gathereth*)

דַּד [*dad*], m. 1717

Pro. 5:19. let *her breasts* satisfy thee
Eze.23: 3. they bruised *the teats of* their virginity.
8. they bruised *the breasts of* her
21. bruising *thy teats* by the Egyptians

דָּדָה [*dāh-dāh'*]. 1718

* HITHPAEL.—*Future.* *

Ps. 42: 4(5). *I went with them* to the house of God,
Isa. 38:15. *I shall go softly* all my years

1722 דְּהַב *d'hav*, Ch. m.

Ezr. 5:14. the vessels also of *gold* and
6: 5. also let *the golden* and silver vessels
7:15. And to carry the silver *and gold*,
16. And all the silver *and gold* that
18. with the rest of the silver *and the gold*,
Dan 2:32. This image's head (was) of fine *gold*,
35. the brass, the silver, *and the gold*,
38. Thou (art) this head of *gold*.
45. the clay, the silver, *and the gold;*
3: 1. the king made an image of *gold*,
5. and worship the *golden* image
7. (and) worshipped the *golden* image
10. and worship the *golden* image:
12. nor worship the *golden* image
14. nor worship the *golden* image which I
18. nor worship the *golden* image which thou
5: 2. commanded to bring the *golden* and silver
3. they brought the *golden* vessels
4. and praised the gods of *gold*,
7. and (have) a chain of *gold* about his neck,
16. and (have) a chain of *gold* about thy neck,
23. thou hast praised the gods of silver, *and gold*,
29. and (put) a chain of *gold* about his neck,

1724 דָּהַם [*dāh-ham'*].

* NIPHAL.—*Participle.* *

Jer. 14: 9. shouldest thou be as a man *astonied*,

1725 דָּהַר [*dāh-har'*].

* KAL.—*Participle.* Poel. *

Nah 3. 2. of the *pransing* horses,

1726 דַּהֲרָה [*dah-hărāh'*], f.

Jud. 5:22. *by the means of the pransings, the pransings of* their mighty ones. (marg. *tramplings*, or, *plungings*)

See 1677 דּוֹב see דֹּב

1727 דּוּב [*doov*].

* HIPHIL.—*Participle.* *

Lev.26:16. *and cause sorrow of* heart:

1728 דַּוָּג [*dav-vāhg'*], m.

Jer. 16:16. (כתיב) I will send for many *fishers*,
Eze.47:10. *the fishers* shall stand

1729 דּוּגָה *doo-gāh'*, f.

Am. 4: 2. your posterity with *fish*hooks.

1730 דּוֹד *dōhd*, m.

Lev.10: 4. *the uncle of* Aaron,
20:20. uncovered *his uncle*'s nakedness:
25:49. Either *his uncle*, or *his uncle*'s son,
Nu. 36:11. unto *their father's brothers'* sons:
1Sa.10:14. Saul's *uncle* said unto him
15. Saul's *uncle* said, Tell me,
16. Saul said unto *his uncle*,
14:50. the son of Ner, Saul's *uncle*.
2K. 24:17. made Mattaniah *his father's brother*
1Ch 27:32. Also Jonathan David's *uncle*
Est. 2: 7. *his uncle*'s daughter:
15. *the uncle of* Mordecai,
Pro. 7:18. let us take our fill of *love*
Cant.1: 2. for *thy love* (is) better than wine. (marg. *loves*)
4. remember *thy love* more than wine.
13. A bundle of myrrh (is) *my wellbeloved*
14. *My beloved* (is) unto me
16. thou (art) fair, *my beloved*,
2: 3. so (is) *my beloved* among the sons.
8. The voice of *my beloved!*
9. *My beloved* is like a roe
10. *My beloved* spake,
16. *My beloved* (is) mine,
17. turn, *my beloved*, and be thou like
4:10. How fair is *thy love*, my sister, (my) spouse! how much better is *thy love*
16. Let *my beloved* come into his
5: 1. drink abundantly, *O beloved*.
2. the voice of *my beloved*
4. *My beloved* put in his hand
5. I rose up to open *to my beloved;*
6. I opened *to my beloved; but my beloved* had withdrawn
8. if ye find *my beloved*,
9, 9. What (is) *thy beloved more than* (another) *beloved*,
10. *My beloved* (is) white and ruddy,
16. This (is) *my beloved*,
6: 1. Whither is *thy beloved* gone,
— whither is *thy beloved* turned
2. *My beloved* is gone down
3. I (am) *my beloved's, and my beloved* (is) mine:
7: 9(10). the best wine *for my beloved*,
10(11). I (am) *my beloved's*,
11(12). Come, *my beloved*, let us go forth
12(13). there will I give thee *my loves*.
13(14). for thee, *O my beloved*.
8: 5. leaning upon *her beloved?*
14. Make haste, *my beloved*,
Isa. 5: 1. a song of *my beloved*
Jer.32: 7. the son of Shallum *thine uncle* shall come
8. Hanameel *mine uncle*'s son
9. Hanameel *my uncle*'s son,
12. in the sight of Hanameel *mine uncle's* (son),
Eze.16: 8. thy time (was) the time of *love;*
23:17. came to her into the bed of *love*,
Am. 6:10. *a man's uncle* shall take him up, (lit. *his uncle*)

דּוֹדָה [*dōh-dāh'*], f. 1733

Ex. 6:20. Jochebed *his father's sister* to wife;
Lev.18:14. she (is) *thine aunt*.
20:20. shall lie with *his uncle's wife*,

דּוּד *dood*, m. 1731

1Sa. 2:14. into the pan, or *kettle*,
2K. 10: 7. put their heads *in baskets*,
2Ch 35:13. sod they in pots, *and in caldrons*,
Job 41:20(12). *as* (out) of a seething *pot*
Ps. 81: 6(7). his hands were delivered *from the pots*.
Jer. 24: 2. One *basket* (had) very good figs,
— *and the* other *basket* (had) very naughty figs,

דּוּדַי [*doo-dahy',*] m. 1736

Gen30:14. found *mandrakes* in the field,
— *of* thy son's *mandrakes*.
15. take away my son's *mandrakes*
— to night for thy son's *mandrakes*.
16. hired thee *with* my son's *mandrakes*.
Cant.7:13(14). *The mandrakes* give a smell,
Jer. 24: 1. two *baskets of* figs

דָּוָה [*dāh-vāh'*]. 1738

* KAL.—*Infinitive.* *

Lev.12: 2. the separation for *her infirmity*

1739 **דָּוֶה** *dāh-veh'*, adj.

Lev.15:33. *And of her that is sick*
20:18. lie with a woman *having her sickness*,
Isa. 30:22. as *a menstruous cloth;*
Lam. 1:13. desolate (and) *faint* all the day.
5:17. For this our heart is *faint;*

1740 **דּוּחַ** [*dooăgh*].

* HIPHIL.—*Preterite.* *

Jer.51:34. *he hath cast me out.*

HIPHIL.—*Future.*

2Ch 4: 6. *they washed* in them;
Isa. 4: 4. *shall have purged* the blood
Eze.40:38. where *they washed* the burnt offering.

1742 **דַּוָּי** *dav-vāhy'*, adj.

Isa. 1: 5. the whole heart *faint*.
Jer. 8:18. my heart (is) *faint* in me.
Lam. 1:22. my sighs (are) many, and my heart (is) *faint*.

1741 **דְּוַי** [*d'vahy*], m.

Job 6: 7. *as* my *sorrowful* meat.
Ps. 41: 3(4). upon the bed of *languishing:*

1743 **דּוּךְ** [*dooch*].

* KAL.—*Preterite.* *

Nu. 11: 8. ground (it) in mills, or *beat* (it) in a mortar,

1744 **דּוּכִיפַת** *doo-chee-phath'*, f.

Lev.11:19. *the lapwing*, and the bat.
Deu14:18. *and the lapwing*, and the bat.

1745 **דּוּמָה** *doo-māh'*, f.

Ps. 94:17. my soul had almost dwelt *in silence*.
115:17. neither any that go down into *silence*.

1747 **דּוּמִיָּה** *doo-meey-yāh'*, f.

Ps. 22: 2(3). in the night season, and am not *silent*. (marg. (there is) no *silence* to me)
39: 2(3). I was dumb *with silence*,
62: 1(2) Truly my soul *waiteth* upon God: (marg. is *silent*)
65: 1(2). Praise *waiteth* for thee, (marg. is *silent*)

1748 **דּוּמָם** *doo-māhm'*, adv.

Isa. 47: 5. Sit thou *silent*, and get thee into
Lam. 3:26. *and quietly wait* for the salvation
Hab 2:19. Awake; to the *dumb* stone,

1777 **דּוּן** [*doon*].

* KAL.—*Future.* *

Gen 6: 3. My spirit *shall* not always *strive*

1779 **דּוּן** *doon*, m.

Job 19:29. that ye may know (there is) *a judgment*.

1749 **דּוֹנַג** *dōh-nag'*, m.

Ps. 22:14(15). my heart is *like wax;*
68: 2(3). as *wax* melteth before the fire,
97: 5. The hills melted *like wax*
Mic 1: 4. *as wax* before the fire,

דּוּץ [*dootz*]. 1750

* KAL.—*Future.* *

Job 41:22 (14). sorrow *is turned into joy* (marg. *rejoiceth*)

דּוּק [*dook*], Ch. 1751

* P'AL.—*Preterite.* *

Dan 2:35. Then *was* the iron, the clay, the brass, the silver, and the gold, *broken to pieces* together,

דּוֹר *dōhr*, m. 1755

Gen. 6: 9. a just man (and) perfect *in his generations*,
7: 1. before me *in* this *generation*.
9:12. *for* perpetual *generations:*
15:16. *But in the* fourth *generation*
17: 7, 9. after thee *in their generations*
12. every man child *in your generations*,
Ex. 1: 6. and all that *generation*.
3:15. this (is) my memorial *unto all generations*. (lit. *to generation of generation*)
12:14. *throughout your generations;* ye shall keep
17. observe this day *in your generations*
42. of Israel *in their generations*.
16:32, 33. to be kept *for your generations;*
17:16. *from generation to generation*.
27:21. for ever *unto their generations*
29:42. offering *throughout your generations*
30: 8. before the Lord *throughout your generations*.
10. upon it *throughout your generations:*
21. to his seed *throughout their generations*.
31. unto me *throughout your generations*.
31:13. me and you *throughout your generations;*
16. the sabbath *throughout their generations*,
40:15. priesthood *throughout their generations*.
Lev. 3:17. a perpetual statute *for your generations*
6:18(11). for ever *in your generations*
7:36. for ever *throughout their generations*.
10: 9. for ever *throughout your generations:*
17: 7. *throughout their generations*.
21:17. of thy seed *in their generations*
22: 3. all your seed *among your generations*,
23:14, 31. for ever *throughout your generations*
21. dwellings *throughout your generations*.
41. a statute for ever *in your generations:*
43. That *your generations* may know
24: 3. a statute for ever *in your generations*.
25:30. *throughout his generations:*
Nu. 9:10. or *of your posterity*
10: 8. for ever *throughout your generations*.
15:14. among you *in your generations*,
15. for ever *in your generations:*
21. heave offering *in your generations*.
23. henceforward *among your generations;*
38. *throughout their generations*,
18:23. for ever *throughout your generations*,
32:13. until all *the generation*, that had
35:29. *throughout your generations*
Deu 1:35. of these men of this evil *generation*
2:14. all *the generation of* the men of war
7: 9. to a thousand *generations;*
23: 2(3). even to his tenth *generation*
3(4). even to their tenth *generation*
8(9). in their third *generation*.
29:22(21). So that *the generation* to come
32: 5. *a* perverse and crooked *generation*.
7. consider the years of *many generations:* (marg. *generation and generation*)
20. *a* very froward *generation*,
Jos. 22:27. *our generations* after us,
28. to *our generations* in time to come,
Jud. 2:10. also all that *generation* were
— there arose another *generation*
3: 2. Only that *the generations of*
1Ch 16:15. commanded to a thousand *generations;*

Est. 9:28. kept *throughout every generation*, (lit. in all *generation and generation*)
Job 8: 8. I pray thee, *of the* former *age*,
42:16. (even) four *generations.*
Ps. 10: 6. for (I shall) *never* (be) in adversity. (marg. *unto generation and generation*)
12: 7(8). from this *generation* for ever.
14: 5. God (is) *in the generation of* the righteous.
22:30(31). accounted to the Lord *for a generation.*
24: 6. *the generation of* them that seek him,
33:11. the thoughts of his heart *to all generations.* (marg. *to generation and generation*)
45:17(18). to be remembered in all *generations:* (lit. in all *generation and generation*)
48:13(14). tell (it) *to the generation* following.
49:11(12). their dwelling places *to all generations;* (marg. *to generation and generation*)
19(20). He shall go to *the generation of* his fathers;
61: 6(7). his years as *many generations.* (marg. *generation and generation*)
71:18. thy strength *unto* (this) *generation*,
72: 5. *throughout all generations.* (lit. *generation of generations*)
73:15. I should offend (against) *the generation of*
77: 8(9). doth (his) promise fail for *evermore?* (marg. *to generation and generation*)
78: 4. shewing *to the generation* to come
6. That *the generation* to come
8. *a* stubborn and rebellious *generation; a generation* (that) set not their
79:13. thy praise *to all generations.* (lit. *to generation and generation*)
85: 5(6). draw out thine anger *to all generations?* (lit. *to generation and generation*)
89: 1(2). thy faithfulness *to all generations.* (marg. *to generation and generation*)
4(5). build up thy throne *to all generations.* (lit. *to generation and generation*)
90: 1. hast been our dwelling place in *all generations.* (marg. *in generation and generation*)
95:10. was I grieved *with* (this) *generation*,
100: 5. his truth (endureth) to *all generations.* (marg. *generation and generation*)
102:12(13). thy remembrance *unto all generations.* (lit. *unto generation and generation*)
18(19). be written *for the generation* to come:
24(25). thy years (are) *throughout all generations.* (lit. *in generation of generations*)
105: 8. (which) he commanded to a thousand *generations.*
106:31. for righteousness *unto all generations* (lit. *unto generation and generation*)
109:13. *in the generation* following
112: 2. *the generation of* the upright
119:90. Thy faithfulness (is) *unto all generations:* (marg. *to generation and generation*)
135:13. thy memorial, O Lord, *throughout all generations.* (lit. *to generation and generation*)
145: 4. *One generation* shall praise thy works *to another*, (lit. *generation to generation*)
13. thy dominion (endureth) throughout all *generations.* (lit. throughout all *generation and generation*)
146:10. *unto all generations.* (lit. *unto generation and generation*)
Pro. 27:24. doth the crown (endure) *to every generation?* (marg. *to generation and generation?*)
30:11. *a generation* (that) curseth their father,
12. *a generation* (that are) pure
13. *a generation*, O how lofty are their eyes!
14. *a generation*, whose teeth (are as)
Ecc. 1: 4. *generation* passeth away, *and* (another) *generation* cometh:
Isa. 13:20. from *generation to generation:* (lit. unto *generation and generation*)
34:10. *from generation to generation* it shall
17. *from generation to generation* shall they
38:12. *Mine age* is departed,
41: 4. calling *the generations* from the
51: 8. *from generation to generation.*
9. in *the generations of* old.
Isa. 53: 8. who shall declare *his generation?*
58:12. the foundations of *many generations;* (lit. *generation and generation*)
60:15. a joy of *many generations.* (lit. *generation and generation*)
61: 4. the desolations of *many generations.* (lit. *generation and generation*)
Jer. 2:31. *O generation*, see ye the word
7:29. forsaken *the generation of* his
50:39. dwelt in *from generation* to *generation.*
Lam. 5:19. thy throne *from generation to generation.*
Joel 1: 3. their children another *generation.*
2: 2. the years of *many generations.* (marg. *generation and generation*)
3:20(4:20). *from generation to generation.*

דּוּר *door.* 1752

* KAL.—*Infinitive.* *

Ps. 84:10(11). *than to dwell* in the tents of wickedness.

דּוּר [*door*], Ch. 1753

* P'AL.—*Future.* *

Dan 4:12(9). fowls of the heaven *dwelt* in the boughs
21(18). under which the beasts of the field *dwelt*,

P'AL.—*Participle.*

Dan 2:38. wheresoever the children of men *dwell*,
4: 1(3:31). that *dwell* in all the earth;
35(32). all *the inhabitants* of the earth
—(—). *and* (among) *the inhabitants* of the earth:
6:25(26). that *dwell* in all the earth;

דּוּר *door*, m. 1754

Isa. 22:18. and toss thee (like) *a ball*
29: 3. I will camp against thee *round about*,
Eze. 24: 5. *burn* also the bones under it, (marg. or, *heap*—perhaps, *the heap of the* bones)

דּוּשׁ *doosh* & דּוֹשׁ *dōhsh.* 1758

* KAL.—*Preterite.* *

Jud. 8: 7. *then I will tear* your flesh (marg. *thresh*)
1Ch 21:20. Now Ornan *was threshing* wheat.

KAL.—*Infinitive.*

2K. 13: 7. made them like the dust *by threshing.*
Hos 10:11. loveth *to tread out* (the corn);
Am. 1: 3. *they have threshed* Gilead

KAL.—*Imperative.*

Mic. 4:13. Arise *and thresh*, O daughter

KAL.—*Future.*

Job 39:15. the wild beast *may break them.*
Isa. 28:28. *he will* not ever *be threshing it*, (lit. in threshing *will thresh it*)
41:15. *thou shalt thresh* the mountains,
Hab 3:12. *thou didst thresh* the heathen

* NIPHAL.—*Preterite.* *

Isa. 25:10. *shall be trodden down* under him, (marg. *threshed*)

NIPHAL.—*Infinitive.*

Isa. 25:10. *even as* straw *is trodden down* (marg. *threshed*)

* HOPHAL.—*Future.* *

Isa. 28:27. the fitches *are* not *threshed*

דּוּשׁ [*doosh*], Ch. 1759

* P'AL.—*Future.* *

Dan 7:23. *and shall tread it down*,

1760 **דָּחָה [*dāh-ghāh'*].**

∗ KAL. *Preterite.* ∗

Ps.118:13. *Thou hast thrust* sore *at me*

KAL.—*Infinitive.*

Ps.118:13. Thou hast thrust *sore* at me (lit. *thrusting* thou hast thrust)
140: 4(5). have purposed *to overthrow* my goings.

KAL.—*Participle.* Poel.

Ps. 35: 5. *let* the angel of the Lord *chase* (lit. *and... chasing*)

KAL.—*Participle.* Paül.

Ps. 62: 3(4). a *tottering* fence.

∗ NIPHAL.—*Future.* ∗

Pro. 14:32. The wicked *is driven away*
Jer. 23:12. *they shall be driven on,* and fall therein:

NIPHAL.—*Participle.*

Ps.147: 2. he gathereth together *the outcasts of* Israel.
Isa. 11:12. shall assemble *the outcasts of* Israel,
56: 8. gathereth *the outcasts of* Israel

∗ PUAL.—*Preterite.* ∗

Ps. 36:12(13). *they are cast down,* and shall not

1761 **דַּחֲוָן *dah-ghăvāhn',* Ch. f. pl.**

Dan 6:18(19). *neither* (lit. *and* not) were *instruments of musick* (marg. or, *table*—perhaps, lit. *concubines*)

See 1760 **דָּחָה see דָּחַח**

1762 **דְּחִי [*d'ghee*], m.**

Ps. 56:13(14). my feet *from falling,*
116: 8. my feet *from falling.*

1763 **דְּחַל [*d'ghal*], Ch.**

∗ P'AL.—*Participle.* Active. ∗

Dan 5:19. trembled *and feared* before him:
6:26(27). men tremble *and fear* before the God of Daniel:

P'AL.—*Participle.* P'il.

Dan 2:31. the form thereof (was) *terrible.*
7: 7. a fourth beast, *dreadful* and terrible,
19. diverse from all the others, exceeding *dreadful,*

∗ PAEL.—*Future.* ∗

Dan 4: 5(2). I saw a dream *which made me afraid,*

1764 **דֹּחַן *dōh'-ghan,* m.**

Eze. 4: 9. lentiles, *and millet,* and fitches,

1765 **דָּחַף [*dāh-ghaph'*].**

∗ KAL.—*Participle.* Paül. ∗

Est. 3:15. The posts went out, *being hastened*
8:14. being hastened *and pressed on*

∗ NIPHAL.—*Preterite.* ∗

2Ch 26:20. himself *hasted* also to go out,
Est. 6:12. *hasted* to his house mourning,

1766 **דָּחַק [*dāh-ghak'*].**

∗ KAL.—*Future.* ∗

Joel. 2: 8. Neither *shall* one *thrust* another ·

KAL.—*Participle.* Poel.

Jud. 2:18. oppressed them *and vexed them.*

דַּי *dahy,* m. 1767

Ex. 36: 5. bring much *more than enough*
7. the stuff *they had* was *sufficient*
Lev. 5: 7. if he be not *able* to bring (marg. his hand cannot reach to *the sufficiency of*)
12: 8. if she be not *able* to bring (marg. her hand find not *sufficiency of*)
25:26. himself be *able to* redeem (lit. find *according to sufficiency*)
28. if he be not *able* to restore
Deu 15: 8. lend him *sufficient for* his need
25: 2. *according to* his fault,
Jud. 6: 5. they came *as* grasshoppers
1Sa. 1: 7. *when* she went up (marg. *from* her going up, or, *from the time that* she, &c.)
7:16. he went *from* year to year
18:30. *after* they went forth,
1K. 14:28. *when* the king went into
2K. 4: 8. *as oft as* he passed by,
2Ch 12:11. *when* the king entered
24: 5. the house of your God *from* year to year,
30: 3. sanctified themselves *sufficiently,*
Neh 5: 8. We *after* our *ability*
Est. 1:18. *Thus* (shall there arise) *too much* contempt
Job 39:25. He saith *among* the trumpets,
Pro. 25:16. eat *so much as is sufficient* for thee,
27:27. *And...*goats' milk *enough* for thy food,
Isa. 28:19. *From* the time that it goeth
40:16. Lebanon (is) not *sufficient to* burn, nor the beasts thereof *sufficient for*
66:23. *from* one new moon to another, *and from* one sabbath to another,
Jer. 20: 8. For *since* I spake, I cried out,
31:20. for *since* I spake against him,
48:27. for *since* thou spakest of him,
49: 9. they will destroy *till they have enough.* (marg. *their sufficiency*)
51:58. the people shall labour *in* vain, and the folk *in* the fire,
Obad. 5. have stolen *till they had enough?*
Nah. 2:12(13). *enough* for his whelps,
Hab. 2:13. in the *very* fire,
— for *very* vanity?
Zec. 14:16. *from* year to year to worship
Mal. 3:10. that (there shall) not (be room) *enough*

NOTE.—דַּי is in several of the above passages omitted in translation, the prefix alone being expressed.

דִּי *dee,* Ch. part. 1768

NOTE.—In the passages marked [a] this word is combined with others in translation.

Ezr. 4:10. the nations *whom* the great and noble Asnapper
11. the letter *that* they sent unto him,
12. *that* the Jews *which* came up from thee
14. Now[a] because we have maintenance
23. Now [a]when the copy of king Artaxerxes' letter
6: 8. I make a decree [a]what ye shall do
7:14. [a]Forasmuch as thou art sent of the king,
15. the God of Israel, *whose* habitation
18. And what*soever* shall seem good to thee,
23. *for* why should there be wrath
Dan 2: 9. *But* if ye will not make known
10. *therefore* (there is) no king, lord, nor ruler,
47. *seeing* thou couldest reveal this secret.
3:19. more[a] than it was wont to be heated.
7:22. [a]Until the Ancient of days came,
&c. &c. &c.

With prefix כְּדִי.

Dan 2:43. even *as* iron is not mixed with clay.
3: 7. *when* all the people heard
&c.

דִּי is also used to mark the genitive.

Ezr. 5:14. And the vessels also *of* gold and silver *of* the house of God,
Dan 2:14. the captain of the king's guard,
&c. &c. &c.

1770 דִּיג [*deeg*].

* KAL.—*Preterite.* *

Jer. 16:16. *and they shall fish them;*

1771 דַּיָּג [*dahy-yāhg'*], m.

Isa. 19: 8. *The fishers* also shall mourn,
Jer. 16:16. I will send for many *fishers,*

1772 דַּיָּה *dahy-yāh'*, f.

Deu 14:13. *and the vulture* after his kind,
Isa. 34:15. *the vultures* also be gathered,

1773 דְּיוֹ *d'yōh*, m.

Jer. 36:18. I wrote (them) *with ink*

1777 דִּין *deen.*

* KAL.—*Preterite.* *

Gen 30: 6. God *hath judged me,*
Jer. 5:28. *they judge* not the cause,
22:16. *He judged* the cause of the poor

KAL.—*Infinitive.*

Ps. 50: 4. *that he may judge* his people.
Ecc. 6:10. neither may he *contend* with him
Isa. 3:13. standeth *to judge* the people.

KAL.—*Imperative.*

Pro. 31: 9. *and plead the cause* of the poor
Jer. 21:12. *Execute* judgment in the morning,

KAL.—*Future.*

Gen 49:16. Dan *shall judge* his people,
Deu 32:36. the Lord *shall judge* his people,
1 Sa. 2:10. the Lord *shall judge* the ends of the
Job 36:31. by them *judgeth he* the people;
Ps. 7: 8(9). The Lord *shall judge* the people:
9: 8(9). *he shall minister judgment* to the people
54: 1(3). *judge me* by thy strength.
72: 2. *He shall judge* thy people
96:10. *he shall judge* the people
110: 6. *He shall judge* among the heathen,
135:14. the Lord *will judge* his people,
Zec. 3: 7. then thou *shalt* also *judge*

KAL.—*Participle.* Poel.

Gen 15:14. whom they shall serve, *will I judge:*
Jer. 30:13. none *to plead* thy cause,

* NIPHAL.—*Participle.* *

2 Sa. 19: 9(10). all the people were *at strife*

1778 דִּין *deen*, Ch.

* P'AL.—*Participle.* Active. *

Ezr. 7:25. which may *judge* all the people

1779 דִּין *deen*, m.

Deu 17: 8. between *plea and plea,*
Est. 1:13. that knew law *and judgment:*
Job 19:29. (כתיב) ye may know (there is) *a judgment.*
35:14. *judgment* (is) before him;
36:17. *But* thou hast fulfilled *the judgment of* the wicked: *judgment* and justice take hold
Ps. 9: 4(5). maintained my right *and my cause;*
76: 8(9). Thou didst cause *judgment*
140:12(13). maintain *the cause of* the afflicted,
Pro. 20: 8. sitteth in the throne of *judgment*
22:10. yea, *strife* and reproach shall cease.
29: 7. considereth *the cause of* the poor
31: 5. pervert *the judgment of* any
8. in *the cause of* all such
Isa. 10: 2. To turn aside the needy *from judgment,*
Jer. 5:28. they judge not *the cause, the cause of* the fatherless,
22:16. He judged *the cause of*
30:13. none to plead *thy cause,*

דִּין *deen*, Ch. m. 1780

Ezr. 7:26. let *judgment* be executed speedily
Dan 4:37(34). and his ways *judgment:*
7:10. *the judgment* was set, and the books
22. *and judgment* was given to the saints
26. *But the judgment* shall sit,

דַּיָּן *dahy-yāhn'*, m. 1781

1 Sa. 24:15(16). The Lord therefore *be judge,* (lit. *for a judge*)
Ps. 68: 5(6). *and a judge of* the widows,

דַּיָּן [*dahy-yāhn'*], m. Ch. 1782

Ezr. 7:25. set magistrates *and judges,*

דָּיֵק *dāh-yĕhk'*, m. 1785

2 K. 25: 1. they built *forts* against it
Jer. 52: 4. built *forts* against it
Eze. 4: 2. build *a fort* against it,
17:17. casting up mounts, and building *forts,*
21:22(27). to cast a mount, (and) to build *a fort.*
26: 8. he shall make *a fort* against thee,

דִּישׁ [*deesh*]. 1758

* KAL.—*Infinitive.* *

Deu 25: 4. muzzle the ox *when he treadeth out* (the corn). (marg. *thresheth*)

דַּיִשׁ *dah'-yeesh*, m. 1786

Lev. 26: 5. your *threshing* shall reach

דִּישׁוֹן *dee-shōhn'*, m. 1788

Deu 14: 5. the wild goat, *and the pygarg,* (marg. *dishon,* or, *bison*)

דַּךְ *dach*, adj. 1790

Ps. 9: 9(10). a refuge *for the oppressed,*
10:18. the fatherless *and the oppressed.*
74:21. O let not *the oppressed*
Pro. 26:28. hateth (those that are) *afflicted by it;*

דֵּךְ *dĕhch*, & דָּךְ *dāhkh*, m. & f. Ch. 1791

Ezr. 4:13, 16. that, if *this* city be builded,
15. and know that *this* city (is) a rebellious
— was *this* city destroyed.
19. it is found that *this* city of old
21. and that *this* city be not builded
5: 8. and *this* work goeth fast on,
16. Then came *the same* Sheshbazzar,
17. to build *this* house of God at Jerusalem,
6: 7. Let the work of *this* house of God alone;
— build *this* house of God in his place.
8. for the building of *this* house of God:
12. to alter (and) to destroy *this* house of God

דָּכָא [*dāh-chāh'*]. 1792

* NIPHAL.—*Participle.* *

Isa. 57:15. to revive the heart of *the contrite ones.*

* PIEL.—*Preterite.* *

Ps. 89:10(11). *Thou hast broken* Rahab
143: 3. *he hath smitten* my life

PIEL.—*Infinitive.*

Isa. 53:10. Yet it pleased the Lord *to bruise him;*
Lam. 3:34. *To crush* under his feet all the prisoners

PIEL.—*Future.*

Job 4:19. *are crushed* before the moth?
6: 9. it would please God *to destroy me;*
19: 2. *and break me in pieces* with words?
Ps. 72: 4. *and shall break in pieces* the oppressor.
94: 5. *They break in pieces* thy people,
Pro.22:22. neither *oppress* the afflicted
Isa. 3:15. *ye beat* my people *to pieces,*

* PUAL.—*Preterite.* *

Jer. 44:10. *They are* not *humbled*

PUAL.—*Future.*

Job 22: 9. of the fatherless *have been broken.*

PUAL.—*Participle.*

Isa. 19:10. they shall be *broken*
53: 5. (he was) *bruised* for our iniquities:

* HITHPAEL.—*Future.* *

Job 5: 4. *and they are crushed* in the
34:25. *so that they are destroyed.* (marg. *crushed*)

1793 **דַּכָּא** *dak-kāh'*, adj.

Ps. 34:18(19). *such as be of a contrite* spirit. (marg. *contrite of* spirit)
90: 3. Thou turnest man to *destruction;*
Isa. 57:15. of a *contrite* and humble spirit,

1794 **דָּכָה** [*dāh-chāh'*].

* KAL.—*Future.* *

Ps. 10:10. *He croucheth,* (and) humbleth (marg. *breaketh himself*)

* NIPHAL.—*Preterite.* *

Ps. 38: 8(9). I am feeble *and sore broken:*

NIPHAL.—*Participle.*

Ps. 51:17(19). a broken *and a contrite* heart,

* PIEL.—*Preterite.* *

Ps. 44:19(20). Though *thou hast sore broken us*
51: 8(10). the bones (which) *thou hast broken*

1795 **דַּכָּה** *dak-kāh'*, f.

Deu23: 1(2). He that is wounded in the stones, (lit. wounded *by bruising*)

1796 **דֳּכִי** [*dŏchee*], m.

Ps. 93: 3. the floods lift up *their waves.*

1797 **דִּכֵּן** *dik-kēhn*, Ch. pron.

Dan 2:31. *This* great image, whose brightness
7:20. even (of) *that* horn that had eyes,
21. and *the same* horn made war with the

1798 **דְּכַר** [*d'char*], Ch. m.

Ezr. 6: 9. both young bullocks, *and rams,* and
17. two hundred *rams,*
7:17. with this money bullocks, *rams,*

1799 **דִּכְרוֹן** [*dich-rōhn'*], Ch. m.

Ezr. 6: 2. and therein (was) *a record* thus written:

1799 **דָּכְרָן** *doch-rāhn'*, Ch. m.

Ezr. 4:15. search may be made in the book of *the records* of thy fathers: so shalt thou find in the book of *the records,*

דַּל *dal*, m. 1817

Ps. 141: 3. keep *the door of* my lips.

דַּל *dal*, adj. 1800

Ex. 23: 3. *Neither* (lit. *and* not) shalt thou countenance *a poor man*)
30:15. *and the poor* shall not give less
Lev.14:21. And if he (be) *poor,*
19:15. respect the person of *the poor,*
Jud. 6:15. my family (is) *poor* in Manasseh,
Ru. 3:10. whether *poor* or rich.
1Sa. 2: 8. He raiseth up *the poor*
2Sa. 3: 1. house of Saul waxed weaker *and weaker* (lit. going *and weak*)
13: 4. king's son, *lean* from day to day? (marg. *thin*)
Job 5:16. So *the poor hath* hope, (lit. *to the poor* is hope)
20:10. shall seek to please *the poor,*
19. hath forsaken *the poor;*
31:16. If I have withheld *the poor*
34:19. the rich more than *the poor?*
28. the cry of the *poor* to come unto him,
Ps. 41: 1(2). he that considereth *the poor:* (marg. *weak,* or, *sick*)
72:13. He shall spare *the poor* and needy,
82: 3. Defend *the poor* and fatherless:
4. Deliver *the poor* and needy:
113: 7. He raiseth up *the poor* out of the
Pro.10:15. the destruction of *the poor*
14:31. He that oppresseth *the poor*
19: 4. *but the poor* is separated
17. He that hath pity upon *the poor*
21:13. stoppeth his ears at the cry of *the poor,*
22: 9. he giveth of his bread *to the poor.*
16. He that oppresseth *the poor*
22. Rob not *the poor,* because he (is) *poor*
28: 3. A poor man that oppresseth *the poor*
8. for him that will pity *the poor.*
11. *but the poor* that hath understanding
15. a wicked ruler over *the poor* people.
29: 7. considereth the cause of *the poor:*
14. that faithfully judgeth *the poor,*
Isa. 10: 2. To turn aside *the needy* from
11: 4. righteousness shall he judge *the poor,*
14:30. the firstborn of *the poor* shall feed,
25: 4. been a strength *to the poor,*
26: 6. the steps of *the needy.*
Jer. 5: 4. Surely these (are) *poor;*
39:10. left of *the poor* of the people,
Am. 2: 7. on the head of *the poor,*
4: 1. which oppress *the poor,*
5:11. your treading (is) upon *the poor,*
8: 6. That we may buy *the poor*
Zep 3:12. an afflicted *and poor* people,

דָּלַג [*dāh-lag'*]. 1801

* KAL.—*Participle.* Poel. *

Zep 1: 9. all *those that leap* on the threshold,

* PIEL.—*Future.* *

2Sa.22:30. by my God *have I leaped* over a wall.
Ps. 18:29(30). by my God *have I leaped* over a wall
Isa. 35: 6. Then *shall* the lame (man) *leap*

PIEL.—*Participle.*

Cant.2: 8. he cometh *leaping* upon the mountains,

דָּלָה *dāh-lāh'*. 1802

* KAL.—*Preterite.* *

Ex. 2:19. also *drew* (water) enough for us,

KAL.—*Infinitive.*

Ex. 2:19. also drew (water) *enough* for us, (lit. *drawing* he drew)

KAL.—*Future.*

Ex. 2:16. they came *and drew* (water),
Pro.20: 5. a man of understanding *will draw it out.*

* PIEL.—*Preterite.* *

Ps. 30: 1(2). *for thou hast lifted me up,*

1817 דָּלָה [*dāh-lāh'*], f.

Isa. 26:20. and shut *thy doors* about thee:

1803 דַּלָּה *dal-lāh'*, f.

Gen41:19. *poor* and very ill favoured
2K. 24:14. save *the poorest sort of* the people
25:12. *But* the captain of the guard left *of the poor of*
Cant.7: 5(6). *and the hair of* thine head
Isa. 38:12. will cut me off *with pining sickness:* (marg. or, *from the thrum*)
Jer.40: 7. *and of the poor of* the land,
52:15. *Then*...away captive (certain) *of the poor of*
16. *But*...left (certain) *of the poor of*

1804 דָּלַח [*dāh-lagh'*].

* KAL.—*Future.* *

Eze.32: 2. *and troubledst* the waters with thy feet,
13. neither shall the foot of man *trouble them*
— nor the hoofs of beasts *trouble them.*

1805 דְּלִי *d'lee*, m.

Isa. 40:15. the nations (are) as a drop *of a bucket,*

1805 דֳּלִי [*dŏlee*], m.

Nu. 24: 7. pour the water *out of his buckets,*

1808 דָּלִיּוֹת [*dāh-leey-yōhth'*], f. pl.

Jer.11:16. *the branches of it* are broken.
Eze.17: 6. *whose branches* turned toward him,
7. *and* shot forth *her branches* toward him,
23. the shadow of *the branches thereof*
19:11. the multitude of *her branches.*
31: 7. in the length of *his branches:*
9. by the multitude of *his branches:*
12. in all the valleys *his branches* are

1809 דָּלַל [*dāh-lal'*].

* KAL.—*Preterite.* *

Job 28: 4. *they are dried up*, they are gone away
Ps. 79: 8. for *we are brought* very *low.*
116: 6. *I was brought low*, and he helped me.
142: 6(7). for *I am brought* very *low:*
Pro.26: 7. The legs of the lame *are not equal:* (marg. *are lifted up*)
Isa. 19: 6. *shall be emptied* and dried up:
38:14. mine eyes *fail* (with looking) upward:

* NIPHAL.—*Future.* *

Jud. 6: 6. *And* Israel *was* greatly *impoverished*
Isa. 17: 4. the glory of Jacob *shall be made thin,*

1811 דָּלַף [*dāh-laph'*].

* KAL.—*Preterite.* *

Job 16:20. mine eye *poureth out* (tears) unto God,
Ps.119:28. My soul *melteth* for heaviness: (marg. *droppeth*)

KAL.—*Future.*

Ecc.10:18. the house *droppeth through.*

1812 דֶּלֶף *deh'-leph*, m.

Pro.19:13. and the contentions of a wife (are) *a* continual *dropping.*
27:15. A continual *dropping* in a very rainy day

דָּלַק [*dāh-lak'*]. 1814

* KAL.—*Preterite.* *

Gen31:36. that *thou hast so hotly pursued* after
Lam.4:19. *they pursued us* upon the mountains,
Obad 18. *and they shall kindle* in them,

KAL.—*Infinitive.*

1Sa.17:53. of Israel returned *from chasing*

KAL.—*Future.*

Ps. 10: 2. *doth persecute* the poor:

KAL.—*Participle.*

Ps. 7:13(14). his arrows *against the persecutors.*
Pro.26:23. *Burning* lips and a wicked heart

* HIPHIL.—*Infinitive.* *

Eze.24:10. Heap on wood, *kindle* the fire,

HIPHIL.—*Future.*

Isa. 5:11. wine *inflame them!* (marg. or, *pursue them*)

דְּלַק [*d'lak*], Ch. 1815

* P'AL.—*Participle.* Active. *

Dan 7: 9. his wheels (as) *burning* fire.

דַּלֶּקֶת *dal-leh'-keth*, f. 1816

Deu28:22. with a fever, *and with an inflammation,*

דֶּלֶת *deh'-leth*, f. 1817

Gen19: 6. *and* shut *the door* after him,
9. came near to break *the door.*
10. and shut to *the door.*
Ex. 21: 6. bring him to *the door,*
Deu 3: 5. with high walls, *gates*, and bars
15:17. through his ear *unto the door,*
Jos. 2:19. go *out of the doors of* thy house
6:26. shall he set up *the gates of it.*
Jud. 3:23. shut *the doors of* the parlour
24. *the doors of* the parlour (were) locked,
25. he opened not *the doors of* the
11:31. cometh *forth of the doors of* my house
16: 3. took *the doors of* the gate
19:22. beat at *the door,*
27. opened *the doors of* the house,
1Sa. 3:15. opened *the doors of* the house
21:13(14). scrabbled on *the doors of* the gate,
23: 7. that hath *gates* and bars.
2Sa.13:17. bolt *the door* after her.
18. bolted *the door* after her.
1K. 6:31. he made *doors* (of) olive tree:
32. The two *doors* also (were of)
34. the two *doors* (were of) fir tree: the two leaves of *the* one *door*
— the two leaves of *the* other *door*
7:50. *for the doors of* the inner house,
— *for the doors of* the house,
16:34. set up *the gates thereof*
2K. 4: 4. thou shalt shut *the door*
5. shut *the door* upon her
33. shut *the door* upon them twain,
6:32. shut *the door*, and hold him fast *at the door:*
9: 3. Then open *the door*, and flee,
10. he opened *the door*, and fled.
12: 9(10). bored a hole *in the lid of it,*
18:16. *the doors of* the temple of the Lord,
1Ch 22: 3. the nails *for the doors of* the gates,
2Ch 3: 7. *and the doors thereof,*
4: 9. *and doors* for the court, and overlaid *the doors of them*
22. *the* inner *doors thereof*
— *and the doors of* the house
8: 5. with walls, *gates*, and bars;
14: 7(6). towers, *gates*, and bars,
28:24. shut up *the doors of* the house
29: 3. opened *the doors of* the house
7. they have shut up *the doors of* the porch,
Neh 3: 1. set up *the doors of it;*

Neh 3: 3, 6, 13. set up *the doors thereof*,
14, 15. set up *the doors thereof*,
6: 1. had not set up *the doors*
10. let us shut *the doors of* the
7: 1. I had set up *the doors*,
3. let them shut *the doors*,
13: 19. *the gates* should be shut,
Job 3: 10. Because it shut not up *the doors of*
31: 32. I opened *my doors* to the traveller.
38: 8. Or (who) shut up the sea *with doors*,
10. set bars *and doors*,
41: 14(6). Who can open *the doors of* his face?
Ps. 78: 23. *and* opened *the doors of* heaven,
107: 16. he hath broken *the gates of* brass,
Pro. 8: 34. watching daily at *my gates*,
26: 14. *the door* turneth upon his hinges,
Ecc. 12: 4. *the doors* shall be shut
Cant. 8: 9. if she (be) *a door*,
Isa. 26: 20. shut *thy doors* about thee:
45: 1. open before him *the two leaved gates;*
2. I will break in pieces *the gates of* brass,
57: 8. Behind *the doors* also and the posts
Jer. 36: 23. had read three or four *leaves*,
49: 31. which have neither *gates* nor bars,
Eze. 26: 2. *the gates of* the people:
38: 11. having neither bars *nor gates*,
41: 23. temple and the sanctuary had two *doors*.
24. *the doors had* two *leaves* (apiece), two turning *leaves;* two (leaves) *for the* one *door*, and two *leaves* for the other (door).
25. on *the doors of* the temple,
Zec. 11: 1. Open *thy doors*, O Lebanon,
Mal. 1: 10. that would shut *the doors*

1818 ## דָּם *dāhm*, m.

Gen. 4: 10. the voice of thy brother's *blood* (marg. *bloods*)
11. to receive thy brother's *blood*
9: 4. life thereof, (which is) *the blood thereof*,
5. surely *your blood* of your lives
6. Whoso sheddeth man's *blood*, by man shall *his blood* be shed:
37: 22. Shed no *blood*,
26. and conceal *his blood?*
31. dipped the coat *in the blood;*
42: 22. also *his blood* is required.
49: 11. *and* his clothes *in the blood of* grapes:
Ex. 4: 9. shall become *blood* upon the dry
25. Surely a *bloody* husband (art) thou
26. A *bloody* husband (thou art),
7: 17. they shall be turned *to blood*.
19. that they may become *blood;* and (that) there may be *blood*
20. in the river were turned *to blood*.
21. *blood* throughout all the land
12: 7. they shall take of *the blood*,
13. *the blood* shall be to you
— when I see *the blood*,
22. dip (it) *in the blood*
— *the blood* that (is) in the bason;
23. when he seeth *the blood*
22: 2(1). no *blood* (be shed) for him.
3(2). *blood* (shed) for him;
23: 18. Thou shalt not offer *the blood of*
24: 6. Moses took half of *the blood*,
— half of *the blood* he sprinkled
8. Moses took *the blood*,
— Behold *the blood of* the covenant,
29: 12. thou shalt take *of the blood of*
— pour all *the blood* beside the
16. thou shalt take *his blood*,
20. kill the ram, and take *of his blood*,
— sprinkle *the blood* upon the altar
21. thou shalt take of *the blood*
30: 10. *with the blood of* the sin offering
34: 25. Thou shalt not offer *the blood of*
Lev. 1: 5. bring *the blood*, and sprinkle *the blood* round about
11. sprinkle *his blood* round about
15. *the blood thereof* shall be wrung
3: 2. sprinkle *the blood* upon the altar
8. shall sprinkle *the blood thereof*
13. Aaron shall sprinkle *the blood thereof*

Lev. 3: 17. that ye eat neither fat nor *blood*.
4: 5. shall take *of* the bullock's *blood*,
6. dip his finger *in the blood*, and sprinkle of *the blood* seven times
7. *the blood* upon the horns
— pour all *the blood of* the bullock
16. shall bring *of the* bullock's *blood*
17. dip his finger (in some) of *the blood*,
18. *And* he shall put (some) of *the blood*
— pour out all *the blood* at the bottom
25, 34. the priest shall take *of the blood of*
— shall pour out *his blood*
30. shall take *of the blood thereof*
—, 34. shall pour out all *the blood thereof*
5: 9. he shall sprinkle *of the blood*
— the rest *of the blood* shall be
6: 27(20). is sprinkled *of the blood thereof*
30(23). *whereof* (any) *of the blood* is brought
7: 2. *the blood thereof* shall he sprinkle
14. the priest's that sprinkleth *the blood of*
26. ye shall eat no manner of *blood*,
27. that eateth any manner of *blood*,
33. offereth *the blood of* the peace offerings,
8: 15. Moses took *the blood*,
— poured *the blood* at the bottom
19, 24. Moses sprinkled *the blood*
23. and Moses took *of the blood of it*,
24. Moses put of *the blood*
30. *the blood* which (was) upon
9: 9. the sons of Aaron brought *the blood* unto him: and he dipped his finger *in the blood*,
— poured out *the blood*
12, 18. presented unto him *the blood*,
10: 18. *the blood of it* was not brought
12: 4. shall then continue *in the blood of* her
5. shall continue in *the blood of* her
7. from the issue of *her blood*.
14: 6. the living bird *in the blood of*
14, 25. the priest shall take (some) *of the blood of* the trespass offering,
17. upon *the blood of* the trespass offering:
28. upon the place of *the blood of*
51. dip them *in the blood of*
52. *with the blood of* the bird,
15: 19. her issue in her flesh be *blood*,
25. if a woman have an issue of *her blood*
16: 14. he shall take *of the blood of*
— shall he sprinkle of *the blood*
15. bring *his blood* within the vail, and do with *that blood* as he did *with the blood of* the bullock,
18. take *of the blood of* the bullock, *and of the blood of* the goat,
19. he shall sprinkle of *the blood*
27. whose *blood* was brought in (lit. who *their blood*)
17: 4. *blood* shall be imputed unto that man; he hath shed *blood;*
6. the priest shall sprinkle *the blood*
10. that eateth any manner of *blood;*
— against that soul that eateth *blood*,
11. the life of the flesh (is) *in the blood:*
— *the blood* (that) maketh an atonement
12. No soul of you shall eat *blood*,
— sojourneth among you eat *blood*.
13. shall even pour out *the blood thereof*,
14. *the blood of it* (is) for the life
— Ye shall eat *the blood of* no
— the life of all flesh (is) *the blood thereof:*
19: 16. against *the blood of* thy neighbour:
26. not eat (any thing) with *the blood:*
20: 9. *his blood* (shall be) upon him.
11, 12, 13, 16, 27. *their blood* (shall be) upon
18. uncovered the fountain of *her blood:*
Nu. 18: 17. thou shalt sprinkle *their blood*
19: 4. shall take *of her blood* with his finger, and sprinkle *of her blood*
5. her flesh, and *her blood*,
23: 24. *and* drink *the blood of* the slain.
35: 19. The revenger of *blood* himself
21. the revenger of *blood* shall slay
24. the slayer and the revenger of *blood*
25. out of the hand of the revenger of *blood*,
27. the revenger of *blood* find him
— the revenger of *blood* kill the slayer; he shall not be guilty of *blood:*

Nu. 35:33. for *blood* it defileth the land: and the land cannot be cleansed *of the blood* that is shed therein, but *by the blood of* him that shed it.
Deu 12:16. Only ye shall not eat *the blood;*
23. be sure that thou eat not *the blood:* for *the blood* (is) the life;
27. the flesh *and the blood,*
— *and the blood of* thy sacrifices
15:23. thou shalt not eat *the blood thereof;*
17: 8. between *blood and blood,*
19: 6. Lest the avenger of *the blood* pursue
10. That innocent *blood* be not shed
— (so) *blood* be upon thee.
12. into the hand of the avenger of *blood,*
13. innocent *blood* from Israel,
21: 7. Our hands have not shed this *blood,*
8. lay not innocent *blood* unto
— And *the blood* shall be forgiven
9. put away the (guilt of) innocent *blood*
22: 8. that thou bring not *blood*
27:25. taketh reward to slay an innocent person. (lit. a soul of innocent *blood*)
32:14. *and* thou didst drink *the* pure *blood of* the grape.
42. make mine arrows drunk *with blood,*
— *with the blood of* the slain
43. for he will avenge *the blood of*
Jos. 2:19. *his blood* (shall be) upon his head,
— *his blood* (shall be) on our head,
20: 3. refuge from the avenger of *blood.*
5. if the avenger of *blood* pursue
9. die by the hand of the avenger of *blood,*
Jud. 9:24. *and their blood* be laid upon Abimelech
1Sa. 14:32. did eat (them) with *the blood.*
33. in that they eat with *the blood.*
34. in eating with *the blood.*
19: 5. wilt thou sin *against* innocent *blood,*
25:26, 33. from coming *to* (shed) *blood,*
31. either that thou hast shed *blood*
26:20. let not *my blood* fall to the earth
2Sa. 1:16. *Thy blood* (be) upon thy head;
22. *From the blood of* the slain,
3:27. *for the blood of* Asahel
28. *from the blood of* Abner (marg. *bloods*)
4:11. therefore now require *his blood*
14:11. the revengers of *blood* to destroy
16: 7. come out, thou *bloody* man, (marg. man of *blood*)
8. all *the blood of* the house of Saul,
— because thou (art) a *bloody* man.
20:12. Amasa wallowed *in blood*
21: 1. for Saul, and for (his) *bloody* house,
23:17. *the blood of* the men
1K. 2: 5. shed *the blood of* war in peace, and put *the blood of* war upon his girdle
9. down to the grave *with blood.*
31. take away *the* innocent *blood,*
32. the Lord shall return *his blood*
33. *Their blood* shall therefore return
37. *thy blood* shall be upon
18:28. till *the blood* gushed out
21:19. where dogs licked *the blood of* Naboth shall dogs lick *thy blood,*
22:35. and *the blood* ran out of
38. the dogs licked up *his blood;*
2K. 3:22. on the other side (as) red *as blood:*
23. they said, This (is) *blood:*
9: 7. that I may avenge *the blood of* my servants the prophets, *and the blood of* all the servants
26. I have seen yesterday *the blood of* Naboth, and *the blood of* his sons, (marg. *bloods*)
33. and (some) *of her blood* was sprinkled
16:13. sprinkled *the blood of*
15. sprinkle upon it all *the blood of* the burnt offering, and all *the blood of* the sacrifice:
21:16. shed innocent *blood* very much,
24: 4. for the innocent *blood* that he shed: for he filled Jerusalem with innocent *blood;*
1Ch 11:19. shall I drink *the blood of* these
22: 8. Thou hast shed *blood* abundantly,
— thou hast shed much *blood*
28: 3. *and* hast shed *blood.* (marg. *bloods*)
2Ch 19:10. between *blood and blood,*
24:25. conspired against him *for the blood of*
2Ch 29:22. the priests received *the blood,*
—, 22. they sprinkled *the blood*
24. reconciliation with *their blood*
30:16. the priests sprinkled *the blood,*
Job 16:18. cover not thou *my blood,*
39:30. Her young ones also suck up *blood:*
Ps. 5: 6(7). *the bloody* and deceitful man. (marg. man of *bloods* and deceit)
9:12(13). When he maketh inquisition for *blood,*
16: 4. their drink offerings *of blood*
26: 9. nor my life with *bloody* men: (marg. men of *blood*)
30: 9(10). What profit (is there) *in my blood,*
50:13. *or* drink *the blood of* goats?
51:14(16). Deliver me *from bloodguiltiness,* (marg. *bloods*)
55:23(24). *bloody* and deceitful men (marg. men of *bloods* and deceit)
58:10(11). *in the blood of* the wicked.
59: 2(3). save me from *bloody* men.
68:23(24). dipped *in the blood* of (thine) enemies,
72:14. precious shall *their blood* be
78:44. turned their rivers *into blood;*
79: 3. *Their blood* have they shed
10. the revenging of *the blood of*
94:21. *and* condemn *the* innocent *blood.*
105:29. turned their waters *into blood,*
106:38. shed innocent *blood,* (even) *the blood of* their sons
— the land was polluted *with blood.*
139:19. depart from me therefore, ye *bloody* men.
Pro. 1:11. let us lay wait *for blood,*
16. make haste to shed *blood.*
18. they lay wait *for their* (own) *blood;*
6:17. hands that shed innocent *blood,*
12: 6. to lie in wait for *blood:*
28:17. violence *to the blood of* (any) person
29:10. The *blood*thirsty hate the upright: (marg. Men of *blood*)
30:33. wringing of the nose bringeth forth *blood.*
Isa. 1:11. *and* I delight not in *the blood of* bullocks,
15. your hands are full of *blood.* (marg. *bloods*)
4: 4. have purged *the blood of* Jerusalem
9: 5(4). garments rolled *in blood;*
15: 9. of Dimon shall be full of *blood:*
26:21. the earth also shall disclose *her blood* (marg. *bloods*)
33:15. stoppeth his ears from hearing of *blood* (marg. *bloods*)
34: 3. shall be melted *with their blood.*
6. The sword of the Lord is filled with *blood,*
— *with the blood of* lambs
7. their land shall be soaked *with blood,*
49:26. drunken with *their own blood,*
59: 3. your hands are defiled *with blood,*
7. make haste to shed innocent *blood:*
66: 3. (as if he offered) swine's *blood;*
Jer. 2:34. is found *the blood of* the souls
7: 6. *and* shed not innocent *blood*
19: 4. with *the blood of* innocents;
22: 3. *neither* shed innocent *blood* in this place.
17. and for to shed innocent *blood,*
26:15. shall surely bring innocent *blood*
46:10. made drunk *with their blood:*
48:10. keepeth back his sword *from blood.*
51:35. *and my blood* upon the inhabitants
Lam 4:13. have shed *the blood of* the just
14. polluted themselves *with blood,*
Eze. 3:18, 20. *but his blood* will I require
5:17. pestilence *and blood* shall pass
7:23. the land is full of *bloody* crimes,
9: 9. the land is full of *blood,*
14:19. pour out my fury upon it *in blood,*
16: 6. polluted *in thine own blood,*
—, 6. (when thou wast) *in thy blood,* Live;
9. washed away *thy blood* from thee, (marg *bloods*)
22. wast polluted *in thy blood.*
36. *and by the blood of* thy children,
38. break wedlock and shed *blood*
— will give thee *blood in* fury
18:10. (that is) a robber, a shedder of *blood,*
13. *his blood* shall be upon him. (marg. *bloods*)
19:10. like a vine *in thy blood,* (marg. or, *in thy quietness,* or, *in thy likeness*)
21:32(37). *thy blood* shall be in the midst
22: 2. wilt thou judge the *bloody* city?

Eze.22: 3. The city sheddeth *blood*
4. Thou art become guilty *in thy blood*
6. their power to shed *blood*.
9. that carry tales to shed *blood:*
12. have they taken gifts to shed *blood;*
13. at *thy blood* which hath been
27. to shed *blood*, (and) to destroy souls,
23:37, 45. *and blood* (is) in their hands,
45. manner of women that shed *blood;*
24: 6, 9. Woe to the *bloody* city,
7. *her blood* is in the midst of her;
8. I have set *her blood* upon
28:23. *and blood* into her streets;
32: 6. I will also water *with thy blood*
33: 4. *his blood* shall be upon his own
5. *his blood* shall be upon him.
6. *but his blood* will I require
8. *but his blood* will I require
25. Ye eat with *the blood*,
— *and* shed *blood:*
35: 6. I will prepare thee *unto blood, and blood* shall pursue thee: sith thou hast not hated *blood, even blood* shall pursue thee.
36:18. *the blood* that they had shed
38:22. with pestilence *and with blood;*
39:17. eat flesh, and drink *blood*.
18. *and* drink *the blood of* the princes
19. and drink *blood* till ye be drunken,
43:18. and to sprinkle *blood* thereon.
20. thou shalt take *of the blood thereof*,
44: 7. my bread, the fat *and the blood*,
15. offer unto me the fat *and the blood*,
45:19. the priest shall take *of the blood of*
Hos. 1: 4. I will avenge *the blood of*
4: 2. *and blood* toucheth *blood*. (marg. *bloods*)
6: 8. polluted *with blood*.
12:14(15). *therefore* shall he leave *his blood* (marg. *bloods*)
Joel 2:30(3:3). *blood*, and fire, and pillars of smoke.
31(3:4). and the moon *into blood*,
3:19(4:19). they have shed innocent *blood*
21(4:21). For I will cleanse *their blood*
Jon. 1:14. lay not upon us innocent *blood:*
Mic. 3:10. They build up Zion *with blood*, (marg. *bloods*)
7: 2. they all lie in wait *for blood;*
Nah 3: 1. Woe to the *bloody* city! (marg. city of *bloods*)
Hab. 2: 8, 17. *because of* men's *blood*, (marg. *bloods*)
12. that buildeth a town *with blood*, (marg. *bloods*)
Zep. 1:17. and *their blood* shall be
Zec. 9: 7. I will take away *his blood* (marg. *bloods*)
11. *by the blood of* thy covenant

1818 ## דָּם [*dāhm*], m.

Eze.19:10. like a vine *in thy blood*, (marg. or, *in thy quietness*, or, *in thy likeness*)

[Compare the preceding.]

1819 ## דָּמָה *dāh-māh'*.

* KAL.—*Preterite.* *

Ps.102: 6(7). *I am like* a pelican of the wilderness:
144: 4. Man *is like* to vanity:
Cant.7: 7(8). This thy stature *is like* to a
Isa. 1: 9. *we should have been like* unto
Eze.31: 2. Whom *art thou like* in thy greatness?
8. *were* not *like* his boughs,
— *was like* unto him in his beauty.
18. To whom *art thou* thus *like*

KAL.—*Imperative.*

Cant.2:17. and *be* thou *like* a roe
8:14. *and be* thou *like* to a roe

KAL.—*Future.*

Ps. 49:12(13), 20(21). is like the beasts (that) *perish*. (probably, lit. *they are alike*)
89: 6(7). *can be likened* unto the Lord?
Isa. 46: 5. compare me, *that we may be like?*

KAL.—*Participle.* Poel.

Cant.2: 9. My beloved *is like* a roe

* NIPHAL.—*Preterite.* *

Eze.32: 2. *Thou art like* a young lion

* PIEL.—*Preterite.* *

Nu. 33:56. as *I thought* to do unto them.
Jud.20: 5. *thought* to have slain me:
2Sa.21: 5. that *devised* against us (marg. or, *cut us off*)
Ps. 48: 9(10). *We have thought* of thy lovingkindness,
50:21. *thou thoughtest* that I was
Cant.1: 9. *I have compared thee*, O my love,
Isa. 14:24. Surely as *I have thought*,

PIEL.—*Future.*

Est. 4:13. *Think* not with thyself
Isa. 10: 7. Howbeit *he meaneth* not so,
40:18. To whom then *will ye liken* God?
25. To whom then *will ye liken me*,
46: 5. To whom *will ye liken me*,
Lam.2:13. what thing *shall I liken* to thee,
Hos.12:10(11). and *used similitudes*,

* HITHPAEL.—*Future.* *

Isa. 14:14. *I will be like* the most High.

דָּמָה [*dāh-māh'*]. 1820

* KAL.—*Preterite.* *

Jer. 6: 2. *I have likened* the daughter of (probably, lit. *I have cut off*)
Hos 4: 5. *and I will destroy* thy mother. (marg. *cut off*)

KAL.—*Future.*

Jer. 14:17. *let them* not *cease:*
Lam. 3:49. and *ceaseth* not,

* NIPHAL.—*Preterite.* *

Isa. 6: 5. for *I am undone;* (marg. *cut off*)
15: 1, 1. is laid waste, (and) *brought to silence;* (marg. or, *cut off*)
Jer. 47: 5. Ashkelon *is cut off*
Hos 4: 6. My people *are destroyed* (marg. *cut off*)
10: 7. her king *is cut off*
15. *shall* the king of Israel utterly *be cut off*.
Obad. 5. how *art thou cut off!*
Zep 1:11. the merchant people *are cut down;*

NIPHAL.—*Infinitive.*

Hos 10:15. shall the king of Israel *utterly* be cut off. (lit. *being cut off* be cut off)

דְּמָה [*d'māh*], Ch. 1821

* P'AL.—*Participle. Active.* *

Dan 3:25. the fourth *is like* the Son of God.
7: 5. a second, *like* to a bear,

דֻּמָּה *doom-māh'*, f. 1822

Eze.27:32. *like the destroyed* in the midst

דְּמוּת *d'mooth*, f. 1823

Gen 1:26. in our image, *after our likeness:*
5: 1. *in the likeness of* God made he him;
3. begat (a son) *in his own likeness*,
2K. 16:10. *the fashion of* the altar,
2Ch 4: 3. *And* under it (was) *the similitude of*
Ps. 58: 4(5). *like* the poison of a serpent: (marg *according to the likeness of*)
Isa. 13: 4. *like as of* a great people; (marg. *the likeness of*)
40:18. or what *likeness* will ye compare
Eze. 1: 5. *the likeness of* four living creatures.
— they had *the likeness of* a man.
10. *As for the likeness of* their faces,
13. *As for the likeness of* the living
16. *and* they four had one *likeness:*
22. *And the likeness* of the firmament
26. over their heads (was) *the likeness of*
— *the likeness of* the throne (was) *the likeness* as the appearance of a man
28. *the likeness of* the glory of the Lord.
8: 2. *a likeness* as the appearance of fire

Eze.10: 1. *the likeness of* a throne.
10. they four had one *likeness*,
21. *and the likeness of* the hands
22. *And the likeness of* their faces
23:15. *after the manner of* the Babylonians
Dan 10:16. *like the similitude of* the sons of men

1824 **דְּמִי** *d'mee*, m.

Isa. 38:10. I said *in the cutting off of* my days.

1824 **דֳּמִי** [*dŏmee*], m.

Ps. 83: 1(2). Keep not thou *silence*, O God: (lit. not *silence* to thee)
Isa. 62: 6. keep not *silence*, (lit. not *silence* to you)
7. And give him no *rest*,

1825 **דִּמְיוֹן** [*dim-yōhn'*], m.

Ps. 17:12. *Like* as a lion (that) is greedy (marg. *The likeness of him*)

1826 **דָּמַם** [*dāh-mam'*].

* KAL.—*Preterite.* *

Job 30:27. My bowels boiled, and *rested* not:
Ps. 35:15. they did tear (me), and *ceased* not:

KAL.—*Imperative.*

Jos. 10:12. Sun, *stand thou still* upon Gibeon;
1Sa. 14: 9. *Tarry* until we come to you; (marg. *Be still*)
Ps. 4: 4(5). upon your bed, *and be still.*
37: 7. *Rest* in the Lord, (marg. *Be silent* to)
62: 5(6). *wait thou* only upon God;
Isa. 23: 2. *Be still*, ye inhabitants (marg. *be silent*)
Jer. 47: 6. rest, *and be still.*
Eze.24:17. *Forbear* to cry, (marg. *Be silent*)

KAL.—*Future.*

Ex. 15:16. *they shall be* (as) *still* as a stone;
Lev.10: 3. *And* Aaron *held his peace.*
Jos. 10:13. *And* the sun *stood still*,
Job 29:21. *and kept silence* at my counsel.
31:34. *that I kept silence*, (and) went not
Ps. 30:12(13). and not *be silent.*
31:17(18). *let them be silent* in the grave.
Lam.2:10. sit upon the ground, (and) *keep silence:*
18. *let* not the apple of thine eye *cease.*
3:28. He sitteth alone *and keepeth silence*,
Am. 5:13. the prudent *shall keep silence*

* NIPHAL.—*Preterite.* *

Jer. 25:37. *And* the peaceable habitations *are cut down*

NIPHAL.—*Future.*

1Sa. 2: 9. the wicked *shall be silent* in darkness;
Jer. 8:14. *and let us be silent* there:
48: 2. Also *thou shalt be cut down*, (marg. or, *brought to silence*)
49:26. all the men of war *shall be cut off*
50:30. all her men of war *shall be cut off*
51: 6. *be* not *cut off* in her iniquity;

* POAL.—*Preterite.* *

Ps. 131: 2. Surely I have behaved *and quieted myself*,

* HIPHIL.—*Preterite.* *

Jer. 8:14. our God *hath put us to silence*,

1827 **דְּמָמָה** *d'māh-māh'*, f.

1K. 19:12. after the fire a *still* small voice.
Job 4:16. (there was) *silence*, and I heard a voice, (marg. or, I heard a *still* voice)
Ps. 107:29. He maketh the storm *a calm*,

1828 **דֹּמֶן** *dōh'-men*, m.

2K. 9:37. Jezebel shall be *as dung*
Ps. 83:10(11). they became (as) *dung* for the
Jer. 8: 2. they shall be *for dung*
9:22(21). shall fall *as dung* upon the
16: 4. they shall be *as dung*
25:33. they shall be *dung* upon the

דָּמַע [*dāh-mag'*]. 1830

* KAL.—*Infinitive.* *

Jer. 13:17. *and* mine eye shall weep *sore*, (lit. *and weeping* shall weep)

KAL.—*Future.*

Jer. 13:17. and mine eye *shall weep* sore,

דֶּמַע [*deh'-mag*], m. 1831

Ex. 22:29(28). of thy ripe fruits, *and of thy liquors:*

דִּמְעָה *dim-gāh'*, f. 1832

2K. 20: 5. I have seen *thy tears:*
Ps. 6: 6(7). I water my couch *with my tears.*
39:12(13). hold not thy peace at *my tears:*
42: 3(4). *My tears* have been my meat
56: 8(9). put thou *my tears* into thy bottle:
80: 5(6). feedest them with the bread of *tears*; and givest them *tears* to drink
116: 8. mine eyes from *tears*,
126: 5. They that sow *in tears*
Ecc. 4: 1. *the tears of* (such as were) oppressed,
Isa. 16: 9. I will water thee *with my tears*,
25: 8. the Lord God will wipe away *tears*
38: 5. I have seen *thy tears:*
Jer. 9: 1(8:23). mine eyes a fountain of *tears*,
18(17). our eyes may run down with *tears*,
13:17. run down with *tears*,
14:17. Let mine eyes run down with *tears*
31:16. thine eyes *from tears:*
Lam. 1: 2. *and her tears* (are) on her
2:11. Mine eyes do fail *with tears*,
18. let *tears* run down
Eze.24:16. neither shall *thy tears*
Mal. 2:13. covering the altar of the Lord with *tears*,

דְּמֶשֶׁק *d'meh'-shek*. 1833

Am. 3:12. *and in Damascus* (in) a couch. (marg. **or**, *on* the bed's *feet*)

דֵּן [*dēhn*], Ch. pron. 1836

Ezr. 4:11. *This* (is) the copy of the letter
14. *therefore* have we sent and certified (lit. on account of *this*)
15. for *which* cause was this city destroyed.
16. by *this* means thou shalt have no
22. that ye fail not to do *this:*
5: 3. Who hath commanded you to build *this* house, and to make up *this* wall?
4. the men that make *this* building?
5. answer by letter concerning *this*
7. wherein was written *thus;*
9. Who commanded you to build *this* house, and to make up *these* walls?
11. builded *these* many years ago,
12. the Chaldean, who destroyed *this* house,
13. Cyrus made a decree to build *this* house
17. his pleasure to us concerning *this matter.*
6:11. whosoever shall alter *this* word,
— let his house be made a dunghill for *this.*
15. And *this* house was finished
16. kept the dedication of *this* house
17. And offered at the dedication of *this* house
7:17. *That* thou mayest buy speedily with *this* money
24. ministers of *this* house of God,
Jer. 10:11. *Thus* shall ye say unto them,
Dan 2:10. nor ruler, (that) asked *such* things
12. For *this* cause the king was angry
18. concerning *this* secret;
24. *Therefore* Daniel went in unto Arioch,
28. the visions of thy head upon thy bed, are *these;*
29. what should come to pass *hereafter:*

Dan 2:30. *this* secret is not revealed to me for
36. *This* (is) the dream; and we will tell
43. but they shall not cleave *one* to *another*, (marg. *this* with *this*)
45. what shall come to pass *here*after: (marg. after *this*)
47. seeing thou couldest reveal *this* secret.
3: 7. *There*fore at that time, when all the people heard
8. *Where*fore at that time
16. we (are) not careful to answer thee in *this*
22. *There*fore because the king's commandment
29. other God that can deliver *after this sort*.
4:18(15). *This* dream I king Nebuchadnezzar
24(21). *This* (is) the interpretation, O king,
5: 7. Whosoever shall read *this* writing,
15. that they should read *this* writing,
22. though thou knewest all *this*;
24. and *this* writing was written.
25. *And this* (is) the writing
26. *This* (is) the interpretation of the thing:
6: 3(4). Then *this* Daniel was preferred
5(6). any occasion against *this* Daniel,
9(10). *Where*fore king Darius signed the
10(11). before his God, as he did afore*time*.
28(29). So *this* Daniel prospered in the
7: 6. After *this* I beheld, and lo another,
7. After *this* I saw in the night visions,
16. and asked him the truth of all *this*.

1843 דֵּעַ [*dēh'ăg*], m.

Job 32: 6. durst not shew you *mine opinion*.
10, 17. I also will shew *mine opinion*.
36: 3. I will fetch *my knowledge* from afar,
37:16. him which is perfect in *knowledge*?

1844 דֵּעָה *dēh-gāh'*, f.

1Sa. 2: 3. the Lord (is) a God of *knowledge*,
Job 36: 4. he that is perfect in *knowledge*
Ps. 73:11. is there *knowledge* in the most high?
Isa. 11: 9. the earth shall be full of *the knowledge* of the Lord,
28: 9. Whom shall he teach *knowledge*?
Jer. 3:15. shall feed you with *knowledge* and understanding.

1846 דָּעַךְ [*dāh-găch'*].

* KAL.—*Preterite*. *

Isa. 43:17. *they are extinct*, they are quenched

KAL.—*Future*.

Job 18: 5. the light of the wicked *shall be put out*,
6. his candle *shall be put out*
21:17. *is* the candle of the wicked *put out*?
Pro. 13: 9. the lamp of the wicked *shall be put out*.
20:20. his lamp *shall be put out* in obscure
24:20. the candle of the wicked *shall be put out*.

* NIPHAL.—*Preterite*. *

Job 6:17. *they are consumed* out of their place. (marg. *extinguished*)

* PUAL.—*Preterite*. *

Ps. 118:12. *they are quenched* as the fire of thorns:

1847 דַּעַת *dah'-gath*, f.

Gen 2: 9. the tree of *knowledge of* good and evil.
17. the tree of *the knowledge of* good and evil,
Ex. 31: 3 & 35:31. in understanding, *and in knowledge*,
Nu. 24:16. *the knowledge of* the most High,
Deu 4:42. should kill his neighbour un*awares*, (lit. without *knowledge*)
19: 4. Whoso killeth his neighbour ig*norantly*, (lit. *id.*)
Jos. 20: 3. unawares (and) un*wittingly* (lit. without *knowledge*)
5. he smote his neighbour un*wittingly*, (lit. *id.*)
1K. 7:14. *cunning* to work all works
Job 10: 7. *Thou knowest* that I am not wicked; (marg. (It is) upon *thy knowledge*)
13: 2. *What ye know*, (the same) do I know (lit. *as your knowledge*)
15: 2. Should a wise man utter vain *knowledge*,
21:14. *for* we desire not *the knowledge of* thy ways.
22. Shall (any) teach God *knowledge*?
33: 3. *and* my lips shall utter *knowledge*
34:35. Job hath spoken *with*out *knowledge*,
35:16. he multiplieth words without *knowledge*.
36:12. they shall die without *knowledge*.
38: 2. darkeneth counsel by words without *knowledge*?
42: 3. he that hideth counsel without *knowledge*?
Ps. 19: 2(3). night unto night sheweth *knowledge*.
94:10. he that teacheth man *knowledge*,
119:66. Teach me good judgment *and knowledge*:
139: 6. (Such) *knowledge* (is) too wonderful
Pro. 1: 4. to the young man *knowledge*
7. the beginning of *knowledge*:
22. fools hate *knowledge*?
29. For that they hated *knowledge*,
2: 5. *and* find *the knowledge of* God.
6. out of his mouth (cometh) *knowledge*
10. *and knowledge* is pleasant unto thy soul;
3:20. *By his knowledge* the depths are
5: 2. *and* (that) thy lips may keep *knowledge*.
8: 9. right to them that find *knowledge*.
10. *and knowledge* rather than choice gold.
12. *and* find out *knowledge* of witty inventions.
9:10. *and* the *knowledge* of the holy (is) understanding.
10:14. Wise (men) lay up *knowledge*:
11: 9. *but through knowledge* shall the just
12: 1. Whoso loveth instruction loveth *knowledge*:
23. A prudent man concealeth *knowledge*:
13:16. Every prudent (man) dealeth *with knowledge*:
14: 6. *but knowledge* (is) easy unto him that understandeth.
7. the lips of *knowledge*.
18. the prudent are crowned with *knowledge*.
15: 2. of the wise useth *knowledge* aright:
7. The lips of the wise disperse *knowledge*:
14. him that hath understanding seeketh *knowledge*:
17:27. He that hath *knowleage* spareth his words:
18:15. of the prudent getteth *knowledge*;
— of the wise seeketh *knowledge*.
19: 2. (that) the soul (be) without *knowledge*,
25. he will understand *knowledge*.
27. the words of *knowledge*.
20:15. the lips of *knowledge*
21:11. he receiveth *knowledge*.
22:12. The eyes of the Lord preserve *knowledge*,
17. apply thine heart *unto my knowledge*.
20. excellent things in counsels *and knowledge*,
23:12. thine ears to the words of *knowledge*.
24: 4. *And* by *knowledge* shall the chambers be filled
5. a man of *knowledge* increaseth
29: 7. the wicked regardeth not *to know* (it).
30: 3. *nor* have *the knowledge of* the holy.
Ecc. 1:16. experience of wisdom *and knowledge*.
18. increaseth *knowledge* increaseth sorrow.
2:21. in wisdom, *and in knowledge*,
26. wisdom, *and knowledge*, and joy:
7:12. the excellency of *knowledge*
9:10. *nor knowledge*, nor wisdom, in the grave,
12: 9. he still taught the people *knowledge*;
Isa. 5:13. because (they have) no *knowledge*:
11: 2. the spirit of *knowledge* and of the fear
32: 4. the rash shall understand *knowledge*,
33: 6. wisdom *and knowledge* shall be the stability
40:14. taught him *knowledge*,
44:19. *knowledge* nor understanding to say,
25. *and* maketh their *knowledge* foolish;
47:10. Thy wisdom *and thy knowledge*,
48: 4. *Because I knew* that thou (art) obstinate,
53:11. *by his knowledge* shall my righteous servant
58: 2. *and* delight *to know* my ways,

Jer. 10:14. Every man is brutish *in* (his) *knowledge:* (marg. or, more brutish *than to know*)
22:16. (was) not this *to know* me?
51:17. Every man is brutish *by* (his) *knowledge;* (marg. or, more brutish *than to know*)
Dan 1: 4. cunning *in knowledge,*
12: 4. *knowledge* shall be increased.
Hos. 4: 1. nor *knowledge of* God in the land.
6. are destroyed for lack of *knowledge:* because thou hast rejected *knowledge,*
6: 6. *and the knowledge* of God more than burnt offerings.
Mal. 2: 7. the priest's lips should keep *knowledge,*

1848 **דָּפִי** [*dŏphee*], m.

Ps. 50:20. thou *slander*est thine own mother's son. (lit. thou wilt give *slander* against)

1849 **דָּפַק** [*dāh-phak'*].

* KAL.—*Preterite.* *

Gen33:13. and *if men should overdrive them*

KAL.—*Participle.*—Poel.

Cant.5: 2. the voice of my beloved that *knocketh,*

* HITHPAEL.—*Participle.* *

Jud.19:22. *beat* at the door, (lit. *beating*)

1851 **דַּק** *dak*, adj.

Gen41: 3. ill favoured *and lean*fleshed;
4. the ill favoured *and lean*fleshed kine
6. behold, seven *thin* ears
7. the seven *thin* ears devoured
23. seven ears, withered, *thin,*
24. *the thin* ears devoured
Ex. 16:14. a *small* round thing, (as) *small* as the hoar-frost
Lev.13:30. in it a yellow *thin* hair;
16:12. full of sweet incense beaten *small,*
21:20. Or crookbackt, or *a dwarf,* (marg. or, *too slender*)
1K. 19:12. after the fire a still *small* voice.
Isa. 29: 5. shall be like *small* dust,
40:15. he taketh up the isles *as a very little thing.*

1852 **דֹּק** *dōhk*, m.

Isa. 40:22. stretcheth out the heavens *as a curtain,*

1854 **דָּקַק** [*dāh-kak'*].

* KAL.—*Preterite.* *

Ex. 32:20. ground (it) to powder, (lit. till that *it was made small*)
Deu 9:21. until it *was as small* as dust:

KAL.—*Future.*

Isa. 28:28. nor *bruise it* (with) his horsemen.
41:15. *and beat* (them) *small,* and shalt make

* HIPHIL.—*Preterite.* *

2K. 23:15. *stamped* (it) *small* to powder,
2Ch 34: 4. *and made dust* (of them), and strowed
Mic. 4:13. *and thou shalt beat in pieces* many people:

HIPHIL.—*Infinitive.*

Ex. 30:36. thou shalt beat (some) of it *very small,*
2Ch 34: 7. beaten the graven images *into powder,* (marg. *to make powder*)

HIPHIL.—*Future.*

2Sa.22:43. *I did stamp them* as the mire
2K. 23: 6. *and stamped* (it) *small* to powder,
2Ch 15:16. *and stamped* (it), and burnt (it)

* HOPHAL.—*Future.* *

Isa. 28:28. Bread (corn) *is bruised;*

דְּקַק [*d'kak,*] Ch. 1855

* P'AL.—*Preterite.* *

Dan 2:35. Then *was* the iron, the clay,...*broken to pieces* together,

* APHEL.—*Preterite.* *

Dan 2:34. *and brake* them *to pieces.*
45. *and* that it *brake in pieces* the iron,
6:24(25). and *brake* all their bones *in pieces*

APHEL.—*Future.*

Dan 2:40. *shall it break in pieces* and bruise.
44. *it shall break in pieces* and
7:23. *and break it in pieces.*

APHEL.—*Participle.*

Dan 2:40. forasmuch as iron *breaketh in pieces*
7: 7. it devoured *and brake in pieces,*
19. (which) devoured, *brake in pieces,* and

דָּקַר [*dāh-kar'*]. 1856

* KAL.—*Preterite.* *

1Sa.31: 4. come *and thrust me through,*
Zec.12:10. upon me whom *they have pierced,*
13: 3. *and* his father...*shall thrust him through*

KAL.—*Imperative.*

1Sa.31: 4. Draw thy sword, *and thrust me through*
1Ch 10: 4. *and thrust me through* therewith;

KAL.—*Future.*

Nu. 25: 8. *and thrust* both of them *through,*
Jud. 9:54. *And* his young man *thrust him through,*

* NIPHAL.—*Future.* *

Isa. 13:15. that is found *shall be thrust through;*

* PUAL.—*Participle.* *

Jer. 37:10. there remained (but) *wounded* men (marg. men *thrust through*)
51: 4. *and* (they that are) *thrust through*
Lam. 4: 9. *stricken through* for (want of) the

דַּר *dar*, m. 1858

Est. 1: 6. *and white,* and black, marble.

דָּר *dāhr*, Ch. m. 1859

Dan 4: 3(3:33). his dominion (is) *from generation to generation.*
34(31). his kingdom (is) *from generation to generation:*

דְּרָאוֹן [*d'rāh-ōhn'*], m. 1860

Dan12: 2. shame (and) everlasting *contempt.*

דֵּרָאוֹן *dēh-rāh-ōhn'*, m. 1860

Isa. 66:24. shall be *an abhorring* unto all

דָּרְבוֹנוֹת *dor-vōh-nōhth'*, f. pl. 1861

Ecc.12:11. The words of the wise (are) *as goads,*

דָּרְבָן *dor-vāhn'* m. 1861

1Sa.13:21. to sharpen *the goads.*

דַּרְדַּר *dar-dar'*, m. 1863

Gen 3:18. Thorns also *and thistles* shall it bring
Hos.10: 8. the thorn *and the thistle*

1864 ## דָּרוֹם *dāh-rōhm'*, m.

Deu33:23. possess thou the west *and the south.*
Job 37:17. he quieteth the earth *by the south* (wind)?
Ecc. 1: 6. The wind goeth toward *the south,*
11: 3. *and* if the tree fall *toward the south,*
Eze.20:46(21:2). and drop (thy word) toward *the south,*
40:24. he brought me toward *the south,* and behold a gate toward *the south:*
27. the inner court toward *the south:*
— from gate to gate toward *the south*
28. the inner court by *the south* gate: and he measured *the south* gate
44. their prospect (was) toward *the south:*
45. whose prospect (is) toward *the south,*
41:11. another door *toward the south:*
42:12. that (were) toward *the south*
13. *the south* chambers, which (are) before
18. He measured *the south* side,

1865 ## דְּרוֹר *d'rōhr*, m.

Ex. 30:23. of *pure* myrrh five hundred
Lev.25:10. proclaim *liberty* throughout
Isa. 61: 1. to proclaim *liberty* to the captives,
Jer.34: 8. to proclaim *liberty* unto them;
15, 17. in proclaiming *liberty*
17. I proclaim *a liberty* for you,
Eze.46:17. it shall be his to the year of *liberty;*

1866 ## דְּרוֹר *d'rōhr*, m.

Ps. 84: 3(4). *and the swallow* a nest
Pro.26: 2. *as the swallow* by flying,

1875 ## דַּרְיוֹשׁ *dar-yōhsh'.*

[Perhaps for דְּרוֹשׁ inf. of דָּרַשׁ.]

Ezr.10:16. *to examine* the matter.

1869 ## דָּרַךְ *dāh-rach'.*

*** KAL.—*Preterite.* ***

Nu.24:17. *there shall come* a Star out of Jacob,
Deu 1:36. I give the land that *he hath trodden*
Jos. 14: 9. whereon thy feet *have trodden*
Job 22:15. which wicked men *have trodden?*
24:11. *tread* (their) winepresses,
Ps. 7:12(13). *he hath bent* his bow,
37:14. *and have bent* their bow,
64: 3(4). *bend* (their bows to shoot) their arrows,
Isa. 63: 3. *I have trodden* the winepress alone;
Lam.1:15. the Lord *hath trodden* the virgin,
2: 4. *He hath bent* his bow like an enemy:
3:12. *He hath bent* his bow, and set me
Mic. 1: 3. *and tread* upon the high places
Hab. 3:15. *Thou didst walk* through the sea
Zec. 9:13. When *I have bent* Judah

KAL.—*Future.*

Deu11:24. the soles of your feet *shall tread*
25. all the land that *ye shall tread*
33:29. *thou shalt tread* upon their high places.
Jos. 1: 3. that the sole of your foot *shall tread*
Jud. 5:21. *thou hast trodden* down strength.
9:27. *and trode* (the grapes),
1Sa. 5: 5. *tread* on the threshold of Dagon
Ps. 11: 2. the wicked *bend* (their) bow,
58: 7(8). *he bendeth* (his bow to shoot)
91:13. *Thou shalt tread* upon the lion
Isa. 16:10. the treaders *shall tread out* no wine
63: 3. *for I will tread* them in mine anger,
Jer. 48:33. none *shall tread* with shouting;
51: 3.(כ׳ ולא ק׳) Against (him that) *bendeth let* the archer *bend* his bow,
Mic. 5: 5(4). *he shall tread* in our palaces,
6(5). when *he treadeth* within our
6:15. thou *shalt tread* the olives,

KAL.—*Participle.* Poel.

1Ch 5:18. *and to shoot* with bow,
1Ch 8:40. were mighty men of valour, archers, (lit. *benders of* the bow)
2Ch 14: 8(7). bare shields *and drew* bows,
Neh 13:15. *treading* wine presses on the
Job 9: 8. *and treadeth* upon the waves
Isa. 16:10. *the treaders* shall tread out no wine
59: 8. whosoever *goeth* therein
63: 2. *like him that treadeth* in the
Jer. 25:30. *as they that tread*
46: 9. that handle (and) *bend* the bow.
50:14. all *ye that bend* the bow,
29. Call together the archers against Babylon: all ye *that bend* the bow
51: 3. let *the archer* bend his bow,
Am. 4:13. *and treadeth* upon the high places
9:13. *and the treader of* grapes

KAL.—*Participle.* Paül.

Isa. 5:28. all their bows *bent,*
21:15. from the *bent* bow,

*** HIPHIL.—*Preterite.* ***

Jud.20:43. *trode them down* with ease
Job 28: 8. The lion's whelps *have* not *trodden* it,
Pro. 4:11. *I have led* thee in right paths.
Isa. 11:15. *and make* (men) *go over* dryshod.

HIPHIL.—*Infinitive.*

Jer. 51:33. time *to thresh her:* (marg. or, in the time that *he thresheth her*)

HIPHIL.—*Imperative.*

Ps. 25: 5. *Lead* me in thy truth,
119:35. *Make me to go* in the path

HIPHIL.—*Future.*

Ps. 25: 9. The meek *will he guide*
107: 7. *And he led them forth* by the
Isa. 42:16. *I will lead* them in paths
Jer. 9: 3(2). *And they bend* their tongues
Hab. 3:19. *he will make me to walk*

HIPHIL.—*Participle.*

Isa. 48:17. *which leadeth thee* by the way

דֶּרֶךְ *deh'-rech*, com. 1870

Gen 3:24. to keep *the way of* the tree of life.
6:12. all flesh had corrupted *his way*
16: 7. by the fountain *in the way*
18:19. they shall keep *the way of* the Lord,
19: 2. go *on your ways.*
31. *after the manner of* all the earth:
24:21. had made *his journey* prosperous
27. I (being) *in the way,*
40. and prosper *thy way;*
42. if now thou do prosper *my way*
48. which had led me *in the* right *way*
56. seeing the Lord hath prospered *my way;*
28:20. will keep me *in* this *way*
30:36. he set three days' *journey* betwixt
31:23. pursued after him seven days' *journey;*
35. for *the custom of* women (is) upon me.
32: 1(2). Jacob went *on his way,*
33:16. *on his way* unto Seir.
35: 3. was with me *in the way*
19. was buried *in the way*
38:14. which (is) by *the way*
16. he turned unto her by *the way,*
21. openly by *the way* side?
42:25. give them provision *for the way:*
38. if mischief befall him *by the way*
45:21. gave them provision *for the way.*
23. meat for his father *by the way.*
24. See that ye fall not out *by the way.*
48: 7. in the land of Canaan *in the way,*
— I buried her there *in the way*
49:17. Dan shall be a serpent by *the way,*
Ex. 3:18. three days' *journey* into the wilderness,
4:24. it came to pass *by the way*
5: 3. three days' *journey* into the desert,
8:27(23). We will go three days' *journey*
13:17. led them not (through) *the way*
18. *the way of* the wilderness
21. to lead them *the way;*
18: 8. had come upon them *by the way,*
20. *the way* wherein they must walk,

Ex. 23:20. to keep thee *in the way*,
32: 8. turned aside quickly out of *the way*
33: 3. lest I consume thee *in the way*.
13. shew me now *thy way*,
Lev.26:22. *your* (high) *ways* shall be desolate.
Nu. 9:10. or (be) *in a journey* afar off,
13. *and* is not *in a journey*,
10:33. from the mount of the Lord three days' *journey*:
— before them *in* the three days' *journey*,
11:31. *as it were* a day's *journey* (marg. *the way of* a day)
— *and as it were* a day's *journey*
14.25. *the way of* the Red sea.
20:17. go by the king's (high) *way*,
21: 1. came *by the way of* the spies;
4. *by the way of* the Red sea,
— discouraged *because of the way*.
22. go along *by* the king's (high) *way*,
33. *by the way of* Bashan:
22:22. the angel of the Lord stood *in the way*
23,31. the angel of the Lord standing *in the way*,
— the ass turned aside out of *the way*,
— to turn her into *the way*.
26. where (was) no *way* to turn
32. because (thy) *way* is perverse
34. I knew not that thou stoodest *in the way*
24:25. Balak also went *his way*.
33: 8. went three days' *journey*
Deu 1: 2. *by the way of* mount Seir
19. *by the way of* the mountain
22. by what *way* we must go up,
31. in all *the way* that ye went,
33. Who went *in the way* before you,
— *by* what *way* ye should go,
40. *by the way of* the Red sea.
2: 1. *by the way of* the Red sea,
8. *through the way of* the plain
— *by the way of* the wilderness
27. I will go *along by the high way*, (lit. *by the way, by the way*)
3: 1. *the way to* Bashan:
5:33(30). Ye shall walk *in* all *the ways*
6: 7. when thou walkest *by the way*,
8: 2. thou shalt remember all *the way*
6. to walk *in his ways*,
9:12. quickly turned aside out of *the way*
16. turned aside quickly out of *the way*
10:12. to walk in all *his ways*,
11:19. when thou walkest *by the way*,
22. to walk in all *his ways*, and to cleave
28. but turn aside out of *the way*
30. by *the way* where the sun goeth
13: 5(6). to thrust thee out of *the way*
14:24. if *the way* be too long for thee,
17:16. return no more that *way*.
19: 3. Thou shalt prepare thee *a way*,
6. because *the way* is long,
9. to walk ever *in his ways*;
22: 4. fall down *by the way*,
6. to be before thee *in the way*
23: 4(5). with water *in the way*,
24: 9. unto Miriam *by the way*,
25:17. what Amalek did unto thee *by the way*,
18. How he met thee *by the way*,
26:17. to walk *in his ways*,
27:18. maketh the blind to wander *out of the way*.
28: 7. come out against thee one *way*, and flee before thee seven *ways*.
9. walk *in his ways*.
25. thou shalt go out one *way*
— flee seven *ways* before them:
29. thou shalt not prosper in *thy ways*:
68. *by the way* whereof I spake
30:16. to walk *in his ways*,
31:29. turn aside from *the way*
32: 4. all *his ways* (are) judgment:
Jos. 1: 8. then thou shalt make *thy way*
2: 7. *the way* to Jordan unto the fords:
16. afterward may ye go *your way*.
22. sought (them) throughout all *the way*,
3: 4. that ye may know *the way*
— for ye have not passed (this) *way*
5: 4, 5. in the wilderness *by the way*,
7. circumcised them *by the way*.
8:15. *by the way of* the wilderness.
9:11. victuals with you *for the journey*,
Jos. 9:13. by reason of *the* very long *journey*.
10:10. chased them along *the way*
12: 3. *the way to* Beth-jeshimoth;
22: 5. to walk in all *his ways*,
23:14. I (am) going *the way of* all the earth:
24:17. preserved us in all *the way*
Jud. 2:17. turned quickly out of *the way*
19. *nor from their* stubborn *way*.
22. keep *the way of* the Lord
4: 9. *the journey* that thou takest
5:10. walk by *the way*.
8:11. Gideon went up *by the way*
9:25. all that came *along that way*
37. *along by* the plain of Meonenim.
17: 8. to the house of Micah, as *he journeyed*. (marg. in making *his way*)
18: 5. whether *our way* which we go
6. before the Lord (is) *your way*
26. the children of Dan went *their way*:
19: 9. get you early *on your way*,
27. went out to go *his way*:
20:42. *the way of* the wilderness;
Ru. 1: 7. they went *on the way*
1Sa. 1:18. So the woman went *her way*,
4:13. Eli sat upon a seat by *the way*side
6: 9. if it goeth up *by the way of*
12. the kine took the straight *way* to *the way of* Beth-shemesh,
8: 3. his sons walked not *in his ways*,
5. thy sons walk not *in thy ways*:
9: 6. he can shew us *our way*
8. to tell us *our way*.
12:23. the good and *the* right *way*:
13:17. one company turned unto *the way*
18. *the way* (to) Beth-horon:
— turned (to) *the way of* the border
15: 2. he laid (wait) for him *in the way*,
18. the Lord sent thee *on a journey*,
20. have gone *the way* which the
17:52. *by the way to* Shaaraim,
18:14. behaved himself wisely in all *his ways*;
21: 5(6). in *a manner* common,
24: 3(4). the sheepcotes by *the way*,
7(8). went *on* (his) *way*.
19(20). will he let him go well *away?* (lit. *in a* good *way*)
25:12. David's young men turned *their way*,
26: 3. before Jeshimon, by *the way*.
25. David went *on his way*,
28:22. when thou goest *on thy way*.
30: 2. went *on their way*.
2Sa. 2:24. *the way of* the wilderness
4: 7. *through* the plain all night.
11:10. Camest thou not *from* (thy) *journey*?
13:30. while they were *in the way*,
34. there came much people *by the way*
15: 2. stood beside *the way of* the gate:
23. toward *the way of* the wilderness.
16:13. David and his men went *by the way*,
18:23. *the way of* the plain,
22:22. *the ways of* the Lord,
31. *his way* (is) perfect;
33. he maketh *my way* perfect.
1K. 1:49. went every man *his way*.
2: 2. I go *the way of* all the earth:
3. to walk *in his ways*, to keep his statutes,
4. If thy children take heed to *their way*,
3:14. if thou wilt walk *in my ways*,
8:25. thy children take heed to *their way*,
32. bring *his way* upon his head;
36. teach them *the* good *way*
39. to every man according to *his ways*,
44. *whither*soever (lit. *in the way* which) thou shalt send
— *toward* the city which thou
48. pray unto thee *toward* their land,
58. to walk in all *his ways*,
11:29. found him *in the way*;
33. have not walked *in my ways*,
38. wilt walk *in my ways*,
13: 9. *by* the same *way*
10. So he went another *way*, and returned not *by the way*
12. What *way* went he? For his sons had seen what *way*
17. nor turn again to go *by the way*
24. a lion met him *by the way*,

1K. 13:24. his carcase was cast *in the way*,
25. saw the carcase cast *in the way*,
26. brought him back from *the way*
28. found his carcase cast *in the way*,
33. returned not *from his* evil *way*,
15:26. walked *in the way of* his father,
34. walked *in the way of* Jeroboam,
16: 2. hast walked *in the way of* Jeroboam,
19. in walking *in the way of* Jeroboam,
26. walked in all *the way of* Jeroboam
18: 6. Ahab went one *way*
— Obadiah went another *way*
7. as Obadiah was *in the way*,
27. or he is in *a journey*,
43. look *toward* the sea.
19: 4. he himself went a day's *journey*
7. *the journey* (is) too great for thee.
15. return *on thy way* to the wilderness of
20:38. waited for the king by *the way*,
22:43. he walked in all *the ways of* Asa
52(53). walked *in the way of* his father, *and in the way of* his mother, *and in the way of* Jeroboam
2K. 2:23. he was going up *by the way*,
3: 8. Which *way* shall we go up?
— *The way* through the wilderness of Edom.
9. they fetched a compass of seven days' *journey*:
20. *by the way of* Edom,
6:19. This (is) not *the way*,
7:15. all *the way* (was) full of garments
8:18, 27. he walked *in the way of* the
9:27. he fled by *the way of* the garden
10:12. he (was) at the shearing house *in the way*,
11:16. she went *by the way*
19. came *by the way of* the gate
16: 3. But he walked *in the way*
17:13. Turn ye *from your* evil *ways*,
19:28. *by the way* by which thou camest.
33. *By the way* that he came,
21:21. he walked in all *the way*
22. walked not *in the way of* the Lord.
22: 2. walked in all *the way of* David
25: 4. *by the way of* the gate
— *the way toward* the plain.
2Ch 6:16. that thy children take heed to *their way*
23. by recompensing *his way* upon his own
27. thou hast taught them *the* good *way*,
30. according unto all *his ways*,
31. to walk *in thy ways*,
34. *by the way* that thou shalt
— pray unto thee *toward* this city
38. and pray *toward* their land,
7:14. turn *from their* wicked *ways*;
11:17. they walked *in the way of* David
13:22. *and his ways*, and his sayings,
17: 3. he walked *in the* first *ways of*
6. was lifted up *in the ways of* the Lord:
18:23. Which *way* went the Spirit
20:32. he walked *in the way of* Asa
21: 6. he walked *in the way of* the kings of
12. walked *in the ways of* Jehoshaphat
— *nor in the ways of* Asa
13. But hast walked *in the way of*
22: 3. He also walked *in the ways of*
27: 6. because he prepared *his ways*
7. all his wars, *and his ways*,
28: 2. he walked *in the ways of* the
26. and of all *his ways*,
34: 2. walked *in the ways of* David
Ezr. 8:21. to seek of him *a* right *way* for us,
22. against the enemy *in the way*:
31. such as lay in wait *by the way*.
Neh 9:12. to give them light in *the way*
19. to lead them *in the way*;
— to shew them light, and *the way*
Job 3:23. to a man *whose way* is hid,
4: 6. the uprightness of *thy ways*?
6:18. The paths of *their way*
8:19. this (is) the joy of *his way*,
12:24. in a wilderness (where there is) no *way*.
13:15. maintain *mine own ways*
17: 9. The righteous also shall hold on *his way*,
19:12. raise up *their way* against me,
21:14. the knowledge of *thy ways*.
29. asked them that go by *the way*?

Job 21:31. Who shall declare *his way*
22: 3. that thou makest *thy ways* perfect?
28. the light shall shine upon *thy ways*.
23:10. But he knoweth *the way*
11. *his way* have I kept,
24: 4. They turn the needy *out of the way*:
13. they know not *the ways thereof*,
18. he beholdeth not *the way*
23. yet his eyes (are) upon *their ways*.
26:14. these (are) parts of *his ways*:
28:23. God understandeth *the way thereof*,
26. *and a way* for the lightning
29:25. I chose out *their way*,
31: 4. Doth not he see *my ways*,
7. If my step hath turned out of *the way*,
34:21. his eyes (are) upon *the ways of* man,
27. consider any of *his ways*:
36:23. Who hath enjoined him *his way*?
38:19. Where (is) *the way*
24. By what *way* is the light parted,
25. *or a way* for the lightning
40:19. He (is) the chief of *the ways of* God:
Ps. 1: 1. *nor* standeth *in the way*
6. For the Lord knoweth *the way of* the righteous: *but the way of* the ungodly
2:12. ye perish (from) *the way*,
5: 8(9). make *thy way* straight
10: 5. *His ways* are always grievous;
18:21(22). *the ways of* the Lord,
30(31). *his way* (is) perfect:
32(33). maketh *my way* perfect.
25: 4. Shew me *thy ways*,
8. will he teach sinners *in the way*.
9. the meek will he teach *his way*.
12. him shall he teach *in the way*
27:11. Teach me *thy way*,
32: 8. instruct thee and teach thee *in the way*
35: 6. Let *their way* be dark
36: 4(5). he setteth himself in *a way*
37: 5. Commit *thy way* unto the Lord;
7. who prospereth in *his way*,
14. such as be of upright *conversation*. (marg. the upright of *way*)
23. *and* he delighteth *in his way*.
34. and keep *his way*,
39: 1(2). I will take heed to *my ways*,
49:13(14). This *their way* (is) their folly:
50:23. ordereth (his) *conversation* (marg. disposeth (his) *way*)
51:13(15). teach transgressors *thy ways*;
67: 2(3). That *thy way* may be known
77:13(14). *Thy way*, O God,
19(20). *Thy way* (is) in the sea,
80:12(13). all they which pass by *the way*
81:13(14). Israel had walked *in my ways*!
85:13(14). shall set (us) *in the way*
86:11. Teach me *thy way*,
89:41(42). All that pass by *the way* spoil him:
91:11. to keep thee in all *thy ways*.
95:10. they have not known *my ways*:
101: 2. behave myself wisely *in a* perfect *way*.
6. he that walketh *in a* perfect *way*,
102:23(24). He weakened my strength *in the way*;
103: 7. He made known *his ways*
107: 4. in *a* solitary *way*;
7. led them forth *by the* right *way*,
17. *because of* their transgression,
40. the wilderness, (where there is) no *way*.
110: 7. shall drink of the brook *in the way*:
119: 1. the undefiled in *the way*,
3. they walk *in his ways*.
5. O that *my ways* were directed
14. I have rejoiced *in the way of*
26. I have declared *my ways*,
27. Make me to understand *the way of*
29. Remove from me *the way of* lying:
30. I have chosen *the way of* truth:
32. I will run *the way of* thy commandments,
33. *the way of* thy statutes;
37. quicken thou me *in thy way*.
59. I thought on *my ways*,
168. all *my ways* (are) before thee.
128: 1. that walketh *in his ways*.
138: 5. sing *in the ways of* the Lord:
139: 3. art acquainted (with) all *my ways*.
24. see if (there be any) wicked *way* in me, and lead me *in the way* everlasting.

Ps.143: 8. cause me to know *the way*
145:17. righteous in all *his ways*,
146: 9. *but the way of* the wicked
Pro. 1:15 walk not thou *in the way*
31. eat of the fruit of *their own way*,
2: 8. *and* preserveth *the way of* his saints.
12. To deliver thee *from the way of*
13. to walk *in the ways of* darkness;
20. That thou mayest walk *in the way of*
3: 6. In all *thy ways* acknowledge
17. *Her ways* (are) *ways of* pleasantness,
23. Then shalt thou walk *in thy way*
31. choose none of *his ways*.
4:11. I have taught thee *in the way of*
14. go not *in the way of* evil
19. *The way of* the wicked
26. let all *thy ways* be established.
5: 8. Remove *thy way* far from her,
21. For *the ways of* man
6: 6. consider *her ways*,
23. *and* reproofs of instruction (are) *the way of* life:
7: 8. *and* he went *the way to* her house,
19. he is gone *a long journey*:
25. Let not thine heart decline to *her ways*,
27. Her house (is) *the way to* hell,
8: 2. by *the way* in the places
13. *and the* evil *way*,
22. in the beginning of *his way*,
32. blessed (are they that) keep *my ways*.
9: 6. go *in the way of* understanding.
15. To call passengers (lit. passers of *the way*)
10: 9. he that perverteth *his ways*
29. *The way of* the Lord
11: 5. the perfect shall direct *his way*:
20. upright in (their) *way*
12:15. *The way of* a fool
26. *but the way of* the wicked
28. *and* (in) *the* path*way* (thereof there is)
13: 6. upright in *the way*:
15. *but the way of* transgressors
14: 2. but (he that is) perverse in *his ways*
8. to understand *his way*:
12. There is *a way* which seemeth
— but the end thereof (are) *the ways of*
14. shall be filled *with his own ways*:
15: 9. *The way of* the wicked
19. *The way of* the slothful
16: 2. All *the ways of* a man
7. When a man's *ways* please
9. A man's heart deviseth *his way*:
17. he that keepeth *his way*
25. There is *a way* that seemeth
— but the end thereof (are) *the ways of*
29. leadeth him *into the way*
31. it be found *in the way of*
19: 3. The foolishness of man perverteth *his way*:
16. he that despiseth *his ways*
20:24. can a man then understand *his own way*?
21: 2. Every *way of* a man (is) right
8. *The way of* man (is) froward
16. The man that wandereth *out of the way*
29. he directeth *his way*.
22: 5. snares (are) *in the way of* the froward:
6. Train up a child in *the way* he should go: (marg. *his way*)
23:19. guide thine heart *in the way*.
26. let thine eyes observe *my ways*.
26:13. a lion *in the way*;
28: 6. perverse (in his) *ways*, though he (be)
10. to go astray *in an* evil *way*,
18. perverse (in his) *ways* shall fall at
29:27. upright in *the way*
30:19. *The way of* an eagle in the air; *the way of* a serpent upon a rock; *the way of* a ship in the midst of the sea; *and the way of* a man with a maid.
20. Such (is) *the way of* an adulterous
31: 3. *nor thy ways* to that which destroyeth
Ecc.10: 3. a fool walketh *by the way*,
11: 5. what (is) *the way of* the spirit,
9. walk *in the ways of* thine heart,
12: 5. fears (shall be) *in the way*,
Isa. 2: 3. he will teach us *of his ways*,
3:12. *and* destroy *the way of* thy paths.
8:11. that I should not walk *in the way of*
9: 1(8:23). *the way of* the sea,

Isa. 10:24. against thee, *after the manner of* Egypt.
26. shall he lift it up *after the manner of*
15: 5. *for in the way of* Horonaim
30:11. Get you out of *the way*,
21. This (is) *the way*,
35: 8. And an highway shall be there, *and a way*, *and* it shall be called *The way of*
— the *way*faring men,
37:29. I will turn thee back *by the way*
34. *By the way* that he came,
40: 3. *the way of* the Lord,
14. *and* shewed to him *the way of*
27. *My way* is hid from the Lord,
42:16. I will bring the blind *by a way*
24. they would not walk *in his ways*,
43:16. *a way* in the sea,
19. *a way* in the wilderness,
45:13. I will direct all *his ways*:
48:15. and he shall make *his way* prosperous.
17. which leadeth thee *by the way*
49: 9. They shall feed in *the ways*,
11. I will make all my mountains *a way*,
51:10. *a way* for the ransomed to pass
53: 6. every one *to his own way*;
55: 7. Let the wicked forsake *his way*,
8. neither (are) *your ways my ways*,
9. so are *my ways* higher *than your ways*,
56:11. they all look *to their own way*,
57:10. in the greatness of *thy way*;
14. prepare *the way*, take up the stumbling block *out of the way of*
17. he went on frowardly *in the way of*
18. I have seen *his ways*,
58: 2. delight to know *my ways*,
13. not doing *thine own ways*,
59: 8. *The way of* peace they know not;
62:10. prepare ye *the way of* the people;
63:17. thou made us to err *from thy ways*
64: 5(4). remember thee *in thy ways*:
65: 2. walketh *in a way* (that was) not good,
66: 3. they have chosen *their own ways*,
Jer. 2:17. when he led thee *by the way*?
18. *in the way of* Egypt,
— *in the way of* Assyria,
23. see *thy way* in the valley, know what
— a swift dromedary traversing *her ways*;
33. Why trimmest thou *thy way* to seek love?
— taught the wicked ones *thy ways*.
36. so much to change *thy way*?
3: 2. In *the ways* hast thou sat
13. hast scattered *thy ways*
21. they have perverted *their way*,
4:11. *toward* the daughter of my people,
18. *Thy way* and thy doings have procured
5: 4, 5. *the way of* the Lord,
6:16. Stand ye in *the ways*,
— where (is) *the* good *way*,
25. *nor* walk *by the way*;
27. mayest know and try *their way*.
7: 3. Amend *your ways*
5. if ye throughly amend *your ways*
23. walk ye in all *the ways*
10: 2. Learn not *the way of* the heathen,
23. *the way* of man (is) not in himself: (lit. to a man *his way* (is) not)
12: 1. Wherefore doth *the way of* the
16. will diligently learn *the ways of*
15: 7. (since) they return not *from their ways*.
16:17. mine eyes (are) upon all *their ways*:
17:10. every man *according to his ways*,
18:11. every one *from his* evil *way*, and make *your ways*
15. caused them to stumble *in their ways*
— *a way* not cast up;
21: 8. set before you *the way of* life, and *the way of* death.
22:21. This (hath been) *thy manner*
23:12. Wherefore *their way* shall be
22. have turned them *from their* evil *way*,
25: 5. every one *from his* evil *way*,
26: 3. every man *from his* evil *way*,
13 Therefore now amend *your ways*
28:11. the prophet Jeremiah went *his way*.
31: 9. *in a* straight *way*,
21. *the way* (which) thou wentest:
32:19. upon all *the ways of* the sons of men: to give every one *according to his ways*,

Jer.32:39. one heart, *and* one *way*,
35:15 & 36:3. every man *from his* evil *way*
36: 7. every one *from his* evil *way*.
39: 4. *by the way of* the king's garden
— *the way of* the plain.
42: 3. thy God may shew us *the way*
48:19. stand by *the way*,
50: 5. They shall ask *the way* to Zion
52: 7. *by the way of* the gate
— and they went *by the way of* the plain.
Lam. 1: 4. *The ways of* Zion do mourn,
12. all ye that pass by? (marg. pass by *the way*)
2:15. All that pass by clap (their) hands (marg. pass by *the way*)
3: 9. He hath inclosed *my ways*
11. He hath turned aside *my ways*,
40. Let us search and try *our ways*,
Eze. 3:18. *from his* wicked *way*,
19. *nor from his* wicked *way*,
7: 3, 8. judge thee *according to thy ways*,
4. will recompense *thy ways* upon thee,
9. I will recompense thee *according to thy ways*
27. I will do unto them *after their way*,
8: 5. *the way* toward the north. So I lifted up mine eyes *the way* toward the north,
9: 2. six men came *from the way of*
10 & 11:21. I will recompense *their way*
13:22. return *from his* wicked *way*,
14:22. ye shall see *their way*
23. when ye see *their ways*
16:25. at every head of *the way*,
27. which are ashamed *of thy* lewd *way*.
31. in the head of every *way*,
43. I also will recompense *thy way*
47. hast thou not walked *after their ways*,
— more than they in all *thy ways*.
61. thou shalt remember *thy ways*,
18:23. should return *from his ways*,
25. *The way of* the Lord is not equal.
— Is not *my way* equal? are not *your ways* unequal?
29. *The way of* the Lord is not equal. O house of Israel, are not *my ways* equal? are not *your ways* unequal?
30. every one *according to his ways*,
20:30. *after the manner of* your fathers?
43. shall ye remember *your ways*,
44. *according to your* wicked *ways*,
46(21:2). set thy face *toward* the south,
21:19(24). appoint thee two *ways*,
—(—). at the head of *the way*
20(25). Appoint *a way*, that the sword
21(26). stood at the parting of *the way*, at the head of *the* two *ways*,
22:31. *their own way* have I recompensed
23:13. they (took) both one *way*,
31. Thou hast walked *in the way of*
24:14. *according to thy ways*, and according
28:15. Thou (wast) perfect *in thy ways*
33: 8. warn the wicked *from his way*,
9. warn the wicked *of his way* to turn from it; if he do not turn *from his way*,
11. that the wicked turn *from his way*
— turn ye *from your* evil *ways*;
17. *The way of* the Lord is not equal:
— *their way* is not equal.
20. ye say, *The way of* the Lord is not equal.
— every one *after his ways*.
36:17. defiled it *by their own way*
— *their way* was before me
19. *according to their way* and according
31. remember *your own* evil *ways*,
32. *for your own ways*, O house of Israel.
40: 6. which looketh *toward* the east,
10. the little chambers of the gate east*ward* (lit. *the way of* the east)
20. that looked *toward* the north,
22. the gate that looketh *toward* the east;
24. brought me *toward* the south, and behold a gate *toward* the south:.
27. a gate in the inner court *toward*
— *toward* the south an hundred
32. the inner court *toward* the east:
44. their prospect (was) *toward* the south:
— the prospect *toward* the north.
Eze.40:45. whose prospect (is) *toward* the south,
46. whose prospect (is) *toward* the north
41:11. one door *toward* the north,
12. at the end *toward* the west
42: 1. *the way toward* the north: (lit. *the way, the way of* the north)
4. *a way of* one cubit;
7. *toward* the utter court
10. the wall of the court *toward* the east,
11. *And the way* before them
— which (were) *toward* the north,
12. the chambers that (were) *toward* the south (was) a door in the head of *the way*, (even) *the way* directly before the wall *toward* the east,
15. brought me forth *toward* the gate whose prospect (is) *toward* the east,
43: 1. the gate that looketh *toward* the east:
2. came *from the way of* the east:
4. by *the way of* the gate whose prospect (is) *toward* the east.
44: 1. brought me back *the way of* the gate
3. *by the way of* the porch of (that) gate, *and* shall go out *by the way of the same*.
4. brought he me *the way of* the north gate
46: 2. shall enter *by the way of* the porch
8. go in *by the way of* the porch of (that) gate, *and* he shall go forth *by the way thereof*.
9. entereth in *by the way of* the north gate to worship shall go out *by the way of* the south gate; and he that entereth *by the way of* the south gate shall go forth *by the way of* the north gate: he shall not return *by the way of* the gate
47: 2. Then brought he me out of *the way*
— led me about *the way*
— *by the way* that looketh eastward;
15. *the way of* Hethlon,
48: 1. to the coast of *the way of* Hethlon,
Hos 2: 6(8). I will hedge up *thy way*
4: 9. I will punish them for *their ways*,
6: 9. murder in *the way* by consent:
9: 8. a fowler in all *his ways*,
10:13. because thou didst trust *in thy way*,
12: 2(3). punish Jacob *according to his ways*;
13: 7. as a leopard by *the way*
14: 9(10). *the ways of* the Lord (are) right,
Joel 2: 7. march every one *on his ways*,
Am. 2: 7. *and* turn aside *the way of* the meek:
4:10. *after the manner of* Egypt: (marg. or, *in the way*)
8:14. *The manner of* Beer-sheba
Jon. 3: 8. turn every one *from his* evil *way*,
10. that they turned *from their* evil *way*;
Mic. 4: 2. he will teach us *of his ways*,
Nah 1: 3. the Lord (hath) *his way* in the
2: 1(2). watch *the way*,
Hag 1: 5, 7. Consider *your ways*.
Zec. 1: 4. Turn ye now *from your* evil *ways*,
6. *according to our ways*,
3: 7. If thou wilt walk *in my ways*,
Mal. 2: 8. But ye are departed out of *the way*;
9. according as ye have not kept *my ways*,
3: 1. he shall prepare *the way* before me.

דַּרְכְּמוֹנִים *dar-k'mōh-neem'*, m. pl. 1871

Ezr. 2:69. threescore and one thousand *drams* of gold,
Neh. 7:70. a thousand *drams* of gold,
71, 72. twenty thousand *drams* of gold,

דְּרָע [*d'rāhg*], Ch. f. 1872

Dan. 2:32. his breast *and his arms* of silver,

דָּרַשׁ *dāh-rash'*. 1875

* KAL.—*Preterite.* *

Lev.10:16. Moses diligently *sought* the goat
Deu 13:14(15). *Then shalt thou enquire*, and make
17: 4. *and enquired* diligently,

Deu 17: 9. *and enquire;* and they shall shew thee
19:18. *And* the judges *shall make* diligent *inquisition:*
2K. 8: 8. *and enquire* of the Lord by him,
1Ch 10:14. *enquired* not of the Lord:
13: 3. for *we enquired* not *at it*
15:13. *we sought him* not after
2Ch 14: 7(6). because *we have sought* the Lord our God, *we have sought* (him),
16:12. *he sought* not to the Lord,
17: 3. *sought* not unto Baalim;
4. But *sought* to the (Lord) God of his
22: 9. who *sought* the Lord with all
24: 6. Why *hast thou* not *required*
25:15. Why *hast thou sought after*
20. because *they sought after* the gods
Ps. 34: 4(5). *I sought* the Lord,
77: 2(3). In the day of my trouble *I sought* the Lord:
78:34. *then they sought him:* and they returned
109:10. *let them seek* (their bread) *also*
119:10. With my whole heart *have I sought thee:*
45. for *I seek* thy precepts.
94. for *I have sought* thy precepts.
155. for *they seek* not thy statutes.
Pro.31:13. *She seeketh* wool, and flax,
Isa. 9:13(12). neither *do they seek* the Lord
19: 3. *and they shall seek* to the idols,
31: 1. neither *seek* the Lord!
65:10. for my people that *have sought me.*
Jer. 8: 2. whom *they have sought,*
10:21. *have* not *sought* the Lord:
Eze.34: 8. *did* my shepherds *search for*
10. *and I will require* my flock
11. I, *will both search* my sheep,
Zep. 1: 6. nor *enquired for him.*

KAL.—*Infinitive.*

Gen 25:22. she went *to enquire of* the Lord.
Ex. 18:15. come unto me *to enquire of* God:
Lev.10:16. Moses *diligently* sought the goat (lit. *seeking* sought)
Deu 22: 2. until thy brother *seek* after it,
23:21(22). God will *surely* require it of thee; (lit. *requiring* will require)
1Sa. 9: 9. went *to enquire of* God,
1K. 14: 5. cometh *to ask* a thing of thee
22: 8. by whom *we may enquire* of the Lord: (lit. *to enquire*)
2K. 1: 3. ye go *to enquire* of Baal-zebub
6. thou sendest *to enquire* of Baal-zebub
16. *to enquire* of Baal-zebub
— no God in Israel *to enquire* of his word?
22:18. sent you *to enquire of* the Lord,
1Ch 10:13. a familiar spirit, *to enquire*
21:30. go before it *to enquire of* God:
22:19. your soul *to seek* the Lord
2Ch 12:14. prepared not his heart *to seek* the Lord.
14: 4(3). commanded Judah *to seek* the Lord
15:12. entered into a covenant *to seek*
18: 7. by whom *we may enquire* (lit. *to enquire*)
19: 3. prepared thine heart *to seek* God.
20: 3. set himself *to seek* the Lord,
26: 5. he *sought* God in the days of (lit. he was *to seek*)
— as long as *he sought* the Lord, (lit. in the days of *his seeking*)
30:19. prepareth his heart *to seek* God,
31:21. *to seek* his God,
32:31. who sent unto him *to enquire of*
34: 3. he began *to seek* after the God
26. who sent you *to enquire* of the Lord,
Ezr. 6:21. *to seek* the Lord God of Israel,
7:10. *to seek* the law of the Lord,
Ecc. 1:13. I gave my heart *to seek*
Jer. 37: 7. sent you unto me *to enquire of me;*
Eze.14: 7. *to enquire* of him concerning me;
20: 1. came *to enquire of* the Lord,
3. Are ye come *to enquire of* me?
Hos.10:12. for (it is) time *to seek* the Lord,

KAL.—*Imperative.*

1K. 22: 5. *Enquire,* I pray thee,
2K. 1: 2. Go, *enquire* of Baal-zebub
22:13. *enquire of* the Lord for me,
1Ch 16:11. *Seek* the Lord and his strength,
28: 8. *and seek* for all the commandments
2Ch 18: 4. *Enquire,* I pray thee,
2Ch 34:21. Go, *enquire of* the Lord for me,
Ps.105: 4. *Seek* the Lord, and his strength:
Isa. 1:17. *seek* judgment,
8:19. *Seek* unto them that have
34:16. *Seek ye* out of the book of the Lord,
55: 6. *Seek ye* the Lord while he may
Jer. 21: 2. *Enquire,* I pray thee,
29: 7. *And seek* the peace of the city
Am. 5: 4. *Seek ye me,* and ye shall live:
6. *Seek* the Lord, and ye shall live;
14. *Seek* good, and not evil,

KAL.—*Future.*

Gen 9: 5. blood of your lives *will I require;* at the hand of every beast *will I require it,*
— *will I require* the life of man.
Deu 4:29. if *thou seek him* with all thy
12: 5. his habitation *shall ye seek,*
30. that *thou enquire* not after
18:19. *I will require* (it) of him.
23: 6(7). *Thou shalt* not *seek* their peace
21(22). thy God *will* surely *require it*
Jud. 6:29. And *when they enquired* and asked,
1Sa.28: 7. *and enquire* of her.
2Sa.11: 3. sent *and enquired* after the woman.
1K. 22: 7. *that we might enquire* of him?
2K. 3:11. *that we may enquire of* the Lord
1Ch 28: 9. if *thou seek him,* he will be found
2Ch 1: 5. *and* the congregation *sought* unto it.
15: 2. if *ye seek him,* he will be found
13. whosoever *would* not *seek* the Lord
18: 6. *that we might enquire* of him?
24:22. The Lord look upon (it), *and require*
31: 9. *Then* Hezekiah *questioned* with
Ezr. 4: 2. for *we seek* your God,
9:12. nor *seek* their peace
Job 3: 4. *let* not God *regard it*
5: 8. *I would seek* unto God,
10: 6. and *searchest* after my sin?
39: 8. *he searcheth* after every green thing.
Ps. 10: 4. *will* not *seek* (after God):
13. *Thou wilt* not *require*
15. *seek out* his wickedness
119: 2. *seek him* with the whole heart.
Isa. 8:19. *should* not a people *seek*
11:10. to it *shall* the Gentiles *seek:*
58: 2. Yet *they seek me* daily,
Jer.29:13. when *ye shall search for me*
30:14. *they seek* thee not;
Lam 3:25. to the soul (that) *seeketh him.*
Eze.20:40. there *will I require* your offerings,
33: 6. but his blood *will I require*
Am. 5: 5. But *seek* not Beth-el,

KAL.—*Participle.* Poel.

Deu 11:12. the Lord thy God *careth for:* (marg. *seeketh*)
18:11. or a wizard, *or a* necro*mancer.* (lit. *one that enquireth of* the dead)
1Ch 28: 9. for the Lord *searcheth* all hearts,
Est. 10: 3. *seeking* the wealth of his people,
Ps. 9:10(11). forsaken *them that seek thee.*
12(13). When *he maketh inquisition* for blood,
14: 2. did understand, (and) *seek* God.
22:26(27). shall praise the Lord *that seek him:*
24: 6. the generation of *them that seek him,*
34:10(11). *but they that seek* the Lord
38:12(13). *and they that seek* my hurt
53: 2(3). *that did seek* God.
69:32(33). your heart shall live *that seek* God.
142: 4(5). no man *cared* for my soul. (marg. *sought* after)
Pro.11:27. *but he that seeketh* mischief,
Isa. 16: 5. *and seeking* judgment,
Jer. 30:17. whom no man *seeketh after.*
38: 4. this man *seeketh* not the welfare
Eze.14:10. the punishment of him *that seeketh*
34: 6. none *did search* or seek
Mic. 6: 8. what *doth* the Lord *require*

KAL.—*Participle.* Paül.

Ps.111: 2. *sought out* of all them
Isa. 62:12. shalt be called, *Sought out,*

* NIPHAL.—*Preterite.* *

Gen 42:22. also his blood *is required.*
1Ch 26:31. *they were sought for,* and there were
Isa. 65: 1. *I am sought* of (them that) asked

NIPHAL.—*Infinitive.*

Eze.14: 3. should I be enquired of *at all* (lit. should I be enquired of *to be enquired*)

NIPHAL.—*Future.*

Eze.14: 3. *should I be enquired of* at all
20: 3, 31. *I will* not *be enquired of* by you.
31. *shall I be enquired of* by you,
36:37. *I will* yet (for) this *be enquired of*

1876 דָּשָׁא [*dāh-shāh'*].

* KAL.—*Preterite.* *

Joel 2:22. the pastures of the wilderness *do spring*,

* HIPHIL.—*Future.* *

Gen 1:11. *Let* the earth *bring forth* grass,

1877 דָּשָׁא *dāh-shāh'*, adj.

Jer.50:11. as the heifer *at grass*,

Note.—This is by some regarded as the Participle Poel fem. of דּוּשׁ with א in the place of ה.

1877 דֶּשֶׁא *deh'-sheh*, m.

Gen 1:11. Let the earth bring forth *grass*, (marg. *tender grass*)
12. the earth brought forth *grass*,
Deu32: 2. as the small rain upon *the tender herb*,
2Sa.23: 4. *the tender grass* (springing) out
2K.19:26. and (as) the green *herb*,
Job 6: 5. Doth the wild ass bray when he hath *grass?*
38:27. *the tender herb* to spring forth?
Ps. 23: 2. He maketh me to lie down in *green* pastures: (marg. pastures of *tender grass*)
37: 2. wither as the green *herb*.
Pro.27:25. *the tender grass* sheweth itself,
Isa. 15: 6. *the grass* faileth,
37:27. and (as) the green *herb*,
66:14. your bones shall flourish *like an herb:*
Jer. 14: 5. because there was no *grass*.

1878 דָּשֵׁן [*dāh-shēhn'*].

* KAL.—*Preterite.* *

Deu31:20. and filled themselves, *and waxen fat;*

* PIEL.—*Preterite.* *

Nu. 4:13. And they *shall take away the ashes from* the altar,
Ps. 23: 5. *thou anointest* my head with oil; (marg. *makest fat*)

PIEL.—*Infinitive.*

Ex. 27: 3. pans *to receive his ashes*,

PIEL.—*Future.*

Ps. 20: 3(4). *accept* thy burnt sacrifice. (marg. *turn to ashes:* or, *make fat*)
Pro.15:30. a good report *maketh* the bones *fat*.

* PUAL.—*Future.* *

Pro.11:25. The liberal soul *shall be made fat:*
13: 4. of the diligent *shall be made fat*.
28:25. trust in the Lord *shall be made fat*.
Isa. 34: 7. and their dust *made fat*

* HOTHPAEL.—*Preterite.* *

Isa. 34: 6. *it is made fat* with fatness,

1879 דָּשֵׁן *dāh-shēhn'*, adj.

Ps. 22:29(30). All (they that be) *fat upon* earth
92:14(15). they shall be *fat* and flourishing;
Isa. 30:23. it shall be *fat* and plenteous:

1880 דֶּשֶׁן *deh'-shen*, m.

Jud. 9: 9. Should I leave *my fatness*,
Job 36:16. thy table (should be) full of *fatness*.
Ps. 36: 8(9). *with the fatness of* thy house;
63: 5(6). as (with) marrow *and fatness;*
65:11(12). thy paths drop *fatness*.
Isa. 55: 2. let your soul delight itself *in fatness*.
Jer. 31:14. satiate the soul of the priests with *fatness*

דֶּשֶׁן *deh'-shen*, m. 1880

Lev. 1:16. by the place of *the ashes:*
4:12. where *the ashes* are poured out,
— where *the ashes* are poured out
6:10(3). take up *the ashes*
11(4). carry forth *the ashes*
1K. 13: 3. *the ashes* that (are) upon it
5. *the ashes* poured out
Jer. 31:40. *and of the ashes*, and all the fields

דָּת *dāhth*, f. 1881

Deu33: 2. *a* fiery *law* for them.
Ezr. 8:36. delivered the king's *commissions*
Est. 1: 8. the drinking (was) *according to the law;*
13. all that knew *law* and judgment:
15. the queen Vashti *according to law*,
19. let it be written *among the laws of*
2: 8. *and his decree* was heard,
12. *according to the manner of* the women,
3: 8. *and their laws* (are) diverse
— neither keep they the king's *laws:*
14. for *a commandment* to be given
15. *and the decree* was given
4: 3. the king's commandment *and his decree*
8. the copy of the writing of *the decree*
11. one *law of his* to put (him) to death,
16. not *according to the law:*
8:13. for *a commandment* to be given
14. *And the decree* was given
17. *and his decree* came,
9: 1. *and his decree* drew near
13. *according unto* this day's *decree*,
14. *the decree* was given at Shushan;

דָּת *dāhth*, Ch. f. 1882

Ezr. 7:12, 21. scribe of *the law* of the God of heaven,
14. *according to the law of* thy God
25. all such as know *the laws of* thy God;
26. whosoever will not do *the law* of thy God, *and the law* of the king, let judgment
Dan 2: 9. (there is but) one *decree for you:*
13. *And the decree* went forth that
15. Why (is) *the decree* (so) hasty from the king?
6: 5(6). *concerning the law of* his God.
8(9), 12(13). *according to the law of* the Medes
15(16). that *the law* of the Medes and
7:25. and think to change times *and laws:*

דֶּתֶא *deh'-theh*, Ch. m. 1883

Dan 4:15(12). *in the tender grass* of the field;
23(20). *in the tender grass* of the field;

דְּתָבָר [*d'thāh-vāhr'*], Ch. m. 1884

Dan 3: 2, 3. the treasurers, *the counsellors*, the

ה *hēh.*

The fifth letter of the Alphabet.

הָא *hāh*, Ch. interj. 1888

Dan 3:25. *Lo*, I see four men loose, walking

הֶא *hēh*, interj. 1887

Gen47:23. *lo*, (here is) seed for you,
Eze.16:43. *behold*, therefore I also

1888 **הֵא** *kĕh*, Ch. interj.

Dan. 2:43. *even* as iron is not mixed with clay.

1889 **הֶאָח** *heh-āhgh'*, interj.

Job 39:25. *Ha, ha;* and he smelleth the battle afar off,
Ps. 35:21. said, *Aha, aha,* our eye hath seen (it).
25. *Ah,* so would we have it: (marg. *Ah, ah,* our soul)
40:15(16). that say unto me, *Aha, aha.*
70: 3(4). a reward of their shame that say, *Aha, aha.*
Isa. 44:16. saith, *Aha,* I am warm,
Eze. 25: 3. Because thou saidst, *Aha,*
26: 2. *Aha,* she is broken
36: 2. the enemy hath said against you, *Aha,*

1890 **הַבְהָבִים** [*hav-hāh-veem'*], m. pl.

Hos 8:13. the sacrifices of *mine offerings,*

1891 **הָבַל** [*hāh-val'*].

* KAL.—*Future.* *

2K. 17:15. *and became vain,* and went after
Job 27:12. why then *are ye* thus altogether *vain?*
Ps. 62:10(11). *become* not *vain* in robbery:
Jer. 2: 5. after vanity, *and are become vain?*

* HIPHIL. *Participle.* *

Jer. 23:16. they *make* you *vain:*

1892 **הֶבֶל** *heh'-vel.* com.

Deu 32:21. me to anger *with their vanities:*
1K. 16:13, 26. to anger *with their vanities.*
2K. 17:15. they followed *vanity,*
Job 7:16. for my days (are) *vanity.*
9:29. why then labour I *in vain?*
21:34. How then comfort ye me *in vain,*
27:12. why then are ye thus *altogether* vain? (lit. are ye vain *in vanity*)
35:16. Job open his mouth *in vain;*
Ps. 31: 6(7). them that regard lying *vanities:*
39: 5(6). at his best state (is) altogether *vanity.*
6(7). surely they are disquieted *in vain:*
11(12). surely every man (is) *vanity.*
62: 9(10). men of low degree (are) *vanity,*
—(—). they (are) altogether (lighter) *than vanity.*
78:33. their days did he consume *in vanity,*
94:11. that they (are) *vanity.*
144: 4. Man is like *to vanity:*
Pro. 13:11. Wealth (gotten) *by vanity*
21: 6. *a vanity* tossed to and fro
31:30. *and* beauty (is) *vain:*
Ecc. 1: 2. Vanity of *vanities,* saith the Preacher, vanity of *vanities;* all (is) *vanity.*
14. all (is) *vanity* and vexation of spirit.
2: 1. this also (is) *vanity.*
11, 17, 26. *vanity* and vexation of spirit,
15. that this also (is) *vanity.*
19. This (is) also *vanity.*
21. This also (is) *vanity*
23. This is also *vanity.*
3:19. for all (is) *vanity.*
4: 4, 8. This (is) also *vanity*
7. I saw *vanity* under the sun.
16. Surely this also (is) *vanity*
5: 7(6). many words (there are) *also* (divers) *vanities:*
10(9). this (is) also *vanity.*
6: 2. this (is) *vanity,* and it (is) an evil
4. For he cometh in *with vanity,*
9. this (is) also *vanity* and vexation
11. many things that increase *vanity,*
12. all the days of *his vain* life (marg. the life of *his vanity*)
7: 6. this also (is) *vanity.*
15. have I seen in the days of *my vanity:*
8:10. this (is) also *vanity.*
Ecc. 8:14. There is *a vanity* which is done
— that this also (is) *vanity.*
9: 9. the days of the life of *thy vanity,*
— all the days of *thy vanity:*
11: 8. All that cometh (is) *vanity.*
10. childhood and youth (are) *vanity.*
12: 8. Vanity of *vanities,* saith the preacher; all (is) *vanity.*
Isa. 30: 7. the Egyptians shall help *in vain,*
49: 4. for nought, *and in vain:*
57:13. *vanity* shall take (them):
Jer. 2: 5. from me, and have walked after *vanity,*
8:19. *with* strange *vanities?*
10: 3. For the customs of the people (are) *vain:* (marg. *vanity*)
8. the stock (is) a doctrine of *vanities.*
15. They (are) *vanity,* (and) the work
14:22. *among the vanities of* the Gentiles
16:19. have inherited lies, *vanity,*
51:18. They (are) *vanity,* the work of errors:
Lam 4:17. failed for our *vain* help:
Jon. 2: 8(9). They that observe lying *vanities*
Zec. 10: 2. they comfort *in vain:*

הֲבֵל *hăvēhl*, m. 1892

Ecc. 1: 2. *Vanity of* vanities, saith the Preacher, *vanity of* vanities; all (is) vanity.
12: 8. *Vanity of* vanities, saith the preacher;

הָבְנִים *hov-neem*, m. pl. 1894

Eze. 27:15. horns of ivory *and ebony.*

הָבַר [*hāh-var'*]. 1895

* KAL.—*Participle.* Poel. *

Isa. 47:13. Let now the astrologers, (marg. *viewers of* the heavens)

הָגָה [*hāh-gāh'*]. 1897

* KAL.—*Preterite.* *

Jos. 1: 8. *but thou shalt meditate* therein
Ps. 77:12(13). *I will meditate also* of all thy work,
143: 5. *I meditate* on all thy works;

KAL.—*Infinitive.*

Isa. 59:11. mourn *sore* like doves: (lit. *mourning* we mourn)

KAL.—*Future.*

Job 27: 4. nor my tongue *utter* deceit.
Ps. 1: 2. in his law *doth he meditate*
2: 1. the people *imagine* a vain thing? (marg. *meditate*)
35:28. my tongue *shall speak*
37:30. of the righteous *speaketh* wisdom,
38:12(13). *imagine* deceits all the day long.
63: 6(7). *meditate* on thee in the (night)
71:24. My tongue also *shall talk*
115: 7. neither *speak they* through their throat.
Pro. 8: 7. my mouth *shall speak* truth;
15:28. of the righteous *studieth* to answer:
24: 2. For their heart *studieth* destruction,
Isa. 16: 7. foundations of Kir-hareseth *shall ye mourn;* (marg. or, *mutter*)
31: 4. the young lion *roaring* on his prey,
33:18. Thine heart *shall meditate* terror.
38:14. *I did mourn* as a dove:
59: 3. your tongue *hath muttered* perverseness.
11. and *mourn* sore like doves:
Jer. 48:31. *shall mourn* for the men of Kir-heres.

* POAL.—*Infinitive.* *

Isa. 59:13. conceiving *and uttering* from the heart

* HIPHIL.—*Participle.* *

Isa. 8:19. that peep, *and that mutter:*

הָגָה *hāh-gāh'*. 1898

* KAL.—*Preterite.* *

Isa. 27: 8. *he stayeth* his rough wind

KAL.—*Infinitive.*

Pro.25: 4. *Take away* the dross
5. *Take away* the wicked

1899 הֶגֶה *heh'-geh*, m.

Job 37: 2. *and the sound* (that) goeth
Ps. 90: 9. we spend our years as *a tale* (marg. *meditation*)
Eze. 2:10. lamentations, *and mourning*, and woe.

1900 הָגוּת *hāh-gooth'*, f.

Ps. 49: 3(4). *and the meditation of* my heart

1901 הָגִיג [*hāh-geeg'*], m.

Ps. 5: 1(2). consider *my meditation.*
39: 3(4). *while I was musing* the fire burned:

1902 הִגָּיוֹן *hig-gāh-yōhn'*, m.

Ps. 9:16(17). the work of his own hands. *Higgaion.*
19:14(15). *and the meditation of* my heart,
92: 3(4). upon the harp with *a solemn sound.*
Lam 3:62. *and their device* against me

1903 הָגִין [*hāh-geen'*], adj.

Eze.42:12. the way *directly* before the wall

1906 הֵד *hēhd*, m.

Eze. 7: 7. *the sounding again of* the mountains. (marg. or, *echo*)

1907 הַדָּבְרִין [*had-dāh-v'reen'*], Ch. m. pl.

Dan. 3:24. and said *unto his counsellors*, (marg. or, *governors*)
27. *and* the king's *counsellors*, being gathered
4:36(33). and *my counsellors* and my lords sought unto me;
6: 7(8). *the counsellors*, and the captains, have

1911 הָדָה *hāh-dāh'*.

✻ KAL.—*Preterite.* ✻

Isa. 11: 8. the weaned child *shall put* his hand

1916 הֲדוֹם *hădōhm*, m.

1Ch 28: 2. *and for the* footstool
Ps. 99: 5. worship *at* his footstool;
110: 1. until I make thine enemies thy footstool.
132: 7. we will worship *at* his footstool.
Isa. 66: 1. the earth (is) my footstool:
Lam 2: 1. remembered not his footstool

1915 הָדַךְ [*hāh-dach'*].

✻ KAL.—*Imperative.* ✻

Job 40:12. *and tread down* the wicked

1917 הַדָּם [*had-dāhm'*], Ch. m.

Dan. 2: 5. ye shall be cut *in pieces*,
3:29. shall be cut *in pieces*,

1918 הֲדַס *hădas* & הֲדָס *hădāhs*, m.

Neh 8:15. and *myrtle* branches,
Isa. 41:19. the shittah tree, *and the myrtle*,
55:13. shall come up *the myrtle tree*:
Zec. 1: 8. he stood among *the myrtle trees*

Zec. 1:10. the man that stood among *the myrtle trees*
11. of the Lord that stood among *the myrtle trees*,

הָדַף [*hāh-daph'*]. 1920

✻ KAL.—*Preterite.* ✻

Nu. 35:22. But if *he thrust him* suddenly
Isa. 22:19. *And I will drive thee* from
Jer. 46:15. because the Lord *did drive them.*

KAL.—*Infinitive.*

Deu. 6:19. *To cast out* all thine enemies
9: 4. *after that* the Lord thy God *hath cast* them *out*
2K. 4:27. Gehazi came near *to thrust her away.*

KAL.—*Future.*

Nu. 35:20. But if *he thrust him* of hatred,
Jos. 23: 5. *he shall expel them* from before you,
Job 18:18. *He shall be driven* from light (marg. *They shall drive him*)
Pro. 10: 3. but *he casteth away* the
Eze. 34:21. Because *ye have thrust* with

הָדַר [*hāh-dar'*]. 1921

✻ KAL.—*Preterite.* ✻

Lev.19:32. *and honour* the face of the old man,

KAL.—*Future.*

Ex. 23: 3. Neither *shalt thou countenance*
Lev.19:15. nor *honour* the person of the mighty:

KAL.—*Participle.* Paül.

Isa. 45: 2. *and* make *the crooked places* straight:
63: 1. *glorious* in his apparel, (marg. *decked*)

✻ NIPHAL.—*Preterite.* ✻

Lam 5:12. the faces of elders *were* not *honoured.*

✻ HITHPAEL.—*Future.* ✻

Pro 25: 6. *Put* not *forth thyself* (marg. *Set* not *out thy glory*)

הֲדַר [*hădar*], Ch. 1922

✻ PAEL.—*Preterite.* ✻

Dan. 4:34(31). and I praised *and honoured* him that liveth for ever,
5:23. *hast thou* not *glorified*:

PAEL.—*Participle.*

Dan. 4:37(34). *and honour* the King of heaven,

הָדָר *hāh-dāhr'*, m. 1926

Lev.23:40. the boughs of *goodly* trees,
Deu33:17. His *glory* (is like) the firstling of
1Ch 16:27. Glory *and honour* (are) in his presence
Job 40:10. array thyself with glory *and beauty.*
Ps. 8: 5(6). crowned him with glory *and honour.*
21: 5(6). honour *and majesty* hast thou
29: 4. the voice of the Lord (is) *full of majesty* (marg. *in majesty*)
45: 3(4). with thy glory *and thy majesty.*
4(5). *And in thy majesty* ride
90:16. *and thy glory* unto their children.
96: 6. Honour *and majesty* (are) before him:
104: 1. clothed with honour *and majesty.*
110: 3. *in the beauties of* holiness
111: 3. His work (is) honourable *and glorious*:
145: 5. the glorious *honour of* thy majesty,
12. the *glorious* majesty of his kingdom.
149: 9. this *honour* have all his saints.
Pro.20:29. *and the beauty of* old men
31:25. Strength *and honour*
Isa. 2:10, 19, 21. *and for the glory of* his majesty.
5:14. and *their glory*, and their multitude,
35: 2. *the excellency of* Carmel
— *the excellency of* our God.
53: 2. he hath no form nor *comeliness*;
Lam 1: 6. all *her beauty* is departed:
Eze.16:14. perfect *through my comeliness*,

Eze.27:10. they set forth *thy comeliness.*
Mic. 2: 9. have ye taken away *my glory*

1925 הֶדֶר *heh'-der*, m.

Dan 11:20. *the glory of* the kingdom:

1923 הֲדַר [*hĕder*], Ch.

Dan 4:30(27). for the honour of *my majesty?*
36(33). *mine honour* and brightness returned
5:18. majesty, and glory, *and honour:*

1927 הֲדָרָה [*hădāh-rāh'*], f.

1Ch 16:29. *in the beauty of* holiness.
2Ch 20:21. should praise *the beauty of* holiness,
Ps. 29: 2. *in the beauty of* holiness. (marg. or, *in* (his) *glorious* sanctuary)
96: 9. *in the beauty of* holiness: (marg. *in* the *glorious* sanctuary)
Pro.14:28. people (is) *the king's honour:*

1929 הָהּ *hāh*, interj.

Eze.30: 2. Howl ye, *Woe worth* the day!

1930 הוֹ *hōh*, interj.

Am. 5:16. say in all the highways, *Alas! alas!*

1931 הוּא *hoo*, part. pron. m.

Gen 2:11. Pison: *that* (is) *it* which compasseth
19. called every living creature, *that* (was) the name
3: 6. and that *it* (was) pleasant to the eyes,
4: 4. And Abel, *he* also brought of the firstlings
26. And to Seth, *to him* also there was born
9:18. and Ham)((is) the father of Canaan.
14: 3. the vale of Siddim, *which is* the salt sea.
17. the valley of Shaveh, *which* (is) the king's dale.
15: 2. the steward of my house (is) *this* Eliezer
19:37. *the same* (is) the father of the Moabites
36: 1. the generations of Esau, *who* (is) Edom.
Ex. 1:10. *they* join also unto our enemies,
6:26. *These* (are) that Aaron and Moses, to whom
Nu. 35:19. The revenger of blood *himself* shall slay
Job 39:30. where the slain (are), there (is) *she.*
Isa. 9:15(14). The ancient and honourable, *he* (is) the head; and the prophet that teacheth lies, *he* (is) the tail.
&c. &c. &c.

With prefixes, as הַהוּא.

Gen 15:18. In *the same* day the Lord made a covenant
19:35. drink wine *that* night also:
Nu. 11: 3. And he called the name of the place)(Taberah:
Deu 3:13. all Bashan, *which* was called the land of giants.
1Sa. 1: 3. And *this* man went up out of his city
30:20. (which) they drave before *those* (other) cattle,
1K. 10:10. there came no more *such* abundance
&c. &c.

שֶׁהוּא.

Ecc. 2:22. *wherein he* hath laboured under the sun?

See 1931-32 הוּא see הִיא

1935 הוֹד *hōhd*, m.

Nu. 27:20. put (some) *of thine honour* upon him,
1Ch 16:27. *Glory* and honour (are) in his presence;
29:11. the victory, *and the majesty:*
1Ch 29:25. bestowed upon him (such) royal *majesty*
Job 37:22. with God (is) terrible *majesty.*
39:20. *the glory of* his nostrils
40:10. *and* array thyself with *glory*
Ps. 8: 1(2). hast set *thy glory* above the heavens.
21: 5(6). *honour* and majesty hast thou laid
45: 3(4). with *thy glory* and thy majesty.
96: 6. *Honour* and majesty (are) before him:
104: 1. thou art clothed with *honour*
111: 3. His work (is) *honourable* and glorious:
145: 5. the glorious honour of *thy majesty,*
148:13. *his glory* (is) above the earth
Pro. 5: 9. Lest thou give *thine honour* unto
Isa. 30:30. the Lord shall cause his *glorious* voice (marg. *the glory of* his voice)
Jer. 22:18. Ah lord! or, Ah *his glory!*
Dan10: 8. *for my comeliness* was turned (marg. or, *vigour*)
11:21. they shall not give *the honour of*
Hos 14: 6. *his beauty* shall be as the olive tree,
Hab. 3: 3. *His glory* covered the heavens,
Zec. 6:13. he shall bear *the glory,*
10: 3. as *his goodly* horse in the battle.

הָוָה & הָוָא [*hāh-vāh'*]. 1933

* KAL.—*Imperative.* *

Gen 27:29. *be* lord over thy brethren,
Job 37: 6. *Be thou* (on) the earth;
Isa. 16: 4. *be thou* a covert to them

KAL.—*Future.*

Ecc. 11: 3. where the tree falleth, there *it shall be.*

KAL.—*Participle.* Poel.

Neh 6: 6. that thou *mayest be* their king,
Ecc. 2:22. what *hath* man of all his labour, (lit. *being* to a man)

הֲוָה & הֲוָא *hăvāh*, Ch. 1934

NOTE.—The verb when followed by a participle is often combined with it in translation; these passages are marked[2].

* P'AL.—*Preterite.* *

Ezr. 4:20. *There have been* mighty kings also over Jerusalem,
24. *So it ceased*[2] unto the second year of the reign (lit. *and it was* ceasing, &c.)
5: 5. the eye of their God *was* upon the elders
11. and build the house that *was* builded
6: 6. *be ye* far from thence:
Dan 2:31. Thou, O king, *sawest*[2], and behold (marg. *wast* seeing)
34. *Thou sawest*[2] till that a stone
35. *and became* like the chaff
— *became* a great mountain,
4: 4(1). *I* Nebuchadnezzar *was* at rest
10(7). *I saw*[2], and behold a tree (marg. *was* seeing)
13(10). *I saw*[2] in the visions of my head
29(26). *he walked*[2] in the palace
5:19. and languages, *trembled*[2] and feared before him: whom *he would*[2] *he slew;*[2] and whom *he would*[2] *he kept*[2] alive; and whom *he would*[2] *he set*[2] up; and whom *he would*[2] *he put*[2] down.
6: 3(4). Then this Daniel *was* preferred
4(5). *sought*[2] to find occasion against Daniel
10(11). as *he did*[2] aforetime.
14(15). and *he laboured*[2] till the going down of the sun
7: 2. *I saw*[2] in my vision by night,
4. *I beheld*[2] till the wings thereof were
6. *I beheld*[2], and lo another, like a leopard,
7. *I saw*[2] in the night visions,
8. *I considered*[2] the horns,
9. *I beheld*[2] till the thrones were cast down,
11. *I beheld*[2] then because of the voice
— *I beheld*[2] (even) till the beast was slain,
13. *I saw*[2] in the night visions, and, behold, (one) like the Son of man *came*[2]
19. which *was* diverse from all the others,
21. *I beheld*[2], and the same horn made war

P'AL.—*Imperative.*

Ezr. 4:22. *Take heed*[2] now that ye fail not to do this:

P'AL.—*Future.*

Ezr. 4:12. *Be it* known unto the king,
13. *Be it* known now unto the king,
5: 8. *Be it* known unto the king,
6: 8. expences *be* given unto these men,
9. *let it be* given them day by day
10. That *they may offer*[2] sacrifices
7:23. for why *should* there *be* wrath against
25. which *may judge*[2] all the people
26. whosoever *will* not *do*[2] the law of thy God,
— *let* judgment *be* executed speedily
Dan 2:20. Blessed *be* the name of God for ever
28. what *shall be* in the latter days.
29. what *should come to pass* hereafter:
— maketh known to thee what *shall come to pass.*
40. the fourth kingdom *shall be* strong
41. the kingdom *shall be* divided;
— *there shall be* in it of the strength of the iron,
42. the kingdom *shall be* partly strong, and partly (lit. *shall be*) broken.
43. *shall mingle themselves*[2] with the seed of men:
— they *shall* not *cleave*[2] one to another,
45. what *shall come to pass* hereafter:
3:18. *be it* known unto thee, O king,
4:25(22). thy dwelling *shall be* with the beasts
27(24). if it *may be* a lengthening of thy tranquillity.
5:17. *Let* thy gifts *be* to thyself,
29. *that he should be* the third ruler
6: 1(2). which *should be* over the whole kingdom;
2(3). that the princes *might give*[2] accounts
—(-). the king *should have* no damage.
26(27). men *tremble*[2] and fear before the God of
7:23. The fourth beast *shall be* the fourth

1942 הַוָּה [*hav-vāh'*], f.

Job 6: 2. *and my calamity* laid in the
30. my taste discern *perverse things?*
30:13. they set forward *my calamity,*
Ps. 5: 9(10). their inward part (is) *very wickedness;* (marg. *wickednesses*)
38:12(13). that seek my hurt speak *mischievous things,*
52: 2(4). Thy tongue deviseth *mischiefs;*
7(9). strengthened himself *in his wickedness.* (marg. or, *substance*)
55:11(12). *Wickedness* (is) in the midst thereof:
57: 1(2). until (these) *calamities* be overpast.
91: 3. from the *noisome* pestilence.
94:20. Shall the throne of *iniquity* have
Pro.10: 3. *but* he casteth away *the substance of* the wicked. (marg. or, wicked for (their) *wickedness*)
11: 6. *but* transgressors shall be taken *in* (their own) *naughtiness.*
17: 4. a liar giveth ear to a *naughty* tongue.
19:13. A foolish son (is) *the calamity*
Mic. 7: 3. he uttereth his *mischievous* desire: (marg. *the mischief of* his soul)

1943 הֹוָה *hōh-vāh'*, f.

Isa. 47:11. *mischief* shall fall upon thee;
Eze. 7:26. *Mischief* shall come upon *mischief,*

1945 הוֹי *hōh'y*, part. interj.

1K. 13:30. *Alas,* my brother!
Isa. 1: 4. *Ah* sinful nation,
24. *Ah,* I will ease me of mine
5: 8. *Woe* unto them that join
11. *Woe* unto them that rise up early
18. *Woe* unto them that draw
20. *Woe* unto them that call evil good,
21. *Woe* unto (them that are) wise
Isa. 5:22. *Woe* unto (them that are) mighty
10: 1. *Woe* unto them that decree
5. *O* Assyrian, the rod of mine anger,
17:12. *Woe* to the multitude of many
18: 1. *Woe* to the land shadowing
28: 1. *Woe* to the crown of pride,
29: 1. *Woe* to Ariel, to Ariel,
15. *Woe* unto them that seek deep
30: 1. *Woe* to the rebellious children,
31: 1. *Woe* to them that go down
33: 1. *Woe* to thee that spoilest,
45: 9. *Woe* unto him that striveth
10. *Woe* unto him that saith
55: 1. *Ho,* every one that thirsteth,
Jer. 22:13. *Woe* unto him that buildeth
18. *Ah* my brother! *or, Ah* sister!
— lament for him, (saying), *Ah* lord! *or, Ah* his glory!
23: 1. *Woe* be unto the pastors
30: 7. *Alas!* for that day (is) great,
34: 5. *and* they will lament thee, (saying), *Ah* lord!
47: 6. *O* thou sword of the Lord,
48: 1. *Woe* unto Nebo! for it is spoiled:
50:27. *woe* unto them!
Eze.13: 3. *Woe* unto the foolish prophets,
18. *Woe* to the (women) that sew pillows
34: 2. *Woe* (be) to the shepherds of Israel
Am. 5:18. *Woe* unto you that desire
6: 1. *Woe* to them (that are) at ease
Mic. 2: 1. *Woe* to them that devise iniquity,
Nah. 3: 1. *Woe* to the bloody city!
Hab. 2: 6. *Woe* to him that increaseth
9. *Woe* to him that coveteth
12. *Woe* to him that buildeth a town
15. *Woe* unto him that giveth
19. *Woe* unto him that saith
Zep. 2: 5. *Woe* unto the inhabitants
3: 1. *Woe* to her that is filthy
Zec. 2: 6(10). *Ho, ho,* (come forth), and flee
7(11). Deliver thyself, *O* Zion,
11:17. *Woe* to the idol shepherd

הוּךְ [*hooch*], Ch. 1946

* P'AL.—*Infinitive.* *

Ezr. 7:13. of their own freewill *to go up* to Jerusalem,

P'AL.—*Future.*

Ezr. 5: 5. till the matter *came* to Darius:
6: 5. *and brought again* unto the temple
7:13. *go* with thee.

הוֹלֵלָה [*hōh-lēh-lāh'*], f. 1947

Ecc. 1:17. to know *madness* and folly:
2:12. wisdom, *and madness,* and folly:
7:25. even of foolishness (and) *madness:*
9: 3. *and madness* (is) in their heart

הוֹלֵלוּת *hōh-lēh-looth'*, f. 1948

Ecc.10:13. talk (is) mischievous *madness.*

הוֹלֵם see הָלַם See 1986

הוּם [*hoom*]. 1949

* KAL.—*Preterite.* *

Deu 7:23. *and shall destroy them* with a mighty

* NIPHAL.—*Future.* *

Ru. 1:19. *that* all the city *was moved* about them,
1Sa. 4: 5. *so that* the earth *rang again.*
1K. 1:45. *so that* the city *rang again.*

* HIPHIL—*Future.* *

Ps. 55: 2(3). in my complaint, *and make a noise;*
Mic. 2:12. *they shall make great noise*

1951 ## הון [*hoon*].

* HIPHIL.—*Future.* *

Deu 1:41. *ye were ready* to go up into the hill.

1952 ## הוֹן *hōhn*, m.

Ps. 44:12(13). sellest thy people for *nought*, (marg. without *riches*)
112: 3. *Wealth* and riches (shall be) in his house:
119:14. as (much as) in all *riches*.
Pro. 1:13. We shall find all precious *substance*,
3: 9. Honour the Lord *with thy substance*,
6:31. give all *the substance of* his house.
8:18. durable *riches* and righteousness.
10:15. The rich man's *wealth*
11: 4. *Riches* profit not in the day of wrath:
12:27. *but the substance of* a diligent man
13: 7. *yet* (hath) great *riches*.
11. *Wealth* (gotten) by vanity
18:11. The rich man's *wealth* (is) his strong city,
19: 4. *Wealth* maketh many friends;
14. House *and riches* (are) the inheritance
24: 4. with all precious and pleasant *riches*.
28: 8. gain increaseth *his substance*,
22. He that hasteth *to be rich*
29: 3. with harlots spendeth (his) *substance*.
30:15. four (things) say not, (It is) *enough*:
16. the fire (that) saith not, (It is) *enough*.
Cant. 8: 7. give all *the substance of* his house for love,
Eze. 27:12. the multitude of all (kind of) *riches*;
18. for the multitude of all *riches*;
27. *Thy riches*, and thy fairs,
33. with the multitude of *thy riches*

1957 ## הָזָה [*hāh-zāh'*].

* KAL.—*Participle.* Poel. *

Isa. 56:10. *sleeping*, lying down, (marg. or, *dreaming*, or, *talking in their sleep*)

1958 ## הִי *hee*, m.

Eze. 2:10. lamentations, and mourning, *and woe*.

1931 ## הִיא *hee*, part. pron. fem.

Note.—This pronoun is, in the Pentateuch, written הִוא, and read as though there were a קרי continually accompanying the word; with the exception of the following passages, in which it is written with [י]:—Gen. 14:2, & 20:5, & 38:25; Lev. 11:39, & 13:10, 21, & 16:31, & 20:17, & 21:9; Num. 5:13, 14; and also in some copies Gen. 38:1.

Gen. 3:12. *she* gave me of the tree, and I did eat.
7: 2. and of beasts that (are) not clean)(
14: 2. and the king of Bela, *which is* Zoar.
8. and the king of Bela, *the same* (is) Zoar;
19:20. near to flee unto, *and it* (is) a little one:
20: 5. *She* (is) my sister? *and she*, even *she herself*
Jos. 10:13. (Is) not *this* written in the book of Jasher?
1K. 3: 4. for *that* (was) the great high place:
Jer. 29:28. *This* (captivity is) long: build ye houses,
Eze. 30:18. *as for her*, a cloud will cover her,
&c. &c. &c.

With prefix הַהִיא.

Gen. 2:12. And the gold of *that* land (is) good:
Nu. 5:31. and *this* woman shall bear her iniquity.
2K. 8:22. Then Libnah revolted at *the same* time.
&c. &c.

הִיא *hee*, Ch. pron. f. 1932

Ezr. 6:15. which was in the sixth year of the (lit. which *it*)
Dan. 2: 9. (there is but) one)(decree for you:
20. for wisdom and might *are* his: (lit. and wisdom and might *it* his)
44. *and it* shall stand for ever.
4:24(21). and *this* (is) the decree of the most High,
30(27). Is not *this* great Babylon,
7: 7. *and it* (was) diverse from all the beasts

הֻיְּדוֹת *hooy-y'dōhth'*, f. pl. 1960

Neh 12: 8. (which was) over *the thanksgiving*,

הֵידָד *hēh-dāhd'*, m. 1959

Isa. 16: 9. *the shouting* for thy summer fruits (marg. or, *the alarm*, &c.)
10. made (their vintage) *shouting* to cease.
Jer. 25:30. he shall give *a shout*,
48:33. none shall tread *with shouting*; (their) *shouting* (shall be) no *shouting*.
51:14. shall lift up *a shout* against thee.

הָיָה *hāh-yāh'*. 1961

A few only of the occurrences of this verb are given as examples of its use; the whole of the passages in which it occurs, would be too numerous for insertion.

* KAL.—*Preterite.* *

Gen. 1: 2. *And* the earth *was* without form
3: 1. Now the serpent *was* more subtil
4:14. *and it shall come to pass*, (that) every one
11: 3. and slime *had* they for morter. (lit. *was* to them)
13: 3. where his tent *had been* at the beginning,
15: 1. the word of the Lord *came* unto Abram
31: 5. the God of my father *hath been* with me.
Ex. 3: 1. Now Moses kept (lit. *was* keeping) the flock
Nu. 10: 2. that thou mayest use them for the calling (lit. *and they shall be* for thee to call)
15:40. *and be* holy unto your God.
31:16. Behold, these *caused* the children of Israel,
Jos. 22:20. and wrath *fell* on all the congregation of Israel?
Jud. 12: 2. I and my people *were* at great strife
14:17. the seven days, while their feast *lasted*:
1Sa. 2:11. And the child *did* minister
6: 9. it (was) a chance (that) *happened* to us.
21: 8(9). because the king's business *required* haste.
2Sa. 3:17. And Abner had communication (lit. the word of Abner *was*)
4: 2. And Saul's son *had* two men
7:24. and thou, Lord, *art become* their God.
9: 9. all that *pertained* to Saul and to all his house.
1K. 16:21. half of the people followed (lit. *were* after) Tibni
20: 6. *and it shall be*, (that) whatsoever
Isa. 1: 9. *we should have been* as Sodom,
&c. &c.

KAL.—*Infinitive.*

Gen. 2:18. (It is) not good *that* the man *should be* alone;
10: 8. he began *to be* a mighty one in the earth.
Ex. 5:13. *as when there was* straw.
8:22(18). that no swarms (of flies) *shall be* there;
12: 4. if the houshold be too little)(for the lamb,
Jud. 18:19. (is it) better *for thee to be* a priest
Ps. 50:21. thou thoughtest that I was *altogether*
&c. &c.

KAL.—*Imperative.*

Gen24:60. *be thou* (the mother) of thousands of millions,
Ex. 18:19. *Be* thou for the people to God-ward,
19:15. *Be* ready against the third day:
1Sa. 4: 9. Be strong, *and quit yourselves* like men, &c. &c.

KAL.—*Future.*

Gen. 1: 3. *Let there be* light: *and there was* light.
29. to you *it shall be* for meat.
9:26. *and* Canaan *shall be* his servant.
13: 8. *Let there be* no strife, I pray thee,
27: 1. *And it came to pass,* that when Isaac
34:10. and the land *shall be* before you;
41:40. Thou *shalt be* over my house,
Ex. 3:14. *I AM* THAT *I AM:*
25:15. The staves *shall be* in the rings
Lev.23:15. seven sabbaths *shall be* complete:
26:12. *and will be* your God, and ye *shall be* my people.
Jer. 48: 6. *and be like* the heath in the wilderness.
Eze. 2: 8. *Be* not *thou* rebellious
16:34. *therefore thou art* contrary.
20:32. ye say, *We will be* as the heathen,
Hos. 3: 3. and *thou shalt* not *be* for (another) man: &c. &c.

KAL.—*Participle.* Poel.

Ex. 9: 3. Behold, the hand of the Lord *is* upon thy cattle

* NIPHAL.—*Preterite.* *

Ex. 11: 6. such as *there was* none like it,
Deu 4:32. *whether there hath been* (any such thing)
27: 9. this day *thou art become* the people of the Lord
Jud.19:30. *There was* no such *deed done* nor seen
20: 3. Tell (us), how *was* this wickedness?
12. What wickedness (is) this that *is done*
1K. 1:27. *Is* this thing *done* by my lord the king,
12:24. for this thing *is* from me.
2Ch 11: 4. for this thing *is done* of me.
Neh 6: 8. *There are* no such things *done* as thou sayest,
Pro. 13:19. The desire *accomplished* is sweet to the soul:
Jer. 5:30. and horrible thing *is committed* in the land;
48:19. (and) say, What *is done?*
Eze.21: 7(12). behold, it cometh, *and shall be brought to pass,*
39: 8. Behold, it is come, *and it is done,*
Dan 2: 1. and his sleep *brake* from him.
8:27. And I Daniel *fainted,* and was sick
12: 1. a time of trouble, such as never *was*
Joel 2: 2. *there hath* not *been* ever the like,
Zec. 8:10. *there was* no hire for man, (marg. the hire of man *became* nothing)

1962 הַיָּה [*hay-yāh'*], f.

Job 6: 2. (כתיב) *and my calamity* laid in the
30:13. (כתיב) they set forward *my calamity,*

1963 הֵיךְ *hēhch,* adv.

1Ch 13:12. *How* shall I bring the ark
Dan 10:17. *For how* can the servant

1964 הֵיכָל *hēh-chāhl',* com.

1Sa. 1: 9. by a post of *the temple of* the Lord.
3: 3. *in the temple of* the Lord,
2Sa.22: 7. hear my voice *out of his temple,*
1K. 6: 3. the porch before *the temple of*
5. *of the temple* and of the oracle:
17. that (is), *the temple* before it,
33. for the door of *the temple*
7:21. in the porch of *the temple:*
50. doors of the house, (to wit), *of the temple.*
21: 1. hard by *the palace of* Ahab
2K. 18:16. the doors of *the temple of* the Lord,
20:18. eunuchs *in the palace of* the king of Babylon.
2K. 23: 4. to bring forth *out of the temple of*
24:13. had made *in the temple of*
2Ch 3:17. the pillars before *the temple,*
4: 7. set (them) *in the temple,*
8. placed (them) *in the temple,*
22. the doors of the house *of the temple,*
26:16. went into *the temple of* the Lord
27: 2. he entered not into *the temple of*
29:16. that they found *in the temple of*
36: 7. and put them *in his temple* at Babylon.
Ezr. 3: 6. *But* the foundation of *the temple of*
10. laid the foundation of *the temple of*
4: 1. the children of the captivity builded *the temple*
Neh 6:10. within *the temple,* and let us shut the doors of *the temple:*
11. would go into *the temple*
Ps. 5: 7(8). will I worship toward thy holy *temple.*
11: 4. The Lord (is) *in* his holy *temple,*
18: 6(7). heard my voice *out of his temple,*
27: 4. to enquire *in his temple.*
29: 9. *and in his temple* doth every one
45: 8(9). out of the ivory *palaces,*
15(16). they shall enter *into* the king's *palace.*
48: 9(10). in the midst of *thy temple.*
65: 4(5). of *thy* holy *temple.*
68:29(30). *Because of thy temple* at Jerusalem
79: 1. thy holy *temple* have they defiled;
138: 2. I will worship toward thy holy *temple,*
144:12. the similitude of *a palace:*
Pro.30:28. and is *in* kings' *palaces.*
Isa. 6: 1. his train filled *the temple.*
13:22. dragons *in* (their) pleasant *palaces:*
39: 7. *in the palace of* the king of Babylon.
44:28. *and* to *the temple,* Thy foundation
66: 6. a voice *from the temple,*
Jer. 7: 4. *The temple of* the Lord, *The temple of* the Lord, *The temple of* the Lord, (are) these.
24: 1. before *the temple of* the Lord,
50:28 & 51:11. the vengeance of *his temple.*
Eze. 8:16. at the door of *the temple of*
— with their backs toward *the temple of*
41: 1. he brought me to *the temple,*
4. before *the temple:*
15. *with the* inner *temple,* and the porches of the court;
20. the wall of *the temple.*
21. The posts of *the temple*
23. And *the temple* and the sanctuary *had* (lit (were) *to the temple*)
25. on the doors of *the temple,*
42: 8. before *the temple*
Dan 1: 4. to stand *in* the king's *palace,*
Hos. 8:14. and buildeth *temples;*
Joel 3: 5(4:5). have carried *into your temples*
Am. 8: 3. the songs of *the temple*
Jon. 2: 4(5). look again toward thy holy *temple.*
7(8). into thine holy *temple.*
Mic. 1: 2. the Lord *from* his holy *temple.*
Nah 2: 6(7). *and the palace* shall be dissolved.
Hab. 2:20. But the Lord (is) *in* his holy *temple:*
Hag. 2:15. was laid upon a stone *in the temple of*
18. the foundation of *the* Lord's *temple*
Zec. 6:12. he shall build *the temple of* the Lord:
13. Even he shall build *the temple of*
14. for a memorial *in the temple of* the Lord.
15. build *in the temple of* the Lord,
8: 9. that *the temple* might be built.
Mal. 3: 1. shall suddenly come to *his temple,*

הֵיכַל *hēh-chal',* Ch. 1965

Ezr. 4:14. we have maintenance from (the king's) *palace,*
5:14. which Nebuchadnezzar took out of *the temple*
— and brought them *into the temple* of Babylon,
— Cyrus the king take out of *the temple*
15. go, carry them *into the temple*
6: 5. which Nebuchadnezzar took forth out of *the temple*
— and brought again *unto the temple*
Dan 4: 4(1). and flourishing *in my palace:*
29(26). he walked in *the palace of*

Dan 5: 2. had taken out of *the temple*
3. that were taken out of *the temple*
5. upon the plaister of the wall of the king's *palace:*
6:18(19). the king went *to his palace,*

1966 **הֵילֵל** *hēh-lēhl′*, m.

Isa. 14:12. *O Lucifer*, son of the morning! (marg. or, *O day star*)

1979 **הֵילְכָה** [*hēh-lee-ċhāh′*], f.

Pro.31:27. (כתיב) She looketh well to *the ways of*

1969 **הִין** *heen*, m.

Ex. 29:40. with the fourth part of *an hin*
— the fourth part of *an hin* of wine
30:24. of oil olive *an hin:*
Lev.19:36. *and a* just *hin,*
23:13. the fourth (part) of *an hin.*
Nu. 15: 4. with the fourth (part) of *an hin*
5. the fourth (part) of *an hin*
6. the third (part) of *an hin* of oil.
7. the third (part) of *an hin* of wine,
9. mingled with half *an hin* of oil.
10. half *an hin* of wine,
28: 5. mingled with the fourth (part) of *an hin*
7. the fourth (part) of *an hin* for the one
14. half *an hin* of wine
— the third (part) of *an hin*
— a fourth (part) of *an hin*
Eze. 4:11. the sixth part of *an hin:*
45:24. *an hin* of oil for an ephah.
46: 5, 7, 11. *an hin* of oil to an ephah.
14. the third part of *an hin* of oil,

1970 **הָכַר** [*hāh-ċhar′*].

* HIPHIL.—*Future.* *

Job 19: 3. *ye make yourselves strange* to me. (marg. or, *harden yourselves* against me)

1971 **הַכָּרָה** [*hak-kāh-rāh′*], f.

Isa. 3: 9. *The shew of* their countenance

See 1973 **הַל** *hal*, adv. interrog.

Deu 32: 6.)(Do ye thus requite the Lord,

1972 **הָלָא** [*hāh-lāh′*].

* NIPHAL.—*Participle.* *

Mic. 4: 7. *and her that was cast far off* a strong nation:

1973 **הָלְאָה** [*hāh′-l′āh*], adv.

Gen19: 9. they said, Stand *back.*
35:21. spread his tent *beyond* the tower
Lev.22:27. *and thenceforth* it shall be
Nu. 15:23. *and henceforward* among your
16:37(17:2). scatter thou the fire *yonder;*
32:19. on yonder side Jordan, *or forward;*
1Sa.10: 3. Then shalt thou go on *forward*
18: 9. Saul eyed David from that day *and forward.*
20:22. the arrows (are) *beyond* thee;
37. (Is) not the arrow *beyond* thee?
Isa. 18: 2, 7. terrible from their beginning *hitherto;*
Jer.22:19. *beyond* the gates of Jerusalem.
Eze.39:22. from that day *and forward.*
43:27. *and* (so) *forward,* the priests shall make
Am. 5:27. go into captivity *beyond* Damascus,

הִלּוּלִים *hil-loo-leem′*, m. pl. 1974

Lev.19:24. holy to *praise* the Lord (marg. holiness of *praises* to the Lord)
Jud. 9:27. and made *merry,* (marg. or, *songs*)

הַלָּז *hal-lāhz′*, pron. com. 1975

Jud. 6:20. lay (them) upon *this* rock,
1Sa.14: 1. that (is) on *the* other *side.* (lit. beyond *this*)
17:26. the man that killeth *this* Philistine,
2K. 4:25. *that* Shunammite:
23:17. What title (is) *that* that I see?
Dan 8:16. make *this* (man) to understand
Zec. 2: 4(8). speak to *this* young man,

הַלָּזֶה *hal-lāh-zeh′*, pron. m. 1976

Gen24:65. What man (is) *this* that walketh
37:19. *this* dreamer cometh.

הַלֵּזוּ *hal-lēh-zoo′*, pron. f. 1977

Eze.36:35. *This* land that was desolate

הָלִיךְ [*hāh-leeċh′*], m. 1978

Job 29: 6. When I washed *my steps* with butter,

הֲלִיכָה [*hălee-ċhāh′*], f. 1979

Job 6:19. *the companies of* Sheba waited
Ps. 68:24(25). They have seen *thy goings,* O God; (even) *the goings of* my God,
Pro.31:27. She looketh well to *the ways of*
Nah 2: 5(6). they shall stumble *in their walk;*
Hab 3: 6. his *ways* (are) everlasting.

הָלַךְ *hāh-laċh′*. 1980

* KAL.—*Preterite.* *

Gen14:24. the men which *went* with me,
19: 2. *and go on* your ways.
26:26. Then Abimelech *went* to him
31:19. Laban *went* to shear his sheep:
30. *thou wouldest* needs *be gone,*
32: 1(2). Jacob *went* on his way,
34:17. our daughter, *and we will be gone.*
35: 3. in the way which *I went.*
Ex. 14:29. the children of Israel *walked*
15:19. Israel *went* on dry (land) in the
17: 5. take in thine hand, *and go.*
Lev.26:23. *but will walk* contrary unto me;
24. *Then will I* also *walk* contrary
27. *but walk* contrary unto me;
28. *Then I will walk* contrary unto you
40. *they have walked* contrary unto me;
Nu. 22:37. wherefore *camest thou* not
24: 1. *he went* not, as at other times,
25. Balak also *went* his way.
32:41. Jair the son of Manasseh *went*
42. Nobah *went* and took Kenath,
Deu 1:31. in all the way that *ye went,*
2:14. the space in which *we came*
4: 3. for all the men that *followed* Baal-peor, (lit. *went* after)
8:19. *and walk* after other gods,
14:25. *and shalt go* unto the place
16: 7. *and go* unto thy tents.

Deu 24: 2. *And* when she is departed...*she may go*
26: 2. *and shalt go* unto the place
28: 9. *and walk* in his ways.
Jos. 2: 5. whither the men *went* I wot not:
3: 3, *and go* after it.
5: 6. Israel *walked* forty years in the
10: 24. the men of war *which went*
14: 10. Israel *wandered* in the wilderness: (marg. *walked*)
17: 7. *and* the border *went along*
23: 16. *and have gone* and served
24: 17. all the way wherein *we went*,
Jud. 1: 3. *and I* likewise *will go*
2: 17. which their fathers *walked* in,
4: 8. If thou wilt go with me, *then I will go :*
6: 21. the angel of the Lord *departed*
8: 1. when *thou wentest* to fight
9: 8. The trees *went* forth
9, 11, 13. *and go* to be promoted
11: 8. *that thou mayest go* with us,
19: 9. *that thou mayest go* home.
21: 21. *and go* to the land of Benjamin.
Ru. 1: 21. *I went out* full,
2: 9. *and go thou* after them:
— *and* when thou art athirst, *go*
1Sa 2: 20. *And they went* unto their own
6: 8. send it away, *that it may go.*
12. *went* along the highway,
7: 16. *And he went* from year to year
8: 3. his sons *walked* not in his ways,
5. thy sons *walk* not in thy ways:
9: 6. shew us our way that *we should go.*
10: 2. The asses which *thou wentest* to seek
14. Whither *went ye ?*
26. Saul also *went* home to Gibeah ;
14: 3. knew not that Jonathan *was gone.*
17. see who *is gone* from us.
46. the Philistines *went* to their own place.
17: 13. *followed* (lit. *went* after) Saul to the battle: and the names of his three sons that *went*
14. the three eldest *followed* Saul. (lit. *went* after)
20: 13. *that thou mayest go* in peace:
23: 18. Jonathan *went* to his house.
23. *and I will go* with you:
30: 22. those that *went* with David,
— Because *they went* not with us,
2Sa 2: 29. Abner and his men *walked*
7: 9. whithersoever *thou wentest*,
23. whom God *went* to redeem
8: 6, 14. preserved David whithersoever *he went.*
10: 11. *then I will come* and help thee.
15: 11. with Absalom *went* two hundred men
16: 17. why *wentest thou* not with
17: 17. *and* a wench *went* and told them ;
19: 25(26). *wentest* not *thou* with me,
1K. 2: 41. Shimei *had gone* from Jerusalem
42. *and walkest* abroad any whither,
3: 6. according as *he walked* before thee
14. as thy father David *did walk*,
8: 25. they walk before me as *thou hast walked*
9: 4. as David thy father *walked*,
6. *but go* and serve other gods,
11: 33. *have* not *walked* in my ways,
38. *and wilt walk* in my ways,
13: 9. by the same way that *thou camest.*
12. What way *went he?* For his sons had seen what way the man of God *went*,
17. by the way that *thou camest.*
14: 2. *and get thee* to Shiloh:
8. who *followed* me (lit. *went* after)
18: 6. Ahab *went* one way by himself, and Obadiah *went* another way
19: 4. But *he* himself *went* a day's journey
22: 13. the messenger that *was gone*
48(49). but *they went* not;
2K. 2: 7. the sons of the prophets *went*,
5: 25. Thy servant *went* no whither.
26. *Went* not mine heart
13: 6. who made Israel sin, (but) *walked*
11. he *walked* therein.
20: 9. *shall* the shadow *go forward*
21: 21. in all the way that his father *walked* in,
22. *walked* not in the way
1Ch 4: 42. *went* to mount Seir,
6: 15(5: 41). Jehozadak *went* (into captivity),
1Ch 17: 8. whithersoever *thou hast walked*,
21. whom God *went* to redeem
18: 6, 13. preserved David whithersoever *he went.*
2Ch 6: 16. as *thou hast walked* before me.
7: 17. as David thy father *walked*,
19. *and shall go* and serve other gods,
8: 17. Then *went* Solomon to Ezion-geber,
11: 17. *they walked* in the way of David
17: 3. because *he walked* in the first ways
4. *walked* in his commandments,
18: 12. the messenger that *went*
21: 12. Because *thou hast* not *walked*
22: 3. *He* also *walked* in the ways
5. *He walked* also after their
Neh 2: 16. the rulers knew not whither *I went*,
Job. 1: 4. *And* his sons *went*
31: 5. If *I have walked* with vanity,
7. and mine heart *walked* after mine eyes,
Ps. 1: 1. that *walketh* not in the counsel of the
26: 1. I *have walked* in mine integrity:
105: 41. *they ran* in the dry places
119: 3. *they walk* in his ways.
Pro. 7: 19. *he is gone* a long journey:
Cant. 2: 11. the rain is over (and) *gone ;*
6: 1. Whither is thy beloved *gone*,
Isa. 2: 3. *And* many people *shall go*
8: 7. *and go* over all his banks:
20: 3. as my servant Isaiah *hath walked*
35: 9. *but* the redeemed *shall walk*
45: 16. *they shall go* to confusion
46: 2. but themselves *are gone* into captivity.
50: 10. that *walketh* (in) darkness,
58: 8. *and* thy righteousness *shall go*
60: 3. *And* the Gentiles *shall come*
14. *also* of them that afflicted thee *shall come*
Jer. 2: 8. *walked* after (things that) do not profit.
23. *I have* not *gone* after Baalim ?
3: 1. *and she go* from him,
7: 23. *and walk ye* in all the ways
8: 2. after whom *they have walked*,
9: 10(9). are fled ; *they are gone.*
13(12). neither *walked* therein ;
11: 10. *they went* after other gods
12. *Then shall* the cities of Judah...*go*,
29: 12. *and ye shall go* and pray unto me,
31: 21. the way (which) *thou wentest :*
32: 23. neither *walked* in thy law ;
44: 10. nor *walked* in my law,
23. the voice of the Lord, nor *walked*
48: 11. neither *hath he gone* into captivity:
50: 3. *they shall depart*, both man and beast.
6. *they have gone* from mountain to hill,
Lam 1: 5. her children *are gone* into captivity
18. my young men *are gone*
Eze. 5: 6. *they have* not *walked* in them.
7. *have* not *walked* in my statutes,
11: 12. *ye have* not *walked* in my statutes,
16: 47. Yet *hast thou* not *walked* after
18: 17. *hath walked* in my statutes ;
20: 13, 21. *they walked* not in my statutes,
16. and *walked* not in my statutes,
23: 31. *Thou hast walked* in the way
25: 3. when *they went* into captivity ;
33: 15. *walk* in the statutes of life,
37: 21. whither they *be gone*,
Hos 5: 11. because *he* willingly *walked*
7: 11. *they go* to Assyria.
9: 6. *they are gone* because of destruction:
11: 2. so *they went* from them:
Am. 1: 15. *And* their king *shall go*
2: 4. after the which their fathers *have walked:*
Mic 4: 2. *And* many nations *shall come*,
Nah 2: 11(12). the old lion, *walked*,
3: 10. *she went* into captivity:
Zep 1: 17. *that they shall walk* like blind men,
Zec. 8: 21. *And* the inhabitants of one (city) *shall go*
9: 14. *and shall go* with whirlwinds of the south.
Mal. 2: 6. *he walked* with me in peace
3: 14. *we have walked* mournfully

KAL.—*Infinitive.*

Gen 8: 3. returned from off the earth *continually :* (marg. *in going* and returning)
5. the waters decreased *continually* (marg. were *in going* and decreasing)
12: 9. *going* on still toward the south. (marg. *going* and journeying)

Gen26:13. went *forward*, (lit. went *going*)
31:30. thou wouldest *needs* be gone, (lit. *going* thou hast gone)
Ex. 3:19. the king of Egypt will not let you *go*,
Nu.22:13. give me leave *to go* with you.
14. Balaam refuseth *to come* with us.
16. hinder thee *from coming* unto
Jos. 6: 9. after the ark, (the priests) *going on*,
13. went *on continually*, (lit. going *to go*)
— (the priests) *going on*, and blowing
Jud. 4: 9. I will *surely* go with thee: (lit. *going* I will go)
24. the hand of the children of Israel prospered, (lit. *going* went)
9: 8. The trees went *forth* (lit. *going* went)
14: 9. went *on* eating, (lit. *going* went)
1Sa. 6:12. went *along* the highway, (lit. went *going* in)
14:19. went *on* and increased: (lit. *going* went)
19:23. went *on*, and prophesied, (lit. *going* went)
2Sa. 3:16. went with her *along* weeping (marg. *going* and weeping)
24. and he is *quite* gone?
5:10. David went *on*, and grew great, (marg. *going* and growing)
13:19. went *on* crying. (lit. *going* and crying)
16:13. cursed *as he went*,
18:25. And he came *apace*, (lit. he went *going*)
24:12. *Go* and say unto David,
2K. 2:11. as they *still* went on,
5:10. *Go* and wash in Jordan
1Ch 11: 9. David waxed greater and greater: (marg. went *in going* and increasing)
Job 34:23. *that he should enter* into judgment (marg. *go*)
Ps.126: 6. He that goeth *forth* and weepeth,
Ecc. 6: 8. that knoweth *to walk*
9. *than the wandering of* the desire: (marg. *than the walking of* the soul)
Isa. 3:16. *walking* and mincing (as) they go,
20: 2. *walking* naked and barefoot.
38: 5. *Go*, and say to Hezekiah,
42:24. for they would not *walk*
Jer. 2: 2. *Go* and cry in the ears of Jerusalem,
3:12. *Go* and proclaim these words
7: 9. *and walk* after other gods whom
13: 1. *Go* and get thee a linen girdle,
17:19. *Go* and stand in the gate
19: 1. *Go* and get a potter's earthen bottle,
23:14. *and walk* in lies:
28:13. *Go* and tell Hananiah,
31: 2. *when I went* to cause him to rest.
34: 2. *Go* and speak to Zedekiah
35: 2. *Go* unto the house of the
13. *Go* and tell the men of Judah
37: 9. The Chaldeans shall *surely* depart
39:16. *Go* and speak to Ebed-melech
41: 6. weeping *all along* as he went: (marg. *in going* and weeping)
50: 4. *going* and weeping:
Zec. 8:21. Let us go *speedily* to pray before the Lord, (marg. *going*; or, *continually*)

KAL.—*Imperative.*

Jer.51:50. *ye* that have escaped the sword, *go away*,

KAL.—*Future.*

Ex. 9:23. *and* the fire *ran along*
Job 14:20. *and he passeth*: thou changest
16: 6. and (though) I forbear, what am I *eased*? (marg. what *goeth* from me?)
22. then *I shall go* the way
20:25. the glittering sword *cometh* out of his
23: 8. Behold, *I go* forward,
41:19(11). Out of his mouth *go* burning lamps,
Ps. 58: 8(9). As a snail (which) melteth, *let* (every one of them) *pass away*:
73: 9. their tongue *walketh* through the
91: 6. the pestilence (that) *walketh* in darkness;
Jer. 9: 4(3). every neighbour *will walk* with

KAL.—*Participle.* Poel.

Gen 2:14. that (is) it *which goeth*
13: 5. *which went* with Abram,
15: 2. seeing I *go* childless,
18:16. Abraham *went* with them
24:42. my way which I *go*:
65. What man (is) this *that walketh*

Gen25:32. I (am) *at the point* to die: (marg. *going* to die)
28:20. in this way that I *go*,
32: 6(7). *he cometh* to meet thee,
19(20). all *that followed* (lit. *that came* after)
20(21). with the present *that goeth* before
37:25. *going* to carry (it) down to Egypt.
Ex. 2: 5. her maidens *walked along*
10: 8. who (are) they *that shall go*?
13:21. the Lord *went* before
14:19. *which went* before the camp
19:19. the trumpet sounded long, (lit. *going* and mighty)
33:15. If thy presence *go* not
Lev.11:20. *going* upon (all) four,
21. *that goeth* upon (all) four,
27. whatsoever *goeth* upon his paws,
— *that go* on (all) four,
42. Whatsoever *goeth* upon the belly, and whatsoever *goeth* upon (all) four,
Nu. 14:14. thou *goest* before them,
38. *that went* to search the land,
22:22. because he *went*:
24:14. I *go* unto my people:
Deu 1:30. *which goeth* before you,
33. *Who went* in the way
20: 4. he *that goeth* with you,
31: 6. he (it is) *that doth go* with thee;
8. he (it is) *that doth go* before thee;
Jos. 6: 8. of the Lord *followed* them. (lit. *going* after)
9, 13. the armed men *went*
—, —. the rereward *came* after the ark,
13. *went* on continually,
8:35. *that were conversant* among them. (marg. *walked*)
18: 8. and Joshua charged *them that went*
23:14. I (am) *going* the way of
Jud. 4: 9. the journey that thou *takest*
5: 6. and the travellers (marg. *and the walkers of* paths) walked through byways.
10. *and walk* by the way.
14: 3. that thou *goest*
17: 9. I *go* to sojourn
18: 5. our way which we *go*
14. *that went* to spy out the country
17. *that went* to spy out the land
19:18. *going* to the house of the Lord;
1Sa. 2:26. the child Samuel grew *on*, (lit. *going* and grew)
6:12. of the Philistines *went* after them
17: 7. one bearing a shield *went* before him.
15. But David *went*
41. the Philistine came *on* and drew near (lit. went *going* and drew near)
25:42. five damsels of her's *that went*
2Sa. 3: 1. David *waxed* stronger and stronger (lit. *going* and strong), and the house of Saul *waxed* weaker and weaker. (lit. *going* and weak)
31. David (himself) *followed* the bier. (lit. *going* after)
6: 4. Ahio *went* before the ark.
12:23. I *shall go* to him, but he shall not return
13:34. there *came* much people
15:11. *and they went* in their simplicity,
12. the people increased *continually* (lit. *going* and was many)
20. seeing I *go* whither I *may*, (lit. *going*)
30. he *went* barefoot:
16:13. Shimei *went* along on the
17:11. that thou *go* to battle
23:17. *that went* in jeopardy
1K. 2: 2. I *go* the way of all
8:23. with thy servants *that walk*
20:36. as soon as thou *art departed*
2K. 1: 3. ye *go* to enquire of Baal-zebub
2:11. it came to pass, *as* they still *went on*,
4:23. Wherefore *wilt* thou *go*
1Ch 15:25. *went* to bring up the ark
2Ch 6:14. *that walk* before thee
9:21. the king's ships *went* to Tarshish
17:12. Jehoshaphat waxed great (lit. was *going* and great)
Neh 6:17. sent many letters unto Tobiah, (marg. multiplied their letters *passing to*)
12:38. *went* over against (them),
Est. 9: 4. his fame *went out* throughout

Est. 9: 4. Mordecai *waxed* greater and greater. (lit. *going* and great)
Job 31:26. or the moon *walking* (in) brightness;
Ps. 15: 2. *He that walketh* uprightly,
78:39. a wind *that passeth away*,
84:11(12). *from them that walk* uprightly.
101: 6. *he that walketh* in a perfect way,
119: 1. *who walk* in the law of the Lord.
128: 1. *that walketh* in his ways.
Pro. 2: 7. a buckler *to them that walk*
4:18. that shineth *more and more* (lit. *going* and shineth)
6:12. *walketh* with a froward mouth.
7:22. *He goeth* after her
10: 9. *He that walketh* uprightly
11:13. A talebearer revealeth secrets: (marg. *He that walketh*, (being) a talebearer)
13:20. *He that walketh* with wise (men)
14: 2. *He that walketh* in his uprightness
19: 1. the poor *that walketh* in his integrity,
20:19. *He that goeth about* (as) a talebearer
28: 6. the poor *that walketh* in his uprightness,
18. *Whoso walketh* uprightly
26. *but whoso walketh* wisely,
Ecc. 1: 4. (One) generation *passeth away*,
6. The wind *goeth* toward the south,
— it *whirleth* about continually,
7. All the rivers *run* into the sea;
— from whence the rivers *come*,
2:14. the fool *walketh* in darkness:
3:20. All *go* unto one place;
6: 6. *do* not all *go* to one place?
9:10. whither thou *goest*.
10: 3. he that is a fool *walketh* by the way,
7. princes *walking* as servants
12: 5. man *goeth* to his long home,
Cant. 7: 9(10). *that goeth* (down) sweetly,
Isa. 8: 6. the waters of Shiloah *that go* softly,
9: 2(1). The people *that walked* in darkness
30: 2. *That walk* to go down into Egypt,
29. *as when one goeth* with a pipe
33:15. *He that walketh* righteously,
35: 8. the way*faring men*,
42: 5. spirit *to them that walk* therein:
52:12. the Lord *will go* before you;
57: 2. *walking* (in) his uprightness.
65: 2. *which walketh* in a way
Jer. 3: 6. she *is gone up* upon every high
6:28. *walking with* slanders:
10:23. *walketh* to direct his steps.
13:10. *which walk* in the imagination
16:12. ye *walk* every one
19:10. the men *that go* with thee,
22:10. weep sore *for him that goeth away*:
23:17. say unto every one that *walketh*
41: 6. weeping all along *as he went*:
Eze. 7:14. none *goeth* to the battle:
11:21. whose heart *walketh* after
13: 3. that *follow* their own spirit, (marg. *that walk* after)
20:16. their heart *went* after their idols.
31: 4. her rivers *running* round about
33:31. their heart *goeth* after
Hos 6: 4. as the early dew *it goeth away*.
13: 3. as the early dew that *passeth away*,
Jon. 1:11, 13. for the sea *wrought*, (marg. *went*)
Mic 2: 7. to him *that walketh* uprightly?
11. *walking* in the spirit and falsehood
Hab 1: 6. *which shall march* through
Zec. 2: 2(6). Whither *goest* thou?

* NIPHAL.—*Preterite.* *

Ps. 109:23. *I am gone* like the shadow

* PIEL.—*Preterite.* *

Job 24:10. *They cause* (him) *to go* naked
30:28. *I went* mourning without
Ps. 38: 6(7). *I go* mourning all the day long.
131: 1. neither *do I exercise myself* (marg. *walk*)
Lam. 5:18. the foxes *walk* upon it.

PIEL.—*Imperative.*

Ecc. 11: 9. *and walk* in the ways of thine

PIEL.—*Future.*

1K. 21:27. *and went* softly.
Ps. 55:14(15). (and) *walked* into the house of God in company.

Ps. 81:13(14). Israel *had walked* in my ways!
85:13(14). Righteousness *shall go* before him;
86:11. *I will walk* in thy truth:
89:15(16). *they shall walk*, O Lord,
104:10. *run* among the hills. (marg. *walk*)
26. There *go* the ships:
115: 7. but *they walk* not:
142: 3(4). In the way wherein *I walked*
Pro. 6:28. *Can* one *go* upon hot coals,
8:20. *I lead* in the way of righteousness, (marg. or, *walk*)
Ecc. 8:10. *gone* from the place of the holy,
Isa. 59: 9. *we walk* in darkness.
Eze. 18: 9. *Hath walked* in my statutes,
Hab 3:11. at the light of thine arrows *they went*, (marg. or, thine arrows *walked* in the light)

PIEL.—*Participle.*

Ps. 104: 3. *who walketh* upon the wings
Pro. 6:11. come *as one that travelleth*,
Ecc. 4:15. all the living *which walk*

* HIPHIL.—*Participle.* *

Zec. 3: 7. I will give thee *places to walk* (marg. *walks*)

* HITHPAEL.—*Preterite.* *

Gen 6: 9. Noah *walked* with God.
24:40. before whom *I walk*,
48:15. Abraham and Isaac *did walk*,
Ex. 21:19. *and walk abroad* upon his staff,
Lev. 26:12. *And I will walk* among you,
1Sa. 2:35. *and he shall walk* before
12: 2. *I have walked* before you
25:15. as long as *we were conversant*
30:31. his men *were wont to haunt*.
2Sa. 7: 7. wherein *I have walked*
2K. 20: 3. how *I have walked* before thee
1Ch 17: 6. *I have walked* with all Israel,
Job 38:16. *hast thou walked* in the search
Ps. 26: 3. *and I have walked* in thy truth.
35:14. *I behaved myself* as though (marg. *walked*)
Isa. 38: 3. how *I have walked* before thee
Eze. 28:14. *thou hast walked up and down*
Zec 1:11. *We have walked to and fro*

* HITHPAEL.—*Infinitive* *.

Job 1: 7 & 2:2. *and from walking up and down* in it.
Ps. 56:13(14). *that I may walk* before God in the light
Pro. 6:22. *When thou goest*, it shall lead thee;
Zec. 1:10. *to walk to and fro* through the earth.
6: 7. *that they might walk to and fro*

HITHPAEL.—*Imperative.*

Gen 13:17. Arise, *walk* through the land
17: 1. *walk* before me,
Jos. 18: 8. Go *and walk* through the land,
Zec. 6: 7. *walk to and fro* through the earth.

HITHPAEL.—*Future.*

Gen 5:22, 24. *And* Enoch *walked* with God
Jos. 18: 4. they shall rise, *and go* through the land,
Jud. 21:24. *And* the children of Israel *departed*
1Sa. 2:30. the house of thy father, *should walk*
23:13. *and went* whithersoever *they could go*.
2Sa. 11: 2. *and walked* upon the roof
1Ch 16:20. *And* (when) *they went* from nation to
21: 4. *and went* throughout all Israel,
Job 18: 8. *he walketh* upon a snare.
22:14. *he walketh* in the circuit of
Ps. 12: 8(9). The wicked *walk* on every side,
39: 6(7). every man *walketh* in a vain shew:
43: 2. why *go I* mourning
58: 7(8). as waters (which) *run* continually:
77:17(18). thine arrows also *went abroad*.
82: 5. *they walk on* in darkness:
101: 2. *I will walk* within my house
105:13. *When they went* from one nation to
116: 9. *I will walk* before the Lord
119:45. *And I will walk* at liberty:
Pro. 23:31. *it moveth itself* aright.
Eze. 19: 6. *And he went up and down* among
Zec. 6: 7. *So they walked to and fro*
10:12. and *they shall walk up and down* in his name,

HITHPAEL.—*Participle.*

Gen 3: 8. the Lord God *walking* in the garden

Deu 23:14(15). For the Lord thy God *walketh*
1Sa. 12: 2. the king *walketh* before
25:27. the young men *that follow* my lord. (marg. *that walk* at the feet of)
2Sa. 7: 6. but have *walked* in a tent (lit. but was *walking*)
Est. 2:11. Mordecai *walked* every day
Ps. 68:21(22). such an one *as goeth on still*
Pro. 20: 7. The just (man) *walketh* in his
24:34. poverty come (as) *one that travelleth;*
Eze. 1:13. *it went up and down* among the

1981 הֲלַךְ [*hălach*], Ch.

* P'AL.—*Participle.* *

Dan 4:29(26). he *walked* in the palace (lit. was *walking*)

* APHEL.—*Participle.* *

Dan 3:25. *walking* in the midst of the fire,
4:37(34). those that *walk* in pride he is able

1982 הֵלֶךְ *heh'-lech*, m.

1Sa. 14:26. behold, the honey *dropped;* (lit. *a dropping of* honey)
2Sa. 12: 4. there came *a traveller* unto the

1983 הֲלָךְ *hălāhch*, Ch. m.

Ezr. 4:13. will they not pay toll, tribute, *and custom,*
20. and toll, tribute, *and custom,*
7:24. toll, tribute, *or custom,* upon them.

1984 הָלַל [*hāh-lal'*].

* KAL.—*Infinitive.* *

Job 29: 3. *When* his candle *shined* (lit. *in its shining*)

KAL.—*Future.*

Ps. 75: 4(5). *Deal* not *foolishly:*

KAL.—*Participle.* Poel.

Ps. 5: 5(6). *The foolish* shall not stand
73: 3. For I was envious *at the foolish,*
75: 4(5). I said *unto the fools,*

* PIEL.—*Preterite.* *

Ps. 10: 3. the wicked *boasteth* of his
44: 8(9). In God *we boast* all the day long,
119:164. Seven times a day *do I praise thee*
Isa. 62: 9. *and praise* the Lord;
64:11(10). where our fathers *praised thee,*
Joel 2:26. *and praise* the name of the Lord

PIEL.—*Infinitive.*

2Sa. 14:25. none *to be* so much *praised* (marg. *to praise* greatly)
1Ch 16: 4. to thank *and praise* the Lord
36. *and praised* the Lord.
23: 5. *to praise* (therewith).
30. to thank *and praise* the Lord,
25: 3. to give thanks *and to praise* the Lord.
2Ch 5:13. *in praising* and thanking the Lord;
— *and praised* the Lord,
7: 6. *when* David *praised*
8:14. *to praise* and minister before the
20:19. stood up *to praise* the Lord God
23:13. such as taught *to sing praise.*
29:30. *to sing praise* unto the Lord
31: 2. *and to praise* in the gates
Ezr. 3:10. *to praise* the Lord,
11. *in praising* and giving thanks
— *when they praised* the Lord,
Neh 12:24. *to praise* (and) to give thanks,

PIEL.—*Imperative.*

Ps. 22:23(24). Ye that fear the Lord, *praise him;*
104:35 & 105:45 & 106:1, 48 & 111:1 & 112:1 & 113:1. *Praise ye* the Lord. (marg. *Hallelujah*)
113: 1. *Praise,* O *ye* servants of the Lord, *praise* the name of the Lord.
9. *Praise ye* the Lord.
115:18. *Praise* the Lord.
116:19. *Praise ye* the Lord.
Ps. 117: 1. O *praise* the Lord,
2. *Praise ye* the Lord.
135: 1. *Praise ye* the Lord. *Praise ye* the name of the Lord; *praise* (him), O *ye* servants
3. *Praise* the Lord; for the Lord
21. *Praise ye* the Lord.
146: 1. *Praise ye* the Lord. *Praise* the Lord,
10 & 147:1, 20. *Praise ye* the Lord.
147.12. *praise* thy God, O Zion.
148: 1, 14. *Praise ye* the Lord.
— *praise ye* the Lord from the heavens: *praise him* in the heights.
2. *Praise ye him,* all his angels: *praise ye him,* all his hosts.
3. *Praise ye him,* sun and moon: *praise him,*
4. *Praise him,* ye heavens of heavens,
7. *Praise* the Lord from the earth,
149: 1, 9. *Praise ye* the Lord.
150: 1, 6. *Praise ye* the Lord.
— *Praise* God in his sanctuary: *praise him*
2. *Praise him* for his mighty acts: *praise him*
3. *Praise him* with the sound of the trumpet: *praise him* with the psaltery
4. *Praise him* with the timbrel and dance: *praise him* with stringed instruments
5. *Praise him* upon the loud cymbals: *praise him* upon the high sounding
Jer. 20:13. *praise ye* the Lord:
31: 7. publish ye, *praise ye,* and say,

PIEL.—*Future.*

Gen 12:15. *and commended* her before Pharaoh:
Jud. 16:24. *And* when the people saw him, *they praised*
2Ch 29:30. *And they sang praises* with gladness,
Neh 5:13. *and praised* the Lord.
Ps. 22:22(23). of the congregation *will I praise thee.*
26(27). *they shall praise* the Lord
35:18. *I will praise thee* among much people.
56: 4(5). In God *I will praise* his word,
10(11). In God *will I praise* (his) word: in the Lord *will I praise* (his) word.
63: 5(6). my mouth *shall praise* (thee)
69:30(31). *I will praise* the name of God
34(35). *Let* the heaven and earth *praise him,*
74:21. *let* the poor and needy *praise* thy name.
84: 4(5). *they will be* still *praising thee.*
102:18(19). shall be created *shall praise* the Lord.
107:32. and *praise him* in the assembly
109:30. *I will praise him* among the
115:17. The dead *praise* not the Lord,
119:175. *and it shall praise thee;*
145: 2. *and I will praise* thy name for ever
146: 2. While I live *will I praise* the Lord:
148: 5, 13. *Let them praise* the name of the
149: 3. *Let them praise* his name
150: 6. *Let* every thing that hath breath *praise*
Pro. 27: 2. *Let* another man *praise thee,* and not
28: 4. They that forsake the law *praise* the
31:28. her husband (also), *and he praiseth her.*
31. *and let* her own works *praise her* in the gates.
Cant. 6: 9. and the concubines, *and they praised her.*
Isa. 38:18. death *can* (not) *celebrate thee:*

PIEL.—*Participle.*

1Ch 23: 5. and four thousand *praised* the Lord
29:13. *and praise* thy glorious name.
2Ch 20:21. *and that should praise* (marg. *praisers*)
23:12. running *and praising* the king,
30:21. *and* the Levites and the priests *praised* the

* POEL.—*Future.* *

Job 12:17. *maketh* the judges *fools.*
Ecc. 7: 7. oppression *maketh* a wise man *mad;*
Isa. 44:25. *maketh* diviners *mad;*

POEL.—*Participle.*

Ps. 102: 8(9). *they that are mad against me* are sworn
Ecc. 2: 2. I said of laughter, (It is) *mad:*

* PUAL.—*Preterite.* *

Ps. 78:63. and their maidens *were* not *given to marriage.* (marg. *praised*)

PUAL.—*Future.*

Pro. 12: 8. A man *shall be commended*

PUAL.—*Participle.*

2Sa. 22: 4. the Lord, (who is) *worthy to be praised:*
1Ch 16:25. *and* greatly *to be praised:*

Ps. 18: 3(4). the Lord, (who is) *worthy to be praised:*
48: 1(2) & 96:4. *and* greatly *to be praised*
113: 3. the Lord's name (is) *to be praised.*
145: 3. *and* greatly *to be praised;*
Eze. 26:17. the *renowned* city,

* HIPHIL.—*Future.* *

Job 31:26. If I beheld the sun when *it shined,*
41:18(10). By his neesings a light *doth shine,*
Isa. 13:10. *shall* not *give* their light:

* HITHPAEL.—*Infinitive.* *

Ps. 106: 5. *that I may glory* with thine inheritance.

HITHPAEL.—*Imperative.*

1Ch 16:10. *Glory ye* in his holy name:
Ps. 105: 3. *Glory ye* in his holy name:

HITHPAEL.—*Future.*

1K. 20:11. *Let* not him that girdeth on (his harness) *boast*
Ps. 34: 2(3). My soul *shall make her boast*
49: 6(7). trust in their wealth, and *boast themselves*
52: 1(3). Why *boastest thou thyself* in mischief,
63:11(12). sweareth by him *shall glory:*
64:10(11). *and* all the upright in heart *shall glory.*
Pro. 20:14. then *he boasteth.*
27: 1. *Boast* not *thyself* of to morrow;
31:30. feareth the Lord, *she shall be praised.*
Isa. 41:16. *shalt glory* in the Holy One of Israel.
45:25. be justified, *and shall glory.*
Jer. 4: 2. in him *shall they glory.*
9:23(22). *Let* not the wise (man) *glory* in his wisdom, neither *let* the mighty man *glory* in his might, *let* not the rich (man) *glory*
24(23). *let* him that glorieth *glory* in this,
49: 4. Wherefore *gloriest thou* in the valleys,

HITHPAEL.—*Participle.*

Ps. 97: 7. *that boast themselves* of idols:
Pro. 25:14. Whoso *boasteth himself* of a false
Jer. 9:24(23). But let *him that glorieth*

* HITHPOEL.—*Imperative.* *

Jer. 25:16. be moved, *and be mad,*
46: 9. *and rage,* ye chariots;

HITHPOEL.—*Future.*

1Sa. 21:13(14). *and feigned himself mad* in their hands,
Jer. 50:38. *they are mad* upon (their) idols.
51: 7. therefore the nations *are mad.*
Nah 2: 4(5). The chariots *shall rage*

1986 **הלם** [*hāh-lam'*].

* KAL.—*Preterite.* *

Jud. 5:22. Then *were* the horsehoofs *broken*
26. *and with the hammer she smote* (marg. *and she hammered*)
Pro. 23:35. *they have beaten me,* (and) I felt
Isa. 16: 8. of the heathen *have broken down*

KAL.—*Infinitive.*

1Sa. 14:16. they went on *beating down*

KAL.—*Future.*

Ps. 74: 6. But now *they break down* the carved work
141: 5. *Let* the righteous *smite me;*

KAL.—*Participle.* Poel.

Isa. 41: 7. *him that smote* the anvil, (marg. or, *the smiting*)

KAL.—*Participle.* Paül.

Isa. 28: 1. *them that are overcome with* wine! (marg. *broken*)

1988 **הֲלֹם** *hălōhm,* adv.

Gen 16:13. Have I also *here* looked after
Ex. 3: 5. Draw not nigh *hither:*
Jud. 18: 3. Who brought thee *hither?*
20: 7. give *here* your advice and counsel.
Ru. 2:14. At mealtime come thou *hither,*
1Sa. 10:22. if the man should yet come *thither.*
1Sa. 14:36. Let us draw near *hither* unto God.
38. Draw ye near *hither,* all the chief
2Sa. 7:18. that thou hast brought me *hither*to?
1Ch 17:16. that thou hast brought me *hither*to?
Ps. 73:10. Therefore his people return *hither:*

הַלְמוּת *hal-mooth',* f. 1989

Jud. 5:26. her right hand *to* the workmen's *hammer;*

הָם [*hāhm*], m. 1991

Eze. 7:11. nor *of any of their's:* (marg. or, *their tumultuous persons*)

הֵם *hēhm,* part. pron. m. pl. 1992

Gen 3: 7. and they knew that *they* (were) naked;
14:24. let *them* take their portion.
Ex. 6:27. *These* (are) *they* which spake to Pharaoh
18:26. every small matter they judged *themselves.*
Lev. 11:27. *those* (are) unclean unto you:
16: 4. *these* (are) holy garments;
Nu. 1:16. heads of thousands in Israel)(.
3:20. These)((are) the families of the Levites
Deu 2:11. *Which* also were accounted giants,
2K. 4: 5. her sons, *who* brought (the vessels) to her;
Ps. 38:10(11). the light of mine eyes, *it* also is gone
Isa. 30: 7. *Their* strength (is) to sit still.
Eze. 10:16. the *same* wheels also turned not
&c. &c. &c.

With prefixes, as הָהֵם.

Gen 6: 4. There were giants in the earth in *those* days;
Ex. 2:23. in process of time, (lit. in *those* many days)
Nu. 14:38. of the men)(that went to search
Deu 28:65. And among *these* nations
&c. &c.

כָּהֵם.

2Sa. 24: 3. *how many soever they be,* (lit. *as they and as they*)
1Ch 21: 3. an hundred times *so many more as they* (be):
2Ch 9:11. and there were none *such* seen before
Ecc. 9:12. *so* (are) the sons of men snared

שֶׁהֵם, שֶׁהֶם־, שֶׁהֵם.

Ecc. 3:18. might see *that they* themselves are beasts.
Cant. 6: 5. *for they* have overcome me:
Lam. 4: 9. *for these* pine away, stricken through

הֵמָּה *hēhm-māh',* part. pron. m. pl. 1992

i. q. הֵם.

Gen 6: 4. *the same* (became) mighty men
7:14. *They,* and every beast after his kind,
Nu. 13: 3. all those men (were) heads of the children of Israel)(.
20:13. *This* (is) the water of Meribah;
Jud. 10:14. let *them* deliver you in the time of your
1Ch 2:55. *These* (are) the Kenites that came
8:13. *who* drove away the inhabitants of Gath:
9:22. *whom* David and Samuel the seer
Ps. 9: 6(7). their memorial is perished *with them.*
16: 3. to the saints that (are) in the earth)(,
Eze. 10:22. of their faces (was) *the same* faces
Zep. 2:12. Ye Ethiopians also, *ye* (shall be) slain
&c. &c. &c.

With prefixes, as בָּהֵמָּה.

Ex. 30: 4. for places for the staves to bear it *withal.*
36: 1. man, *in whom* the Lord put wisdom
Hab. 1:16. because *by them* their portion (is) fat,

הָהֵמָּה.

Nu. 9: 7. And *those* men said unto him,
Zec. 14:15. all the beasts that shall be in *these* tents,
&c. &c.

כָּהֵמָּה.

Jer. 36:32. added besides unto them many *like* words. (marg. words *as they*)

לָהֵמָּה.

Jer. 14:16. and they shall have none to bury *them,*

מֵהֵמָּה.

Ecc.12:12. *by these*, my son, be admonished:
Jer. 10: 2. for the heathen are dismayed *at them.*

1993 ## הָמָה [*hāh-māh'*].

* KAL.—*Preterite.* *

Ps. 46: 6(7). The heathen *raged*,
Cant.5: 4. my bowels *were moved* for him.
Jer. 5:22. *though they roar*, yet can they not
31:20. my bowels *are troubled* (marg. *sound*)
51:55. *when* her waves *do roar*
Zec. 9:15. *make a noise* as through wine;

KAL.—*Infinitive.*

Isa. 17:12. *like the noise of* the seas;

KAL.—*Future.*

Ps. 39: 6(7). surely *they are disquieted* in vain:
42: 5(6). *and* (why) *art thou disquieted* in me?
11(12) & 43:5. why *art thou disquieted* within
46: 3(4). the waters thereof *roar*
55:17(18). will I pray, *and cry aloud:*
59: 6(7). *they make a noise* like a dog,
14(15). *let them make a noise* like a dog,
77: 3(4). I remembered God, *and was troubled:*
83: 2(3). thine enemies *make a tumult:*
Isa. 16:11. my bowels *shall sound* like an harp
17:12. *make a noise* like the noise of the seas;
51:15. whose waves *roared:*
59:11. *We roar* all like bears,
Jer. 6:23. their voice *roareth* like the sea;
31:35. *when* the waves thereof *roar;*
48:36. mine heart *shall sound* for Moab
— mine heart *shall sound* like pipes
50:42. their voice *shall roar* like the sea,

KAL.—*Participle.* Poel.

1K. 1:41. the city *being in an uproar?*
Pro. 1:21. crieth in the chief place of *concourse*,
7:11. She (is) *loud* and stubborn;
9:13. A foolish woman (is) *clamorous:*
20: 1. strong drink (is) *raging:*
Isa. 22: 2. a *tumultuous* city,
Jer. 4:19. my heart *maketh a noise* in me;
Eze. 7:16. all of them *mourning*,

1994 ## הִמּוֹ *him-mōh'* & הִמּוֹן *him-mōhn'*.

Ch. pron.

Ezr. 4:10. the nations whom the great...and set)(
23. and made *them* to cease by force
5: 5. they could not cause *them* to cease,
11. We *are* the servants of the God of
12. he gave *them* into the hand
14. and brought *them* into the temple of Babylon, *those* did Cyrus the king
15. carry *them* into the temple
7:17. and offer *them* upon the altar
Dan 2:34. and brake *them* to pieces.
35. and the wind carried *them* away,
3:22. the flame of the fire slew those men (lit. those men...the flame...slew *them*).

1995 ## הָמוֹן *hāh-mōhn'*.

Gen 17: 4. shalt be a father of *many* nations. (marg. *multitude of* nations)
5. a father of *many* nations
Jud. 4: 7. with his chariots and *his multitude;*
1Sa. 4:14. What (meaneth) the noise of this *tumult?*
14:16. *the multitude* melted away,
19. *that the noise* that (was) in (marg. or, *tumult*)
2Sa. 6:19. among *the* whole *multitude of*
18:29. I saw *a* great *tumult*,
1K. 18:41. a sound of *abundance of* rain.
20:13. Hast thou seen all this great *multitude?*
28. deliver all this great *multitude*
2K. 7:13. as all *the multitude of* Israel
— even as all *the multitude of* the Israelites
25:11. with the remnant of *the multitude*,
1Ch 29:16. all this *store* that we have prepared
2Ch 11:23. he desired *many* wives. (marg. *a multitude of* wives)
13: 8. ye (be) *a* great *multitude*,
14:11(10). we go against this *multitude.*
20: 2. There cometh *a* great *multitude*
12. against this great *company*
15. by reason of this great *multitude;*
24. they looked unto *the multitude*,
31:10. that which is left (is) this great *store.*
32: 7. nor for all *the multitude*
Job 31:34. Did I fear *a* great *multitude*,
39: 7. He scorneth *the multitude of*
Ps. 37:16. better *than the riches of* many
42: 4(5). with *a multitude* that kept holyday.
65: 7(8). *and the tumult of* the people.
Ecc. 5:10(9). nor he that loveth *abundance*
Isa. 5:13. *and their multitude* dried up
14. *and their multitude*, and their pomp,
13: 4. The noise of *a multitude*
16:14. with all *that* great *multitude;*
17:12. Woe to *the multitude of* many people, (marg. or, *noise*)
29: 5. *Moreover the multitude of* thy strangers
— *the multitude of* the terrible
7, 8. *the multitude of* all the nations
31: 4. *nor* abase himself *for the noise of them:* (marg. or, *multitude*)
32:14. *the multitude of* the city shall be
33: 3. At the noise of *the tumult*
60: 5. *the abundance of* the sea (marg. or, *noise*)
63:15. *the sounding of* thy bowels (marg. or, *the multitude*)
Jer. 3:23. *the multitude of* mountains:
10:13. *a multitude of* waters (marg. or, *noise*)
47: 3. *the rumbling of* his wheels,
49:32. *and the multitude of* their cattle a spoil:
51:16. *a multitude of* waters
42. covered *with the multitude of* the waves
Eze. 7:11. nor *of their multitude*, (marg. *tumult*)
12, 14. upon all *the multitude thereof.*
13. touching *the* whole *multitude thereof*,
23:42. a voice of *a multitude* being at
26:13. I will cause *the noise of* thy songs
29:19. he shall take *her multitude*,
30: 4. they shall take away *her multitude*,
10. make *the multitude of* Egypt to cease
15. I will cut off *the multitude of* No.
31: 2. and to *his multitude;*
18. This (is) Pharaoh and all *his multitude*,
32:12. will I cause *thy multitude* to fall,
— all *the multitude thereof*
16. for all *her multitude*,
18. wail for *the multitude of* Egypt,
20. draw her and all *her multitudes.*
24. There (is) Elam and all *her multitude*
25. the slain with all *her multitude:*
26. Tubal, and all *her multitude:*
31. shall be comforted over all *his multitude*
32. Pharaoh and all *his multitude*,
39:11. Gog and all *his multitude:*
— The valley of *Hamon*-gog. (marg. i. e. *The multitude of* Gog)
15. in the valley of *Hamon*-gog.
Dan 10: 6. his words like the voice of *a multitude.*
11:10. shall assemble *a multitude*
11. he shall set forth *a* great *multitude;* but *the multitude* shall be given
12. he hath taken away *the multitude*,
13. shall set forth *a multitude*
Joel 3:14(4:14). *Multitudes, multitudes* in the valley
Am. 5:23. *the noise of* thy songs;

הֶמְיָה [*hem-yāh'*], f. 1998

Isa. 14:11. *the noise of* thy viols:

הֲמֻלָּה *hămool-lāh'*, f. 1999

Jer. 11:16. the noise of *a* great *tumult*
Eze. 1:24. the voice of *speech*,

הָמַם *hāh-mam'*. 2000

* KAL.—*Preterite.* *

Ex. 23:27. *and will destroy* all the people
2Ch 15: 6. for God *did vex them*

Isa. 28:28. *nor break* (it with) the wheel
Jer. 51:34. *he hath crushed me*, he hath made

KAL.—*Infinitive.*

Deu 2:15. *to destroy them* from among
Est. 9:24. *to consume them*, and to destroy them; (marg. *crush*)

KAL.—*Future.*

Ex. 14:24. *and troubled* the host of the Egyptians,
Jos. 10:10. *And* the Lord *discomfited* them
Jud. 4:15. *And* the Lord *discomfited* Sisera,
1Sa. 7:10. the Philistines, *and discomfited them;*
2Sa. 22:15. lightning, *and discomfited them.*
Ps. 18:14(15). lightnings, *and discomfited them.*
144: 6. thine arrows, *and destroy them.*

1995 הָמַן [*hāh-man'*].

* KAL.—*Infinitive.* *

Eze. 5: 7. Because *ye multiplied* more

2002 הַמְנִיךְ [*ham-neech'*], Ch.

[כתיב ׀ הַמְנוּךְ]

Dan 5: 7. *and* (have) *a chain* of gold about his
16. *and* (have) *a chain* of gold about thy
29. *and* (put) *a chain* of gold about his neck,

2003 הֲמָסִים *hămāh-seem'*, m. pl.

Isa. 64: 2(1). As (when) the *melting* fire burneth, (marg. fire of *meltings*—perhaps, lit. *brushwood*)

2004 הֵן *hēhn*, part. pron. f.

Gen 19:29. *in the which* Lot dwelt.
30:26. *for whom* I have served thee,
Ex. 25:29. to cover *withal:*
37:16. his covers to cover *withal*,
Lev. 10: 1. and put fire *therein*,
11:21. to leap *withal* upon the earth;
14:40. the stones *in* which (lit. which *in them*)
Nu. 10: 3. they shall blow *with them*,
16: 7. And put fire *therein*,
Deu 28:52. wherein (lit. which *in them*) thou trustedst,
Jer. 4:29. not a man dwell *therein.*
48: 9. without any to dwell *therein.*
51:43. *wherein* no man dwelleth, neither doth (any) son of man pass *thereby.*
Eze. 16:47. thou wast corrupted *more than they*
52. more abominable *than they:*
18:14. doeth not *such like*,

2005 הֵן *hēhn*, part. interj.

Gen 3:22. *Behold*, the man is become as one of us,
29: 7. And he said, *Lo*, (it is) yet high day,
Ex. 8:26(22). *lo*, shall we sacrifice the abomination
Lev. 10:18. *Behold*, the blood of it was not brought in
2Ch 7:13. *If* I shut up heaven that there be no rain, *or if*
Job 13:15. *Though* he slay me, yet will I trust in
Isa. 59: 1. *Behold*, the Lord's hand is not shortened,

&c. &c.

2006 הֵן *hēhn*, Ch. part. conj.

Ezr. 4:13, 16. *that, if* this city be builded,
5:17. therefore, *if* (it seem) good to the king, — *whether* it be (so), that a decree
7:26. *whether* (it be) unto death, *or* to banishment, *or* to confiscation of goods,
Dan 2: 5. *if* ye will not make known unto me the
6. *But if* ye shew the dream,
9. *But if* ye will not make known unto me
3:15. Now *if* ye be ready that at what time ye — *but if* ye worship not,
17. *If* it be (so), our God whom we serve
18. *But if* not, be it known unto thee,
4:27(24). *if* it may be a lengthening of thy tranquillity.
5:16. now *if* thou canst read the writing,

הֵנָּה *hēhn'-nāh*, part. pron. f. pl. 2007

Gen 6: 2. saw the daughters of men that *they* (were)
Ex. 9:32. and the rie were not smitten: for *they* (were) not grown up.
Lev. 18:10. for *their's* (is) thine own nakedness.
Nu. 31:16. Behold, *these* caused the children of Israel,
Deu 20:15. which)((are) not of the cities of these
1Sa. 27: 8. for *those* (nations were) of old the

&c. &c.

With prefixes, as בָּהֵנָּה.

Lev. 6: 3(5:22). that a man doeth, sinning *therein:*
Nu. 13:19. what cities (they be) that they dwell *in*,
Jer. 5:17. thy fenced cities, *wherein* thou trustedst,

הֲהֵנָּה.

1Sa. 17:28. and with whom hast thou left *those* few

כָּהֵנָּה.

Gen 41:19. *such* as I never saw in all the land of
2Sa. 12: 8. I would moreover have given unto thee *such and such things.*
Job 23:14. *and* many *such* (things are) with him.

לָהֵנָּה.

Eze. 1: 5. *they had* (lit. *to them*) the likeness of a
23. *on this side*, and every one had two, which covered *on that side*,
42: 9. as one goeth *into them* from the utter
Zec. 5: 9. *for they had* wings like the wings of a

מֵהֵנָּה.

Lev. 4: 2. and shall do against any *of them:*
1Ch 21:10. choose thee one *of them*, that I may do (it)
Ps. 34:20(21). He keepeth all his bones: not one *of them* is broken.
Isa. 34:16. no one *of these* shall fail, none shall
Jer. 5: 6. every one that goeth out *thence* shall be
Eze. 16:51. multiplied thine abominations *more than they*,
42: 5. for the galleries were higher *than these*,

הֵנָּה *hēhn'-nāh*, part. adv. 2008

Gen 15:16. they shall come *hither* again:
21:23. swear unto me *here* by God
29. What)((mean) these seven ewe lambs,
Nu. 14:19. from Egypt even until *now.*
Jos. 8:20. no power to flee *this way or that way:*
2K. 4:35. walked in the house *to* and *fro*; (marg once *hither*, and once *thither*)
Jer. 50: 5. to Zion with their faces *thitherward*,
Dan 12: 5. the one *on this side* of the bank of the river, and the other *on that side*

&c. &c.

It is sometimes combined in translation with עַד preceding it.

Gen 15:16. the iniquity of the Amorites (is) not *yet*
44:28. torn in pieces; and I saw him not *since:*
Jud. 16:13. *Hitherto* thou hast mocked me, and told
2K. 8: 7. saying, The man of God is come *hither.*
Jer. 48:47. *Thus far* (is) the judgment of Moab.

&c. &c

הִנֵּה *hin-nēh'*, part. interj. 2009

Gen 1:29. And God said, *Behold*, I have given you
12:11. *Behold* now, I know that thou (art)
19:21. *See*, I have accepted thee concerning
42:28. and, *lo*, (it is) even in my sack:
50: 5. My father made me swear, saying, *Lo*, I

&c. &c.

With pronominal suffixes הִנְּךָ, הִנְנִי, &c.

Gen 6:17. And, *behold*, *I*, even I, do bring a flood
16:11. *Behold*, *thou* (art) with child, and shalt
Nu. 14:40. *Lo*, *we* (be here), and will go up
Jos. 9:25. And now, *behold*, *we* (are) in thine hand:
1Sa. 3: 5. and said, *Here* (am) *I*; for thou calledst
14:43. (and), *lo*, *I* must die.
1Ch 11:25. *Behold*, *he* was honourable among the
Isa. 41:27. (shall say) to Zion, Behold, *behold them:*
Jer. 16:12. *for*, *behold*, *ye* walk every one after
18: 3. *and*, *behold*, *he* wrought a work
Eze. 13:10. *and*, *lo*, *others* daubed it with untempered

&c. &c.

2010 ## הֲנָחָה hănāh-ghāh', f.

Est. 2:18. *and* he made *a release* to the provinces,

2013 ## הָסָה [hāh-sāh'].

✱ PIEL.—*Imperative.* ✱

Jud. 3:19. who said, *Keep silence.*
Neh 8:11. saying, *Hold your peace,*
Am. 6:10. Then shall he say, *Hold thy tongue :*
8: 3. cast (them) forth *with silence.* (marg. *be silent*)
Hab 2:20. *let* all the earth *keep silence* (marg. *be silent*)
Zep 1: 7. *Hold thy peace* at the presence
Zec. 2:13(17). *Be silent,* O all flesh,

✱ HIPHIL.—*Future.* ✱

Nu. 13:30. *And* Caleb *stilled* the people

2014 ## הֲפוּגָה [hăphoo-gāh'], f.

Lam. 3:49. without any *intermission,*

2015, 2017 ## הָפַךְ hāh-phach'.

✱ KAL.—*Preterite.* ✱

Lev. 13: 3. the hair in the plague *is turned*
4. the hair thereof *be* not *turned*
10. *have turned* the hair white,
13. *it is* all *turned* white:
20. the hair thereof *be turned* white;
55. the plague *have* not *changed*
Deu 29:23(22). Zeboim, which the Lord *overthrew*
Jos. 7: 8. when Israel *turneth* their backs
Jud. 20:41. the men of Israel *turned again,*
2K. 5:26. when the man *turned again*
21:13. *and turning* (it) upside down.
Job 9: 5. *overturneth them* in his anger.
28: 9. *he overturneth* the mountains
34:25. *and he overturneth* (them) in the
Ps. 30:11(12). *Thou hast turned* for me
41: 3(4). *thou wilt make* all his bed (marg. *turn*)
66: 6. *He turned* the sea into dry (land):
78: 9. *turned back* in the day of battle.
105:25. *He turned* their heart to hate his
29. *He turned* their waters into blood,
Jer. 20:16. the cities which the Lord *overthrew,*
23:36. *for ye have perverted* the words
31:13. *for I will turn* their mourning into joy,
Am. 4:11. *I have overthrown* (some) of you,
6:12. *ye have turned* judgment into gall,
8:10. *And I will turn* your feasts into
Hag 2:22. *And I will overthrow* the throne of
— *and I will overthrow* the chariots,

KAL.—*Infinitive.*

Gen 19:21. *I will* not *overthrow* this city,
29. *when he overthrew* the cities
2Sa. 10: 3. to spy it out, *and to overthrow* it?
1Ch 19: 3. to search, *and to overthrow,*
Pro. 12: 7. The wicked *are overthrown,*
Isa. 29:16. *your turning of things upside down*

KAL.—*Imperative.*

1K. 22:34. *Turn* thine hand, and carry me
2Ch 18:33. *Turn* thine hand, that thou

KAL.—*Future.*

Gen 19:25. *And he overthrew* those cities,
Ex. 10:19. *And* the Lord *turned* a mighty
Deu 23: 5(6). *but* the Lord thy God *turned* the
Jud. 7:13. *and* over*turned it,* that the tent
20:39. *And when* the men of Israel *retired*
1Sa. 10: 9. *that* when he had turned...God *gave* him another heart: (marg. *turned*)
25:12. *So* David's young men *turned* their way,
2K. 9:23. *And* Joram *turned* his hands,
2Ch 9:12. *So she turned,* and went away
Neh 13: 2. *howbeit* our God *turned* the curse
Job 12:15. *and they overturn* the earth.
Ps. 78:44. *And had turned* their rivers
Jer. 13:23. *Can* the Ethiopian *change* his skin,
Lam. 3: 3. *he turneth* his hand (against me)
Zep 3: 9. then *will I turn* to the people

KAL.—*Participle.* Poel.

Ps. 114: 8. *Which turned* the rock (into) a standing
Am. 5: 7. Ye *who turn* judgment to wormwood,
8. *and turneth* the shadow of death

KAL.—*Participle.* Paül.

Lam. 4: 6. *that was overthrown* as in a moment,
Hos 7: 8. Ephraim is a cake not *turned.*

✱ NIPHAL.—*Preterite.* ✱

Ex. 7:15. the rod which *was turned*
17. *and they shall be turned* to blood.
Lev. 13:16. *and be changed* unto white,
17. the plague *be turned* into white;
25. the bright spot *be turned* white,
Jos. 8:20. *turned back* upon the pursuers.
1Sa. 4:19. pains *came* upon her. (marg. *were turned*)
10: 6. *and shalt be turned* into another
Est. 9:22. the month which *was turned*
Job 19:19. they whom I loved *are turned*
20:14. his meat in his bowels *is turned,*
28: 5. under it *is turned up*
41:28(20) slingstones *are turned* with him
Ps. 32: 4. *is turned* into the drought of summer.
78:57. *they were turned aside* like a
Pro. 17:20. *and he that hath a perverse* tongue (lit. *and he that is turned* in his tongue)
Isa. 34: 9. *And* the streams thereof *shall be turned*
Jer. 2:21. how then *art thou turned*
30: 6. *and* all faces *are turned*
Lam. 1:20. mine heart *is turned* within me;
5: 2. Our inheritance *is turned*
15. our dance *is turned* into mourning.
Dan 10: 8. for my comeliness *was turned*
16. my sorrows *are turned* upon me,
Hos 11: 8. mine heart *is turned* within me,

NIPHAL.—*Infinitive.*

Est. 9: 1. *though* it *was turned to the contrary,*

NIPHAL.—*Future.*

Ex. 7:20. *and* all the waters that (were) in the river *were turned*
14: 5. *and* the heart of Pharaoh...*was turned*
Job 30:21. *Thou art become* cruel to me: (marg. *turned* to be)
Isa. 60: 5. the sea *shall be converted* unto thee,
63:10. *therefore he was turned* to be their enemy,
Eze. 4: 8. and *thou shalt* not *turn*
Joel 2:31(3:4). The sun *shall be turned*

NIPHAL.—*Participle.*

Jon. 3: 4. Nineveh *shall be overthrown.*

✱ HOPHAL.—*Preterite.* ✱

Job 30:15. Terrors *are turned* upon me:

✱ HITHPAEL.—*Future.* ✱

Job 38:14. *It is turned* as clay (to) the seal;

HITHPAEL.—*Participle.*

Gen 3:24. a flaming sword *which turned every way,*
Jud. 7:13. *tumbled* into the host of Midian,
Job 37:12. *it is turned* round about

הֵפֶךְ hĕh'-phĕch & הֶפֶךְ heh'-phĕch, m. 2016

Eze. 16:34. *the contrary* is in thee
— therefore thou art *contrary.*

הֲפֵכָה hăphēh-chāh', f. 2018

Gen 19:29. the midst of *the overthrow,*

הֲפַכְפַּךְ hăphach-pach', adj. 2019

Pro. 21: 8. The way of man (is) *froward*

הַצָּלָה hatz-tzāh-lāh', f. 2020

Est. 4:14. shall there enlargement *and deliverance*

הֹצֶן hōh'-tzen, m. 2021

Eze. 23:24. come against thee *with chariots,*

2022 # הַר *har*, m.

Gen 7:19. all *the* high *hills*,
20. *the mountains* were covered.
8: 4. upon *the mountains of* Ararat.
5. were the tops of *the mountains* seen.
10:30. *a mount of* the east.
12: 8. *unto a mountain* on the east
14:10. they that remained fled *to the mountain.*
19:17. escape *to the mountain,*
19. I cannot escape *to the mountain,*
30. dwelt *in the mountain,*
22: 2. offering upon one of *the mountains*
14. *In the mount of* the Lord
31:21. set his face (toward) *the mount*
23. they overtook him *in the mount*
25. Jacob had pitched his tent *in the mount:*
— pitched *in the mount of* Gilead.
54. offered sacrifice *upon the mount,*
— tarried all night *in the mount.*
36: 8. Thus dwelt Esau *in mount* Seir:
9. the Edomites *in mount* Seir:
Ex. 3: 1. and came to *the mountain of* God,
12. ye shall serve God upon this *mountain.*
4:27. and met him *in the mount of* God,
15:17. plant them *in the mountain of*
18: 5. where he encamped at *the mount of* God:
19: 2. Israel camped before *the mount.*
3. called unto him out of *the mountain,*
11. of all the people upon *mount* Sinai.
12. go (not) up *into the mount,*
— whosoever toucheth *the mount*
13. shall come up *to the mount.*
14. Moses went down from *the mount*
16. a thick cloud upon *the mount,*
17. at the nether part of *the mount.*
18. *And mount* Sinai was altogether on a smoke,
— *the* whole *mount* quaked greatly.
20. the Lord came down upon *mount* Sinai, on the top of *the mount:* and the Lord called Moses (up) to the top of *the mount;*
23. The people cannot come up to *mount* Sinai:
— Set bounds about *the mount,*
20:18. *the mountain* smoking:
24: 4. builded an altar under *the hill,*
12. Come up to me *into the mount,*
13. Moses went up into *the mount of* God.
15. Moses went up into *the mount,* and a cloud covered *the mount.*
16. the glory of the Lord abode upon *mount* Sinai,
17. fire on the top of *the mount*
18. gat him up into *the mount:* and Moses was *in the mount*
25:40. which was shewed thee *in the mount.*
26:30. which was shewed thee *in the mount.*
27: 8. as it was shewed thee *in the mount,*
31:18. of communing with him *upon mount* Sinai,
32: 1. to come down out of *the mount,*
12. to slay them *in the mountains,*
15. went down from *the mount,*
19. brake them beneath *the mount.*
33: 6. of their ornaments *by the mount* Horeb.
34: 2. come up in the morning unto *mount* Sinai,
— in the top of *the mount.*
3. seen throughout all *the mount;*
— feed before that *mount.*
4. and went up unto *mount* Sinai,
29. when Moses came down *from mount*
— when he came down from *the mount,*
32. had spoken with him *in mount* Sinai.
Lev. 7:38. the Lord commanded Moses *in mount* Sinai,
25: 1. spake unto Moses *in mount* Sinai,
26:46. *in mount* Sinai by the hand of Moses.
27:34. for the children of Israel *in mount* Sinai.
Nu. 3: 1. the Lord spake with Moses *in mount* Sinai.
10:33. they departed *from the mount of* the Lord
13:17. go up into *the mountain:*
29. dwell *in the mountains:*
14:40. up into the top of *the mountain,*
44. to go up unto *the hill* top:
45. which dwelt *in* that *hill,*
Nu. 20:22. from Kadesh, and came unto *mount* Hor.
23. unto Moses and Aaron in *mount* Hor,
25. bring them up unto *mount* Hor:
27. and they went up into *mount* Hor
28. Aaron died there in the top of *the mount:* and Moses and Eleazar came down from *the mount.*
21: 4. they journeyed from *mount* Hor
27:12. Get thee up into this *mount*
28: 6. which was ordained *in mount* Sinai
33:23. pitched *in mount* Shapher.
24. removed *from mount* Shapher,
37. from Kadesh, and pitched in *mount* Hor,
38. Aaron the priest went up into *mount* Hor
39. when he died in *mount* Hor.
41. they departed from *mount* Hor,
47. pitched *in the mountains of*
48. they departed *from the mountains of*
34: 7. ye shall point out for you *mount* Hor:
8. From *mount* Hor ye shall point out
Deu 1: 2. from Horeb by the way of *mount* Seir
6. dwelt long enough *in* this *mount:*
7. go to *the mount of* the Amorites,
— in the plain, *in the hills,*
19. *the mountain of* the Amorites,
20. come unto *the mountain of*
24. went up *into the mountain,*
41. ready to go up *into the hill.*
43. went presumptuously up *into the hill.*
44. which dwelt *in* that *mountain,*
2: 1. we compassed *mount* Seir many days.
3. Ye have compassed this *mountain*
5. I have given *mount* Seir unto Esau
37. the cities in *the mountains,*
3: 8. Arnon unto *mount* Hermon;
12. and half *mount* Gilead,
25. that goodly *mountain,*
4:11. stood under *the mountain; and the mountain* burned with fire
48. even unto *mount* Sion, which (is) Hermon,
5: 4. face to face *in the mount*
5. went not up *into the mount;*
22(19). unto all your assembly *in the mount*
23(20). *for the mountain* did burn
8: 7. that spring out of valleys *and hills;*
9: 9. I was gone up *into the mount*
— I abode *in the mount* forty days
10. spake with you *in the mount*
15. came down from *the mount, and the mount* burned with fire:
21. that descended out of *the mount.*
10: 1. come up unto me *into the mount,*
3. went up *into the mount,*
4. spake unto you *in the mount*
5. came down from *the mount,*
10. I stayed *in the mount,*
11:11. a land of *hills* and valleys,
29. put the blessing upon *mount* Gerizim, and the curse upon *mount* Ebal.
12: 2. upon *the* high *mountains,*
27: 4. *in mount* Ebal,
12. stand upon *mount* Gerizim
13. these shall stand *upon mount* Ebal
32:22. set on fire the foundations of *the mountains.*
49. Get thee up into this *mountain* Abarim, (unto) *mount* Nebo,
50. die *in the mount* whither thou
— as Aaron thy brother died in *mount* Hor,
33: 2. he shined forth *from mount* Paran,
19. call the people unto *the mountain;*
34: 1. unto *the mountain of* Nebo,
Jos. 2:16. Get you *to the mountain,*
22. came *unto the mountain,*
23. descended *from the mountain,*
8:30. God of Israel *in mount* Ebal,
33. over against *mount* Gerizim; and half of them over against *mount* Ebal;
9: 1. on this side Jordan, *in the hills,*
10: 6. the kings of the Amorites that dwell in *the mountains*
40. smote all the country of *the hills,*
11: 2. on the north *of the mountains,*
3. the Jebusite *in the mountains,*
16. *the hills,* and all the south country,
— and *the mountain of* Israel,
17. from *the mount* Halak,

Jos. 11:17. under *mount* Hermon:
21. cut off the Anakims from *the mountains*,
— from all *the mountains of* Judah, and from all *the mountains of* Israel:
12: 1. unto *mount* Hermon,
5. reigned *in mount* Hermon,
7. even unto *the mount* Halak,
8. *In the mountains*, and in the valleys,
13. 5. Baal-gad under *mount* Hermon
6. the inhabitants of *the hill country*
11. and all *mount* Hermon,
19. *in the mount of* the valley,
14:12. therefore give me this *mountain*,
15: 8. to the top of *the mountain*
9. drawn from the top of *the hill*
— to the cities of *mount* Ephron;
10. westward unto *mount* Seir,
— along unto the side of *mount* Jearim,
11. passed along to *mount* Baalah,
48. *And in the mountains*, Shamir,
16: 1. *throughout mount* Beth-el,
17:15. if *mount* Ephraim be too narrow
16. *The hill* is not enough for us:
18. But *the mountain* shall be thine;
18:12. went up *through the mountains*
13. near *the hill* that (lieth) on the
14. from *the hill* that (lieth) before
16. to the end of *the mountain*
19:50. Timnath-serah *in mount* Ephraim:
20: 7. Kedesh in Galilee *in mount* Naphtali, and Shechem *in mount* Ephraim,
— *in the mountain of* Judah.
21:11. *in the hill* (country) *of* Judah,
21. her suburbs *in mount* Ephraim,
24: 4. I gave unto Esau *mount* Seir,
30. which (is) *in mount* Ephraim, on the north side *of the hill of* Gaash.
33. was given him *in mount* Ephraim.
Jud. 1: 9. that dwelt in *the mountain*,
19. drave out (the inhabitants of) *the mountain;*
34. the children of Dan *into the mountain*.
35. the Amorites would dwell *in mount*
2: 9. *in the mount of* Ephraim, on the north side *of the hill* Gaash.
3: 3. Hivites that dwelt in *mount* Lebanon, *from mount* Baal-hermon
27. he blew a trumpet *in the mountain of*
— went down with him from *the mount*,
4: 5. Beth-el *in mount* Ephraim:
6. draw *toward mount* Tabor,
12. was gone up to *mount* Tabor.
14. Barak went down *from mount* Tabor,
5: 5. *The mountains* melted from
6: 2. the dens which (are) *in the mountains*,
7: 3. depart early *from mount* Gilead.
24. sent messengers throughout all *mount*
9: 7. stood in the top of *mount* Gerizim,
25. in the top of *the mountains*,
36. down from the top of *the mountains*.
— seest the shadow of *the mountains*
48. gat him up to *mount* Zalmon,
10: 1. Shamir *in mount* Ephraim.
11:37. go up and down upon *the mountains*,
38. bewailed her virginity upon *the mountains*.
12:15. *in the mount of* the Amalekites.
16: 3. carried them up to the top of *an hill*
17: 1. a man *of mount* Ephraim,
8. he came to *mount* Ephraim
18: 2. when they came to *mount* Ephraim,
13. they passed thence unto *mount*
19: 1. on the side of *mount* Ephraim,
16. which (was) also *of mount* Ephraim
18. toward the side of *mount* Ephraim;
1Sa. 1: 1. *of mount* Ephraim,
9: 4. he passed *through mount* Ephraim,
13: 2. *and in mount* Beth-el,
14:22. hid themselves *in mount* Ephraim,
17: 3. the Philistines stood on *a mountain*
— Israel stood on *a mountain*
23:14. remained *in a mountain*
26. And Saul went on this side of *the mountain*,
— on that side of *the mountain:*
25 20. by the covert of *the hill*,
26. 13. stood on the top of *an hill*

1Sa. 26:20. a partridge *in the mountains*.
31: 1. fell down slain *in mount* Gilboa.
8. his three sons fallen *in mount* Gilboa
2Sa. 1: 6. by chance *upon mount* Gilboa,
21. *Ye mountains* of Gilboa,
13:34. by the way of the *hill* side
16:13. Shimei went along on *the hill*'s side
20:21. but a man *of mount* Ephraim,
21: 9. they hanged them *in the hill*
1K. 4: 8. The son of Hur, *in mount* Ephraim:
5:15(29). hewers *in the mountains;*
11: 7. *in the hill* that (is) before Jerusalem,
12:25. Jeroboam built Shechem *in mount* Ephraim,
16:24. he bought *the hill* Samaria
— and built on *the hill*,
— owner of *the hill*, Samaria.
18:19. all Israel unto *mount* Carmel,
20. prophets together unto *mount* Carmel.
19: 8. Horeb *the mount of* God.
11. stand *upon the mount*
— strong wind rent *the mountains*,
20:23. Their gods (are) gods of *the hills;*
28. The Lord (is) God of *the hills*,
22:17. I saw all Israel scattered upon *the hills*,
2K. 1: 9. he sat on the top of *an hill*.
2:16. upon some *mountain*, (marg. one of *the mountains*)
25. went from thence to *mount* Carmel,
4:25. the man of God to *mount* Carmel.
27. came to the man of God to *the hill*,
5:22. *from mount* Ephraim two young men
6:17. *the mountain* (was) full of horses
19:23. come up to the height of *the mountains*,
31. they that escape *out of mount* Zion:
23:13. *of the mount of* corruption,
16. that (were) there *in the mount*,
1Ch 4:42. went *to mount* Seir,
5:23. *and unto mount* Hermon.
6:67(52). Shechem *in mount* Ephraim with her suburbs;
10: 1. fell down slain *in mount* Gilboa.
8. his sons fallen *in mount* Gilboa.
12: 8. as swift as the roes upon *the mountains;*
2Ch 2: 2(1). to hew *in the mountain*,
18(17). (to be) hewers *in the mountain*,
3: 1. Jerusalem *in mount* Moriah,
13: 4. stood up upon *mount* Zemaraim, which (is) *in mount* Ephraim,
15: 8. which he had taken *from mount* Ephraim,
18:16. Israel scattered upon *the mountains*,
19: 4. from Beer-sheba to *mount* Ephraim,
20:10,22. Moab *and mount* Seir,
23. the inhabitants of *mount* Seir,
21:11. he made high places *in the mountains of*
26:10. vine dressers *in the mountains*,
27: 4. *in the mountains of* Judah,
33:15. the altars that he had built *in the mount of*
Neh 8:15. Go forth unto *the mount*,
9:13. Thou camest down also upon *mount* Sinai
Job 9: 5. Which removeth *the mountains*,
14:18. *the mountain* falling cometh to nought,
24: 8. wet with the showers of *the mountains*,
28: 9. he overturneth *the mountains*
39: 8. The range of *the mountains*
40:20. Surely *the mountains* bring him
Ps. 2: 6. set my king upon my holy *hill* of Zion.
3: 4(5). he heard me *out of* his holy *hill*.
11: 1. Flee (as) a bird to *your mountain?*
15: 1. who shall dwell *in* thy holy *hill?*
18: 7(8). the foundations also of *the hills*
24. 3. Who shall ascend *into the hill of*
42: 6(7). *from the hill* Mizar.
43: 3. bring me unto thy holy *hill*,
46: 2(3). though *the mountains* be carried
3(4). *the mountains* shake
48: 1(2). *the mountain of* his holiness.
2(3). the joy of the whole earth, (is) *mount* Zion,
11(12). Let *mount* Zion rejoice,
50:11. I know all the fowls of *the mountains:*
65: 6(7). his strength setteth fast *the mountains*·
68:15(16). *The hill of* God (is as) *the hill of* Bashan; *an* high *hill* (as) *the hill of* Bashan.
16(17). Why leap ye, *ye* high *hills?* (this is) *the hill* (which) God desireth

Ps. 72: 3. *The mountains* shall bring peace
16. upon the top of *the mountains ;*
74: 2. this *mount* Zion, wherein thou hast dwelt.
75: 6(7). *promotion* (cometh) neither...nor from the south.
78:54. (even to) this *mountain*,
68. *the mount* Zion which he loved.
80:10(11). *The hills* were covered
83:14(15). setteth *the mountains* on fire;
90: 2. Before *the mountains* were
95: 4. the strength of *the hills* (is) his also.
97: 5. *The hills* melted like wax
98: 8. let *the hills* be joyful together
99: 9. worship *at* his holy *hill ;*
104: 6. the waters stood above *the mountains.*
8. They go up by *the mountains ;*
10. run among *the hills.*
13. He watereth *the hills*
18. *The* high *hills* (are) a refuge for
32. he toucheth *the hills*, and they smoke.
114: 4. *The mountains* skipped like rams,
6. *Ye mountains*, (that) ye skipped
121: 1. I will lift up mine eyes unto *the hills*,
125: 1. that trust in the Lord (shall be) *as mount* Zion,
2. *the mountains* (are) round about
144: 5. touch *the mountains*,
147: 8. grass to grow upon *the mountains.*
148: 9. *Mountains*, and all hills;
Pro. 8:25. Before *the mountains* were
27:25. herbs of *the mountains* are gathered.
Cant. 2: 8. cometh leaping upon *the mountains*,
17. upon *the mountains of* Bether.
4: 1. that appear *from mount* Gilead.
6. I will get me to *the mountain*
8:14. upon *the mountains of* spices.
Isa. 2: 2. *the mountain of* the Lord's house
— in the top of *the mountains*,
3. let us go up to *the mountain of* the Lord,
14. upon all *the* high *mountains*,
4: 5. upon every dwelling place of *mount* Zion,
5:25. *the hills* did tremble,
7:25. all *hills* that shall be digged
8:18. which dwelleth *in mount* Zion.
10:12. his whole work *upon mount* Zion
32. *the mount of* the daughter of Zion,
11: 9. nor destroy in all my holy *mountain :*
13: 2. a banner upon *the* high *mountain*,
4. noise of a multitude *in the mountains*,
14:13. I will sit also *upon the mount of*
25. and upon *my mountains*
16: 1. unto *the mount of* the daughter of
17:13. be chased as the chaff of *the mountains*
18: 3. an ensign on *the mountains ;*
6. unto the fowls of *the mountains*,
7. the name of the Lord of hosts, *the mount* Zion.
22: 5. crying to *the mountains.*
24:23. the Lord of hosts shall reign *in mount* Zion,
25: 6. *in* this *mountain* shall the Lord
7. he will destroy *in* this *mountain*
10. For *in* this *mountain* shall the
27:13. *in the* holy *mount* at Jerusalem.
28:21. rise up *as* (in) *mount* Perazim,
29: 8. that fight against *mount* Zion.
30:17. upon the top of *a mountain*,
25. upon every high *mountain*,
29. to come *into the mountain of* the Lord,
31: 4. come down to fight for *mount* Zion,
34: 3. *the mountains* shall be melted
37:24. come up to the height of *the mountains*,
32. that escape *out of mount* Zion:
40: 4. every *mountain* and hill shall be
9. get thee up into the high *mountain ;*
12. weighed *the mountains* in scales,
41:15. thou shalt thresh *the mountains*,
42:11. shout from the top of *the mountains.*
15. I will make waste *mountains* and hills,
44:23. break forth into singing, *ye mountains*,
49:11. I will make all *my mountains*
13. break forth into singing, *O mountains :*
52: 7. How beautiful upon *the mountains*
54:10. For *the mountains* shall depart,
55:12. *the mountains* and the hills
56: 7. them will I bring to my holy *mountain*,
57: 7. Upon *a* lofty and high *mountain*

Isa. 57:13. shall inherit my holy *mountain ;*
64: 1(63:19). that *the mountains* might flow
3(2). *the mountains* flowed down
65: 7. burned incense upon *the mountains*,
9. an inheritor of *my mountains :*
11. that forget my holy *mountain*,
25. nor destroy in all my holy *mountain*.
66:20. to my holy *mountain* Jerusalem,
Jer. 3: 6. gone up upon every high *mountain*
23. the multitude of *mountains :*
4:15. publisheth affliction *from mount* Ephraim.
24. I beheld *the mountains*,
9:10(9). For *the mountains* will I take
13:16. feet stumble upon *the* dark *mountains*,
16:16. hunt them from every *mountain*,
17:26. and from *the mountains*,
26:18. *and the mountain of* the house
31: 5. plant vines *upon the mountains of*
6. the watchmen *upon the mount* Ephraim
23. *mountain of* holiness.
32:44 & 33:13. in the cities of *the mountains*,
46:18. Tabor (is) *among the mountains*,
50: 6. turned them away (on) *the mountains :* they have gone *from mountain* to hill,
19. satisfied *upon mount* Ephraim and Gilead.
51:25. *O* destroying *mountain*,
— will make thee *a* burnt *mountain.*
Lam. 4:19. they pursued us upon *the mountains*,
5:18. Because of *the mountain of* Zion,
Eze. 6: 2. *the mountains of* Israel,
3. *Ye mountains of* Israel,
— *to the mountains*, and to the hills,
13. in all the tops of *the mountains*,
7: 7. the sounding again of *the mountains.*
16. shall be on *the mountains*
11:23. stood upon *the mountain*
17:22. will plant (it) upon *an* high *mountain*
23. *In the mountain of* the height
18: 6, 15. hath not eaten upon *the mountains*,
11. even hath eaten upon *the mountains*,
19: 9. no more be heard upon *the mountains of* Israel.
20:40. For *in* mine holy *mountain*, *in the mountain of* the height of Israel,
22: 9. in thee they eat upon *the mountains :*
28:14. thou wast *upon the* holy *mountain* of God;
16. as profane *out of the mountain of* God:
31:12. upon *the mountains*
32: 5. I will lay thy flesh upon *the mountains*,
6. (even) to *the mountains ;*
33:28. *the mountains of* Israel shall be
34: 6. wandered through all *the mountains*,
13. feed them upon *the mountains of*
14. *and upon the* high *mountains of*
— shall they feed upon *the mountains of*
35: 2. set thy face against *mount* Seir,
3. Behold, *O mount* Seir,
7. Thus will I make *mount* Seir
8. I will fill *his mountains*
12. against *the mountains of* Israel,
15. thou shalt be desolate, *O mount* Seir,
36: 1. prophesy unto *the mountains of* Israel, and say, *Ye mountains of* Israel,
4. Therefore, *ye mountains of* Israel,
— Thus saith the Lord God *to the mountains*,
6. say *unto the mountains*,
8. But ye, *O mountains of* Israel,
37:22. the land *upon the mountains of*
38: 8. against *the mountains of*
20. *the mountains* shall be thrown
21. throughout all *my mountains*,
39: 2. will bring thee upon *the mountains of*
4. Thou shalt fall upon *the mountains of*
17. sacrifice upon *the mountains of*
40: 2. set me upon *a* very high *mountain*,
43:12. Upon the top of *the mountain*
Dan 9:16. thy holy *mountain :*
20. for *the* holy *mountain* of my God;
11:45. *in the* glorious holy *mountain ;*
Hos. 4:13. sacrifice upon the tops of *the mountains*,
10: 8. they shall say *to the mountains*,
Joel 2: 1. sound an alarm *in* my holy *mountain :*
2. as the morning spread upon *the mountains :*
5. chariots on the tops of *mountains*
32(3:5). *in mount* Zion and in Jerusalem
3:17(4:17). in Zion, my holy *mountain :*

Joel. 3:18(4:18). *the mountains* shall drop down
Am. 3: 9. Assemble yourselves upon *the mountains of* Samaria,
4: 1. *in the mountain of* Samaria,
13. he that formeth *the mountains*,
6: 1. trust *in the mountain of* Samaria,
9:13. and *the mountains* shall drop
Obad. 8. *out of the mount of* Esau ?
9. every one *of the mount of* Esau
16. have drunk upon my holy *mountain*,
17. *But upon mount* Zion shall be
19. shall possess *the mount of* Esau ;
21. And saviours shall come up *on mount* Zion to judge *the mount of* Esau ;
Jon. 2: 6(7). I went down to the bottoms of *the mountains* ;
Mic. 1: 4. *the mountains* shall be
3:12. *and the mountain of* the house
4: 1. *the mountain of* the house of the Lord shall be established in the top of *the mountains*,
2. let us go up to *the mountain of* the Lord,
7. the Lord shall reign over them *in mount* Zion
6: 1. contend thou before *the mountains*,
2. Hear ye, *O mountains*,
7:12. *and* (from) *mountain to mountain.*
Nah. 1: 5. *The mountains* quake at him,
15(2:1). Behold upon *the mountains*
3:18. thy people is scattered upon *the mountains*,
Hab. 3: 3. the Holy One *from mount* Paran.
10. *The mountains* saw thee,
Zep. 3:11. *because of* my holy *mountain.* (marg. *in*, &c.)
Hag. 1: 8. Go up to *the mountain*,
11. and upon *the mountains*,
Zec. 4: 7. *O* great *mountain ?*
6: 1. out from between two *mountains ; and the mountains* (were) *mountains of* brass.
8: 3. *and the mountain of* the Lord of hosts *the* holy *mountain.*
14: 4. upon *the mount of* Olives,
— *the mount of* Olives shall cleave
— half of *the mountain* shall remove
5. flee (to) the valley of *the mountains ;* (marg. *my mountains*) for the valley of *the mountains*
Mal. 1: 3. and laid *his mountains*

NOTE.—הָרִים in Ps. 75:6(7) may be Infinitive Hiphil of רוּם, as it is taken in the English version ; otherwise the literal rendering of the end of the verse would be " nor from the desert of *the mountains.*"

2025 הַרְאֵל *har-ēhl'*, m.

Eze.43:15. *So the altar* (shall be) four cubits ;

2026 הָרַג *hāh-rag'.*

* KAL.—*Preterite.* *

Gen. 4:23. *I have slain* a man to my wounding, (marg. or, *I would slay*)
25. Abel, *whom* Cain *slew.* (lit. for Cain *slew him*)
12:12. *and they will kill* me, but they will
20:11. *and they will slay me* for my wife's sake.
34:26. *they slew* Hamor and Shechem
49: 6. in their anger *they slew* a man,
Ex. 2:14. as *thou killedst* the Egyptian ?
22:24(23). *and I will kill* you with the sword ;
Lev. 20:16. *And* if a woman...*thou shalt kill* the woman,
Nu. 22:29. for now *would I kill thee.*
33. now also *I had slain* thee,
31: 8. *they slew* the kings of Midian,
— *they slew* with the sword.
Jos. 9:26. that *they slew them* not.
10:11. whom the children of Israel *slew*
13:22. *did* the children of Israel *slay*
Jud. 7:25. *they slew* at the winepress
8:18. whom *ye slew* at Tabor ?
19. *I would* not *slay* you.
Jud. 9:24. which *slew* them ;
45. *slew* the people
54. A woman *slew him.*
16: 2. *when* it is day, *we shall kill him.*
1Sa. 16: 2. if Saul hear (it), *he will kill me.*
22:21. Saul *had slain* the Lord's priests.
24:11(12). and *killed thee* not, know thou
18(19). *thou killedst me* not.
2Sa. 3:30. Joab and Abishai his brother *slew* Abner,
4:11. when wicked men *have slain* a righteous
12: 9. *hast slain* him with the sword
14: 7. the life of his brother whom *he slew ;*
1K. 9:16. *and slain* the Canaanites
12:27. *and they shall kill me*, and go again
18:12. *and* (so) when I come...*he shall slay me :*
14. Elijah (is here): *and he shall slay me.*
19: 1. how *he had slain* all the prophets
10, 14. and *slain* thy prophets
2K. 11:18. *slew* Mattan the priest of Baal
1Ch. 7:21. *whom* the men of Gath...*slew*,
2Ch 21:13. also *hast slain* thy brethren
22: 1. *had slain* all the eldest.
23:17. *slew* Mattan the priest of Baal
Neh. 4:11(5). *and slay them*, and cause
9:26. and *slew* thy prophets
Est. 9: 6. the Jews *slew* and destroyed five hundred
10. the enemy of the Jews, *slew they ;*
12. The Jews *have slain* and destroyed
Ps. 78:34. When *he slew them*,
135:10. *and slew* mighty kings ;
Isa. 14:20. destroyed thy land, (and) *slain* thy people :
27: 1. *and he shall slay* the dragon
Lam. 2:21. *thou hast slain* (them) in the day
3:43. *thou hast slain*, thou hast not
Eze. 23:10. *and slew* her with the sword:
Hos. 6: 5. *I have slain them* by the words of my mouth:
Am. 4:10. your young men *have I slain*
9: 4. *and it shall slay them :*

KAL.—*Infinitive.*

Gen27:42. (purposing) *to kill thee.*
Ex. 2:14. intendest thou *to kill me*,
15. he sought *to slay* Moses.
5:21. to put a sword in their hand *to slay us.*
21:14. *to slay him* with guile ;
32:12. *to slay* them in the mountains,
Nu. 11:15. kill me, I pray thee, *out of hand*, (lit. kill me—*in killing*)
Deu 13: 9(10). But thou shalt *surely* kill him ;
Jos. 8:24. when Israel had made an end *of slaying*
Jud. 9:24. aided him *in the killing* of his brethren. (marg. strengthened his hands *to kill*)
56. *in slaying* his seventy brethren:
20: 5. thought *to have slain* me:
1Sa. 24:10(11). and (some) bade (me) *kill thee :*
1K. 11:24. *when* David *slew* them
18:13. *when* Jezebel *slew* the prophets
Neh 6:10. they will come *to slay thee ;* yea, in the night will they come *to slay thee.*
Est. 3:13. *to kill*, and to cause to perish,
7: 4. to be destroyed, *to be slain*,
8:11. *to slay*, and to cause to perish,
9:16. *and slew* of their foes
Ecc. 3: 3. A time *to kill*, and a time to heal ;
Isa. 22:13. *slaying* oxen, and killing sheep,
Jer. 15: 3. the sword *to slay*,
Hab 1:17. *to slay* the nations ?

KAL.—*Imperative.*

Ex. 32:27. *and slay* every man his brother,
Nu. 11:15. *kill me*, I pray thee, out of hand,
25: 5. *Slay ye* every one his men
31:17. *kill* every male among the little ones, and *kill* every woman
Jud. 8:20. Up, (and) *slay them.*

KAL.—*Future.*

Gen. 4: 8. against Abel his brother, *and slew him.*
14. every one that findeth me *shall slay me.*
20: 4. *wilt thou slay* also a righteous nation ?
26: 7. the men of the place *should kill me*
27:41. *then will I slay* my brother
34:25. *and slew* all the males.
37:20. *and let us slay him*, and cast him
26. What profit (is it) if *we slay* our
Ex. 13:15. *that* the Lord *slew* all the firstborn
23: 7. righteous *slay thou* not:

Lev.20:15. *ye shall slay* the beast.
Nu.31: 7. *and they slew* all the males.
Deu13: 9(10). *thou shalt* surely *kill him;*
Jud. 7:25. *and they slew* Oreb
8:17. *and slew* the men of the city.
21. *and slew* Zebah and Zalmunna,
9: 5. *and slew* his brethren
18. *and have slain* his sons,
2Sa. 4:10. *and slew him* in Ziklag,
12. *and they slew them*, and cut off
10:18. *and* David *slew* (the men of)
23:21. *and slew him* with his own
1K. 2: 5. *whom he slew*, and shed
32. *and slew them* with the sword,
2K. 8:12. their young men *wilt thou slay*
10: 9. against my master, *and slew him:*
1Ch 11:23. *and slew him* with his own
19:18. *and* David *slew* of the Syrians
2Ch 21: 4. *and slew* all his brethren
22: 8. that ministered to Ahaziah, *he slew them.*
24:22. *but slew* his son.
25. *and slew him* on his bed,
25: 3. *that he slew* his servants
28: 6. *For* Pekah...*slew* in Judah
7. *And* Zichri,...*slew* Maaseiah the king's son,
9. *and ye have slain* them in a rage
36:17. *who slew* their young men
Est. 9:15. *and slew* three hundred men
Job 5: 2. wrath *killeth* the foolish man,
20:16. the viper's tongue *shall slay him.*
Ps. 10: 8. *doth he murder* the innocent:
59:11(12). *Slay them* not, lest my people
78:31. *and slew* the fattest of them,
47. *He destroyed* their vines (marg. *killed*)
94: 6. *They slay* the widow and the stranger,
136:18. *And slew* famous kings:
Pro. 1:32. of the simple *shall slay them,*
Isa. 14:30. *he shall slay* thy remnant.
Lam. 2: 4. *and slew* all (that were) pleasant
Eze. 9: 6. *Slay* utterly old (and) young,
23:47. *they shall slay* their sons
26: 8. *He shall slay* with the sword
11. *he shall slay* thy people by the sword,
Am. 2: 3. *will slay* all the princes thereof
9: 1. *I will slay* the last of them
Zec.11: 5. Whose possessors *slay them,*

KAL.—*Participle.* Poel.

Gen.4:15. whosoever *slayeth* Cain,
Ex. 4:23. I *will slay* thy son,
Nu. 31:19. whosoever *hath killed* any person,
2K. 9:31. *who slew* his master?
17:25. which *slew* (some) of them. (lit. were *slayers*)
Jer. 4:31. my soul is wearied *because of murderers.*
Eze.21:11(16). to give it into the hand of *the slayer.*
28: 9. before him *that slayeth thee,*
Hos. 9.13. bring forth his children to *the murderer.*

KAL.—*Participle.* Paül.

Est. 9:11. the number of *those that were slain*
Pro. 7:26. strong (men) *have been slain by her.*
Isa. 10: 4. they shall fall under *the slain.*
14:19. the raiment of those *that are slain,*
26:21. shall no more cover *her slain.*
27: 7. them *that are slain by him?*
Jer.18:21. *be put to* death; (lit. *the slain of* death)
Eze.37: 9. breathe *upon* these *slain,*

* NIPHAL.—*Infinitive.* *

Eze.26:15. *when* the slaughter *is made* (lit. *when* the slaughter *is slaughtered*)

NIPHAL.—*Future.*

Lam.2:20. *shall* the priest and the prophet *be slain*
Eze.26: 6. *shall be slain* by the sword;

* PUAL.—*Preterite.* *

Ps. 44:22(23). for thy sake *are we killed*
Isa. 27: 7. *is he slain* according to the slaughter

2027 ## הֶרֶג *heh'-reg*, m.

Est. 9: 5. *and slaughter*, and destruction,
Pro.24:11. ready *to be slain;*
Isa 27: 7. slain *according to the slaughter*
30:25. in the day of *the* great *slaughter,*
Eze.26:15. when *the slaughter* is made

הֲרֵגָה *hărēh-gāh'*, f. 2028

Jer. 7:32. but the valley of *slaughter:*
12: 3. prepare them for the day of *slaughter.*
19: 6. The valley of *slaughter.*
Zec.11: 4. Feed the flock of *the slaughter;*
7. I will feed the flock of *slaughter,*

הָרָה *hāh-rāh'*. 2029

* KAL.—*Preterite.* *

Gen16:4, 5. when she saw that *she had conceived,*
Nu.11:12. *Have I conceived* all this people?
Jud.13: 3. *but thou shalt* conceive, and bear a son.
Ps. 7:14(15). *and hath conceived* mischief,
Isa. 26:18. *We have been with child,*

KAL.—*Infinitive.*

Job 15:35. *They conceive* (lit. *to conceive*) mischief
Isa. 59: 4. *they conceive* mischief, and bring forth

KAL.—*Future.*

Gen 4: 1. *and she conceived*, and bare Cain,
17. *and she conceived*, and bare Enoch:
16: 4. went in unto Hagar, *and she conceived:*
19:36. *Thus were* both the daughters of Lot *with child*
21: 2. *For* Sarah *conceived*, and bare
25:21. *and* Rebekah his wife *conceived.*
29:32. *And* Leah *conceived*, and bare a son,
33, 34, 35. *And she conceived* again,
30: 5. *And* Bilhah *conceived*, and bare
7. *And* Bilhah Rachel's maid *conceived* again,
17. *and she conceived*, and bare Jacob
19. *And* Leah *conceived* again,
23. *And she conceived*, and bare a son;
38: 3. *And she conceived*, and bare a son;
4. *And she conceived* again,
18. *and she conceived* by him.
Ex. 2: 2. *And* the woman *conceived,*
1Sa. 1:20. *after* Hannah *had conceived,*
2:21. *so that she conceived*, and bare
2Sa.11: 5. *And* the woman *conceived,*
2K. 4:17. *And* the woman *conceived,*
1Ch 4:17. *and she bare* Miriam,
7:23. *And* when he went...*she conceived*, and bare a son,
Isa. 8: 3. *and she conceived*, and bare a son.
33:11. *Ye shall conceive* chaff,
Hos. 1: 3. *which conceived*, and bare him a son.
6. *And she conceived* again,
8. *Now* when she had weaned...*she conceived,*

KAL.—*Participle.* Poel.

Gen49:26. the blessings of *my progenitors*
Cant.3: 4. into the chamber of *her that conceived me.*
Hos. 2: 5(7). *she that conceived them* hath done

* PUAL.—*Preterite.* *

Job 3: 3. *There is* a man child *conceived.*

* POEL.—*Infinitive.* *

Isa. 59:13. *conceiving* and uttering from the heart

הָרָה *hāh-rāh'*, adj. fem. 2030

Gen16:11. Behold, thou (art) *with child,*
38:24. *she* (is) *with child* by whoredom.
25. (am) I *with child:*
Ex. 21:22. hurt a woman *with child,*
Jud.13: 5, 7. thou *shalt conceive*, and bear
1Sa. 4:19. *was with child*, (near) to be delivered:
2Sa.11: 5. told David, and said, I (am) *with child.*
2K. 8:12. *and* rip up *their women with child.*
15:16. all *the women therein that were with child*
Isa. 7:14. a virgin *shall conceive*, and bear a son,
26:17. Like as *a woman with child,*
Jer.20:17. her womb (to be) always *great*
31: 8. the lame, *the woman with child*
Am. 1:13. ripped up *the women with child of* (marg. or, divided *the mountains*)

הַרְהֹר [*har-hōhr'*], Ch. m. 2031

Dan 4: 5(2). *and the thoughts* upon my bed

2032 **הֵרוֹן** [*hēh-rōhn'*], m.

Gen 3:16. thy sorrow *and thy conception;*

2030 **הָרִיָּה** [*hāh-reey-yāh'*], adj. f.

Hos.13:16(14:1). *and their women with child* shall be ripped up.

2032 **הֵרָיוֹן** *hēh-rāh-yōhn'*, m.

Ru. 4:13. the Lord gave her *conception,*
Hos. 9:11. from the womb, *and from the conception.*

2034 **הֲרִיסָה** [*hăree-sāh'*], f.

Am. 9:11. *and* I will raise up *his ruins,*

2035 **הֲרִיסוּת** [*hăree-sooth'*], f.

Isa. 49:19. the land of *thy destruction,*

2038 **הַרְמוֹן** [*har-mōhn'*], m.

Am. 4: 3. ye shall cast (them) *into the palace,*

2040 **הָרַס** *hāh-ras'*.

* KAL.—*Preterite.* *

Jud. 6:25. *and throw down* the altar
1K. 19:10, 14. *thrown down* thine altars,
Isa. 14:17. *destroyed* the cities thereof;
Lam.2: 2. *he hath thrown down* in his wrath
17. *he hath thrown down,* and hath not
Eze.13:14. *So will I break down* the wall
16:39. *and they shall throw down*
26: 4. *and break down* her towers:
12. *and they shall break down* thy walls,
Mic. 5:11(10). *and throw down* all thy strong holds:

KAL.—*Infinitive.*

Jer. 1:10. to destroy, *and to throw down,*
31:28. *and to throw down,* and to destroy,

KAL.—*Imperative.*

2Sa.11:25. against the city, *and overthrow it:*
Ps. 58: 6(7). *Break* their teeth, O God,

KAL.—*Future.*

Ex. 15: 7. *thou hast overthrown* them that rose
19:21. lest *they break through*
24. the people *break through*
2K. 3:25. *they beat down* the cities,
1Ch 20: 1. Joab smote Rabbah, *and destroyed it.*
Job 12:14. Behold, *he breaketh down,*
Ps. 28: 5. *he shall destroy them,* and not build
Pro.14: 1. but the foolish *plucketh it down*
29: 4. receiveth gifts *overthroweth it.*
Isa. 22:19. from thy state *shall he pull thee down.*
Jer. 24: 6. and not *pull* (them) *down;*
42:10. build you, and not *pull* (you) *down,*
Mal. 1: 4. but *I will throw down;*

KAL.—*Participle.* Poel.

Jer. 45: 4. which I have built *will* I *break down,*

KAL.—*Participle.* Paül.

1K. 18:30. the altar of the Lord (that was) *broken down.*

* NIPHAL.—*Preterite.* *

Pro.24:31. the stone wall thereof *was broken down.*
Jer. 50:15. her walls *are thrown down:*
Eze.30: 4. *and* her foundations *shall be broken down.*
38:20. *and* the mountains *shall be thrown down,*
Joel 1:17. the barns *are broken down;*

NIPHAL.—*Future.*

Ps. 11: 3. If the foundations *be destroyed,*
Pro.11:11. but *it is overthrown* by the mouth
Jer. 31:40. nor *thrown down* any more

NIPHAL.—*Participle.*

Eze.36:35. desolate *and ruined* cities
36. that I the Lord build *the ruined* (places),

* PIEL.—*Infinitive.* *

Ex. 23:24. thou shalt *utterly* overthrow them,

PIEL.—*Future.*

Ex. 23:24. *thou shalt* utterly *overthrow them,*

PIEL.—*Participle.*

Isa. 49:17. *thy destroyers* and they that made

הֶרֶס *heh'-res*, m. 2041

Isa. 19:18. The city of *destruction.* (marg. or, *Heres,* or, *the sun*)

הָרָר [*hāh-rāhr'*] & **הֶרֶר** [*heh'-rer*], m. 2042

Gen14: 6. Horites *in their mount* Seir,
Nu. 23: 7. *out of the mountains of* the east,
Deu 8: 9. *and out of whose hills* thou mayest dig
33:15. chief things of *the* ancient *mountains,*
Ps. 30: 7(8). made *my mountain* (marg. *for my mountain*)
36. 6(7). *like the* great *mountains;*
50:10. the cattle *upon* a thousand *hills.*
76: 4(5). *than the mountains of* prey.
87: 1. His foundation (is) *in the* holy *mountains.*
133: 3. descended upon *the mountains of* Zion:
Cant.4: 8. *from the mountains of* the leopards.
Jer. 17: 3. *O my mountain* in the field,
Hab 3: 6. *the* everlasting *mountains*

הַשְׁמָעוּת *hash-māh-ğooth'*, f. 2045

Eze.24:26. *to cause* (thee) *to hear*

הִתּוּךְ *hit-tooch'*. 2046

Eze.22:22. *As* silver *is melted* (lit. *as the melting of* silver)

הָתַל [*hāh-thal'*]. 2048

* PIEL.—*Preterite.* *

Gen31: 7. your father *hath deceived* me,
Jud.16:10, 13, 15. *thou hast mocked* me,

PIEL.—*Infinitive.*

Ex. 8:29(25). let not Pharaoh *deal deceitfully* any more (lit. add *to mock*)
Job 13: 9. *as* one man *mocketh* another,

PIEL.—*Future.*

1K. 18:27. *that* Elijah *mocked* them,
Job 13: 9. *do ye* (so) *mock* him?
Jer. 9: 5(4). *they will deceive* every one his neighbour, (marg. *mock*)

* PUAL.—*Preterite.* *

Isa. 44:20. *a deceived* heart hath turned him

הֲתֻלִּים *hăthool-leem'*, m. pl. 2049

Job 17: 2. (Are there) not *mockers* with me?

הָתַת [*hāh-thath'*]. 2050

* POEL.—*Future.* *

Ps. 62: 3(4). How long *will ye imagine mischief* against a man?

ו vāhv.

The sixth letter of the Alphabet.

2052 **וָהֵב** *vāh-hēhv'.*

Nu. 21:14. What *he did* in the Red sea, (marg. or, *Vaheb* in Suphah)

NOTE.—Perhaps this obscure word is a verb in Kal, preterite, or perhaps it is a proper name.

2053 **וָו** [*vāhv*], m.

Ex. 26:32, 37. *their hooks* (shall be of) gold,
27:10, 11. *the hooks of* the pillars
17. *their hooks* (shall be of) silver,
36:36. *their hooks* (were of) gold;
38. five pillars of it with *their hooks*:
38:10, 11, 12, 17. *the hooks of* the pillars
19. *their hooks* (of) silver,
28. he made *hooks* for the pillars,

2054 **וָזָר** *vāh-zāhr'*, m.

Pro. 21: 8. The way of man (is) froward *and strange*: (lit. The way of a *guilty* man (is) froward. The English Version renders it as זָר with ו copulative prefixed.)

2056 **וָלָד** *vāh-lāhd'*, m.

Gen11:30. she (had) no *child*.

2056 **וֶלֶד** *veh'-led.*

2Sa. 6:23. had no *child* unto the day of her death.

ז zah'-yin.

The seventh letter of the Alphabet.

2061 **זְאֵב** *z'ēhv*, m.

Gen49:27. Benjamin shall ravin (as) *a wolf*:
Isa. 11: 6. *The wolf* also shall dwell with
65:25. *The wolf* and the lamb shall feed
Jer. 5: 6. *a wolf of* the evenings shall
Eze.22:27. *like wolves* ravening the prey,
Hab 1: 8. more fierce *than the* evening *wolves*:
Zep. 3: 3. her judges (are) evening *wolves*;

2063 **זֹאת** *zōhth*, part. pron. f.

Gen 2:23. And Adam said, *This* (is) now bone of my
— because *she* was taken out of Man.
29:27. Fulfil *her* week, and we will give thee *this*
44:17. God forbid that I should do *so*:
Ex. 14:11. wherefore hast thou dealt *thus* with us,
Lev.11: 2. *These* (are) the beasts which ye shall
26:44. And yet for all *that*, when they be in the
Nu. 14:35. I will surely do *it* unto all
1K. 3:23. *The one* saith, This (is) my son
— *and the other* saith, Nay; but thy son
1Ch 11:19. that I should do *this thing*:
2Ch 27: 5. *So much* (marg. *This*) did the children of
Eze.21:26(31). take off the crown: *this* (shall) not (be) *the same*:
&c. &c.

With prefixes, as בְּזֹאת.

Gen34:15. But *in this* will we consent
22. Only *herein* will the men consent
42:15. *Hereby* ye shall be proved:
Lev.16: 3. *Thus* shall Aaron come
26:27. And if ye will not *for all this* hearken
1Sa.11: 2. *On this* (condition) will I make (a covenant)
Isa. 27: 9. *By this* therefore shall the iniquity
Eze.16:29. and yet thou wast not satisfied *herewith*,
&c. &c.

בַּזֹּאת.

1Ch 27.24. because there fell wrath *for it*
2Ch 19: 2. *therefore* (is) wrath upon thee
20:17. shall not (need) to fight *in this* (battle):
Mal. 3:10. and prove me now *herewith*,

הַזֹּאת.

Gen12: 7. Unto thy seed will I give *this* land:
43:15. And the men took *that* present,
Deu 6:25. to do all *these* commandments
13:14(15). (that) *such* abomination is wrought among you;
Jud.19:24. do not *so* vile a thing. (marg. the matter of *this* folly)
&c. &c.

כְּזֹאת.

Gen45:23. to his father he sent *after this* (manner);

כָּזֹאת.

Jud. 8: 8. and spake unto them *likewise*:
13:23. have told us (such things) *as these*.
15: 7. Though ye have done *this*,
19:30. There was no *such deed* done nor seen
&c. &c.

לְזֹאת.

Gen 2:23. *she* shall be called Woman,
Job 37: 1. *At this* also my heart trembleth,

לָזֹאת.

Ex. 7:23. neither did he set his heart *to this* also.
Isa. 30: 7. therefore have I cried *concerning this*, (marg. or, *to her*)
Jer. 5: 7. How shall I pardon thee *for this*?

מִזֹּאת.

2Sa. 6:22. And I will yet be *more* vile *than thus*,

זָבַד [*zāh-vad'*]. 2064

* KAL.—*Preterite.* *

Gen30:20. God *hath endued me* (with) a good dowry;

זֶבֶד *zeh'-ved*, m. 2065

Gen30:20. hath endued me (with) *a* good *dowry*;

זְבוּב *z'voov*, m. 2070

Ecc.10: 1. Dead *flies* cause the ointment of the
Isa. 7:18. shall hiss *for the fly* that (is) in the

זְבֻל & זְבוּל *z'vool*, m. 2073

1K. 8:13. built thee an house *to dwell in*, (lit. house of *habitation*)
2Ch 6: 2. built an house of *habitation*
Ps. 49:14(15). in the grave *from* their *dwelling*.
Isa. 63:15. behold *from the habitation of* thy
Hab 3:11. stood still *in their habitation*:

זָבַח *zāh-vagh'.* 2076

* KAL.—*Preterite.* *

Ex. 8:27(23). *and sacrifice* to the Lord our God,
28(24). *that ye may sacrifice* to the Lord
20:24. *and shalt sacrifice* thereon
34:15. *and do sacrifice* unto their gods,
Lev.17: 5. *and offer* them (for) peace offerings
Deu12:21. *then thou shalt kill* of thy herd
16: 2. *Thou shalt therefore sacrifice* the passover
27: 7. *And thou shalt offer* peace offerings,
1K. 8:63. which *he offered* unto the Lord,
13: 2. *and* upon thee *shall he offer*
Eze.39:19. of my sacrifice which *I have sacrificed* for

KAL.—*Infinitive.*

Ex. 8:29(25). letting the people go *to sacrifice*
Lev. 9: 4. *to sacrifice* before the Lord;
Deu16. 5. Thou mayest not *sacrifice* the passover (marg. or, *kill*)
Jud.16:23. *for to offer* a great sacrifice
1Sa. 1: 3. *and to sacrifice* unto the Lord
21. went up *to offer* unto the Lord
2:19. *to offer* the yearly sacrifice.
10: 8. *to sacrifice* sacrifices of peace offerings:
15:15. to *sacrifice* unto the Lord thy God;
21. *to sacrifice* unto the Lord
16: 2, 5. I am come *to sacrifice*
2Sa.15:12. *while he offered* sacrifices.
1K. 3: 4. the king went to Gibeon *to sacrifice*
2Ch 11:16. *to sacrifice* unto the Lord
Isa. 57: 7. wentest thou up *to offer* sacrifice.
Mal. 1: 8. if ye offer the blind *for sacrifice,* (marg. *to*)

KAL.—*Imperative.*

Ex. 8:25(21). Go ye, *sacrifice* to your God
Ps. 4: 5(6). *Offer* the sacrifices of righteousness,
50:14. *Offer* unto God thanksgiving;

KAL.—*Future.*

Gen31:54. *Then* Jacob *offered* sacrifice (marg. or, *killed* beasts)
46: 1. *and offered* sacrifices unto
Ex. 3:18. *that we may sacrifice* to the Lord
5: 3. *and sacrifice* unto the Lord
8. Let us go (and) *sacrifice* to our God.
17. Let us go (and) *do sacrifice*
8: 8(4). *that they may do sacrifice* unto the
26(22). for *we shall sacrifice* the abomination
—(—). *shall we sacrifice* the abomination
23:18. *Thou shalt* not *offer* the blood
24: 5. *and sacrificed* peace offerings
32: 8. *and have sacrificed* thereunto,
Lev.17: 7. *they shall* no more *offer* their
19: 5. if *ye offer* a sacrifice of peace offerings
— *ye shall offer it* at your own will.
22:29. when *ye will offer* a sacrifice
— *offer* (it) at your own will.
Nu. 22:40. *And* Balak *offered* oxen and sheep,
Deu12:15. *thou mayest kill* and eat flesh
15:21. *thou shalt* not *sacrifice it*
16: 4. which *thou sacrificedst*
6. there *thou shalt sacrifice*
17: 1. *Thou shalt* not *sacrifice*
32:17. *They sacrificed* unto devils,
33:19. there *they shall offer* sacrifices
Jos. 8:31. *and sacrificed* peace offerings.
Jud. 2: 5. *and they sacrificed* there
1Sa. 1: 4. *And* when the time was that Elkanah *offered,*
6:15. *and sacrificed* sacrifices
11:15. *and* there *they sacrificed* sacrifices
28:24. she hasted, *and killed it,*
2Sa. 6:13. it was (so), *that...he sacrificed* oxen and
1K. 1: 9. *And* Adonijah *slew* sheep
19. *And he hath slain* oxen
25. *and hath slain* oxen and fat cattle.
8:63. Solomon *offered* a sacrifice
19:21. took a yoke of oxen, *and slew them,*
2K. 17:35. nor serve them, nor *sacrifice* to them:
36. to him *shall ye do sacrifice.*
23:20. *And he slew* all the priests (marg. or, *sacrificed*)
1Ch 15:26. *that they offered* seven bullocks
21:28. *then he sacrificed* there.
29:21. *And they sacrificed* sacrifices
2Ch 7: 5. *And* king Solomon *offered* a sacrifice
15:11. *And they offered* unto the Lord
18: 2. *And* Ahab *killed* sheep and oxen
28:23. *For he sacrificed* unto the gods
33:16. *and sacrificed* thereon peace offerings
Neh 4: 2(3:34). *will they sacrifice?* will they make
12:43. *Also* that day *they offered* great sacrifices,
Ps. 27: 6. *therefore will I offer* in his tabernacle
54: 6(8). *I will* freely *sacrifice* unto thee:
106:37. *Yea, they sacrificed* their sons
107:22. *And let them sacrifice* the sacrifices
116:17. *I will offer* to thee the sacrifice
Eze.16:20. *and these hast thou sacrificed* unto them
20:28. *and they offered* there
34: 3. *ye kill* them that are fed:
Hos. 8:13. *They sacrifice* flesh (for) the

Jon. 1:16. *and offered* a sacrifice unto the Lord, (marg. *sacrificed*)
2: 9(10). But *I will sacrifice* unto thee

KAL.—*Participle.* Poel.

Ex. 13:15. therefore I *sacrifice* to the Lord
22:20(19). *He that sacrificeth* unto (any) god,
Lev.17: 5. may bring their sacrifices, which they *offer*
Deu 18: 3. from *them that offer* a sacrifice,
1Sa. 2:13. when any man *offered* sacrifice,
15. said to the man *that sacrificed,*
1K. 8:62. *offered* sacrifice before
2Ch 7: 4. the people *offered* sacrifices
33:17. Nevertheless the people *did sacrifice* still
34: 4. *them that had sacrificed* unto them.
Ezr. 4: 2. we *do sacrifice* unto him
Ps. 50:23. *Whoso offereth* praise glorifieth
Ecc. 9: 2. *to him that sacrificeth,* and to him that *sacrificeth* not:
Isa. 65: 3. *that sacrificeth* in gardens,
66: 3. *he that sacrificeth* a lamb,
Eze.39:17. to my sacrifice that I *do sacrifice*
Hos13: 2. Let the men *that sacrifice* kiss (marg. or, *sacrificers of* men)
Zec.14:21. all *they that sacrifice*
Mal. 1:14. *and sacrificeth* unto the Lord

* PIEL.—*Preterite.* *

2Ch 33:22. Amon *sacrificed* unto all the
Ps.106:38. *they sacrificed* unto the idols
Hos.12:11(12). *they sacrifice* bullocks in Gilgal;

PIEL.—*Infinitive.*

1K. 12:32. *sacrificing* unto the calves that he had (marg. or, *to sacrifice*)

PIEL.—*Future.*

2K. 16: 4. *And he sacrificed* and burnt incense
2Ch 28: 4. *He sacrificed also* and burnt incense
23. *will I sacrifice* to them,
Hos. 4:13. *They sacrifice* upon the tops
14. *they sacrifice* with harlots:
11: 2. *they sacrificed* unto Baalim,
Hab 1:16. *they sacrifice* unto their net,

PIEL.—*Participle.*

1K. 3: 2. Only the people *sacrificed* in high places,
3. he *sacrificed* and burnt incense
8: 5. *sacrificing* sheep and oxen,
11: 8. burnt incense *and sacrificed*
22:43(44). the people *offered* and burnt incense
2K. 12: 3(4). the people still *sacrificed*
14: 4. as yet the people *did sacrifice*
15: 4. the people *sacrificed* and burnt incense
35. the people *sacrificed* and burned incense
2Ch 5: 6. *sacrificed* sheep and oxen,
30:22. *offering* peace offerings,

זֶבַח *zeh'-vagh,* m. 2077

Gen31:54. Then Jacob offered *sacrifice* (marg. or, killed *beasts*)
46: 1. to Beer-sheba, and offered *sacrifices*
Ex. 10:25. give us also *sacrifices*
12:27. It (is) *the sacrifice of* the Lord's
18:12. took a burnt offering *and sacrifices*
23:18. shalt not offer the blood of *my sacrifice*
24: 5. sacrificed peace *offerings*
29:28. *of the sacrifice of* their peace offerings,
34:15. thou eat *of his sacrifice;*
25. shalt not offer the blood of *my sacrifice*
— *the sacrifice of* the feast
Lev. 3: 1. if his oblation (be) *a sacrifice of*
3, 9. he shall offer *of the sacrifice of*
6. if his offering *for a sacrifice of*
4:10. *the sacrifice of* peace offerings:
26. as the fat of *the sacrifice of*
31. is taken away from off *the sacrifice of*
35. *from the sacrifice of* the peace offerings;
7:11. this (is) the law of *the sacrifice of*
12. then he shall offer with *the sacrifice of*
13. leavened bread with *the sacrifice of*
15. the flesh of *the sacrifice of* his
16. But if *the sacrifice of* his offering
— the same day that he offereth *his sacrifice*
17. the remainder of the flesh of *the sacrifice*
18. if (any) of the flesh of *the sacrifice of*
20. that eateth (of) the flesh of *the sacrifice of*
21. eat of the flesh of *the sacrifice of*

Lev. 7:29. He that offereth *the sacrifice of*
— *of the sacrifice of* his peace offerings.
32. *of the sacrifices of* your peace offerings.
34. *from off the sacrifices of* their peace offerings,
37. *and of the sacrifice of* the peace offerings;
9:18. the ram (for) *a sacrifice of* peace offerings,
10:14. *out of the sacrifices of* peace offerings
17: 5. bring *their sacrifices*, which they offer
— offer them (for) peace *offerings*
7. they shall no more offer *their sacrifices*
8. that offereth a burnt offering or *sacrifice*,
19: 5. if ye offer *a sacrifice of* peace offerings
6. eaten the same day *ye offer it*, (lit. in the day of *your sacrifice*)
22:21. whosoever offereth *a sacrifice of*
29. when ye will offer *a sacrifice of*
23:19. *for a sacrifice of* peace offerings.
37. a meat offering, *a sacrifice*,
Nu. 6:17. he shall offer the ram (for) *a sacrifice of*
18. the fire which (is) under *the sacrifice of*
7:17, 23, 29, 35, 41, 47, 53, 59, 65, 71, 77, 83. *And for a sacrifice of* peace offerings,
88. all the oxen for *the sacrifice of*
10:10. *the sacrifices of* your peace offerings;
15: 3. a burnt offering, or *a sacrifice*
5. with the burnt offering or *sacrifice*,
8. a burnt offering, or (for) *a sacrifice*
25: 2. they called the people *unto the sacrifices of*
Deu 12: 6, 11. your burnt offerings, *and your sacrifices*,
27. the blood of *thy sacrifices*
18: 3. from them that offer *a sacrifice*,
32:38. did eat the fat of *their sacrifices*,
33:19. there they shall offer *sacrifices of*
Jos. 22:23. or if to offer peace *offerings*
26. not for burnt offering, nor *for sacrifice*:
27. *and with our sacrifices*,
28. not for burnt offerings, nor *for sacrifices*;
29. for meat offerings, *or for sacrifices*,
Jud. 16:23. for to offer *a great sacrifice*
1Sa. 1:21. to offer unto the Lord *the* yearly *sacrifice*,
2:13. when any man offered *sacrifice*,
19. to offer *the* yearly *sacrifice*.
29. Wherefore kick ye *at my sacrifice*
3:14. shall not be purged *with sacrifice*
6:15. and sacrificed *sacrifices*
9:12. for (there is) *a sacrifice of* the people (marg. or, *feast*)
13. because he doth bless *the sacrifice*;
10: 8. to sacrifice *sacrifices of* peace offerings:
11:15. there they sacrificed *sacrifices*
15:22. in burnt offerings *and sacrifices*,
— to obey (is) better *than sacrifice*,
16: 3. call Jesse *to the sacrifice*,
5. come with me *to the sacrifice*.
— and called them *to the sacrifice*.
20: 6. (there is) *a* yearly *sacrifice* (marg. or, *feast*)
29. for our family hath *a sacrifice*
2Sa. 15:12. while he offered *sacrifices*.
1K. 8:62. offered *sacrifice* before the Lord.
63. Solomon offered *a sacrifice of*
12:27. If this people go up to do *sacrifice*
2K. 5:17. neither burnt offering *nor sacrifice*
10:19. I have *a* great *sacrifice* (to do) to Baal;
24. they went in to offer *sacrifices*
16:15. and all the blood of *the sacrifice*:
1Ch 29:21. they sacrificed *sacrifices* unto the Lord,
— their drink offerings, *and sacrifices*
2Ch 7: 1. the burnt offering *and the sacrifices*;
4. all the people offered *sacrifices*
5. king Solomon offered *a sacrifice of*
12. to myself for an house of *sacrifice*.
29:31. bring *sacrifices* and thank offerings
— the congregation brought in *sacrifices*
30:22. seven days, offering peace *offerings*,
33:16. sacrificed thereon peace *offerings*
Neh 12:43. that day they offered great *sacrifices*,
Ps. 4: 5(6). Offer *the sacrifices of* righteousness,
27: 6. offer in his tabernacle *sacrifices of* joy;
40: 6(7). *Sacrifice* and offering thou didst
50: 5. made a covenant with me by *sacrifice*.
8. I will not reprove thee for *thy sacrifices*
51:16(18). For thou desirest not *sacrifice*;
17(19). *The sacrifices of* God (are) a broken spirit.
Ps. 51:19(21). with *the sacrifices of* righteousness,
106:28. ate *the sacrifices of* the dead.
107:22. *the sacrifices of* thanksgiving,
116:17. I will offer to thee *the sacrifice of*
Pro. 7:14. (I have) peace *offerings* with me;
15: 8. *The sacrifice of* the wicked
17: 1. an house full of *sacrifices* (with) strife. (lit. *sacrifices of* strife; marg. *good cheer*)
21: 3. more acceptable to the Lord *than sacrifice*.
27. *The sacrifice of* the wicked
Ecc. 5: 1(4:17). than to give *the sacrifice* of fools:
Isa. 1:11. the multitude of *your sacrifices*
19:21. shall do *sacrifice* and oblation;
34: 6. the Lord hath *a sacrifice* in Bozrah,
43:23. *neither* hast thou honoured me *with thy sacrifices*.
24. filled me with the fat of *thy sacrifices*:
56: 7. *and their sacrifices* (shall be) accepted
57: 7. wentest thou up to offer *sacrifice*.
Jer. 6:20. *nor your sacrifices* sweet unto me.
7:21. Put your burnt offerings unto *your sacrifices*,
22. concerning burnt offerings *or sacrifices*:
17:26. bringing burnt offerings, *and sacrifices*,
33:18. to do *sacrifice* continually.
46:10. the Lord God of hosts hath *a sacrifice*
Eze. 20:28. they offered there *their sacrifices*,
39:17. on every side to *my sacrifice* (marg. or, *slaughter*)
— *a* great *sacrifice* upon the mountains
19. *of my sacrifice* which
40:42. the burnt offering *and the sacrifice*.
44:11. the burnt offering and *the sacrifice*
46:24. shall boil *the sacrifice of* the people.
Dan 9:27. he shall cause *the sacrifice*
Hos 3: 4. and without *a sacrifice*,
4:19. ashamed *because of their sacrifices*.
6: 6. I desired mercy, and not *sacrifice*;
8:13. flesh (for) *the sacrifices of* mine offerings,
9: 4. *their sacrifices* (shall be) unto them
Am. 4: 4. bring *your sacrifices* every morning,
5:25. Have ye offered unto me *sacrifices*
Jon. 1:16. offered *a sacrifice* unto the Lord,
Zep. 1: 7. for the Lord hath prepared *a sacrifice*,
8. in the day of the Lord's *sacrifice*,

זָבַל [*zāh-val'*]. 2082

* KAL.—*Future.* *

Gen 30:20. now *will* my husband *dwell with me*,

זְבַן [*z'van*], Ch. 2084

* P'AL.—*Participle.* *

Dan 2: 8. that ye *would gain* the time, (marg. *buy*)

זָג *zāhg*, m. 2085

Nu. 6: 4. from the kernels even to *the husk*.

זֵד *zēhd*, adj. 2086

Ps. 19:13(14). thy servant also *from presumptuous* (sins);
86:14. *the proud* are risen against me,
119:21. Thou hast rebuked *the proud*
51. *The proud* have had me greatly
69. *The proud* have forged a lie
78. Let *the proud* be ashamed;
85. *The proud* have digged pits
122. let not *the proud* oppress me.
Pro. 21:24. *Proud* (and) haughty scorner
Isa. 13:11. arrogancy of *the proud* to cease,
Jer. 43: 2. all the *proud* men,
Mal 3:15. now we call *the proud* happy;
4: 1(3:19). all *the proud*, yea, and all that do wickedly,

זָדוֹן *zāh-dōhn'*, m. 2087

Deu 17:12. the man that will do *presumptuously*,

Deu 18:22. the prophet hath spoken it *presumptuously:*
1Sa.17:28. I know *thy pride*, and the naughtiness of
Pro.11: 2. (When) *pride* cometh, then cometh shame:
13:10. Only *by pride* cometh contention:
21:24. scorner (is) his name, who dealeth in *proud* wrath. (marg. the wrath of *pride*)
Jer. 49:16. *the pride of* thine heart,
50:31. against thee, (O thou) *most proud*, (marg. *pride*)
32. *the most proud* shall stumble (marg. *pride*)
Eze. 7:10. the rod hath blossomed, *pride* hath budded.
Obad 3. *The pride of* thine heart

2088 **זֶה** *zeh*, part. pron. m.

Gen. 5: 1. *This* (is) the book of the generations
25:22. If (it be) so, why (am) I *thus?*
27:21. whether thou (be) my *very* son Esau
36. he hath supplanted me *these* two times:
32:29(30). Wherefore (is) *it* (that) thou dost ask
Ex. 13: 8. because of *that* (which) the Lord did
14:20. so that *the one* came not near *the other*
15: 2. *he* (is) my God, and I will prepare him
Deu 5:29(26). O that there were *such* an heart in them,
1K. 17:24. Now *by this* I know that thou (art)
2K. 1: 5. Why are ye *now* turned back?
5: 7. that *this man* doth send unto me
Job. 14: 3. dost thou open thine eyes upon *such an one*,
Ps. 68: 8(9). (even) Sinai *itself* (was moved)
104: 8. the place *which* thou hast founded
Ecc. 3:19. as *the one* dieth, so dieth *the other;*
&c. &c.

With prefixes, as בָּזֶה.

1Sa.21: 9(10). for (there is) no other save that *here.*

בָּזֶה.

Gen38:21. There was no harlot *in this* (place).
Ex. 24:14. Tarry ye *here* for us, until
Ecc. 7:18. (It is) good that thou shouldest take hold *of this;*
&c. &c.

הַזֶּה.

Gen 7: 1. righteous before me in *this* generation.
11. *the same* day were all the fountains
24: 9. and sware to him concerning *that* matter.
Lev.23:14. until the *selfsame* day that ye
1Sa.17:17. and *these* ten loaves,
2K. 6: 9. Beware that thou pass not *such* a place;
&c. &c.

כָּזֶה.

Gen41:38. Can we find (such a one) *as this* (is),
&c. &c.

לָזֶה.

1Sa.21:11(12). did they not sing one to another *of him*
25:21. have I kept all that *this* (fellow) *hath*
Ecc. 6: 5. *this hath* more rest than the other.
Isa. 58: 5. wilt thou call *this* a fast,

מִזֶּה.

Gen37:17. They are departed *hence;*
50:25. ye shall carry up my bones *from hence.*
Ex. 13: 3. the Lord brought you out *from this* (place):
25:19. one cherub *on the one* end, and the other cherub *on the other* end:
26:13. *on this side and on that* side, to cover it.
Ps. 75: 8(9). he poureth *out of the same:*
Ecc. 6: 5. this hath more rest *than the other.*
&c. &c.

2090 **זֹה** *zōh*, pron. f.

Jud.18: 4. *Thus and thus* dealeth Micah
2Sa 11:25. devoureth one *as well as another:*
1K. 14: 5. *thus and thus* shalt thou say
2K. 6:19. This (is) not the way, neither (is) *this* the city:
Ps. 132:12. my testimony *that* I shall teach them,
Ecc. 2: 2. of mirth, What doeth *it?*
Ecc. 2:24. *This* also I saw, that it (was) from
5:16(15). *this* also (is) a sore evil,
19(18). *this* (is) the gift of God.
7:23. All *this* have I proved by wisdom:
9:13. *This* wisdom have I seen
Eze.40:45. *This* chamber, whose prospect (is) toward the south,

---

זָהָב *zāh-hāhv'*, m. 2091

Gen 2:11. whole land of Havilah, where (there is) *gold;*
12. *And the gold of* that land
13: 2. in cattle, in silver, *and in gold.*
24:22. the man took a *golden* earring
— ten (shekels) weight of *gold;*
35. flocks, and herds, and silver, *and gold,*
53. jewels of silver, and jewels of *gold,*
41:42. put a *gold* chain about his neck;
44: 8. thy lord's house silver or *gold?*
Ex. 3:22 & 11:2 & 12:35. jewels of silver, and jewels of *gold,*
20:23. neither shall ye make unto you gods of *gold.*
25: 3. *gold*, and silver, and brass,
11, 24. overlay it with pure *gold,*
— make upon it a crown of *gold*
12. thou shalt cast four rings of *gold*
13, 28. overlay them with *gold.*
17. make a mercy seat (of) pure *gold:*
18. make two cherubims (of) *gold,*
24. make thereto a crown of *gold*
25. thou shalt make a *golden* crown
26. make for it four rings of *gold,*
29. (of) pure *gold* shalt thou make them.
31. shalt make a candlestick (of) pure *gold:*
36. it (shall be) one beaten work (of) pure *gold.*
38. snuffdishes thereof, (shall be of) pure *gold.*
39. (Of) a talent of pure *gold* shall he make
26: 6. thou shalt make fifty taches of *gold,*
29. overlay the boards with *gold*, and make their rings (of) *gold*
— overlay the bars with *gold.*
32. pillars of shittim (wood) overlaid with *gold:* their hooks (shall be of) *gold,*
37. overlay them with *gold*, (and) their hooks (shall be of) *gold:*
28: 5. they shall take *gold*, and blue,
6. they shall make the ephod (of) *gold,*
8. *gold*, (of) blue, and purple,
11. make them to be set in ouches of *gold.*
13. thou shalt make ouches (of) *gold;*
14. two chains (of) pure *gold* at the ends;
15. *gold*, (of) blue, and (of) purple,
20. they shall be set in *gold*
22. (of) wreathen work (of) pure *gold.*
23. upon the breastplate two rings of *gold,*
24. put the two wreathen (chains) of *gold*
26. thou shalt make two rings of *gold,*
27. And two (other) rings of *gold*
33. bells of *gold* between them
34, 34. A *golden* bell and a pomegranate,
36. thou shalt make a plate (of) pure *gold,*
30: 3. thou shalt overlay it with pure *gold,*
— make unto it a crown of *gold*
4. two *golden* rings shalt thou make
5. overlay them with *gold.*
31: 4. to work *in gold*, and in silver,
32: 2. Break off the *golden* earrings,
3. brake off the *golden* earrings
24. Whosoever hath any *gold,*
31. have made them gods of *gold.*
35: 5. an offering of the Lord; *gold*, and silver,
22. rings, and tablets, all jewels of *gold:*
— an offering of *gold* unto the Lord.
32. to work *in gold*, and in silver,
36:13. he made fifty taches of *gold,*
34. he overlaid the boards with *gold*, and made their rings (of) *gold*
— overlaid the bars with *gold.*
36. overlaid them with *gold:* their hooks (were of) *gold;*
38. and their fillets with *gold:*
37: 2, 26. he overlaid it with pure *gold*

Ex. 37: 2. made a crown of *gold* to it
3. four rings of *gold*,
4, 15, 28. overlaid them with *gold*.
6, 11, 16, 17, 22, 23, 24. pure *gold*:
7. he made two cherubims (of) *gold*,
11. made thereunto a crown of *gold*
12. made a crown of *gold* for the border
13. he cast for it four rings of *gold*,
26. made unto it a crown of *gold*
27. he made two rings of *gold*
38:24. All *the gold* that was occupied
— even *the gold of* the offering,
39: 2. he made the ephod (of) *gold*,
3. they did beat *the gold* into thin plates,
5, 8. (of) *gold*, blue, and purple,
6, 13. inclosed in ouches of *gold*,
15, 25, 30. (of) pure *gold*.
16. they made two ouches (of) *gold*, and two *gold* rings,
17. put the two wreathen chains of *gold*
19. they made two rings of *gold*,
20. they made two (other) *golden* rings,
38. the *golden* altar, and the anointing oil,
40: 5. thou shalt set the altar of *gold*
26. he put the *golden* altar
Lev. 8: 9. did he put the *golden* plate,
Nu. 4:11. upon the *golden* altar they shall
7:14. One spoon of ten (shekels) of *gold*,
20. One spoon of *gold*
26, 32, 38, 44, 50, 56, 62, 68, 74, 80. One *golden* spoon
84. twelve spoons of *gold*:
86. The *golden* spoons (were) twelve,
— all *the gold of* the spoons
8: 4. the candlestick (was of) beaten *gold*,
22:18 & 24:13. his house full of silver *and gold*,
31:22. Only *the gold*, and the silver,
50. of jewels of *gold*, chains, and bracelets,
51. Eleazar the priest took *the gold*
52. all *the gold of* the offering
54. the priest took *the gold* of the captains
Deu 7:25. thou shalt not desire the silver *or gold*
8:13. *and* thy *gold* is multiplied,
17:17. multiply to himself silver *and gold*.
29:17(16). idols, wood and stone, silver *and gold*,
Jos. 6:19. But all the silver, *and gold*,
24. only the silver, *and the gold*,
7:21. a wedge of *gold* of fifty shekels
24. the garment, and the wedge of *gold*,
22: 8. with silver, *and with gold*,
Jud. 8:24. For they had *golden* earrings,
26. the weight of the *golden* earrings
— a thousand and seven hundred (shekels) of *gold*;
1Sa. 6: 4. Five *golden* emerods, and five *golden* mice,
8. put the jewels of *gold*,
11. the coffer with the mice of *gold*
15. wherein the jewels of *gold* (were),
17. these (are) the *golden* emerods
18. And the *golden* mice,
2Sa. 1:24. who put on ornaments of *gold*
8: 7. David took the shields of *gold*
10. vessels of *gold*, and vessels of brass:
11. the silver *and gold* that he had dedicated
12:30. weight whereof (was) a talent of *gold*
21: 4. We will have no silver *nor gold*
1K. 6:20. and he overlaid it with pure *gold*;
21. overlaid the house within with pure *gold*: and he made a partition by the chains of *gold* before the oracle; and he overlaid it with *gold*.
22, 22. he overlaid with *gold*,
28. he overlaid the cherubims with *gold*.
30. of the house he overlaid with *gold*,
32. overlaid (them) with *gold*, and spread *gold* upon the cherubims,
35. covered (them) with *gold*
7:48. the altar of *gold*, and the table of *gold*,
49. the candlesticks of pure *gold*,
— the tongs (of) *gold*,
50. and the censers (of) pure *gold*, and the hinges (of) *gold*,
51. the silver, and *the gold*, and the vessels,
9:11. cedar trees and fir trees, *and with gold*,
14. Hiram sent to the king sixscore talents of *gold*.
28. fetched from thence *gold*,

1K. 10: 2. spices, *and* very much *gold*,
10. an hundred and twenty talents of *gold*,
11. that brought *gold* from Ophir,
14. the weight of *gold* that came
— six hundred threescore and six talents of *gold*,
16. two hundred targets (of) beaten *gold*: six hundred (shekels) of *gold*
17. three hundred shields (of) beaten *gold*, three pound of *gold* went
18. overlaid it with the best *gold*.
21. Solomon's drinking vessels (were of) *gold*,
— of the forest of Lebanon (were of) pure *gold*;
22. the navy of Tharshish, bringing *gold*,
25. vessels of silver, and vessels of *gold*,
12:28. made two calves (of) *gold*,
14:26. he took away all the shields of *gold*
15:15. silver, *and gold*, and vessels.
18. Asa took all the silver *and the gold*
19. sent unto thee a present of silver *and gold*;
20: 3, 5. Thy silver *and thy gold*
7. for my silver, *and for my gold*;
22:48(49). of Tharshish to go to Ophir *for gold*:
2K. 5: 5. six thousand (pieces) of *gold*,
7: 8. carried thence silver, *and gold*,
10:29. the *golden* calves that (were) in Beth-el,
12:13(14). any vessels of *gold*, or vessels of silver,
18(19). all *the gold* (that was) found
14:14. And he took all *the gold*
16: 8. Ahaz took the silver and *gold* that was
18:14. of silver and thirty talents of *gold*.
20:13. the silver, and *the gold*, and the spices,
23:33. talents of silver, and a talent of *gold*.
35. gave the silver *and the gold*
— he exacted the silver and *the gold*
24:13. cut in pieces all the vessels of *gold*
25:15. such things as (were) of *gold*, (in) *gold*,
1Ch. 18: 7. David took the shields of *gold*
10. all manner of vessels of *gold* and silver
11. *and the gold* that he brought
20: 2. and found it to weigh a talent of *gold*,
21:25. six hundred shekels of *gold*
22:14. an hundred thousand talents of *gold*,
16. *Of the gold*, the silver, and the brass,
28:14. (He gave) *of gold* by weight for (things) *of gold*,
15. the weight for the candlesticks of *gold*, and for their lamps of *gold*,
16. by weight (he gave) *gold*
17. Also pure *gold* for the flesh-hooks,
— and for the *golden* basons (he gave gold)
18. the altar of incense refined *gold* by weight and *gold* for the pattern
29: 2. *the gold for* (things to be made) *of gold*,
3. mine own proper good, of *gold* and silver,
4. three thousand talents of *gold*, *of the gold of* Ophir,
5. *The gold for* (things) *of gold*,
7. of *gold* five thousand talents
2Ch 1:15. the king made silver and *gold* at Jerusalem
2: 7(6). a man cunning to work *in gold*,
14(13). skilful to work *in gold*,
3: 4. he overlaid it within with pure *gold*.
5. which he overlaid with fine *gold*,
6. *and the gold* (was) *gold of* Parvaim.
7. and the doors thereof, with *gold*;
8. he overlaid it with fine *gold*,
9. the nails (was) fifty shekels of *gold*.
— the upper chambers with *gold*.
10. overlaid them with *gold*.
4: 7. he made ten candlesticks of *gold*
8. he made an hundred basons of *gold*.
19. the *golden* altar also,
20. before the oracle, of pure *gold*;
21. the tongs, (made he of) *gold*, (and) that perfect *gold*;
22. spoons, and the censers, (of) pure *gold*:
— house of the temple, (were of) *gold*.
5: 1. the silver, and *the gold*,
8:18. four hundred and fifty talents of *gold*,
9: 1. spices, *and gold* in abundance,
9. an hundred and twenty talents of *gold*,
10. which brought *gold* from Ophir,
13. Now the weight of *gold* that came
— six hundred and threescore and six talents of *gold*;

2Ch. 9:14. brought *gold* and silver
15, 15, 16. beaten *gold:*
16. three hundred (shekels) of *gold*
17. throne of ivory, and overlaid it with pure *gold.*
18. with a footstool *of gold,*
20. vessels of king Solomon (were of) *gold,*
— (were of) pure *gold:* none (were of) silver;
21. bringing *gold,* and silver, ivory,
24. vessels of silver, and vessels of *gold,*
12: 9. he carried away also the shields of *gold*
13: 8. (there are) with you *golden* calves,
11. the candlestick of *gold*
15:18. himself had dedicated, silver, *and gold,*
16: 2. Asa brought out silver *and gold*
3. I have sent thee silver *and gold;*
21: 3. gave them great gifts of silver, *and of gold,*
24:14. and spoons, and vessels of *gold* and silver.
25:24. all *the gold* and the silver,
32:27. made himself treasuries for silver, *and for gold,*
36: 3. an hundred talents of silver and a talent of *gold.*
Ezr. 1: 4. help him with silver, *and with gold,*
6. vessels of silver, *with gold,* with goods,
9. thirty chargers of *gold,*
10. Thirty basons of *gold,*
11. All the vessels *of gold* and of silver
2:69. threescore and one thousand drams of *gold,*
8:25. unto them the silver, and *the gold,*
26. of *gold* an hundred talents;
27. Also twenty basons of *gold,*
— fine copper, precious *as gold.*
28. the silver *and the gold*
30. of the silver, *and the gold,*
33. *and the gold* and the vessels weighed
Neh. 7:70. a thousand drams of *gold,*
71. twenty thousand drams of *gold,*
72. gave (was) twenty thousand drams of *gold,*
Est. 1: 6. the beds (were of) *gold*
7. gave (them) drink in vessels of *gold,*
4:11. shall hold out the *golden* sceptre,
5: 2. held out to Esther the *golden* sceptre
8: 4. held out the *golden* sceptre toward Esther.
15. with a great crown of *gold,*
Job 3:15. Or with princes that had *gold,*
23:10. I shall come forth *as gold.*
28: 1. a place *for gold* (where) they fine
6. it hath dust of *gold.*
17. *The gold* and the crystal cannot equal it:
31:24. If I have made *gold* my hope,
37:22. *Fair weather* cometh out of the north: (marg. *Gold*)
42:11. every one an earring of *gold.*
Ps. 19:10(11). More to be desired (are they) *than gold,*
45:13(14). her clothing (is) of wrought *gold.*
72:15. shall be given *of the gold of* Sheba:
105:37. brought them forth also with silver *and gold:*
115: 4. Their idols (are) silver *and gold,*
119:72. better unto me than thousands of *gold*
127. thy commandments *above gold;*
135:15. The idols of the heathen (are) silver *and gold,*
Pro. 11:22. a jewel of *gold* in a swine's snout,
17: 3. the furnace *for gold:*
20:15. There is *gold,* and a multitude of rubies:
22: 1. loving favour rather than silver *and gold.*
25:11. apples of *gold* in pictures of silver.
12. an earring of *gold,* and an ornament
27:21. and the furnace *for gold;*
Ecc. 2: 8. I gathered me also silver *and gold,*
12: 6. or the *golden* bowl be broken,
Cant. 1:11. We will make thee borders of *gold*
3.10. the bottom thereof (of) *gold,*
5:14. His hands (are as) *gold* rings set with
Isa. 2: 7. Their land also is full of silver *and gold,*
20. and *his* idols of *gold,*
13:17. *and* (as for) *gold,*
30:22. *thy* molten images of *gold:*
31: 7. and *his* idols of *gold,* (marg. the idols of *his gold*)
39: 2. the silver, and *the gold,*
40:19. spreadeth it over *with gold,*
46: 6. They lavish *gold* out of the bag,
Isa. 60: 6. they shall bring *gold*
9. their silver *and their gold*
17. For brass I will bring *gold,*
Jer. 4:30. deckest thee with ornaments of *gold,*
10: 4. They deck it with silver *and with gold,*
9. *and gold* from Uphaz,
51: 7. Babylon (hath been) a *golden* cup
52:19. which (was) of *gold* (in) *gold,*
Lam. 4: 1. How is *the gold* become dim!
Eze. 7:19. *and their gold* shall be removed: their silver *and their gold*
16:13. Thus wast thou decked with *gold*
17. taken thy fair jewels *of my gold*
27:22. with all precious stones, *and gold.*
28: 4. and hast gotten *gold* and silver
13. the carbuncle, *and gold:*
38:13. to carry away silver *and gold,*
Dan 11: 8. vessels of silver *and of gold;*
38. shall he honour *with gold,* and silver,
43. have power over the treasures of *gold*
Hos. 2: 8(10). multiplied her silver *and gold,*
8: 4. their silver *and their gold*
Joel 3: 5(4:5). ye have taken my silver *and my gold,*
Nah. 2: 9(10). take the spoil of *gold:*
Hab. 2:19. it (is) laid over with *gold* and silver,
Zep. 1:18. Neither their silver nor *their gold*
Hag. 2: 8. The silver (is) mine, and *the gold*
Zec. 4: 2. a candlestick all (of) *gold,*
12. which through the two *golden* pipes empty *the golden* (oil) out (marg. *the gold*)
6:11. Then take silver *and gold,* and make crowns,
13: 9. will try them as *gold* is tried:
14:14. shall be gathered together, *gold,* and silver,
Mal. 3: 3. and purge them *as gold* and silver,

זָהַם [*zāh-ham'*]. 2092

* PIEL.—*Preterite.* *

Job 33:20. *So that* his life *abhorreth* bread,

זָהַר [*zāh-har'*]. 2094

* NIPHAL.—*Infinitive.* *

Ecc. 4:13. who will no more *be admonished.*

NIPHAL.—*Imperative.*

Ecc. 12:12. by these, my son, *be admonished:*

NIPHAL.—*Participle.*

Ps. 19:11(12). by them *is* thy servant *warned:*
Eze. 3:21. because *he is warned;*
33: 4. and *taketh* not *warning;*
5. *took* not *warning;*
— he *that taketh warning*
6. the people *be* not *warned;*

* HIPHIL.—*Preterite.* *

Ex. 18:20. *And thou shalt teach* them ordinances
2K. 6:10. of God told him *and warned him of,*
2Ch 19:10. *ye shall even warn* them
Eze. 3:17. *and give* them *warning* from me.
18. *thou givest him* not *warning,*
19. Yet if thou *warn* the wicked,
20. because *thou hast* not *given him warning,*
21. if *thou warn* the righteous (man),
33: 3. he blow the trumpet, *and warn* the people;
7. *and warn* them from me.
9. if *thou warn* the wicked of his way

HIPHIL.—*Infinitive.*

Eze. 3:18. nor speakest *to warn* the wicked
33: 8. if thou dost not speak *to warn* the wicked

HIPHIL.—*Future.*

Dan 12: 3. *they* that be wise *shall shine*

זְהַר [*z'har*], Ch. 2095

* P'AL.—*Participle.* *

Ezr. 4:22. *Take heed now* that ye fail not

זֹהַר *zōh'-har*, m. 2096

Eze. 8: 2. as the appearance of *brightness,*
Dan 12: 3. shine *as the brightness of* the firmament;

2097 **זוֹ** *zōh*, part. pron.

Ps.132:12. my testimony *that* I shall teach them,
Hos. 7:16. *this* (shall be) their derision in the land of Egypt.

2098 **זוּ** *zoo*, part. pron.

Ex. 15:13. the people *which* thou hast redeemed:
16. till the people pass over, *which* thou hast
Ps. 9:15(16). in the net *which* they hid is their own
10: 2. in the devices *that* they have imagined.
12: 7(8). from *this* generation for ever.
17: 9. From the wicked *that* oppress me,
31: 4(5). Pull me out of the net *that* they have
32: 8. and teach thee in the way *which* thou
62:11(12). twice have I heard *this;* that power
68:28(29). strengthen, O God, *that which* thou
142: 3(4). In the way *wherein* I walked
143: 8. to know the way *wherein* I should walk;
Isa. 42:24. he against *whom* we have sinned?
43:21. *This* people have I formed for myself;
Hab 1:11. (imputing) *this* his power unto his god.

2099 **זִו** *ziv*, m.

1K. 6: 1,37. in the month *Zif*,

2100 **זוּב** [*zoov*].

* KAL.—*Future.* *

Lev.15:25. if a woman *have an issue* (lit. *shall run* a running)
— or if *it run* beyond the time
Ps. 78:20. *that* the waters *gushed out*,
105:41. *and* the waters *gushed out;*
Isa. 48:21. *and* the waters *gushed out.*
Lam.4: 9. with hunger: for these *pine away*, (marg. *flow out*)

KAL.—*Participle.* Poel.

Ex. 3: 8, 17 & 13:5 & 33:3. a land *flowing* with milk and honey;
Lev.15: 2. *hath a running issue* out of his flesh, (marg. or, *running of the reins*)
4. whereon he lieth *that hath the issue*,
6. whereon he sat *that hath the issue*
7. the flesh of *him that hath the issue*
8. if he *that hath the issue* spit
9. he rideth upon *that hath the issue*
11. he toucheth *that hath the issue*,
12. he toucheth *which hath the issue*,
13. when *he that hath an issue*
19. if a woman *have an issue*, (lit. be *having*, &c.)
32. This (is) the law of *him that hath an issue*,
33. *and* of *him that hath* an issue, (lit. *and* of *him that runneth* his running)
20:24. a land *that floweth* with milk and honey:
22: 4. or *hath a running issue;*
Nu. 5: 2. every one *that hath an issue*,
13:27. surely it *floweth* with milk and honey;
14: 8. a land *which floweth* with milk
16:13, 14. *that floweth* with milk and honey,
Deu 6: 3 & 11:9 & 26:9, 15 & 27:3 & 31:20. *that floweth* with milk and honey.
Jos. 5: 6. *that floweth* with milk and honey.
2Sa. 3:29. from the house of Joab *one that hath an issue*,
Jer. 11: 5 & 32:22. a land *flowing* with milk and
49: 4. thy *flowing* valley, O backsliding daughter? (marg. or, valley *floweth away*)
Eze.20: 6, 15. *flowing* with milk and honey,

2101 **זוֹב** *zōhv*, m.

Lev.15: 2. (because of) *his issue* he (is) unclean.
3. shall be his uncleanness *in his issue:* whether his flesh run with *his issue*, or his flesh be stopped *from his issue*,
13. hath an issue is cleansed *of his issue;*
15. for him before the Lord *for his issue.*
19. (and) *her issue* in her flesh be blood,
Lev.15:25. if a woman have *an issue of*
— all the days of *the issue of* her
26. whereon she lieth all the days of *her issue*
28. if she be cleansed *of her issue*,
30. for her before the Lord *for the issue of*
33. and of him that hath *an issue*, (lit. that runneth *his running*)

זוּד [*zood*] or **זִיד** [*zeed*]. 2102

* KAL.—*Preterite.* *

Ex. 18:11. the thing wherein *they dealt proudly*
Jer. 50:29. for *she hath been proud*

* HIPHIL.—*Preterite.* *

Neh 9:10. knewest that *they dealt proudly*
16. they and our fathers *dealt proudly*,
29. yet *they dealt proudly*,

HIPHIL.—*Future.*

Gen 25:29. *And* Jacob *sod* pottage:
Ex. 21:14. if a man *come presumptuously*
Deu 1:43. *and* went *presumptuously* up (marg. *ye were presumptuous* and went up)
17:13. and *do* no more *presumptuously.*
18:20. which *shall presume* to speak

זוּד [*zood*], Ch. 2103

* APHEL.—*Infinitive.* *

Dan 5:20. and his mind hardened *in pride*, (marg. or, *to deal proudly*)

זָוִיּוֹת *zāh-veey-yōhth'*, f. pl. 2106

Ps.144:12. our daughters (may be) *as corner stones*,
Zec. 9:15. *as the corners of* the altar.

זוּל [*zool*]. 2107

* KAL.—*Participle.* *

Isa. 46: 6. *They lavish* gold out of the bag,

* HIPHIL.—*Preterite.* *

Lam. 1: 8. all that honoured her *despise her*,

זוּלָה [*zoo-lāh'*], f. 2108

Deu 1:36. *Save* Caleb the son of Jephunneh;
4:12. *only* (ye heard) a voice. (marg. *save* a voice)
Jos. 11:13. burned none of them, *save* Hazor
Ru. 4: 4. none to redeem (it) *beside thee;*
1Sa.21: 9(10). no other *save that* here.
2Sa. 7:22. neither (is there any) God *beside thee*,
1K. 3:18. *save* we two in the house.
12:20. *but* the tribe of Judah only.
2K. 24:14. *save* the poorest sort of the people
1Ch 17:20. neither (is there any) God *beside thee*,
Ps. 18:31(32). or who (is) a rock *save* our God?
Isa. 26:13. lords *beside thee* have had dominion
45: 5. no God *beside me:*
21. no God else *beside me;*
64: 4(3). neither hath the eye seen, O God, *beside thee*,
Hos13: 4. thou shalt know no god *but me:*

זוּן [*zoon*]. 2109

* HOPHAL.—*Participle.* *

Jer. 5: 8. (כתיב) They were (as) *fed* horses

זוּן [*zoon*], Ch. 2110

* ITHP'EL.—*Future.* *

Dan 4:12(9). and all flesh *was fed* of it.

זוֹנָה see **זָנָה** part. poel. See 2181

2111 **זוּעַ** [zooăg].

* KAL.—*Preterite.* *

Est. 5: 9. nor *moved* for him,

KAL.—*Future.*

Ecc.12: 3. *when* the keepers of the house *shall tremble*,

* PILPEL.—*Participle.* *

Hab 2: 7. awake *that shall vex thee*,

2112 **זוּעַ** [zooăg], Ch.

* P'AL.—*Participle.* *

Dan 5:19. and languages, *trembled* and feared (lit. were *trembling*)
6:26(27). men *tremble* and fear before the God

2113 **זְוָעָה** z'vāh-gāh', f.

2Ch 29: 8. (כתיב) delivered them *to trouble*, (marg. *commotion*)
Isa. 28:19. it shall be *a vexation* only
Jer. 15: 4. (כתיב) cause them *to be removed* (marg. *for a removing*)
24: 9 & 29:18. (כתיב) deliver them *to be removed* (marg. *for removing*, or, *vexation*)
34:17. (כתיב) I will make you *to be removed* (marg. *for a removing*)

2115 **זוּר** [zoor].

* KAL.—*Preterite.* *

Isa. 1: 6. *they have* not *been closed*,

KAL.—*Future.*

Jud. 6:38. *and thrust* the fleece *together*,
Job 39:15. forgetteth that the foot *may crush them*,

2114 **זוּר** [zoor].

* KAL.—*Preterite.* *

Job 19:13. *are* verily *estranged* from me.
17. My breath *is strange* to my wife,
Ps. 58: 3(4). The wicked *are estranged* from
78:30. *They were* not *estranged*

KAL.—*Participle.*

Ex. 29:33. *but a stranger* shall not eat
30: 9. Ye shall offer no *strange* incense
33. whosoever putteth (any) of it upon *a stranger*,
Lev.10: 1. offered *strange* fire before the Lord,
22:10. There shall no *stranger* eat
12. daughter also be (married) unto *a stranger*, (marg. a man *a stranger*)
13. but there shall no *stranger*
Nu. 1:51. *and the stranger* that cometh nigh
3: 4. when they offered *strange* fire
10,38. *and the stranger* that cometh
16:40(17:5). that no *stranger*, which (is) not
18: 4. *and a stranger* shall not come
7. *and the stranger* that cometh nigh
26:61. when they offered *strange* fire
Deu 25: 5. shall not marry without unto *a stranger*:
32:16. provoked him to jealousy *with strange* (gods),
1K. 3:18. no *stranger* with us in the house,
2K. 19 24. I have digged and drunk *strange* waters,
Job 15:19. no *stranger* passed among them.
19:15. count me *for a stranger*:
27. mine eyes shall behold, and not *another*; (marg. *a stranger*)
Ps. 44:20(21). stretched out our hands to *a strange*
54: 3(5). For *strangers* are risen up
81: 9(10). There shall no *strange* god be in
109:11. let *the strangers* spoil his labour.
Pro. 2:16. To deliver thee from the *strange* woman,
5: 3. For the lips of a *strange woman*
10. Lest *strangers* be filled with thy
17. be only thine own, and not *strangers'*
20. be ravished *with a strange woman*,
6: 1. hast stricken thy hand *with a stranger*,
7: 5. keep thee from the *strange* woman
11:15. He that is surety for *a stranger*
Pro.14:10. and *a stranger* doth not intermeddle
20:16. garment that is surety (for) *a stranger*:
22:14. The mouth of *strange women*
23:33. Thine eyes shall behold *strange women*,
27: 2. Let *another man* praise thee,
13. garment that is surety for *a stranger*,
Isa. 1: 7. *strangers* devour it in your presence,
— desolate, as overthrown by *strangers*.
17:10. shalt set it with *strange* slips:
25: 2. a palace of *strangers* to be no city;
5. bring down the noise of *strangers*,
28:21. do his work, his *strange* work;
29: 5. the multitude of *thy strangers*
43:12. when (there was) no *strange* (god)
61: 5. *strangers* shall stand and feed
Jer. 2:25. for I have loved *strangers*,
3:13. scattered thy ways *to the strangers*
5:19. so shall ye serve *strangers*
18:14. waters *that come from another place*
30: 8. *strangers* shall no more serve
51: 2. will send unto Babylon *fanners*,
51. *strangers* are come into the
Lam.5: 2. Our inheritance is turned *to strangers*,
Eze. 7:21. into the hands of *the strangers*
11: 9. deliver you into the hands of *strangers*,
16:32. taketh *strangers* instead of her husband!
28: 7. I will bring *strangers* upon thee,
10. uncircumcised by the hand of *strangers*:
30:12. by the hand of *strangers*:
31:12. *strangers*, the terrible of the nations,
Hos. 5: 7. for they have begotten *strange* children:
7: 9. *Strangers* have devoured his strength,
8: 7. *the strangers* shall swallow it up.
12. they were counted as *a strange thing*.
Joel 3:17(4:17). *and* there shall no *strangers* pass
Obad 11. in the day that *the strangers* carried

* NIPHAL.—*Preterite.* *

Isa. 1: 4. *they are gone away* backward. (marg. *alienated*, or, *separated*)
Eze.14: 5. *they are* all *estranged* from me

* HOPHAL.—*Participle.* *

Ps. 69: 8(9). I am become *a stranger*

זוּרֶה zoo-reh', m. 2116

Isa. 59: 5. *and that which is crushed* (marg. *sprinkled*)

זָחַח [zāh-ghagh']. 2118

* NIPHAL.—*Future.* *

Ex. 28:28. the breastplate *be* not *loosed*
39:21. the breastplate *might* not *be loosed*

זָחַל [zāh-ghal']. 2119

* KAL.—*Preterite.* *

Job 32: 6. wherefore *I was afraid*,

KAL.—*Participle.*

Deu 32:24. with the poison of *serpents of* the dust.
Mic. 7:17. move out of their holes *like worms of* (marg. *creeping things*)

זֵידוֹן [zēh-dōhn'], adj. 2121

Ps.124: 5. the *proud* waters had gone over

זִיו [zeev], Ch. 2122

Dan 2:31. This great image, *whose brightness*
4:36(33). mine honour *and brightness* returned
5: 6. Then the king's *countenance* was changed, (marg. *brightnesses*)
9. *and his countenance* was changed (marg. *id.*)
10. nor let *thy countenance* be changed:
7:28. *and my countenance* changed in me:

זִיז zeez, m. 2123

Ps. 50:11. *and the wild beasts of* the field
80:13(14). *and the wild beast of* the field
Isa. 66:11. *with the abundance of* her glory. (marg. or *brightness*)

2131 **זִיקוֹת** *zee-kōhth'*, f. pl.

Isa. 50:11. compass (yourselves) about *with sparks:*
— *and in the sparks* (that) ye have

2132 **זַיִת** *zah'-yith*, m.

Gen 8:11. in her mouth (was) an *olive* leaf
Ex. 23:11. thy vineyard, (and) *with thy oliveyard.* (marg. or, *olive trees*)
27:20. they bring thee pure oil *olive* beaten
30:24. and of oil *olive* an hin:
Lev.24: 2. bring unto thee pure oil *olive*
Deu 6:11. vineyards *and olive trees,*
8: 8. a land of oil *olive*, and honey; (marg. of *olive tree of* oil)
24:20. When thou beatest *thine olive tree,*
28:40. Thou shalt have *olive trees*
— for *thine olive* shall cast (his fruit).
Jos. 24:13. of the vineyards *and oliveyards*
Jud. 9: 8. they said *unto the olive tree,*
9. But *the olive tree* said unto them,
15: 5. with the vineyards (and) *olives.*
1Sa. 8:14. your vineyards, *and your oliveyards*
2Sa. 15:30. by the ascent of (mount) *Olivet,*
2K. 5:26. to receive garments, *and oliveyards,*
18:32. a land of oil *olive* and of honey,
1Ch 27:28. over the *olive trees*
Neh 5:11. *their oliveyards,* and their houses,
8:15. fetch *olive* branches,
9:25. vineyards, *and oliveyards,*
Job 15:33. cast off his flower *as the olive.*
Ps. 52: 8(10). I (am) *like a* green *olive tree*
128: 3. thy children like *olive* plants
Isa. 17: 6 & 24:13. as the shaking of *an olive tree,*
Jer. 11:16. called thy name, *A* green *olive tree,*
Hos.14: 6(7). his beauty shall be *as the olive tree,*
Am. 4: 9. your fig trees *and your olive trees*
Mic. 6:15. thou shalt tread *the olives,*
Hab. 3:17. the labour of *the olive* shall fail,
Hag. 2:19. the pomegranate, and *the olive* tree,
Zec. 4: 3. two *olive trees* by it,
11. What (are) these two *olive trees*
12. What (be these) two *olive* branches
14: 4. in that day upon the mount of *Olives,*
— the mount of *Olives* shall cleave

2134 **זַךְ** *zāhch* & **זַךְ** *zach*, adj.

Ex. 27:20. that they bring thee *pure* oil olive
30:34. spices with *pure* frankincense:
Lev.24: 2. they bring unto thee *pure* oil olive
7. put *pure* frankincense upon (each) row,
Job 8: 6. If thou (wert) *pure* and upright;
11: 4. thou hast said, My doctrine (is) *pure,*
16:17. also my prayer (is) *pure.*
33: 9. I am *clean* without transgression,
Pro.16: 2. ways of a man (are) *clean* in his own eyes;
20:11. whether his work (be) *pure,*
21: 8. *but* (as for) *the pure,* his work (is) right.

2135 **זָכָה** [*zāh-chāh'*].

* KAL.—*Future.* *

Job 15:14. man, that *he should be clean?*
25: 4. or how *can he be clean*
Ps. 51: 4(6). (and) *be clear* when thou judgest.
Mic. 6:11. *Shall I count* (them) *pure* (marg. or, *Shall I be pure*)

* PIEL.—*Preterite.* *

Ps. 73:13. Verily *I have cleansed* my heart (in) vain,
Pro.20: 9. Who can say, *I have made* my heart *clean,*

PIEL.—*Future.*

Ps.119: 9. *shall* a young man *cleanse* his way?

* HITHPAEL.—*Imperative.* *

Isa. 1:16. Wash you, *make you clean;*

2136 **זָכוּ** *zāh-choo'*, Ch. f.

Dan 6:22(23). before him *innocency* was found in me;

זְכוּכִית *z'choo-cheeth'*, f. 2137

Job 28:17. The gold *and the crystal* cannot equal it:

זָכוּר [*zāh-choor'*], m. 2138

Ex. 23:17. all *thy males* shall appear before the Lord
34:23. Thrice in the year shall all *your menchildren*
Deu 16:16. Three times in a year shall all *thy males*
20:13. thou shalt smite every *male thereof*

זָכַךְ [*zāh-chach'*]. 2141

* KAL.—*Preterite.* *

Job 15:15. the heavens *are* not *clean* in his sight.
25: 5. the stars *are* not *pure* in his sight.
Lam.4: 7. Her Nazarites *were purer* than snow,

* HIPHIL.—*Preterite.* *

Job 9:30. *and make* my hands never so *clean;*

זָכַר *zāh-char'*. 2142

* KAL.—*Preterite.* *

Gen 9:15. *And I will remember* my covenant,
40:14. *think on me* when it shall be well (marg. *remember me*)
23. *did* not the chief butler *remember*
Lev.26:42. *Then will I remember* my covenant
45. *But I will* for their sakes *remember*
Nu. 11: 5. *We remember* the fish, which we did eat
15:39. *and remember* all the commandments
Deu 5:15. *And remember* that thou wast a servant
8: 2. *And thou shalt remember* all the way
18. *But thou shalt remember* the Lord
15:15 & 16:12. *And thou shalt remember* that thou
24:18. *But thou shalt remember* that thou
22. *And thou shalt remember* that thou
Jud. 8:34. the children of Israel *remembered* not
9: 2. *remember also* that I (am) your bone
1Sa. 1:11. *and remember me,* and not forget
25:31. *then remember* thine handmaid.
2Ch 24:22. Joash the king *remembered* not the kindness
Neh 9:17. neither *were mindful of* thy wonders
Est. 2: 1. *he remembered* Vashti, and what
Job 21: 6. when *I remember* I am afraid,
Ps. 9:12(13). *he remembereth* them:
63: 6(7). When *I remember thee* upon my bed,
78:42. *They remembered* not his hand,
88: 5(6). whom *thou rememberest* no more: (lit. *rememberest them*)
98: 3. *He hath remembered* his mercy
105: 8. *He hath remembered* his covenant
42. *he remembered* his holy promise,
106: 7. *they remembered* not the multitude
109:16. Because that *he remembered* not
115:12. The Lord *hath been mindful of us:*
119:52. *I remembered* thy judgments
55. *I have remembered* thy name,
136:23. Who *remembered* us in our low estate:
143: 5. *I remember* the days of old;
Ecc. 9:15. yet no man *remembered* that same poor man.
Isa. 17:10. *hast* not *been mindful* of the rock
47: 7. neither *didst remember* the latter end
57:11. *hast* not *remembered* me,
Jer. 2: 2. Thus saith the Lord; *I remember* thee,
44:21. *did* not the Lord *remember* them,
Lam.1: 7. Jerusalem *remembered* in the days
9. *she remembereth* not her last end;
2: 1. *remembered* not his footstool
Eze. 6: 9. *And they* that escape of you *shall remember*
16:22, 43. *thou hast* not *remembered* the days
60. *Nevertheless* I *will remember*
61. *Then thou shalt remember* thy ways,
20:43. *And* there *shall ye remember* your ways,
36:31. *Then shall ye remember* your own
Hos. 7: 2. *I remember* all their wickedness:
Am. 1: 9. *remembered* not the brotherly covenant:
Jon. 2: 7(8). *I remembered* the Lord:

KAL.—*Infinitive.*

Gen 9:16. *that I may remember* the everlasting covenant

Ex. 13: 3. unto the people, *Remember* this day,
20: 8. *Remember* the sabbath day,
Deu 7:18. shalt *well* remember (lit. *remembering* remember)
24: 9. *Remember* what the Lord thy God did
25:17. *Remember* what Amalek did
Jos. 1:13. *Remember* the word which Moses
Ps. 137: 1. *when we remembered* Zion.
Jer. 17: 2. *Whilst* their children *remember*
31:20. I do *earnestly* remember (lit. *remembering* remember)
Lam 3:20. hath (them) *still* in remembrance, (lit. *remembering* remembereth)
Eze. 23:19. in *calling to remembrance* the days

KAL.—*Imperative.*

Ex. 32:13. *Remember* Abraham, Isaac, and Israel,
Deu. 9: 7. *Remember*, (and) forget not,
27. *Remember* thy servants, Abraham,
32. 7. *Remember* the days of old,
Jud. 16:28. *remember me*, I pray thee,
2K. 9:25. for *remember* how that, when I and thou
20: 3. *remember* now how I have walked
1Ch 16:12. *Remember* his marvellous works that
15. *Be ye mindful* always *of* his
2Ch 6:42. *remember* the mercies of David
Neh 1: 8. *Remember*, I beseech thee,
4:14(8). *remember* the Lord, (which is) great
5:19. *Think* upon me, my God,
6:14. My God, *think thou* upon
13:14, 22, 31. *Remember* me, O my God,
29. *Remember* them, O my God,
Job 4: 7. *Remember*, I pray thee,
7: 7. *O remember* that my life (is) wind:
10: 9. *Remember*, I beseech thee,
36:24. *Remember* that thou magnify
41: 8(40:32). *remember* the battle, do no more.
Ps. 25: 6. *Remember*, O Lord, thy tender mercies
7. to thy mercy *remember* thou me
74: 2. *Remember* thy congregation,
18. *Remember* this, (that) the enemy
22. *remember* how the foolish man
89:47(48). *Remember* how short my time is
50(51). *Remember*, Lord, the reproach
105: 5. *Remember* his marvellous
106: 4. *Remember me*, O Lord,
119:49. *Remember* the word unto thy servant,
132: 1. Lord, *remember* David,
137: 7. *Remember*, O Lord, the children of Edom
Ecc. 12: 1. *Remember now* thy Creator
Isa. 38: 3. *Remember* now, O Lord,
44:21. *Remember* these, O Jacob
46: 8. *Remember* this, and shew
9. *Remember* the former things
Jer. 14:21. *remember*, break not thy covenant
15:15. *remember me*, and visit me,
18:20. *Remember* that I stood
51:50. *remember* the Lord afar off,
Lam 3:19. *Remembering* mine affliction (marg. or, *Remember*)
5: 1. *Remember*, O Lord, what is
Mic. 6: 5. *remember* now what Balak
Mal. 4: 4(3:22). *Remember* ye the law of Moses

KAL.—*Future.*

Gen 8: 1. *And* God *remembered* Noah,
19:29. *that* God *remembered* Abraham,
30:22. *And* God *remembered* Rachel,
42: 9. *And* Joseph *remembered* the dreams
Ex. 2:24. *and* God *remembered* his covenant
6: 5. *and I have remembered* my covenant.
Lev. 26:42. my covenant with Abraham *will I remember; and I will remember* the land
Nu. 15:40. That *ye may remember*, and do
Deu 7:18. *shalt* well *remember* what
16: 3. that *thou mayest remember*
1Sa. 1:19. *and* the Lord *remembered her.*
2Sa. 14:11. *let* the king *remember* the Lord
19:19(20). neither *do thou remember*
Job 11:16. *remember* (it) as waters (that) pass away:
14:13. appoint me a set time, *and remember me!*
Ps. 8: 4(5). man, that *thou art mindful of him?*
20: 3(4). *Remember* all thy offerings,
22:27(28). All the ends of the world *shall remember*
25: 7. *Remember* not the sins of my youth,
42: 4(5). When *I remember* these (things),
Ps. 42: 6(7). therefore *will I remember thee*
77: 3(4). *I remembered* God, and was troubled:
6(7). *I call to remembrance* my song
11(12). *I will remember* the works of the Lord:
—(—). *I will remember* thy wonders of old.
78:35. *And they remembered* that God
39. *For he remembered* that they
79: 8. *O remember* not against us
106:45. *And he remembered* for them
111: 5. *he will* ever *be mindful* of his covenant.
137: 6. If *I do* not *remember thee*,
Pro. 31: 7. *remember* his misery no more.
Ecc. 5:20(19). *he shall* not much *remember*
11: 8. *yet let him remember* the days of
Isa. 43:18. *Remember ye* not the former things,
25. and *will* not *remember* thy sins.
54: 4. *shalt* not *remember* the reproach
63:11. *Then he remembered* the days
64: 5(4). *remember thee* in thy ways:
9(8). neither *remember* iniquity
Jer. 3:16. neither *shall they remember* it;
14:10. *he will* now *remember* their iniquity,
20: 9. *I will* not *make mention* of him,
23:36. the burden of the Lord *shall ye mention* no more:
31:20. *I do* earnestly *remember* him still:
34. *and I will remember* their sin no more.
Lam. 3:20. My soul *hath* (them) still *in remembrance*,
Eze. 16:63. That *thou mayest remember*,
23:27. nor *remember* Egypt any more.
Hos. 8:13. now *will he remember* their iniquity,
9: 9. *he will remember* their iniquity,
Nah. 2: 5(6). *He shall recount* his worthies:
Hab. 3: 2. in wrath *remember* mercy.
Zec. 10: 9. *they shall remember me* in far

KAL.—*Participle.* Poel.

Ps. 103:18. *and to those that remember* his commandments

KAL.—*Participle.* Paül.

Ps. 103:14. *he remembereth* that we (are) dust.

* NIPHAL.—*Preterite.* *

Nu. 10: 9. *and ye shall be remembered* before

NIPHAL.—*Infinitive.*

Eze. 21:24(29). that *ye are come to remembrance*,

NIPHAL.—*Future.*

Ex. 34:19. ox or sheep, *that is male.*
Job 24:20. *he shall be* no more *remembered;*
28:18. No *mention shall be made of* coral, (lit. *shall* not *be remembered*)
Ps. 83: 4(5). Israel *may be* no more *in remembrance.*
109:14. iniquity of his fathers *be remembered*
Isa. 23:16. that *thou mayest be remembered.*
65:17. the former *shall* not *be remembered*,
Jer. 11:19. his name *may be* no more *remembered.*
Eze. 3:20. hath done *shall* not *be remembered;*
18:22. *they shall* not *be mentioned* unto him:
24. that he hath done *shall* not *be mentioned:*
21:32(37). *thou shalt be* no (more) *remembered:*
25:10. Ammonites *may* not *be remembered*
33:13. his righteousnesses *shall* not *be remembered*
16. he hath committed *shall be mentioned*
Hos 2:17(19). *they shall* no more *be remembered*
Zec 13: 2. *they shall* no more *be remembered:*

NIPHAL.—*Participle.*

Est. 9:28. these days (should be) *remembered*

* HIPHIL.—*Preterite.* *

Gen 40:14. *and make mention of me* unto Pharaoh,
Isa. 49: 1. *hath he made mention of* my name.

HIPHIL.—*Infinitive.*

1Sa. 4:18. *when he made mention of* the ark
2Sa. 18:18. no son *to keep* my name *in remembrance:*
1K. 17:18. *to call* my sin *to remembrance*,
1Ch 16: 4. *and to record*, and to thank and praise
Ps. 38:[title](1) & 70:[title](1). *to bring to remembrance.*
Eze. 21:24(29). Because *ye have made* your iniquity *to be remembered*,
Am. 6:10. for *we may* not *make mention* (marg. or, *they will* not, or. *have* not)

HIPHIL.—*Imperative.*

Isa. 12: 4. *make mention* that his name is exalted.

Isa. 43:26. *Put me in remembrance:* let us plead
Jer. 4:16. *Make ye mention* to the nations;

HIPHIL.—*Future.*

Ex. 20:24. in all places where *I record* my name
23:13. *make* no *mention of* the name
Jos. 23: 7. neither *make mention of* the name
Ps. 20: 7(8). *we will remember* the name of the Lord
45:17(18). *I will make* thy name *to be remembered*
71:16. *I will make mention of* thy righteousness,
77:11(12). (כתיב) *I will remember* the works of the Lord:
87: 4. *I will make mention of* Rahab
Cant 1: 4. *we will remember* thy love
Isa. 19:17. every one that *maketh mention*
26:13. by thee only *will we make mention of*
48: 1. *make mention of* the God of Israel,
63: 7. *I will mention* the lovingkindnesses

HIPHIL.—*Participle.*

Gen41: 9. I *do remember* my faults this day:
Nu. 5:15. *bringing* iniquity *to remembrance.*
2Sa. 8:16. the son of Ahilud (was) *recorder;* (marg. or, *remembrancer*, or, *writer of chronicles*)
20:24. the son of Ahilud (was) *recorder:* (marg. or, *remembrancer*)
1K. 4: 3. the son of Ahilud, *the recorder.* (marg. *id*)
2K. 18:18, 37. the son of Asaph *the recorder.*
1Ch 18:15. Jehoshaphat the son of Ahilud, *recorder.* (marg. or, *remembrancer*)
2Ch 34: 8. Joah the son of Joahaz *the recorder,*
Isa. 36: 3. Joah, Asaph's son, *the recorder.*
22. Joah, the son of Asaph, *the recorder,*
62: 6. *ye that make mention of* the Lord, (marg. or, *ye that are* the Lord's *remembrancers*)
66: 3. *he that burneth* incense, (marg. *maketh a memorial of*)
Eze. 21:23(28). he *will call to remembrance*
29:16. *which bringeth* (their) iniquity *to remembrance,*

2145 **זָכָר** *zāh-ċhāhr'*, m.

Gen. 1:27 & 5:2. *male* and female created he them.
6:19. they shall be *male* and female.
7: 3, 9. *the male* and the female;
16. went in *male* and female
17:10. Every *man child* among you
12. every *man child* in your generations,
14. the uncircumcised *man child*
23. every *male* among the men
34:15. that every *male* of you be circumcised;
22. if every *male* among us be circumcised,
24. every *male* was circumcised,
25. slew all *the males.*
Ex. 12: 5. *a male* of the first year:
48. let all *his males* be circumcised,
13:12. *the males* (shall be) the Lord's.
15. all that openeth the matrix, *being males;*
Lev. 1: 3. let him offer *a male* without blemish:
10. he shall bring it *a male*
3: 1. whether (it be) *a male* or female,
6. *male* or female, he shall offer it
4:23. goats, *a male* without blemish:
6:18(11). All *the males* among the children
29(22). All *the males* among the priests
7: 6. Every *male* among the priests
12: 2. and born *a man child:*
7. that hath born *a male* or a female.
15:33. *of the man*, and of the woman,
18:22. Thou shalt not lie with *mankind*,
20:13. If a man also lie with *mankind*,
22:19. at your own will *a male*
27: 3. of *the male* from twenty years
5. shall be of *the male* twenty shekels,
6. shall be of *the male* five shekels
7. if (it be) *a male*,
Nu. 1: 2. every *male* by their polls;
20, 22. every *male* from twenty years old
3:15. every *male* from a month old
22. to the number of all *the males*,
28, 34, 39. all *the males*, from a month old
40. Number all the firstborn of *the males*
43. all *the* firstborn *males*
5: 3. *Both male* and female (lit. *from the male* to the female)
Nu. 18:10. every *male* shall eat it:
26:62. all *males* from a month old
31: 7. they slew all *the males.*
17. Now therefore kill every *male*
— hath known man by lying with *him.* (marg. *a male*)
18. not known *a man* by lying *with him*, (lit. the lying of *a male*)
35. not known *man* by lying *with him.* (lit. *id.*)
Deu 4:16. the likeness of *male* or female,
15:19. All the firstling *males* that come
Jos. 5: 4. came out of Egypt, (that were) *males*,
17: 2. these (were) *the male* children
Jud. 21:11. Ye shall utterly destroy every *male*, and every woman that hath lain by *man.*
12. known no man by lying with any *male:*
1K. 11:15. after he had smitten every *male*
16. until he had cut off every *male*
2Ch 31:16. Beside their genealogy *of males*,
19. give portions to all *the males*
Ezr. 8: 3. reckoned by genealogy *of the males*
4, 5, 6, 7, 8, 9, 10, 11, 12. and with him...*males.*
13, 14. with them...*males.*
Isa. 66: 7. she was delivered of *a man child.*
Jer. 20:15. A *man* child is born unto thee;
30: 6. see whether *a man* doth travail (marg. *male*)
Eze. 16:17. madest to thyself images of *men*, (marg. *a male*)
Mal. 1:14. which hath in his flock *a male*,

זֵכֶר *zēh'-ċher*, & **זֶכֶר** *zeh'-ċher*, m. 2143

Ex. 3:15. this (is) *my memorial* unto all generations.
17:14. will utterly put out *the remembrance of*
Deu 25:19. thou shalt blot out *the remembrance of*
32:26. make *the remembrance of them* to cease
Est. 9:28. *nor the memorial of them* perish
Job 18:17. *His remembrance* shall perish
Ps. 6: 5(6). in death (there is) no *remembrance of thee:*
9: 6(7). *their memorial* is perished with them.
30: 4(5). give thanks *at the remembrance of* his (marg. or, *to the memorial*)
34:16(17). to cut off *the remembrance of them*
97:12. give thanks *at the remembrance of* his holiness. (marg. or, *to the memorial*)
102:12(13). *and thy remembrance* unto all generations.
109:15. cut off *the memory of them* from the earth.
111: 4. made his wonderful works to be *remembered:* (lit. *a memorial* for his, &c.)
112: 6. the righteous shall be *in* everlasting *remembrance.*
135:13. *thy memorial*, O Lord,
145: 7. utter *the memory of* thy great goodness,
Pro 10: 7. *The memory of* the just (is) blessed:
Ecc. 9: 5. *the memory of them* is forgotten.
Isa. 26: 8. *and to the remembrance of thee.*
14. made all *their memory* to perish.
Hos 12: 5(6). the Lord (is) *his memorial.*
14: 7(8). *the scent thereof* (shall be) as the wine (marg. or, *memorial*)

זִכָּרוֹן *zik-kāh-rōhn'*, m. 2146

Ex. 12:14. this day shall be unto you *for a memorial*,
13: 9. *and for a memorial* between thine eyes,
17:14. (for) *a memorial* in a book,
28:12. the ephod (for) stones of *memorial*
— upon his two shoulders *for a memorial.*
29. *for a memorial* before the Lord
30:16. that it may be *a memorial*
39: 7. stones for *a memorial* to the children
Lev 23:24. *a memorial of* blowing of trumpets,
Nu. 5:15. an offering of *memorial*,
18. put the offering of *memorial*
10:10. that they may be to you *for a memorial*
16:40(17:5). *a memorial* unto the children of Israel,
31:54. *a memorial* for the children
Jos. 4: 7. these stones shall be *for a memorial*
Neh. 2:20. nor right, *nor memorial*,

Est. 6: 1. he commanded to bring the book of *records*
Job 13:12. *Your remembrances* (are) like unto ashes,
Ecc. 1:11. no *remembrance* of former (things); neither shall there be (any) *remembrance*
2:16. For (there is) no *remembrance* of the wise
Isa. 57: 8. hast thou set up *thy remembrance:*
Zec. 6:14. *for a memorial* in the temple
Mal. 3:16. a book of *remembrance* was written

2149 **זֻלּוּת** *zool-looth'*, f.

Ps. 12: 8(9). when *the vilest* men are exalted.

2150 **זַלְזַלִּים** *zal-zal-leem'*, m. pl.

Isa. 18: 5. he shall both cut off *the sprigs*

2151 **זָלַל** [*zāh-lal'*].

* KAL.—*Participle.* Poel. *

Deu 21:20. *a glutton*, and a drunkard.
Pro. 23:20. *among riotous eaters of* flesh:
21. the drunkard *and the glutton*
28: 7. he that is a companion of *riotous* (men) (marg. or, feedeth *gluttons*)
Jer. 15:19. take forth the precious *from the vile*,
Lam. 1:11. for I am become *vile*.

* NIPHAL.—*Preterite.* *

Isa. 64: 1(63:19). the mountains *might flow down*
3(2). the mountains *flowed down*

2152 **זַלְעָפָה** *zal-gāh-phāh'*, f.

Ps. 11: 6. and an *horrible* tempest: (marg. *burning*)
119:53. *Horror* hath taken hold upon me
Lam. 5:10. because of the *terrible* famine. (marg. or, *terrors*, or, *storms*)

2154 **זִמָּה** *zim-māh'*, f.

Lev. 18:17. her near kinswomen: it (is) *wickedness*.
19:29. the land become full of *wickedness*.
20:14. it (is) *wickedness:*
— there be no *wickedness* among you.
Jud. 20: 6. for they have committed *lewdness*
Job 17:11. *my purposes* are broken off,
31:11. For this (is) *an heinous crime;*
Ps. 26:10. In whose hands (is) *mischief*,
119:150. nigh that follow after *mischief:*
Pro. 10:23. (It is) as sport to a fool to do *mischief:*
21:27. he bringeth it *with a wicked mind?* (marg. *in wickedness*)
24: 9. *The thought of* foolishness (is) sin:
Isa. 32: 7. he deviseth *wicked devices* to destroy
Jer. 13:27. *the lewdness of* thy whoredom,
Eze. 16:27. which are ashamed of thy *lewd* way.
43. thou shalt not commit this *lewdness*
58. Thou hast borne *thy lewdness*
22: 9. in the midst of thee they commit *lewdness*.
11. another hath *lewdly* defiled
23:21. calledst to remembrance *the lewdness of*
27. make *thy lewdness* to cease
29. *both thy lewdness* and thy whoredoms.
35. therefore bear thou also *thy lewdness*
44. Aholah and unto Aholibah, the *lewd*
48. Thus will I cause *lewdness* to cease
— taught not to do *after your lewdness*.
49. they shall recompense *your lewdness*
24:13. In thy filthiness (is) *lewdness:*
Hos. 6: 9. for they commit *lewdness*. (marg. or, *enormity*)

2156 **זְמוֹרָה** *z'mōh-rāh'*, f.

Nu. 13:23. cut down from thence *a branch*
Isa. 17:10. *and* shalt set it with strange *slips*.
Eze. 8:17. they put *the branch* to their nose.
Eze. 15: 2. *a branch* which is among the trees
Nah 2: 2(3). *and* marred *their vine branches*.

זָמִיר *zāh-meer'*, m. 2158

Cant. 2:12. the time of *the singing* (of birds) is come,

זְמִיר *z'meer*, m. 2158-59

2Sa. 23: 1. sweet *psalmist of* Israel, (lit. of *Psalms*)
Job 35:10. who giveth *songs* in the night;
Ps. 95: 2. make a joyful noise unto him *with psalms*.
119:54. Thy statutes have been my *songs*
Isa. 24:16. of the earth have we heard *songs*,
25: 5. *the branch of* the terrible ones

זָמַם *zāh-mam'*. 2161

* KAL.—*Preterite.* *

Deu 19:19. do unto him, as *he had thought*
Ps. 31:13(14). *they devised* to take away my life.
Pro. 30:32. or if *thou hast thought evil,*
31:16. *She considereth* a field,
Jer. 4:28. I have spoken (it), *I have purposed*
51:12. the Lord *hath* both *devised* and done
Lam. 2:17. hath done (that) which *he had devised;*
Zec. 1: 6. the Lord of hosts *thought* to do unto us,
8:14. As *I thought* to punish you,
15. So again *have I thought* in these days

KAL.—*Infinitive.*

Ps. 17: 3. *I am purposed* (that) my mouth (lit. *my purpose*)

KAL.—*Future.*

Gen 11: 6. which *they have imagined* to do.

KAL.—*Participle.* Poel.

Ps. 37:12. The wicked *plotteth* against the just, (marg. or, *practiseth*)

זָמָם [*zāh-māhm'*], m. 2162

Ps. 140: 8(9). further not *his wicked device;*

זָמַן [*zāh-man'*]. 2163

* PUAL.—*Participle.* *

Ezr. 10:14. come at *appointed* times,
Neh 10:34(35). at times *appointed*
13:31. the wood offering, at times *appointed*,

זְמַן [*z'man*], Ch. 2164

* ITHPAEL.—*Preterite.* *

Dan 2: 9. *ye have prepared* lying and corrupt words [Note, כתיב Aphel].

זְמָן *z'māhn*, m. 2165

Neh 2: 6. and I set him *a time*.
Est. 9:27. *and according to their* (appointed) *time*
31. Purim *in their times* (appointed),
Ecc. 3: 1. To every (thing there is) *a season*,

זְמָן *z'māhn*, Ch. 2166

Ezr. 5: 3. At the same *time* came
Dan 2:16. that he would give him *time*,
21. he changeth the times *and the seasons:*
3: 7. Therefore at that *time*, when all the people
8. Wherefore at that *time* certain Chaldeans
4:36(33). At the same *time* my reason
6:10(11). kneeled upon his knees three *times* a
13(14). *but* maketh his petition three *times* a
7:12. their lives were prolonged for *a season*
22. *and the time* came that the saints
25. and think to change *times* and laws,

2167-68 ## זָמַר [*zāh-mar'*].

* KAL.—*Future.* *

Lev.25: 3. *thou shalt prune* thy vineyard,
4. nor *prune* thy vineyard.

* NIPHAL.—*Future.* *

Isa. 5: 6. *it shall* not *be pruned,* nor digged;

* PIEL.—*Infinitive.* *

Ps. 92: 1(2). *and to sing praises* unto thy name,
147: 1. for (it is) good *to sing praises*

PIEL.—*Imperative.*

1Ch 16: 9. *sing psalms* unto him,
Ps. 9:11(12). *Sing praises* to the Lord,
30: 4(5) *Sing* unto the Lord, O ye saints
33: 2. *sing* unto him with the psaltery
47: 6(7). *Sing praises to* God, *sing praises: sing praises* unto our King, *sing praises.*
7(8). *sing ye praises* with understanding.
66: 2. *Sing forth* the honour of his name:
68: 4(5). *sing praises to* his name:
32(33). *O sing praises unto* the Lord;
98: 4. rejoice, *and sing praise.*
5. *Sing* unto the Lord with the harp;
105: 2. Sing unto him, *sing psalms* unto him.
135: 3. *sing praises* unto his name;
147: 7. *sing praise* upon the harp
Isa. 12: 5. *Sing unto* the Lord;

PIEL.—*Future.*

Jud. 5: 3. *I will sing* (praise) to the Lord
2Sa.22:50. *I will sing praises* unto thy name.
Ps. 7:17(18). *and will sing praise to* the name of
9: 2(3). *I will sing praise to* thy name,
18:49(50). and *sing praises* unto thy name.
21:13(14). (so) will we sing *and praise* thy
27: 6. *yea, I will sing praises*
30:12(13). that (my) glory *may sing praise to thee,*
57: 7(8). I will sing *and give praise.*
9(10). *I will sing unto thee* among
59:17(18). Unto thee, O my strength, *will I sing:*
61: 8(9). So *will I sing praise unto* thy name
66: 4. *and shall sing* unto thee; *they shall sing* (to) thy name.
71:22. unto thee *will I sing* with the harp,
23. greatly rejoice when *I sing* unto thee;
75: 9(10). *I will sing praises* to the God of
101: 1. unto thee, O Lord, *will I sing.*
104:33. *I will sing praise* to my God
108: 1(2). I will sing *and give praise,*
3(4). *and I will sing praises* unto thee
138: 1. the gods *will I sing praise unto thee.*
144: 9. of ten strings *will I sing praises* unto
146: 2. *I will sing praises* unto my God
149: 3. *let them sing praises* unto him with the

2170 ## זְמָר [*z'māhr*], Ch. m.

Dan 3: 5, 7, 10, 15. and all kinds of *musick,*

2171 ## זַמָּר [*zam-māhr'*], Ch. m.

Ezr. 7:24. Levites, *singers,* porters, Nethinims,

2169 ## זֶמֶר [*zeh'-mer*], m.

Deu 14: 5. the wild ox, *and the chamois.*

2172-73 ## זִמְרָה *zim-rāh'*, f.

Gen43:11. take *of the best fruits in* the land
Ps. 81: 2(3). Take *a psalm,* and bring hither the
98: 5. with the harp, and the voice of *a psalm.*
Isa. 51: 3. thanksgiving, and the voice of *melody.*
Am. 5:23. *for* I will not hear *the melody of* thy viols.

2176 ## זִמְרָת *zim-rāhth'*, f.

Ex. 15: 2. The Lord (is) my strength *and song,*
Ps.118:14. The Lord (is) my strength *and song,*
Isa. 12: 2. my strength *and* (my) *song;*

זַן *zan*, m. 2177

2Ch 16:14. with sweet odours *and divers kinds*
Ps.144:13. affording *all manner of store:* (marg. *from kind to kind*)

זַן [*zan*], Ch. m. 2178

Dan 3: 5, 7, 10, 15. and all *kinds of* musick,

זָנָב *zāh-nāhv'*, m. 2180

Ex. 4: 4. Put forth thine hand, and take it *by the tail.*
Deu28:13. make thee the head, and not *the tail;*
44. he shall be the head, and thou shalt be *the tail.*
Jud.15: 4. took firebrands, and turned *tail* to *tail,*
— in the midst between two *tails.*
Job 40:17. He moveth *his tail* like a cedar:
Isa. 7: 4. the two *tails of* these smoking firebrands,
9:14(13). cut off from Israel head *and tail,*
15(14). prophet that teacheth lies, he (is) *the tail.*
19:15. which the head *or tail,* branch

זָנַב [*zāh-nav'*]. 2179

* PIEL.—*Preterite.* *

Jos. 10:19. *and smite the hindmost* of them; (marg. *cut off the tail*)

PIEL.—*Future.*

Deu25:18. *and smote the hindmost* of thee,

זָנָה *zāh-nāh'*. 2181

* KAL.—*Preterite.* *

Gen38:24. thy daughter in law *hath played the harlot;*
Ex. 34:15. *and they go a whoring* after their gods,
16. *and* their daughters *go a whoring*
Deu31:16. *and go a whoring* after the gods
Jud. 2:17. but *they went a whoring*
Isa. 23:17. *and shall commit fornication* with all
Jer. 3: 1. but thou *hast played the harlot*
Eze.23: 3. *they committed whoredoms* in their youth:
19. wherein *she had played the harlot*
Hos. 2: 5(7). their mother *hath played the harlot:*
9: 1. for *thou hast gone a whoring*

KAL.—*Infinitive.*

Lev.20: 5. *to commit whoredom* with Molech,
6. *to go a whoring* after them,
21: 9. profane herself *by playing the whore,*
Nu. 25: 1. the people began *to commit whoredom*
Deu22:21. *to play the whore* in her father's house:
Eze.23:30. *because thou hast gone a whoring*
Hos. 1: 2. the land hath committed *great* whoredom, (lit. *in whoring* hath whored)

KAL.—*Future.*

Lev.19:29. lest the land *fall to whoredom,*
Jud. 8:27. *and* all Israel *went* thither *a whoring* after it:
33. *and went a whoring* after Baalim,
19: 2. *And* his concubine *played the whore*
1Ch 5:25. *and went a whoring* after the gods
Ps.106:39. *and went a whoring* with their own inventions.
Isa. 57: 3. seed of the adulterer *and the whore.* (lit. *and she will commit whoredom*)
Jer. 3: 6. *and* there *hath played the harlot.*
8. but went *and played the harlot* also.
Eze.16:15. *and playedst the harlot* because of
16. *and playedst the harlot* thereupon:
17. *and didst commit whoredom* with them,
26. *Thou hast also committed fornication*
28. *Thou hast played the whore also*

Eze.16:28. *yea, thou hast played the harlot with them,*
23: 3. *And they committed whoredoms* in Egypt;
5. *And* Aholah *played the harlot*
43. *Will they* now *commit* whoredoms with her,
Hos. 1: 2. the land *hath committed* great *whoredom,*
3: 3. *thou shalt* not *play the harlot,*
4:12. *and they have gone a whoring*
13. your daughters *shall commit whoredom,*
14. when *they commit whoredom,*
Am. 7:17. Thy wife *shall be an harlot*

KAL.—*Participle.* Poel.

([1] lit. a woman *a harlot*).

Gen34:31. deal with our sister *as with an harlot?*
38:15. he thought her *to* (be) *an harlot;*
Lev.17: 7. after whom they *have gone a whoring.*
20: 5. all that *go a whoring* after him,
21: 7. shall not take a wife (that is) *a whore,*
14. or profane, (or) *an harlot,*
Nu. 15:39. ye *use to go a whoring:*
Deu23:18(19). shalt not bring the hire of *a whore,*
Jos. 2: 1. came into [1]*an harlot*'s house,
6:17. only Rahab *the harlot* shall live,
22. Go into [1]*the harlot*'s house,
25. Joshua saved Rahab *the harlot*
Jud.11: 1. he (was) the son of [1]*an harlot:*
16: 1. saw there [1]*an harlot,*
1K. 3:16. two women, (that were) *harlots,*
Ps. 73:27. *them that go a whoring* from thee.
Pro. 6:26. For by means of a *whorish* woman
7:10. a woman (with) the attire of *an harlot,*
23:27. For *a whore* (is) a deep ditch;
29: 3. he that keepeth company with *harlots*
Isa. 1:21. the faithful city become *an harlot!*
23:15. shall Tyre sing as *an harlot.*
16. thou *harlot* that hast been forgotten;
Jer. 2:20. thou wanderest, *playing the harlot.*
3: 3. thou hadst [1]*a whore*'s forehead,
5: 7. by troops in *the harlots'* houses.
Eze. 6: 9. I am broken with their *whorish* heart,
— which *go a whoring* after their idols:
16:30. the work of an imperious *whorish* woman.
31. hast not been *as an harlot,*
33. They give gifts to all *whores:*
35. *O harlot,* hear the word of the Lord:
41. cause thee to cease *from playing the harlot,*
20:30. *commit* ye *whoredom* after their
23:44. as they go in unto a woman *that playeth the harlot:*
Hos 4:14. themselves are separated with *whores,*
15. Though thou, Israel, *play the harlot,*
Joel 3: 3(4:3). have given a boy *for an harlot,*
Mic. 1: 7. she gathered (it) of the hire of *an harlot,* and they shall return to the hire of *an harlot.*
Nah 3: 4. of *the* wellfavoured *harlot,*

* PUAL.—*Preterite.* *

Eze.16:34. none followeth thee *to commit whoredoms:*

* HIPHIL.—*Preterite.* *

Ex. 34:16. *and make* thy sons *go a whoring*
Hos. 4:10. *they shall commit whoredom,*
18. *they have committed whoredom* continually:
5: 3. O Ephraim, *thou committest whoredom,*

HIPHIL.—*Infinitive.*

Lev.19:29. *to cause her to be a whore;*
2Ch 21:13. *like to the whoredoms of* the house of Ahab,
Hos. 4:18. they have committed whoredom *continually:* (lit. *in committing whoredom* they have committed whoredom)

HIPHIL.—*Future.*

2Ch 21:11. *and caused* the inhabitants of Jerusalem *to commit fornication,*
13. *and hast made* Judah...*to go a whoring,*

2184 **זְנוּנִים** *z'noo-neem',* m. pl.

Gen38:24. she (is) with child *by whoredom.*
2K. 9:22. so long as *the whoredoms of* thy mother
Eze.23:11. *more than* her sister in (her) *whoredoms.* (marg. *the whoredoms of* her sister)
29. the nakedness of *thy whoredoms*
Hos. 1: 2. take unto thee a wife of *whoredoms* and children of *whoredoms:*
Hos. 2: 2(4). let her therefore put away *her whoredoms*
4(6). for they (be) the children of *whoredoms.*
4:12 & 5:4. for the spirit of *whoredoms*
Nah. 3: 4. *the whoredoms of* the wellfavoured harlot,
— selleth nations *through her whoredoms,*

זֹנוֹת *zōh-nōhth',* f. pl. 2185

1K. 22:38. *and* they washed *his armour;*

זְנוּת *z'nooth,* f. 2184

Nu. 14:33. and bear *your whoredoms,*
Jer. 3: 2. polluted the land *with thy whoredoms*
9. through the lightness of *her whoredom,*
13:27. the lewdness of *thy whoredom,*
Eze.23:27. *thy whoredom* (brought) from
43: 7. nor their kings, *by their whoredom,*
9. let them put away *their whoredom,*
Hos. 4:11. *Whoredom* and wine and new wine
6:10. there (is) *the whoredom* of Ephraim,

זָנַח *zāh-nagh'.* 2186

* KAL.—*Preterite.* *

Ps. 43: 2. why *dost thou cast me off?*
44: 9(10). But *thou hast cast off,* and put us
60: 1(3). O God, *thou hast cast us off,*
10(12). thou, O God, (which) *hadst cast us off?*
74: 1. why *hast thou cast* (us) *off* for ever?
89:38(39). But thou *hast cast off* and abhorred,
108:11(12). O God, (who) *hast cast us off?*
Lam. 2: 7. The Lord *hath cast off* his altar,
Hos. 8: 3. Israel *hath cast off* (the thing that is) good:
5. Thy calf, O Samaria, *hath cast* (thee) *off;*
Zec.10: 6. though *I had* not *cast them off:*

KAL.—*Future.*

Ps. 44:23(24). arise, *cast* (us) not *off* for ever.
77: 7(8). *Will* the Lord *cast off* for ever?
88:14(15). Lord, why *castest thou off* my soul?
Lam.3:17. *And thou hast removed* my soul *far off*
31. the Lord *will* not *cast off* for ever:

* HIPHIL.—*Preterite.* *

2Ch 11:14. and his sons *had cast them off*
29:19. king Ahaz in his reign *did cast away*
Isa. 19: 6. *And they shall turn* the rivers *far away;*

* HIPHIL.—*Future.* *

1Ch 28: 9. if thou forsake him, *he will cast thee off*

זָנַק [*zāh-nak'*]. 2187

* PIEL.—*Future.* *

Deu 33:22. *he shall leap* from Bashan.

זֵעָה [*zēh-"gāh'*], f. 2188

Gen 3:19. *In the sweat of* thy face shalt thou eat bread,

זַעֲוָה *zah-"găvāh',* f. 2189

Deu 28:25. shalt be *removed* into all the kingdoms of the earth. (marg. *for a removing*)
2Ch 29: 8. he hath delivered them *to trouble,* (marg. *commotion*)
Jer. 15: 4. I will cause them *to be removed* into all (marg. *for a removing*)
24: 9 & 29:18. will deliver them *to be removed* (marg. *for removing,* or, *vexation*)
34:17. I will make you *to be removed* (marg. *for a removing*)
Eze.23:46. and will give them *to be removed* (marg. *id.*)

זְעֵיר *z'"gēhr,* m. 2191

Job 36: 2. Suffer me *a little,* and I will shew thee
Isa. 28:10, 13. line upon line; here *a little,* (and) there *a little:*

2192 זְעֵיר [z'g̃ehr], Ch. adj.

Dan 7: 8. among them another *little* horn,

2193 זָעַךְ [zāh-g̃ach'].

* NIPHAL.—*Preterite.* *

Job 17: 1. My breath is corrupt, my days *are extinct,*

2194 זָעַם zāh-g̃am'.

* KAL.—*Preterite.* *

Nu. 23: 8. the Lord *hath* not *defied?*
Isa. 66:14. *and* (his) *indignation* toward his enemies. (lit. *and he shall be angry*)
Dan 11:30. *and have indignation* against the
Zec. 1:12. against which *thou hast had indignation*
Mal. 1: 4. the Lord *hath indignation* for ever.

KAL.—*Imperative.*

Nu. 23: 7. curse me Jacob, and come, *defy* Israel.

KAL.—*Future.*

Nu. 23: 8. hath not cursed? or how *shall I defy,*
Pro. 24:24. nations *shall abhor him:*

KAL.—*Participle.*—Poel.

Ps. 7:11(12). God *is angry* (with the wicked) every day.

KAL.—*Participle.* Paül.

Pro. 22:14. *he that is abhorred of* the Lord
Mic. 6:10. the scant measure (that is) *abominable?*

* NIPHAL.—*Participle.* *

Pro. 25:23. so (doth) an *angry* countenance

2195 זַעַם zah'-g̃am.

Ps. 38: 3(4). in my flesh because of *thine anger;*
69:24(25). Pour out *thine indignation* upon them,
78:49. anger, wrath, *and indignation,*
102:10(11). Because of *thine indignation*
Isa. 10: 5. the staff in their hand is *mine indignation.*
25. *the indignation* shall cease,
13: 5. the weapons of *his indignation,*
26:20. until *the indignation* be overpast.
30:27. his lips are full of *indignation,*
Jer. 10:10. shall not be able to abide *his indignation.*
15:17. thou hast filled me with *indignation.*
50:25. brought forth the weapons of *his indignation:*
Lam 2: 6. *in the indignation of* his anger
Eze. 21:31(36). I will pour out *mine indignation*
22:24. nor rained upon in the day of *indignation.*
31. have I poured out *mine indignation* upon them;
Dan 8:19. shall be in the last end of *the indignation:*
11:36. till *the indignation* be accomplished:
Hos. 7:16. fall by the sword *for the rage of*
Nah. 1: 6. Who can stand before *his indignation?*
Hab 3:12. didst march through the land *in indignation,*
Zep. 3: 8. to pour upon them *mine indignation,*

2196 זָעַף [zāh-g̃aph'].

* KAL.—*Infinitive.* *

2Ch 26:19. *and while he was wroth* with the priests,

KAL.—*Future.*

2Ch 26:19. *Then* Uzziah *was wroth,*
Pro. 19: 3. his heart *fretteth* against the Lord.

KAL.—*Participle.* Poel.

Gen 40: 6. behold, they (were) *sad.*
Dan 1:10. should he see your faces *worse liking* (marg. *sadder*)

2198 זָעֵף zāh-g̃ehph', adj.

1K. 20:43. went to his house heavy *and displeased,*
21: 4. came into his house heavy *and displeased*

זַעַף zah'-g̃aph, m. 2197

2Ch 16:10. for (he was) *in a rage* with him
28: 9. ye have slain them *in a rage*
Pro. 19:12. The king's *wrath* (is) as the roaring of a lion;
Isa. 30:30. *with the indignation of* (his) anger,
Jon. 1:15. the sea ceased *from her raging.*
Mic. 7: 9. I will bear *the indignation of* the Lord,

זָעַק [zāh-g̃ak']. 2199

* KAL.—*Preterite.* *

Jud. 6: 7. when the children of Israel *cried*
1Sa. 8:18. *And ye shall cry out* in that day
2Sa. 13:19. her hand on her head, *and* went on *crying.* (lit. going *and cried*)
1Ch 5:20. *they cried* to God in the battle,
Ps. 22: 5(6). *They cried* unto thee,
142: 5(6). *I cried* unto thee, O Lord:
Jer 11:11. *and though they shall cry* unto me,
12. go, *and cry* unto the gods
47: 2. *then* the men *shall cry,*
Hos. 7:14. And *they have* not *cried*

KAL.—*Infinitive.*

1Sa. 7: 8. Cease not *to cry* unto the Lord (marg. Be not silent from us *from crying*)
2Sa. 19:28(29). What right *therefore* have I yet *to cry*
Isa. 30:19. at the voice of *thy cry;*
57:13. *When thou criest,* let thy companies

KAL.—*Imperative.*

Jud. 10:14. Go *and cry* unto the gods
Isa. 14:31. Howl, O gate; *cry,* O city;
Jer. 25:34. Howl, ye shepherds, *and cry;*
48:20. it is broken down: howl *and cry;*
Eze. 21:12(17). *Cry* and howl, son of man:
Joel 1:14. *and cry* unto the Lord,

KAL.—*Future.*

Ex. 2:23. *and they cried,* and their cry came up
Jud. 3: 9, 15. *when* the children of Israel *cried*
6: 6 & 10:10. *and* the children of Israel *cried* unto
12: 2. and *when I called* you, ye delivered
1Sa. 4:13. *And* when the man came...all the city *cried out.*
5:10. *that* the Ekronites *cried out,*
7: 9. *and* Samuel *cried* unto the Lord for Israel;
12: 8. *and* your fathers *cried* unto the Lord,
10. *And they cried* unto the Lord,
15:11. *and he cried* unto the Lord
28:12. *And* when the woman saw Samuel, *she cried*
2Sa. 19: 4(5). *and* the king *cried* with a loud voice,
1K. 22:32. *and* Jehoshaphat *cried out.*
2Ch 18:31. *but* Jehoshaphat *cried out,*
20: 9. *and cry* unto thee in our affliction,
32:20. prayed *and cried* to heaven.
Neh 9: 4. *and cried* with a loud voice
28. returned, *and cried unto thee,*
Est. 4: 1. *and cried* with a loud and a bitter cry;
Job 31:38. If my land *cry* against me,
Ps. 107:13. *Then they cried* unto the Lord
19. *Then they cry* unto the Lord
142: 1(2). *I cried* unto the Lord
Isa. 15: 4. *And* Heshbon *shall cry,*
5. My heart *shall cry out* for Moab;
26:17. *crieth out* in her pangs;
Jer. 20: 8. For since I spake, *I cried out,*
30:15. Why *criest thou* for thine affliction?
48:31. *I will cry out* for all Moab;
Lam. 3: 8. Also when *I cry* and shout,
Eze. 9: 8. I fell upon my face, *and cried,*
11:13. fell I down upon my face, *and cried*
27:30. *and shall cry* bitterly,
Hos. 8: 2. Israel *shall cry* unto me,
Jon. 1: 5. *and cried* every man unto his god,
Mic. 3: 4. Then *shall they cry* unto the Lord,
Hab 1: 2. *cry out* unto thee (of) violence,
2:11. the stone *shall cry out* of the wall,

* NIPHAL.—*Preterite.* *

Jud. 18:22. Micah's house *were gathered together,*

Jud.18:23. that *thou comest with such a company?* (marg. *art gathered together?*)

NIPHAL.—*Future.*

Jos. 8:16. *And* all the people...*were called together*
Jud. 6:34. *and* Abi-ezer *was gathered* after him. (marg. *called*)
35. who also *was gathered* after him:
1Sa.14:20. *And* Saul and all the people...*assembled themselves*, (marg. *were cried together*)

* HIPHIL.—*Infinitive.* *

2Sa.20: 5. So Amasa went *to assemble*

HIPHIL.—*Imperative.*

2Sa.20: 4. *Assemble* me the men of Judah (marg. *Call*)

HIPHIL.—*Future.*

Jud. 4:10. *And* Barak *called* Zebulun
13. *And* Sisera *gathered together* (marg. *gathered by cry*, or, *proclamation*)
Job 35: 9. *they make* (the oppressed) *to cry:*
Jon. 3: 7. *And he caused* (it) *to be proclaimed*
Zec. 6: 8. *Then cried he* upon me,

2200 **זְעִק** *z'geek*, Ch.

* P'AL.—*Preterite.* *

Dan 6:20(21). *he cried* with a lamentable voice

2201 **זְעָקָה** *z'gāh-kāh'*, f.

Gen18:20. *the cry of* Sodom and Gomorrah is great,
Neh 5: 6. when I heard *their cry* and these words.
9: 9. heardest *their cry* by the Red sea;
Est. 4: 1. cried with a loud and *a* bitter *cry;*
9:31. the matters of the fastings *and their cry.*
Job 16:18. let *my cry have* no place. (lit. let be *to my cry*)
Pro.21:13. stoppeth his ears *at the cry of* the poor,
Ecc. 9:17. *more than the cry of* him that ruleth
Isa. 15: 5. they shall raise up *a cry of* destruction.
8. For *the cry* is gone round about
65:19. nor the voice of *crying.*
Jer. 18:22. Let *a cry* be heard from their houses,
20:16. and let him hear *the cry* in the morning,
48: 4. her little ones have caused *a cry*
34. *From the cry of* Heshbon
50:46. *and the cry* is heard among the nations.
51:54. A sound of *a cry* (cometh) from Babylon,
Eze.27:28. shall shake at the sound of *the cry of*

2203 **זֶפֶת** *zeh'-pheth*, f.

Ex. 2: 3. daubed it with slime *and with pitch,*
Isa. 34: 9, shall be turned *into pitch,*
— shall become burning *pitch.*

2131 **זִקִּים** *zik-keem'*, m. pl.

Job 36: 8. if (they be) bound *in fetters,*
Ps.149: 8. To bind their kings *with chains,*
Pro.26:18. As a mad (man) who casteth *firebrands,* (marg. *flames*, or, *sparks*)
Isa. 45:14. *in chains* they shall come over,
Nah 3:10. all her great men were bound *in chains.*

2206 **זָקָן** *zāh-kāhn'*, com.

Lev.13:29. a plague upon the head or *the beard;*
30. a leprosy upon the head or *beard.*
14: 9. all his hair off his head and *his beard*
19:27. mar the corners of *thy beard.*
21: 5. they shave off the corner of *their beard,*
1Sa.17:35. I caught (him) *by his beard,*
21:13(14). let his spittle fall down upon *his beard.*
2Sa.10: 4. shaved off the one half of *their beards,*
5. until *your beards* be grown,
20: 9. Joab took Amasa *by the beard*
1Ch 19: 5. until *your beards* be grown,
Ezr. 9: 3. the hair of my head *and of my beard,*
Ps.133: 2. that ran down *upon the beard,* (even) Aaron's *beard:*
Isa. 7:20. it shall also consume *the beard.*
15: 2. every *beard* cut off.
Jer.41: 5. having their *beards* shaven,
48:37. and every *beard* clipped:
Eze. 5: 1. upon thine head and upon *thy beard:*

זָקֵן *zāh-kēhn'*. 2204

* KAL.—*Preterite.* *

Gen18:12. my lord *being old* also?
13. bear a child, which *am old?*
19:31. said unto the younger, Our father (is) *old,*
24: 1. Abraham *was old,* (and) well stricken
27: 1. that when Isaac *was old,*
2. he said, Behold now, *I am old,*
Jos.13: 1. Joshua *was old* (and) stricken in years;
— Thou *art old* (and) stricken in years,
23: 1. that Joshua *waxed old*
2. I *am old* (and) stricken in age:
Ru. 1:12. for *I am* too *old* to have an husband.
1Sa. 2:22. Now Eli *was* very *old,*
4:18. for *he was* an *old* man,
8: 1. when Samuel *was old,*
5. said unto him, Behold, thou *art old,*
12: 2. I *am old* and grayheaded;
17:12. went among men (for) *an old man*
2Sa.19:32(33). Barzillai *was* a very *aged man,*
1K. 1: 1. Now king David *was old*
15. the king *was* very *old;*
2K. 4:14. no child, and her husband *is old.*
1Ch 23: 1. when David *was old* and full of days,
Ps. 37:25. I have been young, and (now) *am old;*
Pro.23:22. despise not thy mother when *she is old.*

KAL.—*Future.*

2Ch 24:15. *But* Jehoiada *waxed old,*

* HIPHIL.—*Future.* *

Job 14: 8. Though the root thereof *wax old*
Pro.22: 6. when *he is old,* he will not depart

זָקֵן *zāh-kehn'*, adj. 2205

Gen18:11. Now Abraham and Sarah (were) *old*
19: 4. both *old* and young,
24: 2. Abraham said unto his *eldest* servant *of*
25: 8. *an old man,* and full (of years);
35:29. *old* and full of days:
43:27. *the old man* of whom ye spake?
44:20. We have a father, *an old man,*
50: 7. *the elders of* his house, and all *the elders of*
Ex. 3:16. Go, and gather *the elders of* Israel
18. thou *and the elders of* Israel,
4:29. gathered together all *the elders of*
10: 9. go with our young *and with our old,*
12:21. Moses called for all *the elders of*
17: 5. take with thee of *the elders of*
6. did so in the sight of *the elders of*
18:12. all *the elders of* Israel,
19: 7. called *for the elders of* the people,
24: 1,9. seventy *of the elders of* Israel;
14. he said unto *the elders,*
Lev. 4:15. *the elders of* the congregation
9: 1. *and the elders of* Israel;
19:32. honour the face of *the old man,*
Nu. 11:16. seventy men *of the elders of* Israel, whom thou knowest to be *the elders of* the
24. seventy men of *the elders of* the people,
25. gave (it) unto *the* seventy *elders:*
30. he *and the elders of* Israel.
16:25. and *the elders of* Israel
22: 4. Moab said unto *the elders of*
7. And *the elders of* Moab *and the elders of* Midian departed
Deu 5:23(20). heads of your tribes, *and your elders;*
19:12. Then *the elders of* his city
21: 2. Then *thy elders* and thy judges
3. even *the elders of* that city
4. And *the elders of* that city
6. And all *the elders of* that city,
19. bring him out unto *the elders of*
20. they shall say unto *the elders of* his city
22:15. the damsel's virginity unto *the elders of*

Deu 22:16. damsel's father shall say unto *the elders*,
17. shall spread the cloth before *the elders of*
18. And *the elders of* that city
25: 7. go up to the gate unto *the elders*,
8. Then *the elders of* his city
9. in the presence of *the elders*,
27: 1. Moses *with the elders of* Israel commanded
28:50. shall not regard the person *of the old*,
29:10(9). *your elders*, and your officers,
31: 9. unto all *the elders of* Israel.
28. Gather unto me all *the elders of*
32: 7. *thy elders*, and they will tell thee.
Jos. 6:21. man and woman, young and *old*,
7: 6 & 8:10. he *and the elders of* Israel,
8:33. all Israel, *and their elders*,
9:11. Wherefore *our elders* and all the
20: 4. declare his cause in the ears of *the elders of*
23: 2. *for their elders*, and for their heads,
24: 1. called *for the elders of* Israel,
31. all the days of *the elders*
Jud. 2: 7. and all the days of *the elders*
8:14. and *the elders thereof*,
16. he took *the elders of* the city,
11: 5. *the elders of* Gilead went to fetch
7. Jephthah said *unto the elders of*
8, 10. *the elders of* Gilead said
9. Jephthah said unto *the elders of*
11. Jephthah went with *the elders of*
19:16. there came an *old* man
17, 20. and the *old* man said,
22. the master of the house, the *old* man,
21:16. Then *the elders of* the congregation
Ru. 4: 2. ten men *of the elders of* the city,
4. before *the elders of* my people.
9. Boaz said *unto the elders*,
11. *and the elders*, said, (We are) witnesses.
1Sa. 2:31. there shall not be *an old man*
32. and there shall not be *an old man*
4: 3. *the elders of* Israel said,
8: 4. Then all *the elders of* Israel gathered
11: 3. *the elders of* Jabesh said unto him,
15:30. before *the elders of* my people,
16: 4. *the elders of* the town trembled
28:14. she said, *An old man* cometh up;
30:26. he sent of the spoil *unto the elders of*
2Sa. 3:17. communication with *the elders of*
5: 3. So all *the elders of* Israel came
12:17. *the elders of* his house arose,
17: 4. Absalom well, and all *the elders of*
15. Absalom and *the elders of* Israel;
19:11(12). Speak unto *the elders of* Judah,
1K. 8: 1. Solomon assembled *the elders of*
3. all *the elders of* Israel came,
12: 6. Rehoboam consulted with *the old men*,
8. forsook the counsel of *the old men*,
13. forsook *the old men*'s counsel
13:11. Now there dwelt an *old* prophet
25. where the *old* prophet dwelt.
29. and the *old* prophet came to the city,
20: 7. king of Israel called all *the elders of*
8. all *the elders* and all the people
21: 8. sent the letters unto *the elders*
11. *the elders* and the nobles
2K. 6:32. *and the elders* sat with
— messenger came to him, he said to *the elders*,
10: 1. unto the rulers of Jezreel, to *the elders*,
5. *the elders also*, and the bringers up
19: 2. *the elders of* the priests,
23: 1. gathered unto him all *the elders of* Judah
1Ch 11: 3. Therefore came all *the elders of*
15:25. So David, *and the elders of* Israel,
21:16. Then David *and the elders*
2Ch 5: 2. Solomon assembled *the elders of*
4. all *the elders of* Israel came;
10: 6. Rehoboam took counsel with *the old men*
8. the counsel which *the old men* gave
13. forsook the counsel of *the old men*,
34:29. gathered together all *the elders of*
36:17. young man or maiden, *old man*,
Ezr. 3:12. the fathers, (who were) *ancient men*,
10: 8. the princes *and the elders*,
14. with them *the elders of* every city,
Est. 3:13. all Jews, both young and *old*,
Job 12:20. taketh away the understanding of *the aged*.
32: 4. because they (were) *elder* than he. (marg. *elder* for days)
Job 32: 9. *neither* do *the aged* understand
42:17. So Job died, (being) *old* and full of days.
Ps. 105:22. *and* teach *his senators* wisdom.
107:32. praise him in the assembly of *the elders*.
119:100. I understand more *than the ancients*,
148:12. *old men*, and children:
Pro. 17: 6. children (are) the crown of *old men*;
20:29. the beauty of *old men* (is) the grey head.
31:23. when he sitteth among *the elders of*
Ecc. 4:13. than an *old* and foolish king,
Isa. 3: 2. the prudent, *and the ancient*,
5. behave himself proudly *against the ancient*,
14. enter into judgment with *the ancients of*
9:15(14). *The ancient* and honourable,
20: 4. young *and old*, naked and barefoot,
24:23. before *his ancients* gloriously.
37: 2. and *the elders of* the priests
47: 6. upon *the ancient* hast thou
65:20. *nor an old man* that hath
Jer. 6:11. *the aged* with (him that is) full
19: 1. *and* (take) *of the ancients of* the people, *and of the ancients of* the priests;
26:17. Then rose up certain of *the elders of* the land,
29: 1. unto the residue of *the elders*
31:13. both young men *and old* together:
51:22. will I break in pieces *old* and young;
Lam 1:19. my priests *and mine elders* gave
2:10. *The elders of* the daughter of Zion
21. The young *and the old*
4:16. they favoured not *the elders*.
5:12. the faces of *elders* were not honoured.
14. *The elders* have ceased from the gate,
Eze. 7:26. counsel *from the ancients*.
8: 1. *and the elders of* Judah sat before me,
11. seventy men *of the ancients of*
12. *the ancients of* the house of Israel
9: 6. Slay utterly *old* (and) young,
— Then they began at the *ancient* men
14: 1. Then came certain of *the elders of*
20: 1. certain *of the elders of* Israel came
3. speak unto *the elders of* Israel,
27: 9. *The ancients of* Gebal
Joel 1: 2. Hear this, *ye old men*, and give ear,
14. gather *the elders* (and) all the inhabitants
2:16. sanctify the congregation, assemble *the elders*,
28(3:1). *your old men* shall dream dreams,
Zec. 8: 4. There shall yet *old men and old women*

זֹקֶן *zōh'-ken*, m. 2207

Gen48:10. the eyes of Israel were dim *for age*,

זִקְנָה *zik-nāh'*, f. 2209

Gen24:36. bare a son to my master when *she was old*: (lit. after *her old age*)
1K. 11: 4. when Solomon *was old*, (lit. in the time of *the old age of*)
15:23. Nevertheless in the time of *his old age*
Ps. 71: 9. Cast me not off in the time of *old age*;
18. when *I am old* and greyheaded, (marg. unto *old age* and grey hairs)
Isa. 46: 4. to (your) *old age* I (am) he;

זְקֻנִים *z'koo-neem'*, m. pl. 2208

Gen21: 2. bare Abraham a son *in his old age*,
7. have born (him) a son *in his old age*.
37: 3. the son of *his old age*:
44:20. child of *his old age*,

זָקַף [*zāh-kaph'*]. 2210

* KAL.—*Participle.* Poel. *

Ps. 145:14. *and raiseth up* all (those that be) bowed down.
146: 8. the Lord *raiseth* them that are bowed down;

2211 זְקַף [z'kaph], Ch.

* P'AL.—*Participle.* Passive. *

Ezr. 6:11. *and being set up*, let him be hanged

2212 זָקַק [zāh-kak'].

* KAL.—*Future.* *

Job 28: 1. a place for gold (where) *they fine*
36:27. *they pour down* rain

* PIEL.—*Preterite.* *

Mal. 3: 3. *and purge* them as gold and silver,

* PUAL.—*Participle.* *

1Ch 28:18. for the altar of incense *refined* gold
29: 4. seven thousand talents of *refined* silver,
Ps. 12: 6(7). *purified* seven times.
Isa. 25: 6. wines on the lees *well refined.*

2213 זֵר zēhr, m.

Ex. 25:11. make upon it *a crown of* gold
24. make thereto *a crown of* gold
25. thou shalt make *a* golden *crown*
30: 3. thou shalt make unto it *a crown of* gold
4. make to it under *the crown of it*,
37: 2. and made *a crown of* gold to it
11. thereunto *a crown of* gold
12. and made *a crown of* gold
26. he made unto it *a crown of* gold
27. gold for it under *the crown thereof*,

2214 זָרָא zāh-rāh', f.

Nu. 11:20. it be *loathsome* unto you:

2215 זָרַב [zāh-rav'].

* PUAL.—*Future.* *

Job 6:17. What time *they wax warm*,

2219 זָרָה [zāh-rāh'].

* KAL.—*Infinitive.* *

Jer. 4:11. not *to fan*, nor to cleanse,

KAL.—*Imperative.*

Nu. 16:37(17:2). *scatter* thou the fire yonder;

KAL.—*Future.*

Ex. 32:20. *and strawed* (it) upon the water,
Isa. 30:22. *thou shalt cast them away* (marg. *scatter*)
41:16. *Thou shalt fan them*, and the wind
Jer. 15: 7. *And I will fan them* with a fan
Eze. 5: 2. a third part *thou shalt scatter*

KAL.—*Participle.* Poel.

Ru. 3: 2. *he winnoweth* barley to night
Isa. 30:24. which *hath been winnowed*

* NIPHAL.—*Infinitive.* *

Eze. 6: 8. *when ye shall be scattered*

NIPHAL.—*Future.*

Eze.36:19. *and they were dispersed*

* PIEL.—*Preterite.* *

1K. 14:15. *and shall scatter them* beyond
Ps. 44:11(12). *hast scattered us* among the heathen.
139: 3. *Thou compassest* my path
Jer. 49:32. *and I will scatter* into all winds
36. *and will scatter them* toward all
51: 2. fanners, *that shall fan her*,
Eze. 5:10. *and* the whole remnant of thee *will I scatter*
6: 5. *and I will scatter* your bones
12:15. *and disperse* them in the countries.
22:15. *and disperse thee* in the countries,
29:12 & 30:23. *and will disperse them* through the
30:26. *and disperse* them among the countries;
Zec. 1:19(2:2), 21(2:4). horns which *have scattered* Judah,
Mal. 2: 3. *and spread* dung upon your faces, (marg. *scatter*)

PIEL.—*Infinitive.*

Ps. 106:27. *and to scatter them* in the lands.
Eze.20:23. *and disperse* them through the countries;
Zec. 1:21(2:4). over the land of Judah *to scatter it.*

PIEL.—*Future.*

Lev.26:33. *I will scatter* you among the heathen,
Pro.15: 7. lips of the wise *disperse* knowledge:
Eze. 5:12. *I will scatter* a third part
12:14. *I will scatter* toward every wind

PIEL.—*Participle.*

Pro.20: 8. *scattereth away* all evil with his eyes.
26. A wise king *scattereth* the wicked,
Jer. 31:10. He *that scattered* Israel will gather

* PUAL.—*Future.* *

Job 18:15. brimstone *shall be scattered* upon

PUAL.—*Participle.*

Pro. 1:17. Surely in vain the net *is spread*

זְרוֹעַ z'rōh'ăg, com. 2220

Gen49:24. and *the arms of* his hands were made
Ex. 6: 6. redeem you *with a* stretched out *arm*,
15:16. by the greatness of *thine arm*
Nu. 6:19. the priest shall take *the* sodden *shoulder*
Deu. 4:34 & 5:15. *and by a* stretched out *arm*,
7:19. *and the* stretched out *arm*,
9:29. *and* by *thy* stretched out *arm.*
11: 2. and *his* stretched out *arm*,
18: 3. shall give unto the priest *the shoulder*,
26: 8. *and with an* outstretched *arm*,
33:20. teareth *the arm* with the crown
27. underneath (are) *the* everlasting *arms:*
Jud.15:14. the cords that (were) upon *his arms*
16:12. he brake them from off *his arms*
1Sa. 2:31. that I will cut off *thine arm*, and *the arm of* thy father's house,
2Sa. 1:10. the bracelet that (was) on *his arm*,
22:35. a bow of steel is broken by *mine arms.*
1K. 8:42. *and of thy* stretched out *arm;*
2K. 9:24. smote Jehoram between *his arms*,
17:36. with great power *and a* stretched out *arm*,
2Ch 6:32. *and thy* stretched out *arm;*
32: 8. With him (is) *an arm of* flesh;
Job 22: 8. But (as for) the *mighty* man, (marg. man of *arm*)
9. *and the arms of* the fatherless
26: 2. *the arm* (that hath) no strength?
35: 9. they cry out *by reason of the arm*
38:15. *and the* high *arm* shall be broken.
40: 9. Hast thou *an arm* like God?
Ps. 10:15. Break thou *the arm of* the wicked
18:34(35). a bow of steel is broken by *mine arms.*
37:17. For *the arms of* the wicked shall be
44: 3(4). *neither* did *their own arm* save them: but thy right hand, *and thine arm*,
71:18. until I have shewed *thy strength* (marg. *thine arm*)
77:15(16). hast *with* (thine) *arm* redeemed
79:11. according to the greatness of *thy power* (marg. *thine arm*)
83: 8(9). they have holpen the children of Lot. (marg. they have been *an arm* to)
89:10(11). scattered thine enemies *with* thy strong *arm.*
13(14). Thou hast *a* mighty *arm:*
21(22). *mine arm* also shall strengthen him.
98: 1. *and* his holy *arm*,
136:12. *and with a* stretched out *arm:*
Pro.31:17. strengtheneth *her arms.*
Cant 8: 6. as a seal upon *thine arm:*
Isa. 9:20(19). eat every man the flesh of *his own arm:*
17: 5. *and* reapeth the ears *with his arm*,
30:30. shew the lighting down of *his arm*,
33: 2. be thou *their arm* every morning,
40:10. *and his arm* shall rule for him:

Isa 40:11. gather the lambs *with his arm*,
44:12. worketh it with the strength of his *arms:* (lit. *with the arm of* his strength)
48:14. *and his arm* (shall be on) the Chaldeans.
51: 5. *and mine arms* shall judge the people;
— on *mine arm* shall they trust.
9. put on strength, *O arm of* the Lord;
52:10. The Lord hath made bare his holy *arm*
53: 1. *and* to whom is *the arm of* the Lord revealed?
59:16. therefore *his arm* brought salvation
62: 8. *and by the arm of* his strength,
63: 5. *mine own arm* brought salvation
12. Moses with his glorious *arm*,
Jer. 17: 5. and maketh flesh *his arm*,
21: 5. *and with a* strong *arm*,
27: 5. *and by my* outstretched *arm*,
32:17. by thy great power *and* stretched out *arm*,
48:25. *and his arm* is broken,
Eze. 4: 7. *and thine arm* (shall be) uncovered,
13:20. I will tear them from *your arms*,
17: 9. even *without* great *power* (lit. not *with a* great *arm*)
20:33, 34. *and with a* stretched out *arm*,
22: 6. *to their power* to shed blood. (marg. *arm*)
30:21. I have broken *the arm of* Pharaoh
22. and will break *his arms*,
24, 25. I will strengthen *the arms of* the king
— I will break Pharaoh's *arms*,
25. *and the arms of* Pharaoh shall fall
31:17. *and* (they that were) *his arm*,
Dan 10: 6. *and his arms* and his feet like
11: 6. shall not retain the power of *the arm;* neither shall he stand, *nor his arm:*
15. *and the arms of* the south shall not
22. *And with the arms of* a flood
31. *And arms* shall stand on his part,
Hos. 7:15. bound (and) strengthened *their arms*,
11: 3. taking them by *their arms;*
Zec 11:17. the sword (shall be) upon *his arm*,
— *his arm* shall be clean dried up,

2221 **זֵרוּעַ** *zēh-roo'ăg̃*, m.

Lev. 11:37. their carcase fall upon any *sowing* seed
Isa. 61:11. causeth *the things that are sown in it*

2222 **זַרְזִיף** *zar-zeeph'*, m.

Ps. 72: 6. as showers (that) *water* the earth.

2223 **זַרְזִיר** *zar-zeer'*, adj.

Pro. 30:31. A greyhound; (marg. *girt in* the loins, or, horse)

2224 **זָרַח** *zāh-ragh'*.

* KAL.—*Preterite.* *

Ex. 22: 3(2). If the sun *be risen* upon him,
Deu 33: 2. *and rose up* from Seir unto them;
2K. 3:22. the sun *shone* upon the water,
2Ch 26:19. the leprosy even *rose up* in his forehead
Ps. 112: 4. Unto the upright there *ariseth* light
Ecc. 1: 5. The sun *also ariseth*,
Isa. 58:10. *then shall* thy light *rise*
60: 1. the glory of the Lord *is risen* upon thee.
Nah 3:17. when the sun *ariseth* they flee
Mal. 4: 2(3:20). *But* unto you...*shall* the Sun of righteousness *arise*

KAL.—*Infinitive.*

Jud. 9:33. *as soon as* the sun *is up*,
Jon. 4: 8. *when* the sun *did arise*,

KAL.—*Future.*

Gen 32:31(32). *And* as he passed over Penuel the sun *rose*
2Sa. 23: 4. the morning, (when) the sun *riseth*,
Job 9: 7. commandeth the sun, and *it riseth* not;
Ps. 104:22. The sun *ariseth*, they gather themselves
Isa. 60: 2. but the Lord *shall arise* upon thee,

KAL.—*Participle.* Poel.

Ecc. 1: 5. hasteth to his place where he *arose.*

זֶרַח [*zeh'-ragh*], m. 2225

Isa. 60: 3. kings to the brightness of *thy rising.*

זָרַם [*zāh-ram'*]. 2229

* KAL.—*Preterite.* *

Ps. 90: 5. *Thou carriest them away as with a flood;*

* POAL.—*Preterite.* *

Ps. 77:17(18). The clouds *poured out* water: (marg. *were poured forth* with water)

זֶרֶם *zeh'-rem*, m. 2230

Job 24: 8. They are wet *with the showers of*
Isa. 4: 6. for a covert *from storm*
25: 4. a refuge *from the storm*,
— *as a storm* (against) the wall.
28: 2. *as a tempest of* hail
— *as a flood of* mighty waters
30:30. scattering, *and tempest*, and hailstones.
32: 2. a covert from *the tempest;*
Hab 3:10. *the overflowing of* the water passed by:

זִרְמָה [*zir-māh'*], f. 2231

Eze. 23:20. *and whose issue* (is like) *the issue of* horses.

זָרַע *zāh-rag̃'*. 2232

* KAL.—*Preterite.* *

Gen 47:23. *and ye shall sow* the land.
Lev. 25:22. *And ye shall sow* the eighth year,
26:16. *and ye shall sow* your seed in vain,
Jud. 6: 3. when Israel *had sown*,
Jer. 12:13. *They have sown* wheat,
31:27. *that I will sow* the house of Israel
Hos 2:23(25). *And I will sow her* unto me
Hag 1: 6. *Ye have sown* much,

KAL.—*Infinitive.*

Isa. 28:24. the plowman plow all day *to sow?*

KAL.—*Imperative.*

2K. 19:29. in the third year *sow ye*,
Ecc. 11: 6. In the morning *sow* thy seed,
Isa. 37:30. in the third year *sow ye*,
Hos 10:12. *Sow* to yourselves in righteousness,

KAL.—*Future.*

Gen 26:12. *Then* Isaac *sowed* in that land,
Ex. 23:10. six years *thou shalt sow* thy land,
16. which *thou hast sown* in the field:
Lev 19:19. *thou shalt* not *sow* thy field
25: 3. Six years *thou shalt sow*
4. *thou shalt* neither *sow* thy field,
11. *ye shall* not *sow*, neither reap
20. behold, *we shall* not *sow*,
Deu 11:10. where *thou sowedst* thy seed,
22: 9. *Thou shalt* not *sow* thy vineyard
— of thy seed which *thou hast sown*,
Jud. 9:45. *and sowed it* with salt.
Job 31: 8. *let me sow*, and let another eat;
Ps. 107:37. *And sow* the fields,
Ecc 11: 4. He that observeth the wind *shall* not *sow;*
Isa. 17:10. and *shalt set it with* strange slips:
30:23. that *thou shalt sow* the ground
Jer. 4: 3. *sow* not among thorns.
35: 7. build house, nor *sow* seed,
Hos 8: 7. *they have sown* the wind,
Mic 6:15. Thou *shalt sow*, but thou
Zec 10: 9. *And I will sow them* among

KAL.—*Participle.* Poel.

Gen 1:29. given you every herb *bearing* seed,
— the fruit of a tree *yielding* seed;
Job 4: 8. plow iniquity, *and sow* wickedness,

Ps.126: 5. *They that sow* in tears shall reap in joy.
Pro.11:18. *but to him that soweth* righteousness
22: 8. *He that soweth* iniquity
Isa. 32:20. *ye that sow* beside all waters,
55:10. that it may give seed *to the sower,*
Jer. 50:16. Cut off *the sower* from Babylon,

KAL.—*Participle.* Paül.

Ps. 97:11. Light is *sown* for the righteous,
Jer. 2: 2. in a land (that was) not *sown.*

* NIPHAL.—Preterite. *

Nu. 5:28. *and shall conceive* seed.
Eze.36: 9. ye shall be tilled *and sown:*

NIPHAL.—*Future.*

Lev.11:37. sowing seed which *is to be sown,*
Deu21: 4. which is neither eared nor *sown,*
29:23(22). burning, (that) *it is* not *sown,*
Nah. 1:14. no more of thy name *be sown:*

* PUAL.—Preterite. *

Isa. 40:24. yea, *they shall* not *be sown:*

* HIPHIL.—Future. *

Lev.12: 2. If a woman *have conceived seed,*

HIPHIL.—*Participle.*

Gen 1:11 12. herb *yielding* seed,

2233 **זֶרַע** *zeh'-rag̃,* m.

Gen 1:11. the herb yielding *seed,*
— whose *seed* (is) in itself, upon the earth: (lit. which *its seed*)
12. herb yielding *seed* after his kind,
— whose *seed* (was) in itself, after his kind: (lit. which *its seed*)
29. every herb bearing *seed,*
— the fruit of a tree yielding *seed;*
3:15. between *thy seed* and *her seed;*
4:25. appointed me another *seed*
7: 3. to keep *seed* alive upon the face of
8:22. *seedtime* and harvest, and cold and heat,
9: 9. and with *your seed* after you;
12: 7. *Unto thy seed* will I give this land:
13:15. to thee will I give it, *and to thy seed*
16. I will make *thy seed* as the dust
— shall *thy seed* also be numbered.
15: 3. to me thou hast given no *seed:*
5. he said unto him, So shall *thy seed* be.
13. Know of a surety that *thy seed*
18. *Unto thy seed* have I given this land,
16:10. I will multiply *thy seed* exceedingly,
17: 7. me and thee and *thy seed* after thee
—, 8. *and to thy seed* after thee.
9. thou, *and thy seed* after thee
10. between me and you and *thy seed*
12. which (is) not *of thy seed.*
19. *with his seed* after him.
19:32, 34. that we may preserve *seed*
21:12. in Isaac shall thy *seed* be called.
13. a nation, because he (is) *thy seed.*
22:17. I will multiply *thy seed* as the stars
— and *thy seed* shall possess the gate
18. And *in thy seed* shall all the nations
24: 7. *Unto thy seed* will I give this land;
60. let *thy seed* possess the gate of those
26: 3. unto thee, *and unto thy seed,*
4. I will make *thy seed* to multiply
— will give *unto thy seed* all these countries; and *in thy seed* shall all the nations
24. multiply *thy seed* for my servant
28: 4. to thee, *and to thy seed* with thee;
13. to thee will I give it, *and to thy seed;*
14. And *thy seed* shall be as the dust
— in thee *and in thy seed* shall all
32:12(13). make *thy seed* as the sand of the sea,
35:12. *and to thy seed* after thee
38: 8. raise up *seed* to thy brother.
9. Onan knew that *the seed* should not
— lest that he should give *seed*
46: 6. Jacob, and all *his seed* with him:
7. all *his seed* brought he with him
47:19. give (us) *seed,* that we may live,
23. lo, (here is) *seed* for you,
24. *for seed of* the field,
48: 4. will give this land *to thy seed*

Gen48:11. God hath shewed me also *thy seed.*
19. *and his seed* shall become a multitude
Ex. 16:31. and it (was) *like* coriander *seed,*
28:43. *and his seed* after him.
30:21. to him *and to his seed*
32:13. I will multiply *your seed*
— will I give *unto your seed,*
33: 1. *Unto thy seed* will I give it:
Lev.11:37. carcase fall upon any sowing *seed*
38. if (any) water be put upon *the seed,*
15:16, 17, 18. *seed* of copulation
32. whose *seed* goeth from him,
18:20. thou shalt not lie *carnally* with (lit. giving thy lying *for seed*)
21. *And* thou shalt not let *any of thy seed*
19:20. whosoever lieth *carnally* with a woman, (lit. with the lying of *seed*)
20: 2. giveth (any) *of his seed* unto Molech,
3. he hath given *of his seed* unto Molech,
4. he giveth *of his seed* unto Molech,
21:15. Neither shall he profane *his seed*
17. Whosoever (he be) *of thy seed*
21. hath a blemish *of the seed of* Aaron
22: 3. Whosoever (he be) of all *your seed*
4. What man soever *of the seed of* Aaron
— or a man whose *seed* goeth from him; (lit. lying of *seed*)
13. *and* have no *child,*
26: 5. the vintage shall reach unto the *sowing time:*
16. ye shall sow *your seed* in vain,
27:16. shall be according to *the seed thereof:* an homer of barley *seed*
30. *of the seed of* the land,
Nu. 5:13. a man lie with her *carnally,* (lit. with the lying of *seed*)
28. and shall conceive *seed.*
11: 7. the manna (was) *as* coriander *seed,*
14:24. *and his seed* shall possess it.
16:40(17:5). which (is) not *of the seed of* Aaron,
18:19. *and to thy seed* with thee.
20: 5. it (is) no place of *seed,*
24: 7. *and his seed* (shall be) in many waters,
25:13. he shall have it, *and his seed* after him,
Deu 1: 8. *and to their seed* after them.
4:37. therefore he chose *their seed*
10:15. he chose *their seed* after them,
11: 9. unto them *and to their seed,*
10. where thou sowedst *thy seed,*
14:22. tithe all the increase of *thy seed,*
22: 9. lest the fruit of *thy seed* which thou
28:38. Thou shalt carry much *seed* out
46. a wonder, *and upon thy seed* for ever.
59. the plagues of *thy seed,*
30: 6. the heart of *thy seed,*
19. that both thou *and thy seed* may live:
31:21. forgotten out of the mouths of *their seed:*
34: 4. I will give it *unto thy seed:*
Jos. 24: 3. and multiplied *his seed,*
Ru. 4:12. *the seed* which the Lord shall give
1Sa. 1:11. give unto thine handmaid *a* man *child,* (marg. *seed of* men)
2:20. The Lord give thee *seed* of this woman
8:15. *And* he will take the tenth of *your seed,*
20:42. between *my seed* and *thy seed* for ever.
24:21(22). that thou wilt not cut off *my seed*
2Sa. 4: 8. this day of Saul, *and of his seed.*
7:12. I will set up *thy seed* after thee,
22:51. David, *and to his seed* for evermore.
1K. 2:33. upon the head of *his seed* for ever: but upon David, *and upon his seed,*
11:14. he (was) *of the* king's *seed* in Edom.
39. I will for this afflict *the seed of* David,
18:32. contain two measures of *seed.*
2K. 5:27. *and unto thy seed* for ever.
11: 1. she arose and destroyed all *the seed* royal.
17:20. rejected all *the seed of* Israel,
25:25. son of Elishama, *of the seed* royal,
1Ch 16:13. *O ye seed of* Israel his servant,
17:11. that I will raise up *thy seed*
2Ch 20: 7. gavest it *to the seed of* Abraham
22:10. she arose and destroyed all *the seed* royal
Ezr. 2:59. their father's house, *and their seed,* (marg. or, *pedigree*)
9: 2. so that *the* holy *seed* have mingled
Neh 7:61. their fathers' house, *nor their seed,* (marg. or, *pedigree*)

Neh 9: 2. And *the seed of* Israel separated
8. to give (it, I say), *to his seed,*
Est. 6:13. If Mordecai (be) *of the seed of* the Jews,
9:27. took upon them, and upon *their seed,*
28. memorial of them perish *from their seed.*
31. themselves and for *their seed,*
10: 3. speaking peace to all *his seed.*
Job 5:25. know also that *thy seed* (shall be) great,
21: 8. *Their seed* is established in their sight
39:12. that he will bring home *thy seed,*
Ps. 18:50(51). *and to his seed* for evermore.
21:10(11). *and their seed* from among the children
22:23(24). all *ye the seed of* Jacob, glorify him; and fear him, all *ye the seed of* Israel.
30(31). *A seed* shall serve him;
25:13. *and his seed* shall inherit the earth.
37:25. *nor his seed* begging bread.
26. *and his seed* (is) blessed.
28. *but the seed of* the wicked
69:36(37). *The seed also of* his servants
89: 4(5). *Thy seed* will I establish for ever,
29(30). *His seed* also will I make (to endure)
36(37). *His seed* shall endure for ever,
102:28(29). *and their seed* shall be established
105: 6. *O ye seed of* Abraham his servant,
106:27. To overthrow *their seed* also among
112: 2. *His seed* shall be mighty upon earth:
126: 6. bearing precious *seed,*
Pro 11:21. *but the seed of* the righteous
Ecc 11: 6. In the morning sow *thy seed,*
Isa. 1: 4. *a seed of* evildoers,
5:10. *and the seed of* an homer
6:13. *the* holy *seed* (shall be) the substance
14:20. *the seed of* evildoers
17:11. in the morning shalt thou make *thy seed* to
23: 3. by great waters *the seed of* Sihor,
30:23. Then shall he give the rain of *thy seed,*
41: 8. *the seed of* Abraham my friend.
43: 5. I will bring *thy seed* from the east,
44: 3. I will pour my spirit upon *thy seed,*
45:19. I said not *unto the seed of* Jacob,
25. In the Lord shall all *the seed of* Israel
48:19. *Thy seed* also had been as the sand,
53:10. he shall see (his) *seed,*
54: 3. *and thy seed* shall inherit the Gentiles,
55:10. that it may give *seed* to the sower,
57: 3. *the seed of* the adulterer
4. *a seed of* falsehood,
59:21. out of the mouth of *thy seed,* nor out of the mouth of *thy seed's seed,*
61: 9. And *their seed* shall be known
— they (are) *the seed* (which) the Lord
65: 9. bring forth *a seed* out of Jacob,
23. *the seed of* the blessed of the Lord,
66:22. so shall *your seed* and your name remain.
Jer. 2:21. a noble vine, wholly *a* right *seed:*
7:15. *the* whole *seed of* Ephraim.
22:28. are they cast out, he *and his seed,*
30. for no man *of his seed* shall prosper,
23: 8. which led *the seed of* the house of Israel
29:32. Shemaiah the Nehelamite, and *his seed:*
30:10. and *thy seed* from the land of their captivity;
31:27. with *the seed of* man, *and* with *the seed of* beast.
36. *the seed of* Israel also shall cease
37. cast off all *the seed of* Israel
33:22. so will I multiply *the seed of* David
26. Then will I cast away *the seed of* Jacob,
— that I will not take (any) *of his seed* (to be) rulers over *the seed of* Abraham,
35: 7. build house, *nor* sow *seed,*
9. vineyard, nor field, *nor seed:*
36:31. I will punish him and *his seed*
41: 1. the son of Elishama, *of the seed* royal,
46:27. and *thy seed* from the land of their captivity;
49:10. *his seed* is spoiled,
Eze 17: 5. He took also *of the seed of* the land, and planted it in a *fruitful* field; (marg. field of *seed*)
13. And hath taken *of* the king's *seed,*
20: 5. *unto the seed of* the house of Jacob,
43:19. the Levites that be *of the seed of* Zadok,
44:22. maidens *of the seed of* the house of Israel,
Dan 1: 3. of Israel, *and of* the king's *seed,*
Dan 9: 1. Ahasuerus, *of the seed of* the Medes,
Am. 9:13. him that soweth *seed;*
Hag 2:19. Is *the seed* yet in the barn?
Zec. 8:12. *the seed* (shall be) prosperous;
Mal. 2: 3. I will corrupt your *seed,*
15. That he might seek *a* godly *seed.*

זְרַע *z'rag̃*, Ch. m. 2234

Dan. 2:43. mingle themselves *with the seed of* men:

זֵרֹעִים *zēh-rōh-g̃eem′*, m. pl. 2235

Dan. 1:12. and let them give us *pulse*

זֵרְעֹנִים *zēh-r'g̃ōh-neem′*, m. pl. 2235

Dan. 1:16. and gave them *pulse.*

זָרַק *zāh-rak′*. 2236

* KAL.—*Preterite.* *

Ex. 9: 8. *and let* Moses *sprinkle it*
24: 6. the blood *he sprinkled* on the altar.
29:16. *and sprinkle* (it) round about
20. *and sprinkle* the blood upon the altar
Lev. 1: 5. *and sprinkle* the blood
11. *and* the priests, Aaron's sons, *shall sprinkle*
3: 2. *and* Aaron's sons the priests *shall sprinkle*
8. *and* Aaron's sons *shall sprinkle*
13. *and* the sons of Aaron *shall sprinkle*
17: 6. *And* the priest *shall sprinkle* the blood
Eze.36:25. *Then will I sprinkle* clean water
Hos. 7: 9. gray hairs *are here and there* upon him, (marg. *sprinkled*)

KAL.—*Infinitive.*

Eze.43:18. *and to sprinkle* blood thereon.

KAL.—*Imperative.*

Eze.10: 2. *and scatter* (them) over the city.

KAL.—*Future.*

Ex. 9:10. *and* Moses *sprinkled* it up toward
24: 8. *and sprinkled* (it) on the people,
Lev. 7: 2. the blood thereof *shall he sprinkle*
8:19, 24. *and* Moses *sprinkled* the blood
9:12. *which he sprinkled* round about
18. *which he sprinkled* upon the altar
Nu. 18:17. *thou shalt sprinkle* their blood
2K. 16:13. *and sprinkled* the blood
15. *sprinkle* upon it all the blood
2Ch 29:22. *and sprinkled* (it) on the altar:
— *likewise,...they sprinkled* the blood
— *and they sprinkled* the blood
34: 4. *and strowed* (it) upon the graves
35:11. *and* the priests *sprinkled* (the blood)
Job 2:12. *and sprinkled* dust upon their heads
Isa. 28:25. cast abroad the fitches, and *scatter* the cummin,

KAL.—*Participle.* Poel.

Lev. 7:14. the priest's *that sprinkleth* the blood
2Ch 30:16. the priests *sprinkled* the blood,

* PUAL.—*Preterite.* *

Nu. 19:13. the water of separation *was* not *sprinkled*
20. *hath* not *been sprinkled* upon him;

זָרַר [*zāh-rar′*]. 2237

* POEL.—*Future.* *

2K. 4:35. *and* the child *sneezed* seven times,

זֶרֶת *zeh′-reth*, f. 2239

Ex. 28:16. *a span* (shall be) the length thereof, *and a span* (shall be) the breadth thereof.
39: 9. *a span* (was) the length thereof, *and a span* the breadth thereof,

1Sa.17: 4. height (was) six cubits *and a span.*
Isa. 40:12. meted out heaven *with the span,*
Eze 43:13. edge thereof round about (shall be) *a span:*

ח
The eighth letter of the Alphabet.

2243 **חֹב** [*ghōhv*], m.

Job 31:33. by hiding mine iniquity *in my bosom:*

2244 **חָבָא** [*ghāh-vāh'*].

* NIPHAL.—*Preterite.* *

Gen31:27. *didst thou* flee away *secretly*, (lit. *didst thou hide thyself* to flee away)
Jos. 10:27. cave wherein *they had been hid,*
Jud. 9: 5. for *he hid himself.*
1Sa.19: 2. in a secret (place), *and hide thyself:*
Job 29: 8. men saw me, *and hid themselves:*
10. The nobles *held* their peace, (marg. The voice of the nobles *was hid*)

NIPHAL.—*Infinitive.*

2Ch 18:24. an inner chamber *to hide thyself.*
Dan 10: 7. so that they fled *to hide themselves.*

NIPHAL.—*Future.*

Gen 3:10. I (was) naked; *and I hid myself.*
Jos. 10:16. five kings fled, *and hid themselves*
Job 5:21. *Thou shalt be hid* from
Am. 9: 3. though *they hide themselves*

NIPHAL.—*Participle.*

Jos. 10:17. The five kings are found *hid*
1Sa.10:22. he *hath hid himself* among the stuff.
2Sa.17: 9. he *is hid* now in some pit,

* PUAL.—*Preterite.* *

Job 24: 4. the poor of the earth *hide themselves*

* HIPHIL.—*Preterite.* *

Jos. 6:17. because *she hid* the messengers
25. because *she hid* the messengers,
Isa. 49: 2. in the shadow of his hand *hath he hid me,*

HIPHIL.—*Future.*

1K. 18: 4. *and hid them* by fifty in a cave,
13. *how I hid* an hundred men
2K. 6:29. *and she hath hid* her son.

* HOPHAL.—*Preterite.* *

Isa. 42:22. *they are hid* in prison houses:

* HITHPAEL.—*Preterite.* *

1Sa.14:11. where *they had hid themselves.*

HITHPAEL.—*Future.*

Gen 3: 8. *and* Adam and his wife *hid themselves*
1Sa.13: 6. *then* the people *did hide themselves*
23:23. where *he hideth himself,*
Job 38:30. The waters *are hid* as (with) a stone,

HITHPAEL.—*Participle.*

1Sa.14:22. *which had hid themselves*
2K. 11: 3. he was with her *hid* in the house
1Ch 21:20. his four sons with him *hid themselves.*
2Ch 22: 9. for he *was hid* in Samaria,
12. *hid* in the house of God

2245 **חָבַב** [*ghāh-vav'*].

* KAL.—*Participle.* *

Deu 33: 3. Yea, *he loved* the people;

2247 **חָבָה** [*ghāh-vāh'*].

* KAL.—*Imperative.* *

Isa. 26:20. *hide thyself* as it were for a little moment,

* NIPHAL.—*Preterite.* *

Jos. 2:16. *and hide yourselves* there

NIPHAL.—*Infinitive.*

1K. 22:25. an inner chamber *to hide thyself.*
2K. 7:12. out of the camp *to hide themselves*
Jer. 49:10. *and* he shall not be able *to hide himself:*

חֲבוּלָה *ghăvoo-lāh'*, Ch. f. 2248

Dan 6:22(23). O king, have I done no *hurt.*

חַבּוּרָה *ghab-boo-rāh'*, & **חֲבֻרָה**, [*ghăvoo-rāh'*], f. 2250

Gen 4:23. a young man *to my hurt:*
Ex. 21:25. wound for wound, *stripe* for *stripe.*
Ps. 38: 5(6). *My wounds* stink (and) are corrupt
Pro.20:30. *The blueness of* a wound cleanseth
Isa. 1: 6. wounds, *and bruises,*
53: 5. *and with his stripes* we are healed. (marg. *bruise*)

חָבַט [*ghāh-vat'*]. 2251

* KAL.—*Future.* *

Deu 24:20. When *thou beatest* thine olive tree,
Ru. 2:17. *and beat out* that she had gleaned:
Isa. 27:12. the Lord *shall beat off* from the channel

KAL.—*Participle.* Poel.

Jud. 6:11. his son Gideon *threshed* wheat

* NIPHAL.—*Future.* *

Isa. 28:27. the fitches *are beaten out* with a staff,

חֶבְיוֹן *ghev-yōhn'*, m. 2253

Hab 3: 4. there (was) *the hiding of* his power.

חָבַל [*ghāh-val'*]. 2254

* KAL.—*Preterite.* *

Neh 1: 7. *We have dealt* very *corruptly*
Eze.18:16. *hath* not *withholden* the pledge, (marg. *pledged*, or, *taken to pledge*)

KAL.—*Infinitive.*

Ex. 22:26(25). If thou *at all* take thy neighbour's raiment to pledge, (lit. *in pledging* shalt pledge)
Neh 1: 7. We have dealt *very* corruptly (lit. *in dealing corruptly* we have dealt corruptly)

KAL.—*Imperative.*

Pro.20:16 & 27:13. *take a pledge of him* for a strange woman.

KAL.—*Future.*

Ex. 22:26(25). If *thou* at all *take* thy neighbour's raiment *to pledge,*
Deu 24: 6. *shall take* the nether or the upper milstone *to pledge:*
17. *nor take* the widow's raiment *to pledge:*
Job 22: 6. For *thou hast taken a pledge*
24: 3. *they take* the widow's ox *for a pledge.*
9. *take a pledge* of the poor.
34:31. I *will* not *offend*

KAL.—*Participle.* Poel.

Deu 24: 6. he *taketh* (a man's) life *to pledge.*
Zec.11: 7. the other I called *Bands;* (marg. *Binders*)
14. I cut asunder mine other staff, (even) *Bands,*

KAL.—*Participle.* Paül.

Am. 2: 8. *laid to pledge* by every altar,

* NIPHAL.—*Future.* *

Pro.13:13. Whoso despiseth the word *shall be destroyed:*

* PIEL.—*Preterite.* *

Ecc. 5: 6(5). *and destroy* the work of thine hands?
Cant.8: 5. there thy mother *brought thee forth:* there she *brought* thee *forth*

PIEL.—*Infinitive.*

Isa. 13: 5. indignation, *to destroy* the whole land.
32: 7. wicked devices *to destroy* the poor
54:16. I have created the waster *to destroy.*

PIEL—*Future.*

Ps. 7:14(15). *he travaileth with* iniquity,
Mic. 2:10. it is polluted, *it shall destroy*

PIEL.—*Participle.*

Cant.2:15. the little foxes, *that spoil* the vines:

* PUAL.—*Preterite.* *

Job 17: 1. My breath *is corrupt,*
Isa. 10:27. *and* the yoke *shall be destroyed*

2255 חֲבַל [*ghăval*], Ch.

* PAEL.—*Preterite.* *

Dan 6:22(23). lions' mouths, that *they have* not *hurt me:*

PAEL.—*Infinitive.*

Ezr. 6:12. to alter (and) *to destroy* this house

PAEL.—*Imperative.*

Dan 4:23(20). Hew the tree down, *and destroy it;*

* ITHPAEL.—*Future.* *

Dan 2:44. which *shall* never *be destroyed:*
6:26(27) & 7:14. (that) which *shall* not *be destroyed,*

2256 חֶבֶל *ghĕh'-vel,* & חֵבֶל *gheh'-vel,* com.

Deu 3: 4, 13. all *the region of* Argob,
14. Manasseh took all *the country of*
32: 9. Jacob (is) *the lot of* his inheritance.
Jos. 2:15. she let them down *by a cord*
17: 5. there fell ten *portions to* Manasseh,
14. and one *portion* to inherit,
19: 9. *Out of the portion of* the children of
29. from *the coast* to Achzib:
1Sa.10: 5. thou shalt meet *a company of* prophets
10. *a company of* prophets met him;
2Sa. 8: 2. measured them *with a line,*
— even with two *lines* measured he
— with one full *line* to keep alive.
17:13. then shall all Israel bring *ropes*
22: 6. *The sorrows of* hell compassed me (marg. or, *cords*)
1K. 4:13. *the region of* Argob,
20:31. *and ropes* upon our heads.
32. *and* (put) *ropes* on their heads,
1Ch 16:18. *the lot of* your inheritance; (marg. *cord*)
Est. 1: 6. fastened *with cords of* fine linen
Job 18:10. *The snare* (is) laid *for him* in the ground,
21:17. distributeth *sorrows* in his anger.
36: 8. be holden *in cords of* affliction;
39: 3. they cast out *their sorrows.*
41: 1(40:25). *or* his tongue *with a cord*
Ps. 16: 6. *The lines* are fallen unto me
18: 4(5). *The sorrows of* death compassed me,
5(6). *The sorrows of* hell compassed me (marg. or, *cords*)
78:55. divided them an inheritance *by line,*
105:11. *the lot of* your inheritance: (marg. *cord*)
116: 3. *The sorrows of* death compassed me,
119:61. *The bands of* the wicked have (marg. or, *companies*)
140: 5(6). hid a snare for me, *and cords;*
Pro. 5:22. *and* he shall be holden *with the cords of*
Ecc.12: 6. Or ever *the* silver *cord* be loosed,
Isa. 5:18. that draw iniquity *with cords of* vanity,
13: 8. pangs *and sorrows* shall take
26:17. crieth out *in her pangs;*
33:20. shall any of *the cords thereof* be broken.
23. *Thy tacklings* are loosed;
66: 7. brought forth; before her *pain* came,
Jer. 13:21. shall not *sorrows* take thee,
Jer. 22:23. when *pangs* come upon thee,
38: 6. they let down Jeremiah *with cords.*
11. let them down *by cords*
12. under thine armholes *under the cords.*
13. they drew up Jeremiah *with cords,*
49:24. anguish *and sorrows* have taken her,
Eze.27:24. rich apparel, bound *with cords,*
47:13. Joseph (shall have two) *portions.*
Hos 11: 4. I drew them *with cords of* a man,
13:13. *The sorrows of* a travailing woman
Am. 7:17. thy land shall be divided *by line;*
Mic. 2: 5. none that shall cast *a cord* by lot
10. *even with a* sore *destruction.*
Zep. 2: 5. the inhabitants of *the* sea *coast,*
6. *the* sea *coast* shall be dwellings
7. *the coast* shall be for the remnant
Zec. 2: 1(5). behold a man with *a* measuring *line*

חֲבֹל *ghăvōhl,* m. 2258

Eze.18:12. hath not restored *the pledge,*
16. hath not withholden *the pledge,*
33:15. the wicked restore *the pledge,*

חֲבַל *ghăval,* Ch. 2257

Dan 3:25. *and* they have no *hurt;*

חֲבָל *ghăvāhl,* Ch. m. 2257

Ezr. 4:22. why should *damage* grow to the hurt of
Dan 6:23(24). no manner of *hurt* was found upon

חִבֵּל *ghib-bēhl'.* 2260

Pro.23:34. as he that lieth upon the top of *a mast.*

חֹבֵל *ghōh'-vēhl,* m. 2259

Eze.27: 8. were in thee, were *thy pilots.*
27. thy mariners, *and thy pilots,*
28. at the sound of the cry of *thy pilots.*
29. all *the pilots of* the sea,
Jon. 1: 6. So the *ship*master came to him, (lit. *the* great *pilot*)

חֲבֹלָה [*ghăvōh-lāh'*], f. 2258

Eze.18: 7. hath restored to the debtor *his pledge,*

חֲבַצֶּלֶת *ghăvatz-tzeh'-leth,* f. 2261

Cant.2: 1. I (am) *the rose of* Sharon,
Isa. 35: 1. blossom *as the rose.*

חָבַק [*ghāh-vak'*]. 2263

* KAL.—*Infinitive.* *

Ecc. 3: 5. a time *to embrace,*

KAL.—*Participle.* Poel.

2K. 4:16. thou *shalt embrace* a son.
Ecc. 4: 5. The fool *foldeth* his hands together,

* PIEL.—*Preterite.* *

Job 24: 8. *embrace* the rock for want of
Lam 4: 5. brought up in scarlet *embrace*

PIEL.—*Infinitive.*

Ecc. 3: 5. a time to refrain *from embracing;*

PIEL.—*Future.*

Gen29:13. he ran to meet him, *and embraced* him,
33: 4. Esau ran to meet him, *and embraced him,*
48:10. he kissed them, *and embraced* them.
Pro. 4: 8. when *thou dost embrace her.*
5:20. *and embrace* the bosom of a stranger?
Cant.2: 6. his right hand *doth embrace me.*
8: 3. his right hand *should embrace me.*

2264 חִבֻּק *ghib-book'*, m.

Pro. 6:10 & 24:33. *a* little *folding of* the hands

2266 חָבַר [*ghāh-vār'*].

* KAL.—*Preterite.* *

Gen14: 3. All these *were joined together*

KAL.—*Participle.* Poel.

Ex. 26: 3. five curtains shall be *coupled together*
— *coupled* one to another.
28: 7. have the two shoulderpieces thereof *joined*
39: 4. for it, *to couple* (it) *together:*
Deu18:11. *Or a charmer*, or a consulter (lit. *one that charms* charming)
Ps. 58: 5(6). hearken to the voice of charmers, charming (lit. enchanters *charming* charms)
Eze. 1: 9. Their wings (were) *joined* one to another;
11. two (wings) of every one (were) *joined*

KAL.—*Participle.* Paül.

Hos 4:17. Ephraim (is) *joined* to idols:

* PIEL.—*Preterite.* *

Ex. 26: 6. *and couple* the curtains together
9. *And thou shalt couple* five curtains
11. *and couple* the tent together,
36:10. curtains *he coupled* one unto another.

PIEL.—*Infinitive.*

Ex. 36:18. *to couple* the tent together,

PIEL.—*Future.*

Ex. 36:10. *And he coupled* the five curtains
13. *and coupled* the curtains
16. *And he coupled* five curtains
2Ch 20:36. *And he joined himself* with him

* PUAL.—*Preterite.* *

Ex. 28: 7. and (so) *it shall be joined together.*
39: 4. by the two edges *was it coupled together.*
Ps. 122: 3. as a city *that is compact* together:

PUAL.—*Future.*

Ps. 94:20. *Shall* the throne of iniquity *have fellowship with thee*,
Ecc. 9: 4. For to him that *is joined* to all the living

* HIPHIL.—*Future.* *

Job 16: 4. *I could heap up* words against you,

* HITHPAEL.—*Preterite.* *

2Ch 20:35. *did* Jehoshaphat king of Judah *join himself*

HITHPAEL.—*Infinitive.*

2Ch 20:37. *Because thou hast joined thyself*
Dan 11:23. after *the league* (made) with him he shall work

HITHPAEL.—*Future.*

Dan11: 6. *they shall join themselves together;*

2271 חַבָּר [*ghab-bāhr'*], m.

Job 41: 6(40:30). Shall *the companions* make a banquet

2270 חָבֵר *ghāh-vēhr*, adj.

Jud.20:11. *knit together* as one man. (marg. *fellows*)
Ps. 45: 7(8). the oil of gladness *above thy fellows.*
119:63. I (am) *a companion* of all (them) that fear thee,
Pro.28:24. the same (is) *the companion* of a destroyer.
Ecc. 4:10. the one will lift up *his fellow:*
Cant.1: 7. by the flocks of *thy companions?*
8:13. *the companions* hearken to thy voice:
Isa. 1:23. *and companions of* thieves:
44:11. all *his fellows* shall be ashamed:
Eze.37:16. the children of Israel *his companions:*
— all the house of Israel *his companions:*
19. the tribes of Israel *his fellows*,

חֲבַר [*ghăvar*], Ch. m. 2269

Dan 2:13. sought Daniel *and his fellows* to be slain.
17. Hananiah, Mishael, and Azariah, *his companions:*
18. that Daniel *and his fellows* should not perish

חֶבֶר *gheh'-ver*, m. 2267

Deu18:11. Or a charmer (lit. one that charms *a charming*), or a consulter
Ps. 58: 5(6). hearken to the voice of charmers, charming (lit. charming *charmings*)
Pro.21: 9. a brawling woman in a *wide* house. (marg. house of *society*)
25:24. a brawling woman and in a *wide* house.
Isa. 47: 9. great abundance of *thine enchantments.*
12. Stand now *with thine enchantments*,
Hos. 6: 9. *the company of* priests murder

חֲבַרְבֻּרוֹת [*ghăvar-boo-rōhth'*], f. pl. 2272

Jer. 13:23. or the leopard *his spots?*

חַבְרָה [*ghav-rāh'*], f. Ch. 2273

Dan 7:20. whose look (was) more stout than *his fellows.*

חֶבְרָה *ghev-rāh'*, f. 2274

Job 34: 8. Which goeth *in company*

חֲבֶרֶת [*ghăveh'-reth*], f. 2278

Mal. 2:14. yet (is) she *thy companion*,

חֹבֶרֶת *ghōh-veh'-reth*, f. 2279

Ex. 26: 4. the selvedge *in the coupling;*
10. outmost *in the coupling*,
— & 36:17. the curtain *which coupleth*

חָבַשׁ [*ghāh-vash'*]. 2280

* KAL.—*Preterite.* *

Ex. 29: 9. *and put* the bonnets on them: (marg. *bind*)
Eze.34: 4. neither *have ye bound up*

KAL.—*Infinitive.*

Isa. 30:26. in the day that the Lord *bindeth up*
61: 1. *to bind up* the brokenhearted,
Eze.30:21. to put a roller *to bind it*,

KAL.—*Imperative.*

1K. 13:13. he said unto his sons, *Saddle* me
27. *Saddle* me the ass. And they saddled
Job 40:13. *bind* their faces in secret.
Eze.24:17. *bind* the tire of thine head

KAL.—*Future.*

Gen22: 3. *and saddled* his ass,
Lev. 8:13. *and put* bonnets upon them; (marg. *bound*)
Nu. 22:21. *and saddled* his ass,
2Sa.17:23. *he saddled* (his) ass, and arose,
19:26(27). *I will saddle* me an ass,
1K. 2:40. Shimei arose, *and saddled* his ass,
13:13. *So they saddled* him the ass:
23. *that he saddled* for him the ass,
27. *And they saddled* (him).
2K. 4:24. *Then she saddled* an ass, and said to her servant,
Job 5:18. he maketh sore, *and bindeth up:*
34:17. *Shall* even he that hateth right *govern?* (marg. *bind*)
Eze.16:10. *and I girded thee about* with fine linen,
34:16. *and will bind up*
Hos. 6: 1. *and he will bind us up.*

KAL.—*Participle.* Poel.

Isa. 3: 7. I will not be *an healer;* (marg. *binder up*)

KAL.—*Participle.* Paül.

Jud. 19:10. with him two asses *saddled,*
2Sa. 16: 1. with a couple of asses *saddled,*
Eze. 27:24. *bound* with cords, and made of cedar,
Jon. 2: 5(6). the weeds *were wrapped* about

* PIEL.—*Preterite.* *

Job 28:11. *He bindeth* the floods from overflowing;

PIEL.—*Participle.*

Ps. 147: 3. *and bindeth up* their wounds.

* PUAL.—*Preterite.* *

Isa. 1: 6. have not been closed, neither *bound up,*
Eze. 30:21. *it shall* not *be bound up*

2281 חֲבִתִּים *g'hăvit-teem',* m. pl.

1Ch 9:31. things that were made in *the pans.* (marg. or, on *flat plates,* or, *slices*)

2282 חַג *g'hāhg,* & חָג *g'hag,* m.

Ex. 10: 9. we (must hold) *a feast* unto the Lord.
12:14. ye shall keep it *a feast* to the Lord
13: 6. the seventh day (shall be) *a feast*
23:15. Thou shalt keep *the feast*
16. *And the feast of* harvest,
— *and the feast of* ingathering,
18. the fat of *my sacrifice* (marg. or, *feast*)
32: 5. To morrow (is) *a feast* to the Lord.
34:18. *The feast of* unleavened bread
22. *And* thou shalt observe *the feast of*
— *and the feast of* ingathering
25. the sacrifice of *the feast of* the passover
Lev. 23: 6. *the feast of* unleavened bread
34. *the feast of* tabernacles
39. ye shall keep *a feast* unto the Lord
41. ye shall keep it *a feast*
Nu. 28:17. fifteenth day of this month (is) *the feast.*
29:12. ye shall keep *a feast* unto the Lord
Deu 16:10. thou shalt keep *the feast of* weeks
13. shalt observe *the feast of* tabernacles
14. thou shalt rejoice *in thy feast,*
16. *in the feast of* unleavened bread, *and in the feast of* weeks, *and in the feast of* tabernacles:
31:10. *in the feast of* tabernacles,
Jud. 21:19. Behold, (there is) *a feast of* the Lord
1K. 8: 2. *at the feast* in the month Ethanim,
65. at that time Solomon held *a feast,*
12:32. Jeroboam ordained *a feast*
— *like unto the feast* that (is) in Judah,
33. ordained *a feast* unto the children of
2Ch 5: 3. assembled themselves unto the king *in the feast*
7: 8. Solomon kept *the feast* seven days,
9. *and the feast* seven days.
8:13. *in the feast of* unleavened bread, *and in the feast of* weeks, *and in the feast of* tabernacles
30:13. to keep *the feast of* unleavened bread
21. kept *the feast of* unleavened bread
35:17. and *the feast of* unleavened bread
Ezr. 3: 4. They kept also *the feast of* tabernacles,
6:22. kept *the feast of* unleavened bread
Neh 8:14. Israel should dwell in booths *in the feast*
18. they kept *the feast* seven days;
Ps. 81: 3(4). on *our solemn feast* day.
118:27. bind *the sacrifice* with cords,
Isa. 29: 1. let them kill *sacrifices.*
30:29. *a* holy *solemnity* is kept;
Eze. 45:17. drink offerings, *in the feasts,*
21. *a feast of* seven days;
23. seven days of *the feast* he shall
25. shall he do the like *in the feast*
46:11. *And in the feasts* and in the solemnities
Hos 2:11(13). *her feast days,* her new moons,
9: 5. in the day of *the feast of* the Lord?
Am. 5:21. I hate, I despise *your feast days,*
8:10. I will turn *your feasts* into mourning,
Nah 1:15(2:1). keep *thy solemn feasts,*
Zec. 14:16. to keep *the feast of* tabernacles.
18, 19. that come not up to keep *the feast of*
Mal. 2: 3. the dung of *your solemn feasts;*

חָגָּא *g'hog-gāh',* f. 2283

Isa. 19:17. the land of Judah shall be *a terror*

חָגָב *g'hāh-gāhv',* m. 2284

Lev. 11:22. *the grasshopper* after his kind.
Nu. 13:33. we were in our own sight *as grasshoppers,*
2Ch 7:13. or if I command *the locusts*
Ecc. 12: 5. *the grasshopper* shall be a burden,
Isa. 40:22. the inhabitants thereof (are) *as grasshoppers;*

חָגַג [*g'hāh-gag'*]. 2287

* KAL.—*Preterite.* *

Ex. 12:14. *and ye shall keep* it a feast
Lev. 23:41. *And ye shall keep* it a feast
Nu. 29:12. *and ye shall keep* a feast unto the

KAL.—*Infinitive.*

Zec. 14:16. *and to keep* the feast
18, 19. that come not up *to keep* the feast

KAL.—*Imperative.*

Nah. 1:15(2:1). *keep* thy solemn feasts, (marg. *feast*)

KAL.—*Future.*

Ex. 5: 1. *that they may hold a feast* unto me
12:14. and *ye shall keep it* a feast
23:14. Three times *thou shalt keep a feast*
Lev. 23:39. *ye shall keep* a feast unto the Lord
41. *ye shall celebrate* it in the seventh month
Deu 16:15. Seven days *shalt thou keep a solemn feast*
Ps. 107:27. *They reel to and fro,* and stagger

KAL.—*Participle.* Poel.

1Sa. 30:16. eating and drinking, *and dancing,*
Ps. 42: 4(5). with a multitude *that kept holyday.*

חֲגָוִים [*g'hăgāh-veem'*], m. pl. 2288

Cant 2:14. *in the clefts of* the rock,
Jer. 49:16. O thou that dwellest *in the clefts of*
Obad 3. dwellest *in the clefts of* the rock,

חֲגוֹר *g'hăgōhr,* m. 2289

1Sa. 18: 4. to his bow, and to *his girdle.*
2Sa. 20: 8. upon it *a girdle* (with) a sword
Pro. 31:24. *and* delivereth *girdles* unto the merchant.
Eze. 23:15. *Girded with* girdles upon their loins,

חֲגוֹרָה *g'hăgōh-rāh',* f. 2290

Gen. 3: 7. made themselves *aprons.* (marg. *things to gird about*)
2Sa. 18:11. ten (shekels) of silver, *and a girdle.*
1K. 2: 5. put the blood of war *upon his girdle*
2K. 3:21. all that were able to put on *armour,* (marg. gird himself with *a girdle*)
Isa. 3:24. instead of *a girdle* a rent;
32:11. *and gird* (sackcloth) upon (your) loins. (lit. *and a girdle,* &c.)

חָגַר [*g'hāh-gar'*]. 2296

* KAL.—*Preterite.* *

Ex. 29: 9. *And thou shalt gird* them
Pro 31:17. *She girdeth* her loins with strength,
Isa. 15: 3. *they shall gird themselves* with sackcloth:
Lam 2:10. *they have girded themselves*
Eze. 7:18. *They shall also gird* (themselves)
27:31. *and gird them* with sackcloth,

KAL.—*Infinitive.*

Isa. 22:12. *and to girding* with sackcloth:

KAL.—*Imperative.*

1Sa.25:13. *Gird ye on* every man his sword.
2Sa. 3:31. *and gird you* with sackcloth,
2K. 4:29. said to Gehazi, *Gird up* thy loins,
9: 1. *Gird up* thy loins, and take this box
Ps. 45: 3(4). *Gird* thy sword upon (thy) thigh,
Jer. 4: 8. For this *gird you* with sackcloth,
6:26. *gird* (thee) with sackcloth,
49: 3. *gird you* with sackcloth;
Joel 1:13. *Gird yourselves*, and lament,

KAL.—*Future.*

Lev. 8: 7. *and girded* him with the girdle,
— *and he girded* him with the curious girdle
13. *and girded* them with girdles,
16: 4. *shall be girded* with a linen girdle,
Deu 1:41. *And when ye had girded on* every
Jud. 3:16. *and he did gird* it under his raiment
1Sa.17:39. *And* David *girded* his sword
25:13. *And they girded on* every man his sword; *and* David also *girded on* his sword:
2Sa.22:46. *and they shall be afraid*
1K. 20:32. *So they girded* sackcloth on their loins,
Ps. 65:12(13). the little hills rejoice *on every side.* (marg. *are girded* with joy)
76:10(11). the remainder of wrath *shalt thou restrain.*
109:19. for a girdle *wherewith he is girded*
Eze 44:18. *they shall* not *gird* (themselves)

KAL.—*Participle.* Poel.

1K. 20:11. Let not him *that girdeth on*
2K. 3:21. all *that were able to put on* armour, (marg. *gird himself* with a girdle)

KAL.—*Participle.* Paül.

Ex. 12:11. (with) your loins *girded*,
Jud.18:11. *appointed* with weapons of war. (marg. *girded*)
16. the six hundred men *appointed*
17. men (that were) *appointed* with
1Sa. 2:18. a child, *girded* with a linen ephod.
2Sa. 6:14. David (was) *girded* with
20: 8. garment that he had put on was *girded*
21:16. he *being girded* with a new (sword),
Dan10: 5. whose loins (were) *girded*
Joel 1: 8. Lament like a virgin *girded* with sackcloth

2298 חַד *g̔had*, Ch. adj. num.

Ezr. 4: 8. wrote *a* letter against Jerusalem
5:13. But in the *first* year of Cyrus
6: 2. *a* roll, and therein (was) a record
3. In the *first* year of Cyrus
Dan. 2: 9. (there is but) *one* decree for you:
31. and behold *a* great image.
35. and the gold, broken to pieces *together*,
3:19. heat the furnace *one* seven times more
4:19(16). was astonied for *one* hour,
6: 2(3). three presidents; of whom Daniel (was) *first:*
17(18). And *a* stone was brought, and laid
7: 1. In the *first* year of Belshazzar
5. and it raised up itself on *one* side,
16. I came near unto *one* of them that stood

2299 חַד *g̔had*, adj.

Ps. 57: 4(5). their tongue a *sharp* sword.
Pro. 5: 4. *sharp* as a twoedged sword.
Isa. 49: 2. made my mouth like a *sharp* sword;
Eze. 5: 1. take thee a *sharp* knife,

2297 חַד *g̔had*, adj. num.

Eze.33:30. and speak *one* to another,

2300 חָדַד [*g̔hāh-dad'*].

* KAL.—*Preterite.* *

Hab 1: 8. *and are* more *fierce* than the evening wolves: (marg. *sharp*)

KAL.—*Future.*

Pro.27:17. Iron *sharpeneth* iron;

* HIPHIL.—*Future.* *

Pro.27:17. so a man *sharpeneth* the countenance

* HOPHAL.—*Preterite.* *

Eze.21: 9(14). A sword, a sword *is sharpened*,
10(15). *It is sharpened* to make a sore
11(16). this sword *is sharpened*,

חָדָה [*g̔hāh-dāh'*]. 2302

* KAL.—*Future.* *

Ex. 18: 9. *And* Jethro *rejoiced* for all the
Job 3: 6. *let it* not *be joined* unto the days (marg. or, *rejoice* among)

* PIEL.—*Future.* *

Ps. 21: 6(7). *thou hast made him* exceeding *glad*

חַדּוּדִים [*g̔had doo-deem'*], m. pl. 2303

Job 41:30(22). *Sharp* stones (are) under him:

חֶדְוָה *g̔hed-vāh'*, f. 2304

1Ch 16:27. strength *and gladness* (are) in his place.
Neh 8:10. for *the joy of* the Lord is your

חֶדְוָה *g̔hed-vāh'*, Ch. f. 2305

Ezr. 6:16. dedication of this house of God *with joy*,

חֲדִין [*g̔hădeen*], Ch. m. pl. 2306

Dan 2:32. *his breast* and his arms of silver,

חָדַל *g̔hāh-dal'*. 2308

* KAL.—*Preterite.* *

Gen18:11. *it ceased* to be with Sarah
41:49. until *he left* numbering;
Ex. 9:34. hail and the thunders *were ceased*,
23: 5. *and wouldest forbear* to help him, (marg. or, *wilt thou cease*)
Nu. 9:13. *and forbeareth* to keep the passover,
Jud. 5: 6. the highways *were unoccupied*,
7. the villages *ceased, they ceased* in Israel,
9: 9. *Should I leave* my fatness,
11. *Should I forsake* my sweetness,
13. *Should I leave* my wine,
1Sa. 2: 5. and (they that were) hungry *ceased.*
Job 3:17. There the wicked *cease* (from) troubling;
19:14. My kinsfolk *have failed*,
Ps. 36: 3(4). *he hath left off* to be wise,
49: 8(9). *and it ceaseth* for ever:
Isa. 24: 8. the noise of them that rejoice *endeth*,
Jer. 44:18. since *we left off* to burn incense
51:30. of Babylon *have forborn* to fight,

KAL.—*Infinitive.*

1Sa.12:23. *in ceasing* to pray for you:

KAL.—*Imperative.*

Ex. 14:12. tell thee in Egypt, saying, *Let* us *alone*,
2Ch 25:16. *forbear;* why shouldest thou be smitten?
35:21. *forbear* thee from (meddling with) God,
Job 7:16. *let* me *alone;* for my days (are) vanity.
10:20. *cease* (then, and) let me alone,
Pro.19:27. *Cease*, my son, to hear the instruction
23: 4. *cease* from thine own wisdom.
Isa. 1:16. *cease* to do evil;
2:22. *Cease ye* from man,
Jer. 40: 4. to come with me into Babylon, *forbear:*
Am. 7: 5. O Lord God, *cease*, I beseech thee:
Zec.11:12. and if not, *forbear.*

KAL.—*Future.*

Gen11: 8. *and they left off* to build the city.
Ex. 9:29. the thunder *shall cease*,
33. *and* the thunders and hail *ceased*,

Deu 15:11. the poor *shall* never *cease* out of the land:
23:22(23). But if *thou shalt forbear* to vow,
Jud.15: 7. after that *I will cease.*
20:28. or *shall I cease?*
Ru. 1:18. *then she left* speaking unto her.
1Sa. 9: 5. lest my father *leave* (caring) for the
23:13. *and he forbare* to go forth.
1K. 15:21. *that he left off* building of Ramah,
22: 6. to battle, or *shall I forbear?*
15. to battle, or *shall we forbear?*
2Ch 16: 5. *that he left off* building of Ramah,
18: 5, 14. to battle, or *shall I forbear?*
25:16. *Then* the prophet *forbare*,
Job 10:20. (כתיב) *cease* (then, and) let me alone,
14: 6. Turn from him, *that he may rest*, (marg. *cease*)
7. the tender branch thereof *will* not *cease.*
16: 6. *and* (though) *I forbear*,
Pro.10:19. multitude of words *there wanteth* not sin:
Jer. 41: 8. *So he forbare*, and slew them not
Eze. 2: 5, 7 & 3:11. or whether *they will forbear*,
3:27. he that forbeareth, *let him forbear:*

2310 **חָדֵל** *ghāh-dēhl'*, adj.

Ps. 39: 4(5). may know how *frail* I (am). (marg. or, what *time* I have (here))
Isa. 53: 3. He is despised *and rejected of* men;
Eze. 3:27. *and he that forbeareth*, let him forbear:

2309 **חֶדֶל** [*gheh'-del*], m.

Isa. 38:11. with the inhabitants of *the world.*

2312 **חֵדֶק** *ghēh'-dek*, m.

Pro.15:19. slothful (man is) as an hedge of *thorns:*
Mic. 7: 4. The best of them (is) *as a brier:*

2314 **חָדַר** [*ghāh-dar'*].

* KAL.—*Participle.* Poel. *

Eze.21:14(19). *entereth* into their *privy chambers.*

2315 **חֶדֶר** *gheh'-der*, m.

Gen43:30. he entered *into* (his) *chamber*,
Ex. 8: 3(7:28). *and into* thy bed*chamber*,
Deu32:25. The sword without, and terror *within*, (marg. *from the chambers*)
Jud. 3:24. covereth his feet *in* his summer *chamber.*
15: 1. I will go in to my wife *into the chamber.*
16: 9. abiding with her *in the chamber.*
12. liers in wait abiding *in the chamber.*
2Sa. 4: 7. he lay on his bed *in* his bed*chamber*,
13:10. Bring the meat *into the chamber*,
— brought (them) *into the chamber*
1K. 1:15. went in unto the king *into the chamber:*
20:30. into the city, into *an inner chamber.* (marg. *a chamber within a chamber*, or, *from chamber to chamber*)
22:25. when thou shalt go into *an inner chamber* (marg. *a chamber in a chamber*)
2K. 6:12. that thou speakest *in* thy bed*chamber.*
9: 2. carry him to *an inner chamber;* (marg. *chamber in a chamber*)
11: 2. *in the* bed*chamber* from Athaliah,
1Ch 28:11. *and of the* inner *parlours thereof*,
2Ch 18:24. when thou shalt go into *an inner chamber* (marg. *a chamber in a chamber*)
22:11. put him and his nurse *in a* bed*chamber.*
Job 9: 9. *and the chambers of* the south.
37: 9. Out of *the south* (marg. *chamber*) cometh
Ps.105:30. *in the chambers of* their kings.
Pro. 7:27. going down to *the chambers of* death.
18: 8. go down *into the innermost parts of* the belly. (marg. *chambers*)
20:27. searching all *the inward parts of* the belly.
30. so (do) stripes *the inward parts of* the
24: 4. by knowledge shall *the chambers*
Pro.26:22. they go down into *the innermost parts of* the belly. (marg. *chambers*)
Ecc.10:20. *and* curse not the rich *in* thy bed*chamber:*
Cant. 1: 4. hath brought me into *his chambers:*
3: 4. into *the chamber of* her that conceived me.
Isa. 26:20. enter thou *into thy chambers*,
Eze. 8:12. every man *in the chambers of* his imagery?
Joel 2:16. the bridegroom go forth *of his chamber*,

חָדַשׁ [*ghāh-dash'*]. 2318

* PIEL.—*Preterite.* *

Isa. 61: 4. *and they shall repair* the waste cities,

PIEL.—*Infinitive.*

2Ch 24: 4. Joash was minded *to repair* the house (marg. *renew*)
12. and carpenters *to repair* the house of the

PIEL.—*Imperative.*

Ps. 51:10(12). *renew* a right spirit within me.
Lam. 5:21. *renew* our days as of old.

PIEL.—*Future.*

1Sa.11:14. *and renew* the kingdom there.
2Ch 15: 8. *and renewed* the altar of the Lord,
Job 10:17. *Thou renewest* thy witnesses
Ps.104:30. *and thou renewest* the face of the earth.

* HITHPAEL.—*Future.* *

Ps.103: 5. thy youth *is renewed* like the eagle's.

חָדָשׁ *ghāh-dāhsh'*, adj. 2319

Ex. 1: 8. there arose up a *new* king over Egypt,
Lev.23:16. ye shall offer a *new* meat offering
26:10. bring forth the old because of *the new.*
Nu. 28:26. when ye bring a *new* meat offering
Deu 20: 5. that hath built a *new* house,
22: 8. When thou buildest a *new* house,
24: 5. When a man hath taken a *new* wife,
32:17. to *new* (gods that) came newly up,
Jos. 9:13. which we filled, (were) *new;*
Jud. 5: 8. They chose *new* gods;
15:13. they bound him with two *new* cords,
16:11. bind me fast with *new* ropes
12. Delilah therefore took *new* ropes,
1Sa. 6: 7. Now therefore make a *new* cart,
2Sa. 6: 3. set the ark of God upon a *new* cart,
— drave the *new* cart.
21:16. he being girded with a *new* (sword),
1K. 11:29. had clad himself with a *new* garment;
30. Ahijah caught the *new* garment
2K. 2:20. Bring me a *new* cruse,
1Ch 13: 7. carried the ark of God in a *new* cart
2Ch 20: 5. before the *new* court,
Job 29:20. My glory (was) *fresh* in me, (marg. *new*)
32:19. it is ready to burst like *new* bottles.
Ps. 33: 3. Sing unto him a *new* song;
40: 3(4). he hath put a *new* song in my
96: 1 & 98:1. Sing unto the Lord a *new* song:
144: 9. I will sing a *new* song unto thee,
149: 1. Sing unto the Lord a *new* song,
Ecc. 1: 9. no *new* (thing) under the sun.
10. may be said, See, this (is) *new?*
Cant.7:13(14). pleasant (fruits), *new* and old,
Isa. 41:15. I will make thee a *new* sharp threshing instrument
42: 9. *and new things* do I declare:
10. Sing unto the Lord a *new* song,
43:19. Behold, I will do *a new thing;*
48: 6. I have shewed thee *new things*
62: 2. thou shalt be called by a *new* name,
65:17. I create *new* heavens and a *new* earth:
66:22. For as the *new* heavens and the *new* earth,
Jer. 26:10. in the entry of the *new* gate
31:22. hath created *a new thing* in the earth,
31. that I will make a *new* covenant
36:10. at the entry of the *new* gate
Lam. 3:23. (They are) *new* every morning:
Eze.11:19. I will put a *new* spirit within you;
18:31 make you a *new* heart and a *new* spirit:
36:26. A *new* heart also will I give you, and a *new* spirit will I put within you:

2320 **חֹדֶשׁ** *ghōh'-desh*, m.

Gen 7:11. *in the* second *month*, the seventeenth day *of the month*,
8: 4. the ark rested *in the* seventh *month*, on the seventeenth day *of the month*,
5. decreased continually until *the* tenth *month*: in the tenth (month), on the first (day) *of the month*,
13. in the first (month), the first (day) *of the month*,
14. *And in the* second *month*, on the seven and twentieth day *of the month*,
29:14. abode with him the space of *a month*.
38:24. it came to pass about three *months* after,
Ex. 12: 2. This *month* (shall be) unto you the beginning *of months*: it (shall be) the first *month of* the year (lit. the first *in the months of* the year)
3. In the tenth (day) *of* this *month*
6. until the fourteenth day *of the* same *month*:
18. on the fourteenth day *of the month* at even,
— until the one and twentieth day *of the month*
13: 4. This day came ye out *in the month* Abib.
5. thou shalt keep this service *in* this *month*.
16: 1. on the fifteenth day *of the* second *month*
19: 1. *In the* third *month*, when the children of
23:15. in the time appointed of *the month* Abib;
34:18. in the time of *the month* Abib: for *in the month* Abib thou camest out
40: 2. On the first day *of the* first *month* (lit. in the first day of *the month*, in the first *of the month*)
17. *in the* first *month* in the second year, on the first (day) *of the month*,
Lev.16:29. *in the* seventh *month*, on the tenth (day) *of the month*,
23: 5. In the fourteenth (day) *of the* first *month* (lit. *in the* first *month*, in the fourteenth *of the month*)
6. on the fifteenth day *of the* same *month*
24. *In the* seventh *month*, in the first (day) *of the month*,
27. on the tenth (day) *of* this seventh *month*
32. in the ninth (day) *of the month* at even,
34. The fifteenth day *of this* seventh *month*
39. in the fifteenth day *of the* seventh *month*,
41. ye shall celebrate it *in the* seventh *month*.
25: 9. on the tenth (day) *of the* seventh *month*, (lit. *in the* seventh *month*, on the tenth *of the month*)
27: 6. if (it be) from *a month* old
Nu. 1: 1, 18. on the first (day) *of the* second *month*,
3:15, 22, 28, 34, 39, 40, 43. from *a month* old and upward
9: 1. *in the* first *month* of the second year
3. In the fourteenth day *of* this *month*,
5. on the fourteenth day *of the* first *month*
11. The fourteenth day *of the* second *month*
22. two days, or *a month*,
10:10. the beginnings of *your months*,
11. on the twentieth (day) *of the* second *month*, (lit. *in the* second *month*, in the twentieth *of the month*)
11:20. even *a* whole *month*,
21. that they may eat *a* whole *month*.
18:16. from *a month* old shalt thou redeem,
20: 1. into the desert of Zin *in the* first *month*:
26:62. from *a month* old and upward:
28:11. in the beginnings of *your months*
14. the burnt offering of *every month* (lit. of *the month in its month*) *throughout the months of* the year.
16. *And in* the fourteenth day of the first *month* (lit. *and in the* first *month*, in the fourteenth day *of the month*)
17. And in the fifteenth day *of* this *month*
29: 1. *And in the* seventh *month*, on the first (day) *of the month*,
6. Beside the burnt offering of *the month*,
7. on the tenth (day) *of* this seventh *month*
12. on the fifteenth day *of the* seventh *month*
33: 3. departed from Rameses *in the* first *month*, on the fifteenth day *of the* first *month*;
38. in the first (day) *of the* fifth *month*. (lit. *in the* fifth *month*, in the first *of the month*)

Deu 1: 3. in *the* eleventh *month*, on the first (day) *of the month*,
16: 1. Observe *the month of* Abib,
— for *in the month of* Abib the Lord thy God
Jos. 4:19. on the tenth (day) *of the* first *month*,
5:10. on the fourteenth day *of the month*
Jud.11:37. let me alone two *months*,
38. he sent her away (for) two *months*:
39. it came to pass at the end of two *months*,
19: 2. and was there four whole *months*.
20:47. abode in the rock Rimmon four *months*.
1Sa. 6: 1. in the country of the Philistines seven *months*.
20: 5. Behold, to morrow (is) *the new moon*,
18. To morrow (is) *the new moon*: and thou
24. when *the new moon* was come,
27. (which was) the second (day) *of the month*,
34. did eat no meat the second day *of the month*:
27: 7. a full year and four *months*.
2Sa. 2:11 & 5:5. seven years and six *months*.
6:11. in the house of Obed-edom the Gittite three *months*:
24: 8. they came to Jerusalem at the end of nine *months*
13. flee three *months* before thine enemies,
1K. 4: 7. each man his *month* in a year
27(5:7). every man in *his month*:
5:14(28). ten thousand *a month* by courses: *a month* they were in Lebanon, (and) two *months* at home:
6: 1. *in the month* Zif, which (is) *the* second *month*,
38. in the month Bul, which (is) *the* eighth *month*,
8: 2. at the feast in the month Ethanim, which (is) *the* seventh *month*.
11:16. For six *months* did Joab remain
12:32. Jeroboam ordained a feast *in the* eighth *month*, on the fifteenth day *of the month*,
33. the fifteenth day of *the* eighth *month*, (even) *in the month* which he had devised
2K. 4:23. (it is) neither *new moon*, nor sabbath.
15: 8. reign over Israel in Samaria six *months*.
23:31. he reigned three *months* in Jerusalem.
24: 8. he reigned in Jerusalem three *months*.
25: 1. *in the* tenth *month*, in the tenth (day) *of the month*,
3. on the ninth (day) *of the* (fourth) *month*
8. *And in the* fifth *month*, on the seventh (day) *of the month*,
25. it came to pass *in the* seventh *month*,
27. in *the* twelfth *month*, on the seven and twentieth (day) *of the month*,
1Ch. 3: 4. he reigned seven years and six *months*:
12:15. that went over Jordan *in the* first *month*,
13:14. of Obed-edom in his house three *months*.
21:12. three *months* to be destroyed before thy
23:31. *in the new moons*, and on the set feasts
27: 1. came in and went out *month by month*, throughout *all the months of* the year,
2. *for the* first *month* (was) Jashobeam
3. the captains of the host *for the* first *month*
4. over the course of *the* second *month* (was)
5. *for the* third *month* (was) Benaiah
7. *for the* fourth *month* (was) Asahel
8. *for the* fifth *month* (was) Shamhuth
9. *for the* sixth *month* (was) Ira
10. *for the* seventh *month* (was) Helez
11. *for the* eighth *month* (was) Sibbecai
12. *for the* ninth *month* (was) Abiezer
13. *for the* tenth *month* (was) Maharai
14. for *the* eleventh *month* (was) Benaiah
15. for *the* twelfth *month* (was) Heldai
2Ch 2: 4(3). *and on the new moons*, and on the solemn feasts
3: 2. in the second (day) *of the* second *month*,
5: 3. in the feast which (was) in *the* seventh *month*.
7:10. the three and twentieth day *of the* seventh *month*
8:13. on the sabbaths, *and on the new moons*,
15:10. *in the* third *month*, in the fifteenth year
29: 3. the first year of his reign, *in the* first *month*,
17. on the first (day) *of the* first *month* to sanctify, and on the eighth day *of the month*

2Ch 29:17. in the sixteenth day *of the* first *month*
30: 2. to keep the passover *in the* second *month*.
13. of unleavened bread *in the* second *month*,
15. on the fourteenth (day) *of the* second *month*:
31: 3. *and for the new moons*, and for the set
7. *In the* third *month* they began
— *and* finished (them) *in the* seventh *month*.
35: 1. on the fourteenth (day) *of the* first *month*.
36: 2. he reigned three *months* in Jerusalem.
9. he reigned three *months* and ten days
Ezr. 3: 1. when *the* seventh *month* was come,
5. burnt offering, *both of the new moons*,
6. From the first day *of the* seventh *month*
8. *in the* second *month*, began Zerubbabel
6:19. upon the fourteenth (day) *of the* first *month*.
7: 8. he came to Jerusalem *in the* fifth *month*,
9. upon the first (day) *of the* first *month*
— on the first (day) *of the* fifth *month*
8:31. on the twelfth (day) *of the* first *month*,
10: 9. It (was) *the* ninth *month*, on the twentieth (day) *of the month*;
16. in the first day *of the* tenth *month*
17. by the first day *of the* first *month*.
Neh. 1: 1. it came to pass *in the month* Chisleu,
2: 1. it came to pass *in the month* Nisan,
7:73. and when *the* seventh *month* came,
8: 2. upon the first day *of the* seventh *month*.
14. in the feast *of the* seventh *month*:
9: 1. in the twenty and fourth day *of* this *month*
10:33(34). of the sabbaths, of *the new moons*,
Est. 2:12. after that she had been twelve *months*,
— six *months* with oil of myrrh, and six *months*
16. *in the* tenth *month*, which (is) *the month* Tebeth,
3: 7. *In the* first *month*, that (is), *the month* Nisan,
— *and from month to month*, (to) the twelfth (month), that (is), *the month* Adar.
12. on the thirteenth day *of the* first *month*,
13. upon the thirteenth (day) *of the* twelfth *month*, which (is) *the month* Adar,
8: 9. called at that time *in the* third *month*, that (is), *the month* Sivan,
12. upon the thirteenth (day) *of the* twelfth *month*, which (is) *the month* Adar.
9: 1. in *the* twelfth *month*, that (is), *the month* Adar,
15. the fourteenth day also *of the month* Adar,
17. On the thirteenth day *of the month* Adar;
19. made the fourteenth day *of the month* Adar
21. keep the fourteenth day *of the month* Adar,
22. *and the month* which was turned unto
Job 14: 5. the number of *his months* (are) with thee,
21:21. the number of *his months* is cut off
Ps. 81: 3(4). Blow up the trumpet *in the new moon*,
Isa. 1:13. *the new moons* and sabbaths,
14. *Your new moons* and your appointed feasts
47:13. the *monthly* prognosticators, (marg. that give knowledge concerning *the months*)
66:23. from *one new moon to another*, (marg. *new moon to his new moon*)
Jer. 1: 3. captive *in the* fifth *month*.
2:24. *in her month* they shall find her.
28: 1. the fourth year, (and) *in the* fifth *month*,
17. died the same year *in the* seventh *month*.
36: 9. *in the* ninth *month*, (that) they proclaimed
22. in the winterhouse *in the* ninth *month*:
39: 1. *in the* tenth *month*, came Nebuchadrezzar
2. *in the* fourth *month*, the ninth (day) *of the month*,
41: 1. it came to pass *in the* seventh *month*,
52: 4. *in the* tenth *month*, in the tenth (day) *of the month*,
6. And *in the* fourth *month*, in the ninth (day) *of the month*,
12. *Now in the* fifth *month*, in the tenth (day) *of the month*,
31. in *the* twelfth *month*, in the five and twentieth (day) *of the month*,
Eze. 1: 1, 2 & 8:1. in the fifth (day) *of the month*,
20: 1. the tenth (day) *of the month*, (that) certain
24: 1. *in the* tenth *month*, in the tenth (day) *of the month*,
Eze.26: 1. the eleventh year, in the first (day) *of the month*,
29: 1. in the twelfth (day) *of the month*,
17. in the first (day) *of the month*,
30:20. in the seventh (day) *of the month*,
31: 1. in the first (day) *of the month*,
32: 1. in *the* twelfth *month*, in the first (day) *of the month*,
17. in the fifteenth (day) *of the month*,
33:21. in the fifth (day) *of the month*,
39:12. And seven *months* shall the house
14. after the end of seven *months* shall
40: 1. in the tenth (day) *of the month*,
45:17. in the feasts, *and in the new moons*,
18. in the first (day) *of the month*,
20. shalt do the seventh (day) *of the month*
21. in the fourteenth day *of the month*
25. in the fifteenth day *of the month*,
46: 1. in the day of *the new moon*
3. in the sabbaths *and in the new moons*.
6. in the day of *the new moon*
47:12. new fruit *according to his months*,
Dan 10: 4. in the four and twentieth day *of the* first *month*,
Hos. 2:11(13). her feast days, *her new moons*.
5: 7. now shall *a month* devour them
Am. 4: 7. (there were) yet three *months* to the harvest:
8: 5. When will *the new moon* be gone, (marg. or, *month*)
Hag. 1: 1. *in the* sixth *month*, in the first day *of the month*,
15. In the four and twentieth day *of the* sixth *month*,
2: 1. in the one and twentieth (day) *of the month*,
20. in the four and twentieth (day) *of the month*,
Zec. 1: 1. *In the* eighth *month*, in the second year
7. the four and twentieth day of *the* eleventh *month*, which (is) *the month* Sebat,
7: 1. in the fourth (day) *of the* ninth *month*,
3. Should I weep *in the* fifth *month*,

חֲדַת 'g̣hădath, Ch. adj. 2323

Ezr. 6: 4. and a row of *new* timber:

חוֹב 'g̣hōhv, m. 2326

Eze.18: 7. hath restored to *the debtor* his pledge,

חוּב ['g̣hoov]. 2325

* PIEL.—*Preterite.* *

Dan 1:10. *then shall ye make* (me) *endanger* my head

חוּג ['g̣hoog]. 2328

* KAL.—*Preterite.* *

Job 26:10. *He hath compassed* the waters

חוּג 'g̣hoog, m. 2329

Job 22:14. *and* he walketh *in the circuit of* heaven.
Pro. 8:27. he set *a compass* upon the face of the (marg. *circle*)
Isa. 40:22. he that sitteth upon *the circle of* the earth,

חוּד 'g̣hood. 2330

* KAL.—*Preterite.* *

Jud.14:16. *thou hast put forth* a riddle

KAL.—*Imperative.*

Jud.14:13. *Put forth* thy riddle,
Eze.17: 2. Son of man, *put forth* a riddle,

KAL.—*Future.*

Jud. 14:12. *I will* now *put forth* a riddle

2331 חָוָה [g̔hāh-vāh'].

* PIEL.—*Infinitive.* *

Job 32: 6. durst *not shew you* mine opinion. (lit. was afraid *from shewing* you)

PIEL.—*Future.*

Job 15:17. *I will shew thee,* hear me;
32:10, 17. I also *will shew* mine opinion.
36: 2. *and I will shew thee* that (I have)
Ps. 19: 2(3). night unto night *sheweth* knowledge.

2324 חֲוָה & חֲוָא [g̔hăvāh], Ch.

* PAEL.—*Future.* *

Dan 2: 4. *and we will shew* the interpretation.
11. there is none other that *can shew it*
24. *I will shew* unto the king the interpretation.
5: 7. Whosoever shall read this writing, and *shew me* the interpretation

* APHEL.—*Infinitive.* *

Dan 2:10. not a man upon the earth that can *shew*
16. he would *shew* the king the interpretation.
27. cannot the wise (men),...*shew* unto the
4: 2(3:32). I thought it good *to shew* the signs
5:15. they could not *shew* the interpretation

APHEL.—*Imperative.*

Dan 2: 6. therefore *shew me* the dream,

APHEL.—*Future.*

Dan 2: 6. But if *ye shew* the dream,
7. and *we will shew* the interpretation
9. and I shall know that *ye can shew me*
5:12. *he will shew* the interpretation.

2333 חַוּוֹת g̔hav-vōhth', f. pl.

Nu. 32:41. took *the small towns thereof,* and called them *Havoth*-jair.
Deu 3:14. Bashan-*havoth*-jair,
Jos. 13:30. all *the towns of* Jair,
Jud.10: 4. which are called *Havoth*-jair (marg. or, *The villages of* Jair)
1K. 4:13. to him (pertained) *the towns of* Jair
1Ch 2:23. with *the towns of* Jair,

2336-37 חוֹחַ g̔hōh'ăg̔h, m.

1Sa.13: 6. hide themselves in caves, *and in thickets,*
2K. 14: 9. *The thistle* that (was) in Lebanon — trode down *the thistle.*
2Ch 25:18. *The thistle* that (was) in Lebanon — trode down *the thistle.*
33:11. took Manasseh *among the thorns,*
Job 31:40. Let *thistles* grow instead of wheat,
41: 2(40:26). *or* bore his jaw through *with a thorn?*
Pro.26: 9. *a thorn* goeth up into the hand
Cant.2: 2. As the lily among *thorns,*
Isa. 34:13. nettles *and brambles* in the fortresses
Hos. 9: 6. *thorns* (shall be) in their tabernacles.

2338 חוּט [g̔hoot], Ch.

* APHEL.—*Future.* *

Ezr. 4:12. and *joined* the foundations. (marg. *sewed together*)

2339 חוּט g̔hoot, m.

Gen 14:23. That I will not (take) *from a thread*
Jos. 2:18. bind this line of scarlet *thread*
Jud.16:12. brake them from off his arms *like a thread.*
1K. 7:15. *and a line of* twelve cubits
Ecc. 4:12. *and a* threefold *cord*
Cant.4: 3. Thy lips (are) *like a thread of* scarlet,
Jer. 52:21. *and a fillet of* twelve cubits

חוּל g̔hool & חִיל [g̔heel]. 2342

* KAL.—*Preterite.* *

Deu 2:25. *and be in anguish* because of thee.
Isa. 23: 4. *I travail* not, nor bring forth children,
26:18. *we have been in pain,*
54: 1. *thou* (that) *didst* not *travail with child:*
66: 8. for as soon as Zion *travailed,*
Jer. 5: 3. but *they have* not *grieved;*
Lam.4: 6. no hands *stayed* on her.
Hos 11: 6. *And* the sword *shall abide*
Mic. 1:12. Maroth *waited carefully* for good: (marg. or, *was grieved*)

KAL.—*Infinitive.*

Jud.21:21. daughters of Shiloh come out *to dance*
Eze.30:16. Sin shall have *great* pain, (lit. *in having pain* shall have pain)

KAL.—*Imperative.*

1Ch 16:30. *Fear* before him, all the earth:
Ps. 96: 9. *fear* before him, all the earth.
114: 7. *Tremble,* thou earth, at the presence of
Mic. 4:10. *Be in pain,* and labour to bring forth,

KAL & HIPHIL.—*Future.*

Gen 8:10. *And he stayed* yet other seven days;
Jud. 3:25. *And they tarried* till they were
1Sa.31: 3. *and he was* sore *wounded*
2Sa. 3:29. *Let it rest* on the head of Joab,
1Ch 10: 3. *and he was wounded* of the archers.
Job 20:21. therefore *shall* no man *look* for his goods.
Ps. 10: 5. His ways *are* always *grievous;*
29: 8. the Lord *shaketh* the wilderness; the Lord *shaketh* the wilderness
55: 4(5). My heart *is sore pained* within me:
77:16(17). *they were afraid:* the depths also
97: 4. the earth saw, *and trembled.*
Isa. 13: 8. *they shall be in pain* as a woman
23: 5. *shall they be* sorely *pained*
26:17. the time of her delivery, *is in pain,*
45:10. What *hast thou brought forth?*
66: 7. Before *she travailed,* she brought forth;
Jer. 4:19. *I am pained* at my very heart;
5:22. *will ye* not *tremble* at my presence,
23:19. *it shall fall grievously* upon the head
30:23. *it shall fall with pain* (marg. or, *remain*)
51:29. the land shall tremble *and sorrow:*
Lam.3:26. good that (a man) *should both hope* [See יָחִיל adj.]
Eze.30:16. Sin *shall have* great *pain,*
Joel 2: 6. the people *shall be much pained:*
Hab 3:10. The mountains saw thee, (and) *they trembled:*
Zec. 9: 5. *and be* very *sorrowful,*

* POLEL.—*Preterite.* *

Job 26:13. his hand *hath formed* the crooked serpent.
39: 1. canst thou mark *when* the hinds *do calve?*

POLEL.—*Future.*

Job 26; 5. Dead (things) *are formed* from under
35:14. *therefore trust thou* in him.
Ps. 29: 9. the Lord *maketh* the hinds *to calve,* (marg. or, *to be in pain*)
90: 2. *or ever thou hadst formed* the
Pro.25:23. The north wind *driveth away* rain: (marg. or, *bringeth forth*)
Isa. 51: 2. unto Sarah (that) *bare you:*

POLEL.—*Participle.*

Deu32:18. hast forgotten God *that formed thee,*
Jud.21:23. to their number, of *them that danced,*
Pro.26:10. The great (God) that *formed* all (marg. a great man *grieveth* all)

* PULAL.—*Preterite.* *

Job 15: 7. *wast thou made* before the hills?

Ps. 51: 5(7). *I was shapen* in iniquity;
Pro. 8:24. no depths, *I was brought forth;*
25. before the hills was *I brought forth:*

* HIPHIL.—*Future.* *

See under KAL.

* HOPHAL.—*Future.* *

Isa. 66: 8. *Shall* the earth *be made to bring forth*

* HITHPOLEL.—*Imperative.* *

Ps. 37: 7. *and wait patiently* for him:

HITHPOLEL.—*Participle.*

Job 15:20. wicked man *travaileth with pain*
Jer. 23:19. even a *grievous* whirlwind:

* HITHPALPEL.—*Future.* *

Est. 4: 4. *Then was* the queen exceedingly *grieved;*

2344 חוֹל *ghōhl*, m.

Gen22:17. *and as the sand* which (is) upon
32:12(13). make thy seed *as the sand of* the sea,
41:49. Joseph gathered corn *as the sand*
Ex. 2:12. hid him *in the sand.*
Deu33:19. treasures hid in *the sand.*
Jos. 11: 4. *as the sand* that (is) upon the sea
Jud. 7:12. *as the sand* by the sea side
1Sa.13: 5. people *as the sand* which (is) on
2Sa.17:11. *as the sand* that (is) by the sea
1K. 4:20. *as the sand* which (is) by the sea
29(5:9). even *as the sand* that (is) on the
Job 6: 3. heavier *than the sand of* the sea:
29:18. *and* I shall multiply (my) days *as the sand.*
Ps. 78:27. *and* feathered fowls *like as the sand of* the
139:18. are more in number *than the sand:*
Pro.27: 3. and *the sand* weighty;
Isa. 10:22. Israel be *as the sand of* the sea,
48:19. Thy seed also had been *as the sand,*
Jer. 5:22. have placed *the sand* (for) the bound
15: 8. *above the sand of* the seas:
33:22. neither *the sand of* the sea measured:
Hos. 1:10(2:1). Israel shall be *as the sand of* the sea,
Hab 1: 9. shall gather the captivity *as the sand.*

2345 חוּם *ghoom*, adj.

Gen30:32. all the *brown* cattle among the sheep,
33. *and brown* among the sheep,
35. all *the brown* among the sheep,
40. all *the brown* in the flock

2346 חוֹמָה *ghōh-māh'*, f.

Ex. 14:22, 29. the waters (were) *a wall* unto them
Lev.25:29. a dwelling house in a *walled* city,
30. the house that (is) in the *walled* city (lit. which (has) *a wall* to it)
31. which have no *wall* round about
Deu. 3: 5. cities (were) fenced with high *walls,*
28:52. until *thy* high and fenced *walls* come down,
Jos. 2:15. her house (was) upon *the* town *wall,* and she dwelt upon *the wall.*
6: 5. *the wall of* the city shall fall
20. that *the wall* fell down
1Sa.25:16. were *a wall* unto us both by night and day,
31:10. they fastened his body *to the wall of*
12. bodies of his sons *from the wall of*
2Sa.11:20. that they would shoot from *the wall?*
21. a millstone upon him from *the wall,*
— why went ye nigh *the wall?*
24. the shooters shot from off *the wall*
18:24. to the roof over the gate unto *the wall,*
20:15. battered *the wall,* to throw it down.
21. thrown to thee over *the wall.*
1K. 3: 1. and *the wall of* Jerusalem round about.
4:13. threescore great cities with *walls*
9:15. Millo, and *the wall of* Jerusalem,
20:30. *a wall* fell upon 27,000
2K. 3:27. offered him (for) a burnt offering upon *the wall.*
2K. 6:26. was passing by upon *the wall,*
30. and he passed by upon *the wall,*
14:13. brake down *the wall of* Jerusalem
18:26. the people that (are) on *the wall.*
27. to the men which sit on *the wall,*
25: 4. way of the gate between *two walls,*
10. brake down *the walls of* Jerusalem
2Ch 8: 5. cities, with *walls,* gates, and bars;
14: 7(6). make about (them) *walls,*
25:23. brake down *the wall of* Jerusalem
26: 6. *the wall of* Gath, and *the wall of* Jabneh, and *the wall of* Ashdod,
27: 3. *and on the wall of* Ophel
32: 5. built up all *the wall* that was broken,
— and another *wall* without,
18. people of Jerusalem that (were) on *the wall,*
33:14. Now after this he built *a wall*
36:19. brake down *the wall of* Jerusalem,
Neh 1: 3. *the wall* of Jerusalem *also* (is) broken
2: 8. *and for the wall of* the city,
13. viewed *the walls of* Jerusalem,
15. by the brook, and viewed *the wall,*
17. let us build up *the wall of* Jerusalem,
3: 8. Jerusalem unto *the* broad *wall.*
13. a thousand cubits *on the wall*
15. and *the wall of* the pool of Siloah
27. even unto *the wall of* Ophel.
4: 1(3:33). Sanballat heard that we builded *the wall,*
3(3:35). even break down their stone *wall.*
6(3:38). So built we *the wall;* and all *the wall* was joined together
7(1). that *the walls of* Jerusalem were
10(4). we are not able to build *the wall.*
13(7). set I in the lower places behind *the wall,*
15(9). we returned all of us to *the wall,*
17(11). They which builded *on the wall,*
19(13). we are separated upon *the wall,*
5:16. I continued in the work of this *wall,*
6: 1. that I had builded *the wall,*
6. thou buildest *the wall,*
15. So *the wall* was finished
7: 1. when *the wall* was built,
12:27. at the dedication of *the wall of*
30. the gates, and *the wall.*
31. princes of Judah upon *the wall,*
— right hand upon *the wall*
37. at the going up *of the wall,*
38. half of the people upon *the wall,*
— the furnaces even unto *the* broad *wall;*
13:21. Why lodge ye about *the wall?*
Ps. 51:18(20). build thou *the walls of* Jerusalem.
55:10(11). go about it upon *the walls thereof:*
Pro.18:11. *and as an* high *wall* in his own
25:28. broken down, (and) without *walls.*
Cant 5: 7. the keepers of *the walls* took away
8: 9. If she (be) *a wall,* we will build
10. I (am) *a wall,* and my breasts like towers:
Isa. 2:15. upon every fenced *wall,*
22:10. broken down to fortify *the wall.*
11. a ditch between the *two walls*
25:12. fortress of the high fort of *thy walls*
26: 1. salvation will (God) appoint (for) *walls*
30:13. swelling out *in a* high *wall,*
36:11. the people that (are) on *the wall.*
12. the men that sit upon *the wall,*
49:16. *thy walls* (are) continually before me.
56: 5. *and within my walls* a place
60:10. strangers shall build up *thy walls,*
18. thou shalt call *thy walls* Salvation,
62: 6. I have set watchmen upon *thy walls,*
Jer. 1:15. against all *the walls thereof*
18. *and* brasen *walls* against the whole
15:20. this people *a* fenced brasen *wall:*
21: 4. which besiege you without *the walls,*
39: 4. the gate betwixt *the two walls:*
8. brake down *the walls of* Jerusalem.
49:27. I will kindle a fire *in the wall of*
50:15. *her walls* are thrown down:
51:12. Set up the standard upon *the walls of*
44. *the wall of* Babylon shall fall.
58. *The* broad *walls of* Babylon
52: 7. the gate between *the two walls,*
14. brake down all *the walls*
Lam 2: 7. enemy *the walls of* her palaces;

Lam 2: 8. destroy *the wall of* the daughter of Zion:
— made the rampart *and the wall*
18. *O wall of* the daughter of Zion,
Eze.26: 4. they shall destroy *the walls of* Tyrus,
9. set engines of war *against thy walls,*
10. *thy walls* shall shake at the noise
12. they shall break down *thy walls,*
27:11. thine army (were) upon *thy walls*
— hanged their shields upon *thy walls*
38:11. all of them dwelling without *walls,*
20. every *wall* shall fall to the ground.
40: 5. behold *a wall* on the outside
42:20. it had *a wall* round about,
Joel 2: 7. shall climb *the wall* like men of war;
9. they shall run *upon the wall,*
Am. 1: 7. will send a fire *on the wall of* Gaza,
10. will send a fire *on the wall of* Tyrus,
14. will kindle a fire *in the wall of*
7: 7. the Lord stood upon *a wall* (made) *by* a plumbline,
Nah 2: 5(6). make haste to *the wall thereof,*
3: 8. *her wall* (was) from the sea?
Zec. 2: 5(9). the Lord, will be unto her *a wall of*

2347 ## חוּס [*ghoos*].

*** KAL.—*Preterite.* ***

Eze.16: 5. None eye *pitied* thee,
Jon. 4:10. *Thou hast had pity* on the gourd, (marg. or, *spared*)

KAL.—*Imperative.*

Neh 13:22. *and spare* me according
Joel 2:17. *Spare* thy people, O Lord,

KAL.—*Future.*

Gen45:20. Also *regard* not your stuff; (marg. *let* not your eye *spare*)
Deu 7:16. thine eye *shall have* no *pity*
13: 8(9). neither *shall* thine eye *pity* him,
19:13, 21 & 25:12. Thine eye *shall* not *pity*
1Sa.24:10(11). but (mine eye) *spared* thee;
Ps. 72:13. *He shall spare* the poor and needy,
Isa. 13:18. their eye *shall* not *spare* children.
Jer. 13:14. I will not pity, nor *spare,*
21: 7. *he shall* not *spare* them,
Eze. 5:11. neither *shall* mine eye *spare,*
7: 4, 9 & 8:18. mine eye *shall* not *spare*
9: 5. *let* not your eye *spare,*
10. mine eye *shall* not *spare,*
20:17. *Nevertheless* mine eye *spared* them
24:14. neither *will I spare,*
Jon. 4:11. *should* not I *spare* Nineveh,

2348 ## חוֹף *ghōhph*, m.

Gen49:13. Zebulun shall dwell *at the haven of* the sea; and he (shall be) *for an haven of* ships;
Deu. 1: 7. *and by the* sea *side,*
Jos. 9: 1. in all *the coasts of* the great sea
Jud. 5:17. Asher continued *on the* sea *shore,* (marg. or, *port*)
Jer. 47: 7. against *the* sea *shore?*
Eze.25:16. destroy the remnant of *the* sea *coast.*

2351 ## חוּץ *ghootz*, m.

[Used also adverbially.]

Gen. 6:14. pitch it within *and without*
9:22. told his two brethren *without.*
15: 5. he brought him forth *abroad,*
19:16. set him *without* the city.
17. had brought them forth *abroad,*
24:11. camels to kneel down *without* the city
29. Laban ran *out* unto the man,
31. wherefore standest thou *without?*
39:12, 15. fled, and got him *out.*
13. garment in her hand, and was fled *forth,*
18. he left his garment with me, and fled *out.*
Ex. 12:46. carry forth ought of the flesh *abroad*
21:19. walk *abroad* upon his staff,
25:11. within *and without* shalt thou overlay it,
Ex. 26:35. thou shalt set the table *without*
27:21. the congregation *without* the vail,
29:14. burn with fire *without* the camp:
33: 7. pitched it *without* the camp,
— the congregation, which (was) *without*
37: 2. with pure gold within *and without,*
40:22. tabernacle northward, *without* the vail.
Lev. 4:12. carry forth *without* the camp
21. forth the bullock *without* the camp,
6:11(4). forth the ashes *without* the camp
8:17 & 9:11. he burnt with fire *without* the camp;
10: 4. before the sanctuary *out of* the camp.
5. in their coats *out of* the camp;
13:46. *without* the camp
14: 3. the priest shall go forth *out of* the camp;
8. shall tarry *abroad out of* his tent
40. an unclean place *without* the city:
41. *without* the city into an unclean place:
45. carry (them) forth *out of* the city
53. let go the living bird *out of* the city
16:27. carry forth *without* the camp;
17: 3. or that killeth (it) *out of* the camp,
18: 9. or born *abroad,*
24: 3. *Without* the vail of the testimony,
14. him that hath cursed *without*
23. him that had cursed *out of* the camp,
Nu. 5: 3. *without* the camp shall ye put them;
4. and put them out *without* the camp:
12:14. let her be shut *out from* the camp seven
15. Miriam was shut *out from* the camp
15:35. stone him with stones *without* the camp.
36. the congregation brought him *without* the camp,
19: 3. bring her forth *without* the camp,
9. lay (them) up *without* the camp in a clean place,
22:39. they came unto Kirjath-*huzoth.* (marg. or, a city of *streets*)
31:13. went forth to meet them *without* the camp.
19. abide *without* the camp seven days:
35: 4. (shall reach) from the wall of the city *and outward*
5. ye shall measure *from without* the city
27. find him *without* the borders of the city
Deu 23:10(11). then shall he go *abroad*
12(13). have a place also *without* the camp, whither thou shalt go forth *abroad:*
13(14). when thou wilt ease thyself *abroad,*
24:11. Thou shalt stand *abroad,*
— shall bring out the pledge *abroad*
25: 5. shall not marry *without* unto a stranger:
32:25. The sword *without,* and terror within,
Jos. 2:19. the doors of thy house *into the street,*
6:23. left them *without* the camp
Jud.12: 9. thirty daughters, (whom) he sent *abroad,*
— took in thirty daughters from *abroad*
19:25. brought her *forth* unto them;
1Sa. 9:26. he and Samuel, *abroad.*
2Sa. 1:20. publish (it) not *in the streets of* Askelon;
13:17. Put now this (woman) *out* from me,
18. Then his servant brought her *out,*
22:43. stamp them as the mire of *the street,*
1K. 6: 6. *without* (in the wall) of the house
7: 9. within *and without,*
— *and* (so) *on the outside*
8: 8. they were not seen *without:*
20:34. *and* thou shalt make *streets* for thee
21:13. carried him forth *out of* the city,
2K. 4: 3. Go, borrow thee vessels *abroad*
10:24. Jehu appointed fourscore men *without,*
23: 4. he burned them *without* Jerusalem
6. *without* Jerusalem, unto the brook
2Ch 5: 9. but they were not seen *without.*
24: 8. set it *without* at the gate
29:16. carry (it) out *abroad* into the brook
32: 3. fountains which (were) *without*
5. the towers, *and* another wall *without,*
33:15. and cast (them) *out of* the city.
Ezr. 10:13. we are not able to stand *without,*
Neh 13: 8. stuff of Tobiah *out* of the chamber.
20. lodged *without* Jerusalem
Job 5:10. sendeth waters upon *the fields:* (marg. *outplaces*)
18:17. he shall have no name in *the street.*
31:32. The stranger did not lodge *in the street:*
Ps. 18:42(43). cast them out as the dirt in *the streets.*

Ps. 31:11(12). they that did see me *without*
41: 6(7). he goeth *abroad*, he telleth (it).
144:13. thousands and ten thousands *in our streets:*
Pro. 1:20. Wisdom crieth *without;*
5:16. Let thy fountains be dispersed *abroad*,
7:12. Now (is she) *without*, now in the streets,
8:26. made the earth, *nor the fields*, (marg. *open places*)
22:13. slothful (man) saith, (There is) a lion *without*,
24:27. Prepare thy work *without*,
Ecc. 2:25. who else can hasten (hereunto), *more* than I?
Cant. 8: 1. I should find thee *without*,
Isa. 5:25. torn in the midst of *the streets.*
10: 6. down like the mire of *the streets.*
15: 3. *In their streets* they shall gird
24:11. a crying for wine *in the streets;*
33: 7. their valiant ones shall cry *without:*
42: 2. cause his voice to be heard *in the street.*
51:20. lie at the head of all *the streets*,
23. as the ground, *and as the street*,
Jer. 5: 1. Run ye to and fro *through the streets of*
6:11. pour it out upon the children *abroad*,
7:17. *and in the streets of* Jerusalem?
34. *and from the streets of* Jerusalem,
9:21(20). cut off the children *from without*,
11: 6. *and in the streets of* Jerusalem,
13. the number of *the streets of* Jerusalem
14:16. cast out *in the streets of* Jerusalem
21: 4. which besiege you *without* the walls,
33:10. *and in the streets of* Jerusalem,
37:21. bread out of the bakers' *street*,
44: 6, 17, 21. in the cities of Judah *and in the streets of* Jerusalem;
9. in the land of Judah, *and in the streets of*
51: 4. thrust through *in her streets.*
Lam. 1:20. *abroad* the sword bereaveth,
2:19. faint for hunger in the top of every *street.*
21. lie on the ground *in the streets:*
4: 1. poured out in the top of every *street.*
5. that did feed delicately are desolate *in the streets:*
8. they are not known *in the streets:*
14. They have wandered (as) blind (men) *in the streets*,
Eze. 7:15. The sword (is) *without*,
19. shall cast their silver *in the streets*,
11: 6. ye have filled *the streets thereof*
26:11. shall he tread down all *thy streets:*
28:23. blood *into her streets;*
34:21. till ye have scattered them *abroad;*
40: 5. behold a wall *on the outside*
19. the forefront of the inner court *without*,
40. at the side *without*,
44. *And without* the inner gate
41: 9. for the side chamber *without*,
17. unto the inner house, *and without*,
25. the face of the porch *without.*
42: 7. the wall that (was) *without*
43:21. *without* the sanctuary.
46: 2. way of the porch of (that) gate *without*,
47: 2. led me about the way *without* unto the *utter* gate by the way
Hos. 7: 1. the troop of robbers spoileth *without.*
Am. 5:16. they shall say in all *the highways*,
Mic. 7:10. trodden down as the mire of *the streets.*
Nah. 2: 4(5). The chariots shall rage *in the streets*,
3:10. dashed in pieces at the top of all *the streets:*
Zep. 3: 6. I made *their streets* waste,
Zec. 9: 3. fine gold as the mire of *the streets.*
10: 5. the mire of *the streets* in the battle:

2436 חוֹק [*g̣hōhk*], m.

Ps. 74:11. (כתיב) pluck (it) out of *thy bosom.*

2357 חָוַר [*g̣hāh-var'*].

* KAL.—*Future.* *

Isa 29:22. neither *shall* his face now *wax pale.*

חוּר [*g̣hūhr*], m. 2355

Isa. 19: 9. they that weave *networks*, (marg. or, *white works*)

חוֹר *g̣hōhr*, m. 2356

1 Sa. 14:11. the Hebrews come forth out of *the holes*
2K. 12: 9(10). bored *a hole* in the lid of it,
Job 30: 6. cliffs of the valleys, (in) *caves of* the earth, (marg. *holes*)
Cant. 5: 4. put in his hand by *the hole*
Eze. 8: 7. behold a *hole* in the wall.
Nah. 2:12(13). filled *his holes* with prey,
Zec. 14:12. shall consume away *in their holes*,

חוּר *g̣hoor*, m. 2353

Est. 1: 6. (Where were) *white*, green, and blue,
8:15. in royal apparel of blue *and white*,

חוּר *g̣hoor*, m. 2352

Isa. 11: 8. shall play on *the hole of* the asp,
42:22. all of them snared *in holes*, (marg. or, in snaring all *the young men* of them, [as if from בָּחוּר])

חִוָּר *g̣hiv-vāhr'*, Ch. adj. 2358

Dan 7: 9. whose garment (was) *white* as snow,

חוֹרִים *g̣hōh-reem'*, m. pl. 2715

1K. 21: 8. to *the nobles* that (were) in his city,
11. the elders *and the nobles*
Neh 2:16. to the priests, *nor to the nobles*,
4:14(8), 19(13). said unto *the nobles*,
5: 7. I rebuked *the nobles*, and the rulers,
6:17. *the nobles of* Judah sent many letters
7: 5. mine heart to gather together *the nobles*,
13:17. I contended with *the nobles of* Judah,
Ecc. 10:17. when thy king (is) the son of *nobles*,
Isa. 34:12. They shall call *the nobles thereof*
Jer. 27:20. all *the nobles of* Judah
39: 6. the king of Babylon slew all *the nobles of* Judah.

חוּשׁ [*g̣hoosh*]. 2363

* KAL.—*Preterite.* *

Deu 32:35. *and* the things that shall come upon them *make haste.*
Ps. 119:60. *I made haste*, and delayed not
Isa. 8: 1. concerning Maher-shalal-*hash*-baz. (marg. in making speed to the spoil *he hasteneth* the prey)
Hab. 1: 8. fly as the eagle (that) *hasteth* to eat

KAL.—*Infinitive.*

Job 20: 2. for (this) I *make haste.* (marg. *my haste* (is) in me)

KAL.—*Imperative.*

1 Sa. 20:38. Make speed, *haste*, stay not.
Ps. 22:19(20). *haste thee* to help me.
38:22(23). *Make haste* to help me, O Lord
40:13(14). O Lord, *make haste* to help me.
70: 1(2). *make haste* to help me, O Lord.
5(6). *make haste* unto me, O God:
71:12. *make haste* for my help.
141: 1. I cry unto thee: *make haste* unto me;

KAL.—*Future.*

Job 31: 5. *or* if my foot *hath hasted* to deceit;
Ecc. 2:25. or who else *can hasten*

KAL.—*Participle.* Paül.

Nu. 32:17. we ourselves will go *ready* armed

* HIPHIL.—*Preterite.* *

Jud.20:37. the liers in wait *hasted,*

HIPHIL.—*Future.*

Ps. 55: 8(9). *I would hasten* my escape
Isa. 5:19. Let him make speed, (and) *hasten*
28:16. he that believeth *shall* not *make haste.*
60:22. I the Lord *will hasten it* in his time.

See 2865 חוּת see חָתַת

2368 חוֹתָם *ġhōh-thāhm',* m.

Gen38:18. *Thy signet,* and thy bracelets,
Ex. 28:11, 21, 36. the engravings of *a signet,*
39: 6. graven, as *signets* are graven,
14, 30. the engravings of *a signet,*
1K. 21: 8. sealed (them) *with his seal,*
Job 38:14. It is turned as clay (to) *the seal;*
41:15(7). shut up together (as with) *a close seal.*
Cant.8: 6. Set me *as a seal* upon thine heart, *as a seal* upon thine arm:
Jer. 22:24. were *the signet* upon my right hand,
Hag. 2:23. will make thee *as a signet:*

2372 חָזָה *ġhāh-zāh'.*

* KAL.—*Preterite.* *

Job 15:17. that (which) *I have seen* I will declare;
24: 1. *do they* that know him not *see*
27:12. all ye yourselves *have seen*
36:25. Every man *may see* it;
Ps. 58: 8(9). *they may* not *see* the sun.
10(11). rejoice when *he seeth* the vengeance:
63: 2(3). *I have seen thee* in the sanctuary.
Pro.22:29. *Seest thou* a man diligent in his business?
29:20. *Seest thou* a man (that is) hasty in his words?
Isa. 1: 1. which *he saw* concerning Judah
2: 1. Isaiah the son of Amoz *saw*
13: 1. Isaiah the son of Amoz *did see.*
57: 8. lovedst their bed where *thou sawest*
Lam.2:14. Thy prophets *have seen* vain
Eze.13: 6. *They have seen* vanity and lying
7. *Have ye* not *seen* a vain vision,
8. spoken vanity, *and seen* lies,
Am. 1: 1. which *he saw* concerning Israel
Mic. 1: 1. which *he saw* concerning Samaria and
Hab. 1: 1. which Habakkuk the prophet *did see.*
Zec.10: 2. the diviners *have seen* a lie,

KAL.—*Infinitive.*

Ps. 27: 4. *to behold* the beauty of the Lord,
Eze.21:29(34). *Whiles they see* vanity unto thee,

KAL.—*Imperative.*

Ps. 46: 8(9). *behold* the works of the Lord,
Isa. 30:10. smooth things, *prophesy* deceits:
33:20. *Look* upon Zion, the city of our
48: 6. Thou hast heard, *see* all this;

KAL.—*Future.*

Ex. 18:21. thou *shalt provide* out of all
24:11. *also they saw* God, and did eat and drink.
Nu. 24: 4, 16. *saw* the vision of the Almighty,
Job 8:17. *seeth* the place of stones.
19:26. yet in my flesh *shall I see* God:
27. Whom *I shall see* for myself,
23: 9. but *I cannot behold*
34:32. *I see* not teach thou me:
Ps. 11: 4. his eyes *behold,* his eyelids try,
7. his countenance *doth behold* the upright.
17: 2. *let* thine eyes *behold* the things
15. *I will behold* thy face in righteousness:
Pro.24:32. *Then I saw,* (and) considered (it) well:
Cant.6:13(7:1). that *we may look* upon thee. What *will ye see* in the Shulamite?
Isa. 26:11. is lifted up, *they will* not *see:* (but) *they shall see,* and be ashamed
Isa. 30:10. *Prophesy* not unto us right things.
33:17. Thine eyes *shall see* the king
Lam. 2:14. *but have seen* for thee false burdens
Eze.13:23. *ye shall see* no more vanity,
Mic. 4:11. *and let* our eye *look* upon Zion.

KAL.—*Participle.* Poel.

Eze.12:27. The vision that he *seeth* (is) for many

חֲזָה & חֲזָא *ġhăzāh,* Ch. 2370

* P'AL.—*Preterite.* *

Dan 2: 8. because *ye see* the thing is gone from me.
26. the dream which *I have seen,*
41. whereas *thou sawest* the feet and toes,
— forasmuch as *thou sawest* the iron
43. whereas *thou sawest* iron mixed
45. Forasmuch as *thou sawest* that the stone
4: 5(2). *I saw* a dream which made me afraid,
9(6). dream that *I have seen,*
18(15). This dream *I* king Nebuchadnezzar *have seen.*
20(17). The tree that *thou sawest,* which grew,
23(20). whereas the king *saw* a watcher and
7: 1. Daniel *had* a dream (marg. *saw*)

P'AL.—*Infinitive.*

Ezr. 4:14. not meet for us *to see* the king's dishonour,

P'AL.—*Participle.* Active.

Dan 2:31. Thou, O king, *sawest,* and behold
34. Thou *sawest* till that a stone
3:25. Lo, I *see* four men loose, walking
27. *saw* these men, upon whose bodies
4:10(7). I *saw,* and behold a tree
13(10). I *saw* in the visions of my head
5: 5. and the king *saw* the part of the hand that wrote.
23. gods of silver,...which *see* not, nor hear,
7: 2. I *saw* in my vision by night,
4. I *beheld* till the wings thereof were plucked.
6. I *beheld,* and lo another, like a leopard,
7, 13. I *saw* in the night visions, and behold
9. I *beheld* till the thrones were cast down,
11. I *beheld* then because of the voice
— I *beheld* (even) till the beast was slain,
21. I *beheld,* and the same horn made war with the saints,

P'AL.—*Participle.* Passive.

Dan 3:19. seven times more than *it was wont*

חָזֶה *ġhāh-zeh',* m. 2373

Ex. 29:26. thou shalt take *the breast*
27. sanctify *the breast of* the wave offering,
Lev. 7:30. the fat with *the breast,*
— that *the breast* may be waved
31. but *the breast* shall be Aaron's
34. *the* wave *breast* and the heave shoulder
8:29. Moses took *the breast,*
9:20. they put the fat upon *the breasts,*
21. *the breasts* and the right shoulder
10:14. *the* wave *breast* and heave shoulder
15. The heave shoulder *and the* wave *breast*
Nu. 6:20. *the* wave *breast* and heave shoulder:
18:18. *as the* wave *breast*

חֹזֶה *ġhōh-zeh',* m 2374

2Sa.24:11. the prophet Gad, David's *seer,*
2K. 17:13. the prophets, (and by) all *the seers,*
1Ch 21: 9. spake unto Gad, David's *seer,*
25: 5. the sons of Heman the king's *seer*
29:29. in the book of Gad *the seer,*
2Ch 9:29. in the visions of Iddo *the seer*
12:15. Iddo *the seer* concerning genealogies?
19: 2. Hanani *the seer* went out to meet him,
29:25. David, and of Gad the king's *seer,*
30. David, and of Asaph *the seer.*
33:18. the words of *the seers* that spake
19. written among the sayings of *the seers.* (marg. or, *Hosai*)

2Ch 35:15. Jeduthun the king's *seer;*
Isa. 28:15. with hell are we at *agreement;*
29:10. *the seers* hath he covered.
30:10. *and to the prophets,* Prophesy not
47:13. astrologers, *the stargazers,*
Eze.13: 9. the prophets *that see* vanity,
16. *and which see* visions of peace
22:28. *seeing* vanity, and divining lies
Am. 7:12. *O thou seer,* go, flee thee away
Mic. 3: 7. Then shall *the seers* be ashamed,

2376 ## חֵזֵו [*gheh'-zev*], Ch. m.

Dan 2:19. unto Daniel in *a* night *vision.*
28. *and the visions of* thy head
4: 5(2). *and the visions of* my head
9(6). tell me *the visions of* my dream
10(7). *Thus* (were) *the visions of* mine
13(10). I saw *in the visions of* my head
7: 1. *and visions of* his head upon his bed:
2. I saw *in my vision* by night,
7, 13. I saw *in the* night *visions,* and behold
15. *the visions of* my head troubled me.
20. *whose look* (was) more stout

2377 ## חָזוֹן *ghāh-zōhn',* m.

1Sa. 3: 1. those days; (there was) no open *vision.*
1Ch 17:15. according to all this *vision,*
2Ch 32:32. written *in the vision of* Isaiah
Ps. 89:19(20). Then thou spakest *in vision*
Pro.29:18. Where (there is) no *vision,*
Isa. 1: 1. *The vision of* Isaiah the son of Amoz,
29: 7. shall be as a dream of *a* night *vision.*
Jer. 14:14. they prophesy unto you *a* false *vision*
23:16. they speak *a vision of* their own heart,
Lam.2: 9. find no *vision* from the Lord.
Eze. 7:13. *the vision* (is) touching the whole
26. then shall they seek *a vision*
12:22. every *vision* faileth?
23. the effect of every *vision.*
24. there shall be no more any vain *vision*
27. *The vision* that he seeth
13:16. which see *visions of* peace
Dan 1:17. understanding in all *visions*
8: 1. *a vision* appeared unto me,
2. And I saw *in a vision;* and it came
— and I saw *in a vision,* and I was by the river
13. How long (shall be) *the vision*
15. I Daniel, had seen *the vision,*
17. time of the end (shall be) *the vision.*
26. wherefore shut thou up *the vision;*
9:21. whom I had seen *in the vision*
24. to seal up *the vision* and prophecy,
10:14. for yet *the vision* (is) for (many) days.
11:14. exalt themselves to establish *the vision;*
Hos.12:10(11). I have multiplied *visions,*
Obad 1. *The vision of* Obadiah.
Mic. 3: 6. *that ye shall not have a vision;* (marg. *from a vision*)
Nah 1: 1. The book of *the vision of* Nahum
Hab 2: 2. Write *the vision,* and make (it) plain
3. *the vision* (is) yet for an appointed time,

2378 ## חָזוֹת [*ghāh-zōhth'*], f.

2Ch 9:29. *and in the visions of* Iddo

2379 ## חֲזוֹת [*ghăzōhth*], Ch. f.

Dan 4:11(8). *and the sight thereof* to the end of all the earth:
20(17). *and the sight thereof* to all the earth;

2380 ## חָזוּת *ghāh-zooth',* f.

Isa. 21: 2. *A* grievous *vision* is declared unto me;
28:18. *and your agreement* with hell
29:11. *the vision of* all is become unto you
Dan 8: 5. the goat (had) a *notable* horn (marg. a horn of *sight*)
8. for it came up four *notable* ones

חִזָּיוֹן *ghiz-zāh-yōhn',* m. 2384

2Sa. 7:17. according to all this *vision,*
Job 4:13. In thoughts *from the visions of* the night,
7:14. *and* terrifiest me *through visions:*
20: 8. chased away *as a vision of* the night.
33:15. in *a vision of* the night,
Isa. 22: 1. The burden of the valley of *vision.*
5. the Lord God of hosts in the valley of *vision,*
Joel 2:28(3:1). your young men shall see *visions:*
Zec.13: 4. be ashamed every one *of his vision,*

חֲזִיז *ghāh-zeez',* m. 2385

Job 28:26. a way *for the lightning of* the thunder:
38:25. a way *for the lightning of* thunder;
Zec.10: 1. the Lord shall make *bright clouds,* (marg. or, *lightnings*)

חֲזִיר *ghăzeer,* m. 2386

Lev.11: 7. *the swine,* though he divide the hoof,
Deu14: 8. *the swine,* because it divideth the hoof,
Ps. 80:13(14). *The boar* out of the wood doth
Pro.11:22. a jewel of gold in *a swine's* snout,
Isa. 65: 4. which eat *swine's* flesh,
66: 3. oblation, (as if he offered) *swine's* blood;
17. eating *swine's* flesh, and the abomination,

חָזַק *ghāh-zak'.* 2388

* KAL.—*Preterite.* *

Gen41:57. the famine *was* (so) *sore* in all lands.
47:20. because the famine *prevailed*
Jos. 17:13. Israel *were waxen strong,*
23: 6. *Be ye therefore* very *courageous*
Jud. 1:28. came to pass, when Israel *was strong,*
2Sa.16:21. *then shall* the hands of all that (are) with thee *be strong.*
1K. 2: 2. *be thou strong therefore,*
20:23. *they were stronger* than we;
2K. 3:26. saw that the battle *was* too *sore*
14: 5. as soon as the kingdom *was confirmed*
1Ch 21: 4. Nevertheless the king's word *prevailed*
2Ch 25: 3. when the kingdom *was established* (marg. *confirmed*)
26:15. marvellously helped, till *he was strong.*
28:20. but *strengthened him* not.
Jer. 20: 7. *thou art stronger than I,*
Eze. 3:14. the hand of the Lord *was strong*
Mal. 3:13. Your words *have been stout*

KAL.—*Infinitive.*

Eze.30:21. *to make it strong* to hold

KAL.—*Imperative.*

Deu12:23. *be sure* that thou eat not the blood:
31: 6. *Be strong* and of a good courage:
7, 23. *Be strong* and of a good courage:
Jos. 1: 6, 9, 18. *Be strong* and of a good courage:
7. Only *be thou strong*
10:25. *be strong* and of good courage:
2Sa.10:12. *Be of good courage,*
13:28. I commanded you? *be courageous,*
1Ch 19:13. *Be of good courage,*
22:13. *be strong,* and of good courage;
28:10. *be strong,* and do
20. *Be strong* and of good courage,
2Ch 15: 7. *Be ye strong* therefore, and let not your
19:11. Deal *courageously,* (marg. *Take courage* and do)
25: 8. *be strong* for the battle.
32: 7. *Be strong* and courageous, be not afraid
Ezr.10: 4. *be of good courage,*
Ps. 27:14. Wait on the Lord: *be of good courage,*
31:24(25). *Be of good courage,* and he shall
Isa. 35: 4. *Be strong,* fear not:
41: 6. *Be of good courage.* (marg. *strong*)
Dan10:19. *be strong, yea, be strong.*
Hag 2: 4. Yet now *be strong,* O Zerubbabel, saith the Lord; *and be strong,* O Joshua, son of Josedech, the high priest; *and be strong,* all ye people

KAL.—*Future.*

Gen41:56. *and* the famine *waxed sore* in the land
Ex. 7:13. *And he hardened* Pharaoh's heart,
22 & 8:19(15). *and* Pharaoh's heart *was hardened,*
9:35. *And* the heart of Pharaoh *was hardened,*
12:33. *And* the Egyptians *were urgent*
Deu 11: 8. that *ye may be strong,*
Jud. 7:11. afterward *shall* thine hands *be strengthened*
1Sa.17:50. *So* David *prevailed* over the Philistine
2Sa. 2: 7. *let* your hands *be strengthened,*
10:11. If the Syrians *be* too *strong* for me,
— if the children of Ammon *be* too *strong*
13:14. *but, being stronger* than she,
18: 9. *and* his head *caught hold* of the oak,
24: 4. *Notwithstanding* the king's word *prevailed*
1K. 16:22. *But* the people that followed Omri *prevailed*
20:23, 25. *we shall be stronger* than they.
2K. 25: 3. And on the ninth (day)... the famine *prevailed*
1Ch 19:12. If the Syrians *be* too *strong*
— but if the children of Ammon *be* too *strong*
28: 7. if *he be constant* to do my commandments (marg. *strong*)
2Ch 8: 3. *and prevailed* against it.
27: 5. *and prevailed* against them.
31: 4. that *they might be encouraged*
Ezr. 9:12. that *ye may be strong,*
Isa. 28:22. lest your bands *be made strong:*
39: 1. had been sick, *and was recovered.*
Jer. 52: 6. the famine *was sore* in the city,
Eze.22:14. *can* thine hands *be strong,*
Dan11: 5. *And* the king of the south *shall be strong,*
—, *and he shall be strong* above him,
Zec. 8: 9, 13. *Let* your hands *be strong,*

* PIEL.—*Preterite.* *

Ex. 14: 4. *And I will harden* Pharaoh's
Jud. 9:24. which *aided* him (marg. *strengthened* his hands)
2K. 12: 6(7). the priests *had* not *repaired*
14(15). *and repaired* therewith the house
Ezr. 1: 6. *strengthened* their hands with vessels of
Ps.147:13. *he hath strengthened* the bars of thy gates;
Jer. 5: 3. *they have made* their faces *harder*
23:14. *they strengthen also* the hands of evildoers,
Eze.30:24. *And I will strengthen* the arms of the king
34: 4. The diseased *have ye* not *strengthened,*
Dan 10:19. my lord speak; for *thou hast strengthened me.*
Hos. 7:15. I have bound (and) *strengthened*

PIEL.—*Infinitive.*

Jos. 11:20. it was of the Lord *to harden* their hearts,
2K. 12: 8(9). neither *to repair* the breaches
12(13). *to repair* the breaches of the house
22: 5. *to repair* the breaches of the house,
6. hewn stone *to repair* the house.
1Ch 26:27. did they dedicate *to maintain*
29:12. *and to give strength* unto all.
2Ch 24: 5. *to repair* the house of your God
12. iron and brass *to mend* the house of the
34: 8. *to repair* the house of the Lord
10. to repair *and amend* the house:
Ezr. 6:22. *to strengthen* their hands
Eze.13:22. *and strengthened* the hands of

PIEL.—*Imperative.*

Deu 1:38. he shall go in thither: *encourage* him:
3:28. charge Joshua, *and encourage him,*
Jud.16:28. *and strengthen me,* I pray thee,
2Sa.11:25. *and encourage thou him.*
Neh 6: 9. therefore, (O God), *strengthen* my hands.
Isa. 35: 3. *Strengthen ye* the weak hands,
54: 2. and *strengthen* thy stakes;
Nah 2: 1(2). *make* (thy) loins *strong,*
3:14. *fortify* thy strong holds:

PIEL.—*Future.*

Ex. 4:21. but I *will harden* his heart,
9:12. *And* the Lord *hardened* the heart
10:20, 27. *But* the Lord *hardened* Pharaoh's
11:10. *and* the Lord *hardened* Pharaoh's heart,
14: 8. *And* the Lord *hardened* the heart
Jud. 3:12. *and* the Lord *strengthened* Eglon
1Sa.23:16. *and strengthened* his hand in God.

2K. 12: 5(6). *let them repair* the breaches of the
2Ch 11:11. *And he fortified* the strong holds,
12. *and made them* exceeding *strong,*
17. *So they strengthened* the kingdom.
26: 9. turning (of the wall), *and fortified them.*
29: 3. house of the Lord, *and repaired them.*
34. *wherefore* their brethren the Levites *did help them,* (marg. *strengthened*)
32: 5. *and repaired* Millo (in) the city
35: 2. *and encouraged them* to the service
Neh 2:18. *So they strengthened* their hands
3:19. next to him *repaired* Ezer
Job 4: 3. *thou hast strengthened* the weak hands.
Ps. 64: 5(6). *They encourage* themselves (in) an
Isa. 22:21. and *strengthen him* with thy girdle,
33:23. *they could* not well *strengthen*
41: 7. *So* the carpenter *encouraged*
— *and he fastened it* with nails,
Jer. 10: 4. *they fasten it* with nails
Eze.34:16. and *will strengthen* that which was sick:
Dan 10:18. *and he strengthened me,*

PIEL.—*Participle.*

Ex. 14:17. I *will harden* the hearts of the Egyptians,
2K. 12: 7(8). Why *repair* ye not the breaches

* HIPHIL.—*Preterite.* *

Lev.25:35. *then thou shalt relieve* him: (marg. *strengthen*)
Deu22:25. *and* the man *force* her, (marg. or, *take strong hold* of her)
25:11. *and taketh* him by the secrets:
Jud. 7: 8. *retained* those three hundred men:
1Sa.17:35. *and* when he arose against me, *I caught* (him)
2Sa.15: 5. he put forth his hand, *and took* him,
2Ch 26: 8. *he strengthened* (himself) exceedingly.
Neh 3: 4, 4, 4, 7, 9, 10. next unto them *repaired*
5. the Tekoites *repaired;*
6. the old gate *repaired* Jehoiada
8, 10, 12, 17. Next unto him *repaired*
— Next unto him also *repaired*
11. *repaired* the other piece, and the tower
13. The valley gate *repaired* Hanun,
14. the dung gate *repaired* Malchiah
15. the gate of the fountain *repaired* Shallun
16. After him *repaired* Nehemiah the son of
17, 18, 22, 29, 30, 30, 31. After him *repaired*
20. the son of Zabbai earnestly *repaired*
21, 23, 23, 24. after him *repaired*
27. the Tekoites *repaired* another piece,
28. above the horse gate *repaired* the priests,
29. After them *repaired* Zadok
32. the sheep gate *repaired* the goldsmiths
5:16. also *I continued* in the work
Job 27: 6. My righteousness *I hold fast,*
Pro. 7:13. *So she caught* him, and kissed him,
Isa. 4: 1. *And* in that day seven women *shall take hold*
41: 9. whom *I have taken* from the ends of
45: 1. whose right hand *I have holden,* (marg. or, *strengthened*)
Jer. 6:24. anguish *hath taken hold of us,*
8: 5. *they hold fast* deceit,
21. astonishment *hath taken hold on me.*
49:24. fear *hath seized on* (her):
50:33. that took them captives *held* them *fast;*
43. anguish *took hold of him,*
Eze.16:49. neither *did she strengthen* the hand
30:25. *But I will strengthen* the arms
Dan 11: 7. deal against them, *and shall prevail:*
21. *and obtain* the kingdom by flatteries.
Mic. 4: 9. pangs *have taken thee* as a woman in
7:18. *he retaineth* not his anger
Zec. 8:23. *even shall take hold* of the skirt
14:13. *and they shall lay hold* every one

HIPHIL.—*Infinitive.*

2K. 15:19. might be with him *to confirm* the kingdom
Isa. 64: 7(6). stirreth up himself *to take hold* of thee:
Jer. 31:32. *I took* them by the hand

HIPHIL.—*Imperative.*

Gen21:18. *and hold* him in thine hand;
2Sa.11:25. *make* thy battle more *strong*
Ps. 35: 2. *Take hold* of shield and buckler,
Pro. 4:13. *Take fast hold* of instruction;
Jer. 51:12. *make* the watch *strong,*
Nah 3:14. *make strong* the brickkiln.

HIPHIL.—*Future.*

Gen19:16. *And* while he lingered, the men *laid hold*
Ex. 4: 4. put forth his hand, *and caught* it,
Jud. 7:20. *and held* the lamps in their left hands,
19: 4. *And* his father in law, the damsel's father, *retained*
25. *so* the man *took* his concubine,
29. *and laid hold* on his concubine,
1Sa.15:27. *And* as Samuel turned...*he laid hold* upon
2Sa. 1:11. *Then* David *took hold* on his clothes,
2:16. *And they caught* every one his fellow
13:11. *he took hold* of her,
1K. 1:50 & 2:28. *and caught hold* on the horns of the
9: 9. *and have taken hold* upon other gods,
2K. 2:12. *and he took hold* of his own clothes,
4: 8. *and she constrained* him to eat bread. (marg. *laid hold* on him)
27. *she caught* him by the feet:
2Ch 7:22. *and laid hold* on other gods,
28:15. rose up, *and took* the captives,
Job 8:15. *he shall hold* it *fast*,
20. neither *will he help* the evil doers: (marg. *will he take* the ungodly by the hand)
18: 9. the robber *shall prevail* against him.
Isa. 27: 5. Or *let him take hold* of my strength,
42: 6. *and will hold* thine hand,
56: 2. the son of man (that) *layeth hold* on it;
Jer. 6:23. *They shall lay hold* on bow and spear;
50:42. *They shall hold* the bow and the lance:
Dan11:32. that do know their God *shall be strong*, and do (exploits).
Zec. 8:23. ten men *shall take hold*

HIPHIL.—*Participle.*

Ex. 9: 2. wilt *hold* them still,
Jud.16:26. the lad *that held* him by the hand,
2Sa. 3:29. *or that leaneth* on a staff,
2Ch 4: 5. *received* and held three thousand baths.
Neh 4:16(10). *held* both the spears, the shields,
17(11). with the other (hand) *held* a weapon.
21(15). half of them *held* the spears
10:29(30). They *clave* to their brethren,
Job 2: 3. still he *holdeth fast* his integrity,
9. Dost thou still *retain* thine integrity?
Pro. 3:18. life *to them that lay hold* upon her:
26:17. one *that taketh* a dog by the ears.
Isa. 41:13. I the Lord thy God *will hold* thy right
51:18. neither (is there any) *that taketh* her
56: 4. *and take hold* of my covenant;
6. *and taketh hold* of my covenant;
Eze.27: 9. were in thee thy calkers: (marg. *strengtheners*, or, *stoppers of* chinks)
27. thy mariners, and thy pilots, thy calkers, (lit. *repairers of* thy chinks)
Dan11: 1. I, stood *to confirm* and to strengthen him.
6. *and he that strengthened her*

* HITHPAEL.—*Preterite.* *

Nu. 13:20. *And be ye of good courage*,
2Ch 13: 7. *could* not *withstand* them.
15: 8. Oded the prophet, *he took courage*,
23: 1. Jehoiada *strengthened himself*,
25:11. Amaziah *strengthened himself*,
Ezr. 7:28. And I *was strengthened*
Dan10:19. *I was strengthened*, and said,

HITHPAEL.—*Infinitive.*

2Ch 13: 8. now ye think *to withstand* the kingdom
16: 9. *to shew himself strong* in the behalf

HITHPAEL.—*Imperative.*

1Sa. 4: 9. *Be strong*, and quit yourselves like men,
1K. 20:22. Go, *strengthen thyself*, and mark,

HITHPAEL.—*Future.*

Gen48: 2. *and* Israel *strengthened himself*,
Jud.20:22. *And*...the men of Israel *encouraged themselves*,
1Sa.30: 6. *but* David *encouraged himself*
2Sa.10:12. *and let us play the men* for our people,
1Ch 19:13. *and let us behave ourselves valiantly*
2Ch 1: 1. *And* Solomon the son of David *was strengthened*
12:13. *So* king Rehoboam *strengthened himself*
13:21. *But* Abijah *waxed mighty*,
17: 1. *and strengthened himself* against Israel.
21: 4. *Now* when Jehoram...*he strengthened himself*,
27: 6. *So* Jotham *became mighty*,
32: 5. *Also he strengthened himself*,
Eze. 7:13. neither *shall* any *strengthen himself*

HITHPAEL.—*Participle.*

2Sa. 3: 6. that Abner *made himself strong* (lit. was *making himself strong*)
1Ch 11:10. *who strengthened themselves* (marg. or, *held strongly*)
Dan 10:21. none *that holdeth* with me (marg. *strengtheneth himself*)

חָזָק *ghāh-zāhk'*, adj. 2389

Ex. 3:19. let you go, no, not by a *mighty* hand.
6: 1, 1. with a *strong* hand
10:19. the Lord turned a mighty *strong* west wind,
13: 9. with a *strong* hand
19:16. the voice of the trumpet exceeding *loud*;
32:11. with a *mighty* hand?
Nu. 13:18. *whether* they (be) *strong* or weak,
31. for they (are) *stronger* than we.
20:20. with a *strong* hand.
Deu. 3:24. and thy *mighty* hand:
4:34. by war, and by a *mighty* hand,
5:15. out thence through a *mighty* hand
6:21. out of Egypt with a *mighty* hand:
7: 8. brought you out with a *mighty* hand.
19. the wonders, and the *mighty* hand,
9:26. forth out of Egypt with a *mighty* hand.
11: 2. his greatness, his *mighty* hand,
26: 8. out of Egypt with a *mighty* hand,
34:12. in all that *mighty* hand,
Jos. 4:24. that it (is) *mighty*:
14:11. As yet I (am as) *strong* this day
17:18. though they (be) *strong*.
Jud.18:26. Micah saw that they (were) too *strong*
1Sa.14:52. there was *sore* war against the
2Sa.11:15. Uriah in the forefront of the *hottest* battle, (marg. *strong*)
1K. 8:42. of thy *strong* hand,
17:17. his sickness was so *sore*, (lit. very *strong*)
18: 2. And (there was) a *sore* famine
19:11. great *and strong* wind rent the mountains,
2Ch 6:32. thy *mighty* hand, and thy stretched out
Neh. 1:10. by thy great power, and by thy *strong* hand.
Job 5:15. from the hand of the *mighty*.
37:18. spread out the sky, (which is) *strong*,
Ps. 35:10. the poor *from him that is* too *strong*
136:12. With a *strong* hand,
Pro.23:11. For their redeemer (is) *mighty*;
Isa. 27: 1. great *and strong* sword shall punish
28: 2. the Lord hath a *mighty* and strong one,
40:10. the Lord God will come *with strong* (hand),
Jer. 21: 5. outstretched hand and with a *strong* arm,
31:11. hand of (him that was) *stronger*
32:21. wonders, and with a *strong* hand,
50:34. Their Redeemer (is) *strong*;
Eze. 2: 4. impudent children *and stiff* hearted.
3: 7. house of Israel (are) impudent (lit. *stiff of* forehead)
8. thy face *strong* against their faces,
— thy forehead *strong* against their
9. As an adamant *harder* than flint
20:33. surely with a *mighty* hand,
34. scattered, with a *mighty* hand,
26:17. which wast *strong* in the sea,
30:22. *the strong*, and that which was broken;
34:16. I will destroy the fat and *the strong*;
Dan 9:15. out of the land of Egypt with a *mighty* hand,
Am. 2:14. *and the strong* shall not strengthen

חָזֵק *ghāh-zēhk'*, adj. 2390

Ex. 19:19. *and waxed louder* and louder, (lit. *and* very *strong*)
2Sa. 3: 1. but David waxed stronger *and stronger*, (lit. was going *and strong*)

2391 **חֵזֶק** [*g̣hēh'-zek*], m.

Ps. 18: 1(2). I will love thee, O Lord, *my strength.*

2392 **חֹזֶק** *g̣hōh'-zek*, m.

Ex. 13: 3. *by strength of* hand the Lord
14, 16. *By strength of* hand the Lord
Am. 6:13. taken to us horns *by our own strength?*
Hag. 2:22. I will destroy *the strength of* the kingdoms

2394 **חֶזְקָה** [*g̣hez-kāh'*], f.

Jud. 4: 3. twenty years he *mightily* oppressed
8: 1. they did chide with him *sharply.* (marg. *strongly*)
1Sa. 2:16. I will take (it) *by force.*
2K. 12:12(13). for the house *to repair* (it).
Eze.34: 4. but *with force* and with cruelty
Jon. 3: 8. cry *mightily* unto God:

2393 **חָזְקָה** *g̣hoz-kāh'*, f.

2Ch 12: 1. *and had strengthened himself,*
26:16. *But when he was strong,*
Isa. 8:11. the Lord spake thus to me *with a strong* hand, (marg. *in strength of*)
Dan 11: 2. *and by his strength* through his

2397 **חָח** *g̣hāhg̣h*, m.

Ex. 35:22. brought *bracelets,* and earrings,
2K. 19:28. I will put *my hook* in thy nose,
Isa. 37:29. will I put *my hook* in thy nose,
Eze.19: 4. brought him *with chains* unto the land
9. put him in ward *in chains,* (marg. *hooks*)
29: 4. But I will put *hooks* in thy jaws,
38: 4. put *hooks* into thy jaws,

2397 **חַחִי** [*g̣hah-g̣hee'*], m.

Eze.29: 4. (כתיב) But I will put *hooks* in thy jaws,

2398 **חָטָא** *g̣hāh-tāh'*.

* KAL.—*Preterite.* *

Gen20: 9. what *have I offended* thee,
39: 9. wickedness, *and sin* against God?
40: 1. baker *had offended* their lord
43: 9. *then let me bear the blame* for ever:
44:32. *then I shall bear the blame*
Ex. 5:16. *but the fault* (is) *in* thine own people.
9:27. *I have sinned* this time:
10:16. *I have sinned* against the Lord
32:30. Ye *have sinned* a great sin:
31. this people *have sinned* a great sin,
33. Whosoever *hath sinned* against me,
Lev. 4: 3. his sin, which *he hath sinned,*
14. *they have sinned* against it,
23. his sin, wherein *he hath sinned.*
28, 28. his sin, which *he hath sinned,*
35. sin that *he hath committed,*
5: 5. shall confess that *he hath sinned*
6. for his sin which *he hath sinned,*
7. trespass, which *he hath committed,*
10. for his sin which *he hath sinned,*
11. then he that *sinned* shall bring
13. touching his sin that *he hath sinned*
15. *and sin* through ignorance,
16. for *the harm that he hath done*
19:22. for his sin which *he hath done:* and the sin which *he hath done*
Nu. 6:11. that *he sinned* by the dead,
12:11. wherein *we have sinned.*
14:40. for *we have sinned.*
21: 7. *We have sinned,* for we have spoken
22:34. *I have sinned;* for I knew not
32:23. *ye have sinned* against the Lord:
Deu 1:41. *We have sinned* against the Lord,
9:16. *ye had sinned* against the Lord
18. all your sins which *ye sinned,*
20:18. *so should ye sin* against the Lord
Jos. 7:11. Israel *hath sinned,*
20. Indeed I *have sinned* against the Lord
Jud.10:10. *We have sinned* against thee,
15. *We have sinned:* do thou
11:27. Wherefore I *have* not *sinned*
1Sa. 7: 6. *We have sinned* against the Lord.
12:10. *We have sinned,* because we
15:24. Saul said unto Samuel, *I have sinned:*
30. Then he said, *I have sinned:*
19: 4. *he hath* not *sinned* against thee,
24:11(12). *I have* not *sinned* against thee;
26:21. Then said Saul, *I have sinned:*
2Sa.12:13. *I have sinned* against the Lord.
19:20(21). doth know that I *have sinned:*
24:10. *I have sinned* greatly
17. Lo, I *have sinned,* and I
1K. 8:47. *We have sinned,* and have done
50. forgive thy people that *have sinned*
14:16. the sins of Jeroboam, who *did sin,*
22. to jealousy with their sins which *they had committed,*
15:30. sins of Jeroboam which *he sinned,*
16:13. and the sins of Elah his son, by which *they sinned,*
19. his sins which *he sinned*
18: 9. What *have I sinned,* that thou wouldest
2K. 17: 7. Israel *had sinned* against the Lord
18:14. *I have offended;* return from me:
21:17. his sin that *he sinned,*
1Ch 21: 8. *I have sinned* greatly,
17. even I it is that *have sinned*
2Ch 6:37. *We have sinned,* we have done amiss,
39. forgive thy people which *have sinned*
Neh. 1: 6. which *we have sinned* against thee: both I and my father's house *have sinned.*
6:13. I should be afraid, and do so, *and sin,*
9:29. *but sinned* against thy judgments,
13:26. *Did* not Solomon king of Israel *sin*
Job 1: 5. It may be that my sons *have sinned,*
22. In all this Job *sinned* not,
2:10. In all this *did* not Job *sin*
7:20. *I have sinned;* what shall I do
8: 4. If thy children *have sinned*
10:14. If *I sin,* then thou markest me,
24:19. the grave (those which) *have sinned.*
33:27. and (if any) say, *I have sinned,*
35: 6. If *thou sinnest,* what doest thou
Ps. 41: 4(5). for *I have sinned* against thee.
51: 4(6). Against thee, thee only, *have I sinned,*
78:32. For all this *they sinned* still,
106: 6. *We have sinned* with our fathers,
Isa. 42:24. he against whom *we have sinned?*
43:27. Thy first father *hath sinned,*
Jer. 2:35. because thou sayest, *I have* not *sinned.*
3:25. *we have sinned* against the Lord
8:14. because *we have sinned*
14: 7. *we have sinned* against thee.
20. for *we have sinned* against thee.
16:10. our sin that *we have committed*
33: 8. their iniquity, whereby *they have sinned*
— their iniquities, whereby *they have sinned,*
37:18. *have I offended* against thee,
40: 3 & 44:23. *ye have sinned* against the Lord,
50: 7. because *they have sinned*
14. for *she hath sinned* against
Lam 1: 8. Jerusalem *hath* grievously *sinned;*
5: 7. Our fathers *have sinned,*
16. that *we have sinned!*
Eze. 3:21. and he *doth* not *sin,*
16:51. Neither *hath* Samaria *committed*
18:24. in his sin that *he hath sinned,*
33:16. None of his sins that *he hath committed*
37:23. wherein *they have sinned,*
Dan 9: 5. *We have sinned,* and have committed
8. because *we have sinned* against thee.
11. because *we have sinned* against him.
15. *we have sinned,* we have done wickedly
Hos. 4: 7. so *they sinned* against me:
10: 9. O Israel, *thou hast sinned*
Mic. 7: 9. because *I have sinned* against him,
Zep. 1:17. *they have sinned* against the Lord:

KAL.—*Infinitive.*

Gen20: 6. I also withheld thee *from sinning*
Ex. 9:34. he *sinned* yet more, (lit. added *to sin*)
Lev. 6: 3(5:22). that a man doeth, *sinning* therein:
Nu. 15:28. *when he sinneth* by ignorance

1Sa.12:23. God forbid *that I should sin* (lit. *from sinning*)
Job 31:30. Neither have I suffered my mouth *to sin*
Ps. 39: 1(2). *that I sin not* with my tongue:
78:17. they *sinned* yet more (lit. added *to sin*)
Eze. 3:21. that the righteous *sin* not,
33:12. in the day that *he sinneth.*
Hos 8:11. hath made many altars *to sin*, altars shall be unto him *to sin.*
13: 2. now they *sin* more and more, (marg. add *to sin*)

KAL.—*Future.*

Gen42:22. *Do* not *sin* against the child;
Ex. 20:20. be before your faces, that *ye sin* not
Lev. 4: 2. If a soul *shall sin* through ignorance
3. If the priest that is anointed *do sin*
22. When a ruler *hath sinned*,
27. if any one of the common people *sin*
5: 1. a soul *sin*, and hear the voice of swearing,
17. if a soul *sin*, and commit any
6: 2(5:21). If a soul *sin*, and commit a trespass
4(-:23). it shall be, because *he hath sinned*,
Nu. 15:27. if any soul *sin* through ignorance,
16:22. *shall* one man *sin*,
Deu19:15. in any sin that *he sinneth:*
1Sa. 2:25. If one man *sin* against another,
— but if a man *sin* against the Lord,
14:34. slay (them) here, and eat; and *sin* not
19: 4. *Let* not the king *sin*
5. wherefore then *wilt thou sin*
1K. 8:31. If any man *trespass* against
33 because *they have sinned*
35. because *they have sinned* against thee;
46. If *they sin* against thee, for (there is) no man that *sinneth* not,
2Ch 6:22. If a man *sin* against his neighbour,
24, 26. because *they have sinned*
36. If *they sin* against thee, for (there is) no man which *sinneth* not,
Job 5:24. visit thy habitation, and *shalt* not *sin.* (marg. or, *err*)
Ps. 4: 4(5). Stand in awe, and *sin* not:
119:11. that *I might* not *sin* against thee.
Ecc. 7:20. that doeth good, and *sinneth* not.
Isa. 64: 5(4). *for we have sinned:*
Eze.14:13. when the land *sinneth*
28:16. *and thou hast sinned:*

KAL.—*Participle.* Poel.

1Sa.14:33. the people *sin* against the Lord,
Pro. 8:36. he that *sinneth against me* wrongeth
11:31. much more the wicked *and the sinner.*
13:22. the wealth of *the sinner* (is) laid up
14:21. He that despiseth his neighbour *sinneth:*
19: 2. he that hasteth with (his) feet *sinneth.*
20: 2. provoketh him to anger *sinneth*
Ecc. 2:26. *but to the sinner* he giveth travail,
7:26. *but the sinner* shall be taken by her.
8:12. Though *a sinner* do evil an hundred times,
9: 2. as (is) the good, *so* (is) *the sinner;*
18. *but* one *sinner* destroyeth much good.
Isa. 1: 4. Ah *sinful* nation,
65:20. *but the sinner* (being) an hundred
Eze.18: 4, 20. the soul *that sinneth*, it shall die.
Hab 2:10. and *hast sinned* (against) thy soul.

* PIEL.—*Preterite.* *

Ex. 29:36. *and thou shalt cleanse* the altar,
Lev.14:52. *And he shall cleanse* the house
Nu. 19:19. *and* on the seventh day *he shall purify himself*,
Eze.43:20. *thus shalt thou cleanse* and purge
22. *and they shall cleanse* the altar, as *they did cleanse* (it) with
45:18. *and cleanse* the sanctuary:

PIEL.—*Infinitive.*

Lev.14:49. he shall take *to cleanse* the house
Eze.43:23. When thou hast made an end *of cleansing*

PIEL.—*Future.*

Gen31:39. I *bare the loss of it;*
Lev. 8:15. with his finger, *and purified* the altar,
9:15. slew it, *and offered it for sin*,
2Ch 29:24. *and they made reconciliation*
Ps. 51: 7(9). *Purge me* with hyssop,

PIEL.—*Participle.*

Lev. 6:26(19). The priest *that offereth it for sin*

* HIPHIL.—*Preterite.* *

1K. 14:16. who *made* Israel *to sin.*
15:26, 34. *he made* Israel *to sin.*
30. *he made* Israel *sin*,
16:13. *they made* Israel *to sin*,
26. *he made* Israel *to sin*,
22:52(53). who *made* Israel *to sin:*
2K. 3: 3. which *made* Israel *to sin;*
10:29. who *made* Israel *to sin*,
31 & 13:2. which *made* Israel *to sin.*
13: 6, 11. who *made* Israel *sin*,
14:24 & 15:9, 18, 24, 28. who *made* Israel *to sin.*
17:21. and *made them sin* a great sin.
21:16. wherewith *he made* Judah *to sin*,
23:15. who *made* Israel *to sin*,
Neh 13:26. him *did* outlandish women *cause to sin.*

HIPHIL.—*Infinitive.*

1K. 16:19. *to make* Israel *to sin.*
Ecc. 5: 6(5). Suffer not thy mouth *to cause* thy flesh *to sin;*
Jer. 32:35. to *cause* Judah *to sin.*

HIPHIL.—*Future.*

Ex. 23:33. lest *they make* thee *sin* against me:
Deu24: 4. *thou shalt* not *cause* the land *to sin*,
Jud.20:16. sling stones at an hair (breadth), and not *miss.*
1K. 16: 2. *and hast made* my people Israel *to sin*,
21:22. *and made* Israel *to sin.*
2K. 21:11. and *hath made* Judah also *to sin*

HIPHIL.—*Participle.*

Isa. 29:21. That *make* a man *an offender*

* HITHPAEL.—*Future.* *

Nu. 8:21. *And* the Levites *were purified*,
19:12. *He shall purify himself* with it
— but if *he purify* not *himself*
13. *purifieth* not *himself*,
20. be unclean, *and shall not purify himself*,
31:19. *purify* (both) yourselves and your captives
20. *purify* all (your) raiment,
23. nevertheless *it shall be purified*
Job 41:25(17). *they purify themselves.*

חֵטְא *ghēht*, m. 2399

Gen41: 9. I do remember *my faults* this day:
Lev.19:17. and not suffer *sin* upon him.
20:20. they shall bear *their sin;*
22: 9. lest they bear *sin* for it,
24:15. Whosoever curseth his God shall bear *his sin.*
Nu. 9:13. that man shall bear *his sin.*
18:22. lest they bear *sin*, and die.
32. ye shall bear no *sin* by reason
27: 3. but died *in his own sin*,
Deu15: 9. it be *sin* unto thee.
19:15. in any *sin* that he sinneth:
21:22. if a man have committed *a sin*
22:26. in the damsel no *sin* (worthy) *of* death:
23:21(22). it would be *sin* in thee.
22(23). it shall be no *sin* in thee.
24:15. it be *sin* unto thee.
16. shall be put to death *for his own sin.*
2K. 10:29. Howbeit (from) *the sins of* Jeroboam
14: 6. man shall be put to death *for his own sin.*
2Ch 25: 4. every man shall die *for his own sin.*
Ps. 51: 5(7). *and in sin* did my mother conceive me.
9(11). Hide thy face *from my sins*,
103:10. dealt with us *after our sins;*
Ecc.10: 4. for yielding pacifieth great *offences.*
Isa. 1:18. though *your sins* be as scarlet,
31: 7. hands have made unto you (for) *a sin.*
38:17. hast cast all *my sins* behind thy back.
53:12. and he bare *the sin of* many, and made
Lam 1: 8. Jerusalem hath *grievously* sinned; (lit hath sinned *a sin*)
3:39. a man for *the punishment of his sins?*
Eze.23:49. *and* ye shall bear *the sins of* your idols:
Dan. 9:16. *because for our sins*, and for
Hos12: 8(9). find none iniquity in me that (were) *sin.*

2400 **חַטָּא [ghat-tāh'], m.**

Gen 13:13. *and sinners* before the Lord
Nu. 16:38(17:3). The censers of these *sinners*
32:14. an increase of *sinful* men,
1Sa. 15:18. destroy *the sinners* the Amalekites,
1K. 1:21. I and my son Solomon shall be counted *offenders.* (marg. *sinners*)
Ps. 1: 1. nor standeth in the way of *sinners,*
5. *nor sinners* in the congregation
25: 8. therefore will he teach *sinners* in the way.
26: 9. Gather not my soul with *sinners,*
51:13(15). *and sinners* shall be converted
104:35. Let *the sinners* be consumed out of
Pro. 1:10. if *sinners* entice thee, consent thou not.
13:21. Evil pursueth *sinners:*
23:17. Let not thine heart envy *sinners:*
Isa. 1:28. transgressors *and of the sinners*
13: 9. *and* he shall destroy *the sinners thereof*
33:14. *The sinners* in Zion are afraid;
Am. 9:10. All *the sinners of* my people

2403 **חַטָּאָה ghat-tāh-āh', f.**

Ex. 34: 7. iniquity and transgression *and sin,*
Isa. 5:18. *sin* as it were with a cart rope:
Am. 9: 8. upon the *sinful* kingdom,

2402 **חַטָּאָה ghat-tāh-āh', Ch. f.**

Ezr. 6:17. and *for a sin offering* for all Israel,

2401 **חֲטָאָה ghătāh-āh', f.**

Gen20: 9. on my kingdom *a great sin?*
Ex. 32:21. hast brought so great *a sin* upon them?
30. Ye have sinned *a great sin:*
31. this people have sinned *a great sin,*
2K. 17:21. made them sin *a great sin.*
Ps. 32: 1. forgiven, (whose) *sin* (is) covered.
40: 6(7). *and sin offering* hast thou not required.
109: 7. let his prayer become *sin.*

2403 **חַטָּאת ghat-tāhth', f.**

Gen 4: 7. *sin* lieth at the door.
18:20. *and* because *their sin* is very grievous;
31:36. What (is) my trespass? what (is) *my sin,*
50:17. trespass of thy brethren, *and their sin;*
Ex. 10:17. forgive, I pray thee, *my sin* only
29:14. without the camp: it (is) *a sin offering.*
36. a bullock (for) *a sin offering*
30:10. with the blood of *the sin offering of*
32:30. I shall make an atonement for *your sin.*
32. if thou wilt forgive *their sin—;*
34. I will visit *their sin* upon them.
34: 9. pardon our iniquity *and our sin,*
Lev. 4: 3. for *his sin,* which he hath sinned,
— unto the Lord *for a sin offering.*
8. fat of the bullock *for the sin offering;*
14. When *the sin,* which they have sinned
— offer a young bullock *for the sin,*
20. the bullock for *a sin offering,*
21. it (is) *a sin offering for* the congregation.
23. if *his sin,* wherein he hath sinned,
24. it (is) *a sin offering.*
25. take of the blood of *the sin offering*
26. for him *as concerning his sin,*
28. Or if *his sin,* which he hath sinned,
— a female without blemish, for *his sin*
29, 33. his hand upon the head of *the sin offering,*
— slay *the sin offering* in the place
32. bring a lamb *for a sin offering,*
33. slay it *for a sin offering*
34. the blood of *the sin offering*
35. make an atonement for *his sin*
5: 6. for *his sin* which he hath sinned,
— a kid of the goats, *for a sin offering;*
— an atonement for him *concerning his sin.*
7. one *for a sin offering,*
8. *for the sin offering* first,
9. the blood of *the sin offering*

Lev. 5: 9. bottom of the altar: it (is) *a sin offering.*
10. *for his sin* which he hath sinned,
11. an ephah of fine flour *for a sin offering:*
—, 12. it (is) *a sin offering.*
13. touching *his sin* that he hath sinned
6:17(10). *as* (is) *the sin offering,*
25(18). This (is) the law of *the sin offering:*
—(—). shall *the sin offering* be killed
30(23). no *sin offering,* whereof (any) of the
7: 7. *As the sin offering*
37. *and of the sin offering,*
8: 2, 14, 14. bullock for *the sin offering,*
9: 2. a young calf *for a sin offering,*
3. a kid of the goats *for a sin offering;*
7. offer *thy sin offering,*
8. slew the calf of *the sin offering,*
10. above the liver of *the sin offering,*
15. the goat, which (was) *the sin offering*
22. from offering of *the sin offering,*
10:16. sought the goat of *the sin offering,*
17. have ye not eaten *the sin offering*
19. have they offered *their sin offering*
— I had eaten *the sin offering* to day,
12: 6. a turtledove, *for a sin offering,*
8. the other *for a sin offering:*
14:13. where he shall kill *the sin offering*
— *as the sin offering* (is) the priest's,
19. the priest shall offer *the sin offering,*
22. the one shall be *a sin offering,*
31 & 15:15, 30. the one (for) *a sin offering,*
16: 3. a young bullock *for a sin offering,*
5. two kids of the goats *for a sin offering,*
6. offer his bullock of *the sin offering,*
9. offer him (for) *a sin offering.*
11, 11. the bullock of *the sin offering,*
15. the goat of *the sin offering,*
16, 21. transgressions in all *their sins:*
25. the fat of *the sin offering*
27. the bullock (for) *the sin offering,* and the goat (for) *the sin offering,*
30. may be clean from all *your sins*
34. for all *their sins* once a year.
19:22. for *his sin* which he hath done: and *the sin* which he hath
23:19. one kid of the goats *for a sin offering,*
26:18. seven times more for *your sins.*
21. *according to your sins.*
24, 28. seven times for *your sins.*
Nu. 5: 6. shall commit any *sin* that men commit,
7. Then they shall confess *their sin*
6:11. offer the one *for a sin offering,*
14. without blemish *for a sin offering,*
16. shall offer *his sin offering,*
7:16, 22, 28, 34, 40, 46, 52, 58, 64, 70, 76, 82. One kid of the goats *for a sin offering:*
87. kids of the goats *for sin offering*
8: 7. Sprinkle water of *purifying*
8. bullock shalt thou take *for a sin offering.*
12. offer the one (for) *a sin offering,*
12:11. lay not *the sin* upon us,
15:24. one kid of the goats *for a sin offering.*
25. *and their sin offering* before the Lord,
27. a she goat of the first year *for a sin offering.*
16:26. lest ye be consumed in all *their sins.*
18: 9. every *sin offering of their's,*
19: 9. it (is) *a purification for sin.*
17. burnt heifer of *purification for sin,*
28:15. one kid of the goats *for a sin offering*
22. one goat (for) *a sin offering,*
29: 5, 11. one kid of the goats (for) *a sin offering,*
11. beside *the sin offering of*
16, 19, 25. one kid of the goats (for) *a sin offering;*
22, 28, 31, 34, 38. one goat (for) *a sin offering:*
32:23. be sure *your sin* will find you out.
Deu 9:18. because of all *your sins*
21. I took *your sin,* the calf
27. nor to their wickedness, nor to *their sin:*
19:15. any iniquity, or for any *sin,*
Jos. 24:19. transgressions *nor your sins.*
1Sa. 2:17. *the sin of* the young men was very great
12:19. we have added unto all *our sins*
14:38. see wherein this *sin* hath been
15:23. rebellion (is as) *the sin of* witchcraft,
25. I pray thee, pardon *my sin,*
20: 1. what (is) *my sin* before thy father,
2Sa. 12:13. The Lord also hath put away *thy sin;*

1K. 8:34. forgive *the sin of* thy people Israel,
35. *and* turn *from their sin*,
36. forgive *the sin of* thy servants,
12:30. And this thing became *a sin:* for the people went
13:34. became *sin* unto the house of Jeroboam,
14:16. because of *the sins of* Jeroboam,
22. provoked him to jealousy *with their sins*
15: 3. he walked in all *the sins of* his father,
26, 34. *and in his sin* wherewith he made
30. Because of *the sins of* Jeroboam
16: 2. provoke me to anger *with their sins;*
13. *the sins of* Baasha, *and the sins of* Elah
19. For *his sins* which he sinned
— *and in his sin* which he did,
26. *and in his sin* wherewith he made
31. walk *in the sins of* Jeroboam
2K. 3: 3. he cleaved *unto the sins of* Jeroboam
10:31. he departed not from *the sins of*
12:16(17). *sin* money was not brought into the
13: 2. followed *the sins of* Jeroboam
6. *from the sins of* the house of Jeroboam,
11 & 14:24. from all *the sins of* Jeroboam
15: 9, 24. *from the sins of* Jeroboam the son of
18. from *the sins of* Jeroboam the son of
28. *the sins of* Jeroboam the son of Nebat,
17:22. walked in all *the sins of*
21:16. *beside his sin* wherewith
17. *and his sin* that he sinned,
24: 3. *for the sins of* Manasseh,
2Ch 6:25. forgive *the sin of* thy people
26. and turn *from their sin*,
27. forgive *the sin of* thy servants,
7:14. will forgive *their sin*,
28:13. ye intend to add (more) to *our sins*
29:21. *for a sin offering* for the kingdom,
23. *the sin offering* before the king
24. burnt offering *and the sin offering*
33:19. and all *his sins*, and his trespass,
Ezr. 8:35. twelve he goats (for) *a sin offering:*
Neh 1: 6. confess *the sins of* the children of Israel,
4: 5(3:37). *and* let not *their sin* be blotted
9: 2. confessed *their sins*,
37. hast set over us *because of our sins:*
10:33(34). *and for the sin offerings*
Job 10: 6. *and* searchest *after my sin?*
13:23. many (are) mine iniquities *and sins:*
— know my transgression *and my sin.*
14:16. dost thou not watch over *my sin?*
34:37. he addeth rebellion unto *his sin*,
35: 3. I have, (if I be cleansed) *from my sin?*
Ps. 25: 7. Remember not *the sins of* my youth,
18. forgive all *my sins.*
32: 5. I acknowledged *my sin* unto thee,
— thou forgavest the iniquity of *my sin.*
38: 3(4). rest in my bones because of *my sin.*
18(19). I will be sorry *for my sin.*
51: 2(4). *and* cleanse me *from my sin.*
3(5). *and my sin* (is) ever before me.
59: 3(4). not (for) my transgression, nor (for) *my sin*,
12(13). *the sin of* their mouth
79: 9. purge away *our sins*,
85: 2(3). thou hast covered all *their sin.*
109:14. *and* let not *the sin of* his mother
Pro. 5:22. shall be holden with the cords of *his sins.* (marg. *sin*)
10:16. the fruit of the wicked *to sin.*
13: 6. wickedness overthroweth *the sinner.* (marg. *sin*)
14:34. but *sin* (is) a reproach to any people.
20: 9. I am pure *from my sin?*
21: 4. the plowing of the wicked, (is) *sin.*
24: 9. The thought of foolishness (is) *sin:*
Isa. 3: 9. *and* they declare *their sin*
6: 7. *and thy sin* purged.
27: 9. all the fruit to take away *his sin*·
30: 1. that they may add *sin* to *sin:*
40: 2. of the Lord's hand double for all *her sins.*
43:24. thou hast made me to serve *with thy sins,*
25. *and* will not remember *thy sins.*
44:22. as a cloud, *thy sins:*
58: 1. the house of Jacob *their sins.*
59: 2. *and your sins* have hid (his) face
12. *and our sins* testify against us:
Jer. 5:25. *and your sins* have withholden good
14:10. and visit *their sins.*
Jer. 15:13. and (that) for all *thy sins*,
16:10. or what (is) *our sin* that we have committed
18. their iniquity *and their sin* double;
17: 1. *The sin of* Judah (is) written
3. thy high places *for sin*,
18:23. *neither* blot out *their sin*
30:14, 15. *thy sins* were increased.
31:34. *and* I will remember *their sin* no more.
36: 3. forgive their iniquity *and their sin.*
50:20. and *the sins of* Judah,
Lam. 4: 6. greater *than the punishment of the sin of* Sodom, (marg. or, *iniquity*)
13. *For the sins of* her prophets,
22. he will discover *thy sins.*
Eze 3:20. he shall die *in his sin*,
16:51. hath Samaria committed half of *thy sins:*
52. *for thy sins* that thou hast committed
18:14. that seeth all his father's *sins*
21. the wicked will turn from all *his sins*
24. *and in his sin* that he hath sinned,
21:24(29). in all your doings *your sins* do appear;
33:10. If our transgressions *and our sins*
14. if he turn *from his sin*,
16. None of *his sins* that he hath committed
40:39. burnt offering *and the sin offering*
42:13. meat offering, *and the sin offering*,
43:19. young bullock *for a sin offering.*
21. the bullock also of *the sin offering*,
22. without blemish *for a sin offering;*
25. a goat (for) *a sin offering:*
44:27. he shall offer *his sin offering*,
29. meat offering, *and the sin offering*,
45:17. he shall prepare *the sin offering*,
19. take of the blood of *the sin offering*,
22. a bullock (for) *a sin offering.*
23. *and* a kid of the goats daily (for) *a sin offering.*
25. *according to the sin offering*,
46:20. trespass offering and *the sin offering*,
Dan 9:20. praying, and confessing *my sin and the sin of* my people Israel,
24. to make an end of *sins*,
Hos. 4: 8. They eat up *the sin of* my people,
8:13. their iniquity, and visit *their sins:*
9: 9. he will visit *their sins.*
10: 8. Aven, *the sin of* Israel,
13:12. Ephraim (is) bound up; *his sin* (is) hid.
Am. 5:12. transgressions and *your* mighty *sins:*
Mic. 1: 5. *and for the sins of* the house of Israel.
13. beginning of *the sin* to the daughter of Zion:
3: 8. to Israel *his sin.*
6: 7. the fruit of my body (for) *the sin of* my soul?
13. desolate because of *thy sins.*
7:19. cast all *their sins* into the depths
Zec.13: 1. *for sin* and for uncleanness.
14:19. shall be *the punishment of* Egypt, *and the punishment of* all nations (marg. or, *sin*)

חָטַב [*ghāh-tav'*]. 2404

*** KAL.—*Infinitive.* ***

Deu 19: 5. with his neighbour *to hew* wood,

KAL.—*Future.*

Eze.39:10. no wood out of the field, neither *cut down*

KAL.—*Participle.* Poel.

Deu 29:11(10). *from the hewer of* thy wood
Jos. 9:21. let them be *hewers of* wood
23. bondmen, *and hewers of* wood
27. made them that day *hewers of*
2Ch. 2:10(9). *the hewers* that cut timber,
Jer. 46:22. with axes, *as hewers of* wood.

*** PUAL.—*Participle.* ***

Ps. 144:12. *polished* (after) the similitude of a palace: (marg. cut)

חֲטֻבוֹת *ghătoo-vōhth'*, f. pl. 2405

Pro. 7:16. with *carved* (works),

2406 **חִטָּה** *ghit-tāh'*, f.

Gen30:14. went in the days of *wheat* harvest,
Ex. 9:32. *But the wheat* and the rie
29: 2. *wheaten* flour shalt thou make
34:22. the firstfruits of *wheat* harvest,
Deu 8: 8. A land of *wheat*, and barley,
32:14. with the fat of kidneys of *wheat;*
Jud. 6:11. his son Gideon threshed *wheat*
15: 1. in the time of *wheat* harvest,
Ru. 2:23. barley harvest and of *wheat* harvest;
1Sa. 6:13. reaping their *wheat* harvest
12:17. (Is it) not *wheat* harvest to day?
2Sa. 4: 6. they would have fetched *wheat;*
17:28. basons, and earthen vessels, *and wheat,*
1K. 5:11(25). twenty thousand measures of *wheat*
1Ch 21:20. Now Ornan was threshing *wheat.*
23. *and the wheat* for the meat offering;
2Ch 2:10(9). twenty thousand measures of beaten *wheat,*
15(14). *the wheat*, and the barley, the oil,
27: 5. ten thousand measures of *wheat,*
Job 31:40. Let thistles grow instead of *wheat,*
Ps. 81:16(17). fed them also with the finest of *the wheat:*
147:14. filleth thee with the finest of *the wheat.*
Cant 7: 2(3). an heap of *wheat* set about with lilies.
Isa. 28:25. cast in the principal *wheat*
Jer. 12:13. They have sown *wheat,*
41: 8. of *wheat*, and of barley, and of oil,
Eze. 4: 9. Take thou also unto thee *wheat,*
27:17. traded in thy market *wheat of* Minnith,
45:13. an ephah of an homer of *wheat,*
Joel. 1:11. for *the wheat* and for the barley;

2408 **חֲטָי** [*ghătāh'y*], Ch. m.

Dan. 4:27(24). *and* break off *thy sins* by righteousness,

2409 **חַטָּיָא** *ghat-tāh-yāh'*, Ch. f.

Ezr. 6:17. (כתיב) and for *a sin offering* for all Israel,

2413 **חָטַם** [*ghāh-tam'*].

* KAL.—*Future.* *

Isa. 48: 9. for my praise *will I refrain* for thee,

2414 **חָטַף** [*ghāh-taph'*].

* KAL.—*Preterite.* *

Jud.21:21. *and catch* you every man his wife

KAL.—*Infinitive.*

Ps. 10: 9. he lieth in wait *to catch* the poor:

KAL.—*Future.*

Ps. 10: 9. *he doth catch* the poor,

2415 **חֹטֶר** *ghōh'-ter*, m.

Pro.14: 3. In the mouth of the foolish (is) *a rod of* pride:
Isa. 11: 1. there shall come forth *a rod* out of

2416 **חַי** *ghah'y*, adj.

Gen. 1:20. the moving creature that hath *life*, (lit. *living* soul)
21. every *living* creature that moveth,
24. bring forth the *living* creature
— *and beast of* the earth after his kind:
25. God made *the beast of* the earth
28. and over every *living thing* that moveth
30. and to every *beast of* the earth,
— wherein (there is) life, (marg. a *living* soul)
2: 7. breathed into his nostrils the breath of *life;* and man became a *living* soul.
Gen. 2: 9. the tree of *life* also in the midst
19, 20. every *beast of* the field,
— Adam called every *living* creature,
3: 1. than any *beast of* the field
14. above every *beast of* the field;
— shalt thou eat all the days of *thy life.*
17. eat (of) it all the days of *thy life;*
20. she was the mother of all *living.*
22. take also of the tree of *life*, and
24. the way of the tree of *life.*
6:17. all flesh, wherein (is) the breath of *life,*
19. every *living thing of* all flesh,
7:11. the six hundredth year *of* Noah's *life,*
14. every *beast* after his kind,
15. two of all flesh, wherein (is) the breath of *life.*
21. of cattle, *and of beast*, and of every creeping thing
22. in whose nostrils (was) the breath of *life,*
8: 1. remembered Noah, and every *living* thing,
17. every *living* thing that (is) with thee,
19. Every *beast*, every creeping thing,
21. smite any more every thing *living,*
9: 2. shall be upon every *beast of* the earth,
3. Every moving thing that *liveth*
5. at the hand of every *beast* will I require it,
10. with every *living* creature that (is) with
— every *beast of* the earth with you;
— to every *beast of* the earth.
12. and every *living* creature that (is) with you,
15, 16. and every *living* creature of all flesh;
16:14. the well was called Beer-*lahai*-roi; (marg. The well *of him that liveth* (and) seeth me)
18:10, 14. according to the time of *life;*
23: 1. Sarah *was* an hundred and seven and twenty years *old:* (lit. *the life of* Sarah was)
— the years of *the life of* Sarah.
25: 6. while he yet *lived,*
7. the years of Abraham's *life* which he lived,
17. these (are) the years of *the life of* Ishmael,
26:19. found there a well of *springing* water. (marg. *living*)
27:46. I am weary *of my life* because of
— what good shall *my life* do me?
37:20. Some evil *beast* hath devoured him:
33. *an* evil *beast* hath devoured him;
42:15, 16. By *the life of* Pharaoh
43: 7. (Is) your father yet *alive?*
27. of whom ye spake? (Is) he yet *alive?*
28. he (is) yet *alive.*
45: 3. *doth* my father yet *live?*
26. told him, saying, Joseph, (is) yet *alive,*
28. Joseph my son (is) yet *alive:*
46:30. because thou (art) yet *alive.*
47: 8. How old (art) thou? (marg. How many (are) the days of the years of *thy life*)
9. have the days of the years of *my life* been,
— the years of *the life of* my fathers
28. the whole age of Jacob was an hundred forty and seven (marg. the days of the years of *his life*)
Ex. 1:14. they made *their lives* bitter
4:18. see whether they be yet *alive.*
6:16, 18, 20. the years of *the life of*
21:35. then they shall sell the *live* ox,
22: 4(3). be certainly found in his hand *alive,*
23:11. what they leave *the beasts of* the field
29. *the beast of* the field multiply
Lev. 5: 2. a carcase of an unclean *beast,*
11: 2. These (are) *the beasts* which ye shall eat
10. of any *living* thing which (is) in the waters,
27. among all manner of *beasts*
46. and of every *living* creature that moveth
47. between *the beast* that may be eaten and *the beast* that may not be eaten.
13:10. quick *raw* flesh in the rising; (marg. the quickening of *living* flesh)
14. But when *raw* flesh appeareth
15. the priest shall see the *raw* flesh,
— the *raw* flesh (is) unclean:
16. Or if the *raw* flesh turn again,
14: 4. cleansed two birds *alive*
5. in an earthen vessel over *running* water:

Lev.14: 6. As for the *living* bird, he shall take it,
— and the *living* bird in the blood of the bird (that was) killed over the *running* water:
7. shall let the *living* bird loose
50. in an earthen vessel over *running* water:
51. the scarlet, and the *living* bird, and dip
— of the slain bird, and in the *running*
52. with the *running* water, and with the *living*
53. he shall let go the *living* bird
15:13. bathe his flesh in *running* water,
16:10. presented *alive* before
20. he shall bring the *live* goat:
21. hands upon the head of the *live* goat,
17:13. which hunteth and catcheth any *beast*
18:18. beside the other *in her life* (time).
25: 7. for thy cattle, *and for the beast*
35. *that he may live* with thee.
36. *that* thy brother *may live*
26: 6. I will rid evil *beasts* out of the land,
22. I will also send wild *beasts*
Nu. 14:21. But (as) truly (as) I *live*,
28. (As truly as) I *live*,
16:30. they go down *quick* into the pit;
33. went down *alive* into the pit,
48(17:13). he stood between the dead and *the living;*
19:17. *running* water shall be put thereto (marg. *living*)
35: 3. goods, and for all *their beasts*.
Deu 4: 4. *alive* every one of you this day.
9. all the days of *thy life:*
10. all the days that they *shall live* upon the
5: 3. who (are) all of us here *alive*
26(23). heard the voice of the *living* God
6: 2. and thy son's son, all the days of *thy life;*
7:22. lest the *beasts of* the field increase
12: 1. all the days that ye *live* upon the earth.
16: 3. the land of Egypt all the days of *thy life*.
17:19. read therein all the days of *his life:*
28:66. And *thy life* shall hang in doubt
— have none assurance *of thy life:*
30: 6. that *thou mayest live*. (lit. on account of *thy life*)
15. I have set before thee this day *life*
19. I have set before you *life* and death,
— therefore choose *life*,
20. for he (is) *thy life*,
31:13. as long as ye *live* in the land whither ye
27. while I am yet *alive* with you
32:40. say, I *live* for ever.
47. because it (is) *your life:*
Jos. 1: 5. stand before thee all the days of *thy life:*
3:10. know that the *living* God (is) among
4:14. all the days of *his life*.
8:23. the king of Ai they took *alive*,
Jud. 8:19. (as) the Lord *liveth*, if ye had saved
16:30. than (they) which he slew *in his life*.
Ru. 2:20. hath not left off his kindness to *the living*
3:13. the Lord *liveth:* lie down until the
1Sa. 1:11. all the days of *his life*,
26. Oh my lord, (as) thy soul *liveth*,
2:15. have sodden flesh of thee, but *raw*.
7:15. all the days of *his life*.
14:39, 45. (as) the Lord *liveth*,
15: 8. he took Agag...*alive*,
17:26, 36. the armies of the *living* God?
46. *and to the wild beasts of* the earth;
55. Abner said, (As) thy soul *liveth*,
18:18. what (is) *my life*,
19: 6. Saul sware, (As) the Lord *liveth*,
20: 3. (as) the Lord *liveth, and* (as) thy soul *liveth*,
14. shalt not only while yet I *live*
21. no hurt; (as) the Lord *liveth*.
25: 6. thus shall ye say *to him that liveth*
26. my lord, (as) the Lord *liveth, and* (as) thy soul *liveth*,
29. shall be bound in the bundle of *life*
34. the Lord God of Israel *liveth*,
26:10, 16 & 28:10 & 29:6. (As) the Lord *liveth*,
2Sa. 1:23. lovely and pleasant *in their lives*,
2:27. Joab said, (As) God *liveth*,
4: 9. (As) the Lord *liveth*,
11:11. *thou livest, and* (as) thy soul *liveth*,
12: 5. said to Nathan, (As) the Lord *liveth*,
18. while the child was yet *alive*,
21. the child, (while it was) *alive;*

2Sa. 12:22. While the child was yet *alive*,
— *that* the child *may live?*
14:11. he said, (As) the Lord *liveth*,
19. (As) thy soul *liveth*,
15:21. (As) the Lord *liveth, and* (as) my lord the king *liveth*,
— the king shall be, whether in death or *life*,
18:14. while he (was) yet *alive* in the midst
18. Now Absalom *in his lifetime*
19: 6(7). that if Absalom *had lived*,
34(35). How long have *I to live*, (marg. how many days (are) the years of *my life*)
21:10. nor *the beasts of* the field by night.
22:47. The Lord *liveth;* and blessed (be) my
23:11. were gathered together into *a troop*, (marg. or, *for foraging*)
13. *and the troop of* the Philistines pitched
1K. 1:29. said, (As) the Lord *liveth*,
2:24. (as) the Lord *liveth*, which hath established
3:22. but *the living* (is) my son,
— and *the living* (is) my son.
23. This (is) my son *that liveth*,
— my son (is) *the living*.
25. Divide the *living* child in two,
26. Then spake the woman whose the *living* child (was)
— O my lord, give her the *living* child,
27. Give her the *living* child, and in no wise
4:21(5:1). Solomon all the days of *his life*.
8:40. fear thee all the days that they *live* in the land
11:34. prince all the days of *his life*
12: 6. Solomon his father while he yet *lived*,
15: 5, 6. all the days of *his life*,
17: 1. the Lord God of Israel *liveth*,
12. (As) the Lord thy God *liveth*,
23. Elijah said, See, thy son *liveth*.
18:10. the Lord thy God *liveth*,
15. the Lord of hosts *liveth*,
20:18. be come out for peace, take them *alive;*
— for war, take them *alive*.
32. he said, (Is) he yet *alive?* he (is) my
21:15. for Naboth is not *alive*, but dead.
22:14. Micaiah said, (As) the Lord *liveth*,
2K 2: 2, 4, 6. (As) the Lord *liveth, and* (as) thy soul *liveth*,
3:14. (As) the Lord of hosts *liveth*,
4:16, 17. according to the time of *life*,
30. (As) the Lord *liveth, and* (as) thy soul *liveth*,
5:16, 20. (As) the Lord *liveth*,
7:12. we shall catch them *alive*,
10:14. he said, Take them *alive*. And they took them *alive*,
14: 9. there passed by *a* wild *beast*
19: 4. hath sent to reproach the *living* God;
16. sent him to reproach the *living* God.
25:29. before him all the days of *his life*.
30. for every day, all the days of *his life*.
2Ch 6:31. so long as they *live* in the land
10: 6. Solomon his father while he yet *lived*,
18:13. (As) the Lord *liveth*,
25:12. ten thousand (left) *alive*
18. passed by *a* wild *beast* (marg. *beast of* the field)
Job 3:20. misery, *and life* unto the bitter (in) soul,
5:22. *neither* shalt thou be afraid *of the beasts of*
23. *and the beasts of* the field shall be
7: 7. O remember that *my life* (is) wind:
9:21. I would despise *my life*.
10: 1. My soul is weary *of my life;* (marg. *while I live*)
12. Thou hast granted me *life* and favour,
12:10. In whose hand (is) the soul of every *living*
19:25. For I know (that) my redeemer *liveth*,
24:22. no (man) is sure *of life*.
27: 2. God *liveth*, (who) hath taken away
28:13. neither is it found in the land of *the living*.
21. it is hid from the eyes of all *living*,
30:23. the house appointed for all *living*.
33:18. *and his life* from perishing
20. So that *his life* abhorreth bread,
22. *and his life* to the destroyers.
28. *and his life* shall see the light.
30. be enlightened with the light of *the living*.
36:14. *and their life* (is) among the unclean.
37: 8. Then *the beasts* go into dens,

Job 38:39. *or* fill *the appetite of* the young lions, (marg. *life*)
39:15. *or* that *the* wild *beast* may break
40:20. where all *the beasts of* the field play.
Ps. 7: 5(6). let him tread down *my life*
16:11. wilt shew me the path of *life:*
17:14. their portion *in* (this) *life,*
18:46(47). The Lord *liveth;* and blessed (be) my
21: 4(5). He asked *life* of thee,
23: 6. shall follow me all the days of *my life:*
26: 9. nor *my life* with bloody men:
27: 1. the Lord (is) the strength of *my life;*
4. all the days of *my life,*
13. the Lord in the land of *the living.*
30: 5(6). in his favour (is) *life:*
31:10(11). For *my life* is spent with grief,
34:12(13). What man (is he that) desireth *life,*
36: 9(10). with thee (is) the fountain of *life:*
38:19(20). But mine enemies (are) *lively,* (marg. (being) *living*)
42: 2(3). for God, for the *living* God:
8(9). my prayer unto the God of *my life.*
49:18(19). *while he lived* he blessed his soul:
50:10. every *beast of* the forest (is) mine,
52: 5(7). root thee out of the land of *the living.*
55:15(16). let them go down *quick* into hell:
56:13(14). before God in the light of *the living?*
58: 9(10). both *living,* and in (his) wrath.
63: 3(4). lovingkindness (is) better *than life,*
4(5). Thus will I bless thee *while I live:* (lit. *in my life*)
64: 1(2). preserve *my life* from fear of the
66: 9. Which holdeth our soul *in life,*
68:10(11). *Thy congregation* hath dwelt therein:
30(31). Rebuke *the company of* spearmen, (marg. *the beasts of* the reeds)
69:28(29). blotted out of the book of *the living,*
74:19. soul of thy turtledove unto *the multitude*
— forget not *the congregation of* thy poor
78:50. *but* gave *their life* over to the pestilence; (marg. or, *beasts* to the murrain)
79: 2. thy saints *unto the beasts of* the earth.
84: 2(3). crieth out for the *living* God.
88: 3(4). *and my life* draweth nigh unto
103: 4. Who redeemeth *thy life* from destruction;
104:11. They give drink to every *beast of*
20. all *the beasts of* the forest do creep
25. both small and great *beasts.*
33. I will sing unto the Lord *as long as I live:* (lit. *in my life*)
116: 9. before the Lord in the land of *the living.*
124: 3. Then they had swallowed us up *quick,*
128: 5. Jerusalem all the days of *thy life.*
133: 3. the blessing, (even) *life* for evermore.
142: 5(6). my portion in the land of *the living.*
143: 2. in thy sight shall no man *living* be
3. he hath smitten *my life* down
145:16. satisfiest the desire of every *living* thing.
146: 2. *While I live* will I praise the Lord: (lit. *in my life*)
148:10. *Beasts,* and all cattle;
Pro. 1:12. Let us swallow them up *alive*
2:19. take they hold of the paths of *life.*
3: 2. For length of days, and long *life,*
18. She (is) a tree of *life* to them
22. So shall they be *life* unto thy soul,
4:10. the years of thy *life* shall be many.
13. keep her; for she (is) *thy life.*
22. they (are) *life* unto those that find
23. for out of it (are) the issues of *life.*
5: 6. thou shouldest ponder the path of *life,*
6:23. reproofs of instruction (are) the way of *life:*
8:35. For whoso findeth me findeth *life,*
9:11. the years of thy *life* shall be increased.
10:11. a righteous (man is) a well of *life:*
16. the righteous (tendeth) *to life:*
17. He (is in) the way *of life* that keepeth
11:19. As righteousness (tendeth) *to life:*
30. fruit of the righteous (is) a tree of *life;*
12:28. In the way of righteousness (is) *life;*
13:12. but (when) the desire cometh, (it is) a tree of *life.*
14. The law of the wise (is) a fountain of *life,*
14:27. fear of the Lord (is) a fountain of *life,*
30. A sound heart (is) *the life of* the flesh:
15: 4. A wholesome tongue (is) a tree of *life:*

Pro. 15:24. The way of *life* (is) above to the wise,
31. The ear that heareth the reproof of *life*
16:15. light of the king's countenance (is) *life;*
22. Understanding (is) a wellspring of *life*
18:21. Death *and life* (are) in the power of the
19:23. The fear of the Lord (tendeth) *to life:*
21:21. righteousness and mercy findeth *life,*
22: 4. fear of the Lord (are) riches, and honour, *and life.*
27:27. *and* (for) the *maintenance* for thy maidens. (marg. *life*)
31:12. good and not evil all the days of *her life.*
Ecc. 2: 3. all the days of *their life.*
17. Therefore I hated *life;*
3:12. to do good *in his life.*
4: 2. dead more than *the living* which are yet alive.
15. I considered all *the living*
5:18(17). all the days of *his life,*
20(19). much remember the days of *his life;*
6: 8. knoweth to walk before *the living?*
12. what (is) good for man *in* (this) *life,* all the days of his vain *life*
7: 2. *and the living* will lay (it) to his heart.
8:15. him of his labour the days of *his life,*
9: 3. madness (is) in their heart *while they live,*
4. him that is joined to all *the living*
— a *living* dog is better
5. *the living* know that they shall die:
9. *Live* joyfully with the wife whom thou lovest (marg. See, or, enjoy *life*) all the days of *the life of* thy vanity,
— for that (is) thy portion *in* (this) *life,*
10:19. wine maketh merry: (marg. glad *the life*)
Cant. 4:15. a well of *living* waters,
Isa. 4: 3. written *among the living* (marg. or, *to life*)
8:19. for *the living* to the dead?
35: 9. nor (any) ravenous *beast* shall go
37: 4, 17. to reproach the *living* God,
38:11. the Lord, in the land of *the living:*
12. I have cut off like a weaver *my life:*
16. in all these (things is) *the life of* my
19. *The living, the living,* he shall praise thee,
20. all the days of *our life*
40:16. *nor the beasts thereof* sufficient
43:20. *The beast of* the field shall honour me,
46: 1. their idols were *upon the beasts,*
49:18. (As) I *live,* saith the Lord,
53: 8. he was cut off out of the land of *the living:*
56: 9. All ye *beasts of* the field,
— all ye *beasts* in the forest.
57:10. hast found *the life of* thine hand; (marg. or, *living*)
Jer. 2:13. forsaken me the fountain of *living* waters,
4: 2. thou shalt swear, The Lord *liveth,*
5: 2. though they say, The Lord *liveth;*
8: 3. death shall be chosen rather *than life*
10:10. God, he (is) the *living* God,
11:19. cut him off from the land of *the living*
12: 9. assemble all *the beasts of* the field, come
16. to swear by my name, The Lord *liveth;*
16:14. it shall no more be said, The Lord *liveth.*
15. The Lord *liveth,* that brought up the
17:13. the Lord, the fountain of *living* waters.
21: 8. I set before you the way of *life,*
22:24. (As) I *live,* saith the Lord,
23: 7. they shall no more say, The Lord *liveth,*
8. But, The Lord *liveth,* which brought up
36. perverted the words of the *living* God,
27: 6. and *the beasts of* the field have I given him
28:14. I have given him *the beasts of* the field
38:16. saying, (As) the Lord *liveth,*
44:26. The Lord God *liveth.*
46:18. I *live,* saith the king,
52:33. before him all the days of *his life,*
34. until the day of his death, all the days of *his life.*
Lam. 3:39. Wherefore doth a *living* man complain,
53. They have cut off *my life*
58. thou hast redeemed *my life.*
Eze. 1: 5. the likeness of four *living creatures.*
13. the likeness of *the living creatures,*
— up and down among *the living creatures;*
14. *And the living creatures* ran
15. as I beheld *the living creatures,* behold one wheel upon the earth by *the living creatures,*

Eze. 1:19. when *the living creatures* went,
— and when *the living creatures* were lifted
20, 21. the spirit of *the living creature* (was) in the wheels.
22. upon the heads of *the living creature* (was)
3:13. the wings of *the living creatures*
5:11. Wherefore, (as) I *live*, saith the Lord
17. famine *and* evil *beasts*,
7:13. although *they* were yet *alive*: (marg. *their life* (were) yet *among the living*)
— in the iniquity of *his life*.
10:15, 20. This (is) *the living creature* that I saw
17. the spirit of *the living creature* (was) in them. (marg. *life*)
14:15. cause noisome *beasts* to pass through
— pass through because of *the beasts*:
16, 18, 20. (as) I *live*, saith the Lord God,
21. the famine, *and the* noisome *beast*,
16:48 & 17:16. (As) I *live*, saith the Lord God,
17:19. thus saith the Lord God; (As) I *live*,
18: 3. (As) I *live*, saith the Lord God,
20: 3. (As) I *live*, saith the Lord God,
31, 33. (As) I *live*, saith the Lord God,
26:20. in the land of *the living*;
29: 5. for meat *to the beasts of* the field
31: 6. under his branches did all *the beasts of*
13. all *the beasts of* the field
32: 4. I will fill *the beasts of* the whole earth
23, 24. 25, 26, 27, 32. in the land of *the living*.
33:11. (As) I *live*, saith the Lord God,
15. walk in the statutes of *life*,
27. Thus saith the Lord God; (As) I *live*,
— give *to the beasts* to be devoured,
34: 5. became meat to all *the beasts of* the field,
8. (As) I *live*, saith the Lord God,
— became meat to every *beast of* the field,
25. will cause *the* evil *beasts* to cease
28. *neither* shall *the beast of* the land devour
35: 6, 11. (as) I *live*, saith the Lord God,
38:20. *and the beasts of* the field,
39: 4. *and* (to) *the beasts of* the field
17. to every *beast of* the field,
47: 9. every thing that *liveth*,
Dan 8: 4. so that no *beasts* might stand before
12: 2. some *to* everlasting *life*,
7. sware *by him that liveth* for ever
Hos. 1:10(2:1). (Ye are) the sons of *the living* God.
2:12(14). *the beasts of* the field shall eat
18(20). make a covenant for them with *the beasts of*
4: 3. *with the beasts of* the field,
15. nor swear, The Lord *liveth*.
13: 8. *the* wild *beast* shall tear them. (marg. *beast of* the field)
Am. 8:14. Thy god, O Dan, *liveth*; *and*, The manner of Beer-sheba *liveth*;
Jon. 2: 6(7). yet hast thou brought up *my life*
4: 3, 8. better for me to die *than to live*.
Zep. 2: 9. (as) I *live*, saith the Lord of hosts,
14. all *the beasts of* the nations:
15. a place *for beasts* to lie down in!
Zec.14: 8. *living* waters shall go out from Jerusalem;
Mal. 2: 5. My covenant was with him of *life*

2417 חַי *g̱hah'y*, Ch. adj.

Ezr. 6:10. and pray *for the life of* the king,
Dan 2:30. wisdom that I have more than any *living*,
4:17(14). to the intent that *the living*
34(31). *and* I praised and honoured him *that liveth* for ever,
6:20(21). O Daniel, servant of the *living* God,
26(27). for he (is) the *living* God,
7:12. yet their *lives* were prolonged (marg. *in life*)

2420 חִידָה *ghee-dāh'*, f.

Nu. 12: 8. and not *in dark speeches*;
Jud.14:12. put forth *a riddle* unto you:
13. Put forth *thy riddle*,
14. could not in three days expound *the riddle*.
15. that he may declare unto us *the riddle*,
16. thou hast put forth *a riddle*
17. she told *the riddle* to the children
Jud. 14:18. ye had not found out *my riddle*.
19. unto them which expounded *the riddle*.
1K. 10: 1. to prove him *with hard questions*.
2Ch 9: 1. to prove Solomon *with hard questions*
Ps. 49: 4(5). I will open *my dark saying*
78: 2. I will utter *dark sayings* of old:
Pro. 1: 6. the wise, *and their dark sayings*.
Eze.17: 2. Son of man, put forth *a riddle*,
Dan 8:23. understanding *dark sentences*,
Hab. 2: 6. *a* taunting *proverb* against him,

חָיָה *g̱hāh-yāh'*. 2421

* KAL.—*Preterite*. *

Gen12:13. *and* my soul *shall live* because of thee.
Nu. 4:19. thus do unto them, *that they may live*,
14:38. that went to search the land, *lived*
Deu30:16. *that thou mayest live* and multiply:
Neh 9:29. *he shall live* in them;
Est. 4:11. the golden sceptre, *that he may live*:
Ecc. 6: 6. though *he live* a thousand years
Jer. 21: 9. *he shall live*, [קרי lit. *and he shall live*] and his life shall be
38: 2. that goeth forth to the Chaldeans *shall live*; [קרי lit. *id*.]
17. *then* thy soul *shall live*,
— *and thou shalt live*, and thine house:
Eze.18:23. return from his ways, *and live*?
33:11. turn from his way *and live*:
37: 5. enter into you, *and ye shall live*:
6. breath in you, *and ye shall live*;
14. spirit in you, *and ye shall live*,
Zec.10: 9. *and they shall live* with their children,

KAL.—*Infinitive*.

Jos. 5: 8. till *they were whole*.
2K. 8:10. Thou mayest *certainly* recover: (lit. *in living* mayest live)
14. told me (that) thou shouldest *surely* recover. (lit. *in living* shalt live)
Eze. 3:21 & 18:9, 17, 19, 21, 28. he shall *surely* live, (lit. *in living* shall live)
33:12. shall the righteous be able *to live*
13, 15, 16. he shall *surely* live; (lit. *in living* shall live)

KAL.—*Imperative*.

Gen20: 7. *and thou shalt live*:
42:18. This do, *and live*; (for) I fear God:
2K. 18:32. *that ye may live*, and not die:
Pro. 4: 4 & 7:2. keep my commandments, *and live*.
9: 6. Forsake the foolish, *and live*;
Jer. 27:12. serve him and his people, *and live*.
17. serve the king of Babylon, *and live*:
Eze.16: 6. in thy blood, *Live*; yea, I said unto thee (when thou wast) in thy blood, *Live*.
18:32. wherefore turn (yourselves), *and live ye*.
Am. 5: 4. Seek ye me, *and ye shall live*:
6. Seek the Lord, *and ye shall live*;

KAL.—*Future*.

Gen 5: 3. *And* Adam *lived* an hundred and thirty years,
6. *And* Seth *lived* an hundred and five years,
7. *And* Seth *lived* after he begat Enos
9. *And* Enos *lived* ninety years,
10. *And* Enos *lived* after he begat
12. *And* Cainan *lived* seventy years,
13. *And* Cainan *lived* after he begat
15. *And* Mahalaleel *lived* sixty and five years,
16. *And* Mahalaleel *lived* after he begat
18. *And* Jared *lived* an hundred sixty and two years,
19. *And* Jared *lived* after he begat
21. *And* Enoch *lived* sixty and five years,
25. *And* Methuselah *lived* an hundred
26. *And* Methuselah *lived* after he
28. *And* Lamech *lived* an hundred
30. *And* Lamech *lived* after he begat Noah
9:28. *And* Noah *lived* after the flood
11:11. *And* Shem *lived* after he begat
13. *And* Arphaxad *lived* after he begat
15. *And* Salah *lived* after he begat
16. *And* Eber *lived* four and thirty
17. *And* Eber *lived* after he begat
18. *And* Peleg *lived* thirty years,

Gen 11:19 *And* Peleg *lived* after he begat
20. *And* Reu *lived* two and thirty
21. *And* Reu *lived* after he begat
22. *And* Serug *lived* thirty years,
23. *And* Serug *lived* after he begat
24. *And* Nahor *lived* nine and twenty
25. *And* Nahor *lived* after he begat
26. *And* Terah *lived* seventy years,
17:18. O that Ishmael *might live* before thee!
19:20. *and* my soul *shall live.*
27:40. by thy sword *shalt thou live,*
31:32. findest thy gods, *let him* not *live:*
42: 2 & 43:8. *that we may live,* and not die.
45:27. *and* when he saw...the spirit of Jacob their father *revived:*
47:19. *that we may live,* and not die,
28. *And* Jacob *lived* in the land of Egypt
50:22. *and* Joseph *lived* an hundred and ten years.
Ex. 19:13. beast or man, *it shall* not *live:*
Nu. 24:23. who *shall live* when God doeth this!
Deu 4: 1. *that ye may live,* and go in
33. as thou hast heard, *and live?*
5:26(23). the fire, as we (have), *and lived?*
33(30). that *ye may live,*
8: 1. that *ye may live,* and multiply,
3. man *doth* not *live* by bread only,
— mouth of the Lord *doth* man *live.*
16:20. that *thou mayest live,*
30:19. thy seed *may live:*
33: 6. *Let* Reuben *live,* and not die;
Jos. 6:17. only Rahab the harlot *shall live,*
9:21. princes said unto them, *Let them live;*
Jud. 15:19. his spirit came again, *and he revived:*
1Sa. 10:24. the people shouted, and said, *God save* the king. (marg. *Let* the king *live*)
2Sa. 1:10. I was sure that *he could* not *live*
16:16, 16. *God save* the king, (marg. *Let* the king *live*)
1K. 1:25. say, *God save* king Adonijah. (marg. *Let* king Adonijah *live*)
31. *Let* my lord king David *live* for ever.
34, 39. *God save* king Solomon. (lit. *let* the king *live*)
17:22. came into him again, *and he revived.*
20:32. *let* me *live.* And he said, (Is) he yet alive?
2K. 1: 2. whether *I shall recover* of this disease.
4: 7. *live* thou and thy children
7: 4. if they save us alive, *we shall live;*
8: 8, 9. *Shall I recover* of this disease?
10. *Thou mayest* certainly *recover:*
14. *thou shouldest* surely *recover.*
10:19. shall be wanting, *he shall* not *live.*
11:12. said, *God save* the king. (marg. *Let* the king *live*)
13:21. *and* when the man...touched the bones of Elisha, *he revived,*
14:17. *And* Amaziah the son of Joash king of Judah *lived*
20: 1. for thou shalt die, and not *live.*
7. laid (it) on the boil, *and he recovered.*
2Ch 23:11. said, *God save* the king. (marg. *Let* the king *live*)
25:25. *And* Amaziah the son of Joash king of Judah *lived*
Neh 2: 3. *Let* the king *live* for ever:
5: 2. that we may eat, *and live.*
Job 7:16. *I would* not *live* alway:
14:14. If a man die, *shall he live* (again)?
21: 7. Wherefore *do* the wicked *live,*
42:16. After this *lived* Job an hundred and forty years,
Ps. 22:26(27). your heart *shall live* for ever.
49: 9(10). *That he should* still *live* for ever,
69:32(33). *and* your heart *shall live* that seek God.
72:15. *And he shall live,* and to him
89:48(49). What man (is he that) *liveth,*
118:17. I shall not die, but *live,*
119:17. *I may live,* and keep thy word.
77. come unto me, *that I may live:*
116. *that I may live:* and let me
144. give me understanding, *and I shall live.*
175. *Let* my soul *live,*
Pro. 15:27. he that hateth gifts *shall live.*
Ecc. 6: 3. *live* many years,
11: 8. But if a man *live* many years,

Isa. 26:14. dead, *they shall* not *live;*
19. Thy dead (men) *shall live*
38: 1. for thou shalt die, and not *live.*
9. *and was recovered* of his sickness:
16. O Lord, by these (things men) *live,*
21. a plaister upon the boil, *and he shall recover.*
55: 3. hear, *and* your soul *shall live;*
Jer. 21: 9. (כתיב) *he shall live,* and his life
35: 7. that *ye may live* many days
38: 2. (כתיב) that goeth forth to the Chaldeans *shall live;*
20. *and* thy soul *shall live.*
Lam 4:20. Under his shadow *we shall live*
Eze. 3:21. *he shall* surely *live,*
13:19. save the souls alive that *should* not *live,*
18: 9. he (is) just, *he shall* surely *live,*
13. shall he then live? *he shall* not *live;*
17, 19, 21, 28. *he shall* surely *live.*
22. that he hath done *he shall live.*
20:25. judgments whereby *they should* not *live:*
33:10. how *should we* then *live?*
13, 15, 16. *he shall* surely *live;*
19. *he shall live* thereby.
37: 3. Son of man, *can* these bones *live?*
9. breathe upon these slain, *that they may live.*
10. breath came into them, *and they lived,*
47: 9. rivers shall come, *shall live:*
Hos 6: 2. *and we shall live* in his sight.
Am. 5:14. Seek good, and not evil, that *ye may live:*
Hab 2: 4. the just *shall live* by his faith.
Zec. 1: 5. the prophets, *do they live* for ever?
13: 3. *Thou shalt* not *live;*

* PIEL.—*Preterite.* *

Nu. 31:15. *Have ye saved* all the women *alive?*
Jud. 21:14. which *they had saved alive* of the women
Ps. 22:29(30). none *can keep alive* his own soul.
30: 3(4). *thou hast kept me alive,*
119:50. for thy word *hath quickened me.*
93. with them *thou hast quickened me.*

PIEL.—*Infinitive.*

Gen. 7: 3. *to keep* seed *alive* upon the face
Deu. 6:24. *that he might preserve us alive,*
Jos. 9:15. *to let them live:*
Ps. 33:19. *and to keep them alive* in famine.
Eze. 3:18. from his wicked way, *to save his life;*
13:19. *and to save* the souls *alive*

PIEL.—*Imperative.*

Ps. 119:25. *quicken thou me* according to thy word.
37. *quicken thou me* in thy way.
40. *quicken me* in thy righteousness.
88. *Quicken me* after thy lovingkindness;
107. *quicken me,* O Lord,
149. *quicken me* according to thy judgment.
154. *quicken me* according to thy word.
156. *quicken me* according to thy judgments.
159. *quicken me,* O Lord,
Hab. 3: 2. *revive* thy work in the midst (marg. or, *preserve alive*)

PIEL.—*Future.*

Gen 12:12. but *they will save* thee *alive.*
19:32, 34. *that we may preserve* seed
Ex. 1:17. *but saved* the men children *alive.*
18. *and have saved* the men children *alive?*
22. every daughter *ye shall save alive.*
22:18(17). *Thou shalt* not *suffer* a witch *to live.*
Deu 20:16. *thou shalt save alive* nothing
32:39. I kill, *and I make alive;*
1Sa. 27: 9. *left* neither man nor woman *alive,*
11. David *saved* neither man nor woman *alive.*
2Sa. 12: 3. which he had bought *and nourished up:*
1K. 18: 5. *to save* the horses and mules *alive,* (lit *and we shall save,* &c.)
20:31. peradventure *he will save* thy life.
2K. 7: 4. if *they save us alive,* we shall live;
1Ch 11: 8. Joab *repaired* the rest of the city. (marg. *revived*)
Neh 4: 2(3:34). *will they revive* the stones
Job 33: 4. the Almighty *hath given me life.*
36: 6. *He preserveth* not *the life of* the wicked:
Ps. 41: 2(3). preserve him, *and keep him alive;*
71:20. troubles, *shalt quicken me* again,
80:18(19). *quicken us,* and we will call

Ps. 85. 6(7). *Wilt thou* not *revive us* again:
138: 7. *thou wilt revive me :*
143:11. *Quicken me*, O Lord,
Ecc. 7:12. wisdom *giveth life* to them that have it.
Isa. 7:21. a man *shall nourish* a young cow,
Jer.49:11. *I will preserve* (them) *alive ;*
Eze.13:18. *will ye save* the souls *alive*
18:27. *he shall save* his soul *alive.*
Hos 6: 2. After two days *will he revive us :*
14: 7(8). *they shall revive* (as) the corn,

PIEL.—*Participle.*

1Sa. 2: 6. The Lord killeth, *and maketh alive :*
Neh. 9: 6. thou *preservest* them all ;

* HIPHIL.—*Preterite.* *

Gen47:25. *Thou hast saved our lives :*
Nu. 22:33. I had slain thee, and *saved* her *alive.*
Jos. 2:13. *And* (that) *ye will save alive* my father,
6:25. Joshua *saved* Rahab the harlot *alive,*
14:10. the Lord *hath kept* me *alive,*
Jud. 8:19. if *ye had saved* them *alive,*
2K. 8: 1. whose son *he had restored to life,*
5. how *he had restored* a dead body *to life,*
— whose son *he had restored to life,*
— whom Elisha *restored to life.*

HIPHIL.—*Infinitive.*

Gen.6:19, 20. *to keep* (them) *alive*
19:19. hast shewed unto me *in saving* my life ;
45: 7. *and to save your lives* by a great deliverance.
50:20. *to save* much people *alive.*
Jos. 9:20. *we will even let* them *live,*
2Sa. 8: 2. with one full line *to keep alive.*
2K. 5: 7. to kill *and to make alive,*
Isa. 57:15. *to revive* the spirit of the humble, *and to revive* the heart of the contrite ones.
Eze.13:22. *by promising him life :* (marg. *quickening him*)

HIPHIL.—*Imperative.*

Nu. 31:18. *keep alive* for yourselves.
Isa. 38:16. *and make me to live.*

2418 חֲיָה & חֲיָא [*ghăyāh*], Ch.

* P'AL.—*Imperative.* *

Dan. 2: 4 & 3:9 & 5:10. O king, *live* for ever:
6: 6(7). King Darius, *live* for ever.
21(22). O king, *live* for ever.

* APHEL.—*Participle.* *

Dan. 5:19. whom he would *he kept alive ;*

2422 חָיֶה [*ghāh-yeh'*], adj.

Ex. 1:19. for they (are) *lively,*

See 2416 חַיָּה see חַי

2423 חֵיוָא *ghēh-vāh'*, Ch. f.

Dan. 2:38. *the beasts of* the field and the fowls
4:12(9). *the beasts of* the field had shadow under it,
14(11). let *the beasts* get away from under it,
15(12). (let) his portion (be) with *the beasts*
16(13). and let *a beast*'s heart be given unto him ;
21(18). under which *the beasts of* the field dwelt,
23(20). (let) his portion (be) with *the beasts of*
25(22). and thy dwelling shall be with *the beasts of*
32(29). thy dwelling (shall be) with *the beasts of*
5:21. his heart was made like *the beasts,*
7: 3. four great *beasts* came up from the sea,
5. And behold another *beast,*
6. *the beast had* also four heads ;

Dan. 7: 7. behold *a* fourth *beast*, dreadful
— diverse from all *the beasts* that (were) before it ;
11. I beheld (even) till *the beast* was slain,
12. concerning the rest of *the beasts,*
17. These great *beasts*, which are four,
19. I would know the truth of *the* fourth *beast,*
23. *The* fourth *beast* shall be the fourth kingdom

חַיּוּת *ghay-yooth'*, f. 2424

2Sa.20: 3. *living* in widowhood. (marg. in widowhood of *life*)

חָיַי [*ghāh-yah'y*]. 2425

* KAL.—*Preterite.* *

Gen.3:22. and eat, *and live* for ever:
5: 5. all the days that Adam *lived*
11:12. Arphaxad *lived* five and thirty years,
14. Salah *lived* thirty years,
25: 7. of Abraham's life which *he lived,*
Ex. 1:16. it (be) a daughter, *then she shall live.*
33:20. there shall no man see me, *and live.*
Lev.18: 5. *he shall live* in them:
Nu. 21: 8. when he looketh upon it, *shall live.*
9. beheld the serpent of brass, *he lived.*
Deu. 4:42. unto one of these cities *he might live :*
5:24(21). God doth talk with man, *and he liveth.*
19: 4. flee thither, *that he may live :*
5. flee unto one of those cities, *and live :*
1Sa.20:31. as long as the son of Jesse *liveth*
Neh 6:11. go into the temple *to save his life?* (lit. *and live*)
Jer. 38: 2. shall have his life for a prey, *and shall live.*
Eze.18:13. *shall he then live ?*
24. the wicked (man) doeth, *shall he live?*
20:11, 13, 21. *he shall even live* in them.
47: 9. *and* every thing *shall live*

חַיִל *ghah'-yil*, m. 2428

Gen34:29. And all *their wealth,*
47: 6. if thou knowest (any) men of *activity*
Ex. 14: 4, 17. Pharaoh, and upon all *his host;*
9. his horsemen, *and his army,*
28. all *the host of* Pharaoh that came
15: 4. Pharaoh's chariots *and his host*
18:21. thou shalt provide out of all the people *able* men,
25. Moses chose *able* men
Nu. 24:18. Israel shall do *valiantly.*
31: 9. all their flocks, and all *their goods.*
14. wroth with the officers of *the host,*
Deu 3:18. all (that are) meet for *the war.* (marg. sons of *power*)
8:17. hath gotten me this *wealth.*
18. he that giveth thee power to get *wealth,*
11: 4. what he did *unto the army of* Egypt,
33:11. Bless, Lord, *his substance,*
Jos. 1:14 & 6:2 & 8:3 & 10:7. mighty men of *valour,*
Jud. 3:29. all lusty, and all men of *valour;*
6:12. thou mighty man of *valour.*
11: 1. a mighty man of *valour,*
18: 2. from their coasts, men of *valour,*
20:44, 46. all these (were) men of *valour.*
21:10. sent thither twelve thousand men of the *valiant*est, (lit. out of the sons of *valour*)
Ru. 2: 1. a mighty man of *wealth,*
3:11. that thou (art) a *virtuous* woman.
4:11. do thou *worthily* in Ephratah, (marg. or, get thee *riches*, or, *power*)
1Sa. 2: 4. stumbled are girded with *strength.*
9: 1. a Benjamite, a mighty man of *power.* (marg. or, *substance*)
10:26. there went with him *a band of men.*
14:48. he gathered *an host,* (marg. or, wrought *mightily*)
52. or any *valiant* man,
16:18. a mighty *valiant* man,

1Sa. 17:20. *as the host* was going forth to the fight,
18:17. only be thou *valiant* for me, (lit. be a son of *valour*)
31:12. All the *valiant* men arose,
2Sa. 2: 7. be ye *valiant:* for your master Saul is dead, (lit. be sons of *valour*)
8: 9. David had smitten all *the host of*
11:16. knew that *valiant* men
13:28. be courageous, and be *valiant.* (lit. be sons of *valour*)
17:10. he also (that is) *valiant,* (lit. son of *valour*)
— and (they) which (be) with him (are) *valiant* men.
22:33. God (is) my strength (and) *power:*
40. thou hast girded me with *strength*
23:20. the son of a *valiant* man,
24: 2. Joab the captain of *the host,*
4, 4. the captains of *the host.*
9. in Israel eight hundred thousand *valiant* men
1K. 1:42. Come in; for thou (art) a *valiant* man,
52. If he will shew himself a *worthy* man,
10: 2. *with a* very great *train,*
11:28. a mighty man of *valour:*
15:20. sent the captains of *the hosts*
20: 1. gathered all *his host* together:
19. *and the army* which followed them.
25. number thee *an army, like the army* that thou hast lost,
2K. 2:16. with thy servants fifty *strong* men; (marg. sons of *strength*)
5: 1. a mighty man in *valour,*
6:14. chariots, *and a* great *host:*
15. *an host* compassed the city
7: 6. the noise of *a* great *host:*
9: 5. the captains of *the host* (were) sitting;
11:15. the officers of *the host,*
15:20. all the mighty men of *wealth,*
24:14. all the mighty men of *valour,*
16. all the men of *might,*
25: 1. came, he, and all *his host,*
5. And *the army of* the Chaldees pursued
— all *his army* were scattered
10. And all *the army of* the Chaldees,
23, 26. the captains of *the armies,*
1Ch. 5:18. of *valiant* men, (marg. sons of *valour*)
24. mighty men of *valour,*
7: 2. valiant men of *might*
5. Issachar (were) valiant men of *might,*
7, 11, 40. mighty men of *valour;*
9. mighty men of *valour,*
8:40. of Ulam were mighty men of *valour,*
9:13. very *able* men for the work (marg. mighty men of *valour*)
10:12. They arose, all the *valiant* men,
11:22. the son of a *valiant* man (lit. of *valour*)
26. Also the valiant men of *the armies*
12: 8. to the wilderness men of *might,*
21. all mighty men of *valour,*
25. Simeon, mighty men of *valour*
28. Zadok, a young man mighty of *valour,*
30. mighty men of *valour,* famous throughout
18: 9. David had smitten all *the host of* Hadarezer
20: 1. Joab led forth *the power of* the army,
26: 6. they (were) mighty men of *valour.*
7. whose brethren (were) *strong* men,
8. *able* men for strength for the service,
9. sons and brethren, *strong* men,
30, 32. his brethren, men of *valour,*
31. among them mighty men of *valour*
28: 1. with all the *valiant* men,
2Ch 9: 1. *with a* very great *company,*
13: 3. in array *with an army* of valiant men
— mighty men of *valour.*
14: 8(7). Asa had *an army* (of men) that bare
—(–). all these (were) mighty men of *valour.*
9(8). *with an host* of a thousand thousand,
16: 4. sent the captains of his *armies*
7. is *the host of* the king of Syria escaped
8. Ethiopians and the Lubims *a* huge *host,*
17: 2. he placed *forces* in all the fenced cities
13, 14. mighty men of *valour,*
16. thousand mighty men of *valour.*
17. Eliada a mighty man of *valour,*
23:14. that were set over *the host,*
24:23. *the host of* Syria came up
24. For *the army of* the Syrians

2Ch 24:24. the Lord delivered *a* very great *host*
25: 6. mighty men of *valour* out of Israel
26:11. Uzziah had *an host* of fighting men,
12. the mighty men of *valour*
13. under their hand (was) an army, (marg *the power of* an army)
— that made war with *mighty* power,
17. priests of the Lord, (that were) *valiant* men:
28: 6. all *valiant* men; (marg. sons of *valour*)
32:21. cut off all the mighty men of *valour,*
33:14. put captains of *war* in all
Ezr. 8:22. to require of the king *a band of soldiers*
Neh 2: 9. had sent captains of *the army*
4: 2(3:34). *and the army of* Samaria,
11: 6. four hundred threescore and eight *valiant* men.
14. mighty men of *valour,*
Est. 1: 3. *the power of* Persia and Media,
8:11. all *the power of* the people
Job 5: 5. swalloweth up *their substance.*
15:29. neither shall *his substance* continue,
20:15. He hath swallowed down *riches,*
18. *according to* (his) *substance*
21: 7. yea, are mighty in *power?*
31:25. If I rejoiced because *my wealth*
Ps. 18:32(33). God that girdeth me with *strength,*
39(40). thou hast girded me with *strength*
33:16. saved by the multitude of *an host:*
17. deliver (any) by *his* great *strength.*
49: 6(7). They that trust in *their wealth,*
10(11). leave *their wealth* to others.
59:11(12). scatter them *by thy power;*
60:12(14). Through God we shall do *valiantly:*
62:10(11). if *riches* increase, set not your
73:12. they increase (in) *riches.*
76: 5(6). none of the men of *might*
84: 7(8). They go *from strength* to *strength,* (marg. or, *company* to *company*)
108:13(14). Through God we shall do *valiantly:*
110: 3. willing in the day of *thy power,*
118:15, 16. hand of the Lord doeth *valiantly.*
136:15. overthrew Pharaoh *and his host*
Pro. 12: 4. A *virtuous* woman (is) a crown to her husband:
13:22. *the wealth of* the sinner (is) laid up
31: 3. Give not *thy strength* unto women,
10. Who can find a *virtuous* woman?
29. Many daughters have done *virtuously,* (marg. or, gotten *riches*)
Ecc. 10:10. *then* must he put to more *strength:*
12: 3. the *strong* men shall bow themselves,
Isa. 5:22. men of *strength* to mingle
8: 4. *the riches of* Damascus
10:14. *the riches of* the people:
30: 6. they will carry *their riches*
43:17. horse, *the army* and the power;
60: 5, 11. *the forces of* the Gentiles (marg. or *wealth*)
61: 6. shall eat *the riches of* the Gentiles,
Jer. 15:13. *Thy substance* and thy treasures
17: 3. I will give *thy substance*
32: 2. then the king of Babylon's *army*
34: 1. king of Babylon, and all *his army,*
7. *When* the king of Babylon's *army*
21. into the hand of the king of Babylon's *army,*
35:11. for fear of *the army of* the Chaldeans, and for fear of *the army of* the Syrians:
37: 5. *Then* Pharaoh's *army* was come
7. Pharaoh's *army,* which is come
10. though ye had smitten *the* whole *army of*
11. when *the army of* the Chaldeans
— for fear of Pharaoh's *army,*
38: 3. the king of Babylon's *army,*
39: 1. all *his army* against Jerusalem,
5. the Chaldeans' *army* pursued after them,
40: 7, 13 & 41:11, 13, 16 & 42:1, 8 & 43:4, 5. all the captains of *the forces*
46: 2. against *the army of* Pharaoh-necho
22. they shall march *with an army,*
48:14. We (are) mighty and *strong* men for the war?
52: 4. he and all *his army,*
8. *the army of* the Chaldeans pursued
— all *his army* was scattered from him.
14. all *the army of* the Chaldeans,

Eze.17:17. Pharaoh *with* (his) mighty *army*
26:12. they shall make a spoil of *thy riches,*
27:10. Lud and of Phut were *in thine army,*
11. The men of Arvad *with thine army*
28: 4. thou hast gotten thee *riches,*
5. hast thou increased *thy riches,*
— heart is lifted up *because of thy riches:*
29:18. caused *his army* to serve a great service
— yet had he no wages, *nor his army,*
19. and it shall be the wages *for his army.*
32:31. Pharaoh and all *his army* slain
37:10. *an* exceeding great *army.*
38: 4. all *thine army,* horses and horsemen,
15. *and a* mighty *army:*
Dan 11: 7. which shall come with *an army,*
10. shall assemble a multitude of *great forces:*
13. after certain years *with a* great *army*
25. of the south *with a* great *army;*
— *with a* very great and mighty *army;*
26. *and his army* shall overflow:
Joel 2:11. shall utter his voice before *his army:*
22. the vine do yield *their strength.*
25. *my* great *army* which I sent
Obad. 11. carried away captive *his forces,* (marg. or, *his substance*)
13. have laid (hands) *on their substance* (marg. or, *forces*)
Mic. 4:13. *and their substance* unto the Lord
Nah 2: 3(4). the *valiant* men (are) in scarlet:
Hab 3:19. The Lord God (is) *my strength,*
Zep. 1:13. *their goods* shall become a booty,
Zec. 4: 6. Not *by might* (marg. or, *army*) nor by power,
9: 4. he will smite *her power* in the sea;
14:14. *the wealth of* all the heathen

2429 **חֵיל** *ghah'-yil,* Ch. m.

Ezr. 4:23. made them to cease by force *and power.*
Dan 3: 4. Then an herald cried *aloud,* (marg. *with might*)
20. commanded the *most* mighty men (marg. mighty of *strength*) that (were) *in his army* to bind
4:14(11). He cried *aloud* (marg. *with might*), and said thus, Hew
35(32). according to his will *in the army of*
5: 7. The king cried *aloud* (marg. *with might*) to bring in the astrologers,

---

2426 **חֵל** *ghēhl,* m.

2Sa. 20:15. it stood *in the trench:* (marg. or, *against the outmost wall*)
1K. 21:23. eat Jezebel *by the wall of* Jezreel. (marg. or, *ditch*)
2K. 18:17. Hezekiah *with a* great *host*
Ps. 10:10. the poor (lit. *the host of* the miserable) may fall by his strong ones.
122: 7. Peace be *within thy walls,*
Isa. 26: 1. walls *and bulwarks.*
36: 2. *with a* great *army.*
Lam. 2: 8. he made *the rampart* and the wall
Obad 20. captivity of this *host* of the children
Nah 3: 8. whose *rampart* (was) the sea,

See 2342 **חִיל** see **חוּל**

2427 **חִיל** *gheel,* m.

Ex. 15:14. *sorrow* shall take hold on the inhabitants
Ps. 48: 6(7). *pain,* as of a woman in travail.
Jer. 6:24. anguish hath taken hold of us, (and) *pain,*
22:23. *the pain* as of a woman in travail!
50:43. anguish took hold of him, (and) *pangs*
Mic. 4: 9. for *pangs* have taken thee as a woman

2427 **חִילָה** *ghee-lāh',* f.

Job 6:10. I would harden myself *in sorrow:*

חֵילָה *ghēh-lāh'.* 2430

Ps. 48:13(14). Mark ye well *her bulwarks,* (lit. *the bulwark*)

NOTE.—Perhaps the true reading is חֵילָהּ (as the English translation renders it); from חֵיל above.

חִין *gheen,* m. 2433

Job 41:12(4). *nor* his *comely* proportion. (lit. *nor the grace of* his structure)

חַיִץ *ghah'-yitz,* m. 2434

Eze.13:10. one built up *a wall,* (marg. or, *a slight wall*)

חִיצוֹן *ghee-tzōhn',* adj. 2435

1K. 6:29. open flowers, within *and without.*
30. overlaid with gold, within *and without.*
2K. 16:18. the king's entry *without,*
1Ch 26:29. for the *outward* business over Israel,
2Ch 33:14. he built a wall *without* the city
Neh 11:16. the oversight of the *outward* business
Est. 6: 4. Haman was come into the *outward* court
Eze.10: 5. was heard (even) to the *outer* court,
40:17. brought he me into the *outward* court,
20. the gate of the *outward* court
31. arches thereof (were) toward the *utter*
34. arches thereof (were) toward the *outward*
37. posts thereof (were) toward the *utter*
41:17. within *and without,* by measure.
42: 1. forth into the *utter* court,
3. the pavement which (was) for the *utter*
7. toward the *utter* court on the forepart
8. the chambers that (were) in the *utter*
9. goeth into them from the *utter* court.
14. of the holy (place) into the *utter* court,
44: 1. the gate of the *outward* sanctuary
19. they go forth into the *utter* court, (even) into the *utter* court to the people,
46:20. bear (them) not out into the *utter* court,
21. brought me forth into the *utter* court.

חֵיק *ghēhk,* m. 2436

Gen16: 5. I have given my maid *into thy bosom;*
Ex. 4: 6. Put now thine hand *into thy bosom.* And he put his hand *into his bosom:*
7. Put thine hand into *thy bosom* again. And he put his hand into *his bosom* again; and plucked it *out of his bosom,*
Nu. 11:12. Carry them *in thy bosom,*
Deu 13: 6(7). or the wife of *thy bosom,*
28:54. toward the wife of *his bosom,*
56. evil toward the husband of *her bosom,*
Ru. 4:16. laid it *in her bosom,*
2Sa. 12: 3. *and* lay *in his bosom,*
8. thy master's wives *into thy bosom,*
1K. 1: 2. let her lie *in thy bosom,*
3.20. and laid it *in her bosom,* and laid her dead child *in my bosom.*
17:19. he took him *out of her bosom,*
22:35. ran out of the wound into *the midst of* the chariot. (marg. *bosom*)
Job 19:27. my reins be consumed *within me.* (marg. *in my bosom*)
Ps. 35:13. prayer returned into *mine own bosom.*
74:11. pluck (it) out of *thy bosom.*
79:12. sevenfold into *their bosom*
89:50(51). I do bear *in my bosom*
Pro. 5:20. embrace *the bosom of* a stranger?
6:27. Can a man take fire *in his bosom,*
16:33. The lot is cast *into the lap;*
17:23. wicked (man) taketh a gift *out of the bosom*
21:14. a reward *in the bosom* strong
Ecc. 7: 9. for anger resteth *in the bosom of* fools.
Isa. 40:11. *and* carry (them) *in his bosom,*
65: 6. even recompense into *their bosom,*
7. their former work into *their bosom.*
Jer. 32:18. into *the bosom of* their children
Lam. 2:12. poured out into their mothers' *bosom.*
Eze. 43:13. *even the bottom* (shall be) a cubit, (marg. *bosom*)
14. *And from the bottom* (upon) the ground
17. *and the bottom* thereof
Mic. 7: 5. from her that lieth in *thy bosom.*

2439 חִישׁ [*g'heesh*].

* KAL.—*Imperative.* *

Ps. 71:12. (כתיב) O my God, *make haste* for my help.

2440 חִישׁ *g'heesh*, adv.

Ps. 90:10. for it is *soon* cut off,

2441 חֵךְ *g'hĕhch*, m.

Job 6:30. cannot *my taste* discern perverse things? (marg. *palate*)
12:11. *and the mouth* taste his meat? (marg. *palate*)
20:13. but keep it still within *his mouth*: (marg. *palate*)
29:10. cleaved *to the roof of their mouth*.
31:30. Neither have I suffered *my mouth*
33: 2. my tongue hath spoken *in my mouth*.
34: 3. *as the mouth* tasteth meat. (marg. *palate*)
Ps. 119:103. sweet are thy words *unto my taste!* (marg. *palate*)
137: 6. cleave *to the roof of my mouth*;
Pro. 5: 3. *her mouth* (is) smoother than oil:
8: 7. For *my mouth* shall speak truth;
24:13. honeycomb, (which is) sweet to *thy taste*: (marg. *palate*)
Cant. 2: 3. his fruit (was) sweet *to my taste*. (marg. *palate*)
5:16. *His mouth* (marg. *palate*) (is) most sweet: yea, he (is) altogether
7: 9(10). *And the roof of thy mouth* like the
Lam. 4: 4. cleaveth to *the roof of his mouth* for thirst:
Eze. 3:26. tongue cleave *to the roof of thy mouth*,
Hos. 8: 1. (Set) the trumpet to *thy mouth*. (marg. *the roof of thy mouth*)

2442 חָכָה [*g'hāh-chāh'*].

* KAL.—*Participle.* Poel. *

Isa. 30:18. blessed (are) all *they that wait* for him.

* PIEL.—*Preterite.* *

2K. 7: 9. *if we tarry* till the morning light,
Job 32: 4. Elihu *had waited* till Job had spoken, (marg. *expected* Job in words)
Ps. 33:20. Our soul *waiteth* for the Lord:
106:13. *they waited* not for his counsel:
Isa. 8:17. *And I will wait* upon the Lord,

PIEL.—*Infinitive.*

Hos. 6: 9. *And as* troops of robbers *wait*

PIEL.—*Imperative.*

Hab 2: 3. though it tarry, *wait* for it;
Zep. 3: 8. Therefore *wait ye* upon me,

PIEL.—*Future.*

2K. 9: 3. open the door, and flee, and *tarry* not.
Isa. 30:18. therefore *will* the Lord *wait*,

PIEL.—*Participle.*

Job 3:21. *Which long* for death, (marg. *wait*)
Isa. 64: 4(3). hath prepared *for him that waiteth*
Dan 12:12. Blessed (is) *he that waiteth*,

2443 חַכָּה *g'hak-kāh'*, f.

Job 41: 1(40:25). draw out leviathan *with an hook?*
Isa. 19: 8. all they that cast *angle* into the brooks
Hab 1:15. take up all of them *with the angle*,

2445 חַכִּים [*g'hak-keem'*], Ch. adj.

Dan 2:12. commanded to destroy all *the wise* (men) *of*
13. *that the wise* (men) should be slain;
14. was gone forth to slay *the wise* (men) *of*
18. perish with the rest of *the wise* (men) *of*
21. he giveth wisdom *unto the wise*,
24. whom the king had ordained to destroy *the wise* (men) *of*
— Destroy not *the wise* (men) *of*
27. cannot *the wise* (men), the astrologers,
48. over all *the wise* (men) *of* Babylon.
4: 6(3). decree to bring in all *the wise* (men) *of*
18(15). forasmuch as all *the wise* (men) *of* my
5: 7. king spake, and said *to the wise* (men) *of*
8. came in all the king's *wise* (men):
15. And now *the wise* (men),

חַכְלִילִי *g'hach-lee-lee'*, adj. 2447

Gen 49:12. His eyes (shall be) *red* with wine,

חַכְלִלוּת *g'hach-lee-looth'*, f. 2448

Pro. 23:29. who hath *redness of* eyes?

חָכַם *g'hāh-cham'*. 2449

* KAL.—*Preterite.* *

Deu 32:29. O that *they were wise*,
Pro. 9:12. If *thou be wise, thou shalt be wise* for thyself:
23:15. My son, if thine heart *be wise*,
Ecc. 2:15. why *was* I then more *wise?*
19. *and wherein I have shewed myself wise*
Zec. 9: 2. Zidon, though *it be* very *wise*.

KAL.—*Imperative.*

Pro. 6: 6. consider her ways, *and be wise*:
8:33. Hear instruction, *and be wise*,
23:19. Hear thou, my son, *and be wise*,
27:11. *be wise*, and make my heart glad,

KAL.—*Future.*

1K. 4:31(5:11). *For he was wiser* than all men;
Job 32: 9. Great men *are* not (always) *wise*:
Pro. 9: 9. *and he will be* yet *wiser*:
13:20. walketh with wise (men) *shall be wise*:
19:20. that *thou mayest be wise*
20: 1. whosoever is deceived thereby *is* not *wise*.
21:11. the simple *is made wise*:
Ecc. 7:23. I said, *I will be wise*;

* PIEL.—*Future.* *

Job 35:11. and *maketh us wiser* than the fowls
Ps. 105:22. *teach* his senators *wisdom*.
119:98. *Thou* through...*hast made me wiser*

* PUAL.—*Participle.* *

Ps. 58: 5(6). charming *never so wisely*. (marg. or, (be) the charmer *never so cunning*)
Pro. 30:24. but they (are) *exceeding* wise: (marg. wise, *made wise*)

* HIPHIL.—*Participle.* *

Ps. 19: 7(8). *making wise* the simple.

* HITHPAEL.—*Future.* *

Ex. 1:10. *let us deal wisely* with them;
Ecc. 7:16. neither *make thyself* over *wise*:

חָכָם *g'hāh-chāhm'*, adj. 2450

Gen 41: 8. *the wise men thereof*:
33. look out a man discreet *and wise*,
39. none so discreet *and wise* as thou
Ex. 7:11. Pharaoh also called *the wise men*
28: 3. speak unto all (that are) *wise* hearted,
31: 6. hearts of all that are *wise* hearted
35:10. every *wise* hearted among you
25. all the women that were *wise* hearted
36: 1, 2. every *wise* hearted man,
4. And all *the wise men*,
8. *And* every *wise* hearted *man*
Deu. 1:13. Take you *wise* men,
15. chief of your tribes, *wise* men,
4: 6. a *wise* and understanding people.
16:19. a gift doth blind the eyes of *the wise*,
32: 6. O foolish people and un*wise?*
Jud. 5:29. Her *wise* ladies answered her,
2Sa. 13: 3. Jonadab (was) a very *subtil* man.
14: 2. fetched thence a *wise* woman,
20. and my lord (is) *wise*,
20:16. Then cried a *wise* woman
1K. 2: 9. for thou (art) a *wise* man,

1K. 3:12. a *wise* and an understanding heart;
5: 7(21). hath given unto David a *wise* son
1Ch 22:15. all manner of *cunning men*
2Ch 2: 7(6). a man *cunning* to work in gold,
—(-). skill to grave with *the cunning men*
12(11). hath given to David the king a *wise* son,
13(12). now I have sent a *cunning* man,
14(13). with *thy cunning men, and* with *the cunning men of* my lord
Est. 1:13. the king said *to the wise men,*
6:13. Then said *his wise men*
Job 5:13. He taketh *the wise* in their own craftiness:
9: 4. *wise in* heart, and mighty
15: 2. Should *a wise man* utter vain knowledge,
18. Which *wise men* have told
17:10. I cannot find (one) *wise* (man) among you.
34: 2. Hear my words, *O ye wise*
34. let *a wise man* hearken unto me.
37:24. not any (that are) *wise of* heart.
Ps. 49:10(11). For he seeth (that) *wise men* die,
107:43. Whoso (is) *wise*, and will observe these
Pro. 1: 5. *A wise* (man) will hear,
6. the words of *the wise,*
3: 7. Be not *wise* in thine own eyes:
35. *The wise* shall inherit glory:
9: 8. rebuke *a wise man*, and he will love
9. Give (instruction) *to a wise* (man),
10: 1. A *wise* son maketh a glad father:
8. *wise in* heart will receive commandments:
14. *Wise* (men) lay up knowledge:
11:29. servant *to the wise of* heart.
30. he that winneth souls (is) *wise.*
12:15. he that hearkeneth unto counsel (is) *wise.*
18. the tongue of *the wise* (is) health.
13: 1. A *wise* son (heareth) his father's instruction:
14. The law of *the wise* (is) a fountain
20. He that walketh with *wise* (men) shall be
14: 3. the lips of *the wise* shall preserve them.
16. *A wise* (man) feareth,
24. The crown of *the wise* (is) their riches:
15: 2. The tongue of *the wise* useth knowledge
7. The lips of *the wise* disperse knowledge:
12. neither will he go unto *the wise.*
20. A *wise* son maketh a glad father:
31. abideth among *the wise.*
16:14. but a *wise* man will pacify it.
21. *The wise in* heart shall be called prudent:
23. The heart of *the wise* teacheth his mouth,
17:28. holdeth his peace, is counted *wise:*
18:15. the ear of *the wise* seeketh knowledge.
20:26. A *wise* king scattereth the wicked,
21:11. when *the wise* is instructed,
20. oil in the dwelling of *the wise;*
22. *A wise* (man) scaleth the city
22:17. hear the words of *the wise,*
23:24. he that begetteth *a wise* (child) shall
24: 5. A *wise* man (is) strong;
23. These (things) also (belong) *to the wise.*
25:12. a *wise* reprover upon an obedient ear.
26: 5. lest he be *wise* in his own conceit.
12. Seest thou a man *wise* in his own conceit?
16. The sluggard (is) *wiser* in his own
28:11. The rich man (is) *wise* in his own conceit;
29: 8. *but wise* (men) turn away wrath.
9. a *wise* man contendeth with a foolish man,
11. *but a wise* (man) keepeth it
30:24. but they (are) exceeding *wise:*
Ecc. 2:14. *The wise man's* eyes (are) in his head;
16. no remembrance *of the wise*
— how dieth *the wise* (man)? as the fool.
19. whether he shall be *a wise* (man) or a fool?
4:13. Better (is) a poor *and a wise* child
6: 8. what *hath the wise* more than the fool?
7: 4. The heart of *the wise* (is) in the house of mourning;
5. better to hear the rebuke of *the wise,*
7. oppression maketh *a wise man* mad;
19. Wisdom strengtheneth *the wise*
8: 1. Who (is) *as the wise* (man)?
5. *a wise man's* heart discerneth
17. though *a wise* (man) think to know
Ecc. 9: 1. that the righteous, *and the wise,*
11. neither yet bread *to the wise,*
15. there was found in it a poor *wise* man,
17. The words of *wise* (men are) heard
10: 2. *A wise man's* heart (is) at his right hand;
12. words of *a wise man's* mouth (are) gracious;
12: 9. because the preacher was *wise,*
11. The words of *the wise*
Isa. 3: 3. the counsellor, *and the cunning*
5:21. Woe unto (them that are) *wise*
19:11. the *wise* counsellors of Pharaoh
— I (am) the son of *the wise,*
12. where (are) *thy wise* (men)?
29:14. the wisdom of *their wise* (men)
31: 2. Yet he also (is) *wise,*
40:20. seeketh unto him a *cunning* workman
44:25. that turneth *wise* (men) backward,
Jer. 4:22. they (are) *wise* to do evil,
8: 8. How do ye say, We (are) *wise,*
9. *The wise* (men) are ashamed,
9:12(11). Who (is) the *wise* man,
17(16). send for *cunning* (women),
23(22). Let not *the wise* (man) glory in his
10: 7. among all *the wise* (men) *of* the nations,
9. all the work of *cunning* (men).
18:18. nor counsel *from the wise,*
50:35. her princes, and upon *her wise* (men).
51:57. her princes, *and her wise* (men),
Eze.27: 8. thy mariners: *thy wise* (men), O Tyrus,
9. Gebal *and the wise* (men) *thereof*
28: 3. thou (art) *wiser* than Daniel;
Hos13:13. he (is) an un*wise* son;
14: 9(10). Who (is) *wise*, and he shall understand
Obad 8. even destroy *the wise* (men) out of Edom,

חָכְמָה *ghoch-māh'*, f. 2451

Ex. 28: 3. have filled with the spirit of *wisdom,*
31: 3. *in wisdom*, and in understanding,
6. that are wise hearted I have put *wisdom,*
35:26. whose heart stirred them up *in wisdom*
31. with the spirit of God, *in wisdom,*
35. Them hath he filled with *wisdom of*
36: 1. in whom the Lord put *wisdom*
2. in whose heart the Lord had put *wisdom,*
Deu 4: 6. for this (is) *your wisdom*
34: 9. was full of the spirit of *wisdom;*
2Sa 14:20. *according to the wisdom of* an angel
20:22. went unto all the people *in her wisdom.*
1K. 2: 6. Do therefore *according to thy wisdom,*
3:28. saw that *the wisdom of* God (was) in him,
4:29(5:9). God gave Solomon *wisdom*
30(5:10). Solomon's *wisdom* excelled *the wisdom of* all the children of the east country, and all *the wisdom of* Egypt.
34(5:14). all people to hear *the wisdom of*
—(-:—). which had heard of *his wisdom.*
5:12(26). the Lord gave Solomon *wisdom,*
7:14. he was filled with *wisdom,*
10: 4. Sheba had seen all Solomon's *wisdom,*
6. thy acts and of *thy wisdom.*
7. thy *wisdom* and prosperity
8. that hear *thy wisdom.*
23. of the earth for riches *and for wisdom.*
24. sought to Solomon, to hear *his wisdom,*
11:41. all that he did, *and his wisdom,*
1Ch 28:21. every willing *skilful* man, (lit. *in wisdom*)
2Ch 1:10. Give me now *wisdom*
11. but hast asked *wisdom* and knowledge
12. *Wisdom* and knowledge (is) granted
9: 3. Sheba had seen *the wisdom of* Solomon,
5. of thine acts, and of *thy wisdom:*
6. the one half of the greatness of *thy wisdom*
7. before thee, and hear *thy wisdom.*
22. kings of the earth in riches *and wisdom.*
23. to hear *his wisdom,*
Job 4:21. they die, even without *wisdom.* (lit. not *in wisdom*)
11: 6. shew thee the secrets of *wisdom,*
12: 2. *wisdom* shall die with you.
12. With the ancient (is) *wisdom;*
13. With him (is) *wisdom* and strength,
13: 5. it should be your *wisdom.* (lit. to you *for wisdom*)

Job 15: 8. dost thou restrain *wisdom*
26: 3. counselled (him that hath) no *wisdom?*
28:12. *But* where shall *wisdom* be found?
18. the price of *wisdom* (is) above rubies.
20. Whence *then* cometh *wisdom?*
28. the fear of the Lord, that (is) *wisdom;*
32: 7. multitude of years should teach *wisdom.*
13. We have found out *wisdom:*
33:33. I shall teach thee *wisdom.*
38:36. Who hath put *wisdom* in the inward parts?
37. Who can number the clouds *in wisdom?*
39:17. God hath deprived her of *wisdom,*
Ps. 37:30. the righteous speaketh *wisdom,*
51: 6(8). thou shalt make me to know *wisdom.*
90:12. may apply (our) hearts *unto wisdom.*
104:24. *in wisdom* hast thou made them all:
107:27. are at *their wit*'s end. (marg. all *their wisdom* is swallowed up)
111:10. The fear of the Lord (is) the beginning of *wisdom:*
Pro. 1: 2. To know *wisdom* and instruction;
7. fools despise *wisdom* and instruction.
2: 2. incline thine ear *unto wisdom,*
6. For the Lord giveth *wisdom:*
10. When *wisdom* entereth into thine heart,
3:13. Happy (is) the man (that) findeth *wisdom.*
19. The Lord *by wisdom* hath founded
4: 5. Get *wisdom,* get understanding:
7. *Wisdom* (is) the principal thing; (therefore) get *wisdom:*
11. I have taught thee in the way of *wisdom;*
5: 1. My son, attend *unto my wisdom,*
7: 4. Say *unto wisdom,* Thou (art) my sister;
8: 1. Doth not *wisdom* cry?
11. For *wisdom* (is) better than rubies;
12. I *wisdom* dwell with prudence,
9:10. of the Lord (is) the beginning of *wisdom:*
10:13. hath understanding *wisdom* is found:
23. *but* a man of understanding hath *wisdom.*
31. mouth of the just bringeth forth *wisdom:*
11: 2. but with the lowly (is) *wisdom.*
13:10. but with the well advised (is) *wisdom.*
14: 6. A scorner seeketh *wisdom,*
8. *The wisdom of* the prudent
33. *Wisdom* resteth in the heart
15:33. the Lord (is) the instruction of *wisdom;*
16:16. better (is it) to get *wisdom* than gold?
17:16. price in the hand of a fool to get *wisdom,*
24. *Wisdom* (is) before him that hath
18: 4. the wellspring of *wisdom*
21:30. no *wisdom* nor understanding
23:23. *wisdom,* and instruction, and
24: 3. *Through wisdom* is an house builded;
14. So (shall) the knowledge of *wisdom*
28:26. whoso walketh *wisely,* he shall be
29: 3. Whoso loveth *wisdom* rejoiceth
15. The rod and reproof give *wisdom:*
30: 3. I neither learned *wisdom,*
31:26. She openeth her mouth *with wisdom;*
Ecc. 1:13. seek and search out *by wisdom*
16. have gotten more *wisdom* than all
— my heart had great experience of *wisdom*
17. I gave my heart to know *wisdom,*
18. in much *wisdom* (is) much grief:
2: 3. yet acquainting mine heart *with wisdom;*
9. also *my wisdom* remained with me.
12. I turned myself to behold *wisdom,*
13. Then I saw that *wisdom* excelleth folly, (lit. there is excellency *to wisdom*)
21. a man whose labour (is) *in wisdom,*
26. that (is) good in his sight *wisdom,*
7:10. thou dost not enquire *wisely* concerning this. (marg. *out of wisdom*)
11. *Wisdom* (is) good with an inheritance:
12. For *wisdom* (is) a defence,
— *wisdom* giveth life to them
19. *Wisdom* strengtheneth the wise
23. All this have I proved *by wisdom:*
25. to seek out *wisdom,*
8: 1. a man's *wisdom* maketh his face to shine,
16. I applied mine heart to know *wisdom,*
9:10. nor knowledge, *nor wisdom,*
13. This *wisdom* have I seen also
15. he *by his wisdom* delivered the city;
16. *Wisdom* (is) better than strength: *nevertheless* the poor man's *wisdom*
18. *Wisdom* (is) better than weapons of war:

Ecc.10: 1. in reputation *for wisdom* (and) honour.
10. but *wisdom* (is) profitable to direct.
Isa. 10:13. *and by my wisdom;*
11: 2. the spirit of *wisdom* and understanding,
29:14. for *the wisdom of* their wise (men)
33: 6. *wisdom* and knowledge shall be
47:10. *Thy wisdom* and thy knowledge,
Jer. 8: 9. *and* what *wisdom* (is) in them? (marg. *the wisdom of* what thing)
9:23(22). the wise (man) glory *in his wisdom,*
10:12. established the world *by his wisdom,*
49: 7. (Is) *wisdom* no more in Teman?
— is *their wisdom* vanished?
51:15. established the world *by his wisdom,*
Eze.28: 4. *With thy wisdom* and with thine understanding
5. By *thy* great *wisdom*
7. against the beauty of *thy wisdom,*
12. full of *wisdom,* and perfect in beauty.
17. thou hast corrupted *thy wisdom*
Dan 1: 4. skilful in all *wisdom,*
17. skill in all learning *and wisdom:*
20. in all matters of *wisdom* (marg. *wisdom of* understanding)

חָכְמָה *ghoch-māh'*, Ch. f. 2452

Ezr. 7:25. And thou, Ezra, *after the wisdom of*
Dan 2:20. for *wisdom* and might are his:
21. he giveth *wisdom* unto the wise,
23. who hast given me *wisdom*
30. not revealed to me *for* (any) *wisdom*
5:11. understanding *and wisdom, like the wisdom of* the gods,
14. and excellent *wisdom* is found in thee.

חָכְמוֹת *ghoch-mōhth'*, f. 2454

Ps. 49: 3(4). My mouth shall speak of *wisdom;*
Pro. 1:20. *Wisdom* crieth without; (marg. *Wisdoms*)
9: 1. *Wisdom* hath builded her house,
24: 7. *Wisdom* (is) too high for a fool:

חַכְמוֹת *ghach-mōhth'*, f. 2454

Pro.14: 1. *Every wise* woman buildeth her house: (lit. *wisdom of* women)

חֹל *ghōhl*, adj. 2455

Lev.10:10. difference between holy and *unholy,*
1Sa.21: 4(5). no *common* bread under mine hand,
5(6). and (the bread is) in a manner *common,*
Eze.22:26. difference between the holy *and profane,*
42:20. the sanctuary *and the profane place.*
44:23. between the holy *and profane,*
48:15. shall be *a profane place* for the city,

חָלָא [*ghāh-lāh'*]. 2456

* KAL.—*Future.* *

2Ch 16:12. *And Asa...was diseased* in his feet,

חֶלְאָה [*ghel-āh'*], f. 2457

Eze.24: 6. the pot *whose scum* (is) therein, *and whose scum* is not gone
11. *the scum of it* may be consumed.
12. *her* great *scum* went not forth
— *her scum* (shall be) in the fire.

חֲלָאִים see חֲלִי· See 2481

חָלָב *ghāh-lāhv'*, m. 2461

Gen18: 8. he took butter, *and milk,*
49:12. his teeth white *with milk.*
Ex. 3: 8, 17 & 13: 5. a land flowing with *milk* and honey;
23:19. shalt not seethe a kid *in* his mother's *milk.*

Ex. 33: 3. a land flowing with *milk* and honey:
34:26 shalt not seethe a kid *in* his mother's *milk*.
Lev.20:24. a land that floweth with *milk*
Nu. 13:27 & 14:8 & 16:13, 14. floweth with *milk*
Deu 6: 3 & 11:9. land that floweth with *milk*
14:21. shalt not seethe a kid *in* his mother's *milk*.
26: 9, 15 & 27:3 & 31:20. that floweth with *milk*
32:14. Butter of kine, *and milk of* sheep,
Jos. 5: 6. a land that floweth with *milk*
Jud. 4:19. she opened a bottle of *milk*,
5:25. He asked water, (and) she gave (him) *milk;*
1Sa. 7: 9. Samuel took a *sucking* lamb,
17:18. carry these ten cheeses unto the captain (marg. cheeses of *milk*)
Job 10:10. Hast thou not poured me out *as milk*,
21:24. His breasts are full of *milk*,
Pro. 27:27. goats' *milk* enough for thy food,
30:33. Surely the churning of *milk*
Cant. 4:11. honey *and milk* (are) under thy tongue;
5: 1. I have drunk my wine with *my milk:*
12. rivers of waters, washed *with milk*,
Isa. 7:22. for the abundance of *milk*
28: 9. weaned *from the milk*,
55: 1. buy wine *and milk* without money
60:16. suck *the milk of* the Gentiles,
Jer. 11: 5, & 32:22. a land flowing with *milk* and honey,
Lam. 4: 7. they were whiter *than milk*,
Eze. 20: 6, 15. flowing with *milk* and honey,
25: 4. they shall drink *thy milk*.
Joel 3:18(4:18). the hills shall flow with *milk*,

2459 חֵלֶב *g'hĕh'-lev*, m.

Gen 4: 4. *and of the fat thereof.*
45:18. ye shall eat *the fat of* the land.
Ex. 23:18. shall *the fat of* my sacrifice
29:13. thou shalt take all *the fat*
— the two kidneys, and *the fat*
22. thou shalt take of the ram *the fat*
— *the fat* that covereth the inwards,
— and *the fat* that (is) upon them,
Lev. 3: 3, 9, 14. *the fat* that covereth the inwards (marg. or, *suet*), and all *the fat* that (is) upon the inwards,
4. and *the fat* that (is) on them,
9. *the fat thereof*, (and) the whole
10, 15. the two kidneys, and *the fat*
16. all *the fat* (is) the Lord's.
17. that ye eat neither *fat* nor blood.
4: 8. shall take off from it all *the fat of*
— *the fat* that covereth the inwards, and all *the fat* that (is) upon the
9. the two kidneys, and *the fat*
19. he shall take all *his fat* from him,
26. he shall burn all *his fat*
— *as the fat of* the sacrifice
31. he shall take away all *the fat thereof*, *as the fat* is taken away
35. he shall take away all *the fat thereof*, as *the fat of* the lamb is taken
6:12(5). he shall burn thereon *the fat of*
7: 3. offer of it all *the fat thereof;*
— *the fat* that covereth the inwards,
4. the two kidneys, and *the fat*
23. Ye shall eat no manner of *fat*,
24. *And the fat of* the beast
— *and the fat of* that which
25. whosoever eateth *the fat of* the beast,
30. *the fat* with the breast,
31. the priest shall burn *the fat*
33. the peace offerings, and *the fat*,
8:16. he took all *the fat* that (was) upon
— the two kidneys, and *their fat*,
25. he took *the fat*, and the rump, and all *the fat* that (was) upon the inwards,
— the two kidneys, and *their fat*,
26. and put (them) on *the fat*,
9:10. But *the fat*, and the kidneys,
19. And *the fat* of the bullock
20. they put *the fat* upon the breasts, and he burnt *the fat* upon the altar:
24. altar the burnt offering and *the fat:*
10:15. made by fire of *the fat*,
16:25. *the fat of* the sin offering
Lev. 17: 6. burn *the fat* for a sweet savour
Nu. 18:12. All *the best* (marg. *fat*) *of* the oil, and all *the best of* the wine,
17. shalt burn *their fat* (for) an offering
29. of all *the best thereof*, (marg. *fat*)
30. When ye have heaved *the best thereof*
32. heaved from it *the best of it:*
Deu 32:14. with *fat of* lambs,
— with *the fat of* kidneys of wheat;
38. did eat *the fat of* their sacrifices,
Jud. 3:22. and *the fat* closed upon the blade,
1Sa. 2:15. Also before they burnt *the fat*,
16. Let them not fail to burn *the fat*
15:22. to hearken *than the fat of* rams.
2Sa. 1:22. *from the fat of* the mighty,
1K. 8:64, 64. meat offerings, and *the fat of*
2Ch 7: 7. *the fat of* the peace offerings,
— the meat offerings, and *the fat*.
29:35. *with the fat of* the peace offerings,
35:14. burnt offerings *and the fat*
Job 15:27. covereth his face *with his fatness*,
Ps. 17:10. They are inclosed in *their own fat:*
63: 5(6). satisfied as (with) *marrow* and fatness (marg. *fatness*)
73: 7. Their eyes stand out *with fatness:*
81:16(17). fed them also *with the finest of* the wheat: (marg. *fat*)
119:70. Their heart is as fat *as grease;*
147:14. filleth thee with *the finest of* the wheat (marg. *fat of* wheat)
Isa. 1:11. *and the fat of* fed beasts;
34: 6. it is made fat *with fatness*,
— *with the fat of* the kidneys
7. their dust made fat *with fatness*.
43:24. *neither* hast thou filled me with *the fat of*
Eze. 34: 3. Ye eat *the fat*, and ye clothe you
39:19. ye shall eat *fat* till ye be full,
44: 7. *the fat* and the blood,
15. to offer unto me *the fat*

חֶלְבְּנָה *g'hel-b'nah'*, f. 2464

Ex. 30:34. onycha, *and galbanum;*

חֶלֶד *g'heh'-led*, m. 2465

Job 11:17. And (thine) *age* shall be clearer
Ps. 17:14. from men *of the world*,
39: 5(6). *and mine age* (is) as nothing
49: 1(2). all (ye) inhabitants of *the world:*
89:47(48). Remember how *short* my *time* is: (lit. how *transitory* I am)

חֹלֶד *g'hōh'-led*, m. 2467

Lev. 11:29. *the weasel*, and the mouse,

חָלָה *g'hāh-lāh'*. 2470

* KAL.—*Preterite.* *

Jud. 16: 7, 11. *then shall I be weak*,
17. *and I shall become weak*,
1Sa. 30:13. three days agone *I fell sick*.
1K. 14: 1. the son of Jeroboam *fell sick*.
15:23. old age *he was diseased* in his feet.
17:17. the mistress of the house, *fell sick;*
2K 13:14. Elisha *was fallen sick* of his sickness
20: 1. In those days *was* Hezekiah *sick* unto death.
12. heard that Hezekiah *had been sick*.
2Ch 32:24. In those days Hezekiah *was sick*
Pro. 23:35. *I was* not *sick;*
Isa. 33:24. the inhabitant shall not say, *I am sick:*
38: 1. In those days *was* Hezekiah *sick*
39: 1. had heard that *he had been sick*,
57:10. therefore *thou wast* not *grieved*.

KAL.—*Infinitive.*

Ps. 35:13. as for me, *when they were sick*,
Isa. 38: 9. *when he had been sick*,

KAL.—*Future.*

2K. 1: 2. that (was) in Samaria, *and was sick:*

KAL.—*Participle.* Poel.

Gen48: 1. Behold, thy father (is) *sick:*
1Sa. 19:14. to take David, she said, He (is) *sick.*
22: 8. none of you *that is sorry* for me,
1K. 14: 5. of thee for her son; for he (is) *sick:*
2K. 8: 7. Ben-hadad the king of Syria *was sick;*
29. in Jezreel, because he *was sick.* (marg. *wounded*)
2Ch22: 6. at Jezreel, because he *was sick.*
Neh 2: 2. seeing thou (art) not *sick?*
Ecc. 5:13(12). There is a *sore* evil (which) I have
16(15). this also (is) a *sore* evil,
Cant 2: 5. for I (am) *sick of* love.
5: 8. *that* I (am) *sick of* love.
Jer. 4:31. a voice *as of a woman in travail,*
Eze 34: 4. healed *that which was sick,*
16. strengthen *that which was sick:*
Mal. 1: 8. if ye offer the lame *and sick,*
13. the lame, and *the sick;*

✻ NIPHAL.—*Preterite.* ✻

Jer. 12:13. *they have put themselves to pain,*
Dan 8:27. *and was sick* (certain) days;
Am. 6: 6. but *they are* not *grieved*

NIPHAL.—*Participle.*

Isa. 17:11. harvest (shall be) a heap in the day of *grief*
Jer. 10:19. my wound *is grievous:*
14:17. with a very *grievous* blow.
30:12. thy wound (is) *grievous.*
Eze.34: 4. *The diseased* have ye not strengthened,
21. pushed all *the diseased* with your horns,
Nah 3:19. thy wound *is grievous:*

✻ PIEL.—*Preterite.* ✻

Deu 29:22(21). which the Lord *hath laid* upon it;
1Sa.13:12. *I have* not *made supplication* (marg. *intreated* the face)
2Ch 33:12. in affliction, *he besought* the Lord
Job 11:19. *yea,* many *shall make suit* unto thee. (marg. *intreat* thy face)
Ps.119:58. *I intreated* thy favour with (my)
Dan 9:13. yet *made we* not *our prayer* (marg. *intreated we* not the face, &c.)

PIEL.—*Infinitive.*

Ps. 77:10(11). I said, This (is) *my infirmity:*
Zec. 7: 2. Regemmelech, and their men, *to pray* (marg. *to intreat* the face of)
8:21. *to pray* before the Lord, (marg. *id.*)
22. Lord of hosts in Jerusalem, *and to pray* before the Lord.

PIEL.—*Imperative.*

1K. 13: 6. *Intreat* now the face of the Lord
Mal. 1: 9. *beseech* God that he will be gracious

PIEL.—*Future.*

Ex. 32:11. *And* Moses *besought* the Lord
1K. 13: 6. *And* the man of God *besought* the Lord,
2K. 13: 4. *And* Jehoahaz *besought* the Lord,
Ps. 45:12(13). the rich among the people *shall intreat*
Pro.19: 6. Many *will intreat* the favour of the prince:
Jer.26:19. *and besought* the Lord,

✻ PUAL.—*Preterite.* ✻

Isa. 14:10. *Art* thou also *become weak* as we?

✻ HIPHIL.—*Preterite.* ✻

Isa. 53:10. *he hath put* (him) *to grief:*
Hos 7: 5. the princes *have made* (him) *sick*
Mic 6:13. Therefore also *will I make* (thee) *sick*

HIPHIL.—*Participle.*

Pro.13:12. Hope deferred *maketh* the heart *sick:*

✻ HOPHAL.—*Preterite.* ✻

1K. 22:34. carry me out of the host; for *I am wounded* (marg. *made sick*)
2Ch 18:33. for *I am wounded* (marg. *made sick*)
35:23. for *I am* sore *wounded.* (marg. *made sick*)

✻ HITHPAEL.—*Infinitive.* ✻

2Sa 13: 2. *that he fell sick* for his sister Tamar;

HITHPAEL.—*Imperative.*

2Sa 13: 5. *and make thyself sick:*

HITHPAEL.—*Future.*

2Sa 13: 6. Amnon lay down, *and made himself sick:*

חַלָּה *g̣hal-lāh'*, f.

Ex. 29: 2. unleavened bread, *and cakes*
23. *and* one *cake of* oiled bread,
Lev. 2: 4. unleavened *cakes of* fine flour
7:12. unleavened *cakes* mingled with oil,
— and *cakes* mingled with oil,
13. Besides *the cakes,* he shall offer
8:26. he took one unleavened *cake, and a cake of* oiled bread,
24: 5. bake twelve *cakes* thereof: two tenth deals shall be in one *cake.*
Nu. 6:15. *cakes* of fine flour mingled with oil,
19. *and* one unleavened *cake*
15:20. Ye shall offer up *a cake* of the first
2Sa. 6:19. to every one *a cake of* bread,

חֲלוֹם *g̣hălōhm*, m. 2472

Gen20: 3. to Abimelech *in a dream* by night,
6. And God said unto him *in a dream,*
31:10. and saw *in a dream,* and, behold,
11. spake unto me *in a dream,*
24. came to Laban the Syrian *in a dream*
37: 5. Joseph dreamed *a dream,*
6. this *dream* which I have dreamed:
8. hated him yet the more for *his dreams,*
9. he dreamed yet another *dream,*
— Behold, I have dreamed *a dream*
10. What (is) this *dream* that thou hast dreamed?
19. Behold, this *dreamer* cometh. (marg. master of *dreams*)
20. see what will become of *his dreams.*
40: 5. they dreamed *a dream* both of them, each man *his dream* in one night,
— according to the interpretation of *his dream,*
8. We have dreamed *a dream,*
9. the chief butler told *his dream*
— *In my dream,* behold, a vine
16. I also (was) *in my dream,*
41: 7. Pharaoh awoke, and, behold, (it was) *a dream.*
8. Pharaoh told them *his dream;*
11. we dreamed *a dream* in one night,
— according to the interpretation of *his dream.*
12. he interpreted to us *our dreams;* to each man *according to his dream*
15. I have dreamed *a dream,*
— thou canst understand *a dream*
17. *In my dream,* behold, I stood
22. I saw *in my dream,*
25. *The dream of* Pharaoh (is) one:
26. seven years: *the dream* (is) one.
32. for that *the dream* was doubled
42: 9. Joseph remembered *the dreams*
Nu. 12: 6. will speak unto him *in a dream.*
Deu 13: 1(2). or a dreamer of *dreams,*
3(4), 5(6). or that dreamer of *dreams:*
Jud. 7:13. a man that told *a dream* unto his fellow, and said, Behold, I dreamed *a dream,*
15. Gideon heard the telling of *the dream,*
1Sa 28: 6. neither *by dreams,* nor by Urim,
15. neither by prophets, nor *by dreams:*
1K. 3: 5. the Lord appeared to Solomon *in a dream*
15. Solomon awoke; and, behold, (it was) *a dream.*
Job 7:14. Then thou scarest me *with dreams,*
20: 8. He shall fly away *as a dream,*
33:15. *In a dream,* in a vision of the night,
Ps. 73:20. *As a dream* when (one) awaketh;
Ecc. 5: 3(2). *a dream* cometh through the multitude
7(6). in the multitude of *dreams* and many words
Isa. 29: 7. shall be *as a dream of* a night
Jer. 23:27. to forget my name *by their dreams*
28. The prophet that hath *a dream,* let him tell *a dream;*
32. against them that prophesy false *dreams,*
27: 9. nor to *your dreamers,* (marg. *dreams*)
29: 8. neither hearken to *your dreams*
Dan 1:17. understanding in all visions *and dreams*
2: 1. Nebuchadnezzar dreamed *dreams.*

Dan 2: 2. for to shew the king *his dreams.*
3. I have dreamed *a dream*, and my spirit was troubled to know *the dream.*
Joel 2:28(3:1). your old men shall dream *dreams*,
Zec. 10: 2. *and* have told false *dreams;*

2474 **חַלּוֹן** *ghal-lohn'*, com.

Gen 8: 6. that Noah opened *the window of* the ark
26: 8. looked out at *a window*,
Jos. 2:15. by a cord through *the window:*
18. scarlet thread *in the window*
21. bound the scarlet line *in the window.*
Jud. 5:28. The mother of Sisera looked out at *a window*,
1 Sa. 19:12. David down through *a window:*
2 Sa. 6:16. looked through *a window*,
1 K. 6: 4. he made *windows of* narrow lights.
2 K. 9:30. looked out at *a window.*
32. he lifted up his face to *the window*,
13:17. Open *the window* eastward.
1 Ch 15:29. looking out at *a window*
Pro. 7: 6. For *at the window* of my house
Cant. 2: 9. he looketh forth at *the windows*,
Jer. 9:21(20). death is come up *into our windows*,
22:14. cutteth him out *windows;* (marg. or, *my windows*)
Eze. 40:16. *And* (there were) narrow *windows*
— *and windows* (were) round about
22. *And their windows*, and their arches,
25. *And* (there were) *windows*
— round about, *like* those *windows:*
29. *and* (there were) *windows* in it
33. *and* (there were) *windows*
36. *and the windows* to it round about.
41:16. door posts, *and the* narrow *windows*,
— from the ground up to *the windows, and the windows* (were) covered;
26. *And* (there were) narrow *windows*
Joel 2: 9. they shall enter in at *the windows*
Zep. 2:14. voice shall sing *in the windows;*

2475 **חֲלוֹף** *ghălohph*, m.

Pro. 31: 8. all such as are appointed to *destruction.* (lit. the sons of *leaving behind*)

2476 **חֲלוּשָׁה** *ghăloo-shah'*, f.

Ex. 32:18. the voice of (them that) cry for *being overcome:* (marg. *weakness*)

2479 **חַלְחָלָה** *ghal-ghah-lah'*, f.

Isa. 21: 3. are my loins filled with *pain:*
Eze. 30: 4. *great pain* shall be in Ethiopia, (marg. or, *fear*)
9. *great pain* shall come upon them,
Nah 2:10(11). *and much pain* (is) in all loins,

2480 **חָלַט** [*ghah-lat'*].

* HIPHIL.—*Future.* *

1 K. 20:33. from him, and did hastily *catch* (it): (lit. did haste *and catch* (it))

2481 **חֲלִי** *ghălee*, m.

Pro. 25:12. *and an ornament of* fine gold,
Cant. 7: 1(2). the joints of thy thighs (are) like *jewels*,

2483 **חֳלִי** *ghŏlee*, m.

Deu 7:15. take away from thee all *sickness*,
28:59. long continuance, *and* sore *sicknesses*,
61. Also every *sickness*, and every plague,
1 K. 17:17. *his sickness* was so sore,
2 K. 1: 2. whether I shall recover *of* this *disease.*
2 K. 8: 8, 9. Shall I recover *of* this *disease?*
13:14. Elisha was fallen sick of *his sickness*
2 Ch 16:12. until *his disease* (was) exceeding (great): yet *in his disease* he sought not
21:15. thou (shalt have) great *sickness*
— bowels fall out by reason of *the sickness*
18. his bowels with *an* incurable *disease.*
19. bowels fell out by reason of *his sickness:*
Ps. 41: 3(4). wilt make all his bed *in his sickness.*
Ecc. 5:17(16). sorrow and wrath *with his sickness.*
6: 2. *and* it (is) *an* evil *disease.*
Isa. 1: 5. the whole head *is sick*,
38: 9. was recovered *of his sickness:*
53: 3. sorrows, and acquainted with *grief:*
4. he hath borne *our griefs*,
Jer. 6: 7. before me continually (is) *grief*
10:19. Truly this (is) *a grief*,
Hos. 5:13. When Ephraim saw *his sickness*,

חֶלְיָה [*ghel-yah'*], f. 2484

Hos. 2:13(15). her earrings *and her jewels*,

חָלִיל *ghah-leel'*, m. 2485

1 Sa. 10: 5. a tabret, *and a pipe*,
1 K. 1:40. the people piped *with pipes*,
Isa. 5:12. the tabret, *and pipe*,
30:29. as when one goeth *with a pipe*
Jer. 48:36. shall sound for Moab *like pipes*, and mine heart shall sound *like pipes*

חָלִילָה *ghah-lee'-lah'*, interj. 2486

Gen 18:25, 25. That *be far* from thee
44: 7. *God forbid* that thy servants
17. *God forbid* that I should do so:
Jos. 22:29. *God forbid* that we should rebel
24:16. *God forbid* that we should forsake
1 Sa. 2:30. *Be it far* from me;
12:23. *God forbid* that I should sin
14:45. *God forbid:* (as) the Lord liveth,
20: 2. he said unto him, *God forbid;*
9. Jonathan said, *Far be it* from thee:
22:15. *be it far* from me:
24: 6(7) & 26:11. The Lord *forbid* that I should
2 Sa. 20:20. Joab answered and said, *Far be it, far be it* from me,
23:17. he said, *Be it far* from me,
1 K. 21: 3. The Lord *forbid* it me,
1 Ch 11:19. My God *forbid* it me,
Job 27: 5. *God forbid* that I should
34:10. *far be it* from God,

חֲלִיפָה [*ghălee-phah'*], f. 2487

Gen 45:22. he gave each man *changes of* raiment;
— five *changes of* raiment.
Jud. 14:12, 13. thirty *change of* garments:
19. and gave *change of* garments unto
1 K. 5:14(28). ten thousand a month *by courses:*
2 K. 5: 5. ten *changes of* raiment.
22, 23. two *changes of* garments.
Job 10:17. *changes* and war (are) against me.
14:14. will I wait, till *my change* come.
Ps. 55:19(20). Because they have no *changes*,

חֲלִיצָה [*ghălee-tzah'*], f. 2488

Jud. 14:19. slew thirty men of them, and took *their spoil*, (marg. or, *apparel*)
2 Sa. 2:21. take thee *his armour.* (marg. or, *spoil*)

חֶלְכָה *gheh-l'chah'*, adj. 2489

Ps. 10: 8. his eyes are privily set *against the poor.*
10. (כתיב) that *the poor* may fall
14. *the poor* committeth himself unto thee;

2490 **חָלַל** *'g'hāh-lal'.*

* KAL.—*Preterite.* *

Ps.109:22. my heart *is wounded* within me.

KAL.—*Participle.* Poel.

Ps. 87: 7. *as the players on instruments*

* NIPHAL.—*Preterite.* *

Eze. 7:24. *and* their holy places *shall be defiled.* (marg. or, *they shall inherit,* [as from נָחַל])
22:16. *And thou shalt take thine inheritance* ([as from נָחַל] marg. or, *be profaned*)
25: 3. my sanctuary, when *it was profaned;*

NIPHAL.—*Infinitive.*

Lev.21: 4. his people, *to profane himself.*
Eze.20: 9, 14, 22. that *it should* not *be polluted*

NIPHAL.—*Future.*

Lev.21: 9. if *she profane herself*
Isa. 48:11. how *should* (my name) *be polluted?*
Eze.22:26. *and I am profaned* among them.

* PIEL.—*Preterite.* *

Gen49: 4. then *defiledst thou* (it):
Lev.19: 8. *he hath profaned* the hallowed thing
12. *neither shalt thou profane* the name
Deu20: 6. hath planted a vineyard, and *hath* not (yet) *eaten of it?* (marg. *made it common*)
Ps. 55:20(21). *he hath broken* his covenant. (marg. *profaned*)
74: 7. *they have defiled* (by casting down) the
89:39(40). *thou hast profaned* his crown
Isa. 47: 6. *I have polluted* mine inheritance,
Jer. 31: 5. *and shall eat* (them) *as common things.* (marg. *profane* (them))
Lam. 2: 2. *he hath polluted* the kingdom
Eze. 7:21. *and they shall pollute it.*
22. *and they shall pollute*
— robbers shall enter into it, *and defile it.*
20:13. my sabbaths *they* greatly *polluted:*
16. but *polluted* my sabbaths:
21. *they polluted* my sabbaths:
24. and *had polluted* my sabbaths,
22: 8. *hast profaned* my sabbaths.
23:38. *have profaned* my sabbaths.
28: 7. *and they shall defile* thy brightness.
18. *Thou hast defiled* thy sanctuaries
36:21. Israel *had profaned* among the heathen,
22. which *ye have profaned* among the heathen,
23. which *ye have profaned* in the midst of them;
Dan 11:31. *and they shall pollute* the sanctuary
Zep. 3: 4. her priests *have polluted*
Mal. 2:11. *hath profaned* the holiness of the Lord

PIEL.—*Infinitive.*

Lev.20: 3. *and to profane* my holy name.
1Ch 5: 1. *but, forasmuch as he defiled*
Neh13:18. *by profaning* the sabbath.
Isa. 23: 9. *to stain* the pride of all glory, (marg. *pollute*)
56: 2, 6. keepeth the sabbath *from polluting it,*
Jer. 16:18. because *they have defiled* my land,
Eze.23:39. into my sanctuary *to profane it;*
44: 7. *to pollute it,* (even) my house,
Am. 2: 7. *to profane* my holy name:
Mal. 2:10. *by profaning* the covenant

PIEL.—*Future.*

Ex. 20:25. thy tool upon it, *thou hast polluted it.*
Lev.18:21. neither *shalt thou profane* the name
19:29. *Do* not *prostitute* thy daughter, (marg. *profane*)
21: 6. unto their God, and not *profane*
12. out of the sanctuary, nor *profane*
15. Neither *shall he profane* his seed
23. that *he profane* not my sanctuaries:
22: 2. that *they profane* not my holy name
9. if *they profane it:*
15. *they shall* not *profane* the holy things
32. Neither *shall ye profane* my holy name;
Nu. 18:32. neither *shall ye pollute* the holy things
Deu20: 6. another man *eat of it.*
28:30. *shalt* not *gather the grapes thereof.* (marg. *profane,* or, *use it as common meat*)

Ps. 89:31(32). If *they break* my statutes,
34(35). My covenant *will I* not *break,*
Isa. 43:28. *Therefore I have profaned* the princes
Jer. 34:16. But ye turned *and polluted* my name,
Eze.13:19. *And will ye pollute* me among my people
20:39. *pollute ye* my holy name no more
22:26. *and have profaned* mine holy things:
28:16. *therefore I will cast thee as profane*
36:20. *And* when they entered...*they profaned*

PIEL.—*Participle.*

Ex. 31:14. every one *that defileth it*
Lev.21: 9. *she profaneth* her father:
1K. 1:40. the people *piped* with pipes,
Neh 13:17. *and profane* the sabbath
Eze.24:21. I *will profane* my sanctuary,
28: 9. in the hand of him *that slayeth thee.* (marg. or, *woundeth*)
Mal. 1:12. But ye *have profaned* it,

* PUAL.—*Participle.* *

Eze.32:26. *slain by* the sword,
36:23. *which was profaned* among the heathen,

* POEL.—*Participle.* *

Isa. 51: 9. that hath cut Rahab, (and) *wounded* the dragon?

* POAL.—*Participle.* *

Isa. 53: 5. he (was) *wounded* (marg. or, *tormented*) for our transgressions,

* HIPHIL.—*Preterite.* *

Gen 6: 1. when men *began* to multiply
10: 8. *he began* to be a mighty one
44:12. he searched, (and) *began* at the eldest,
Nu. 16:46(17:11). the plague *is begun.*
47(—:12). the plague *was begun* among
Deu 2:31. *I have begun* to give Sihon
3:24. *thou hast begun* to shew thy servant
Jud.20:39. Benjamin *began* to smite
40. when the flame *began* to arise
1Sa. 3: 2. his eyes *began* to wax dim,
14:35. the same was the *first* altar that he built (marg. that altar *he began* to build)
22:15. *Did I* then *begin* to enquire of God
2K. 10:32. the Lord *began* to cut Israel short:
15:37. In those days the Lord *began* to send
1Ch 1:10. *he began* to be mighty upon the earth.
27:24. Joab the son of Zeruiah *began* to number,
2Ch 20:22. when *they began* to sing and to praise,
29:27. when the burnt offering *began,* the song of the Lord *began*
31: 7. *they began* to lay the foundation
21. in every work that *he began*
34: 3. *he began* to seek after the God of David
— in the twelfth year *he began*
Ezr. 3: 6. *began* they to offer burnt offerings
8. *began* Zerubbabel the son of
Neh 4: 7(1). that the breaches *began* to be stopped,
Est. 6:13. before whom *thou hast begun* to fall,
9:23. the Jews undertook to do as *they had begun.*

HIPHIL.—*Infinitive.*

Gen11: 6. this *they begin* to do:
Deu16: 9. *from* (such time as) thou *beginnest*
1Sa. 3:12. *when I begin,* I will also make an end. (marg. *beginning*)
2Ch 31:10. *Since* (the people) *began* to bring

HIPHIL.—*Imperative.*

Deu 2:24. *begin* to possess
31. his land before thee: *begin* to possess,

HIPHIL.—*Future.*

Gen 9:20. *And* Noah *began* (to be) an husbandman,
41:54. *And* the seven years of dearth *began* to come,
Nu. 25: 1. *and* the people *began* to commit whoredom
30: 2(3). *he shall* not *break* his word, (marg. *profane*)
Deu 2:25. This day *will I begin* to put
16: 9. *begin* to number the seven weeks
Jos. 3: 7. This day *will I begin* to magnify
Jud.10:18. What man (is he) that *will begin*
13: 5. *he shall begin* to deliver Israel
25. *And* the Spirit of the Lord *began* to move
16:19. *and she began* to afflict him,

Jud 16:22. *Howbeit* the hair of his head *began*
20:31. *and they began* to smite
2Ch 3: 1. *Then* Solomon *began* to build
2. *And he began* to build
29:17. *Now they began* on the first
Eze. 9: 6. and *begin* at my sanctuary. *Then they began* at the ancient
39: 7. *I will* not (let them) *pollute* my holy name
Hos. 8:10. *and they shall sorrow* a little (marg. or, *begin*)
Jon. 3: 4. *And* Jonah *began* to enter

HIPHIL.—*Participle.*

Jer. 25:29. I *begin* to bring evil on the city

* HOPHAL.—*Preterite.* *

Gen 4:26. then *began men* (lit. *was begun*) to call upon the

---

2491 **חָלָל** *ghāh-lāhl'*, adj.

Gen34:27. of Jacob came upon *the slain*,
Lev.21: 7. shall not take a wife (that is) a whore, *or profane;*
14. a divorced woman, *or profane*,
Nu. 19:16. toucheth *one that is slain with* a sword
18. *or one slain*, or one dead,
23:24. drink the blood of *the slain*.
31: 8. beside the rest of *them that were slain;*
19. whosoever hath touched *any slain*,
Deu21: 1. If (one) be found *slain* in the land
2. round about him *that is slain:*
3. next unto *the slain man*,
6. next unto *the slain* (man),
32:42. with the blood of *the slain*
Jos 11: 6. deliver them up all *slain* before Israel:
13:22. among *them that were slain by them.*
Jud. 9:40. many were overthrown (and) *wounded*,
16:24. *slew* many *of us.* (marg. multiplied *our slain*)
20:31. began to smite of the people, (and) *kill*, (marg. *wounded*)
39. began to smite (and) *kill* (marg. *the wounded*)
1Sa.17:52. *the wounded of* the Philistines
31: 1. fell down *slain* in mount Gilboa. (marg. or, *wounded*)
8. the Philistines came to strip *the slain*,
2Sa. 1:19. The beauty of Israel is *slain*
22. From the blood of *the slain*,
25. O Jonathan, (thou wast) *slain*
23: 8. *whom he slew* at one time. (marg. *slain*)
18. against three hundred, (and) *slew* (them),
1K. 11:15. was gone up to bury *the slain*,
1Ch 5:22. For there fell down many *slain*,
10: 1. fell down *slain* in mount Gilboa. (marg. or, *wounded*)
8. Philistines came to strip *the slain*,
11:11. *slain* (by him) at one time.
20. three hundred, *he slew* (them),
2Ch 13:17. so there fell down *slain*
Job 24:12. the soul of *the wounded*
39:30. where *the slain* (are),
Ps. 69:26(27). *those whom thou hast wounded.* (marg. *thy wounded*)
88: 5(6). like *the slain* that lie in the grave,
89:10(11). *as one that is slain;*
Pro 7:26. hath cast down many *wounded:*
Isa. 22: 2. *thy slain* (men are) not *slain with* the sword,
34: 3. *Their slain also* shall be cast
66:16. *the slain of* the Lord shall be many.
Jer. 9: 1(8:23). for *the slain of* the daughter of my people!
14:18. then behold *the slain with* the sword!
25:33. *the slain of* the Lord shall be
41: 9. filled it with *them that were slain.*
51: 4. Thus *the slain* shall fall in the land of the Chaldeans,
47. all *her slain* shall fall in the midst
49. Babylon (hath caused) *the slain of* Israel
— shall fall *the slain of* all the earth.
52. her land *the wounded* shall groan.
Lam 2:12. when they swooned *as the wounded* in the streets
Lam. 4: 9. *They that be slain with* the sword are better than *they that be slain with* hunger:
Eze. 6: 4. I will cast down *your slain*
7. *the slain* shall fall in the midst
13. *their slain* (men) shall be among
9: 7. fill the courts with *the slain:*
11: 6. Ye have multiplied *your slain*
— filled the streets thereof with *the slain.*
7. *Your slain* whom ye have laid
21:14(19). the sword of *the slain:* it (is) the sword of the great men *that are slain*,
25(30). thou, *profane* wicked prince of Israel,
29(34). the necks of *them that are slain, of*
26:15. when *the wounded* cry,
28: 8. the deaths of *them that are slain*
23. *the wounded* shall be judged
30: 4. when *the slain* shall fall in Egypt,
11. fill the land with *the slain.*
24. the groanings of *a deadly wounded*
31:17. unto *them that be slain with* the sword;
18. with *them that be slain by* the sword.
32:20. midst of *them that are slain by*
21. uncircumcised, *slain by* the sword.
22, 23, 24. all of them *slain*, fallen by the sword:
25. a bed in the midst of *the slain*
— uncircumcised, *slain by* the sword:
— is put in the midst of *them that be slain.*
28. lie with *them that are slain with* the sword.
29. laid by *them that were slain by* the sword:
30. gone down with *the slain;*
— with *them that be slain by* the
31. Pharaoh and all his army *slain by* the
32. with *them that are slain with*
35: 8. fill his mountains with *his slain*
— fall that *are slain with* the sword.
Dan 11:26. many shall fall down *slain.*
Nah 3: 3. a multitude of *slain*,
Zep 2:12. Ethiopians also, ye (shall be) *slain by*

חָלַם *ghāh-lam'*. 2492

* KAL.—*Preterite.* *

Gen37: 6. this dream which *I have dreamed:*
9. *I have dreamed* a dream more;
10. this dream that *thou hast dreamed?*
40: 8. *We have dreamed* a dream,
41:11. *we dreamed* each man according
15. *I have dreamed* a dream,
42: 9. dreams which *he dreamed* of them,
Jud. 7:13. said, Behold, *I dreamed* a dream,
Jer. 23:25. *I have dreamed, I have dreamed.*
Dan 2: 1. Nebuchadnezzar *dreamed* dreams,
3. *I have dreamed* a dream,

KAL.—*Future.*

Gen28:12. *And he dreamed*, and behold a ladder
37: 5. *And* Joseph *dreamed* a dream,
9. *And he dreamed* yet another
40: 5. *And they dreamed* a dream
41: 5. he slept *and dreamed* the second time:
11. *And we dreamed* a dream
Isa. 29: 8. as when an hungry (man) *dreameth*,
— as when a thirsty man *dreameth*,
Joel 2:28(3:1). your old men *shall dream*

KAL.—*Participle.* Poel.

Gen41: 1. that Pharaoh *dreamed:*
Deu13: 1(2). prophet, or *a dreamer of* dreams,
3(4). that prophet, or that *dreamer of* dreams:
5(6). that prophet, or that *dreamer of* dreams,
Ps.126: 1. we were *like them that dream.*

* HIPHIL.—*Participle.* *

Jer.29: 8. which ye *cause to be dreamed.*

חָלַם [*ghāh-lam'*]. 2492

* KAL.—*Future.* *

Job 39: 4. Their young ones *are in good liking*,

* HIPHIL.—*Future.* *

Isa. 38:16. *so wilt thou recover me*,

2493 חֵלֶם *g'heh'-lem*, Ch. m.

Dan. 2: 4. tell thy servants *the dream*, and
5. if ye will not make known unto me *the dream*,
6. But if ye shew *the dream*,
— therefore shew me *the dream*,
7. Let the king tell his servants *the dream*,
9. not make known unto me *the dream*,
— therefore tell me *the dream*,
26. Art thou able to make known unto me *the dream*
28. *Thy dream*, and the visions of thy head
36. This (is) *the dream;* and we will tell the
45. and *the dream* (is) certain, and the
4: 5(2). I saw *a dream* which made me afraid,
6(3). known unto me the interpretation of *the dream.*
7(4). *and* I told *the dream* before them;
8(5). *and* before him I told *the dream*,
9(6). tell me the visions of *my dream* that I have seen,
18(15). This *dream* I king Nebuchadnezzar
19(16). let not *the dream*, or the interpretation
—(—). *the dream* (be) to them that hate thee,
5:12. interpreting of *dreams*, and
7: 1. Daniel had *a dream*
— then he wrote *the dream*,

2495 חַלָּמוּת *g'hal-lah-mooth'*, f.

Job 6: 6. taste in the white of *an egg?*

2496 חַלָּמִישׁ *g'hal-lah-meesh'*, m.

Deu. 8:15. water out of the rock of *flint;*
32:13. oil *out of the flinty* rock;
Job 28: 9. putteth forth his hand *upon the rock;* (marg. or, *flint*)
Ps. 114: 8. *the flint* into a fountain of waters.
Isa. 50: 7. therefore have I set my face *like a flint*,

2498 חָלַף *g'hah-laph'.*

* KAL.—*Preterite.* *

Jud. 5:26. she had pierced *and stricken through*
1Sa. 10: 3. *Then shalt thou go on forward*
Job 9:26. *They are passed away* as the swift ships:
Ps. 90: 6. it flourisheth, *and groweth up;*
Cant 2:11. the rain *is over*
Isa. 8: 8. *And he shall pass* through Judah;
24: 5. they have transgressed the laws, *changed*
Hab 1:11. Then *shall* (his) mind *change*,

KAL.—*Infinitive.*

Isa. 21: 1. whirlwinds in the south *pass through;*

KAL.—*Future.*

Job 4:15. Then a spirit *passed* before my face;
9:11. *he passeth on also*, but I perceive
11:10. If *he cut off*, and shut up,
20:24. the bow of steel *shall strike him through.*
Ps. 90: 5. like grass (which) *groweth up.* (marg. or, *is changed*)
102:26(27). *and they shall be changed:*
Isa. 2:18. the idols *he shall* utterly *abolish.* (marg. or, *shall* utterly *pass away*)

* PIEL.—*Future.* *

Gen41:14. *and changed* his raiment,
2Sa 12:20. *and changed* his apparel,

* HIPHIL.—*Preterite.* *

Gen31: 7. *and changed* my wages ten times;

HIPHIL.—*Imperative.*

Gen35: 2. be clean, *and change* your garments:

HIPHIL.—*Future.*

Gen31:41. *and thou hast changed* my wages
Lev.27:10. *He shall* not *alter it*,
Job 14: 7. that *it will sprout* again,
Job 29:20. my bow *was renewed* in my hand. (marg. *changed*)
Ps.102:26(27). as a vesture *shalt thou change them*,
Isa. 9:10(9). *we will change* (them into) cedars.
40:31. *shall renew* (their) strength; (marg. *change*)
41: 1. *let* the people *renew* (their) strength:

חֲלַף [*g'halaph*], Ch. 2499

* P'AL.—*Future.* *

Dan 4:16(13). *let* seven times *pass* over him.
23(20). till seven times *pass* over him;
25(22), 32(29). and seven times *shall pass*

חֵלֶף *g'heh'-leph*, m. 2500

Nu. 18:21. *for* their service which they serve, (lit. *the exchange of*)
31. *for* your service in the tabernacle

חָלַץ *g'hah-latz'.* 2502

* KAL.—*Preterite.* *

Deu 25: 9. *and loose* his shoe from off his foot,
Lam. 4: 3. the sea monsters *draw out* the breast,
Hos 5: 6. *he hath withdrawn himself*

KAL.—*Future.*

Isa. 20: 2. *put off* thy shoe from thy foot.

KAL.—*Participle.* Paül.

Nu. 31: 5. twelve thousand *armed for* war.
32:21. go all of you *armed* over Jordan
27. every man *armed for* war,
29. every man *armed to* battle,
30. pass over with you *armed*,
32. We will pass over *armed*
Deu 3:18. ye shall pass over *armed*
25:10. The house of him *that hath* his shoe *loosed.*
Jos. 4:13. forty thousand *prepared for* war (marg. or, *ready armed*)
6: 7. *and* let *him that is armed* pass
9, 13. *And the armed men* went
1Ch 12:23. bands (that were) *ready armed*
24. *ready armed to* the war. (marg. or, *prepared*)
2Ch 17:18. an hundred and fourscore thousand *ready prepared for*
20:21. they went out before *the army*,
28:14. So *the armed men* left the captives
Isa. 15: 4. *the armed soldiers of* Moab

* NIPHAL.—*Preterite.* *

Pro.11: 8. The righteous *is delivered*

NIPHAL.—*Imperative.*

Nu. 31: 3. *Arm* some of yourselves unto the war,

NIPHAL.—*Future.*

Nu. 32:17. we ourselves *will go* ready *armed*
20. if *ye will go armed* before
Ps. 60: 5(7). That thy beloved *may be delivered;*
108: 6(7). That thy beloved *may be delivered:*
Pro.11: 9. through knowledge *shall* the just *be delivered.*

* PIEL.—*Preterite.* *

Lev.14:40. *that they take away* the stones
43. after that *he hath taken away*
Ps.116: 8. For *thou hast delivered* my soul

PIEL.—*Imperative.*

Ps. 6: 4(5). Return, O Lord, *deliver* my soul:
119:153. Consider mine affliction, *and deliver me:*
140: 1(2). *Deliver me*, O Lord, from the evil

PIEL.—*Future.*

2Sa.22:20. *he delivered me*, because he
Job 36:15. *He delivereth* the poor
Ps. 7: 4(5). *yea, I have delivered* him
18:19(20). *he delivered me*,
34: 7(8). that fear him, *and delivereth them.*
50:15. in the day of trouble: *I will deliver thee*,
81: 7(8). calledst in trouble, *and I delivered thee;*
91:15. in trouble; *I will deliver him*,

* HIPHIL.—*Future.* *

Isa. 58:11. the Lord shall guide thee...and *make fat* thy bones:

2504 חֲלָצַיִם [ghălāh-tzah'-yim], f. dual.

Gen35:11. kings shall come out *of thy loins;*
1K. 8:19. son that shall come forth *out of thy loins,*
2Ch 6: 9. which shall come forth *out of thy loins,*
Job 31:20. If *his loins* have not blessed me,
38: 3. Gird up now *thy loins* like a man;
40: 7. Gird up *thy loins* now
Isa. 5:27. the girdle of *their loins* be loosed,
11: 5. faithfulness the girdle of *his reins.*
32:11. gird (sackcloth) upon (your) *loins.*
Jer. 30: 6. every man with his hands on *his loins,*

2505 חָלַק ghāh-lak'.

* KAL.—*Preterite.* *

Deu 4:19. which the Lord thy God *hath divided* (marg. or, *imparted*)
29:26(25). *he had* not *given* unto them: (marg. *divided*)
Jos. 18: 2. *had* not yet *received* their inheritance.
2Ch 23:18. whom David *had distributed*
28:21. For Ahaz *took away a portion*
Job 39:17. neither *hath he imparted* to her
Ps. 55:21(22). (The words) of his mouth *were smoother* than butter,
Hos 10: 2. Their heart *is divided;*

KAL.—*Infinitive.*

Neh 13:13. *to distribute* unto their brethren.

KAL.—*Imperative.*

Jos. 22: 8. *divide* the spoil of your enemies

KAL.—*Future.*

Jos. 14: 5. *and they divided* the land.
1Sa. 30:24. by the stuff: *they shall part* alike.
2Sa. 19:29(30). Thou and Ziba *divide* the land.
1Ch 24: 4. *and* (thus) *were they divided.*
5. *Thus were they divided*
Neh 9:22. *and didst divide them*
Job 27:17. and the innocent *shall divide* the silver.
Pro. 17: 2. and *shall have part* of the inheritance

KAL.—*Participle.* Poel.

Pro. 29:24. *Whoso is partner* with a thief

* NIPHAL.—*Future.* *

Gen14:15. *And he divided himself*
Nu. 26:53. Unto these the land *shall be divided*
55. the land *shall be divided* by lot:
56. *shall* the possession thereof *be divided*
1K. 16:21. Then *were* the people of Israel *divided*
1Ch 23: 6. *And* David *divided them*
24: 3. *And* David *distributed them,*
Job 38:24. By what way *is* the light *parted,*

* PIEL.—*Preterite.* *

Isa. 34:17. his hand *hath divided it*
Lam. 4:16. the Lord *hath divided them;*
Eze. 5: 1. *and divide* the (hair).
47:21. *So shall ye divide*
Joel 3: 2(4:2). whom they have...*parted* my land.

PIEL.—*Infinitive.*

Jos. 19:51. So they made an end *of dividing*
Pro. 16:19. *than to divide* the spoil
Isa. 9: 3(2). rejoice *when they divide* the spoil.

PIEL.—*Imperative.*

Jos. 13: 7. Now therefore *divide* this land

PIEL.—*Future.*

Gen49: 7. *I will divide them* in Jacob,
27. at night *he shall divide* the spoil.
Ex. 15: 9. I will overtake, *I will divide* the spoil;
Jos. 18:10. *and* there Joshua *divided* the land
Jud. 5:30. *have they* (not) *divided* the prey;
2Sa. 6:19. *And he dealt* among all the people,
1K. 18: 6. *So they divided* the land
1Ch 16: 3. *And he dealt* to every one of Israel,
Job 21:17. *distributeth* sorrows in his anger.
Ps. 22:18(19). *They part* my garments among them,
60: 6(8). *I will divide* Shechem,
68:12(13). tarried at home *divided* the spoil.
108: 7(8). *I will divide* Shechem,
Isa. 53:12. Therefore *will I divide* him
— *he shall divide* the spoil
Dan 11:39. and *shall divide* the land
Mic. 2: 4. *he hath divided* our fields.

* PUAL.—*Preterite.* *

Isa. 33:23. *is* the prey of a great spoil *divided;*
Zec. 14: 1. *and* thy spoil *shall be divided*

PUAL.—*Future.*

Am. 7:17. thy land *shall be divided*

* HIPHIL.—*Preterite.* *

Ps. 36: 2(3). *he flattereth* himself in his own eyes,
Pro. 2:16 & 7:5. the stranger (which) *flattereth*

HIPHIL.—*Infinitive.*

Jer. 37:12. *to separate himself* thence (marg. or, *slip away*)

HIPHIL.—*Future.*

Ps. 5: 9(10). *they flatter* with their tongue.

HIPHIL.—*Participle.*

Pro. 28:23. *than he that flattereth* with the tongue.
29: 5. A man *that flattereth* his neighbour
Isa. 41: 7. *he that smootheth* (with) the hammer

* HITHPAEL.—*Preterite.* *

Jos. 18: 5. *And they shall divide* it

חָלָק ghāh-lāhk', adj. 2509

Gen27:11. I (am) a *smooth* man:
Jos. 11:17 & 12:7. the mount *Halak,* (lit. *smooth* mountain)
Pro. 5: 3. *and* her mouth (is) *smoother* than oil:
26:28. a *flattering* mouth worketh ruin.
Eze. 12:24. vain vision nor *flattering* divination

חֲלָק ghălāhk, Ch. m. 2508

Ezr. 4:16. thou shalt have no *portion* on this side the river.
Dan 4:15(12), 23(20). and (let) *his portion* (be) with

חֵלֶק ghēh'-lek, m. 2506, 2511

Gen 14:24. *and the portion of* the men
— let them take *their portion.*
31:14. yet *any portion* or inheritance
Lev. 6:17(10). given it (unto them for) *their portion*
Nu. 18:20. *neither* shalt thou have *any part*
— I (am) *thy part* and thine inheritance
31:36. *the portion of* them that went
Deu 10: 9 & 12:12 & 14:27, 29 & 18:1. no *part* nor inheritance
18: 8. They shall have *like portions* to eat, (lit. *part like part*)
32: 9. the Lord's *portion* (is) his people;
Jos. 14: 4. they gave no *part* unto the Levites
15:13. he gave *a part* among the children of
18: 5. divide it into seven *parts:*
6. describe the land (into) seven *parts,*
7. But the Levites have no *part*
9. by cities into seven *parts* in a book,
19: 9. *the part of* the children of Judah
22:25, 27. ye have no *part* in the Lord:
1Sa. 30:24. *as* his *part* (is) that goeth down to the battle, *so* (shall) his *part* (be) that tarrieth
2Sa. 20: 1. We have no *part* in David,
1K. 12:16. What *portion* have we in David?
2K. 9:10. eat Jezebel *in the portion of* Jezreel,
36. *In the portion of* Jezreel shall dogs eat

2K. 9:37. the field *in the portion of* Jezreel;
2Ch 10:16. What *portion* have we in David?
Neh 2:20. but ye have no *portion*,
Job 17: 5. He that speaketh *flattery*
20:29 & 27:13. This (is) *the portion of* a wicked man.
31: 2. what *portion of* God (is there) from above?
32:17. I will answer also *my part*,
Ps. 16: 5. The Lord (is) the portion of *mine inheritance* (marg. *my part*)
17:14. (which have) *their portion* in (this) life,
50:18. hast been *partaker* with adulterers. (marg. *thy portion* (was) with)
73:26. *and my portion* for ever.
119:57. *my portion*, O Lord:
142: 5(6). Thou (art) my refuge (and) *my portion*
Pro. 7:21. *with the flattering of* her lips
Ecc. 2:10. this was *my portion* of all my labour.
21. shall he leave it (for) *his portion*.
3:22. for that (is) *his portion*:
5:18(17). for it (is) *his portion*.
19(18). to eat thereof, and to take *his portion*,
9: 6. *neither* have they any more *a portion*
9. for that (is) *thy portion*
11: 2. Give *a portion* to seven,
Isa. 17:14. This (is) *the portion of* them
57: 6. *Among the smooth* (stones) *of* the stream (is) *thy portion*;
61: 7. they shall rejoice in *their portion*:
Jer. 10:16 & 51:19. *The portion of* Jacob (is) not like
Lam. 3:24. The Lord (is) *my portion*,
Eze. 45: 7. over against one of *the portions*,
48: 8. length as one of *the* (other) *parts*,
21. over against *the portions*
Hos. 5: 7. devour them with *their portions*.
Am. 7: 4. did eat up *a part*.
Mic. 2: 4. hath changed *the portion of* my people:
Hab. 1:16. because by them *their portion* (is) fat,
Zec. 2:12(16). Judah *his portion* in the holy land,

2512 **חַלֻּק** [*ghal-look'*], adj.

1Sa. 17:40. chose him five *smooth* stones

2513 **חֶלְקָה** *ghel-kāh'*, f.

Gen 27:16. upon *the smooth of* his neck:
33:19. he bought *a parcel of* a field,
Deu 33:21. *a portion of* the lawgiver,
Jos. 24:32. *in a parcel of* ground which Jacob bought
Ru. 2: 3. was to light on *a part of* the field
4: 3. selleth *a parcel of* land,
2Sa. 2:16. that place was called *Helkath*-hazzurim, (marg. *The field of* strong men)
14:30. See, Joab's *field* is near mine,
— Absalom's servants set *the field* on fire.
31. have thy servants set my *field* on fire?
23:11. where was *a piece of* ground
12. stood in the midst of *the ground*,
2K. 3:19. mar every good *piece of land*
25. on every good *piece of land*
9:21. met him *in the portion of*
25. *in the portion of* the field of Naboth
26. I will requite thee *in* this *plat*, (marg. or, *portion*)
— (and) cast him *into the plat* (of ground),
1Ch 11:13. where was *a parcel of* ground
14. in the midst of (that) *parcel*,
Job 24:18. *their portion* is cursed in the earth:
Ps. 12: 2(3). (with) *flattering* lips (lit. of *flatteries*)
3(4). The Lord shall cut off all *flattering* lips, (lit. of *flatteries*)
73:18. thou didst set them *in slippery places*:
Pro. 6:24. *from the flattery of* the tongue
Isa. 30:10. speak unto us *smooth things*,
Jer. 12:10. they have trodden *my portion* under foot,
— made my pleasant *portion* a desolate wilderness.
Am. 4: 7. one *piece* was rained upon, *and the piece* whereupon it rained

---

2515 **חֲלֻקָּה** [*ghălook-kāh'*], f.

2Ch 35: 5. *and* (after) *the division of* the families

חֲלַקּוֹת *ghălak-kohth'*, f. pl. 2514

Dan 11:32. shall he corrupt *by flatteries*:

חֲלַקְלַקּוֹת *ghălak-lak-kohth'*, f. pl. 2519

Ps. 35: 6. Let their way be dark *and slippery*: (marg. *slipperiness*)
Jer. 23:12. way shall be unto them *as slippery* (ways)
Dan 11:21. obtain the kingdom *by flatteries*.
34. shall cleave to them *with flatteries*.

חָלַשׁ [*ghāh-lash'*]. 2522

* KAL.—*Future*. *

Ex. 17:13. *And* Joshua *discomfited* Amalek
Job 14:10. But man dieth, *and wasteth away*: (marg. *is weakened*, or, *cut off*)

KAL.—*Participle*. Poel.

Isa. 14:12. *which didst weaken* the nations!

חַלָּשׁ *ghal-lāhsh'*, m. 2523

Joel 3:10(4:10). let *the weak* say, I (am) strong.

חָם [*ghāhm*], m. 2524

Gen 38:13. *thy father in law* goeth up to Timnath
25. she sent to *her father in law*,
1Sa. 4:19. that *her father in law* and her husband
21. because of *her father in law*

חָם *ghāhm*, adj. 2525

Jos. 9:12. bread we took *hot* (for) our provision
Job 37:17. How thy garments (are) *warm*,

חֹם *ghōhm*, m. 2527

Gen 8:22. cold *and heat*, and summer
18: 1. sat in the tent door *in the heat of* the day;
1Sa. 11: 9. *by* (that time) the sun *be hot*,
11. until *the heat of* the day:
21: 6(7). to put *hot* bread in the day
2Sa. 4: 5. came *about the heat of* the day
Neh 7: 3. until the sun *be hot*;
Job 6:17. *when it is hot*, they are consumed (marg. *in the heat thereof*)
24:19. Drought and *heat* consume the snow
Isa. 18: 4. *like a* clear *heat* upon herbs,
— a cloud of dew *in the heat of* harvest.
Jer. 17: 8. shall not see when *heat* cometh,
51:39. *In their heat* I will make their
Hag. 1: 6. but there is none *warm*;

חֵמָא *ghēh-māh'*, f. 2534

Dan 11:44. go forth *with* great *fury* to destroy,

חֱמָא *ghĕmāh* & **חֲמָא** *ghămāh*, Ch. f. 2528

Dan 3:13. in (his) rage *and fury* commanded
19. Then was Nebuchadnezzar full of *fury*,

חֶמְאָה *ghem-āh'*, f. 2529

Gen 18: 8. he took *butter*, and milk,
Deu 32:14. *Butter of* kine, and milk of sheep,
Jud. 5:25. she brought forth *butter*

2Sa.17:29. honey, *and butter*, and sheep,
Job 20:17. the brooks of honey *and butter*.
Pro.30:33. churning of milk bringeth forth *butter*,
Isa. 7:15. *Butter* and honey shall he eat,
22. give he shall eat *butter*: for *butter* and honey shall every one

---

2530 חָמַד *'ghāh-mad'*.

* KAL.—*Preterite.* *

Ps. 68:16(17). the hill (which) God *desireth*
Pro. 1:22. the scorners *delight* in their scorning,
12:12. The wicked *desireth* the net
Isa. 1:29. the oaks which *ye have desired*,
Mic. 2: 2. *And they covet* fields,

KAL.—*Future.*

Ex. 20:17, 17. *Thou shalt* not *covet*
34:24. neither *shall* any man *desire*
Deu 5:21(18). Neither *shalt thou desire*
7:25. *thou shalt* not *desire* the silver
Jos. 7:21. *then I coveted them*,
Pro. 6:25. *Lust* not after her beauty
Isa. 53: 2. no beauty *that we should desire him*.

KAL.—*Participle.* Paül.

Job 20:20. save *of that which he desired*.
Ps. 39:11(12). thou makest *his beauty* to consume
Isa. 44: 9. *and their delectable things* (marg. *desirable*)

* NIPHAL.—*Participle.* *

Gen 2: 9. every tree *that is pleasant* to the sight
3: 6. *and* a tree *to be desired*
Ps. 19:10(11). *More to be desired* (are they) than
Pro.21:20. treasure *to be desired*

* PIEL.—*Preterite.* *

Cant.2: 3. *I* sat down under his shadow *with great delight*, (marg. *I delighted* and sat down)

2531 חֶמֶד *'gheh'-med*, m.

Isa. 27: 2. A vineyard of *red wine*.
32:12. lament for the teats, for the *pleasant* fields, (marg. fields of *desire*)
Eze.23: 6, 12, 23. *desirable* young men, (lit. young men of *desire*)
Am. 5:11. ye have planted *pleasant* vineyards, (marg. vineyards of *desire*)

[N.B. In Isa. 27:2, most copies read חֶמֶר.]

2532 חֶמְדָּה *'ghem-dāh'*, f.

1Sa. 9:20. on whom (is) all *the desire of* Israel?
2Ch 21:20. departed without *being desired*. (marg. *desire*)
32:27. for all manner of *pleasant* jewels; (marg. of *desire*)
36:10. with the *goodly* vessels (marg. of *desire*)
Ps.106:24. they despised the *pleasant* land, (marg. of *desire*)
Isa. 2:16. upon all *pleasant* pictures. (marg. of *desire*)
Jer. 3:19. give thee a *pleasant* land, (marg. of *desire*)
12:10. have made *my pleasant* portion a desolate (lit. the portion of *my desire*)
25:34. fall like a *pleasant* vessel. (marg. of *desire*)
Eze.26:12. destroy *thy pleasant* houses: (marg. houses of *thy desire*)
Dan 11: 8. with *their precious* vessels of silver (lit. vessels of *their desire*)
37. nor *the desire of* women,
Hos.13:15. all *pleasant* vessels. (marg. of *desire*)
Nah 2: 9(10). all the *pleasant* furniture. (marg. of *desire*)
Hag. 2: 7. *the desire of* all nations
Zec. 7:14. laid the *pleasant* land desolate. (marg. of *desire*)

See 2530 חֲמוּדָה see חֶמְדָּה

חַמָּה *'gham-māh'*, f. 2535

Job 30:28. I went mourning without *the sun*:
Ps. 19: 6(7). nothing hid *from the heat thereof*.
Cant.6:10. clear *as the sun*,
Isa. 24:23. and *the sun* ashamed,
30:26. moon shall be as the light of *the sun*, and the light of *the sun* shall be sevenfold,

---

חֵמָה *'ghēh-māh'*, f. 2534

Gen27:44. until thy brother's *fury* turn away;
Lev.26:28. Then I will walk contrary unto you also *in fury*;
Nu. 25:11. hath turned *my wrath* away
Deu 9:19. was afraid of the anger *and hot displeasure*,
29:23(22). the Lord overthrew in his anger, *and in his wrath*:
28(27). *and in wrath*, and in great
32:24. *the poison of* serpents of the dust.
33. Their wine (is) *the poison of* dragons,
2Sa.11:20. if so be that the king's *wrath* arise,
2K. 5:12. So he turned and went away *in a rage*.
22:13. great (is) *the wrath of* the Lord
17. therefore *my wrath* shall be kindled
2Ch 12: 7. *my wrath* shall not be poured out
28: 9. *because* the Lord God of your fathers *was wroth* (lit. *in the wrath of*)
34:21. great (is) *the wrath of* the Lord
25. *my wrath* shall be poured out
36:16. *the wrath of* the Lord arose
Est. 1:12. *and his anger* burned in him.
2: 1. when *the wrath of* king Ahasuerus was
3: 5. then was Haman full of *wrath*.
5: 9. he was full of *indignation* against
7: 7. from the banquet of wine *in his wrath*
10. *Then* was the king's *wrath* pacified.
Job 6: 4. *the poison whereof* drinketh up my spirit:
19:29. *wrath* (bringeth) the punishments of the
21:20. *and* he shall drink *of the wrath of* the
36:18. Because (there is) *wrath*,
Ps. 6: 1(2). chasten me *in thy hot displeasure*.
37: 8. Cease from anger, and forsake *wrath*:
38: 1(2). neither chasten me *in thy hot displeasure*.
58: 4(5). Their *poison* (is) like *the poison of* a
59:13(14). Consume (them) *in wrath*, consume (them),
76:10(11). *the wrath of* man shall praise thee: the remainder of *wrath* shalt thou
78:38. did not stir up all *his wrath*.
79: 6. Pour out *thy wrath* upon the heathen
88: 7(8). *Thy wrath* lieth hard upon me,
89:46(47). shall *thy wrath* burn like fire?
90: 7. *and by thy wrath* are we troubled.
106:23. to turn away *his wrath*,
140: 3(4). adders' *poison* (is) under their lips.
Pro. 6:34. jealousy (is) *the rage of* a man:
15: 1. A soft answer turneth away *wrath*:
18. A *wrathful* man (lit. a man of *wrath*) stirreth up strife:
16:14. *The wrath of* a king (is as) messengers of
19:19. A man of great *wrath* shall suffer
21:14. a reward in the bosom strong *wrath*.
22:24. a *furious* man (lit. a man of *wraths*)
27: 4. *Wrath* (is) cruel, and anger (is)
29:22. a *furious* man (lit. a master of *wrath*)
Isa. 27: 4. *Fury* (is) not in me:
34: 2. *and* (his) *fury* upon all their armies:
42:25. he hath poured upon him *the fury of* his
51:13. because of *the fury of* the oppressor,
— where (is) *the fury of* the oppressor?
17. of the Lord the cup of *his fury*;
20. they are full of *the fury of* the Lord,
22. the dregs of the cup of *my fury*;
59:18. *fury* to his adversaries,
63: 3. trample them *in my fury*;
5. *and my fury*, it upheld me.
6. make them drunk *in my fury*,
66:15. to render his anger *with fury*,
Jer. 4: 4. lest *my fury* come forth like fire,
6:11. I am full of *the fury of* the Lord;
7:20. mine anger *and my fury* shall be poured
10:25. Pour out *thy fury* upon the heathen
18:20. turn away *thy wrath* from them.

Jer.21: 5. even in anger, *and in fury,*
12. lest *my fury* go out like fire,
23:19. the Lord is gone forth in *fury,*
25:15. Take the wine cup of this *fury* at my
30:23. the whirlwind of the Lord goeth forth *with fury,*
32:31. provocation of mine anger and of *my fury*
37. *and in my fury,* and in great wrath;
33: 5. in mine anger *and in my fury,*
36: 7. *and the fury* that the Lord hath
42:18. *and my fury* hath been poured forth
— so shall *my fury* be poured forth upon
44: 6. *my fury* and mine anger was poured
Lam.2: 4. he poured out *his fury* like fire.
4:11. The Lord hath accomplished *his fury;*
Eze. 3:14. *in the heat of* my spirit; (marg. *hot anger*)
5:13. I will cause *my fury* to rest upon them,
— I have accomplished *my fury*
15. in anger *and in fury* and in *furious* rebukes. (lit. rebukes of *wrath*)
6:12. thus will I accomplish *my fury*
7: 8. Now will I shortly pour out *my fury*
8:18. Therefore will I also deal *in fury:*
9: 8. thy pouring out of *thy fury*
13:13. with a stormy wind *in my fury;*
— great hailstones *in* (my) *fury*
15. Thus will I accomplish *my wrath*
14:19. pour out *my fury* upon it
16:38. I will give thee blood *in fury*
42. So will I make *my fury*
19:12. she was plucked up *in fury,*
20: 8. I will pour out *my fury*
13, 21. I would pour out *my fury*
33, 34. *and with fury* poured out,
21:17(22). I will cause *my fury* to rest:
22:20. in mine anger *and in my fury,*
22. have poured out *my fury*
23:25. they shall deal *furiously* with thee:
24: 8. That it might cause *fury* to come up
13. I have caused *my fury* to rest
25:14. *according to my fury;*
17. with *furious* rebukes; (lit. rebukes of *wrath*)
30:15. I will pour *my fury* upon Sin,
36: 6. spoken in my jealousy *and in my fury,*
18. I poured *my fury* upon them
38:18. *my fury* shall come up in my face.
Dan 8: 6. *in the fury of* his power.
9:16. let thine anger *and thy fury* be turned
Hos 7: 5. sick with *bottles* (marg. *heat*) of wine;
Mic. 5:15(14). anger *and fury* upon the heathen,
Nah 1: 2. the Lord revengeth, and (is) *furious;* (lit. a master of *wrath*)
6. *his fury* is poured out like fire,
Zec. 8: 2. *and* I was jealous for her *with* great *fury.*

2529 חֶמָה *'ghĕh-māh'*, f.

Job 29: 6. When I washed my steps *with butter,*

2532 חֲמוּדוֹת *'ghămoo-dōhth'*, f. pl.

Gen27:15. Rebekah took *goodly* raiment (marg. *desirable*)
2Ch 20:25. with the dead bodies, and *precious* jewels,
Ezr. 8:27. copper, *precious* as gold. (marg. *desirable*)
Dan 9:23. for thou (art) *greatly beloved:* (marg. (a man) of *desires*)
10: 3. I ate no *pleasant* bread, (marg. bread of *desires*)
11. a man *greatly beloved,* (marg. of *desires*)
19. O man *greatly beloved,*
11:38. precious stones, *and pleasant things.* (marg. *things desired*)
43. over all *the precious things of* Egypt:

2541 חָמוֹץ *'ghāh-mōhtz'*, m.

Isa. 1:17. relieve *the oppressed,*

2542 חָמוּק [*'gham-mook'*], m.

Cant 7: 1(2). *the joints of* thy thighs (are) like jewels,

חֲמוֹר *'ghămōhr*, m. 2543

Gen12:16. and he had sheep, and oxen, *and he asses,*
22: 3. saddled *his ass,* and took two
5. Abide ye here with *the ass;*
24:35. maidservants, and camels, *and asses.*
30:43. menservants, and camels, *and asses.*
32: 5(6). I have oxen, *and asses,* flocks,
34:28. their oxen, and *their asses,*
36:24. as he fed *the asses* of Zibeon
42:26. they laded *their asses* with the corn,
27. to give *his ass* provender
43:18. take us for bondmen, and *our asses.*
24. he gave *their asses* provender.
44: 3. sent away, they *and their asses.*
13. laded every man *his ass,*
45:23. ten *asses* laden with the good things
47:17. herds, *and for the asses:*
49:14. Issachar (is) *a* strong *ass* couching
Ex. 4:20. set them upon *an ass,*
9: 3. upon the horses, *upon the asses,*
13:13. every firstling of *an ass*
20:17. nor his ox, *nor his ass,*
21:33. an ox or *an ass* fall therein;
22: 4(3). whether it be ox, or *ass,* or sheep;
9(8). for ox, for *ass,* for sheep,
10(9). deliver unto his neighbour *an ass,*
23: 4. meet thine enemy's ox or *his ass*
5. If thou see *the ass of* him that hateth thee
12. that thine ox *and thine ass* may
34:20. But the firstling of *an ass*
Nu. 16:15. I have not taken one *ass*
31:28. of the beeves, and of *the asses,*
30. of *the asses,* and of the flocks,
34. *And* threescore and one thousand *asses,*
39. *And the asses* (were) thirty thousand
45. *And* thirty thousand *asses* and five hundred,
Deu 5:14. nor thine ox, *nor thine ass,*
21(18). his ox, *or his ass,*
22: 3. shalt thou do *with his ass;*
4. see thy brother's *ass* or his ox fall
10. plow with an ox *and an ass* together.
28:31. *thine ass* (shall be) violently
Jos. 6:21. ox, and sheep, *and ass,*
7:24. his oxen, and *his asses,*
9: 4. took old sacks *upon their asses,*
15:18. she lighted off (her) *ass;*
Jud. 1:14. she lighted from off (her) *ass;*
6: 4. neither sheep, nor ox, *nor ass.*
15:15. found a new jawbone of *an ass,*
16. With the jawbone of *an ass, heaps* upon heaps, with the jaw of *an ass*
19: 3. servant with him, and a couple of *asses:*
10. with him two *asses* saddled,
19. straw and provender *for our asses;*
21. gave provender *unto the asses:*
28. the man took her (up) upon *an ass,*
1Sa. 8:16. your goodliest young men, and *your asses,*
12: 3. *or* whose *ass* have I taken?
15: 3. ox and sheep, camel and *ass.*
16:20. Jesse took *an ass* (laden) *with* bread,
22:19. oxen, *and asses,* and sheep,
25:18. laid (them) on *asses.*
20. she rode on *the ass,*
23. she hasted, and lighted off *the ass,*
42. arose, and rode upon *an ass,*
27: 9. the oxen, *and the asses,*
2Sa.16: 1. with a couple of *asses* saddled,
2. *The asses* (be) for the king's houshold
17:23. he saddled (his) *ass,* and arose,
19:26(27). I will saddle me *an ass,*
1K. 2:40. Shimei arose, and saddled *his ass,*
13:13. Saddle me *the ass.* So they saddled him *the ass:*
23. that he saddled for him *the ass,*
24. cast in the way, *and the ass* stood by it,
27. Saddle me *the ass.*
28. *and the ass* and the lion standing
— the carcase, nor torn *the ass.*
29. laid it upon *the ass,*
2K. 6:25. until an *ass's* head was (sold)
7: 7. their horses, and *their asses,*
10. horses tied, *and asses* tied,
1Ch 5:21. *and of asses* two thousand,
12:40. brought bread *on asses,*
2Ch 28:15. carried all the feeble of them *upon asses,*

Ezr. 2:67. asses, six thousand seven hundred and twenty.
Neh 7:69. seven hundred and twenty *asses.*
13:15. bringing in sheaves, and lading *asses;*
Job 24: 3. They drive away *the ass of* the fatherless,
Pro 26: 3. a bridle *for the ass,*
Isa. 1: 3. *and the ass* his master's crib:
21: 7. a chariot of *asses,*
32:20. the feet of the ox *and the ass.*
Jer. 22:19. buried with the burial of *an ass,*
Eze. 23:20. whose flesh (is as) the flesh of *asses,*
Zec. 9: 9. lowly, and riding upon *an ass,*
14:15. the mule, of the camel, *and of the ass,*

2565 **חֲמוֹרָתַיִם** [*ghămōh-rāh-thah'-yim*], f. dual.

Jud. 15:16. the jawbone of an ass, heaps upon *heaps,* (marg. an heap, *two heaps*)

2545 **חָמוֹת** [*ghămōhth*], f.

Ru. 1:14. Orpah kissed *her mother in law;*
2:11. thou hast done unto *thy mother in law*
18. *her mother in law* saw what she had
19. *her mother in law* said unto her,
— shewed *her mother in law* with whom
23. dwelt with *her mother in law.*
3: 1. Naomi *her mother in law* said
6. all that *her mother in law* bade her.
16. when she came to *her mother in law,*
17. Go not empty unto *thy mother in law.*
Mic 7: 6. daughter in law *against her mother in law;*

2546 **חֹמֶט** *ghōh'-met*, m.

Lev. 11:30. the lizard, *and the snail,*

2548 **חָמִיץ** *ghāh-meetz'*, adj.

Isa. 30:24. shall eat *clean* provender, (marg. *leavened,* or, *savoury*)

2549 **חֲמִישִׁי** *ghămee-shee'* & **חֲמִשִׁי** *ghă-mish-shee'*, ordinal num.

Gen. 1:23. the evening and the morning were the *fifth* day.
30:17. bare Jacob the *fifth* son.
47:24. that ye shall give *the fifth* (part)
Lev. 5:16. add *the fifth part* thereto,
6: 5(5:24). add *the fifth part* more thereto,
19:25. in the *fifth* year shall ye eat
22:14. he shall put *the fifth* (part) *thereof*
27:13. he shall add *a fifth* (part) *thereof*
15, 19. he shall add *the fifth* (part) *of*
27. shall add *a fifth* (part) *of it*
31. shall add thereto *the fifth* (part) *thereof.*
Nu. 5: 7. *and* add unto it *the fifth* (part) *thereof,*
7:36. On the *fifth* day Shelumiel
29:26. on the *fifth* day nine bullocks,
33:38. in the first (day) of the *fifth* month.
Jos. 19:24. the *fifth* lot came out for the tribe
Jud. 19: 8. on the *fifth* day to depart:
2Sa. 3: 4. *and the fifth,* Shephatiah
1K. 6:31. side posts (were) *a fifth part* (marg. or, *fivesquare*)
14:25. in the *fifth* year of king Rehoboam,
2K. 25: 8. And in the *fifth* month,
1Ch 2:14. Nethaneel the fourth, Raddai the *fifth,*
3: 3. *The fifth,* Shephatiah of Abital:
8: 2. Nohah the fourth, and Rapha *the fifth.*
12:10. Jeremiah *the fifth,*
24: 9. *The fifth* to Malchijah,
25:12. *The fifth* to Nethaniah,
26: 3. Elam *the fifth,* Jehohanan the sixth,
4. Nethaneel *the fifth,*
27: 8. The *fifth* captain for the *fifth* month
2Ch 12: 2. in the *fifth* year of king Rehoboam
Ezr. 7: 8. came to Jerusalem in the *fifth* month,
9. on the first (day) of the *fifth* month
Neh 6: 5. in like manner *the fifth time*
Jer. 1: 3. Jerusalem captive in the *fifth* month.
28: 1. fourth year, (and) in the *fifth* month,
36: 9. in the *fifth* year of Jehoiakim
52:12. Now in the *fifth* month,
Eze. 1: 2. the *fifth* year of king Jehoiachin's
20: 1. seventh year, *in the fifth* (month),
Zec. 7: 3. Should I weep in the *fifth* month,
5. mourned in the *fifth* and seventh
8:19. the fast of *the fifth,*

חָמַל *ghāh-mal'*. 2550

✱ KAL.—*Preterite.* ✱

1Sa. 15:15. for the people *spared* the best
23:21. for *ye have compassion* on me.
2Sa. 12: 6. because *he had* no *pity.*
2Ch 36:15. because *he had compassion*
17. *had* no *compassion* upon young man
Lam. 2: 2, 17. and *hath* not *pitied:*
21. thou hast killed, (and) not *pitied.*
3:43. hast slain, *thou hast* not *pitied.*
Mal. 3:17. *and I will spare* them,

KAL.—*Infinitive.*

Eze. 16: 5. *to have compassion* upon thee;

KAL.—*Future.*

Ex. 2: 6. *And she had compassion* on him,
Deu 13: 8(9). neither *shalt thou spare,*
1Sa. 15: 3. they have, and *spare* them not;
9. *But* Saul and the people *spared* Agag,
2Sa. 12: 4. *and he spared* to take of his own flock
21: 7. *But* the king *spared* Mephibosheth,
Job 6:10. *let him* not *spare;*
16:13. my reins asunder, and *doth* not *spare*
20:13. *he spare* it, and forsake it not;
27:22. cast upon him, and not *spare:*
Pro. 6:34. *he will* not *spare* in the day of vengeance.
Isa. 9:19(18). no man *shall spare* his brother.
30:14. *he shall* not *spare:*
Jer. 13:14. *I will* not *pity,* nor spare,
15: 5. who *shall have pity* upon thee,
21: 7. neither *have pity,* nor have mercy.
50:14. shoot at her, *spare* no arrows:
51: 3. *spare ye* not her young men;
Eze. 5:11. neither *will* I *have any pity.*
7: 4. neither *will I have pity:*
9 & 8:18. neither *will I have pity:*
9: 5. neither *have ye pity:*
10. neither *will I have pity,*
36:21. *But I had pity* for mine holy name,
Joel 2:18. *and pity* his people.
Hab. 1:17. empty their net, and not *spare*
Zec. 11: 5. their own shepherds *pity* them not.
6. *I will* no more *pity* the inhabitants
Mal. 3:17. as a man *spareth* his own son

חֶמְלָה [*ghem-lāh'*], f. 2551

Gen 19:16. the Lord *being merciful* unto him: (lit. *in the mercy of*)
Isa. 63: 9. in his love *and in his pity*

חָמַם [*ghāh-mam'*]. 2552

✱ KAL.—*Preterite.* ✱

Ex. 16:21. *when* the sun *waxed hot,*
1K. 1: 2. *that* my lord the king *may get heat.*
Ps. 39: 3(4). My heart *was hot* within me,
Ecc. 4:11. if two lie together, *then they have heat:*
Isa. 44:16. Aha, *I am warm,* I have seen the fire:

KAL.—*Infinitive.*

Isa. 47:14. a coal *to warm at,* (nor) fire

KAL.—*Future.*

2K. 4:34. *and* the flesh of the child *waxed warm.*
Isa. 44:15. take thereof, *and warm himself;*
16. yea, *he warmeth* (himself),

✱ NIPHAL.—*Future.* ✱

Hos 7:7. *They are* all *hot* as an oven,

NIPHAL.—*Participle.*

Isa. 57: 5. *Enflaming yourselves* with idols

* PIEL—*Future.* *

Job 39:14. and *warmeth them* in dust,

* HITHPAEL.—*Future.* *

Job 31:20. *he were* (not) *warmed* with the fleece

2553 חַמָּנִים *gham-māh-neem'*, m. pl.

Lev.26:30. cut down *your images*,
2Ch 14: 5(4). the high places and *the images*: (marg. *sun images*)
34: 4. *and the images*, that (were) on high (marg. *id.*)
7. cut down all *the idols*
Isa. 17: 8. either the groves, *or the images*. (marg. or, *sun images*)
27: 9. the groves *and images* shall not stand (marg. *id.*)
Eze. 6: 4. *your images* shall be broken: (marg. *id.*)
6. *your images* may be cut down,

2554 חָמַס [*ghāh-mas'*].

* KAL.—*Preterite.* *

Eze.22:26. Her priests *have violated* my law, (marg. *offered violence to*)
Zep. 3: 4. *they have done violence to* the law.

KAL.—*Future.*

Job 15:33. *He shall shake off* his unripe grape
21:27. devices (which) *ye wrongfully imagine*
Jer. 22: 3. *do* no *violence* to the stranger,
Lam. 2: 6. *And he hath violently taken away*

KAL.—*Participle.* Poel.

Pro. 8:36. sinneth against me *wrongeth* his own soul:

* NIPHAL.—*Preterite.* *

Jer. 13:22. are thy skirts discovered, (and) thy heels *made bare.* (marg. or, *shall be violently taken away*)

2555 חָמָס *ghāh-māhs'*, m.

Gen 6:11. the earth was filled with *violence.*
13. the earth is filled with *violence*
16: 5. *My wrong* (be) upon thee:
49: 5. instruments of *cruelty* (are in)
Ex. 23: 1. wicked to be an *unrighteous* witness. (lit. witness of *violence*)
Deu19:16. If a *false* witness rise up against
Jud. 9:24. That *the cruelty* (done) *to* the threescore
2Sa.22: 3. thou savest me *from violence.*
49. thou hast delivered me from the *violent* man. (lit. the man of *violences*)
1Ch 12:17. seeing (there is) no *wrong* in mine hands, (marg. *violence*)
Job 16:17. Not for (any) *injustice* in mine hands:
19: 7. Behold, I cry out of *wrong*, (marg. *violence*)
Ps. 7:16(17). *his violent dealing* shall come down
11: 5. him that loveth *violence* his soul
18:48(49). thou hast delivered me from the *violent* man, (marg. man of *violence*)
25:19. they hate me with *cruel* hatred. (marg. hatred of *violence*)
27:12. such as breathe out *cruelty.*
35:11. *False* witnesses did rise up; (marg. Witnesses of *wrong*)
55: 9(10). I have seen *violence* and strife
58: 2(3). ye weigh *the violence of* your hands
72:14. soul from deceit *and violence:*
73: 6. *violence* covereth them
74:20. full of the habitations of *cruelty.*
140: 1(2). preserve me from the *violent* man; (marg. man of *violences*)
4(5). preserve me from the *violent* man;
11(12). evil shall hunt the *violent* man
Pro. 3:31. Envy thou not the oppressor, (marg. man of *violence*)
4:17. drink the wine of *violence.*
Pro.10: 6, 11. but *violence* covereth the mouth
13: 2. the transgressors (shall eat) *violence.*
16:29. A *violent* man enticeth his neighbour,
26: 6. (and) drinketh *damage.* (marg. *violence*)
Isa. 53: 9. because he had done no *violence*,
59: 6. the act of *violence* (is) in their hands.
60:18. *Violence* shall no more be heard
Jer. 6: 7. *violence* and spoil is heard in her;
20: 8. I cried *violence* and spoil;
51:35. *The violence done to me* (marg. *My violence*)
46. a rumour, *and violence* in the land,
Eze. 7:11. *Violence* is risen up into a rod of wickedness:
23. the city is full of *violence.*
8:17. they have filled the land with *violence*,
12:19. *because of the violence of* all them
28:16. have filled the midst of thee with *violence*,
45: 9. remove *violence* and spoil,
Joel 3:19(4:19). *for the violence* (against) the
Am. 3:10. who store up *violence* and robbery
6: 3. cause the seat of *violence* to come
Obad. 10. *For* (thy) *violence against* thy brother
Jon. 3: 8. *the violence* that (is) in their hands.
Mic. 6:12. rich men thereof are full of *violence*,
Hab. 1: 2. cry out unto thee (of) *violence*,
3. spoiling *and violence* (are) before me:
9. They shall come all *for violence:*
2: 8. *and* (for) *the violence of* the land,
17. For *the violence of* Lebanon
— *and* for *the violence of* the land,
Zep. 1: 9. fill their masters' houses with *violence*
Mal. 2:16. covereth *violence* with his garment,

חָמֵץ *ghāh-mehtz'*. 2556

* KAL.—*Preterite.* *

Ex. 12:39. for *it was* not *leavened;*

KAL.—*Infinitive.*

Hos. 7: 4. dough, until *it be leavened.*

KAL.—*Future.*

Ex. 12:34. dough before *it was leavened*,

KAL.—*Participle.* Poel.

Ps. 71: 4. the unrighteous *and cruel man.*

KAL.—*Participle.* Paül.

Isa. 63: 1. with *dyed* garments from Bozrah?

* HIPHIL.—*Participle* *

Ex. 12:19. whosoever eateth *that which is leavened*
20. Ye shall eat nothing *leavened;*

* HITHPAEL.—*Future.* *

Ps. 73:21. Thus my heart *was grieved*,

חָמֵץ *ghāh-mehtz'*, m. 2557

Ex. 12:15. whosoever eateth *leavened bread*
13: 3, 7. there shall no *leavened bread*
23:18. of my sacrifice with *leavened bread;*
34:25. the blood of my sacrifice with *leaven;*
Lev. 2:11. shall be made with *leaven:*
6:17(10). It shall not be baken with *leaven.*
7:13. offer (for) his offering *leavened* bread
23:17. they shall be baken with *leaven;*
Deu16: 3. Thou shalt eat no *leavened bread*
Am. 4: 5. a sacrifice of thanksgiving *with leaven*,

חֹמֶץ *ghōh'-metz*, m. 2558

Nu. 6: 3. shall drink no *vinegar of* wine, *or vinegar of* strong drink,
Ru. 2:14. dip thy morsel *in the vinegar.*
Ps. 69:21(22). in my thirst they gave me *vinegar*
Pro.10:26. *As vinegar* to the teeth,
25:20. *vinegar* upon nitre,

חָמַק *ghāh-mak'*. 2559

* KAL.—*Preterite.* *

Cant.5: 6. my beloved *had withdrawn himself*,

* HITHPAEL.—*Future.* *

Jer. 31:22. How long *wilt thou go about*,

2560 חָמַר *ghāh-mar'*

* KAL.—*Preterite.* *

Ps. 75: 8(9). the wine *is red*; it is full of mixture;

KAL.—*Future.*

Ex. 2: 3. *and daubed it* with slime
Ps. 46: 3(4). waters thereof roar (and) *be troubled*,

* POALAL.—*Preterite.* *

Job 16:16. My face *is foul* with weeping,
Lam. 1:20 & 2:11. my bowels *are troubled*;

2564 חֵמָר *ghēh-māhr'*, m.

Gen11: 3. *and slime* had they for morter.
14:10. vale of Siddim (was full of) *slime*pits;
Ex. 2: 3. daubed it *with slime*

2561 חֶמֶר *gheh'-mer*, m.

Deu32:14. the *pure* blood of the grape.
Isa. 27: 2. A vineyard of *red wine*. [Some copies read חֶמֶד.]

2562 חֲמַר *ghămar*, Ch. m.

Ezr. 6: 9. offerings of the God of heaven, wheat, salt, *wine*,
7:22. and to an hundred baths of *wine*,
Dan 5: 1. and drank *wine* before the thousand.
2. Belshazzar, whiles he tasted *the wine*,
4. They drank *wine*, and praised the gods
23. and thy concubines, have drunk *wine* in them;

2563 חֹמֶר *ghōh'-mer*, m.

Gen11: 3. slime had they *for morter*.
Ex. 1:14. *in morter*, and in brick,
8:14(10). they gathered them together upon *heaps*: (lit. *heaps heaps*)
Lev.27:16. *an homer of* barley seed
Nu. 11:32. gathered least gathered ten *homers*:
Job 4:19. them that dwell in houses of *clay*,
10: 9. thou hast made me *as the clay*;
13:12. your bodies to bodies of *clay*.
27:16. *and* prepare raiment *as the clay*;
30:19. He hath cast me *into the mire*,
33: 6. I also am formed *out of the clay*.
38:14. It is turned *as clay* (to) the seal;
Isa. 5:10. *an homer* shall yield an ephah.
10: 6. tread them down *like the mire of*
29:16. be esteemed *as the* potter's *clay*:
41:25. come upon princes as (upon) *morter*,
45: 9. Shall *the clay* say to him
64: 8(7). thou (art) our father; we (are) *the clay*,
Jer. 18: 4. the vessel that he made of *clay* was marred (marg. was marred, *as clay*)
6. *as the clay* (is) in the potter's hand, so (are) ye in
Eze.45:11. contain the tenth part of *an homer*, and the ephah the tenth part of *an homer*: the measure thereof shall be after *the homer*.
13, 13. an ephah of *an homer of*
14. *an homer* of ten baths; for ten baths (are) *an homer*:
Hos. 3: 2. *and* (for) *an homer of* barley,
Nah. 3:14. go into clay, and tread *the morter*,
Hab. 3:15. *the heap of* great waters. (marg. or, *mud*)

2567 חָמַשׁ [*ghāh-mash'*].

* PIEL.—*Preterite.* *

Gen41:34. *and take up the fifth part of* the land

חָמֵשׁ *ghāh-mehsh'*, f. & חֲמִשָּׁה *ghămish-shāh'*, m. num. adj. 2568

Gen.5: 6. Seth lived an hundred and *five* years,
10. eight hundred and *fif*teen years, (lit. *five* ten)
11. nine hundred and *five* years:
15. Mahalaleel lived sixty and *five* years,
17. eight hundred ninety and *five* years:
21. Enoch lived sixty and *five* years,
23. three hundred sixty and *five* years:
30. *five* hundred ninety *and five*
32. Noah was *five* hundred years old:
7:20. *Fif*teen cubits upward did the waters prevail;
11:11. *five* hundred years, and begat
12. Arphaxad lived *five* and thirty
32. were two hundred and *five* years:
12: 4. Abram (was) seventy and *five* years
14: 9. four kings with *five*.
18.28. Peradventure there shall lack *five*
— destroy all the city *for* (lack of) *five?*
— If I find there forty *and five*,
25: 7. threescore *and fif*teen years. (lit. seventy years *and five* years)
43:34. Benjamin's mess was *five* times so much
45: 6. and yet (there are) *five* years,
11. for yet (there are) *five* years of famine;
22. *and five* changes of raiment.
47: 2. some of his brethren, (even) *five* men,
Ex. 16: 1. *on* the *fif*teenth day (lit. *on five* ten)
22: 1(21:37). he shall restore *five* oxen
26: 3. The *five* curtains shall be
— *and* (other) *five* curtains
9. thou shalt couple *five* curtains
26. *five* for the boards of the one
27, 27. *And five* bars for the boards
37. make for the hanging *five* pillars
— thou shalt cast *five* sockets
27: 1. *five* cubits long, *and five* cubits broad;
14. one side (of the gate shall be) *fif*teen cubits: (lit. *and five* ten)
15. (shall be) hangings *fif*teen (cubits): (lit. *id.*)
18. the height *five* cubits
30:23. of pure myrrh *five* hundred
24. of cassia *five* hundred
36:10. he coupled the *five* curtains
— *and* (the other) *five* curtains
16. he coupled *five* curtains
31. *five* for the boards of the one
32, 32. *And five* bars for the boards
38. the *five* pillars of it
— their *five* sockets (were of) brass.
38: 1. *five* cubits (was) the length thereof, *and five* cubits the breadth
14. side (of the gate were) *fif*teen (lit. *five* ten)
15. hangings of *fif*teen cubits; (lit. *five* ten)
18. in the breadth (was) *five* cubits,
25. a thousand seven hundred and threescore *and fif*teen shekels, (lit. *and five* and seventy)
26. three thousand *and five* hundred
28. the thousand seven hundred seventy *and five*
Lev.23: 6. *And on* the *fif*teenth day of the same month (lit. *and on five* ten)
34. The *fif*teenth day of this seventh month (lit. *in five* ten)
39. *in* the *fif*teenth day
26: 8. *five* of you shall chase an hundred,
27: 5. if (it be) from *five* years old
6. even unto *five* years old,
— *five* shekels of silver,
7. shall be *fif*teen shekels, (lit. *five* ten)
Nu. 1:21. forty and six thousand *and five* hundred.
25. forty and *five* thousand six hundred and
33. forty thousand *and five* hundred.
37. Benjamin, (were) thirty and *five* thousand and four hundred.
41. forty and one thousand *and five* hundred.
46. six hundred thousand and three thousand *and five* hundred and fifty.
2:11. forty and six thousand *and five* hundred.
15. forty and *five* thousand and six hundred and fifty.

Nu 2:19. forty thousand *and five* hundred.
23. that were numbered of them, (were) thirty and *five* thousand and four hundred.
28. that were numbered of them, (were) forty and one thousand *and five* hundred.
32. six hundred and three thousand *and five* hundred and fifty.
3:22. (were) seven thousand *and five* hundred.
47. Thou shalt even take *five* shekels *apiece* (lit. *five five* shekels)
50. a thousand three hundred and threescore and *five* (shekels),
4:48. eight thousand *and five* hundred and fourscore.
7:17, 23, 29, 35, 41, 47, 53, 59, 65, 71, 77, 83. *five* rams, *five* he goats, *five* lambs
8:24. from twenty and *five* years old
11:19. two days, nor *five* days,
18:16. for the money of *five* shekels,
26:18. forty thousand *and five* hundred.
22. threescore and sixteen thousand *and five* hundred.
27. threescore thousand *and five* hundred.
37. that were numbered of them, thirty and two thousand *and five* hundred.
41. forty and *five* thousand and six hundred.
50. that were numbered of them (were) forty and *five* thousand and four hundred.
28:17. *And in* the *fif*teenth day of this month (lit. *and on five* ten)
29:12. *And on* the *fif*teenth day of the seventh month (lit. *and on five* ten)
31: 8. *five* kings of Midian:
28. one soul *of five* hundred,
32. six hundred thousand and seventy thousand *and five* thousand sheep,
36. three hundred thousand and seven and thirty thousand *and five* hundred
37. six hundred and threescore and *fif*teen. (lit. *five* and seventy)
39. thirty thousand *and five* hundred;
43. seven thousand *and five* hundred sheep,
45. thirty thousand asses *and five* hundred,
33: 3. *on the fif*teenth day of the first month; (lit. *on five* ten)
Jos. 8:12. he took *about five* thousand men,
10: 5. the *five* kings of the Amorites,
16. But these *five* kings fled,
17. The *five* kings are found hid
22. bring out those *five* kings
23. brought forth those *five* kings
26. hanged them on *five* trees:
13: 3. *five* lords of the Philistines;
14:10. these forty *and five* years,
— fourscore and *five* years old.
Jud. 3: 3. *five* lords of the Philistines,
8:10. *about fif*teen thousand (lit. *about five* ten)
18: 2. Dan sent of their family *five* men
7. Then the *five* men departed,
14. Then answered the *five* men
17. the *five* men that went
20:35. twenty *and five* thousand and an hundred
45. in the highways *five* thousand men;
46. twenty *and five* thousand men
1Sa. 6: 4. *Five* golden emerods, *and five* golden mice,
16. *when* the *five* lords of the Philistines
18. Philistines (belonging) *to* the *five* lords,
17: 5. *five* thousand shekels of brass.
40. chose him *five* smooth stones
21: 3(4). give (me) *five* (loaves of) bread
22:18. fourscore *and five* persons
25:18. *and five* sheep ready dressed, *and five* measures of parched (corn),
42. *with five* damsels of her's
2Sa. 4: 4. He was *five* years old
9:10. Ziba had *fif*teen sons (lit. *five* ten)
19:17(18). *and* his *fif*teen sons (lit. *and five* ten)
21: 8. the *five* sons of Michal
24: 9. and the men of Judah (were) *five* hundred thousand men.
1K. 4:32(5:12). his songs were a thousand and *five*.
6: 6. chamber (was) *five* cubits broad,
10. against all the house, *five* cubits
24. *And five* cubits (was) the one
— *and five* cubits the other
7: 3. that (lay) on forty *five* pillars, *fif*teen (in) a row. (lit. *and five* ten)

1K. 7:16. one chapiter (was) *five* cubits, *and* the height of the other chapiter (was) *five*
23. *and* his height (was) *five* cubits:
39. put *five* bases on the right side of the house, *and five* on the left side of the house:
49. *five* on the right (side), *and five* on the left,
9:23. over Solomon's work, *five* hundred *and* fifty, (lit. fifty, *and five* hundred)
12:32. *on* the *fif*teenth day of the month, (lit. *on five* ten)
33. *the fif*teenth day of the eighth month,
22:42. Jehoshaphat (was) thirty *and five* years
— he reigned twenty *and five* years
2K. 6:25. a cab of dove's dung *for five* (pieces)
7:13. *five* of the horses that remain,
8:16. in the *fifth* year of Joram
13:19. shouldest have smitten *five*
14: 2. twenty *and five* years old
17. king of Israel *fif*teen years. (lit. *five* ten)
23. In the *fif*teenth year (lit. *five* ten)
15:33. *Five and* twenty years old was he when he began to reign,
18: 2. Twenty *and five* years old
19:35. an hundred fourscore *and five*
20: 6. I will add unto thy days *fif*teen years; (lit. *five* ten)
21: 1. reigned fifty *and five* years
23:36. twenty *and five* years old
25:19. *and five* men of them that were in
1Ch 2: 4. All the sons of Judah (were) *five*.
6. *five* of them in all.
3:20. Hasadiah, Jushab-hesed, *five*.
4:32. Tochen, and Ashan, *five* cities:
42. sons of Simeon, *five* hundred men,
7: 3. *five*: all of them chief men.
7. and Jerimoth, and Iri, *five*;
11:23. a man of (great) stature, *five* cubits high;
24:14. *The fif*teenth to Bilgah, (lit. *five* ten)
25:22. *The fif*teenth to Jeremoth, (lit. *the five* tenth)
29: 7. *five* thousand talents
2Ch 3:11. wing (of the one cherub was) *five*
— other wing (was likewise) *five* cubits,
12. of the other cherub (was) *five* cubits,
— the other wing (was) *five* cubits
15. pillars of thirty *and five* cubits
— the top of each of them (was) *five*
4: 2. *and five* cubits the height thereof;
6. put *five* on the right hand, *and five* on the left,
7. *five* on the right hand, *and five* on the left.
8. *five* on the right side, *and five* on the left.
6:13. brasen scaffold, of *five* cubits long, *and five* cubits broad,
13:17. slain of Israel *five* hundred thousand
15:10. in the *fif*teenth year (lit. *five* ten)
19. no (more) war unto the *five and* thirtieth year of the reign
20:31. thirty *and five* years old
— he reigned twenty *and five* years
25: 1. Amaziah (was) twenty *and five* years old
25. king of Israel *fif*teen years. (lit. *five* ten)
26:13. and seven thousand *and five* hundred,
27: 1. Jotham (was) twenty *and five* years old
8. He was *five* and twenty years old
29: 1. *five and* twenty years old
33: 1. he reigned fifty *and five* years
35: 9. *five* thousand (small cattle), and *five* hundred oxen.
36: 5. twenty *and five* years old
Ezr. 1:11. *five* thousand and four hundred.
2: 5. Arah, seven hundred seventy *and five*.
8. The children of Zattu, nine hundred forty *and five*.
20. The children of Gibbar, ninety *and five*.
33. and Ono, seven hundred twenty *and five*.
34. The children of Jericho, three hundred forty *and five*.
66. their mules, two hundred forty *and five*;
67. Their camels, four hundred thirty *and five*;
69. *five* thousand pound of silver,
Neh. 6:15. finished in the twenty *and fifth*
7:13. Zattu, eight hundred forty *and five*.
20. Adin, six hundred fifty *and five*.

Neh 7:25. Gibeon, ninety *and five.*
36. Jericho, three hundred forty *and five.*
67. two hundred forty *and five*
68. two hundred forty *and five :*
69. four hundred thirty *and five :*
70. *five* hundred and thirty priests' (lit. thirty *and five* hundred)
Est. 9: 6, 12. destroyed *five* hundred men.
16. foes seventy and *five* thousand,
18. and *on* the *fif*teenth (day) of the same they rested, (lit. *on five* ten)
21. Adar, and the *fif*teenth (lit. *five* ten)
Job 1: 3. *and five* hundred yoke of oxen, *and five* hundred she asses,
Isa. 7: 8. within threescore *and five* years
17: 6. four (or) *five* in the outmost
19:18. In that day shall *five* cities
30:17. at the rebuke of *five* shall ye flee:
37:36. a hundred and fourscore *and five* thousand:
38: 5. I will add unto thy days *fif*teen years. (lit. *five* ten)
Jer. 52:22. one chapiter (was) *five* cubits,
30. seven hundred forty *and five*
31. in the *five* and twentieth (day) of the month, (lit. twenty *and five*)
Eze. 1: 1, 2 & 8:1. *in the fifth* (day) of the month,
8:16 & 11:1. *five and* twenty men, (lit. twenty *and five*)
32:17. *in* the *fif*teenth (day) of the month, (lit. *in five* ten)
33:21. *in the fifth* (day) of the month,
40: 1. In the *five and* twentieth year of our captivity, (lit. twenty *and five*)
7. the little chambers (were) *five* cubits ;
13. the breadth (was) *five and* twenty cubits, (lit. twenty *and five*)
21, 25. and the breadth *five* and twenty
29. and *five and* twenty cubits broad. (lit. twenty *and five*)
30. *five and* twenty cubits long (lit. *id.*), and *five* cubits broad.
33. and *five* and twenty cubits broad.
36. and the breadth *five* and twenty
48. *five* cubits on this side, *and five* cubits on that side:
41: 2. the sides of the door (were) *five* cubits on the one side, *and five* cubits on
9. chamber without, (was) *five* cubits:
11. left (was) *five* cubits round about.
12. the building (was) *five* cubits thick
42:16, 17, 18, 19. *five* hundred reeds,
20. *five* hundred (reeds) long, and *five* hundred broad,
45: 1. the length of *five* and twenty thousand
2. *five* hundred (in length), *with five* hundred (in breadth),
3. the length of *five* and twenty thousand,
5. the *five* and twenty thousand of length,
6. the city *five* thousand broad, and *five* and twenty thousand long,
12. *five and* twenty shekels, *fif*teen shekels, shall be your maneh.
25. *in* the *fif*teenth day of the month, (lit. *in five* ten)
48: 8, 9, 10, 10, 13, 13. *five* and twenty thousand
15. And the *five* thousand, that are left
— against the *five and* twenty thousand,
16, 16, 16, 16, 30, 32, 33, 34. four thousand and *five* hundred,
— (כתיב ולא קרי) the south side four thousand and five)(hundred,
20. *five* and twenty thousand *by five* and twenty thousand:
21, 21. against the *five* and twenty thousand
Dan 12:12. three hundred *and five* and thirty days.
Hos 3: 2. So I bought her to me *for fif*teen (pieces) of silver, (lit. *for five* ten)

2569 חֹמֶשׁ *ghōh'-mesh*, m.

Gen 47:26. Pharaoh should have *the fifth part;*

2570 חֹמֶשׁ *ghōh'-mesh*, m.

2Sa. 2:23. smote him under *the fifth* (rib),
3:27. smote him there under *the fifth* (rib),
2Sa. 4: 6. and they smote him under *the fifth* (rib):
20:10. smote him therewith in *the fifth* (rib),

חֲמִשִּׁים *ghămish-sheem'*, num. adj. pl. 2572

Gen 6:15. the breadth of it *fifty* cubits,
7:24. an hundred and *fifty* days.
8: 3. end of the hundred and *fifty* days
9:28. three hundred *and fifty* years.
29. of Noah were nine hundred *and fifty*
18:24. Peradventure there be *fifty* righteous
— spare the place for the *fifty* righteous
26. If I find in Sodom *fifty* righteous
28. there shall lack five of the *fifty*
Ex. 18:21. rulers of *fifties*, and rulers of tens:
25. rulers of hundreds, rulers of *fifties*,
26: 5. *Fifty* loops shalt thou make in the one curtain, *and fifty* loops
6. thou shalt make *fifty* taches
10. thou shalt make *fifty* loops
— *and fifty* loops in the edge
11. thou shalt make *fifty* taches
27:12. hangings of *fifty* cubits:
13. side eastward (shall be) *fifty* cubits.
18. the breadth *fifty every where*, (marg. *fifty by fifty*)
30:23, 23. two hundred and *fifty*
36:12. *Fifty* loops made he in one curtain, *and fifty* loops made he
13. he made *fifty* taches of gold,
17. he made *fifty* loops upon the
— *and fifty* loops made he upon the edge
18. he made *fifty* taches (of) brass
38:12. hangings of *fifty* cubits,
13. east side eastward *fifty* cubits.
26. five hundred *and fifty*
Lev. 23:16. shall ye number *fifty* days ;
25:10. ye shall hallow the *fiftieth* year,
11. A jubile shall that *fiftieth* year be
27: 3. estimation shall be *fifty* shekels
16. *at fifty* shekels of silver.
Nu. 1:23. *fifty and* nine thousand and three hundred. (lit. nine *and fifty*)
25. forty and five thousand six hundred *and fifty*.
29. *fifty and* four thousand and four hundred. (lit. four *and fifty*)
31. *fifty and* seven thousand and four hundred. (lit. seven *and fifty*)
43. *fifty and* three thousand and four hundred. (lit. three *and fifty*)
46. six hundred thousand and three thousand and five hundred *and fifty.*
2: 6. *fifty and* four thousand and four hundred. (lit. four *and fifty*)
8. *fifty and* seven thousand and four hundred. (lit. seven *and fifty*)
13. *fifty and* nine thousand (lit. nine *and fifty*) and three hundred.
15. forty and five thousand and six hundred *and fifty*.
16. an hundred thousand *and fifty* and one thousand and four hundred *and fifty*,
30. *fifty and* three thousand and four hundred. (lit. three *and fifty*)
31. an hundred thousand *and fifty* and seven thousand and six hundred.
32. six hundred thousand and three thousand and five hundred *and fifty.*
4: 3. even until *fifty* years old,
23. until *fifty* years old
30, 35, 39, 43, 47. even unto *fifty* years old
36. seven hundred *and fifty.*
8:25. from the age of *fifty* years
16: 2. two hundred and *fifty* princes
17. two hundred and *fifty* censers ;
35 & 26:10. two hundred and *fifty* men
26:34. *fifty and* two thousand and seven hundred. (lit. two *and fifty*)
47. *fifty and* three thousand and four hundred. (lit. three *and fifty*)
31:30. take one portion of *fifty*,
47. Moses took one portion of *fifty*,
52. sixteen thousand seven hundred *and fifty* shekels.
Deu 1:15. captains over *fifties*,
22:29. give unto the damsel's father *fifty*

Jos 7:21. a wedge of gold of *fifty* shekels
1Sa. 6:19. smote of the people *fifty* thousand and threescore and ten
8:12. captains over *fifties;*
2Sa. 15: 1. *and fifty* men to run before him.
24:24. the oxen for *fifty* shekels of silver.
1K. 1: 5. *and fifty* men to run before him.
7: 2. *and* the breadth thereof *fifty* cubits,
6. the length thereof (was) *fifty* cubits,
9:23. five hundred and *fifty*,
10:29. an horse *for* an hundred and *fifty:* (lit. *for fifty* and a hundred)
18: 4. hid them *by fifty* in a cave,
13. *by fifty* in a cave, (lit. *fifty fifty*)
19. of Baal four hundred *and fifty*,
22. Baal's prophets (are) four hundred *and fifty*
2K. 1: 9. sent unto him a captain of *fifty with his fifty*. And he went up
10. said to the captain of *fifty*,
— consume thee and *thy fifty*.
— consumed him and *his fifty*.
11. sent unto him another captain of *fifty with his fifty*.
12. consume thee and *thy fifty*.
— consumed him and *his fifty*.
13. sent again a captain of the third *fifty with his fifty*. And the third captain of *fifty*
— the life of these *fifty* thy servants,
14. two captains of the former *fifties* with *their fifties:*
2: 7. *And fifty* men of the sons of the prophets
16. there be with thy servants *fifty* strong
17. They sent therefore *fifty* men;
13: 7. people to Jehoahaz but *fifty* horsemen,
15: 2. he reigned two *and fifty* years
20. of each man *fifty* shekels of silver,
23. In the *fiftieth* year of Azariah
25. with him *fifty* men of the Gileadites:
27. In the two and *fiftieth* year
21: 1. *and* reigned *fifty* and five years
1Ch 5:21. of their camels *fifty* thousand,
— two hundred *and fifty* thousand,
8:40. an hundred *and fifty*.
9: 9. nine hundred *and fifty* and six.
12:33. instruments of war, *fifty* thousand,
2Ch 1:17. and an horse *for* an hundred and *fifty:*
2:17(16). an hundred *and fifty* thousand and three thousand and six hundred.
3: 9. of the nails (was) *fifty* shekels of gold.
8:10. two hundred and *fifty*,
18. four hundred *and fifty* talents
26: 3. reigned *fifty and* two years (lit. two *and fifty*)
33: 1. *and* he reigned *fifty* and five years in
Ezr. 2: 7. a thousand two hundred *fifty* and four.
14. two thousand *fifty* and six.
15. Adin, four hundred *fifty* and four.
22. The men of Netophah, *fifty* and six.
29. The children of Nebo, *fifty* and two.
30. Magbish, an hundred *fifty* and six.
31. a thousand two hundred *fifty* and four.
37. Immer, a thousand *fifty* and two.
60. Nekoda, six hundred *fifty* and two.
8: 3. the males an hundred *and fifty*.
6. Jonathan, and with him *fifty* males.
26. six hundred *and fifty* talents
Neh 5:17. an hundred *and fifty* of the Jews
6:15. in *fifty* and two days.
7:10. Arah, six hundred *fifty* and two.
12. a thousand two hundred *fifty* and four.
20. The children of Adin, six hundred *fifty* and five.
33. Nebo, *fifty* and two.
34. a thousand two hundred *fifty* and four.
40. Immer, a thousand *fifty* and two.
70. *fifty* basons, five hundred and thirty
Est. 5:14. gallows be made of *fifty* cubits high,
7: 9. the gallows *fifty* cubits high,
Isa. 3: 3. The captain of *fifty*, and the honourable
Eze. 40:15. the inner gate (were) *fifty* cubits.
21. the length thereof (was) *fifty* cubits,
25. the length (was) *fifty* cubits,
29, 33. *fifty* cubits long,
36. the length (was) *fifty* cubits,
42: 2. the breadth (was) *fifty* cubits.
7. the length thereof (was) *fifty* cubits.
Eze. 42: 8. in the utter court (was) *fifty* cubits:
45: 2. *and fifty* cubits round
48:17. the north two hundred and *fifty*, and toward the south two hundred and *fifty*, and toward the east two hundred and *fifty*, and toward the west two hundred and *fifty*.
Hag. 2:16. *fifty* (vessels) out of the press,

חֲמֻשִׁים *ghămoo-sheem'*, adj. pl. 2571

Ex. 13:18. *and* the children of Israel went up *harnessed* (marg. or, *by five in a rank*)
Jos. 1:14. pass before your brethren *armed*, (marg. *marshalled by five*)
4:12. Manasseh, passed over *armed*
Jud. 7:11. *the armed men* that (were) in the host. (marg. *ranks by five*)

חֵמֶת *ghēh'-meth*, m. 2573

Gen 21:14. took bread, *and a bottle of* water,
15. the water was spent in *the bottle*,
19. filled *the bottle* with water,
Hab 2:15. that puttest *thy bottle* to (him),

חֵן *ghēhn*, m. 2580

Gen 6: 8. But Noah found *grace*
18: 3. if now I have found *favour*
19:19. Behold now, thy servant hath found *grace*
30:27. if I have found *favour* in thine eyes,
32: 5(6). that I may find *grace* in thy sight.
33: 8. to find *grace* in the sight of my lord.
10. if now I have found *grace*
15. let me find *grace*
34:11. Let me find *grace* in your eyes,
39: 4. Joseph found *grace* in his sight,
21. gave *him favour* in the sight
47:25. let us find *grace* in the sight
29 & 50:4. If now I have found *grace*
Ex. 3:21. I will give this people *favour*
11: 3. the Lord gave the people *favour*
12:36. the Lord gave the people *favour*
33:12. thou hast also found *grace*
13. if I have found *grace* in thy sight,
— I may find *grace* in thy sight:
16. have found *grace* in thy sight?
17. thou hast found *grace* in my sight,
34: 9. If now I have found *grace* in thy sight,
Nu. 11:11, 15. found *favour* in thy sight,
32: 5. if we have found *grace*
Deu 24: 1. she find no *favour* in his eyes,
Jud. 6:17. If now I have found *grace* in thy sight,
Ru. 2: 2. in whose sight I shall find *grace*.
10. Why have I found *grace* in thine eyes,
13. Let me find *favour* in thy sight,
1Sa. 1:18. handmaid find *grace* in thy sight.
16:22. he hath found *favour* in my sight.
20: 3. I have found *grace* in thine eyes;
29. if I have found *favour* in thine eyes,
25: 8. let the young men find *favour*
27: 5. If I have now found *grace*
2Sa. 14:22. knoweth that I have found *grace*.
15:25. if I shall find *favour*
16: 4. I may find *grace* in thy sight,
1K. 11:19. Hadad found great *favour*
Est. 2:15. Esther obtained *favour* in the sight of
17. she obtained *grace* and favour
5: 2. she obtained *favour* in his sight:
8. If I have found *favour* in the sight
7: 3. If I have found *favour* in thy sight,
8: 5. if I have found *favour* in his sight,
Ps. 45: 2(3). *grace* is poured into thy lips:
84:11(12). the Lord will give *grace* and glory:
Pro. 1: 9. (be) an ornament of *grace* unto thy head
3: 4. So shalt thou find *favour*
22. and *grace* to thy neck.
34. but he giveth *grace* unto the lowly.
4: 9. to thine head an ornament of *grace:*
5:19. the loving hind and *pleasant* roe; (lit. roe *of favour*)
11:16. A *gracious* woman retaineth honour: (lit. a woman of *favour*)

Pro. 13:15. Good understanding giveth *favour :*
17: 8. A gift (is as) a *precious* stone (marg. stone of *grace*)
22: 1. loving *favour* rather than silver
11. *the grace of* his lips
28:23. shall find more *favour* than
31:30. *Favour* (is) deceitful, and beauty (is)
Ecc. 9:11. nor yet *favour* to men of skill;
10:12. of a wise man's mouth (are) *gracious ;* (marg. *grace*)
Jer. 31: 2. the sword found *grace* in the wilderness;
Nah 3: 4. the whoredoms of the well*favoured* harlot, (lit. of good *favour*)
Zec. 4: 7. (crying), *Grace, grace* unto it.
12:10. the spirit of *grace* and of supplications:

2583 חָנָה *g'hāh-nāh'.*

* KAL.—*Preterite.* *

Nu. 1:52. *And* .... Israel *shall pitch their tents,*
2:34. so *they pitched* by their standards,
1Sa. 4: 1. the Philistines *pitched* in Aphek.
13:16. the Philistines *encamped* in Michmash.
26: 5. the place where Saul *had pitched:*
Isa. 29: 1. the city (where) David *dwelt!*
3. *And I will camp* against thee round about,
Zec. 9: 8. *And I will encamp* about mine house

KAL.—*Infinitive.*

Nu. 1:51. *and when* the tabernacle *is to be pitched,*
10:31. how *we are to encamp*
Deu 1:33. a place *to pitch your tents*
Jud. 19: 9. the day *groweth to an end,* (marg. (it is) *the pitching* (time) of the day)

KAL.—*Imperative.*

Nu. 31:19. *do* ye *abide* without the camp
2Sa. 12:28. *and encamp* against the city,
Jer. 50:29. *camp* against it round about;

KAL.—*Future.*

Gen 26:17. *and pitched* **his** *tent* in the valley
33:18. *and pitched* **his** *tent* before the city.
Ex. 13:20. *and encamped* in Etham,
14: 2. turn *and encamp* before Pi-hahiroth,
— *shall ye encamp* by the sea.
15:27. *and they encamped* there by the waters.
17: 1. *and pitched* in Rephidim:
19: 2. *and had pitched* in the wilderness; *and* there Israel *camped* before the mount.
Nu. 1:50. shall minister unto it, and *shall encamp*
53. But the Levites *shall pitch* round
2: 2. Israel *shall pitch* by his own standard,
— of the congregation *shall they pitch.*
17. as *they encamp,*
3:23. the Gershonites *shall pitch* behind
29. Kohath *shall pitch* on the side
35. *shall pitch* on the side of the
9:17. Israel *pitched their tents.*
18. commandment of the Lord *they pitched :*
— *they rested in their tents.*
20. *they abode in their tents,*
22. the children of Israel *abode in their tents,*
23. *they rested in the tents,*
12:16. *and pitched* in the wilderness of
21:10. *and pitched* in Oboth.
11. *and pitched* at Ije-abarim,
12. *and pitched* in the valley of Zared.
13. *and pitched* on the other side
22: 1. *and pitched* in the plains of Moab
33: 5. *and pitched* in Succoth.
6, 8, 15, 16, 18, 19, 20, 21, 22, 23, 25, 27, 28, 29, 31, 33, 36, 37, 41, 42, 43, 44, 45, 47, 48. *and pitched*
7, 9, 49. *and they pitched*
10, 11, 12, 13, 14, 17, 24, 26, 30, 32, 34, 35, 46. *and encamped*
Jos. 4:19. *and encamped* in Gilgal.
5:10. *And* the children of Israel *encamped* in Gilgal,
8:11. *and pitched* on the north side
10: 5. *and encamped* before Gibeon,
31. *and encamped* against it,
34. *and they encamped* against it,
11: 5. came *and pitched* together
Jud. 6: 4. *And they encamped* against them,
33. *and pitched* in the valley
7: 1. *and pitched* beside the well
9:50. *and encamped* against Thebez,
10:17. *and encamped* in Gilead.
— *and encamped* in Mizpeh.
11:18. *and pitched* on the other side
20. *and pitched* in Jahaz,
15: 9. *and pitched* in Judah,
18:12. *and pitched* in Kirjath-jearim,
20:19. *and encamped* against Gibeah.
1Sa. 4: 1. *and pitched* beside Eben-ezer:
11: 1. *and encamped* against Jabesh-gilead:
13: 5. came up, *and pitched* in Michmash,
17: 1. *and pitched* between Shochoh and
2. *and pitched* by the valley of Elah,
26: 3. *And* Saul *pitched* in the hill
28: 4. came *and pitched* in Shunem:
— *and they pitched* in Gilboa.
2Sa. 17:26. *So* Israel and Absalom *pitched*
24: 5. *and pitched* in Aroer,
1K. 20:27. *and* the children of Israel *pitched* before
29. *And they pitched* one over against the
2K. 25: 1. *and pitched* against it;
1Ch 19: 7. came *and pitched* before Medeba.
2Ch 32: 1. *and encamped* against the fenced cities,
Ezr. 8:15. *and* there *abode we in tents* (marg. or, *pitched*)
Neh 11:30. *And they dwelt* from Beer-sheba
Job 19:12. *and encamp* round about
Ps. 27: 3. Though an host *should encamp*
Jer. 52: 4. *and pitched* against it,

KAL.—*Participle.* Poel.

Ex. 14: 9. overtook them *encamping* by the sea,
18: 5. where he *encamped* at the mount
Nu. 2: 3. *And...shall* they of the standard...*pitch*
5. *And those that do pitch* next
12. *And those which pitch*
27. *And those that encamp* by him
3:38. *But those that encamp* before
10: 5. the camps *that lie* on the east
6. the camps *that lie* on the south
1Sa. 26: 5. the people *pitched* round about
29: 1. the Israelites *pitched* by a fountain
2Sa. 11:11. *are encamped* in the open fields;
23:13. the Philistines *pitched* in the valley
1K. 16:15. the people (were) *encamped*
16. the people (that were) *encamped*
1Ch 11:15. the Philistines *encamped* in the valley
Ps. 34: 7(8). The angel of the Lord *encampeth* round
53: 5(6). bones of him *that encampeth* (against) *thee:*
Nah 3:17. *which camp* in the hedges

חַנּוּן *g'han-noon',* adj. 2587

Ex. 22:27(26). I will hear; for I (am) *gracious.*
34: 6. The Lord God, merciful *and gracious,*
2Ch 30: 9. the Lord your God (is) *gracious*
Neh 9:17. a God ready to pardon, *gracious* and merciful,
31. thou (art) a *gracious* and merciful God.
Ps. 86:15. a God full of compassion, *and gracious,*
103: 8. The Lord (is) merciful *and gracious,*
111: 4 & 112:4. *gracious* and full of compassion.
116: 5. *Gracious* (is) the Lord,
145: 8. The Lord (is) *gracious,*
Joel 2:13. for he (is) *gracious* and merciful,
Jon. 4: 2. I knew that thou (art) a *gracious* God,

חָנוּת [*g'hāh-nooth'*], f. 2588

Jer. 37:16. and into *the cabins,* (marg. or, *cells*)

חָנַט [*g'hāh-nat'*]. 2590

* KAL.—*Preterite.* *

Cant 2:13. The fig tree *putteth forth* her green figs,

KAL.—*Infinitive.*

Gen 50: 2. the physicians *to embalm* his father:

KAL.—*Future.*

Gen50: 2. *and* the physicians *embalmed* Israel.
26. *and they embalmed* him,

KAL.—*Participle.* Paül.

Gen50: 3. the days of *those which are embalmed:*

2591 **חִנְטִין** *ghin-teen'*, Ch. m. pl.

Ezr. 6: 9. offerings of the God of heaven, *wheat*, salt,
7:22. and to an hundred measures of *wheat*,

2593 **חָנִיךְ** [*ghāh-neech'*], adj.

Gen14:14. he armed *his trained* (servants), (marg. or, *instructed*)

2594 **חֲנִינָה** *ghănee-nāh'*, f.

Jer. 16:13. where I will not shew you *favour*.

2595 **חֲנִית** *ghăneeth*, f.

1Sa 13:19. make (them) swords or *spears:*
22. there was neither sword *nor spear*
17: 7. the staff of *his spear*
— *his spear*'s head (weighed)
45. with a sword, *and with a spear*,
47. saveth not with sword *and spear:*
18:10. *and* (there was) *a javelin* in Saul's hand.
11. Saul cast *the javelin;*
19: 9. *with his javelin* in his hand:
10. even to the wall *with the javelin;*
— smote *the javelin* into the wall:
20:33. Saul cast *a javelin* at him
21: 8(9). under thine hand *spear* or sword?
22: 6. *having his spear* in his hand,
26: 7. *and his spear* stuck in the ground
8. *with the spear* even to the earth
11. take thou now *the spear* that (is) at
12. So David took *the spear*
16. now see where the king's *spear* (is),
22. Behold the king's *spear!*
2Sa 1: 6. Saul leaned upon *his spear;*
2:23. with the hinder end of *the spear*
— *the spear* came out behind him;
21:19. *whose spear* (was) like a weaver's beam.
23: 7. the staff of *a spear;*
18. he lifted up *his spear* against
21. the Egyptian had *a spear* in his hand;
— plucked *the spear* out of the Egyptian's hand, and slew him *with his own spear*.
2K. 11:10. give king David's *spears* and shields,
1Ch 11:11. he lifted up *his spear* against
20. for lifting up *his spear* against
23. in the Egyptian's hand (was) *a spear*
— plucked *the spear* out of the Egyptian's hand, and slew him *with his own spear*.
12:34. with shield *and spear*
20: 5. *whose spear* staff (was) like
2Ch 23: 9. to the captains of hundreds *spears*,
Job 39:23. the glittering *spear* and the shield.
41:26(18). *the spear*, the dart,
Ps. 35: 3. Draw out also *the spear*,
46: 9(10). cutteth *the spear* in sunder;
57: 4(5). whose teeth (are) *spears* and arrows,
Isa. 2: 4. *and their spears* into pruninghooks:
Mic 4: 3. *and their spears* into pruninghooks:
Nah 3: 3. bright sword and *the* glittering *spear:*
Hab 3:11. at the shining of *thy* glittering *spear*.

2596 **חָנַךְ** [*ghāh-nach'*].

* KAL.—*Preterite.* *

Deu20: 5. *hath* not *dedicated it?*

KAL.—*Imperative.*

Pro.22: 6. *Train up* a child in the way he should go: (marg. or, *Catechise*)

KAL.—*Future.*

Deu 20: 5. and another man *dedicate it.*
1K. 8:63. *So* the king and all the children of Israel *dedicated*
2Ch 7: 5. *so* the king and all the people *dedicated* the house

---

חֲנֻכָּה *ghănook-kāh'*, f. 2598

Nu. 7:10. the princes offered for *dedicating*
11. *for the dedicating of* the altar.
84, 88. This (was) *the dedication of* the altar,
2Ch 7: 9. they kept *the dedication of* the altar
Neh 12:27. *And at the dedication of* the wall
— to keep *the dedication* with gladness,
Ps. 30[title](1). Song (at) *the dedication of* the house of David.

חֲנֻכָּה [*ghănook-kāh'*], Ch. f. 2597

Ezr. 6:16. kept *the dedication of* this house
17. And offered *at the dedication of*
Dan. 3: 2. come *to the dedication of* the image
3. were gathered together *unto the dedication of*

חִנָּם *ghin-nāhm'*, adv. 2600

Gen29:15. thou therefore serve me *for nought?*
Ex. 21: 2. he shall go out free *for nothing*.
11. then shall she go out *free*
Nu. 11: 5. which we did eat in Egypt *freely;*
1Sa 19: 5. to slay David *without a cause?*
25:31. either that thou hast shed blood *causeless*,
2Sa 24:24. of *that which doth cost me nothing*.
1K. 2:31. take away the *innocent* blood,
1Ch 21:24. nor offer burnt offerings *without cost*.
Job 1: 9. Doth Job fear God *for nought?*
2: 3. to destroy him *without cause*.
9:17. multiplieth my wounds *without cause*.
22: 6. a pledge from thy brother *for nought*,
Ps. 35: 7. For *without cause* have they hid for me
— *without cause* they have digged
19. the eye that hate me *without a cause*.
69: 4(5). They that hate me *without a cause*
109: 3. fought against me *without a cause*.
119:161. Princes have persecuted me *without a cause:*
Pro. 1:11. privily for the innocent *without cause:*
17. Surely *in vain* the net is spread
3:30. Strive not with a man *without cause*,
23:29. who hath wounds *without cause?*
24:28. witness against thy neighbour *without cause;*
26: 2. so the curse *causeless* shall not come.
Isa. 52: 3. Ye have sold yourselves *for nought;*
5. my people is taken away *for nought?*
Jer. 22:13. useth his neighbour's service *without wages*,
Lam. 3:52. like a bird, *without cause*.
Eze. 6:10. I have not said *in vain*
14:23. that I have not done *without cause*
Mal. 1:10. kindle (fire) on mine altar *for nought*.

חֲנָמַל *ghănāh-māhl'*, m. 2602

Ps. 78:47. their sycomore trees *with frost*. (marg. or, *great hailstones*)

חָנַן *ghāh-nan'*. 2589, 2603

* KAL.—*Preterite.* *

Gen33: 5. which God *hath graciously given*
11. God *hath dealt graciously with me*,
Ex. 33:19. *and will be gracious* to whom
2Sa. 12:22. God *will be gracious* to me,
Lam. 4:16. *they favoured* not the elders.

KAL.—*Infinitive.*

Job 19:17. *though I intreated* for the children's (sake)
Ps. 77: 9(10). Hath God forgotten *to be gracious?*
102:13(14). for the time *to favour her,*
Isa. 30:18. *that he may be gracious unto you,*
19. he will be *very* gracious unto thee (lit. *being gracious* he will be gracious)

KAL.—*Imperative.*

Jud. 21:22. *Be favourable* unto them *for our sakes:* (marg. or, *Gratify us* in them)
Job 19:21. *Have pity upon me, have pity upon me,*
Ps. 4: 1(2) & 6:2(3) & 9:13(14) & 25:16. *have mercy upon me,* (marg. or, *be gracious unto me*)
25:16. *and have mercy upon me;*
26:11. redeem me, *and be merciful unto me.*
27: 7. *have mercy also upon me,*
30:10(11). *and have mercy upon me:*
31: 9(10). *Have mercy upon me,*
41: 4(5), 10(11). Lord, *be merciful unto me:*
51: 1(3). *Have mercy upon me,* O God
56: 1(2) & 57:1(2), 1(2) & 86:3. *Be merciful unto me,*
86:16. O turn unto me, *and have mercy upon me;*
119:29. *grant me* thy law *graciously.*
58. *be merciful unto me* according to
132. *and be merciful unto me,*
123: 3. *Have mercy upon us,* O Lord, *have mercy upon us:*
Isa. 33: 2. O Lord, *be gracious unto us;*

KAL.—*Future.*

Gen 43:29. God *be gracious unto thee,*
Ex. 33:19. gracious to whom *I will be gracious,*
Nu. 6:25. *and be gracious unto thee:*
Deu 7: 2. thou shalt make no covenant...*nor shew mercy unto them:*
28:50. shall not regard...nor *shew favour*
2K. 13:23. *And* the Lord *was gracious* unto them,
Job 33:24. *Then he is gracious unto him,*
Ps. 59: 5(6). *be* not *merciful* to any wicked
67: 1(2). God *be merciful unto us,*
123: 2. until *that he have mercy upon us.*
Isa. 27:11. *will shew them* no *favour.*
30:19. *he will be* very *gracious unto thee*
Am. 5:15. the Lord God of hosts *will be gracious unto* the remnant
Mal. 1: 9. beseech God *that he will be gracious unto us:*

KAL.—*Participle.* Poel.

Ps. 37:21. the righteous *sheweth mercy,*
26. (He is) ever *merciful,*
109:12. neither let there be *any to favour*
112: 5. A good man *sheweth favour,*
Pro. 14:31. honoureth him *hath mercy on* the poor.
19:17. *He that hath pity upon* the poor
28: 8. *for him that will pity* the poor.

* NIPHAL.—*Preterite.* *

Jer. 22:23. how *gracious shalt thou be*

* PIEL.—*Future.* *

2Sa. 12:22. (כתיב) God *will be gracious to me,*
Pro. 26:25. When *he* speaketh *fair,* (marg. *maketh* his voice *gracious*)

* POEL.—*Future.* *

Ps. 102:14(15). *favour* the dust thereof.

POEL.—*Participle.*

Pro. 14:21. *but he that hath mercy on* the poor,

* HOPHAL.—*Preterite.* *

Pro. 21:10. his neighbour *findeth* no *favour*
Isa. 26:10. *Let favour be shewed* to the wicked,

* HITHPAEL.—*Preterite.* *

1K. 8:33, 47. *and make supplication* unto thee
59. wherewith *I have made supplication*
9: 3. supplication, that *thou hast made*
2Ch 6:24. pray *and make supplication*
37. turn *and pray* unto thee

HITHPAEL.—*Infinitive.*

Gen 42:21. *when he besought* us,
Est. 4: 8. *to make supplication* unto him,

HITHPAEL.—*Future.*

Deu 3:23. *And I besought* the Lord
2K. 1:13. *and besought* him,
Est. 8: 3. *and besought* him with tears
Job 8: 5. and *make thy supplication*
9:15. *I would make supplication* to my judge.
19:16. *I intreated* him with my mouth.
Ps. 30: 8(9). unto the Lord *I made supplication.*
142: 1(2). unto the Lord *did I make my supplication.*
Hos. 12: 4(5). wept, *and made supplication* unto him:

חֲנַן [*g̱hănāhn*], Ch. 2604

* P'AL.—*Infinitive.* *

Dan 4:27(24). *by shewing mercy* to the poor;

* ITHPAEL.—*Participle.* *

Dan 6:11(12). praying *and making supplication*

חָנֵף [*g̱hāh-nēhph'*]. 2610

* KAL.—*Preterite.* *

Isa. 24 5. The earth also *is defiled*
Jer. 23 11. both prophet and priest *are profane;*

KAL.—*Infinitive.*

Jer. 3: 1. shall not that land be *greatly* polluted (lit. *in polluting* be polluted)

KAL.—*Future.*

Ps. 106:38. *and* the land *was polluted*
Jer. 3: 1. *shall* not that land *be* greatly *polluted?*
9. *that she defiled* the land,
Mic. 4:11. that say, *Let her be defiled,*

* HIPHIL.—*Future.* *

Nu. 35:33. So *ye shall* not *pollute* the land
— for blood it *defileth* the land:
Jer. 3: 2. *and thou hast polluted* the land
Dan 11:32. covenant *shall he corrupt* by flatteries (marg. or, *cause to dissemble*)

חָנֵף *g̱hāh-nēhph'*, adj. 2611

Job 8:13. *the hypocrite*'s hope shall perish:
13:16. for *an hypocrite* shall not come
15:34. the congregation of *hypocrites*
17: 8. shall stir up himself against *the hypocrite.*
20: 5. the joy of *the hypocrite* (but) for a moment?
27: 8. what (is) the hope of *the hypocrite,*
34:30. That *the hypocrite* reign not, lest the people (lit. *hypocritical* man)
36:13. *But the hypocrites in* heart
Ps. 35:16. *With hypocritical* mockers
Pro. 11: 9. *An hypocrite* with (his) mouth destroyeth
Isa. 9:17(16). for every one (is) *an hypocrite* and an evildoer,
10: 6. I will send him against an *hypocritical* nation,
33:14. fearfulness hath surprised *the hypocrites.*

חֹנֶף *g̱hōh'-neph*, m. 2612

Isa. 32: 6. work iniquity, to practise *hypocrisy,*

חֲנֻפָּה *g̱hănoo-phāh'*, f. 2613

Jer. 23:15. from the prophets of Jerusalem is *profaneness* (marg. or, *hypocrisy*)

חָנַק [*g̱hāh-nak'*]. 2614

* NIPHAL.—*Future.* *

2Sa. 17:23. *and hanged himself,* and died,

* PIEL.—*Participle.* *

Nah 2:12(13). *and strangled* for his lionesses,

חָסַד [*g̱hāh-sad'*]. 2616

* PIEL.—*Future.* *

Pro. 25:10. he that heareth (it) *put thee to shame,*

* HITHPAEL.—*Future.* *

2Sa.22:26. With the merciful *thou wilt shew thyself merciful,*
Ps. 18:25(26). With the merciful *thou wilt shew thyself merciful;*

2617 חֶסֶד *gheh'-sed*, m.

Gen19:19. thou hast magnified *thy mercy,*
20:13. This (is) *thy kindness* which thou
21:23. *according to the kindness* that I have
24:12. shew *kindness* unto my master
14. I know that thou hast shewed *kindness*
27. destitute my master of *his mercy*
49. if ye will deal *kindly* (lit. do *kindness to*)
32.10(11). the least of all *the mercies,*
39:21. and shewed him *mercy,* (marg. *kindness*)
40:14. well with thee, and shew *kindness,*
47:29. deal *kindly* and truly (lit. do *kindness* to)
Ex. 15:13. Thou *in thy mercy* hast led forth
20: 6. shewing *mercy* unto thousands
34: 6. abundant in *goodness* and truth,
7. Keeping *mercy* for thousands,
Lev.20:17. it (is) *a wicked thing;*
Nu. 14:18. longsuffering, and of great *mercy,*
19. according unto the greatness of *thy mercy,*
Deu 5:10. shewing *mercy* unto thousands
7: 9. keepeth covenant *and mercy*
12. the covenant and *the mercy*
Jos. 2:12. since I have shewed you *kindness,* that ye will also shew *kindness*
14. that we will deal *kindly* and truly with thee. (lit. do *kindness* to)
Jud. 1:24. we will shew thee *mercy.*
8:35. Neither shewed they *kindness*
Ru. 1: 8. the Lord deal *kindly* with you, (lit. do *kindness* to)
2:20. who hath not left off *his kindness*
3:10. thou hast shewed more *kindness* (lit. thou hast bettered *thy kindness*)
1Sa.15: 6. for ye shewed *kindness* to all
20: 8. thou shalt *deal kindly* (lit. do *kindness* to)
14. shew me *the kindness of* the Lord,
15. thou shalt not cut off *thy kindness*
2Sa. 2: 5. that ye have shewed *this kindness*
6. the Lord shew *kindness*
3: 8. Judah do shew *kindness* this day
7:15. *But my mercy* shall not depart
9: 1. that I may shew him *kindness*
3. shew *the kindness of* God unto him?
7. for I will surely shew thee *kindness*
10: 2. I will shew *kindness* unto Hanun the son of Nahash, as his father shewed *kindness*
15:20. *mercy* and truth (be) with thee.
16:17. (Is) this *thy kindness* to thy friend?
22:51. sheweth *mercy* to his anointed,
1K. 2: 7. But shew *kindness* unto the sons of
3: 6. David my father great *mercy,* (marg. or, *bounty*)
— hast kept for him this great *kindness.*
8:23. who keepest covenant and *mercy*
20:31. house of Israel (are) *merciful* kings: (lit. of *mercy*)
1Ch 16:34. for *his mercy* (endureth) for ever.
41. because *his mercy* (endureth)
17:13. *and* I will not take *my mercy*
19: 2. I will shew *kindness* unto Hanun
— because his father shewed *kindness*
2Ch 1: 8. hast shewed great *mercy* unto David
5:13. for *his mercy* (endureth) for ever:
6:14. *and* (shewest) *mercy* unto thy servants,
42. remember *the mercies of* David
7: 3,6 & 20:21. *his mercy* (endureth) for ever.
24:22. the king remembered not *the kindness*
32:32. acts of Hezekiah, *and his goodness,* (marg. *kindnesses*)
35:26. the acts of Josiah, *and his goodness,* (marg. *kindnesses*)
Ezr. 3:11. *his mercy* (endureth) for ever
7:28. hath extended *mercy* unto me
9: 9. hath extended *mercy* unto us
Neh 1: 5. that keepeth covenant *and mercy*
9:17. of great *kindness,*
32. who keepest covenant *and mercy,*
13:14. wipe not out *my good deeds* (marg. *kindnesses*)
Neh 13:22. me according to the greatness of *thy mercy.*
Est. 2: 9. she obtained *kindness*
17. she obtained grace *and favour* (marg. or, *kindness*)
Job 6:14. To him that is afflicted *pity*
10:12. hast granted me life *and favour,*
37:13. for his land, or *for mercy.*
Ps. 5: 7(8). house in the multitude of *thy mercy;*
6: 4(5). oh save me for *thy mercies'* sake.
13: 5(6). But I have trusted *in thy mercy;*
17: 7. Shew *thy* marvellous *lovingkindness,*
18:50(51). sheweth *mercy* to his anointed,
21: 7(8). *and through the mercy of* the most High
23: 6. Surely goodness *and mercy* shall follow
25: 6. mercies *and thy lovingkindnesses;*
7. *according to thy mercy*
10. paths of the Lord (are) *mercy* and truth
26: 3. *thy lovingkindness* (is) before mine eyes:
31: 7(8). I will be glad and rejoice *in thy mercy:*
16(17). save me *for thy mercies'* sake.
21(22). *his* marvellous *kindness* in a strong
32:10. *mercy* shall compass him about.
33: 5. earth is full of *the goodness of* the Lord. (marg. or, *mercy*)
18. them that hope *in his mercy;*
22. Let *thy mercy,* O Lord, be upon us,
36: 5(6). *Thy mercy,* O Lord, (is) in the
7(8). How excellent (is) *thy lovingkindness,*
10(11). O continue *thy lovingkindness*
40:10(11). have not concealed *thy lovingkindness*
11(12). let *thy lovingkindness*
42: 8(9). will command *his lovingkindness*
44:26(27). redeem us for *thy mercies'* sake.
48: 9(10). have thought of *thy lovingkindness,*
51: 1(3). O God, *according to thy lovingkindness:*
52: 1(3). *the goodness of* God (endureth)
8(10). I trust *in the mercy of* God
57: 3(4). God shall send forth *his mercy*
10(11). For *thy mercy* (is) great
59:10(11). The God of *my mercy* shall
16(17). I will sing aloud of *thy mercy*
17(18). the God of *my mercy.*
61: 7(8). O prepare *mercy* and truth,
62:12(13). thee, O Lord, (belongeth) *mercy:*
63: 3(4). *thy lovingkindness* (is) better
66:20. *nor his mercy* from me.
69:13(14). in the multitude of *thy mercy*
16(17). for *thy lovingkindness* (is) good:
77: 8(9). Is *his mercy* clean gone for ever?
85: 7(8). Shew us *thy mercy,* O Lord,
10(11). *Mercy* and truth are met together;
86: 5. plenteous in *mercy* unto all them
13. For great (is) *thy mercy* toward me:
15. plenteous in *mercy* and truth.
88:11(12). Shall *thy lovingkindness* be declared
89: 1(2). I will sing of *the mercies of* the Lord
2(3). *Mercy* shall be built up for ever:
14(15). *mercy* and truth shall go before
24(25). my faithfulness *and my mercy*
28(29). *My mercy* will I keep for him
33(34). *Nevertheless my lovingkindness*
49(50). *thy* former *lovingkindnesses,*
90.14. O satisfy us early with *thy mercy;*
92: 2(3). To shew forth *thy lovingkindness*
94:18. *thy mercy,* O Lord, held me up.
98: 3. He hath remembered *his mercy*
100: 5. *his mercy* (is) everlasting;
101: 1. I will sing of *mercy* and judgment:
103: 4. who crowneth thee with *lovingkindness*
8. slow to anger, and plenteous in *mercy*
11. great is *his mercy* toward them
17. *But the mercy of* the Lord
106: 1. for *his mercy* (endureth) for ever.
7. the multitude of *thy mercies;*
45. the multitude of *his mercies.*
107: 1. for *his mercy* (endureth) for ever.
8, 15, 21, 31. praise the Lord (for) *his goodness,*
43. *the lovingkindness of* the Lord.
108: 4(5). *thy mercy* (is) great above the heavens:
109:12. Let there be none to extend *mercy*
16. he remembered not to shew *mercy,*
21. because *thy mercy* (is) good,
26. O save me *according to thy mercy.*
115: 1. for *thy mercy,* (and) for thy truth's
117: 2. For *his merciful kindness* is great
118: 1 2, 3, 4, 29. *his mercy* (endureth) for ever.

Ps.119:41. Let *thy mercies* come also unto me,
64. The earth, O Lord, is full of *thy mercy:*
76. *thy merciful kindness* be for
88. Quicken me *after thy lovingkindness;*
124. thy servant *according unto thy mercy,*
149. *according unto thy lovingkindness:*
159. *according to thy lovingkindness.*
130: 7. with the Lord (there is) *mercy,*
136: 1, 2, 3, 4, 5, 6, 7, 8, 9, 10, 11, 12, 13, 14, 15, 16, 17, 18, 19, 20, 21, 22, 23, 24, 25, 26. for *his mercy* (endureth) for ever.
138: 2. for *thy lovingkindness*
8. *thy mercy,* O Lord, (endureth) for ever:
141: 5. smite me; (it shall be) *a kindness:*
143: 8. Cause me to hear *thy lovingkindness*
12. *And of thy mercy* cut off mine enemies,
144: 2. *My goodness,* and my fortress;
145: 8. slow to anger, and of great *mercy.*
147:11. in those that hope *in his mercy.*
Pro. 3: 3. Let not *mercy* and truth forsake thee:
11:17. The *merciful* man (lit. of *mercy*)
14:22. *but mercy* and truth (shall be) to them
34. *but* sin (is) *a reproach* to any people.
16: 6. *By mercy* and truth iniquity is purged:
19:22. The desire of a man (is) *his kindness:*
20: 6. proclaim every one *his own goodness:* (marg. or, *bounty*)
28. *Mercy* and truth preserve the king: and his throne is upholden *by mercy.*
21:21. *and mercy* findeth life,
31:26. in her tongue (is) the law of *kindness.*
Isa. 16: 5. *in mercy* shall the throne be established:
40: 6. all *the goodliness thereof* (is) as
54: 8. *but with* everlasting *kindness*
10. *but my kindness* shall not depart
55: 3. *the* sure *mercies of* David.
57: 1. *merciful* men (are) taken (marg. men of *kindness,* or, *godliness*)
63: 7. *the lovingkindnesses of* the Lord,
— multitude of *his lovingkindnesses.*
Jer. 2: 2. *the kindness of* thy youth.
9:24(23). Lord which exercise *lovingkindness,*
16: 5. *lovingkindness* and mercies.
31: 3. with *lovingkindness* have I drawn
32:18. Thou shewest *lovingkindness*
33:11. for *his mercy* (endureth) for ever:
Lam. 3:22. (It is of) the Lord's *mercies*
32. the multitude of *his mercies.*
Dan 1: 9. God had brought Daniel *into favour*
9: 4. keeping the covenant *and mercy*
Hos. 2:19(21). *and in lovingkindness,*
4: 1. because (there is) no truth, nor *mercy,*
6: 4. *for your goodness* (is) as a morning (marg. or, *mercy,* or, *kindness*)
6. For I desired *mercy,* and not sacrifice;
10:12. reap in *mercy;* break up your fallow
12: 6(7). keep *mercy* and judgment,
Joel 2:13. slow to anger, and of great *kindness,*
Jon. 2: 8(9). forsake *their own mercy.*
4: 2. slow to anger, and of great *kindness,*
Mic. 6: 8. to do justly, and to love *mercy,*
7:18. because he delighteth (in) *mercy.*
20. *the mercy* to Abraham,
Zec. 7: 9. *and* shew *mercy* and compassions

2620 חָסָה *ghāh-sāh'.*

* KAL.—*Preterite.* *

Deu 32:37. rock in whom *they trusted,*
Ps. 7: 1(2). in thee *do I put my trust:*
11: 1. In the Lord *put I my trust:* how say ye
16: 1. for in thee *do I put my trust*
25:20. for *I put my trust* in thee.
31: 1(2). In thee, O Lord, *do I put my trust;*
37:40. save them, because *they trust* in him.
57: 1(2). my soul *trusteth* in thee:
64:10(11). *and shall trust* in him;
71: 1. In thee, O Lord, *do I put my trust:*
141: 8. in thee *is my trust;*
144: 2. my shield, and (he) in whom *I trust;*
Zep. 3:12. *and they shall trust* in the name

KAL.—*Infinitive.*

Ru. 2:12. under whose wings thou art come *to trust.*
Ps. 118: 8, 9. better *to trust* in the Lord
Isa. 30: 2. *and to trust* in the shadow of Egypt!

KAL.—*Imperative.*

Jud. 9:15. come (and) *put your trust* in my shadow

KAL.—*Future.*

2Sa 22: 3. my rock; in him *will I trust:*
Ps. 18: 2(3). my strength, in whom *I will trust;*
34: 8(9). blessed (is) the man (that) *trusteth*
36: 7(8). the children of men *put their trust*
57: 1(2). thy wings *will I make my refuge,*
61: 4(5). *I will trust* in the covert of thy wings. (marg. or, *make my refuge*)
91: 4. under his wings *shalt thou trust:*
Isa. 14:32. the poor of his people *shall trust* (marg. *betake themselves*)

KAL.—*Participle.* Poel.

2Sa 22:31. a buckler to all *them that trust*
Ps. 2:12. Blessed (are) all *they that put their trust*
5:11(12). But let all those *that put their trust*
17: 7. *them which put their trust*
18:30(31). buckler to all *those that trust*
31:19(20). *for them that trust* in thee
34:22(23). none of *them that trust* in him
Pro. 14:32. *but* the righteous *hath hope*
30: 5. shield *unto them that put their trust*
Isa. 57:13. *but he that putteth his trust*
Nah 1: 7. he knoweth *them that trust* in him.

חָסוּת *ghāh-sooth',* f. 2622

Isa. 30: 3. *and the trust* in the shadow

חָסִיד *ghāh-seed',* adj. 2623

Deu 33: 8. thy Urim (be) with *thy holy* one,
1Sa 2: 9. He will keep the feet of *his saints,*
2Sa 22:26. With *the merciful* thou wilt
2Ch 6:41. *and* let *thy saints* rejoice
Ps. 4: 3(4). hath set apart *him that is godly*
12: 1(2). for *the godly man* ceaseth;
16:10. suffer *thine Holy One* to see
18:25(26). With *the merciful* thou wilt
30: 4(5). Sing unto the Lord, *O ye saints of his,*
31:23(24). O love the Lord, all *ye his saints:*
32: 6. For this shall every one *that is godly*
37:28. and forsaketh not *his saints;*
43: 1. an un*godly* nation: (lit. not *godly*) (marg. or, un*merciful*)
50: 5. Gather *my saints* together
52: 9(11). for (it is) good before *thy saints.*
79: 2. the flesh of *thy saints* unto the beasts
85: 8(9). peace unto his people, and to *his saints:*
86: 2. Preserve my soul; for I (am) *holy:* (marg. or, *one whom thou favourest*)
89:19(20). spakest in vision *to thy holy one,*
97:10. he preserveth the souls of *his saints;*
116:15. in the sight of the Lord (is) the death *of his saints.*
132: 9. *and* let *thy saints* shout for joy.
16. *and her saints* shall shout aloud
145:10. *and thy saints* shall bless thee.
17. *and holy* in all his works. (marg. *merciful,* or, *bountiful*)
148:14. the praise of all *his saints;*
149: 1. his praise in the congregation of *saints.*
5. Let *the saints* be joyful in glory:
9. this honour have all *his saints.*
Pro. 2: 8. preserveth the way of *his saints.*
Jer. 3:12. for I (am) *merciful,*
Mic. 7: 2. *The good* (man) is perished (marg. or, *godly,* or, *merciful*)

חֲסִידָה *ghăsee-dāh',* f. 2624

Lev 11:19. And *the stork,* the heron
Deu 14:18. And *the stork,* and the heron
Job 39:13. wings and *feathers* unto the ostrich? (marg. or, the feathers of *the stork* and ostrich)
Ps. 104:17. *the stork,* the fir trees (are) her house.
Jer. 8: 7. *the stork* in the heaven knoweth
Zec. 5: 9. they had wings like the wings of *a stork:*

2625 **חָסִיל** *ghāh seel'*, m.

1K. 8:37. if there be *caterpiller;*
2Ch 6:28. mildew, locusts, *or caterpillers;*
Ps. 78:46. their increase *unto the caterpiller*,
Isa. 33: 4. the gathering of *the caterpiller:*
Joel 1: 4. left hath *the caterpiller* eaten.
2:25. cankerworm, *and the caterpiller*,

2626 **חָסִין** *ghăseen*, adj.

Ps. 89: 8(9). who (is) a *strong* Lord like unto thee?

2627 **חַסִּיר** *ghas-seer'*, Ch. adj.

Dan. 5:27. and art found *wanting.*

2628 **חָסַל** [*ghāh-sal'*].

* KAL.—*Future.* *

Deu 28:38. for the locust *shall consume it.*

2629 **חָסַם** [*ghāh-sam'*].

* KAL.—*Future.* *

Deu 25: 4. *Thou shalt* not *muzzle* the ox

KAL.—*Participle.*—Poel.

Eze 39:11. *and* it *shall stop* the (noses)

2630 **חָסַן** [*ghāh-san'*].

* NIPHAL.—*Future.* *

Isa. 23:18. it shall not be treasured nor *laid up;*

2631 **חֲסַן** [*ghăsan*], Ch.

* APHEL. *Preterite.* *

Dan. 7:22. that the saints *possessed* the kingdom.

APHEL.—*Future.*

Dan. 7:18. *and possess* the kingdom for ever,

2634 **חָסֹן** *ghāh-sōhn'*, adj.

Isa. 1:31. *the strong* shall be as tow,
Am. 2: 9. *and* he (was) *strong* as the oaks;

2632 **חֵסֶן** [*ghĕh'-sen*], Ch. m.

Dan. 2:37. the God of heaven hath given thee a kingdom, *power*, and strength,
4:30(27). by the might of *my power*,

2633 **חֹסֶן** *ghōh'-sen*, m.

Pro. 15: 6. house of the righteous (is) much *treasure:*
27:24. For *riches* (are) not for ever: (marg. *strength*)
Isa. 33: 6. *strength of* salvation:
Jer. 20: 5. I will deliver all *the strength of* this city,
Eze 22:25. they have taken *the treasure*

2635 **חֲסַף** *ghăsaph*, Ch. m.

Dan. 2:33. his feet part of iron and part of *clay.*
34. his feet (that were) of iron *and clay*, and brake them
35. Then was the iron, *the clay*, the
41. feet and toes, part of potters' *clay*, and
— the iron mixed *with* miry *clay*
42. toes of the feet (were) part of iron, and part of *clay*,
Dan 2:43. thou sawest iron mixed *with* miry *clay*,
— even as iron is not mixed with *clay.*
45. brake in pieces the iron, the brass, *the clay*,

חַסְפַּס [*ghas-pas'*]. 2636

* *Participle.* Passive. *

Ex. 16:14. *a* small *round thing*,

חָסֵר [*ghāh-sĕhr'*]. 2637

* KAL.—*Preterite.* *

Deu. 2: 7. *thou hast lacked* nothing.
Neh. 9:21. *they lacked* nothing;
Jer. 44:18. *we have wanted* all

KAL.—*Infinitive.*

Gen. 8: 5. the waters *decreased* continually (marg. were in going *and decreasing*)

KAL.—*Future.*

Gen. 8: 3. *and* after the end of the hundred and fifty days the waters *were abated.*
18:28. Peradventure *there shall lack*
Deu 8: 9. *thou shalt* not *lack* any (thing) in it;
15: 8. need, (in that) which *he wanteth.*
1K. 17:14. neither *shall* the cruse of oil *fail*,
Ps. 23: 1. my shepherd; *I shall* not *want.*
34:10(11). *shall* not *want* any good
Pro 13:25. the belly of the wicked *shall want.*
31:11. *he shall have* no *need* of spoil.
Ecc. 9: 8. *let* thy head *lack* no ointment.
Cant. 7: 2(3). goblet, (which) *wanteth* not liquor:
Isa. 51:14. nor that his bread *should fail.*
Eze. 4:17. That *they may want* bread

* PIEL.—*Future.* *

Ps. 8: 5(6). *For thou hast made him* a little *lower*

PIEL.—*Participle.*

Ecc. 4: 8. *and bereave* my soul of good?

* HIPHIL.—*Preterite.* *

Ex. 16:18. gathered little *had* no *lack;*

HIPHIL.—*Future.*

Isa. 32: 6. *he will cause* the drink of the thirsty *to fail.*

חָסֵר *ghāh-sĕhr'*, adj. 2638

1Sa 21:15(16). *Have* I *need* of mad men,
2Sa 3:29. *or that lacketh* bread.
1K. 11:22. what *hast* thou *lacked* with me,
17:16. neither *did* the cruse of oil *fail*,
Pro 6:32. woman *lacketh* understanding:
7: 7. a young man *void of* understanding,
9: 4. *him that wanteth* understanding,
16. *and* (as for) *him that wanteth*
10:13. *him that is void of* understanding.
21. fools die *for want of* wisdom.
11:12. *He that is void of* wisdom (marg. *destitute*)
12: 9. honoureth himself, *and lacketh* bread.
11. vain (persons is) *void of* understanding.
15:21. joy *to* (him that is) *destitute of* wisdom:
17:18. A man *void of* understanding striketh hands,
24:30. the man *void of* understanding;
28:16. The prince *that wanteth* understanding
Ecc. 6: 2. so that he *wanteth* nothing
10: 3. his wisdom *faileth* (him),

חֶסֶר *gheh'-ser*, m. 2639

Job 30: 3. *For want* and famine
Pro. 28:22. considereth not that *poverty*

חֹסֶר *ghōh'-ser*, m. 2640

Deu 28:48. in nakedness, *and in want of*

Deu28:57. she shall eat them *for want of*
Am. 4: 6. *and want of* bread in all your places:

2642 ## חֶסְרוֹן *ghes-rōhn'*, m.

Ecc. 1:15. *and that which is wanting* (marg. *defect*)

2643 ## חַף *ghaph*, adj.

Job 33: 9. without transgression, I (am) *innocent;*

2644 ## חָפָא [*ghāh-phāh'*].

* PIEL.—*Future.* *

2K. 17: 9. *And* the children of Israel *did secretly*

2645 ## חָפָה [*ghāh-phāh'*].

* KAL.—*Preterite.* *

2Sa 15:30. *covered* every man his head,
Est. 7: 8. *they covered* Haman's face.
Jer. 14: 3. *and covered* their heads.
4. *they covered* their heads.

KAL.—*Participle.* Poel.

2Sa 15:30. *had* his head *covered,*
Est. 6:12. *and having* his head *covered.*

* NIPHAL.—*Participle.* *

Ps. 68:13(14). wings of a dove *covered* with silver,

* PIEL.—*Preterite.* *

2Ch. 3: 5. the greater house *he cieled*
9. *he overlaid* the upper chambers

PIEL.—*Future.*

2Ch 3: 5. *which he overlaid* with fine gold,
7. *He overlaid also* the house,
8. *and he overlaid it* with fine gold,

2646 ## חֻפָּה *ghoop-pāh'*, f.

Ps. 19: 5(6). as a bridegroom coming out *of his chamber,*
Isa. 4: 5. upon all the glory (shall be) *a defence.* (marg. *covering*)
Joel 2:16. go forth of his chamber, and the bride out *of her closet.*

2648 ## חָפַז [*ghāh-phaz'*].

* KAL.—*Infinitive.* *

2Sa 4: 4. *as she made haste* to flee,(lit. *in her hastening*)
2K. 7:15. the Syrians had cast away *in their haste.*
Ps. 31:22(23). For I said *in my haste,*
116:11. I said *in my haste,* All men (are) liars.

KAL.—*Future.*

Deu 20: 3. fear not, and *do* not *tremble,* (marg. *make haste*)
Job 40:23. drinketh up a river, (and) *hasteth* not:

* NIPHAL.—*Preterite.* *

Ps. 48: 5(6). they were troubled, (and) *hasted away.*

NIPHAL.—*Future.*

Ps. 104: 7. voice of thy thunder *they hasted away.*

NIPHAL.—*Participle.*

1Sa 23:26. David *made haste* to get away

2649 ## חִפָּזוֹן *ghip-pāh-zōhn'*, m.

Ex. 12:11. ye shall eat it *in haste:*
Deu 16: 3. out of the land of Egypt *in haste:*
Isa. 52:12. ye shall not go out *with haste,*

2651 ## חָפְנַיִם *ghoph-nah'-yim*, dual.

Ex. 9: 8. Take to you *hand*fuls of ashes (lit. the fill of *your hands*)
Lev. 16:12. *his hands* full of sweet incense
Pro 30: 4. who hath gathered the wind *in his fists?*
Ecc. 4: 6. than *both the hands* full
Eze. 10: 2. fill *thine hand* with coals
7. and put (it) into *the hands of* (him)

חָפַף [*ghāh-phaph'*]. 2653

* KAL.—*Participle.* Poel. *

Deu 33:12. Lord *shall cover him* all the day

חָפֵץ *ghāh-phēhtz'*. 2654

* KAL.—*Preterite.* *

Gen34:19. *he had delight* in Jacob's daughter:
Nu. 14: 8. If the Lord *delight* in us,
Deu 21:14. if *thou have* no *delight* in her,
25: 8. *I like* not to take her;
Jud 13:23. If the Lord *were pleased* to kill us,
1Sa 2:25. because the Lord *would* slay them.
18:22. the king *hath delight* in thee,
19: 2(1). Saul's son *delighted* much in David:
2Sa 15:26. *I have* no *delight* in thee;
20:11. He that *favoureth* Joab,
22:20. because *he delighted* in me.
24: 3. why *doth* my lord the king *delight*
1K. 9: 1. desire which *he was pleased*
10: 9. which *delighted* in thee,
2Ch 9: 8. which *delighted* in thee
Est. 2:14. except the king *delighted* in her,
6: 6, 7, 9, 9, 11. whom the king *delighteth* to honour?
Job 21:14. *we desire* not the knowledge
33:32. for *I desire* to justify thee.
Ps. 18:19(20). because *he delighted* in me.
22: 8(9). seeing *he delighted* in him.
40: 6(7). Sacrifice and offering *thou didst* not *desire;*
8(9). *I delight* to do thy will,
41:11(12). I know that *thou favourest* me,
51: 6(8). *thou desirest* truth in the inward parts:
73:25. upon earth (that) *I desire* beside thee.
109:17. as *he delighted* not in blessing,
112: 1. *delighteth* greatly in his commandments.
115: 3. done whatsoever *he hath pleased.*
119:35. for therein *do I delight.*
135: 6. Whatsoever the Lord *pleased,*
Isa. 1:11. *I delight* not in the blood of bullocks,
42:21. The Lord *is well pleased* for his
53:10. *it pleased* the Lord to bruise him;
55:11. shall accomplish that which *I please,*
56: 4. choose (the things) that *please me,*
62: 4. the Lord *delighteth* in thee,
65:12. choose (that) wherein *I delighted* not.
66: 3. their soul *delighteth* in their abominations.
4. chose (that) in which *I delighted* not.
Jer. 9:24(23). for in these (things) *I delight,*
42:22. the place whither *ye desire* to go
Hos 6: 6. For *I desired* mercy,
Jon 1:14. hast done as *it pleased thee.*
Mic. 7:18. because *he delighteth* (in) mercy.
Mal. 2:17. *he delighteth* in them;

KAL.—*Infinitive.*

Eze 18:23. Have I *any* pleasure *at all* (lit. *in desiring* do I desire)

KAL.—*Future.*

Deu 25: 7. if the man *like* not to take
Ru. 3:13. if *he will* not do the part of a
Est. 6: 6. To whom *would* the king *delight* to do
Job 9: 3. If *he will* contend with him,
13: 3. *I desire* to reason with God.
40:17. *He moveth* his tail like a cedar:
Ps. 37:23. *he delighteth* in his way.
51:16(18). For *thou desirest* not sacrifice;
19(21). Then *shalt thou be pleased*
68:30(31). the people (that) *delight* in war
147:10. *He delighteth* not in the strength
Pro 18: 2. A fool *hath* no *delight* in understanding,
21: 1. he turneth it whithersoever *he will.*
Ecc. 8: 3. he doeth whatsoever *pleaseth him.*
Cant. 2: 7 & 3:5. nor awake (my) love, till *he please.*
8: 4. nor awake (my) love, until *he please.*

Isa. 13:17. *they shall* not *delight* in it.
58: 2. they seek me daily, and *delight* to know
— *they take delight* in approaching
Jer. 6:10. *they have* no *delight* in it.
Eze 18:23. *Have I* any *pleasure* at all
32. For *I have* no *pleasure* in the death
33:11. *I have* no *pleasure* in the death

2655 **חָפֵץ** *ghāh-phēhtz'*, adj.

1K. 13:33. *whosoever would*, he consecrated
21: 6. or else, *if it please* thee,
1Ch 28: 9. perfect heart and with a *willing* mind:
Neh 1:11. *who desire* to fear thy name:
Ps. 5: 4(5). not a God *that hath pleasure*
34:12(13). What man (is he that) *desireth* life,
35:27. *that favour* my righteous cause:
— *which hath pleasure* in the prosperity of
40:14(15). put to shame *that wish* me evil.
70: 2(3). put to confusion, *that desire* my hurt.
Mal. 3: 1. whom ye *delight in*:

2656 **חֵפֶץ** *ghĕh'-phetz*, m.

1Sa 15:22. Hath the Lord (as great) *delight*
18:25. The king *desireth* not any dowry,
2Sa 23: 5. and all (my) *desire*,
1K. 5: 8(22). I will do all *thy desire*
9(23). thou shalt accomplish *my desire*,
10(24). fir trees (according to) all *his desire*.
9:11. according to all *his desire*,
10:13. the queen of Sheba all *her desire*,
2Ch 9:12. the queen of Sheba all *her desire*,
Job 21:21. For what *pleasure* (hath) he in his (lit. what is *his pleasure*)
22: 3. *any pleasure* to the Almighty,
31:16. If I have withheld the poor *from* (their) *desire*,
Ps. 1: 2. But *his delight* (is) in the law
16: 3. in whom (is) all *my delight*.
107:30. so he bringeth them unto *their desired* haven. (lit. of *their desire*)
111: 2. all them *that have pleasure therein*.
Pro 3:15. all *the things thou canst desire* are not to be compared
8:11. all *the things that may be desired*
31:13. worketh *willingly* with her hands.
Ecc. 3: 1. time to every *purpose* under the heaven:
17. a time there for every *purpose*
5: 4(3). for (he hath) no *pleasure* in fools:
8(7). marvel not at *the matter*: (marg. *will*, or, *purpose*)
8: 6. to every *purpose* there is time
12: 1. I have no *pleasure* in them;
10. The preacher sought to find out *acceptable* words: (marg. words of *delight*)
Isa. 44:28. shall perform all *my pleasure*:
46:10. I will do all *my pleasure*:
48:14. he will do *his pleasure* on Babylon,
53:10. *and the pleasure of* the Lord
54:12. all thy borders of *pleasant* stones. (lit. stones of *delight*)
58: 3. in the day of your fast ye find *pleasure*,
13. doing *thy pleasure* on my holy day;
— nor finding *thine own pleasure*,
62: 4. thou shalt be called *Hephzi*-bah, (marg. *My delight* (is) in her)
Jer. 22:28 & 48:38. a vessel wherein (is) no *pleasure*?
Hos 8: 8. a vessel wherein (is) no *pleasure*.
Mal. 1:10. I have no *pleasure* in you,
3:12. for ye shall be a *delightsome* land, (lit. a land of *delight*)

2658 **חָפַר** *ghāh-phar'*.

* KAL.—*Preterite*. *

Gen21:30. that *I have digged* this well.
26:15. *had digged* in the days of Abraham
18. which *they had digged*
32. the well which *they had digged*,
Nu. 21:18. The princes *digged* the well
Deu 23:13(14). *thou* (lit. *and thou*) *shalt dig* therewith,
Job 11:18. *yea, thou shalt dig*
39:29. From thence *she seeketh* the prey,
Ps. 35: 7. *they have digged* for my soul.

KAL.—*Infinitive*.

Jos. 2: 2. *to search out* the country.
3. *to search out* all the country.

KAL.—*Future*.

Gen26:18. *And* Isaac *digged* again the wells
19. *And* Isaac's servants *digged*
21. *And they digged* another well,
22. *and digged* another well;
Ex. 7:24. *And* all the Egyptians *digged*
Deu 1:22. *and they shall search* us *out*
Job 3:21. *and dig for it* more than for hid treasures;
39:21. *He paweth* in the valley, (marg. or, (His feet) *dig*)
Ps. 7:15(16). He made a pit, *and digged it*,
Jer. 13: 7. Then I went to Euphrates, *and digged*.

KAL.—*Participle*. Poel.

Ecc. 10: 8. *He that diggeth* a pit shall fall into it;

חָפֵר [*ghāh-phēhr'*]. 2659

* KAL.—*Preterite*. *

Ps. 71:24. for *they are brought unto shame*,
Isa. 24:23. *Then* the moon *shall be confounded*,
Jer. 15: 9. she hath been ashamed *and confounded*:
50:12. she that bare you *shall be ashamed*:
Mic. 3: 7. *and* the diviners *confounded*:

KAL.—*Future*.

Job 6:20. they came thither, *and were ashamed*.
Ps. 34: 5(6). their faces *were* not *ashamed*.
35: 4. turned back *and brought to confusion*
26. be ashamed *and brought to confusion*
40:14(15) & 70:2(3). Let them be ashamed *and confounded*
83:17(18). *yea, let them be put to shame*,
Isa. 1:29. *and ye shall be confounded*

* HIPHIL.—*Preterite*. *

Isa. 33: 9. Lebanon *is ashamed* (and) hewn down:

HIPHIL.—*Future*.

Pro. 13: 5. loathsome, *and cometh to shame*.
Isa. 54: 4. for *thou shalt* not *be put to shame*:

HIPHIL.—*Participle*.

Pro. 19:26. *and bringeth reproach*.

חֲפֹר [*gh'phōhr*], m. 2661

Isa. 2:20. to the moles (perhaps, lit. *to the hole of* mice) and to the bats;

חֲפַרְפֵּרוֹת see **חֲפֹר** and **פֵּרוֹת**. See 2661

חָפַשׂ [*ghāh-phas'*]. 2664

* KAL.—*Future*. *

Ps. 64: 6(7). *They search out* iniquities;
Pro. 2: 4. and *searchest for her* as (for) hid
Lam. 3:40. *Let us search* and try our ways,

KAL.—*Participle*. Poel.

Pro. 20:27. *searching* all the inward parts

* NIPHAL.—*Preterite*. *

Obad. 6. How *are* (the things) of Esau *searched out*!

* PIEL.—*Preterite*. *

1Sa. 23:23. *that I will search* him *out*
1K. 20: 6. *and they shall search* thine house,

PIEL.—*Imperative*.

2K. 10:23. *Search*, and look that there be here

PIEL.—*Future*.

Gen 31:35. *And he searched*, but found not
44:12. *And he searched*, (and) began at
Ps. 77: 6(7). *and* my spirit *made diligent search*.
Am. 9: 3. *I will search* and take them out
Zep. 1:12. *I will search* Jerusalem with candles.

* PUAL.—*Future.* *

Pro.28:12. but when the wicked rise, a man *is hidden.* (marg. or, *sought for*)

PUAL.—*Participle.*

Ps. 64: 6(7). they accomplish a *diligent* search: (lit. a search *searched*)

* HITHPAEL.—*Preterite.* *

2Ch 35:22. but *disguised himself,*

HITHPAEL.—*Infinitive.*

1K. 22:30. *I will disguise myself,*
2Ch 18:29. *I will disguise myself,*

HITHPAEL.—*Future.*

1Sa.28: 8. *And* Saul *disguised himself,*
1K. 20:38. *and disguised himself* with ashes
22:30. *And* the king of Israel *disguised himself,*
2Ch 18:29. *So* the king of Israel *disguised himself;*
Job 30:18. force (of my disease) *is* my garment *changed:*

2665 **חֵפֶשׂ** *ghĕh'-phes*, m.

Ps. 64: 6(7). they accomplish *a* diligent *search:*

2666 **חָפַשׁ** [*ghāh-phash'*].

* PUAL.—*Preterite.* *

Lev.19:20. because *she was* not *free.*

2667 **חֹפֶשׁ** *ghōh'-phesh*, m.

Eze.27:20. Dedan (was) thy merchant in *precious* clothes (marg. clothes of *freedom*)

2668 **חֻפְשָׁה** *ghooph-shāh'*, f.

Lev.19:20. nor *freedom* given her;

2669 **חָפְשׁוּת** *ghoph-shooth'*, f.

2Ch 26:21. (כתיב) and dwelt in a *several* house, (marg. *free*)

2670 **חָפְשִׁי** *ghoph-shee'*, adj.

Ex. 21: 2. the seventh he shall go out *free* (lit. *for free*)
5. I will not go out *free:*
26, 27. he shall let him go *free* (lit. *for free*)
Deu 15:12. thou shalt let him go *free*
13. when thou sendest him out *free*
18. when thou sendest him away *free*
1Sa.17:25. make his father's house *free*
Job 3:19. the servant (is) *free* from his master.
39: 5. Who hath sent out the wild ass *free?*
Ps. 88: 5(6). *Free* among the dead,
Isa. 58: 6. to let the oppressed go *free,*
Jer. 34: 9. an Hebrew or an Hebrewess, go *free;*
10. every one his maidservant, go *free,*
11. whom they had let go *free,*
14. thou shalt let him go *free*
16. whom he had set at *liberty*

2669 **חָפְשִׁית** *ghoph-sheeth'*, f.

2K. 15: 5. dwelt in a *several* house.
2Ch 26:21. and dwelt in a *several* house, (marg. *free*)

2671 **חֵץ** *ghēhtz*, m.

Gen49.23. The archers (lit. *arrow* masters) have
Nu. 24: 8. pierce (them) through *with his arrows.*
Deu32:23. I will spend *mine arrows* upon them.
42. make *mine arrows* drunk with blood,
1Sa.17: 7. (כתיב) *And the staff of* his spear
20:20. I will shoot three *arrows*
21. Go, find out *the arrows.*
— *the arrows* (are) on this side
22. *the arrows* (are) beyond thee;
36. find out now *the arrows* which I shoot.
38. Jonathan's lad gathered up *the arrows,*
2Sa.22:15. he sent out *arrows,* and scattered them;
2K. 13:15. Take bow *and arrows.* And he took unto him bow *and arrows.*
17. *The arrow of* the Lord's deliverance, *and the arrow of* deliverance
18. he said, Take *the arrows.*
19:32. nor shoot *an arrow* there,
1Ch 12: 2. in (hurling) stones *and* (shooting) *arrows*
2Ch 26:15. to shoot *arrows* and great stones
Job 6: 4. For *the arrows of* the Almighty
34: 6. *my wound* (is) incurable (marg. *arrow*)
Ps. 7:13(14). he ordaineth *his arrows*
11: 2. they make ready *their arrow*
18:14(15). Yea, he sent out *his arrows,*
38: 2(3). For *thine arrows* stick fast in me,
45: 5(6). *Thine arrows* (are) sharp
57: 4(5). whose teeth (are) spears *and arrows,*
58: 7(8). he bendeth (his bow to shoot) *his arrows,*
64: 3(4). bend (their bows to shoot) *their arrows*
7(8). shall shoot at them (with) *an arrow;*
91: 5. *for the arrow* (that) flieth by day;
120: 4. Sharp *arrows of* the mighty,
127: 4. *As arrows* (are) in the hand of a
144: 6. shoot out *thine arrows,*
Pro. 7:23. Till *a dart* strike through his liver;
25:18. a sword, *and a* sharp *arrow.*
26:18. who casteth firebrands, *arrows,* and death,
Isa. 5:28. Whose *arrows* (are) sharp, (lit. who *his arrows*)
7:24. *With arrows* and with bows
37:33. nor shoot *an arrow* there,
49: 2. made me *a* polished *shaft;*
Jer. 9: 8(7). Their tongue (is as) *an arrow*
50: 9. *their arrows* (shall be) as of a mighty
14. shoot at her, spare no *arrows:*
51:11. Make bright *the arrows;*
Lam.3:12. set me as a mark for *the arrow.*
Eze. 5:16. shall send upon them *the* evil *arrows of*
21:21(26). he made (his) *arrows* bright, he consulted (marg. or, *knives*)
39: 3. *and* will cause *thine arrows* to fall
9. the bows *and the arrows,*
Hab 3:11. at the light of *thine arrows*
Zec. 9:14. *his arrow* shall go forth

חָצַב [*ghāh-tzav'*] & **חָצֵב** *ghāh-tzēhv'*. 2672

* KAL.—*Preterite.* *

Deu 6:11. wells digged, which *thou diggedst* not,
Pro. 9: 1. *she hath hewn out* her seven pillars:
Isa. 5: 2. also *made* a winepress (marg. *hewed*)
22:16. *thou hast hewed* thee *out*
Hos. 6: 5. *have I hewed* (them) by the prophets;

KAL.—*Infinitive.*

1Ch 22: 2. he set masons *to hew* wrought stones
Jer. 2:13. *hewed* them *out* cisterns,

KAL.—*Future.*

Deu 8: 9. out of whose hills thou *mayest dig*
2Ch 26:10. *and digged* many wells: (marg. or, *cut out,* &c.)

KAL.—*Participle.* Poel.

1K. 5:15(29). fourscore thousand *hewers*
2K. 12:12(13). masons, *and hewers* of stone,
1Ch 22: 2. he set *masons* to hew
15. *hewers* and workers of stone
2Ch 2: 2(1). fourscore thousand *to hew*
18(17). fourscore thousand (to be) *hewers*
24:12. hired *masons* and carpenters
Ezr. 3: 7. gave money also *unto the masons,*
Ps. 29: 7. the Lord *divideth* the flames of fire.
Isa. 10:15. against him *that heweth*
22:16. (as) *he that heweth him out* a sepulchre

KAL.—*Participle.* Paül.

Deu 6:11. wells *digged,* which thou diggedst not,
Neh 9:25. full of all goods, wells *digged,*

* NIPHAL.—*Future.* *

Job 19:24. *they were graven* with an iron pen

* PUAL.—*Preterite.* *

Isa. 51: 1. look unto the rock (whence) *ye are hewn,*

* HIPHIL.—*Participle.* *

Isa. 51: 9. (Art) thou not it *that hath cut* Rahab,

2673 ## חָצָה *g̔hāh-tzāh'.*

✱ KAL.—*Preterite.* ✱

Ex. 21:35. *and divide* the money of it;
Nu. 31:27. *And divide* the prey into two parts;
42. which Moses *divided* from the men

KAL.—*Future.*

Gen32: 7(8). *and he divided* the people
33: 1. *And he divided* the children unto
Ex. 21:35. the dead (ox) also *they shall divide.*
Jud. 7:16. *And he divided* the three hundred
9:43. *and divided them* into three companies,
Job 41: 6(40:30). *shall they part him* among
Ps. 55:23(24). bloody and deceitful men *shall* not *live out half* their days; (marg. *shall* not *half* their days)
Isa. 30:28. *shall reach to the midst of* the neck,

✱ NIPHAL.—*Future.* ✱

2K. 2: 8. *and they were divided* hither
14. *And...they parted* hither and thither:
Eze.37:22. neither *shall they be divided*
Dan11: 4. *and shall be divided*

2676 ## חָצוֹת [*g̔hāh-tzōhth'*], f.

Ex. 11: 4. *About mid*night will I go
Job 34:20. people shall be troubled *at mid*night,
Ps.119:62. *At mid*night I will rise to give thanks

2677 ## חֵצִי *g̔hēh-tzee'* & חֲצִי *g̔hătzee*, m.

Ex. 12:29. *at mid*night the Lord smote
24: 6. Moses took *half of* the blood,
— *and half of* the blood he sprinkled
25:10. two cubits *and a half* (shall be) the length thereof, and a cubit *and a half* the breadth thereof, and a cubit *and a half*
17. two cubits *and a half* (shall be) the length thereof, and a cubit *and a half*
23. a cubit *and a half* the height
26:12. the *half* curtain that remaineth,
16. a cubit *and a half* (shall be) the breadth
27: 5. even to *the midst of* the altar.
36:21. a board one cubit *and a half.*
37: 1. two cubits *and a half* (was) the length of it, and a cubit *and a half* the breadth of it, and a cubit *and a half*
6. two cubits *and a half* (was) the length thereof, and one cubit *and a half*
10. a cubit *and a half* the height thereof:
38: 4. beneath unto *the midst of it.*
Nu. 12:12. whom the flesh is *half* consumed
15: 9. mingled with *half* an hin of oil.
10. for a drink offering *half* an hin
28:14. their drink offerings shall be *half* an hin
32:33. *and unto half* the tribe of Manasseh
34:13. *and to the half* tribe:
14. *and half* the tribe of Manasseh
15. The two tribes *and the half* tribe
Deu 3:12. *and half* mount Gilead,
13. gave I *unto* the *half* tribe of Manasseh;
29: 8(7). *and to* the *half* tribe of Manasseh.
Jos. 1:12. *and to half* the tribe of Manasseh,
4:12. *and half* the tribe of Manasseh,
8:33. *half of them* over against mount Gerizim, *and half of them*
10:13. *in the midst of* heaven,
12: 2. *and from half* Gilead,
5. Maachathites, *and half* Gilead,
6. *and* the *half* tribe of Manasseh.
13: 7. *and* the *half* tribe of Manasseh,
25. *and half* the land of the children
29. *unto* the *half* tribe of Manasseh:
— *of* the *half* tribe of the children of
31. *And half* Gilead, and Ashtaroth,
— *to the one half of* the children of Machir
14: 2. *and* (for) the *half* tribe.
3. two tribes *and an half* tribe
18: 7. Reuben, *and half* the tribe of Manasseh,
Jos.21: 5, 6. *and out of* the *half* tribe
27. *out of* the (other) *half* tribe
22: 1. *and* the *half* tribe of Manasseh,
7. *Now to the* (one) *half of* the tribe
— *but unto the* (other) *half thereof*
9. the children of Gad *and* the *half* tribe
10. Gad *and* the *half* tribe of Manasseh
11. the children of Gad *and* the *half* tribe
13, 15. and *to* the *half* tribe of Manasseh,
21. *and* the *half* tribe of Manasseh
Jud.16: 3. Samson lay till *mid*night, and arose *at mid*night,
Ru. 3: 8. it came to pass *at mid*night,
1Sa.14:14. *within as it were* an *half* acre
2Sa.10: 4. shaved off *the* one *half of* their beards,
— cut off their garments *in the middle,*
18: 3. neither if *half of us* die,
19:40(41). also *half* the people of Israel.
1K. 3:25. give *half* to the one, and *half* to the other.
7:31. a cubit *and an half:*
32. a wheel (was) a cubit *and half* a cubit.
35. a round compass of *half* a cubit
10: 7. *the half* was not told me:
13: 8. If thou wilt give me *half* thine house,
16:21. Israel divided *into two parts: half of* the people followed Tibni
— *and half* followed Omri.
1Ch 2:52. Haroeh, (and) *half of* the Manahethites.
54. *and half of* the Manahethites.
5:18. *and half* the tribe of Manasseh,
23. the children of the *half* tribe
26. *and* the *half* tribe of Manasseh.
6:61(46). (of) the *half* (tribe) of Manasseh,
71(56). the *half* tribe of Manasseh,
12:31. *And of* the *half* tribe of Manasseh
37. *and of* the *half* tribe of Manasseh,
19: 4. cut off their garments *in the midst*
26:32. *and* the *half* tribe of Manasseh,
27:20. *of* the *half* tribe of Manasseh,
21. *Of the half* (tribe) *of* Manasseh
2Ch 9: 6. *the one half of* the greatness of thy
Neh 3: 9, 12, 16, 17, 18. the ruler of the *half* part of
4: 6(3:38). joined together unto *the half thereof:*
16(10). *the half of* my servants wrought in
—(—). *and the other half of them* held
21(15). *and half of them* held the spears
12:32. *and half of* the princes of Judah,
38. *and the half of* the people
40. I, *and the half of* the rulers with me:
13:24. their children spake *half* in the
Est. 5: 3. given thee to *the half of* the kingdom.
6 & 7:2. to *the half of* the kingdom
Ps.102:24(25). take me not away *in the midst of* my days:
Isa. 44:16. He burneth *part thereof* in the fire; with *part thereof* he eateth flesh;
19. I have burned *part of it* in the fire;
Jer. 17:11. shall leave them *in the midst of*
Eze.16:51. Neither hath Samaria committed *half of*
40:42. a cubit *and an half* long, and a cubit *and an half* broad,
43:17. the border about it (shall be) *half* a
Dan 9:27. *and in the midst of* the week
12: 7. for a time, times, *and an half;* (marg. or, *part*)
Zec.14: 2. *half of* the city shall go forth
4. shall cleave *in the midst thereof*
— *half of* the mountain shall remove
— *and half of it* toward the south.
8. *half of them* toward the former sea, *and half of them* toward the hinder sea:

חֵצִי *g̔hēh-tzee'*, m. 2678

1Sa.20:36. he shot *an arrow* beyond him.
37. was come to the place of *the arrow*
— (Is) not *the arrow* beyond thee?
38. (כתיב) Jonathan's lad gathered up *the arrows,*
2K. 9:24. *the arrow* went out at his heart,

חָצִיר *g̔hāh-tzeer'*, m. 2681

Isa. 34:13. dragons, (and) *a court* for owls.

2682 **חָצִיר** *g'hāh-tzeer'*, m.

Nu. 11: 5. cucumbers, and the melons, and *the leeks,*
1K. 18: 5. peradventure we may find *grass*
2K. 19:26. *the grass on* the house tops,
Job 8:12. withereth before any (other) *herb.*
40:15. he eateth *grass* as an ox.
Ps. 37: 2. shall soon be cut down *like the grass,*
90: 5. in the morning (they are) *like grass*
103:15. man, his days (are) *as grass:*
104:14. He causeth *the grass* to grow
129: 6. *as the grass* (upon) the housetops,
147: 8. who maketh *grass* to grow
Pro. 27:25. *The hay* appeareth,
Isa. 15: 6. for *the hay* is withered away,
35: 7. *grass* with reeds and rushes.
37:27. *the grass on* the housetops,
40: 6. What shall I cry? All flesh (is) *grass,*
7. *The grass* withereth, the flower fadeth:
— surely the people (is) *grass.*
8. *The grass* withereth, the flower fadeth:
44: 4. they shall spring up (as) among *the grass,*
51:12. man (which) shall be made (as) *grass;*

2683 **חֵצֶן** [*g'hĕh'-tzen*], m.

Ps. 129: 7. *nor* he that bindeth sheaves *his bosom.*

2684 **חֹצֶן** *g'hōh'-tzen*, m.

Neh 5:13. Also I shook *my lap,*
Isa. 49:22. bring thy sons *in* (their) *arms,* (marg. *bosom*)

2685 **חֲצַף** [*g'hătzaph*], Ch.

* APHEL.—*Participle.* *

Dan 2:15. Why (is) the decree (so) *hasty* from the
3:22. the king's commandment *was urgent,*

2686 **חָצַץ** [*g'hāh-tzatz'*].

* KAL.—*Participle.* Poel. *

Pro. 30:27. go they forth all of them *by bands;* (marg. *gathered together*)

* PIEL.—*Participle.* *

Jud. 5:11. from the noise of *archers*

* PUAL.—*Preterite.* *

Job 21:21. the number of his months *is cut off in the midst?*

2687 **חָצָץ** *g'hāh-tzāhtz'*, m.

Ps. 77:17(18). *thine arrows* also went abroad.
Pro. 20:17. his mouth shall be filled with *gravel.*
Lam. 3:16. broken my teeth *with gravel stones,*

2690 **חֲצֹצֵר** [*g'hătzōh-tzēhr'*].

* PIEL.—*Participle.* *

1Ch 15:24. (כתיב) the priests, *did blow* (lit. (were) *trumpeting*)
2Ch 5:13. (——) *as the trumpeters* and singers
7: 6. (——) the priests *sounded* trumpets
13:14. (——) the priests *sounded* with the trumpets.
29:28. (——) the trumpeters *sounded:*

2689 **חֲצֹצְרָה** *g'hătzōh-tz'rāh*, f.

Nu. 10: 2. Make thee two *trumpets of* silver;
8. shall blow *with the trumpets;*
9. blow an alarm *with the trumpets;*
10. ye shall blow *with the trumpets*
31: 6. *and the trumpets* to blow
2K. 11:14. the princes *and the trumpeters*
— rejoiced, and blew *with trumpets:*
12:13(14). snuffers, basons, *trumpets,*
1Ch 13: 8. with cymbals, *and with trumpets.*
15:24. the priests, did blow *with the trumpets*
28. sound of the cornet, *and with trumpets,*
1Ch 16: 6. the priests *with trumpets*
42. with *trumpets* and cymbals
2Ch 5:12. twenty priests sounding *with trumpets:*
13. lifted up (their) voice *with the trumpets*
13:12. priests *with* sounding *trumpets*
14. the priests sounded *with the trumpets.*
15:14. with shouting, *and with trumpets,*
20:28. psalteries and harps *and trumpets*
23:13. the princes *and the trumpets*
— rejoiced, and sounded *with trumpets,*
29:26. the priests *with the trumpets.*
27. began (also) *with the trumpets,*
28. *and the trumpeters* sounded:
Ezr. 3:10. priests in their apparel *with trumpets,*
Neh 12:35. the priests' sons *with trumpets;*
41. Hananiah, *with trumpets;*
Ps. 98: 6. *With trumpets* and sound of cornet
Hos. 5: 8. *the trumpet* in Ramah:

חָצַר [*g'hāh-tzar'*]. 2690

* PIEL.—*Participle.* *

2Ch 5:13. *as the trumpeters* and singers

* HIPHIL.—*Participle.* *

1Ch 15:24. the priests, *did blow* (lit. (were) *trumpeting*) with the trumpets before the ark
2Ch 5:12. an hundred and twenty priests *sounding*
7: 6. the priests *sounded* trumpets
13:14. the priests *sounded* with the trumpets.
29:28. the trumpeters *sounded:*

חָצֵר *g'hāh-tzēhr'*, m. 2691

Gen 25:16. these (are) their names, *by their towns,*
Ex. 8:13(9). out of *the villages,*
27: 9. make *the court of* the tabernacle:
— hangings *for the court*
12, 13. breadth of *the court* on the
16. for the gate of *the court*
17. the pillars round about *the court*
18. The length of *the court* (shall be)
19. all the pins of *the court,*
35:17. The hangings of *the court,*
— the hanging for the door of *the court,*
18. the pins of *the court,*
38: 9. he made *the court:* on the south
— the hangings of *the court*
15. for the other side of the *court* gate,
16. All the hangings of *the court*
17. all the pillars of *the court*
18. the hanging for the gate of *the court*
— answerable to the hangings of *the court.*
20. *and of the court* round about,
31. the sockets of *the court* round about, and the sockets of the *court* gate,
— all the pins of *the court*
39:40. The hangings of *the court,*
— the hanging for the *court* gate,
40: 8. thou shalt set up *the court*
— hang up the hanging at *the court*
33. he reared up *the court* round about
— set up the hanging of *the court*
Lev. 6:16(9), 26(19). *in the court of* the tabernacle
25:31. But the houses of *the villages*
Nu. 3:26. the hangings of *the court,* and the curtain for the door of *the court,*
37. the pillars of *the court* round about,
4:26. the hangings of *the court,*
— the door of the gate of *the court,*
32. the pillars of *the court*
Jos. 13:23. the cities *and the villages thereof.*
28. the cities, *and their villages.*
15:32, 36, 41, 44. *with their villages:*
45. Ekron, with her towns *and her villages:*
46. Ashdod, *with their villages:*
47, 47. with her towns *and her villages,*
51, 54, 57, 59, 60, 62 & 16:9 & 18:24, 28. *with their villages:*
19: 6. thirteen cities *and their villages:*
7. four cities *and their villages:*
8. all *the villages* that (were)
15, 16, 22, 30, 31, 38. cities *with their villages.*
23. the cities *and their villages.*
39. the cities *and their villages.*
48. these cities *with their villages.*

Jos.21:12. fields of the city, and *the villages thereof*,
2Sa.17:18. which had a well *in his court;*
1K. 6:36. he built *the* inner *court*
7: 8. another *court* within the porch,
9. the outside toward *the* great *court*.
12. *And the* great *court* round about
— *both for the* inner *court*
8:64. hallow the middle of *the court*
2K. 20: 4. Isaiah was gone out into *the* middle *court*,
21: 5. in *the* two *courts of* the house
23:12. Manasseh had made in *the* two *courts of*
1Ch 4:32. *And their villages* (were), Etam, and Ain,
33. all *their villages* that (were)
6:56(41). the fields of the city, and *the villages thereof*,
9:16. dwelt *in the villages of* the Netophathites.
22. by their genealogy *in their villages*,
25. brethren, (which were) *in their villages*,
23:28. in *the courts*, and in the chambers,
28: 6. he shall build my house *and my courts:*
12. *of the courts of* the house of the Lord,
2Ch 4: 9. he made *the court of* the priests,
7: 7. hallowed the middle of *the court*
20: 5. before *the* new *court*,
23: 5. all the people (shall be) *in the courts of*
24:21. *in the court of* the house of the Lord.
29:16. *into the court of* the house of the Lord.
33: 5. in *the* two *courts of* the house
Neh 3:25. that (was) *by the court of* the prison.
8:16. *and in their courts, and in the courts of* the house of God,
11:25. for *the villages*, with their fields,
— Jekabzeel, *and* (in) *the villages thereof*,
30. *and* (in) *their villages*,
12:28. from *the villages of* Netophathi;
29. the singers had builded them *villages*
13: 7. preparing him a chamber *in the courts of*
Est. 1: 5. *in the court of* the garden
2:11. before *the court of* the women's house,
4:11. come unto the king into *the* inner *court*,
5: 1. stood *in the* inner *court*
2. the queen standing *in the court*,
6: 4. the king said, Who (is) *in the court?*
— *into the* outward *court of* the king's house,
5. Haman standeth *in the court*.
Ps. 10: 8. in the lurking places of *the villages:*
65: 4(5). he may dwell in *thy courts:*
84: 2(3). even fainteth *for the courts of* the Lord:
10(11). For a day *in thy courts* (is) better
92:13(14). shall flourish *in the courts of* our
96: 8. bring an offering, and come *into his courts*.
100: 4. into *his courts* with praise:
116:19. *In the courts of* the Lord's house,
135: 2. *in the courts of* the house of our God,
Isa. 1:12. to tread *my courts?*
42:11. *the villages* (that) Kedar doth inhabit:
62: 9. drink it *in the courts of* my holiness.
Jer. 19:14. he stood *in the court of* the Lord's
26: 2. Stand *in the court of*
32: 2. was shut up *in the court of* the prison,
8. came to me in *the court of* the prison
12. that sat *in the court of* the prison.
33: 1. shut up *in the court of* the prison,
36:10. *in the* higher *court*,
20. went in to the king *into the court*,
37:21. *into the court of* the prison,
— & 38:6, 13, 28. *in the court of* the prison.
39:14. took Jeremiah *out of the court of* the
15. shut up *in the court of* the prison,
Eze. 8: 7. brought me to the door of *the court;*
16. brought me into *the* inner *court of*
9: 7. fill *the courts* with the slain:
10: 3. the cloud filled *the* inner *court*.
4. *and the court* was full of the
5. was heard (even) to *the* outer *court*,
40:14. even unto the post of *the court*
17. brought he me into *the* outward *court*,
— a pavement made *for the court*
19. unto the forefront of *the* inner *court*
20. the gate *of the* outward *court*
23. the gate *of the* inner *court*
27. a gate *in the* inner *court*
28. he brought me to *the* inner *court*
31. toward *the* utter *court;*
32. brought me into *the* inner *court*
34. *toward the* outward *court;*
37. *toward the* utter *court;*

Eze.40:44. the singers *in the* inner *court*,
47. So he measured *the court*,
41:15. the porches of *the court;*
42: 1. brought me forth into *the* utter *court*,
3. which (were) *for the* inner *court*,
— which (was) *for the* utter *court*,
6. pillars as the pillars of *the courts:*
7. toward *the* utter *court*
8. chambers that (were) *in the* utter *court*
9. goeth into them *from the* utter *court*.
10. the thickness of the wall of *the court*
14. the holy (place) into *the* utter *court*,
43: 5. brought me into *the* inner *court;*
44:17, 17. the gates of *the* inner *court*,
19, 19. into *the* utter *court*,
21. drink wine, when they enter into *the* inner *court*.
27. unto *the* inner *court*,
45:19 & 46:1. the gate of *the* inner *court*.
46:20. out into *the* utter *court*,
21. he brought me forth into *the* utter *court*,
— corners of *the court;* and, behold, in every corner of *the court* (there was) *a court*. (marg. *a court* in a corner of a *court, and a court* in a corner of *a court*)
22. In the four corners of *the court* (there were) *courts* joined of forty (cubits) long
47:16. *Hazar*-hatticon, which (is) by (marg. or, the middle *village*)
Zec. 3: 7. shalt also keep *my courts*,

חֲצֹרֵר *[g'hătzōh-rēhr]*. 2690

* PIEL.—*Participle*. *

2Ch 5:12. (כתיב) an hundred and twenty priests *sounding*

חֵק see חֵיק See 2436

חֹק *g'hōhk*, m. 2706

Gen47:22. for the priests had *a portion*
— did eat *their portion* which
26. Joseph made it *a law*
Ex. 5:14. have ye not fulfilled *your task*
12:24. observe this thing *for an ordinance*
15:25. there he made for them *a statute*
26. keep all *his statutes*,
18:16. I do make (them) know *the statutes of*
20. thou shalt teach them *ordinances*
29:28. Aaron's and his sons' *by a statute for* ever
30:21. it shall be *a statute for* ever
Lev. 6:18(11). *a statute for* ever in your
22(15). *a statute for* ever unto the Lord;
7:34. unto his sons *by a statute for* ever
10:11. all *the statutes* which the Lord hath
13. because it (is) *thy due, and* thy sons' *due*,
14. for (they be) *thy due, and* thy sons' *due*,
15. *by a statute for* ever;
24: 9. by fire by *a* perpetual *statute*.
26:46. These (are) *the statutes* and judgments
Nu. 18: 8. *by an ordinance for* ever.
11, 19. *by a statute for* ever:
30:16(17). *the statutes*, which the Lord commanded
Deu 4: 1. hearken, O Israel, unto *the statutes*
5. I have taught you *statutes* and judgments,
6. which shall hear all these *statutes*,
8. that hath *statutes* and judgments
14. commanded me at that time to teach you *statutes*
40. Thou shalt keep therefore *his statutes*,
45. testimonies, *and the statutes*,
5: 1. Hear, O Israel, *the statutes* and judgments
31(28). the commandments, *and the statutes*,
6: 1. *the statutes*, and the judgments,
17. his testimonies, *and his statutes*,
20. the testimonies, *and the statutes*,
24. commanded us to do all these *statutes*,
7:11. the commandments, and *the statutes*,
11:32. observe to do all *the statutes*
12: 1. These (are) *the statutes* and judgments,
16:12. thou shalt observe and do these *statutes*.
17:19. words of this law and these *statutes*,
26:16. commanded thee to do these *statutes*

Deu 26:17. to keep *his statutes*,
27:10. his commandments and *his statutes*,
Jos. 24:25. set them *a statute* and an ordinance
Jud. 11:39. was *a custom* in Israel, (marg. *ordinance*)
1Sa. 30:25. that he made it *a statute*
1K. 3:14. keep *my statutes* and my commandments,
8:58. commandments, *and his statutes*,
61. to walk *in his statutes*,
9: 4. wilt keep *my statutes* and my judgments:
2K. 17:15. they rejected *his statutes*,
37. And *the statutes*, and the ordinances,
1Ch 16:17. the same to Jacob *for a law*,
22:13. to fulfil *the statutes* and judgments
29:19. thy testimonies, *and thy statutes*,
2Ch 7:17. *and* shalt observe *my statutes*
19:10. *statutes* and judgments,
33: 8. the whole law *and the statutes*
34:31. his testimonies, *and his statutes*,
35:25. made them *an ordinance*
Ezr. 7:10. to teach in Israel *statutes*
11. *and of his statutes* to Israel.
Neh 1: 7. commandments, nor *the statutes*,
9:13. good *statutes* and commandments:
14. precepts, *statutes*, and laws,
10:29(30). his judgments *and his statutes*;
Job 14: 5. thou hast appointed *his bounds* that he
13. wouldest appoint me *a set time*,
23:12. *more than my necessary* (food). (marg. *appointed portion*)
14. (the thing that is) *appointed for me*:
26:10. compassed the waters with *bounds*,
28:26. When he made *a decree*
38:10. brake up for it *my decreed* (place),
Ps. 2: 7. I will declare *the decree*:
50:16. What hast thou to do to declare *my statutes*,
81: 4(5). this (was) *a statute* for Israel,
94:20. which frameth mischief by *a law*?
99: 7. *and the ordinance* (that) he gave
105:10. the same unto Jacob *for a law*,
45. That they might observe *his statutes*,
119: 5. ways were directed to keep *thy statutes*!
8. I will keep *thy statutes*:
12, 26, 68. teach me *thy statutes*.
23. thy servant did meditate *in thy statutes*.
33. the way of *thy statutes*;
48. I will meditate *in thy statutes*.
54. *Thy statutes* have been my songs
64. teach me *thy statutes*.
71. that I might learn *thy statutes*.
80. Let my heart be sound *in thy statutes*;
83. do I not forget *thy statutes*.
112. inclined mine heart to perform *thy statutes*
117. I will have respect *unto thy statutes*
118. all them that err *from thy statutes*:
124. *and* teach me *thy statutes*.
135. teach me *thy statutes*.
145. I will keep *thy statutes*.
155: for they seek not *thy statutes*.
171. when thou hast taught me *thy statutes*.
147:19. *his statutes* and his judgments unto Israel.
148: 6. he hath made *a decree*
Pro. 8:29. When he gave to the sea *his decree*,
30: 8. feed me with food *convenient for me*:
31:15. *and a portion* to her maidens.
Isa. 5:14. opened her mouth without *measure*:
24: 5. changed *the ordinance*,
Jer. 5:22. the sea by *a* perpetual *decree*,
31:36. If those *ordinances* depart
32:11. sealed (according) to the law *and custom*,
Eze. 11:12. for ye have not walked *in my statutes*,
16:27. have diminished *thine ordinary* (food),
20:18. Walk ye not *in the statutes of*
25. Wherefore I gave them also *statutes*
36:27. cause you to walk *in my statutes*,
45:14. *Concerning the ordinance of* oil,
Am. 2: 4. *and* have not kept *his commandments*,
Mic. 7:11. that day shall *the decree* be far removed.
Zep. 2: 2. Before *the decree* bring forth,
Zec. 1: 6. But my words *and my statutes*,
Mal. 3: 7. ye are gone away *from mine ordinances*,
4: 4(3:22). *the statutes* and judgments.

2707 חָקָה [*ghāh-kāh'*].

* PUAL.—*Participle.* *
1K. 6:35. gold fitted upon *the carved work*.
Eze. 8:10. Israel, *pourtrayed* upon the wall
Eze. 23:14. when she saw men *pourtrayed*

* HITHPAEL.—*Future.* *
Job 13:27. *thou settest a print* upon the heels

חֻקָּה *ghook-kāh'*, f. 2708

Gen 26: 5. *my statutes*, and my laws.
Ex. 12:14. keep it a feast by *an ordinance for* ever.
17. generations by *an ordinance for* ever.
43. This (is) *the ordinance of* the passover:
13:10. keep this *ordinance* in his season
27:21. *a statute for* ever unto their
28:43. *a statute for* ever unto him
29: 9. be their's *for a* perpetual *statute*:
Lev. 3:17. *a* perpetual *statute* for your generations
7:36. *a statute for* ever throughout their generations.
10: 9. *a statute for* ever throughout
16:29. And (this) shall be *a statute for* ever
31. by *a statute for* ever.
34. this shall be *an* everlasting *statute*
17: 7. This shall be *a statute for* ever
18: 3. *neither* shall ye walk *in their ordinances*.
4. keep *mine ordinances*,
5. Ye shall therefore keep *my statutes*,
26. Ye shall therefore keep *my statutes*
30. *of* these abominable *customs*,
19:19. Ye shall keep *my statutes*.
37. Therefore shall ye observe all *my statutes*,
20: 8. ye shall keep *my statutes*,
22. shall therefore keep all *my statutes*,
23. ye shall not walk *in the manners of*
23:14, 21, 31, 41 & 24:3. *a statute for* ever
25:18. Wherefore ye shall do *my statutes*,
26: 3. If ye walk *in my statutes*,
15. if ye shall despise *my statutes*,
43. their soul abhorred *my statutes*.
Nu. 9: 3. according to all *the rites of it*,
12. all *the ordinances of* the passover
14. *according to the ordinance of*
— ye shall have one *ordinance*,
10: 8. they shall be to you *for an ordinance for*
15:15. One *ordinance* (shall be both) for you
— *an ordinance for* ever in your generations:
18:23. *a statute for* ever throughout
19: 2. This (is) *the ordinance of* the law
10. *for a statute for* ever.
21. it shall be *a* perpetual *statute*
27:11. the children of Israel *a statute of*
31:21. This (is) *the ordinance of* the law
35:29. shall be *for a statute of* judgment
Deu 6: 2. to keep all *his statutes*
8:11. judgments, *and his statutes*,
10:13. *his statutes*, which I command thee
11: 1. keep his charge, *and his statutes*,
28:15, 45 & 30:10, 16. commandments *and his statutes*
2Sa. 22:23. *and* (as for) *his statutes*,
1K. 2: 3. to keep *his statutes*,
3: 3. walking *in the statutes of* David
6:12. if thou wilt walk *in my statutes*,
9: 6. *my statutes* which I have set
11:11. kept my covenant *and my statutes*,
33. *and* (to keep) *my statutes*
34. my commandments *and my statutes*:
38. keep *my statutes* and my commandments,
2K. 17: 8. walked *in the statutes of* the heathen,
13. commandments (and) *my statutes*,
19. walked *in the statutes of* Israel
34. neither do they *after their statutes*,
23: 3. his testimonies and *his statutes*
2Ch 7:19. turn away, and forsake *my statutes*
Job 38:33 Knowest thou *the ordinances of* heaven?
Ps. 18:22(23). *and* I did not put away *his statutes* from me.
89:31(32). If they break *my statutes*,
119:16. I will delight myself *in thy statutes*:
Jer. 5:24. reserveth unto us the *appointed* weeks
10: 3. *the customs of* the people (are) vain: (marg. *statutes*, or, *ordinances*)
31:35. *the ordinances of* the moon
33:25. appointed *the ordinances of* heaven
44:10. *nor in my statutes*,
23. *nor in his statutes*,

Eze. 5: 6. and *my statutes* more than the countries
— refused my judgments *and my statutes*,
7. have not walked *in my statutes*,
11:20. That they may walk *in my statutes*,
18: 9, 17. Hath walked *in my statutes*,
19. hath kept all *my statutes*,
21. keep all *my statutes*,
20:11. I gave them *my statutes*,
13. they walked not *in my statutes*,
16. and walked not in *my statutes*,
19. walk *in my statutes*,
21. they walked not *in my statutes*,
24. *but* had despised *my statutes*,
33:15. walk *in the statutes of* life,
37:24. *and* observe *my statutes*,
43:11, 11. all *the ordinances thereof*,
18. *the ordinances of* the altar
44: 5. concerning all *the ordinances of*
24. keep my laws and *my statutes*
46:14. by *a* perpetual *ordinance*
Mic. 6:16. *the statutes of* Omri are kept,

2710 חָקַק [*g̣hāh-kak'*].

* KAL.—*Preterite.* *

Isa. 49:16. *I have graven thee* upon the palms
Eze. 4: 1. *and pourtray* upon it the city,

KAL.—*Infinitive.*

Pro. 8:27. *when he set* a compass
29. *when he appointed* the foundations

KAL.—*Imperative.*

Isa. 30: 8. and *note it* in a book,

KAL.—*Participle.* Poel

Jud. 5: 9. *toward the governors of* Israel,
Isa. 10: 1. Woe unto them *that decree*
22:16. *that graveth* an habitation

KAL.—*Participle.* Paül.

Eze. 23:14. Chaldeans *pourtrayed* with vermilion,

* POEL.—*Future.* *

Pro. 8:15. kings reign, and princes *decree* justice.

POEL.—*Participle.*

Gen 49:10. *nor a lawgiver* from between his feet,
Nu. 21:18. *by* (the direction of) *the lawgiver*,
Deu 33:21. a portion of *the lawgiver*,
Jud. 5:14. out of Machir came down *governors*,
Ps. 60: 7(9). Judah (is) *my lawgiver;*
108: 8(9). Judah (is) *my lawgiver;*
Isa. 33:22. the Lord (is) *our lawgiver*,

* PUAL.—*Participle.* *

Pro. 31: 5. Lest they drink, and forget *the law*,

* HOPHAL.—*Future.* *

Job 19:23. oh *that they were printed*

2711 חֵקֶק [*g̣hēh'-kek*], m.

Jud. 5:15. great *thoughts of* heart. (marg. *impressions*)
Isa. 10: 1. that decree unrighteous *decrees*,

2713 חָקַר [*g̣hāh-kar'*].

* KAL.—*Preterite.* *

Deu 13:14(15). enquire, *and make search*,
Job 5:27. Lo this, *we have searched it*,
28:27. yea, and *searched it out*.
Ps. 139: 1. O Lord, *thou hast searched me*,
Pro 18:17. cometh *and searcheth him*.

KAL.—*Infinitive.*

Jud 18: 2. to spy out the land, *and to search it;*
2Sa 10: 3. *to search* the city, and to spy
1Ch 19: 3. his servants come unto thee *for to search*,
Pro 23:30. they that go *to seek* mixed wine.
25: 2. honour of kings (is) *to search out* a matter.

KAL.—*Imperative.*

Jud 18: 2. Go, *search* the land:
Ps. 139:23. *Search me*, O God, and know my heart:

KAL.—*Future.*

1Sa 20:12. when *I have sounded* my father (marg. *searched*)
Job 13: 9. Is it good that *he should search*
29:16. I knew not *I searched out*.
32:11. *ye searched out* what to say.
Ps. 44:21(22). *Shall* not God *search* this *out?*
Pro 28:11. hath understanding *searcheth him out*.
Lam. 3:40. Let us search *and try* our ways,
Eze 39:14. seven months *shall they search*.

KAL.—*Participle.* Poel.

Job 28: 3. *searcheth out* all perfection:
Jer. 17:10. I the Lord *search* the heart,

* NIPHAL.—*Preterite.* *

1K. 7:47. neither *was* the weight of the brass *found out*. (marg. *searched*)
2Ch 4:18. the brass *could* not *be found out*.

NIPHAL.—*Future.*

Jer. 31:37. *and* the foundations of the earth *searched out*
46:23. though *it cannot be searched;*

* PIEL.—*Preterite.* *

Ecc. 12: 9. he gave good heed, *and sought out*,

חֵקֶר *g̣hēh'-ker*, m. 2714

Jud 5:16. great *searchings of* heart.
Job 5: 9. great things and *unsearchable;* (marg. no *search*)
8: 8. *to the search of* their fathers:
9:10. doeth great things past *finding out;*
11: 7. Canst thou by *searching* find out God?
34:24. break in pieces mighty men without *number*,
36:26. number of his years *be searched out*.
38:16. *or* hast thou walked *in the search of*
Ps. 145: 3. his greatness (is) *unsearchable*. (marg. no *search*)
Pro 25: 3. heart of kings (is) *unsearchable*. (marg. no *searching*)
27. *so* (for men) *to search* their own glory
Isa. 40:28. no *searching* of his understanding.

חֹר see חוֹר See 2715

חֹר see חוּר See 2352

חֲרָאִים [*g̣hărāh-eem'*], m. pl. 2716

Isa. 36:12. may eat *their own dung*,

חָרַב [*g̣hāh-rav'*] & חָרֵב [*g̣hāh-rēhv'*]. 2717

* KAL.—*Preterite.* *

Gen. 8:13. the waters *were dried up*
— the face of the ground *was dry*.
Isa. 19: 6. shall be emptied *and dried up:*

KAL.—*Infinitive.*

Isa. 60:12. shall be *utterly* wasted. (lit. *in wasting* shall be wasted)

KAL.—*Imperative.*

Isa. 44:27. That saith to the deep, *Be dry*,
Jer. 2:12. *be ye* very *desolate*,
50:21. *waste* and utterly destroy after them,
27. *Slay* all her bullocks;

KAL.—*Future.*

Job 14:11. the flood *decayeth* and drieth up:
Ps. 106: 9. the Red sea also, *and it was dried up:*
Isa. 19: 5. the river *shall be wasted*

Isa. 34:10. to generation *it shall lie waste*,
60:12. nations *shall be* utterly *wasted.*
Jer. 26: 9. this city *shall be desolate*
Eze 6: 6. the cities *shall be laid waste*,
— your altars *may be laid waste*
12:20. inhabited *shall be laid waste*,
Hos 13:15. *and* his fountain *shall be dried up*:
Am 7: 9. Israel *shall be laid waste*;

* NIPHAL.—*Preterite.* *

2K. 3:23. the kings *are* surely *slain*, (marg. *destroyed*)

NIPHAL.—*Participle.*

Eze 26:19. I shall make thee a *desolate* city,
30: 7. of the cities (that are) *wasted.*

* PUAL.—*Preterite.* *

Jud 16: 7. green withs that *were* never *dried*,
8. withs which *had* not *been dried*,

* HIPHIL.—*Preterite.* *

2K. 19:17. the kings of Assyria *have destroyed*
Isa. 37:18. the kings of Assyria *have laid waste*
Jer. 51:36. *and I will dry up* her sea,
Eze 19: 7. *he laid waste* their cities;
Nah 1: 4. and maketh it dry, and *drieth up* all the rivers:
Zep 3: 6. *I made* their streets *waste*,

HIPHIL.—*Future.*

2K. 19:24. *and* with the sole of my feet *have I dried up*
Isa. 37:25. *and* with the sole of my feet *have I dried up*
42:15. *I will make waste* mountains
50: 2. at my rebuke *I dry up* the sea,

HIPHIL.—*Participle.*

Jud 16:24. *the destroyer of* our country,
Isa. 49:17. *and they that made thee waste*
51:10. (Art) thou not it *which hath dried* the sea,

* HOPHAL.—*Preterite.* *

Eze 26: 2. replenished, (now) *she is laid waste*:

HOPHAL.—*Infinitive.*

2K. 3:23. the kings are *surely* slain, (lit. *slain* are slain)

HOPHAL.—*Participle.*

Eze 29:12. the cities (that are) *laid waste*

2718 חֲרַב [*ghărav*], Ch.

* HOPHAL.—*Preterite.* *

Ezr. 4:15. for which cause *was* this city *destroyed.*

2720 חָרֵב *ghāh-rēhv'*, adj.

Lev. 7:10. mingled with oil, *and dry*,
Neh. 2: 3. of my fathers' sepulchres, (lieth) *waste*,
17. how Jerusalem (lieth) *waste*,
Pro 17: 1. Better (is) a *dry* morsel, and quietness
Jer. 33:10. which ye say (shall be) *desolate*
12. Again in this place, *which is desolate*
Eze 36:35. *the waste* and desolate
38. so shall the *waste* cities be filled
Hag 1: 4. this house (lie) *waste?*
9. Because of mine house that (is) *waste*,

2719 חֶרֶב *gheh'-rev*, f.

Gen. 3:24. *a* flaming *sword* which turned
27:40. by *thy sword* shalt thou live,
31:26. as captives (taken) with *the sword?*
34:25. took each man *his sword*,
26. his son with the edge of *the sword*,
48:22. *with my sword* and with my bow.
Ex. 5: 3. with pestilence, or *with the sword*.
21. to put *a sword* in their hand
15: 9. I will draw *my sword*,
17:13. his people with the edge of *the sword.*
18: 4. delivered me *from the sword of*
20:25. if thou lift up *thy tool* upon it,
22:24(23). I will kill you *with the sword*
Ex. 32:27. Put every man *his sword*
Lev. 26: 6. *neither* shall *the sword* go through
7. they shall fall before you *by the sword.*
8. fall before you *by the sword.*
25. I will bring *a sword* upon you,
33. will draw out *a sword* after you:
36. as fleeing from *a sword*;
37. as it were before *a sword*,
Nu. 14: 3. to fall *by the sword*,
43. ye shall fall *by the sword*:
19:16. toucheth one that is slain with *a sword*
20:18. come out against thee *with the sword.*
21:24. Israel smote him with the edge of *the sword*,
22:23. *and his sword* drawn in his hand:
29. I would there were *a sword*
31. *and his sword* drawn in his hand:
31: 8. they slew *with the sword.*
Deu 13:15(16). that city with the edge of *the sword*,
—(—). with the edge of *the sword.*
20:13. with the edge of *the sword*:
28:22. *and with the sword*,
32:25. *The sword* without, and terror within,
41. If I whet *my* glittering *sword*,
42. *and my sword* shall devour
33:29. who (is) *the sword of* thy excellency!
Jos. 5: 2. Make thee sharp *knives*,
3. Joshua made him sharp *knives*,
13. *with his sword* drawn
6:21. with the edge of *the sword.*
8:24. all fallen on the edge of *the sword*,
— smote it with the edge of *the sword.*
10:11. Israel slew *with the sword.*
28, 30, 32, 35, 37, 39. with the edge of *the sword*,
11:10. smote the king thereof *with the sword*:
11, 12, 14. with the edge of *the sword*,
13:22. Israel slay *with the sword*
19:47. smote it with the edge of *the sword*,
24:12. not *with thy sword*,
Jud. 1: 8, 25. with the edge of *the sword*,
3:16. Ehud made him *a dagger*
21. took *the dagger* from his right
22. he could not draw *the dagger* out
4:15. with the edge of *the sword*
16. Sisera fell upon the edge of *the sword*;
7:14. *the sword of* Gideon
20. *The sword* of the Lord,
22. every man's *sword* against his fellow,
8:10. twenty thousand men that drew *sword.*
20. But the youth drew not *his sword*:
9:54. Draw *thy sword*, and slay me,
18:27. smote them with the edge of *the sword*,
20: 2, 15, 17. that drew *sword.*
25, 35. all these drew *the sword.*
37. all the city with the edge of *the sword.*
46. five thousand men that drew *the sword*;
48. smote them with the edge of *the sword.*
21:10. smite the inhabitants of Jabesh-gilead with the edge of *the sword*,
1Sa 13:19. Lest the Hebrews make (them) *swords*
22. there was neither *sword* nor spear
14:20. every man's *sword* was against his fellow,
15: 8. with the edge of *the sword.*
33. As *thy sword* hath made women childless,
17:39. David girded *his sword* upon his armour,
45. Thou comest to me *with a sword*,
47. the Lord saveth not *with sword*
50. *but* (there was) no *sword* in the hand of David.
51. took *his sword*, and drew it out
18: 4. his garments, even to *his sword*,
21: 8(9). here under thine hand spear or *sword?* for I have neither brought *my sword*
9(10). *The sword of* Goliath the Philistine,
22:10. gave him *the sword of* Goliath
13. given him bread, *and a sword*,
19, 19. with the edge of *the sword*,
25:13. Gird ye on every man *his sword.* And they girded on every man *his sword*; and David also girded on *his sword*:
31: 4. Draw *thy sword*, and thrust me
— Saul took *a sword*, and fell upon it.
5. he fell likewise upon *his sword*,
2Sa 1:12. they were fallen *by the sword.*
22. *and the sword of* Saul returned
2:16. *and* (thrust) *his sword* in his fellow's side;

2Sa. 2:26. Shall *the sword* devour for ever?
3:29. or that falleth *on the sword,*
11:25. for *the sword* devoureth one
12: 9. killed Uriah the Hittite *with the sword,*
— hast slain him *with the sword*
10. therefore *the sword* shall never depart
15:14. smite the city with the edge of *the sword.*
18: 8. that day than *the sword* devoured.
20: 8. upon it a girdle (with) *a sword*
10. Amasa took no heed *to the sword*
23:10. his hand clave unto *the sword:*
24: 9. valiant men that drew *the sword;*
1K. 1:51. will not slay his servant *with the sword.*
2: 8. put thee to death *with the sword.*
32. slew them *with the sword,*
3:24. the king said, Bring me *a sword.* And they brought *a sword* before the king.
18:28. after their manner *with knives*
19: 1. slain all the prophets *with the sword.*
10, 14. slain thy prophets *with the sword;*
17. that escapeth *the sword of* Hazael
— escapeth *from the sword of* Jehu
2K. 3:26. seven hundred men that drew *swords,*
6:22. thou hast taken captive *with thy sword*
8:12. their young men wilt thou slay *with the sword,*
10:25. smote them with the edge of *the sword;*
11:15. him that followeth her kill *with the sword.*
20. they slew Athaliah *with the sword*
19: 7. fall *by the sword* in his own land.
37. his sons smote him *with the sword:*
1Ch 5:18. able to bear buckler *and sword,*
10: 4. Draw *thy sword,* and thrust me through
— Saul took *a sword,* and fell upon it.
5. he fell likewise on *the sword,*
21: 5. hundred thousand men that drew *sword:*
— ten thousand men that drew *sword.*
12. *while that the sword of* thine enemies
— or else three days *the sword of*
16. *having a* drawn *sword* in his hand (lit. *and his sword* drawn)
27. he put up *his sword* again
30. he was afraid because of *the sword of*
2Ch 20: 9. cometh upon us, (as) *the sword,*
21: 4. slew all his brethren *with the sword,*
23:14. let him be slain *with the sword.*
21. had slain Athaliah *with the sword.*
29: 9. our fathers have fallen *by the sword,*
32:21. slew him there *with the sword.*
34: 6. *with their mattocks* round about. (marg. or, *mauls*)
36:17. slew their young men *with the sword*
20. them that had escaped from *the sword*
Ezr. 9: 7. *to the sword,* to captivity,
Neh 4:13(7). after their families with *their swords,*
18(12). every one had *his sword*
Est. 9: 5. with the stroke of *the sword,*
Job 1:15, 17. servants with the edge of *the sword;*
5:15. he saveth the poor *from the sword,*
20. in war from the power of *the sword.*
15:22. he is waited for of *the sword.*
19:29. Be ye afraid of *the sword:*
— the punishments of *the sword,*
27:14. multiplied, (it is) for *the sword:*
39:22. neither turneth he back from *the sword.*
40:19. he that made him can make *his sword*
41:26(18). *The sword of* him that layeth
Ps. 7:12(13). he will whet *his sword;*
17:13. from the wicked, (which is) *thy sword:*
22:20(21). Deliver my soul *from the sword;*
37:14. The wicked have drawn out *the sword,*
15. *Their sword* shall enter into their own
44: 3(4). in possession *by their own sword,*
6(7). *neither* shall *my sword* save me.
45: 3(4). Gird *thy sword* upon (thy) thigh,
57: 4(5). their tongue *a* sharp *sword.*
59: 7(8). *swords* (are) in their lips:
63:10(11). They shall fall by *the sword:*
64: 3(4). Who whet their tongue *like a sword,*
76: 3(4). the shield, *and the sword,*
78:62. his people over also *unto the sword;*
64. Their priests fell *by the sword;*
89:43(44). also turned the edge of *his sword,*
144:10. David his servant *from the* hurtful *sword.*
149: 6. *and a* twoedged *sword* in their hand;
Pro 5: 4. sharp *as a* twoedged *sword.*
12:18. speaketh like the piercings of *a sword:*
Pro 25:18. a maul, *and a sword,*
30:14. whose teeth (are as) *swords,*
Cant 3: 8. They all hold *swords,*
— every man (hath) *his sword*
Isa. 1:20. ye shall be devoured with *the sword:*
2: 4. they shall beat *their swords* into
— nation shall not lift up *sword*
3:25. Thy men shall fall *by the sword,*
13:15. shall fall *by the sword.*
14:19. thrust through with *a sword,*
21:15. For they fled from *the swords,* from *the* drawn *sword,*
22: 2. thy slain (men are) not slain with *the sword,*
27: 1. *with his* sore and great and strong *sword*
31: 8. the Assyrian fall *with the sword,*
— *and the sword,* not of a mean man,
— but he shall flee from *the sword,*
34: 5. For *my sword* shall be bathed
6. *The sword of* the Lord
37: 7. fall *by the sword* in his own land.
38. his sons smote him *with the sword;*
41: 2. as the dust to *his sword,*
49: 2. made my mouth *like a* sharp *sword;*
51:19. the famine, *and the sword:*
65:12. I number you *to the sword,*
66:16. For by fire *and by his sword*
Jer. 2:30. *your own sword* hath devoured
4:10. whereas *the sword* reacheth unto
5:12. *neither* shall we see *sword* nor famine;
17. wherein thou trustedst, *with the sword.*
6:25. for *the sword* of the enemy
9:16(15). I will send *a sword* after them,
11:22. the young men shall die *by the sword;*
12:12. *the sword of* the Lord
14:12. I will consume them *by the sword,*
13. Ye shall not see *the sword,*
15. *Sword* and famine shall not be
— *By sword* and famine shall those
16. because of the famine *and the sword;*
18. behold the slain with *the sword!*
15: 2. such as (are) *for the sword, to the sword;*
3. *the sword* to slay, and the dogs to tear,
9. will I deliver *to the sword*
16: 4. *and* they shall be consumed *by the sword,*
18:21. their (blood) by the force of *the sword;*
— their young men (be) slain by *the sword*
19: 7. I will cause them to fall *by the sword*
20: 4. they shall fall *by the sword*
— shall slay them *with the sword.*
21: 7. from *the sword,* and from the famine,
— smite them with the edge of *the sword;*
9. abideth in this city shall die *by the sword,*
24:10. I will send *the sword,* the famine,
25:16, 27. because of *the sword*
29. for I will call for *a sword*
31. give them (that are) wicked *to the sword,*
26:23. who slew him *with the sword,*
27: 8. *with the sword,* and with the famine,
13. die, thou and thy people, *by the sword,*
29:17. I will send upon them *the sword,*
18. persecute them *with the sword,*
31: 2. people (which were) left of *the sword*
32:24. because of *the sword,*
36. king of Babylon *by the sword,*
33: 4. by the mounts, and by *the sword;*
34: 4. Thou shalt not die *by the sword:*
17. to *the sword,* to the pestilence,
38: 2. this city shall die *by the sword,*
39:18. *and* thou shalt not fall *by the sword,*
41: 2. the son of Shaphan *with the sword,*
42:16. *the sword,* which ye feared,
17. they shall die *by the sword,*
22. that ye shall die *by the sword,*
43:11. such (as are) *for the sword to the sword.*
44:12. *by the sword* (and) by the famine:
— *by the sword* and by the famine:
13. *by the sword,* by the famine,
18. *and* have been consumed *by the sword*
27. *by the sword* and by the famine,
28. a small number that escape *the sword*
46:10. and *the sword* shall devour,
14. for *the sword* shall devour
16. from *the* oppressing *sword.*
47: 6. *thou sword of* the Lord,
48: 2. *the sword* shall pursue thee.
10. keepeth back *his sword* from blood.

Jer. 49:37. I will send *the sword* after them,
50:16. for fear of *the* oppressing *sword*
35. *A sword* (is) upon the Chaldeans,
36. *A sword* (is) upon the liars;
— *a sword* (is) upon her mighty men;
37. *A sword* (is) upon their horses,
— *a sword* (is) upon her treasures;
51:50. Ye that have escaped *the sword*,
Lam 1:20. abroad *the sword* bereaveth,
2:21. my young men are fallen *by the sword;*
4: 9. slain with *the sword*
5: 9. because of *the sword*
Eze 5: 1. take thee *a* sharp *knife*,
2. smite about it *with a knife:*
—, 12. *and* I will draw out *a sword* after them.
12. a third part shall fall *by the sword*
17. *and* I will bring *the sword* upon thee.
6: 3. I, will bring *a sword* upon you,
8. that shall escape *the sword*
11. for they shall fall *by the sword*,
12. that is near shall fall *by the sword;*
7:15. *The sword* (is) without,
— in the field shall die *with the sword;*
11: 8. Ye have feared *the sword; and* I will bring *a sword* upon you,
10. Ye shall fall *by the sword;*
12:14. *and* I will draw out *the sword* after
16. a few men of them *from the sword*,
14:17. Or (if) I bring *a sword* upon that land,
— say, *Sword*, go through the land;
21. *the sword*, and the famine,
16:40. thrust thee through *with their swords*.
17:21. all his bands shall fall *by the sword*,
21: 3(8). draw forth *my sword* out of
4(9). therefore shall *my sword* go forth
5(10). I the Lord have drawn forth *my sword*
9(14). *A sword, a sword* is sharpened,
11(16). this *sword* is sharpened,
12(17). by reason of *the sword*
14(19). let *the sword* be doubled the third time, *the sword of* the slain: it (is) *the sword* of the great (men)
15(20). I have set the point of *the sword*
19(24). that *the sword of* the king of
20(25). that *the sword* may come to Rabbath
28(33). even say thou, *The sword, the sword* (is) drawn:
23:10. slew her *with the sword:*
25. thy remnant shall fall *by the sword:*
47. dispatch them *with their swords;*
24:21. whom ye have left shall fall *by the sword*.
25:13. Dedan shall fall *by the sword.*
26: 6. shall be slain *by the sword;*
8. He shall slay *with the sword*
9. *with his axes* he shall break down
11. shall slay thy people *by the sword*,
28: 7. they shall draw *their swords*
23. *by the sword* upon her on every side;
29: 8. I will bring *a sword* upon thee,
30: 4. And *the sword* shall come upon Egypt,
5. shall fall with them *by the sword*.
6. shall they fall in it *by the sword*,
11. shall draw *their swords* against Egypt,
17. shall fall *by the sword:*
21. make it strong to hold *the sword*.
22. cause *the sword* to fall out of his hand.
24. put *my sword* in his hand:
25. put *my sword* into the hand of
31:17. (them that be) slain with *the sword;*
18. (them that be) slain by *the sword*.
32:10. when I shall brandish *my sword*
11. *The sword of* the king of Babylon
12. *By the swords of* the mighty
20. slain by *the sword:* she is delivered to *the sword:*
21. uncircumcised, slain by *the sword*.
22, 23, 24. slain, fallen *by the sword:*
25, 29, 30, 31. slain by *the sword:*
26. slain by *the sword*,
27. have laid *their swords* under their heads,
28, 32. slain with *the sword*.
33: 2. When I bring *the sword* upon a land,
3. when he seeth *the sword* come
4. if *the sword* come, and take him away,
6. if the watchman see *the sword* come,
— if *the sword* come, and take (any) person
26. Ye stand upon *your sword*,
Eze 33:27. the wastes shall fall *by the sword*.
35: 5. Israel by the force of *the sword*
8. fall that are slain with *the sword*.
38: 4. all of them handling *swords:*
8. brought back *from the sword*,
21. I will call for *a sword*
— every man's *sword* shall be against
39:23. so fell they all *by the sword*.
Dan 11:33. yet they shall fall *by the sword*,
Hos 1: 7. save them by bow, *nor by sword*,
2:18(20). break the bow *and the sword*
7:16. princes shall fall *by the sword*
11: 6. *the sword* shall abide on his cities,
13:16(14:1). they shall fall *by the sword:*
Joel 3:10(4:10). Beat your plowshares *into swords*.
Am. 1:11. pursue his brother *with the sword*,
4:10. have I slain *with the sword*,
7: 9. Jeroboam *with the sword*.
11. Jeroboam shall die *by the sword*,
17. shall fall *by the sword*,
9: 1. slay the last of them *with the sword:*
4. thence will I command *the sword*,
10. my people shall die *by the sword*,
Mic. 4: 3. they shall beat *their swords* into
— nation shall not lift up *a sword*
5: 6(5). waste the land of Assyria *with the sword*,
6:14. deliverest will I give up *to the sword*.
Nah 2:13(14). and *the sword* shall devour
3: 3. lifteth up both *the* bright *sword*
15. *the sword* shall cut thee off,
Zep 2:12. ye (shall be) slain by *my sword*.
Hag 2:22. every one *by the sword of* his
Zec 9:13. made thee *as the sword*
11:17. *the sword* (shall be) upon his arm,
13: 7. Awake, *O sword*, against my shepherd,

חֹרֶב *ghōh'-rev*, m. 2721

Gen31:40. in the day *the drought* consumed me,
Jud 6:37. *dry* upon all the earth (lit. *dryness*)
39. let it now be *dry* only (lit. *dryness*)
40. it was *dry* upon the fleece (lit. *dryness*)
Job 30:30. my bones are burned with *heat*.
Isa. 4: 6. a shadow in the daytime *from the heat*,
25: 4. a shadow *from the heat*,
5. *as the heat* in a dry place; (even) *the heat* with the shadow
61: 4. shall repair the *waste* cities,
Jer. 36:30. cast out in the day *to the heat*,
49:13. Bozrah shall become *a waste*,
50:38. *A drought* (is) upon her waters;
Eze 29:10. Egypt *utterly* waste (and) desolate, (marg. wastes of *waste*)
Zep 2:14. *desolation* (shall be) in the thresholds:
Hag 1:11. I called for *a drought* upon the land,

חָרְבָּה *ghor-bāh'*, f. 2723

Lev 26:31. make your cities *waste*, (lit. *a desolation*)
33. your cities *waste*. (lit. *a desolation*)
Ezr. 9: 9. to repair *the desolations thereof*,
Job 3:14. which built *desolate places*
Ps. 9: 6(7). *destructions* are come to a perpetual end:
102: 6(7). I am like an owl of *the desert*.
109:10. also *out of their desolate places*.
Isa. 5:17. *and the waste places of* the fat ones
44:26. *and* I will raise up *the decayed places thereof:* (marg. *wastes*)
48:21. he led them *through the deserts:*
49:19. *thy waste* and thy desolate places,
51: 3. he will comfort all *her waste places;*
52: 9. ye *waste places of* Jerusalem:
58:12. shall build *the old waste places:*
61: 4. they shall build *the* old *wastes*,
64:11(10). all our pleasant things are *laid waste*. (lit. *to desolation*)
Jer. 7:34. for the land shall be *desolate*. (lit. *for desolation*)
22: 5. this house shall become *a desolation*.
25: 9. *and* perpetual *desolations*.
11. this whole land shall be *a desolation*,
18. to make them *a desolation*,

Jer. 27:17. wherefore should this city be *laid waste?* (lit. *a desolation*)
44: 2. this day they (are) *a desolation,*
6. they are *wasted* (and) desolate,
22. therefore is your land *a desolation,*
49:13. shall be perpetual *wastes.*
Eze 5:14. I will make thee *waste,*
13: 4. are like the foxes *in the deserts.*
25:13. I will make it *desolate* from Teman;
26:20. *in places desolate* of old,
29: 9. Egypt shall be desolate *and waste;*
10. Egypt utterly *waste* (and) desolate, (lit. *wastes of* waste)
33:24. they that inhabit those *wastes*
27. they that (are) *in the wastes*
35: 4. I will lay thy cities *waste,*
36: 4. *to the* desolate *wastes,*
10. *and the wastes* shall be builded:
33. *the wastes* shall be builded.
38: 8. which have been always *waste:*
12. thine hand upon *the desolate places*
Dan 9: 2. seventy years *in the desolations of* Jerusalem.
Mal 1: 4. return and build *the desolate places;*

2724 **חָרָבָה** *g̣hāh-rāh-vāh'*, f.

Gen. 7:22. all that (was) *in the dry land,*
Ex. 14:21. made the sea *dry land,*
Jos. 3:17. stood firm *on dry ground*
— Israelites passed over *on dry ground,*
4:18. lifted up unto *the dry land,*
2K. 2: 8. they two went over *on dry ground.*
Eze 30:12. I will make the rivers *dry,*(marg. *drought*)
Hag 2: 6. the sea, and *the dry land;*

2725 **חֲרָבוֹן** [*g̣hărāh-vōhn'*], m.

Ps. 32: 4. moisture is turned *into the drought of*

2727 **חָרַג** [*g̣hāh-rag'*].

* KAL.—*Future.* *

Ps. 18:45(46). shall fade away, *and be afraid*

2728 **חַרְגֹּל** *g̣har-gōhl'*, m.

Lev. 11:22. *the beetle* after his kind,

2729 **חָרַד** *g̣hāh-rad'*.

* KAL.—*Preterite.* *

1Sa. 13: 7. all the people followed him *trembling.* (marg. *trembled* after him)
14:15. the spoilers, *they* also *trembled,*
2K. 4:13. *thou hast been careful* for us
Isa. 10:29. Ramah *is afraid;*
19:16. *and it shall be afraid* and fear
Eze. 26:16. *and shall tremble* at (every)
32:10. *and they shall tremble* at (every)

KAL.—*Imperative.*

Isa. 32:11. *Tremble,* ye women that are at ease;

KAL.—*Future.*

Gen 27:33. *And* Isaac *trembled* very exceedingly,
42:28. *and they were afraid,*
Ex. 19:16. *so* that all the people that (was) in the camp *trembled.*
18. *and* the whole mount *quaked*
Ru. 3: 8. *that* the man *was afraid,*
1Sa. 16: 4. *And* the elders of the town *trembled*
21: 1(2). *and* Ahimelech *was afraid*
28: 5. *and* his heart greatly *trembled.*
1K. 1:49. *And* all the guests that (were) with Adonijah *were afraid,*
Job 37. 1. At this also my heart *trembleth,*
Isa. 41: 5. the ends of the earth *were afraid,*
Eze 26:18. Now *shall* the isles *tremble*
Hos 11:10. *then* the children *shall tremble*
11. *They shall tremble* as a bird
Am. 3: 6. the people not *be afraid?*

* HIPHIL.—*Preterite.* *

Jud. 8:12. *discomfited* all the host. (marg. *terrified*)
2Sa. 17: 2. *and will make* him *afraid:*

HIPHIL.—*Infinitive.*

Eze. 30: 9. *to make* the careless Ethiopians *afraid,*
Zec. 1:21(2:4). these are come *to fray* them,

HIPHIL.—*Participle.*

Lev. 26: 6. none *shall make* (you) *afraid:*
Deu 28:26. no man *shall fray* (them) *away.*
Job 11:19. none *shall make* (thee) *afraid;*
Isa. 17: 2. none *shall make* (them) *afraid.*
Jer. 7:33. none *shall fray* (them) *away.*
30:10 & 46:27. none *shall make* (him) *afraid.*
Eze. 34:28. none *shall make* (them) *afraid.*
39:26. none *made* (them) *afraid.*
Mic. 4: 4. none *shall make* (them) *afraid:*
Nah 2:11(12). none *made* (them) *afraid?*
Zep. 3:13. none *shall make* (them) *afraid.*

חָרֵד *g̣hāh-rēhd'*, adj. 2730

Jud. 7: 3. Whosoever (is) fearful *and afraid,*
1Sa. 4:13. his heart *trembled* for the ark
Ezr. 9: 4. every one *that trembled* at
10: 3. *and of those that tremble*
Isa. 66: 2. *and trembleth* at my word.
5. *ye that tremble* at his word;

חֲרָדָה *g̣hărāh-dāh'*, f. 2731

Gen 27:33. Isaac trembled very *exceedingly,* (marg. with *a* great *trembling* greatly)
1Sa. 14:15. there was *trembling* in the host,
— so it was *a* very great *trembling.*
2K. 4:13. careful for us with all this *care;*
Pro. 29:25. *The fear of* man bringeth a snare:
Isa. 21: 4. my pleasure hath he turned *into fear*
Jer. 30: 5. We have heard a voice of *trembling,*
Eze. 26:16. clothe themselves with *trembling;* (marg. *tremblings*)
Dan 10: 7. but *a* great *quaking* fell upon them,

חָרָה *g̣hāh-rāh'*. 2734

* KAL.—*Preterite.* *

Gen 4: 6. Why *art* thou *wroth?* (lit. *does it kindle* to thee)
Ex. 22:24(23). *And* my wrath *shall wax hot,*
Nu. 11:33. the wrath of the Lord *was kindled*
Deu 7: 4. *so* will the anger of the Lord *be kindled*
11:17. *And* (then) the Lord's wrath *be kindled*
31:17. *Then* my anger *shall be kindled*
Jos. 23:16. *then shall* the anger of the Lord *be kindled*
2Sa. 19:42(43). wherefore then *be* ye *angry*
22: 8. because he *was wroth.*
2K. 23:26. wherewith his anger *was kindled*
Job 32: 2. against Job *was* his wrath *kindled,*
3. against his three friends *was* his wrath *kindled,*
42: 7. My wrath *is kindled* against thee,
Ps. 18: 7(8). because he *was wroth.*
Isa. 5:25. is the anger of the Lord *kindled*
Hos. 8: 5. mine anger *is kindled* against them:
Jon 4: 4, 9. Doest thou well *to be angry?*
9. I do well *to be angry,*
Hab 3: 8. *Was* the Lord *displeased*
Zec. 10: 3. Mine anger *was kindled*

KAL.—*Infinitive.*

1Sa 20: 7. but if he be *very* wroth, (lit. wroth *in being wroth*)
2Sa. 24: 1. again the anger of the Lord *was kindled*
Ps. 124: 3. *when* their wrath *was kindled*

KAL.—*Future.*

Gen 4: 5. *And* Cain *was* very *wroth,*
18:30, 32. Oh *let* not the Lord *be angry,*
30: 2. *And* Jacob's anger *was kindled*
31:35. *Let it* not *displease* my lord
36. *And* Jacob *was wroth,*
34: 7. *and* they *were* very *wroth,*
39:19. *that* his wrath *was kindled.*
44:18. *let* not thine anger *burn*

Gen45: 5. be not grieved, nor *angry*
Ex. 4:14. *And* the anger of the Lord *was kindled*
32:10. *that* my wrath *may wax hot*
11. why *doth* thy wrath *wax hot*
19. *and* Moses' anger *waxed hot,*
22. *Let* not the anger of my lord *wax hot:*
Nu. 11: 1. *and* his anger *was kindled;*
10 & 12:9. *and* the anger of the Lord *was kindled*
16:15. *And* Moses *was* very *wroth,*
22:22. *And* God's anger *was kindled*
27. *and* Balaam's anger *was kindled,*
24:10. *And* Balak's anger *was kindled*
25: 3. *and* the anger of the Lord *was kindled*
32:10, 13. *And* the Lord's anger *was kindled*
Deu 6:15. of the Lord thy God *be kindled*
29:27(26). *And* the anger of the Lord *was kindled*
Jos. 7: 1. *and* the anger of the Lord *was kindled*
Jud. 2:14, 20. *And* the anger of the Lord *was hot*
3: 8. *Therefore* the anger of the Lord *was hot*
6:39. *Let* not thine anger *be hot*
9:30. *And* when...his anger *was kindled.* (marg. or, *hot*)
10: 7. *And* the anger of the Lord *was hot*
14:19. *And* his anger *was kindled,*
1Sa. 11: 6. *and* his anger *was kindled*
15:11. *And it grieved* Samuel;
17:28. *and* Eliab's anger *was kindled*
18: 8. *And* Saul *was* very *wroth,*
20: 7. but if he *be* very *wroth,*
30. *Then* Saul's anger *was kindled*
2Sa. 3: 8. *Then was* Abner very *wroth*
6: 7. *And* the anger of the Lord *was kindled*
8. *And* David *was displeased,*
12: 5. *And* David's anger *was* greatly *kindled*
13:21. *But* when...he *was* very *wroth.*
2K. 13: 3. *And* the anger of the Lord *was kindled*
1Ch 13:10. *And* the anger of the Lord *was kindled*
11. *And* David *was displeased,*
2Ch 25:10. *wherefore* their anger *was* greatly *kindled*
15. *Wherefore* the anger of the Lord *was kindled*
Neh 4: 1(3:33). *when* Sanballat heard...he *was wroth,*
7(1). *then* they *were* very *wroth,*
5: 6. *And* I *was* very *angry*
Job 32: 2. *Then was kindled* the wrath
5. *then* his wrath *was kindled.*
Ps.106:40. *Therefore was* the wrath of the Lord *kindled*
Jon. 4: 1. *and* he *was very angry.*

* NIPHAL.—*Participle.* *

Isa. 41:11. all *they that were incensed*
45:24. all *that are incensed* against

* HIPHIL.—*Preterite.* *

Neh 3:20. *earnestly* repaired the other piece, (lit. *made hot* to repair)

HIPHIL.—*Future.*

Job 19:11. *He hath also kindled* his wrath

* TIPHEL.—*Future.* *

Jer. 12: 5. how *canst thou contend* with horses?

TIPHEL.—*Participle.*

Jer. 22:15. because thou *closest* (thyself) in cedar?

* HITHPAEL.—*Future.* *

Ps. 37: 1. *Fret* not *thyself* because of evildoers,
7. *fret* not *thyself* because of him
8. *fret* not *thyself* in any wise
Pro.24:19. *Fret* not *thyself* because of evil (men), (marg. or, *Keep* not *company* with)

2737 חֲרוּזִים *ghăroo-zeem'*, m. pl.

Cant 1:10. thy neck *with chains* (of gold).

2738 חָרוּל *ghāh-rool'*, m.

Job. 30: 7. under *the nettles* they were gathered
Pro. 24:31. *nettles* had covered the face thereof,
Zep. 2: 9. the breeding of *nettles,*

חָרוֹן *ghāh-rōhn'*, m. 2740

Ex. 15: 7. thou sentest forth *thy wrath,*
32:12. Turn *from* thy *fierce* wrath, (lit. *heat of* anger)
Nu. 25: 4. that the *fierce* anger of the Lord may be (lit. *heat of* anger)
32:14. to augment yet the *fierce* anger of the Lord (lit. *heat of* anger)
Deu 13:17(18). turn *from the fierceness of* his anger,
Jos. 7:26. *from the fierceness of* his anger.
1Sa. 28:18. nor executedst his *fierce* wrath (lit. *heat of* wrath)
2K. 23:26. turned not *from the fierceness of*
2Ch 28:11. for the *fierce* wrath of the Lord (is) upon you. (lit. *heat of* wrath)
13. *and* (there is) *fierce* wrath
29:10. that his *fierce* wrath may turn away (lit. *heat of* wrath)
30: 8. *the fierceness of* his wrath
Ezr. 10:14. until the *fierce* wrath (lit. *heat of* anger)
Neh 13:18. bring more *wrath* upon Israel
Job 20:23. (God) shall cast *the fury of* his wrath
Ps. 2: 5. *and* vex them *in his sore displeasure.*
58: 9(10). both living, and in (his) *wrath.*
69:24(25). *and* let thy *wrathful* anger
78:49. cast upon them *the fierceness of* his anger,
85: 3(4). *from the fierceness of* thine anger.
88:16(17). *Thy fierce wrath* goeth over
Isa. 13: 9. with wrath *and fierce* anger,
13. in the day of his *fierce* anger.
Jer. 4: 8. the *fierce* anger of the Lord is not turned
26. by his *fierce* anger.
12:13. *because of* the *fierce* anger of the Lord.
25:37. because of the *fierce* anger of the
38. because of *the fierceness of* the oppressor and because of his *fierce* anger.
30:24. The *fierce* anger of the Lord shall not return,
49:37. my *fierce* anger,
51:45. every man his soul *from* the *fierce* anger of
Lam. 1:12. the day of his *fierce* anger.
4:11. hath poured out his *fierce* anger,
Eze. 7:12. *wrath* (is) upon all the multitude
14. for *my wrath* (is) upon all the
Hos. 11: 9. execute *the fierceness of* mine anger,
Jon. 3: 9. turn away *from* his *fierce* anger,
Nah 1: 6. who can abide *in the fierceness of* his
Zep. 2: 2. before the *fierce* anger of the Lord come
3: 8. all my *fierce* anger:

חָרוּץ *ghāh-rootz'*, m. 2742

Job 41:30(22). he spreadeth *sharp pointed things*
Ps. 68:13(14). her feathers with yellow *gold.*
Pro. 3:14. *and* the gain thereof *than fine gold.*
8:10. knowledge *rather than* choice *gold.*
19. My fruit (is) better *than gold,*
16:16. to get wisdom *than gold?*
Isa. 28:27. threshed *with a threshing instrument,*
41:15. a new *sharp* threshing instrument
Dan 9:25. built again, *and the wall,* (marg. or *breach,* or, *ditch*)
Joel 3:14(4:14), 14(4:14). in the valley of *decision.*
Am. 1: 3. threshed Gilead *with threshing instruments of* iron:
Zec. 9: 3. *and fine gold* as the mire

חָרוּץ *ghāh-rootz'*, m. 2742

Pro. 10: 4. the hand of *the diligent* maketh rich.
12:24. of *the diligent* shall bear rule:
27. substance of a *diligent* man (is) precious.
13: 4. the soul of *the diligent* shall be made
21: 5. The thoughts of *the diligent*

חַרְחֻר *ghar-ghoor*, m. 2746

Deu 28:22. *and with an extreme burning,*

חֶרֶט *gheh'-ret*, m. 2747

Ex. 32: 4. fashioned it *with a graving tool,*
Isa. 8: 1. write in it *with* a man's *pen*

2749 **חַרְטֹם** *ghar-tōhm'*, Ch. m.

Dan 2:10. (that) asked such things at any *magician*,
27. the wise (men), the astrologers, *the magicians*,
4: 7(4). Then came in *the magicians*,
9(6). Belteshazzar, master of *the magicians*,
5:11. thy father, made master of *the magicians*,

2748 **חַרְטֻמִּים** *ghar-toom-meem'*, m. pl.

Gen41: 8. called for all *the magicians of*
24. I told (this) unto *the magicians*;
Ex. 7:11, 22. *the magicians of* Egypt,
8: 7(3), 18(14). *the magicians* did so with their
19(15). Then *the magicians* said
9:11. *the magicians* could not stand
— the boil was *upon the magicians*,
Dan 1:20. ten times better than all *the magicians*
2: 2. king commanded to call *the magicians*,

2750 **חֳרִי** *ghŏree*, m.

Ex. 11: 8. from Pharaoh *in* a *great* anger. (marg. *heat of* anger)
Deu29:24(23). *the heat of* this great anger?
1Sa.20:34. arose from the table *in fierce* anger, (lit. *heat of* anger)
2Ch 25:10. returned home *in great* anger. (marg. *heat of* anger)
Isa. 7: 4. *for* the *fierce* anger of Rezin (lit. *heat of* anger)
Lam. 2: 3. He hath cut off *in* (his) *fierce* anger

2751 **חֹרִי** *ghōh-ree'*.

Gen40:16. (I had) three *white* baskets on my head: (marg. *full of holes*)

2754 **חָרִיטִים** *ghāh-ree-teem'*, m. pl.

2K. 5:23. bound two talents of silver in two *bags*,
Isa. 3:22. wimples, *and the crisping pins*,

2755 **חֲרִים** [*ghăreem*], m. pl.

2K. 6:25. (כתיב) the fourth part of a cab of doves' *dung*
18:27. (——) that they may eat *their own dung*,

2757 **חָרִיץ** [*ghāh-reetz'*], m.

1Sa.17:18. carry these ten *cheeses* (marg. *cheeses of* milk)
2Sa.12:31. saws, *and under harrows of* iron,
1Ch 20: 3. *and with harrows of* iron,

2758 **חָרִישׁ** *ghāh-reesh'*, m.

Gen45: 6. neither (be) *earing* nor harvest.
Ex. 34:21. *in earing time* and in harvest
1Sa. 8:12. and (will set them) to ear *his ground*,

2759 **חֲרִישִׁי** [*ghăree-shee'*], adj.

Jon. 4: 8. God prepared a *vehement* east wind; (marg. or, *silent*)

2760 **חָרַךְ** [*ghāh-rach'*].

* KAL.—*Future.* *

Pro.12:27. The slothful (man) *roasteth* not

חֲרַךְ [*ghărach*], Ch. 2761

* ITHPAEL.—*Preterite.* *

Dan 3:27. nor *was* an hair of their head *singed*,

חֲרַכִּים *ghărak-keem'*, m. pl. 2762

Cant.2: 9. shewing himself through *the lattice*.

חָרַם [*ghāh-ram'*]. 2763

* KAL.—*Participle.* Paül. *

Lev.21:18. or *he that hath a flat nose*,

* HIPHIL.—*Preterite.* *

Nu. 21: 2. *then I will utterly destroy* their cities.
Jos. 2:10. Og, whom *ye utterly destroyed*.
8:26. until *he had utterly destroyed*
10:28. the king thereof *he utterly destroyed*,
35. *he utterly destroyed* that day,
40. but *utterly destroyed* all that breathed.
11:12. *he utterly destroyed* (them),
21. Joshua *destroyed them utterly*
1Sa.15: 3. smite Amalek, *and utterly destroy* all
8. and *utterly destroyed* all the people
9. that *they destroyed utterly*.
15. the rest *we have utterly destroyed*.
18. Go *and utterly destroy* the sinners
20. *have utterly destroyed* the Amalekites.
2Ch 32:14. that my fathers *utterly destroyed*,
Isa. 11:15. *And* the Lord *shall utterly destroy*
34: 2. *he hath utterly destroyed them*,
Jer. 25: 9. *and will utterly destroy them*,
Mic. 4:13. *and I will consecrate* their gain

HIPHIL.—*Infinitive.*

Deu 3: 6. *utterly destroying* the men,
7: 2. *utterly* destroy them; (lit. *utterly destroying* thou shalt utterly destroy)
20:17. thou shalt *utterly* destroy (lit. *id.*)
Jos. 11:11. *utterly destroying* (them):
20. that *he might destroy them utterly*,
1Sa.15: 9. would not *utterly destroy them*:
1K. 9:21. Israel also were not able *utterly to destroy*,
2K. 19:11. *by destroying them utterly*:
2Ch 20:23. mount Seir, *utterly to slay* and destroy (them):
Isa. 37:11. *by destroying them utterly*;
Jer. 50:21. waste *and utterly destroy* after them,
Dan 11:44. *and utterly to make away* many.

HIPHIL.—*Imperative.*

Deu13:15(16). *destroying* it *utterly*,
Jer. 50:26. *and destroy her utterly*:
51: 3. *destroy ye utterly* all her host.

HIPHIL.—*Future.*

Lev.27:28. that a man *shall devote* unto the Lord
Nu. 21: 3. *and they utterly destroyed* them
Deu 2:34. *and utterly destroyed* the men,
3: 6. *And we utterly destroyed* them,
7: 2. utterly *destroy* them;
20:17. But *thou shalt* utterly *destroy them*;
Jos. 6:18. lest *ye make* (yourselves) *accursed*,
21. *And they utterly destroyed* all
10: 1. taken Ai, *and had utterly destroyed it*;
37. *but destroyed* it *utterly*,
39. *and utterly destroyed* all
Jud. 1:17. *and utterly destroyed* it.
21:11. *Ye shall utterly destroy* every male,
1Ch 4:41. *and destroyed them utterly*

* HOPHAL.—*Future.* *

Ex. 22:20(19). *he shall be utterly destroyed*.
Lev.27:29. which *shall be devoted* of men,
Ezr.10: 8. all his substance *should be forfeited*, (marg. *devoted*)

חֵרֶם *ghĕh'-rem*, m. 2764

Lev.27:21. as a field *devoted*,
28. no *devoted thing*, that a man shall devote
— every *devoted thing* (is) most holy
29. None *devoted*, which shall be devoted
Nu. 18:14. Every *thing devoted* in Israel

Deu 7:26. lest thou be *a cursed thing*
— for it (is) *a cursed thing.*
13:17(18). cleave nought of *the cursed thing* (marg. *devoted*)
Jos. 6:17. the city shall be *accursed*, (marg. *id.*)
18. keep (yourselves) from *the accursed thing*,
— when ye take of *the accursed thing*, and make the camp of Israel *a curse*,
7: 1. a trespass *in the accursed thing:*
— took of *the accursed thing:*
11. have even taken of *the accursed thing*,
12. because they were *accursed:*
— except ye destroy *the accursed*
13. *an accursed thing* in the midst of thee,
— until ye take away *the accursed thing*
15. taken *with the accursed thing*
22:20. commit a trespass *in the accursed thing*,
1Sa.15:21. *things which should have been utterly destroyed*,
1K. 20:42. whom *I appointed to utter destruction*,
1Ch 2: 7. who transgressed *in the thing accursed.*
Ecc. 7:26. whose heart (is) snares *and nets*,
Isa. 34: 5. upon the people of *my curse*,
43:28. have given Jacob *to the curse*,
Eze.26: 5. shall be (a place for) the spreading of *nets*
14. thou shalt be (a place) to spread *nets*
32: 3. bring thee up *in my net.*
44:29. every *dedicated thing* in Israel (marg. *devoted*)
47:10. a (place) to spread forth *nets;* (lit. of *nets*)
Mic. 7: 2. hunt every man his brother with *a net.*
Hab. 1:15. they catch them *in their net*,
16. they sacrifice *unto their net*,
17. Shall they therefore empty *their net*,
Zec.14:11. *and* there shall be no more *utter destruction;*
Mal. 4: 6(3:24). lest I come and smite the earth with *a curse.*

2770 **חֶרְמֵשׁ** *'gher-mĕhsh'*, m.

Deu16: 9. beginnest (to put) *the sickle* to the corn.
23:25(26). *but* thou shalt not move *a sickle*

2775 **חֶרֶס** *'gheh'-res*, m.

Deu 28:27. the scab, *and with the itch*,
Jud. 8:13. returned from battle before *the sun*
14:18. before *the sun* went down,
Job 9: 7. Which commandeth *the sun*,

2777 **חַרְסִית** *'ghar-seeth'* (קרי) or **חַרְסוּת** *'ghar-sooth'* (כתיב) f.

Jer. 19: 2. which (is) by the entry of the *east* gate, (marg. the *sun* gate)

2778 **חָרַף** [*'ghāh-raph'*].

* KAL.—*Future.* *

Job 27: 6. my heart *shall not reproach*
Isa. 18: 6. beasts of the earth *shall winter* upon them.

KAL.—*Participle.* Poel.

Ps. 69:9(10). reproaches of *them that reproached thee*
119:42. to answer *him that reproacheth me:*
Pro.27:11. answer *him that reproacheth me.*

* NIPHAL.—*Participle.* *

Lev.19:20. *betrothed* to an husband, (marg. *reproached* by, or, for man; or, *abused* by any)

* PIEL.—*Preterite.* *

Jud. 5:18. a people (that) *jeoparded* their lives (marg. *exposed to reproach*)
8:15. with whom *ye did upbraid* me,
1Sa. 17:10. I *defy* the armies of Israel this day;
26. that *he should defy* the armies of
36. seeing *he hath defied*
45. Israel, whom *thou hast defied.*
2K. 19:22. Whom *hast thou reproached*
23. *thou hast reproached* the Lord,

Ps. 42:10(11). mine enemies *reproach me;*
57: 3(4). save me (from) *the reproach* of him (marg. *he reproacheth*)
74:18. the enemy *hath reproached*,
79:12. wherewith *they have reproached thee*,
89:51(52). Wherewith thine enemies *have reproached*, O Lord; wherewith *they have reproached* the footsteps
102: 8(9). Mine enemies *reproach me*
Pro.14:31. oppresseth the poor *reproacheth* his
17: 5. mocketh the poor *reproacheth* his Maker:
Isa. 37:23. Whom *hast thou reproached*
24. *hast thou reproached* the Lord,
65: 7. upon the mountains, and *blasphemed me*
Zep. 2: 8. whereby *they have reproached* my people,
10. because *they have reproached*

PIEL.—*Infinitive.*

1Sa.17:25. surely *to defy* Israel is he come up:
2Sa.23: 9. *when they defied* the Philistines
2K. 19: 4, 16. *to reproach* the living God;
2Ch 32:17. He wrote also letters *to rail* on the Lord
Isa. 37: 4, 17. hath sent *to reproach* the living God,

PIEL.—*Future.*

2Sa.21:21. And *when he defied* Israel, (marg. *reproached*)
1Ch 20: 7. But *when he defied* Israel, (marg. *id.*)
Neh 6:13. that *they might reproach me.*
Ps. 55:12(13). an enemy (that) *reproached me;*
74:10. how long *shall* the adversary *reproach?*

PIEL.—*Participle.*

Ps. 44:16(17). the voice of *him that reproacheth*

חֹרֶף *'ghōh'-reph*, m. 2779

Gen 8:22. cold and heat, and summer *and winter*,
Job 29: 4. As I was in the days of *my youth*,
Ps. 74:17. thou hast made summer *and winter.*
Pro.20: 4. wilt not plow *by reason of the cold;* (marg. or, *winter*)
Jer. 36:22. the king sat in the *winter*house
Am. 3:15. I will smite the *winter* house
Zec.14: 8. in summer *and in winter*

חֶרְפָּה *'gher-pāh'*, f. 2781

Gen30:23. God hath taken away *my reproach:*
34:14. that (were) *a reproach* unto us:
Jos. 5: 9. have I rolled away *the reproach of*
1Sa.11: 2. lay it (for) *a reproach* upon all Israel.
17:26. taketh away *the reproach* from Israel?
25:39. hath pleaded the cause of *my reproach*
2Sa.13:13. whither shall I cause *my shame* to go?
Neh 1: 3. in great affliction *and reproach:*
2:17. that we be no more *a reproach.*
4: 4(3:36). turn *their reproach* upon their
5: 9. *because of the reproach of* the heathen
Job 16:10. smitten me upon the cheek *reproachfully;*
19: 5. plead against me *my reproach:*
Ps. 15: 3. *nor* taketh up *a reproach*
22: 6(7). no man; *a reproach of* men,
31:11(12). I was *a reproach* among all
39: 8(9). make me not *the reproach of*
44:13(14). Thou makest us *a reproach*
69: 7(8). for thy sake I have borne *reproach;*
9(10). *and the reproaches of* them
10(11). that was *to* my *reproach.*
19(20). Thou hast known *my reproach*,
20(21). *Reproach* hath broken my heart;
71:13. let them be covered (with) *reproach*
74:22. how the foolish man *reproacheth thee* (lit. *thy reproach* from the foolish man)
78:66. put them to *a* perpetual *reproach.*
79: 4. We are become *a reproach*
12. sevenfold into their bosom *their reproach*,
89:41(42). he is *a reproach* to his neighbours.
50(51). Remember, Lord, *the reproach of*
109:25. I became also *a reproach* unto them:
119:22. Remove from me *reproach*
39. Turn away *my reproach*
Pro. 6:33. *and his reproach* shall not be wiped
18: 3. with ignominy *reproach.*
Isa. 4: 1. to take away *our reproach.*

Isa. 25: 8. *and the rebuke of* his people
30: 5. but a shame, and also *a reproach.* (lit. *for a reproach*)
47: 3. yea, *thy shame* shall be seen:
51: 7. fear ye not *the reproach of* men,
54: 4. *and* shalt not remember *the reproach of*
Jer. 6:10. the word of the Lord is unto them *a reproach;* (lit. *for a reproach*)
15:15. for thy sake I have suffered *rebuke.*
20: 8. word of the Lord was made *a reproach* (lit. *for a reproach*)
23:40. bring *an* everlasting *reproach*
24: 9. *a reproach* and a proverb, a taunt and a curse, (lit. *for a reproach*)
29:18. an hissing, *and a reproach,*
31:19. I did bear *the reproach of* my youth.
42:18. an astonishment, and a curse, *and a reproach;*
44: 8. curse *and a reproach* among all the
12. astonishment, and a curse, *and a reproach.*
49:13. Bozrah shall become a desolation, *a reproach,* (lit. *for a reproach*)
51:51. because we have heard *reproach:*
Lam. 3:30. he is filled full *with reproach.*
61. Thou hast heard *their reproach,*
5: 1. consider, and behold *our reproach.*
Eze. 5:14. *and a reproach* among the nations
15. So it shall be *a reproach*
16:57. as at the time of (thy) *reproach of*
21:28(33). concerning *their reproach;*
22: 4. have I made thee *a reproach*
36:15. *neither* shalt thou bear *the reproach of*
30. ye shall receive no more *reproach of*
Dan 9:16. thy people (are become) *a reproach* (lit. *for a reproach*)
11:18. shall cause *the reproach offered by him* (marg. *his reproach*)
— without *his own reproach*
12: 2. some *to shame* (and) everlasting contempt.
Hos 12:14(15). *and his reproach* shall his Lord
Joel 2:17. give not thine heritage *to reproach,*
19. I will no more make you *a reproach*
Mic. 6:16. *therefore* ye shall bear *the reproach of*
Zep. 2: 8. I have heard *the reproach of* Moab,
3:18. *the reproach* of it (was) a burden.

2782 **חָרַץ** *ghāh-ratz'.*

* KAL.—*Preterite.* *

Jos. 10:21. none *moved* his tongue against
1K. 20:40. thyself *hast decided* (it).

KAL.—*Future.*

Ex. 11: 7. *shall* not a dog *move* his tongue,
2Sa. 5:24. then *thou shalt bestir thyself:*

KAL.—*Participle.* Paül.

Lev. 22:22. Blind, or broken, or *maimed,* or having a wen,
Job 14: 5. Seeing his days (are) *determined,*
Isa. 10:22. the consumption *decreed* shall overflow with righteousness.

* NIPHAL.—*Participle.* *

Isa. 10:23. *even determined,* in the midst
28:22. *even determined* upon the whole earth.
Dan 9:26. unto the end of the war desolations *are determined.*
27. *and that determined* shall be
11:36. for *that that is determined* shall be done.

2783 **חֲרַץ** [*ghărats*], Ch. f.

Dan 5: 6. the joints of *his loins* were loosed,

2784 **חַרְצֻבּוֹת** *ghar-tzoob-bōhth',* f. pl.

Ps. 73: 4. For (there are) no *bands* in their death:
Isa. 58: 6. loose *the bands of* wickedness,

חַרְצַנִּים *ghar-tzan-neem',* m. pl. 2785

Nu. 6: 4. *from the kernels* even to the husk.

חָרַק *ghāh-rak'.* 2786

* KAL.—*Preterite.* *

Job 16: 9. *he gnasheth* upon me with his teeth;

KAL.—*Infinitive.*

Ps. 35:16. *they gnashed* (lit. *to gnash*) upon me

KAL.—*Future.*

Ps. 112:10. *he shall gnash* with his teeth,
Lam. 2:16. they hiss *and gnash* the teeth:

KAL.—*Participle.* Poel.

Ps. 37:12. *and gnasheth* upon him

חָרַר [*ghāh-rar'*]. 2787

* KAL.—*Preterite.* *

Job 30:30. my bones *are burned* with heat.
Isa. 24: 6. inhabitants of the earth *are burned,*
Eze. 24:11. may be hot, *and may burn,*

* NIPHAL.—*Preterite.* *

Ps. 69: 3(4). my throat *is dried:*
102: 3(4). my bones *are burned* as an hearth.
Cant. 1: 6. my mother's children *were angry*
Jer. 6:29. The bellows *are burned,*

NIPHAL.—*Future.*

Eze. 15: 5. devoured it, *and it is burned?*
24:10. *let* the bones *be burned.*

NIPHAL.—*Participle.*

Eze. 15: 4. the midst of it *is burned.*

* PILPEL.—*Infinitive.* *

Pro. 26:21. a contentious man *to kindle* strife.

חֲרֵרִים *ghărĕh-reem',* m. pl. 2788

Jer. 17: 6. shall inhabit *the parched places*

חֶרֶשׂ *gheh'-res,* m. 2789

Lev. 6:28(21). But the *earthen* vessel
11:33. every *earthen* vessel,
14: 5. be killed in an *earthen* vessel
50. the one of the birds in an *earthen* vessel
15:12. the vessel of *earth,*
Nu. 5:17. holy water in an *earthen* vessel;
Job 2: 8. he took him *a potsherd*
41:30(22). Sharp *stones* (are) under him: (marg. pieces of *potsherd*)
Ps. 22:15(16). strength is dried up *like a potsherd;*
Pro. 26:23. and a wicked heart (are like) *a potsherd*
Isa. 30:14. found in the bursting of it *a sherd*
45: 9. (Let) *the potsherd* (strive) with *the potsherds of* the earth.
Jer. 19: 1. Go and get a potter's *earthen* bottle,
32:14. put them in an *earthen* vessel,
Lam. 4: 2. esteemed as *earthen* pitchers,
Eze. 23:34. thou shalt break *the sherds thereof,*

חָרַשׁ [*ghāh-rash'*]. 2790

* KAL.—*Preterite.* *

Jud. 14:18. If *ye had* not *plowed* with my heifer,
Ps. 129: 3. The plowers *plowed* upon my back:
Hos. 10:13. *Ye have plowed* wickedness,

KAL.—*Infinitive.*

1Sa. 8:12. *and* (will set them) *to ear* his ground,

KAL.—*Future.*

Deu 22:10. *Thou shalt* not *plow* with
Ps. 28: 1. *be* not *silent* to me:
35:22. *keep* not *silence:* O Lord,

Ps. 39:12(13). *hold* not *thy peace* at my tears:
50: 3. *shall* not *keep silence:*
83: 1(2). *hold* not *thy peace*, and be
109: 1. *Hold* not *thy peace*, O God
Pro. 3:29. *Devise* not evil against (marg. *Practise*)
20: 4. The sluggard *will* not *plow*
Isa. 28:24. *Doth* the plowman *plow* all day
Hos.10:11. I will make Ephraim to ride; Judah *shall plow*,
Am. 6:12. *will* (one) *plow* (there) with oxen?
Mic. 7:16. their ears *shall be deaf*.

KAL.—*Participle.* Poel.

1K. 7:14. *a worker in* brass:
19:19. *plowing* (with) twelve yoke (of oxen)
Job 1:14. The oxen were *plowing*,
4: 8. *they that plow* iniquity,
Ps.129: 3. *The plowers* plowed upon my back:
Pro. 6:14. he *deviseth* mischief continually;
18. heart *that deviseth* wicked imaginations,
12:20. Deceit (is) in the heart of *them that imagine* evil:
14:22. Do they not err *that devise* evil? but mercy and truth (shall be) to *them that devise* good.
Isa. 28:24. Doth *the plowman* plow all day
Am. 9:13. *the plowman* shall overtake the reaper,

KAL.—*Participle.* Paül.

Jer. 17: 1. *graven* upon the table of their heart,

* NIPHAL.—*Future.* *

Jer. 26:18. Zion *shall be plowed*
Mic. 3:12. *shall* Zion for your sake *be plowed*

* HIPHIL.—*Preterite.* *

Gen34: 5. *and* Jacob *held his peace*
Nu. 30: 4(5). *and* her father *shall hold his peace*
7(8), 11(12). *and held his peace* at her
14(15). because *he held his peace*
2K. 18:36. *But* the people *held their peace*,
Est. 7: 4. bondwomen, *I had held my tongue*,
Ps. 32: 3. When *I kept silence*,
50:21. done, *and I kept silence;*

HIPHIL.—*Infinitive.*

Nu. 30:14(15). *altogether* hold his peace (lit. *in holding his peace* shall hold his peace)
Est. 4:14. if thou *altogether* holdest thy peace (lit. *in holding* thy peace shalt hold thy peace)
Job 13: 5. would *altogether* hold your peace! (lit. *in holding your peace* shall hold your peace)

HIPHIL.—*Imperative.*

Jud.18:19. said unto him, *Hold thy peace*,
2Sa.13:20. but *hold* now *thy peace*,
Job 13:13. *Hold your peace*, let me alone, (marg. *Be silent* from me)
33:31. *hold thy peace*, and I will speak.
33. *hold thy peace*, and I shall teach thee
Isa. 41: 1. *Keep silence* before me, O islands;

HIPHIL.—*Future.*

Ex. 14:14. ye *shall hold your peace*.
Nu. 30:14(15). altogether *hold his peace*
1Sa. 7: 8. *Cease* not to cry unto the Lord (marg. *Be* not *silent* from us from crying)
Neh 5: 8. *Then held they their peace*,
Est. 4:14. if *thou* altogether *holdest thy peace*
Job 6:24. I *will hold my tongue:*
11: 3. thy lies *make* men *hold their peace?*
13: 5. O that *ye would* altogether *hold your peace!*
19. for now, if *I hold my tongue*,
41:12(4). *I will* not *conceal* his parts,
Pro.11:12. man of understanding *holdeth his peace*.
Isa. 36:21. *But they held their peace*,
42:14. *I have been still*, (and) refrained
Jer. 4:19. *I cannot hold my peace*,
38:27. *So they left off speaking* (marg. *were silent*)
Hab 1:13. *holdest thy tongue* when the
Zep 3:17. *he will rest* in his love, (marg. *be silent*)

HIPHIL.—*Participle.*

Gen24:21. wondering at her *held his peace*,
1Sa.10:27. But he *held his peace*. (marg. was *as though he had been deaf*)
23: 9. Saul *secretly practised* mischief

2Sa.19:10(11). why *speak* ye *not a word* (marg. (are) ye *silent*)
Pro.17:28. a fool, *when he holdeth his peace*,

* HITHPAEL.—*Future.* *

Jud.16: 2. *and were quiet* all the night, (marg. *silent*)

חָרָשׁ *ghāh-rāhsh'*, m. 2796

Ex. 28:11. With the work of *an engraver*
35:35. all manner of work, of *the engraver*,
38:23. *an engraver*, and a cunning workman,
Deu27:15. work of the hands of *the craftsman*,
1Sa.13:19. *Now* there was no *smith* found
2Sa. 5:11. and carpenters, and masons: (lit. *and workers of* wood, *and workers of* stone)
2K. 12:11(12). they laid it out to the carpenters (lit. *workers of* wood)
22: 6. *Unto carpenters*, and builders,
24:14. all *the craftsmen* and smiths:
16. *and craftsmen* and smiths a thousand,
1Ch 14: 1. *with masons and carpenters*, (lit. *and workers of* wall, *and workers of* wood)
22:15. *and workers of* stone and timber,
29: 5. by the hands of *artificers*.
2Ch 24:12. hired masons *and carpenters*
— also *such as wrought* iron
34:11. Even *to the artificers* and builders
Ezr. 3: 7. the masons, *and to the carpenters;* (marg. or, *workmen*)
Isa. 40:19. *The workman* melteth a graven image,
20. seeketh unto him a cunning *workman*
41: 7. *the carpenter* encouraged the goldsmith,
44:11. *and the workmen*, they (are) of men:
12. The smith (lit. *the workman of* iron) with the tongs both worketh
13. The carpenter (lit. *the workman of* wood) stretcheth out (his) rule;
45:16. together (that are) *makers of* idols.
54:16. I have created *the smith*
Jer. 10: 3. work of the hands of *the workman*,
9. the work of *the workman*,
24: 1. with *the carpenters* and smiths,
29: 2. *and the carpenters*, and the smiths,
Eze 21:31(36). brutish men, (and) *skilful to* destroy.
Hos. 8: 6. *the workman* made it;
13: 2. all of it the work of *the craftsmen:*
Zec. 1:20(2:3). the Lord shewed me four *carpenters*.

חֵרֵשׁ *ghēh-rēhsh'*, adj. 2795

Ex. 4:11. who maketh the dumb, or *deaf*,
Lev.19:14. Thou shalt not curse *the deaf*,
Ps. 38:13(14). But I, *as a deaf* (man), heard not;
58: 4(5). like the *deaf* adder (that) stoppeth her ear;
Isa. 29:18. in that day shall *the deaf* hear
35: 5. the ears of *the deaf* shall be unstopped.
42:18. Hear, ye *deaf;* and look, ye blind,
19. *or deaf*, as my messenger
43: 8. *and the deaf* that have ears.

חֶרֶשׁ *gheh'-resh*, m. 2791

Jos. 2: 1. two men to spy *secretly*,
1Ch 4:14. of the valley of *Charashim;* (marg. *Craftsmen*) for they were *craftsmen*.
Neh 11:35. Ono, the valley of *craftsmen*.
Isa. 3: 3. the cunning *artificer*,

חֹרֵשׁ *ghōh-rēhsh'*, m. 2794

Gen 4:22. an instructer of every *artificer*

חֹרֶשׁ *ghōh'-resh*, m. 2793

1Sa.23:15. in the wilderness of Ziph *in a wood*.
16. went to David *into the wood*,
18. David abode *in the wood*,
19. in strong holds *in the wood*,
2Ch 27: 4. *and in the forests* he built
Isa. 17: 9. strong cities be as *a* forsaken *bough*,
Eze 31: 3. *and with a* shadowing *shroud*,

2799 **חֲרֹשֶׁת** *g̣hărōh'-sheth*, f.

Ex. 31: 5. *And in cutting of* stones,
— *and in carving of* timber,
35:33. *And in the cutting of* stones, to set (them), *and in carving of* wood,

---

2801 **חָרַת** [*g̣hāh-rath'*].

* KAL.—*Participle.* Paül. *

Ex. 32:16. *graven* upon the tables.

2820 **חָשַׂךְ** *g̣hāh-sach'*.

* KAL.—*Preterite.* *

Gen22:12. seeing thou *hast* not *withheld*
16. *hast* not *withheld* thy son,
39: 9. neither *hath he kept back* any thing
1Sa.25:39. *hath kept* his servant from evil:
2Sa.18:16. Joab *held back* the people.
2K. 5:20. my master *hath spared* Naaman
Ezr. 9:13. God *hast punished* us less (marg. *withheld*)
Job 30:10. they flee far from me, and *spare* not (marg. *withhold* not)
38:23. Which *I have reserved*
Ps. 78:50. *he spared* not their soul
Isa. 14: 6. persecuted, (and) none *hindereth.*
Jer. 14:10. *they have* not *refrained* their feet,
Eze.30:18. day *shall be darkened*, [Some copies read חָשַׂךְ] (marg. *restrained*)

KAL.—*Imperative.*

Ps. 19:13(14). *Keep back* thy servant also

KAL.—*Future.*

Gen20: 6. *for I* also *withheld* thee
Job 7:11. *I will* not *refrain* my mouth;
16: 5. my lips *should asswage*
33:18. *He keepeth back* his soul
Pro.21:26. righteous giveth and *spareth* not.
24:11. If *thou forbear* to deliver
Isa. 54: 2. *spare* not, lengthen thy cords,
58: 1. Cry aloud, *spare* not,

KAL.—*Participle.* Poel.

Pro.10:19. but he *that refraineth* his lips
11:24. *and* (there is) *that withholdeth*
13:24. *He that spareth* his rod
17:27. He that hath knowledge *spareth*

* NIPHAL.—*Future.* *

Job 16: 6. my grief *is* not *asswaged:*
21:30. the wicked *is reserved* to the day

2834 **חָשַׂף** *g̣hāh-saph'*.

* KAL.—*Preterite.* *

Isa. 52:10. The Lord *hath made bare* his holy arm
Jer. 13:26. Therefore *will I discover* thy skirts
49:10. *I have made* Esau *bare*,
Joel 1: 7. *he hath made it* clean *bare*,

KAL.—*Infinitive.*

Isa. 30:14. *or to take* water (withal) out of the pit.
Joel 1: 7. he hath made it *clean* bare, (lit. *in making bare* he hath made it bare)
Hag. 2:16. the pressfat *for to draw out*

KAL.—*Imperative.*

Isa. 47: 2. *make bare* the leg,

KAL.—*Future.*

Ps. 29: 9. *and discovereth* the forests:

KAL.—*Participle.* Paül.

Isa. 20: 4. *even* with (their) buttocks *uncovered*,
Eze. 4: 7. thine arm (shall be) *uncovered*,

2835 **חֲשִׂף** [*g̣hăseeph*], m.

1K. 20:27. like two *little flocks of* kids;

חָשַׁב *g̣hāh-shav'*. 2803

* KAL.—*Preterite.* *

Gen50:20. *ye thought* evil against me; (but) God *meant it* unto good,
1Sa.18:25. Saul *thought* to make David fall
2Sa.14:13. Wherefore then *hast thou thought*
14. *yet doth he devise* means,
Est. 8: 3. his device that *he had devised*
9:24. *had devised* against the Jews
25. *he devised* against the Jews,
Job 35: 2. *Thinkest thou* this to be right,
Ps. 10: 2. devices that *they have imagined.*
21:11(12). *they imagined* a mischievous
140: 2(3). Which *imagine* mischiefs
4(5). who *have purposed* to overthrow
Isa. 33: 8. *he regardeth* no man.
53: 3. *we esteemed him* not.
4. yet *we did esteem him* stricken,
Jer. 11:19. I knew not that *they had devised*
18: 8. the evil that *I thought* to do
48: 2. in Heshbon *they have devised* evil
49:20. purposes, that *he hath purposed*
30. *and hath conceived* a purpose
50:45. purposes, that *he hath purposed*
Lam.2: 8. The Lord *hath purposed* to destroy
Eze.38:10. *and thou shalt think* an evil thought:
Am. 6: 5. *invent* to themselves instruments of musick,

KAL.—*Infinitive.*

Ex. 31: 4. *To devise* cunning works,
35:32. *And to devise* curious works,
2Ch 2:14(13). *and to find out* every device
Pro.16:30. shutteth his eyes *to devise* froward things.

KAL.—*Future.*

Gen15: 6. *and he counted it* to him
38:15. *he* (lit. *and he*) *thought her* to (be) an
1Sa. 1:13. *therefore* Eli *thought* she had been drunken.
2Sa.19:19(20). *Let* not my lord *impute*
Job 6:26. *Do ye imagine* to reprove words,
13:24. *and holdest me* for thine enemy?
19:11. *and he counteth me* unto him
15. in mine house, and my maids, *count me*
33:10. *he counteth me* for his enemy,
41:27(19). *He esteemeth* iron as straw,
32(24). *would think* the deep (to be) hoary.
Ps. 32: 2. whom the Lord *imputeth* not iniquity,
35:20. but *they devise* deceitful matters
36: 4(5). *He deviseth* mischief upon his bed;
40:17(18). the Lord *thinketh* upon me:
41: 7(8). against me *do they devise* my hurt.
52: 2(4). Thy tongue *deviseth* mischiefs;
Isa. 10: 7. neither *doth* his heart *think* so;
13:17. which *shall* not *regard* silver;
Jer. 18:18. Come, *and let us devise* devices
Dan11:25. *they shall forecast* devices
Zec. 7:10 & 8:17. *let* none of you *imagine* evil

KAL.—*Participle.* Poel.

Ex 26: 1. cherubims of *cunning* work shalt thou make (marg. work of *a cunning* workman)
31. fine twined linen of *cunning* work:
28: 6. fine twined linen, with *cunning* work.
15. the breastplate of judgment with *cunning* work;
35:35. *and of the cunning workman*,
— *and of those that devise* cunning work.
36: 8. cherubims of *cunning* work made he them.
35. cherubims made he it of *cunning* work.
38:23. *and a cunning workman*,
39: 3. in the fine linen, (with) *cunning* work.
8. the breastplate (of) *cunning* work,
2Ch 26:15. engines, invented by *cunning men*,
Neh 6: 2. But they *thought* to do me mischief.
6. thou and the Jews *think* to rebel:
Ps. 35: 4. confusion *that devise* my hurt.
Jer. 18:11. *and devise* a device against you: (lit. *and* (I am) *devising*)
23:27. *Which think* to cause my people
26: 3. repent me of the evil, which I *purpose*
29:11. the thoughts that I *think* toward you,
36: 3. the evil which I *purpose*
Eze.11: 2. the men *that devise* mischief,

Mic. 2: 1. Woe to *them that devise* iniquity,
3. against this family *do I devise*
Nah. 1:11. come out of thee, *that imagineth* evil
Mal. 3:16. *and that thought upon* his name.

* NIPHAL.—*Preterite.* *

Gen31:15. *Are we* not *counted* of him
Nu. 18:27. *And* (this) your heave offering *shall be reckoned*
30. *then it shall be counted*
Neh 13:13. for *they were counted* faithful,
Job 18: 3. Wherefore *are we counted* as beasts,
41:29(21). Darts *are counted* as stubble:
Ps. 44:22(23). *we are counted* as sheep
88: 4(5). *I am counted* with them that
Isa. 5:28. horses' hoofs *shall be counted*
40:15. *are counted* as the small dust
17. *they are counted* to him less
Lam. 4: 2. how *are they esteemed* as earthen pitchers,
Hos. 8:12. *they were counted* as a strange thing.

NIPHAL.—*Future.*

Lev. 7:18. neither *shall it be imputed*
17: 4. blood *shall be imputed* unto that man;
25:31. *shall be counted* as the fields
Deu 2:11. Which also *were accounted* giants,
20. That also *was accounted* a land
Jos. 13: 3. *is counted* to the Canaanite:
2Sa. 4: 2. Beeroth also *was reckoned*
2K. 22: 7. there *was* no *reckoning made*
Ps. 106:31. *And* that *was counted* unto him
Pro. 17:28. holdeth his peace, *is counted* wise:
27:14. *it shall be counted* a curse to him.
Isa. 29:16. *shall be esteemed* as the potter's clay:
17. fruitful field *shall be esteemed* as a forest?
32:15. and the fruitful field *be counted* for a forest.

NIPHAL.—*Participle.*

1K. 10:21. *it was* nothing *accounted*
2Ch 9:20. *it was* (not) any thing *accounted*
Isa. 2:22. wherein *is* he *to be accounted of?*

* PIEL.—*Preterite.* *

Lev. 25:27. *Then let him count* the years
50. *And he shall reckon* with him
52. *then he shall count* with him,
27:18, 23. *then* the priest *shall reckon*
Ps. 77: 5(6). *I have considered* the days of old,
119:59. *I thought on* my ways,
Jon. 1: 4. so that the ship *was like* to be broken. (marg. *thought*)

PIEL.—*Future.*

2K. 12:15(16). *they reckoned* not with the men,
Ps. 73:16. *When I thought* to know this,
144: 3. the son of man, *that thou makest account of him!*
Pro. 16: 9. A man's heart *deviseth* his way:
Dan 11:24. *he shall forecast* his devices (marg. *think* his thoughts)
Hos. 7:15. yet *do they imagine* mischief
Nah. 1: 9. What *do ye imagine* against

PIEL.—*Participle.*

Pro. 24: 8. *He that deviseth* to do evil

* HITHPAEL.—*Future.* *

Nu. 23: 9. *shall* not *be reckoned* among

2804 חֲשַׁב [*g'hăshav*], Ch.

* P'AL.—*Participle.* Passive. *

Dan 4:35(32). inhabitants of the earth (are) *reputed* as nothing:

2805 חֵשֶׁב *g'hēh'-shev*, m.

Ex. 28: 8. *And the curious girdle of* (marg. *embroidered*)
27. above *the curious girdle of* the ephod.
28. *the curious girdle of* the ephod,
29: 5. *with the curious girdle of* the ephod:
39: 5. *And the curious girdle of* his ephod,
20. above *the curious girdle of* the ephod.
21. above *the curious girdle of* the ephod,
Lev. 8: 7. *with the curious girdle of* the ephod,

חֶשְׁבּוֹן *g'hesh-bōhn'*, m. 2808

Ecc. 7:25. seek out wisdom, *and the reason*
27. one by one, to find out *the account:*
9:10. for (there is) no work, *nor device,*

חִשְּׁבֹנוֹת *g'hish-sh'vōh-nōhth'*, f. pl. 2810

2Ch 26:15. he made in Jerusalem *engines,*
Ecc. 7:29. have sought out many *inventions.*

חָשָׁה [*g'hāh-shāh'*]. 2814

* KAL.—*Infinitive.* *

Ecc. 3: 7. a time *to keep silence,*

KAL.—*Future.*

Ps. 28: 1. lest, (if) *thou be silent* to me,
107:29. *so* that the waves thereof *are still.*
Isa. 62: 1. For Zion's sake *will I* not *hold my peace,*
6. *shall* never *hold their peace*
64:12(11). *wilt thou hold thy peace,*
65: 6. *I will* not *keep silence,*

* HIPHIL.—*Preterite.* *

Ps. 39: 2(3). with silence, *I held my peace,*
Isa. 42:14. *I have* long time *holden my peace;*

HIPHIL.—*Imperative.*

2K. 2: 3, 5. *hold ye your peace.*

HIPHIL.—*Participle.*

Jud. 18: 9. and (are) ye *still?*
1K. 22: 3. Gilead (is) our's, and we (be) *still,* (and) take it not (marg. *silent* from taking it)
2K. 7: 9. and we *hold our peace:*
Neh 8:11. So the Levites *stilled* all the people,
Isa. 57:11. *have* not I *held my peace*

חֲשׁוֹךְ [*g'hăshōhch*], Ch. m. 2816

Dan 2:22. he knoweth what (is) *in the darkness,*

חֲשֻׁקִים see חֲשׁוּקִים See 2838

חֲשַׁח [*g'hăshag'h*], Ch. 2818

* P'AL.—*Participle.* *

Ezr. 6: 9. And that which *they have need of,*
Dan 3:16. we (are) not *careful* to answer thee in this matter.

חַשְׁחוּת *g'hash-g'hooth'*, f. 2819

Ezr. 7:20. whatsoever more *shall be needful*

חֲשֵׁיכָה *g'hăshēh-chāh'*, f. 2825

Gen 15:12. an horror of great *darkness* fell
Ps. 82: 5. they walk on *in darkness:*
139:12. *the darkness* and the light (are) both *alike* (marg. *as* (is) *the darkness,* so (is) the light)
Isa. 8:22. behold trouble *and darkness,*
50:10. walketh (in) *darkness,*

חָשַׁךְ *g'hāh-shach'*. 2821

* KAL.—*Preterite.* *

Job 18: 6. The light *shall be dark*
Ecc. 12: 3. *and* those that look out of the windows *be darkened,*
Isa. 5:30. the light *is darkened* in the heavens
13:10. the sun *shall be darkened*
Lam. 4: 8. Their visage *is blacker* than a coal;
5:17. for these (things) our eyes *are dim.*

Eze 30:18. the day *shall be darkened*, (marg. *restrained* as from חָשַׂךְ which some copies read)
Mic. 3: 6. *and it shall be dark* unto you, [See also חֲשֵׁכָה].

KAL.—*Future.*

Ex. 10:15. *so* that the land *was darkened;*
Job 3: 9. *Let* the stars of the twilight thereof *be dark;*
Ps. 69:23(24). *Let* their eyes *be darkened,*
Ecc. 12: 2. the stars, *be not darkened,*

* HIPHIL.—*Preterite.* *

Am. 5: 8. *maketh* the day *dark*
8: 9. *and I will darken* the earth

HIPHIL.—*Future.*

Ps. 105:28. sent darkness, *and made it dark;*
139:12. the darkness *hideth* not from thee;
Jer. 13:16. before *he cause darkness*, and before your

HIPHIL.—*Participle.*

Job 38: 2. Who (is) this *that darkeneth* counsel

2823 חָשֹׁךְ [*ghāh-shōhch'*], adj.

Pro. 22:29. he shall not stand before *mean* (marg. *obscure*) (men).

2822 חֹשֶׁךְ *ghōh'-shech*, m.

Gen 1: 2. *and darkness* (was) upon the face
4. divided the light from *the darkness.*
5. *and the darkness* he called Night.
18. divide the light from *the darkness:*
Ex. 10:21. that there may be *darkness*
— even *darkness* (which) may be felt.
22. there was *a* thick *darkness*
14:20. it was a cloud *and darkness*
Deu 4:11. with *darkness*, clouds, and thick darkness.
5:23(20). voice out of the midst of *the darkness*,
Jos. 2: 5. *when it was dark*, that the men
1Sa. 2: 9. the wicked shall be silent *in darkness;*
2Sa. 22:12. he made *darkness* pavilions
29. the Lord will lighten *my darkness.*
Job 3: 4. Let that day be *darkness;*
5. Let *darkness* and the shadow of death
5:14. They meet with *darkness*
10:21. to the land of *darkness*
12:22. discovereth deep things out of *darkness*,
25. They grope in *the dark*
15:22. that he shall return out of *darkness*,
23. knoweth that the day of *darkness*
30. He shall not depart out of *darkness;*
17:12. the light (is) short because of *darkness*,
13. I have made my bed *in the darkness.*
18:18. be driven from light into *darkness*,
19: 8. he hath set *darkness* in my paths.
20:26. All *darkness* (shall be) hid
22:11. *darkness*, (that) thou canst not see;
23:17. I was not cut off before *the darkness*,
24:16. *In the dark* they dig through
26:10. until the day and *night* come to an end.
28: 3. He setteth an end *to darkness*,
29: 3. by his light I walked (through) *darkness;*
34:22. no *darkness*, nor shadow of death,
37:19. order (our speech) by reason of *darkness.*
38:19. *and* (as for) *darkness*, where (is) the
Ps. 18:11(12). He made *darkness* his secret place;
28(29). my God will enlighten *my darkness.*
35: 6. Let their way be *dark* and slippery: (marg. *darkness*)
88:12(13). Shall thy wonders be known *in the dark?*
104:20. Thou makest *darkness*,
105:28. He sent *darkness*, and made it dark;
107:10. Such as sit in *darkness*
14. He brought them out *of darkness*
112: 4. there ariseth light *in the darkness:*
139:11. Surely *the darkness* shall cover me;
12. Yea, *the darkness* hideth not
Pro. 2:13. to walk in the ways of *darkness;*
20:20. lamp shall be put out in obscure *darkness.*
Ecc. 2:13. as far as light excelleth *darkness.*
14. but the fool walketh *in darkness:*
Ecc. 5:17(16). his days also he eateth *in darkness*,
6: 4. *and* departeth *in darkness*, and his name shall be covered *with darkness.*
11: 8. let him remember the days of *darkness;*
Isa. 5:20. that put *darkness* for light, and light *for darkness;*
30. behold *darkness* (and) sorrow,
9: 2(1). The people that walked *in darkness*
29:18. out of obscurity, *and out of darkness.*
42: 7. them that sit in *darkness*
45: 3. give thee the treasures of *darkness*,
7. form the light, and create *darkness:*
19. in a *dark* place of the earth:
47: 5. get thee *into darkness*,
49: 9. to them that (are) *in darkness*,
58:10. then shall thy light rise *in obscurity*,
59: 9. wait for light, but behold *obscurity;*
60: 2. *the darkness* shall cover the earth,
Lam. 3: 2. brought (me into) *darkness*,
Eze 8:12. the house of Israel do *in the dark*,
32: 8. set *darkness* upon thy land,
Joel 2: 2. A day of *darkness* and of gloominess,
31(3:4). The sun shall be turned *into darkness*,
Am. 5:18. the day of the Lord (is) *darkness*,
20. the day of the Lord (be) *darkness*,
Mic. 7: 8. when I sit *in darkness*,
Nah 1: 8. and *darkness* shall pursue his enemies.
Zep 1:15. a day of *darkness* and gloominess,

חֶשְׁכָה [*ghesh-kāh'*], f. 2824

Ps. 18:11(12). round about him (were) *dark* waters (lit. *darkness of* water)

חֲשֵׁכָה *ghosh-chāh'*, f. 2821

Mic. 3: 6. *and* it shall be *dark* unto you, [see also חָשַׁךְ, some copies read חֲשֵׁכָה].

חָשַׁל [*ghāh-shal'*]. 2826

* NIPHAL.—*Participle.* *

Deu 25:18. all (that were) *feeble*

חֲשַׁל [*ghăshal*], Ch. 2827

* P'AL.—*Participle.* Active. *

Dan 2:40. breaketh in pieces *and subdueth* all (things):

חַשְׁמַל *ghash-mal'*, m. 2830

Eze 1: 4. as the colour of *amber*,
27. I saw as the colour of *amber*,
8: 2. as the colour of *amber.*

חַשְׁמַנִּים *ghash-man-neem'*, m. pl. 2831

Ps. 68:31(32). *Princes* shall come out of Egypt;

חֹשֶׁן *ghōh'-shen*, m. 2833

Ex. 25: 7. the ephod, *and in the breastplate.*
28: 4. they shall make; *a breastplate*,
15. thou shalt make *the breastplate of*
22. make upon *the breastplate* chains
23. make upon *the breastplate* two rings
— on the two ends of *the breastplate.*
24, 26. ends of *the breastplate.*
28. they shall bind *the breastplate*
— that *the breastplate* be not loosed
29. children of Israel *in the breastplate of*
30. put in *the breastplate of* judgment
29: 5. the ephod, and *the breastplate*,
35: 9, 27. ephod, *and for the breastplate.*
39: 8. he made *the breastplate*
9. they made *the breastplate* double:
15. made upon *the breastplate* chains

Ex. 39:16. rings in the two ends of *the breastplate.*
17, 19. ends of *the breastplate.*
21. bind *the breastplate* by his rings
— that *the breastplate* might not be loosed
Lev. 8. 8. he put *the breastplate* upon him: also he put in *the breastplate*

2836 חָשַׁק *ghāh-shak'*.

* KAL.—*Preterite.* *

Gen34: 8. The soul of my son Shechem *longeth*
Deu 7: 7. The Lord *did* not *set his love*
10:15. the Lord *had a delight* in thy fathers
21:11. *and hast a desire* unto her,
1K. 9:19. that which Solomon *desired*
2Ch 8: 6. all that Solomon *desired*
Ps. 91:14. Because *he hath set his love* upon me,
Isa. 38:17. but *thou hast in love to* my soul (marg. *thou hast loved* my soul from)

* PIEL.—*Preterite.* *

Ex. 38:28. *and filleted* them.

* PUAL.—*Participle.* *

Ex. 27:17. the court (shall be) *filleted* with silver;
38:17. pillars of the court (were) *filleted*

2837 חֵשֶׁק *ghēh'-shek*, m.

1K. 9: 1. all Solomon's *desire*
19. and *that* which Solomon desired (marg. *the desire of* Solomon which he desired)
2Ch. 8: 6. and all that Solomon desired (marg. all *the desire of* Solomon which he desired)
Isa. 21: 4. the night of *my pleasure*

2838 חֲשֻׁקִים [*ghăshoo-keem'*], m. pl.

Ex. 27:10. the pillars *and their fillets*
11. *their fillets* (of) silver.
36:38. *and their fillets*
38:10, 11, 12, 17. the pillars *and their fillets*
19. their chapiters *and their fillets*

2839 חִשֻּׁקִים [*ghish-shoo-keem'*], m. pl.

1K. 7:33. their naves, *and their felloes,*

2841 חַשְׁרָה [*ghash-rāh'*], f.

2Sa. 22:12. about him, *dark* waters, (marg. *binding*)

2840 חִשֻּׁרִים [*ghish-shoo-reem'*], m. pl.

1K. 7:33. their felloes, *and their spokes,*

2842 חֲשַׁשׁ *ghăshash*, m.

Isa. 5:24. *and* the flame consumeth *the chaff,*
33:11. Ye shall conceive *chaff,*

2844 חַת [*ghath*], m.

Gen. 9: 2. fear of you *and the dread of you*
1Sa. 2: 4. The bows of the mighty men (are) *broken,*
Job 41:33(25). who is made without *fear.*
Jer. 46: 5. Wherefore have I seen them *dismayed*

2846 חָתָה [*ghāh-thāh'*].

* KAL.—*Infinitive.* *

Isa. 30:14. a sherd *to take* fire

KAL.—*Future.*

Ps. 52: 5(7). *he shall take thee away,*
Pro 6:27. *Can* a man *take* fire in his bosom,

KAL.—*Participle.* Poel.

Pro 25:22. For thou *shalt heap* coals of fire

חִתָּה [*ghit-tāh'*], f. 2847

Gen35: 5. *the terror of* God was upon the cities

חִתּוּל *ghit-tool'*, m. 2848

Eze. 30:21. to put *a roller* to bind it,

חַתְחַתִּים *ghath-ghat-teem'*, m. pl. 2849

Ecc 12: 5. *and fears* (shall be) in the way,

חִתִּית *ghit-teeth'*, f. 2851

Eze 26:17. cause *their terror* (to be) on all
32:23. caused *terror* in the land (marg. *dismaying*)
24. which caused *their terror*
25. though *their terror* was caused
26. though they caused *their terror*
27. though (they were) *the terror of*
30. *with their terror* they are ashamed
32. For I have caused *my terror*

חָתַךְ [*ghāh-thach'*]. 2852

* NIPHAL.—*Preterite.* *

Dan 9:24. Seventy weeks *are determined* (lit. *are divided*)

חָתַל [*ghāh-thal'*]. 2853

* PUAL.—*Preterite.* *

Eze 16: 4. not salted at all, nor *swaddled* at all. (lit. in swaddling *thou wast* not *swaddled*)

* HOPHAL.—*Infinitive.* *

Eze 16: 4. *nor* swaddled *at all.*

חֲתֻלָּה [*ghăthool-lāh'*], f. 2854

Job 38: 9. thick darkness *a swaddlingband for it,*

חָתַם [*ghāh-tham'*]. 2856

* KAL.—*Infinitive.* *

Jer. 32:44. subscribe evidences, *and seal*
Dan 9:24. (כתיב) *and to make an end* of sins, (marg. *to seal up,* so כתיב)
— *and to seal up* the vision and prophecy,

KAL.—*Imperative.*

Est. 8: 8. *and seal* (it) with the king's ring:
Isa. 8:16. *seal* the law among my disciples.
Dan12: 4. shut up the words, *and seal* the book,

KAL.—*Future.*

1K. 21: 8. *and sealed* (them) with his seal,
Est. 8:10. *and sealed* (it) with the king's ring,
Job 9: 7. *sealeth up* the stars.
33:16. *sealeth* their instruction,
37: 7. *He sealeth up* the hand of every man;
Jer. 32:10. I subscribed the evidence, *and sealed* (it),

KAL.—*Participle.* Poel.

Eze 28:12. Thou *sealest up* the sum,

KAL.—*Participle.* Paül.

Deu 32:34. *sealed up* among my treasures?
Neh 9:38(10:1). princes, Levites, (and) priests, *seal* (unto it). (marg. (are) at *the sealing,* or, *sealed*)
10: 1(2). Now *those that sealed* (marg. at *the sealings*)
Job 14:17. My transgression (is) *sealed up*
Cant. 4:12. a spring shut up, a fountain *sealed.*
Isa. 29:11. words of a book *that is sealed,*
— I cannot; for it (is) *sealed:*
Jer. 32:11. *that which was sealed* (according)

Jer. 32:14. both *which is sealed,*
Dan 12: 9. the words (are) closed up *and sealed*

* NIPHAL.—*Preterite.* *

Est. 3:12. *and sealed* with the king's ring.

NIPHAL.—*Participle.*

Est. 8: 8. *and sealed* with the king's ring,

* PIEL.—*Preterite.* *

Job 24:16. *they had marked* for themselves

* HIPHIL.—*Preterite.* *

Lev 15: 3. or his flesh *be stopped* from his issue,

2857 **חֲתַם** [*g'hăthăm*], Ch.

* P'AL.—*Preterite.* *

Dan. 6:17(18). *and* the king *sealed it* with his own signet,

---

See 2368 **חוֹתָם** see **חֹתָם**

2858 **חֹתֶמֶת** *g'hōh-theh'-meth*, f.

Gen 38:25. *the signet,* and bracelets, and staff.

2859 **חָתַן** [*g'hāh-than'*].

* KAL.—*Participle.* Poel. *

Ex. 3: 1. flock of Jethro *his father in law,*
4:18. returned to Jethro *his father in law,*
18: 1. Moses' *father in law,*
2. Then Jethro, Moses' *father in law,*
5. Jethro, Moses' *father in law,*
6. I *thy father in law* Jethro am come
7. went out to meet *his father in law,*
8. Moses told *his father in law*
12. Jethro, Moses' *father in law,*
— to eat bread with Moses' *father in law*
14. when Moses' *father in law* saw
15. Moses said *unto his father in law,*
17. Moses' *father in law* said
24. hearkened to the voice of *his father in law,*
27. Moses let *his father in law* depart;
Nu. 10:29. Moses' *father in law,*
Deu 27:23. that lieth with *his mother in law.*
Jud 1:16. Moses' *father in law,* went up
4:11. *the father in law of* Moses,
19: 4. And *his father in law,* the damsel's father,
7. *his father in law* urged him:
9. his servant, *his father in law,* the damsel's father,

* HITHPAEL.—*Preterite.* *

Jos. 23:12. *and shall make marriages*

HITHPAEL.—*Infinitive.*

1 Sa 18:23. *to be* a king's *son in law,*
26. *to be* the king's *son in law:*
27. *he might be* the king's *son in law.*
Ezr. 9:14. *and join in affinity* with the people

HITHPAEL.—*Imperative.*

Gen 34: 9. *And make ye marriages* with us,
1 Sa 18:22. therefore *be* the king's *son in law.*

HITHPAEL.—*Future.*

Deu 7: 3. Neither *shalt thou make marriages*
1 Sa 18:21. *Thou shalt* this day *be* my *son in law*
1 K. 3: 1. *And* Solomon *made affinity*
2 Ch 18: 1. *and joined affinity* with Ahab.

2860 **חָתָן** *g'hāh-thāhn'*, m.

Gen 19:12. *son in law,* and thy sons,
14. spake unto *his sons in law,*
— one that mocked unto *his sons in law.*
Ex. 4:25. *a* bloody *husband* (art) thou to me.
26. *A* bloody *husband* (thou art),
Jud 15: 6. Samson, *the son in law of* the Timnite,
19: 5. damsel's father said unto *his son in law,*
1 Sa 18:18. that I should be *son in law* to the king?
22:14. *which* is the king's *son in law,*
2 K. 8:27. for he (was) *the son in law of* the
Neh 6:18. he (was) *the son in law* of Shechaniah
13:28. *son in law* to Sanballat
Ps. 19: 5(6). *as a bridegroom* coming out of
Isa. 61:10. *as a bridegroom* decketh (himself)
62: 5. *the bridegroom* rejoiceth over the bride,
Jer. 7:34 & 16:9 & 25:10 & 33:11. the voice of *the bridegroom,*
Joel 2:16. let *the bridegroom* go forth

חֲתֻנָּה [*g'hăthoon-nāh'*], f. 2861

Cant 3:11. in the day of *his espousals,*

חָתַף [*g'hāh-thaph'*]. 2862

* KAL.—*Future.* *

Job 9:12. Behold, *he taketh away,*

חֶתֶף *g'heh'-theph*, m. 2863

Pro 23:28. She also lieth in wait *as* (for) *a prey,*

חָתַר *g'hāh-thar'*. 2864

* KAL.—*Preterite.* *

Job 24:16. In the dark *they dig through*
Eze 12: 7. even *I digged* through the wall

KAL.—*Imperative.*

Eze 8: 8. Son of man, *dig* now in the wall:
12: 5. *Dig thou* through the wall

KAL.—*Future.*

Eze 8: 8. and *when I had digged*
12:12. *they shall dig* through the wall
Am 9: 2. Though *they dig* into hell,
Jon 1:13. *Nevertheless* the men *rowed* (marg. *digged*)

חָתַת [*g'hāh-thath'*]. 2865

* KAL.—*Preterite.* *

2 K. 19:26. *they were dismayed* and confounded;
Job 32:15. *They were amazed,* they answered no
Isa. 20: 5. *And they shall be afraid*
31: 9. *and...shall be afraid* of the ensign,
37:27. *they were dismayed* and confounded:
Jer. 8: 9. *they are dismayed* and taken:
14: 4. Because the ground *is chapt,*
48: 1. Misgab is confounded *and dismayed.*
20. for *it is broken down:*
39. howl, (saying), How *is it broken down!*
50: 2. Merodach *is broken in pieces;*
— her images *are broken in pieces.*
36. *and they shall be dismayed.*
Obad 9. *And* thy mighty men, O Teman, *shall be dismayed,*

KAL.—*Imperative.*

Isa. 8: 9. *and ye shall be broken in pieces;*
— *and ye shall be broken in pieces:* gird yourselves, *and ye shall be broken in pieces.*

* NIPHAL.—*Preterite.* *

Mal 2: 5. *was afraid* before my name.

NIPHAL.—*Future.*

Deu 1:21. fear not, neither *be discouraged.*
31: 8. fear not, neither *be dismayed.*
Jos. 1: 9 & 8:1. neither *be thou dismayed:*
10:25. Fear not, nor *be dismayed,*
1 Sa. 2:10. *shall be broken to pieces;*
17:11. *they* (lit. *and they*) *were dismayed,*
1 Ch 22:13 & 28:20. nor *be dismayed.*
2 Ch 20:15. Be not afraid nor *dismayed*
17. fear not, nor *be dismayed;*
32: 7. be not afraid nor *dismayed*
Job 21:13. They spend their days in wealth, and in a moment *go down*
39:22. at fear, and *is* not *affrighted;*
Isa. 7: 8. five years *shall* Ephraim *be broken,*
30:31. *shall* the Assyrian *be beaten down,*
31: 4. *he will* not *be afraid* of their voice,
51: 6. my righteousness *shall* not *be abolished.*
7. neither *be ye afraid* of their revilings.
Jer. 1:17. *be* not *dismayed* at their faces,
10: 2. *and be* not *dismayed* at the signs of heaven; for the heathen *are dismayed* at them.

Jer. 17:18. *let them be dismayed*, but *let* not *me be dismayed:*
23: 4. they shall fear no more, nor *be dismayed*,
30:10. neither *be dismayed*,
46:27. *be* not *dismayed*, O Israel:
Eze 2: 6 & 3:9. *be dismayed* at their looks,

* PIEL.—*Preterite.* *

Job 7:14. *Then thou scarest me* with dreams,
Jer. 51:56. every one of their bows *is broken:*

* HIPHIL.—*Preterite.* *

Isa. 9: 4(3). *thou hast broken* the yoke of his burden,
Jer. 49:37. For *I will cause* Elam *to be dismayed*

HIPHIL.—*Future.*

Job 31:34. *did* the contempt of families *terrify me*,
Jer. 1:17. lest *I confound thee* before them.
Hab 2:17. beasts, (which) *made them afraid*,

2866 **חִתַּת** *ghăthath*, m.

Job 6:21. ye see (my) *casting down*,

ט *tēhth.*

The ninth letter of the Alphabet.

2868 **טְאֵב** *t'ēhv*, Ch.

* P'AL.—*Preterite.* *

Dan 6:23(24). Then *was* the king exceeding *glad* for him,

See 2894 **טוּא** see **טֵאטֵא**

2869 **טָב** *tāhv*, Ch. m.

Ezr. 5:17. if (it seem) *good* to the king,
Dan 2:32. This image's head (was) of *fine* gold,

2871 **טְבוּלִים** *t'voo-leem'*, m. pl.

Eze. 23:15. exceeding in *dyed attire*

2872 **טַבּוּר** *tab-boor'*, m.

Jud. 9:37. down by *the middle of* the land, (marg. *navel*)
Eze. 38:12. that dwell in *the midst of* the land. (marg. *navel*)

2873 **טָבַח** [*tāh-vagh'*].

* KAL.—*Preterite.* *

Ex. 22: 1(21:37). or a sheep, *and kill it*,
1 Sa. 25:11. my flesh that *I have killed*
Pro. 9: 2. *She hath killed* her beasts;
Lam. 2:21. *thou hast killed*, (and) not pitied.

KAL.—*Infinitive.*

Gen43:16. *and slay*, and make ready; (marg. *kill* a killing)
Ps. 37:14. *to slay* such as be of upright conversation.
Jer. 11:19. an ox (that) is brought *to the slaughter;*
25:34. for the days *of* your *slaughter* (marg. your days *for slaughter*)
51:40. down like lambs *to the slaughter*,
Eze. 21:10(15). It is sharpened to *make a sore slaughter;*

KAL.—*Participle.* Paül.

Deu 28:31. Thine ox (shall be) *slain*

טַבָּח *tab-bāhgh'*, m. 2876

Gen37:36. captain of *the guard*. (marg. chief of the *slaughtermen*, or, *executioners*)
39: 1. captain of *the guard*, an Egyptian,
40: 3. the house of the captain of *the guard*,
4. of *the guard* charged Joseph with them,
41:10. ward in the captain of *the guard*'s house,
12. servant to the captain of *the guard;*
1 Sa. 9:23. Samuel said *unto the cook*,
24. *the cook* took up the shoulder,
2K. 25: 8. Nebuzar-adan, captain of *the guard*, (marg. or, chief *marshal*)
10. the captain of *the guard*, brake down
11. the captain of *the guard* carry away.
12. the captain of *the guard* left of the poor
15. the captain of *the guard* took away.
18. the captain of *the guard* took Seraiah
20. captain of *the guard* took these,
Jer. 39: 9. the captain of *the guard* carried away captive (marg. chief of *the executioners*, or, *slaughtermen*, or, chief *marshal*)
10. the captain of *the guard* left of the poor
11. Nebuzar-adan the captain of *the guard*,
13. Nebuzar-adan the captain of *the guard* sent,
40: 1. the captain of *the guard* had let him go
2. the captain of *the guard* took Jeremiah,
5. the captain of *the guard* gave him victuals
41:10. the captain of *the guard* had committed
43: 6. the captain of *the guard* had left with Gedaliah
52:12. captain of *the guard*,
14. the captain of *the guard*, brake down all the walls
15. captain of *the guard* carried away captive
16. the captain of *the guard* left (certain) of the poor
19. took the captain of *the guard*
24. the captain of *the guard* took Seraiah
26. the captain of *the guard* took them,
30. captain of *the guard* carried away captive

טַבָּח [*tab-bāhgh'*], Ch. m. 2877

Dan 2:14. and wisdom to Arioch the captain of the king's *guard*, (marg. chief of *the executioners*, or, *slaughtermen*, or, chief *marshal*)

טֶבַח *teh'-vagh*, m. 2874

Gen43:16. Bring (these) men home, and slay, (marg. kill *a killing*)
Pro. 7:22. as an ox goeth to *the slaughter*,
9: 2. She hath killed *her beasts;* (marg. *killing*)
Isa. 34: 2. hath delivered them *to the slaughter*.
6. *and a* great *slaughter*
53: 7. brought as a lamb *to the slaughter*,
65:12. all bow down *to the slaughter:*
Jer. 48:15. men are gone down *to the slaughter*,
50:27. let them go down *to the slaughter:*
Eze. 21:10(15). to make a *sore* slaughter; (lit. to slay *a slaughter*)
15(20). (it is) wrapped up *for the slaughter*.
28(33). *for the slaughter* (it is) furbished,

טִבְחָה *tiv-ghāh'*, f. 2878

1 Sa. 25:11. *my flesh* that I have killed
Ps. 44:22(23). counted as sheep for *the slaughter*.
Jer. 12: 3. like sheep *for the slaughter*,

טַבָּחוֹת *tab-bāh-ghōhth'*, f. pl. 2879

1 Sa. 8:13. confectionaries, *and* (to be) *cooks*,

טָבַל *tāh-val'*. 2881

* KAL.—*Preterite.* *

Ex. 12:22. *and dip* (it) in the blood
Lev. 4: 6, 17. *And* the priest *shall dip* his finger

Lev.14: 6. *and shall dip* them and the living bird
16. *And* the priest *shall dip* his right finger
51. *and dip* them in the blood
Nu. 19:18. *and dip* (it) in the water,
Ru. 2:14. *and dip* thy morsel in the vinegar.

KAL.—*Future.*

Gen37:31. *and dipped* the coat in the blood;
Lev. 9: 9. *and he dipped* his finger in the blood,
1Sa.14:27. *and dipped* it in an honeycomb,
2K. 5:14. *and dipped* himself seven times
8:15. *and dipped* (it) in water,
Job 9:31. Yet *shalt thou plunge me* in the ditch,

KAL.—*Participle.* Poel.

Deu33:24. *and let him dip* his foot in oil.

* NIPHAL.—*Preterite.* *

Jos. 3:15. *were dipped* in the brim of the water,

2883 טָבַע [*tāh-vag'*].

* KAL.—*Preterite.* *

Ps. 9:15(16). The heathen *are sunk* down
69: 2(3). *I sink* in deep mire,
Lam. 2: 9. Her gates *are sunk* into the ground;

KAL.—*Future.*

1Sa.17:49. *that* the stone *sunk* into his forehead;
Ps. 69:14(15). *let me not sink:*
Jer. 38: 6. *so* Jeremiah *sunk* in the mire.

* PUAL.—*Preterite.* *

Ex. 15: 4. his chosen captains also *are drowned*

* HOPHAL.—*Preterite.* *

Job 38: 6. the foundations thereof *fastened?* (marg. *made to sink*)
Pro. 8:25. Before the mountains *were settled*,
Jer. 38:22. thy feet *are sunk* in the mire,

2885 טַבַּעַת *tab-bah'-gath*, f.

Gen41:42. Pharaoh took off *his ring*
Ex. 25:12. thou shalt cast four *rings of* gold
— two *rings* (shall be) in the one side of it, and two *rings* in the other side
14. the staves *into the rings*
15. The staves shall be *in the rings of*
26. thou shalt make for it four *rings of* gold, and put *the rings* in the four corners
27. against the border shall *the rings*
26:24. above the head of it unto one *ring:*
29. make *their rings* (of) gold
27: 4. make four brasen *rings*
7. the staves shall be put *into the rings*,
28:23. upon the breastplate two *rings*
— put the two *rings* on the two ends
24. wreathen (chains) of gold in the two *rings*
26. thou shalt make two *rings of* gold,
27. two (other) *rings of* gold
28. bind the breastplate *by the rings thereof* unto *the rings of* the ephod
30: 4. two golden *rings* shalt thou make
35:22. bracelets, and earrings, *and rings*,
36:29. the head thereof, to one *ring:*
34. made *their rings* (of) gold
37: 3, 13. he cast for it four *rings of* gold,
— even two *rings* upon the one side of it, and two *rings* upon the other side
5. he put the staves *into the rings*
13. put *the rings* upon the four corners
14. against the border were *the rings*,
27. he made two *rings of* gold
38: 5. he cast four *rings* for the four ends
7. he put the staves *into the rings*
39:16. ouches (of) gold, and two gold *rings*, and put *the* two *rings* in the two ends
17. chains of gold in *the* two *rings*
19. they made two *rings of* gold,
20. they made two (other) golden *rings*,
21. *by his rings* unto *the rings of* the ephod
Nu. 31:50. chains, and bracelets, *rings*,
Est. 3:10. the king took *his ring* from his hand,
12. sealed *with* the king's *ring*.
8: 2. the king took off *his ring*,
8. seal (it) *with* the king's *ring:*
Est. 8: 8. sealed *with* the king's *ring*,
10. sealed (it) *with* the king's *ring*,
Isa. 3:21. *The rings*, and nose jewels,

טֵבֵת *tēh-vēhth'*. 2887

Est. 2:16. which (is) the month *Tebeth*,

טָהוֹר *tāh-hōhr'*, adj. 2889

Gen 7: 2. Of every *clean* beast thou shalt
— of beasts that (are) not *clean*
8. Of *clean* beasts, and of beasts that (are) not *clean*,
8:20. took of every *clean* beast, and of every *clean* fowl,
Ex. 25:11. shalt overlay it with *pure* gold,
17. make a mercy seat (of) *pure* gold:
24. shalt overlay it with *pure* gold,
29. to cover withal: (of) *pure* gold
31. make a candlestick (of) *pure* gold:
36. one beaten work (of) *pure* gold.
38. snuffdishes thereof, (shall be of) *pure* gold.
39. a talent of *pure* gold shall he make
28:14. two chains (of) *pure* gold
22. wreathen work (of) *pure* gold.
36. shalt make a plate (of) *pure* gold,
30: 3. thou shalt overlay it with *pure* gold,
35. tempered together, *pure* (and) holy:
31: 8. the *pure* candlestick with all
37: 2. he overlaid it with *pure* gold
6. made the mercy seat (of) *pure* gold:
11, 26. he overlaid it with *pure* gold,
16. covers to cover withal, (of) *pure* gold.
17. he made the candlestick (of) *pure* gold:
22. all of it (was) one beaten work (of) *pure* gold.
23. his snuffdishes, (of) *pure* gold.
24. a talent of *pure* gold made he it,
29. the *pure* incense of sweet spices,
39:15. wreathen work (of) *pure* gold.
25. they made bells (of) *pure* gold,
30. plate of the holy crown (of) *pure* gold,
37. The *pure* candlestick,
Lev. 4:12 & 6:11(4). without the camp unto a *clean* place,
7:19. all *that be clean* shall eat
10:10. between unclean and *clean;*
14. shall ye eat in a *clean* place;
11:36. plenty of water, shall be *clean:*
37. fall upon any sowing seed...it (shall be) *clean*.
47. between the unclean and *the clean*,
13:13. it is all turned white: he (is) *clean*.
17. (that hath) the plague: he (is) *clean*.
37. the scall is healed, he (is) *clean:*
39. groweth in the skin; he (is) *clean*.
40. he (is) bald; (yet is) he *clean*.
41. he (is) forehead bald: (yet is) he *clean*.
14: 4. cleansed two birds alive (and) *clean*,
57. unclean, and when (it is) *clean:*
15: 8. spit *upon him that is clean;*
20:25. between *clean* beasts and unclean, and between unclean fowls *and clean:*
24: 4. order the lamps upon the *pure* candlestick
6. upon the *pure* table before the Lord.
Nu. 5:28. be not defiled, *but be clean;*
9:13. But the man that (is) *clean*,
18:11, 13. every one *that is clean*
19: 9. a man (that is) *clean* shall gather
— without the camp in a *clean* place,
18. a *clean* person shall take hyssop,
19. And *the clean* (person) shall
Deu 12:15. unclean *and the clean* may eat
22. the unclean *and the clean* shall eat
14:11. all *clean* birds ye shall eat.
20. all *clean* fowls ye may eat.
15:22. unclean *and the clean*
23:10(11). not *clean* by reason of uncleanness
1Sa.20:26. he (is) not *clean;* surely he (is) not *clean*.
1Ch 28:17. Also *pure* gold for the fleshhooks,
2Ch 3: 4. he overlaid it within with *pure* gold.
9:17. overlaid it with *pure* gold.
13:11. upon the *pure* table;
30:17. for every one (that was) not *clean*,

Ezr. 6:20. all of them (were) *pure*,
Job 14: 4. Who can bring *a clean* (thing)
28:19. neither shall it be valued with *pure* gold.
Ps. 12: 6(7). The words of the Lord (are) *pure* words:
19: 9(10). The fear of the Lord (is) *clean*,
51:10(12). Create in me a *clean* heart,
Pro. 15:26. *but* (the words) of *the pure* (are) pleasant words.
22:11. (כתיב) He that loveth *pureness of* heart,
30:12. a generation (that are) *pure*
Ecc. 9: 2. to the good *and to the clean*,
Isa. 66:20. bring an offering in a *clean* vessel
Eze. 22:26. between the unclean *and the clean*,
36:25. Then will I sprinkle *clean* water
44:23. between the unclean *and the clean*.
Hab 1:13. (Thou art) of *purer* eyes than to behold evil, (lit. *pure of* eyes)
Zec. 3: 5. Let them set a *fair* mitre upon his head. So they set a *fair* mitre upon
Mal. 1:11. unto my name, and a *pure* offering:

2891 טָהֵר *tāh-hēhr'*.

* KAL.—*Preterite.* *

Lev. 11:32. *so it shall be cleansed.*
12: 7. *and she shall be cleansed* from
8. *and she shall be clean.*
13: 6, 34. wash his clothes, *and be clean.*
58. second time, *and shall be clean.*
14: 8. *that he may be clean:*
9, 20. *and he shall be clean.*
53. *and it shall be clean.*
15:13. *and shall be clean.*
28. if *she be cleansed* of her issue,
17:15. *then shall he be clean.*
22: 7. *And* when the sun is down, *he shall be clean*,
Nu. 19:19. *and shall be clean* at even.
31:23. *and it shall be clean:*
24. *and ye shall be clean*,
2K. 5:12. wash in them, *and be clean?*
Pro. 20: 9. *I am pure* from my sin?
Eze. 24:13. *thou wast* not *purged*,
36:25. *and ye shall be clean:*

KAL.—*Imperative.*

2K. 5:10. *and thou shalt be clean.*
13. Wash, *and be clean?*

KAL.—*Future.*

Lev. 15:13. he that hath an issue *is cleansed*
28. after that *she shall be clean.*
16:30. *ye may be clean* from all your sins
22: 4. the holy things, until *he be clean.*
Nu. 19:12. seventh day *he shall be clean:*
— seventh day *he shall* not *be clean.*
2K. 5·14. *and he was clean.*
Job 4:17. *shall* a man *be more pure*
Ps. 51: 7(9). with hyssop, *and I shall be clean:*
Jer. 13:27. *wilt thou* not *be made clean?*
Eze. 24:13. *thou shalt* not *be purged*

* PIEL.—*Preterite.* *

Lev. 13: 6. the priest *shall pronounce him clean:*
13. *he shall pronounce* (him) *clean*
17. *then* the priest *shall pronounce* (him) *clean*
23, 28. *and* the priest *shall pronounce him clean*,
34. *then* the priest *shall pronounce* him *clean:*
37. *and* the priest *shall pronounce him clean.*
14: 7. *and shall pronounce him clean*,
48. *then* the priest *shall pronounce* the house *clean*,
16:19. seven times, *and cleanse it*,
Nu. 8: 6. of Israel, *and cleanse* them.
15. *and thou shalt cleanse* them,
2Ch 29:18. *We have cleansed* all the house
Neh 13:30. *Thus cleansed I them*
Jer. 33: 8. *And I will cleanse them*
Eze 24:13. because *I have purged thee*,
37:23. *and will cleanse* them:
39:16. *Thus shall they cleanse* the land.
43:26. Seven days shall they purge the altar *and purify* it;
Mal. 3: 3. *and he shall purify* the sons

PIEL.—*Infinitive.*

Lev. 13:59. *to pronounce it clean*,
Lev. 16:30. an atonement for you, *to cleanse*
Nu. 8: 7. do unto them, *to cleanse them:*
21. atonement for them *to cleanse them.*
2Ch 29:15. *to cleanse* the house of the Lord.
16. house of the Lord, *to cleanse* (it),
34: 3. *to purge* Judah and Jerusalem
8. *when he had purged* the land,
Eze. 36:33. In the day that *I shall have cleansed*
39:12. that *they may cleanse* the land.
14. face of the earth, *to cleanse it:*

PIEL.—*Imperative.*

Ps. 51: 2(4). *cleanse me* from my sin.

PIEL.—*Future.*

2Ch 34: 5. *and cleansed* Judah and Jerusalem.
Neh 12:30. purified themselves, *and purified* the
13: 9. I commanded, *and they cleansed*
Job 37:21. the wind passeth, *and cleanseth them.*
Eze 36:25. from all your idols, *will I cleanse* you.

PIEL.—*Participle.*

Lev. 14:11. the priest *that maketh* (him) *clean*
Mal. 3: 3. a refiner *and purifier of* silver:

* PUAL.—*Participle.* *

Eze 22:24. the land *that is* not *cleansed*,

* HITHPAEL.—*Preterite.* *

Nu. 8: 7. *and* (so) *make themselves clean.*
Jos. 22:17. from which *we are* not *cleansed*
2Ch 30:18. *had* not *cleansed themselves*,
Ezr. 6:20. the Levites *were purified*

HITHPAEL.—*Imperative.*

Gen35: 2. among you, *and be clean*,

HITHPAEL.—*Future.*

Neh 12:30. *And* the priests and the Levites *purified themselves*,

HITHPAEL.—*Participle.*

Lev. 14: 4. take *for him that is to be cleansed*
7. upon *him that is to be cleansed*
8. *he that is to be cleansed*
11. the man *that is to be made clean*,
14, 17. ear of *him that is to be cleansed*,
18. head of *him that is to be cleansed:*
19. for *him that is to be cleansed*
25, 28. right ear of *him that is to be cleansed*,
29. the head of *him that is to be cleansed*,
31. atonement for *him that is to be cleansed*
Neh 13:22. that they should *cleanse themselves*, (lit. should be *cleansing*, &c.)
Isa. 66:17. *and purify themselves* in the gardens

טְהֹר [*t'hōhr*], m. 2890-91

Job 17: 9. *and he that hath clean* hands shall be
Pro. 22:11. He that loveth *pureness of* heart,

טֹהַר *tōh'-har*, m. 2892

Ex. 24:10. the body of heaven *in* (his) *clearness.*
Lev. 12: 4. the days of *her purifying* be fulfilled.
6. when the days of *her purifying* are

טְהָר [*tŏhāhr*], m. 2892

Ps. 89:44(45). Thou hast made *his glory* to cease, (marg. *brightness*)

טָהֳרָה *toh-hŏrāh'*, f. 2893

Lev. 12: 4. in the blood of *her purifying* (lit. of *purifying*)
5. in the blood of *her purifying* (lit. *id.*)
13: 7. seen of the priest *for his cleansing*,
35. in the skin after *his cleansing;*
14: 2. the leper in the day of *his cleansing:*
23. on the eighth day *for his cleansing*
32. (which pertaineth) *to his cleansing.*
15:13. seven days *for his cleansing*,
Nu. 6: 9. in the day of *his cleansing*,

1Ch 23:28. in *the purifying of* all holy things,
2Ch 30:19. *according to the purification of*
Neh 12:45. the ward of *the purification,*
Eze.44:26. after *he is cleansed,* they shall reckon

2894 **טוּא** [*too*].

* PILPEL.—*Preterite.* *

Isa. 14:23. *and I will sweep it* with the besom

2895 **טוֹב** *tōhv.*

* KAL.—*Preterite.* *

Nu. 11:18. for *it was well* with us
24: 1. Balaam saw that *it pleased* (lit. *was good* in the eyes of) the Lord
5. How *goodly are* thy tents, O Jacob,
Deu 5:33(30). and (that) *it may be well* with you,
15:16. because *he is well* with thee;
19:13. that *it may go well* with thee.
1Sa 16:16. *and* thou *shalt be well.* (lit. *it shall be well* with thee)
23. refreshed, *and was well,*
20:12. behold, (if) *there be good* toward David,
1Ch 13: 2. If *it seem good* unto you,
Neh 2: 5,7. said unto the king, if *it please* the king,
Est. 1:19. If *it please* (marg. *be good* with) the king,
3: 9. If *it please* the king,
5: 4. If *it seem good* unto the king,
8. if *it please* the king to grant my petition,
7: 3. if *it please* the king, let my life be given
Job 10: 3. *Is it good* unto thee that thou
13: 9. *Is it good* that he should search you out?
Cant.4:10. how much *better is* thy love than wine!

* HIPHIL.—*Preterite.* *

Nu. 10:29. come thou with us, *and we will do* thee *good:*
32. the same *will we do* unto thee.
1K. 8:18. *thou didst well* that it was
2K. 10:30. Because *thou hast done well*
2Ch 6: 8. *thou didst well* in that
Eze 36:11. *and will do better* (unto you)
Hos.10: 1. *they have made goodly* images.

HIPHIL.—*Infinitive.*

Jer. 32:41. rejoice over them *to do* them *good,*

HIPHIL.—*Imperative.*

Ps.125: 4. *Do good,* O Lord, unto (those that be)

HIPHIL.—*Future.*

Ecc.11: 9. *and let* thy heart *cheer thee*

HIPHIL.—*Participle.*

Ps.119:68. Thou (art) good, *and doest good;*
Pro.30:29. There be three (things) which go *well,*
Eze.33:32. *and can play well on* an instrument:

2896 **טוֹב** *tōhv,* adj.

Gen 1: 4. saw the light, that (it was) *good:*
10, 12, 18, 21, 25. God saw that (it was) *good.*
31. behold, (it was) very *good.*
2: 9. pleasant to the sight *and good*
— the tree of knowledge of *good* and evil.
12. the gold of that land (is) *good:*
17. tree of the knowledge of *good* and evil,
18. not *good* that the man should be alone;
3: 5. knowing *good* and evil.
6. that the tree (was) *good* for food,
22. to know *good* and evil:
6: 2. daughters of men that they (were) *fair;*
15:15. thou shalt be buried in a *good* old age.
16: 6. do to her *as it pleaseth* thee. (marg. (that which is) *good* in thine eyes)
18: 7. fetcht a calf tender *and good,*
19: 8. do ye to them *as* (is) *good*
20:15. dwell *where it pleaseth* thee. (marg. *as* (is) *good* in thine eyes)
24:16. the damsel (was) very *fair*
50. we cannot speak unto thee bad or *good.*
25: 8. died in a *good* old age,
26: 7. because she (was) *fair* to look upon.
29. done unto thee nothing but *good,*
Gen27: 9. fetch me from thence two *good* kids
29:19. *better* that I give her to thee,
30:20. God hath endued me (with) a *good* dowry;
31:24, 29. speak not to Jacob *either good* or bad. (marg. *from good* to bad)
40:16. saw that the interpretation was *good,*
41: 5. upon one stalk, rank *and good.*
22. came up in one stalk, full *and good:*
24. devoured the seven *good* ears:
26. The seven *good* kine (are) seven years, and the seven *good* ears (are) seven
35. all the food of those *good* years
44: 4. have ye rewarded evil for *good?*
49:15. he saw that rest (was) *good,*
50:20. God meant it *unto good,*
Ex. 2: 2. saw him that he (was a) *goodly* (child),
3: 8. unto a *good* land and a large,
14:12. *better* for us to serve
18: 9. Jethro rejoiced for all *the goodness*
17. The thing that thou doest (is) not *good.*
Lev.27:10. nor change it, *a good* for a bad, or a bad *for a good:*
12, 14. whether it be *good* or bad:
33. whether it be *good* or bad,
Nu. 10:29. for the Lord hath spoken *good*
32. *what goodness* the Lord shall do
13:19. *whether* it (be) *good* or bad;
14: 3. *better* for us to return into Egypt?
7. an exceeding *good* land.
24:13. to do (either) *good* or bad
36: 6. marry *to* whom they think *best;*
Deu 1:14. thing which thou hast spoken (is) *good*
25. a *good* land which the Lord
35. evil generation see that *good* land,
39. no knowledge between *good* and evil,
3:25. see the *good* land
— that *goodly* mountain,
4:21. I should not go in unto that *good* land,
22. possess that *good* land.
6:10. to give thee great *and goodly* cities,
18. right *and good* in the sight of the Lord:
— possess the *good* land which the Lord
24. *for* our *good* always,
8: 7. God bringeth thee into a *good* land,
10. for the *good* land which he hath
12. and hast built *goodly* houses,
9: 6. God giveth thee not this *good* land
10:13. I command thee this day *for* thy *good?*
11:17. perish quickly from off the *good* land
12:28. doest (that which is) *good* and right
23: 6(7). seek their peace *nor their prosperity* (marg. *good*)
16(17). *where it liketh* him *best:* (marg. *is good* for him.)
26:11. thou shalt rejoice in every *good*
28:11. make thee plenteous *in goods,*
12. open unto thee his *good* treasure,
30: 9. in the fruit of thy land, *for good:*
— will again rejoice over thee *for good,*
15. set before thee this day life and *good,*
Jos. 7:21. among the spoils a *goodly* Babylonish
9:25. *as* it seemeth *good* and right
21:45(43). failed not ought of any *good* thing
23:13. perish from off this *good* land
14. hath failed of all the *good* things
15. as all *good* things are come upon you,
— destroyed you from off this *good* land
16. perish quickly from off the *good* land
Jud. 8: 2. the grapes of Ephraim *better* than the vintage of Abi-ezer?
32. died in a *good* old age,
35. all *the goodness* which he had shewed
9: 2. Whether (is) *better* for you, (marg. What (is) *good?* whether, &c.)
11. my sweetness, and my *good* fruit,
16. if ye have dealt *well* with
10:15. whatsoever seemeth *good* unto thee;
11:25. now (art) thou *any thing better* (lit. *good, good* rather, &c.)
15: 2. her younger sister *fairer* than she?
16:25. *when* their hearts were *merry,*
18: 9. behold, it (is) very *good:*
19. (is it) *better* for thee to be a priest
19:24. what seemeth *good* unto you:
Ru. 2:22. *good,* my daughter, that thou go
3:13. unto thee the part of a kinsman, *well; let* him do

Ru. 4:15. which is *better* to thee
1Sa. 1: 8. *better* to thee than ten sons?
23. Do what seemeth thee *good*;
2:24. for (it is) no *good* report that I hear:
26. *and was in favour* both with
3:18. let him do what seemeth him *good*.
8:14. your oliveyards, (even) *the best*
16. your *goodliest* young men,
9: 2. a choice young man, *and a goodly*:
— a *goodlier* person than he:
10. *Well* said; come, let us go. (marg. Thy word (is) *good*)
11:10. all *that* seemeth *good* unto you.
12:23. teach you the *good* and the right way:
14:36. Do whatsoever seemeth *good* unto thee.
40. Do *what* seemeth *good* unto thee.
15: 9. all (that was) *good*,
22. to obey (is) *better* than sacrifice,
28. (that is) *better* than thou.
16:12. *and goodly* to look to.
19: 4. Jonathan spake *good* of David
— works (have been) to theeward very *good*:
20: 7. If he say thus, (It is) *well*;
24:17(18). for thou hast rewarded me *good*,
18(19). how that thou hast dealt *well*
19(20). will he let him go *well* away? wherefore the Lord reward thee *good*
25: 3. a woman of *good* understanding,
8. for we come in a *good* day:
15. But the men (were) very *good*
21. hath requited me evil for *good*.
30. according to all *the good*
36. Nabal's heart (was) *merry* within him,
26:16. This thing (is) not *good*
27: 1. nothing *better* for me
29: 6. *and* thy going out and thy coming in...(is) *good*
— nevertheless the lords *favour* thee not. (marg. thou (art) not *good* in the eyes of)
9. I know that thou (art) *good*
2Sa. 2: 6. I also will requite you this *kindness*,
3:13. he said, *Well*; I will make a league
19. all that seemed *good* to Israel,
36. whatsoever the king did *pleased* (lit. was *good* in the eyes)
7:28. thou hast promised this *goodness*
10:12. do *that* which seemeth him *good*.
11: 2. the woman (was) very *beautiful*
13:22. brother Amnon neither *good* nor bad.
28. *when* Amnon's heart is *merry*
14:17. to discern *good* and bad:
32. *good* for me (to have been) there
15: 3. See, thy matters (are) *good* and right;
26. let him do to me as seemeth *good*
16:12. the Lord will requite me *good*
17: 7. Ahithophel hath given (is) not *good*
14. *better* than the counsel of Ahithophel.
— appointed to defeat the *good* counsel
18: 3. *better* that thou succour
27. He (is) a *good* man, and cometh with *good*
19:18(19). to do *what* he thought *good*.
27(28). do therefore (what is) *good* in thine
35(36). can I discern between *good* and evil?
37(38). what shall seem *good* unto thee.
38(39). *that* which shall seem *good*
24:22. *what* (seemeth) *good* unto him:
1K. 1: 6. he also (was a) very *goodly* (man);
42. *and* bringest *good* tidings.
2:18. *Well*; I will speak for thee
32. more righteous *and better* than he,
38. The saying (is) *good*:
42. The word (that) I have heard (is) *good*.
3: 9. discern between *good* and bad:
8:36. teach them the *good* way
56. word of all his *good* promise,
66. joyful *and glad of* heart for all *the goodness* that the Lord
10: 7. thy wisdom *and prosperity*
12: 7. speak *good* words to them,
14:13. there is found (some) *good* thing
15. root up Israel out of this *good* land,
18:24. It is *well* spoken.
19: 4. for I (am) not *better* than my fathers.
20: 3. thy children, (even) *the goodliest*,
21: 2. I will give thee for it a *better* vineyard than it; (or), if it seem *good* to thee,
1K. 22: 8. for he doth not prophesy *good*
13. the prophets (declare) *good* unto the king
— speak (that which is) *good*.
18. that he would prophesy no *good*
2K. 2:19. the situation of this city (is) *pleasant*,
3:19. fell every *good* tree,
— mar every *good* piece of land
25. on every *good* piece of land
— and felled all the *good* trees:
5:12. *better* than all the waters
10: 3. Look even out *the best* and meetest
5. do thou (that which is) *good*
20: 3. *and* have done (that which is) *good*
13. and the *precious* ointment,
19. *Good* (is) the word of the Lord
25:28. And he spake *kindly* to him, and set his (marg. *good things*)
1Ch 4:40. they found fat pasture *and good*,
16:34. thanks unto the Lord; for (he is) *good*;
17:26. hast promised this *goodness*
19:13. do (that which is) *good* in his sight.
21:23. do (that which is) *good* in his eyes:
28: 8. that ye may possess this *good* land,
29:28. he died in a *good* old age,
2Ch 3: 5. which he overlaid with *fine* gold,
8. and he overlaid it with *fine* gold,
5:13. For (he is) *good*;
6:27. hast taught them the *good* way,
41. let thy saints rejoice *in goodness*.
7: 3. For (he is) *good*;
10. glad *and merry in* heart for *the goodness* that the Lord had shewed
10: 7. If thou be *kind* to this people,
— speak *good* words to them,
12:12. also in Judah things went *well*. (marg. or. and yet in Judah there were *good* things)
14: 2(1). Asa did (that which was) *good*
18: 7. he never prophesied *good*
12. prophets (declare) *good* to the king
— speak thou *good*.
17. he would not prophesy *good*
19: 3. there are *good* things found in thee,
11. the Lord shall be with *the good*.
21:13. *better* than thyself:
24:16. because he had done *good* in Israel,
30:18. The *good* Lord pardon every one
22. that taught the *good* knowledge
31:20. wrought (that which was) *good*
Ezr. 3:11. because (he is) *good*,
7: 9. according to the *good* hand
8:18. by the *good* hand of our God
22. upon all them *for good*
27. two vessels of *fine* copper,
9:12. their peace *or their wealth*
Neh 2: 8. according to the *good* hand of my God
10. to seek *the welfare* of the children of
18. my God which was *good* upon me;
— *for* (this) *good* (work).
5: 9. It (is) not *good* that ye do:
19. Think upon me, my God, *for good*,
6:19. they reported *his good deeds*
9:13. *good* statutes and commandments:
20. Thou gavest also thy *good* spirit
13:31. Remember me, O my God, *for good*.
Est. 1:10. *when* the heart of the king was *merry*
11. for she (was) *fair* to look on. (marg. *good of* countenance)
19. unto another *that is better* than she.
2: 2. Let there be fair (lit. *good of* countenance) young virgins sought for
3. gather together all the *fair* young virgins
7. the maid (was) fair *and beautiful*;
9. her maids unto *the best* (place)
3:11. do with them *as* it seemeth *good*
5: 9. joyful *and with* a *glad* heart:
7: 9. who had spoken *good* for the king,
8: 5. And said, If it *please* the king,
— *and* I (be) *pleasing* in his eyes,
8. for the Jews, *as it liketh* you, (lit. *as* (is) *good* in your eyes)
17. a feast and a *good* day.
9:13. Then said Esther, If it *please* the king,
19. feasting, and a *good* day,
22. from mourning into a *good* day:
10: 3. seeking *the wealth of* his people,
Job 2:10. receive *good* at the hand of God,
7: 7. mine eye shall no more see *good*.

Job 9:25. they see no *good*.
21:13. They spend their days *in wealth*,
25. never eateth *with pleasure*.
22:18. he filled their houses with *good*
21. thereby *good* shall come unto thee.
30:26. When I looked for *good*, then evil
34: 4. let us know among ourselves what (is) *good*.
36:11. spend their days *in prosperity*,
Ps. 4: 6(7). Who will shew us (any) *good?*
14: 1,3. none that doeth *good*.
16: 2. *my goodness* (extendeth) not to thee;
21: 3(4). with the blessings of *goodness:*
23: 6. Surely *goodness* and mercy shall follow
25: 8. *Good* and upright (is) the Lord:
13. His soul shall dwell *at ease*; (marg. *in goodness*)
34: 8(9). taste and see that the Lord (is) *good:*
10(11). seek the Lord shall not want any *good*
12(13). days, that he may see *good?*
14(15). Depart from evil, and do *good;*
35:12. They rewarded me evil for *good*
36: 4(5). setteth himself in a way (that is) not *good;*
37: 3. Trust in the Lord, and do *good;*
16. *better* than the riches of
27. Depart from evil, and do *good;*
38:20(21). They also that render evil for *good*
—(—). I follow (the thing that) *good* (is).
39: 2(3). I held my peace, (even) *from good;*
45: 1(2). My heart is inditing a *good* matter:
52: 3(5). Thou lovest evil *more than good;*
9(11). for (it is) *good* before thy saints.
53: 1(2), 3(4). none that doeth *good*.
54: 6(8). O Lord; for (it is) *good*.
63: 3(4). lovingkindness (is) *better* than life,
65:11(12). crownest the year with *thy goodness;*
68:10(11). hast prepared *of thy goodness*
69:16(17). for thy lovingkindness (is) *good:*
73: 1. Truly God (is) *good* to Israel,
28. But (it is) *good* for me to draw near
84:10(11). a day in thy courts (is) *better* than a
11(12). no *good* (thing) will he withhold
85:12(13). Lord shall give (that which is) *good;*
86: 5. For thou, Lord, (art) *good*,
17. Shew me a token *for good;*
92: 1(2). (a) *good* (thing) to give thanks
100: 5. For the Lord (is) *good;*
103: 5. satisfieth thy mouth *with good*
104:28. they are filled with *good*.
106: 1. unto the Lord; for (he is) *good:*
5. That I may see *the good of*
107: 1. unto the Lord, for (he is) *good:*
9. filleth the hungry soul with *goodness*.
109: 5. have rewarded me evil for *good*,
21. because thy mercy (is) *good*,
111:10. a *good* understanding have all
112: 5. A *good* man sheweth favour,
118: 1. thanks unto the Lord; for (he is) *good:*
8,9. *better* to trust in the Lord than to put
29. for (he is) *good:* for his mercy
119:39. for thy judgments (are) *good*.
65. Thou hast dealt *well* with thy servant,
68. Thou (art) *good*,
71. (It is) *good* for me that I have
72. The law of thy mouth (is) *better*
122. Be surety for thy servant *for good*.
122: 9. I will seek thy *good*.
125: 4. *unto* (those that be) *good*,
128: 2. *and* (it shall be) *well* with thee.
133: 1. how *good* and how pleasant
2. like the *precious* ointment upon
135: 3. for the Lord (is) *good:*
136: 1. unto the Lord; for (he is) *good:*
143:10. thy spirit (is) *good;*
145: 9. The Lord (is) *good* to all:
147: 1. for (it is) *good* to sing praises
Pro. 2: 9. equity; (yea), every *good* path.
20. mayest walk in the way of *good* (men),
3: 4. find favour and *good* understanding
14. *better* than the merchandise
27. Withhold not *good* from them
4: 2. For I give you *good* doctrine,
8:11. wisdom (is) *better* than rubies;
19. My fruit (is) *better*
11:23. desire of the righteous (is) only *good:*
27. He that diligently seeketh *good*

Pro. 12: 2. *A good* (man) obtaineth favour
9. *better* than he that honoureth
14. A man shall be satisfied with *good*
25. a *good* word maketh it glad.
13: 2. A man shall eat *good* by the fruit
15. *Good* understanding giveth favour:
21. but to the righteous *good*
22. *A good* (man) leaveth an inheritance
14:14. and a *good* man (shall be satisfied)
19. The evil bow before *the good;*
22. truth (shall be) to them that devise *good*.
15: 3. beholding the evil *and the good*.
15. *but* he that is of a *merry* heart
16. *Better* (is) little with the fear of
17. *Better* (is) a dinner of herbs
23. word (spoken) in due season, how *good*
30. a *good* report maketh the bones fat.
16: 8. *Better* (is) a little with
16. *better* (is it) to get wisdom
19. *Better* (it is to be) of an humble spirit
20. handleth a matter wisely shall find *good:*
29. leadeth him into the way (that is) not *good*.
32. slow to anger (is) *better*
17: 1. *Better* (is) a dry morsel,
13. Whoso rewardeth evil for *good*,
20. a froward heart findeth no *good:*
26. to punish the just (is) not *good*,
18: 5. not *good* to accept the person of the
22. findeth a wife findeth a *good*
19: 1. *Better* (is) the poor
2. without knowledge, (it is) not *good;*
8. keepeth understanding shall find *good*.
22. *and* a poor man (is) *better* than a liar.
20:23. a false balance (is) not *good*.
21: 9. *better* to dwell in a corner
19. *better* to dwell in the wilderness,
22: 1. *loving* favour rather than silver
9. He that hath a *bountiful* eye
24:13. eat thou honey, because (it is) *good;*
23. not *good* to have respect of persons
25. a *good* blessing shall come
25: 7. *better* (it is) that it be said
24. *better* to dwell in the corner
25. so (is) *good* news from a far country.
27. not *good* to eat much honey:
27: 5. Open rebuke (is) *better* than secret love.
10. *better* (is) a neighbour
28: 6. *Better* (is) the poor that walketh
10. the upright shall have *good*
21. respect of persons (is) not *good:*
31:12. She will do him *good* and not evil
18. that her merchandise (is) *good:*
Ecc. 2: 1. therefore enjoy *pleasure:*
3. what (was) that *good* for the sons of men
24. nothing *better* for a man,
— he should make his soul enjoy *good*
26. giveth to a man *that* (is) *good*
— he may give *to* (him that is) *good*
3:12. I know that (there is) no *good* in them,
— rejoice, and to do *good* in his life.
13. enjoy *the good of* all his labour,
22. that (there is) nothing *better*,
4: 3. *Yea, better* (is he) than both they, which
6. *Better* (is) an handful (with) quietness,
8. bereave my soul *of good?*
9. Two (are) *better* than one;
— they have a *good* reward for their labour.
13. *Better* (is) a poor and a wise child
5: 5(4). *Better* (is it) that thou
11(10). When *goods* increase,
18(17). *good* and comely (for one) to eat
—(—). to enjoy *the good* of all his labour
6: 3. his soul be not filled with *good*,
— an untimely birth (is) *better* than he.
6. *yet* hath he seen no *good:*
9. *Better* (is) the sight of the eyes
12. who knoweth what (is) *good* for man
7: 1. A *good* name (is) *better*
2. *better* to go to the house of mourning,
3. Sorrow (is) *better* than laughter:
5. *better* to hear the rebuke
8. *Better* (is) the end of a thing
— *better* than the proud in spirit.
10. What is (the cause) that the former days were *better*
11. Wisdom (is) *good* with an inheritance:

Ecc. 7:14. In the day of *prosperity* be *joyful*, (lit. *in good*)
18. *good* that thou shouldest take hold
20. just man upon earth, that doeth *good*,
26. whoso *pleaseth* God shall escape from her; (marg. (he that is) *good* before God)
8:12. that it shall be *well* with them
13. *But* it shall not be *well*
15. man hath no *better* thing
9: 2. *to the good* and to the clean,
— *as* (is) *the good*, so (is) the sinner;
4. a living dog is *better* than a dead lion.
7. drink thy wine with a *merry* heart;
16. Wisdom (is) *better* than strength:
18. Wisdom (is) *better* than weapons of war: but one sinner destroyeth much *good*.
11: 6. whether they both (shall be) alike *good*.
7. *and a pleasant* (thing it is)
12:14. whether (it be) *good*,
Cant. 1: 2. thy love (is) *better* than wine.
3. the savour of thy *good* ointments
7: 9(10). roof of thy mouth like the *best* wine
Isa. 3:10. that (it shall be) *well*
5: 9. shall be desolate, (even) great *and fair*,
20. Woe unto them that call evil *good*, *and good* evil;
7:15, 16. refuse the evil, and choose *the good*.
38: 3. *and* have done (that which is) *good*
39: 2. and the *precious* ointment,
8. *Good* (is) the word of the Lord
41: 7. It (is) *ready* for the sodering: (marg. of the soder, It (is) *good*)
52: 7. that bringeth good tidings of *good*,
55: 2. eat ye (that which is) *good*,
56: 5. a name *better* than of sons
65: 2. walketh in a way (that was) not *good*,
Jer. 5:25. your sins have withholden *good*
6:16. where (is) the *good* way,
20. and the *sweet* cane from a far country?
8:15. for peace, but no *good*
12: 6. they speak *fair words* unto thee. (marg. *good things*)
14:11. Pray not for this people *for* (their) *good*.
19. and (there is) no *good*;
15:11. Verily *it shall be well* (lit. *for good*)
17: 6. shall not see when *good* cometh;
18:10. then I will repent of *the good*,
20. Shall evil be recompensed for *good*?
— I stood before thee to speak *good*
21:10. not *for good*,
22:15, 16. then (it was) *well*
24: 2. One basket (had) very *good* figs,
3. I said, Figs; the *good* figs, very *good*; and the evil,
5. Like these *good* figs,
— land of the Chaldeans *for* (their) *good*.
6. set mine eyes upon them *for good*,
26:14. *as* seemeth *good* and meet
29:10. perform my *good* word
32. shall he behold *the good*
32:39. *for the good of* them,
42. bring upon them all *the good*
33: 9. hear all *the good* that I do
— fear and tremble for all *the goodness*
11. for the Lord (is) *good*;
14. I will perform that *good* thing
39:16. for evil, and not *for good*;
40: 4. If it seem *good* unto thee
— whither it seemeth *good*
42: 6. Whether (it be) *good*,
44:17. plenty of victuals, and were *well*,
27. for evil, and not *for good*:
52:32. spake *kindly* unto him, (marg. *good things*)
Lam. 3:17. my soul far off from peace: I forgat *prosperity*. (marg. *good*)
25. The Lord (is) *good* unto them
26. *good* that (a man) should
27. (It is) *good* for a man
38. proceedeth not evil *and good*?
4: 1. is the *most* fine gold changed! (lit. *good* fine gold)
9. *better* than (they that be) slain
Eze. 17: 8. It was planted in a *good* soil
18:18. did (that) which (is) not *good*
20:25. statutes (that were) not *good*,
24: 4. every *good* piece, the thigh,
31:16. the choice *and best of* Lebanon,
Eze. 34:14. I will feed them in a *good* pasture,
— there shall they lie in a *good* fold,
18. have eaten up the *good* pasture,
36:31. your doings that (were) not *good*,
Dan 1: 4. no blemish, *but well* favoured,
15. *fairer* and fatter in flesh
Hos. 2: 7(9). *better* with me than now.
4:13. the shadow thereof (is) *good*:
8: 3. cast off (the thing that is) *good*:
10: 1. *according to the goodness*
14: 2(3). receive (us) *graciously*:
Joel 3: 5(4:5). temples my *goodly* pleasant things:
Am. 5:14. Seek *good*, and not evil,
15. Hate the evil, and love *the good*,
6: 2. (be they) *better* than these
9: 4. for evil, and not *for good*.
Jon. 4: 3, 8. *better* for me to die than to live.
Mic. 1:12. Maroth waited carefully *for good*:
3: 2. Who hate *the good*,
6: 8. shewed thee, O man, what (is) *good*;
7: 4. *The best of them* (is) as a brier:
Nah 1: 7. The Lord (is) *good*,
3: 4. the whoredoms of the *well*favoured harlot, (lit. *good of* favour)
Zec. 1:13. *good* words (and) comfortable
17. My cities *through prosperity* (marg. *good*)
8:19. gladness, and *cheerful* feasts;
11:12. If ye think *good*,
Mal. 2:17. Every one that doeth evil (is) *good*

טוּב *toov*, m. 2898

Gen24:10. all *the goods of* his master
45:18. I will give you *the good of* the land
20. for *the good of* all the land
23. laden with *the good things of* Egypt,
Ex. 33:19. I will make all *my goodness* pass before
Deu 6:11. houses full of all *good* (things),
28:47. joyfulness, *and with gladness of* heart,
2K. 8: 9. even of every *good thing* of Damascus,
Ezr. 9:12. eat *the good of* the land,
Neh 9:25. houses full of all *goods*,
— delighted themselves *in thy* great *goodness*.
35. *and in thy* great *goodness*
36. and *the good thereof*,
Job 20:21. shall no man look for *his goods*.
21:16. *their good* (is) not in their hand:
Ps. 25: 7. remember thou me for *thy goodness'* sake,
27:13. see *the goodness of* the Lord
31:19(20). how great (is) *thy goodness*,
65: 4(5). satisfied *with the goodness of* thy house,
119:66. Teach me *good* judgment
128: 5. thou shalt see *the good of* Jerusalem
145: 7. utter the memory of *thy* great *goodness*,
Pro. 11:10. *When it goeth well with* the righteous, (lit. *in the good of*)
Isa. 1:19. ye shall eat *the good of* the land:
63: 7. great *goodness* toward the house of Israel,
65:14. my servants shall sing *for joy of* heart,
Jer. 2: 7. *and the goodness thereof*;
31:12. flow together to *the goodness of* the Lord,
14. shall be satisfied with *my goodness*,
Hos. 3: 5. fear the Lord and *his goodness*
10:11. but I passed over upon her *fair* neck: (marg. *the beauty of* her neck)
Zec 9:17. For how great (is) *his goodness*,

טוֹבָה see טוֹב See 2896

טָוָה [*tāh-vāh'*]. 2901

* KAL.—*Preterite.* *

Ex. 35:25. the women that were wise hearted *did spin*
26. stirred them up in wisdom *spun* goats' (hair).

טוּחַ *tooăgh*. 2902

* KAL.—*Preterite.* *

Lev 14:42. *and shall plaister* the house.

Isa. 44:18. for *he hath shut* their eyes, (marg. *daubed*)
Eze 13:12. daubing wherewith *ye have daubed*
14. the wall that *ye have daubed*
22:28. her prophets *have daubed* them

KAL.—*Infinitive.*

1Ch 29: 4. *to overlay* the walls of the houses

KAL.—*Participle.* Poel.

Eze 13:10. *daubed* it with untempered (morter):
11. Say unto *them which daub* (it) *with*
15. *and upon them that have daubed*
— neither *they that daubed*

* NIPHAL.—*Infinitive.* *

Lev 14:43. after *it is plaistered;*
48. after the house *was plaistered:*

2903 **טוֹטָפוֹת** *tōh-tāh-phōhth'*, f. pl.

Ex. 13:16. *and for frontlets* between thine eyes:
Deu 6: 8. they shall be *as frontlets*
11:18. they may be *as frontlets*

2904 **טוּל** [*tool*].

* PILPEL.—*Participle.* *

Isa. 22:17. the Lord *will carry thee away* (marg. or, *who covered thee*)

* HIPHIL.—*Preterite.* *

Jer. 16:13. *Therefore will I cast* you *out*
22:26. *And I will cast* thee *out,*
Jon 1: 4. the Lord *sent out* a great wind (marg. *cast forth*)

HIPHIL.—*Imperative.*

Jon 1:12. *and cast me forth* into the sea;

HIPHIL.—*Future.*

1Sa 18:11. *And* Saul *cast* the javelin;
20:33. *And* Saul *cast* a javelin
Eze 32: 4. *I will cast thee forth* upon
Jon 1: 5. *and cast forth* the wares
15. *and cast him forth* into the sea:

* HOPHAL.—*Preterite.* *

Jer. 22:28. wherefore *are they cast out,*

HOPHAL.—*Future.*

Job 41: 9(1). *shall* not (one) *be cast down*
Ps. 37:24. *he shall* not *be utterly cast down:*
Pro 16:33. The lot *is cast* into the lap;

2905 **טוּר** *toor*, m.

Ex. 28:17. four *rows* of stones:
— *row* (shall be) a sardius,
— (this shall be) *the* first *row.*
18. *And the* second *row*
19. *And the* third *row* a ligure,
20. *And the* fourth *row* a beryl,
39:10. they set in it four *rows of* stones: (the first) *row* (was) a sardius,
— this (was) *the* first *row.*
11. *And the* second *row,*
12. *And the* third *row,* a ligure,
13. *And the* fourth *row,* a beryl,
1K. 6:36. the inner court with three *rows of*
— *and a row of* cedar beams.
7: 2. upon four *rows of* cedar pillars,
3. forty five pillars, fifteen (in) *a row.*
4. windows (in) three *rows,*
12. with three *rows* of hewed stones,
— *and a row of* cedar beams,
18. two *rows* round about
20. two hundred in *rows* round about
24. knops (were) cast in two *rows,*
42. two *rows* of pomegranates
2Ch 4: 3. Two *rows* of oxen (were) cast,
13. two *rows* of pomegranates
Eze 46:23. *And* (there was) *a row*

טוּר *toor*, Ch. m. 2906

Dan 2:35. that smote the image became *a great mountain,*
45. cut out *of the mountain* without hands,

טוּשׁ [*toosh*]. 2907

* KAL.—*Future.* *

Job 9:26. as the eagle (that) *hasteth*

טְוָת *t'vāhth*, Ch. adv. 2908

Dan 6:18(19). and passed the night *fasting:*

טָחָה [*tāh-ghāh'*]. 2909

* PIEL.—*Participle.* *

Gen 21:16. *as it were a* bowshot:

טְחוֹן *t'ghōhn*, m. 2911

Lam 5:13. They took the young men *to grind,*

טְחוֹרִים *t'ghōh-reem'*, m. pl. 2914

Deu 28:27. *and with the emerods,*
1Sa 5: 6. smote them *with emerods,*
9. they had *emerods* in their secret parts.
12. were smitten *with the emerods:*
6: 4. Five golden *emerods,*
5. make images of *your emerods,*
11. the images of *their emerods.*
17. these (are) *the* golden *emerods*

טֻחוֹת *too-ghōhth'*, f. pl. 2910

Job 38:36. put wisdom *in the inward parts?*
Ps. 51: 6(8). desirest truth *in the inward parts:*

טָחַן [*tāh-ghan'*]. 2912

* KAL.—*Preterite.* *

Nu. 11: 8. *and ground* (it) in mills,

KAL.—*Infinitive.*

Deu 9:21. *ground* (it) very small,

KAL.—*Imperative.*

Isa. 47: 2. Take the millstones, *and grind* meal:

KAL.—*Future.*

Ex. 32:20. *and ground* (it) to powder,
Job 31:10. *let* my wife *grind* unto another,
Isa. 3:15. to pieces, and *grind* the faces of the poor?

KAL.—*Participle.* Poel.

Jud 16:21. he *did grind* in the prison house.
Ecc 12: 3. *the grinders* cease because they are few,

טַחֲנָה *tah-ghănāh'*, f. 2913

Ecc 12: 4. when the sound of *the grinding*

טִיחַ *tee'ăgh*, m. 2915

Eze 13:12. Where (is) *the daubing*

טִיט *teet*, m. 2916

2Sa 22:43. did stamp them *as the mire of*
Job 41:30(22). sharp pointed things upon *the mire.*
Ps. 18:42(43). cast them out *as the dirt in* the streets.
40: 2(3). *out of the* miry *clay,*
69:14(15). Deliver me *out of the mire,*

Isa. 41:25. as the potter treadeth *clay.*
57:20. whose waters cast up mire *and dirt.*
Jer. 38: 6. no water, but *mire:* so Jeremiah sunk *in the mire.*
Mic. 7:10. be trodden down *as the mire of*
Nah 3:14. go *into clay,* and tread the morter,
Zec 9: 3. fine gold *as the mire of* the streets.
10: 5. *in the mire of* the streets

2917 טִין [*teen*], Ch. m.

Dan 2:41. sawest the iron mixed with *miry* clay.
43. thou sawest iron mixed with *miry* clay,

2918 טִירָה [*tee-rāh'*], f.

Gen25:16. towns, *and by their castles;*
Nu. 31:10. and all *their goodly castles,*
1Ch 6:54(39). dwelling places *throughout their castles*
Ps. 69:25(26). Let *their habitation* be desolate; (marg. *palace*)
Cant 8: 9. build upon her *a palace of* silver:
Eze 25: 4. they shall set *their palaces*
46:23. with boiling places under *the rows* round about.

2919 טַל *tal*, m.

Gen27:28. God give thee *of the dew of* heaven,
39. *and of the dew of* heaven
Ex. 16:13. *the dew* lay round about
14. when *the dew* that lay was gone
Nu. 11: 9. when *the dew* fell upon the camp
Deu32: 2. my speech shall distil *as the dew,*
33:13. *for the dew,* and for the deep
28. his heavens shall drop down *dew.*
Jud 6:37. if *the dew* be on the fleece
38. wringed *the dew* out of the fleece,
39. upon all the ground let there be *dew.*
40. there was *dew* on all the ground.
2Sa 1:21. Gilboa, (let there be) no *dew,*
17:12. light upon him as *the dew*
1K. 17: 1. there shall not be *dew* nor rain
Job 29:19. *and the dew* lay all night
38:28. who hath begotten the drops of *dew?*
Ps.110: 3. thou hast *the dew of* thy youth.
133: 3. *As the dew of* Hermon,
Pro 3:20. the clouds drop down *the dew.*
19:12. *but* his favour (is) *as dew* upon the grass.
Cant 5: 2. for my head is filled with *dew,*
Isa. 18: 4. like a cloud of *dew* in the heat
26:19. for *thy dew* (is as) *the dew of* herbs,
Hos 6: 4. *and as the* early *dew* it goeth away.
13: 3. *and as the* early *dew* that passeth away,
14: 5(6). I will be *as the dew* unto Israel:
Mic. 5: 7(6). *as a dew* from the Lord,
Hag 1:10. the heaven over you is stayed *from dew,*
Zec. 8:12. the heavens shall give *their dew;*

2920 טַל *tal*, Ch. m.

Dan 4:15(12), 23(20). *and* let it be wet *with the dew of*
25(22). *and* they shall wet thee *with the dew*
33(30) & 5:21. *and* his body was wet *with the dew*

2921 טָלָא [*tāh-lāh'*].

* KAL.—*Participle.* Paül. *

Gen30:32. all the speckled *and spotted* cattle,
— *and the spotted* and speckled
33. every one that (is) not speckled *and spotted*
35. that were ringstraked *and spotted,*
— that were speckled *and spotted,*
39. speckled, *and spotted.*
Eze.16:16. thy high places *with divers colours,*

* PUAL.—*Participle.* *

Jos. 9: 5. old shoes *and clouted* upon

טְלָאִים *t'lāh-eem'*, m. pl. 2922

Isa. 40:11. he shall gather *the lambs* with his arm,

טָלֶה *tāh'-leh*, m. 2924

1Sa 7: 9. Samuel took *a* sucking *lamb,*
Isa. 65:25. The wolf *and the lamb* shall feed

טַלְטֵלָה *tal-tēh-lāh'*, f. 2925

Isa. 22:17. with *a* mighty *captivity,*

טָלַל [*tāh-lal'*]. 2926

* PIEL.—*Future.* *

Neh 3:15. he built it, *and covered it,*

טְלַל [*t'lal*], Ch. 2927

* APHEL.—*Future.* *

Dan 4:12(9). the beasts of the field *had shadow* under it,

טָמֵא *tāh-mēh'*. 2930

* KAL.—*Preterite.* *

Lev.11:25, 28, 40, 40. *and be unclean* until the even.
32. *and it shall be unclean* until the even;
12: 2. *then she shall be unclean* seven days;
5. *then she shall be unclean* two weeks,
15: 5, 6, 7, 8, 10, 11, 16, 17, 21, 22, 27. *and be unclean* until the even.
18. *and be unclean* until the even.
24. *he shall be unclean* seven (lit. *and he shall*)
17:15. *and be unclean* until the even:
22: 6. any such *shall be unclean* (lit. *and, &c.*)
Nu. 6:12. because his separation *was defiled.*
19: 7. *and* the priest *shall be unclean*
8. *and shall be unclean* until the even.
10. *and be unclean* until the even:
11. *shall be unclean* seven (lit. *and he shall*)
Eze.22: 4. *hast defiled thyself* in thine idols

KAL.—*Infinitive.*

Lev.15:32. *and is defiled* therewith;
18:20. *to defile thyself* with her.
23. lie with any beast *to defile thyself*
19:31. wizards, *to be defiled* by them:
22: 8. *to defile himself* therewith:
Eze 22: 3. idols against herself *to defile herself.*
44:25. *to defile themselves.*
Mic. 2:10. because *it is polluted,* it shall destroy

KAL.—*Future.*

Lev. 5: 3. that a man *shall be defiled*
11:24. *shall be unclean* until the even.
26. that toucheth them *shall be unclean.*
27. toucheth their carcase *shall be unclean*
31. *shall be unclean* until the even.
32. doth fall, *it shall be unclean;*
33. whatsoever (is) in it *shall be unclean;*
34. water cometh *shall be unclean:*
— every (such) vessel *shall be unclean.*
35. carcase falleth *shall be unclean;*
36. toucheth their carcase *shall be unclean.*
39. *shall be unclean* until the even.
12: 2. for her infirmity *shall she be unclean.*
13:14. *he shall be unclean.*
46. in him *he shall be defiled;*
14:36. the house *be not made unclean:*
46. *shall be unclean* until the even.
15: 4. lieth that hath the issue, *is unclean:*
—, 9, 10, 19, 20, 20, 23, 24, 27. *shall be unclean.*
18:25, 27. *And* the land *is defiled:*
22: 5. whereby *he may be made unclean,* or a man of whom *he may take uncleanness,*
Nu. 19:14, 16, 20, 21, 22, 22. *shall be unclean*
Ps 106:39. *Thus were they defiled*
Eze 23:17. *and she was polluted*

Hag 2:13. *shall it be unclean?* And the priests answered and said, *It shall be unclean.*

*** NIPHAL.—*Preterite.* ***

Lev.18:24. in all these the nations *are defiled*
Nu. 5:13. kept close, and she *be defiled,*
14. jealous of his wife, and she *be defiled*
— and she *be* not *defiled:*
20. if *thou be defiled,*
27. if she *be defiled,*
28. if the woman *be* not *defiled,*
29. instead of her husband, *and is defiled;*
Jer. 2:23. canst thou say, *I am* not *polluted,*
Eze 20:43. wherein *ye have been defiled;*
23: 7. with all their idols *she defiled herself.*
13. Then I saw that *she was defiled,*
30. *thou art polluted* with their idols.
Hos 5: 3 & 6:10. Israel *is defiled.*

NIPHAL.—*Participle.*

Eze 20:30. Are ye *polluted* after the
31. ye *pollute yourselves* with all

*** PIEL.—*Preterite.* ***

Gen34: 5. Jacob heard that *he had defiled*
13. because *he had defiled* Dinah
27. *they had defiled* their sister.
Lev.13: 3. *and pronounce* him *unclean.*
8. *then* the priest *shall pronounce him unclean:*
11. *and* the priest *shall pronounce him unclean,*
15. *and pronounce him to be unclean:*
20. the priest *shall pronounce him unclean:*
22, 27, 30. *then* the priest *shall pronounce* him *unclean:*
25. *wherefore* the priest *shall pronounce* him *unclean:*
Nu. 6: 9. *and he hath defiled* the head
19:13. *defileth* the tabernacle of the Lord;
20. *he hath defiled* the sanctuary
2K. 23:10. *And he defiled* Topheth,
13. *did* the king *defile.*
Ps. 79: 1. thy holy temple *have they defiled;*
Isa. 30:22. *Ye shall defile also* the covering
Eze 5:11. *thou hast defiled* my sanctuary
18: 6. neither *hath defiled* his neighbour's wife,
11. and *defiled* his neighbour's wife,
15. *hath* not *defiled* his neighbour's wife,
22:11. *hath* lewdly *defiled* his daughter in law;
23:38. *they have defiled* my sanctuary
33:26. *ye defile* every one his neighbour's wife:
36:18. idols (wherewith) *they had polluted it:*
43: 8. *they have even defiled* my holy name

PIEL.—*Infinitive.*

Lev.13:44. shall pronounce him *utterly* unclean;
59. *to pronounce it unclean.*
15:31. *when they defile* my tabernacle
18:28. *when ye defile* it,
20: 3. to *defile* my sanctuary,
25. have separated from you *as unclean.*
Jer. 7:30. called by my name, *to pollute it.*
32:34. called by my name, *to defile it.*

PIEL.—*Imperative.*

Eze 9: 7. said unto them, *Defile* the house,

PIEL.—*Future.*

Lev.11:44. neither *shall ye defile* yourselves
13:44. *shall pronounce him* utterly *unclean;*
Nu. 5: 3. that *they defile* not their camps,
35:34. *Defile* not therefore the land
Deu21:23. that thy land *be* not *defiled,*
2K. 23: 8. *and defiled* the high places
16. upon the altar, *and polluted it,*
2Ch 36:14. *and polluted* the house of the Lord
Jer. 2: 7. *but* when ye entered, *ye defiled*
Eze 20:26. *And I polluted* them
23:17. *and they defiled* her
36:17. *when* the house...*they defiled* it by their own way
43: 7. *shall* the house of Israel no more *defile,*

*** PUAL.—*Participle.* ***

Eze. 4:14. my soul *hath* not *been polluted:*

*** HITHPAEL.—*Future.* ***

Lev.11:24. for these *ye shall be unclean:*
43. neither *shall ye make yourselves unclean*
18:24. *Defile* not *ye yourselves*
30. that *ye defile* not *yourselves*
Lev 21: 1. There *shall* none *be defiled*
3. for her *may he be defiled.*
4. *he shall* not *defile himself,*
11. nor *defile himself* for his father,
Nu. 6: 7. *He shall* not *make himself unclean*
Eze 14:11. neither *be polluted* any more
20: 7. *defile* not *yourselves*
18. nor *defile yourselves* with their idols:
37:23. Neither *shall they defile themselves*
44:25. *they may defile themselves.*
Hos 9: 4. eat thereof *shall be polluted:*

*** HOTHPAEL.—*Preterite.* ***

Deu24: 4. after that *she is defiled;*

טָמֵא *tāh-mēh'*, adj. 2931

Lev. 5: 2. touch any *unclean* thing, whether (it be) a carcase of an *unclean* beast, or a carcase of *unclean* cattle, or the carcase of *unclean* creeping things,
— he also shall be *unclean,*
7:19. that toucheth any *unclean* (thing)
21. soul that shall touch any *unclean* (thing),
— or (any) *unclean* beast, or any abominable *unclean* (thing),
10:10. between *unclean* and clean;
11: 4, 5. he (is) *unclean* unto you.
6. he (is) *unclean* unto you.
7. he (is) *unclean* to you.
8. they (are) *unclean* to you.
26, 27, 28. (are) *unclean* unto you:
29. These also (shall be) *unclean*
31. These (are) *unclean* to you
35. broken down: (for) they (are) *unclean, and* shall be *unclean* unto you.
38. it (shall be) *unclean* unto you.
47. make a difference between *the unclean*
13:11. for he (is) *unclean.*
15. the raw flesh (is) *unclean:*
36. for yellow hair; he (is) *unclean.*
44. a leprous man, he (is) *unclean:*
45. *and* shall cry, *Unclean, unclean.*
46. shall be defiled; he (is) *unclean:*
51. a fretting leprosy; it (is) *unclean.*
55. plague be not spread; it (is) *unclean;*
14:40. cast them into an *unclean* place
41. without the city into an *unclean* place:
44. leprosy in the house: it (is) *unclean.*
45. out of the city into an *unclean* place.
57. To teach when (it is) *unclean,*
15: 2. his issue he (is) *unclean.*
25. she (shall be) *unclean.*
26. sitteth upon shall be *unclean,*
33. lieth with her that is *unclean.*
20:25. between clean beasts *and unclean,*
— between *unclean* fowls and clean:
22: 4. toucheth any thing (that is) *unclean*
27:11. if (it be) any *unclean* beast,
27. if (it be) of an *unclean* beast,
Nu. 5: 2. whosoever is *defiled* by the dead:
9: 6. men, who were *defiled*
7. We (are) *defiled* by the dead body
10. shall be *unclean* by reason of
18:15. the firstling of *unclean* beasts
19:13. he shall be *unclean;*
15. covering bound upon it, (is) *unclean.*
17. *for an unclean* (person)
19. shall sprinkle upon *the unclean*
20. sprinkled upon him; he (is) *unclean.*
22. whatsoever *the unclean* (person) toucheth
Deu12:15. *the unclean* and the clean may eat
22. *the unclean* and the clean
14: 7. they (are) *unclean* unto you.
8, 10. it (is) *unclean* unto you:
19. creeping thing that flieth (is) *unclean*
15:22. *the unclean* and the clean
26:14. thereof *for* (any) *unclean*
Jos. 22:19. the land of your possession (be) *unclean,*
Jud 13: 4. eat not any *unclean* (thing):
2Ch 23:19. none (which was) *unclean* in any
Job 14: 4. a clean (thing) *out of an unclean?*
Ecc. 9: 2. to the clean, *and to the unclean;*
Isa. 6: 5. I (am) a man of *unclean* lips, and I dwell in the midst of a people of *unclean*
35: 8. *the unclean* shall not pass

Isa. 52: 1. the uncircumcised *and the unclean.*
11. touch no *unclean* (thing);
64: 6(5). But we are all *as an unclean*
Jer. 19:13. shall be *defiled* as the place of Tophet,
Lam 4:15. Depart ye; (it is) *unclean;*
Eze 4:13. Israel eat their *defiled* bread
22: 5. mock thee, (which art) infamous (marg. *polluted of* name)
10. her that was set apart for *pollution.*
26. between *the unclean* and the clean,
44:23. discern between *the unclean* and the clean.
Hos 9: 3. they shall eat *unclean* (things)
Am 7:17. thou shalt die in a *polluted* land:
Hag 2:13. If (one that is) *unclean by* a dead
14. which they offer there (is) *unclean.*

2932 **טֻמְאָה** *toom-āh'*, f.

Lev. 5: 3. if he touch *the uncleanness of* man, whatsoever *uncleanness* (it be)
7:20. *having his uncleanness* upon him,
21. (as) *the uncleanness of* man,
14:19. be cleansed *from his uncleanness;*
15: 3. this shall be *his uncleanness*
— it (is) *his uncleanness.*
25. the days of the issue of *her uncleanness*
26. *as the uncleanness of* her separation.
30. for the issue of *her uncleanness.*
31. Israel *from their uncleanness;* that they die not *in their uncleanness,*
16:16. *because of the uncleanness of* the
— in the midst of *their uncleanness.*
19. hallow it *from the uncleanness of*
18:19. she is put apart for *her uncleanness.*
22: 3. *having his uncleanness* upon him,
5. whatsoever *uncleanness he hath;*
Nu. 5:19. gone aside to *uncleanness*
19:13. *his uncleanness* (is) yet upon him.
Jud.13: 7. neither eat any *unclean* (thing):
14. nor eat any *unclean* (thing):
2Sa 11: 4. she was purified *from her uncleanness:*
2Ch 29:16. brought out all *the uncleanness*
Ezr. 6:21. *from the filthiness of* the heathen
9:11. to another *with their uncleanness.*
Lam. 1: 9. *Her filthiness* (is) in her skirts;
Eze 22:15. will consume *thy filthiness*
24:11. *the filthiness of it* may be molten
13. *In thy filthiness* (is) lewdness:
— shalt not be purged *from thy filthiness*
36:17. *as the uncleanness of* a removed woman.
25. clean: from all *your filthiness,*
29. from all *your uncleannesses:*
39:24. *According to their uncleanness*
Zec 13: 2. the *unclean* spirit to pass out of the land. (lit. spirit of *uncleanness*)

2933 **טָמָה** [*tāh-māh'*].

* NIPHAL.—*Preterite.* *

Lev.11:43. *that ye should be defiled*
Job 18: 3. are we counted as beasts, (and) *reputed vile*

2934 **טָמַן** *tāh-man'.*

* KAL.—*Preterite.* *

Ps. 9:15(16). in the net which *they hid*
31: 4(5). the net that *they have laid privily*
35: 7. without cause *have they hid*
8. net that *he hath hid*
140: 5(6). The proud *have hid* a snare
142: 3(4). *have they privily laid* a snare
Pro 19:24. A slothful (man) *hideth* his hand
26:15. The slothful *hideth* his hand
Jer. 13: 7. from the place where *I had hid it:*
18:22. *hid* snares for my feet.
43: 9. *and hide them* in the clay
10. upon these stones that *I have hid*

KAL.—*Infinitive.*

Job 31:33. as Adam, *by hiding* mine iniquity
Ps. 64: 5(6). commune *of laying* snares *privily;* (marg. *to hide*)

Jer. 13: 6. which I commanded thee *to hide* there.

KAL.—*Imperative.*

Job 40:13. *Hide them* in the dust together;
Jer. 13: 4. go to Euphrates, *and hide it*

KAL.—*Future.*

Gen35: 4. *and* Jacob *hid* them under
Ex. 2:12. Egyptian, *and hid him* in the sand.
Jos. 2: 6. *and hid them* with the stalks
Jer. 13: 5. So I went, *and hid it*

KAL.—*Participle.* Paül.

Deu33:19. and (of) treasures *hid in* the sand.
Jos. 7:21. they (are) *hid* in the earth
22. behold, (it was) *hid* in his tent,
Job 3:16. as an *hidden* untimely birth
18:10. The snare (is) *laid* for him (marg. *hidden*)
20:26. All darkness (shall be) *hid*
40:13. bind their faces *in secret.*

* NIPHAL.—*Imperative.* *

Isa. 2:10. *and hide thee* in the dust,

* HIPHIL.—*Future.* *

2K. 7: 8. raiment, and went *and hid* (it);
— thence (also), and went *and hid* (it).

טֶנֶא *teh'-neh*, m. 2935

Deu 26: 2. shalt put (it) *in a basket,*
4. the priest shall take *the basket*
28: 5. Blessed (shall be) *thy basket*
17. Cursed (shall be) *thy basket*

טָנַף [*tāh-naph'*]. 2936

* PIEL.—*Future.* *

Cant.5: 3. how *shall I defile them?*

טָעָה [*tāh-ğāh'*]. 2937

* HIPHIL.—*Preterite.* *

Eze.13:10. *they have seduced* my people,

טָעַם *tāh-ğam'.* 2938

* KAL.—*Preterite.* *

1Sa.14:24. So none of the people *tasted* (any) food.
29. because *I tasted* a little of this honey.
43. *I did* but *taste* a little honey
Pro.31:18. *She perceiveth* (marg. *tasteth*) that her merchandise (is) good:

KAL.—*Infinitive.*

1Sa.14:43. I did *but* taste a little honey (lit. *in tasting* I did taste)

KAL.—*Imperative.*

Ps. 34: 8(9). *O taste* and see that the Lord (is) good:

KAL.—*Future.*

2Sa. 3:35. if *I taste* bread, or ought else,
19:35(36). *can* thy servant *taste* what I eat
Job 12:11. the mouth *taste* his meat?
34: 3. the mouth *tasteth* meat.
Jon. 3: 7. *Let* neither man nor beast, herd nor flock, *taste*

טְעֵם [*t'ğam*], Ch. 2939

* P'AL.—*Future.* *

Dan 4:25(22), 32(29). *they shall make* thee *to eat* grass
5:21. *they fed him* with grass like oxen,

טַעַם *tah'-ğam*, m. 2940

Ex. 16:31. *and the taste of it* (was) like wafers
Nu. 11: 8. and *the taste of it* was *as the taste* of fresh oil.

1Sa.21:13(14). he changed *his behaviour*
25:33. blessed (be) *thy advice*,
Job 6: 6. is there (any) *taste* in the white of an egg?
12:20. *and* taketh away *the understanding*
Ps. 34 [title](1). when he changed *his behaviour*
119:66. Teach me good *judgment*
Pro 11:22. a fair woman which is without *discretion.*
26:16. seven men that can render *a reason.*
Jer. 48:11. therefore *his taste* remained in him,
Jon. 3: 7. *by the decree of* the king and his nobles,

2941 **טַעַם** *tah'-ğam*, Ch. m.

Ezr. 4:21. until (another) *commandment* shall be given from me.
5: 5. till *the matter* came to Darius:
6:14. according to *the commandment of*
7:23. is commanded by the God of (lit. is from *the decree*)
Dan 6: 2(3). that the princes might give *accounts*

2942 **טְעֵם** *t'ğēhm*, Ch. m.

Ezr. 4: 8, 9, 17. Rehum the chancellor (lit. master of *decrees*)
19. And I *commanded*, (marg. by me *a decree* is set)
21. Give ye now *commandment* (marg. *decree*)
5: 3. Who hath *commanded* you to build this house, (lit. set *a decree*)
9. Who *commanded* you to build this house, (lit. set *a decree*)
13. Cyrus made *a decree* to build this house
17. that *a decree* was made of Cyrus
6: 1. Darius the king made *a decree*,
3. Cyrus the king made *a decree*
8. I make *a decree* what ye shall do
11. I have made *a decree*, that whosoever
12. I Darius have made *a decree*;
14. of Israel, *and according to the commandment of* Cyrus,
7:13. I make *a decree*, that all they of the people of Israel,
21. I Artaxerxes the king, do make *a decree*
Dan 2:14. Daniel answered with counsel *and wisdom*
3:10. Thou, O king, hast made *a decree*,
12. these men, O king, have not *regard*ed thee: (marg. set no *regard* upon thee)
29. I make *a decree*, That every people,
4: 6(3). Therefore made I *a decree* to bring in all the wise (men)
5: 2. Belshazzar, *whiles he tasted* the wine,
6:13(14). *regardeth* not thee, O king, (lit. setteth no *regard*
26(27). I make *a decree*, That in every dominion

2943 **טְעַן** [*tāh-ğan'*].

* KAL.—*Imperative.* *

Gen 45:17. *lade* your beasts, and go,

2944 **טָעַן** [*tāh-ğan'*].

* PUAL.—*Participle.* *

Isa. 14:19. *thrust through* with a sword,

2945 **טַף** *taph*, m.

Gen 34:29. wealth, and all *their little ones*,
43: 8. thou, (and) also *our little ones.*
45:19. Egypt *for your little ones*,
46: 5. their father, and *their little ones*,
47:12. according to (their) *families.* (marg. according to *the little ones*)
24. food *for your little ones.*
50: 8. only *their little ones*,
21. nourish you, and *your little ones.*
Ex. 10:10. let you go, and *your little ones:*
24. let *your little ones* also go
Ex. 12:37. men, beside *children.*
Nu. 14: 3. our wives *and our children*
31. *But your little ones*, which ye said
16:27. *and their little children.*
31: 9. captives, and *their little ones*,
17. kill every male *among the little ones*,
18. But all *the* women *children*,
32:16. cities *for our little ones:*
17. *our little ones* shall dwell
24. cities *for your little ones*,
26. *Our little ones*, our wives,
Deu 1:39. *Moreover your little ones*, which ye said
2:34. the women, *and the little ones*,
3: 6. men, women, *and children*,
19. your wives, *and your little ones*,
20:14. the women, *and the little ones*,
29:11(10). *Your little ones*, your wives,
31:12. men, and women, *and children*,
Jos. 1:14. Your wives, *your little ones*,
8:35. the women, *and the little ones*,
Jud. 18:21. put *the little ones* and the cattle
21:10. with the women *and the children.*
2Sa. 15:22. all *the little ones* that (were) with him.
2Ch 20:13. with *their little ones*,
31:18. genealogy of all *their little ones*,
Ezr. 8:21. for us, *and for our little ones*,
Est. 3:13. *little children* and women,
8:11. *little ones* and women,
Jer. 40: 7. men, and women, *and children*,
41:16. the women, *and the children*,
43: 6. men, and women, and *children*,
Eze. 9: 6. both maids, *and little children*,

טָפַח [*tāh-phağh'*]. 2946

* PIEL.—*Preterite.* *

Isa. 48:13. my right hand *hath spanned* the heavens:
Lam. 2:22. those that *I have swaddled*

טֶפַח *teh'-phağh*, m. 2947

1K. 7: 9. from the foundation unto *the coping*,
26. it (was) *an hand breadth* thick,
2Ch 4: 5. the thickness of it (was) *an hand breadth*,
Ps. 39: 5(6). made my days (as) *an hand breadth;*

טֹפַח *tōh'-phağh*, m. 2948

Ex. 25:25. a border of *an hand breadth*
37:12. *an hand breadth* round about;
Eze. 40: 5. by the cubit *and an hand breadth:*
43. hooks, an *hand broad*,
43:13. a cubit *and an hand breadth;*

טִפֻּחִים *tip-poo-ğheem'*, m. pl. 2949

Lam. 2:20. children of *a span long?* (marg. or, *swaddled with their hands*)

טָפַל [*tāh-phal'*]. 2950

* KAL.—*Preterite.* *

Ps. 119:69. The proud *have forged* a lie

KAL.—*Future.*

Job 14:17. *and thou sewest up* mine iniquity.

KAL.—*Participle.* Poel.

Job 13: 4. But ye (are) *forgers of* lies,

טִפְסַר [*tiph-sar'*], m. 2951

Jer. 51:27. appoint *a captain* against her;
Nah 3:17. the locusts, *and thy captains*

טָפַף [*tāh-phaph'*]. 2952

* KAL.—*Infinitive.* *

Isa. 3:16. walking *and mincing* (as) they go, (marg. or, *tripping nicely*)

2953 **טְפַר [t'phar], Ch. m.**

Dan 4:33(30). *and his nails* like birds' (claws).
7:19. *and his nails* (of) brass;

2954 **טָפַשׁ tāh-phash'.**

* KAL.—*Preterite.* *

Ps.119:70. Their heart *is* as *fat* as grease;

2956 **טָרַד [tāh-rad'].**

* KAL.—*Participle.* Poel. *

Pro.19:13. of a wife (are) a *continual* dropping.
27:15. A *continual* dropping in a very rainy day

2957 **טְרַד t'rad, Ch.**

* P'AL.—*Participle.* Active. *

Dan 4:25(22). *they shall drive* thee from men,
32(29). And *they shall drive* thee from men,

P'AL.—*Participle.* Passive.

Dan 4:33(30). *he was driven* from men,
5:21. *he was driven* from the sons of men;

2958 **טְרוֹם t'rōhm.**

Ru. 3:14. (כתיב) she rose up *before* one could know another.

2959 **טָרַח [tāh-ragh'].**

* HIPHIL.—*Future.* *

Job 37:11. Also by watering *he wearieth*

2960 **טֹרַח tōh'-ragh', m.**

Deu 1:12. How can I myself alone bear *your cumbrance*,
Isa. 1:14. they are *a trouble* unto me;

2961 **טָרִי [tāh-ree'], adj.**

Jud.15:15. he found a *new* jawbone of an ass,
Isa. 1: 6. bruises, and *putrifying* sores:

2962 **טֶרֶם teh'-rem, part.**

Gen 2: 5. *before* it was in the earth, and every herb of the field *before* it grew:
Nu. 11:33. yet between their teeth, *ere* it was chewed,
1Sa. 3: 7. Now Samuel did *not yet* know the Lord, *neither* was the word of the Lord yet revealed unto him.
&c. &c.

With prefixes, as בְּטֶרֶם

Gen27: 4. may bless thee *before* I die.
Ex. 1:19. are delivered *ere* the midwives
Jer. 1: 5. *Before* I formed thee in the belly I knew thee; *and before* thou camest forth
&c. &c.

הֲטֶרֶם

Ex. 10: 7. knowest thou *not yet* that Egypt is destroyed?

מִטֶּרֶם

Hag 2:15. *from before* a stone was laid upon a stone

טָרַף tāh-raph'. 2963

* KAL.—*Preterite.* *

Deu33:20. *and teareth* the arm with the
Job 16: 9. *He teareth* (me) in his wrath,
Hos. 6: 1. for he *hath torn*,
Mic. 5: 8(7). treadeth down, *and teareth in pieces*,

KAL.—*Infinitive.*

Gen37:33. Joseph is *without doubt* rent in pieces. (lit. *in rending* is rent in pieces)
44:28. *Surely* he is torn in pieces; (lit. *in rending* is rent in pieces)
Ex. 22:13(12). If it be)(torn in pieces, (lit. *in rending* is rent in pieces)
Ps. 17:12. a lion (that) is greedy *of his prey*,
Eze.19: 3. it learned *to catch* the prey;
6. and learned *to catch* the prey,

KAL.—*Future.*

Gen49:27. Benjamin *shall ravin* (as) a wolf:
Ps. 7: 2(3). Lest *he tear* my soul like a lion,
50:22. lest *I tear* (you) *in pieces*,
Hos. 5:14. I, (even) I, *will tear* and go away;
Am. 1:11. *and* his anger *did tear* perpetually,

KAL.—*Participle.* Poel.

Job 18: 4. He *teareth* himself in his anger:
Ps. 22:13(14). a *ravening* and a roaring lion.
Eze.22:25. like a roaring lion *ravening* the prey;
27. like wolves *ravening* the prey,
Nah. 2:12(13). The lion *did tear in pieces*

* NIPHAL.—*Future.* *

Ex. 22:13(12). If *it be torn in pieces*,
Jer. 5: 6. *shall be torn in pieces*:

* POAL.—*Preterite.* *

Gen37:33. Joseph *is* without doubt *rent in pieces*.
44:28. Surely *he is torn in pieces*;

* HIPHIL.—*Imperative.* *

Pro.30: 8. *feed me* with food convenient for me:

טָרָף tāh-rāhph', adj. 2965

Gen 8:11. an olive leaf *pluckt off*:

טֶרֶף teh'-reph, m. 2964

Gen49: 9. a lion's whelp: *from the prey*,
Nu. 23:24. not lie down until he eat (of) *the prey*,
Job 4:11. The old lion perisheth for lack of *prey*,
24: 5. rising betimes *for a prey*:
29:17. plucked *the spoil* out of his teeth.
38:39. Wilt thou hunt *the prey*
Ps. 76: 4(5). excellent than the mountains of *prey*.
104:21. The young lions roar *after* their *prey*, (lit. *the prey*)
111: 5. He hath given *meat* unto them that fear him: (marg. *prey*)
124: 6. hath not given us (as) *a prey*
Pro.31:15. giveth *meat* to her houshold,
Isa. 5:29. lay hold of *the prey*,
31: 4. the young lion roaring *on his prey*,
Eze.17: 9. wither in all *the leaves of* her spring
19: 3. it learned to catch *the prey*;
6. and learned to catch *the prey*,
22:25. like a roaring lion ravening *the prey*;
27. like wolves ravening *the prey*,
Am. 3: 4. *when* he hath no *prey*?
Nah. 2:12(13). filled his holes with *prey*,
13(14). I will cut off *thy prey*
3: 1. *the prey* departeth not;
Mal. 3:10. that there may be *meat* in mine house,

טְרֵפָה t'rēh-phāh', f. 2966

Gen31:39. *That which was torn* (of beasts)
Ex. 22:13(12). make good *that which was torn*.
31(30). flesh (that is) *torn of beasts*
Lev. 7:24. the fat of *that which is torn*
17:15. *or that which was torn*
22: 8. dieth of itself, *or is torn*
Eze. 4:14. dieth of itself, *or is torn in pieces*;
44:31. that is dead of itself, *or torn*,
Nah. 2:12(13). his dens *with ravin*.

י *yōhd*,

The tenth letter of the Alphabet.

2968 ## יָאַב [*yāh-av'*].

* KAL.—*Preterite.* *

Ps.119:131. for *I longed* for thy commandments.

2969 ## יָאָה [*yāh-āh'*].

* KAL.—*Preterite.* *

Jer. 10: 7. for to thee *doth it appertain:* (marg. *it liketh* thee)

2975 ## יְאוֹר *y'ōhr*, m.

Gen41: 1. behold, he stood by *the river.*
2, 18. there came up out of *the river*
3. came up after them out of *the river,*
— kine upon the brink of *the river.*
17. I stood upon the bank of *the river:*
Ex. 1:22. born ye shall cast *into the river,*
2: 3. in the flags by *the river's* brink.
5. to wash (herself) at *the river;* and her maidens walked along by *the river's* side;
4: 9. take of the water of *the river,*
— which thou takest out of *the river*
7:15. shalt stand by *the river's* brink
17. the waters which (are) *in the river,*
18. the fish that (is) *in the river* shall die, and *the river* shall stink;
— shall lothe to drink of the water of *the river.*
19. streams, upon *their rivers,*
20, 20. the waters that (were) *in the river,*
21. the fish that (was) *in the river* died; and *the river* stank,
— could not drink of the water of *the river;*
24. digged round about *the river*
— could not drink of the water of *the river.*
25. after that the Lord had smitten *the river.*
8: 3(7:28). *the river* shall bring forth frogs
5(1). over the streams, over *the rivers,*
9(5). may remain *in the river* only?
11(7). they shall remain *in the river*
17: 5. wherewith thou smotest *the river,*
2K. 19:24. dried up all *the rivers of* besieged places.
Job 28:10. He cutteth out *rivers* among
Ps. 78:44. turned *their rivers* into blood;
Isa. 7:18. uttermost part of *the rivers of*
19: 6. (and) *the brooks of* defence shall be
7. The paper reeds by *the brooks,* by the mouth of *the brooks,* and every thing sown by *the brooks,*
8. they that cast angle *into the brooks*
23: 3. Sihor, the harvest of *the river,*
10. Pass through thy land *as a river,*
33:21. unto us a place of broad rivers (and) *streams;*
37:25. I dried up all *the rivers of*
Jer. 46: 7. Who (is) this (that) cometh up *as a flood,*
8. Egypt riseth up *like a flood,*
Eze 29: 3. lieth in the midst of *his rivers,*
— *My river* (is) mine own,
4. will cause the fish of *thy rivers*
— up out of the midst of *thy rivers,* and all the fish of *thy rivers*
5. thee and all the fish of *thy rivers:*
9. hath said, *The river* (is) mine,
10. against thee, and against *thy rivers,*
30:12. I will make *the rivers* dry,
Dan12: 5. on this side of the bank of *the river,* and the other on that side of the bank of *the river.*
6, 7. which (was) upon the waters of *the river,*
Am. 8: 8. *as* (by) *the flood of* Egypt.
9: 5. rise up wholly *like a flood;*
— *as* (by) *the flood of* Egypt.
Nah 3. 8. No, that was situate *among the rivers,*
Zec 10:11. all the deeps of *the river* shall dry

יָאַל [*yāh-al'*]. 2973

* NIPHAL.—*Preterite.* *

Nu. 12:11. wherein *we have done foolishly,*
Isa. 19:13. The princes of Zoan *are become fools,*
Jer. 5: 4. *they are foolish:* for they know not
50:36. *and they shall dote:*

יָאַל [*yāh-al'*]. 2974

* HIPHIL.—*Preterite.* *

Gen18:27, 31. *I have taken upon me* to speak
Deu 1: 5. *began* Moses to declare this law,
Jos. 7: 7. would to God *we had been content,*
1Sa 12:22. because *it hath pleased* the Lord
1Ch 17:27. *let it please thee* to bless (marg. or, *it hath pleased*)
Hos 5:11. because *he willingly* walked (lit. *he was willing* to walk)

HIPHIL.—*Imperative.*

Jud.19: 6. *Be content,* I pray thee,
2Sa. 7:29. *let it please thee* to bless the house
2K. 5:23. Naaman said, *Be content,*
6: 3. one said, *Be content,*
Job 6:28. Now therefore *be content,*

HIPHIL.—*Future.*

Ex. 2:21. *And* Moses *was content* to dwell
Jos. 17:12. *but* the Canaanites *would* dwell
Jud. 1:27. *but* the Canaanites *would* dwell
35. *But* the Amorites *would* dwell
17:11. *And* the Levite *was content*
1Sa. 17:39. *and he assayed* to go;
Job 6: 9. *Even that it would please* God

יָאַשׁ [*yāh-ash'*]. 2976

* NIPHAL.—*Preterite.* *

1Sa.27: 1. *and* Saul *shall despair* of me,

NIPHAL.—*Participle.*

Job 6:26. speeches of *one that is desperate,*
Isa. 57:10. *There is no hope:*
Jer. 2:25. thou saidst, *There is no hope:* (marg. or, *Is the case desperate*)
18:12. they said, *There is no hope:*

* PIEL.—*Infinitive.* *

Ecc. 2:20. *to cause* my heart *to despair*

יָבַב [*yāh-vav'*]. 2980

* PIEL.—*Future.* *

Jud. 5:28. *and cried* through the lattice,

יְבוּל *y'vool*, m. 2981

Lev.26: 4. the land shall yield *her increase,*
20. shall not yield *her increase,*
Deu11:17. land yield not *her fruit;*
32:22. the earth *with her increase,*
Jud. 6: 4. destroyed *the increase of* the earth,
Job 20:28. *The increase of* his house shall
Ps. 67: 6(7). the earth yield *her increase;*
78:46. He gave also *their increase* unto
85:12(13). our land shall yield *her increase.*
Eze.34:27. earth shall yield *her increase,*
Hab 3:17. neither (shall) *fruit* (be) in the
Hag 1:10. earth is stayed (from) *her fruit.*
Zec. 8:12. ground shall give *her increase,*

יָבַל [*yāh-val'*]. 2986

* HIPHIL.—*Future.* *

Ps. 60: 9(11). Who *will bring me*(into) the strong

Ps. 68:29(30). *shall* kings *bring* presents unto thee.
76:11(12). *let* all that be round about him *bring*
108:10(11). Who *will bring me* into the strong city?
Isa. 23: 7. her own feet *shall carry her* afar off
Jer. 31: 9. with supplications *will I lead them:*
Zep 3:10. *shall bring* mine offering.

* HOPHAL.—*Future.* *

Job 10:19. *I should have been carried* from the
21:30. *they shall be brought forth* to the
32. Yet *shall he be brought* to the grave,
Ps. 45:14(15). *She shall be brought* unto the king
15(16). rejoicing *shall they be brought:*
Isa. 18: 7. *shall* the present *be brought* unto
53: 7. *he is brought* as a lamb to the
55:12. ye shall go out with joy, and *be led forth*
Jer. 11:19. an ox (that) *is brought* to the slaughter;
Hos.10: 6. *It shall be* also *carried* unto Assyria
12: 1(2). oil *is carried* into Egypt.

2987 ## יְבַל [*y'val*]. Ch.

* APHEL.—*Preterite.* *

Ezr. 5:14. *and brought* them into the temple of Babylon,
6: 5. *and brought* unto Babylon,

APHEL.—*Infinitive.*

Ezr. 7:15. *And to carry* the silver and gold,

2988 ## יָבָל [*yāh-vāhl'*], m.

Isa. 30:25. rivers (and) *streams of* waters in the
44: 4. as willows by *the* water *courses.*

2990 ## יַבָּל [*yab-bāhl'*], adj.

Lev.22:22. maimed, or *having a wen,*

2993 ## יָבָם [*yāh-vāhm'*], m.

Deu 25: 5. *her husband's brother* shall go (marg. or, *next kinsman*)
7. *My husband's brother* refuseth

2992 ## יָבַם [*yāh-vam'*].

* PIEL.—*Infinitive.* *

Deu 25: 7. *perform the duty of my husband's brother.*

PIEL.—*Imperative.*

Gen 38: 8. thy brother's wife, *and marry* her,

PIEL.—*Future.*

Deu 25: 5. *and perform the duty of an husband's brother unto her.*

2994 ## יְבֶמֶת [*y'veh'-meth*], f.

Deu 25: 7. to take *his brother's wife,* (marg. or, *next kinsman's*) then let *his brother's wife* go up to
9. Then shall *his brother's wife*
Ru. 1:15. *thy sister in law* is gone back
— thou after *thy sister in law.*

3001 ## יָבַשׁ [*yāh-vash'*].

* HIPHIL.—*Preterite.* *

2Sa.19: 5(6). *Thou hast shamed* this day
Isa. 30: 5. *They were* all *ashamed*
Jer. 2:26. so *is* the house of Israel *ashamed*
6:15. *Were they ashamed*
8: 9. The wise men *are ashamed,*
12. *Were they ashamed* when they
10:14. every founder *is confounded*
Jer. 46:24. The daughter of Egypt *shall be confounded*
48: 1. Kiriathaim *is confounded* (and) taken; Misgab *is confounded* and dismayed.
20. Moab *is confounded:*
50: 2. Bel *is confounded,*
— her idols *are confounded,*
51:17. every founder *is confounded*
Hos 2: 5(7). conceived them *hath done shamefully:*
Zec. 9: 5. her expectation *shall be ashamed;*
10: 5. *and* the riders on horses *shall be confounded.*

HIPHIL.—*Imperative.*

Joel 1:11. *Be ye ashamed,* O ye

יָבֵשׁ *yāh-vēhsh'*. 3001

* KAL.—*Preterite.* *

Gen 8:14. of the month, *was* the earth *dried.*
Jos. 9: 5. their provision *was dry* (and)
12. now, behold, *it is dry,* and it is
Job 14:11. flood decayeth *and drieth up:*
Ps. 22:15(16). My strength *is dried up* like a potsherd;
90: 6. it is cut down, *and withereth.*
129: 6. which *withereth* afore it groweth
Isa. 15: 6. for the hay *is withered away,*
19: 5. shall be wasted *and dried up.*
40: 7, 8. The grass *withereth,* the flower
Jer. 23:10. of the wilderness *are dried up,*
50:38. *and they shall be dried up:*
Lam. 4: 8. *it is withered,* it is become
Eze.17: 9. the fruit thereof, *that it wither?*
19:12. were broken *and withered;*
37:11. they say, Our bones *are dried,*
Hos. 9:16. their root *is dried up,* they shall
Joel 1:12. trees of the field, *are withered:*
20. the rivers of waters *are dried up,*
Am. 1: 2. *and* the top of Carmel *shall wither.*

KAL.—*Infinitive.*

Gen 8: 7. until the waters *were dried up*
Isa. 27:11. *When* the boughs thereof *are withered,*
Eze.17:10. shall it not *utterly* wither, (lit. *in withering* shall it not wither)
Zec.11:17. his arm shall be *clean* dried up,

KAL.—*Future.*

1K. 13: 4. *And* his hand,...*dried up,*
17: 7. *that* the brook *dried up,* because
Job 8:12. *it withereth* before any (other) herb.
12:15. the waters, *and they dry up:*
18:16. His roots *shall be dried up*
Ps.102: 4(5). My heart is smitten, *and withered*
11(12). *I am withered* like grass.
Isa. 19: 7. every thing sown...*shall wither,*
40:24. blow upon them, *and they shall wither,*
Jer. 12: 4. the herbs of every field *wither,*
Eze.17: 9. *it shall wither* in all the leaves of
10. *shall it* not utterly *wither,*
— *it shall wither* in the furrows where
Am. 4: 7. and the piece whereupon it rained not *withered.*
Jon. 4: 7. smote the gourd *that it withered.*
Zec.11:17. his arm *shall be* clean *dried up,*

* PIEL.—*Future.* *

Job 15:30. the flame *shall dry up* his branches,
Pro.17:22. a broken spirit *drieth* the bones.
Nah 1: 4. He rebuketh the sea, *and maketh it dry,*

* HIPHIL.—*Preterite.* *

Jos. 2:10. *dried up* the water of the Red sea
4:23. God *dried up* the waters of Jordan
— the Red sea, which *he dried up* from
5: 1. the Lord *had dried up* the waters of Jordar
Ps. 74:15. *thou driedst up* mighty rivers.
Jer. 51:36. *make* her springs *dry.*
Eze.17:24. I the Lord...*have dried up* the green tree,
19:12. the east wind *dried up* her fruit:
Joel 1:10. the new wine *is dried up,* the
12. The vine *is dried up,*
— joy *is withered away* from the sons of men.
17. broken down; for the corn *is withered.*
Zec.10:11. *and* all the deeps of the river *shall dry up,*

HIPHIL.—*Future.*

Isa. 42:15. and *dry up* all their herbs;
— rivers islands, and *I will dry up* the pools.
44:27. Be dry, and *I will dry up* thy rivers:

3002 יָבֵשׁ *yāh-vēhsh'*, adj.

Nu. 6: 3. nor eat moist grapes, *or dried.*
11: 6. now our soul (is) *dried away:* (there is)
Job 13:25. wilt thou pursue the *dry* stubble?
Isa. 56: 3. the eunuch say, Behold, I (am) a *dry* tree.
Eze. 17:24. have made the *dry* tree to flourish:
20:47(21:3). every green tree in thee, and every *dry* tree:
37: 2. the open valley; and, lo, (they were) very *dry.*
4. O ye *dry* bones, hear the word of the
Nah 1:10. shall be devoured as stubble fully *dry.*

3004 יַבָּשָׁה *yab-bāh-shāh'*, f.

Gen 1: 9. let *the dry* (land) appear: and it was so.
10. God called *the dry* (land) Earth;
Ex. 4: 9. pour (it) upon *the dry* (land): and the
14:16. children of Israel shall go *on dry* (ground)
22. midst of the sea *upon the dry* (ground):
29. children of Israel walked *upon dry* (land)
15:19. the children of Israel went *on dry* (land)
Jos. 4:22. Israel came over this Jordan *on dry land.*
Neh 9:11. the midst of the sea *on the dry land;*
Ps. 66: 6. He turned the sea *into dry* (land):
Isa. 44: 3. and floods upon *the dry ground:*
Jon. 1: 9. hath made the sea and *the dry* (land).
13. rowed hard to bring (it) to *the land;*
2:10(11). it vomited out Jonah upon *the dry* (land).

3006 יַבֶּשֶׁת *yab-beh'-sheth*, f.

Ex. 4: 9. shall become blood *upon the dry* (land).
Ps. 95: 5. *and* his hands formed *the dry* (land).

3007 יַבֶּשֶׁת [*yab-beh'-sheth*], Ch. f.

Dan 2:10. There is not a man upon *the earth* that can

3009 יָגַב [*yāh-gav'*].

* KAL.—*Participle.* Poel. *

2K. 25:12. (to be) vinedressers *and husbandmen.*
Jer. 52:16. for vinedressers *and for husbandmen.*

3010 יְגֵבִים *y'gēh-veem'*, m. pl.

Jer. 39:10. gave them vineyards *and fields* at the

3013 יָגָה [*yāh-gāh'*].

* NIPHAL.—*Participle.* *

Lam. 1: 4. her priests sigh, her virgins *are afflicted,*
Zep. 3:18. I will gather (them that are) *sorrowful*

* PIEL.—*Future.* *

Lam. 3:33. *nor grieve* the children of men.

* HIPHIL.—*Preterite.* *

Lam. 1: 5. for the Lord *hath afflicted her* for the
12. wherewith the Lord *hath afflicted* (me)
3:32. though *he cause grief,* yet will he

HIPHIL.—*Future.*

Job 19: 2. How long *will ye vex* my soul,

HIPHIL.—*Participle.*

Isa. 51:23. into the hand of *them that afflict thee:*

יָגָה [*yāh-gāh'*]. 3014

* HIPHIL.—*Preterite.* *

2Sa. 20:13. When *he was removed* out of the highway,

יָגוֹן *yāh-gōhn'*, m. 3015

Gen 42:38. my gray hairs *with sorrow* to the grave.
44:31. our father *with sorrow* to the grave.
Est. 9:22. turned unto them *from sorrow* to joy,
Ps. 13: 2(3). (having) *sorrow* in my heart daily?
31:10(11). For my life is spent *with grief,*
107:39. through oppression, affliction, *and sorrow.*
116: 3. upon me: I found trouble *and sorrow.*
Isa. 35:10. *sorrow* and sighing shall flee away.
51:11. *sorrow* and mourning shall flee away.
Jer. 8:18. I would comfort myself against *sorrow,*
20:18. out of the womb to see labour *and sorrow,*
31:13. make them rejoice *from their sorrow.*
45: 3. the Lord hath added *grief* to my sorrow;
Eze. 23:33. be filled with drunkenness *and sorrow,*

יָגוּר adj. or part. see יָגֻר part. See 3025

יָגִיעַ [*yāh-gee'ag̃*], adj. 3019

Job 3:17. there *the weary* be at rest. (marg. *wearied* (in) strength)

יְגִיעַ *y'gee'ag̃*, m. 3018

Gen 31:42. mine affliction and *the labour of* my hands,
Deu 28:33. fruit of thy land, and all *thy labours,* shall
Neh 5:13. man from his house, *and from his labour,*
Job 10: 3. shouldest despise *the work of* thine hands,
39:11. wilt thou leave *thy labour* to him?
16. *her labour* is in vain without fear;
Ps. 78:46. *and their labour* unto the locust.
109:11. let the strangers spoil *his labour.*
128: 2. thou shalt eat *the labour of* thine hands:
Isa. 45:14. *The labour of* Egypt, and merchandise
55: 2. *and your labour* for (that which) satisfieth not?
Jer. 3:24. shame hath devoured *the labour of*
20: 5. strength of this city, and all *the labours thereof,*
Eze. 23:29. shall take away all *thy labour,*
Hos. 12: 8(9). (in) all *my labours* they shall find
Hag. 1:11. upon all *the labour of* the hands.

יָגַע [*yāh-gag̃'*]. 3021

* KAL.—*Preterite.* *

Jos. 24:13. a land for which *ye did* not *labour,*
2Sa. 23:10. until his hand *was weary,* and his
Ps. 6: 6(7). *I am weary* with my groaning;
69: 3(4). *I am weary* of my crying: my
Isa. 43:22. *thou hast been weary* of me, O Israel.
47:12. wherein *thou hast laboured* from
15. with whom *thou hast laboured,*
49: 4. Then I said, *I have laboured* in vain,
57:10. *Thou art wearied* in the greatness
62: 8. thy wine, for the which *thou hast laboured:*
Jer. 45: 3. *I fainted* in my sighing,
Lam. 5: 5. *we labour,* (and) have no rest.

KAL.—*Future.*

Job 9:29. why then *labour I* in vain?
Pro. 23: 4. *Labour* not to be rich: cease from
Isa. 40:28. fainteth not, neither *is weary?*
30. the youths shall faint *and be weary,*
31. they shall run, and not *be weary;*
65:23. *They shall* not *labour* in vain, nor
Jer. 51:58. *and* the people *shall labour* in vain,
Hab 2:13. *that* the people *shall labour* in the

* PIEL.—*Future.* *

Jos. 7: 3. *make* not all the people *to labour* thither;
Ecc. 10:15. labour of the foolish *wearieth every one of them,*

* HIPHIL.—*Preterite.* *

Isa. 43:23. *wearied thee* with incense.
24. *thou hast wearied me* with thine iniquities.

Mal. 2:17. *Ye have wearied* the Lord with your words. Yet ye say, Wherein *have we wearied* (him)?

3022 **יְגַע** *yāh-gāhğ′*, m.

Job 20:18. *That which he laboured for*

3023 **יָגֵעַ** *yāh-gēh′ağ*, adj.

Deu25:18. when thou (wast) faint *and weary;*
2Sa.17: 2. while he (is) *weary* and weak handed,
Ecc. 1: 8. All things (are) *full of labour;* man

3024 **יְגִעָה** [*y′gee-ğāh′*], f.

Ecc.12:12. much study (is) *a weariness of* the flesh.

3026 **יְגַר** *y′gar*, Ch. m.

Gen31:47. And Laban called it *Jegar*-sahadutha: (marg. *The heap of* witness)

3025 **יָגֹר** [*yāh-gōhr′*].

* KAL.—*Preterite.* *

Deu 9:19. For *I was afraid* of the anger and hot
28:60. diseases of Egypt, which *thou wast afraid* of;
Job 3:25. that which *I was afraid* of is come
9:28. *I am afraid* of all my sorrows, I
Ps.119:39. Turn away my reproach which *I fear:*

KAL.—*Participle.*

Jer. 22:25. (of them) whose face thou *fearest,*
39:17. of the men of whom thou (art) *afraid.*

3027 **יָד** *yāhd*, com.

Gen 3:22. now, lest he put forth *his hand,* and
4:11. thy brother's blood *from thy hand;*
5:29. toil of *our hands,*
8: 9. then he put forth *his hand,* and took
9: 2. fishes of the sea; *into your hand* are they
5. *at the hand of* every beast will I require it, *and at the hand of* man; *at the hand of* every man's
14:20. delivered thine enemies *into thy hand.*
22. I have lift up *mine hand* unto
16: 6. Behold, thy maid (is) *in thy hand;*
9. submit thyself under *her hands.*
12. *his hand* (will be) against every man, *and* every man's *hand* against him;
19:10. the men put forth *their hand,* and
16. the men laid hold *upon his hand, and upon the hand of* his wife, *and upon the hand of* his two daughters;
21:18. hold him in *thine hand;* for I
30. lambs shalt thou take *of my hand,*
22: 6. he took the fire *in his hand,* and a knife;
10. Abraham stretched forth *his hand,*
12. Lay not *thine hand* upon the lad,
24: 2. Put, I pray thee, *thy hand* under my
9. the servant put *his hand* under
10. goods of his master (were) *in his hand:*
18. down her pitcher upon *her hand,*
22. two bracelets for *her hands*
30. bracelets upon his sister's *hands,*
47. the bracelets upon *her hands.*
25:26. *and his hand* took hold on Esau's heel;
27:16. she put the skins of the kids of the goats upon *his hands,*
17. *into the hand of* her son Jacob.
22. *but the hands* (are) *the hands of* Esau.
23. *his hands* were hairy, *as* his brother Esau's *hands:*
30:35. gave (them) *into the hand of* his sons.
31:29. It is in the power of *my hand* to do
39. *of my hand* didst thou require it,
32:11(12). Deliver me, I pray thee, *from the hand of* my brother, *from the hand of* Esau:

Gen32:13(14). that which came *to his hand*
16(17). delivered (them) *into the hand of*
33:10. receive my present *at my hand:*
19. *at the hand of* the children of Hamor,
34:21. (it is) large *enough* (lit. large of *hands,* or *spaces,* or *sides*)
35: 4. strange gods which (were) *in their hand,*
37:21. delivered him *out of their hands;*
22. *and* lay no *hand* upon him; that he might rid him *out of their hands,*
27. *and* let not *our hand* be upon him;
38:18. thy staff that (is) *in thine hand.*
20. sent the kid *by the hand of* his friend the Adullamite, to receive (his) pledge *from* the woman's *hand:*
28. put out (his) *hand:* and the midwife took and bound upon *his hand* a
29. as he drew back *his hand,* that,
30. had the scarlet thread upon *his hand:*
39: 1. bought him *of the hands of* the
3. that he did to prosper *in his hand.*
4. all (that) he had he put *into his hand.*
6. left all that he had *in* Joseph's *hand;*
8. committed all that he hath *to my hand;*
12. left his garment *in her hand,*
13. he had left his garment *in her hand,*
22. committed *to* Joseph's *hand* all the
23. any thing (that was) *under his hand;*
40:11. Pharaoh's cup (was) *in my hand:*
13. deliver Pharaoh's cup *into his hand,*
41:35. lay up corn under *the hand of*
42. took off his ring from *his hand,* and put it upon Joseph's *hand,* and arrayed
44. shall no man lift up *his hand*
42:37. deliver him into *my hand,* and I will
43: 9. *of my hand* shalt thou require him:
12. take double money *in your hand;*
— carry (it) again *in your hand;*
15. they took double money *in their hand,*
21. have brought it again *in our hand.*
22. money have we brought down *in our hands*
26. present which (was) *in their hand*
34. five *times* so much as any of their's.
44:16. *with whom* the cup is found. (lit. who... *in his hand*)
17. *in* whose *hand* the cup is found, (lit. *id.*)
46: 4. Joseph shall put *his hand* upon thine eyes.
47:24. four *parts* shall be your own,
29. put, I pray thee, *thy hand* under my
48:14. guiding *his hands* wittingly;
17. laid his right *hand* upon the head
— he held up his father's *hand,* to
22. which I took *out of the hand of* the
49: 8. *thy hand* (shall be) in the neck of thine
24. the arms of *his hands* were made strong *by the hands of* the mighty (God)
Ex. 2: 5. walked along by the river's *side;*
19. delivered us *out of the hand of* the
3: 8. deliver them *out of the hand of* the
19. let you go, no, not *by a* mighty *hand.*
20. I will stretch out *my hand,* and smite
4: 2. What (is) that *in thine hand?* And he
4. Put forth *thine hand,* and take it by the tail. And he put forth *his hand,* and
6. Put now *thine hand* into thy bosom. And he put *his hand* into his bosom:
— behold, *his hand* (was) leprous as snow.
7. Put *thine hand* into thy bosom again. And he put *his hand* into his bosom
13. send, I pray thee, *by the hand* (of him)
17. shalt take this rod *in thine hand,*
20. took the rod of God *in his hand.*
21. which I have put *in thine hand*
5:21. to put a sword *in their hand* to slay us.
6: 1. for *with a* strong *hand* shall he let them go, *and with a* strong *hand* shall he drive
8. which I did swear (marg. lift up *my hand*)
7: 4. that I may lay *my hand* upon
5. when I stretch forth *mine hand*
15. to a serpent shalt thou take *in thine hand.*
17. with the rod that (is) *in mine hand*
19. stretch out *thine hand* upon the
8: 5(1). Stretch forth *thine hand* with thy rod
6(2), 17(13). Aaron stretched out *his hand*
9: 3. *the hand of* the Lord is upon thy cattle
15. now I will stretch out *my hand,*
22. Stretch forth *thine hand* toward heaven,

Ex. 9:35. the Lord had spoken *by* Moses. (marg. *by the hand of* Moses)
10:12. Stretch out *thine hand* over the land
21. Stretch out *thine hand* toward heaven,
22. Moses stretched forth *his hand* toward
25. give *us* (marg. give *into our hands*) also sacrifices and burnt offerings,
12:11. your staff *in your hand;* and ye
13: 3. for by strength of *hand* the Lord brought
9. a sign unto thee upon *thine hand,*
— for *with a* strong *hand* hath the Lord
14, 16. By strength of *hand* the Lord brought
16. for a token upon *thine hand,*
14: 8. children of Israel went out *with an* high *hand.*
16, 26. stretch out *thine hand* over the sea,
21. Moses stretched out *his hand* over the
27. Moses stretched forth *his hand* over
30. saved Israel that day *out of the hand of*
31. Israel saw *that* great *work* which the (marg. *hand*)
15: 9. *my hand* shall destroy them.
17. (which) *thy hands* have established.
20. took a timbrel *in her hand;*
16: 3. we had died *by the hand of* the Lord
17: 5. thy rod,...take *in thine hand,* and go.
9. with the rod of God *in mine hand.*
11. Moses held up *his hand,* that Israel prevailed: and when he let down *his hand,*
12. *But* Moses' *hands* (were) heavy;
— Hur stayed up *his hands,*
— *his hands* were steady
16. the Lord hath sworn (marg. *the hand* upon the throne of the Lord)
18: 9. delivered *out of the hand of* the Egyptians.
10. delivered you *out of the hand of* the Egyptians, *and out of the hand of* Pharaoh,
— from under *the hand of* the Egyptians.
19:13. There shall not *an hand* touch it,
21:13. God deliver (him) *into his hand;*
16. selleth him, or if he be found *in his hand,*
20. and he die under *his hand;*
24. tooth for tooth, *hand* for *hand,* foot
22: 4(3). If the theft be certainly found *in his hand*
8(7). have put *his hand* unto his neighbour's
11(10). hath not put *his hand* unto his
23: 1. put not *thine hand* with the wicked
31. inhabitants of the land *into your hand;*
24:11. upon the nobles...he laid not *his hand:*
26:17. Two *tenons* (shall there be) in one board, (marg. *hands*)
19. one board for *his* two *tenons,* and two sockets under another board for *his* two *tenons.*
28:41. consecrate)(them, (marg. fill *their hand*)
29: 9. and thou shalt consecrate)(Aaron and)(his sons. (lit. fill *the hand of* Aaron *and the hand of* his sons)
10, 15, 19. his sons shall put *their hands*
20. upon the thumb of *their* right *hand,*
25. thou shalt receive them *of their hands,*
29. to be consecrated)((lit. to fill *their hand*)
33. to consecrate)((and) to sanctify them: (lit. *id.*)
35. seven days shalt thou consecrate)(them. (lit. *id.*)
30:19. his sons shall wash *their hands*
21. they shall wash *their hands*
32: 4. he received (them) *at their hand,*
11. with great power, *and with a* mighty *hand?*
15. the two tables of the testimony (were) *in his hand:*
19. he cast the tables *out of his hands,*
29. Consecrate)(yourselves (marg. Fill *your hands*)
34: 4. took *in his hand* the two tables of stone.
29. tables of testimony *in* Moses' *hand,*
35:25. did spin *with their hands,*
29. to be made *by the hand of* Moses.
36:22. One board had two *tenons,*
24. one board for *his* two *tenons,* and two sockets under another board for *his* two *tenons.*
38:21. *by the hand of* Ithamar, son to Aaron
40:31. washed *their hands*

Lev. 1: 4. he shall put *his hand* upon the head
3: 2. he shall lay *his hand* upon the head
8. he shall lay *his hand* upon the head
13. he shall lay *his hand* upon the head
4: 4. shall lay *his hand* upon the bullock's
15. lay *their hands* upon the head
24. lay *his hand* upon the head
29, 33. he shall lay *his hand* upon the head
5: 7. *he* be not able (marg. *his hand* cannot reach) to bring a lamb,
11. he be not able (lit. *his hand* reach not)
6: 2(5:21). or in fellowship, (marg. putting of *the hand*)
7:30. *His own hands* shall bring the offerings
8:14, 18, 22. laid *their hands* upon the head
23. upon the thumb of *his* right *hand,*
24. upon the thumbs of *their* right *hands,*
33. seven days shall he consecrate)(*you.* (lit. fill *your hand*)
36. the Lord commanded *by the hand of*
9:22. Aaron lifted up *his hand*
10:11. spoken unto them *by the hand of* Moses.
12: 8. she be not able (lit. *her hand* find) to bring a lamb, then she
14:14, 17, 25, 28. upon the thumb of *his* right *hand,*
21. he (be) poor, and cannot get (marg. *his hand* reach not)
22, 31. such as he is able to get; (lit. *his hand* can reach)
30. such as he can get; (lit. *his hand* find)
32. *whose hand* is not able to get (that) (lit. who *his hand*)
15:11. *and* hath not rinsed *his hands*
16:21. Aaron shall lay both *his hands*
— send (him) away *by the hand of* a fit man
32. whom he shall consecrate)((marg. fill *his hand*) to minister
21:10. that is consecrated)((lit. filled *his hand*) to put on the garments,
19. brokenfooted, or broken*handed,*
22:25. *Neither from a* stranger's *hand* shall
24:14. lay *their hands* upon his head,
25:14. buyest (ought) *of* thy neighbour's *hand,*
26. and *himself* be able (marg. *his hand* hath attained) to redeem
28. if *he* be not able (lit. *his hand* find)
— shall remain *in the hand of* him
35. fallen in decay with thee; (marg. *his hand* faileth)
47. if a sojourner or stranger wax rich (lit. *the hand of* a stranger gain)
49. if he be able, (lit. *his hand* find)
26:25. ye shall be delivered *into the hand of* the
46. *by the hand of* Moses.
27: 8. according to his ability (lit. as *the hand of* him, &c. can attain)

Nu. 2:17. every man in *his place*
3: 3. whom he consecrated)((marg. *whose hand* he filled)
4:28, 33. *under the hand of* Ithamar the son of
37. the commandment of the Lord *by the hand of* Moses.
45. word of the Lord *by the hand of* Moses.
49. they were numbered *by the hand of*
5:18. *and* the priest shall have *in his hand* the
25. the priest shall take the jealousy offering *out of* the woman's *hand,*
6:21. beside (that) that *his hand* shall get:
7: 8. *under the hand of* Ithamar
8:10. put *their hands* upon the Levites:
12. the Levites shall lay *their hands*
9:23 & 10:13. the commandment of the Lord *by the hand of* Moses.
11:23. Is the Lord's *hand* waxed short?
13:29. by *the coast of* Jordan.
14:30. I sware (marg. lifted up *my hand*)
15:23. *by the hand of* Moses,
30. the soul that doeth (ought) *presumptuously,* (lit. *with an* high *hand*)
16:40(17:5). as the Lord said to him *by the hand of* Moses.
20:11. Moses lifted up *his hand,*
20. *and with a* strong *hand.*
21: 2. deliver this people *into my hand,*
26. taken all his land *out of his hand,*
34. I have delivered him *into thy hand,*

Nu. 22: 7. the rewards of divination *in their hand;*
23. 31. his sword drawn *in his hand:*
29. I would there were a sword *in mine hand,*
24: 24. ships (shall come) *from the coast of*
25: 7. took a javelin *in his hand;*
27: 18. lay *thine hand* upon him;
23. he laid *his hands* upon him,
— *by the hand of* Moses.
31: 6. the trumpets to blow *in his hand.*
49. which (are) *under our charge,* (marg. *hand*)
33: 1. *under the hand of* Moses and Aaron.
3. the children of Israel went out *with an* high *hand*
34: 3. along by *the coast of* Edom,
35: 17. if he smite him with *throwing* a stone, (marg. a stone of *the hand*)
18. (if) he smite him with an *hand* weapon
21. in enmity smite him *with his hand,*
25. *out of the hand of* the revenger of blood,
36: 13. *by the hand of* Moses
Deu 1: 25. they took of the fruit of the land *in their hands,*
27. deliver us *into the hand of* the Amorites,
2: 7. the works of *thy hand:*
15. *the hand of* the Lord was against them,
24. I have given *into thine hand*
30. deliver him *into thy hand,*
37. unto any *place of* the river
3: 2. and his land, *into thy hand;*
3. God delivered *into our hands* Og also,
8. *out of the hand of* the two kings
24. *thy* mighty *hand:*
4: 28. the work of men's *hands,*
34. *and by a* mighty *hand,*
5: 15. *through a* mighty *hand*
6: 8. a sign upon *thine hand,*
21 & 7: 8. *with a* mighty *hand:*
7: 8. *from the hand of* Pharaoh
19. *and the* mighty *hand,* and the stretched out arm,
24. shall deliver their kings *into thine hand,*
8: 17. the might of *mine hand*
9: 15. of the covenant (were) in *my* two *hands.*
17. cast them out of *my* two *hands,*
26. *with a* mighty *hand.*
10: 3. the two tables *in mine hand.*
11: 2. *his* mighty *hand,* and his stretched out arm,
18. a sign upon *your hand,*
12: 6. heave offerings of *your hand,*
7. all that ye put *your hand* unto,
11. the heave offering of *your hand,*
17. heave offering of *thine hand:*
18. in all that thou puttest *thine hands* unto.
13: 9(10). *thine hand* shall be first
—(—). *and* afterwards *the hand of* all the
17(18). the cursed thing *to thine hand:*
14: 25. bind up the money *in thine hand,*
29. the work of *thine hand*
15: 2. Every creditor (marg. master of the lending of *his hand*) that lendeth
3. *thine hand* shall release;
7. nor shut *thine hand*
8, 11. thou shalt open *thine hand*
10. all that thou puttest *thine hand* unto.
16: 10. a freewill offering of *thine hand,*
15. all the works of *thine hands,*
17. Every man (shall give) as he is able, (marg. according to the gift of *his hand*)
17: 7. *The hands of* the witnesses
— *and* afterward *the hands of* all the people.
19: 5. *his hand* fetcheth a stroke
12. *into the hand of* the avenger
21. *hand for hand,* foot for foot.
20: 13. delivered it *into thine hands,*
21: 6. shall wash *their hands*
7. *Our hands* have not shed this blood,
10. delivered them *into thine hands,*
23: 12(13). Thou shalt have *a place also*
20(21). all that thou settest *thine hand* to
25(26). pluck the ears *with thine hand;*
24: 1. give (it) *in her hand,*
3. giveth (it) *in her hand,*
19. all the work of *thine hands.*
25: 11. *out of the hand of* him
— putteth forth *her hand,*
26: 4. take the basket *out of thine hand,*

Deu 26: 8. *with a* mighty *hand,*
27: 15. the work of *the hands of*
28: 8. all that thou settest *thine hand* unto;
12. bless all the work of *thine hand:*
20. all that thou settest *thine hand* unto
32. (there shall be) no might in *thine hand.*
30: 9. every work of *thine hand,*
31: 29. the work of *your hands.*
32: 27. *Our hand* (is) high,
36. (their) *power* is gone, (marg. *hand*)
39. deliver out *of my hand.*
40. I lift up *my hand* to heaven,
41. *mine hand* take hold on judgment;
33: 3. all his saints (are) *in thy hand:*
7. let *his hands* be sufficient for him;
11. accept the work of *his hands:*
34: 9. Moses had laid *his hands* upon him:
12. in all *that* mighty *hand,*
Jos. 2: 19. if (any) *hand* be upon him.
24. the Lord hath delivered *into our hands*
4: 24. *the hand of* the Lord,
5: 13. his sword drawn *in his hand:*
6: 2. I have given *into thine hand* Jericho,
7: 7. *into the hand of* the Amorites,
8: 1. I have given *into thy hand*
7. deliver it *into your hand.*
18. the spear that (is) *in thy hand* toward Ai; for I will give it *into thine hand.*
— the spear that (he had) *in his hand*
19. he had stretched out *his hand:*
20. they had no *power* to flee (marg. *hand*)
26. Joshua drew not *his hand* back,
9: 11. Take victuals *with you* for the journey, (marg. *in your hand*)
25. we (are) *in thine hand:*
26. *out of the hand of* the children of Israel,
10: 6. Slack not *thy hand* from thy servants;
8. delivered them *into thine hand;*
19. delivered them *into your hand.*
30. the king thereof, *into the hand of* Israel;
32. Lachish *into the hand of* Israel,
11: 8. the Lord delivered them *into the hand of* Israel,
14: 2. *by the hand of* Moses,
15: 46. all that (lay) *near* (marg. *by the place of*) Ashdod,
20: 2. *by the hand of* Moses:
5. not deliver the slayer up *into his hand;*
9. *by the hand of* the avenger
21: 2, 8. *by the hand of* Moses
44(42). their enemies *into their hand.*
22: 9. *by the hand of* Moses.
31. *out of the hand of* the Lord.
24: 8. I gave them *into your hand.*
10. I delivered you *out of his hand.*
11. I delivered them *into your hand.*
Jud. 1: 2. delivered the land *into his hand.*
4. the Perrizzites *into their hand:*
6. cut off his thumbs (lit. the thumbs of *his hands*)
7. having their thumbs (marg. the thumbs of *their hands*)
35. *the hand of* the house of Joseph
2: 14. he delivered them *into the hands of* spoilers that spoiled them, and he sold them *into the hands of* their enemies
15. *the hand of* the Lord was against them
16. *out of the hand of* those that spoiled them.
18. *out of the hand of* their enemies
23. *into the hand of* Joshua.
3: 4. *by the hand of* Moses.
8. *into the hand of* Chushan-rishathaim
10. *into his hand;* and *his hand* prevailed against Chushan-rishathaim.
15. a man left*handed* (marg. shut of his right *hand*): and *by him* (lit. *in his hand*) the children of Israel
21. Ehud put forth his left *hand,*
28. the Moabites *into your hand.*
30. under *the hand of* Israel.
4: 2. the Lord sold them *into the hand of*
7. I will deliver him *into thine hand.*
9. *into the hand of* a woman.
14. the Lord hath delivered Sisera *into thine hand:*
21. took an hammer *in her hand,*
24. *the hand of* the children of Israel

Jud. 5:26. She put *her hand* to the nail,
6: 1. the Lord delivered them *into the hand of* Midian
2. *the hand of* Midian prevailed
9. *out of the hand of* the Egyptians, *and out of the hand of* all that oppressed you,
21. the staff that (was) *in his hand,*
36. If thou wilt save Israel *by mine hand,*
37. thou wilt save Israel *by mine hand,*
7: 2. give the Midianites *into their hands,*
— *Mine own hand* hath saved me.
6. (putting) *their hand* to their mouth,
7. deliver the Midianites *into thine hand:*
8. the people took victuals *in their hand,*
9. I have delivered it *into thine hand.*
11. afterward shall *thine hands* be strengthened
14. *into his hand* hath God delivered Midian,
15. the Lord hath delivered *into your hand*
16. he put a trumpet *in* every man's *hand,*
19. brake the pitchers that (were) *in their hands.*
20. held the lamps *in* their left *hands,* and the trumpets *in* their right *hands*
8: 3. God hath delivered *into your hands*
6, 15. Zebah and Zalmunna now *in thine hand,*
7. and Zalmunna *into mine hand,*
22. thou hast delivered us *from the hand of*
34. *out of the hands of* all their enemies
9:16. according to the deserving of *his hands;*
17. delivered you *out of the hand of* Midian:
24. the men of Shechem, which aided *him* (marg. strengthened *his hands*)
29. this people were *under my hand!*
33. as *thou* shalt find occasion. (marg. as *thine hand* shall find)
48. Abimelech took an ax *in his hand,*
10: 7. *into the hands of* the Philistines, *and into the hands of* the children of Ammon.
12. I delivered you *out of their hand.*
11:21. *into the hand of* Israel,
26. by *the coasts of* Arnon,
30. deliver the children of Ammon *into mine hands,*
32. the Lord delivered them *into his hands.*
12: 2. ye delivered me not *out of their hands.*
3. the Lord delivered them *into my hand:*
13: 1. the Lord delivered them *into the hand of*
5. *out of the hand of* the Philistines.
23. a meat offering *at our hands,*
14: 6. (he had) nothing *in his hand:*
15:12. deliver thee *into the hand of* the Philistines.
13. deliver thee *into their hand:*
14. his bands loosed from off *his hands.*
15. put forth *his hand,* and took it,
17. he cast away the jawbone *out of his hand,*
18. *into the hand of* thy servant: and now shall I...fall *into the hand of* the uncircumcised?
16:18. brought money *in their hand.*
23. delivered Samson our enemy *into our hand.*
24. hath delivered *into our hands* our enemy,
26. the lad that held him *by the hand,*
17: 3. *from my hand* for my son,
5. consecrated (marg. filled *the hand*)
12. And Micah consecrated (lit. filled *the hand of*)
18:10. a large land (lit. large of *hands*): for God hath given it *into your hands;*
19. lay *thine hand* upon thy mouth,
19:27. *and her hands* (were) upon the
20:16. (there were) seven hundred chosen men left*handed;*
28. I will deliver them *into thine hand.*
Ru. 1:13. *the hand of* the Lord is gone out against me.
4: 5. thou buyest the field *of the hand of* Naomi,
9. *of the hand of* Naomi.
1 Sa. 2:13. a fleshhook of three teeth *in his hand;*
4: 8. *out of the hand of* these mighty Gods?
13. a seat by *the* wayside
18. by *the side of* the gate,
5: 4. both the palms of *his hands*
6. *the hand of* the Lord was heavy upon them
7. *his hand* is sore upon us,
9. *the hand of* the Lord was against the city
11. *the hand of* God was very heavy there.
6: 3. why *his hand* is not removed

1 Sa. 6: 5. peradventure he will lighten *his hand*
9. we shall know that (it is) not *his hand*
7: 3. he will deliver you *out of the hand of* the
8. he will save us *out of the hand of* the
13. *the hand of* the Lord was against the
14. *out of the hands of* the Philistines.
9: 8. *I* have here *at hand* (marg. there is found *in my hand*)
16. *out of the hand of* the Philistines:
10: 4. thou shalt receive *of their hands.*
7. as occasion serve *thee;* (marg. as *thine hand* shall find)
18. *out of the hand of* the Egyptians, *and out of the hand of* all kingdoms,
11: 7. *by the hands of* messengers,
12: 3. *or of* whose *hand* have I received (any) bribe
4. taken ought *of* any man's *hand.*
5. ye have not found ought *in my hand.*
9. he sold them *into the hand of* Sisera,
— *and into the hand of* the Philistines, *and into the hand of* the king of Moab,
10. deliver us *out of the hand of* our enemies,
11. delivered you *out of the hand of* your enemies
15. then shall *the hand of* the Lord be against you,
13:22. *in the hand of* any of the people
14:10. the Lord hath delivered them *into our hand:*
12. the Lord hath delivered them *into the hand of* Israel.
13. Jonathan climbed up upon *his hands*
19. Withdraw *thine hand.*
26. no man put *his hand* to his mouth:
27. the rod that (was) *in his hand,*
— and put *his hand* to his mouth;
34. the people brought every man his ox *with him* (marg. *in his hand*)
37. wilt thou deliver them *into the hand of* Israel?
43. the rod that (was) *in mine hand,*
48. *out of the hands of* them that spoiled them.
15:12. behold, he set him up *a place,*
16: 2. Take an heifer *with thee,* (marg. *in thine hand*)
16. he shall play *with his hand,*
20. sent (them) *by* David (lit. *by the hand of* David)
23. David took an harp, and played *with his hand:*
17:22. David left his carriage in *the hand of* the keeper
37. delivered me *out of the paw of* the lion, *and out of the paw of* the bear, he will deliver me *out of the hand of* this Philistine.
40. took his staff *in his hand,*
— his sling (was) *in his hand:*
46. the Lord deliver thee *into mine hand;*
47. he will give you *into our hands.*
49. David put *his hand* in his bag,
50. (there was) no sword *in the hand of* David.
57. the head of the Philistine *in his hand.*
18:10. David played *with his hand,*
— (there was) a javelin *in* Saul's *hand.*
17. Let not *mine hand* be upon him, but let *the hand of* the Philistines be upon him.
21. that *the hand of* the Philistines may be against him.
25. *by the hand of* the Philistines.
19: 3. I will go out and stand *beside* my father
9. with his javelin *in his hand:* and David played *with* (his) *hand.*
20:16. *at the hand of* David's enemies.
21: 3(4). what is under *thine hand?* give (me) five (loaves of) bread *in mine hand,*
4(5). (There is) no common bread under *mine hand,*
8(9). is there not here under *thine hand*
—(–). my weapons *with me,* (lit. *in my hand*)
13(14). feigned himself mad *in their hands,*
22: 6. having his spear *in his hand,*
17. *their hand* also (is) with David,
— would not put forth *their hand*
23: 4. I will deliver the Philistines *into thine hand.*
6. he came down (with) an ephod *in his hand.*
7. God hath delivered him *into mine hand*

1Sa.23:11. Will the men of Keilah deliver me up *into his hand?*
12. me and my men *into the hand of* Saul?
14. God delivered him not *into his hand.*
16. strengthened *his hand* in God.
17. *the hand of* Saul my father shall not find
20. deliver him *into* the king's *hand.*
24: 4(5). deliver thine enemy *into thine hand,*
6(7). to stretch forth *mine hand* against him,
10(11). the Lord had delivered thee to day *into mine hand*
—(—). I will not put forth *mine hand*
11(12). see the skirt of thy robe *in my hand:*
—(—). nor transgression *in mine hand,*
12(13), 13(14). *but mine hand* shall not be upon thee.
15(16). deliver me *out of thine hand.*
18(19). the Lord had delivered me *into thine hand,*
20(21). shall be established *in thine hand.*
25: 8. whatsoever cometh to *thine hand*
26. avenging thyself with *thine own hand,*
33. avenging myself with *mine own hand.*
35. David received *of her hand*
39. the cause of my reproach *from the hand of*
26: 8. delivered thine enemy *into thine hand*
9. who can stretch forth *his hand*
11. The Lord forbid that I should stretch forth *mine hand*
18. what evil (is) *in mine hand?*
23. delivered thee *into* (my) *hand* to day, but I would not stretch forth *mine hand*
27: 1. now perish one day *by the hand of* Saul:
— so shall I escape *out of his hand.*
28:15. neither *by* prophets, (marg. *by the hand of* prophets)
17. as he spake *by me* (marg. *by mine hand*): for the Lord hath rent the kingdom *out of thine hand,*
19, 19. *into the hand of* the Philistines:
30:15. deliver me *into the hands of* my master,
23. delivered the company...*into our hand.*
2Sa. 1:14. wast thou not afraid to stretch forth *thine hand*
2: 7. now let *your hands* be strengthened,
3: 8. have not delivered thee *into the hand of* David,
12. behold, *my hand* (shall be) with thee,
18. *By the hand of* my servant David I will save my people Israel *out of the hand of* the Philistines, *and out of the hand of* all their enemies.
34. *Thy hands* (were) not bound,
4: 1. *his hands* were feeble,
11. require his blood *of your hand,*
12. cut off *their hands*
5:19. wilt thou deliver them *into mine hand?*
— doubtless deliver the Philistines *into thine hand.*
8: 1. *out of the hand of* the Philistines.
3. he went to recover *his border*
10. *And* (Joram) brought *with him* vessels of
10: 2. sent to comfort him *by the hand of* his servants
10. he delivered *into the hand of* Abishai
11:14. sent (it) *by the hand of* Uriah.
12: 7. I delivered thee *out of the hand of* Saul;
25. he sent *by the hand of* Nathan the prophet;
13: 5. eat (it) *at her hand.*
6. that I may eat *at her hand.*
10. that I may eat *of thine hand.*
19. laid *her hand* on her head, and went on
14:19. (Is not) *the hand of* Joab with thee
30. Joab's field is near *mine,* (lit. *my hand,* marg. *my place*)
15: 2. stood *beside* the way of the gate:
5. he put forth *his hand,* and took him,
18. servants passed on *beside him;* (lit. at *his hand*)
36. *by them* ye shall send unto me
16: 8. *into the hand of* Absalom thy son:
21. *the hands of* all that (are) with thee
17: 2. he (is) weary and weak *handed,* (lit. weak of *hands*)
18: 2. *under the hand of* Joab, and a third part *under the hand of* Abishai...and a third part *under the hand of* Ittai

2Sa.18: 4. the king stood by *the* gate *side,*
12. (yet) would I not put forth *mine hand*
18. it is called unto this day, Absalom's *place.*
19. avenged him (marg. judged him *from the hand*) *of* his enemies.
28. that lifted up *their hand* against my lord
31. avenged thee (lit. judged thee *from the hand*) this day *of* all them that rose up
19:43(44). We have ten *parts* in the king,
20: 9. Joab took Amasa by the beard with *the* right *hand*
10. the sword that (was) *in* Joab's *hand:*
21. hath lifted up *his hand* against the king,
21: 9. he delivered them *into the hands of* the
20. had on *every hand* six fingers, (lit. fingers on *his hands*)
22. fell *by the hand of* David, *and by the hand* of his servants.
22:21. the cleanness of *my hands*
35. He teacheth *my hands* to war;
23: 6. they cannot be taken *with hands:*
10. smote the Philistines until *his hand* was weary, and *his hand*
21. *and* the Egyptian had a spear *in his hand;*
— plucked the spear *out of* the Egyptian's *hand,*
24:14. let us fall now *into the hand of* the Lord; for his mercies (are) great: *and* let me not fall *into the hand of* man.
16. when the angel stretched out *his hand*
— It is enough: stay now *thine hand.*
17. let *thine hand,* I pray thee, be against me,
1K. 2:25. king Solomon sent *by the hand of*
46. the kingdom was established *in the hand of* Solomon.
7:32. *and the axletrees of* the wheels
33. *their axletrees,* and their naves,
35. on the top of the base *the ledges thereof*
36. on the plates of *the ledges thereof,*
8:15. *and* hath *with his hand* fulfilled (it),
24. *and* hast fulfilled (it) *with thine hand,*
42. of *thy* strong *hand,*
53. *by the hand of* Moses thy servant,
56. *by the hand of* Moses his servant.
10:13. Solomon gave her of his royal bounty. (marg. gave her *according to the hand of* king Solomon)
19. *and* (there were) *stays* on either side on the (marg. *hands*)
— two lions stood beside *the stays.*
29. bring (them) out *by their means.* (marg. *hand*)
11:12. I will rend it *out of the hand of* thy son.
26. he lifted up (his) *hand* against the king.
27. the cause that he lifted up (his) *hand*
31. I will rend the kingdom *out of the hand of*
34. I will not take the whole kingdom *out of his hand:*
35. I will take the kingdom *out of* his son's *hand,*
12:15. the Lord spake *by* (lit. *by the hand of*) Ahijah
13: 4. he put forth *his hand* from the altar,
— *his hand,* which he put forth
6. that *my hand* may be restored
— the king's *hand* was restored him again,
33. whosoever would, he consecrated *him,* (marg. he filled *his hand*)
14: 3. take *with thee* ten loaves, (marg. *in thine hand*)
18. *by the hand of* his servant Ahijah
27. *the hands of* the chief of the guard,
15:18. delivered them *into the hand of* his servants:
29. spake *by* (lit. *by the hand of*) his servant Ahijah
16: 7. *by the hand of* the prophet Jehu
— the work of *his hands,*
12. he spake against Baasha *by* (marg. *by the hand of*) Jehu,
34. he spake *by* (lit. *by the hand of*) Joshua
17:11. a morsel of bread *in thine hand.*
16. he spake *by* (marg. *by the hand of*) Elijah.
18: 9. deliver thy servant *into the hand of* Ahab,
46. *And the hand of* the Lord was on Elijah;
20: 6. they shall put (it) *in their hand,*
13. I will deliver it *into thine hand*
28. deliver all this great multitude *into thine hand,*

1K. 20:42. thou hast let go *out of* (thy) *hand*
22: 3. take it not *out of the hand of* the king
6. deliver (it) *into the hand of* the king.
12. the Lord shall deliver (it) *into* the king's *hand.*
15. deliver (it) *into the hand of* the king.
34. Turn *thine hand*, and carry me out of the
2K. 3:10, 13. deliver them *into the hand of* Moab!
11. *the hands of* Elijah.
15. *the hand of* the Lord came upon him.
18. deliver the Moabites also *into your hand.*
4:29. take my staff *in thine hand,*
5: 5. took *with him* ten talents of silver, (marg. *in his hand*)
11. strike *his hand* over the place, and recover
18. he leaneth on *my hand,*
20. in not receiving *at his hands* that which
24. he took (them) *from their hand,*
6: 7. he put out *his hand*, and took it.
7: 2. a lord on *whose hand* the king leaned
17. the lord on *whose hand* he leaned
8: 8. Take a present *in thine hand,*
9. took a present *with him*, (marg. *in his hand*)
20, 22. under *the hand of* Judah,
9: 1. take this box of oil *in thine hand,*
7. *at the hand of* Jezebel.
23. Joram turned *his hands*, and fled,
24. Jehu drew a bow with his full strength, (marg. filled *his hand* with a bow)
35. the palms of (her) *hands.*
36 & 10:10. *by* his servant Elijah (marg. *by the hand of*)
10:15. If it be, give (me) *thine hand.* And he gave (him) *his hand;*
24. the men whom I have brought into *your hands*
11: 7. two *parts* of all you that go forth (marg. *hands*, or, *companies*)
8, 11. his weapons *in his hand:*
16. they laid *hands* on her;
12:11(12). *the hands of* them that did the work,
15(16). into *whose hand* they delivered
13: 3. *into the hand of* Hazael king of Syria, *and into the hand of* Ben-hadad
5. under *the hand of* the Syrians:
16. Put *thine hand* upon the bow. And he put *his hand* (upon it): and Elisha put *his hands* upon the king's *hands.*
25. took again *out of the hand of* Ben-hadad... the cities, which he had taken *out of the hand of* Jehoahaz
14: 5. the kingdom was confirmed *in his hand,*
25. *by the hand of* his servant Jonah,
27. *by the hand of* Jeroboam
15:19. that *his hand* might be with him to confirm the kingdom *in his hand.*
17: 7. from under *the hand of* Pharaoh
13. *by* (marg. *by the hand of*) all the prophets,
— *by* (lit. *id.*) my servants the prophets.
20. delivered them *into the hand of* spoilers,
23. *by* (lit. *by the hand of*) all his servants the prophets.
39. *out of the hand of* all your enemies.
18:29. to deliver you *out of his hand:*
30. delivered *into the hand of* the king
33. *out of the hand of* the king of Assyria?
34. have they delivered Samaria *out of mine hand?*
35. delivered their country *out of mine hand,*
— deliver Jerusalem *out of mine hand?*
19:10. delivered *into the hand of* the king
14. *of the hand of* the messengers,
18. the work of men's *hands,*
19. save thou us *out of his hand,*
23. *By* (lit. *by the hand of*) thy messengers
26. their inhabitants were of small *power,*
21:10. *by* (lit. *by the hand of*) his servants the prophets,
14. *into the hand of* their enemies;
22: 5. let them deliver it into *the hand of* the doers
7. delivered into *their hand,*
9. *the hand of* them that do the work,
17. the works of *their hands;*
24: 2. *by* (lit. *by the hand of*) his servants the prophets.

1Ch 4:10. that *thine hand* might be with me,
40. the land (was) wide, (lit. large of *hands*)
5:10. who fell *by their hand:*
20. the Hagarites were delivered *into their hand,*
6:15(5:41). *by the hand of* Nebuchadnezzar.
31(16). *the service of* song
7:29. *the borders of* the children of Manasseh.
11: 3. *by* (marg. *by the hand of*) Samuel.
23. *and in* the Egyptian's *hand* (was) a spear
— plucked the spear *out of* the Egyptian's *hand,*
13: 9. Uzza put forth *his hand*
10. because he put *his hand* to the ark:
14:10. wilt thou deliver them *into mine hand?*
— I will deliver them *into thine hand.*
11. *by mine hand* like the breaking
16: 7. *into the hand of* Asaph
18: 1. *out of the hand of* the Philistines.
3. he went to stablish *his dominion* (lit. *his hand*)
17. the sons of David (were) chief *about* the king. (marg. *at the hand of*)
19:11. delivered *unto the hand of* Abishai
20: 8. they fell *by the hand of* David, *and by the hand of* his servants.
21:13. let me fall now *into the hand of* the Lord;
— *but* let me not fall *into the hand of* man.
15. It is enough, stay now *thine hand.*
16. having a drawn sword *in his hand*
17. let *thine hand*, I pray thee,
22:18. the land *into mine hand;*
23:28. their office (was) *to wait on* (marg. *at the hand of*) the sons of Aaron
24:19. *under* (lit. *by the hand of*) Aaron
25: 2. under *the hands of* Asaph,
— *the order of* the king. (marg. *hands*)
3, 6. *the hands of* their father
6. according to the king's *order* (marg. by *the hands of*)
26:28. (it was) under *the hand of* Shelomith,
28:19. by (his) *hand* upon me,
29: 5. (made) *by the hands of* artificers.
— to consecrate his service (lit. to fill *his hand*)
8. by *the hand of* Jehiel
12. *and in thine hand* (is) power and might; *and in thine hand* (it is) to make great,
14. *and of thine own* have we given (marg. *hand*)
16. (cometh) *of thine hand*, and (is) all thine
24. submitted (lit. gave *the hand* under) themselves
2Ch 1:17. for the kings of Syria, *by their means.* (marg. *hand*)
6: 4. *who hath with his hands*
15. *and* hast fulfilled (it) *with thine hand,*
32. *and thy* mighty *hand*, and thy stretched out arm;
7: 6. when David praised *by their ministry;* (marg. *hand*)
8:18. *by the hands of* his servants
9:18. *and stays* (marg. *hands*) on each side of
— and two lions standing by *the stays:*
10:15. he spake *by the hand of* Ahijah
12: 5. I also left you *in the hand of* Shishak.
7. *by the hand of* Shishak.
10. *the hands of* the chief of the guard,
13: 8. *in the hand of* the sons of David;
9. to consecrate *himself* (marg. to fill *his hand*)
16. God delivered them *into their hand.*
15: 7. let not *your hands* be weak:
16: 7. the king of Syria escaped *out of thine hand.*
8. he delivered them *into thine hand.*
17: 5. stablished the kingdom *in his hand;*
15. next *to him* (marg. at *his hand*)
16. next *him* (was) Amasiah (lit. *id.*)
18. next *him* (was) Jehozabad, (lit. *id.*)
18: 5. God will deliver (it) *into* the king's *hand.*
11. the Lord shall deliver (it) *into the hand of* the king.
14. they shall be delivered *into your hand.*
33. Turn *thine hand,*
20: 6. *and in thine hand* (is there not) power
21: 8. from under *the dominion* (marg. *hand*) *of*
10. from under *the hand of* Judah
— from under *his hand;*

2 Ch21:16. that (were) *near* (lit. by *the place of*) the Ethiopians:
23: 7. every man with his weapons *in his hand;*
10. having his weapon *in his hand,*
15. they laid *hands* on her;
18. *by the hand of* the priests the Levites,
— (as it was ordained) *by* David. (marg. *by the hands of* David)
24:11. *by the hand of* the Levites,
13. the work was perfected *by them,*
24. a very great host *into their hand,*
25:15. their own people *out of thine hand?*
20. *into the hand* (of their enemies),
26:11. *by the hand of* Jeiel the scribe
— under *the hand of* Hananiah,
13. under *their hand* (was) an army,
19. *and* (had) a censer *in his hand*
28: 5. *into the hand of* the king of Syria;
— *into the hand of* the king of Israel,
9. he hath delivered them *into your hand,*
29:23. they laid *their hands* upon them:
25. the commandment of the Lord (lit. *by the hand of* the Lord) by his prophets. (lit. *by the hand of* his prophets)
27. with the instruments (ordained) by David (marg. *hands of* instruments)
31. ye have consecrated *yourselves* (marg. filled *your hand*)
30: 6. *from* (*lit. from the hand of*) the king.
8. yield (marg. give *the hand*) yourselves unto the Lord,
12. *the hand of* God was to give them one heart
16. *of the hand of* the Levites.
31:13. *under the hand of* Cononiah and Shimei
15. next *him* (marg. at *his hand*) (were) Eden,
32:13. deliver their lands *out of mine hand?*
14. deliver his people *out of mine hand,*
— deliver you *out of mine hand?*
15. deliver his people *out of mine hand, and out of the hand of* my fathers:
— deliver you *out of mine hand?*
17. delivered their people *out of mine hand,*
— deliver his people *out of mine hand.*
19. the work of *the hands of* man.
22. *from the hand of* Sennacherib the king of Assyria, *and from the hand of* all (other),
33: 8. the ordinances *by the hand of* Moses.
34: 9. had gathered *of the hand of* Manasseh
10. they put (it) in *the hand of* the workmen
14. the law of the Lord (given) *by* (marg. *to the hand of*) Moses.
16. committed to thy servants, (marg. *to the hand of* thy servants)
17. into *the hand of* the overseers, and to *the hand of* the workmen.
25. the works of *their hands;*
35: 6. the word of the Lord *by the hand of* Moses.
11. sprinkled (the blood) *from their hands,*
36:15. *by* his messengers, (marg. *by the hand of* his messengers)
17. he gave (them) all *into his hand.*
Ezr. 1: 6. they that (were) about them strengthened *their hands*
8. by *the hand of* Mithredath
3:10. after *the ordinance of* David
4: 4. weakened *the hands of* the people
6:22. to strengthen *their hands*
7: 6. *according to the hand of* the Lord his God
9. *according to the* good *hand of* his God
28. *as the hand of* the Lord my God (was)
8:18. *by the* good *hand of* our God upon us
22. *The hand of* our God (is) upon all
26. I even weighed unto *their hand*
31. *and the hand of* our God was upon us,
33. by *the hand of* Meremoth
9: 2. *yea, the hand of* the princes and rulers
7. *into the hand of* the kings of the lands,
11. *by* (marg. *by the hand of*) thy servants the prophets,
10:19. they gave *their hands* that they would put
Neh 1:10. *and by thy* strong *hand.*
2: 8. *according to the* good *hand of* my God
18. Then I told them of *the hand of* my God
— they strengthened *their hands*
3: 2. And next *unto him* (marg. at *his hand*) builded the men of Jericho. And next *to them*

Neh 3: 4. next *unto them* repaired Meremoth (lit. at *their hand*)
— next *unto them* repaired Meshullam (lit. *id.*)
— next *unto them* repaired Zadok (lit. *id.*)
5. next *unto them* the Tekoites (lit. *id.*)
7. next *unto them* repaired Melatiah (lit. *id.*)
8. Next *unto him* repaired Uzziel (lit. *id.*)
— Next *unto him* also repaired Hananiah
9. next *unto them* repaired Rephaiah (lit. at *their hand*)
10. next *unto them* repaired Jedaiah (lit. *id.*)
— next *unto him* repaired Hattush (lit. *id.*)
12. next *unto him* repaired Shallum (lit. *id.*)
17. Next *unto him* repaired Hashabiah, (lit. *id.*)
19. next *to him* repaired Ezer (lit. *id.*)
4:17(11). one of *his hands* wrought in the work,
5: 5. neither (is it) in *our* power (lit. in the power of *our hands*)
6: 5. an open letter *in his hand;*
9. *Their hands* shall be weakened
— (O God), strengthen *my hands.*
7: 4. the city (was) large (marg. broad in *spaces*)
8: 6. with lifting up *their hands:*
14. *by* Moses, (marg. *by the hand of* Moses)
9:14. *by the hand of* Moses thy servant:
15. thou hadst sworn (marg. thou hadst lift up *thine hand*)
24. and gavest them *into their hands,*
27. *into the hand of* their enemies,
— *out of the hand of* their enemies.
28. *in the hand of* their enemies,
30. thy spirit *in* thy prophets: (marg. *in the hand of* thy)
— *into the hand of* the people of the lands.
10:29(30). *by* Moses (marg. *by the hand of* Moses)
31(32). exaction of every *debt.* (marg. *hand*)
11: 1. nine *parts* (to dwell) in (other) cities.
24. (was) *at* the king's *hand*
13:13. *next to them* (was) Hanan
21. if ye do (so) again, I will lay *hands* on you.
Est. 1: 7. *according to the state of* the king.
12. *by* (marg. *by the hand of*) (his) chamber lains:
15. *by* (lit. *id.*) the chamberlains?
2: 3. unto *the custody* (marg. *hand*) *of* Hege
8, 8. to *the custody of* Hegai,
14. to *the custody of* Shaashgaz,
18. *according to the state of* the king.
21. sought to lay *hand* on the king
3: 6. he thought scorn to lay *hands* on Mordecai
9. *the hands of* those that have the charge
10. the king took his ring *from his hand,*
13. the letters were sent *by* posts (lit. *by the hand of* posts)
5: 2. the golden sceptre that (was) *in his hand.*
6: 2. who sought to lay *hand* on the king
9. *the hand of* one of the king's most noble
8: 7. he laid *his hand* upon the Jews.
10. sent letters *by* posts (lit. *by the hand of* posts)
9: 2. to lay *hand* on such as sought their hurt:
10. on the spoil laid they not *their hand.*
15. on the prey they laid not *their hand.*
16. but they laid not *their hands* on the prey,
Job 1:10. thou hast blessed the work of *his hands,*
11. put forth *thine hand*
12. all that he hath (is) *in thy power;* only upon himself put not forth *thine hand.*
14. the asses feeding *beside them:* (lit. at *their hands*)
2: 5. put forth *thine hand*
6. Behold, he (is) *in thine hand;*
4: 3. *and* thou hast strengthened *the* weak *hands.*
5:12. *their hands* cannot perform
15. *and from the hand of* the mighty.
18. *and his hands* make whole.
20. *from the power of* the sword.
6: 9. that he would let loose *his hand,*
23. Deliver me *from* the enemy's *hand? or,* Redeem me *from the hand of* the mighty?
8: 4. *for* their (marg. *in the hand of* their) transgression;
20. neither will he help (lit. take *by the hand*) the evil doers:
9:24. The earth is given *into the hand of* the wicked:

Job 9:33. (that) might lay *his hand* upon us both.
10: 7. (there is) none that can deliver *out of thine hand.*
8. *Thine hands* have made me
11:14. If iniquity (be) *in thine hand,*
12: 6. *into whose hand* God bringeth (abundantly).
9. *the hand of* the Lord hath wrought this?
10. *In whose hand* (is) the soul of every living
14:15. the work of *thine hands.*
15:23. the day of darkness is ready *at his hand.*
25. he stretcheth out *his hand* against God,
16:11. *the hands of* the wicked.
17: 3. strike *hands with me?* (lit. strike *at my hand*)
9. he that hath clean *hands*
19:21. *the hand of* God hath touched me.
20:10. *and his hands* shall restore their goods.
22. every *hand of* the wicked shall come upon
21: 5. lay (your) *hand* upon (your) mouth.
16. their good (is) not *in their hand:*
23: 2. *my stroke* is heavier than my groaning. (marg. *hand*)
26:13. *his hand* hath formed the crooked serpent.
27:11. I will teach you *by the hand* of God:
22. he would fain flee *out of his hand.*
28: 9. He putteth forth *his hand*
29:20. my bow was renewed *in my hand.*
30: 2. the strength of *their hands*
21. with *thy* strong *hand* thou opposest thyself
24. not stretch out (his) *hand* to the grave,
31:21. lifted up *my hand* against the fatherless,
25. because *mine hand* had gotten much;
27. my mouth hath kissed *my hand:*
34:19. the work of *his hands.*
20. the mighty shall be taken away *with*out *hand.*
35: 7. what receiveth he *of thine hand?*
37: 7. He sealeth up *the hand of* every man;
40: 4. I will lay *mine hand* upon my mouth.
Ps. 8: 6(7). the works of *thy hands;*
10:12. O God, lift up *thine hand:*
14. to requite (it) *with thy hand:*
17:14. From men (which are) *thy hand,*
18[title](1). *and from the hand of* Saul:
20(21), 24(25). the cleanness of *my hands*
34(35). He teacheth *my hands* to war,
19: 1(2). *his hand*ywork. (lit. the work of *his hands*)
21: 8(9). *Thine hand* shall find out all thine enemies:
22:16(17). they pierced *my hands* and my feet.
20(21). my darling *from the power of* the dog. (marg. *hand*)
26:10. *In whose hands* (is) mischief,
28: 2. when I lift up *my hands*
4. the work of *their hands;*
5. the operation of *his hands,*
31: 5(6). *Into thine hand* I commit my spirit:
8(9). *into the hand of* the enemy:
15(16). My times (are) *in thy hand:* deliver me *from the hand of* mine enemies,
32: 4. day and night *thy hand* was heavy upon
36:11(12). *and* let not *the hand of* the wicked remove me.
37:24. Lord upholdeth (him with) *his hand.*
33. The Lord will not leave him *in his hand,*
38: 2(3). *thy hand* presseth me sore.
39:10(11). I am consumed by the blow of *thine hand.*
44: 2(3). drive out the heathen with *thy hand,*
49:15(16). *from the power of* the grave:
55:20(21). He hath put forth *his hands*
58: 2(3). the violence of *your hands*
63:10(11). They shall fall *by* the sword: (marg. by *the hands of* the sword)
68:31(32). Ethiopia shall soon stretch out *her hands*
71: 4. O my God, *out of the hand of* the wicked.
73:23. thou hast holden (me) *by* my right *hand.*
74:11. Why withdrawest thou *thy hand,*
75: 8(9). *in the hand of* the Lord (there is) a
76: 5(6). the men of might have found *their hands.*
77: 2(3). *my sore* ran in the night, (marg. *hand*)
20(21). *by the hand of* Moses and Aaron.

Ps. 78:42. They remembered not *his hand,*
61. his glory *into* the enemy's *hand.*
80:17(18). Let *thy hand* be upon the man
81:14(15). *my hand* against their adversaries.
82: 4. *out of the hand of* the wicked.
88: 5(6). they are cut off *from thy hand.*
89:13(14). strong is *thy hand,*
21(22). *my hand* shall be established
25(26). I will set *his hand* also in the sea,
48(49). *from the hand of* the grave?
90:17. the work of *our hands* upon us; yea, the work of *our hands* establish thou
92: 4(5). the works of *thy hands.*
95: 4. *In his hand* (are) the deep places
5. *his hands* formed the dry (land).
7. the sheep of *his hand.*
97:10. *out of the hand of* the wicked.
102:25(26). the work of *thy hands.*
104:25. great and wide sea, (lit. wide of *spaces*)
28. thou openest *thine hand,*
106:10. *from the hand of* him that hated (them), and redeemed them *from the hand* of
26. he lifted up *his hand* against them,
41. *into the hand of* the heathen;
42. under *their hand.*
107: 2. *from the hand of* the enemy;
109:27. that this (is) *thy hand;*
111: 7. The works of *his hands*
115: 4. the work of men's *hands.*
7. *They have hands,* but they handle not:
119:73. *Thy hands* have made me
173. Let *thine hand* help me;
121: 5. the Lord (is) thy shade upon thy right *hand.*
123: 2. *the hand of* their masters,
— *the hand of* her mistress;
125: 3. put forth *their hands* unto iniquity.
127: 4. As arrows (are) *in the hand of* a mighty
134: 2. Lift up *your hands* (in) the sanctuary,
135:15. the work of men's *hands.*
136:12. *With a* strong *hand,* and with a stretched out arm:
138: 7. stretch forth *thine hand*
8. the works of *thine own hands.*
139:10. there shall *thy hand* lead me,
140: 4(5). *from the hands of* the wicked;
5(6). they have spread a net *by the wayside*
141: 6. judges are overthrown *in* stony *places,*
9. Keep me *from* the snares (lit. *from the hands of* the snare)
143: 5. I muse on the work of *thy hands.*
6. I stretch forth *my hands* unto thee:
144: 1. teacheth *my hands* to war,
7. Send *thine hand* from above; (marg. *hands*)
—, 11. *from the hand of* strange children;
145:16. Thou openest *thine hand,*
149: 6. a twoedged sword *in their hand;*
Pro 1:24. I have stretched out *my hand,*
3:27. the power of *thine hand* to do (it).
6: 5. as a roe *from the hand* (of the hunter), and as a bird *from the hand of* the
10. a little folding of *the hands* to sleep:
17. *and hands* that shed innocent blood,
7:20. He hath taken a bag of money *with him,* (marg. *in his hand*)
8: 3. She crieth *at* the gates,
10: 4. *but the hand of* the diligent maketh rich.
11:21. (Though) *hand* (join) *in hand,*
12:14. the recompence of a man's *hands*
24. *The hand of* the diligent shall bear rule:
13:11. he that gathereth *by labour* shall increase. (marg. *with the hand*)
14: 1. plucketh it down *with her hands.*
16: 5. (though) *hand* (join) *in hand,*
17:16. (is there) a price *in the hand of* a fool
18:21. Death and life (are) *in the power of* the tongue:
19:24. A slothful (man) hideth *his hand*
21: 1. The king's heart (is) *in the hand of* the Lord,
25. *his hands* refuse to labour.
24:33. a little folding of *the hands* to sleep:
26: 6. a message *by the hand of* a fool
9. *into the hand of* a drunkard,
15. The slothful hideth *his hand* in (his) bosom;

Pro.30:28. The spider taketh hold *with her hands*,
32. (lay) *thine hand* upon thy mouth.
31:19. She layeth *her hands* to the spindle,
20. *yea*, she reacheth forth *her hands* to the needy.
31. Give her of the fruit of *her hands*;
Ecc 2:11. the works that *my hands* had wrought,
24. it (was) *from the hand of* God.
4: 1. *and on the side of* their oppressors (there was) power; (marg. *hand*)
5. The fool foldeth *his hands* together,
5: 6(5). the work of *thine hands?*
14(13). (there is) nothing *in his hand*.
15(14). carry away *in his hand*.
7:18. from this withdraw not *thine hand:*
26. *her hands* (as) bands:
9: 1. their works, (are) *in the hand of* God:
10. Whatsoever *thy hand* findeth to do,
10:18. through idleness of *the hands*
11: 6. withhold not *thine hand:*
Cant 5: 4. My beloved put in *his hand*
5. *and my hands* dropped (with) myrrh,
14. *His hands* (are as) gold rings
7: 1(2). the work of *the hands of* a cunning
Isa. 1:12. who hath required this *at your hand*,
15. *your hands* are full of blood.
25. I will turn *my hand* upon thee,
2: 8. the work of *their own hands*,
3: 6. (let) this ruin (be) under *thy hand:*
11. the reward of *his hands*
5:12. the operation of *his hands*.
25. he hath stretched forth *his hand*
— *his hand* (is) stretched out still.
6: 6. *having* (lit. *and*) a live coal *in his hand*,
8:11. with *a* strong *hand*,
9:12(11), 17(16), 21(20) & 10:4. *his hand* (is) stretched out still.
10: 5. the staff *in their hand*
10. *my hand* hath found the kingdoms
13. the strength of *my hand*
14. *my hand* hath found as a nest
32. he shall shake *his hand*
11: 8. put *his hand* on the cockatrice' den.
11. the Lord shall set *his hand* again
14. they shall lay *their hand* upon Edom
15. shake *his hand* over the river,
13: 2. shake *the hand*,
7. Therefore shall all *hands* be faint,
14:26. this (is) *the hand* that is stretched out
27. *and his hand* (is) stretched out,
17: 8. the work of *his hands*,
19: 4. *into the hand of* a cruel lord;
16. the shaking of *the hand of* the Lord
25. the work of *my hands*,
20: 2. spake the Lord *by* Isaiah (marg. *by the hand of* Isaiah)
22:18. a large country: (marg. large of *spaces*)
21. commit thy government *into his hand:*
23:11. He stretched out *his hand* over the sea,
25:10. mountain shall *the hand of* the Lord
11. And he shall spread forth *his hands*
— the spoils of *their hands*.
26:11. (when) *thy hand* is lifted up,
28: 2. cast down to the earth *with the hand*.
29:23. the work of *mine hands*,
31: 3. the Lord shall stretch out *his hand*,
7. *your own hands* have made
33:21. a place of broad rivers (marg. broad of *spaces*, or, *hands*)
34:17. *and his hand* hath divided it
35: 3. Strengthen ye *the* weak *hands*,
36:15. *into the hand of* the king of Assyria.
18. *out of the hand of* the king of Assyria?
19. they delivered Samaria *out of my hand?*
20. delivered their land *out of my hand*,
— deliver Jerusalem *out of my hand?*
37:10. *into the hand of* the king of Assyria.
14. *from the hand of* the messengers,
19. the work of men's *hands*,
20. save us *from his hand*,
24. *By* thy servants (lit. *by the hand of* thy servants)
27. their inhabitants (were) of small *power*, (marg. short of *hand*)
40: 2. received *of* the Lord's *hand* double
41:20. *the hand of* the Lord hath done this,
42: 6. will hold *thine hand*,

Isa. 43:13. deliver *out of my hand:*
44: 5. another shall subscribe (with) *his hand*
45: 9. He hath no *hands?*
11. the work of *my hands*
12. I, (even) *my hands*,
47: 6. given them *into thine hand:*
14. themselves *from the power of* the flame:
48:13. *Mine hand* also hath laid the foundation
49: 2. in the shadow of *his hand* hath he hid me,
22. I will lift up *mine hand* to the Gentiles,
50: 2. Is *my hand* shortened at all,
11. This shall ye have *of mine hand;*
51:16. the shadow of *mine hand*,
17. hast drunk *at the hand of* the Lord
18. that taketh her *by the hand*
22. I have taken *out of thine hand*
23. *into the hand of* them that afflict
53:10. the pleasure of the Lord shall prosper *in his hand*.
56: 2. keepeth *his hand* from doing any evil.
5. *a place* and a name
57: 8. *where* (lit. *the place*) thou sawest (it).
10. thou hast found the life of *thine hand;*
59: 1. the Lord's *hand* is not shortened,
60:21. the work of *my hands*,
62: 3. a crown of glory *in the hand of* the Lord,
64: 7(6). *because of* (lit. *by the hand of*) our iniquities.
8(7). we all (are) the work of *thy hand*.
65: 2. I have spread out *my hands*
22. the work of *their hands*.
66: 2. all those (things) hath *mine hand* made,
14. *the hand of* the Lord shall be known
Jer 1: 9. the Lord put forth *his hand*,
16. the works of *their own hands*.
2:37. *and thine hands* upon thine head:
5:31. the priests bear rule by *their means*; (marg. take into *their hands*)
6: 3. every one in *his place*.
9. turn back *thine hand*
12. I will stretch out *my hand*
24. *our hands* wax feeble:
10: 3. the work of *the hands of*
9. *and of the hands of* the founder:
11:21. that thou die not *by our hand:*
15: 6. therefore will I stretch out *my hand*
17. I sat alone because of *thy hand:*
21. *out of the hand of* the wicked,
16:21. I will cause them to know *mine hand*
18: 4. clay was marred *in the hand of* the potter:
6. as the clay (is) *in* the potter's *hand*, so (are) ye *in mine hand*,
21. *the force of* the sword;
19: 7. *and by the hands of* them that seek their lives:
20: 4. *into the hand of* the king of Babylon,
5. *into the hand of* their enemies,
13. *from the hand of* evildoers.
21: 4. the weapons of war that (are) *in your hands*,
5. *with an* outstretched *hand*
7. *into the hand of* Nebuchadrezzar king of Babylon, *and into the hand of* their enemies, *and into the hand of* those that
10. *into the hand of* the king of Babylon,
12. *out of the hand of* the oppressor,
22: 3. *out of the hand of* the oppressor:
24. the signet upon my right *hand*,
25. *into the hand of* them that seek thy life, *and into the hand* (of them) whose face thou fearest, *even into the hand of* Nebuchadrezzar king of Babylon, *and into the hand of* the Chaldeans.
23:14. they strengthen also *the hands of*
25: 6, 7. with the works of *your hands;*
14. the works of *their own hands*.
15. the wine cup of this fury *at my hand*,
17. the cup *at* the Lord's *hand*,
28. the cup *at thine hand*
26:14. I (am) *in your hand:*
24. *the hand of* Ahikam
— *into the hand of* the people
27: 3. *by the hand of* the messengers
6. *into the hand of* Nebuchadnezzar
8. until I have consumed them *by his hand*
29: 3. *By the hand of* Elasah
21. *into the hand of* Nebuchadrezzar

Jer. 30: 6. *his hands* on his loins,
31:11. *from the hand of* (him that was) stronger
32. the day (that) I took *them by the hand*
32: 3, 4, 36. *into the hand of* the king of Babylon,
4. *out of the hand of* the Chaldeans, but shall
21. *and with a* strong *hand,*
24, 25, 28, 43. *into the hand of* the Chaldeans,
28. *and into the hand of* Nebuchadrezzar
30. the work of *their hands,*
33:13. *the hands of* him that telleth (them),
34: 1. his dominion, (marg. the dominion of *his hand*)
2. *into the hand of* the king of Babylon,
3. thou shalt not escape *out of his hand,*
— and delivered *into his hand;*
20, 21. *into the hand of* their enemies, *and into the hand of* them that seek their life:
21. *and into the hand of* the king of Babylon's
36:14. Take *in thine hand* the roll
— took the roll *in his hand,*
37: 2. *by* the prophet Jeremiah. (lit. *by the hand of* the prophet Jeremiah)
17. *into the hand of* the king of Babylon.
38: 3. *into the hand of* the king of Babylon's
4. he weakeneth *the hands of* the men
— and *the hands of* all the people,
5. he (is) *in your hand:*
10. Take from hence thirty men *with thee,* (marg. *in thine hand*)
11. took the men *with him,*
12. rotten rags under thine armholes (lit. armholes of *thine hands*)
16. *into the hand of* these men
18. *into the hand of* the Chaldeans,
—, 23. thou shalt not escape *out of their hand.*
19. lest they deliver me *into their hand,*
23. *by the hand of* the king of Babylon:
39:11. *to* Nebuzar-adan (marg. *by the hand of*)
17. *into the hand of* the men of whom thou (art) afraid.
40: 4. the chains which (were) upon *thine hand.*
41: 5. offerings and incense *in their hand,*
9. *because of* Gedaliah, (lit. *in the hand of* Gedaliah)
42:11. deliver you *from his hand.*
43: 3. *into the hand of* the Chaldeans,
9. Take great stones *in thine hand,*
44: 8. the works of *your hands,*
25. *and* fulfilled with *your hand,*
30. *into the hand of* his enemies, *and into the hand of* them that seek his life;
— *into the hand of* Nebuchadrezzar
46: 6. by the river Euphrates. (lit. by *the hand of* the river Euphrates)
24. *into the hand of* the people of the north.
26. *into the hand of* those that seek their lives, *and into the hand of* Nebuchadrezzar king of Babylon, *and into the hand of*
47: 3. for feebleness of *hands;*
48:37. upon all *the hands* (shall be) cuttings,
50: 1. *by* Jeremiah (marg. *by the hand of* Jeremiah)
15. she hath given *her hand:*
43. *his hands* waxed feeble:
51: 7. a golden cup *in* the Lord's *hand,*
25. I will stretch out *mine hand* upon thee,
Lam 1: 7. her people fell *into the hand of* the enemy,
10. The adversary hath spread out *his hand*
14. of my transgressions is bound *by his hand.*
— hath delivered me *into* (their) *hands,*
17. Zion spreadeth forth *her hands,*
2: 7. *into the hand of* the enemy
8. he hath not withdrawn *his hand*
3: 3. he turneth *his hand* (against me)
64. the work of *their hands.*
4: 2. the work of *the hands of* the potter!
6. no *hands* stayed on her.
10. *The hands of* the pitiful women
5: 6. We have given *the hand*
8. deliver (us) *out of their hand.*
12. Princes are hanged up *by their hand:*
Eze 1: 3. *the hand of* the Lord was there upon him.
8. *And* (they had) *the hands of* a man
2: 9. *an hand* (was) sent unto me;
3:14. *but the hand of* the Lord was strong upon
18, 20. his blood will I require *at thine hand.*
Eze. 3:22. *the hand of* the Lord was there upon me.
6:14. So will I stretch out *my hand*
7:17. All *hands* shall be feeble,
21. *into the hands of* the strangers
27. *and the hands of* the people
8: 1. *the hand of* the Lord God fell there upon
3. he put forth the form of *an hand,*
11. every man his censer *in his hand;*
9: 1. his destroying weapon *in his hand.*
2. a slaughter weapon *in his hand;*
10: 7. (one) cherub stretched forth *his hand*
8. the form of a man's *hand*
12. *and their hands,* and their wings,
21. *the hands of* a man
11: 9. *into the hands of* strangers,
12: 7. I digged through the wall *with* mine *hand;*
13: 9. *mine hand* shall be upon the prophets
18. the (women) that sew pillows to all armholes, (lit. armholes of *my hands*)
21. deliver my people *out of your hand,* and they shall be no more *in your hand*
22. strengthened *the hands of* the wicked,
23. my people *out of your hand:*
14: 9. I will stretch out *my hand* upon him,
13. then will I stretch out *mine hand* upon it,
16:11. I put bracelets upon *thy hands,*
27. I have stretched out *my hand* over thee,
39. I will also give thee *into their hand,*
49. neither (lit. *and* not)...*the hand of* the poor and needy.
17:18. he had given *his hand,*
18: 8. hath withdrawn *his hand* from iniquity,
17. hath taken off *his hand*
20: 5. and lifted up *mine hand*
— I lifted up *mine hand*
6. I lifted up *mine hand*
15. I lifted up *my hand* unto them
22. I withdrew *mine hand,*
23. I lifted up *mine hand* unto them
28, 42. (for) the which I lifted up *mine hand*
33, 34. *with a* mighty *hand,*
21: 7(12). all *hands* shall be feeble,
11(16). *into the hand of* the slayer.
19(24). *and* choose thou *a place,*
31(36). deliver thee *into the hand of* brutish men,
22:14. can *thine hands* be strong,
23: 9. I have delivered her *into the hand of* her lovers, *into the hand of*
28. *into the hand* (of them) whom thou hatest, *into the hand* (of them) from whom thy
31. will I give her cup *into thine hand.*
37, 45. blood (is) *in their hands,*
42. which put bracelets upon *their hands,*
25: 6. thou hast clapped (thine) *hands,*
7. I will stretch out *mine hand* upon thee,
13. I will also stretch out *mine hand*
14. *by the hand of* my people Israel:
16. I will stretch out *mine hand*
27:15. the merchandise of *thine hand:*
21. they occupied *with thee* (marg. (were) the merchants of *thy hand*)
28: 9. *in the hand of* him that slayeth thee.
10. *by the hand of* strangers:
30:10. *by the hand of* Nebuchadrezzar
12. *into the hand of* the wicked:
— *by the hand of* strangers:
22. to fall *out of his hand.*
24. put my sword *in his hand:*
25. *into the hand of* the king of Babylon,
31:11. *into the hand of* the mighty one
33: 6. *at* the watchman's *hand.*
8. his blood will I require *at thine hand.*
22. *Now the hand of* the Lord was upon me
34:10. I will require my flock *at their hand,*
27. *out of the hand of* those that served themselves
35: 3. I will stretch out *mine hand*
5. *the force of* the sword (marg. *hands*)
36: 7. I have lifted up *mine hand,*
37: 1. *The hand of* the Lord was upon me,
17. they shall become one *in thine hand.*
19. *in the hand of* Ephraim,
— they shall be one *in mine hand.*
20. shall be *in thine hand* before their eyes.
38:12. turn *thine hand* upon the desolate places

Eze.38:17. *by* my servants the prophets (lit. *by the hand of*)
39: 3. *out of* thy left *hand*, and will cause thine arrows to fall *out of* thy right *hand*.
9. the *hand*staves, and the spears,
21. *my hand* that I have laid upon them.
23. *into the hand of* their enemies:
40: 1. *the hand of* the Lord
3. a line of flax *in his hand*,
5. *and in* the man's *hand*
43:26. they shall consecrate *themselves*. (marg. shall fill *their hands*)
44:12. I lifted up *mine hand*
46: 5. as he shall *be able* to give, (marg. the gift of *his hand*)
7. according as *his hand* shall attain
11. he is *able* to give, (lit. the gift of *his hand*)
47: 3. the man that had the line *in his hand*
14. I lifted up *mine hand*
48: 1. *the coast of* the way of Hethlon,
— *the coast of* Hamath;
Dan 1: 2. *into his hand*,
20. he found them ten *times* better
8: 4. deliver *out of his hand;*
7. deliver the ram *out of his hand*.
25. cause craft to prosper *in his hand;*
— he shall be broken without *hand*.
9:10. *by* (lit. *by the hand of*) his servants the prophets.
15. *with a* mighty *hand*,
10: 4. *the side of* the great river,
10. *an hand* touched me,
— the palms of *my hands*.
11:11. given *into his hand*.
16. *by his hand* shall be consumed.
41. escape *out of his hand*,
42. He shall stretch forth *his hand*
12: 7. *the power of* the holy people,
Hos 2:10(12). *out of mine hand*.
7: 5. he stretched out *his hand*
12: 7(8). the balances of deceit (are) *in his hand:*
10(11). *and* used similitudes, *by the ministry of* the prophets.
13:14. *from the power of* the grave; (marg. *hand*)
14: 3(4). the work of *our hands*,
Joel 3: 8(4:8). *into the hand of* the children
Am. 1: 8. I will turn *mine hand*
5:19. leaned *his hand* on the wall,
7: 7. *with* a plumbline *in his hand*.
9: 2. thence shall *mine hand* take them;
Mic. 2: 1. the power of *their hand*.
5: 9(8). *Thine hand* shall be lifted up
12(11). *out of thine hand;*
13(12). the work of *thine hands*.
7:16. lay (their) *hand* upon (their) mouth,
Hab 3: 4. he had horns (coming) *out of his hand:*
10. lifted up *his hands*
Zep 1: 4. I will also stretch out *mine hand*
2:13. he will stretch out *his hand*
15. shall hiss, (and) wag *his hand*.
3:16. Let not *thine hands* be slack.
Hag 1: 1, 3. *by* (marg. *by the hand of*) Haggai the prophet
2: 1. *by* the prophet Haggai, (marg. *id.*)
10. *by* Haggai the prophet, (lit. *id.*)
14. so (is) every work of *their hands;*
17. the labours of *your hands;*
Zec 2: 1(5). *with* a measuring line *in his hand*.
9(13). I will shake *mine hand* upon them,
4: 9. *The hands of* Zerubbabel have laid the foundation of this house; *his hands* shall *also* finish it;
10. *in the hand of* Zerubbabel
12. *through* (marg. *by the hand*) the two golden
7: 7, 12. *by* the former prophets. (marg. *by the hand of*)
8: 4. his staff *in his hand*
9, 13. Let *your hands* be strong,
11: 6. *into* his neighbour's *hand*, *and into the hand of* his king: and they shall smite the land, and *out of their hand*
13: 6. What (are) these wounds in *thine hands?*
7. I will turn *mine hand*
14:13. *the hand of* his neighbour, and *his hand* shall rise up against *the hand of*

Mal. 1: 1. *by* Malachi. (marg. *by the hand of* Malachi)
9. this hath been *by your means:* (marg. *from your hand*)
10. an offering *at your hand*.
13. should I accept this *of your hand?*
2:13. with good will *at your hand*.

יַד *yad*, Ch. com. 3028

Ezr. 5: 8. and prospereth *in their hands*.
12. he gave them *into the hand of* Nebuchadnezzar
6:12. that shall put to *their hand* to alter
7:14. of thy God which (is) *in thine hand;*
25. of thy God, that (is) *in thine hand*,
Dan 2:34. till that a stone was cut out *without hands*, (marg. not in *hands*)
38. hath he given *into thine hand*,
45. was cut out of the mountain *with*out *hands*, (marg. not in *hand*)
3:15. that shall deliver you out of *my hands?*
17. he will deliver (us) out of *thine hand*,
4:35(32). none can stay *his hand*, or say
5: 5. came forth fingers of a man's *hand*,
— saw the part of *the hand* that wrote.
23. and the God *in whose hand* thy breath (is),
24. Then was the part of *the hand* sent from
6:27(28). hath delivered Daniel from *the power of* the lions. (marg. *hand*)
7:25. and they shall be given *into his hand*

יְדָא [*y'dāh*], Ch. 3029

* APHEL.—*Participle.* *

Dan 2:23. I *thank* thee, and praise thee,
6:10(11). *and gave thanks* before his God,

יָדַד [*yāh-dad'*]. 3032

* KAL.—*Preterite.* *

Joel 3: 3(4:3). *they have cast* lots for my people;
Obad 11. *cast* lots upon Jerusalem,
Nah 3:10. *they cast* lots for her honourable men,

יְדִדוּת *y'dee-dooth'*, f. 3033

Jer. 12: 7. *the dearly beloved* (marg. *love*) *of* my soul

יָדָה [*yāh-dāh'*]. 3034

* KAL.—*Imperative.* *

Jer. 50:14. *shoot* at her, spare no arrows:

* PIEL.—*Infinitive.* *

Zec. 1:21(2:4). *to cast out* the horns of the Gentiles,

PIEL.—*Future.*

Lam 3:53. *and cast* a stone upon me.

יָדָה [*yāh-dāh'*]. 3034

* HIPHIL.—*Preterite.* *

1K. 8:33, 35. *and confess* thy name,
2Ch 6:24, 26. *and confess* thy name,
Ps. 75: 1(2). Unto thee, O God, *do we give thanks*, (unto thee) *do we give thanks:*

HIPHIL.—*Infinitive.*

1Ch 16: 4. *and to thank* and praise the Lord God
7. *to thank* the Lord
35. *that we may give thanks* to thy holy name,
41. *to give thanks* to the Lord,
23:30. *to thank* and praise the Lord,
25: 3. *to give thanks* and to praise the Lord.
2Ch 5:13. praising *and thanking* the Lord;

2Ch 7: 3. worshipped, *and praised* the Lord,
6. *to praise* the Lord,
31: 2. to minister, *and to give thanks,*
Ezr. 3:11. praising *and giving thanks* unto the Lord;
Neh 12:24. to praise (and) *to give thanks,*
46. songs of praise *and thanksgiving*
Ps. 92: 1(2). (It is a) good (thing) *to give thanks*
106:47. *to give thanks* unto thy holy name,
119:62. I will rise *to give thanks* unto thee
122: 4. *to give thanks* unto the name of the Lord.
142: 7(8). *that I may praise* thy name:

HIPHIL.—*Imperative.*

1Ch 16: 8. *Give thanks* unto the Lord,
34. *O give thanks* unto the Lord;
2Ch 20:21. *Praise* the Lord;
Ps. 30: 4(5). *and give thanks* at the remembrance of
33: 2. *Praise* the Lord with harp:
97:12. *and give thanks* at the remembrance of his
100: 4. *be thankful* unto him,
105: 1 & 106:1 & 107:1 & 118:1, 29 & 136:1. *O give thanks* unto the Lord;
136: 2. *O give thanks* unto the God of gods:
3. *O give thanks* to the Lord of lords:
26. *O give thanks* unto the God of heaven:
Isa. 12: 4. *Praise* the Lord, call upon his name,
Jer. 33:11. *Praise* the Lord of hosts:

HIPHIL.—*Future.*

Gen 29:35. Now *will I praise* the Lord:
49: 8. thou (art he) *whom* thy brethren *shall praise:*
2Sa. 22:50. Therefore *I will give thanks* unto thee,
Neh 11:17. the principal to begin *the thanksgiving* (lit. *he shall give thanks*)
Job 40:14. Then *will I* also *confess unto thee*
Ps. 6: 5(6). in the grave who *shall give* thee *thanks?*
7:17(18). *I will praise* the Lord
9: 1(2). *I will praise* (thee), O Lord,
18:49(50). Therefore *will I give thanks* unto thee, (marg. or, *confess*)
28: 7. with my song *will I praise him.*
30: 9(10). *Shall* the dust *praise thee?*
12(13). *I will give thanks unto thee* for ever.
32: 5. *I will confess* my transgressions
35:18. *I will give thee thanks* in the great congregation:
42: 5(6), 11(12). *I shall* yet *praise him* (marg. *give thanks*)
43: 4. *yea,* upon the harp *will I praise thee,*
5. *I shall* yet *praise him,*
44: 8(9). *praise* thy name for ever.
45:17(18). therefore *shall* the people *praise thee*
49:18(19). *and* (men) *will praise thee,*
52: 9(11). *I will praise thee* for ever,
54: 6(8). *I will praise* thy name, O Lord;
57: 9(10). *I will praise thee,* O Lord,
67: 3(4), 5(6). *Let* the people *praise thee,* O God; *let* all the people *praise thee.*
71:22. *I will* also *praise thee* with the psaltery,
76:10(11). the wrath of man *shall praise thee:*
79:13. *will give* thee *thanks* for ever:
86:12. *I will praise thee,* O Lord my God,
88:10(11). shall the dead arise (and) *praise thee?*
89: 5(6). *And* the heavens *shall praise* thy wonders,
99: 3. *Let them praise* thy great and terrible
107: 8, 15, 21, 31. *Oh that* (men) *would praise* the
108: 3(4). *I will praise thee,* O Lord,
109:30. *I will* greatly *praise* the Lord with my
111: 1. *I will praise* the Lord with (my) whole
118:19. into them, (and) *I will praise* the Lord:
21. *I will praise thee:* for thou hast heard
28. Thou (art) my God, *and I will praise thee:*
119: 7. *I will praise thee* with uprightness of heart,
138: 1. *I will praise thee* with my whole heart:
2. *and praise* thy name for thy lovingkindness
4. All the kings of the earth *shall praise thee,*
139:14. *I will praise thee;* for I am
140:13(14). the righteous *shall give thanks* unto thy name:
145:10. All thy works *shall praise thee,*
Isa. 12: 1. O Lord, *I will praise thee:*
25: 1. *I will praise* thy name;
38:18. the grave *cannot praise thee,*
19. The living, the living, he *shall praise thee,*

HIPHIL.—*Participle.*

1Ch 29:13. our God, we *thank* thee,
Pro 28:13. *but whoso confesseth* and forsaketh (them) shall have mercy.

* HITHPAEL.—*Preterite.* *

Lev 5: 5. *that he shall confess* that he hath sinned
16:21. *and confess* over him all the iniquities
26:40. *If they shall confess* their iniquity,
Num 5: 7. *Then they shall confess* their sin

HITHPAEL.—*Infinitive.*

Ezr. 10: 1. when Ezra had prayed, *and when he had confessed,*

HITHPAEL.—*Future.*

Neh 9: 2. stood *and confessed* their sins,
Dan 9: 4. I prayed unto the Lord my God, *and made my confession,*

HITHPAEL.—*Participle.*

2Ch 30:22. *and making confession* to the Lord God
Neh 1: 6. *and confess* the sins of the children of Israel,
9: 3. (another) fourth part *they confessed,*
Dan 9:20. praying, *and confessing* my sin

יְדִיד *y'deed,* adj. const. 3039

Deu 33:12. *The beloved of* the Lord
Ps. 45[title](1). A Song of *loves.*
60: 5(7). That *thy beloved* may be delivered;
84: 1(2). How *amiable* (are) thy tabernacles,
108: 6(7). That *thy beloved* may be delivered:
127: 2. so he giveth *his beloved* sleep.
Isa. 5: 1. Now will I sing *to my wellbeloved*
— *My wellbeloved* hath a vineyard
Jer. 11:15. What *hath my beloved to do* in mine house,

יְדִידוּת see יְדִדוּת See 3033

יָדַע *yāh-dag'.* 3045

* KAL.—*Preterite.* *

Gen 4: 1. Adam *knew* Eve his wife;
9. And he said, *I know* not:
12:11. *I know* that thou (art) a fair woman
18:19. For *I know him,* that he will command his children
19: 8. two daughters which *have* not *known*
33, 35. *he perceived* not when she lay down,
20: 6. Yea, *I know* that thou didst this
21:26. *I wot* not who hath done this thing:
22:12. now *I know* that thou fearest God,
24:16. neither *had* any man *known her:*
27: 2. *I know* not the day of my death:
28:16. Surely the Lord is in this place; and I *knew* (it) not.
29: 5. *Know ye* Laban the son of Nahor? And they said, *We know* (him).
30:26. thou *knowest* my service
29. Thou *knowest* how I have served thee,
31: 6. ye *know*...I have served your father.
32. Jacob *knew* not that Rachel had stolen
38:16. *he knew* not that she (was) his daughter in law.
39: 6. *he knew* not ought he had,
8. my master *wotteth* not what (is) with me
42:23. *they knew* not that Joseph understood
43:22. *we cannot tell* who put our money in our
44:15. *wot ye* not that...I can certainly divine?
27. *Ye know* that my wife bare me two (sons):
47: 6. if *thou knowest* (any) men of activity
48:19. *I know* (it), my son, *I know* (it):
Ex. 1: 8. which *knew* not Joseph.
3: 7. *I know* their sorrows;
19. *I am sure* that the king of Egypt will not
4:14. *I know* that he can speak well.
5: 2. *I know* not the Lord,
6: 7. *and ye shall know* that I (am) the Lord
7: 5. *And* the Egyptians *shall know*
9:30. *I know* that ye will not yet fear the Lord
10: 2. *that ye may know* how that I (am) the Lord.

Ex. 14: 4. *that* the Egyptians *may know* that I (am) the Lord.
18. *And* the Egyptians *shall know* that I (am)
16: 6. *then ye shall know* that the Lord
12. *and ye shall know* that I (am) the Lord
15. *they wist* not what it (was).
18:11. *I know* that the Lord (is) greater than all
23: 9. *ye know* the heart of a stranger,
29:46. *And they shall know* that I (am) the Lord
32: 1, 23. *we wot* not what is become of him.
22. *thou knowest* the people,
33:12. *I know thee* by name,
34:29. Moses *wist* not that the skin of his face
Lev. 5: 1. whether he hath seen or *known* (of it);
3, 4. when *he knoweth* (of it),
17. though *he wist* (it) not, yet is he guilty,
18. he erred and *wist* (it) not,
Nu. 10:31. *thou knowest* how we are to encamp
11:16. whom *thou knowest* to be the elders
14:31. *and they shall know* the land
34. *and ye shall know* my breach of promise.
16:30. *then ye shall understand* that these men
20:14. *Thou knowest* all the travel that hath
22: 6. *I wot* that he whom thou blessest (is)
34. *I knew* not that thou stoodest in the way
31:18. all the women children, that *have* not *known* a man
35. women that *had* not *known* man
Deu 1:39. *had* no *knowledge* between good and evil,
2: 7. *he knoweth* thy walking through this
3:19. *I know* that ye have much cattle,
4:39. *Know therefore* this day,
7: 9. *Know therefore* that the Lord thy God,
15. the evil diseases of Egypt, which *thou knowest*,
8: 3. fed thee with manna, which *thou knewest not*, neither *did* thy fathers *know;*
5. *Thou shalt also consider* in thine heart,
16. thy fathers *knew* not,
9: 2. the children of the Anakims, whom thou *knowest*,
3. *Understand therefore* this day,
6. *Understand therefore*, that the Lord
11: 2. *And know ye* this day:
— your children which *have* not *known*,
28. other gods, which *ye have* not *known*.
13: 2(3). other gods, which *thou hast* not *known*,
6(7). other gods, which *thou hast* not *known*,
13(14). other gods, which *ye have* not *known;*
22: 2. if *thou know him* not,
28:33. a nation which *thou knowest* not
36, 64. neither thou nor thy fathers *have known;* (lit. thou *hast* not *known* nor thy fathers)
29:16(15). *ye know* how we have dwelt in the
26(25). gods whom *they knew* (lit. *they knew them*) not,
31:13. which *have* not *known* (any thing),
21. *I know* their imagination
27. *I know* thy rebellion, and thy stiff neck:
29. *I know* that after my death ye will
32:17. gods *whom they knew* not,
33: 9. nor *knew* his own children:
34: 6. no man *knoweth* of his sepulchre
10. whom the Lord *knew*
Jos. 2: 4. *I wist* not whence they (were):
5. whither the men went *I wot* not:
9. *I know* that the Lord hath given you the
8:14. *he wist* not that (there were) liers in
14: 6. *Thou knowest* the thing that the Lord
22:31. *we perceive* that the Lord (is) among us,
23:14. *and ye know* in all your hearts
24:31. which *had known* all the works of the
Jud. 2:10. which *knew* not the Lord,
3: 1. *had* not *known* all the wars of Canaan;
2. such as before *knew* nothing *thereof;*
6:37. *then shall I know* that thou wilt save
11:39. *she knew* no man.
13:16. Manoah *knew* not that he (was) an angel
21. Manoah *knew* that he (was) an angel
14: 4. and his mother *knew* not that it (was) of
15:11. *Knowest thou* not that the Philistines (are) rulers over us?
16:20. *he wist* not that the Lord was departed
17:13. Now *know I* that the Lord will do me
18:14. *Do ye know* that there is in these houses
20:34. *they knew* not that evil (was) near them.
Jud. 21:12. that *had known* no man
Ru. 2:11. a people which *thou knewest* not heretofore,
3: 4. *that thou shalt mark* the place where he
1Sa. 2:12. *they knew* not the Lord.
3: 7. Samuel *did* not yet *know* the Lord,
13. the iniquity which *he knoweth;*
6: 9. *then we shall know* that (it is) not his
14: 3. the people *knew* not that Jonathan was
17:28. I *know* thy pride, and the naughtiness of
55. O king, *I cannot tell.* (lit. if *I know*)
20: 3. Thy father certainly *knoweth* that I have
30. *do* not *I know* that thou hast chosen the
39. the lad *knew* not any thing: only Jonathan and David *knew* the matter.
22:15. thy servant *knew* nothing of all this,
17. because *they knew* when he fled,
22. *I knew* (it) that day,
24:20(21). *I know* well that thou shalt surely be
25:11. *I know* not whence they (be)?
28: 9. *thou knowest* what Saul hath done,
29: 9. *I know* that thou (art) good in my sight,
2Sa. 1: 5. How *knowest thou* that Saul and Jonathan
10. *I was sure* that he could not live
2:26. *knowest thou* not that it will be bitterness
3:25. *Thou knowest* Abner the son of Ner,
26. David *knew* (it) not.
7:20. for thou, Lord God, *knowest* thy servant.
11:16. *he knew* that valiant men (were).
20. *knew ye* not that they would shoot
14:22. thy servant *knoweth* that I have found
15:11. *they knew* not any thing.
17: 8. *thou knowest* thy father and his men,
18:29. *I knew* not what (it was).
19: 6(7). for this day *I perceive*, that if Absalom
20(21). thy servant *doth know* that I have
22(23). *do* not *I know* that I (am) this day
22:44. a people (which) *I knew* not shall serve
24: 2. *that I may know* the number of the
1K. 1: 4. the king *knew her* not.
11. David our lord *knoweth* (it) not?
18. *thou knowest* (it) not:
2: 5. *thou knowest* also what Joab
9. *and knowest* what thou oughtest to do
15. *Thou knowest* that the kingdom was mine,
32. my father David not *knowing* (thereof),
44. Thou *knowest* all the wickedness which thine heart *is privy to*,
5: 3(17). Thou *knowest* how that David my
6(20). thou *knowest* that (there is) not among
8:39. thou only, *knowest* the hearts
17:24. *I know* that thou (art) a man of God,
20:13. *and thou shalt know* that I (am) the Lord.
28. *and ye shall know* that I (am) the Lord.
22: 3. *Know ye* that Ramoth in Gilead (is) our's,
2K. 2: 3, 5. *Knowest thou* that the Lord will take
—, –. Yea, I *know* (it); hold ye your peace.
4: 1. *thou knowest* that thy servant did fear the
9. *I perceive* that this (is) an holy man of
39. *they knew* (them) not.
5:15. *I know* that (there is) no God in all the
7:12. *They know* that we (be) hungry;
8:12. *I know* the evil that thou wilt do
9:11. Ye *know* the man, and his communication.
17:26. *know* not the manner of the God
19:27. *I know* thy abode,
1Ch 17:18. thou *knowest* thy servant.
29:17. *I know also*, my God,
2Ch 2: 8(7). I *know* that thy servants can skill to
6:30. for thou only *knowest* the hearts
25:16. *I know* that God hath determined to
Neh 2:16. the rulers *knew* not whither I went,
9:10. *thou knewest* that they dealt proudly
Est. 4: 1. Mordecai *perceived* all that was done,
Job 5:24. *And thou shalt know* that thy tabernacle (shall be) in peace;
25. *Thou shalt know also* that thy seed (shall be) great,
9: 2. *I know* (it is) so of a truth:
5. *they know* not:
28. *I know* that thou wilt not hold me
10:13. *I know* that this (is) with thee.
11:11. *he knoweth* vain men:
12: 9. Who *knoweth* not in all these
13: 2. (the same) *do I know* also:
18. *I know* that I shall be justified.
15: 9. What *knowest thou*, that we know not?
23. *he knoweth* that the day of darkness is

Job 18:21. (him that) *knoweth* not God.
19:25. I *know* (that) my redeemer liveth,
20: 4. *Knowest thou* (not) this of old,
20. *he shall* not *feel* quietness (marg. *know*)
21:27. Behold, *I know* your thoughts,
22:13. How *doth* God *know?*
23: 3. Oh that *I knew* where I might find him!
10. *he knoweth* the way that I take:
24:16. *they know* not the light.
28: 7. no fowl *knoweth*,
13. Man *knoweth* not the price thereof;
23. he *knoweth* the place thereof.
29:16. the cause (which) *I knew* not
30:23. *I know* (that) thou wilt bring me (to)
32:22. *I know* not to give flattering titles;
34:33. speak what *thou knowest*.
35:15. *he knoweth* (it) not
38: 4. declare, if *thou hast* (marg. *knowest*) understanding.
18. declare if *thou knowest* it all.
21. *Knowest thou* (it),
33. *Knowest thou* the ordinances of heaven?
39: 1. *Knowest thou* the time
2. *or knowest thou* the time when they bring
42: 2. *I know* that thou canst do every (thing),
Ps. 14: 4. *Have* all the workers of iniquity no *knowledge?*
18:43(44). a people (whom) *I have* not *known*
20: 6(7). Now *know I* that the Lord saveth his
31: 7(8). *thou hast known* my soul
35:11. (things) that *I knew* not.
15. *I knew* (it) not;
40: 9(10). O Lord, *thou knowest*.
41:11(12). By this *I know* that thou favourest me,
50:11. *I know* all the fowls of the mountains:
53: 4(5). *Have* the workers of iniquity no *knowledge?*
56: 9(10). this *I know;* for God (is) for me.
69: 5(6). thou *knowest* my foolishness;
19(20). Thou *hast known* my reproach,
71:15. *I know* not the numbers (thereof).
73:11. How *doth* God *know?*
79: 6. the heathen that *have* not *known* thee,
81: 5(6). a language (that) *I understood* not.
82: 5. *They know* not, neither will they understand;
91:14. *he hath known* my name.
95:10. *they have* not *known* my ways:
103:14. *he knoweth* our frame;
104:19. the sun *knoweth* his going down.
119:75. *I know*, O Lord, that thy judgments (are)
79. (כתיב) *and those that have known*
152. *I have known* of old
135: 5. I *know* that the Lord (is) great,
139: 2. Thou *knowest* my downsitting
4. *thou knowest* it altogether.
140:12(13). *I know* that the Lord will maintain
142: 3(4). thou *knewest* my path.
147:20. *they have* not *known them*.
Pro. 4:19. *they know* not at what they stumble.
7:23. *knoweth* not that it (is) for his life.
9:13. (she is) simple, and *knoweth* nothing.
18. *he knoweth* not that the dead (are) there;
14: 7. when *thou perceivest* not (in him) the lips
23:35. *I felt* (it) not: (marg. *knew*)
24:12. Behold, *we knew* it not;
30:18. four *which I know* not:
Ecc. 1:17. *I perceived* that this also is vexation of
2:14. *and I* myself *perceived* also
3:12. *I know* that (there is) no good in them,
14. *I know* that, whatsoever God doeth,
4:13. who *will* no more *be* admonished. (marg. *knoweth* not to be)
6: 5. he hath not seen the sun, nor *known* (any thing):
7:22. thine own heart *knoweth*
10:15. *he knoweth* not how to go to the city.
Cant. 6:12. Or ever *I was aware*,
Isa. 1: 3. The ox *knoweth* his owner, and the ass his master's crib: (but) Israel *doth* not *know*,
9: 9(8). *And* all the people *shall know*,
19:21. *and* the Egyptians *shall know*
29:12. him that *is* not *learned*, (lit. *knoweth* not a book)
— *I am* not *learned*. (lit. *I know* not a book)
24. They *also...shall come to* understanding, (marg. *shall know* understanding)

Isa. 37:28. *I know* thy abode,
40:28. *Hast thou* not *known?*
42:16. a way (that) *they knew* not;
— paths (that) *they have* not *known:*
25. yet *he knew* not;
44: 8. *I know* not (any).
18. *They have* not *known*
45: 4, 5. *thou hast* not *known me*.
20. *they have* no *knowledge*
48: 6. *thou didst* not *know them*.
7. Behold, *I knew them*.
8. *thou knewest* not;
— *I knew* that thou wouldest deal very
49:23. *and thou shalt know* that I (am) the Lord:
26. *and* all flesh *shall know*
55: 5. nations (that) *knew* not *thee*
56:10. His watchmen (are) blind: they *are* all *ignorant*, (lit. *they know* not)
11. greedy dogs (which) *can* never *have* enough, (marg. *know* not to be satisfied)
— shepherds (that) *can*not understand: (lit. *know* not to understand)
59: 8. The way of peace *they know* not;
— *shall* not *know* peace.
12. (as for) our iniquities, *we know them;*
60:16. *and thou shalt know* that I the Lord (am)
63:16. though Abraham *be ignorant of us*, (lit. *know us* not)
Jer. 1: 5. Before I formed thee in the belly *I knew thee;*
6. Ah, Lord God! behold, *I can*not speak: (lit. *I know* not to speak)
2: 8. they that handle the law *knew me* not:
4:22. they *have* not *known* me;
— *they have* no *knowledge*.
5: 4. *they know* not the way of the Lord,
5. *they have known* the way of the Lord,
6:15. neither *could they* blush: (lit. *they knew* not to blush)
7: 9. other gods whom *ye know* not;
8: 7. the stork...*knoweth* her appointed times;
— my people *know* not the judgment of the
12. neither *could they* blush: (lit. *they knew* not to blush)
9: 3(2). *they know* not me,
16(15). neither they nor their fathers *have known:*
10:23. *I know* that the way of man
25. the heathen that *know thee* not,
11:19. *I knew* not that they had devised devices
12: 3. thou, O Lord, *knowest me:*
14:18. a land that *they know* not.
20. *We acknowledge*, O Lord, our wickedness,
15:14. a land (which) *thou knowest* not:
15. O Lord, thou *knowest:*
16:13. a land that ye *know* not,
21. *and they shall know* that my name (is)
17: 4. the land which *thou knowest* not:
16. thou *knowest:* that which came
18:23. thou *knowest* all their counsel against me
19: 4. whom neither they nor their fathers *have known*, (lit. *known them*)
22:28. a land which *they know* not?
29:11. I *know* the thoughts
33: 3. mighty things, *which thou knowest* not.
41: 4. no man *knew* (it),
44: 3. other gods, whom *they knew* (lit. *knew them*) not,
28. *and* all the remnant...*shall know* whose words shall stand,
48:30. I *know* his wrath, saith the Lord;
50:24. *thou wast* not *aware:*
Eze. 2: 5. *yet shall know* that there hath been a
5:13. *and they shall know* that I the Lord have spoken (it)
6: 7. *and ye shall know* that I (am) the Lord.
10, 14. *And they shall know* that I (am) the
13. *Then shall ye know* that I (am) the Lord,
7: 4, 9. *and ye shall know* that I (am) the Lord.
27. *and they shall know* that I (am) the Lord.
11: 5. I *know* the things that come into your
10, 12. *and ye shall know* that I (am) the Lord.
12:15, 16. *And they shall know* that I (am) the
20. *and ye shall know* that I (am) the Lord.
13: 9, 14. *and ye shall know* that I (am) the Lord
21, 23. *and ye shall know* that I (am) the Lord.
14: 8. *and ye shall know* that I (am) the Lord.

Eze.14:23. *and ye shall know* that I have not done
15: 7. *and ye shall know* that I (am) the Lord,
16:62. *and thou shalt know* that I (am) the Lord:
17:12. *Know ye* not what these (things mean)?
21. *and ye shall know* that I the Lord have spoken (it).
24. *And* all the trees of the field *shall know*
20:38, 42, 44. *and ye shall know* that I (am) the
21: 5(10). *That* all flesh *may know*
22:16. *and thou shalt know* that I (am) the Lord.
22. *and ye shall know* that I the Lord have poured out my fury
23:49. *and ye shall know* that I (am) the Lord God.
24:24. *and* when this cometh, *ye shall know*
27. *and they shall know* that I (am) the Lord.
25: 5. *and ye shall know* that I (am) the Lord.
7. *and thou shalt know* that I (am) the Lord.
11, 17. *and they shall know* that I (am) the
14. *and they shall know* my vengeance,
26: 6 & 28:22, 23, 24, 26. *and they shall know* that I (am) the Lord.
29: 6. *And* all the inhabitants of Egypt *shall know*
9, 21. *and they shall know* that I (am) the
16. *but they shall know* that I (am) the Lord
30: 8, 19, 25, 26. *And they shall know* that I (am)
32: 9. the countries which *thou hast* not *known*.
15 & 33:29. *then shall they know* that I (am)
33:33. *then shall they know* that a prophet hath been among them.
34:27. *and shall know* that I (am) the Lord,
30. *Thus shall they know* that I the Lord their God (am) with them,
35: 4, 12. *and thou shalt know* that I (am) the
9. *and ye shall know* that I (am) the Lord.
15. *and they shall know* that I (am) the Lord.
36:11. *and ye shall know* that I (am) the Lord.
23. *and* the heathen *shall know* that I (am) the
36. *Then* the heathen...*shall know* that I the
38. *and they shall know* that I (am) the Lord.
37: 3. O Lord God, thou *knowest*.
6, 13. *and ye shall know* that I (am) the Lord.
14. *then shall ye know* that I the Lord have
28. *And* the heathen *shall know* that I the Lord
38:23 & 39:6. *and they shall know* that I (am) the
39: 7. *and* the heathen *shall know* that I (am) the
22. *So* the house of Israel *shall know*
23. *And* the heathen *shall know* that the house of
28. *Then shall they know* that I (am) the Lord
Dan 10:20. *Knowest thou* wherefore I come unto thee?
11:38. a god whom his fathers *knew* not
Hos. 2: 8(10). *she did* not *know* that I gave her corn,
20(22). *and thou shalt know* the Lord.
5: 3. *I know* Ephraim,
4. *they have* not *known* the Lord.
7: 9. *he knoweth* (it) not: yea, gray hairs
— yet *he knoweth* not.
8: 2. My God, *we know thee*.
4. they have made princes, and *I knew* (it)
11: 3. *they knew* not that I healed them.
13: 5. I *did know thee* in the wilderness,
Joel 2:27. *And ye shall know* that I (am) in the midst
3:17(4:17). *So shall ye know* that I (am) the
Am. 3: 2. You only *have I known*
10. *they know* not to do right,
5:12. *I know* your manifold transgressions
Jon. 1:10. the men *knew* that he fled
4: 2. *I knew* that thou (art) a gracious God,
11. that cannot *discern* between their right hand and their left hand;
Mic. 4:12. they *know* not the thoughts of the Lord,
Zec. 2: 9(13). *and ye shall know* that the Lord
11(15). *and thou shalt know* that the Lord
4: 5. *Knowest thou* not what these be?
9. *and thou shalt know* that the Lord of hosts hath sent
13. *Knowest thou* not what these (be)?
6:15. *and ye shall know* that the Lord of hosts
7:14. the nations whom *they knew* (lit. *knew them*) not.
Mal. 2: 4. *And ye shall know* that I have sent this commandment

KAL.—*Infinitive.*

Gen 3:22. *to know* good and evil:
15:13. Know *of a surety* (lit. *knowing* thou shalt know)
Gen24:21. *to wit* whether the Lord had made his
38:26. he *knew her* again no more. (lit. he added not *to know her*)
43: 7. could we *certainly* know (marg. *knowing* could we know)
Ex. 2: 4. *to wit* what would be done
31:13. *that* (ye) *may know* that I (am) the Lord
36: 1. *to know* how to work
Deu 4:35. *that* thou *mightest know*
8: 2. *to know* what (was) in thine heart,
9:24. the day that *I knew* you.
13: 3(4). *to know* whether ye love the Lord
29: 4(3). an heart *to perceive*,
Jos. 4:24. the people of the earth *might know*
23:13. Know *for a certainty* (lit. *knowing* ye shall know)
Jud. 3: 2. the children of Israel *might know*,
4. *to know* whether they would hearken
1Sa 20: 3. Thy father *certainly* knoweth (lit. *knowing* he knoweth)
9. if I knew *certainly*
28: 1. Know thou *assuredly*,
2Sa. 3:25. *and to know* thy going out and thy coming in, *and to know* all that thou doest.
14:20. *to know* all (things) that (are) in the earth.
1K. 2:37. thou shalt know *for certain*
42. Know *for a certain*,
8:43. *and that they may know* that this house,
60. That all the people of the earth *may know*
1Ch 12:32. *to know* what Israel ought to do;
2Ch 6:33. *and may know* that this house which I have
13: 5. Ought ye not *to know* that the Lord
32:31. *that he might know* all (that was) in his
Est. 2:11. *to know* how Esther did,
4: 5. *to know* what it (was),
Job 37: 7. all men *may know* his work.
Ps. 67: 2(3). *That* thy way *may be known* upon earth,
73:16. When I thought *to know* this,
Pro. 1: 2. *To know* wisdom and instruction;
4: 1. attend *to know* understanding.
27:23. Be thou diligent *to know* the state of thy flocks, (lit. *knowing* thou shalt know)
Ecc. 1:17. *to know* madness and folly:
7:25. I applied mine heart *to know*,
— *and to know* the wickedness of folly,
8:16. I applied mine heart *to know* wisdom,
17. though a wise (man) think *to know* (it),
Isa. 7:15. *that he may know* to refuse the evil,
50: 4. *that I should know* how to speak
Jer. 9: 6(5). through deceit they refuse *to know* me,
24(23). that he understandeth *and knoweth* me,
13:12. Do we not *certainly* know
24: 7. I will give them an heart *to know* me,
26:15. know ye *for certain*, that if ye
40:14. Dost thou *certainly* know
42:19. know *certainly* that I have
22. Now therefore know *certainly* (lit. *in knowing* know)
Eze.20:12. *that they might know* that I (am) the Lord
20. *that ye may know* that I (am) the Lord your God.
38:16. that the heathen *may know* me,
Dan 2: 3. my spirit was troubled *to know* the dream.
Hos. 6: 3. (if) we follow on *to know* the Lord:
Mic. 3: 1. (Is it) not for you *to know* judgment?
6: 5. *that ye may know* the righteousness of the
Hab 2:14. the earth shall be filled *with the knowledge* of the glory of the Lord, (lit. *to know*)

KAL.—*Imperative.*

Gen20: 7. *know thou* that thou shalt surely die,
Nu. 32:23. *and be sure* your sin will find you out.
Jud.18:14. *consider* what ye have to do.
1Sa 12:17. *that ye may perceive* and see
14:38. *and know* and see wherein this sin hath
20: 7. *be sure* that evil is determined
23:22. *and know* and see his place
23. *and take knowledge* of all the lurking places
24:11(12). *know thou* and see
25:17. *know* and consider what thou wilt do;
2Sa 24:13. *advise*, and see what answer I shall return
1K. 20: 7. *Mark*, I pray you, and see
22. *and mark*, and see what thou doest:
2K. 5: 7. wherefore *consider*, I pray you,
10:10. *Know* now that there shall fall unto the earth nothing
1Ch 28: 9. *know thou* the God of thy father,

Job 5:27. *know* thou (it) for thy good.
11: 6. *Know therefore* that God exacteth
19: 6. *Know* now that God hath overthrown me,
Ps. 4: 3(4). *But know* that the Lord hath set apart
46:10(11). *and know* that I (am) God:
100: 3. *Know ye* that the Lord he (is) God:
139.23. Search me, O God, *and know* my heart: try me, *and know* my thoughts:
Pro 3: 6. In all thy ways *acknowledge him*,
24:14. So (shall) *the knowledge of* wisdom (be) unto thy soul: (lit. *know* that such is wisdom unto thy soul)
Ecc.11: 9. *but know* thou,...God will bring thee into
Isa. 33:13. *and*, ye (that are) near, *acknowledge* my
Jer. 2:19. *know therefore* and see
23. *know* what thou hast done:
3:13. Only *acknowledge* thine iniquity,
5: 1. see now, *and know*,
6:18. *and know*, O congregation,
15:15. *know* that for thy sake I have suffered
31:34. *Know* the Lord:

KAL.—*Future*.

Gen 3: 7. *and they knew* that they (were) naked;
4:17. *And* Cain *knew* his wife;
25. *And* Adam *knew* his wife again;
8:11. *so* Noah *knew* that the waters
9:24. *and knew* what his younger son
15: 8. whereby *shall I know* that I shall inherit
13. *Know* of a surety that
18:21. if not, *I will know*.
19: 5. bring them out unto us, *that we may know*
24:14. thereby *shall I know* that thou hast shewed
38: 9. *And* Onan *knew* that the seed should not
42:33. Hereby *shall I know* that ye (are) true
34. *then shall I know* that ye (are) no spies,
43: 7. *could we* certainly *know* that he would say,
Ex. 2:25. *and* God *had respect* unto (them). (marg. *knew*)
7:17. In this *thou shalt know* that I (am) the Lord:
8:10(6). that *thou mayest know*
22(18). *thou mayest know* that I (am)
9:14. that *thou mayest know*
29. that *thou mayest know*
10: 7. *knowest thou* not yet that Egypt is destroyed?
26. *we know* not with what we must serve the
11: 7. that *ye may know*
33: 5. *that I may know* what to do unto thee.
13. *that I may know thee*,
17. *and I know thee* by name.
Lev.23:43. That your generations *may know*
Nu. 16:28. Hereby *ye shall know* that the Lord hath
22:19. *that I may know* what the Lord will say
Deu 18:21. How *shall we know* the word
20:20. the trees which *thou knowest*
29: 6(5). that *ye might know* that I (am) the Lord
Jos. 3: 4. that *ye may know* the way
7. that *they may know* that,
10. Hereby *ye shall know* that the living God
22:22. and Israel he *shall know*;
23:13. *Know* for a certainty
Jud 18: 5. *that we may know*
19:22. *that we may know him*.
25. *and they knew* her,
Ru. 3:18. until *thou know* how the matter will fall:
4: 4. tell me, *that I may know*:
1Sa. 1:19. *and* Elkanah *knew* Hannah his wife;
3:20. *And* all Israel...*knew* that Samuel
4: 6. *And they understood* that the ark of the
17:46. *that* all the earth *may know* that there is a
47. *And* all this assembly *shall know*
18:28. Saul saw *and knew* that the Lord (was)
20: 3. *Let* not Jonathan *know* this,
9. *I knew* certainly that evil were determined
33. *whereby* Jonathan *knew* that it was
21: 2(3). *Let* no man *know* any thing of the
22: 3. till *I know* what God will do for me.
23: 9. *And* David *knew* that Saul secretly practised
26: 4. *and understood* that Saul was come
28: 1. *Know thou* assuredly,
2. thou *shalt know* what thy servant
14. *And* Saul *perceived* that it (was) Samuel,
2Sa. 3:37. *For*...all Israel *understood* that day
38. *Know ye* not that there is a prince
5:12. *And* David *perceived* that the Lord had
14: 1. *Now* Joab... *perceived* that the king's heart
19:35(36). *can I discern* between good and evil?

1K. 2:37. *thou shalt know* for certain
42. *Know* for a certain, on the day thou
3: 7. *I know* not (how) to go out or come in.
8:38. which *shall know* every man
39. whose heart *thou knowest*;
43. the earth *may know* thy name,
14: 2. that *thou be* not *known* (lit. *they may* not *know* thee)
18:12. carry thee whither *I know* not;
37. *that* this people *may know*
2K. 5: 8. *and he shall know* that there is a prophet
19:19. *that* all the kingdoms of the earth *may know* that thou (art) the Lord
1Ch 14: 2. *And* David *perceived* that the Lord had
21: 2. to me, *that I may know* (it).
2Ch 6:29. every one *shall know* his own sore
30. whose heart *thou knowest*;
33. all people of the earth *may know* thy
12: 8. *that they may know* my service,
20:12. neither *know we* what to do:
32:13. *Know ye* not what I and my fathers have
33:13. *Then* Manasseh *knew* that the Lord he
Neh 4:11(5). *They shall* not *know*,
6:16. *for they perceived* that this work was
13:10. *And I perceived* that the portions of the
Job 8: 9. we (are but of) yesterday, and *know*
9:21. (yet) *would I* not *know* my soul:
11: 8. deeper than hell; what *canst thou know?*
14:21. His sons come to honour, and *he knoweth*
15: 9. that *we know* not?
19:29. that *ye may know* (there is) a judgment.
21:19. he rewardeth him, *and he shall know* (it).
23: 5. *I would know* the words
31: 6. *that* God *may know* mine integrity.
34: 4. *let us know* among ourselves
36:26. God (is) great, and *we know* (him) not,
37: 5. great things doeth he, which *we cannot comprehend*.
15. *Dost thou know* when God disposed them,
16. *Dost thou know* the balancings
38: 5. if *thou knowest?*
42: 3. things...which *I knew* not.
Ps. 9:20(21). (that) the nations *may know*
35: 8. Let destruction come upon him *at unawares*; (marg. (which) *he knoweth* not)
39: 4(5). (that) *I may know* how frail I (am).
6(7). *knoweth* not who shall gather them.
51: 3(5). *I acknowledge* my transgressions:
59:13(14). *and let them know* that God ruleth
73:22. So foolish (was) I, and *ignorant*: (marg. *I knew* not)
78: 3. Which we have heard *and known*,
6. That the generation to come might *know*
83:18(19). *That* (men) *may know*
92: 6(7). A brutish man *knoweth* not;
101: 4. *I will* not *know* a wicked (person).
109:27. *That they may know* that this (is) thy
119:125. *that I may know* thy testimonies.
138: 6. the proud *he knoweth* afar off.
139: 1. thou hast searched me, *and known* (me).
144: 3. what (is) man, *that thou takest knowledge of him!*
Pro 5: 6. *thou canst* not *know* (them).
10:32. The lips of the righteous *know* what is
24:12. *doth* (not) *he know* (it)?
27: 1. *thou knowest* not what a day may bring
23. *Be thou diligent* to know (lit. in knowing *know*) the state of thy flocks,
28:22. *considereth* not that poverty shall come
30: 3. nor *have* (marg. *know*) the knowledge of
4. what (is) his son's name, if *thou canst tell?*
Ecc. 8: 5. Whoso keepeth the commandment *shall feel* (marg. *know*) no evil thing: and a wise man's heart *discerneth*
9:12. man also *knoweth* not his time:
10:14. a man *cannot tell* what shall be;
11: 2. *thou knowest* not what evil shall be
5. *thou knowest* not the works
Cant. 1: 8. If *thou know* not, O thou fairest among
Isa. 5:19. *that we may know* (it)!
6: 9. see ye indeed, but *perceive* not.
7:16. the child *shall know* to refuse the evil,
8: 4. the child *shall have knowledge*
19:12. *and let them know* what the Lord of hosts
37:20. *that* all the kingdoms of the earth *may know*
40:21. *Have ye* not *known?*

Isa. 41:20. That they may see, and *know*,
22. *and know* the latter end of them ;
23. *that we may know* that ye (are) gods:
26. *that we may know?* and beforetime,
43:10. that *ye may know and* believe me,
19. *shall ye* not *know* it?
44: 9. they see not, nor *know;*
45: 3. that *thou mayest know* that I, the Lord,
6. That *they may know* from the rising of the
47: 8. *shall I know* the loss of children:
11. thou *shalt* not *know* from whence it riseth:
— (which) *thou shalt* not *know*.
50: 7. *and I know* that I shall not be ashamed.
52: 6. my people *shall know* my name:
55: 5. Behold, thou shalt call a nation (that) *thou knowest* not,
58: 3. *thou takest* no *knowledge?*
Jer. 5:15. a nation whose language *thou knowest* not,
6:27. *that thou mayest know* and try their way.
11:18. *and I know* (it):
13:12. *Do we* not certainly *know* that every bottle
17: 9. who *can know it?*
26:15. *know ye* for certain,
31:34. *they shall* all *know* me,
32: 8. *Then I knew* that this (was) the word of
36:19. *let* no man *know* where ye be.
38:24. *Let* no man *know* of these words,
40:14. *Dost thou* certainly *know*
15. no man *shall know* (it):
42:19. *know* certainly that I have admonished
22. Now therefore *know* certainly
44:29. that *ye may know* that my words shall
Eze 10:20. *and I knew* that they (were) the cherubims.
19: 7. *And he knew* their desolate palaces,
20:26. that *they might know* that I (am) the Lord.
38:14. *shalt thou* not *know* (it)?
Dan 9:25. *Know therefore* and understand,
Hos 6: 3. *Then shall we know*, (if) we follow on
9: 7. Israel *shall know* (it):
13: 4. *thou shalt know* no god but me:
14: 9(10). prudent, *and he shall know them?*
Jon 1: 7. *that we may know* for whose cause
Zec 11:11. *and* so the poor...*knew* that it (was) the

KAL.—*Participle.* Poel.

Gen 3: 5. God *doth know* that in the day
— ye shall be as gods, *knowing* good and evil.
25:27. Esau was a *cunning* hunter,
33:13. My lord *knoweth* that the children (are)
Nu. 24:16. *and knew* the knowledge of the most High,
31:17. kill every woman *that hath known* man
Jos. 22:22. the Lord God of gods, he *knoweth*,
Jud 21:11. every woman that hath lain by man. (lit. *that knoweth* the lying with man)
Ru. 3:11. the city of my people *doth know*
1Sa. 10:11. all *that knew him* beforetime
16:16. seek out a man, (who is) a *cunning* player
18. (that is) *cunning* in playing,
23:17. that also Saul my father *knoweth*.
26:12. no man saw (it), nor *knew* (it),
2Sa. 12:22. Who *can tell* (whether) God will be gracious
17:10. all Israel *knoweth* that thy father
1K. 5: 6(20). any *that can skill* to hew
9:27. shipmen *that had knowledge of* the sea,
2K. 17:26. because they *know* not the manner of the
1Ch 12:32. (men) *that had understanding* (lit. *knew* the knowledge) of the times,
2Ch 2: 7(6). *and that can skill* to grave
8(7). I know that thy servants *can skill*
12(11). *endued with* prudence and understanding, (marg. *knowing*)
13(12). *endued with* understanding,
14(13). *skilful* to work in gold,
8:18. servants *that had knowledge of* the sea;
Neh 10:28(29). every one *having knowledge*, and having understanding;
Est. 1:13. the wise men, *which knew* the times,
— all *that knew* law and judgment:
4:11. the people of the king's provinces, *do know*,
14. who *knoweth* whether thou art come
Job 19:13. *and mine acquaintance* are verily estranged
24: 1. do *they that know him* not see his days?
34: 2. *and* give ear unto me, ye *that have knowledge*.
42:11. all *they that had been of his acquaintance*
P. 1: 6. the Lord *knoweth* the way of the righteous:
9:10(11). *they that know* thy name
Ps. 36:10(11). *unto them that know thee;*
37:18. The Lord *knoweth* the days of the upright
44:21(22). *he knoweth* the secrets of the heart.
74: 9. any *that knoweth* how long.
87: 4. *to them that know me:*
89:15(16). the people *that know* the joyful sound:
90:11. Who *knoweth* the power of thine anger?
94:11. The Lord *knoweth* the thoughts of man,
119:79. *and those that have known* thy testimonies.
139:14. my soul *knoweth* right well.
Pro. 12:10. A righteous (man) *regardeth* the life of his
14:10. The heart *knoweth* his own bitterness;
17:27. *He that hath* knowledge spareth his words: (lit. *he that knoweth* knowledge)
24:22. who *knoweth* the ruin of them both?
28: 2. a man of understanding (and) *knowledge*
29: 7. The righteous *considereth* the cause of the
Ecc. 2:19. who *knoweth* whether he shall be a wise
3:21. Who *knoweth* the spirit of man
5: 1(4:17). they *consider* not that they do evil.
6: 8. *that knoweth* to walk before the living?
12. who *knoweth* what (is) good
8: 1. who *knoweth* the interpretation
7. he *knoweth* not that which shall be:
12. yet surely I *know*
9: 1. no man *knoweth* either love or hatred
5. the living *know* that they shall die: but the dead *know* not any thing,
11. nor yet favour *to men of skill;*
11: 5. thou *knowest* not what (is) the way of the
6. thou *knowest* not whether shall prosper,
Isa. 29:11. which (men) deliver to *one that is learned*, (lit. *that knoweth* a book)
15. Who seeth us? and who *knoweth us?*
51: 7. *ye that know* righteousness,
Jer. 29:23. even I *know*, and (am) a witness,
44:15. the men *which knew* that their wives had
48:17. all ye *that know* his name,
Eze. 28:19. *they that know thee* among the people
Dan 1: 4. *and cunning in* knowledge,
11:32. the people *that do know* their God
Joel 2:14. Who *knoweth* (if) he will return and repent,
Am. 5:16. *such as are skilful of* lamentation
Jon. 1:12. I *know* that for my sake
3: 9. Who *can tell* (if) God will turn and repent,
Nah. 1: 7. *and he knoweth* them that trust in him.
Zep. 3: 5. the unjust *knoweth* no shame.

KAL.—*Participle.* Paül.

Deu 1:13. *and known* among your tribes,
15. wise men, *and known*,
Isa. 53: 3. man of sorrows, *and acquainted with* grief:

* NIPHAL.—*Preterite.* *

Gen 41:21. *it could* not *be known* that they had eaten
Ex. 2:14. Surely this thing *is known*.
6: 3. *was I* not *known* to them.
21:36. if *it be known* that the ox hath used to push
Lev. 4:14. *When* the sin,...*is known*,
Deu 21: 1. it *be* not *known* who hath slain him:
Jud. 16: 9. So his strength *was* not *known*.
1Sa. 6: 3. *and it shall be known* to you
22: 6. Saul heard that David *was discovered*,
2Sa. 17:19. the thing *was* not *known*.
Neh 4:15(9). our enemies heard that *it was known*
Ps. 9:16(17). The Lord *is known* (by) the judgment
48: 3(4). God *is known* in her palaces
77:19(20). thy footsteps *are* not *known*.
Isa. 19:21. *And* the Lord *shall be known* to Egypt,
61: 9. *And* their seed *shall be known* among the
66:14. *and* the hand of the Lord *shall be known*
Eze 20: 9. in whose sight *I made myself known*
35:11. *and I will make myself known* among them,
38:23. *and I will be known* in the eyes of many
Nah 3:17. their place *is* not *known*

NIPHAL.—*Infinitive.*

Jer. 31:19. after that *I was instructed*,

NIPHAL.—*Future.*

Gen 41:31. the plenty *shall* not *be known* in the land
Ex. 33:16. wherein *shall it be known*
Ru. 3: 3. *make* not *thyself known* unto the man,
14. *Let it* not *be known* that a woman came
1K. 18:36. *let it be known* this day that thou (art) God
Est. 2:22. *And* the thing *was known* to Mordecai,
Ps. 74: 5. (A man) *was famous* according as he had

Ps. 79:10. *let him be known* among the heathen
88:12(13). *Shall* thy wonders *be known* in the
Pro 10: 9. he that perverteth his ways *shall be known.*
12:16. A fool's wrath *is* presently *known:*
14:33. in the midst of fools *is made known.*
Jer. 28: 9. (then) *shall* the prophet *be known,*
Eze. 20: 5. *and made myself known* unto them
36:32. *be it known* unto you:
Zec. 14: 7. one day which *shall be known* to the

NIPHAL.—*Participle.*

Ps. 76: 1(2). In Judah (is) God *known:*
Pro 31:23. Her husband *is known* in the gates,
Ecc. 6:10. *and it is known* that it (is) man:

* PIEL.—*Preterite.* *

Job 38:12. *caused* the dayspring *to know* his place;

* POAL.—*Preterite.* *

1 Sa. 21: 2(3). *I have appointed* (my) servants

* PUAL.—*Participle.* *

2K. 10:11. all his great men, *and his kinsfolks,*
Ru. 2: 1. (כתיב) Naomi had *a kinsman*
Job 19:14. *and my familiar friends* have forgotten
Ps. 31:11(12). a fear *to mine acquaintance:*
55:13(14). my guide, *and mine acquaintance.*
88: 8(9). Thou hast put away *mine acquaintance*
18(19). *mine acquaintance* into darkness.
Isa. 12: 5. (כתיב) this (is) *known* in all the earth.

* HIPHIL.—*Preterite.* *

Ex. 18:16. *and I do make* (them) *know* the statutes
20. *and shalt shew* them the way wherein they
33:12. *thou hast* not *let me know* whom thou wilt
Deu 4: 9. *but teach them* thy sons, and thy sons' sons;
Jos. 4:22. *Then ye shall let* your children *know,*
1 Sa. 10: 8. *and shew* thee what thou shalt do.
1 K. 1:27. *thou hast* not *shewed* (it) unto thy servant,
Neh 8:12. the words that *were declared* unto them.
9:14. *madest known* unto them thy holy sabbath,
Job 26: 3. (how) *hast thou* plentifully *declared* the
Ps. 77:14(15). *thou hast declared* thy strength among
98: 2. The Lord *hath made known* his salvation:
Pro 22:19. *I have made known to thee* this day,
Jer. 11:18. the Lord *hath given me knowledge* (of it),
Eze. 20:11. *shewed* them my judgments, (marg. *made* them *to know*)
22: 2. *yea, thou shalt shew her* all her abominations. (marg. *make her know*)
26. neither *have they shewed* (difference)
Hos 5: 9. *have I made known* that which shall surely

HIPHIL.—*Infinitive.*

Gen 41:39. Forasmuch as God *hath shewed* thee all
Deu 8: 3. that he *might make thee know* that man
1 Sa 28:15. *that thou mayest make known unto me* what
2 Sa 7:21. *to make* thy servant *know* (them).
1 Ch 17:19. *in making known* all (these) great things.
Ps. 25:14. he *will shew them* his covenant. (marg. *to make them know* (it))
78: 5. *that they should make them known* to their
106: 8. *that he might make* his mighty power *to be known.*
145:12. *To make known* to the sons of men
Pro 22:21. *That I might make thee know* the certainty
Isa. 64: 2(1). *to make* thy name *known* to thine

HIPHIL.—*Imperative.*

Ex. 33:13. *shew me* now thy way,
1 Sa. 6: 2. *tell us* wherewith we shall send it to his
1 Ch 16: 8. *make known* his deeds among the people.
Job 10: 2. *shew me* wherefore thou contendest with
13:23. *make me to know* my transgression
37:19. *Teach us* what we shall say unto him;
38: 3. I will demand of thee, *and answer thou me.* (marg. *make me know*)
40: 7 & 42:4. of thee, *and declare thou unto me.*
Ps. 25: 4. *Shew me* thy ways, O Lord;
39: 4(5). *make me to know* mine end,
90:12. So *teach* (us) to number our days,
105: 1. *make known* his deeds among the people.
143: 8. *cause me to know* the way wherein I should
Pro 9: 9. *teach* a just (man), and he will increase
Isa. 12: 4. *declare* his doings among the people,
Eze. 16: 2. *cause* Jerusalem *to know* her abominations,
20: 4. *cause them to know* the abominations
43:11. *shew* them the form of the house,

HIPHIL.—*Future.*

Nu. 16: 5. *Even* to morrow the Lord *will shew* who
Jud. 8:16. *and* with them *he taught* the men of Succoth. (marg. *made to know*)
1 Sa. 14:12. Come up to us, *and we will shew* you a
16: 3. I *will shew thee* what thou shalt do:
Job 32: 7. multitude of years *should teach* wisdom.
Ps. 16:11. *Thou wilt shew me* the path of life:
32: 5. *I acknowledged* my sin *unto thee,*
51: 6(8). *thou shalt make me to know* wisdom.
89: 1(2). with my mouth *will I make known* thy
103: 7. *He made known* his ways unto Moses,
Pro 1:23. *I will make known* my words unto you.
Isa. 5: 5. *I will tell* you what I will do
38:19. to the children *shall make known* thy truth.
40:13. (being) his counsellor *hath taught him?*
14. *shewed to him* the way of understanding?
Jer. 16:21. *I will cause them to know* mine hand and
Eze. 39: 7. So *will I make* my holy name *known*
44:23. *cause them to discern* between the unclean
Hab 3: 2. in the midst of the years *make known;*

HIPHIL.—*Participle.*

2 Ch 23:13. *and such as taught* to sing praise.
Isa. 47:13. the monthly *prognosticators,* (marg. *that give knowledge* concerning the months)
Jer. 16:21. I will this once *cause them to know,*
Dan 8:19. I will *make thee know* what shall be in the

* HOPHAL.—*Preterite.* *

Lev. 4:23, 28. if his sin,...*come to his knowledge;*

HOPHAL.—*Participle.*

Isa. 12: 5. this (is) *known* in all the earth.

* HITHPAEL.—*Infinitive.* *

Gen 45: 1. *while* Joseph *made himself known* unto his

HITHPAEL.—*Future.*

Nu. 12: 6. *I* the Lord *will make myself known*

יְדַע *y'dag*, Ch. 3046

* P'AL.—*Preterite.* *

Dan 4: 9(6). I *know* that the spirit of the holy gods
5:21. till *he knew* that the most high God ruled
22. though *thou knewest* all this;
6:10(11). Now when Daniel *knew* that the

P'AL.—*Imperative.*

Dan 6:15(16). *Know,* O king, that the law of the

P'AL.—*Future.*

Ezr. 4:15. *and know* that this city (is) a rebellious
Dan 2: 9. *and I shall know* that ye can shew me
30. that *thou mightest know* the thoughts
4:17(14). to the intent that the living *may know*
25(22). till *thou know* that the most High
26(23). *thou shalt have known* that the
32(29). until *thou know* that the most High

P'AL.—*Participle.* Active.

Ezr. 7:25. all *such as know* the laws of thy God; and teach ye *them that know* (them) not.
Dan 2: 8. I *know* of certainty that ye would gain
21. knowledge *to them that know*
22. *he knoweth* what (is) in the darkness,
5:23. which see not, nor hear, nor *know:*

P'AL.—*Participle.* Passive.

Ezr. 4:12. Be it *known* unto the king,
13. Be it *known* now unto the king,
5: 8. Be it *known* unto the king,
Dan 3:18. be it *known* unto thee, O king, that

* APHEL.—*Preterite.* *

Ezr. 4:14. have we sent *and certified* the king;
Dan 2:15. Arioch *made* the thing *known* to Daniel.
17. and *made* the thing *known* to Hananiah,
23. and *hast made known unto me*
— *thou hast* (now) *made known unto us*
28. *and maketh known* to the king (marg. *hath made known*)
29. *maketh known to thee* what shall come to
45. the great God *hath made known*

APHEL.—*Infinitive.*

Ezr. 5:10. their names also, *to certify thee,*
Dan 2:26. Art thou able *to make known unto me*
4:18(15). not able *to make known unto me*
5: 8. *nor make known* to the king the
15. and *make known unto me* the
16. and *make known to me* the

APHEL.—*Future.*

Ezr. 7:25. *teach ye* them that know (them) not.
Dan 2: 5, 9. if *ye will* not *make known unto me*
25. that *will make known* unto the king
30. that *shall make known* the
4: 6(3). that *they might make known unto me*
5:17. and *make known to him* the interpretation.
7:16. and *made me know* the interpretation

APHEL.—*Participle.*

Ezr. 4:16. We *certify* the king that, if this city
7:24. Also *we certify* you, that touching any of
Dan 4: 7(4). but *they did* not *make known* unto me

3049 **יִדְּעֹנִי** *yid-d'ˉgōh-nee'*, m.

Lev.19:31. neither seek after *wizards,*
20: 6. and after *wizards,*
27. that is *a wizard,*
Deu 18:11. *or a wizard,* or a necromancer.
1Sa.28: 3. and *the wizards,* out of the land.
9. and *the wizards,* out of the land:
2K. 21: 6. dealt with familiar spirits *and wizards:*
23:24. the (workers with) familiar spirits, and *the wizards,*
2Ch 33: 6. with a familiar spirit, *and with wizards:*
Isa. 8:19. unto *wizards* that peep, and that mutter:
19: 3. have familiar spirits, and to *the wizards.*

3051, 3053 **יָהַב** [*yāh-hav'*].

* KAL.—*Preterite.* *

Ps. 55:22(23). Cast *thy burden* upon the Lord, (lit. which *he hath given thee, i. e.* thy lot)

KAL.—*Imperative.*

Gen 11: 3. *Go to,* let us make brick,
4. *Go to,* let us build us a city
7. *Go to,* let us go down,
29:21. *Give* (me) my wife, for my days are
30: 1. *Give* me children, or else I die.
38:16. *Go to,* I pray thee,
47:15. came unto Joseph, and said, *Give* us
16. And Joseph said, *Give* your cattle;
Ex. 1:10. *Come on,* let us deal wisely
Deu 1:13. *Take* you wise men, (marg. *Give*)
32: 3. *ascribe ye* greatness unto our God.
Jos. 18: 4. *Give* out from among you three men
Jud. 1:15. *Give* me a blessing:
20: 7. *give* here your advice and counsel.
Ru. 3:15. *Bring* the vail that (thou hast) upon
1Sa.14:41. *Give* a perfect (lot).
2Sa.11:15. *Set ye* Uriah in the forefront of the hottest
16:20. *Give* counsel among you what we shall
1Ch 16:28. *Give* unto the Lord, ye kindreds of the people, *give* unto the Lord
29. *Give* unto the Lord the glory
Job 6:22. Did I say, *Bring* unto me?
Ps. 29: 1. *Give* unto the Lord, O ye mighty, *give* unto the Lord glory and strength.
2. *Give* unto the Lord the glory
60:11(13). *Give* us help from trouble:
96: 7. *Give* unto the Lord, O ye kindreds of the people, *give* unto the Lord
8. *Give* unto the Lord the glory
108:12(13). *Give* us help from trouble:
Pro 30:15. horseleach hath two daughters, (crying), *Give, give.*
Hos 4:18. rulers (with) shame do love, *Give ye.*
Zec.11:12. If ye think good, *give* (me) my price;

3052 **יְהַב** *y'hav*, Ch.

* P'AL.—*Preterite.* *

Ezr. 5:12. *he gave* them into the hand of
16. (and) *laid* the foundation of the house
Dan 2:23. who *hast given* me wisdom and might,
37. the God of heaven *hath given* thee a
38. *hath he given* into thine hand,
48. and *gave* him many great gifts,
3:28. *and yielded* their bodies,
5:18. the most high God *gave* Nebuchadnezzar
19. for the majesty that *he gave* him,

P'AL.—*Imperative.*

Dan 5:17. and *give* thy rewards to another;

P'AL.—*Participle.* Active.

Dan 2:21. *he giveth* wisdom unto the wise,
6: 2(3). princes *might give* accounts unto them,

P'AL.—*Participle.* P'il.

Ezr. 5:14. *and they were delivered* unto (one),
Dan 5:28. *and given* to the Medes and Persians.
7: 4. and a man's heart *was given* to it.
6. and dominion *was given* to it.
11. *and given* to the burning flame.
12. lives were prolonged for a season (marg. a prolonging in life *was given* them)
14. And there *was given* him dominion,
22. and judgment *was given* to the saints
27. *shall be given* to the people of the saints

* ITHP'AL.—*Future.* *

Ezr. 6: 4. and *let* the expences *be given* out of the
Dan 4:16(13). and *let* a beast's heart *be given* unto
7:25. *and they shall be given* into his hand

ITHP'AL.—*Participle.*

Ezr. 4:20. and custom, *was paid* unto them.
6: 8. forthwith expences *be given* unto these
9. *let it be given* them day by day
7:19. The vessels also that *are given* thee

יָהַד [*yāh-had'*]. 3054

* HITHPAEL.—*Participle.* *

Est. 8:17. people of the land *became Jews;*

יָהִיר *yāh-heer'*, adj. 3093

Pro.21:24. Proud (and) *haughty* scorner
Hab. 2: 5. (he is) a *proud* man,

יַהֲלֹם *yah - hălōhm'*, m. 3095

Ex. 28:18 & 39:11. a sapphire, *and a diamond.*
Eze.28:13. sardius, topaz, *and the diamond,*

יוֹבֵל *yōh-vēhl'*, com. 3104

Ex. 19:13. when *the trumpet* soundeth (marg. or, *cornet*)
Lev.25:10. it shall be *a jubile* unto you;
11. *A jubile* shall that fiftieth year
12. For it (is) *the jubile;* it shall
13. In the year of *this jubile* ye shall
15. after *the jubile* thou shalt
28. until the year of *jubile:* and *in the jubile* it shall go out,
30. not go out *in the jubile.*
31. *and* they shall go out *in the jubile.*
33. go out *in* (the year of) *jubile:*
40. unto the year of *jubile:*
50. him unto the year of *jubile:*
52. years unto the year of *jubile,*
54. go out in the year of *jubile,*
27:17. from the year of *jubile,*
18. sanctify his field after *the jubile,*
—, 23. unto the year of *the jubile,*
21. it goeth out *in the jubile,*
24. In the year of *the jubile* the
Nu. 36: 4. when *the jubile of* the children
Jos. 6: 4, 8, 13. seven trumpets of *rams' horns:*
5. a long (blast) with *the ram's* horn,
6. seven trumpets of *rams' horns*

יוּבַל *yoo-val'*, m. 3105

Jer. 17: 8. (that) spreadeth out her roots by *the river*

3117 **יוֹם** *yōhm*, m.

Gen 1: 5. God called the light *Day*,
— evening and the morning were *the* first *day*.
8. the evening and the morning were *the* second *day*.
13. the evening and the morning were *the* third *day*.
14. divide *the day* from the night;
— for seasons, *and for days*,
16. the greater light to rule *the day*,
18. to rule *over the day*
19. the evening and the morning were *the* fourth *day*.
23. evening and the morning were *the* fifth *day*.
31. evening and the morning were *the* sixth *day*.
2: 2. *on the* seventh *day* God ended his work
— he rested *on the* seventh *day*
3. God blessed *the* seventh *day*,
4. *in the day that* the Lord God made
17. *in the day that* thou eatest thereof
3: 5. *in the day* ye eat thereof,
8. the cool of *the day*:
14. dust shalt thou eat all *the days of* thy life:
17. (of) it all *the days of* thy life;
4: 3. in process of *time* it came to pass,
14. thou hast driven me out *this day*
5: 1. *In the day that* God created man,
2. *in the day when* they were created.
4. *the days of* Adam
5. all *the days* that Adam lived
8. all *the days of* Seth
11. all *the days of* Enos
14. all *the days of* Cainan
17. all *the days of* Mahalaleel
20. all *the days of* Jared
23. all *the days of* Enoch
27. all *the days of* Methuselah
31. all *the days of* Lamech
6: 3. *his days* shall be an hundred and
4. giants in the earth *in* those *days*;
5. evil continually. (marg. every *day*)
7: 4. For yet seven *days*,
— to rain upon the earth forty *days*
10. it came to pass after seven *days*,
11. *the* seventeenth *day* of the month, *the* same *day* were all the fountains
12. the rain was upon the earth forty *days*
13. In *the* selfsame *day* entered Noah,
17. the flood was forty *days* upon the earth;
24. an hundred and fifty *days*.
8: 3. the end of *the* hundred and fifty *days*
4. *the* seventeenth *day* of the month,
6. at the end of forty *days*,
10, 12. he stayed yet other seven *days*;
14. *the* seven and twentieth *day* of the month, was the earth dried.
22. While the earth remaineth, (marg. as yet all *the days of* the earth)
— *and day* and night shall not cease.
9:29. all *the days of* Noah were 950 years:
10:25. *in his days* was the earth divided;
11:32. *the days of* Terah were 205 years:
14: 1. to pass *in the days of* Amraphel
15:18. *In* the same *day* the Lord made a covenant
17:12. he that is eight *days* old
23. in *the* selfsame *day*, as God had said
26. *the* selfsame *day* was Abraham
18: 1. the heat of *the day*;
11. well stricken *in age*;
19:37. the father of the Moabites unto *this day*.
38. children of Ammon unto *this day*.
21: 4. being eight *days* old,
8. made a great feast *the* (same) *day*
26. neither yet heard I (of it), but *to day*.
34. in the Philistines' land many *days*.
22: 4. *on the* third *day* Abraham lifted up his eyes,
14. as it is said (to) *this day*,
24: 1. well stricken *in age*:
12. send me good speed *this day*,
42. I came *this day* unto the well,
55. Let the damsel abide with us (a few) *days*,
25: 7. these (are) *the days of* the years
24. when *her days* to be delivered
31. Sell me *this day* thy birthright.
33. Swear to me *this day*;
26: 1. *in the days of* Abraham.

Gen26: 8. when he had been there *a* long *time*, (lit. when *days* were prolonged to him there)
15, 18. *in the days of* Abraham his father,
32. it came to pass *the* same *day*,
33. of the city (is) Beer-sheba unto this *day*.
27: 2. I know not *the day of* my death:
41. *The days of* mourning for my father
44. tarry with him a few *days*,
45. deprived also of you both in one *day*?
29: 7. (it is) yet high *day*,
14. he abode with him the *space* of a month. (marg. a month of *days*)
20. they seemed unto him (but) a few *days*,
21. *my days* are fulfilled,
30:14. *in the days of* wheat harvest,
32. I will pass through all thy flock *to day*,
33. answer for me *in time* to come, (lit. *in the day of* to-morrow)
35. he removed that *day* the he goats
36. he set three *days'* journey betwixt
31:22. it was told Laban *on the* third *day*
23. pursued after him seven *days'* journey;
39. (whether) stolen by *day*,
40. *in the day* the drought consumed me,
43. what can I do *this day* unto these
48. witness between me and thee *this day*.
32:32(33). unto this *day*:
33:13. if men should overdrive them one *day*,
16. Esau returned that *day*
34:25. it came to pass *on the* third *day*,
35: 3. answered me *in the day of* my distress,
20. the pillar of Rachel's grave unto *this day*.
28. *the days of* Isaac were 180 years.
29. (being) old and full of *days*:
37:34. mourned for his son many *days*.
38:12. And in process of *time* (lit. *the days* were multiplied)
39:10. spake to Joseph *day by day*, (lit. *day*, *day*,)
11. it came to pass *about* this *time*,
40: 4. they continued *a season* in ward.
7. Wherefore look ye (so) sadly *to day*?
12. three branches (are) three *days*:
13, 19. Yet within three *days*
18. The three baskets (are) three *days*:
20. it came to pass *the* third *day*, (which was) Pharaoh's birth*day*,
41: 1. at the end of two *full* years,
9. I do remember my faults *this day*:
42:13. the youngest (is) *this day* with our father,
17. all together into ward three *days*.
18. Joseph said unto them *the* third *day*,
32. the youngest (is) *this day* with our father
43: 9. bear the blame for ever: (lit. all *the days*)
44:32. I shall bear the blame to my father for ever. (lit. all *the days*)
47: 8. How old (art) thou? (marg. How many (are) *the days of* the years of thy life)
9. *The days of* the years of my pilgrimage
— few and evil have *the days of* the years of my life been, and have not attained unto *the days of*
— *in the days of* their pilgrimage.
23. I have bought you *this day*
26. a law over the land of Egypt unto this *day*,
28. the whole age (marg. *the days of* the years of his life) of Jacob
29. *the time* drew nigh that Israel must die:
48:15. all my life long unto this *day*,
20. he blessed them that *day*,
49: 1. which shall befall you in *the* last *days*.
50: 3. forty *days* were fulfilled for him;
— so are fulfilled *the days of*
— threescore and ten *days*.
4. when *the days of* his mourning were past,
10. made a mourning for his father seven *days*.
20. *as* (it is) this *day*,
Ex. 2:11. it came to pass *in* those *days*,
13. he went out *the* second *day*,
18. How (is it that) ye are come so soon *to day*?
23. *in* process of *time*, (lit. *in* those many *days*)
3:18 & 5:3. three *days'* journey into the
5: 6. Pharaoh commanded *the* same *day*
13. (your) *daily* tasks, (marg. a matter of *a day in his day*)
14. both yesterday and *to day*,
19. your *daily* task. (lit. the affair of *the day in its day*)

Ex. 6:28. *on the day* (when)the Lord spake unto
7:25. seven *days* were fulfilled,
8:22(18). I will sever *in* that *day*
27(23). three *days'* journey into the wilderness,
9:18. since the foundation thereof (lit. from *the day* it was founded)
10: 6. *since the day* that they were upon the earth unto this *day*.
13. an east wind upon the land all that *day*,
22. in all the land of Egypt three *days:*
23. any from his place for three *days:*
28. *in* (that) *day* thou seest my face
12: 6. *the* fourteenth *day* of the same month:
14. this *day* shall be unto you for a memorial;
15. Seven *days* shall ye eat unleavened bread;
— *the* first *day* ye shall put away
— *from the* first *day* until *the* seventh *day*,
16. *And in the* first *day* (there shall be) an holy convocation, *and in the* seventh *day*
17. in this selfsame *day*
— observe this *day* in your generations
18. *the* fourteenth *day* of the month
— *the* one and twentieth *day* of the month
19. Seven *days* shall there be no leaven
41. *the* selfsame *day* it came to pass,
51. it came to pass *the* selfsame *day*,
13: 3. Remember this *day*, in which ye came out
4. *This day* came ye out
6. Seven *days* thou shalt eat unleavened bread, *and in the* seventh *day* (shall be) a
7. Unleavened bread shall be eaten seven *days;*
8. thou shalt shew thy son *in* that *day*,
10. *from year to year.*
14:13. which he will shew to you *to day:* for the Egyptians whom ye have seen *to day*,
30. the Lord saved Israel that *day*
15:22. they went three *days* in the wilderness,
16: 1. *the* fifteenth *day* of the second month
4. gather a certain rate *every day*, (marg. the portion of *a day in his day*)
5. *on the* sixth *day* they shall prepare
— as they gather *daily*. (lit. *a day, a day*)
22. *on the* sixth *day* they gathered twice as
25. Eat that *to day;* for *to day* (is) a sabbath unto the Lord: *to day* ye shall not find
26. Six *days* ye shall gather it; *but on the* seventh *day*,
27. *on the* seventh *day* for to gather,
29. he giveth you *on the* sixth *day* the bread of *two days;*
— let no man go out of his place *on the* seventh *day*.
30. the people rested *on the* seventh *day*.
19: 1. *the* same *day* came they (into) the
10. sanctify them *to day* and to morrow,
11. be ready *against the* third *day:* for *the* third *day* the Lord will come down
15. Be ready against *the* third *day:*
16. it came to pass *on the* third *day*
20: 8. Remember *the* sabbath *day*,
9. Six *days* shalt thou labour,
10. *But the* seventh *day* (is) the sabbath
11. (in) six *days* the Lord made
— rested *the* seventh *day:* wherefore the Lord blessed *the* sabbath *day*,
12. that *thy days* may be long upon the land
21:21. if he continue *a day* or *two*, (lit. *two days*)
22:30(29). seven *days* it shall be with his dam; *on the* eighth *day* thou shalt give it me.
23:12. Six *days* thou shalt do thy work, *and on the* seventh *day* thou shalt rest:
15. thou shalt eat unleavened bread seven *days*,
26. the number of *thy days* I will fulfil.
24:16. the cloud covered it six *days:* and *the* seventh *day* he called unto Moses
18. Moses was in the mount forty *days*
29:30. shall put them on seven *days*,
35. seven *days* shalt thou consecrate them.
36. thou shalt offer *every day* a bullock
37. Seven *days* thou shalt make an atonement
38. two lambs of the first year *day by day*
31:15. Six *days* may work be done; *but in the* seventh (lit. seventh *day*)
— (any) work *in the* sabbath *day*,
17. (in) six *days* the Lord made heaven and earth, *and on the* seventh *day* he rested,

Ex. 32:28. there fell of the people that *day*
29. Consecrate yourselves *to day*
— that he may bestow upon you a blessing *this day*.
34. *nevertheless in the day when* I visit
34:11. I command thee *this day:*
18. Seven *days* thou shalt eat unleavened
21. Six *days* thou shalt work, *but on the* seventh *day* thou shalt rest:
28. he was there with the Lord forty *days*
35: 2. Six *days* shall work be done, *but on the* seventh *day* there shall be to you
3. *upon the* sabbath *day*.
40: 2. *On the* first *day* of the first month
37. they journeyed not till *the day*
Lev. 6: 5(5:24). *in the day of* his trespass offering.
20(13). *in the day* when he is anointed;
7:15. shall be eaten *the* same *day*
16. *the* same *day* that he offereth
17. the sacrifice *on the* third *day* shall be burnt
18. eaten at all on *the* third *day*,
35. *in the day* (when) he presented them
36. *in the day that* he anointed them,
38. *in the day that* he commanded the children
8:33. (in) seven *days*, until *the days of* your consecration be at an end (lit. until *the day* of the fulfilling of *the days of*, &c.): for seven *days*
34. As he hath done this *day*,
35. Therefore shall ye abide...seven *days*,
9: 1. it came to pass *on the* eighth *day*,
4. *to day* the Lord will appear unto you.
10:19. *this day* have they offered
— I had eaten the sin offering *to day*,
12: 2. she shall be unclean seven *days; according to the days of* the separation
3. *And in the* eighth *day*
4. her purifying three and thirty *days;* (lit. thirty *days* and three *days*)
— until *the days of* her purifying be fulfilled.
5. her purifying threescore and six *days*. (lit. sixty *days* and six *days*)
6. when *the days of* her purifying are fulfilled,
13: 4. the priest shall shut up (him)...seven *days:*
5. priest shall look on him *the* seventh *day:*
—, 21, 26. priest shall shut him up seven *days*
6. the priest shall look on him again *the* seventh *day:*
14. *But when* raw flesh appeareth (lit. *and in the day of* appearing, &c.)
27. priest shall look upon him *the* seventh *day:*
31. the plague of the scall seven *days:*
32. *in the* seventh *day* the priest shall look on
33. the priest shall shut up (him)...seven *days*
34. *in the* seventh *day* the priest shall look on
46. All *the days* wherein the plague
50. shut up (it)...seven *days:*
51. he shall look...*on the* seventh *day:*
54. he shall shut it up seven *days* more:
14: 2. *in the day of* his cleansing:
8. abroad out of his tent seven *days*.
9. it shall be *on the* seventh *day*,
10. *And on the* eighth *day* he shall take two he
23. he shall bring them *on the* eighth *day*
38. shut up the house seven *days:*
39. priest shall come again *the* seventh *day*,
46. all *the while that* it is shut up
57. To teach *when* (it is) unclean, *and when* (it is) clean: (marg. *in the day of* the *unclean, and in the day of* the clean)
15:13. he shall number to himself seven *days*
14. *And on the* eighth *day* he shall take
19. she shall be put apart seven *days:*
24. he shall be unclean seven *days;*
25. many *days* out of the time
— *the days of* the issue of her uncleanness shall be *as the days of* her separation
26. *the days of* her issue
28. she shall number to herself seven *days*,
29. *And on the* eighth *day* she shall take
16:30. *on* that *day* shall (the priest) make an
19: 6. It shall be eaten *the* same *day*
— if ought remain until *the* third *day*,
7. if it be eaten at all *on the* third *day*,
22:27. it shall be seven *days* under the dam; *and from the* eighth *day* and thenceforth
28. her young both *in* one *day*.

Lev.22:30. *On the* same *day* it shall be eaten
23: 3. Six *days* shall work be done:
— *but the* seventh *day* (is) the sabbath of rest,
6. *the* fifteenth *day* of the same month
— seven *days* ye must eat unleavened bread.
7. *In the* first *day* ye shall have an holy
8. ye shall offer an offering...seven *days: in the* seventh *day* (is) an holy convocation:
12. ye shall offer *that day*
14. until *the* selfsame *day*
15. *from the day* that ye brought the sheaf
16. shall ye number fifty *days;*
21. ye shall proclaim on *the* selfsame *day*,
27. *a day of* atonement:
28. ye shall do no work in that same *day:* for it (is) *a day of* atonement,
29. shall not be afflicted in that same *day*,
30. doeth any work in that same *day*,
34. *The* fifteenth *day* of this seventh month
— seven *days* unto the Lord.
35. *On the* first *day* (shall be) an holy
36. Seven *days* ye shall offer an offering
— *on the* eighth *day* shall be an holy
37. every thing upon *his day:* (lit. the matter of *a day in his day*)
39. in *the* fifteenth *day* of the seventh month,
— a feast unto the Lord seven *days: on the* first *day* (shall be) a sabbath, *and on the* eighth *day* (shall be) a sabbath.
40. ye shall take you *on the first day*
— before the Lord your God seven *days.*
41. seven *days* in the year.
42. Ye shall dwell in booths seven *days;*
24: 8. *Every* sabbath he shall set it (lit. *on the* sabbath *day, on the* sabbath *day*)
25: 8. *the space of* the seven sabbaths
9. *in the day of* atonement shall ye make the
29. (within) *a full year* may he redeem it.
50. *according to the time of* an hired servant
26:34, 35. *as long as* (lit. all *the days of*) it lieth
27:23. he shall give thine estimation *in* that *day*,
Nu. 3: 1. *in the day* (that) the Lord spake with
13. *on the day that* I smote all the firstborn
6: 4, 8. All *the days of* his separation
5. *the days of* the vow of his separation
— until *the days* be fulfilled,
6. *the days that* he separateth
9. *in the day of* his cleansing, *on the* seventh *day* shall he shave it.
10. *And on the* eighth *day* he shall bring two
11. shall hallow his head *that* same *day.*
12. *the days of* his separation,
— *but the days* that were before shall
13. *when the days of* his separation are fulfilled: (lit. *in the day of* the fulfilling of *the days of*)
7: 1. it came to pass *on the day that*
10. *in the day that* it was anointed,
11. each prince *on his day*, (lit. a prince *on a day*, a prince *on a day*)
12. he that offered his offering *the* first *day*
18. *On the* second *day* Nethaneel
24. *On the* third *day* Eliab
30. *On the* fourth *day* Elizur
36. *On the* fifth *day* Shelumiel
42. *On the* sixth *day* Eliasaph
48. *On the* seventh *day* Elishama
54. *On the* eighth *day* (offered) Gamaliel
60. *On the* ninth *day* Abidan
66. *On the* tenth *day* Ahiezer
72. *On the* eleventh *day* Pagiel (lit. *on the day, the* eleventh *day*)
78. *On the* twelfth *day* Ahira (lit. *id.*)
84. *in the day when* it was anointed,
8:17. *on the day that* I smote every firstborn
9: 3. In *the* fourteenth *day* of this month,
5. *the* fourteenth *day* of the first month
6. could not keep the passover *on* that *day:*
— before Aaron *on* that *day:*
11. *The* fourteenth *day* of the second month
15. *And on the day that* the tabernacle was
18. as long as (lit. all *the days of*) the cloud
19. upon the tabernacle many *days*,
20. when the cloud was a few *days*
22. Or (whether it were) *two days*, or a month, or *a year*,
10:10. *Also in the day of* your gladness,

Nu. 10:33, 33. three *days'* journey:
11:19. Ye shall not eat one *day*, nor two *days*, nor five *days*, neither ten *days*, nor twenty *days;*
20. a *whole* month, (marg. month of *days*)
21. eat a *whole* month. (lit. a month of *days*)
31. as it were *a day*'s journey on this side, and as it were *a day*'s journey on the
32. the people stood up all that *day*, and all (that) night, and all *the* next *day*,
12:14. should she not be ashamed seven *days?* let her be shut out from the camp seven *days*,
15. shut out from the camp seven *days:*
13:20. *Now the time* (was) *the time of* the first-ripe grapes.
25. searching of the land after forty *days.*
14:34. After the number of *the days*
— (even) forty *days, each day* for a year, (lit. *a day* for a year, *a day* for a year)
15:23. *the day* that the Lord commanded (Moses),
32. that gathered sticks *upon the* sabbath *day.*
19:11. shall be unclean seven *days.*
12. He shall purify himself with it *on the* third *day, and on the* seventh *day* he shall be clean: but if he purify not himself *the* third *day, then the* seventh *day* he shall not be clean.
14, 16. shall be unclean seven *days.*
19. sprinkle upon the unclean *on the* third *day, and on the* seventh *day:* and *on the* seventh *day* he shall purify himself,
20:15. *a* long *time;* (lit. many *days*)
29. they mourned for Aaron thirty *days*,
22:30. since (I was) thine unto this *day?*
24:14. in *the* latter *days.*
25:18. *the day of* the plague for Peor's sake.
28: 3. without spot *day by day*, (marg. *in a day*)
9. *And on the* sabbath *day* two lambs
16. in *the* fourteenth *day* of the first month
17. in *the* fifteenth *day* of this month
— seven *days* shall unleavened bread be
18. *In the* first *day*
24. After this manner ye shall offer *daily*, throughout *the* seven *days*,
25. *And on the* seventh *day*
26. *Also in the day of* the firstfruits,
29: 1. it is *a day of* blowing the trumpets
12. *the* fifteenth *day* of the seventh month
— a feast unto the Lord seven *days:*
17. *And on the* second *day*
20. *And on the* third *day* eleven bullocks,
23. *And on the* fourth *day* ten bullocks,
26. *And on the* fifth *day* nine bullocks,
29. *And on the* sixth *day* eight bullocks,
32. *And on the* seventh *day* seven bullocks,
35. *On the* eighth *day* ye shall have a solemn
30: 5(6). *in the day that* he heareth;
7(8). *in the day that* he heard (it):
8(9). *on the day* that he heard (it);
12(13). *on the day* he heard (them);
14(15). *from day* to *day;*
—(—). at her *in the day that* he heard (them).
31:19. abide without the camp seven *days:*
— purify (both) yourselves and your captives *on the* third *day, and on the* seventh *day.*
24. wash your clothes *on the* seventh *day*,
32:10. Lord's anger was kindled *the* same *time*,
33: 3. *the* fifteenth *day* of the first month;
8. went three *days'* journey
Deu 1: 2. (There are) eleven *days'* (journey)
10. ye (are) *this day* as the stars of heaven
39. which in *that day* had no knowledge
46. ye abode in Kadesh many *days, according unto the days* that ye abode
2: 1. we compassed mount Seir many *days.*
14. *And the space* in which we came
18. Thou art to pass...*this day:*
22. even unto this *day:*
25. *This day* will I begin to put the dread of
30. *as* (appeareth) this *day.*
3:14. Bashan-havoth-jair, unto this *day.*
4: 4. every one of you *this day.*
8. which I set before you *this day?*
9. all *the days of* thy life:
10. *the day* that thou stoodest before the Lord

Deu 4:10. all *the days* that they shall live
15. *on the day* (that) the Lord spake unto you
20. *as* (ye are) this *day*.
26. heaven and earth to witness against you *this day*,
— ye shall not prolong (your) *days* upon it,
30. (even) in the latter *days*,
32. ask now *of the days* that are past,
— *the day* that God created man
38. *as* (it is) this *day*.
39. Know therefore *this day*,
40. I command thee *this day*,
— that thou mayest prolong (thy) *days* upon the earth, which the Lord thy God giveth thee, *for ever*. (lit. all *the days*)
5: 1. I speak in your ears *this day*,
3. who (are) all of us here alive *this day*.
12. Keep *the* sabbath *day* to sanctify it,
13. Six *days* thou shalt labour,
14. *But the* seventh *day* (is) the sabbath
15. commanded thee to keep *the* sabbath *day*.
16. that *thy days* may be prolonged,
24(21). we have seen this *day*
29(26). keep all my commandments always, (lit. all *days*)
33(30). (that) ye may prolong (your) *days*
6: 2. all *the days of* thy life; and that *thy days*
6. I command thee *this day*,
24. for our good *always*, (lit. all *days*)
— *as* (it is) at this *day*.
7:11 & 8:1, 11. I command thee *this day*,
8:18. *as* (it is) this *day*.
19. I testify against you *this day*
9: 1. Thou (art) to pass over Jordan *this day*,
3. Understand therefore *this day*,
7. *the day* that thou didst depart
9. I abode in the mount forty *days*
10. *in the day of* the assembly.
11. at the end of forty *days*
18. before the Lord, as at the first, forty *days*
24. *from the day* that I knew you.
25. I fell down before the Lord forty *days*
10: 4. *in the day of* the assembly:
8. to bless in his name, unto this *day*.
10. *according to the* first *time*, forty *days*
13. I command thee *this day*
15. *as* (it is) this *day*.
11: 1. his commandments, alway. (lit. all *days*)
2. know ye *this day*:
4. hath destroyed them unto this *day*;
8. I command you *this day*,
9. that ye may prolong (your) *days*
13, 27, 28. I command you *this day*,
21. That *your days* may be multiplied, *and the days of* your children,
— *as the days of* heaven
26, 32. I set before you *this day*
12: 1. all *the days* that ye live
8. (the things) that we do here *this day*,
19. as long as thou livest (marg. all *thy days*)
13:18(19). I command thee *this day*,
14:23. the Lord thy God always. (lit. all *days*)
15: 5. I command thee *this day*.
15. I command thee this thing *to day*.
16: 3. seven *days* shalt thou eat unleavened
— that thou mayest remember *the day*
— all *the days of* thy life.
4. in all thy coast seven *days*,
— *the* first *day* at even,
8. Six *days* thou shalt eat unleavened bread: *and on the* seventh *day* (shall be) a
13. the feast of tabernacles seven *days*,
15. Seven *days* shalt thou keep a solemn
17: 9. the judge that shall be *in* those *days*,
19. all *the days of* his life:
20. that he may prolong (his) *days*
18: 5. him and his sons for ever. (lit. all *days*)
16. *in the day of* the assembly,
19: 9. I command thee *this day*,
— to walk ever (lit. all *the days*) in his
17. the judges, which shall be *in* those *days*;
20: 3. ye approach *this day* unto battle
19. shalt besiege a city *a* long *time*,
21:13. a *full* month: (lit. a month of *days*)
16. *when* (lit. *in the day*) he maketh his sons
23. shalt in any wise bury him that *day*;
22: 7. (that) thou mayest prolong (thy) *days*.

Deu 22:19. he may not put her away all *his days*.
29. he may not put her away all *his days*.
23: 6(7). their prosperity all *thy days*
24:15. *At his day* thou shalt give (him) his hire,
25:15. that *thy days* may be lengthened
26: 3. the priest that shall be *in* those *days*,
— I profess *this day* unto the Lord
16. This *day* the Lord thy God hath
17. Thou hast avouched the Lord *this day*
18. the Lord hath avouched thee *this day*
27: 1, 4. I command you *this day*.
2. *on the day* when ye shall pass over
9. this *day* thou art become the people of
10. I command thee *this day*.
11. Moses charged the people *the* same *day*,
28: 1, 13, 15. I command thee *this day*,
14. I command thee *this day*,
29. spoiled evermore, (lit. all *days*)
32. fail (with longing) for them all *the day*
33. oppressed and crushed alway: (lit. all *days*)
29: 4(3). ears to hear, unto this *day*.
10(9). Ye stand *this day* all of you
12(11). thy God maketh with thee *this day*:
13(12). That he may establish thee *to day*
15(14). (him) that standeth here with us *this day*
—(—). (him) that (is) not here with us *this day*:
18(17). whose heart turneth away *this day*
28(27). *as* (it is) this *day*.
30: 2, 8, 11, 16. I command thee *this day*,
15. I have set before thee *this day*
18. I denounce unto you *this day*,
— ye shall not prolong (your) *days*
19. I call heaven and earth to record *this day*
20. the length of *thy days*:
31: 2. I (am) an hundred and twenty years old *this day*;
13. *as long as* (lit. all *the days*) ye live in
14. *thy days* approach that thou must die:
17. kindled against them *in* that *day*,
— so that they will say *in* that *day*,
18. I will surely hide my face *in* that *day*
21. *even now*, before I have brought them
22. therefore wrote this song *the* same *day*,
27. I am yet alive with you *this day*,
29. evil will befall you in *the* latter *days*;
32: 7. Remember *the days of* old,
35. *the day of* their calamity (is) at hand,
46. I testify among you *this day*,
47. ye shall prolong (your) *days*
48. Lord spake unto Moses that selfsame *day*,
33:12. (the) Lord shall cover him all *the day*
25. *and as thy days*, (so shall) thy strength
34: 6. knoweth of his sepulchre unto this *day*.
8. wept for Moses...thirty *days*: *so the days of* weeping (and) mourning

Jos. 1: 5. all *the days of* thy life:
11. within three *days* ye shall pass over
2:16. hide yourselves there three *days*.
22. abode there three *days*,
3: 2. it came to pass after three *days*,
7. This *day* will I begin to magnify thee
15. all *the time of* harvest,
4: 9. they are there unto this *day*.
14. *On* that *day* the Lord magnified Joshua
— all *the days of* his life.
24. Lord your God for *ever*. (marg. all *days*)
5: 9. *This day* have I rolled away the reproach
— is called Gilgal unto this *day*.
10. *the* fourteenth *day* of the month
11. *the* selfsame *day*.
6: 3. Thus shalt thou do six *days*.
4. *and the* seventh *day* ye shall compass the
10. *the day* I bid you shout;
14. *the* second *day* they compassed the city
— so they did six *days*.
15. it came to pass *on the* seventh *day*,
— *on* that *day* they compassed the city
25. (even) unto this *day*;
7:25. the Lord shall trouble thee this *day*.
26. a great heap of stones unto this *day*.
— The valley of Achor, unto this *day*.
8:25. all that fell that *day*,
28. a desolation unto this *day*.
29. (that remaineth) unto this *day*.
9:12. *on the day* we came forth

Jos. 9:16. at the end of three *days*
17. came unto their cities *on the* third *day.*
27. Joshua made them that *day*
— even unto this *day,*
10:12. *in the day when* the Lord delivered
13. not to go down *about a* whole *day.*
14. there was no *day like* that
27. (which remain) until this very *day.*
28. that *day* Joshua took Makkedah,
32. took it *on the* second *day,*
35. they took it *on* that *day,*
— he utterly destroyed that *day,*
11:18. made war *a* long *time* (lit. many *days*)
13: 1. Joshua was old (and) stricken *in years;*
— Thou art old (and) stricken *in years,*
13. until this *day.*
14: 9. Moses sware *on* that *day,*
10. *this day* fourscore and five years old.
11. strong *this day* as (I was) *in the day that*
12. the Lord spake *in* that *day;* for thou heardest *in* that *day*
14. unto this *day,* because
15:63. at Jerusalem unto this *day.*
16:10. unto this *day,* and serve under tribute.
20: 6. the high priest that shall be *in* those *days:*
22: 3. left your brethren these many *days* unto this *day,*
16. to turn away *this day*
— that ye might rebel *this day*
17. we are not cleansed until this *day,*
18. ye must turn away *this day*
— (seeing) ye rebel *to day*
22. save us not this *day,*
29. turn *this day* from following the Lord,
31. *This day* we perceive that the Lord (is)
23: 1. it came to pass *a* long *time after* (lit. *after* many *days*)
— Joshua waxed old (and) stricken *in age.* (marg. come *into days*)
2. I am old (and) stricken *in age:*
8. as ye have done unto this *day.*
9. stand before you unto this *day.*
14. *this day* I (am) going the way of all the
24: 7. wilderness *a* long *season.* (lit. many *days*)
15. choose you *this day* whom ye will serve;
25. a covenant with the people that *day,*
31. Israel served the Lord all *the days of* Joshua, and all *the days of* the elders that overlived Joshua, (marg. prolonged (their) *days* after Joshua)
Jud. 1:21. in Jerusalem unto this *day.*
26. the name thereof unto this *day.*
2: 7. the people served the Lord all *the days of* Joshua, and all *the days of* the elders that outlived Joshua, (marg. prolonged *days* after Joshua)
18. all *the days of* the judge:
3:30. So Moab was subdued that *day*
4:14. this (is) *the day*
23. God subdued *on* that *day* Jabin
5: 1. Then sang Deborah...*on* that *day,*
6. *In the days of* Shamgar the son of Anath, *in the days of* Jael,
6:24. unto this *day* it (is) yet
32. *on* that *day* he called him Jerubbaal,
8:28. *in the days of* Gideon.
9:18. against my father's house *this day,*
19. with his house this *day,*
45. fought against the city all that *day;*
10: 4. are called Havoth-jair unto this *day,*
15. deliver us only, we pray thee, this *day.*
11: 4. *in process of time,* (marg. *after days*)
27. the Judge be judge *this day*
40. daughters of Israel went *yearly* (lit. *from days to days;* marg. *from year to year*)
— to lament...four *days*
12: 3. are ye come up unto me this *day,*
13: 7. from the womb to *the day of* his death.
10. that came unto me *the* (other) *day.*
14: 8. *after a time* he returned to take her,
12. *the* seven *days of* the feast,
14. they could not in three *days* expound
15, 17. it came to pass *on the* seventh *day,*
17. she wept before him *the* seven *days,*
18. said unto him *on the* seventh *day*
15: 1. it came to pass *within a while after, in the time of* wheat harvest,
Jud. 15:19. which (is) in Lehi unto this *day.*
20. *in the days of* the Philistines
16:16. when she pressed him *daily* (lit. all *days*)
17: 6. *In* those *days* (there was) no king
10. thee ten (shekels) of silver *by the year,*
18: 1. *In* those *days* (there was) no king in Israel: *and in* those *days* the tribe of
— unto that *day* (all their) inheritance had
12. Mahaneh-dan unto this *day:*
30. *the day of* the captivity of the land.
31. all *the time that* the house of God was in
19: 1. it came to pass *in* those *days,*
2. was there four *whole* months. (marg. *days* four months)
4. he abode with him three *days:*
5. it came to pass *on the* fourth *day,*
8. the morning *on the* fifth *day*
— they tarried until afternoon, (marg. till *the day* declined)
9. *the day* draweth toward evening,
— *the day* groweth to an end,
11. *the day* was far spent;
30. *from the day* that the children of Israel came up out of the land of Egypt unto this *day:*
20:15. of Benjamin were numbered *at* that *time*
21. that *day* twenty and two thousand men.
22. they put themselves in array *the* first *day.*
24. of Israel came near...*the* second *day.*
25. Benjamin went forth...*the* second *day,*
26. fasted that *day* until even,
27. the ark...(was) there *in* those *days,*
28. stood before it *in* those *days,*
30. And the children of Israel went up...*the* third *day,*
35. that *day* twenty and five thousand
46. all which fell that *day*
21: 3. that there should be *to day*
6. one tribe cut off from Israel *this day.*
19. (there is) a feast of the Lord in Shiloh *yearly* (lit. *from days to days*)
25. *In* those *days* (there was) no king
Ru. 1: 1. *in the days when* the judges ruled,
2:19. Where hast thou gleaned *to day?*
— with whom I wrought *to day*
3:18. until he have finished the thing *this day.*
4: 5. *What day* thou buyest the field
9, 10. Ye (are) witnesses *this day,*
14. which hath not left thee *this day*
1Sa. 1: 3. this man went up out of his city *yearly* (lit. *from days to days*)
4. when *the time* was that Elkanah offered,
11. all *the days of* his life,
20. it came to pass, when *the time* was come about (marg. in revolution of *days*)
21. the Lord the *yearly* (lit. of *days*) sacrifice,
28. as long as (lit. all *the days*) he liveth
2:16. burn the fat *presently,* (marg. as *on the day*)
19. brought (it) to him *from year to year,*
— to offer the *yearly* (lit. of *days*) sacrifice.
31. *days* come, that I will cut off thine arm,
32. thine house for ever. (lit. all *the days*)
34. *in* one *day* they shall die both of them.
35. mine anointed for ever. (lit. all *the days*)
3: 1. the Lord was precious *in* those *days;*
2. it came to pass *at* that *time,*
12. *In* that *day* I will perform
4: 3. the Lord smitten us *to day*
12. came to Shiloh *the* same *day*
16. I fled *to day* out of the army.
5: 5. unto this *day.*
6:15. *the* same *day* unto the Lord.
16. they returned to Ekron *the* same *day.*
18. (which stone remaineth) unto this *day*
7: 2. *while* the ark abode in Kirjath-jearim, (lit. *from the day of* abiding)
— that *the time* was long; (lit. *the days* were multiplied)
6. fasted *on* that *day,*
10. a great thunder *on* that *day*
13. all *the days of* Samuel.
15. Samuel judged Israel all *the days of* his
8: 8. *since the day* that I brought them up out of Egypt even unto this *day,*
18. ye shall cry out *in* that *day*
— the Lord will not hear you *in* that *day.*
9. 9. (he that is) *now* (called) a Prophet

1Sa. 9:12. he came *to day* to the city; for (there is) a sacrifice of the people *to day*
13. *about this time* (marg. *to day*) ye shall find
15. *a day* before Saul came,
19. ye shall eat with me *to day*,
20. three *days ago*, (marg. *to day* three *days*)
24. Saul did eat with Samuel that *day*.
27. stand thou still *a while*, (marg. *to day*)
10: 2. art departed from me *to day*,
8. seven *days* shalt thou tarry,
9. those signs came to pass that *day*.
19. ye have *this day* rejected your God,
11: 3. Give us seven *days'* respite,
11. the heat of *the day*:
13. be put to death this *day*: for *to day* the Lord hath wrought salvation
12: 2. from my childhood unto this *day*.
5. his anointed (is) witness this *day*,
17. (Is it) not wheat harvest *to day*?
18. the Lord sent thunder and rain that *day*:
13: 8. he tarried seven *days*,
11. thou camest not within *the days*
22. it came to pass *in the day of* battle,
14: 1. it came to pass upon *a day*,
18. the ark of God was *at* that *time*
23. the Lord saved Israel that *day*:
24. men of Israel were distressed that *day*:
28. the man that eateth (any) food *this day*.
30. the people had eaten freely *to day*
31. they smote the Philistines that *day*
33. roll a great stone unto me *this day*.
37. he answered him not that *day*.
38. see wherein this sin hath been *this day*.
45. he hath wrought with God this *day*.
52. all *the days of* Saul:
15:28. from thee *this day*,
35. *the day of* his death:
16:13. *from* that *day* forward.
17:10. I defy the armies of Israel this *day*;
12. *in the days of* Saul.
16. presented himself forty *days*.
46. This *day* will the Lord deliver thee
— the host of the Philistines this *day*
18: 2. Saul took him that *day*,
9. Saul eyed David *from* that *day*
10. David played with his hand, *as at other times*: (lit. *as the day in the day*)
21. Thou shalt *this day* be my son
26. *the days* were not expired.
29. Saul became David's enemy continually. (lit. all *the days*)
19:24. lay down naked all that *day*
20: 6. (there is) a *yearly* (lit. of *days*) sacrifice
19. *when* the business was (in hand), (marg. *in the day of* the business)
26. Saul spake not any thing that *day*:
27. neither yesterday, nor *to day*?
31. as long *as* (lit. all *the days*) the son of
34. did eat no meat *the* second *day of*
21: 5(6). though it were sanctified *this day*
6(7). *in the day when* it was taken away.
7(8). servants of Saul (was) there that *day*,
10(11). fled that *day* for fear of Saul,
22: 4. all *the while* that David was in the hold.
8. to lie in wait, *as at* this *day*?
13. to lie in wait, *as at* this *day*?
15. Did I *then* begin to enquire of God
18. slew *on* that *day* fourscore and five
22. I knew (it) that *day*,
23:14. Saul sought him every *day*, (lit. all *days*)
24: 4(5). Behold *the day* of which the Lord said
10(11). this *day* thine eyes have seen how that the Lord had delivered thee *to day*
18(19). thou hast shewed *this day*
19(20). that thou hast done unto me this *day*.
25: 7. all *the while* they were in Carmel.
8. we come in *a* good *day*:
10. there be many servants *now a days*
15. as long as (lit. all *the days*) we were
16. all *the while* we were with them
28. not been found in thee (all) *thy days*.
32. sent thee this *day* to meet me:
33. which hast kept me this *day*
38. it came to pass about ten *days* (after),
26: 8. thine enemy into thine hand *this day*:
10. *his day* shall come to die;
19. they have driven me out *this day*

1Sa. 26:21. soul was precious in thine eyes this *day*:
23. Lord delivered thee into (my) hand *to day*
24. thy life was much set by this *day*
27: 1. I shall now perish one *day*
6. Achish gave him Ziklag that *day*:
— unto the kings of Judah unto this *day*.
7. the time (marg. the number of *days*) that
— a full year (marg. (a year of) *days*) and
10. Whither have ye made a road *to day*?
11. all *the while* he dwelleth in the country
28: 1. it came to pass *in* those *days*,
2. of mine head for ever. (lit. all *the days*)
18. done this thing unto thee this *day*.
20. he had eaten no bread all *the day*,
29: 3. which hath been with me these *days*,
— *since* (lit. *from the day*) he fell (unto me) unto this *day*?
6. *since the day of* thy coming unto me unto this *day*:
8. *so long* (lit. *from the day*) as I have been with thee unto this *day*,
30: 1. were come to Ziklag *on the* third *day*,
12. had eaten no bread,...three *days* and three
13. three *days agone* I fell sick.
25. it was (so) *from* that *day* forward,
— an ordinance for Israel unto this *day*.
31: 6. all his men, that same *day* together.
13. fasted seven *days*.
2Sa. 1: 1. David had abode two *days* in Ziklag;
2. It came even to pass *on the* third *day*,
2:11. the time (marg. the number of *days*) that
17. was a very sore battle that *day*;
3: 8. shew kindness *this day* unto the house of
— thou chargest me *to day* with a fault
35. eat meat while it was yet *day*,
37. all Israel understood that *day*
38. a great man fallen this *day* in Israel?
39. I (am) *this day* weak,
4: 3. were sojourners there until this *day*.
5. about the heat of *the day*
8. hath avenged my lord the king this *day*
5: 8. David said *on* that *day*,
6: 8. Perez-uzzah to this *day*.
9. David was afraid of the Lord that *day*,
20. How glorious was the king of Israel *to day*, who uncovered himself *to day*
23. had no child unto *the day of* her death.
7: 6. *since the time* that I brought up the
— even to this *day*,
11. since *the time* that I commanded judges
12. when *thy days* be fulfilled,
11:12. Tarry here *to day* also,
— Uriah abode in Jerusalem that *day*,
12:18. it came to pass *on the* seventh *day*,
13:23. it came to pass after two *full* years,
32. *from the day* that he forced his sister
37. (David) mourned for his son every *day*.
14: 2. be as a woman that had *a* long *time* (lit. many *days*)
22. *To day* thy servant knoweth
26. it was at *every year*'s end (lit. the end of *days to days*) that he polled (it):
28. Absalom dwelt two *full* years in
15:20. should I *this day* make thee go up
16: 3. *To day* shall the house of Israel restore
12. good for his cursing this *day*.
23. which he counselled *in* those *days*,
18: 7. there was there a great slaughter that *day*
8. the wood devoured more people that *day*
18. it is called unto this *day*,
20. Thou shalt not bear tidings this *day*, but thou shalt bear tidings another *day*: *but* this *day* thou shalt bear no tidings,
31. the Lord hath avenged thee *this day*
19: 2(3). the victory that *day* was (turned) into
—(–). the people heard say *that day*
3(4). the people gat them by stealth that *day*
5(6). Thou hast shamed *this day* the faces
—(–). *this day* have saved thy life,
6(7). thou hast declared *this day*,
—(–). *this day* I perceive, that if Absalom had lived, and all we had died *this day*,
13(14). of the host before me continually (lit. all *the days*)
19(20). *the day* that my lord the king went out
20(21). I am come the first *this day*
22(23). ye should *this day* be adversaries

2Sa.19:22(23). put to death *this day* in Israel? for do not I know that I (am) *this day* king
24(25). from *the day* the king departed until *the day*
34(35). How long have I to live, (marg. How many *days* (are) the years of my life)
35(36). I (am) *this day* fourscore years old:
20: 3. they were shut up unto *the day of* their
4. the men of Judah within three *days*,
21: 1. there was a famine *in the days of* David
9. put to death *in the days of* harvest,
12. *when* (lit. *in the day that*) the Philistines had slain Saul
22: 1. *in the day* (that) the Lord had delivered
19. They prevented me *in the day of* my
23: 10. the Lord wrought a great victory that *day;*
20. slew a lion in the midst of a pit *in time of*
24: 8. nine months and twenty *days*.
13. three *days'* pestilence in thy land?
18. Gad came that *day* to David,
1K. 1: 1. king David was old (and) stricken *in years;*
6. his father had not displeased him *at any time* (marg. *from his days*)
25. he is gone down *this day*,
30. so will I certainly do this *day*.
48. sit on my throne *this day*,
51. Let king Solomon swear unto me *to day*
2: 1. *the days of* David drew nigh
8. *in the day when* I went to Mahanaim:
11. *And the days* that David reigned over Israel
24. Adonijah shall be put to death this *day*.
26. *but* I will not *at* this *time* put thee to death,
37, 42. *on the day* thou goest out,
38. Shimei dwelt in Jerusalem many *days*.
3: 2. no house built...until those *days*.
6. *as* (it is) this *day*.
11. hast not asked for thyself long *life;* (marg. many *days*)
13. like unto thee all *thy days*.
14. then I will lengthen *thy days*.
18. it came to pass *the* third *day*
4:21(5:1). served Solomon all *the days of* his
22(5:2). Solomon's provision *for* one *day*
25(5:5). all *the days of* Solomon.
5: 1(15). Hiram was ever (lit. all *the days*) a lover of David.
7(21). Blessed (be) the Lord *this day*,
8: 8. there they are unto this *day*.
16. Since *the day* that I brought forth my
24. *as* (it is) this *day*.
28. thy servant prayeth before thee *to day:*
29. toward this house night *and day*,
40. all *the days* that they live
59. the cause of his people Israel *at all times*, as the matter shall require: (marg. the thing of *a day in his day*)
61. keep his commandments, *as at* this *day*.
64. *The* same *day* did the king hallow
65. seven *days* and seven *days*, (even) fourteen *days*.
66. *On the* eighth *day* he sent the people away:
9: 3. shall be there perpetually. (lit. all *the days*)
13. the land of Cabul unto this *day*.
21. a tribute of bondservice unto this *day*.
10: 12. nor were seen unto this *day*.
21. nothing accounted of *in the days of*
11: 12. *in thy days* I will not do it
25. to Israel all *the days of* Solomon,
34. prince all *the days of* his life
36. have a light alway (lit. all *the days*)
39. I will for this afflict the seed of David, but not for ever. (lit. all *the days*)
42. *And the time* (marg. *days*) that Solomon
12: 5. Depart yet (for) three *days*,
7. a servant unto this people *this day*,
— thy servants for ever. (lit. all *the days*)
12. people came to Rehoboam *the* third *day*,
— Come to me again *the* third *day*.
19. against the house of David unto this *day*.
32. *the* fifteenth *day* of the month,
33. *the* fifteenth *day* of the eighth month,
13: 3. he gave a sign *the* same *day*,
11. that the man of God had done *that day*
14: 14. cut off the house of Jeroboam that *day:*
19, 29. written in the book of the chronicles (lit. the words of *the days*)
20. *And the days* which Jeroboam reigned

1K. 14:30. there was war between Rehoboam and Jeroboam all (their) *days*.
15: 5, 6. all *the days of* his life,
7, 23, 31. (are) they not written in the book of the chronicles (lit. words of *the days*)
14. perfect with the Lord all *his days*.
16, 32. Baasha king of Israel all *their days*.
16: 5, 14, 20, 27. (are) they not written in the book of the chronicles (lit. words of *days*)
15. did Zimri reign seven *days* in Tirzah.
16. king over Israel that *day* in the camp.
34. *In his days* did Hiel the Bethelite
17: 7. after *a while*, (marg. at the end of *days*)
14. *the day* (that) the Lord sendeth rain
15. her house, did eat (many) *days*. (marg. *a full year*)
18: 1. it came to pass (after) many *days*,
15. surely shew myself unto him *to day*.
36. known *this day* that thou (art) God
19: 4. he himself went *a day's* journey
8. strength of that meat forty *days*
20: 13. deliver it into thine hand *this day;*
29. over against the other seven *days*.
— *in the* seventh *day* the battle was joined:
— an hundred thousand footmen *in* one *day*.
21: 29. evil *in his days:* (but) *in* his son's *days*
22: 5. the word of the Lord *to day*.
25. thou shalt see *in* that *day*,
35. the battle increased that *day:*
39, 45(46). (are) they not written in the book of the chronicles (lit. words of *days*)
46(47). *in the days of* his father
2K. 1: 18. written in the book of the chronicles (lit. words *of days*)
2: 3, 5. thy master from thy head *to day?*
17. they sought three *days*, but found him
22. the waters were healed unto this *day*,
3: 6. went out of Samaria *the* same *time*,
9. a compass of seven *days'* journey:
4: 8. it fell on *a day*, that Elisha
11. it fell on *a day*, that he came thither,
18. it fell on *a day*, that he went out
23. Wherefore wilt thou go to him *to day?*
6: 28. Give thy son, that we may eat him *to day*,
29. I said unto her *on the* next *day*,
31. shall stand on him *this day*.
7: 9. this *day* (is) *a day of* good tidings,
8: 6. *since the day* that she left the land,
19. to give him alway (lit. all *the days*) a
20. *In his days* Edom revolted
22. unto this *day*.
23. of the chronicles (lit. words of *the days*)
10: 27. made it a draught house unto *this day*.
32. *In* those *days* the Lord began
34. of the chronicles (lit. words of *the days*)
36. *And the time* that Jehu reigned over
12: 2(3). all *his days* wherein Jehoiada
19(20). in the book of the chronicles (lit. words of *the days*)
13: 3. all (their) *days*.
8, 12. (are) they not written in the book of the chronicles (lit. words of *the days*)
22. all *the days of* Jehoahaz.
14: 7. the name of it Joktheel unto this *day*.
15, 18, 28. the book of the chronicles (lit. the words of *the days*)
15: 5. he was a leper unto *the day of* his death,
6, 11, 15, 21, 26, 31, 36. the book of the chronicles (lit. the words of *the days*)
13. he reigned a *full* month (marg. a month of *days*) in Samaria.
18. he departed not all *his days*
29. *In the days of* Pekah king of Israel
37. *In* those *days* the Lord began to send
16: 6. dwelt there unto this *day*.
19. of the chronicles (lit. words of *the days*)
17: 23. unto this *day*.
34. Unto this *day* they do after the former
37. to do *for evermore;* (lit. all *the days*)
41. so do they unto this *day*.
18: 4. unto those *days* the children of Israel
19: 3. This *day* (is) *a day* of trouble,
25. *of* ancient *times* that I have formed it?
20: 1. *In* those *days* was Hezekiah sick
5. *on the* third *day* thou shalt go up
6. I will add unto *thy days* fifteen years;
8. I shall go up...*the* third *day?*

2K. 20:17. Behold, *the days* come,
— laid up in store unto this *day*,
19. if peace and truth be *in my days?*
20. in the book of the chronicles (lit. words of *the days*)
21:15. since *the day* their fathers came forth out of Egypt, even unto this *day*.
17, 25. in the book of the chronicles (lit. words of *the days*)
23:22. *from the days of* the judges that judged Israel, nor in all *the days of* the kings
28. book of the chronicles (lit. words of *the days*)
29. *In his days* Pharaoh-nechoh
24: 1. *In his days* Nebuchadnezzar
5. of the chronicles (lit. words of *the days*)
25:29, 30. all *the days of* his life.
30. *a daily* rate *for every day*, (lit. the affair of *the day in his day*)
1Ch. 1:19. because *in his days* the earth was divided:
4:41. *in the days of* Hezekiah king of Judah,
— destroyed them utterly unto this *day*,
43. dwelt there unto this *day*.
5:10. *And in the days of* Saul they made war
17. *in the days of* Jotham king of Judah, *and in the days of* Jeroboam king of Israel.
26. to the river Gozan, unto this *day*.
7: 2. *in the days of* David
22. their father mourned many *days*,
9:25. (were) to come after seven *days*
10:12. fasted seven *days*.
11:22. slew a lion in a pit *in a* snowy *day*.
12:22. For at (that) time *day by day* there came
39. they were with David three *days*,
13: 3. we enquired not at it *in the days of* Saul.
11. called Perez-uzza to this *day*.
12. David was afraid of God that *day*,
16: 7. *on* that *day* David delivered
23. shew forth *from day* to *day* his salvation.
37. *as every day*'s work *required:* (lit. the affair of *the day in his day*)
17: 5. since *the day* that I brought up Israel unto this *day;*
10. *And since the time* that I commanded
11. when *thy days* be expired
21:12. or else three *days* the sword of the Lord,
22: 9. quietness unto Israel *in his days*.
23: 1. when David was old and full of *days*,
26:17. northward four *a day*, southward four *a day*,
27:24. the chronicles (lit. the words of *the days*)
28: 7. my judgments, *as at* this *day*.
29: 5. consecrate his service *this day*
15. *our days* on the earth (are) as a shadow,
21. on the morrow after that *day*,
22. drink before the Lord *on* that *day*
27. *And the time* that he reigned over Israel
28. full of *days*, riches, and honour:
2Ch. 1:11. yet hast asked long *life;* (lit. many *days*)
5: 9. there it is unto this *day*.
6: 5. Since *the day* that I brought
15. *as* (it is) this *day*.
31. so long as (marg. all *the days*) they live
7: 8. Solomon kept the feast seven *days*,
9. *in the* eighth *day* they made
— seven *days*, and the feast seven *days*.
10. *And on the* three and twentieth *day*
16. shall be there perpetually. (lit. all *the days*)
8: 8. pay tribute until this *day*.
13. after a certain rate *every day*, (lit. the affair of *a day in a day*)
14. *as* the duty of *every day required:* (lit. the affair of *a day in his day*)
16. *the day of* the foundation of the house
9:20. *in the days of* Solomon.
10: 5. Come again unto me after three *days*.
7. be thy servants for ever. (lit. all *the days*)
12. came to Rehoboam *on the* third *day*,
— Come again to me *on the* third *day*.
19. Israel rebelled...unto this *day*.
12:15. Jeroboam continually. (lit. all *the days*)
13:20. *in the days of* Abijah:
14: 1(13:23). *In his days* the land was quiet
15: 3. *for a* long *season* Israel
11. Lord *the* same *time*, (marg. *in* that *day*)
17. Asa was perfect all *his days*.
18: 4. the word of the Lord *to day*.

2Ch.18: 7. unto me, but always (lit. all *his days*) evil:
24. thou shalt see *on* that *day*
34. the battle increased that *day:*
20:25. they were three *days* in gathering
26. *And on the* fourth *day* they assembled
— The valley of Berachah, unto this *day*.
21: 7. to his sons for ever. (lit. all *the days*)
8. *In his days* the Edomites revolted
10. the Edomites revolted...unto this *day*.
15. by reason of the sickness *day* by *day*.
19. it came to pass, that *in process of time*, (lit. *to days from days*) after the end *of* two *years*,
24: 2, 14. all *the days of* Jehoiada
11. Thus they did *day by day*, and gathered
15. was full of *days* when he died;
26: 5. he sought God *in the days of* Zechariah,
— *and as long as* he sought the Lord,
21. *the day of* his death,
28: 6. twenty thousand *in* one *day*,
29:17. *and on the* eighth *day* of the month
— the house of the Lord *in* eight *days; and in the* sixteenth *day* of the first
30:21. feast of unleavened bread seven *days*
— the priests praised the Lord *day by day*,
22. eat throughout the feast seven *days*,
23. took counsel to keep other seven *days:* and they kept (other) seven *days*
26. *since the time of* Solomon
31:16. *his daily* portion for their service (lit. the affair of *the day in his day*)
32:24. *In* those *days* Hezekiah was sick
26. *in the days of* Hezekiah.
34:33. all *his days* they departed not
35:16. of the Lord was prepared *the* same *day*,
17. the feast of unleavened bread seven *days*.
18. *from the days of* Samuel the prophet;
21. (I come) not against thee *this day*,
25. their lamentations to *this day*,
36: 9. he reigned three months and ten *days*
21. as long as (lit. all *the days*) she lay
Ezr. 3: 4. the *daily* burnt offerings (lit. of *a day in a day*)
— as the duty of *every day* required; (marg. the matter of *the day in his day*)
6. *From the* first *day* of the seventh month
4: 2. *since the days of* Esar-haddon
5. all *the days of* Cyrus
7. *And in the days of* Artaxerxes
6:22. the feast of unleavened bread seven *days*
8:15. there abode we in tents three *days:*
32. abode there three *days*.
33. *Now on the* fourth *day* was the silver
9: 7. *Since the days of* our fathers
— a great trespass unto this *day*,
—, 15. *as* (it is) this *day*.
10: 8. would not come within three *days*,
9. gathered themselves...within three *days*.
13. a work *of* one *day* or two:
16. *in the* first *day of* the tenth month
17. *the* first *day* of the first month.
Neh. 1: 4. wept, and mourned (certain) *days*,
6. I pray before thee *now*, (lit. *this day*)
11. prosper, I pray thee, thy servant *this day*,
2:11. to Jerusalem, and was there three *days*.
4: 2(3:34). will they make an end *in a day?*
16(10). it came to pass from that *time* forth,
22(16). a guard to us, *and* labour *on the day*.
5:11. Restore, I pray you, to them, *even this day*,
14. *from the time* that I was appointed
18. prepared (for me) *daily* (lit. *for* one *day*)
— once in ten *days* store of all sorts of wine:
6:15. in fifty and two *days*.
17. *in* those *days* the nobles of Judah
8: 2. *upon the* first *day of* the seventh month.
3. from the morning until mid*day*,
9. *This day* (is) holy unto the Lord
10. (this) *day* (is) holy unto our Lord:
11. Hold your peace, for *the day* (is) holy;
13. *And on the* second *day* were gathered
17. *since the days of* Jeshua
— unto that *day* had not the children of
18. Also *day by day*, from *the* first *day* unto *the* last *day*,
— they kept the feast seven *days; and on the* eighth *day*
9: 1. *Now in the* twenty and fourth *day*

Neh 9: 3. (one) fourth part of *the day;*
10. *as* (it is) this *day.*
32. *since the time of* the kings of Assyria unto this *day.*
36. we (are) servants *this day,*
10:31(32). *on the* sabbath *day*
—(—). *or on the* holy *day:*
11:23. due *for every day.* (lit. the affair of *the day in his day*)
12: 7. *in the days of* Jeshua.
12. *And in the days of* Joiakim
22. *in the days of* Eliashib,
23. the book of the chronicles (lit. the words of *days*), even until *the days of* Johanan
26. *in the days of* Joiakim
— *and in the days of* Nehemiah
43. that *day* they offered great sacrifices,
44. *at* that *time* were some appointed
46. *in the days of* David
47. *in the days of* Zerubbabel, *and in the days of*
— *every day his* portion: (lit. the affair of *the day in his day*)
13: 1. *On* that *day* they read in the book
6. after certain *days* obtained I leave
15. *In* those *days* saw I in Judah
— into Jerusalem *on the* sabbath *day:*
— *in the day wherein* they sold victuals.
17. profane *the* sabbath *day?*
19. *on the* sabbath *day.*
22. to sanctify *the* sabbath *day.*
23. *In* those *days* also saw I Jews
Est. 1: 1. it came to pass *in the days of* Ahasuerus,
2. (That) *in* those *days,* when the king
4. excellent majesty many *days,* (even) an hundred and fourscore *days.*
5. when these *days* were expired,
— both unto great and small, seven *days,*
10. *On the* seventh *day,*
18. ladies of Persia and Media say this *day*
2:11. walked every *day* (lit. every *day and day*)
12. so were *the days of* their purifications
21. *In* those *days,* while Mordecai
23. the chronicles (lit. the words of *the days*)
3: 4. when they spake *daily* (lit. *day and day*)
7. *from day to day,* and from month to
12. *the* thirteenth *day* of the first month,
13. *in* one *day,*
14. ready *against* that *day.*
4:11. in unto the king these thirty *days.*
16. neither eat nor drink three *days,* night *or day:*
5: 1. it came to pass *on the* third *day,*
4. let the king and Haman come *this day*
9. Then went Haman forth that *day*
6: 1. the chronicles; (lit. the words of *the days*)
7: 2. unto Esther *on* the second *day*
8: 1. *On* that *day* did the king Ahasuerus
12. *Upon* one *day*
13. Jews should be ready *against* that *day*
17. a feast *and a* good *day.*
9: 1. on *the* thirteenth *day of* the same,
— *in the day* that the enemies of the Jews
11. *On* that *day* the number of those that
13. according unto this *day*'s decree,
15. *on the* fourteenth *day*
17. *On the* thirteenth *day*
—, 18. made it *a day of* feasting
19. *the* fourteenth *day* of the month
— gladness and feasting, *and a* good *day,*
21. *the* fourteenth *day* of the month Adar, and *the* fifteenth *day* of the same,
22. *As the days* wherein the Jews rested
— from mourning *into a* good *day:* that they should make them *days of* feasting
26. they called these *days* Purim
27. that they would keep these two *days*
28. *And* (that) these *days* (should be)
— *and* (that) these *days of* Purim should
31. To confirm these *days of* Purim
10: 2. the chronicles (lit. words of *the days*)
Job 1: 4. every one *his day;*
5. when *the days of* (their) feasting were
— did Job continually. (marg. all *the days*)
6. there was *a day* when the sons of God
13. there was *a day* when his sons
2: 1. Again there was *a day*
13. with him upon the ground seven *days*

Job 3: 1. cursed *his day.*
3. Let *the day* perish wherein I was born,
4. Let that *day* be darkness;
5. let the blackness of *the day* terrify it.
6. let it not be joined *unto the days of* the
8. Let them curse it that curse *the day,*
7: 1. (are not) *his days also like the days of* an
6. *My days* are swifter than a weaver's
16. *my days* (are) vanity.
8: 9. *our days* upon earth (are) a shadow:
9:25. *Now my days* are swifter than a post:
10: 5. (Are) *thy days as the days* of man? (are) thy years *as* man's *days,*
20. (Are) not *my days* few?
12:12. in length of *days* understanding.
14: 1. born of a woman (is) of few *days,*
5. Seeing *his days* (are) determined,
6. as an hireling, *his day.*
14. all *the days of* my appointed time
15:10. much elder (lit. more advanced (in) *days*)
20. man travaileth with pain all (his) *days,*
23. *the day of* darkness is ready
32. accomplished before *his time,*
17: 1. *my days* are extinct,
11. *My days* are past, my purposes are
12. They change the night *into day:*
18:20. shall be astonied at *his day,*
20:28. *in the day of* his wrath.
21:13. They spend *their days* in wealth,
30. *to the day of* destruction? they shall be brought forth *to the day of* wrath.
23: 2. Even *to day* (is) my complaint bitter:
24: 1. do they that know him not see *his days?*
27: 6. shall not reproach (me) *so long as I live.*
29: 2. *as* (in) *the days* (when) God preserved
4. As I was *in the days of* my youth,
18. I shall multiply (my) *days* as the sand.
30: 1. But now (they that are) younger (marg. of fewer *days*) than I
16. *the days of* affliction have taken hold
25. was in trouble? (marg. hard of *day*)
27. *the days of* affliction prevented me.
32: 4. they (were) elder (marg. elder *for days*)
6. I (am) young, (marg. few *of days*) and ye
7. I said, *Days* should speak,
33:25. he shall return *to the days of* his youth:
36:11. they shall spend *their days* in prosperity,
38:12. commanded the morning *since thy days;*
21. (because) the number of *thy days* (is)
23. *against the day of* battle and war?
42:17. Job died, (being) old and full of *days.*
Ps. 2: 7. *this day* have I begotten thee.
7:11(12). angry (with the wicked) every *day.*
18[title](1). *in the day* (that) the Lord delivered
18(19). *in the day of* my calamity:
19: 2(3). *Day unto day* uttereth speech,
20: 1(2). The Lord hear thee *in the day of*
9(10). let the king hear us *when* we call.
21: 4(5). length of *days* for ever and ever.
23: 6. goodness and mercy shall follow me all *the days of* my life: and I will dwell in the house of the Lord *for ever.* (marg. to length of *days*)
25: 5. on thee do I wait all *the day.*
27: 4. all *the days of* my life,
5. *in the time of* trouble he shall hide me
32: 3. my roaring all *the day* long.
34:12(13). loveth (many) *days,*
35:28. thy praise all *the day* long.
37:13. for he seeth that *his day* is coming.
18. The Lord knoweth *the days of* the
19. *and in the days of* famine they shall be
26. (He is) ever merciful, (marg. all *the day*
38: 6(7). I go mourning all *the day* long.
12(13). imagine deceits all *the day* long.
39: 4(5). the measure of *my days,*
5(6). thou hast made *my days* (as) an
41: 1(2). the Lord will deliver him *in time of*
42: 3(4). while they continually (lit. all *the day*) say unto me,
10(11). say *daily* unto me, (lit. all the *day*)
44: 1(2). (what) work thou didst *in their days, in the times of* old.
8(9). In God we boast all *the day* long,
15(16). (is) continually (lit. all *the day*)
22(23). for thy sake are we killed all *the day*
49: 5(6). Wherefore should I fear *in the days of*

Ps. 50:15. call upon me *in the day of* trouble:
52: 1(3). the goodness of God (endureth) continually. (lit. every *day*)
55:23(24). shall not live out half *their days;*
56: 1(2). he fighting *daily* oppresseth me.
2(3). enemies would *daily* swallow (me)
3(4). *What time* I am afraid,
5(6). Every *day* they wrest my words:
9(10). *When* I cry (unto thee), (lit. *In the day*)
59:16(17). *in the day of* my trouble.
61: 6(7). Thou wilt prolong the king's life: (lit. add *days* upon the king's *days*)
8(9). that I may *daily* perform my vows. (lit. *day, day*)
68:19(20). (who) *daily* (lit. *day, day*) loadeth
71: 8. thy honour all *the day.*
15. thy salvation all *the day;*
24. thy righteousness all *the day* long:
72: 7. *In his days* shall the righteous flourish;
15. *daily* shall he be praised. (lit. all *the day*)
73:14. all *the day* long have I been plagued,
74:16. *The day* (is) thine, the night also (is)
22. the foolish man reproacheth thee *daily.* (lit. every *day*)
77: 2(3). *In the day of* my trouble
5(6). I have considered *the days* of old,
78: 9. turned back *in the day of* battle.
33. *their days* did he consume in vanity,
42. *the day* when he delivered them
81: 3(4). *on* our solemn feast *day.*
84:10(11). *a day* in thy courts (is) better
86: 3. I cry unto thee *daily.* (marg. all *the day*)
7. *In the day of* my trouble I will call
88: 1(2). I have cried *day* (and) night before
9(10). Lord, I have called *daily* upon thee,
17(18). They came round about me *daily* (marg. all *the day*) like water;
89:16(17). In thy name shall they rejoice all *the day:*
29(30). his throne *as the days of* heaven.
45(46). *The days of* his youth hast thou
90: 4. in thy sight (are but) *as yesterday*
9. all *our days* are passed away in thy wrath:
10. *The days of* our years (are) threescore
12. So teach (us) to number *our days,*
14. we may rejoice and be glad all *our days.*
15. *according to the days* (wherein) thou hast
91:16. With long *life* (marg. length of *days*) will
92[title](1). A Psalm (or) Song *for the* sabbath *day.*
93: 5. holiness becometh thine house, O Lord, for ever. (marg. length of *days*)
94:13. *from the days of* adversity,
95: 7. *To day* if ye will hear his voice,
8. *as* (in) *the day of* temptation in the
96: 2. shew forth his salvation *from day to day.*
102: 2(3). *in the day* (when) I am in trouble;
—(–). *in the day* (when) I call
3(4). *my days* are consumed like smoke,
8(9). Mine enemies reproach me all *the day;*
11(12). *My days* (are) like a shadow that
23(24). he shortened *my days.*
24(25). me not away in the midst of *my days:*
103:15. (As for) man, *his days* (are) as grass:
109: 8. Let *his days* be few;
110: 3. *in the day of* thy power,
5. *in the day of* his wrath.
116: 2. *therefore* will I call upon (him) *as long as I live.* (marg. *in my days*)
118:24. This (is) *the day* (which) the Lord hath
119:84. How many (are) *the days of* thy servant?
91. They continue *this day*
97. it (is) my meditation all *the day.*
164. Seven times *a day* do I praise thee
128: 5. all *the days of* thy life.
136: 8. The sun to rule *by day:*
137: 7. *the day of* Jerusalem;
138: 3. *In the day when* I cried thou
139:12. the night shineth *as the day:*
16. (which) in *continuance* were fashioned, (marg. or, (what) *days* they should be)
140: 2(3). continually (lit. all *day*) are they
7(8). thou hast covered my head *in the day of*
143: 5. I remember *the days* of old;
144: 4. *his days* (are) as a shadow
145: 2. Every *day* will I bless thee;

Ps. 146: 4. *in* that very *day* his thoughts perish.
Pro. 3: 2. length of *days,* and long life,
16. Length of *days* (is) in her right hand;
4:18. more and more unto *the* perfect *day.*
6:34. he will not spare *in the day of* vengeance.
7: 9. in the evening, (marg. evening of *the day*)
14. *this day* have I payed my vows.
20. will come home *at the day* appointed.
8:30. and I was *daily* (lit. *day, day*) (his)
34. watching *daily* (lit. *day, day*) at my gates,
9:11. by me *thy days* shall be multiplied,
10:27. The fear of the Lord prolongeth *days:*
11: 4. Riches profit not *in the day of* wrath:
12:16. A fool's wrath is *presently* (marg. *in that day*) known:
15:15. All *the days of* the afflicted (are) evil:
16: 4. the wicked *for the day of* evil.
21:26. He coveteth greedily all *the day* long:
31. The horse (is) prepared *against the day of*
22:19. I have made known to thee *this day,*
23:17. the fear of the Lord all *the day* long.
24:10. (If) thou faint *in the day of* adversity,
25:13. As the cold of snow *in the time of* harvest,
19. an unfaithful man *in time of* trouble
20. a garment *in* cold *weather,*
27: 1. Boast not thyself of to morrow (lit. *in the day of* to morrow); for thou knowest not what *a day* may bring forth.
10. *in the day of* thy calamity:
15. A continual dropping *in a* very rainy *day*
28:16. he that hateth covetousness shall prolong (his) *days.*
31:12. all *the days of* her life.
25. she shall rejoice *in time to* come.
Ecc. 2: 3. all *the days of* their life.
16. in *the days* to come shall all be forgotten.
23. all *his days* (are) sorrows,
5:17(16). All *his days* also he eateth in darkness,
18(17). all *the days of* his life,
20(19). not much remember *the days of* his
6: 3. *the days of* his years be many,
12. all *the days of* his vain life
7: 1. *and the day of* death *than the day of* one's
10. *that the* former *days* were better than these?
14. *In the day of* prosperity be joyful, *but in the day of* adversity consider:
15. *in the days of* my vanity:
8: 8. power *in the day of* death:
13. neither shall he prolong (his) *days,*
15. *the days of* his life,
16. neither *day* nor night seeth sleep
9: 9. *the days of* the life of thy vanity,
— all *the days of* thy vanity:
11: 1. thou shalt find it after many *days.*
8. let him remember *the days of* darkness;
9. let thy heart cheer thee *in the days of* thy
12: 1. Remember now thy Creator *in the days of* thy youth, while *the* evil *days* come not,
3. *In the day* when the keepers
Cant 2:17. Until *the day* break,
3:11. *in the day of* his espousals, *and in the day of* the gladness of his heart.
4: 6. Until *the day* break,
8: 8. *in the day* when she shall be spoken for?
Isa. 1: 1. *in the days of* Uzziah,
2: 2. it shall come to pass in *the* last *days,*
11, 17. Lord alone shall be exalted *in* that *day.*
12. *the day of* the Lord of hosts
20. *In* that *day* a man shall cast his idols
3: 7. *In* that *day* shall he swear,
18. *In* that *day* the Lord will take away
4: 1. *in* that *day* seven women shall take
2. *In* that *day* shall the branch of the Lord be
5:30. *in* that *day* they shall roar
7: 1. it came to pass *in the days of* Ahaz
17. *days* that have not come, *from the day that* Ephraim departed from
18. it shall come to pass *in* that *day,*
20. *In the* same *day* shall the Lord shave
21, 23. it shall come to pass *in* that *day,*
9: 4(3). *as in the day of* Midian.
14(13). branch and rush, in one *day.*
10: 3. what will ye do *in the day of* visitation,
17. his thorns and his briers *in* one *day;*
20, 27. it shall come to pass *in* that *day,*
32. As yet shall he remain at Nob *that day:*
11:10. *in* that *day* there shall be a root of Jesse,

Isa 11:11. It shall come to pass *in* that *day*,
16. *in the day* that he came up
12: 1. *in* that *day* thou shalt say,
4. *in* that *day* shall ye say,
13: 6. *the day of* the Lord (is) at hand
9. *the day of* the Lord cometh,
13. *and in the day of* his fierce anger.
22. *and her days* shall not be prolonged.
14: 3. it shall come to pass *in the day that*
17: 4. *in* that *day* it shall come to pass,
7. *At* that *day* shall a man look
9. *In* that *day* shall his strong cities
11. *In the day* shalt thou make thy plant
— *in the day of* grief and of desperate
19:16. *In* that *day* shall Egypt be like
18. *In* that *day* shall five cities...speak
19. *In* that *day* shall there be an altar
21. shall know the Lord *in* that *day*,
23. *In* that *day* shall there be a highway
24. *In* that *day* shall Israel be the third
20: 6. shall say *in* that *day*,
22: 5. (it is) *a day of* trouble,
8. thou didst look *in* that *day*
12. *in* that *day* did the Lord God of hosts
20. it shall come to pass *in* that *day*,
25. *In* that *day*, saith the Lord of hosts,
23: 7. antiquity (is) *of* ancient *days?*
15. it shall come to pass *in* that *day*,
— *according to the days of* one king:
24:21. it shall come to pass *in* that *day*,
22. after many *days* shall they be visited.
25: 9. it shall be said *in* that *day*,
26: 1. *In* that *day* shall this song be sung
27: 1. *In* that *day* the Lord
2. *In* that *day* sing ye unto her,
3. I will keep it night *and day*.
8. *in the day of* the east wind.
12, 13. it shall come to pass *in* that *day*,
28: 5. *In* that *day* shall the Lord of hosts
19. *by day* and by night:
24. Doth the plowman plow all *day*
29:18. *in* that *day* shall the deaf hear
30: 8. be *for the time* to come (marg. latter **day**)
23. *in* that *day* shall thy cattle feed
25. *in the day of* the great slaughter,
26. as the light of seven *days*, *in the day that* the Lord bindeth up
31: 7. *in* that *day* every man shall cast away
32:10. Many *days* and years shall ye be
34: 8. (it is) *the day of* the Lord's vengeance,
37: 3. This *day* (is) *a day of* trouble,
26. *of* ancient *times*, that I have formed it?
38: 1. *In* those *days* was Hezekiah sick unto
5. I will add unto *thy days* fifteen years.
10. I said in the cutting off of *my days*,
12, 13. *from day* (even) to night wilt thou
19. he shall praise thee, as I (do) *this day:*
20. all *the days of* our life
39: 6. Behold, *the days* come,
— have laid up in store until this *day*,
8. shall be peace and truth *in my days*.
43:13. *before the day* (was) I (am) he;
47: 9. come to thee in a moment *in* one *day*,
48: 7. before *the day* when thou heardest
49: 8. *and in a day of* salvation have I helped
51: 9. awake, *as* in *the* ancient *days*,
13. hast feared continually every *day*
52: 5. continually every *day* (is) blasphemed.
6. (they shall know) *in* that *day*
53:10. he shall prolong (his) *days*,
56:12. to morrow shall be as this *day*,
58: 2. Yet they seek me *daily*, (lit. *day, day*)
3. *in the day of* your fast
4. ye shall not fast *as* (ye do this) *day*,
5. *a day* for a man to afflict his soul?
— *and an* acceptable *day* to the Lord?
13. doing thy pleasure *on* my holy *day;*
60:20. *the days of* thy mourning shall be ended.
61: 2. *and the day of* vengeance of our God;
62: 6. shall never hold their peace *day* nor
63: 4. *the day of* vengeance (is) in mine heart,
9. carried them all *the days of* old.
11. be remembered *the days of* old,
65: 2. I have spread out my hands all *the day*
5. a fire that burneth all *the day*.
20. thence an infant of *days*, nor an old man that hath not filled *his days:*

Isa. 65:22. *as the days of* a tree (are) *the days of* my
66: 8. be made to bring forth *in* one *day?*
Jer. 1: 2. *in the days of* Josiah
3. *in the days of* Jehoiakim
10. I have *this day* set thee over the nations
18. I have made thee *this day* a defenced
2:32. have forgotten me *days* without number.
3: 6. *in the days of* Josiah the king,
16. *in* those *days*, saith the Lord,
18. *In* those *days* the house of Judah
25. from our youth even unto this *day*,
4: 9. it shall come to pass *at* that *day*,
5:18. *in* those *days*, saith the Lord,
6: 4. *the day* goeth away,
11. the aged with (him that is) full of *days*.
7:22. *in the day that* I brought them out
25. Since *the day* that your fathers came forth out of the land of Egypt unto this *day*
— *daily* rising up early
32 & 9:25(24). *the days* come, saith the Lord,
11: 4. *in the day* (that) I brought them forth
5. *as* (it is) this *day*.
7. *in the day* (that) I brought them up out of the land of Egypt, (even) unto this *day*,
12: 3. prepare them *for the day of* slaughter.
13: 6. it came to pass after many *days*,
15: 9. is gone down while (it was) yet *day:* (lit. *their day;* see also יוֹמָם)
16: 9. *and in your days*,
14. *the days* come, saith the Lord,
19. my refuge *in the day of* affliction,
17:11. leave them in the midst of *his days*,
16. *neither* have I desired *the* woeful *day;*
17. thou (art) my hope *in the day of* evil.
18. bring upon them *the day of* evil,
21. bear no burden *on the* sabbath *day*,
22. carry forth a burden out...*on the* sabbath *day*,
— hallow ye *the* sabbath *day*,
24. bring in no burden...*on the* sabbath *day*,
—, 27. hallow *the* sabbath *day*,
27. the gates of Jerusalem *on the* sabbath *day;*
18:17. *in the day of* their calamity.
19: 6. *the days* come, saith the Lord,
20: 7. I am in derision *daily*, (lit. every *day*)
8. a derision, *daily*. (lit. every *day*)
14. Cursed (be) *the day* wherein I was born: let not *the day* wherein
18. that *my days* should be consumed
22:30. a man (that) shall not prosper *in his days:*
23: 5, 7. *the days* come, saith the Lord,
6. *In his days* Judah shall be saved,
20. in *the* latter *days* ye shall consider it
25: 3. even unto this *day*,
18. *as* (it is) this *day;*
33. the slain of the Lord shall be *at* that *day*
34. *the days* of *your* slaughter (marg. *your days* for slaughter)
26:18. *in the days of* Hezekiah
27:22. until *the day* that I visit them,
28: 3. two *full* years (marg. years of *days*)
11. within the space of two *full* years. (lit. *id.*)
30: 3. *the days* come, saith the Lord,
7. that *day* (is) great,
8. it shall come to pass *in* that *day*.
24. in *the* latter *days* ye shall consider it.
31: 6. there shall be *a day*,
27, 31, 38. *the days* come, saith the Lord,
29. *In* those *days* they shall say no more,
32. *in the day* (that) I took them by the
33. After those *days*, saith the Lord,
36. before me for ever. (lit. all *the days*)
32:14. that they may continue many *days*.
20. (even) unto this *day*,
— hast made thee a name, *as at* this *day;*
31. *the day* that they built it even unto this *day;*
39. may fear me for ever, (marg. all *days*)
33:14. *the days* come, saith the Lord,
15. *In* those *days*, and at that time,
16. *In* those *days* shall Judah be saved,
18. do sacrifice continually. (lit. all *the days*)
20. If ye can break my covenant of *the day*,
34:13. *in the day that* I brought them forth
15. ye were *now* (marg. *to day*) turned,
35: 1. *in the days of* Jehoiakim

Jer. 35: 7. all *your days* ye shall dwell in tents; that ye may live many *days*
8. drink no wine all *our days*,
14. unto this *day* they drink none,
19. before me for ever. (lit. all *the days*)
36: 2. from *the day* I spake unto thee, *from the days of* Josiah, even unto this *day*.
6. *upon the* fasting *day*:
30. his dead body shall be cast out *in the day*
37:16. Jeremiah had remained there many *days*;
21. *daily* a piece of bread out of the bakers'
38:28. *the day* that Jerusalem was taken:
39:10. vineyards and fields *at the* same *time*. (marg. that *day*)
16. *in* that *day* before thee.
17. I will deliver thee *in* that *day*,
40: 4. I loose thee this *day*
41: 4. *the* second *day* after he had slain Gedaliah,
42: 7. it came to pass after ten *days*,
19. I have admonished you *this day*.
21. I have *this day* declared (it) to you;
44: 2. this *day* they (are) a desolation,
6. wasted (and) desolate, *as* at this *day*.
10. (even) unto this *day*,
22. without an inhabitant, *as* at this *day*.
23. happened unto you, *as* at this *day*.
46:10. *For* this (is) *the day* of the Lord God of hosts, *a day of* vengeance,
21. *the day of* their calamity was come
26. *as in the days of* old,
47: 4. *the day* that cometh to spoil
48:12. *the days* come, saith the Lord,
41. men's hearts in Moab *at* that *day*
47. in *the* latter *days*, saith the Lord.
49: 2. *the days* come, saith the Lord,
22. *at* that *day* shall the heart of the mighty
26. shall be cut off *in* that *day*,
39. it shall come to pass in *the* latter *days*,
50: 4, 20. *In* those *days*, and in that time,
27. *their day* is come,
30. men of war shall be cut off *in* that *day*,
31. *thy day* is come, the time
51: 2. *in the day of* trouble they shall be
47. behold, *the days* come,
52. *the days* come, saith the Lord,
52:11. *the day of* his death.
33, 34. all *the days of* his life.
34. *every day* a portion (marg. the matter of *the day in his day*) until *the day of*
Lam. 1: 7. *the days of* her affliction
— *in the days of* old,
12. *in the day of* his fierce anger.
13. made me desolate (and) faint all *the day*.
21. *the day* (that) thou hast called,
2: 1. *in the day of* his anger!
7. *as in the day of* a solemn feast.
16. *the day* that we looked for;
17. *in the days of* old:
21. *in the day of* thine anger;
22. *as in a* solemn *day* my terrors round about, so that *in the day of* the Lord's anger
3: 3. his hand (against me) all *the day*.
14. their song all *the day*.
57. Thou drewest near *in the day*
62. their device against me all *the day*.
4:18. *our days* are fulfilled;
5:20. (and) forsake us so long *time*? (lit. to the length of *days*)
21. renew *our days* as of old.
Eze. 1:28. the cloud *in the day of* rain
2: 3. (even) unto this *very day*.
3:15. astonished among them seven *days*.
16. it came to pass at the end of seven *days*,
4: 4, 9. (according) to the number of *the days*
5. according to the number of *the days*, three hundred and ninety *days*:
6. iniquity of the house of Judah forty *days*
— *each day* for a year. (marg *a day* for a year, *a day* for a year)
8. thou hast ended *the days of* thy siege.
9. three hundred and ninety *days*
10. twenty shekels *a day*:
5: 2. when *the days of* the siege are fulfilled:
7: 7. *the day of* trouble (is) near,
10. Behold *the day*, behold, it is come:
12. *the day* draweth near:
19. *in the day of* the wrath of the Lord:
Eze. 12:22. *The days* are prolonged,
23. *The days* are at hand,
25. *in your days*, O rebellious house,
27. *for* many *days* (to come),
13: 5. *in the day of* the Lord.
16: 4. *in the day* thou wast born
5. *in the day that* thou wast born.
22, 43. thou hast not remembered *the days of*
56. *in the day of* thy pride,
60. with thee *in the days of* thy youth,
20: 5. *In the day when* I chose Israel,
6. *In the day* (that) I lifted up mine hand
29. is called Bamah unto this *day*.
31. even unto *this day*:
21:25(30). *whose day* is come,
29(34). *whose day* is come,
22: 4. thou hast caused *thy days* to draw near,
14. *in the days* that I shall deal with thee?
24. *in the day of* indignation.
23:19. calling to remembrance *the days of* her
38. defiled my sanctuary *in the* same *day*,
39. they came *the* same *day* into my sanctuary
24: 2. name of *the day*, (even) of this same *day*:
— against Jerusalem this same *day*.
25. *in the day when* I take from them
26. he that escapeth *in* that *day*
27. *In* that *day* shall thy mouth be opened
26:18. *the day of* thy fall;
27:27. *in the day of* thy ruin.
28:13. *in the day that* thou wast created.
15. *from the day* that thou wast created,
29:21. *In* that *day* will I cause the horn
30: 2. Howl ye, Woe worth *the day!*
3. For *the day* (is) near, even *the day of* the Lord (is) near, *a* cloudy *day*;
9. *In* that *day* shall messengers go forth
— come upon them, *as* in *the day of* Egypt:
18. *the day* shall be darkened,
31:15. *In the day when* he went down to the grave
32:10. *in the day of* thy fall.
33:12. *in the day of* his transgression:
— *in the day that* he turneth from
— *in the day that* he sinneth.
34:12. *in the day that* he is among his sheep
— *in the* cloudy and dark *day*.
36:33. *In the day that* I shall have cleansed
38: 8. *After* many *days* thou shalt be visited:
10. *at the* same *time* shall things come
14. *In* that *day* when my people of Israel
16. it shall be in *the* latter *days*,
17. he of whom I have spoken *in* old *time*
— which prophesied *in* those *days*
18. it shall come to pass *at the* same *time when* Gog shall come (lit. *in* that *day*, *the day*)
19. *in* that *day* there shall be a great
39: 8. this (is) *the day* whereof I have spoken.
11. it shall come to pass *in* that *day*,
13. *the day* that I shall be glorified,
22. from that *day* and forward.
40: 1. in the selfsame *day*
43:18. *in the day when* they shall make
22. *And on the* second *day* thou shalt offer
25. Seven *days* shalt thou prepare *every day* a goat (for) a sin offering:
26. Seven *days* shall they purge the altar
27. when these *days* are expired,
— *upon the* eighth *day*,
44:26. they shall reckon unto him seven *days*.
27. *And in the day that* he goeth into the
45:21. in the fourteenth *day* of the month,
— a feast of seven *days*;
22. *upon* that *day* shall the prince prepare
23. seven *days of* the feast he shall prepare
— seven rams without blemish *daily the* seven *days*; and a kid of the goats *daily*
25. *the* fifteenth *day* of the month,
— the feast of *the* seven *days*,
46: 1. six working *days*; *but on the* sabbath (lit. *and on the* sabbath *day*) it shall be opened, *and in the day of* the
4. *in the* sabbath *day*
6. *And in the day of* the new moon
12. as he did *on the* sabbath *day*:
13. Thou shalt *daily* prepare a burnt offering
48:35. *from* (that) *day* (shall be),
Dan 1: 5. *daily* provision (lit. the affair of *the day, in his day*)

Dan 1:12. thy servants, I beseech thee, ten *days;*
14. proved them ten *days.*
15. at the end of ten *days*
18. at the end of *the days*
8:26. for it (shall be) *for* many *days.*
27. Daniel fainted, and was sick (certain) *days;*
9: 7. *as* at this *day;*
15. hast gotten thee renown, *as* at this *day;*
10: 2. *In* those *days* I Daniel was mourning three *full* weeks. (lit. three weeks *days*)
3. three *whole* weeks (lit. three weeks *days*)
4. *And in the* four and twentieth *day*
12. from *the* first *day* that thou didst set
13. withstood me one and twenty *days:*
14. shall befall thy people in *the* latter *days:* for yet the vision (is) *for* (many) *days.*
11:20. *but within* few *days* he shall be destroyed,
33. by captivity, and by spoil, (many) *days.*
12:11. a thousand two hundred and ninety *days.*
12. *to the* thousand three hundred and five and thirty *days.*
13. stand in thy lot at the end of *the days.*
Hos. 1: 1. *in the days of* Uzziah,
— *and in the days of* Jeroboam
5. it shall come to pass *at* that *day,*
11(2:2). great (shall be) *the day of* Jezreel.
2: 3(5). *as in the day that* she was born,
13(15). I will visit upon her *the days of*
15(17). *as* in *the days of* her youth, *and as* in *the day when* she came up
16(18). it shall be *at* that *day,*
18(20). *in* that *day* will I make a covenant
21(23). it shall come to pass *in* that *day,*
3: 3. Thou shalt abide for me many *days;*
4. children of Israel shall abide many *days*
5. his goodness in *the* latter *days.*
4: 5. Therefore shalt thou fall in *the day,*
5: 9. Ephraim shall be desolate *in the day of*
6: 2. *After two days* will he revive us:
— *in the* third *day* he will raise us up,
7: 5. In *the day of* our king
9: 5. What will ye do *in the* solemn *day, and in the day of* the feast
7. *The days of* visitation are come, *the days of* recompence are come;
9. *as in the days of* Gibeah:
10: 9. thou hast sinned *from the days of* Gibeah:
14. *in the day of* battle:
12: 1(2). he *daily* (lit. every *day*) increaseth
9(10). *as in the days of* the solemn feast.
Joel 1: 2. *in your days,* or even *in the days of* your
15. Alas *for the day!* for *the day of* the Lord
2: 1. *the day of* the Lord cometh,
2. *A day of* darkness and of gloominess, *a day of* clouds and of thick darkness,
11. *the day of* the Lord (is) great
29(3:2). *in* those *days* will I pour out my
31(3:4). *the* great and the terrible *day of* the
3: 1(4:1). behold, *in* those *days,*
14(4:14). *the day of* the Lord (is) near
18(4:18). it shall come to pass *in* that *day,*
Am. 1: 1. *in the days* of Uzziah king of Judah, *and in the days of* Jeroboam
14. shouting *in the day of* battle, with a tempest *in the day of* the whirlwind:
2:16. shall flee away naked *in* that *day,*
3:14. *in the day that* I shall visit
4: 2. *the days* shall come upon you,
4. after three *years:* (marg. (years) of *days*)
5: 8. *and* maketh *the day* dark with night:
18. Woe unto you that desire *the day* of the
— *the day of* the Lord (is) darkness,
20. not *the day of* the Lord (be) darkness,
6: 3. Ye that put far away *the* evil *day,*
8: 3. the temple shall be howlings *in* that *day,*
9. it shall come to pass *in* that *day,*
— I will darken the earth *in the* clear *day:*
10. the end thereof *as a* bitter *day.*
11. *the days* come, saith the Lord
13. *In* that *day* shall the fair virgins
9:11. *In* that *day* will I raise up the
— I will build it *as in the days of* old:
13. *the days* come, saith the Lord,
Obad. 8. Shall I not *in* that *day,*
11. *In the day that* thou stoodest on the other side, *in the day that* the strangers
12. *on the day of* thy brother *in the day that*

Obad. 12. *in the day of* their destruction;
—, 14. *in the day of* distress.
13. *in the day of* their calamity;
—, 13. *in the day of* their calamity,
15. *the day of* the Lord (is) near
Jon. 1:17(2:1). the belly of the fish three *days*
3: 3. great city of three *days'* journey.
4. *a day's* journey, and he cried, and said, Yet forty *days,*
Mic. 1: 1. *in the days of* Jotham,
2: 4. *In* that *day* shall (one) take up a
3: 6. *the day* shall be dark over them.
4: 1. in *the* last *days* it shall come to pass,
6. *In* that *day,* saith the Lord,
5: 2(1). goings forth (have been)...*from* everlasting. (marg. *from the days of* eternity)
10(9). it shall come to pass *in* that *day,*
7: 4. *the day of* thy watchmen
11. (In) *the day* that thy walls are to be built, (in) that *day* shall the decree be far
12. (In) that *day* (also) he shall come
14. *as in the days of* old.
15. *According to the days of* thy coming out
20. unto our fathers *from the days of* old.
Nah 1: 7. a strong hold *in the day of* trouble;
2: 3(4). *in the day of* his preparation,
8(9). Nineveh (is) *of old* (lit. *of days*) like a
3:17. camp in the hedges *in the* cold *day,*
Hab 1: 5. (I) will work a work *in your days,*
3:16. that I might rest *in the day of* trouble:
Zep 1: 1. *in the days of* Josiah
7. *the day of* the Lord (is) at hand:
8. it shall come to pass *in the day of*
9. *In the* same *day* also
10. it shall come to pass *in* that *day,*
14. *The* great *day of* the Lord (is) near,
— the voice of *the day of* the Lord:
15. That *day* (is) *a day of* wrath, *a day of* trouble and distress, *a day of* wasteness and desolation, *a day of* darkness and gloominess, *a day of* clouds and thick
16. *A day of* the trumpet and alarm
18. *in the day of* the Lord's wrath;
2: 2. (before) *the day* pass as the chaff,
— *the day of* the Lord's anger
3. *in the day of* the Lord's anger.
3: 8. *until the day* that I rise up to the prey:
11. *In* that *day* shalt thou not be ashamed
16. *In* that *day* it shall be said
Hag 1: 1. *in the* first *day* of the month,
15. *In the* four and twentieth *day*
2:15. consider from this *day* and upward,
18. from this *day* and upward, *from the* four and twentieth *day* of the ninth (month, even) from *the day* that the foundation
19. from this *day* will I bless (you).
23. *In* that *day,* saith the Lord of hosts,
Zec. 1: 7. *Upon the* four and twentieth *day*
2:11(15). be joined to the Lord *in* that *day,*
3: 9. the iniquity of that land *in* one *day.*
10. *In* that *day,* saith the Lord of hosts,
4:10. who hath despised *the day of* small
6:10. come thou *the* same *day,*
8: 4. every man with his staff in his hand for very *age.* (marg. multitude of *days*)
6. remnant of this people *in* these *days,*
9. ye that hear *in* these *days*
— *in the day* (that) the foundation
10. before these *days* there was no hire
11. *as* in *the* former *days,*
15. have I thought *in* these *days* to do well
23. *In* those *days* (it shall come to pass),
9:12. even *to day* do I declare
16. their God shall save them *in* that *day*
11:11. it was broken *in* that *day:*
12: 3. *in* that *day* will I make Jerusalem
4. *In* that *day,* saith the Lord,
6. *In* that *day* will I make the governors
8. *In* that *day* shall the Lord defend
— he that is feeble among them *at* that *day*
9. it shall come to pass *in* that *day,*
11. *In* that *day* shall there be a great
13: 1. *In* that *day* there shall be a fountain
2, 4. it shall come to pass *in* that *day,*
14: 1. *the day of* the Lord cometh,
3. *as when* (lit. *as the day*) he fought *in the day of* battle

Zec.14: 4. his feet shall stand *in* that *day*
5. *in the days of* Uzziah
6. it shall come to pass *in* that *day*,
7. it shall be one *day* which shall be known to the Lord, not *day*, nor night:
8. it shall be *in* that *day*,
9. *in* that *day* shall there be one Lord,
13. it shall come to pass *in* that *day*,
20. *In* that *day* shall there be
21. *in* that *day* there shall be no more
Mal. 3: 2. who may abide *the day of* his coming?
4. *as in the days of* old,
7. *from the days of* your fathers
17. *in that day* when I make up my jewels;
4: 1(3:19). *the day* cometh, that shall burn as an oven;
—(-:—). *the day* that cometh shall burn
3(-:21). *in the day* that I shall do (this),
5(-:23). *the* great and dreadful *day of* the

3118 **יוֹם** *yōhm*, Ch. m.

Ezr. 4:15. sedition within the same of old *time:*
19. it is found that this city of old *time*
6: 9. let it be given them *day by day*
15. was finished on *the* third *day* of the month
Dan 2:28. what shall be in *the* latter *days*.
44. *And in the days* of these kings
4:34(31). And at the end of *the days* I
5:11. *and in the days of* thy father
6: 7(8). of any God or man for thirty *days*,
10(11). he kneeled upon his knees three times *a day*,
12(13). of any God or man within thirty *days*,
13(14). maketh his petition three times *a day*.
7: 9. and the Ancient of *days* did sit,
13. and came to the Ancient of *days*,
22. Until the Ancient of *days* came,

3119 **יוֹמָם** *yōh-māhm'*, adv.

Ex. 13:21. the Lord went before them *by day*
— to go *by day* and night:
22. the pillar of the cloud *by day*,
40:38. cloud...(was) upon the tabernacle *by day*,
Lev. 8:35. *day* and night seven days,
Nu. 9:21. whether (it was) *by day* or by night
10:34. the cloud...(was) upon them *by day*,
14:14. *by day time* in a pillar of a cloud,
Deu 1:33. in a cloud *by day*.
28:66. thou shalt fear *day* and night, (lit. night *and day*)
Jos. 1: 8. shalt meditate therein *day* and night,
Jud. 6:27. he could not do (it) *by day*,
1Sa.25:16. both by night and *day*,
2Sa.21:10. birds of the air to rest on them *by day*,
1K. 8:59. unto the Lord our God *day* and night,
1Ch 9:33. they were employed in (that) work *day* and
2Ch 6:20. be open upon this house *day* and night,
Neh 1: 6. I pray before thee now, *day* and night,
4: 9(3). set a watch against them *day* and
9:12. them *in the day* by a cloudy pillar;
19. the cloud departed not from them *by day*,
Job 5:14. They meet with darkness *in the daytime*,
24:16. marked for themselves *in the daytime:*
Ps. 1: 2. in his law doth he meditate *day* and night.
13: 2(3). (having) sorrow in my heart *daily?*
22: 2(3). O my God, I cry *in the daytime*,
32: 4. *day* and night thy hand was heavy
42: 3(4). My tears have been my meat *day* and
8(9). his lovingkindness *in the daytime*,
55:10(11). *Day* and night they go about it
78:14. *In the daytime* also he led them with a
91: 5. for the arrow (that) flieth *by day;*
121: 6. The sun shall not smite thee *by day*,
Isa. 4: 5. a cloud and smoke *by day*,
6. a shadow *in the daytime* from the heat,
21: 8. upon the watchtower *in the daytime*,
34:10. It shall not be quenched night *nor day;*
60:11. they shall not be shut *day* nor night;
19. The sun shall be no more thy light *by day:*
Jer. 9: 1(8:23). that I might weep *day* and night
14:17. Let mine eyes run down with tears night *and day*,
Jer.15: 9. her sun is gone down while (it was) yet *day:* [see also יום]
16:13. there shall ye serve other gods *day* and
31:35. which giveth the sun for a light *by day*,
33:20. that there should not be *day* and night
25. If my covenant (be) not with *day* and
Lam.2:18. let tears run down like a river *day* and
Eze 12: 3. remove *by day* in their sight;
4. bring forth thy stuff *by day*
7. I brought forth my stuff *by day*,
30:16. Noph (shall have) distresses *daily*.

יָוֵן *yāh-vēhn'*, m. 3121

Ps. 40: 2(3). out of the *miry* clay,
69: 2(3). I sink *in* deep *mire*,

יוֹנָה *yōh-nāh'*, f. 3123, 3128

Gen. 8: 8. he sent forth *a dove* from him,
9. *the dove* found no rest
10. again he sent forth *the dove*
11. *the dove* came in to him in the evening;
12. other seven days; and sent forth *the dove;*
Lev. 1:14. of turtledoves, or of young *pigeons*.
5: 7. committed, two turtledoves, or two young *pigeons*,
11. two turtledoves, or two young *pigeons*,
12: 6. *a* young *pigeon*, or a turtledove,
8. two turtles, or two young *pigeons;*
14:22. two turtledoves, or two young *pigeons*,
30. of the turtledoves, or of *the* young *pigeons*,
15:14. two turtledoves, or two young *pigeons*,
29. two turtles, or two young *pigeons*,
Nu. 6:10. two turtles, or two young *pigeons*,
2K. 6:25. (כתיב) fourth part of a cab of *doves'* dung
Ps. 55: 6(7). Oh that I had wings *like a dove!*
56[title](1). To the chief Musician upon *Jonath*-elem-rechokim,
68:13(14). (yet shall ye be as) the wings of *dove*
Cant. 1:15. thou (art) fair; thou (hast) *doves'* eyes.
2:14. *O my dove*, (that art) in the clefts of the
4: 1. thou (hast) *doves'* eyes within thy locks.
5: 2. Open to me, my sister, my love, *my dove*,
12. His eyes (are) *as* (the eyes) of *doves*
6: 9. *My dove*, my undefiled is (but) one;
Isa. 38:14. I did mourn *as a dove:*
59:11. all like bears, *and* mourn sore *like doves:*
60: 8. *and as the doves* to their windows?
Jer. 48:28. be *like the dove* (that) maketh her nest
Eze. 7:16. shall be on the mountains *like doves of*
Hos 7:11. Ephraim also is *like a* silly *dove*
11:11. *and as a dove* out of the land of Assyria:
Nah 2: 7(8). lead (her) as with the voice of *doves*,

יוֹנֵק *yōh-nēhk'*, m. 3126

Isa. 53: 2. grow up before him *as a tender plant*,

יוֹנֶקֶת [*yōh-neh'-keth*], f. 3127

Job 8:16. *his branch* shooteth forth in his garden.
14: 7. *that the tender branch thereof* will not
15:30. the flame shall dry up *his branches*,
Ps. 80:11(12). *her branches* unto the river.
Eze.17:22. the top of *his young twigs*
Hos 14: 6(7). *His branches* shall spread,

יוֹצֵד see **יָצַד** See 3334

יוֹרֶה *yōh-reh'*, m. 3138

Deu 11:14. *the first rain* and the latter rain,
Jer. 5:24. rain, *both the former* and the latter,

יוֹתֵר *yōh-thēhr'*, m. 3148

Est. 6: 6. *more* than to myself?
Ecc. 2:15. why was I then *more* wise?

Ecc. 6: 8. For what hath the wise *more* than the fool?
11. what (is) man *the better?*
7:11. *and* (by it there is) *profit* to them
16. neither make thyself *over* wise:
12: 9. *And moreover*, because the preacher was wise, (marg. or, the *more* wise, &c.)
12. *And further*, by these, my son, be

See 3508 יְתֶרֶת see יוֹתֶרֶת

See 2161 יָזֻם (Gen. 11:6) see זָמַם

2109 יָזַן [*yāh-zan'*].

* HOPHAL.—*Participle.* *

Jer. 5: 8. They were (as) *fed* horses in the

3154 יֶזַע [*yeh'-zag*], m.

Eze 44:18. they shall not gird (themselves) *with any thing that causeth sweat.* (marg. *in*, or, *with sweat*; or, *in sweating* (places))

3161 יָחַד [*yāh-ghad'*].

* KAL.—*Future.* *

Gen49: 6. mine honour, *be* not *thou united*:
Isa. 14:20. *Thou shalt* not *be joined* with them in

* PIEL.—*Imperative.* *

Ps. 86:11. *unite* my heart to fear thy name.

3162 יַחַד *yah'-ghad*, m., יַחְדָּו *yagh-dāhv'*, & יַחְדָּיו *yagh-dāhv'*.

Gen13: 6. that they might dwell *together*:
— they could not dwell *together*.
22: 6, 8. they went both of them *together*.
19. and went *together* to Beer-sheba;
36: 7. that they might dwell *together*;
Ex. 19: 8. all the people answered *together*,
26:24. *and* they shall be coupled *together* above
36:29. *and* coupled *together* at the head thereof,
Deu12:22. and the clean shall eat (of) them *alike*.
15:22. and the clean (person shall eat it) *alike*,
22:10. an ox and an ass *together*.
11. (as) of woollen and linen *together*.
25: 5. If brethren dwell *together*,
11. When men strive *together*
33: 5. the tribes of Israel were gathered *together*.
17. he shall push the people *together*
Jos. 9: 2. they gathered themselves *together*,
11: 5. they came and pitched *together* at the
Jud. 6:33. children of the east were gathered *together*,
19: 6. did eat and drink both of them *together*:
1Sa.11:11. so that two of them were not left *together*.
17:10. me a man, that we may fight *together*.
30:24. they shall part *alike*.
31: 6. that same day *together*.
2Sa. 2:13. met *together* by the pool of Gibeon:
16. so they fell down *together*:
10:15. they gathered themselves *together*.
12: 3. it grew up *together* with him,
14:16. destroy me and my son *together*
21: 9. they fell (all) seven *together*,
1K. 3:18. we (were) *together*;
1Ch 10: 6. all his house died *together*.
12:17. mine heart shall be *knit* unto you:
Ezr. 4: 3. we ourselves *together* will build
Neh 4: 8(2). conspired all of them *together*
6: 2. Come, let us meet *together*
7. let us take counsel *together*.
Job 2:11. they had made an appointment *together*
3:18. (There) the prisoners rest *together*;
6: 2. my calamity laid in the balances *together*!
9:32. we should come *together* in judgment.
10: 8. made me and fashioned me *together*
16:10. they have gathered themselves *together*
Job 17:16. (our) rest *together* (is) in the dust.
19:12. His troops come *together*,
21:26. They shall lie down *alike* in the dust,
24: 4. of the earth hide themselves *together*.
17. *even as* the shadow of death:
31:38. *or* that the furrows *likewise* thereof
34:15. All flesh shall perish *together*,
29. against a man *only*:
38: 7. When the morning stars sang *together*,
40:13. Hide them in the dust *together*;
Ps. 2: 2. the rulers take counsel *together*,
4: 8(9). I will *both* lay me down in peace,
14: 3. they are (all) *together* become filthy:
19: 9(10). (are) true (and) righteous *altogether*.
31:13(14). they took counsel *together* against
33:15. He fashioneth their hearts *alike*;
34: 3(4). let us exalt his name *together*.
35:26. brought to confusion *together*
37:38. transgressors shall be destroyed *together*:
40:14(15). be ashamed and confounded *together*
41: 7(8). All that hate me whisper *together*
48: 4(5). they passed by *together*.
49: 2(3). rich and poor, *together*.
10(11). *likewise* the fool and the brutish
53: 3(4). they are *altogether* become filthy;
55:14(15). We took sweet counsel *together*,
62: 9(10). they (are) *altogether* (marg. *alike*)
71:10. wait for my soul take counsel *together*,
74: 6. down the carved work thereof *at once*
8. Let us destroy them *together*:
83: 5(6). they have consulted *together*
88:17(18). they compassed me about *together*.
98: 8. let the hills be joyful *together*
102:22(23). the people are gathered *together*,
122: 3. a city that is compact *together*:
133: 1. *together* in unity! (marg. even *together*)
141:10. whilst that I *withal* escape.
Pro 22:18. they shall *withal* be fitted in thy lips.
Isa. 1:28. the sinners (shall be) *together*,
31. they shall both burn *together*,
9:21(20). they *together* (shall be) against Judah.
10: 8. (Are) not my princes *altogether* kings?
11: 6. the fatling *together*;
7. their young ones shall lie down *together*:
14. they shall spoil them of the east *together*:
18: 6. They shall be left *together*
22: 3. All thy rulers are fled *together*,
— that are found in thee are bound *together*,
27: 4. I would burn them *together*.
31: 3. *and* they all shall fail *together*.
40: 5. all flesh shall see (it) *together*:
41: 1. let us come near *together* to judgment.
19. the pine, and the box tree *together*:
20. consider, and understand *together*,
23. behold (it) *together*.
42:14. I will destroy and devour *at once*.
43: 9. Let all the nations be gathered *together*,
17. they shall lie down *together*,
26. let us plead *together*:
44:11. (and) they shall be ashamed *together*.
45: 8. let righteousness spring up *together*;
16. they shall go to confusion *together*
20. draw near *together*,
21. let them take counsel *together*:
46: 2. they bow down *together*;
48:13. I call unto them, they stand up *together*,
50: 8. let us stand *together*:
52: 8. with the voice *together* shall they sing:
9. Break forth into joy, sing *together*,
60:13. the pine tree, and the box *together*,
65: 7. the iniquities of your fathers *together*,
66:17. the mouse, shall be consumed *together*,
Jer. 3:18. they shall come *together* out of the land
5: 5. these have *altogether* broken the yoke,
6:11. the assembly of young men *together*:
12. (their) fields and wives *together*:
21. the sons *together* shall fall upon them;
13:14. the fathers and the sons *together*,
31: 8. her that travaileth with child *together*:
13. both young men and old *together*:
24. all the cities thereof *together*,
41: 1. they did eat bread *together*
46:12. they are fallen both *together*.
21. are fled away *together*:
48: 7 & 49:3. his priests and his princes *together*.
50: 4. they and the children of Judah *together*,
33. of Judah (were oppressed *together*:

Jer. 51:38. They shall roar *together* like lions:
Lam. 2: 8. they languished *together*.
Hos. 1:11(2:2). of Israel be gathered *together*,
11: 7. none *at all* would exalt (him). (marg. *together* they exalted not)
8. my repentings are kindled *together*.
Am 1:15. he and his princes *together*,
3: 3. Can two walk *together*, except they be
Mic 2:12. I will put them *together* as the sheep
Zec 10: 4. out of him every oppressor *together*.

3173 **יָחִיד** *yāh-'gheed'*, adj.

Gen22: 2. Take now thy son, *thine only* (son) Isaac,
12, 16. hast not withheld thy son, *thine only*
Jud. 11:34. she (was his) *only child*;
Ps. 22:20(21). *my darling* (marg. *only one*) from the
25:16. I (am) *desolate* and afflicted.
35:17. *my darling* (marg. *only one*) from the
68: 6(7). God setteth *the solitary* in families:
Pro 4: 3. tender *and only* (beloved) in the sight of
Jer. 6:26. make thee mourning, (as for) an *only son*,
Am 8:10. I will make it as the mourning of an *only*
Zec 12:10. as one mourneth for (his) *only* (son),

3175 **יָחִיל** *yāh-'gheel*, adj.

Lam. 3:26. (It is) good that (a man) *should both hope* (lit. *and expecting*)

3176 **יָחַל** [*yāh-'ghal'*].

* NIPHAL.—*Preterite.* *

Eze 19: 5. when she saw that *she had waited*,

NIPHAL.—*Future.*

Gen 8:12. *And he stayed* yet other seven days;
1Sa. 13: 8. (כתיב) *And he tarried* seven days,

* PIEL.—*Preterite.* *

Job 29:21. Unto me (men) gave ear, *and waited*,
23. *And they waited* for me as for the rain;
Ps. 33:22. according as *we hope* in thee.
119:43. *I have hoped* in thy judgments.
49. upon which *thou hast caused me to hope*.
74. *I have hoped* in thy word.
81, 114. *I hope* in thy word.
147. *I hoped* in thy word.
Eze 13: 6. *and they have made* (others) *to hope*

PIEL.—*Imperative.*

Ps. 130: 7 & 131:3. *Let* Israel *hope* in the Lord:

PIEL.—*Future.*

Job 6:11. (is) my strength, that *I should hope*?
13:15. Though he slay me, yet *will I trust* in
14:14. days of my appointed time *will I wait*,
30:26. *when I waited* for light, there came
Ps. 71:14. But I *will hope* continually,
Isa. 42: 4. the isles *shall wait* for his law.
51: 5. and on mine arm *shall they trust*.
Mic 5: 7(6). nor *waiteth* for the sons of men.

PIEL.—*Participle.*

Ps. 31:24(25). all *ye that hope* in the Lord.
33:18. *upon them that hope* in his mercy;
69: 3(4). mine eyes fail *while I wait* for my
147:11. *those that hope* in his mercy.

* HIPHIL.—*Preterite.* *

Job 32:11. *I waited* for your words;
16. *When I had waited*,
Ps. 38:15(16). in thee, O Lord, *do I hope*:
130: 5. in his word *do I hope*.

HIPHIL.—*Imperative.*

Ps. 42: 5(6), 11(12). *hope thou* in God: for I shall
43: 5. *hope* in God: for I shall yet

HIPHIL.—*Future.*

1Sa. 10: 8. seven days *shalt thou tarry*,
13: 8. *And he tarried* seven days,
2Sa. 18:14. *I may* not *tarry* thus with thee.
2K. 6:33. *should I wait* for the Lord any longer?
Jer. 4:19. *I am pained* at my very heart; (see also חול)

Lam. 3:21. therefore *have I hope*.
24. therefore *will I hope* in him.
Mic 7: 7. *I will wait* for the God of my salvation:

יָחַם [*yāh-'gham'*]. 3179

* KAL.—*Future.* *

Gen30:38. *that they should conceive* when they came
39. *And* the flocks *conceived* before the rods,
Deu 19: 6. while his heart *is hot*,
1K. 1: 1. they covered him with clothes, but he *gat no heat*. (lit. *it was* not *hot* to him)
Ecc. 4:11. how *can* one *be warm* (alone)?
Eze 24:11. that the brass of it *may be hot*,

* PIEL.—*Preterite.* *

Ps. 51: 5(7). in sin *did* my mother *conceive* me. (marg. *warm*)

PIEL.—*Infinitive.*

Gen30:41. whensoever the stronger cattle *did conceive*,
— *that they might conceive* among the rods.
31:10. the time *that* the cattle *conceived*,

יַחְמוּר *yagh-moor'*, m. 3180

Deu 14: 5. the roebuck, *and the fallow deer*,
1K. 4:23(5:3). roebucks, *and fallowdeer*,

יָחֵף *yāh-'ghēhph'*, adj. 3182

2Sa. 15:30. he went *barefoot*:
Isa. 20: 2. he did so, walking naked *and barefoot*.
3. Isaiah hath walked naked *and barefoot*
4. young and old, naked *and barefoot*,
Jer. 2:25. Withhold thy foot *from being unshod*,

יָחַר [*yāh-'ghar'*]. 3186

* KAL.—*Future.* *

2Sa. 20: 5. (כתיב) *but he tarried longer* than the set

יָחַשׂ [*yāh-'ghas'*]. 3187

* KAL.—*Preterite.* *

1Ch 5:17. All these *were reckoned by genealogies*
9: 1. all Israel *were reckoned by genealogies*;

HITHPAEL.—*Infinitive.*

1Ch 4:33. These (were) their habitations, *and their genealogy*. (marg. or, *as they divided themselves by nations* among them)
5: 1. *the genealogy is* not *to be reckoned*
7. *when the genealogy* of their generations *was reckoned*,
7: 5. *reckoned* in all *by their genealogies*
7. *and were reckoned by their genealogies*
9. *And the number of them, after their genealogy* by their generations,
40. *And the number throughout the genealogy of them*
9:22. These *were reckoned by their genealogy*
2Ch 12:15. Iddo the seer *concerning genealogies*?
31:16. Beside *their genealogy* of males,
17. *the genealogy* of the priests
18. *And to the genealogy* of all their little ones,
19. all *that were reckoned by genealogies*
Ezr. 8: 1. *and* (this is) *the genealogy of them*
3. with him *were reckoned by genealogy*
Neh 7: 5. *that they might be reckoned by genealogy*.

HITHPAEL.—*Participle.*

Ezr. 2:62. those *that were reckoned by genealogy*,
Neh. 7:64. those *that were reckoned by genealogy*,

יַחַשׂ *yah'-ghas*. m. 3188

Neh. 7: 5. I found a register of *the genealogy*

3190 יָטַב [*yāh-tav'*].

*** KAL.—*Future.* ***

Gen 12:13. that *it may be well* with me for thy sake;
34:18. *And* their words *pleased* Hamor,
40:14. think on me when *it shall be well* with
41:37. *And* the thing *was good* in the eyes of
45:16. *and it pleased* Pharaoh well,
Lev. 10:19. *should it have been accepted* in the sight
20. when Moses heard (that), *he was content.* (lit. *and it was good* in his eyes)
Deu 1:23. *And* the saying *pleased* me *well:* (lit. *was good* in my eyes)
4:40. that *it may go well* with thee,
5:16. that *it may go well* with thee,
29(26). that *it might be well* with them,
6: 3. that *it may be well* with thee,
18. that *it may be well* with thee,
12:25, 28. that *it may go well* with thee,
22: 7. that *it may be well* with thee,
Jos. 22:30. *it pleased* them. (marg. *was good* in their eyes)
33. *And* the thing *pleased* the children of
Jud. 18:20. *And* the priest's heart *was glad,*
19: 6. *and let* thine heart *be merry.*
9. lodge here, *that* thine heart *may be merry;*
Ru. 3: 1. that *it may be well* with thee?
7. *and* his heart *was merry,*
1Sa 18: 5. *and he was accepted* in the sight of all the
24: 4(5). do to him as *it shall* seem *good* (lit. *be good* in thine eyes)
2Sa 3:36. *and it pleased* them: (marg. *was good* in their eyes)
18: 4. What *seemeth* you *best* I will do. (lit. *is good* in your eyes)
1K. 3:10. *And* the speech *pleased* the Lord, (lit. *was good* in the eyes of)
21: 7. *and let* thine heart *be merry:*
2K. 25:24. *and it shall be well* with you.
Neh 2: 5. if thy servant *have found favour*
6. *So it pleased* the king to send me;
Est. 1:21. *And* the saying *pleased* the king (lit. *was good* in the eyes of)
2: 4. the maiden which *pleaseth* the king (lit. *id.*)
— *And* the thing *pleased* the king; (lit. *id.*)
9. *And* the maiden *pleased* him, (lit. *id.*)
5:14. *And* the thing *pleased* Haman; (lit. *was good* before)
Ps. 69:31(32). (This) *also shall please* the Lord *better*
Ecc. 7: 3. the countenance the heart *is made better.*
Jer. 7:23. that *it may be well* unto you.
38:20. *so it shall be well* unto thee,
40: 9. *and it shall be well* with you.
42: 6. that *it may be well* with us,

*** HIPHIL.—*Preterite.* ***

Gen 12:16. *he entreated* Abram *well* for her sake:
Deu 5:28(25). *they have well* said all that they
18:17. *They have well* (spoken that) which they
30: 5. *and he will do thee good,* and multiply
Jos. 24:20. after that *he hath done* you *good.*
Ru. 3:10. *thou hast shewed more* kindness in the latter end (lit. *thou hast made good* thy kindness)
1Sa. 25:31. *when* the Lord *shall have dealt well* with my
Jer. 1:12. *Thou hast well* seen:

HIPHIL.—*Infinitive.*

Gen 32:12(13). I will *surely* do thee good, (lit. *in doing good* I will do good)
Ex. 30: 7. *when he dresseth* the lamps,
Lev. 5: 4. to do evil, or *to do good,*
Deu 8:16. *to do thee good* at thy latter end;
9:21. stamped it, (and) ground (it) *very small,*
13:14(15). make search, and ask *diligently;*
17: 4. hast heard (of it), and enquired *diligently,*
19:18. the judges shall make *diligent* inquisition:
27: 8. thou shalt write...*very* plainly. (lit. by declaring *well*)
28:63. the Lord rejoiced over you *to do* you *good,*
2K. 11:18. his images brake they in pieces *thoroughly,*
Ps. 36: 3(4). he hath left off to be wise, (and) *to do good.*
Isa. 1:17. Learn *to do well;*
Jer. 4:22. *but to do good* they have no knowledge.
7: 5. if ye *throughly* amend your ways (lit. *in mending* amend)
Jer. 10: 5. neither also (is it) in them *to do good.*
13:23. (then) may ye also *do good,*
18:10. the good, wherewith I said *I would benefit them.*
32:40. that I will not turn away from them, *to do* them *good;*
Jon. 4: 4. *Doest* thou *well* to be angry? (marg. or, *Art* thou *greatly* angry)
9. *Doest* thou *well* to be (marg. or, *Art* thou *greatly*) angry for the gourd? And he said, I *do well* (marg. *I am greatly*) to be angry,
Mic. 7: 3. That they may do evil with both hands *earnestly,*
Zec. 8:15. I thought in these days *to do well*

HIPHIL.—*Imperative.*

Ps. 33: 3. play *skilfully* with a loud noise. (lit. *do good* to play)
51:18(20). *Do good* in thy good pleasure unto
Isa. 23:16. *make sweet* melody, sing many songs,
Jer. 7: 3. *Amend* your ways and your doings,
18:11. *and make* your ways and your doings *good.*
26:13. *amend* your ways and your doings,
35:15. *and amend* your doings,

HIPHIL.—*Future.*

Gen 4: 7. If *thou doest well,* shalt thou not be accepted? and if *thou doest* not *well,* sin lieth
32: 9(10). *and I will deal well* with thee:
12(13). *I will* surely *do* thee *good,*
Ex. 1:20. *Therefore* God *dealt well* with the midwives:
Nu. 10:32. what goodness the Lord *shall do* unto us,
Jud. 17:13. Now know I that the Lord *will do* me *good,*
1Sa. 2:32. all (the wealth) which (God) *shall give*
20:13. if *it please* my father (to do) thee evil,
1K. 1:47. God *make* the name of Solomon *better* than
2K. 9:30. *and tired* her head,
Job 24:21. and *doeth* not *good* to the widow.
Ps. 49:18(19). when *thou doest well* to thyself.
Pro. 15: 2. of the wise *useth* knowledge *aright:*
13. A merry heart *maketh* a *cheerful*
17:22. A merry heart *doeth good*
Isa. 41:23. yea, *do good,* or do evil, that we may be
Jer. 2:33. Why *trimmest* thou thy way
7: 5. if *ye* throughly *amend* your ways
Mic. 2: 7. *do* not my words *do good*
Nah. 3: 8. *Art* thou *better* than populous No,
Zep. 1:12. say in their heart, The Lord *will* not *do good,*

HIPHIL.—*Participle.*

Jud. 19:22. *as* they *were making* their hearts *merry,*
1Sa. 16:17. Provide me now a man *that can* play *well,*
Pro. 30:29. yea, four *are comely* in going:

יְטַב [*y'tav*], Ch. 3191

*** P'AL.—*Future.* ***

Ezr. 7:18. whatsoever *shall seem good* to thee,

יַיִן *yah'-yin,* m. 3196

Gen 9:21. he drank of *the wine,* and was drunken;
24. Noah awoke *from his wine,*
14:18. And Melchizedek king of Salem brought forth bread *and wine:*
19:32. let us make our father drink *wine,*
33. they made their father drink *wine*
34. let us make him drink *wine*
35. they made their father drink *wine*
27:25. he brought him *wine,* and he drank.
49:11. he washed his garments *in wine,*
12. His eyes (shall be) red *with wine,*
Ex. 29:40. the fourth part of an hin of *wine*
Lev. 10: 9. Do not drink *wine*
23:13. drink offering thereof (shall be) of *wine,*
Nu. 6: 3. He shall separate (himself) *from wine*
— shall drink no vinegar of *wine,*
4. that is made of the *vine* tree, (marg. vine of *the wine*)

Nu. 6:20. after that the Nazarite may drink *wine*.
15: 5. *And* the fourth (part) of an hin of *wine*
7. *And*...the third (part) of an hin of *wine*,
10. *And* thou shalt bring...half an hin of *wine*,
28:14. And their drink offerings shall be half an hin of *wine*
Deu 14:26. for sheep, *or for wine*,
28:39. *but* shalt neither drink (of) *the wine*,
29: 6(5). *neither* have ye drunk *wine*
32:33. *Their wine* (is) the poison of dragons,
38. drank *the wine of* their drink offerings?
Jos. 9: 4. *wine* bottles, old, and rent,
13. these bottles of *wine*,
Jud. 13: 4. drink not *wine* nor strong drink,
7. drink no *wine* nor strong drink,
14. any (thing) that cometh of *the vine*, (lit. vine of *the wine*) *neither* let her drink *wine* or strong drink,
19:19. there is bread *and wine* also
1Sa. 1:14. put away *thy wine* from thee.
15. I have drunk *neither wine* nor strong drink,
24. and a bottle of *wine*,
10: 3. another carrying a bottle of *wine:*
16:20. a bottle of *wine*, and a kid,
25:18. two bottles of *wine*,
37. when *the wine* was gone out of Nabal,
2Sa. 13:28. when Amnon's heart is merry *with wine*,
16: 1. a bottle of *wine*.
2. *and the wine*, that such as be faint
1Ch 9:29. the fine flour, *and the wine*, and the oil,
12:40. bunches of raisins, *and wine*,
27:27. the increase of the vineyards for *the wine*
2Ch 2:10(9). *and* twenty thousand baths of *wine*,
15(14). the barley, the oil, *and the wine*,
11:11. store of victual, and of oil *and wine*.
Neh 2: 1. *wine* (was) before him: and I took up *the wine*,
5:15. had taken of them bread *and wine*,
18. store of all sorts of *wine:*
13:15. as also *wine*, grapes, and figs,
Est. 1: 7. *and* royal *wine* in abundance,
10. the heart of the king was merry *with wine*,
5: 6. the king said unto Esther at the banquet of *wine*,
7: 2. the second day at the banquet of *wine*,
7. arising from the banquet of *wine*
8. the place of the banquet of *wine;*
Job 1:13, 18. drinking *wine* in their eldest
32:19. belly (is) *as wine* (which) hath no vent;
Ps. 60: 3(5). to drink *the wine* of astonishment.
75: 8(9). *and the wine* is red;
78:65. man that shouteth *by reason of wine*.
104:15. *And wine* (that) maketh glad the heart of
Pro. 4:17. *and* drink *the wine of* violence.
9: 2. she hath mingled *her wine;*
5. drink *of the wine* (which) I have mingled.
20: 1. *Wine* (is) a mocker,
21:17. he that loveth *wine* and oil
23:20. Be not among *wine*bibbers;
30. They that tarry long at *the wine;*
31. Look not thou upon *the wine*
31: 4. (it is) not for kings to drink *wine;*
6. *and wine* unto those that be of heavy hearts.
Ecc. 2: 3. to give myself *unto wine*,
9: 7. drink *thy wine* with a merry heart;
10:19. *and wine* maketh merry:
Cant. 1: 2. thy love (is) better *than wine*.
4. we will remember thy love *more than wine:*
2: 4. He brought me to the *banqueting* house, (marg. house of *wine*)
4:10. how much better is thy love *than wine!*
5: 1. I have drunk *my wine* with my milk:
7: 9(10). *like the* best *wine* for my beloved,
8: 2. I would cause thee to drink *of* spiced *wine*
Isa. 5:11. (till) *wine* inflame them!
12. *and wine*, are in their feasts:
22. (them that are) mighty to drink *wine*,
16:10. the treaders shall tread out no *wine*
22:13. eating flesh, and drinking *wine:*
24: 9. They shall not drink *wine* with a song;
11. (There is) a crying for *wine*
28: 1. them that are overcome with *wine!*
7. they also have erred *through wine*,
— they are swallowed up of *wine*,
29: 9. they are drunken, but not with *wine;*
51:21. drunken, but not *with wine:*
55. 1. buy *wine* and milk without money
Isa. 56:12. Come ye, (say they), I will fetch *wine*,
Jer. 13:12, 12. Every bottle shall be filled with *wine:*
23: 9. a man whom *wine* hath overcome,
25:15. Take the *wine* cup of this fury
35: 2. give them *wine* to drink.
5. pots full of *wine*, and cups, and I said unto them, Drink ye *wine*.
6. We will drink no *wine:*
— Ye shall drink no *wine*,
8. to drink no *wine* all our days,
14. he commanded his sons not to drink *wine*,
40:10. gather ye *wine*, and summer fruits,
12. gathered *wine* and summer fruits
48:33. *and* I have caused *wine* to fail
51: 7. the nations have drunken *of her wine;*
Lam. 2:12. Where (is) corn *and wine?*
Eze. 27:18. *in the wine of* Helbon,
44:21. *Neither* shall any priest drink *wine*,
Dan 1: 5. *and of the wine which* he drank:
8. *nor with the wine which* he drank:
16. *and the wine that* they should drink;
10: 3. neither came flesh *nor wine* in my mouth,
Hos. 4:11. Whoredom *and wine*
7: 5. the princes have made (him) sick with bottles *of wine;*
9: 4. They shall not offer *wine* (offerings)
14: 7(8). scent thereof (shall be) *as the wine of*
Joel 1: 5. howl, all ye drinkers of *wine*,
3: 3(4:3). sold a girl *for wine*,
Am. 2: 8. *and* they drink *the wine of* the condemned
12. ye gave the Nazarites *wine*
5:11. ye shall not drink *wine of them*.
6: 6. That drink *wine* in bowls,
9:14. drink *the wine thereof;*
Mic. 2:11. I will prophesy unto thee *of wine*
6:15. shalt not drink *wine*.
Hab. 2: 5. he transgresseth by *wine*,
Zep. 1:13. not drink *the wine thereof*.
Hag. 2:12. *wine*, or oil, or any meat,
Zec. 9:15. make a noise as through *wine;*
10: 7. their heart shall rejoice as through *wine:*

יַךְ *yach*. 3197

1Sa. 4:13. (כתיב) a seat *by* the way*side* (see יַד [קרי])

יָכַח [*yāh-chagh'*]. 3198

* NIPHAL.—*Future.* *

Isa. 1:18. Come now, *and let us reason together*,

NIPHAL.—*Participle.*

Gen 20:16. *thus she was reproved*.
Job 23: 7. There the righteous *might dispute* with him;

* HIPHIL.—*Preterite.* *

Gen 21:25. *And* Abraham *reproved* Abimelech
24:14. (that) *thou hast appointed* for thy servant
44. the woman whom the Lord *hath appointed*
2Sa. 7:14. *I will chasten him* with the rod
2K. 19: 4. *and will reprove* the words
Pro. 19:25. *and reprove* one that hath understanding,
Isa. 2: 4. *and shall rebuke* many people:
11: 4. *and reprove* with equity for the meek
37: 4. *and will reprove* the words which the Lord
Mic. 4: 3. *and rebuke* strong nations afar off;

HIPHIL.—*Infinitive.*

Lev. 19:17. thou shalt *in any wise* rebuke (lit. *in rebuking* thou shalt rebuke)
Job 6:25. what doth your *arguing* reprove?
26. Do ye imagine *to reprove* words,
13: 3. *and* I desire *to reason* with God.
10. He will *surely* reprove you,
15: 3. *Should* he *reason* with unprofitable talk?
Pro. 15:12. A scorner loveth not *one that reproveth* him:
Hab 1:12. thou hast established them *for correction*.

HIPHIL.—*Imperative.*

Pro. 9: 8. *rebuke* a wise man, and he will love thee.

HIPHIL.—*Future.*

Gen31:37. *that they may judge* betwixt us both.
42. *and rebuked* (thee) yesternight.
Lev.19:17. *thou shalt* in any wise *rebuke* thy neighbour,
1Ch12:17. the God of our fathers look (thereon), *and rebuke* (it).
16:21. *yea, he reproved* kings for their sakes,
Job 5:17. happy (is) the man *whom* God *correcteth*:
6:25. what *doth* your arguing *reprove?*
13:10. *He will* surely *reprove* you,
15. *I will maintain* mine own ways (marg. *prove*, or, *argue*)
16:21. *O that one might plead* for a man with God,
19: 5. *and plead* against me my reproach:
22: 4. *Will he reprove thee* for fear of thee?
Ps. 6: 1(2). O Lord, *rebuke me* not in thine anger,
38: 1(2). O Lord, *rebuke me* not in thy wrath:
50: 8. *I will* not *reprove thee*
21. *I will reprove thee*, and set (them) in order
94:10. He that chastiseth the heathen, *shall* not *he correct?*
105:14. *yea, he reproved* kings for their sakes;
141: 5. *and let him reprove me;*
Pro. 3:12. whom the Lord loveth *he correcteth;*
9: 8. *Reprove* not a scorner, lest he hate thee:
30: 6. *he reprove* thee, and thou be found a liar.
Isa. 11: 3. neither *reprove* after the hearing of his ears:
Jer. 2:19. thy backslidings *shall reprove thee:*
Hos. 4: 4. let no man strive, nor *reprove* another:

HIPHIL.—*Participle.*

Job 9:33. Neither is there *any daysman* (marg. *umpire*) betwixt us,
32:12. (there was) none of you *that convinced* Job,
40: 2. *he that reproveth* God,
Pro. 9: 7. *and he that rebuketh* a wicked (man)
24:25. *But to them that rebuke* (him) shall he
25:12. (so is) *a* wise *reprover* upon an obedient
28:23. *He that rebuketh* a man
Isa. 29:21. *and* lay a snare *for him that reproveth*
Eze. 3:26. shalt not be to them *a reprover:* (marg. a man *reproving*)
Am. 5:10. They hate him *that rebuketh*

* HOPHAL.—*Preterite.* *

Job 33:19. *He is chastened also* with pain

* HITHPAEL.—*Future.* *

Mic. 6: 2. *he will plead* with Israel.

3201 יָכֹל *yāh-chōhl′.*

* KAL.—*Preterite.* *

Gen 13: 6. *they could* not dwell together.
30: 8. and *I have prevailed:*
32:25(26). when he saw that *he prevailed* not
36: 7. the land...*could* not bear them
37: 4. they hated him, and *could* not speak
45: 1. Joseph *could* not refrain himself
3. his brethren *could* not answer him;
Ex. 2: 3. *she could* not longer hide him,
7:21. the Egyptians *could* not drink of the water
24. *they could* not drink of the water
8:18(14). the magicians did so...but *they could*
9:11. the magicians *could* not stand before Moses
12:39. thrust out of Egypt, and *could* not tarry,
15:23. *they could* not drink of the waters
18:23. *then thou shalt be able* to endure,
40:35. Moses *was* not *able* to enter
Nu. 9: 6. *they could* not keep the passover
Jos. 15:63. the children of Judah *could* not drive them
17:12. the children of Manasseh *could* not drive
Jud. 2:14. *they could* not any longer stand
8: 3. what *was I able* to do
14:14. *they could* not in three days expound
1Sa. 4:15. his eyes were dim, that *he could* not see.
2Sa. 3:11. *he could* not answer Abner
1K. 5: 3(17). my father *could* not build an house
8:11. the priests *could* not stand to minister
9:21. *were* not *able* utterly to destroy,
13: 4. *he could* not pull it in again
14: 4. Ahijah *could* not see;
2K. 3:26. but *they could* not.
4:40. *they could* not eat (thereof).
2K. 16: 5. *could* not overcome (him).
1Ch 21:30. David *could* not go before it
2Ch 5:14. the priests *could* not stand to minister
7: 2. the priests *could* not enter into the house
7. the brasen altar...*was* not *able* to receive
29:34. *they could* not flay all the burnt offerings:
30: 3. *they could* not keep it at that time,
32:13. *were* the gods...any ways *able*
14. that *could* deliver his people out of mine
Ezr. 2:59. *they could* not shew their father's house,
Neh 7:61. *they could* not shew their father's house,
Ps. 13: 4(5). *I have prevailed against him;*
36:12(13). *shall* not *be able* to rise.
40:12(13). *I am* not *able* to look up;
129: 2. *they have* not *prevailed* against me.
Isa. 7: 1. *could* not prevail against it.
46: 2. *they could* not deliver the burden,
Jer. 38:22. *and have prevailed* against thee:
Obad. 7. (and) *prevailed* against thee;
Jon. 1:13. but *they could* not:

KAL.—*Infinitive.*

Nu. 13:30. we are well able *to overcome* it.
14:16. the Lord *was* not *able* to bring this people
22:38. have I now *any* power *at all* (lit. in *having power* have I power)
Deu 9:28. the Lord *was* not *able* to bring them into
1Sa. 26:25. shalt *still* prevail. (lit. in *prevailing* shall prevail)
2Ch 32:13. were the gods...*any ways* able

KAL.—*Future.*

Gen13:16. if a man *can* number the dust
15: 5. if *thou be able* to number them:
19:19. *I can*not escape to the mountain,
22. *I can*not do any thing till thou be come
24:50. *we can*not speak unto thee
29: 8. *We can*not, until all the flocks be gathered
31:35. *I can*not rise up before thee;
32:28(29). and with men, *and hast prevailed.*
34:14. *We can*not do this thing,
43:32. the Egyptians *might* not eat bread with the
44: 1. as much as *they can* carry,
22. The lad *can*not leave his father:
26. *We can*not go down
— *we may* not see the man's face,
48:10. *he could* not see.
Ex. 10: 5. *one can*not *be able* to see the earth:
18:18. thou *art not able* to perform it
19:23. people *can*not come up to mount Sinai:
33:20. *Thou canst* not see my face:
Nu. 11:14. *I am* not *able* to bear all this people
13:30. *we are* well *able* to overcome it.
31. *We be* not *able* to go up
22: 6. peradventure *I shall prevail,*
11. *I shall be able* to overcome them,
18. *I can*not go beyond the word of the Lord
37. *am I* not *able* indeed to promote thee
38. *have I* now any *power* at all
24:13. *I can*not go beyond the commandment of
Deu 1: 9. *I am* not *able* to bear you myself alone:
7:17. how *can I* dispossess them?
22. *thou mayest* not consume them at once,
12:17. *Thou mayest* not eat within thy gates
14:24. *thou art* not *able* to carry it;
16: 5. *Thou mayest* not sacrifice the passover
17:15. *thou mayest* not set a stranger over thee,
21:16. *he may* not make the son
22: 3. *thou mayest* not hide thyself.
19. *he may* not put her away all his days.
29. *he may* not put her away all his days.
24: 4. *may* not take her again to be his wife,
28:27. *thou canst* not be healed.
35. a sore botch that *can*not *be* healed,
31: 2. *I can* no more go out and come in:
Jos. 7:12. the children of Israel *could* not stand
13. *thou canst* not stand before thine enemies,
9:19. *we may* not touch them.
15:63. (כתיב) the children of Judah *could* not drive
24:19. *Ye can*not serve the Lord:
Jud. 11:35. *I can*not go back.
14:13. if *ye can*not declare (it) me,
16: 5. by what (means) *we may prevail* against
21:18. *we may* not give them wives
Ru. 4: 6. *I can*not redeem (it) for myself,
— *I can*not redeem (it).

1Sa. 3: 2. *he could* not see;
6:20. Who *is able* to stand before this holy Lord
17: 9. If *he be able* to fight with me,
— if *I prevail* against him, and kill him,
33. *Thou art* not *able* to go against this
39. *I can*not go with these;
26:25. also *shalt* still *prevail*.
2Sa. 12:23. *can I* bring him back again?
17:17. *they might* not be seen to come into the city:
1K. 3: 9. who *is able* to judge this...people?
13:16. *I may* not return with thee,
20: 9. this thing *I may* not do.
22:22. shalt persuade (him), and *prevail* also:
2K. 18:23. if *thou be able* on thy part
29. *he shall* not *be able* to deliver you
2Ch 18:21. entice (him), and thou *shalt also prevail:*
32:14. your God *should be able* to deliver
15. no god...*was able* to deliver his people
Neh 4:10(4). *we are* not *able* to build the wall.
6: 3. so that *I can*not come
Est. 6:13. *thou shalt* not *prevail* against him,
8: 6. how *can I endure* to see the evil (marg. *be able* that I may see)
— how *can I endure* to see the destruction
Job 4: 2. who *can* withhold himself from speaking?
31:23. reason of his highness *I could* not endure.
33: 5. If *thou canst* answer me,
42: 2. I know that *thou canst* do every (thing),
Ps. 18:38(39). that *they were* not *able* to rise:
21:11(12). *they are* not *able* (to perform).
78:19. *Can* God furnish a table
20. *can he* give bread also?
101: 5. a proud heart *will* not *I suffer*.
139: 6. *I can*not (attain) unto it.
Pro. 30:21. four (which) *it can*not bear:
Ecc. 1: 8. man *can*not utter (it):
15. crooked *can*not be made straight: and that which is wanting *can*not be numbered.
6:10. neither *may he* contend with him
7:13. who *can* make (that) straight,
8:17. a man *can*not find out the work
— yet *shall he* not *be able* to find (it).
Cant. 8: 7. Many waters *can*not quench love,
Isa. 1:13. the calling of assemblies, *I can*not *away with;*
16:12. *he shall* not *prevail*.
29:11. *I can*not; for it (is) sealed:
36: 8. if *thou be able* on thy part
14. *he shall* not *be able* to deliver you.
47:11. *thou shalt* not *be able* to put it off:
12. if so be *thou shalt be able* to profit,
56:10. they (are) all dumb dogs, *they can*not bark;
57:20. the troubled sea, when *it can*not rest,
59:14. equity *can*not enter.
Jer. 1:19. *they shall* not *prevail* against thee;
3: 5. and done evil things *as thou couldest*.
5:22. yet *can they* not *prevail;*
6:10. *they can*not hearken:
11:11. *they shall* not *be able* to escape;
13:23. *may ye* also do good,
14: 9. a mighty man (that) *can*not save?
15:20. *they shall* not *prevail* against thee:
18: 6. *can*not *I* do with you as this potter?
19:11. that *can*not be made whole again:
20: 7. thou art stronger than I, *and hast prevailed:*
9. *I could* not (stay).
10. *and we shall prevail* against him,
11. *they shall* not *prevail:*
36: 5. *I can*not go into the house
38: 5. (he that) *can* do (any) thing against you.
44:22. the Lord *could* no longer bear,
49:10. *he shall* not *be able* to hide himself:
23. *it can*not be quiet.
Lam. 1:14. *I am* not *able* to rise up.
4:14. men *could* not touch their garments.
Eze. 7:19. their gold *shall* not *be able* to deliver them
33:12. neither *shall* the righteous *be able* to live
47: 5. a river that *I could* not pass over:
Dan 10:17. how *can* the servant of this my lord
Hos. 5:13. *could he* not heal you,
8: 5. how long (will it be) ere *they attain* to
12: 4(5). he had power over the angel, *and prevailed:*
Am. 7:10. the land *is* not *able* to bear all his words.
Hab 1:13. *canst* not look on iniquity:
Zep. 1:18. nor their gold *shall be able* to deliver them

יְכִל *y'cheel*, Ch. 3202

* P'AL.—*Preterite*. *

Dan 2:47. seeing *thou couldest* reveal this
6:20(21). *is* thy God,...*able* to deliver thee

P'AL.—*Future*.

Dan 2:10. not a man upon the earth that *can*
3:29. there is no other God that *can* deliver
5:16. that *thou canst* make interpretations,
— now if *thou canst* read the writing,

P'AL.—*Participle*.

Dan 2:27. *can*not the wise (men), the astrologers,
3:17. our God whom we serve *is able*
4:18(15). *are* not *able* to make known
37(34). that walk in pride *he is able* to abase.
6: 4(5). *they could* find none occasion
7:21. made war with the saints, *and prevailed*

יָלַד *yāh-lad'*. 3205

* KAL.—*Preterite*. *

Gen 4:18. Irad *begat* Mehujael: and Mehujael *begat* Methusael: and Methusael *begat*
22. *she* also *bare* Tubal-cain,
6: 4. *and they bare* (children) to them,
10: 8. Cush *begat* Nimrod:
13. Mizraim *begat* Ludim,
15. Canaan *begat* Sidon
24. Arphaxad *begat* Salah; and Salah *begat* Eber.
26. Joktan *begat* Almodad,
16: 1. Sarai...*bare* him no children:
15. called his son's name, which Hagar *bare*,
19:38. *she* also *bare* a son,
21: 3. whom Sarah *bare* to him,
7. *I have born* (him) a son in his old age.
9. which *she had born* unto Abraham,
22:20. *she hath* also *born* children
23. Bethuel *begat* Rebekah: these eight Milcah *did bear* to Nahor,
24:24. which *she bare* unto Nahor.
47. whom Milcah *bare* unto him:
25: 3. Jokshan *begat* Sheba,
12. whom Hagar...*bare* unto Abraham:
29:34. *I have born* him three sons:
30: 1. *she bare* Jacob no children,
20. *I have born* him six sons:
21. afterwards *she bare* a daughter,
25. Rachel *had born* Joseph,
31: 8. *then* all the cattle *bare* speckled:
— *then bare* all the cattle ringstraked.
43. their children which *they have born?*
34: 1. which *she bare* unto Jacob,
36: 4. and Bashemath *bare* Reuel;
5. Aholibamah *bare* Jeush,
41:50. which Asenath...*bare* unto him.
44:27. know that my wife *bare* me two (sons):
46:15. which she *bare* unto Jacob
20. which Asenath...*bare* unto him.
Ex. 1:19. *and are delivered* ere the midwives come
21: 4. *and she have born* him sons or daughters;
Lev. 12: 2. *and born* a man child:
Nu. 11:12. *have I begotten them,*
26:59. whom (her mother) *bare* to Levi
Deu 21:15. *and they have born* him children,
32:18. the Rock (that) *begat thee*
Jud. 8:31. *she* also *bare* him a son,
13: 2. his wife (was) barren, *and bare* not.
3. thou (art) barren, and *bearest* not: but thou shalt conceive, *and bear* a son.
Ru. 1:12. *should* also *bear* sons;
4:12. whom Tamar *bare* unto Judah,
15. thy daughter in law,...*hath born him*.
1Sa. 2: 5. the barren *hath born* seven;
4:20. *thou hast born* a son.
2Sa. 12:15. the child that Uriah's wife *bare*
21: 8. whom she *bare* unto Saul,
— whom she *brought up* for Adriel (marg. *she bare* to)
1K. 1: 6. (his mother) *bare* him after Absalom.
3:21. it was not my son, which *I did bear*.
1Ch 1:10. Cush *begat* Nimrod:
11. Mizraim *begat* Ludim,

1Ch 1:13. Canaan *begat* Zidon
18. Arphaxad *begat* Shelah, and Shelah *begat*
20. Joktan *begat* Almodad,
32. *she bare* Zimran, and Jokshan,
2: 4. Tamar...*bare* him Pharez and Zerah.
17. Abigail *bare* Amasa:
46. Ephah,...*bare* Haran,
48. Maachah,...*bare* Sheber,
4: 9. *I bare* him with sorrow.
18. his wife Jehudijah *bare* Jered
7:14. Ashriel, whom *she bare:* (but) his concubine the Aramitess *bare* Machir
18. his sister...*bare* Ishod,
Job 38:29. hoary frost of heaven, who *hath gendered it?*
Ps. 2: 7. this day *have I begotten thee.*
7:14(15). *and brought forth* falsehood.
Pro.23:22. Hearken unto thy father that *begat thee,*
Cant.8: 5. she brought thee forth (that) *bare thee.*
Isa. 23: 4. I travail not, nor *bring forth children,*
26:18. *we have* as it were *brought forth* wind;
49:21. Who *hath begotten* me these,
51:18. the sons (whom) *she hath brought forth;*
54: 1. Sing, O barren, *thou* (that) *didst* not *bear;*
66: 7. Before she travailed, *she brought forth;*
8. *she brought forth* her children.
Jer. 2:27. (כתיב) *Thou hast brought me forth:* (marg. or, *hast begotten me*) (קרי, *hast begotten us*)
14: 5. the hind also *calved* in the field,
15:10. *thou hast borne me* a man of strife
17:11. (As) the partridge sitteth (on eggs), and *hatcheth* (them) not;
20:14. the day wherein my mother *bare me*
22:26. thy mother that *bare thee,*
Eze.16:20. whom *thou hast borne* unto me,
23:37. their sons, whom *they bare*
31: 6. *did* all the beasts of the field *bring forth* their *young,*
Hos. 5: 7. *they have begotten* strange children:
Mic. 5: 3(2). she which travaileth *hath brought forth:*

KAL.—*Infinitive.*

Gen 4: 2. she again *bare* his brother Abel. (lit. added *to bear*)
16: 2. the Lord hath restrained me *from bearing:*
16. *when* Hagar *bare* Ishmael to Abram.
25:24. when her days *to be delivered* were
26. Isaac (was) threescore years old *when she bare* them.
29:35. *left bearing.* (lit. stood *from bearing*)
30: 9. had left *bearing,* (lit. stood *from bearing*)
35:16. she had hard *labour.* (lit. she had difficulty *in her labour*)
17. when she was in hard *labour,* (lit. she had difficulty *in her labour*)
38: 5. he was at Chezib, *when she bare* him.
27. in the time of *her travail,*
28. it came to pass, *when she travailed,*
1Sa. 4:19. Phinehas' wife, was with child, (near) *to be delivered:*
1K. 3:18. the third day *after that I was delivered,*
2K. 19: 3. (there is) not strength *to bring forth.*
Job 15:35. conceive mischief, *and bring forth* vanity,
39: 1. time when the wild goats...*bring forth?*
2. thou the time *when they bring forth?*
Ecc. 3: 2. A time *to be born,* (marg. *to bear*)
Isa. 26:17. draweth near *the time of her delivery,* (lit. *to bear*)
37: 3. (there is) not strength to *bring forth.*
Jer. 13:21. sorrows take thee, as a woman *in travail?*
Hos. 9:11. *from the birth,* and from the womb,
Zep. 2: 2. Before the decree *bring forth,*

KAL.—*Future.*

Gen 3:16. in sorrow *thou shalt bring forth* children;
4: 1. she conceived, *and bare* Cain,
17. she conceived, *and bare* Enoch:
20. *And* Adah *bare* Jabal:
25. *and she bare* a son, and called his name
16:15. *And* Hagar *bare* Abram a son:
17:17. *shall* Sarah, that is ninety years old, *bear?*
21. Sarah *shall bear* unto thee at this set
18:13. *Shall I* of a surety *bear a child,*
19:37. *And* the firstborn *bare* a son,
20:17. *and they bare* (children).
21: 2. Sarah conceived, *and bare* Abraham a
22:24. *she bare* also Tebah,
24:36. *And* Sarah...*bare* a son to my master
25: 2. *And she bare* him Zimran, and Jokshan,
Gen 29:32. Leah conceived, *and bare* a son,
33, 34, 35. she conceived again, *and bare* a
30: 3. *and she shall bear* upon my knees,
5. Bilhah conceived, *and bare* Jacob a son.
7. Rachel's maid conceived again, *and bare*
10. *And* Zilpah Leah's maid *bare* Jacob a son.
12. *And* Zilpah Leah's maid *bare* Jacob a
17. she conceived, *and bare* Jacob the fifth
19. Leah conceived again, *and bare* Jacob the sixth son.
23. she conceived, *and bare* a son;
39. *and brought forth* cattle ringstraked,
35:16. *and* Rachel *travailed,* and she had hard
36: 4. *And* Adah *bare* to Esau Eliphaz;
12. *and she bare* to Eliphaz Amalek:
14. *and she bare* to Esau Jeush,
38: 3. she conceived, *and bare* a son;
4. she conceived again, *and bare* a son;
5. she yet again conceived, *and bare* a son;
46:18. *and* these *she bare* unto Jacob,
25. *and she bare* these unto Jacob:
Ex. 2: 2. the woman conceived, *and bare* a son:
22. *And she bare* (him) a son,
6:20. *and she bare* him Aaron and Moses:
23. *and she bare* him Nadab, and Abihu,
25. *and she bare* him Phinehas:
Lev.12: 5. if *she bear* a maid child,
Nu. 26:59. *and she bare* unto Amram Aaron
Deu25: 6. the firstborn which *she beareth*
28:57. toward her children which *she shall bear:*
Jud.11: 2. *And* Gilead's wife *bare* him sons;
13:24. *And* the woman *bare* a son,
Ru. 4:13. *and she bare* a son.
1Sa. 1:20. *that she bare* a son,
2:21. she conceived, *and bare* three sons and two daughters.
4:19. she bowed herself *and travailed;*
2Sa.11:27. she became his wife, *and bare* him a son.
12:24. *and she bare* a son,
1K. 3:17. *and I was delivered of a child* with her in
18. *that* this woman *was delivered* also:
11:20. *And* the sister of Tahpenes *bare* him
2K. 4:17. the woman conceived, *and bare* a son
1Ch 2:19. *which bare* him Hur.
21. *and she bare* him Segub.
24. *then* Abiah Hezron's wife *bare* him
29. *and she bare* him Ahban,
35. *and she bare* him Attai.
49. *She bare also* Shaaph
4: 6. *And* Naarah *bare* him Ahuzam,
7:16. *And* Maachah the wife of Machir *bare* a
23. she conceived, *and bare* a son,
2Ch 11:19. *Which bare* him children;
20. *which bare* him Abijah,
Job 24:21. the barren (that) *beareth* not:
Pro.27: 1. knowest not what a day *may bring forth.*
Isa. 8: 3. she conceived, *and bare* a son.
33:11. *ye shall bring forth* stubble:
65:23. labour in vain, nor *bring forth* for trouble;
Jer. 29: 6. *that they may bear* sons and daughters;
Eze.23: 4. *and they bare* sons and daughters.
Hos. 1: 3. conceived, *and bare* him a son.
6. she conceived again, *and bare* a
8. she conceived, *and bare* a son.
9:16. though *they bring forth,*

KAL.—*Participle.* Poel.

Gen16:11. thou (art) with child, *and shalt bear*
17:19. Sarah thy wife *shall bear* thee a son
Lev.12: 7. This (is) the law for her *that hath born*
Jud.13: 5, 7. thou shalt conceive, *and bear* a son;
Ps. 48: 6(7). pain, *as of a woman in travail.*
Pro.17:21. *He that begetteth* a fool (doeth it) to his
25. bitterness *to her that bare him.*
23:24. *and he that begetteth* a wise (child) shall
25. *she that bare thee* shall rejoice.
Cant.6: 9. the choice (one) *of her that bare her.*
Isa. 7:14. a virgin shall conceive, *and bear* a son,
13: 8. be in pain *as a woman that travaileth:*
21: 3. the pangs of *a woman that travaileth:*
42:14. (now) will I cry *like a travailing woman;*
Jer. 6:24. pain, *as of a woman in travail.*
15: 9. *She that hath borne* seven languisheth:
16: 3. their mothers *that bare* them,
22:23. the pain *as of a woman in travail!*
30: 6. see whether a man *doth travail with child?*
— *as a woman in travail,*

Jer. 31. 8. *and her that travaileth with child* together:
49:24. *as a woman in travail.*
50:12. *she that bare you* shall be ashamed:
43. pangs *as of a woman in travail.*
Dan 11: 6. they that brought her, *and he that begat her*, (marg. or, *whom she brought forth*)
Hos. 13:13. The sorrows of *a travailing woman* shall
Mic. 4: 9. have taken thee *as a woman in travail:*
10. Be in pain,...*like a woman in travail:*
5: 3(2). *she which travaileth* hath brought forth:
Zec. 13: 3. his father and his mother *that begat him*
— his father and his mother *that begat him*

KAL.—*Participle.* Paül.

1K. 3:26, 27. give her *the* living *child*,
1Ch 14: 4. these (are) the names of (his) *children*
Job 14: 1. Man (that is) *born of* a woman
15:14. (he which is) *born of* a woman,
25: 4. how can he be clean (that is) *born of* a

* NIPHAL.—*Preterite.* *

1Ch 2: 3. (which) three *were born* unto him
9. that *were born* unto him;
3: 1. which *were born* unto him in Hebron;
4. (These) six *were born* unto him in Hebron;
5. these *were born* unto him in Jerusalem;
20: 6. he also *was the son of* (marg. *was born* to) the giant.
8. These *were born* unto the giant in Gath;
26: 6. Also unto Shemaiah his son *were* sons *born*,
Ecc. 4:14. (he that is) *born* in his kingdom becometh

NIPHAL.—*Infinitive.*

Gen 21: 5. *when* his son Isaac *was born*
Ecc. 7: 1. the day of death than the day of *one's birth.*
Hos. 2: 3(5). set her as in the day *that she was born*,

NIPHAL.—*Future.*

Gen 4:18. *And* unto Enoch *was born* Irad:
10: 1. *and* unto them *were* sons *born* after the
17:17. *Shall* (a child) *be born* unto him
46:20. *And* unto Joseph...*were born* Manasseh and
Lev. 22:27. When a bullock,...*is brought forth*,
Nu. 26:60. *And* unto Aaron *was born* Nadab, and
Deu 15:19. the firstling males that *come* of thy herd
23: 8(9). The children that *are begotten*
2Sa. 3: 2. *And* unto David *were* sons *born* in Hebron:
5:13. *and there were* yet sons and daughters *born*
14:27. *And* unto Absalom *there were born* three
Job 1: 2. *And there were born* unto him seven sons
3: 3. Let the day perish wherein *I was born*,
11:12. though man *be born* (like) a wild ass's colt.
15: 7. (Art) thou the first man (that) *was born?*
38:21. because *thou wast* then *born?*
Ps. 78: 6. the children (which) *should be born;*
Pro. 17:17. a brother *is born* for adversity.
Isa. 66: 8. *shall* a nation *be born* at once?

NIPHAL.—*Participle.*

Gen 21: 3. his son *that was born* unto him,
48: 5. thy two sons,...*which were born* unto thee
1K. 13: 2. child *shall be born* unto the house of David,
1Ch 7:21. the men of Gath *that were born* in (that)
22: 9. a son *shall be born* to thee,
Ezr. 10: 3. *and such as are born* of them,
Ps. 22:31(32). a people *that shall be born*,

* PIEL.—*Infinitive.* *

Ex. 1:16. *When ye do the office of a midwife*

PIEL.—*Participle.*

Gen 35:17. *the midwife* said unto her, Fear not;
38:28. *the midwife* took and bound upon his hand
Ex. 1:15. the king of Egypt spake *to the* Hebrew *midwives*,
17. *the midwives* feared God, and did not
18. the king of Egypt called *for the midwives*,
19. *the midwives* said unto Pharaoh,
— ere *the midwives* come in
20. God dealt well *with the midwives:*
21. because *the midwives* feared God,

* PUAL.—*Preterite.* *

Gen 4:26. to him also *there was born* a son;
6: 1. daughters *were born* unto them,
10:21. even to him *were* (children) *born.*
25. unto Eber *were born* two sons:
24:15. who *was born* to Bethuel,
35:26. which *were born* to him in Padan-aram.

Gen 36: 5. *were born* unto him in the land of Canaan.
41:50. unto Joseph *were born* two sons
46:22. which *were born* to Jacob:
27. which *were born* him in Egypt,
50:23. *were brought up* (marg. *borne*) upon Joseph's knees.
Jud. 13: 8. the child *that shall be born.*
18:29. Dan...who *was born* unto Israel:
Ru. 4:17. *There is* a son *born* to Naomi;
2Sa. 3: 2. (כתיב) *And* unto David *were* sons *born* in
5. These *were born* to David in Hebron.
21:20. he also *was born* to the giant.
22. These four *were born* to the giant
1Ch 1:19. unto Eber *were born* two sons:
Job 5: 7. man *is born* unto trouble,
Ps. 87: 4. this (man) *was born* there.
5. that man *was born* in her:
6. (that) this (man) *was born* there.
90: 2. Before the mountains *were brought forth*,
Isa. 9: 6(5). unto us a child *is born*,
Jer. 20:14. Cursed (be) the day wherein *I was born:*
15. A man child *is born* unto thee;
22:26. another country, where *ye were* not *born;*

* HIPHIL.—*Preterite.* *

Gen 11:27. Terah *begat* Abram, Nahor, and Haran; and Haran *begat* Lot.
25:19. Abraham *begat* Isaac:
48: 6. thy issue, which *thou begettest* after them,
Lev. 25:45. which *they begat* in your land:
Nu. 26:29. Machir *begat* Gilead:
58. Kohath *begat* Amram.
Ru. 4:18. Pharez *begat* Hezron,
19. Hezron *begat* Ram, and Ram *begat*
20. Amminadab *begat* Nahshon, and Nahshon *begat* Salmon,
21. Salmon *begat* Boaz, and Boaz *begat* Obed,
22. Obed *begat* Jesse, and Jesse *begat* David.
1Ch 2:10. Ram *begat* Amminadab; and Amminadab *begat* Nahshon,
11. Nahshon *begat* Salma, and Salma *begat*
12. Boaz *begat* Obed, and Obed *begat* Jesse,
13. Jesse *begat* his firstborn Eliab,
18. Caleb...*begat* (children) of Azubah
20. Hur *begat* Uri, and Uri *begat* Bezaleel.
22. Segub *begat* Jair,
36. Attai *begat* Nathan, and Nathan *begat*
37. Zabad *begat* Ephlal, and Ephlal *begat*
38. Obed *begat* Jehu, and Jehu *begat* Azariah,
39. Azariah *begat* Helez, and Helez *begat*
40. Eleasah *begat* Sisamai, and Sisamai *begat*
41. Shallum *begat* Jekamiah, and Jekamiah *begat* Elishama.
44. Shema *begat* Raham, the father of Jorkoam: and Rekem *begat* Shammai.
46. Haran *begat* Gazez.
4: 2. Reaiah the son of Shobal *begat* Jahath; and Jahath *begat* Ahumai,
8. Coz *begat* Anub,
11. Chelub...*begat* Mehir,
12. Eshton *begat* Beth-rapha,
14. Meonothai *begat* Ophrah: and Seraiah *begat* Joab,
6: 4(5:30). Eleazar *begat* Phinehas, Phinehas *begat* Abishua,
5(-:31). And Abishua *begat* Bukki, and Bukki *begat* Uzzi,
6(-:32). And Uzzi *begat* Zerahiah, and Zerahiah *begat* Meraioth,
7(-:33). Meraioth *begat* Amariah, and Amariah *begat* Ahitub,
8(-:34). And Ahitub *begat* Zadok, and Zadok *begat* Ahimaaz,
9(-:35). And Ahimaaz *begat* Azariah, and Azariah *begat* Johanan,
10(-:36). And Johanan *begat* Azariah,
11(-:37). and Amariah *begat* Ahitub,
12(-:38). And Ahitub *begat* Zadok, and Zadok *begat* Shallum,
13(-:39). And Shallum *begat* Hilkiah, and Hilkiah *begat* Azariah,
14(-:40). And Azariah *begat* Seraiah, and Seraiah *begat* Jehozadak,
7:32. Heber *begat* Japhlet,
8: 1. Benjamin *begat* Bela
7. *and begat* Uzza, and Ahihud.
8. Shaharaim *begat* (children) in the country

1Ch 8:11. of Hushim *he begat* Abitub,
32. Mikloth *begat* Shimeah.
33. Ner *begat* Kish, and Kish *begat* Saul, and Saul *begat* Jonathan,
34. Merib-baal *begat* Micah.
36. Ahaz *begat* Jehoadah; and Jehoadah *begat* Alemeth, and Azmaveth, and Zimri; and Zimri *begat* Moza,
37. Moza *begat* Binea:
9:38. Mikloth *begat* Shimeam.
39. Ner *begat* Kish; and Kish *begat* Saul; and Saul *begat* Jonathan,
40. Merib-baal *begat* Micah.
42. Ahaz *begat* Jarah; and Jarah *begat* Alemeth, and Azmaveth, and Zimri; and Zimri *begat* Moza;
43. Moza *begat* Binea;
Neh12:10. Jeshua *begat* Joiakim, Joiakim also *begat* Eliashib, and Eliashib *begat* Joiada,
11. Joiada *begat* Jonathan, and Jonathan *begat*
Job 38:28. who *hath begotten* the drops of dew?
Ecc. 5:14(13). *and he begetteth* a son,
Isa. 55:10. *and maketh it bring forth* and bud,
Eze.18:10. *If he beget* a son (that is) a robber,
14. (if) *he beget* a son,
47:22. which *shall beget* children among you:

HIPHIL.—*Infinitive.*

Gen 5: 4. the days of Adam after *he had begotten* Seth
7. And Seth lived after *he begat* Enos
10. And Enos lived after *he begat* Cainan
13. And Cainan lived after *he begat*
16. And Mahalaleel lived after *he begat*
19. And Jared lived after *he begat*
22. walked with God after *he begat*
26. And Methuselah lived after *he begat*
30. And Lamech lived after *he begat* Noah
11:11. Shem lived after *he begat* Arphaxad
13. Arphaxad lived after *he begat* Salah
15. Salah lived after *he begat* Eber
17. Eber lived after *he begat* Peleg
19. Peleg lived after *he begat* Reu
21. Reu lived after *he begat* Serug
23. Serug lived after *he begat* Nahor
25. Nahor lived after *he begat* Terah
Isa. 59: 4. they conceive mischief, *and bring forth*

HIPHIL.—*Imperative.*

Jer. 29: 6. Take ye wives, *and beget* sons and

HIPHIL.—*Future.*

Gen 5: 3. *and begat* (a son) in his own
4. *and he begat* sons and daughters:
6. And Seth lived...*and begat* Enos:
7, 10, 13, 16, 19, 22, 26, 30. *and begat* sons
9. Enos...*and begat* Cainan:
12. Cainan...*and begat* Mahalaleel:
15. Mahalaleel...*and begat* Jared:
18. Jared...*and he begat* Enoch:
21. Enoch...*and begat* Methuselah:
25. Methuselah...*and begat* Lamech:
28. Lamech...*and begat* a son:
32. *and* Noah *begat* Shem, Ham, and Japheth.
6:10. *And* Noah *begat* three sons,
11:10. Shem...*and begat* Arphaxad
11, 13, 15, 17, 19, 21, 23, 25. *and begat* sons and
12. *and begat* Salah:
14. *and begat* Eber:
16. *and begat* Peleg:
18. *and begat* Reu:
20. *and begat* Serug:
22. *and begat* Nahor:
24. *and begat* Terah:
26. Terah...*and begat* Abram,
17:20. twelve princes *shall he beget*,
Deu 4:25. When *thou shalt beget* children,
28:41. *Thou shalt beget* sons and daughters,
Jud.11: 1. *and* Gilead *begat* Jephthah.
2K. 20:18. thy sons...which *thou shalt beget*,
1Ch 1:34. *And* Abraham *begat* Isaac.
6:11(5:37). *And* Azariah *begat* Amariah,
8: 9. *And he begat*...Jobab, and Zibia,
14: 3. *and* David *begat* more sons and daughters.
2Ch 11:21. *and begat* twenty and eight sons,
13:21. *and begat* twenty and two sons,
24: 3. *and he begat* sons and daughters.
Ecc. 6: 3. If a man *beget* an hundred (children),
Isa. 39: 7. thy sons...which *thou shalt beget*,

Isa. 45:10. saith unto (his) father, What *begettest thou?*
66: 9. to the birth, and not *cause to bring forth?*

HIPHIL.—*Participle*

Isa. 66: 9. *shall* I *cause to bring forth*, and shut
Jer. 16: 3. their fathers *that begat* them

* HOPHAL.—*Infinitive.* *

Gen40:20. third day, (which was) Pharaoh's *birth*day,
Eze.16: 4. in the day thou *wast born*
5. in the day *that* thou *wast born*.

* HITHPAEL.—*Future.* *

Nu. 1:18. *and they declared their pedigrees* after their

יֶלֶד *yeh'-led*, m. 3206

Gen 4:23. *and a young man* to my hurt:
21: 8. *the child* grew, and was weaned:
14. gave (it) unto Hagar,...and *the child*,
15. she cast *the child* under one of the shrubs.
16. Let me not see the death of *the child*.
30:26. Give (me) my wives and *my children*,
32:22(23). womenservants, and *his* eleven *sons*,
33: 1. he divided *the children* unto Leah,
2. the handmaids *and their children* foremost, and Leah *and her children* after,
5. saw the women and *the children*;
— *The children* which God hath graciously
6. they *and their children*,
7. And Leah also *with her children*
13. knoweth that *the children* (are) tender,
14. and *the children* be able to endure,
37:30. *The child* (is) not; and I,
42:22. Do not sin *against the child*;
44:20. *and a child of* his old age,
Ex. 1:17. but saved *the* men *children* alive.
18. have saved *the* men *children* alive?
2: 3. and put *the child* therein;
6. had opened (it), she saw *the child*:
— This (is one) *of* the Hebrews' *children*.
7. that she may nurse *the child*
8. the maid went and called *the child*'s
9. Take this *child* away, and nurse it for me,
— the woman took *the child*, and nursed it.
10. And *the child* grew,
21: 4. the wife *and her children* shall be her
22. so that *her fruit* depart (from her),
Ru. 1: 5. *her* two *sons* and her husband.
4:16. Naomi took *the child*, and laid it in her
1Sa. 1: 2. Peninnah had *children*, but Hannah had no *children*.
2Sa. 6:23. (כתיב) the daughter of Saul had no *child*
12:15. the Lord struck *the child*
18. on the seventh day, that *the child* died.
— feared to tell him that *the child* was dead:
— *the child* was yet alive,
— tell him that *the child* is dead?
19. David perceived that *the child* was dead:
— Is *the child* dead?
21. thou didst fast and weep for *the child*,
— when *the child* was dead,
22. While *the child* was yet alive, I fasted and
— that *the child* may live?
1K. 3:25. Divide *the* living *child* in two,
12: 8. consulted with *the young men*
10. *the young men* that were grown up
14. the counsel of *the young men*,
14:12. thy feet enter into the city, *the child* shall
17:21. he stretched himself upon *the child*
— let this *child*'s soul come into him again.
22. the soul of *the child* came into him
23. Elijah took *the child*,
2K. 2:24. forty and two *children* of them.
4: 1. is come to take unto him *my* two *sons*
18. when *the child* was grown,
26. (is it) well *with the child?*
34. he went up, and lay upon *the child*,
— the flesh of *the child* waxed warm.
2Ch 10: 8. took counsel with *the young men*
10. *the young men* that were brought up
14. the advice of *the young men*,
Ezr.10: 1. women *and children*:
Neh 12:43. the wives also and *the children* rejoiced:
Job 21:11. *and their children* dance.
38:41. when *his young ones* cry unto God,

Job 39: 3. they bring forth *their young ones*,
Ecc. 4:13. Better (is) a poor and *a wise child*
15. *the* second *child* that shall stand up
Isa. 2: 6. *and* they please themselves *in the children of*
8:18. *and the children* whom the Lord hath
9: 6(5). unto us *a child* is born,
11: 7. *their young ones* shall lie down together:
29:23. when he seeth *his children*,
57: 4. (are) ye not *children of* transgression,
5. slaying *the children* in the valleys
Jer. 31:20. (is he) *a pleasant child?*
Lam. 4:10. the pitiful women have sodden *their own children:*
Dan 1: 4. *Children* in whom (was) no blemish,
10. *the children* which (are) of your sort?
13. the countenance of *the children*
15. *the children* which did eat the portion
17. *As for* these four *children*,
Hos. 1: 2. *and children of* whoredoms:
Joel 3: 3(4:3). have given *a boy* for an harlot,
Zec. 8: 5. *boys* and girls playing in the streets

3207 ## יַלְדָּה *yal-dāh'*, f.

Gen 34: 4. Get me this *damsel* to wife.
Joel 3: 3(4:3). *and* sold *a girl* for wine,
Zec. 8: 5. *and girls* playing in the streets

3208 ## יַלְדוּת *yal-dooth'*, f.

Ps. 110: 3. thou hast the dew of *thy youth*.
Ecc. 11: 9. Rejoice, O young man, *in thy youth;*
10. *childhood* and youth (are) vanity.

3209 ## יִלּוֹד *yil-lōhd'*, adj.

Ex. 1:22. Every son *that is born*
Jos. 5: 5. the people (that were) *born* in the
2Sa. 5:14. the names of those that were *born*
12:14. the child also (that is) *born* unto thee
Jer. 16: 3. the daughters that are *born* in this place,

3211 ## יְלִיד *y'leed*, m. const.

Gen 14:14. *born in* his own house,
17:12. *he that is born in* the house,
13. *He that is born in* thy house,
23. all *that were born in* his house,
27. men of his house, *born in* the house,
Lev. 22:11. *and he that is born in* his house:
Nu. 13:22. *the children of* Anak, (were).
28. we saw *the children of* Anak
Jos. 15:14. *the children of* Anak,
2Sa. 21:16, 18. (was) *of the sons of* the giant,
1Ch 20: 4. *of the children of* the giant:
Jer. 2:14. (is) he a home*born* (slave)?

3212 ## יָלַךְ [*yāh-lach'*].

* KAL.—*Infinitive.* *

Gen 11:31. *to go* into the land of Canaan;
12: 5. they went forth *to go* into the land of
24: 5. the woman will not be willing *to follow* (lit. *to go* after) me
8. if the woman will not be willing *to follow* (lit. *to go* after) thee,
Ex. 4:21. *When thou goest* to return into Egypt,
8:28(24). only ye shall not *go* very far
13:21. *to go* by day and night:
33:16. (is it) not *in that thou goest* with us?
Lev. 18: 4. keep mine ordinances, *to walk* therein:
Deu 2: 7. he knoweth *thy walking* through this
6: 7. *and when thou walkest* by the way,
8: 6. *to walk* in his ways, and to fear him.
10:12. *to walk* in all his ways,
11:19. *and when thou walkest* by the way,
22. *to walk* in all his ways,
28. *to go* after other gods,
Deu 13: 5(6). which the Lord thy God commanded thee *to walk* in.
19: 9. *and to walk* ever in his ways,
26:17. *and to walk* in his ways,
28:14. *to go* after other gods to serve them.
29:18(17). *to go* (and) serve the gods of these
30:16. *to walk* in his ways,
Jos. 9:12. the day we came forth *to go* unto you;
22: 5. *and to walk* in all his ways,
9. *to go* unto the country of Gilead,
Jud. 2:19. *in following* (lit. *going* after) other gods to
22. the way of the Lord *to walk* therein,
12: 1. didst not call us *to go* with thee?
18: 9. be not slothful *to go*,
19: 5. he rose up *to depart:*
7, 9. the man rose up *to depart*,
8. arose early in the morning...*to depart:*
27. went out *to go* his way:
Ru. 1:18. she was stedfastly minded *to go*
3:10. as thou *followedst* not young men, (lit. *in* not *going* after)
1Sa. 9: 9. *when* a man *went* to enquire of God,
10: 2. *When thou art departed* from me to day,
9. when he had turned his back *to go* from
15:27. Samuel turned about *to go away*,
17:33. Thou art not able *to go*
39. he assayed *to go;*
— I cannot *go* with these;
23:26. David made haste *to get away*
29:11. David and his men rose up early *to depart*
30:21. were so faint that they *could not follow* (lit. *go* after) David,
2Sa. 2:19. *in going* he turned not
8: 3. *as he went* to recover his border
13:25. howbeit he would not *go*,
15:14. make speed *to depart*,
20. make thee *go* up and down
17:21. after *they were departed*,
18:33(19:1). *as he went*, thus he said,
19:15(16). *to go* to meet the king,
24(25). the day the king *departed*
1K. 2: 3. *to walk* in his ways,
4. *to walk* before me in truth
8. when *I went* to Mahanaim:
3: 3. *walking* in the statutes of David
6:12. keep all my commandments *to walk* in
8:25. *that they walk* before me
58. *to walk* in all his ways,
61. *to walk* in his statutes,
11:10. that he *should* not *go* after other gods:
22. thou seekest *to go* to thine own country?
12:24. returned *to depart*,
13:17. turn again *to go* by the way
16:19. *walking* in the way of Jeroboam,
31. a light thing *for him to walk* in the sins
21:26. he did very abominably *in following* (lit. *in going* after) idols,
22:48(49). ships of Tharshish *to go* to Ophir for
2K. 9:15. *to go* to tell (it) in Jezreel.
10:31. *to walk* in the law of the Lord
23: 3. *to walk* after the Lord,
1Ch 12:20. *As he went* to Ziklag,
17:11. *that* thou *must go* (to be) with thy fathers,
18: 3. *as he went* to stablish his dominion
21:30. David could not *go* before it
2Ch 6:16. *to walk* in my law,
31. *to walk* in thy ways,
11: 4. returned *from going* against Jeroboam.
20:36. to make ships *to go* to Tarshish:
37. they were not able *to go* to Tarshish.
24:25. *And when they were departed* from him,
25:10. the army...*to go* home again:
13. *that they should not go* with him to battle,
34:31. *to walk* after the Lord,
Ezr. 8:31. *to go* unto Jerusalem:
Neh 10:29(30). *to walk* in God's law,
Job 34: 8. *and walketh* with wicked men.
Ps. 78:10. refused *to walk* in his law;
107: 7. *that they might go* to a city of habitation.
Pro. 2:13. *to walk* in the ways of darkness;
4:12. *When thou goest*, thy steps shall not be
15:21. a man of understanding *walketh* uprightly.
30:29. four are comely in *going:*
Ecc. 1: 7. thither they return *again*. (marg return *to go*)
5:15(14). naked shall he return *to go* as he came,

Ecc. 7: 2. (It is) better *to go* to the house of mourning, *than to go* to the house of feasting:
10:15. he knoweth not how *to go* to the city.
Isa. 8:11. *that* I *should not walk* in the way
Jer. 2: 2. *when thou wentest* after me
18:15. *to walk* in paths,
26: 4. *to walk* in my law,
37:12. *to go* into the land of Benjamin,
40: 4. good and convenient for thee *to go*,
5. it seemeth convenient unto thee *to go*.
41:17. *to go* to enter into Egypt,
44: 3. *in that* they *went* to burn incense,
51:59. *when he went* with Zedekiah
Lam. 4:18. They hunt our steps, *that we cannot go*
Eze. 1: 9. they turned not *when they went;*
12. whither the spirit was *to go*, they went; (and) they turned not *when they went*.
17. *When they went*, they went upon their four sides: (and) they turned not *when they went*.
19. *And when* the living creatures *went*, the
20. Whithersoever the spirit was *to go*, they went, thither (was their) spirit *to go;*
21. *When those went*,
24. And *when they went*,
10:11. *When they went*, they went upon their four sides; they turned not *as they went*, — they turned not *as they went*.
16. And *when* the cherubims *went*, the wheels
Dan 9:10. *to walk* in his laws,
Mic. 6: 8. *to walk* humbly with thy God?
Zec. 6: 7. the bay went forth, and sought *to go*

KAL.—*Imperative.*

Gen 12: 1. *Get* thee out of thy country,
19. take (her), *and go* thy way.
19:32. *Come*, let us make our father drink wine,
22: 2. *and get* thee into the land of Moriah;
24:51. (is) before thee, take (her), *and go*,
26:16. Abimelech said unto Isaac, *Go* from us;
27: 9. *Go* now to the flock,
13. obey my voice, *and go* fetch me (them).
28: 2. Arise, *go* to Padan-aram,
29: 7. water ye the sheep, *and go* (and) feed
31:44. *come thou*, let us make a covenant,
37:13. *come*, and I will send thee unto them.
14. he said to him, *Go*, I pray thee,
20. *Come* now therefore,
27. *Come*, and let us sell him to the
41:55. Pharaoh said unto all the Egyptians, *Go*
42:19. *go ye*, carry corn for the famine of your
33. (food for) the famine of your housholds, *and be gone:*
45:17. *and go*, get you unto the land of Canaan;
Ex. 2: 8. Pharaoh's daughter said to her, *Go*.
3:10. *Come* now therefore,
16. *Go*, and gather the elders of Israel
4:12. Now therefore *go*,
18. Jethro said to Moses, *Go* in peace.
19. *Go*, return into Egypt:
27. *Go* into the wilderness to meet Moses.
5: 4. *get you* unto your burdens.
11. *Go ye*, get you straw
18. *Go* therefore now, (and) work;
7:15. *Get thee* unto Pharaoh in the morning;
8:25(21). *Go ye*, sacrifice to your God
10: 8. *Go*, serve the Lord your God:
11. *go* now *ye* (that are) men,
24. *Go ye*, serve the Lord;
28. *Get* thee from me,
12:31. *and go*, serve the Lord,
32. flocks and your herds,...*and be gone;*
19:10. *Go* unto the people,
24. *Away*, get thee down,
32: 7. *Go*, get thee down;
34. Therefore now *go*,
33: 1. *Depart*, (and) go up hence,
Nu. 10:29. *come thou* with us, and we will do thee
22: 6. *Come* now therefore, I pray thee,
11. *come* now, curse me them;
13. *Get you* into your land:
17. *come therefore*, I pray thee,
20. rise up, (and) *go* with them;
35. *Go* with the men:
23: 7. *Come*, curse me Jacob, *and come*, defy
13. *Come*, I pray thee,
27. *Come*, I pray thee,
Nu. 24:14. *come* (therefore, and) I will advertise
Deu 5:30(27). *Go* say to them, Get you
10:11. Arise, *take* (thy) journey before the
Jos. 2: 1. *Go* view the land, even Jericho.
16. *Get you* to the mountain,
9:11. *and go* to meet them,
18: 8. *Go* and walk through the land,
22: 4. *and get* you unto your tents,
Jud. 4: 6. *Go* and draw toward mount Tabor,
22. *Come*, and I will shew thee the man
6:14. *Go* in this thy might,
9:10, 12. *Come* thou, (and) reign over us.
14. *Come* thou, (and) reign over us.
10:14. *Go* and cry unto the gods
11: 6. *Come*, and be our captain,
38. And he said, *Go*.
18: 2. *Go*, search the land:
6. the priest said unto them, *Go* in peace:
19. *and go* with us, and be to us a father and
19:11. *Come*, I pray thee, and let us turn in
13. *Come*, and let us draw near to one of
21:10. *Go* and smite the inhabitants of
20. *Go* and lie in wait in the vineyards;
Ru. 1: 8. *Go*, return each to her mother's house:
12. Turn again, my daughters, *go* (your way);
2: 2. she said unto her, *Go*, my daughter.
1Sa. 1:17. Eli answered and said, *Go* in peace:
3: 9. Eli said unto Samuel, *Go*, lie down:
8:22. *Go ye* every man unto his city.
9: 3. arise, *go* seek the asses.
5. *Come*, and let us return;
9. *Come*, and let us go to the seer:
10. Well said; *come*, let us go.
11:14. *Come*, and let us go to Gilgal,
14: 1, 6. *Come*, and let us go over
15: 3. Now *go and* smite Amalek,
6. *Go*, depart, get you down
18. *Go* and utterly destroy the sinners the
16: 1. fill thine horn with oil, *and go*,
17:37. Saul said unto David, *Go*,
44. *Come* to me, and I will give thy flesh unto the fowls
20:11. *Come*, and let us go out into the field.
21. *Go*, find out the arrows.
22. *go thy way:* for the Lord hath sent thee
40. *Go*, carry (them) to the city.
42. Jonathan said to David, *Go* in peace,
22: 5. *depart*, and get thee into the land of Judah.
23: 2. *Go* and smite the Philistines,
22. *Go*, I pray you, prepare yet,
27. Haste thee, *and come;*
26:19. *Go*, serve other gods.
29: 7. Wherefore now return, *and go* in peace,
10. as soon as ye be up early...*depart*.
2Sa. 3:16. Then said Abner unto him, *Go*, return.
7: 3. *Go*, do all that (is) in thine heart;
5. *Go* and tell my servant David,
13: 7. *Go* now to thy brother Amnon's house,
15. Amnon said unto her, Arise, *be gone*.
14: 8. the king said...*Go* to thine house,
21. *go therefore*, bring the young man Absalom
30. *go* and set it on fire.
15: 9. the king said unto him, *Go* in peace.
22. David said to Ittai, *Go* and pass over.
18:21. *Go* tell the king what thou hast seen.
24: 1. *Go*, number Israel and Judah.
1K. 1:12. Now therefore *come*,
13. *Go* and get thee in unto king David,
53. Solomon said unto him, *Go* to thine house.
2:26. *Get thee* to Anathoth,
29. *Go*, fall upon him.
12: 5. *Depart* yet (for) three days,
13:15. *Come* home with me, and eat bread.
14: 7. *Go*, tell Jeroboam,
12. *get thee* to thine own house:
15:19. *come* and break thy league with Baasha
17: 3. *Get thee* hence, and turn thee eastward,
9. Arise, *get thee* to Zarephath,
18: 1. *Go*, shew thyself unto Ahab;
5. *Go* into the land,
8. *go*, tell thy lord, Behold, Elijah (is here).
11, 14. now thou sayest, *Go*, tell thy lord,
21. if the Lord (be) God, *follow* (lit. *go* after) him: but if Baal, (then) *follow* (lit. *go* after) him.
19:15. *Go*, return on thy way
20. he said unto him, *Go* back again:

1K. 20:22. *Go*, strengthen thyself, and mark,
2K. 1: 2. *Go*, enquire of Baal-zebub
6. *Go*, turn again unto the king that sent you,
3:13. *get thee* to the prophets of thy father,
4: 3. *Go*, borrow thee vessels
7. *Go*, sell the oil, and pay thy debt,
24. Drive, *and go* forward;
29. take my staff in thine hand, *and go* thy way:
5: 5. the king of Syria said, *Go* to,
19. he said unto him, *Go* in peace.
6: 2. he answered, *Go ye*.
3. *and go* with thy servants.
13. *Go* and spy where he (is),
19. *follow* (marg. *come ye* after) me,
7: 4, 9. Now therefore *come*,
14. the king sent...saying, *Go* and see.
8: 1. Arise, *and go* thou and thine houshold,
8. *and go*, meet the man of God,
10. *Go*, say unto him,
9: 1. *and go* to Ramoth-gilead:
10:16. he said, *Come* with me,
14: 8. *Come*, let us look one another in the face.
22:13. *Go ye*, enquire of the Lord
1Ch 17: 4. *Go* and tell David my servant,
21: 2. *Go*, number Israel from Beer-sheba even
10. *Go* and tell David, saying,
2Ch 16: 3. *go*, break thy league with Baasha
25:17. *Come*, let us see one another in the face.
34:21. *Go*, enquire of the Lord for me,
Neh. 2:17. *come*, and let us build up the wall
6: 2. *Come*, let us meet together
7. *Come* now therefore,
8:10. *Go your way*, eat the fat,
Est. 4:16. *Go*, gather together all the Jews
Job 42: 8. *and go* to my servant
Ps. 34:11(12). *Come*, ye children, hearken unto me:
46: 8(9). *Come*, behold the works of the Lord,
66: 5. *Come* and see the works of God:
16. *Come* (and) hear, all ye that fear God,
80: 2(3). *and come* (and) save us.
83: 4(5). *Come*, and let us cut them off
95: 1. *O come*, let us sing unto the Lord:
Pro. 1:11. *Come* with us, let us lay wait for blood,
3:28. Say not unto thy neighbour, *Go*,
6: 3. *go*, humble thyself,
6. *Go* to the ant, thou sluggard;
7:18. *Come*, let us take our fill of love
9: 5. *Come*, eat of my bread,
14: 7. *Go* from the presence of a foolish man,
Ecc. 2: 1. I said in mine heart, *Go to* now,
9: 7. *Go thy way*, eat thy bread with joy,
Cant. 2:10. my love, my fair one, *and come away*.
13. Arise, my love, my fair one, *and come away*.
7:11(12). *Come*, my beloved, let us go forth
Isa. 1:18. *Come* now, and let us reason together,
2: 3. *Come ye*, and let us go up to the mountain
5. O house of Jacob, *come ye*,
6: 9. *Go*, and tell this people,
18: 2. *Go*, *ye* swift messengers,
20: 2. *Go* and loose the sackcloth from off thy
21: 6. *Go*, set a watchman,
22:15. *Go*, get thee unto this treasurer,
26:20. *Come*, my people, enter thou into thy
30:21. This (is) the way, *walk ye* in it,
50:11. *walk* in the light of your fire,
55: 1. *come ye* to the waters, and he that hath no money; *come ye*, buy, and eat; *yea*, *come*, buy wine and milk
3. Incline your ear, and *come* unto me:
Jer. 6:16. *and walk* therein, and ye shall find rest
7:12. *go ye* now unto my place
12: 9. *come ye*, assemble all the beasts of the field,
13: 4, 6. arise, *go* to Euphrates,
18:18. *Come*, and let us devise devices
— *Come*, and let us smite him
36:14. Take in thine hand the roll...*and come*.
19. *Go*, hide thee, thou and Jeremiah;
40: 4. thither *go*.
5. or *go* wheresoever it seemeth
48: 2. *come*, and let us cut it off
Eze. 3: 1. *and go* speak unto the house of Israel.
4. Son of man, *go*,
11. *And go*, get thee to them of the captivity,
20:19. *walk* in my statutes, and keep my
39. *Go ye*, serve ye every one his idols,
Dan 12: 9. he said, *Go thy way*, Daniel:
13. *go* thou *thy way* till the end (be):

Hos. 1: 2. *Go*, take unto thee a wife of whoredoms
3: 1. *Go* yet, love a woman
6: 1. *Come*, and let us return unto the Lord:
Am. 6: 2. *and* from thence *go ye* to Hamath
7:12. *go*, flee thee away into the land of Judah,
15. *Go*, prophesy unto my people Israel.
Jon. 1: 2. Arise, *go* to Nineveh,
7. *Come*, and let us cast lots,
3: 2. Arise, *go* unto Nineveh,
Mic. 2:10. Arise ye, *and depart;*
4: 2. *Come*, and let us go up to the mountain
Zec. 6: 7. *Get you hence*, walk to and fro

KAL. *Future.*

Gen 3:14. upon thy belly *shalt thou go*,
7:18. *and* the ark *went* upon the face of the
9:23. *and went* backward, and covered
12: 4. *So* Abram *departed*, as the Lord had spoken unto him; *and* Lot *went* with him:
13: 3. *And he went* on his journeys
14:11. *and went their way*.
12. they took Lot,...*and departed*.
16: 8. whither *wilt thou go?*
18:22. the men turned...*and went* toward Sodom.
33. *And* the Lord *went his way*,
21:14. *and she departed*, and wandered in the
16. *And she went*, and sat her down
19. *and she went*, and filled the bottle
22: 3. *and went* unto the place
5. I and the lad *will go* yonder
6. *and they went* both of them together.
8. *so they went* both of them together.
13. *and* Abraham *went* and took the ram,
19. rose up *and went* together to Beer-sheba;
24: 4. *thou shalt go* unto my country,
10. the camels of his master, *and departed;*
— he arose, *and went* to Mesopotamia,
38. *thou shalt go* unto my father's house,
39. the woman *will* not *follow* me. (lit. *will* not *go* after)
55. after that *she shall go*.
56. send me away *that I may go* to my master.
58. *Wilt thou go* with this man? And she said, *I will go*.
61. *and followed* (lit. *and went* after) the man: and the servant took Rebekah, *and went his way*.
25:22. *And she went* to enquire of the Lord.
34. rose up, *and went his way:*
26: 1. *And* Isaac *went* unto Abimelech
13. the man waxed great, *and went* forward,
17. *And* Isaac *departed* thence,
31. *and they departed* from him in peace.
27: 5. *And* Esau *went* to the field to hunt
14. *And he went*, and fetched,
28: 5. *and he went* to Padan-aram
7. *and was gone* to Padan-aram;
9. *Then went* Esau unto Ishmael,
10. *and went* toward Haran.
15. all (places) whither *thou goest*,
29: 1. on his journey, *and came* into the land
30:14. *And* Reuben *went* in the days of wheat
25. *that I may go* unto mine own place,
26. I have served thee, *and let me go:*
31:55(32:1). *and* Laban *departed*, and returned
32:17(18). Whose (art) thou? and whither *goest thou?*
33:12. Let us take our journey, *and let us go*, *and I will go* before thee.
35:22. *that* Reuben *went* and lay with Bilhah
36: 6. *and went* into the country
37:12. *And* his brethren *went* to feed their father's
17. *Let us go* to Dothan. *And* Joseph *went* after his brethren,
38:11. *And* Tamar *went* and dwelt in her father's
19. she arose, *and went away*,
42:26. they laded their asses...*and departed*
38. the way in the which ye *go*,
43: 8. we will arise *and go;*
45:24. sent his brethren away, *and they departed:*
28. *I will go* and see him before I die.
50:18. *And* his brethren also *went* and fell down
Ex. 2: 1. *And there went* a man of the house of Levi,
7. *Shall I go* and call to thee a nurse
8. *And* the maid *went* and called the child's
3:11. (am) I, that *I should go* unto Pharaoh
18. now *let us go*, we beseech thee,

Ex. 3:21. it shall come to pass, that, when *ye go, ye shall* not *go* empty:
4:18. *And* Moses *went* and returned to Jethro his father in law, and said unto him, *Let me go*, I pray thee,
27. *And he went*, and met him
29. *And* Moses and Aaron *went* and gathered
5: 3. *let us go*, we pray thee,
7. *let them go* and gather straw
8. *Let us go* (and) sacrifice to our God.
17. *Let us go* (and) do sacrifice to the Lord.
8:27(23). *We will go* three days' journey
10: 9. *We will go* with our young
— our flocks and with our herds *will we go;*
24. *let* your little ones also *go* with you.
26. Our cattle also *shall go* with us;
12:28. *And* the children of Israel *went away*,
14:19. removed *and went* behind them;
15:22. *and they went* three days in the wilderness,
16: 4. *whether they will walk* in my law, or no.
18:20. shew them the way wherein *they must walk*,
27. *and he went* his way into his own land.
23:23. mine Angel *shall go* before thee,
32: 1, 23. make us gods, which *shall go* before us;
34. mine Angel *shall go* before thee:
33:14. My presence *shall go* (with thee),
34: 9. *let* my Lord, I pray thee, *go* among us;
Lev. 18: 3. neither *shall ye walk* in their ordinances.
19:16. *Thou shalt* not *go up* and *down*
20:23. *ye shall* not *walk* in the manners of
26: 3. If *ye walk* in my statutes,
21. *ye walk* contrary unto me,
41. I also *have walked* contrary unto them,
Nu. 10:30. he said unto him, *I will* not *go;* but *I will depart* to mine own land,
32. if *thou go* with us,
12: 9. kindled against them; *and he departed.*
13:26. *And they went* and came to Moses,
16:25. Moses rose up *and went* unto Dathan
— *and* the elders of Israel *followed* (lit. *went* after) him.
20:17. *we will go* by the king's (high) way,
21:22. *we will go* along by the king's (high)way,
22: 7. *and* the elders of Midian *departed*
12. *Thou shalt* not *go* with them;
21. *and went* with the princes of Moab.
23. out of the way, *and went* into the field:
35. *So* Balaam *went* with the princes of Balak.
39. *And* Balaam *went* with Balak,
23: 3. Stand by thy burnt offering, *and I will go:*
— *And he went* to an high place.
24:25. Balaam rose up, *and went*
32:39. *And* the children of Machir...*went* to Gilead,
33: 8. *and went* three days' journey in the
Deu. 1:19. *And* when...*we went* through all that great
33. what way *ye should go*,
2:27. *I will go* along by the high way,
5:33(30). *Ye shall walk* in all the ways
6:14. *Ye shall* not *go* after other gods,
13: 2(3). *Let us go* after other gods,
4(5). *Ye shall walk* after the Lord
6(7), 13(14). *Let us go* and serve other gods,
17: 3. *And hath gone* and served other gods,
20: 5. *let him go* and return to his house,
6. *let him* (also) *go* and return unto his house,
7, 8. *let him go* and return unto his house,
28:41. *they shall go* into captivity.
29:19(18). though *I walk* in the imagination of
26(25). *For they went* and served other gods,
31: 1. *And* Moses *went* and spake these words
14. *And* Moses and Joshua *went*,
Jos. 1: 7, 9. whithersoever *thou goest.*
16. whithersoever thou sendest us, *we will go.*
2: 1. *And they went*, and came into an harlot's
16. afterward *may ye go* your way.
21. she sent them away, *and they departed:*
22. *And they went*, and came unto the
3: 4. the way by which *ye must go:*
6. *and went* before the people.
4:18. *and flowed* (marg. *went*) over all his banks,
5:13. *and* Joshua *went* unto him,
8: 9. *and they went* to lie in ambush,
13. *And* when...Joshua *went* that night
9: 4. *and went* and made as if they had been
6. *And they went* to Joshua unto the camp
16: 8. The border *went out* from Tappuah
18: 8. the men arose, *and went away:*

Jos. 18: 9. *And* the men *went* and passed through the
22: 6. *and they went* unto their tents.
9. *and departed* from the children of Israel
Jud. 1: 3. *So* Simeon *went* with him.
10. *And* Judah *went* against the Canaanites
11. *And* from thence *he went* against...Debir:
16. *and they went* and dwelt among the people.
17. *And* Judah *went* with Simeon his brother,
26. *And* the man *went* into the land of the
2: 6. *And* when...the children of Israel *went*
12. *and followed* (lit. *and went* after) other gods,
3:13. *and went* and smote Israel,
4: 8. If *thou wilt go* with me,
— if *thou wilt* not *go* with me, (then) *I will* not *go.*
9. *I will* surely *go* with thee:
— Deborah arose, *and went*
24. *And* the hand of the children of Israel *prospered,*
5: 6. and the travellers *walked* through byways.
7: 4. This *shall go* with thee, the same *shall go* with thee; and of whomsoever I say unto thee, This *shall* not *go* with thee, the same *shall* not *go.*
7. *let* all the (other) people *go*
8:29. *And* Jerubbaal...*went* and dwelt in his own
9: 1. *And* Abimelech...*went* to Shechem
4. *which followed* him. (lit. *and went* after)
6. *and went*, and made Abimelech king,
7. *And* when...*he went* and stood in the top
21. and fled, *and went* to Beer,
49. *and followed* (lit. *and went* after)
50. *Then went* Abimelech to Thebez,
55. *And* when the men...*they departed* every
11: 5. the elders of Gilead *went* to fetch
11. *Then* Jephthah *went* with the elders of
16. *and walked* through the wilderness
18. *Then they went* along through the
37. *that I may go* up and down upon the
38. *and she went* with her companions,
40. the daughters of Israel *went* yearly
13:11. Manoah arose, *and went* after his wife,
14: 9. he took thereof...*and went* on eating, *and came* to his father and mother,
15: 4. *And* Samson *went* and caught three
16: 1. *Then went* Samson to Gaza,
17: 8. *And* the man *departed* out of the city
10. *So* the Levite *went in.*
18: 6. your way wherein *ye go.*
7. *Then* the five men *departed*,
21. So they turned *and departed*,
24. *and ye are gone away:*
26. *And* the children of Dan *went* their way:
19: 2. *and went away* from him unto her father's
3. her husband arose, *and went* after her,
5. afterward *go your way.*
10. he rose up *and departed*,
14. they passed on *and went their way;*
17. the old man said, Whither *goest thou?*
18. *and I went* to Beth-lehem-judah,
28. Up, *and let us be going.*
— man rose up, *and gat* him unto his place.
20: 8. *We will* not any (of us) *go* to his tent,
21:23. *and they went* and returned unto their
Ru. 1: 1. *And* a certain man...*went* to sojourn
7. *and they went* on the way
11. why *will ye go* with me?
16. whither *thou goest, I will go;*
19. *So they* two *went* until they came to
2: 2. *Let me* now *go* to the field,
3. *And she went*, and came, and gleaned
8. *Go* not to glean in another field,
11. *and art come* unto a people which thou
1Sa. 1:18. *So* the woman *went* her way,
2:11. *And* Elkanah *went* to Ramah to his house.
3: 5. *And he went* and lay down.
6. Samuel arose *and went* to Eli,
8. he arose *and went* to Eli,
9. *So* Samuel *went* and lay down
6: 6. did they not let the people go, *and they departed?*
9: 6. now *let us go* thither;
7. behold, (if) *we go*,
9. Come, *and let us go* to the seer:
10. Well said; come, *let us go. So they went* unto the city
10:26. *and there went* with him a band of men,

1Sa. 11:14. Come, *and let us go* to Gilgal,
15. *And* all the people *went* to Gilgal;
14:16. *and they went* on beating down (one another).
19. in the host of the Philistines *went* on
15:20. *and have gone* the way which the Lord sent
32. *And* Agag *came* unto him delicately.
34. *Then* Samuel *went* to Ramah;
16: 2. Samuel said, How *can I go?*
13. Samuel rose up, *and went* to Ramah.
17:13. *And* the three eldest sons of Jesse *went*
20. *and went*, as Jesse had commanded him;
32. *will go* and fight with this Philistine.
41. *And* the Philistine *came* on
48. the Philistine arose, *and came*
18:27. Wherefore David arose *and went*,
19:12. *and he went*, and fled, and escaped.
18. *And* he and Samuel *went* and dwelt
22. *Then went he* also to Ramah,
23. *And he went* thither to Naioth in Ramah:
— *and he went* on, and prophesied,
20:42(21:1). And he arose *and departed:*
22: 1. David *therefore departed* thence,
3. *And* David *went* thence to Mizpeh
5. *Then* David *departed*,
23: 2. *Shall I go* and smite these Philistines?
3. how much more then if *we come* to Keilah
5. *So* David and his men *went* to Keilah,
16. *and went* to David into the wood,
24. they arose, *and went* to Ziph
25. Saul *also* and his men *went* to seek (him).
26. *And* Saul *went* on this side of the mountain,
28. Saul...*and went* against the Philistines:
24: 2(3). *and went* to seek David
7(8). out of the cave, *and went* on (his)
22(23). *And* Saul *went* home;
25:42. *and she went* after the messengers
26:11. take thou now the spear...*and let us go.*
12. *and they gat* them *away*,
25. *So* David *went* on his way,
28: 7. *that I may go* to her,
8. *and he went*, and two men with him,
22. mayest have strength, when *thou goest*
25. they rose up, *and went away* that night.
30: 2. *and went* on their way.
9. *So* David *went*, he and the six hundred
22. they may lead (them) away, *and depart.*
31:12. the valiant men arose, *and went*
2Sa. 2:29. *and went* through all Bithron,
32. *And* Joab and his men *went* all night,
3:16. *And* her husband *went* with her
19. *and* Abner *went* also to speak
21. I will arise *and go*,
— *and he went* in peace.
22. *and he was gone* in peace.
23. *and he is gone* in peace.
24. *and he is* quite *gone?*
4: 5. *And* the sons...Rechab and Baanah, *went*,
7. *and gat them away* through the plain
5: 6. *And* the king and his men *went* to
10. *And* David *went* on, and grew great,
6: 2. David arose, *and went*
12. *So* David *went* and brought up the ark
19. *So* all the people *departed*
11:22. *So* the messenger *went*,
12:15. *And* Nathan *departed* unto his house.
29. *and went* to Rabbah, and fought
13: 8. *So* Tamar *went* to her brother
19. *and went* on crying.
24. *let* the king,...*go* with thy servant.
25. *let us* not all now *go*,
26. *let* my brother Amnon *go* with us.
— Why *should he go* with thee?
37. Absalom fled, *and went* to Talmai,
38. Absalom fled, *and went* to Geshur,
14:23. Joab arose *and went* to Geshur,
15: 7. *let me go* and pay my vow,
9. he arose, *and went* to Hebron.
19. Wherefore *goest thou* also with us?
16:13. *And* as David and his men *went* by the
17:17. they *went* and told king David.
18. *but they went* both of them *away* quickly,
21. *and went* and told king David,
23. *and gat him* home to his house,
18:24. *and* the watchman *went up* to the roof
25. *And he came* apace, and drew near
19:26(27). *and go* to the king:

2Sa. 20: 5. *So* Amasa *went* to assemble (the men of)
21. *and I will depart* from the city.
21:12. *And* David *went* and took the bones
1K. 1:49. *and went* every man his way.
50. Adonijah...arose, *and went*,
2:40. *and went* to Gath to Achish
— *and* Shimei *went*, and brought his
3: 4. *And* the king *went* to Gibeon
14. if *thou wilt walk* in my ways,
6:12. if *thou wilt walk* in my statutes,
8:36. the good way wherein *they should walk*,
66. *and went* unto their tents joyful
9: 4. if thou *wilt walk* before me,
10:13. So she turned *and went* to her own
11: 5. *For* Solomon *went* after Ashtoreth
21. *that I may go* to mine own country.
24. *and they went* to Damascus,
12: 1. *And* Rehoboam *went* to Shechem:
5. *And* the people *departed*.
16. *So* Israel *departed* unto their tents.
30. *for* the people *went* (to worship)
13:10. *So he went* another way,
14. *And went* after the man of God,
24. *when he was gone*, a lion met him
28. *And he went* and found his carcase
14: 4. arose, *and went* to Shiloh,
9. *for thou hast gone* and made thee other
17. Jeroboam's wife arose, *and departed*,
15: 3. *And he walked* in all the sins of his
26. *and walked* in the way of his father,
34. *and walked* in the way of Jeroboam,
16: 2. *and thou hast walked* in the way of
26. *For he walked* in all the way of Jeroboam
31. *and went* and served Baal,
17: 5. *So he went* and did according unto the word of the Lord: *for he went* and
10. he arose *and went* to Zarephath.
11. *as she was going* to fetch (it),
15. *And she went* and did according
18: 2. *And* Elijah *went* to shew himself unto
12. (as soon as) I *am gone* from thee,
16. *So* Obadiah *went* to meet Ahab, and told him: *and* Ahab *went* to meet Elijah.
18. *and thou hast followed* (lit. *gone* after)
35. *And* the water *ran* round about the
45. Ahab rode, *and went* to Jezreel.
19: 3. he arose, *and went* for his life,
8. *and went* in the strength of that meat
19. *So he departed* thence,
20. *and* (then) *I will follow* (lit. *I will go* after) thee.
21. he arose, *and went* after Elijah,
20: 9. *And* the messengers *departed*,
27. *and went* against them:
36. *And as soon as he was departed*
38. *So* the prophet *departed*,
43. *And* the king of Israel *went* to his house
22: 4. *Wilt thou go* with me to battle
6. *Shall I go* against Ramoth-gilead
15. *shall we go* against Ramoth-gilead
43. *And he walked* in all the ways of Asa
49(50). *Let* my servants *go* with thy servants
52(53). *and walked* in the way of his father,
2K. 1: 4. *And* Elijah *departed*.
2: 1. *that* Elijah *went* with Elisha from Gilgal.
6. *And they* two *went on*.
16. *let them go*, we pray thee,
18. Did I not say unto you, *Go* not?
25. *And he went* from thence to mount
3: 7. *And he went* and sent to Jehoshaphat
— *wilt thou go* with me against Moab
9. *So* the king of Israel *went*,
4: 5. *So she went* from him,
25. *So she went* and came unto the man of
30. *and followed* (lit. *went* after) her.
35. *and walked* in the house to and fro;
5: 5. *And he departed*, and took
11. Naaman was wroth, *and went away*,
12. So he turned *and went away* in a rage.
19. *So he departed* from him
24. he let the men go, *and they departed*.
6: 2. *Let us go*, we pray thee,
3. he answered, I *will go*.
4. *So he went* with them.
22. *and go* to their master.
23. *and they went* to their master.
7: 8, 8. *and went* and hid (it);

2K. 7:15. *And they went* after them unto Jordan:
8: 2. *and she went* with her houshold,
9. *So* Hazael *went* to meet him,
14. *So he departed* from Elisha, and came to
18. *And he walked* in the way of the kings of
27. *And he walked* in the way of the house of
28. *And he went* with Joram the son of Ahab
9: 4. *So* the young man...*went* to Ramoth-gilead.
16. Jehu rode in a chariot, *and went* to
18. *So there went* one on horseback
35. *And they went* to bury her:
10:12. he arose and departed *and came*
15. *when he was departed* thence,
25. *and went* to the city of the house of Baal.
13: 2. *and followed* (marg. *walked* after) the sins
21. when the man *was let down*, (lit. *and went* (down))
16: 3. *But he walked* in the way of the kings of
10. *And* king Ahaz *went* to Damascus
17: 8. *And walked* in the statutes of the heathen, (lit. *went* after)
15. *and they followed* vanity,
19. *but walked* in the statutes of Israel
22. *For* the children of Israel *walked*
27. *and let them go* and dwell there,
19:36. *and went* and returned,
21:21. *And he walked* in all the way
22: 2. *and walked* in all the way of David
14. *So* Hilkiah...*went* unto Huldah the
23:29. *and* king Josiah *went* against him;
25: 4. *and* (the king) *went* the way toward the
1Ch. 4:39. *And they went* to the entrance of Gedor,
11: 4. *And* David...*went* to Jerusalem,
9. *So* David *waxed* greater (marg. *so* David *went* in going)
16:43. *And* all the people *departed*
19: 5. *Then there went* (certain),
2Ch. 1: 3. *So* Solomon,...*went* to the high place
6:27. the good way, wherein *they should walk;*
7:17. if *thou wilt walk* before me,
8: 3. *And* Solomon *went* to Hamath-zobah,
9:12. So she turned, *and went away*
10: 1. *And* Rehoboam *went* to Shechem:
5. *And* the people *departed.*
16. *So* all Israel *went* to their tents.
11:14. *and came* to Judah and Jerusalem:
18: 3. *Wilt thou go* with me to Ramoth-gilead?
5, 14. *Shall we go* to Ramoth-gilead
20:32. *And he walked* in the way of Asa
21: 6. *And he walked* in the way of the kings of
13. *But hast walked* in the way of the kings of
20. *and departed* without being desired.
22: 5. *and went* with Jehoram
25:11. *and went* to the valley of salt,
26: 8. *and* his name *spread* (marg. *went*) abroad
28: 2. *For he walked* in the ways of the kings of
30: 6. *So* the posts *went* with the letters
34: 2. *and walked* in the ways of David his father,
22. *And* Hilkiah...*went* to Huldah the
Ezr. 10: 6. *and went* into the chamber of Johanan the son of Eliashib: *and* (when) *he came*
Neh. 5: 9. *ought ye* not *to walk* in the fear of our God
8:12. *And* all the people *went* their way
9:12, 19. the way wherein *they should go.*
12:32. *And* after them *went* Hoshaiah,
Job 7: 9. (As) the cloud is consumed *and vanisheth*
10:21. Before *I go* (whence) I shall not return,
19:10. *and I am gone:*
27:21. The east wind carrieth him away, *and he departeth:*
29: 3. *I walked* (through) darkness;
38:35. thou send lightnings, *that they may go,*
42: 9. *So* Eliphaz...*went*, and did according
Ps. 23: 4. though *I walk* through the valley
26:11. *I will walk* in mine integrity:
32: 8. the way which *thou shalt go:*
34[title](1). who drove him away, *and he departed.*
39:13(14). before *I go* hence, and be no more.
42: 9(10). why *go I* mourning
81:12(13). *they walked* in their own counsels.
84: 7(8). *They go* from strength to strength,
89:30(31). *walk* not in my judgments;
97: 3. A fire *goeth* before him,
122: 1. *Let us go* into the house of the Lord.
126: 6. *He that goeth* forth and weepeth,
138: 7. *I walk* in the midst of trouble,
Ps. 139: 7. Whither *shall I go* from thy spirit?
143: 8. the way wherein *I should walk;*
Pro. 1:15. *walk* not *thou* in the way with them;
2:20. *thou mayest walk* in the way of good (men),
3:23. Then *shalt thou walk* in thy way safely,
10: 9. He that walketh uprightly *walketh* surely:
15:12. neither *will he go* unto the wise.
Ecc. 5: 1(4:17). when *thou goest* to the house of God,
16(15). so *shall he go:*
6: 4. and *departeth* in darkness,
8: 3. Be not hasty to *go* out of his sight:
Cant. 4: 6. *I will get me* to the mountain
Isa. 2: 3. *and we will walk* in his paths:
5. *and let us walk* in the light
3:16. *and walk* with stretched forth necks
— walking and mincing (as) *they go,*
6: 8. who *will go* for us?
28:13. that *they might go*, and fall backward,
33:21. wherein *shall go* no galley with oars,
37:37. Sennacherib...departed, *and went*
38:10. *I shall go* to the gates of the grave:
40:31. *they shall walk*, and not faint.
43: 2. when *thou walkest* through the fire,
45: 2. *I will go* before thee,
14. *they shall come* after thee;
48:17. thee by the way (that) *thou shouldest go.*
52:12. nor *go* by flight:
57:17. *and he went on* frowardly in the way
Jer. 1: 7. *thou shalt go* to all
2: 5. *and have walked* after vanity,
25. after them *will I go.*
3: 8. *but went* and played the harlot
17. neither *shall they walk* any more
18. the house of Judah *shall walk*
5: 5. *I will get me* unto the great men,
23. they are revolted *and gone.*
6:16. *We will* not *walk* (therein).
25. nor *walk* by the way;
7: 6. neither *walk* after other gods
24. *but walked* in the counsels
9: 2(1). *and go* from them!
14(13). *But have walked* after the imagination
11: 8. *but walked* every one in the imagination
12: 2. they have taken root: *they grow*, (marg. *go on*)
13: 5. *So I went*, and hid it
7. *Then I went* to Euphrates,
10. *and walk* after other gods,
15: 6. *thou art gone* backward:
16: 5. neither *go* to lament nor bemoan them:
11. *and have walked* after other gods,
18:12. *we will walk* after our own devices,
20: 6. dwell in thine house *shall go* into captivity:
22:22. thy lovers *shall go* into captivity:
25: 6. *go* not after other gods
28:11. *And* the prophet Jeremiah *went* his way.
30:16. every one of them, *shall go* into captivity;
35:15. *go* not after other gods
37: 9. The Chaldeans *shall* surely *depart* from us: for *they shall* not *depart.*
40:15. *Let me go*, I pray thee,
41:10. *and departed* to go over to the Ammonites.
12. *and went* to fight with Ishmael
14. returned, *and went* unto Johanan
15. *and went* to the Ammonites.
17. *And they departed*, and dwelt in the
42: 3. the way wherein *we may walk,*
45: 5. a prey in all places whither *thou goest.*
46:22. The voice thereof *shall go* like a serpent; for *they shall march* with an army,
48: 2. the sword *shall pursue* (lit. *shall go* after) thee.
49: 3. their king *shall go* into captivity,
50: 4. *they shall go*, and seek the Lord their God.
51: 9. *and let us go* every one into his own
52: 7. *and they went* by the way of the plain.
Lam. 1: 6. *and they are gone* without strength
Eze. 1: 9. *they went* every one straight forward.
12. *they went* every one straight forward: whither the spirit was to go, *they went;*
17. *they went* upon their four sides:
19. the wheels *went* by them:
20. the spirit was to go, *they went,*
21. When those went, (these) *went;*
3:14. *and I went* in bitterness,
7:17. all knees *shall be weak* (as) water. (marg. *go* into water)

Eze 10:11. *they went* upon their four sides;
— whither the head looked *they followed* it; (lit. *they went* after it)
16. the wheels *went* by them:
22. *they went* every one straight forward.
11:20. That *they may walk* in my statutes,
12:11. they shall remove (and) *go* into captivity.
20:18. *Walk ye* not in the statutes of your fathers,
21: 7(12). all knees *shall be weak* (as) water:
30:17. these (cities) *shall go* into captivity.
18. her daughters *shall go* into captivity.
36:27. cause you to *walk* in my statutes,
37:24. *they shall* also *walk* in my judgments,
Hos. 1: 3. *So he went* and took Gomer
2: 5(7). *I will go* after my lovers,
7(9). *I will go* and return to my first husband;
13(15). *and she went* after her lovers,
5: 6. They *shall go* with their flocks
13. *then went* Ephraim to the Assyrian,
14. I, (even) I, will tear *and go away;*
15. *I will go* (and) return to my place,
7:12. When *they shall go*, I will spread my net
11:10. *They shall walk* after the Lord:
14: 6(7). branches *shall spread*, (marg. *shall go*)
9(10). the just *shall walk* in them:
Joel 2: 7. *they shall march* every one
8. *they shall walk* every one
3:18(4:18). the hills *shall flow* with milk, and all the rivers of Judah *shall flow* (marg. *shall go*) with waters,
Am. 2: 7. his father *will go* in unto the (same) maid,
3: 3. *Can* two *walk* together,
9: 4. though *they go* into captivity
Jon. 3: 3. So Jonah arose, *and went* unto Nineveh,
Mic. 1: 8. *I will go* stripped and naked:
2: 3. neither *shall ye go* haughtily:
4: 2. *and we will walk* in his paths:
5. all people *will walk* every one
— *and we will walk* in the name of the Lord
6:16. *and ye walk* in their counsels;
Hab. 3: 5. Before him *went* the pestilence,
Zec. 3: 7. If *thou wilt walk* in my ways,
8:21. *Let us go* speedily to pray
— *I will go* also.
23. *We will go* with you:

* HIPHIL.—*Preterite.* *

Deu 8: 2. thy God *led thee* these forty years
2K. 24:15. (those) *carried he* into captivity
Pro.16:29. *and leadeth him* into the way (that is) not
Isa. 42:16. *And I will bring* the blind by a way
48:21. *he led them* through the deserts:
Eze.36:12. *Yea, I will cause* men *to walk* upon you,
Hos. 2:14(16). *and bring* her into the wilderness,

HIPHIL.—*Infinitive.*

2Ch 36: 6. *to carry him* to Babylon.

HIPHIL.—*Imperative.*

Ex. 2: 9. *Take* this child *away*,
Nu. 16:46(17:11). *and go* quickly unto the
2K. 17:27. *Carry* thither one of the priests

HIPHIL.—*Future.*

Ex. 14:21. *and* the Lord *caused* the sea *to go* (back)
Lev.26:13. *and made* you *go* upright.
Deu28:36. The Lord *shall bring* thee,
29: 5(4). *And I have led* you forty years
Jos. 24: 3. *and led* him throughout all the land of
2Sa.13:13. whither *shall I cause* my shame *to go?*
1K. 1:38. *and brought* him to Gihon.
2K. 6:19. *and I will bring* you to the man whom ye seek. *But he led* them to Samaria.
25:20. *and brought* them to the king of Babylon
2Ch 33:11. *and carried him* to Babylon.
35:24. *and they brought him* to Jerusalem,
Ps.106: 9. *so he led them* through the depths,
125: 5. the Lord *shall lead them forth* with the
Ecc. 5:15(14). *which he may carry away* in his hand.
10:20. a bird of the air *shall carry* the voice,
Jer. 31: 9. *I will cause them to walk* by the rivers
32: 5. *he shall lead* Zedekiah to Babylon,
52:26. *and brought* them to the king of Babylon
Lam. 3: 2. *and brought* (me into) darkness,
Eze.32:14. and *cause* their rivers *to run* like oil,
40:24. *After that he brought me* toward the south,
43: 1. *Afterward he brought me* to the gate,
Eze.47: 6. *Then he brought me*, and caused me to
Am. 2:10. *and led* you forty years through the

HIPHIL.—*Participle.*

Deu 8:15. *Who led thee* through that great and terrible
Job 12:17. *He leadeth* counsellors away spoiled,
19. *He leadeth* princes away spoiled,
Ps.136:16. *To him which led* his people
Isa. 63:12. *That led* (them) by the right hand of Moses
13. *That led them* through the deep,
Jer. 2: 6. *that led* us through the wilderness,
17. when *he led thee* by the way?
Zec. 5:10. Whither *do* these *bear* the ephah?

יָלַל [*yāh-lal'*]. 3213

* HIPHIL.—*Preterite.* *

Jer. 47: 2. *and* all the inhabitants of the land *shall howl.*
Am. 8: 3. *And* the songs of the temple *shall be howlings*

HIPHIL.—*Imperative.*

Isa. 13: 6. *Howl ye;* for the day of the Lord (is) at
14:12. O *Lucifer*, son of the morning! (marg. or, *day star;* perhaps, lit. *Howl;* see also הֵילֵל)
31. *Howl*, O gate; cry, O city;
23: 1, 14. *Howl, ye* ships of Tarshish;
6. *howl, ye* inhabitants of the isle.
Jer. 4: 8. gird you with sackcloth, lament *and howl:*
25:34. *Howl, ye* shepherds, and cry;
48:20. *howl* and cry; tell ye it in Arnon,
39. *They shall howl*, (lit. *Howl ye*)
49: 3. *Howl*, O Heshbon, for Ai is spoiled:
51: 8. Babylon is suddenly fallen and destroyed: *howl* for her;
Eze.21:12(17). Cry *and howl*, son of man:
30: 2. Thus saith the Lord God; *Howl ye*,
Joel 1: 5. *and howl*, all ye drinkers of wine,
11. *howl*, O ye vinedressers,
13. *howl*, ye ministers of the altar:
Zep. 1:11. *Howl, ye* inhabitants of Maktesh,
Zec.11: 2. *Howl*, fir tree; for the cedar is fallen;
— *howl*, O ye oaks of Bashan;

HIPHIL.—*Future.*

Isa. 15: 2. Moab *shall howl* over Nebo,
3. every one *shall howl*,
16: 7. Therefore shall Moab *howl* for Moab, every one *shall howl:*
52: 5. they that rule over them *make* them *to howl*,
65:14. and *shall howl* for vexation of spirit.
Jer. 48:31. Therefore *will I howl* for Moab,
Hos. 7:14. when *they howled* upon their beds:
Mic. 1: 8. I will wail *and howl*,

יְלֵל *y'lēhl*, m. 3214

Deu32:10. the waste *howling* wilderness;

יְלָלָה *y'lāh-lāh'*, f. 3215

Isa. 15: 8. *the howling thereof* unto Eglaim, and *the howling thereof* unto Beer-elim.
Jer. 25:36. *and an howling of* the principal of the flock,
Zep. 1:10. *and an howling* from the second,
Zec.11: 3. *the howling of* the shepherds;

יָלַע *yāh-lag'*. 3216

* KAL.—*Preterite.* *

Pro.20:25. man (who) *devoureth* (that which is) holy,

יַלֶּפֶת *yal-leh'-pheth*, f. 3217

Lev.21:20. or be scurvy, or *scabbed*,
22:22. or scurvy, or *scabbed*,

יֶלֶק *yeh'-lek*, m. 3218

Ps.105:34. the locusts came, *and caterpillers*,

Jer. 51:14. will fill thee with men, *as* with *caterpillers;*
27. horses to come up *as the* rough *caterpillers.*
Joel 1: 4. hath *the cankerworm* eaten; and that which *the cankerworm* hath left
2:25. *the cankerworm,* and the caterpiller,
Nah. 3:15. it shall eat thee up *like the cankerworm:* make thyself many *as the cankerworm,*
16. *the cankerworm* spoileth, and fleeth away.

3219 יַלְקוּט *yal-koot',* m.

1Sa. 17:40. in a shepherd's bag which he had, *even in a scrip;*

3220 יָם *yāhm,* m.

Gen. 1:10. gathering together of the waters called he *Seas:*
22. fill the waters *in the seas,*
26, 28. the fish of *the sea,*
9: 2. all the fishes of *the sea;*
12: 8. (having) Beth-el *on the west,*
13:14. eastward, and *westward:*
14: 3. which is *the* salt *sea.*
22:17. the sand which (is) upon the *sea* shore;
28:14. thou shalt spread abroad *to the west,*
32:12(13). make thy seed as the sand of *the sea,*
41:49. Joseph gathered corn as the sand of *the sea,*
49:13. Zebulun shall dwell at the haven of *the sea;*
Ex. 10:19. a mighty strong *west* wind,
— cast them *into the* Red *sea:*
13:18. the wilderness of *the* Red *sea:*
14: 2. between Migdol and *the sea,*
— before it shall ye encamp by *the sea.*
9. overtook them encamping by *the sea,*
16, 26. stretch out thine hand over *the sea,*
— through the midst of *the sea.*
21. Moses stretched out his hand over *the sea;* and the Lord caused *the sea* to go (back)
— made *the sea* dry (land),
22. into the midst of *the sea*
23. went in after them to the midst of *the sea,*
27. Moses stretched forth his hand over *the sea,* and *the sea* returned to his strength
— the Egyptians in the midst of *the sea.*
28. the host of Pharaoh that came *into the sea*
29. in the midst of *the sea;*
30. the Egyptians dead upon the *sea* shore.
15: 1, 21. and his rider hath he thrown *into the sea.*
4. his host hath he cast *into the sea:* his chosen captains also are drowned *in the* Red *sea.*
8. the heart of *the sea.*
10. *the sea* covered them:
19. his horsemen *into the sea,* and the Lord brought again the waters of *the sea*
— the midst of *the sea.*
22. Moses brought Israel *from the* Red *sea,*
20:11. *the sea,* and all that in them (is),
23:31. I will set thy bounds *from the* Red *sea* even unto *the sea of* the Philistines,
26:22. the sides of the tabernacle *westward*
27. for the two sides *westward.*
27:12. the breadth of the court on the *west* side
36:27. the sides of the tabernacle *westward*
32. the tabernacle for the sides *westward.*
38:12. for the *west* side (were) hangings
Lev. 11: 9. *in the seas,* and in the rivers,
10. all that have not fins and scales *in the seas,*
Nu. 2:18. *On the west side* (shall be) the standard
3:23. shall pitch behind the tabernacle *westward.*
11:22. shall all the fish of *the sea* be gathered
31. brought quails from *the sea,*
13:29. the Canaanites dwell by *the sea,*
14:25 & 21:4. by the way of *the* Red *sea.*
33: 8. passed through the midst of *the sea*
10. encamped by *the* Red *sea.*
11. they removed *from the* Red *sea,*
34: 3. the outmost coast of *the* salt *sea*
5. it shall be *at the sea.*
6. (as for) the *western* border, ye shall even have *the* great *sea* for a border: this shall be your *west* border.
7. from *the* great *sea* ye shall point
11. the side of *the sea of* Chinnereth
12. it shall be at *the* salt *sea:*
Nu. 35: 5. on the *west* side two thousand cubits,
Deu 1: 7. in the south, and by the *sea* side,
40 & 2:1. by the way of *the* Red *sea.*
3:17. *the sea of* the plain, (even) *the* salt *sea,*
27. lift up thine eyes *westward,*
4:49. *the sea of* the plain,
11: 4. the water of *the* Red *sea*
24. even unto *the* uttermost *sea*
30:13. Neither (is) it beyond *the sea,* (lit. from the passage *of the sea*)
— Who shall go over *the sea*
33:19. the abundance of *the seas,*
23. possess thou *the west*
34: 2. unto the utmost *sea,*
Jos. 1: 4. unto *the* great *sea*
2:10. the water of *the* Red *sea*
3:16. came down toward *the sea of* the plain (even) *the* salt *sea,*
4:23. the Lord your God did *to the* Red *sea,*
5: 1. on the side of Jordan *westward,*
— which (were) by *the sea,*
8: 9. *on the west side* of Ai:
12. *on the west side* of the city.
13. liers in wait *on the west* of the city,
9: 1. in all the coasts of *the* great *sea*
11: 2. in the borders of Dor *on the west,*
3. on the east *and on the west,*
4. the sand that (is) upon the *sea* shore
12: 3. from the plain to *the sea of* Chinneroth on the east, and unto *the sea of* the plain, (even) *the* salt *sea* on the east,
7. on this side Jordan *on the west,*
13:27. the edge of *the sea of* Chinnereth
15: 2. the shore of *the* salt *sea,*
4. the goings out of that coast were *at the sea:*
5. the east border (was) *the* salt *sea,*
— the bay of *the sea*
8. the valley of Hinnom *westward,*
10. border compassed from Baalah *westward*
11. the goings out of the border were *at the sea.*
12. *the west* border (was) *to the* great *sea,*
46. From Ekron *even unto the sea,*
47. *and the* great *sea,* and the border (thereof):
16: 3. goeth down *westward* to the coast
— the goings out thereof are *at the sea.*
6. the border went out *toward the sea*
8. border went out from Tappuah *westward*
— the goings out thereof were *at the sea.*
17: 9. the outgoings of it were *at the sea:*
10. *the sea* is his border;
18:12. went up through the mountains *westward;*
14. compassed the corner of *the sea*
— this (was) the *west* quarter.
15. the border went out *on the west,*
19. the north bay of *the* salt *sea*
19:11. their border went up *toward the sea,*
26. reacheth to Carmel *westward,*
29. the outgoings thereof are *at the sea*
34. the coast turneth *westward*
— reacheth to Asher *on the west* side,
22: 7. on this side Jordan *westward.*
23: 4. *even unto the* great *sea*
24: 6. ye came *unto the sea;*
— chariots and horsemen unto *the* Red *sea.*
7. brought *the sea* upon them,
Jud. 5:17. Asher continued on the *sea* shore,
7:12. as the sand by the *sea* side
11:16. through the wilderness unto *the* Red *sea,*
1Sa. 13: 5. the sand which (is) on the *sea*shore
2Sa. 17:11. the sand that (is) by *the sea*
22:16. the channels of *the sea* appeared,
1K. 4:20. the sand which (is) by *the sea*
29(5:9). the sand that (is) on the *sea* shore.
5: 9(23). from Lebanon *unto the sea:* and I will convey them *by sea*
7:23. he made *a* molten *sea,*
24. compassing *the sea* round about:
25. three looking *toward the west,*
— *and the sea* (was set) above
39. he set *the sea* on the right side
44. one *sea,* and twelve oxen under *the sea;*
9:26. the shore of *the* Red *sea,*
27. shipmen that had knowledge of *the sea,*
10:22. the king had *at sea* a navy
18:43. Go up now, look toward *the sea.*
44. there ariseth a little cloud *out of the sea,*
2K. 14:25. *the sea of* the plain,

2K. 16:17. took down *the sea* from off the brasen
25:13. *the* brasen *sea* that (was) in the house
16. The two pillars, one *sea*,
1Ch 9:24. toward the east, *west*,
16:32. Let *the sea* roar, and the fulness thereof:
18: 8. Solomon made *the* brasen *sea*,
2Ch 2:16(15). bring it to thee in flotes by *sea*
4: 2. Also he made *a* molten *sea*
3. compassing *the sea* round about.
4. three looking *toward the west*,
— *and the sea* (was set) above
6. *but the sea* (was) for the priests
10. he set *the sea* on the right side
15. One *sea*, and twelve oxen under it.
8:17. at the *sea* side in the land of Edom.
18. servants that had knowledge of *the sea*;
20: 2. from beyond *the sea*
Ezr. 3: 7. from Lebanon to *the sea of* Joppa,
Neh 9: 6. *the seas*, and all that (is) therein,
9. heardest their cry by *the* Red *sea*;
11. *And* thou didst divide *the sea* before them, so that they went through the midst of *the sea*
Est. 10: 1. the isles of *the sea*.
Job 6: 3. heavier than the sand of *the sea*:
7:12. (Am) I *a sea*, or a whale,
9: 8. treadeth upon the waves of *the sea*.
11: 9. broader than *the sea*.
12: 8. the fishes of *the sea* shall declare
14:11. (As) the waters fail from *the sea*,
26:12. He divideth *the sea* with his power,
28:14. *and the sea* saith, (It is) not with me.
36:30. covereth the bottom of *the sea*.
38: 8. (who) shut up *the sea* with doors,
16. thou entered into the springs of *the sea*?
41:31(23). he maketh *the sea* like a pot of
Ps. 8: 8(9). the fish of *the sea*,
—(-). passeth through the paths of *the seas*.
24: 2. he hath founded it upon *the seas*,
33: 7. He gathereth the waters of *the sea* together
46: 2(3). the midst of *the sea*;
65: 5(6). *and* of them that are afar off (upon) *the sea*:
7(8). Which stilleth the noise of *the seas*,
66: 6. He turned *the sea* into dry (land):
68:22(23). the depths of *the sea*:
69:34(35). *the seas*, and every thing that moveth
72: 8. shall have dominion also *from sea* to *sea*,
74:13. Thou didst divide *the sea*
77:19(20). Thy way (is) *in the sea*,
78:13. He divided *the sea*,
27. the sand of *the sea*:
53. *the sea* overwhelmed their enemies.
80:11(12). She sent out her boughs unto *the sea*,
89: 9(10). Thou rulest the raging of *the sea*:
25(26). I will set his hand also *in the sea*,
93: 4. the mighty waves of *the sea*.
95. 5. *The sea* (is) his, and he made it:
96:11 & 98:7. let *the sea* roar, and the fulness
104:25. (So is) this great and wide *sea*,
106: 7. (him) at *the sea*, (even) *at the* Red *sea*.
9. He rebuked *the* Red *sea* also,
22. terrible things by *the* Red *sea*.
107: 3. *and from the south*.
23. They that go down to *the sea*
114: 3. *The sea* saw (it), and fled:
5. What (ailed) thee, *O thou sea*,
135: 6. *in the seas*, and all deep places.
136:13. divided *the* Red *sea* into parts:
15. Pharaoh and his host *in the* Red *sea*:
139: 9. dwell in the uttermost parts of *the sea*;
146: 6. *the sea*, and all that therein (is):
Pro. 8:29. When he gave *to the sea* his decree,
23:34. the midst of *the sea*,
30:19. the way of a ship in the midst of *the sea*;
Ecc. 1: 7. All the rivers run into *the sea*; *yet the sea* (is) not full;
Isa. 5:30. the roaring of *the sea*:
9: 1(8:23). the way of *the sea*,
10:22. the sand of *the sea*,
26. (as) his rod (was) upon *the sea*,
11: 9. as the waters cover *the sea*.
11. from the islands of *the sea*.
14. they shall fly...*toward the west*;
15. the tongue of *the* Egyptian *sea*;
16: 8. they are gone over *the sea*.
17:12. like the noise of *the seas*;

Isa. 18: 2. That sendeth ambassadors *by the sea*,
19: 5. the waters shall fail *from the sea*,
21: 1. The burden of the desert of *the sea*.
23: 2. that pass over *the sea*,
4. *the sea* hath spoken, (even) the strength of *the sea*,
11. He stretched out his hand over *the sea*,
24:14. they shall cry aloud *from the sea*
15. the isles of *the sea*.
27: 1. the dragon that (is) *in the sea*.
42:10. ye that go down to *the sea*,
43:16. which maketh a way *in the sea*,
48:18. the waves of *the sea*:
49:12. *and from the west*;
50: 2. at my rebuke I dry up *the sea*,
51:10. which hath dried *the sea*,
— made the depths of *the sea* a way
15. that divided *the sea*,
57:20. the wicked (are) *like the* troubled *sea*,
60: 5. abundance of *the sea* shall be converted
63:11. brought them up *out of the sea*
Jer. 5:22. the sand (for) the bound *of the sea*
6:23. their voice roareth *like the sea*;
15: 8. above the sand of *the seas*:
25:22. the isles which (are) beyond *the sea*,
27:19. concerning *the sea*,
31:35. which divideth *the sea*
33:22. neither the sand of *the sea* measured:
46:18. as Carmel *by the sea*,
47: 7. against the *sea* shore?
48:32. thy plants are gone over *the sea*, they reach (even) to *the sea of* Jazer:
49:21. the noise thereof was heard *in the* Red *sea*.
23. (there is) sorrow *on the sea*;
50:42. their voice shall roar *like the sea*,
51:36. I will dry up *her sea*,
42. *The sea* is come up upon Babylon:
52:17. *the* brasen *sea* that (was) in the house
20. The two pillars, one *sea*,
Lam. 2:13. thy breach (is) great *like the sea*:
Eze. 25:16. destroy the remnant of the *sea* coast.
26: 3. *the sea* causeth his waves to come up.
5. the midst of *the sea*:
16. the princes of *the sea* shall come
17. (wast) inhabited *of seafaring men*, (marg. *the seas*)
— wast strong *in the sea*,
18. that (are) *in the sea* shall be troubled
27: 3. the entry of *the sea*,
4. Thy borders (are) in the midst of *the seas*,
9. the ships of *the sea* with their mariners
25. glorious in the midst of *the seas*.
26. broken thee in the midst of *the seas*.
27. shall fall into the midst of *the seas*
29. all the pilots of *the sea*,
32. the midst of *the sea*?
33. When thy wares went forth *out of the seas*,
34. thou shalt be broken *by the seas*
28: 2. of God, in the midst of *the seas*;
8. slain in the midst of *the seas*.
32: 2. thou (art) as a whale *in the seas*:
38:20. the fishes of *the sea*,
39:11. the east of *the sea*:
41:12. at the end toward *the west*
42:19. He turned about to the *west* side,
45: 7. from *the west* side *westward*,
— from the *west* border
46:19. the two sides *westward*.
47: 8. go *into the sea*: (which being) brought forth *into the sea*,
10. the fish of *the* great *sea*,
15. from *the* great *sea*,
17. the border from *the sea*
18. from the border unto *the* east *sea*.
19. the river to *the* great *sea*.
20. The *west* side also (shall be) *the* great *sea*
— This (is) the *west* side.
48: 1. these are his sides east (and) *west*;
2, 8. from the east side unto the *west* side,
3. from the east side even unto the *west* side,
4, 5, 8. from the east side unto the *west* side,
6. from the east side even unto the *west* side,
7. from the east side unto the *west* side
10. *and toward the west* ten thousand in
16. the *west* side four thousand and five
17. *and toward the west* two hundred and
18. ten thousand *westward*:

Eze.48:21. *and westward* over against the five and
— toward the *west* border,
23, 24, 25, 26, 27. from the east side *unto the west* side
28. toward *the* great *sea.*
34. At the *west* side four thousand
Dan 8: 4. I saw the ram pushing *westward,*
11:45. his palace between *the seas*
Hos. 1:10(2:1). the sand of *the sea,*
4: 3. the fishes of *the sea* also shall be taken
11:10. the children shall tremble *from the west.*
Joel 2:20. his face toward *the* east *sea,* and his hinder part toward *the* utmost *sea,*
Am. 5: 8. that calleth for the waters of *the sea,*
8:12. they shall wander *from sea* to *sea,*
9: 3. in the bottom of *the sea,*
6. that calleth for the waters of *the sea,*
Jon. 1: 4. a great wind into *the sea,* and there was a mighty tempest *in the sea,*
5. wares that (were) in the ship into *the sea,*
9. which hath made *the sea*
11. that *the sea* may be calm unto us? for *the sea* wrought,
12. into *the sea;* so shall *the sea* be calm unto
13. *the sea* wrought, and was tempestuous
15. forth into *the sea:* and *the sea* ceased
2: 3(4). in the midst of *the seas;*
Mic. 7:12. *and from sea to sea,*
19. the depths of *the sea.*
Nah 1: 4. He rebuketh *the sea,*
3: 8. whose rampart (was) *the sea,* (and) her wall (was) *from the sea?*
Hab 1:14. makest men as the fishes of *the sea,*
2:14. as the waters cover *the sea.*
3: 8. (was) thy wrath *against the sea,*
15. Thou didst walk *through the sea*
Zep. 1: 3. the fishes of *the sea,*
2: 5. Woe unto the inhabitants of the *sea* coast,
6. the *sea* coast shall be dwellings
Hag. 2: 6. I will shake the heavens, and the earth, and *the sea,*
Zec. 9: 4. he will smite her power *in the sea;*
10. his dominion (shall be) *from sea* (even) to *sea,*
10:11. pass *through the sea* with affliction, and shall smite the waves *in the sea,*
14: 4. toward the east *and toward the west,*
8. half of them toward *the* former *sea,* and half of them toward *the* hinder *sea:*

3221 יָם [*yāhm*], Ch. m.

Dan 7: 2. winds of the heaven strove *upon the* great *sea.*
3. four great beasts came up from *the sea,*

See 3222 יֵמִים see יֵמִם

3225 יָמִין *yāh-meen',* m.

Gen 13: 9. if (thou depart) to *the right hand,*
24:49. that I may turn to *the right hand,*
48:13. Ephraim *in his right hand*
— *toward* Israel's *right hand,*
14. Israel stretched out *his right hand,*
17. his father laid *his right* hand
18. put *thy right hand* upon his head.
Ex. 14:22. *on their right hand,*
29. a wall unto them *on their right hand,*
15: 6. *Thy right hand,* O Lord, is become glorious in power: *thy right hand,* O Lord,
12. Thou stretchedst out *thy right hand,*
29:22. and the *right* shoulder;
Lev. 7:32. the *right* shoulder shall ye give
33. shall have the *right* shoulder
8:25. and the *right* shoulder:
26. upon the *right* shoulder:
9:21. the breasts and the *right* shoulder
Nu. 18:18. and as the *right* shoulder are thine
20:17. we will not turn to *the right hand*
22:26. to *the right hand* or to the left.
Deu 2:27. I will neither turn unto *the right hand*
5:32(29). turn aside to *the right hand*
Deu 17:11. (to) *the right hand,* nor (to) the left.
20 & 28:14. (to) *the right hand,* or (to) the left:
33: 2. *from his right hand* (went) a fiery law
Jos. 1: 7. (to) *the right hand* or (to) the left,
17: 7. the border went along on *the right hand*
23: 6. turn not aside therefrom (to) *the right hand*
Jud. 3:15. a man lefthanded: (marg. shut of *his right* hand)
16. he did gird it...upon *his right* thigh.
21. took the dagger from *his right* thigh,
5:26. *and her right hand* to the workmen's
7:20. the trumpets in *their right* hands
16:29. the one *with his right hand,*
20:16. seven hundred chosen men lefthanded; (lit. bound of *their right* hand)
1Sa. 6:12. turned not aside (to) *the right hand*
11: 2. I may thrust out all your *right* eyes,
23:19. *on the south of* Jeshimon? (marg. *on the right hand*)
24. the plain on *the south of* Jeshimon.
2Sa. 2:19. he turned not to *the right hand*
21. Turn thee aside to *thy right hand*
16: 6. the mighty men (were) *on his right hand*
20: 9. with the *right* hand to kiss him.
24: 5. on *the right side of* the city
1K. 2:19. she sat *on his right hand.*
7:39. on the *right* side of the house,
49. five *on the right* (side),
22:19. *on his right hand* and on his left.
2K. 12: 9(10). set it beside the altar, *on the right side*
22: 2. turned not aside to *the right hand*
23:13. *on the right hand* of the mount
1Ch 6:39(24). who stood on *his right hand,*
2Ch 3:17. one *on the right hand,*
4: 6. put five *on the right hand,*
7. in the temple, five *on the right hand,*
8. five *on the right side,* and five
18:18. host of heaven standing on *his right hand*
34: 2. to *the right hand,* nor to the left.
Neh 8: 4. on *his right hand;*
12:31. (one) went *on the right hand*
Job 23: 9. he hideth himself on *the right hand,*
30:12. Upon (my) *right* (hand) rise the youth;
40:14. *thine own right hand* can save thee.
Ps. 16: 8. (he is) *at my right hand,*
11. *at thy right hand* (there are) pleasures
17: 7. O thou that savest *by thy right hand*
18:35(36). *and thy right hand* hath holden me
20: 6(7). the saving strength of *his right hand.*
21: 8(9). *thy right hand* shall find out those
26:10. *and their right hand* is full of bribes.
44: 3(4). but *thy right hand,*
45: 4(5). thy *right hand* shall teach thee terrible
9(10). *upon thy right hand* did stand the queen
48:10(11). *thy right hand* is full of righteousness.
60: 5(7). save (with) *thy right hand,*
63: 8(9). *thy right hand* upholdeth me.
73:23. thou hast holden (me) by *my right* hand.
74:11. *even thy right hand?*
77:10(11). *the right hand of* the most high.
78:54. (which) *his right hand* had purchased.
80:15(16). which *thy right hand* hath planted,
17(18). the man of *thy right hand,*
89:12(13). north *and the south* thou hast created
13(14). high is *thy right hand.*
25(26). *his right hand* in the rivers.
42(43). Thou hast set up *the right hand of* his adversaries;
91: 7. ten thousand *at thy right hand;*
98: 1. *his right hand,* and his holy arm,
108: 6(7). save (with) *thy right hand,*
109: 6. let Satan stand at *his right hand.*
31. *at the right hand of* the poor,
110: 1. Sit thou *at my right hand,*
5. The Lord at *thy right hand*
118:15. *the right hand of* the Lord doeth valiantly.
16. *The right hand of* the Lord is exalted: *the right hand of* the Lord doeth valiantly.
121: 5. Lord (is) thy shade upon *thy right* hand.
137: 5. let *my right hand* forget (her cunning).
138: 7. *thy right hand* shall save me.
139:10. *thy right hand* shall hold me.
142: 4(5). I looked on (my) *right hand,*
144: 8, 11. *and their right hand* (is) *a right hand of*
Pro. 3:16. Length of days (is) *in her right hand;*
4:27. Turn not to *the right hand*
27:16. the ointment of *his right hand,*

Ecc.10: 2. A wise man's heart (is) *at his right hand;*
Cant.2: 6. *and his right hand* doth embrace me.
8: 3. *and his right hand* should embrace me.
Isa. 9:20(19). he shall snatch on *the right hand,*
41:10. *the right hand of* my righteousness.
13. thy God will hold *thy right hand,*
44:20. (Is there) not a lie *in my right hand?*
45: 1. *whose right hand* I have holden,
48:13. *and my right hand* hath spanned the
54: 3. thou shalt break forth on *the right hand*
62: 8. The Lord hath sworn *by his right hand,*
63:12. That led (them) *by the right hand of* Moses
Jer. 22:24. the signet upon *my right* hand,
Lam.2: 3. he hath drawn back *his right hand*
4. stood with *his right hand* as an adversary,
Eze. 1:10. the face of a lion, on *the right side:*
10: 3. the cherubims stood *on the right side*
16:46. dwelleth *at thy right hand,*
21:22(27). *At his right hand* was the divination
39: 3. thine arrows to fall out of *thy right* hand.
Dan 12: 7. he held up *his right hand*
Jon. 4:11. between *their right hand* and their left
Hab. 2:16. the Lord's *right hand* shall be turned
Zec. 3: 1. Satan standing at *his right hand*
4: 3. one *upon the right* (side)
11. *the right* (side) *of* the candlestick
11:17. upon *his right* eye:
— *his right* eye shall be utterly darkened.
12: 6. on *the right hand*

3227 **יְמִינִי** *y'mee-nee'*, adj.

2Ch 3:17. (כתיב) the name of *that on the right hand*
Eze. 4: 6. (כתיב) lie again on thy *right* side,

3222 **יֵמִם** *yĕh-meem'*, m. pl.

Gen 36:24. found *the mules* in the wilderness,

3231 **יָמַן** [*yāh-man'*].

* HIPHIL.—*Infinitive.* *

2Sa. 14:19. none *can turn to the right hand*

HIPHIL.—*Imperative.*

Eze. 21:16(21). *Go* thee one way or other, (either) *on the right hand,*

HIPHIL.—*Future.*

Gen 13: 9. *then I will go to the right;*

HIPHIL.—*Participle.*

1Ch 12: 2. *could use* both *the right hand* and the left

3233 **יְמָנִי** *y'māh-nee'*, adj.

Ex. 29:20. the tip of the *right* ear of his sons, and upon the thumb of their *right* hand, and upon the great toe of their *right* foot,
Lev. 8:23. the tip of Aaron's *right* ear, and upon the thumb of his *right* hand, and upon the great toe of his *right* foot.
24. the tip of their *right* ear, and upon the thumbs of their *right* hands, and upon the great toes of their *right* feet:
14:14, 17, 25, 28. the tip of the *right* ear of him that is to be cleansed, and upon the thumb of his *right* hand, and upon the great toe of his *right* foot:
16. priest shall dip his *right* finger
27. priest shall sprinkle with his *right* finger
1K. 6: 8. *the right* side of the house:
7:21. he set up the *right* pillar,
39. the *right* side of the house,
2K. 11:11. from the *right* corner of the temple
2Ch 3:17. the name of *that on the right hand* Jachin,
4:10. he set the sea on *the right* side
23:10. *the right* side of the temple
Eze. 4: 6. accomplished them, lie again on thy *right*
47: 1. *the right* side of the house,
2. there ran out waters on *the right* side.

יָמַר [*yāh-mar'*]. 3235

* HIPHIL.—*Preterite.* *

Jer. 2:11. *Hath* a nation *changed* (their) gods,

* HITHPAEL.—*Future.* *

Isa. 61: 6. in their glory *shall ye boast yourselves.*

יָמַשׁ [*yāh-mash'*]. 3237

* HIPHIL.—*Imperative.* *

Jud.16:26. (כתיב) Suffer me *that I may feel* the pillars

יָנָה [*yāh-nāh'*]. 3238

* KAL.—*Future.* *

Ps. 74: 8. *Let us destroy them* together: (marg. *break*)

KAL.—*Participle.* Poel.

Ps.123: 4. the contempt of *the proud.*
Jer. 25:38. the fierceness of *the oppressor,*
46:16. the *oppressing* sword.
50:16. for fear of the *oppressing* sword
Zep. 3: 1. the *oppressing* city!

* HIPHIL.—*Preterite.* *

Eze.18:12. *Hath oppressed* the poor and needy,
16. Neither *hath oppressed* any,
22: 7. in thee *have they vexed* the fatherless
29. *have vexed* the poor and needy:

HIPHIL.—*Infinitive.*

Eze.46:18. the people's inheritance *by oppression, to thrust them out*

HIPHIL.—*Future.*

Ex. 22:21(20). *Thou shalt* neither *vex* a stranger,
Lev.19:33. *ye shall* not *vex* him. (marg. or, *oppress*)
25:14. *ye shall* not *oppress* one another:
17. *Ye shall* not therefore *oppress* one another;
Deu 23:16(17). *thou shalt* not *oppress him.*
Jer. 22: 3. and *do no wrong,* do no violence
Eze.18: 7. *hath* not *oppressed* any,
45: 8. my princes *shall* no more *oppress*

HIPHIL.—*Participle.*

Isa. 49:26. I will feed them *that oppress thee*

יָנַח [*yāh-nagh'*]. 3240

* HIPHIL.—*Preterite.* *

Lev.16:23. *and shall leave them* there:
Nu. 17: 4(19). *And thou shalt lay them up* in the
19: 9. *and lay* (them) *up* without the camp
Deu 14:28. *and shalt lay* (it) *up* within thy gates:
26: 4. *and set it down* before the altar of the Lord
10. *And thou shalt set it* before the Lord
Jos. 4: 3. *and leave* them in the lodging place,
Jud. 3: 1. the nations which the Lord *left,*
6:18. *and set* (it) before thee.
1Sa. 6:18. whereon *they set down* the ark of the Lord:
2Sa.16:21. which *he hath left* to keep the house;
20: 3. whom *he had left* to keep the house,
1K. 8: 9. which Moses *put* there at Horeb,
1Ch 16:21. *He suffered* no man to do them wrong:
Ps. 17:14. *and leave* the rest of their (substance)
105:14. *He suffered* no man to do them wrong:
Isa. 14: 1. *and set them* in their own land:
28: 2. *shall cast down* to the earth
65:15. *And ye shall leave* your name for a curse
Jer. 27:11. *those will I let remain* still in their own
43: 6. the captain of the guard *had left*
Eze.16:39. *and leave thee* naked and bare.
22:20. *and I will leave* (you there),
37:14. *and I shall place* you in your own land:
44:19. *and lay* them in the holy chambers,
Am. 5: 7. *leave off* righteousness in the earth,

HIPHIL.—*Infinitive.*

Nu. 32:15. he will yet again *leave them*
Est. 3: 8. it (is) not for the king's profit *to suffer them*

HIPHIL.—*Imperative.*

Gen 42:33. *leave* one of your brethren (here)
Ex. 16:23. that which remaineth over *lay up*

Ex. 16:33. *and lay* it *up* before the Lord,
32:10. Now therefore *let* me *alone*,
Jud. 6:20. *and lay* (them) upon this rock,
16:26. *Suffer* me that I may feel the pillars
2Sa. 16:11. *let* him *alone*, and let him curse;
1K. 13:31. *lay* my bones beside his bones:
2K. 23:18. And he said, *Let* him *alone;*
Hos 4:17. *let* him *alone*.

HIPHIL.—*Future*.

Gen 2:15. *and put him* into the garden of
19:16. *and set him* without the city.
39:16. *And she laid up* his garment by her,
Ex. 16:24. *And they laid it up* till the morning,
34. *so* Aaron *laid it up*
Lev. 7:15. *he shall* not *leave* any of it
24:12. *And they put him* in ward,
Nu. 15:34. *And they put* him in ward,
17: 7(22). *And* Moses *laid up* the rods
Jos. 4: 8. *and laid them down* there.
6:23. *and left them* without the camp
Jud. 2:23. *Therefore* the Lord *left* those nations,
1Sa. 10:25. *and laid* (it) *up* before the Lord.
1K. 7:47. *And* Solomon *left* all the vessels
13:29. *and laid it* upon the ass,
30. *And he laid* his carcase in his own grave;
19: 3. *and left* his servant there.
2K. 17:29. *and put* (them) in the houses
2Ch 1:14. *which he placed* in the chariot cities,
4: 8. *and placed* (them) in the temple,
9:25. *whom he bestowed* in the chariot cities,
Ps. 119:121. *leave me* not to mine oppressors.
Ecc. 2:18. *because I should leave it* unto the man
7:18. *withdraw* not thine hand:
10: 4. *leave* not thy place; for yielding *pacifieth*
11: 6. in the evening *withhold* not thine hand:
Isa. 46: 7. *and set him* in his place,
Jer. 14: 9. we are called by thy name; *leave us* not.
Eze. 40:42. *also they laid* the instruments
42:13. there *shall they lay* the most holy things,
14. there *they shall lay* their garments

HIPHIL.—*Participle*.

Ecc. 5:12(11). abundance of the rich *will* not *suffer*

* HOPHAL.—*Preterite*. *

Zec. 5:11. *and set* there upon her own base.

HOPHAL.—*Participle*.

Eze. 41: 9. (that) which (was) *left*
11. *toward* (the place that was) *left*,
— the place *that was left*

3242 **יְנִיקוֹת** [*y'nee-kōhth'*], f. pl.

Eze. 17: 4. the top of *his young twigs*,

3243 **יָנַק** [*yāh-nak'*].

* KAL.—*Preterite*. *

Isa. 60:16. *Thou shalt also suck* the milk
66:12. *then shall ye suck*,

KAL.—*Future*.

Deu 33:19. *they shall suck* (of) the abundance of the
Job 3:12. the breasts that *I should suck?*
20:16. *He shall suck* the poison of asps:
Isa. 60:16. and *shalt suck* the breast of kings:
66:11. That *ye may suck*, and be satisfied

KAL.—*Participle*. Poel.

Nu. 11:12. a nursing father beareth *the sucking child*,
Deu 32:25. the virgin, *the suckling* (also) with the man
1Sa. 15: 3. infant and *suckling*,
22:19. children and *sucklings*,
Ps. 8: 2(3). Out of the mouth of babes *and sucklings*
Cant. 8: 1. *that sucked* the breasts
Isa. 11: 8. *the sucking child* shall play
Jer. 44: 7. child *and suckling*,
Lam. 2:11. the children *and the sucklings*
4: 4. The tongue of *the sucking child*
Joel 2:16. *and those that suck* the breasts:

* HIPHIL.—*Preterite*. *

Gen 21: 7. that Sarah *should have given* children *suck?*
Lam. 4: 3. *they give suck* to their young ones:

HIPHIL.—*Infinitive*.

1K. 3:21. *to give* my child *suck*,

HIPHIL.—*Imperative*.

Ex. 2: 9. Take this child away, *and nurse it* for me,

HIPHIL.—*Future*.

Ex. 2: 7. *that she may nurse* the child
Deu 32:13. *and he made him to suck* honey
1Sa. 1:23. *and gave* her son *suck*

HIPHIL.—*Participle*.

Gen 24:59. they sent away Rebekah their sister, and *her nurse*,
32:15(16). Thirty *milch* camels
35: 8. Deborah Rebekah's *nurse* died,
Ex. 2: 7. Shall I go and call to thee *a nurse*
2K. 11: 2. him and *his nurse*,
2Ch 22:11. put him and *his nurse* in a bedchamber.
Isa. 49:23. their queens *thy nursing mothers:*

יַנְשׁוּף *yan-shooph'* & **יַנְשֹׁוף** *yan-shōhph'*, m. 3244

Lev. 11:17. the cormorant, and *the great owl*,
Deu 14:16. *the great owl*, and the swan,
Isa. 34:11. *the owl also* and the raven

יָסַד *yāh-sad'*. 3245

* KAL.—*Preterite*. *

Ps. 24: 2. he *hath founded it* upon the seas,
78:69. the earth *which he hath established* for ever. (marg. *founded*)
89:11(12). *thou hast founded them*.
102:25(26). Of old *hast thou laid the foundation*
104: 5. (Who) *laid* the foundations of the earth (marg. *He hath founded* the earth upon her bases)
8. the place which *thou hast founded*
119:152. *thou hast founded them* for ever.
Pro. 3:19. Lord by wisdom *hath founded* the earth;
Isa. 23:13. the Assyrian *founded it* for them
48:13. Mine hand also *hath laid the foundation*
54:11. *and lay thy foundations* with sapphires.
Am. 9: 6. *hath founded* his troop in the earth;
Hab. 1:12. *thou hast established them* for correction. (marg. *founded*)

KAL.—*Infinitive*.

2Ch 31: 7. they began *to lay the foundation*
Ezr. 3:12. *when the foundation* of this house *was laid*
Job 38: 4. Where wast thou *when I laid the foundations*
Isa. 51:16. *and lay the foundations* of the earth,

KAL.—*Participle*.

Isa. 51:13. *and laid the foundations* of the earth;
Zec. 12: 1. *and layeth the foundation* of the earth,

* NIPHAL.—*Preterite*. *

Ps. 2: 2. the rulers *take counsel* together,

NIPHAL.—*Infinitive*.

Ex. 9:18. since *the foundation thereof* even until now.
Ps. 31:13(14). *while they took counsel* together

NIPHAL.—*Future*.

Isa. 44:28. *Thy foundation shall be laid*.

* PIEL.—*Preterite*. *

1K. 16:34. *he laid the foundation thereof*
1Ch 9:22. Samuel the seer *did ordain* (marg. *founded*)
Ezr. 3:10. *when* the builders *laid the foundation*
Est. 1: 8. so the king *had appointed*
Ps. 8: 2(3). Out of the mouth of babes...*hast* thou *ordained* strength (marg. *founded*)
Isa. 14:32. the Lord *hath founded* Zion,
28:16. *I lay* in Zion *for a foundation*
Zec. 4: 9. *have laid the foundation* of this house;

PIEL.—*Infinitive*.

1K. 5:17(31). *to lay the foundation* of the house.

PIEL.—*Future*.

Jos. 6:26. *he shall lay the foundation thereof*

* PUAL.—*Preterite.* *

1K. 6:37. In the fourth year *was the foundation...laid,*
Ezr. 3: 6. *the foundation* of the temple of the Lord *was* not (yet) *laid.*
Hag. 2:18. the day that *the foundation* of the Lord's temple *was laid,*
Zec. 8: 9. the day (that) *the foundation...was laid,*

PUAL.—*Participle.*

1K. 7:10. *And the foundation* (was of) costly stones,
Cant. 5:15. *set* upon sockets of fine gold:

* HOPHAL.—*Preterite.* *

2Ch 3: 3. Solomon *was instructed* (marg. *founded*)
Ezr. 3:11. *the foundation* of the house of the Lord *was laid.*

HOPHAL.—*Participle.*

Isa. 28:16. a *sure* foundation: (lit. a *founded* foundation)

3246 **יְסֻד** *y'sood,* m.

Ezr. 7: 9. the first month *began* he to go up (marg. (was) *the foundation of* the going up)

3247 **יְסוֹד** *y'sōhd,* m.

Ex. 29:12. beside *the bottom of* the altar.
Lev. 4: 7. shall pour all the blood...at *the bottom of*
18. the blood at *the bottom of* the altar
25. pour out his blood at *the bottom of* the altar
30, 34. pour out all the blood thereof at *the bottom of* the altar.
5: 9. blood shall be wrung out at *the bottom of*
8:15 & 9:9. the blood at *the bottom of* the altar,
2Ch 23: 5. the gate of *the foundation:*
24:27. *and the repairing of* the house
Job 4:19. whose *foundation* (is) in the dust,
22:16. *whose foundation* was overflown
Ps. 137: 7. to *the foundation* thereof.
Pro. 10:25. righteous (is) *an* everlasting *foundation.*
Lam. 4:11. it hath devoured *the foundations thereof.*
Eze. 13:14. *the foundation thereof* shall be discovered,
30: 4. *her foundations* shall be broken down.
Mic. 1: 6. *and* I will discover *the foundations thereof.*
Hab. 3:13. discovering *the foundation*

3248 **יְסוּדָה** [*y'soo-dāh'*], f.

Ps. 87: 1. *His foundation* (is) in the holy mountains.

3249 **יָסוּר** [*yāh-soor'*], m.

Jer 17:13. (כתיב) *they that depart from me*

3250 **יִסּוֹר** *yis-sōhr',* m.

Job 40: 2. Shall he...*instruct* (him)? (or, lit. (be) a *reprover*)

3251 **יָסַךְ** [*yāh-sach'*].

* KAL.—*Future.* *

Ex. 30:32. Upon man's flesh *shall it* not *be poured,*

3254 **יָסַף** *yāh-saph'.*

* KAL.—*Preterite.* *

Gen 8:12. return*ed* not *again* (lit. *added* not to return)
38:26. he knew her *again* (lit. *he added* to know her) no more.
Lev. 22:14. *then he shall put* the fifth (part)
26:18. *then I will* punish you seven times *more* (lit. *and I will add* to punish)
21. *I will bring* seven times *more* (lit. *and I will add*) plagues
Lev. 27:13. *then he shall add* a fifth (part)
15, 19. *then he shall add* the fifth (part)
27. *and shall add* a fifth (part)
Nu. 11:25. they prophesied, and *did* not *cease.* (lit. and *added* not)
32:15. *he will* yet *again* leave (lit. *and he will add* to leave)
Deu 5:22(19). *he added* no *more.*
19: 9. *then shalt thou add* three cities
20: 8. *And* the officers *shall* speak *further* (lit. *shall add* to speak)
Jud. 8:28. *they* lifted up their heads no *more.* (lit. *they added* not to lift up)
13:21. the angel of the Lord *did* no *more* appear (lit. *added* not to appear)
1Sa. 7:13. *they* came no more (lit. *they added* not yet to come)
12:19. *we have added* unto all our sins
15:35. Samuel *came* no *more* to see (lit. *added* not to see) Saul
27: 4. *he* sought no *more* (lit. *he added* not to seek)
2Sa. 2:28. neither fought *they* any *more.* (lit. *added they* yet to fight)
2K. 6:23. the bands of Syria came no more (lit. *added* not yet to come)
19:30. *And* the remnant...*shall yet again* take
2Ch. 9: 6. *thou exceedest* the fame that I heard
Isa. 26:15. *Thou hast increased* the nation, O Lord, *thou hast increased* the nation:
29:19. The meek *also shall increase* (marg. *add*)
37:31. *And* the remnant...*shall again* take root
Jer. 45: 3. the Lord *hath added* grief

KAL.—*Participle.* Poel.

Deu 5:25(22). if we hear the voice of the Lord our God *any more,* (marg. *add* to hear)
Isa. 29:14. I *will proceed* to do a marvellous work
38: 5. I *will add* unto thy days fifteen years.

* NIPHAL.—*Preterite.* *

Ex. 1:10. *they join* also unto our enemies,
Nu. 36: 3. *and shall be put* to the inheritance
4. *then shall* their inheritance *be put*
Jer. 36:32. *there were added* besides unto them

NIPHAL.—*Participle.*

Pro. 11:24. There is that scattereth, *and* yet *increaseth;*
Isa. 15: 9. I will bring *more* (marg. *additions*) upon

* HIPHIL.—*Preterite.* *

1K. 10: 7. thy wisdom and prosperity *exceedeth* (lit. *thou hast added* wisdom and prosperity)
2K. 20: 6. *And I will add* unto thy days
24: 7. the king of Egypt came not *again* (lit. *added* not to come)
Ps. 71:14. *and will yet* praise thee *more and more.* (lit. *I will add* unto all thy praise)
Ecc. 1:16. *and have gotten more* wisdom
2: 9. So I was great, *and increased* more

HIPHIL.—*Infinitive.*

Lev. 19:25. *that it may yield* unto you the increase
2Ch 28:13. ye intend *to add* (more) to our sins
Ezr. 10:10. *to increase* the trespass of Israel.
Ecc. 3:14. nothing *can be put to it,*

HIPHIL.—*Future.*

Gen 4: 2. *And she again* bare (lit. *and she added* to bear)
12. *it shall* not *henceforth* yield (lit. *it shall* not *add* to give)
8:10. *and again he* sent (lit. *and he added* to send) forth the dove
21. *I will* not *again* curse the ground any more — neither *will I again* smite any more
18:29. *And he* spake unto him yet *again,* (lit. *and added* to speak)
25: 1. *Then again* Abraham took (lit. *added* to take)
30:24. The Lord *shall add* to me another son.
37: 5, 8. *and they* hated him yet *the more.* (lit. *and they added* to hate)
38: 5. *And she* yet *again conceived,* and bare (lit. *and she added* yet and bare)
44:23. *ye shall* see my face no *more.* (lit. *ye shall* not *add* to see)
Ex. 5: 7. *Ye shall* no *more* give (lit. *ye shall* not *add* to give) the people straw

Ex. 8:29(25). *let* not Pharaoh deal deceitfully *any more* (lit. *let...add* to deal)
9:28. *ye shall* stay no *longer.* (lit. *ye shall* not *add* to stay)
34. *And* when...*he* sinned *yet more,* (lit. *he added* to sin)
10:28. see my face no *more;* (lit. *add* not to see)
29. *I will* see thy face *again* no more. (lit. *I will* not *add* to)
11: 6. nor *shall be* like it *any more.*
14:13. *ye shall* see them *again* (lit. *ye shall add* to see) no more
Lev. 5:16. *shall add* the fifth part thereto,
6: 5(5:24). *shall add* the fifth part
27:31. *he shall add* thereto the fifth (part)
Nu. 5: 7. *add* unto it the fifth (part)
22:15. *And* Balak sent yet *again* princes, (lit. *added* to send)
19. the Lord *will* say unto me *more.* (lit. *will add* to say)
25. *and he* smote her *again.* (lit. *and added* to smite)
26. *And* the angel of the Lord went *further,* (lit. *added* to pass on)
Deu 1:11. *make* you a thousand times so many *more*
3:26. speak no *more* (lit. *add* not to speak)
4: 2. *Ye shall* not *add* unto the word
12:32(13:1). *thou shalt* not *add* thereto,
13:11(12). *shall* do no *more* any such wickedness (lit. *they shall* not *add* to do)
17:16. *Ye shall* henceforth return no *more* (lit. *Ye shall* not *add* to return)
18:16. *Let me* not hear *again* (lit. *let me* not *add* to hear)
19:20. *shall* henceforth commit no *more* any such
25: 3. Forty stripes he may give him, (and) not *exceed:* lest, (if) *he should exceed,*
28:68. *Thou shalt* see it no *more* again;
Jos. 7:12. neither *will I* be with you *any more,*
23:13. *will* no *more* drive (lit. *will* not *add* to drive)
Jud. 2:21. I also *will* not *henceforth* drive out (lit. *will* not *add* to drive out)
3:12. *And* the children of Israel did evil *again* (lit. *added* to do evil)
4: 1. *And* the children of Israel *again* did evil (lit. *added* to do evil)
9:37. *And* Gaal spake *again* (lit. *and added* to speak) and said,
10: 6. *And* the children of Israel did evil *again* (lit. *added* to do evil)
13. *I will* deliver you no *more.* (lit. *I will* not *add* to deliver you)
11:14. *And* Jephthah sent messengers *again*
13: 1. *And* the children of Israel did evil *again* (lit. *added* to do evil)
20:22. *and* set their battle *again* in array
23. *Shall I* go up *again* to battle
28. *Shall I* yet *again* go out to battle
Ru. 1:17. the Lord do so to me, and *more* also, (lit. so *may he add*)
1Sa. 3: 6. *And* the Lord called yet *again,*
8. *And* the Lord called Samuel *again*
17. God do so to thee, and *more* also, (marg. and so *add*)
21. *And* the Lord appeared *again* in Shiloh:
9: 8. *And* the servant answered Saul *again,* (lit. *added* to answer)
14:44. do so and *more* also: (lit. so *may he add*)
18:29. *And* Saul *was yet the more* afraid (lit. *And ...added* to fear)
19: 8. *And there* was war *again:* (lit. *And* war *added* to be)
21. *And* Saul sent messengers *again*
20:13. do so and *much more* (lit. so *may he add*)
17. *And* Jonathan caused David to swear *again,* (lit. *and added* to cause)
23: 4. *Then* David enquired of the Lord yet *again.* (lit. *and added* yet to enquire)
25:22. So and *more* also (lit. so *may he add*)
27: 4. (כתיב) *he* sought no more *again* (lit. *added* no more to seek)
2Sa. 2:22. *And* Abner said *again* (lit. *and added* to say) to Asahel,
3: 9. So do God to Abner, and *more* also, (lit. and so *may he add*)
34. *And* all the people wept *again* (lit. *and added* to weep) over him.

2Sa. 3:35. So do God to me, and *more* also, (lit. and so *may he add*)
5:22. *And* the Philistines came up yet *again,* (lit. *and added* to come)
6: 1. Again, David *gathered together* [see also אָסַף.]
7:10. neither *shall* the children of wickedness afflict them *any more,* (lit. *shall* not *add* to afflict)
20. *can* David say *more* (lit. *shall add* to say)
12: 8. *I would moreover have given* unto thee
14:10. *he shall* not touch thee *any more.* (lit. *he shall* not *add* to touch)
18:22. *Then* said Ahimaaz...yet *again* (lit. *and added* to say)
19:13(14). God do so to me, and *more* also, (lit. and so *may he add*)
24: 1. *And again* the anger of the Lord *was* kindled (lit. *And* the anger...*added* to be kindled)
3. *Now* the Lord thy God *add* unto the
1K. 2:23. God do so to me, and *more* also, (lit. and so *may he add*)
12:11, 14. *I will add* to your yoke:
16:33. *and* Ahab did *more* to provoke the Lord
19: 2. So let the gods do (to me), and *more* also, (lit. and so *may they add*)
20:10. The gods do so unto me, and *more* also, (lit. so *may they add*)
2K. 6:31. God do so and *more* also (lit. and so *may he add*) to me,
21: 8. Neither *will I* make the feet of Israel move *any more*
1Ch 14:13. *And* the Philistines yet *again* spread (lit. *and they added* yet to spread) themselves
17: 9. neither *shall* the children of wickedness waste them *any more,* (lit. *they shall* not *add* to waste)
18. *can* David (speak) *more* (lit. *can add*)
21: 3. The Lord *make* his people an hundred times so many *more*
22:14. *thou mayest add* thereto.
2Ch 10:11. *I will put more* to your yoke:
14. *I will add* thereto:
28:22. in the time of his distress *did he* trespass *yet more*
33: 8. Neither *will I any more* remove the foot
Est. 8: 3. *And* Esther spake yet *again* (lit. Esther *added* and spake) before the king,
Job 17: 9. he that hath clean hands *shall be* stronger and stronger. (lit. *shall add* strength)
20: 9. The eye also (which) saw him *shall* (see him) no *more;*
27: 1 & 29:1. *Moreover* Job *continued* (marg. *added* to take up) his parable,
34:32. if I have done iniquity, *I will do* no *more.*
37. *he addeth* rebellion unto his sin,
36: 1. Elihu *also proceeded,* and said,
38:11. Hitherto shalt thou come, but no *further:* (lit. *but shalt* not *add*)
40: 5. *I will proceed* no *further.*
41: 8(40:32). remember the battle, *do* no *more.*
42:10. *also* the Lord *gave* (marg. *added*) Job twice
Ps. 10:18. that the man of the earth *may* no *more* oppress. (lit. *may* not *add* to oppress)
41: 8(9). *he shall* rise up no *more.* (lit. *he shall* not *add* to rise up)
61: 6(7). *Thou wilt prolong* (marg. *Thou shalt add* days to) the king's life:
77:7(8). *will he* be favourable no *more?* (lit. *will he* not *add* to be favourable)
78:17. *And they* sinned yet *more* against him
115:14. The Lord *shall increase* you *more and more,*
120: 3. what *shall be done* unto thee, (marg. *added*)
Pro. 1: 5. A wise (man) will hear, *and will increase*
3: 2. peace, *shall they add* to thee.
9: 9. *and he will increase* in learning.
11. *and* the years of thy life *shall be increased.*
10:22. *he addeth* no sorrow with it.
27. The fear of the Lord *prolongeth* days:
16:21. sweetness of the lips *increaseth* learning.
23. *addeth* learning to his lips.
19: 4. Wealth *maketh* many friends;
19. yet thou must *do it again.* (marg. *add*)
23:28. *increaseth* the transgressors among men.
35. *I will* seek it *yet* again.

Pro.30: 6. *Add thou* not unto his words,
Ecc. 1:18. *and he that increaseth* knowledge *increaseth*
Isa. 1: 5. *ye will* revolt *more and more:* (marg. *increase* revolt)
13. *Bring* no *more* (lit. *add* not to bring) vain
7:10. *Moreover* the Lord spake *again* (lit. *added* to speak) unto Ahaz,
8: 5. The Lord spake *also* unto me *again*, (lit. *and added* to speak)
10:20. *shall* no *more* again stay upon him (lit. *he shall* not *add* to stay)
11:11. the Lord *shall* set his hand *again*
23:12. *Thou shalt* no *more* (lit. *thou shalt* not *add*)
24:20. it shall fall, and not rise *again*. (lit. *shall* not *add* to rise)
47: 1, 5. *thou shalt* no *more* be (lit. *thou shalt* not *add* to be) called
51:22. *thou shalt* no *more* drink (lit. *thou shalt* not *add* to drink) it again:
52: 1. henceforth *there shall* no *more* come (lit. *shall* not *add* to come) into thee
Jer. 31:12. *they shall* not sorrow *any more* (lit. *they shall* not *add* to sorrow)
Lam. 4:15. *They shall* no *more* sojourn (lit. *they shall* not *add* to sojourn)
16. *he will* no *more* regard (lit. *he will* not *add* to regard) them:
22. *he will* no *more* carry (lit. *he will* not *add* to carry) thee away
Eze. 5:16. *I will increase* the famine upon you,
23:14. *And* (that) *she increased* her whoredoms:
36:12. *thou shalt* no *more* henceforth bereave (lit. *thou shalt* not *add* to bereave) them
Dan10:18. *Then there came again* and touched me
Hos. 1: 6. *I will* no *more* (marg. *I will* not *add*) have mercy upon the house of Israel;
9:15. *I will* love them no *more:*
13: 2. *they* sin *more and more*, (lit. *they add* to sin)
Joel 2: 2. neither *shall* be *any more* after it,
Am. 5: 2. *she shall* no *more* rise: (lit. *she shall* not *add* to rise)
7: 8. *I will* not *again* pass by them any more:
13. prophesy not *again* (lit. *add* not to prophesy) any more at Beth-el:
8: 2. *I will* not *again* pass by them any more.
Jon. 2: 4(5). *I will* look *again* toward thy holy
Nah. 1:15(2:1). the wicked *shall* no *more* pass (lit. *shall* not *add* to pass) through thee;
Zep. 3:11. *thou shalt* no *more* be haughty (lit. *thou shalt* not *add* to be haughty)

HIPHIL.—*Participle.*

Neh 13:18. ye *bring more* wrath upon Israel

3255 יְסַף [*y'saph*], Ch.

* HOPHAL.—*Preterite.* *

Dan 4:36(33). excellent majesty *was added* unto me.

3256 יָסַר [*yāh-sar'*].

* KAL.—*Future.* *

Hos.10:10. in my desire *that I should chastise them;*

KAL.—*Participle.* Poel.

Ps. 94:10. *He that chastiseth* the heathen,
Pro. 9: 7. *He that reproveth* a scorner

* NIPHAL.—*Imperative.* *

Ps. 2:10. *be instructed*, ye judges of the earth.
Jer. 6: 8. *Be thou instructed*, O Jerusalem,

NIPHAL.—*Future.*

Lev.26:23. if *ye will* not *be reformed*
Pro.29:19. A servant *will* not *be corrected* by words:
Jer. 31:18. *and I was chastised*, as a bullock

* NITHPAEL.—*Preterite.* *

Eze.23:48. *that* all women *may be taught*

* PIEL.—*Preterite.* *

Lev.26:28. *and I*, even I, *will chastise* you seven times
Deu 21:18. *when they have chastened* him,
22:18. take that man *and chastise* him;
1K. 12:11. my father *hath chastised* you with whips,
14. my father (also) *chastised* you with whips,
2Ch 10:11, 14. my father *chastised* you with whips,
Job 4: 3. *thou hast instructed* many,
Ps. 16: 7. my reins also *instruct me*
39:11(12). When *thou* with rebukes *dost correct*
118:18. The Lord *hath chastened me* sore:
Pro.31: 1. the prophecy that his mother *taught him.*
Isa. 8:11. *and instructed me* that I should not
28:26. *For* his God *doth instruct him*
Jer. 30:11. *but I will correct thee* in measure,
31:18. *Thou hast chastised me*,
46:28. *but correct thee* in measure;
Hos. 7:15. *I have bound* (marg. *chastened*) (and) strengthened their arms,

PIEL.—*Infinitive.*

Lev.26:18. I will *punish* you seven times more (lit. I will add *to punish*)
Deu 4:36. *that he might instruct thee:*
Ps.118:18. The Lord hath chastened me *sore:* (lit. *in chastening* hath chastened)

PIEL.—*Imperative.*

Pro.19:18. *Chasten* thy son while there is hope,
29:17. *Correct* thy son, and he shall give thee rest;
Jer. 10:24. O Lord, *correct me*, but with judgment;

PIEL.—*Future.*

Deu 8: 5. a man *chasteneth* his son,
1K. 12:11, 14. *I will chastise* you with scorpions.
Ps. 6: 1(2). *chasten me* in thy hot displeasure.
38: 1(2). *chasten me* in thy hot displeasure.
94:12. Blessed (is) the man *whom thou chastenest*,
Jer. 2:19. Thine own wickedness *shall correct thee*,

PIEL.—*Participle.*

Deu 8: 5. the Lord thy God *chasteneth thee.*

* HIPHIL.—*Future.* *

Hos. 7:12. *I will chastise them*, as their congregation

יָע see יָעִים 3257

יָעַד [*yāh-gad'*]. 3259

* KAL.—*Preterite.* *

Ex. 21: 8. who *hath betrothed her* to himself,
2Sa.20: 5. the set time which *he had appointed him.*
Jer. 47: 7. there *hath he appointed it.*
Mic. 6: 9. who *hath appointed it.*

KAL.—*Future.*

Ex. 21: 9. if *he have betrothed* her unto his son,

* NIPHAL.—*Preterite.* *

Ex. 25:22. *And* there *I will meet* with thee,
29:43. *And* there *I will meet* with the children of
Nu. 10: 3. the assembly *shall assemble themselves*
4. *then* the princes,...*shall gather themselves*
Ps. 48: 4(5). the kings *were assembled*,
Am. 3: 3. two walk together, except *they be agreed?*

NIPHAL.—*Future.*

Ex. 29:42. where *I will meet* you,
30: 6, 36. where *I will meet* with thee.
Nu. 17: 4(19). where *I will meet* with you.
Jos. 11: 5. *And when* all these kings *were met together*,
Neh 6: 2. *let us meet* together in (some one of) the villages
10. *Let us meet together* in the house of God,
Job 2:11. *for they had made an appointment* together

NIPHAL.—*Participle.*

Nu. 14:35. *that are gathered together* against me:
16:11. thy company (are) *gathered together*
27: 3. *them that gathered themselves together*
1K. 8: 5. *that were assembled* unto him,
2Ch 5: 6. *that were assembled* unto him

* HIPHIL.—*Future.* *

Job 9:19. who *shall set me a time* (to plead)?
Jer. 49:19. who *will appoint me the time?* (marg. or, *convent me in judgment*)
50:44. who *will appoint me the time?* (marg. or, *convent me to plead*)

* HOPHAL.—*Participle.* *

Jer. 24: 1. two baskets of figs (were) *set* before the
Eze.21:16(21). whithersoever thy face (is) *set.*

3261 **יָעָה** *yāh-gāh'.*

* KAL.—*Preterite.* *

Isa. 28:17. *and* the hail *shall sweep away* the refuge

3264 **יְעוֹרִים** *y'gōh-reem'*, m. pl.

Eze.34:25. (כתיב) and sleep *in the woods.*

3267 **יָעַז** [*yāh-gaz'*].

* NIPHAL.—*Participle.* *

Isa. 33:19. Thou shalt not see a *fierce* people,

3271 **יָעַט** [*yāh-gat'*].

* KAL.—*Preterite.* *

Isa. 61:10. *he hath covered me* with the robe of

3272 **יְעַט** [*y'gat*], Ch.

* P'AL.—*Participle.* *

Ezr. 7:14. and of *his* seven *counsellors,*
15. which the king *and his counsellors*

* ITHPAEL.—*Preterite.* *

Dan 6: 7(8). *have consulted together* to establish

3257 **יָעִים** *yāh-geem'*, m. pl.

Ex. 27: 3. *and his shovels,* and his basons,
38: 3. the pots, and *the shovels,*
Nu. 4:14. the fleshhooks, and *the shovels,*
1K. 7:40. *the shovels,* and the basons.
45. the pots, and *the shovels,*
2K. 25:14. the pots, and *the shovels,*
2Ch 4:11. Huram made the pots, and *the shovels,*
16. The pots also, and *the shovels,*
Jer. 52:18. The caldrons also, and *the shovels,* (marg. or, *instruments to remove the ashes*)

3276 **יָעַל** [*yāh-gal'*].

* HIPHIL.—*Preterite.* *

Hab 2:18. What *profiteth* the graven image

HIPHIL.—*Infinitive.*

Isa. 30: 5. nor be an help nor *profit,*
44:10. (that) *is profitable* for nothing?
47:12. if so be thou shalt be able *to profit,*
48:17. thy God which teacheth thee *to profit,*
Jer. 7: 8. trust in lying words, that cannot *profit.*
23:32. *therefore* they shall not profit this people *at all,* (lit. *therefore in profiting* they shall not profit)

HIPHIL.—*Future.*

1Sa.12:21. vain (things), which *cannot profit* nor
Job 15: 3. speeches wherewith *he can do* no *good?*
21:15. what *profit should we have,* if we pray
30:13. *they set forward* my calamity,
35: 3. What *profit shall I have,* (if I be cleansed) from my sin?
Pro.10: 2. Treasures of wickedness *profit* nothing:
11: 4. Riches *profit* not in the day of wrath:
Isa. 30: 5. a people (that) *could* not *profit* them,
6. a people (that) *shall* not *profit* (them).
44: 9. their delectable things *shall* not *profit;*
57:12. *they shall* not *profit thee.*
Jer. 2: 8. (things that) *do* not *profit.*
11. (that which) *doth* not *profit.*
12:13. *shall* not *profit:*
23:32. *they shall* not *profit* this people at all,

HIPHIL.—*Participle.*

Jer. 16:19. (things) wherein (there is) no *profit.*

יַעֲלָה [*yah-gălāh'*], f. 3280

Pro. 5:19. the loving hind *and* pleasant *roe;*

יְעֵלִים *y'gēh-leem'*, m. pl. 3277

1Sa.24: 2(3). the rocks of *the wild goats.*
Job 39: 1. *the wild goats of* the rock
Ps.104:18. high hills (are) a refuge *for the wild goats;*

יַעַן *yah'-gan*, part. 3282

Lev.26:43. *because, even because* (וּבְיַעַן) they despised my judgments,
Nu. 11:20. *because* that ye have despised the Lord
Eze. 5: 9. *because of* all thine abominations.
21: 4(9). *Seeing then* that I will cut off from
25: 8. *Because that* Moab and Seir do say,
Am. 5:11. *Forasmuch* therefore as your treading (is) upon the poor,
&c. &c.

It is also combined with a following word in translation:—as,

I. With אֲשֶׁר

Gen22:16. for *because* thou hast done this thing,
1K. 8:18. *Whereas* it was in thine heart to build
14: 7. *Forasmuch as* I exalted thee from
Eze.12:12. he shall cover his face, *that* he see not
&c. &c.

II. With כִּי

1K. 13:21. *Forasmuch as* thou hast disobeyed
21:29. *because* he humbleth himself before me,
Isa. 3:16. *Because* the daughters of Zion are
8: 6. *Forasmuch as* this people refuseth
29:13. *Forasmuch as* this people draw near

III With מָה

Hag 1: 9. *Why?* saith the Lord of hosts.

יַעֲנָה *yah-gănāh'*, f. 3284

Lev.11:16. *the owl,* (lit. daughter of *the owl*)
Deu14:15. *the owl,* (lit. daughter of *the owl*)
Job 30:29. a companion to *owls.* (lit. daughters of the *owl;* marg. or, *ostriches*)
Isa. 13:21. *owls* (marg. daughters of *the owl*) shall
34:13. for *owls.* (marg. daughters of *the owl*)
43:20. dragons and *the owls:* (marg. daughters of *the owl*)
Jer 50:39. *the owls* (lit. daughters of *the owl*) shall
Mic. 1: 8. mourning as *the owls.* (marg. daughters of *the owl*)

יְעֵנִים *y'gēh-neem'*, m. pl. 3283

Lam. 4: 3. *like the ostriches* in the wilderness.

יָעַף [*yāh-gaph'*]. 3286

* KAL.—*Preterite.* *

Jer. 51:58. in the fire, *and they shall be weary.*
64. upon her: *and they shall be weary.*

KAL.—*Future.*

Isa. 40:28. Creator of the ends of the earth, *fainteth*
30. *Even* the youths *shall faint*
31. they shall walk, and not *faint.*
44:12. he drinketh no water, *and is faint.*
Jer. 2:24. that seek her *will* not *weary themselves;*
Hab 2:13. the people *shall weary themselves*

* HOPHAL.—*Participle.* *

Dan 9:21. *being caused to fly* swiftly,

יָעֵף *yāh-gēhph'*, adj. 3287

Jud. 8:15. bread unto thy men (that are) *weary?*
2Sa.16: 2. that *such as be faint* in the wilderness

Isa 40:29. He giveth power *to the faint;*
50: 4. word in season to (him that is) *weary:*

3288 **יְעָף** [*y'ghāhph*], m.

Dan 9:21. being caused to fly *swiftly*, (marg. *with weariness*, or, *flight*)

3289 **יָעַץ** *yāh-ghatz'.*

*** KAL.—*Preterite.* ***

2Sa. 16:23. *he counselled* in those days,
17: 7. The counsel that Ahithophel *hath given* (lit. *counselled*)
11. *I counsel* that all Israel be generally
15. Thus and thus *did* Ahithophel *counsel* — thus and thus *have I counselled.*
21. thus *hath* Ahithophel *counselled* against
1K. 12: 8. which *they had given him,* (lit. *counselled*)
13. the old men's counsel that *they gave him;*
2Ch 10: 8. the counsel which the old men *gave him,*
25:16. know that God *hath determined* to destroy thee, (marg. *counselled*)
Job 26: 3. How *hast thou counselled* (him)
Ps. 16: 7. bless the Lord, who *hath given me counsel:*
62: 4(5). *They* only *consult* to cast (him) down
Isa. 7: 5. *have taken* evil *counsel* against thee,
14:24. as *I have purposed,* (so) shall it stand:
27. the Lord of hosts *hath purposed,*
19:12. the Lord of hosts *hath purposed*
23: 8. Who *hath taken* this *counsel* against Tyre,
9. The Lord of hosts *hath purposed it,*
32: 7. *he deviseth* wicked devices
8. the liberal *deviseth* liberal things;
Jer. 49:20. *he hath taken* against Edom; (lit. *counselled*)
30. king of Babylon *hath taken counsel*
50:45. the counsel of the Lord, that *he hath taken*
Mic. 6: 5. what Balak...*consulted,*
Hab 2:10. *Thou hast consulted* shame

KAL.—*Future.*

Ex. 18:19. *I will give thee counsel,* and God shall be
Nu. 24:14. *I will advertise thee* what this people shall
1K. 1:12. *let me,* I pray thee, *give thee counsel,*
Ps. 32: 8. *I will guide* thee with mine eye.
Jer. 38:15. if *I give thee counsel,* wilt thou not hearken

KAL.—*Participle.* Poel.

2Sa. 15:12. Absalom sent for...David's *counsellor,*
1Ch 26:14. for Zechariah his son, *a* wise *counsellor,*
27:32. Jonathan David's uncle was *a counsellor,*
33. Ahithophel (was) the king's *counsellor:*
2Ch 22: 3. his mother was *his counsellor*
4. they were his *counsellors*
25:16. Art thou made of the king's *counsel?* (lit. *for counsellor* to the king)
Ezr. 4: 5. hired *counsellors* against them, to frustrate
7:28. before the king, *and his counsellors,*
8:25. which the king, *and his counsellors,*
Job 3:14. With kings *and counsellors of* the earth,
12:17. He leadeth *counsellors* away spoiled.
Pro. 11:14. in the multitude of *counsellors* (there is)
12:20. *but to the counsellors of* peace (is) joy.
15:22. in the multitude of *counsellors* they are
24: 6. in multitude of *counsellors* (there is)
Isa. 1:26. *and thy counsellors* as at the beginning:
3: 3. *and the counsellor,* and the cunning
9: 6(5). his name shall be called Wonderful, *Counsellor,*
19:11. *the* wise *counsellors of* Pharaoh
17. he *hath determined* against it.
41:28. (there was) no *counsellor,*
Eze. 11: 2. *and give* (lit. *and counsellors* of) wicked counsel in this city:
Mic. 4: 9. is *thy counsellor* perished?
Nah 1:11. *a* wicked *counsellor.*

KAL.—*Participle.* Paül.

Isa. 14:26. This (is) the purpose *that is purposed*

*** NIPHAL.—*Preterite.* ***

Ps. 71:10. they that lay wait for my soul *take counsel*
83: 5(6). *they have consulted* together with one
Isa. 40:14. With whom *took he counsel,*

NIPHAL.—*Future.*

1K. 12: 6. *And* king Rehoboam *consulted* with the
8. *and consulted* with the young men
28. *Whereupon* the king *took counsel,*
2K. 6: 8. *Then* the king of Syria...*took counsel* with
1Ch 13: 1. *And* David *consulted* with the captains
2Ch 10: 6. *And* king Rehoboam *took counsel* with the
8. *and took counsel* with the young men
20:21. *when he had consulted* with the people,
25:17. *Then* Amaziah king of Judah *took advice,*
30: 2. *For* the king *had taken counsel,*
23. *And* the whole assembly *took counsel*
32: 3. *He took counsel* with his princes
Neh 6: 7. *and let us take counsel* together.
Isa. 45:21. *let them take counsel* together:

NIPHAL.—*Participle.*

1K. 12: 6. How *do* ye *advise* that I may answer this
9. What *counsel give* ye
2Ch 10: 6. What *counsel give* ye (me)
9. What *advice give* ye
Pro. 13:10. with *the well advised* (is) wisdom.

*** HITHPAEL.—*Future.* ***

Ps. 83: 3(4). *and consulted* against thy hidden ones.

יַעַר *yah'-ghar*, m. 3293

Deu 19: 5. when a man goeth *into the wood*
Jos. 17:15. get thee up *to the wood* (country),
18. mountain shall be thine; for it (is) *a wood,*
1Sa. 14:25. (they of) the land came *to a wood;*
26. the people were come into *the wood,*
22: 5. *the forest of* Hareth.
2Sa. 18: 6. the battle was *in the wood of* Ephraim;
8. *the wood* devoured more people
17. cast him into a great pit *in the wood,*
1K. 7: 2. *the forest of* Lebanon;
10:17, 21. the house of *the forest of* Lebanon.
2K. 2:24. came forth two she bears out of *the wood,*
19:23. *the forest of* his Carmel.
1Ch 16:33. Then shall the trees of *the wood* sing
2Ch 9:16, 20. the house of *the forest of* Lebanon.
Ps. 50:10. every beast of *the forest* (is) mine,
80:13(14). The boar *out of the wood* doth waste it,
83:14(15). As the fire burneth *a wood,*
96:12. then shall all the trees of *the wood* rejoice
104:20. all the beasts of *the forest* do creep
132: 6. we found it in the fields of *the wood.*
Ecc. 2: 6. *the wood* that bringeth forth trees:
Cant. 2: 3. the trees of *the wood,*
5: 1. I have eaten *my* honey*comb*
Isa. 7: 2. the trees of *the wood* are moved
9:18(17). the thickets of *the forest,*
10:18. consume the glory of *his forest,*
19. the trees of *his forest* shall be few,
34. he shall cut down the thickets of *the forest*
21:13. *In the forest* in Arabia shall ye lodge,
22: 8. the armour of the house of *the forest.*
29:17. fruitful field shall be esteemed *as a forest?*
32:15. the fruitful field be counted *for a forest.*
19. coming down on *the forest;*
37:24. *the forest of* his Carmel.
44:14. the trees of *the forest:*
23. *O forest,* and every tree therein:
56: 9. all ye beasts *in the forest.*
Jer. 5: 6. a lion *out of the forest* shall slay them,
10: 3. (one) cutteth a tree *out of the forest,*
12: 8. a lion *in the forest;*
21:14. I will kindle a fire *in the forest thereof,*
26:18. the high places of *a forest.*
46:23. They shall cut down *her forest,*
Eze. 15: 2. the trees of *the forest?*
6. the trees of *the forest,*
20:46(21:2). prophesy against *the forest*
47(21:3). say *to the forest of* the south,
34:25. sleep *in the woods.*
39:10. neither cut down (any) out of *the forests*
Hos. 2:12(14). I will make them *a forest,*
Am. 3: 4. Will a lion roar *in the forest,*
Mic. 3:12. the high places of *the forest.*

Mic. 5: 8(7). the beasts of *the forest*,
7:14. dwell solitarily (in) *the wood*,
Zec.11: 2. *the forest of* the vintage is come down.

3295 **יַעְרָה** [*yah-găr-āh'*], f.

1Sa.14:27. dipped it *in an* honeycomb,
Ps. 29: 9. discovereth *the forests*:

3302 **יָפָה** [*yāh-phāh'*].

* KAL.—*Preterite.* *

Cant.4:10. How *fair is* thy love,
7: 1(2). How *beautiful are* thy feet
6(7). How *fair* and how pleasant art thou,

KAL.—*Future.*

Eze.16:13. *thou wast* exceeding *beautiful*,
31: 7. *Thus was he fair* in his greatness,

* PIEL.—*Future.* *

Jer. 10: 4. *They deck it* with silver and with gold;

* PUAL.—*Preterite.* *

Ps. 45: 2(3). *Thou art fairer* than the children of

* HITHPAEL.—*Future.* *

Jer. 4:30. in vain *shalt thou make thyself fair*;

3303 **יָפֶה** *yāh-pheh'*, adj.

Gen 12:11. I know that thou (art) a *fair* woman
14. she (was) very *fair*.
29:17. Rachel was *beautiful* (lit. *fair of* form) *and well* favoured. (lit. *and beautiful of* countenance)
39: 6. Joseph was (a) *goodly* (lit. *beautiful of* form) (person), and *well* favoured. (lit. *and beautiful of* countenance)
41: 2. *well* favoured (lit. *fair of* appearance) kine
4. the seven *well* favoured (lit. *fair of* appearance) and fat kine.
18. fatfleshed *and well* favoured; (lit. *fair of* appearance)
Deu21:11. a *beautiful* (lit. *fair of* form) woman,
1Sa.16:12. withal of a *beautiful* countenance, (marg. *fair of* eyes)
17:42. ruddy, and of a *fair* countenance.
25: 3. *and* of a *beautiful* countenance:
2Sa.13: 1. Absalom...had a *fair* sister,
14:25. there was none to be so much praised as Absalom for his *beauty*: (lit. there was not a *beautiful* man)
27. she was a woman of a *fair* countenance.
1K. 1: 3. they sought for a *fair* damsel
4. the damsel (was) very *fair*,
Est. 2: 7. the maid (was) *fair* (lit. *fair of* form) and
Job 42:15. *fair* as the daughters of Job:
Ps. 48: 2(3). *Beautiful for* situation,
Pro.11:22. a *fair* woman which is without discretion.
Ecc. 3:11. *beautiful* in his time:
5:18(17). (it is) good and *comely* (for one) to eat
Cant.1: 8. *O thou fairest* among women,
15. Behold, thou (art) *fair*, my love; behold, thou (art) *fair*;
16. Behold, thou (art) *fair*,
2:10. Rise up, my love, *my fair one*,
13. Arise, my love, *my fair one*,
4: 1. Behold, thou (art) *fair*, my love; behold, thou (art) *fair*;
7. Thou (art) all *fair*, my love;
5: 9 & 6:1. *O thou fairest* among women?
6: 4. Thou (art) *beautiful*, O my love,
10. *fair* as the moon, clear as the sun,
Jer.11:16. *fair*, (and) of goodly fruit:
Eze.31: 3. a cedar in Lebanon with *fair* branches,
9. I have made him *fair*
33:32. song of one that hath a *pleasant* voice,
Am. 8:13. In that day shall the *fair* virgins

יְפֵה־פִיָּה *y'phēh-pheey-yāh'*, adj. 3304

Jer. 46:20. Egypt (is like) a *very fair* heifer,

יָפַח [*yāh-phăgh'*]. 3306

* HITHPAEL.—*Future.* *

Jer. 4:31. daughter of Zion, (that) *bewaileth herself*,

יָפֵחַ [*yāh-phēh'ăgh*], adj. 3307

Ps. 27:12. *and such as breathe out* cruelty.

יְפִי *y'phee*, m. 3308

Eze.28: 7. *the beauty of* thy wisdom,

יֳפִי [*yŏphee*], m. 3308

Est. 1:11. shew the people and the princes *her beauty*:
Ps. 45:11(12). the king greatly desire *thy beauty*:
50: 2. the perfection of *beauty*,
Pro. 6:25. Lust not after *her beauty*
31:30. Favour (is) deceitful, and *beauty* (is) vain:
Isa. 3:24. burning instead of *beauty*.
33:17. Thine eyes shall see the king *in his beauty*:
Lam. 2:15. The perfection of *beauty*,
Eze.16:14. thy renown went forth...*for thy beauty*:
15. thou didst trust *in thine own beauty*,
25. hast made *thy beauty* to be abhorred,
27: 3. I (am) of perfect *beauty*.
4. thy builders have perfected *thy beauty*.
11. they have made *thy beauty* perfect.
28:12. full of wisdom, and perfect in *beauty*.
17. heart was lifted up *because of thy beauty*,
31: 8. like unto him *in his beauty*.
Zec. 9:17. how great (is) *his beauty*!

יָפַע [*yāh-phag'*]. 3313

* HIPHIL.—*Preterite.* *

Deu33: 2. *he shined forth* from mount Paran,
Job 10: 3. *and shine* upon the counsel of the wicked?
37:15. *and caused* the light of his cloud *to shine*?
Ps. 50: 2. Out of Zion,...God *hath shined*.

HIPHIL.—*Imperative.*

Ps. 80: 1(2). thou that dwellest (between) the cherubims, *shine forth*.
94: 1. O God,...*shew thyself*. (marg. *shine forth*)

HIPHIL.—*Future.*

Job 3: 4. neither *let* the light *shine* upon it.
10:22. *and* (where) *the light is* as darkness.

יִפְעָה [*yiph-gāh'*], f. 3314

Eze.28: 7. they shall defile *thy brightness*.
17. by reason of *thy brightness*:

יָצָא *yāh-tzāh'*. 3318

* KAL.—*Preterite.* *

Gen. 8:19. *went forth* out of the ark.
10:11. Out of that land *went forth* Asshur,
14. out of whom *came* Philistim,
19:23. The sun *was risen* upon the earth (marg. *gone forth*)
24: 5. the land from whence *thou camest*?
50. The thing *proceedeth* from the Lord:
25:26. after that *came* his brother *out*,
27:30. Jacob *was* yet scarce *gone out*
38:28. This *came out* first.
29. behold, his brother *came out*:
30. afterward *came out* his brother,
44: 4. when they *were gone out*
Ex. 12:41. all the hosts of the Lord *went out*

Ex. 13: 3. *ye came out* from Egypt,
16: 4. *and* the people *shall go out*
27. *there went out* (some) of the people
17: 6. *and there shall* come water *out* of it,
21: 3. *then* his wife *shall go out*
11. *then shall she go out* free
22. *so that* her fruit *depart* (from her),
23:15. in it *thou camest out* from Egypt:
34:18. *thou camest out* from Egypt.
34. *And he came out*, and spake unto the
Lev.14: 3. *And* the priest *shall go forth* out of the
38. *Then* the priest *shall go out*
16:18. *And he shall go out* unto the altar
24. put on his garments, *and come forth*,
25:28. *and* in the jubile it *shall go out*,
33. *then...shall go out* in (the year of) jubile:
41. *And* (then) *shall* he *depart* from thee,
54. *then he shall go out* in the year of jubile,
Nu. 11:20. Why *came we forth* out of Egypt?
26. but *went* not *out* unto the tabernacle:
16:27. Dathan and Abiram *came out*,
35. *there came out* a fire from the Lord,
46(17:11). *there is* wrath *gone out* from the
21:28. *there is* a fire *gone out* of Heshbon,
22: 5. *there is* a people *come out* from Egypt:
32. *I went out* to withstand thee,
33: 1. which *went forth* out of the land of Egypt
3. the children of Israel *went out*
34: 4. *and shall go on* to Hazar-addar,
9. *And* the border *shall go on* to Ziphron,
Deu 9: 7. from the day that *thou didst depart*
11:10. from whence *ye came out*,
13:13(14). the children of Belial, *are gone out* from
16: 3. *thou camest forth* out of the land of Egypt
21: 2. *Then* thy elders and thy judges *shall come forth*,
23:10(11). *then shall he go abroad* out of the camp,
12(13). whither *thou shalt go forth* abroad:
24: 2. *when she is departed* out of his house,
Jos. 2: 5. that the men *went out:*
7. as soon as they...*were gone out*,
8: 6. *For they will come out* after us
17. that *went* not *out* after Israel:
22. the other *issued out* of the city
15: 3. *And it went out* to the south side
4. *and went out* unto the river of Egypt;
9. *and went out* to the cities of mount Ephron;
11. *And* the border *went out* unto the side of
— *and went out* unto Jabneel;
16: 2. *And goeth out* from Beth-el to Luz,
6. *And* the border *went out* toward the sea
7. *and went out* at Jordan.
18:15. *and* the border *went out* on the west, *and went out* to the well of waters
17. *and went forth* to En-shemesh, *and went forth* toward Geliloth,
19:12. *and then goeth out* to Daberath,
13. *and goeth out* to Remmon-methoar
17. the fourth lot *came out* to Issachar,
27. *and goeth out* to Cabul
32. The sixth lot *came out* to the children of
34. *and goeth out* from thence to Hukkok,
40. the seventh lot *came out* for the tribe
Jud. 2:15. Whithersoever *they went out*,
3:24. When he *was gone out*,
4:14. *is* not the Lord *gone out* before thee?
11:36. that which *hath proceeded* out of thy mouth;
14:14. Out of the eater *came forth* meat, and out of the strong *came forth* sweetness.
21:21. *then come ye out* of the vineyards,
Ru. 1:13. the hand of the Lord *is gone out* against me.
1Sa. 8:20. *and go out* before us, and fight our battles
11: 3. *we will come out* to thee.
14:41. Saul and Jonathan were taken: but the people *escaped*.
17:35. *And I went out* after him, and smote him,
23:15. Saul *was come out* to seek his life:
24:14(15). whom *is* the king of Israel *come out?*
26:20. the king of Israel *is come out* to seek a flea,
2Sa. 2:13. the servants of David, *went out*,
5:24. then *shall* the Lord *go out* before thee,
16:11. my son, which *came forth* of my bowels,
18: 4. all the people *came out* by hundreds
19:19(20). the day that my lord the king *went out*
20: 8. as he *went forth* it fell out.
1K. 11:29. Jeroboam *went out* of Jerusalem,
20:17. *There are* men *come out* of Samaria.
1K. 20:18. Whether *they be come out* for peace, take them alive; or whether *they be come out*
19. So these young men...*came out*
39. Thy servant *went out* into the midst of the
2K. 2:23. *there came forth* little children
5: 2. the Syrians *had gone out* by companies,
9:11. Jehu *came forth* to the servants
19: 9. *he is come out* to fight against thee:
20: 4. afore Isaiah *was gone out* into the middle
21:15. the day their fathers *came forth*
1Ch. 1:12. of whom *came* the Philistines,
2:53. of them *came* the Zareathites,
14:15. God *is gone forth* before thee
2Ch.21:19. his bowels *fell out* by reason of his sickness:
22: 7. *he went out* with Jehoram
31: 1. all Israel...*went out* to the cities
Est. 3:15. The posts *went out*,
7: 8. the word *went out* of the king's mouth,
8:14. (So) the posts...*went out*,
15. Mordecai *went out* from the presence of the
Job 1:21. Naked *came I out* of my mother's womb,
3:11. *I came out* of the belly?
14: 2. *He cometh forth* like a flower,
24: 5. (as) wild asses in the desert, *go they forth*
26: 4. whose spirit *came* from thee?
38:29. *Out* of whose womb *came* the ice?
39: 4. *they go forth*, and return not unto them.
Ps. 19: 4(5). Their line *is gone out* through all the
73: 7. Their eyes *stand out* with fatness:
Pro. 7:15. Therefore *came I forth* to meet thee,
Ecc. 4:14. out of prison *he cometh* to reign;
5:15(14). As *he came forth* of his mother's womb,
Cant.5: 6. my soul *failed* when he spake:
Isa. 11: 1. *And there shall come forth* a rod
28:29. This also *cometh forth* from the Lord
37: 9. *He is come forth* to make war with thee.
45:23. the word *is gone out* of my mouth
48: 1. *are come forth* out of the waters of Judah,
3. *they went forth* out of my mouth,
51: 5. my salvation *is gone forth*,
66:24. *And they shall go forth*, and look
Jer. 4: 7. *he is gone forth* from his place
7:25. the day that your fathers *came forth*
9: 3(2). *they proceed* from evil to evil,
10:20. my children *are gone forth of me*,
14:18. If *I go forth* into the field,
19: 2. *And go forth* unto the valley
20:18. Wherefore *came I forth* out of the womb
22:11. which *went forth* out of this place;
23:15. the prophets...*is* profaneness *gone forth*
19. a whirlwind of the Lord *is gone forth*
29:16. your brethren that *are* not *gone forth*
30:19. *And* out of them *shall proceed* thanksgiving
23. the whirlwind of the Lord *goeth forth*
31: 4. *and shalt go forth* in the dances
39. *And* the measuring line *shall* yet *go forth*
37: 5. Then Pharaoh's army *was come forth*
43:12. *and he shall go forth* from thence in peace.
44:17. whatsoever thing *goeth forth*
48: 7. *and* Chemosh *shall go forth* into captivity
45. a fire *shall come forth* out of Heshbon,
Eze. 7:10. the morning *is gone forth*;
9: 7. *And they went forth*, and slew in the city.
15: 7. *they shall go out* from (one) fire,
24: 6. whose scum *is* not *gone out* of it!
36:20. *are gone forth* out of his land.
39: 9. *And* they that dwell...*shall go forth*,
46: 2. *then he shall go forth;* but the gate
12. *then he shall go forth;* and after
Dan. 8: 9. out of one of them *came forth* a little horn,
9:22. *I am* now *come forth* to give thee skill
23. the commandment *came forth*,
11:11. *and shall come forth* and fight with him,
44. *therefore he shall go forth* with great fury
Mic. 1:11. the inhabitant of Zaanan *came* not *forth*
Nah. 1:11. *There is* (one) *come out* of thee,
Hab. 3:13. *Thou wentest forth* for the salvation of thy
Zec. 6: 6. the white *go forth* after them; and the grisled *go forth* toward the south
7. And the bay *went forth*,
9:14. *and* his arrow *shall go forth* as the lightning:
14: 2. *and* half of the city *shall go forth* into
3. *Then shall* the Lord *go forth*,
Mal. 4: 2(3:20). *and ye shall go forth*, and grow up as

KAL.—*Infinitive.*

Gen 8: 7. *to* and fro, (marg. *going forth* and returning

Gen 12: 4. *when he departed* out of Haran.
24:11. the time that women *go out* to draw (water).
27:30. was yet *scarce* gone (lit. *going* was gone)
35:18. as her soul was *in departing*,
Ex. 5:20. *as they came forth* from Pharaoh:
9:29. As soon *as I am gone out* of the city,
13: 8. *when I came forth* out of Egypt.
16: 1. *after their departing* out of the land of
19: 1. *when* the children of Israel *were gone forth*
21: 7. she shall not go out *as* the menservants *do.* (lit. *as.. go out*)
23:16. *in the end of* the year,
28:35. *and when he cometh out*, that he die not.
33: 8. *when* Moses *went out* unto the tabernacle,
34:34. until *he came out.*
Lev. 16:17. *he come out*, and have made an atonement
27:21. *when it goeth out* in the jubile,
Nu. 1: 1 & 9:1. *after they were come out* of the land
12:12. *when he cometh out* of his mother's womb.
33:38. *after* the children of Israel *were come out*
35:26. if the slayer shall *at any time* come without (lit. *going out* shall go out)
Deu 4:45. *after they came forth* out of Egypt,
46. *after they were come forth* out of Egypt:
16: 3. *thou camest forth* out of the land of Egypt
6. season that *thou camest forth out* of Egypt.
23: 4(5). *when ye came forth* out of Egypt;
24: 9. *after that ye were come forth* out of Egypt.
25:17. *when ye were come forth* out of Egypt;
28: 6, 19. (shalt) thou (be) *when thou goest out.*
31: 2. I can no more *go out* and come in:
33:18. Rejoice, Zebulun, *in thy going out;*
Jos. 2:10. *when ye came out* of Egypt;
5: 4. *after they came out* of Egypt.
5. *as they came forth* out of Egypt,
9:12. *we came forth* to go unto you;
14:11. *both to go out*, and to come in.
Jud. 5: 4. *when thou wentest out* of Seir,
31. as the sun *when he goeth forth* in his might.
20:14. *to go out* to battle against the children of
28. Shall I yet again *go out* to battle
1Sa. 18:30. it came to pass, after *they went forth*,
21: 5(6). these three days, *since I came out*,
23:13. he forbare *to go forth.*
25:37. *when* the wine *was gone out* of Nabal,
29: 6. *thy going out* and thy coming in
2Sa. 11: 1. the time when kings *go forth* (to battle),
13:39. David longed *to go forth* unto Absalom:
16: 5. cursed *still* as he came.
18: 2. I will *surely* go forth (lit. *going* I will go forth)
1K. 2:37, 42. on the day *thou goest out*,
3: 7. I know not (how) *to go out*
6: 1. *after* the children of Israel *were come out*
8: 9. *when they came out* of the land of Egypt.
10. *when* the priests *were come out* of the holy
2K. 5:11. He will *surely* come out (lit. *coming* he will come out)
11: 8. be ye with the king *as he goeth out*
19:27. I know thy abode, *and thy going out*,
24: 7. the king of Egypt *came* not again (lit. added not *to come*)
1Ch 20: 1. the time that kings *go out* (to battle),
2Ch 5:10. *when they came out* of Egypt
11. *when* the priests *were come out* of the holy
20:20. *and as they went forth*, Jehoshaphat stood
21. *as they went out* before the army,
21:19. *after* the end (lit. *the going out of* the end) of two years,
23: 7. when he cometh in, *and when he goeth out.*
26:20. himself hasted also *to go out*,
Neh. 4:21(15). till the stars *appeared.* (lit. *the coming forth of* the stars)
Job 29: 7. *When I went out* to the gate
Ps. 68: 7(8). *when thou wentest forth* before thy people,
81: 5(6). *when he went out* through the land
105:38. Egypt was glad *when they departed:*
114: 1. *When* Israel *went out* of Egypt,
121: 8. The Lord shall preserve *thy going out*
Isa. 13:10. the sun shall be darkened *in his going forth*,
37:28. I know thy abode, *and thy going out*,
Jer. 11:11. they shall not be able *to escape;*
29: 2. *were departed* from Jerusalem;
38:17. If thou wilt *assuredly* go forth (lit. *going* wilt go forth)
21. if thou refuse *to go forth*,
Eze. 10:19. *when they went out*,
Eze. 26:18. the isles...shall be troubled *at thy departure.*
27:33. *When* thy wares *went forth* out of the seas,
44:19. *And when they go forth* into the utter court,
46:10. *and when they go forth*, shall go forth.
12. *his going forth* (one) shall shut the gate.
47: 3. And *when* the man...*went forth* eastward,
Mic. 7:15. According to the days of *thy coming out*
Hag. 2: 5. *when ye came out* of Egypt,

KAL.—*Imperative.*

Gen 8:16. *Go forth* of the ark,
19:14. Up, *get you out* of this place;
27: 3. *and go out* to the field, and take me (some)
31:13. *get thee out* from this land,
Ex. 11: 8. *Get* thee *out*, and all the people
12:31. *get you forth* from among my people,
17: 9. Choose us out men, *and go out*,
Nu. 12: 4. *Come out* ye three unto the tabernacle
Jud. 9:29. Increase thine army, *and come out.*
38. *go out*, I pray now, and fight with them.
2Sa. 16: 7. *Come out, come out*, thou bloody man,
19: 7(8). Now therefore arise, *go forth*,
1K. 2:30. Thus saith the king, *Come forth.*
19:11. *Go forth*, and stand upon the mount
22:22. *go forth*, and do so.
2K. 18:31. (an agreement) with me...*and come out* to
2Ch. 18:21. *go out*, and do (even) so.
20:17. to morrow *go out* against them:
24: 5. *Go out* unto the cities of Judah,
26:18. *go out* of the sanctuary;
Neh 8:15. *Go forth* unto the mount,
Cant. 1: 8. *go* thy way *forth* by the footsteps of the
3:11. *Go forth*, O ye daughters of Zion,
Isa. 7: 3. *Go forth* now to meet Ahaz,
30:22. thou shalt say unto it, *Get thee hence.*
36:16. Make (an agreement)...*and come out* to me:
48:20. *Go ye forth* of Babylon,
49: 9. thou mayest say to the prisoners, *Go forth;*
52:11. *go ye out* from thence,
— *go ye out* of the midst of her;
Jer. 50: 8. *go forth* out of the land of the Chaldeans,
51:45. *go ye out* of the midst of her,
Eze. 3:22. Arise, *go forth* into the plain,
9: 7. he said unto them,...*go ye forth.*

KAL.—*Future.*

Gen 4:16. *And* Cain *went out* from the presence of the
8: 7. *which went forth* to and fro,
18. *And* Noah *went forth*, and his sons,
11:31. *and they went forth* with them
12: 5. *and they went forth* to go into the land
14: 8. *And there went out* the king of Sodom,
17. *And* the king of Sodom *went out* to meet
15: 4. he that *shall come forth*
14. *shall they come out* with great substance.
17: 6. kings *shall come out* of thee.
19: 6. *And* Lot *went out* at the door unto them,
14. *And* Lot *went out*, and spake unto his
24:63. *And* Isaac *went out* to meditate
25:25. *And* the first *came out* red,
28:10. *And* Jacob *went out* from Beer-sheba,
30:16. *and* Leah *went out* to meet him,
31:33. *Then went he out* of Leah's tent,
34: 1. *And* Dinah...*went out* to see the daughters
6. *And* Hamor...*went out* unto Jacob
26. took Dinah out...*and went out.*
35:11. kings *shall come out* of thy loins;
39:12, 15. fled, *and got him* out.
41:45. *And* Joseph *went out* over (all) the land of
46. *And* Joseph *went out* from the presence of
42:15. *ye shall* not *go forth* hence,
28. *and* their heart *failed* (them),
43:31. he washed his face, *and went out*,
44:28. *And* the one *went out* from me,
47:10. Jacob...*and went out* from before Pharaoh.
Ex. 2:11. *that he went out* unto his brethren,
13. *And* when *he went out* the second day,
5:10. *And* the taskmasters of the people *went out*,
8:12(8). *And* Moses and Aaron *went out* from
30(26). *And* Moses *went out* from Pharaoh,
9:33. *And* Moses *went out* of the city
10: 6. he turned himself, *and went out* from
18. *And he went out* from Pharaoh,
11: 8. after that *I will go out.* *And he went out*
12:22. none of you *shall go out* at the door
15:20. *and* all the women *went out* after her
22. *and they went out* into the wilderness

Ex. 16:29. *let* no man *go out* of his place
18: 7. *And* Moses *went out* to meet his
21: 2. *he shall go out* free for nothing.
3. *he shall go out* by himself:
4. he *shall go out* by himself.
5. *I will* not *go out* free:
7. *she shall* not *go out* as the menservants do.
22: 6(5). If fire *break out*, and catch in thorns,
32:24. *and there came out* this calf.
33: 7. every one which sought the Lord *went out*
35:20. *And* all the congregation of the children of Israel *departed*
Lev. 8:33. *ye shall* not *go out* of the door
9:23. *and came out*, and blessed the people:
24. *And there came* a fire *out* from before the
10: 2. *And there went out* fire from the Lord,
7. *ye shall* not *go out* from the door
15:16. if any man's seed...*go out*
32. (him) whose seed *goeth* from him,
21:12. Neither *shall he go out* of the sanctuary,
22: 4. a man whose seed *goeth* from him;
24:10. *And* the son...*went out* among the children
25:30. *it shall* not *go out* in the jubile.
31. *they shall go out* in the jubile.
Nu. 11:20. until it *come out* at your nostrils,
24. *And* Moses *went out*, and told the people
12: 4. *And* they three *came out*.
5. *and they* both *came forth*.
20:11. *and* the water *came out* abundantly,
18. lest *I come out* against thee with the sword.
20. *And* Edom *came out* against him
21:23. *and went out* against Israel
33. *and* Og the king of Bashan *went out* against
22:36. *And* when...*he went out* to meet him
27:17. Which *may go out* before them,
21. at his word *shall they go out*,
31:13. *And* Moses,...*went forth* to meet them
33:54. the place where his lot *falleth;*
35:26. if the slayer *shall* at any time *come without*
Deu. 1:44. *And* the Amorites,...*came out* against you,
2:32. *Then* Sihon *came out* against us,
3: 1. *and* Og the king of Bashan *came out* against
15:16. *I will* not *go away* from thee;
20: 1. When *thou goest out* to battle
21:10. When *thou goest forth* to war
23: 9(10). When the host *goeth forth*
24: 5. *he shall* not *go out* to war,
28: 7. *they shall come out* against thee one way,
25. *thou shalt go out* one way against them,
29: 7(6). *And*...Sihon...and Og...*came out*
Jos. 2:19. whosoever *shall go out* of the doors
6:10. *shall* (any) word *proceed* out of your mouth,
8: 5. when *they come out* against us,
14. *and* the men of the city *went out* against
11: 4. *And they went out*, they and all their hosts
16: 1. *And* the lot...*fell* from Jordan by
18:11. *and* the coast of their lot *came forth*
19: 1. *And* the second lot *came forth* to Simeon,
24. *And* the fifth lot *came out* for the tribe
47. *And* the coast of the children of Dan *went out*
21: 4. *And* the lot *came out* for the families
Jud. 3:10. he judged Israel, *and went out* to war:
19. *And* all that stood by him *went out* from
22. *and* the dirt *came out*.
23. *Then* Ehud *went forth* through the porch,
4:18. *And* Jael *went out* to meet Sisera,
22. Jael *came out* to meet him,
9:15. *let* fire *come out* of the bramble,
20. *let* fire *come out* from Abimelech,
— *and* let fire *come out* from the men of
27. *And they went out* into the fields,
35. *And* Gaal the son of Ebed *went out*,
39. *And* Gaal *went out* before the men
42. *that* the people *went out* into the field;
11: 3. *and went out* with him.
31. whatsoever *cometh forth* of the doors
13:14. any (thing) that *cometh* of the vine,
15:19. *and there came* water *thereout;*
16:20. *I will go out* as at other times before,
19:23. *And* the man, the master of the house, *went out* unto them,
27. *and went out* to go his way:
20: 1. *Then* all the children of Israel *went out*,
20. *And* the men of Israel *went out* to battle
21. *And* the children of Benjamin *came forth*
25. *And* Benjamin *went forth* against them

Jud. 20:31. *And* the children of Benjamin *went out*
21:21. if the daughters of Shiloh *come out*
24. *and they went out* from thence every man
Ru. 1: 7. *Wherefore she went forth* out of the place
2:22. that *thou go out* with his maidens,
1Sa. 2: 3. (not) arrogancy *come out* of your mouth:
4: 1. *Now* Israel *went out* against the Philistines
7:11. *And* the men of Israel *went out*
9:26. *and they went out* both of them,
11: 7. *and they came out* with one consent.
10. To morrow *we will come out* unto you,
13:10. *and* Saul *went out* to meet him,
17. *And* the spoilers *came out* of the camp
23. *And* the garrison of the Philistines *went out*
17: 4. *And there went out* a champion
8. Why *are ye come out* to set (your) battle in
18: 5. *And* David *went out* whithersoever
6. *that* the women *came out* of all cities
13. *and he went out* and came in before the
30. *Then* the princes...*went forth:*
19: 3. I *will go out* and stand beside my father
8. *and* David *went out*, and fought with the
20:11. *and let us go out* into the field. *And they went out* both of them into the field.
35. *that* Jonathan *went out* into the field
22: 3. *Let* my father and my mother, I pray thee, *come forth*,
23:13. David...arose *and departed* out of Keilah,
24: 8(9). *and went out* of the cave,
13(14). Wickedness *proceedeth* from the
28: 1. *thou shalt go out* with me to battle,
30:21. *and they went forth* to meet David,
2Sa. 2:12. *And* Abner...*went out* from Mahanaim
23. *that* the spear *came out* behind him;
3:26. *And when* Joab *was come out* from David,
6:20. *And* Michal...*came out* to meet David,
7:12. which *shall proceed* out of thy bowels,
10: 8. *And* the children of Ammon *came out*,
11: 8. *And* Uriah *departed* out of the king's house, *and there followed* (marg. *went out* after) him a mess (of meat)
13. *and* at even *he went out* to lie on his bed
17. *And* the men of the city *went out*,
23. *and came out* unto us into the field,
13: 9. *And they went out* every man from him.
15:16. *And* the king *went forth*, and all his
17. *And* the king *went forth*, and all the people
18: 2. *I will* surely *go forth* with you myself
3. *Thou shalt* not *go forth:*
6. *So* the people *went out* into the field
20: 7. *And there went out* after him Joab's men,
— *and they went out* of Jerusalem,
21:17. *Thou shalt go* no more *out* with us to battle,
24: 4. *And* Joab and the captains of the host *went out*
7. *and they went out* to the south of Judah,
20. *and* Araunah *went out*, and bowed himself
1K. 2:36. *go* not *forth* thence any whither.
46. *which went out*, and fell upon him,
8:44. If thy people *go out* to battle
9:12. *And* Hiram *came out* from Tyre
10:29. And a chariot came up *and went out* of
12:25. *and went out* from thence, and built Penuel.
19:13. wrapped his face in his mantle, *and went out*,
20:16. *And they went out* at noon.
17. *And* the young men...*went out* first;
21. *And* the king of Israel *went out*,
31. *and go out* to the king of Israel:
33. *Then* Ben-hadad *came forth* to him;
22:21. *And there came forth* a spirit,
22. *I will go forth*, and I will be a lying spirit
2K. 2: 3. *And* the sons of the prophets...*came forth*
21. *And he went forth* unto the spring
24. *And there came forth* two she bears
3: 6. *And* king Jehoram *went out* of Samaria
4:18. *that he went out* to his father
21. shut (the door) upon him, *and went out*.
37. took up her son, *and went out*.
39. *And* one *went out* into the field
5:11. *He will* surely *come out* to me,
27. *And he went out* from his presence a leper
6:15. servant...was risen early, *and gone forth*,
7:12. *therefore are they gone out* of the camp
— When *they come out* of the city,
16. *And* the people *went out*, and spoiled the
8: 3. *and she went forth* to cry unto the king
9:15. *let* none *go forth*

2K. 9:21. *And* Joram...and Ahaziah...*went out*, each in his chariot, *and they went out* against
24. *and* the arrow *went out* at his heart,
10: 9. *that he went out*, and stood,
25. *let* none *come forth.*
12:12(13). all that *was laid out* for the house
13: 5. *so that they went out* from under the hand
18: 7. he prospered whithersoever *he went forth:*
18. *And...there came out* to them Eliakim
19:31. out of Jerusalem *shall go forth* a remnant,
35. *that* the angel of the Lord *went out*,
20:18. thy sons that *shall issue* from thee,
24:12. *And* Jehoiachin...*went out*
1Ch 12:17. *And* David *went out* to meet them,
14: 8. *and went out* against them.
15. then *thou shalt go out* to battle:
17. *And* the fame of David *went out*
19: 9. *And* the children of Ammon *came out*,
21: 4. *Wherefore* Joab *departed*, and went
21. *and went out* of the threshingfloor,
24: 7. *Now* the first lot *came forth* to Jehoiarib,
25: 9. *Now* the first lot *came forth* for Asaph
26:14. *and* his lot *came out* northward.
2Ch 1:10. *that I may go out* and come in
6:34. If thy people *go out* to war
14: 9(8). *And there came out* against them Zerah
10(9). *Then* Asa *went out* against him,
15: 2. *And he went out* to meet Asa,
18:20. *Then there came out* a spirit,
21. *I will go out*, and be a lying spirit
19: 2. *And* Jehu...*went out* to meet him,
4. *and he went out* again
20:20. they rose...*and went forth* into the
21:15. thy bowels *fall out* by reason of the
26: 6. *And he went forth* and warred against the
15. *And* his name *spread* (marg. *went forth*) far
28: 9. *and he went out* before the host
35:20. *and* Josiah *went out* against him.
Neh 2:13. *And I went out* by night
8:16. *So* the people *went forth*,
Est. 1:17. (this) deed...*shall come abroad* unto all
19. *let there go* a royal commandment
4: 1. *and went out* into the midst of the city,
6. *So* Hatach *went forth* to Mordecai
5: 9. *Then went* Haman *forth* that day
Job 1:12. *So* Satan *went forth* from the presence of
2: 7. *So went* Satan *forth* from the presence
5: 6. affliction *cometh* not *forth* of the dust,
8:16. his branch *shooteth forth* in his garden.
20:25. It is drawn, *and cometh out* of the body;
23:10. *I shall come forth* as gold.
28: 5. out of it *cometh* bread:
31:34. *went* not *out* of the door?
40. *Let* thistles *grow* instead of wheat,
37: 2. the sound (that) *goeth out* of his mouth.
38: 8. *it had issued out* of the womb?
39:21. *he goeth on* to meet the armed men.
41:20(12). Out of his nostrils *goeth* smoke,
21(13). a flame *goeth out* of his mouth.
Ps. 17: 2. *Let* my sentence *come forth*
41: 6(7). (when) *he goeth* abroad, he telleth (it).
44: 9(10). and *goest* not *forth* with our armies.
60:10(12). (which) *didst* not *go out* with our
88: 8(9). *I cannot come forth.*
104:23. Man *goeth forth* unto his work
108:11(12). *wilt* not thou, O God, *go forth* with
109: 7. *let him be* condemned: (marg. *let him go out* guilty)
146: 4. His breath *goeth forth*,
Pro. 12:13. *but* the just *shall come out* of trouble.
22:10. *and* contention *shall go out;*
25: 4. *and there shall come forth* a vessel
8. *Go* not *forth* hastily to strive,
30:27. *yet go they forth* all of them
Ecc. 7:18. he that feareth God *shall come forth*
Cant. 7:11(12). *let us go forth* into the field;
Isa. 2: 3. out of Zion *shall go forth* the law,
14:29. out of the serpent's root *shall come forth*
36: 3. *Then came forth* unto him Eliakim,
37:32. out of Jerusalem *shall go forth* a remnant,
36. *Then* the angel of the Lord *went forth*,
39: 7. thy sons that *shall issue* from thee,
42:13. The Lord *shall go forth* as a mighty man,
49:17. they that made thee waste *shall go forth*
51: 4. a law *shall proceed* from me,
52:12. *ye shall* not *go out* with haste,
55:11. So shall my word be that *goeth forth*
Isa. 55:12. *ye shall go out* with joy,
62: 1. the righteousness thereof *go forth* as
Jer. 1: 5. before *thou camest forth* out of the womb
2:37. *thou shalt go forth* from him,
4: 4. lest my fury *come forth* like fire,
6:25. *Go* not *forth* into the field,
15: 1. *and let them go forth.*
2. Whither *shall we go forth?*
17:19. by the which *they go out*,
21:12. lest my fury *go out* like fire,
30:21. their governor *shall proceed* from the
37:12. *Then* Jeremiah *went forth* out of
38: 8. Ebed-melech *went forth* out of the king's
17. If *thou wilt* assuredly *go forth*
18. if *thou wilt* not *go forth*
39: 4. *and went forth* out of the city by night,
— *and he went out* the way of the plain.
41: 6. *And* Ishmael...*went forth* from Mizpah
46: 9. *and let* the mighty men *come forth;*
48: 9. that it may flee and *get away:*
50: 8. (כתיב) *go forth* out of the land of the
52: 7. *and went forth* out of the city by night
Lam. 1: 6. *And*...all her beauty *is departed:*
3: 7. that *I cannot get out:*
38. *proceedeth* not evil and good?
Eze. 3:23. I arose, *and went forth* into the plain:
25. *thou shalt* not *go out* among them:
5: 4. thereof *shall* a fire *come forth*
10: 7. took (it), *and went out.*
18. *Then* the glory of the Lord *departed*
12: 4. *thou shalt go forth* at even
12. *and shall go forth:*
16:14. *And* thy renown *went forth* among the
19:14. *And* fire *is gone out* of a rod
21: 4(9). therefore *shall* my sword *go forth*
19(24). both twain *shall come forth* out of one
24:12. her great scum *went* not *forth* out of her:
30: 9. In that day *shall* messengers *go forth*
42:14. *shall they* not *go out* of the holy (place)
44: 3. *shall go out* by the way of the same.
46: 8. *he shall go forth* by the way thereof.
9. *shall go out* by the way of the south gate;
— *shall go forth* by the way of the north
— *shall go forth* over against it.
10. when they go forth, *shall go forth.*
Hos. 6: 5. (are as) the light (that) *goeth forth.*
Joel 2:16. let the bridegroom *go forth* of his chamber,
3:18(4:18). a fountain *shall come forth* of the
Am. 4: 3. *ye shall go out* at the breaches,
Jon. 4: 5. *So* Jonah *went out* of the city,
Mic. 2:13. *and are gone out* by it:
4: 2. the law *shall go forth* of Zion,
10. now *shalt thou go forth* out of the city,
5: 2(1). out of thee *shall he come forth*
Hab 1: 4. judgment *doth* never *go forth:*
— therefore wrong judgment *proceedeth.*
7. their dignity *shall proceed* of themselves.
3: 5. *and* burning coals *went forth* at his feet.
Zec. 5: 5. *Then* the angel that talked with me *went forth*,
10: 4. Out of him *came forth* the corner,
14: 8. living waters *shall go out* from Jerusalem;

KAL.—*Participle.* Poel.

Gen 2:10. a river *went out* of Eden
9:10. all *that go out of* the ark,
18. *that went forth* of the ark,
24:13. the daughters...*come out* to draw water:
15. behold, Rebekah *came out*,
43. when the virgin *cometh forth* to draw
45. Rebekah *came forth* with her pitcher
34:24, 24. all *that went out of* the gate
46:26. *which came out of* his loins,
Ex. 1: 5. all the souls *that came out of*
4:14. he *cometh forth* to meet thee:
7:15. he *goeth out* unto the water;
8:20(16). he *cometh forth* to the water;
29(25). Behold, I *go out* from thee,
11: 4. About midnight *will* I *go out*
13: 4. This day *came* ye *out*
14: 8. the children of Israel *went out*
25:32. six branches *shall come out* of the sides
33. the six branches *that come out*
35. the six branches *that proceed*
37:18. six branches *going out* of the sides
19. branches *going out* of the candlestick.
21. the six branches *going out* of it.

Nu. 1: 3. all *that are able to go forth* to war
20, 22, 24, 26, 28, 30, 32, 34, 36, 38, 40, 42, 45. all *that were able to go forth* to war;
21:13. *that cometh out* of the coasts of the
22:11. a people *come out* of Egypt,
26: 2. all *that are able to go* to war
4. *which went forth* out of the land of Egypt.
30: 2(3). all *that proceedeth* out of his mouth.
31:27. *who went out* to battle,
28. the men of war *which went out* to battle:
36. them *that went out* to war,
32:24. *and* do *that which hath proceeded* out of
Deu 2:23. *which came forth* out of Caphtor,
8: 7. depths *that spring out* of valleys
14:22. *that* the field *bringeth forth*
28:57. *cometh out* from between her feet,
Jos. 5: 4. All the people *that came out* of Egypt,
5. all the people *that came out*
6. *which came out* of Egypt,
6: 1. none *went out*, and none came in.
Jud. 1:24. the spies saw a man *come forth*
8:30. had threescore and ten sons of his body *begotten*: (marg. *going out of* his thigh)
9:33. the people...*come out* against thee,
43. the people (were) *come forth* out of the
11:31. *whatsoever* cometh forth (marg. *that which cometh forth*, which shall come forth)
34. his daughter *came out* to meet him
1Sa. 9:11. they found young maidens *going out*
14. Samuel *came out* against them,
11: 7. Whosoever *cometh* not *forth* after Saul
14:11. the Hebrews *come forth* out of the holes
17:20. the host *was going forth* to the fight,
55. Saul saw David *go forth*
18:16. he *went out* and came in before them.
2Sa. 16: 5. thence *came out* a man
— he *came forth*, and cursed
19: 7(8). swear by the Lord, if thou *go* not *forth*,
1K. 4:33(5:13). the hyssop *that springeth out* of the
8:19. thy son *that shall come forth* out of thy
15:17. that he might not suffer *any to go out*
2K. 11: 7. two parts of all you *that go forth on* the sabbath,
9. them *that should go out on* the sabbath,
1Ch 5:18. *that went out to* the war.
7:11. fit to *go out for* war (and) battle.
12:33, 36. *such as went forth to* battle,
27: 1. which came in *and went out* month by
2Ch 6: 9. thy son *which shall come forth* out of thy
15: 5. (there was) no peace *to him that went out*,
16: 1. let none *go out* or come in
23: 8. them *that were to go out on* the sabbath:
25: 5. (able) *to go forth to* war,
26:11. *that went out to* war by bands,
Neh 3:25. the tower *which lieth out*
26. the tower *that lieth out*.
27. against the great tower *that lieth out*,
Ps. 19: 5(6). a bridegroom *coming out* of his
144:14. (that there be) no breaking in, nor *going out*;
Ecc. 10: 5. an error (which) *proceedeth* from the
Isa. 26:21. the Lord *cometh out* of his place
Jer. 5: 6. every one *that goeth out* thence shall be
21: 9. *but he that goeth out*, and falleth to the
25:32. evil *shall go forth* from nation to nation,
37: 4. Jeremiah came in *and went out*
7. *which is come forth* to help you,
38: 2. *but he that goeth forth* to the Chaldeans
Eze. 1:13. out of the fire *went forth* lightning.
14:22. they *shall come forth* unto you,
33:30. the word *that cometh forth* from the Lord.
47: 1. waters *issued out* from under the
8. These waters *issue out* toward the east
12. they *issued out* of the sanctuary:
Dan 10:20. *when* I *am gone forth*, lo, the prince of
Am. 5: 3. The city *that went out*
— *and that which went forth* (by) an hundred
Mic. 1: 3. the Lord *cometh forth* out of his place,
Zec. 2: 3(7). the angel that talked with me *went forth*, and another angel *went out* to
5: 3. This (is) the curse *that goeth forth*
5. see what (is) this *that goeth forth*.
6. This (is) an ephah *that goeth forth*.
9. *there came out* two women,
6: 1. *there came* four chariots *out*
5. which *go forth* from standing
6. *go forth* into the north country

Zec. 6: 8. these *that go* toward the north country
8:10. *neither...to him that went out* or came in

* HIPHIL.—*Preterite.* *

Gen 14:18. Melchizedek...*brought forth* bread and
15: 7. I (am) the Lord that *brought thee out* of
40:14. *and bring me out* of this house:
Ex. 6: 6. *and I will bring* you *out* from under the
7: 4. *and bring forth* mine armies, (and) my
5. *and bring out* the children of Israel
12:17. in this selfsame day *have I brought* your armies *out*
39. the dough which *they brought forth*
51. Lord *did bring* the children of Israel *out*
13: 3. the Lord *brought* you *out* from this
9. strong hand *hath* the Lord *brought thee out*
14. the Lord *brought us out* from Egypt,
16. the Lord *brought us forth* out of Egypt.
16: 3. *ye have brought* us *forth* into this
6. the Lord *hath brought* you *out*
18: 1. the Lord *had brought* Israel *out*
20: 2. *have brought thee out* of the land of Egypt,
29:46. that *brought* them *forth* out of the land of
32:11. which thou *hast brought forth* out of the
12. For mischief *did he bring them out*,
Lev. 4:12. *Even* the whole bullock *shall he carry forth*
21. *And he shall carry forth* the bullock
6:11(4). *and carry forth* the ashes without the
14:45. *and he shall carry* (them) *forth* out of the
19:36. which *brought* you *out* of the land of
25:38. which *brought* you *forth* out of the land
42. which *I brought forth* out of the land of
55. whom *I brought forth* out of the land of
26:13. which *brought* you *forth* out of the land
45. whom *I brought forth* out of the land of
Nu. 15:41. which *brought* you *out* of the land of
19: 3. *that he may bring* her *forth* without the
20: 8. *and thou shalt bring forth* to them water
Deu 1:27. *he hath brought us forth* out of the land of
5: 6. which *brought thee out* of the land of
6:12. *brought thee forth* out of the land of
23. *he brought* us *out* from thence,
7: 8. *brought* you *out* with a mighty hand,
19. the Lord thy God *brought thee out*:
9:12. thy people which *thou hast brought forth*
26. which *thou hast brought forth* out of
28. the land whence *thou broughtest us out*
— *he hath brought them out* to slay them
29. which *thou broughtest out* by thy mighty
16: 1. the Lord thy God *brought thee forth*
17: 5. *Then shalt thou bring forth* that man
21:19. *and bring* him *out* unto the elders of his
22:14. *and bring up* an evil name upon her,
15. *and bring forth* (the tokens of) the
19. *he hath brought up* an evil name upon a
21. *Then they shall bring out* the damsel
24. *Then ye shall bring* them both *out*
Jos. 6:23. *they brought out* all her kindred,
24: 5. afterward *I brought* you *out*.
Jud. 6:18. *and bring forth* my present,
2Sa. 12:30. *he brought forth* the spoil of the city
31. *he brought forth* the people that (were)
1K. 8:16. the day that *I brought forth* my people
51. *thou broughtest forth* out of Egypt,
9: 9. who *brought forth* their fathers
17:13. *and bring* (it) unto me,
21:10. *And* (then) *carry him out*, and stone him,
1Ch 20: 2. *he brought* also exceeding much spoil *out*
3. *he brought out* the people that (were) in
2Ch 6: 5. Since the day that *I brought forth* my
7:22. which *brought them forth* out of the land
18:33. *that thou mayest carry me out* of the host;
Ezr. 1: 7. the king *brought forth* the vessels
— *which* Nebuchadnezzar *had brought forth*
Neh 9: 7. *and broughtest him forth* out of Ur
15. *broughtest forth* water for them
Job 10:18. Wherefore then *hast thou brought me forth*
15:13. *and lettest* (such) words *go out* of thy
Ps. 37: 6. *And he shall bring forth* thy righteousness
Isa. 65: 9. *And I will bring forth* a seed out of Jacob,
Jer. 51:10. The Lord *hath brought forth* our
44. *and I will bring forth* out of his mouth
Eze. 11: 7. *I will bring* you *forth* out of the midst of
9. *And I will bring* you *out* of the midst
12: 4. *Then shalt thou bring forth* thy stuff
5. *and carry out* thereby.
7. *I brought forth* my stuff by day,

Eze.12: 7. *I brought*(it) *forth* in the twilight,
20:14. in whose sight *I brought them out.*
22. in whose sight *I brought* them *forth.*
34. *And I will bring* you *out* from the people,
21: 3(8). *and will draw forth* my sword
5(10). I the Lord *have drawn forth* my sword
34:13. *And I will bring them out* from the people,
38: 4. *and I will bring* thee *forth,*
42:15. *he brought me forth* toward the gate
Dan 9:15. that *hast brought* thy people *forth*
Zec. 4: 7. *and he shall bring forth* the headstone
5: 4. *I will bring it forth,* saith the Lord

HIPHIL.—*Infinitive.*

Gen19:17. *when they had brought* them *forth* abroad,
Ex. 3:12. *When thou hast brought forth* the people
6:13. *to bring* the children of Israel *out*
27. *to bring out* the children of Israel
8:18(14). the magicians did so...*to bring forth*
12:42. *for bringing them out* from the land of
14:11. *to carry us forth* out of Egypt?
16:32. *when I brought* you *forth* from the land of
Lev.23:43. *when I brought* them *out* of the land of
Nu. 14:36. *bringing up* a slander upon the land,
Deu29:25(24). *when he brought them forth* out of the
Jos. 10:24. *when they brought out* those kings
1K. 8:21. *when he brought* them *out* of the land of
53. *when thou broughtest* our fathers *out* of
2K. 23: 4. *to bring forth* out of the temple
2Ch29:16. the Levites took (it), *to carry* (it) *out*
34:14. *And when they brought out* the money
Ezr.10: 3. *to put away* all the wives,
19. *that they would put away* their wives;
Ps.104:14. *that he may bring forth* food
Ecc. 5: 2(1). let not thine heart be hasty *to utter*
Isa. 42: 7. *to bring out* the prisoners
Jer. 7:22. the day that *I brought* them *out*
11: 4. the day (that) *I brought* them *forth*
31:32. *to bring them out* of the land of
34:13. the day that *I brought* them *forth*
39:14. *that he should carry him* home:
Eze.12:12. dig through the wall *to carry out*
20: 6. *to bring them forth* of the land
9. *in bringing them forth* out of the land
41. *when I bring* you *out* from the people,
46:20. *they bear* (them) not *out* into the utter court,
Hos. 9:13. Ephraim *shall bring forth* his children
Am. 6:10. *to bring out* the bones

HIPHIL.—*Imperative.*

Gen 8:17. *Bring forth* with thee every living thing
19: 5. *bring them out* unto us,
12. *bring* (them) *out* of this place:
38:24. *Bring her forth,* and let her be burnt.
45: 1. *Cause* every man *to go out* from me.
Ex. 3:10. *that thou mayest bring forth* my people
6:26. *Bring out* the children of Israel
Lev.24:14. *Bring forth* him that hath cursed
Jos. 2: 3. *Bring forth* the men that are come to thee,
6:22. *and bring out* thence the woman,
10:22. *and bring out* those five kings unto me
Jud. 6:30. *Bring out* thy son, that he may die:
19:22. *Bring forth* the man that came into thine
2Sa.13: 9. *Have out* all men from me.
1K. 22:34. *and carry me out* of the host;
2K. 10:22. *Bring forth* vestments for all the
11:15. *Have* her *forth* without the ranges:
2Ch23:14. *Have her forth* of the ranges:
29: 5. *and carry forth* the filthiness
Ps. 25:17. (O) *bring thou me out* of my distresses.
142: 7(8). *Bring* my soul *out* of prison,
Isa. 43: 8. *Bring forth* the blind people
48:20. *utter it* (even) to the end of the earth;
Eze.24: 6. *bring it out* piece by piece;

HIPHIL.—*Future.*

Gen 1:12. *And* the earth *brought forth* grass,
24. *Let* the earth *bring forth* the living creature
15: 5. *And he brought* him *forth* abroad,
19: 8. *let me,* I pray you, *bring* them *out* unto you,
16. *and they brought him forth,* and set him
24:53. *And* the servant *brought forth* jewels
43:23. *And he brought* Simeon *out* unto them.
48:12. *And* Joseph *brought* them *out*
Ex. 3:11. *I should bring forth* the children of Israel
4: 6. and *when he took it out,* behold, his hand
7. *and plucked it out* of his bosom,
12:46. *thou shalt* not *carry forth* ought of the flesh

Ex. 19:17. *And* Moses *brought forth* the people
Lev.16:27. *shall* (one) *carry forth* without the camp;
24:23. *that they should bring forth* him that had
26:10. *bring forth* the old because of the new.
Nu. 13:32. *And they brought up* an evil report
15:36. *And* all the congregation *brought* him
17: 8(23). *and brought forth* buds, and bloomed
9(24). *And* Moses *brought out* all the rods
20:10. *must we fetch* you water *out* of this rock?
16. *and hath brought us forth* out of Egypt:
27:17. and which *may lead them out,*
Deu 4:20. *and brought* you *forth* out of the iron
37. *and brought thee out* in his sight
5:15. *and* (that) the Lord thy God *brought thee out* thence
6:21. *and* the Lord *brought us out* of Egypt
14:28. *thou shalt bring forth* all the tithe
24:11. *shall bring out* the pledge abroad
26: 8. *And* the Lord *brought us forth* out of Egypt
28:38. *Thou shalt carry* much seed *out* into the
Jos. 6:23. *and brought out* Rahab,
10:23. they did so, *and brought forth* those five
24: 6. *And I brought* your fathers *out* of Egypt:
Jud. 6: 8. *and brought* you *forth* out of the house of
19. *and brought* (it) *out* unto him
19:24. *I will bring out* now, and humble ye them,
25. the man took his concubine, *and brought* her *forth*
Ru. 2:18. *and she brought forth,* and gave to her
1Sa.12: 8. *which brought forth* your fathers out of
2Sa.10:16. *and brought out* the Syrians that (were)
13:18. *Then* his servant *brought* her *out,*
22:20. *He brought* me *forth also* into a large place:
1K. 10:29. *did they bring* (them) *out* by their means.
21:13. *Then they carried him forth* out of the city,
2K. 10:22. *And he brought* them *forth* vestments.
26. *And they brought forth* the images
11:12. *And he brought forth* the king's son,
12:11(12). *and they laid it out* to the carpenters
15:20. *And* Menahem *exacted* (marg. *And caused to come forth*)
23: 6. *And he brought out* the grove
24:13. *And he carried out* thence all the treasures
1Ch. 9:28. that they should bring them in and *out* by tale. (marg. bring them in by tale, and *carry them out* by tale)
19:16. *and drew forth* the Syrians that (were)
2Ch. 1:17. *and brought forth* out of Egypt a chariot — so *brought they out* (horses)
16: 2. *Then* Asa *brought out* silver and gold
23:11. *Then they brought out* the king's son,
14. *Then* Jehoiada...*brought out* the captains
29:16. *and brought out* all the uncleanness
Ezr. 1: 8. *Even those did* Cyrus...*bring forth*
8:17. (כתיב)*And I sent* them *with commandment* (lit. according to כתיב, *and I brought* them)
Job 8:10. *Shall* not *they...utter* words out of their
12:22. *and bringeth out* to light the shadow of
28:11. (the thing that is) hid *bringeth he forth* to
38:32. *Canst thou bring forth* Mazzaroth
Ps. 18:19(20). *He brought me forth also* into a large
25:15. *he shall pluck* my feet *out* of the net. (marg. *bring forth*)
31: 4(5). *Pull me out* of the net that they have
66:12. *but thou broughtest us out* into a wealthy
78:16. *He brought* streams *also out* of the rock,
105:37. *He brought them forth also* with silver
43. *And he brought forth* his people with joy,
107:14. *He brought them out* of darkness
28. *he bringeth them out* of their distresses.
136:11. *And brought out* Israel from among them:
143:11. *bring* my soul *out* of trouble.
Pro.29:11. A fool *uttereth* all his mind:
30:33. the churning of milk *bringeth forth* butter, and the wringing of the nose *bringeth forth* blood: so the forcing of wrath *bringeth forth* strife.
Isa. 42: 1. *he shall bring forth* judgment to the
3. *he shall bring forth* judgment unto truth.
61:11. as the earth *bringeth forth* her bud,
Jer. 8: 1. *they shall bring out* the bones (כתיב *and they shall,* &c.)
10:13. *and bringeth forth* the wind
15:19. if *thou take forth* the precious
17:22. Neither *carry forth* a burden
20: 3. *that* Pashur *brought forth* Jeremiah

Jer. 26:23. *And they fetched forth* Urijah out of Egypt,
32:21. *And hast brought forth* thy people Israel
50:25. *and hath brought forth* the weapons
51:16. *and bringeth forth* the wind
52:31. *and brought* him *forth* out of prison,
Eze. 12: 6. *carry* (it) *forth* in the twilight:
20:10. *Wherefore I caused them to go forth* out of
38. *I will bring* them *forth* out of the country
28:18. *therefore will I bring forth* a fire
37: 1. *and carried me out* in the spirit
42: 1 & 46:21. *Then he brought me forth* into the
47: 2. *Then brought he me out* of the way
Mic. 7: 9. *he will bring me forth* to the light,
Hag. 1:11. (that) which the ground *bringeth forth*,

HIPHIL.—*Participle.*

Ex. 6: 7. *bringeth* you *out* from under the burdens
Lev. 22:33. *That brought* you *out* of the land of
Nu. 14:37. *that did bring up* the evil report
23:22. God *brought them out* of Egypt;
24: 8. God *brought him forth* out of Egypt;
Deu 8:14. *which brought thee forth* out of the land
15. *who brought* thee *forth* water
13: 5(6). *which brought* you *out* of the land of
10(11). *which brought thee out* of the land of
Jud. 2:12. *which brought* them *out* of the land of
2Sa. 5: 2. thou wast he *that leddest out*...Israel:
22:49. *And that bringeth* me *forth* from mine
1Ch 11: 2. thou (wast) he *that leddest out*...Israel:
2Ch 9:28. *And they brought* unto Solomon horses *out*
Neh 6:19. *uttered* (lit. had been *uttering*) my words to him.
Ps. 68: 6(7). he *bringeth out* those which are bound
135: 7. *he bringeth* the wind *out* of his treasuries.
Pro. 10:18. *and he that uttereth* a slander,
Isa. 40:26. *that bringeth out* their host by number:
43:17. *Which bringeth forth* the chariot
54:16. *and that bringeth forth* an instrument
Jer. 38:23. *they shall bring out* all thy wives

* HOPHAL.—*Preterite.* *

Eze. 38: 8. *it is brought forth* out of the nations,

HOPHAL.—*Participle.*

Gen 38:25. When she (was) *brought forth*,
Jer. 38:22. *brought forth* to the king of Babylon's
Eze. 14:22. a remnant *that shall be brought forth*,
47: 8. *brought forth* into the sea,

3319 **יְצָא** [*y'tzāh*], Ch.

* SHAPHEL.—*Preterite.* *

Ezr. 6:15. *And* this house *was finished* on the third

3320 **יָצַב** [*yāh-tzav'*].

* HITHPAEL.—*Preterite.* *

Nu. 11:16. *that they may stand* there with thee.
2Ch 11:13. all Israel *resorted* to him (marg. *presented themselves*)

HITHPAEL.—*Infinitive.*

2Sa. 21: 5. we should be destroyed *from remaining*
2Ch 20: 6. none is able *to withstand* thee?
Job 1: 6 & 2:1. sons of God came *to present themselves*
2: 1. Satan came...*to present himself*
Zec. 6: 5. which go forth *from standing* before the

HITHPAEL.—*Imperative.*

Ex. 8:20(16) & 9:13. *and stand* before Pharaoh;
14:13. Fear ye not, *stand still*,
Nu. 23: 3. *Stand* by thy burnt offering,
15. *Stand* here by thy burnt offering,
Deu 31:14. *and present yourselves* in the tabernacle
1Sa. 10:19. *present yourselves* before the Lord
12: 7. Now therefore *stand still*,
16. *stand* and see this great thing,
2Sa. 18:30. Turn aside, (and) *stand* here.
2Ch 20:17. *set yourselves*, stand ye (still),
Job 33: 5. (thy words) in order before me, *stand up*.
Jer. 46: 4. *and stand forth* with (your) helmets;
14. *Stand fast*, and prepare thee;

HITHPAEL.—*Future.*

Ex. 2: 4. *And* his sister *stood* afar off,
19:17. *and they stood* at the nether part of the
34: 5. *and stood* with him there,
Nu. 22:22. *and* the angel of the Lord *stood* in the way
Deu 7:24. *there shall* no man *be able to stand* before
9: 2. *can stand* before the children of Anak!
11:25. *There shall* no man *be able to stand* before
31:14. *and presented themselves* in the tabernacle
Jos. 1: 5. *There shall* not any man *be able to stand*
24: 1. *and they presented themselves* before God.
Jud. 20: 2. *And* the chief...*presented themselves* in the
1Sa. 3:10. the Lord came, *and stood*,
10:23. *when he stood* among the people,
17:16. *and presented himself* forty days.
2Sa. 18:13. thou thyself *wouldest have set thyself*
23:12. *But he stood* in the midst of the ground,
1Ch 11:14. *And they set themselves* in the midst of (that)
Job 38:14. *and they stand* as a garment.
41:10(2). who then *is able to stand* before me?
Ps. 2: 2. The kings of the earth *set themselves*,
5: 5(6). The foolish *shall* not *stand* in thy
36: 4(5). *he setteth himself* in a way (that is) not
94:16. who *will stand up* for me
Pro. 22:29. *he shall stand* before kings; *he shall* not *stand* before mean (men).
Hab 2: 1. *and set me* upon the tower,

יְצַב [*y'tzēhv*], Ch. 3321

* PAEL.—*Infinitive.* *

Dan 7:19. Then I would know *the truth* of the fourth

יָצַג [*yāh-tzag'*]. 3322

* HIPHIL.—*Preterite.* *

Gen 43: 9. *and set him* before thee,
Job 17: 6. *He hath made me also* a byword
Jer. 51:34. *he hath made me* an empty vessel, (כתיב *made us*, &c.)
Hos. 2: 3(5). *and set her* as in the day that she was

HIPHIL.—*Infinitive.*

Deu 28:56. would not adventure *to set* the sole of her

HIPHIL.—*Imperative.*

Am. 5:15. *and establish* judgment in the gate:

HIPHIL.—*Future.*

Gen 30:38. *And he set* the rods which he had pilled
33:15. *Let me* now *leave* with thee (some) of the
47: 2. *and presented them* unto Pharaoh.
Jud. 7: 5. him *shalt thou set* by himself;
8:27. *and put* it in his city,
1Sa. 5: 2. *and set* it by Dagon.
2Sa. 6:17. *and set* it in his place,
1Ch 16: 1. *and set* it in the midst of the tent

HIPHIL.—*Participle.*

Jud. 6:37. I *will put* a fleece of wool in the floor;

* HOPHAL.—*Future.* *

Ex. 10:24. *let* your flocks and your herds *be stayed*:

יִצְהָר *yitz-hāhr'*, m. 3323

Nu. 18:12. All the best of *the oil*,
Deu 7:13 & 11:14. thy wine, *and thine oil*,
12:17. or of thy wine, *or of thy oil*,
14:23 & 18:4. of thy wine, *and of thine oil*,
28:51. (either) corn, wine, *or oil*,
2K. 18:32. a land of *oil* olive and of honey,
2Ch 31: 5. the firstfruits of corn, wine, *and oil*,
32:28. the increase of corn, and wine, *and oil*;
Neh 5:11. the corn, the wine, *and the oil*,
10:37(38). of wine *and of oil*,
39(40) & 13:5, 12. the new wine, *and the oil*,
Jer. 31:12. for wine, and for *oil*,
Hos. 2: 8(10). I gave her corn, and wine, *and oil*,
22(24). and the wine, and *the oil*;
Joel 1:10. *the oil* languisheth.
2:19. I will send you corn, and wine, *and oil*,
24. the fats shall overflow with wine *and oil*.
Hag. 1:11. upon the new wine, and upon *the oil*,
Zec. 4:14. the two *anointed* ones, (lit. two sons of *oil*)

יָצוּעַ [*yāh-tzoo'ăg*], m. 3326

Gen 49: 4. he went up to *my couch*.

1K. 6: 5. (כתיב) he built *chambers* round about,
6. (——) The nethermost *chamber* (was)
10. (——) (then) he built *chambers*
1Ch 5: 1. he defiled his father'*s bed*,
Job 17:13. I have made *my bed* in the darkness.
Ps. 63: 6(7). I remember thee upon *my bed*,
132: 3. up into *my bed;* (lit. the couch of *my bed*)

3329 **יָצִיא** [*yāh-tzee′*], adj.

2Ch 32:21. *And...they that came forth of* his own

3330 **יַצִּיב** *yatz-tzeev′*, Ch. adj.

Dan 2: 8. I know of *certainty* that ye would gain the
45. *and* the dream (is) *certain*, and the
3:24. *True*, O king.
6:12(13). The thing (is) *true*, according to the
7:16. *and* asked him *the truth* of all this.

3326 **יָצִיעַ** *yāh-tzee′ag̃*, com.

1K. 6: 5. built *chambers* round about, (marg. *floors*)
6. *The* nethermost *chamber* (was) five cubits
10. (then) he built *chambers*

3331 **יָצַע** [*yāh-tzag̃′*].

* HIPHIL.—*Future.* *

Ps. 139: 8. *if I make my bed* in hell,
Isa. 58: 5. *to spread* sackcloth and ashes (under him)?

* HOPHAL.—*Future.* *

Est. 4: 3. many *lay* in sackcloth and ashes. (marg. *were laid* under many)
Isa. 14:11. the worm *is spread* under thee,

3332 **יָצַק** *yāh-tzak′*.

* KAL.—*Preterite.* *

Ex. 25:12. *And thou shalt cast* four rings
26:37. *and thou shalt cast* five sockets of brass
29: 7. *and pour* (it) upon his head,
Lev. 2: 1. *and he shall pour* oil upon it,
6. *and pour* oil thereon:
8:15. and *poured* the blood at the bottom of
9: 9. and *poured out* the blood
14:15. *and pour* (it) into the palm
1K. 7:46. plain of Jordan *did* the king *cast them*,
2K. 3:11. which *poured* water on the hands of
4: 4. *and shalt pour out* into all those vessels,
9: 3. take the box of oil, *and pour* (it) on his
2Ch 4:17. plain of Jordan *did* the king *cast them*,

KAL.—*Infinitive.*

Ex. 38:27. the hundred talents of silver were *cast*
Job 38:38. *When* the dust *groweth* into hardness,

KAL.—*Imperative.*

1K. 18:33(34). *and pour* (it) on the burnt sacrifice,
2K. 4:41. *Pour out* for the people, that they may
Eze. 24: 3. also *pour* water into it:

KAL.—*Future.*

Gen 28:18. *and poured* oil upon the top of it.
35:14. *and he poured* oil thereon.
Ex. 36:36. *and he cast* for them four sockets of
37: 3, 13. *And he cast* for it four rings
38: 5. *And he cast* four rings
Lev. 8:12. *And he poured* of the anointing oil upon
14:26. the priest *shall pour* of the oil
Nu. 5:15. *he shall pour* no oil upon it,
1Sa. 10: 1. Samuel took a vial of oil, *and poured* (it)
2Sa. 13: 9. she took a pan, *and poured* (them) out
1K. 22:35. *and* the blood *ran out* of the wound
2K. 4:40. *So they poured out* for the men to eat.
9: 6. *and he poured* the oil on his head,
Isa. 44: 3. *I will pour* water upon him that is thirsty,
— *I will pour* my spirit upon thy seed,

KAL.—*Participle.* Paül.

1K. 7:24. the knops (were) *cast* in two rows,
30. the laver (were) undersetters *molten*,
2Ch 4: 3. Two rows of oxen (were) *cast*,

Job 41:23(15). *they are firm* in themselves;
24(16). His heart *is as firm* as a stone; *yea, as hard* as a piece of the nether (millstone).
Ps. 41: 8(9). disease, (say they), *cleaveth fast* unto him:

* HIPHIL.—*Future.* *

Jos. 7:23. *and laid them out* before the Lord.
2Sa. 15:24. *and they set down* the ark of God;

* HOPHAL.—*Preterite.* *

Ps. 45: 2(3). grace *is poured* into thy lips:

HOPHAL.—*Future.*

Lev. 21:10. whose head the anointing oil *was poured*,
Job 22:16. whose foundation *was overflown* with a flood:

HOPHAL.—*Participle.*

1K. 7:16. he made two chapiters (of) *molten* brass,
23. he made a *molten* sea,
33. their spokes, (were) all *molten*.
2K. 4: 5. she went from him,...and she *poured out*.
2Ch 4: 2. he made a *molten* sea
Job 11:15. yea, thou shalt be *stedfast*,
37:18. as a *molten* looking glass?

יְצֻקָה [*y′tzoo-kāh′*], f. 3333

1K. 7:24. in two rows, *when it was cast*.

יָצַר *yāh-tzar′*. 3335

* KAL.—*Preterite.* *

Gen 2: 8. the man whom *he had formed*.
2K. 19:25. of ancient times *that I have formed it?*
Ps. 74:17. thou *hast made* summer and winter.
95: 5. his hands *formed* the dry (land).
104:26. (whom) *thou hast made* to play therein.
Isa. 37:26. of ancient times, *that I have formed it?*
43: 7. *I have formed him;* yea, I have made him.
21. This people *have I formed* for myself;
44:10. Who *hath formed* a god.
21. *I have formed thee;* thou (art) my servant:
45:18. *he formed it* to be inhabited:
46:11. *I have purposed* (it), I will also do it.

KAL.—*Future.*

Gen 2: 7. *And* the Lord God *formed* man
19. *And*...the Lord God *formed* every beast
Isa. 44:12. *fashioneth it* with hammers,
Jer. 1: 5. *I formed thee* in the belly

KAL.—*Participle.* Poel.

2Sa. 17:28. *earthen* vessels, (lit. vessels of *the potter*)
1Ch. 4:23. These (were) *the potters*,
Ps. 2: 9. shalt dash them in pieces like *a potter*'s
33:15. *He fashioneth* their hearts alike;
94: 9. *he that formed* the eye,
20. *which frameth* mischief by a law?
Isa. 22:11. *neither* had respect unto him *that fashioned it*
27:11. *and he that formed them* will shew them no
29:16. shall be esteemed as *the potter*'s clay:
— the thing framed say *of him that framed it*,
30:14. *the potters*' vessel that is broken in pieces;
41:25. as *the potter* treadeth clay.
43: 1. *and he that formed thee*, O Israel,
44: 2. *and formed thee* from the womb,
9. *They that make* a graven image
24. *and he that formed thee* from the womb,
45: 7. *I form* the light, and create darkness: (lit. *forming*)
9. Woe unto him that striveth with *his Maker!*
— Shall the clay say *to him that fashioneth it*,
11. the Holy One of Israel, *and his Maker*,
18. God himself *that formed* the earth
49: 5. the Lord *that formed me* from the womb
64: 8(7). we (are) the clay, and thou *our potter;*
Jer. 10:16. he (is) *the former of* all (things);
18: 2. go down to *the potter*'s house,
3. I went down to *the potter*'s house,
4. the hand of *the potter:*
— as seemed good to *the potter*
6. cannot I do with you *as this potter?*
— as the clay (is) in *the potter*'s hand,

Jer. 18:11. I *frame* evil against you,
19: 1. Go and get *a potter*'s earthen bottle,
11. as (one) breaketh *a potter*'s vessel,
33: 2. the Lord *that formed* it,
51:19. he (is) *the former of* all things:
Lam. 4: 2. the work of the hands of *the potter!*
Am. 4:13. *he that formeth* the mountains,
7: 1. *he formed* grasshoppers in the beginning
Hab. 2:18. *the maker thereof* hath graven it;
— *the maker of* his work trusteth therein, (marg. *fashioner*)
Zec. 11:13. Cast it unto *the potter:*
— cast them to *the potter*
12: 1. *and formeth* the spirit of man

* NIPHAL.—*Preterite.* *

Isa. 43:10. *there was* no God *formed*,

* PUAL.—*Preterite.* *

Ps. 139:16. (which) in continuance *were fashioned*,

* HOPHAL.—*Future.* *

Isa. 54:17. No weapon *that is formed* against thee shall

3334 **יָצַר** [*yāh-tzar'*].

* KAL.—*Future.* *

Gen 32: 7(8). Jacob was greatly afraid *and distressed:*
Jud. 2:15. *and they were* greatly *distressed.*
10: 9. *so that* Israel *was* sore *distressed.*
1 Sa. 30: 6. *And* David *was* greatly *distressed;*
2Sa. 13: 2. *And* Amnon *was* so *vexed*,
Job 18: 7. The steps of his strength *shall be straitened*,
20:22. In the fulness of his sufficiency he *shall be in straits:*
Pro. 4:12. thy steps *shall* not *be straitened;*
Isa. 49:19. *shall* even now *be* too *narrow* by reason

3336 **יֵצֶר** *yĕh'-tzer*, m.

Gen 6: 5. every *imagination of* the thoughts
8:21. *the imagination of* man's heart (is) evil
Deu 31:21. I know *their imagination*
1Ch 28: 9. all *the imaginations of* the thoughts:
29:18. keep this for ever *in the imagination of*
Ps. 103:14. For he knoweth *our frame;*
Isa. 26: 3. (whose) *mind* (is) stayed (on thee): (marg. or, *thought*, or, *imagination*)
29:16. *or* shall *the thing framed* say
Hab. 2:18. the maker of *his work* trusteth therein, (marg. *his fashion*)

3338 **יְצֻרִים** [*y'tzoo-reem'*], m. pl.

Job 17: 7. *and* all *my members* (are) as a shadow. (marg. or, *thoughts*)

3341 **יָצַת** [*yāh-tzath'*].

* KAL.—*Future.* *

Isa. 9:18(17). *and shall kindle* in the thickets
33:12. (as) thorns cut up *shall they be burned*
Jer. 49: 2. her daughters *shall be burned* with fire:
51:58. her high gates *shall be burned* with fire;

* NIPHAL.—*Preterite.* *

2K. 22:13. wrath of the Lord that *is kindled* against us,
17. *therefore* my wrath *shall be kindled*
Neh 1: 3 & 2:17. gates thereof *are burned* with fire.
Jer. 2:15. his cities *are burned* without inhabitant.
9:10(9). *they are burned up*, (marg. *desolate*)
12(11). the land perisheth (and) *is burned up*
46:19. Noph shall be waste *and desolate* without

* HIPHIL.—*Preterite.* *

2Sa. 14:31. *have* thy servants *set* my field *on fire?*
Jer. 11:16. *he hath kindled* fire upon it,
17:27. *then will I kindle* a fire in the gates
21:14. *and I will kindle* a fire in the forest
32:29. shall come *and set* fire on this city,
43:12. *And I will kindle* a fire in the houses
49:27. *And I will kindle* a fire in the wall
Jer. 50:32. *and I will kindle* a fire in his cities,
51:30. *they have burned* her dwellingplaces;
Am. 1:14. *But I will kindle* a fire in the wall

HIPHIL.—*Imperative.*

2Sa. 14:30. go *and set it* on fire.

HIPHIL.—*Future.*

Jos. 8: 8. (that) *ye shall set* the city on fire:
19. hasted *and set* the city on fire.
Jud. 9:49. *and set* the hold on fire upon them;
2Sa. 14:30. *And* Absalom's servants *set* the field on fire.
Lam. 4:11. *and hath kindled* a fire in Zion,

HIPHIL.—*Participle.*

Eze. 20:47(21:3). I *will kindle* a fire in thee,

יֶקֶב *yeh'-kev*, m. 3342

Nu. 18:27. as the fulness of *the winepress.*
30. as the increase of *the winepress.*
Deu 15:14. *and out of thy winepress:*
16:13. hast gathered in thy corn *and thy wine:*
Jud. 7:25. they slew *at the winepress of* Zeeb,
2K. 6:27. out of *the winepress?*
Job 24:11. tread (their) *winepresses*,
Pro. 3:10. *thy presses* shall burst out with new wine.
Isa. 5: 2. also made *a winepress* therein:
16:10. shall tread out no wine *in* (their) *presses;*
Jer. 48:33. caused wine to fail *from the winepresses:*
Hos. 9: 2. The floor *and the winepress* shall not feed them, (marg. or, *winefat*)
Joel 2:24. *the fats* shall overflow with wine and oil.
3:13(4:13). the press is full, *the fats* overflow;
Hag. 2:16. when (one) came to *the pressfat*
Zec. 14:10. the king's *winepresses.*

יָקַד [*yāh-kad'*]. 3344

* KAL.—*Future.* *

Deu 32:22. *and shall burn* unto the lowest hell,
Isa. 10:16. *he shall kindle* a burning like the burning

KAL.—*Participle.* Poel.

Isa. 65: 5. a fire *that burneth* all the day.

KAL.—*Participle.* Paül.

Isa. 30:14. a sherd to take fire *from the hearth*,

* HOPHAL.—*Future.* *

Lev. 6: 9(2). the fire of the altar *shall be burning*
12(5). the fire upon the altar *shall be burning*
13(6). The fire *shall* ever *be burning*
Jer. 15:14. (which) *shall burn* upon you.
17: 4. (which) *shall burn* for ever.

יְקַד [*y'kad*], Ch. 3345

* P'AL.—*Participle.* Active. *

Dan 3: 6. into the midst of a *burning* fiery furnace.
11. should be cast into the midst of a *burning*
15. shall be cast...into the midst of a *burning*
17. is able to deliver us from the *burning* fiery
20. (and) to cast (them) into the *burning* fiery
21. were cast into the midst of the *burning*
23. bound into the midst of the *burning* fiery
26. came near to the mouth of the *burning*

יְקֵדָה [*y'kēh-dāh'*], Ch. f. 3346

Dan 7:11. and given *to the burning* flame.

יִקְּהָה [*yik-k'hāh'*], f. 3349

Gen 49:10. him (shall) *the gathering of* the people (be).
Pro. 30:17. despiseth *to obey* (his) mother,

יְקוֹד *y'kōhd*, m. 3350

Isa. 10:16. shall kindle *a burning like the burning of* a

3351 יְקוּם *y'koom*, m.

Gen 7: 4. every *living substance* that I have made will
23. every *living substance* was destroyed
Deu 11: 6. all *the substance* that (was) in their possession, (marg. or, *living substance*)

3352 יָקוֹשׁ *yāh-kōhsh'*, m.

Hos. 9: 8. the prophet (is) a snare of *a fowler*

3353 יָקוּשׁ *yāh-koosh'*, m.

Ps. 91: 3. deliver thee from the snare of *the fowler*,
Pro. 6: 5. a bird from the hand of *the fowler*.
Jer. 5:26. he that setteth *snares;*

3357 יַקִּיר *yak-keer'*, adj.

Jer. 31:20. (Is) Ephraim my *dear* son?

3358 יַקִּיר [*yak-keer'*], Ch. adj.

Ezr. 4:10. the nations whom the great *and noble*
Dan 2:11. (it is) a *rare* thing that the king requireth,

3363 יָקַע [*yāh-kag'*].

* KAL—*Future*. *

Gen 32:25(26). *and*...Jacob's thigh *was out of joint*,
Jer. 6: 8. lest my soul *depart* from thee; (marg. *be loosed*, or, *disjointed*)
Eze. 23:17. *and* her mind *was alienated* from them. (marg. *id*).
18. *then* my mind *was alienated* from her,

* HIPHIL.—*Preterite*. *

2Sa. 21: 6. *and we will hang them up* unto the Lord

HIPHIL.—*Imperative*.

Nu. 25: 4. *and hang* them *up* before the Lord

HIPHIL.—*Future*.

2Sa. 21: 9. *and they hanged them* in the hill

* HOPHAL.—*Participle*. *

2Sa. 21:13. they gathered the bones of them *that were hanged*.

3364 יָקַץ [*yāh-katz'*].

* KAL.—*Future*. *

Gen 9:24. *And* Noah *awoke* from his wine,
28:16. *And* Jacob *awaked* out of his sleep,
41: 4. *So* Pharaoh *awoke*.
7. *And* Pharaoh *awoke*, and, behold, (it was)
21. as at the beginning. *So I awoke*.
Jud. 16:14. *And he awaked* out of his sleep,
20. *And he awoke* out of his sleep,
1K. 3:15. *And* Solomon *awoke;* and, behold, (it was)
18:27. he sleepeth, *and must be awaked*.
Ps. 78:65. *Then* the Lord *awaked* as one out of sleep,
Hab. 2: 7. *and awake* that shall vex thee,

3365 יָקַר [*yāh-kar'*].

* KAL.—*Preterite*. *

1 Sa. 26:21. my soul *was precious* in thine eyes
Ps. 139:17. How *precious* also *are* thy thoughts
Isa. 43: 4. Since *thou wast precious* in my sight,
Zec. 11:13. a goodly price *that I was prised* at of them.

KAL.—*Future*.

1 Sa. 18:30. *so that* his name *was* much *set by*. (marg. *precious*)
2K. 1:13. *let* my life,...*be precious* in thy sight.
14. *let* my life now *be precious* in thy sight.
Ps. 49: 8(9). *For* the redemption of their soul (is) *precious*,
72:14. *and precious shall* their blood *be* in his sight.

* HIPHIL.—*Imperative*. *

Pro. 25:17. *Withdraw* thy foot from thy neighbour's

HIPHIL.—*Future*.

Isa. 13:12. *I will make* a man more *precious*

יָקָר *yāh-kāhr'*, adj. 3368

1 Sa. 3: 1. the word of the Lord was *precious*
2Sa. 12:30. a talent of gold with the *precious* stones:
1K. 5:17(31). *costly* stones, (and) hewed stones,
7: 9. All these (were of) *costly* stones,
10. the foundation (was of) *costly* stones,
11. above (were) *costly* stones,
10: 2. very much gold, and *precious* stones:
10. spices very great store, *and precious* stones:
11. the navy...brought in...*precious* stones.
1 Ch 20: 2. (there were) *precious* stones in it;
29: 2. all manner of *precious* stones,
2Ch 3: 6. he garnished the house with *precious* stones
9: 1. gold in abundance, and *precious* stones:
9. of spices great abundance, and *precious*
10. the servants...brought...*precious* stones.
32:27. he made himself treasuries...for *precious*
Job 28:16. with the *precious* onyx, or the sapphire.
31:26. the moon walking (in) *brightness;*
Ps. 36: 7(8). How *excellent* (is) thy lovingkindness, (marg. *precious*)
37:20. the enemies...(shall be) *as the fat of* lambs:
45: 9(10). Kings' daughters (were) *among thy honourable women:*
116:15. *Precious* in the sight of the Lord (is) the
Pro. 1:13. We shall find all *precious* substance,
3:15. She (is) more *precious* than rubies:
6:26. the adulteress will hunt for the *precious* life.
12:27. substance of a diligent man (is) *precious*.
17:27. a man of understanding is of an *excellent*
24: 4. all *precious* and pleasant riches.
Ecc. 10: 1. him that is in *reputation*
Isa. 28:16. a *precious* corner (stone),
Jer. 15:19. take forth *the precious* from the vile,
Lam. 4: 2. The *precious* sons of Zion,
Eze. 27:22. with all *precious* stones, and gold.
28:13. every *precious* stone (was) thy covering,
Dan 11:38. with *precious* stones, and pleasant things.
Zec. 14: 6. light shall not be *clear*, (marg. *precious*)

יְקָר *y'kāhr*, m. 3366

Est. 1: 4. *the honour of* his excellent majesty
20. wives shall give to their husbands *honour*,
6: 3. What *honour* and dignity hath been done
6. What shall be done unto the man whom the king delighteth *to honour?* (lit. delighteth *in his honour*)
— whom would the king delight to do *honour*
7. the man whom the king delighteth *to honour*, (lit. delighteth *in his honour*)
9. man (withal) whom the king delighteth *to honour*, (lit. delighteth *in his honour*)
—, 11. the man whom the king delighteth *to honour*. (lit. delighteth *in his honour*)
8:16. The Jews had light, and gladness, and joy, *and honour*.
Job 28:10. his eye seeth every *precious thing*.
Ps. 49:12(13). man (being) *in honour* abideth not:
20(21). Man (that is) *in honour*,
Pro. 20:15. lips of knowledge (are) a *precious* jewel.
Jer. 20: 5. all *the precious things thereof*,
Eze. 22:25. have taken the treasure *and precious things;*
Zec. 11:13. *a* goodly *price* that I was prised at

יְקָר [*y'kāhr*], Ch. m. 3367

Dan 2: 6. shall receive of me gifts...*and* great *honour:*
37. God of heaven hath given thee...*and glory*.
4:30(27). *and for the honour of* my majesty?
36(33). *and for the glory of* my kingdom,
5:18. gave Nebuchadnezzar thy father a kingdom, and majesty, *and glory*,
20. *and* they took *his glory* from him:
7:14. there was given him dominion, *and glory*,

3369 ## יָקֹשׁ [yāh-kōsh'].

*** KAL.—*Preterite.* ***

Ps. 141: 9. the snares (which) *they have laid*
Jer. 50:24. *I have laid a snare* for thee,

KAL.—*Participle.* Poel.

Ps. 124: 7. the snare of *the fowlers:*

*** NIPHAL.—*Preterite.* ***

Pro. 6: 2. *Thou art snared* with the words of thy
Isa. 8:15. *and be snared*, and be taken.
28:13. be broken, *and snared*, and taken.

NIPHAL.—*Future.*

Deu 7:25. lest *thou be snared* therein:

*** HOPHAL.—*Participle.* ***

Ecc. 9:12. so (are) the sons of men *snared*

3384 ## יָרָא [yāh-rāh'].

*** KAL.—*Infinitive.* ***

2Ch. 26:15. *to shoot* arrows and great stones withal.

*** HIPHIL.—*Future.* ***

2Sa. 11:24. *And* the shooters *shot* from off the wall
Pro. 11:25. he that watereth *shall be watered* also (lit. he that moisteneth *will* also *pour*. This, others have taken for Hophal).

HIPHIL.—*Participle.*

2Sa. 11:24. And *the shooters* shot from off the wall

3372 ## יָרֵא yāh-rēh'.

*** KAL.—*Preterite.* ***

Gen 18:15. I laughed not; for *she was afraid.*
19:30. *he feared* to dwell in Zoar:
26: 7. *he feared* to say, (She is) my wife;
31:31. Because *I was afraid:*
Ex. 1:21. the midwives *feared* God,
3: 6. *he was afraid* to look upon God.
Lev. 19:14. *but shalt fear* thy God:
32. *and fear* thy God:
25:17. *but thou shalt fear* thy God:
36. *but fear* thy God;
43. *but shalt fear* thy God.
Nu. 12: 8. wherefore then *were ye* not *afraid*
Deu 5: 5. *ye were afraid* by reason of the fire,
28:10. *and they shall be afraid* of thee.
31:12. that they may learn, *and fear* the Lord
Jos. 4:14. as *they feared* Moses,
24. that *ye might fear* the Lord your God
Jud. 6:27. *he feared* his father's houshold,
8:20. *he feared*, because he (was) yet a youth.
1Sa. 3:15. Samuel *feared* to shew Eli the vision.
14:26. the people *feared* the oath.
15:24. because *I feared* the people,
31: 4. *he was* sore *afraid.*
2Sa. 1:14. How *wast thou* not *afraid* to stretch forth
1K. 1:50. Adonijah *feared* because of Solomon,
51. Adonijah *feareth* king Solomon:
18:12. *I* thy servant *fear* the Lord from my youth.
2K. 17:25. *they feared* not the Lord:
25:26. *they were afraid* of the Chaldees.
1Ch 10: 4. would not; for *he was* sore *afraid.*
Neh 7: 2. *and feared* God above many.
Job 1: 9. *Doth* Job *fear* God for nought?
37:24. Men *do* therefore *fear him:*
Ps. 55:19(20). therefore *they fear* not God.
76: 8(9). the earth *feared*, and was still,
112: 1. Blessed (is) the man (that) *feareth* the
119:63. all (them) that *fear thee,*
120. *I am afraid* of thy judgments.
Jer. 3: 8. her treacherous sister Judah *feared* not,
41:18. *they were afraid* of them,
44:10. *have they feared*, nor walked in my law,
Eze. 11: 8. *Ye have feared* the sword;
Hos. 10: 3. because *we feared* not the Lord;
Hab. 3: 2. I have heard thy speech, (and) *was afraid:*
Mal. 3: 5. and *fear* not *me*, saith the Lord

KAL.—*Infinitive.*

Deu 4:10. that they may learn *to fear* me
5:29(26). *that they would fear* me,
6:24. *to fear* the Lord our God,
8: 6. to walk in his ways, *and to fear* him.
10:12. *to fear* the Lord thy God,
14:23. that thou mayest learn *to fear* the Lord
17:19. that he may learn *to fear* the Lord
28:58. *that thou mayest fear* this glorious and
31:13. learn *to fear* the Lord your God,
Jos. 22:25. our children cease from *fearing* the Lord.
1Sa. 18:29. Saul was yet the more *afraid* (lit. added *to fear*) of David;
2Sa. 3:11. not answer Abner...*because he feared* him.
1K. 8:43. *to fear* thee, as (do) thy people Israel;
2Ch. 6:33. *and fear* thee, as (doth) thy people Israel,
Neh 1:11. who desire *to fear* thy name:
Ps. 86:11. unite my heart *to fear* thy name.
Jer. 32:39. *that they may fear* me for ever,

KAL.—*Imperative.*

Jos. 24:14. Now therefore *fear* the Lord,
1Sa. 12:24. Only *fear* the Lord,
Ps. 34: 9(10). *O fear* the Lord, ye his saints:
Pro. 3: 7. *fear* the Lord, and depart from evil.
24:21. My son, *fear thou* the Lord
Ecc. 5: 7(6). but *fear thou* God.
12:13. *Fear* God, and keep his commandments:

KAL.—*Future.*

Gen 3:10. *and I was afraid*, because I (was) naked;
15: 1. *Fear* not, Abram: I (am) thy shield,
20: 8. *and* the men *were* sore *afraid.*
21:17. What aileth thee, Hagar? *fear* not;
26:24. *fear* not, for I (am) with thee,
28:17. *And he was afraid*, and said,
32: 7(8). *Then* Jacob *was* greatly *afraid*
35:17. *Fear* not; thou shalt have this son also.
42:35. *and* when (both) they...*they were afraid.*
43:18. *And* the men *were afraid,*
23. Peace (be) to you, *fear* not:
46: 3. *fear* not to go down into Egypt;
50:19. Joseph said unto them, *Fear* not:
21. Now therefore *fear ye* not:
Ex. 1:17. *But* the midwives *feared* God,
2:14. *And* Moses *feared,*
9:30. I know that *ye will* not yet *fear* the Lord
14:10. *and they were* sore *afraid:*
13. *Fear ye* not, stand still,
31. *and* the people *feared* the Lord,
20:20. Moses said unto the people, *Fear* not:
34:30. *and they were afraid* to come nigh him.
Lev. 19: 3. *Ye shall fear* every man his mother,
30 & 26:2. Ye shall keep my sabbaths, and *reverence* my sanctuary:
Nu. 14: 9. neither *fear ye* the people of the land;
— *fear them* not.
21:34. the Lord said unto Moses, *Fear* him not:
Deu 1:21. *fear* not, neither be discouraged.
29. Dread not, neither *be afraid* of them.
2: 4. *and they shall be afraid* of you:
3: 2. the Lord said unto me, *Fear* him not:
22. *Ye shall* not *fear them:*
6: 2. That *thou mightest fear* the Lord
13. *Thou shalt fear* the Lord thy God,
7:18. *Thou shalt* not *be afraid* of them:
10:20. *Thou shalt fear* the Lord thy God;
13: 4(5). after the Lord your God, and *fear* him,
11(12). all Israel shall hear, *and fear,*
17:13. all the people shall hear, *and fear,*
19:20. those which remain shall hear, *and fear,*
20: 1. *be* not *afraid* of them:
3. *fear* not, and do not tremble,
21:21. all Israel shall hear, *and fear.*
31: 6. *fear* not, nor be afraid of them:
8. *fear* not, neither be dismayed.
Jos. 4:14. *and they feared* him,
8: 1. *Fear* not, neither be thou dismayed:
9:24. *therefore we were* sore *afraid* of our lives
10: 2. *That they feared* greatly,
8. the Lord said unto Joshua, *Fear* them not:
25. *Fear* not, nor be dismayed,
11: 6. *Be* not *afraid* because of them:
Jud. 4:18. turn in to me; *fear* not.
6:10. *fear* not the gods of the Amorites,
23. Peace (be) unto thee; *fear* not:
Ru. 3:11. my daughter, *fear* not;
1Sa. 4: 7. *And* the Philistines *were afraid,*
20. *Fear* not; for thou hast born a son.
7: 7. *they were afraid* of the Philistines.
12:14. If *ye will fear* the Lord,

1Sa.12:18. *and* all the people greatly *feared* the Lord
20. Samuel said unto the people, *Fear* not:
17:11. they were dismayed, *and* greatly *afraid.*
24. fled from him, *and were* sore *afraid.*
18:12. *And* Saul *was afraid* of David,
21:12(13). *and was* sore *afraid* of Achish
22:23. Abide thou with me, *fear* not:
23:17. he said unto him, *Fear* not:
28: 5. *he was afraid*, and his heart greatly
13. the king said unto her, *Be* not *afraid:*
20. *and was* sore *afraid*, because of the words
2Sa. 6: 9. *And* David *was afraid* of the Lord
9: 7. David said unto him, *Fear* not:
10:19. *So* the Syrians *feared* to help
12:18. *And* the servants of David *feared* to tell
13:28. then kill him, *fear* not:
1K. 3:28. *and they feared* the king:
8:40. That *they may fear thee*
17:13. Elijah said unto her, *Fear* not;
2K. 1:15. *be* not *afraid* of him.
6:16. he answered, *Fear* not:
10: 4. *But they were* exceedingly *afraid,*
17: 7. *and had feared* other gods,
28. taught them how *they should fear* the Lord.
35, 37. *Ye shall* not *fear* other gods,
36. him *shall ye fear,*
38. neither *shall ye fear* other gods.
39. the Lord your God *ye shall fear;*
19: 6. *Be* not *afraid* of the words
25:24. *Fear* not to be the servants of the
1Ch 13:12. *And* David *was afraid* of God
22:13. *dread* not, nor be dismayed.
28:20. *fear* not, nor be dismayed:
2Ch 6:31. That *they may fear thee,*
20: 3. *And* Jehoshaphat *feared,*
15. *Be* not *afraid* nor dismayed
17. *fear* not, nor be dismayed;
32: 7. *be* not *afraid* nor dismayed
Neh 2: 2. *Then I was* very sore *afraid,*
4:14(8). *Be* not *ye afraid* of them:
6:13. (was) he hired, that *I should be afraid,*
Job 5:21. neither *shalt thou be afraid* of destruction
22. neither *shalt thou be afraid* of the beasts
6:21. ye see (my) casting down, *and are afraid.*
9:35. (Then) would I speak, and not *fear him;*
11:15. thou shalt be stedfast, and *shalt* not *fear:*
32: 6. wherefore I was afraid, *and durst not* shew
Ps. 3: 6(7). *I will* not *be afraid* of ten thousands of
23: 4. *I will fear* no evil:
27: 1. whom *shall I fear?*
3. my heart *shall* not *fear:*
33: 8. *Let* all the earth *fear* the Lord:
40: 3(4). many shall see (it), *and fear,*
46: 2(3). Therefore *will* not *we fear,*
49: 5(6). Wherefore *should I fear* in the days of
16(17). *Be* not *thou afraid* when one is made
52: 6(8). The righteous also shall see, *and fear,*
56: 3(4). What time *I am afraid,*
4(5). *I will* not *fear* what flesh can do unto
11(12). *I will* not *be afraid* what man can do
64: 4(5). suddenly do they shoot at him, and *fear*
9(10). *And* all men *shall fear,*
65: 8(9). They *also...are afraid* at thy tokens:
67: 7(8). *and* all the ends of the earth *shall fear*
72: 5. *They shall fear* thee as long as the sun and
91: 5. *Thou shalt* not *be afraid* for the terror by
102:15(16). *So* the heathen *shall fear*...the Lord,
112: 7. *He shall* not *be afraid* of evil tidings:
8. heart (is) established, *he shall* not *be afraid,*
118: 6. The Lord (is) on my side; *I will* not *fear:*
Pro. 3:25. *Be* not *afraid* of sudden fear,
31:21. She *is* not *afraid* of the snow
Ecc. 3:14. God doeth (it), *that* (men) *should fear*
8:12. which *fear* before him:
12: 5. *they shall be afraid* of (that which is) high,
Isa. 7: 4. Take heed, and be quiet; *fear* not,
8:12. neither *fear ye* their fear,
10:24. *be* not *afraid* of the Assyrian:
25: 3. city of the terrible nations *shall fear thee.*
35: 4. Be strong, *fear* not:
37: 6. *Be* not *afraid* of the words
40: 9. lift (it) up, *be* not *afraid;*
41: 5. The isles saw (it), *and feared;*
10. *Fear thou* not; for I (am) with thee:
13. *Fear* not; I will help thee.
14. *Fear* not, thou worm Jacob,
43: 1. *Fear* not: for I have redeemed thee,

Isa. 43: 5. *Fear* not: for I (am) with thee:
44: 2. *Fear* not, O Jacob, my servant;
51: 7. *fear ye* not the reproach of men,
12. *that thou shouldest be afraid* of a man
54: 4. *Fear* not; for thou shalt not be ashamed:
14. from oppression; for *thou shalt* not *fear:*
57:11. of whom hast thou been afraid *or feared,*
— *and thou fearest* me not?
59:19. *So shall they fear* the name of the Lord
60: 5. Then *thou shalt see,* and flow [see also רָאָה]
Jer. 1: 8. *Be* not *afraid* of their faces:
5:22. *Fear ye* not me? saith the Lord:
24. *Let us* now *fear* the Lord our God,
10: 5. *Be* not *afraid* of them;
7. Who *would* not *fear thee,*
23: 4. *they shall fear* no more,
26:21. *he was afraid*, and fled, and went into
30:10. Therefore *fear* thou not,
40: 9. *Fear* not to serve the Chaldeans:
42:11. *Be* not *afraid* of the king of Babylon,
— *be* not *afraid* of him,
46:27. *fear* not thou, O my servant Jacob,
28. *Fear* thou not, O Jacob my servant,
51:46. lest your heart faint, *and ye fear*
Lam. 3:57. I called upon thee: thou saidst, *Fear* not.
Eze. 2: 6. *be* not *afraid* of them, neither *be afraid* of
— *be* not *afraid* of their words,
3: 9. *fear* them not, neither be dismayed
Dan 10:12. Then said he unto me, *Fear* not,
19. O man greatly beloved, *fear* not:
Joel 2:21. *Fear* not, O land; be glad and rejoice:
22. *Be* not *afraid*, ye beasts of the field:
Am. 3: 8. The lion hath roared, who *will* not *fear?*
Jon. 1: 5. *Then* the mariners *were afraid,*
10. *Then were* the men exceedingly *afraid,*
16. *Then* the men *feared* the Lord
Mic. 7:17. *and shall fear* because of thee.
Zep. 3: 7. Surely *thou wilt fear* me,
16. day it shall be said to Jerusalem, *Fear thou*
Hag. 1:12. *and* the people *did fear* before the Lord.
2: 5. spirit remaineth among you: *fear ye* not.
Zec. 8:13. *fear* not, (but) let your hands be strong.
15. *fear ye* not.
9: 5. Ashkelon shall see (it), *and fear;*
Mal. 2: 5. the fear *wherewith he feared me,*

* NIPHAL.—*Future.* *

Ps.130: 4. (there is) forgiveness with thee, that *thou mayest be feared.*

NIPHAL.—*Participle.*

Gen 28:17. How *dreadful* (is) this place!
Ex. 15:11. *fearful* (in) praises, doing wonders?
34:10. it (is) a *terrible* thing that I will do
Deu 1:19. that great *and terrible* wilderness,
7:21. a mighty God *and terrible.*
8:15. that great *and terrible* wilderness,
10:17. a great God, a mighty, *and a terrible,*
21. these great and *terrible* things,
28:58. this glorious *and fearful* name,
Jud. 13: 6. an angel of God, very *terrible:*
2Sa. 7:23. to do for you great things *and terrible,*
1Ch 16:25. he *also* (is) *to be feared* above all gods.
17:21. a name of greatness *and terribleness,*
Neh 1: 5. the great *and terrible* God,
4:14(8). the Lord, (which is) great *and terrible,*
9:32. the mighty, *and the terrible* God,
Job 37:22. with God (is) *terrible* majesty.
Ps. 45: 4(5). hand shall teach thee *terrible things.*
47: 2(3). the Lord most high (is) *terrible;*
65: 5(6). *terrible things* in righteousness
66: 3. How *terrible* (art thou in) thy works!
5. (he is) *terrible* (in his) doing
68:35(36). (thou art) *terrible* out of thy holy
76: 7(8). Thou, (even) thou, (art) *to be feared*
12(13). (he is) *terrible* to the kings
89: 7(8). *and to be had in reverence* of all
96: 4. he (is) *to be feared* above all gods.
99: 3. Let them praise thy great *and terrible*
106:22. *terrible things* by the Red sea.
111: 9. holy *and reverend* (is) his name.
139:14. I am *fearfully* (and) wonderfully made:
145: 6. the might of *thy terrible acts:*
Isa. 18: 2, 7. a people *terrible* from their beginning
21: 1. from a *terrible* land.
64: 3(2). thou didst *terrible things*

Eze. 1:22. the colour of the *terrible* crystal,
Dan 9: 4. the great *and dreadful* God,
Joel 2:11. of the Lord (is) great *and* very *terrible;*
31(3:4). the great *and* the *terrible* day of the
Hab 1: 7. They (are) terrible and *dreadful:*
Zep. 2:11. The Lord (will be) *terrible*
Mal. 1:14. my name (is) *dreadful* among the
4: 5(3:23). the great *and dreadful* day of the

* PIEL.—*Preterite.* *

2Sa. 14:15. the people *have made me afraid:*

PIEL.—*Infinitive.*

2Ch 32:18. *to affright them,* and to trouble them;
Neh 6:19. Tobiah sent letters *to put me in fear.*

PIEL.—*Participle.*

Neh 6: 9. they all *made* us *afraid,*
14. that would have *put* me *in fear.*

3373 יָרֵא *yāh-rēh',* adj.

Gen22:12. now I know that thou *fearest* God,
32:11(12). I *fear* him, lest he will come and
42:18. This do, and live; (for) I *fear* God:
Ex. 9:20. *He that feared* the word of the Lord
18:21. *such as fear* God, men of truth,
Deu 7:19. the people of whom thou *art afraid.*
20: 8. What man (is there) *that* (is) *fearful*
25:18. *he feared* not God.
Jud. 7: 3. Whosoever (is) *fearful*
10. if thou *fear* to go down,
1Sa. 23: 3. we *be afraid* here in Judah:
1K. 18: 3. Obadiah *feared* the Lord greatly:
2K. 4: 1. thou knowest that thy servant did *fear*
17:32. So they *feared* the Lord,
33. They *feared* the Lord, and served their
34. they *fear* not the Lord,
41. So these nations *feared* the Lord,
Job 1: 1. *and one that feared* God, and eschewed
8 & 2:3. *one that feareth* God, and escheweth
Ps. 15: 4. he honoureth *them that fear* the Lord.
22:23(24). *Ye that fear* the Lord, praise him;
25(26). my vows before *them that fear him.*
25:12. *he that feareth* the Lord?
14. of the Lord (is) *with them that fear him;*
31:19(20). hast laid up *for them that fear thee;*
33:18. of the Lord (is) upon *them that fear* him,
34: 7(8). round *about them that fear him,*
9(10). no want *to them that fear him.*
60: 4(6). Thou hast given a banner *to them that feared thee,*
61: 5(6). the heritage of *those that fear* thy
66:16. Come (and) hear, all *ye that fear* God,
85: 9(10). salvation (is) nigh *them that fear him;*
103:11. is his mercy toward *them that fear him.*
13. the Lord pitieth *them that fear him.*
17. of the Lord (is)...upon *them that fear him,*
111: 5. hath given meat *unto them that fear him:*
115:11. *Ye that fear* the Lord, trust in the Lord:
13. He will bless *them that fear* the Lord,
118: 4. Let them now *that fear* the Lord say,
119:74. *They that fear thee* will be glad
79. Let *those that fear thee* turn unto me,
128: 1. (is) every one *that feareth* the Lord;
4. shall the man be blessed *that feareth* the
135:20. *ye that fear* the Lord, bless the Lord.
145:19. fulfil the desire of *them that fear him:*
147:11. Lord taketh pleasure in *them that fear him,*
Pro. 13:13. *but he that feareth* the commandment
14: 2. that walketh in his uprightness *feareth*
16. A wise (man) *feareth,*
31:30. a woman (that) *feareth* the Lord,
Ecc. 7:18. *he that feareth* God shall come forth
8:12. it shall be well *with them that fear* God,
13. he *feareth* not before God.
9: 2. (he) *that feareth* an oath.
Isa. 50:10. Who (is) among you *that feareth* the
Jer. 26:19. *did he* not *fear* the Lord,
42:11. of whom ye *are afraid;*
16. the sword, which ye *feared,* shall
Dan 1:10. I *fear* my lord the king,
Jon. 1: 9. I *fear* the Lord,
Mal. 3:16. *they that feared* the Lord
— *for them that feared* the Lord,
4: 2(3:20). *you that fear* my name

יִרְאָה *yee-r'āh',* f.

Gen20:11. *the fear of* God (is) not in this place;
Ex. 20:20. that *his fear* may be before your faces,
Deu 2:25. the dread of thee *and the fear of thee*
2Sa. 23: 3. ruling in *the fear of* God.
2Ch 19: 9. Thus shall ye do *in the fear of* the Lord,
Neh 5: 9. ought ye not to walk *in the fear of* our
15. so did not I, because of *the fear of* God.
Job 4: 6. (Is) not (this) *thy fear,*
6:14. *but* he forsaketh *the fear of* the Almighty.
15: 4. thou castest off *fear,*
22: 4. Will he reprove thee *for fear of thee?*
28:28. *the fear of* the Lord, that (is) wisdom;
Ps. 2:11. Serve the Lord *with fear,*
5: 7(8). *in thy fear* will I worship
19: 9(10). *The fear of* the Lord (is) clean,
34:11(12). I will teach you *the fear of* the Lord.
55: 5(6). *Fearfulness* and trembling are come
90:11. *even according to thy fear,* (so is) thy
111:10. *The fear of* the Lord (is) the beginning
119:38. who (is devoted) *to thy fear.*
Pro. 1: 7. *The fear of* the Lord (is) the beginning
29. *and* did not choose *the fear of* the Lord:
2: 5. Then shalt thou understand *the fear of*
8:13. *The fear of* the Lord (is) to hate evil:
9:10. *The fear of* the Lord (is) the beginning
10:27. *The fear of* the Lord prolongeth days:
14:26. *In the fear of* the Lord (is) strong
27. *The fear of* the Lord (is) a fountain of
15:16. Better (is) little *with the fear of* the Lord
33. *The fear of* the Lord (is) the instruction
16: 6. *and by the fear of* the Lord (men) depart
19:23. *The fear of* the Lord (tendeth) to life:
22: 4. By humility (and) *the fear of* the Lord
23:17. (be thou) *in the fear of* the Lord
Isa. 7:25. *the fear of* briers and thorns:
11: 2. the spirit of knowledge *and* of *the fear of*
3. *in the fear of* the Lord:
29:13. *their fear* toward me is taught
33: 6. *the fear of* the Lord (is) his treasure.
63:17. hardened our heart *from thy fear?*
Jer. 32:40. I will put *my fear* in their hearts,
Eze. 1:18. they were so high *that* they were *dreadful;* (lit. *and fear* was to them)
30:13. I will put *a fear* in the land of Egypt.
Jon. 1:10. Then were the men exceedingly (lit. *a* great *fear*) afraid,
16. Then the men feared the Lord exceedingly, (lit. *a* great *fear*)

יָרַד *yāh-rad'.* 3381

* KAL.—*Preterite.* *

Gen43:20. *we came* indeed *down* at the first time
44:26. brother be with us, *then will we go down:*
Ex. 9:19. hail *shall come down* upon them,
11: 8. *And* all these thy servants *shall come down*
15: 5. *they sank* into the bottom as a stone.
19:18. the Lord *descended* upon it in fire:
Nu. 11:17. *And I will come down* and talk with thee
16:30. *and they go down* quick into the pit;
34:11. *And* the coast *shall go down* from
— *and* the border *shall descend,*
12. *And* the border *shall go down* to Jordan,
Deu 10:22. Thy fathers *went down* into Egypt
Jos. 15:10. *and went down* to Beth-shemesh,
16: 3. *And goeth down* westward to the coast
7. *And it went down* from Janohah to
17: 9. *And* the coast *descended* unto the river
18:13. *and* the border *descended* to Ataroth-adar,
16. *And* the border *came down* to the end of
— *and descended* to the valley of Hinnom,
— *and descended* to En-rogel,
17. *and descended* to the stone of Bohan
18. *and went down* unto Arabah:
24: 4. Jacob and his children *went down* into
Jud. 1: 9. the children of Judah *went down* to fight
5:11. then *shall* the people of the Lord *go down*
14. out of Machir *came down* governors,
7:11. shall thine hands be strengthened *to go down* (lit. *and thou shalt go down*) unto
11:37. that I may go up *and down* upon the mountains, (marg. go, *and go down*)
15:12. *We are come down* to bind thee,
Ru. 3: 3. *and get thee down* to the floor:

1Sa. 10: 8. *And thou shalt go down* before me to
17:28. Why *camest thou down* hither?
— *thou art come down* that thou mightest see
23: 6. *he came down* (with) an ephod in his hand
2Sa. 11: 9. Uriah...*went* not *down* to his house.
10. Uriah *went* not *down* unto his house,
— why (then) *didst thou* not *go down* unto
13. *went* not *down* to his house.
19:24(25). Mephibosheth...*came down* to meet
31(32). Barzillai...*came down* from Rogelim,
23:20. *he went down* also and slew a lion
1K. 1:25. *he is gone down* this day,
2: 8. *he came down* to meet me at Jordan,
21:18. whither *he is gone down* to possess it.
2K. 1:14. there *came* fire *down* from heaven,
8:29. And Ahaziah...*went down* to see Joram
9:16. Ahaziah...*was come down* to see Joram.
20:11. by which *it had gone down* in the dial of
1Ch 7:21. *they came down* to take away their cattle.
11:22. *he went down* and slew a lion
2Ch 7: 1. the fire *came down* from heaven,
22: 6. Azariah...*went down* to see Jehoram
Neh 6: 3. whilst I leave it, *and come down* to you?
9:13. *Thou camest down* also upon mount Sinai,
Ps. 119:136. Rivers of waters *run down* mine eyes,
Pro. 18: 8 & 26:22. *they go down* into the innermost
Cant. 6: 2. My beloved *is gone down* into his garden,
11. *I went down* into the garden
Isa. 5:14. *and* he that rejoiceth, *shall descend* into it.
34: 7. *And* the unicorns *shall come down* with
38: 8. which *is gone down* in the sun dial of
— by which degrees *it was gone down.*
52: 4. My people *went down* aforetime
64: 1(63:19). that *thou wouldest come down,*
3(2). *thou camest down,* the mountains
Jer. 13:18. your principalities *shall come down,*
18: 2. Arise, *and go down* to the potter's house,
48:15. his chosen young men *are gone down* to
Eze. 26:16. *Then* all the princes of the sea *shall come down* from their thrones,
27:29. *shall come down* from their ships,
30: 6. *and* the pride of her power *shall come down:*
31:17. *They* also *went down* into hell
32:21. *they are gone down,*
24. which *are gone down* uncircumcised
27. which *are gone down* to hell
30. which *are gone down* with the slain;
47: 8. *and go down* into the desert,
Jon. 1: 5. Jonah *was gone down* into the sides of the
2: 6(7). *I went down* to the bottoms of the
Mic. 1: 3. and *will come down,* and tread upon
12. evil *came down* from the Lord
Hag. 2:22. *and* the horses and their riders *shall come down,*
Zec. 11: 2. the forest of the vintage *is come down.*

KAL.—*Infinitive.*

Gen 43:20. O sir, we came *indeed* down (lit. *coming* we came down)
44:26. We cannot *go down*
46: 3. fear not *to go down* into Egypt;
Ex. 32: 1. Moses delayed *to come down*
34:29. *when* Moses *came down* from mount Sinai
— *when he came down* from the mount,
Nu. 11: 9. *And when* the dew *fell* upon the camp
Deu 20:20. until *it be subdued.* (marg. *come down*)
28:52. thy high and fenced walls *come down,*
Jud. 1:34. they would not suffer them *to come down*
7:10. if thou fear *to go down,*
1Sa. 23: 8. Saul called all the people...*to go down* to
20. the desire of thy soul *to come down;*
2Sa. 19:20(21). *to go down* to meet my lord the king.
1K. 21:16. Ahab rose up *to go down* to the vineyard
2K. 7:17. *when* the king *came down* to him.
2Ch 7: 3. *when* all the children of Israel saw how the fire *came down,*
Neh. 6: 3. so that I cannot *come down:*
Job 33:24. Deliver him *from going down* to the pit:
Ps. 30: 3(4). *that I should not go down* to the pit.
9(10). *when I go down* to the pit?
Isa. 30: 2. That walk *to go down* into Egypt,
32:19. When it shall hail, *coming down* on the
Eze. 31:15. In the day *when he went down* to the grave

KAL.—*Imperative.*

Gen 42: 2. *get you down* thither,
45: 9. *come down* unto me, tarry not:
Ex. 19:21. *Go down,* charge the people,
24. Away, *get thee down,*
32: 7. Go, *get thee down;*
Deu 9:12. Arise, *get thee down* quickly from hence;
Jud. 7: 9. Arise, *get thee down* unto the host;
10. *go thou* with Phurah thy servant *down*
24. *Come down* against the Midianites,
1Sa. 6:21. *come ye down,* (and) fetch it up to you.
15: 6. *get you down* from among the Amalekites,
23: 4. Arise, *go down* to Keilah;
20. Now therefore, O king, *come down*
2Sa. 11: 8. *Go down* to thy house, and wash thy feet.
1K. 18:44. Prepare (thy chariot), *and get thee down,*
21:18. Arise, *go down* to meet Ahab
2K. 1: 9. Thou man of God,...*Come down.*
11. O man of God,...*Come down* quickly.
15. *Go down* with him: be not afraid of him.
2Ch. 20:16. To morrow *go ye down* against them:
Isa. 47: 1. *Come down,* and sit in the dust,
Jer. 22: 1. *Go down* to the house of the king of Judah,
48:18. *come down* from (thy) glory,
Eze. 32:19. *go down,* and be thou laid with the
Joel 3:13(4:13). come, *get you down;* for the press
Am. 6: 2. *then go down* to Gath of the Philistines:

KAL.—*Future.*

Gen 11: 5. *And* the Lord *came down* to see the city
7. *let us go down,* and there confound their
12:10. *and* Abram *went down* into Egypt to sojourn
15:11. *And* when the fowls *came down* upon the
18:21. *I will go down* now, and see
24:16. *and she went down* to the well,
45. *and she went down* unto the well,
26: 2. *Go* not *down* into Egypt;
37:35. *I will go down* into the grave unto my son
38: 1. *that* Judah *went down* from his brethren,
42: 3. *And* Joseph's ten brethren *went down* to
38. My son *shall* not *go down* with you;
43: 4. *we will go down* and buy thee food:
5. wilt not send (him), *we will* not *go down:*
15. rose up, *and went down* to Egypt,
44:23. Except your youngest brother *come down*
46: 4. *I will go down* with thee into Egypt;
Ex. 2: 5. *And* the daughter of Pharaoh *came down*
3: 8. *And I am come down* to deliver them
19:11. the third day the Lord *will come down*
14. *And* Moses *went down* from the mount
20. *And* the Lord *came down* upon mount Sinai,
25. *So* Moses *went down* unto the people,
32:15. Moses turned, *and went down* from the
33: 9. the cloudy pillar *descended,*
34: 5. *And* the Lord *descended* in the cloud,
Lev. 9:22. *and came down* from offering of the
Nu. 11: 9. the manna *fell* upon it.
25. *And* the Lord *came down* in a cloud,
12: 5. *And* the Lord *came down* in the pillar of
14:45. *Then* the Amalekites *came down,*
16:33. They,...*went down* alive into the pit,
20:15. *How* our fathers *went down* into Egypt,
28. *and* Moses and Eleazar *came down* from the
Deu 9:15. So I turned *and came down* from the mount,
10: 5. I turned myself *and came down* from the
26: 5. *and he went down* into Egypt,
28:24. from heaven *shall it come down* upon thee,
43. *thou shalt come down* very low.
Jos. 2:23. the two men returned, *and descended* from
Jud. 3:27. *and* the children of Israel *went down* with
28. *And they went down* after him,
4:14. *So* Barak *went down* from mount Tabor,
15. *so that* Sisera *lighted down* off (his) chariot,
7:11. *Then went he down* with Phurah
14: 1. *And* Samson *went down* to Timnath,
5. *Then went* Samson *down,*
7. *And he went down,* and talked with the
10. *So* his father *went down* unto the woman:
19. *and he went down* to Ashkelon,
15: 8. *and he went down* and dwelt in the top of
11. *Then* three thousand men of Judah *went*
16:31. *Then* his brethren and all the house of his father *came down,*
Ru. 3: 6. *And she went down* unto the floor,
1Sa. 9:25. *when they were come down* from the high
13:12. The Philistines *will come down* now upon
20. *But* all the Israelites *went down* to the
14:36. *Let us go down* after the Philistines
37. *Shall I go down* after the Philistines?
15:12. passed on, *and gone down* to Gilgal.

1Sa.17: 8. *and let him come down* to me.
20:19. *thou shalt go down* quickly,
22: 1. *they went down* thither to him.
23:11. *will* Saul *come down*, as thy servant hath
— the Lord said, *He will come down*.
25. *wherefore he came down* into a rock,
25: 1. *and went down* to the wilderness of Paran.
23. she hasted, *and lighted* off the ass,
26: 2. *and went down* to the wilderness of Ziph,
6. Who *will go down* with me to Saul to the camp? And Abishai said, *I will go down*
10. *he shall descend* into battle, and perish.
29: 4. *let him* not *go down* with us to battle,
2Sa. 5:17. David heard (of it), *and went down* to the
17:18. whither *they went down*.
19:16(17). *and came down* with the men of Judah
21:15. *and* David *went down*, and his servants with
22:10. He bowed the heavens also, *and came down;*
23:13. *And* three of the thirty chief *went down*,
21. *but he went down* to him with a staff,
1K. 1:38. *So* Zadok...*went down*,
22: 2. *that* Jehoshaphat the king of Judah *came down*
2K. 1: 4, 6. *Thou shalt* not *come down* from that bed
10, 12. *let* fire *come down* from heaven,
— *And there came down* fire from heaven,
12. *And* the fire of God *came down* from heaven,
15. he arose, *and went down* with him
16. *thou shalt* not *come down* off that bed
2: 2. *So they went down* to Beth-el.
3:12. *So* the king of Israel...*went down* to him.
5:14. *Then went he down*, and dipped himself
6:18. *when they came down* to him,
10:13. *and we go down* to salute the children of
13:14. *And* Joash the king of Israel *came down*
1Ch 11:15. *Now* three of the thirty captains *went down*
23. *and he went down* to him with a staff,
2Ch 18: 2. *And* after (certain) years *he went down* to
Job 17:16. *They shall go down* to the bars of the pit,
Ps. 7:16(17). his violent dealing *shall come down*
18: 9(10). the heavens also, *and came down:*
49:17(18). his glory *shall* not *descend* after him.
55:15(16). *let them go down* quick into hell:
72: 6. *He shall come down* like rain
104: 8. *they go down* by the valleys
107:26. *they go down* again to the depths:
144: 5. Bow thy heavens, O Lord, *and come down:*
Pro.30: 4. ascended up into heaven, *or descended?*
Isa. 31: 4. so *shall* the Lord of hosts *come down*
34: 5. *it shall come down* upon Idumea,
55:10. as the rain *cometh down*,
63:14. As a beast *goeth down* into the valley,
Jer. 9:18(17). *that* our eyes *may run down* with tears,
13:17. mine eye shall weep sore, *and run down*
14:17. *Let* mine eyes *run down* with tears
18: 3. *Then I went down* to the potter's house,
36:12. *Then he went down* into the king's house,
50:27. *let them go down* to the slaughter:
Lam.1: 9. *therefore she came down* wonderfully:
3:48. Mine eye *runneth down* with rivers of water
Eze.26:11. thy strong garrisons *shall go down* to the
31:12. *and* all the people of the earth *are gone down*
Jon. 1: 3. *and went down* to Joppa;
— so he paid the fare thereof, *and went down*

KAL.—*Participle*. Poel.

Gen28:12. angels of God ascending *and descending*
Deu 9:21. the brook *that descended* out of the mount.
Jos. 3:13. (from) the waters *that come down* from
16. the waters *which came down* from above
— *and those that came down* toward the sea
Jud. 9:36. there *come* people *down* from the top of the
37. there *come* people *down* by the middle
1Sa. 9:27. *as* they *were going down* to the end of the
10: 5. meet a company of prophets *coming down*
8. I *will come down* unto thee,
25:20. *that she came down* by the covert of the hill,
— his men *came down* against her;
30:24. as his part (is) *that goeth down* to the battle,
2K. 6:33. the messenger *came down* unto him:
12:20(21). *which goeth down* to Silla.
Neh. 3:15. the stairs *that go down* from the city
Job 7: 9. *he that goeth down* to the grave
Ps. 22:29(30). all *they that go down to* the dust
28: 1. become like *them that go down into* the pit.
30: 3(4). (כתיב) *that I should not go down* to the
88: 4(5). with *them that go down into* the pit:
Ps.107:23. *They that go down to* the sea
115:17. any *that go down into* silence.
133: 2. *that ran down* upon the beard,
— *that went down* to the skirts of his garments;
3. *that descended* upon the mountains
143: 7. be like unto *them that go down into* the pit.
Pro. 1:12. *as those that go down into* the pit:
5: 5. Her feet *go down* to death;
7:27. *going down* to the chambers of death.
Ecc. 3:21. the spirit of the beast *that goeth downward*
Isa. 14:19. *that go down* to the stones of the pit;
15: 3. every one shall howl, weeping *abundantly*. (lit. *descending* into weeping)
31: 1. Woe to them *that go down* to Egypt
38:18. *they that go down* into the pit
42:10. *ye that go down* to the sea,
Lam. 1:16. mine eye *runneth down* with water,
Eze.26:20. *them that descend into* the pit,
— *them that go down to* the pit,
31:14. *them that go down to* the pit.
16. *them that descend into* the pit:
32:18. *them that go down into* the pit.
24, 25, 29, 30. *them that go down to* the pit.
47: 1. the waters *came down* from under

* HIPHIL.—*Preterite*. *

Gen39: 1. which *had brought him down* thither.
42:38. *then shall ye bring down* my gray hairs
43:22. other money *have we brought down*
44:29. *And* if ye take...*ye shall bring down* my gray
31. *and* thy servants *shall bring down* the gray
45:13. ye shall haste *and bring down* my father
Nu. 4: 5. *and they shall take down* the covering vail,
Deu21: 4. *And* the elders of that city *shall bring down*
Jos. 2:18. window which *thou didst let us down* by:
1Sa. 6:15. And the Levites *took down* the ark
1K. 1:33. *and bring* him *down* to Gihon:
2: 9. *but* his hoar head *bring* thou *down* to the
2K. 16:17. *took down* the sea from off the brasen oxen
Isa. 43:14. *and have brought down* all their nobles,
Lam.2:10. the virgins of Jerusalem *hang down* their
Eze.26:20. *When I shall bring thee down* with them
34:26. *and I will cause* the shower *to come down* in
Joel 3: 2(4:2). *and will bring them down* into the
Am. 3:11. *and he shall bring down* thy strength

HIPHIL.—*Infinitive*.

Gen37:25. going *to carry* (it) *down* to Egypt.
Eze.31:16. *when I cast* him *down* to hell

HIPHIL.—*Imperative*.

Gen43: 7. *Bring* your brother *down?*
11. *and carry down* the man a present,
44:21. *Bring him down* unto me,
Ex. 33: 5. therefore now *put off* thy ornaments
Jud. 7: 4. *bring* them *down* unto the water,
Ps. 56: 7(8). in (thine) anger *cast down* the people,
59:11(12). *and bring them down*, O Lord our
Lam.2:18. *let* tears *run down* like a river
Eze.32:18. *and cast them down*, (even) her,

HIPHIL.—*Future*.

Gen24:18. she hasted, *and let down* her pitcher
46. she made haste, *and let down* her pitcher
44:11. *Then they* speedily *took down* every man
Nu. 1:51. the Levites *shall take* it *down:*
Deu 1:25. *and brought* (it) *down* unto us,
Jos. 2:15. *Then she let them down* by a cord
8:29. *that they should take* his carcase *down*
10:27. *and they took them down* off the trees,
Jud. 7: 5. *So he brought down* the people
16:21. *and brought* him *down* to Gaza,
1Sa.19:12. *So* Michal *let* David *down*
21:13(14). *and let* his spittle *fall down* upon his
30:15. *Canst thou bring me down* to this company?
— *and I will bring thee down* to this company.
16. *And when he had brought him down*,
1K. 1:53. *and they brought him down* from the altar.
2: 6. *let not* his hoar head *go down* to the grave
5: 9(23). My servants *shall bring* (them) *down*
17:23. *and brought him down* out of the chamber
18:40. *and* Elijah *brought them down* to the brook
2K. 11:19. *and they brought down* the king
2Ch 23:20. *and brought down* the king from the house
Ps. 55:23(24). thou, O God, *shalt bring them down*
78:16. *and caused* waters *to run down* like rivers.
Pro.21:22. *and casteth down* the strength of the
Isa. 10:13. *and I have put down* the inhabitants

Isa. 63: 6. *and I will bring down* their strength
Jer. 49:16. *I will bring thee down* from thence,
51:40. *I will bring them down* like lambs to the
Eze.28: 8. *They shall bring thee down* to the pit,
Hos. 7:12. *I will bring them down* as the fowls of the
Joel 2:23. *and he will cause to come down* for you the
Am. 9: 2. thence *will I bring them down:*
Obad. 3. Who *shall bring me down* to the ground?
4. thence *will I bring thee down,*

HIPHIL.—*Participle.*

1Sa. 2: 6. *he bringeth down* to the grave,
2Sa.22:48. *and that bringeth down* the people

* HOPHAL.—*Preterite.* *

Gen39: 1. Joseph *was brought down* to Egypt;
Nu. 10:17. *And* the tabernacle *was taken down;*
1Sa.30:24. (כתיב) as his part (is) *that goeth down*
Isa. 14:11. Thy pomp *is brought down* to the grave,
Eze.31:18. *yet shalt thou be brought down* with the trees
Zec.10:11. *and* the pride of Assyria *shall be brought down,*

HOPHAL.—*Future.*

Isa. 14:15. *thou shalt be brought down* to hell,

3384 ## יָרָה *yāh-rāh'.*

* KAL.—*Preterite.* *

Gen31:51. behold (this) pillar, which *I have cast*
Ex. 15: 4. his host *hath he cast* into the sea:
Jos. 18: 6. *that I may cast* lots for you
1Sa.20:36. he *shot* an arrow beyond him.
37. the arrow which Jonathan *had shot,*
Job 38: 6. who *laid* the corner stone thereof;

KAL.—*Infinitive.*

Ex. 19:13. he shall surely be stoned, or shot *through;* (lit. *shooting* shall be shot)
Ps. 11: 2. *that* they *may* privily *shoot* at the upright
64: 4(5). *That* they *may shoot* in secret at the

KAL.—*Imperative.*

2K. 13:17. Then Elisha said, *Shoot.*

KAL.—*Future.*

Nu. 21:30. *We have shot at them;* Heshbon is perished

KAL.—*Participle.* Poel.

1Ch 10: 3. he was wounded of *the archers.*
2Ch 35:23. *the archers* shot at king Josiah;
Pro.26:18. *who casteth* firebrands,
Hos. 6: 3. as the latter (and) *former rain* unto the earth. [perhaps, as the latter rain *sprinkling* the earth]

* NIPHAL.—*Future.* *

Ex. 19:13. he shall surely be stoned, or *shot* through;

* HIPHIL.—*Preterite.* *

Ex. 4:12. *and teach thee* what thou shalt say.
15. *and will teach* you what ye shall do.
1Sa.12:23. *but I will teach* you the good...way:
2K. 12: 2(3). the priest *instructed him.*
Job 30:19. *He hath cast* me into the mire,
Ps.119:102. thou *hast taught me.*
Pro. 4:11. *I have taught thee* in the way of wisdom;

HIPHIL.—*Infinitive.*

Gen46:28. *to direct* his face unto Goshen;
Ex. 24:12. *that thou mayest teach them.*
35:34. *And...that* he *may teach,*
Lev.10:11. *And that ye may teach* the children of Israel
14:57. *To teach* when (it is) unclean,

HIPHIL.—*Imperative.*

Job 6:24. *Teach me,* and I will hold my tongue:
34:32. (That which) I see not *teach* thou *me:*
Ps. 27:11 & 86:11. *Teach me* thy way, O Lord,
119:33. *Teach me,* O Lord, the way of thy statutes;

HIPHIL.—*Future.*

Ex. 15:25. *and* the Lord *shewed him* a tree,
Deu17:10. all that *they inform thee:*
11. the law which *they shall teach thee,*
24: 8. all that the priests the Levites *shall teach*
33:10. *They shall teach* Jacob thy judgments,
Jud.13: 8. *and teach us* what we shall do
1Sa.20:20. *I will shoot* three arrows
2Sa.11:20. knew ye not that *they would shoot*
1K. 8:36. that *thou teach them* the good way
2K. 13:17. Elisha said, Shoot. *And he shot.*
17:27. *and let him teach them* the manner
19:32. He shall not come into this city, nor *shoot*
2Ch 6:27. *thou hast taught them* the good way,
35:23. *And* the archers *shot* at king Josiah;
Job 8:10. *Shall* not *they teach thee,*
12: 7. now the beasts, *and they shall teach thee;*
8. speak to the earth, *and it shall teach thee:*
27:11. *I will teach* you by the hand of God:
Ps. 25: 8. therefore *will he teach* sinners in the way.
12. *him shall he teach* in the way
32: 8. I will instruct thee *and teach thee*
45: 4(5). *and* thy right hand *shall teach thee*
64: 4(5). suddenly *do they shoot at him,*
7(8). *But* God *shall shoot at them*
Pro. 4: 4. *He taught me also,* and said unto me,
Isa. 2: 3. *and he will teach us* of his ways,
28: 9. Whom *shall he teach* knowledge?
26. God...*doth teach him.*
37:33. He shall not come into this city, nor *shoot*
Eze.44:23. *they shall teach* my people
Hos10:12. till he come *and rain* righteousness
Mic. 3:11. the priests thereof *teach* for hire,
4: 2. *and he will teach us* of his ways,
Hab. 2:19. Arise, *it shall teach!*

HIPHIL.—*Participle.*

1Sa.20:36. find out now the arrows which I *shoot.*
31: 3. *the archers* (marg. *shooters,* men with bows) hit him; and he was sore wounded *of the archers.*
2K. 17:28. *taught* (lit. was *teaching*) them how they
1Ch 10: 3. and *the archers* (marg. *the shooters* with bows) hit him,
2Ch 15: 3. without a *teaching* priest,
Job 36:22. who *teacheth* like him?
Pro. 5:13. have not obeyed the voice of *my teachers,*
6:13. he *teacheth* with his fingers;
Isa. 9:15(14). the prophet *that teacheth* lies,
30:20. yet shall not *thy teachers* be removed
— thine eyes shall see *thy teachers:*
Hab. 2:18. the molten image, *and a teacher of* lies,

יָרַה [*yāh-rah'*]. 7297

* KAL.—*Future.* *

Isa. 44: 8. Fear ye not, neither *be afraid:* [see also רָהָה]

יָרוֹק *yāh-rōhk',* m. 3387

Job 39: 8. he searcheth after every *green thing.*

יָרֵחַ *yāh-rēh'ăgh,* m. 3394

Gen37: 9. the sun *and the moon* and the eleven stars
Deu 4:19. the sun, and *the moon,* and the stars,
17: 3. either the sun, or *moon,*
Jos. 10:12. *and thou, Moon,* in the valley of Ajalon.
13. the sun stood still, *and the moon* stayed,
2K. 23: 5. to the sun, *and to the moon,*
Job 25: 5. Behold even to *the moon,*
31:26. *or the moon* walking (in) brightness;
Ps. 8: 3(4). *the moon* and the stars, which thou hast
72: 5. thee as long as the sun and *moon* endure,
7. abundance of peace so long as *the moon*
89:37(38). be established for ever *as the moon,*
104:19. He appointed *the moon* for seasons:
121: 6. *nor the moon* by night.
136: 9. *The moon* and stars to rule by night:
148: 3. Praise ye him, sun *and moon:*
Ecc.12: 2. *or the moon,* or the stars,
Isa. 13:10. *and the moon* shall not cause her light to
60:19. *the moon* give light unto thee:
Jer. 8: 2. before the sun, *and the moon,*
31:35. the ordinances of *the moon*
Eze.32: 7. *and the moon* shall not give her light.
Joel 2:10. the sun *and the moon* shall be dark,
31(3:4). *and the moon* into blood,
3:15(4:15). The sun and the *moon* shall be darkened,
Hab. 3:11. The sun (and) *moon* stood still

3391 **יֶרַח** *yeh'-ragh*, m.

Ex. 2: 2. she hid him three *months*.
Deu 21:13. her father and her mother *a* full *month*:
33:14. the precious things put forth by *the moon*, (marg. *moons*)
1K. 6:37. *in the month* Zif:
38. in the eleventh year, *in the month* Bul,
8: 2. *in the month* Ethanim,
2K. 15:13. he reigned *a* full *month* in Samaria.
Job 3: 6. it not come into the number of *the months*.
7: 3. So am I made to possess *months of* vanity,
29: 2. Oh that I were *as* (in) *months* past,
39: 2. Canst thou number *the months* (that) they
Isa. 60:20. *neither* shall *thy moon* withdraw
Zec. 11: 8. shepherds also I cut off *in* one *month*;

3393 **יְרַח** [*y'ragh*], Ch. m.

Ezr. 6:15. was finished on the third day *of the month*
Dan 4:29(26). At the end of twelve *months* he walked

3399 **יָרַט** *yāh-rat'*.

* KAL.—*Preterite*. *

Nu. 22:32. (thy) way *is perverse* before me:
Job 16:11. and *turned me over* into the hands of the

3401 **יָרִיב** [*yāh-reev'*], m.

Ps. 35: 1. O Lord, with *them that strive with me*:
Isa. 49:25. with *him that contendeth with thee*.
Jer. 18:19. the voice of *them that contend with me*.

3407 **יְרִיעָה** *y'ree-gāh'*, f.

Ex. 26: 1. ten *curtains* (of) fine twined linen,
2, 8. The length of one *curtain*
—, 8. the breadth of one *curtain*
— every one of *the curtains*
3. *The* five *curtains* shall be coupled
— (other) five *curtains* (shall be) coupled
4, 10. the edge of *the* one *curtain*
— the uttermost edge of (another) *curtain*,
5. loops shalt thou make *in the* one *curtain*,
— the edge of *the curtain*
6. couple *the curtains* together
7. thou shalt make *curtains* (of) goats' (hair)
— eleven *curtains* shalt thou make.
8. the eleven *curtains* (shall be all) of one
9. thou shalt couple five *curtains*
— six *curtains* by themselves, and shalt double *the* sixth *curtain*
10. the edge of *the curtain*
12. *of the curtains of* the tent, *the* half *curtain* that remaineth,
13. the length of *the curtains of* the tent,
36: 8. ten *curtains* (of) fine twined linen,
9, 15. The length of one *curtain*
— the breadth of one *curtain*
— *the curtains* (were) all of one size.
10. he coupled *the* five *curtains*
— (the other) five *curtains* he coupled
11. the edge of one *curtain*
— the uttermost side of (another) *curtain*,
12. Fifty loops made he *in* one *curtain*,
— the edge of *the curtain*
13. coupled *the curtains* one unto another
14. he made *curtains* (of) goats' (hair)
— eleven *curtains* he made them.
15. the breadth of one *curtain*: *the* eleven *curtains* (were) of one size.
16. he coupled five *curtains*
— six *curtains* by themselves.
17. the uttermost edge of *the curtain*
— loops made he upon the edge of *the curtain*
Nu. 4:25. they shall bear *the curtains of*
2Sa. 7: 2. the ark of God dwelleth within *curtains*.
1Ch. 17: 1. the ark...(remaineth) under *curtains*.
Ps. 104: 2. stretchest out the heavens *like a curtain*:
Cant. 1: 5. *as the curtains of* Solomon.
Isa. 54: 2. *and* let them stretch forth *the curtains*
Jer. 4:20. *my curtains* in a moment.
10:20. (there is) none...to set up *my curtains*.
49:29. they shall take to themselves *their curtains*,
Hab. 3: 7. *the curtains of* the land of Midian did

יָרֵךְ *yāh-rēch'*, f. 3409

Gen 24: 2. Put, I pray thee, thy hand under *my thigh*:
9. the servant put his hand under *the thigh of*
32:25(26). he touched the hollow of *his thigh*; and the hollow of Jacob's *thigh* was out
31(32). he halted upon *his thigh*.
32(33). the hollow of *the thigh*,
—(—). the hollow of Jacob's *thigh*
46:26. which came out of *his loins*, (marg. *thigh*)
47:29. put, I pray thee, thy hand under *my thigh*,
Ex. 1: 5. the souls that came out of *the loins* (marg. *thigh*) *of* Jacob
25:31. *his shaft*, and his branches,
28:42. from the loins even unto *the thighs*
32:27. Put every man his sword by *his side*,
37:17. *his shaft*, and his branch,
40:22. *the side of* the tabernacle northward,
24. *the side of* the tabernacle southward.
Lev. 1:11. *the side of* the altar northward
Nu. 3:29. *the side of* the tabernacle southward.
35. *the side of* the tabernacle northward.
5:21. the Lord doth make *thy thigh* to rot,
22. make (thy) belly to swell, and (thy) *thigh*
27. *her thigh* shall rot:
8: 4. unto *the shaft thereof*,
Jud. 3:16. upon his right *thigh*.
21. took the dagger from his right *thigh*,
8:30. had threescore and ten sons of *his body* begotten: (marg. going out of *his thigh*)
15: 8. he smote them hip and *thigh*
2K. 16:14. put it on *the* north *side of* the altar.
Ps. 45: 3(4). Gird thy sword upon (thy) *thigh*,
Cant. 3: 8. every man (hath) his sword upon *his thigh*
7: 1(2). the joints of *thy thighs* (are) like jewels,
Jer. 31:19. I smote upon (my) *thigh*:
Eze. 21:12(17). smite therefore upon (thy) *thigh*.
24: 4. *the thigh*, and the shoulder;

יַרְכָה [*yar-chāh'*], f. 3411

Gen 49:13. *and his border* (shall be) unto Zidon.
Ex. 26:22. *And for the sides of* the tabernacle
23. corners of the tabernacle *in the two sides*.
27. *for the two sides* westward.
36:27. *And for the sides of* the tabernacle westward
28. corners of the tabernacle *in the two sides*.
32. *for the sides* westward.
Jud. 19: 1. sojourning *on the side of* mount Ephraim,
18. toward *the side of* mount Ephraim;
1Sa. 24: 3(4). his men remained *in the sides of* the
1K. 6:16. *on the sides of* the house,
2K. 19:23. to *the sides of* Lebanon,
Ps. 48: 2(3). (on) *the sides of* the north,
128: 3. *by the sides of* thine house:
Isa. 14:13. *in the sides of* the north:
15. to *the sides of* the pit.
37:24. to *the sides of* Lebanon;
Jer. 6:22. great nation shall be raised *from the sides of*
25:32. *from the coasts of* the earth.
31: 8. gather them *from the coasts of* the earth,
50:41. raised up *from the coasts of* the earth.
Eze. 32:23. Whose graves are set *in the sides of* the pit,
38: 6. Togarmah of *the* north *quarters*,
15. thy place *out of the* north *parts*,
39: 2. cause thee to come up *from the* north *parts*, (marg. *sides of* the north)
46:19. (was) a place *on the two sides* westward.
Am. 6:10. him that (is) *by the sides of* the house,
Jon. 1: 5. Jonah was gone down into *the sides of* the

יַרְכָה [*yar-chāh'*], Ch. f. 3410

Dan 2:32. his belly *and his thighs* of brass, (marg. or, *sides*)

3415 **יָרַע** [*yāh-rag'*].

* KAL.—*Preterite.* *

Isa. 15: 4. his life *shall be grievous* unto him.

KAL.—*Future.*

Gen21:11. *And* the thing *was* very *grievous* in
12. *Let* it not *be grievous* in thy sight
38:10. *And* the thing which he did *displeased* the Lord: (lit. *was evil* in the eyes of)
48:17. *And* when Joseph...*it displeased* (lit. *id.*)
Deu15:10. thine heart *shall* not *be grieved*
28:54. his eye *shall be evil* toward his brother
56. her eye *shall be evil* toward the husband
1Sa. 1: 8. why eatest thou not? and why *is* thy heart *grieved?*
8: 6. *But* the thing *displeased* Samuel, (marg. *was evil* in the eyes of)
18: 8. *and* the saying *displeased* him; (lit. *id.*)
2Sa.11:25. *Let* not this thing *displease* thee, (lit. *id.*)
27. *But* the thing that David had done *displeased* the Lord. (marg. *id.*)
20: 6. Now *shall* Sheba...*do* us more *harm*
1Ch 21: 7. *And* God *was displeased* with this thing; (marg. *it was evil* in the eyes of)
Neh. 2: 3. why *should* not my countenance *be sad,*
10. *it grieved* them exceedingly
13: 8. *And it grieved* me sore:
Job 20:26. *it shall go ill* with him
Ps.106:32. *so that it went ill* with Moses for their
Isa. 59:15. *and it displeased* him that (there was) no judgment. (marg. *was evil* in his eyes)
Jon. 4: 1. *But it displeased* Jonah exceedingly,

3417 **יָרַק** *yāh-rak'.*

* KAL.—*Preterite.* *

Nu. 12:14. If her father *had* but *spit* in her face,
Deu25: 9. *and spit* in his face,

KAL.—*Infinitive.*

Nu. 12:14. If her father had *but* spit in her face, (lit. *spitting* had spit)

3419 **יָרָק** *yāh-rāhk'*, m.

Deu11:10. as a garden of *herbs:*
1K. 21: 2. that I may have it for a garden of *herbs,*
2K. 19:26. *and* (as) the *green* herb,
Pro. 15:17. Better (is) a dinner of *herbs*
Isa. 37:27. *and* (as) the *green* herb,

3418 **יֶרֶק** *yeh'-rek*, m.

Gen 1:30. (I have given) every *green* herb for meat:
9: 3. even *as the green* herb
Ex. 10:15. there remained not any *green thing*
Nu. 22: 4. the ox licketh up *the grass of* the field.
Ps. 37: 2. *and* wither as the *green* herb.
Isa. 15: 6. there is no *green thing.*

3420 **יֵרָקוֹן** *yēh-rāh-kōhn'*, m.

Deu28:22. with blasting, *and with mildew;*
1K. 8:37. blasting, *mildew,* locust,
2Ch. 6:28. if there be blasting, *or mildew,*
Jer. 30: 6. all faces are turned *into paleness?*
Am. 4: 9. smitten you with blasting *and mildew:*
Hag. 2:17. smote you with blasting *and with mildew*

3422 **יְרַקְרַק** *y'rak-rak'*, adj.

Lev.13:49. if the plague be *greenish*
14:37. *greenish* or reddish,
Ps. 68.13(14). her feathers *with yellow* gold.

3423 **יָרַשׁ** *yāh-rash'.*

* KAL.—*Preterite.* *

Nu.13:30. Let us go up at once, *and possess* it;
Nu. 27:11. *and he shall possess* it:
Deu 3:12. *we possessed* at that time,
20. *and* (until) *they* also *possess* the land
4: 1. go in *and possess* the land
22. shall go over, *and possess* that good land.
6:18. that thou mayest go in *and possess* the good
8: 1 & 11:8. go in *and possess* the land
11:23. *and ye shall possess* greater nations
31. *and ye shall possess* it, and dwell therein.
12:29. *and thou succeedest* them, and dwellest in
16:20. that thou mayest live, *and inherit* the land
17:14. *and shalt possess it,* and shalt dwell therein,
19: 1. *and thou succeedest them,* and dwellest in
26: 1. *and possessest it,* and dwellest therein;
30: 5. the land which thy fathers *possessed, and thou shalt possess it;*
31: 3. *and thou shalt possess them:*
Jos. 1:15. *and they* also *have possessed* the land
— ye shall return unto the land...*and enjoy it,*
23: 5. *and ye shall possess* their land,
1K. 21:19. Hast thou killed, and also *taken possession?*
Ps. 44: 3(4). *they got* not the land *in possession*
69:35(36). *and have it in possession.*
Isa. 14:21. that they do not rise, *nor possess* the land,
34:11. *But* the cormorant and the bittern *shall possess* it;
63:18. The people of thy holiness *have possessed*
65: 9. *and* mine elect *shall inherit it,*
Jer. 30: 3. *and they shall possess it.*
49: 1. why (then) *doth* their king *inherit* Gad,
2. *then shall* Israel *be heir*
Eze. 7:24. *and they shall possess* their houses:
35:10. *and we will possess it;*
36:12. *and they shall possess thee,*
Obad. 17. *and* the house of Jacob *shall possess*
19. *And* (they of) the south *shall possess* the
— *and they shall possess* the fields of Ephraim,

KAL.—*Infinitive.*

Gen15: 7. to give thee this land *to inherit it.*
28: 4. *that thou mayest inherit* the land
Lev.20:24. I will give it unto you *to possess* it,
25:46. *to inherit* (them for) a possession;
Nu. 33:53. I have given you the land *to possess* it.
Deu 2:31. *that* thou *mayest inherit* his land.
3:18. God hath given you this land *to possess it:*
4: 5. the land whither ye go *to possess it.*
14. the land whither ye go over *to possess it.*
26. whereunto ye go over Jordan *to possess it;*
5:31(28). land which I give them *to possess it.*
6: 1. the land whither ye go *to possess it:*
7: 1. the land whither thou goest *to possess it,*
9: 1. to go in *to possess* nations
4. the Lord hath brought me in *to possess* this
5. dost thou go *to possess* their land:
6. *to possess it* for thy righteousness;
11: 8, 11. whither ye go *to possess it;*
10. whither thou goest in *to possess it,*
29. the land whither thou goest *to possess it,*
31. to go in *to possess* the land
12: 1. of thy fathers giveth thee *to possess it,*
29. whither thou goest *to possess* them,
15: 4. an inheritance *to possess it:*
19: 2, 14 & 21:1. thy God giveth thee *to possess it.*
23:20(21). land whither thou goest *to possess it.*
25:19. an inheritance *to possess it,*
28:21, 63 & 30:16. whither thou goest *to possess it.*
30:18. thou passest over Jordan to go *to possess it.*
31:13 & 32:47. ye go over Jordan *to possess it.*
Jos. 1:11. to go in *to possess* the land, which the Lord your God giveth you *to possess it.*
13: 1. very much land *to be possessed.* (marg. *to possess it*)
18: 3. to go *to possess* the land,
24: 4. I gave unto Esau mount Seir, *to possess* it;
Jud. 2: 6. children of Israel went...*to possess* the land.
14:15. have ye called us *to take that we have?* (marg. *possess us*)
18: 9. to enter *to possess* the land.
1K. 21:16. Ahab rose up...*to take possession of it.*
18. whither he is gone down *to possess it.*
Ezr. 9:11. The land, unto which ye go *to possess it,*
Neh. 9:15. that they should go in *to possess* the land
23. that they should go in *to possess* (it).
Ps. 37:34. he shall exalt thee *to inherit* the land:
Am. 2:10. *to possess* the land of the Amorite.
Hab. 1: 6. *to possess* the dwellingplaces

KAL.—*Imperative.*

Deu 1: 8. go in *and possess* the land
21. go up (and) *possess* (it),
2:24, 31. begin *to possess* (marg. *possess*)
9:23. Go up *and possess* the land which I have
33:23. *possess thou* the west and the south.
1K. 21:15. *take possession* of the vineyard of Naboth

KAL.—*Future.*

Gen15: 4. This *shall* not *be thine heir;*
— he...*shall be thine heir.*
8. whereby shall I know that *I shall inherit it?*
21:10. the son of this bondwoman *shall* not *be heir*
22:17. *and* thy seed *shall possess* the gate
24:60. *and let* thy seed *possess* the gate
Lev.20:24. Ye *shall inherit* their land,
Nu. 21:24. *and possessed* his land from Arnon
32. (כתיב) *and drove out* the Amorites
35. *and they possessed* his land.
36: 8. that the children of Israel *may enjoy*
Deu 1:39. and *they shall possess it.*
2:12. the children of Esau *succeeded them,* (marg. *inherited them*)
21, 22. *and they succeeded them,* and dwelt in
4:47. *And they possessed* his land,
5:33(30). the land which *ye shall possess.*
10:11. that they may go in *and possess* the land,
Jos. 12: 1. *and possessed* their land on the other side
19:47. with the edge of the sword, *and possessed*
21:43(41). *and they possessed it,* and dwelt
24: 8. *that ye might possess* their land;
Jud. 3:13. *and possessed* the city of palm trees.
11:21. *so* Israel *possessed* all the land of the
22. *And they possessed* all the coasts
23. and *shouldest* thou *possess it?*
24. *Wilt* not *thou possess*
— them *will we possess.*
2K. 17:24. *and they possessed* Samaria, and dwelt in
1Ch 28: 8. that *ye may possess* this good land,
Neh. 9:22. *so they possessed* the land of Sihon,
24. the children went in *and possessed* the land,
25. *and possessed* houses full of all goods,
Ps. 25:13. his seed *shall inherit* the earth.
37: 9. they *shall inherit* the earth.
11. the meek *shall inherit* the earth;
22. (such as be) blessed of him *shall inherit*
29. The righteous *shall inherit* the land,
83:12(13). *Let us take* to ourselves the houses of God *in possession.*
105:44. *they inherited* the labour of the people;
Pro.30:23. an handmaid that *is heir* to her mistress.
Isa. 34:17. *they shall possess it* for ever,
54: 3. thy seed *shall inherit* the Gentiles,
57:13. *and shall inherit* my holy mountain;
60:21. *they shall inherit* the land for ever,
61: 7. in their land *they shall possess* the double:
Jer. 32:23. they came in, *and possessed* it;
Eze.33:24. *and he inherited* the land:
25, 26. and *shall ye possess* the land?
Hos. 9: 6. nettles *shall possess them:*
Am. 9:12. That *they may possess* the remnant
Obad. 20. *shall possess* the cities of the south.

KAL.—*Participle.* Poel.

Gen15: 3. one born in my house *is* mine *heir.*
Nu. 36: 8. daughter, *that possesseth* an inheritance
Deu12: 2. the nations which ye *shall possess*
18:14. For these nations, which thou *shalt possess,*
Jud.18: 7. (there was) no magistrate (marg. *possessor* of restraint) in the land,
2Sa.14: 7. we will destroy *the heir* also:
Isa. 65: 9. *an inheritor of* my mountains:
Jer. 8:10. fields *to them that shall inherit* (them):
49: 1. hath he no *heir?*
2. them *that were his heirs,*
Mic. 1:15. Yet will I bring *an heir* unto thee,

* NIPHAL.—*Future.* *

Gen45:11. all that thou hast, *come to poverty.*
Pro.20:13. Love not sleep, lest *thou come to poverty;*
23:21. the glutton *shall come to poverty:*
30: 9. lest *I be poor,* and steal,

* PIEL.—*Future.* *

Deu28:42. fruit of thy land *shall* the locust *consume.*

* HIPHIL.—*Preterite.* *

Nu. 33:52. *Then ye shall drive out* all the inhabitants
Nu. 33:53. *And ye shall dispossess* (the inhabitants)
Deu 9: 3. *so shalt thou drive them out,*
11:23. *Then will* the Lord *drive out* all these
Jos. 8: 7. *and seize upon* the city:
13:13. the children of Israel *expelled* not the
14:12. *then I shall be able to drive them out,*
16:10. *they drave* not *out* the Canaanites
17:13. *did* not utterly *drive them out.*
23: 5. *and drive* them from out of your sight;
Jud. 1:21. the children of Benjamin *did* not *drive out*
27. *did* Manasseh *drive out* (the inhabitants)
28. *did* not utterly *drive them out.*
29. *did* Ephraim *drive out* the Canaanites
30. *did* Zebulun *drive out* the inhabitants
31. *did* Asher *drive out* the inhabitants
32. *they did* not *drive them out.*
33. *did* Naphtali *drive out* the inhabitants
11:23. Lord God...*hath dispossessed* the Amorites
24. Lord our God *shall drive out* from before
1K. 14:24. the nations which the Lord *cast out*
21:26. whom the Lord *cast out*
2K. 16: 3. whom the Lord *cast out*
17: 8 & 21:2. whom the Lord *cast out*
2Ch 20: 7. *didst drive out* the inhabitants
11. which *thou hast given us to inherit.*
28: 3 & 33:2. whom the Lord *had cast out*
Ezr. 9:12. *and leave* (it) *for an inheritance* to your
Ps. 44: 2(3). *thou didst drive out* the heathen

HIPHIL.—*Infinitive.*

Nu. 32:21. until he *hath driven out* his enemies from
Deu 4:38. *To drive out* nations from before thee
7:17. how can I *dispossess them?*
Jos. 3:10. *and* (that) he will *without fail* drive out (lit. *driving* he will drive out) from
15:63. children of Judah could not *drive them out:*
17:12. children of Manasseh could not *drive out*
13. *but* did not *utterly* drive them out. (lit. *driving* did not drive them out)
23:13. your God will no more *drive out* (any of)
Jud. 1:19. *could* not *drive out* the inhabitants
28. *and* did not *utterly* drive them out. (lit. *driving* did not utterly drive them out)
2:21. I also will not henceforth *drive out*
23. without *driving them out* hastily;

HIPHIL.—*Future.*

Ex. 15: 9. hand *shall destroy them.* (marg. *repossess*)
34:24. *I will cast out* the nations before thee,
Nu. 14:12. I will smite them...*and disinherit them,*
24. his seed *shall possess it.*
21:32. *and drove out* the Amorites that (were)
32:39. *and dispossessed* the Amorite which (was)
33:55. if *ye will* not *drive out* the inhabitants
Jos. 3:10. and (that) *he will* without fail *drive out*
13: 6. *them will* I *drive out* from before the
12. these did Moses smite, *and cast them out.*
15:14. *And* Caleb *drove* thence the three sons of
17:18. *thou shalt drive out* the Canaanites,
23: 9. *For* the Lord *hath driven out*
Jud. 1:19. *and he drave out* (the inhabitants of) the
20. *and he expelled* thence the three sons of
11:24. Chemosh thy god *giveth thee to possess?*
Job 13:26. *and makest me to possess* the iniquities of
20:15. God *shall cast them out* of his belly.
Zec. 9: 4. the Lord *will cast her out,*

HIPHIL.—*Participle.*

Deu 9: 4. the Lord *doth drive them out*
5. the Lord thy God *doth drive them out*
18:12. the Lord thy God *doth drive* them *out*
1Sa. 2: 7. The Lord *maketh poor,* and maketh rich.

יְרֵשָׁה *y'rēh-shāh',* f. 3424

Nu. 24:18. Edom shall be *a possession,* Seir also shall be *a possession*

יְרֻשָּׁה *y'roosh-shāh',* f. 3425

Deu 2: 5. mount Seir unto Esau (for) *a possession.*
9. I will not give thee of their land (for) *a possession;* because I have given Ar... (for) *a possession.*
12. the land of *his possession,*

Deu 2:19. I will not give thee...(any) *possession;* because I have given it unto the children of Lot (for) *a possession.*
3:20. return every man *unto his possession,*
Jos. 1:15. return unto the land of *your possession,*
12: 6. it (for) *a possession* unto the Reubenites,
7. unto the tribes of Israel (for) *a possession*
Jud. 21:17. (There must be) *an inheritance* for them
2Ch 20:11. to cast us *out of thy possession,*
Ps. 61: 5(6). thou hast given (me) *the heritage of*
Jer. 32: 8. the right of *inheritance* (is) thine,

3455 יָשַׂם [*yāh-sam'*].

* KAL.—*Future.* *

Gen 24:33. (כתיב) *And there was set* (meat) before
50:26. *and he was put* in a coffin in Egypt.

3426 יֵשׁ *yēhsh.*

Gen 18:24. Peradventure *there be* fifty righteous
23: 8. If *it be* your mind
24:23. *is there* room (in) thy father's house
42. if now *thou do* prosper my way
49. *ye will* deal (lit. if *you are* dealing) kindly
28:16. Surely the Lord *is* in this place;
31:29. *It is* in the power of my hand to do you
33: 9. said, I *have* (lit. *there is* to me) enough,
11. and because I *have* enough.
39: 4. all (that) he *had* he put into his hand.
5. over all that he *had,*
— of the Lord was upon all that he *had*
8. committed all that he *hath* to my hand;
42: 1. Jacob saw that *there was* corn in Egypt,
2. I have heard that *there is* corn in Egypt:
43: 4. If *thou wilt* send our brother with us,
7. *have* ye (another) brother?
44:19. *Have* ye a father, or a brother?
20. We *have* a father, an old man,
26. if our youngest brother *be* with us,
47: 6. if thou knowest (any) men (lit. if thou knowest *that there are* men)
Ex. 17: 7. *Is* the Lord among us, or not?
Nu. 9:20,21. *And* (so) *it was,*
13:20. *whether there be* wood therein,
22:29. I would *there were* a sword in mine hand,
Deu 13: 3(4). to know *whether ye* love (lit. *whether ye are* loving) the Lord your God
29:15(14). (him) that standeth (lit. him *that is* standing) here with us this day
18(17). Lest *there should be* among you man,
—(—). lest *there should be* among you a root
Jud. 4:20. *Is there* any man here?
6:13. *if* the Lord *be* with us,
36. If *thou wilt* save (lit. if *thou art* saving) Israel by mine hand,
18:14. there *is* in these houses an ephod,
19:19. Yet *there is* both straw and provender for our asses; and *there is* bread and wine
Ru. 1:12. If I should say, I *have* hope,
3:12. *there is* a kinsman nearer than I.
1Sa. 9:11. said unto them, *Is* the seer here?
12. they answered them, and said, *He is;*
14:39. though *it be* in Jonathan my son,
17:46. *there is* a God in Israel.
20: 8. if *there be* in me iniquity,
21: 3(4). Now therefore what *is* under thine
4(5). *there is* hallowed bread;
8(9). *is there* not here under thine hand
23:23. if *he be* in the land,
2Sa. 9: 1. *Is there* yet any that is left of the house of
14:32. if *there be* (any) iniquity in me,
19:28(29). What right therefore *have* I yet to cry
1 K. 17:12. I *have* not a cake,
18:10. *there is* no nation or kingdom,
2 K. 2:16. *there be* with thy servants fifty strong men;
3:12. The word of the Lord *is* with him.
4: 2. tell me, what *hast* thou in the house?
13. *wouldest* thou be spoken for to the king,
5: 8. shall know that *there is* a prophet in Israel.
9:15. Jehu said, If *it be* your minds,
10:15. *Is* thine heart right,
— Jehonadab answered, *It is.* *If it be,*
23. look that *there be* here with you none of
1Ch 29:3. I *have* of mine own proper good,
2Ch 15: 7. your work *shall be* rewarded. (lit. *there is* reward)
16: 9. thou *shalt have* wars.
25: 8. for God *hath* power to help,
9. The Lord *is* able to give thee much more
Ezr. 10: 2. *there is* hope in Israel concerning this thing.
4. *and* (some) of them *had* wives
Neh. 5: 2. *For there were* that said,
3. (Some) *also there were* that said,
4. *There were also* that said,
5. our daughters *are* brought unto bondage
Est. 3: 8. *There is* a certain people scattered abroad
Job. 5: 1. if *there be* any that will answer thee;
6: 6. *is there* (any) taste in the white of an egg?
30. *Is there* iniquity in my tongue?
9:33. Neither *is* there any daysman betwixt us,
11:18. thou shalt be secure, because *there is* hope;
14: 7. For *there is* hope of a tree, if it be cut
16: 4. if your soul *were* in my soul's stead,
25: 3. *Is there* any number of his armies?
28: 1. Surely *there is* a vein for the silver,
33:23. If *there be* a messenger with him,
32. If thou *hast* any thing to say, answer
38:28. *Hath* the rain a father?
Ps. 7: 3(4). if *there be* iniquity in my hands;
14: 2. to see if *there were* any that did understand,
53: 2(3). if *there were* (any) that did understand,
58:11(12). he *is* a God that judgeth in the earth.
73:11. *and is there* knowledge in the most high?
135:17. neither *is there* (any) breath in their
Pro. 3:28. *when* thou *hast it* by thee.
8:21. That I may cause those that love me to inherit *substance;*
11:24. *There is* that scattereth, and yet increaseth;
12:18. *There is* that speaketh like the piercings of
13: 7. *There is* that maketh himself rich,
23. *but there is* (that is) destroyed for want of
14:12. *There is* a way which seemeth right unto
16:25. *There is* a way that seemeth right unto a
18:24. *and there is* a friend (that) sticketh closer
19:18. Chasten thy son while *there is* hope,
20:15. *There is* gold, and a multitude of rubies:
23:18. For surely *there is* an end;
24:14. *then there shall be* a reward,
Ecc. 1:10. *Is there* (any) thing
2:13. I saw that wisdom excelleth (lit. *that there is* excellence to wisdom)
21. *there is* a man whose labour (is) in wisdom,
4: 8. *There is* one (alone),
9. they *have* a good reward for their labour.
5:13(12). *There is* a sore evil
6: 1. *There is* an evil which I have seen
11. Seeing *there be* many things that increase
7:15. *there is* a just (man) that perisheth in his righteousness, *and there is* a wicked
8: 6. to every purpose *there is* time
14. *There is* a vanity which is done upon the earth; that *there be* just (men),
— *again, there be* wicked (men), to whom it
9: 4. to him that is joined to all the living *there is* hope:
10: 5. *There is* an evil (which) I have seen
Isa. 43: 8. the deaf *that have* ears.
44: 8. *Is there* a God beside me?
Jer. 5: 1. if *there be* (any) that executeth judgment,
14:22. *Are there* (any) among the vanities of the
23:26. How long *shall* (this) *be*
27:18. if the word of the Lord *be* with them.
31: 6. *there shall be* a day, (that) the watchmen
16. thy work *shall be* rewarded,
17. *And there is* hope in thine end,
37:17. *Is there* (any) word from the Lord? And Jeremiah said, *There is:*
41: 8. *have* treasures in the field, of wheat,
Lam. 1:12. see if *there be* any sorrow like unto my
3:29. if so be *there may be* hope.
Jon. 4:11. city, wherein *are* more
Mic. 2: 1. because it *is* in the power of their hand.
Mal. 1:14. *which hath* in his flock a male,

יָשַׁב *yāh-shav'.* 3427

* KAL.—*Preterite.* *

Gen 13:12. Abram *dwelled* in the land of Canaan, and Lot *dwelled* in the cities of the plain,
19:29. the cities in the which Lot *dwelt.*

Gen27:44. *And tarry* with him a few days,
34:16. *and we will dwell* with you,
45:10. *And thou shalt dwell* in the land of Goshen,
Ex. 12:40. children of Israel, who *dwelt* in Egypt,
Lev.14: 8. *and shall tarry* abroad out of his tent
18: 3. the land of Egypt, wherein *ye dwelt*,
25:18. *and ye shall dwell* in the land in safety.
19. *and dwell* therein in safety.
26: 5. *and dwell* in your land safely.
Nu. 32:17. *and* our little ones *shall dwell* in the fenced
33:53. *and dwell* therein:
35:25. *and he shall abide* in it unto the death of
Deu. 1:46. the days that *ye abode* (there).
2:10. The Emims *dwelt* therein in times past,
12. The Horims also *dwelt* in Seir
20. giants *dwelt* therein in old time;
8:12. built goodly houses, *and dwelt* (therein);
11:31. ye shall possess it, *and dwell* therein.
12:10. *and dwell* in the land which the Lord your
— *so that ye dwell* in safety;
29. thou succeedest them, *and dwellest* in their
17:14. shalt possess it, *and shalt dwell* therein,
19: 1. thou succeedest them, *and dwellest* in their
21:13. *and shall remain* in thine house,
26: 1. possessest it, *and dwellest* therein;
29:16(15). *we have dwelt* in the land of Egypt;
Jos. 20: 4. *that he may dwell* among them.
6. *And he shall dwell* in that city,
24: 2. Your fathers *dwelt* on the other side of
Jud. 3: 5. the children of Israel *dwelt* among the
5:16. Why *abodest* thou among the sheepfolds,
17. Asher *continued* on the sea shore,
1Sa. 1:22. *and* there *abide* for ever.
19: 2. *and abide* in a secret (place), and hide
20:19. *and shalt remain* by the stone Ezel.
25:13. two hundred *abode* by the stuff.
27: 7. David *dwelt* in the country of the
11. *he dwelleth* in the country of the
2Sa. 7: 1. the king *sat* in his house,
6. *I have* not *dwelt* in (any) house
1 K. 1:35. that he may come *and sit* upon my throne;
46. Solomon *sitteth* on the throne
2:12. Then *sat* Solomon upon the throne
36. an house in Jerusalem, *and dwell* there,
11:16. six months *did* Joab *remain* there:
17: 9. get thee to Zarephath,...*and dwell* there:
2 K. 7: 4. if *we sit still* here, we die also.
13:13. Jeroboam *sat* upon his throne:
1Ch. 2:55. (כתיב) the scribes *which dwelt* at Jabez;
4:23. there *they dwelt* with the king
5: 9. eastward *he inhabited* unto the entering
11. the children of Gad *dwelt* over against
23. the half tribe of Manasseh *dwelt* in the
7:29. In these *dwelt* the children of Joseph
8:28. These *dwelt* in Jerusalem.
29. at Gibeon *dwelt* the father of Gibeon;
32. these also *dwelt* with their brethren
9: 3. in Jerusalem *dwelt* of the children of
34. these *dwelt* at Jerusalem.
35. in Gibeon *dwelt* the father of Gibeon,
38. *they* also *dwelt* with their brethren
17: 1. David *sat* in his house,
5. *I have* not *dwelt* in an house
Neh. 1: 4. *I sat down* and wept,
11: 3. of the province that *dwelt* in Jerusalem: but in the cities of Judah *dwelt* every
4. at Jerusalem *dwelt* (certain) of the
25. children of Judah *dwelt* at Kirjath-arba,
13:16. There *dwelt* men of Tyre also therein,
Est. 3:15. the king and Haman *sat down* to drink;
Job.24:13. *abide* in the paths thereof.
Ps. 1: 1. nor *sitteth* in the seat of the scornful.
9: 4(5). *thou satest* in the throne judging right.
23: 6. *and I will dwell* in the house of the Lord
26: 4. *I have* not *sat* with vain persons,
29:10. The Lord *sitteth* upon the flood;
47: 8(9). God *sitteth* upon the throne
68:10(11). Thy congregation *hath dwelt* therein:
69:35(36). *that they may dwell* there,
119:23. Princes also *did sit* (and) speak against
122: 5. *there are set* thrones of judgment, (marg. *do sit*)
137: 1. By the rivers of Babylon, there *we sat down*,
Pro. 9:14. *For she sitteth* at the door of her house,
Cant.2: 3. *I sat down* under his shadow with great delight, (marg. I delighted *and sat down*)
Isa. 16: 5. *and he shall sit* upon it in truth
32:18. *And* my people *shall dwell* in a peaceable
65:21. shall build houses, *and inhabit* (them);
Jer. 2: 6. where no man *dwelt?*
3: 2. In the ways *hast thou sat* for them,
15:17. *I sat* not in the assembly of the mockers, nor rejoiced; *I sat* alone because of thy
17:25. *and* this city *shall remain* for ever.
23: 8. *and they shall dwell* in their own land.
27:11. they shall till it, *and dwell* therein.
31:24. *And there shall dwell* in Judah itself,
49: 1. his people *dwell* in his cities?
50:39. *and* the owls *shall dwell* therein:
51:30. *they have remained* in (their) holds:
Lam. 1: 1. How *doth* the city *sit* solitary,
3. *she dwelleth* among the heathen,
Eze.23:41. *And satest* upon a stately bed,
28: 2. *I sit* (in) the seat of God,
25. *then shall they dwell* in their land
26. *And they shall dwell* safely therein,
— *yea, they shall dwell* with confidence,
31:17. (that) *dwelt* under his shadow
34:25. *and they shall dwell* safely
28. *but they shall dwell* safely,
36:28. *And ye shall dwell* in the land
35. (are become) fenced, (and) *are inhabited.*
37:25. *And they shall dwell* in the land
— wherein your fathers *have dwelt; and they shall dwell* therein,
38: 8. *and they shall dwell* safely all of them.
Am. 9:14. the waste cities, *and inhabit* (them);
Mic. 4: 4. *But they shall sit* every man under his vine
5: 4(3). *and they shall abide:*
Zec. 6:13. *and shall sit* and rule upon his throne;
9: 6. *And* a bastard *shall dwell* in Ashdod,
12: 6. *and* Jerusalem *shall be inhabited* again
14:10. *and inhabited* in her place, (marg. or, *shall abide*)
11. *And* (men) *shall dwell* in it,
— *but* Jerusalem *shall be* safely *inhabited.*
Mal. 3: 3. *And he shall sit* (as) a refiner

KAL.—*Infinitive.*

Gen13: 6. *that they might dwell* together:
— *so that* they could not *dwell* together.
16: 3. *after* Abram *had dwelt* ten years
19:30. he feared *to dwell* in Zoar:
34:22. the men consent unto us for *to dwell* with
36: 7. *than that* they *might dwell* together;
Ex. 2:21. Moses was content *to dwell* with the man:
15:17. (which) thou hast made *for thee to dwell in*,
16: 3. *when we sat* by the flesh pots,
Lev.20:22. whither I bring you *to dwell* therein,
26:35. *when ye dwelt* upon it.
Nu. 21:15. that goeth down *to the dwelling of* Ar,
35: 2. of their possession cities *to dwell in;*
3. the cities shall they have *to dwell in;*
32. come again *to dwell* in the land,
Deu 1: 6. Ye have *dwelt* long enough in this mount:
6: 7 & 11:19. *when thou sittest* in thine house,
13:12(13). God hath given thee *to dwell* there,
17:18. *when he sitteth* upon the throne
23:13(14). *when thou wilt ease thyself* abroad,
30:20. *that thou mayest dwell* in the land
Jos. 14: 4. save cities *to dwell* (in),
17:12. the Canaanites would *dwell* in that land.
21: 2. to give us cities *to dwell in*,
Jud. 1:27. the Canaanites would *dwell* in that land.
35. the Amorites would *dwell* in mount Heres
9:41. *that* they *should not dwell* in Shechem.
11:26. *While* Israel *dwelt* in Heshbon
17:11. the Levite was content *to dwell* with the
18: 1. sought them an inheritance *to dwell in;*
Ru. 2: 7. *that she tarried* a little in the house.
1Sa. 7: 2. while the ark *abode* in Kirjath-jearim,
20: 5. I should not *fail* to sit with the king at
2Sa. 7: 5. thou build me an house *for me to dwell in?*
15: 8. *while I abode* at Geshur
23: 7. burned with fire *in the* (same) *place.*
1K. 8:13. a settled place *for thee to abide in*
30. hear thou in heaven *thy dwelling* place:
39, 43. hear thou in heaven *thy dwelling*
49. Then hear...in heaven *thy dwelling* place,
10:19. the place of *the seat*,
16:11. *as soon as he sat* on his throne,
2K. 6: 2. where we *may dwell.*
17:25. the beginning of *their dwelling*

2K. 19:27. *But* I know *thy abode*, (marg. *sitting*)
1Ch 17: 4. shalt not build me an house *to dwell in:*
28: 5. *to sit* upon the throne of the kingdom
2Ch 2: 3(2). build him an house *to dwell* therein,
6: 2. a place *for thy dwelling* for ever.
21. hear thou from *thy dwelling* place,
30. hear thou from heaven *thy dwelling* place,
33, 39. (even) from *thy dwelling* place,
9:18. each side of the *sitting* place,
Neh 11: 1. *to dwell* in Jerusalem the holy city,
2. *to dwell* at Jerusalem.
Est. 1: 2. *when* the king Ahasuerus *sat* on the throne
Ps. 27: 4. *that I may dwell* in the house of the Lord
33:14. the place of *his habitation*
68:16(17). God desireth *to dwell in;*
101: 6. *that* they *may dwell* with me:
113: 5. who *dwelleth* on high, (marg. exalteth (himself) *to dwell*)
127: 2. *to sit up* late, to eat the bread
133: 1. *to dwell* together in unity!
139: 2. Thou knowest *my downsitting*
Pro. 21: 9. (It is) better *to dwell* in a corner of the
19. (It is) better *to dwell* in the wilderness,
25:24. (It is) better *to dwell* in the corner of the
31:23. *when he sitteth* among the elders
Isa. 37:28. *But* I know *thy abode*, (marg. or, *sitting*)
40:22. spreadeth them out as a tent *to dwell in:*
44:13. *that* it *may remain* in the house.
45:18. he formed it *to be inhabited:*
47:14. (nor) fire *to sit* before it.
58:12. The restorer of paths *to dwell in.*
Jer. 9: 6(5). *Thine habitation* (is) in the midst of
16: 8. *to sit* with them to eat and to drink.
35: 9. Nor to build houses *for us to dwell in:*
43: 4. *to dwell* in the land of Judah.
44:14. they have a desire to return *to dwell* there:
49: 8. Flee ye, turn back, *dwell* deep,
30. Flee, get you far off, *dwell* deep,
Lam. 3:63. Behold *their sitting down*,
Eze. 38:14. *when* my people of Israel *dwelleth* safely,
39:26. *when they dwelt* safely in their land,
Am. 6: 3. cause *the seat of* violence to come near; (marg. or, *habitation*)
Obad. 3. *whose habitation* (is) high;
Hag. 1: 4. *to dwell* in your cieled houses,

KAL.—*Imperative.*

Gen 20:15. *dwell* where it pleaseth thee.
22: 5. *Abide ye* here with the ass;
27:19. *sit* and eat of my venison,
29:19. *abide* with me.
34:10. *dwell* and trade ye therein,
35: 1. go up to Beth-el, *and dwell* there:
38:11. *Remain* a widow at thy father's house,
Ex. 16:29. *abide ye* every man in his place,
24:14. *Tarry ye* here for us,
Nu. 22:19. *tarry ye* also here this night,
Jud. 17:10. Micah said unto him, *Dwell* with me,
Ru. 3:18. *Sit still*, my daughter,
4: 1. turn aside, *sit down* here.
2. *Sit ye down* here.
1Sa. 1:23. *tarry* until thou have weaned him,
22:23. *Abide thou* with me, fear not:
2Sa. 10: 5. *Tarry* at Jericho until your beards be
11:12. *Tarry* here to day also,
15:19. return to thy place, *and abide* with the
2K. 2: 2, 4. *Tarry* here, I pray thee;
6. *Tarry*, I pray thee, here;
14:10. glory (of this), *and tarry* at home:
25:24. *dwell* in the land, and serve the king of
1Ch 19: 5. *Tarry* at Jericho until your beards be
2Ch 25:19. *abide* now at home;
Ps. 110: 1. *Sit thou* at my right hand,
Isa. 47: 1. Come down, *and sit* in the dust, O virgin daughter of Babylon, *sit* on the ground:
5. *Sit thou* silent, and get thee into darkness,
52: 2. *sit down*, O Jerusalem:
Jer. 13:18. Humble yourselves, *sit down:*
25: 5. *and dwell* in the land that the Lord hath
29: 5, 28. Build ye houses, *and dwell* (in them);
35:15. *and ye shall dwell* in the land which I have given to you and your fathers:
36:15. *Sit down* now, and read it in our ears.
40: 5. *and dwell* with him among the people:
9. *dwell* in the land, and serve the king of
10. *and dwell* in your cities
48:18. down from (thy) glory, *and sit* in thirst;

KAL.—*Future.*

Gen 4:16. *and dwelt* in the land of Nod,
11: 2. *and they dwelt* there.
31. they came unto Haran, *and dwelt* there.
13:18. came *and dwelt* in the plain of Mamre,
19:30. *and dwelt* in the mountain,
— *and he dwelt* in a cave,
20: 1. *and dwelled* between Kadesh and Shur,
21:16. *and sat her down* over against (him)
— *And she sat* over against (him),
20. *and dwelt* in the wilderness,
21. *And he dwelt* in the wilderness of Paran:
22:19. *and* Abraham *dwelt* at Beer-sheba.
24:55. *Let* the damsel *abide* with us
25:11. *and* Isaac *dwelt* by the well
26: 6. *And* Isaac *dwelt* in Gerar:
17. in the valley of Gerar, *and dwelt* there.
29:14. *And he abode* with him the space of a
31:34. *and sat* upon them.
34:10. *ye shall dwell* with us:
21. *therefore let them dwell* in the land,
23. *and they will dwell* with us.
36: 8. *Thus dwelt* Esau in mount Seir:
37: 1. *And* Jacob *dwelt* in the land
25. *And they sat down* to eat bread:
38:11. Tamar went *and dwelt* in her father's
14. *and sat* in an open place,
43:33. *And they sat* before him,
44:33. *let* thy servant *abide* instead of the lad
46:34. that *ye may dwell* in the land of Goshen;
47: 4. *let* thy servants *dwell* in the land of
6. in the land of Goshen *let them dwell:*
27. *And* Israel *dwelt* in the land of Egypt,
48: 2. Israel strengthened himself, *and sat* upon
49:24. *But* his bow *abode* in strength,
50:22. *And* Joseph *dwelt* in Egypt,
Ex. 2:15. *and dwelt* in the land of Midian: *and he sat down* by a well.
17:12. *and he sat* thereon;
18:13. *that* Moses *sat* to judge the people:
23:33. *They shall* not *dwell* in thy land,
32: 6. *and* the people *sat down* to eat and to
Lev. 8:35. Therefore *shall ye abide* (at) the door of
12: 4. *she shall then continue* in the blood of her
5. *she shall continue* in the blood of her
13:46. *he shall dwell* alone;
15: 4. every thing, whereon *he sitteth*,
6. whereon *he sat* that hath the issue
20. every thing also that *she sitteth* upon
22. any thing that *she sat* upon
26. whatsoever *she sitteth* upon shall be
23:42. *Ye shall dwell* in booths seven days; all... *shall dwell* in booths:
Nu. 20: 1. *and* the people *abode* in Kadesh;
15. *and we have dwelt* in Egypt a long time;
21:25. *and* Israel *dwelt* in all the cities of the
31. *Thus* Israel *dwelt* in the land of the
22: 8. *and* the princes of Moab *abode* with
25: 1. *And* Israel *abode* in Shittim,
32: 6. *shall ye sit* here?
40. *and he dwelt* therein.
35:28. *he should have remained* in the city of
Deu 1:46. *So ye abode* in Kadesh many days,
2:12. *and dwelt* in their stead;
21. they succeeded them, *and dwelt* in their
22. *and dwelt* in their stead even unto this
23. destroyed them, *and dwelt* in their stead.
3:19. your wives,...*shall abide* in your cities
29. *So we abode* in the valley
9: 9. *then I abode* in the mount forty days
23:16(17). *He shall dwell* with thee,
25: 5. If brethren *dwell* together,
28:30. build an house, and *thou shalt* not *dwell*
Jos. 1:14. Your wives,...*shall remain* in the land
2:22. *and abode* there three days,
5: 8. *that they abode* in their places
6:25. *and she dwelleth* in Israel (even) unto
7: 7. *and dwelt* on the other side Jordan!
8: 9. *and abode* between Beth-el and Ai,
13:13. *but* the Geshurites and the Maachathites *dwell* among the Israelites
15:63. *but* the Jebusites *dwell* with the children
16:10. *but* the Canaanites *dwell* among the
19:47. possessed it, *and dwelt* therein,
50. he built the city, *and dwelt* therein.
21:43(41). they possessed it, *and dwelt* therein.
24: 7. *and ye dwelt* in the wilderness a long

Jos. 24:13. cities which ye built not, *and ye dwell*
Jud. 1:16. they went *and dwelt* among the people.
21. *but* the Jebusites *dwell* with the children
29. *but* the Canaanites *dwelt* in Gezer
30. *but* the Canaanites *dwelt* among them,
32. *But* the Asherites *dwelt* among the
33. *but he dwelt* among the Canaanites,
6:11. *and sat* under an oak
18. I *will tarry* until thou come again.
8:29. *and dwelt* in his own house.
9:21. went to Beer, *and dwelt* there,
41. *And* Abimelech *dwelt* at Arumah:
11: 3. *and dwelt* in the land of Tob:
17. *and* Israel *abode* in Kadesh.
15: 8. *and dwelt* in the top of the rock Etam.
18:28. they built a city, *and dwelt* therein.
19: 4. *and he abode* with him three days:
6. *And they sat down*, and did eat and drink
15. *and* when...*he sat him down* in a street
20:26. *and sat* there before the Lord,
47. *and abode* in the rock Rimmon
21: 2. *and abode* there till even before God,
23. repaired the cities, *and dwelt* in them.
Ru. 1: 4. *and they dwelled* there about ten years.
2:14. *And she sat* beside the reapers:
23. *and dwelt* with her mother in law.
4: 1. Then went Boaz up to the gate, *and sat him down* there:
— he turned aside, *and sat down*.
2. *And they sat down*.
1Sa. 1:23. *So* the woman *abode*,
5: 7. of the God of Israel *shall* not *abide* with
12:11. *and ye dwelled* safe.
19:18. he and Samuel went *and dwelt* in Naioth.
20: 5. I *should* not fail to *sit* with the king at
24. *and* when...the king *sat him down* to eat
25. *And* the king *sat* upon his seat,
— *and* Abner *sat* by Saul's side,
22: 4. *and they dwelt* with him all the while
5. *Abide* not in the hold;
23:14. *And* David *abode* in the wilderness
— *and remained* in a mountain
18. *and* David *abode* in the wood,
25. *and abode* in the wilderness of Maon.
29(24:1). *and dwelt* in strong holds at
27: 3. *And* David *dwelt* with Achish
5. *that I may dwell* there: for why *should* thy servant *dwell*
28:23. So he arose from the earth, *and sat* upon
31: 7. the Philistines came *and dwelt* in them.
2Sa. 1: 1. *and* David *had abode* two days in Ziklag;
2: 3. *and they dwelt* in the cities of Hebron.
13. *and they sat down*, the one on the one
5: 9. *So* David *dwelt* in the fort,
6:11. *And* the ark of the Lord *continued* in the
7:18. *and sat* before the Lord,
11:12. *So* Uriah *abode* in Jerusalem that day,
13:20. *So* Tamar *remained* desolate in her
14:28. *So* Absalom *dwelt* two full years in
15:29. *and they tarried* there.
16:18. with him *will I abide*.
19: 8(9). Then the king arose, *and sat* in the
1K. 1:13, 17, 24, 30. he *shall sit* upon my throne?
20. who *shall sit* on the throne of my lord
27. who *should sit* on the throne of my lord
2:19. *and sat down* on his throne,
— *and she sat* on his right hand.
38. *And* Shimei *dwelt* in Jerusalem many
4:25(5:5). *And* Judah and Israel *dwelt* safely,
7: 8. his house where *he dwelt*
8:20. *and sit* on the throne of Israel,
27. *will* God indeed *dwell* on the earth?
11:24. they went to Damascus, *and dwelt* therein,
12: 2. *and* Jeroboam *dwelt* in Egypt;
25. Jeroboam built Shechem...*and dwelt*
15:21. *and dwelt* in Tirzah.
17: 5. he went *and dwelt* by the brook Cherith,
19: 4. *and sat down* under a juniper tree:
21:13. *and sat* before him:
22: 1. *And they continued* three years without war
2K. 4:20. *And* when...*he sat* on her knees till noon,
10:30. *shall sit* on the throne of Israel.
11:19. *And he sat* on the throne
13: 5. *and* the children of Israel *dwelt* in their
15: 5. *and dwelt* in a several house.
12. Thy sons *shall sit* on the throne
16: 6. *and dwelt* there unto this day.
2K. 17:24. *and dwelt* in the cities thereof.
27. let them go *and dwell* there,
28. came *and dwelt* in Beth-el,
19:36. went and returned, *and dwelt* at Nineveh.
1Ch 4:28. *And they dwelt* at Beer-sheba,
41. *and dwelt* in their rooms:
43. *and dwelt* there unto this day.
5:10. *and they dwelt* in their tents
16. *And they dwelt* in Gilead in Bashan,
22. *And they dwelt* in their steads
10: 7. the Philistines came *and dwelt* in them.
11: 7. *And* David *dwelt* in the castle;
13:14. *And* the ark of God *remained*
17:16. the king came *and sat* before the Lord,
29:23. *Then* Solomon *sat* on the throne
2Ch 6:10. *and am set* on the throne of Israel,
18. *will* God in very deed *dwell* with men
8:11. My wife *shall* not *dwell* in the house of
11: 5. *And* Rehoboam *dwelt* in Jerusalem,
19: 4. *And* Jehoshaphat *dwelt* at Jerusalem:
20: 8. *And they dwelt* therein,
26:21. *and dwelt* in a several house,
28:18. *and they dwelt* there.
Ezr. 2:70. *So* the priests,...*dwelt* in their cities,
8:32. *and abode* there three days.
9: 3. *and sat down* astonied.
10: 9. *and* all the people *sat* in the street
16. *and sat down* in the first day
Neh 7:73. *So* the priests,...*dwelt* in their cities;
8:14. the children of Israel *should dwell* in booths
17. *and sat* under the booths:
11: 1. *And* the rulers of the people *dwelt* at
Job 2:13. *So they sat down* with him
15:28. in houses which no man *inhabiteth*,
22: 8. the honourable man *dwelt* in it.
29:25. I chose out their way, *and sat* chief,
38:40. (and) *abide* in the covert to lie in wait?
Ps. 9: 7(8). the Lord *shall endure* for ever:
10: 8. *He sitteth* in the lurking places of the
26: 5. *will* not *sit* with the wicked.
29:10. *yea*, the Lord *sitteth* King for ever.
50:20. *Thou sittest* (and) speakest against thy
61: 7(8). *He shall abide* before God for ever:
101: 7. He that worketh deceit *shall* not *dwell*
102:12(13). thou, O Lord, *shalt endure* for ever;
125: 1. *abideth* for ever.
132:12. their children *shall* also *sit* upon thy throne
14. here *will I dwell*;
140:13(14). the upright *shall dwell* in thy presence.
Pro. 23: 1. When *thou sittest* to eat with a ruler,
Ecc. 10: 6. the rich *sit* in low place.
Isa. 3:26. *she* (being) desolate *shall sit* upon the
13:20. *It shall* never *be inhabited*,
14:13. *I will sit also* upon the mount
30:19. the people *shall dwell* in Zion
32:16. and righteousness *remain* in the fruitful
37:37. went and returned, *and dwelt* at Nineveh.
42:11. the villages (that) Kedar *doth inhabit*:
47: 8. *I shall* not *sit* (as) a widow,
49:20. give place to me *that I may dwell*.
65:22. They shall not build, and another *inhabit*;
Jer. 17: 6. a salt land and not *inhabited*.
26:10. *and sat down* in the entry of the new gate
30:18. the palace *shall remain* after the manner
35: 7. all your days *ye shall dwell* in tents;
10. *But we have dwelt* in tents,
11. *so we dwell* at Jerusalem.
37:16. *and* Jeremiah *had remained* there many
21. *Thus* Jeremiah *remained* in the court of
38:13. *and* Jeremiah *remained* in the court of the
28. *So* Jeremiah *abode* in the court of the
39: 3. *and sat* in the middle gate,
14. *so he dwelt* among the people.
40: 6. *and dwelt* with him among the people
41:17. they departed, *and dwelt* in the habitation
42:10. If *ye will* still *abide* in this land,
13. *We will* not *dwell* in this land,
14. there *will we dwell*:
49:18. no man *shall abide* there,
33. *there shall* no man *abide* there,
50:13. *it shall* not *be inhabited*,
39. the wild beasts...*shall dwell* (there),
— *it shall be* no more *inhabited* for ever;
40. (so) *shall* no man *abide* there,
51:43. a land wherein no man *dwelleth*,
Lam. 2:10. The elders...*sit* upon the ground,
3:28. *He sitteth* alone and keepeth silence,

Lam. 5:19. Thou, O Lord, *remainest* for ever;
Eze. 3:15. *and I sat* where they sat, *and remained* there astonished among them
14: 1. of the elders of Israel unto me, *and sat*
20: 1. to enquire of the Lord, *and sat* before me.
26:16. *they shall sit* upon the ground,
20. that *thou be* not *inhabited;*
29:11. neither *shall it be inhabited* forty years.
31: 6. under his shadow *dwelt* all great nations.
33:31. *and they sit* before thee (as) my people,
35: 9. (כתיב) thy cities *shall* not *return:*
44: 3. *he shall sit* in it to eat bread
Hos. 3: 3. *Thou shalt abide* for me many days;
4. the children of Israel *shall abide* many
9: 3. *They shall* not *dwell* in the Lord's land;
Joel 3:12(4:12). there *will I sit* to judge all the
20(-:20). Judah *shall dwell* for ever,
Am. 5:11. *ye shall* not *dwell* in them;
Jon. 3: 6. covered (him) with sackcloth, *and sat* in
4: 5. *and sat* on the east side of the city,
— *and sat* under it in the shadow,
Mic. 7: 8. when *I sit* in darkness,
Zep. 1:13. shall also build houses, and not *inhabit*
Zec. 2: 4(8). Jerusalem *shall be inhabited*
8: 4. there *shall* yet old men...*dwell* in the streets
9: 5. Ashkelon *shall* not *be inhabited.*

KAL.—*Participle.* Poel.

Gen. 4:20. the father of *such as dwell in* tents,
13: 7. *dwelled* then in the land.
14: 7. *that dwelt* in Hazezon-tamar.
12. who *dwelt* in Sodom,
18: 1. he *sat* in the tent door
19: 1. Lot *sat* in the gate of Sodom:
25. *the inhabitants of* the cities,
23:10. Ephron *dwelt* among the children of Heth:
24: 3. among whom I *dwell:*
37. in whose land I *dwell:*
62. he *dwelt* in the south country.
25:27. Jacob (was) a plain man, *dwelling* in tents.
34:30. *among the inhabitants of* the land,
36:20. *who inhabited* the land;
50:11. *the inhabitants of* the land,
Ex. 11: 5. of Pharaoh *that sitteth* upon his throne,
12:29. of Pharaoh *that sat* on his throne
15:14. *the inhabitants of* Palestina.
15. all *the inhabitants of* Canaan shall melt
18:14. why *sittest* thou thyself alone,
23:31. I will deliver *the inhabitants of* the land
34:12,15. *with the inhabitants of* the land
Lev. 15: 6. *And he that sitteth* on (any) thing
23. any thing whereon she *sitteth,*
18:25. the land itself vomiteth out *her inhabitants.*
25:10. all *the inhabitants thereof:*
26:32. your enemies *which dwell* therein
Nu. 13:18. the people *that dwelleth* therein,
19. what the land (is) that they *dwell* in,
— that they *dwell* in,
28. the people (be) strong *that dwell* in the
29. The Amalekites *dwell* in the land
— the Amorites, *dwell* in the mountains: and the Canaanites *dwell* by the sea,
32. a land that eateth up *the inhabitants thereof;*
14:14. *the inhabitants of* this land:
25. the Canaanites *dwelt* in the valley.
45. the Canaanites *which dwelt* in that hill,
21: 1. *which dwelt* in the south,
34. which *dwelt* at Heshbon.
22: 5. they *abide* over against me:
32:17. *the inhabitants of* the land.
33:40. which *dwelt* in the south
52. *the inhabitants of* the land
55. *the inhabitants of* the land
— shall vex you in the land wherein ye *dwell.*
35:34. the land which ye *shall inhabit,*
Deu. 1: 4. which *dwelt* in Heshbon,
— which *dwelt* at Astaroth
44. *which dwelt* in that mountain,
2: 4. *which dwell* in Seir;
8,22. *which dwelt* in Seir,
23. the Avims *which dwelt* in Hazerim,
29. the children of Esau *which dwell* in Seir, and the Moabites *which dwell* in Ar,
3: 2. which *dwelt* at Heshbon.
4:46. who *dwelt* at Heshbon,
11:30. *which dwell* in the champaign
13:13(14). *the inhabitants of* their city,
Deu. 13:15(16). shalt surely smite *the inhabitants of*
Jos. 2: 9. all *the inhabitants of* the land faint
15. she *dwelt* upon the wall.
24. all *the inhabitants of* the country do faint
7: 9. all *the inhabitants of* the land shall hear
8:24, 26. all *the inhabitants of* Ai
9: 3. *And* when *the inhabitants of* Gibeon heard
7. Peradventure ye *dwell* among us;
11. all *the inhabitants of* our country
16. they *dwelt* among them.
22. when ye *dwell* among us?
24. *the inhabitants of* the land
10: 1. *the inhabitants of* Gibeon
6. *that dwell in* the mountains
11:19. *the inhabitants of* Gibeon:
12: 2. *who dwelt* in Heshbon,
4. *that dwelt* at Ashtaroth
13: 6. All *the inhabitants of* the hill country
21. *dwelling in* the country.
15:15. *the inhabitants of* Debir
63. *the inhabitants of* Jerusalem,
16:10. the Canaanites *that dwelt* in Gezer:
17: 7. *the inhabitants of* En-tappuah.
11. *the inhabitants of* Dor and her towns, *and the inhabitants of* En-dor and her towns, *and the inhabitants of* Taanach and her towns, *and the inhabitants of* Megiddo
16. *that dwell* in the land of the valley
22:33. the children of Reuben and Gad *dwelt.*
24: 8. *which dwelt* on the other side Jordan;
15. in whose land ye *dwell:*
18. the Amorites *which dwelt* in the land:
Jud. 1: 9. *that dwelt* in the mountain,
10. the Canaanites *that dwelt* in Hebron:
11. *the inhabitants of* Debir:
17. the Canaanites *that inhabited* Zephath,
19. *the inhabitants of* the valley,
21. the Jebusites *that inhabited* Jerusalem;
27. *the inhabitants of* Dor and her towns, nor *the inhabitants of* Ibleam and her towns, nor *the inhabitants of* Megiddo
29. the Canaanites *that dwelt* in Gezer;
30. *the inhabitants* of Kitron, nor *the inhabitants of* Nahalol;
31. *the inhabitants of* Accho, nor *the inhabitants of* Zidon,
32. *the inhabitants of* the land:
33. *the inhabitants of* Beth-shemesh, nor *the inhabitants of* Beth-anath;
— *the inhabitants of* the land: *nevertheless the inhabitants of* Beth-shemesh
2: 2. *with the inhabitants of* this land;
3: 3. the Hivites *that dwelt* in mount Lebanon,
20. he *was sitting* in a summer parlour,
4: 2. *which dwelt* in Harosheth of the Gentiles.
5. she *dwelt* under the palm tree of Deborah
5:10. *ye that sit* in judgment,
23. curse ye bitterly *the inhabitants thereof;*
6:10. in whose land ye *dwell:*
10: 1. he *dwelt* in Shamir
18 & 11:8. *the inhabitants of* Gilead.
11:21. *the inhabitants of* that country.
13: 9. came again unto the woman *as* she *sat* in
16: 9. *abiding* with her in the chamber.
12. *abiding* in the chamber.
18: 7. how they *dwelt* careless,
20:15. *the inhabitants of* Gibeah,
21: 9. *of the inhabitants of* Jabesh-gilead
10. and smite *the inhabitants of* Jabesh-gilead
12. *among the inhabitants of* Jabesh-gilead
Ru. 4: 4. Buy (it) before *the inhabitants,*
1Sa. 1: 9. Eli the priest *sat* upon a seat
4: 4. *which dwelleth* (between) the cherubims;
13. Eli *sat* upon a seat
6:21. *the inhabitants of* Kirjath-jearim,
13:16. *abode* in Gibeah of Benjamin:
14: 2. Saul *tarried* in the uttermost part of
19: 9. as he *sat* in his house
22: 6. now Saul *abode* in Gibeah
23: 5. David saved *the inhabitants of* Keilah.
24: 3(4). his men *remained* in the sides of the
26: 3. David *abode* in the wilderness,
27: 8. *the inhabitants of* the land,
30:24. *that tarrieth* by the stuff:
31:11. *the inhabitants of* Jabesh-gilead
2Sa. 5: 6. *the inhabitants of* the land:
6: 2. *that dwelleth* (between) the cherubims.

2Sa. 7: 2. I *dwell* in an house of cedar, but the ark of God *dwelleth* within curtains.
9:13. So Mephibosheth *dwelt* in Jerusalem:
11: 1. David *tarried* still at Jerusalem.
11. The ark, and Israel, and Judah, *abide* in
16: 3. he *abideth* at Jerusalem:
18:24. David *sat* between the two gates:
19: 8(9). the king *doth sit* in the gate.
23: 8. The Tachmonite *that sat* in the seat,
1K. 1:48. hath given (one) *to sit* (lit. *sitting*) on my
3: 6. a son *to sit* on his throne,
17. I and this woman *dwell* in one house;
8:25. *to sit* (lit. *sitting*) on the throne of Israel;
9:16. the Canaanites *that dwelt* in the city,
12:17. *which dwelt* in the cities of Judah,
13:11. *there dwelt* an old prophet in Beth-el;
14. found him *sitting* under an oak:
20. it came to pass, as they *sat* at the table,
25. the city where the old prophet *dwelt*.
15:18. *that dwelt* at Damascus,
17:19. carried him up into a loft, where he *abode*,
21: 8. *dwelling* with Naboth.
11. *the inhabitants* in his city,
22:10. the king of Israel...the king of Judah *sat* each on his throne,
19. I saw the Lord *sitting* on his throne,
2K. 1: 9. he *sat* on the top of an hill.
2:18. he *tarried* at Jericho,
4:13. I *dwell* among mine own people.
38. the sons of the prophets (were) *sitting*
6: 1. the place where we *dwell*
32. Elisha *sat* in his house, and the elders *sat*
7: 3. Why *sit* we here until we die?
9: 5. the captains of the host (were) *sitting*;
17:29. their cities wherein they *dwelt*.
18:27. the men *which sit* on the wall,
19:15. *which dwellest* (between) the cherubims,
26. *Therefore their inhabitants* were of small
22:14. she *dwelt* in Jerusalem in the college;
16. upon *the inhabitants thereof*,
19. against *the inhabitants thereof*,
23: 2. *the inhabitants of* Jerusalem
1Ch. 2:55. the scribes *which dwelt* at Jabez;
4:23. *and those that dwelt among* plants
40. (they) of Ham *had dwelt* there of old.
5: 8. who *dwelt* in Aroer,
8: 6. *of the inhabitants of* Geba,
13. *of the inhabitants of* Aijalon, who drove away *the inhabitants of* Gath:
9: 2. *Now the* first *inhabitants* that (dwelt)
16. *that dwelt* in the villages
11: 4. *the inhabitants of* the land.
5. *the inhabitants of* Jebus
13: 6. *that dwelleth* (between) the cherubims,
17: 1. I *dwell* in an house of cedars,
20: 1. David *tarried* at Jerusalem.
22:18. *the inhabitants of* the land
2Ch. 6:16. *to sit* (lit. *sitting*) upon the throne of
10:17. *that dwelt* in the cities of Judah,
15: 5. *the inhabitants of* the countries.
16: 2. *that dwelt* at Damascus,
18: 9. *sat* either of them on his throne,
— *and* they *sat* in a void place
18. I saw the Lord *sitting* upon his throne,
19:10. your brethren *that dwell* in their cities,
20: 7. *the inhabitants of* this land
15,20. *and ye inhabitants of* Jerusalem,
18. *and the inhabitants of* Jerusalem fell
23. against *the inhabitants of* mount Seir,
— made an end *of the inhabitants of* Seir,
21:11. *the inhabitants of* Jerusalem to commit
13. *the inhabitants of* Jerusalem to go a
22: 1. *the inhabitants of* Jerusalem made
26: 7. the Arabians *that dwelt* in Gur-baal,
30:25. *and that dwelt* in Judah,
31: 4. the people *that dwelt* in Jerusalem
6. *that dwelt* in the cities of Judah,
32:10. *that ye abide* in the siege in Jerusalem?
22. *the inhabitants of* Jerusalem
26. he *and the inhabitants of* Jerusalem,
33. *and the inhabitants of* Jerusalem did him
33: 9. *and the inhabitants of* Jerusalem to err,
34: 9. (כתיב) *and they returned* to Jerusalem. (lit. according to כתיב—*and the inhabitants of* Jerusalem)
22. she *dwelt* in Jerusalem in the college:
24. upon *the inhabitants thereof*,
2Ch 34:27. against *the inhabitants thereof*,
28. upon *the inhabitants of the same*.
30. *and the inhabitants of* Jerusalem, and the
32. *the inhabitants of* Jerusalem did
35:18. present, *and the inhabitants of* Jerusalem.
Ezr. 4: 6. *the inhabitants of* Judah and Jerusalem.
9: 4. I *sat* astonied until the evening sacrifice.
Neh. 2: 6. the queen also *sitting* by him,
3:13. *and the inhabitants of* Zanoah;
26. the Nethinims *dwelt* in Ophel, (lit. were *dwelling*)
4:12(6). the Jews *which dwelt* by them
7: 3. *the inhabitants of* Jerusalem,
9:24. *the inhabitants of* the land,
11: 6. the sons of Perez *that dwelt* at Jerusalem
21. the Nethinims *dwelt* in Ophel:
Est. 1:14. *which sat* the first in the kingdom;
2:19,21. Mordecai *sat* in the king's gate.
5: 1. the king *sat* upon his royal throne
13. *sitting* at the king's gate.
6:10. *that sitteth* at the king's gate:
9:19. *that dwelt* in the unwalled towns,
Job. 2: 8. he *sat down* among the ashes.
Ps. 2: 4. He *that sitteth* in the heavens
9:11(12). which *dwelleth* in Zion:
17:12. *lurking* in secret places.
22: 3(4). *that inhabitest* the praises of Israel.
24: 1. *and they that dwell* therein.
33: 8. *the inhabitants of* the world
14. *the inhabitants of* the earth.
49: 1(2). all (ye) *inhabitants of* the world:
55:19(20). *even he that abideth* of old.
65: 8(9). *They* also *that dwell in* the uttermost
69:12(13). *They that sit in* the gate
25(26). let none *dwell* (lit. let there not be *a dweller*) in their tents.
75: 3(4). all *the inhabitants thereof* are dissolved:
80: 1(2). thou *that dwellest* (between) the
83: 7(8). *the inhabitants of* Tyre;
84: 4(5). Blessed (are) *they that dwell* in thy
91: 1. *He that dwelleth* in the secret place
98: 7. *and they that dwell* therein.
99: 1. he *sitteth* (between) the cherubims;
107:10. *Such as sit in* darkness
34. the wickedness of *them that dwell* therein.
123: 1. *O thou that dwellest* in the heavens.
Pro. 3:29. seeing he *dwelleth* securely
20: 8. A king *that sitteth* in the throne
Cant 5:12. washed with milk, (and) fitly *set*.
8:13. *Thou that dwellest* in the gardens,
Isa. 5: 3. *O inhabitants of* Jerusalem,
9. many houses shall be...without *inhabitant*.
6: 1. I saw also the Lord *sitting* upon a throne,
5. I *dwell* in the midst of a people of unclean
11. the cities be wasted without *inhabitant*,
8:14. a snare *to the inhabitants of* Jerusalem.
9: 2(1). *they that dwell* in the land
9(8). *and the inhabitant of* Samaria,
10:13. I have put down *the inhabitants*
24. O my people *that dwellest in* Zion,
31. *the inhabitants of* Gebim
12: 6. *inhabitant of* Zion: (marg. *inhabitress*)
18: 3. All ye *inhabitants of* the world,
20: 6. *the inhabitant of* this isle
21:14. *The inhabitants of* the land of Tema
22:21. *to the inhabitants of* Jerusalem,
23: 2, 6. ye *inhabitants of* the isle;
18. them *that dwell* before the Lord,
24: 1. scattereth abroad *the inhabitants thereof*.
5. under *the inhabitants thereof*;
6. they *that dwell* therein are desolate: therefore *the inhabitants of* the earth
17. *O inhabitant of* the earth.
26: 5. them *that dwell* on high;
9, 18. *the inhabitants of* the world
21. to punish *the inhabitants of* the earth
28: 6. *to him that sitteth* in judgment,
33:24. the people *that dwell* therein
36:12. the men *that sit* upon the wall,
37:16. *that dwellest* (between) the cherubims,
27. *Therefore their inhabitants* (were) of small
38:11. *the inhabitants of* the world.
40:22. *that sitteth* upon the circle of the earth, *and the inhabitants thereof* (are) as
42: 7. them *that sit* in darkness
10. the isles, *and the inhabitants thereof*.
11. let *the inhabitants of* the rock sing,

Isa. 47: 8. (thou)...*that dwellest* carelessly,
49:19. *by reason of the inhabitants,*
51: 6. *and they that dwell therein* shall die in like
65: 4. *Which remain* among the graves,
Jer. 1:14. *the inhabitants of* the land.
2:15. his cities are burned without *inhabitant.*
4: 4. *and inhabitants of* Jerusalem:
7. without *an inhabitant.*
29. not a man *dwell* therein.
6:12. *the inhabitants of* the land,
8: 1. the bones of *the inhabitants of* Jerusalem,
14. Why do we *sit still?*
16. *and those that dwell* therein.
9:11(10). without *an inhabitant.*
26(25). *that dwell* in the wilderness:
10:17. *O inhabitant of* the fortress. (marg. *inhabitress*)
18. I will sling out *the inhabitants of* the land
11: 2. *the inhabitants of* Jerusalem;
9. *and among the inhabitants of* Jerusalem.
12. *and inhabitants of* Jerusalem
12: 4. the wickedness of them *that dwell* therein?
13:13. I will fill all *the inhabitants of* this land, even the kings *that sit* upon David's
— *the inhabitants of* Jerusalem,
17:20. all *the inhabitants of* Jerusalem,
25. *sitting* upon the throne of David,
— *and the inhabitants of* Jerusalem:
18:11. *the inhabitants of* Jerusalem,
19: 3. *and inhabitants of* Jerusalem;
12. *and to the inhabitants thereof,*
20: 6. all *that dwell in* thine house
21: 6. I will smite *the inhabitants of* this city,
9. He *that abideth* in this city shall die
13. *O inhabitant of* the valley, (marg. *inhabitress*)
22: 2. *that sittest* upon the throne of David,
4. *sitting* upon the throne of David,
23. *O inhabitant of* Lebanon,
30. *sitting* upon the throne of David,
23:14. *and the inhabitants thereof as* Gomorrah.
24: 8. *and them that dwell* in the land of Egypt:
25. 2. all *the inhabitants of* Jerusalem,
9. against *the inhabitants thereof,*
29, 30. all *the inhabitants of* the earth,
26: 9. without *an inhabitant?*
15. upon *the inhabitants thereof:*
29:16. *that sitteth* upon the throne of David, and of all the people *that dwelleth* in this
32. not have a man *to dwell* (lit. *dwelling*)
32:12. *that sat* in the court of the prison.
32. *and the inhabitants of* Jerusalem.
33:10. without *inhabitant,*
17. never want a man *to sit* (lit. *sitting*) upon
34:22. without *an inhabitant.*
35:13. *and the inhabitants of* Jerusalem,
17. *the inhabitants of* Jerusalem
36:12. all the princes *sat* there,
22. the king *sat* in the winterhouse
30. He shall have none *to sit* (lit. *sitting*)
31. *the inhabitants of* Jerusalem,
38: 2. He *that remaineth* in this city shall die
7. the king then *sitting* in the gate of
40:10. I *will dwell* at Mizpah,
42:18. *the inhabitants of* Jerusalem;
44: 1. *which dwell* in the land of Egypt, *which dwell* at Migdol,
2. no man *dwelleth* therein,
13. I will punish them *that dwell* in the land
15. all the people *that dwelt* in the land of
22. without *an inhabitant,*
26. all Judah *that dwell* in the land of Egypt;
46: 8. I will destroy the city *and the inhabitants*
19. O thou daughter *dwelling* in Egypt,
— without *an inhabitant.*
47: 2. *and them that dwell* therein: then the men shall cry, and all *the inhabitants of* the
48: 9. without any *to dwell* (lit. *dwelling*) therein.
18. Thou daughter *that dost inhabit* Dibon,
— (כתיב) come down from (thy) glory, and *sit* in thirst;
19. *O inhabitant of* Aroer,
28. *O ye that dwell in* Moab,
43. *O inhabitant of* Moab,
49: 8. *O inhabitants of* Dedan;
20. *the inhabitants of* Teman:
30. *O ye inhabitants of* Hazor,

Jer. 49:31. *that dwelleth* without care,
50: 3. none *shall dwell* therein:
21. against *the inhabitants of* Pekod:
34. disquiet *the inhabitants of* Babylon.
35. upon *the inhabitants of* Babylon,
51: 1. against *them that dwell*
12. *the inhabitants of* Babylon.
24. *the inhabitants of* Chaldea
29. without *an inhabitant.*
35. *the inhabitant of* Zion say; and my blood upon *the inhabitants of* Chaldea,
37. without *an inhabitant.*
62. none shall *remain* in it,
Lam. 4:12. *the inhabitants of* the world,
21. *that dwellest* in the land of Uz;
Eze. 2: 6. thou *dost dwell* among scorpions:
3:15. *that dwelt* by the river of Chebar, and I sat where they *sat,*
7: 7. O thou *that dwellest in* the land:
8: 1. I *sat* in mine house, and the elders of Judah *sat* before me,
14. there *sat* women weeping
11:15. *the inhabitants of* Jerusalem
12: 2. thou *dwellest* in the midst of a rebellious
19. *of the inhabitants of* Jerusalem,
— all them *that dwell* therein.
15: 6. *the inhabitants of* Jerusalem.
16:46. her daughters *that dwell* at thy left hand:
— *that dwelleth* at thy right hand,
26:17. she *and her inhabitants,*
— on all *that haunt it!*
27: 3. O thou *that art situate* at the entry of the
8. *The inhabitants of* Zidon
35. *the inhabitants of* the isles
29: 6. *the inhabitants of* Egypt
32:15. I shall smite all them *that dwell* therein,
33:24. they *that inhabit* those wastes
36:17. the house of Israel *dwelt* in their own land,
38:11. I will go to them...*that dwell* safely, all of them *dwelling* without walls,
12. *that dwell* in the midst of the land.
39: 6. *and among them that dwell* carelessly
9. *they that dwell* in the cities of Israel
Dan 9: 7. *and to the inhabitants of* Jerusalem,
Hos. 4: 1. *the inhabitants of* the land,
3. every one *that dwelleth* therein
14: 7(8). *They that dwell* under his shadow shall
Joel 1: 2. all *ye inhabitants of* the land.
14. *the inhabitants of* the land
2: 1. let all *the inhabitants of* the land tremble:
Am. 1: 5. cut off *the inhabitant* from the plain
8. I will cut off *the inhabitant* from Ashdod,
3:12. *that dwell* in Samaria
8: 8. every one mourn *that dwelleth* therein?
9: 5. all *that dwell* therein shall mourn:
Mic. 1:11. *inhabitant of* Saphir, (marg. *inhabitress*)
— *the inhabitant of* Zaanan
12. *the inhabitant of* Maroth
13. *O* thou *inhabitant of* Lachish,
15. *O inhabitant of* Mareshah:
6:12. *and the inhabitants thereof* have spoken lies,
16. *and the inhabitants* thereof an hissing:
7:13. because of them *that dwell* therein,
Nah 1: 5. all *that dwell* therein.
3: 8. *that was situate* among the rivers,
Hab. 2: 8, 17. all *that dwell* therein.
Zep. 1: 4. *the inhabitants of* Jerusalem;
11. ye *inhabitants of* Maktesh,
18. all them *that dwell in* the land.
2: 5. *the inhabitants of* the sea coast,
— that there shall be no *inhabitant.*
15. the rejoicing city *that dwelt* carelessly,
3: 6. that there is none *inhabitant.*
Zec. 1:11. all the earth *sitteth still,*
2: 7(11). *that dwellest* (with) the daughter of
3: 8. thy fellows *that sit* before thee:
5: 7. a woman *that sitteth* in the midst
7: 7. when Jerusalem was *inhabited*
— when (men) *inhabited* the south
8:20. *and the inhabitants of* many cities.
21. *the inhabitants of* one (city)
11: 6. no more pity *the inhabitants of* the land,
12: 5. *The inhabitants of* Jerusalem (shall be)
7. *the inhabitants of* Jerusalem do not
8. shall the Lord defend *the inhabitants of*
10. upon *the inhabitants of* Jerusalem,
13: 1. *and to the inhabitants of* Jerusalem

* NIPHAL.—*Preterite.* *

Jer. 6: 8. a land not *inhabited.*
22: 6. cities (which) *are* not *inhabited.*
Eze.26:19. the cities that *are* not *inhabited;*
36:10. *and* the cities *shall be inhabited,*

NIPHAL.—*Participle.*

Ex. 16:35. they came to a land *inhabited,*
Jer. 22: 6. (כתיב) cities (which) *are* not *inhabited.*
Eze.12:20. the cities *that are inhabited*
26:17. (that wast) *inhabited* of seafaring men,
38:12. desolate places (that are now) *inhabited,*

* PIEL.—*Preterite.* *

Eze.25: 4. *and they shall set* their palaces in thee,

* HIPHIL.—*Preterite.* *

Lev.23.43. *I made* the children of Israel *to dwell* in
1K. 21:12. *and set* Naboth on high among the people.
Ezr.10:14. all them *which have taken* strange wives
17. the men *that had taken* strange wives
18. that *had taken* strange wives:
Neh 13:23. *had married* wives of Ashdod, (marg. *made to dwell* (with them))
Ps.143: 3. *he hath made me to dwell* in darkness,
Jer. 32:37. *and I will cause them to dwell* safely:
Lam.3: 6. *He hath set me* in dark places,
Eze.26:20. *and shall set thee in* the low parts of the
36:11. *and I will settle you* after your old estates,
33. *I will also cause* (you) *to dwell* in the cities,
Hos.11:11. *and I will place them* in their houses,
Zec.10: 6. *I will bring them again to place them;*

HIPHIL.—*Infinitive.*

1Sa. 2: 8. *to set* (them) among princes,
Neh 13:27. *in marrying* strange wives?
Ps.113: 8. *That he may set* (him) with princes,

HIPHIL.—*Imperative.*

Gen47: 6. *make* thy father and brethren *to dwell;*
1K. 21: 9. *and set* Naboth on high among the people:
10. *And set* two men, sons of Belial, before

HIPHIL.—*Future.*

Gen47:11. *And* Joseph *placed* his father
1Sa.12: 8. *and made them dwell* in this place.
30:21. *whom they had made also to abide* at the
1K. 2:24. *and set me* on the throne of David
2K. 17: 6. *and placed* them in Halah
24. *and placed* (them) in the cities of Samaria
26. *and placed* in the cities of Samaria,
2Ch 8: 2. *and caused* the children of Israel *to dwell*
23:20. *and set* the king upon the throne
Ezr.10: 2. *and have taken* strange wives
10. *and have taken* strange wives,
Job 36: 7. *yea, he doth establish them* for ever,
Ps. 4: 8(9). thou, Lord, only *makest me dwell*
107:36. *And* there *he maketh* the hungry *to dwell,*
Isa. 54: 3. *make* the desolate cities *to be inhabited.*
Hos.12: 9(10). *will* yet *make thee to dwell* in tabernacles,

HIPHIL.—*Participle.*

Ps. 68: 6(7). God *setteth* the solitary in families:
113: 9. He *maketh* the barren woman *to keep* house, (marg. *dwell in*)

* HOPHAL.—*Preterite.* *

Isa. 5: 8. *that they may be placed* alone in the midst

HOPHAL.—*Future.*

Isa. 44:26. saith to Jerusalem, *Thou shalt be inhabited;*

3444 יְשׁוּעָה *y'shoo-gāh'*, f.

Gen49:18. I have waited *for thy salvation,*
Ex. 14:13. see *the salvation of* the Lord,
15: 2. he is become my *salvation:* (lit. *for salvation* to me)
Deu32:15. the Rock of *his salvation.*
1Sa. 2: 1. I rejoice *in thy salvation.*
14:45. who hath wrought this great *salvation*
2Sa.10:11. shalt *help* me: (lit. shalt be *for help* to me)
22:51. the tower of *salvation*
1Ch 16:23. shew forth from day to day *his salvation.*
2Ch 20:17. see *the salvation of* the Lord
Job 13:16. He also (shall be) my *salvation:* (lit. *for salvation* to me)
30:15. *my welfare* passeth away as a cloud.
Ps. 3: 2(3). (There is) no *help* for him in God.
Ps. 3: 8(9). *Salvation* (belongeth) unto the Lord:
9:14(15). I will rejoice *in thy salvation.*
13: 5(6). my heart shall rejoice *in thy salvation,*
14: 7. *the salvation of* Israel
18:50(51). Great *deliverance* giveth he to his king;
20: 5(6). We will rejoice *in thy salvation,*
21: 1(2). *and in thy salvation* how greatly shall
5(6). His glory (is) great *in thy salvation:*
22: 1(2). (why art thou so) far *from helping me,*
28: 8. he (is) the *saving* strength (marg. strength of *salvations*) of his anointed.
35: 3. say unto my soul, I (am) *thy salvation.*
9. it shall rejoice *in his salvation.*
42: 5(6). *the help of* his countenance.
11(12) & 43:5. *the health of* my countenance,
44: 4(5). command *deliverances for* Jacob.
53: 6(7). *the salvation of* Israel
62: 1(2). from him (cometh) *my salvation.*
2(3), 6(7). (is) my rock *and my salvation;*
67: 2(3). *thy saving health* among all nations.
68:19(20). the God of *our salvation.*
69:29(30). let *thy salvation,* O God, set me up on
70: 4(5). let such as love *thy salvation*
74:12. working *salvation* in the midst of the earth.
78:22. trusted not *in his salvation:*
80: 2(3). come (and) *save* us. (marg. *for salvation* to us)
88: 1(2). O Lord God of *my salvation,*
89:26(27). the rock of *my salvation.*
91:16. shew him *my salvation.*
96: 2. shew forth *his salvation* from day to day.
98: 2. The Lord hath made known *his salvation:*
3. *the salvation of* our God.
106: 4. O visit me *with thy salvation;*
116:13. I will take the cup of *salvation,*
118:14. is become my *salvation.* (lit. *for salvation* to me)
15. The voice of rejoicing *and salvation*
21. my *salvation.* (lit. *for salvation* to me)
119:123. Mine eyes fail *for thy salvation,*
155. *Salvation* (is) far from the wicked:
166. I have hoped *for thy salvation,*
174. I have longed *for thy salvation,*
140: 7(8). the strength of *my salvation,*
149: 4. he will beautify the meek *with salvation.*
Isa. 12: 2. God (is) *my salvation;*
— he also is become my *salvation.* (lit. *for salvation* to me)
3. the wells of *salvation.*
25: 9. we will be glad and rejoice *in his salvation.*
26: 1. *salvation* will (God) appoint (for) walls
18. we have not wrought any *deliverance*
33: 2. *our salvation* also in the time of trouble.
6. strength of *salvation:* (marg. *salvations*)
49: 6. that thou mayest be *my salvation*
8. in a day of *salvation* have I helped thee:
51: 6. *but my salvation* shall be for ever,
8. *and my salvation* from generation to
52: 7. that publisheth *salvation,*
10. all the ends of the earth shall see *the salvation of* our God.
56: 1. *my salvation* (is) near to come,
59:11. *for salvation,* (but) it is far off from us.
17. an helmet of *salvation* upon his head;
60:18. thou shalt call thy walls *Salvation,*
62: 1. *and the salvation thereof* as a lamp
Jon. 2: 9(10). *Salvation* (is) of the Lord.
Hab. 3: 8. thy chariots of *salvation?*

יֶשַׁח *[yeh'-shagh]*, m. 3445

Mic. 6:14. *and thy casting down* (shall be) in the

יָשַׁט *[yāh-shat']*. 3447

* HIPHIL.—*Future.* *

Est. 4:11. to whom the king *shall hold out* the
5: 2. *and* the king *held out* to Esther the
8: 4. *Then* the king *held out* the golden

יְשִׁימוֹן *[y'shee-mōhn']*, m. 3452

Nu. 21:20. which looketh toward *Jeshimon,* (marg. or, *the wilderness*)

Nu. 23:28. that looketh toward *Jeshimon.*
Deu32:10. in the waste howling *wilderness ;*
1Sa.23:19. which (is) on the south of *Jeshimon ?* (marg. or, *the wilderness*)
24. in the plain on the south of *Jeshimon.*
26: 1. (which is) before *Jeshimon ?*
3. which (is) before *Jeshimon,*
Ps. 68: 7(8). didst march *through the wilderness ;*
78:40. grieve him *in the desert !*
106:14. tempted God *in the desert.*
107: 4. *in a solitary* way; (lit. *in the solitude of* the way)
Isa. 43:19. rivers *in the desert.*
20. rivers *in the desert,*

3451 **יְשִׁימוֹת** *y'shee-mōhth'*, f. pl.

Ps. 55:15(16). (כתיב) *Let death seize* upon them, (or, *destructions* (are) upon them,—so כתיב)

3453 **יָשִׁישׁ** *yāh-sheesh'*, m.

Job 12:12. *With the ancient* (is) wisdom ;
15:10. the grayheaded and *very aged men,*
29: 8. *and the aged* arose, (and) stood up.
32: 6. I (am) young, and ye (are) *very old;*

3456 **יָשַׁם** [*yāh-sham'*].

* KAL.—*Future.* *

Gen47:19. that the land *be* not *desolate.*
Eze. 6: 6. the high places *shall be desolate ;*
12:19. that her land *may be desolate*
19: 7. *and* the land *was desolate,*

3462 **יָשַׁן** [*yāh-shan'*].

* NIPHAL.—*Preterite.* *

Deu 4:25. *and ye shall have remained long* in the

NIPHAL.—*Participle.*

Lev.13:11. It (is) an *old* leprosy
26:10. ye shall eat *old store,*

3465 **יָשָׁן** *yāh-shāhn'*, adj.

Lev.25:22. eat (yet) of *old* fruit
— ye shall eat (of) the *old* (store).
26:10. ye shall eat *old* store, *and* bring forth *the old* because of the new.
Neh 3: 6. the *old* gate repaired
12:39. above the *old* gate,
Cant.7:13(14). new and *old,*
Isa. 22:11. the water of the *old* pool:

3462 **יָשֵׁן** [*yāh-shēhn'*].

* KAL.—*Preterite.* *

Job 3:13. *I should have slept:*
Jer. 51:39. *and sleep* a perpetual sleep,
57. *and they shall sleep* a perpetual sleep,
Eze.34:25. *and sleep* in the woods.

KAL.—*Infinitive.*

Ecc. 5:12(11). of the rich will not suffer him *to sleep.*

KAL.—*Future.*

Gen 2:21. to fall upon Adam, *and he slept:*
41: 5. *And he slept* and dreamed the second
1K. 19: 5. as he lay *and slept* under a juniper tree,
Ps. 3: 5(6). I laid me down *and slept;*
4: 8(9). both lay me down in peace, *and sleep:*
13: 3(4). lest *I sleep* the (sleep of) death ;
44:23(24). why *sleepest thou,* O Lord?
121: 4. shall neither slumber nor *sleep.*
Pro. 4:16. For *they sleep* not,
Isa. 5:27. none shall slumber nor *sleep;*

* PIEL.—*Future.* *

Jud.16:19. *And she made him sleep* upon her knees;

יָשֵׁן *yāh-shēhn'*, adj. 3463

1Sa.26: 7. Saul lay *sleeping* within the trench,
12. for they (were) all *asleep ;*
1K. 3:20. while thine handmaid *slept,*
18:27. peradventure he *sleepeth,* and must be
Ps. 78:65. Then the Lord awaked *as one out of sleep,*
Cant.5: 2. I *sleep,* but my heart waketh:
7: 9(10). those that are *asleep*
Dan 12: 2. many *of them that sleep*
Hos. 7: 6. their baker *sleepeth* all the night;

יָשַׁע [*yāh-shag'*]. 3467

* NIPHAL.—*Preterite.* *

Nu. 10: 9. *and ye shall be saved* from your enemies.
Isa. 45:17. Israel *shall be saved* in the Lord
Jer. 8:20. we *are* not *saved.*

NIPHAL.—*Imperative.*

Isa. 45:22. Look unto me, *and be ye saved,*

NIPHAL.—*Future.*

2Sa.22: 4. so *shall I be saved* from mine enemies.
Ps. 18: 3(4). so *shall I be saved* from mine enemies.
80: 3(4), 7(8), 19(20). cause thy face to shine; *and we shall be saved.*
119:117. Hold thou me up, *and I shall be safe:*
Pro.28:18. Whoso walketh uprightly *shall be saved :*
Isa. 30:15. In returning and rest *shall ye be saved;*
64: 5(4). is continuance, *and we shall be saved.*
Jer. 4:14. that *thou mayest be saved.*
17:14. save me, *and I shall be saved:*
23: 6. In his days Judah *shall be saved,*
30: 7. *he shall be saved* out of it.
33:16. In those days *shall* Judah *be saved,*

NIPHAL.—*Participle.*

Deu33:29. O people *saved* by the Lord,
Ps. 33:16. *There is* no king *saved* by the multitude
Zec. 9: 9. he (is) just, *and having salvation;*

* HIPHIL.—*Preterite.* *

Jud. 2:18. *and delivered them* out of the hand of
6:14. *and thou shalt save* Israel from the hand
7: 2. Mine own hand *hath saved* me.
8:22. *thou hast delivered us* from the hand of
12: 2. *ye delivered* me not out of their hands.
1Sa. 9:16. *that he may save* my people out of
23: 2. Go and smite the Philistines, *and save*
1Ch 19:12. *then I will help thee.*
Job 26: 2. (how) *savest thou* the arm (that hath) no
Ps. 20: 6(7). that the Lord *saveth* his anointed;
34: 6(7). *saved him* out of all his troubles.
44: 3(4). neither *did* their own arm *save* them:
7(8). *thou hast saved us* from our enemies,
98: 1. holy arm, *hath gotten* him *the victory.*
Isa. 43:12. I have declared, *and have saved,*
63: 9. the angel of his presence *saved them :*
Eze.34:22. *Therefore will I save* my flock,
36:29. *I will also save* you from all your
37:23. *but I will save* them out of all their
Hos. 1: 7. *and will save them* by the Lord their God,
Zep. 3:19. *and I will save* her that halteth,
Zec. 9:16. *And* the Lord their God *shall save them* in
12: 7. The Lord *also shall save* the tents of

HIPHIL.—*Infinitive.*

Deu20: 4. against your enemies, *to save* you.
Jud.10: 1. *to defend* Israel (marg. *save,* or, *deliver*)
13. I will *deliver* you no more. (lit. I will not add *to deliver*)
13: 5. he shall begin *to deliver* Israel
1Sa.14: 6. *to save* by many or by few.
25:26. *and* from *avenging* thyself with thine own hand, (marg. *saving*)
31. *or that* my lord *hath avenged* himself:
33. *and* from *avenging* myself with mine
2Sa. 3:18. *I will save* my people Israel
10:11. I will come *and help* thee.
19. the Syrians feared *to help* the children of
2K. 19:34. I will defend this city, *to save it,*
1Ch 19:19. neither would the Syrians *help* the

Ps. 31: 2(3). an house of defence *to save me.*
71: 3. thou hast given commandment *to save me;*
76: 9(10). *to save* all the meek of the earth.
109:31. *to save* (him) from those that condemn
Isa. 37:35. I will defend this city *to save it*
38:20. The Lord (was ready) *to save me:*
59: 1. is not shortened, *that* it *cannot save;*
63: 1. speak in righteousness, mighty *to save.*
Jer. 11:12. *but* they shall not save them *at all* (lit. *saving* they shall save)
14: 9. as a mighty man (that) cannot *save?*
15:20. I (am) with thee *to save thee*
30:11. I (am) with thee,...*to save thee:*
42:11. I (am) with you *to save* you,

HIPHIL.—*Imperative.*

Jos. 10: 6. come up to us quickly, *and save* us,
2Sa. 14: 4. *Help*, O king. (marg. *Save*)
2K. 6:26. *Help*, my lord, O king.
16: 7. *and save me* out of the hand of the king
19:19. *save thou us* out of his hand,
1Ch 16:35. *Save us*, O God of our salvation,
Ps. 3: 7(8). *save me*, O my God:
6: 4(5). oh *save me* for thy mercies' sake.
7: 1(2). *save* me from all them that persecute
12: 1(2). *Help*, Lord; for the godly man
20: 9(10). *Save*, Lord.
22:21(22). *Save me* from the lion's mouth:
28: 9. *Save* thy people, and bless thine
31:16(17). *save me* for thy mercies' sake.
54: 1(3). *Save me*, O God, by thy name,
59: 2(3). *save me* from bloody men.
60: 5(7). *save* (with) thy right hand,
69: 1(2). *Save me*, O God;
71: 2. incline thine ear unto me, *and save me.*
86: 2. *save* thy servant that trusteth in thee.
16. *and save* the son of thine handmaid.
106:47. *Save us*, O Lord our God,
108: 6(7). *save* (with) thy right hand,
109:26. O *save me* according to thy mercy:
118:25. *Save* now, I beseech thee, O Lord:
119:94. I (am) thine, *save me;*
146. I cried unto thee; *save me,*
Isa. 37:20. *save us* from his hand,
Jer. 2:27. Arise, *and save us.*
17:14. *save me*, and I shall be saved:
31: 7. O Lord, *save* thy people,

HIPHIL.—*Future.*

Ex. 2:17. Moses stood up *and helped them,*
14:30. *Thus* the Lord *saved* Israel
Jos. 22:22. *save us* not this day,
Jud. 2:16. *which delivered them* out of the hand (marg. *saved*)
3: 9. Lord raised up a deliverer...*who delivered them,*
31. *and* he also *delivered* Israel.
6:15. Oh my Lord, wherewith *shall I save*
31. *will ye save* him?
37. shall I know that *thou wilt save* Israel
7: 7. By the three hundred men...*will I save*
10:12. *and I delivered* you out of their hand.
14. *let them deliver* you
1Sa. 4: 3. *that,...it may save us* out of the hand of
7: 8. *that he will save us* out of the hand of
10:27. How *shall* this man *save us?*
14:23. *So* the Lord *saved* Israel that day:
17:47. the Lord *saveth* not with sword and
23: 5. *So* David *saved* the inhabitants of Keilah.
2Sa. 8: 6, 14. *And* the Lord *preserved* David
22: 3. *thou savest me* from violence.
28. the afflicted people *thou wilt save:*
2K. 6:27. If the Lord *do* not *help thee*, whence *shall I help thee?*
14:27. *but he saved them* by the hand of
1Ch 11:14. *and* the Lord *saved* (them) by a great
18: 6. *Thus* the Lord *preserved* David
13. *Thus* the Lord *preserved* David
2Ch 20: 9. then thou wilt hear *and help.*
32:22. *Thus* the Lord *saved* Hezekiah
Neh 9:27. *who saved them* out of the hand of their
Job 5:15. *But he saveth* the poor from the sword,
22:29. *he shall save* the humble person.
40:14. thine own right hand *can save* thee.
Ps. 18:27(28). For *thou wilt save* the afflicted
34:18(19). *saveth* such as be of a contrite spirit.
36: 6(7). *thou preservest* man and beast.
Ps. 37:40. from the wicked, *and save them,*
44: 6(7). neither *shall* my sword *save me.*
55:16(17). the Lord *shall save me.*
57: 3(4). shall send from heaven, *and save me*
69:35(36). For God *will save* Zion,
72: 4. *he shall save* the children of the needy,
13. *shall save* the souls of the needy.
106: 8. *Nevertheless he saved them* for his name's
10. *And he saved them* from the hand of him
107:13. *he saved them* out of their distresses.
19. *he saveth them* out of their distresses.
116: 6. I was brought low, and *he helped* me.
138: 7. *and* thy right hand *shall save me.*
145:19. hear their cry, *and will save them.*
Pro. 20:22. wait on the Lord, *and he shall save* thee.
Isa. 25: 9. waited for him, *and he will save us:*
33:22. the Lord (is) our king; *he will save us.*
35: 4. he will come *and save you.*
45:20. pray unto a god (that) *cannot save.*
46: 7. nor *save him* out of his trouble.
47:13. prognosticators, stand up, *and save thee*
49:25. *I will save* thy children.
59:16. *therefore* his arm *brought salvation*
63: 5. *therefore* mine own arm *brought salvation*
Jer. 2:28. let them arise, *if they can save thee*
11:12. *they shall* not *save* them at all
Lam. 4:17. nation (that) *could* not *save* (us).
Hos. 1: 7. and *will* not *save them* by bow,
13:10. where (is any other) *that may save thee*
14: 3(4). Asshur *shall* not *save us;*
Hab 1: 2. *thou wilt* not *save!*
Zep. 3:17. *he will save*, he will rejoice over thee
Zec. 8:13. so *will I save* you,
10: 6. *I will save* the house of Joseph,

HIPHIL.—*Participle.*

Deu 22:27. the betrothed damsel cried, and (there was) none *to save* her. (lit. no *saviour*)
28:29. no man *shall save* (thee).
31. none *to rescue* (them). (lit. no *saviour*)
Jud. 3: 9. raised up *a deliverer* (marg. *saviour*)
15. the Lord raised them up *a deliverer,*
6:36. If thou wilt *save* (lit. if thou wilt be *saving*) Israel by mine hand,
12: 3. I saw that ye *delivered* (me) not,
1Sa. 10:19. who himself *saved* you out of all your
11: 3. if (there be) no *man to save* us,
14:39. (as) the Lord liveth, *which saveth* Israel,
2Sa. 22: 3. my refuge, *my saviour;*
42. They looked, but (there was) none *to save;* (lit. no *saviour*)
2K. 13: 5. the Lord gave Israel *a saviour,*
Neh 9:27. thou gavest them *saviours,*
Ps. 7:10(11). *which saveth* the upright in heart.
17: 7. O thou *that savest* by thy right hand
18:41(42). They cried, but (there was) *none to save* (lit. no *saviour*)
106:21. They forgat God *their saviour,*
Isa. 19:20. he shall send them *a saviour,*
43: 3. the Holy One of Israel, *thy Saviour:*
11. beside me (there is) no *saviour.*
45:15. O God of Israel, *the Saviour.*
21. a just God *and a Saviour;*
47:15. none *shall save thee.* (lit. *thy saviour*)
49:26 & 60:16. I the Lord (am) *thy Saviour*
63: 8. so he was their *Saviour.* (lit. *for a saviour* to them)
Jer. 14: 8. *the saviour thereof* in time of trouble,
30:10 & 46:27. I *will save thee* from afar,
Hos. 13: 4. *for* (there is) no *saviour* beside me.
Obad. 21. *saviours* shall come up on mount Zion
Zec. 8: 7. I *will save* my people from the east

יֶשַׁע & יֵשַׁע *yĕh'-shag*, m. 3468

2Sa. 22: 3. the horn of *my salvation,*
36. the shield of *thy salvation:*
47. the rock of *my salvation.*
23: 5. for (this is) all *my salvation,*
1Ch 16:35. Save us, O God of *our salvation,*
Job. 5: 4. His children are far *from safety,*
11. those which mourn may be exalted *to safety.*
Ps. 12: 5(6). I will set (him) *in safety*
18: 2(3). the horn of *my salvation,*
35(36). the shield of *thy salvation:*

Ps. 18:46(47). let the God of *my salvation* be exalted.
20: 6(7). the *saving* strength (marg. the strength of *the salvation*) *of* his right hand.
24: 5. the God of *his salvation.*
25: 5. thou (art) the God of *my salvation ;*
27: 1. The Lord (is) my light *and my salvation ;*
9. O God of *my salvation.*
50:23. *the salvation of* God.
51:12(14). unto me the joy of *thy salvation;*
62: 7(8). In God (is) *my salvation*
65: 5(6). O God of *our salvation ;*
69:13(14). in the truth of *thy salvation.*
79: 9. Help us, O God of *our salvation,*
85: 4(5). Turn us, O God of *our salvation,*
7(8). *and* grant us *thy salvation.*
9(10). Surely *his salvation* (is) nigh
95: 1. the rock of *our salvation.*
132:16. I will also clothe her priests *with salvation :*
Isa. 17:10. hast forgotten the God of *thy salvation,*
45: 8. let them bring forth *salvation,*
51: 5. *my salvation* is gone forth,
61:10. clothed me with the garments of *salvation,*
62:11. Behold, *thy salvation* cometh ;
Mic. 7: 7. I will wait for the God of *my salvation :*
Hab 3:13. Thou wentest forth *for the salvation of* thy people, (even) *for salvation* with thine
18. I will joy in the God of *my salvation.*

3471 ## יָשְׁפֵה *yāh-sh'phēh'*, m.

Ex. 28:20. a beryl, and an onyx, *and a jasper :*
39:13. a beryl, an onyx, *and a jasper :*
Eze. 28:13. the onyx, *and the jasper,*

3474 ## יָשַׁר *yāh-shar'.*

* KAL.—*Preterite.* *

Jud. 14: 3. she *pleaseth* me *well.* (marg. (is) *right* in mine eyes)
1 K. 9:12. *they pleased* him not. (marg. *were* not *right* in his eyes)
1 Ch. 13: 4. the thing *was right* in the eyes of all the
Jer. 18: 4. as *seemed good* to the potter
27: 5. have given it unto whom *it seemed meet*
Hab. 2: 4. his soul...*is* not *upright* in him:

KAL.—*Future.*

Nu. 23:27. peradventure *it will please* God (lit. *it will be right* in the eyes of God)
Jud. 14: 7. *and she pleased* Samson *well.* (lit. *and she was right* in the eyes of Samson)
1 Sa. 6:12. *And* the kine *took the straight way*
18:20. *and* the thing *pleased* him. (marg. *and was right* in his eyes)
26. *it pleased* David *well* (lit. *it was right* in the eyes of David)
2 Sa. 17: 4. *And* the saying *pleased* Absalom *well,* (marg. *and was right* in the eyes)
2 Ch 30: 4. *And* the thing *pleased* the king (marg. *and was right* in the eyes)

* PIEL.—*Preterite.* *

Job. 37: 3. *He directeth it* under the whole heaven,
Ps. 119:128. *I esteem* all (thy) precepts...(to be) *right;*

PIEL.—*Imperative.*

Isa. 40: 3. *make straight* in the desert a highway for

PIEL.—*Future.*

2 Ch 32:30. *and brought it straight* down to the west
Pro. 3: 6. *he shall direct* thy paths.
11: 5. The righteousness of the perfect *shall direct* his way: (marg. *rectify*)
15:21. a man of understanding walketh *uprightly.*
Isa. 45: 2. *I will...make* the crooked places *straight :*
13. *I will direct* all his ways: (marg. or, *make straight*)

PIEL.—*Participle.*

Pro. 9:15. To call passengers *who go right on* their

* PUAL.—*Participle.* *

1 K. 6:35. covered (them) with gold *fitted* upon the

* HIPHIL.—*Imperative.* *

Ps. 5: 8(9). *make* thy way *straight* before my face.

HIPHIL.—*Future.*

Pro. 4:25. *let* thine eyelids *look straight* before thee.
Isa. 45: 2. (כתיב) *make* the crooked places *straight :*

יָשָׁר *yāh-shāhr'*, adj. 3477

Ex. 15:26. *and* wilt do *that which is right* in his sight,
Nu. 23:10. Let me die the death of *the righteous,*
Deu. 6:18. thou shalt do (that which is) *right*
12: 8. every man whatsoever (is) *right* in his
25. when thou shalt do (that which is) *right*
28. *when* thou doest (that which is)...*right*
13:18(19). to do (that which is) *right*
21: 9. when thou shalt do (that which is) *right*
32: 4. just *and right* (is) he.
Jos. 9:25. as it seemeth good *and right* unto thee to
10:13. (Is) not this written in the book of *Jasher ?* (marg. *the upright*)
Jud. 17: 6 & 21:25. man did (that which was) *right*
1 Sa. 12:23. I will teach you the good *and* the *right*
29: 6. thou hast been *upright,*
2 Sa. 1:18. (it is) written in the book of *Jasher.* (marg. or, *the upright*)
19: 6(7). then it had *pleased* thee *well.* (lit. been *right* in thine eyes)
1 K. 11:33. to do (that which is) *right* in mine eyes,
38. and do (that is) *right* in my sight,
14: 8. to do (that) only (which was) *right*
15: 5. David did (that which was) *right*
11. Asa did (that which was) *right*
22:43. doing (that which was) *right* in the eyes
2 K. 10: 3. Look even out the best *and meetest* of your
15. Is thine heart *right,*
30. executing (that which is) *right*
12: 2(3). Jehoash did (that which was) *right*
14: 3 & 15:3,34. he did (that which was) *right*
16: 2. Ahaz...did not (that which was) *right*
18: 3 & 22:2. he did (that which was) *right*
2 Ch. 14: 2(1). Asa did (that which was) good *and right*
20:32. doing (that which was) *right* in the sight
24: 2. Joash did (that which was) *right* in the
25: 2 & 26:4 & 27:2. he did (that which was) *right*
28: 1. he did not (that which was) *right*
29: 2. he did (that which was) *right*
34. the Levites (were) more *upright in* heart
31:20. wrought (that which was) good *and right*
34: 2. he did (that which was) *right*
Ezr. 8:21. to seek of him a *right* way for us,
Neh. 9:13. gavest them *right* judgments, and true laws,
Job. 1: 1. that man was perfect *and upright,*
8 & 2:3. a perfect *and* an *upright* man,
4: 7. where were *the righteous* cut off ?
8: 6. If thou (wert) pure *and upright ;*
17: 8. *Upright* (men) shall be astonied at this,
23: 7. There *the righteous* might dispute with
33:27. *and* perverted (that which was) *right,*
Ps. 7:10(11). which saveth *the upright in* heart.
11: 2. that they may privily shoot *at the upright in*
7. his countenance doth behold the *upright.*
19: 8(9). The statutes of the Lord (are) *right,*
25: 8. Good *and upright* (is) the Lord:
32:11. all (ye that are) *upright in* heart.
33: 1. praise is comely *for the upright.*
4. the word of the Lord (is) *right ;*
36:10(11). thy righteousness *to the upright in*
37:14. slay such as be of *upright* conversation.
37. the perfect (man), and behold *the upright :*
49:14(15). *the upright* shall have dominion
64:10(11). all *the upright in* heart shall glory
92:15(16). To shew that the Lord (is) *upright :*
94:15. all *the upright in* heart shall follow it.
97:11. *and* gladness *for the upright in* heart.
107: 7. he led them forth by *the right* way,
42. *The righteous* shall see (it), and rejoice:
111: 1. the assembly of *the upright,*
8. (are) done in truth *and uprightness.*
112: 2. the generation of *the upright* shall be
4. *Unto the upright* there ariseth light
119:137. *and upright* (are) thy judgments.
125: 4. *and* to (them that are) *upright* in their
140:13(14). *the upright* shall dwell in thy presence.
Pro. 2: 7. layeth up sound wisdom *for the righteous :*
21. *the upright* shall dwell in the land,
3:32. his secret (is) with *the righteous.*
8: 9. *and right* to them that find knowledge.

Pro.11: 3. The integrity of *the upright* shall guide
6. The righteousness of *the upright* shall
11. the blessing of *the upright*
12: 6. the mouth of *the upright* shall deliver
15. The way of a fool (is) *right* in his own
14: 9. among *the righteous* (there is) favour.
11. the tabernacle of *the upright* shall flourish.
12. There is a way which seemeth *right* unto
15: 8. the prayer of *the upright* (is) his delight.
19. the way of *the righteous* (is) made plain.
16:13. they love him that speaketh *right*.
17. The highway of *the upright*
25. There is a way that seemeth *right* unto a
20:11. whether (it be) *right*.
21: 2. Every way of a man (is) *right* in his own
8. (as for) the pure, his work (is) *right*.
18. and the transgressor for *the upright*.
29. *but* (as for) *the upright*, he directeth his
28:10. Whoso causeth *the righteous* to go astray
29:10. *but the just* seek his soul.
27. (he that is) *upright in* the way
Ecc. 7:29. God hath made man *upright*;
Isa. 26: 7. thou, *most upright*, dost weigh the path of
Jer. 26:14. as seemeth good *and meet* unto you.
31: 9. I will cause them to walk...in a *straight*
34:15. had done *right* in my sight,
40: 4. whither it seemeth good *and convenient* for
5. go wheresoever it seemeth *convenient* unto
Eze. 1: 7. their feet (were) *straight* feet;
23. (were) their wings *straight*,
Dan11:17. *and upright ones* with him;
Hos14: 9(10). the ways of the Lord (are) *right*,
Mic. 2: 7. him that walketh *uprightly?* (marg: *upright*)
3: 9. pervert all *equity*.
7: 2. *and* (there is) none *upright* among men:
4. *the most upright* (is sharper) than a thorn

3476 **יֹשֶׁר** *yōh'-sher*, m.

Deu. 9: 5. *or for the uprightness of* thine heart,
1 K. 9: 4. in integrity of heart, *and in uprightness*,
1Ch 29:17. *in the uprightness* of mine heart
Job. 6:25. How forcible are *right* words!
33: 3. *the uprightness of* my heart:
23. to shew unto man *his uprightness*:
Ps. 25:21. Let integrity and *uprightness* preserve me;
119: 7. I will praise thee *with uprightness of* heart,
Pro. 2:13. Who leave the paths of *uprightness*,
4:11. I have led thee in *right* paths.
11:24. withholdeth *more than is meet*,
14: 2. He that walketh *in his uprightness*
17:26. to strike princes *for equity*.
Ecc.12:10. (that which was) written (was) *upright*,

3483 **יִשְׁרָה** [*yish-rāh'*], f.

1 K. 3: 6. *and in uprightness of* heart with thee;

3486 **יָשֵׁשׁ** *yāh-shēhsh'*, m.

2Ch 36:17. *or him that stooped for age*:

3487 **יַת** [*yath*] Ch. part.

Dan. 3:12. Jews *whom* thou hast set over the affairs [דִּי–יָתְהוֹן]

3488 **יְתִב** *y'theev*, Ch.

* P'AL.—*Preterite*. *

Dan 7: 9. and the Ancient of days *did sit*,
10. the judgment *was set*, and the books
26. But the judgment *shall sit*,

P'AL.—*Participle*.

Ezr. 4:17. their companions that *dwell* in Samaria,

* APHEL.—*Preterite*. *

Ezr. 4:10. Asnapper brought over, *and set* in the cities

יָתֵד *yah-thēhd'*, f. 3489

Ex. 27:19. all *the pins thereof*, and all *the pins of* the
35:18. *The pins of* the tabernacle, and *the pins of*
38:20. all *the pins* of the tabernacle,
31. all *the pins of* the tabernacle, and all *the pins of* the court round about.
39:40. his cords, *and his pins*,
Nu. 3:37 & 4:32. *and their pins*, and their cords.
Deu23:13(14). *And* thou shalt have *a paddle* upon thy
Jud. 4:21. Then Jael Heber's wife took *a nail of* the
— smote *the nail* into his temples,
22. *and the nail* (was) in his temples.
5:26. She put her hand *to the nail*,
16:14. she fastened (it) *with the pin*,
— went away with *the pin of* the beam,
Ezr. 9: 8. *a nail* in his holy place, (marg. or, *a pin*)
Isa. 22:23. will fasten him (as) *a nail* in a sure place;
25. *the nail* that is fastened
33:20. not one of *the stakes thereof* shall ever be
54: 2. *and* strengthen *thy stakes*;
Eze.15: 3. will (men) take *a pin* of it
Zec.10: 4. out of him *the nail*,

יָתוֹם *yāh-thōhm'*, m. 3490

Ex. 22:22(21). afflict any widow, *or fatherless child*.
24(23). widows, and your children *fatherless*.
Deu10:18. the judgment of *the fatherless* and widow,
14:29 & 16:11, 14. the stranger, *and the fatherless*,
24:17. (nor) of *the fatherless*;
19, 20, 21. for the stranger, *for the fatherless*,
26:12. unto the Levite, the stranger, *the fatherless*,
13. *to the fatherless*, and to the widow,
27:19. the judgment of the stranger, *fatherless*,
Job 6:27. ye overwhelm *the fatherless*,
22: 9. the arms of *the fatherless* have been broken.
24: 3. They drive away the ass of *the fatherless*,
9. They pluck *the fatherless* from the breast,
29:12. the poor that cried, *and the fatherless*,
31:17. *the fatherless* hath not eaten thereof;
21. lifted up my hand against *the fatherless*,
Ps. 10:14. thou art the helper of *the fatherless*.
18. To judge *the fatherless*
68: 5(6). A father of *the fatherless*,
82: 3. Defend the poor *and fatherless*:
94: 6. *and* murder *the fatherless*.
109: 9. Let his children be *fatherless*,
12. to favour *his fatherless children*.
146: 9. he relieveth *the fatherless* and widow:
Pro.23:10. enter not into the fields of *the fatherless*:
Isa. 1:17. judge *the fatherless*,
23. they judge not *the fatherless*,
9:17(16). shall have mercy on *their fatherless*
10. 2. (that) they may rob *the fatherless!*
Jer. 5:28. the cause of *the fatherless*,
7: 6. *the fatherless*, and the widow,
22: 3. *the fatherless*, nor the widow,
49:11. Leave *thy fatherless children*,
Lam. 5: 3. We are *orphans* and fatherless,
Eze.22: 7. in thee have they vexed *the fatherless*
Hos.14: 3(4). in thee *the fatherless* findeth mercy.
Zec. 7:10. oppress not the widow, *nor the fatherless*,
Mal. 3: 5. the widow, *and the fatherless*,

יְתוּר *y'thoor*, m. 3491

Job 39: 8. *The range of* the mountains

יַתִּיר *yat-teer'*, Ch. adj. 3493

Dan 2:31. whose brightness (was) *excellent*,
3:22. and the furnace *exceeding* hot,
4:36(33). and *excellent* majesty was added unto
5:12. Forasmuch as an *excellent* spirit,
14. and *excellent* wisdom is found in thee.
6: 3(4). because an *excellent* spirit (was) in him;
7: 7. and strong *exceedingly*;
19. *exceeding* dreadful, whose teeth (were of)

יִתֹּם (Ps. 19:13(14).) see **תָּמַם** See 8552

3498 יָתַר [*yāh-thar'*].

* KAL.—*Participle.* Poel. *

1Sa.15:15. *the rest* we have utterly destroyed.

* NIPHAL.—*Preterite.* *

Ex. 10:15. *there remained* not any green thing
Nu. 26:65. And *there was* not *left* a man of them,
Jos.11:11. *there was* not any *left* to breathe:
22. *There was* none of the Anakims *left*
1Sa.25:34. surely *there had* not *been left* unto Nabal
2Sa. 9: 1. any that *is left* of the house of Saul,
13:30. *there is* not one of them *left.*
17:12. *there shall* not *be left* so much as one.
1K. 9:21. Their children that *were left* after them
17:17. *there was* no breath *left* in him.
18:22. I only, *remain* a prophet of the Lord;
2Ch 8: 8. who *were left* after them in the land,
Neh. 6: 1. *there was* no breach *left* therein;
Ps.106:11. *there was* not one of them *left.*
Isa. 1: 8. *And* the daughter of Zion *is left*
30:17. till *ye be left* as a beacon upon the top
Eze.14:22. therein *shall be left* a remnant
Dan10:13. *I remained* there with the kings of Persia.

NIPHAL.—*Future.*

Gen32:24(25). *And* Jacob *was left* alone;
44:20. *and* he alone *is left* of his mother,
Ex. 29:34. if ought...*remain* unto the morning,
Jos. 18: 2. *And there remained* among the children of
Jud. 9: 5. *notwithstanding* yet Jotham...*was left;*
1K. 19:10, 14. *and* I, (even) I only, *am left;*
2K. 20:17. nothing *shall be left,*
Pro. 2:21. the perfect *shall remain* in it.
Isa. 39: 6. nothing *shall be left,* saith the Lord.
Am. 6: 9. if there *remain* ten men in one house,
Zec.13: 8. the third *shall be left* therein.

NIPHAL.—*Participle.*

Gen30:36. Jacob fed *the rest* of Laban's flocks.
Ex. 12:10. *and that which remaineth* of it until the
28:10. (the other) six names of *the rest*
29:34. thou shalt burn *the remainder* with fire:
Lev. 2: 3. *And the remnant* of the meat offering
10. *And that which is left* of the meat offering
6:16(9). *And the remainder* thereof shall Aaron
7:16. *also the remainder* of it shall be eaten:
17. *But the remainder* of the flesh
8:32. *And that which remaineth* of the flesh
10:12. and unto Ithamar, his sons *that were left,* Take the meat offering *that remaineth*
16. sons of Aaron (which were) *left* (alive),
14:18. *And the remnant* of the oil
29. *And the rest* of the oil
19: 6. *if ought remain* until the third day,
27:18. according to the years *that remain,*
Jos. 17: 2. *the rest* of the children of Manasseh
6. *the rest* of Manasseh's sons
21: 5. *the rest* of the children of Kohath
20. the Levites *which remained*
26. the children of Kohath *that remained.*
34. *the rest* of the Levites,
40(38). *which were remaining* of the families
Jud. 8:10. all *that were left* of all the hosts
21: 7. shall we do for wives *for them that remain,*
16. shall we do for wives *for them that remain,*
1Sa. 2:36. every one *that is left* in thine house
30: 9. *where those that were left behind* stayed.
1K. 9:20. all the people (that were) *left*
15:18. and the gold (that were) *left* in the
20:30. But *the rest* fled to Aphek,
— seven thousand of the men (that were) *left.*
2K. 4: 7. live thou and thy children *of the rest.*
1Ch 6:61(46). (which were) *left* of the family of that
70(55). *the remnant* of the sons of Kohath.
77(62). Unto *the rest* of the children of Merari
24:20. *the rest* of the sons of Levi
2Ch 8: 7. the people (that were) *left* of the Hittites,
31:10. *and that which is left* (is) this great store.
Isa. 4: 3. *and* (he that) *remaineth* in Jerusalem,
7:22. that is *left* in the land.
Jer. 27:18. the vessels *which are left* in the house of
19. the vessels *that remain* in this city,
21. the vessels *that remain* (in) the house of the Lord,
34: 7 all the cities of Judah *that were left,*
Eze.34:18. ye must foul *the residue* with your feet?
39:14. *that remain* upon the face of the earth,
48:15. five thousand, *that are left* in the breadth
18. *And the residue* in length
21. *And the residue* (shall be) for the prince.
Zec.14:16. every one *that is left* of all the nations

* HIPHIL.—*Preterite.* *

Ex. 10:15. the trees which the hail *had left:*
Deu28:11. *And* the Lord *shall make thee plenteous*
30: 9. *And* the Lord thy God *will make thee plenteous*
Ru. 2:18. gave to her that *she had reserved*
Isa. 1: 9. Except the Lord of hosts *had left* unto us
Eze. 6: 8. *Yet will I leave a remnant,*
12:16. *But I will leave* a few men of them

HIPHIL.—*Infinitive.*

Ex. 36: 7. stuff they had was sufficient...*and too much.*
2K. 4:43. They shall eat, *and shall leave* (thereof).
2Ch 31:10. *and have left* plenty:
Jer. 44: 7. *to leave* you none to remain;

HIPHIL.—*Imperative.*

Ps. 79:11. *preserve* thou those that are appointed to

HIPHIL.—*Future.*

Gen49: 4. Unstable as water, *thou shalt* not *excel;*
Ex. 12:10. *ye shall let* nothing of it *remain* until the
16:19. *Let* no man *leave* of it till the morning.
20. *but* some of them *left* of it until the
Lev.22:30. *ye shall leave* none of it until the morrow:
Nu. 33:55. those which *ye let remain* of them
Deu28:54. his children which *he shall leave:*
Ru. 2:14. she did eat, and was sufficed, *and left.*
2Sa. 8: 4. *but reserved* of them (for) an hundred
2K. 4:44. they did eat, *and left* (thereof),
1Ch 18: 4. *but reserved* of them an hundred chariots.
Eze.39.28. *have left* none of them any more there.

יֶתֶר *yeh'-ther,* m. 3499

Gen49: 3. *the excellency of* dignity, *and the excellency of*
Ex. 10: 5. shall eat *the residue of* that which is escaped,
23:11. *and what they leave* the beasts of the field
Lev.14:17. *And of the rest of* the oil
Nu. 31:32. *the rest of* the prey which the men of war
Deu 3:11. *of the remnant of* giants;
13. *And the rest of* Gilead,
28:54. *and toward the remnant of* his children
Jos. 12: 4. *of the remnant of* the giants,
13:12. who remained *of the remnant of* the giants
27. *the rest of* the kingdom of Sihon
23:12. cleave *unto the remnant of* these nations,
Jud. 7: 6. *the rest of* the people bowed down
1Sa.13: 2. *and the rest of* the people he sent every man
2Sa.10:10. *the rest of* the people he delivered into
12:28. gather *the rest of* the people together,
21: 2. *of the remnant of* the Amorites;
1K. 11:41. *And the rest of* the acts of Solomon,
12:23. *and to the remnant of* the people,
14:19. *And the rest of* the acts of Jeroboam,
29. *Now the rest of* the acts of Rehoboam,
15: 7. *Now the rest of* the acts of Abijam,
23. *The rest of* all the acts of Asa,
31. *Now the rest of* the acts of Nadab,
16: 5. *Now the rest of* the acts of Baasha,
14. *Now the rest of* the acts of Elah,
20. *Now the rest of* the acts of Zimri,
27. *Now the rest of* the acts of Omri
22:39. *Now the rest of* the acts of Ahab,
45(46). *Now the rest of* the acts of Jehoshaphat,
46(47). *And the remnant of* the sodomites,
2K. 1:18. *Now the rest of* the acts of Ahaziah
8:23. *And the rest of* the acts of Joram,
10:34. *Now the rest of* the acts of Jehu,
12:19(20). *And the rest of* the acts of Joash,
13: 8. *Now the rest of* the acts of Jehoahaz
12. *And the rest of* the acts of Joash,
14:15. *Now the rest of* the acts of Jehoash
18. *And the rest of* the acts of Amaziah,
28. *Now the rest of* the acts of Jeroboam,
15: 6. *And the rest of* the acts of Azariah,
11. *And the rest of* the acts of Zachariah,
15. *And the rest of* the acts of Shallum,
21. *And the rest of* the acts of Menahem,

2K. 15:26. *And the rest of* the acts of Pekahiah,
31. *And the rest of* the acts of Pekah,
36. *Now the rest of* the acts of Jotham,
16:19. *Now the rest of* the acts of Ahaz
20:20. *And the rest of* the acts of Hezekiah,
21:17. *Now the rest of* the acts of Manasseh,
25. *Now the rest of* the acts of Amon
23:28. *Now the rest of* the acts of Josiah,
24: 5. *Now the rest of* the acts of Jehoiakim,
25:11. Now *the rest of* the people
— with *the remnant of* the multitude,
1Ch 19:11. And *the rest of* the people he delivered
2Ch 13:22. *And the rest of* the acts of Abijah,
20:34. *Now the rest of* the acts of Jehoshaphat,
25:26. *Now the rest of* the acts of Amaziah,
26:22. *Now the rest of* the acts of Uzziah,
27: 7. *Now the rest of* the acts of Jotham,
28:26. *Now the rest of* his acts
32:32. *Now the rest of* the acts of Hezekiah,
33:18. *Now the rest of* the acts of Manasseh,
35:26. *Now the rest of* the acts of Josiah,
36: 8. *Now the rest of* the acts of Jehoiakim,
Neh. 2:16. *nor to the rest* that did the work.
4:14(8), 19(13). and to *the rest of* the people,
6: 1. *and the rest of* our enemies,
14. *and the rest of* the prophets,
Job. 4:21. Doth not *their excellency*...go away?
22:20. *but the remnant of them* the fire consumeth.
Ps. 17:14. leave *the rest of their* (substance) to their babes.
31:23(24). *plentifully* rewardeth the proud doer.
Pro.17: 7. *Excellent* speech (lit. a lip of *excellency*) becometh not a fool:
Isa. 38:10. I am deprived of *the residue of* my years.
44:19. *and* shall I make *the residue thereof* an
56:12. much more abundant. (lit. *a* very great *residue*)
Jer. 27:19. concerning *the residue of* the vessels
29: 1. *the residue of* the elders
39: 9. *the remnant of* the people that remained
— *the rest of* the people that remained.
52:15. *the residue of* the people
— *the rest of* the multitude.
Eze.34:18. *but* ye must tread down...*the residue of*
48:23. *As for the rest of* the tribes,
Dan 8: 9. which waxed *exceeding* great,
Joel 1: 4. *That* which the palmerworm *hath left*
— *and that* which the locust *hath left*
— *and that* which the cankerworm *hath left*
Mic. 5: 3(2). *then the remnant of* his brethren
Hab. 2: 8. all *the remnant of* the people shall spoil
Zep. 2: 9. *and the remnant of* my people shall possess them.
Zec.14: 2. *and the residue of* the people

3499 יֶתֶר *yeh'-ther*, m.

Jud.16: 7. bind me with seven green *withs* (marg. moist, or, new *cords*)
8. brought up to her seven green *withs*
9. And he brake *the withs*,
Job 30:11. Because he hath loosed *my cord*,
Ps. 11: 2. make ready their arrow upon *the string*,

3502 יִתְרָה *yith-rāh'*, f.

Isa. 15: 7. *the abundance* they have gotten,
Jer. 48:36. *the riches* (that) he hath gotten are

3504 יִתְרוֹן *yith-rōhn'*, f.

Ecc. 1: 3. What *profit* hath a man
2:11. (there was) no *profit* under the sun.
13. Then I saw that wisdom *excelleth* (marg. there is *an excellency* in wisdom)
— as far as light *excelleth* (lit. as much as *the excellency of* light above darkness)
3: 9. What *profit* hath he that worketh
5: 9(8). *Moreover the profit* of the earth is for
16(15). what *profit* hath he that hath laboured
7:12. *but the excellency of* knowledge
10:10. *but* wisdom (is) *profitable* to direct.
11. and a babbler is no *better*.

יֹתֶרֶת *yōh-theh'-reth*. 3508

Ex. 29:13. *the caul* (that is) above the liver, (marg. or, *midriff*)
22. *the caul* (above) the liver,
Lev. 3: 4, 10, 15 & 4:9. *the caul* above the liver, (marg. or, *midriff*)
7: 4. *the caul* (that is) above the liver,
8:16, 25. *the caul* (above) the liver,
9:10. *the caul* above the liver
19. *and the caul* (above) the liver:

כ *kāhph*.

The eleventh letter of the Alphabet.

כָּאַב [*kāh-av'*]. 3510

* KAL.—*Future.* *

Job 14:22. his flesh upon him *shall have pain*,
Pro.14:13. Even in laughter the heart *is sorrowful*;

KAL.—*Participle.* Poel.

Gen34:25. when they were *sore*,
Ps. 69:29(30). But I (am) poor *and sorrowful*:

* HIPHIL.—*Preterite.* *

Eze.13:22. *whom* I *have* not *made sad*;

HIPHIL.—*Future.*

2K. 3:19. and *mar* (marg. *grieve*) every good piece
Job 5:18. For he *maketh sore*, and bindeth up:

HIPHIL.—*Participle.*

Eze.28:24. nor (any) *grieving* thorn

כְּאֵב *k'ēhv*, m. 3511

Job 2:13. they saw that (his) *grief* was very great.
16: 6. *my grief* is not asswaged:
Ps. 39:2(3). *and my sorrow* was stirred.
Isa. 17:11. the day of grief *and* of desperate *sorrow*.
65:14. ye shall cry *for sorrow of* heart,
Jer. 15:18. Why is *my pain* perpetual,

כָּאָה [*kāh-āh'*]. 3512

* NIPHAL.—*Preterite.* *

Job 30: 8. *they were viler* than the earth.
Dan 11:30. *therefore he shall be grieved*, and return,

NIPHAL.—*Participle.*

Ps. 109:16. *that* he might even slay *the broken* in heart.

* HIPHIL.—*Infinitive.* *

Eze.13:22. ye *have made* the heart of the righteous *sad*,

כָּאִים *kāh-eem'*, m. pl. 2489

Ps. 10:10. that the *poor* may fall (lit. host of *the afflicted*; but the translators have followed the כתיב)

כָּבֵד *kāh-vēhd'* & כָּבַד *kāh-vad'*. 3513

* KAL.—*Preterite.* *

Gen13: 2. Abram *was* very *rich*
18:20. because their sin *is* very *grievous*;
48:10. the eyes of Israel *were dim* for age, (marg. *heavy*)
Jud.20:34. the battle *was sore*:
1Sa. 4:18. he was an old man, *and heavy*.
5:11. the hand of God *was* very *heavy* there.
2Sa.14:26. (the hair) *was heavy* on him,
Neh. 5:18. the bondage *was heavy* upon this people.
Job 23: 2. my stroke *is heavier* than my groaning.
Isa. 24:20. *and* the transgression thereof *shall be heavy*
59: 1. neither his ear *heavy*, that it cannot hear:

KAL.—*Future.*

Ex. 5: 9. *Let there more* work *be laid* upon the men, (marg. *Let* the work *be heavy*)
9: 7. *And* the heart of Pharaoh *was hardened,*
Jud. 1:35. *yet* the hand of the house of Joseph *prevailed,* (marg. *was heavy*)
1Sa. 5: 6. *But* the hand of the Lord *was heavy* upon
31: 3. *And* the battle *went sore* against Saul,
2Sa.13:25. lest *we be chargeable* unto thee.
1Ch 10: 3. *And* the battle *went sore* against Saul,
Job 6: 3. For now *it would be heavier* than the sand
14:21. His sons *come to honour,*
33: 7. neither *shall* my hand *be heavy* upon thee.
Ps. 32: 4. thy hand *was heavy* upon me:
38: 4(5). *they are* too *heavy* for me.
Isa. 66: 5. *Let* the Lord *be glorified:*
Eze.27:25. wast replenished, *and made* very *glorious*

* NIPHAL.—*Preterite.* *

2Sa. 6:20. How *glorious was* the king of Israel to day,
Isa. 26:15. increased the nation: *thou art glorified:*
43: 4. *thou hast been honourable,*
Eze.28:22. *and I will be glorified* in the midst of thee:

NIPHAL.—*Infinitive.*

Ex. 14:18. *when I have gotten me honour* upon Pharaoh,
Eze.39:13. the day that *I shall be glorified,*

NIPHAL.—*Imperative.*

2K. 14:10. *glory* (of this), and tarry at home:

NIPHAL.—*Future.*

Ex. 14: 4. *and I will be honoured* upon Pharaoh,
17. *and I will get* me *honour* upon Pharaoh,
Lev.10: 3. before all the people *I will be glorified.*
2Sa. 6:22. of them *shall I be had in honour.*
Isa. 49: 5. *yet shall I be glorious* in the eyes of the
Hag. 1: 8. *and I will be glorified,* saith the Lord.

NIPHAL.—*Participle.*

Gen34:19. he (was) more *honourable* than all the house
Nu. 22:15. *and* more *honourable* than they.
Deu28:58. mayest fear this *glorious* and fearful name,
1Sa. 9: 6. (he is) an *honourable* man;
22:14. *and is honourable* in thine house?
2Sa.23:19. Was he not most *honourable* of three?
23. He was more *honourable* than the thirty,
1Ch 4: 9. was more *honourable* than his brethren:
11:21. he *was* more *honourable* than the two;
25. he *was honourable* among the thirty,
Ps. 87: 3. *Glorious things* are spoken of thee,
149: 8. *and their nobles* with fetters of iron;
Pro. 8:24. no fountains *abounding with* water.
Isa. 3: 5. the base *against the honourable.*
23: 8, 9. *the honourable of* the earth?
Nah. 3:10. they cast lots for *her honourable men,*

* PIEL.—*Preterite.* *

Jud.13:17. *that* when thy sayings come to pass *we may do thee honour?*
1Sa. 6: 6. and Pharaoh *hardened* their hearts?
Isa. 29:13. with their lips *do honour me,*
43:23. *hast thou honoured me* with thy sacrifices.
58:13. *and shalt honour him,* not doing thine own

PIEL.—*Infinitive.*

Nu. 22:17. I will promote thee unto *very great* honour, (lit. *honouring* I will honour thee)
37. not able indeed *to promote thee to honour?*
24:11. to promote thee unto *great* honour; (lit. *honouring* I will honour thee)

PIEL.—*Imperative.*

Ex. 20:12. *Honour* thy father and thy mother:
Deu 5:16. *Honour* thy father and thy mother,
1Sa.15:30. (yet) *honour me* now, I pray thee,
Ps. 22:23(24). all ye the seed of Jacob, *glorify him;*
Pro. 3: 9. *Honour* the Lord with thy substance,
Isa. 24:15. Wherefore *glorify ye* the Lord

PIEL.—*Future.*

Nu. 22:17. *I will promote thee unto* very great *honour,*
24:11. thought *to promote thee* unto great honour;
Jud. 9: 9. by me *they honour* God and man,
1Sa. 2:29. *and honourest* thy sons above me,
30. them that honour me *I will honour,*
6: 6. Wherefore then *do ye harden* your hearts,
Ps 15: 4. *he honoureth* them that fear the Lord.
50:15. will deliver thee, *and thou shalt glorify me*
23. Whoso offereth praise *glorifieth me:*
Ps. 86: 9. *and shall glorify* thy name.
12. *and I will glorify* thy name for evermore.
91:15. I will deliver him, *and honour him.*
Pro. 4: 8. *she shall bring thee to honour,*
Isa. 25: 3. *shall* the strong people *glorify thee,*
43:20. The beast of the field *shall honour me,*
60:13. *I will make* the place of my feet *glorious.*
Dan 11:38. *shall he honour* the God of forces: and a god whom his fathers knew not *shall he honour*
Mal. 1: 6. A son *honoureth* (his) father,

PIEL.—*Participle.*

1Sa. 2:30. *them that honour me* I will honour,
2Sa.10: 3. Thinkest thou that David *doth honour* thy
1Ch 19: 3. Thinkest thou that David *doth honour* thy
Pro.14:31. *but he that honoureth him* hath mercy on
Lam. 1: 8. all *that honoured her* despise her,

* PUAL.—*Future.* *

Pro.13:18. he that regardeth reproof *shall be honoured.*
27:18. waiteth on his master *shall be honoured.*

PUAL.—*Participle.*

Isa. 58:13. the holy of the Lord, *honourable;*

* HIPHIL.—*Preterite.* *

Ex. 10: 1. I *have hardened* his heart,
1K. 12:10. Thy father *made* our yoke *heavy,*
14. My father *made* your yoke *heavy,*
2Ch 10:10. Thy father *made* our yoke *heavy,*
14. My father *made* your yoke *heavy,*
Neh. 5:15. *were chargeable* unto the people,
Isa. 9: 1(8:23). afterward *did more grievously afflict*
47: 6. upon the ancient *hast thou* very *heavily laid*
Jer. 30:19. *I will also glorify them,* and they shall
Lam.3: 7. *he hath made* my chain *heavy.*
Zec. 7:11. and *stopped* their ears, that they should not hear. (marg. *made heavy*)

HIPHIL.—*Infinitive.*

Ex. 8:15(11). *he hardened* his heart,
2Ch 25:19. thine heart lifteth thee up *to boast:*

HIPHIL.—*Imperative.*

Isa. 6:10. *make* their ears *heavy,*

HIPHIL.—*Future.*

Ex. 8:32(28). *And* Pharaoh *hardened* his heart at this
9:34. sinned yet more, *and hardened* his heart,

HIPHIL.—*Participle.*

Hab. 2: 6. *and to him that ladeth* himself with thick

* HITHPAEL.—*Imperative.* *

Nah. 3:15. *make thyself many* as the cankerworm, *make thyself many* as the locusts.

HITHPAEL.—*Participle.*

Pro.12: 9. (is) better *than he that honoureth himself,*

כָּבֵד *kāh-vēhd',* adj. 3515

Gen12:10. the famine (was) *grievous* in the land.
41:31. it (shall be) very *grievous.* (marg. *heavy*)
43: 1. the famine (was) *sore* in the land.
47: 4. the famine (is) *sore* in the land
13. the famine (was) very *sore,*
50: 9. it was a very *great* company.
10. a great *and* very *sore* lamentation:
11. This (is) a *grievous* mourning
Ex. 4:10. (am) *slow of* speech, *and* of a *slow* tongue.
7:14. Pharaoh's heart (is) *hardened,*
8:24(20). there came a *grievous* swarm (of flies)
9: 3. (there shall be) a very *grievous* murrain.
18. I will cause it to rain a very *grievous* hail,
24. fire mingled with the hail, very *grievous,*
10:14. very *grievous* (were they);
12:38. (even) very *much* cattle.
17:12. Moses' hands (were) *heavy;*
18:18. this thing (is) too *heavy* for thee;
19:16. a *thick* cloud upon the mount,
Nu. 11:14. because (it is) *too heavy* for me.
20:20. Edom came out against him with *much*
1K. 3: 9. who is able to judge this thy *so great* a
10: 2. she came to Jerusalem with a very *great*
12: 4. his *heavy* yoke which he put upon us,
11. my father did lade you with a *heavy* yoke,
2K. 6:14. and a *great* host: (marg. *heavy*)

2K. 18:17. with a *great* host against Jerusalem. (marg. *heavy*)
2Ch 9: 1. with a very *great* company,
10: 4. his *heavy* yoke that he put upon us,
11. my father put a *heavy* yoke upon you,
Ps. 38: 4(5). as an *heavy* burden
Pro. 27: 3. a fool's wrath (is) *heavier* than them both.
Isa. 1: 4. a people *laden with* iniquity, (marg. of *heaviness*)
32: 2. as the shadow of a *great* rock (marg. *heavy*)
36: 2. with a *great* army.
Eze. 3: 5. *and* of an *hard* language, (marg. and *heavy of* language)
6. *and* of an *hard* language, (marg. *and heavy of* language)

3516 **כָּבֵד** *kāh-vēhd′*, m.

Ex. 29:13. the caul (that is) above *the liver*,
22. the caul (above) *the liver*,
Lev. 3: 4, 10, 15 & 4:9. the caul above *the liver*,
7: 4. the caul (that is) above *the liver*,
8:16, 25. the caul (above) *the liver*,
9:10. the caul above *the liver* of the sin offering,
19. the caul (above) *the liver*:
Pro. 7:23. Till a dart strike through *his liver*;
Lam. 2:11. *my liver* is poured upon the earth,
Eze. 21:21(26). he looked *in the liver*.

See 3520 **כָּבֹד** see **כְּבוּדָּה**

3514 **כֹּבֶד** *kōh′-ved*, m.

Pro. 27: 3. A stone (is) *heavy*, (marg. *heaviness*)
Isa. 21:15. from *the grievousness of* war.
30:27. *and* the burden (thereof is) *heavy*: (marg. *heaviness*)
Nah. 3: 3. *and a great number of* carcases;

3517 **כְּבֵדֻת** *k′vēh-dooth′*, f.

Ex. 14:25. drave them *heavily*: (lit. *with heaviness*)

3518 **כָּבָה** [*kāh-vāh′*].

* KAL.—*Preterite*. *

Isa. 43:17. *they are quenched* as tow.

KAL.—*Future*.

Lev. 6:12(5). *it shall* not *be put out*:
13(6). *it shall* never *go out*.
1Sa. 3: 3. ere the lamp of God *went out*
2K. 22:17. and *shall* not *be quenched*.
2Ch 34:25. and *shall* not *be quenched*.
Pro. 26:20. (there) the fire *goeth out*:
31:18. her candle *goeth* not *out* by night.
Isa. 34:10. *It shall* not *be quenched*
66:24. neither *shall* their fire *be quenched*;
Jer. 7:20. it shall burn, and *shall* not *be quenched*.
17:27. *it shall* not *be quenched*.
Eze. 20:47(21:3). flaming flame *shall* not *be quenched*,
48(—:4). *it shall* not *be quenched*.

* PIEL.—*Preterite*. *

2Sa. 14: 7. *so they shall quench* my coal which is left,

PIEL.—*Infinitive*.

Cant. 8: 7. Many waters cannot *quench* love,
Eze. 32: 7. *when I shall put thee out*, (marg. *extinguish thee*)

PIEL.—*Future*.

2Sa. 21:17. that *thou quench* not the light of Israel.
2Ch 29: 7. *and put out* the lamps,
Isa. 42: 3. the smoking flax *shall* he not *quench*:

PIEL.—*Participle*.

Isa. 1:31. none *shall quench* (them).
Jer. 4: 4 & 21:12. burn that none *can quench* (it),
Am. 5: 6. (there be) none *to quench* (it)

כָּבוֹד *kāh-vōhd′*, m. 3519

Gen 31: 1. hath he gotten all this *glory*.
45:13. ye shall tell my father of all *my glory*
49: 6. *mine honour*, be not thou united:
Ex. 16: 7. ye shall see *the glory of* the Lord;
10. *the glory of* the Lord appeared
24:16. *the glory of* the Lord abode upon mount
17. *the glory of* the Lord (was) like
28: 2, 40. *for glory* and for beauty.
29:43. shall be sanctified *by my glory*.
33:18. I beseech thee, shew me *thy glory*.
22. while *my glory* passeth by,
40:34, 35. *and the glory of* the Lord filled the
Lev. 9: 6. *the glory of* the Lord shall appear unto you.
23. *the glory of* the Lord appeared unto all the
Nu. 14:10. *And the glory of* the Lord appeared
21. shall be filled with *the glory of* the Lord.
22. all those men which have seen *my glory*,
16:19. and *the glory of* the Lord appeared
42(17:7). *the glory of* the Lord appeared.
20: 6. *the glory of* the Lord appeared
24:11. the Lord hath kept thee back *from honour*.
Deu 5:24(21). Lord our God hath shewed us *his glory*
Jos. 7:19. *glory* to the Lord God of Israel,
1Sa. 2: 8. make them inherit the throne of *glory*:
4:21, 22. *The glory* is departed from Israel:
6: 5. ye shall give *glory* unto the God of Israel:
1K. 3:13. both riches, and *honour*:
8:11. *the glory of* the Lord had filled the house
1Ch 16:24. Declare *his glory* among the heathen;
28. give unto the Lord *glory* and strength.
29. Give unto the Lord *the glory* (due) *unto*
17:18. *for the honour* of thy servant?
29:12. Both riches *and honour* (come) of thee,
28. full of days, riches, *and honour*:
2Ch 1:11. hast not asked riches, wealth, or *honour*,
12. give thee riches, and wealth, *and honour*,
5:14. *the glory of* the Lord had filled the house
7: 1. *and the glory of* the Lord filled the house.
2. *the glory of* the Lord had filled the Lord's
3. *and the glory of* the Lord upon the house,
17: 5. he had riches *and honour* in abundance.
18: 1. had riches *and honour* in abundance,
26:18. neither (shall it be) *for* thine *honour*
32:27. had exceeding much riches *and honour*:
33. inhabitants of Jerusalem did him *honour*
Neh. 9: 5. blessed be *thy glorious* name,
Est. 1: 4. the riches of his *glorious* kingdom
5:11. Haman told them of *the glory of* his riches,
Job 19: 9. He hath stripped me of *my glory*,
29:20. *My glory* (was) fresh in me,
Ps. 3: 3(4). *my glory*, and the lifter up of mine head.
4: 2(3). how long (will ye turn) *my glory* into
7: 5(6). *and* lay *mine honour* in the dust.
8: 5(6). crowned him *with glory* and honour.
16: 9. *my glory* rejoiceth:
19: 1(2). The heavens declare *the glory of* God;
21: 5(6). *His glory* (is) great in thy salvation:
24: 7, 9. the King of *glory* shall come in.
8. Who (is) this King of *glory?*
10. Who is this King of *glory?* The Lord of hosts, he (is) the King of *glory*.
26: 8. the place where *thine honour* dwelleth.
29: 1. give unto the Lord *glory* and strength.
2. Give unto the Lord *the glory due unto* (marg. *honour of*) his
3. the God of *glory* thundereth:
9. doth every one speak of (his) *glory*.
30:12(13). (my) *glory* may sing praise to thee,
49:16(17). *the glory of* his house is increased;
17(18). *his glory* shall not descend after him
57: 5(6). (let) *thy glory* (be) above all the earth.
8(9). Awake up, *my glory*;
11(12). (let) *thy glory* (be) above all the
62: 7(8). (is) my salvation *and my glory*:
63: 2(3). To see thy power *and thy glory*,
66: 2. Sing forth *the honour of* his name: make his praise *glorious*.
72:19. (be) *his glorious* name for ever: and let the whole earth be filled (with) *his glory*;
73:24. afterward receive me (to) *glory*.
79: 9. *the glory of* thy name:
84:11(12). the Lord will give grace *and glory*:
85: 9(10). that *glory* may dwell in our land.
96: 3. Declare *his glory* among the heathen,
7. give unto the Lord *glory* and strength.

Ps. 96: 8. Give unto the Lord *the glory* (due unto) (marg. *of*) his name:
97: 6. all the people see *his glory.*
102:15(16). the kings of the earth *thy glory.*
16(17). he shall appear *in his glory.*
104:31. *The glory of* the Lord shall endure for
106:20. Thus they changed *their glory*
108: 1(2). even with *my glory.*
5(6). *thy glory* above all the earth;
112: 9. his horn shall be exalted *with honour.*
113: 4. *his glory* above the heavens.
115: 1. unto thy name give *glory,*
138: 5. great (is) *the glory of* the Lord.
145: 5. I will speak of the *glorious* honour of
11. They shall speak of *the glory of* thy
12. *and* the *glorious* majesty of his kingdom. (lit. *and the glory of* the honour of, &c.)
149: 5. Let the saints be joyful *in glory:*
Pro. 3:16. in her left hand riches *and honour.*
35. The wise shall inherit *glory:*
8:18. Riches *and honour* (are) with me;
11:16. A gracious woman retaineth *honour:*
15:33 & 18:12. before *honour* (is) humility.
20: 3. (It is) *an honour* for a man to cease from
21:21. findeth life, righteousness, *and honour.*
22: 4. riches, *and honour,* and life.
25: 2. (It is) *the glory of* God to conceal a thing: *but the honour of* kings (is) to search
27. (for men) to search *their own glory* (is not) *glory.*
26: 1. *honour* is not seemly for a fool.
8. he that giveth *honour* to a fool.
29:23. *honour* shall uphold the humble in spirit.
Ecc. 6: 2. riches, wealth, *and honour,*
10: 1. is in reputation for wisdom (and) *honour.*
Isa. 3: 8. to provoke the eyes of *his glory.*
4: 2. the branch of the Lord be beautiful *and glorious,* (lit. for beauty *and for glory*)
5. upon all *the glory* (shall be) a defence.
5:13. *and their honourable* men (are) famished, (marg. *and their glory* (are) men of famine.)
6: 3. the whole earth (is) full of *his glory.*
8: 7. and all *his glory:*
10: 3. where will ye leave *your glory?*
16. under *his glory* he shall kindle a burning
18. *And* shall consume *the glory of* his forest,
11:10. his rest shall be *glorious.*
14:18. All the kings of the nations,...lie *in glory,*
16:14. *the glory of* Moab shall be contemned,
17: 3. they shall be *as the glory of* the children
4. *the glory of* Jacob shall be made thin,
21:16. all *the glory of* Kedar shall fail:
22:18. the chariots of *thy glory*
23. he shall be for a *glorious* throne
24. all *the glory of* his father's house,
24:23. before his ancients *gloriously.* (marg. or, *glory* before his ancients)
35: 2. *the glory of* Lebanon shall be given unto
— they shall see *the glory of* the Lord,
40: 5. *the glory of* the Lord shall be revealed,
42: 8. *and my glory* will I not give to another,
12. Let them give *glory* unto the Lord,
43: 7. *for* I have created him *for my glory,*
48:11. *and* I will not give *my glory* unto
58: 8. *the glory of* the Lord shall be thy
59:19. *his glory* from the rising of the sun.
60: 1. *and the glory of* the Lord is risen upon
2. *and his glory* shall be seen upon thee.
13. *The glory of* Lebanon shall come unto
61: 6. *and in their glory* shall ye boast
62: 2. all kings *thy glory:*
66:11. the abundance of *her glory.*
12. *the glory of* the Gentiles like a flowing
18. they shall come, and see *my glory.*
19. neither have seen *my glory;* and they shall declare *my glory* among the Gentiles.
Jer. 2:11. my people have changed *their glory*
13:16. Give *glory* to the Lord your God,
14:21. do not disgrace the throne of *thy glory:*
17:12. A *glorious* high throne
48:18. come down *from* (thy) *glory,*
Eze. 1:28. the likeness of *the glory of* the Lord.
3:12. Blessed (be) *the glory of* the Lord
23. *the glory of* the Lord stood there, *as the glory* which I saw by the river
8: 4. *the glory of* the God of Israel (was)
Eze. 9: 3. *And the glory of* the God of Israel
10: 4. *the glory of* the Lord went up from the
— full of the brightness of the Lord's *glory.*
18. *the glory of* the Lord
19 & 11:22. *and the glory of* the God of Israel
11:23. *the glory of* the Lord
31:18. To whom art thou thus like *in glory*
39:21. I will set *my glory* among the heathen,
43: 2. *the glory of* the God of Israel
— the earth shined *with his glory.*
4. *And the glory of* the Lord came into the
5. *the glory of* the Lord filled the house.
44: 4. *the glory of* the Lord filled the house
Dan 11:39. acknowledge (and) increase with *glory:*
Hos. 4: 7. (therefore) will I change *their glory* into
9:11. *their glory* shall fly away like a bird,
10: 5. for *the glory thereof,*
Mic. 1:15. he shall come unto Adullam *the glory of*
Nah 2: 9(10). (there is) none end of the store (and) *glory*
Hab 2:14. the knowledge of *the glory of* the Lord,
16. Thou art filled with shame *for glory:*
— shameful spewing (shall be) on *thy glory.*
Hag. 2: 3. that saw this house *in her* first *glory?*
7. I will fill this house with *glory,*
9. *The glory of* this latter house
Zec. 2: 5(9). *and* will be *the glory* in the midst of
8(12). After *the glory* hath he sent
Mal. 1: 6. I (be) a father, where (is) *mine honour?*
2: 2. to give *glory* unto my name,

כְּבוּדָּה *k'vood-dāh'*, adj. f. 3520

Jud. 18:21. *the carriage* before them.
Ps. 45:13(14). The king's daughter (is) *all glorious*
Eze. 23:41. satest upon a *stately* bed, (marg. *honourable*)

כַּבִּיר *kab-beer'*, adj. 3524

Job 8: 2. thy mouth (be like) a *strong* wind?
15:10. aged men, *much* elder than thy father.
31:25. mine hand had gotten *much;*
34:17. him that is *most* just?
24. He shall break in pieces *mighty* men
36: 5. Behold, God (is) *mighty,* and despiseth not (any): (he is) *mighty* in strength
Isa. 10:13. I have put down the inhabitants *like a valiant* (man): (כתיב כַּאַבִּיר;—marg. *many* people)
16:14. the remnant (shall be) very small (and) feeble. (marg. or, not *many*)
17:12. of *mighty* waters! (marg. or, *many*)
28: 2. as a flood of *mighty* waters

כְּבִיר *k'veer*, m. 3523

1 Sa. 19:13. and put *a pillow of* goats' (hair)
16. *with a pillow of* goats' (hair)

כֶּבֶל *keh'-vel*, m. 3525

Ps. 105:18. Whose feet they hurt *with fetters:*
149: 8. their nobles *with fetters of* iron;

כָּבַס [*kāh-vas'*]. 3526

* KAL.—*Participle.* *

2K. 18:17. in the highway of *the fuller*'s field.
Isa. 7: 3. in the highway of *the fuller*'s field;
36: 2. in the highway of *the fuller*'s field.

* PIEL.—*Preterite.* *

Gen 49:11. *he washed* his garments in wine,
Ex. 19:10. *and let* them *wash* their clothes,
Lev. 13: 6, 34. *and he shall wash* his clothes,
54. the priest shall command *that they wash*
14: 8. *And* he that is to be cleansed *shall wash*
9. *and he shall wash* his clothes,
15: 8. *then he shall wash* his clothes,
11. *he shall wash* his clothes,
13. *and wash* his clothes.

Lev.15:27. *and shall wash* his clothes,
17:15. *he shall both wash* his clothes,
Nu. 8: 7. *and let them wash* their clothes,
19: 7. *Then* the priest *shall wash* his clothes,
10. *And* he that gathereth the ashes of the heifer *shall wash* his clothes,
19. *and wash* his clothes,
31:24. *And ye shall wash* your clothes
2Sa.19:24(25). nor trimmed his beard, *nor washed*

PIEL.—*Imperative.*

Ps. 51: 2(4). *Wash me* throughly from mine iniquity,
Jer. 4:14. O Jerusalem, *wash* thine heart from

PIEL.—*Future.*

Ex. 19:14. *and they washed* their clothes.
Lev. 6:27(20). *thou shalt wash* that whereon it was
11:25. whosoever beareth (ought) of the carcase of them *shall wash* his clothes,
28. that beareth the carcase of them *shall wash*
40. that eateth of the carcase of it *shall wash*
— that beareth the carcase of it *shall wash*
13:58. which *thou shalt wash*, if the plague
14:47. he that lieth in the house *shall wash* his clothes; and he that eateth in the house *shall wash* his clothes.
15: 5. whosoever toucheth his bed *shall wash* his
6. he that sitteth...*shall wash* his clothes,
7. he that toucheth...*shall wash* his clothes,
10. he that beareth...*shall wash* his clothes,
21. whosoever toucheth her bed *shall wash*
22. *shall wash* his clothes, and bathe
16:26. let go the goat for the scapegoat *shall wash*
28. that burneth them *shall wash* his clothes,
17:16. But if *he wash* (them) not,
Nu. 8:21. *they washed* their clothes;
19: 8. he that burneth her *shall wash* his clothes
21. he that sprinkleth...*shall wash* his clothes;
Ps. 51: 7(9). *wash me*, and I shall be whiter than
Jer. 2:22. though *thou wash* thee with nitre,

PIEL.—*Participle.*

Mal. 3: 2. he (is) like a refiner's fire, and like *fullers'*

* PUAL.—*Preterite.* *

Lev.13:58. *then it shall be washed*
15:17. *shall be washed* with water,

* HOTHPAEL.—*Infinitive.* *

Lev.13:55. after that *it is washed:*
56. after *the washing* of it;

3527, 4342 **כָּבַר** [*kāh-var'*].

* HIPHIL.—*Future.* *

Job 35:16. *he multiplieth* words without knowledge.

HIPHIL.—*Participle.*

Job 36:31. he giveth meat *in abundance.*

3528 **כְּבָר** *k'vāhr*, part. adv.

Ecc. 1:10. it hath been *already* of old time,
2:12. (even) that which hath been *already* done.
16. *seeing that* which *now* (is)
3:15. That which hath been is *now;* and that which is to be hath *already* been;
4: 2. the dead *which* are *already* dead
6:10. That which hath been is named *already*,
9: 6. their envy, is *now* perished;
7. God *now* accepteth thy works.

3531 **כְּבָרָה** *k'vāh-rāh'*, f.

Am. 9: 9. like as (corn) is sifted *in a sieve*,

3530 **כִּבְרָה** [*kiv-rāh'*], f.

Gen35:16. there was but a *little* way (marg. *a little piece of* ground) to come
48: 7. (there was) but a *little* way (lit. *a little piece of* ground) to come
2K. 5:19. he departed from him a *little* way. (marg. *a little piece of* ground)

כֶּבֶשׂ *keh'-ves*, m. 3532

Ex. 12: 5. ye shall take (it) out from *the sheep*,
29:38. two *lambs* of the first year
39. *The* one *lamb* thou shalt offer in the morning; and *the* other *lamb* thou shalt offer
40. *with the* one *lamb* a tenth deal
41. *the* other *lamb* thou shalt offer at even,
Lev. 4:32. if he bring *a lamb*
9: 3. a calf *and a lamb*,
12: 6. *a lamb of* the first year
14:10. he shall take two *he lambs*
12. the priest shall take one *he lamb*,
13. he shall slay *the lamb*
21. he shall take one *lamb*
24. the priest shall take *the lamb*
25. he shall kill *the lamb*
23:12. *an he lamb* without blemish
18. seven *lambs* without blemish
19. two *lambs* of the first year
20. with *the* two *lambs:*
Nu. 6:12. *a lamb* of the first year
14. one *he lamb* of the first year
7:15, 21, 27, 33, 39, 45, 51, 57, 63, 69, 75, 81. one *lamb* of the first year,
17, 23, 29, 35, 41, 47, 53, 59, 65, 71, 77, 83, 87. *lambs* of the first year:
88. *the lambs* of the first year sixty.
15: 5. the fourth (part) of an hin...*for* one *lamb.*
11. or for a lamb, or a kid. (lit. a lamb *in the sheep* or in the goats)
28: 3. two *lambs* of the first year
4. *The* one *lamb* shalt thou offer in the morning, and *the* other *lamb* shalt thou offer
7. fourth (part) of an hin *for the* one *lamb:*
8. *the* other *lamb* shalt thou offer
9. two *lambs* of the first year
11. seven *lambs* of the first year
13. a meat offering *unto* one *lamb;*
14. a fourth (part) of an hin *unto* a *lamb:*
19. seven *lambs* of the first year:
21. shalt thou offer *for* every *lamb*, throughout *the* seven *lambs:*
27. seven *lambs* of the first year;
29. A several tenth deal *unto* one *lamb*, throughout *the* seven *lambs;*
29: 2, 8, 36. seven *lambs* of the first year
4. one tenth deal *for* one *lamb*,
—, 10. throughout *the* seven *lambs:*
10. A several tenth deal *for* one *lamb*,
13, 17, 20, 23, 26, 29, 32. fourteen *lambs* of the first year;
15. a several tenth deal *to* each *lamb* of *the* fourteen *lambs:*
18, 21, 24, 27, 30, 33. for the rams, *and for the lambs*,
37. for the ram, *and for the lambs*,
1Ch 29:21. a thousand rams, (and) a thousand *lambs*,
2Ch 29:21. *and* seven *lambs*, and seven he goats,
22. they killed also *the lambs*,
32. two hundred *lambs:*
35: 7. Josiah gave to the people,...*lambs* and
Ezr. 8:35. seventy and seven *lambs*,
Job 31:20. the fleece of *my sheep;*
Pro.27:26. *The lambs* (are) for thy clothing,
Isa. 1:11. the blood of bullocks, *or* of *lambs*,
5:17. Then shall *the lambs* feed
11: 6. The wolf also shall dwell with *the lamb*,
Jer. 11:19. I (was) *like a lamb*
Eze.46: 4. six *lambs* without blemish,
5. *and* the meat offering *for the lambs*
6. six *lambs*, and a ram:
7. *and for the lambs* according as
11. *and to the lambs* as he is able
13. *a lamb* of the first year
15. Thus shall they prepare *the lamb*,
Hos. 4:16. *as a lamb* in a large place.

כִּבְשָׂה *kiv-sāh'* & **כַּבְשָׂה** *kav-sāh'*, f. 3535

Gen21:28. Abraham set seven *ewe lambs of* the flock
29. What (mean) these seven *ewe lambs*
30. For (these) seven *ewe lambs*
Lev.14:10. *and* one *ewe lamb* of the first year
Nu. 6:14. *and* one *ewe lamb* of the first year

2Sa.12: 3. one little *ewe lamb*,
4. but took the poor man's *lamb*,
6. he shall restore *the lamb*

3533 ## כָּבַשׁ [*kāh-vash'*].

* KAL.—*Preterite.* *

Zec. 9:15. they shall devour, *and subdue*

KAL.—*Infinitive.*

2Ch 28:10. *to keep under* the children of Judah
Est. 7: 8. *Will he force* the queen

KAL.—*Imperative.*

Gen 1:28. replenish the earth, *and subdue it:*

KAL.—*Future.*

Jer. 34:11. *and brought them into subjection*
16. *and brought* them *into subjection*,
Mic. 7:19. *he will subdue* our iniquities;

KAL.—*Participle.* Poel.

Neh. 5: 5. we *bring into bondage* our sons

* NIPHAL.—*Preterite.* *

Nu. 32:22. *And* the land *be subdued*
29. *and* the land *shall be subdued*
Jos. 18: 1. And the land *was subdued*
1Ch 22:18. *and* the land *is subdued*

NIPHAL.—*Participle.*

Neh 5: 5. our daughters *are brought unto bondage*

* PIEL.—*Preterite.* *

2Sa. 8:11. all nations which *he subdued;*

* HIPHIL.—*Future.* *

Jer. 34:11. (כתיב) *and brought them into subjection*

3534 ## כֶּבֶשׁ *keh'-vesh*, m.

2Ch 9:18. *with a footstool* of gold,

3536 ## כִּבְשָׁן *kiv-shāhn'*, m.

Gen 19:28. as the smoke of *a furnace*.
Ex. 9: 8. handfuls of ashes of *the furnace*,
10. they took ashes of *the furnace*,
19:18. as the smoke of *a furnace*,

3537 ## כַּד *kad*, f.

Gen 24:14. Let down *thy pitcher*,
15. *with her pitcher* upon her shoulder.
16. and filled *her pitcher*,
17. drink a little water *of thy pitcher*.
18. hasted, and let down *her pitcher*
20. and emptied *her pitcher* into the trough,
43. I pray thee, a little water *of thy pitcher*
45. Rebekah came forth *with her pitcher*
46. made haste, and let down *her pitcher*
Jud. 7:16. *with* empty *pitchers*, and lamps within *the pitchers*.
19. and brake *the pitchers*
20. and brake *the pitchers*,
1K. 17:12. an handful of meal *in a barrel*,
14. *The barrel of* meal shall not waste,
16. *the barrel of* meal wasted not,
18:33(34). Fill four *barrels* with water,
Ecc.12: 6. or *the pitcher* be broken at the fountain,

3538 ## כְּדַב [*k'dav*], Ch. adj.

Dan 2: 9. *lying* and corrupt words

3539 ## כַּדְכֹּד *kad-kōhd'*, m.

Isa. 54:12. I will make thy windows of *agates*,
Eze.27:16. and coral, *and agate*. (marg. *chrysoprase*.)

כֹּה *kōh*, part. 3541

Gen 15: 5. said unto him, *So* shall thy seed be.
24:30. saying, *Thus* spake the man unto me;
31:37. set (it) *here* before my brethren
Ex. 2:12. And he looked *this way and that way*, [כֹּה וָכֹה]
Nu. 6:23. *On this wise* ye shall bless the children
11:31. a day's journey *on this side*, and as it were a day's journey *on the other side*,
23:15. Stand *here* by thy burntoffering, while I meet (the Lord) *yonder*
1Sa.20:13. The Lord do *so and much* more (lit. *So* may the Lord do *and so* may he add)
25:22. *So and* more *also* do God (lit. *so* may God do...*and so* may he add)
2Sa.18:30. Turn aside, (and) stand *here*.
2Ch 19:10. *this* do, and ye shall not trespass.
Isa. 7: 7. *Thus* saith the Lord God,
18: 4. For *so* the Lord said unto me,
20: 6. Behold, *such* (is) our expectation,
Jer. 23:29. (Is) not my word *like* as a fire?
Lam. 2:20. consider to whom thou hast done *this*.
&c. &c. &c.

It is sometimes combined in translation with עַד.

Gen22: 5. I and the lad will go *yonder*
Ex. 7:16. behold, *hitherto* thou wouldest not hear.
Jos. 17:14. as the Lord hath blessed me *hitherto?*
1K. 18:45. And it came to pass *in the mean while*,

With prefix בְּכֹה.

1K. 22:20. And one said *on this manner*, and another said *on that manner*.

כָּה *kāh*, Ch. adv. 3542

Dan 7:28. *Hither*to [עַד־כָּה] (is) the end of the

כָּהָה [*kāh-hāh'*]. 3543

* KAL.—*Preterite.* *

Deu 34: 7. his eye *was* not *dim*,

KAL.—*Infinitive.*

Zec.11:17. his right eye shall be *utterly* darkened. (lit. *darkening* shall be darkened)

KAL.—*Future.*

Gen27: 1. *and* his eyes *were dim*,
Job 17: 7. Mine eye *also is dim*
Isa. 42: 4. *He shall* not *fail*
Zec.11:17. his right eye *shall be* utterly *darkened*.

* PIEL.—*Preterite.* *

1Sa. 3:13. and *he restrained* them not. (marg. *frowned* not upon them)
Eze.21: 7(12). *and* every spirit *shall faint*,

כֵּהֶה *kēh-hāh'*, adj. f. 3544

Lev.13: 6. (if) the plague (be) *somewhat dark*,
21, 26. but (be) *somewhat dark;*
28. but it (be) *somewhat dark;*
39. the skin of their flesh (be) *darkish*
56. the plague (be) *somewhat dark*
1Sa. 3: 2. his eyes began *to wax dim*,
Isa. 42: 3. *smoking* flax shall he not quench: (marg. or, *dimly burning*)
61: 3. the spirit of *heaviness;*

כֵּהָה *kēh-hāh'*, f. 3545

Nah 3:19. (There is) no *healing* of thy bruise; (marg. *wrinkling*)

כְּהַל [*k'hal*], Ch. 3546

* P'AL.—*Participle.* Active. *

Dan 2:26. Art thou *able* to make known unto me
4:18(15). but thou (art) *able;* for the spirit

Dan 5: 8. but *they could* not read the writing,
15. *they could* not shew the interpretation

3547 **כִּהֵן [*kāh-han'*].**

* PIEL.—*Preterite.* *

Ex. 28:41. *that they may minister* unto me *in the priest's office.*
40:13. *that he may minister* unto me *in the priest's office.*
15. *that they may minister* unto me *in the priest's office:*
1Ch 6:10(5:36). he (it is) that *executed the priest's office* in the temple

PIEL.—*Infinitive.*

Ex. 28: 1, 3, 4. *that he may minister* unto me *in the priest's office,*
29: 1. *to minister* unto me *in the priest's office:*
44. *to minister* to me *in the priest's office.*
30:30. *that* (they) *may minister...in the priest's office.*
31:10 & 35:19 & 39:41. *to minister in the priest's office,*
Lev. 7:35. *to minister...in the priest's office;*
16:32. *to minister in the priest's office*
Nu. 3: 3. *to minister in the priest's office.*
2Ch 11:14. *from executing the priest's office*
Eze.44:13. *to do the office of a priest*
Hos. 4: 6. *that thou shalt be no priest*

PIEL.—*Future.*

Nu. 3: 4. *and* Eleazar and Ithamar *ministered in the priest's office*
Deu 10: 6. *and* Eleazar his son *ministered in the priest's office*
1Ch 24: 2. *therefore* Eleazar and Ithamar *executed the priest's office.*
Isa. 61:10. as a bridegroom *decketh* (himself) (marg. *decketh as a priest*)

3548 **כֹּהֵן *kōh-hēhn'*, m.**

Gen14:18. he (was) *the priest* of the most high God.
41:45, 50 & 46:20. Poti-pherah *priest of* On. (marg. or, *prince*)
47:22. the land of *the priests* (marg. or, *princes*)
— *the priests had* (lit. there was *to the priests*) a portion
26. the land of *the priests* (marg. or, *princes*)
Ex. 2:16. *Now the priest of* Midian *had* seven daughters: (marg. or, *prince*)
3: 1. his father in law, *the priest of* Midian:
18: 1. Jethro, *the priest of* Midian,
19: 6. a kingdom of *priests,*
22. let *the priests...*sanctify themselves,
24. *but* let not *the priests...*break through
29:30. that son that is *priest* in his stead
31:10 & 35:19. holy garments for Aaron *the priest,*
38:21. son to Aaron *the priest.*
39:41. holy garments for Aaron *the priest,*
Lev. 1: 5. *the priests,* Aaron's sons,
7. the sons of Aaron *the priest*
8. And *the priests,* Aaron's sons,
9. *the priest* shall burn all on the altar,
11. and *the priests,* Aaron's sons,
12. *the priest* shall lay them in order
13. *the priest* shall bring (it) all,
15. *the priest* shall bring it unto the altar,
17. *the priest* shall burn it upon the altar,
2: 2. Aaron's sons *the priests:*
—, 16. *the priest* shall burn the memorial of
8. when it is presented unto *the priest,*
9. *the priest* shall take from the meat
3: 2. Aaron's sons *the priests*
11. *the priest* shall burn it
16. *the priest* shall burn them upon the
4: 3. *the priest* that is anointed do sin
5. *the priest* that is anointed shall take
6. *the priest* shall dip his finger in the
7. *the priest* shall put (some) of the blood
10. *the priest* shall burn them upon the
16. *the priest* that is anointed shall bring
17. *the priest* shall dip his finger (in some)
20. *the priest* shall make an atonement
25. *the priest* shall take of the blood

Lev. 4:26, 31, 35. *the priest* shall make an atonement for him
30. *the priest* shall take of the blood
31. *the priest* shall burn (it) upon the altar
34. *the priest* shall take of the blood
35. *the priest* shall burn them upon the altar,
5: 6, 10, 13. *the priest* shall make an atonement
8. he shall bring them unto *the priest,*
12. bring it to *the priest,* and *the priest* shall
13. (the remnant) shall be *the priest's,*
16. give it *unto the priest: and the priest* shall make an atonement
18. unto *the priest:* and *the priest* shall make
6: 6(5:25). a trespass offering, unto *the priest:*
7(-:26). *the priest* shall make an atonement
10(3). And *the priest* shall put on his linen
12(5). *the priest* shall burn wood on it every
22(15). *And the priest* of his sons that is
23(16). every meat offering for *the priest*
26(19). *The priest* that offereth it
29(22). All the males *among the priests*
7: 5. *the priest* shall burn them
6. Every male *among the priests*
7. *the priest* that maketh atonement
8. *And the priest* that offereth any
— *the priest* shall *have* (lit. *to the priest* shall be) to himself the skin
9. all the meat offering...shall be *the priest's*
14. it shall be *the priest's*
31. *the priest* shall burn the fat
32. right shoulder shall ye give *unto the priest*
34. have given them unto Aaron *the priest*
12: 6. she shall bring a lamb...unto *the priest:*
8. *the priest* shall make an atonement
13: 2. he shall be brought unto Aaron *the priest*
— one of his sons *the priests:*
3. *the priest* shall look on the plague
— *the priest* shall look on him,
4. *the priest* shall shut up (him)
5. *the priest* shall look on him the seventh
— *the priest* shall shut him up
6. *the priest* shall look on him again the
— *the priest* shall pronounce him clean:
7. after that he hath been seen of *the priest*
— he shall be seen of *the priest* again:
8. (if) *the priest* see that,
— *the priest* shall pronounce him
9. he shall be brought unto *the priest;*
10. And *the priest* shall see (him):
11. *the priest* shall pronounce him unclean,
12. wheresoever *the priest* looketh;
13. Then *the priest* shall consider:
15. *the priest* shall see the raw flesh,
16. he shall come unto *the priest;*
17. *the priest* shall see him:
— *the priest* shall pronounce (him) clean
19. it be shewed to *the priest;*
20. when *the priest* seeth it,
— *the priest* shall pronounce him unclean:
21, 26. if *the priest* look on it,
— *the priest* shall shut him up
22, 25, 27, 30. *the priest* shall pronounce him unclean:
23, 28, 37. and *the priest* shall pronounce him
25. *the priest* shall look upon it:
26. *the priest* shall shut him up
27. *the priest* shall look upon him
30. *the priest* shall see the plague:
31. if *the priest* look on the plague
—, 33. *the priest* shall shut up (him)
32. *the priest* shall look on the plague:
34. *the priest* shall look on the scall:
— *the priest* shall pronounce him clean:
36. *the priest* shall look on him:
— *the priest* shall not seek for yellow hair;
39. Then *the priest* shall look:
43. *the priest* shall look upon it:
44. *the priest* shall pronounce him utterly
49. shall be shewed unto *the priest:*
50. *the priest* shall look upon the plague,
53. if *the priest* shall look,
54. Then *the priest* shall command
55. *the priest* shall look on the plague,
56. And if *the priest* look,
14: 2. He shall be brought unto *the priest,*
3. *the priest* shall go forth
— *the priest* shall look,

Lev.14: 4. Then shall *the priest* command
5. *the priest* shall command
11. *the priest* that maketh (him) clean
12. *the priest* shall take one he lamb,
13. the sin offering (is) *the priest's*,
14, 25. *the priest* shall take (some) of the
— *the priest* shall put (it) upon the tip
15. *the priest* shall take (some) of the log
— the palm of *his own* (lit. *the priest's*) left
16. *the priest* shall dip his right finger in
17. the rest...shall *the priest* put upon the
18. the oil that (is) in *the priest's* hand
—, 20. *the priest* shall make an atonement
19. *the priest* shall offer the sin offering,
20. *the priest* shall offer the burnt offering
23. he shall bring them...unto *the priest*,
24. *the priest* shall take the lamb
— *the priest* shall wave them
26. *the priest* shall pour of the oil into the palm of *his own* (lit. *the priest's*) left
27. *the priest* shall sprinkle
28. *the priest* shall put of the oil
29. the oil that (is) in *the priest's* hand
31. *the priest* shall make an atonement
35. shall come and tell *the priest*,
36. Then *the priest* shall command
— before *the priest* go (into it)
— *the priest* shall go in to see the house:
38. *the priest* shall go out of the house
39. And *the priest* shall come again
40. Then *the priest* shall command
44. Then *the priest* shall come and look,
48. *the priest* shall come in,
— *the priest* shall pronounce the house
15:14. give them unto *the priest:*
15. *the priest* shall offer them,
— *the priest* shall make an atonement
29. bring them unto *the priest*,
30. *the priest* shall offer the one
— *the priest* shall make an atonement
16:32. *the priest*, whom he shall anoint,
33. an atonement for *the priests*,
17: 5. they may bring them...unto *the priest*,
6. *the priest* shall sprinkle the blood
19:22. *the priest* shall make an atonement
21: 1. Speak unto *the priests*
9. the daughter of any *priest*,
10. *And* (he that is) *the* high *priest*
21. the seed of Aaron *the priest*
22:10. a sojourner of *the priest*,
11. *But* if *the priest* buy (any) soul
12. If *the priest's* daughter also be (married)
13. if *the priest's* daughter be a widow,
14. shall give (it) *unto the priest*
23:10. ye shall bring a sheaf...unto *the priest:*
11. *the priest* shall wave it.
20. *the priest* shall wave them
— shall be holy to the Lord *for the priest*.
27: 8. present himself before *the priest*, and *the priest* shall value him;
— shall *the priest* value him.
11. shall present the beast before *the priest:*
12. *the priest* shall value it,
— (who art) *the priest*,
14. then *the priest* shall estimate it
— as *the priest* shall estimate it,
18. *the priest* shall reckon unto him the
21. possession thereof shall be *the priest's*.
23. *the priest* shall reckon unto him the
Nu. 3: 3. *the priests* which were anointed,
6. present them before Aaron *the priest*,
32. And Eleazar the son of Aaron *the priest*
4:16. of Eleazar the son of Aaron *the priest*
28, 33. Ithamar the son of Aaron *the priest*.
5: 8. (even) *to the priest;*
9. which they bring *unto the priest*,
10. whatsoever any man giveth *the priest*,
15. the man bring his wife unto *the priest*,
16. *the priest* shall bring her near,
17. *the priest* shall take holy water
— of the dust... *the priest* shall take,
18. *the priest* shall set the woman
— *the priest* shall have in his hand
19. *the priest* shall charge her by an oath,
21. *the priest* shall charge the woman
— *the priest* shall say unto the woman,
23. *the priest* shall write these curses in a

Nu. 5:25. *the priest* shall take the
26. *the priest* shall take an handful of the
30. *the priest* shall execute upon her all this
6:10. he shall bring two turtles,... to *the priest*,
11. *the priest* shall offer the one for a sin
16. *the priest* shall bring (them) before the
17. *the priest* shall offer also his meat offering,
19. *the priest* shall take the sodden shoulder
20. *the priest* shall wave them
— this (is) holy *for the priest*,
7: 8. Ithamar the son of Aaron *the priest*.
10: 8. the sons of Aaron, *the priests*,
15:25. *the priest* shall make an atonement for
28. *the priest* shall make an atonement for the
16:37(17:2). Eleazar the son of Aaron *the priest*,
39(—:4). Eleazar *the priest* took the brasen
18:28. ye shall give thereof... to Aaron *the priest*.
19: 3. ye shall give her unto Eleazar *the priest*,
4. Eleazar *the priest* shall take of her blood
6. *the priest* shall take cedar wood,
7. *the priest* shall wash his clothes,
— *the priest* shall be unclean
25: 7, 11 & 26:1. the son of Aaron *the priest*,
26: 3, 63. Moses and Eleazar *the priest*
64. Moses and Aaron *the priest*
27: 2. before Moses, and before Eleazar *the priest*,
19. set him before Eleazar *the priest*,
21. he shall stand before Eleazar *the priest*,
22. set him before Eleazar *the priest*,
31: 6. Phinehas the son of Eleazar *the priest*,
12. unto Moses, and Eleazar *the priest*,
13, 31, 51, 54. Moses, and Eleazar *the priest*,
21. Eleazar *the priest* said unto the men of
26. thou, and Eleazar *the priest*,
29. give (it) unto Eleazar *the priest*,
41. unto Eleazar *the priest*,
32: 2. to Eleazar *the priest*,
28. Moses commanded Eleazar *the priest*,
33:38. And Aaron *the priest* went up into mount Hor
34:17. Eleazar *the priest*, and Joshua
35:25. abide in it unto the death of *the* high *priest*,
28. until the death of *the* high *priest:* but after the death of *the* high *priest*
32. until the death of *the priest*.
Deu17: 9. unto *the priests* the Levites,
12. will not hearken unto *the priest*
18. before *the priests* the Levites:
18: 1. *The priests*... shall *have* (lit. there is *to the priests*) no part
3. this shall be *the priests'* due
— they shall give *unto the priest*
19:17. *the priests* and the judges,
20: 2. *the priest* shall approach
21: 5. *the priests* the sons of Levi
24: 8. *the priests* the Levites
26: 3. thou shalt go unto *the priest*
4. *the priest* shall take the basket
27: 9. Moses *and the priests* the Levites
31: 9. *the priests* the sons of Levi,
Jos. 3: 3. *and the priests* the Levites
6. Joshua spake unto *the priests*,
8. thou shalt command *the priests*
13. the feet of *the priests* that bear
14. *and the priests* bearing the ark
15. the feet of *the priests* that bare
17. *the priests* that bare the ark
4: 3. where *the priests'* feet stood firm,
9. *the priests* which bare the ark
10. *For the priests* which bare the ark
11. the Lord passed over, *and the priests*,
16. Command *the priests*
17. Joshua therefore commanded *the priests*.
18. *the priests* that bare the ark
— the soles of *the priests'* feet
6: 4. seven *priests* shall bear... trumpets
— *and the priests* shall blow with the trumpets.
6. Joshua... called *the priests*,
— let seven *priests* bear seven trumpets
8. *the* seven *priests* bearing the seven
9. *the priests* that blew with the trumpets
12. *the priests* took up the ark
13. seven *priests* bearing seven trumpets
16. when *the priests* blew
8:33. *the priests* the Levites,
14: 1. which Eleazar *the priest*,

Jos. 17: 4. they came near before Eleazar *the priest*,
19:51. Eleazar *the priest*, and Joshua the son of
20: 6. the death of *the* high *priest*
21: 1. unto Eleazar *the priest*,
4, 13. the children of Aaron *the priest*,
19. the children of Aaron, *the priests*,
22: 13, 31, 32. the son of Eleazar *the priest*,
30. when Phinehas *the priest*,
Jud. 17: 5. who became his *priest*.
10. be unto me a father *and a priest*,
12. the young man became his *priest*,
13. seeing I have a Levite *to* (my) *priest*.
18: 4. I am his *priest*.
6. *the priest* said unto them,
17. *and the priest* stood in the entering of the
18. Then said *the priest* unto them,
19. be to us a father *and a priest:* (is it) better for thee to be *a priest*
— *a priest* unto a tribe and a family
20. And *the priest*'s heart was glad,
24. Ye have taken away... *the priest*,
27. *the priest* which he had,
30. *priests* to the tribe of Dan
1Sa. 1: 3. *the priests* of the Lord,
9. Eli *the priest* sat upon a seat
2: 11. child did minister...before Eli *the priest*.
13. *the priests*' custom with the people
— *the priest*'s servant came,
14. all that the fleshhook brought up *the priest*
15. *the priest*'s servant came, and said to the man that sacrificed, Give flesh to roast *for the priest;*
28. did I choose him out...(to be) my *priest*,
35. I will raise me up *a* faithful *priest*,
5: 5. *the priests of* Dagon,
6: 2. the Philistines called *for the priests*
14: 3. the Lord's *priest* in Shiloh,
19. Saul talked unto *the priest*,
— Saul said unto *the priest*,
36. Then said *the priest*,
21: 1(2). to Ahimelech *the priest:*
2(3). David said unto Ahimelech *the priest*,
4(5). And *the priest* answered David,
5(6). And David answered *the priest*,
6(7). *the priest* gave him hallowed (bread):
9(10). And *the priest* said,
22: 11. the king sent to call Ahimelech *the priest*,
— *the priests* that (were) in Nob:
17. slay *the priests of* the Lord;
— to fall *upon the priests of* the Lord.
18. fall *upon the priests.*
— he fell *upon the priests*,
19. the city of *the priests*,
21. Saul had slain the Lord's *priests*.
23: 9. said to Abiathar *the priest*,
30: 7. David said to Abiathar *the priest*,
2Sa. 8: 17. Zadok... and Ahimelech... (were) *the priests;*
18. David's sons were *chief rulers*. (marg. or, *princes*)
15: 27. The king said also unto Zadok *the priest*,
35. with thee Zadok and Abiathar *the priests?*
— to Zadok and Abiathar *the priests*.
17: 15. unto Zadok and to Abiathar *the priests*,
19: 11(12). to Zadok and to Abiathar *the priests*,
20: 25. Zadok and Abiathar (were) *the priests:*
26. Ira...was *a chief ruler* (marg. or, *a prince*)
1K. 1: 7. and with Abiathar *the priest:*
8. But Zadok *the priest*,
19. Abiathar *the priest*, and Joab
25. and Abiathar *the priest;*
26. and Zadok *the priest*,
32. Call me Zadok *the priest*,
34. Zadok *the priest* and Nathan the prophet
38. So Zadok *the priest*,
39. Zadok *the priest* took an horn
42. the son of Abiathar *the priest*
44. Zadok *the priest*, and Nathan the prophet.
45. Zadok *the priest* and Nathan the prophet
2: 22. and for Abiathar *the priest*,
26. unto Abiathar *the priest* said the king,
27. thrust out Abiathar from being *priest*
35. Zadok *the priest*
4: 2. Azariah the son of Zadok *the priest*, (marg. or, *the chief officer*)
4. Zadok and Abiathar (were) *the priests:*
5. Zabud...(was) *principal officer*,

1K. 8: 3. *the priests* took up the ark.
4. *the priests* and the Levites
6. *the priests* brought in the ark
10. when *the priests* were come out
11. *the priests* could not stand
12: 31. and made *priests* of the lowest of
32. *the priests of* the high places which
13: 2. *the priests of* the high places that burn
33. of the people *priests of* the high places.
— he became (one) of *the priests of* the high
2K. 10: 11. his kinsfolks, *and his priests*,
19. all his servants, and all *his priests;*
11: 9. Jehoiada *the priest* commanded:
— and came to Jehoiada *the priest*.
10. did *the priest* give king David's spears
15. Jehoiada *the priest* commanded
— *the priest* had said,
18. Mattan *the priest* of Baal
— *the priest* appointed officers
12: 2(3). Jehoiada *the priest* instructed
4(5). Jehoash said to *the priests*,
5(6). Let *the priests* take (it) to them,
6(7). *the priests* had not repaired
7(8). *the priest, and the* (other) *priests*,
8(9). And *the priests* consented to receive
9(10). Jehoiada *the priest* took a chest,
—(—). *the priests* that kept the door
10(11). *and the* high *priest* came up,
16(17). it was *the priests*'.
16: 10. sent to Urijah *the priest*
11. Urijah *the priest* built an altar
— Urijah *the priest* made (it)
15. Ahaz commanded Urijah *the priest*,
16. Thus did Urijah *the priest*,
17: 27. Carry thither one *of the priests*
28. one *of the priests* whom they had carried
32. *priests of* the high places,
19: 2. the elders of *the priests*,
22: 4. Go up to Hilkiah *the* high *priest*,
8. Hilkiah *the* high *priest* said
10. Hilkiah *the priest* hath delivered
12. the king commanded Hilkiah *the priest*,
14. So Hilkiah *the priest*,
23: 2. *and the priests*, and the prophets,
4. the king commanded Hilkiah *the* high *priest*, and *the priests of* the second order,
8. he brought all *the priests*
— where *the priests* had burned incense,
9. *the priests of* the high places
20. he slew all *the priests of* the high
24. Hilkiah *the priest*
25: 18. Seraiah *the* chief *priest*, and Zephaniah *the* second *priest*,
1Ch 9: 2. *the priests*, Levites, and the Nethinims.
10. And of *the priests;* Jedaiah, and
30. the sons of *the priests*
13: 2. *the priests* and Levites
15: 11. Zadok and Abiathar *the priests*,
14. *the priests* and the Levites sanctified
24. *the priests*, did blow with the trumpets
16: 6. Benaiah also and Jahaziel *the priests*
39. *the priest*, and his brethren *the priests*,
18: 16. And Zadok...and Abimelech...(were) *the priests;*
23: 2. *with the priests* and the Levites.
24: 6. the princes, and Zadok *the priest*,
—, 31. the chief of the fathers *of the priests*
27: 5. Benaiah the son of Jehoiada, *a* chief *priest:* (marg. or, principal *officer*)
28: 13, 21. the courses of *the priests*
29: 22. and Zadok (to be) *priest*.
2Ch 4: 6. the sea (was) *for the priests* to wash in.
9. the court of *the priests*,
5: 5. these did *the priests*
7. *the priests* brought in the ark
11. when *the priests* were come out
— *the priests* (that were) present
12. hundred and twenty *priests* sounding with
14. *the priests* could not stand to minister
6: 41. let *thy priests*, O Lord God, be clothed
7: 2. *the priests* could not enter
6. *And the priests* waited on their offices:
— *and the priests* sounded trumpets
8: 14. the courses of *the priests*
— to praise and minister before *the priests*,
15. *the priests* and Levites
11: 13. *And the priests* and the Levites

2Ch 11:15. he ordained him *priests*
13: 9. *the priests of* the Lord,
— and have made you *priests*
— *a priest* of (them that are) no gods.
10. *and the priests*, which minister
12. *and his priests* with sounding trumpets
14. *and the priests* sounded with the trumpets.
15: 3. and without *a* teaching *priest*,
17: 8. Elishama and Jehoram, *priests*.
19: 8. of the Levites, *and* (of) *the priests*,
11. Amariah *the* chief *priest*
22:11. the wife of Jehoiada *the priest*,
23: 4. *of the priests* and of the Levites,
6. *the priests*, and they that minister
8. Jehoiada *the priest* had commanded,
— Jehoiada *the priest* dismissed not
9. Jehoiada *the priest* delivered to
14. Jehoiada *the priest* brought out
— *the priest* said, Slay her not in
17. Mattan *the priest of* Baal
18. by the hand of *the priests*
24: 2. all the days of Jehoiada *the priest*.
5. *the priests* and the Levites,
11. *the* high *priest*'s officer
20. Zechariah the son of Jehoiada *the priest*,
25. the sons of Jehoiada *the priest*,
26:17. Azariah *the priest*
— fourscore *priests* of the Lord,
18. *to the priests* the sons of Aaron,
19. he was wroth with *the priests*,
— before *the priests* in the house of the Lord,
20. Azariah *the* chief *priest*, and all *the priests*,
29: 4. *the priests* and the Levites,
16. *the priests* went into the inner part
21. *the priests* the sons of Aaron
22. *the priests* received the blood,
24. *the priests* killed them,
26. *and the priests* with the trumpets.
34. *the priests* were too few,
— *the* (other) *priests* had sanctified
— to sanctify themselves *than the priests*.
30: 3. *the priests* had not sanctified themselves
15. *and the priests* and the Levites
16. *the priests* sprinkled the blood,
21. *and the priests* praised the Lord
24. a great number of *priests*
25. *with the priests* and the Levites,
27. *the priests* the Levites
31: 2. the courses of *the priests* and the Levites
— *the priests* and Levites for burnt offerings
4. the portion of *the priests*
9. *the priests* and the Levites
10. Azariah *the* chief *priest*
15. the cities of *the priests*,
17. the genealogy of *the priests*
19. the sons of Aaron *the priests*,
— the males *among the priests*,
34: 5. the bones of *the priests*
9. Hilkiah *the* high *priest*,
14. Hilkiah *the priest* found a book
18. Hilkiah *the priest* hath given me a book.
30. *and the priests*, and the Levites,
35: 2. *the priests* in their charges,
8. *to the priests*, and to the Levites:
— *unto the priests* for the passover offerings
10. *the priests* stood in their place,
11. *the priests* sprinkled (the blood)
14. for themselves, *and for the priests:* because *the priests* the sons of Aaron
— *and for the priests* the sons of
18. *and the priests*, and the Levites,
36:14. the chief of *the priests*,
Ezr. 1: 5. *and the priests*, and the Levites,
2:36. *The priests:* the children of Jedaiah,
61. the children of *the priests:*
63. till there stood up *a priest*
69. one hundred *priests*' garments.
70. So *the priests*, and the Levites, and (some)
3: 2. his brethren *the priests*,
8. *the priests* and the Levites,
10. they set *the priests* in their apparel
12. *of the priests* and Levites
6:20. *the priests* and the Levites
— their brethren *the priests*,
7: 5. the son of Aaron *the* chief *priest:*
7. and of *the priests*,

Ezr. 7:11. Ezra *the priest*, the scribe
8:15. I viewed the people, *and the priests*,
24, 29. the chief of *the priests*,
30. *the priests* and the Levites
33. Uriah *the priest;*
9: 1. The people of Israel, *and the priests*,
7. our kings, (and) *our priests*,
10: 5. *the* chief *priests*, the Levites,
10. Ezra *the priest* stood up,
16. And Ezra *the priest*,
18. the sons of *the priests*
Neh. 2:16. *nor to the priests*, nor to the nobles,
3: 1. Eliashib *the* high *priest* rose up with his brethren *the priests*,
20. the house of Eliashib *the* high *priest*.
22. after him repaired *the priests*,
28. above the horse gate repaired *the priests*,
5:12. Then I called *the priests*,
7:39. *The priests:* the children of Jedaiah,
63. And of *the priests:*
65. till there stood (up) *a priest*
70. five hundred and thirty *priests*' garments.
72. threescore and seven *priests*' garments.
73. *the priests*, and the Levites,
8: 2. Ezra *the priest* brought the law
9. Ezra *the priest* the scribe,
13. *the priests*, and the Levites,
9:32. *and on our priests*, and on our prophets,
34. *our priests*, nor our fathers,
38(10:1). our princes, Levites, (and) *priests*,
10: 8(9). these (were) *the priests*.
28(29). *the priests*, the Levites,
34(35). we cast the lots among *the priests*,
36(37). *unto the priests* that minister in the
37(38). *unto the priests*, to the chambers
38(39). *the priest* the son of Aaron
39(40). *and the priests* that minister,
11: 3. *the priests*, and the Levites,
10. Of *the priests:*
20. *the priests*, (and) the Levites,
12: 1. these (are) *the priests*
7. These (were) the chief of *the priests*
12. in the days of Joiakim were *priests*,
22. *also the priests*, to the reign
26. Ezra *the priest*, the scribe.
30. *the priests* and the Levites purified
35. (certain) of *the priests*' sons
41. *And the priests;* Eliakim,
44. *for the priests* and Levites: for Judah rejoiced for *the priests*
13: 4. Eliashib *the priest*,
5. the offerings of *the priests*.
13. Shelemiah *the priest*,
28. Eliashib *the* high *priest*,
30. the wards *of the priests*
Job 12:19. He leadeth *princes* away spoiled,
Ps. 78:64. *Their priests* fell by the sword;
99: 6. Moses and Aaron *among his priests*,
110: 4. Thou (art) *a priest* for ever
132: 9. *thy priests* be clothed with righteousness;
16. I will *also* clothe *her priests* with salvation:
Isa. 8: 2. Uriah *the priest*,
24: 2. as with the people, *so* with *the priest;* (marg. or, *prince*)
28: 7. *the priest* and the prophet have erred
37: 2. the elders of *the priests*
61: 6. *the Priests of* the Lord:
66:21. *for priests* (and) for Levites,
Jer. 1: 1. *the priests* that (were) in Anathoth
18. *against the priests thereof*,
2: 8. *The priests* said not,
26. *and their priests*, and their prophets,
4: 9. *the priests* shall be astonished,
5:31. *and the priests* bear rule by their means;
6:13. from the prophet even unto *the priest*
8: 1. the bones of *the priests*,
10. even unto *the priest*
13:13. and *the priests*, and the prophets,
14:18. the prophet and *the priest* go about
18:18. the law shall not perish *from the priest*,
19: 1. the ancients of *the priests;*
20: 1. Pashur the son of Immer *the priest*,
21: 1. Zephaniah the son of Maaseiah *the priest*,
23:11. both prophet and *priest* are profane;
33. the prophet, or *a priest*,
34. *and the priest*, and the people,
26: 7, 8. *the priests* and the prophets

Jer. 26:11. Then spake *the priests*
16. unto *the priests* and to the prophets;
27:16. I spake to *the priests*
28: 1, 5. in the presence of *the priests*
29: 1. to *the priests*, and to the prophets,
25. Zephaniah the son of Maaseiah *the priest*, and to all *the priests*,
26. The Lord hath made thee *priest* in the stead of Jehoiada *the priest*,
29. Zephaniah *the priest*
31:14. I will satiate the soul of *the priests*
32:32. *their priests*, and their prophets,
33:18. *Neither* shall *the priests*
21. with the Levites *the priests*,
34:19. the eunuchs, *and the priests*,
37: 3. Zephaniah the son of Maaseiah *the priest*
48: 7 & 49:3. *his priests* and his princes together.
52:24. Seraiah *the* chief *priest*, and Zephaniah *the* second *priest*,
Lam. 1: 4. *her priests* sigh,
19. *my priests* and mine elders gave up the
2: 6. the king *and the priest*.
20. shall *the priest* and the prophet be slain
4:13. the iniquities of *her priests*,
16. respected not the persons of *the priests*,
Eze. 1: 3. Ezekiel *the priest*,
7:26. the law shall perish *from the priest*,
22:26. *Her priests* have violated my law,
40:45, 46. (is) *for the priests*,
42:13. *the priests* that approach unto the Lord
14. When *the priests* enter therein,
43:19. thou shalt give to *the priests*
24. *the priests* shall cast salt upon them,
27. *the priests* shall make your burnt offerings
44:15. *But the priests* the Levites,
21. Neither shall any *priest* drink wine,
22. *that had a priest before*. (marg. *from a priest*)
30. shall be *the priests*: ye shall also give *unto the priest*
31. *The priests* shall not eat of any thing...dead
45: 4. the land shall be *for the priests*
19. *the priest* shall take of the blood
46: 2. *the priests* shall prepare his burnt offering
19. the holy chambers of *the priests*,
20. *the priests* shall boil the trespass offering
48:10. (even) *for the priests*,
11. (It shall be) *for the priests*
13. the border of *the priests*
Hos. 4: 4. they that strive with *the priest*.
9. like people, *like priest*:
5: 1. Hear ye this, *O priests*;
6: 9. the company of *priests*
Joel 1: 9. *the priests*, the Lord's ministers,
13. Gird yourselves, and lament, *ye priests*:
2:17. Let *the priests*, the ministers of the Lord,
Am. 7:10. Amaziah *the priest of* Beth-el
Mic. 3:11. *and the priests thereof* teach for hire,
Zep. 1: 4. name of the Chemarims with *the priests*;
3: 4. *her priests* have polluted the sanctuary,
Hag. 1: 1, 12, 14 & 2:2. Joshua the son of Josedech, *the* high *priest*,
2: 4. O Joshua, son of Josedech, *the* high *priest*;
11. Ask now *the priests*
12. *the priests* answered and said, No.
13. *the priests* answered and said,
Zec. 3: 1. Joshua *the* high *priest*
8. O Joshua *the* high *priest*,
6:11. Joshua the son of Josedech, *the* high *priest*;
13. he shall be *a priest*
7: 3. to speak unto *the priests*
5. Speak...to *the priests*,
Mal. 1: 6. *O priests*, that despise my name.
2: 1. *O ye priests*, this commandment
7. *the priest*'s lips should keep knowledge,

3549 ## כָּהֵן [*kāh-hēhn'*], Ch. m.

Ezr. 6: 9. according to the appointment of *the priests*
16. And the children of Israel, *the priests*,
18. they set *the priests* in their divisions,
7:12. unto Ezra *the priest*, a scribe
13. *and* (of) *his priests* and Levites,
16. *and* of *the priests*, offering willingly
21. that whatsoever Ezra *the priest*,
24. that touching any of *the priests*

כְּהֻנָּה *k'hoon-nāh'*, f. 3550

Ex. 29: 9. *the priest's office* shall be their's
40:15. be *an* everlasting *priesthood*
Nu. 3:10. they shall wait on *their priest's office*:
16:10. seek ye *the priesthood* also?
18: 1. the iniquity of *your priesthood*.
7. keep *your priest's office*
— I have given *your priest's office*
25:13. the covenant of *an* everlasting *priesthood*;
Jos. 18: 7. *the priesthood of* the Lord
1Sa. 2:36. one of *the priest's offices*,
Ezr. 2:62. put from *the priesthood*.
Neh. 7:64. put from *the priesthood*.
13:29. they have defiled *the priesthood*, and the covenant of *the priesthood*,

---

כּוֹבַע *kōh'-vag̃*, m. 3553

1Sa. 17: 5. *And* (he had) *an helmet of* brass
2Ch 26:14. spears, *and helmets*, and habergeons,
Isa. 59:17. *and an helmet of* salvation upon his head;
Jer. 46: 4. stand forth *with* (your) *helmets*;
Eze. 27:10. they hanged the shield *and helmet*
38: 5. all of them with shield *and helmet*:

כָּוָה [*kāh-vāh'*]. 3554

* NIPHAL.—*Future*. *

Pro. 6:28. upon hot coals, and his feet not *be burned*?
Isa. 43: 2. *thou shalt* not *be burned*;

כּוֹחַ see כֹּחַ See 3581

כְּוִיָּה *k'veey-yāh'*, f. 3555

Ex. 21:25. *Burning* for *burning*,

כַּוִּין *kav-veen'*, Ch. m. pl. 3551

Dan 6:10(11). *and* his *windows* being open

כּוֹכָב *kōh-chāhv'*. 3556

Gen 1:16. (he made) *the stars* also.
15: 5. now toward heaven, and tell *the stars*,
22:17. *as the stars of* the heaven,
26: 4. *as the stars of* heaven,
37: 9. the sun and the moon and *the* eleven *stars*
Ex. 32:13. multiply your seed *as the stars of* heaven,
Nu. 24:17. there shall come *a Star* out of Jacob,
Deu 1:10. *as the stars of* heaven for multitude.
4:19. the sun, and the moon, and *the stars*,
10:22. God hath made thee *as the stars of*
28:62. ye were *as the stars of* heaven
Jud. 5:20. *the stars* in their courses fought
1Ch 27:23. *like to the stars of* the heavens.
Neh 4:21(15). till *the stars* appeared.
9:23. multipliedst thou *as the stars of* heaven,
Job. 3: 9. *the stars of* the twilight
9: 7. and sealeth up *the stars*.
22:12. the height of *the stars*,
25: 5. *yea, the stars* are not pure
38: 7. When *the* morning *stars* sang together,
Ps. 8: 3(4). the moon *and the stars*,
136: 9. The moon *and stars* to rule
147: 4. He telleth the number *of the stars*;
148: 3. praise him, all ye *stars of* light.
Ecc 12: 2. or the moon, *or the stars*,
Isa. 13:10. *the stars of* heaven
14:13. I will exalt my throne above *the stars of*
47:13. the astrologers, the *star*gazers, (lit. who contemplate *upon the stars*)
Jer. 31:35. ordinances of the moon *and* of *the stars*
Eze 32: 7. and make *the stars thereof* dark;
Dan 8:10. (some) of the host and of *the stars* to the
12: 3. *as the stars* for ever and ever.

Joel 2:10, & 3:15(4:15). *and the stars* shall withdraw
Am. 5:26. *the star of* your god,
Obad. 4. though thou set thy nest among *the stars*,
Nah 3:16. *above the stars of* heaven:

3557 **כּוּל [*kool*].**

* KAL.—*Preterite.* *

Isa. 40:12. *and comprehended* the dust of the earth

* PILPEL.—*Preterite.* *

Gen 45:11. *And* there *will I nourish thee;*
2Sa. 19:32(33). he *had provided* the king *of sustenance*
33(34). *and I will feed* thee with me
1 K. 4: 7. twelve officers ... *which provided victuals*
27(5:7). *And* those officers *provided victual*
18: 4. *and fed them with* bread and water.
Neh 9:21. forty years *didst thou sustain them*

PILPEL.—*Infinitive.*

Ru. 4:15. *and a nourisher* of thine old age: (marg. *to nourish*)
1 K. 4: 7. man his month in a year *made provision.*
17: 4. I have commanded the ravens *to feed thee*
9. have commanded a widow...*to sustain thee.*
Jer. 20: 9. I was weary *with forbearing*,

PILPEL.—*Future.*

Gen 47:12. *And* Joseph *nourished* his father,
50:21. *I will nourish* you, and your little ones.
2Sa. 20: 3. put them in ward, *and fed them*,
1 K. 8:27. heaven of heavens *cannot contain thee;*
18:13. *and fed them with* bread and water?
2Ch. 2: 6(5). heaven of heavens *cannot contain him?*
6:18. the heaven of heavens *cannot contain thee;*
Ps. 55:22(23). *he shall sustain thee:*
112: 5. *he will guide* his affairs with discretion.
Pro. 18:14. The spirit of a man *will sustain*
Zec 11:16. nor *feed* (marg. *bear*) that that standeth

PILPEL.—*Participle.*

Mal. 3: 2. who *may abide* the day of his coming?

* POLPAL.—*Preterite.* *

1 K. 20:27. Israel were numbered, and *were all present*, (marg. or, *victualled*)

* HIPHIL.—*Infinitive.* *

1 K. 8:64. brasen altar ... (was) *too little to receive*
2Ch. 7: 7. brasen altar ... was not able *to receive*
Jer. 6:11. I am weary *with holding in:*
Eze. 23:32. it *containeth* much. (lit. it is great *to contain*)
Am. 7:10. the land is not able *to bear* all his words.

HIPHIL.—*Future.*

1 K. 7:26. *it contained* two thousand baths.
38. one laver *contained* forty baths:
2Ch 4: 5. and *held* three thousand baths.
Jer. 2:13. broken cisterns, that *can hold* no water.
10:10. the nations *shall* not *be able to abide*
Joel 2:11. and who *can abide it?*

3558 **כּוּמָז *koo-māhz'*, m.**

Ex. 35:22. earrings, and rings, *and tablets*,
Nu. 31:50. earrings, *and tablets*,

3559 **כּוּן [*koon*].**

* NIPHAL.—*Preterite.* *

1 K. 2:46. the kingdom *was established*
Pro 19:29. Judgments *are prepared* for
Eze 16: 7. (thy) breasts *are fashioned*,

NIPHAL.—*Imperative.*

2Ch 35: 4. (כתיב) *And prepare* (yourselves) by the
Eze 38: 7. *Be thou prepared*, and prepare for thyself,
Am 4:12. *prepare* to meet thy God, O Israel.

NIPHAL.—*Future.*

1 Sa. 20:31. *thou shalt* not *be established*,
1 K. 2:12. *and* his kingdom *was established*
1 Ch 16:30. the world also *shall be stable*,
2Ch 8:16. *Now* all the work ... *was prepared*
2Ch. 29:35. *So* the service ... *was set in order.*
35:10. *So* the service *was prepared*,
16. *So* all the service ... *was prepared*
Ps. 89:21(22). my hand *shall be established:*
37(38). *It shall be established* for ever
93: 1. the world also *is stablished*,
96:10. the world also *shall be established*
101: 7. he that telleth lies *shall* not *tarry* in my sight. (marg. *be established*)
102:28(29). their seed *shall be established*
119: 5. O that my ways *were directed*
140:11(12). *Let* not an evil speaker *be established*
141: 2. *Let* my prayer *be set forth* (marg. *directed*)
Pro. 4:26. *let* all thy ways *be established.*
12: 3. A man *shall* not *be established*
19. The lip of truth *shall be established*
16: 3. *and* thy thoughts *shall be established.*
12. the throne *is established* by righteousness.
20:18. (Every) purpose *is established*
22:18. *they shall* withal *be fitted* in thy lips.
25: 5. *and* his throne *shall be established*
29:14. his throne *shall be established*
Jer. 30:20. their congregation *shall be established*

NIPHAL.—*Participle.*

Gen 41:32. the thing (is) *established* by God, (marg. or, *prepared* of God)
Ex. 8:26(22). It *is* not *meet* so to do;
19:11. be *ready* against the third day:
15. Be *ready* against the third day:
34: 2. And be *ready* in the morning,
Deu 13:14(15). (and) the thing *certain*,
17: 4. (it be) true, (and) the thing *certain*,
Jos. 8: 4. but be ye all *ready:*
Jud 16:26. whereupon the house *standeth*,
29. pillars upon which the house *stood*,
1 Sa. 23:23. come ye again to me with *the certainty*,
26: 4. Saul was come in *very deed.*
2Sa. 7:16. thy throne shall be *established*
26. house of thy servant David be *established*
1 K. 2:45. the throne of David shall be *established*
1 Ch. 17:14. his throne shall be *established*
24. (let) the house of David ... (be) *established*
Neh 8:10. unto them for whom nothing is *prepared.*
Job. 12: 5. He that is *ready* to slip
15:23. the day of darkness is *ready* at his hand.
18:12. destruction (shall be) *ready* at his side.
21: 8. Their seed is *established* in their sight
42: 7, 8. ye have not spoken of me ... *right*,
Ps. 5: 9(10). (there is) no *faithfulness* in their mouth; (marg. or, *stedfastness*)
38:17(18). I (am) *ready* to halt,
51:10(12). renew a *right* spirit within me. (marg. or, *constant*)
57: 7(8). My heart is *fixed* (marg. or, *prepared*), O God, my heart is *fixed:*
78:37. their heart *was* not *right*
93: 2. Thy throne (is) *established* of old:
108: 1(2). O God, my heart is *fixed;*
112: 7. his heart is *fixed*,
Pro. 4:18. shineth more and more unto the *perfect*
Isa. 2: 2. of the Lord's house shall be *established*
Hos 6: 3. his going forth is *prepared*
Mic 4: 1. the house of the Lord shall be *established* in the top of the mountains,

* POLEL.—*Preterite.* *

Ex. 15:17. thy hands *have established.*
2Sa. 7:13. *and I will stablish* the throne of
1 Ch 17:12. *and I will stablish* his throne
Ps. 8: 3(4). the stars, which *thou hast ordained;*
9: 7(8). *he hath prepared* his throne
11: 2. *they make ready* their arrow
40: 2(3). (and) *established* my goings.
68: 9(10). whereby thou *didst confirm* thine inheritance,
99: 4. thou *dost establish* equity,
119:90. *thou hast established* the earth,
Pro. 3:19. by understanding *hath he established*
Isa. 45:18. he *hath established it*,
51:13. as if *he were ready* to destroy? (marg. or, *made* (himself) *ready*)
Hab 2:12. *and stablisheth* a city by iniquity!

POLEL.—*Imperative.*

Job 8: 8. *and prepare thyself* to the search
Ps. 90:17. and *establish thou* the work of our hands
— the work of our hands *establish thou it.*

POLEL.—*Future.*

Deu32: 6. he not made thee, *and established thee?*
2Sa. 7:24. *For thou hast confirmed* to thyself
Job 31:15. *and did* not one *fashion us*
Ps. 7: 9(10). *but establish* the just:
12(13). hath bent his bow, *and made* it *ready.*
21:12(13). *thou shalt make ready* (thine arrows)
24: 2. *and established it* upon the floods.
48: 8(9). God *will establish it* for ever.
87: 5. the highest himself *shall establish her.*
107:36. *that they may prepare* a city
119:73. hands have made me *and fashioned me:*
Isa. 62: 7. give him no rest, till *he establish,*

* PULAL.—*Preterite.* *

Ps. 37:23. The steps of a (good) man *are ordered* by the Lord: (marg. or, *established*)
Eze.28:13. *was prepared* in thee in the day that

* HIPHIL.—*Preterite.* *

Ex. 16: 5. *that.. they shall prepare* (that) which
23:20. the place which *I have prepared.*
Jos. 4: 4. the twelve men, whom *he had prepared*
1Sa.13:13. *would* the Lord *have established* thy
2Sa. 5:12. the Lord *had established him*
7:12. *and I will establish* his kingdom.
1K. 2:24. the Lord liveth, which *hath established me,*
6:19. the oracle *he prepared*
1Ch 12:39. their brethren *had prepared*
14: 2. the Lord *had confirmed him*
15: 3. his place, which *he had prepared*
12. (the place that) *I have prepared* for it.
17:11. *and I will establish* his kingdom.
22: 3. David *prepared* iron in abundance
10. *and I will establish* the throne of his
14. *I have prepared* for the house
— timber also and stone *have I prepared;*
28: 2. *and had made ready* for the building:
7. *Moreover I will establish* his kingdom
29: 2. *I have prepared* with all my might
3. all that *I have prepared*
16. all this store that *we have prepared*
19. (for) the which *I have made provision.*
2Ch 2: 7(6). whom David my father *did provide.*
3: 1. the place that David *had prepared*
12:14. *he prepared* (marg. or, *fixed*) not his heart
19: 3. *and hast prepared* thine heart
20:33. the people *had* not *prepared*
27: 6. *he prepared* his ways before the Lord (marg. or, *established*)
29:19. all the vessels,...*have we prepared*
36. *that* God *had prepared* the people:
30:19. *prepareth* his heart to seek God,
35:14. *they made ready* for themselves,
— the Levites *prepared* for themselves,
15. the Levites *prepared* for them.
20. when Josiah *had prepared* the temple,
Ezr. 7:10. Ezra *had prepared* his heart
Est. 6: 4 & 7:10. the gallows that *he had prepared*
Job 11:13. If *thou prepare* thine heart,
28:27. *he prepared it,* yea, and searched it out.
Ps. 7:13(14). *He hath* also *prepared* for him
57: 6(7). *They have prepared* a net
74:16. *thou hast prepared* the light
78: 8. *set* not their heart *aright,*
103:19. The Lord *hath prepared* his throne
Eze. 4: 3. *and set* thy face against it,
Zep. 1: 7. the Lord *hath prepared* a sacrifice,

HIPHIL.—*Infinitive.*

Jos. 3:17. And the priests...stood *firm*
4: 3. where the priests' feet stood *firm,*
1Ch 9:32. *to prepare* (it) every sabbath.
2Ch 1: 4. *to* (the place which) David *had prepared*
2: 9(8). *Even to prepare* me timber
12: 1. *when* Rehoboam *had established*
31:11. Hezekiah commanded *to prepare*
Pro. 8:27. *When he prepared* the heavens,
Isa. 9: 7(6). *to order* it, and to establish it
40:20. *to prepare* a graven image,
Jer. 10:23. (it is) not in man that walketh *to direct* his
33: 2. formed it, *to establish it;*
Eze. 7:14. *even to make* all *ready;*
Nah. 2: 3(4). in the day of *his preparation,*

HIPHIL.—*Imperative.*

Gen43:16. slay, *and make ready;*
Nu. 23: 1. *and prepare* me here seven oxen
Nu. 23:29. *and prepare* me here seven bullocks
Jos. 1:11. *Prepare* you victuals;
1Sa. 7: 3. *and prepare* your hearts unto the Lord,
23:22. Go, I pray you, *prepare* yet,
1Ch 29:18. *and prepare* their heart unto thee: (marg. or, *stablish*)
2Ch 35: 4. *And prepare* (yourselves) by the houses of
6. *prepare* your brethren,
Ps.119:133. *Order* my steps in thy word:
Pro. 24:27. *Prepare* thy work without,
Isa. 14:21. *Prepare* slaughter for his children
Jer. 46:14. Stand fast, *and prepare* thee;
51:12. *prepare* the ambushes:
Eze.38: 7. *and prepare* for thyself,

HIPHIL.—*Future.*

Gen43:25. *And they made ready* the present
Deu 19: 3. *Thou shalt prepare* thee a way,
Jud.12: 6. *he could* not *frame* to pronounce
1K. 5:18(32). *so they prepared* timber
1Ch 15: 1. *and prepared* a place for the ark
22: 5. *I will* (therefore) now *make preparation* for it. *So* David *prepared* abundantly
2Ch 17: 5. *Therefore* the Lord *stablished* the kingdom
26:14. *And* Uzziah *prepared* for them
31:11. *and they prepared* (them),
Ezr. 3: 3. *And they set* the altar upon his bases;
Job 15:35. their belly *prepareth* deceit.
27:16. *and prepare* raiment as the clay;
17. *He may prepare* (it), but the just
29: 7. *I prepared* my seat in the street!
38:41. Who *provideth* for the raven
Ps. 10:17. *thou wilt prepare* (marg. *establish*) their heart,
65: 9(10). *thou preparest* them corn, when *thou hast* so *provided for it.*
68:10(11). *thou,* O God, *hast prepared*
78:20. *can he provide* flesh for his people?
89: 2(3). thy faithfulness *shalt thou establish*
4(5). Thy seed *will I establish* for ever,
Pro. 6: 8. *Provideth* her meat in the summer,
16: 9. but the Lord *directeth* his steps.
21:29. (כתיב) the upright, he *directeth* his way. (marg. or, *considereth* [so קרי])
30:25. *yet they prepare* their meat in the summer;
Eze. 4: 7. *thou shalt set* thy face toward the siege

HIPHIL.—*Participle.*

Ps. 65: 6(7). his strength *setteth fast* the mountains;
147: 8. *who prepareth* rain for the earth,
Jer. 10:12 & 51:15. *he hath established* the world

* HOPHAL.—*Preterite.* *

Isa. 16: 5. *And* in mercy *shall* the throne *be established:*
30:33. for the king *it is prepared;*
Nah. 2: 5(6). *and* the defence *shall be prepared.*
Zec. 5:11. *and it shall be established,*

HOPHAL.—*Participle.*

Pro.21:31. The horse (is) *prepared* against the day of
Eze.40:43. (were) hooks, a hand broad, *fastened*

* HITHPOLEL.—*Future.* *

Nu. 21:27. the city of Sihon be built *and prepared:*
Ps. 59: 4(5). They run *and prepare themselves*
Pro.24: 3. by understanding *it is established:*
Isa. 54:14. In righteousness *shalt thou be established:*

כַּוָּנִים *kav-vāh-neem',* m. pl. 3561

Jer. 7:18. to make *cakes* to the queen of heaven,
44:19. did we make her *cakes* to worship her,

כּוֹס *kōhs,* f. 3563

Gen40:11. *And* Pharaoh's *cup* (was) in my hand:
— and pressed them into Pharaoh's *cup,* and I gave *the cup* into Pharaoh's hand.
13. thou shalt deliver Pharaoh's *cup*
21. he gave *the cup* into Pharaoh's hand:
Lev.11:17. And *the little owl,*
Deu 14:16. *The little owl,* and the great owl,
2Sa.12: 3. *and* drank *of his own cup,*
1K. 7:26. wrought like the brim of *a cup,*
2Ch 4: 5. the work of the brim of *a cup,*
Ps. 11: 6. the portion of *their cup.*

Ps. 16: 5. of mine inheritance *and* of *my cup:*
23: 5. *my cup* runneth over.
75: 8(9). the hand of the Lord (there is) *a cup,*
102: 6(7). I am *like an owl of* the desert.
116:13. I will take *the cup of* salvation,
Pro.23:31. when it giveth his colour *in the cup,*
Isa. 51:17. *the cup of* his fury; thou hast drunken the dregs of *the cup of* trembling,
22. *the cup of* trembling, (even) the dregs of *the cup of* my fury;
Jer. 16: 7. *the cup of* consolation
25:15. *the* wine *cup* of this fury
17. Then took I *the cup*
28. if they refuse to take *the cup*
35: 5. pots full of wine, *and cups,*
49:12. to drink of *the cup*
51: 7. Babylon (hath been) *a* golden *cup*
Lam. 4:21. *the cup* also shall pass through
Eze.23:31. therefore will I give *her cup*
32. Thou shalt drink of thy sister's *cup*
33. *the cup of* astonishment and desolation, with *the cup of* thy sister Samaria.
Hab. 2:16. *the cup of* the Lord's right hand

3564 כּוּר *koor*, m.

Deu 4:20. brought you forth *out of the* iron *furnace,*
1K. 8:51. from the midst of *the furnace of* iron:
Pro.17: 3 & 27:21. *and the furnace* for gold:
Isa. 48:10. I have chosen thee *in the furnace of*
Jer. 11: 4. *from the* iron *furnace,*
Eze.22:18, 22. in the midst of *the furnace;*
20. into the midst of *the furnace,*

3734 כּוֹרִין *kōh-reen'*, Ch. m. pl.

Ezr. 7:22. hundred *measures* (marg. *cors*) of wheat,

3574 כּוֹשָׁרוֹת *kōh-shāh-rōhth'*, f. pl.

Ps. 68: 6(7). those which are bound *with chains:* [perhaps *into prosperity*]

See 3805 כּוֹתֶרֶת see כֹּתֶרֶת

3576 כָּזַב [*kāh-zav'*].

* KAL.—*Participle.* Poel. *

Ps.116:11. I said in my haste, All men (are) *liars.*

* NIPHAL.—*Preterite.* *

Job 41: 9(1). the hope of him *is in vain:*
Pro.30: 6. *and thou be found a liar.*

* PIEL.—*Preterite.* *

Mic. 2:11. walking in the spirit and falsehood *do lie,*

PIEL.—*Infinitive.*

Eze.13:19. *by your lying* to my people

PIEL.—*Future.*

Nu. 23:19. God (is) not a man, *that he should lie;*
2K. 4:16. *do* not *lie* unto thine handmaid.
Job 6:28. evident unto you if *I lie.*
34: 6. *Should I lie* against my right?
Ps. 78:36. *they lied* unto him with their tongues.
89:35(36). *I will* not *lie* unto David.
Pro.14: 5. A faithful witness *will* not *lie:*
Isa. 57:11. *thou hast lied,* and hast not remembered
58:11. a spring of water, whose waters *fail* not.
Hab. 2: 3. it shall speak, and not *lie:*

* HIPHIL.—*Future.* *

Job 24:25. who *will make me a liar,*

3577 כָּזָב *kāh-zahv'*, m.

Jud.16:10, 13. hast mocked me, and told me *lies:*
Ps. 4: 2(3). (and) seek after *leasing?*
5: 6(7). destroy them that speak *leasing:*
40: 4(5). nor such as turn aside to *lies.*
58: 3(4). they go astray...speaking *lies.*
62: 4(5). they delight in *lies:*
9(10). men of high degree (are) *a lie:*
Pro. 6:19. A false witness (that) speaketh *lies,*
14: 5. a false witness will utter *lies.*
25. a deceitful (witness) speaketh *lies.*
19: 5. (he that) speaketh *lies* shall not escape.
9. (he that) speaketh *lies* shall perish.
22. a poor man (is) better than *a liar.* (lit. man of *a lie*)
21:28. A *false* witness (marg. A witness of *lies*) shall perish:
23: 3. (are) *deceitful* meat. (lit. meat of *lies*)
30: 8. Remove far from me vanity and *lies:* (lit. word of *a lie*)
Isa. 28:15. we have made *lies* our refuge,
17. sweep away the refuge of *lies,*
Eze.13: 6. They have seen vanity and *lying* divination, (lit. divination of *a lie*)
7. a *lying* divination, (lit. divination of *a lie*)
8. ye have spoken vanity, and seen *lies,*
9. that see vanity, and that divine *lies:*
19. my people that hear (your) *lies?*
21:29(34). they divine *a lie* unto thee,
22:28. divining *lies* unto them,
Dan 11:27. they shall speak *lies* at one table;
Hos. 7:13. they have spoken *lies*
12: 1(2). he daily increaseth *lies*
Am. 2: 4. *their lies* caused them to err,
Zep. 3:13. shall not do iniquity, nor speak *lies;*

כֹּחַ *kōhăgh*, m. 3581

Gen 4:12. henceforth yield unto thee *her strength;*
31: 6. with all *my power* I have served
49: 3. thou (art) my firstborn, *my might,*
Ex. 9:16. to shew (in) thee *my power;*
15: 6. O Lord, is become glorious *in power:*
32:11. thou hast brought forth...*with* great *power,*
Lev.11:30. the ferret, *and the chameleon,*
26:20. *your strength* shall be spent
Nu. 14:13. thou broughtest up this people *in thy might*
17. let *the power of* my Lord be great,
Deu 4:37. *with his* mighty *power*
8:17. *My power* and the might of mine hand
18. he that giveth thee *power*
9:29. *by thy* mighty *power*
Jos. 14:11. *as my strength* (was) then, *even so* (is) *my strength* now,
17:17. a great people, *and* hast great *power:*
Jud 6:14. Go *in* this *thy might,*
16: 5. wherein *his* great *strength* (lieth),
6,15. wherein *thy* great *strength* (lieth),
9. *his strength* was not known.
17. *my strength* will go from me,
19. *his strength* went from him.
30. bowed himself *with* (all his) *might;*
1Sa. 2: 9. *by strength* shall no man prevail.
28:20. there was no *strength* in him;
22. that thou mayest have *strength,*
30: 4. they had no more *power* to weep.
1 K.19: 8. and went *in the strength of* that meat
2 K.17:36. *with* great *power*
19: 3. *and* (there is) not *strength* to bring forth.
1Ch.26: 8. able men *for strength* for the service,
29: 2. I have prepared with all *my might*
12. in thine hand (is) *power* and might;
14. that we should be *able* (marg. obtain *strength*) to offer so willingly
2Ch 2: 6(5). is *able* (marg. hath obtained *strength*) to build him an house,
13:20. Neither did Jeroboam recover *strength*
14:11(10). them that have no *power:*
20: 6. in thine hand (is there not) *power* and
12. we have no *might*
22: 9. the house of Ahaziah had no *power*
25: 8. God hath *power* to help,
26:13. made war *with* mighty *power,*
Ezr. 2:69. They gave *after their ability*
10:13. we are not *able* (lit. not *power*) to stand
Neh 1:10. redeemed *by thy* great *power,*
4:10(4). *The strength of* the bearers
Job 3:17. the weary (marg. wearied (in) *strength*)
6:11. What (is) *my strength,*
12. (Is) *my strength the strength of* stones?
22. *or,* Give a reward for me *of your substance?*
9: 4. wise in heart, and mighty in *strength.*

Job 9:19. If (I speak) *of strength*,
23: 6. plead against me with (his) great *power?*
24:22. He draweth also the mighty *with his power:*
26: 2. helped (him that is) without *power?*
12. He divideth the sea *with his power,*
30: 2. *the strength of* their hands
18. By *the* great *force* (of my disease)
31:39. eaten *the fruits thereof* (marg. *strength*)
36: 5. (he is) mighty in *strength*
19. all the forces of *strength.*
22. God exalteth *by his power:*
37:23. (he is) excellent in *power,*
39:11. because *his strength* (is) great?
21. and rejoiceth *in* (his) *strength:*
40:16. *his strength* (is) in his loins,
Ps. 22:15(16). *My strength* is dried up
29: 4. the Lord (is) *powerful;* (marg. *in power*)
31:10(11). *my strength* faileth
33:16. is not delivered by much *strength.*
38:10(11). *my strength* faileth me:
65: 6(7). *by his strength* setteth fast the
71: 9. forsake me not when *my strength* faileth.
102:23(24). He weakened *my strength*
103:20. ye his angels, that excel in *strength,*
111: 6. shewed his people *the power of* his works,
147: 5. Great (is) our Lord, and of great *power:*
Pro. 5:10. Lest strangers be filled *with thy wealth;* (marg. *strength*)
14: 4. *by the strength of* the ox.
20:29. The glory of young men (is) *their strength:*
24: 5. a man of knowledge increaseth *strength.*
10. *thy strength* (is) small.
Ecc. 4: 1. side of their oppressors (there was) *power;*
9:10. do (it) *with thy might;*
Isa. 10:13. *By the strength of* my hand
37: 3. *and* (there is) not *strength* to bring forth.
40: 9. lift up thy voice *with strength;*
26. (he is) strong in *power;*
29. He giveth *power* to the faint;
31. shall renew (their) *strength;*
41: 1. let the people renew (their) *strength:*
44:12. worketh it with *the strength* of his arms: (lit. the arm of *his strength*)
— and his *strength* faileth:
49: 4. I have spent *my strength*
50: 2. have I no *power* to deliver?
63: 1. in the greatness of *his strength?*
Jer. 10:12. He hath made the earth *by his power,*
27: 5. *by my* great *power*
32:17. *by thy* great *power*
48:45. of Heshbon *because of the force:*
51:15. He hath made the earth *by his power,*
Lam 1: 6. they are gone without *strength*
14. he hath made *my strength* to fall,
Dan. 1: 4. such as (had) *ability* in them
8: 6. in the fury of *his power.*
7. there was no *power* in the ram
22. not *in his power.*
24. And *his power* shall be mighty, but not *by his own power:*
10: 8. there remained no *strength* in me:
— I retained no *strength.*
16. I have retained no *strength.*
17. there remained no *strength* in me,
11: 6. she shall not retain *the power of* the arm;
15. neither (shall there be any) *strength*
25. he shall stir up *his power*
Hos. 7: 9. Strangers have devoured *his strength,*
Am. 2:14. the strong shall not strengthen *his force,*
Mic. 3: 8. I am full of *power* by the spirit
Nah 1: 3. (is) slow to anger, and great in *power,*
2: 1(2). fortify (thy) *power* mightily.
Hab. 1:11. (imputing) this *his power* unto his god.
Zec. 4: 6. Not by might, nor *by power,*

3582 **כָּחַד** [*kāh-ghad'*].

* NIPHAL.—*Preterite.* *

Job 4: 7. where *were* the righteous *cut off?*
22:20. our substance *is* not *cut down,*
Ps. 69: 5(6). my sins *are* not *hid* from thee.
139:15. My substance *was* not *hid*
Hos. 5: 3. Israel *is* not *hid* from me:

NIPHAL.—*Future.*

Ex. 9:15. *and thou shalt be cut off* from the earth.
2Sa.18:13. *there is* no matter *hid* from the king,
Zec.11: 9. to be cut off, *let it be cut off;*

NIPHAL.—*Participle.*

Job 15:28. he dwelleth in *desolate* cities,
Zec.11: 9. *and that that is to be cut off,*
16. *those that be cut off,* (marg. or, *hidden*)

* PIEL.—*Preterite.* *

1Sa. 3:18. and *hid* nothing from him.
Job 6:10. *I have* not *concealed* the words
15:18. from their fathers, and *have* not *hid* (it):
Ps. 40:10(11). *I have* not *concealed* thy lovingkindness
Isa. 3: 9. *they hide* (it) not.

PIEL.—*Future.*

Gen47:18. *We will* not *hide* (it) from my lord,
Jos. 7:19. *hide* (it) not from me.
1Sa. 3:17. I pray thee *hide* (it) not from me:
— if *thou hide* (any) thing from me
2Sa.14:18. *Hide* not from me, I pray thee,
Job 27:11. with the Almighty *will I* not *conceal.*
Ps. 78: 4. *We will* not *hide* (them) from
Jer. 38:14. *hide* nothing from me.
25. *hide it* not from us,
50: 2. publish, (and) *conceal* not:

* HIPHIL.—*Preterite.* *

Ex. 23:23. *and I will cut them off.*

HIPHIL.—*Infinitive.*

1K. 13:34. *even to cut* (it) *off,* and to destroy

HIPHIL.—*Future.*

2Ch 32:21. the Lord sent an angel, *which cut off*
Job 20:12. (though) *he hide it* under his tongue;
Ps. 83: 4(5). Come, *and let us cut them off*
Zec.11: 8. Three shepherds *also I cut off*

כָּחַל [*kāh-ghal'*]. 3583

* KAL.—*Preterite.* *

Eze.23:40. *paintedst* thy eyes, and deckedst thyself

כָּחַשׁ *kāh-ghash'*. 3584

* KAL.—*Preterite.* *

Ps.109:24. my flesh *faileth* of fatness.

* NIPHAL.—*Future.* *

Deu33:29. *and* thine enemies *shall be found liars* (marg. *be subdued*)

* PIEL.—*Preterite.* *

Lev. 6: 2(5:21). *and lie* unto his neighbour
3(-:22). *and lieth* concerning it,
Jos. 7:11. have also stolen, and *dissembled*
1K. 13:18. (But) *he lied* unto him.
Job 8:18. *then* (it) *shall deny* him,
31:28. *I should have denied* the God (that)
Pro.30: 9. be full, *and deny* (thee), (marg. *belie*)
Jer. 5:12. *They have belied* (lit. *lied* against) the Lord,
Hab. 3:17. labour of the olive *shall fail,* (marg. *lie*)

PIEL.—*Infinitive.*

Isa. 59:13. transgressing *and lying* against the Lord,
Hos. 4: 2. By swearing, *and lying,* and killing,
Zec.13: 4. neither shall they wear a rough garment *to deceive:* (marg. *lie*)

PIEL.—*Future.*

Gen18:15. *Then* Sarah *denied,*
Lev.19:11. Ye shall not steal, neither *deal falsely,*
Jos. 24:27. lest *ye deny* your God.
Ps. 18:44(45). *shall submit themselves* unto me. (marg. *lie;* or, *yield feigned obedience*)
66: 3. *shall* thine enemies *submit themselves* (marg. *lie;* or, *yield feigned obedience*)
81:15(16). The haters of the Lord *should have submitted themselves* (marg. *lied* &c.)
Hos. 9: 2. the new wine *shall fail*

* HITHPAEL.—*Future.* *

2Sa.22:45. Strangers *shall submit themselves* (marg. *lie;* or, *yield feigned obedience*)

כַּחַשׁ *kah'-ghash*, m. 3585

Job 16: 8. *my leanness* rising up in me

Ps. 59:12(13). and for cursing *and lying* (which)
Hos. 7: 3. *and* the princes *with their lies.*
10:13. ye have eaten the fruit of *lies:*
11:12(12:1). compasseth me about *with lies,*
Nah. 3: 1. to the bloody city! it (is) all full of *lies*

3586 כֶּחָשִׁים *keh-ghāh-sheem'*, m. pl.

Isa. 30: 9. a rebellious people, *lying* children,

3587 כִּי *kee*, m.

Isa. 3:24. *burning* instead of beauty.

3588 כִּי *kee*, part.

Gen 1: 4. And God saw the light, *that* (it was)
2: 3. *because that* in it he had rested
5. *for* the Lord God had not caused it to rain
4:12. *When* thou tillest the ground,
24. *If* Cain shall be avenged sevenfold,
25. instead of Abel, *whom* Cain slew.
17:15. shalt not call her name Sarai, *but* Sarah
27:36. Is not he *rightly* named Jacob?
29:32. *for* she said, *Surely* the Lord hath looked upon my affliction; now *therefore* my
31:37. *Whereas* thou hast searched all my stuff,
Ex. 3:12. And he said, *Certainly* I will be with
5:11. *yet* not ought of your work shall be
10: 4. *Else*, if thou refuse to let my people go,
13:17. *although* that (was) near; *for* God said,
23: 9. *seeing* ye were strangers in the land
32:29. *even* every man upon his son,
Lev.13:18. The flesh also,)(in which, (lit. *for* in it)
40. And the man)(whose hair (lit. *if* his hair)
20:27. A man also or woman that hath (lit. *if* there be in them)
24:15. Whosoever curseth (lit. a man a man *if* he curse)
Nu. 16:13. *except* thou make thyself altogether
Deu 12:12. *forasmuch as* he hath no part
14:24. too long for thee, *so that* thou art not
19: 6. pursue the slayer, *while* his heart is hot,
— *inasmuch as* he hated him not
29:19(18). I shall have peace, *though* I walk
31:18. *in that* they are turned unto other gods.
32:30. except)(their Rock had sold them,
Jos. 2:12. *since* I have shewed you kindness,
24. *Truly* the Lord hath delivered
5: 5. *Now* all the people that came out
10: 1. heard *how* Joshua had taken Ai,
1Sa. 2:21. *And* the Lord visited Hannah,
15:35. *nevertheless* Samuel mourned for Saul:
27: 1. better for me *than that* I should speedily
1K. 1:13. *Assuredly* Solomon thy son shall reign
Job 22: 2. *as* he that is wise may be profitable
34:33. *whether* thou refuse, *or whether* thou choose;
Isa. 5:10. *Yea*, ten acres of vineyard shall yield
63:16. *Doubtless* thou (art) our father,
Jer. 8:22. why *then* is not the health
&c. &c. &c.

Observe the meaning of עַד כִּי

Gen 49:10. The sceptre shall not depart...*until* Shiloh
2Sa. 23:10. smote the Philistines *until* his hand was
2Ch. 26:15. marvellously helped, *till* he was strong.

For the other combinations of כִּי, such as כִּי אִם, אֶפֶס כִּי, &c., see the respective words with which it is so joined.

3589 כִּיד [*keed*], m.

Job 21:20. His eyes shall see *his destruction,*

3590 כִּידוֹד [*kee-dōhd'*], m.

Job 41:19(11). *sparks of* fire leap out.

כִּידוֹן *kee-dōhn'*, m. 3591

Jos. 8:18. Stretch out *the spear*
— And Joshua stretched out *the spear*
26. he stretched out *the spear,*
1Sa. 17: 6. *and a target* of brass between his shoulders. (marg. or, *gorget*)
45. with a spear, *and with a shield:*
Job 39:23. the glittering spear *and the shield.*
41:29(21). he laugheth at the shaking of *a spear.*
Jer. 6:23. They shall lay hold on bow *and spear;*
50:42. They shall hold the bow *and the lance:*

כִּידוֹר *kee-dōhr'*, m. 3593

Job 15:24. as a king ready *to the battle.*

כִּיּוֹר *keey-yōhr'*, m. 3595

Ex. 30:18. Thou shalt also make *a laver*
28 & 31:9 & 35:16. *the laver* and his foot.
38: 8. he made *the laver* (of) brass,
39:39. *the laver* and his foot,
40: 7. thou shalt set *the laver* between
11. thou shalt anoint *the laver*
30. he set *the laver* between
Lev. 8:11. *the laver* and his foot,
1Sa. 2:14. he struck (it) *into the pan,*
1K. 7:30. under *the laver* (were) undersetters
38. Then made he ten *lavers* of brass: one *laver* contained forty baths: (and) every *laver* was four cubits: (and) upon every one of the ten bases one *laver.*
40. And Hiram made *the lavers,*
43. ten *lavers* on the bases;
2K. 16:17. and removed *the laver* from off them;
2Ch 4: 6. He made also ten *lavers,*
14. *lavers* made he upon the bases; (marg. or, *caldrons*)
6:13. Solomon had made *a* brasen *scaffold,*
Zec. 12: 6. *like an hearth of* fire

כִּילַי *kee-lah'y*, m. 3596

[see also כֵּלַי]

Isa. 32: 5. *nor the churl* said (to be) bountiful.

כֵּילַפּוֹת *kēh-lap-pōhth'*, f. pl. 3597

Ps. 74: 6. with axes *and hammers.*

כִּימָה *kee-māh'*, f. 3598

Job 9: 9. maketh Arcturus, Orion, *and Pleiades,*
38:31. the sweet influences of *Pleiades,*
Am. 5: 8. (him) that maketh *the seven stars*

כִּיס *kees*, m. 3599

Deu 25:13. Thou shalt not have *in thy bag* divers
Pro. 1:14. let us all have one *purse:*
16:11. all the weights *of the bag*
23:31. (כתיב) when it giveth his colour *in the cup,*
Isa. 46: 6. They lavish gold *out of the bag,*
Mic. 6:11. *and with the bag of* deceitful weights?

כִּירַיִם *kee-rah'-yim*, m. dual. 3600

Lev. 11:35. oven, *or ranges for pots,*

כִּישׁוֹר *kee-shōhr'*, m. 3601

Pro. 31:19. She layeth her hands *to the spindle,*

3602 ## כָּכָה *kāh'-chāh*, part.

Ex. 12:11. *And thus* shall ye eat it;
Nu. 15:12. *so* shall ye do to every one
2Ch18:19. And one spake saying *after this manner*, and another saying *after that manner*.
Est. 9:26. they had seen concerning *this matter*,
Jer. 19:11. *Even so* will I break this people
Hos10:15. *So* shall Beth-el do unto you
&c.

With prefix שֶׁכָּכָה

Ps. 144:15. Happy (is that) people, *that* is *in such a case*
Cant.5: 9. *that* thou dost *so* charge us?

3603 ## כִּכָּר *kik-kāhr'*, f.

Gen13:10, 11. all *the plain of* Jordan,
12. the cities of *the plain*,
19:17. neither stay thou in all *the plain*;
25. and all *the plain*,
28. all the land of *the plain*,
29. the cities of *the plain*,
Ex. 25:39. *a talent of* pure gold
29:23. *And* one *loaf of* bread,
37:24. *a talent* of pure gold
38:24. twenty and nine *talents*,
25. an hundred *talents*,
27. the hundred *talents* of silver
— the hundred *talents*, *a talent* for a socket.
29. brass of the offering (was) seventy *talents*,
Deu34: 3. *the plain* of the valley
Jud. 8: 5. Give, I pray you, *loaves of* bread
1Sa. 2:36. *and a morsel of* bread,
10: 3. another carrying three *loaves of* bread,
2Sa. 12:30. *a talent of* gold
18:23. by the way of *the plain*,
1K. 7:46. *In the plain of* Jordan
9:14. sixscore *talents of* gold.
28. four hundred and twenty *talents*,
10:10. an hundred and twenty *talents of* gold,
14. six hundred threescore and six *talents*
16:24. the hill Samaria of Shemer *for two talents*
20:39. thou shalt pay *a talent of* silver.
2K. 5: 5. and took with him ten *talents of* silver,
22. give them, I pray thee, *a talent of* silver,
23. And Naaman said,...take *two talents*. And he urged him, and bound *two talents* of
15:19. a thousand *talents of* silver,
18:14. three hundred *talents of* silver and thirty *talents of* gold.
23:33. an hundred *talents of* silver, *and a talent*
1Ch 16: 3. to every one *a loaf of* bread,
19: 6. a thousand *talents of* silver
20: 2. *a talent of* gold,
22:14. an hundred thousand *talents* of gold, and a thousand thousand *talents* of silver;
29: 4. three thousand *talents of* gold,
— seven thousand *talents of* refined silver,
7. of gold five thousand *talents*
— of silver ten thousand *talents*, and of brass eighteen thousand *talents*, and one hundred thousand *talents* of iron.
2Ch 3: 8. (amounting) *to* six hundred *talents*.
4:17. *In the plain of* Jordan
8:18. four hundred and fifty *talents of* gold,
9: 9. an hundred and twenty *talents of* gold,
13. six hundred and threescore and six *talents of* gold;
25: 6. an hundred *talents of* silver.
9. the hundred *talents* which I have given
27: 5. an hundred *talents of* silver,
36: 3. an hundred *talents of* silver *and a talent of*
Ezr. 8:26. six hundred and fifty *talents* of silver, and silver vessels an hundred *talents*, (and) of gold an hundred *talents*;
Neh 3:22. the men of *the plain*.
12:28. *the plain* country
Est. 3: 9. I will pay ten thousand *talents of*
Pro. 6:26. *a piece of* bread:
Jer. 37:21. *a piece of* bread
Zec. 5: 7. there was lifted up *a talent of* lead: (marg. or, *weighty piece*)

כַּכְּרִין *kak-k'reen'*, Ch. f. pl. 3604

Ezr. 7:22. Unto an hundred *talents* of silver,

כֹּל *kōhl*, part. 3605

Properly a noun, but used very extensively as a particle.

Gen 3:17. shalt thou eat (of) it *all* the days of
6:17. *every thing* that (is) in the earth shall die.
7: 4. *every* living substance that I have made
8:19. *whatsoever* creepeth upon the earth,
30:33. *every one* that (is) not speckled
33:11. because I have *enough*. (lit. *all*)
Ex. 12: 6. the *whole* assembly of the congregation
16:23. and)(that which remaineth over lay
35: 5. *whosoever* (is) of a willing heart,
22. *as many as* were willing hearted,
35. to work *all manner of* work,
Lev. 7:27. that eateth *any manner of* blood,
11:27. *whoso* toucheth their carcase shall be
Nu. 31:35. thirty and two thousand persons *in all*,
Deu 4:23. the likeness of *any* (thing),
2Sa. 3:35. if I taste bread, or *ought* else,
Ps. 39: 5(6). *every* man at his best state (is) *altogether*
Isa. 3: 1. *the whole* stay of bread, *and the whole*
8: 9. give ear, *all* ye of far countries:
30:32. And (in) *every place* where the grounded staff shall pass, (marg. *every* passing of the rod founded)
43: 7. *every one* that is called by my name:
Zep 3: 7. howsoever (lit *all* that) I punished
&c. &c. &c.

It is sometimes combined in translation with an accompanying negative:—

Gen11: 6. *nothing* will be restrained from them,
Pro. 13: 7. maketh himself rich, *yet* (hath) *nothing*:
&c.

It is often found with the article and with other prefixes, the meaning of the word itself being unchanged. The pronominal suffixes with which it is also often combined, do not influence the meaning of the word itself.

כֹּל *kōhl*, Ch. 3606

כ״ ק״ דְּנָה or כָּל־קֳבֵל דִּי marked [2].

Ezr. 4:14. Now because[2] we have
20. which have ruled *over all* (countries)
5: 7. Unto Darius the king, *all* peace.
6:11. a decree, that *whosoever* shall alter this
12. destroy *all* kings and people,
17. for a sin offering for *all* Israel,
7:13. a decree, that *all* they of the people of
14. Forasmuch as[2] thou art sent
16. *And all* the silver and gold that thou canst find *in all* the province of
17. That[2] thou mayest buy
21. do make a decree *to all* the treasurers which (are) beyond the river, that *whatsoever*
23. *Whatsoever* is commanded by the God
24. that touching *any* of the priests
25. judges, which may judge *all* the people that (are) beyond the river, *all* such as
26. *And whosoever* will not do the law
Dan 2: 8. because[2] ye see the thing
10. therefore[2] (there is) *no* (lit. not *any*) king, lord, nor ruler, (that) asked such things *at any* magician, or
12. For this cause[2] the king
— commanded to destroy *all* the wise
24. Therefore[2] Daniel went in
30. that I have more than *any* living,
35. *that no* (lit. *any* not) place was found for
— a great mountain, and filled the *whole*
38. *And wheresoever* the children of men
— and hath made thee ruler *over them all*.
39. which shall bear rule *over all* the earth.
40. forasmuch as[2] iron breaketh in pieces and subdueth *all* (things): and as iron that breaketh *all* these,

Dan 2:41. forasmuch as[2] thou sawest the iron
44. and consume *all* these kingdoms,
45. Forasmuch as[2] thou sawest that the stone
48. made him ruler over the *whole* province
— over *all* the wise (men) of Babylon.
3: 2, 3. *and all* the rulers of the provinces,
5, 7, 10, 15. *and all* kinds of musick,
7. Therefore[2] at that time, when *all* the people heard the sound
— *all* the people, the nations,
8. Wherefore[2] at that time
10. that *every* man that shall hear
22. Therefore[2] because the
28. that they might not serve nor worship *any*
29. That *every* people, nation, and language,
— because[2] there is no other
4: 1(3:31). *unto all* people, nations, and languages, that dwell *in all* the earth;
6(3). to bring in *all* the wise (men)
9(6). *and no* secret troubleth thee,
11(8). thereof to the end of *all* the earth:
12(9),21(18). and in it (was) meat *for all:*
—(-). *all* flesh was fed of it.
18(15). forasmuch as[2] *all* the wise (men)
20(17). and the sight thereof to *all* the earth;
28(25). *All* this came upon the king
35(32). *And all* the inhabitants of the earth
37(34). *all* whose works (are) truth,
5: 7. Whosoever (lit. *any* man that) shall read
8. Then came in *all* the king's wise (men):
12. Forasmuch as[2] an excellent spirit,
19. *all* people, nations, and languages,
22. though[2] thou knewest *all*
23. *and* whose (are) *all* thy ways,
6: 1(2). which should be *over the whole*
3(4). because[2] an excellent
—(-). to set him over the *whole* realm.
4(5). *but* they could find none (lit. not *any*)
—(-). forasmuch as[2] he (was) faithful, neither was there *any* error or
5(6). We shall not find *any* occasion against
7(8). *All* the presidents of the kingdom,
—(-). that *whosoever* shall ask a petition of *any* God or man for thirty days,
9(10). Wherefore[2] king Darius
10(11). as[2] he did aforetime.
12(13). that *every* man that shall ask (a petition) of *any* God or man
15(16). That no (lit. not *any*) decree nor
22(23). forasmuch as[2] before him innocency
23(24). *and no manner* of hurt was found
24(25). *and* brake *all* their bones in pieces
25(26). unto *all* people, nations, and languages, that dwell *in all* the earth;
26(27). That *in every* dominion of my
7: 7. it (was) diverse from *all* the beasts
14. *that all* people, nations, and languages,
16. and asked him the truth of *all* this.
19. which was diverse from *all* the others,
23. which shall be diverse from *all* kingdoms, and shall devour the *whole* earth,
27. the kingdom under the *whole* heaven,
— *and all* dominions shall serve and obey

3607

כָּלָא [*kāh-lāh'*].

* KAL.—*Preterite.* *

1Sa. 6:10. and *shut up* their calves at home:
25:33. *hast kept me* this day
Ps. 119:101. *I have refrained* my feet
Jer. 32: 3. Zedekiah ... *had shut him up,*
Hag 1:10. the heaven over you *is stayed* from dew, and the earth *is stayed* (from) her fruit.

KAL.—*Infinitive.*

Ecc. 8: 8. hath power over the spirit *to retain*

KAL.—*Imperative.*

Nu. 11:28. My lord Moses, *forbid them.*

KAL.—*Future.*

Gen 23: 6. none of us *shall withhold* from thee
Ps. 40: 9(10). *I have* not *refrained* my lips,
11(12). *Withhold* not *thou* thy tender mercies
Isa. 43: 6. *Keep* not *back:*

KAL.—*Participle.* Paül.

Ps. 88: 8(9). (I am) *shut up,* and I cannot come
Jer. 32: 2. Jeremiah the prophet was *shut up*

* NIPHAL.—*Future.* *

Gen 8: 2. *and* the rain from heaven *was restrained;*
Ex. 36: 6. *So* the people *were restrained*
Eze. 31:15. *and* the great waters *were stayed:*

* PIEL.—*Infinitive.* *

Dan 9:24. *to finish* the transgression, (marg. or, *restrain*)

N. B. See also כָּלָה, with which this word is connected in forms, as well as often in signification.

כֶּלֶא *keh'-leh,* m. 3608

1 K. 22:27. Put this (fellow) in *the prison,* (lit. house of *restraint*)
2 K. 17: 4. him in *prison.* (lit. house of *restraint*)
25:27. out of *prison;* (lit. house of *restraint*)
29. And changed *his prison* garments:
2Ch 18:26. Put this (fellow) in *the prison,* (lit. house of *restraint*)
Isa. 42: 7. out of the *prison* house.
22. they are hid in *prison* houses:
Jer. 37:15. that *the prison.* (lit. the house of *restraint*)
18. ye have put me in *prison?* (lit. *id.*)
52:33. And changed *his prison* garments:

כִּלְאַיִם *kil-ah'-yim,* dual. 3610

Lev. 19:19. gender *with a diverse kind:* thou shalt not sow thy field *with mingled seed:* neither shall a garment *mingled* of linen and
Deu 22: 9. Thou shalt not sow ... *with divers seeds:*

כֶּלֶב *keh'-lev,* m. 3611

Ex. 11: 7. shall not *a dog* move his tongue,
22:31(30). ye shall cast it *to the dogs.*
Deu 23:18(19). the price of *a dog,*
Jud. 7: 5. as *a dog* lappeth,
1Sa. 17:43. (Am) I *a dog,* that thou comest to me
24:14(15). after *a* dead *dog,*
2Sa. 3: 8. (Am) I *a dog*'s head,
9: 8. such *a* dead *dog* as I (am)?
16: 9. Why should this dead *dog* curse
1K. 14:11. dieth of Jeroboam ... shall *the dogs* eat;
16: 4. dieth of Baasha ... shall *the dogs* eat;
21:19. where *dogs* licked the blood of Naboth shall *dogs* lick thy blood,
23. *The dogs* shall eat Jezebel
24. Him that dieth of Ahab ... *the dogs* shall
22:38. *the dogs* licked up his blood;
2K. 8:13. (is) thy servant *a dog,*
9:10. *the dogs* shall eat Jezebel
36. shall *dogs* eat the flesh of Jezebel:
Job. 30: 1. *the dogs of* my flock.
Ps. 22:16(17). For *dogs* have compassed me:
20(21). from the power of *the dog.*
59: 6(7). they make a noise *like a dog,*
14(15). let them make a noise *like a dog,*
68:23(24). the tongue of *thy dogs*
Pro. 26:11. *As a dog* returneth to his vomit,
17. one that taketh *a dog* by the ears.
Ecc. 9: 4. *a* living *dog* is better than a dead lion.
Isa. 56:10. they (are) all dumb *dogs,*
11. *Yea,* (they are) greedy *dogs*
66: 3. he cut off *a dog*'s neck;
Jer. 15: 3. and *the dogs* to tear,

כָּלָה *kāh-lāh'.* 3615

* KAL.—*Preterite.* *

1Sa. 20: 7. evil *is determined* by him.
9. evil *were determined* by my father
25:17. evil *is determined* against our master,
1K. 6:38. the eighth month, *was* the house *finished*

1 K. 17:16. the barrel of meal *wasted* not,
Est. 7: 7. *there was* evil *determined* against him
Job. 7: 9. (As) the cloud *is consumed*
19:27. my reins *be consumed*
Ps. 31:10(11). my life *is spent* with grief,
37:20. *they shall consume;* into smoke *shall they consume away.*
39:10(11). *I am consumed* by the blow of
69: 3(4). mine eyes *fail* while I wait
73:26. My flesh and my heart *faileth:*
84: 2(3). My soul longeth, yea, even *fainteth*
90: 7. *we are consumed* by thine anger,
102: 3(4). my days *are consumed*
119:81. My soul *fainteth* for thy salvation:
82. Mine eyes *fail* for thy word,
123. Mine eyes *fail* for thy salvation,
143: 7. O Lord: my spirit *faileth:*
Isa. 10:25. *and* the indignation *shall cease,*
15: 6. the grass *faileth,*
16: 4. the spoiler *ceaseth,*
21:16. *and* all the glory of Kedar *shall fail:*
24:13. when the vintage *is done,*
29:20. *and* the scorner *is consumed,*
32:10. the vintage *shall fail,*
Jer. 8:20. the summer *is ended,*
14: 6. their eyes *did fail,*
Lam 2:11. Mine eyes *do fail* with tears,
3:22. his compassions *fail* not.
Eze. 5:13. *Thus shall* mine anger *be accomplished,*
13:14. and *ye shall be consumed* in the midst
Dan 11:36. till the indignation *be accomplished:*
Mal 3: 6. ye sons of Jacob *are* not *consumed.*

KAL.—*Infinitive.*

Ru. 2:23. unto *the end of* barley harvest
1 Ch. 28:20. until thou *hast finished* all the work
2Ch. 8:16. until *it was finished.*
29:28. until the burnt offering *was finished.*
34. till the work *was ended,*
36:22. *that* the word of the Lord... *might be accomplished,*
Ezr. 1: 1. *that* the word of the Lord... *might be fulfilled,*
Ps. 71: 9. *when* my strength *faileth.*
Pro 5:11. *when* thy flesh and thy body *are consumed,*
Jer. 44:27. until *there be an end of them.*

KAL.—*Future.*

Gen 21:15. *And* the water *was spent* in the bottle,
41:53. *And* the seven years of plenteousness,... *were ended.*
Ex. 39:32. *Thus was* all the work... *finished:*
1 K. 17:14. The barrel of meal *shall* not *waste,*
Job 4: 9. breath of his nostrils *are they consumed.*
7: 6. *and are spent* without hope.
11:20. the eyes of the wicked *shall fail,*
17: 5. the eyes of his children *shall fail.*
33:21. His flesh *is consumed away,*
Ps. 71:13. Let them be confounded (and) *consumed*
Pro. 22: 8. the rod of his anger *shall fail.*
Isa. 1:28. that forsake the Lord *shall be consumed.*
31: 3. *they* all *shall fail* together.
Jer. 16: 4. *they shall be consumed*
20:18. *that* my days *should be consumed*
Lam 4:17. our eyes as yet *failed*
Eze. 5:12. with famine *shall they be consumed*
Dan 12: 7. all these (things) *shall be finished.*

* PIEL.—*Preterite.* *

Gen 18:33. as soon as *he had left* communing
24:15. before *he had done* speaking,
19. until *they have done* drinking.
22. as the camels *had done* drinking,
27:30. as soon as Isaac *had made an end*
41:30. *and* the famine *shall consume* the land;
43: 2. when *they had* eaten up (lit. *had made an end* of eating) the corn
44:12. began at the eldest, and *left* at the
Ex. 5:14. Wherefore *have ye* not *fulfilled*
33: 5. I will come up... *and consume thee:*
Lev. 16:20. And *when he hath made an end*
Nu. 4:15. And *when* Aaron and his sons *have made an end.*
25:11. *I consumed* not the children of Israel
Jos. 24:20. he will turn... *and consume* you,
Jud. 3:18. when *he had made an end* to offer
Ru. 2:21. until *they have ended* all my harvest.
3:18. until *he have finished* the thing

2Sa. 21: 5. The man that *consumed us,*
1 K. 1:41. as *they had made an end* of eating.
1 Ch 27:24. Joab... began to number, but *he finished* not
2Ch 8: 8. whom the children of Israel *consumed* not,
29:17. in the sixteenth day... *they made an end.*
31: 7. and *finished* (them) in the seventh month.
Ps. 90: 9. *we spend* our years as a tale (that is told).
119:87. *They had* almost *consumed me*
Pro. 16:30. moving his lips *he bringeth* evil *to pass.*
Isa. 27:10. *and consume* the branches thereof.
49: 4. *I have spent* my strength for nought,
Jer. 5: 3. *thou hast consumed them,*
Lam. 2:22. *hath* mine enemy *consumed.*
4:11. The Lord *hath accomplished* his fury;
Eze. 4: 6. And *when thou hast accomplished*
6:12. *thus will I accomplish* my fury
7: 8. *and accomplish* mine anger upon thee:
13:15. *Thus will I accomplish* my wrath
22:31. *I have consumed them* with the fire
42:15. *Now when he had made an end* of
Hos. 11: 6. *and shall consume* his branches,
Am. 7: 2. *when they had made an end* of eating
Zec. 5: 4. *and shall consume it* with the timber

PIEL.—*Infinitive.*

Ex. 31:18. *when he had made an end* of communing
32:12. *and to consume them* from the face of the
Lev. 26:44. *to destroy them utterly,*
Nu. 7: 1. Moses had *fully* set up the tabernacle,
16:31. *as he had made an end* of speaking
Deu 7:22. thou mayest not *consume them*
20: 9. *when* the officers *have made an end*
28:21. until *he have consumed* thee
31:24. *when* Moses *had made an end*
Jos. 8:24. *when* Israel *had made an end* of slaying
10:20. *when* Joshua... *had made an end*
Jud. 15:17. *when he had made an end* of speaking,
Ru. 3: 3. until *he shall have done* eating
1 Sa. 2:33. *to consume* thine eyes,
3:12. *I will also make an end.* (marg. *and ending*)
13:10. *as soon as he had made an end*
15:18. until *they be consumed.*
18: 1. *when he had made an end* of speaking
24:16(17). *when* David *had made an end*
2Sa. 11:19. *When thou hast made an end*
13:36. *as soon as he had made an end*
22:38. until *I had consumed them.*
1 K. 3: 1. until *he had made an end*
8:54. *when* Solomon *had made an end*
9: 1. *when* Solomon *had finished* the building
22:11. until thou *have consumed them.*
2K. 10:25. *as soon as he had made an end*
13:17. till thou *have consumed* (them).
19. till thou *hadst consumed* (it):
2Ch 7: 1. Now *when* Solomon *had made an end*
18:10. until *they be consumed.*
20:23. *and when they had made an end*
24:10. until *they had made an end.*
14. *And when they had finished* (it),
29:29. *And when* they *had made an end*
31: 1. *Now when* all this *was finished,*
— until *they had utterly destroyed them all.*
Ezr. 9: 1. *Now when* these things *were done,*
14. till *thou hadst consumed* (us),
Ps. 18:37(38). till *they were consumed.*
Jer. 9:16(15). till *I have consumed* them.
26: 8 & 43:1. *when* Jeremiah *had made an end*
49:37. till *I have consumed* them:
51:63. *when thou hast made an end*
Eze. 4: 8. till *thou hast ended* the days of
5:13. *when I have accomplished* my fury
20: 8, 21. *to accomplish* my anger
13. would pour out my fury... *to consume them.*
43:23. *When thou hast made an end*
Dan 12: 7. *and when he shall have accomplished*

PIEL.—*Imperative.*

Ex. 5:13. *Fulfil* your works, (your) daily tasks,
Ps. 59:13(14). *Consume* (them) in wrath, *consume* (them), that they (may) not (be):
74:11. thy right hand? *pluck* (it) out

PIEL.—*Future.*

Gen 2: 2. *And* on the seventh day God *ended*
6:16. in a cubit *shalt thou finish it*
17:22. *And he left off* talking
24:19. And *when she had done* giving him drink,

Gen24:45. before *I had done* speaking
49:33. And *when* Jacob *had made an end*
Ex. 32:10. *that I may consume them:*
33: 3. lest *I consume thee* in the way.
34:33. *And* (till) Moses *had done* speaking
40:33. *So* Moses *finished* the work.
Lev.19: 9. *thou shalt* not *wholly reap* the corners of
23:22. *thou shalt* not *make clean riddance* of
Nu. 16:21. *that I may consume* them in a moment.
45(17:10). *that I may consume* them as in a
17:10(25). *and thou shalt quite take away* their
Deu26:12. When *thou hast made an end* of tithing
32:23. *I will spend* mine arrows upon them.
45. *And* Moses *made an end* of speaking
Jos. 19:49. *When they had made an end* of dividing
51. *So they made an end* of dividing the
1Sa.10:13. *when he had made an end* of prophesying,
2Sa. 6:18. *as soon as* David *had made an end* of
13:39. *And* (the soul of) king David *longed*
22:39. *And I have consumed them,*
1K. 6: 9. he built the house, *and finished it;*
14. Solomon built the house, *and finished it.*
7: 1. *and he finished* all his house.
40. *So* Hiram *made an end*
1Ch 16: 2. And *when* David *had made an end*
2Ch 4:11. *And* Huram *finished* the work (marg. *finished* to make)
7:11. *Thus* Solomon *finished* the house
Ezr.10:17. *And they made an end*
Neh 4: 2(3:34). *will they make an end* in a day?
Job 21:13. *They spend* their days in wealth,
31:16. *have caused* the eyes of the widow *to fail;*
36:11. *they shall spend* their days in prosperity,
Ps. 78:33. *Therefore* their days *did he consume*
Isa. 10:18. And *shall consume* the glory of
Jer. 10:25. and devoured him, *and consumed him,*
Eze.43: 8. *wherefore I have consumed* them
27. And *when* these days *are expired,*

PIEL.—*Participle.*

Lev.26:16. *that shall consume* the eyes,
Job 9:22. He *destroyeth* the perfect and the wicked.
Jer. 14:12. I *will consume* them by the sword,

* PUAL.—*Preterite.* *

Ps. 72:20. The prayers of David the son of Jesse *are ended.*

PUAL.—*Future.*

Gen. 2: 1. *Thus* the heavens and the earth *were finished,*

[N. B. See also כָּלָא, and the note at the end of the passages under that word.]

3617 **כָּלָה** *kāh-lāh'*, f.

Gen.18:21. whether they have done *altogether*
Ex. 11: 1. thrust you out hence *altogether.*
1 Sa.20:33. Jonathan knew that it *was determined*
2Ch. 12:12. he would not destroy (him) *altogether:*
Neh. 9:31. thou didst not *utterly consume* them, (lit. madest not *a destruction*)
Isa. 10:23. the Lord...shall make *a consumption,*
28:22. *a consumption,* even determined
Jer. 4:27. *yet* will I not make *a full end.*
5:10. *but* make not *a full end:*
18. I will not make *a full end*
30:11. though I make *a full end*
— yet will I not make *a full end*
46:28. I will make *a full end*
— I will not make *a full end*
Eze.11:13. Ah Lord God! wilt thou make *a full end*
13:13. great hailstones in (my) fury *to consume*
20:17. neither did I make *an end* of them
Dan. 9:27 until *the consummation,*
11:16. *which* by his hand *shall be consumed.* (lit. *and destruction* in his hand)
Nah. 1: 8. he will make *an utter end*
9. he will make *an utter end:*
Zep 1:18. he shall make even *a speedy riddance*

3616 **כָּלֶה** [*kāh-leh'*] adj.

Deu.28:32. thine eyes shall look, *and fail*

כַּלָּה *kal-lāh'*, f. 3618

Gen11:31. and Sarai *his daughter in law,*
38:11. said Judah to Tamar *his daughter in law,*
16. not that she (was) *his daughter in law.*
24. Tamar *thy daughter in law* hath played
Lev.18:15. the nakedness of *thy daughter in law:*
20:12. if a man lie with *his daughter in law,*
Ru. 1: 6. she arose *with her daughters in law,*
7. *her* two *daughters in law* with her;
8. Naomi said unto *her* two *daughters in law,*
22. and Ruth...*her daughter in law,*
2:20. Naomi said *unto her daughter in law,*
22. Ruth *her daughter in law,*
4:15. *thy daughter in law,* which loveth thee,
1Sa. 4:19. *And his daughter in law,* Phinehas' wife,
1Ch 2: 4. Tamar *his daughter in law*
Cant. 4: 8. with me from Lebanon, (my) *spouse,*
9. ravished my heart, my sister, (my) *spouse;*
10. fair is thy love, my sister, (my) *spouse!*
11. Thy lips, O (my) *spouse,*
12. inclosed (is) my sister, (my) *spouse;*
5: 1. into my garden, my sister, (my) *spouse:*
Isa. 49:18. bind them (on thee), *as a bride* (doeth).
61:10. and *as a bride* adorneth (herself)
62: 5. the bridegroom rejoiceth over *the bride,*
Jer. 2:32. a maid forget her ornaments, (or) *a bride'*
7:34 & 16:9 & 25:10 & 33:11. voice of *the bride:*
Eze.22:11. defiled *his daughter in law;*
Hos. 4:13. *and your spouses* shall commit adultery.
14. *your spouses* when they commit adultery:
Joel 2:16. *and the bride* out of her closet.
Mic. 7: 6. *the daughter in law* against her mother in

כְּלוּא *k'loo*, m. (קרי) 3628

Jer. 37: 4. they had not put him into *prison.* (lit. house of *restraint*)
52:31. brought him forth out of *prison,* (lit. house of *restraint*)

כְּלוּב *k'loov*, m. 3619

Jer. 5:27. *As a cage* (marg. or, *coop*) is full of birds,
Am. 8: 1, 2. *a basket of* summer fruit.

כְּלוּלוֹת [*k'loo-lōhth'*], f. pl. 3623

Jer. 2: 2. the love of *thine espousals,*

כֶּלַח *keh'-lagh*, m. 3624

Job 5:26. shalt come to (thy) grave *in a full age,*
30: 2. in whom *old age* was perished?

כֵּלַי *kēh-lah'y*, m. 3596

[see also כִּילַי]

Isa. 32: 7. The instruments *also of the churl*

כְּלִי *k'lee*, m. 3627

Gen24:53. the servant brought forth *jewels of* silver, *and jewels of* gold,
27: 3. therefore take, I pray thee, *thy weapons,*
31:37. thou hast searched all *my stuff,* what hast thou found of all thy houshold *stuff?*
42:25. Joseph commanded to fill *their sacks*
43:11. take of the best fruits ... *in your vessels,*
45:20. Also regard not *your stuff;*
49: 5. *instruments of* cruelty (are in) their
Ex. 3:22. shall borrow...*jewels of* silver, *and jewels of*
11: 2. neighbour, *jewels of* silver, *and jewels of*
12:35. borrowed...*jewels of* silver, *and jewels of*
22: 7(6). money or *stuff* to keep,
25: 9. all *the instruments thereof,*
39. with all these *vessels.*
27: 3. all *the vessels thereof*
19. All *the vessels of* the tabernacle

Ex. 30:27. all *his vessels*, and the candlestick and *his vessels*,
28. the altar...with all *his vessels*,
31: 7. all *the furniture of* the tabernacle, (marg. *vessels*)
8. the table and *his furniture*, and the pure candlestick with all *his furniture*,
9. the altar...with all *his furniture*,
35:13. The table,...and all *his vessels*,
14. The candlestick...and *his furniture*,
16. his staves, and all *his vessels*,
22. all *jewels of* gold:
37:16. he made *the vessels*
24. all *the vessels thereof*.
38: 3, 30. all *the vessels of* the altar,
— all *the vessels thereof*
39:33. all *his furniture*,
36. The table, (and) all *the vessels thereof*,
37. all *the vessels thereof*,
39. his staves, and all *his vessels*,
40. all *the vessels of* the service
40: 9. all *the vessels thereof*:
10. the altar...and all *his vessels*,
Lev. 6:28(21). *But the* earthen *vessel* wherein it is
—(—). and if it be sodden *in a* brasen *pot*,
8:11. the altar and all *his vessels*,
11:32. any *vessel of* wood,
— whatsoever *vessel* (it be),
33. every earthen *vessel*,
34. in every (such) *vessel*
13:49. in any *thing of* skin; (marg. *vessel*, or, *instrument*)
52. or any *thing of* skin,
53, 57. or in any *thing of* skin;
58. whatsoever *thing of* skin (it be),
59. or any *thing of* skins,
14: 5, 50. in *an* earthen *vessel*
15: 4. every *thing*, whereon he sitteth,
6. he that sitteth on (any) *thing*
12. *And the vessel of* earth,
— and every *vessel of* wood
22. whosoever toucheth any *thing*
23. any *thing* whereon she sitteth,
26. whatsoever (lit. what *thing* soever) she
Nu. 1:50, 50. all *the vessels thereof*,
3: 8. all *the instruments of* the tabernacle
31. *and the vessels of* the sanctuary
36. all *the vessels thereof*,
4: 9. all *the* oil *vessels thereof*,
10. all *the vessels thereof*
12. all *the instruments of* ministry,
14. all *the vessels thereof*,
— all *the vessels of* the altar;
15. all *the vessels of* the sanctuary,
16. *and in the vessels thereof*.
26. *the instruments of* their service,
32. all *their instruments*,
— *the instruments of* the charge
5:17. *in an* earthen *vessel;*
7: 1. all *the instruments thereof*, both the altar and all *the vessels thereof*,
85. all *the* silver *vessels*
18: 3. *the vessels of* the sanctuary
19:15. And every open *vessel*,
17. water shall be put thereto *in a vessel:*
18. and upon all *the vessels*,
31: 6. *with the* holy *instruments*,
20. all *that is made of* skins,
— all *things* made of wood.
50. *jewels of* gold, chains, and bracelets,
51. all wrought *jewels*.
35:16. *with an instrument of* iron,
18. *with an* hand *weapon of* wood,
22. or have cast upon him any *thing*
Deu 1:41. every man his *weapons of* war,
22: 5. *that which pertaineth unto* a man,
23:24(25). thou shalt not put (any) in *thy vessel*.
Jos. 6:19. *and vessels of* brass and iron,
24. *and the vessels of* brass and of iron,
7:11. *among their own stuff*.
Jud. 9:54. the young man *his armour*bearer,
18:11. six hundred men appointed with *weapons of*
16. men appointed with their *weapons of*
17. appointed with *weapons of* war.
Ru. 2: 9. go unto *the vessels*, and drink
1 Sa. 6: 8. and put *the jewels of* gold,...in a coffer
15. the coffer...wherein *the jewels of* gold

1Sa. 8:12. to make his *instruments of* war, *and instruments of* his chariots.
9: 7. the bread is spent *in our vessels*,
10:22. he hath hid himself among *the stuff*.
14: 1, 6. the young man that bare *his armour*,
7. *his armour*bearer said unto him,
12. Jonathan and *his armour*bearer,
— Jonathan said unto *his armour*bearer,
13. and *his armour*bearer after him:
— and *his armour*bearer slew after him.
14, 17. Jonathan and *his armour*bearer
16:21. and he became his *armour*bearer.
17:22. David left his *carriage* (marg. *vessels*) in the hand of the keeper of *the carriage*,
40. them *in* a shepherd's *bag* (marg. *vessel*)
49. David put his hand in his *bag*,
54. he put *his armour* in his tent.
20:40. Jonathan gave *his artillery* unto his lad,
21: 5(6). *the vessels of* the young men are holy.
—(—). sanctified this day *in the vessel*.
8(9). brought my sword nor *my weapons*
25:13. two hundred abode by *the stuff*.
30:24. that tarrieth by *the stuff:*
31: 4. said Saul unto *his armour*bearer,
— But *his armour*bearer would not;
5. when *his armour*bearer saw
6. and *his armour*bearer,
9. and stripped off *his armour*,
10. they put *his armour* in the house
2Sa. 1:27. and *the weapons of* war perished!
8:10. *vessels of* silver, *and vessels of* gold, *and vessels of* brass:
17:28. beds, and basons, *and* earthen *vessels*,
18:15. young men that bare Joab's *armour*
23:37. *armour*bearer to Joab
24:22. and (other) *instruments of* the oxen
1K. 6: 7. (nor) any *tool of* iron heard in the house,
7:45. and all these *vessels*,
47. Solomon left all *the vessels* (unweighed),
48. Solomon made all *the vessels*
51. gold, and *the vessels*, did he put among
8: 4. all *the* holy *vessels*
10:21. king Solomon's drinking *vessels*
— and all *the vessels of* the house of
25. *vessels of* silver, *and vessels of* gold,
15:15. silver, and gold, *and vessels*.
17:10. a little water *in a vessel*,
19:21. *and* boiled their flesh *with the instruments of*
2K. 4: 3. Go, borrow thee *vessels*
— (even) empty *vessels;*
4. pour out into all those *vessels*,
6. when *the vessels* were full,
— Bring me yet *a vessel*.
— (There is) not *a vessel* more.
7:15. full of garments *and vessels*,
11: 8, 11. every man *with his weapons*
12:13(14). any *vessels of* gold, *or vessels of* silver,
14:14. all *the vessels* that were found
20:13. of *his armour*, (marg. *vessels*, or, *jewels*)
23: 4. all *the vessels* that were made
24:13. all *the vessels of* gold
25:14. all *the vessels of* brass
16. of all these *vessels* was without weight.
1Ch. 9:28. *the* ministering *vessels*,
29. *the vessels*, and all *the instruments of* the
10: 4. Then said Saul to *his armour*bearer,
— But *his armour*bearer would not;
5. when *his armour*bearer saw
9. they took his head, and *his armour*,
10. they put *his armour* in the house of
11:39. the *armour*bearer of Joab
12:33. all *instruments of* war,
37. all manner of *instruments of* war
15:16. *with instruments of* musick,
16: 5. *with* psalteries (marg. *with instruments of* psalteries) and with harps;
42. *and with* musical *instruments*
18: 8. and *the vessels of* brass.
10. all manner of *vessels of* gold
22:19. *and the* holy *vessels of* God,
23: 5. *with the instruments* which I made
26. any *vessels of it* for the service
28:13. all *the vessels of* service
14. gold, for all *instruments of* all manner of service; (silver also) for all *instruments of* silver by weight, for all *instruments of*
2Ch. 4:16. and all *their instruments*,

2Ch. 4:18. Thus Solomon made all these *vessels*
19. Solomon made all *the vessels*
5: 1. and all *the instruments*,
5. all *the* holy *vessels*
13. *and instruments of* musick,
7: 6. *with instruments of* musick
9:20. all *the* drinking *vessels* of king Solomon (were of) gold, and all *the vessels of*
24. *vessels of* silver, *and vessels of* gold,
15:18. silver, and gold, *and vessels.*
20:25. *and* precious *jewels*,
23: 7. every man *with his weapons*
13. *with instruments of* musick,
24:14. *vessels* for the house of the Lord, (even) *vessels to* minister, and to offer (withal), and spoons, *and vessels of* gold and
25:24. all *the vessels* that were found in
28:24. *the vessels of* the house of God, and cut in pieces *the vessels of* the house of
29:18. with all *the vessels thereof*, and the shew-bread table, with all *the vessels thereof.*
19. Moreover all *the vessels*,
26. the Levites stood *with the instruments of*
27. with *the instruments* (ordained) *by*
30:21. (singing) *with* loud *instruments*
32:27. all manner of pleasant *jewels;* (marg. *instruments of* desire)
34:12. that could skill *of instruments of* musick.
36: 7. Nebuchadnezzar *also* carried *of the vessels of*
10. *the* goodly *vessels of* the house of
18. all *the vessels of* the house of God,
19. all *the* goodly *vessels* thereof.
Ezr 1: 6. *with vessels of* silver,
7. *the vessels of* the house of the Lord,
10. other *vessels* a thousand.
11. All *the vessels* of gold
8:25. the silver, and the gold, and *the vessels*,
26. *and* silver *vessels* an hundred
27. *and* two *vessels of* fine copper,
28. *the vessels* (are) holy *also ;*
30. and the gold, *and the vessels*,
33. the silver and the gold *and the vessels*
Neh 10:39(40). *the vessels of* the sanctuary,
12:36. *with the* musical *instruments of* David
13: 5. the frankincense, *and the vessels*,
8. all *the* houshold *stuff*
9. *the vessels of* the house of God,
Est. 1: 7. gave (them) drink *in vessels of* gold, *the vessels* being diverse *one from another*, (lit. *and vessels* different *from vessels*)
Job 28:17. *jewels of* fine gold.
Ps. 2: 9. *like* a potter's *vessel.*
7:13(14). *the instruments of* death ;
31:12(13). I am *like a* broken *vessel.*
71:22. I will also praise thee *with the* psaltery, (marg. *with the instrument of* psaltery)
Pro. 20:15. *but* the lips of knowledge (are) *a* precious *jewel.*
25: 4. there shall come forth *a vessel* for the
Ecc. 9:18. Wisdom (is) better *than weapons of* war:
Isa. 10:28. he hath laid up *his carriages :*
13: 5. *and the weapons of* his indignation,
18: 2. *even in vessels of* bulrushes
22:24. all *vessels of* small quantity, *from the vessels of* cups, even to all *the vessels of* flagons. (marg. or, *instruments of* viols)
32: 7. *The instruments* also of the churl
39: 2. all the house of *his armour*, (marg. *vessels*, or, *instruments*, or, *jewels*)
52:11. *the vessels of* the Lord.
54:16. *an instrument* for his work ;
17. No *weapon* that is formed against thee
61:10. adorneth (herself) with *her jewels.*
65: 4. of abominable (things is in) *their vessels*,
66:20. an offering *in a* clean *vessel*
Jer. 14: 3. they returned with *their vessels* empty ;
18: 4. *the vessel* that he made of clay
— he made it again another *vessel*,
19:11. as (one) breaketh a potter's *vessel*,
21: 4. I will turn back *the weapons of* war
22: 7. every one *with his weapons :*
28. *a vessel* wherein (is) no pleasure ?
25:34. ye shall fall *like a* pleasant *vessel.*
27:16. *the vessels of* the Lord's house
18. *the vessels* which are left
19. and concerning the residue of *the vessels*
21. concerning *the vessels* that remain
Jer. 28: 3. bring again into this place all *the vessels of*
6. *the vessels of* the Lord's house,
32:14. and put them *in an* earthen *vessel*,
40:10. and put (them) *in your vessels*,
46:19. *furnish* thyself to go into captivity: (marg. make thee *instruments of* captivity)
48:11. hath not been emptied *from vessel to vessel*,
12. *and* shall empty *his vessels*,
38. I have broken Moab *like a vessel*
49:29. all *their vessels*, and their camels ;
50:25. *the weapons of* his indignation:
51:20. (art) my battle ax (and) *weapons of* war:
34. he hath made me *an* empty *vessel*,
52:18. all *the vessels of* brass wherewith they
20. the brass of all these *vessels*
Eze. 4: 9. and put them *in* one *vessel*,
9: 1. his destroying *weapon* in his hand.
2. every man *a* slaughter *weapon* in his hand ;
12: 3. *stuff* (marg. *instruments*) *for* removing,
4. Then shalt thou bring forth *thy stuff*
— *as stuff for* removing:
7. I brought forth *my stuff* by day, *as stuff for*
15: 3. to hang any *vessel* thereon ?
16:17. Thou hast also taken thy fair *jewels*
39. and shall take thy fair *jewels*, (marg. *instruments of* thine ornament)
23:26. and take away thy fair *jewels.*
27:13. *and vessels of* brass in thy market.
32:27. *with* their *weapons of* war:
40:42. *the instruments* wherewith they slew
Dan 1: 2. *the vessels of* the house of God:
— he brought *the vessels* into the treasure
11: 8. their precious *vessels of* silver
Hos 8: 8. *as a vessel* wherein (is) no pleasure.
13:15. the treasure of all pleasant *vessels.*
Am. 6: 5. invent to themselves *instruments of* musick,
Jon. 1: 5. and cast forth *the wares*
Nah 2: 9(10). all *the* pleasant *furniture.* (marg. *vessels of* desire)
Zec 11:15. *the instruments of* a foolish shepherd.

כְּלִיא *k'lee*, m. (כתיב) 3628

Jer. 37: 4. for they had not put him into *prison.* (lit. house of *restraint*)
52:31. brought him forth out of *prison*, (lit. *id.*)

כִּלָּיוֹן *kil-lāh-yōhn'*, m. 3631

Deu 28:65. a trembling heart, *and failing of* eyes,
Isa. 10:22. *the consumption* decreed

כְּלָיוֹת *k'lāh-yōhth'*, f. pl. 3629

Ex. 29:13. and *the* two *kidneys*, and the fat
22. the caul...and *the* two *kidneys*,
Lev. 3: 4, 10, 15. And *the* two *kidneys*,
—, 10, 15. the caul...with *the kidneys*,
4: 9. And *the* two *kidneys*,
— and the caul...with *the kidneys*,
7: 4. And *the* two *kidneys*,
— and the caul...with *the kidneys*,
8:16, 25. and *the* two *kidneys*,
9:10. the fat, and *the kidneys*,
19. *and the kidneys*, and the caul
Deu 32:14. the fat of *kidneys of* wheat ;
Job 16:13. he cleaveth *my reins* asunder,
19:27. (though) *my reins* be consumed
Ps. 7: 9(10). God trieth the hearts *and reins.*
16: 7. *my reins* also instruct me
26: 2. try *my reins* and my heart.
73:21. *and* I was pricked *in my reins.*
139:13. thou hast possessed *my reins :*
Pro. 23:16. *my reins* shall rejoice,
Isa. 34: 6. the fat of *the kidneys of* rams:
Jer. 11:20. that triest *the reins* and the heart,
12: 2. and far *from their reins.*
17:10. the Lord search the heart, (I) try *the reins*
20:12. *the reins* and the heart,
Lam 3:13. to enter *into my reins.*

3632 כָּלִיל *kāh-leel'*, adj.

Ex. 28:31. thou shalt make the robe...*all* (of) blue.
39:22. he made the robe...*all* (of) blue.
Lev. 6:22(15). it shall be *wholly* burnt.
23(16). every meat offering...shall be *wholly*
Nu. 4: 6. a cloth *wholly of* blue,
Deu 13:16(17). the spoil thereof *every whit*,
33:10. *and whole burnt sacrifice* upon thine altar.
Jud. 20:40. *the flame of* the city ascended up (marg. *whole consumption*)
1 Sa. 7: 9. a burnt offering *wholly* unto the Lord:
Ps. 51:19(21). offering *and whole burnt offering :*
Isa. 2:18. the idols he shall *utterly* abolish.
Lam 2:15. *The perfection of* beauty,
Eze. 16:14. it (was) *perfect* through my comeliness,
27: 3. I (am) of *perfect* beauty.
28:12. full of wisdom, *and perfect in* beauty.

3634 כָּלַל [*kāh-lal'*].

* KAL.—*Preterite.* *

Eze. 27: 4. thy builders *have perfected* thy beauty.
11. *they have made* thy beauty *perfect*.

3635 כְּלַל [*k'lal*], Ch.

* SHAPHEL.—*Preterite.* *

Ezr. 4:12. and *have set up* the walls (thereof), (marg. *finished*)
5:11. a great king of Israel builded *and set up*.
6:14. And they builded, *and finished* (it),

SHAPHEL.—*Infinitive.*

Ezr. 5: 3. and *to make up* this wall?
9. and *to make up* these walls?

* ISHTAPHEL.—*Future.* *

Ezr. 4:12. (כתיב) and *have set up* the walls (thereof), (marg. *finished*)
13. and the walls *set up* (again),
16. and the walls thereof *set up*,

3637 כָּלַם [*kāh-lam'*].

* NIPHAL.—*Preterite.* *

2Ch. 30:15. and the Levites *were ashamed*,
Ezr. 9: 6. I am ashamed *and blush*
Isa. 45:16. They shall be ashamed, and also *confounded*,
50: 7. therefore *shall I* not *be confounded :*
Jer. 22:22. then shalt thou be ashamed *and confounded*,
31:19. I was ashamed, yea, even *confounded*,
Eze. 16:54. *and mayest be confounded*
61. shalt remember thy ways, *and be ashamed*,
43:11. if *they be ashamed* of all that

NIPHAL.—*Infinitive.*

Jer. 3: 3. thou refusedst *to be ashamed*.
8:12. *neither* could they *blush:*

NIPHAL.—*Imperative.*

Eze. 36:32. be ashamed *and confounded*

NIPHAL.—*Future.*

Nu. 12:14. *should she* not *be ashamed*
Ps. 35: 4. Let them be confounded *and put to shame*
40:14(15). *and put to shame* that wish me evil.
69: 6(7). *let* not those that seek thee *be confounded*
70: 2(3). *and put to confusion*, that desire my
Isa. 41:11. shall be ashamed *and confounded :*
45:17. ye shall not be ashamed nor *confounded*
54: 4. neither *be thou confounded ;*
Eze. 43:10. *that they may be ashamed* of their

NIPHAL.—*Participle.*

2Sa. 10: 5. the men were greatly *ashamed :*
19: 3(4). as people *being ashamed*
1Ch 19: 5. the men were greatly *ashamed*.
Ps. 74:21. let not the oppressed return *ashamed :*
Eze 16:27. of the Philistines, *which are ashamed*

* HIPHIL.—*Preterite.* *

1Sa. 20:34. his father *had done him shame*.
25: 7. *we hurt them* not, (marg. *shamed*)

HIPHIL.—*Infinitive.*

Pro. 25: 8. *when* thy neighbour *hath put* thee *to shame*.
Jer. 6:15. neither could they *blush :*

HIPHIL.—*Future.*

Ru. 2:15. glean...and *reproach her* not: (marg. *shame*)
Job. 19: 3. These ten times *have ye reproached me :*
Ps. 44: 9(10). hast cast off, *and put us to shame ;*
Pro. 28: 7. a companion of riotous (men) *shameth*

HIPHIL.—*Participle.*

Jud. 18: 7. *that might put* (them) *to shame*
Job. 11: 3. *shall* no man *make* thee *ashamed ?*

* HOPHAL.—*Preterite.* *

1 Sa. 25:15. *we were* not *hurt*, (marg. *shamed*)
Jer. 14: 3. they were ashamed *and confounded*,

כְּלִמָּה *k'lim-māh'*, f. 3639

Job. 20: 3. I have heard the check of *my reproach*,
Ps. 4: 2(3). (will ye turn) my glory *into shame ?*
35:26. them be clothed with shame *and dishonour*
44:15(16). *My confusion* (is) continually before
69: 7(8). *shame* hath covered my face.
19(20). my shame, *and my dishonour :*
71:13. be covered (with) reproach *and dishonour*
109:29. Let mine adversaries be clothed with *shame*,
Pro. 18:13. it (is) folly *and shame* unto him.
Isa. 30: 3. the shadow of Egypt (your) *confusion*.
45:16. they shall go *to confusion*
50: 6. I hid not my face *from shame* and spitting.
61: 7. *and* (for) *confusion* they shall rejoice
Jer. 3:25. *our confusion* covereth us:
20:11. (their) everlasting *confusion* shall never
51:51. *shame* hath covered our faces:
Eze 16:52. bear *thine own shame*
— and bear *thy shame*,
54. That thou mayest bear *thine own shame*,
63. because of *thy shame*,
32:24, 25. yet have they borne *their shame*
30. and bear *their shame*
34:29. neither bear *the shame of* the heathen
36: 6. *the shame of* the heathen:
7. they shall bear *their shame*.
15. *the shame of* the heathen
39:26. After that they have borne *their shame*,
44:13. but they shall bear *their shame*,
Mic. 2: 6. they shall not take *shame*.

כְּלִמּוּת *k'lim-mooth'*, f. 3640

Jer. 23:40. *and a* perpetual *shame*,

כָּמַהּ *kāh-mah'*. 3642

* KAL.—*Preterite.* *

Ps. 63: 1(2). my flesh *longeth* for thee

כְּמוֹ *k'mōh*, part. 3644

Gen 19:15. *And when* the morning arose,
Ex. 15: 5. they sank into the bottom *as* a stone.
Ps. 73:15. If I say, I will speak *thus ;*
Isa. 26:17. *Like as* a woman with child,
18. we have *as it were* brought forth wind;
51: 6. therein shall die *in like* manner:
&c. &c.

With suffixes :—

Ex. 9:18. such *as* hath not been (lit. which was not *like it*)
Lev. 19:18. love thy neighbour *as thyself :*
Jud. 8:18. *As thou* (art), *so* (were) *they ;* each one
9:48. make haste, (and) do *as I* (have done).
2Sa. 18: 3. *worth* (marg. *as*) ten thousand *of us :*
1K. 22: 4. *I* (am) *as thou* (art), my people as
2Ch 35:18. there was no passover *like to* that kept
Neh 6:11. Should *such* a man *as I* flee?
Job 12: 3. I have understanding *as well as you ;*
Isa. 46: 9. (I am) God, and (there is) none *like me*,
Lam 1:21. and they shall be *like unto me*.
Hag 2: 3. *in comparison of it* as nothing?
Zec 5: 3. on this side *according to it ;*
&c. &c.

3646 **כַּמֹּן** *kam-mōhn'*, m.

Isa. 28.25. *and* scatter *the cummin*,
27. a cart wheel turned about upon *the cummin*;
— *and the cummin* with a rod.

3647 **כָּמַס** [*kāh-mas'*].

* KAL.—*Participle.* Paül. *

Deu 32:34. (Is) not this *laid up in store*

3648 **כָּמַר** [*kāh-mar'*].

* NIPHAL.—*Preterite.* *

Gen 43:30. his bowels *did yearn* upon his brother:
1K. 3:26. *yearned* upon her son, (marg. *were hot*)
Lam 5:10. Our skin *was black* like an oven
Hos 11: 8. my repentings *are kindled* together.

3649 **כְּמָרִים** *k'māh-reem'*, m. pl.

2K. 23: 5. *the idolatrous priests*, (marg. *chemarim*)
Hos 10: 5. *the priests thereof* (that) rejoiced (marg. *id.*)
Zep 1: 4. *the Chemarims* with the priests;

3650 **כִּמְרִירִים** [*kim-ree-reem'*], m. pl.

Job 3: 5. *the blackness of* the day

3653 **כֵּן** *kēhn*, m.

Gen40:13. and restore thee unto *thy place*:
41:13. me he restored unto *mine office*,
Ex. 30:18. a laver (of) brass, *and his foot*
28 & 31:9 & 35:16. the laver and *his foot*.
38: 8. the laver (of) brass, and *the foot of it*
39:39 & 40:11. the laver and *his foot*,
Lev 8:11. the laver and *his foot*,
1K. 7:29. upon the ledges (there was) *a base*
31. the work of *the base*,
Isa. 33:23. they could not *well* strengthen their mast,
Dan11: 7. shall (one) stand up in *his estate*,
20. Then shall stand up in *his estate*
21. in *his estate* shall stand up a vile person,
38. in *his estate* shall he honour

3654 **כֵּן** *kēhn*, m.

Ex. 8:16(12). that it may become *lice*
17(13). the dust of the land became *lice*
18(14). to bring forth *lice*,
Ps. 105:31. *lice* in all their coasts.
Isa. 51: 6. die in like *manner*: [perhaps, like as *a louse*]

3651 **כֵּן** *kēhn*, part.

Gen 1: 7. above the firmament: and it was *so*.
42:25. and *thus* did he unto them.
44:10. according unto your words:)(he with
Ex. 1:12. *the more* (marg. *so*) they multiplied *and*)(grew.
7:11. they also did *in like manner*
10:14. there were no *such* locusts as they,
29. Thou hast spoken *well*, I will see
22:30(29). *Likewise* shalt thou do with thine
39:43. *even so* had they done it:
Nu. 27: 7. the daughters of Zelophehad speak *right*:
Deu22: 3. *In like manner* shalt thou do with his ass; *and so* shalt thou do with his raiment; *and*)(with all lost thing
1Sa. 9:13. ye shall *straightway* find him,
2Sa. 13:12. no *such thing* ought to be done (marg. it ought not *so* to be done)
1K. 10:20. there was not *the like* (marg. *so*) made
2Ch 32:31. *Howbeit* in (the business of) the
Pro. 28: 2. *the state* (thereof) shall be prolonged.
Eze. 42:11. as long as they, (and) *as* broad *as* they:
Am. 4: 5. for *this* liketh you, (marg. *so* ye love)
&c. &c.

It is sometimes combined with another word in translation :—

I. **אַחֲרֵי**

Gen 6: 4. and also *after that*, when the sons of God
15:14. *and afterward* shall they come out
23:19. *And after this*, Abraham buried Sarah
41:31. by reason of that famine *following*;
1Sa. 9:13. *afterwards* they eat that be bidden.
&c. &c.

II. **עַל**

Gen 2:24. *Therefore* shall a man leave
10: 9. *wherefore* it is said, Even as Nimrod
Nu. 10:31. for*asmuch as* thou knowest
Jud. 6:22. for *because* I have seen an angel of the
Neh 6: 6. *for which cause* thou buildest the wall,
Jer. 38: 4. for *thus* he weakeneth the hands
&c. &c.

III. **עַד**

Neh 2:16. neither had I *as yet* told (it) to the Jews,

With prefixes: as **וּבְכֵן**

Est. 4:16. *and so* will I go in unto the king,
Ecc 8:10. *And so* I saw the wicked buried,

לָכֵן

Gen 4:15. *Therefore* whosoever slayeth Cain,
Ex. 6: 6. *Wherefore* say unto the children of Israel,
Nu. 16:11. *For which cause* (both) thou and all thy
1Sa. 28: 2. *Surely* thou shalt know what thy servant
Zec 11: 7. the flock of slaughter, (even) *you*, O poor of the flock. [The English Translation takes this for a pronominal suffix.] (marg. *verily* the poor)
&c. &c.

כֵּן adj. see **כֵּנִים** See 3651

כֵּן *kēhn*, Ch. part. 3652

Ezr. 5: 3. and their companions, *and* said *thus* unto
6: 2. *and* therein (was) a record *thus* written:
Dan 2:24. and said *thus* unto him;
25. *and* said *thus* unto him,
4:14(11). He cried aloud, *and* said *thus*,
6: 6(7). *and* said *thus* unto him,
7: 5. and they said *thus* unto it,
23. *Thus* he said, The fourth beast

כָּנָה [*kāh-nāh'*]. 3655

* PIEL.—*Future.* *

Job 32:21. neither *let me give flattering titles* unto man
22. I know not *to give flattering titles*;
Isa. 44: 5. and *surname* (himself) by the name of
45: 4. *I have surnamed thee*,

כַּנָּה *kan-nāh'*, f. 3657

Ps. 80:15(16). *And the vineyard* which thy right hand [perhaps a verb imperative of **כָּנַן**, which see]

כִּנּוֹר *kin-nōhr'*, m. 3658

Gen 4:21. such as handle *the harp* and organ.
31:27. with tabret, *and with harp*?
1Sa. 10: 5. a pipe, *and a harp*,
16:16. a cunning player *on an harp*:
23. David took *an harp*, and played
2Sa. 6: 5. *even on harps*, and on psalteries,
1K. 10:12. *harps also* and psalteries for singers:
1Ch 13: 8. *and with harps*, and with psalteries,
15:16. psalteries *and harps*
21. *with harps* on the Sheminith
28. making a noise with psalteries *and harps*
16: 5. with psalteries *and with harps*;

1Ch 25: 1. who should prophesy *with harps*,
3. who prophesied *with a harp*,
6. with cymbals, palteries, *and harps*,
2Ch 5:12. having cymbals and psalteries *and harps*,
9:11. *and harps* and psalteries for singers:
20:28. with psalteries *and harps*
29:25. with psalteries, *and with harps*,
Neh 12:27. psalteries, *and with harps*.
Job 21:12. They take the timbrel *and harp*,
30:31. *My harp* also is (turned) to mourning,
Ps. 33: 2. Praise the Lord *with harp:*
43: 4. *upon the harp* will I praise thee,
49: 4(5). open my dark saying upon *the harp*.
57: 8(9). awake, psaltery *and harp:*
71:22. unto thee will I sing with *the harp*,
81: 2(3). *the* pleasant *harp* with the psaltery.
92: 3(4). *upon the harp* with a solemn sound.
98: 5. Sing unto the Lord *with the harp; with the harp*, and the voice of a psalm.
108: 2(3). Awake, psaltery *and harp:*
137: 2. We hanged *our harps* upon the willows
147: 7. sing praise *upon the harp*
149: 3. with the timbrel *and harp*.
150: 3. praise him with the psaltery *and harp*.
Isa. 5:12. *the harp*, and the viol,
16:11. my bowels shall sound *like an harp*
23:16. Take *an harp*, go about the city,
24: 8. the joy of *the harp* ceaseth.
30:32. (it) shall be with tabrets *and harps:*
Eze.26:13. the sound of *thy harps*

3651 **כֵּנִים** *keh-neem'*, adj. pl. m.

Gen 42:11. we (are) *true* (men), thy servants
19. If ye (be) *true* (men),
31. We (are) *true* (men); we are no spies:
33. shall I know that ye (are) *true* (men);
34. but (that) ye (are) *true* (men):

3654 **כִּנָּם** *kin-nāhm'*, f.

Ex. 8:17(13). it became *lice* in man,
18(14). so there were *lice* upon man,

3660 **כְּנֵמָא** *k'nēh-māh'*, Ch. adv.

Ezr. 4: 8. to Artaxerxes the king *in this sort:*
5: 4. Then said we unto them after *this manner*,
9. said unto them *thus*,
11. *And thus* they returned us answer,
6:13. *so* they did speedily.

3661 **כָּנַן** [*kāh-nan'*].

* KAL.—*Imperative.* *

Ps. 80:15(16). *And the vineyard* which thy right hand hath planted, [perhaps, *and protect* that which:—see also כַּנָּה]

3664 **כָּנַס** [*kāh-nas'*].

* KAL.—*Preterite.* *

Ecc. 2: 8. *I gathered* me also silver and gold,

KAL.—*Infinitive.*

1Ch 22: 2. David commanded *to gather together* the
Neh 12:44. *to gather* into them
Ecc. 2:26. to gather *and to heap up*,
3: 5. a time *to gather* stones *together;*

KAL.—*Imperative.*

Est. 4:16. *gather together* all the Jews

KAL.—*Participle.* Poel.

Ps. 33: 7. He *gathereth* the waters of the sea

* PIEL.—*Preterite.* *

Eze.22:21. *Yea, I will gather* you,
39:28. *but I have gathered them*

PIEL.—*Future.*

Ps.147. 2. *he gathereth together* the outcasts of Israel.

* HITHPAEL.—*Infinitive.* *

Isa. 28:20. *than that he can wrap himself* (in)

כָּנַע [*kāh-nag'*]. 3665

* NIPHAL.—*Preterite.* *

1K. 21:29. how Ahab *humbleth himself* before me? because *he humbleth himself* before me,
2Ch 12: 7. the Lord saw that *they humbled themselves*,
— *They have humbled themselves;*
30:11. *humbled themselves*, and came to Jerusalem.
33:23. *humbled* not *himself* before the Lord,
36:12. *humbled* not *himself* before Jeremiah

NIPHAL.—*Infinitive.*

2Ch 12:12. *And when he humbled himself*,
33:19. before *he was humbled:*
23. *as* Manasseh his father *had humbled himself;*

NIPHAL.—*Future.*

Lev.26:41. their uncircumcised hearts *be humbled*,
Jud. 3:30. *So* Moab *was subdued* that day
8:28. *Thus was* Midian *subdued*
11:33. *Thus* the children of Ammon *were subdued*
1Sa. 7:13. *So* the Philistines *were subdued*.
2K. 22:19. *and thou hast humbled thyself* before the
1Ch 20: 4. *and they were subdued*.
2Ch 7:14. *If* my people,...*shall humble themselves*,
12: 6. *Whereupon* the princes of Israel...*humbled themselves;*
13:18. *Thus* the children of Israel *were brought under*
32:26. *Notwithstanding* Hezekiah *humbled* himself
33:12. *and humbled himself* greatly
34:27. *and thou didst humble thyself* before God,
— *and humbledst thyself* before me,
Ps.106:42. *and they were brought into subjection*

* HIPHIL.—*Preterite.* *

1Ch 17:10. *Moreover I will subdue* all thine enemies,
2Ch 28:19. the Lord *brought* Judah *low*

HIPHIL.—*Imperative.*

Job 40:12. (and) *bring him low;*

HIPHIL.—*Future.*

Deu 9: 3. *he shall bring them down* before thy face:
Jud. 4:23. *So* God *subdued* on that day Jabin
2Sa. 8: 1. smote the Philistines, *and subdued them:*
1Ch 18: 1. smote the Philistines, *and subdued them*,
Neh. 9:24. *and thou subduedst* before them the
Ps. 81:14(15). *I should* soon *have subdued* their
107:12. *Therefore he brought down* their heart
Isa. 25: 5. *Thou shalt bring down* the noise of

כִּנְעָה [*kin-gāh'*]. 3666

Jer. 10:17. Gather up *thy wares* out of the land,

כְּנַעַן *k'nah'-gan*, m. 3667

Isa. 23: 8. *whose traffickers* (are) the honourable
Eze.17: 4. carried it into a land of *traffick;*
Hos.12: 7(8). (He is) *a merchant*, (marg. *Canaan*)
Zep. 1:11. all the *merchant* people are cut down;

כְּנַעֲנִי *k'nah-gănee'*, m. 3669

Job 41: 6(40:30). part him among *the merchants?*
Pro.31:24. delivereth girdles *unto the merchant*.
Zec. 14:21. there shall be no more *the Canaanite* [or perhaps, *merchant*]

כָּנַף [*kāh-naph'*]. 3670

* NIPHAL.—*Future.* *

Isa. 30:20. *shall...be removed into a corner*

כָּנָף *kāh-nāhph'*, com. 3671

Gen 1:21. every *winged* fowl after his kind: (lit. fowl of *wing*)
7:14. every bird of every *sort*. (marg. *wing*)
Ex. 19: 4. I bare you on eagles' *wings*,

Ex. 25:20. the cherubims shall stretch forth (their) *wings* on high, covering the mercy seat *with their wings*,
37: 9. the cherubims spread out (their) *wings* on high, (and) covered *with their wings*
Lev. 1:17. he shall cleave it *with the wings thereof*,
Nu. 15:38. in *the borders of* their garments
— upon the fringe of *the borders*
Deu 4:17. the likeness of any *wing*ed fowl
22:12. *the* four *quarters of* thy vesture, (marg. *wings*)
30(23:1). nor discover his father's *skirt*.
27:20. he uncovereth his father's *skirt*.
32:11. As an eagle...spreadeth abroad *her wings*,
Ru. 2:12. under *whose wings* thou art come
3: 9. spread therefore *thy skirt*
1Sa. 15:27. he laid hold *upon the skirt of* his mantle,
24: 4(5). cut off *the skirt of* Saul's robe privily.
5(6). he had cut off Saul's *skirt*.
11(12). see *the skirt of* thy robe in my hand: for in that I cut off *the skirt of* thy robe,
2Sa. 22:11. he was seen upon *the wings of* the wind.
1K. 6:24. *the* one *wing of* the cherub, and five cubits the other *wing of* the cherub: from the uttermost part of *the one wing* unto the uttermost part of *the other* (lit. from the uttermost part of *his wings* to the uttermost part of *his wings*)
27. stretched forth *the wings of* the cherubims, so that *the wing of* the one touched the (one) wall, *and the wing of* the other cherub touched the other wall; *and their wings* touched *one another* (lit. *wing* to *wing*)
8: 6. *the wings of* the cherubims.
7. cherubims spread forth (their) two *wings*
2Ch 3:11. *And the wings of* the cherubims (were) twenty cubits long: one *wing* (of the one cherub)
— *and the* other *wing* (was likewise) five cubits, reaching *to the wing of* the other
12. *And* (one) *wing of* the other cherub
— *and the* other *wing* (was) five cubits (also), joining *to the wing of* the other cherub.
13. *The wings of* these cherubims
5: 7. *the wings of* the cherubims:
8. the cherubims spread forth (their) *wings*
Job 37: 3. unto *the ends* (marg. *wings*) *of* the earth.
38:13. hold *of the ends* (marg. *wings*) *of* the earth,
39:13. (Gavest thou) *the* goodly *wings* unto the
26. Doth the hawk...stretch *her wings*
Ps. 17: 8. under the shadow of *thy wings*,
18:10(11). he did fly upon *the wings of* the wind.
36: 7(8). under the shadow of *thy wings*.
57: 1(2). in the shadow of *thy wings*
61: 4(5). I will trust in the covert of *thy wings*.
63: 7(8). in the shadow of *thy wings*
68:13(14). *the wings of* a dove
78:27. *feathered* fowls like as the sand
91: 4. under *his wings* shalt thou trust:
104: 3. who walketh upon *the wings of* the wind:
139: 9. (If) I take *the wings of* the morning,
148:10. creeping things, and *flying* fowl: (marg. birds of *wing*)
Pro. 1:17. in vain the net is spread in the sight of any *bird*. (lit. master of *wing*)
23: 5. (riches) certainly make themselves *wings*;
Ecc. 10:20. that which hath *wings* shall tell the matter.
Isa. 6: 2. each one had six *wings*; (lit. six *wings*, six *wings* to one)
8: 8. the stretching out of *his wings*
10:14. there was none that moved *the wing*,
11:12. *the* four *corners of* the earth. (marg. *wings*)
18: 1. the land shadowing with *wings*,
24:16. *From the uttermost part* (marg. *wing*) *of* the earth
Jer. 2:34. *in thy skirts* is found the blood of
48:40. shall spread *his wings* over Moab.
49:22. and spread *his wings* over Bozrah:
Eze. 1: 6. every one had four *wings*.
8. the hands of a man under *their wings*
— their faces *and their wings*.
9. *Their wings* (were) joined
11. *and their wings* (were) stretched upward;
23. under the firmament (were) *their wings*
24. I heard the noise of *their wings*,
— they let down *their wings*.
Eze. 1:25. had let down *their wings*.
3:13. the noise of *the wings of*
5: 3. and bind them *in thy skirts*. (marg. *wings*)
7: 2. *the* four *corners of* the land.
10: 5. the sound of the cherubims' *wings*
8. a man's hand under *their wings*.
12. and their hands, *and their wings*.
16. when the cherubims lifted up *their wings*
19. the cherubims lifted up *their wings*,
21. and every one four *wings*;
— hands of a man (was) under *their wings*.
11:22. the cherubims lift up *their wings*,
16: 8. I spread *my skirt* over thee,
17: 3. A great eagle with great *wings*,
7. another great eagle with great *wings*
23. it shall dwell all fowl of every *wing*;
39: 4. ravenous birds of every *sort*, (marg. *wing*)
17. Speak unto every *feathered* fowl. (marg. fowl of every *wing*)
Dan 9:27. *the overspreading of* abominations
Hos. 4:19. The wind hath bound her up *in her wings*,
Hag. 2:12. one bear holy flesh *in the skirt of* his garment, and *with his skirt* do touch bread,
Zec. 5: 9. the wind (was) *in their wings*; for they had *wings like the wings of* a stork:
8:23. *of the skirt of* him that is a Jew,
Mal. 4: 2(3:20). the Sun of righteousness arise with healing *in his wings*;

כְּנַשׁ [*k'nash*], Ch. 3673

* P'AL.—*Infinitive*. *

Dan 3: 2. the king sent *to gather together* the

* ITHPAEL.—*Participle*. *

Dan 3: 3. *were gathered together* unto the dedication
27. *And...being gathered together*, saw these

כְּנָת [*k'nāhth*], m. 3674

Ezr. 4: 7. rest of *their companions*, (marg. *societies*)

כְּנָת [*k'nāhth*], Ch. m. 3675

Ezr. 4: 9,17. the rest of *their companions*; (marg. *societies*)
23. Shimshai the scribe, *and their companions*,
5: 3. Shethar-boznai, *and their companions*,
6. Shethar-boznai, *and his companions*
6: 6. Shethar-boznai, *and your companions* (marg. *societies*)
13. Shethar-boznai, *and their companions*,

כֵּס *kēhs*, m. 3676

Ex. 17:16. the Lord hath sworn (marg. the hand upon *the throne of* the Lord)

כֶּסֶא *keh'-seh*, m. 3677

Pro. 7:20. the day *appointed*. (marg. or, *new moon*)

כִּסֵּא *kis-sēh'*, m. 3678

Gen 41:40. only in *the throne* will I be greater than
Ex. 11: 5. Pharaoh that sitteth upon *his throne*,
12:29. Pharaoh that sat on *his throne*
Deu 17:18. *the throne of* his kingdom,
Jud. 3:20. And he arose out of (his) *seat*.
1Sa. 1: 9. Eli the priest sat upon *a seat*
2: 8. *and* to make them inherit *the throne of*
4:13. Eli sat upon *a seat*
18. he fell from off *the seat*
2Sa. 3:10. to set up *the throne of* David
7:13. I will stablish *the throne of*
16. *thy throne* shall be established
14: 9. the king *and his throne* (be) guiltless.
1K. 1:13,17,24,30. he shall sit upon *my throne*?
20. who shall sit on *the throne of*
27. who should sit on *the throne of* my lord
35. that he may come and sit upon *my throne*;

1K. 1:37. make *his throne* greater *than the throne of*
46. Solomon sitteth on *the throne of* the
47. make *his throne* greater *than thy throne.*
48. hath given (one) to sit on *my throne*
2: 4. *the throne of* Israel.
12. Then sat Solomon upon *the throne of* David
19. sat down on *his throne*, and caused *a seat*
24. set me on *the throne of* David
33. *and upon his throne*, shall there be peace
45. *the throne of* David shall be established
3: 6. hast given him a son to sit on *his throne*,
5: 5(19). whom I will set upon *thy throne*
7: 7. Then he made a porch for *the throne*
8:20. sit on *the throne of* Israel,
25. to sit on *the throne of* Israel;
9: 5. Then I will establish *the throne of*
— upon *the throne of* Israel.
10: 9. to set thee on *the throne of* Israel:
18. the king made *a* great *throne of* ivory,
16:11. as soon as he sat on *his throne*,
22:10. sat each on *his throne*,
19. I saw the Lord sitting on *his throne*,
2K. 4:10. a table, *and a stool*,
10: 3. set (him) on his father's *throne*,
30. shall sit on *the throne of* Israel.
11:19. he sat on *the throne of* the kings.
13:13. Jeroboam sat upon *his throne*:
15:12. Thy sons shall sit on *the throne of* Israel
25:28. and set *his throne* above *the throne of* the
1Ch.17:12. I will stablish *his throne*
14. *and his throne* shall be established
22:10. I will establish *the throne of*
28: 5. upon *the throne of* the kingdom
29:23. Solomon sat on *the throne*
2Ch. 6:10. and am set on *the throne of* Israel,
16. to sit upon *the throne of* Israel;
7:18. will I stablish *the throne of* thy kingdom,
9: 8. to set thee on *his throne*,
17. the king made *a* great *throne of* ivory,
18. six steps *to the throne*, with a footstool of gold, (which were) fastened *to the throne*,
18: 9. sat either of them on *his throne*,
18. I saw the Lord sitting upon *his throne*,
23:20. upon *the throne of* the kingdom.
Neh 3: 7. *unto the throne of* the governor
Est. 1: 2. Ahasuerus sat on *the throne*
3: 1. and set *his seat* above all the princes
5: 1. the king sat upon his royal *throne*
Job 36: 7. with kings (are they) *on the throne*;
Ps. 9: 4(5). thou satest *in the throne*
7(8). he hath prepared *his throne*
11: 4. the Lord's *throne* (lit. *his throne*) (is) in
45: 6(7). *Thy throne*, O God, (is) for ever and
47: 8(9). God sitteth upon *the throne of* his
89: 4(5). and build up *thy throne* to all
14(15). the habitation of *thy throne*:
29(30). *and his throne* as the days of heaven.
36(37). *and his throne* as the sun before me.
44(45). *and* cast *his throne* down to the
93: 2. *Thy throne* (is) established of old:
94:20. Shall *the throne of* iniquity have fellowship
97: 2. the habitation of *his throne*.
103:19. The Lord hath prepared *his throne*
122: 5. set *thrones* of judgment, *the thrones* of the
132:11. of thy body will I set *upon* thy *throne*.
12. their children shall also sit *upon* thy *throne*
Pro. 9:14. on *a seat* in the high places
16:12. *the throne* is established by righteousness.
20: 8. A king that sitteth in *the throne*
28. *his throne* is upholden by mercy.
25: 5. *his throne* shall be established
29:14. *his throne* shall be established
Isa. 6: 1. I saw also the Lord sitting upon *a throne*,
9: 7(6). upon *the throne of* David,
14: 9. raised up *from their thrones* all the kings
13. I will exalt *my throne*
16: 5. in mercy shall *the throne* be established:
22:23. he shall be *for a* glorious *throne*
47: 1. (there is) no *throne*, O daughter
66: 1. The heaven (is) *my throne*,
Jer. 1:15. they shall set every one *his throne*
3:17. *the throne of* the Lord;
13:13. the kings that sit upon David's *throne*, (lit. for David upon *his throne*)
14:21. do not disgrace *the throne of* thy glory:
17:12. *A* glorious high *throne*
25. sitting upon *the throne of* David,
Jer. 22: 2. sittest upon *the throne of* David,
4. sitting upon *the throne* of David, (marg. for David upon *his throne*)
30. sitting upon *the throne of* David,
29:16. sitteth upon *the throne of* David,
33:17. *the throne of* the house of Israel;
21. a son to reign upon *his throne*;
36:30. to sit upon *the throne of* David:
43:10. and will set *his throne* upon these stones
49:38. I will set *my throne* in Elam,
52:32. and set *his throne* above *the throne of* the
Lam 5:19. *thy throne* from generation
Eze. 1:26. the likeness of *a throne*,
— and upon the likeness of *the throne*
10: 1. the likeness of *a throne*.
26:16. shall come down from *their thrones*,
43: 7. the place of *my throne*,
Jon. 3: 6. he arose *from his throne*,
Hag 2:22. I will overthrow *the throne of* kingdoms.
Zec 6:13. shall sit and rule upon *his throne*; and he shall be a priest upon *his throne*:

כָּסָה [*kāh-sāh'*]. 3680

* KAL.—*Participle.* Poel. *

Pro.12:16. *but* a prudent (man) *covereth* shame.
23. A prudent man *concealeth* knowledge:

KAL.—*Participle.* Paül.

Ps. 32: 1. (whose) sin (is) *covered*.

* NIPHAL.—*Preterite.* *

Jer.51:42. *she is covered* with the multitude

NIPHAL.—*Infinitive.*

Eze 24: 8. that it *should* not *be covered*.

* PIEL.—*Preterite.* *

Gen 37:26. if we slay our brother, *and conceal* his
38:15. *she had covered* her face.
Ex. 10: 5. *And they shall cover* the face of the earth,
15:10. the sea *covered them*:
Lev.13:12. *and* the leprosy *cover* all the skin
13. (if) the leprosy *have covered*
16:13. *that* the cloud of the incense *may cover*
17:13. *and cover it* with dust.
Nu. 4: 5. *and cover* the ark of testimony
8. *and cover* the same with a covering
9. *and cover* the candlestick
11. *and cover* it with a covering
12. *and cover* them with a covering
9:15. the cloud *covered* the tabernacle,
16:42(17:7). the cloud *covered it*,
22: 5. *they cover* the face of the earth,
Deu 23:13(14). and shalt turn back *and cover* that
Job 15:27. *he covereth* his face with his fatness,
23:17. (neither) *hath he covered* the darkness
31:33. If *I covered* my transgressions
36:30. and *covereth* the bottom of the sea.
32. With clouds *he covereth* the light;
Ps. 32: 5. mine iniquity *have I* not *hid*.
40:10(11). *I have* not *hid* thy righteousness
44:15(16). the shame of my face *hath covered me*,
69: 7(8). shame *hath covered* my face.
78:53. the sea *overwhelmed* their enemies. (marg. *covered*)
85: 2(3). *thou hast covered* all their sin.
104: 6. *Thou coveredst it* with the deep
143: 9. *I flee* unto thee *to hide me*. (marg. *hide me* with thee)
Isa. 29:10. the seers *hath he covered*.
51:16. *I have covered thee* in the shadow of
58: 7. the naked, *that thou cover him*;
Jer. 51:51. shame *hath covered* our faces:
Eze. 7:18. *and* horror *shall cover* them;
18:16. and *hath covered* the naked
26:19. *and* great waters *shall cover thee*;
31:15. *I covered* the deep for him,
32: 7. *And...I will cover* the heaven,
Hab 3: 3. His glory *covered* the heavens,
Mal 2:16. *for* (one) *covereth* violence

PIEL.—*Infinitive.*

Ex. 26:13. it shall hang over...*to cover it*.
28:42. breeches *to cover* their nakedness;
Nu. 4:15. have made an end *of covering*
1 K. 7:18. network, *to cover* the chapiters

1 K. 7:41. networks, *to cover* the two bowls
42. *to cover* the two bowls of the chapiters
2Ch 4:12, 13. *to cover* the two pommels
Ps. 104: 9. that they turn not again *to cover*
Eze 24: 7. *to cover* it with dust;
38: 9. like a cloud *to cover* the land,
16. as a cloud *to cover* the land;
Hos 2: 9(11). *to cover* her nakedness.
Mal 2:13. *covering* the altar of the Lord

PIEL.—*Imperative.*

Hos 10: 8. they shall say to the mountains, *Cover us*;

PIEL.—*Future.*

Gen 9:23. *and covered* the nakedness of their father;
38:14. *and covered* her with a vail,
Ex. 8: 6(2). the frogs came up, *and covered* the
10:15. *For they covered* the face of the whole
14:28. the waters returned, *and covered*
15: 5. The depths *have covered them*:
16:13. the quails came up, *and covered* the camp:
21:33. if a man shall dig a pit, and not *cover it*,
24:15. *and* a cloud *covered* the mount.
16. *and* the cloud *covered it* six days:
40:34. *Then* a cloud *covered* the tent
Nu. 9:16. the cloud *covered it* (by day),
16:33. *and* the earth *closed* upon them:
22:11. *which covereth* the face of the earth:
Deu 13: 8(9). neither *shalt thou conceal* him:
22:12. wherewith *thou coverest* (thyself).
Jos. 24: 7. the sea upon them, *and covered them*;
Jud. 4:18. *and* when...*she covered him* with a mantle.
19. and gave him drink, *and covered him*.
1 Sa 19:13. *and covered* (it) with a cloth.
1 K. 1: 1. *and they covered him* with clothes,
2Ch 5: 8. *and* the cherubims *covered* the ark
Neh 4: 5(3:37). And *cover* not their iniquity,
Job. 9:24. *he covereth* the faces of the judges
16:18. *cover* not *thou* my blood,
21:26. the worms *shall cover* them.
22:11. abundance of waters *cover thee*.
33:17. and *hide* pride from man.
38:34. that abundance of waters *may cover thee*?
Ps. 44:19(20). *and covered* us with the shadow of
55: 5(6). *and* horror *hath overwhelmed me*.
106:11. *And* the waters *covered* their enemies:
17. *and covered* the company of Abiram.
140: 9(10). *let* the mischief of their own lips *cover them*.
Pro. 10: 6, 11. violence *covereth* the mouth of the
12. but love *covereth* all sins.
Isa. 6: 2. with twain *he covered* his face, and with twain *he covered* his feet,
26:21. *shall* no more *cover* her slain.
60: 2. darkness *shall cover* the earth,
6. The multitude of camels *shall cover thee*,
Jer. 3:25. *and* our confusion *covereth us*:
46: 8. I will go up, (and) *will cover* the earth;
Eze 12: 6. *thou shalt cover* thy face,
12. *he shall cover* his face, that he see not
16: 8. *and covered* thy nakedness:
10. *and I covered thee* with silk.
18. *and coveredst them*:
18: 7. *hath covered* the naked
26:10. their dust *shall cover thee*:
30:18. a cloud *shall cover her*,
32: 7. *I will cover* the sun with a cloud,
Obad 10. shame *shall cover thee*,
Jon. 3: 6. *and covered* (him) with sackcloth,
Mic. 7:10. *and* shame *shall cover her*
Hab 2:14. as the waters *cover* the sea.
17. the violence of Lebanon *shall cover thee*,

PIEL.—*Participle.*

Gen 18:17. *Shall* I *hide* from Abraham that thing
Ex. 29:13, 22. the fat *that covereth* the inwards,
Lev. 3: 3, 9, 14 & 4:8 & 7:3. the fat *that covereth* the
Ps. 147: 8. *Who covereth* the heaven with clouds,
Pro. 10:18. *He that hideth* hatred
11:13. a faithful spirit *concealeth* the matter.
17: 9. *He that covereth* a transgression
28:13. *He that covereth* his sins
Isa. 11: 9. as the waters *cover* the sea.
Eze. 1:11. and two *covered* their bodies.
23. two, *which covered* on this side,
— two, *which covered* on that side,

* PUAL.—*Preterite.* *

Ps. 80:10(11). The hills *were covered*
Pro. 24:31. nettles *had covered* the face thereof,

PUAL.—*Future.*

Gen 7:19. *and* all the high hills,...*were covered*.
20. *and* the mountains *were covered*.
Ecc. 6: 4. his name *shall be covered* with

PUAL.—*Participle.*

1 Ch 21:16. the elders (of Israel, who were) *clothed* in
Eze. 41:16. the windows (were) *covered*;

* HITHPAEL.—*Future.* *

Gen 24:65. she took a vail, *and covered herself*.
2K. 19: 1. *and covered himself* with sackcloth,
Pro. 26:26. (Whose) hatred *is covered* by deceit,
Isa. 37: 1. *and covered himself* with sackcloth,
59: 6. neither *shall they cover themselves*
Jon 3: 8. *But* let man and beast *be covered*

HITHPAEL.—*Participle.*

1K. 11:29. he *had clad himself* with a new garment;
2K. 19: 2. the elders of the priests, *covered* with
Isa. 37: 2. the elders of the priests *covered*

כֶּסֶה *keh'-seh*, m. 3677

[see also כֶּסֶא]

Ps. 81: 3(4). in the new moon, *in the time appointed*,

כִּסֵּה *kis-sēh'*, m. 3678

[see also כִּסֵּא]

1K. 10:19. *The throne had* six steps, and the top of *the throne*
Job. 26: 9. He holdeth back the face of (his) *throne*,

כָּסוּי [*kāh-soo'y*], m. 3681

Nu. 4: 6. *the covering of* badgers' skins,
14. *a covering of* badgers' skins,

כְּסוּת *k'sooth*, f. 3682

Gen 20:16. he (is) to thee *a covering of* the eyes,
Ex. 21:10. her food, *her raiment*, and her duty of
22:27(26) For that (is) *his covering* only:
Deu 22:12. the four quarters of *thy vesture*,
Job 24: 7. (they have) no *covering* in the cold.
26: 6. destruction hath no *covering*.
31:19. or any poor without *covering*;
Isa. 50: 3. I make sackcloth *their covering*.

כָּסַח [*kāh-sagh'*]. 3683

KAL.—*Participle* Paül.

Ps. 80:16(17). burned with fire, (it is) *cut down*:
Isa. 33:12. (as) thorns *cut up* shall they be

כְּסִיל *k'seel*, m. 3684

Job 9: 9. Which maketh Arcturus, *Orion*, and Pleiades, (marg. Ash, *Cesil*, and Cimah)
38:31. loose the bands of *Orion*?
Ps. 49:10(11). *the fool* and the brutish person
92: 6(7). *neither* doth *a fool* understand
94: 8. *and* (ye) *fools*, when will ye be wise?
Pro. 1:22. *and fools* hate knowledge?
32. the prosperity of *fools* shall destroy them.
3:35. *but* shame shall be the promotion of *fools*.
8: 5. *and, ye fools*, be ye of an understanding
10: 1. a *foolish* son (is) the heaviness of his
18. he that uttereth a slander, (is) *a fool*.
23. sport *to a fool* to do mischief:
12:23. the heart of *fools* proclaimeth foolishness.
13:16. *but a fool* layeth open (his) folly.
19. (it is) abomination to *fools* to depart from
20. a companion of *fools* shall be destroyed.
14: 7. Go from the presence of a *foolish* man,
8. the folly of *fools* (is) deceit.
16. *but the fool* rageth, and is confident.
24. the foolishness of *fools* (is) folly.

Pro.14:33.(that which is) in the midst of *fools*
15: 2.the mouth of *fools* poureth out foolishness.
7.the heart of *the foolish* (doeth) not so.
14.the mouth of *fools* feedeth on foolishness.
20.*but* a *foolish* man despiseth his mother.
17:10.an hundred stripes into *a fool.*
12.rather than *a fool* in his folly.
16.the hand of *a fool*
21.He that begetteth *a fool*
24.the eyes of *a fool* (are) in the ends of the
25.A *foolish* son (is) a grief to his father,
18: 2.*A fool* hath no delight in understanding,
6.*A fool*'s lips enter into contention,
7.*A fool*'s mouth (is) his destruction,
19: 1.(he that is) perverse ... and is *a fool.*
10.Delight is not seemly *for a fool ;*
13.A *foolish* son (is) the calamity of his
29.stripes for the back of *fools.*
21:20.*but a foolish* man spendeth it up.
23: 9.Speak not in the ears of *a fool :*
26: 1.honour is not seemly *for a fool.*
3.a rod for *the fools*' back.
4.Answer not *a fool* according to his folly,
5.Answer *a fool* according to his folly,
6.sendeth a message by the hand of *a fool*
7.so (is) a parable in the mouth of *fools.*
8.he that giveth honour *to a fool.*
9.so (is) a parable in the mouth of *fools.*
10.both rewardeth *the fool,*
11.*a fool* returneth to his folly.
12.(there is) more hope *of a fool*
28:26.that trusteth in his own heart is *a fool :*
29:11.*A fool* uttereth all his mind:
20.(there is) more hope *of a fool*
Ecc. 2:14.*but the fool* walketh in darkness:
15.As it happeneth to *the fool,*
16.of the wise more than of *the fool*
— how dieth the wise (man)? as *the fool.*
4: 5.*The fool* foldeth his hands together,
13.an old *and foolish* king,
5: 1(4:17).than to give the sacrifice of *fools :*
3(2).*a fool*'s voice (is known)
4(3).(he hath) no pleasure *in fools :*
6: 8.For what hath the wise more than *the fool?*
7: 4.the heart of *fools*
5.for a man to hear the song of *fools.*
6.so (is) the laughter of *the fool :*
9.anger resteth in the bosom of *fools.*
9:17.him that ruleth *among fools.*
10: 2.*a fool*'s heart at his left.
12.the lips of *a fool* will swallow up himself.
15.The labour of *the foolish*
Isa. 13:10.heaven and *the constellations thereof*
Am. 5: 8.that maketh the seven stars *and Orion,*

3687 **כְּסִילוּת** *k'see-looth'*, f.

Pro. 9:13.A *foolish* woman (is) clamorous:

3688 **כָּסַל** [*kāh-sal'*].

* KAL.—*Future.* *

Jer. 10: 8.they are altogether brutish *and foolish :*

3689 **כֶּסֶל** *keh'-sel*, m.

Lev. 3: 4,10,15.which (is) by *the flanks,*
4: 9.the fat ... which (is) by *the flanks,*
7: 4.which (is) by *the flanks,*
Job 8:14.*Whose hope* shall be cut off,
15:27.maketh collops of fat on (his) *flanks.*
31:24.If I have made gold *my hope,*
Ps. 38: 7(8).*my loins* are filled with a loathsome
49:13(14).their way (is) their *folly :*
78: 7.That they might set *their hope* in God,
Pro. 3:26.the Lord shall be *thy confidence,*
Ecc. 7:25.to know the wickedness of *folly,*

3690 **כִּסְלָה** *kis-lāh'*, f.

Job 4: 6.thy fear, *thy confidence,* thy hope,
Ps. 85: 8(9).let them not turn again *to folly.*

כִּסְלֵו *kis-lēhv'*, m. 3691

Neh 1: 1.in the month *Chisleu,*
Zec 7: 1.(even) *in Chisleu ;*

כָּסַם [*kāh-sam'*]. 3697

* KAL.—*Infinitive.* *

Eze.44:20.they shall *only* poll (lit. *in polling* they shall poll) their heads.

KAL.—*Future.*

Eze.44:20.*they shall* only *poll* their heads.

כֻּסֶּמֶת *koos-seh'-meth*, f. 3698

Ex. 9:32.the wheat *and the rie* were not smitten:
Isa. 28:25.*and the rie* in their place? (marg. or *spelt*)
Eze. 4: 9.lentiles, and millet, *and fitches,* (marg.*id.*)

כָּסַס [*kāh-sas'*]. 3699

* KAL—*Future.* *

Ex. 12: 4.every man...*shall make your count*

כָּסַף [*kāh-saph'*]. 3700

* KAL.—*Future.* *

Job 14:15.*thou wilt have a desire* to the work of
Ps. 17:12.Like as a lion (that) *is greedy* of his prey,

* NIPHAL.—*Preterite.* *

Gen31:30.*thou* sore *longedst* after thy father's house,
Ps. 84: 2(3).My soul *longeth,* yea, even fainteth

NIPHAL.—*Infinitive.*

Gen31:30.thou *sore* longedst (lit. *in longing* thou longedst) after thy father's house,

NIPHAL.—*Participle.*

Zep. 2: 1.gather together, O nation not *desired,* (marg. *desirous*)

כֶּסֶף *keh'-seph*, m. 3701

Gen13: 2.Abram (was) very rich in cattle, *in silver,*
17:12.or bought with *money* of any stranger,
13.he that is bought with *thy money,*
23.all that were bought with *his money,*
27.bought with *money* of the stranger,
20:16.thy brother a thousand (pieces) of *silver :*
23: 9.*for* as much *money* as it is worth
13.I will give thee *money* for the field ;
15.(is worth) four hundred shekels of *silver ;*
16.Abraham weighed to Ephron *the silver,*
— four hundred shekels of *silver,*
24:35.flocks, and herds, *and silver,* and gold,
53.jewels of *silver,* and jewels of gold,
31:15.hath quite devoured also *our money.*
37:28.sold Joseph...for twenty (pieces) of *silver :*
42:25.to restore every man's *money*
27.he espied *his money ;*
28.*My money* is restored ;
35.every man's bundle of *money*
— the bundles of *money,* (lit. *their money*)
43:12.*And* take double *money* in your hand ; and *the money* that was brought again
15.and they took double *money*
18.Because of *the money* that was returned
21.(every) man's *money* (was) in the mouth of his sack, *our money* in full weight:
22.*And* other *money* have we brought
— who put *our money* in our sacks.
23.I had *your money.*
44: 1.put every man's *money* in his sack's mouth.
2.my cup, the *silver* cup, in the sack's mouth of the youngest, and his corn *money.*
8.Behold, *the money,* which we found
— we steal out of thy lord's house *silver*
45:22.three hundred (pieces) of *silver,*

Gen47:14. Joseph gathered up all *the money*
— Joseph brought *the money*
15. when *money* failed in the land
— for *the money* faileth.
16. will give you for your cattle, if *money* fail.
18. that *our money* (lit. *the money*) is spent;
Ex. 3:22 & 11:2 & 12:35. jewels of *silver*, and jewels
12:44. servant that is bought for *money*,
20:23. Ye shall not make with me gods of *silver*,
21:11. she go out free without *money*.
21. he (is) *his money*.
32. thirty shekels of *silver*,
34. give *money* unto the owner
35. and divide *the money of it;*
22: 7(6). deliver unto his neighbour *money*
17(16). he shall pay *money* according to
25(24). If thou lend *money*
25: 3. gold, *and silver*, and brass,
26:19. forty sockets of *silver*
21. their forty sockets (of) *silver;*
25. and their sockets (of) *silver*,
32. the four sockets of *silver*.
27:10. their fillets (shall be of) *silver*.
11. and their fillets (of) *silver*.
17. filleted with *silver;* their hooks (shall be of) *silver*,
30:16. thou shalt take *the* atonement *money*
31: 4. to work in gold, *and in silver*,
35. 5. gold, *and silver*, and brass,
24. an offering of *silver* and brass
32. to work in gold, *and in silver*,
36:24. forty sockets of *silver* he made
26. their forty sockets of *silver;*
30. sixteen sockets of *silver*,
36. four sockets of *silver*.
38:10. their fillets (were of) *silver*.
11, 12. the hooks...and their fillets (of) *silver*.
17. and their fillets (of) *silver;* and the overlaying of their chapiters (of) *silver;* and all the pillars of the court (were) filleted with *silver*.
19. their hooks (of) *silver*,
— and their fillets (of) *silver*.
25. *And the silver of* them that were numbered
27. the hundred talents of *silver*
Lev. 5:15. thy estimation by shekels of *silver*,
22:11. if the priest buy (any) soul with *his money*,
25:37. not give him *thy money* upon usury,
50. *the price of* his sale
51. *out of the money* that he was bought for.
27: 3. estimation shall be fifty shekels of *silver*,
6. estimation shall be...five shekels of *silver*,
— estimation (shall be) three shekels of *silver*.
15, 19. *the money* of thy estimation
16. fifty shekels of *silver*.
18: the priest shall reckon unto him *the money*
Nu. 3:48. thou shalt give *the money*,
49. Moses took *the* redemption *money*
50. of the children of Israel took he *the money;*
51. Moses gave *the money of* them
7:13, 19, 25, 31, 37, 49, 55, 61, 67, 73, 79. one *silver* charger,...one *silver* bowl
43. one *silver* charger...a *silver* bowl
84. twelve chargers of *silver*, twelve *silver*
85. Each charger of *silver*
— all the *silver* vessels
10: 2. Make thee two trumpets of *silver;*
18:16. for *the money of* five shekels,
22:18 & 24:13. his house full of *silver*,
31:22. Only the gold, and *the silver*,
Deu 2: 6. Ye shall buy meat of them *for money*,
— buy water of them *for money*,
28. Thou shalt sell me meat *for money*, that I may eat; and give me water *for money*,
7:25. thou shalt not desire *the silver*
8:13. *and* thy *silver* and thy gold is multiplied,
14:25. Then shalt thou turn (it) *into money*, and bind up *the money* in thine hand,
26. thou shalt bestow *that money*
17:17. *neither* shall he greatly multiply...*silver*
21:14. thou shalt not sell her at all *for money*,
22:19. an hundred (shekels) of *silver*,
29. fifty (shekels) of *silver*,
23:19(20). usury of *money*,
29:17(16). *silver* and gold,
Jos. 6:19. all *the silver*, and gold,
24. only *the silver*, and the gold,

Jos. 7:21. two hundred shekels of *silver*,
—, 22. *and the silver* under it.
24. *the silver*, and the garment,
22: 8. *with silver*, and with gold,
Jud. 5:19. they took no gain of *money*.
9: 4. him threescore and ten (pieces) of *silver*
16: 5. eleven hundred (pieces) of *silver*
18. brought *money* in their hand.
17: 2. The eleven hundred (shekels) of *silver*
— *the silver* (is) with me;
3. the eleven hundred (shekels) of *silver*
— wholly dedicated *the silver* unto the Lord
4. Yet he restored *the money*
— two hundred (shekels) of *silver*,
10. I will give thee ten (shekels) of *silver*,
1 Sa. 2:36. crouch to him for a piece of *silver*
9: 8. the fourth part of a shekel of *silver:*
2 Sa. 8:10. (Joram) brought with him vessels of *silver*,
11. with *the silver* and gold
18:11. have given thee ten (shekels) of *silver*,
12. a thousand (shekels) of *silver*
21: 4. We will have no *silver* nor gold
24:24. *for* fifty shekels of *silver*.
1 K. 7:51. (even) *the silver*, and the gold,
10:21. none (were of) *silver:*
22. bringing gold, *and silver*,
25. vessels of *silver*, and vessels of gold,
27. the king made *silver*...as stones,
29. six hundred (shekels) of *silver*,
15:15. *silver*, and gold,
18. Then Asa took all *the silver*
19. I have sent unto thee a present of *silver*
16:24. two talents of *silver*,
20: 3. *Thy silver* and thy gold (is) mine;
5. Thou shalt deliver me *thy silver*,
7. *and for my silver*, and for my gold;
39. else thou shalt pay a talent of *silver*.
21: 2. I will give thee the worth of it *in money*.
6. Give me thy vineyard *for money;*
15. which he refused to give thee *for money:*
2K. 5: 5. and took with him ten talents of *silver*,
22. give them, I pray thee, a talent of *silver*,
23. bound two talents of *silver* in two bags,
26. (Is it) a time to receive *money*,
6:25. fourscore (pieces) of *silver*,
— five (pieces) of *silver*.
7: 8. carried thence *silver*, and gold,
12: 4(5). *the money of* the dedicated things
—(-). *the money of* every one that passeth (the account), *the money* that every man is set at, (and) all *the money* that cometh into any man's heart.
7(8). receive no (more) *money*
8(9). consented to receive no (more) *money*
9(10). all *the money* (that was) brought into
10(11). they saw that (there was) much *money*
—(—). told *the money* that was found
11(12). And they gave *the money*,
13(14). bowls of *silver*,
—(—). vessels of *silver*, of *the money* (that was) brought into the house
15(16). whose hand they delivered *the money*
16(17). *The* trespass *money and* sin *money* was
14:14. he took all the gold *and silver*,
15:19. gave Pul a thousand talents of *silver*,
20. Menahem exacted *the money*
— of each man fifty shekels of *silver*,
16: 8. Ahaz took *the silver* and gold,
18:14. three hundred talents of *silver*
15. Hezekiah gave (him) all *the silver*
20:13. *the silver*, and the gold,
22: 4. that he may sum *the silver*
7. no reckoning made with them of *the money*
9. Thy servants have gathered *the money*
23:33. an hundred talents of *silver*,
35. *And* Jehoiakim gave *the silver*
— he taxed the land to give *the money*
— he exacted *the silver* and the gold
25:15. things as (were)...of *silver*, (in) *silver*,
1Ch 18:10. all manner of vessels of gold *and silver*
11. with *the silver* and the gold
19: 6. a thousand talents of *silver*
21:22. thou shalt grant it me *for the* full *price:*
24. I will verily buy it *for the* full *price:*
22:14. *and* a thousand thousand talents of *silver*,
16. Of the gold, *the silver*, and the brass.
28:14. all instruments of *silver*

1Ch.28: 15. the candlesticks of *silver*
16. *and* (likewise) *silver* for the tables of *silver:*
17. every bason of *silver:*
29: 2. *and the silver for* (things) of *silver*,
3. of gold *and silver*,
4. seven thousand talents of refined *silver*,
5. *the silver for* (things) of *silver*,
7. *and of silver* ten thousand talents,
2Ch. 1: 15. the king made *silver*...as stones,
17. six hundred (shekels) of *silver*,
2: 7(6). *and in silver* and in brass,
14(13). skilful to work in gold, *and in silver*,
5: 1. and *the silver*, and the gold,
9: 14. brought gold *and silver* to Solomon.
20. none (were of) *silver;*
21. *and silver*, ivory, and apes,
24. vessels of *silver*, and vessels of gold,
27. the king made *silver*...as stones,
15: 18. *silver*, and gold, and vessels.
16: 2. Then Asa brought out *silver*
3. I have sent thee *silver* and gold;
17: 11. Jehoshaphat presents, *and* tribute *silver*,
21: 3. their father gave them great gifts of *silver*,
24: 5. gather of all Israel *money*
11. they saw that (there was) much *money*,
— gathered *money* in abundance.
14. they brought the rest of *the money*
— vessels of gold *and silver*.
25: 6. an hundred talents of *silver*.
24. (he took) all the gold *and the silver*,
27: 5. an hundred talents of *silver*,
32: 27. he made himself treasuries *for silver*,
34: 9. they delivered *the money*,
14. when they brought out *the money*
17. they have gathered together *the money*
36: 3. an hundred talents of *silver*
Ezr. 1: 4. the men of his place help him *with silver*,
6. their hands with vessels of *silver*,
9. a thousand chargers of *silver*,
10. *silver* basons of a second (sort)
11. All the vessels of gold *and of silver*
2: 69. *and* five thousand pound of *silver*,
3: 7. They gave *money* also unto the masons,
8: 25. weighed unto them *the silver*,
26. six hundred and fifty talents of *silver*, and *silver* vessels an hundred talents,
28. *and the silver* and the gold (are) a freewill
30. the weight of *the silver*,
33. *the silver* and the gold
Neh. 5: 4. We have borrowed *money*
10. might exact of them *money*
11. the hundredth (part) of *the money*,
15. beside forty shekels of *silver;*
7: 71. *and* two thousand and two hundred pound of *silver*.
72. *and* two thousand pound of *silver*,
Est. 1: 6. *silver* rings and pillars of marble:
— the beds (were of) gold *and silver*,
3: 9. I will pay ten thousand talents of *silver*
11. *The silver* (is) given to thee,
4: 7. the sum of *the money*
Job 3: 15. who filled their houses with *silver:*
22: 25. *and* thou shalt have plenty of *silver*.
27: 16. Though he heap up *silver* as the dust,
17. *and* the innocent shall divide *the silver*.
28: 1. Surely there is a vein *for the silver*,
15. neither shall *silver* be weighed
31: 39. eaten the fruits thereof without *money*
Ps. 12: 6(7). (as) *silver* tried in a furnace of earth,
15: 5. putteth not out *his money* to usury,
66: 10. as *silver* is tried.
68: 13(14) a dove covered *with silver*,
30(31) submit himself with pieces of *silver:*
105: 37. He brought them forth also *with silver*
115: 4. Their idols (are) *silver* and gold,
119: 72. thousands of gold *and silver*.
135: 15. The idols of the heathen (are) *silver*
Pro. 2: 4. If thou seekest her *as silver*,
3: 14. the merchandise of *silver*,
7: 20. He hath taken a bag of *money*
8: 10. Receive my instruction, and not *silver;*
19. my revenue *than* choice *silver*.
10: 20. tongue of the just (is as) choice *silver:*
16: 16. rather to be chosen *than silver?*
17: 3. The fining pot (is) *for silver*,
22: 1. loving favour rather *than silver*
Pro. 25: 4. Take away the dross *from the silver*,
11. (like) apples of gold in pictures of *silver*
26: 23. a potsherd covered with *silver* dross.
27: 21. (As) the fining pot *for silver*,
Ecc. 2: 8. I gathered me also *silver*
5: 10(9). He that loveth *silver* shall not be satisfied with *silver;*
7: 12. *money* (is) a defence;
10: 19. *but money* answereth all (things).
12: 6. Or ever the *silver* cord be loosed,
Cant. 1: 11. with studs of *silver*.
3: 10. He made the pillars thereof (of) *silver*,
8: 9. we will build upon her a palace of *silver:*
11. a thousand (pieces) of *silver*.
Isa. 1: 22. *Thy silver* is become dross,
2: 7. Their land also is full of *silver*
20. *his* idols of *silver*,
7: 23. a thousand vines at a thousand *silverlings*,
13: 17. which shall not regard *silver;*
30: 22. *thy* graven images of *silver*,
31: 7. cast away *his* idols of *silver*,
39: 2. *the silver*, and the gold, and the spices,
40: 19. and casteth *silver* chains.
43: 24. bought me no sweet cane *with money*,
46: 6. *and* weigh *silver* in the balance,
48: 10. I have refined thee, but not *with silver;*
52: 3. ye shall be redeemed *without money*.
55: 1. he that hath no *money;*
— without *money* and without price.
2. Wherefore do ye spend *money*
60: 9. *their silver* and their gold
17. for iron I will bring *silver*,
Jer. 6: 30. Reprobate *silver* shall (men) call them,
10: 4. They deck it *with silver*
9. *Silver* spread into plates
32: 9. and weighed him *the money*, (even) seventeen shekels of *silver*.
10. and weighed (him) *the money*
25. Buy thee the field *for money*,
44. Men shall buy fields *for money*,
52: 19. (that) which (was) of *silver* (in) *silver*,
Lam. 5: 4. We have drunken our water *for money;*
Eze. 7: 19. They shall cast *their silver*
— *their silver* and their gold
16: 13. thou decked with gold *and silver*,
17. of my gold *and of my silver*,
22: 18. they are (even) the dross of *silver*.
20. they gather *silver*,
22. As *silver* is melted in the...furnace,
27: 12. *with silver*, iron, tin, and lead,
28: 4. hast gotten gold *and silver*
38: 13. to carry away *silver* and gold,
Dan 11: 8. their precious vessels of *silver*
38. shall he honour with gold, *and silver*,
43. the treasures of gold *and* of *silver*,
Hos 2: 8(10). multiplied *her silver* and gold,
3: 2. fifteen (pieces) of *silver*,
8: 4. *their silver* and their gold
9: 6. pleasant (places) *for their silver*,
13: 2. molten images *of their silver*,
Joel 3: 5(4: 5). ye have taken *my silver*
Am. 2: 6. sold the righteous *for silver*,
8: 6. That we may buy the poor *for silver*,
Mic 3: 11. the prophets thereof divine *for money:*
Nah 2: 9(10). Take ye the spoil of *silver*,
Hab 2: 19. laid over with gold *and silver*,
Zep 1: 11. all they that bear *silver*
18. Neither *their silver* nor their gold
Hag 2: 8. *The silver* (is) mine,
Zec 6: 11. Then take *silver* and gold,
9: 3. heaped up *silver* as the dust,
11: 12. for my price thirty (pieces) of *silver*.
13. I took the thirty (pieces) of *silver*,
13: 9. refine them as *silver* is refined,
14: 14. gold, *and silver*, and apparel,
Mal. 3: 3. (as) a refiner and purifier of *silver*.
— and purge them as gold *and silver*,

כְּסַף *k'saph*, Ch. m. 3702

Ezr. 5: 14. the vessels also of gold *and silver*
6: 5. also let the golden *and silver vessels*
7: 15. And to carry *the silver* and gold,
16. And all *the silver* and gold that
17. mayest buy speedily *with* this *money*
18. to do with the rest of *the silver*

Ezr. 7:22. Unto an hundred talents of *silver*,
Dan 2:32. his breast and his arms of *silver*,
35. the brass, *the silver*, and the gold,
45. the clay, *the silver*, and the gold;
5: 2. to bring the golden *and silver* vessels
4. and praised the gods of gold, *and of silver*,
23. thou hast praised the gods of *silver*, and

3704 **כְּסָתוֹת** *k'sāh-thōhth'*, f. pl.

Eze.13:18. the (women) that sew *pillows*
20. I (am) against *your pillows*,

3705 **כְּעַן** *k'^{n}gan*, Ch. adv.

Ezr. 4:13. Be it known *now* unto the king,
14. *Now* because we have maintenance
21. Give ye *now* commandment to cause
5:16. and since that time even until *now*
17. *Now therefore*, if (it seem) good to the
6: 6. *Now* (therefore), Tatnai, governor
Dan 2:23. *and* hast made known unto me *now*
3:15. *Now* if ye be ready that at what time
4:37(34). *Now* I Nebuchadnezzar praise and
5:12. *now* let Daniel be called,
15. *And now* the wise (men), the astrologers,
16. *now* if thou canst read the writing,
6: 8(9). *Now*, O king, establish the decree,

3706 **כְּעֶנֶת** *k'^{n}geh'-neth*, Ch. part.

Ezr. 4:10, 11. the river, *and at such a time*. (marg. *Cheeneth*)
7:12. perfect (peace), *and at such a time*.

3707 **כָּעַס** *kāh-^{n}gas'*.

* KAL.—*Preterite*. *

Ps.112:10. The wicked shall see (it), *and be grieved*;
Ecc. 5:17(16). *and he hath* much *sorrow* and wrath

KAL.—*Infinitive*.

Ecc. 7: 9. Be not hasty in thy spirit *to be angry*:

KAL.—*Future*.

2Ch.16:10. *Then* Asa *was wroth*
Neh 4: 1(3:33). *and took* great *indignation*,
Eze 16:42. and *will be* no more *angry*.

* PIEL.—*Preterite*. *

Deu32:21. *they have provoked me to anger*
1Sa. 1: 6. *And* her adversary also *provoked her*

* HIPHIL.—*Preterite*. *

1K. 15:30. *he provoked* the Lord God of Israel *to anger*.
21:22. *thou hast provoked* (me) *to anger*,
2K. 23:26. Manasseh *had provoked him*
Neh. 4: 5(3:37). *they have provoked* (thee) *to anger*
Jer. 8:19. Why *have they provoked me to anger*
Eze.32: 9. *I will also vex* the hearts of (marg. *provoke to anger*, or, *grief*)
Hos.12:14(15). Ephraim *provoked* (him) *to anger*

HIPHIL.—*Infinitive*.

Deu 4:25. *to provoke him to anger*:
9:18. the Lord, *to provoke him to anger*.
31:29. *to provoke him to anger*
1K. 14: 9. images, *to provoke me to anger*,
16: 2. to sin, *to provoke me to anger*
7. *in provoking him to anger*
13. *in provoking* the Lord God of Israel *to anger*
26, 33. *to provoke* the Lord God of Israel *to anger*
2K. 17:11. *to provoke* the Lord *to anger*:
17. the Lord, *to provoke him to anger*.
21: 6. *to provoke* (him) *to anger*.
22:17. that they *might provoke me to anger*
23:19. *to provoke* (the Lord) *to anger*,
2Ch 33: 6. *to provoke him to anger*.
34:25. that they *might provoke me to anger*
Jer. 7:18. that they *may provoke me to anger*.
11:17. *to provoke me to anger*
25: 7. that ye *might provoke me to anger*
32:29, 32 & 44:3. *to provoke me to anger*.
44: 8. *In that* ye *provoke me unto wrath*
Eze. 8:17 & 16:26. *to provoke me to anger*:

HIPHIL.—*Future*.

Deu32:16. *provoked they him to anger*.
21. *I will provoke them to anger*
Jud. 2:12. *and provoked* the Lord *to anger*.
1Sa. 1: 7. *so she provoked her*;
1K. 22:53(54). *and provoked to anger* the Lord
2Ch 28:25. *and provoked to anger* the Lord
Ps. 78:58. *For they provoked him to anger*
106:29. *Thus they provoked* (him) *to anger*
Jer. 25: 6. *provoke* me not *to anger*

HIPHIL.—*Participle*.

1K. 14:15. *provoking* the Lord *to anger*.
2K. 21:15. *have provoked* me *to anger*,
Isa. 65: 3. A people *that provoketh* me *to anger*
Jer. 7:19. *Do* they *provoke* me *to anger?*
32:30. *have* only *provoked* me *to anger*

כַּעַס *kah'-^{n}gas*, m. 3708

Deu32:19. *because of the provoking of* his sons,
27. I feared *the wrath of* the enemy,
1Sa. 1: 6. her adversary also provoked her *sore*, (lit. provoked her even *to vexation*)
16. the abundance of my complaint *and grief*
1K. 15:30. *by his provocation* wherewith he provoked
21:22. *the provocation* wherewith thou hast
2K. 23:26. of all *the provocations* (marg. *angers*)
Ps. 6: 7(8). Mine eye is consumed *because of grief*;
10:14. thou beholdest mischief *and spite*,
31: 9(10). mine eye is consumed *with grief*,
85: 4(5). cause *thine anger* toward us to cease.
Pro.12:16. A fool's *wrath* is presently known:
17:25. A foolish son (is) *a grief* to his father,
21:19. a contentious *and* an *angry* woman. (lit. a woman of contentions *and* of *anger*)
27: 3. *but* a fool's *wrath* (is) heavier than
Ecc. 1:18. in much wisdom (is) much *grief*:
2:23. *and* his travail *grief*;
7: 3. *Sorrow* (is) better than laughter: (marg. or, *Anger*)
9. *anger* resteth in the bosom of fools.
11:10. remove *sorrow* from thy heart, (marg. or, *anger*
Eze.20:28. *the provocation of* their offering:

כַּעַשׂ *kah'-^{n}gas*, m. 3708

Job 5: 2. *wrath* killeth the foolish man,
6: 2. Oh that *my grief* were throughly weighed,
10:17. increasest *thine indignation*
17: 7. Mine eye also is dim *by reason of sorrow*,

כְּעֶת *k'^{n}geth*, Ch, part. 3706

Ezr. 4:17. Peace, *and at such a time*.

כַּף *kaph*, f. 3709

Gen 8: 9. no rest *for the sole of* her foot,
20: 5. innocency of *my hands*
31:42. the labour of *my hands*,
32:25(26). he touched *the hollow of* his thigh; and *the hollow of* Jacob's thigh
32(33). *the hollow of* the thigh, unto this day: because he touched *the hollow of* Jacob's
40:11. I gave the cup into Pharaoh's *hand*.
21. he gave the cup into Pharaoh's *hand*:
Ex. 4: 4. it became a rod *in his hand*:
9:29. I will spread abroad *my hands*
33. spread abroad *his hands* unto the Lord:
25:29. the dishes thereof, *and spoons thereof*,
29:24. *in the hands of* Aaron, and *in the hands of*
33:22. will cover thee with *my hand*
23. I will take away *mine hand*,
37:16. the table, his dishes, and *his spoons*,
Lev. 8:27. he put all upon Aaron's *hands*, and upon his sons' *hands*,
28. Moses took them from off *their hands*,
9:17. took an *handful* (marg. filled *his hand*)
11:27. whatsoever goeth upon *his paws*,
14:15. *the palm of* his own left hand:
16, 27. the oil that (is) in *his* left *hand*,

Lev.14:17, 28. the oil that (is) in *his hand*
18. the oil that (is) in the priest's *hand*
26. *the palm of* his own left hand:
29. the oil that (is) in the priest's *hand*
23:40. *branches of* palm trees,
Nu. 4: 7. the dishes, and *the spoons*, and the bowls,
5:18. the offering of memorial in *her hands*,
6:19. upon *the hands of* the Nazarite,
7:14. One *spoon* of ten (shekels)
20. One *spoon* of gold of ten (shekels),
26, 32, 38, 44, 50, 56, 62, 68, 74, 80. One golden *spoon* of ten (shekels),
84. twelve *spoons of* gold:
86. The golden *spoons* (were) twelve,
— (weighing) ten (shekels) *apiece*, (lit. *the spoon*)
— all the gold of *the spoons* (was)
24:10. he smote *his hands* together:
Deu 2: 5. a foot breadth; (marg. the treading of *the sole of* the foot)
11:24. whereon *the soles of* your feet shall tread
25:12. Then thou shalt cut off *her hand*,
28:35. *from the sole of* thy foot
56. to set *the sole of* her foot upon
65. shall *the sole of* thy foot have rest:
Jos. 1: 3. *the sole of* your foot shall tread
3:13. *the soles of* the feet of the priests
4:18. *the soles of* the priests' feet
Jud. 6:13. *into the hands of* the Midianites.
14. *from the hand of* the Midianites:
8: 6, 15. *the hands of* Zebah and Zalmunna now
12: 3. I put my life *in my hands*,
14: 9. he took thereof *in his hands*,
1Sa. 4: 3. *out of the hand of* our enemies.
5: 4. both *the palms of* his hands
19: 5. he did put his life *in his hand*,
25:29. the middle of (lit. of *the hollow of*) a sling.
28:21. I have put my life *in my hand*,
2Sa.14:16. *out of the hand of* the man (that)
25. *from the sole of* his foot
18:12. thousand (shekels) of silver in *mine hand*,
14. he took three darts *in his hand*,
19: 9(10). *out of the hand of* our enemies, and he delivered us *out of the hand of* the
22: 1. *out of the hand of* all his enemies, *and out of the hand of* Saul:
1K. 5: 3(17). under *the soles of* his feet.
7:50. and the basons, *and the spoons*,
8:22. spread forth *his hands* toward heaven:
38. and spread forth *his hands*
54. *with his hands* spread
17:12. *an hand*ful of meal in a barrel,
18:44. ariseth a little cloud...*like* a man's *hand*.
2K. 4:34. *and his hands* upon *his hands*:
9:35. *and the palms of* (her) hands.
11:12. they clapped their *hands*,
16: 7. *out of the hand of* the king of Syria, *and out of the hand of* the king of Israel,
18:21. if a man lean, it will go *into his hand*,
19:24. *with the sole of* my feet have I dried up
20: 6. *and* I will deliver...*out of the hand of* the
25:14. and the snuffers, and *the spoons*,
1Ch 12:17. (there is) no wrong *in mine hands*,
2Ch 4:22. *and the spoons*, and the censers,
6:12. and spread forth *his hands*:
13. and spread forth *his hands* toward heaven,
29. and shall spread forth *his hands*
24:14. *and spoons*, and vessels of gold and silver.
30: 6. *out of the hand of* the kings of Assyria.
32:11. *out of the hand of* the king of Assyria?
Ezr. 8:31. *from the hand of* the enemy,
9: 5. and spread out *my hands*
Job 2: 7. *from the sole of* his foot unto his crown.
9:30. and make *my hands* never so clean;
10: 3. the work of *thine hands*,
11:13. stretch out *thine hands* toward him;
13:14. and put my life *in mine hand?*
21. Withdraw *thine hand* far from me:
16:17. (any) injustice *in mine hands*:
22:30. the pureness of *thine hands*.
27:23. (Men) shall clap *their hands*
29: 9. *and* laid (their) *hand* on their mouth.
31: 7. *and* if any blot hath cleaved *to mine hands*;
36:32. With *clouds* he covereth the light;
41: 8(40:32). Lay *thine hand* upon him,
Ps. 7: 3(4). if there be iniquity *in my hands*;
9:16(17). the work of *his own hands*.

Ps. 18 [title](1). *from the hand of* all his enemies,
24: 4. He that hath clean *hands*,
26: 6. I will wash *mine hands* in innocency:
44:20(21). stretched out *our hands*
47: 1(2). O clap your *hands*, all ye people;
63: 4(5). I will lift up *my hands* in thy name.
71: 4. *out of the hand of* the unrighteous
73:13. washed *my hands* in innocency.
78:72. by the skilfulness of *his hands*.
81: 6(7). *his hands* were delivered from
88: 9(10). I have stretched out *my hands*
91:12. They shall bear thee up in (their) *hands*,
98: 8. Let the floods clap (their) *hands*:
119:48. *My hands* also will I lift up
109. My soul (is) continually *in my hand*:
128: 2. thou shalt eat the labour of *thine hands*:
129: 7. the mower filleth not *his hand*;
139: 5. and laid *thine hand* upon me.
141: 2. the lifting up of *my hands*
Pro. 6: 1. (if) thou hast stricken *thy hand* with
3. *into the hand of* thy friend;
10: 4. poor that dealeth (with) *a slack hand*:
17:18. man void of understanding striketh *hands*,
22:26. (one) of them that strike *hands*,
31:13. worketh willingly with *her hands*.
16. the fruit of *her hands*
19. *and her hands* hold the distaff.
20. She stretcheth out *her hand* to the poor;
Ecc. 4: 6. *an hand*ful (with) quietness,
Cant.5: 5. upon *the handles of* the lock.
Isa. 1: 6. *From the sole of* the foot even unto the
15. when ye spread forth *your hands*,
28: 4. while it is yet *in his hand*
33:15. shaketh *his hands* from holding of bribes,
36: 6. it will go *into his hand*, and pierce
37:25. *with the sole of* my feet have I dried up
38: 6. *And* I will deliver...*out of the hand of* the
49:16. upon *the palms of* (my) *hands*;
55:12. all the trees...shall clap (their) *hands*.
59: 3. *your hands* are defiled with blood,
6. the act of violence (is) *in their hands*.
60:14. bow themselves down at *the soles of* thy
62: 3. *in the hand of* thy God.
Jer. 4:31. (that) spreadeth *her hands*,
12: 7. *into the hand of* her enemies.
15:21. *out of the hand of* the terrible.
52:18. the bowls, and *the spoons*,
19. *the spoons*, and the cups;
Lam.2:15. All that pass by clap (their) *hands*
19. lift up *thy hands* toward him
3:41. lift up our heart with (our) *hands*
Eze. 1: 7. *and the sole of* their feet (was) *like the sole of* a calf's foot:
6:11. Smite *with thine hand*,
21:11(16). that it may be *hand*led: (lit. to be held *in the hand*)
14(19). smite (thine) *hands together*, (marg. *hand* to *hand*)
17(22). I will also smite *mine hands together*, (lit. *my hand* to *my hand*)
24(29). ye shall be taken *with the hand*.
22:13. I have smitten *mine hand*
29: 7. they took hold of thee *by thy hand*,
43: 7. the place of *the soles of* my feet,
Dan 10:10. *and* (upon) *the palms of* my hands.
Jon. 3: 8. the violence that (is) *in their hands*.
Mic. 4:10. *from the hand of* thine enemies.
7: 3. That they may do evil with *both hands*
Nah. 3:19. shall clap *the hands* over thee:
Hab. 2: 9. *from the power* (marg. *palm of the hand*) *of* evil!
Hag. 1:11. all the labour of *the hands*.
Mal. 4: 3(3:21). under *the soles of* your feet

כָּפָה [*kāh-phāh'*]. 3711

*** KAL.—*Future.* ***

Pro.21:14. A gift in secret *pacifieth* anger:

כִּפָּה *kip-pāh'*, f. 3712

Job 15:32. *and his branch* shall not be green.
Isa. 9:14(13). head and tail, *branch* and rush,
19:15. the head or tail, *branch* or rush,

3713 **כְּפוֹר** *k'phōhr*, m.

Ex. 16:14. (as) small *as the hoarfrost* on the ground.
1Ch 28:17. *and for the* golden *basons* (he gave gold) by weight *for every bason;* (lit. *for bason and bason*). *and* (likewise silver) by weight *for every bason of* silver (lit. *and for the basons of* silver *for bason and bason*)
Ezr. 1:10. Thirty *basons of* gold, silver *basons of* a
8:27. Also twenty *basons of* gold,
Job 38:29. *and the hoary frost of* heaven,
Ps. 147:16. he scattereth *the hoarfrost* like ashes.

3710 **כֵּפִים** *kēh-pheem'*, m. pl.

Job 30: 6. (in) caves of the earth, *and* (in) *the rocks.*
Jer. 4:29. *and* climb up *upon the rocks:*

3714 **כָּפִיס** *kāh-phees'*, m.

Hab 2:11. *and the beam* out of the timber shall answer (marg. or, *piece*, or, *fastening*)

3715 **כְּפִיר** *k'pheer*, m.

Jud. 14: 5. *a young* lion (lit. *a whelp of* lionesses)
Neh. 6: 2. *in* (some one of) *the villages*
Job 4:10. the teeth of *the young lions,*
38:39. fill the appetite of *the young lions,*
Ps. 17:12. and as it were *a young lion*
34:10(11). *The young lions* do lack, and suffer
35:17. my darling *from the lions.*
58: 6(7). the great teeth of *the young lions,*
91:13. *the young lion* and the dragon
104:21. *The young lions* roar after their prey,
Pro. 19:12. king's wrath (is) *as* the roaring of *a lion;*
20: 2. of a king (is) *as* the roaring of *a lion:*
28: 1. the righteous are bold *as a lion.*
Isa. 5:29. they shall roar *like young lions:*
11: 6. *and the young lion* and the fatling together;
31: 4. Like as the lion *and the young lion* roaring
Jer. 2:15. *The young lions* roared upon him,
25:38. He hath forsaken his covert, *as the lion:*
51:38. They shall roar together *like lions:*
Eze. 19: 2. nourished her whelps among *young lions.*
3. it became *a young lion,*
5. made him *a young lion.*
6. he became *a young lion,*
32: 2. Thou art like *a young lion*
38:13. all *the young lions thereof,*
41:19. the face of *a young lion*
Hos 5:14. *and as a young lion* to the house of Judah:
Am. 3: 4. will *a young lion* cry out of his den,
Mic 5: 8(7). *as a young lion* among the flocks of
Nah 2:11(12). the feedingplace *of the young lions,*
13(14). *and* the sword shall devour *thy young lions:*
Zec. 11: 3. a voice of the roaring of *young lions;*

3717 **כָּפַל** [*kāh-phal'*].

* KAL.—*Preterite.* *

Ex. 26: 9. *and shalt double* the sixth curtain

KAL.—*Participle.* Paül.

Ex. 28:16. Foursquare it shall be (being) *doubled;*
39: 9. they made the breastplate *double:*
— a span the breadth thereof, (being) *doubled.*

* NIPHAL.—*Future.* *

Eze. 21:14(19). and *let* the sword *be doubled*

3718 **כֶּפֶל** *keh'-phel*, m.

Job. 11: 6. secrets of wisdom, that (they are) *double*
41:13(5). who can come (to him) *with* his *double*
Isa. 40: 2. received of the Lord's hand *double*

3719 **כָּפַן** [*kāh-phan'*].

* KAL.—*Preterite.* *

Eze. 17: 7. this vine *did bend* her roots toward

כָּפָן *kāh-phāhn'*, m. 3720

Job. 5:22. At destruction *and famine* thou shalt
30: 3. For want *and famine* (they were) solitary;

כָּפַף *kāh-phaph'*. 3721

* KAL.—*Preterite.* *

Ps. 57: 6(7). my soul *is bowed down:*

KAL.—*Infinitive.*

Isa. 58: 5. *to bow down* his head as a bulrush,

KAL.—*Participle.* Paül.

Ps. 145:14. all (those that be) *bowed down.*
146: 8. *them that are bowed down:*

* NIPHAL.—*Future.* *

Mic 6: 6. (and) *bow myself* before the high God?

כָּפַר [*kāh-phar'*]. 3722

* KAL.—*Preterite.* *

Gen 6:14. *and shalt pitch* it within

* PIEL.—*Preterite.* *

Ex. 30:10. *And* Aaron *shall make an atonement*
Lev. 4:20. *and* the priest *shall make an atonement* for
26, 31. *and* the priest *shall make an atonement*
35. *and* the priest *shall make an atonement* for
5: 6,10,13,18 & 6:7(5:26). *and* the priest *shall make an atonement* for him
12: 7. *and make an atonement* for her;
8. *and* the priest *shall make an atonement* for
14:18, 20. *and* the priest *shall make an atonement*
19. *and make an atonement* for him
31. *and* the priest *shall make an atonement* for
53. *and make an atonement* for the house:
15:15. *and* the priest *shall make an atonement* for
30. *and* the priest *shall make an atonement* for
16: 6. *and make an atonement* for himself,
11. *and shall make an atonement* for himself,
16. *And he shall make an atonement* for the
17. *and have made an atonement* for himself,
18. *and make an atonement* for it;
24. *and make an atonement* for himself,
32. *And* the priest,...*shall make the atonement,*
33. *And he shall make an atonement* for the
19:22. *And* the priest *shall make an atonement* for
Nu. 6:11. *and make an atonement* for him,
15:25, 28. *And* the priest *shall make an atonement*
Deu 32:43. *and will be merciful unto* his land,
Eze. 43:20. thus shalt thou cleanse *and purge it.*
45:20. *so shall ye reconcile* the house.

PIEL.—*Infinitive.*

Ex. 29:36. *when thou hast made an atonement* for it,
30:15, 16. *to make an atonement* for your souls.
Lev. 1: 4. *to make atonement* for him.
6:30(23). *to reconcile* (withal) in the holy
8:15. *to make reconciliation* upon it.
34. *to make an atonement* for you.
10:17. *to make atonement* for them
14:21. *to make an atonement* for him,
29. *to make an atonement* for him
16:10. *to make an atonement* with him,
17. *to make an atonement* in the holy (place),
20. when he hath made an end *of reconciling*
27. blood was brought in *to make atonement*
34. *to make an atonement* for the children of
17:11. *to make an atonement* for your souls:
23:28. *to make an atonement* for you
Nu. 8:12. *to make an atonement* for the Levites.
19. *and to make an atonement* for the children
15:28. *to make an atonement* for him;
28:22, 30 & 29:5. *to make an atonement* for you.
31:50. *to make an atonement* for our souls
1Ch 6:49(34). *and to make an atonement* for Israel,
2Ch 29:24. *to make an atonement* for all Israel:
Neh 10:33(34). *to make an atonement* for Israel,
Isa. 47:11. be able *to put it off:* (marg. *expiate*)
Eze. 16:63. *when I am pacified* toward thee
45:15. *to make reconciliation* for them,
17. *to make reconciliation* for the house of
Dan 9:24. *and to make reconciliation* for iniquity,

PIEL.—*Imperative.*

Lev. 9: 7. *and make an atonement* for thyself,
— *and make an atonement* for them;
Nu. 16:46 (17:11). *and make an atonement* for them:
Deu 21: 8. *Be merciful*, O Lord, unto thy people
Ps. 79: 9. deliver us, *and purge away* our sins,

PIEL.—*Future.*

Gen 32:20 (21). *I will appease* him with the present
Ex. 29:37. *thou shalt make an atonement*
30:10. once in the year *shall he make atonement*
32:30. *I shall make an atonement*
Lev. 5:16. the priest *shall make an atonement*
7: 7. the priest *that maketh atonement*
16:30. *shall* (the priest) *make an atonement*
33. *shall make an atonement* for the tabernacle
— and *he shall make an atonement* for the
17:11. the blood (that) *maketh an atonement*
Nu. 5: 8. *atonement shall be made* for him.
8:21. *and* Aaron *made an atonement*
16:47 (17:12). *and made an atonement* for the
25:13. *and made an atonement* for the children of
2Sa. 21: 3. wherewith *shall I make the atonement*,
2Ch 30:18. The good Lord *pardon* every one
Ps. 65: 3 (4). *thou shalt purge them away.*
78:38. *forgave* (their) iniquity,
Pro. 16:14. a wise man *will pacify it.*
Jer. 18:23. *forgive* not their iniquity,
Eze. 43:26. *shall they purge* the altar

* PUAL.—*Preterite.* *

Ex. 29:33. things wherewith *the atonement was made*,
Isa 28:18. *And* your covenant with death *shall be disannulled*,

PUAL.—*Future.*

Nu. 35:33. the land *cannot be cleansed*
Pro. 16: 6. By mercy and truth iniquity *is purged*:
Isa. 6: 7. and thy sin *purged.*
22:14. this iniquity *shall* not *be purged*
27: 9. *shall* the iniquity of Jacob *be purged*;

* HITHPAEL.—*Future.* *

1Sa. 3:14. of Eli's house *shall* not *be purged*

* NITHPAEL.—*Preterite.* *

Deu 21: 8. *And* the blood *shall be forgiven* them.

3723 **כָּפָר** [*kāh-phāhr'*], m.

Jos. 18:24. *And Chephar*-haammonai, (or, *and the village of* Ammonai)
1Ch 27:25. in the cities, *and in the villages*,
Cant. 7:11 (12). let us lodge *in the villages.*

3724 **כֹּפֶר** *kōh'-pher*, m.

Gen 6:14. pitch it within and without *with pitch.*
Ex. 21:30. If there be laid on him *a sum of money*,
30:12. then shall they give every man *a ransom*
Nu. 35:31. ye shall take no *satisfaction* for the life of
32. ye shall take no *satisfaction* for him
1Sa. 6:18. and of country *villages*,
12: 3. of whose hand have I received (any) *bribe* (marg. *ransom*)
Job 33:24. found *a ransom.* (marg. or, *atonement*)
36:18. *a* great *ransom* cannot deliver thee.
Ps. 49: 7 (8). nor give to God *a ransom* for him:
Pro. 6:35. He will not regard any *ransom*;
13: 8. *The ransom* of a man's life (are) his riches:
21:18. The wicked (shall be) *a ransom* for the
Cant. 1:14. a cluster of *camphire*
4:13. *camphire*, with spikenard,
Isa. 43: 3. I gave Egypt (for) *thy ransom*,
Am. 5:12. they take *a bribe*, (marg. or, *ransom*)

3725 **כִּפֻּרִים** *kip-poo-reem'*, pl. m.

Ex 29:36. a sin offering for *atonement*:
30:10. the sin offering of *atonements*:
16. thou shalt take the *atonement* money
Lev. 23:27. (there shall be) a day of *atonement*:
28. it (is) a day of *atonement*,
25: 9. the day of *atonement*
Nu. 5: 8. the ram of *the atonement*,
29:11. the sin offering of *atonement*,

כַּפֹּרֶת *kap-pōh'-reth*, f. 3727

Ex. 25:17. thou shalt make *a mercy seat*
18. the two ends of *the mercy seat.*
19. of *the mercy seat* shall ye make
20. covering *the mercy seat*
— toward *the mercy seat*
21. put *the mercy seat* above upon the ark;
22. from above *the mercy seat*,
26:34. put *the mercy seat* upon the ark
30: 6. before *the mercy seat*
31: 7. *the mercy seat* that (is) thereupon,
35:12. The ark,...(with) *the mercy seat*,
37: 6. he made *the mercy seat*
7. on the two ends of *the mercy seat*,
8. out of *the mercy seat*
9. over *the mercy seat*,
— to *the mercy seat*ward
39:35. The ark...and *the mercy seat*,
40:20. and put *the mercy seat* above
Lev. 16: 2. the vail before *the mercy seat*,
— in the cloud upon *the mercy seat.*
13. of the incense may cover *the mercy seat*
14. upon *the mercy seat* eastward; and before *the mercy seat* shall he
15. sprinkle it upon *the mercy seat*, and before *the mercy seat*:
Nu. 7:89. from off *the mercy seat*
1Ch 28:11. the place of *the mercy seat*,

כָּפַשׁ [*kāh-phash'*]. 3728

* HIPHIL.—*Preterite.* *

Lam. 3:16. *he hath covered me* with ashes. (marg. *rolled me* in)

כְּפַת [*k'phath*], Ch. 3729

* P'IL.—*Preterite.* *

Dan 3:21. Then these men *were bound* in their coats,

* PAEL.—*Infinitive.* *

Dan 3:20. mighty men that (were) in his army *to bind*

PAEL.—*Participle.*

Dan 3:23. fell down *bound* into the midst
24. Did not we cast three men *bound*

כַּפְתּוֹר *kaph-tōhr'*, m. 3730

Ex. 25:31. his bowls, *his knops*, and his flowers,
33. *a knop* and a flower
— *a knop* and a flower:
34. *their knops* and their flowers.
35. *And* (there shall be) *a knop* under two branches of the same, *and a knop* under two branches of the same, *and a knop*
36. *Their knops* and their branches
37:17. his bowls, *his knops*, and his flowers,
19. *a knop* and a flower;
— *a knop* and a flower:
20. *his knops*, and his flowers:
21. *And a knop* under two branches of the same, *and a knop* under two branches of the same, *and a knop* under two branches
22. *Their knops* and their branches
Am. 9: 1. Smite *the lintel* of the door, (marg. or, *chapiter*, or, *knop*)
Zep. 2:14. in *the upper lintels* of it; (marg. *id.*)

כַּר *kar*, m. 3733

Gen 31:34. put them *in* the camel's *furniture*,
Deu 32:14. with fat of *lambs*,
1Sa. 15: 9. of the fatlings, and *the lambs*,
2K. 3: 4. an hundred thousand *lambs*,
Ps. 37:20. as the fat of *lambs*:
65:13 (14). *The pastures* are clothed with flocks;
Isa. 16: 1. Send ye *the lamb* to the ruler of the land

Isa. 30:23. day shall thy cattle feed in *large pastures.*
34: 6. the blood of *lambs* and goats,
Jer. 51:40. I will bring them down *like lambs*
Eze. 4: 2. set (battering) *rams* against it (marg. or, *chief leaders*)
21:22(27). to appoint *captains,* (marg. *rams,* or, (battering) *rams*)
—(—). to appoint (battering) *rams*
27:21. occupied with thee *in lambs,* and rams,
39:18. of rams, of *lambs,* and of goats,
Am. 6: 4. eat *the lambs* out of the flock,

3734 ## כֹּר *kōhr,* m.

1K. 4:22(5:2). thirty *measures* of fine flour, and threescore *measures* of meal, (marg. *cors*)
5:11(25). twenty thousand *measures* of wheat
—(—). and twenty *measures* of pure oil:
2Ch 2:10(9). twenty thousand *measures* of beaten wheat, and twenty thousand *measures* of
27: 5. ten thousand *measures* of wheat,
Eze.45:14. the tenth part of a bath out of *the cor,*

See 3734 ## כֹּר Ch. see כּוֹרִין

3735 ## כְּרָא [*k'rāh*], Ch.

* ITHP'EL.—*Preterite.* *

Dan. 7:15. I Daniel *was grieved* in my spirit

3736 ## כִּרְבֵּל [*kir-bēhl'*].

* *Participle.* Passive. *

1Ch 15:27. (was) *clothed* with a robe of fine linen,

3737 ## כַּרְבְּלָא [*kar-b'lāh'*], Ch. f.

Dan. 3:21. their hosen, *and their hats,* and their (marg. or, *turbans*)

3738-39 ## כָּרָה *kāh-rāh'.*

* KAL.—*Preterite.* *

Gen50: 5. my grave which *I have digged*
Nu. 21:18. the nobles of the people *digged it,*
2Ch 16:14. sepulchres, which *he had made* (marg. *digged*)
Ps. 7:15(16). *He made* (marg. *digged*) a pit, and
22:16(17). *they pierced* my hands and my feet.
40: 6(7). ears *hast thou opened:* (marg. *digged*)
57: 6(7). *they have digged* a pit
119:85. The proud *have digged* pits
Jer. 18:20. *they have digged* a pit for my soul.
22. *they have digged* a pit to take me,

KAL.—*Future.*

Gen26:25. *and* there Isaac's servants *digged* a well.
Ex. 21:33. if a man *shall dig* a pit,
Deu 2: 6. *Ye shall* also *buy* water
2K. 6:23. *And he prepared* great provision
Job 6:27. *and ye dig* (a pit) for your friend.
41: 6(40:30). *Shall* the companions *make a banquet*
Hos. 3: 2. *So I bought her* to me

KAL.—*Participle.* Poel.

Pro.16:27. An ungodly man *diggeth* up evil:
26:27. Whoso *diggeth* a pit shall fall

* NIPHAL.—*Future.* *

Ps. 94:13. until the pit *be digged*

NOTE.—In Ps. 22:16(17). the reading of the printed Hebrew copies is כָּאֲרִי (*like a lion*) some MSS. however read כָּאֲרוּ, others כָּארוּ or כָּרוּ, this is evidently the true reading, and is followed by the English version.

כֵּרָה *kēh-rāh'.* 3740

2K. 6:23. he prepared great *provision*

כְּרוּב *k'roov,* m. 3742

Gen 3:24. the east of the garden of Eden *Cherubims,*
Ex. 25:18. thou shalt make two *cherubims*
19. one *cherub* on the one end, *and the* other *cherub* on the other end: (even) of the mercy seat shall ye make *the cherubims*
20. *the cherubims* shall stretch forth (their)
— the faces of *the cherubims*
22. between *the* two *cherubims*
26: 1. *cherubims* of cunning work
31. with *cherubims* shall it be made:
36: 8. *cherubims* of cunning work
35. *cherubims* made he it of cunning work.
37: 7. he made two *cherubims* (of) gold,
8. One *cherub* on the end on this side, *and* another *cherub* on the (other) end on that side: out of the mercy seat made he *the cherubims*
9. *the cherubims* spread out (their) wings
— the faces of *the cherubims.*
Nu. 7:89. from between *the* two *cherubims:*
1Sa. 4: 4. which dwelleth (between) *the cherubims:*
2Sa. 6: 2. that dwelleth (between) *the cherubims.*
22:11. he rode upon *a cherub,*
1K. 6:23. he made two *cherubims*
24. the one wing of *the cherub,* and five cubits the other wing of *the cherub:*
25. *the* other *cherub* (was) ten cubits: both *the cherubims* (were) of one measure
26. height of *the* one *cherub* (was) ten cubits, and so (was it) of *the* other *cherub.*
27. he set *the cherubims* within the inner house: and they stretched forth the wings of *the cherubims,*
— of *the* other *cherub* touched the other wall;
28. he overlaid *the cherubims* with gold.
29. about with carved figures of *cherubims*
32. carvings of *cherubims*
— spread gold upon *the cherubims,*
35. he carved (thereon) *cherubims*
7:29. lions, oxen, *and cherubims:*
36. he graved *cherubims,*
8: 6. the wings of *the cherubims.*
7. *the cherubims* spread forth (their) two
— *the cherubims* covered the ark
2K. 19:15. which dwellest (between) *the cherubims,*
1Ch 13: 6. that dwelleth (between) *the cherubims,*
28:18. the chariot of *the cherubims,*
2Ch 3: 7. graved *cherubims* on the walls.
10. he made two *cherubims* of image work,
11. the wings of *the cherubims*
— reaching to the wing of *the* other *cherub.*
12. (one) wing of *the* other *cherub*
— the wing of *the* other *cherub.*
13. The wings of these *cherubims*
14. wrought *cherubims* thereon.
5: 7. under the wings of *the cherubims:*
8. *the cherubims* spread forth (their) wings
— *the cherubims* covered the ark
Ps. 18:10(11). he rode upon *a cherub,*
80: 1(2). that dwellest (between) *the cherubims,*
99: 1. he sitteth (between) *the cherubims;*
Isa. 37:16. that dwellest (between) *the cherubims,*
Eze. 9: 3. the glory...was gone up from *the cherub,*
10: 1. the head of *the cherubims*
2. (even) under *the cherub,*
— from between *the cherubims,*
3. *Now the cherubims* stood on the right side
4. the glory...went up from *the cherub,*
5. the sound of *the cherubims'* wings
6. from between *the cherubims;*
7. And (one) *cherub* stretched forth his hand from between *the cherubims* unto the fire that (was) between *the cherubims,*
8. there appeared *in the cherubims*
9. behold the four wheels by *the cherubims,* one wheel by one *cherub,* and another wheel by another *cherub:*
14. the first face (was) the face of *a cherub,*
15. *the cherubims* were lifted up.

Eze.10:16. when *the cherubims* went, the wheels went by them: and when *the cherubims* lifted
18. stood over *the cherubims.*
19. *the cherubims* lifted up their wings,
20. I knew that they (were) *the cherubims.*
11:22. *the cherubims* lift up their wings,
28:14. Thou (art) *the* anointed *cherub*
16. I will destroy thee, O covering *cherub,*
41:18. And (it was) made with *cherubims* and palm trees, so that a palm tree (was) between *a cherub and a cherub;* and (every) *cherub* had two faces;
20. *cherubims* and palm trees made,
25. *cherubims* and palm trees, like as

3744 כָּרוֹז [*kāh-rōhz'*], Ch. m.

Dan 3: 4. *Then an herald* cried aloud, To you

3745 כְּרַז [*k'raz*], Ch.

* APHEL.—*Preterite.* *

Dan 5:29. *and made a proclamation* concerning him,

3746 כָּרִי *kāh-ree'*, m. pl.

2Sa.20:23. (כתיב) (was) over *the Cherethites*
2 K.11: 4. *with the captains* and the guard,
19. *the captains,* and the guard,

3748 כְּרִיתוּת *k'ree-thooth'*, f.

Deu24: 1. bill of *divorcement,* (marg. *cutting off*)
3. and write her a bill of *divorcement,*
Isa. 50: 1. the bill of your mother's *divorcement,*
Jer. 3: 8. given *her* a bill of *divorce;*

3749 כַּרְכֹּב *kar-kōhv'*, m.

Ex. 27: 5. *the compass of* the altar
38: 4. under *the compass thereof*

3750 כַּרְכֹּם *kar-kōhm'*, m.

Cant 4:14. Spikenard *and saffron;*

3753 כִּרְכָּרוֹת *kir-kāh-rōhth'*, f. pl.

Isa. 66:20. upon mules, *and upon swift beasts,*

3754 כֶּרֶם *keh'-rem*, com.

Gen 9:20. and he planted *a vineyard:*
Ex. 22: 5(4). a field or *vineyard*
— the best of *his own vineyard,*
23:11. thou shalt deal *with thy vineyard,*
Lev.19:10. *And* thou shalt not glean *thy vineyard,* neither shalt thou gather (every) grape of *thy vineyard;*
25: 3. thou shalt prune *thy vineyard,*
4. *nor* prune *thy vineyard.*
Nu. 16:14. inheritance of fields *and vineyards:*
20:17. through the fields, *or through the vineyards,*
21:22. *or into the vineyards;*
22:24. in a path of *the vineyards,*
Deu 6:11. *vineyards* and olive trees,
20: 6. (he) that hath planted *a vineyard,*
22: 9. Thou shalt not sow *thy vineyard* with
— the fruit of (thy) *vineyard,*
23:24(25). *into* thy neighbour's *vineyard,*
24:21. the grapes of *thy vineyard,*
28:30. thou shalt plant *a vineyard,*
39. Thou shalt plant *vineyards,*
Jos. 24:13. *the vineyards* and oliveyards
Jud. 9:27. and gathered *their vineyards,*
11:33. unto the plain of *the vineyards,*
14: 5. *the vineyards of* Timnath:
Jud.15: 5. *the vineyards* (and) olives.
21:20. lie in wait *in the vineyards;*
21. then come ye out of *the vineyards,*
1Sa. 8:14. your fields, and *your vineyards,*
15. *and* of *your vineyards,*
22: 7. give every one of you fields *and vineyards,*
1K. 21: 1. Naboth the Jezreelite had *a vineyard,*
2, 6. Give me *thy vineyard,*
— a better *vineyard* than it;
6. I will give thee (another) *vineyard* for it: and he answered, I will not give thee *my vineyard.*
7. I will give thee *the vineyard of*
15, 16. *the vineyard of* Naboth
18. *in the vineyard of* Naboth,
2K. 5:26. garments, and oliveyards, *and vineyards,*
18:32. a land of bread *and vineyards,*
19:29. sow ye, and reap, and plant *vineyards,*
1Ch.27:27. over *the vineyards* (was) Shimei the Ramathite: over *the increase of the vineyards* (marg. *that which* (was) *of the vineyards*)
Neh 3:14. the ruler of part of Beth-*haccerem;* (lit. house of *the vineyard*)
5: 3. our lands, *vineyards,* and houses,
4. our lands *and vineyards.*
5. other men have our lands *and vineyards.*
11. their lands, *their vineyards,*
9:25. wells digged, *vineyards,* and oliveyards,
Job.24: 6. *and* they gather *the vintage* of the wicked.
18. he beholdeth not the way of *the vineyards.*
Ps.107:37. sow the fields, and plant *vineyards,*
Pro.24:30. *the vineyard of* the man void of
31:16. she planteth *a vineyard.*
Ecc. 2: 4. I planted me *vineyards:*
Cant 1: 6. they made me keeper of *the vineyards;* (but) *mine own vineyard* have I not
14. *in the vineyards of* En-gedi.
2:15. the little foxes, that spoil *the vines: for our vines* (have) tender grapes.
7:12(13). Let us get up early *to the vineyards;*
8:11. Solomon had *a vineyard* at Baal-hamon; he let out *the vineyard* unto keepers;
12. *My vineyard,* which (is) mine,
Isa. 1: 8. as a cottage *in a vineyard,*
3:14. ye have eaten up *the vineyard;*
5: 1. my beloved *touching his vineyard.* My wellbeloved hath *a vineyard*
3. betwixt me and *my vineyard.*
4. been done more *to my vineyard,*
5. what I will do *to my vineyard:*
7. *the vineyard of* the Lord of hosts
10. ten acres of *vineyard*
16:10. *and in the vineyards* there shall be no
27: 2. *A vineyard of* red wine.
36:17. a land of bread *and vineyards.*
37:30. sow ye, and reap, and plant *vineyards,*
65:21. they shall plant *vineyards,*
Jer. 6: 1. a sign of fire in Beth-*haccerem:* (lit. house of *the vineyard*)
12:10. Many pastors have destroyed *my vineyard,*
31: 5. Thou shalt yet plant *vines*
32:15. Houses and fields *and vineyards*
35: 7. nor sow seed, *nor* plant *vineyard,*
9. neither (lit. *and* not) have we *vineyard,*
39:10. and gave them *vineyards* and fields
Eze.28:26. build houses, and plant *vineyards;*
Hos. 2:15(17). I will give her *her vineyards*
Am. 4: 9. your gardens *and your vineyards*
5:11. ye have planted pleasant *vineyards,*
17. in all *vineyards* (shall be) wailing:
9:14. they shall plant *vineyards,*
Mic. 1: 6. as plantings of *a vineyard;*
Zep 1:13. they shall plant *vineyards,*

כַּרְמִיל *kar-meel'*, m. 3758

2Ch. 2: 7(6). in purple, *and crimson,* and blue,
14(13). in fine linen, *and in crimson;*
3:14. purple, *and crimson,* and fine linen,

כֹּרְמִים *kōh-r'meem'*, m. pl. 3755

2K. 25:12. (to be) *vinedressers* and husbandmen.
2Ch 26:10. *and vine dressers* in the mountains.

Isa. 61: 5. your plowmen *and your vinedressers.*
Jer. 52:16. the poor of the land *for vinedressers*
Joel 1:11. howl, *O ye vinedressers,*

3759-60 ## כַּרְמֶל *kar-mel'*, m.

Lev. 2:14. beaten out of *full ears.*
23:14. nor parched corn, *nor green ears,*
2K. 4:42. *and full ears of corn* in the husk thereof.
19:23. forest of *his Carmel.* (or, *fruitful field*)
2Ch.26:10. in the mountains, *and in Carmel:* (marg. or, *fruitful fields*)
Cant 7: 5(6). Thine head upon thee (is) *like Carmel,* (marg. or, *crimson*)
Isa. 10:18. of his forest, *and of his fruitful field,*
16:10. and joy out of *the plentiful field;*
29:17. Lebanon shall be turned into *a fruitful field, and the fruitful field* shall be
32:15. the wilderness be *a fruitful field, and the fruitful field* be counted for a forest.
16. righteousness remain *in the fruitful field.*
37:24. the forest of *his Carmel.* (marg. or *his fruitful field*)
Jer. 2: 7. I brought you in to a *plentiful* country,
4:26. *the fruitful place* (was) a wilderness,
48:33. gladness is taken from *the plentiful field,*
Am. 1: 2. the top of *Carmel* shall wither.
9: 3. they hide themselves in the top of *Carmel,*
Mic. 7:14. in the midst of *Carmel:*

3764 ## כָּרְסֵא *kor-sēh'*, Ch. m

Dan 5:20. he was deposed from his kingly *throne,*
7: 9. I beheld till *the thrones* were cast down,
— *his throne* (was like) the fiery flame,

3765 ## כִּרְסֵם [*keer-sēhm',*].

Future.

Ps. 80:13(14). boar out of the wood *doth waste it,*

3766 ## כָּרַע *kāh-rag'.*

* KAL.—*Preterite.* *

Gen49: 9. *he stooped down,* he couched
Nu. 24: 9. *He couched,* he lay down as a lion,
Jud. 5:27. At her feet *he bowed,* he fell, he lay down: at her feet *he bowed,* he fell: where *he bowed,* there he fell
7: 6. the rest of the people *bowed down*
1 K.19:18. all the knees which *have* not *bowed*
2Ch.29:29. all that were present...*bowed themselves,*
Ps. 20: 8(9). *They are brought down*
Isa. 10: 4. Without me *they shall bow down*
46: 1. Bel *boweth down,*
2. *they bow down* together;

KAL.—*Infinitive.*

1 K. 8:54. *from kneeling* on his knees

KAL.—*Future.*

Jud. 7: 5. every one that *boweth down*
1 Sa. 4:19. *and* when...*she bowed herself* and
2K. 1:13. *and fell* on his knees before Elijah, (marg. *bowed*)
9:24. *and he sunk down* in his chariot. (marg. *bowed*)
2Ch. 7: 3. *And* when all...*they bowed themselves* with
Ezr. 9: 5. *I fell* upon my knees,
Est. 3: 2. Mordecai *bowed* not,
Job 31:10. *let* others *bow down* upon her.
39: 3. *They bow themselves,* they bring
Ps. 22:29(30). all they that go down...*shall bow*
72: 9. They that dwell in the wilderness *shall bow*
95: 6. let us worship *and bow down:*
Isa. 45:23. unto me every knee *shall bow,*
65:12. *ye shall* all *bow down*

KAL.—*Participle.* Poel.

Est. 3: 2. *bowed,* and reverenced Haman:
5. Haman saw that Mordecai *bowed* not,
Job 4: 4. thou hast strengthened the *feeble* knees. (marg. *bowing*)

* HIPHIL.—*Preterite.* *

Jud.11:35. daughter! *thou hast brought me* very *low,*
Ps. 78:31. *smote down* the chosen (men)

HIPHIL.—*Infinitive.*

Jud.11:35. hast brought me *very* low, (lit. *bringing low* hast brought me low)

HIPHIL.—*Imperative.*

Ps. 17:13. disappoint him, *cast him down:*

HIPHIL.—*Future.*

2Sa. 22:40. *hast thou subdued* under me. (marg. *caused to bow*)
Ps. 18:39(40). *thou hast subdued* under (marg. *id.*)

כְּרָעַיִם *k'rāh-ğah'-yim*, f. 3767

Ex. 12: 9. his head with *his legs,*
29:17. the inwards of him, *and his legs,*
Lev. 1: 9. his inwards *and his legs*
13. the inwards *and the legs*
4:11. with his head, and with *his legs,*
8:21 & 9:14. the inwards and *the legs*
11:21. which have *legs* above their feet,
Am. 3:12. out of the mouth of the lion *two legs,*

כַּרְפַּס *kar-pas'*, m. 3768

Est. 1: 6. white, *green,* and blue, (hangings),

כָּרַר [*kāh-rar'*]. 3769

* PILPEL.—*Participle.* *

2Sa. 6:14. David *danced* before the Lord
16. saw king David leaping *and dancing*

כְּרֵשׂ [*k'rēhs*] m. 3770

Jer. 51:34: he hath filled *his belly* with

כָּרַת *kāh-rath'.* 3772

* KAL.—*Preterite.* *

Gen15:18. the Lord *made* a covenant
Ex. 24: 8. the covenant, which the Lord *hath made*
34:27. *I have made* a covenant with thee
Nu. 13:24. the children of Israel *cut down*
Deu 4:23. the covenant...which *he made*
5: 2. The Lord our God *made* a covenant
3. The Lord *made* not this covenant
9: 9. the covenant which the Lord *made*
20:20. thou shalt destroy *and cut* them *down,*
29: 1(28:69). the covenant which *he made*
25(24). the covenant of the Lord God...which *he made*
31:16. my covenant which *I have made*
Jos. 9:16. *they had made* a league
Jud. 6:30. *he hath cut down* the grove
1Sa. 24: 5(6). *he had cut off* Saul's skirt.
1K. 8: 9. the Lord *made* (a covenant)
21. the covenant of the Lord, which *he made*
2K. 17:15. his covenant that *he made*
38. the covenant that *I have made*
18: 4. *and cut down* the groves,
1Ch16:16. (the covenant) which *he made*
2Ch 5:10. the Lord *made* (a covenant)
6:11. the covenant of the Lord, that *he made*
7:18. *I have covenanted* with David
21: 7. the covenant that *he had made*
Job 31: 1. *I made* a covenant with mine eyes;
Ps. 89: 3(4). *I have made* a covenant with
105: 9. (covenant) *he made* with Abraham,
Isa. 18: 5. *he shall both cut off* the sprigs
28:15. *We have made* a covenant
Jer. 10: 3. (one) *cutteth* a tree out of the forest,
11:10. my covenant which *I made*
22: 7. *and they shall cut down* thy choice cedars,
31:31. *that I will make* a new covenant
32. the covenant that *I made*
32:40. *And I will make* an everlasting covenant
34:13. *I made* a covenant with your fathers

Jer. 34:18. the covenant which *they had made*
— *they cut* the calf in twain,
46:23. *They shall cut down* her forest,
Eze.34:25. *And I will make* with them a covenant
37:26. *Moreover I will make* a covenant
Hos. 2:18(20). *will I make* a covenant
Hag. 2: 5. *I covenanted* with you
Zec.11:10. my covenant which *I had made*

KAL.—*Infinitive.*

Deu 19: 5. *to cut down* the tree,
29: 1(28:69). covenant, which the Lord commanded Moses *to make*
1 Sa.22: 8. *that* my son *hath made a league*
24:11(12). *in that I cut off* the skirt
1 K. 5: 6(20). *to hew* timber like unto the Sidonians.
2 Ch 2: 8(7). *to cut* timber in Lebanon;
29:10. *to make* a covenant with the Lord
Neh 9: 8. *and madest* a covenant with him
Isa. 44:14. *He heweth* him *down* cedars,
Jer. 34: 8. after *that* the king Zedekiah *had made* a
Hos10: 4. *in making* a covenant:

KAL.—*Imperative.*

Jos. 9: 6, 11. *make ye* a league with us.
1 Sa.11: 1. *Make* a covenant with us,
2 Sa. 3:12. *Make* thy league with me,
Jer. 6: 6. *Hew ye down* trees,
50:16. *Cut off* the sower from Babylon,

KAL.—*Future.*

Gen21:27. *and* both of them *made* a covenant,
32. *Thus they made* a covenant
26:28. *and let us make* a covenant
31:44. *let us make* a covenant,
Ex. 4:25. *and cut off* the foreskin of her son,
23:32. *Thou shalt make* no covenant
34:12, 15. lest *thou make* a covenant
13. and *cut down* their groves:
Nu. 13:23. *and cut down* from thence a branch
Deu 7: 2. *thou shalt make* no covenant
20:19. *thou shalt* not *cut* them *down*
Jos. 9: 7. how *shall we make* a league
15. *and made* a league with them,
24:25. *So* Joshua *made* a covenant
Jud. 2: 2. *ye shall make* no league
6:25. and *cut down* the grove
26. the grove which *thou shalt cut down.*
9:48. *and cut down* a bough from the trees,
49. *And* all the people...*cut down* every man
1 Sa.11: 2. *will I make* (a covenant) with you,
17:51. *and cut off* his head
18: 3. *Then* Jonathan and David *made* a covenant,
20:16. *So* Jonathan *made* (a covenant) (marg. *cut*)
23:18. *And they* two *made* a covenant
24: 4(5). *and cut off* the skirt of Saul's robe
31: 9. *And they cut off* his head,
2 Sa. 3:13. *I will make* a league with thee:
21. *that they may make* a league
5: 3. *and* king David *made* a league
10: 4. *and cut off* their garments
20:22. *And they cut off* the head of Sheba
1 K. 5: 6(20). *that they hew* me cedar trees
12(26). *and they* two *made* a league
15:13. *and* Asa *destroyed* her idol, (marg. *cut off*)
20:34. *So he made* a covenant with him,
2 K. 11: 4. *and made* a covenant with them,
17. *And* Jehoiada *made* a covenant
17:35. With whom (lit. *And* with them) the Lord *had made* a covenant
19:23. *and will cut down* the tall cedar trees
23: 3. *and made* a covenant before the Lord,
14. *and cut down* the groves,
1 Ch11: 3. *and* David *made* a covenant
19: 4. *and cut off* their garments
2 Ch 2:16(15). we *will cut* wood out of Lebanon,
15:16. she had made an idol...*and* Asa *cut down*
23: 3. *And* all the congregation *made* a covenant
16. *And* Jehoiada *made* a covenant
34:31. *and made* a covenant before the Lord,
Ezr.10: 3. *let us make* a covenant
Job 41: 4(40:28). *Will he make* a covenant
Ps. 83: 5(6). *they are confederate* (lit. *they have made* a covenant)
Isa. 37:24. *and I will cut down* the tall cedars
55: 3. *and I will make* an everlasting covenant
57: 8. *and made a covenant* with them; (marg. or, *hewed* it)
Isa. 61: 8. *I will make* an everlasting covenant
Jer. 11:19. *and let us cut him off* from the land
31:33. the covenant that *I will make*
34:15. *and ye had made* a covenant
Eze.17:13. *and made* a covenant with him,
31:12. *And* strangers, the terrible of the nations, *have cut him off,*
Hos.12: 1(2). *they do make* a covenant

KAL.—*Participle.* Poel.

Ex. 34:10. Behold, I *make* a covenant:
Deu29: 12(11). oath, which the Lord thy God *maketh*
14(13). *do* I *make* this covenant
2 Ch 2:10(9). the hewers *that cut* timber,
Neh 9:38(10:1). we *make* a sure (covenant),
Ps. 50: 5. *those that have made* a covenant
Isa. 14: 8. no *feller* is come up against us.

KAL.—*Participle.* Paül.

Lev.22:24. is bruised, or crushed, or broken, *or cut;*
Deu23: 1(2). *or hath* his privy member *cut off,*
1 Sa. 5: 4. the palms of his hands (were) *cut off*

* NIPHAL.—*Preterite.* *

Gen17:14. that soul *shall be cut off*
Ex. 12:15. that soul *shall be cut off* from Israel.
19. *even* that soul *shall be cut off* from the
30:33, 38. *shall even be cut off* from his people.
31:14. that soul *shall be cut off*
Lev. 7:20, 21. *even* that soul *shall be cut off*
25. *even* the soul...*shall be cut off* from
27. *even* that soul *shall be cut off*
17: 4. *and* that man *shall be cut off*
9. *shall be cut off* from among
18:29. *even* the souls that commit (them) *shall be cut off*
19: 8. *and* that soul *shall be cut off*
20:17. *and they shall be cut off*
18. *and* both of them *shall be cut off*
22: 3. that soul *shall be cut off*
23:29. *he shall be cut off* from among
Nu. 9:13. *even* the same soul *shall be cut off*
15:30. *and* that soul *shall be cut off*
19:13. *and* that soul *shall be cut off*
20. that soul *shall be cut off*
Jos. 3:16. the waters...toward the sea of the plain,... *were cut off:*
4: 7. the waters of Jordan *were cut off*
— the waters of Jordan *were cut off:*
Ps. 37:28. the seed of the wicked *shall be cut off.*
38. the end of the wicked *shall be cut off.*
Isa. 22:25. *and* the burden that (was) upon it *shall be cut off:*
29:20. *and* all that watch for iniquity *are cut off:*
Jer. 7:28. truth is perished, *and is cut off*
Joel 1: 5. the new wine; for *it is cut off*
16. *Is* not the meat *cut off*
Obad. 10. *and thou shalt be cut off*
Nah. 1:15(2:1). the wicked...*he is* utterly *cut off.*
Zep. 1:11. they that bear silver *are cut off.*
Zec. 9:10. *and* the battle bow *shall be cut off:*

NIPHAL.—*Infinitive.*

Nu. 15:31. that soul shall *utterly* be cut off; (lit. *being cut off* shall be cut off)
Ps. 37:34. *when* the wicked *are cut off,*

NIPHAL.—*Future.*

Gen 9:11. neither *shall* all flesh *be cut off*
41:36. the land *perish* not (marg. *be* not *cut off*)
Lev.17:14. whosoever eateth it *shall be cut off.*
Nu. 11:33. the flesh...ere *it was chewed,*
15:31. that soul *shall* utterly *be cut off;*
Jos. 3:13. the waters of Jordan *shall be cut off*
9:23. *there shall* none of you *be freed* (marg. not *be cut off* from you)
Ru. 4:10. that the name of the dead *be* not *cut off*
2 Sa. 3:29. *let there* not *fail* from the house of Joab
1 K. 2: 4. *there shall* not *fail* thee...a man (marg. *be cut off*)
8:25 & 9:5. *There shall* not *fail* thee a man (marg. *id.*)
2 Ch 6:16 & 7:18. *There shall* not *fail* thee a man (marg. *id.*)
Job 14: 7. there is hope of a tree, if *it be cut down,*
Ps. 37: 9. evildoers *shall be cut off:*
22. (they that be) cursed...*shall be cut off.*

Pro. 2:22. the wicked *shall be cut off*
10:31. the froward tongue *shall be cut out.*
23:18. thine expectation *shall* not *be cut off.*
24:14. thy expectation *shall* not *be cut off.*
Isa. 11:13. the adversaries of Judah *shall be cut off:*
48:19. his name *should* not *have been cut off*
55:13. everlasting sign (that) *shall* not *be cut off.*
56: 5. everlasting name, that *shall* not *be cut off.*
Jer. 33:17. David *shall* never *want* (marg. *There shall* not *be cut off* from David)
18. *shall* the priests the Levites *want* (lit. *there shall* not *be cut off* from the priests)
35:19. Jonadab the son of Rechab *shall* not *want* a man (marg. *There shall* not a man *be cut off* from Jonadab)
Dan. 9:26. *shall* Messiah *be cut off,*
Hos. 8: 4. that *they may be cut off.*
Obad. 9. *may be cut off* by slaughter.
Mic. 5: 9(8). all thine enemies *shall be cut off.*
Zep. 3: 7. their dwelling *should* not *be cut off,*
Zec.13: 8. two parts therein *shall be cut off*
14: 2. the people *shall* not *be cut off*

* PUAL.—*Preterite.* *

Jud. 6:28. the grove *was cut down* that (was) by it,
Eze.16: 4. thy navel *was* not *cut,*

* HIPHIL.—*Preterite.* *

Lev.17:10. *and will cut* him *off* from among his people.
20: 3. *and will cut* him *off* from among his people;
5. *and will cut* him *off,* and all
6. *and will cut* him *off* from among
26:22. *and destroy* your cattle, and make you few
30. *and cut down* your images,
Jos. 7: 9. *and cut off* our name from the earth:
23: 4. all the nations that *I have cut off,*
Jud. 4:24. until *they had destroyed* Jabin
1Sa.28: 9. *he hath cut off* those that have familiar
1K. 9: 7. *Then will I cut off* Israel
11:16. until *he had cut off* every male
14:10. *and will cut off* from Jeroboam
21:21. *and will cut off* from Ahab
2K. 9: 8. *and I will cut off* from Ahab
Isa. 14:22. *and cut off* from Babylon the name,
Eze.14: 8. *and I will cut him off* from the midst
13. *and will cut off* man and beast
17. *so that I cut off* man and beast
21: 3(8). *and will cut off* from thee the righteous
4(9). *I will cut off* from thee the righteous
25: 7. *and I will cut thee off* from the people,
13. *and will cut off* man and beast
16. *and I will cut off* the Cherethims,
29: 8. *and cut off* man and beast
30:15. *and I will cut off* the multitude of No.
35: 7. *and cut off* from it him that passeth out
Am. 1: 5. *and cut off* the inhabitant
8. *And I will cut off* the inhabitant
2: 3. *And I will cut off* the judge
Mic. 5:10(9). *that I will cut off* thy horses
11(10). *And I will cut off* the cities
12(11). *And I will cut off* witchcrafts
13(12). Thy graven images *also will I cut off,*
Nah. 2:13(14). *and I will cut off* thy prey
Zep. 1: 3. *and I will cut off* man
4. *and I will cut off* the remnant of Baal
3: 6. *I have cut off* the nations:
Zec. 9: 6. *and I will cut off* the pride of the
10. *And I will cut off* the chariot

HIPHIL.—*Infinitive.*

Ex. 8: 9(5). *to destroy* the frogs from thee
1Sa.20:15. *when* the Lord *hath cut off*
1K. 18: 4. *when* Jezebel *cut off* the prophets
2Ch 22: 7. the Lord had anointed *to cut off*
Ps. 34:16(17). *to cut off* the remembrance of them
101: 8. *that I may cut off* all wicked doers
109:13. Let his posterity *be cut off;*
Isa. 10: 7. to destroy *and cut off* nations
48: 9. *that I cut thee* not *off.*
Jer. 9:21(20). *to cut off* the children
44: 7. *to cut off* from you man and woman,
8. that ye *might cut* yourselves *off,*
11. *and to cut off* all Judah.
47: 4. *to cut off* from Tyrus and Zidon
51:62. spoken against this place, *to cut it off,*
Eze.14:19, 21. *to cut off* from it man and beast:
17:17. *to cut off* many persons:
Obad. 14. *to cut off* those...that did escape;

HIPHIL.—*Future.*

Nu. 4:18. *Cut ye* not *off* the tribe of
Deu 12:29. the Lord thy God *shall cut off* the nations
19: 1. the Lord thy God *hath cut off* the nations,
Jos. 11:21. *and cut off* the Anakims from the
1Sa. 2:33. *I shall* not *cut off* from mine altar,
20:15. *thou shalt* not *cut off* thy kindness
24:21(22). *thou wilt* not *cut off* my seed
2Sa. 7: 9. *and have cut off* all thine enemies
1K. 14:14. who *shall cut* off the house of Jeroboam
18: 5. that *we lose* not (marg. *we cut* not *off*) all
1Ch 17: 8. *and have cut off* all thine enemies
Ps. 12: 3(4). The Lord *shall cut off* all flattering lips,
109:15. *that he may cut off* the memory
Isa. 9:14(13). *Therefore* the Lord *will cut off* from
Jer. 48: 2. *and let us cut it off* from (being) a nation.
Nah. 1:14. *will I cut off* the graven image
3:15. the sword *shall cut thee off,*
Zec.13: 2. *I will cut off* the names of the idols
Mal. 2:12. The Lord *will cut off* the man

* HOPHAL.—*Preterite.* *

Joel 1: 9. the drink offering *is cut off*

כְּרֹת *k'rōhth,* f. pl. const. 3741

Zep. 2: 6. *cottages for* shepherds,

כְּרֻתוֹת *k'roo-thōhth',* f. pl. 3773

1K. 6:36. a row of cedar *beams.*
7: 2. *with* cedar *beams* upon the pillars.
12. a row of cedar *beams,*

כְּרֵתִי *k'rēh-thee',* m. 3774

2Sa. 8:18. *both the Cherethites* and the Pelethites;
15:18. all *the Cherethites,*
20: 7. *and the Cherethites,* and the Pelethites,
23. over *the Cherethites*
1K. 1:38, 44. *and the Cherethites,* and the Pelethites,
1Ch 18:17. *the Cherethites* and the Pelethites;
Eze. 25:16. I will cut off *the Cherethims,*
Zep. 2: 5. the nation of *the Cherethites!*

כֶּשֶׂב *keh'-sev,* m. 3775

Gen30:32. all the brown cattle *among the sheep,*
33. the goats, and brown *among the sheep,*
35. all the brown *among the sheep,*
40. *And* Jacob did separate *the lambs,*
Lev. 1:10. of *the sheep,* or of the goats,
3: 7. If he offer *a lamb*
4:35. as the fat of *the lamb* is taken away
7:23. *or* of *sheep,* or of goat.
17: 3. that killeth an ox, or *lamb,*
22:19. *of the sheep,* or of the goats.
27. a bullock, or *a sheep,*
Nu. 18:17. the firstling of *a sheep,*
Deu 14: 4. the ox, *the sheep,* (lit. the lamb of *sheep*)

כִּשְׂבָּה *kis-bāh',* f. 3776

Lev. 5: 6. *a lamb* or a kid of the goats,

כָּשָׂה [*kāh-sāh'*]. 3780

* KAL.—*Preterite.* *

Deu 32:15. *thou art covered* (with fatness);

כַּשִּׁיל *kash-sheel',* m. 3781

Ps. 74: 6. *with axes* and hammers.

3782 כָּשַׁל *kāh-shal'.*

✱ KAL.—*Preterite.* ✱

Lev.26:37. *And they shall fall* one upon another,
Neh. 4:10(4). The strength...*is decayed,*
Ps. 27: 2. they *stumbled* and fell.
31:10(11). my strength *faileth* because of mine
107:12. *they fell down,* and (there was) none to
109:24. My knees *are weak* through fasting;
Isa. 3: 8. For Jerusalem *is ruined,*
8:15. *And* many among them *shall stumble,*
28:13. that they might go, *and fall* backward,
31: 3. *both* he that helpeth *shall fall,*
59:10. *we stumble* at noon day as in the night;
14. truth *is fallen* in the street,
Jer. 6:21. *and* the fathers and the sons together *shall fall*
46: 6. *they shall stumble,* and fall toward the north
12. the mighty man *hath stumbled*
50:32. *And* the most proud *shall stumble*
Lam. 5:13. the children *fell* under the wood.
Hos. 4: 5. *Therefore shalt thou fall* in the day, *and* the prophet *also shall fall* with thee
5: 5. Judah also *shall fall* with them.
14: 1(2). *thou hast fallen* by thine iniquity.
Nah. 3: 3. *they* (lit. *and they*) *stumble* upon their corpses:

KAL.—*Infinitive.*

Isa. 40:30. the young men shall *utterly* fall: (lit. *falling* shall fall)

KAL.—*Future.*

Pro. 4:16. (כתיב) unless *they cause* (some) *to fall.*

KAL.—*Participle.* Poel.

2Ch 28:15. carried all *the feeble* of them upon asses,
Job 4: 4. him *that was falling,*
Ps.105:37. (there was) not one *feeble* (person)
Isa. 5:27. None shall be weary nor *stumble* among
35: 3. confirm the *feeble* knees.
Jer. 46:16. He made many *to fall,* (marg. multiplied *the faller*)

✱ NIPHAL.—*Preterite.* ✱

Dan 11:14. to establish the vision; *but they shall fall.*
19. *but he shall stumble* and fall,
33. *yet they shall fall* by the sword,

NIPHAL.—*Infinitive.*

Pro.24:17. *and* let not thine heart be glad *when he stumbleth:*
Dan 11:34. *Now when they shall fall,* they shall be

NIPHAL.—*Future.*

Ps. 9: 3(4). *they shall fall* and perish at thy
Pro. 4:12. when thou runnest, *thou shalt* not *stumble.*
19. they know not at what *they stumble.*
24:16. the wicked *shall fall* into mischief.
Isa 40:30. the young men *shall* utterly *fall:*
63:13. (that) *they should* not *stumble?*
Jer. 6:15. (that) I visit them *they shall be cast down,*
8:12. of their visitation *they shall be cast down,*
20:11. therefore my persecutors *shall stumble,*
31: 9. wherein *they shall* not *stumble:*
Eze.33:12. *he shall* not *fall* thereby
Dan 11:35. (some) of them of understanding *shall fall,*
41. many (countries) *shall be overthrown:*
Hos. 5: 5. therefore *shall* Israel and Ephraim *fall*
14: 9(10). the transgressors *shall fall* therein.
Nah. 2: 5(6). *they shall stumble* in their walk;
3: 3. (כתיב) *they stumble* upon their corpses:

NIPHAL.—*Participle.*

1Sa. 2: 4. *and they that stumbled* are girded with
Zec.12: 8. *he that is feeble* among them (marg. *fallen,* or, *abject*)

✱ PIEL.—*Future.* ✱

Eze.36:14. neither *bereave* thy nations any more, (marg. *cause to fall*)

✱ HIPHIL.—*Preterite.* ✱

Lam. 1:14. *he hath made* my strength *to fall,*
Mal. 2: 8. *ye have caused* many *to stumble* (marg. *fall*) at the law;

HIPHIL.—*Infinitive.*

2Ch 25: 8. God hath power to help, *and to cast down.*
28:23. they *were the ruin of him,*

HIPHIL.—*Future.*

2Ch 25: 8. God *shall make thee fall*
Ps. 64: 8(9). *So they shall make* their own tongue *to fall*
Pro. 4:16. unless *they cause* (some) *to fall.*
Jer. 18:15. *and they have caused them to stumble* in their
Eze.36:15. neither *shalt thou cause* thy nations *to fall*

✱ HOPHAL.—*Participle.* ✱

Jer. 18:23. let them be *overthrown* before thee;

כִּשָּׁלוֹן *kish-shāh-lōhn',* m. 3783

Pro.16:18. an haughty spirit before *a fall.*

כָּשַׁף [*kāh-shaph'*]. 3784

✱ PIEL.—*Preterite.* ✱

2Ch 33: 6. used enchantments, *and used witchcraft,*

PIEL.—*Participle.*

Ex. 7:11. the wise men *and the sorcerers:*
22:18(17). Thou shalt not suffer *a witch* to live.
Deu 18:10. or an enchanter, *or a witch,*
Dan. 2: 2. *and the sorcerers,* and the Chaldeans,
Mal. 3: 5. will be a swift witness *against the sorcerers,*

כַּשָּׁף [*kash-shāhph'*], m. 3786

Jer. 27: 9. nor to *your sorcerers,*

כְּשָׁפִים *k'shāh-pheem',* m. pl. 3785

2K. 9:22. *and her witchcrafts* (are so) many?
Isa. 47: 9, 12. the multitude of *thy sorceries,*
Mic. 5:12(11). I will cut off *witchcrafts*
Nah. 3: 4. the mistress of *witchcrafts,*
— families *through her witchcrafts.*

כָּשֵׁר *kāh-shēhr'.* 3787

✱ KAL.—*Preterite.* ✱

Est. 8: 5. *and* the thing (seem) *right* before the

KAL.—*Future.*

Ecc.11: 6. thou knowest not whether *shall prosper,*

✱ HIPHIL.—*Infinitive.* ✱

Ecc.10:10. wisdom (is) profitable *to direct.*

כִּשְׁרוֹן *kish-rōhn',* m. 3788

Ecc. 2:21. in knowledge, *and in equity;*
4: 4. I considered all travail, and every *right* (marg. all *the rightness of*) work,
5:11(10). *good* (is there) to the owners thereof,

כָּתַב *kāh-thav'.* 3789

✱ KAL.—*Preterite.* ✱

Ex. 24:12. commandments which *I have written;*
32:32. thy book which *thou hast written.*
34: 1. *and I will write* upon (these) tables
Nu. 5:23. *And* the priest *shall write* these curses
Deu 6: 9. *And thou shalt write them* upon the posts of
11:20. *And thou shalt write them* upon the door
17:18. *that he shall write* him a copy
24: 1. *then let him write* her a bill of
3. *and write* her a bill of divorcement,
27: 3. *And thou shalt write* upon them
8. *And thou shalt write* upon the stones
Jos. 8:32. *he wrote* in the presence of
2K. 17:37. which *he wrote* for you,
2Ch 26:22. *did* Isaiah the prophet,...*write.*
30: 1. *wrote* letters also to Ephraim
32:17. *wrote* also letters to rail on the Lord God
Ezr. 4: 6. *wrote they* (unto him) an accusation
7. *wrote* Bishlam, Mithredath, Tabeel,
Est. 8: 5. *he wrote* to destroy the Jews
9:23. as Mordecai *had written* unto them;
Job 31:35. mine adversary *had written*

Pro.22: 20. *Have* not *I written* to thee
Jer. 36: 2. *and write* therein all the words
6. *thou hast written* from my mouth,
17. How *didst thou write* all these words
27. the words which Baruch *wrote*
29. Why *hast thou written* therein,

KAL.—*Infinitive.*

Deu 31: 24. Moses had made an end *of writing*
Jos. 18: 8. them that went *to describe* the land,
Ps. 87: 6. *when he writeth up* the people,
Jer. 32: 44. *and subscribe* evidences,
45: 1. *when he had written* these words

KAL.—*Imperative.*

Ex. 17: 14. *Write* this (for) a memorial
34: 27. *Write* thou these words:
Deu 31: 19. Now therefore *write ye* this song
Jos. 18: 8. walk through the land, *and describe it,*
Est. 8: 8. *Write ye* also for the Jews,
Pro. 3: 3 & 7: 3. *write them* upon the table of
Isa. 8: 1. *and write* in it with a man's pen
30: 8. *write it* before them in a table,
Jer. 22: 30. *Write ye* this man childless,
30: 2. *Write* thee all the words
36: 28. *and write* in it all the former words
Eze. 24: 2. *write* thee the name of the day,
37: 16. take thee one stick, *and write* upon it,
— take another stick, *and write* upon it,
43: 11. *and write* (it) in their sight,
Hab. 2: 2. *Write* the vision,

KAL.—*Future.*

Ex. 24: 4. *And* Moses *wrote* all the words
34: 28. *And he wrote* upon the tables
39: 30. *and wrote* upon it a writing,
Nu. 17: 2(17). *write thou* every man's name
3(18). *And thou shalt write* Aaron's name
33: 2. *And* Moses *wrote* their goings out
Deu 4: 13. *and he wrote them* upon two tables
5: 22(19). *And he wrote them* in two tables
10: 2. *And I will write* on the tables
4. *And he wrote* on the tables,
31: 9. *And* Moses *wrote* this law,
22. Moses *therefore wrote* this song
Jos. 8: 32. *And he wrote* there upon the stones
18: 4. and go through the land, *and describe* it
6. *Ye shall* therefore *describe* the land
9. *and describe it* by cities
24: 26. *And* Joshua *wrote these* words
Jud. 8: 14. *and he described* (marg. *writ*) unto him
1 Sa. 10: 25. *and wrote* (it) in a book,
2 Sa. 11: 14. *that* David *wrote* a letter to Joab,
15. *And he wrote* in the letter,
1 K. 21: 8. *So she wrote* letters in Ahab's name,
9. *And she wrote* in the letters saying,
2 K. 10: 1. *And* Jehu *wrote* letters, and sent to
6. *Then he wrote* a letter
1Ch 24: 6. *And* Shemaiah...(one) of the Levites, *wrote them*
Est. 8: 10. *And he wrote* in the king Ahasuerus' name,
9: 20. *And* Mordecai *wrote* these things,
29. *Then* Esther...and Mordecai...*wrote* with
Job 13: 26. *thou writest* bitter things
Isa. 10: 19. that a child *may write them.*
44: 5. another *shall subscribe*
Jer. 31: 33. *write it* in their hearts;
32: 10. *And I subscribed* the evidence,
36: 4. *and* Baruch *wrote* from the mouth of
32. *who wrote* therein from the mouth of
51: 60. *So* Jeremiah *wrote* in a book
Eze 37: 20. the sticks whereon *thou writest*
Hos. 8: 12. *I have written* to him the great things

KAL.—*Participle.* Poel.

Neh. 9: 38(10: 1). make a sure (covenant), *and write*
Jer. 32: 12. the witnesses *that subscribed*
36: 18. I *wrote* (them) with ink

KAL.—*Participle.* Paül.

Ex. 31: 18. *written* with the finger of God.
32: 15. the tables (were) *written* on both their
— on the other (were) they *written.*
Nu. 11: 26. they (were) *of them that were written,*
Deu 9: 10. *written* with the finger of God;
28: 58. *that are written* in this book,
61. (is) not *written* in the book of this law,
29: 20(19). the curses *that are written* in this book
21(20). *that are written* (marg. *is written*) in
Deu 29: 27(26). the curses *that are written* in this book.
30: 10. his statutes *which are written* in this book
Jos. 1: 8. all *that is written* therein:
8: 31. *as it is written* in the book
34. according to all *that is written*
10: 13. (Is) not this *written* in the book of Jasher?
23: 6. all *that is written* in the book of the law
2 Sa. 1: 18. (it is) *written* in the book of Jasher,
1 K. 2: 3. *as it is written* in the law of Moses,
11: 41. (are) they not *written* in the book
14: 19. (are) *written* in the book of the chronicles
29. not *written* in the book of the chronicles
15: 7, 23, 31 & 16: 5, 14, 20, 27. *written* in the book
21: 11. as it (was) *written* in the letters
22: 39, 45(46). *written* in the book of the
2 K. 1: 18 & 8: 23 & 10: 34 & 12: 19(20) & 13: 8, 12. *written* in the book of the chronicles
14: 6. *according unto that which is written*
15, 18, 28 & 15: 6, 11, 15, 21, 26, 31, 36, & 16: 19 & 20: 20 & 21: 17, 25. *written* in the book of the chronicles
22: 13. *that which is written* concerning us.
23: 3. words of this covenant *that were written*
21. *as* (it is) *written* in the book
24. the words of the law *which were written*
28 & 24: 5. *written* in the book of the chronicles
1 Ch 4: 41. these *written* by name came
9: 1. *written* in the book of the kings
16: 40. *that is written* in the law
29: 29. *written* in the book of Samuel
2 Ch 9: 29. *written* in the book of Nathan
12: 15. *written* in the book of Shemaiah
13: 22. *written* in the story of the prophet Iddo.
16: 11. *written* in the book of the kings
20: 34. *written* in the book of Jehu
23: 18. *as* (it is) *written* in the law of Moses,
24: 27. *written* in the story of the book of
25: 4. *as* (it is) *written* in the law in the book of
26 & 27: 7 & 28: 26. *written* in the book of the
30: 5. (in such sort) *as it was written.*
18. the passover otherwise *than it was written.*
31: 3. *as* (it is) *written* in the law of the Lord.
32: 32. *written* in the vision of Isaiah
33: 19. *written* among the sayings of the seers.
34: 21. all *that is written* in this book.
24. the curses *that are written* in the book
31. words of the covenant *which are written*
35: 12. *as* (it is) *written* in the book of Moses.
25. *written* in the lamentations.
26 *according to* (that which was) *written*
27 & 36: 8. *written* in the book of the kings
Ezr. 3: 2. *as* (it is) *written* in the law of Moses
4. They kept also the feast...*as* (it is) *written,*
4: 7. *written* in the Syrian tongue,
Neh. 6: 6. Wherein (was) *written,*
7: 5. and found *written* therein,
8: 14. And they found *written* in the law
15. to make booths *as* (it is) *written.*
10: 34(35), 36(37). *as* (it is) *written* in the law:
12: 22. *recorded* chief of the fathers
23. *written* in the book of the chronicles,
13: 1. therein was found *written,*
Est. 6: 2. it was found *written,*
10: 2. *written* in the book of the chronicles
Ps. 40: 7(8). the volume of the book (it is) *written*
149: 9. execute upon them the judgment *written.*
Ecc. 12: 10. *and* (that which was) *written* (was)
Isa. 4: 3. every one *that is written* among
65: 6. (it is) *written* before me:
Jer. 17: 1. The sin of Judah (is) *written* with a pen
25: 13. all *that is written* in this book,
51: 60. all these words *that are written*
Eze. 2: 10. it (was) *written* within and without: *and* (there was) *written* therein lamentations,
Dan. 9: 11. *written* in the law of Moses
13. *written* in the law of Moses,
12: 1. that shall be found *written*

* NIPHAL....*Future.* *

Ezr. 8: 34. *and* all the weight was *written*
Est. 1: 19. *and let it be written* among the laws
2: 23. *and it was written* in the book of the
3: 9. *let it be written* that they may be destroyed:
12. *and there was written* according to all that
8: 5. *let it be written* to reverse the letters
9. *and it was written* according to all that
Job 19: 23. Oh *that* my words *were* now *written!*

Ps. 69:28(29). not *be written* with the righteous.
102:18(19). This *shall be written* for the generation
139:16. in thy book all (my members) *were written*,
Jer. 17:13. they that depart from me *shall be written*
Eze.13: 9. neither shall *they be written*
Mal. 3:16. *and* a book of remembrance *was written*

NIPHAL.—*Participle.*

Est. 3:12. the name of king Ahasuerus *was it written*,
8: 8. the writing *which is written*
9:32. *and it was written* in the book.

∗ PIEL.—*Preterite.* ∗

Isa. 10: 1. (which) *they have prescribed;*

PIEL.—*Participle.*

Isa. 10: 1. *and that write* grievousness

3791 **כְּתָב** *k'thāhv*, m.

1 Ch28:19. the Lord made me understand *in writing*
2 Ch 2:11(10). the king of Tyre answered *in writing*,
35: 4. *according to the writing of* David
Ezr. 2:62. These sought *their register*
4: 7. *and the writing of* the letter
Neh. 7:64. These sought *their register*
Est. 1:22 & 3:12. *according to the writing thereof*,
3:14. The copy of *the writing* for a
4: 8. the copy of *the writing of* the decree
8: 8. for *the writing* which is written in the
9. *according to the writing thereof*,
— to the Jews *according to their writing*,
13. copy of *the writing* for a commandment
9:27. *according to their writing*,
Eze.13: 9. *neither* shall they be written *in the writing of* the house of Israel,
Dan 10:21. which is noted *in the scripture of* truth:

3792 **כְּתָב** *k'thāhv*, m. Ch.

Ezr. 6:18. *as it is written* in the book of Moses, (marg. according to *the writing*)
7:22. and salt without *prescribing* (how much).
Dan 5: 7. Whosoever shall read this *writing*,
8. but they could not read *the writing*,
15. that they should read this *writing*,
16. now if thou canst read *the writing*,
17. yet I will read *the writing*
24. *and* this *writing* was written,
25. And this (is) *the writing* that was written,
6: 8(9). the decree, and sign *the writing*.
9(10). king Darius signed *the writing*
10(11). when Daniel knew that *the writing*

3790 **כְּתַב** *k'thav*, Ch.

∗ P'AL.—*Preterite.* ∗

Ezr. 4: 8. and Shimshai the scribe *wrote* a letter
Dan 6:25(26). Then king Darius *wrote* unto all
7: 1. then *he wrote* the dream,

P'AL.—*Future.*

Ezr. 5:10. that *we might write* the names

P'AL.—*Participle.* Active.

Dan 5: 5. forth fingers of a man's hand, *and wrote*
— king saw the part of the hand that *wrote*.

P'AL.—*Participle.* Passive.

Ezr. 5: 7. sent a letter unto him, wherein was *written*
6: 2. and therein (was) a record thus *written*:

3793 **כְּתֹבֶת** *k'thōh'-veth*, f.

Lev.19:28. nor print *any* marks (lit. *and an inscription of* a mark) upon you:

3795 **כָּתִית** *kāh-theeth'*, f.

Ex. 27:20. pure oil olive *beaten* for the light,
29:40. fourth part of an hin of *beaten* oil;
Lev.24: 2. pure oil olive *beaten* for the light,
Nu. 28: 5 fourth (part) of an hin of *beaten* oil.
1 K. 5:11(25). twenty measures of *pure* oil:

כֹּתֶל [*kōh'-thel*], m. 3796

Cant.2: 9. he standeth behind *our wall*,

כְּתַל [*k'thal*], Ch. m. 3797

Ezr. 5: 8. and timber is laid *in the walls*,
Dan 5: 5. upon the plaster *of the wall of* the

כָּתַם [*kāh-tham'*]. 3799

∗ NIPHAL.—*Participle.* ∗

Jer. 2:22. thine iniquity *is marked* before me,

כֶּתֶם *keh'-them*, m. 3800

Job 28:16. It cannot be valued *with the gold of* Ophir,
19. neither shall it be valued *with pure gold*.
31:24. *or* have said *to the fine gold*,
Ps. 45: 9(10). hand did stand the queen *in gold of*
Pro.25:12. an ornament of *fine gold*,
Cant.5:11. *the most* fine gold, (lit. *gold* fine gold)
Isa. 13:12. *than the golden wedge of* Ophir.
Lam 4: 1. (how) is the most *fine gold* changed!
Dan 10: 5. *with fine gold of* Uphaz:

כְּתֹנֶת *k'thōh'-neth* & **כֻּתֹּנֶת** *koot-tōh-neth*, f. 3801

Gen 3:21. did the Lord God make *coats of* skins,
27: 3. he made him *a coat of* (many) colours,
23. stript Joseph out of *his coat* (his) *coat of*
31. they took Joseph's *coat*,
— dipped *the coat* in the blood;
32. they sent *the coat of* (many) colours,
— know now whether it (be) thy son's *coat* or
33. (It is) my son's *coat;*
Ex. 28: 4. *and a* broidered *coat*, a mitre, and a
39. thou shalt embroider *the coat*
40. for Aaron's sons thou shalt make *coats*,
29: 5. put upon Aaron *the coat*,
8. and put *coats* upon them.
39:27. they made *coats* (of) fine linen
40:14. and clothe them with *coats*,
Lev. 8: 7. he put upon him *the coat*,
13. put *coats* upon them,
10: 5. carried them *in their coats*
16: 4 He shall put on *the* holy linen *coat*,
2 Sa.13:18. (she had) *a garment of* divers colours
19. *and* rent her *garment of* divers colours
15:32. Hushai...came to meet him with *his coat*
Ezr. 2:69. *and* one hundred priests' *garments*.
Neh 7:70. five hundred and thirty priests' *garments*.
72. *and* threescore and seven priests' *garments*.
Job 30:18. bindeth me about as the collar of *my coat*.
Cant 5: 3. I have put off *my coat;*
Isa. 22:21. I will clothe him with *thy robe*,

כָּתֵף *kāh-thēhph'*, f. 3802

Ex. 27:14. The hangings *of one side*
15. *And on the* other *side*
28: 7. It shall have *the* two *shoulderpieces* thereof
12. *the shoulders of* the ephod
— upon *his* two *shoulders*
25. on *the shoulderpieces of* the ephod
27. *the* two *sides of* the ephod
38:14. The hangings of *the one side*
15. *And for the* other *side* of the court gate,
39: 4. They made *shoulderpieces* for it,
7. he put them on *the shoulders of* the ephod,
18. *the shoulderpieces of* the ephod,
20. *the* two *sides of* the ephod
Nu. 7: 9. they should bear upon their *shoulders*.
34:11. *the side of* the sea of Chinnereth
Deu 33:12. he shall dwell between *his shoulders*.
Jos. 15: 8. *the* south *side of* the Jebusite;
10. unto *the side of* mount Jearim,
11. *the side of* Ekron northward:

Jos. 18:12. to *the side of* Jericho
13. to *the side of* Luz,
16. to *the side of* Jebusi
18. And passed along toward *the side*
19. to *the side of* Beth-hoglah
Jud.16: 3. put (them) upon *his shoulders*,
1Sa.17: 6. a target of brass between *his shoulders*.
1K. 6: 8. *the* right *side of* the house: (marg. *shoulder*)
7:30. the four corners thereof had *undersetters:* under the laver (were) *undersetters*
34. And (there were) four *undersetters* to the four corners of one base: (and) *the undersetters* (were) of the very base itself.
39. *the* right *side of* the house, and five *on the* left *side of* the house: and he set the sea on *the* right *side of* the house
2K. 11:11. *from the* right *corner of* the temple to *the* left *corner of* the temple,
1Ch15:15. bare the ark of God *upon their shoulders*
2Ch 4:10. he set the sea *on the* right *side*
23:10. *from the* right *side of* the temple to *the* left *side of* the temple,
35: 3. a burden *upon* (your) *shoulders :*
Neh 9:29. and withdrew *the shoulder*,
Job 31:22. (Then) let *mine arm* fall from my shoulder
Isa. 11:14. *upon the shoulders of* the Philistines
30: 6. *the shoulders of* young asses,
46: 7. They bear him upon *the shoulder*,
49:22. shall be carried upon (their) *shoulders*.
Eze.12: 6. bear (it) upon (thy) *shoulders*,
7. I bare (it) upon (my) *shoulder*
12. shall bear upon (his) *shoulder*
24: 4. the thigh, *and the shoulder ;*
25: 9. open *the side* (marg. *shoulder*) *of* Moab
29: 7. rend all their *shoulder :*
18. every *shoulder* (was) peeled:
34:21. have thrust with side *and with shoulder*,
40:18. *the side of* the gates
40. at *the side* without, as one goeth
— and on *the* other *side*, which (was) at the
41. *by the side of* the gate;
44. *the side of* the north gate;
— at *the side of* the east gate
41: 2. *and the sides of* the door (were) five
26. on *the sides of* the porch,
46:19. at *the side of* the gate,
47: 1. *from the* right *side of* the house,
2. there ran out waters on *the* right *side*.
Zec. 7:11. to hearken, and pulled away *the shoulder*,

3803 כָּתַר [*kāh-thar'*].

* PIEL.—*Preterite.* *

Jud.20:43. (Thus) *they inclosed* the Benjamites *round about*,
Ps. 22:12(13). (bulls) of Bashan *have beset me round.*

PIEL.—*Imperative.*

Job 36: 2. *Suffer me* a little, and I will shew thee

* HIPHIL.—*Future.* *

Ps.142: 7(8). the righteous *shall compass* me *about ;*
Pro.14:18. the prudent *are crowned* with knowledge.

HIPHIL.—*Participle.*

Hab 1: 4. the wicked *doth compass about* the

3804 כֶּתֶר *keh'-ther*, m.

Est. 1:11. the queen before the king *with the crown*
2:17. he set *the* royal *crown* upon her head,
6: 8. *the crown* royal which is set upon his

3805 כֹּתֶרֶת *kōh-theh'-reth*, f.

1K. 7:16. And he made two *chapiters*
— the height of *the* one *chapiter* (was) five cubits, and the height of *the* other *chapiter*
17. *for the chapiters* which (were) upon the
— seven *for the* one *chapiter*, and seven *for the* other *chapiter*.
18. to cover *the chapiters*
— so did he *for the* other *chapter*.
19. *And the chapiters* that (were) upon the

1K. 7:20. *And the chapiters* upon the two pillars
— round about upon *the* other *chapiter*.
31. the mouth of it *within the chapiter*
41. the (two) bowls of *the chapiters*
— the two bowls of *the chapiters*
42. the two bowls of *the chapiters*
2K. 25:17. *and the chapiter* upon it (was) brass: and the height of *the chapiter* three cubits; and the wreathen work, and pomegranates upon *the chapiter*
2Ch. 4:12. the pommels, *and the chapiters*
—, 13. the two pommels of *the chapiters*
Jer. 52:22. *And a chapiter of* brass (was) upon it; and the height of one *chapiter* (was) five cubits, with network and pomegranates upon *the chapiters*

כָּתַשׁ [*kāh-thash'*]. 3806

* KAL.—*Future.* *

Pro.27:22. Though *thou shouldest bray* a fool

כָּתַת [*kāh-thath'*]. 3807

* KAL.—*Preterite.* *

Ps. 89:23(24). *And I will beat down* his foes

KAL.—*Infinitive.*

Isa.30:14. the potters' vessel *that is broken in pieces ;*

KAL.—*Imperative.*

Joel 3:10(4:10). *Beat* your plowshares into swords,

KAL.—*Future.*

Deu 9:21. burnt it with fire, *and stamped* it,

KAL.—*Participle.* Paül.

Lev 22:24. *or crushed*, or broken, or cut;

* PIEL.—*Preterite.* *

2K. 18: 4. *and brake in pieces* the brasen serpent
2Ch34: 7. *had beaten* the graven images into powder,
Isa. 2: 4. *and they shall beat* their swords into
Mic 4: 3. *and they shall beat* their swords into
Zec.11: 6. *and they shall smite* the land,

* PUAL.—*Preterite.* *

2Ch.15: 6. *And* nation *was destroyed* of nation,

* HIPHIL.—*Future.* *

Nu. 14:45. smote them, *and discomfited them*,
Deu 1:44. *and destroyed* you in Seir,

* HOPHAL.—*Future.* *

Job. 4:20. *They are destroyed* from morning to
Isa. 24:12. the gate *is smitten* with destruction.
Jer. 46: 5. their mighty ones *are beaten down*, (marg. *broken in pieces*)
Mic. 1: 7. images thereof *shall be beaten to pieces*,

ל *lāh'-med.*

The twelfth letter of the Hebrew Alphabet.

לָא *lāh*, Ch. part. 3809

Ezr. 4:13. (then) will they *not* pay toll, tribute,
14. and it was *not* meet for us to see the king's
16. by this means thou shalt have *no* portion
21. and that this city be *not* builded,
5: 5. that they could *not* cause them to cease,
16. and (yet) it is *not* finished.
6: 8. that they be *not* hindered.
9. be given them day by day with*out* fail: (lit. so that *not*)
7:22. and salt *without* prescribing (how much).
24. it shall *not* be lawful to impose toll,
25. and teach ye them that know (them) *not*.
26. And whosoever will *not* do
Jer. 10:11. The gods that have *not* made the heavens
Dan 2: 5, 9. if ye will *not* make known unto me the
10. There is *not* a man upon the earth that
— (there is) *no* king, lord, nor ruler, (that)
11. there is *none* other that can shew it
— whose dwelling is *not* with flesh.
18. should *not* perish with the rest

Dan. 2:27. cannot the wise (men), the astrologers,
30. this secret is *not* revealed to me for
34. a stone was cut out with*out* hands, (lit. *not* in hands)
35. that *no* place was found for them:
43. but they shall *not* cleave one to another, even as iron is *not* mixed with clay.
44. kingdom, which shall never (lit. *not* ever) be destroyed:
— kingdom shall *not* be left to other people,
45. cut out of the mountain with*out* hands,
3: 6, 11. falleth *not* down and worshippeth
12. these men, O king, have *not* regarded thee: they serve *not* thy gods, *nor* (lit. and *not*) worship the golden image
14. do *not* ye serve my gods, *nor* worship the
15. but if ye worship *not*,
16. we (are) *not* careful to answer thee
18. But if *not*, be it known unto thee, O king, that we will *not* serve thy gods, *nor*
24. Did *not* we cast three men bound
25. and they have *no* hurt;
27. upon whose bodies the fire had *no* power, *nor* was an hair of their head singed, *neither* were their coats changed, *nor* the smell of fire had passed on them.
28. that they might *not* serve *nor* worship any
29. there is *no* other God that can deliver
4: 7(4). but they did *not* make known
9(6). and *no* secret troubleth thee,
18(15). are *not* able to make known unto me
30(27). Is *not* this great Babylon, that I
35(32). of the earth (are) reputed as *nothing:*
—(—). *and none* can stay his hand,
5: 8. but they could *not* read the writing,
15. but they could *not* shew the
22. hast *not* humbled thine heart,
23. which see *not*, *nor* hear, *nor* know:
6: 2(3). the king should have *no* damage.
4(5). they could find *none* occasion *nor* fault;
5(6). We shall *not* find any occasion against
8(9). that it be *not* changed, according to the law of...which altereth *not*.
12(13). Hast thou *not* signed a decree,
—(—). and Persians, which altereth *not*.
13(14). regardeth *not* thee, O king,
17(18). that the purpose might *not* be changed
18(19). *neither* were instruments of musick
22(23). that they have *not* hurt me:
—(—). thee, O king, have I done *no* hurt.
23(24). *no* manner of hurt was found upon
24(25). *or ever* they came at the bottom of the
26(27). his kingdom (that) which shall *not* be
7:14. which shall *not* pass away, and his kingdom (that) which shall *not* be destroyed.

3808 **לֹא & לוֹא** *lōh*, part. adv.

Gen 2: 5. the Lord God had *not* caused it
11: 6. *nothing* will be restrained (lit. every thing will *not* be)
15: 3. to me thou hast given *no* seed:
16: 1. Abram's wife bare him *no* children:
18:15. he said, *Nay;* but thou didst laugh.
21:26. *n*either didst thou (lit. and moreover thou didst *not*) tell me, *n*either yet heard I
22:12. *seeing* thou hast *not* withheld thy son,
16. *and* hast *not* withheld thy son,
23: 6. *n*one of us shall (lit. a man of us shall *not*) withhold from thee
11. *Nay*, my lord, hear me: the field
34:14. We can*not* do this thing,
38:22. and said, I can*not* find her;
39: 9. *neither* hath he kept back any thing
41:19. such as I *never* saw in all the land
Ex. 9:24. such as there was *none* like it
11: 6. *n*or (lit. and *not*) shall be like it any
Lev 27:29. *N*one devoted,...shall be (lit. all...shall *not* be)
Nu. 7: 9. unto the sons of Kohath he gave *none:*
14:11. how long will it be *ere* they believe me,
19: 2. upon which *never* came yoke:
Deu 8: 9. thou shalt eat bread with*out* scarceness,
Jud. 1:19. but could *not* drive out the inhabitants
2Sa. 19:24(25). *and* had *neither* dressed his feet, *nor* trimmed his beard, nor (lit. and *not*)
2Sa. 19:28(29). For all (of) my father's house were but dead men (lit. were *not* but &c.
23: 4. (even) a morning *without* clouds;
2K. 25:16. of all these vessels was *without* weight.
2Ch. 32:15. how *much less* shall your God deliver
Ps. 35: 8. come upon him at *un*awares; (marg. (which) he knoweth *not* of)
43: 1. my cause against an *un*godly nation:
49:19(20). they shall *n*ever (lit. *not* for ever) see
Pro. 27:20. Hell and destruction are *never* (marg. *not*)
Ecc. 12: 6. Or ever (lit. until that *not*) the silver cord
Isa. 16:14. small (and) feeble. (marg. or, *not* many)
63:16. though Abraham be *ig*norant of us,
Jer. 31:18. as a bullock *un*accustomed (to the yoke)
33:17. David shall *never* want (marg. There shall *not* be cut off from David) a man
47: 6. how long (will it be) *ere* thou be quiet?
Hos. 8: 5. how long (will it be) *ere* they attain
Am. 3: 8. God hath spoken, who can *but* prophesy?
Zep. 2: 2. before)(the fierce anger of the Lord come upon you, before)(the day
&c. &c.

It occurs with prefixes: as,

I. **בְּלֹא**

Lev. 15:25. many days *out of* the time
Nu. 35:22. thrust him suddenly *without* enmity,
23. a man may die, seeing (him) *not*,
Deu 32:21. to jealousy *with* (that which is) *not* God;
1Ch. 12:17. *seeing* (there is) *no* wrong in mine hands,
2Ch. 30:18. eat the passover *otherwise* than it was
Job. 15:32. It shall be accomplished *before* his time,
Psa. 17: 1. (that goeth) *not out of* (marg. *without*)
Pro. 13:23. destroyed *for want of* judgment.
Isa. 55: 2. money *for* (that which is) *not* bread? and your labour *for* (that which) satisfieth *not?*
Jer. 5: 7. sworn *by* (them that are) *no* gods:
22:13. buildeth his house *by un*righteousness,
Lam 4:14. *so that* men could *not* touch (marg. or, *in that* they could *not* (but))
&c. &c.

II. **כְּלוֹא**

Obad 16. they shall be *as though* they had *not* been.

III. **לְלֹא**

2Ch. 13: 9. a priest *of* (them that are) *no* gods.
15: 3. *without* the true God, *and without* a teaching priest, *and without* law.
Job 26: 2. helped (him that is) *without* power?
3. counselled (him that hath) *no* wisdom?
39:16. *as though* (they were) *not* her's:
Isa. 65: 1. I am sought *of* (them that) asked *not* (for me); I am found *of* (them that) sought me *not:*
Am. 6:13. Ye which rejoice in a thing *of nought*,

It is sometimes combined in translation with another word, when it commonly retains its negative force without farther affecting the sense. Some combinations require a particular notice: as,

אִם לֹא

Gen 42:16. *or else* by the life of Pharaoh surely ye
44:23. *Except* your youngest brother come
Ex. 22: 8(7). (to see) *whether* he have put his hand
Nu. 14:28. *As truly as* I live saith the Lord,
35. I the Lord have said, I will *surely* do it
Jos. 7:12. *except* ye destroy the accursed
1K. 20:23. *and surely* we shall be stronger than they.
Job 1:11. *and* he will curse thee (marg. *if* he curse thee *not*) to thy face.
Isa. 5: 9. *Of a truth* (marg. *If not*) many houses
Jer. 15:11. *Verily* it shall be well with thy remnant;
&c. &c.

אִם לֹא כִּי

Deu 32:30. *except* their Rock had sold them,

לֻא *loo*, (כתיב). 3863

2Sa. 18:12. *Though* I should receive
19: 6(7). I perceive, that *if* Absalom had lived,

3811 **לָאָה** [*lāh-āh'*].

* KAL.—*Future.* *

Gen19:11. *so that they wearied themselves* to find
Job 4: 2. commune with thee, *wilt thou be grieved?*
5. it is come upon thee, *and thou faintest;*

* NIPHAL.—*Preterite.* *

Ex. 7:18. *and* the Egyptians *shall lothe* to drink
Ps. 68: 9(10). thine inheritance, *when it was weary.*
Pro.26:15. *it grieveth him* to bring it again (marg. or, *he is weary*)
Isa. 1:14. *I am weary* to bear (them).
16:12. Moab *is weary* on the high place,
47:13. *Thou art wearied* in the multitude
Jer. 6:11. *I am weary* with holding in:
9: 5(4). *weary themselves* to commit iniquity.
15: 6. *I am weary* with repenting.
20: 9. *and I was weary* with forbearing,

* HIPHIL.—*Preterite.* *

Job 16: 7. *he hath made me weary:*
Eze.24:12. *She hath wearied* (herself) with lies,
Mic. 6: 3. wherein *have I wearied thee?*

HIPHIL.—*Infinitive.*

Isa. 7:13. (Is it) a small thing for you *to weary* men,

HIPHIL.—*Future.*

Isa. 7:13. *will ye weary* my God also?
Jer. 12: 5. *and they have wearied thee,*

3816 **לְאֹם & לְאוֹם** *l'ōhm*, m.

[In the singular it occurs only five times, marked [1]]

Gen25:23. two manner of *people*
— *and* (the one) *people*[1] shall be stronger *than* (the other) *people*[1];
27:29. *nations* bow down to thee:
Ps. 2: 1. *and the people* imagine a vain thing?
7: 7(8). the congregation of *the people*
9: 8(9). minister judgment to *the people*
44: 2(3). thou didst afflict *the people,*
14(15). shaking of the head *among the people.*
47: 3(4). *and the nations* under our feet.
57: 9(10). sing unto thee *among the nations.*
65: 7(8). and the tumult of *the people.*
67: 4(5). O let *the nations* be glad
—(-). *and* govern *the nations* upon earth.
105:44. inherited the labour of *the people;*
108: 3(4). praises unto thee *among the nations.*
148:11. Kings of the earth, and all *people;*
149: 7. punishments *upon the people;*
Pro.11:26. *the people*[1] shall curse him:
14:28. but in the want of *people*[1]
34. sin (is) a reproach to any *people.*
24:24. *nations* shall abhor him:
Isa. 17:12. to the rushing of *nations,*
13. *The nations* shall rush like
34: 1. *and* hearken, *ye people:* let the earth
41: 1. *and* let *the people* renew (their) strength:
43: 4. *and people* for thy life.
9. let *the people* be assembled:
49: 1. hearken, *ye people,* from far;
51: 4. *and* give ear unto me, *O my nation:*[1]
55: 4. given him (for) a witness to *the people,* a leader and commander to *the people.*
60: 2. gross darkness *the people:*
Jer. 51:58. *and the people* shall labour in vain,
Hab. 2:13. *that the people* shall labour

3813 **לָאַט** *lāh-at'.*

* KAL.—*Preterite.* *

2Sa.19: 4(5). the king *covered* his face,

3814 **לָאט** *lāht*, m.

Jud. 4:21. and went *softly* (lit. *with secresy*) unto

See 328 **לְאַט** see **אַט**

לֵב *lēhv*, m. 3820

Gen 6: 5. imagination of the thoughts of *his heart*
6. it grieved him at *his heart.*
8:21. the Lord said in *his heart,*
— the imagination of man's *heart*
17:17. and said *in his heart,*
18: 5. and comfort ye *your hearts;*
24:45. before I had done speaking in *mine heart,*
27:41. Esau said *in his heart,*
31:20. Jacob stole away *unawares to* Laban (marg. *the heart of* Laban)
34: 3. and spake *kindly* unto (marg. to *the heart of*) the damsel.
42:28. *their heart* failed (them),
45:26. Jacob's *heart* (marg. *his heart*) fainted,
50:21. *kindly unto them.* (lit. to *their hearts*)
Ex. 4:14. he will be glad *in his heart.*
21. I will harden *his heart,*
7: 3. I will harden Pharaoh's *heart,*
13. he hardened Pharaoh's *heart,*
14. Pharaoh's *heart* (is) hardened,
22. Pharaoh's *heart* was hardened,
23. neither did he set *his heart* to
8:15(11). he hardened *his heart,*
19(15). Pharaoh's *heart* was hardened,
32(28). Pharaoh hardened *his heart*
9: 7. *the heart of* Pharaoh was hardened,
12. the Lord hardened *the heart of* Pharaoh,
14. send all my plagues upon *thine heart,*
21. he that *regarded* not (marg. set not *his heart* unto) the word of the Lord
34. and hardened *his heart,*
35. *the heart of* Pharaoh was hardened,
10: 1. I have hardened *his heart,* and *the heart of*
20, 27 & 11:10. Lord hardened Pharaoh's *heart,*
14: 4. I will harden Pharaoh's *heart,*
8. the Lord hardened *the heart of* Pharaoh
17. I will harden *the hearts of* the Egyptians,
15: 8. *in the heart of* the sea.
25: 2. giveth it willingly with *his heart* (lit. whom *his heart* will make liberal)
28: 3. (that are) wise *heart*ed, (lit. wise of *heart*)
29. the breastplate of judgment upon *his heart,*
30. they shall be upon Aaron's *heart,*
— upon *his heart* before the Lord
31: 6. *and in the hearts of* all that are wise *heart*ed (lit. wise of *heart*)
35: 5. whosoever (is) of *a* willing *heart,* (lit. willing of *his heart*)
10. every wise *heart*ed
21. every one whose *heart* stirred him up, (lit. whom *his heart* stirred up)
22. as many as were willing *heart*ed,
25. the women that were wise *hearted*
26. the women whose *heart* stirred them up (lit. whom *their heart* stirred up)
29. whose *heart* made them willing (lit. whom *their heart* made willing)
34. he hath put *in his heart*
35. hath he filled with wisdom of *heart,*
36: 1. every wise *heart*ed man,
2. every wise *heart*ed man, *in whose heart* the Lord had put wisdom, (even) every one *whose heart* (lit. whom *his heart*) stirred
8. every wise *heart*ed man
Nu. 16:28. (I have) not (done them) *of mine own mind.*
24:13. do (either) good or bad *of mine own mind;*
32: 7. *the heart of* the children of Israel
9. they discouraged *the heart of*
Deu 4:11. unto *the midst* (marg. *heart*) *of* heaven,
28:65. *a* trembling *heart,* and failing of eyes,
29: 4(3). the Lord hath not given you *an heart*
19(18). walk in the imagination of *mine heart,*
Jos. 11:20. of the Lord to harden *their hearts,*
14: 8. made *the heart of* the people melt:
Jud. 5: 9. *My heart* (is) toward the governors of
15. (there were) great thoughts of *heart.*
16. (there were) great searchings of *heart.*
9: 3. *their hearts* inclined to follow
16:15. *when thine heart* (is) not with me?
17. That he told her all *his heart,*
18. he had told her all *his heart,*
— he hath shewed me all *his heart.*
25. when *their hearts* were merry,
18:20. the priest's *heart* was glad,
19: 3. to speak *friendly* (marg. to *her heart*) unto

Jud.19: 5. Comfort *thine heart* with a morsel of
6. let *thine heart* be merry.
22. they were making *their hearts* merry,
Ru. 2:13. thou hast spoken *friendly* (marg. to *the heart*) unto thine handmaid,
3: 7. *his heart* was merry,
1Sa. 1:13. Hannah, she spake in *her heart;*
2: 1. *My heart* rejoiceth in the Lord,
4:13. *his heart* trembled for the ark of God.
20. she answered not, neither did she regard (lit. set not *her heart*)
6: 6. and Pharaoh hardened *their hearts?*
9:20. set not *thy mind* on them;
10: 9. God gave him another *heart:*
26. men, whose *hearts* (lit. *in their hearts*)
17:32. Let no man's *heart* fail
24: 5(6). David's *heart* smote him,
25:25. not my lord,...regard (lit. set *his heart*)
31. nor offence of *heart* unto my lord,
36. *and* Nabal's *heart* (was) merry
37. *his heart* died within him,
27: 1. David said in *his heart,*
28: 5. *his heart* greatly trembled.
2Sa. 6:16. she despised him *in her heart.*
7:21. *and according to thine own heart,*
27. thy servant found in *his heart* to pray
13:20. regard not (marg. set not *thine heart*) this
28. when Amnon's *heart* is merry
33. not my lord...take the thing to *his heart,*
14: 1. the king's *heart* (was) toward Absalom.
15: 6. Absalom stole *the hearts of* the men
13. *The hearts of* the men of Israel
17:10. he also (that is) valiant, whose (lit. who *his*) *heart* (is) *as the heart of* a lion,
18: 3. they will not care for (marg. set (their) *heart* on) us; neither if half of us die, will they care for us: (lit. *id.*)
14. thrust them *through the heart of* Absalom, while he (was) yet alive *in the midst* (marg. *heart*) *of* the oak.
19: 7(8). speak *comfortably* unto (marg. to *the heart of*) thy servants:
19(20). the king should take it to *his heart.*
24:10. David's *heart* smote him
1K. 3: 9. thy servant *an* understanding *heart*
12. thee a wise and *an* understanding *heart;*
4:29(5:9). and largeness of *heart,*
8:23. walk before thee with all *their heart:*
47. if they shall bethink *themselves* (marg. bring back to *their heart*)
66. joyful and glad of *heart*
9: 3. mine eyes *and mine heart* shall be there
10:24. God had put *in his heart.*
11: 3. his wives turned away *his heart.*
12:26. Jeroboam said *in his heart,*
27. *the heart of* this people turn again
33. devised *of his own heart;*
18:37. thou hast turned *their heart*
21: 7. let *thine heart* be merry:
2K. 5:26. Went not *mine heart* (with thee),
6:11. *the heart of* the king of Syria
9:24. the arrow went out *at his heart,*
12: 4(5). that cometh into any man's *heart*
14:10. *thine heart* hath lifted thee up:
23: 3. with all (their) *heart* and all (their) soul,
1Ch.12:33. (they were) not of *double heart.* (marg. without *a heart and a heart*)
38. the rest also of Israel (were) of one *heart*
15:29. she despised him *in her heart.*
16:10. let *the heart of* them rejoice that seek the
17:19. *and according to thine own heart,*
28: 9. serve him *with a* perfect *heart*
29: 9. *with* perfect *heart* they offered
2Ch. 6:14. walk before thee with all *their hearts:*
38. return to thee with all *their heart*
7:10. glad and merry in *heart*
11. all that came into Solomon's *heart*
16. mine eyes *and mine heart* shall be there
9:23. God had put *in his heart.*
12:14. he prepared not *his heart*
17: 6. *his heart* was lifted up
24: 4. Joash was *minded* (lit. it was in *the heart of* Joash) to repair the house
25:19. *thine heart* lifteth thee up
26:16. *his heart* was lifted up
29:31. as many as were of *a* free *heart*
30:12. to give them one *heart*

2Ch.30:22. Hezekiah spake *comfortably* unto (marg. to *the heart of*)
32:25. *his heart* was lifted up:
26. the pride of *his heart,*
Ezr. 6:22. *the heart of* the king of Assyria
7:27. *in* the king's *heart,*
Neh 2: 2. nothing (else) but sorrow of *heart.*
12. God had put in *my heart*
4: 6(3:38). the people had *a mind* to work.
5: 7. *I* consulted (marg. *my heart* consulted)
6: 8. thou feignest them out *of thine own heart.*
7: 5. my God put into *mine heart*
Est. 1:10. *the heart of* the king was merry with wine,
5: 9. joyful and with *a* glad *heart:*
6: 6. Now Haman thought *in his heart,*
7: 5. that durst presume in *his heart*
Job 1: 8. Hast thou considered (marg. set *thy heart* on) my servant Job,
2: 3. Hast thou considered (lit. *id.*) my
7:17. set *thine heart* upon him?
8:10. *and* utter words out *of their heart?*
11:13. If thou prepare *thine heart,*
12:24. *the heart of* the chief of the people
15:12. Why doth *thine heart* carry thee away?
17: 4. thou hast hid *their heart*
23:16. God maketh *my heart* soft,
29:13. *and* I caused the widow's *heart* to sing
31: 7. *mine heart* walked after mine eyes,
9. If *mine heart* have been deceived
27. *my heart* hath been secretly enticed,
33: 3. the uprightness of *my heart:*
34:14. If he set *his heart* upon man,
36: 5. (he is) mighty in strength (and) *wisdom.* (marg. *heart*)
13. the hypocrites in *heart* heap up wrath:
37: 1. At this also *my heart* trembleth,
24. any (that are) wise of *heart.*
41:24(16). *His heart* is as firm as a stone;
Ps. 4: 7(8). Thou hast put gladness *in my heart,*
7:10(11). which saveth the upright in *heart.*
9: 1(2). with *my* whole *heart;*
10: 6, 11, 13. He hath said *in his heart.*
17. thou wilt prepare *their heart,*
11: 2. the upright in *heart.*
12: 2(3). with *a double heart* do they speak. (marg. *an heart and an heart*)
13: 5(6). *my heart* shall rejoice in thy salvation.
14: 1. The fool hath said *in his heart,*
16: 9. Therefore *my heart* is glad,
17: 3. Thou hast proved *mine heart;*
19: 8(9). rejoicing *the heart:*
14(15). the meditation of *my heart,*
21: 2(3). Thou hast given him *his heart's* desire,
22:14(15). *my heart* is like wax;
26: 2. try my reins *and my heart.*
27: 3. *my heart* shall not fear:
8. *my heart* said unto thee,
14. he shall strengthen *thine heart:*
28: 7. *my heart* trusted in him, and I am helped: therefore *my heart* greatly rejoiceth;
31:12(13). a dead man *out of mind:*
32:11. (ye that are) upright in *heart.*
33:11. the thoughts of *his heart*
15. He fashioneth *their hearts* alike;
21. *our heart* shall rejoice in him,
34:18(19). them that are of *a* broken *heart;*
35:25. Let them not say *in their hearts,*
36: 1(2). saith within *my heart,*
10(11). the upright in *heart.*
37: 4. the desires of *thine heart.*
15. enter *into their own heart,*
31. The law of his God (is) *in his heart;*
38: 8(9). the disquietness of *my heart.*
10(11). *My heart* panteth,
39: 3(4). *My heart* was hot within me,
40:10(11). thy righteousness within *my heart;*
12(13). *therefore my heart* faileth me.
41: 6(7). *his heart* gathereth iniquity
44:18(19). *Our heart* is not turned back,
21(22). the secrets of *the heart.*
45: 1(2). *My heart* is inditing a good matter:
5(6). *in the heart of* the king's enemies;
46: 2(3). *into the midst of* the sea; (marg. *heart of* the seas)
48:13(14). Mark ye well (marg. Set *your heart* to) her bulwarks,
49: 3(4). the meditation of *my heart*

Ps. 51:10(12). Create in me *a* clean *heart*,
17(19). a broken and *a* contrite *heart*,
53: 1(2). The fool hath said *in his heart*,
55: 4(5). *My heart* is sore pained
21(22). war (was) in *his heart:*
57: 7(8). *My heart* is fixed, O God, *my heart* is
58: 2(3). *in heart* ye work wickedness;
61: 2(3). *my heart* is overwhelmed:
62:10(11). set not your *heart* (upon them).
64: 6(7). *and the heart*, (is) deep.
10(11). all the upright in *heart* shall glory.
66:18. If I regard iniquity *in my heart*,
69:20(21). Reproach hath broken *my heart;*
74: 8. They said *in their hearts*,
76: 5(6). The stout*hearted* (lit. stout of *heart*)
78: 8. (that) set not *their heart* aright,
37. *For their heart* was not right with him,
81:12(13). I gave them up unto *their own heart*'s
83: 5(6). consulted together with one *consent:*
84: 2(3). *my heart* and my flesh crieth out
94:15. all the upright in *heart*
97:11. gladness for the upright in *heart*.
102: 4(5). *My heart* is smitten,
105: 3. *the heart of* them rejoice that
25. He turned *their heart* to hate his people,
107:12. he brought down *their heart*
108: 1(2). O God, *my heart* is fixed;
109:22. *and my heart* is wounded within me.
112: 7. *his heart* is fixed,
8. *His heart* (is) established,
119: 2. seek him with *the* whole *heart*.
10. With *my* whole *heart* have I sought thee:
11. Thy word have I hid *in mine heart*,
32. thou shalt enlarge *my heart*.
34. observe it with (my) whole *heart*.
36. Incline *my heart* unto thy testimonies.
58. favour with (my) whole *heart:*
69. thy precepts with (my) whole *heart*.
70. *Their heart* is as fat as grease;
80. Let *my heart* be sound
111. the rejoicing of *my heart*.
112. I have inclined *mine heart*
145. I cried with (my) whole *heart;*
161. *my heart* standeth in awe
131: 1. *my heart* is not haughty,
138: 1. with *my* whole *heart:*
140: 2(3). imagine mischiefs *in* (their) *heart*,
141: 4. Incline not *my heart*
143: 4. *my heart* within me is desolate.
147: 3. He healeth the broken in *heart*,
Pro. 2: 2. apply *thine heart* to understanding;
10. wisdom entereth *into thine heart*,
3: 1. let *thine heart* keep my commandments:
3. the table of *thine heart:*
5. Trust in the Lord with all *thine heart;*
4: 4. Let *thine heart* retain my words:
23. Keep *thy heart* with all diligence;
5:12. *my heart* despised reproof;
6:14. Frowardness (is) *in his heart*,
18. *An heart* that deviseth wicked imaginations,
21. Bind them continually upon *thine heart*,
32. whoso committeth adultery...lacketh *understanding:* (marg. *heart*)
7: 3. the table of *thine heart*.
7. a young man void of *understanding*,
10. and subtil of *heart*.
25. Let not *thine heart* decline to her ways,
8: 5. be ye of *an* understanding *heart*.
9: 4, 16. him that wanteth *understanding*,
10: 8. wise in *heart* will receive commandments:
13. that is void of *understanding*. (marg. *heart*)
20. *the heart of* the wicked (is) little worth.
21. fools die for want of *wisdom*. (marg. *heart*)
11:12. He that is void of *wisdom* (marg. *id.*)
20. They that are of *a* froward *heart*
29. the wise of *heart*.
12: 8. *a* perverse *heart* shall be despised.
11. he that followeth vain (persons is) void of *understanding*.
20. *in the heart of* them that imagine evil:
23. *but the heart of* fools proclaimeth
25. Heaviness *in the heart of* man
13:12. Hope deferred maketh *the heart* sick:
14:10. *The heart* knoweth his own bitterness;
13. Even in laughter *the heart* is sorrowful;
14. The backslider in *heart*
30. *A* sound *heart* (is) the life of the flesh:

Pro.14:33. Wisdom resteth *in the heart of*
15: 7. *but the heart of* the foolish
13. *A* merry *heart* maketh a chearful countenance: but by sorrow of *the heart* the
14. *The heart of* him that hath
15. he that is of *a* merry *heart*
21. to (him that is) destitute of *wisdom*. (marg. *heart*)
28. *The heart of* the righteous
30. The light of the eyes rejoiceth *the heart:*
32. that heareth reproof getteth *understanding*
16: 1. The preparations of *the heart*
5. Every one (that is) proud in *heart*
9. A man's *heart* deviseth his way:
21. The wise in *heart* shall be called prudent:
23. *The heart of* the wise teacheth
17:16. *seeing* (he hath) no *heart* (to it)?
18. A man void of *understanding* (marg. *heart*)
20. He that hath *a* froward *heart*
22. *A* merry *heart* doeth good
18: 2. that *his heart* may discover itself.
12. *the heart of* man is haughty,
15. *The heart of* the prudent getteth knowledge;
19: 3. *his heart* fretteth against the Lord.
8. He that getteth *wisdom* (marg. *an heart*)
21. many devices *in* a man's *heart;*
20: 5. Counsel *in the heart of* man
9. I have made *my heart* clean,
21: 1. The king's *heart* (is) in the hand of
4. An high look, and *a* proud *heart*,
22:11. He that loveth pureness of *heart*,
15. Foolishness (is) bound *in the heart of*
17. *and* apply *thine heart* unto my knowledge.
23: 7. but *his heart* (is) not with thee.
12. Apply *thine heart* unto instruction,
15. *thine heart* be wise, *my heart* shall rejoice,
17. Let not *thine heart* envy sinners:
19. guide *thine heart* in the way.
26. My son, give me *thine heart*,
33. *and thine heart* shall utter perverse things.
34. lieth down *in the midst of* (marg. *heart*)
24: 2. *their heart* studieth destruction,
17. let not *thine heart* be glad when
30. the man void of *understanding;*
32. I...considered (marg. set *my heart*) (it) well:
25: 3. *and the heart of* kings (is) unsearchable.
20. he that singeth songs to *an* heavy *heart*.
26:23. Burning lips *and a* wicked *heart*
25. seven abominations *in his heart*.
27: 9. Ointment and perfume rejoice *the heart:*
11. make *my heart* glad,
19. *the heart of* man to man.
23. look well (marg. set *thy heart*) to thy
28:14. he that hardeneth *his heart*
26. He that trusteth *in his own heart*
30:19. ship *in the midst* (marg. *heart*) *of* the sea;
31:11. *The heart of* her husband
Ecc. 1:13. I gave *my heart* to seek and search
16. I communed with *mine own heart*,
— *yea, my heart* had great experience
17. I gave *my heart* to know wisdom,
2: 1. I said *in mine heart*,
3. I sought *in mine heart* to give myself unto wine, *yet* acquainting *mine heart* with
10. I withheld not *my heart* from any joy; for *my heart* rejoiced in all my labour:
15. Then said I *in my heart*,
— Then I said *in my heart*,
20. to cause *my heart* to despair
22. and of the vexation of *his heart*,
23. *his heart* taketh not rest in the night.
3:11. he hath set the world *in their heart*,
17. I said *in mine heart*,
18. I said *in mine heart*
5: 2(1). *and* let not *thine heart* be hasty to utter
20(19). in the joy of *his heart*.
7: 2. the living will lay (it) to *his heart*.
3. the sadness of the countenance *the heart*
4. *The heart of* the wise (is) in the house of mourning; *but the heart of* fools
7. a gift destroyeth *the heart*.
21. take no heed (marg. give not *thine heart*) unto all words that are spoken;
22. *thine own heart* knoweth that
25. I applied *mine heart* to know, (lit. I *and my heart* compassed)

Ecc. 7:26. the woman, *whose heart* (is) snares
8: 5. a wise man's *heart* discerneth
9. and applied *my heart* unto every work
11. *the heart of* the sons of men
16. I applied *mine heart* to know wisdom,
9: 1. I considered in *my heart*
3. *the heart of* the sons of men
7. drink thy wine *with a* merry *heart*;
10: 2. A wise man's *heart* (is) at his right hand; *but* a fool's *heart*
3. *his wisdom* (marg. *heart*) faileth (him),
11: 9. let *thy heart* cheer thee in the days of thy youth, and walk in the ways of *thine heart*,
10. remove sorrow *from thy heart*,
Cant. 3:11. in the day of the gladness of *his heart*.
5: 2. I sleep, *but my heart* waketh:
8: 6. Set me as a seal upon *thine heart*,
Isa. 6:10. Make *the heart of* this people fat,
15: 5. *My heart* shall cry out for Moab;
24: 7. all the merry*hearted* (lit. merry of *heart*)
29:13. *but* have removed *their heart* far from me,
32: 6. *and his heart* will work iniquity,
33:18. *Thine heart* shall meditate terror.
35: 4. them (that are) of *a* fearful *heart*,
38: 3. *and with a* perfect *heart*,
40: 2. Speak ye *comfortably* (marg. to *the heart*)
41:22. we may consider (marg. set *our heart*)
42:25. yet he laid (it) not to *heart*.
44:19. none considereth in *his heart*,
20. *a* deceived *heart* hath turned him aside,
46: 8. (it) again to *mind*, O ye transgressors.
12. Hearken unto me, ye stout*heart*ed,
47: 7. didst not lay these (things) to *thy heart*,
10. thou hast said *in thine heart*,
51: 7. the people *in whose heart* (is) my law;
57: 1. no man layeth (it) to *heart*:
11. nor laid (it) to *thy heart*?
15. *the heart of* the contrite ones.
17. frowardly in the way of *his heart*.
59:13. uttering *from the heart* words of
61: 1. to bind up the broken*heart*ed,
63: 4. the day of vengeance (is) *in mine heart*,
17. hardened *our heart* from thy fear?
65:14. my servants shall sing for joy of *heart*, but ye shall cry for sorrow of *heart*,
17. come into *mind*. (marg. upon *the heart*)
66:14. *your heart* shall rejoice,
Jer 3:10. not turned unto me with *her* whole *heart*,
15. *according to mine heart*,
16. neither shall it come to *mind*: (marg. upon *the heart*)
17. the imagination of *their* evil *heart*.
4: 9. *the heart of* the king shall perish, *and the heart of* the princes;
14. O Jerusalem, wash *thine heart*
18. it reacheth unto *thine heart*.
19. I am pained at *my* very *heart*; *my heart* maketh a noise in me;
5:21. O foolish people, and without *understanding*; (marg. *heart*)
23. hath a revolting and *a* rebellious *heart*;
7:24. the imagination of *their* evil *heart*,
31. neither came it into *my heart*.
8:18. *my heart* (is) faint in me.
9:14(13). the imagination of *their own heart*,
26(25). the house of Israel (are) uncircumcised in *the heart*.
11: 8. the imagination of *their* evil *heart*:
20. that triest the reins and *the heart*,
12: 3. and tried *mine heart* toward thee:
11. no man layeth (it) to *heart*.
13:10. the imagination of *their heart*,
14:14. the deceit of *their heart*.
16:12. the imagination of *his* evil *heart*,
17: 1. graven upon the table of *their heart*,
5. *whose heart* departeth from
9. *The heart* (is) deceitful above all (things),
10. I the Lord search *the heart*,
18:12. the imagination of *his* evil *heart*.
19: 5. neither came (it) into *my mind*:
20: 9. (his word) was *in mine heart*
12. seest the reins *and the heart*,
22:17. thine eyes *and thine heart*
23: 9. *Mine heart* within me is broken
16. they speak a vision of *their own heart*,
17. after the imagination of *his own heart*,

Jer. 23:20. performed the thoughts of *his heart*:
26. *in the heart of* the prophets
— the deceit of *their own heart*;
24: 7. I will give them *an heart* to know
— return unto me with *their* whole *heart*.
30:21. engaged *his heart* to approach unto me?
24. performed the intents of *his heart*:
31:21. set *thine heart* toward the highway.
33. and write it in *their hearts*;
32:35. neither came it into *my mind*,
39. I will give them one *heart*,
41. with *my* whole *heart*
44:21. and came it (not) into *his mind*?
48:29. the haughtiness of *his heart*.
36. *mine heart* shall sound for Moab like pipes, *and mine heart* shall sound like pipes
41. the mighty men's *hearts* in Moab at that day shall be *as the heart of* a woman in
49:16. the pride of *thine heart*,
22. *the heart of* the mighty men of Edom be *as the heart of* a woman in her pangs.
51: 1. against them that dwell in *the midst* (marg. *heart*) *of* them that
Lam. 1:20. *mine heart* is turned within me;
22. my sighs (are) many, *and my heart* (is)
2:18. *Their heart* cried unto the Lord,
19. pour out *thine heart* like water
3:21. This I recall to *my mind*,
33. he doth not afflict *willingly* (marg. *from his heart*)
65. Give them sorrow of *heart*,
5:15. The joy of *our heart* is ceased;
17. For this *our heart* is faint;
Eze. 2: 4. impudent children and stiff*heart*ed.
3: 7. of Israel (are) impudent and hard*heart*ed.
6: 9. I am broken with *their* whorish *heart*,
11:19. I will give them one *heart*,
— I will take *the* stony *heart* out of their flesh, and will give them *an heart of*
21. (as for them) *whose heart* walketh after *the heart of*
13: 2. them that prophesy *out of their own hearts*,
17. which prophesy *out of their own heart*;
22. ye have made *the heart of* the righteous
14: 3. set up their idols in *their heart*,
4. setteth up his idols in *his heart*,
5. take the house of Israel *in their own heart*.
7. setteth up his idols in *his heart*,
18:31. make you *a* new *heart*
20:16. *their heart* went after their idols.
21: 7(12). every *heart* shall melt,
15(20). that (their) *heart* may faint,
22:14. Can *thine heart* endure,
27: 4. Thy borders (are) *in the midst* (marg *heart*) *of* the seas,
25. made very glorious *in the midst of*
26. broken thee *in the midst of* the seas.
27. thy company...shall fall *into the midst* (marg. *heart*) *of*
28: 2. *thine heart* is lifted up,
— *in the midst of* the seas; (marg. *heart*)
— though thou set *thine heart as the heart of*
6. *as the heart of* God;
8. (them that are) slain *in the midst of* the
17. *Thine heart* was lifted up
32: 9. I will also vex *the hearts of*
33:31. *their heart* goeth after their covetousness.
36:26. *A* new *heart* also will I give you,
— I will take away *the* stony *heart* out of your flesh, and I will give you *an heart of*
40: 4. set *thine heart* upon all that
44: 5. Son of man, mark well, (marg. set *thine heart*)
— and mark well (lit. *id.*) the entering in
7. strangers, uncircumcised in *heart*,
9. No stranger, uncircumcised in *heart*,
Dan. 1: 8. Daniel purposed in *his heart*
10:12. thou didst set *thine heart* to
Hos. 2:14(16). speak *comfortably* (marg. to *her heart*)
4:11. and new wine take away *the heart*.
7: 6. they have made ready *their heart* like an
11. is like a silly dove without *heart*:
14. have not cried unto me *with their heart*,
10: 2. *Their heart* is divided;
11: 8. *mine heart* is turned within me,
13: 6. *their heart* was exalted;
8. will rend the caul of *their heart*,

Am. 2:16. (he that is) *courageous* (marg. strong of *his heart*)
Obad. 3. The pride of *thine heart*
— that saith *in his heart*,
Nah. 2:10(11). *and the heart* melteth,
Zep. 3:14. be glad and rejoice with all *the heart*,
Zec. 7:12. *Yea*, they made *their hearts* (as) an
10: 7. *their heart* shall rejoice as through
— *their heart* shall rejoice in
12: 5. governors of Judah shall say *in their heart*,
Mal. 2: 2. if ye will not lay (it) to *heart*,
— ye do not lay (it) to *heart*.
4: 6(3:24). he shall turn *the heart of* the fathers to the children, *and the heart of* the

3821 לְבֵ [*lēhv*], Ch. m.

Dan 7:28. but I kept the matter *in my heart*.

3833 לְבָאוֹת [*l'vāh-ōhth'*], f. pl.

Nah. 2:12(13). and strangled *for his lionesses*,

3833 לְבָאִים *l'vāh-eem'*, m. pl.

Ps. 57: 4(5). My soul (is) among *lions* :

3823 לָבַב [*lāh-vav'*].

* NIPHAL.—*Future*. *

Job 11:12. vain man *would be wise*,

* PIEL.—*Preterite*. *

Cant. 4: 9. *Thou hast ravished* (marg. *taken away*) *my heart*, my sister,
— *thou hast ravished my heart* with one of

PIEL.—*Future*.

2Sa. 13: 6. *and make* me a couple of cakes
8. *and made cakes* in his sight,

3824 לֵבָב *lēh-vāhv'*, m.

Gen20: 5. in the integrity of *my heart*
6. in the integrity of *thy heart* ;
31:26. stolen away *unawares to me* (lit. stolen from *my heart*)
Ex. 14: 5. *the heart of* Pharaoh
Lev. 19:17. shalt not hate thy brother *in thine heart* :
26:36. I will send a faintness *into their hearts*
41. if then *their* uncircumcised *hearts* be
Nu. 15:39. ye seek not after *your own heart*
Deu 1:28. our brethren have discouraged *our heart*,
2:30. and made *his heart* obstinate,
4: 9. lest they depart *from thy heart*
29. seek him with all *thy heart*
39. consider (it) in *thine heart*,
5:29(26). that there were such *an heart* in them, (lit. *their heart* this to them)
6: 5. love the Lord...with all *thine heart*,
6. these words,...shall be in *thine heart* :
7:17. If thou shalt say *in thine heart*,
8: 2. to know what (was) *in thine heart*,
5. Thou shalt also consider in *thine heart*,
14. *thine heart* be lifted up,
17. And thou say *in thine heart*,
9: 4. Speak not thou *in thine heart*,
5. the uprightness of *thine heart*,
10:12. serve the Lord thy God with all *thy heart*
16. the foreskin of *your heart*,
11:13. serve him with all *your heart*
16. that *your heart* be not deceived,
18. lay up these my words *in your heart*
13: 3(4). love the Lord...with all *your heart*
15: 7. thou shalt not harden *thine heart*,
9. a thought in *thy* wicked *heart*,
10. *thine heart* shall not be grieved
17:17. that *his heart* turn not away:
20. That *his heart* be not lifted up
18:21. if thou say *in thine heart*,
19: 6. while *his heart* is hot,
20: 3. let not *your hearts* faint,
Deu20: 8. and faint*hearted*? (lit. tender of *heart*)
— brethren's *heart* faint as well *as his heart*.
26:16. and do them with all *thine heart*,
28:28. and astonishment of *heart* :
47. with gladness of *heart*,
67. for the fear of *thine heart*
29:18(17). *whose heart* turneth away
19(18). he bless himself *in his heart*,
30: 1. thou shalt call (them) to *mind*
2. and thy children, with all *thine heart*,
6. will circumcise *thine heart*, and *the heart of* thy seed, to love the Lord thy God with all *thine heart*,
10. turn unto the Lord...with all *thine heart*,
14. in thy mouth, *and in thy heart*,
17. if *thine heart* turn away,
32:46. Set *your hearts* unto all the words
Jos. 2:11. *our hearts* did melt,
5: 1. *their heart* melted,
7: 5. *the hearts of* the people
14: 7. as (it was) in *mine heart*.
22: 5. to serve him with all *your heart*
23:14. ye know in all *your hearts*
24:23. incline *your heart* unto the Lord
Jud. 19: 8. Comfort *thine heart*,
9. that *thine heart* may be merry;
1Sa. 1: 8. why is *thy heart* grieved?
2:35. *in mine heart* and in my mind:
6: 6. Wherefore then do ye harden *your hearts*,
7: 3. return unto the Lord with all *your hearts*,
— prepare *your hearts* unto the Lord,
9:19. all that (is) *in thine heart*.
12:20. serve the Lord with all *your heart* ;
24. serve him in truth with all *your heart* :
13:14. a man *after his own heart*,
14: 7. all that (is) *in thine heart* : turn thee; behold, I (am) with thee *according to thy heart*.
16: 7. the Lord looketh *on the heart*.
17:28. the naughtiness of *thine heart* ;
21:12(13). David laid up these words *in his heart*,
2Sa. 7: 3. do all that (is) *in thine heart* ;
19:14(15). *the heart of* all the men of Judah,
1 K. 2: 4. with all *their heart*
44. wickedness which *thine heart* is privy to,
3: 6. uprightness of *heart*
8:17. in *the heart of* David
18. it was in *thine heart* to build
— that it was in *thine heart*.
38. every man the plague of *his own heart*,
39. *whose* (lit. who *his*) *heart* thou knowest; for thou, (even) thou only, knowest *the hearts of*
48. return unto thee with all *their heart*,
58. That he may incline *our hearts*
61. Let *your heart* therefore be perfect
9: 4. in integrity of *heart*,
10: 2. all that was in *her heart*.
11: 2. they will turn away *your heart*
4. his wives turned away *his heart* after other gods: and *his heart* was not perfect with the Lord his God, *as* (was) *the heart of*
9. *his heart* was turned from the Lord
14: 8. followed me with all *his heart*,
15: 3. *his heart* was not perfect with the Lord his God, *as the heart of* David
14. Asa's *heart* was perfect
2K. 10:15. Is *thine heart* right, as *my heart* (is) with *thy heart* ?
30. all that (was) *in mine heart*,
31. with all *his heart* :
20: 3. in truth *and with a* perfect *heart*,
22:19. *thine heart* was tender,
23:25. that turned to the Lord with all *his heart*,
1Ch 12:17. *mine heart* shall be knit unto you:
38. came *with a* perfect *heart*
17: 2. Do all that (is) *in thine heart* ;
22: 7. in *my mind* to build an house
19. set *your heart* and your soul to seek
28: 2. I (had) in *mine heart* to build
9. the Lord searcheth all *hearts*,
29:17. thou triest *the heart*,
— in the uprightness of *mine heart*
18. the thoughts of *the heart of* thy people, and prepare *their heart* unto thee:
19. give unto Solomon my son *a* perfect *heart*,
2Ch. 1:11. Because this was in *thine heart*,

2Ch. 6: 7. it was in *the heart of* David
8. Forasmuch as it was in *thine heart*
— in that it was in *thine heart:*
30. *whose* (lit. who *his*) *heart* thou knowest; for thou only knowest *the hearts of*
37. (if) *they bethink themselves* (marg. bring back to *their heart*)
9: 1. all that was in *her heart.*
11:16. such as set *their hearts* to seek the Lord
13: 7. Rehoboam was young and tender*heart*ed, (lit. tender of *heart*)
15:12. with all *their heart* and with all their soul;
15. they had sworn with all *their heart,*
17. *the heart of* Asa was perfect
16: 9. (them) *whose heart* (is) perfect
19: 3. hast prepared *thine heart* to seek God.
9. *and with a* perfect *heart.*
20:33. the people had not prepared *their hearts*
22: 9. sought the Lord with all *his heart.*
25: 2. not *with a* perfect *heart.*
29:10. (it is) in *mine heart* to make a covenant
34. the Levites (were) more upright in *heart*
30:19. prepareth *his heart* to seek God,
31:21. he did (it) with all *his heart,*
32: 6. spake *comfortably* (marg. to *their heart*) to
31. all (that was) *in his heart.*
34:27. Because *thine heart* was tender,
31. his commandments,...with all *his heart,*
36:13. hardened *his heart* from turning unto
Ezr. 7:10. Ezra had prepared *his heart*
Neh. 9: 8. foundest *his heart* faithful
Job. 1: 5. and cursed God *in their hearts.*
9: 4. (He is) wise in *heart,*
10:13. these (things) hast thou hid *in thine heart:*
12: 3. I have *understanding* as well as you; (marg. *an heart*)
17:11. the thoughts of *my heart.*
22:22. lay up his words *in thine heart.*
27: 6. *my heart* shall not reproach (me)
34:10. ye men of *understanding:* (marg. *heart*)
34. men of *understanding* (marg. *heart*) tell me,
Ps. 4: 4(5). commune *with your own heart*
13: 2(3). sorrow *in my heart* daily?
15: 2. and speaketh the truth *in his heart.*
20: 4(5). *according to thine own heart,*
22:26(27). *your heart* shall live for ever.
24: 4. that hath clean hands, and *a* pure *heart;*
25:17. The troubles of *my heart* are enlarged:
28: 3. mischief (is) *in their hearts.*
31:24(25). he shall strengthen *your heart,*
62: 8(9). pour out *your heart* before him:
69:32(33). *your heart* shall live that seek God.
73: 1. such as are of *a* clean *heart.*
7. they have more than *heart* could wish.
13. I have cleansed *my heart* (in) vain,
21. Thus *my heart* was grieved,
26. My flesh *and my heart* faileth: (but) God (is) the strength of *my heart,*
77: 6(7). I commune with *mine own heart:*
78:18. they tempted God *in their heart*
72. according to the integrity of *his heart;*
84: 5(6). *in whose heart* (are) the ways (of them).
86:11. unite *my heart* to fear thy name.
12. I will praise thee,...with all *my heart:*
90:12. that we may apply (our) *hearts* unto
95: 8. Harden not *your heart,*
10. a people that do err in *their heart,*
101: 2. walk within my house with *a* perfect *heart.* (lit. in the perfection of *my heart*)
4. *A* froward *heart* shall depart from me:
5. an high look and *a* proud *heart*
104:15. maketh glad *the heart of* man,
— bread (which) strengtheneth man's *heart.*
109:16. the broken in *heart.*
111: 1. praise the Lord with (my) whole *heart,*
119: 7. with uprightness of *heart,*
139:23. Search me, O God, and know *my heart:*
Pro. 4:21. in the midst of *thine heart.*
6:25. Lust not after her beauty *in thine heart;*
Ecc. 9: 3. and madness (is) *in their heart*
Isa. 1: 5. and *the* whole *heart* faint.
6:10. *and* understand with *their heart,*
7: 2. And *his heart* was moved, *and the heart of*
4. *neither* be faint*hearted* (marg. & lit. *and* let not *thy heart* be tender)
9: 9(8). in the pride and stoutness of *heart,*
Isa. 10: 7. *neither* doth *his heart* think so; but (it is) *in his heart* to destroy
12. *the* stout *heart of* the king of Assyria,
13: 7. every man's *heart* shall melt:
14:13. thou hast said *in thine heart,*
19: 1. *and the heart of* Egypt shall melt
21: 4. *My heart* panted,
30:29. and gladness of *heart,*
32: 4. *The heart also of* the rash
47: 8. that sayest *in thine heart,*
49:21. Then shalt thou say *in thine heart,*
60: 5. and *thine heart* shall fear,
Jer. 4: 4. the foreskins of *your heart,*
5:24. say they *in their heart,*
13:22. if thou say *in thine heart,*
15:16. the joy and rejoicing of *mine heart:*
29:13. search for me with all *your heart.*
32:40. put my fear *in their hearts,*
51:46. lest *your heart* faint,
50. let Jerusalem come into *your mind.*
Lam 3:41. Let us lift up *our heart*
Eze. 3:10. receive *in thine heart,*
28: 5. *thine heart* is lifted up
6. thou hast set *thine heart*
31:10. *his heart* is lifted up
36: 5. the joy of all (their) *heart,*
38:10. shall things come into *thy mind,*
Dan. 8:25. *and* he shall magnify (himself) *in his heart.*
11:12. *his heart* shall be lifted up;
25. he shall stir up his power *and his courage*
27. both these kings' *hearts* (marg. *their hearts*)
28. *and his heart* (shall be) against the holy
Hos. 7: 2. they consider not *in their hearts*
Joel 2:12. turn ye (even) to me with all *your heart,*
13. And rend *your heart,*
Jon. 2: 3(4). *in the midst* (marg. *heart*) *of* the seas;
Nah. 2: 7(8). tabering upon *their breasts.*
Zep. 1:12. that say *in their heart,*
2:15. that said *in her heart,*
Hag 1: 5, 7. Consider (marg. Set *your heart* on) your ways.
2:15. consider (lit. set *your heart* on) from
18. Consider (lit. Set *your heart* on) now from
— consider (lit. *id.*) (it.)
Zec. 7:10. none of you imagine evil...*in your heart.*
8:17. let none of you imagine evil *in your hearts*

לְבַב *l'vav*, Ch. m. 3825

Dan. 2:30. mightest know the thoughts of *thy heart.*
4:16(13). Let *his heart* be changed from man's, *and* let a beast's *heart* be given unto him;
5:20. But when *his heart* was lifted up,
21. *and his heart* was made like the beasts,
22. O Belshazzar, hast not humbled *thine heart,*
7: 4. *and* a man's *heart* was given to it.

לְבִבוֹת *l'vee-vōhth'*, f. pl. 3834

2Sa. 13: 6. make me a couple of *cakes*
8. and did bake *the cakes.*
10. Tamar took *the cakes* which she had made,

לַבָּה [*lab-bāh'*], f. 3827

Ex. 3: 2. angel of the Lord appeared...*in a flame of*

לִבָּה [*lib-bāh'*], f. 3826

Ps. 7: 9(10). the righteous God trieth *the hearts*
125: 4. (them that are) upright *in their hearts.*
Pro. 15:11. *the hearts of* the children of men?
17: 3. the Lord trieth *the hearts.*
21: 2. the Lord pondereth *the hearts.*
24:12. he that pondereth *the heart*
Isa. 44:18. he hath shut their eyes,...(and) *their hearts,*
Eze. 16:30. How weak is *thine heart,*

לְבוֹנָה *l'vōh-nāh'*, f. 3828

Ex. 30:34. sweet spices *with* pure *frankincense:*
Lev. 2: 1. and put *frankincense* thereon:

Lev. 2: 2, 16. with all *the frankincense thereof;*
15. and lay *frankincense* thereon:
5. 11. shall he put (any) *frankincense* thereon:
6: 15(8). all *the frankincense* which (is) upon
24: 7. thou shalt put pure *frankincense* upon
Nu. 5: 15. nor put *frankincense* thereon;
1Ch. 9: 29. *and the frankincense,* and the spices.
Neh 13: 5. *the frankincense,* and the vessels,
9. the meat offering *and the frankincense.*
Cant 3: 6. perfumed with myrrh *and frankincense,*
4: 6. the hill of *frankincense.*
14. with all trees of *frankincense;*
Isa. 43: 23. nor wearied thee *with incense.*
60: 6. they shall bring gold *and incense;*
66: 3. he that burneth *incense,*
Jer. 6: 20. cometh there to me *incense*
17: 26. meat offerings, *and incense,*
41: 5. with offerings *and incense* in their **hand,**

3830 **לְבוּשׁ** *l'voosh,* m.

Gen 49: 11. he washed *his garments* in wine,
2Sa. 1: 24. ornaments of gold upon *your apparel.*
20: 8. Joab's garment *that he had put on*
2K. 10: 22. Bring forth *vestments* for
Est. 4: 2. none (might) enter into the king's gate *clothed with* (lit. *in clothing of*) sackcloth.
6: 8. Let *the* royal *apparel* be brought
9. let *this apparel* and horse be delivered to
10. take *the apparel* and the horse,
11. Then took Haman *the apparel*
8: 15. *in* royal *apparel* of blue and white,
Job 24: 7. cause the naked to lodge without *clothing,*
10. cause (him) to go naked without *clothing,*
30: 18. is *my garment* changed:
31: 19. have seen any perish for want of *clothing,*
38: 9. I made the cloud *the garment thereof,*
14. they stand as *a garment.*
41: 13(5). can discover the face of *his garment?*
Ps. 22: 18(19). cast lots upon *my vesture.*
35: 13. *my clothing* (was) sackcloth.
45: 13(14). *her clothing* (is) of wrought gold.
69: 11(12). I made sackcloth also *my garment;*
102: 26(27). *as a vesture* shalt thou change them,
104: 6. it with the deep *as* (with) *a garment:*
Pro. 27: 26. The lambs (are) *for thy clothing,*
31: 22. *her clothing* (is) silk and purple.
25. Strength and honour (are) *her clothing;*
Isa. 14: 19. *the raiment* of those that are slain,
63: 1. this (that is) glorious *in his apparel,*
2. Wherefore (art thou) red *in thine apparel,*
Jer. 10: 9. blue and purple (is) *their clothing:*
Lam 4: 14. men could not touch *their garments.*
Mal. 2: 16. (one) covereth violence with *his garment,*

3831 **לְבוּשׁ** [*l'voosh*], Ch. m.

Dan. 3: 21. *and their* (other) *garments,* and were cast
7: 9. *whose garment* (was) white as snow,

3832 **לָבַט** [*lāh-vat'*].

* NIPHAL.—*Future.* *

Pro. 10: 8, 10. a prating fool *shall fall.* (marg. *be beaten*)
Hos. 4: 14. the people (that) doth not understand *shall fall.* (marg. or, *be punished*)

3833 **לָבִיא** *lāh-vee',* com.

Gen 49. 9. he couched as a lion, and *as an old lion;*
Nu. 23: 24. the people shall rise up *as a great lion,*
24: 9. he lay down as a lion, *and as a great lion:*
Deu 33: 20. he dwelleth *as a lion,*
Job 4: 11. *the stout lion's* whelps are scattered
38: 39. Wilt thou hunt the prey *for the lion?*
Isa. 5: 29. Their roaring (shall be) *like a lion,*
30: 6. whence (come) *the young* and old lion,
Hos. 13: 8. there will I devour them *like a lion:*
Joel 1: 6. the cheek teeth of *a great lion.*
Nah. 2: 11(12). the lion, (even) *the old lion,*

לְבִיָּא *l'veey-yāh',* f. 3833

Eze. 19: 2. What (is) thy mother? *A lioness:*

לָבֵן [*lāh-vehn'*]. 3835

* KAL.—*Infinitive.* *

Ex. 5: 7. give the people straw *to make* brick,
14. fulfilled your task *in making brick*

KAL.—*Future.*

Gen 11: 3. Go to, *let us make* brick,

* HIPHIL.—*Preterite.* *

Joel 1: 7. the branches thereof *are made white.*

HIPHIL.—*Infinitive.*

Dan. 11: 35. to purge, and *to make* (them) *white,*

HIPHIL.—*Future.*

Ps. 51: 7(9). *I shall be whiter* than snow.
Isa. 1: 18. *they shall be as white* as snow;

* HITHPAEL.—*Future.* *

Dan 12: 10. Many shall be purified, *and made white,*

לָבָן *lāh-vāhn',* adj. 3836

Gen 30: 35. every one that had (some) *white*
37. and pilled *white* strakes in them, and made *the white* appear
Ex. 16: 31. like coriander seed, *white;*
Lev. 13: 3. the hair in the plague is turned *white,*
4. If the bright spot (be) *white*
— the hair thereof be not turned *white;*
10. (if) the rising (be) *white* in the skin, and it have turned the hair *white,*
13. it is all turned *white:*
16. and be changed *unto white,*
17. (if) the plague be turned *into white;*
19. a *white* rising, or a bright spot, *white,*
20. the hair thereof be turned *white;*
21. (there be) no *white* hairs therein,
24. have a *white* bright spot, somewhat reddish, or *white;*
25. (if) the hair...be turned *white,*
26. (there be) no *white* hair
38. (even) *white* bright spots;
39. the skin of their flesh (be) darkish *white;*
42. a *white* reddish sore;
43. (if) the rising of the sore (be) *white*
Ecc. 9: 8. Let thy garments be always *white;*
Zec. 1: 8. red horses, speckled, *and white.*
6: 3. in the third chariot *white* horses;
6. *and the white* go forth after them;

לָבֵן [*lāh-vehn'*], adj. 3836

Gen 49: 12. *and* his teeth *white* with milk.

לְבָנָה *l'vāh-nāh',* f. 3842

Cant 6: 10. fair *as the moon,* clear as the sun,
Isa. 24: 23. Then *the moon* shall be confounded,
30: 26. the light of *the moon* shall be as the light

לְבֵנָה *l'vēh-nāh',* f. 3843

Gen 11: 3. Go to, let us make *brick,*
— they had *brick* for stone,
Ex. 1: 14. in morter, *and in brick,*
5: 7. give the people straw to make *brick,*
8. the tale of *the bricks,*
16. *and* they say to us, Make *brick:*
18. yet shall ye deliver the tale of *bricks.*
19. *from your bricks* of your daily task.
Isa. 9: 10(9). *The bricks* are fallen down,
65: 3. burneth incense upon *altars of brick;* (marg. *bricks*)
Eze. 4: 1. son of man, take thee *a tile*

3839 **לִבְנֶה** *liv-neh'*, m.

Gen 30:37. Jacob took him rods of green *poplar*,
Hos. 4:13. oaks *and poplars* and elms,

3840 **לִבְנָה** [*liv-nāh'*], f.

Ex. 24:10. a *paved* work of a sapphire stone,

See 3828 **לְבוֹנָה** see **לְבֹנָה**

3847 **לָבַשׁ** *lāh-vash'* & **לָבֵשׁ** *lāh-vēhsh'*.

* KAL.—*Preterite.* *

Lev. 6:10(3). *And* the priest *shall put on* his linen
11(4). *and put on* other garments,
16: 4. *and* (so) *put them on.*
23. the linen garments, which *he put on*
24. *and put on* his garments,
32. *and shall put on* the linen clothes,
Jud. 6:34. the Spirit of the Lord *came upon* (marg. *clothed*) Gideon,
1Ch 12:18. the spirit *came upon* (marg. *id.*) Amasai,
2Ch 24:20. the Spirit of God *came upon* (marg. *id.*) Zechariah
Est. 6: 8. the royal apparel...which the king (useth) *to wear*, (lit. *clotheth* with it)
Job 7: 5. My flesh *is clothed with* worms
29:14. *I put on* righteousness,
Ps. 65:13(14). The pastures *are clothed with* flocks;
93: 1. *he is clothed with* majesty; the Lord *is clothed with* strength,
104: 1. *thou art clothed with* honour and majesty.
Eze.42:14. *and shall put on* other garments,
44:19. *and they shall put on* other garments;

KAL.—*Infinitive.*

Gen28:20. bread to eat, and raiment *to put on*,
Lev.21:10. *to put on* the garments,
Hag. 1: 6. ye *clothe* you,

KAL.—*Imperative.*

2Sa.14: 2. *and put on* now mourning apparel,
1K. 22:30. *put* thou *on* thy robes.
2Ch 18:29. *put* thou *on* thy robes.
Isa. 51: 9. Awake, awake, *put on* strength,
52: 1. Awake, awake; *put on* thy strength, O Zion; *put on* thy beautiful
Jer. 46: 4. *put on* the brigandines.

KAL.—*Future.*

Gen38:19. *and put on* the garments of her widowhood.
Ex. 29:30. *shall put them on* seven days,
Lev. 6:10(3). his linen breeches *shall he put* upon
16: 4. *He shall put on* the holy linen
Deu22: 5. *shall* a man *put on* a woman's garment:
11. *Thou shalt* not *wear* a garment of
1Sa.28: 8. *and put on* other raiment,
2Sa.13:18. *were* the king's daughters...*apparelled.*
2Ch 6:41. *let* thy priests, O Lord God, *be clothed with*
Est. 4: 1. rent his clothes, *and put on* sackcloth
5: 1. *that* Esther *put on* (her) royal (apparel),
Job 8:22. They that hate thee *shall be clothed with*
27:17. the just *shall put* (it) *on*,
29:14. I put on righteousness, *and it clothed me:*
40:10. and *array thyself with* glory and beauty.
Ps. 35:26. *let* them *be clothed with* shame
109.18. *As he clothed himself with* cursing
29. *Let* mine adversaries *be clothed with* shame,
132: 9. *Let* thy priests *be clothed with*
Cant.5: 3. how *shall I put it on?*
Isa. 4: 1. eat our own bread, and *wear* our own
49.18. *thou shalt* surely *clothe thee with*
59:17. *For he put on* righteousness
— *and he put on* the garments of
Jer. 4:30. *thou clothest thyself with* crimson,
Eze. 7:27. the prince *shall be clothed with*
26:16. *they shall clothe themselves with*
34: 3. *ye clothe you with* the wool,
42:14. (כתיב) *and shall put on* other garments,
44:17. *they shall be clothed with* linen garments;
Jon. 3: 5. proclaimed a fast, *and put on* sackcloth,
Zec.13: 4. neither *shall they wear* a rough garment

KAL.—*Participle.* Poel.

Zep. 1: 8. all such *as are clothed with* strange

KAL.—*Participle.* Paül.

1Sa.17: 5. he (was) *armed with* a coat of mail; (marg. *clothed*)
Pro.31:21. all her houshold (are) *clothed with* scarlet
Eze. 9: 2. one man...(was) *clothed with* linen,
3. the man *clothed with* linen,
11 & 10:2, 6. the man *clothed with* linen,
10: 7. (him that was) *clothed with* linen:
23: 6. (Which were) *clothed with* blue,
12. and rulers *clothed* most gorgeously,
38: 4. *clothed with* all sorts (of armour),
Dan 10: 5. a certain man *clothed in* linen,
12: 6. said to the man *clothed in* linen,
7. I heard the man *clothed in* linen,
Zec. 3: 3. Joshua was *clothed with* filthy garments,

* PUAL.—*Participle.* *

1K. 22:10. *having put on* their robes,
2Ch 5:12. *arrayed in* white linen,
18: 9. *clothed in* (their) robes,
Ezr. 3:10. they set the priests *in their apparel*

* HIPHIL.—*Preterite.* *

Gen27:16. *she put* the skins of the kids
Ex. 28:41. *And thou shalt put* them upon Aaron
29: 5. *and put* upon Aaron the coat,
8. *and put* coats *upon them.*
40:13. *And thou shalt put* upon Aaron
14. his sons, *and clothe* them *with* coats:
Nu. 20:26. *and put them* upon Eleazar
2Ch 28:15. *clothed* all that were naked
Est. 6: 9. *that they may array* the man
Isa. 22:21. *And I will clothe him with* thy robe,
61:10. *he hath clothed me with* the garments of

HIPHIL.—*Infinitive.*

Est. 4: 4. sent raiment *to clothe* Mordecai,
Zec. 3: 4. *and I will clothe* (lit. *and to clothe*)...*with*

HIPHIL.—*Future.*

Gen 3:21. did the Lord God make coats of skins, *and clothed them.*
27:15. *and put them* upon Jacob her younger son:
41:42. *and arrayed* him *in* vestures of fine linen,
Lev. 8: 7. *and clothed* him *with* the robe,
13. *and put* coats *upon them,*
Nu. 20:28. *and put* them upon Eleazar
1Sa.17:38. *And* Saul *armed* (marg. *clothed*) D. *with*
— *also he armed* him *with* a coat of mail.
2Ch 28:15. *and arrayed them,* and shod them,
Est. 6:11. *and arrayed* Mordecai,
Job 10:11. *Thou hast clothed me with* skin
39:19. *hast thou clothed* his neck *with* thunder?
Ps.132:16. *I will* also *clothe* her priests *with*
18. His enemies *will I clothe with* shame:
Pro.23:21. drowsiness *shall clothe* (a man) *with* rags.
Isa. 50: 3. *I clothe* the heavens *with* blackness,
Eze.16:10. *I clothed thee also with* broidered work,
Zec. 3: 5. *and clothed him with* garments.

HIPHIL.—*Participle.*

2Sa. 1:24. Saul, *who clothed you in scarlet,* with

לְבַשׁ [*l'vash*], Ch. 3848

* P'AL.—*Future.* *

Dan 5: 7. *shall be clothed with* scarlet,
16. *thou shalt be clothed with* scarlet,

* APHEL.—*Preterite.* *

Dan 5:29. *and they clothed* Daniel *with* scarlet,

לֹג *lōhg*, m. 3849

Lev.14:10. *and* one *log of* oil.
12, 24. and *the log of* oil,
15. (some) *of the log of* oil,
21. *and a log of* oil;

לָה *lāh*, Ch. part. (כתיב) 3809

Dan 4:35(32). (are) reputed *as nothing:*

3808 **לֹה** *lōh*, part. (כתיב)

Deu 3:11. (is) it *not* in Rabbath

3851 **לַהַב** *lah'-hav*, m.

Jud. 3:22. the haft also went in after *the blade;* and the fat closed upon *the blade*,
13:20. when *the flame* went up toward heaven from off the altar, that the angel of the Lord ascended *in the flame of*
Job 39:23. the *glittering* spear and the shield.
41:21(13). *and a flame* goeth out of his mouth.
Isa. 13: 8. their faces (shall be as) *flames*. (marg. faces of *the flames*)
29: 6. *and the flame of* devouring fire.
30:30. *and* (with) *the flame of* a devouring fire,
66:15. his rebuke *with flames of* fire.
Joel 2: 5. like the noise of *a flame of* fire
Nah. 3: 3. *both the bright* (marg. *the flame of* the) sword and the glittering spear:

3852 **לֶהָבָה** *leh-hāh-vāh'* & **לַהֶבֶת** *lāh-heh'-veth*, f.

Nu. 21:28. *a flame* from the city of Sihon:
1Sa.17: 7. *and* his spear's *head* (weighed) six hundred
Ps. 29: 7. The voice of the Lord divideth *the flames*
83:14(15). *and as the flame* setteth the mountains
105:32. *flaming* fire in their land.
106:18. *the flame* burned up the wicked.
Isa. 4: 5. the shining of a *flaming* fire
5:24. *the flame* consumeth the chaff,
10:17. his Holy One *for a flame:*
43: 2. *neither* (lit. *and* not) shall *the flame* kindle
47:14. themselves from the power of *the flame:*
Jer. 48:45. *a flame* from the midst of Sihon,
Lam. 2: 3. burned against Jacob like a *flaming* fire,
Eze.20:47(21:3). the *flaming* flame shall not be
Dan11:33. they shall fall by the sword, *and by flame*,
Hos. 7: 6. in the morning it burneth as a *flaming* fire.
Joel 1:19. *the flame* hath burned all the trees
2: 3. behind them *a flame* burneth:
Obad. 18. the house of Joseph *a flame*,

3854 **לַהַג** *lah'-hag*, m.

Ecc.12:12. *and* much *study* (marg. *reading*) (is) a weariness of the flesh.

3856 **לָהַהּ** [*lāh-hah*,]

* KAL.—*Future.* *

Gen47:13. *so that*...(all) the land of Canaan *fainted*

* HITHPALPEL.—*Participle.* *

Pro.26:18. *As a mad* (man) who casteth firebrands,

3857 **לָהַט** [*lāh-hat*].

* KAL.—*Participle.* Poel. *

Ps. 57: 4(5). (even among) *them that are set on fire*,
104: 4. Who maketh...his ministers a *flaming* fire:

* PIEL.—*Preterite.* *

Joel 1:19. the flame *hath burned* all the trees
Mal. 4: 1.(3.19). *and* the day that cometh *shall burn* them *up*.

PIEL.—*Future.*

Deu32:22. *and set on fire* the foundations of the
Job 41:21.(13). His breath *kindleth* coals,
Ps. 83:14(15). the flame *setteth* the mountains *on fire;*
97: 3. A fire goeth before him, *and burneth up*
106:18. the flame *burned up* the wicked.
Isa. 42:25. *and it hath set him on fire*
Joel 2: 3. behind them a flame *burneth*

לַהַט *lah'-hat*, m. 3858

Gen 3:24. a *flaming* sword which turned every way,

לְהָטִים [*l'hāh-teem'*], m. pl. 3858

Ex. 7:11. did in like manner *with their enchantments.*

לָהַם [*lāh-ham'*]. 3859

* HITHPAEL.—*Participle.* *

Pro.18: 8 & 26:22. of a talebearer (are) *as wounds*, (marg. *like as when men are wounded*)

לָהֵן *lāh-hēhn'*, part. 3860

Ru. 1:13. Would ye tarry *for them* till they were grown? would ye stay *for them* [perhaps lit. *therefore...therefore*]

לָהֵן *lāh-hēhn'*, Ch. part. 3861

Ezr. 5:12. *But* after that our fathers had
Dan 2: 6. *therefore* shew me the dream,
9. *therefore* tell me the dream,
11. *except* the gods, whose dwelling is not
30. *but* for (their) sakes that shall
3:28. *except* their own God.
4:27(24). *Wherefore*, O king, let my counsel
6: 5(6). *except* we find (it) against him
7(8),12(13). thirty days, *save* of thee, O king,

לַהֲקָה [*lah-hăkāh'*], f. 3862

1Sa.19:20. *the company of* the prophets

לוּ *loo*, part. 3863

Gen17:18. *O that* Ishmael might live
23:13. if thou (wilt give it), *I pray thee*, hear me:
30:34. *I would* it might be according to thy word.
50:15. Joseph will *peradventure* hate us,
Nu. 14: 2. *Would God that* we had died
— *would God* we had died in this wilderness!
20: 3. *Would God that* we had died
22:29. *I would* there were a sword
Deu 32:29. *O that* they were wise,
Jos. 7: 7. *would to God* we had been content,
Jud. 8:19. *if* ye had saved them alive,
13:23. *If* the Lord were pleased to kill us,
1 Sa.14:30. *if haply* the people had eaten
2Sa.18:12. *Though* I should receive a thousand
19: 6(7). *if* Absalom had lived,
Job 6: 2. *Oh that* my grief were
16: 4. *if* your soul were in
Ps. 81:13(14). *Oh that* my people had hearkened
Eze.14:15. *If* I cause noisome beasts to pass
Mic. 2:11. *If* a man walking in the spirit

לוּא *loo*, part. 3863

1Sa.14:30. (כתיב) *if haply* the people had eaten
Isa. 48:18. *O that* thou hadst hearkened
64: 1(63:19). *Oh that* thou wouldest rend the

לָוָה [*lāh-vāh'*]. 3867

*KAL.—*Preterite.* *

Neh 5: 4. *We have borrowed* money

KAL.—*Future.*

Deu28:12. thou *shalt* not *borrow*.
Ecc. 8:15. that *shall abide with him*

KAL.—*Participle.*

Ps. 37:21. The wicked *borroweth*,
Pro.22: 7. *the borrower* (is) servant to the lender
Isa. 24: 2. *so with the borrower;*

* NIPHAL.—*Preterite.* *

Nu. 18: 4. *And they shall be joined* unto thee,
Ps. 83: 8(9). Assur also *is joined* with them:

Isa. 14: 1. *and* the strangers *shall be joined*
56: 3. the stranger, *that hath joined himself* to
Jer. 50: 5. *and let us join ourselves* to the Lord
Dan 11:34. *but* many *shall cleave* to them
Zec. 2:11(15). *And* many nations *shall be joined* to the

NIPHAL.—*Future.*

Gen 29:34. this time *will* my husband *be joined* unto
Nu. 18: 2. *that they may be joined* unto thee,

NIPHAL.—*Participle.*

Est. 9:27. all *such as joined themselves*
Isa. 56: 6. *that join themselves* to the Lord,

* HIPHIL.—*Preterite.* *

Deu 28:12. *and thou shalt lend* unto many nations,

HIPHIL.—*Future.*

Ex. 22:25(24). If *thou lend* money
Deu 28:44. He *shall lend to thee*, and thou *shalt* not *lend to him:*

HIPHIL.—*Participle.*

Ps. 37:26. (He is) ever merciful, *and lendeth;*
112: 5. A good man sheweth favour, *and lendeth:*
Pro. 19:17. pity upon the poor *lendeth* unto the Lord;
22: 7. the borrower (is) servant to the *lender.* (marg. to the man *that lendeth*)
Isa. 24: 2. *as with the lender*, so with the borrower;

3868 ## לוּז [*looz*].

* KAL.—*Future.* *

Pro. 3:21. *let* not *them depart* from thine eyes:

* NIPHAL.—*Participle.* *

Pro. 2:15. *and* (they) *froward* in their paths:
3:32. *the froward* (is) abomination to the Lord:
14: 2. *but* (he that is) *perverse* in his ways
Isa. 30:12. trust in oppression *and perverseness*,

* HIPHIL.—*Future.* *

Pro. 4:21. *Let them* not *depart* from thine eyes;

3869 ## לוּז *looz*, m.

Gen 30:37. *and of the hazel* and chesnut tree;

3871 ## לוּחַ *loo'ăgh*, m.

Ex. 24:12. I will give thee *tables of* stone,
27: 8. with *boards* shalt thou make it:
31:18. two *tables of* testimony, *tables of* stone,
32:15. the two *tables of* the testimony (were) in his hand: *the tables* (were) written on
16. *And the tables* (were) the work of God, and the writing (was) the writing of God, graven upon *the tables.*
19. he cast *the tables* out of his hands,
34: 1. Hew thee two *tables of* stone like unto the first: and I will write upon (these) *tables* the words that were in *the* first *tables*,
4. he hewed two *tables of* stone
— took in his hand *the* two *tables of*
28. he wrote upon *the tables*
29. *the* two *tables of* testimony
38: 7. he made the altar hollow with *boards.*
Deu 4:13. he wrote them upon two *tables of* stone.
5:22(19). he wrote them in two *tables of*
9: 9. to receive *the tables of* stone, (even) *the tables of* the covenant
10. the Lord delivered unto me two *tables of*
11. the Lord gave me *the* two *tables of* stone, (even) *the tables of* the covenant.
15. *the* two *tables of* the covenant
17. I took *the* two *tables*,
10: 1. Hew thee two *tables of* stone
2. I will write on *the tables* the words that were in *the* first *tables* which thou
3. and hewed two *tables of* stone
— *the* two *tables* in mine hand.
4. he wrote on *the tables*,
5. and put *the tables* in the ark
1K. 7:36. *the plates* of the ledges thereof,
8: 9. *the* two *tables of* stone,
2Ch. 5:10. *the* two *tables* which Moses put

Pro. 3: 3 & 7:3. write them upon *the table of* thine
Cant. 8: 9. we will inclose her with *boards*
Isa. 30: 8. write it before them in *a table*,
Jer. 17: 1. *the table of* their heart,
Eze. 27: 5. thy (ship) *boards* of fir trees
Hab. 2: 2. make (it) plain upon *tables*,

לוּט [*loot*]. 3874

* KAL.—*Participle.* Poel. *

Isa. 25: 7. the covering *cast* over all people,

KAL.—*Participle.* Paül.

1Sa. 21: 9(10). *wrapped* in a cloth behind the ephod:

* HIPHIL.—*Future.* *

1K. 19:13. *that he wrapped* his face in his mantle,

לוֹט *lōht*, m. 3875

Isa. 25: 7. *the covering* cast over all people,

לִוְיָה [*liv-yāh'*], f. 3880

Pro. 1: 9. they (shall be) *an ornament* (marg. *adding*) *of* grace
4: 9. to thine head *an ornament of* grace:

לִוְיָתָן *liv-yāh-thāhn'*, m. 3882

Job 3: 8. ready to raise up *their mourning.* (marg. or, *a leviathan*)
41: 1(40:25). Canst thou draw out *leviathan* (marg. i. e. *a whale*, or, *a whirlpool*)
Ps. 74:14. Thou brakest the heads of *leviathan*
104:26. (there is) that *leviathan*,
Isa. 27: 1. *leviathan* the piercing serpent, even *leviathan* that crooked serpent;

לוּלֵא *loo-lēh'*, part. 3884

Gen 43:10. *except* we had lingered,
Jud. 14:18. *If* ye had *not* plowed with my heifer,
2Sa. 2:27. *unless* thou hadst spoken,
Ps. 27:13. (I had fainted), *unless* I had believed

לוּלֵי *loo-lēh'y*, part. 3884

Gen 31:42. *Except* the God of my father,...had been
Deu 32:27. *Were it not that* I feared the wrath of
1Sa. 25:34. *except* thou hadst hasted
2K. 3:14. *were it not that* I regard
Ps. 94:17. *Unless* the Lord (had been) my help,
106:23. *had not* Moses his chosen stood before
119:92. *Unless* thy law (had been) my delights,
124: 1, 2. *If* (it had not been) the Lord
Isa. 1: 9. *Except* the Lord of hosts had left

לוּלִים *loo-leem'*, m. pl. 3883

1K. 6: 8. *and* they went up *with winding stairs*

לוּן *loon* & לִין *leen.* 3885

* KAL.—*Preterite.* *

Gen 32:21(22). himself *lodged* that night
Jud. 19:13. *to lodge all night*, (lit. *and we will lodge*) in Gibeah,
2Sa. 12:16. *and lay all night* upon the earth.
Zec. 5: 4. *and it shall remain* in the midst of

KAL.—*Infinitive.*

Gen 24:23. is there room...for us *to lodge in?*
25. and room *to lodge in.*
Jud. 19:10. the man would not *tarry that night*,
15. *to lodge* in Gibeah:
— took them into his house *to lodging.*
20: 4. I and my concubine, *to lodge.*

Jer. 14: 8. turneth aside *to tarry for a night?*

KAL.—*Imperative.*

Gen19: 2. *and tarry all night,*
Nu. 22: 8. *Lodge* here *this night,*
Jud.19: 6. *and tarry all night,*
9. I pray you *tarry all night:*
— *lodge* here, that thine heart may be merry;
Ru. 3:13. *Tarry this night,*
Joel 1:13. *lie all night* in sackcloth,

KAL.—*Future.*

Gen19: 2. *we will abide* in the street *all night.*
24:54. *and tarried all night;*
28:11. *and tarried* there *all night,*
31:54. *and tarried all night* in the mount.
32:13(14). *And he lodged* there that same night;
Ex. 23:18. neither *shall* the fat...*remain*
34:25. neither *shall* the sacrifice...*be left*
Lev.19:13. *shall* not *abide* with thee *all night*
Deu16: 4. neither *shall* there (any thing)...*remain*
21:23. His body *shall* not *remain*
Jos. 3: 1. *and lodged* there before they passed over.
4: 3. *ye shall lodge* this night.
6:11. came into the camp, *and lodged* in the
8: 9. *but* Joshua *lodged* that night
Jud.18: 2. *who* when...*they lodged* there.
19: 4. so they did eat and drink, *and lodged* there.
7. *therefore he lodged* there
11. and let us turn in into this city...*and lodge*
20. *lodge* not in the street.
Ru. 1:16. where *thou lodgest, I will lodge:*
2Sa.17: 8. *will* not *lodge* with the people.
16. *Lodge* not this night in the plains
19: 7(8). there *will* not *tarry* one with thee
1K. 19: 9. he came thither unto a cave, *and lodged*
1Ch. 9:27. *they lodged* round about
Neh. 4:22(16). *Let* every one with his servant *lodge*
13:20. *So* the merchants and sellers of all kind of ware *lodged*
Job 17: 2. *doth* not mine eye *continue* (marg. *lodge*)
19: 4. mine error *remaineth* with myself.
29:19. the dew *lay all night* upon
31:32. The stranger *did* not *lodge* in the street:
39: 9. Will the unicorn...*abide* by thy crib?
41:22(14). In his neck *remaineth* strength,
Ps. 25:13. soul *shall dwell* at ease; (marg. *lodge* in goodness)
30: 5(6). weeping *may endure* for a night,
49:12(13). man (being) in honour *abideth* not:
55: 7(8). (and) *remain* in the wilderness.
59:15(16). *and grudge* if they be not satisfied.
Pro.15:31. that heareth the reproof of life *abideth*
19:23. (he that hath it) *shall abide* satisfied;
Cant.1:13. *he shall lie all night* betwixt my breasts
7:11(12). *let us lodge* in the villages
Isa. 1:21. righteousness *lodged* in it;
21:13. in Arabia *shall ye lodge,*
65: 4. and *lodge* in the monuments,
Zep. 2:14. the bittern *shall lodge* in the upper lintels

KAL.—*Participle.*

Neh 13:21. Why *lodge ye* about the wall?

* NIPHAL.—*Future.* *

Ex. 15:24. *And* the people *murmured*
16: 2. *And*...the children of Israel *murmured*
7. (כתיב) *ye murmur* against us?
Nu. 14: 2. *And* all the children of Israel *murmured*
36. (כתיב) *and made* all the congregation *to murmur*
16:11. (כתיב) *ye murmur* against him?
41(17:6). *But*...the children of Israel *murmured*
Jos. 9:18. *And* all the congregation *murmured*

* HIPHIL.—*Preterite.* *

Nu. 14:29. which *have murmured* against me,

HIPHIL.—*Future.*

Ex. 16: 7. *ye murmur* against us?
17: 3. *and* the people *murmured* against Moses,
Nu. 14:36. *and made* all the congregation *to murmur*
16:11. *ye murmur* against him?
Job 24: 7. *They cause* the naked *to lodge*
Jer. 4:14. How long *shall* thy vain thoughts *lodge* [Gesen. how long *wilt thou harbour* vain thoughts]

HIPHIL.—*Participle.*

Ex. 16: 8. ye *murmur* against him:

Nu. 14:27. this evil congregation, which *murmur*
— they *murmur* against me.
17: 5(20). they *murmur* against you.

* HITHPALPEL.—*Future.* *

Job 39:28. She dwelleth *and abideth* on the rock,
Ps. 91: 1. *shall abide* (marg. *lodge*) under the shadow

לוּעַ *[loo'ag̃]*. 3886

* KAL.—*Preterite.* *

Job 6: 3. my words *are swallowed up.*
Obad. 16. *and they shall swallow down,* (marg. *sup up*)

לוּץ *[lootz]*. 3887

* KAL.—*Preterite.* *

Pro. 9:12. *but* (if) *thou scornest,*

KAL.—*Participle.*

Ps. 1: 1. nor sitteth in the seat of *the scornful.*
Pro. 1:22. *and the scorners* delight in their scorning,
3:34. he scorneth *the scorners:*
9: 7. He that reproveth *a scorner*
8. Reprove not *a scorner,*
13: 1. *but a scorner* heareth not rebuke.
14: 6. *A scorner* seeketh wisdom,
15:12. *A scorner* loveth not one that reproveth
19:25. Smite *a scorner,*
29. Judgments are prepared *for scorners,*
20: 1. Wine (is) *a mocker,*
21:11. When *the scorner* is punished,
24. Proud (and) haughty *scorner*
22:10. Cast out *the scorner,*
24: 9. *the scorner* (is) an abomination
Isa. 29:20. and *the scorner* is consumed

* HIPHIL.—*Preterite.* *

Ps. 119:51. proud *have had me* greatly *in derision*

HIPHIL.—*Future.*

Pro. 3:34. he *scorneth* the scorners:
14: 9. Fools *make a mock* at sin:
19:28. An ungodly witness *scorneth*

HIPHIL.—*Participle.*

Gen42:23. he spake unto them by *an interpreter.*
2Ch.32:31. *in* (the business of) *the ambassadors* (marg. *interpreters*)
Job 16:20. My friends *scorn me:* (marg. (are) *my scorners*)
33:23. *an interpreter,* one among a thousand,
Isa. 43:27. *and thy teachers* (marg. *interpreters*) have

* HITHPALPEL.—*Future.* *

Isa. 28:22. *be ye* not *mockers,*

לוּשׁ *loosh.* 3888

* KAL.—*Infinitive.* *

Hos. 7: 4. *after he hath kneaded* the dough,

KAL.—*Imperative.*

Gen 18: 6. three measures of fine meal, *knead* (it),

KAL.—*Future.*

1Sa.28:24. and took flour, *and kneaded* (it),
2Sa.13: 8. she took flour, *and kneaded* (it),

KAL.—*Participle.* Poel.

Jer. 7:18. the women *knead* (their) dough,

לְוָת *[l'vāhth]*, Ch. part. 3890

Ezr. 4:12. the Jews which came up from *thee* (lit. from *with thee*)

לְזוּת *l'zooth*, f. 3891

Pro. 4:24. *and perverse* (lit. *and perverseness of*) lips

לַח *lagh*, adj. 3892

Gen30:37. Jacob took him rods of *green* poplar,
Nu. 6: 3. nor eat *moist* grapes,

Jud.16: 7. bind me with seven *green* withs (marg. *moist*, or, *new* cords)
8. seven *green* withs which had not been
Eze.17:24. have dried up the *green* tree,
20:47(21:3). shall devour every *green* tree

3893 לֵחַ [*lēh-agh'*], m.

Deu 34: 7. nor *his natural force* abated. (marg. *moisture* fled)

3894 לְחוּם [*l'ghoom*], m.

Job 20:23. shall rain (it) upon him *while he is eating.*
Zep. 1:17. *and their flesh* as the dung.

3895 לְחִי *l'ghee*, m.

Deu 18: 3. the shoulder, *and the two cheeks,*
Jud. 15:15. he found *a new jawbone*
16. *With the jawbone of* an ass, heaps upon heaps, *with the jaw of* an ass
17. he cast away *the jawbone* out of his hand, and called that place Ramath-*lehi.* (marg. The lifting up of *the jawbone*)
19. an hollow place that (was) *in the jaw,* (marg. or, *Lehi*)
— *in Lehi* unto this day.
1K. 22:24. and smote Micaiah on *the cheek,*
2Ch.18:23. and smote Micaiah upon *the cheek,*
Job 16:10. they have smitten me upon *the cheek* (lit. *my cheeks*)
41: 2(40:26). or bore *his jaw* through
Ps. 3: 7(8). mine enemies (upon) *the cheek bone ;*
Cant 1:10. *Thy cheeks* are comely
5:13. *His cheeks* (are) as a bed of spices,
Isa. 30:28. a bridle in *the jaws of* the people,
50: 6. *and my cheeks* to them that plucked off the
Lam. 1: 2. her tears (are) on *her cheeks :*
3:30. He giveth (his) *cheek* to him that smiteth
Eze.29: 4. I will put hooks *in thy jaws,*
38: 4. and put hooks *into thy jaws,*
Hos.11: 4. take off the yoke on *their jaws,*
Mic. 5: 1(4:14). the judge of Israel...upon *the cheek.*

3897 לָחַךְ [*lāh-ghach'*].

* KAL.—*Infinitive.* *

Nu. 22: 4. *as* the ox *licketh up* the grass

* PIEL.—*Preterite.* *

1K. 18:38. and *licked up* the water

PIEL.—*Future.*

Nu. 22: 4. Now *shall* this company *lick up*
Ps. 72: 9. his enemies *shall lick* the dust.
Isa. 49:23. and *lick up* the dust of thy feet ;
Mic. 7:17. *They shall lick* the dust

3898 לָחַם [*lāh-gham'*].

* KAL.—*Preterite.* *

Pro. 4:17. *they eat* the bread of wickedness,

KAL.—*Infinitive.*

Pro.23: 1. When thou sittest *to eat* with a ruler,

KAL.—*Imperative.*

Ps. 35: 1. *fight* against them that fight
Pro. 9: 5. Come, *eat* of my bread,

KAL.—*Future.*

Ps.141: 4. *let me* not *eat* of their dainties.
Pro.23: 6. *Eat thou* not the bread of (him that)

KAL.—*Participle.* Poel.

Ps. 35: 1. fight against them *that fight against me.*
56: 1(2). he *fighting* daily oppresseth me.
2(3). (they be) many *that fight* against me,

KAL.—*Participle.* Paül.

Deu 32:24. *and devoured* with burning heat,

* NIPHAL.—*Preterite.* *

Ex. 1:10. they join also unto our enemies, *and fight*
Nu. 21:26. who *had fought* against the former king
Deu 1:41. we will go up *and fight,*
Jud. 5:19. The kings came (and) *fought,* then *fought*
20. *They fought* from heaven; the stars in their courses *fought*
9:17. my father *fought* for you,
45. Abimelech *fought* against the city
11: 5. when the children of Ammon *made war*
8. *and fight* against the children of Ammon,
25. *did he* ever *fight* against them,
1Sa. 4: 9. quit yourselves like men, *and fight.*
8:20. *and fight* our battles.
15:18. *and fight* against them until they be
17:32. thy servant will go *and fight*
29: 8. that I may not go *fight* (lit. *and fight*)
2Sa. 8:10. *he had fought* against Hadadezer,
12:27. *I have fought* against Rabbah,
1K. 14:19. the acts of Jeroboam, how *he warred,*
22:45(46). that he shewed, and how *he warred,*
2K. 13:12. *he fought* against Amaziah
14:15. how *he fought* with Amaziah
28. how *he warred,*
1Ch.10: 1. the Philistines *fought* against Israel;
18:10. *he had fought* against Hadarezer,
2Ch.17:10. *they made* no *war* against Jehoshaphat.
20:29. the Lord *fought* against the enemies
27: 5. He *fought* also with the king
Isa. 19: 2. *and they shall fight* every one
30:32. in battles of shaking *will he fight*
63:10. *he fought* against them.
Jer. 1:19 & 15:20. *And they shall fight* against thee;
21: 5. *And I* myself *will fight*
34:22. *and they shall fight* against it,
37: 8. *and fight* against this city,
Dan 11:11. shall come forth *and fight*
Zec.10: 5. *and they shall fight,*
14: 3. *and fight* against those nations,

NIPHAL.—*Infinitive.*

Ex. 17:10. *and fought* (lit. *to fight*) with Amalek:
Nu. 22:11. I shall be able *to overcome* (marg. shall prevail *in fighting* against him)
Deu 20: 4. *to fight* for you against your enemies,
10. comest nigh unto a city *to fight*
19. *in making war* against it
Jos. 9: 2. *to fight* with Joshua and with Israel,
11: 5. *to fight* against Israel.
Jud. 1: 1. the Canaanites first, *to fight* against them?
9. Judah went down *to fight*
8: 1. when thou wentest *to fight*
10: 9. *to fight* also against Judah,
18 & 11:9. *to fight* against the children of
11:12. come against me *to fight*
25. did he *ever* fight (lit. *fighting* did he fight)
27. thou dost me wrong *to war* against me:
32. children of Ammon *to fight* against
12: 1. Wherefore passedst thou over *to fight*
3. *to fight* against me?
1Sa.13: 5. gathered themselves together *to fight*
17: 9. If he be able *to fight* with me,
33. to go against this Philistine *to fight*
28: 1. *to fight* with Israel.
2Sa. 2:28. neither *fought* they any more. (lit. added *to fight*)
11:20. approached ye so nigh ... *when ye did fight?*
1K. 12:21. *to fight* against the house of Israel,
22:32. they turned aside *to fight*
2K. 3:21. the kings were come up *to fight*
8:29. *when he fought* against Hazael
9:15. *when he fought* with Hazael
16: 5. besieged Ahaz, but could not *overcome*
19: 9. he is come out *to fight*
2Ch.11: 1. *to fight* against Israel,
18:31. they compassed about him *to fight :*
20:17. Ye shall not (need) *to fight*
22: 6. *when he fought* with Hazael
32: 8. *and to fight* our battles.
35:20. Necho king of Egypt came up *to fight*
22. *that he might fight* with him,
— came *to fight* in the valley of Megiddo.
Neh 4: 8(2). *to fight* against Jerusalem,
Isa. 7: 1. to war against it, but could not *prevail*
37: 9. He is come forth *to make war* with thee,
Jer. 33: 5. They come *to fight* with the Chaldeans,
41:12. *to fight* with Ishmael the son of
51:30. men of Babylon have forborn *to fight,*

Dan 10:20. now will I return *to fight*
Zec.14: 3. as when *he fought* in the day of battle.

NIPHAL.—*Imperative.*

Ex. 17: 9. go out, *fight* with Amalek:
Jud. 9:38. go out, I pray now, *and fight*
1Sa.18:17. *and fight* the Lord's battles.
2K. 10: 3. *and fight* for your master's house.
Neh 4:14(8). *and fight* for your brethren,

NIPHAL.—*Future.*

Ex. 14:14. The Lord *shall fight* for you,
17: 8. came Amalek, *and fought* with Israel
Nu. 21: 1. *then he fought* against Israel,
23. *and fought* against Israel.
Deu 1:30. he *shall fight* for you,
42. Go not up, neither *fight;*
Jos. 10: 5. *and made war* against it.
29. *and fought* against Libnah:
31. *and fought* against it:
34. *and fought* against it:
36. *and they fought* against it:
38. *and fought* against it:
19:47. the children of Dan went up *to fight*
24: 8. *and they fought* with you:
9. Balak...arose *and warred* against Israel,
11. *and* the men of Jericho *fought* against you,
Jud. 1: 3. *that we may fight* against the Canaanites;
5. *and they fought* against him,
8. *Now* the children of Judah *had fought*
9:39. *and fought* with Abimelech.
52. *and fought* against it,
11: 4. *that* the children of Ammon *made war*
6. *that we may fight* with the children
20. *and fought* against Israel.
12: 4. *and fought* with Ephraim:
1Sa. 4:10. *And* the Philistines *fought,*
12: 9. *and they fought* against them.
14:47. *and fought* against all his enemies
17:10. *that we may fight* together.
19: 8. David went out, *and fought*
23: 5. *and fought* with the Philistines,
2Sa.10:17. in array against David, *and fought*
11:17. the men of the city went out, *and fought*
12:26. *And* Joab *fought* against Rabbah
29. Rabbah, *and fought* against it,
21:15. David went down,...*and fought*
1K. 12:24. nor *fight* against your brethren
20: 1. besieged Samaria, *and warred*
23. *let us fight* against them in the plain,
25. *and we will fight* against them
22:31. *Fight* neither with small nor great,
2K. 12:17(18). king of Syria went up, *and fought*
1Ch.19:17. *they fought* with him.
2Ch 11: 4. nor *fight* against your brethren:
13:12. *fight ye* not against the Lord
18:30. *Fight ye* not with small or great,
26: 6. he went forth *and warred*
Neh 4:20(14). our God *shall fight* for us.
Ps.109: 3. *and fought against me* without a cause.
Isa. 20: 1. *and fought* against Ashdod, and took it;
Jer. 32: 5. though *ye fight* with the Chaldeans,
Zec.14:14. Judah also *shall fight*

NIPHAL.—*Participle.*

Ex. 14:25. the Lord *fighteth* for them
Deu 3:22. your God he *shall fight*
Jos. 10:14. the Lord *fought* for Israel.
25. your enemies against whom ye *fight.*
42. the Lord God of Israel *fought* for Israel.
23: 3. he *that hath fought* for you.
10. he (it is) *that fighteth* for you,
1Sa.17:19. *fighting* with the Philistines.
23: 1. the Philistines *fight* against Keilah,
25:28. my lord *fighteth* the battles of the Lord,
28:15. the Philistines *make war* against me,
31: 1. the Philistines *fought* against Israel:
2K. 6: 8. king of Syria *warred* (lit. was *warring*)
19: 8. found the king of Assyria *warring*
Isa. 37: 8. found the king of Assyria *warring*
Jer. 21: 2. king of Babylon *maketh war* against us;
4. ye *fight* against the king of Babylon,
32:24. the Chaldeans, *that fight* against it,
29. the Chaldeans, *that fight* against this city,
34: 1. all the people, *fought*
7. the king of Babylon's army *fought*
37:10. the Chaldeans *that fight*

לָחֶם *lāh-ġhem'*, m. 3901

Jud. 5: 8. then (was) *war in* the gates:

לֶחֶם *leh'-ġhem*, m. 3899

Gen 3:19. the sweat of thy face shalt thou eat *bread,*
14:18. of Salem brought forth *bread* and wine:
18: 5. I will fetch a morsel of *bread,*
21:14. and took *bread,* and a bottle of water,
25:34. Jacob gave Esau *bread* and pottage
27:17. she gave the savoury meat and *the bread,*
28:20. and will give me *bread* to eat,
31:54. called his brethren to eat *bread:* and they did eat *bread,*
37:25. they sat down to eat *bread:*
39: 6. *the bread* which he did eat.
41:54. in all the land of Egypt there was *bread.*
55. the people cried to Pharaoh *for bread:*
43:25. they heard that they should eat *bread*
31. Set on *bread.*
32. the Egyptians might not eat *bread* with
45:23. laden with corn *and bread*
47:12. Joseph nourished his father,...with *bread,*
13. *And* (there was) no *bread* in all the land;
15. Give us *bread:*
17. Joseph gave them *bread*
— he fed them *with bread*
19. buy us and our land *for bread,*
49:20. Out of Asher *his bread* (shall be) fat,
Ex. 2:20. call him, that he may eat *bread.*
16: 3. when we did eat *bread* to the full;
4. I will rain *bread* from heaven
8. *and* in the morning *bread* to the full;
12. the morning ye shall be filled with *bread;*
15. *the bread* which the Lord hath given
22. they gathered twice as much *bread,*
29. on the sixth day *the bread of* two days;
32. *the bread* wherewith I have fed you
18:12. to eat *bread* with Moses'
23:25. he shall bless *thy bread,*
25:30. set upon the table shew*bread*
29: 2. *And* unleavened *bread,* and cakes
23. loaf of *bread,* and one cake of oiled *bread,*
32. *the bread* that (is) in the basket,
34. if ought...of *the bread,* remain
34:28. he did neither eat *bread,* nor drink water.
35:13. his vessels, and *the* shew*bread,*
39:36. the vessels thereof, and *the* shew*bread,*
40:23. he set *the bread* in order
Lev. 3:11, 16. *the food of* the offering made by fire
7:13. leavened *bread* with the sacrifice
8:26. the basket of unleavened *bread,*
31. *the bread* that (is) in the basket
32. that which remaineth...*and of the bread*
21: 6. *the bread of* their God,
8. he offereth *the bread of* thy God:
17. to offer *the bread* (marg. *food*) *of* his God.
21. to offer *the bread of* his God.
22. He shall eat *the bread of* his God,
22: 7. because it (is) *his food.*
11. they shall eat *of his meat.*
13. she shall eat *of* her father's *meat:*
25. *the bread of* your God
23:14. ye shall eat *neither bread,* nor
17. two wave *loaves*
18. offer with *the bread* seven lambs
20. *the bread of* the firstfruits
24: 7. *on the bread* for a memorial,
26: 5. ye shall eat *your bread* to the full,
26. the staff of your *bread,* ten women shall bake *your bread* in one oven, and they shall deliver (you) *your bread*
Nu. 4: 7. *and the* continual *bread* shall be
14: 9. for they (are) *bread for us:*
15:19. when ye eat *of the bread of* the land,
21: 5. for (there is) no *bread,*
— our soul loatheth this light *bread.*
28: 2. *my bread* for my sacrifices
24. *the meat of* the sacrifice
Deu 8: 3. man doth not live by *bread* only,
9. A land wherein thou shalt eat *bread*
9: 9. I neither did eat *bread*
18. I did neither eat *bread,*
10:18. in giving him *food* and raiment.

Deu 16: 3. *the bread of* affliction ;
23: 4(5). they met you not *with bread*
29: 6(5). Ye have not eaten *bread*,
Jos. 9: 5. all *the bread of* their provision
12. This *our bread* we took hot
Jud. 7:13. a cake of barley *bread*
8: 5. Give, I pray you, loaves of *bread*
6. that we should give *bread* unto thine army?
15. that we should give *bread* unto thy men
13:16. I will not eat *of thy bread:*
19: 5. Comfort thine heart with a morsel of *bread*,
19. there is *bread* and wine also for me,
Ru. 1: 6. visited his people in giving them *bread*.
2:14. eat of *the bread*,
1Sa. 2: 5. hired out themselves *for bread;*
36. and a morsel of *bread*,
— that I may eat a piece of *bread*.
9: 7. *the bread* is spent in our vessels,
10: 3. another carrying three loaves of *bread*,
4. and give thee two (loaves) of *bread;*
14:24, 28. (be) the man that eateth (any) *food*
— none of the people tasted (any) *food*.
16:20. an ass (laden) with *bread*,
17:17. this parched (corn), and these ten *loaves*,
20:24. the king sat him down to eat *meat*.
27. cometh not the son of Jesse to *meat*,
34. and did eat no *meat*
21: 3(4). give (me) five (loaves of) *bread*
4(5). (There is) no common *bread* under mine hand, but there is hallowed *bread;*
6(7). there was no *bread* there but *the* shew-*bread*, that was taken from before the Lord, to put hot *bread* in the day
22:13. in that thou hast given him *bread*,
25:11. Shall I then take *my bread*,
18. and took two hundred *loaves*,
28:20. he had eaten no *bread* all the day,
22. let me set a morsel of *bread* before thee;
30:11. and gave him *bread*, and he did eat ;
12. for he had eaten no *bread*,
2Sa. 3:29. or that lacketh *bread*.
35. to cause David to eat *meat*
— if I taste *bread*,...till the sun be down.
6:19. to every one a cake of *bread*,
9: 7. thou shalt eat *bread* at my table
10. that thy master's son may have *food* to eat: but Mephibosheth...shall eat *bread*
12:17. neither did he eat *bread*
20. they set *bread* before him,
21. thou didst rise and eat *bread*.
13: 5. my sister Tamar come, and give me *meat*,
16: 1. two hundred (loaves) of *bread*,
2. *and the bread* and summer fruit for the
1K. 4:22(5:2). Solomon's *provision* (marg. *bread*)
5: 9(23). in giving *food for* my houshold.
7:48. table of gold, whereupon *the* shew*bread*
11:18. *and* appointed him *victuals*,
13: 8, 16. neither will I eat *bread*
9. Eat no *bread*, nor drink water,
15. Come home with me, and eat *bread*.
17. Thou shalt eat no *bread*
18. that he may eat *bread* and drink water.
19. he went back with him, and did eat *bread*
22. and hast eaten *bread* and drunk water
— Eat no *bread*, and drink no water ;
23. after he had eaten *bread*,
14: 3. take with thee ten *loaves*,
17: 6. the ravens brought him *bread*
— *and bread* and flesh in the evening ;
11. Bring me, I pray thee, a morsel of *bread*
18: 4. fed them with *bread* and water.
13. and fed them with *bread* and water?
21: 4. and would eat no *bread*.
5. that thou eatest no *bread?*
7. arise, (and) eat *bread*,
22:27. feed him with *bread* of affliction
2K. 4: 8. she constrained him to eat *bread*.
— he turned in thither to eat *bread*.
42. *bread of* the firstfruits, twenty *loaves of*
6:22. set *bread* and water before them,
18:32. a land of *bread* and vineyards,
25: 3. there was no *bread* for the people
29. he did eat *bread* continually
1Ch. 9:32. the Kohathites, (were) over *the* shew*bread*,
12:40. *bread* on asses, and on camels,
16: 3. to every one a loaf of *bread*,
23:29. *Both for the* shewbread, and for the fine
2Ch. 4:19. tables whereon *the* shew*bread* (was set);
13:11. *the* shew*bread* also (set they in order)
18:26. feed him with *bread* of affliction
Ezr. 10: 6. he did eat no *bread*,
Neh. 5:14. *the bread of* the governor.
15. and had taken of them *bread* and wine,
18. *the bread of* the governor,
9:15. *And* gavest them *bread* from heaven
10:33(34). *For the* shew*bread*,
13: 2. met not the children of Israel *with bread*
Job 3:24. cometh before *I eat*, (lit. before *my bread*)
6: 7. as *my* sorrowful *meat*.
15:23. He wandereth abroad *for bread*,
20:14. *his meat* in his bowels is turned,
22: 7. withholden *bread* from the hungry.
24: 5. the wilderness (yieldeth) *food* for them
27:14. offspring shall not be satisfied with *bread*.
28: 5. the earth, out of it cometh *bread:*
30: 4. cut up...juniper roots (for) *their meat*.
33:20. his life abhorreth *bread*,
42:11. and did eat *bread* with him
Ps. 14: 4. eat up my people (as) they eat *bread*,
37:25. forsaken, nor his seed begging *bread*.
41: 9(10). which did eat of *my bread*,
42: 3(4). My tears have been my *meat*
53: 4(5). eat up my people (as) they eat *bread:*
78:20. can he give *bread* also?
25. Man did eat angels' *food:* (marg. Every one did eat *the bread of* the mighty)
80: 5(6). Thou feedest them with *the bread of*
102: 4(5). I forget to eat *my bread*.
9(10). I have eaten ashes *like bread*,
104:14. he may bring forth *food* out of the earth ;
15. *and bread* (which) strengtheneth man's
105:16. he brake the whole staff of *bread*.
40. *and* satisfied them with *the bread of*
127: 2. to eat *the bread of* sorrows:
132:15. I will satisfy her poor with *bread*.
136:25. Who giveth *food* to all flesh:
146: 7. which giveth *food* to the hungry.
147: 9. He giveth to the beast *his food*,
Pro. 4:17. they eat *the bread of* wickedness,
6: 8. Provideth *her meat* in the summer,
26. (a man is brought) to a piece of *bread*.
9: 5. Come, eat *of my bread*,
17. *and bread* (eaten) in secret is pleasant.
12: 9. that honoureth himself, and lacketh *bread*.
11. He that tilleth his land shall be satisfied with *bread:*
20:13. thou shalt be satisfied with *bread*.
17. *Bread of* deceit (is) sweet to a man ;
22: 9. he giveth *of his bread* to the poor.
23: 3. dainties: for they (are) deceitful *meat*.
6. *the bread of* (him that hath) an evil eye,
25:21. If thine enemy be hungry, give him *bread*
27:27. goats' milk enough *for thy food, for the food of* thy houshold,
28: 3. a sweeping rain which leaveth no *food*.
19. tilleth his land shall have plenty of *bread*.
21. a piece of *bread* (that) man will transgress.
30: 8. feed me with *food* convenient for me:
22. a fool when he is filled with *meat;*
25. they prepare *their meat* in the summer;
31:14. she bringeth *her food* from afar.
27. *and* eateth not *the bread of* idleness.
Ecc. 9: 7. eat *thy bread* with joy,
11. neither yet *bread* to the wise,
10:19. *A feast* is made for laughter,
11: 1. Cast *thy bread* upon the waters:
Isa. 3: 1. the whole stay of *bread*,
7. neither *bread* nor clothing:
4: 1. We will eat *our own bread*,
21:14. they prevented *with their bread*
28:28. *Bread* (corn) is bruised ;
30:20. *the bread of* adversity,
23. *and bread of* the increase of the earth,
33:16. *bread* shall be given *him;*
36:17. a land of *bread* and vineyards.
44:15. he kindleth (it), and baketh *bread*,
19. I have baked *bread* upon the coals
51:14. nor that *his bread* should fail.
55: 2. (that which is) not *bread?*
10. seed to the sower, *and bread* to the eater:
58: 7. to deal *thy bread* to the hungry,
65:25. dust (shall be) the serpent's *meat*.
Jer. 5:17. eat up thine harvest, *and thy bread*,
11:19. Let us destroy the tree *with the fruit thereof*

Jer. 37:21. give him daily a piece of *bread* out of the bakers' street, until all *the bread* in the
38: 9. no more *bread* in the city.
41: 1. they did eat *bread* together
42:14. *nor* have hunger *of bread;*
44:17. had we plenty of *victuals*, (marg. *bread*)
52: 6. there was no *bread* for the people
33. he did continually eat *bread*
Lam 1:11. All her people sigh, they seek *bread;*
4: 4. the young children ask *bread*,
5: 6. to be satisfied with *bread*.
9. We gat *our bread* with (the peril of)
Eze. 4: 9. make thee *bread* thereof,
13. *their* defiled *bread* among the Gentiles,
15. thou shalt prepare *thy bread*
16. I will break the staff of *bread* in Jerusalem: and they shall eat *bread* by weight,
17. That they may want *bread*
5:16. will break your staff of *bread:*
12:18. Son of man, eat *thy bread* with quaking,
19. They shall eat *their bread* with carefulness,
13:19. handfuls of barley and for pieces of *bread*,
14:13. will break the staff of *the bread* thereof,
16:19. *My meat also* which I gave thee,
49. fulness of *bread*, and abundance of
18: 7. given *his bread* to the hungry,
16. hath given *his bread* to the hungry,
24:17. *and* eat not *the bread of* men.
22. *nor* eat *the bread* of men.
44: 3. to eat *bread* before the Lord;
7. when ye offer *my bread*,
48:18. *for food* unto them that serve the city.
Dan 10: 3. I ate no pleasant *bread*,
Hos. 2: 5(7). give (me) *my bread* and my water,
9: 4. *as the bread of* mourners;
— *their bread* for their soul
Am. 4: 6. want of *bread* in all your places:
7:12. and there eat *bread*,
8:11. not a famine *of bread*,
Obad. 7. (they that eat) *thy bread* have laid
Hag 2:12. with his skirt do touch *bread*,
Mal. 1: 7. Ye offer polluted *bread*

3900 **לְחֶם** *l'ghem*, Ch. m.

Dan 5: 1. Belshazzar the king made *a great feast*

3904 **לְחֵנָה** [*l'ghēh-nāh'*], Ch. f.

Dan 5: 2. *and his concubines*, might drink therein.
3. *and his concubines*, drank in them.
23. *and thy concubines*, have drunk wine in

3905 **לָחַץ** *lāh-ghatz'*.

* KAL.—*Preterite.* *

Jud. 4: 3. mightily *oppressed* the children of Israel.
10:12. and the Maonites, *did oppress* you;
2K. 6:32. *and hold* him *fast* at the door:
13: 4. the king of Syria *oppressed* them.
22. Hazael king of Syria *oppressed*
Am. 6:14. *and they shall afflict* you

KAL.—*Future.*

Ex. 22:21(20). vex a stranger, nor *oppress him:*
23: 9. *thou shalt* not *oppress* a stranger:
Nu. 22:25. *and crushed* Balaam's foot
Jud. 1:34. *And* the Amorites *forced* the children of
Ps. 56: 1(2). he fighting daily *oppresseth me*.
106:42. Their enemies *also oppressed them*,

KAL.—*Participle.*

Ex. 3: 9. the Egyptians *oppress* them.
Jud. 2:18. them *that oppressed them*
6: 9. all *that oppressed you*,
1Sa. 10:18. *them that oppressed* you:
Isa. 19:20. because of *the oppressors*,
Jer. 30:20. I will punish all *that oppress them*.

* NIPHAL.—*Future.* *

Nu. 22:25. *And* when the ass...*she thrust herself* unto

3906 **לַחַץ** *lah'-ghatz*, m.

Ex. 3: 9. *the oppression* wherewith the Egyptians
Deu26: 7. and our labour, and *our oppression:*
1K. 22:27. feed him with bread of *affliction* and with water of *affliction*,
2K. 13: 4. he saw *the oppression of* Israel,
2Ch 18:26. feed him with bread of *affliction* and with water of *affliction*,
Job 36:15. and openeth their ears *in oppression*.
Ps. 42: 9(10) & 43:2. *because of the oppression of* the
44:24(25). our affliction *and our oppression?*
Isa. 30:20. water of *affliction*, (marg. or, *oppression*)

3907 **לָחַשׁ** [*lāh-ghash'*].

* PIEL.—*Participle.* *

Ps. 58: 5(6). the voice of *charmers*,

* HITHPAEL.—*Future.* *

Ps. 41: 7(8). All that hate me *whisper together*

HITHPAEL.—*Participle.*

2Sa. 12:19. David saw that his servants *whispered*,

3908 **לַחַשׁ** *lah'-ghash*, m.

Ecc. 10:11. the serpent will bite without *enchantment;*
Isa. 3: 3. eloquent *orator*. (marg. skilful of *speech*)
20. the tablets, *and the earrings*,
26:16. poured out *a prayer* (marg. *secret speech*)
Jer. 8:17. which (will) not (be) *charmed*, (lit. for whom (there is) no *charm*)

3909 **לָט** *lāht*, adj.

Ex. 7:22. of Egypt did so *with their enchantments:*
8: 7(3), 18(14). did so *with their enchantments*
Ru. 3: 7. she came *softly*,
1Sa. 18:22. Commune with David *secretly*,
24: 4(5). cut off the skirt of Saul's robe *privily*.

3910 **לֹט** *lōht*, m.

Gen37:25. bearing spicery and balm *and myrrh*,
43:11. spices, *and myrrh*, nuts, and almonds:

3911 **לְטָאָה** *l'tāh-āh'*, f.

Lev. 11:30. the chameleon, *and the lizard*,

3913 **לָטַשׁ** [*lāh-tash'*].

* KAL.—*Infinitive.* *

1Sa. 13:20. *to sharpen* every man his share,

KAL.—*Future.*

Job 16: 9. mine enemy *sharpeneth* his eyes
Ps. 7:12(13). *he will whet* his sword;

KAL.—*Participle.* Paül.

Gen 4:22. *an instructer* (marg. *whetter*) *of* every artificer

* PUAL.—*Participle.* *

Ps. 52: 2(4). like a *sharp* razor,

3914 **לֹיוֹת** *lōh-yōhth'*, f. pl.

1K. 7:29. *certain additions* made of thin work.
30. at the side of every *addition*.
36. *and additions* round about.

3915 **לַיִל** *lah'-yil*, m.

[More commonly found with ה Paragogic, לַיְלָה.]

Gen 1: 5. the darkness he called *Night*.
14. to divide the day from *the night;*

Gen 1:16. the lesser light to rule *the night:*
18. to rule over the day *and over the night,*
7: 4, 12. forty days and forty *nights;*
8:22. summer and winter, and day *and night*
14:15. he and his servants, *by night,*
19: 5. the men which came in to thee *this night?*
33. made their father drink wine that *night:*
34. make him drink wine *this night*
35. made their father drink wine that *night*
20: 3. came to Abimelech in a dream by *night,*
26:24. Lord appeared unto him *the* same *night,*
30:15. he shall lie with thee *to night*
16. he lay with her that *night.*
31:24. God came to Laban...in a dream *by night,*
39. stolen by day, or stolen by *night.*
40. and the frost *by night;*
32:13(14). lodged there that same *night;*
21(22). himself lodged that *night*
22(23). he rose up that *night,*
40: 5. each man his dream *in* one *night,*
41:11. we dreamed a dream *in* one *night,*
46: 2. in the visions of *the night,*
Ex. 10:13. all that day, and all (that) *night;*
11: 4. About mid*night* will I go out
12: 8. they shall eat the flesh *in* that *night,*
12. I will pass through...this *night,*
29. at mid*night* the Lord smote all
30. Pharaoh rose up *in the night,*
31. he called for Moses and Aaron *by night,*
42. *a night* to be much observed (marg. *a night of* observations)
— that *night* of the Lord
13:21. *and by night* in a pillar of fire, to give them light; to go by day *and night:*
22. the pillar of fire *by night,*
14:20. it gave light *by night*
— one came not near the other all *the night.*
21. a strong east wind all that *night,*
24:18 & 34:28. forty days and forty *nights.*
40:38. fire was on it *by night,*
Lev. 6: 9(2). burning upon the altar all *night*
8:35. day *and night* seven days,
Nu. 9:16. the appearance of fire *by night.*
21. whether (it was) by day *or by night*
11: 9. the dew fell upon the camp *in the night,*
32. all that day, and all (that) *night,*
14: 1. the people wept that *night.*
14. in a pillar of fire *by night.*
22: 8. Lodge here *this night,*
19. tarry ye also here *this night,*
20. God came unto Balaam *at night,*
Deu 1:33. in fire *by night,*
9: 9. in the mount forty days and forty *nights,*
11. at the end of forty days and forty *nights,*
18. as at the first, forty days and forty *nights:*
25. before the Lord forty days and forty *nights,*
10:10. first time, forty days and forty *nights;*
16: 1. brought thee forth out of Egypt *by night.*
23:10(11). that chanceth him *by night,*
28:66. thou shalt fear day and *night,*
Jos. 1: 8. meditate therein day *and night,*
2: 2. there came men in hither *to night*
4: 3. where ye shall lodge *this night.*
8: 3. and sent them away *by night.*
9. Joshua lodged that *night*
13. Joshua went that *night*
10: 9. went up from Gilgal all *night.*
Jud. 6:25. it came to pass *the* same *night,*
27. that he did (it) *by night.*
40. God did so that *night:*
7: 9. it came to pass *the* same *night,*
9:32. Now therefore up *by night,*
34. Abimelech rose up,...*by night,*
16: 2. laid wait for him all *night* in the gate of the city, and were quiet all *the night,*
3. lay till mid*night*, and arose at mid*night,*
19:25. abused her all *the night*
20: 5. beset the house round about...*by night,*
Ru. 1:12. I should have an husband also *to night,*
3: 2. he winnoweth barley *to night*
8. it came to pass at mid*night,*
13. Tarry this *night,*
1Sa. 14:34. every man his ox with him that *night,*
36. us go down after the Philistines *by night,*
15:11. he cried unto the Lord all *night.*
16. what the Lord hath said to me *this night.*
19:10. David fled, and escaped that *night.*

1Sa. 19:11. If thou save not thy life *to night,*
24. all that day and all *that night.*
25:16. a wall unto us both *by night* and day,
26: 7. and Abishai came to the people *by night.*
28: 8. they came to the woman *by night:*
20. all the day, nor all *the night.*
25. and went away that *night.*
30:12. three days and three *nights.*
31:12. the valiant men arose, and went all *night,*
2Sa. 2:29. Abner and his men walked all that *night*
32. Joab and his men went all *night,*
4: 7. gat them away through the plain all *night.*
7: 4. it came to pass that *night,*
17: 1. and pursue after David *this night:*
16. Lodge not *this night* in the plains
19: 7(8). will not tarry one with thee *this night:*
21:10. nor the beasts of the field *by night.*
1K. 3: 5. Solomon in a dream *by night:*
19. this woman's child died *in the night;*
20. she arose at mid*night,*
8:29. That thine eyes may be open...*night* and
59. nigh unto the Lord our God day *and night,*
19: 8. forty days and forty *nights*
2K. 6:14. and they came *by night,*
7:12. the king arose *in the night,*
8:21. and he rose *by night,*
19:35. it came to pass that *night,*
25: 4. all the men of war (fled) *by night*
1Ch 9:33. employed in (that) work day *and night.*
17: 3. it came to pass *the* same *night,*
2Ch 1: 7. In that *night* did God appear
6:20. thine eyes may be open...day *and night,*
7:12. the Lord appeared to Solomon *by night,*
21: 9. he rose up *by night,*
35:14. offering...the fat until *night;*
Neh. 1: 6. I pray before thee now, day *and night,*
2:12. I arose *in the night,*
13. I went out *by night*
15. Then went I up *in the night*
4: 9(3). set a watch against them day *and night,*
22(16). *in the night* they may be a guard
6:10. *yea, in the night* will they come
9:12. *in the night* by a pillar of fire,
19. the pillar of fire *by night,*
Est. 4:16. eat nor drink three days, *night* or day:
6: 1. *On* that *night* could not the king sleep,
Job 2:13. seven days and seven *nights,*
3: 3. *and the night* (in which) it was said,
6. (As for) that *night,*
7. let that *night* be solitary,
4:13. the visions of *the night,*
5:14. *and* grope in the noonday *as in the night.*
7: 3. *and* wearisome *nights* are appointed to me.
17:12. They change *the night* into day:
20: 8. as a vision *of the night.*
24:14. *and in the night* is as a thief.
27:20. a tempest stealeth him away *in the night.*
30:17. bones are pierced in me *in the night season:*
33:15. in a vision of *the night,*
34:20. the people shall be troubled *at* mid*night,*
25. overturneth (them) *in the night,*
35:10. giveth songs *in the night;*
36:20. Desire not *the night,*
Ps. 1: 2. he meditate day *and night.*
6: 6(7). all *the night* make I my bed to swim;
16: 7. reins also instruct me *in the night seasons.*
17: 3. visited (me) *in the night;*
19: 2(3). *and night* unto *night* sheweth
22: 2(3). *and in the night* season, and am not
32: 4. day *and night* thy hand was heavy
42: 3(4). my meat day *and night,*
8(9). *and in the night* his song
55:10(11). Day *and night* they go about
74:16. *the night* also (is) thine:
77: 2(3). my sore ran *in the night,*
6(7). to remembrance my song *in the night.*
78:14. all *the night* with a light of fire.
88: 1(2). I have cried day (and) *night*
90: 4. (as) a watch *in the night.*
91: 5. the terror *by night;*
92: 2(3). and thy faithfulness *every night,* (marg. *in the nights*)
104:20. Thou makest darkness, and it is *night:*
105:39. fire to give light *in the night.*
119:55. remembered thy name, O Lord, *in the night,*
62. At mid*night* I will rise
121: 6. nor the moon *by night.*

Ps. 134: 1. *by night* stand in the house of the Lord.
136: 9. The moon and stars to rule *by night:*
139:11. *even the night* shall be light
12. *but the night* shineth as the day:
Pro. 7: 9. in the black and dark *night:*
31:15. She riseth also while it is yet *night,*
18. her candle goeth not out *by night.*
Ecc. 2:23. his heart taketh not rest *in the night.*
8:16. neither day *nor night* seeth sleep
Cant.3: 1. *By night* on my bed I sought him
8. because of fear *in the night.*
5: 2. with the drops of *the night.*
Isa. 4: 5. a flaming fire *by night:*
15: 1. *in the night* Ar
— *in the night* Kir
16: 3. make thy shadow *as the night*
21: 8. I am set in my ward whole *nights:* (marg. or, every *night*)
11. Watchman, what *of the night?* Watchman, what *of the night?*
12. The morning cometh, and also *the night:*
26: 9. I desired thee *in the night;*
27: 3. I will keep it *night* and day.
28:19. by day *and by night:*
29: 7. as a dream of a *night* vision.
30:29. have a song, *as in the night*
34:10. It shall not be quenched *night* nor day;
38:12, 13. from day (even) to *night*
60:11. they shall not be shut day *nor night;*
62: 6. never hold their peace day nor *night:*
Jer. 6: 5. let us go *by night,*
9: 1(8:23). that I might weep day and *night*
14:17. eyes run down with tears *night* and day,
16:13. serve other gods day and *night;*
31:35. the stars for a light *by night,*
33:20. my covenant of *the night,* and that there should not be day *and night*
25. my covenant (be) not with day *and night,*
36:30. *in the night* to the frost.
39: 4. went forth out of the city *by night,*
49: 9. if thieves *by night,*
52: 7. went forth out of the city *by night*
Lam. 1: 2. She weepeth sore *in the night,*
2:18. tears run down like a river day and *night:*
19. Arise, cry out *in the night:*
Hos. 4: 5. the prophet also shall fall...*in the night,*
7: 6. their baker sleepeth all *the night;*
Am. 5: 8. maketh the day dark with *night:*
Obad. 5. If thieves came to thee, if robbers *by night,*
Jon. 1:17(2:1). of the fish three days and three *nights.*
4:10. came up in *a night,* and perished in *a night:*
Mic. 3: 6. *night* (shall be) unto you,
Zec. 1: 8. I saw *by night,*
14: 7. not day, nor *night:*

3916 לֵילְיָא *lēh-l'yāh',* Ch. f.

Dan. 2:19. revealed unto Daniel in a *night* vision.
5:30. *In* that *night* was Belshazzar
7: 2. I saw in my vision by *night,*
7, 13. I saw in the *night* visions,

3917 לִילִית *lee-leeth',* f.

Isa. 34:14. *the screech owl* (marg. or, *nightmonster*) also

---

See 3885 לין see לון

3918 לַיִשׁ *lah'-yish,* m.

Job 4:11. *The old lion* perisheth for lack of prey,
Pro.30:30. *A lion* (which is) strongest among beasts,
Isa. 30: 6. the young *and old lion,*

3920 לָכַד *lāh-chad'.*

* KAL.—*Preterite.* *

Deu 2:35. the spoil of the cities which *we took.*
Jos. 8:21. the ambush *had taken* the city,
10: 1. Joshua *had taken* Ai,
28. Joshua *took* Makkedah,
42 their land *did* Joshua *take*
Jos. 11:12. all the kings of them, *did* Joshua *take,*
17. all their kings *he took,*
15:16. that smiteth Kirjath-sepher, *and taketh it,*
Jud. 1:12. that smiteth Kirjath-sepher, *and taketh it,*
1Sa.14:47. Saul *took* the kingdom
2Sa.12:27. and *have taken* the city of waters.
2K. 17: 6. the king of Assyria *took* Samaria,
2Ch 15: 8. the cities which *he had taken*
17: 2. cities of Ephraim, which Asa...*had taken.*
Jer.32: 3, 28. king of Babylon, *and he shall take it;*
34:22. they shall fight against it, *and take it,*
37: 8. and fight against this city, *and take it,*
38: 3. Babylon's army, *which shall take it.*
Dan 11:15. *and take* the most fenced cities:
18. *and shall take* many:
Am. 3: 4. if *he have taken* nothing?

KAL.—*Infinitive.*

Jer. 18:22. they have digged a pit *to take me,*
32:24. they are come unto the city *to take it:*
Am. 3: 5. *and* have taken nothing *at all?* (lit. *and taking* have taken nothing)

KAL.—*Imperative.*

Jud. 7:24. *and take* before them the waters
2Sa.12:28. encamp against the city, *and take it:*

KAL.—*Future.*

Nu. 21:32. *and they took* the villages thereof,
32:39. went to Gilead, *and took it,*
41. *and took* the small towns thereof,
42. Nobah went *and took* Kenath,
Deu 2:34&3:4. *And we took* all his cities at that time,
Jos. 6:20. *and they took* the city.
7:14. tribe which the Lord *taketh* (lit. *taketh it*)
— family which the Lord *shall take* (lit. *id.*)
— houshold which the Lord *shall take* (lit. *id.*)
17. *and he took* the family of the Zarhites:
8:19. they entered into the city, *and took it,*
10:32. *which took it* on the second day,
35. *And they took it* on that day,
37. *And they took it,* and smote it
39. *And he took it,* and the king thereof,
11:10. Joshua at that time turned back, *and took*
15:17. *And* Othniel...*took it:*
19:47. to fight against Leshem, *and took* it,
Jud. 1: 8. fought against Jerusalem, *and had taken* it,
13. *And* Othniel the son of Kenaz,...*took it:*
18. *Also* Judah *took* Gaza
3:28. *and took* the fords of Jordan
7:24. *and took* the waters unto Beth-barah
25. *And they took* two princes
8:12. *and took* the two kings of Midian,
14. *And caught* a young man
9:45. *and he took* the city,
50. Then went Abimelech...*and took it.*
12: 5. *And* the Gileadites *took* the passages
15: 4. And Samson went *and caught* three
2Sa. 5: 7. *Nevertheless* David *took* the strong hold
8: 4. *And* David *took* from him a thousand
12:26. *and took* the royal city.
28. lest I *take* the city,
29. and fought against it, *and took it.*
1K. 9:16. king of Egypt had gone up, *and taken*
2K. 12:17(18). fought against Gath, *and took it:*
18:10. *And* at the end of three years *they took it.*
1Ch.11: 5. *Nevertheless* David *took* the castle
18: 4. *And* David *took* from him a thousand
2Ch.12: 4. *And he took* the fenced cities
13:19. *and took* cities from him,
22: 9. he sought Ahaziah: *and they caught him,*
28:18. *and had taken* Beth-shemesh,
32:18. that *they might take* the city.
33:11. the captains of the host...*which took*
Neh 9:25. *And they took* strong cities,
Ps. 35: 8. *let* his net that he hath hid *catch himself:*
Pro. 5:22. His own iniquities *shall take* the wicked
Isa. 20: 1. fought against Ashdod, *and took it;*
Jer. 5:26. they set a trap, *they catch* men.
Am. 3: 5. *have taken* nothing at all?
Hab. 1:10. they shall heap dust, *and take it.*

KAL.—*Participle.* Poel.

Job 5:13. *He taketh* the wise in their own
Pro.16:32. *than he that taketh* a city.

* NIPHAL.—*Preterite.* *

1K. 16:18. when Zimri saw that the city *was taken,*

2K. 18:10. Samaria *was taken.*
Ps. 9:15(16). which they hid *is* their own foot *taken.*
Pro. 6: 2. *thou art taken* with the words of thy
Isa. 8:15. and be snared, *and be taken.*
28:13. be broken, and snared, *and taken.*
Jer. 38:28. the day that Jerusalem *was taken:* and he was (there) when Jerusalem *was taken.*
48: 1. Kiriathaim is confounded (and) *taken:*
41. Kerioth *is taken,*
50: 2. Babylon *is taken,*
24. *thou art* also *taken,*
51:31. the king of Babylon that his city *is taken*
41. How *is* Sheshach *taken!*
56. her mighty men *are taken,*
Lam 4:20. the anointed of the Lord, *was taken*
Zec. 14: 2. *and* the city *shall be taken,*

NIPHAL.—*Future.*

Jos. 7:16. *and* the tribe of Judah *was taken:*
17. *and* Zabdi *was taken:*
18. *and* Achan, the son of Carmi,...*was taken.*
1Sa. 10:20. *And* when...the tribe of Benjamin *was taken*
21. the family of Matri *was taken, and* Saul the son of Kish *was taken:*
14:41. *And* Saul and Jonathan *were taken:*
42. *And* Jonathan *was taken.*
Job 36: 8. *be holden* in cords of affliction;
Ps. 59:12(13). *let them even be taken* in their pride:
Pro. 11: 6. transgressors *shall be taken*
Ecc. 7:26. the sinner *shall be taken* by her.
Isa. 24:18. out of the midst of the pit *shall be taken*
Jer. 6:11. the husband with the wife *shall be taken,*
8: 9. they are dismayed *and taken:*
48: 7. thou *shalt* also *be taken:*
44. *shall be taken* in the snare:
50: 9. *she shall be taken:*

NIPHAL.—*Participle.*

Jos. 7:15. *he that is taken* with the accursed thing

* HITHPAEL.—*Future.* *

Job 38:30. face of the deep *is frozen.* (marg. *taken*)
41:17(9). *they stick together,*

3921 לֶכֶד [*leh'-ched*], m.

Pro. 3:26. shall keep thy foot *from being taken.*

3924 לֻלָאֹת *loo-lāh-ōhth'*, f. pl.

Ex. 26: 4. thou shalt make *loops of* blue
5. Fifty *loops* shalt thou make in the one curtain, and fifty *loops* shalt thou make in
— that *the loops* may take hold
10. thou shalt make fifty *loops*
— fifty *loops* in the edge
11. put the taches *into the loops,*
36:11. he made *loops of* blue
12. Fifty *loops* made he in one curtain, and fifty *loops* made he in the edge
— *the loops* held one (curtain) to another.
17. fifty *loops* upon the uttermost edge
— fifty *loops* made he upon the edge

3925 לָמַד *lāh-mad'.*

* KAL.—*Preterite.* *

Deu. 5: 1. *that ye may learn* them,
31:13. may hear, *and learn* to fear the Lord
Pro. 30: 3. *I* neither *learned* wisdom,
Isa. 26: 9. the inhabitants of the world *will learn.*
10. *will he* not *learn* righteousness:

KAL.—*Infinitive.*

Ps. 119: 7. *when I shall have learned* thy righteous
Jer. 12:16. they will *diligently* learn (lit. *learning* they will learn)

KAL.—*Imperative.*

Isa. 1:17. *Learn* to do well;

KAL.—*Future.*

Deu 4:10. that *they may learn* to fear me
14.23. that *thou mayest learn* to fear
17:19. that *he may learn* to fear
Deu 18: 9. *thou shalt* not *learn* to do after
31:12. that *they may learn,* and fear
Ps. 106:35. *and learned* their works.
119:71. that *I might learn* thy statutes.
73. *that I may learn* thy commandments.
Isa. 2: 4. neither *shall they learn* war any more.
29:24. they that murmured *shall learn*
Jer. 10: 2. *Learn* not the way of the heathen,
12:16. if *they will* diligently *learn*
Eze. 19: 3. *and it learned* to catch the prey;
6. *and learned* to catch the prey,
Mic. 4: 3. neither *shall they learn* war

KAL.—*Participle.* Paül.

1Ch. 5:18. *and skilful in* war,

* PIEL.—*Preterite.* *

Deu 4: 5. *I have taught* you statutes
11:19. *And ye shall teach* them your children,
Ps. 71:17. *thou hast taught me* from my youth:
Ecc. 12: 9. *he* still *taught* the people
Jer. 2:33. *hast thou* also *taught* the wicked
9: 5(4). *they have taught* their tongue to speak
14(13). their fathers *taught them:*
12:16. *they taught* my people to swear
13:21. *thou hast taught* them (to be) captains,

PIEL.—*Infinitive.*

Deu 4:14. *to teach* you statutes
6: 1. commanded *to teach* you,
Jud. 3: 2. *to teach them* war,
2Sa. 1:18. he bade them *teach* the children of Judah
2Ch 17: 7. *to teach* in the cities of Judah.
Ezr. 7:10. *and to teach* in Israel statutes
Ps. 60[title](1). Michtam of David, *to teach;*
Jer. 32:33. *though* I *taught* them, rising up early *and teaching* (them),
Dan 1: 4. *and whom they might teach*

PIEL.—*Imperative.*

Deu 31:19. *and teach it* the children of Israel:
Ps. 25: 4. O Lord; *teach me* thy paths.
5. Lead me in thy truth, *and teach me:*
119:12, 26, 68, 124. *teach me* thy statutes.
64. *teach me* thy statutes.
66. *Teach me* good judgment
108. *teach me* thy judgments.
135. *and teach me* thy statutes.
143:10. *Teach me* to do thy will;
Jer. 9:20(19). *and teach* your daughters wailing,

PIEL.—*Future.*

Deu 4:10. *they may teach* their children.
5:31(28). *thou shalt teach them,*
20:18. *they teach* you not
31:22. *and taught it* the children of Israel.
2Ch 17: 9. *And they taught* in Judah,
— *and taught* the people.
Job 21:22. *Shall* (any) *teach* God knowledge?
Ps. 25: 9. *and* the meek *will he teach*
34:11(12). *I will teach you* the fear of the Lord.
51:13(15). (Then) *will I teach* transgressors
94:12. *teachest him* out of thy law;
119:171. *thou hast taught me* thy statutes.
132:12. my testimony that *I shall teach them,*
Cant 8: 2. (who) *would instruct me:*
Isa. 40:14. *and taught him* in the path of judgment, *and taught him* knowledge,
Jer. 31:34. *they shall teach* no more

PIEL.—*Participle.*

Deu 4: 1. the judgments, which I *teach* you,
2Sa. 22:35. *He teacheth* my hands to war;
Ps. 18:34(35). *He teacheth* my hands to war,
94:10. *he that teacheth* man knowledge,
119:99. more understanding than all *my teachers:*
144: 1. *which teacheth* my hands to war,
Pro. 5:13. *nor* (lit. *and* not)...*to them that instructed me!*
Isa. 48:17. *which teacheth thee* to profit,

* PUAL.—*Preterite.* *

Jer. 31:18. a bullock un*accustomed* (to the yoke):

PUAL.—*Participle.*

1Ch. 25: 7. their brethren *that were instructed*
Cant. 3: 8. (being) *expert* in war:

Isa. 29:13. their fear toward me *is taught*
Hos.10:11. Ephraim (is as) an heifer (that is) *taught,*

See 4100 לָמָּה, לָמָה, לְמָה see מָה

3926 **לְמוֹ** *l'mōh,* part.

Job 27:14. be multiplied: (it is) *for* the sword,
29:21. and kept silence *at* my counsel.
38:40. abide in the covert *to* lie in wait?
40: 4. I will lay mine hand *upon* my mouth.

3928 **לִמּוּד** *lim-mood',* adj.

Isa. 8:16. the law *among my disciples.*
50: 4. the tongue of *the learned,* (lit. *disciples*)
— to hear *as the learned.* (lit. *id.*)
54:13. all thy children (shall be) *taught of* the
Jer. 2:24. A wild ass *used* (marg. *taught*) to the
13:23. *that are accustomed* (marg. *taught*) to do

See 4616 לְמַעַן see מַעַן

3930 **לֹעַ** [*lōh'ăg*], m.

Pro. 23: 2. And put a knife *to thy throat,*

3931 **לָעַב** [*lāh-găv'*].

* HIPHIL.—*Participle.* *

2Ch.36:16. they *mock*ed (lit. were *mocking*) the

3932 **לָעַג** [*lāh-găg'*].

* KAL.—*Preterite.* *

2K. 19:21. of Zion hath...*laughed thee to scorn;*
Isa. 37:22. of Zion, hath...*laughed thee to scorn;*

KAL.—*Future.*

Job 9:23. *he will laugh* at the trial of the innocent.
11: 3. and *when thou mockest,*
22:19. the innocent *laugh* them *to scorn.*
Ps. 2: 4. the Lord *shall have* them *in derision.*
59: 8(9). *thou shalt have* all the heathen *in derision.*
80: 6(7). our enemies *laugh* among themselves.
Pro. 1:26. *I will mock* when your fear cometh;
30:17. The eye (that) *mocketh* at (his) father,

KAL.—*Participle.* Poel.

Pro.17: 5. Whoso *mocketh* the poor
Jer. 20: 7. every one *mocketh* me.

* NIPHAL.—*Participle.* *

Isa. 33:19. *stammering* (marg. or, *ridiculous*) tongue,

* HIPHIL.—*Future.* *

Neh 2:19. *they laughed* us *to scorn,*
4: 1(3:33). *and mocked* the Jews.
Job 21: 3. after that I have spoken, *mock on.*
Ps. 22: 7(8). they that see me *laugh* me *to scorn:*

HIPHIL.—*Participle.*

2Ch 30:10. laughed them to scorn, *and mocked* them.

3933 **לַעַג** *lah'-găg,* m.

Job 34: 7. drinketh up *scorning* like water?
Ps. 44:13(14). *a scorn* and a derision to them that
79: 4. *a scorn* and derision to them
123: 4. *the scorning of* those that are at ease,
Eze.23:32. laughed to scorn *and had in derision;*
36: 4. became a prey *and derision*
Hos. 7:16. *their derision* in the land of Egypt.

לָעֵג [*lāh-gēhg'*], adj. 3934

Ps. 35:16. With hypocritical *mockers*
Isa. 28:11. *with stammering* (marg. *stammerings of*) lips

לָעַז [*lāh-găz'*]. 3937

* KAL.—*Participle.* Poel. *

Ps.114: 1. from a people of *strange language;*

לָעַט [*lāh-găt'*]. 3938

* HIPHIL.—*Imperative.* *

Gen 25:30. *Feed me,* I pray thee, with

לַעֲנָה *lah-gănāh',* f. 3939

Deu 29:18(17). root that beareth gall *and wormwood;*
Pro. 5: 4. her end is bitter *as wormwood,*
Jer. 9:15(14). I will feed them,...with *wormwood,*
23:15. I will feed them with *wormwood,*
Lam 3:15. made me drunken with *wormwood.*
19. *the wormwood* and the gall.
Am. 5: 7. who turn judgment *to wormwood,*
6:12. the fruit of righteousness *into hemlock:*

לַפִּיד *lap-peed',* m. 3940

Gen15:17. *and a* burning *lamp* that passed between
Ex. 20:18. saw the thunderings, and *the lightnings,*
Jud. 7:16. *and lamps* within the pitchers. (marg. *firebrands,* or, *torches*)
20. and held *the lamps* in their left hands,
15: 4. and took *firebrands* (marg. *torches*), and turned tail to tail, and put *a firebrand*
5. when he had set *the brands* on fire,
Job 12: 5. (as) *a lamp* despised
41:19(11). Out of his mouth go *burning lamps,*
Isa. 62: 1. the salvation thereof *as a lamp*
Eze. 1:13. like the appearance of *lamps:*
Dan 10: 6. his eyes *as lamps of* fire,
Nah 2: 4(5). they shall seem *like torches,*
Zec.12: 6. *and like a torch of* fire

לִפְנֵי *liph-nāh'y,* adj. 3942

1K. 6:17. the temple *before it,* was forty cubits

לָפַת [*lāh-phath'*]. 3943

* KAL.—*Future.* *

Jud.16:29. *And* Samson *took hold of* the two middle

* NIPHAL.—*Future.* *

Ru. 3: 8. the man was afraid, *and turned himself:* (marg. or, *took hold on*)
Job 6:18. The paths of their way *are turned aside;*

לָצוֹן *lāh-tzōhn',* m. 3944

Pro. 1:22. the scorners delight in their *scorning,*
29: 8. *Scornful* men (lit. men of *scorning*) bring
Isa. 28:14. ye *scornful* men, that rule this people

לָצַץ [*lāh-tzatz'*]. 3945

* KAL.—*Participle.* Poel. *

Hos. 7: 5. he stretched out his hand with *scorners.*

לָקַח *lāh-kăgh'.* 3947

* KAL.—*Preterite.* *

Gen 2:22. the rib, which the Lord God *had taken*
3:22. *and take* also of the tree of life,

Gen 5:24. for God *took* him.
20: 3. the woman which *thou hast taken ;*
24: 4, 38. *and take* a wife unto my son
7. *took me* from my father's house,
— *and thou shalt take* a wife unto my son
40. *and thou shalt take* a wife for my son
27:36. *he took away* my birthright ; and, behold, now *he hath taken away* my blessing.
45. I will send, *and fetch thee*
31: 1. Jacob *hath taken away* all
34. Rachel *had taken* the images,
33:10. *then receive* my present
34:17. *then will we take* our daughter,
28. *They took* their sheep,
36: 2. Esau *took* his wives
43:15. and *they took* double money in their
44:29. *And* if *ye take* this also from me,
47: 2. *he took* some of his brethren,
48:22. *I took* out of the hand of the Amorite
Ex. 4: 9. *that thou shalt take* of the water
6: 7. *And I will take* you to me
25. Eleazar...*took* him (one) of the daughters
12: 4. *let* him and his neighbour...*take* (it)
7. *And they shall take* of the blood,
22. *And ye shall take* a bunch of hyssop,
14: 6. and *took* his people with him:
11. *hast thou taken us away* to die
22:11(10). *and* the owner of it *shall accept*
28: 9. *And thou shalt take* two onyx stones,
29: 5. *And thou shalt take* the garments,
7. *Then shalt thou take* the anointing oil,
12. *And thou shalt take* of the blood
13. *And thou shalt take* all the fat
16. *and thou shalt take* his blood,
19. *And thou shalt take* the other ram ;
20. *and take* of his blood,
21. *And thou shalt take* of the blood
22. *Also thou shalt take* of the ram
25. *And thou shalt receive* them
26. *And thou shalt take* the breast
30:16. *And thou shalt take* the atonement money
34:16. *And thou take* of their daughters
40: 9. *And thou shalt take* the anointing oil,
Lev. 4: 5. *And* the priest...*shall take* of the bullock's
25, 30, 34. *And* the priest *shall take* of the blood
7:34. the heave shoulder *have I taken*
8:26. *he took* one unleavened cake,
12: 8. *then she shall bring* two turtles,
14: 4. the priest command *to take* (lit. *and take*)
12. *And* the priest *shall take* one he lamb,
14, 25. *And* the priest *shall take* (some) of the
15. *And* the priest *shall take* (some) of the log
21. *then he shall take* one lamb
24. *And* the priest *shall take* the lamb
42. *And they shall take* other stones,
49. *And he shall take* to cleanse the house
51. *And he shall take* the cedar wood,
16: 7. *And he shall take* the two goats,
12. *And he shall take* a censer
14. *And he shall take* of the blood
18. *and shall take* of the blood
23:40. *And ye shall take* you on the first day
24: 5. *And thou shalt take* fine flour,
Nu. 3:12. *I have taken* the Levites
41. *And thou shalt take* the Levites
47. *Thou shalt even take* five shekels
50. firstborn of the children of Israel *took he*
4: 9. *And they shall take* a cloth
12. *And they shall take* all the instruments
5:17. *And* the priest *shall take* holy water
25. *Then* the priest *shall take* the jealousy
6:18. *and shall take* the hair of the head
19. *And* the priest *shall take* the sodden
8: 8. *Then let them take* a young bullock
16. *have I taken* them unto me.
11:16. *and bring* them unto the tabernacle
12: 1. Ethiopian woman whom *he had married :* for *he had married* (marg. *taken*) an
13:20. *and bring* of the fruit of the land.
18: 6. *I have taken* your brethren
19: 4. *And* Eleazar the priest *shall take* of her
6. *And* the priest *shall take* cedar wood,
17. *And* for an unclean (person) *they shall take* of the ashes
18. *And* a clean person *shall take* hyssop,
23:11. *I took thee* to curse mine enemies,
20. *I have received* (commandment) to

Nu. 34:14. *have received* (their inheritance) ;
—, 15. *have received* their inheritance:
Deu 3: 4. not a city which *we took* not
14. Jair the son of Manasseh *took* all the
4:20. the Lord *hath taken* you,
7:25. *nor take* (it) unto thee,
9:21. *I took* your sin,
15:17. *Then thou shalt take* an aul,
19:12. the elders of his city shall send *and fetch*
20: 7. betrothed a wife, and *hath* not *taken her?*
21: 3. *even* the elders of that city *shall take* an
11. *that thou wouldest have her* to thy wife ;
22:14. *I took* this woman,
15. *Then shall* the father of the damsel,...*take*
18. *And* the elders of that city *shall take*
24: 3. the latter husband die, which *took her*
5. cheer up his wife which *he hath taken.*
25: 5. *and take her* to him to wife,
26: 2. *That thou shalt take* of the first of
4. *And* the priest *shall take* the basket
Jos. 4:20. twelve stones, which *they took*
6:18. *when ye take* of the accursed thing,
7:11. *they have* even *taken* of the accursed thing
11:19. all (other) *they took* in battle.
13: 8. the Gadites *have received* their inheritance,
18: 7. the tribe of Manasseh, *have received* their
Jud. 4: 6. *and take* with thee ten thousand men
5:19. *they took* no gain of money.
6:26. *and take* the second bullock,
11:13. Israel *took* away my land,
15. Israel *took* not away
13:23. *he would* not *have received*
15: 6. because *he had taken* his wife,
17: 2. the silver (is) with me ; I *took it.*
18:17. (and) *took* the graven image,
24. *Ye have taken away* my gods
27. And they *took* (the things)
20:10. *And we will take* ten men
21:22. *we reserved* not to each man his wife
1Sa. 2:16. *I will take* (it) by force.
5: 1. the Philistines *took* the ark
6: 8. *And take* the ark of the Lord,
7:14. the cities which the Philistines *had taken*
10: 4. *which thou shalt receive* of their hands.
12: 3. *have I taken?* or whose ass *have I taken?*
— of whose hand *have I received* (any) bribe
4. neither *hast thou taken* ought
16:23. *that* David *took* an harp,
21: 8(9). *I have* neither *brought* my sword nor
25:11. *Shall I then take* my bread,
43. David also *took* Ahinoam
27: 9. *and took away* the sheep,
30:16. the great spoil that *they had taken*
18. the Amalekites *had carried away :*
19. *they had taken* to them:
2Sa. 2: 8. Abner the son of Ner,...*took* Ish-bosheth
4:12. *they took* the head of Ish-bosheth,
7: 8. *I took thee* from the sheepcote,
8: 8. David *took* exceeding much brass.
12: 9. *hast taken* his wife
11. *and I will take* thy wives
18:18. Absalom in his lifetime *had taken* and
1K. 4:15. he also *took* Basmath the daughter of
7: 8. whom *he had taken* (to wife),
11:35. *But I will take* the kingdom
14: 3. *And take* with thee ten loaves,
26. *he* even *took away* all:
20: 6. *and take* (it) *away.*
34. The cities, which my father *took*
2K. 5:20. *and take* somewhat of him.
9: 3. *Then take* the box of oil,
13:25. the cities, which *he had taken*
14:14. *And he took* all the gold and silver,
18:32. Until I come *and take* you *away*
23:34. and *took* Jehoahaz *away :*
24: 7. the king of Babylon *had taken*
25:14. all the vessels...*took they away.*
15. the captain of the guard *took away.*
19. out of the city *he took* an officer
1Ch 2:21. the daughter of Machir...*whom* he *married* (lit. *and* he *took her*)
4:18. daughter of Pharaoh, which Mered *took.*
7:15. Machir *took* to wife (the sister) of Huppim
17: 7. I *took thee* from the sheepcote,
18: 8. *brought* David very much brass,
2Ch 11:20. *he took* Maachah the daughter of Absalom,
12: 9. *he took* all;

2Ch 16: 6. Then Asa the king *took* all Judah;
36: 4. Necho *took* Jehoahaz his brother,
Ezr. 2:61. *took* a wife of the daughters of Barzillai
Neh. 6:18. Johanan *had taken* the daughter of
7:63. *took* (one) of the daughters of Barzillai
Est. 2: 7. *whom* Mordecai,...*took* for his own
15. who *had taken* her for his daughter,
Job 1:21. Lord gave, and the Lord *hath taken away*,
Ps. 15: 5. nor *taketh* reward against the innocent.
68:18(19). *thou hast received* gifts for men;
Pro. 7:20. *He hath taken* a bag of money
22:25. *and get* a snare to thy soul.
24:32. upon (it, and) *received* instruction.
Isa. 6: 6. coal in his hand, (which) *he had taken*
14: 2. *And* the people *shall take them*,
36:17. Until I come *and take* you away
40: 2. *she hath received* of the Lord's hand
51:22. *I have taken* out of thine hand
Jer. 2:30. *they received* no correction:
3:14. *I will take* you one of a city,
7:28. nor *receiveth* correction:
20: 5. shall spoil them, *and take them*,
25: 9. I will send *and take* all the families
27:20. Which Nebuchadnezzar king of Babylon *took* (lit. *took them*) not,
28: 3. king of Babylon *took away*
36:32. *Then took* Jeremiah another roll,
43:10. I will send *and take* Nebuchadrezzar
44:12. *And I will take* the remnant of Judah,
52:18. all the vessels...*took they away*.
19. *took* the captain of the guard away.
25. *He took* also out of the city an eunuch,
Eze. 5: 1. *then take* thee balances to weigh,
2. *and thou shalt take* a third part,
3. *Thou shalt also take* thereof
16:39. *and shall take* thy fair jewels.
17: 5. *he placed* (it) by great waters,
13. *he hath* also *taken* the mighty
22. *I will also take* of the highest branch
18:13. and *hath taken* increase:
17. *hath* not *received* usury
22:12. In thee *have they taken* gifts
— *thou hast taken* usury and increase,
23:10. *they took* her sons and her daughters,
26. *and take away* thy fair jewels.
29. *and shall take away* all thy labour,
27: 5. *they have taken* cedars from Lebanon
30: 4. *and they shall take away* her multitude,
33: 2. *if* the people of the land *take* a man
36:24. *For I will take* you from among the
43:20. *And thou shalt take* of the blood
21. *Thou shalt take* the bullock *also*
45:19. *And* the priest *shall take* of the blood
Hos. 2: 9(11). *and take away* my corn
Joel 3: 5(4:5). *ye have taken* my silver and my gold,
Am. 6:13. *Have we* not *taken* to us horns
9: 3. I will search *and take them*
Zep. 3: 2. *she received* not correction;
Zec. 6:11. *Then take* silver and gold,
14:21. that sacrifice shall come *and take* of them,

KAL.—*Infinitive.*

Gen 4:11. *to receive* thy brother's blood
24:48. *to take* my master's brother's daughter
25:20. *when he took* Rebekah to wife,
28: 6. *to take* him a wife from thence;
30:15. *that thou hast taken* my husband? *and wouldest thou take away* my son's
38:20. *to receive* (his) pledge from
43:18. *and take us* for bondmen,
Deu 4:34. to go (and) *take* him a nation
9: 9. *to receive* the tables of stone,
24: 4. Her former husband,...may not *take her*
19. thou shalt not go again *to fetch it:*
25: 7. if the man like not *to take*
8. I like not *to take her;*
31:26. *Take* this book of the law,
Jud.11: 5. elders of Gilead went *to fetch* Jephthah
14: 3. thou goest *to take* a wife
8. he returned *to take her*,
20:10. *to fetch* victual for the people,
1Sa.19:14, 20. Saul sent messengers *to take* David,
24:11(12). thou huntest my soul *to take it.*
25:39. *to take her* to him to wife.
40. *to take* thee to him to wife.
2Sa.12: 4. he spared *to take* of his own flock
1K. 17:11. as she was going *to fetch* (it),
1K. 19:10, 14. they seek my life, *to take it away.*
22: 3. we (be) still, (and) *take* it *not* (marg. silent *from taking*)
2K. 4: 1. the creditor is come *to take*
5:16. he urged him *to take* (it);
20. *in not receiving* at his hands
26. *to receive* money, *and to receive* garments,
12: 8(9). consented *to receive* no (more) money
1Ch 7:21. they came down *to take away* their cattle.
Ps. 31:13(14). they devised *to take away* my life.
Pro. 1: 3. *To receive* the instruction of wisdom,
Jer. 5: 3. they have refused *to receive* correction:
17:23. nor *receive* instruction.
25:28. if they refuse *to take* the cup
32:14. *Take* these evidences,
33. have not hearkened *to receive* instruction.
33:26. I will not *take* (any) of his seed
36:21. the king sent Jehudi *to fetch* the roll:
26. *to take* Baruch the scribe
40: 1. *when he had taken* him being bound
Eze.16:61. *when thou shalt receive* thy sisters,
24: 5. *Take* the choice of the flock,
25. *when I take* from them their strength,
38:13. *to take away* cattle and goods,
Hos 11: 3. *taking them* by their arms;
Zec. 6:10. *Take* of (them of) the captivity,
Mal. 2:13. *or receiveth* (it) with good will

KAL.—*Imperative.*

Gen 6:21. *take* thou unto thee of all food
12:19. behold thy wife, *take* (her),
14:21. and *take* the goods to thyself.
15: 9. *Take* me an heifer of three years old,
19:15. *take* thy wife, and thy two daughters,
22: 2. *Take* now thy son,
23:13. *take* (it) of me, and I will bury my dead
24:51. Rebekah (is) before thee, *take* (her),
27: 9. *and fetch* me from thence two good kids
13. obey my voice, and go *fetch* me (them).
28: 2. *and take* thee a wife from thence
31:32. *and take* (it) to thee.
33:11. *Take*, I pray thee, my blessing
34: 4. *Get* me this damsel to wife.
42:33. *take* (food for) the famine
43:11. *take* of the best fruits
12. *take* double money
13. *Take* also your brother,
45:18. *And take* your father and your housholds,
19. *take* you wagons out of the land
48: 9. *Bring them*, I pray thee,
Ex. 5:11. *get* you straw where ye can find it:
7: 9. *Take* thy rod, and cast (it) before
19. *Take* thy rod, and stretch out thine hand
9: 8. *Take* to you handfuls of ashes
12:21. Draw out *and take* you a lamb
32. *take* your flocks and your herds,
16:33. Moses said unto Aaron, *Take* a pot,
17: 5. *and take* with thee of the elders of Israel;
— *take* in thine hand, and go.
29: 1. *Take* one young bullock,
30:23. *Take* thou also unto thee principal spices,
34. *Take* unto thee sweet spices,
35: 5. *Take ye* from among you
Lev. 8: 2. *Take* Aaron and his sons
9: 2. *Take* thee a young calf
3. *Take ye* a kid of the goats
10:12. *Take* the meat offering
Nu. 3:45. *Take* the Levites
7: 5. *Take* (it) of them,
8: 6. *Take* the Levites from among
16: 6. *Take* you censers,
17. *And take* every man his censer,
46(17:11). Moses said unto Aaron, *Take* a
17: 2(17). *and take* of every one of them a rod
20: 8. *Take* the rod, and gather thou the
25. *Take* Aaron and Eleazar
25: 4. *Take* all the heads of the people,
27:18. *Take* thee Joshua the son of Nun,
Jos. 3:12. *take* you twelve men
4: 2. *Take* you twelve men
8: 1. *take* all the people of war
9:11. *Take* victuals with you for the journey,
Jud. 6:20. *Take* the flesh and the unleavened cakes,
25. *Take* thy father's young bullock,
14: 2. *get* her for me to wife.
3. *Get* her for me;
1Sa. 2:16. *and* (then) *take* (as much) as thy soul

1Sa. 6: 7. *take* two milch kine,
9: 3. *Take* now one of the servants
16:11. Send *and fetch him:*
17:17. *Take* now for thy brethren
20:21. (are) on this side of thee, *take them;*
31. send *and fetch* him unto me,
21: 9(10). if thou wilt take that, *take* (it):
26:11. *take thou* now the spear
2Sa. 2:21. *and take* thee his armour.
20: 6. *take thou* thy lord's servants,
1K. 1:33. *Take* with you the servants of your lord,
3:24. the king said, *Bring* me a sword.
11:31. *Take* thee ten pieces:
17:10. *Fetch* me, I pray thee, a little water
11. *Bring* me, I pray thee, a morsel of bread
19: 4. O Lord, *take away* my life;
20:33. Go ye, *bring him.*
22:26. *Take* Micaiah, and carry him back
2K. 2:20. *Bring* me a new cruse,
3:15. *bring* me a minstrel.
4:29. *and take* my staff in thine hand,
41. he said, *Then bring* meal.
5:15. *take* a blessing of thy servant.
23. Be content, *take* two talents.
8: 8. *Take* a present in thine hand,
9: 1. *and take* this box of oil in thine hand,
17. Joram said, *Take* an horseman,
10: 6. *take ye* the heads of the men
13:15. *Take* bow and arrows.
18. he said, *Take* the arrows.
20: 7. *Take* a lump of figs.
1Ch 21:23. Ornan said unto David, *Take* (it)
2Ch 18:25. *Take ye* Micaiah, and carry him back
Est. 6:10. *take* the apparel and the horse,
Job 22:22. *Receive*, I pray thee, the law
42: 8. *take* unto you now seven bullocks
Pro. 4:10. Hear, O my son, *and receive* my sayings;
8:10. *Receive* my instruction,
20:16. *Take* his garment that is surety
27:13. *Take* his garment that is surety
Isa. 8: 1. *Take* thee a great roll,
23:16. *Take* an harp, go about the city,
47: 2. *Take* the millstones,
Jer. 13: 4. *Take* the girdle that thou hast got,
6. *and take* the girdle from thence,
25:15. *Take* the wine cup of this fury
29: 6. *Take ye* wives, and beget sons
— *and take* wives for your sons,
36: 2. *Take* thee a roll of a book,
14. *Take* in thine hand the roll
28. *Take* thee again another roll,
38:10. *Take* from hence thirty men
39:12. *Take him*, and look well to him,
43: 9. *Take* great stones
46:11. Go up into Gilead, *and take* balm,
51: 8. *take* balm for her pain,
Eze. 3:10. all my words...*receive* in thine heart,
4: 1. son of man, *take* thee a tile,
3. *take* thou unto thee an iron pan,
9. *Take* thou also unto thee wheat,
5: 1. *take* thee a sharp knife,
10: 6. *Take* fire from between the wheels,
37:16. thou son of man, *take* thee one stick,
— *then take* another stick,
Hos. 1: 2. *take* unto thee a wife
14: 2(3). *Take* with you words,
—(–). *and receive* (us) graciously: (marg. or, *give* good)
Jon. 4: 3. O Lord, *take*, I beseech thee, my life
Zec. 11:15. *Take* unto thee yet the instruments of

KAL.—*Future.*

Gen. 2:15. *And* the Lord God *took* the man,
21. *and he took* one of his ribs,
3: 6. *And* when the woman saw...*she took* of
4:19. *And* Lamech *took* unto him two wives:
6: 2. *and they took* them wives
7: 2. Of every clean beast *thou shalt take* to thee
8: 9. he put forth his hand, *and took her*,
20. *and took* of every clean beast,
9:23. *And* Shem and Japheth *took* a garment,
11:29. *And* Abram and Nahor *took* them wives:
31. *And* Terah *took* Abram his son,
12: 5. *And* Abram *took* Sarai his wife,
19. *so I might have taken* her
14:11. *And they took* all the goods of Sodom
12. *And they took* Lot,
Gen 14:23. *I will* not *take* any thing
24. *let them take* their portion.
15:10. *And he took* unto him all these,
16: 3. *And* Sarai...*took* Hagar her maid
17:23. *And* Abraham *took* Ishmael his son,
18: 5. *And I will fetch* a morsel of bread,
7. *and fetcht* a calf tender and good,
8. *And he took* butter, and milk,
20: 2. king of Gerar sent, *and took* Sarah.
14. *And* Abimelech *took* sheep, and oxen,
21:14. Abraham rose up early...*and took* bread,
21. *and* his mother *took* him a wife
27. *And* Abraham *took* sheep and oxen
30. *shalt thou take* of my hand,
22: 3. *and took* two of his young men
6. *And* Abraham *took* the wood
— *and he took* the fire
10. *and took* the knife to slay his son.
13. Abraham went *and took* the ram,
24: 3. *thou shalt* not *take* a wife unto my son
10. *And* the servant *took* ten camels
22. *that* the man *took* a golden earring
37. *Thou shalt* not *take* a wife to my son
61. *and* the servant *took* Rebekah,
65. *therefore she took* a vail,
67. *and took* Rebekah, and she became
25: 1. Then again Abraham *took* (lit. added *and took*) a wife,
26:34. *when he took* to wife Judith
27:14. he went, *and fetched*,
15. *And* Rebekah *took* goodly raiment
35. *and hath taken away* thy blessing.
28: 1, 6. *Thou shalt* not *take* a wife of
9. Then went Esau unto Ishmael, *and took*
11. *and he took* of the stones of that place,
18. *and took* the stone that he had put
29:23. *that he took* Leah his daughter,
30: 9. *she* (lit. *and she*) *took* Zilpah her maid,
37. *And* Jacob *took* him rods
31:23. *And he took* his brethren with him,
45. *And* Jacob *took* a stone,
46. *and they took* stones,
50. if *thou shalt take* (other) wives
32:13(14). *and took* of that which came
22(23). *and took* his two wives,
23(24). *And he took them*,
33:11. And he urged him, *and he took* (it).
34: 2. *And* when...*he took* her, and lay with her,
9. *take* our daughters unto you.
16. *we will take* your daughters
21. *let us take* their daughters
25. *that* two of the sons...*took* each man his
26. *and took* Dinah out of Shechem's house,
36: 6. *And* Esau *took* his wives,
37:24. *And they took him*,
31. *And they took* Joseph's coat,
38: 2. *and he took her*, and went in unto her.
6. *And* Judah *took* a wife for Er
23. *Let her take* (it) to her,
28. *and* the midwife *took* and bound upon his
39:20. *And* Joseph's master *took* him,
40:11. *and I took* the grapes,
42:16. *and let him fetch* your brother,
24. *and took* from them Simeon,
36. *ye will take* Benjamin (away):
43:15. *And* the men *took* that present,
46: 6. *And they took* their cattle,
48: 1. *and he took* with him his two sons,
13. *And* Joseph *took* them both,
Ex. 2: 1. *and took* (to wife) a daughter of Levi.
3. *And* when she could...*she took* for him an
5. she sent her maid *to fetch it.*
9. *And* the woman *took* the child,
4: 9. the water which *thou takest*
17. *thou shalt take* this rod
20. *And* Moses *took* his wife
— *and* Moses *took* the rod of God
25. *Then* Zipporah *took* a sharp stone,
6:20. *And* Amram *took* him Jochebed
23. *And* Aaron *took* him Elisheba,
7:15. the rod...*shalt thou take* in thine hand.
9:10. *And they took* ashes of the furnace,
10:26. thereof *must we take* to serve the Lord
12: 3. *they shall take* to them...a lamb,
5. *ye shall take* (it) out from the sheep,
13:19. *And* Moses *took* the bones of Joseph
14: 7. *And he took* six hundred chosen chariots,

Ex. 15:20. *And* Miriam...*took* a timbrel
16:16. *take ye* every man for (them)
17:12. *and they took* a stone,
18: 2. *Then* Jethro,...*took* Zipporah, Moses' wife,
12. *And* Jethro,...*took* a burnt offering
21:10. If *he take* him another (wife);
14. *thou shalt take him* from mine altar,
23: 8. *thou shalt take* no gift:
24: 6. *And* Moses *took* half of the blood,
7. *And he took* the book of the covenant,
8. *And* Moses *took* the blood,
25: 2. *that they bring* (marg. *take*) me an
— *ye shall take* my offering.
3. the offering which *ye shall take* of them;
27:20. *that they bring* thee pure oil
28: 5. they *shall take* gold,
29:15. *Thou shalt* also *take* one ram;
31. *thou shalt take* the ram
32: 4. *And he received* (them) at their hand,
20. *And he took* the calf which they had made,
33: 7. Moses *took* the tabernacle,
34: 4. *and took* in his hand the two tables
36: 3. *And they received* of Moses
40:20. *And he took* and put the testimony into the
Lev. 8:10. *And* Moses *took* the anointing oil,
15. *and* Moses *took* the blood,
16. *And he took* all the fat
23. *and* Moses *took* of the blood
25. *And he took* the fat,
28. *And* Moses *took* them from off their hands,
29. *And* Moses *took* the breast,
30. *And* Moses *took* of the anointing oil,
9: 5. *And they brought* (that) which Moses
15. *and took* the goat,
10: 1. *And* Nadab and Abihu,...*took* either of
14: 6. the living bird, *he shall take* it,
10. *he shall take* two he lambs
42. *he shall take* other morter,
15:14. *he shall take* to him two turtledoves,
29. *she shall take* unto her two turtles,
16: 5. *he shall take* of the congregation
18:17. neither *shalt thou take* her son's daughter,
18. Neither *shalt thou take* a wife to
20:14. if a man *take* a wife and her mother,
17. if a man *shall take* his sister,
21. if a man *shall take* his brother's wife,
21: 7. *They shall* not *take* a wife (that is) a
— neither *shall they take* a woman put away
13. he *shall take* a wife in her virginity.
14. *shall he* not *take:* but *he shall take* a virgin
24: 2. *that they bring* unto thee pure oil olive
25:36. *Take* thou no usury of him,
Nu. 1:17. *And* Moses and Aaron *took* these men
3:47. *shalt thou take* (them):
49. *And* Moses *took* the redemption money
5:17. the priest *shall take*, and put
7: 6. *And* Moses *took* the wagons
8: 8. and another young bullock *shalt thou take*
18. *And I have taken* the Levites
16: 1. *Now* Korah,...and Dathan and Abiram,...
took (men):
18. *And they took* every man his censer,
39(17:4). *And* Eleazar the priest *took* the
47(—:12). *And* Aaron *took* as Moses
17: 9(24). *and took* every man his rod.
18:26. When *ye take* of the children of Israel
28. your tithes, which *ye receive*
19: 2. *that they bring* thee a red heifer
20: 9. *And* Moses *took* the rod from before the
21:25. *And* Israel *took* all these cities:
26. *and taken* all his land
22:41. *that* Balak *took* Balaam,
23:14. *And he brought him* into the field of
27. *I will bring thee* unto another place;
28. *And* Balak *brought* Balaam unto
25: 7. *and took* a javelin in his hand;
27:22. *and he took* Joshua,
31:11. *And they took* all the spoil,
29. *Take* (it) of their half,
30. *thou shalt take* one portion
47. *Even*...Moses *took* one portion
51, 54. *And* Moses and Eleazar the priest *took*
34:18. *ye shall take* one prince
35:31, 32. *ye shall take* no satisfaction
Deu 1:15. *So I took* the chief of your tribes,
23. *and I took* twelve men of you,
25. *And they took* of the fruit

Deu 3: 8. *And we took* at that time
7: 3. nor his daughter *shalt thou take*
10:17. regardeth not persons, nor *taketh* reward:
16:19. neither *take* a gift:
20: 7. and another man *take her*
22: 6. *thou shalt* not *take* the dam with
7. and *take* the young to thee;
13. If any man *take* a wife,
30(23:1). A man *shall* not *take* his father's
24: 1. When a man *hath taken* a wife,
5. When a man *hath taken* a new wife,
29: 8(7). *And we took* their land,
30: 4. from thence *will he fetch thee:*
12. Who shall go up...*and bring it* unto us,
13. over the sea for us, *and bring it* unto us,
32:11. *taketh them*, beareth them on her wings:
Jos. 2: 4. *And* the woman *took* the two men,
7: 1. *for* Achan,...*took* of the accursed thing:
21. I coveted them, *and took them;*
23. *And they took them* out of the midst
24. *And* Joshua,...*took* Achan
8:12. *And he took* about five thousand men,
9: 4. *and took* old sacks upon their asses,
14. *And* the men *took* of their victuals, (marg.
or, *they received* the men by reason of)
11:16. *So* Joshua *took* all that land,
23. *So* Joshua *took* the whole land,
24: 3. *And I took* your father Abraham
26. *and took* a great stone,
Jud. 3: 6. *And they took* their daughters
21. *and took* the dagger from his right thigh,
25. *therefore they took* a key,
4:21. *Then* Jael Heber's wife *took* a nail
6:27. *Then* Gideon *took* ten men
7: 8. *So* the people *took* victuals
8:16. *And he took* the elders of the city,
21. *and took away* the ornaments
9:43. *And he took* the people,
48. *and* Abimelech *took* an ax
13:19. *So* Manoah *took* a kid
14:11. *that they brought* thirty companions
19. slew thirty men of them, *and took* their
15: 4. *and took* firebrands,
15. he found a new jawbone of an ass,...*and
took it,*
16:12. Delilah *therefore took* new ropes,
17: 4. *and* his mother *took* two hundred (shekels)
18:18. *and fetched* the carved image,
20. *and he took* the ephod,
19: 1. *who took* to him a concubine
28. *Then* the man *took her* (up)
29. *And* when...*he took* a knife,
Ru. 4: 2. *And he took* ten men
13. *So* Boaz *took* Ruth,
16. *And* Naomi *took* the child,
1 Sa. 2:14. the priest *took* for himself.
15. *he will* not *have* sodden flesh
4: 3. *Let us fetch* (marg. *take* unto us) the ark
5: 2. *When* the Philistines *took* the ark
3. *And they took* Dagon,
6:10. *and took* two milch kine,
7: 9. *And* Samuel *took* a sucking lamb,
12. *Then* Samuel *took* a stone,
8: 3. turned aside after lucre, *and took* bribes,
11. *He will take* your sons,
13. *he will take* your daughters
14. *he will take* your fields,
16. *he will take* your menservants,
9:22. *And* Samuel *took* Saul
10: 1. *Then* Samuel *took* a vial
23. they ran *and fetched him*
11: 7. *And he took* a yoke of oxen,
14:32. the people flew upon the spoil, *and took*
15:21. *But* the people *took* of the spoil,
16: 2. *Take* an heifer with thee,
13. *Then* Samuel *took* the horn
20. *And* Jesse *took* an ass
17:18. and *take* their pledge.
31. *and he sent for* (marg. *took*) *him.*
40. *And he took* his staff
49. *and took* thence a stone,
51. stood upon the Philistine, *and took* his
54. *And* David *took* the head of the Philistine,
57. Abner *took* him, and brought him before
18: 2. *And* Saul *took* him that day,
19:13. *And* Michal *took* an image,
21: 9(10). if *thou wilt take* that

1Sa.24: 2(3). *Then* Saul *took* three thousand chosen
25:18. Abigail made haste, *and took* two hundred
35. *So* David *received* of her hand
26:12. *So* David *took* the spear
22. the young men come over *and fetch it.*
28:24. *and took* flour, and kneaded (it),
30:11. they found...*and brought him* to David,
20. *And* David *took* all the flocks
31: 4. *Therefore* Saul *took* a sword,
12. *and took* the body of Saul
13. *And they took* their bones,
2Sa. 1:10. *and I took* the crown that (was) upon his
3:15. Ish-bosheth sent, *and took her*
4: 7. and beheaded him, *and took* his head,
5:13. *And* David *took* (him) more concubines
8: 1. *and* David *took* Metheg-ammah
7. *And* David *took* the shields
9: 5. king David sent, *and fetched* him
10: 4. *Wherefore* Hanun *took* David's servants,
11: 4. David sent messengers, *and took her;*
12: 4. *but took* the poor man's lamb,
10. *and hast taken* the wife of Uriah
30. *And he took* their king's crown
13: 8. *And she took* flour,
9. *And she took* a pan,
10. *And* Tamar *took* the cakes
19. *And* Tamar *put* ashes on her head,
14: 2. *and fetched* thence a wise woman,
17:19. *And* the woman *took* and spread a covering
18:14. *And he took* three darts in his hand,
17. *And they took* Absalom,
19:30(31). Yea, *let him take* all,
20: 3. *and* the king *took* the ten women
21: 8. *But* the king *took* the two sons
10. *And* Rizpah the daughter of Aiah *took*
12. David went *and took* the bones of Saul
22:17. He sent from above, *he took me;*
23: 6. *they cannot be taken* with hands:
24:22. *Let* my lord the king *take*
1K. 1:39. *And* Zadok the priest *took* an horn
3: 1. *and took* Pharaoh's daughter,
20. *and took* my son from beside me,
7:13. king Solomon sent *and fetched* Hiram
9:28. *and fetched* from thence gold,
10:28. king's merchants *received* the linen yarn
11:18. *they took* men with them
34. *I will* not *take* the whole kingdom
37. *I will take* thee,
14:26. *And he took away* the treasures
— *and he took away* all the shields
15:18. *Then* Asa *took* all the silver
16:31. *that he took* to wife Jezebel
17:19. *And he took* him out of her bosom,
23. *And* Elijah *took* the child,
18: 4. *that* Obadiah *took* an hundred prophets,
26. *And they took* the bullock
31. *And* Elijah *took* twelve stones,
19:21. *and took* a yoke of oxen,
2K. 2: 8. *And* Elijah *took* his mantle,
14. *And he took* the mantle of Elijah
20. *And they brought* (it) to him.
3:26. *And* when...*he took* with him seven hundred
27. *Then he took* his eldest son
5: 5. *and took* with him ten talents
16. *I will receive* none.
24. *And* when...*he took* (them) from their
6: 2. *and take* thence every man a beam,
7. he put out his hand, *and took it.*
13. that I may send *and fetch him.*
7:13. *Let* (some) *take,* I pray thee,
14. *They took therefore* two chariot
8: 9. *and took* a present with him,
15. *that he took* a thick cloth,
9:13. *and took* every man his garment,
10: 7. *that they took* the king's sons,
11: 2. *But* Jehosheba,...*took* Joash the son
4. Jehoiada sent *and fetched*
9. *and they took* every man his men
19. *And he took* the rulers over hundreds,
12: 5(6). *Let* the priests *take*
7(8). *receive* no (more) money
9(10). *But* Jehoiada the priest *took* a chest,
18(19). *And* Jehoash king of Judah *took* all
13:15. *And he took* unto him bow and arrows.
18. Take the arrows. *And he took* (them).
25. son of Jehoahaz *took* again (marg. returned *and took*)

2K. 14:21. *And* all the people of Judah *took* Azariah,
15:29. came Tiglath-pileser king of Assyria, *and took* Ijon,
16: 8. *And* Ahaz *took* the silver and gold
19:14. *And* Hezekiah *received* the letter
20: 7. *And they took* and laid (it) on the boil,
18. thy sons...*shall they take away;*
23:16. *and took* the bones out of the sepulchres,
30. *And* the people of the land *took* Jehoahaz
24:12. *and* the king of Babylon *took* him
25:18. *And* the captain of the guard *took* Seraiah
20. *And* Nebuzar-adan captain of the guard *took*
1Ch. 2:19. *And* when...Caleb *took* unto him Ephrath,
23. *And he took* Geshur,
10: 4. *So* Saul *took* a sword,
14: 3. *And* David *took* more wives
18: 1. *and took* Gath and her towns
7. *And* David *took* the shields
19: 4. *Wherefore* Hanun *took* David's servants,
20: 2. *And* David *took* the crown
2Ch. 1:16. the king's merchants *received* the linen
8:18. *and took* thence four hundred and fifty
11:18. *And* Rehoboam *took* him Mahalath
12: 9. *and took* away the treasures
— *he carried away also* the shields
22:11. *But* Jehoshabeath...*took* Joash
23: 1. *and took* the captains of hundreds,
8. *and took* every man his men
20. *And he took* the captains
26: 1. *Then* all the people of Judah *took* Uzziah,
36: 1. *Then* the people of the land *took* Jehoahaz
Neh. 5: 2. *therefore we take* up corn
3. *that we might buy* corn,
15. *and had taken* of them bread and wine,
10:30(31). nor *take* their daughters for
31(32). *we would* not *buy* it of them
Est. 6:11. *Then took* Haman the apparel
Job. 1:15. the Sabeans fell (upon them), *and took them away;*
17. *and have carried them away,*
2: 8. *And he took* him a potsherd
3: 6. *let* darkness *seize upon it;*
4:12. *and* mine ear *received* a little
5: 5. and *taketh it* even out of the thorns,
12:20. and *taketh away* the understanding
15:12. Why *doth* thine heart *carry thee away?*
27:13. *they shall receive* of the Almighty.
35: 7. what *receiveth he* of thine hand?
38:20. That *thou shouldest take it*
40:24. *He taketh it* with his eyes:
41: 4(40:28). *wilt thou take him* for a servant
Ps. 6: 9(10). the Lord *will receive* my prayer.
18:16(17). He sent from above, *he took me,*
49:15(16). *he shall receive me.*
17(18). *he shall carry* nothing *away:*
50: 9. *I will take* no bullock out of
51:11(13). *take* not thy holy spirit from me.
73:24. and afterward *receive me* (to) glory.
75: 2(3). When *I shall receive* the congregation
78:70. *and took him* from the sheepfolds:
109: 8. *let* another *take* his office.
Pro. 1:19. *taketh away* the life of the owners
2: 1. if *thou wilt receive* my words,
6:25. neither *let her take thee* with her eyelids.
10: 8. wise in heart *will receive* commandments:
17:23. A wicked (man) *taketh* a gift
21:11. when the wise is instructed, *he receiveth* knowledge.
22:27. why *should he take away* thy bed from
31:16. She considereth a field, *and buyeth it:*
Isa. 28:19. it goeth forth *it shall take* you:
37:14. *And* Hezekiah *received* the letter
39: 7. thy sons...*shall they take away;*
44:14. *and taketh* the cypress and the oak,
15. *for he will take* thereof,
47: 3. *I will take* vengeance,
56:12. *I will fetch* wine,
57:13. vanity *shall take* (them):
66:21. *I will* also *take* of them
Jer. 9:20(19). *and let* your ear *receive* the word
13: 7. *and took* the girdle from the place
15:15. *take me* not *away* in thy longsuffering:
16: 2. *Thou shalt* not *take* thee a wife,
20:10. *and we shall take* our revenge
25:17. *Then took I* the cup
28:10. *Then* Hananiah the prophet *took* the yoke
32:11. *So I took* the evidence

Jer.35: 3. *Then I took* Jaazaniah
13. *Will ye* not *receive* instruction
36:14. *So* Baruch the son of Neriah *took* the roll
21. *and he took it* out of Elishama the scribe's
37:17. Zedekiah the king sent, *and took him out:*
38: 6. *Then took* they Jeremiah,
11. *So* Ebed-melech *took* the men
— *and took* thence old cast clouts
14. *and took* Jeremiah the prophet
39: 5. *when they had taken* him,
14. they sent, *and took* Jeremiah
40: 2. *And* the captain of the guard *took*
41:12. *Then they took* all the men,
16. *Then took* Johanan the son of Kareah,
43: 5. *But* Johanan...*took* all the remnant of
49:29. their flocks *shall they take away:*
51:26. *they shall* not *take* of thee a stone
52:24. *And* the captain of the guard *took*
26. *So* Nebuzar-adan the captain of the guard *took*
Eze. 3:14. the spirit lifted me up, *and took me away,*
5: 1. *take* thee a barber's razor,
4. Then *take* of them again,
8: 3. *and took me* by a lock of mine head;
10: 7. *who took* (it), and went out.
15: 3. *will* (men) *take* a pin of it
16:16. *And* of thy garments *thou didst take,*
17. *Thou hast also taken* thy fair jewels
18. *And tookest* thy broidered garments,
20. *Moreover thou hast taken* thy sons
32. *taketh* strangers instead of her husband!
17: 3. *and took* the highest branch of the cedar:
5. *He took also* of the seed of the land,
12. *and hath taken* the king thereof,
13. *And hath taken* of the king's seed,
18: 8. neither *hath taken* any increase,
19: 5. *then she took* another of her whelps,
22:25. *they have taken* the treasure
23:25. *they shall take* thy sons and
33: 4. if the sword come, *and take him away,*
6. if the sword come, *and take* (any) person
36:30. *ye shall receive* no more reproach
44:22. Neither *shall they take* for their wives a
— *they shall take* maidens
45:18. *thou shalt take* a young bullock
46:18. the prince *shall* not *take* of the people's
Hos. 1: 3. So he went *and took* Gomer
4:11. and new wine *take away* the heart.
10: 6. Ephraim *shall receive* shame,
13:11. *and took* (him) *away* in my wrath.
Am. 5:11. *ye take* from him burdens of wheat:
7:15. *And* the Lord *took me*
9: 2. *shall* mine hand *take them;*
Mic. 1:11. *he shall receive* of you his standing.
2: 9. their children *have ye taken away*
Zep 3: 7. *thou wilt receive* instruction;
Hag 2:23. In that day,...*will I take thee,*
Zec.11: 7. *And I took* unto me two staves;
10. *And I took* my staff,
13. *And I took* the thirty (pieces)

KAL.—*Participle.* Poël.

Gen 19:14. his sons in law, *which married* his
27:46. if Jacob *take* a wife
Deu 27:25. *he that taketh* reward to slay an innocent
2Sa. 4: 6. (as though) *they would have fetched* wheat;
2K. 2: 3, 5. the Lord *will take away* thy master
Pro. 9: 7. that reproveth a scorner *getteth*...shame:
11:30. *and he that winneth* (marg. *taketh*) souls
Jer. 23:31. *that use* (marg. or, *smooth*) their tongues,
Eze.24:16. I *take away* from thee the desire of
37:19. I *will take* the stick of Joseph,
21. I *will take* the children of Israel
Am. 5:12. they afflict the just, *they take* a bribe,

KAL.—*Participle.* Paül.

Pro.24:11. (them that are) *drawn* unto death,

* NIPHAL.—*Preterite.* *

1Sa. 4:11. the ark of God *was taken;*
17. the ark of God *is taken.*
22. for the ark of God *is taken.*
Eze.33: 6. he *is taken away* in his iniquity;

NIPHAL.—*Infinitive.*

1Sa. 4:19, 21. the ark of God *was taken,*
21: 6(7). *when it was taken away.*

NIPHAL.—*Future.*

2K. 2: 9. before *I be taken away* from thee.
Est. 2: 8. *that* Esther *was brought also*
16. *So* Esther *was taken* unto king Ahasuerus

* PUAL.—*Preterite.* *

Gen 2:23. she *was taken* out of Man.
3:19. out of it *wast thou taken:*
23. the ground from whence *he was taken.*
Jud.17: 2. (shekels) of silver that *were taken*
2K. 2:10. (when I am) *taken* from thee,
Isa. 52: 5. my people *is taken away*
53: 8. *He was taken* from prison
Jer. 29:22. *And* of them *shall be taken up*
48:46. thy sons *are taken* captives,

* HOPHAL.—*Future.* *

Gen12:15. *and* the woman *was taken* into Pharaoh's
18: 4. *Let* a little water, I pray you, *be fetched,*
Job 28: 2. Iron *is taken* out of the earth,
Isa. 49:24. *Shall* the prey *be taken* from the mighty,
25. of the mighty *shall be taken away,*
Eze.15: 3. *Shall* wood *be taken* thereof

* HITHPAEL.—*Participle.* *

Ex. 9:24. fire *mingled* with the hail,
Eze. 1: 4. a fire *infolding* (marg. *catching*) *itself,*

לֶקַח *leh'-kagh,* m. 3948

Deu 32: 2. *My doctrine* shall drop as the rain,
Job 11: 4. *My doctrine* (is) pure,
Pro. 1: 5. and will increase *learning;*
4: 2. I give you good *doctrine,*
7:21. With *her* much *fair speech*
9: 9. he will increase in *learning.*
16:21. sweetness of the lips increaseth *learning.*
23. and addeth *learning* to his lips.
Isa. 29:24. they that murmured shall learn *doctrine.*

לָקַט [*lāh-kat'*]. 3950

* KAL.—*Preterite.* *

Ex. 16: 4. the people shall go out *and gather*
18. *they gathered* every man
22. the sixth day *they gathered* twice as much
Nu. 11: 8. the people went about, *and gathered*

KAL.—*Infinitive.*

Ex. 16:27. on the seventh day *for to gather,*
Ru. 2: 8. Go not *to glean* in another field,
Cant.6: 2. to feed in the gardens, *and to gather* lilies.

KAL.—*Imperative.*

Gen31:46. Jacob said unto his brethren, *Gather*
Ex. 16:16. *Gather* of it every man

KAL.—*Future.*

Ex. 16: 5. twice as much as *they gather* daily.
17. the children of Israel did so, *and gathered,*
21. *And they gathered* it every morning,
26. Six days *ye shall gather it;*
Ps.104:28. thou givest them *they gather:*

* PIEL.—*Preterite.* *

Ru. 2:16. *that she may glean* (them),
17. and beat out that *she had gleaned:*
18. mother in law saw what *she had gleaned:*
19. Where *hast thou gleaned* to day?

PIEL.—*Infinitive.*

Ru. 2:15. when she was risen up *to glean,*
23. *to glean* unto the end of barley harvest
2K. 4:39. one went out...*to gather* herbs,

PIEL.—*Future.*

Gen47:14. *And* Joseph *gathered up* all the money
Lev.19: 9. neither *shalt thou gather* the gleanings
10. neither *shalt thou gather* (every) grape
23:22. neither *shalt thou gather* any gleaning
Ru. 2: 2. *and glean* ears of corn
3. *and gleaned* in the field
7. *let me glean* and gather
15. *Let her glean* even among the sheaves,
17. *So she gleaned* in the field
1Sa.20:38. *And* Jonathan's lad *gathered up* the arrows,
2K. 4:39. *and gathered* thereof wild gourds

PIEL.—*Participle.*

Jud. 1: 7. *gathered* (marg. *gleaned*) (their meat)
Isa. 17: 5. *as he that gathereth* ears in the valley
Jer. 7:18. The children *gather* wood,

* PUAL.—*Future.* *

Isa. 27:12. *ye shall be gathered* one by one,

* HITHPAEL.—*Future.* *

Jud.11: 3. *and there were gathered* vain men

3951 לֶקֶט *leh'-ket*, m.

Lev.19: 9. neither (lit. *and* not). *the gleanings of*
23:22. neither (lit. *and* not)...*any gleaning of* thy

3952 לָקַק [*lāh-kak'*].

* KAL.—*Preterite.* *

1K. 21:19. where dogs *licked* the blood of Naboth

KAL.—*Future.*

Jud. 7: 5. Every one that *lappeth*
— as a dog *lappeth*,
1K. 21:19. *shall* dogs *lick* thy blood,
22:38. *and* the dogs *licked* up his blood;

* PIEL.—*Participle.* *

Jud. 7: 6. the number of them *that lapped*,
7. the three hundred men *that lapped*

3953 לָקַשׁ [*lāh-kash'*].

* PIEL.—*Future.* *

Job 24: 6. *they gather* the vintage of the wicked. (marg. the wicked *gather* the vintage)

3954 לֶקֶשׁ *leh'-kesh*, m.

Am. 7: 1. the shooting up *of the latter growth*; and, lo, (it was) *the latter growth* after

3955 לְשַׁד *l'shad*, m.

Nu. 11: 8. as the taste of *fresh* oil.
Ps. 32: 4. *my moisture* is turned into the drought

3956 לָשׁוֹן *lāh-shōhn'*, com.

Gen10: 5. every one after *his tongue*,
20. after their families, *after their tongues*,
31. *after their tongues*, in their lands,
Ex. 4:10. I (am) slow of speech, and of *a* slow *tongue*.
11: 7. shall not a dog move *his tongue*,
Deu28:49. a nation whose (lit. who *its*) *tongue*
Jos. 7:21. *and a wedge* (marg. *tongue*) *of* gold of
24. *the wedge of* gold,
10:21. none moved *his tongue*
15: 2. *the bay* (marg. *tongue*) that looketh
5. *from the bay of* the sea
18:19. *the* north *bay* (marg. *tongue*) *of* the salt sea
Jud. 7: 5. Every one that lappeth...*with his tongue*,
2Sa.23: 2. his word (was) in *my tongue*.
Neh13:24. *but according to the language of* each people.
Est. 1:22. to every people *after their language*,
— *according to the language of* every people.
3:12. (to) every people *after their language*;
8: 9. unto every people *after their language*,
— *and according to their language*.
Job 5:21. the scourge *of the tongue*:
6:30. Is there iniquity *in my tongue*?
15: 5. thou choosest *the tongue of* the crafty.
20:12. he hide it under *his tongue*;
16. the viper's *tongue* shall slay him.
27: 4. *nor my tongue* utter deceit.
29:10. *and their tongue* cleaved to the roof of
33: 2. *my tongue* hath spoken
41: 1(40:25). or *his tongue* with a cord
Ps. 5: 9(10). they flatter *with their tongue*.
10: 7. under *his tongue* (is) mischief
12: 3(4). *the tongue* that speaketh proud things:
4(5). *With our tongue* will we prevail;
15: 3. backbiteth not with *his tongue*,
22:15(16). *and my tongue* cleaveth to my jaws;
31:20(21). from the strife of *tongues*.
34:13(14). Keep *thy tongue* from evil,
35:28. *And my tongue* shall speak of
37:30. *and his tongue* talketh of judgment.
39: 1(2). that I sin not with *my tongue*:
3(4). spake I *with my tongue*,
45: 1(2). *my tongue* (is) the pen of a ready
50:19. *and thy tongue* frameth deceit.
51:14(16). *my tongue* shall sing aloud
52: 2(4). *Thy tongue* deviseth mischiefs;
4(6). O (thou) deceitful *tongue*.
55: 9(10). divide *their tongues*:
57: 4(5). *and their tongue* a sharp sword.
64: 3(4). whet *their tongue* like a sword,
8(9). they shall make *their own tongue* to fall
66:17. he was extolled with *my tongue*.
68:23(24). *the tongue* of thy dogs
71:24. *My tongue* also shall talk of
73: 9. *their tongue* walketh through
78:36. *and* they lied unto him *with their tongues*.
109: 2. spoken against me with *a* lying *tongue*.
119:172. *My tongue* shall speak
120: 2. *from a* deceitful *tongue*.
3. what shall be done unto thee, thou false *tongue*?
126: 2. *and our tongue* with singing:
137: 6. let *my tongue* cleave to the roof of my
139: 4. not a word *in my tongue*,
140: 3(4). They have sharpened *their tongues*
11(12). Let not an evil speaker (marg. a man of *tongue*) be established
Pro. 6:17. A proud look, *a* lying *tongue*,
24. *the tongue of* a strange woman.
10:20. *The tongue of* the just
31. *but the* froward *tongue* shall be cut out.
12:18. *but the tongue of* the wise (is) health.
19. *a* lying *tongue* (is) but for a moment.
15: 2. *The tongue of* the wise
4. *A* wholesome *tongue*
16: 1. the answer *of the tongue*,
17: 4. a liar giveth ear to *a* naughty *tongue*.
20. he that hath *a* perverse *tongue* (lit. is perverse *in his tongue*)
18:21. in the power of *the tongue*:
21: 6. The getting of treasures *by a* lying *tongue*
23. Whoso keepeth his mouth *and his tongue*
25:15. *and a* soft *tongue* breaketh the bone.
23. angry countenance *a* backbiting *tongue*.
26:28. *A* lying *tongue* hateth
28:23. he that flattereth *with the tongue*.
31:26. in *her tongue* (is) the law of kindness.
Ecc.10:11. a babbler (marg. the master of *the tongue*)
Cant.4:11. honey and milk (are) under *thy tongue*;
Isa. 3: 8. *their tongue* and their doings
5:24. the fire (marg. *the tongue of* fire) devoureth
11:15. *the tongue of* the Egyptian sea;
28:11. with stammering lips *and* another *tongue*
30:27. *his tongue* as a devouring fire:
32: 4. *and the tongue* of the stammerers
33:19. of *a* stammering *tongue*,
35: 6. *the tongue of* the dumb sing:
41:17. *their tongue* faileth for thirst,
45:23. every *tongue* shall swear.
50: 4. *the tongue of* the learned,
54:17. every *tongue* (that) shall rise against thee
57: 4. draw out *the tongue*?
59: 3. *your tongue* hath muttered perverseness.
66:18. I will gather all nations *and tongues*;
Jer. 5:15. a nation *whose language* thou knowest not.
9: 3(2). they bend *their tongues*
5(4). they have taught *their tongue*
8(7). *Their tongue* (is as) an arrow
18:18. let us smite him *with the tongue*,
23:31. the prophets,...that use *their tongues*,
Lam 4: 4. *The tongue of* the sucking child
Eze. 3: 5. a people...of *an* hard *language*,
6. many people...of *an* hard *language*,
26. *And* I will make *thy tongue* cleave to
36: 3. ye are taken up in the lips of *talkers*, (lit. of *the tongue*)
Dan 1: 4. *and the tongue of* the Chaldeans.
Hos. 7:16. the rage of *their tongue*:

Mic. 6:12. *and their tongue* (is) deceitful
Zep. 3:13. neither shall *a* deceitful *tongue* be found
Zec. 8:23. out of all *languages*
14:12. *their tongue* shall consume away

3957 לִשְׁכָּה *lish-kāh'*, f.

1Sa. 9:22. and brought them *into the parlour*,
2K. 23:11. *the chamber of* Nathan-melech the
1Ch 9:26. over *the chambers* (marg. or, *storehouses*)
33. Levites, (who remaining) *in the chambers*
23:28. in the courts, and in *the chambers*,
28:12. all *the chambers* round about,
2Ch 31:11. to prepare *chambers* (marg. *storehouses*)
Ezr. 8:29. *in the chambers of* the house
10: 6. *the chamber of* Johanan
Neh 10:37(38). to *the chambers of* the house of
38(39). to *the chambers*, into the treasure
39(40). unto *the chambers*, where (are) the
13: 4. *of the chamber of* the house of our God,
5. he had prepared for him *a* great *chamber*,
8. out of *the chamber*.
9. they cleansed *the chambers* :
Jer. 35: 2. into one of *the chambers*,
4. *the chamber of* the sons of Hanan,
— by *the chamber of* the princes, which (was) above *the chamber of* Maaseiah
36:10. *in the chamber of* Gemariah
12. into the scribe's *chamber* :
20. *in the chamber* of Elishama
21. it *out of* Elishama the scribe's *chamber*.
Eze. 40:17. (there were) *chambers*,
— thirty *chambers* (were) upon the pavement.
38. *And the chambers* and the entries
44. *the chambers of* the singers
45. This *chamber*, whose prospect
46. *And the chamber* whose prospect
41:10. And between *the chambers*
42: 1. into *the chamber* that (was) over
4. And before *the chambers*
5. *the* upper *chambers*
7. over against *the chambers*, toward the utter court on the forepart of *the chambers*,
8. the length of *the chambers*
9. from under these *chambers*
10. *The chambers* (were) in the thickness
11. the appearance of *the chambers*
12. the doors of *the chambers*
13. *The* north *chambers* (and) *the* south *chambers*, which (are) before the separate place, they (be) *holy chambers*,
44:19. *in the* holy *chambers*,
45: 5. a possession for twenty *chambers*.
46:19. into *the* holy *chambers*

3958 לֶשֶׁם *leh'-shem*, m.

Ex. 28:19 & 39:12. the third row *a ligure*,

3960 לָשַׁן [*lāh-shan'*].

* PIEL.—*Participle.* *

Ps.101: 5. Whoso privily *slandereth* his neighbour,

* POEL.—*Participle.* *

Ps.101: 5. (כתיב) Whoso privily *slandereth* his

* HIPHIL.—*Future.* *

Pro.30:10. *Accuse* not (marg. *Hurt* not *with thy tongue*) a servant unto his master,

3961 לִשָּׁן *lish-shāhn'*, com. Ch.

Dan 3: 4. O people, nations, *and languages*,
7. the people, the nations, *and the languages*,
29. That every people, nation, *and language*,
4: 1(3:31). all people, nations, *and languages*,
5:19. people, nations, *and languages*, trembled
6:25(26). all people, nations, *and languages*,
7:14. that all people, nations, *and languages*,

לֶתֶךְ *leh'-thech*, m. 3963

Hos. 3: 2. *and an half homer* (marg. *lethech*) *of* barley:

מ *mem*.

The thirteenth letter of the alphabet.

מָא *māh*, Ch. part. 3964

Ezr. 6: 8. I make a decree *what* (לְמָא דִי) ye shall

מַאֲבוּס [*mah-ăvoos'*], m. 3965

Jer. 50:26. open *her storehouses* :

מְאֹד *m'ōhd*, m. 3966

[Commonly used as an adverb].

Gen 1:31. and, behold, (it was) *very* good.
4: 5. And Cain was *very* wroth, and his
7:18. were increased *greatly* upon the earth;
19. And the waters prevailed *exceedingly* (מְאֹד מְאֹד) upon
12:14. beheld the woman that she (was) *very* fair.
13: 2. And Abram (was) *very* rich in cattle,
13. and sinners before the Lord *exceedingly*.
15: 1. (and) thy *exceeding* great reward.
17: 2. and will multiply thee *exceedingly*. (בִּמְאֹד מְאֹד)
6. I will make thee *exceeding* (*id.*) fruitful,
20. and will multiply him *exceedingly*; (*id.*)
18:20. and because their sin is *very* grievous;
19: 3. he pressed upon them *greatly*; and they
9. pressed *sore* upon the man, (even) Lot,
20: 8. and the men were *sore* afraid.
21:11. thing was *very* grievous in Abraham's sight
24:16. the damsel (was) *very* fair to look upon,
35. the Lord hath blessed my master *greatly*;
26:13. and grew until he became *very* great:
16. for thou art *much* mightier than we.
27:33. Isaac trembled very *exceedingly*, (marg. trembled with a great trembling *greatly*)
34. with a great and *exceeding* bitter cry,
30:43. And the man increased *exceedingly*, (מְאֹד מְאֹד)
32: 7(8). Then Jacob was *greatly* afraid
34: 7. were *very* wroth, because he had wrought
12. Ask me *never so much* dowry and gift,
41:19. poor and *very* ill favoured and leanfleshed,
31. for it (shall be) *very* grievous.
49. *very* much, until he left numbering;
47:13. for the famine (was) *very* sore, so that
27. and grew, and multiplied *exceedingly*.
50: 9. and it was a *very* great company.
10. with a great and *very* sore lamentation:
Ex. 1: 7. waxed *exceeding* (בִּמְאֹד מְאֹד) mighty;
20. people multiplied, and waxed *very* mighty.
9: 3. (there shall be) a *very* grievous murrain.
18. cause it to rain a *very* grievous hail,
24. fire mingled with the hail, *very* grievous,
10:14. of Egypt: *very* grievous (were they);
19. Lord turned a *mighty* strong west wind,
11: 3. (was) *very* great in the land of Egypt,
12:38. and herds, (even) *very* much cattle.
14:10. marched after them; and they were *sore*
19:16. the voice of the trumpet *exceeding* loud;
18. and the whole mount quaked *greatly*.
19. and waxed *louder and louder*,
Nu. 11:10. anger of the Lord was kindled *greatly*;
33. smote the people with a *very* great plague.
12: 3. the man Moses (was) *very* meek, above all
13:28. and the cities (are) walled, (and) *very*

Nu. 14: 7. to search it, (is) an *exceeding* (מְאֹד מְאֹד) good land.
39. and the people mourned *greatly*.
16:15. And Moses was *very* wroth, and said
22: 3. And Moab was *sore* afraid of the people,
17. will promote thee unto *very* great honour,
32: 1. children of Gad had a *very* great multitude
Deu 2: 4. ye *good* heed unto yourselves therefore:
3: 5. beside unwalled towns a *great* many.
4: 9. and keep thy soul *diligently*, lest
15. ye therefore *good* heed unto yourselves;
6: 3. and that ye may increase *mightily*,
5. with all thy soul, and with all *thy might*.
9:20. And the Lord was *very* angry with Aaron
17:17. neither shall he *greatly* multiply to himself
20:15. cities (which are) *very* far off from thee,
24: 8. leprosy, that thou observe *diligently*,
28:54. tender among you, and *very* delicate,
30:14. But the word (is) *very* nigh unto thee,
Jos. 1: 7. be thou strong and *very* courageous,
3:16. an heap *very* far from the city Adam,
8: 4. go not *very* far from the city, but be
9: 9. From a *very* far country thy servants
13. by reason of the *very* long journey.
22. We (are) *very* far from you;
24. therefore we were *sore* afraid of our lives
10: 2. That they feared *greatly*, because Gibeon
20. slaying them with a *very* great slaughter,
11: 4. with horses and chariots *very* many.
13: 1. *very* much land to be possessed.
22: 5. take *diligent* heed to do the commandment
8. and with *very* much cattle, with silver,
— and with *very* much raiment:
23: 6. Be ye therefore *very* courageous to keep
11. Take *good* heed therefore unto yourselves,
Jud. 2:15. and they were *greatly* distressed.
3:17. and Eglon (was) a *very* fat man.
6: 6. And Israel was *greatly* impoverished
10: 9. so that Israel was *sore* distressed.
11:33. the vineyards, with a *very* great slaughter.
12: 2. I and my people were at *great* strife
13: 6. of an angel of God, *very* terrible:
15:18. And he was *sore* athirst, and called
18: 9. the land, and, behold, it (is) *very* good:
19:11. by Jebus, the day was *far* spent;
Ru. 1:13. for it grieveth me *much* for your
20. hath dealt *very* bitterly with me.
1Sa. 2:17. the sin of the young men was *very* great
22. Now Eli was *very* old, and heard all that
4:10. and there was a *very* great slaughter;
5: 9. the city with a *very* great destruction:
11. the hand of God was *very* heavy there.
11: 6. and his anger was kindled *greatly*.
15. the men of Israel rejoiced *greatly*.
12:18. and all the people *greatly* feared the Lord
14:20. (and there was) a *very* great discomfiture.
31. and the people were *very* faint.
16:21. and he loved him *greatly*;
17:11. they were dismayed, and *greatly* afraid.
24. fled from him, and were *sore* afraid.
18: 8. And Saul was *very* wroth,
15. that he behaved himself *very* wisely,
30. so that his name was *much* set by.
19: 2(1). Saul's son delighted *much* in David:
4. (have been) to thee-ward *very* good:
20:19. (then) thou shalt go down *quickly*, (marg. *greatly*, or, *diligently*)
21:12(13). and was *sore* afraid of Achish
25: 2. and the man (was) *very* great,
15. But the men (were) *very* good unto us,
36. for he (was) *very* (עַד מְאֹד) drunken:
26:21. the fool, and have erred *exceedingly*..
28: 5. and his heart *greatly* trembled.
15. Saul answered, I am *sore* distressed;
20. on the earth, and was *sore* afraid,
21. and saw that he was *sore* troubled,
30: 6. And David was *greatly* distressed;
31: 3. and he was *sore* wounded of the archers.
4. would not; for he was *sore* afraid.
2Sa. 1:26. *very* pleasant hast thou been unto me:
2:17. there was a *very* sore battle that day;
3: 8. Then was Abner *very* wroth for the
8: 8. king David took *exceeding* much brass.
10: 5. because the men were *greatly* ashamed:
11: 2. and the woman (was) *very* beautiful
12: 2. The rich (man) had *exceeding* many flocks

2Sa. 12: 5. David's anger was *greatly* kindled
30. spoil of the city in *great* abundance.
13: 3. and Jonadab (was) a *very* subtil man.
15. Amnon hated her exceedingly; (marg. with great hatred *greatly*)
21. all these things, he was *very* wroth.
36. and all his servants wept *very* sore.
14:25. to be *so much* praised as Absalom
18:17. laid a *very* great heap of stones upon him:
19:32(33). Barzillai was a *very* aged man,
—(—). for he (was) a *very* great man.
24:10. I have sinned *greatly* in that I have done:
— for I have done *very* foolishly.
14. I am in a *great* strait:
1K. 1: 4. And the damsel (was) *very* fair,
6. and he also (was a) *very* goodly (man);
15. and the king was *very* old;
2:12. his kingdom was established *greatly*.
4:29(5:9). and understanding *exceeding* much,
5: 7(21). of Solomon, that he rejoiced *greatly*,
7:47. because they were *exceeding* (מְאֹד מְאֹד) many:
10: 2. to Jerusalem with a *very* great train,
— and *very* much gold, and precious stones:
10. and of spices *very* great store,
11. from Ophir *great* plenty of almug trees,
11:19. And Hadad found *great* favour in the
17:17. and his sickness was *so sore*, that there
18: 3. Now Obadiah feared the Lord *greatly*:
21:26. And he did *very* abominably in following
2 K. 10: 4. But they were *exceedingly* (מְאֹד מְאֹד) afraid,
14:26. affliction of Israel, (that it was) *very* bitter:
17:18. Therefore the Lord was *very* angry
21:16. Manasseh shed innocent blood *very* much,
23:25. and with all *his might*, according to
1Ch 10: 4. for he was *sore* afraid.
16:25. and *greatly* to be praised:
18: 8. brought David *very* much brass,
19: 5. for the men were *greatly* ashamed.
20: 2. *exceeding* much spoil out of the city.
21: 8. David said unto God, I have sinned *greatly*,
— for I have done *very* foolishly.
13. I am in a *great* strait:
— for *very* great (are) his mercies:
2Ch 4:18. these vessels in *great* abundance:
7: 8. a *very* great congregation,
9: 1. with a *very* great company,
9. and of spices *great* abundance,
11:12. and made them exceeding strong, (lit. and strengthened them to a multitude of *strength*)
14:13(12). they carried away *very* much spoil.
16: 8. with *very* many chariots and horsemen?
14. they made a *very* (עַד מְאֹד) great burning for him.
24:24. a *very* great host into their hand,
25:10. was *greatly* kindled against Judah,
30:13. second month, a *very* great congregation.
32:27. Hezekiah had *exceeding* much riches
29. had given him substance *very* much.
33:12. and humbled himself *greatly* before
14. raised it up a *very* great height,
35:23. for I am *sore* wounded.
Ezr. 10: 1. a *very* great congregation of men and
Neh 2: 2. Then I was *very* sore afraid,
4: 7(1). then they were *very* wroth,
5: 6. And I was *very* angry when I heard
6:16. were *much* cast down in their own eyes:
8:17. And there was *very* great gladness.
13: 8. And it grieved me *sore*:
Est. 1:12. therefore was the king *very* wroth.
4: 4. Then was the queen *exceedingly* grieved;
Job 1: 3. and a *very* great houshold;
2:13. they saw that (his) grief was *very* great.
8: 7. thy latter end should *greatly* increase.
35:15. knoweth (it) not in *great* extremity:
Ps. 6: 3(4). My soul is also *sore* vexed:
10(11). enemies be ashamed and *sore* vexed:
21: 1(2). salvation how *greatly* shall he rejoice!
31:11(12). but *especially* among my neighbours,
38: 6(7). I am bowed down *greatly*; (עַד מְאֹד)
8(9). I am feeble and *sore* (*id.*) broken:
46: 1(2). a *very* present help in trouble.
47: 9(10). he is *greatly* exalted.

Ps. 48: 1(2). and *greatly* to be praised in the city
50: 3. and it shall be *very* tempestuous
78:29. So they did eat, and were *well* filled:
59. was wroth, and *greatly* abhorred Israel:
79: 8. for we are brought *very* low.
92: 5(6). (and) thy thoughts are *very* deep.
93: 5. Thy testimonies are *very* sure:
96: 4. and *greatly* to be praised:
97: 9. thou art exalted *far* above all gods.
104: 1. Lord my God, thou art *very* great;
105:24. And he increased his people *greatly*;
107:38. so that they are multiplied *greatly*;
109:30. I will *greatly* praise the Lord
112: 1. delighteth *greatly* in his commandments.
116:10. I was *greatly* afflicted:
119: 4. to keep thy precepts *diligently*.
8. O forsake me not *utterly*.
43. truth *utterly* out of my mouth;
51. have had me *greatly* in derision:
96. thy commandment (is) *exceeding* broad.
107. I am afflicted *very much*: (עַד מְאֹד)
138. (are) righteous and *very* faithful.
140. Thy word (is) *very* pure:
167. and I love them *exceedingly*.
139:14. and (that) my soul knoweth *right well*. (marg. *greatly*)
142: 6(7). for I am brought *very* low:
145: 3. the Lord, and *greatly* to be praised;
Isa. 16: 6. pride of Moab; (he is) *very* proud:
31: 1. because they are *very* strong;
47: 6. hast thou *very* heavily laid thy yoke.
9. for the *great* abundance of thine
52:13. and extolled, and be *very* high.
56:12. as this day, (and) *much* more abundant.
64: 9(8). Be not wroth *very sore*, O Lord,
12(11). hold thy peace, and afflict us *very sore*?
Jer. 2:10. and consider *diligently*, and see if there
12. be ye *very* desolate, saith the Lord.
36. Why gaddest thou about *so much*
9:19(18). we are *greatly* confounded, because
14:17. a great breach, with a *very* grievous blow.
18:13. Israel hath done a *very* horrible thing.
20:11. they shall be *greatly* ashamed;
24: 2. One basket (had) *very* good figs,
— the other basket (had) *very* naughty figs.
3. the good figs, *very* good; and the evil, *very* evil, that cannot be eaten,
40:12. wine and summer fruits *very* much.
48:16. and his affliction hasteth *fast*.
29. pride of Moab, he is *exceeding* proud
49:30. Flee, get you *far* off, dwell deep,
50:12. Your mother shall be *sore* confounded;
Lam. 5:22. thou art *very* (עַד מְאֹד) wroth against
Eze. 9: 9. and Judah (is) *exceeding* (בִּמְאֹד מְאֹד) great,
16:13. and thou wast *exceeding* (*id.*) beautiful,
20:13. and my sabbaths they *greatly* polluted:
27:25. made *very* glorious in the midst of the
37: 2. *very* many in the open valley; and, lo, (they were) *very* dry.
10. an *exceeding* (מְאֹד מְאֹד) great army.
40: 2. and set me upon a *very* high mountain,
47: 7. of the river (were) *very* many trees
9. shall be a *very* great multitude of fish,
10. fish of the great sea, *exceeding* many.
Dan. 8: 8. Therefore the he goat waxed *very* (עַד מְאֹד) great:
11:25. with a *very* (*id.*) great and mighty army;
Joel 2:11. for his camp (is) *very* great:
— of the Lord (is) great and *very* terrible;
Obad. 2. thou art *greatly* despised.
Nah 2: 1(2). fortify (thy) power *mightily*.
Zep. 1:14. (it is) near, and hasteth *greatly*,
Zec. 9: 2. and Zidon, though it be *very* wise.
5. (shall see it), and be *very* sorrowful,
9. Rejoice *greatly*, O daughter of Zion;
14: 4. (and there shall be) a *very* great valley;
14. and apparel, in *great* abundance.

3967 **מֵאָה** *mēh-āh'*, f.

Gen 5: 3. Adam lived *an hundred and* thirty (lit. thirty *and an hundred*) years,
4. begotten Seth were eight *hundred* years:
5. nine *hundred* and thirty years:
6. Seth lived *an hundred and* five years,
7. eight *hundred* and seven years,
8. nine *hundred* and twelve years:
10. eight *hundred* and fifteen years,
11. nine *hundred* and five years:
13. eight *hundred* and forty years,
14. nine *hundred* and ten years:
16. eight *hundred* and thirty years,
17. eight *hundred* ninety and five years:
18. Jared lived *an hundred* sixty and two years, (lit. sixty and two *and an hundred* years)
19. begat Enoch eight *hundred* years,
20. nine *hundred* sixty and two years:
22. he begat Methuselah three *hundred* years,
23. three *hundred* sixty and five years:
25. Methuselah lived *an hundred* eighty and seven years, (lit. eighty and seven *and an hundred* years)
26. seven *hundred* eighty and two years,
27. nine *hundred* sixty and nine years:
28. Lamech lived *an hundred* eighty and two years, (lit. eighty and two *and an hundred* years)
30. five *hundred* ninety and five years,
31. seven *hundred* seventy and seven years:
32. Noah was five *hundred* years old:
6: 3. his days shall be *an hundred* and twenty
15. (shall be) three *hundred* cubits,
7: 6. And Noah (was) six *hundred* years old
11. In the six *hundredth* year of Noah's life,
24. prevailed upon the earth *an hundred and*
8: 3. after the end of the *hundred and* fifty days
13. in the six *hundredth* and first year,
9:28. three *hundred* and fifty years.
29. nine *hundred* and fifty years:
11:10. Shem (was) *an hundred* years old,
11. after he begat Arphaxad five *hundred*
13, 15. four *hundred* and three years,
17. four *hundred* and thirty years,
19. *two hundred and* nine years,
21. *two hundred and* seven years,
23. he begat Nahor *two hundred* years,
25. Nahor lived...*an hundred and* nineteen
32. *two hundred and* five years:
14:14. three *hundred* and eighteen,
15:13. shall afflict them four *hundred* years;
17:17. unto him that is *an hundred* years old?
21: 5. Abraham was *an hundred* years
23: 1. was *an hundred* and seven and twenty years
15. the land (is worth) four *hundred* shekels
16. four *hundred* shekels of silver,
25: 7. *an hundred* threescore and fifteen years.
17. *an hundred* and thirty and seven years:
26:12. received in the same year *an hundredfold*:
32: 6(7). and four *hundred* men with him.
14(15). *Two hundred* she goats, and twenty he goats, *two hundred* ewes,
33: 1. Esau came, and with him four *hundred*
19. father, *for an hundred* pieces of money.
35:28. of Isaac were *an hundred* and fourscore
45:22. three *hundred* (pieces) of silver,
47: 9. of my pilgrimage (are) *an hundred and*
28. was *an hundred* forty and seven years. (lit. forty and seven *and an hundred* years)
50:22. Joseph lived *an hundred* and ten years.
26. (being) *an hundred* and ten years old:
Ex. 6:16. (were) *an hundred* thirty and seven years. (lit. thirty and seven *and an hundred*)
18. *an hundred*) (thirty and three years.
20. Amram (were) *an hundred and* thirty
12:37. about six *hundred* thousand on foot
40, 41. four *hundred* and thirty years.
14: 7. he took six *hundred* chosen chariots,
18:21, 25. rulers of *hundreds*, rulers of fifties,
27: 9. (of) fine twined linen of *an hundred* cubits
11. (there shall be) hangings of *an hundred*
18. of the court (shall be) *an hundred* cubits,
30:23. of pure myrrh five *hundred*
—, 23. *two hundred and* fifty (shekels),
24. And of cassia five *hundred* (shekels),
38: 9. (of) fine twined linen, *an hundred* cubits:
11. (the hangings were) *an hundred* cubits,
24. seven *hundred* and thirty shekels,
25. *an hundred* talents, and a thousand seven *hundred* and threescore and fifteen

Ex. 38:26. six *hundred* thousand and three thousand and five *hundred* and fifty
27. of *the hundred* talents of silver were cast
— *an hundred* sockets *of the hundred* talents,
28. seven *hundred* seventy and five
29. two thousand and four *hundred* shekels.
Lev.26: 8. five of you shall chase *an hundred, and an hundred* of you shall put ten thousand
Nu. 1:21. 46,000 and five *hundred.*
23. 59,000 and three *hundred.*
25. 45,000 six *hundred* and fifty.
27. 74,000 and six *hundred.*
29. 54,000 and four *hundred.*
31. 57,000 and four *hundred.*
33. forty thousand and five *hundred.*
35. 32,000 *and two hundred.*
37. 35,000 and four *hundred.*
39. 62,000 and seven *hundred.*
41. 41,000 and five *hundred.*
43. 53,000 and four *hundred.*
46. six *hundred* thousand and three thousand and five *hundred* and fifty.
2: 4. 74,000 and six *hundred.*
6. 54,000 and four *hundred.*
8. 57,000 and four *hundred.*
9. *an hundred* thousand and 86,000 and four *hundred,*
11. 46,000 and five *hundred.*
13. 59,000 and three *hundred.*
15. 45,000 and six *hundred*
16. numbered in the camp of Reuben (were) *an hundred* thousand and 51,000 and four *hundred* and 50,
19. forty thousand and five *hundred.*
21. 32,000 *and two hundred.*
23. 35,000 and four *hundred.*
24. *an hundred* thousand and eight thousand *and an hundred,*
26. 62,000 and seven *hundred.*
28. 41,000 and five *hundred.*
30. fifty and three thousand and four *hundred.*
31. *an hundred* thousand and 57,000 and six *hundred.*
32. six *hundred* thousand and three thousand and five *hundred* and fifty.
3:22. seven thousand and five *hundred.*
28. eight thousand and six *hundred,*
34. upward, (were) 6,000 *and two hundred.*
43. 22,000 *two hundred and* 73.
46. *the two hundred and* threescore and thirteen
50. a thousand three *hundred* and 65
4:36. two thousand seven *hundred* and fifty.
40. two thousand and six *hundred* and thirty.
44. families, were 3000 *and two hundred.*
48. eight thousand and five *hundred* and 80.
7:13, 19, 25, 31, 37, 43, 49, 55, 61, 67, 73, 79, 85. *an hundred* and thirty (shekels),
85. all the silver vessels (weighed) 2000 and four *hundred* (shekels),
86. *an hundred and* twenty (shekels).
11:21. six *hundred* thousand footmen;
16: 2. *two hundred and* fifty princes of the
17. his censer, *two hundred and* fifty censers;
35. consumed the *two hundred and* fifty men
49(17:14). they that died in the plague were 14,000 and seven *hundred,*
26: 7. 43,000 and seven *hundred* and thirty.
10. devoured *two hundred and* fifty men:
14. Simeonites, 22,000 *and two hundred.*
18. forty thousand and five *hundred.*
22. 76,000 and five *hundred.*
25. 64,000 and three *hundred.*
27. threescore thousand and five *hundred.*
34. 52,000 and seven *hundred.*
37. 32,000 and five *hundred.*
41. 45,000 and six *hundred.*
43. 64,000 and four *hundred.*
47. 53,000 and four *hundred.*
50. 45,000 and four *hundred.*
51. six *hundred* thousand and a thousand seven *hundred* and thirty.
31:14. captains over *hundreds,*
28. one soul of five *hundred,* (both) of the
32. six *hundred* thousand and 75,000
36. three *hundred* thousand and seven and thirty thousand and five *hundred*
37. six *hundred* and threescore and fifteen.

Nu. 31:39. thirty thousand and five *hundred;*
43. three *hundred* thousand and thirty thousand (and) seven thousand and five *hundred*
45. thirty thousand asses and five *hundred,*
48, 52. captains of *hundreds,*
52. sixteen thousand seven *hundred* and fifty
54. captains of thousands and of *hundreds,*
33:39. Aaron (was) *an hundred and* 23 years old
Deu 1:15. captains over *hundreds,*
22:19. amerce him in *an hundred* (shekels)
31: 2. I (am) *an hundred* and twenty years old
34: 7. Moses (was) *an hundred* and 20 years old
Jos. 7:21. Babylonish garment, *and two hundred*
24:29. *an hundred* and ten years old.
32. of Shechem *for an hundred* pieces of
Jud. 2: 8. *an hundred* and ten years old.
3:31. slew of the Philistines six *hundred* men
4: 3, 13. nine *hundred* chariots of iron;
7: 6. to their mouth, were three *hundred* men:
7. By the three *hundred* men that lapped
8. and retained those three *hundred* men:
16. he divided the three *hundred* men
19. Gideon, *and the hundred* men
22. And the three *hundred* blew the trumpets,
8: 4. and the three *hundred* men that (were)
10. *an hundred* and twenty thousand men
26. a thousand and seven *hundred*
11:26. by the coasts of Arnon, three *hundred*
15: 4. Samson went and caught three *hundred*
16: 5. we will give thee every one of us eleven *hundred* (lit. a thousand *and a hundred*)
17: 2. The eleven *hundred* (lit. *id.*) (shekels) of
3. when he had restored the eleven *hundred* (lit. *id.*) (shekels) of silver
4. his mother took *two hundred* (shekels) of
18:11. six *hundred* men appointed
16. And the six *hundred* men appointed
17. the six *hundred* men (that were) appointed
20: 2. four *hundred* thousand footmen
10. take ten men *of an hundred* throughout all the tribes of Israel, *and an hundred*
15, 16. seven *hundred* chosen men.
17. four *hundred* thousand men
35. that day 25,000 *and an hundred* men:
47. But six *hundred* men turned and fled
21:12. four *hundred* young virgins, that had
1Sa. 11: 8. Israel were three *hundred* thousand,
13:15 & 14:2. about six *hundred* men.
15: 4. in Telaim, *two hundred* thousand footmen,
17: 7. spear's head (weighed) six *hundred* shekels
18:25. but *an hundred* foreskins of the Philistines,
27. slew of the Philistines *two hundred* men;
22: 2. were with him about four *hundred* men.
7. captains of *hundreds;*
23:13. about six *hundred,* arose
25:13. went up after David about four *hundred* men; *and two hundred* abode by the
18. took *two hundred* loaves,
— *and an hundred* clusters of raisins, *and two hundred* cakes of figs,
27: 2. he passed over with the six *hundred* men
29: 2. of the Philistines passed on *by hundreds,*
30: 9. David went, he and the six *hundred* men
10. David pursued, he and four *hundred* men: for *two hundred* abode behind,
17. four *hundred* young men, which rode
21. David came to the *two hundred* men,
2Sa. 2:31. three *hundred* and threescore men
3:14. which I espoused to me *for an hundred*
8: 4. seven *hundred* horsemen,
— reserved of them (for) *an hundred* chariots.
10:18. David slew (the men of) seven *hundred*
14:26. hair of his head at *two hundred* shekels
15:11. with Absalom went *two hundred* men
18. the Gittites, six *hundred* men
16: 1. upon them *two hundred* (loaves) of bread, *and an hundred* bunches of raisins, *and an hundred* of summer fruits,
18: 1. captains of *hundreds*
4. all the people came out *by hundreds*
21:16. (weighed) three *hundred* (shekels) of
23: 8. against eight *hundred,* whom he slew
18. lifted up his spear against three *hundred,*
24: 3. soever they be, *an hundredfold,*
9. eight *hundred* thousand valiant men
— five *hundred* thousand men.
1K. 4:23(5:3). *and an hundred* sheep, beside harts,

1K. 5:16(30). three thousand and three *hundred*,
6: 1. in the four *hundred* and eightieth year
7: 2. the length thereof (was) *an hundred*
20. the pomegranates (were) *two hundred*
42. And four *hundred* pomegranates for
8:63. *an hundred* and twenty thousand sheep.
9:14. Hiram sent to the king sixscore (lit. *a hundred* and twenty) talents of gold.
23. five *hundred* and fifty,
28. four *hundred* and twenty talents,
10:10. *an hundred* and twenty talents of gold,
14. six *hundred* threescore and six talents of
16. Solomon made *two hundred* targets (of) beaten gold: six *hundred* (shekels)
17. (he made) three *hundred* shields
26. a thousand and four *hundred* chariots,
29. for six *hundred* (shekels) of silver, and an horse for *an hundred and* fifty:
11: 3. he had seven *hundred* wives, princesses, and three *hundred* concubines:
12:21. *an hundred* and fourscore thousand
18: 4. Obadiah took *an hundred* prophets,
13. how I hid *an hundred* men
19. of Baal four *hundred* and fifty, and the prophets of the groves four *hundred*,
22. four *hundred* and fifty men.
20:15. they were *two hundred* and thirty two:
29. *an hundred* thousand footmen in one day.
22: 6. the prophets together, about four *hundred*
2K. 3: 4. *an hundred* thousand lambs, *and an hundred* thousand rams,
26. he took with him seven *hundred* men
4:43. should I set this before *an hundred* men?
11: 4, 19. the rulers over *hundreds*,
9. the captains over *the hundreds*
10. the captains over *hundreds*
15. the captains of *the hundreds*,
14:13. unto the corner gate, four *hundred* cubits.
18:14. of Judah three *hundred* talents
19:35. *an hundred* fourscore and five thousand:
23:33. a tribute of *an hundred* talents
1Ch. 4:42. of the sons of Simeon, five *hundred* men,
5:18. 44,000 seven *hundred* and threescore,
21. sheep *two hundred* and 50,000, and of asses 2000, and of men *an hundred* thousand.
7: 2. two and twenty thousand and six *hundred*.
9. valour, (was) 20,000 *and two hundred*.
11. 17,000 *and two hundred* (soldiers), fit to
8:40. sons, and sons' sons, *an hundred* and fifty.
9: 6. six *hundred* and ninety.
9. nine *hundred* and fifty and six.
13. seven *hundred* and threescore;
22. the gates (were) *two hundred* and twelve.
11:11. lifted up his spear against three *hundred*
20. lifting up his spear against three *hundred*,
12:14. one of the least (was) *over an hundred*,
24. six thousand and eight *hundred*,
25. for the war, 7000 *and one hundred*.
26. four thousand and six *hundred*.
27. three thousand and seven *hundred*;
30. twenty thousand and eight *hundred*,
32. the heads of them (were) *two hundred*;
35. twenty and eight thousand and six *hundred*.
37. *an hundred* and twenty thousand.
13: 1. captains of thousands *and hundreds*,
15: 5. his brethren *an hundred* and twenty:
6. his brethren *two hundred* and twenty:
7. his brethren *an hundred* and thirty:
8. the chief, and his brethren *two hundred*:
10. his brethren *an hundred* and twelve.
18: 4. but reserved of them *an hundred* chariots.
21: 3. The Lord make his people *an hundred* times
5. a thousand thousand *and an hundred* thousand men that drew sword: and Judah (was) four *hundred*
25. gave to Ornan for the place six *hundred*
22:14. Lord *an hundred* thousand talents of gold,
25: 7. was *two hundred* fourscore and eight.
26:26. captains over thousands *and hundreds*,
30. of valour, a thousand and seven *hundred*,
32. two thousand and seven *hundred* chief
27: 1. captains of thousands *and hundreds*,
28: 1. captains over *the hundreds*,
29: 6. captains of thousands *and* of *hundreds*,
7. *one hundred* thousand talents of iron.
2Ch. 1: 2. the captains of thousands *and* of *hundreds*,
14. a thousand and four *hundred* chariots,
17. a chariot for six *hundred* (shekels) of silver, and an horse for *an hundred and*
2: 2(1). three thousand and six *hundred*
17(16). found *an hundred* and fifty thousand and three thousand and six *hundred*.
18(17). three thousand and six *hundred*
3: 4. the height (was) *an hundred* and twenty:
8. gold, (amounting) to six *hundred* talents.
16. and made *an hundred* pomegranates,
4: 8. And he made *an hundred* basons of gold.
13. four *hundred* pomegranates on
5:12. *an hundred* and twenty priests sounding
7: 5. *an hundred* and twenty thousand sheep:
8:10. officers, (even) *two hundred and* fifty,
18. four *hundred* and fifty talents of gold,
9: 9. *an hundred* and twenty talents of gold,
13. six *hundred* and threescore and six talents
15. Solomon made *two hundred* targets (of) beaten gold: six *hundred* (shekels)
16. three *hundred* shields (made he of) beaten gold: three *hundred* (shekels) of gold
11: 1. *an hundred* and fourscore thousand
12: 3. With twelve *hundred* (lit. a thousand *and two hundred*) chariots,
13: 3. four *hundred* thousand chosen men:
— eight *hundred* thousand chosen men,
17. five *hundred* thousand chosen men.
14: 8(7). of Judah three *hundred* thousand;
—(–). *two hundred* and fourscore thousand:
9(8). and three *hundred* chariots;
15:11. had brought, seven *hundred* oxen
17:11. 7000 and seven *hundred* rams, and 7000 and seven *hundred* he goats.
14. men of valour three *hundred* thousand.
15. and with him *two hundred* and 80,000.
16. and with him *two hundred* thousand
17. with bow and shield *two hundred* thousand.
18. *an hundred* and fourscore thousand
18: 5. together of prophets four *hundred* men,
23: 1, 9, 14, 20. the captains of *hundreds*,
24:15. *an hundred* and thirty years old
25: 5. captains over *hundreds*,
— three *hundred* thousand choice (men),
6. *an hundred* thousand mighty men of valour out of Israel *for an hundred*
9. *for the hundred* talents which I have given
23. to the corner gate, four *hundred* cubits.
26:12. two thousand and six *hundred*.
13. three *hundred* thousand and seven thousand and five *hundred*,
27: 5. gave him the same year *an hundred* talents
28: 6. *an hundred* and twenty thousand
8. of their brethren *two hundred* thousand.
29:32. *an hundred* rams, (and) *two hundred*
33. consecrated things (were) six *hundred*
35: 8. two thousand and six *hundred* (small cattle), and three *hundred* oxen.
9. thousand (small cattle), and five *hundred*
36: 3. condemned the land in *an hundred* talents
Ezr. 1:10. silver basons...four *hundred* and ten,
11. five thousand and four *hundred*.
2: 3. of Parosh, 2000 *an hundred* 72.
4. of Shephatiah, three *hundred* 72.
5. of Arah, seven *hundred* seventy and five.
6. of Pahath-moab,...2000 eight *hundred* and
7. of Elam, 1000 *two hundred* 54.
8. of Zattu, nine *hundred* forty and five.
9. of Zaccai, seven *hundred* and threescore.
10. of Bani, six *hundred* forty and two.
11. of Bebai, six *hundred* twenty and three.
12. Azgad, 1000 *two hundred* twenty and two.
13. of Adonikam, six *hundred* sixty and six.
15. of Adin, four *hundred* fifty and four.
17. of Bezai, three *hundred* twenty and three.
18. of Jorah, *an hundred* and twelve.
19. of Hashum, *two hundred* twenty and three.
21. Beth-lehem, *an hundred* twenty and three.
23. of Anathoth, *an hundred* twenty and eight.
25. Beeroth, seven *hundred* and 43.
26. of Ramah and Gaba, six *hundred* 21.
27. of Michmas, *an hundred* twenty and two.
28. Beth-el and Ai, *two hundred* 23.
30. of Magbish, *an hundred* fifty and six.
31. of the other Elam,...1000 *two hundred* 54.
32. of Harim, three *hundred* and twenty.
33. and Ono, seven *hundred* twenty and five.
34. of Jericho, three *hundred* forty and five.

Ezr. 2:35. of Senaah, 3000 and six *hundred* and 30.
36. of Jeshua, nine *hundred* seventy and three.
38. of Pashur, 1000 *two hundred* 47.
41. of Asaph, *an hundred* twenty and eight.
42. (in) all *an hundred* thirty and nine.
58. (were) three *hundred* ninety and two.
60. of Nekoda, six *hundred* fifty and two.
64. 42,000 three *hundred* (and) threescore,
65. 7000 three *hundred* thirty and seven: and (there were) among them *two hundred*
66. Their horses (were) seven *hundred* 36; their mules, *two hundred* 45;
67. Their camels, four *hundred* 35; (their) asses, 6000 seven *hundred* and twenty.
69. and *one hundred* priests' garments.
8: 3. of the males *an hundred* and fifty.
4. and with him *two hundred* males.
5. and with him three *hundred* males.
9. with him *two hundred* and eighteen males.
10. *an hundred* and threescore males.
12. and with him *an hundred* and ten males.
20. *two hundred* and twenty Nethinims:
26. six *hundred* and fifty talents of silver, and silver vessels *an hundred* talents, (and) of gold *an hundred* talents;
Neh 3: 1. even unto the tower of *Meah* (lit. the tower of *the hundred*)
5:11. *also the hundredth* (part) of the money,
17. *an hundred* and fifty of the Jews
7: 8. Parosh, 2000 *an hundred* seventy and two.
9. Shephatiah, three *hundred* seventy and two.
10. of Arah, six *hundred* fifty and two.
11. of Pahath-moab,...2000 and eight *hundred* (and) 18.
12. of Elam, 1000 *two hundred* fifty and four.
13. of Zattu, eight *hundred* forty and five.
14. of Zaccai, seven *hundred* and threescore.
15. of Binnui, six *hundred* forty and eight.
16. of Bebai, six *hundred* twenty and eight.
17. Azgad, 2000 three *hundred* twenty and two.
18. of Adonikam, six *hundred* 67.
20. of Adin, six *hundred* fifty and five.
22. Hashum, three *hundred* twenty and eight.
23. of Bezai, three *hundred* twenty and four.
24. of Hariph, *an hundred* and twelve.
26. and Netophah, *an hundred* 88.
27. of Anathoth, *an hundred* twenty and eight.
29. Beeroth, seven *hundred* forty and three.
30. and Gaba, six *hundred* twenty and one.
31. Michmas, *an hundred* and twenty and two.
32. and Ai, *an hundred* twenty and three.
34. of the other Elam, 1000 *two hundred* 54.
35. of Harim, three *hundred* and twenty.
36. of Jericho, three *hundred* forty and five.
37. and Ono, seven *hundred* twenty and one.
38. of Senaah, 3000 nine *hundred* and thirty.
39. of Jeshua, nine *hundred* seventy and three.
41. of Pashur, 1000 *two hundred* 47.
44. of Asaph, *an hundred* forty and eight.
45. of Shobai, *an hundred* thirty and eight.
60. three *hundred* ninety and two.
62. six *hundred* forty and two.
66. 42,000 three *hundred* and threescore,
67. (there were) 7000 three *hundred* 37: and they had *two hundred* 45 singing men
68. Their horses, seven *hundred* 36: their mules, *two hundred* 45:
69. camels, four *hundred* thirty and five: 6000 seven *hundred* and twenty asses.
70. five *hundred* and thirty priests' garments.
71. and 2000 *and two hundred* pound of silver.
11: 6. four *hundred* threescore and eight valiant
8. Sallai, nine *hundred* twenty and eight.
12. eight *hundred* twenty and two:
13. of the fathers, *two hundred* forty and two:
14. *an hundred* twenty and eight:
18. (were) *two hundred* fourscore and four.
19. *an hundred* seventy and two.
12:39. the tower of *Meah*, (lit. *the hundred*)
Est. 1: 1. *an hundred* and seven and twenty
4. *an hundred and* fourscore days.
8: 9. *an hundred*)(twenty and seven provinces,
9: 6. slew and destroyed five *hundred* men.
12. have slain and destroyed five *hundred* men
15. and slew three *hundred* men at Shushan;
30. *the hundred*)(twenty and seven provinces
Job 1: 3. five *hundred* yoke of oxen, and five *hundred*
Job 42:16. lived Job *an hundred* and forty years,
Pro.17:10. than *an hundred* stripes into a fool.
Ecc. 6: 3. If a man beget *an hundred* (children),
8:12. Though a sinner do evil *an hundred* times,
Cant.8:12. *and* those that keep the fruit thereof *two hundred*.
Isa. 37:36. *a hundred* and fourscore and five
65:20. the child shall die *an hundred* years old; but the sinner (being) *an hundred*
Jer. 52:23. upon the network (were) *an hundred*
29. from Jerusalem eight *hundred* thirty and
30. seven *hundred* forty and five persons: all the persons (were) four thousand and six *hundred*.
Eze. 4: 5, 9. three *hundred* and ninety days:
40:19. *an hundred* cubits eastward and northward.
23. from gate to gate *an hundred* cubits.
27. toward the south *an hundred* cubits.
47. measured the court, *an hundred* cubits long, and *an hundred* cubits broad,
41:13. the house, *an hundred* cubits long;
— the walls thereof, *an hundred* cubits long;
14. place toward the east, *an hundred* cubits.
15. on the other side, *an hundred* cubits,
42: 2. Before the length of *an hundred* cubits
8. before the temple (were) *an hundred*
16, 17, 18, 19. five *hundred* reeds,
20. five *hundred* (reeds) long, and five *hundred*
45: 2. for the sanctuary five *hundred* (in length), with five *hundred* (in breadth), square
15. out of the flock, out of *two hundred*,
48:16, 16, 16, 16, 30, 32, 33, 34. four thousand and five *hundred*,
17, 17, 17, 17. *two hundred and* fifty,
Dan 8:14. two thousand and three *hundred* days;
12:11. a thousand *two hundred* and ninety days.
12. the thousand three *hundred* and five and
Am. 5: 3. thousand shall leave *an hundred*, and that which went forth (by) *an hundred*

מְאָה *m'āh*, Ch. f. 3969

Ezr. 6:17. *an hundred* bullocks, *two hundred* rams, four *hundred* lambs;
7:22. Unto *an hundred* talents of silver, and to *an hundred* measures of wheat, and to *an hundred* baths of wine, and to *an hundred* baths of oil,
Dan 6: 1(2). *an hundred* and twenty princes,

מַאֲוַיִּים [*mah-ăvahy-yeem'*], m. pl. 3970

Ps. 140: 8(9). Grant not, O Lord, *the desires of* the

מאום *moom*, m. 3971

Job 31: 7. if *any blot* hath cleaved to
Dan 1: 4. (כתיב) Children in whom (was) no *blemish*,

מְאוּמָה *m'oo-māh'*, f. 3972

Gen22:12. neither do thou *any thing* unto him:
30:31. Thou shalt not give me *any thing*:
39: 6. he knew not *ought* he had,
9. neither hath he kept back *any thing*
23. looked not to *any thing*
40:15. have I done no*thing*
Nu. 22:38. I now any power at all to say *any thing*?
Deu 13:17(18). shall cleave n*ought* (lit. not *any thing*)
24:10. dost lend thy brother *any thing*,
Jud. 14: 6. (he had) no*thing* (lit. not *any thing*) in
1Sa. 12: 4. neither hast thou taken *ought*
5. ye have not found *ought*
20:26. Saul spake not *any thing*
39. the lad knew not *any thing*:
21: 2(3). Let no man know *any thing*
25: 7. neither was there *ought* missing
15. neither missed we *any thing*,
21. no*thing* (lit. not *any thing*) was missed

1Sa.29: 3. I have found no *fault* (lit. not *any thing*)
2Sa. 3:35. if I taste bread, or *ought* else,
13: 2. thought it hard for him to do *any thing*
1K. 10:21. it was no*thing* accounted *of* in the days
18:43. looked, and said, (There is) no*thing*.
2K. 5:20. and take *somewhat* of him.
2Ch. 9:20. it was (not) *any thing* accounted *of* in the
Ecc. 5:14(13). (there is) no*thing* in his hand.
15(14). *and* shall take no*thing* of his labour,
7:14. to the end that man should find no*thing*
9: 5. but the dead know not *any thing*,
Jer. 39:10. the poor...which had no*thing*,
12. do him no harm ; (lit. not *any* harm)
Jon. 3: 7. herd nor flock, taste *any thing* :

3974 **מָאוֹר** *māh-ōhr'*, m.

Gen 1:14. Let there be *lights* in the firmament
15. let them be *for lights* in the firmament
16. God made two great *lights ; the* greater *light* to rule the day, and *the* lesser *light*
Ex. 25: 6. Oil *for the light*, spices for
27:20. pure oil olive beaten *for the light*,
35: 8. And oil *for the light*, and spices for
14. The candlestick also for *the light*,
— with the oil for *the light*,
28. And spice, and oil *for the light*,
39:37. the vessels thereof, and the oil for *light*,
Lev.24: 2. pure oil olive beaten *for the light*,
Nu. 4: 9. cover the candlestick of *the light*,
16. the oil for *the light*,
Ps. 74:16. hast prepared *the light* and the sun.
90: 8. *in the light of* thy countenance.
Pro.15:30. *The light of* the eyes rejoiceth the heart:
Eze.32: 8. All the *bright* lights (marg. *lights of* the light) of heaven will I

3975 **מְאוּרָה** [*m'oo-rāh*], f.

Isa. 11: 8. put his hand on the cockatrice' *den*.

3976 **מֹאזְנַיִם** *mōh-z'nah'-yim*, dual.

Lev.19:36. Just *balances*, just weights,
Job 6: 2. my calamity laid *in the balances*
31: 6. Let me be weighed *in an* even *balance*,
Ps. 62: 9(10). to be laid *in the balance*,
Pro.11: 1. *A* false *balance* (is) abomination to the
16:11. just weight *and balance* (are) the Lord's:
20:23. *and a* false *balance* (is) not good.
Isa. 40:12. and the hills *in a balance?*
15. counted as the small dust of *the balance :*
Jer.32:10. weighed (him) the money *in the balances*.
Eze. 5: 1. then take thee *balances to* weigh,
45:10. Ye shall have just *balances*,
Hos 12: 7(8). *the balances of* deceit (are) in his hand:
Am. 8: 5. falsifying *the balances by* deceit?
Mic. 6:11. pure *with the* wicked *balances*,

3977 **מֹאזְנַיִן** [*mōh-z'nah'-yin*], Ch. dual.

Dan 5:27. Thou art weighed *in the balances*,

3978 **מַאֲכָל** *mah-ăchāhl'*, m.

Gen 2: 9. pleasant to the sight and good *for food ;*
3: 6. saw that the tree (was) good *for food*,
6:21. unto thee of all *food* that is eaten,
40:17. all manner of bake*meats for* Pharaoh ; (marg. *meat of* Pharaoh, the work of a baker)
Lev.19:23. planted all manner of trees for *food*,
Deu 20:20. that they (be) not trees for *meat*,
28:26. thy carcase shall be (lit. *for*) *meat*
Jud. 14:14. Out of the eater came forth *meat*,
1K. 10: 5. *And the meat of* his table,
1Ch 12:40. on oxen, (and) *meat*, meal, (marg. or, *victual of* meal)
2Ch 9: 4. *And the meat of* his table,
11:11. put captains in them, and store of *victual*,
Ezr. 3: 7. *and meat*, and drink, and oil,
Neh 9:25. *fruit* trees (marg. tree of *food*) in
Job 33:20. his soul dainty *meat*.
Ps. 44:11(12). like sheep (appointed) for *meat ;*
74:14. gavest him (to be) *meat*
79: 2. servants have they given (to be) *meat*
Pro. 6: 8. gathereth *her food* in the harvest.
Isa. 62: 8. give thy corn (to be) *meat*
Jer. 7:33 & 16:4. shall be *meat* for the fowls
19: 7. will I give to be (lit. *for*) *meat*
34:20. their dead bodies shall be *for meat*
Eze. 4:10. *And thy meat* which thou
47:12. shall grow all trees *for meat*,
— the fruit thereof shall be *for meat*,
Dan 1:10. who hath appointed *your meat*
Hab. 1:16. *and their meat* plenteous.
Hag. 2:12. or wine, or oil, or any *meat*,

מַאֲכֶלֶת *mah-ăcheh'-leth*, f. 3979

Gen22: 6. took the fire in his hand, and *a knife ;*
10. took *the knife* to slay his son.
Jud.19:29. he took *a knife*, and laid hold
Pro.30:14. *and* their jaw teeth (as) *knives*,

מַאֲכֹלֶת *mah-ăchōh'-leth*, f. 3980

Isa. 9: 5(4). shall be with burning (and) *fuel* (marg. *meat*) *of* fire.
19(18). shall be *as the fuel* (marg. *meat*) *of*

מַאֲמַצִּים [*mah-ămatz-tzeem'*], m. pl. 3981

Job 36:19. nor all *the forces of* strength.

מַאֲמַר *mah-ămar'*, m. 3982

Est. 1:15. hath not performed *the commandment of*
2:20. Esther did *the commandment of* Mordecai,
9:32. *And the decree of* Esther confirmed

מֵאמַר *mēh-mar'*, Ch. m. 3983

Ezr. 6: 9. *according to the appointment of* the
Dan 4:17(14). *and* the demand *by the word of* the

מָאן [*māhn*], Ch. m. 3984

Ezr. 5:14. And *the vessels* also of gold and silver
15. Take these *vessels*, go, carry them into
6: 5. golden and silver *vessels of* the house
7:19. *The vessels also* that are given thee
Dan 5: 2. to bring the golden and silver *vessels*
3. Then they brought *the* golden *vessels*
23. *and* they have brought *the vessels* of his

מָאֵן *māh-ēhn'*. 3985

* PIEL.—*Preterite.* *

Ex. 7:14. *he refuseth* to let the people go.
10: 3. How long *wilt thou refuse* to humble
16:28. How long *refuse ye* to keep my
Nu. 22:13. the Lord *refuseth* to give me leave
14. Balaam *refuseth* to come with us.
Deu 25: 7. My husband's brother *refuseth*
1K. 21:15. *he refused* to give thee for money:
Job 6: 7. The things (that) my soul *refused*

Ps. 77: 2(3). my soul *refused* to be comforted.
78:10. *refused* to walk in his law;
Pro.21: 7. *they refuse* to do judgment.
25. his hands *refuse* to labour.
Jer. 3: 3. *thou refusedst* to be ashamed.
5: 3. *they have refused* to receive correction:
— *they have refused* to return.
8: 5. *they refuse* to return.
9: 6(5). through deceit *they refuse* to know
11:10. forefathers, which *refused* to hear my
15:18. *refuseth* to be healed?
31:15. *refused* to be comforted for her children,
50:33. held them fast; *they refused* to let them
Hos 11: 5. *they refused* to return.

PIEL.—*Infinitive.*

Ex. 22:17(16). If her father *utterly* refuse (lit. *refusing* shall refuse)

PIEL.—*Future.*

Gen37:35. *but he refused* to be comforted;
39: 8. *But he refused*, and said
48:19. *And* his father *refused*, and said,
Ex. 4:23. *if thou refuse* to let him go,
22:17(16). If her father utterly *refuse*
Nu. 20:21. *Thus* Edom *refused* to give Israel passage
1Sa. 8:19. *Nevertheless* the people *refused*
28:23. *But he refused*, and said,
2Sa. 2:23. *Howbeit he refused* to turn aside:
13: 9. before him; *but he refused* to eat.
1K. 20:35. *And* the man *refused* to smite him.
2K. 5:16. he urged him to take (it); *but he refused.*
Neh 9:17. *And refused* to obey,
Est. 1:12. *But* the queen Vashti *refused* to come
Pro. 1:24. I have called, *and ye refused;*
Isa. 1:20. But if *ye refuse* and rebel,
Jer. 25:28. if *they refuse* to take the cup
Zec. 7:11. *But they refused* to hearken,

3986 **מָאֵן** *māh-ēhn'*, adj.

Ex. 8: 2(7:27) & 9:2. if thou *refuse* (lit. *refusing*)
10: 4. if thou *refuse* to let my people go,
Jer. 38:21. if thou *refuse* to go forth,

3987 **מֵאֲנִים** *mēh-ăneem'*, adj. pl.

Jer. 13:10. This evil people, *which refuse* to hear

3973, 3988 **מָאַס** *māh-as'.*

∗ KAL.—*Preterite.* ∗

Lev.26:43. *they despised* my judgments,
44. *I will* not *cast them away*,
Nu. 11:20. *ye have despised* the Lord
14:31. the land which *ye have despised.*
Jud. 9:38. the people that *thou hast despised?*
1Sa. 8: 7. *they have* not *rejected* thee, but *they have rejected* me,
10:19. *ye have* this day *rejected* your God,
15:23, 26. *thou hast rejected* the word of the Lord,
16: 1. *I have rejected him* from reigning
7. because *I have refused him:*
2K. 23:27. *and will cast off* this city
Job 7:16. *I loathe* (it); I would not live alway:
19:18. young children *despised* me;
30: 1. whose fathers *I would have disdained*
34:33. whether *thou refuse*, or whether thou
Ps. 53: 5(6). God *hath despised them.*
118:22. The stone (which) the builders *refused*
Isa. 5:24. *they have cast away* the law
8: 6. this people *refuseth* the waters of Shiloah
33: 8. *he hath despised* the cities,
41: 9. I have chosen thee, and not *cast thee away.*
Jer. 2:37. the Lord *hath rejected* thy confidences,
4:30. (thy) lovers *will despise* thee,
6:30. the Lord *hath rejected* them.
7:29. the Lord *hath rejected* and forsaken
8: 9. *they have rejected* the word of the Lord;
14:19. *Hast thou* utterly *rejected* Judah?
Lam. 5:22. *thou hast* utterly *rejected us;*
Eze. 5: 6. *they have refused* my judgments
20:13. *they despised* my judgments,
16. *they despised* my judgments,
24. but *had despised* my statutes,
Hos. 4: 6. *thou hast rejected* knowledge,
Am. 5:21. *I despise* your feast days,

KAL.—*Infinitive.*

Isa. 7:15. that he may know *to refuse*
16. before the child shall know *to refuse*
30:12. Because *ye despise* this word,
Jer. 14:19. Hast thou *utterly* rejected Judah?
Lam. 3:45. the offscouring *and refuse* in the midst
5:22. thou hast *utterly* rejected us;
Am. 2: 4. *they have despised* the law

KAL.—*Future.*

Lev.26:15. if *ye shall despise* my statutes,
1Sa. 15:23. *he hath also rejected thee* from (being)
26. *and* the Lord *hath rejected thee*
2K. 17:15. *And they rejected* his statutes,
20. *And* the Lord *rejected* all the seed of
Job 5:17. *despise* not *thou* the chastening of
8:20. God *will* not *cast away* a perfect (man),
9:21. *I would despise* my life.
10: 3. that *thou shouldest despise* the work
31:13. If *I did despise* the cause of
36: 5. God (is) mighty, and *despiseth* not (any):
42: 6. Wherefore *I abhor* (myself), and repent
Ps. 36: 4(5). *he abhorreth* not evil.
78:59. *and* greatly *abhorred* Israel:
67. *Moreover he refused* the tabernacle of
89:38(39). thou hast cast off *and abhorred*,
106:24. *Yea, they despised* the pleasant land,
Pro. 3:11. *despise* not the chastening of the Lord;
Isa. 31: 7. every man *shall cast away* his idols
Jer. 6:19. nor to my law, *but rejected* it.
31:37. I *will* also *cast off* all the seed of Israel
33:24. *he hath even cast them off?*
26. Then *will I cast away* the seed of Jacob,
Hos. 4: 6. *I will also reject thee*,
9:17. My God *will cast them away*,

KAL.—*Participle.* Poël.

Pro.15:32. He that refuseth instruction *despiseth*
Isa. 33:15. *he that despiseth* the gain of
Eze.21:10(15). *it contemneth* the rod of my son,
13(18). if (the sword) *contemn* even the rod?

∗ NIPHAL.—*Future.* ∗

Isa. 54: 6. when *thou wast refused*,

NIPHAL.—*Participle.*

Ps. 15: 4. In whose eyes *a vile person* is contemned;
Jer. 6:30. *Reprobate* (marg. or, *Refuse*) silver shall

מָאַס [*māh-as'*]. 3988

∗ NIPHAL.—*Future.* ∗

Job 7: 5. my skin is broken, *and become loathsome.*
Ps. 58: 7(8). *Let them melt away* as waters

מַאֲפֶה [*mah-ăpheh'*], m. 3989

Lev. 2: 4. a meat offering *baken in* the oven,

מַאֲפֵל *mah-ăphēhl'*, m. 3990

Jos. 24: 7. he put *darkness* between you

מַאְפֵּלְיָה *mah-pēh-l'yāh'*, f. 3991

Jer. 2:31. a land of *darkness?*

מָאַר [*māh-ar'*]. 3992

∗ HIPHIL.—*Participle.* ∗

Lev. 13:51. the plague (is) a *fretting* leprosy;

Lev.13:52 & 14:44. it (is) a *fretting* leprosy;
Eze.28:24. there shall be no more a *pricking* brier

3993 **מַאֲרָב** *mah-ărāhv'*, m.

Jos. 8: 9. they went to *lie in ambush*,
Jud. 9:35. from *lying in wait*-
2Ch 13:13. Jeroboam caused *an ambushment*
— *and the ambushment* (was) behind them.
Ps. 10: 8. He sitteth *in the lurking places of*

3994 **מְאֵרָה** *m'ēh-rāh'*, f.

Deu28:20. The Lord shall send upon thee *cursing*,
Pro. 3:33. *The curse of* the Lord (is) in the
28:27. shall have many *a curse*.
Mal. 2: 2. I will even send *a curse* upon you,
3: 9. Ye (are) cursed *with a curse:*

3995 **מִבְדָּלוֹת** *miv-dāh-lohth'*, f. pl.

Jos. 16: 9. And *the separate cities* for the children of

3996-97 **מָבוֹא** *māh-vōh'*, com.

Deu 11:30. *where* the sun *goeth* down,
Jos. 1: 4. toward *the going down of* the sun,
23: 4. unto the great sea westward. (marg. at *the sunset;* lit. *the going down of* the sun)
Jud. 1:24. Shew us,...*the entrance into* the city,
25. when he shewed them *the entrance into*
2Sa. 3:25. (כתיב) thy going out and *thy coming in*,
2K. 11:16. the way *by the which* the horses *came* (lit. *the Entrance of* the horses)
16:18. the king's *entry* without,
1Ch 4:39. they went *to the entrance of* Gedor,
9:19. keepers of *the entry*.
2Ch 23:13. at his pillar *at the entering in*,
15. when she was come to *the entering of*
Ps. 50: 1. unto *the going down thereof*.
104:19. the sun knoweth *his going down*.
113: 3. unto *the going down of the same*
Pro. 8: 3. at *the coming in* at the doors.
Jer. 38:14. prophet unto him into *the* third *entry*
Eze.26:10. *as men enter into* (marg. *according to the enterings of*) a city
27: 3. situate at *the entry of* the sea,
33:31. *as* the people *cometh*, (marg. *according to the coming of* the people)
42: 9. (כתיב) *the entry* on the east side,
44: 5. mark well *the entering in of*
46:19. he brought me *through the entry*,
Zec. 8: 7. from the west country; (marg. the country of *the going down of* the sun)
Mal. 1:11. unto *the going down of the same*

3998 **מְבוּכָה** *m'voo-chāh'*, f.

Isa. 22: 5. *and of perplexity* by the Lord
Mic. 7: 4. now shall be *their perplexity*.

3999 **מַבּוּל** *mab-bool'*, m.

Gen 6:17. I, do bring *a flood of* waters
7: 6. *when the flood* of waters was upon
7. because of the waters of *the flood*.
10. the waters of *the flood* were upon
17. *the flood* was forty days upon the earth;
9:11. by the waters of *a flood;* neither shall there any more be *a flood*
15. the waters shall no more become *a flood*
28. Noah lived after *the flood*
10: 1. sons born after *the flood*.
Gen 10:32. nations divided in the earth after *the flood*.
11:10. two years after *the flood:*
Ps. 29:10. The Lord sitteth *upon the flood;*

מְבוֹנִים *m'vōh-neem'*, m. pl. 4000

2Ch 35: 3. (כתיב) the Levites *that taught* all Israel,

מְבוּסָה *m'voo-sāh'*, f. 4001

Isa. 18: 2. a nation meted out *and trodden down*, (marg. *and treading under foot*)
7. meted out and *trodden under foot*,
22: 5. of trouble, *and of treading down*,

מַבּוּעַ *mab-boo'ăg*, m. 4002

Ecc.12: 6. or the pitcher be broken at *the fountain*,
Isa. 35: 7. the thirsty land *springs of* water:
49:10. *the springs of* water shall he guide them.

מְבוּקָה *m'voo-kāh'*, f. 4003

Nah. 2:10(11). She is empty, *and void*,

מִבְחוֹר *miv-ghōhr'*, m. 4004

2K. 3:19. fenced city, and every *choice* city,
19:23. the *choice* fir trees thereof:

מִבְחָר [*miv-ghāhr'*], m. 4005

Gen23: 6. *in the choice of* our sepulchres
Ex. 15: 4. his *chosen* captains *also* are drowned
Deu12:11. your *choice* vows (marg. *choice of* your vows) which ye vow
Isa. 22: 7. *choicest* (marg. *the choice of* thy) valleys
37:24. the *choice* fir trees thereof:
Jer. 22: 7. shall cut down thy *choice* cedars,
48:15. *and* his *chosen* (marg. *the choice of*) young
Eze.23: 7. with all them (that were) the *chosen* (marg. *id.*) men
24: 4. fill (it) with the *choice* bones.
5. Take *the choice of* the flock,
31:16. *the choice* and best of Lebanon,
Dan 11:15. neither *his chosen* people, (marg. the people of *his choices*)

מַבָּט [*mab-bāht'*], m. 4007

Isa. 20: 5. Ethiopia *their expectation*,
6. such (is) *our expectation*,

מֶבָּט [*meh'-vat*], m. 4007

Zec. 9: 5. Ekron; for *her expectation*

מִבְטָא *miv-tāh'*, m. 4008

Nu. 30: 6(7). *uttered ought out of* her lips,
8(9). *that which she uttered with* her lips,

מִבְטָח *miv-tāh'gh*, m. 4009

Job 8:14. *whose trust* (shall be) a spider's web.
18:14. *His confidence* shall be rooted out
31:24. fine gold, (Thou art) *my confidence;*
Ps. 40: 4(5). that maketh the Lord *his trust*,
65: 5(6). *the confidence of* all the ends of the
71: 5. *my trust* from my youth.
Pro. 14:26. the fear of the Lord (is) strong *confidence:*

Pro.21:22. the strength of *the confidence thereof.*
22:19. That *thy trust* may be in the Lord,
25:19. *Confidence in* an unfaithful man
Isa. 32:18. and in *sure* dwellings,
Jer. 2:37. the Lord hath rejected *thy confidences,*
17: 7. *whose hope* the Lord is.
48:13. Beth-el *their confidence.*
Eze.29:16. it shall be no more *the confidence*

4010 מַבְלִיגִית *mav-lee-geeth'*, f.

Jer. 8:18. (When) *I would comfort myself* (lit. *my consolation*) against sorrow,

---

4011 מִבְנֶה [*miv-neh'*], m.

Eze.40: 2. by which (was) *as the frame of* a city

4013 מִבְצָר *miv-tzāhr'*, m.

Nu. 13:19. in tents, or *in strong holds;*
32:17. shall dwell in the *fenced* cities
36. *fenced* cities: and folds for sheep.
Jos. 10:20. entered into *fenced* cities.
19:29. to the *strong* city Tyre;
35. the *fenced* cities (are) Ziddim, Zer,
1Sa. 6:18. *fenced* cities, and of country villages,
2Sa.24: 7. came to *the strong hold of* Tyre,
2K. 3:19. ye shall smite every *fenced* city,
8:12. *their strong holds* wilt thou set on fire,
10: 2. a *fenced* city also, and armour;
17: 9 & 18:8. the watchmen to the *fenced* city.
2Ch 17:19. the king put in the *fenced* cities
Ps. 89:40(41). hast brought *his strong holds* to ruin.
108:10(11). will bring me into the *strong* city?
Isa. 17: 3. *The fortress* also shall cease
25:12. *And the fortress of* the high fort
34:13. brambles *in the fortresses thereof:*
Jer. 1:18. I have made thee this day a *defenced* city,
4: 5. let us go into the *defenced* cities.
5:17. impoverish *thy fenced* cities,
6:27. *a fortress* among my people,
8:14. let us enter into the *defenced* cities,
34: 7. for these *defenced* cities remained
48:18. he shall destroy *thy strong holds.*
Lam. 2: 2. *the strong holds of* the daughter of Judah;
5. he hath destroyed *his strong holds,*
Dan 11:15. take the *most fenced* cities: (marg. city of *munitions*)
24. devices against *the strong holds,*
39. Thus shall he do *in the most strong* holds (marg. *in the fortresses of* munitions)
Hos 10:14. all *thy fortresses* shall be spoiled,
Am. 5: 9. shall come against *the fortress.*
Mic. 5:11(10). throw down all *thy strong holds:*
Nah. 3:12. All *thy strong holds*
14. fortify *thy strong holds:*
Hab. 1:10. they shall deride every *strong hold;*

4015 מִבְרָח [*miv-rāhğh'*].

Eze.17:21. *his fugitives* with all his bands

4016 מְבֻשִׁים [*m'voo-sheem'*] m. pl.

Deu 25:11. taketh him *by the* (lit. *his*) *secrets:*

4018 מְבַשְּׁלוֹת *m'vash-sh'lōhth'*, f. pl.

Eze.46:23. *and* (it was) made *with boiling places*

7248 מָג *māhg*, m.

Jer. 39: 3, 13. Nergal-sharezer, Rab-*mag*, (perhaps lit. chief *Magian*)

מִגְבָּלֹת *mig-bāh-lōhth'*, f. pl. 4020

Ex. 28:14. pure gold *at the ends;*

מִגְבָּעוֹת *mig-bāh-ğōhth'*, f. pl. 4021

Ex. 28:40. *and bonnets* shalt thou make
29: 9. put *the bonnets* on them:
39:28. goodly *bonnets* (of) fine linen,
Lev. 8:13. put *bonnets* upon them;

מֶגֶד *meh'-ged*, m. 4022

Deu 33:13. *for the precious things* of heaven,
14. *And for the precious fruits* (brought forth) by the sun, *and for the precious things*
15. *and for the precious things* of the lasting
16. *And for the precious things of* the earth
Cant. 4:13. an orchard of pomegranates, with *pleasant*
16. and eat *his pleasant* fruits.
7:13(14). all manner of *pleasant* (fruits),

מִגְדָּל *mig-dāhl'*, m. 4026

Gen 11: 4. let us build us a city *and a tower,*
5. to see the city and *the tower,*
35:21. beyond *the tower of* Edar.
Jos. 15:37. *and Migdal-*gad, (or, *the tower of* Gad)
19:38. Iron, *and Migdal-*el, (or, *the tower of* El)
Jud. 8: 9. I will break down this *tower.*
17. he beat down *the tower of* Penuel,
9:46, 47. all the men of *the tower of* Shechem
49. all the men of *the tower of* Shechem
51. *But* there was *a* strong *tower*
— gat them up to the top of *the tower.*
52. Abimelech came unto *the tower,*
— went hard unto the door of *the tower*
2K. 9:17. there stood a watchman on *the tower*
17: 9 & 18:8. *from the tower of* the watchmen
1Ch 27:25. in the villages, *and in the castles,*
2Ch 14: 7(6). make about (them) walls, *and towers,*
26: 9. Uzziah built *towers* in Jerusalem
10. Also he built *towers* in the desert,
15. to be on *the towers*
27: 4. he built castles *and towers.*
32: 5. and raised (it) up to *the towers,*
Neh. 3: 1. even unto *the tower of* Meah they sanctified it, unto *the tower of* Hananeel.
11. *the tower of* the furnaces.
25. *and the tower* which lieth out
26. *and the tower* that lieth out.
27. over against *the* great *tower*
8: 4. stood upon *a pulpit* (marg. *tower*) *of* wood,
12:38. from *beyond the tower of*
39. *and the tower of* Hananeel, *and the tower of*
Ps. 48:12(13). tell *the towers thereof.*
61: 3(4). *a* strong *tower* from the enemy.
Pro.18:10. the Lord (is) *a* strong *tower:*
Cant. 4: 4. Thy neck (is) *like the tower of* David
5:13. as a bed of spices, (as) sweet *flowers:* (marg. *towers* of perfumes)
7: 4(5). Thy neck (is) *as a tower of* ivory;
—(–). thy nose (is) *as the tower of* Lebanon
8:10. my breasts *like towers:*
Isa. 2:15. upon every high *tower,*
5: 2. built *a tower* in the midst of it,
30:25. great slaughter, when *the towers* fall.
33:18. where (is) he that counted *the towers?*
Jer. 31:38. *from the tower of* Hananeel
Eze.26: 4. break down *her towers:*
9. *and* with his axes he shall break down *thy towers.*
27:11. the Gammadims were *in thy towers:*
Mic. 4: 8. thou, *O tower of* the flock,
Zec.14:10. *and* (from) *the tower of* Hananeel

מִגְדּוֹל *mig-dōhl'*, m. 4024

2Sa.22:51. (He is) *the tower of* salvation
Eze.29:10. *from the tower of* Syene even unto
30: 6. *from the tower of* Syene shall

4030 **מִגְדָּנוֹת** *mig-dāh-nōhth'*, f. pl.

Gen24:53. he gave *also* to her brother and to her mother *precious things*.
2Ch 21: 3. of gold, *and of precious things*,
32:23. *and presents* (marg. *precious things*) to
Ezr. 1: 6. *and with precious things*,

4032 **מָגוֹר** *māh-gōhr'*, m.

Ps. 31:13(14). *fear* (was) on every side:
Isa. 31: 9. over to his strong hold *for fear*,
Jer. 6:25. *fear* (is) on every side.
20: 3. *Magor*-missabib. (marg. *Fear* round about)
4. I will make thee *a terror* to thyself,
10. *fear* on every side.
46: 5. *fear* (was) round about,
49:29. *Fear* (is) on every side.
Lam. 2:22. *my terrors* round about,

4033 **מָגוּר** [*māh-goor'*], m.

Gen17: 8 & 28:4. the land wherein *thou art a stranger*, (marg. the land of *thy sojournings*)
36: 7. the land wherein *they were strangers*
37: 1. the land wherein his father *was a stranger*, (marg. of his father's *sojournings*)
47: 9. the years of *my pilgrimage*
— in the days of *their pilgrimage*.
Ex. 6: 4. the land of *their pilgrimage*,
Job 18:19. nor any remaining *in his dwellings*.
Ps. 55:15(16). wickedness (is) *in their dwellings*,
119:54. in the house of *my pilgrimage*.
Eze.20:38. the country *where they sojourn*,

4034 **מְגוֹרָה** [*m'gōh-rāh'*], f.

Pro.10:24. *The fear of* the wicked,

4035 **מְגוּרָה** *m'goo-rāh'*, f.

Ps. 34: 4(5). delivered me from all *my fears*.
Isa. 66: 4. *and* will bring *their fears* upon them;
Hag. 2:19. Is the seed yet in *the barn?*

4037 **מַגְזֵרָה** [*mag-zēh-rāh'*], f.

2Sa.12:31. *and under axes of* iron,

4038 **מַגָּל** *mag-gāhl'*, m.

Jer. 50:16. that handleth *the sickle* (marg. or, *scythe*)
Joel 3:13(4:13). Put ye in *the sickle*,

4039 **מְגִלָּה** *m'gil-lāh'*, f.

Ps. 40: 7(8). *in the volume of* the book
Jer. 36: 2. Take thee *a roll of* a book,
4. upon *a roll of* a book.
6. and read *in the roll*,
14. Take in thine hand *the roll*
— took *the roll* in his hand,
20. but they laid up *the roll*
21. sent Jehudi to fetch *the roll:*
23. until all *the roll* was consumed
25. that he would not burn *the roll:*
27. the king had burned *the roll*,
28. Take thee again another *roll*,
— that were in *the* first *roll*,
29. Thou hast burned this *roll*,
32. Then took Jeremiah another *roll*,
Eze. 2: 9. *a roll of* a book (was) therein;
3: 1. eat that thou findest; eat this *roll*,
2. he caused me to eat that *roll*.
3. fill thy bowels with this *roll*
Zec. 5: 1. behold *a* flying *roll*.
2. I see *a* flying *roll;*

מְגִלָּה *m'gil-lāh'*, Ch. f. 4040

Ezr. 6: 2. *a roll*, and therein (was) a record thus

מְגַמָּה [*m'gam-māh'*], f. 4041

Hab. 1: 9. *shall sup up* (as) the east wind, (marg. *the opposition of* their faces toward the east)

מָגַן [*māh-gan'*]. 4042

* PIEL.—*Preterite.* *

Gen14:20. *hath delivered* thine enemies into thy hand.

PIEL.—*Future.*

Pro. 4: 9. a crown of glory *shall she deliver to thee.* (marg. or, *she shall compass thee with* &c.)
Hos.11: 8. (how) *shall I deliver thee*,

מָגֵן *māh-gēhn'*, m. 4043

Gen15: 1. Fear not, Abram: I (am) thy *shield*,
Deu33:29. *the shield of* thy help,
Jud. 5: 8. was there *a shield* or spear
2Sa. 1:21. there *the shield of* the mighty is vilely cast away, *the shield of* Saul,
22: 3. *my shield*, and the horn of my
31. he (is) *a buckler* to all them
36. given me *the shield of* thy salvation:
1K. 10:17. three hundred *shields*
— of gold went to one *shield:*
14:26. he took away all *the shields of*
27. made in their stead brasen *shields*,
2K. 19:32. nor come before it with *shield*,
1Ch 5:18. men able to bear *buckler*
2Ch 9:16. three hundred *shields*
— of gold went to one *shield*.
12: 9. carried away also *the shields of* gold
10. Rehoboam made *shields of* brass,
14: 8(7). that bare *shields* and drew bows,
17:17. bow *and shield* two hundred
23: 9. spears, *and bucklers*, and shields,
26:14. throughout all the host *shields*,
32: 5. made darts *and shields*
27. for spices, *and for shields*,
Neh 4:16(10). the spears, *the shields*,
Job 15:26. the thick bosses of *his bucklers:*
41:15(7). (His) scales (marg. strong pieces of *shields*) (are his) pride,
Ps. 3: 3(4). thou, O Lord, (art) *a shield*
7:10(11). *My defence* (is) of God, (marg. *My buckler* (is) upon)
18: 2(3). *my buckler*, and the horn of my
30(31). he (is) *a buckler* to all
35(36). given me *the shield of* thy salvation:
28: 7. The Lord (is) my strength *and my shield;*
33:20. he (is) our help *and our shield*.
35: 2. Take hold of *shield* and buckler,
47: 9(10). for *the shields of* the earth
59:11(12). O Lord *our shield*.
76: 3(4). *the shield*, and the sword,
84: 9(10). Behold, O God *our shield*,
11(12). the Lord God (is) a sun *and shield:*
89:18(19). For the Lord (is) *our defence;* (marg. or, *our shield* (is) of the Lord)
115: 9, 10, 11. he (is) their help *and their shield*.
119:114. my hiding place *and my shield:*
144: 2. my deliverer; *my shield*,
Pro. 2: 7. *a buckler* to them that walk
6:11. as an *armed* man. (lit. man of *a shield*)
24:34. as an *armed* man. (marg. a man of *shield*)
30: 5. he (is) *a shield* unto them
Cant.4: 4. there hang a thousand *bucklers*,
Isa. 21: 5. arise, ye princes, (and) anoint *the shield*.
22: 6. Kir uncovered *the shield*.
37:33. nor come before it with *shields*, (lit. *shield*)
Jer. 46: 3. Order ye *the buckler* and shield,
9. that handle *the shield;*
Eze.23:24. buckler *and shield* and helmet
27:10. hanged *the shield* and helmet
38: 4. company (with) bucklers *and shields*,
5. all of them with *shield* and helmet:
39: 9. *both the shields* and the bucklers,

Hos. 4:18. *her rulers* (marg. *shields*) (with) shame
Nah. 2: 3(4). *The shield of* his mighty men

4044 **מְגִנָּה** [*m'gin-nāh'*], f.

Lam. 3:65. Give them *sorrow* (marg. or, *obstinacy*) *of*

4045 **מִגְעֶרֶת** *mig-geh'-reth*, f.

Deu 28:20. *rebuke*, in all that thou settest

4046 **מַגֵּפָה** *mag-gēh-phāh'*, f.

Ex. 9:14. I will at this time send all *my plagues*
Nu. 14:37. died *by the plague*
16:48(17:13). and *the plague* was stayed.
49(—:14). they that died *in the plague*
50(—:15). *and the plague* was stayed.
25: 8. So *the plague* was stayed
9. those that died *in the plague*
18. in the day of *the plague*
26: 1(25:19). it came to pass after *the plague*,
31:16. there was *a plague* among
1Sa. 4:17. there hath been also *a* great *slaughter*
6: 4. one *plague* (was) on you all,
2Sa.17: 9. There is *a slaughter* among the people
18: 7. there was there *a* great *slaughter*
24:21. that *the plague* may be stayed
25. and *the plague* was stayed
1Ch 21:17. not on thy people, *that they should be plagued*. (lit. *for plague*)
22. that *the plague* may be stayed
2Ch 21:14. with *a* great *plague* (marg. *stroke*) will the
Ps. 106:29. *the plague* brake in upon them.
30. *the plague* was stayed.
Eze.24:16. the desire of thine eyes *with a stroke:*
Zec.14:12. this shall be *the plague*
15. *the plague of* the horse,
— in these tents, *as* this *plague*.
18. there shall be *the plague*,

4048 **מָגַר** [*māh-gar'*].

* KAL.—*Participle*. Paül. *

Eze.21:12(17). *terrors* by reason of the sword (marg. *they are thrust down to* the sword. See מָגוֹר.

* PIEL.—*Preterite*. *

Ps. 89:44(45). *cast* his throne *down* to the ground.

4049 **מְגַר** [*m'gar'*], Ch.

* PAEL.—*Future*. *

Ezr. 6:12. *destroy* all kings and people, that

4050 **מְגֵרָה** *m'gēh-rāh'*, f.

2Sa.12:31. put (them) *under saws*,
1K. 7: 9. hewed stones, sawed *with saws*,
1Ch 20: 3. cut (them) *with saws*, and with harrows of iron, *and with axes*.

4052 **מִגְרָעוֹת** *mig-rāh-gōhth'*, f. pl.

1K. 6: 6. he made *narrowed rests* (marg. *narrowings*, or, *rebatements*)

4053 **מֶגְרָפָה** [*meg-rāh-phāh'*], f.

Joel 1:17. is rotten under *their clods*,

4054 **מִגְרָשׁ** *mig-rāhsh'*, m.

Lev.25:34. But the field of *the suburbs of*
Nu. 35: 2. *and* ye shall give (also) unto the Levites *suburbs*
3. *and the suburbs of them* shall be
4. *And the suburbs of* the cities,
5. *the suburbs of* the cities.
7. with *their suburbs*.
Jos. 14: 4. *with their suburbs* for their cattle
21: 2. *with the suburbs thereof*
3. these cities and *their suburbs*.
8. these cities with *their suburbs*,
11. with *the suburbs thereof*
13. Hebron with *her suburbs*,
— and Libnah with *her suburbs*,
14. Jattir with *her suburbs*, and Eshtemoa with *her suburbs*,
15. Holon with *her suburbs*, and Debir with *her suburbs*,
16. Ain with *her suburbs*, and Juttah with *her suburbs*, (and) Beth-shemesh with *her suburbs;*
17. Gibeon with *her suburbs*, Geba with *her suburbs*,
18. Anathoth with *her suburbs*, and Almon with *her suburbs;*
19. thirteen cities *with their suburbs*.
21. Shechem with *her suburbs*
— and Gezer with *her suburbs*,
22. Kibzaim with *her suburbs*, and Beth-horon with *her suburbs;*
23. Eltekeh with *her suburbs*, Gibbethon with *her suburbs*,
24. Aijalon with *her suburbs*, Gath-rimmon with *her suburbs;*
25. Tanach with *her suburbs*, and Gath-rimmon with *her suburbs;*
26. ten *with their suburbs*
27. Golan in Bashan with *her suburbs*,
— Beesh-terah with *her suburbs;*
28. Kishon with *her suburbs*, Dabareh with *her suburbs*,
29. Jarmuth with *her suburbs*, En-gannim with *her suburbs;*
30. Mishal with *her suburbs*, Abdon with *her suburbs*,
31. Helkath with *her suburbs*, and Rehob with *her suburbs;*
32. Kedesh in Galilee with *her suburbs*,
— Hammoth-dor with *her suburbs*, and Kartan with *her suburbs;*
33. thirteen cities *with their suburbs*.
34. Jokneam with *her suburbs*, and Kartah with *her suburbs*,
35. Dimnah with *her suburbs*, Nahalal with *her suburbs;*
38(36). Ramoth in Gilead with *her suburbs*,
—(—). Mahanaim with *her suburbs*,
39(37). Heshbon with *her suburbs*, Jazer with *her suburbs;*
41(39). forty and eight cities *with their suburbs*.
42(40). every one *with their suburbs*
1Ch 5:16. in all *the suburbs of* Sharon,
6:55(40). *the suburbs thereof*
57(42). Libnah with *her suburbs*, and Jattir, and Eshtemoa, with *their suburbs*,
58(43). Hilen with *her suburbs*, Debir with *her suburbs*,
59(44). Ashan with *her suburbs*, and Beth-shemesh with *her suburbs:*
60(45). Geba with *her suburbs*, and Alemeth with *her suburbs*, and Anathoth with *her suburbs*.
64(49). (these) cities with *their suburbs*.
67(52). Shechem in mount Ephraim with *her suburbs;*
—(—). Gezer with *her suburbs*,
68(53). Jokmeam with *her suburbs*, and Beth-horon with *her suburbs*,
69(54). Aijalon with *her suburbs*, and Gath-rimmon with *her suburbs*.
70(55). Aner with *her suburbs*, and Bileam with *her suburbs*,
71(56). Golan in Bashan with *her suburbs*, and Ashtaroth with *her suburbs:*
72(57). Kedesh with *her suburbs*, Daberath with *her suburbs*,
73(58). Ramoth with *her suburbs*, and Anem with *her suburbs:*

1Ch 6:74(59). Mashal with *her suburbs*, and Abdon with *her suburbs*,
75(60). Hukok with *her suburbs*, and Rehob with *her suburbs:*
76(61). Kedesh in Galilee with *her suburbs*, and Hammon with *her suburbs*, and Kirjathaim with *her suburbs*.
77(62). Rimmon with *her suburbs*, Tabor with *her suburbs:*
78(63). Bezer in the wilderness with *her suburbs*, and Jahzah with *her suburbs*,
79(64). Kedemoth also with *her suburbs*, and Mephaath with *her suburbs:*
80(65). Ramoth in Gilead with *her suburbs*, and Mahanaim with *her suburbs*,
81(66). Heshbon with *her suburbs*, and Jazer with *her suburbs*.
13: 2. (which are) in their cities (and) *suburbs*,
2Ch 11:14. left *their suburbs* and their possession,
31:19. in the fields of *the suburbs of*
Eze. 27:28. *The suburbs* (marg. or, *waves*) shall shake
36: 5. to *cast it out* for a prey.
45: 2. round about for *the suburbs* (marg. *void places*)
48:15. for dwelling, *and for suburbs:*
17. *the suburbs* of the city

4055 מַד [*mad*], m.

Lev. 6:10(3). priest shall put on *his* linen *garment*,
Jud. 3:16. he did gird it under *his raiment*
5:10. ye that sit *in judgment*,
1Sa. 4:12. *with his clothes* rent, and with earth
17:38. Saul armed David with *his armour*, (marg. clothed David with *his clothes*)
39. David girded his sword *upon his armour*,
18: 4. *and his garments*, even to his sword,
2Sa. 20: 8. Joab's *garment* that he had put
21:20. (כתיב) where was a man of (great) *stature*,
Job 11: 9. *The measure thereof* (is) longer
Ps. 109:18. with cursing *like as with his garment*,
Jer. 13:25. of *thy measures*

4056 מַדְבַּח [*mad-bagh'*], Ch. m.

Ezr. 7:17. and offer them upon *the altar*

4057 מִדְבָּר *mid-bāhr'*, m.

Gen14: 6. which (is) by *the wilderness*.
16: 7. a fountain of water *in the wilderness*,
21:14. wandered *in the wilderness of* Beer-sheba.
20. he grew, and dwelt *in the wilderness*,
21. he dwelt *in the wilderness of* Paran:
36:24. found the mules *in the wilderness*,
37:22. into this pit that (is) *in the wilderness*,
Ex. 3: 1. to the backside of *the desert*,
18. three days' journey *into the wilderness*,
4:27. Go *into the wilderness* to meet Moses.
5: 1. hold a feast unto me *in the wilderness*.
3. three days' journey *into the desert*,
7:16. they may serve me *in the wilderness:*
8:27(23). three days' journey *into the wilderness*,
28(24). the Lord your God *in the wilderness;*
13:18. the way of *the wilderness* of the Red sea:
20. in Etham, in the edge of *the wilderness*.
14: 3. *the wilderness* hath shut them in.
11. away to die *in the wilderness?*
12. that we should die *in the wilderness*.
15:22. they went out into *the wilderness of*
— they went three days *in the wilderness*,
16: 1. came unto *the wilderness of*
2. Moses and Aaron *in the wilderness:*
3. brought us forth into this *wilderness*,
10. they looked toward *the wilderness*,
14. upon the face of *the wilderness*
32. I have fed you *in the wilderness*,
17: 1. journeyed *from the wilderness of* Sin,
18: 5. his wife unto Moses into *the wilderness*,
19: 1. came they (into) *the wilderness of* Sinai.
2. were come (to) *the desert of* Sinai, and had pitched *in the wilderness;*
23:31. *and from the desert* unto the river:
Lev. 7:38. *in the wilderness of* Sinai.
16:10. for a scapegoat *into the wilderness*.
21. a fit man *into the wilderness:*
22. let go the goat *in the wilderness*.
Nu. 1: 1. unto Moses *in the wilderness of* Sinai,
19. he numbered them *in the wilderness of*
3: 4. before the Lord, *in the wilderness of* Sinai,
14. spake unto Moses *in the wilderness of*
9: 1. unto Moses *in the wilderness of* Sinai,
5. at even *in the wilderness of* Sinai:
10:12. journeys *out of the wilderness of* Sinai; and the cloud rested *in the wilderness of*
31. we are to encamp *in the wilderness*,
12:16. pitched *in the wilderness of* Paran.
13: 3. sent them *from the wilderness of*
21. *from the wilderness of* Zin
26. unto *the wilderness of* Paran,
14: 2. we had died *in* this *wilderness!*
16. hath slain them *in the wilderness*.
22. in Egypt *and in the wilderness*,
25. get you *into the wilderness*
29. shall fall *in* this *wilderness;*
32. they shall fall *in* this *wilderness*.
33. shall wander *in the wilderness*
— be wasted *in the wilderness*.
35. *in* this *wilderness* they shall be
15:32. were *in the wilderness*,
16:13. to kill us *in the wilderness*,
20: 1. *into the desert of* Zin in the first
4. into this *wilderness*, that we
21: 5. out of Egypt to die *in the wilderness?*
11. Ije-abarim, *in the wilderness*
13. which (is) *in the wilderness* that cometh
18. *And from the wilderness* (they went)
23. out against Israel *into the wilderness:*
24: 1. set his face toward *the wilderness*.
26:64. of Israel *in the wilderness of* Sinai.
65. They shall surely die *in the wilderness*.
27: 3. Our father died *in the wilderness*,
14. *in the desert of* Zin, in the strife
— in Kadesh in *the wilderness of* Zin.
32:13. made them wander *in the wilderness*
15. leave them *in the wilderness;*
33: 6. which (is) in the edge of *the wilderness*.
8. *into the wilderness*, and went three days journey *in the wilderness of*
11. encamped *in the wilderness of* Sin.
12. journey *out of the wilderness of* Sin,
15. pitched *in the wilderness of* Sinai.
16. removed *from the desert of* Sinai,
36. pitched *in the wilderness of* Zin,
34: 3. *from the wilderness of* Zin
Deu 1: 1. Jordan *in the wilderness*,
19. that great and terrible *wilderness*,
31. *And in the wilderness*, where thou
40. take your journey *into the wilderness*
2: 1. took our journey *into the wilderness*
7. walking through this great *wilderness:*
8. by the way of *the wilderness of*
26. sent messengers *out of the wilderness of*
4:43. Bezer *in the wilderness*,
8: 2. these forty years *in the wilderness*,
15. *through* that great and terrible *wilderness*,
16. Who fed thee *in the wilderness*
9: 7. thy God to wrath *in the wilderness:*
28. to slay them *in the wilderness*.
11: 5. what he did unto you *in the wilderness*,
24. from *the wilderness* and Lebanon,
29: 5(4). led you forty years *in the wilderness:*
32:10. He found him in a *desert* land,
51. in *the wilderness of* Zin;
Jos. 1: 4. *From the wilderness* and this Lebanon
5: 4. died *in the wilderness* by the way,
5. born *in the wilderness*
6. walked forty years *in the wilderness*,
8:15. fled by the way of *the wilderness*.
20. that fled to *the wilderness*
24. *in the wilderness* wherein
12: 8. *and in the wilderness*, and in the south
14:10. wandered *in the wilderness:*
15: 1. *the wilderness of* Zin southward
61. *In the wilderness*, Beth-arabah,
16: 1. to *the wilderness* that goeth up
18:12. *at the wilderness of* Beth-aven.
20: 8. Bezer *in the wilderness*
24: 7. ye dwelt *in the wilderness* a long season.
Jud. 1:16. of Judah into *the wilderness of* Judah,

Jud. 8: 7. with the thorns of *the wilderness*
16. and thorns of *the wilderness* and briers,
11:16. walked *through the wilderness*
18. went along *through the wilderness*,
22. from *the wilderness* even unto Jordan.
20:42. unto the way of *the wilderness*;
45. fled *toward the wilderness*
47. turned and fled *to the wilderness*
1Sa. 4: 8. with all the plagues *in the wilderness*.
13:18. of Zeboim *toward the wilderness*.
17:28. left those few sheep *in the wilderness*?
23:14. David abode *in the wilderness*
— in a mountain *in the wilderness of* Ziph.
15. David (was) *in the wilderness of* Ziph
24. and his men (were) *in the wilderness of*
25. abode *in the wilderness of* Maon.
— after David *in the wilderness of* Maon.
24: 1(2). David (is) *in the wilderness*
25: 1. went down to *the wilderness of* Paran.
4. David heard *in the wilderness*
14. sent messengers *out of the wilderness*
21. hath *in the wilderness*,
26: 2. went down to *the wilderness of* Ziph,
— to seek David *in the wilderness of* Ziph.
3. *in the wilderness*, and he saw that Saul came after him *into the wilderness*.
2Sa. 2:24. by the way of *the wilderness of* Gibeon.
15:23. toward the way of *the wilderness*.
28. tarry in the plain of *the wilderness*,
16: 2. such as be faint *in the wilderness*
17:16. in the plains of *the wilderness*,
29. thirsty, *in the wilderness*.
1K. 2:34. in his own house *in the wilderness*.
9:18. Tadmor *in the wilderness*,
19: 4. a day's journey *into the wilderness*,
15. on thy way *to the wilderness* of Damascus:
2K. 3: 8. The way through *the wilderness of* Edom.
1Ch 5: 9. the entering in of *the wilderness*
6:78(63). Bezer *in the wilderness*
12: 8. into the hold to *the wilderness*
21:29. Moses made in *the wilderness*,
2Ch 1: 3. had made *in the wilderness*.
8: 4. Tadmor *in the wilderness*,
20:16. before *the wilderness of* Jeruel.
20. went forth *into the wilderness of*
24. the watch tower *in the wilderness*,
24: 9. (laid) upon Israel *in the wilderness*.
26:10. he built towers *in the desert*,
Neh 9:19. forsookest them not *in the wilderness*:
21. sustain them *in the wilderness*,
Job 1:19. a great wind from *the wilderness*,
24: 5. wild asses *in the desert*,
38:26. *the wilderness*, wherein (there is) no man;
Ps. 29: 8. the Lord shaketh *the wilderness*; the Lord shaketh *the wilderness of*
55: 7(8). remain *in the wilderness*.
63: [title](1). when he was *in the wilderness of*
65:12(13). the pastures of *the wilderness*:
75: 6(7). nor *from the south*. (marg. *desert*)
78:15. He clave the rocks *in the wilderness*,
19. God furnish a table *in the wilderness*?
40. they provoke him *in the wilderness*,
52. guided them *in the wilderness*
95: 8. the day of temptation *in the wilderness*:
102: 6(7). I am like a pelican of *the wilderness*:
106: 9. the depths, *as through the wilderness*.
14. exceedingly *in the wilderness*,
26. overthrow them *in the wilderness*:
107: 4. They wandered *in the wilderness*
33. He turneth rivers *into a wilderness*,
35. He turneth *the wilderness*
136:16. led his people *through the wilderness*:
Pro. 21:19. better to dwell in *the wilderness*, (marg. land of *the desert*)
Cant. 3: 6. that cometh out of *the wilderness*
4: 3. *and thy speech* (is) comely:
8: 5. that cometh up from *the wilderness*,
Isa. 14:17. made the world *as a wilderness*,
16: 1. from Sela *to the wilderness*,
8. they wandered (through) *the wilderness*:
21: 1. The burden of *the desert of* the sea.
— cometh *from the desert*,
27:10. forsaken, and left *like a wilderness*:
32:15. *the wilderness* be a fruitful field,
16. judgment shall dwell *in the wilderness*,
35: 1. *The wilderness* and the solitary place
6. *in the wilderness* shall waters

Isa. 40: 3. of him that crieth *in the wilderness*,
41:18. make *the wilderness* a pool of water,
19. I will plant *in the wilderness*
42:11. Let *the wilderness* and the cities
43:19. make a way *in the wilderness*,
20. I give waters *in the wilderness*,
50: 2. I make the rivers *a wilderness*:
51: 3. will make *her wilderness* like Eden,
63:13. as an horse *in the wilderness*,
64:10(9). Thy holy cities are *a wilderness*, Zion is *a wilderness*,
Jer. 2: 2. wentest after me *in the wilderness*,
6. led us *through the wilderness*,
24. A wild ass used to *the wilderness*,
31. Have I been *a wilderness*
3: 2. as the Arabian *in the wilderness*;
4:11. the high places *in the wilderness*
26. fruitful place (was) *a wilderness*,
9: 2(1). Oh that I had *in the wilderness*
10(9). habitations of *the wilderness*
12(11). is burned up *like a wilderness*,
26(25). that dwell *in the wilderness*:
12:10. pleasant portion *a* desolate *wilderness*.
12. high places *through the wilderness*:
13:24. by the wind of *the wilderness*.
17: 6. the parched places *in the wilderness*,
22: 6. I will make thee *a wilderness*,
23:10. the pleasant places of *the wilderness*
25:24. people that dwell *in the desert*,
31: 2. found grace *in the wilderness*;
48: 6. be like the heath *in the wilderness*.
50:12. of the nations (shall be) *a wilderness*,
Lam. 4: 3. like the ostriches *in the wilderness*.
19. laid wait for us *in the wilderness*.
5: 9. the sword of *the wilderness*.
Eze. 6:14. more desolate *than the wilderness*
19:13. she (is) planted *in the wilderness*,
20:10. brought them into *the wilderness*.
13. rebelled against me *in the wilderness*:
— my fury upon them *in the wilderness*,
15. unto them *in the wilderness*,
17. an end of them *in the wilderness*.
18. their children *in the wilderness*,
21. anger against them *in the wilderness*.
23. unto them also *in the wilderness*,
35. bring you into *the wilderness of*
36. with your fathers *in the wilderness of*
23:42. Sabeans *from the wilderness*,
29: 5. leave thee (thrown) *into the wilderness*,
34:25. dwell safely *in the wilderness*,
Hos. 2: 3(5). make her *as a wilderness*,
14(16). bring her into *the wilderness*,
9:10. like grapes *in the wilderness*;
13: 5. I did know thee *in the wilderness*,
15. come up *from the wilderness*,
Joel 1:19, 20. the pastures of *the wilderness*,
2: 3. behind them *a* desolate *wilderness*;
22. the pastures of *the wilderness* do spring,
3:19(4:19). Edom shall be *a* desolate *wilderness*,
Am. 2:10. forty years *through the wilderness*,
5:25. sacrifices and offerings *in the wilderness*
Zep. 2:13. dry *like a wilderness*.
Mal. 1: 3. the dragons of *the wilderness*.

מָדַד *māh-dad'*. 4058

* KAL.—*Preterite*. *

Nu. 35: 5. *And ye shall measure* from without
Deu 21: 2. *and they shall measure* unto the cities
Isa. 40:12. Who *hath measured* the waters
65: 7. *therefore will I measure* their former work
Eze. 40:20. *he measured* the length thereof,
24. *and he measured* the posts thereof
35. *and measured* (it) according to
41:13. *So he measured* the house,
15. *And he measured* the length
42:15. *and measured* it round about.
16. *He measured* the east side
17. *He measured* the north side,
18. *He measured* the south side,
19. (and) *measured* five hundred reeds
20. *He measured it* by the four sides:
43:10. *and let them measure* the pattern.

KAL.—*Infinitive*.

Zec. 2: 2(6). *To measure* Jerusalem,

KAL.—*Future.*

Ex. 16:18. *And when they did mete* (it)
Ru. 3:15. *And* when...*he measured* six (measures) of
Eze.40: 5. *so he measured* the breadth
6. *and measured* the threshold of the gate,
8. *He measured also* the porch
9. *Then measured he* the porch
11. *And he measured* the breadth
13. *He measured then* the gate
19. *Then he measured* the breadth
23, 27. *and he measured* from gate to gate
28. *and he measured* the south gate
32. *and he measured* the gate
47. *So he measured* the court,
48. *and measured* (each) post
41: 1. *and measured* the posts,
2. *and he measured* the length thereof,
3. *and measured* the post of the door,
4. *So he measured* the length
5. *After he measured* the wall of the house,
45: 3. *shalt thou measure* the length
47: 3. *And* when the man...*he measured* a
4, 4. *Again he measured* a thousand,
5. *Afterward he measured* a thousand;
18. *ye shall measure* from Hauran,

* NIPHAL.—*Future.* *

Jer. 31:37. If heaven above *can be measured,*
33:22. neither the sand of the sea *measured:*
Hos. 1:10(2:1). which *cannot be measured*

* PIEL.—*Future.* *

2Sa. 8: 2. *and measured them* with a line,
— *even* with two lines *measured he*
Ps. 60: 6(8) & 108:7(8). and *mete out* the valley of

* POLEL.—*Future.* *

Hab. 3: 6. He stood, *and measured* the earth:

* HITHPOLEL.—*Future.* *

1K. 17:21. *And he stretched* (marg. *measured*) *himself* upon the child

---

4059 **מִדַּד** *mid-dad′*, m.

Job 7: 4. *and* the night *be gone?* (lit. *the flight of* the night; marg. the evening *be measured*)

4060 **מִדָּה** *mid-dāh′*, f.

Ex. 26: 2. the curtains shall have one *measure.*
8. (all) of one *measure.*
36: 9. the curtains (were) all of one *size.*
15. the eleven curtains (were) of one *size.*
Lev.19:35. *in meteyard*, in weight,
Nu. 13:32. all the people...(are) men of *a great stature.* (marg. of *statures*)
Jos. 3: 4. about two thousand cubits *by measure:*
1K. 6:25. of one *measure* and one size.
7: 9. *according to the measures of* hewed stones,
11. *after the measures of* hewed stones,
37. one *measure,* (and) one size.
1Ch 11:23 & 20:6. a man of (great) *stature,* (marg. of *measure*)
23:29. all manner of measure *and size;*
2Ch 3: 3. *after the* first *measure*
Neh 3:11. repaired *the* other *piece,* (marg. second *measure*)
19. another *piece* over against
20. earnestly repaired *the* other *piece,*
21. the son of Koz another *piece,*
24. the son of Henadad another *piece,*
27. the Tekoites repaired another *piece,*
30. the sixth son of Zalaph, another *piece.*
5: 4. borrowed money *for* the king's *tribute,*
Job 28:25. he weigheth the waters *by measure.*
Ps. 39: 4(5). *and the measure of* my days,
133: 2. went down to the skirts of *his garments;*
Isa. 45:14. the Sabeans, men of *stature,*
Jer. 22:14. I will build me a *wide* house (lit. a house of *measures*)
31:39 the *measuring* line shall yet go
Eze.40: 3. in his hand, and a *measuring* reed;
5. in the man's hand a *measuring* reed
10. they three (were) of one *measure: and* the posts had one *measure*
21. *after the measure of* the first gate:
22. *after the measure of* the gate
24, 28, 29, 32, 33, 35. *according to* these *measures.*
41:17. within and without, *by measure.* (marg. *measures*)
42:15. when he had made an end of *measuring*
16, 16, 17, 18, 19. with the *measuring* reed,
43:13. *the measures of* the altar
45: 3. of this *measure* shalt thou measure
46:22. these four corners (were) of one *measure.*
48:16. these (shall be) *the measures thereof;*
30, 33. four thousand and five hundred *measures.*
Zec. 2: 1(5). a man with a *measuring* line

מִדָּה *mid-dāh′*, f. Ch. 4061

Ezr. 4:20. *and toll,* tribute, and custom, was paid
6: 8. (even) of *the tribute* beyond the river,
(See also מִנְדָּה).

מַדְהֵבָה *mad-hĕh-vāh′*, f. 4062

Isa. 14: 4. *the golden city* (marg. *exactress of gold*)

מֶדֶו [*meh′-dev*], m. 4063

2Sa.10: 4. cut off *their garments*
1Ch 19: 4. cut off *their garments*

מַדְוֶה [*mad-veh′*], m. 4064

Deu 7:15. none of *the* evil *diseases of* Egypt,
28:60. bring upon thee all *the diseases of* Egypt,

מַדּוּחִים *mad-doo-ghheem′*, m. pl. 4065

Lam.2:14. false burdens *and causes of banishment.*

מָדוֹן *māh-dōhn′*, m. 4066

Ps. 80: 6(7). Thou makest us *a strife*
Pro. 6:14. he soweth *discord.*
15:18. A wrathful man stirreth up *strife:*
16:28. A froward man soweth *strife:*
17:14. The beginning of *strife* (is as) when
18:19. (כתיב)*and* (their) *contentions* (are) like
21: 9. (——) than with a *brawling* woman (marg. a woman of *contentions*) in a wide house.
19. (כתיב) than with a *contentious* and an angry woman. (lit. a woman of *contentions*)
22:10. *contention* shall go out;
23:29. (כתיב) who hath *contentions?*
25:24. (——) than with a *brawling* woman
26:20. no talebearer, *the strife* ceaseth.
21. (כתיב) so (is) a *contentious* man (lit. a man of *contentions*) to kindle strife.
27:15. (כתיב) and a *contentious* woman (lit. a woman of *contentions*) are alike.
28:25. a proud heart stirreth up *strife:*
29:22. An angry man stirreth up *strife,*
Jer. 15:10. a man of *contention* to the whole earth!
Hab. 1: 3. raise up strife *and contention.*

מָדוֹן *māh-dōhn′*, m. 4067

2Sa.21:20. where was a man of (great) *stature,*

מַדּוּעַ *mad-doo′ăg*, part. adv. 4069

Gen26:27. Isaac said unto them, *Wherefore* come ye
Ex. 1:18. *Why* have ye done this thing,
2:18. *How* (is it that) ye are come so soon to day?
3: 3. this great sight, *why* the bush is not burnt.
Isa. 5: 4. *wherefore*...brought it forth wild grapes?
Jer. 2:14. *why* is he spoiled?
&c.

4070 מְדוֹר [*m'dōhr*], Ch. m.

Dan 4:25(22). *thy dwelling* shall be with the beasts
32(29). *thy dwelling* (shall be) with the beasts
5:21. and *his dwelling* (was) with the wild asses:

4071 מְדוּרָה *m'doo-rāh'*, f.

Isa. 30:33. *the pile thereof* (is) fire
Eze. 24: 9. even make *the pile for fire* great.

4072 מִדְחֶה *mid-gheh'*, m.

Pro. 26:28. a flattering mouth worketh *ruin*.

4073 מַדְחֵפֹת *mad-ghēh-phōhth'*, f. pl.

Ps. 140:11(12). the violent man *to overthrow* (him).

4078 מַדַּי *mad-dah'y*, adv.

2Ch 30: 3. had not sanctified themselves *sufficiently*,

4082 מְדִינָה *m'dee-nāh'*, f.

1K. 20:14, 15, 17, 19. the princes of *the provinces*.
Ezr. 2: 1. the children of *the province*
Neh 1: 3. The remnant that are left...*in the province*
7: 6. the children of *the province*,
11: 3. the chief of *the province*
Est. 1: 1. an hundred and seven and twenty *provinces:*
3. and princes of *the provinces*,
16. *the provinces of* the king Ahasuerus.
22. all the king's *provinces*, into *every province* (lit. *province and province*)
2: 3. in all *the provinces of* his kingdom,
18. he made a release *to the provinces*,
3: 8. *the provinces of* thy kingdom;
12. the governors that (were) over *every province*, (lit. *province and province*) and to the rulers of every people of *every province* (lit. *id.*)
13. all the king's *provinces*,
14. The copy...to be given in every *province* (lit. every *province and province*)
4: 3. And in every *province*, (lit. *id.*)
11. the people of the king's *provinces*,
8: 5. in all the king's *provinces:*
9. rulers of *the provinces*
— an hundred twenty and seven *provinces*, unto *every province* (lit. *province and province*) according to the writing
11. all the power of the people *and province*
12. *the provinces of* king Ahasuerus,
13. The copy...to be given in every *province* (lit. every *province and province*)
17. And in every *province*, (lit. every *province and province*)
9: 2. throughout all *the provinces of* the king
3. the rulers of *the provinces*,
4. throughout all *the provinces:*
12. the rest of the king's *provinces?*
16. *in* the king's *provinces*
20. *the provinces of* the king
28. every family, *every province*, (lit. *province and province*)
30. the hundred twenty and seven *provinces*
Ecc. 2: 8. treasure of kings *and of the provinces:*
5: 8(7). of judgment and justice *in a province*,
Lam. 1: 1. princess *among the provinces*,
Eze. 19: 8. *from the provinces*,
Dan 8: 2. *in the province* of Elam;
11:24. the fattest places of *the province;*

4083 מְדִינָה [*m'dee-nāh'*], Ch. f.

Ezr 4:15. and hurtful unto kings *and provinces*,
5: 8. that we went into *the province*
6: 2. that (is) in *the province* of the Medes,
Ezr. 7:16. canst find in all *the province of* Babylon,
Dan 2:48. over *the* whole *province of* Babylon,
49. the affairs of *the province of* Babylon:
3: 1. Dura, *in the province of* Babylon.
2, 3. and all the rulers of *the provinces*,
12. the affairs of *the province of* Babylon,
30. and Abed-nego, in *the province of* Babylon.

מְדָנִים *mid-yāh-neem'*, m. pl. 4079

Pro. 18:18. The lot causeth *contentions*
19. *and* (their) *contentions* (are) like
19:13. *the contentions of* a wife
21: 9. than with a *brawling* woman (marg. a woman of *contentions*)
19. a *contentious* and an angry woman.
23:29. who hath *contentions?*
25:24. than with a *brawling* woman
26:21. a *contentious* man to kindle strife.
27:15. and a *contentious* woman are alike.

מְדֹכָה *m'dōh-chāh'*, f. 4085

Nu. 11: 8. or beat (it) *in a mortar*,

מַדְמֵנָה *mad-mēh-nāh'*, f. 4087

Isa. 25:10. trodden down for *the dunghill*.

מְדָנִים *m'dāh-neem'*, m. pl. 4090

Pro. 6:14(כתיב). he soweth *discord*.
19. he that soweth *discord* among
10:12. Hatred stirreth up *strifes:*

מַדָּע *mad-dāhn̄g'* & מַדַּע *mad-dan̄g'*, m. 4093

2Ch 1:10. Give me now wisdom *and knowledge*,
11. hast asked wisdom *and knowledge*
12. Wisdom *and knowledge* (is) granted unto
Ecc. 10:20. Curse not the king, no not *in thy thought;* (marg. *conscience*)
Dan 1: 4. understanding *science*,
17. God gave them *knowledge* and skill

מַדְקְרוֹת [*mad-kāh-rōhth'*], f. pl. 4094

Pro. 12:18. *like the piercings of* a sword:

מְדָר *m'dāhr*, Ch. m. 4070

Dan 2:11. *whose dwelling* is not with flesh.

מַדְרֵגָה *mad-rēh-gāh'*, f. 4095

Cant. 2:14. in the secret (places) of *the stairs*,
Eze. 38:20. *the steep places* (marg. or, *towers*, or, *stairs*) shall fall,

מִדְרָךְ *mid-rach'*, m. 4096

Deu 2: 5. not so much as a foot *breadth;* (marg. *the treading of* the sole of the foot)

מִדְרָשׁ *mid-rash'*, m. 4097

2Ch 13:22. written *in the story* (marg. or, *commentary*) *of* the prophet Iddo.
24:27. written in *the story of* the book (marg. *id.*)

מְדֻשָּׁה [*m'doosh-shāh'*], f. 4098

Isa. 21:10. *O my threshing*, and the corn of my floor:

4100 ## מָה *māh*, part.

Gen20:10. *What* sawest thou, that thou hast done
Nu. 23: 8. *How* shall I curse, whom God hath not
Jud. 8: 1. Why (marg. *What* thing) hast thou
1Sa.19: 3. and *what* I see, that I will tell thee.
2Sa.18:22. But *how*soever, (marg. be *what* (may))
Pro. 9:13. (she is) simple, and knoweth no*thing*.
Lam. 2:13. *What thing* shall I take to witness for thee?
Mal. 2:14. Yet ye say, *Where*fore? (עַל מָה)
&c.

With prefixes; as,

I. בַּמָּה.

Gen15: 8. *whereby* shall I know that I shall
Jud. 6:15. *wherewith* shall I save Israel?
1Sa.14:38. *wherein* this sin hath been this day.
&c.

II. כַּמָּה.

Gen47: 8. *How* old (art) thou? (marg. *How many* (are) the days &c.)
Job 7:19. *How long* wilt thou not depart
Ps. 78:40. *How oft* did they provoke him
Zec. 2: 2(6). to see *what* (is) the breadth thereof, *and what* (is) the length thereof.

III. לָמָה, לָמָּה.

Gen18:13. *Wherefore* did Sarah laugh, saying,
27:45. *why* should I be deprived also
46. *what good* shall my life do me?
33:15. *What* needeth it? (marg. *Wherefore* (is) this)
Job 30: 2. *whereto* (might) the strength of their hands
Isa. 1:11. *To what purpose* (is) the multitude
Am. 5:18. *to what end* (is) it for you?
&c.

IV. שַׁלָּמָה.

Cant.1: 7. *for why* should I be as one that turneth

4100 ## מֶה *meh*, part.

[i. q. מָה].

Gen 4:10. And he said, *What* hast thou done?
Jos. 7:25. *Why* hast thou troubled us?
2Sa. 1: 4. *How* went (marg. *What* was) the matter?
Jer. 5:19. *Wherefore* doeth the Lord our God
&c.

It occurs with the prefixes ב, כ, ל, which affect its sense just as they do that of מָה.

4101 ## מָה *māh*, Ch. part.

Ezr. 4:22. *why* should damage grow to the hurt
6: 9. *And that which* they have need of,
7:18. *And whatsoever* shall seem good to thee,
23. for *why* should there be wrath against
Dan. 2:15. *Why* (lit. upon *what*) (is) the decree (so)
22. he knoweth *what* (is) in the darkness,
28. *what* shall be in the latter days.
29. *what* should come to pass hereafter:
— known to thee *what* shall come to pass.
45. *what* shall come to pass hereafter:
4: 3(3:33). *How great* (are) his signs! and *how mighty* (are) his wonders!
35(32). or say unto him, *What* doest thou?

4102 ## מָהַהּ [*māh-hah'*].

* HITHPALPEL.—*Preterite.* *

Gen43:10. For except *we had lingered*, surely
Jud.19: 8. *And they tarried* until afternoon,
Ps.119:60. I made haste, and *delayed* not

HITHPALPEL.—*Infinitive.*

Ex. 12:39. and could not *tarry*,
Jud. 3:26. Ehud escaped while *they tarried*,

HITHPALPEL.—*Imperative.*

Isa. 29: 9. *Stay yourselves*, and wonder;

HITHPALPEL.—*Future.*

Gen19:16. *And while he lingered*,
Hab. 2: 3. though *it tarry*, wait for it;

HITHPALPEL.—*Participle.*

2Sa.15:28. I *will tarry* in the plain

מְהוּמָה *m'hoo-māh'*, f. 4103

Deu 7:23. destroy them with *a* mighty *destruction*,
28:20. send upon thee cursing, *vexation*,
1Sa. 5: 9. with *a* very great *destruction*:
11. there was *a* deadly *destruction*
14:20. *a* very great *discomfiture*.
2Ch 15: 5. great *vexations* (were) upon all
Pro.15:16. *and trouble* therewith.
Isa. 22: 5. For (it is) a day of *trouble*,
Eze. 7: 7. the day of *trouble* (is) near,
22: 5. infamous (and) much *vexed*.
Am. 3: 9. *the* great *tumults* in the midst thereof,
Zec.14:13. *a* great *tumult from* the Lord

מָהִיר *māh-heer'*, adj. 4106

Ezr. 7: 6. he (was) a *ready* scribe
Ps. 45: 1(2). tongue (is) the pen of a *ready* writer.
Pro.22:29. Seest thou a man *diligent*
Isa. 16: 5. *and hasting* righteousness.

מָהַל [*māh-hal'*]. 4107

* KAL.—*Participle.* Paül. *

Isa. 1:22. thy wine *mixed* with water:

מַהֲלָךְ *mah-hălach'*, m. 4109

Neh. 2: 6. how long shall *thy journey* be?
Eze.42: 4. before the chambers (was) *a walk of*
Jon. 3: 3. great city of three days' *journey*.
4. enter into the city a day'*s journey*,

מַהֲלָל [*mah-hălāhl'*], m. 4110

Pro.27:21. so (is) a man to *his praise*. (lit. to the mouth of *his praise*)

מַהֲלֻמּוֹת *mah-hăloom-mōhth'*, f. pl. 4112

Pro.18: 6. his mouth calleth *for strokes*.
19:29. *and stripes* for the back of fools.

מַהֲמֹרוֹת *mah-hămōh-rōhth'*, f. pl. 4113

Ps.140:10(11). into the fire; *into deep pits*,

מַהְפֵּכָה [*mah-pēh-chāh'*], f. 4114

Deu 29:23(22). *like the overthrow of* Sodom,
Isa. 1: 7. *as overthrown by* strangers. (marg. *as the overthrow of*)
13:19. *as when* God *overthrew* Sodom (lit. *as the overthrowing of* God)
Jer. 49:18. *As* in *the overthrow of* Sodom
50:40. *As* God *overthrew* Sodom (lit. *as the overthrowing of* God)
Am. 4:11. *as* God *overthrew* Sodom (lit. *id.*)

מַהְפֶּכֶת *mah-peh'-cheth*, f. 4115

2Ch 16:10. put him in a *prison* house;
Jer. 20: 2. put him in *the stocks*
3. Jeremiah out of *the stocks*.
29:26. that thou shouldest put him in *prison*,

4116 ## מָהַר [*māh-har'*].

* KAL.—*Preterite.* *

Ps. 16: 4. (that) *hasten* (after) another (god): (marg. or, *give gifts* to another)

* NIPHAL.—*Participle.* *

Job 5:13. counsel of the froward *is carried headlong.*
Isa. 32: 4. The heart also of *the rash* (marg. *hasty*)
35: 4. *to them that are of* a *fearful* heart, (marg. *hasty*)
Hab. 1: 6. (that) bitter *and hasty* nation,

* PIEL.—*Preterite.* *

Gen27:20. How (is it) that *thou hast* found (it) *so quickly*, (lit. that *thou hast hasted* to find)
45:13. *and ye shall haste* and bring down
Ex. 2:18. How (is it that) *ye are* come *so soon* to day? (lit. *ye have hastened* to come)
1Sa. 4:14. And the man came in *hastily*, (lit. *hasted* and came in)
25:34. except *thou hadst hasted* and come
2Ch 24: 5. the Levites *hastened* (it) not.
Ps.106:13. *They soon* forgat (marg. *They made haste*, they forgat) his works;
Isa. 49:17. Thy children *shall make haste;*
51:14. The captive exile *hasteneth*
Jer. 48:16. his affliction *hasteth* fast.

PIEL.—*Infinitive.*

Ex. 12:33. send them out of the land *in haste;*
1Ch 12: 8. *as swift* (marg. *to make haste*) as the roes
Pro. 7:23. *as* a bird *hasteth* to the snare,
Isa. 8: 1. *concerning Maher-shalal-hash-baz.* (marg. *in making speed* to the spoil &c.)

PIEL.—*Imperative.*

Gen18: 6. *Make ready quickly* (marg. *Hasten*) three
19:22. *Haste thee*, escape thither;
45: 9. *Haste ye*, and go up to my father,
Jud. 9:48. *make haste*, (and) do as I (have done).
1Sa. 9:12. *make haste* now, for he came
23:27. *Haste thee*, and come;
2Sa. 15:14. *make speed* to depart,
1K. 22: 9. *Hasten* (hither) Micaiah
2Ch 18: 8. *Fetch quickly* (marg. *Hasten*) Micaiah
Est. 5: 5. *Cause* Haman *to make haste*,
6:10. *Make haste*, (and) take the apparel

PIEL.—*Future.*

Gen18: 6. *And* Abraham *hastened* into the tent
7. *and he hasted* to dress it.
24:18. *and she hasted*, and let down her pitcher
20. *And she hasted*, and emptied her pitcher
46. *And she made haste*, and let down her
43:30. *And* Joseph *made haste;*
44:11. *Then they speedily* took down (lit. *and they hasted* and took down)
Ex. 10:16. *Then* Pharaoh called for Moses and Aaron *in haste;* (lit. *and hasted* to call)
34: 8. *And* Moses *made haste*,
Jos. 4:10. *and* the people *hasted* and passed over.
8:14. *that they hasted* and rose up early,
19. *and hasted* and set the city on fire.
Jud.13:10. *And* the woman *made haste*,
1Sa.17:48. *that* David *hasted*,
25:18. *Then* Abigail *made haste*,
23. *And* when Abigail saw David, *she hasted*,
42. *And* Abigail *hasted*, and arose,
28:20. *Then* Saul fell *straightway* (marg. *made haste*, and fell) all along on the earth,
24. *and she hasted*, and killed it,
2Sa. 15:14. lest *he* overtake us *suddenly*, (lit. lest *he make haste* and overtake us)
19:16(17). *And* Shimei...*hasted* and came down
1K. 20:33. *and* did *hastily* catch (lit. *and they hasted* and caught)
41. *And he hasted*, and took the ashes
2K. 9:13. *Then they hasted*, and took
2Ch 24: 5. and see that ye *hasten* the matter.
Pro. 1:16. *and make haste* to shed blood.
Ecc. 5: 2(1). *let* not thine heart *be hasty* to utter
Isa. 5:19. *Let him make speed*, (and) hasten his
32: 4. tongue of the stammerers *shall be ready*
59: 7. *and they make haste* to shed innocent
Jer. 9:18(17). *And let them make haste*, and take
Nah. 2: 5(6). *they shall make haste* to the wall

PIEL.—*Participle.*

Gen41:32. *and* God *will shortly* (lit. *and* (is) *hastening* to) bring it to pass.
Pro. 6:18. feet *that be swift* in running to
Mal. 3: 5. I will be a *swift* witness

מָהַר [*māh-har'*]. 4117

* KAL.—*Infinitive.* *

Ex. 22:16(15). he shall *surely* endow (lit. *endowing* he shall endow) her

KAL.—*Future.*

Ex. 22:16(15). *he shall* surely *endow her*

מַהֵר *mah-hēhr'*, adj. 4118

Zep. 1:14. The great day of the Lord (is) near,...*and hasteth*

מַהֵר *mah-hēhr'*, adv. 4118

Ex. 32: 8. They have turned aside *quickly*
Deu 4:26. ye shall *soon* utterly perish
7: 4 against you, and destroy thee *suddenly.*
22. thou mayest not consume them *at once*,
9: 3. and destroy them *quickly*,
12. get thee down *quickly*
— they are *quickly* turned aside
16. ye had turned aside *quickly*
28:20. until thou perish *quickly;*
Jos. 2: 5. pursue after them *quickly;*
Jud. 2:17. they turned *quickly* out of the way
23. without driving them out *hastily;*
Ps. 69:17(18). I am in trouble: hear me *speedily.* (marg. *haste* to hear me)
79: 8. let thy tender mercies *speedily* prevent us:
102: 2(3). (when) I call answer me *speedily.*
143: 7. Hear me *speedily*, O Lord:
Pro.25: 8. Go not forth *hastily* to strive,

מֹהַר *mōh'-har*, m. 4119

Gen34:12. Ask me never so much *dowry*
Ex. 22:17(16). *according to the dowry of* virgins.
1Sa.18:25. The king desireth not *any dowry*,

מְהֵרָה *m'hēh-rāh'*, f. 4120

Nu. 16:46(17:11). go *quickly* unto the congregation,
Deu11:17. (lest) ye perish *quickly*
Jos. 8:19. the ambush arose *quickly*
10: 6. come up to us *quickly*,
23:16. ye shall perish *quickly*
Jud. 9:54. he called *hastily* unto the young man
1Sa.20:38. *Make speed*, haste, stay not.
2Sa.17:16. Now therefore send *quickly*, and tell
18. they went both of them away *quickly*,
21. and pass *quickly* over the water:
2K. 1:11. Come down *quickly.*
Ps. 31: 2(3). deliver me *speedily:*
37: 2. they shall *soon* be cut down
147:15. his word runneth very *swiftly.*
Ecc. 4:12. a threefold cord is not *quickly* broken.
8:11. sentence...is not executed *speedily*,
Isa. 5:26. they shall come *with speed* swiftly:
58: 8. thine health shall spring forth *speedily:*
Jer.27:16. Lord's house shall now *shortly* be brought
Joel 3: 4(4:4). *speedily* will I return

מַהֲתַלּוֹת *mah-hăthal-lōhth'*, f. pl. 4123

Isa. 30:10. unto us smooth things, prophesy *deceits:*

מוֹאל *mōhl.* 4136

[כתיב for מוֹל]

Neh 12:38. the other (company)...went *over against*

4126 **מוֹבָא** *mōh-vāh'*, m.

2Sa. 3:25. thy going out and *thy coming in*,
Eze.43:11. *and the comings in thereof*, and all

4127 **מוּג** *moog*.

* KAL.—*Infinitive*. *

Eze.21:15(20). that (their) heart *may faint*,

KAL.—*Future*.

Ps. 46: 6(7). he uttered his voice, the earth *melted*.
Isa. 64: 7(6). *and hast consumed* (marg. *melted*) *us*,
Am. 9: 5. toucheth the land, *and it shall melt*,

* NIPHAL.—*Preterite*. *

Ex. 15:15. the inhabitants of Canaan *shall melt away*.
Jos. 2: 9. inhabitants of the land *faint* (marg. *melt*)
24. the inhabitants of the country *do faint* (marg. *id.*)
1Sa.14:16. the multitude *melted away*,
Isa. 14:31. thou, whole Palestina, (art) *dissolved*:
Jer. 49:23. *they are fainthearted*; (marg. *melted*)
Nah. 2: 6(7). palace *shall be dissolved*. (marg. *molten*)

NIPHAL.—*Participle*.

Ps. 75: 3(4). the inhabitants thereof *are dissolved*:

* POLEL.—*Future*. *

Job 30:22. *and dissolvest my* substance.
Ps. 65:10(11). *thou makest it soft* (marg. *dissolvest it*)

* HITHPOLEL.—*Preterite*. *

Nah. 1: 5. and the hills *melt*,

HITHPOLEL.—*Future*.

Ps.107:26. their soul *is melted*
Am. 9:13. all the hills *shall melt*.

4129 **מֹדָע** *mōh-dāhg'* & **מוֹדַע** *mōh-dag'*, m.

Ru. 2: 1. Naomi had *a kinsman* of her husband's,
Pro. 7: 4. *and* call understanding (thy) *kinswoman*:

4130 **מוֹדַעַת** [*mōh-dah'-gath*], f.

Ru. 3: 2. (is) not Boaz of *our kindred*,

4131 **מוֹט** *mōht*, f.

* KAL.—*Preterite*. *

Lev.25:35. *and fallen in decay* with thee; (marg. his hand *faileth*)
Ps. 46: 6(7). the kingdoms *were moved*:
60: 2(4). the breaches thereof; for *it shaketh*.
94:18. When I said, My foot *slippeth*;

KAL.—*Infinitive*.

Ps. 38:16(17). *when* my foot *slippeth*,
46: 2(3). *and though* the mountains *be carried*
55:22(23). never suffer the righteous to *be moved*.
Isa. 24:19. the earth is moved *exceedingly*.

KAL.—*Future*.

Deu 32:35. their foot *shall slide*
Isa. 54:10. the hills *be removed*;
— *shall* the covenant of my peace *be removed*,

KAL.—*Participle*.

Pro.24:11. *and those that are ready* to be slain;
25:26. A righteous man *falling down*

* NIPHAL.—*Preterite*. *

Ps. 17: 5. (that) my footsteps *slip* not. (marg. *be* not *moved*)

NIPHAL.—*Future*.

1Ch 16:30. *that it be* not *moved*.
Job 41:23(15). *they* cannot *be moved*.
Ps. 10: 6. *I shall* not *be moved*:
13: 4(5). trouble me rejoice when *I am moved*.
15: 5. doeth these (things) *shall* never *be moved*.
16: 8. *I shall* not *be moved*.
21: 7(8). *he shall* not *be moved*.
30: 6(7). I said, *I shall* never *be moved*.
46: 5(6). *she shall* not *be moved*:
62: 2(3). *I shall* not *be* greatly *moved*.
6(7). *I shall* not *be moved*.
82: 5. foundations of the earth *are out of course*.
93: 1. stablished, *that it* cannot *be moved*.
96:10. established *that it shall* not *be moved*:
104: 5. (that) *it should* not *be removed*
112: 6. *he shall* not *be moved* for ever:
125: 1. as mount Zion, (which) *cannot be removed*,
140:10(11). *Let* burning coals *fall* upon them:
Pro.10:30. The righteous *shall* never *be removed*:
12: 3. root of the righteous *shall* not *be moved*.
Isa. 40:20. a graven image, (that) *shall* not *be moved*.
41: 7. (that) *it should* not *be moved*.

* HIPHIL.—*Future*. *

Ps. 55: 3(4). *they cast* iniquity upon me,
140:10(11). (כתיב) *Let* burning coals *fall* upon

* HITHPAEL.—*Preterite*. *

Isa. 24:19. the earth *is moved* exceedingly.

מוֹט *mōht*, m. 4132

Nu. 4:10. and shall put (it) upon *a bar*.
12. and shall put (them) on *a bar*:
13:23. they bare it between two *upon a staff*;
Ps. 66: 9. suffereth not our feet *to be moved*.
121: 3. He will not suffer thy foot *to be moved*:
Nah. 1:13. now will I break *his yoke*

מוֹטָה *mōh-tāh'*, f. 4133

Lev.26:13. I have broken *the bands* of your yoke,
1Ch 15:15. upon their shoulders *with the staves*
Isa. 58: 6. to undo the *heavy* burdens, (marg. bundles of *the yoke*)
— and that ye break *every yoke*?
9. If thou take away...*the yoke*,
Jer. 27: 2. Make thee bonds *and yokes*,
28:10. Hananiah the prophet took *the yoke*
12. the prophet had broken *the yoke*
13. Thou hast broken *the yokes of* wood; but thou shalt make for them *yokes of* iron.
Eze.30:18. I shall break there *the yokes of* Egypt:
34:27. I have broken *the bands of* their yoke,

מוּךְ [*mooch*]. 4134

* KAL.—*Future*. *

Lev.25:25, 35. If thy brother *be waxen poor*,
39. if thy brother...*be waxen poor*,

KAL.—*Participle*. Poel.

Lev.25:47. *and* thy brother...*wax poor*,
27: 8. if he *be poor*er than thy estimation,

מוּל *mool*. 4135

* KAL.—*Preterite*. *

Ex. 12:44. *when thou hast circumcised* him,
Deu 10:16. *Circumcise therefore* the foreskin of
30: 6. *And* the Lord thy God *will circumcise*
Jos. 5: 4. the cause why Joshua *did circumcise*·
5. (them) *they had* not *circumcised*.
7. them Joshua *circumcised*:
— *they had* not *circumcised* them

KAL.—*Imperative*.

Jos. 5: 2. *circumcise* again the children of Israel

KAL.—*Future*.

Gen17:23. *and circumcised* the flesh of their foreskin
21: 4. *And* Abraham *circumcised* his son
Jos. 5: 3. *and circumcised* the children of Israel

KAL.—*Participle*. Paül.

Jos. 5: 5. people that came out *were circumcised*.
Jer. 9:25(24). all (them which are) *circumcised*

* NIPHAL.—*Preterite*. *

Gen17:26. *was* Abraham *circumcised*,

Gen17:27. all the men...*were circumcised* with him.

NIPHAL.—*Infinitive.*

Gen17:10. Every man child...*shall be circumcised.*
13. He that is born in thy house,...*must needs* be circumcised: (lit. *being circumcised* shall be circumcised)
24, 25. *when he was circumcised*
34:15. *that* every male of you *be circumcised;*
17. if ye will not hearken...*to be circumcised;*
22. *if* every male among us *be circumcised,*
Ex. 12:48. *let* all his males *be circumcised,*
Jos. 5: 8. when they had done *circumcising*

NIPHAL.—*Imperative.*

Jer. 4: 4. *Circumcise yourselves* to the Lord,

NIPHAL.—*Future.*

Gen17:12. that is eight days old *shall be circumcised*
13. must needs *be circumcised:* (lit. being circumcised *shall be circumcised*)
14. flesh of his foreskin *is* not *circumcised,*
34:24. *and* every male *was circumcised,*
Lev.12: 3. flesh of his foreskin *shall be circumcised.*

NIPHAL.—*Participle.*

Gen34:22. circumcised, as they (are) *circumcised.*

* POLEL.—*Future.* *

Ps. 90: 6. in the evening *it is cut down,*

* HIPHIL.—*Future.* *

Ps.118:10. in the name of the Lord *will I destroy them.* (marg. *cut them off*)
11, 12. name of the Lord *I will destroy them.*

* HITHPOLEL.—*Future.* *

Ps. 58: 7(8). let them be as *cut in pieces.*

4136 מוֹל *mōhl*, m.

Deu 1: 1. in the plain *over against* the Red (sea),

4136 מוּל *mool*, m.

Ex. 18:19. Be thou for the people *to* God-*ward*
26: 9. in *the* fore*front* of the tabernacle.
28:25. on the shoulderpieces of the ephod before it. (lit. to *the front of* its face)
27. *toward* the forepart thereof, over against
37. upon *the* fore*front* of the mitre
34: 3. let the flocks...feed be*fore* that mount.
39:18. on the shoulderpieces of the ephod, before (lit. to *the front of* its face) it.
20. *toward* the forepart of it, over against
Lev. 5: 8. wring off his head *from* his neck,
8: 9. (even) upon his fore*front*,
Nu. 8: 2. over against (lit. to *the front of* the face of)
3. the lamps thereof over against (lit. *id.*)
22: 5. they abide *over against me:*
Deu 2:19. *over against* the children of Ammon,
3:29. in the valley *over against* Beth-peor.
4:46. in the valley *over against* Beth-peor,
11:30. in the champaign *over against* Gilgal,
34: 6. of Moab, *over against* Beth-peor:
Jos. 8:33. over *against* mount Gerizim,
— over *against* mount Ebal;
9: 1. over *against* Lebanon,
18:18. *over against* Arabah
19:46. the border *before* (marg. or, *over against*)
22:11. over *against* the land of Canaan,
1Sa.14: 5. northward *over against* Michmash,
— southward *over against* Gibeah.
17:30. from him to*ward* another,
2Sa. 5:23. *over against* the mulberry trees
11:15. in *the* fore*front* of the hottest battle,
1K. 7: 5. light (was) *against* light
39. eastward *over against* the south.
1Ch 14:14. *over against* the mulberry trees.
2Ch 4:10. east end, *over against* the south.
Mic. 2: 8. ye pull off the robe *with* (marg. *over against*) the garment

---

4138 מוֹלֶדֶת *mōh-leh'-deth*, f.

Gen11:28. in the land of *his nativity,*
12: 1. out of thy country, *and from thy kindred,*
Gen24: 4. unto my country, and to *my kindred,*
7. and from the land of *my kindred,*
31: 3. the land of thy fathers, *and to thy kindred;*
13. the land of *thy kindred.*
32: 9(10). unto thy country, *and to thy kindred,*
43: 7. of our state, *and of our kindred,*
48: 6. *And thy issue,* which thou begettest
Lev.18: 9. (whether she be) *born at* home, or *born*
11. *begotten of* thy father,
Nu. 10:30. to mine own land, and to *my kindred.*
Ru. 2:11. thy mother, and the land of *thy nativity,*
Est. 2:10. shewed her people nor *her kindred:*
20. Esther had not (yet) shewed *her kindred*
8: 6. to see the destruction of *my kindred?*
Jer. 22:10. nor see *his native* country.
46:16. the land of *our nativity,*
Eze.16: 3. *thy nativity* (is) of the land of Canaan;
4. *And* (as for) *thy nativity,*
23:15. the land of *their nativity:*

מוּלֹת *moo-lōhth'*, f. pl. 4139

Ex. 4:26. A bloody husband (thou art), *because of the circumcision.*

מוּם *moom*, m. 3971

Lev.21:17. their generations that hath (any) *blemish,*
18. man (he be) that hath *a blemish,*
21. No man that hath *a blemish*
— he hath *a blemish;* he shall not
23. because he hath *a blemish;*
22:20. whatsoever hath *a blemish,*
21. there shall be no *blemish* therein.
25. (and) *blemishes* (be) in them:
24:19. if a man cause *a blemish*
20. he hath caused *a blemish*
Nu. 19: 2. a red heifer...wherein (is) no *blemish,*
Deu 15:21. be (any) *blemish* therein, (as if it be) lame, or blind, (or have) any ill *blemish,*
17: 1. (any) bullock, or sheep, wherein is *blemish,*
32: 5. *their spot* (marg. *their blot*) (is) not
2Sa.14:25. there was no *blemish* in him.
Job 11:15. lift up thy face *without spot;*
Pro. 9: 7. a wicked (man getteth) *himself a blot.*
Cant.4: 7. my love; (there is) no *spot* in thee.
Dan 1: 4. Children in whom (was) no *blemish,*

מוּסַב *moo-sav'*, m. 4141

Eze.41: 7. for *the winding about of* the house went

מוּסָד *moo-sāhd'*, m. 4143-44

2Ch 8:16. the day of *the foundation of*
Isa. 28:16. *a* sure *foundation:* (lit. *a* founded *foundation*)

מוּסָדָה *moo-sāh-dāh'*, f. 4145

Isa. 30:32. every place where the *grounded* staff shall
Eze.41: 8. *the foundations of* the side chambers

מוֹסָדוֹת *mōh-sāh-dōhth'*, f. pl. 4146

Deu 32:22. *the foundations of* the mountains.
2Sa.22: 8. *the foundations of* heaven moved
16. *the foundations of* the world were
Ps. 18: 7(8). *the foundations also of* the hills moved
15(16). *the foundations of* the world were
82: 5. all *the foundations of* the earth
Pro. 8:29. appointed *the foundations of* the earth:
Isa. 24:18. *the foundations of* the earth do shake.
40:21. *the foundations of* the earth?
58:12. *the foundations of* many generations;
Jer. 31:37. *the foundations of* the earth searched out
51:26. a stone *for foundations;*
Mic. 6: 2. ye strong *foundations of* the earth:

4329 **מוּסָךְ** *moo-sach'*, m.

2K. 16:18. *the covert for* the sabbath that they had

4147 **מוֹסֵר** [*mōh-sēhr'*], m.

Job 39: 5. *or* who hath loosed *the bands of* the wild
Ps. 2: 3. Let us break *their bands* asunder,
107:14. *and* brake *their bands* in sunder.
116:16. thou hast loosed *my bonds*.
Isa. 28:22. lest *your bands* be made strong:
52: 2. loose thyself from *the bands of* thy neck,
Jer. 2:20. broken thy yoke, (and) burst *thy bands;*
5: 5. broken the yoke, (and) burst *the bonds*.
27: 2. Make thee *bonds* and yokes,
30: 8. *and* will burst *thy bonds*,
Nah. 1:13. *and* will burst *thy bonds* in sunder.

4148 **מוּסָר** *moo-sāhr'*, m.

Deu11: 2. *the chastisement of* the Lord your God,
Job 5:17. *therefore* despise not thou *the chastening of*
12:18. He looseth *the bond of* kings,
20: 3. I have heard *the check of* my reproach,
36:10. He openeth also their ear *to discipline*,
Ps. 50:17. Seeing thou hatest *instruction*,
Pro. 1: 2. To know wisdom *and instruction;*
3. To receive *the instruction of* wisdom,
7. fools despise wisdom *and instruction*.
8. hear *the instruction of* thy father,
3:11. despise not *the chastening of* the Lord;
4: 1. ye children, *the instruction of* a father,
13. Take fast hold *of instruction;*
5:12. How have I hated *instruction*,
23. He shall die without *instruction;*
6:23. reproofs of *instruction* (are) the way of
7:22. *the correction* of the stocks;
8:10. Receive *my instruction*, and not silver;
33. Hear *instruction*, and be wise,
10:17. the way of life that keepeth *instruction:*
12: 1. loveth *instruction* loveth knowledge:
13: 1. wise son (heareth) his father's *instruction:*
18. him that refuseth *instruction:*
24. he that loveth him *chasteneth* him betimes. (lit. betimes seeketh *correction* for him)
15: 5. A fool despiseth his father's *instruction:*
10. *Correction* (is) grievous unto him
32. refuseth *instruction* (marg. or, *correction*)
33. *the instruction of* wisdom;
16:22. *but the instruction of* fools (is) folly.
19:20. Hear counsel, and receive *instruction*,
27. Cease, my son, to hear *the instruction*
22:15. the rod of *correction* shall drive it far from
23:12. Apply thine heart *unto instruction*,
13. Withhold not *correction* from the child:
23. *and instruction*, and understanding.
24:32. looked upon (it, and) received *instruction*.
Isa. 26:16. *thy chastening* (was) upon them.
53: 5. *the chastisement of* our peace (was) upon
Jer. 2:30. they received no *correction:*
5: 3. they have refused to receive *correction:*
7:28. nor receiveth *correction:*
10: 8. the stock (is) *a doctrine of* vanities.
17:23. might not hear, nor receive *instruction*.
30:14. *the chastisement of* a cruel one,
32:33. have not hearkened to receive *instruction*.
35:13. Will ye not receive *instruction*
Eze. 5:15. *an instruction* and an astonishment
Hos. 5: 2. I (have been) *a rebuker* (marg. *a correction*) of them all.
Zep. 3: 2. not *correction;* (marg. or, *instruction*)
7. thou wilt receive *instruction;*

4150 **מוֹעֵד** *mōh-ğēhd'*, m.

Gen 1:14. let them be for signs, *and for seasons*,
17:21. *at* this *set time* in the next year.
18:14. *At the time appointed* I will return
21: 2. *at the set time* of which God had spoken
Ex. 9: 5. the Lord appointed *a set time*,
13:10. keep this ordinance *in his season*
23:15. *in the time appointed of* the month Abib;
Ex. 27:21 & 28:43 & 29:4, 10, 11, 30, 32, 42, 44 & 30:16, 18, 20, 26, 36 & 31:7 & 33:7, 7. the tabernacle of *the congregation*
34:18. *in the time of* the month Abib:
35:21 & 38:8, 30. tabernacle of *the congregation*,
39:32. the tent of *the congregation*
40. the tent of *the congregation*,
40: 2, 6, 7, 22, 24, 26, 29, 30, 32, 34, 35. the tent of *the congregation*.
12. door of the tabernacle of *the congregation*,
Lev. 1: 1, 3, 5 & 3:2, 8, 13 & 4:4, 5, 7, 7, 14, 16, 18, 18 & 6:16(9), 26(19), 30(23) & 8:3, 4, 31, 33, 35 & 9:5, 23 & 10:7, 9 & 12:6 & 14:11, 23 & 15:14, 29 & 16:7, 16, 17, 20, 23, 33 & 17:4, 5, 6, 9 & 19:21. the tabernacle of *the congregation*,
23: 2. (Concerning) *the feasts of* the Lord,
— these (are) *my feasts*.
4, 37. These (are) *the feasts of* the Lord,
— ye shall proclaim *in their seasons*.
44. of Israel *the feasts of* the Lord.
24: 3. in the tabernacle of *the congregation*,
Nu. 1: 1 & 2:2, 17 & 3:7, 8, 25, 25, 38 & 4:3, 4, 15, 23, 25, 25, 28, 30, 31, 33, 35, 37, 39, 41, 43, 47 & 6:10, 13, 18 & 7:5, 89 & 8:9, 15, 19, 22, 24, 26. the tabernacle of *the congregation*,
9: 2. keep the passover *at his appointed season*.
3. ye shall keep it *in his appointed season:*
7. *in his appointed season* among the children
13. of the Lord *in his appointed season*,
10: 3. the tabernacle of *the congregation*.
10. *and in your solemn days*, and in the
11:16, & 12:4 & 14:10. the tabernacle of *the congregation*,
15: 3. *in your solemn feasts*, to make
16: 2. famous in *the congregation*,
18, 19, 42(17:7), 43(17:8), 50(17:15) & 17:4 (19) & 18:4, 6, 21, 22, 23, 31 & 19:4 & 20:6 & 25:6 & 27:2. the tabernacle of *the congregation*
28: 2. offer unto me *in their due season*.
29:39. ye shall do...*in your set feasts*,
31:54. the tabernacle of *the congregation*,
Deu16: 6. *at the season* that thou camest forth
31:10. *in the solemnity of* the year
14, 14. the tabernacle of *the congregation*,
Jos. 8:14. *at a time appointed*, before the plain;
18: 1 & 19:51. the tabernacle of *the congregation*
Jud. 20:38. *Now* there was *an appointed sign* (marg. or, *time*)
1Sa. 2:22. the tabernacle of *the congregation*.
9:24. *unto this time* hath it been kept
13: 8. *according to the set time* that Samuel
11. thou camest not *within* the days *appointed*,
20:35. *at the time appointed with* David,
2Sa. 20: 5. he tarried longer than *the set time*
24:15. morning even to the time *appointed:*
1K. 8: 4. the tabernacle of *the congregation*,
2K. 4:16. *About* this *season*, (marg. *set time*)
17. bare a son *at that season*
1Ch. 6:32(17) & 9:21. tabernacle of *the congregation*
23:31. *and on the set feasts*, by number,
32. the tabernacle of *the congregation*,
2Ch. 1: 3, 6, 13. the tabernacle of *the congregation*
2: 4(3). *and on the solemn feasts of* the Lord
5: 5. the tabernacle of *the congregation*,
30:22. they did eat throughout *the feast*
31: 3. for the new moons, *and for the set feasts*,
Ezr. 3: 5. all *the set feasts of* the Lord
Neh 10:33(34). *the set feasts*, and for the holy (things),
Job 30:23. the house *appointed* for all living.
Ps. 74: 4. the midst of *thy congregations;*
8. have burned up all *the synagogues of* God
75: 2(3). When I shall receive *the congregation*
102:13(14). yea, *the set time*, is come.
104:19. He appointed the moon *for seasons:*
Isa. 1:14. Your new moons *and your appointed feasts*
14:13. the mount of *the congregation*,
33:20. the city of *our solemnities:*
Jer. 8: 7. in the heaven knoweth *her appointed times*
46:17. he hath passed *the time appointed*.
Lam. 1: 4. none come to *the solemn feasts:*
15. he hath called *an assembly*
2: 6. hath destroyed *his places of the assembly:*
the Lord hath caused *the solemn feasts*
7. the day of *a solemn feast*.
22. Thou hast called as in a *solemn* day

Eze.36:38. of Jerusalem *in her solemn feasts;*
44:24. my statutes in all *mine assemblies;*
45:17. all *solemnities of* the house of Israel:
46: 9. before the Lord *in the solemn feasts,*
11. in the feasts *and in the solemnities*
Dan. 8:19. *at the time appointed* the end (shall be).
11:27. the end (shall be) *at the time appointed.*
29. *At the time appointed* he shall return,
35. (it is) yet *for a time appointed.*
12: 7. (it shall be) *for a time, times,* and an half;
Hos. 2: 9(11). my wine in *the season thereof,*
11(13). her sabbaths, and all *her solemn feasts.*
9: 5. What will ye do in the *solemn* day,
12: 9(10). the days of *the solemn feast.*
Hab. 2: 3. the vision (is) yet *for an appointed time,*
Zep. 3:18. (them that are) sorrowful *for the solemn assembly,*
Zec. 8:19. joy and gladness, *and* cheerful *feasts;* (marg. or, *solemn,* or, *set times*)

4151 **מוֹעָד** [*mōh-ĝāhd'*], m.

Isa. 14:31. (shall be) alone *in his appointed times.*

4150 **מוֹעֲדוֹת** *mōh-ĝădōhth'*, f. pl.

2Ch. 8:13. the new moons, *and on the solemn feasts*

4152 **מוּעָדָה** *moo-ĝāh-dāh'*, f.

Jos. 20: 9. These were the cities *appointed*

4154 **מוּעֶדֶת** [*moo-ĝeh'-deth*], adj. f.

Pro.25:19. and a foot *out of joint.*

4155 **מוּעָף** *moo-ĝāhph'*, m.

Isa. 9: 1(8:23). *the dimness* (shall) not (be) such as

4156 **מוֹעֵצוֹת** *mōh-ĝēh-tzōhth'*, f pl.

Ps. 5:10(11). let them fall *by* (marg. or, *from*) *their own counsels;*
81:12(13). they walked *in their own counsels.*
Pro. 1:31. *and* be filled *with their own devices.*
22:20. excellent things *in counsels*
Jer. 7:24. *in the counsels* (and) in the imagination
Hos 11: 6. (them), *because of their own counsels.*
Mic. 6:16. ye walk *in their counsels;*

4157 **מוּעָקָה** *moo-ĝāh-kāh'*, f.

Ps. 66:11. thou laidst *affliction* upon our loins.

4159 **מוֹפֵת** *mōh-phēhth'*, m.

Ex. 4:21. do all those *wonders* before Pharaoh,
7: 3. *my wonders* in the land of Egypt.
9. Shew *a miracle* for you:
11: 9. that *my wonders* may be multiplied
10. Moses and Aaron did all these *wonders*
Deu 4:34. by signs, *and by wonders,*
6:22. the Lord shewed signs *and wonders,*
7:19. the signs, *and the wonders,*
13: 1(2). giveth thee a sign or *a wonder,*
2(3). the sign *or the wonder* come to pass,
26: 8. with signs, *and with wonders:*
28:46. for a sign *and for a wonder,*
29: 3(2). the signs, *and* those great *miracles:*
34:11. all the signs *and the wonders,*
1K. 13: 3. he gave *a sign* the same day, saying, This (is) *the sign* which the Lord hath spoken;
5. *according to the sign* which the man
1Ch 16:12. *his wonders,* and the judgments of his
2Ch 32:24. *and* he gave him *a sign.*
31. *the wonder* that was (done) in the land,
Neh 9:10. shewedst signs *and wonders* upon Pharaoh
Ps. 71: 7. I am *as a wonder* unto many;
78:43. *and his wonders* in the field of Zoan:
105: 5. *his wonders,* and the judgments of his
27. *and wonders* in the land of Ham.
135: 9. (Who) sent tokens *and wonders*
Isa. 8:18. for signs *and for wonders* in Israel
20: 3. a sign *and wonder* upon Egypt
Jer. 32:20. Which hast set signs *and wonders*
21. with signs, *and with wonders,*
Eze.12: 6. I have set thee (for) *a sign*
11. Say, I (am) *your sign:*
24:24. Ezekiel is unto you *a sign:*
27. thou shalt be *a sign* unto them;
Joel 2:30(3:3). I will shew *wonders* in the heavens
Zec. 3: 8. men *wondered at:* (marg. men of *wonder*)

מוּץ [*mootz*]. 4160

* KAL.—*Participle.* *

Isa. 16: 4. *the extortioner* (marg. *wringer*) is at an

מוּץ see **מִיץ** See 4671

מוֹצָא *mōh-tzāh'*, m. 4161

Nu. 30:12(13). whatsoever *proceeded out of* her lips
33: 2. Moses wrote *their goings out*
— their journeys *according to their goings out.*
Deu 8: 3. every (word) *that proceedeth out of* the
23:23(24). *That which is gone out of* thy lips
2Sa. 3:25. to know *thy going out* and thy coming in,
1K. 10:28. *And* Solomon had horses *brought out of* (marg. *the going forth of* the horses (which was) Solomon's)
2K. 2:21. he went forth unto *the spring of* the waters,
2Ch 1:16. *And* Solomon had horses *brought out of* Egypt, (marg. *the going forth of* the horses which (was) Solomon's)
32:30. the upper water*course* of Gihon,
Job 28: 1. Surely there is *a vein* (marg. or, *mine*) for
38:27. to cause *the bud of* the tender herb
Ps. 19: 6(7). *His going forth* (is) from the end of
65: 8(9). *the outgoings of* the morning and evening
75: 6(7). neither *from the east,*
89:34(35). *nor* alter *the thing that is gone out of*
107:33. *and the* water*springs* into dry ground;
35. dry ground *into* water*springs.*
Isa. 41:18. the dry land *springs of* water.
58:11. *and like a spring of* water,
Jer. 17:16. *that which came out of* my lips
Eze.12: 4. *as they that go forth into* (marg. *the goings forth of*) captivity.
42:11. *their goings out* (were) both according to
43:11. fashion thereof, *and the goings out thereof,*
44: 5. every *going forth of* the sanctuary.
Dan 9:25. *the going forth of* the commandment
Hos. 6: 3. *his going forth* is prepared as the morning;

מוֹצָאוֹת *mōh-tzāh-ōhth'*, f. pl. 4163

2K. 10:27. and made it *a draught house* unto
Mic. 5: 2(1). *whose* (lit. who *his*) *goings forth* (have been) from of old,

מוּצָק *moo-tzāhk'*, m. 4165

1K. 7:37. all of them had one *casting,*
Job 38:38. the dust groweth *into hardness,* (marg. *into mire*)

מוּצָק & **מוּצַק** *moo-tzāhk'*, & *moo-tzak'*, m. 4164

Job 36:16. where (there is) no *straitness;*
37:10. of the waters *is straitened.* (lit. *in straitness,*
Isa. 9:1(8:23) such as (was) in her *vexation.*

4166 מוּצֶקֶת [*moo-tzeh'-keth*], f.

2Ch 4: 3. cast, *when it was cast.*
Zec. 4: 2. seven *pipes* to the seven lamps,

4167 מוּק [*mook*].

* HIPHIL.—*Future.* *

Ps. 73: 8. *They are corrupt*, and speak wickedly

4168 מוֹקֵד *mōh-kēhd'*, m.

Ps. 102: 3(4). my bones are burned *as an hearth.*
Isa. 33:14. who among us shall dwell with everlasting *burnings?*

4169 מוֹקְדָה *mōh-k'dāh'*, f.

Lev. 6: 9(2). because of *the burning*

4170 מוֹקֵשׁ *mōh-kēhsh'*, m.

Ex. 10: 7. How long shall this man be *a snare*
23:33. it will surely be *a snare* unto thee.
34:12. lest it be *for a snare* in the midst of thee:
Deu 7:16. that (will be) *a snare* unto thee.
Jos. 23:13. they shall be snares *and traps* unto you,
Jud. 2: 3. their gods shall be *a snare* unto you.
8:27. which thing became *a snare* unto Gideon,
1Sa. 18:21. that she may be *a snare* to him,
2Sa. 22: 6. *the snares of* death prevented
Job 34:30. *lest* the people *be ensnared.*
40:24. (his) nose pierceth *through snares.*
Ps. 18: 5(6). *the snares of* death prevented me.
64: 5(6). they commune of laying *snares*
69:22(23). welfare (let it become) *a trap.*
106:36. which were *a snare* unto them.
140: 5(6). they have set *gins* for me.
141: 9. *the gins of* the workers of iniquity.
Pro. 12:13. The wicked is *snared* (marg. *The snare* of the wicked (is)) by the transgression of
13:14. depart *from the snares of* death.
14:27. depart from *the snares of* death.
18: 7. his lips (are) *the snare of* his soul.
20:25. (It is) *a snare to* the man
22:25. get *a snare* to thy soul.
29: 6. In the transgression of an evil man (there is) *a snare:*
25. The fear of man bringeth *a snare:*
Isa. 8:14. *and for a snare* to the inhabitants of
Am. 3: 5. *where* no *gin* (is) for him?

See 4753 מוֹר see מֹר

4171 מוּר [*moor*].

* NIPHAL.—*Preterite.* *

Jer. 48:11. and his scent *is* not *changed.*

* HIPHIL.—*Preterite.* *

Jer. 2:11. my people *have changed*

HIPHIL.—*Infinitive.*

Lev. 27:10. if he shall *at all* change (lit. *changing* he shall change)
33. if he change it *at all*, (lit. *id.*)
Ps. 46: 2(3). *though* the earth *be removed*,

HIPHIL.—*Future.*

Lev. 27:10. nor *change* it, a good for a bad,
— if *he shall* at all *change*
33. neither *shall he change it:* and if *he change it* at all,
Ps. 15: 4. (He that) sweareth...and *changeth* not.
106:20. *Thus they changed* their glory
Eze. 48:14. neither *exchange*, nor alienate
Hos. 4: 7. *will I change* their glory
Mic. 2: 4. *he hath changed* the portion

מוֹרָא *mōh-rāh'*, m. 4172

Gen 9: 2. *the fear of you* and the dread of you
Deu 4:34. a stretched out arm, *and by* great *terrors*,
11:25. *and the dread of you* upon all the land
26: 8. *and with* great *terribleness*,
34:12. all *the* great *terror* which Moses shewed
Ps. 9:20(21). Put them in *fear*, O Lord:
76:11(12). bring presents *unto him that ought to be feared.* (marg. *to fear*)
Isa. 8:12. neither fear ye *their fear*,
13. (let) him (be) *your fear*,
Jer. 32:21. a stretched out arm, *and with* great *terror;*
Mal. 1: 6. if I (be) a master, where (is) *my fear?*
2: 5. *the fear* wherewith he feared me,

מוֹרַג *mōh-rag'*, m. 4173

2Sa. 24:22. *and threshing instruments* and (other)
1Ch 21:23. *and the threshing instruments* for wood,
Isa. 41:15. *a* new sharp *threshing instrument*

מוֹרָד *mōh-rāhd'*, m. 4174

Jos. 7: 5. smote them *in the going down:* (marg. or, *in Morad*)
10:11. were in *the going down to* Beth-horon,
1K. 7:29. certain additions made of *thin* work.
Jer. 48: 5. *in the going down of* Horonaim
Mic. 1: 4. the waters (that are) poured down *a steep place.* (marg. *a descent*)

מוֹרָה *mōh-rāh'*, m. 4177

Jud. 13: 5. *and* no *razor* shall come on his head:
16:17. There hath not come *a razor* upon mine
1Sa. 1:11. *and* there shall no *razor* come upon his

מוֹרָה *mōh-rāh'*, m. 4172

Ps. 9:20(21). (כתיב) Put them in *fear*, O Lord:

מוֹרֶה *mōh-reh'*, m. 4175

Ps. 84: 6(7). *the rain* also filleth the pools.
Joel 2:23. he hath given you *the former rain* moderately, (marg. or, *a teacher* of righteousness)
— *the former rain*, and the latter rain

מוֹרָט see מֹרָט 4178

מוֹרָשׁ *mōh-rāhsh'*, m. 4180

Job 17:11. *the thoughts* (marg. *possessions*) *of* my heart.
Isa. 14:23. I will also make it *a possession for* the
Obad. 17. of Jacob shall possess *their possessions.*

מוֹרָשָׁה *mōh-rāh'-shāh*, f. 4181

Ex. 6: 8. I will give it you for *an heritage:*
Deu 33: 4. *the inheritance* of the congregation of
Eze. 11:15. unto us is this land given *in possession.*
25: 4. thee to the men of the east *for a possession*,
10. will give them *in possession*,
33:24. the land is given us *for inheritance.*
36: 2. ancient high places are our's *in possession:*
3. that ye might be *a possession*
5. appointed my land *into* their *possession*

מוּשׁ *moosh.* 4185

* KAL.—*Preterite.* *

Nu. 14:44. and Moses, *departed* not
Zec. 3: 9. *and I will remove* the iniquity
14: 4. *and* half of the mountain *shall remove*

KAL.—*Future.*

Jos. 1: 8. This book of the law *shall* not *depart*
Jud. 6:18. *Depart* not hence,
Pro.17:13. evil *shall* not *depart*
Isa. 22:25. *shall* the nail...*be removed,*
54:10. the mountains *shall depart,*
— my kindness *shall* not *depart*
59:21. my words...*shall* not *depart*
Jer. 31:36. If those ordinances *depart*

* HIPHIL.—*Future.* *

Ex. 13:22. *He took* not *away* the pillar
33:11. Joshua,...*departed* not
Job 23:12. Neither *have I gone back* from
Ps. 55:11(12). deceit and guile *depart* not
Pro.17:13. (כתיב) evil *shall* not *depart*
Isa. 46: 7. from his place *shall he* not *remove:*
Jer.17: 8. neither *shall cease* from yielding
Mic. 2: 3. *ye shall* not *remove* your necks;
4. how *hath he removed* (it) from me!
Nah 3: 1. the prey *departeth* not;

4184 **מוּשׁ** *moosh.*

* KAL.—*Future.* *

Gen27:21. *that I may feel thee,*

* HIPHIL.—*Imperative.* *

Jud.16:26. Suffer me *that I may feel*

HIPHIL.—*Future.*

Ps.115: 7. They have hands, but *they handle* not:

4186 **מוֹשָׁב** *mōh-shāhv',* m.

Gen10:30. *their dwelling* was from Mesha,
27:39. *thy dwelling* shall be the fatness of the
36:43. *according to their habitations* in the land
Ex. 10:23. had light *in their dwellings.*
12:20. in all *your habitations* shall ye eat
40. *Now the sojourning of* the children of
35: 3. kindle no fire throughout *your habitations*
Lev. 3:17. throughout all *your dwellings,*
7:26. in any of *your dwellings.*
13:46. without the camp (shall) *his habitation*
23: 3. of the Lord in all *your dwellings.*
14, 31. your generations in all *your dwellings.*
17. Ye shall bring *out of your habitations*
21. for ever in all *your dwellings*
25:29. if a man sell a *dwelling* house
Nu. 15: 2. the land of *your habitations,*
24:21. Strong is *thy dwellingplace,*
31:10. burnt all their cities *wherein they dwelt,*
35:29. in all *your dwellings.*
1Sa.20:18. because *thy seat* will be empty.
25. the king sat upon *his seat,* as at other times, (even) upon *a seat by* the wall:
2Sa. 9:12. all *that dwelt in* the house of Ziba
1K. 10: 5. *and the sitting of* his servants,
2K. 2:19. *the situation of* this city (is) pleasant,
1Ch 4:33. These (were) *their habitations,*
6:54(39). these (are) *their dwelling places*
7:28. their possessions *and habitations*
2Ch 9: 4. *and the sitting of* his servants,
Job 29: 7. I prepared *my seat* in the street!
Ps. 1: 1. *nor* sitteth *in the seat of* the scornful.
107: 4. they found no city *to dwell in.*
7. that they might go to a city of *habitation.*
32. *and* praise him *in the assembly of* the
36. that they may prepare a city for *habitation;*
132:13. he hath desired (it) for his *habitation.*
Eze. 6: 6. In all *your dwellingplaces*
14. in all *their habitations:*
8: 3. *the seat of* the image of jealousy,
28: 2. I sit (in) *the seat of* God,
34:13. all *the inhabited places of* the country.
37:23. save them out of all *their dwellingplaces,*
48:15. *for dwelling,* and for suburbs:

4189 **מוֹשְׁכוֹת** *mōh-sh'chōhth',* f. pl.

Job 38:31. or loose *the bands of* Orion?

מוֹשָׁעוֹת *mōh-shāh-gōhth',* f. pl. 4190

Ps. 68:20(21). the God *of salvation;*

מוּת *mooth.* 4191

* KAL.—*Preterite.* *

Gen 7:22. all that (was) in the dry land, *died.*
19:19. lest some evil take me, *and I die:*
33:13. them one day, all the flock *will die.*
35:18. as her soul was in departing, for *she died*
42:38. for his brother *is dead,*
44: 9. it be found, *both let him die,*
20. and his brother *is dead,*
22. father, (his father) (lit. *and*) *would die.*
31. the lad (is) not (with us), *that he will die:*
48: 7. Rachel *died* by me
50:15. saw that their father *was dead,*
Ex. 4:19. all the men *are dead*
7:21. the fish that (was) in the river *died;*
9: 6. of the cattle of the children of Israel *died*
7. *there was* not one of the cattle of the Israelites *dead.*
19. hail shall come down...*and they shall die.*
11: 5. *And* all the firstborn...*shall die,*
21:12. He that smiteth a man, *so that he die,*
20. *and he die* under his hand;
28. gore a man or a woman, *that they die:*
35. if one man's ox hurt another's, *that he die;*
22: 2(1). breaking up, and be smitten *that he die,*
10(9). *and it die,* or be hurt,
14(13). and it be hurt, or *die,*
28:43. that they bear not iniquity, *and die:*
Lev.22: 9. lest they bear sin for it, *and die*
Nu. 4:15. not touch (any) holy thing, *lest they die.*
20. they shall not go in...*lest they die.*
14: 2. Would God *that we had died* in
— would God *we had died* in this wilderness!
20:26. gathered (unto his people), *and shall die*
26:11. the children of Korah *died* not.
27: 3. Our father *died* in the wilderness,
— but *died* in his own sin,
Deu 5:25(22). voice of the Lord...*then we shall die.*
10: 6. there Aaron *died,* and there he was
13:10(11). stone him with stones, *that he die;*
17: 5. stone them with stones, *till they die.*
12. *even* that man *shall die:*
18:20. *even* that prophet *shall die.*
19: 5. lighteth upon his neighbour, *that he die;*
11. and smite him mortally *that he die,*
12. and deliver him...*that he may die.*
21:21. stone him with stones, *that he die:*
22:21. stone her with stones *that she die:*
22. *then they shall* both of them *die,*
24. stone them with stones *that they die;*
25. *then* the man only that lay with her *shall die:*
24: 7. *then* that thief *shall die;*
25: 5. dwell together, and one of them *die,*
32:50. Aaron thy brother *died*
Jos. 1: 2. Moses my servant *is dead;*
5: 4. all the men of war, *died*
10:11. more which *died* with hailstones than
24:33. Eleazar the son of Aaron *died;*
Jud. 4: 1. sight of the Lord, when Ehud *was dead.*
8:33. as soon as Gideon *was dead,*
9:55. Israel saw that Abimelech *was dead,*
1Sa. 4:11. the two sons of Eli,...*were slain.*
17. Hophni and Phinehas, *are dead,*
19. *that* her father in law and her husband *were dead,*
5:12. the men that *died* not
14:45. people rescued Jonathan, that *he died* not.
17:51. Philistines saw their champion *was dead,*
25:39. when David heard that Nabal *was dead,*
26:10. his day shall come *to die;* (lit. *and he shall die*)
28: 3. Now Samuel *was dead,*
31: 5. his armourbearer saw that Saul *was dead,*
7. Saul and his sons *were dead,*
2Sa. 1: 4. Saul and Jonathan his son *are dead*
5. Saul and Jonathan his son *be dead?*
2: 7. your master Saul *is dead,*
31. three hundred and threescore men *died.*
4: 1. Abner *was dead* in Hebron,
10. Behold, Saul *is dead,*

2Sa.11:15. that he may be smitten, *and die.*
21, 24. Thy servant Uriah the Hittite *is dead*
26. Uriah her husband *was dead,*
12:18. feared to tell him that the child *was dead:*
— if we tell him that the child *is dead?*
19. David perceived that the child *was dead:*
— *Is* the child *dead?* And they said, *He is dead.*
21. when the child *was dead,*
23. But now *he is dead,* wherefore
13:32. Amnon only *is dead:* for by
33. that all the king's sons *are dead:* for Amnon only *is dead.*
39. Amnon, seeing *he was dead.*
18:20. because the king's son *is dead.*
19:10(11). Absalom,...*is dead* in battle.
1K. 1:52. *but* if wickedness shall be found in him, *he shall die.*
3:21. my child suck, behold, it *was dead:*
11:21. Joab the captain of the host *was dead,*
14:12. into the city, the child *shall die.*
17. came to the threshold...the child *died;*
17:12. that we may eat it, *and die.*
21:15. Naboth is not alive, but *dead.*
16. when Ahab heard that Naboth *was dead,*
2K. 4: 1. Thy servant my husband *is dead;*
7: 3. Why sit we here until *we die?*
4. *and we shall die* there: and if we sit still here, *we die also.*
— if they kill us, *we shall but die.*
11: 1. Athaliah...saw that her son *was dead,*
1Ch 10: 5. his armourbearer saw that Saul *was dead,*
6. and all his house *died* together.
7. Saul and his sons *were dead,*
2Ch 22:10. Athaliah...saw that her son *was dead,*
Ecc. 4: 2. the dead which *are* already *dead*
Jer. 16: 6. *Both* the great and the small *shall die*
Eze.11:13. Pelatiah the son of Benaiah *died.*
18:26. committeth iniquity, *and dieth* in them;
28: 8. *and thou shalt die* the deaths of
33:18. *he shall even die* thereby.
Am. 2: 2. *and* Moab *shall die* with tumult,
6: 9. ten men in one house, *that they shall die.*

KAL.—*Infinitive.*

Gen 2:17. shalt *surely* die. (marg. *dying* shalt die)
3: 4. shall not *surely* die: (lit. *dying* shall not die)
20: 7. thou shalt *surely* die, (lit. *dying* shalt die)
25:32. I (am) at the point *to die:*
26:11. He that toucheth this man or his wife shall *surely* be put to death. (lit. *dying* shall be caused to die)
47:29. the time drew nigh *that* Israel *must die:*
Ex. 14:11. taken us away *to die* in the wilderness?
12. *than* that we *should die* in the wilderness.
16: 3. Would to God *we had died*
19:12. whosoever toucheth the mount shall be *surely* put to death: (lit. *dying* shall be caused to die)
21:12. He that smiteth a man,...shall be *surely* put to death. (lit. *id.*)
14. take him from mine altar, *that he may die.*
15. he that smiteth his father,...shall be *surely* put to death. (lit. *dying* shall be caused to die)
16. he that stealeth a man,...shall *surely* be put to death. (lit. *id.*)
17. he that curseth his father,...shall *surely* be put to death. (lit. *id.*)
22:19(18). Whosoever lieth with a beast shall *surely* be put to death. (lit. *id.*)
31:14. that defileth it shall *surely* be put to death: (lit. *id.*)
15. he shall *surely* be put to death. (lit. *id.*)
Lev.20: 2. he shall *surely* be put to death: (lit. *dying* shall be caused to die)
9. that curseth his father...shall be *surely* put to death: (lit. *id.*)
10. the adulterer...shall *surely* be put to death. (lit. *id.*)
11, 12. both of them shall *surely* be put to death; (lit. *id.*)
13, 16. shall *surely* be put to death; (lit. *id.*)
15. he shall *surely* be put to death: (lit. *id.*)
27. a wizard, shall *surely* be put to death: (lit. *id.*)
24:16. he that blasphemeth...shall *surely* be put to death, (lit. *id.*)
Lev.24:17. he that killeth any man shall *surely* be put to death. (lit. *id.*)
27:29. (but) shall *surely* be put to death. (lit. *id.*)
Nu. 15:35. The man shall be *surely* put to death: (lit. *dying* shall be caused to die)
18:22. lest they bear sin, *and die.* (marg. *to die*)
20: 4. that we and our cattle *should die*
21: 5. *to die* in the wilderness?
26:65. They shall *surely* die in the wilderness. (lit. *dying* they shall die)
35:16, 17, 18. the murderer shall *surely* be put to death. (lit. *dying* shall be caused to die)
21. he that smote (him) shall *surely* be put to death; (lit. *id.*)
30. against any person (to cause him) *to die.*
31. a murderer, which (is) guilty *of death* (marg. *to die*): but he shall be *surely* put to death.
Deu. 2:16. the men of war were consumed *and dead*
31:14. thy days approach *that* thou *must die:*
Jos. 2:14. Our life for your's, (marg. instead of you *to die*)
Jud. 5:18. jeoparded their lives *unto the death*
13:22. Manoah said unto his wife, We shall *surely* die, (lit. *dying* we shall die)
16:16. his soul was vexed *unto death;*
21: 5. He shall *surely* be put to death. (lit. *dying* shall be caused to die)
1Sa. 4:20. about the time of *her death*
14:39. though it be in Jonathan my son, he shall *surely* die. (lit. *dying* shall die)
44. thou shalt *surely* die (lit. *id.*), Jonathan.
22:16. Thou shalt *surely* die, (lit. *dying* shall die)
2Sa.12:14. the child also (that is) born...shall *surely* die. (lit. *dying* shall die)
14:14. For we *must needs* die, (lit. *id.*)
18:33(19:1). would God *I had died* for thee,
20: 3. shut up unto the day of *their death,*
1K. 2: 1. of David drew nigh *that* he *should die;*
37, 42. that thou shalt *surely* die: (lit. *dying* shalt die)
13:31. *When I am dead,* then bury me in
19: 4. requested for himself *that he might die;*
2K. 1: 4, 6, 16. shalt *surely* die. (lit. *dying* shalt die)
8:10. he shall *surely* die. (lit. *dying* he shall die)
20: 1. was Hezekiah sick *unto death.*
2Ch 32:11. *to die* by famine and by thirst,
24. Hezekiah was sick *to the death,*
Ecc. 3: 2. A time to be born, and a time *to die;*
Isa. 38: 1. was Hezekiah sick *unto death.*
Jer. 26: 8. Thou shalt *surely* die. (lit. *dying* shalt die)
38:26. return to Jonathan's house, *to die* there.
Eze. 3:18. When I say unto the wicked, Thou shalt *surely* die; (lit. *dying* shalt die)
18:13. abominations; he shall *surely* die; (lit. *dying* shall be caused to die)
33: 8. O wicked (man), thou shalt *surely* die; (lit. *dying* shalt die)
14. unto the wicked, Thou shalt *surely* die; (lit. *dying* shalt die)
Jon. 4: 8. and wished in himself *to die,* and said,

KAL.—*Imperative.*

Deu 32:50. *And die* in the mount
Job 2: 9. curse God, *and die.*

KAL.—*Future.*

Gen 2:17. *thou shalt* surely *die.*
3: 3. neither shall ye touch it, lest *ye die.*
4. *Ye shall* not surely *die:*
5: 5. Adam lived were 930 years: *and he died.*
8. days of Seth were 912 years: *and he died.*
11. days of Enos were 905 years: *and he died.*
14. days of Cainan were 910 years: *and he died.*
17. of Mahalaleel were 895 years: *and he died.*
20. days of Jared were 962 years: *and he died.*
27. of Methuselah were 969 years: *and he died.*
31. days of Lamech were 777 years: *and he died.*
9:29. days of Noah were 950 years: *and he died.*
11:28. *And* Haran *died* before his father
32. *and* Terah *died* in Haran.
20: 7. *thou shalt* surely *die,*
23: 2. *And* Sarah *died* in Kirjath-arba;
25: 8. *and died* in a good old age,
17. and he gave up the ghost *and died;*
26: 9. Lest *I die* for her.
27: 4. that my soul may bless thee before *I die.*

Gen 35: 8. *But* Deborah Rebekah's nurse *died*,
19. *And* Rachel *died*,
29. Isaac gave up the ghost, *and died*,
36:33. *And* Bela *died*,
34. *And* Jobab *died*,
35. *And* Husham *died*,
36. *And* Hadad *died*,
37. *And* Samlah *died*,
38. *And* Saul *died*,
39. *And* Baal-hanan the son of Achbor *died*,
38:11. Lest peradventure *he die* also,
12. the daughter of Shuah Judah's wife *died;*
42: 2. that we may live, and not *die*.
20. be verified, and *ye shall* not *die*.
43: 8. that we may live, and not *die*,
45:28. I will go and see him before *I die*.
46:12. *but* Er and Onan *died* in the land
30. Now *let me die*, since I have seen
47:15. why *should we die*
19. Wherefore *shall we die*
— that we may live, and not *die*,
50:26. *So* Joseph *died*, (being) an hundred
Ex. 1: 6. *And* Joseph *died*, and all
2:23. *that* the king of Egypt *died :*
7:18. the fish that (is) in the river *shall die*,
8:13(9). *and* the frogs *died* out of the houses,
9: 4. *there shall* nothing *die*
6. *and* all the cattle of Egypt *died:*
10:28. day thou seest my face *thou shalt die*.
20:19. let not God speak with us, lest *we die*.
21:18. one smite another...and *he die* not,
28:35. that *he die* not.
30:20, 21. that *they die* not;
Lev. 8:35. of the Lord, that *ye die* not:
10: 2. *and they died* before the Lord.
6. neither rend your clothes; lest *ye die*,
7. ye shall not go out...lest *ye die :*
9. Do not drink wine...lest *ye die :*
11:39. if any beast,...*die ;*
15:31. that *they die* not in their uncleanness,
16: 1. they offered before the Lord, *and died;*
2, 13. that *he die* not:
20:20. *they shall die* childless.
Nu. 3: 4. *And* Nadab and Abihu *died*
4:19. that they may live, and not *die*,
6: 9. if any man *die* very suddenly
14:35. and there *they shall die*.
37. *Even* those men...*died*
15:36. stoned him with stones, *and he died ;*
16:29. If these men *die* the common death
17:10(25). from me, that *they die* not.
13(28). cometh any thing near...*shall die :*
18: 3. that neither they, nor ye also, *die*.
32. neither shall ye pollute...lest *ye die*.
19:13. body of any man that *is dead*,
14. when a man *dieth* in a tent:
20: 1. *and* Miriam *died* there,
28. *and* Aaron *died* there
21: 6. *and* much people of Israel *died*.
23:10. *Let* me *die* the death of the righteous,
26:19. *and* Er and Onan *died* in the land
61. *And* Nadab and Abihu *died*,
65. *They shall* surely *die*
27: 8. If a man *die*, and have no son,
33:38. the commandment of the Lord, *and died*
35:12. that the manslayer *die* not,
16. if he smite him...*so that he die*,
17. wherewith *he may die*, *and he die*,
18. wherewith *he may die*, *and he die*,
20. if he thrust him...*that he die ;*
21. Or in enmity smite him...*that he die :*
23. wherewith a man *may die*,
— cast (it) upon him, *that he die*,
Deu 5:25(22). Now therefore why *should we die?*
18:16. let me see this great fire...that *I die* not.
20: 5, 6, 7. lest *he die* in the battle,
24: 3. if the latter husband *die*,
33: 6. Let Reuben live, and not *die;*
34: 5. *So* Moses the servant of the Lord *died*
Jos. 10:11. upon them unto Azekah, *and they died :*
20: 9. and not *die* by the hand of the avenger
24:29. *that* Joshua the son of Nun,...*died*,
Jud. 1: 7. him to Jerusalem, *and* there *he died*.
2: 8. *And* Joshua the son of Nun,...*died*,
21. the nations which Joshua left *when he died:*
3:11. *And* Othniel the son of Kenaz *died*.
4:21. he was fast asleep and weary. *So he died*.

Jud. 6:23. fear not: *thou shalt* not *die*.
30. Bring out thy son, *that he may die :*
8:32. *And* Gideon the son of Joash *died*
9:49. *so that* all the men...*died*
54. young man thrust him through, *and he died*.
10: 2. Israel twenty and three years, *and died*,
5. *And* Jair *died*, and was buried
12: 7. *Then died* Jephthah the Gileadite,
10. *Then died* Ibzan,
12. *And* Elon the Zebulonite *died*,
15. *And* Abdon the son of Hillel...*died*,
13:22. *We shall* surely *die*,
15:18. and now *shall I die* for thirst,
16:30. *Let* me *die* with the Philistines.
20: 5. my concubine have they forced, *that she is dead*.
Ru. 1: 3. *And* Elimelech Naomi's husband *died ;*
5. *And* Mahlon and Chilion *died*
17. Where *thou diest, will I die*,
1Sa. 2:33. the increase of thine house *shall die*
34. in one day *they shall die*
4:18. his neck brake, *and he died :*
12:19. Pray for thy servants...that *we die* not:
14:39. *he shall* surely *die*.
43. (and), lo, *I must die*.
44. *thou shalt* surely *die*, Jonathan.
45. *Shall* Jonathan *die*,
20: 2. God forbid; *thou shalt* not *die :*
14. the kindness of the Lord, that *I die* not:
22:16. *Thou shalt* surely *die*, Ahimelech,
25: 1. *And* Samuel *died ;*
37. *that* his heart *died* within him,
38. the Lord smote Nabal, *that he died*.
31: 5. *and died* with him.
6. *So* Saul *died*, and his three sons,
2Sa. 1: 4. of the people also are fallen *and dead*,
15. he smote him *that he died*.
2:23. *and died* in the same place:
— Asahel fell down *and died*
3:27. smote him there...*that he died*,
33. *Died* Abner as a fool dieth?
6: 7. *and* there *he died* by the ark of God.
10: 1. *that* the king of the children of Ammon *died*,
18. the captain of their host, *who died*
11:17. *and* Uriah the Hittite *died*
21. *that he died* in Thebez?
24. *and* (some) of the king's servants *be dead*,
12:13. *thou shalt* not *die*.
14. born unto thee *shall* surely *die*.
18. on the seventh day, *that* the child *died*.
14: 5. *and* mine husband *is dead*.
14. *we* must needs *die*, (lit. dying *we shall die*)
17:23. and hanged himself, *and died*,
18: 3. *if* half of us *die*,
19:23(24). *Thou shalt* not *die*.
37(38). *that I may die* in mine own city,
20:10. struck him not again; *and he died*.
24:15. *and there died* of the people
1K. 2:25. he fell upon him *that he died*.
30. but *I will die* here.
37, 42. *thou shalt* surely *die :*
46. and fell upon him, *that he died*.
3:19. *And* this woman's child *died*
12:18. stoned him with stones, *that he died*.
16:18. king's house over him with fire, *and died*,
22. *so* Tibni *died*, and Omri reigned.
21:10. stone him, *that he may die*.
13. stoned him with stones, *that he died*.
14. Naboth is stoned, *and is dead*.
15. that Naboth was stoned, *and was dead*,
22:35. against the Syrians, *and died* at even:
37. *So* the king *died*,
2K. 1: 4, 6, 16. but *shalt* surely *die*.
17. *So he died* according to the word
4:20. sat on her knees till noon, *and* (then) *died*.
7:17. trode upon him in the gate, *and he died*,
20. trode upon him in the gate, *and he died*.
8:10. *he shall* surely *die*.
15. spread (it) on his face, *so that he died :*
9:27. he fled to Megiddo, *and died* there.
12:21(22). his servants, smote him, *and he died;*
13:14. his sickness whereof *he died*.
20. *And* Elisha *died*, and they buried him.
24. *So* Hazael king of Syria *died :*
14: 6. (כתיב) *shall be put to death* for his own
18:32. that ye may live, and not *die:*

2K. 23:34. he came to Egypt, *and died* there.
25:25. and smote Gedaliah, *that he died*,
1Ch 1:44. And *when* Bela *was dead*,
45. And *when* Jobab *was dead*, Husham
46. And *when* Husham *was dead*, Hadad
47. And *when* Hadad *was dead*, Samlah
48. And *when* Samlah *was dead*, Shaul
49. And *when* Shaul *was dead*, Baal-hanan
50. And *when* Baal-hanan *was dead*,
51. Hadad *died also*.
2:19. And *when* Azubah *was dead*,
30. *but* Seled *died* without children.
32. *and* Jether *died* without children.
10: 5. he fell likewise on the sword, *and died*.
6. *So* Saul *died*, and his three sons,
13. *So* Saul *died* for his transgression
13:10. *and* there *he died* before God.
19: 1. *that* Nahash the king...*died*,
23:22. *And* Eleazar *died*, and had no sons,
24: 2. *But* Nadab and Abihu *died*
29:28. *And he died* in a good old age,
2Ch 10:18. stoned him with stones, *that he died*.
13:20. the Lord struck him, *and he died*.
16:13. *and died* in the one and fortieth year of
18:34. *and* about the time of the sun going down *he died*.
21:19. *so he died* of sore diseases.
24:15. was full of days *when he died*;
25. slew him on his bed, *and he died*:
25: 4. The fathers *shall* not *die* for the children, neither *shall* the children *die* for the fathers, but every man *shall die* for his
35:24. brought him to Jerusalem, *and he died*,
Job 1:19. the young men, *and they are dead*;
3:11. Why *died I* not from the womb?
4:21. *they die*, even without wisdom.
12: 2. wisdom *shall die* with you.
14: 8. the stock thereof *die* in the ground;
10. But man *dieth*, and wasteth away:
14. If a man *die*, shall he live (again)?
21:23. One *dieth* in his full strength,
25. another *dieth* in the bitterness of
34:20. In a moment *shall they die*,
36:14. They *die* (marg. Their soul *dieth*) in youth,
42:17. *So* Job *died*, (being) old and full of days.
Ps. 41: 5(6). When *shall he die*, and his name
49:10(11). he seeth (that) wise men *die*,
82: 7. *ye shall die* like men, and fall like
118:17. *I shall* not *die*, but live.
Pro. 5:23. *He shall die* without instruction;
10:21. fools *die* for want of wisdom.
15:10. he that hateth reproof *shall die*.
19:16. he that despiseth his ways *shall die*.
23:13. him with the rod, *he shall* not *die*.
30: 7. deny me (them) not before *I die*:
Ecc. 2:16. how *dieth* the wise (man)?
7:17. why *shouldest thou die* before
9: 5. the living know *that they shall die*:
Isa. 22:13. let us eat and drink; for to morrow *we shall die*.
14. shall not be purged from you till *ye die*,
18. there *shalt thou die*,
50: 2. their fish stinketh,...*and dieth* for thirst.
51: 6. they that dwell therein *shall die*
12. be afraid of a man (that) *shall die*,
14. that *he should* not *die* in the pit,
59: 5. he that eateth of their eggs *dieth*,
65:20. the child *shall die* an hundred years old;
66:24. their worm *shall* not *die*,
Jer. 11:21. that *thou die* not by our hand:
22. the young men *shall die* by the sword; their sons and their daughters *shall die*
16: 4. *They shall die* of grievous deaths;
20: 6. and there *thou shalt die*,
21: 6. *they shall die* of a great pestilence.
9. He that abideth...*shall die*
22:12. *he shall die* in the place
26. and there *shall ye die*.
26: 8. saying, *Thou shalt* surely *die*.
27:13. Why *will ye die*, thou and thy people,
28:17. *So* Hananiah the prophet *died*
31:30. every one *shall die* for his own .
34: 4. *Thou shalt* not *die* by the sword:
5. *thou shalt die* in peace:
37:20. lest *I die* there.
38: 2. He that remaineth...*shall die*
9. *and he is like to* (marg. *will*) *die* for hunger

Jer. 38:10. take up Jeremiah...before *he die*.
24. and *thou shalt* not *die*.
42:16. and there *ye shall die*.
17. *they shall die* by the sword,
22. know certainly that *ye shall die*
44:12. *they shall die*, from the least
Eze. 3:18. *Thou shalt* surely *die*;
— the same wicked (man) *shall die*
19. *he shall die* in his iniquity;
20. *he shall die*: because thou hast not given him warning, *he shall die* in his sin,
5:12. A third part of thee *shall die* with
6:12. He that is far off *shall die*
— he that remaineth...*shall die*
7:15. he that (is) in the field *shall die*
12:13. though *he shall die* there.
13:19. the souls that *should* not *die*,
17:16. in the midst of Babylon *he shall die*.
18: 4, 20. the soul that sinneth, it *shall die*.
17. *he shall* not *die* for the iniquity
21, 28. surely live, *he shall* not *die*.
24. in them *shall he die*.
26. for his iniquity...*shall he die*.
31. why *will ye die*, O house of Israel?
24:18. *and* at even my wife *died*;
28:10. *Thou shalt die* the deaths of
33: 8, 14. *thou shalt* surely *die*;
— that wicked (man) *shall die*
9. *he shall die* in his iniquity;
11. why *will ye die*, O house of Israel?
13. *he shall die* for it.
15. surely live, *he shall* not *die*.
27. *shall die* of the pestilence.
Hos 13: 1. *but* when he offended in Baal, *he died*.
Am. 7:11. Jeroboam *shall die* by the sword,
17. *thou shalt die* in a polluted land:
9:10. All the sinners of my people *shall die*
Hab. 1:12. *we shall* not *die*.
Zec. 11: 9. that that dieth, *let it die*;

KAL.—*Participle.*

Gen 20: 3. thou (art but) *a dead man*,
23: 3. Abraham stood up from before *his dead*,
4. that I may bury *my dead*
6. choice of our sepulchres bury *thy dead*;
— that thou mayest bury *thy dead*.
8. that I should bury *my dead*
11. give I it thee: bury *thy dead*.
13. I will bury *my dead* there.
15. bury therefore *thy dead*.
30: 1. Give me children, or else I *die*.
48:21. Israel said unto Joseph, Behold, I *die*:
50: 5. made me swear, saying, Lo, I *die*:
24. Joseph said unto his brethren, I *die*:
Ex. 12:30. a house where (there was) not *one dead*.
33. We (be) all *dead* (men).
14:30. Israel saw the Egyptians *dead*
21:34. *and the dead* (beast) shall be his.
35. *the dead* (ox) also they shall divide.
36. *and the dead* shall be his own.
Lev. 21:11. Neither shall he go in to any *dead* body,
Nu. 6: 6. he shall come at no *dead* body.
9. if any man die *very suddenly*
12:12. Let her not be *as one dead*,
16:48(17:13). between *the dead* and the living;
49(—:14). *they that died* in the plague
—(—:—). *them that died* about the matter of
19:11. He that toucheth *the dead body*
13. Whosoever toucheth *the dead body*
16. or *a dead body*, or a bone of a man,
18. or one slain, or *one dead*,
25: 9. *those that died* in the plague
Deu 4:22. I *must die* in this land,
14: 1. nor make any baldness...*for the dead*.
17: 6. shall *he that is worthy of death*
18:11. or a wizard, or a *necromancer*. (lit. one that enquires of *the dead*)
25: 5. the wife of *the dead*
6. the name of his brother (which is) *dead*,
26:14. nor given (ought) thereof *for the dead*:
Jud. 3:25. their lord (was) fallen down *dead*
4:22. Sisera lay *dead*,
16:30. *the dead* which he slew at his death
Ru. 1: 8. as ye have dealt with *the dead*,
2:20. to the living and to *the dead*.
4: 5. wife of *the dead*, to raise up the name of *the dead*

Ru. 4:10. the name of *the dead* upon his inheritance, that the name of *the dead* be not cut off
1Sa.24:14(15). after a *dead* dog, after a flea.
2Sa. 9: 8. such a *dead* dog as I (am)?
14: 2. a long time mourned for *the dead:*
16: 9. Why should this *dead* dog curse
19: 6(7). all we *had died* this day,
1K. 3:20. laid her *dead* child in my bosom.
22. *the dead* (is) thy son. And this said, No; but *the dead* (is) thy son,
23. and thy son (is) *the dead:* and the other saith, Nay; but thy son (is) *the dead,*
14:11. *Him that dieth* of Jeroboam
— *and him that dieth* in the field
16: 4. *Him that dieth* of Baasha
— *and him that dieth* of his in the fields
21:24. *Him that dieth* of Ahab
— *and him that dieth* in the field
2K. 4:32. the child *was dead,*
8: 5. he had restored *a dead body*
19:35. they (were) all *dead* corpses.
20: 1. thou *shalt die,* and not live.
23:30. his servants carried him in a chariot *dead*
Ps. 31:12(13). I am forgotten *as a dead man*
88: 5(6). Free *among the dead,*
10(11). Wilt thou shew wonders *to the dead?*
106:28. and ate the sacrifices of *the dead.*
115:17. *The dead* praise not the Lord,
143: 3. *as those that have been* long *dead.*
Ecc. 4: 2. I praised *the dead*
9: 3. and after that (they go) to *the dead.*
4. a living dog is better than *a dead* lion.
5. *but the dead* know not any thing,
Isa. 8:19. unto their God? for the living to *the dead?*
22: 2. slain with the sword, nor *dead in* battle.
26:14. (They are) *dead,* they shall not live;
19. *Thy dead* (men) shall live,
37:36. they (were) all *dead* corpses.
38: 1. thou *shalt die,* and not live.
59:10. (we are) in desolate places *as dead* (men).
Jer. 16: 7. to comfort them for *the dead;*
22:10. Weep ye not *for the dead,*
28:16. this year thou *shalt die,*
Lam.3: 6. *as* (they that be) *dead* of old.
Eze.18:18. *he shall die* in his iniquity.
32. the death of *him that dieth,*
24:17. make no mourning *for the dead,*
44:25. they shall come at no *dead* person
Zec.11: 9. *that that dieth,* let it die;

* POLEL.—*Preterite.* *

2Sa. 1:16. *I have slain* the Lord's anointed.
Jer. 20:17. *he slew me* not from the womb;

POLEL.—*Infinitive.*

Ps.109:16. *that he might* even *slay* the broken in heart.

POLEL.—*Imperative.*

Jud. 9:54. Draw thy sword, *and slay me,*
2Sa. 1: 9. Stand, I pray thee, upon me, *and slay me:*

POLEL.—*Future.*

1Sa 17:51. *and slew him,* and cut off his head
2Sa. 1:10. I stood upon him, *and slew him,*
Ps. 34:21(22). Evil *shall slay* the wicked:

POLEL.—*Participle.*

1Sa.14:13. and his armourbearer *slew* after him.

* HIPHIL.—*Preterite.* *

Ex. 1:16. if it (be) a son, *then ye shall kill* him:
21:29. *but that he hath killed* a man
Nu. 14:15. *Now* (if) *thou shalt kill* (all) this people
16:41(17:6). *have killed* the people of the Lord.
Jud.16:30. dead which *he slew* at his death were more than (they) which *he slew* in his life.
1Sa.15: 3. *but slay* both man and woman,
17:35. and smote him, *and slew him.*
30: 2. *they slew* not any, either great
2Sa. 3:30. *he had slain* their brother
13:28. *then kill* him, fear not:
32. (that) *they have slain* all the young men
14:32. be (any) iniquity in me, *let him kill me.*
21: 1. because *he slew* the Gibeonites.
2K. 11:20. *they slew* Athaliah with the sword
14: 6. the children of the murderers *he slew* not:
16: 9. to Kir, and *slew* Rezin.
1Ch 19.18. *killed* Shophach the captain of the host.
2Ch 22:11. so that *she slew him* not.
2Ch 23:21. *they had slain* Athaliah
25: 4. *he slew* not their children,
Isa. 14:30. *and I will kill* thy root with famine,
65:15. *for* the Lord God *shall slay thee,*
Jer. 26:19. *Did* Hezekiah...*put him* at all *to death?*
41: 8. *slew them* not among their brethren.
Hos. 2: 3(5). *and slay her* with thirst.
9:16. *yet will I slay* (even) the beloved (fruit)

HIPHIL.—*Infinitive.*

Gen18:25. *to slay* the righteous with the wicked:
37:18. they conspired against him *to slay him.*
Ex. 4:24. met him, and sought *to kill him.*
16: 3. *to kill* this whole assembly
17: 3. *to kill* us and our children
Lev.20: 4. and *kill* him not:
Nu. 16:13. *to kill us* in the wilderness,
Deu 9:28. *to slay them* in the wilderness.
13: 9(10) & 17:7. upon him *to put him to death,*
Jud.13:23. If the Lord were pleased *to kill us,*
15:13. *but surely* we will not kill thee. (lit. *but killing* we will not kill thee)
1Sa. 2:25. because the Lord would *slay them.*
5:10. *to slay us* (lit. *me*) and our people.
19: 1. *that they should kill* David.
2. Saul my father seeketh *to kill thee:*
5. *to slay* David without a cause?
11. *and to slay him* in the morning:
15. Bring him up to me...*that I may slay him.*
20:33. determined of his father *to slay* David.
28: 9. a snare for my life, *to cause me to die?*
2Sa. 3:37. it was not of the king *to slay* Abner
8: 2. with two lines measured he *to put to death,*
20:19. thou seekest *to destroy* a city
21: 4. neither for us *shalt thou kill*
1K. 3:26, 27. *and in no wise* slay it. (lit. *and slaying* slay it not)
11:40. Solomon sought therefore *to kill* Jeroboam.
17:18. to remembrance, *and to slay* my son?
20. brought evil upon the widow...*by slaying*
18: 9. into the hand of Ahab, *to slay me?*
2K. 5: 7. *to kill* and to make alive,
11:15. him that followeth her *kill*
Est. 4:11. one law of his *to put* (him) *to death,*
Ps. 37:32. and seeketh *to slay him.*
59[title](1). they watched the house *to kill him.*
Pro.19:18. spare for *his crying.* (marg. or, to *his destruction:* or, to *cause him to die*)
Jer. 26:19. Hezekiah...put him *at all* to death? (lit. *putting to death* put they him to death)
21. the king sought *to put him to death:*
24. should not give him...*to put him to death.*
38:15. not *surely* put me to death? (lit. *putting to death* wilt thou not put me to death)
41: 4. *after he had slain* Gedaliah,
43: 3. *that they might put* us *to death,*
Eze.13:19. *to slay* the souls that should not die,

HIPHIL.—*Imperative.*

1Sa.20: 8. *slay me* thyself; for why
22:17. Turn, *and slay* the priests of the Lord;

HIPHIL.—*Future.*

Gen38: 7. *and* the Lord *slew him.*
10. *wherefore he slew* him also.
42:37. Reuben spake...saying, *Slay* my two sons,
Nu. 35:19. of blood himself *shall slay* the murderer: when he meeteth him, *he shall slay him.*
21. the revenger of blood *shall slay*
Deu32:39. I *kill,* and I make alive;
Jos. 10:26. Joshua smote them, *and slew them,*
11:17. and smote them, *and slew them.*
Jud.15:13. but surely *we will* not *kill thee.*
20:13. *that we may put them to death,* and put
1Sa. 5:11. that *it slay* us not, and our people:
11:12. the men, *that we may put them to death.*
17:50. smote the Philistine, *and slew him;*
19:17. why *should I kill thee?*
22:18. he fell upon the priests, *and slew*
30:15. that *thou wilt* neither *kill me,*
2Sa. 4: 7. they smote him, *and slew him,*
14: 6. the one smote the other, *and slew* him.
7. *that we may kill him,* for the life
18:15. and smote Absalom, *and slew him.*
21:17. smote the Philistine, *and killed him.*
1K. 1:51. that *he will* not *slay* his servant
2: 8. *I will* not *put thee to death*
26. *I will* not at this time *put thee to death,*

1K. 2:34. and fell upon him, *and slew him:*
3:26, 27. and in no wise *slay it.*
13:24. a lion met him by the way, *and slew him:*
26. hath torn him, *and slain him,*
15:28. *Even* in the third year of Asa...*did* Baasha *slay him,*
16:10. went in and smote him, *and killed him,*
19:17. him that escapeth...*shall* Jehu *slay:* and him that escapeth...*shall* Elisha *slay.*
2K. 7: 4. if *they kill us,* we shall but die.
14:19. *and slew him* there.
15:10. smote him before the people, *and slew him,*
14. smote Shallum...*and slew him,*
25. *and he killed him,* and reigned in his room.
30. smote him, *and slew him,*
21:23. *and slew* the king in his own house.
23:29. *and he slew him* at Megiddo,
25:21. the king...smote them, *and slew them*
1Ch 2: 3. in the sight of the Lord; *and he slew him.*
10:14. *therefore he slew him,* and turned
2Ch 22: 9. and *when they had slain him,* they
23:14. *Slay her* not in the house
15. *and* when...*they slew her* there.
25:27. to Lachish after him, *and slew him* there.
33:24. conspired against him, *and slew him*
Job 5: 2. envy *slayeth* the silly one.
9:23. If the scourge *slay* suddenly,
Ps. 105:29. waters into blood, *and slew* their fish.
Pro. 21:25. The desire of the slothful *killeth him;*
Isa. 11: 4. *shall he slay* the wicked.
Jer. 38:15. *wilt thou* not surely *put me to death?*
16. *I will* not *put thee to death,*
25. *we will* not *put thee to death;*
41: 2. smote Gedaliah...*and slew* him,
8. *Slay us* not: for we have treasures
52:27. smote them, *and put them to death*

HIPHIL.—*Participle.*

1Sa. 2: 6. The Lord *killeth,*
2K. 17:26. and, behold, *they slay* them,
Job 33:22. his life *to the destroyers.*
Jer. 26:15. if ye *put* me *to death,*

* HOPHAL.—*Preterite.* *

Deu 21:22. *and he be to be put to death,*
2Sa. 21: 9. *and were put to death* in the days of harvest,
2K. 11: 2. so that *he was* not *slain.*

HOPHAL.—*Future.*

Gen 26:11. *shall* surely *be put to death.*
Ex. 19:12. whosoever...*shall be* surely *put to death:*
21:12. smiteth a man,...*shall be* surely *put to death.*
15. smiteth his father,...*shall be...put to death.*
16. *he shall* surely *be put to death.*
17. his mother, *shall* surely *be put to death.*
29. his owner also *shall be put to death.*
22:19(18) & 31:14. *shall* surely *be put to death.*
31:15. *he shall* surely *be put to death.*
35: 2. doeth work therein *shall be put to death.*
Lev. 19:20. *they shall* not *be put to death,*
20: 2, 15. *he shall* surely *be put to death:*
9. *shall be* surely *put to death:*
10. the adulteress *shall* surely *be put to death.*
11, 12. of them *shall* surely *be put to death;*
13, 16. *they shall* surely *be put to death;*
27. a wizard, *shall* surely *be put to death:*
24:16. *he shall* surely *be put to death,*
— (of the Lord), *shall be put to death.*
17. any man *shall* surely *be put to death.*
21. *he shall be put to death.*
27:29. (but) *shall* surely *be put to death.*
Nu. 1:51. that cometh nigh *shall be put to death.*
3:10, 38. the stranger...*shall be put to death.*
15:35. The man *shall be* surely *put to death:*
18: 7. the stranger...*shall be put to death.*
35:16, 17, 18. murderer *shall* surely *be put to death.*
21. he that smote (him) *shall* surely *be put to death;*
31. *he shall be* surely *put to death.*
Deu 13: 5(6). *shall be put to death;*
17: 6. *shall he* that is worthy of death *be put to death;*
— *he shall* not *be put to death.*
24:16. The fathers *shall* not *be put to death* for the children, neither *shall* the children *be put to death* for the fathers: every man *shall be put to death*
Jos. 1:18. *he shall be put to death:* only

Jud. 6:31. *let him be put to death* whilst
21: 5. *He shall* surely *be put to death.*
1Sa. 11:13. There *shall* not a man *be put to death*
19: 6. (As) the Lord liveth, *he shall* not *be slain.*
20:32. Wherefore *shall he be slain?*
2Sa. 19:21(22). *Shall* not Shimei *be put to death*
22(23). *shall* there any man *be put to death*
1K. 2:24. Adonijah *shall be put to death*
2K. 11: 8. within the ranges, *let him be slain:*
15. *Let her* not *be slain* in the house of the
16. *and* there *was she slain.*
14: 6. The fathers *shall* not *be put to death* for the children, nor the children *be put to death* for the fathers; but every man *shall be put to death* for
2Ch 15:13. not seek the Lord...*should be put to death,*
23: 7. the house, *he shall be put to death:*
14. *let him be slain* with the sword.
Jer. 38: 4. *let* this man *be put to death:*
Eze. 18:13. *he shall* surely *die;* his blood

HOPHAL.—*Participle.*

1Sa. 19:11. to morrow thou *shalt be slain.*
2K. 11: 2. the king's sons *which were slain;*
2Ch 22:11. the king's sons *that were slain,*

מָוֶת *māh'-veth,* m. 4194

Gen 21:16. Let me not see *the death of* the child.
25:11. after *the death of* Abraham,
26:18. after *the death of* Abraham:
27: 2. I know not the day of *my death:*
7. and bless thee...before *my death.*
10. that he may bless thee before *his death.*
50:16. Thy father did command before *he died,*
Ex. 10:17. take away from me this *death*
Lev. 11:31. *when they be dead,* shall be unclean
32. *when they are dead,* doth fall,
16: 1. after *the death of* the two sons
Nu. 6: 7. or for his sister, *when they die:*
16:29. If these men die *the* common *death of* all men, (marg. *as* every man *dieth*)
23:10. Let me die *the death of* the righteous,
26:10. *when* that company *died,*
33:39. *when he died* in mount Hor.
35:25. *unto the death of* the high priest,
28. *until the death of* the high priest: but after *the death of* the high priest
32. until *the death of* the priest.
Deu 19: 6. he (was) not worthy of *death,*
21:22. man have committed a sin worthy of *death,*
22:26. in the damsel no sin (worthy) of *death:*
30:15. life and good, and *death* and evil;
19. I have set before you life *and death,*
31:27. how much more after *my death?*
29. I know that after *my death*
33: 1. the children of Israel before *his death.*
34: 7. And Moses...*when he died:*
Jos. 1: 1. after *the death of* Moses
2:13. deliver our lives *from death.*
20: 6. until *the death of* the high priest
Jud. 1: 1. after *the death of* Joshua
2:19. *when* the judge *was dead,*
13: 7. from the womb to the day of *his death.*
16:30. the dead which he slew *at his death*
Ru. 1:17. (if ought) but *death* part thee and me.
2:11. since *the death of* thine husband:
1Sa. 5:11. there was a *deadly* destruction (lit. destruction of *death*)
15:32. Surely the bitterness of *death* is past.
35. until the day of *his death:*
20: 3. but a step between me and *death.*
31. for he shall surely *die.* (marg. (is) the son of *death*)
26:16. worthy to *die,* (marg. the sons of *death*)
2Sa. 1: 1. after *the death of* Saul,
23. *and in their death* they were not divided:
3:33. Died Abner *as a fool dieth?*
6:23. Michal...had no child unto the day of *her death.*
12: 5. this (thing) shall surely *die:* (marg. (is) worthy *to die;* lit. (is) a son of *death*)
15:21. whether *in death* or life,
19:28(29). all (of) my father's house were but *dead* men (marg. men of *death*)

2Sa.22: 5. When the waves of *death* compassed me,
6. the snares of *death* prevented me;
1K. 2:26. worthy of *death:* (marg. a man of *death*)
11:40. until *the death of* Solomon.
2K. 1: 1. after *the death of* Ahab.
2:21. any more *death* or barren (land).
3: 5. *when* Ahab *was dead,*
4:40. (there is) *death* in the pot.
14:17. after *the death of* Jehoash
15: 5. a leper unto the day of *his death,*
1Ch 2:24. after that Hezron *was dead*
22: 5. prepared abundantly before *his death.*
2Ch 22: 4. after *the death of* his father
24:15. hundred and thirty years old...*when he died.*
17. after *the death of* Jehoiada
22. *And when he died,* he said,
25:25. after *the death of* Joash
26:21. a leper unto the day of *his death,*
32:33. did him honour *at his death.*
Est. 2: 7. *when* her father and mother *were dead,*
Job 3:21. Which long *for death,*
5:20. he shall redeem thee *from death:*
7:15. *death* rather than my life.
18:13. the firstborn of *death*
27:15. that remain...shall be buried *in death:*
28:22. Destruction *and death* say,
30:23. thou wilt bring me (to) *death,*
38:17. Have the gates of *death* been opened
Ps. 6: 5(6). *in death* (there is) no remembrance of
7:13(14). the instruments of *death;*
9:13(14). liftest me up from the gates of *death:*
13: 3(4). lest I sleep the (sleep of) *death;*
18: 4(5). The sorrows of *death* compassed me,
5(6). the snares of *death* prevented me.
22:15(16). brought me into the dust of *death.*
33:19. To deliver their soul *from death,*
49:14(15). *death* shall feed on them;
17(18). *when he dieth* he shall carry nothing
55: 4(5). the terrors of *death* are fallen upon me.
15(16). Let *death* seize upon them,
56:13(14). hast delivered my soul *from death:*
68:20(21). the issues *from death.*
73: 4. (there are) no bands *in their death:*
78:50. spared not their soul *from death,*
89:48(49). What man...shall not see *death?*
107:18. they draw near unto the gates of *death.*
116: 3. The sorrows of *death* compassed me,
8. delivered my soul *from death,*
15. *the death* of his saints.
118:18. *but* he hath not given me over *unto death.*
Pro. 2:18. her house inclineth unto *death,*
5: 5. Her feet go down *to death;*
7:27. the chambers of *death.*
8:36. all they that hate me love *death.*
10: 2 & 11:4. righteousness delivereth *from death*
11: 7. *When* a wicked man *dieth,*
19. he that pursueth evil...*to his own death.*
12:28. the pathway (thereof there is) no *death.*
13:14. to depart from the snares of *death.*
14:12. the end thereof (are) the ways of *death.*
27. to depart from the snares of *death.*
32. the righteous hath hope *in his death.*
16:14. (as) messengers of *death:*
25. the end thereof (are) the ways of *death.*
18:21. *Death* and life (are) in the power of the
21: 6. tossed to and fro of them that seek *death.*
24:11. (them that are) drawn *unto death,*
26:18. firebrands, arrows, *and death,*
Ecc. 3:19. *as* the one *dieth,* so *dieth* the other;
7: 1. the day of *death* than the day of one's birth.
26. more bitter *than death* the woman,
8: 8. power in the day of *death:*
10: 1. *Dead* flies (marg. Flies of *death*) cause the ointment of the
Cant. 8: 6. love (is) strong *as death;*
Isa. 6: 1. In the year *that* king Uzziah *died*
14:28. In the year *that* king Ahaz *died*
25: 8. He will swallow up *death*
28:15. We have made a covenant with *death,*
18. your covenant with *death*
38:18. *death* can (not) celebrate thee:
53: 9. with the rich *in his death;* (marg. *deaths*)
12. poured out his soul *unto death:*
Jer. 8: 3. *death* shall be chosen
9:21(20). *death* is come up into our windows,
15: 2. Such as (are) *for death, to death;*
18:21. let their men be put *to death;*
Jer. 18:23. all their counsel against me *to slay* (me): (marg. *for death*)
21: 8. the way of life, and the way of *death.*
26:11. This man (is) worthy to *die;* (marg. The judgment of *death* (is) for this man)
16. This man (is) not worthy to *die:* (lit. *id.*)
43:11. such (as are) *for death to death;*
52:11. in prison till the day of *his death.*
34. a portion until the day of *his death,*
Lam. 1:20. at home (there is) *as death.*
Eze. 18:23. *that* the wicked *should die?*
32. no pleasure *in the death of* him
28:10. die *the deaths of* the uncircumcised
31:14. they are all delivered *unto death,*
33:11. no pleasure *in the death of* the wicked;
Hos. 13:14. I will redeem them *from death: O death,*
Jon. 4: 3. (it is) better *for me to die*
8. (It is) better *for me to die* than to live.
9. to be angry, (even) unto *death.*
Hab. 2: 5. his desire as hell, and (is) *as death,*

מוּת *mōhth*, Ch. m. 4193

Ezr. 7:26. whether (it be) *unto death,* or to

מוּת *mooth*, m. 4192

Ps. 9[title](1). chief Musician upon *Muth*-labben,
48:14(15). our guide (even) unto *death.*

מוֹתָר *mōh-thāhr'*, m. 4195

Pro. 14:23. In all labour there is *profit:*
21: 5. (tend) only *to plenteousness;*
Ecc. 3:19. so *that* a man hath no *preeminence*

מִזְבֵּחַ *miz-bēh'ăgh*, m. 4196

Gen 8:20. Noah builded *an altar*
— offered burnt offerings *on the altar.*
12: 7. there builded he *an altar*
8. there he builded *an altar*
13: 4. Unto the place of *the altar,*
18. built there *an altar* unto the Lord.
22: 9. Abraham built *an altar* there,
— laid him on *the altar*
26:25. he builded *an altar* there,
33:20. And he erected there *an altar,*
35: 1. make there *an altar* unto God,
3. I will make there *an altar*
7. he built there *an altar,*
Ex. 17:15. And Moses built *an altar,*
20:24. *An altar of* earth thou shalt make
25. if thou wilt make me *an altar of*
26. go up by steps unto *mine altar,*
21:14. thou shalt take him from *mine altar,*
24: 4. builded *an altar* under the hill,
6. the blood he sprinkled on *the altar.*
27: 1. thou shalt make *an altar*
— *the altar* shall be foursquare:
5. compass of *the altar* beneath, that the net may be even to the midst of *the altar.*
6. thou shalt make staves *for the altar,*
7. be upon the two sides of *the altar,*
28:43. when they come near unto *the altar*
29:12. put (it) upon the horns of *the altar*
— beside the bottom of *the altar.*
13. burn (them) *upon the altar.*
16. sprinkle (it) round about upon *the altar.*
18. burn the whole ram *upon the altar:*
20. sprinkle the blood upon *the altar*
21. the blood that (is) upon *the altar,*
25. burn (them) *upon the altar*
36. thou shalt cleanse *the altar,*
37. an atonement for *the altar,* and sanctify it; and it shall be *an altar* most holy: whatsoever toucheth *the altar* shall be holy.
38. thou shalt offer upon *the altar;*
44. the congregation, and *the altar:*
30: 1. thou shalt make *an altar* to burn
18. the congregation and *the altar,*
20. when they come near to *the altar*
27. and *the altar of* incense,
28. *the altar of* burnt offering
31: 8. *the altar of* incense,

Ex. 31: 9. *the altar of* burnt offering
32: 5. he built *an altar* before it;
34:13. But ye shall destroy *their altars*,
35:15. *the* incense *altar*, and his staves,
16. *The altar of* burnt offering,
37:25. he made *the* incense *altar*
38: 1. he made *the altar of* burnt offering
3. he made all the vessels of *the altar*,
4. he made *for the altar* a brasen grate
7. the rings on the sides of *the altar*,
30. and *the* brasen *altar*,
— all the vessels of *the altar*,
39:38. *the* golden *altar*, and the anointing oil,
39. *The* brasen *altar*, and his grate
40: 5. thou shalt set *the altar of* gold
6. set *the altar of* the burnt offering
7. the tent of the congregation and *the altar*,
10. shalt anoint *the altar of* the burnt offering, and all his vessels, and sanctify *the altar*: and it shall be *an altar* most holy.
26. he put *the* golden *altar* in the tent
29. he put *the altar of* burnt offering
30. tent of the congregation and *the altar*,
32. they came near unto *the altar*,
33. round about the tabernacle *and the altar*,
Lev. 1: 5. blood round about upon *the altar*
7. shall put fire upon *the altar*,
8, 12. the fire which (is) upon *the altar*:
9. the priest shall burn all *on the altar*,
11. kill it on the side of *the altar*
— blood round about upon *the altar*.
13. burn (it) *upon the altar*:
15. the priest shall bring it unto *the altar*,
— *on the altar*; and the blood thereof shall be wrung out at the side of *the altar*:
16. cast it beside *the altar*
17. the priest shall burn it *upon the altar*,
2: 2. burn the memorial of it *upon the altar*,
8. he shall bring it unto *the altar*.
9. shall burn (it) *upon the altar*:
12. shall not be burnt on *the altar*
3: 2. shall sprinkle the blood upon *the altar*
5. shall burn it *on the altar*
8. round about upon *the altar*.
11. the priest shall burn it *upon the altar*;
13. upon *the altar* round about.
16. priest shall burn them *upon the altar*:
4: 7. blood upon the horns of *the altar of*
— the bullock at the bottom of *the altar of*
10. shall burn them upon *the altar of*
18. blood upon the horns of *the altar*
— the blood at the bottom of *the altar of*
19. burn (it) *upon the altar*.
25, 30, 34. (it) upon the horns of *the altar of*
— blood at the bottom of *the altar*
26. burn all his fat *upon the altar*,
30. thereof at the bottom of *the altar*.
31. shall burn (it) *upon the altar*
34. blood thereof at the bottom of *the altar*:
35. shall burn them *upon the altar*,
5: 9. upon the side of *the altar*;
— out at the bottom of *the altar*:
12. burn (it) *on the altar*,
6: 9(2). the burning upon *the altar*
—(–). the fire of *the altar* shall be burning
10(3). with the burnt offering on *the altar*, and he shall put them beside *the altar*.
12(5). the fire upon *the altar* shall be
13(6). shall ever be burning upon *the altar*;
14(7). before the Lord, before *the altar*.
15(8). shall burn (it) upon *the altar*
7: 2. sprinkle round about upon *the altar*.
5. the priest shall burn them *upon the altar*
31. shall burn the fat *upon the altar*:
8:11. he sprinkled thereof upon *the altar*
— and anointed *the altar* and all
15. put (it) upon the horns of *the altar*
— and purified *the altar*, and poured the blood at the bottom of *the altar*,
16. Moses burned (it) *upon the altar*.
19, 24. sprinkled the blood upon *the altar*
21. burnt the whole ram *upon the altar*:
28. burnt (them) *on the altar*
30. the blood which (was) upon *the altar*,
9: 7. Go unto *the altar*,
8. Aaron therefore went unto *the altar*,
9. put (it) upon the horns of *the altar*,

Lev. 9: 9. the blood at the bottom of *the altar*:
10. he burnt *upon the altar*;
12. sprinkled round about upon *the altar*.
13. and he burnt (them) upon *the altar*.
14. the burnt offering *on the altar*.
17. burnt (it) upon *the altar*,
18. which he sprinkled upon *the altar*
20. he burnt the fat *upon the altar*:
24. upon *the altar* the burnt offering
10:12. eat it without leaven beside *the altar*:
14:20. the meat offering *upon the altar*:
16:12. burning coals of fire from off *the altar*
18. he shall go out unto *the altar*
— put (it) upon the horns of *the altar*
20. *the altar*, he shall bring
25. shall he burn *upon the altar*.
33. of the congregation, and for *the altar*,
17: 6. sprinkle the blood upon *the altar of*
11. to you upon *the altar*
21:23. nor come nigh unto *the altar*,
22:22. an offering by fire of them upon *the altar*
Nu. 3:26. by *the altar* round about,
31. the candlestick, *and the altars*,
4:11. upon *the* golden *altar* they shall spread
13. take away the ashes from *the altar*,
14. all the vessels of *the altar*;
26. by *the altar* round about,
5:25. offer it upon *the altar*:
26. and burn (it) *upon the altar*,
7: 1. both *the altar* and all the vessels
10. offered for dedicating of *the altar*
— offered their offering before *the altar*.
11. for the dedicating of *the altar*.
84, 88. This (was) the dedication of *the altar*,
16:38(17: 3). plates (for) a covering *of the altar*:
39(—: 4). (plates for) a covering *of the altar*.
46(—:11). put fire therein from off *the altar*,
18: 3. the vessels of the sanctuary and *the altar*,
5. the charge of *the altar*:
7. for every thing of *the altar*,
17. sprinkle their blood upon *the altar*,
23: 1, 29. Build me here seven *altars*,
2. *on* (every) *altar* a bullock and a ram.
4. I have prepared seven *altars*,
— *upon* (every) *altar* a bullock and a ram.
14. and built seven *altars*,
—, 30. a bullock and a ram *on* (every) *altar*.
Deu 7: 5. ye shall destroy *their altars*,
12: 3. ye shall overthrow *their altars*,
27, 27. upon *the altar of* the Lord
16:21. trees near unto *the altar of*
26: 4. set it down before *the altar of*
27: 5. shalt thou build *an altar*
— *an altar of* stones:
6. build *the altar of* the Lord thy God
33:10. burnt sacrifice upon *thine altar*.
Jos. 8:30. Then Joshua built *an altar*
31. *an altar of* whole stones,
9:27. *and for the altar of* the Lord,
22:10. there *an altar* by Jordan, *a* great *altar*
11. have built *an altar* over against
16. in that ye have builded you *an altar*,
19. in building you *an altar* beside *the altar of* the Lord
23. That we have built us *an altar*
26. prepare to build us *an altar*,
28. Behold the pattern of *the altar of*
29. to build *an altar* for burnt offerings,
— beside *the altar of* the Lord
34. called *the altar* (Ed):
Jud. 2: 2. ye shall throw down *their altars*:
6:24. Then Gideon built *an altar* there
25. throw down *the altar of* Baal
26. And build *an altar* unto the Lord
28. *the altar of* Baal was cast down,
— second bullock was offered upon *the altar*
30. he hath cast down *the altar of* Baal,
31. because (one) hath cast down *his altar*.
32. because he hath thrown down *his altar*.
13:20. toward heaven from off *the altar*,
— in the flame of *the altar*.
21: 4. built there *an altar*,
1 Sa. 2:28. to offer upon *mine altar*,
33. I shall not cut off from *mine altar*,
7:17. and there he built *an altar*
14:35. And Saul built *an altar*...the same was the first *altar*

2Sa.24:18. rear *an altar* unto the Lord
21. to build *an altar* unto the Lord,
25. David built there *an altar*
1K. 1:50, 51. hold on the horns of *the altar.*
53. brought him down from *the altar.*
2:28. caught hold on the horns of *the altar.*
29. behold, (he is) by *the altar.*
3: 4. did Solomon offer upon that *altar.*
6:20. and (so) covered *the altar*
22. also *the* whole *altar*
7:48. *the altar of* gold, and the table of gold,
8:22. Solomon stood before *the altar of* the Lord
31. the oath come before *thine altar*
54. he arose from before *the altar of*
64. *the* brasen *altar* that (was) before the Lord
9:25. upon *the altar* which he built
12:32, 33, 33. he offered upon *the altar.*
13: 1. Jeroboam stood by *the altar*
2. he cried against *the altar* in the word of the Lord, and said, *O altar, altar,*
3. *the altar* shall be rent,
4. which had cried against *the altar* in Bethel, that he put forth his hand from *the altar,*
5. *The altar also* was rent, and the ashes poured out from *the altar,*
32. against *the altar* in Beth-el,
16:32. he reared up *an altar* for Baal
18:26. they leaped upon *the altar*
30. he repaired *the altar of* the Lord
32. And with the stones he built *an altar*
— he made a trench about *the altar,*
35. the water ran round about *the altar;*
19:10, 14. thrown down *thine altars,*
2K. 11:11. *by the altar* and the temple.
18. *his altars* and his images
— the priest of Baal before *the altars.*
12: 9(10). set it beside *the altar,*
16:10. saw *an altar* that (was) at Damascus:
— the fashion of *the altar,*
11. And Urijah the priest built *an altar*
12. the king saw *the altar:* and the king approached to *the altar,*
13. his peace offerings, upon *the altar.*
14. he brought also *the* brasen *altar,*
— from between *the altar*
— put it on the north side of *the altar.*
15. Upon *the* great *altar* burn
— *and the* brasen *altar* shall be for me
18:22. *whose altars* Hezekiah hath taken away,
— Ye shall worship before this *altar*
21: 3. he reared up *altars* for Baal,
4. he built *altars* in the house of the Lord,
5. he built *altars* for all the host of heaven
23: 9. came not up to *the altar of* the
12. *the altars* that (were) on the top
— and *the altars* which Manasseh had made
15. *the altar* that (was) at Beth-el,
— made, both that *altar* and the high place
16. burned (them) upon *the altar,*
17. that thou hast done against *the altar of*
20. that (were) there upon *the altars,*
1Ch. 6:49(34). Aaron and his sons offered upon *the altar of* the burnt offering, and on *the altar of* incense,
16:40. upon *the altar of* the burnt offering
21:18. set up *an altar* unto the Lord
22. that I may build *an altar*
26. David built there *an altar* unto the Lord,
— by fire upon *the altar of* burnt offering.
29. *and the altar of* the burnt offering,
22: 1. this (is) *the altar* of the burnt offering
28:18. *And for the altar of* incense
2Ch. 1: 5. *Moreover the* brasen *altar,* that Bezaleel
6. went up thither to *the* brasen *altar*
4: 1. Moreover he made *an altar of* brass,
19. *the* golden *altar* also,
5:12. stood at the east end *of the altar,*
6:12. he stood before *the altar of*
22. and the oath come before *thine altar*
7: 7. *the* brasen *altar* which Solomon had
9. kept the dedication of *the altar*
8:12. on *the altar of* the Lord,
14: 3(2). For he took away *the altars*
15: 8. renewed *the altar of* the Lord,
23:10. along *by the altar* and the temple,
17. brake *his altars* and his images
— the priest of Baal before *the altars.*

2Ch 26:16. to burn incense upon *the altar of*
19. from beside *the* incense *altar.*
28:24. he made him *altars* in every corner
29:18. *the altar of* burnt offering,
19. they (are) before *the altar of* the Lord.
21. to offer (them) on *the altar of*
22. sprinkled (it) *on the altar:*
—, 22. they sprinkled the blood *upon the altar*
24. their blood *upon the altar,*
27. the burnt offering *upon the altar.*
30:14. they arose and took away *the altars*
31: 1. *the altars* out of all Judah
32:12. taken away his high places and *his altars,*
— Ye shall worship before one *altar,*
33: 3. he reared up *altars* for Baalim,
4. Also he built *altars* in the house
5. he built *altars* for all the host of heaven
15. all *the altars* that he had built
16. he repaired *the altar of* the Lord,
34: 4. they brake down *the altars of* Baalim
5. bones of the priests upon *their altars,*
7. when he had broken down *the altars*
35:16. to offer burnt offerings upon *the altar of*
Ezr. 3: 2. builded *the altar of* the God of Israel,
3. they set *the altar* upon his bases;
Neh 10:34(35). to burn upon *the altar of*
Ps. 26: 6. so will I compass *thine altar,*
43: 4. Then will I go unto *the altar of* God,
51:19(21). they offer bullocks upon *thine altar.*
84: 3(4). (even) *thine altars,* O Lord of hosts,
118:27. unto the horns of *the altar.*
Isa. 6: 6. taken with the tongs from off *the altar:*
17: 8. he shall not look to *the altars,*
19:19. In that day shall there be *an altar*
27: 9. maketh all the stones of *the altar*
36: 7. *whose altars* Hezekiah hath taken away,
— Ye shall worship before this *altar?*
56: 7. accepted upon *mine altar;*
60: 7. with acceptance on *mine altar,*
Jer. 11:13. have ye set up *altars* to (that) shameful thing, (even) *altars* to burn incense
17: 1. upon the horns of *your altars;*
2. their children remember *their altars*
Lam. 2: 7. The Lord hath cast off *his altar,*
Eze. 6: 4. *your altars* shall be desolate,
5. scatter your bones round about *your altars.*
6. that *your altars* may be laid waste
13. round about *their altars,*
8: 5. at the gate of *the altar*
16. between the porch and *the altar,*
9: 2. stood beside *the* brasen *altar.*
40:46. the keepers of the charge of *the altar:*
47. *and the altar* (that was) before
41:22. *The altar* of wood
43:13. measures of *the altar* after the cubits:
— the higher place of *the altar.*
18. These (are) the ordinances of *the altar*
22. they shall cleanse *the altar,*
26. Seven days shall they purge *the altar*
27. make your burnt offerings upon *the altar,*
45:19. the four corners of the settle *of the altar,*
47: 1. at the south (side) *of the altar.*
Hos. 8:11. Ephraim hath made many *altars* to sin, *altars* shall be unto him to sin.
10: 1. he hath increased *the altars;*
2. he shall break down *their altars,*
8. shall come up on *their altars;*
12:11(12). *their altars* (are) as heaps
Joel 1:13. howl, ye ministers of *the altar:*
2:17. between the porch *and the altar,*
Am. 2: 8. laid to pledge by every *altar,*
3:14. I will also visit *the altars of* Beth-el:
— the horns of *the altar* shall be cut off,
9: 1. I saw the Lord standing upon *the altar:*
Zec. 9:15. as the corners of *the altar.*
14:20. be like the bowls before *the altar.*
Mal. 1: 7. Ye offer polluted bread upon *mine altar;*
10. do ye kindle (fire) on *mine altar*
2:13. covering *the altar of* the Lord

מֶזֶג [*meh'-zeg*], m. 4197

Cant. 7: 2(3). a round goblet, (which) wanteth not *liquor:* (marg. *mixture*)

4198 **מָזֶה** [*māh-zeh'*], adj.

Deu 32:24. (They shall be) *burnt with* hunger,

4200 **מֶזֶו** [*meh'-zev*], m.

Ps 144:13. *our garners* (may be) full,

4201 **מְזוּזָה** *m'zoo-zāh'*, f.

Ex. 12: 7. strike (it) on *the* two *side posts*
22. *the* two *side posts* with the blood
23. on *the* two *side posts*,
21: 6. or unto *the door post;*
Deu 6: 9. write them upon *the posts of* thy house,
11:20. write them upon *the door posts of*
Jud.16: 3. and *the* two *posts*,
1Sa. 1: 9. sat upon a seat by *a post of* the temple
1K. 6:31. the lintel (and) side *posts*
33. the door of *the* temple *posts*
7: 5. all the doors *and posts*
Pro. 8:34. waiting at *the posts of* my doors.
Isa. 57: 8. the doors also *and the posts* hast thou set
Eze.41:21. *The posts* (marg. *post*) of the temple
43: 8. *and their post* by *my posts*,
45:19. put (it) upon *the posts of* the house,
— upon *the posts of* the gate
46: 2. shall stand by *the post of* the gate,

4202 **מָזוֹן** *māh-zōhn'*, m.

Gen 45:23. laden with corn and bread *and meat*
2Ch.11:23. he gave them *victual* in abundance.

4203 **מָזוֹן** *māh-zōhn'*, Ch. m.

Dan 4:12(9), 21(18). *and* in it (was) *meat* for all:

4205 **מָזוֹר** *māh-zōhr'*, m.

Jer. 30:13. to plead thy cause, *that thou mayest be bound up:* (marg. *for binding up*, or, *pressing*)
Hos. 5:13. Judah (saw) *his wound*,
— nor cure you of your *wound*.

4204 **מָזוֹר** *māh-zōhr'*, m.

Obad. 7. thy bread have laid *a wound* (perhaps, lit. *a snare*)

4206 **מֵזַח** *mēh'-zagh* & **מְזִיחַ** *m'zee'ăgh*, m.

Job 12:21. weakeneth *the strength of* the mighty.
Ps.109:19. *and for a girdle* wherewith he is girded
Isa. 23:10. (there is) no more *strength*. (marg. *girdle*)

4207 **מַזְלֵג** *maz-lēhg'*, m.

1Sa. 2:13. with *a fleshhook* of three teeth
14. all that *the fleshhook* brought up

4207 **מִזְלָגוֹת** *miz-lāh-gōhth'*, f. pl.

Ex. 27: 3. *and his fleshhooks*,
38: 3. the basons, (and) *the fleshhooks*,
Nu. 4:14. the censers, *the fleshhooks*,
1Ch 28:17. *Also* pure gold for *the fleshhooks*,
2Ch. 4:16. the shovels, and *the fleshhooks*,

4208 **מַזָּלוֹת** *maz-zāh-lōhth'*, f. pl.

2K. 23: 5. to the moon, *and to the planets*, (marg. or, *twelve signs*, or, *constellations*)

מְזִמָּה *m'zim-māh'*, f. 4209

Job 21:27. *and the devices* (which) ye wrongfully
42: 2. no *thought* can be withholden from thee.
Ps. 10: 2. let them be taken *in the devices*
4. God (is) not in all *his thoughts*.
21:11(12). they imagined *a mischievous device*,
37: 7. man who bringeth *wicked devices* to pass.
139:20. they speak against thee *wickedly*,
Pro. 1: 4. the young man knowledge *and discretion*. (marg. or, *advisement*)
2:11. *Discretion* shall preserve thee,
3:21. keep sound wisdom *and discretion:*
5: 2. That thou mayest regard *discretion*,
8:12. find out knowledge of *witty inventions*.
12: 2. a man of *wicked devices* will he condemn.
14:17. a man of *wicked devices* is hated.
24: 8. called a *mischievous* person. (lit. a *mischief* master)
Jer. 11:15. she hath wrought *lewdness*
23:20. have performed *the thoughts of* his heart:
30:24. have performed *the intents of* his heart:
51:11. for his *device* (is) against Babylon,

מִזְמוֹר *miz-mōhr'*, m. 4210

Ps. 3 & 4 & 5 & 6 & 8 & 9 & 12 & 13 & 15 & 19 & 20 & 21 & 22 & 23[title](1). *A Psalm* of David,
24[title](1). *A Psalm* of David.
29[title](1). *A Psalm* of David.
30[title](1). *A Psalm* (and) Song (at) the dedication of the house of David.
31 & 38 & 39[title](1). *A Psalm* of David.
40[title](1). *A Psalm* of David.
41[title](1). *A Psalm* of David.
47[title](1). *A Psalm* for the sons of Korah.
48[title](1). A Song (and) *Psalm* for the sons of Korah.
49[title](1). *A Psalm* for the sons of Korah.
50[title](1). *A Psalm* of Asaph.
51 & 62 & 63 & 64[title](1). *A Psalm* of David,
65[title](1). *A Psalm* (and) Song of David.
66[title](1). To the chief Musician, A Song (or) *Psalm*.
67[title](1). Musician on Neginoth, *A Psalm* (or) Song.
68[title](1). *A Psalm* (or) Song of David.
73[title](1). *A Psalm* of Asaph.
75 & 76[title](1). *A Psalm* (or) Song of Asaph.
77[title](1). *A Psalm* of Asaph.
79[title](1). *A Psalm* of Asaph.
80[title](1). *A Psalm* of Asaph.
82[title](1). *A Psalm* of Asaph.
83[title](1). A Song (or) *Psalm* of Asaph.
84 & 85[title](1). *A Psalm* for the sons of Korah.
87[title](1). *A Psalm* (or) Song for the sons of Korah.
88[title](1). A Song (or) *Psalm* for the sons of Korah,
92[title](1). *A Psalm* (or) Song for the sabbath
98[title](1). *A Psalm.*
100[title](1). *A Psalm* of praise.
101[title](1). *A Psalm* of David.
108[title](1). A Song (or) *Psalm* of David.
109 & 110 & 139[title](1). *A Psalm* of David.
140 & 141 & 143[title](1). *A Psalm* of David.

מַזְמֵרוֹת *maz-mēh-rōhth'*, f. pl. 4211

Isa. 2: 4. their spears *into pruninghooks:* (marg. *scythes*)
18: 5. cut off the sprigs *with pruning hooks*,
Joel 3:10(4:10). *and your pruninghooks* (marg. *scythes*)
Mic. 4: 3. their spears *into pruninghooks:*

מְזַמְּרוֹת *m'zam-m'rōhth'*, f. pl. 4212

1K. 7:50. the bowls, *and the snuffers*,
2K. 12:13(14). bowls of silver, *snuffers*,
25:14. the pots, and the shovels, and *the snuffers*
2Ch. 4:22. *And the snuffers*, and the basons,
Jer. 52:18. and *the snuffers*, and the bowls,

4213 **מִזְעָר** *miz-gāhr′*, adv.

Isa. 10:25. For yet a *very* little while,
16:14. the remnant (shall be) *very* small
24: 6. are burned, and *few* men left.
29:17. it not yet a *very* little while,

4214 **מִזְרֶה** *miz-reh′*, m.

Isa. 30:24. with the shovel *and with the fan.*
Jer. 15: 7. I will fan them *with a fan*

4216 **מַזָּרוֹת** *maz-zāh-rōhth′*, f. pl.

Job 38:32. Canst thou bring forth *Mazzaroth* (marg. or, *the twelve signs*)

4215 **מְזָרִים** *m′zāh-reem′*, m. pl.

Job 37: 9. *and* cold *out of the north.* (marg. *scattering* (winds))

4217 **מִזְרָח** *miz-rāhgh′*, m.

Ex. 27:13 & 38:13. the east side *eastward*
Nu. 2: 3. *toward the rising of the sun* shall
3:38. *eastward*, (shall be) Moses, and Aaron
21:11. before Moab, *toward the* sun*rising.*
32:19. on this side Jordan *eastward.*
34:15. eastward, *toward the sunrising.*
Deu 3:17. under Ashdoth-pisgah *eastward.*
27. northward, and southward, *and eastward*,
4:41. on this side Jordan *toward the* sun *rising;*
47. on this side Jordan *toward the* sun *rising;*
49. the plain on this side Jordan *eastward*,
Jos. 1:15. this side Jordan *toward the* sunrising.
4:19. in the *east* border of Jericho.
11: 3. the Canaanite *on the east*
8. unto the valley of Mizpeh *eastward;*
12: 1. *toward the rising* of the sun,
— Hermon, and all the plain *on the east:*
3. the sea of Chinneroth *on the east*,
— the salt sea *on the east*,
13: 5. all Lebanon, *toward the* sun*rising.*
8. gave them, beyond Jordan *eastward*,
27. other side Jordan *eastward.*
32. other side Jordan, by Jericho, *eastward.*
16: 1. Jericho *on the east*,
5. their inheritance *on the east side*
6. the border went about *eastward*
— passed by it *on the east*
17:10. in Issachar *on the east.*
18: 7. beyond Jordan *on the east*,
19:12. *toward the sunrising*
13. passeth on along on *the east*
27. turneth *toward the sunrising*
34. upon Jordan *toward the sunrising.*
20: 8. Jordan by Jericho *eastward*,
Jud. 11:18. came by *the east side of* the land (lit. *by the rising of* the sun)
20:43. Gibeah *toward the sunrising.*
21:19. *on the east side* (marg. or, *toward the sunrising*) of the highway
1K. 7:25. three looking *toward the east:*
2K. 10:33. From Jordan *eastward*, (marg. *toward the rising of* the sun)
1Ch. 4:39. *unto the east side of* the valley,
5: 9. *And eastward* he inhabited
10. throughout all *the east* (land)
6:78(63). *on the east side of* Jordan,
7:28. *and eastward* Naaran,
9:18. in the king's gate *eastward:*
24. *toward the east*, west, north, and south.
12:15. *toward the east*, and toward the west.
26:14. the lot *eastward* fell to Shelemiah.
17. *Eastward* (were) six Levites,
2Ch. 4: 4. three looking *toward the east:*
5:12. stood *at the east end* of the altar,
29: 4. gathered them together into the *east* street,
31:14. the porter *toward the east*,
Neh. 3:26. the water gate *toward the east*,
29. the keeper of the *east* gate.
Neh 12:37. even unto the water gate *eastward.*
Ps. 50: 1. *from the rising of* the sun
103:12. As far as *the east* is from the west,
107: 3. *from the east*, and from the west,
113: 3. *From the rising of* the sun
Isa. 41: 2. the righteous (man) *from the east*,
25. *from the rising of* the sun
43: 5. I will bring thy seed *from the east*,
45: 6. may know *from the rising of* the sun,
46:11. Calling a ravenous bird *from the east*,
59:19. *and* his glory *from the rising of* the sun
Jer. 31:40. the horse gate *toward the east*,
Dan 8: 9. toward the south, and toward *the east*,
11:44. But tidings *out of the east*
Am. 8:12. from the north even to *the east*,
Zec. 8: 7. save my people from the *east* country,
14: 4. in the midst thereof *toward the east*
Mal. 1:11. For *from the rising of* the sun

מִזְרָע *miz-rag′*, m. 4218

Isa. 19: 7. every *thing sown by* the brooks,

מִזְרָק *miz-rāhk′*, m. 4219

Ex. 27: 3. his shovels, *and his basons*,
38: 3. the shovels, and *the basons*,
Nu. 4:14. the shovels, and *the basons*, (marg. *bowls*)
7:13, 19, 25, 31, 37, 43, 49, 55, 61, 67, 73, 79. silver *bowl* of seventy shekels,
84. twelve silver *bowls*,
85. each *bowl* seventy:
1K. 7:40, 45. the shovels, and *the basons.*
50. the snuffers, *and the basons*,
2K. 12:13(14). bowls of silver, snuffers, *basons*,
25:15. the firepans, and *the bowls*,
1Ch 28:17. the fleshhooks, *and the bowls*,
2Ch 4: 8. he made an hundred *basons of* gold. (marg. *bowls*)
11. the shovels, and *the basons.* (marg. *bowls*)
22. the snuffers, *and the basons*, (marg. *id.*)
Neh. 7:70. thousand drams of gold, fifty *basons*,
Jer. 52:18. the snuffers, and *the bowls*, (marg. or, *basons*)
19. the firepans, and *the bowls*,
Am. 6: 6. That drink wine *in bowls*, (marg. *in bowls of* wine)
Zec. 9:15. they shall be filled *like bowls*,
14:20. be *like the bowls* before the altar.

מֹחַ *mōh′ăgh*, m. 4221

Job 21:24. *and* his bones are moistened *with marrow.*

מֵחִים *mēh-gheem′*, m. pl. 4220

Ps. 66:15. burnt sacrifices of *fatlings*, (marg. *marrow*)
Isa. 5:17. the waste places of *the fat ones*

מָחָא [*māh-ghāh′*]. 4222

* KAL.—*Future.* *

Ps. 98: 8. *Let* the floods *clap* (their) hands:
Isa. 55:12. all the trees of the field *shall clap*

* PIEL.—*Infinitive.* *

Eze. 25: 6. *thou hast clapped* (thine) hands,

מְחָא [*m′ghāh*], Ch. 4223

* P'AL.—*Preterite.* *

Dan. 2:34. *which smote* the image upon his feet
35. the stone that *smote* the image

* PAEL.—*Future.* *

Dan. 4:35(32). and none *can* (lit. there is none who *will*) *stay* his hand,

* ITHP'AL.—*Future.* *

Ezr. 6:11. *let him be hanged* (marg. *destroyed*) thereon;

4224 **מַחֲבֵא** *mah-ghăvēh'*, m.

Isa. 32: 2. a man shall be *as an hiding place*

4224 **מַחֲבֹאִים** *mah-ghăvōh-eem'*, m. pl.

1Sa.23:23. take knowledge of all *the lurking places*

4226 **מְחַבְּרוֹת** *m'ghab-b'rōhth'*, f. pl.

1Ch.22: 3. the gates, *and for the joinings;*
2Ch.34:11. stone, and timber *for couplings,*

4225 **מַחְבֶּרֶת** *magh-beh'-reth*, f.

Ex. 26: 4. curtain, *in the coupling of* the second.
5. that (is) *in the coupling of* the second;
28:27. over against the (other) *coupling thereof,*
36:11. from the selvedge *in the coupling:*
—, 12. *in the coupling of* the second.
17. of the curtain *in the coupling,*
39:20. against *the* (other) *coupling thereof,*

4227 **מַחֲבַת** *mah-ghăvath'*, f.

Lev. 2: 5. a meat offering (baken) in *a pan,* (marg. or, *on a flat plate,* or, *slice*)
6:21(14). In *a pan* it shall be made
7: 9. in the fryingpan, and in *the pan,* (marg. or, on *the flat plate,* or, *slice*)
1Ch 23:29. *and for* (that which is baked in) *the pan,* (marg. or, *flat plate*)
Eze. 4: 3. take thou unto thee *an* iron *pan,* (marg. or, *a flat plate,* or, *slice*)

4228 **מַחֲגֹרֶת** *mah-ghăgōh'-reth*, f.

Isa. 3:24. *a girding of* sackcloth;

4229 **מָחָה** *māh-ghāh'*.

* KAL.—*Preterite.* *

Gen 7: 4. *and* every living substance...*will I destroy* (marg. *blot out*)
Nu. 5:23. *and he shall blot* (them) *out*
Deu 29:20(19). *and* the Lord *shall blot out* his name
2K. 21:13. *and I will wipe* Jerusalem as (a man) wipeth a dish, *wiping* (marg. *he wipeth*)
Ps. 9: 5(6). *thou hast put out* their name
Pro.30:20. she eateth, *and wipeth* her mouth,
Isa. 25: 8. *and* the Lord God *will wipe away* tears
44:22. *I have blotted out,*...thy transgressions,

KAL.—*Infinitive.*

Ex. 17:14. I will *utterly* put out the remembrance (lit. *putting out* I will &c.)
2K. 14:27. *that he would blot out* the name of Israel

KAL.—*Imperative.*

Ex. 32:32. *blot me,* I pray thee, out of
Ps. 51: 1(3). *blot out* my transgressions.
9(11). *blot out* all mine iniquities.

KAL.—*Future.*

Gen 6: 7. And the Lord said, *I will destroy* man
Ex. 17:14. *I will* utterly *put out* the remembrance of
32:33. *him will I blot* out of my book.
Deu 9:14. *and blot out* their name from under
25:19. *thou shalt blot out* the remembrance
2K. 21:13. as (a man) *wipeth* a dish,

KAL.—*Participle.* Poel.

Isa. 43:25. he *that blotteth out* thy transgressions

* NIPHAL.—*Preterite.* *

Eze. 6: 6. *and* your works *may be abolished.*

NIPHAL.—*Future.*

Gen. 7:23. *And* every living substance *was destroyed* — *and they were destroyed* from the earth:
Deu25: 6. that his name *be* not *put out*
Jud.21:17. that a tribe *be* not *destroyed*
Neh. 4: 5(3:37). *let* not their sin *be blotted out*
Ps. 69:28(29). *Let them be blotted out*
109:13. *let* their name *be blotted out.*
14. *let* not the sin of his mother *be blotted out.*
Pro. 6:33. his reproach *shall* not *be wiped away.*

* HIPHIL.—*Infinitive.* *

Pro.31: 3. *to that which destroyeth* kings.

HIPHIL.—*Future.*

Neh 13:14. *wipe* not *out* my good deeds
Jer. 18:23. neither *blot out* their sin

מָחָה [*māh-ghāh*]. 4229

* PUAL.—*Participle.* *

Isa. 25: 6. of fat things *full of marrow,*

מָחָה *māh-ghāh'*. 4229

* KAL.—*Preterite.* *

Nu. 34:11. *and shall reach* unto the side of

מְחוּגָה *m'ghoo-gāh'*, f. 4230

Isa. 44:13. *and* he marketh it out *with the compass,*

מָחוֹז [*māh-ghōhz'*], m. 4231

Ps.107:30. bringeth them unto their desired *haven.*

מָחוֹל *māh-ghōhl'*, m. 4234

Ps. 30:11(12). for me my mourning *into dancing:*
149: 3. praise his name *in the dance:* (marg. *with the pipe*)
150: 4. Praise him with the timbrel *and dance:* (marg. *pipe*)
Jer. 31: 4. shalt go forth *in the dances of* them
13. Then shall the virgin rejoice *in the dance,*
Lam. 5:15. *our dance* is turned into mourning.

מְחוֹלָה [*m'ghōh-lāh'*], f. 4246

Ex. 15:20. with timbrels *and with dances.*
32:19. saw the calf, *and the dancing:*
Jud.11:34. with timbrels *and with dances:*
21:21. come out to dance *in dances,*
1Sa.18: 6. singing *and dancing,*
21:11(12). sing one to another of him *in dances,*
29: 5. whom they sang one to another *in dances,*
Cant.6:13(7:1). *As it were the company of* two armies.

מַחֲזֶה *mah-ghăzeh'*, m. 4236

Gen 15: 1. the Lord came unto Abram *in a vision,*
Nu. 24: 4, 16. saw *the vision of* the Almighty,
Eze.13: 7. Have ye not seen *a* vain *vision,*

מֶחֱזָה *meh-ghĕzāh'*, f. 4237

1K. 7: 4. *and light* (was) against *light* (marg. *sight* against *sight*)
5. and *light* (was) against *light*

מְחִי *m'ghee*, m. 4239

Eze.26: 9. *And* he shall set *engines of* war

4241 מִחְיָה *mee-ghʼyāh'*, f.

Gen45: 5. did send me before you *to preserve life.*
Lev. 13:10. *and* (there be) *quick* raw flesh (marg. *the quickening of* living flesh)
24. *the quick* (flesh) that burneth
Jud. 6: 4. left no *sustenance* for Israel,
17:10. a suit of apparel, *and thy victuals.*
2Ch 14:13(12). that they could not *recover themselves;* (lit. they had no *life*)
Ezr. 9: 8. give us *a little reviving*
9. to give us *a reviving,*

4242 מְחִיר *m'gheer*, m.

Deu23:18(19). *or the price of* a dog,
2Sa.24:24. I will surely buy (it) of thee *at a price:*
1K. 10:28. received the linen yarn *at a price.*
21: 2. I will give thee *the worth*
2Ch. 1:16. received the linen yarn *at a price.*
Job 28:15. be weighed (for) *the price thereof.*
Ps. 44:12(13). increase (thy wealth) *by their price.*
Pro.17:16. *a price* in the hand of a fool
27:26. *and* the goats (are) *the price of* the field.
Isa. 45:13. not *for price* nor reward,
55: 1. without money and without *price.*
Jer. 15:13. will I give to the spoil *without price,*
Lam.5: 4. our wood is *sold* unto us. (marg. cometh *for price*)
Dan 11:39. divide the land *for gain.* (marg. *a price*)
Mic. 3:11. the priests thereof teach *for hire,*

4245 מַחֲלֶה *mah-ghălĕh'*, m.

2Ch 21:15. sickness *by disease of* thy bowels,
Pro.18:14. spirit of a man will sustain *his infirmity;*

4245 מַחֲלָה *mah-ghălāh'*, f.

Ex. 15:26. I will put none of these *diseases*
23:25. I will take *sickness* away
1K. 8:37. plague, whatsoever *sickness*
2Ch 6:28. whatsoever sore or whatsoever *sickness*

See 4246 מְחוֹלָה see מְחֹלָה

4247 מְחִלּוֹת *m'ghil-lōhth'*, f. pl.

Isa. 2:19. *and into the caves of* the earth,

4251 מַחֲלֻיִים *mah-ghăloo-yeem'*, m. pl.

2Ch 24:25. they left him *in* great *diseases,*

4253 מַחְלְפוֹת *magh-l'phōhth'*, f. pl.

Jud.16:13. If thou weavest *the* seven *locks*
19. shave off *the* seven *locks*

4252 מַחֲלָפִים *mah-ghălāh-pheem'*, m. pl.

Ezr. 1: 9. nine and twenty *knives,*

4254 מַחֲלָצוֹת *mah-ghălāh-tzōhth'*, f. pl.

Isa. 3:22. *The changeable suits of apparel,*
Zec. 3: 4. clothe thee with *change of raiment.*

4255 מַחְלְקָה [*magh-l'kāh'*], Ch. f.

Ezr. 6:18. and the Levites *in their courses,*

מַחֲלֹקֶת *mah-ghălōh'-keth*, f. 4256

Jos. 11:23 & 12:7 & 18:10. *according to their divisions*
1Sa.23:28. called that place Sela-*hammahlekoth.* (marg. The rock of *divisions*)
1Ch 23: 6. divided them into *courses* (marg. *divisions*)
24: 1. (these are) the *divisions* of the sons of Aaron. (lit. unto the children of Aaron *their divisions*)
26: 1. *Concerning the divisions* of the
12. Among these (were) *the divisions of*
19. These (are) *the divisions of* the porters
27: 1. in any matter of *the courses,*
— *course* (were) twenty and four thousand.
2. Over *the* first *course*
— *his course* (were) twenty and four thousand.
4. over *the course of* the second month
— *and of his course* (was) Mikloth also the ruler: in *his course* likewise
5, 7, 8, 9, 10, 11, 12, 13, 14, 15. *his course* (were) twenty and four thousand.
6. *and in his course* (was) Ammizabad
28: 1. *companies* that ministered to the king *by course,*
13. *Also for the courses of* the priests
21. behold, *the courses of* the priests
2Ch 5:11. did not (then) wait *by course:*
8:14. *the courses of* the priests
— the porters also *by their courses*
23: 8. the priest dismissed not *the courses.*
31: 2. appointed *the courses of* the priests and the Levites after *their courses,*
15. to give to their brethren *by courses,*
16. in their charges *according to their courses;*
17. their charges *by their courses;*
35: 4. fathers, *after your courses,*
10. the Levites *in their courses,*
Neh 11:36. of the Levites (were) *divisions* (in) Judah,
Eze.48:29. these (are) *their portions,*

מַחֲלַת *mah-ghălath'*, f. 4257

Ps. 53[title](1). To the chief Musician upon *Mahalath,*
88[title](1). the chief Musician upon *Mahalath* Leannoth,

מַחֲמָאֹת *mah-ghămāh-ōhth'*, f. pl. 4260

Ps. 55:21(22). (The words) of his mouth were smoother *than butter,* (lit. smooth are the *milkinesses of* his mouth)

מַחְמָד [*magh-māhd'*], m. 4261

1K. 20: 6. whatsoever is *pleasant in* thine eyes, (marg. *desirable;* lit. *the desire of* thy eyes)
2Ch 36:19. all the *goodly* vessels *thereof.*
Cant 5:16. yea, he (is) altogether *lovely.*
Isa. 64:11(10). all *our pleasant things* are laid
Lam.1:10. his hand upon all *her pleasant things:*
11. they have given *their pleasant things*
2: 4. all (that were) *pleasant to* the eye
Eze.24:16. away from thee *the desire of* thine eyes
21. *the desire of* your eyes,
25. *the desire of* their eyes,
Hos. 9: 6. *the pleasant* (places) for their silver, (lit. *the desire* for the silver)
16. *the beloved* (fruit) (marg. *desires*) *of* their
Joel 3: 5(4:5). *and* have carried into your temples *my* goodly *pleasant things:*

מַחֲמֻדִּים [*mah-ghămood-deem'*], m. pl. 4262

Lam.1: 7. all *her pleasant* (marg. *desirable*) *things*
11. (כתיב) have given *their pleasant things*

מַחְמָל [*magh-māhl'*], m. 4263

Eze.24:21. *and that which* your soul *pitieth;* (marg. *the pity of* your soul)

4264 מַחֲנֶה *mah-ghăneh'*, com.

Gen32: 2(3). This (is) God's *host:* and he called the name of that place *Mahanaim.* (marg. *Two hosts*)
7(8). the camels, into two *bands;*
8(9). If Esau come to *the* one *company,* and smite it, then *the* other *company* which
10(11). now I am become two *bands.*
21(22). lodged that night *in the company.*
33: 8. What (meanest) thou by all this *drove*
50: 9. it was *a* very great *company.*
Ex. 14:19. which went before *the camp of* Israel,
20. it came between *the camp of* the Egyptians and *the camp of* Israel;
24, 24. *the host of* the Egyptians
16:13. covered *the camp:* and in the morning the dew lay round *about the host.*
19:16. people that (was) *in the camp* trembled.
17. the people out of *the camp*
29:14. burn with fire without *the camp:*
32:17. a noise of war *in the camp.*
19. as he came nigh unto *the camp,*
26. stood in the gate of *the camp,*
27. from gate to gate *throughout the camp,*
33. 7. pitched it without *the camp,* afar off from *the camp,*
— which (was) without *the camp.*
11. he turned again into *the camp:*
36: 6. proclaimed *throughout the camp,*
Lev. 4:12. he carry forth without *the camp*
21. the bullock without *the camp,*
6:11(4). the ashes without *the camp*
8:17 & 9:11. burnt with fire without *the camp;*
10: 4. before the sanctuary out of *the camp.*
5. their coats out of *the camp;*
13:46. without *the camp* (shall) his habitation (be).
14: 3. shall go forth out of *the camp;*
8 & 16:26. come into *the camp,*
16:27. carry forth without *the camp;*
28. he shall come into *the camp.*
17: 3. lamb, or goat, *in the camp,* or that killeth (it) out of *the camp,*
24:10. strove together *in the camp;*
14. him that hath cursed without *the camp;*
23. had cursed out of *the camp,*
Nu. 1:52. every man by *his own camp,*
2: 3. the standard of *the camp of* Judah
9. All that were numbered *in the camp of*
10. the standard of *the camp of* Reuben
16. All that were numbered *in the camp of*
17. with *the camp of* the Levites in the midst of *the camp:*
18. standard of *the camp of* Ephraim
24. that were numbered *of the camp of*
25. The standard of *the camp of* Dan
31. they that were numbered *in the camp of*
32. that were numbered of *the camps*
4: 5. when *the camp* setteth forward,
15. as *the camp* is to set forward;
5: 2. put out of *the camp* every leper,
3. without *the camp* shall ye put
— that they defile not *their camps,*
4. put them out without *the camp:*
10: 2. for the journeying of *the camps.*
5, 6. then *the camps* that lie
14, 18, 22, 25. the standard of *the camp of*
25. the rereward of all *the camps*
34. they went out of *the camp.*
11: 1. the uttermost parts of *the camp.*
9. the dew fell upon *the camp*
26. remained two (of the) men *in the camp,*
— prophesied *in the camp.*
27. Eldad and Medad do prophesy *in the camp.*
30. Moses gat him into *the camp,*
31. let (them) fall by *the camp,*
— the other side, round about *the camp,*
32. themselves round about *the camp.*
12:14. let her be shut out from *the camp*
15. Miriam was shut out from *the camp*
13:19. *whether in tents,* or in strong holds;
14:44. departed not out of *the camp.*
15:35. stone him with stones without *the camp.*
36. brought him without *the camp,*
19: 3. bring her forth without *the camp,*
7. afterward he shall come into *the camp,*
9. without *the camp* in a clean place,
Nu. 31:12. unto *the camp* at the plains of Moab,
13. to meet them without *the camp.*
19. do ye abide without *the camp*
24. ye shall come into *the camp.*
Deu. 2:14. wasted out from among *the host,*
15. destroy them from among *the host,*
23: 9(10). When *the host* goeth forth
10(11). shall he go abroad out *of the camp,* he shall not come within *the camp:*
11(12). he shall come into *the camp*
12(13). have a place also without *the camp,*
14(15). God walketh in the midst of *thy camp,*
—(—). therefore shall *thy camp* be holy: (lit. *thy camps*)
29:11(10). thy stranger that (is) in *thy camp,*
Jos. 1:11. Pass through *the host,*
3: 2. that the officers went through *the host;*
5: 8. they abode in their places *in the camp,*
6:11. they came into *the camp,* and lodged *in the camp.*
14. returned into *the camp:*
18. make *the camp of* Israel a curse,
23. left them without *the camp of*
8:13. all *the host* that (was) on the north
9: 6. went to Joshua unto *the camp*
10: 5. they and all *their hosts,*
6. sent unto Joshua to *the camp*
15, 43. all Israel with him, unto *the camp*
21. all the people returned to *the camp*
11: 4. all *their hosts* with them,
18: 9. came (again) to Joshua to *the host*
Jud. 4:15. all (his) chariots, and all (his) *host,*
16. and after *the host,*
— all *the host of* Sisera fell
7: 1. *so that the host of* the Midianites
8. *and the host of* Midian was
9. get thee down *unto the host;*
10. with Phurah thy servant down to *the host:*
11. be strengthened to go down *unto the host.*
— armed men that (were) *in the host.*
13. barley bread tumbled *into the host of*
14. Midian, and all *the host.*
15. and returned into *the host of* Israel,
— *the host of* Midian.
17. when I come to the outside of *the camp,*
18. also on every side of all *the camp,*
19. came unto the outside of *the camp*
21. in his place round *about the camp:* and all *the host* ran,
22. even throughout all *the host:* and *the host*
8:10. *and their hosts* with them,
— all that were left of all *the hosts of*
11. smote *the host: for the host* was secure.
12. discomfited all *the host.*
13:25. him at times *in the camp of* Dan (or, *Mahaneh* Dan)
18:12. called that place *Mahaneh*-dan (lit. *the camp of* Dan)
21: 8. there came none to *the camp*
12. they brought them unto *the camp*
1Sa. 4: 3. the people were come into *the camp,*
5. the Lord came into *the camp,*
6. the noise of this great shout *in the camp of*
— ark of the Lord was come into *the camp.*
7. God is come into *the camp.*
11:11. they came into the midst of *the host*
13:17. spoilers came *out of the camp of*
14:15. there was trembling *in the host,*
19. the noise that (was) *in the host of*
21. went up with them *into the camp*
17: 1. gathered together *their armies*
4. *out of the camp of* the Philistines,
17. run to *the camp* to thy brethren;
46. I will give the carcases of *the host of*
53. they spoiled *their tents.*
26: 6. go down with me to Saul to *the camp?*
28: 1. the Philistines gathered *their armies*
— thou shalt go out with me *to battle,* (lit. *into the camp*)
5. when Saul saw *the host of* the Philistines
19. also shall deliver *the host of* Israel
29: 1. gathered together all *their armies*
6. thy coming in with me *in the host*
2Sa. 1: 2. a man came out of *the camp*
3. *Out of the camp of* Israel
5:24. to smite *the host of* the Philistines.
23:16. brake *through the host of* the Philistines.

1K. 16:16. king over Israel that day *in the camp.*
22:34. carry me out of *the host;*
36. proclamation throughout *the host*
2K. 3: 9. there was no water *for the host,*
24. when they came to *the camp of* Israel,
5:15. he and all *his company,*
6:24. Syria gathered all *his host,*
7: 4. let us fall unto *the host of* the
5. to go unto *the camp of* the Syrians: and when they were come to the uttermost part of *the camp of*
6. For the Lord had made *the host of*
7. even *the camp* as it (was),
8. came to the uttermost part of *the camp,*
10. We came to *the camp of* the Syrians,
12. are they gone out of *the camp*
14. the king sent after *the host of*
16. spoiled *the tents of* the Syrians.
19:35. smote *in the camp of* the Assyrians
1Ch. 9:18. they (were) porters *in the companies of*
19. fathers, (being) over *the host of* the Lord,
11:15. *and the host of* the Philistines
18. the three brake *through the host of*
12:22. (it was) *a great host, like the host of* God.
14:15. to smite *the host of* the Philistines.
16. they smote *the host of* the Philistines
2Ch 14:13(12). before the Lord, and before *his host;*
18:33. carry me out of *the host;*
22: 1. that came with the Arabians *to the camp*
31: 2. *the tents of* the Lord.
32:21. the leaders and captains *in the camp of*
Ps. 27: 3. Though *an host* should encamp
78:28. fall in the midst of *their camp,*
106:16. They envied Moses also *in the camp,*
Cant.6:13(7:1). the company of *two armies.* (marg. or, *Mahanaim*)
Isa. 37:36. smote *in the camp of* the Assyrians
Eze. 1:24. as the noise of *an host:*
4: 2. set *the camp* also against it,
Joel 2:11. for *his camp* (is) very great:
Am. 4:10. the stink of *your camps* to come
Zec. 14:15. that shall be *in* these *tents,*

4267 ## מַחֲנָק *mah-ghănak'*, m.

Job 7:15. So that my soul chooseth *strangling,*

4268 ## מַחְסֶה *magh-seh'*, m.

Job 24: 8. embrace the rock for want of *a shelter.*
Ps. 14: 6. because the Lord (is) *his refuge.*
46: 1(2). God (is) our *refuge* and strength,
61: 3(4). For thou hast been *a shelter*
62: 7(8). rock of my strength, (and) *my refuge,*
8(9). God (is) *a refuge* for us.
71: 7. but thou (art) *my* strong *refuge.*
73:28. I have put *my trust* in the Lord
91: 2. *my refuge* and my fortress:
9. the Lord (which is) *my refuge,*
94:22. my God (is) the rock of *my refuge.*
104:18. The high hills (are) *a refuge*
142: 5(6). Thou (art) *my refuge* (and) my portion
Pro. 14:26. his children shall have *a place of refuge.*
Isa. 4: 6. *and for a place of refuge,* and for
25: 4. *a refuge* from the storm,
28:15. for we have made lies *our refuge,*
17. shall sweep away *the refuge of* lies,
Jer. 17:17. thou (art) *my hope* in the day of evil.
Joel 3:16(4:16). *the hope of* his people,

4269 ## מַחְסוֹם *magh-sōhm'*, m.

Ps. 39: 1(2). I will keep my mouth with *a bridle,*

4270 ## מַחְסוֹר *magh-sōhr'*, m.

Deu15: 8. lend him sufficient for *his need,*
Jud.18:10. a place where (there is) no *want*
19:19. no *want of* any thing.
20. all *thy wants* (lie) upon me;
Ps. 34: 9(10). for (there is) no *want* to them
Pro. 6:11. *and thy want* as an armed man
Pro. 11:24. but (it tendeth) *to poverty.*
14:23. talk of the lips (tendeth) only *to penury.*
21: 5. every one (that is) hasty only *to want.*
17. He that loveth pleasure (shall be) a *poor* man: (lit. a man of *want*)
22:16. to the rich, (shall) surely (come) *to want.*
24:34. *and thy want* as an armed man.
28:27. He that giveth unto the poor shall not *lack:* (lit. shall not have *want*)

מָחַץ *māh-ghatz'*. 4272

* KAL.—*Preterite.* *

Nu. 24:17. *and shall smite* the corners of Moab,
Deu32:39. *I wound,* and I heal:
Jud. 5:26. *when she had pierced* and stricken
Job 26:12. *he smiteth through* the proud.
Ps. 110: 5. at thy right hand *shall strike through*
6. *he shall wound* the heads
Hab. 3:13. *thou woundedst* the head

KAL.—*Imperative.*

Deu33:11. *smite through* the loins of them

KAL.—*Future.*

Nu. 24: 8. and *pierce* (them) *through* with his arrows,
2Sa.22:39. I have consumed them, *and wounded them,*
Job 5:18. *he woundeth,* and his hands make whole.
Ps. 18:38(39). *I have wounded them*
68:21(22). God *shall wound* the head of
23(24). That thy foot *may be dipped* in

מַחַץ *mah'-ghatz*, m. 4273

Isa. 30:26. *and* healeth *the stroke of* their wound.

מַחְצֵב *magh-tzēhv'*, m. 4274

2K. 12:12(13). to buy timber and *hewed* stone (lit. stones of *hewing*)
22: 6. *hewn* stone (lit. *id.*) to repair the house.
2Ch 34:11. to buy *hewn* stone, (lit. *id.*) and timber

מֶחֱצָה *meh-ghĕtzāh'*, f. 4275

Nu. 31:36. *the half,* (which was) the portion
43. *the half* (that pertained unto) the

מַחֲצִית *mah-ghăhtzeeth'*, f. 4276

Ex. 30:13. *half* a shekel after the shekel of the
— *an half* shekel (shall be) the offering
15. give less *than half* a shekel,
23. sweet cinnamon *half so much,*
38:26. *half* a shekel, after the shekel of
Lev. 6:20(13). *half of it* in the morning, *and half thereof* at night.
Nu. 31:29. Take (it) *of their half,*
30, 42. *And of* the children of Israel'*s half,*
47. Even *of* the children of Israel'*s half,*
Jos. 21:25. *And out of the half* tribe
1K. 16: 9. Zimri, captain of *half* (his) chariots,
1Ch. 6:61(46). out *of the half* tribe,
70(55). *And out of the half* tribe
Neh. 8: 3. from the morning until *mid*day,

מָחַק [*māh-ghak'*]. 4277

* KAL.—*Preterite.* *

Jud. 5:26. *she smote off* his head,

מֶחְקָר [*meh-gh'kāhr'*]. 4278

Ps. 95: 4. In his hand (are) *the deep places of*

מָחָר *māh-ghāhr'*, m. 4279

Gen30:33. in time *to come,* (lit. in the day of *to morrow*)

Ex. 8:10(6). And he said, *To morrow.* (marg. or, *Against to morrow*)
23(19). *to morrow* (marg. or, *by to morrow*) shall this sign be.
29(25). that the swarms (of flies) may depart ...*to morrow:*
9: 5. *To morrow* the Lord shall do this
18. *to morrow* about this time
10: 4. *to morrow* will I bring the locusts
13:14. when thy son asketh thee *in time to come,* (marg. *to morrow*)
16:23. *To morrow* (is) the rest of the holy sabbath
17: 9. *to morrow* I will stand on the top
19:10. sanctify them to day *and to morrow,*
32: 5. *To morrow* (is) a feast to the Lord.
Nu. 11:18. Sanctify yourselves *against to morrow,*
14:25. *To morrow* turn you, and get you
16: 7. put incense in them...*to morrow:*
16. thou, and they, and Aaron, *to morrow:*
Deu. 6:20. when thy son asketh thee *in time to come,* (marg. *to morrow*)
Jos. 3: 5. *to morrow* the Lord will do wonders
4: 6. when your children ask...*in time to come.* (marg. *to morrow*)
21. When your children shall ask...*in time to come,* (marg. *id.*)
7:13. Sanctify yourselves *against to morrow:*
11: 6. *to morrow* about this time
22:18. *to morrow* he will be wroth
24. *In time to come* (marg. *To morrow*) your children might speak
27. say to our children *in time to come,*
28. us or to our generations *in time to come,*
Jud.19: 9. *to morrow* get you early on your way,
20:28. *to morrow* I will deliver them
1Sa. 9:16. *To morrow* about this time
11: 9. *To morrow,* by (that time)
10. *To morrow* we will come out
19:11. *to morrow* thou shalt be slain.
20: 5. *to morrow* (is) the new moon,
12. about *to morrow* any time,
18. *To morrow* (is) the new moon:
28:19. *and to morrow* (shalt) thou and thy sons (be) with me:
2Sa. 11:12. *and to morrow* I will let thee depart.
1K. 19: 2. *to morrow* about this time.
20: 6. *to morrow* about this time,
2K. 6:28. we will eat my son *to morrow.*
7: 1, 18. *To morrow* about this time
10: 6. by *to morrow* this time.
2Ch 20:16. *To morrow* go ye down
17. *to morrow* go out against them:
Est. 5: 8. *and* I will do *to morrow* as the king hath
12. *to morrow* am I invited
9:13. to do *to morrow* also
Pro. 3:28. *and to morrow* I will give;
27: 1. Boast not thyself of *to morrow;*
Isa. 22:13. *to morrow* we shall die.
56:12. *to morrow* shall be as this day,

4280 מַחֲרָאוֹת *mah-'ghărāh-ōhth',* f. pl.

2K. 10:27. (כתיב) made it *a draught house*

4281 מַחֲרֵשָׁה *mah-'ghăreh-shāh',* f.

1Sa. 13:20. his ax, *and his mattock.*
21. Yet they had a file *for the mattocks,*

4282 מַחֲרֶשֶׁת [*mah-'ghăreh'-sheth*], f.

1Sa. 13:20. to sharpen every man *his share,*

4283 מָחֳרָת *moh-'ghŏrāhth',* f.

Gen19:34. it came to pass *on the morrow,*
Ex. 9: 6. the Lord did that thing *on the morrow,*
18:13. it came to pass *on the morrow,*
32: 6. they rose up early *on the morrow,*
30. it came to pass *on the morrow,*
Lev. 7:16. *and on the morrow* also the remainder
Lev.19: 6. *and on the morrow:* and if ought
23:11. *on the morrow after* the sabbath
15. *from the morrow after* the sabbath,
16. Even *unto the morrow after* the
Nu. 11:32. and all the *next* day,
16:41(17:6). But *on the morrow*
17: 8(23). *on the morrow* Moses went into
33: 3. *on the morrow after* the passover
Jos. 5:11. *on the morrow after* the passover,
12. the manna ceased *on the morrow*
Jud. 6:38. he rose up early *on the morrow,*
9:42 & 21:4. it came to pass *on the morrow,*
1Sa. 5: 3. of Ashdod arose early *on the morrow,*
4. they arose early *on the morrow*
11:11. it was (so) *on the morrow,*
18:10 & 20:27. it came to pass *on the morrow*
30:17. the evening *of the next day:*
31: 8. it came to pass *on the morrow,*
2Sa. 11:12. in Jerusalem that day, *and the morrow.*
2K. 8:15. it came to pass *on the morrow,*
1Ch 10: 8. it came to pass *on the morrow,*
29:21. *on the morrow after* that day,
Jer. 20: 3. it came to pass *on the morrow,* that Pashur
Jon. 4: 7. when the morning rose *the next day,*

מַחְשֹׂף *magh-sōhph',* m. 4286

Gen30:37. and *made* the white *appear*

מַחֲשָׁבָה *mah-'ghăshāh-vāh',* f. 4284

Jer. 18:11. and devise *a device* against you:
49:30. hath conceived *a purpose*

מַחֲשֶׁבֶת *mah-'ghăsheh'-veth,* f. 4284

Gen 6: 5. imagination of *the thoughts of* his heart
Ex. 31: 4. To devise *cunning works,*
35:32. to devise *curious works,*
33. to make any manner of *cunning* work. (lit. work of *invention*)
35. those that devise *cunning work.*
2Sa. 14:14. yet doth he devise *means,*
1Ch 28: 9. all the imaginations of *the thoughts:*
29:18. in the imagination of *the thoughts of*
2Ch. 2:14(13). to find out every *device*
26:15. engines, *invented by* (lit. *the invention of*) cunning men,
Est. 8: 3. *his device* that he had devised
5. letters *devised by* (lit. *the device of*) Haman
9:25. by letters that *his* wicked *device,*
Job 5:12. He disappointeth *the devices of*
21:27. I know *your thoughts,*
Ps. 33:10. maketh *the devices of* the people
11. *the thoughts of* his heart
40: 5(6). *and thy thoughts* (which are) to us-ward:
56: 5(6). all *their thoughts* (are) against me
92: 5(6). *thy thoughts* are very deep.
94:11. The Lord knoweth *the thoughts of* man,
Pro. 6:18. that deviseth wicked *imaginations,*
12: 5. *The thoughts of* the righteous
15:22. Without counsel *purposes* are
26. *The thoughts of* the wicked
16: 3. and *thy thoughts* shall be established.
19:21. many *devices* in a man's heart;
20:18. (Every) *purpose* is established
21: 5. *The thoughts of* the diligent
Isa. 55: 7. and the unrighteous man *his thoughts:*
8. For *my thoughts* (are) not *your thoughts,*
9. *and my thoughts than your thoughts.*
59: 7. blood: *their thoughts* (are) *thoughts of*
65: 2. after *their own thoughts;*
66:18. their works *and their thoughts:*
Jer. 4:14. How long shall thy vain *thoughts*
6:19. the fruit of *their thoughts,*
11:19. they had devised *devices*
18:12. we will walk after *our own devices,*
18. let us devise *devices* against
29:11. I know *the thoughts* that I think toward you, saith the Lord, *thoughts of* peace,
49:20 & 50:45. *and his purposes,* that he hath
51:29. every *purpose of* the Lord shall be

Lam.3:60. all *their imaginations* against me.
61. all *their imaginations* against me;
Eze.38:10. thou shalt think *an* evil *thought:* (marg. or, conceive *a* mischievous *purpose*)
Dan 11:24. he shall forecast *his devices*
25. they shall forecast *devices*
Mic. 4:12. they know not *the thoughts of* the Lord,

4285 **מַחְשָׁךְ** *măgh-shāhch'*, m.

Ps. 74:20. *for the dark places of* the earth
88: 6(7). *in darkness*, in the deeps.
18(19). mine acquaintance into *darkness.*
143: 3. hath made me to dwell *in darkness*,
Isa. 29:15. their works are *in the dark*,
42:16. I will make *darkness* light before them,
Lam.3: 6. He hath set me *in dark places*,

4289 **מַחְתָּה** *măgh-tāh'*, f.

Ex. 25:38. *and the snuffdishes thereof*,
27: 3. his fleshhooks, *and his firepans:*
37:23. his snuffers, *and his snuffdishes*,
38: 3. the fleshhooks, and *the firepans:*
Lev.10: 1. took either of them *his censer*,
16:12. he shall take *a censer* full
Nu. 4: 9. his tongs, and *his snuffdishes*,
14. *the censers*, the fleshhooks,
16 6. This do; Take you *censers*,
7. take every man *his censer*,
— before the Lord every man *his censer*, two hundred and fifty *censers;*
— each (of you) *his censer.*
18. they took every man *his censer*,
37(17:2). that he take up *the censers*
38(—:3). *The censers of* these sinners
39(—:4). the priest took *the* brasen *censers*,
46(—:11). Take *a censer*, and put fire therein
1K. 7:50. the spoons, *and the censers* (marg. *ash pans*)
2K. 25:15. *the firepans*, and the bowls,
2Ch. 4:22. the spoons, *and the censers*,
Jer. 52:19. the basons, and *the firepans*, (marg. or, *censers*)

4288 **מְחִתָּה** *m'ghit-tāh'*, f.

Ps. 89:40(41). hast brought his strong holds *to ruin.*
Pro.10:14. mouth of the foolish (is) near *destruction.*
15. *the destruction of* the poor
29. *but destruction* (shall be) to the
13: 3. wide his lips shall have *destruction.*
14:28. people (is) *the destruction of* the prince.
18: 7. A fool's mouth (is) his *destruction*,
21:15. *but destruction* (shall be) to the workers
Isa. 54:14. *and from terror;* for it shall not come
Jer. 17:17. Be not *a terror* unto me:
48:39. a derision *and a dismaying*

4290 **מַחְתֶּרֶת** *măgh-teh'-reth*, f.

Ex. 22: 2(1). If a thief be found *breaking up*,
Jer. 2:34. I have not found it *by secret search*, (marg. *digging*)

4291 **מְטָא & מְטָה** *m'tāh'*, Ch.

* P'AL.—*Preterite.* *

Dan. 4:22(19). *and reacheth* unto heaven,
24(21). which *is come* upon my lord the king:
28(25). All this *came* upon the king
6:24(25). or ever *they came* at the bottom of
7:13. and *came* to the Ancient of days,
22. the time *came* that the saints possessed

P'AL.—*Future.*

Dan. 4:11(8). the height thereof *reached* unto heaven,
20(17). whose height *reached* unto the heaven,

4292 **מַטְאֲטֵא** *mat-ătēh'*, m.

Isa. 14:23. sweep it with *the besom of* destruction,

מַטְבֵּחַ *mat-bēh'ăgh*, m. 4293

Isa. 14:21. Prepare *slaughter* for his children

מַטָּה *mat'-tāh*, adv. 4295

Ex. 26:24. coupled together *beneath*,
27: 5. the compass of the altar *beneath*,
28:27. the two sides of the ephod *underneath*,
36:29. they were coupled *beneath*,
38: 4. *beneath* unto the midst of it.
39:20. the two sides of the ephod *underneath*,
Deu 28:13. thou shalt not be *beneath;*
43. thou shalt come down *very low.* (lit. *low, low*)
2K. 19:30. shall yet again take root *downward*,
1Ch 27:23. from twenty years old *and under:*
2Ch 32:30. brought it straight *down*
Ezr. 9:13. thou our God hast punished us *less* (marg. withheld *beneath* our iniquities)
Pro.15:24. that he may depart from hell *beneath.*
Ecc. 3:21. the spirit of the beast that goeth *downward*
Isa. 37:31. shall again take root *downward*,
Jer. 31:37. the foundations of the earth searched out *beneath*,
Eze. 1:27 & 8:2. the appearance of his loins *even downward*.

מַטֶּה *mat-teh'*, com. 4294

Gen38:18. Thy signet, and thy bracelets, *and thy staff*
25. the signet, and bracelets, *and staff.*
Ex. 4: 2. in thine hand? And he said, *A rod.*
4. it became *a rod* in his hand:
17. thou shalt take this *rod*
20. Moses took *the rod of* God
7: 9. Take *thy rod*, and cast (it)
10. Aaron cast down *his rod*
12. they cast down every man *his rod*,
— but Aaron's *rod* swallowed up *their rods.*
15. *and the rod* which was turned to a serpent
17. I will smite *with the rod*
19. Say unto Aaron, Take *thy rod*,
20. he lifted up *the rod*,
8: 5(1). Stretch forth thine hand *with thy rod*
16(12). Stretch out *thy rod*, and smite
17(13). stretched out his hand *with his rod*,
9:23 & 10:13. Moses stretched forth *his rod*
14:16. But lift thou up *thy rod*,
17: 5. *and thy rod*, wherewith thou smotest the
9. *with the rod of* God in mine hand.
31: 2. *of the tribe of* Judah:
6. *of the tribe of* Dan:
35:30. *of the tribe of* Judah;
34. *of the tribe of* Dan.
38:22. *of the tribe of* Judah,
23. *of the tribe of* Dan,
Lev.24:11. *of the tribe of* Dan:
26:26. I have broken *the staff of* your bread
Nu. 1: 4. there shall be a man of *every tribe;*
16. princes of *the tribes*
21. *of the tribe of* Reuben,
23. *of the tribe of* Simeon,
25. *of the tribe of* Gad,
27. *of the tribe of* Judah,
29. *of the tribe of* Issachar,
31. *of the tribe of* Zebulun,
33. *of the tribe of* Ephraim,
35. *of the tribe of* Manasseh,
37. *of the tribe of* Benjamin,
39. *of the tribe of* Dan,
41. *of the tribe of* Asher,
43. *of the tribe of* Naphtali,
47. the Levites *after the tribe of* their fathers
49. *the tribe of* Levi,
2: 5. *the tribe of* Issachar:
7. *the tribe of* Zebulun:
12. *the tribe of* Simeon:
14. *Then the tribe of* Gad:
20. *the tribe of* Manasseh:
22. *Then the tribe of* Benjamin:
27. *the tribe of* Asher:
29. *Then the tribe of* Naphtali:
3: 6. Bring *the tribe of* Levi near,

Nu. 7: 2. the princes of *the tribes*,
12. son of Amminadab, *of the tribe of* Judah:
10:15. *the tribe of* the children of Issachar
16. *the tribe of* the children of Zebulun
19. *the tribe of* the children of Simeon
20. *the tribe of* the children of Gad
23. *the tribe of* the children of Manasseh
24. *the tribe of* the children of Benjamin
26. *the tribe of* the children of Asher
27. *the tribe of* the children of Naphtali
13: 2. *of* every *tribe of* their fathers shall ye send
4. *of the tribe of* Reuben,
5. *Of the tribe of* Simeon,
6. *Of the tribe of* Judah,
7. *Of the tribe of* Issachar,
8. *Of the tribe of* Ephraim,
9. *Of the tribe of* Benjamin,
10. *Of the tribe of* Zebulun,
11. *Of the tribe of* Joseph,
— *of the tribe of* Manasseh,
12. *Of the tribe of* Dan,
13. *Of the tribe of* Asher,
14. *Of the tribe of* Naphtali,
15. *Of the tribe of* Gad,
17: 2(17). take of every one of them *a rod* (lit. *a rod, a rod* according &c.) according to the house of (their) fathers,
—(—). twelve *rods:* write thou every man's name upon *his rod.*
3(18). write Aaron's name upon *the rod of* Levi: for one *rod* (shall be) for the head
5(20). man's *rod* (lit. *his rod*), whom I shall
6(21). every one of their princes gave him *a rod* apiece, (marg. *a rod* for one prince, *a rod* for one prince)
—(—). twelve *rods: and the rod of* Aaron (was) among *their rods.*
7(22). Moses laid up *the rods*
8(23). *the rod of* Aaron for the house of Levi
9(24). Moses brought out all *the rods*
—(—). and took every man *his rod.*
10(25). Bring Aaron's *rod* again
18: 2. And thy brethren also of *the tribe of* Levi,
20: 8. Take *the rod*, and gather thou
9. Moses took *the rod*
11. *with his rod* he smote the rock
26:55. *the tribes of* their fathers
30: 1(2). the heads of *the tribes*
31: 4. *Of every tribe* (marg. A thousand *of a tribe*, a thousand *of a tribe*) a thousand, throughout all *the tribes*
5. a thousand *of* (every) *tribe*,
6. a thousand *of* (every) *tribe*,
32:28. *the tribes* of the children of Israel:
33:54. *according to the tribes of* your fathers
34:13. to give unto *the* nine *tribes*, and to *the* half *tribe:*
14. *the tribe of* the children of Reuben
— *and the tribe of* the children of Gad
— half *the tribe of* Manasseh
15. The two *tribes* and *the* half *tribe*
18. one prince *of* every *tribe*,
19. *Of the tribe of* Judah,
20. *And of the tribe of* the children of Simeon,
21. *Of the tribe of* Benjamin,
22. *And...of the tribe of* the children of Dan,
23. *for the tribe of* the children of Manasseh,
24. *And...of the tribe of* the children of Ephraim,
25. *And...of the tribe of* the children of Zebulun,
26. *And...of the tribe of* the children of Issachar,
27. *And...of the tribe of* the children of Asher,
28. *And...of the tribe of* the children of Naphtali,
36: 3, 4. the inheritance of *the tribe*
4. *the tribe of* our fathers.
5. *The tribe of* the sons of Joseph
6. *the tribe of* their father
7. remove *from tribe to tribe:*
— *the tribe of* his fathers.
8. *in any tribe of* the children of Israel,
— unto one of the family of *the tribe of*
9. *from* (one) *tribe to* another *tribe;* but every one of *the tribes of* the children
12. in *the tribe of* the family
Jos. 7: 1, 18. the son of Zerah, *of the tribe of* Judah,
13:15. gave *unto the tribe of* the children of
24. gave (inheritance) *unto the tribe of* Gad,
29. *the* half *tribe of* the children of Manasseh
14: 1. *the tribes* of the children of Israel,
2. for *the* nine *tribes*, and (for) *the* half *tribe*
3. two *tribes* and *an* half *tribe* on the other side
4. the children of Joseph were two *tribes*,
15: 1, 21. *of the tribe of* the children of Judah
20. *the tribe of* the children of Judah
16: ,8. *the tribe of* the children of Ephraim
17: 1. a lot *for the tribe of* Manasseh;
18:11. *the tribe of* the children of Benjamin
21. *of the tribe of* the children of Benjamin
19: 1. *for the tribe of* the children of Simeon
8. *the tribe of* the children of Simeon
23. *the tribe of* the children of Issachar
24. *for the tribe of* the children of Asher
31. *the tribe of* the children of Asher
39. *the tribe of* the children of Naphtali
40. *for the tribe of* the children of Dan
48. *the tribe of* the children of Dan
51. *of the tribes of* the children of Israel,
20: 8. *out of the tribe of* Reuben,
— *out of the tribe of* Gad,
— *out of the tribe of* Manasseh.
21: 1. *the tribes* of the children of Israel;
4. *out of the tribe of* Judah, *and out of the tribe of* Simeon, *and out of the tribe of* Benjamin,
5. *the tribe of* Ephraim, *and out of the tribe of* Dan,
—, 6. *the* half *tribe of* Manasseh,
6. *the tribe of* Issachar, *and out of the tribe of* Asher, *and out of the tribe of* Naphtali,
7. *out of the tribe of* Reuben, *and out of the tribe of* Gad, *and out of the tribe of* Zebulun,
9. *out of the tribe of* the children of Judah, *and out of the tribe of*
17. *And out of the tribe of* Benjamin,
20. *out of the tribe of* Ephraim.
23. *And out of the tribe of* Dan,
25. *the* half *tribe of* Manasseh,
27. *the* (other) half *tribe of* Manasseh
28. *And out of the tribe of* Issachar,
30. *And out of the tribe of* Asher,
32. *And out of the tribe of* Naphtali,
34. *the tribe of* Zebulun,
38(36). *And out of the tribe of* Gad,
22: 1. and *the* half *tribe of* Manasseh,
14. throughout all *the tribes of* Israel;
1Sa. 14:27. put forth the end of *the rod*
43. *the rod* that (was) in mine hand,
1K. 7:14. a widow's son *of the tribe of* Naphtali,
8: 1. all the heads of *the tribes*,
1Ch. 6:60(45). *And out of the tribe of* Benjamin;
61(46). the family of that *tribe*, (were cities given) out of *the* half *tribe*,
62(47). *out of the tribe of* Issachar, *and out of the tribe of* Asher, *and out of the tribe of* Naphtali, *and out of the tribe of* Manasseh
63(48). *out of the tribe of* Reuben, *and out of the tribe of* Gad, *and out of the tribe of* Zebulun,
65(50). *out of the tribe of* the children of Judah, *and out of the tribe of* the children of Simeon, *and out of the tribe of* the children of Benjamin,
66(51). *out of the tribe of* Ephraim.
70(55). *the* half *tribe of* Manasseh;
71(56). *the* half *tribe of* Manasseh,
72(57). *And out of the tribe of* Issachar;
74(59). *And out of the tribe of* Asher;
76(61). *And out of the tribe of* Naphtali;
77(62). *out of the tribe of* Zebulun,
78(63). *out of the tribe of* Reuben,
80(65). *And out of the tribe of* Gad;
12:31. And of *the* half *tribe of* Manasseh
2Ch. 5: 2. all the heads of *the tribes*,
Ps. 105:16. he brake *the* whole *staff of* bread.
110: 2. The Lord shall send *the rod of* thy strength
Isa. 9: 4(3). thou hast broken.....*the staff of* his shoulder,
10: 5. *and the staff* in their hand
15. as if *the staff* should lift up (itself),

Isa. 10:24. *and* shall lift up *his staff* against
26. *and* (as) *his rod* (was) upon the sea
14: 5. hath broken *the staff of* the wicked.
28:27. the fitches are beaten out *with a staff*,
30:32. where *the* grounded *staff* shall pass,
Jer. 48:17. How is *the* strong *staff* broken,
Eze. 4:16. I will break *the staff of* bread
5:16. will break your *staff of* bread:
7:10. *the rod* hath blossomed,
11. Violence is risen up *into a rod of* wickedness:
14:13. will break *the staff of* the bread
19:11. she had strong *rods*
12. her strong *rods* were broken
14. fire is gone *out of a rod of* her branches,
— she hath no strong *rod*
Mic. 6: 9. hear ye *the rod*, and who hath appointed
Hab. 3: 9. (according) to the oaths of *the tribes*,
14. Thou didst strike through *with his staves*

4296 מִטָּה *mit-tāh*, f.

Gen47:31. Israel bowed himself upon *the bed*'s head.
48: 2. and sat upon *the bed*.
49:33. he gathered up his feet into *the bed*,
Ex. 8: 3(7:28). thy bedchamber, and upon *thy bed*,
1Sa.19:13. Michal took an image, and laid (it) *in the bed*,
15. Bring him up to me *in the bed*,
16. (there was) an image *in the bed*,
28:23. and sat upon *the bed*.
2Sa. 3:31. king David (himself) followed *the bier*. (marg. *bed*)
4: 7. he lay on *his bed* in his bedchamber,
1K. 17:19. and laid him upon *his own bed*.
21: 4. he laid him down upon *his bed*,
2K. 1: 4, 6, 16. that *bed* on which thou art gone up,
4:10. let us set for him there *a bed*,
21. laid him on *the bed of* the man of God,
32. the child was dead, (and) laid upon *his bed*.
11: 2. hid him,...in the *bed*chamber
2Ch 22:11. put him and his nurse in a *bed*chamber.
24:25. and slew him on *his bed*,
Est. 1: 6. *the beds* (were of) gold and silver,
7: 8. Haman was fallen *upon the bed*
Ps. 6: 6(7). all the night make I *my bed* to swim;
Pro.26:14. the slothful upon *his bed*.
Cant.3: 7. Behold *his bed*, which (is) Solomon's;
Eze.23:41. And satest upon *a* stately *bed*,
Am. 3:12. in the corner of *a bed*,
6: 4. That lie upon *beds of* ivory

4297 מֻטֶּה *moot-teh'*, m.

Eze. 9: 9. the city full of *perverseness*: (marg. or, *wresting of* (judgment))

4299 מַטְוֶה *mat-veh'*, m.

Ex. 35:25. and brought *that which they had spun*,

4298 מֻטּוֹת *moot-tōhth'*, f. pl.

Isa. 8: 8. *the stretching out of* his wings

4300 מְטִיל *m'teel*, m.

Job 40:18. his bones (are) *like bars of* iron.

4301 מַטְמוֹן *mat-mōhn'*, m.

Gen43:23. hath given you *treasure*
Job 3:21. dig for it *more than for hid treasures*
Pro. 2: 4. *and* searchest for her *as* (for) *hid treasures*;
Isa. 45: 3. *and hidden riches* of secret places,
Jer. 41: 8. for we have *treasures* in the field,

מַטָּע *mat-tāhg'*, m. 4302

Isa. 60:21. the branch of *my planting*,
61: 3. *the planting of* the Lord,
Eze.17: 7. the furrows of *her plantation*.
31: 4. her rivers running roundabout *his plants*
34:29. I will raise up for them *a plant*
Mic. 1: 6. *as plantings of* a vineyard:

מַטְעַמּוֹת *mat-gam-mōhth'*, f. pl. 4303

Pro.23: 3. Be not desirous *of his dainties*:
6. neither desire thou *his dainty meats*:

מַטְעַמִּים *mat-gam-meem'*, m. pl. 4303

Gen27: 4, 7. make me *savoury meat*,
9. I will make them *savoury meat*
14. his mother made *savoury meat*,
17. she gave *the savoury meat*
31. he also had made *savoury meat*,

מִטְפַּחַת *mit-pah'-ghath*, f. 4304

Ru. 3:15. Bring *the vail* (marg. or, *sheet*, or, *apron*) that (thou hast)
Isa. 3:22. the mantles, *and the wimples*,

מָטַר [*māh-tar'*]. 4305

* NIPHAL.—*Future*. *

Am. 4: 7. one piece *was rained upon*,

* HIPHIL.—*Preterite*. *

Gen 2: 5. the Lord God *had* not *caused it to rain*
19:24. the Lord *rained* upon Sodom and
Am. 4: 7. *and I caused it to rain*

HIPHIL.—*Infinitive*.

Job 38:26. *To cause it to rain* on the earth,
Isa. 5: 6. command the clouds *that they rain* no rain

HIPHIL.—*Future*.

Ex. 9:23. *and* the Lord *rained* hail
Job 20:23. *and shall rain* (it) upon him
Ps. 11: 6. Upon the wicked *he shall rain* snares,
78:24. *And had rained* down manna
27. *He rained* flesh *also* upon them as dust,
Eze.38:22. *I will rain* upon him,
Am. 4: 7. and *caused it* not *to rain*
— the piece whereupon *it rained*

HIPHIL.—*Participle*.

Gen 7: 4. I will *cause it to rain*
Ex. 9:18. I will *cause it to rain*
16: 4. I will *rain* bread from heaven

מָטָר *māh-tāhr'*, m. 4306

Ex. 9:33. *and the rain* was not poured upon the
34. *the rain* and the hail and the thunders
Deu 11:11. drinketh water *of the rain of* heaven:
14. I will give (you) *the rain of* your land
17. the heaven, that there be no *rain*,
28:12. to give *the rain unto* thy land
24. *the rain of* thy land powder
32: 2. My doctrine shall drop *as the rain*,
1Sa.12:17. he shall send thunder *and rain*;
18. the Lord sent thunder *and rain*
2Sa. 1:21. neither (let there be) *rain*,
23: 4. clear shining *after rain*.
1K. 8:35. and there is no *rain*,
36. and give *rain* upon thy land,
17: 1. there shall not be dew nor *rain*
18: 1. I will send *rain* upon the earth.
2Ch 6:26. and there is no *rain*,
27. and send *rain* upon thy land,
7:13. If I shut up heaven that there be no *rain*,
Job 5:10. Who giveth *rain* upon the earth,
28:26. he made a decree *for the rain*,
29:23. they waited for me *as for the rain*;
36:27. they pour down *rain* according to

Job 37: 6. likewise *to* the *small* rain, and *to* the *great* rain of his strength. (marg. and *to* the *shower of* rain, and *to* the *showers of* rain of his strength)
38:28. Hath *the rain* (lit. is there *to the rain*) a father?
Ps. 72: 6. He shall come down *like rain*
135: 7. he maketh lightnings *for the rain;*
147: 8. who prepareth *rain* for the earth,
Pro. 26: 1. *and as rain* in harvest,
28: 3. *a* sweeping *rain* which leaveth no food.
Isa. 4: 6. a covert from storm *and from rain.*
5: 6. that they rain no *rain*
30:23. Then shall he give *the rain of* thy seed,
Jer. 10:13 & 51:16. he maketh lightnings *with rain,* (marg. *for rain*)
Zec. 10: 1. Ask ye of the Lord *rain*
— *and* give them *showers of* rain,

4307 **מַטָּרָא** *mat-tāh-rāh'*, f.

Lam. 3:12. set me *as a mark*

4307 **מַטָּרָה** *mat-tāh-rāh'*, f.

1 Sa. 20:20. as though I shot *at a mark.*
Neh 3:25. by the court of *the prison.*
12:39. they stood still in the *prison* gate.
Job 16:12. set me up *for* his *mark.*
Jer. 32: 2. shut up in the court of *the prison,*
8. to me in the court of *the prison*
12. that sat in the court of *the prison.*
33: 1. shut up in the court of *the prison,*
37:21. into the court of *the prison,*
— remained in the court of *the prison.*
38: 6. that (was) in the court of *the prison:*
13. remained in the court of *the prison.*
28. abode in the court of *the prison*
39:14. out of the court of *the prison,*
15. shut up in the court of *the prison,*

4310 **מִי** *mee*, part. pron.

Gen. 3:11. *Who* told thee that thou (wast) naked?
19:12. Hast thou here *any* besides?
24:23. *Whose* daughter (art) thou?
65. *What* man (is) this that walketh
Ex. 16: 3. Would to God (מִי יִתֵּן) we had died
24:14. *if any man* have any matters to do,
Deu. 5:29(26). O that (מִי יִתֵּן) there were such an
Jos. 24:15. choose you this day *whom* ye will serve;
Jud. 20:18. *Which* of us shall go up first
2Sa. 20:11. *He* that favoureth Joab, *and he* that (is) for David,
Ecc. 9: 4. For to *him* that is joined to all the living
Isa. 54:15. *whosoever* shall gather together against &c.

With prefixes the signification of מִי is not changed.

4315 **מֵיטַב** *mēh-tav'*, m.

Gen 47: 6. *in the best of* the land make thy father
11. *in the best of* the land, in the land
Ex. 22: 5(4). *of the best of* his own field, *and of the best of* his own vineyard,
1 Sa. 15: 9. *the best of* the sheep, and of
15. spared *the best of* the sheep

4323 **מִיכַל** *mee-chal'*, m.

2Sa. 17:20. They be gone over *the brook of* water.

4325 **מַיִם** *mah'-yim*, m. dual.

Gen 1 2. upon the face of *the waters.*
6. in the midst of *the waters,* and let it divide *the waters from the waters.*
7. and divided *the waters* which (were) under the firmament from *the waters*
9. Let *the waters*...be gathered together

Gen 1:10. the gathering together of *the waters*
20. Let *the waters* bring forth
21. *the waters* brought forth
22. fill *the waters* in the seas,
6:17. do bring a flood of *waters*
7: 6. the flood of *waters*
7. because of *the waters of* the flood,
10. *that the waters of* the flood
17. and *the waters* increased,
18. And *the waters* prevailed,
— upon the face of *the waters.*
19. *And the waters* prevailed exceedingly
20. Fifteen cubits upward did *the waters*
24. And *the waters* prevailed upon
8: 1. and *the waters* asswaged.
3. And *the waters* returned from off
— *the waters* were abated.
5. *And the waters* decreased
7. until *the waters* were dried up
8. to see if *the waters* were abated
9. *the waters* (were) on the face of
11. *the waters* were abated
13. *the waters* were dried up
9:11. *by the waters of a* flood;
15. *the waters* shall no more become a flood
16: 7. found her by a fountain of *water*
18: 4. Let a little *water,* I pray you, be
21:14. took bread, and a bottle of *water,*
15. *the water* was spent in the bottle,
19. she saw a well of *water;* and she went, and filled the bottle with *water,*
25. because of a well of *water,*
24:11. by a well of *water* at the time
13. (here) by the well of *water;*
— come out to draw *water:*
17, 43. a little *water* of thy pitcher.
32. *and water* to wash his feet,
43. I stand by the well of *water;*
26:18. digged again the wells of *water,*
19. a well of springing *water.*
20. *The water* (is) our's: and he called
32. said unto him, We have found *water.*
30:38. the gutters in the *watering* troughs (lit. troughs of *water*)
37:24. the pit (was) empty, (there was) no *water*
43:24. and gave (them) *water,* and they
49: 4. Unstable *as water,* thou shalt not
Ex. 2:10. I drew him out of *the water.*
4: 9. take *of the water of* the river,
— and *the water* which thou takest
7:15. he goeth out *unto the water;*
17. upon *the waters* which (are) in the river
18, 21. drink of *the water* of the river.
19. upon *the waters of* Egypt,
— upon all *their* pools of *water,* (marg. gathering of *their waters*)
20. *the waters* that (were) in the river,
— *the waters* that (were) in the river
24. digged round about the river for *water*
— they could not drink *of the water of*
8: 6(2). his hand over *the waters of* Egypt;
20(16). lo, he cometh forth *to the water;*
12: 9. nor sodden at all *with water,*
14:21. *the waters* were divided.
22, 29. *and the waters* (were) a wall unto
26. that *the waters* may come again
28. And *the waters* returned,
15: 8. *the waters* were gathered together,
10. they sank as lead *in the* mighty *waters.*
19. brought again *the waters of* the sea
22. wilderness, and found no *water.*
23. *the waters* of Marah,
25. (which) when he had cast into *the waters, the waters* were made sweet:
27. twelve wells of *water,*
— they encamped there by *the waters.*
17: 1. no *water* for the people
2. Give us *water* that we may drink.
3. the people thirsted there *for water;*
6. there shall come *water* out
20: 4. *in the water* under the earth:
23:25. he shall bless thy bread, and *thy water;*
29: 4. shalt wash them *with water.*
30:18. thou shalt put *water* therein.
20. they shall wash with *water,*
32:20. strawed (it) upon *the water,*
34:28. did neither eat bread, *nor* drink *water.*

Ex. 40: 7. and shalt put *water* therein.
12. wash them *with water*.
30. and put *water* there, to wash
Lev. 1: 9. his inwards...shall he wash *in water* :
13. he shall wash the inwards...*with water* .
6:28(21). both scoured, and rinsed *in water*.
8: 6. and washed them *with water*.
21. he washed the inwards...*in water* ;
11: 9. all that (are) *in the waters* : whatsoever hath fins and scales *in the waters*,
10. all that move in *the waters*, and of any living thing which (is) *in the waters*,
12. hath no fins nor scales *in the waters*,
32. it must be put *into water*,
34. on which (such) *water* cometh
36. (wherein there is) plenty of *water*,
38. if (any) *water* be put upon the seed,
46. every living creature that moveth *in the waters*,
14: 5, 50. an earthen vessel over running *water* :
6. killed over *the* running *water* :
8. and wash himself *in water*,
9. he shall wash his flesh *in water*,
51. *and in the* running *water*,
52. *and with the* running *water*,
15: 5, 6, 7, 8, 10, 11, 21, 22, 27. and bathe (himself) *in water*,
11. hath not rinsed his hands *in water*,
12. vessel of wood shall be rinsed *in water*.
13. and bathe his flesh *in* running *water*,
16. he shall wash all his flesh *in water*,
17. shall be washed *with water*,
18. shall (both) bathe (themselves) *in water*,
16: 4. wash his flesh *in water*,
24. shall wash his flesh *with water*
26, 28. and bathe his flesh *in water*,
17:15. and bathe (himself) *in water*,
22: 6. he wash his flesh *with water*.
Nu. 5:17. the priest shall take holy *water*
— and put (it) into *the water* :
18. *the* bitter *water* that causeth the curse :
19. be thou free *from* this bitter *water*
22. this *water* that causeth the curse
23. blot (them) out with *the* bitter *water* :
24. to drink *the* bitter *water* that causeth the curse: and *the water* that causeth
26. cause the woman to drink *the water*.
27. made her to drink *the water*,
— *the water* that causeth the curse
8: 7. Sprinkle *water of* purifying
19: 7. he shall bathe his flesh *in water*,
8. shall wash his clothes *in water*, and bathe his flesh *in water*,
9. *for a water of* separation:
13. *the water of* separation was not
17. running *water* shall be put thereto
18. take hyssop, and dip (it) *in the water*,
19. and bathe himself *in water*,
20. *the water of* separation hath not
21. he that sprinkleth *the water of*
— he that toucheth *the water of*
20: 2. there was no *water* for the congregation:
5. *neither* (is) there any *water*
8. it shall give forth *his water*, and thou shalt bring forth to them *water* out of the
10. must we fetch you *water*
11. *the water* came out abundantly,
13. *the water of* Meribah; because
17. *the water of* the wells:
19. if I and my cattle drink of *thy water*,
24. *at the water of* Meribah.
21: 5. neither (is there any) *water* ;
16. I will give them *water*.
22. *the waters of* the well:
24: 6. as cedar trees beside *the waters*.
7. He shall pour *the water* out
— his seed (shall be) *in* many *waters*,
27:14. to sanctify me *at the water* before their eyes: that (is) *the water of* Meribah
31:23. *with the water of* separation:
— shall make go *through the water*.
33: 9. twelve fountains of *water*,
14. no *water* for the people
Deu 2: 6. ye shall also buy *water*
28. *and* give me *water* for money,
4:18 & 5:8. *in the waters* beneath the earth:
8: 7. a land of brooks of *water*,

Deu 8:15. where (there was) no *water* ; who brought thee forth *water*
9: 9. I neither did eat bread *nor* drink *water*:
18. I did neither eat bread, *nor* drink *water*,
10: 7. a land of rivers of *waters*.
11: 4. made *the water of* the Red sea to
11. *water* of the rain of heaven:
12:16, 24. pour it upon the earth *as water*.
14: 9. all that (are) *in the waters* :
15:23. pour it upon the ground *as water*.
23: 4(5). met you not with bread *and with water*
11(12). he shall wash (himself) *with water* :
29:11(10). the drawer of *thy water* :
32:51. *at the waters of* Meribah-Kadesh,
33: 8. at *the waters of* Meribah;
Jos. 2:10. *the water of* the Red sea
3: 8. *the water of* Jordan,
13. *in the waters of* Jordan, (that) *the waters of* Jordan shall be cut off (from) *the waters* that come down
15. in the brim of *the water*,
16. *the waters* which came down
4: 7. That *the waters of* Jordan were cut off
— *the waters of* Jordan were cut off:
18. *the waters of* Jordan returned
23. dried up *the waters of* Jordan
5: 1. dried up *the waters of* Jordan
7: 5. hearts of the people...became *as water*.
9:21, 23, 27. hewers of wood and drawers of *water*
11: 5. at *the waters of* Merom,
7. by *the waters of* Merom
8. chased them unto...Misrephoth-*maim*, (lit. of *water*)
13: 6. from Lebanon unto Misrephoth-*maim*,
15: 7. toward *the waters of* En-shemesh,
9. *the water of* Nephtoah,
19. give me also springs of *water*.
16: 1. *unto the water of* Jericho
18:15. the well of *waters of* Nephtoah:
Jud. 1:15. give me also springs of *water*.
4:19. Give me, I pray thee, a little *water*
5: 4. the clouds also dropped *water*.
19. by *the waters of* Megiddo;
25. He asked *water*, (and) she gave (him)
6:38. a bowl full of *water*.
7: 4. bring them down unto *the water*,
5. brought down the people unto *the water* .
— Every one that lappeth of *the water*
6. down upon their knees to drink *water*.
24. before them *the waters* unto Beth-barah
— took *the waters* unto Beth-barah
15:19. there came *water* thereout;
1Sa. 7: 6. they gathered together...and drew *water*,
9:11. young maidens going out to draw *water*,
25:11. Shall I then take my bread, and *my water*,
26:11. and the cruse of *water*,
12. took the spear and the cruse of *water*
16. the cruse of *water* that (was) at his bolster.
30:11. they made him drink *water* ;
12. nor drunk (any) *water*,
2Sa. 5:20. as the breach of *waters*.
12:27. and have taken the city of *waters*.
14:14. *and* (are) *as water* spilt on the ground,
17:20. gone over the brook of *water*.
21. Arise, and pass quickly over *the water* .
21:10. until *water* dropped upon them
22:12. dark *waters*, (and) thick clouds
17. he drew me *out of* many *waters* ;
23:15. *the water* of the well of Beth-lehem,
16. and drew *water* out of the well
1K. 13: 8. neither will I eat bread nor drink *water*
9. Eat no bread, nor drink *water*,
16. will I eat bread nor drink *water*
17. eat no bread nor drink *water*
18. that he may eat bread and drink *water*
19. and did eat bread...and drank *water*.
22. hast eaten bread and drunk *water*
— Eat no bread, and drink no *water* ;
14:15. as a reed is shaken *in the water*,
17:10. Fetch me, I pray thee, a little *water*
18: 4. and fed them with bread *and water*.
5. unto all fountains of *water*,
13. and fed them with bread *and water* ?
33(34). Fill four barrels with *water*,
35. *the water* ran round about
— he filled the trench also with *water*.

1K. 18:38. *the water* that (was) in the trench
19: 6. a cruse of *water* at his head.
22:27. *with water* of affliction,
2K. 2: 8, 14. and smote *the waters*,
14. he also had smitten *the waters*,
19 *but the water* (is) naught,
21. the spring ot *the waters*,
— I have healed these *waters;*
22. So *the waters* were healed unto this day,
3: 9. there was no *water* for the host,
11. poured *water* on the hands of Elijah.
17. that valley shall be filled with *water*,
19. and stop all wells of *water*,
20. there came *water* by the way of Edom, and the country was filled with *water*.
22. the sun shone upon *the water*, and the Moabites saw *the water*
25. they stopped all the wells of *water*,
5:12. all *the waters of* Israel?
6: 5. the ax head fell into *the water:*
22. set bread *and water* before them,
8. 15. a thick cloth, and dipped (it) *in water*,
18:27: and drink their own piss (marg. *the water of* their feet)
31. *the waters of* his cistern:
19:24. I have digged and drunk strange *waters*,
20:20. and brought *water* into the city,
1Ch. 11:17. *the water* of the well of Beth-lehem,
18. and drew *water* out of the well
14:11. like the breaking forth of *waters:*
2Ch 18:26. *and* with *water* of affliction,
32: 3. *the waters of* the fountains
4. and find much *water?*
30. the upper *water*course of Gihon,
Ezr. 10: 6. he did eat no bread, *nor* drink *water:*
Neh 3:26. over against the *water* gate
4:23(17). every one put them off for *washing*. (marg. for *water*)
8: 1, 3. the street that (was) before the *water* gate;
16. in the street of the *water* gate,
9:11. as a stone *into the* mighty *waters*.
15. *and* broughtest forth *water* for them
20. *and* gavest them *water* for their thirst.
12:37. even unto the *water* gate
13: 2. of Israel with bread *and with water*,
Job 3:24. roarings are poured out *like the waters*.
5:10. and sendeth *waters* upon the fields:
8:11. can the flag grow without *water?*
9:30. If I wash myself *with* snow *water*,
11:16. remember (it) *as waters* (that) pass away:
12:15. he withholdeth *the waters*,
14: 9. through the scent of *water*
11. (As) *the waters* fail from the sea,
19. *The waters* wear the stones:
15:16. drinketh iniquity *like water?*
22: 7. hast not given *water* to the weary
11. abundance of *waters* cover thee.
24:18. He (is) swift as *the waters;*
19. Drought and heat consume *the* snow *waters:*
26: 5. from under *the waters*,
8. He bindeth up *the waters*
10. He hath compassed *the waters*
27:20. Terrors take hold on him *as waters*,
28:25. *and* he weigheth *the waters* by measure.
29:19. My root (was) spread out by *the waters*,
34: 7. drinketh up scorning *like water?*
36:27. he maketh small the drops of *water:*
37:10. the breadth of *the waters* is straitened.
38:30. *The waters* are hid as (with) a stone,
34. that abundance of *waters* may cover thee?
Ps. 1: 3. a tree planted by the rivers of *water*,
18:11(12). dark *waters* (and) thick clouds
15(16). the channels of *waters* were seen,
16(17). he drew me *out of* many *waters*.
22:14(15). I am poured out *like water*,
23: 2. he leadeth me beside *the* still *waters*.
29: 3. of the Lord (is) upon *the waters:*
— the Lord (is) upon many *waters*.
32: 6. in the floods of great *waters*
33: 7. He gathereth *the waters of*
42: 1(2). As the hart panteth after the *water* brooks,
46: 3(4). *the waters thereof* roar
58: 7(8). Let them melt away *as waters*
63: 1(2). where no *water* is;

Ps. 65: 9(10). the river of God, (which) is full of *water:*
66:12. we went through fire *and tarough water:*
69: 1(2). *the waters* are come in unto (my) soul
2(3). I am come into deep *waters*,
14(15). out of *the* deep *waters*.
15(16). Let not the *water*flood overflow me,
73:10. *and waters of* a full (cup)
74:13. brakest the heads of the dragons in *the waters*.
77:16(17). *The waters* saw thee, O God, *the waters* saw thee;
17(18). The clouds poured out *water:*
19(20). thy path *in the* great *waters*.
78:13. made *the waters* to stand as an heap.
16. caused *waters* to run down like rivers.
20. *the waters* gushed out,
79: 3. Their blood have they shed *like water*
81: 7(8). I proved thee at *the waters of* Meribah.
88:17(18). They came round about me daily *like water;*
93: 4. the noise of many *waters*,
104: 3. Who layeth the beams of his chambers *in the waters:*
6. *the waters* stood above the mountains,
105:29. He turned *their waters* into blood,
41. *the waters* gushed out;
106:11. *the waters* covered their enemies:
32. *the waters of* strife,
107:23. that do business *in* great *waters;*
33. *the water*springs into dry ground
35. *a* standing *water*, and dry ground into *water*springs.
109:18. let it come into his bowels *like water*,
114: 8. Which turned the rock (into) *a* standing *water*, the flint into a fountain of *waters*.
119:136. Rivers of *waters* run down mine eyes,
124: 4. *the waters* had overwhelmed us,
5. *the* proud *waters* had gone over our soul.
136: 6. that stretched out the earth above *the waters:*
144: 7. deliver me *out of* great *waters*,
147:18. to blow, (and) *the waters* flow.
148: 4. *and ye waters* that (be) above the heavens.
Pro. 5:15. *waters* out of thine own cistern,
16. rivers of *waters* in the streets.
8:24. no fountains abounding with *water*.
29. *that the waters* should not pass his commandment:
9:17. Stolen *waters* are sweet,
17:14. when one letteth out *water:*
18: 4. of a man's mouth (are as) deep *waters*,
20: 5. Counsel...(is like) deep *water;*
21: 1. (as) the rivers of *water:*
25:21. give him *water* to drink:
25. (As) cold *waters* to a thirsty soul,
27:19. *As* in *water* face (answereth) to face,
30: 4. who hath bound *the waters* in a garment?
16. the earth (that) is not filled with *water;*
Ecc. 2: 6. I made me pools of *water*,
11: 1. Cast thy bread upon *the waters:*
Cant. 4:15. a well of living *waters*,
5:12. by the rivers of *waters*,
8: 7. Many *waters* cannot quench love,
Isa. 1:22. thy wine mixed *with water:*
30. as a garden that hath no *water*.
3: 1. the whole stay of *water*,
8: 6. *the waters of* Shiloah that go softly,
7. *the waters of* the river,
11: 9. *as the waters* cover the sea.
12: 3. with joy shall ye draw *water*
14:23. for the bittern, and pools of *water:*
15: 6. *the waters of* Nimrim shall be desolate:
9. *the waters of* Dimon shall be full of blood:
17:12. like the rushing of mighty *waters!*
13. like the rushing of many *waters:*
18: 2. in vessels of bulrushes upon *the waters*,
19: 5. *the waters* shall fail from the sea,
8. they that spread nets upon *the waters*
21:14. brought *water* to him that was thirsty,
22: 9. *the waters of* the lower pool.
11. *for the water of* the old pool:
23: 3. *And by* great *waters* the seed of Sihor,
25:10. (כתיב) trodden down *for* (lit. according to כתיב, *in the water of*) the dunghill.
28: 2. as a flood of mighty *waters*
17. *the waters* shall overflow the hiding place.

Isa. 30:14. to take *water* (withal) out of the pit.
20. *and the water* of affliction,
25. rivers (and) streams of *waters*
32: 2. as rivers of *water* in a dry place,
20. Blessed (are) ye that sow beside all *waters*,
33:16. *his waters* (shall be) sure.
35: 6. in the wilderness shall *waters* break out,
7. the thirsty land springs of *water*;
36:12. and drink their own piss (lit. *water of* their feet)
16. *the waters of* his own cistern;
37:25. I have digged, and drunk *water*;
40:12. Who hath measured *the waters*
41:17. (When) the poor and needy seek *water*
18. I will make the wilderness a pool of *water*, and the dry land springs of *water*
43: 2. When thou passest *through the waters*,
16. in the sea, *and* a path *in the* mighty *waters*;
20. I give *waters* in the wilderness,
44: 3. I will pour *water* upon him that is thirsty,
4. as willows by the *water* courses.
12. he drinketh no *water*, and is faint.
48: 1. *and* are come forth *out of the waters of* Judah,
21. he caused *the waters* to flow out of the rock
— *the waters* gushed out.
49:10. by the springs of *water* shall he guide
50. 2. because (there is) no *water*,
51:10. *the waters of* the great deep;
54: 9. this (is as) *the waters of* Noah unto me: for (as) I have sworn that *the waters of*
55: 1. come ye *to the waters*,
57:20. *whose waters* cast up mire
58:11. and like a spring of *water whose waters* fail not.
63:12. dividing *the water* before them,
64: 2(1). the fire causeth *the waters* to boil,
Jer. 2:13. the fountain of living *waters*,
— that can hold no *water*.
18. to drink *the waters of* Sihor?
— to drink *the waters of* the river?
6: 7. As a fountain casteth out *her waters*,
8:14. given us *water of* gall to drink,
9: 1(8. 23). Oh that my head were *waters*,
15(14). give them *water of* gall to drink.
18(17). our eyelids gush out with *waters*.
10:13. (there is) a multitude of *waters* in the
13: 1. *and* put it not *in water*.
14: 3. their nobles have sent their little ones *to the waters*: they came to the pits, (and) found no *water*;
15:18. (and as) *waters* (that) fail?
17: 8. he shall be as a tree planted by *the waters*,
13. the fountain of living *waters*.
18:14. *the* cold flowing *waters*
23:15. make them drink *the water of* gall:
31: 9. to walk by the rivers of *waters*
38: 6. in the dungeon (there was) no *water*,
41:12. *the* great *waters* that (are) in Gibeon.
46: 7. *whose waters* are moved as the rivers?
8. (his) *waters* are moved like the rivers;
47: 2. *waters* rise up out of the north,
48:34. *the waters* also *of* Nimrim shall be desolate.
50:38. A drought (is) upon *her waters*;
51:13. O thou that dwellest upon many *waters*,
16. (there is) a multitude of *waters* in the heavens;
55. when her waves do roar *like* great *waters*,
Lam. 1:16. mine eye runneth down *with water*,
2:19. pour out thine heart *like water*
3:48. runneth down with rivers of *water*
54. *Waters* flowed over mine head;
5: 4. We have drunken *our water*
Eze. 1:24. like the noise of great *waters*,
4:11. Thou shalt drink *also water* by measure,
16. *and* they shall drink *water* by measure,
17. That they may want bread *and water*,
7:17. all knees shall be weak (as) *water*.
12:18. *and* drink *thy water* with trembling
19. *and* drink *their water* with astonishment,
16: 4. *neither* wast thou washed *in water*,
9. Then washed I thee *with water*;
17: 5. he placed (it) by great *waters*,
8. in a good soil by great *waters*,
19:10. planted by *the waters*: she was fruitful and full of branches *by reason of* many *waters*.
21: 7(12). all knees shall be weak (as) *water*;

Eze. 24: 3. also pour *water* into it:
26:12. and thy dust in the midst of *the water*,
19. great *waters* shall cover thee;
27:26. Thy rowers have brought thee *into* great *waters*:
34. in the depths of *the waters*
31: 4. *The waters* made him great,
5. *because of* the multitude of *waters*,
7. his root was by great *waters*.
14. all the trees by *the waters* exalt themselves
—, 16. all that drink *water*:
15. *the* great *waters* were stayed:
32: 2. troubledst *the waters* with thy feet,
13. from beside *the* great *waters*;
14. Then will I make *their waters* deep,
34:18. to have drunk of *the* deep *waters*,
36:25. will I sprinkle clean *water* upon you,
43: 2. like a noise of many *waters*:
47: 1. *waters* issued out from under
— *and the waters* came down
2. there ran out *waters* on the right side.
3. he brought me *through the waters*; *the waters* (were) *to* the ancles.
4. brought me *through the waters*; *the waters* (were) *to* the knees.
— *the waters* (were) *to* the loins.
5. *the waters* were risen, *waters to* swim in,
8. These *waters* issue out toward the east
— *the waters* shall be healed.
9. because these *waters* shall come thither:
12. *their waters* they issued out
19. *the waters of* strife (in) Kadesh,
48:28. *the waters of* strife (in) Kadesh,
Dan. 1:12. *and water* to drink.
12: 6,7. upon *the waters of* the river,
Hos. 2: 5(7). give (me) my bread *and my water*,
5:10. I will pour out my wrath upon them *like water*.
10: 7. as the foam upon *the water*.
Joel 1:20. the rivers of *waters* are dried up,
3:18. (4:18). of Judah shall flow with *waters*,
Am. 4: 8. wandered unto one city, to drink *water*;
5: 8. that calleth *for the waters of* the sea,
24. let judgment run down *as waters*,
8:11. nor a thirst *for water*.
9: 6. he that calleth *for the waters of* the sea,
Jon. 2: 5. (6). *The waters* compassed me about,
3: 7. let them not feed, *nor* drink *water*:
Mic. 1: 4. *as the waters* (that are) poured down
Nah. 2: 8. (9). Nineveh (is) of old like a pool of *water*:
3: 8. (that had) *the waters* round about it,
14. Draw the *waters for* the siege,
Hab. 2:14. *as the waters* cover the sea.
3:10. the overflowing of *the water* passed by:
15. (through) the heap of great *waters*.
Zec. 9:11. the pit wherein (is) no *water*.
14: 8. living *waters* shall go out from Jerusalem;

מין [*meen*], m. 4327

Gen. 1:11. yielding fruit *after his kind*,
12. herb yielding seed *after his kind*,
— whose seed (was) in itself *after his kind*:
21. forth abundantly, *after their kind*, and every winged fowl *after his kind*:
24. the living creature *after his kind*,
— beast of the earth *after his kind*:
25. the beast of the earth *after his kind*, and cattle *after their kind*, and every thing that creepeth...*after his kind*:
6:20. Of fowls *after their kind*, and of cattle *after their kind*, of every creeping thing ...*after his kind*,
7:14. every beast *after his kind*, and all the cattle *after their kind*, and every creeping thing...*after his kind*, and every fowl *after his kind*,
Lev. 11:14. the kite *after his kind*;
15. Every raven *after his kind*;
16. the hawk *after his kind*,
19. the heron *after her kind*,
22. the locust *after his kind*, and the bald locust *after his kind*, and the beetle *after his kind*, and the grasshopper *after his kind*.

Lev.11:29. the tortoise *after his kind,*
Deu14:13. the vulture *after his kind,*
14. every raven *after his kind,*
15. the hawk *after his kind,*
18. the heron *after her kind,*
Eze.47:10. their fish shall be *according to their kinds,*

4329 **מֵיסַךְ** *mēh-sach'*, m.

2K. 16:18. (כתיב) And *the covert for* the sabbath that they had built

4330 **מִיץ** *meetz*, m.

Pro.30:33. *the churning of* milk bringeth forth butter, *and the wringing of* the nose bringeth forth blood: *so the forcing of* wrath bringeth forth strife.

4334 **מִישׁוֹר** *mee-shōhr'*, m.

Deu. 3:10. All the cities of *the plain,*
4:43. in the *plain* country,
Jos. 13: 9. all *the plain of* Medeba
16. all *the plain* by Medeba;
17. all her cities that (are) *in the plain;*
21. all the cities of *the plain;*
20: 8. the wilderness *upon the plain*
1 K. 20:23. let us fight against them *in the plain,*
25. we will fight against them *in the plain,*
2Ch 26:10. both in the low country, *and in the plains:*
Ps. 26:12. My foot standeth *in an even place:*
27:11. lead me in a *plain* path, (marg. way of *plainness*)
45: 6(7). of thy kingdom (is) a *right* sceptre.
67: 4(5). thou shalt judge the people *righteously,*
143:10. lead me into the land of *uprightness.*
Isa. 11: 4. reprove *with equity* for the meek
40: 4. the crooked shall be *made straight,* (marg. or, *a straight place*)
42:16. and crooked things *straight.* (marg. *into straightness*)
Jer. 21:13. rock of *the plain.*
48: 8. *the plain* shall be destroyed,
21. judgment is come upon the *plain* country;
Zec. 4: 7. (thou shalt become) *a plain;*
Mal. 2: 6. he walked with me in peace *and equity,*

4334, 4339 **מֵישָׁרִים** *mēh-shāh-reem'*, m. pl.

1Ch 29:17. *and* hast pleasure in *uprightness.*
Ps. 9: 8(9). judgment to the people *in uprightness.*
17: 2. thine eyes behold *the things that are equal.*
58: 1(2). do ye judge *uprightly,*
75: 2(3). I will judge *uprightly.*
96:10. he shall judge the people *righteously.*
98: 9. the people *with equity,*
99: 4. thou dost establish *equity,*
Pro. 1: 3. justice, and judgment, *and equity;* (marg. *equities*)
2: 9. righteousness and judgment, *and equity;*
8: 6. opening of my lips (shall be) *right things.*
23:16. when thy lips speak *right things.*
31. it moveth itself *aright.*
Cant.1: 4. *the upright* love thee. (marg. they love thee *uprightly*)
7: 9(10). that goeth (down) *sweetly,* (marg. *straightly*)
Isa. 26: 7. The way of the just (is) *uprightness:*
33:15. speaketh *uprightly;* (marg. *in uprightnesses*)
45:19. I declare *things that are right.*
Dan 11: 6. to make *an agreement:* (marg. *rights*)

4340 **מֵיתָר** [*mēh-thāhr'*], m.

Ex. 35:18. the pins of the court, and *their cords,*
39:40. *his cords,* and his pins,
Nu. 3:26. and *the cords of it*
37. their pins, *and their cords.*
4:26. *their cords,* and all the instruments
Nu. 4:32. their pins, *and their cords,*
Ps. 21:12(13). ready (thine arrows) *upon thy strings*
Isa. 54: 2. lengthen *thy cords,*
Jer. 10:20. all *my cords* are broken:

מַכְאוֹב *mach-ōhv'*, m. 4341

Ex. 3: 7. I know *their sorrows;*
2Ch. 6:29. his own sore *and his own grief,*
Job 33:19. He is chastened also *with pain*
Ps. 32:10. Many *sorrows* (shall be) to the wicked:
38:17(18). *and my sorrow* (is) continually before
69:26(27). they talk to *the grief of* those whom
Ecc. 1:18. increaseth knowledge increaseth *sorrow.*
2:23. For all his days (are) *sorrows,*
Isa. 53: 3. a man of *sorrows,* and acquainted
4. Surely he hath borne our griefs, *and* carried *our sorrows:*
Jer. 30:15. *thy sorrow* (is) incurable
45: 3. the Lord hath added grief to *my sorrow;*
51: 8. take balm *for her pain,*
Lam. 1:12. see if there be any *sorrow* like unto *my sorrow,*
18. behold *my sorrow:* my virgins

מִכְבָּר *mich-bāhr'*, m. 4345

Ex. 27: 4. thou shalt make for it *a grate*
35:16. with his brasen *grate*
38: 4. he made...*a* brasen *grate*
5. the four ends *of the grate*
30. and the brasen *grate*
39:39. The brasen altar, and his *grate*

מַכְבֵּר *mach-bēhr'*, m. 4346

2K. 8:15. he took *a thick cloth,*

מַכָּה *mak-kāh'*, f. 4347

Lev.26:21. I will bring seven times more *plagues*
Nu. 11:33. the people with *a* very great *plague.*
Deu25: 3. beat him above these with many *stripes,*
28:59. the Lord will make *thy plagues* wonderful and *the plagues of* thy seed, (even) great *plagues,*
61. every sickness, and every *plague,*
29:22(21). when they see *the plagues of* that
Jos. 10:10. slew them with *a* great *slaughter*
20. slaying them with *a* very great *slaughter,*
Jud 11:33. with *a* very great *slaughter.*
15: 8. hip and thigh with *a* great *slaughter:*
1Sa. 4: 8. smote the Egyptians with all *the plagues*
10. there was *a* very great *slaughter;*
6:19. of the people with *a* great *slaughter.*
14:14. *that* first *slaughter,* which
30. *a* much greater *slaughter*
19: 8. slew them with *a* great *slaughter;*
23: 5. smote them with *a* great *slaughter.*
1K. 20:21. slew the Syrians with *a* great *slaughter.*
22:35. the blood ran out of *the wound*
2K. 8:29 & 9:15. *the wounds* which the Syrians had
2Ch 2:10(9). measures of *beaten* wheat,
13:17. slew them with *a* great *slaughter:*
22: 6. *the wounds* which were given him
28: 5. who smote him with *a* great *slaughter.*
Est. 9: 5. with *the stroke of* the sword,
Ps. 64: 7(8). suddenly shall *they* be *wounded.* (lit. shall *their wounds* be)
Pro.20:30. *so* (do) *stripes* the inward parts
Isa. 1: 6. and bruises, *and* putrifying *sores:*
10:26. *according to the slaughter of* Midian
14: 6. with *a* continual *stroke,*
27: 7. as he *smote* (marg. *according to the stroke of*) those that smote him?
30: 26. healeth the stroke of *their wound.*
Jer. 6: 7. continually (is) grief *and wounds.*
10:19. *my wound* is grievous:
14:17. with *a* very grievous *blow.*
15:18. *and my wound* incurable,
19: 8. because of all *the plagues thereof.*
30:12. *thy wound* (is) grievous.

Jer. 30:14. I have wounded thee *with the wound of*
17. *and* I will heal thee of *thy wounds,*
49:17. all *the plagues thereof.*
50:13. hiss at all *her plagues.*
Mic. 1: 9. *her wound* (is) incurable;
Nah. 3:19. *thy wound* is grievous:
Zec. 13: 6. What (are) these *wounds* in thine hands?

4348 **מִכְוָה** *mich-vāh',* f.

Lev 13:24. in the skin...*a* hot *burning,* and the quick (flesh) *that burneth*
25. a leprosy broken *out of the burning:*
28. a rising of *the burning,*
— an inflammation of *the burning.*

4349 **מָכוֹן** *māh-chōhn',* m.

Ex. 15:17. *the place,* O Lord, (which) thou hast
1K. 8:13. *a settled place* for thee
39, 43, 49. in heaven thy dwelling *place,*
2Ch. 6: 2. *and a place* for thy dwelling
30. heaven thy dwelling *place,*
33, 39. *from* thy dwelling *place,*
Ezr. 2:68. the house of God to set it up in *his place:*
Ps. 33:14. *From the place of* his habitation
89:14(15). *the habitation* (marg. *establishment*) *of* thy throne:
97: 2. *the habitation of* his throne. (marg. *id.*)
104: 5. *the foundations of* the earth, (marg. *bases*)
Isa. 4: 5. every *dwelling place of* mount Zion,
18: 4. I will consider *in my dwelling place* (marg. *set dwelling*)
Dan. 8:11. *the place of* his sanctuary

4350 **מְכוֹנָה** *m'chōh-nāh',* f.

1K. 7:27. he made ten *bases*
— the length of one *base,*
28. the work of *the bases*
30. every *base had* four brasen wheels,
32. the axletrees...(were joined) *to the base:*
34. the four corners of one *base:* (and) the undersetters (were) of *the* very *base*
35. in the top of *the base*
— on the top of *the base*
37. he made *the* ten *bases:*
38. upon *every* one of *the* ten *bases* (lit. upon one *base* of *the* ten *bases*)
39. he put five *bases* on the right side
43. And *the* ten *bases,* and ten lavers on *the bases;*
2K. 16:17. cut off the borders of *the bases,*
25:13. and *the bases,* and the brasen sea
16. *and the bases* which Solomon had made
2Ch 4:14. He made also *bases,* and lavers made he upon *the bases;*
Ezr. 3: 3. they set the altar upon *his bases;*
Jer. 27:19. and concerning *the bases,*
52:17. *the bases,* and the brasen sea
20. twelve brasen bulls that (were) under *the bases,*

See 4369 **מְכֻנָה** see **מְכוֹנָה**

4351 **מְכוּרָה** [*m'choo-rāh'*], f.

Eze. 16: 3. *Thy birth* (marg. *cutting out,* or, *habitation*) and thy nativity
21:30(35). in the land of *thy nativity.*
29:14. the land of *their habitation;* (marg. or, *birth*)

4355 **מָכַךְ** [*māh-chach'*].

* KAL.—*Future.* *

Ps. 106:43. *and were brought low* for their iniquity. (marg. or, *impoverished,* or, *weakened*)

* NIPHAL.—*Future.* *

Ecc. 10:18. much slothfulness the building *decayeth;*

* HOPHAL.—*Preterite.* *

Job 24:24. are gone *and brought low;*

מִכְלָה *mich-lāh',* f. 4356

Ps. 50: 9. (nor) he goats *out of thy folds.*
78:70. and took him *from the* sheep*folds:*
Hab. 3:17. the flock shall be cut off *from the fold,*

מִכְלוֹל *mich-lōhl',* m. 4358

Eze. 23:12. captains and rulers clothed *most gorgeously*
38: 4. with *all sorts* (of armour),

מִכְלוֹת *mich-lōhth',* f. pl. 4357

2Ch 4:21. (and) that *perfect* (marg. *perfections of*) gold.

מִכְלַל *mich-lal',* m. 4359

Ps. 50: 2. *the perfection of* beauty,

מַכְלֻלִים *mach-loo-leem',* m. pl. 4360

Eze. 27:24. thy merchants *in all sorts* (of things), (marg. or, *excellent things*)

מַכֹּלֶת *mak-kōh'-leth,* f. 4361

1K. 5:11(25). twenty thousand measures of wheat (for) *food*

מִכְמַנִּים [*mich-man-neem'*], m. pl. 4362

Dan 11:43. *over the treasures of* gold and of silver,

מַכְמֹר [*mach-mōhr'*], m. 4364

Ps. 141:10. Let the wicked fall *into their own nets,*

מִכְמָר *mich-māhr',* m. 4364

Isa. 51:20. as a wild bull in *a net:*

מִכְמֶרֶת [*mich-meh'-reth*]. 4365

Hab. 1:15. gather them *in their drag:* (marg. *flue net*)
16. burn incense *unto their drag;*

מִכְמֹרֶת *mich-mōh'-reth,* f. 4365

Isa. 19: 8. they that spread *nets*

מְכֻנָה [*m'choo-nāh'*], f. 4369

Zec. 5:11. set there upon *her own base.*

מִכְנְסַיִם [*mich-n'sah'-yim*], dual, m. 4370

Ex. 28:42. thou shalt make them linen *breeches*
39:28. linen *breeches* (of) fine twined linen,
Lev. 6:10(3). *and* his linen *breeches* shall he put
16: 4. *and* he shall have *the* linen *breeches* upon
Eze. 44:18. *and* shall have linen *breeches* upon their

4371 **מֶכֶס** *meh'-ches*, m.

Nu. 31:28. levy *a tribute* unto the Lord
37. the Lord's *tribute of* the sheep
38. *of which* the Lord's *tribute* (was) threescore
39. *of which the* Lord's *tribute* (was) threescore
40. *of which* the Lord's *tribute* (was) thirty
41. Moses gave *the tribute*,

4373 **מִכְסָה** [*mich-sāh'*], f.

Ex. 12: 4. *according to the number of* the souls;
Lev.27:23. *the worth of* thy estimation,

4372 **מִכְסֶה** *mich-seh'*, m.

Gen 8:13. Noah removed *the covering of* the ark,
Ex. 26:14. make *a covering* for the tent
— *and a covering* above (of) badgers' skins.
35:11. The tabernacle, his tent, and *his covering*,
36:19. he made *a covering* for the tent
— *and a covering of* badgers' skins
39:34. *the covering of* rams' skins dyed red, and *the covering of* badgers' skins,
40:19. *the covering of* the tent
Nu. 3:25. the tent, *the covering thereof*,
4: 8, 11, 12. *with a covering of* badgers' skins,
10. *a covering of* badgers' skins,
25. the tabernacle...*his covering, and the covering of* the badgers' skins

---

4374 **מְכַסֶּה** *m'chas-seh'*, m.

Lev. 9:19. *and that which covereth* (the inwards),
Isa. 14:11. *and* the worms *cover thee*.
23:18. *and for* durable *clothing*.
Eze.27: 7. of Elishah was *that which covered thee*.

4376 **מָכַר** *māh-char'*.

* KAL.—*Preterite*. *

Gen31:15. for *he hath sold us*, and hath
37:36. And the Midianites *sold* him
45: 4. your brother, whom *ye sold* into Egypt.
5. be not grieved,...that *ye sold* me
47:20. the Egyptians *sold* every man his field,
22. *they sold* not their lands.
Ex. 21:16. stealeth a man, *and selleth him*,
35. *then they shall sell* the live ox,
22: 1(21:37). and kill it, or *sell it*;
Lev.25:25. *and hath sold away* (some) of his possession,
27. the man to whom *he sold* it;
27:20. if *he have sold* the field
Deu24: 7. merchandise of him, *or selleth him*;
32:30. except their Rock *had sold them*,
Ru. 4: 3. *selleth* a parcel of land,
Isa. 50: 1. to whom *I have sold* you?
Eze.30:12. *and sell* the land into the hand of
Joel 3: 3(4:3). and *sold* a girl for wine,
6(-:6). *ye sold* unto the Grecians,
7(-:7). the place whither *ye have sold* them,
8(-:8). *And I will sell* your sons
—(-:-). *and they shall sell them* to the Sabeans,

KAL.—*Infinitive*.

Ex. 21: 8. *to sell her* unto a strange nation
Deu14:21. *thou mayest sell* it unto an alien:
21:14. *but* thou shalt not sell her *at all* (lit. *and selling* thou shalt not sell)
Neh 10:31(32). victuals on the sabbath day *to sell*,
13:15. the day *wherein they sold* victuals.
Am. 2: 6. *they sold* the righteous for silver,

KAL.—*Imperative*.

Gen25:31. *Sell* me this day thy birthright.
2K. 4: 7. *sell* the oil, and pay thy debt,

KAL.—*Future*.

Gen25:33. *and he sold* his birthright
37:27. *and let us sell him* to the Ishmeelites,
28. *and sold* Joseph to the Ishmeelites

Ex. 21: 7. if a man *sell* his daughter
Lev.25:14. if *thou sell* (lit. *ye shall sell*) ought unto
15. of the fruits *he shall sell* unto thee:
29. if a man *sell* a dwelling house
Deu21:14. *thou shalt* not *sell her* at all
Jud. 2:14. *and he sold them* into the hands of
3: 8. *and he sold them* into the hand of
4: 2. *And* the Lord *sold them*
9. the Lord *shall sell* Sisera
10: 7. *and he sold them* into the hands of
1Sa.12: 9. *And* when they forgat...*he sold* them into
Neh 5: 8. *will ye* even *sell* your brethren?
Ps. 44:12(13). *Thou sellest* thy people for nought,
Pro.23:23. Buy the truth, and *sell* (it) not;
31:24. She maketh fine linen, *and selleth* (it);
Eze.48:14. *they shall* not *sell* of it,

KAL.—*Participle*. Poël.

Lev.25:16. the fruits *doth* he *sell* unto thee.
Neh 13:16. *and sold* on the sabbath
20. the merchants *and sellers of* all kind of
Isa. 24: 2. as with the buyer, *so with the seller*;
Eze. 7:12. *nor the seller* mourn:
13. *the seller* shall not return
Nah 3: 4. *that selleth* nations
Zec.11: 5. *and they that sell them* say,

* NIPHAL.—*Preterite*. *

Ex. 22: 3(2). *then he shall be sold* for his theft.
Lev.25:39. *and be sold* unto thee;
47. *and sell himself* unto the stranger
48. After that *he is sold*
27:27. *then it shall be sold* according to
Neh 5: 8. *or shall they be sold* unto us?
Est. 7: 4. For *we are sold*, I and my people,
— if *we had been sold* for bondmen
Ps.105:17. Joseph, (who) *was sold* for a servant:
Isa. 50: 1. *have ye sold yourselves*, and for
52: 3. *Ye have sold yourselves* for nought;

NIPHAL.—*Infinitive*.

Lev.25:50. the year *that he was sold*

NIPHAL.—*Future*.

Lev.25:23. The land *shall* not *be sold* for ever:
34. the field...*may* not *be sold*;
42. *they shall* not *be sold*
27:28. no devoted thing,...*shall be sold*
Deu 15:12. if thy brother,...*be sold* unto thee,
Jer. 34:14. which *hath been sold* (marg. or, *hath sold himself*) unto thee;

NIPHAL.—*Participle*.

Neh 5: 8. our brethren...*which were sold*

* HITHPAEL.—*Preterite*. *

Deu28:68. *and* there *ye shall be sold* unto your
1K. 21:25. *did sell himself* to work wickedness

HITHPAEL.—*Infinitive*.

1K. 21:20. *thou hast sold thyself*

HITHPAEL.—*Future*.

2K. 17:17. *and sold themselves* to do evil

מֶכֶר *meh'-cher*, m. 4377

Nu. 20:19. I will *pay for it*: (lit. I will give *the price of them*)
Neh 13:16. all manner of *ware*,
Pro.31:10. *her price* (is) far above rubies.

מַכָּר [*mak-kāhr'*], m. 4378

2K. 12: 5(6). every man of *his acquaintance*:
7(8). receive no (more) money *of your acquaintance*,

מִכְרֶה [*mich-reh'*], m. 4379

Zep. 2: 9. the breeding of nettles, *and saltpits*,

מְכֵרָה [*m'chēh-rāh'*], f. 4380

Gen49: 5. instruments of cruelty (are in) *their habitations*.

See 4351 ## מְכוּרָה see מְכֹרָה

4383 ## מִכְשׁוֹל *mĭch-shōhl*, m.

Lev.19:14. nor put *a stumblingblock* before the blind,
1 Sa.25:31. *nor offence of* heart unto my lord,
Ps.119:165. no*thing* shall *offend* them. (lit. there shall be no *stumbling block* to them)
Isa. 8:14. for a rock of *offence* to both the houses
57:14. take up *the stumbling block*
Jer. 6:21. I will lay *stumbling blocks* before this people,
Eze. 3:20. I lay *a stumblingblock* before him,
7:19. it is *the stumblingblock of* their iniquity.
14: 3. *and* put *the stumblingblock of* their iniquity
4, 7. *and* putteth *the stumblingblock of* his iniquity
18:30. iniquity shall not be your *ruin*. (lit. shall not be *for a stumbling block* to you)
21:15(20). (their) *ruins* be multiplied:
44:12. *caused* the house of Israel *to fall* into iniquity; (marg. were *for a stumbling-block of* iniquity unto)

4384 ## מַכְשֵׁלָה *măch-shēh-lāh'*, f.

Isa. 3: 6. *and* (let) this *ruin* (be) under thy hand:
Zep. 1: 3. *and the stumblingblocks* (marg. or, *idols*) with the wicked:

4385 ## מִכְתָּב *mĭch-tāhv*, m.

Ex. 32:16. *and the writing* (was) *the writing of* God,
39:30. wrote upon it *a writing*,
Deu 10: 4. *according to the* first *writing*,
2Ch 21:12. there came *a writing* to him
35: 4. *and according to the writing of* Solomon his son.
36:22. (put it) also *in writing*,
Ezr. 1: 1. (put it) also *in writing*,
Isa. 38: 9. *The writing* of Hezekiah

4386 ## מְכִתָּה [*m'chit-tāh'*], f.

Isa. 30:14. shall not be found *in the bursting of it*

4387 ## מִכְתָּם *mĭch-tāhm'*, m.

Ps. 16[title](1). *Michtam* of David.
56[title](1). *Michtam* of David, when the Philistines
57[title](1). *Michtam* of David, when he fled
58[title](1) & 59[title](1). Al-taschith, *Michtam* of David.
60[title](1). *Michtam* of David, to teach;

4388 ## מַכְתֵּשׁ *măch-tĕhsh'*, m.

Jud.15:19. God clave *an hollow place*
Pro.27:22. Though thou shouldest bray a fool *in a mortar*

4390 ## מָלֵא *māh-lēh'* & מָלָא [*māh-lāh'*].

* KAL.—*Preterite.* *

Gen 6:13. the earth *is filled* with violence
29:21. my days *are fulfilled*,
Ex. 8:21(17). *and* the houses of the Egyptians *shall be full*
10: 6. *and they shall fill* thy houses,
40:34, 35. the glory of the Lord *filled*
Lev.19:29. *and* the land *become full* of wickedness.
Jos. 3:15. Jordan over*floweth* (lit. *filleth* over) all his banks
Jud.16:27. the house *was full* of men and women;
1 Sa.18:26. the days *were* not *expired*. (marg. *fulfilled*)
1 K. 8:10. the cloud *filled* the house
11. the glory of the Lord *had filled*
2 K. 6:17. the mountain *was full of* horses
1 Ch 17:11. when thy days *be expired*
2 Ch 5:13. the house was *filled* with a cloud,
2Ch 5:14. the glory of the Lord *had filled* the house
7: 1. the glory of the Lord *filled* the house
2. the glory of the Lord *had filled* the Lord's house.
Est. 7: 5. where is he, that *durst presume* (marg. whose heart *hath filled him*)
Job 20:11. His bones *are full of* (the sin) of
21:24. His breasts *are full of* milk,
32:18. *I am full of* matter,
36:16. on thy table *should be full of*
17. *thou hast fulfilled* the judgment of
Ps. 10: 7. His mouth *is full of* cursing
26:10. their right hand *is full of* (marg. *filled with*) bribes.
33: 5. the earth *is full of* the goodness of
38: 7(8). my loins *are filled with* a loathsome
48:10(11). thy right hand *is full of* righteousness.
65: 9(10). the river of God, (which) *is full of* water:
74:20. the dark places of the earth *are full of*
104:24. the earth *is full of* thy riches.
110: 6. *he shall fill* (the places) *with*
119:64. The earth, O Lord, *is full of* thy mercy:
Pro.12:21. the wicked *shall be filled with*
Ecc. 8:11. the heart of the sons of men *is fully set*
9: 3. heart of the sons of men *is full of* evil.
Isa. 1:15. your hands *are full of* blood.
2: 6. *they be replenished* from the east,
11: 9. the earth *shall be full of* the knowledge
13:21. *and* their houses *shall be full of* doleful creatures;
14:21. *nor fill* the face of the world *with*
15: 9. the waters of Dimon *shall be full of* blood:
21: 3. my loins *filled with* pain:
22: 7. thy choicest valleys *shall be full of*
27: 6. *and fill* the face of the world *with*
28: 8. all tables *are full of* vomit
30:27. his lips *are full of* indignation,
34: 6. The sword of the Lord *is filled with* blood
40: 2. her warfare *is accomplished*,
Jer. 6:11. *I am full of* the fury of the Lord;
16:18. *they have filled* mine inheritance *with*
19: 4. *and have filled* this place *with*
23:10. the land *is full of* adulterers;
25:34. your dispersions *are accomplished;*
46:12. thy cry *hath filled* the land:
51: 5. their land *was filled with* sin
Lam.4:18. our days *are fulfilled;*
Eze. 7:23. the land *is full of* bloody crimes, and the city *is full of* violence.
8:17. *they have filled* the land *with* violence,
9: 9. the city *full of* perverseness:
10: 3. the cloud *filled* the inner court.
4. and the court *was full of* the brightness
28:16. *they have filled* the midst of thee *with*
30:11. *and fill* the land *with* the slain.
43: 5. the glory of the Lord *filled* the house.
44: 4. the glory of the Lord *filled* the house
Joel 2:24. *And* the floors *shall be full of* wheat,
3:13(4:13). the press *is full*,
Mic. 3: 8. I *am full of* power by the spirit
6:12. the rich men thereof *are full of* violence,
Hab 3: 3. the earth *was full of* his praise.
Zec. 9:15. *and they shall be filled* (marg. or, *fill both* the) like bowls,

KAL.—*Infinitive.*

Lev. 8:33. the days of your consecration *be at an end:*
12: 4. until the days of her purifying *be fulfilled*,
6. *And when* the days of her purifying *are fulfilled*,
25:30. within *the space* (lit. *the fulfilling*) *of* a full year,
Nu. 6: 5. until the days *be fulfilled*.
13. when the days of his separation *are fulfilled:*
2 K. 4: 6. *when* the vessels *were full*,
Est. 1: 5. *And when* these days *were expired*,
Job 20:22. *In the fulness of* his sufficiency
Jer. 25:12. *when* seventy years *are accomplished*
29:10. after seventy years *be accomplished*
Eze 5: 2. *when* the days of the siege *are fulfilled*
Dan10: 3. till three whole weeks *were fulfilled*.

KAL.—*Imperative.*

Gen 1:22. *and fill* the waters in the seas,
28. *and replenish* the earth,
9: 1. *and replenish* the earth.

Ex. 32:29. *Consecrate* yourselves to day (marg. *Fill* your hands)
1K. 18:33(34). *Fill* four barrels with water,
Jer.51:11. *gather* the shields:

KAL.—*Future.*

Gen25:24. And *when* her days to be delivered *were fulfilled,*
50: 3. *And* forty days *were fulfilled* for him; for so *are fulfilled* the days of those
Ex. 15: 9. my lust *shall be satisfied upon them;* (lit. my soul *shall be full of them*)
2Sa. 7:12. when thy days *be fulfilled,*
Est. 2:12. *were* the days of their purifications *accomplished,*

*NIPHAL.—*Preterite.**

Cant.5: 2. my head *is filled with* dew,

NIPHAL.—*Future.*

Gen 6:11. *and* the earth *was filled with* violence.
Ex. 1: 7. *and* the land *was filled with* them.
7:25. *And* seven days *were fulfilled,*
Nu. 14:21. the earth *shall be filled with*
2Sa.23: 7. the man...*must be fenced* (marg. *filled*) *with*
1K. 7:14. *and he was filled with* wisdom,
2K. 3:17. that valley *shall be filled with*
20. *and* the country *was filled with* water.
10:21. *and* the house of Baal *was full*
Est. 3: 5. *then was* Haman *full of* wrath.
5: 9. *he was full of* indignation
Job 15:32. *It shall be accomplished* (marg. or, *cut off*)
Ps. 71: 8. *Let* my mouth *be filled with*
72:19. *and let* the whole earth *be filled with*
126: 2. Then *was* our mouth *filled with*
Pro. 3:10. *So shall* thy barns *be filled with*
20:17. his mouth *shall be filled with*
24: 4. *shall* the chambers *be filled with*
Ecc. 1: 8. nor the ear *filled with* hearing.
6: 7. the appetite *is* not *filled.*
11: 3. If the clouds *be full of* rain,
Isa. 2: 7. Their land *also is full of* silver
— their land *is also full of* horses,
8. Their land *also is full of* idols;
6: 4. the house *was filled with* smoke.
Jer. 13:12, 12. Every bottle *shall be filled with*
Eze. 9: 9. *and* the land *is full of* (marg. *filled with*)
10: 4. *and* the house *was filled with* the cloud,
23:33. *Thou shalt be filled with* drunkenness
26: 2. *I shall be replenished,* (now) she is
27:25. *and thou wast replenished,* and made
32: 6. the rivers *shall be full of* thee.
Hab 2:14. the earth *shall be filled*
Zec. 8: 5. the streets...*shall be full of* boys and girls

*PIEL.—*Preterite.**

Ex. 28: 3. whom *I have filled with* the spirit
17. *And thou shalt set* (marg. *fill*) in it settings of stones,
41. and shalt anoint them, *and consecrate* them, (marg. *and fill* their hand)
29: 9. *and thou shalt consecrate* Aaron (marg. *and thou shalt fill* the hand of)
35:35. Them *hath he filled with* wisdom
Lev.21:10. *and that is consecrated* (lit. *and that hath filled* his hand)
Nu. 3: 3. whom *he consecrated* (marg. whose hand *he filled*) to minister
32:11. *they have* not *wholly* followed (marg. *fulfilled* after)
12. *they have wholly* followed (lit. *id.*) the Lord.
Deu. 1:36. *he hath wholly* followed (marg. *fulfilled* (to go) after) the Lord.
6:11. houses full of all good (things), which *thou filledst* not,
Jos. 9:13. these bottles of wine, which *we filled,*
14: 8. *I wholly* followed (lit. *filled* after) the Lord
9. *thou hast wholly* followed (lit. *id.*)
14. *he wholly* followed (lit. *id.*)
1K. 1:14. thee, *and confirm* (marg. *fill up*) thy words.
8:15. *hath* with his hand *fulfilled*
24. *and hast fulfilled* (it) with thine hand,
11: 6. *went* not *fully* after (marg. *fulfilled* not after) the Lord,
18:35. *he filled* the trench also *with* water
20:27. the Syrians *filled* the country.
2K. 3:25. cast every man his stone, *and filled it;*
9:24. Jehu *drew* a bow with his *full* strength, (marg. *filled* his hand with a bow)
2K. 21:16. till *he had filled* Jerusalem
2Ch. 6: 4. who *hath* with his hands *fulfilled*
15. and *hast fulfilled* (it) with thine hand,
16:14. the bed which *was filled with* sweet odours
29:31. *ye have consecrated* yourselves (marg. *ye have filled* your hand)
Ezr. 9:11. *have filled it* from one end to another *with*
Job 22:18. he *filled* their houses *with* good (things):
Ps.107: 9. and *filleth* the hungry soul *with*
127: 5. the man that *hath* his quiver *full of*
129: 7. Where*with* the mower *filleth* not his hand;
Isa. 23: 2. *thou whom* the merchants of Zidon,...*have replenished.*
33: 5. *he hath filled* Zion *with* judgment
Jer. 15:17. *thou hast filled me with* indignation.
31:25. *I have replenished* every sorrowful soul.
41: 9. Ishmael the son of Nethaniah *filled* it
44:25. spoken with your mouths, and *fulfilled*
51:14. *I will fill thee with* men,
34. *he hath filled* his belly *with* my delicates,
Eze.11: 6. *and ye have filled* the streets thereof *with*
32: 5. *and fill* the valleys *with* thy height.
35: 8. *and I will fill* his mountains *with*
43:26. *and they shall consecrate* themselves. (marg. *fill* their hands)
Hag. 2: 7. *and I will fill* this house *with* glory,
Zec. 9:13. *filled* the bow *with* Ephraim,

PIEL.—*Infinitive.*

Ex. 29:29. *and to be consecrated* (lit. *and to fill* their hand)
33. *to consecrate* (lit. *to fill* their hands) (and) to sanctify them:
31: 5. in cutting of stones, *to set* (them),
35:33. in the cutting of stones, *to set* (them).
1K. 2:27. *that he might fulfil* the word of the Lord,
1Ch 29: 5. *to consecrate* his service (lit. *to fill* his hand)
2Ch 13: 9. *to consecrate* himself (marg. *to fill* his hand)
36:21. *To fulfil* the word of the Lord
— *to fulfil* threescore and ten years.
Job 20:22. (כתיב). *In the fulness of* his sufficiency
23. (When) he is about *to fill* his belly,
Pro. 6:30. if he steal *to satisfy* his soul
Jer. 33: 5. *but* (it is) *to fill them* with the dead bodies
Dan. 9: 2. *that he would accomplish* seventy years

PIEL.—*Imperative.*

Gen29:27. *Fulfil* her week,
44: 1. *Fill* the men's sacks *with* food,
1Sa.16: 1. *fill* thine horn *with* oil,
Ps. 83:16(17). *Fill* their faces *with* shame;
Jer. 4: 5. *gather together,* and say, Assemble
Eze. 9: 7. *and fill* the courts *with* the slain:
10: 2. *and fill* thine hand *with* coals
24: 4. *fill* (it) *with* the choice bones.

PIEL.—*Future.*

Gen21:19. *and filled* the bottle *with* water,
24:16. *and filled* her pitcher, and came up.
26:15. *and filled them with* earth.
29:28. Jacob did so, *and fulfilled* her week:
42:25. commanded *to fill* (lit. *and they filled*)
Ex. 2:16. *and filled* the troughs to water
23:26. the number of thy days *I will fulfil.*
29:35. *shalt thou consecrate* them. (lit. *fill* their hand)
31: 3. *And I have filled* him *with* the spirit
35:31. *And he hath filled him with* the spirit
39:10. *And they set* (lit. *filled*) in it four rows
Lev. 8:33. *shall he consecrate* you. (lit. *fill* your hand)
9:17. *and took* an hand*ful* (marg. *and filled* his hand)
16:32. whom *he shall consecrate* (lit. whose hands *he shall fill*)
Nu. 14:24. *and hath* followed me *fully,* (lit. *hath filled* after me)
Jud.17: 5. *and consecrated* (marg. *and filled* the hand of) one of his sons,
12. *And* Micah *consecrated* (lit. *filled* the hand of) the Levite;
1Sa. 18:27. *and they gave them in full tale* to the
1K. 13:33. *he consecrated* him, (lit. *he filled* his hand)
2K. 23:14. *and filled* their places *with* the bones of
24: 4. *for he filled* Jerusalem *with* innocent
Job 8:21. Till *he fill* thy mouth *with* laughing,
15: 2. *and fill* his belly *with* the east wind?
23: 4. and *fill* my mouth *with* arguments.

Job 38:39. or *fill* the appetite of the young lions,
39: 2. the months (that) *they fulfil?*
41: 7(40:31). *Canst thou fill* his skin *with* barbed
Ps. 17:14. whose belly *thou fillest with* thy hid
20: 4(5). and *fulfil* all thy counsel.
5(6). the Lord *fulfil* all thy petitions.
80: 9(10). *and it filled* the land.
81:10(11). open thy mouth wide, *and I will fill it.*
Pro. 1:13. *we shall fill* our houses *with* spoil:
8:21. *I will fill* their treasures.
Isa. 65:20. an old man that *hath* not *filled* his days:
Eze. 3: 3. *fill* thy bowels *with* this roll
7:19. neither *fill* their bowels:
Nah. 2:12(13). *and filled* his holes *with* prey,

PIEL.—*Participle.*

1Ch 12:15. when it *had overflown* (marg. *filled* over) all his banks;
Job 3:15. *who filled* their houses *with* silver:
Isa. 65:11. *and that furnish* the drink offering
Jer. 13:13. I will *fill* all the inhabitants
Zep. 1: 9. *which fill* their masters' houses

* PUAL.—*Participle.* *

Cant.5:14. gold rings *set* (lit. *filled*) with the beryl:

* HITHPAEL.—*Future.* *

Job 16:10. *they have gathered themselves* together

4391 מְלָא [*m'lāh*]. Ch.

* P'AL.—*Preterite.* *

Dan 2:35. *and filled* the whole earth.

* ITHP'AL.—*Preterite.* *

Dan 3:19. Then was Nebuchadnezzar *full* (marg. *filled*) *of* fury,

---

4392 מָלֵא *māh-lēh'*, adj.

Gen23: 9. money *as it is worth* (marg. *full* money)
41: 7. the seven rank *and full* ears.
22. seven ears came up...*full* and good:
Nu. 7:13. both of them (were) *full of* fine flour
14, 20. One spoon...of gold, *full of* incense:
19, 25, 31, 37, 43, 49, 55, 61, 67, 73, 79. both of them *full of* fine flour
26, 32, 38, 44, 50, 56, 62, 68, 74, 80. One golden spoon...*full of* incense:
86. The golden spoons (were) twelve, *full of*
Deu 6:11. houses *full of* all good (things),
33:23. *and full with* the blessing of the Lord:
34: 9. *full of* the spirit of wisdom;
Ru. 1:21. I went out *full*,
2Sa.23:11. a piece of ground *full of* lentiles:
2K. 4: 4. *and* thou shalt set aside *that which is full.*
7:15. *full of* garments and vessels,
1Ch 11:13. a parcel of ground *full of* barley;
21:22. grant it me for the *full* price:
24. buy it for the *full* price:
Neh 9:25. possessed houses *full of* all goods,
Ps. 73:10. waters of *a full* (cup)
75: 8(9). it is *full of* mixture;
144:13. (That) our garners (may be) *full*,
Pro.17: 1. an house *full of* sacrifices
Ecc. 1: 7. yet the sea (is) not *full*;
11: 5. the womb of *her that is with child:*
Isa. 1:21. it was *full of* judgment; righteousness
6: 1. his train *filled* the temple.
22: 2. Thou that art *full of* stirs,
51:20. *they are full of* the fury of the Lord,
Jer. 4:12. a *full* wind from those (places)
5:27. As a cage is *full of* birds, so (are) their houses *full of* deceit:
6:11. the aged with (him that is) *full of* days.
12: 6. they have called *a multitude* (marg. or, cried...*fully*)
23:24. Do not I *fill* heaven and earth?
35: 5. pots *full of* wine, and cups,
Eze. 1:18. their rings (were) *full of* eyes
10:12. *full of* eyes round about,
17: 3. longwinged, *full of* feathers,
28:12. *full of* wisdom, and perfect in beauty.
36:38. so shall the waste cities be *filled with*
37: 1. the valley which (was) *full of* bones,
Am. 2:13. as a cart...*full of* sheaves.
Nah 1:10. as stubble *fully* dry.
3: 1. *full of* lies (and) robbery

מְלֹא *m'lōh*, m. 4393

Gen48:19. his seed shall become *a multitude* (marg. *fulness*) *of* nations.
Ex. 9: 8. Take to you hand*fuls* of ashes (lit. *the fulness of* your hands)
16:32. *Fill* an omer of it
33. put an omer *full* (lit. *the fulness of* an omer) of manna
Lev. 2: 2. he shall take thereout his hand*ful* (lit. *the fulness of* his hand)
5:12. the priest shall take his hand*ful* of (lit. *the fulness of* his hand)
16:12. he shall take a censer *full* (lit. *the fulness of* a censer)
— *and* his hands *full* (lit. *and the fulness of* his hands)
Nu. 22:18 & 24:13. If Balak would give me his house *full* (lit. *the fulness of* his house)
Deu 33:16. things of the earth *and fulness thereof*,
Jud. 6:38. a bowl *full* of water.
1Sa. 28:20. Saul fell straightway *all along* (marg *the fulness of* his stature) on the earth,
2Sa. 8: 2. *and with* one *full* line (lit. *the fulness of* a line) to keep alive.
1K. 17:12. an hand*ful* of meal in a barrel,
2K. 4:39. gathered...wild gourds his lap *full*,
1Ch 16:32. Let the sea roar, *and the fulness thereof:*
Ps. 24: 1. The earth (is) the Lord's, *and the fulness thereof;*
50:12. world (is) mine, *and the fulness thereof.*
89:11(12). the world *and the fulness thereof,*
96:11 & 98:7. the sea roar, *and the fulness thereof.*
Ecc. 4: 6. Better (is) an hand*ful* (with) quietness, *than* both the hands *full*
Isa. 6: 3. the whole earth (is) *full of* his glory. (marg. his glory is *the fulness of* the whole earth)
8: 8. shall *fill* the breadth of thy land, (marg. *fulness of* the breadth of thy land shall be)
31: 4. *a multitude of* shepherds
34: 1. the earth hear, *and all that is therein;*
42:10. the sea, *and all that is therein;* (marg *the fulness thereof*)
Jer. 8:16. land, *and all that is in it;* (marg. *id.*)
47: 2. land, *and all that is therein;* (marg. *id.*
Eze.12:19. desolate *from all that is therein,* (marg. *the fulness thereof*)
19: 7. the land...*and the fulness thereof,*
30:12. the land...*and all that is therein,* (marg. *the fulness thereof*)
32:15. *of that whereof it was full,* (marg. *from the fulness thereof*)
41: 8. of the side chambers (were) a *full* reed
Am. 6: 8. the city *with all that is therein.* (marg. *the fulness thereof*)
Mic. 1: 2. O earth, *and all that therein is:* (marg. *id.*)

מְלֵאָה *m'lēh-āh'*, f. 4395

Ex. 22:29(28). *the first of thy ripe fruits,* (marg. *thy fulness*)
Nu. 18:27. *and as the fulness* of the winepress.
Deu 22: 9. *the fruit of* thy seed

מִלֻּאָה [*mil-loo-āh'*], f. 4396

Ex. 28:17. set in it *settings of* stones, (marg. *fillings*)
20. set in gold *in their inclosings.* (marg. *id.*)
39:13. inclosed...*in their inclosings.*

מִלֻּאִים *mil-loo-eem'*, m. pl. 4394

Ex. 25: 7. *to be set* in the ephod,
29:22. a ram of *consecration:*
26. the ram of Aaron's *consecration,*
27, 31. the ram of *the consecration,*
34. the flesh of *the consecrations,*
35: 9, 27. stones *to be set* for the ephod,
Lev. 7:37. *and of the consecrations,* and of the
8:22. the ram of *consecration:*
28. *consecrations* for a sweet savour:
29. of the ram of *consecration*

Lev. 8:31. in the basket of *consecrations,*
33. the days of *your consecration*
1Ch 29: 2. *and* (stones) *to be set,* glistering stones,

4397 **מַלְאָךְ** *mal-āh'ch',* m.

Gen16: 7. *the angel of* the Lord found her
9,10,11. And *the angel of* the Lord said unto her,
19: 1. there came two *angels* to Sodom
15. then *the angels* hastened Lot,
21:17. *the angel of* God called to Hagar
22:11. *the angel of* the Lord called unto him
15. *the angel of* the Lord called unto
24: 7. he shall send *his angel*
40. will send *his angel* with thee,
28:12. *the angels of* God ascending
31:11. *the angel of* God spake unto me
32. 1(2). on his way, and *the angels of* God met him.
3(4). Jacob sent *messengers* before
6(7). *the messengers* returned to Jacob,
48:16. *The Angel* which redeemed me
Ex. 3: 2. *the angel of* the Lord appeared
14:19. *the angel of* God, which went before
23:20. I send *an Angel* before thee,
23. *mine Angel* shall go before thee,
32:34. *mine Angel* shall go before thee:
33: 2. I will send *an angel*
Nu. 20:14. Moses sent *messengers*
16. he heard our voice, and sent *an angel,*
21:21. Israel sent *messengers* unto Sihon
22: 5. He sent *messengers* therefore
22. *the angel of* the Lord stood
23,25,27. the ass saw *the angel of*
24. *the angel of* the Lord stood
26. *the angel of* the Lord went further,
31. he saw *the angel of* the Lord
32. *the angel of* the Lord said unto him,
34. Balaam said unto *the angel of*
35. *the angel of* the Lord said unto Balaam,
24:12. Spake I not also to *thy messengers*
Deu 2:26. I sent *messengers* out of the wilderness
Jos. 6:17. she hid *the messengers* that we sent.
25. she hid *the messengers,* which Joshua
7:22. So Joshua sent *messengers,*
Jud. 2: 1. *an angel* (marg. or, *messenger*) *of* the Lord
4. when *the angel of* the Lord spake
5:23. Curse ye Meroz, said *the angel of* the Lord,
6:11. there came *an angel of* the Lord,
12. *the angel of* the Lord appeared
20. *the angel of* God said unto him,
21. *the angel of* the Lord put forth
— *Then the angel of* the Lord departed
22. perceived that he (was) *an angel of*
— I have seen *an angel of* the Lord
35. *And* he sent *messengers* throughout all
— *and* he sent *messengers* unto Asher,
7:24. *And* Gideon sent *messengers*
9:31. he sent *messengers* unto Abimelech
11:12. Jephthah sent *messengers* unto the king
13. *the messengers of* Jephthah,
14. Jephthah sent *messengers* again
17. Israel sent *messengers* unto the king
19. Israel sent *messengers* unto Sihon
13: 3. *the angel of* the Lord appeared
6. the countenance of *an angel of*
9. *the angel of* God came again
13, 16. *the angel of* the Lord said
15, 17. Manoah said unto *the angel of* the Lord,
16. Manoah knew not that he (was) *an angel of*
18. And *the angel of* the Lord said
20. *the angel of* the Lord ascended
21. *the angel of* the Lord did no more appear
— Manoah knew that he (was) *an angel of*
1Sa. 6:21. they sent *messengers* to the inhabitants
11: 3. that we may send *messengers*
4. Then came *the messengers* to Gibeah
7. by the hands of *messengers,* saying,
9. they said *unto the messengers*
— *the messengers* came and shewed
16:19. Saul sent *messengers* unto Jesse,
19:11. Saul also sent *messengers* unto
14,20. Saul sent *messengers* to take
15. Saul sent *the messengers* (again)
16. when *the messengers* were come

1Sa. 19:20. *the messengers of* Saul, and they
21. he sent other *messengers,* and they
— Saul sent *messengers* again
23:27. *But* there came *a messenger* unto Saul,
25:14. David sent *messengers*
42. she went after *the messengers of*
29: 9. in my sight, *as an angel of* God:
2Sa. 2: 5. David sent *messengers*
3:12. Abner sent *messengers*
14. David sent *messengers*
26. he sent *messengers* after Abner,
5:11. Hiram king of Tyre sent *messengers*
11: 1. (כתיב)when *kings* go forth
4. David sent *messengers,*
19. And charged *the messenger,*
22. So *the messenger* went,
23. *the messenger* said unto David,
25. David said unto *the messenger,*
12:27. Joab sent *messengers*
14:17. *as an angel of* God, so (is) my lord
20. to the wisdom of *an angel of* God,
19:27(28). the king (is) *as an angel of* God:
24:16. when *the angel* stretched out his hand
— *to the angel* that destroyed the people,
— *And the angel of* the Lord was by
17. *the angel* that smote the people,
1K. 13:18. *and an angel* spake unto me
19: 2. Jezebel sent *a messenger*
5. *an angel* touched him,
7. *the angel of* the Lord came again
20: 2. he sent *messengers* to Ahab
5. *the messengers* came again,
9. *unto the messengers of* Ben-hadad,
— *the messengers* departed,
22:13. *And the messenger* that was gone
2K. 1: 2. he sent *messengers,*
3. *But the angel of* the Lord said
— *the messengers of* the king of Samaria,
5. when *the messengers* turned back
15. *the angel of* the Lord said
16. thou hast sent *messengers* to enquire
5:10. Elisha sent *a messenger*
6:32. ere *the messenger* came to him,
— when *the messenger* cometh,
33. *the messenger* came down unto him:
7:15. *the messengers* returned,
9:18. *The messenger* came to them,
10: 8. there came *a messenger,*
14: 8. Amaziah sent *messengers*
16: 7. Ahaz sent *messengers*
17: 4. he had sent *messengers* to So
19: 9. he sent *messengers* again unto
14. letter of the hand of *the messengers,*
23. By *thy messengers* thou hast reproached
35. *the angel of* the Lord went out,
1Ch 14: 1. Hiram king of Tyre sent *messengers*
19: 2. David sent *messengers*
16. they sent *messengers,* and drew
21:12. *and the angel of* the Lord destroying
15. God sent *an angel* unto
— *to the angel* that destroyed,
— *And the angel of* the Lord stood
16. saw *the angel of* the Lord stand
18. *Then the angel of* the Lord commanded
20. Ornan turned back, and saw *the angel;*
27. And the Lord commanded *the angel;*
30. the sword of *the angel of* the Lord.
2Ch 18:12. *And the messenger* that went to call Micaiah
32:21. the Lord sent *an angel,*
35:21. he sent *ambassadors* to him,
36:15. sent to them by *his messengers,*
16. they mocked *the messengers of* God,
Neh 6: 3. And I sent *messengers* unto them,
Job 1:14. *And* there came *a messenger* unto Job,
4:18. *and his angels* he charged with folly:
33:23. If there be *a messenger* with him,
Ps. 34: 7(8). *The angel of* the Lord encampeth
35: 5. *and* let *the angel of* the Lord chase (them).
6. *and* let *the angel of* the Lord persecute them.
78:49. by sending evil *angels* (among them).
91:11. he shall give *his angels* charge over thee,
103:20. Bless the Lord, ye *his angels,*
104: 4. Who maketh *his angels* spirits;
148: 2. Praise ye him, all *his angels:*
Pro. 13:17. *A* wicked *messenger* falleth into mischief
16:14. (as) *messengers of* death:
17:11. *therefore a* cruel *messenger* shall be sent

Ecc. 5: 6(5). neither say thou before *the angel,*
Isa. 14:32. *the messengers of* the nation?
18: 2. Go, ye swift *messengers,*
30: 4. *and his ambassadors* came to Hanes.
33: 7. *the ambassadors of* peace shall weep bitterly.
37: 9. he sent *messengers* to Hezekiah,
14. from the hand of *the messengers,*
36. *the angel of* the Lord went forth,
42:19. *as my messenger* (that) I sent?
44:26. performeth the counsel of *his messengers,*
63: 9. *and the angel of* his presence saved them:
Jer. 27: 3. by the hand of *the messengers*
Eze. 17:15. in sending *his ambassadors* into Egypt,
23:16. sent *messengers* unto them into Chaldea.
40. unto whom *a messenger* (was) sent;
30: 9. In that day shall *messengers* go forth
Hos. 12: 4(5). he had power over *the angel,*
Nah 2:13(14). the voice of *thy messengers*
Hag. 1:13. Haggai the Lord's *messenger*
Zec. 1: 9. *the angel* that talked with me
11. they answered *the angel of* the Lord
12. *the angel of* the Lord answered
13. the Lord answered *the angel*
14. *the angel* that communed with me
19(2:2). I said unto *the angel*
2: 3(7). *the angel* that talked with me went forth, *and* another *angel* went out
3: 1. *the angel of* the Lord, and Satan
3. stood before *the angel.*
5. *And the angel of* the Lord stood by.
6. *the angel of* the Lord protested
4: 1. *the angel* that talked with me came
4. spake to *the angel* that talked with me,
5. *the angel* that talked with me answered
5: 5. *the angel* that talked with me went
10. Then said I to *the angel*
6: 4. I answered and said unto *the angel*
5. *the angel* answered and said
12: 8. *as the angel of* the Lord
Mal. 2: 7. *the messenger of* the Lord of hosts.
3: 1. I will send *my messenger,*
— *even the messenger of* the covenant,

4398 מַלְאַךְ [*mal-ăhch'*], Ch. m.

Dan 3:28. who hath sent *his angel,* and delivered
6:22(23). My God hath sent *his angel,* and hath

4399 מְלָאכָה *m'lāh-chāh'*, f.

Gen 2: 2. on the seventh day God ended *his work*
— on the seventh day from all *his work*
3. he had rested from all *his work*
33:14. according as *the cattle* (marg. according to the foot of *the work*)...be able
39:11. went into the house to do *his business;*
Ex. 12:16. no manner of *work* shall be done
20: 9. and do all *thy work:*
10. (in it) thou shalt not do any *work,*
22: 8(7), 11(10). put his hand *unto* his neighbour's *goods.*
31: 3. and in all manner of *workmanship,*
5. to work in all manner of *workmanship.*
14. whosoever doeth (any) *work* therein,
15. Six days may *work* be done;
— whosoever doeth (any) *work*
35: 2. Six days shall *work* be done,
— whosoever doeth *work* therein
21. to *the work of* the tabernacle
24. for any *work of* the service,
29. to bring for all manner of *work,*
31. in all *manner of workmanship;*
33. to make any manner of cunning *work.*
35. to work all *manner of work, of* the engraver,
— them that do any *work,*
36: 1. all *manner of work for* the service
2. to come unto *the work*
3. *for the work of* the service of the sanctuary,
4. wrought all *the work of* the sanctuary, came every man *from his work*
5. the service *of the work,*
6. nor woman make any more *work*
7. *For the stuff* they had was sufficient for all *the work*

Ex. 36: 8. that wrought *the work* of the tabernacle
38:24. the gold that was occupied *for the work* in all *the work of* the holy (place),
39:43. Moses did look upon all *the work,*
40:33. So Moses finished *the work.*
Lev. 7:24. may be used in any other *use:*
11:32. wherein (any) *work* is done,
13:48. any *thing made of* skin; (marg. any *work of* skin)
51. (or) in any *work* that is made of skin;
16:29. and do no *work* at all,
23: 3. Six days shall *work* be done:
— ye shall do no *work* (therein):
7, 8, 21, 25, 35, 36. ye shall do no servile *work*
28. ye shall do no *work* in that same day:
30. that doeth any *work* in that same day,
31. Ye shall do no manner of *work:*
Nu. 4: 3. to do *the work* in the tabernacle
28:18. ye shall do no manner of servile *work*
25, 26, & 29:1. ye shall do no servile *work.*
29: 7. ye shall not do any *work* (therein):
12, 35. ye shall do no servile *work,*
Deu 5:13. and do all *thy work:*
14. thou shalt not do any *work,*
16: 8. thou shalt do no *work* (therein).
Jud. 16:11. new ropes that never were occupied, (marg. wherewith *work* hath not been done)
1Sa. 8:16. and put (them) *to his work.*
15: 9. every *thing* (that was) vile and refuse,
1K. 5:16(30). officers which (were) over *the work,*
—(—). the people that wrought *in the work.*
7:14. cunning to work all *works*
— and wrought all *his work.*
22. *the work of* the pillars finished.
40. Hiram made an end of doing all *the work*
51. So was ended all *the work*
9:23. that (were) over Solomon's *work,*
— the people that wrought *in the work.*
11:28. that he was *industrious,* (marg. did *work*)
2K. 12:11(12). the hands of them that did *the work,*
14(15). they gave that to the *work*men, (lit. doers of *the work*)
15(16). the money to be bestowed on *work*-men: (lit. doers of *the work*)
22: 5. deliver it into the hand of the doers of *the work,*
— let them give it to the doers of *the work*
9. into the hand of them that do *the work,*
1Ch 4:23. they dwelt with the king *for his work.*
6:49(34). all *the work of* the (place) most holy,
9:13. very able men for *the work of*
19. *the work of* the service,
33. they were employed *in* (that) *work*
22:15. (there are) *work*men (lit. doers of *the work*) with thee
— for every *manner of work.*
23: 4. *the work of* the house of the Lord;
24. that did *the work* for the service
25: 1. the number of the *work*men (lit. men of *work*)
26:29. his sons (were) *for the* outward *business*
30. in all *the business of* the Lord,
27:26. that did *the work of* the field
28:13. for all *the work of* the service
19. (even) all *the works of* this pattern.
20. until thou hast finished all *the work for*
21. for all *manner of workmanship*
29: 1. *and the work* (is) great:
5. for all *manner of work*
6. with the rulers of the king's *work,*
2Ch 4:11. Huram finished *the work*
5: 1. all *the work* that Solomon made
8: 9. make no servants *for his work;*
16. all *the work of* Solomon was prepared
13:10. the Levites (wait) *upon* (their) *business:*
16: 5. and let *his work* cease.
17:13. *And* he had much *business*
24:12. such as did *the work of*
13. So the *work*men (lit. doers of *the work*)
— *the work* was perfected (marg. the healing went up *upon the work*)
29:34. till *the work* was ended,
34:10. they put (it) in the hand of the *work*men
— they gave it to the *work*men
12. the men did *the work* faithfully:
13. all that wrought *the work*
17. to the hand of the *work*men

Ezr. 2:69. the treasure of *the work*
3: 8. to set forward *the work of*
9. to set forward the *work*men
6:22. to strengthen their hands *in the work of*
10:13. *neither* (is this) *a work* of one day or two:
Neh. 2:16. nor to the rest that did *the work.*
4:11(5). cause *the work* to cease.
15(9). every one unto *his work.*
16(10). of my servants wrought *in the work,*
17(11). one of his hands wrought *in the work,*
19(13). *The work* (is) great and large,
21(15). So we laboured *in the work:*
22(16). and *labour* on the day.
5:16. I continued *in the work of* this wall
— gathered thither unto *the work.*
6: 3. I (am) doing *a great work,*
— why should *the work* cease,
9. hands shall be weakened from *the work,*
16. this *work* was wrought of our God.
7:70. the fathers gave *unto the work.*
71. the treasure of *the work*
10:33(34). *the work of* the house of our God.
11:12. their brethren that did *the work*
16. *the* outward *business* of the house of God.
22. *the business of* the house of God.
13:10. Levites and the singers, that did *the work,*
30. every one *in his business;*
Est. 3: 9. those that have the charge of *the business,*
9: 3. officers (marg. those which did *the business*) of the king,
Ps. 73:28. that I may declare all *thy works.*
107:23. that do *business* in great waters;
Pro. 18: 9. He also that is slothful *in his work*
22:29. Seest thou a man diligent *in his business?*
24:27. Prepare *thy work* without,
Jer. 17:22. neither do ye any *work,*
24. to do no *work* therein;
18: 3. he wrought *a work* on the wheels.
48:10. *the work of* the Lord deceitfully,
50:25. this (is) *the work* of the Lord
Eze. 15: 3. wood be taken thereof to do any *work?*
4. Is it meet *for* (any) *work?*
5. it was meet *for* no *work:*
— shall it be meet yet *for* (any) *work,*
28:13. *the workmanship of* thy tabrets
Dan. 8:27. I rose up, and did the king's *business;*
Jon. 1: 8. What (is) *thine occupation?*
Hag. 1:14. they came and did *work*

4400 מַלְאֲכוּת *mal-ăchooth'*, f. const.

Hag. 1:13. *in* the Lord's *message* unto the people,

4402 מִלֵּאת *mil-lēhth'*, f.

Cant. 5:12. His eyes (are) as (the eyes) of doves... *fitly* set. (marg. sitting in *fulness*)

4403 מַלְבּוּשׁ *mal-boosh'*, m.

1K. 10: 5. his ministers, *and their apparel,*
2K. 10:22. he brought them forth *vestments.*
2Ch. 9: 4. his ministers, *and their apparel;* his cupbearers also, *and their apparel;*
Job 27:16. and prepare *raiment* as the clay;
Isa. 63: 3. I will stain all *my raiment.*
Eze. 16:13. *and thy raiment* (was of) fine linen,
Zep. 1: 8. such as are clothed with strange *apparel.*

4404 מַלְבֵּן *mal-bēhn'*, m.

2Sa. 12:31. made them pass *through the brickkiln:*
Jer. 43: 9. the clay *in the brickkiln,*
Nah. 3:14. make strong *the brickkiln.*

4405 מִלָּה *mil-lāh'*, f.

2Sa. 23: 2. *and his word* (was) in my tongue.
Job 4: 2. who can withhold himself *from speaking?* (marg. *from words*)
Job 4: 4. *Thy words* have upholden him
6:26. Do ye imagine to reprove *words,*
8:10. utter *words* out of their heart?
12:11. Doth not the ear try *words?*
13:17. Hear diligently *my speech,*
15: 3. *or with speeches* wherewith
13. lettest (such) *words* go out of thy mouth?
16: 4. I could heap up *words* against you,
18: 2. (ere) ye make an end *of words?*
19: 2. and break me in pieces *with words?*
23. Oh that *my words* were now written!
21: 2. Hear diligently *my speech,*
23: 5. I would know *the words* (which)
24:25. and make *my speech* nothing worth?
26: 4. To whom hast thou uttered *words?*
29: 9. The princes refrained *talking,*
22. *my speech* dropped upon them.
30: 9. I am their *byword.*
32:11. ye searched out *what to say.* (marg. *words*)
14. hath not directed (his) *words* against me:
15. they left off *speaking.* (marg. removed *speeches* from themselves)
18. I am full of *matter,* (marg. *words*)
33: 1. Job, I pray thee, hear *my speeches,*
8. I have heard the voice of (thy) *words,*
32. If thou hast *any thing to say,*
34: 2. Hear *my words,* O ye wise (men);
3. the ear trieth *words,*
16. hearken to the voice of *my words.*
35: 4. I will answer thee, (marg. return to thee *words*)
16. he multiplieth *words* without knowledge.
36: 2. that (I have) yet *to speak* (marg. *words*)
4. *my words* (shall) not (be) false:
38: 2. that darkeneth counsel *by words*
Ps. 19: 4(5). *their words* to the end of the world.
139: 4. not *a word* in my tongue,
Pro. 23: 9. the wisdom of *thy words.*

מִלָּה *mil-lāh'*, Ch. f. 4406

Dan. 2: 5. *The thing* is gone from me: if ye
8. ye see *the thing* is gone from me.
9. prepared lying *and* corrupt *words*
10. that can shew the king's *matter:*
— lord, nor ruler, (that) asked such *things*
11. *And* (it is) *a* rare *thing* that the king
15. Arioch made *the thing* known to Daniel.
17. and made *the thing* known to Hananiah,
23. made known unto us the king's *matter.*
3:22. the king's *commandment* was urgent,
28. *and* have changed the king's *word,*
4:31(28). While *the word* (was) in the king's
33(30). The same hour was *the thing* fulfilled
5:10. the queen by reason of *the words of*
15. not shew the interpretation of *the thing:*
26. This (is) the interpretation of *the thing:*
6:12(13). *The thing* (is) true,
14(15). Then the king, when he heard (these) *words,*
7: 1. (and) told the sum of *the matters.* (marg. or, *words*)
11. the voice of *the* great *words*
16. the interpretation of *the things.*
25. *And* he shall speak (great) *words*
28. Hitherto (is) the end of *the matter.*
— *but* I kept *the matter* in my heart.

מְלוֹ, מְלוֹא, see מְלֹא See 4393

מִלּוּאִים see מִלֻּאִים See 4394

מַלּוּחַ *mal-loo'ăch*, m. 4408

Job 30: 4. Who cut up *mallows* by the bushes,

מְלוּכָה *m'loo-chāh'*, f. 4410

1Sa. 10:16. the matter of *the kingdom,*
25. the manner of *the kingdom,*

1Sa. 11:14. and renew *the kingdom*
14:47. Saul took *the kingdom*
18: 8. (what) can he have more but *the kingdom?*
2Sa. 12:26. and took the *royal* city. (lit. city of *the kingdom*)
16: 8. the Lord hath delivered *the kingdom*
1K. 1:46. the throne of *the kingdom.*
2:15. *the kingdom* was mine,
— *the kingdom* is turned about,
22. ask for him *the kingdom*
11:35. I will take *the kingdom*
12:21. to bring *the kingdom* again
21: 7. *the kingdom* of Israel?
2K. 25:25. the seed *royal*, (marg. *the kingdom*)
1Ch 10:14. turned *the kingdom* unto David
Ps. 22:28(29). *the kingdom* (is) the Lord's:
Isa. 34:12. call the nobles...to *the kingdom*,
62: 3. a *royal* diadem (lit. diadem of *the kingdom*)
Jer. 41: 1. the seed *royal*, (lit. seed of *the kingdom*)
Eze. 16:13. thou didst prosper *into a kingdom.*
17:13. hath taken of *the king's* seed, (lit. of the seed of *the kingdom*)
Dan. 1: 3. and of *the king's* seed, (lit. *id.*)
Obad. 21. *the kingdom* shall be the Lord's.

4411 מָלוֹן *māh-lōhn'*, m.

Gen 42:27. to give his ass provender *in the inn,*
43:21. when we came to *the inn,*
Ex. 4:24. by the way *in the inn,*
Jos. 4: 3. leave them *in the lodging place,*
8. unto *the place where they lodged,*
2K. 19:23. I will enter into *the lodgings of*
Isa. 10:29. they have taken up their *lodging*
Jer. 9: 2(1). *a lodging place of* wayfaring men;

4412 מְלוּנָה *m'loo-nāh'*, f.

Isa. 1: 8. *as a lodge* in a garden
24:20. shall be removed *like a cottage;*

4414 מָלַח [*māh-lağh'*].

* KAL.—*Future.* *

Lev. 2:13. *shalt thou season* (lit. *thou shalt salt*) with

* PUAL.—*Participle.* *

Ex. 30:35. *tempered together,* (marg. *salted*) pure

* HOPHAL.—*Preterite.* *

Eze. 16: 4. *thou wast* not *salted* at all,

HOPHAL.—*Infinitive.*

Eze. 16: 4. thou wast not salted *at all,* (lit. *being salted* thou wast not salted)

4414 מָלַח [*māh-lağh'*].

* NIPHAL.—*Preterite.* *

Isa. 51: 6. the heavens *shall vanish away*

4417 מֶלַח *meh'-lağh*, m.

Gen 14: 3. the vale of Siddim, which is the *salt* sea.
19:26. she became a pillar of *salt.*
Lev. 2:13. shalt thou season *with salt;* neither shalt thou suffer *the salt of*
— all thine offerings thou shalt offer *salt.*
Nu. 18:19. a covenant of *salt* for ever
34: 3. outmost coast of the *salt* sea eastward:
12. at the *salt* sea: this shall be
Deu 3:17. the sea of the plain, (even) the *salt* sea,
29:23(22). land thereof (is) brimstone, *and salt,*
Jos. 3:16. the sea of the plain, (even) the *salt* sea,
12: 3. the *salt* sea on the east,
15: 2. the shore of the *salt* sea,
5. the east border (was) the *salt* sea,
18:19. the north bay of the *salt* sea
Jud. 9:45. down the city, and sowed it with *salt.*
2Sa. 8:13. in the valley of *salt,*
2K. 2:20. Bring me a new cruse, and put *salt*
21. and cast *the salt* in there,
14: 7. in the valley of *salt*
1Ch 18:12. in the valley of *salt*
2Ch 13: 5. by a covenant of *salt?*
25:11. and went to the valley of *salt,*
Job 6: 6. which is unsavoury be eaten without *salt?*
Ps. 60[title](2). in the valley of *salt*
Eze. 43:24. the priests shall cast *salt* upon
47:11. they shall be given *to salt.*
Zep. 2: 9. the breeding of nettles, and *salt*pits,

מְלַח [*m'lağh*], Ch. 4415

* P'AL.—*Preterite.* *

Ezr. 4:14. Now because *we have* maintenance (marg *are salted* with the salt of)

מְלַח *m'lağh*, Ch. m. 4416

Ezr. 4:14. because we have *maintenance from* the (marg. are salted with *the salt of*)
6: 9. wheat, *salt*, wine, and oil,
7:22. *and salt* without prescribing

מַלָּח [*mal-lāhğh'*] m. 4419

Eze. 27: 9. the ships...*with their mariners*
27. *thy mariners*, and thy pilots,
29. *the mariners*, (and) all the pilots
Jon. 1: 5. *the mariners* were afraid,

מְלֵחָה *m'lēh-ğhāh'*, f. 4420

Job 39: 6. *the barren land* (marg. *salt places*) his
Ps. 107:34. A fruitful land *into barrenness,*
Jer. 17: 6. a *salt* land and not inhabited.

מְלָחִים *m'lāh-ğheem'*, m. pl. 4418

Jer. 38:11. old cast clouts and old *rotten rags,*
12. old cast clouts *and rotten rags*

מִלְחָמָה *mil-ğhāh-māh'*, f. 4421

Gen 14: 2. made *war* with Bera king of
8. they joined *battle* with them
Ex. 1:10. when there falleth out any *war,*
13:17. repent when they see *war,*
15: 3. The Lord (is) a man of *war:*
17:16. the Lord (will have) *war* with Amalek
32:17. (There is) a noise of *war* in the camp.
Nu. 10: 9. if ye go to *war* in your land
21:14. in the book of *the wars of* the Lord,
33. *to the battle* at Edrei.
31:14. came from the battle. (marg. host of *war*)
21. the men of war which went to *the battle,*
27. them that took *the war*
28. the men of *war* which went out
49. the sum of the men of *war*
32: 6. Shall your brethren go *to war,*
20. go armed before the Lord *to war,*
27. before the Lord *to battle,*
29. every man armed *to battle,*
Deu 1:41. every man *his* weapons of *war,* (lit. the weapons of *his war*)
2: 9. neither contend with them in *battle:*
14. the generation of the men of *war*
16. all the men of *war* were consumed
24. contend with him in *battle.*
32. Sihon came out...*to fight*
3: 1. he and all his people, *to battle*
4:34. by signs, and by wonders, *and by war,*
20: 1. When thou goest out *to battle*
2. when ye are come nigh *unto the battle,*
3. ye approach this day *unto battle*
5, 6, 7. lest he die *in the battle,*
12. will make *war* against thee,
20. the city that maketh *war*
21:10. When thou goest forth *to war*
29: 7(6). came out against us *unto battle.*
Jos. 4:13. *unto battle,* to the plains

Jos. 5: 4. all the men of *war*, died
6. all the people (that were) men of *war*,
6: 3. all (ye) men of *war*,
8: 1. take all the people of *war*
3. Joshua arose, and all the people of *war*,
11. (even the people) of *war* that (were)
14. went out against Israel *to battle*,
10: 7. all the people of *war*
24. the captains of the men of *war*
11: 7. all the people of *war*
18. Joshua made *war* a long time
19. all (other) they took *in battle*.
20. should come against Israel in *battle*,
23. the land rested *from war*.
14:11. so (is) my strength now, *for war*,
15. the land had rest *from war*.
17: 1. he was a man of *war*,
Jud. 3: 1. all *the wars of* Canaan;
2. to teach them *war*,
10. and went out *to war*:
8:13. Gideon...returned from *battle*
18:11. six hundred men appointed with weapons of *war*.
16. *their* weapons of *war*, (lit. the weapons of *their war*)
17. (that were) appointed with weapons of *war*.
20:14. to go out *to battle*
17. all these (were) men of *war*.
18. Which of us shall go up first *to the battle*
20. the men of Israel went out *to battle*
— the men of Israel put themselves in array *to fight* (lit. arrayed *a battle*)
22. and set their *battle* again in array
23. Shall I go up again *to battle*
28. Shall I yet again go out *to battle*
34. *and the battle* was sore:
39. the men of Israel retired *in the battle*,
— *as* (in) *the* first *battle*.
42. *but the battle* overtook them;
21:22. to each man his wife *in the war*:
1Sa. 4: 1. out against the Philistines *to battle*,
2. when they joined *battle*,
7:10. the Philistines drew near *to battle*
8:12. *his* instruments of *war*, (lit. instruments of *his war*)
20. and fight *our battles*.
13:22. in the day of *battle*,
14:20. and they came to *the battle*:
22. followed hard after them *in the battle*.
23. *and the battle* passed over unto Beth-aven.
52. sore *war* against the Philistines
16:18. a mighty valiant man, and a man of *war*,
17: 1. gathered together their armies *to battle*,
2. and set *the battle* in array
8. come out to set (your) *battle* in array?
13. followed Saul *to the battle*:
— three sons that went *to the battle*
20. and shouted *for the battle*.
28. that thou mightest see *the battle*.
33. he a man of *war* from his youth.
47. *the battle* (is) the Lord's,
18: 5. Saul set him over the men of *war*,
17. fight the Lord's *battles*.
19: 8. And there was *war* again:
23: 8. called all the people together *to war*,
25:28. my lord fighteth *the battles of*
26:10. he shall descend *into battle*,
29: 4. not go down with us *to battle*, lest *in the battle* he be an adversary
9. He shall not go up with us *to the battle*.
30:24. that goeth down *to the battle*,
31: 3. *the battle* went sore against Saul,
2Sa. 1: 4. the people are fled from *the battle*,
25. in the midst of *the battle*!
27. the weapons of *war* perished!
2:17. there was *a* very sore *battle*
3: 1. there was long *war*
6. while there was *war*
30. he had slain their brother...*in the battle*.
8:10. Hadadezer had *wars* with Toi.
10: 8. and put *the battle* in array
9. the front of *the battle*
13. *unto the battle* against the Syrians:
11: 7. and how *the war* prospered.
15. in the forefront of *the* hottest *battle*,
18. all the things concerning *the war*;
19. an end of telling the matters of *the war*

2Sa. 11:25. make *thy battle* more strong
17: 8. thy father (is) a man of *war*,
18: 6. *the battle* was in the wood
8. *the battle* was there scattered
19: 3(4). when they flee *in battle*.
10(11). Absalom,...is dead *in battle*.
21:15. the Philistines had yet *war*
17. go no more out with us *to battle*,
18. that there was again *a battle* with the
19. And there was again *a battle*
20. there was yet *a battle* in Gath,
22:35. He teacheth my hands *to war*; (marg. *for the war*)
40. girded me with strength *to battle*:
23: 9. gathered together *to battle*,
1K. 2: 5. shed the blood of *war* in peace, and put the blood of *war* upon his girdle
5: 3(17). *the wars* which were about him
8:44. If thy people go out *to battle*
9:22. but they (were) men of *war*,
12:21. an hundred and fourscore thousand chosen men, which were *war*riors, (lit. making *war*)
14:30 & 15:6. *And* there was *war* between
15: 7. *And* there was *war* between Abijam
16, 32. *And* there was *war* between
20:14. Who shall order *the battle*?
18. whether they be come out *for war*,
26. *to fight* (marg. *to the war*) against Israel.
29. in the seventh day *the battle* was joined:
39. into the midst of *the battle*;
22: 1. they continued three years without *war*
4. Wilt thou go with me *to battle*
6. Shall I go against Ramoth-gilead *to battle*,
15. go against Ramoth-gilead *to battle*,
30. enter *into the battle*;
— and went *into the battle*.
35. *the battle* increased that day:
2K. 3: 7. wilt thou go with me...*to battle*?
26. the king of Moab saw that *the battle*
8:28. *to the war* against Hazael
13:25. the cities, which he had taken...*by war*.
14: 7. and took Selah *by war*,
16: 5. came up to Jerusalem *to war*:
18:20. (I have) counsel and strength *for the war*.
24:16. strong (and) apt for *war*,
25: 4. the men of *war* (fled)
19. that was set over the men of *war*,
1Ch. 5:10. in the days of Saul they made *war*
18. to shoot with bow, and skilful in *war*,
19. they made *war* with the Hagarites,
20. they cried to God *in the battle*,
22. because *the war* (was) of God.
7: 4. bands of soldiers for *war*,
11. fit to go out for war (and) *battle*.
40. that were apt to the war (and) *to battle*
10: 3. *the battle* went sore against Saul,
11:13. the Philistines were gathered together *to battle*,
12: 1. mighty men, helpers of *the war*.
8. men of war (fit) *for the battle*,
19. Philistines against Saul *to battle*: but they
33. Of Zebulun, such as went forth to battle, expert in *war* (marg. or, rangers of *battle*), with all instruments of *war*,
35. of the Danites expert in *war*
36. went forth to battle, expert in *war*,
37. instruments of war for *the battle*,
38. All these men of *war*,
14:15. then thou shalt go out *to battle*:
18:10. had *war* (marg. was the man of *wars*) with Tou;
19: 7. and came *to battle*.
9. and put *the battle* in array
10. Joab saw that *the battle* was set against him
14. Joab and the people...drew nigh...*unto the battle*;
17. when David had put *the battle* in array
20: 4. there arose *war* at Gezer
5. there was *war* again with
6. yet again there was *war*
22: 8. *and* hast made great *wars*:
26:27. the spoils won in *battles* (marg. *battles* and spoils)
28: 3. thou (hast been) a man of *war*,
2Ch. 6:34. If thy people go out *to war*
8: 9. they (were) men of *war*,

2Ch 11: 1. an hundred and fourscore thousand chosen (men), which were *war*riors, (lit. making *war*)
12:15. *And* (there were) *wars between* Rehoboam
13: 2. *And* there was *war* between Abijah
3. Abijah set *the battle* in array with an army of valiant men of *war*,
— Jeroboam also set *the battle* in array
14. *the battle* (was) before and behind:
14: 6(5). had no *war* in those years;
10(9). they set *the battle* in array
15:19. *And* there was no (more) *war*
16: 9. thou shalt have *wars*.
17:13. the men of *war*, mighty men
18: 3. (we will be) with thee *in the war*.
5, 14. Shall we go to Ramoth-gilead *to battle*,
29. and will go *to the battle*;
— they went *to the battle*.
34. *the battle* increased that day:
20: 1. came against Jehoshaphat *to battle*.
15. *the battle* (is) not your's,
22: 5. went with Jehoram...*to war*
25: 8. be strong *for the battle*:
13. should not go with him *to battle*,
26:11. host of *fighting* men, that went out to war
13. made *war* with mighty power,
27: 7. Jotham, and all *his wars*,
32: 2. he was purposed *to fight* against
6. he set captains of *war* over
8. and to fight *our battles*.
35:21. the house wherewith *I* have *war*: (marg. of *my war*)
Job 5:20. *and in war* from the power of the sword.
38:23. the day of battle *and war*?
39:25. he smelleth *the battle* afar off,
41: 8(40:32). remember *the battle*,
Ps. 18:34(35). He teacheth my hands *to war*,
39(40). girded me with strength *unto the battle*:
24: 8. the Lord mighty in *battle*.
27: 3. though *war* should rise against me,
46: 9(10). He maketh *wars* to cease
76: 3(4). the shield, and the sword, *and the battle*.
89:43(44). made him to stand *in the battle*.
120: 7. when I speak, they (are) *for war*.
140: 2(3). are they gathered together (for) *war*.
144: 1. teacheth my hands to war, (and) my fingers *to fight*.
Pro. 20:18. with good advice make *war*.
21:31. The horse (is) prepared against the day of *battle*:
24: 6. by wise counsel thou shalt make thy *war*:
Ecc. 3: 8. a time of *war*, and a time of peace.
8: 8. no discharge *in* (that) *war*;
9:11. nor *the battle* to the strong,
Cant. 3: 8. They all hold swords, (being) expert in *war*:
Isa. 2: 4. neither shall they learn *war* any more.
3: 2. The mighty man, and the man of *war*,
25. thy mighty *in the war*.
7: 1. went up toward Jerusalem *to war*
13: 4. mustereth the host of *the battle*.
21:15. from the grievousness of *war*.
22: 2. slain with the sword, nor dead in *battle*.
27: 4. set the briers...against me *in battle*?
28: 6. them that turn *the battle*
30:32. *and in battles of* shaking
36: 5. (I have) counsel and strength *for war*:
41:12. they that *war against thee* (marg. the men of *thy war*)
42:13. shall stir up jealousy like a man of *war*:
25. the strength of *battle*:
Jer. 4:19. sound of the trumpet, the alarm of *war*.
6: 4. Prepare ye *war* against her;
23. set in array as men *for war*
8: 6. the horse rusheth *into the battle*.
18:21. slain by the sword *in battle*.
21: 4. I will turn back the weapons of *war*
28: 8. *of war*, and of evil, and of pestilence.
38: 4. the hands of the men of *war*
39: 4. all the men of *war*,
41: 3. (and) the men of *war*.
16. mighty men of *war*,
42:14. where we shall see no *war*,
46: 3. and draw near *to battle*.
48:14. strong men *for the war*?
49: 2. I will cause an alarm of *war*
14. rise up *to the battle*.
Jer. 49:26. all the men of *war*
50:22. A sound of *battle* (is) in the land,
30. *her* men of *war* (lit. the men of *her war*)
42. like a man *to the battle*,
51:20. my battle ax (and) weapons of *war*:
32. the men of *war* are affrighted.
52: 7. all the men of *war* fled,
25. charge of the men of *war*;
Eze. 7:14. none goeth *to the battle*:
13: 5. to stand *in the battle*
17:17. make for him *in the war*,
27:10. thine army, *thy* men of *war*: (lit. the men of *thy war*)
27. and all *thy* men of *war*, (lit. the men of *thy war*)
32:27. *their* weapons of *war*: (lit. the weapons of *their war*)
39:20. with all men of *war*,
Dan 9:26. the end of *the war*
11:20. neither in anger, nor *in battle*.
25. stirred up *to battle*
Hos. 1: 7. nor by sword, *nor by battle*,
2:18(20). the bow and the sword *and the battle*
10: 9. *the battle* in Gibeah
14. in the day of *battle*:
Joel 2: 5. a strong people set in *battle*
7. climb the wall like men of *war*;
3: 9(4:9). Prepare *war*, wake up the mighty men, let all the men of *war* draw near;
Am. 1:14. in the day of *battle*,
Obad. 1. rise up against her *in battle*.
Mic. 2: 8. as men averse from *war*.
3: 5. prepare *war* against him:
4: 3. neither shall they learn *war*
Zec. 9:10. the *battle* bow shall be cut off:
10: 3. as his goodly horse *in the battle*.
4. out of him the *battle* bow,
5. tread down (their enemies)...*in the battle*:
14: 2. against Jerusalem *to battle*;

מָלַט [*māh-lat′*]. 4422

*** NIPHAL.—*Preterite.* ***

Jud. 3:26. Ehud *escaped* while they tarried,
29. and there *escaped* not a man.
1Sa. 23:13. David *was escaped* from Keilah;
27: 1. *so shall I escape* out of his hand.
30:17. there *escaped* not a man
2Sa. 1: 3. Out of the camp of Israel *am I escaped*.
4: 6. Rechab and Baanah his brother *escaped*.
2K. 19:37. and they *escaped* into the land of
2Ch 16: 7. the host of the king of Syria *escaped*
Job 22:30. *and it is delivered* by the pureness of
Ps. 22: 5(6). cried unto thee, *and were delivered*:
124: 7. Our soul *is escaped*
— the snare is broken, and *we are escaped*.
Pro. 11:21. the righteous *shall be delivered*.
Isa. 37:38. and they *escaped* into the land of
Jer. 41:15. Ishmael the son of Nethaniah *escaped*
Eze. 17:15. break the covenant, *and be delivered*?

NIPHAL.—*Infinitive.*

Gen 19:19. I cannot *escape* to the mountain,
1Sa. 27: 1. I should *speedily* escape (lit. *escaping* I should escape)
Est. 4:13. *that thou shalt escape* in the king's house,

NIPHAL.—*Imperative.*

Gen 19:17. *Escape* for thy life;
— *escape* to the mountain,
22. Haste thee, *escape* thither;
Zec. 2: 7(11). *Deliver thyself*, O Zion,

NIPHAL.—*Future.*

Gen 19:20. Oh, *let me escape* thither,
Jud. 3:26. *and escaped* unto Seirath.
1Sa. 19:10. David fled, *and escaped*
12. he went, and fled, *and escaped*.
17. mine enemy, *that he is escaped*?
18. David fled, *and escaped*,
20:29. *let me get away*, I pray thee,
22: 1. *and escaped* to the cave Adullam:
20. *And* one of the sons of Ahimelech...*escaped*, and fled
27: 1. that *I should* speedily *escape*
1K. 18:40. *let* not one of them *escape*.
20:20. *and* Ben-hadad the king of Syria *escaped*

2K. 10:24. (If) any of the men...*escape*,
Job 1:15, 16, 17, 19. *and* I only *am escaped*
Pro.19: 5. (he that) speaketh lies *shall* not *escape*.
28:26. whoso walketh wisely, *he shall be delivered*.
Ecc. 7:26. whoso pleaseth God *shall escape*
Isa. 20: 6. how *shall* we *escape?*
49:24. or the lawful captive *delivered?*
25. the prey of the terrible *shall be delivered:*
Jer. 32: 4. *shall* not *escape* out of the hand
34: 3. thou *shalt* not *escape* out of his hand,
38:18, 23. thou *shalt* not *escape* out of their hand.
46: 6. nor the mighty man *escape;*
48: 8. no city *shall escape:*
Eze.17:15. *shall he escape* that doeth such (things)?
18. *he shall* not *escape*.
Dan 11:41. these *shall escape* out of
12: 1. thy people *shall be delivered*,
Joel 2:32(3:5). whosoever shall call on the name of the Lord *shall be delivered:*
Am. 9: 1. *shall* not *be delivered*.
Mal. 3:15. they that tempt God *are even delivered*.

NIPHAL.—*Participle.*

1K. 19:17. *him that escapeth* the sword of Hazael
— *and him that escapeth* from the sword of
Jer. 48:19. him that fleeth, *and her that escapeth*,

* PIEL.—*Preterite.* *

2Sa.19: 9(10). and he *delivered us* out of the hand of
Ecc. 9:15. *and* he by his wisdom *delivered* the city;
Eze.33: 5. he that taketh warning *shall deliver*

PIEL.—*Infinitive.*

Isa. 46: 2. they could not *deliver* the burden,
Jer.39:18. I will *surely* deliver (lit. *delivering* I will deliver)

PIEL.—*Imperative.*

1K. 1:12. *that thou mayest save* thine own life,
Job 6:23. *Or, Deliver me* from the enemy's hand?
Ps.116: 4. O Lord,...*deliver* my soul.
Jer. 48: 6. Flee, *save* your lives,
51: 6. *and deliver* every man his soul:
45. *and deliver ye* every man his soul

PIEL.—*Future.*

2K. 23:18. *So they let* his bones *alone*, (marg. *to escape*)
Job 20:20. *he shall* not *save* of that
22:30. *He shall deliver* the island
29:12. *I delivered* the poor that cried,
Ps. 33:17. neither *shall he deliver* (any)
41: 1(2). the Lord *will deliver him*
89:48(49). *shall he deliver* his soul
107:20. *and delivered* (them) from
Ecc. 8: 8. neither *shall* wickedness *deliver*
Isa. 34:15. the great owl make her nest, *and lay*,
46: 4. I will carry, *and will deliver* (you).
Jer. 39:18. *I will* surely *deliver thee*,
Am. 2:14. neither *shall* the mighty *deliver* himself:
15. (he that is) swift of foot *shall* not *deliver*
— neither *shall* he that rideth...*deliver*

PIEL.—*Participle.*

1Sa.19:11. If thou *save* (lit. art *saving*) not thy life
2Sa.19: 5(6). *which* this day *have saved* thy life,

* HIPHIL.—*Preterite.* *

Isa. 31: 5. passing over *he will preserve* (it).
66: 7. *she was delivered of* a man child.

* HITHPAEL.—*Future.* *

Job 19:20. *and I am escaped* with the skin of my
41:19(11). sparks of fire *leap out*.

4423 מֶלֶט *meh'-let*, m.

Jer. 43: 9. great stones...and hide them *in the clay*

4425 מְלִילָה [*m'lee-lāh'*], f.

Deu 23:25(26). thou mayest pluck *the ears*

4426 מְלִיצָה *m'lee-tzāh'*, f.

Pro. 1: 6. a proverb, *and the interpretation;* (marg. or, *an eloquent speech*)
Hab. 2: 6. *and* a *taunting* proverb against him,

מָלַךְ *māh-lăch'*. 4427

* KAL.—*Preterite.* *

Gen36:31. the kings that *reigned* in the land
Jos.13:10. which *reigned* in Heshbon,
12. Og...which *reigned* in Ashtaroth
21. Sihon...which *reigned* in Heshbon,
Jud. 4: 2. Jabin king of Canaan, that *reigned*
1Sa.12:14. the king that *reigneth* over you
13: 1. when *he had reigned* two years over
2Sa. 2:10. Saul's son...*reigned* two years.
3:21. *and that thou mayest reign* over all
5: 4. *he reigned* forty years.
5. In Hebron *he reigned* over Judah
— in Jerusalem *he reigned*
15:10. Absalom *reigneth* in Hebron.
16: 8. in whose stead *thou hast reigned;*
1K. 1:11. Adonijah the son of Haggith *doth reign*,
13. why then *doth* Adonijah *reign?*
18. now, behold, Adonijah *reigneth;*
2:11. the days that David *reigned*
— seven years *reigned he* in Hebron, and thirty and three years *reigned he* in
11:37. *and thou shalt reign* according to
42. the time that Solomon *reigned*
14:19. how he warred, and how *he reigned*,
20. the days which Jeroboam *reigned*
21. Rehoboam the son of Solomon *reigned*
— *he reigned* seventeen years
15: 1. *reigned* Abijam over Judah.
2. Three years *reigned he* in Jerusalem.
9. *reigned* Asa over Judah.
10. forty and one years *reigned he*
25. Nadab...*began to reign* (marg. *reigned*)
33. *began* Baasha the son of Ahijah *to reign*
16: 8. *began* Elah the son of Baasha *to reign*
15. *did* Zimri *reign* seven days in Tirzah.
23. *began* Omri *to reign* over Israel,
— six years *reigned he* in Tirzah.
29. *began* Ahab the son of Omri *to reign*
22:41. Jehoshaphat the son of Asa *began to reign*
42. *he reigned* twenty and five years
51(52). Ahaziah the son of Ahab *began to reign*
2K. 3: 1. Jehoram the son of Ahab *began to reign*
8:16. Jehoram the son of Jehoshaphat...*began to reign*. (marg. *reigned*)
17. *he reigned* eight years in
25. *did* Ahaziah...*begin to reign*.
26. and *he reigned* one year,
9:13. blew with trumpets, saying, Jehu *is king*. (marg. *reigneth*)
29. *began* Ahaziah *to reign*
10:36. the time that Jehu *reigned*
12: 1(2). Jehoash *began to reign;* and forty years *reigned he*
13: 1. Jehoahaz the son of Jehu *began to reign*
10. *began* Jehoash the son of Jehoahaz *to reign*
14: 1. *reigned* Amaziah the son of Joash
2. and *reigned* twenty and nine years
23. son of Joash king of Israel *began to reign*
15: 1. *began* Azariah son of Amaziah...*to reign*.
2. *he reigned* two and fifty years
8. *did* Zachariah the son of Jeroboam *reign*
13. Shallum the son of Jabesh *began to reign*
17. *began* Menahem the son of Gadi *to reign*
23. Pekahiah the son of Menahem *began to reign*
27. Pekah the son of Remaliah *began to reign*
32. *began* Jotham the son of Uzziah...*to reign*.
33. *he reigned* sixteen years
16: 1. Ahaz the son of Jotham...*began to reign*.
2. and *reigned* sixteen years in Jerusalem,
17: 1. *began* Hoshea the son of Elah *to reign*
18: 1. Hezekiah the son of Ahaz...*began to reign*.
2. *he reigned* twenty and nine years
21: 1. and *reigned* fifty and five years
19. *he reigned* two years in Jerusalem.
22: 1. *he reigned* thirty and one years
23:31. *he reigned* three months in Jerusalem.
36. and *he reigned* eleven years
24: 8. *he reigned* in Jerusalem three months.
18. *he reigned* eleven years in Jerusalem.
1Ch 1:43. the kings that *reigned* in the land
3: 4. in Jerusalem *he reigned* thirty and three
16:31. let (men) say...The Lord *reigneth*.
29:26. Thus David the son of Jesse *reigned*

1Ch 29:27. the time that *he reigned* over Israel
— seven years *reigned he* in Hebron, and thirty and three (years) *reigned he* in
2Ch 12:13. *he reigned* seventeen years
13: 2. *He reigned* three years in Jerusalem.
20:31. *he reigned* twenty and five years
21: 5. *he reigned* eight years in Jerusalem.
20. *he reigned* in Jerusalem eight years,
22: 2. *he reigned* one year in Jerusalem.
24: 1. *he reigned* forty years in Jerusalem.
25: 1. twenty and five years old (when) *he began to reign*, and *he reigned* twenty and nine
26: 3. *he reigned* fifty and two years
27: 1. *he reigned* sixteen years
8. and *reigned* sixteen years
28: 1. and *he reigned* sixteen years
29: 1. Hezekiah *began to reign*
— *he reigned* nine and twenty years
33: 1. *he reigned* fifty and five years
21. and *reigned* two years in Jerusalem.
34: 1. and *he reigned* in Jerusalem
36: 2. and *he reigned* three months in Jerusalem.
5. and *he reigned* eleven years
9. and *he reigned* three months and ten days
11. and *reigned* eleven years
Ps. 47: 8(9). God *reigneth* over the heathen:
93: 1. The Lord *reigneth*, he is clothed
96:10. Say among the heathen (that) the Lord *reigneth:*
97: 1. The Lord *reigneth;* let the earth
99: 1. The Lord *reigneth;* let the people
Isa. 24:23. when the Lord of hosts *shall reign*
52: 7. that saith unto Zion, Thy God *reigneth!*
Jer. 23: 5. *and* a King *shall reign* and prosper,
52: 1. and *he reigned* eleven years
Mic. 4: 7. *and* the Lord *shall reign* over them

KAL.—*Infinitive.*

Gen36:31. before *there reigned* any king
37: 8. Shalt thou *indeed* reign (lit. *reigning* shalt thou reign)
1Sa. 8: 7. *that I should not reign* over them.
13: 1. Saul *reigned* one year; (marg. one year *in his reigning*)
16: 1. I have rejected him *from reigning*
24:20(21). that thou shalt *surely* be king, (lit. *reigning* thou shalt reign)
2Sa. 2:10. forty years old *when he began to reign*
5: 4. thirty years old *when he began to reign*,
1K. 2:15. on me, *that I should reign:*
6: 1. fourth year *of* Solomon*'s reign*
14:21. *when he began to reign*, and he reigned
15:29. it came to pass, *when he reigned*,
16:11. *when he began to reign*, as soon as
22:42. *when he began to reign;* and he reigned
2K. 8:17, 26. *when he began to reign;* and he reigned
11:21(12:1). Jehoash *when he began to reign.*
14: 2. *when he began to reign*, and reigned
15: 2, 33. *when he began to reign*, and he reigned
16: 2. Ahaz *when he began to reign*,
18: 2. *when he began to reign;* and he reigned
21: 1, 19 & 22:1 & 23:31. years old *when he began to reign*,
23:33. *that he might not reign* (marg. or, *because he reigned*)
36 & 24:8. years old *when he began to reign;*
24:12. in the eighth year *of his reign.*
18. *when he began to reign*,
25: 1. in the ninth year *of his reign*,
27. in the year *that he began to reign*
1Ch. 1:43. before (any) king *reigned*
4:31. unto *the reign* of David.
2Ch 12:13. years old *when he began to reign*,
16:13. the one and fortieth year *of his reign.*
17: 7. in the third year *of his reign*
20:31 & 21:5. years old *when he began to reign*,
21:20. was he *when he began to reign*,
22: 2 & 24:1 & 26:3 & 27:1, 8 & 28:1. *when he began to reign*,
29: 3. in the first year *of his reign*,
33: 1, 21 & 34:1. years old *when he began to reign*,
34: 3. in the eighth year *of his reign*,
8. in the eighteenth year *of his reign*,
36: 2, 5, 9, 11. years old *when he began to reign*,
20. until *the reign of* the kingdom
Est. 1: 3. In the third year *of his reign*,
Job 34:30. *That* the hypocrite *reign not*,
Ecc. 4:14. out of prison he cometh *to reign;*
Jer. 1: 2. in the thirteenth year *of his reign.*
51:59. in the fourth year *of his reign.*
52: 1. *when he began to reign*, (marg. *reigned*)
4. in the ninth year *of his reign*,
Dan 9: 2. In the first year *of his reign*

KAL.—*Imperative.*

Jud. 9: 8. *Reign thou* over us.
10, 12. Come thou, (and) *reign* over us.
14. Come thou, (and) *reign* over us.

KAL.—*Future.*

Gen36:32. *And* Bela the son of Beor *reigned*
33. *and* Jobab the son of Zerah...*reigned*
34. *and* Husham of the land of Temani *reigned*
35. *and* Hadad the son of Bedad,...*reigned*
36. *and* Samlah of Masrekah *reigned*
37. *and* Saul of Rehoboth...*reigned*
38. *and* Baal-hanan the son of Achbor *reigned*
39. *and* Hadar *reigned* in his stead:
37: 8. *Shalt thou* indeed *reign* over us?
Ex. 15:18. The Lord *shall reign* for ever and ever.
1Sa. 8: 9. the king that *shall reign* over them.
11. the king that *shall reign* over you:
11:12. *Shall* Saul *reign* over us?
12:12. a king *shall reign* over us:
23:17. thou *shalt be king* over Israel,
24:20(21). well *that thou shalt* surely *be king*,
2Sa. 8:15. *And* David *reigned* over all Israel;
10: 1. *and* Hanun his son *reigned* in his stead.
1K. 1: 5. himself, saying, *I will be king:* (marg. *reign*)
13, 17, 30. Solomon thy son *shall reign*
24. Adonijah *shall reign* after me,
35. he *shall be king* in my stead:
11:24. *and reigned* in Damascus.
25. *and reigned* over Syria.
43. *and* Rehoboam his son *reigned*
12:17. Rehoboam *reigned* over them.
14:20. *and* Nadab his son *reigned* in his stead.
31. *And* Abijam his son *reigned* in his stead.
15: 8. *and* Asa his son *reigned*
24. *and* Jehoshaphat his son *reigned*
25. *and reigned* over Israel two years.
28. *and reigned* in his stead.
16: 6. *and* Elah his son *reigned*
10. *and reigned* in his stead.
22. Tibni died, *and* Omri *reigned.*
28. *and* Ahab his son *reigned*
29. *and* Ahab the son of Omri *reigned*
22:40. *and* Ahaziah his son *reigned*
50(51). *and* Jehoram his son *reigned*
51(52). *and reigned* two years over Israel.
2K. 1:17. *And* Jehoram *reigned* in his stead
3: 1. *and reigned* twelve years.
27. his eldest son that *should have reigned*
8:15. *and* Hazael *reigned* in his stead.
24. *and* Ahaziah his son *reigned*
10:35. *And* Jehoahaz his son *reigned*
12:21(22). *and* Amaziah his son *reigned*
13: 9. *and* Joash his son *reigned*
24. *and* Ben-hadad his son *reigned* in his stead.
14:16. *and* Jeroboam his son *reigned*
29. *and* Zachariah his son *reigned*
15: 7. *and* Jotham his son *reigned*
10, 14, 30. slew him, *and reigned* in his stead.
13. *and he reigned* a full month in Samaria.
22. *and* Pekahiah his son *reigned*
25. *and reigned* in his room.
38. *and* Ahaz his son *reigned*
16:20. *and* Hezekiah his son *reigned*
19:37. *And* Esarhaddon his son *reigned*
20:21. *and* Manasseh his son *reigned*
21:18. *and* Amon his son *reigned*
26. *and* Josiah his son *reigned*
24: 6. *and* Jehoiachin his son *reigned*
1Ch. 1:44. *And* when Bela was dead, Jobab...*reigned*
45. *And* when Jobab was dead, Husham... *reigned*
46. *And* when Husham was dead, Hadad... *reigned*
47. *And* when Hadad was dead, Samlah... *reigned*
48. *And* when Samlah was dead, Shaul... *reigned*
49. *And* when Shaul was dead, Baal-hanan ...*reigned*

1Ch. 1:50. *And* when Baal-hanan was dead, Hadad *reigned*
3: 4. *and* there *he reigned* seven years and six months:
18:14. *So* David *reigned* over all Israel,
19: 1. of Ammon died, *and* his son *reigned*
29:28. *and* Solomon his son *reigned*
2Ch. 1:13. *and reigned* over Israel.
9:30. *And* Solomon *reigned* in Jerusalem
31. *and* Rehoboam his son *reigned*
10:17. *But* (as for)...Rehoboam *reigned* over
12:13. Rehoboam strengthened himself ... *and reigned:*
16. *and* Abijah his son *reigned*
13: 1. *Now...began* Abijah *to reign*
14: 1(13:23). *and* Asa his son *reigned*
17: 1. *And* Jehoshaphat his son *reigned*
20:31. *And* Jehoshaphat *reigned* over Judah:
21: 1. *And* Jehoram his son *reigned*
22: 1. *So* Ahaziah the son of Jehoram king of Judah *reigned.*
23: 3. Behold, the king's son *shall reign,*
24:27. *And* Amaziah his son *reigned*
26:23. *and* Jotham his son *reigned*
27: 9. *and* Ahaz his son *reigned*
28:27. *and* Hezekiah his son *reigned*
32:33. *And* Manasseh his son *reigned*
33:20. *and* Amon his son *reigned*
36: 8. *and* Jehoiachin his son *reigned*
Est. 2: 4. *let* the maiden...*be queen*
Ps.146:10. The Lord *shall reign* for ever,
Pro 8:15. By me kings *reign,*
30:22. a servant when *he reigneth;*
Isa. 32: 1. a king *shall reign* in righteousness,
37:38. *and* Esar-haddon his son *reigned*
Jer. 22:15. *Shalt thou reign,* because thou closest
37: 1. *And* king Zedekiah the son of Josiah *reigned*
Eze.20:33. with fury poured out, *will I rule*

KAL.—*Participle.* Poel.

2K. 11: 3. Athaliah *did reign* over the land.
2Ch 22:12. Athaliah *reigned* over the land.
Est. 1: 1. this (is) Ahasuerus *which reigned,*
Jer. 22:11. Shallum the son of Josiah...*which reigned*
33:21. a son *to reign* upon his throne;

* NIPHAL.—*Future.* *

Neh. 5: 7. *Then* I *consulted* with myself, (marg. my heart *consulted* in me)

* HIPHIL.—*Preterite.* *

1Sa. 8:22. *and make* them a king. (lit. *cause* a king *to reign*)
15:11. that *I have set up* Saul (to be) king:
35. repented that *he had made* Saul *king*
1K. 1:43. David *hath made* Solomon *king.*
3: 7. *thou hast made* thy servant *king*
2Ch. 1: 8. *and hast made me to reign* in his stead.
9. thou *hast made me king* over
11. over whom *I have made thee king:*
Jer. 37: 1. king of Babylon *made king*
Hos. 8: 4. *They have set up kings,* but not

HIPHIL.—*Infinitive.*

1K. 12: 1. *to make* him *king.*
16:21. followed Tibni...*to make him king;*
1Ch 11:10. strengthened themselves...*to make him king,*
12:31. to come *and make* David *king.*
38. *to make* David *king* over all Israel:
— of one heart *to make* David *king.*
28: 4. *to make* (me) *king* over all Israel:
2Ch 10: 1. were all Israel come *to make* him *king.*
11:22. (he thought) *to make him king.*

HIPHIL.—*Future.*

Jud. 9: 6. *and made* Abimelech king,
16. *in that ye have made* Abimelech *king,*
18. *and have made* Abimelech,...*king*
1Sa.11:15. *and* there *they made* Saul *king*
12: 1. *and have made* a king over you.
2Sa. 2: 9. *And made him king* over Gilead,
1K. 12:20. *and made* him *king* over all Israel:
16:16. *wherefore* all Israel *made* Omri,...*king*
2K. 8:20. *and made* a king over themselves.
10: 5. *we will* not *make* any *king:*
11:12. *and they made* him *king,*
2K. 14:21. *and made* him *king*
17:21. *and they made* Jeroboam...*king:*
21:24. the people of the land *made* Josiah...*king*
23:30. *and made* him *king* in his father's stead.
34. *And* Pharaoh-nechoh *made* Eliakim...*king*
24:17. *And* the king of Babylon *made* Mattaniah ...*king*
1Ch 23: 1. *So* when David was old...*he made* Solomon ...*king*
29:22. *And* they *made* Solomon...*king*
2Ch 21: 8. *and made* themselves a king.
22: 1. *And* the inhabitants of Jerusalem *made* Ahaziah...king
23:11. *and made* him *king.*
26: 1. took Uzziah,...*and made* him *king*
33:25. *and* the people of the land *made* Josiah.. *king*
36: 1. *and made him king* in his father's stead
4. *And* the king of Egypt *made* Eliakim... *king*
10. *and made* Zedekiah...*king*
Est. 2:17. *and made her queen*
Isa. 7: 6. *and set* a king in the midst

HIPHIL.—*Participle.*

Eze.17:16. (where) the king (dwelleth) *that made him king,*

* HOPHAL.—*Preterite.* *

Dan. 9: 1. Darius...which *was made king*

מֶלֶךְ *meh'-lech,* m. 4428

Gen14: 1. in the days of Amraphel *king of* Shinar, Arioch *king of* Ellasar, Chedorlaomer *king of* Elam, and Tidal *king of* nations;
2. with Bera *king of* Sodom, and with Birsha *king of* Gomorrah, Shinab *king of* Admah, and Shemeber *king of* Zeboiim, *and the king of* Bela,
5. *and the kings* that (were) with him,
8. there went out *the king of* Sodom, *and the king of* Gomorrah, *and the king of* Admah, *and the king of* Zeboiim, *and the king of* Bela
9. With Chedorlaomer *the king of* Elam, and with Tidal *king of* nations, and Amraphel *king of* Shinar, and Arioch *king of* Ellasar; four *kings* with five.
10. *the kings of* Sodom and Gomorrah
17. And *the king of* Sodom went out to meet
— and of *the kings* that (were) with him, at the valley of Shaveh, which (is) *the king's* dale.
18. And Melchizedek *king of* Salem brought
21. And *the king of* Sodom said unto Abram,
22. Abram said to *the king of* Sodom,
17: 6. *and kings* shall come out of thee.
16. *kings of* people shall be of her.
20: 2. Abimelech *king of* Gerar sent, and took
26: 1. Abimelech *king of* the Philistines unto
8. Abimelech *king of* the Philistines looked
35:11. *and kings* shall come out of thy loins;
36:31. *the kings* that reigned in the land of Edom, before there reigned any *king*
39:20. *the king's* prisoners (were) bound:
40: 1. the butler of *the king of* Egypt and (his) baker had offended their lord *the king of* Egypt.
5. butler and the baker *of the king of* Egypt,
41:46. he stood before Pharaoh *king of* Egypt.
49:20. and he shall yield *royal* dainties. (lit. dainties of *a king*)
Ex. 1: 8. there arose up *a* new *king* over Egypt,
15. *the king of* Egypt spake to the Hebrew
17. as *the king of* Egypt commanded
18. *the king of* Egypt called for the midwives,
2:23. that *the king of* Egypt died: and the
3:18. elders of Israel, unto *the king of* Egypt,
19. *the king of* Egypt will not let you go,
5: 4. And *the king of* Egypt said unto them,
6:11. speak unto Pharaoh *king of* Egypt,
13. and unto Pharaoh *king of* Egypt,
27. spake to Pharaoh *king of* Egypt,
29. speak thou unto Pharaoh *king of* Egypt
14: 5. it was told *the king of* Egypt
8. the heart of Pharaoh *king of* Egypt,

Nu. 20:14. from Kadesh unto *the king of* Edom,
17. by *the king*'s (high)way,
21: 1. *king* Arad the Canaanite,
21. unto Sihon *king of* the Amorites, saying,
22. by *the king*'s (high)way,
26. Sihon *the king of* the Amorites, who had fought *against the* former *king of* Moab,
29. *unto* Sihon *king of* the Amorites.
33. Og *the king of* Bashan went out against
34. didst unto Sihon *king of* the Amorites,
22: 4. Balak the son of Zippor (was) *king of*
10. *king of* Moab, hath sent unto me,
23: 7. *the king of* Moab hath brought me
21. the shout of *a king* (is) among them.
24: 7. *his king* shall be higher than Agag,
31: 8. they slew *the kings of* Midian,
— five *kings of* Midian:
32:33. kingdom of Sihon *king of* the Amorites, and the kingdom of Og *king of* Bashan,
33:40. *king* Arad the Canaanite,
Deu 1: 4. *the king of* the Amorites, which dwelt in Heshbon, and Og *the king of* Bashan,
2:24. Sihon the Amorite, *king of* Heshbon,
26. unto Sihon *king of* Heshbon with words
30. *king of* Heshbon would not let us pass
3: 1. Og *the king of* Bashan came out against
2. as thou didst unto Sihon *king of* the
3. into our hands Og also, *the king of* Bashan,
6. as we did unto Sihon *king of* Heshbon,
8. out of the hand of *the* two *kings of* the
11. only Og *king of* Bashan remained
21. done unto these two *kings:*
4:46. in the land of Sihon *king of* the Amorites,
47. the land of Og *king of* Bashan, two *kings of* the Amorites,
7: 8. from the hand of Pharaoh *king of* Egypt.
24. he shall deliver *their kings*
11: 3. unto Pharaoh *the king of* Egypt,
17:14. I will set *a king* over me,
15. set (him) *king* over thee,
— shalt thou set *king* over thee:
28:36. The Lord shall bring thee, and *thy king*
29: 7(6). Sihon *the king of* Heshbon, and Og *the king of*
31: 4. as he did to Sihon and to Og, *kings of* the
33: 5. he was *king* in Jeshurun,
Jos. 2: 2. it was told *the king of* Jericho, saying,
3. *the king of* Jericho sent unto Rahab,
10. what ye did unto *the* two *kings of* the
5: 1. all *the kings of* the Amorites, which (were) on the side of Jordan westward, and all *the kings of*
6: 2. Jericho, and *the king thereof,*
8: 1. I have given into thy hand *the king of* Ai,
2. Ai *and her king*
— Jericho *and her king:*
14. when *the king of* Ai saw (it), that they
23. *the king of* Ai they took alive,
29. *the king of* Ai he hanged on a tree
9: 1. *the kings* which (were) on this side Jordan,
10. he did to *the* two *kings of* the Amorites, that (were) beyond Jordan, to Sihon *king of* Heshbon, and to Og *king of* Bashan,
10: 1. Adoni-zedec *king of* Jerusalem had
— as he had done to Jericho *and her king*, so he had done to Ai *and her king;*
3. Adoni-zedec *king of* Jerusalem sent unto Hoham *king of* Hebron, and unto Piram *king of* Jarmuth, and unto Japhia *king of* Lachish, and unto Debir *king of* Eglon,
5. Therefore *the* five *kings of* the Amorites, *the king of* Jerusalem, *the king of* Hebron, *the king of* Jarmuth, *the king of* Lachish, *the king of* Eglon, gathered themselves
6. all *the kings of* the Amorites that
16. these five *kings* fled,
17. *The* five *kings* are found hid
22. bring out those five *kings*
23. brought forth those five *kings* unto him out of the cave, *the king of* Jerusalem, *the king of* Hebron, *the king of* Jarmuth, *the king of* Lachish, (and) *the king of* Eglon.
24. when they brought out those *kings*
— your feet upon the necks of these *kings.*
28. and *the king thereof* he utterly destroyed,
— he did *to the king of* Makkedah as he did *unto the king of* Jericho.

Jos. 10:30. and *the king thereof*, into the hand
— *unto the king thereof* as he did *unto the king of* Jericho.
33. Horam *king of* Gezer came up to help
37. and *the king thereof*, and all
39. he took it, and *the king thereof*, and all
— he did to Debir, *and to the king thereof;* as he had done also to Libnah, *and to her king.*
40. So Joshua smote...all *their kings:*
42. all these *kings* and their land
11: 1. Jabin *king of* Hazor had heard (those things), that he sent to Jobab *king of* Madon, and to *the king of* Shimron, and to *the king of*
2. *the kings* that (were) on the north
5. when all these *kings* were met
10. and smote *the king thereof* with the sword:
12. the cities of those *kings*, and all *the kings of them,*
17. all *their kings* he took,
18. Joshua made war...with all those *kings.*
12: 1. *the kings of* the land,
2. Sihon *king of* the Amorites,
4. the coast of Og *king of* Bashan,
5. the border of Sihon *king of* Heshbon.
7. *the kings of* the country
9. *The king of* Jericho, one; *the king of* Ai, ...one;
10. *The king of* Jerusalem, one; *the king of* Hebron, one;
11. *The king of* Jarmuth, one; *the king of* Lachish, one;
12. *The king of* Eglon, one; *the king of* Gezer, one;
13. *The king of* Debir, one; *the king of* Geder, one;
14. *The king of* Hormah, one; *the king of* Arad, one;
15. *The king of* Libnah, one; *the king of* Adullam, one;
16. *The king of* Makkedah, one; *the king of* Beth-el, one;
17. *The king of* Tappuah, one; *the king of* Hepher, one;
18. *The king of* Aphek, one; *the king of* Lasharon, one;
19. *The king of* Madon, one; *the king of* Hazor, one;
20. *The king of* Shimron-meron, one; *the king of* Achshaph, one;
21. *The king of* Taanach, one; *the king of* Megiddo, one;
22. *The king of* Kedesh, one; *the king of* Jokneam of Carmel, one;
23. *The king of* Dor in the coast of Dor, one; *the king of* the nations
24. *The king of* Tirzah, one: all *the kings*
13:10. the cities of Sihon *king of* the Amorites,
21. kingdom of Sihon *king of* the Amorites,
27. the kingdom of Sihon *king of* Heshbon,
30. the kingdom of Og *king of* Bashan,
24: 9. Balak the son of Zippor, *king of* Moab,
12. (even) *the* two *kings of* the Amorites;
Jud. 1: 7. Threescore and ten *kings,*
3: 8, 10. Chushan-rishathaim *king of* Mesopotamia:
12, 14, 15. Eglon *the king of* Moab
17. Eglon *king of* Moab:
19. a secret errand unto thee, *O king:*
4: 2. into the hand of Jabin *king of* Canaan,
17. Jabin *the king of* Hazor
23. subdued on that day Jabin *the king of*
24. against Jabin *the king of* Canaan, until they had destroyed Jabin *king of* Canaan.
5: 3. Hear, *O ye kings;*
19. *The kings* came (and) fought, then fought *the kings of* Canaan
8: 5. Zebah and Zalmunna, *kings of* Midian.
12. and took *the* two *kings of* Midian,
18. the children of *a king.*
26. raiment that (was) on *the kings of* Midian,
9: 6. and made Abimelech *king,*
8. The trees went forth...to anoint *a king*
15. If in truth ye anoint me *king*
11:12, 13, 14, 28. *the king of* the children of Ammon,

Jud. 11:17. messengers unto *the king of* Edom, saying, Let me, I pray thee, pass through thy land: but *the king of* Edom would not hearken (thereto). And in like manner they sent unto *the king of* Moab:
19. Israel sent messengers unto Sihon *king of* the Amorites, *the king of* Heshbon;
25. Balak the son of Zippor, *king of* Moab?
17: 6 & 18:1. no *king* in Israel,
19: 1. *when* (there was) no *king* in Israel,
21:25. no *king* in Israel:
1Sa. 2:10. he shall give strength *unto his king*,
8: 5. now make us *a king*
6. Give us *a king* to judge us.
9, 11. the manner of *the king*
10. asked of him *a king*.
18. *your king* which ye shall have chosen
19. we will have *a king*
20. that *our king* may judge us,
22. and make them *a king*.
10:19. but set *a king* over us.
24. God save *the king*.
12: 1. have made *a king* over you.
2. *the king* walketh before you:
9. into the hand of *the king of* Moab,
12. *the king of* the children of Ammon
— *a king* shall reign over us: when the Lord your God (was) *your king*.
13. *the king* whom ye have chosen,
— the Lord hath set *a king* over you.
14. *the king* that reigneth over you
17. sight of the Lord, in asking you *a king*.
19. (this) evil, to ask us *a king*.
25. both ye and *your king*.
14:47. against Edom, *and against the kings of* Zobah,
15: 1. *king* over his people,
8. he took Agag *the king of* the Amalekites
11. I have set up Saul (to be) *king:*
17. the Lord anointed thee *king*
20. have brought Agag *the king of* Amalek,
23. rejected thee *from* (being) *king*.
26. from being *king* over Israel.
32. Bring ye hither to me Agag *the king of*
16: 1. I have provided me *a king*
17:25. *the king* will enrich
55. *O king*, I cannot tell.
56. *the king* said, Enquire
18: 6. to meet *king* Saul,
18. son in law *to the king?*
22. *the king* hath delight in thee,
— be *the king's* son in law.
23. to be *a king's* son in law,
25. *The king* desireth not any dowry,
— avenged of *the king*'s enemies.
26. to be *the king's* son in law:
27. in full tale *to the king*, that he might be *the king's* son in law.
19: 4. Let not *the king* sin against his servant,
20: 5. to sit with *the king* at meat:
24. *the king* sat him down to eat
25. *the king* sat upon his seat,
29. cometh not unto *the king*'s table.
21: 2(3). *The king* hath commanded me
8(9). *the king*'s business required haste.
10(11). went to Achish *the king of* Gath.
11(12). (Is) not this David *the king of* the land?
12(13). sore afraid of Achish *the king of* Gath.
22: 3. and he said unto *the king of* Moab,
4. brought them before *the king of* Moab:
11. Then *the king* sent
— they came all of them to *the king*.
14. Ahimelech answered *the king*,
— *the king*'s son in law,
15. let not *the king* impute
16. And *the king* said,
17. *the king* said unto the footmen
— the servants of *the king*
18. *the king* said to Doeg,
23:20. Now therefore, *O king*, come down
— to deliver him into *the king*'s hand.
24: 8(9). My lord *the king*.
14(15). After whom is *the king of* Israel come
25:36. like the feast of *a king;*
26:14. thou (that) criest to *the king?*
15. not kept thy lord *the king?* for there came one...to destroy *the king*

1Sa. 26:16. see where *the king*'s spear (is),
17. (It is) my voice, my lord, *O king*.
19. let my lord *the king* hear
20. *the king of* Israel is come out to seek
22. Behold *the king*'s spear!
27: 2. Achish, the son of Maoch, *king of* Gath.
6. Ziklag pertaineth *unto the kings of* Judah
28:13. *the king* said unto her,
29: 3. the servant of Saul *the king of* Israel,
8. the enemies of my lord *the king?*
2Sa. 2: 4. they anointed David *king*
7. have anointed me *king*
11. the time that David was *king*
3: 3. the daughter of Talmai *king of* Geshur;
17. Ye sought for David...(to be) *king*
21. my lord *the king*,
23. Abner the son of Ner came to *the king*,
24. Joab came to *the king*,
31. *And king* David (himself) followed
32. *the king* lifted up his voice,
33. *the king* lamented over Abner,
36. whatsoever *the king* did
37. it was not *of the king* to slay Abner
38. *the king* said unto his servants,
39. though anointed *king;*
4: 8. and said to *the king*,
— the Lord hath avenged my lord *the king*
5: 2. when Saul *was king* over us,
3. the elders of Israel came to *the king* to Hebron; and *king* David made a league
— they anointed David *king*
6. *the king* and his men went to Jerusalem
11. Hiram *king of* Tyre sent messengers
12. the Lord had established him *king*
17. they had anointed David *king*
6:12. it was told *king* David,
16. and saw *king* David leaping
20. How glorious was *the king of* Israel
7: 1. when *the king* sat in his house,
2. *the king* said unto Nathan
3. Nathan said to *the king*,
18. Then went *king* David in,
8: 3, 12. son of Rehob, *king of* Zobah,
5. to succour Hadadezer *king of* Zobah,
8. *king* David took exceeding much
9. When Toi *king of* Hamath heard
10. Toi sent Joram his son unto *king* David,
11. *king* David did dedicate
9: 2. *the king* said unto him,
3. And *the king* said,
— Ziba said unto *the king*,
4. *the king* said unto him, Where (is) he? And Ziba said unto *the king*,
5. Then *king* David sent,
9. Then *the king* called to Ziba,
11. Then said Ziba unto *the king*,
— my lord *the king* hath commanded
— as one of *the king*'s sons.
13. did eat continually at *the king*'s table;
10: 1. *the king of* the children of Ammon
5. *the king* said, Tarry at Jericho
6. and of *king* Maacah a thousand
19. all *the kings* (that were) servants
11: 1. the time when *kings* go forth (to battle),
2. the roof of *the king*'s house:
8. Uriah departed out of *the king*'s house,
— there followed him a mess...from *the king*.
9. the door of *the king*'s house
19. telling the matters...unto *the king*,
20. that *the king*'s wrath arise,
24. and (some) of *the king*'s servants be dead,
12: 7. I anointed thee *king*
30. he took *their king*'s crown
13: 4. thou, (being) *the king*'s son,
6. when *the king* was come to see him, Amnon said unto *the king*,
13. speak unto *the king;*
18. *the king*'s daughters
21. *when king* David heard
23. invited all *the king*'s sons.
24. Absalom came to *the king*,
— let *the king*,...go with thy servant.
25. And *the king* said to Absalom,
26. *the king* said unto him, Why should
27. he let Amnon and all *the king*'s sons
29. Then all *the king*'s sons arose,
30. Absalom hath slain all *the king*'s sons.

2Sa.13:31. Then *the king* arose, and tare his
32. all the young men *the king*'s sons;
33. let not my lord *the king* take the thing to his heart, to think that all *the king*'s sons are dead:
35. And Jonadab said unto *the king*, Behold, *the king*'s sons come:
36. *the king*'s sons came,
— *the king* also and all his servants wept
37. the son of Ammihud, *king of* Geshur.
39. (the soul of) *king* David longed
14: 1. *the king*'s heart (was) toward Absalom.
3. come to *the king*,
4. the woman of Tekoah spake to *the king*,
— and said, Help, *O king*.
5. *the king* said unto her,
8. *the king* said unto the woman,
9. the woman of Tekoah said unto *the king*, My lord, *O king*, the iniquity (be) on me, and on my father's house: *and the king* and his throne (be) guiltless.
10. And *the king* said, Whosoever
11. let *the king* remember
12. speak (one) word unto my lord *the king*.
13. *the king* doth speak this thing
— *the king* doth not fetch home
15. speak of this thing unto my lord *the king*,
— I will now speak unto *the king*; it may be that *the king* will perform
16. For *the king* will hear,
17. The word of my lord *the king*
— so (is) my lord *the king* to discern
18. Then *the king* answered
— Let my lord *the king* now speak.
19. And *the king* said, (Is not)
— (As) thy soul liveth, my lord *the king*,
— my lord *the king* hath spoken:
21. *the king* said unto Joab,
22. and thanked *the king*:
— grace in thy sight, my lord, *O king*, in that *the king* hath fulfilled
24. And *the king* said, Let him
— saw not *the king*'s face.
26. after *the king*'s weight.
28. and saw not *the king*'s face.
29. to have sent him to *the king*;
32. that I may send thee to *the king*,
— let me see *the king*'s face;
33. Joab came to *the king*,
— he came to *the king*, and bowed himself on his face to the ground before *the king* and *the king* kissed Absalom.
15: 2. when any man...came to *the king*
3. no man (deputed) of *the king*
6. all Israel that came to *the king*
7. Absalom said unto *the king*,
9. *the king* said unto him,
15. *the king*'s servants said unto *the king*, Behold, thy servants (are ready to do) whatsoever my lord *the king* shall appoint.
16, 17. And *the king* went forth,
— And *the king* left ten women,
18. passed on before *the king*.
19. Then said *the king* to Ittai
— and abide with *the king*:
21. Ittai answered *the king*,
— (as) my lord *the king* liveth, surely in what place my lord *the king* shall be,
23. *the king also* himself passed over
25. *the king* said unto Zadok,
27. *The king* said also unto Zadok
34. I will be thy servant, *O king*;
35. out of *the king*'s house,
16: 2. *the king* said unto Ziba,
— *the king*'s houshold
3. And *the king* said, And where
— And Ziba said unto *the king*,
4. Then said *the king* to Ziba,
— find grace in thy sight, my lord, *O king*.
5. when *king* David came
6. the servants of *king* David:
9. unto *the king*, Why should this dead dog curse my lord *the king*?
10. And *the king* said, What
14. *the king*, and all the people
16. God save *the king*, God save *the king*.
17: 2. I will smite *the king* only:

2Sa.17:16. lest *the king* be swallowed up,
17. they went and told *king* David.
21. went and told *king* David,
18: 2. *the king* said unto the people,
4. *the king* said unto them,
— *the king* stood by the gate side,
5. *the king* commanded Joab
— when *the king* gave...charge
12. against *the king*'s son: for in our hearing *the king* charged thee
13. no matter hid from *the king*,
18. in *the king*'s dale:
19. run, and bear *the king* tidings,
20. *the king*'s son is dead.
21. Go tell *the king*
25. the watchman cried, and told *the king*. And *the king* said,
26. *the king* said, He also bringeth tidings.
27. *the king* said, He (is) a good man,
28. And Ahimaaz...said unto *the king*,
— to the earth upon his face *before the king*,
— their hand against my lord *the king*.
29. *the king* said, Is the young man
— When Joab sent *the king*'s servant,
30. And *the king* said (unto him),
31. Tidings, my lord *the king*:
32. And *the king* said unto Cushi,
— The enemies of my lord *the king*,
33(19:1). *the king* was much moved,
19: 1(2). *the king* weepeth and mourneth
2(3). *the king* was grieved for his son.
4(5). *But the king* covered his face, and *the king* cried with a loud voice,
5(6). Joab came...to *the king*,
8(9). Then *the king* arose,
—(-). *the king* doth sit in the gate. And all the people came before *the king*:
9(10). *The king* saved us out of the hand
10(11). not a word of bringing *the king* back?
11(12). And *king* David sent to Zadok
—(—). Why are ye the last to bring *the king* back
—(—). the speech of all Israel is come to *the king*,
12(13). are ye the last to bring back *the king*?
14(15). they sent (this word) unto *the king*,
15(16). So *the king* returned, and came to Jordan. And Judah came to Gilgal, to go to meet *the king*, to conduct *the king*
16(17). the men of Judah to meet *king* David.
17(18). went over Jordan before *the king*.
18(19). to carry over *the king*'s houshold,
—(—). fell down before *the king*, as he
19(20). And said unto *the king*,
—(—). the day that my lord *the king* went out of Jerusalem, that *the king*
20(21). to go down to meet my lord *the king*.
22(23). I (am) this day *king* over Israel?
23(24). *the king* said unto Shimei, Thou shalt not die. And *the king* sware unto him.
24(25). of Saul came down to meet *the king*,
—(—). from the day *the king* departed
25(26). to meet *the king*, that *the king* said
26(27). And he answered, My lord, *O king*,
—(—). ride thereon, and go to *the king*;
27(28). slandered thy servant unto my lord *the king*; but my lord *the king*
28(29). dead men before my lord *the king*:
—(—). to cry any more unto *the king*?
29(30). And *the king* said unto him,
30(31). Mephibosheth said unto *the king*,
—(—). forasmuch as my lord *the king*
31(32). went over Jordan with *the king*,
32(33). and he had provided *the king* of
33(34). And *the king* said unto Barzillai,
34(35). And Barzillai said unto *the king*,
—(—). that I should go up with *the king*
35(36). be yet a burden unto my lord *the king*?
36(37). over Jordan with *the king*: and why should *the king* recompense it
37(38). let him go over with my lord *the king*;
38(39). And *the king* answered, Chimham
39(40). *when the king* was come over, *the king* kissed Barzillai,
40(41). Then *the king* went on to Gilgal,
—(—). all the people of Judah conducted *the king*,

2Sa.19:41(42). all the men of Israel came to *the king*, and said unto *the king*,
—(—). away, and have brought *the king*,
42(43). Because *the king* (is) near of kin to us:
—(—). have we eaten at all of *the king*'s (cost)?
43(44). We have ten parts *in the king*,
—(—). in bringing back *our king*?
20: 2. the men of Judah clave *unto their king*,
3. *the king* took the ten women
4. Then said *the king* to Amasa,
21. lifted up his hand *against the king*,
22. Joab returned to Jerusalem unto *the king*.
21: 2. *the king* called the Gibeonites,
5. And they answered *the king*,
6. And *the king* said, I will give (them).
7. *the king* spared Mephibosheth,
8. *the king* took the two sons of Rizpah
14. all that *the king* commanded.
22:51. the tower of salvation for *his king*:
24: 2. *the king* said to Joab
3. Joab said unto *the king*,
— the eyes of my lord *the king* may see (it): but why doth my lord *the king* delight
4. *the king*'s word prevailed
— went out from the presence of *the king*,
9. Joab gave up the sum...unto *the king*:
20. Araunah looked, and saw *the king*
— bowed himself *before the king*
21. Wherefore is my lord *the king* come
22. Let my lord *the king* take and offer
23. did Araunah (as) *a king* (lit. *the king*), give *unto the king*. And Araunah said unto *the king*,
24. *the king* said unto Araunah,
1K. 1: 1. *Now king* David was old
2. Let there be sought for my lord *the king* a young virgin: and let her stand before *the king*,
— that my lord *the king* may get heat.
3. and brought her *to the king*.
4. and cherished *the king*,
— *but the king* knew her not.
9. his brethren *the king*'s sons, and all the men of Judah *the king*'s servants:
13. get thee in unto *king* David,
— Didst not thou, my lord, *O king*,
14. while thou yet talkest there with *the king*,
15. Bath-sheba went in unto *the king* into the chamber: *and the king* was very old; and Abishag the Shunammite ministered unto *the king*.
16. Bath-sheba...did obeisance *unto the king*. And *the king* said,
18. my lord *the king*, thou knowest (it) not:
19. hath called all the sons of *the king*,
20. And thou, my lord, *O king*,
— on the throne of my lord *the king*
21. when my lord *the king* shall sleep
22. while she yet talked with *the king*,
23. And they told *the king*,
— when he was come in before *the king*, he bowed himself before *the king*
24. Nathan said, My lord, *O king*, hast thou
25. hath called all *the king*'s sons,
— God save *king* Adonijah.
27. Is this thing done by my lord *the king*,
— sit on the throne of my lord *the king*
28. Then *king* David answered and said,
— she came into *the king*'s presence, and stood before *the king*.
29. And *the king* sware, and said,
31. and did reverence *to the king*, and said, Let my lord *king* David live
32. And *king* David said, Call me Zadok
— And they came before *the king*.
33. *The king* also said unto them, Take
34. anoint him there *king* over
—, 39. God save *king* Solomon.
36. Benaiah...answered *the king*,
— Amen: the Lord God of my lord *the king*
37. with my lord *the king*,
— than the throne of my lord *king* David.
38. upon *king* David's mule,
43. our lord *king* David
44. *the king* hath sent with him Zadok

1K. 1:44. upon *the king*'s mule:
45. have anointed him *king*
47. *the king*'s servants came to bless our lord *king* David,
— And *the king* bowed himself
48. also thus said *the king*,
51. Adonijah feareth *king* Solomon:
— Let *king* Solomon swear unto me
53. So *king* Solomon sent,
— bowed himself *to king* Solomon:
2:17. Speak,...unto Solomon *the king*,
18. I will speak for thee unto *the king*.
19. Bath-sheba therefore went unto *king*
— And *the king* rose up to meet her,
— a seat to be set for *the king*'s mother;
20. And *the king* said unto her,
22. *king* Solomon answered
23. Then *king* Solomon sware
25. And *king* Solomon sent
26. unto Abiathar the priest said *the king*,
29. it was told *king* Solomon
30. Thus saith *the king*,
— Benaiah brought *the king*
31. *the king* said unto him,
35. *the king* put Benaiah...in his room
— Zadok the priest did *the king* put
36. *the king* sent and called for Shimei,
38. Shimei said *unto the king*, The saying (is) good: as my lord *the king* hath said,
39. Achish son of Maachah *king of* Gath.
42. *the king* sent and called for Shimei,
44. *The king* said moreover to Shimei,
45. *And king* Solomon (shall be) blessed,
46. So *the king* commanded
3: 1. made affinity with Pharaoh *king of* Egypt,
4. *the king* went to Gibeon
13. there shall not be any *among the kings*
16. came there two women,...unto *the king*,
22. Thus they spake before *the king*.
23. Then said *the king*, The one saith,
24. *the king* said, Bring me a sword. And they brought a sword before *the king*.
25. *the king* said, Divide the living child
26. the living child (was) unto *the king*,
27. *the king* answered and said, Give her
28. the judgment which *the king* had judged; and they feared *the king*:
4: 1. So *king* Solomon was *king* over all Israel.
5. principal officer, (and) *the king*'s friend:
7. provided victuals for *the king*
19. Sihon *king of* the Amorites, and of Og *king of* Bashan;
24(5:4). all *the kings on* this side the river:
27(—:7). provided victual for *king* Solomon, and for all that came unto *king*
34(—:14). all *kings of* the earth.
5: 1(15). And Hiram *king of* Tyre sent his
—(—). they had anointed him *king*
13(27). *king* Solomon raised a levy
17(31). And *the king* commanded,
6: 2. the house which *king* Solomon built
7:13. *king* Solomon sent and fetched
14. he came to *king* Solomon,
40. the work that he made *king* Solomon
45. Hiram made *to king* Solomon
46. did *the king* cast them,
51. the work that *king* Solomon made
8: 1. unto *king* Solomon in Jerusalem,
2. assembled themselves unto *king* Solomon
5. *And king* Solomon, and all the
14. *the king* turned his face
62. *And the king*, and all Israel
63. So *the king* and all the children of Israel
64. did *the king* hallow the middle of the
66. and they blessed *the king*,
9: 1. when Solomon had finished...*the king*'s
10. the house of the Lord, and *the king*'s
11. Hiram *the king of* Tyre had furnished
— *king* Solomon gave Hiram twenty cities
14. Hiram sent *to the king*
15. the levy which *king* Solomon raised;
16. Pharaoh *king of* Egypt had gone up,
26. *king* Solomon made a navy
28. and brought (it) to *king* Solomon.
10: 3. there was not (any) thing hid from *the king*,
6. she said to *the king*,

1K. 10: 9. therefore made he thee *king*,
10. she gave *the king* an hundred and twenty
— queen of Sheba gave *to king* Solomon.
12. *the king* made of the almug trees
— of the Lord, and for *the king*'s house,
13. *And king* Solomon gave unto the queen
— gave her of his *royal* bounty. (lit. as the hand of *the king*)
15. and of all *the kings of* Arabia,
16. *king* Solomon made two hundred targets
17. *the king* put them in the house
18. *the king* made a great throne
21. all *king* Solomon's drinking vessels
22. *the king had* at sea a navy
23. *king* Solomon exceeded all *the kings of*
26. with *the king* at Jerusalem.
27. *the king* made silver (to be)...as stones,
28. *the king*'s merchants received
29. *the kings of* the Hittites, *and for the kings of*
11: 1. *But king* Solomon loved many strange
14. of *the king*'s seed in Edom.
18. unto Pharaoh *king of* Egypt;
23. from his lord Hadadezer *king of* Zobah:
26. he lifted up (his) hand *against the king.*
27. he lifted up (his) hand *against the king:*
37. and shalt be *king* over Israel.
40. unto Shishak *king of* Egypt,
12: 2. fled from the presence of *king* Solomon,
6. *king* Rehoboam consulted
12. as *the king* had appointed,
13. *the king* answered the people
15. Wherefore *the king* hearkened not
16. that *the king* hearkened not
— the people answered *the king*,
18. *king* Rehoboam sent Adoram,
— *Therefore king* Rehoboam made speed
23. Rehoboam, the son of Solomon, *king of*
27. unto Rehoboam *king of* Judah,
— and go again to Rehoboam *king of* Judah.
28. Whereupon *the king* took counsel,
13: 4. when *king* Jeroboam heard the saying
6. *the king* answered and said
— *the king*'s hand was restored
7. *the king* said unto the man of God,
8. the man of God said unto *the king*,
11. he had spoken unto *the king*,
14: 2. told me *that* (I should be) *king* (lit. *for king*)
14. the Lord shall raise him up *a king*
19. of the chronicles *of the kings of* Israel.
25. in the fifth year *of king* Rehoboam, (that) Shishak *king of* Egypt came up
26. the treasures of *the king*'s house;
27. *king* Rehoboam made in their stead
— kept the door of *the king*'s house.
28. when *the king* went into the house
29. of the chronicles *of the kings of* Judah?
15: 1. in the eighteenth year *of king* Jeroboam
7, 23. of the chronicles *of the kings of* Judah?
9. twentieth year of Jeroboam *king of* Israel
16. between Asa and Baasha *king of* Israel
17. And Baasha *king of* Israel went up
— come in to Asa *king of* Judah.
18. the treasures of *the king*'s house,
— *king* Asa sent them to Ben-hadad,...*king of* Syria,
19. thy league with Baasha *king of* Israel,
20. Ben-hadad hearkened unto *king* Asa,
22. *Then king* Asa made a proclamation
— *king* Asa built with them
25. in the second year of Asa *king of* Judah,
28. the third year of Asa *king of* Judah
31. of the chronicles *of the kings of* Israel?
32. between Asa and Baasha *king of* Israel
33. third year of Asa *king of* Judah
16: 5, 14, 20, 27. chronicles *of the kings of* Israel?
8. twenty and sixth year of Asa *king of*
10, 15. twenty and seventh year of Asa *king of*
16. and hath also slain *the king:*
18. the palace of *the king*'s house, and burnt *the king*'s house
23. thirty and first year of Asa *king of*
29. thirty and eighth year of Asa *king of*
31. Ethbaal *king of* the Zidonians,
33. all *the kings of* Israel that were before him.
19: 15. anoint Hazael (to be) *king*
16. anoint (to be) *king* (lit. *for king*) over Israel:

1K. 20: 1. Ben-hadad *the king of* Syria gathered
— (there were) thirty and two *kings*
2. to Ahab *king of* Israel into the city,
4. *the king of* Israel answered and said, My lord, *O king*,
7. Then *the king of* Israel called
9. Tell my lord *the king*, All that
11. *the king of* Israel answered and said,
12. *and the kings* in the pavilions,
13. came a prophet unto Ahab *king of* Israel,
16. he *and the kings, the* thirty and two *kings*
20. Ben-hadad *the king of* Syria escaped
21. *the king of* Israel went out, and smote
22. the prophet came to *the king of* Israel,
— *the king of* Syria will come up against
23. the servants of *the king of* Syria said
24. Take *the kings* away,
28. of God, and spake unto *the king of* Israel,
31. *the kings of* the house of Israel (are) merciful *kings:*
— and go out to *the king of* Israel:
32. on their heads, and came to *the king of*
38. and waited *for the king* by the way,
39. And as *the king* passed by, he cried unto *the king:*
40. *the king of* Israel said unto him,
41. *the king of* Israel discerned him
43. *the king of* Israel went to his house
21: 1. by the palace of Ahab *king of* Samaria.
10. Thou didst blaspheme God *and the king.*
13. Naboth did blaspheme God *and the king.*
18. go down to meet Ahab *king of* Israel,
22: 2. Jehoshaphat *the king of* Judah came down to *the king of* Israel.
3. *the king of* Israel said unto his servants,
— out of the hand of *the king of* Syria?
4. Jehoshaphat said to *the king of* Israel,
5. Jehoshaphat said unto *the king of* Israel,
6. *the king of* Israel gathered the prophets
— into the hand of *the king.*
8. And *the king of* Israel said
— Let not *the king* say so.
9. *the king of* Israel called an officer,
10. *And the king of* Israel and Jehoshaphat *the king of*
12. deliver (it) into *the king*'s hand.
13. (declare) good unto *the king*
15. So he came to *the king.* And *the king* said
— into the hand of *the king.*
16. *the king* said unto him,
18. *the king of* Israel said unto Jehoshaphat,
26. And *the king of* Israel said, Take
— Joash *the king*'s son;
27. Thus saith *the king*,
29. *the king of* Israel and Jehoshaphat *the king of* Judah went
30. *the king of* Israel said unto Jehoshaphat,
— And *the king of* Israel disguised himself,
31. *But the king of* Syria commanded
— save only with *the king of* Israel.
32. they said, Surely it (is) *the king of* Israel.
33. perceived that it (was) not *the king of* Israel,
34. smote *the king of* Israel between
35. *and the king* was stayed up
37. So *the king* died, and was brought to Samaria; and they buried *the king*
39. the chronicles *of the kings of* Israel?
41. in the fourth year of Ahab *king of* Israel.
44(45). Jehoshaphat made peace with *the king of*
45(46). the chronicles *of the kings of* Judah?
47(48). no *king* in Edom: a deputy (was) *king.*
51(52). of Jehoshaphat *king of* Judah,
2K. 1: 3. to meet the messengers of *the king of*
6. turn again unto *the king*
9. *the king* hath said, Come down.
11. thus hath *the king* said,
15. went down with him unto *the king.*
17. Jehoram the son of Jehoshaphat *king of*
18. the book of the chronicles *of the kings of*
3: 1. eighteenth year of Jehoshaphat *king of*
4. Mesha *king of* Moab was a sheepmaster, and rendered *unto the king of* Israel
5. *the king of* Moab rebelled *against the king of*
6. *king* Jehoram went out of Samaria
7. to Jehoshaphat *the king of* Judah, saying, *The king of* Moab hath rebelled

2K. 3: 9. *the king of* Israel went, *and the king of* Judah, *and the king of* Edom:
10. *the king of* Israel said, Alas! that the Lord hath called these three *kings*
11. one of *the king of* Israel's servants
12. *the king of* Israel and Jehoshaphat *and the king of* Edom went down
13. Elisha said unto *the king of* Israel,
— And *the king of* Israel said unto him, Nay: for the Lord hath called these three *kings*
14. the presence of Jehoshaphat *the king of*
21. *the kings* were come up
23. *the kings* are surely slain,
26. when *the king of* Moab saw that the
— to break through (even) unto *the king of*
4:13. wouldest thou be spoken for to *the king*,
5: 1. captain of the host of *the king of* Syria,
5. And *the king of* Syria said, Go to,
— a letter unto *the king of* Israel.
6. he brought the letter to *the king of* Israel,
7. when *the king of* Israel had read
8. heard that *the king of* Israel had rent his clothes, that he sent to *the king*,
6: 8. *Then the king of* Syria warred against
9. the man of God sent unto *the king of*
10. *the king of* Israel sent to the place
11. the heart of *the king of* Syria was
— which of us (is) for *the king of* Israel?
12. None, my lord, *O king:*
— telleth *the king of* Israel
21. *the king of* Israel said unto Elisha,
24. Ben-hadad *king of* Syria gathered
26. as *the king of* Israel was passing
— Help, my lord, *O king.*
28. *the king* said unto her, What
30. when *the king* heard the words
7: 2. a lord on whose hand *the king* leaned
6. *the king of* Israel hath hired against us *the kings of* the Hittites, and *the kings of* the Egyptians,
9. we may go and tell *the king*'s houshold.
11. they told (it) to *the king*'s house
12. *the king* arose in the night,
14. *the king* sent after the host
15. messengers returned, and told *the king.*
17. *And the king* appointed the lord
— when *the king* came down to him.
18. as the man of God had spoken to *the king*,
8: 3. to cry unto *the king*
4. *And the king* talked with Gehazi
5. as he was telling *the king*
— cried to *the king* for her house and for her land. And Gehazi said, My lord, *O king*,
6. when *the king* asked the woman,
— So *the king* appointed
7. Ben-hadad *the king of* Syria was sick;
8. *the king* said unto Hazael,
9. Thy son Ben-hadad *king of* Syria
13. thou (shalt be) *king* over Syria.
16. Joram the son of Ahab *king of* Israel, Jehoshaphat (being) then *king of* Judah, Jehoram the son of Jehoshaphat *king of*
18. he walked in the way of *the kings of* Israel,
20. and made *a king* over themselves.
23. of the chronicles *of the kings of* Judah?
25. Joram the son of Ahab *king of* Israel did Ahaziah the son of Jehoram *king of* Judah
26. the daughter of Omri *king of* Israel.
28. Hazael *king of* Syria in Ramoth-gilead;
29. *king* Joram went back to be healed
— against Hazael *king of* Syria. And Ahaziah the son of Jehoram *king of* Judah
9: 3, 6, 12. I have anointed thee *king*
14. because of Hazael *king of* Syria.
15. *king* Joram was returned
— when he fought with Hazael *king of* Syria.
16. Ahaziah *king of* Judah was come down
18, 19. Thus saith *the king*,
21. Joram *king of* Israel and Ahaziah *king of*
27. when Ahaziah *the king of* Judah saw
34. bury her: for she (is) *a king*'s daughter.
10: 4. two *kings* stood not before him:
6. *the king*'s sons, (being) seventy persons,
7. they took *the king*'s sons,
8. the heads of *the king*'s sons.
13. the brethren of Ahaziah *king of* Judah,
— the children of *the king*

2K. 10:34. the book of the chronicles *of the kings of*
11: 2. the daughter of *king* Joram,
— from among *the king*'s sons
4. and shewed them *the king*'s son.
5. keepers of the watch of *the king*'s house;
7. they shall keep the watch...about *the king*
8. ye shall compass *the king*
— be ye with *the king*
10. *king* David's spears and shields,
11. round about *the king*, from the right
12. he brought forth *the king*'s son,
— God save *the king.*
14. *the king* stood by a pillar,
— and the trumpeters by *the king*,
16. came into *the king*'s house:
17. a covenant between the Lord and *the king*
— between *the king* also and the people.
19. they brought down *the king*
— the gate of the guard to *the king*'s house. And he sat on the throne of *the kings.*
20. with the sword (beside) *the king*'s house.
12: 6(7). three and twentieth year *of king*
7(8). *king* Jehoash called for Jehoiada
10(11). *the king*'s scribe and the high priest
17(18). Hazael *king of* Syria went up,
18(19). Jehoash *king of* Judah took
—(—). *kings of* Judah, had dedicated,
—(—). and in *the king*'s house, and sent (it) to Hazael *king of* Syria:
19(20). the chronicles *of the kings of* Judah?
13: 1. Joash the son of Ahaziah *king of*
3. the hand of Hazael *king of* Syria,
4. *the king of* Syria oppressed them.
7. *the king of* Syria had destroyed them,
8, 12. the chronicles *of the kings of* Israel?
10. thirty and seventh year of Joash *king of*
12. fought against Amaziah *king of*
13. buried in Samaria with *the kings of* Israel.
14. Joash *the king of* Israel came down
16. And he said *to the king of* Israel,
— Elisha put his hands upon *the king*'s hands.
18. And he said *unto the king of* Israel,
22. But Hazael *king of* Syria oppressed
24. So Hazael *king of* Syria died;
14: 1. of Joash son of Jehoahaz *king of* Israel reigned Amaziah the son of Joash *king of* Judah.
5. which had slain *the king* his father.
8. Jehoash, the son of Jehoahaz son of Jehu, *king of*
9. And Jehoash *the king of* Israel sent to Amaziah *king of* Judah,
11. Jehoash *king of* Israel went up; and he and Amaziah *king of* Judah
13. And Jehoash *king of* Israel took Amaziah *king of* Judah,
14. in the treasures of *the king*'s house,
15. fought with Amaziah *king of* Judah,
— of the chronicles *of the kings of* Israel?
16. buried in Samaria with *the kings of*
17. Amaziah the son of Joash *king of* Judah
— Jehoash son of Jehoahaz *king of* Israel
18. the chronicles *of the kings of* Judah?
22. after that *the king* slept
23. Amaziah the son of Joash *king of* Judah Jeroboam the son of Joash *king of* Israel
28. the chronicles *of the kings of* Israel?
29. his fathers, (even) with *the kings of* Israel;
15: 1. the twenty and seventh year of Jeroboam *king of* Israel began Azariah son of Amaziah *king of* Judah
5. the Lord smote *the king*,
— Jotham *the king*'s son (was) over the house,
6, 36. the chronicles *of the kings of* Judah?
8. year of Azariah *king of* Judah
11, 15, 21, 26, 31. the chronicles *of the kings of*
13. year of Uzziah *king of* Judah;
17. year of Azariah *king of* Judah
19. Pul *the king of* Assyria came against
20. to give *to the king of* Assyria. So *the king of* Assyria turned
23. the fiftieth year of Azariah *king of*
25. in the palace of *the king*'s house,
27. two and fiftieth year of Azariah *king of*
29. In the days of Pekah *king of* Israel came Tiglath-pileser *king of* Assyria,
32. Pekah the son of Remaliah *king of* Israel

2K. 15 32. Jotham the son of Uzziah *king of* Judah
37. against Judah Rezin *the king of* Syria,
16: 1. Ahaz the son of Jotham *king of* Judah
3. walked in the way of *the kings of* Israel,
5. Rezin *king of* Syria and Pekah son of Remaliah *king of* Israel came up
6. Rezin *king of* Syria recovered Elath
7. to Tiglath-pileser *king of* Assyria,
— save me out of the hand of *the king of* Syria, and out of the hand of *the king of* Israel,
8. the treasures of *the king*'s house, and sent (it for) a present *to the king of* Assyria.
9. And *the king of* Assyria hearkened unto him: for *the king of* Assyria went up
10. *king* Ahaz went to Damascus to meet Tiglath-pileser *king of* Assyria,
— *king* Ahaz sent to Urijah the priest
11. *king* Ahaz had sent from Damascus:
— *king* Ahaz came from Damascus.
12. when *the king* was come from Damascus, *the king* saw the altar: and *the king* approached to the altar,
15. *king* Ahaz commanded Urijah
— and *the king*'s burnt sacrifice,
16. all that *king* Ahaz commanded.
17. *king* Ahaz cut off the borders
18. *the king*'s entry without,
— of the Lord for *the king of* Assyria.
19. the book of the chronicles *of the kings of*
17: 1. the twelfth year of Ahaz *king of* Judah
2. but not *as the kings of* Israel
3. Shalmaneser *king of* Assyria;
4. *the king of* Assyria found conspiracy
— to So *king of* Egypt, and brought no present *to the king of* Assyria, as (he had done) year by year: therefore *the king of*
5. *the king of* Assyria came up
6. ninth year of Hoshea *the king of* Assyria
7. under the hand of Pharaoh *king of* Egypt,
8. *and of the kings of* Israel, which they had
24. *the king of* Assyria brought (men)
26. they spake *to the king of* Assyria,
27. Then *the king of* Assyria commanded,
18: 1. of Hoshea son of Elah *king of* Israel, (that) Hezekiah the son of Ahaz *king of* Judah
5. like him among all *the kings of* Judah,
7. rebelled *against the king of* Assyria,
9. in the fourth year *of king* Hezekiah,
— of Hoshea son of Elah *king of* Israel, (that) Shalmaneser *king of* Assyria came
10. the ninth year of Hoshea *king of* Israel,
11. *the king of* Assyria did carry away
13. the fourteenth year *of king* Hezekiah did Sennacherib *king of* Assyria come up
14. Hezekiah *king of* Judah sent to *the king of*
— And *the king of* Assyria appointed unto Hezekiah *king of* Judah
15. the treasures of *the king*'s house.
16. which Hezekiah *king of* Judah had overlaid, and gave it *to the king of*
17. *the king of* Assyria sent...to *king* Hezekiah
18. when they had called to *the king*,
19. saith *the* great *king*, *the king of* Assyria,
21. so (is) Pharaoh *king of* Egypt unto all
23. pledges to my lord *the king of* Assyria,
28. Hear the word of *the* great *king*, *the king of* Assyria:
29. Thus saith *the king*, Let not Hezekiah
30. be delivered into the hand of *the king of*
31. for thus saith *the king of* Assyria,
33. out of the hand of *the king of* Assyria?
36. for *the king*'s commandment was,
19: 1. when *king* Hezekiah heard (it),
4. *the king of* Assyria his master hath sent
5. the servants of *king* Hezekiah
6. the servants of *the king of* Assyria have
8. found *the king of* Assyria warring
9. heard say of Tirhakah *king of* Ethiopia,
10. Thus shall ye speak to Hezekiah *king of*
— into the hand of *the king of* Assyria.
11. what *the kings of* Assyria have done
13. *the king of* Hamath, *and the king of* Arpad, *and the king* of the city of Sepharvaim,
17. *the kings of* Assyria have destroyed
20. against Sennacherib *king of* Assyria
32. the Lord concerning *the king of* Assyria,
36. So Sennacherib *king of* Assyria departed,

2K. 20: 6. out of the hand of *the king of* Assyria;
12. Berodach-baladan,...*king of* Babylon,
14. Isaiah the prophet unto *king* Hezekiah,
18. in the palace of *the king of* Babylon.
20. the chronicles *of the kings of* Judah?
21: 3. a grove, as did Ahab *king of* Israel;
11. Manasseh *king of* Judah hath done
17, 25. the book of the chronicles *of the kings of* Judah?
23. and slew *the king* in his own house.
24. conspired against *king* Amon;
22: 3. in the eighteenth year *of king* Josiah, (that) *the king* sent Shaphan
9. came to *the king*, and brought *the king* word
10. Shaphan the scribe shewed *the king*,
— Shaphan read it *before the king*.
11. when *the king* had heard the words
12. *the king* commanded Hilkiah
— Asahiah a servant of *the king*'s,
16. of the book which *the king of* Judah hath
18. to *the king of* Judah which sent you
20. And they brought *the king* word again.
23: 1. And *the king* sent,
2. *the king* went up into the house
3. *the king* stood by a pillar,
4. *the king* commanded Hilkiah
5. whom *the kings of* Judah had ordained
11. that *the kings of* Judah had given to the sun,
12. which *the kings of* Judah had made,
— did *the king* beat down, and brake
13. Solomon *the king of* Israel had builded
— did *the king* defile.
19. which *the kings of* Israel had made
21. *the king* commanded all the people,
22. nor in all the days of *the kings of* Israel, *nor of the kings of* Judah;
23. in the eighteenth year *of king* Josiah,
25. like unto him was there no *king* before
28. the chronicles *of the kings of* Judah?
29. Pharaoh-nechoh *king of* Egypt went up against *the king of* Assyria
— *king* Josiah went against him;
24: 1, 11. Nebuchadnezzar *king of* Babylon came
5. the chronicles *of the kings of* Judah?
7. *the king of* Egypt came not again
— *the king of* Babylon had taken from
— all that pertained *to the king of* Egypt.
10. of Nebuchadnezzar *king of* Babylon
12. Jehoiachin *the king of* Judah went out to *the king of* Babylon,
— and *the king of* Babylon took him
13. and the treasures of *the king*'s house,
— vessels of gold which Solomon *king of*
15. and *the king*'s mother, and *the king*'s wives,
16. them *the king of* Babylon brought captive
17. *the king of* Babylon made Mattaniah
20. Zedekiah rebelled *against the king of*
25: 1. Nebuchadnezzar *king of* Babylon came,
2. the eleventh year *of king* Zedekiah.
4. by *the king*'s garden:
5. of the Chaldees pursued after *the king*,
6. So they took *the king*, and brought him up to *the king of* Babylon
8. the nineteenth year *of king* Nebuchadnezzar *king of* Babylon.
— a servant of *the king of* Babylon,
9. house of the Lord, and *the king*'s house,
11. fell away to *the king of* Babylon,
19. that were in *the king*'s presence,
20. brought them to *the king of* Babylon
21. *the king of* Babylon smote them,
22. whom Nebuchadnezzar *king of* Babylon
23. *the king of* Babylon had made Gedaliah
24. and serve *the king of* Babylon;
27. the captivity of Jehoiachin *king of*
— Evil-merodach *king of* Babylon
— lift up the head of Jehoiachin *king of*
28. above the throne of *the kings*
30. allowance given him of *the king*,
1Ch. 1:43. *the kings* that reigned in the land of Edom before (any) *king* reigned
3: 2. the daughter of Talmai *king of*
4:23. they dwelt with *the king*
41. in the days of Hezekiah *king of* Judah,
5: 6. *king of* Assyria carried away (captive):
17. in the days of Jotham *king of* Judah, and in the days of Jeroboam *king of* Israel.

1Ch. 5:26. the spirit of Pul *king of* Assyria, and the spirit of Tilgath-pilneser *king of*
9: 1. *the kings of* Israel and Judah,
18. hitherto (waited) in *the king*'s gate
11: 2. when Saul was *king*,
3. came all the elders of Israel to *the king*
— they anointed David *king*
14: 1. Hiram *king of* Tyre sent messengers
2. the Lord had confirmed him *king*
8. David was anointed *king*
15:29. saw *king* David dancing
16:21. he reproved *kings* for their sakes,
17:16. David *the king* came and sat
18: 3. smote Hadarezer *king of* Zobah
5. to help Hadarezer *king of* Zobah,
9. Tou *king of* Hamath heard how David
— the host of Hadarezer *king of* Zobah;
10. sent Hadoram his son to *king* David,
11. Them also *king* David dedicated
17. the sons of David (were) chief about *the king.*
19: 1. *the king of* the children of Ammon
5. *the king* said, Tarry at Jericho
7. and *the king of* Maachah and his people;
9. *and the kings* that were come
20: 1. the time that *kings* go out (to battle),
2. David took the crown of *their king*
21: 3. but, my lord *the king*, (are) they not
4. *the king*'s word prevailed
6. *the king*'s word was abominable
23. let my lord *the king* do
24. *king* David said to Ornan,
24: 6. wrote them before *the king*,
31. in the presence of David *the king*,
25: 2. according to the order of *the king.*
5. Heman *the king*'s seer
6. according to *the king*'s order
26:26. David *the king*, and the chief fathers,
30. the service of *the king.*
32. *king* David made rulers
— affairs of *the king.*
27: 1. officers that served *the king* in any
24. the chronicles *of king* David.
25. over *the king*'s treasures (was) Azmaveth
31. the substance which (was) *king* David's.
32. of Hachmoni (was) with *the king*'s sons:
33. Ahithophel (was) *the king's* counsellor: and Hushai the Archite (was) *the king*'s companion:
34. the general of *the king's* army
28: 1. ministered to *the king* by course,
— substance and possession *of the king*,
2. David *the king* stood up
4. to be *king* over Israel for ever:
29: 1. David *the king* said
6. the rulers of *the king*'s work,
9. David *the king* also rejoiced
20. worshipped the Lord, *and the king.*
23. Solomon sat on the throne...*as king*
24. the sons likewise of *king* David, submitted themselves unto Solomon *the king.*
25. as had not been on any *king* before
29. the acts of David *the king*,
2Ch. 1:12. none of *the kings* have *had*
14. with *the king* at Jerusalem.
15. *the king* made silver and gold at
16. *the king*'s merchants received
17. for all *the kings of* the Hittites, *and* for *the kings of* Syria,
2: 3(2). sent to Huram *the king of* Tyre,
11(10). Huram *the king of* Tyre answered
—(—). he hath made thee *king*
12(11). hath given to David *the king*
4:11. the work that he was to make *for king*
16. make *to king* Solomon
17. In the plain of Jordan did *the king* cast
5: 3. assembled themselves unto *the king*
6. *Also king* Solomon, and all the congregation
6: 3. And *the king* turned his face,
7: 4. *Then the king* and all the people
5. *king* Solomon offered
— *the king* and all the people
6. David *the king* had made to praise
11. the house of the Lord, and *the king*'s house:
8:10. the chief of *king* Solomon's officers,
11. in the house of David *king of* Israel,
15. the commandment of *the king*

2Ch. 8:18. brought (them) to *king* Solomon.
9: 5. And she said to *the king*,
8. (to be) *king* for the Lord thy God:
— therefore made he thee *king* over them,
9. she gave *the king* an hundred and twenty talents
— the queen of Sheba gave *king* Solomon.
11. *the king* made (of) the algum trees
— and to *the king*'s palace,
12. *And king* Solomon gave to the queen of
— which she had brought unto *the king.*
14. all *the kings of* Arabia
15. *king* Solomon made two hundred targets
16. *the king* put them in the house of the forest
17. *the king* made a great throne of ivory,
20. all the drinking vessels of *king* Solomon
21. *the king's* ships went to Tarshish
22. And *king* Solomon passed all *the kings of*
23. all *the kings of* the earth sought
25. with *the king* at Jerusalem.
26. he reigned over all *the kings*
27. *the king* made silver in Jerusalem as stones,
10: 2. the presence of Solomon *the king*,
6. *king* Rehoboam took counsel with the old
12. as *the king* bade,
13. *the king* answered them roughly; and *king* Rehoboam forsook
15. So *the king* hearkened not unto the people:
16. *the king* would not hearken unto them the people answered *the king*,
18. Then *king* Rehoboam sent Hadoram
— *But king* Rehoboam made speed to get him up to (his) chariot,
11: 3. Speak unto Rehoboam...*king of* Judah,
12: 2. in the fifth year *of king* Rehoboam Shishak *king of* Egypt came up against Jerusalem,
6. the princes...*and the king* humbled themselves;
9. Shishak *king of* Egypt came up
— the treasures of *the king*'s house;
10. *king* Rehoboam made shields of brass,
— that kept the entrance of *the king*'s house.
11. *the king* entered into the house of the Lord,
13. *king* Rehoboam strengthened himself
13: 1. the eighteenth year *of king* Jeroboam
15:16. the mother of Asa *the king*,
16: 1. Baasha *king of* Israel came up
— to Asa *king of* Judah.
2. and of *the king*'s house, and sent to Ben-hadad *king of*
3. break thy league with Baasha *king of*
4. Ben-hadad hearkened unto *king* Asa,
6. Asa *the king* took all Judah;
7. came to Asa *king of* Judah, and said
— thou hast relied on *the king of* Syria,
— therefore is the host of *the king of* Syria
11. *the kings* of Judah and Israel.
17:19. These waited on *the king*, beside (those) whom *the king* put
18: 3. And Ahab *king of* Israel said unto Jehoshaphat *king of* Judah,
4. Jehoshaphat said unto *the king of*
5. *the king of* Israel gathered together
— God will deliver (it) into *the king*'s hand.
7. *the king of* Israel said unto Jehoshaphat,
— Let not *the king* say so.
8. And *the king of* Israel called for one (of)
9. *And the king of* Israel and Jehoshaphat *king of* Judah sat either of them
11. the hand of *the king.*
12. the words of the prophets (declare) good to *the king*
14. when he was come to *the king*, *the king* said unto him,
15. And *the king* said to him,
17. And *the king of* Israel said
19. Who shall entice Ahab *king of* Israel,
25. Then *the king of* Israel said,
— and to Joash *the king*'s son;
26. Thus saith *the king*,
28. *the king of* Israel and Jehoshaphat *the king of* Judah went up to Ramoth-gilead.
29. *the king of* Israel said unto Jehoshaphat,
— *the king of* Israel disguised himself;
30. *Now the king of* Syria had commanded
— save only with *the king of* Israel.
31. they said, It (is) *the king of* Israel.

2Ch.18:32. perceived that it was not *the king of*
33. smote *the king of* Israel between
34. *howbeit the king of* Israel stayed (himself)
19: 1. Jehoshaphat *the king of* Judah returned
2. and said to *king* Jehoshaphat,
11. for all *the king*'s matters:
20:15. *and thou king* Jehoshaphat,
34. in the book of *the kings of* Israel.
35. after this did Jehoshaphat *king of* Judah join himself with Ahaziah *king of* Israel,
21: 2. the sons of Jehoshaphat *king of* Israel.
6. in the way of *the kings of* Israel,
8. made themselves *a king.*
12. nor in the ways of Asa *king of* Judah,
13. hast walked in the way of *the kings of*
17. that was found in *the king*'s house,
20. the sepulchres of *the kings.*
22: 1. Ahaziah the son of Jehoram *king of* Judah
5. the son of Ahab *king of* Israel to war against Hazael *king of*
6. fought with Hazael *king of* Syria. And Azariah the son of Jehoram *king of* Judah
11. the daughter of *the king*,
— stole him from among *the king*'s sons
— the daughter of *king* Jehoram,
23: 3. made a covenant with *the king*
— *the king*'s son shall reign,
5. a third part (shall be) at *the king*'s house;
7. the Levites shall compass *the king* round
— but be ye with *the king* when he cometh
9. that (had been) *king* David's,
10. by *the king* round about.
11. Then they brought out *the king*'s son,
— God save *the king.*
12. running and praising *the king*,
13. *the king* stood at his pillar
— the princes and the trumpets by *the king:*
15. the horse gate by *the king*'s house,
16. between all the people, and between *the king*,
20. brought down *the king* from the house
— the high gate into *the king*'s house, and set *the king* upon the throne
24: 6. *the king* called for Jehoiada
8. at *the king*'s commandment (lit. *the king* commanded) they made a chest,
11. was brought unto *the king*'s office
— *the king*'s scribe and the high priest's
12. *the king* and Jehoiada gave it to such
14. the rest of the money before *the king*
16. they buried him...among *the kings*,
17. made obeisance *to the king*. Then *the king* hearkened unto them.
21. at the commandment of *the king*
22. Joash *the king* remembered not the kindness
23. the spoil of them *unto the king of*
25. in the sepulchres of *the kings.*
27. the story of the book of *the kings.*
25: 3. that had killed *the king* his father.
7. came a man of God to him, saying. *O king*,
16. Art thou made of *the king's* counsel?
17. Amaziah *king of* Judah took advice, and sent to Joash, the son...*king of* Israel,
18. Joash *king of* Israel sent to Amaziah *king of* Judah saying,
21. Joash *the king of* Israel went up;
— he and Amaziah *king of* Judah,
23. Joash *the king of* Israel took Amaziah *king of* Judah, the son of Joash,
24. the treasures of *the king*'s house,
25. Amaziah the son of Joash *king of* Judah
— death of Joash son of Jehoahaz *king of* Israel
26. *the kings of* Judah and Israel?
26: 2. after that *the king* slept with his fathers.
11. (one) of *the king*'s captains.
13. to help *the king* against the enemy.
18. And they withstood Uzziah *the king*,
21. Uzziah *the king* was a leper
— Jotham his son (was) over *the king*'s house,
23. the field...which (belonged) *to the kings;*
27: 5. He fought also with *the king of* the
7. *the kings of* Israel and Judah.
28. 2. the ways of *the kings of* Israel,
5. into the hand of *the king of* Syria;
— into the hand of *the king of* Israel,
7. slew Maaseiah *the king*'s son,
— Elkanah (that was) next to *the king.*

2Ch.28:16. At that time did *king* Ahaz send unto *the kings of* Assyria
19. low because of Ahaz *king of* Israel;
20. Tilgath-pilneser *king of* Assyria came
21. the house of *the king*, and of the princes, and gave (it) *unto the king of* Assyria:
22. this (is that) *king* Ahaz.
23. the gods of *the kings of* Syria help them,
26. *the kings of* Judah and Israel.
27. into the sepulchres of *the kings of* Israel:
29:15. according to the commandment of *the king*
18. Then they went in to Hezekiah *the king*,
19. which *king* Ahaz in his reign did cast
20. Then Hezekiah *the king* rose early,
23. before *the king and* the congregation;
24. for *the king* commanded
25. of Gad *the king*'s seer,
27. (ordained) by David *king of* Israel.
29. *the king* and all that were present
30. *the king* and the princes commanded
30: 2. For *the king* had taken counsel,
4. the thing pleased *the king*
6. the letters from *the king*
— according to the commandment of *the king*,
— escaped out of the hand of *the kings of*
12. the commandment of *the king*
24. Hezekiah *king of* Judah did give to
26. Solomon the son of David *king of* Israel
31: 3. *the king*'s portion of his substance
13. at the commandment of Hezekiah *the king*,
32: 1. Sennacherib *king of* Assyria came,
4. Why should *the kings of* Assyria come,
7. nor dismayed for *the king of* Assyria,
8. upon the words of Hezekiah *king of*
9. did Sennacherib *king of* Assyria send
— unto Hezekiah *king of* Judah, and
10. Thus saith Sennacherib *king of* Assyria,
11. out of the hand of *the king of* Assyria?
20. Hezekiah *the king*, and the prophet Isaiah
21. captains in the camp of *the king of* Assyria.
22. from the hand of Sennacherib *the king of*
23. and presents to Hezekiah *king of* Judah:
32. *the kings of* Judah and Israel.
33:11. captains of the host *of the king of* Assyria,
18. in the book of *the kings of* Israel.
25. conspired against *king* Amon;
34:11. which *the kings of* Judah had destroyed.
16. Shaphan carried the book to *the king*, and brought *the king* word
18. Shaphan the scribe told *the king*,
— Shaphan read it before *the king.*
19. *the king* had heard the words of the law,
20. *the king* commanded Hilkiah,
— a servant of *the king*'s,
22. (they) that *the king* (had appointed),
24. they have read before *the king of* Judah:
26. as for *the king of* Judah, who sent you
28. So they brought *the king* word again.
29. *the king* sent and gathered together
30. *the king* went up into the house of the Lord,
31. *the king* stood in his place,
35: 3. Solomon the son of David *king of* Israel
4. the writing of David *king of* Israel,
7. these (were) of *the king*'s substance.
10. according to *the king*'s commandment.
15. Jeduthun *the king*'s seer;
16. to the commandment of *king* Josiah.
18. neither did all *the kings of* Israel keep
20. Necho *king of* Egypt came up to fight
21. have I to do with thee, thou *king of* Judah?
23. the archers shot *at king* Josiah; and *the king* said
27. *the kings of* Israel and Judah.
36: 3. *the king of* Egypt put him down at
4. *the king of* Egypt made Eliakim his
6. came up Nebuchadnezzar *king of* Babylon,
8. *the kings of* Israel and Judah:
10. *king* Nebuchadnezzar sent, and brought
13. also rebelled *against king* Nebuchadnezzar,
17. brought upon them *the king of* the Chaldees,
18. the treasures of *the king*,
22. the first year of Cyrus *king of* Persia,
— the spirit of Cyrus *king of* Persia,
23. Thus saith Cyrus *king of* Persia,
Ezr. 1: 1. in the first year of Cyrus *king of* Persia.
— the spirit of Cyrus *king of* Persia,
2. Thus saith Cyrus *king of* Persia,

Ezr 1: 7. *Also* Cyrus *the king* brought forth the vessels
8. those did Cyrus *king of* Persia bring
2: 1. Nebuchadnezzar *the king of* Babylon
3: 7. the grant that they had of Cyrus *king of*
10. after the ordinance of David *king of*
4: 2. the days of Esar-haddon *king of* Assur,
3. as *king* Cyrus *the king of* Persia hath
5. all the days of Cyrus *king of* Persia, even until the reign of Darius *king of* Persia.
7. companions, unto Artaxerxes *king of*
6:22. turned the heart of *the king of* Assyria
7: 1. in the reign of Artaxerxes *king of* Persia,
6. *the king* granted him all his request,
7. in the seventh year of Artaxerxes *the king*.
8. the seventh year *of the king*.
11. the letter that *the king* Artaxerxes
27. (such a thing) as this in *the king*'s heart,
28. hath extended mercy unto me before *the king*, and his counsellors, and before all *the king*'s mighty princes.
8: 1. in the reign of Artaxerxes *the king*.
22. to require of *the king* a band of soldiers
— we had spoken *unto the king*,
25. which *the king*, and his counsellors,
36. they delivered *the king*'s commissions unto *the king*'s lieutenants,
9: 7. have we, *our kings*, (and) our priests, been delivered into the hand of *the kings of* the lands,
9. in the sight of *the kings of* Persia,
Neh. 1:11. I was *the king*'s cupbearer.
2: 1. the twentieth year of Artaxerxes *the king*,
— I took up the wine, and gave (it) *unto the king*.
2. *the king* said unto me, Why (is) thy
3. said *unto the king*, Let *the king* live for ever:
4. *the king* said unto me, For what dost
5, 7. I said *unto the king*, If it please *the king*,
6. *the king* said unto me, the queen also
— So it pleased *the king* to send me;
8. the keeper of *the king*'s forest,
— And *the king* granted me, according
9. and gave them *the king*'s letters. Now *the king* had sent captains
14. and to *the king*'s pool:
18. also *the king*'s words that he had spoken unto me.
19. will ye rebel against *the king?*
3:15. of the pool of Siloah by *the king*'s garden,
25. which lieth out from *the king*'s high house,
5: 4. borrowed money for *the king*'s tribute,
14. the two and thirtieth year of Artaxerxes *the king*,
6: 6. that thou mayest be their *king*,
7. (There is) *a king* in Judah: and now shall it be reported *to the king*
7: 6. Nebuchadnezzar *the king of* Babylon
9:22. the land of *the king of* Heshbon, and the land of Og *king of* Bashan
24. with *their kings*, and the people
32. *on our kings*, on our princes,
— *the kings of* Assyria
34. *our kings*, our princes,
37. *unto the kings* whom thou hast set over us
11:23. (it was) *the king*'s commandment concerning them,
24. Pethahiah...(was) at *the king*'s hand in all
13: 6. in the two and thirtieth year of Artaxerxes *king of* Babylon came I unto *the king*, and after certain days obtained I leave of *the king:*
26. Did not Solomon *king of* Israel sin
— among many nations was there no *king*
— God made him *king* over all Israel:
Est 1: 2. *the king* Ahasuerus sat on the throne
5. *the king* made a feast
— the court of the garden of *the king*'s palace;
7. according to the state of *the king*.
8. for so *the king* had appointed
9. which (belonged) *to king* Ahasuerus.
10. the heart of *the king* was merry
— in the presence of Ahasuerus *the king*,
11. bring Vashti the queen before *the king*
12. refused to come at *the king*'s commandment
— therefore was *the king* very wroth,
13. *the king* said to the wise men, which knew the times, for so (was) *the king*'s manner

Est. 1:14. which saw *the king*'s face,
15. the commandment of *the king* Ahasuerus
16. Memucan answered before *the king* and the princes, Vashti the queen hath not done wrong to *the king* only,
— all the provinces of *the king* Ahasuerus.
17. *The king* Ahasuerus commanded Vashti
18. say this day unto all *the king*'s princes,
19. If it please *the king*,
— before *king* Ahasuerus; and let *the king* give her royal estate
20. *the king*'s decree which he shall
21. the saying pleased *the king* and the princes; and *the king* did according
22. he sent letters into all *the king*'s provinces,
2: 1. the wrath of *king* Ahasuerus was appeased,
2. said *the king*'s servants that ministered
— young virgins sought *for the king:*
3. *the king* appoint officers in all the provinces
— Hege *the king*'s chamberlain,
4. the maiden which pleaseth *the king*
— And the thing pleased *the king;*
6. Jeconiah *king of* Judah, whom Nebuchadnezzar *the king of* Babylon had carried
8. *the king*'s commandment...was heard,
— brought also unto *the king*'s house,
9. out of *the king*'s house:
12. to go in *to king* Ahasuerus,
13. thus came (every) maiden unto *the king;*
— of the women unto *the king*'s house.
14. *the king*'s chamberlain, which kept the concubines: she came in unto *the king* no more, except *the king*
15. to go in unto *the king*, she required nothing but what Hegai *the king*'s chamberlain,
16. So Esther was taken unto *king* Ahasuerus
17. *the king* loved Esther above all the
18. Then *the king* made a great feast
— according to the state of *the king*.
19. then Mordecai sat in *the king*'s gate.
21. while Mordecai sat in *the king*'s gate, two of *the king*'s chamberlains,...sought to lay hand on *the king*
22. Esther certified *the king* (thereof)
23. the book of the chronicles before *the king*.
3: 1. did *king* Ahasuerus promote Haman
2. all *the king*'s servants, that (were) in *the king*'s gate,
— *the king* had so commanded
3. *the king*'s servants, which (were) in *the king*'s gate, said unto Mordecai, Why transgressest thou *the king*'s
7. in the twelfth year *of king* Ahasuerus,
8. Haman said *unto king* Ahasuerus,
— neither keep they *the king*'s laws: *therefore* it (is) not *for the king*'s profit to suffer them.
9. If it please *the king*,
— to bring (it) into *the king*'s treasuries.
10. *the king* took his ring from his hand,
11. *the king* said unto Haman, The silver
12. Then were *the king*'s scribes called
— commanded unto *the king*'s lieutenants,
— in the name of *king* Ahasuerus was it written, and sealed with *the king*'s ring.
13. all *the king*'s provinces,
15. being hastened by *the king*'s commandment,
— *And the king* and Haman sat down to drink;
4: 2. came even before *the king*'s gate: for none (might) enter into *the king*'s gate
3. *the king*'s commandment...came,
5. (one) of *the king*'s chamberlains,
6. which (was) before *the king*'s gate.
7. to pay to *the king*'s treasuries for
8. that she should go in unto *the king*,
11. All *the king*'s servants, and the people of *the king*'s provinces, do know,
— man or woman, shall come unto *the king*
— to whom *the king* shall hold out
— not been called to come in unto *the king*
13. thou shalt escape in *the king*'s house,
16. so will I go in unto *the king*,
5: 1. the inner court of *the king*'s house, over against *the king*'s house: *and the king* sat upon his royal throne
2. when *the king* saw Esther the queen
— and *the king* held out to Esther the golden

Est. 5: 3. Then said *the king* unto her, What wilt
4. If it seem good unto *the king*, let *the king* and Haman come this day
5. Then *the king* said,
— So *the king* and Haman came
6. *the king* said unto Esther
8. found favour in the sight of *the king*, and if it please *the king* to grant
— let *the king* and Haman
— to morrow as *the king* hath said.
9. Haman saw Mordecai in *the king*'s gate,
11. *the king* had promoted him,
— above the princes and servants of *the king*.
12. the queen did let no man come in with *the king*
— am I invited unto her also with *the king*.
13. Mordecai the Jew sitting at *the king*'s gate.
14. speak thou *unto the king*
— go thou in merrily with *the king*
6: 1. could not *the king* sleep,
— and they were read before *the king*.
2. two of *the king*'s chamberlains,
— sought to lay hand *on the king*
3. *the king* said, What honour and dignity
— Then said *the king*'s servants
4. *the king* said, Who (is) in the court? Now Haman was come into the outward court of *the king*'s house, to speak *unto the king*
5. *the king*'s servants said unto him,
— *the king* said, Let him come in.
6. *the king* said unto him, What shall be done unto the man whom *the king*
— To whom would *the king* delight
7. Haman answered *the king*, For the man whom *the king* delighteth to honour,
8. which *the king* (useth) to wear, and the horse that *the king* rideth upon,
9. one of *the king*'s most noble princes,
—, 9, 11. whom *the king* delighteth to honour,
10. Then *the king* said to Haman,
— that sitteth at *the king*'s gate:
12. Mordecai came again to *the king*'s gate.
14. came *the king*'s chamberlains,
7: 1. *the king* and Haman came to banquet
2. *the king* said again unto Esther
3. *O king*, and if it please *the king*,
4. could not countervail *the king*'s
5. *the king* Ahasuerus answered
6. Haman was afraid before *the king*
7. *And the king* arising from the banquet
— determined against him by *the king*.
8. *Then the king* returned out of the palace garden
— Then said *the king*, Will he force
— the word went out of *the king*'s mouth,
9. one of the chamberlains, said before *the king*,
— who had spoken good for *the king*,
— Then *the king* said, Hang him
10. Then was *the king*'s wrath pacified.
8: 1. did *the king* Ahasuerus give the house of
— And Mordecai came before *the king*;
2. *the king* took off his ring,
3. Esther spake yet again before *the king*,
4. *the king* held out the golden sceptre
— So Esther arose, and stood before *the king*.
5. If it please *the king*,
— the thing (seem) right before *the king*,
— which (are) in all *the king*'s provinces:
7. Then *the king* Ahasuerus said
8. in *the king*'s name, and seal (it) with *the king*'s ring: for the writing which is written in *the king*'s name, and sealed with *the king*'s ring,
9. Then were *the king*'s scribes called
10. he wrote in *the king* Ahasuerus' name, and sealed (it) with *the king*'s ring,
11. Wherein *the king* granted the Jews
12. all the provinces of *king* Ahasuerus,
14. pressed on by *the king*'s commandment.
15. Mordecai went out from the presence of *the king*
17. whithersoever *the king*'s commandment... came,
9: 1. *the king*'s commandment and his decree
2, 20. the provinces of *the king* Ahasuerus,
3. officers *of the king*,

Est. 9: 4. Mordecai (was) great in *the king*'s house,
11. was brought before *the king*.
12. And *the king* said unto Esther
— in the rest of *the king*'s provinces?
13. If it please *the king*,
14. *the king* commanded it so to be done:
16. in *the king*'s provinces gathered
25. (Esther) came before *the king*,
10: 1. *the king* Ahasuerus laid a tribute
2. whereunto *the king* advanced him,
— the chronicles *of the kings of* Media
3. next *unto king* Ahasuerus,
Job 3:14. *kings* and counsellors of the earth,
12:18. He looseth the bond of *kings*,
15:24. *as a king* ready to the battle.
18:14. it shall bring him *to the king of* terrors
29:25. dwelt *as a king* in the army,
34:18. (Is it fit) to say *to a king*,
36: 7. with *kings* (are they) on the throne;
41:34(26). he (is) *a king* over all the children of pride.
Ps. 2: 2. *The kings of* the earth set themselves,
6. Yet have I set *my king*
10. Be wise now therefore, *O ye kings*:
5: 2(3). *my King*, and my God:
10:16. The Lord (is) *King* for ever and ever:
18:50(51). Great deliverance giveth he to *his king*
20: 9(10). let *the king* hear us when we call.
21: 1(2). *The king* shall joy in thy strength,
7(8). For *the king* trusteth in the Lord,
24: 7, 9. *the King of* glory shall come in.
8. Who (is) this *King of* glory?
10. Who is this *King of* glory? The Lord of hosts, he (is) *the King of* glory.
29:10. the Lord sitteth *King* for ever.
33:16. There is no *king* saved by the multitude of an host:
44: 4(5). Thou art *my King*,
45: 1(2). the things which I have made *touching the king*:
5(6). the heart of *the king*'s enemies;
9(10). *Kings*' daughters (were) among
11(12). So shall *the king* greatly desire thy beauty:
13(14). *The king*'s daughter (is) all glorious within.
14(15). She shall be brought *unto the king*
15(16). they shall enter into *the king*'s palace.
47: 2(3). (he is) *a* great *King* over all the earth
6(7). sing praises *unto our King*,
7(8). *the King* of all the earth:
48: 2(3). the city of *the* great *King*.
4(5). *the kings* were assembled,
61: 6(7). Thou wilt prolong *the king*'s life:
63:11(12). *But the king* shall rejoice in God:
68:12(13). *Kings of* armies did flee
14(15). When the Almighty scattered *kings*
24(25). the goings of my God, *my King*,
29(30). shall *kings* bring presents
72: 1. Give *the king* thy judgments, O God, and thy righteousness unto *the king*'s son.
10. *The kings of* Tarshish
— *the kings of* Sheba and Seba
11. all *kings* shall fall down before him:
74:12. God (is) *my King* of old,
76:12(13). (he is) terrible *to the kings of* the earth.
84: 3(4). *my King*, and my God.
89:18(19). the Holy One of Israel (is) *our king*.
27(28). higher than *the kings of* the earth.
95: 3. *and a* great *King* above all gods.
98: 6. a joyful noise before the Lord, *the King*.
99: 4. *The king*'s strength also loveth judgment;
102:15(16). all *the kings of* the earth
105:14. he reproved *kings* for their sakes;
20. *The king* sent and loosed him;
30. the chambers of *their kings*.
110: 5. shall strike through *kings*
119:46. I will speak of thy testimonies also before *kings*,
135:10. and slew mighty *kings*;
11. Sihon *king of* the Amorites, and Og *king of* Bashan,
136:17. him which smote great *kings*:
18. And slew famous *kings*:
19. Sihon *king of* the Amorites:
20. And Og *the king of* Bashan:
138: 4. All *the kings of* the earth shall praise thee

Ps.144:10. giveth salvation *unto kings :*
145: 1. I will extol thee, my God, *O king ;*
148:11. *Kings of* the earth, and all people ;
149: 2. children of Zion be joyful *in their King.*
8. To bind *their kings* with chains,
Pro. 1: 1. David, *king of* Israel ;
8:15. By me *kings* reign,
14:28. In the multitude of people (is) *the king*'s honour:
35. *The king*'s favour (is) toward a wise servant:
16:10. divine sentence (is) in the lips of *the king:*
12. an abomination to *kings* to commit wickedness:
13. Righteous lips (are) the delight of *kings ;*
14. The wrath of *a king* (is as) messengers of death:
15. In the light of *the king*'s countenance (is) life ;
19:12. *The king*'s wrath (is) as the roaring of a lion ;
20: 2. The fear of *a king* (is) as the roaring of a lion:
8. *A king* that sitteth in the throne
26. *A* wise *king* scattereth the wicked,
28. Mercy and truth preserve *the king :*
21: 1. *The king*'s heart (is) in the hand of the Lord,
22:11. *the king* (shall be) his friend.
29. he shall stand before *kings ;*
24:21. fear thou the Lord *and the king:*
25: 1. Hezekiah *king of* Judah
2. the honour of *kings*
3. the heart of *kings* (is) unsearchable.
5. Take away the wicked (from) before *the king,*
6. thyself in the presence of *the king,*
29: 4. *The king* by judgment establisheth the land:
14. *The king* that faithfully judgeth the poor,
30:27. The locusts have no *king,*
28. is in *kings'* palaces.
31. *and a king,* against whom (there is) no rising
31: 1. The words of *king* Lemuel,
3. that which destroyeth *kings.*
4. (It is) not *for kings,* O Lemuel, (it is) not *for kings* to drink wine ;
Ecc. 1: 1. *king of* Jerusalem.
12. I the Preacher was *king* over Israel
2: 8. the peculiar treasure of *kings*
12. the man (do) that cometh after *the king ?*
4:13. *than an* old and foolish *king,*
5: 9(8). *the king* (himself) is served by the field.
8: 2. to keep *the king*'s commandment,
4. Where the word of *a king* (is),
9:14. there came *a* great *king*
10:16. Woe to thee, O land, *when thy king* (is) a child,
17. *when thy king* (is) the son of nobles,
20. Curse not *the king,*
Cant. 1: 4. *the king* hath brought me into
12. While *the king* (sitteth) at his table,
3: 9. *King* Solomon made himself a chariot
11. behold *king* Solomon with the crown
7: 5(6). *the king* (is) held in the galleries.
Isa. 1: 1. Ahaz, (and) Hezekiah, *kings of* Judah.
6: 1. In the year that *king* Uzziah died
5. have seen *the King,* the Lord of hosts.
7: 1. Ahaz the son of Jotham, the son of Uzziah, *king of* Judah, (that) Rezin *the king of* Syria, and Pekah the son of Remaliah, *king of* Israel,
6. set *a king* in the midst
16. forsaken of both *her kings.*
17. (even) *the king of* Assyria.
20. beyond the river, by *the king of* Assyria,
8: 4. shall be taken away before *the king of* Assyria.
7. *the king of* Assyria, and all his glory:
21. and curse *their king* and their God,
10: 8. (Are) not my princes altogether *kings ?*
12. the stout heart of *the king of* Assyria,
14: 4. this proverb against *the king of* Babylon,
9. all *the kings of* the nations.
18. All *the kings of* the nations, (even)
28. In the year that *king* Ahaz died
19: 4. *and a* fierce *king* shall rule over them,

Isa. 19:11. the son of ancient *kings ?*
20: 1. Sargon *the king of* Assyria sent
4. So shall *the king of* Assyria lead
6. delivered from *the king of* Assyria:
23:15. according to the days of one *king :*
24:21. and *the kings of* the earth upon the earth.
30:33. *for the king* it is prepared ;
32: 1. *a king* shall reign in righteousness,
33:17. Thine eyes shall see *the king*
22. the Lord (is) *our king ;*
36: 1. in the fourteenth year *of king* Hezekiah, (that) Sennacherib *king of* Assyria
2. *the king* of Assyria...unto *king* Hezekiah
4. Thus saith *the* great *king, the king of* Assyria,
6. so (is) Pharaoh *king of* Egypt to all
8. to my master *the king of* Assyria,
13. Hear ye the words of *the* great *king, the king of* Assyria.
14. Thus saith *the king,* Let not
15. delivered into the hand of *the king of*
16. thus saith *the king of* Assyria,
18. out of the hand of *the king of* Assyria?
21. *the king*'s commandment was,
37: 1. when *king* Hezekiah heard (it),
4. *the king of* Assyria his master
5. the servants of *king* Hezekiah
6. the servants of *the king of* Assyria
8. found *the king of* Assyria warring
9. concerning Tirhakah *king of* Ethiopia,
10. shall ye speak to Hezekiah *king of* Judah,
— given into the hand of *the king of* Assyria.
11. thou hast heard what *the kings of* Assyria
13. Where (is) *the king of* Hamath, *and the king of* Arphad, *and the king of*
18. *the kings of* Assyria have laid waste
21. prayed to me against Sennacherib *king of*
33. concerning *the king of* Assyria,
37. Sennacherib *king of* Assyria departed,
38: 6. out of the hand of *the king of* Assyria:
9. The writing of Hezekiah *king of* Judah,
39: 1. *king of* Babylon, sent letters
3. came Isaiah the prophet unto *king* Hezekiah,
7. in the palace of *the king of* Babylon.
41: 2. *and* made (him) rule over *kings ?*
21. your strong (reasons), saith *the King of* Jacob.
43:15. the creator of Israel, *your King.*
44: 6. the Lord *the King of* Israel,
45: 1. I will loose the loins of *kings,*
49: 7. *Kings* shall see and arise,
23. *kings* shall be thy nursing fathers,
52:15. *the kings* shall shut their mouths
57: 9. thou wentest *to the king*
60: 3. *and kings* to the brightness of
10. *and their kings* shall minister unto thee :
11. *and* (that) *their kings* (may be) brought.
16. shalt suck the breast of *kings :*
62: 2. all *kings* thy glory:
Jer. 1: 2. Josiah the son of Amon *king of* Judah,
3. Jehoiakim the son of Josiah *king of* Judah,
— Zedekiah the son of Josiah *king of* Judah,
18. *against the kings of* Judah,
2:26. *their kings,* their princes,
3: 6. in the days of Josiah *the king,*
4: 9. the heart of *the king* shall perish,
8: 1. the bones of *the kings of* Judah,
19. (is) not *her king* in her?
10: 7. Who would not fear thee, *O King of* nations?
10. living God, *and an* everlasting *king :*
13:13. *the kings* that sit upon David's throne,
18. Say *unto the king* and to the queen,
15: 4. Manasseh the son of Hezekiah *king of* Judah,
17:19. whereby *the kings of* Judah come in,
20. the word of the Lord, *ye kings of* Judah,
25. *kings* and princes sitting upon
19: 3. the word of the Lord, *O kings of* Judah,
4. *nor the kings of* Judah,
13. the houses of *the kings of* Judah, shall be defiled
20: 4. all Judah into the hand of *the king of*
5. all the treasures of *the kings of* Judah
21: 1. when *king* Zedekiah sent unto him Pashur
2. *king of* Babylon maketh war

Jer. 21: 4. ye fight against *the king of* Babylon,
7. I will deliver Zedekiah *king of* Judah,
— into the hand of Nebuchadrezzar *king of*
10. shall be given into the hand of *the king of*
11. touching the house of *the king of* Judah,
22: 1. to the house of *the king of* Judah,
2. the word of the Lord, *O king of* Judah,
4. *kings* sitting upon the throne of David,
6. *the king*'s house of Judah ;
11. Shallum the son of Josiah *king of* Judah,
18. Jehoiakim the son of Josiah *king of*
24. Coniah the son of Jehoiakim *king of*
25. into the hand of Nebuchadrezzar *king of*
23: 5. *a King* shall reign and prosper.
24: 1. *king of* Babylon had carried away captive Jeconiah the son of Jehoiakim *king of*
8. So will I give Zedekiah *the king of* Judah,
25: 1. son of Josiah *king of* Judah, that (was) the first year of Nebuchadrezzar *king of*
3. Josiah the son of Amon *king of* Judah,
9. *the king of* Babylon, my servant,
11. shall serve *the king of* Babylon
12. I will punish *the king of* Babylon,
14. *and* great *kings* shall serve themselves
18. the cities of Judah, and *the kings thereof*,
19. Pharaoh *king of* Egypt, and his servants,
20. all *the kings of* the land of Uz, and all *the kings of* the land of the Philistines,
22. all *the kings of* Tyrus, and all *the kings of* Zidon, and *the kings of* the isles
24. all *the kings of* Arabia, and all *the kings of*
25. all *the kings of* Zimri, and all *the kings of* Elam, and all *the kings of* the Medes.
26. all *the kings of* the north,
— *and the king of* Sheshach shall drink
26: 1. Jehoiakim the son of Josiah *king of*
10. they came up from *the king*'s house
18. prophesied in the days of Hezekiah *king of*
19. Did Hezekiah *king of* Judah and
21. when Jehoiakim *the king*,...heard his words, *the king* sought to put him to death:
22. Jehoiakim *the king* sent men
23. brought him unto Jehoiakim *the king;*
27: 1. Jehoiakim the son of Josiah *king of*
3. send them to *the king of* Edom, and to *the king of* Moab, and to *the king of* the Ammonites, and to *the king of* Tyrus, and to *the king of* Zidon, by the hand of the messengers which come to Jerusalem unto Zedekiah *king of* Judah ;
6, 8. Nebuchadnezzar *the king of* Babylon,
7. *and* great *kings* shall serve themselves
8. neck under the yoke of *the king of*
9, 14. Ye shall not serve *the king of* Babylon:
11, 12. under the yoke of *the king of* Babylon,
12. I spake also to Zedekiah *king of* Judah
13. that will not serve *the king of* Babylon?
17. serve *the king of* Babylon, and live:
18. (in) the house of *the king of* Judah,
20. *king of* Babylon took not,
— the son of Jehoiakim *king of* Judah
21. (in) the house of *the king of* Judah
28: 1. the reign of Zedekiah *king of* Judah,
2. the yoke of *the king of* Babylon.
3. Nebuchadnezzar *king of* Babylon took away
4. Jeconiah the son of Jehoiakim *king of*
— I will break the yoke of *the king of*
11. the yoke of Nebuchadnezzar *king of*
14. serve Nebuchadnezzar *king of* Babylon ;
29: 2. that Jeconiah *the king*, and the queen,
3. whom Zedekiah *king of* Judah sent unto Babylon to Nebuchadnezzar *king of*
16. *the king* that sitteth upon the throne
21. hand of Nebuchadrezzar *king of* Babylon ;
22. whom *the king of* Babylon roasted
30: 9. serve the Lord...and David *their king*,
32: 1. the tenth year of Zedekiah *king of* Judah,
2. then *the king of* Babylon's army
— which (was) in *the king of* Judah's house.
3. Zedekiah *king of* Judah had shut
— into the hand of *the king of* Babylon,
4. Zedekiah *king of* Judah shall not escape
— be delivered into the hand of *the king of*
28. into the hand of Nebuchadrezzar *king of*
32. *their kings*, their princes,
36. be delivered into the hand of *the king of*

Jer. 33: 4. concerning the houses of *the kings of* Judah,
34: 1. *king of* Babylon, and all his army,
2. speak to Zedekiah *king of* Judah,
— into the hand of *the king of* Babylon,
3. shall behold the eyes of *the king of*
4. O Zedekiah *king of* Judah ;
5. *the* former *kings* which were before thee,
6. unto Zedekiah *king of* Judah
7. When *the king of* Babylon's army
8. *the king* Zedekiah had made a covenant
21. Zedekiah *king of* Judah and his princes
— into the hand of *the king of* Babylon's army,
35: 1. Jehoiakim the son of Josiah *king of* Judah,
11. *king of* Babylon came up into
36: 1, 9. Jehoiakim the son of Josiah *king of*
12. went down into *the king*'s house,
16. We will surely tell *the king*
20. they went in to *the king*
— told all the words in the ears of *the king*.
21. *the king* sent Jehudi
— Jehudi read it in the ears of *the king*. and in the ears of all the princes which stood beside *the king*.
22. *Now the king* sat in the winterhouse
24. *the king*, nor any of his servants
25. made intercession *to the king*
26. *the king* commanded Jerahmeel the son of *Hammelech*, (marg. or, *the king*)
27. after that *the king* had burned the roll,
28. Jehoiakim *the king of* Judah hath burned.
29. say to Jehoiakim *king of* Judah,
— *The king of* Babylon shall certainly come
30. thus saith the Lord of Jehoiakim *king of*
32. Jehoiakim *king of* Judah had burned
37: 1. *king* Zedekiah the son of Josiah
— whom Nebuchadrezzar *king of* Babylon
3. Zedekiah *the king* sent Jehucal
7. Thus shall ye say to *the king of* Judah,
17. Zedekiah *the king* sent, and took him out: and *the king* asked him secretly
— be delivered into the hand of *the king of*
18. Jeremiah said unto *king* Zedekiah,
19. *The king of* Babylon shall not come
20. I pray thee, O my lord *the king:*
21. Zedekiah *the king* commanded
38: 3. the hand of *the king of* Babylon's army,
4. the princes said unto *the king*,
5. Then Zedekiah *the king* said,
— *the king* (is) not (he that) can do
6. Malchiah the son of *Hammelech*, (marg. or, *the king*)
7. which was in *the king*'s house,
— *the king then* sitting in the gate
8. went forth out of *the king*'s house, and spake to *the king*,
9. My lord *the king*, these men
10. *the king* commanded Ebed-melech
11. went into the house of *the king*
14. Zedekiah *the king* sent,
— *the king* said unto Jeremiah,
16. Zedekiah *the king* sware
17. go forth unto *the king of* Babylon's
18. not go forth to *the king of* Babylon's
19. And Zedekiah *the king* said
22. that are left in *the king of* Judah's house (shall be) brought forth to *the king of*
23. taken by the hand of *the king of*
25. what thou hast said unto *the king*,
— what *the king* said unto thee:
26. my supplication before *the king*,
27. these words that *the king* had commanded.
39: 1. In the ninth year of Zedekiah *king of*
— came Nebuchadrezzar *king of* Babylon
3, 3. the princes of *the king of* Babylon
4. Zedekiah *the king of* Judah saw them,
— by the way of *the king*'s garden,
5. brought him up to Nebuchadnezzar *king of*
6. *the king of* Babylon slew the sons of
— *the king of* Babylon slew all the
8. the Chaldeans burned *the king*'s house,
11. Nebuchadrezzar *king of* Babylon gave
13. all *the king of* Babylon's princes ;
40: 5. whom *the king of* Babylon hath made
7. *the king of* Babylon had made Gedaliah
9. and serve *the king of* Babylon,
11. that *the king of* Babylon had left
14. Baalis *the king of* the Ammonites

Jer. 41: 1. the princes of *the king*,
2. whom *the king of* Babylon had made
9. which Asa *the king* had made for fear of Baasha *king of* Israel:
10. *the king*'s daughters, and all the people
18. whom *the king of* Babylon made
42:11. Be not afraid of *the king of* Babylon,
43: 6. and children, and *the king*'s daughters,
10. take Nebuchadrezzar *the king of* Babylon,
44: 9. the wickedness of *the kings of* Judah,
17. *our kings*, and our princes,
21. *your kings*, and your princes,
30. Pharaoh-hophra *king of* Egypt
— Zedekiah *king of* Judah into the hand of Nebuchadrezzar *king of* Babylon,
45: 1. Jehoiakim the son of Josiah *king of* Judah,
46: 2. the army of Pharaoh-necho *king of* Egypt,
— Nebuchadrezzar *king of* Babylon smote in
— son of Josiah *king of* Judah.
13. *king of* Babylon should come
17. Pharaoh *king of* Egypt (is but) a noise;
18. (As) I live, saith *the king*,
25. with their gods, and *their kings;*
26. into the hand of Nebuchadrezzar *king of*
48:15. *the king*, whose name (is) the Lord of hosts.
49: 1. why (then) doth *their king* (marg. or, *Melcom*) inherit Gad,
3. *their king* (marg. or, *Melcom*) shall go into captivity,
28. Nebuchadrezzar *king of* Babylon shall
30. Nebuchadrezzar *king of* Babylon hath
34. the reign of Zedekiah *king of* Judah,
38. *the king* and the princes,
50:17. *the king of* Assyria hath devoured him;
— *king of* Babylon hath broken his bones.
18. I will punish *the king of* Babylon and his land, as I have punished *the king of*
41. *and* many *kings* shall be raised up
43. *The king of* Babylon hath heard the
51:11. the spirit of *the kings of* the Medes:
28. nations with *the kings of* the Medes,
31. to shew *the king of* Babylon that his city
34. *king of* Babylon hath devoured me,
57. *the king*, whose name (is) the Lord of hosts.
59. with Zedekiah *the king of* Judah
52: 3. Zedekiah rebelled *against the king of*
4. *king of* Babylon came, he and all
5. the eleventh year *of king* Zedekiah.
7. by *the king*'s garden;
8. the Chaldeans pursued after *the king*,
9. Then they took *the king*, and carried him up unto *the king of* Babylon
10. *the king of* Babylon slew the sons
11. *the king of* Babylon bound him in
12. the nineteenth year of Nebuchadrezzar *king of* (lit. *of king* Nebuchadrezzar *king of*) Babylon,
— (which) served *the king of* Babylon,
13. And burned...*the king*'s house;
15. fell to *the king of* Babylon,
20. which *king* Solomon had made
25. that were near *the king*'s person,
26. brought them to *the king of* Babylon
27. *the king of* Babylon smote them,
31. the captivity of Jehoiachin *king of*
— Evil-merodach *king of* Babylon
— the head of Jehoiachin *king of* Judah,
32. *the kings* that (were) with him
34. diet given him of *the king of* Babylon,
Lam. 2: 6. hath despised...*the king* and the priest.
9. *her king* and her princes (are) among the Gentiles:
4:12. *The kings of* the earth,
Eze. 1: 2. the fifth year of *king* Jehoiachin's
7:27. *The king* shall mourn,
17:12. *the king of* Babylon is come to Jerusalem, and hath taken *the king thereof*,
16. in the place (where) *the king* (dwelleth)
19: 9. brought him to *the king of* Babylon:
21:19(24). the sword of *the king of* Babylon may come:
21(26). *the king of* Babylon stood at the
24: 2. *the king of* Babylon set himself
26: 7. *king of* Babylon, *a king of kings*, from the
27:33. *the kings of* the earth
35. *and their kings* shall be sore afraid,
28:12. a lamentation upon *the king of* Tyrus,
Eze. 28:17. I will lay thee before *kings*,
29: 2. set thy face against Pharaoh *king of*
3. (am) against thee, Pharaoh *king of* Egypt,
18, 19 & 30:10. Nebuchadrezzar *king of*
30:21, 22. Pharaoh *king of* Egypt;
24, 25, 25. *the king of* Babylon,
31: 2 & 32:2. Pharaoh *king of* Egypt,
32:10. *and their kings* shall be horribly afraid
11. The sword of *the king of* Babylon
29. There (is) Edom, *her kings*,
37:22. *and* one *king* shall be *king* to them all:
24. David my servant (shall be) *king*
43: 7. (neither) they, *nor their kings*,
—, 9. the carcases of *their kings*
Dan. 1: 1. of the reign of Jehoiakim *king of* Judah came Nebuchadnezzar *king of* Babylon
2. the Lord gave Jehoiakim *king of*
3. *the king* spake unto Ashpenaz
4. to stand in *the king*'s palace,
5. *the king* appointed them a daily provision of *the king*'s meat,
— they might stand before *the king*.
8. the portion of *the king*'s meat,
10. I fear my lord *the king*,
— endanger my head *to the king*.
13, 15. the portion of *the king*'s meat:
18. *the king* had said he should bring them in,
19. And *the king* communed with them;
— therefore stood they before *the king*.
20. *the king* enquired of them, he found
21. the first year of *king* Cyrus.
2: 2. *the king* commanded to call the magicians,
— to shew *the king* his dreams. So they came and stood *before the king*.
3. *the king* said unto them,
4. Then spake the Chaldeans *to the king*
8: 1. third year of the reign of *king* Belshazzar
20. *the kings of* Media and Persia.
21. the rough goat (is) *the king of* Grecia:
— the great horn...(is) *the* first *king*.
23. *a king* of fierce countenance,
27. I rose up, and did *the king*'s business;
9: 6. to *our kings*, our princes,
8. *to our kings*, to our princes,
10: 1. the third year of Cyrus *king of* Persia
13. I remained there with *the kings of*
11: 2. there shall stand up yet three *kings*
3. *a* mighty *king* shall stand up,
5. *the king of* the south shall be strong,
6. *the king*'s daughter of the south shall come to *the king* of the north
7. the fortress of *the king of* the north,
8. continue (more) years *than the king of*
9. *the king of* the south shall come
11. *the king of* the south shall be moved
— (even) with *the king of* the north:
13. *the king of* the north shall return,
14. stand up against *the king of* the south:
15. So *the king of* the north shall come,
25. against *the king of* the south with a great army; *and the king of* the south
27. both these *kings*' hearts
36. *the king* shall do according
40. shall *the king of* the south push at him: and *the king of* the north shall come
Hos. 1: 1. *kings of* Judah, and in the days of Jeroboam the son of Joash, *king of* Israel.
3: 4. shall abide many days without *a king*,
5. seek the Lord their God, and David *their king;*
5: 1. O house of *the king;*
13. and sent to *king* Jareb:
7: 3. They make *the king* glad
5. In the day of *our king*
7. all *their kings* are fallen:
8:10. the burden of *the king of* princes.
10: 3. We have no *king*,
— what *then* should *a king* do to us?
6. a present *to king* Jareb:
7. Samaria, *her king* is cut off
15. in a morning shall *the king of* Israel
11: 5. the Assyrian shall be *his king*,
13:10. I will be *thy king:*
— Give me *a king* and princes?
11. I gave thee *a king* in mine anger,
Am. 1: 1. of Uzziah *king of* Judah,
— Jeroboam the son of Joash *king of* Israel.

Am. 1:15. *their king* shall go into captivity,
2: 1. burned the bones of *the king of* Edom
5:26. the tabernacle of *your Moloch* (or, *your king*)
7: 1. the latter growth after *the king*'s mowings.
10. Beth-el sent to Jeroboam *king of* Israel,
13. for it (is) *the king*'s chapel,
Jon. 3: 6. word came unto *the king of* Nineveh,
7. the decree of *the king*
Mic. 1: 1. Ahaz, (and) Hezekiah, *kings of*
14. a lie *to the kings of* Israel.
2:13. *their king* shall pass before them,
4: 9. (is there) no *king* in thee?
6: 5. what Balak *king of* Moab consulted,
Nah. 3:18. Thy shepherds slumber, *O king of*
Hab. 1:10. they shall scoff *at the kings*,
Zep. 1: 1. Josiah the son of Amon, *king of* Judah.
5. that swear *by Malcham*; (or, *their king*)
8. the princes, and *the king*'s children,
3:15. *the king of* Israel, (even) the Lord,
Hag. 1: 1, 15. the second year of Darius *the king*,
Zec. 7: 1. the fourth year of *king* Darius,
9: 5. *the king* shall perish from Gaza,
9. behold, *thy King* cometh unto thee:
11: 6. and into the hand of *his king*:
14: 5. in the days of Uzziah *king of* Judah:
9. the Lord shall be *king* over all the earth:
10. unto *the king*'s winepresses.
16, 17. to worship *the King*, the Lord of hosts,
Mal. 1:14. I (am) *a great King*,

4430 מֶלֶךְ *meh'-lech*, Ch. m.

Ezr. 4: 8. Artaxerxes *the king* in this sort:
11. unto Artaxerxes *the king*;
12. Be it known *unto the king*,
13. Be it known now *unto the king*,
— endamage the revenue of *the kings*.
14. it was not meet for us to see *the king*'s
— sent and certified *the king*;
15. hurtful unto *kings* and provinces,
16. We certify *the king* that,
17. (Then) sent *the king* an answer
19. hath made insurrection against *kings*,
20. There have been mighty *kings*
22. grow to the hurt of *the kings*?
23. when the copy of *king* Artaxerxes'
24. of the reign of Darius *king of* Persia.
5: 6. sent unto Darius *the king*:
7. Unto Darius *the king*, all peace.
8. Be it known *unto the king*,
11. *which a* great *king* of Israel builded
12. of Nebuchadnezzar *the king of* Babylon,
13. in the first year of Cyrus *the king* of Babylon (the same) *king* Cyrus
14. those did Cyrus *the king*
17. Now therefore, if (it seem) good to *the king*, let there be search made in *the king*'s treasure house,
— a decree was made of Cyrus *the king*
— let *the king* send his pleasure
6: 1. Then Darius *the king* made a decree,
3. In the first year of Cyrus *the king* (the same) Cyrus *the king*
4. expences be given out of *the king*'s house:
8. that of *the king*'s goods,
10. and pray for the life of *the king*,
12. destroy all *kings* and people, that
13. to that which Darius *the king* had sent,
14. and Artaxerxes *king of* Persia.
15. the reign of Darius *the king*.
7:12. Artaxerxes, *king of kings*,
14. Forasmuch as thou art sent of *the king*,
15. which *the king* and his counsellors
20. out of *the king*'s treasure house.
21. I Artaxerxes *the king*, do make
23. the realm of *the king* and his sons?
26. and the law of *the king*,
Dan. 2: 4. *O king*, live for ever:
5, 8, 26. *The king* answered and said
7. Let *the king* tell his servants
10. Chaldeans answered before *the king*,
— that can shew *the king*'s matter: therefore (there is) no *king*, lord, nor ruler,
11. And (it is) a rare thing that *the king*

Dan. 2:11. that can shew it before *the king*,
12. For this cause *the king* was angry
14. Arioch the captain of *the king*'s guard,
15. to Arioch *the king*'s captain, Why (is) the decree (so) hasty from *the king*?
16. and desired of *the king* that he would give him time, and that he would shew *the king*
21. he removeth *kings*, and setteth up *kings*:
23. known unto us *the king*'s matter.
24. whom *the king* had ordained
— bring me in before *the king*, and I will shew *unto the king*
25. Daniel before *the king* in haste,
— that will make known *unto the king*
27. answered in the presence of *the king*, and said, The secret which *the king*
— the soothsayers, shew *unto the king*;
28. known *to the king* Nebuchadnezzar
29. As for thee, *O king*,
30. the interpretation *to the king*,
31. Thou, *O king*, sawest,
36. interpretation thereof before *the king*.
37. Thou, *O king*, (art) *a king of kings*:
44. in the days of these *kings*
45. made known *to the king*
46. Then *the king* Nebuchadnezzar
47. *The king* answered unto Daniel,
— and a Lord of *kings*,
48. Then *the king* made Daniel
49. Then Daniel requested of *the king*,
— Daniel (sat) in the gate of *the king*.
3: 1. Nebuchadnezzar *the king* made
2. Then Nebuchadnezzar *the king*
— which Nebuchadnezzar *the king* had set up.
3. the image that Nebuchadnezzar *the king*
5. Nebuchadnezzar *the king* hath set up:
7. that Nebuchadnezzar *the king* had set up.
9. They spake and said to *the king* Nebuchadnezzar, *O king*, live for ever.
10. Thou, *O king*, hast made a decree,
12. these men, *O king*, have not regarded
13. they brought these men before *the king*.
16. answered and said *to the king*,
17. out of thine hand, *O king*.
18. be it known unto thee, *O king*,
22. because *the king*'s commandment
24. Nebuchadnezzar *the king* was astonied,
— They answered and said *unto the king*, True, *O king*.
27. and *the king*'s counsellors,
28. and have changed *the king*'s word,
30. Then *the king* promoted Shadrach,
4: 1(3:31). Nebuchadnezzar *the king*, unto all
18(15). This dream I *king* Nebuchadnezzar
19(16), 30(27). *The king* spake, and said,
22(19). It (is) thou, *O king*, that art grown
23(20). And whereas *the king* saw
24(21). This (is) the interpretation, *O king*,
—(—). which is come upon my lord *the king*:
27(24). Wherefore, *O king*, let my counsel
28(25). came upon *the king* Nebuchadnezzar.
31(28). While the word (was) in *the king*'s
—(—). (saying), *O king* Nebuchadnezzar,
37(34). and honour *the King of* heaven,
5: 1. Belshazzar *the king* made a great feast
2. that *the king*, and his princes,
3. and *the king*, and his princes,
5. of the wall of *the king*'s palace: *and the king* saw the part of the hand
6. Then *the king*'s countenance was
7. *The king* cried aloud to bring in
— (And) *the king* spake, and said
8. Then came in all *the king*'s wise
— nor make known *to the king*
9. was *king* Belshazzar greatly troubled,
10. the queen by reason of the words of *the king*
— the queen spake and said, *O king*,
11. *whom the king* Nebuchadnezzar thy father, *the king*, (I say), thy father,
12. whom *the king* named Belteshazzar:
13. Daniel brought in before *the king*. (And) *the king* spake and said unto Daniel,
— whom *the king* my father brought
17. and said before *the king*,

Dan. 5:17. I will read the writing *unto the king*,
18. *O* thou *king*, the most high God gave
30. Belshazzar *the king of* the Chaldeans slain.
6: 2(3). *and the king* should have no damage.
3(4). *and the king* thought to set him over
6(7). assembled together to *the king*, and said thus unto him, *King* Darius,
7(8). to establish a *royal* statute,
—(-). save of thee, *O king*,
8(9). Now, *O king*, establish the decree,
9(10). Wherefore *king* Darius signed
12(13). and spake before *the king* concerning *the king*'s decree;
—(—). *O king*, shall be cast into the den of lions? *The king* answered and said,
13(14). and said before *the king*,
—(—). regardeth not thee, *O king*,
14(15). Then *the king*, when he heard
15(16). these men assembled unto *the king*, and said *unto the king*, Know, *O king*,
—(—). *the king* establisheth may be changed.
16(17). Then *the king* commanded,
—(—). (Now) *the king* spake and said unto
17(18). and *the king* sealed it with his own
18(19). Then *the king* went to his palace,
19(20). Then *the king* arose very early
20(21). *the king* spake and said to Daniel,
21(22). said Daniel unto *the king*, *O king*, live for ever.
22(23). also before thee, *O king*, have I done no hurt.
23(24). Then was *the king* exceeding glad
24(25). And *the king* commanded,
25(26). Then *king* Darius wrote unto all
7: 1. In the first year of Belshazzar *king of*
17. These great beasts, which are four, (are) four *kings*,
24. out of this kingdom (are) ten *kings*
— and he shall subdue three *kings*.

4431 **מְלַךְ** [*m'lach*], Ch. m.

Dan 4:27(24). O king, let *my counsel* be acceptable

4434 **מַלְכֹּדֶת** [*mal-kōh'-deth*], f.

Job 18:10. *and a trap for him* in the way.

4436 **מַלְכָּה** *mal-kāh'*, f.

1K. 10: 1. *when the queen of* Sheba heard
4. when *the queen of* Sheba had seen
10. *the queen of* Sheba gave to king Solomon.
13. Solomon gave *unto the queen of* Sheba
2Ch 9: 1. *when the queen of* Sheba heard
3. when *the queen of* Sheba had seen
9. *the queen of* Sheba gave king Solomon.
12. Solomon gave *to the queen of* Sheba
Est. 1: 9. Vashti *the queen* made a feast
11. To bring Vashti *the queen*
12. *the queen* Vashti refused
15. What shall we do *unto the queen* Vashti
16. Vashti *the queen* hath not done wrong
17. (this) deed of *the queen*
— commanded Vashti *the queen* to be brought
18. the deed of *the queen*.
2:22. told (it) unto Esther *the queen*;
4: 4. Then was *the queen* exceedingly grieved;
5: 2. when the king saw Esther *the queen*
3. What wilt thou, *queen* Esther?
12. Esther *the queen* did let no man come
7: 1. to banquet with Esther *the queen*.
2. What (is) thy petition, *queen* Esther?
3. Esther *the queen* answered
5. and said unto Esther *the queen*,
6. before the king *and the queen*.
7. request for his life to Esther *the queen*;
8. Will he force *the queen* also
8: 1, 7 & 9:12. unto Esther *the queen*.
9:29. Then Esther *the queen*,
31. Mordecai the Jew and Esther *the queen*

Cant.6: 8. There are threescore *queens*,
9. *the queens* and the concubines,

מַלְכָּה [*mal-kāh'*], Ch. f. 4433

Dan 5:10. (Now) *the queen* by reason of the words
— *the queen* spake and said, O king,

מַלְכוּ *mal-choo'*, Ch. f. 4437

Ezr. 4:24. the second year *of the reign of* Darius
6:15. in the sixth year *of the reign of* Darius
7:13. priests and Levites, *in my realm*,
23. why should there be wrath against *the realm*
Dan 2:37. God of heaven hath given thee *a kingdom*,
39. shall arise another *kingdom*
— *and* another third *kingdom* of brass,
40. *And the* fourth *kingdom* shall be strong
41. *the kingdom* shall be divided;
42. *the kingdom* shall be partly strong,
44. the God of heaven set up *a kingdom*,
— *and the kingdom* shall not be left
— and consume all these *kingdoms*,
4: 3(3:33). *his kingdom* (is) *an* everlasting *kingdom*,
17(14), 25(22), 32(29). the most High ruleth *in the kingdom of* men,
18(15). all the wise (men) *of my kingdom*
26(23). *thy kingdom* shall be sure unto thee,
29(26). he walked in the palace of *the kingdom*
30(27). for the house of *the kingdom*
31(28). *The kingdom* is departed from thee
34(31). *and his kingdom* (is) from generation
36(33). and for the glory *of my kingdom*,
—(—). I was established in *my kingdom*,
5: 7. shall be the third ruler *in the kingdom*.
11. There is a man *in thy kingdom*,
16. shalt be the third ruler *in the kingdom*.
18. Nebuchadnezzar thy father *a kingdom*,
20. he was deposed from *his kingly* throne,
21. God ruled *in the kingdom of* men,
26. Mene; God hath numbered *thy kingdom*,
28. Peres; *Thy kingdom* is divided,
29. should be the third ruler *in the kingdom*.
31(6:1). the Median took *the kingdom*,
6: 1(2). Darius to set over *the kingdom*
—(—). should be over *the* whole *kingdom*;
3(4). thought to set him over *the* whole *realm*.
4(5). against Daniel concerning *the kingdom*;
7(8). All the presidents of *the kingdom*,
26(27). That in every dominion of *my kingdom*
—(—). *and his kingdom* (that) which shall not be destroyed,
28(29). So this Daniel prospered *in the reign of* Darius, *and in the reign of* Cyrus
7:14. and glory, *and a kingdom*, that all
— *and his kingdom* (that) which shall not be destroyed.
18. of the most High shall take *the kingdom*, and possess *the kingdom* for ever,
22. *that* the saints possessed *the kingdom*.
23. shall be the fourth *kingdom* upon earth, which shall be diverse from all *kingdoms*,
24. the ten horns out of this *kingdom*
27. *And the kingdom* and dominion, and the greatness of *the kingdom* under
— *whose kingdom* (is) *an* everlasting *kingdom*,

מַלְכוּת *mal-chooth'*, f. 4438

Nu. 24: 7. *his kingdom* shall be exalted.
1Sa.20:31. shalt not be established, *nor thy kingdom*.
1K. 2:12. *his kingdom* was established
1Ch 11:10. with him *in his kingdom*,
12:23. *the kingdom of* Saul to him,
14: 2. *his kingdom* was lifted up
17:11. I will establish *his kingdom*.
14. *and in my kingdom* for ever:

1Ch.22:10. I will establish the throne of *his kingdom*
26:31. In the fortieth year of *the reign of*
28: 5. the throne of *the kingdom of*
7. I will establish *his kingdom* for ever,
29:25. (such) *royal* majesty (lit. majesty of *the kingdom*)
30. *his reign* and his might,
2Ch. 1: 1. Solomon...was strengthened in *his kingdom*,
2: 1(1:18),12(11). an house *for his kingdom*.
3: 2. in the fourth year *of his reign*.
7:18. will I stablish the throne of *thy kingdom*,
11:17. they strengthened *the kingdom of* Judah,
12: 1. Rehoboam had established *the kingdom*,
15:10. in the fifteenth year *of the reign of* Asa.
19. the five and thirtieth year *of the reign of* Asa.
16: 1. the six and thirtieth year *of the reign of* Asa
12. the thirty and ninth year *of his reign*
20:30. *the realm of* Jehoshaphat
29:19. king Ahaz *in his reign*
33:13. brought him...*into his kingdom*.
35:19. *of the reign of* Josiah
36:20. until the reign of *the kingdom of* Persia:
22. throughout all *his kingdom*,
Ezr. 1: 1. throughout all *his kingdom*,
4: 5. *the reign of* Darius
6. *And in the reign of* Ahasuerus, in the beginning of *his reign*,
7: 1 & 8:1. *in the reign of* Artaxerxes
Neh 9:35. have not served thee *in their kingdom*,
12:22. *the reign of* Darius the Persian.
Est. 1: 2. on the throne of *his kingdom*
4. the riches of *his* glorious *kingdom*
7. *royal* wine (marg. wine of *the kingdom*) in abundance,
9. the *royal* house (lit. house of *the kingdom*) which (belonged) to king
11. the crown *royal*, (lit. crown of *the kingdom*)
14. sat the first *in the kingdom* ;
19. let there go a *royal* commandment (lit. commandment of *the kingdom*)
— *and* let the king give *her royal estate*
20. throughout all *his empire*,
2: 3. the provinces of *his kingdom*,
16. into *his* house *royal* (lit. house of *his kingdom*)
— in the seventh year *of his reign*.
17. he set the *royal* crown (lit. crown of *the kingdom*) upon her head,
3: 6. throughout *the* whole *kingdom*
8. the provinces of *thy kingdom* ;
4:14. thou art come *to the kingdom*
5: 1. Esther put on (her) *royal* (apparel),
— the king sat upon *his royal* throne (lit. throne of *his kingdom*) in *the royal* house, (lit. house of *the kingdom*)
3. given thee to the half of *the kingdom*.
6. even to the half of *the kingdom*
6: 8. Let the *royal* apparel (lit. apparel of *the kingdom*) be brought
— the crown *royal* (lit. crown of *the kingdom*) which is
7: 2. to the half of *the kingdom*.
8:15. *royal* apparel (lit. apparel of *the kingdom*) of blue and white,
9:30. provinces of *the kingdom*
Ps. 45: 6(7). the sceptre of *thy kingdom*
103:19. *his kingdom* ruleth over all.
145:11. the glory of *thy kingdom*,
12. the glorious majesty of *his kingdom*.
13. *Thy kingdom* (is) *an* everlasting *kingdom*,
Ecc. 4:14. (he that is) born *in his kingdom*
Jer. 10: 7. in all *their kingdoms*,
49:34. *the reign of* Zedekiah
52:31. in the (first) year of *his reign* lifted
Dan 1: 1. *of the reign of* Jehoiakim
20. astrologers that (were) in all *his realm*.
2: 1. *of the reign of* Nebuchadnezzar
8: 1. *of the reign of* king Belshazzar
22. four *kingdoms* shall stand up
23. in the latter time of *their kingdom*,
9: 1. *the realm of* the Chaldeans ;
10:13. *the kingdom of* Persia
Dan11: 2. against *the realm of* Grecia.
Dan11: 4. *his kingdom* shall be broken,
— *his kingdom* shall be plucked up,
9. shall come *into* (his) *kingdom*,
17. the strength of *his* whole *kingdom*,
20. the glory of *the kingdom*:
21. the honour of *the kingdom*:
— and obtain *the kingdom*

מְלֶכֶת *m'leh'-cheth*, f. 4446

Jer. 7:18. make cakes *to the queen of* heaven, (marg. or, *frame*, or, *workmanship*)
44:17. to burn incense *unto the queen of* heaven, (marg. *frame*)
18, 25. to burn incense *to the queen of* heaven,
19. we burned incense *to the queen of* heaven,

מָלַל [*māh-lal'*]. 4448

* KAL.—*Participle*. Poel.

Pro. 6:13. *he speaketh* with his feet,

* PIEL.—*Preterite*. *

Gen21: 7. Who *would have said* unto Abraham,
Job 33: 3. my lips *shall utter* knowledge

PIEL.—*Future*.

Job 8: 2. How long *wilt thou speak*
Ps.106: 2. Who *can utter* the mighty acts of the Lord?

מְלַל [*m'-lal*], Ch. 4449

* PAEL.—*Preterite*. *

Dan. 6:21(22). Then *said* Daniel unto the king,

PAEL.—*Future*.

Dan. 7:25. *he shall speak* (great) words against the most High,

PAEL.—*Participle*.

Dan. 7: 8. and a mouth *speaking* great things.
11. the great words which the horn *spake*:
20. a mouth *that spake* very great things,

מַלְמָד [*mal-māhd'*], m. 4451

Jud. 3:31. slew of the Philistines six hundred men *with an ox goad*:

מָלַץ [*māh-latz'*]. 4452

* NIPHAL.—*Preterite*. *

Ps.119:103. How *sweet are* thy words unto my taste!

מֶלְצַר *mel-tzar'*, m. 4453

Dan. 1:11. Then said Daniel to *Melzar*, (marg. *the steward*)
16. Thus *Melzar* took away the portion

מָלַק *māh-lak'*. 4454

* KAL.—*Preterite*. *

Lev. 1:15. *and wring off* his head, (marg. or, *pinch off* the head *with the nail*) and burn (it)
5: 8. *and wring off* his head from his neck,

מַלְקוֹחַ *mal-kōh'ăgh*, m. 4455

Nu. 31:11. they took all the spoil, and all *the prey*,
12. they brought the captives, and *the prey*,
26. Take the sum of *the prey*
27. divide *the prey* into two parts;
32. *the booty*, (being) the rest of the prey
Ps. 22:15(16). my tongue cleaveth *to my jaws*;
Isa. 49:24. Shall *the prey* be taken from the mighty,
25. *and the prey of* the terrible

4456 מַלְקוֹשׁ *mal-kōhsh'*, m.

Deu11:14. the first rain *and the latter rain*,
Job 29:23. they opened their mouth wide (as) *for the latter rain*.
Pro.16:15. as a cloud of *the latter rain*.
Jer. 3: 3. *and* there hath been no *latter rain*;
5:24. rain, both the former *and the latter*,
Hos. 6: 3. *as the latter* (and) former *rain*
Joel 2:23. the former rain, *and the latter rain*
Zec.10: 1. in the time of *the latter rain*;

4457 מֶלְקָחַיִם *mel-kāh-ghah'-yim*, m. dual.

1K. 7:49. the lamps, *and the tongs* (of) gold,
2Ch. 4:21. the lamps, *and the tongs*,
Isa. 6: 6. he had taken *with the tongs*

4457 מַלְקָחַיִם [*mal-kāh-ghah'-yim*], m. dual.

Ex. 25:38. *And the tongs thereof*, and the
37:23. he made his seven lamps, *and his snuffers*,
Nu. 4: 9. *his tongs*, and his snuffdishes,

4458 מֶלְתָּחָה *mel-tāh-ghāh'*, f.

2K. 10:22. him that (was) over *the vestry*,

4459 מַלְתָּעוֹת [*mal-tāh-ⁿgōhth'*], f. pl.

Ps. 58: 6(7). break out *the great teeth*

4460 מַמְּגֻרוֹת *mam-m'goo-rōhth'*, f. pl.

Joel 1:17. *the barns* are broken down ;

4461 מְמַדִּים [*m'mad-deem'*], m. pl.

Job 38: 5. Who hath laid *the measures thereof*,

4463 מָמוֹת [*māh-mōhth'*], m.

Jer. 16: 4. They shall die of grievous *deaths*;
Eze.28: 8. *the deaths of* (them that are) slain

4464 מַמְזֵר *mam-zēhr'*, m.

Deu23: 2(3). *A bastard* shall not enter
Zec. 9: 6. *a bastard* shall dwell in Ashdod,

4465 מִמְכָּר *mim-kāhr'*, m.

Lev.25:14. if thou sell *ought* (lit. *a selling*) unto thy neighbour,
25. *that which* his brother *sold*.
27. the years of *the sale thereof*,
28. *that which is sold* shall remain
29. a whole year *after it is sold*;
33. the house *that was sold*,
50. the price of *his sale*
Deu18: 8. *that which cometh of the sale* of *his* patrimony. (marg. *his sales* by the fathers)
Neh 13:20. sellers of all kind of *ware*
Eze. 7:13. return to *that which is sold*,

4466 מִמְכֶּרֶת *mim-keh'-reth*, f.

Lev.25:42. they shall not be sold *as* bondmen. (marg. *with the sale of* a bondman)

מַמְלָכָה *mam-lāh-chāh'*, f. 4467

Gen10:10. the beginning of *his kingdom*
20: 9. on me and on *my kingdom*
Ex. 19: 6. *a kingdom of* priests,
Nu. 32:33. *the kingdom of* Sihon king of the Amorites, and *the kingdom of* Og
Deu. 3: 4, 10. *the kingdom of* Og in Bashan.
13. *the kingdom of* Og, gave I
21. *the kingdoms* whither thou passest.
17:18. the throne of *his kingdom*,
20. prolong (his) days in *his kingdom*,
28:25. all *the kingdoms of* the earth.
Jos. 10: 2. one of the *royal* cities,
11:10. the head of all those *kingdoms*.
1Sa.10:18. out of the hand of all *kingdoms*,
13:13. have established *thy kingdom*
14. *thy kingdom* shall not continue:
24:20(21). *the kingdom of* Israel shall be established
27: 5. should thy servant dwell in the *royal* city
28:17. the Lord hath rent *the kingdom*
2Sa. 3:10. To translate *the kingdom*
28. I *and my kingdom* (are) guiltless
5:12. he had exalted *his kingdom*
7:12. I will establish *his kingdom*.
13. I will stablish the throne of *his kingdom*
16. thine house *and thy kingdom*
1K. 2:46. *And the kingdom* was established
4:21(5:1). Solomon reigned over all *kingdoms*
9: 5. the throne of *thy kingdom*
10:20. not the like made in any *kingdom*.
11:11. I will surely rend *the kingdom*
13. I will not rend away all *the kingdom*;
31. I will rend *the kingdom*
34. I will not take *the* whole *kingdom*
12:26. Now shall *the kingdom* return
14: 8. rent *the kingdom* away
18:10. no nation *or kingdom*,
— he took an oath of *the kingdom*
2K. 11:1. destroyed all the seed *royal*. (marg. of *the kingdom*)
14: 5. as soon as *the kingdom* was confirmed
15:19. to confirm *the kingdom*
19:15, 19. *the kingdoms of* the earth;
1Ch.16:20. *and from* (one) *kingdom* to another people;
29:11. thine (is) *the kingdom*, O Lord,
30. *the kingdoms of* the countries.
2Ch. 9:19. not the like made in any *kingdom*.
11: 1. that he might bring *the kingdom*
12: 8. service of *the kingdoms of* the countries.
13: 5. *the kingdom* over Israel
8. *the kingdom of* the Lord
14: 5(4). *the kingdom* was quiet
17: 5. the Lord stablished *the kingdom*
10. *the kingdoms of* the lands
20: 6. *the kingdoms of* the heathen?
29. *the kingdoms of* (those) countries,
21: 3. *the kingdom* gave he to Jehoram;
4. Jehoram was risen up to *the kingdom of*
22: 9. to keep still *the kingdom*.
10. destroyed all the seed *royal*
23:20. the throne of *the kingdom*.
25: 3. when *the kingdom* was established
29:21. a sin offering for *the kingdom*,
32:15. no god of any nation *or kingdom* was able
36:23. All *the kingdoms of* the earth
Ezr. 1: 2. *the kingdoms of* the earth;
Neh 9:22. gavest them *kingdoms* and nations,
Ps. 46: 6(7). the *kingdoms* were moved:
68:32(33). Sing unto God, *ye kingdoms*
79: 6. the *kingdoms* that have not called upon
102:22(23). When the people are gathered...*and the kingdoms*,
105:13. *from* (one) *kingdom* to another people;
135:11. all *the kingdoms of* Canaan:
Isa. 9:7(6). upon *his kingdom*,
10:10. *the kingdoms of* the idols,
13: 4. *the kingdoms of* nations
19. Babylon, the glory of *kingdoms*,
14:16. that did shake *kingdoms*;
17: 3. *and the kingdom* from Damascus,
19: 2. city against city, (and) *kingdom against kingdom*.
23:11. he shook *the kingdoms*:
17. *the kingdoms of* the world
37:16, 20. *the kingdoms of* the earth:
47: 5. The lady of *kingdoms*.

Isa. 60:12. the nation *and kingdom* that will not serve
Jer. 1:10. over the nations and over *the kingdoms*,
15. the families of *the kingdoms of*
15: 4. all *kingdoms of* the earth,
18: 7, 9. concerning *a kingdom*,
24: 9. *the kingdoms of* the earth
25:26. *the kingdoms of* the world,
27: 1. the beginning of *the reign of* Jehoiakim
8. nation *and kingdom* which will not serve
28: 1. the beginning of *the reign of* Zedekiah
8. against great *kingdoms*,
29:18 & 34:1, 17. all *the kingdoms of* the earth,
49:28. *and concerning the kingdoms of* Hazor,
51:20. with thee will I destroy *kingdoms*;
27. call together against her *the kingdoms of* Ararat,
Lam 2: 2. he hath polluted *the kingdom*
Eze. 17:14. That *the kingdom* might be base,
29:14. they shall be there *a* base *kingdom*.
15. the basest of *the kingdoms*;
37:22. divided into two *kingdoms*
Am. 6: 2. better than these *kingdoms*?
7:13. *king's* court. (marg. house of *the kingdom*)
9: 8. *upon the* sinful *kingdom*,
Mic. 4: 8. *the kingdom* shall come
Nah 3: 5. will shew...*the kingdoms* thy shame.
Zep. 3: 8. that I may assemble *the kingdoms*,
Hag 2:22. the throne of *kingdoms*, and I will destroy the strength of *the kingdoms of*

4468 **מַמְלְכוּת** *[mam-lāh-chooth']*, f.

Jos. 13:12, 31. *the kingdom of* Og in Bashan,
21. *the kingdom of* Sihon king of
27. the rest of *the kingdom of* Sihon
30. *the kingdom of* Og king of Bashan,
1 Sa. 15:28. The Lord hath rent *the kingdom of* Israel
2 Sa. 16: 3. *the kingdom of* my father.
Jer. 26: 1. the beginning of *the reign of*
Hos. 1: 4. *the kingdom of* the house of

4469 **מִמְסָךְ** *mim-sāhch'*, m.

Pro. 23:30. they that go to seek *mixed wine*.
Isa. 65:11. that furnish *the drink offering*

4470 **מֶמֶר** *meh'-mer*, m.

Pro. 17:25. *and bitterness* to her that bare him.

4472 **מַמְרֹרִים** *mam-m'rōh-reem'*, m. pl.

Job 9:18. but filleth me *with bitterness*.

4473 **מִמְשַׁח** *mim-shach'*, m.

Eze. 28:14. the *anointed* cherub

4474 **מִמְשָׁל** *mim-shāhl'*, m.

1 Ch 26: 6. *that ruled* throughout the house
Dan 11: 3. that shall rule with great *dominion*,
5. *a* great *dominion*.

4475 **מֶמְשָׁלָה** *mem-shāh-lāh'*, f.

Gen 1:16. the greater light *to rule* (marg. *for the rule of*) the day, and the lesser light *to rule* the night:
1 K. 9:19. in all the land of *his dominion*.
2 K. 20:13. in all *his dominion*,
2 Ch 8: 6. all the land of *his dominion*.
32: 9. all *his power* (marg. *dominion*) with him,
Ps. 103:22. in all places of *his dominion*:
114: 2. Israel *his dominion*.
Ps. 136: 8. The sun *to rule* by day:
9. The moon and stars *to rule* by night:
145:13. *thy dominion* (endureth)
Isa. 22:21. and I will commit *thy government*
39: 2. in all *his dominion*,
Jer. 34: 1. the kingdoms of the earth of his *dominion*, (marg. *the dominion of* his hand)
51:28. all the land of *his dominion*.
Dan 11: 5. *his dominion* (shall be) a great dominion.
Mic. 4: 8. even *the* first *dominion*;

מִמְשָׁק *mim-shak'*, m. 4476

Zep 2: 9. *the breeding of* nettles,

מַמְתַּקִּים *mam-tak-keem'*, m. pl. 4477

Neh 8:10. eat the fat, and drink *the sweet*,
Cant 5:16. His mouth (is) *most sweet*:

מָן *māhn*, m. 4478

Ex. 16:15. they said one to another, It (is) *manna*: (marg: or, *What* (is) this? or, It (is) *a portion*)
31. called the name thereof *Manna*:
33. put an omer full of *manna* therein,
35. the children of Israel did eat *manna*
— they did eat *manna*, until
Nu. 11: 6. (there is) nothing at all, beside this *manna*,
7. *And the manna* (was) as coriander seed,
9. *the manna* fell upon it.
Deu 8: 3. fed thee with *manna*,
16. Who fed thee in the wilderness with *manna*,
Jos. 5:12. And *the manna* ceased on the morrow
— neither had the children of Israel *manna* any more;
Neh 9:20. *and* withheldest not *thy manna* from their mouth,
Ps. 78:24. had rained down *manna* upon them

מָן *[māhn]*, Ch. pron. interrog. 4479
מַן־דִּי[2]

Ezr. 5: 3. *Who* hath commanded you to build
4. *What* are the names of the men
9. *Who* commanded you to build
Dan 3: 6, 11. *And whoso*[2] falleth not down
15. *and who* (is) that God that shall deliver
4:17(14), 25(22), 32(29). *and* giveth it *to whomsoever* he will,
5:21. he appointeth over it *whomsoever*[2] he will.

מָן see מִנִּים See 4482

מִן *min*, part. prep. 4480

Gen 2: 6. went up a mist *from* the earth,
7. man (of) the dust *of* the ground,
9. *out of* the ground made the Lord God
5:29. *because of* the ground which the Lord
21:15. the water was spent *in* the bottle,
25:30. Feed me, I pray thee, *with* that
Ex. 2:23. sighed *by reason of* the bondage,
Lev. 9:10. caul *above* the liver *of* the sin offering,
11:13. have in abomination *among* the fowls;
14:37. in sight (are) lower *than* the wall;
Nu. 15:30. born in the land (lit. *of* the native), *or* a stranger, (lit. *and of* the stranger)
31:43. seven thousand and five hundred sheep, (lit. *of* sheep, &c.)
Deu 33:11. hate him, *that* they rise *not* again.
1 Sa. 17:50. David prevailed *over* the Philistine
30:19. lacking to them, *neither* small nor great, (lit. *from* small to &c.)
1 K. 6:16. both the floor and the walls (lit. *from* the floor to &c.)
2 K. 21:15. *since* the day their fathers came

1Ch. 8: 8. *after* he had sent them away;
Ps. 104: 7. *At* thy rebuke they fled; *at* the voice
Cant. 5: 4. My beloved put in his hand *by* the hole
Isa. 28: 7. erred *through* strong drink, they are swallowed up *of* wine,
Eze. 36: 24. take you *from among* the heathen,
&c. &c.

With prefix; as, לְמִן

Ex. 9: 18. *since* (lit. *from* the day of) the foundation thereof even until
Deu. 9: 7. *from* the day that thou didst depart
2Ch. 15: 13. *whether* small or great,
&c. &c.

The signification of מִן with pronominal suffixes remains unchanged.

4481 מִן *min*, Ch. part. prep.

[2] Marks קֳדָם as being combined with מִן in translation: [3] marks דִּי similarly combined.

Ezr. 4: 12. Jews which came up *from* thee
15. sedition within the same *of* old
19. *And I* commanded, (marg. *by me* a decree is set)
— *of* old time hath made insurrection
21. commandment shall be given *from me.*
23. *when* [3] the copy of king
5: 12. *after* that our fathers had provoked
14. took *out of* the temple that (was)
— take *out of* the temple of Babylon,
16. *and since* that time
17. a decree was made *of* Cyrus
6: 4. be given *out of* the king's house:
5. took forth *out of* the temple
6. be ye far *from* thence·
8. *Moreover I* make a decree (marg. *by me* a decree is made)
11. *Also I* have made a decree, (lit. *id.*)
— timber be pulled down *from* his
14. *according* to the commandment of the God
7: 13. *I* make (lit. *by me* is made) a decree, that all they *of* the people
14. art sent *of* (marg. *from* before) the king,
20. *out of* the king's treasure house.
21. *And I* (lit. *and by me*), (even) I
23. *commanded by* (marg. *of* the decree of) the God of heaven,
26. judgment be executed speedily *upon him,*
Dan 2: 5. The thing is gone *from me:*
6. ye shall receive *of* me gifts
8. I know *of* certainty that
— the thing is gone *from* me.
15. the decree (so) hasty *from*[2] the king?
16. went in, and desired *of* the king
18. desire mercies *of*[2] the God of heaven
20. Blessed be the name of God *for* ever
23. what we desired *of thee:*
25. a man *of* the captives of Judah,
30. that I have *more than* any living,
33. feet *part* of iron *and part* of clay.
35. chaff *of* the summer threshingfloors;
39. another kingdom inferior *to thee,*
41. *part* of potters' clay, *and part* of
— *but* there shall be in it *of* the strength
42. *part* of iron, *and part* of clay, (so) the kingdom shall be *partly* (lit. *of* part) strong, *and partly*
47. *Of* a truth (it is), that
49. Daniel requested *of* the king,
3: 15. deliver you *out of* my hands?
17. *from* the burning fiery furnace, *and* he will deliver (us) *out of*
22. *because*[3] the king's commandment
26. forth *of* the midst of the fire.
29. *Therefore I* make (marg. made *by me*)
4: 6(3). *Therefore* made *I* (lit. *id.*)
12(9). *and* all flesh was fed *of it.*
13(10). an holy one came down *from*
14(11). beasts get away *from* under it, and the fowls *from*
16(13). his heart be changed *from* man's,
23(20). holy one coming down *from* heaven,
25(22). shall drive thee *from* men,
26(23). *after* that thou shalt have known

Dan 4: 31(28). fell a voice *from* heaven,
—(—). The kingdom is departed *from thee*
32(29). *And* they shall drive thee *from*
33(30). *and* he was driven *from* men,
5: 2. had taken *out of* the temple
3. that were taken *out of* the temple
13. *of* the children of the captivity
— my father brought *out of* Jewry?
19. *And for* the majesty that
— trembled and feared *before*[2] him:
20. deposed *from* his kingly throne, and they took his glory *from him:*
21. *And* he was driven *from* the sons of
24. part of the hand sent *from* him;
6: 2(3). over *these* three presidents; *of whom*
7(8). *of* any God or man for thirty days, save *of thee,*
10(11). as he did aforetime. (lit. *from* the former time of this)
12(13). *of* any God or man within thirty days, save *of thee,*
13(14). which (is) *of* the children of
20(21). able to deliver thee *from* the lions?
23(24). *out of* the den. So Daniel was taken up *out of*
26(27). I make (lit. *from* before me is made) a decree,
—(—). *before*[2] the God of Daniel:
27(28). *from* the power of the lions.
7: 3. *from* the sea, diverse one *from* another.
4. was lifted up *from* the earth,
7. diverse *from* all the beasts
8. *before*[2] whom there were three *of* the first
10. issued and came forth *from* before him:
11. *because of* the voice of the great
16. one *of* them that stood by, and asked *him* the truth
17. shall arise *out of* the earth.
19. which was diverse *from* all the others,
20. and *before*[2] whom three fell;
— *more* stout *than* his fellows.
23. shall be diverse *from* all kingdoms,
24. horns *out of* this kingdom
— shall be diverse *from* the first,

מְנָא see מְנָה See 4483

מַנְגִּינָה [*man-gee-nāh'*], f. 4485

Lam. 3: 63. I (am) *their musick.*

מִנְדָּה *min-dah'*, Ch. f. 4061

Ezr. 4: 13. (then) will they not pay *toll,*
7: 24. it shall not be lawful to impose *toll,*

מַנְדַּע *man-dag'*, Ch. m. 4486

Dan 2: 21. *and knowledge* to them that know understanding:
4: 34(31). *and mine understanding* returned unto
36(33). *my reason* returned unto me;
5: 12. excellent spirit, *and knowledge,*

מָנָה *māh-nāh'*. 4487

* KAL.—*Preterite.* *

Nu. 23: 10. Who *can count* the dust of Jacob,
Isa. 65: 12. *Therefore will I number you* to the

KAL.—*Infinitive.*

Gen 13: 16. if a man can *number* the dust
1Ch. 21: 1. provoked David *to number* Israel.
17. commanded the people *to be numbered* (lit. *to number* the people)
27: 24. Joab...began *to number,*
Ps. 90: 12. teach (us) *to number* our days,

KAL.—*Imperative.*

2Sa. 24: 1. *number* Israel and Judah.

KAL.—*Future.*

1K. 20:25. And *number* thee an army,
2K. 12:10(11). *and told* the money that was found in

KAL.—*Participle.* Poel.

Ps.147: 4. *He telleth* the number of the stars;
Jer. 33:13. the hands of *him that telleth* (them),

* NIPHAL.—*Preterite.* *

Isa. 53:12. *he was numbered* with the transgressors;

NIPHAL.—*Infinitive.*

Ecc. 1:15. that which is wanting cannot *be numbered.*

NIPHAL.—*Future.*

Gen 13:16. (then) *shall* thy seed also *be numbered.*
1K. 3: 8. a great people, that *cannot* be *numbered*
8: 5. that could not be told nor *numbered*
2Ch 5: 6. which could not be told nor *numbered*

* PIEL.—*Preterite.* *

Job. 7: 3. wearisome nights *are appointed* to me.
Dan 1:10. who *hath appointed* your meat
11. the prince of the eunuchs *had set* over

PIEL.—*Imperative.*

Ps. 61: 7(8). *O prepare* mercy and truth,

PIEL.—*Future.*

Dan 1: 5. *And* the king *appointed* them a daily provision
Jon. 1:17(2:1). *Now* the Lord *had prepared* a great fish
4: 6. *And* the Lord God *prepared* a gourd,
7. *But* God *prepared* a worm
8. *that* God *prepared* a vehement east wind;

* PUAL.—*Participle.* *

1Ch. 9:29. (Some) of them also (were) *appointed*

4483-84 מְנָה & מְנָא *m'nāh'*, Ch.

* P'AL.—*Preterite.* *

Dan 5:26. Mene; God *hath numbered* thy kingdom,

P'AL.—*Participle Passive.*

Dan 5:25. *Mene, Mene,* Tekel, Upharsin.

* PAEL.—*Preterite.* *

Dan 2:24. whom the king *had ordained*
49. *and he set* Shadrach, Meshach, and
3:12. whom *thou hast set* over the affairs

PAEL.—*Imperative.*

Ezr. 7:25. *set* magistrates and judges,

4490 מָנָה *māh-nāh'*, f.

Ex. 29:26. and it shall be thy *part.*
Lev. 7:33. have the right shoulder *for* (his) *part.*
8:29. the ram of consecration it was Moses' *part;*
1Sa. 1: 4. and her daughters, *portions:*
5. unto Hannah he gave a worthy *portion;*
9:23. Bring *the portion* which I gave thee,
2Ch 31:19. to give *portions* to all the males
Neh. 8:10. and send *portions* unto them for whom
12. to drink, and to send *portions,*
Est. 2: 9. with *such things as belonged to her,* (marg. *her portions*)
9:19, 22. sending *portions* one to another.
Ps. 16: 5. The Lord (is) *the portion of*
Jer. 13:25. thy lot, *the portion of* thy measures

4488 מָנֶה *māh-neh'*, m.

1K. 10:17. three *pound* of gold went to one shield:
Ezr. 2:69. five thousand *pound* of silver,
Neh 7:71. two thousand and two hundred *pound* of silver.
72. two thousand *pound* of silver,
Eze. 45:12. fifteen shekels, shall be your *maneh.*

See 4489 מֹנִים see מֹנֶה

מִנְהָג *min-hāhg'*, m. 4491

2K. 9:20. *and the driving* (marg. *marching*) (is) *like the driving of* Jehu

---

מִנְהָרוֹת *min-hāh-rōhth'*, f. pl. 4492

Jud. 6: 2. the children of Israel made them *the dens*

מָנוֹד [*māh-nōhd'*], m. 4493

Ps. 44:14(15). *a shaking of* the head among the people.

מָנוֹחַ *māh-nōh'ăgh*, m. 4494

Gen 8: 9. the dove found no *rest*
Deu 28:65. neither shall the sole of thy foot have *rest:*
Ru. 3: 1. shall I not seek *rest* for thee,
1Ch. 6:31(16). *after that* the ark *had rest.* (lit. *after the rest of* the ark)
Ps. 116: 7. Return *unto thy rest,*
Isa. 34:14. find for herself *a place of rest.*
Lam 1: 3. she findeth no *rest:*

מְנוּחָה *m'noo-ghāh'*, f. 4496

Gen 49:15. he saw that *rest* (was) good,
Nu. 10:33. to search out *a resting place*
Deu 12: 9. ye are not as yet come to *the rest*
Jud. 20:43. trode them down *with ease* (marg. or, (from) *Menuchah*)
Ru. 1: 9. that ye may find *rest,*
2Sa. 14:17. shall now be *comfortable:* (marg. *for rest*)
1K. 8:56. the Lord, that hath given *rest*
1Ch 22: 9. who shall be a man of *rest;*
28: 2. to build an house of *rest*
Ps. 23: 2. he leadeth me beside the *still* waters (marg. waters of *quietness*)
95:11. they should not enter into *my rest.*
132: 8. Arise, O Lord, *into thy rest;*
14. This (is) *my rest* for ever:
Isa. 11:10. *his rest* shall be glorious.
28:12. This (is) *the rest* (wherewith)
32:18. *in* quiet *resting places;*
66: 1. where (is) the place of *my rest?*
Jer. 45: 3. *and* I find no *rest.*
51:59. Seraiah (was) a *quiet* prince. (marg. or, prince of *Menucha,* or, chief *chamberlain*)
Mic. 2:10. this (is) not (your) *rest:*
Zec. 9: 1. Damascus (shall be) *the rest thereof:*

מָנוֹן *māh-nōhn'*, m. 4497

Pro. 29:21. shall have him become (his) *son*

מָנוֹס *māh-nōhs'*, m. 4498

2Sa. 22: 3. my high tower, *and my refuge,*
Job. 11:20. *and* they shall not *escape,* (marg. *and flight* shall perish from them)
Ps. 59:16(17). thou hast been my defence *and refuge*
142: 4(5). *refuge* failed me;
Jer. 16:19. *my refuge* in the day of affliction,
25:35. the shepherds shall have no *way to flee,* (marg. *flight* shall perish from the shepherds)
46: 5. *and* their mighty ones...are fled *apace,* (marg. *a flight*)
Am. 2:14. *the flight* shall perish from the swift,

מְנוּסָה *m'noo-sāh'*, f. 4499

Lev. 26:36. flee, *as fleeing from* a sword;
Isa. 52:12. not go out with haste, *nor go by flight:*

מָנוֹר [*māh-nōhr'*], m. 4500

1Sa. 17: 7. the staff...(was) *like a weavers' beam,*

2Sa.21:19. the staff...(was) *like a* weavers' *beam.*
1Ch 11:23. a spear *like a* weavers' *beam;*
20: 5. spear staff (was) *like a* weavers' *beam.*

4501 מְנוֹרָה *m'nōh-rāh'*, f.

Ex. 25:31. thou shalt make *a candlestick* (of) pure gold: (of) beaten work shall *the candlestick* be made:
32, 32. three branches of *the candlestick*
33. six branches that come out of *the candlestick.*
34. *And in the candlestick* (shall be) four bowls
35. six branches...out of *the candlestick.*
26:35. *the candlestick* over against the table
30:27. *the candlestick* and his vessels,
31: 8. *the* pure *candlestick*
35:14. *The candlestick* also *for* the light,
37:17. he made *the candlestick* (of) pure gold: (of) beaten work made he *the candlestick;*
18, 18. three branches of *the candlestick*
19. six branches going out of *the candlestick.*
20. *And in the candlestick* (were) four bowls
39:37. *The* pure *candlestick,* (with) the lamps
40: 4. thou shalt bring in *the candlestick,*
24. he put *the candlestick* in the tent
Lev.24: 4. the lamps upon *the* pure *candlestick*
Nu. 3:31. *and the candlestick,* and the altars,
4: 9. *the candlestick of* the light,
8: 2, 3. over against *the candlestick.*
4. this work of *the candlestick*
— so he made *the candlestick.*
1K. 7:49. *the candlesticks* of pure gold,
2K. 4:10. a table, and a stool, *and a candlestick:*
1Ch 28:15. the weight *for the candlesticks of* gold,
— by weight for *every candlestick,* (lit. *candlestick and candlestick*)
— *and for the candlesticks of* silver by weight, (both) *for the candlestick,*
— the use of *every candlestick.* (lit. *candlestick and candlestick*)
2Ch. 4: 7. he made ten *candlesticks of*
20. *the candlesticks* with their lamps,
13:11. *and the candlestick of* gold
Jer. 52:19. *the candlesticks,* and the spoons,
Zec. 4: 2. *a candlestick* all (of) gold,
11. upon the right (side) of *the candlestick*

4502 מִנְּזָרִים [*min-n'zāh-reem'*], m. pl.

Nah. 3:17. *Thy crowned* (are) as the locusts,

4503 מִנְחָה *min-ghāh'*, f.

Gen. 4: 3. *an offering* unto the Lord.
4. respect unto Abel and to *his offering:*
5. to *his offering* he had not respect.
32:13(14). *a present* for Esau his brother;
18(19). it (is) *a present* sent unto my lord
20(21). I will appease him *with the present*
21(22). So went *the present* over
33:10. then receive *my present* at my hand:
43:11. carry down the man *a present,*
15. the men took that *present,*
25. they made ready *the present*
26. they brought him *the present*
Ex. 29:41. *according to the meat offering of* the
30: 9. *nor meat offering;* neither shall ye
40:29. and *the meat offering;*
Lev. 2: 1. when any will offer a *meat* offering
3. the remnant of *the meat offering*
4. if thou bring an oblation of *a meat offering*
5. And if thy oblation (be) *a meat offering*
6. it (is) *a meat offering.*
7. if thy oblation (be) *a meat offering*
8. thou shalt bring *the meat offering*
9. the priest shall take from *the meat offering*
10. that which is left of *the meat offering*
11. No *meat offering,* which ye shall
13. every oblation of *thy meat offering*
— to be lacking from *thy meat offering:*
14. if thou offer *a meat offering of*

Lev. 2:14. thou shalt offer for *the meat offering of*
15. it (is) *a meat offering.*
5:13. the priest's, *as a meat offering.*
6:14(7). this (is) the law of *the meat offering:*
15(8). the flour of the *meat offering,*
—(-). which (is) upon *the meat offering,*
20(13). for *a meat offering* perpetual,
21(14). the baken pieces of *the meat offering*
23(16). every *meat offering for* the priest
7: 9. all *the meat offering* that is baken
10. every *meat offering,* mingled with oil,
37. the burnt offering, *of the meat offering,*
9: 4. *and a meat offering* mingled with oil:
17. he brought *the meat offering,*
10:12. Take *the meat offering* that remaineth
14:10. deals of fine flour (for) *a meat offering,*
20. *the meat offering* upon the altar:
21. fine flour mingled with oil *for a meat offering,*
31. with *the meat offering:*
23:13. *And the meat offering thereof*
16. ye shall offer *a* new *meat offering*
18. unto the Lord, *with their meat offering,*
37. a burnt offering, *and a meat offering,*
Nu. 4:16. *and the* daily *meat offering,*
5:15. it (is) *an offering of* jealousy, *an offering of* memorial,
18. put *the offering of* memorial in her hands, which (is) *the* jealousy *offering:*
25. the priest shall take *the* jealousy *offering* out of the woman's hand, and shall wave *the offering* before the Lord,
26. the priest shall take an handful of *the offering,*
6:15. *and their meat offering,* and their
17. the priest shall offer also *his meat offering.*
7:13, 19, 25, 31, 37, 43, 49, 55, 61, 67, 73, 79. mingled with oil *for a meat offering:*
87. twelve, *with their meat offering:*
8: 8. a young bullock *with his meat offering,*
15: 4. bring *a meat offering* of
6. thou shalt prepare (for) *a meat offering*
9. *a meat offering* of three tenth deals of flour
24. *with his meat offering,* and his
16:15. Respect not thou *their offering:*
18: 9. every *meat offering of* their's,
28: 5. of flour *for a meat offering,*
8. *as the meat offering of* the morning,
9, 12. two tenth deals of flour (for) *a meat offering,*
12. And three tenth deals of flour (for) *a meat offering,*
13. (for) *a meat offering* unto one lamb;
20. *their meat offering* (shall be of) flour
26. when ye bring *a* new *meat offering*
28. *their meat offering* of flour mingled with
31. burnt offering, *and his meat offering,*
29: 3, 9, 14. *And their meat offering* (shall be of)
6. *and his meat offering,* and the daily burnt offering, *and his meat offering,*
11. *and the meat offering of it,* and their
16, 25, 31, 34. *his meat offering,* and his drink
18, 21, 30, 33. *And their meat offering* and their
19. *and the meat offering thereof,* and their
22, 28, 38. *and his meat offering,* and his drink
24, 37. *Their meat offering* and their drink
27. *And their meat offering*
39. *and for your meat offerings,*
Jos. 22:23. burnt offering *or meat offering,*
29. for burnt offerings, *for meat offerings,*
Jud. 3:15. sent *a present* unto Eglon
17. he brought *the present* unto Eglon
18. to offer *the present,* he sent away the people that bare *the present.*
6:18. and bring forth *my present,* (marg. or, *meat offering*)
13:19. Manoah took a kid with *a meat offering,*
23. *a meat offering* at our hands,
1Sa. 2:17. men abhorred *the offering of* the Lord.
29. at my sacrifice *and at mine offering,*
— the chiefest of all *the offerings of*
3:14. not be purged with sacrifice *nor offering*
10:27. and brought him no *presents.*
26:19. let him accept *an offering:*
2Sa. 8: 2. the Moabites...brought *gifts.*
6. and the Syrians...brought *gifts.*
1K. 4:21(5:1). they brought *presents,*

1K. 8:64. offered burnt offerings, and *meat offerings*,
— to receive the burnt offerings, and *meat offerings*,
10:25. they brought every man *his present*,
18:29, 36. the offering of *the* (evening) *sacrifice*,
2K. 3:20. when *the meat offering* was offered,
8: 8. Take *a present* in thine hand,
9. and took *a present* with him,
16:13, 15. and *his meat offering*,
15. *the* evening *meat offering*,
— *and their meat offering*,
17: 3. and gave him *presents*. (marg. or, *tribute*)
4. brought no *present* to the king of Assyria,
20:12. sent letters *and a present* unto Hezekiah:
1Ch 16:29. bring *an offering*, and come before him:
18: 2. David's servants, (and) brought *gifts*.
6. David's servants, (and) brought *gifts*.
21:23. wheat *for the meat offering*;
23:29. fine flour *for meat offering*,
2Ch 7: 7. and *the meat offerings*, and the fat.
9:24. brought every man *his present*,
17: 5. brought to Jehoshaphat *presents*;
11. Philistines brought Jehoshaphat *presents*,
26: 8. the Ammonites gave *gifts*
32:23. And many brought *gifts*
Ezr. 9: 4. until (lit. until *to*) *the* evening *sacrifice*.
5. *And at the* evening *sacrifice*
Neh 10:33(34). *the* continual *meat offering*,
13: 5. they laid *the meat offerings*,
9. *the meat offering* and the frankincense.
Ps. 20: 3(4). Remember all *thy offerings*,
40: 6(7). Sacrifice *and offering* thou didst not
45:12(13). the daughter of Tyre (shall be there) *with a gift*;
72:10. kings of Tarshish...shall bring *presents*:
96: 8. bring *an offering*, and come
141: 2. the lifting up of my hands (as) *the* evening *sacrifice*.
Isa. 1:13. Bring no more vain *oblations*;
19:21. shall do sacrifice *and oblation*;
39: 1. letters *and a present* to Hezekiah:
43:23. to serve *with an offering*,
57: 6. hast offered *a meat offering*.
66: 3. he that offereth *an oblation*,
20. *an offering* unto the Lord
— bring *an offering* in a clean vessel
Jer. 14:12. offer burnt offering *and an oblation*,
17:26. *and meat offerings*, and incense,
33:18. to kindle *meat offerings*,
41: 5. *with offerings* and incense in their hand,
Eze. 42:13. most holy things, *and the meat offering*,
44:29. They shall eat *the meat offering*,
45:15. *for a meat offering*, and for
17. burnt offerings, *and meat offerings*,
— *the meat offering*, and the burnt offering,
24. *And* he shall prepare *a meat offering*
25. *and according to the meat offering*,
46: 5. *And the meat offering* (shall be)
— *and the meat offering* for the lambs
7. he shall prepare *a meat offering*,
11. *the meat offering* shall be an ephah
14. *And* thou shalt prepare *a meat offering*
— *a meat offering* continually by a perpetual
15. *the meat offering*, and the oil,
20. they shall bake *the meat offering*;
Dan 9:21. the time of *the* evening *oblation*.
27. the sacrifice *and the oblation*
Hos 10: 6. *a present* to king Jareb:
Joel 1: 9, 13. *The meat offering* and the drink offering
2:14. *a meat offering* and a drink offering
Am. 5:22. *and your meat offerings*, I will not
25. *and offerings* in the wilderness
Zep 3:10. shall bring *mine offering*.
Mal. 1:10. *neither* will I accept *an offering*
11. *and a* pure *offering*:
13. thus ye brought *an offering*:
2:12. him that offereth *an offering*
13. he regardeth not *the offering*
3: 3. *an offering* in righteousness.
4. *the offering of* Judah and Jerusalem

4504 מִנְחָה *min-ghāh'*, Ch. f.

Ezr. 7:17. lambs, *with their meat offerings*
Dan 2:46. *and* commanded that they should offer *an oblation*

מְנִי *m'nee'*, m. 4507

[Perhaps a proper name].

Isa. 65:11. furnish the drink offering *unto that number*

מִנִּים *min-neem'*, m. pl. 4482

Ps. 45: 8(9). *whereby* they have made thee glad.
150: 4. praise him *with stringed instruments*

מֹנִים *mōh-neem'*, m. pl. 4489

Gen 31: 7. changed my wages ten *times*;
41. thou hast changed my wages ten *times*.

מִנְיָן [*min-yāhn'*], Ch. m. 4510

Ezr. 6:17. *according to the number of* the tribes

מִנְלֶה [*min-leh'*], m. 4512

Job 15:29. shall he prolong *the perfection thereof*

מָנַע *māh-nag'*. 4513

* KAL.—*Preterite*. *

Gen 30: 2. who *hath withheld* from thee the fruit of
Nu. 24:11. the Lord *hath kept thee back*
1Sa. 25:26. the Lord *hath withholden thee*
34. *hath kept me back* from hurting thee,
1K. 20: 7. and *I denied* him not. (marg. *kept* not *back* from him)
Neh. 9:20. and *withheldest* not thy manna
Ps. 21: 2(3). *hast* not *withholden* the request
Ecc. 2:10. *I withheld* not my heart
Jer. 5:25. your sins *have withholden* good
Am. 4: 7. *I have withholden* the rain

KAL.—*Imperative*.

Pro. 1:15. *refrain* thy foot from their path:
Jer. 2:25. *Withhold* thy foot from being unshod,
31:16. *Refrain* thy voice from weeping,

KAL.—*Future*.

2Sa. 13:13. *he will* not *withhold me*
Job 20:13. *but keep it* still within his mouth:
22: 7. *thou hast withholden* bread from the hungry.
31:16. If *I have withheld* the poor
Ps. 84:11(12). no good (thing) *will he withhold*
Pro. 3:27. *Withhold* not good from them
23:13. *Withhold* not correction from the child:
30: 7. *deny* me (them) not before I die:
Jer. 42: 4. *I will keep* nothing *back*
Eze. 31:15. *and I restrained* the floods thereof,

KAL.—*Participle*. Poel.

Pro. 11:26. *He that withholdeth* corn,
Jer. 48:10. *he that keepeth back* his sword

* NIPHAL.—*Preterite*. *

Joel 1:13. the drink offering *is withholden*

NIPHAL. *Future*.

Nu. 22:16. *Let* nothing,...*hinder thee* (marg. *Be not thou letted*)
Job 38:15. *And* from the wicked their light *is withholden*,
Jer. 3: 3. *Therefore* the showers *have been withholden*,

מַנְעוּל *man-gool'*, m. 4514

Neh. 3: 3, 13, 14, 15. *the locks thereof*, and the bars thereof.
6. *and the locks thereof*, and the bars thereof.
Cant. 5: 5. upon the handles of *the lock*.

מִנְעָל [*min-gāhl'*], m. 4515

Deu 33:25. *Thy shoes* (shall be) iron and brass;

4516 מַנְעַמִּים [man-ğam-meem'], m. pl.

Ps. 141: 4. let me not eat of *their dainties.*

4517 מְנַעַנְעִים m'nah-ğan-ğeem', m. pl.

2Sa. 6: 5. on timbrels, and *on cornets,*

4518 מְנַקִּיּוֹת m'nak-keey-yōhth', f. pl.

Ex. 25:29. covers thereof, *and bowls thereof,*
37:16. his spoons, and *his bowls,*
Nu. 4: 7. the spoons, and *the bowls,*
Jer. 52:19. and the spoons, and *the cups;*

See 3243 מֵנֶקֶת see יָנַק

4521 מְנָת m'nāhth, f.

2Ch 31: 3. (He appointed) *also* the king's *portion*
4. to give *the portion of* the priests
Neh 12:44. *the portions of* the law for the priests
47. gave *the portions of* the singers
13:10. *the portions of* the Levites had not been given
Ps. 11: 6. (this shall be) *the portion of* their cup.
63:10(11). they shall be *a portion* for foxes.

4523 מָס māhs, adj.

Job 6:14. *To him that is afflicted* (marg. *melteth*)

4522 מַס mas, m.

Gen49:15. became a servant *unto tribute.*
Ex. 1:11. they did set over them *task*masters (lit. princes of *tribute*)
Deu20:11. shall *be tributaries* unto thee,
Jos. 16:10. and serve *under tribute.*
17:13. they put the Canaanites *to tribute;*
Jud. 1:28. they put the Canaanites *to tribute,*
30. and became *tributaries.*
33. Beth-anath became *tributaries*
35. so that they became *tributaries.*
2Sa.20:24. Adoram (was) over *the tribute:*
1K. 4: 6. Adoniram...(was) over *the tribute.* (marg. or, *levy*)
5:13(27). king Solomon raised *a levy* (marg. *tribute* (of men)) out of all Israel; and *the levy* was thirty thousand men.
14(28). Adoniram (was) over *the levy.*
9:15. *the levy* which king Solomon raised;
21. did Solomon levy *a tribute* of bondservice
12:18. Adoram, who (was) over *the tribute;*
2Ch. 8: 8. to pay *tribute* until this day.
10:18. Hadoram that (was) over *the tribute;*
Est. 10: 1. the king Ahasuerus laid *a tribute*
Pro.12:24. the slothful shall be *under tribute.*
Isa. 31: 8. his young men shall be *discomfited.* (marg. *for melting,* or, *tribute,* or, *tributary*)
Lam.1: 1. (how) is she become *tributary!*

4524 מֵסַב mēh-sav', m.

1K. 6:29. the walls of the house *round about*
2K. 23: 5. *and in the places round about* Jerusalem;
Job 37:12. it is turned *round about* by his counsels:
Ps.140: 9(10). the head *of those that compass me about,*
Cant.1:12. While the king (sitteth) *at his table,*

4525 מַסְגֵּר mas-gēhr', m.

2K. 24:14. and all the craftsmen *and smiths:*
16. and craftsmen *and smiths* a thousand,
Ps.142: 7(8). Bring my soul *out of prison,*
Isa. 24:22. shall be shut up in *the prison,*
42: 7. to bring out the prisoners *from the prison,*
Jer. 24: 1. with the carpenters and *smiths,*
29: 2. and the carpenters, *and the smiths,*

מִסְגֶּרֶת mis-geh'-reth, f. 4526

Ex. 25:25. make unto it *a border of* an hand breadth
— a golden crown *to the border thereof*
27. Over against *the border* shall the
37:12. made thereunto *a border*
— a crown of gold *for the border thereof*
14. Over against *the border*
2Sa.22:46. afraid *out of their close places.*
1K. 7:28. they had *borders, and the borders* (were) between the ledges:
29. on *the borders* that (were) between the
31. gravings *with their borders,*
32. *under the borders* (were) four wheels;
35. *and the borders thereof* (were) of the same.
36. *the borders thereof,* he graved cherubims,
2K. 16:17. And king Ahaz cut off *the borders of* the bases,
Ps. 18:45(46). and be afraid *out of their close places.*
Mic. 7:17. they shall move *out of their holes*

מַסָּד mas-sad', m. 4527

1K. 7: 9. *even from the foundation* unto the coping,

מִסְדְּרוֹן [mis-d'rōhn'], m. 4528

Jud. 3:23. Then Ehud went forth *through the porch,*

מָסָה [māh-sāh']. 4529

* HIPHIL.—*Preterite.* *

Jos. 14: 8. *made* the heart of the people *melt:*

HIPHIL.—*Future.*

Ps. 6: 6(7). *I water* my couch with my tears.
39:11(12). *thou makest* his beauty *to consume away*
147:18. sendeth out his word, *and melteth them:*

מִסָּה [mis-sāh'], f. 4530

Deu 16:10. *with a tribute of* a freewill offering

מַסָּה mas-sāh', f. 4531-32

Ex. 17: 7. he called the name of the place *Massah,* (marg. i.e. *Tentation*)
Deu. 4:34. *by temptations,* by signs, and by wonders,
6:16. as ye tempted (him) in *Massah.*
7:19. *The* great *temptations* which thine eyes
9:22. *at Massah,* and at Kibroth-hattaavah,
29: 3(2). *The* great *temptations* which thine eyes have seen,
33: 8. whom thou didst prove *at Massah,*
Job 9:23. he will laugh *at the trial of* the innocent.
Ps. 95: 8. the day of *temptation* in the wilderness.

מַסְוֶה mas-veh', m. 4533

Ex. 34:33. he put *a vail* on his face.
34. he took *the vail* off,
35. and Moses put *the vail* upon his face again,

מְסוּכָה m'soo-ċhāh', f. 4534

Mic. 7: 4. the most upright (is sharper) *than a thorn hedge:*

מַסָּח mas-sāhċh', m. 4535

2K. 11: 6. the house, *that it be not broken down.* (marg. from *breaking up*)

מִסְחָר [mis-ğhāhr'], m. 4536

1K. 10:15. *and of the traffick of* the spice merchants,

4537 מָסַךְ *māh-sach'*.

* KAL.—*Preterite.* *

Ps. 102: 9(10). and *mingled* my drink with weeping,
Pro. 9: 2. *she hath mingled* her wine;
5. the wine (which) *I have mingled.*
Isa. 19: 14. The Lord *hath mingled*

KAL.—*Infinitive.*

Isa. 5: 22. men of strength *to mingle* strong drink:

4539 מָסָךְ *māh-sāhch'*, m.

Ex. 26: 36. thou shalt make *an hanging* for the door
37. thou shalt make *for the hanging* five pillars
27: 16. for the gate of the court (shall be) *an hanging*
35: 12. and the vail of *the covering,*
15. and *the hanging for* the door at the entering
17. *the hanging for* the door of the court,
36: 37. he made *an hanging* for the tabernacle
38: 18. *And the hanging for* the gate of the court
39: 34. and the vail of *the covering.*
38. and *the hanging for* the tabernacle door,
40. *the hanging* for the court gate,
40: 5. *the hanging of* the door to the tabernacle.
8. hang up *the hanging* at the court gate.
21. set up the vail of *the covering,*
28. he set up *the hanging* (at) the door of the tabernacle.
33. and set up *the hanging of* the court gate.
Nu. 3: 25. *and the hanging for* the door of the tabernacle
26. *the curtain for* the door of the court,
31. *and the hanging,* and all the service
4: 5. they shall take down the *covering* vail,
25. and *the hanging for* the door of the tabernacle
26. and *the hanging for* the door of the gate
2Sa. 17: 19. the woman took and spread *a covering*
Ps. 105: 39. He spread a cloud *for a covering;*
Isa. 22: 8. he discovered *the covering of* Judah,

4538 מֶסֶךְ *meh'-sech*, m.

Ps. 75: 8(9). it is full of *mixture;*

4540 מְסֻכָּה [*m'sook-kāh'*], f.

Eze. 28: 13. every precious stone (was) *thy covering,*

4541 מַסֵּכָה *mas-sēh-chāh'*, f.

Ex. 32: 4. he had made it a *molten* calf:
8. they have made them a *molten* calf,
34: 17. Thou shalt make thee no *molten* gods.
Lev. 19: 4. nor make to yourselves *molten* gods:
Nu. 33: 52. destroy all *their molten* images,
Deu 9: 12. they have made them *a molten image.*
16. had made you a *molten* calf:
27: 15. that maketh (any) graven *or molten image,*
Jud. 17: 3, 4 & 18: 14. a graven image *and a molten image:*
18: 17, 18. the teraphim, *and the molten image:*
1K. 14: 9. made thee other gods, *and molten images,*
2K. 17: 16. made them *molten images,*
2Ch 28: 2. made also *molten images*
34: 3, 4. the carved images, *and the molten images.*
Neh 9: 18. made them a *molten* calf,
Ps. 106: 19. worshipped *the molten image.*
Isa. 30: 1. that cover *with a covering,*
22. the ornament of thy *molten images of*
42: 17. that say *to the molten images,* Ye (are) our
Hos. 13: 2. have made them *molten images*
Nah 1: 14. the graven image *and the molten image:*
Hab. 2: 18. *the molten image,* and a teacher of lies,

4541 מַסֵּכָה *mas-sēh-chāh'*, f.

Isa. 25: 7. *the vail* that is spread over all nations.
28: 20. *and the covering* narrower than that he can wrap himself

מִסְכֵּן *mis-kēhn'*, adj. 4542

Ecc. 4: 13. Better (is) a *poor* and a wise child than
9: 15. there was found in it a *poor* wise man,
— no man remembered that same *poor* man
16. *the poor man's* wisdom (is) despised,

מִסְכְּנוֹת *mis-k'nōhth'*, f. pl. 4543

Ex. 1: 11. they built for Pharaoh *treasure* cities,
1K. 9: 19. all the cities of *store* that Solomon had,
2Ch 8: 4. all the *store* cities, which he built in Hamath.
6. all the *store* cities that Solomon had,
16: 4. all the *store* cities of Naphtali.
17: 12. he built in Judah castles, and cities of *store.*
32: 28. *Storehouses also* for the increase of corn,

מִסְכֵּנֻת *mis-kēh-nooth'*, f. 4544

Deu 8: 9. wherein thou shalt eat bread *with*out *scarceness,*

מַסֶּכֶת [*mas-seh'-cheth*], f. 4545

Jud. 16: 13. weavest the seven locks of my head with *the web.*
14. with the pin of the beam, and with *the web.*

מְסִלָּה *m'sil-lāh'*, f. 4546

Nu. 20: 19. We will go *by the high way:*
Jud. 5: 20. the stars *in their courses* (marg. *paths*)
20: 31. kill, as at other times, *in the highways,*
32. draw them from the city unto *the highways.*
45. they gleaned of them *in the highways*
21: 19. on the east side *of the highway*
1Sa. 6: 12. went *along the highway,*
2Sa. 20: 12. in blood in the midst of *the highway.*
— he removed Amasa out of *the highway*
13. When he was removed out of *the highway,*
2K. 18: 17. *in the highway of* the fuller's field.
1Ch 26: 16. *by the causeway* of the going up,
18. four *at the causeway,* (and) two at Parbar.
2Ch 9: 11. the king made (of) the algum trees *terraces* (marg. *highways,* or, *stairs*)
Ps. 84: 5(6). in whose heart (are) *the ways* (of them).
Pro. 16: 17. *The highway of* the upright (is) to depart from evil:
Isa. 7: 3. *in the highway of* the fuller's field;
11: 16. there shall be *an highway* for the remnant
19: 23. In that day shall there be *a highway*
33: 8. *The highways* lie waste,
36: 2. *in the highway of* the fuller's field.
40: 3. make straight in the desert *a highway*
49: 11. *and my highways* shall be exalted.
59: 7. wasting and destruction (are) *in their paths.*
62: 10. cast up *the highway;*
Jer. 31: 21. set thine heart *toward the highway,*
Joel 2: 8. they shall walk every one *in his path:*

מַסְלוּל *mas-lool'*, m. 4547

Isa. 35: 8. *an highway* shall be there,

מַסְמֵר [*mas-mēhr'*], m. 4548

1Ch 22: 3. iron in abundance *for the nails*
2Ch 3: 9. the weight *of the nails* (was) fifty shekels of gold.
Isa. 41: 7. he fastened it *with nails,*
Jer. 10: 4. they fasten it *with nails* and with hammers.

מָסַס [*māh-sas'*]. 4549

* KAL.—*Infinitive.* *

Isa. 10: 18. *as when* a standardbearer *fainteth.*

* NIPHAL.—*Preterite.* *

Ex. 16:21. *and* when the sun waxed hot, *it melted.*
1Sa. 15: 9. every thing (that was) vile *and refuse,*
Ps. 22:14(15). *it is melted* in the midst
97: 5. The hills *melted* like wax
112:10. he shall gnash with his teeth, *and melt away:*
Isa. 34: 3. *and* the mountains *shall be melted*
Eze. 21: 7(12). *and* every heart *shall melt,*
Mic. 1: 4. *And* the mountains *shall be molten*
Nah. 2:10(11). and the heart *melteth,*

NIPHAL.—*Infinitive.*

2Sa. 17:10. whose heart...shall *utterly* melt: (lit. *melting* shall melt)
Ps. 68: 2(3). *as* wax *melteth* before the fire,

NIPHAL.—*Future.*

Deu 20: 8. lest his brethren's heart *faint* (marg. *melt*)
Jos. 2:11. our hearts *did melt,*
5: 1. *that* their heart *melted,*
7: 5. *wherefore* the hearts of the people *melted,*
Jud. 15:14. *and* his bands *loosed* (marg. *were melted*)
2Sa. 17:10. whose heart...*shall* utterly *melt:*
Isa. 13: 7. every man's heart *shall melt:*
19: 1. the heart of Egypt *shall melt*

* HIPHIL.—*Preterite.* *

Deu 1:28. our brethren *have discouraged*

4551 מַסָּע *mas-sāh^{n}g′*, m.

Job 41:26(18). the spear, *the dart,* nor the habergeon.

4551 מַסָּע *mas-sāh^{n}g′*, m.

1K. 6: 7. stone made ready *before it was brought*

4550 מַסַּע *mas-sa^{n}g′*, m.

Gen 13: 3. he went *on his journeys*
Ex. 17: 1. *after their journeys,* according
40:36. Israel went onward in all *their journeys:*
38. throughout all *their journeys.*
Nu. 10: 2. *and for the journeying of* the camps.
6. blow an alarm *for their journeys.*
12. the children of Israel took *their journeys*
28. *the journeyings of* the children of Israel
33: 1. *the journeys of* the children of Israel,
2. goings out *according to their journeys*
— *their journeys* according to their goings
Deu 10:11. take (thy) *journey* (lit. go *in journeying*)

4552 מִסְעָד *mis-^{n}gāhd′*, m.

1K. 10:12. the king made of the almug trees *pillars* (marg. *a prop,* or, *rails*)

4553 מִסְפֵּד *mis-pēhd′*, m.

Gen 50:10. *a* great and very sore *lamentation:*
Est. 4: 3. fasting, and weeping, *and wailing;*
Ps. 30:11(12). turned for me *my mourning* into dancing:
Isa. 22:12. call to weeping, *and to mourning,*
Jer. 6:26. most bitter *lamentation:*
48:38. (There shall be) *lamentation* generally
Eze. 27:31. bitterness of heart (and) bitter *wailing.*
Joel 2:12. with fasting, and with weeping, *and with mourning:*
Am. 5:16. *Wailing* (shall be) in all streets;
— *and* such as are skilful of lamentation *to wailing.*
17. in all vineyards (shall be) *wailing:*
Mic. 1: 8. *wailing* like the dragons, and mourning as the owls.
11. came not forth in *the mourning of* Beth-ezel;
Zec. 12:10. *as one mourneth* for (his) only (son),
11. shall there be *a* great *mourning* in Jerusalem, *as the mourning of* Hadadrimmon

---

מִסְפּוֹא *mis-pōh′* m. 4554

Gen 24:25. We have both straw and *provender* enough,
32. and gave straw *and provender* for the camels,
42:27. to give his ass *provender*
43:24. he gave their asses *provender.*
Jud. 19:19. there is both straw and *provender* for our asses;

מִסְפָּחוֹת *mis-pāh-ghōhth′*, f. pl. 4555

Eze. 13:18. make *kerchiefs* upon the head of every stature
21. *Your kerchiefs* also will I tear,

מִסְפַּחַת *mis-pah′-ghath*, f. 4556

Lev. 13: 6. it (is but) *a scab:*
7. if *the scab* spread much abroad in the skin,
8. behold, *the scab* spreadeth in the skin,

מִסְפָּר *mis-pāhr′*, m. 4557

Gen 34:30. I (being) few in *number,* they shall gather themselves
41:49. for (it was) without *number.*
Ex. 16:16. (according to) *the number of* your persons;
23:26. *the number of* thy days I will fulfil.
Lev. 25:15. *According to the number of* years
— *according unto the number of* years
16. (according) to *the number* (of the years) of the fruits
50. *according unto the number of* years,
Nu. 1: 2. *with the number of* (their) names,
18, 20, 22, 24, 26, 28, 30, 32, 34, 36, 38, 40, 42. *according to the number of* the names,
3:22, 34. *according to the number of* all the males,
28. *In the number of* all the males,
40. take *the number of* their names.
43. *by the number of* names,
9:20. when the cloud was *a few* days (lit. days of *number*) upon the tabernacle;
14:29. according to *your* whole *number,*
34. *After the number of* the days
15:12. *According to the number* that ye shall prepare,
— to every one *according to their number.*
23:10. *and the number* of the fourth (part) of Israel?
26:53. *according to the number of* names.
29:18, 21, 24, 27, 30, 33, 37. *according to their number,* after the manner:
31:36. was *in number* three hundred thousand
Deu 4:27. ye shall be left few in *number*
25: 2. to his fault, *by a certain number.*
32: 8. *according to the number of* the children of Israel.
33: 6. let (not) his men be *few.* (lit. let his men be *a number*)
Jos. 4: 5. *according unto the number of* the tribes of
8. *according to the number of* the tribes of
Jud. 6: 5. and their camels were without *number:*
7: 6. *the number of* them that lapped,
12. their camels (were) without *number,*
15. Gideon heard *the telling of* the dream,
21:23. wives, *according to their number,*
1Sa. 6: 4. *the number of* the lords of the Philistines:
18. *the number of* all the cities of the Philistines
27: 7. And the time (marg. *the number of* days) that David dwelt
2Sa. 2:11. the time (marg. *the number of* days) that David was king in Hebron
15. there arose and went over *by number*
21:20. four and twenty in *number;*
24: 2. that I may know *the number of* the people.
9. *the sum of* the number of the people
1K. 18:31. *according to the number of* the tribes
1Ch. 7: 2. *whose number* (was) in the days of David

1Ch 7:40. *the number* throughout the genealogy *of them*
9:28. bring them in *and* out *by tale.* (marg. bring them in *by tale, and* carry them out *by tale*)
11:11. *the number of* the mighty men whom David had;
12:23. *the numbers of* the bands (that were) ready armed
16:19. When ye were but *few,* (marg. men of *number*)
21: 2. bring *the number of them* to me,
5. And Joab gave *the sum of* the number of the people
22: 4. cedar trees *in abundance:* (lit. without *number*)
16. the brass, and the iron, (there is) no *number.*
23: 3. *their number* by their polls,
24. they were counted *by number of* names by their polls,
27. Levites (were) *numbered* (marg. *number*) from twenty years old
31. *by number,* according to the order
25: 1. *the* (lit. *their*) *number* of the workmen
7. *the number of them,* with their brethren
27: 1. the children of Israel *after their number,*
23. David took not *the number of them*
24. neither was *the number* put *in the account of* the chronicles of king David.
2Ch 12: 3. the people (were) without *number*
26:11. *according to the number of* their account
12. *The* whole *number of* the chief of the fathers
29:32. *the number of* the burnt offerings,
35: 7. *to the number of* thirty thousand,
Ezr. 1: 9. And this (is) *the number of them:*
2: 2. *The number of* the men of the people of Israel:
3: 4. the daily burnt offerings *by number,*
8:34. *By number* (and) by weight of every one:
Neh 7: 7. *The number,* (I say), *of* the men of the people
Est. 9:11. *the number of* those that were slain
Job 1: 5. (according) to *the number of* them all:
3: 6. not come *into the number of* the months.
5: 9. marvellous things without *number:*
9:10. and wonders without *number.*
14: 5. *the number of* his months (are) with thee,
15:20. *and the number of* years is hidden
16:22. When *a few* years (marg. years of *number*) are come,
21:21. *when the number of* his months is cut off
33. as (there are) in*numerable* (lit. without *number*)
25: 3. Is there any *number* of his armies?
31:37. I would declare unto him *the number of* my steps;
36:26. neither can *the number of* his years
38:21. *or* (because) *the number of* thy days (is) great?
Ps. 40:12(13). For in*numerable* (lit. without *number*) evils have compassed me about:
104:25. wherein (are) things creeping in*numerable,* (lit. *id.*)
105:12. When there were (but) a few men in *number;*
34. caterpillers, and that without *number,*
147: 4. He telleth *the number* of the stars;
5. his understanding (is) in*finite.* (marg. no *number*)
Ecc. 2: 3. *all* the days (marg. *the number of* the days) of their life.
5:18(17). *all* the days (marg. *id.*) of his life,
6:12. *all* the days (marg. *id.*) of his vain life
Cant 6: 8. and virgins without *number.*
Isa. 10:19. the trees of his forest shall be *few,* (marg. *number*)
21:17. the residue of *the number of* archers,
40:26. that bringeth out their host *by number:*
Jer. 2:28. *the number of* thy cities are thy gods,
32. forgotten me days without *number.*
11:13. (according to) *the number of* thy cities — *and* (according to) *the number of* the streets
44:28. *a* small *number* that escape the sword
46:23. more than the grasshoppers, and (are) in*numerable.* (lit. without *number*)
Eze. 4: 4, 9. (according) to *the number of* the days
Eze. 4: 5. *according to the number of* the days,
5: 3. take thereof a few *in number,*
12:16. I will leave *a few* men (marg. men of *number*)
Dan 9: 2. I Daniel understood by books *the number of* the years,
Hos. 1:10(2:1). *the number of* the children of Israel
Joel 1: 6. strong, and without *number,*

מָסַר [*māh-sar'*]. 4560

* KAL.—*Infinitive.* *

Nu. 31:16. *to commit* trespass against the Lord

* NIPHAL.—*Future.* *

Nu. 31: 5. *So there were delivered* out of the thousands

מֹסָר [*mōh-sāhr'*], m. 4561

Job 33:16. *and* sealeth *their instruction,*

מָסֹרֶת *māh-sōh'-reth*, f. 4562

Eze.20:37. *into the bond of* the covenant:

מִסְתּוֹר *mis-tōhr'*, m. 4563

Isa. 4: 6. and *for a covert* from storm and from rain.

מִסְתָּר *mis-tāhr'*, m. 4565

Ps. 10: 8. *in the secret places* doth he murder
9. He lieth in wait *secretly* (marg. *in the secret places*)
17:12. lurking *in secret places.*
64: 4(5). That they may shoot *in secret* at the perfect:
Isa. 45: 3. hidden riches of *secret places,*
Jer. 13:17. my soul shall weep *in secret places*
23:24. Can any hide himself *in secret places*
49:10. I have uncovered *his secret places,*
Lam 3:10. (as) a lion *in secret places.*
Hab. 3:14. their rejoicing (was) as to devour the poor *secretly.*

מַעְבָד [*mag̃-bāhd'*], m. 4566

Job.34:25. Therefore he knoweth *their works,*

מַעְבַד [*mag̃-bāhd'*], Ch. m. 4567

Dan 4:37(34). all *whose works* (are) truth,

מַעֲבֶה [*mah-g̃āveh'*], m. 4568

1K. 7:46. the king cast them, *in the clay* ground (marg. *in the thickness of* the ground)

מַעֲבָר [*mah-g̃āvāhr'*], m. 4569

Gen32:22(23). passed over *the ford* Jabbok.
1Sa.13:23. of the Philistines went out to *the passage*
Isa. 30:32. *every place where* the grounded staff *shall pass,* (marg. every *passing of* the rod founded)

מַעְבָּרָה *mag̃-bāh-rāh'*, f. 4569

Jos. 2: 7. the way to Jordan unto *the fords:*
Jud. 3:28. took *the fords of* Jordan toward Moab,
12: 5. the Gileadites took *the passages of* Jordan
6. slew him at *the passages of* Jordan:
1Sa.14: 4. between *the passages,*
Isa. 10:29. They are gone over *the passage:*

Isa. 16: 2. Moab shall be at *the fords of* Arnon.
Jer. 51:32. And *that the passages* are stopped,

4570 **מַעְגָּל** *mag̃-^{n}gāhl'*, m.

1Sa.26: 5. Saul lay *in the trench*, (marg. or, *midst of his carriages*)
7. Saul lay sleeping *within the trench*,
Ps. 23: 3. he leadeth me *in the paths of* righteousness
65:11(12). *and thy paths* drop fatness.
140: 5(6). they have spread a net by the *way*side;
Pro. 2: 9. judgment, and equity; (yea), every good *path*.
4:11. I have led thee *in* right *paths*.
26. Ponder *the path of* thy feet,
Isa. 26: 7. dost weigh *the path of* the just.

4570 **מַעְגָּלָה** *mag̃-^{n}gāh-lāh'*, f.

1Sa.17:20. he came *to the trench*, (marg. or, *place of the carriage*)
Ps. 17: 5. Hold up my goings *in thy paths*,
Pro. 2:15. (they) froward *in their paths:*
18. and *her paths* unto the dead.
5: 6. *her ways* are moveable,
21. he pondereth all *his goings*.
Isa. 59: 8. (there is) no judgment *in their goings:*

4571 **מָעַד** [*māh-^{n}gad'*].

* KAL.—*Preterite*. *

2Sa.22:37. my feet *did* not *slip*.
Ps. 18:36(37). my feet *did* not *slip*.

KAL.—*Future*.

Ps. 26: 1. (therefore) *I shall* not *slide*.
37:31. none of his steps *shall slide*.

KAL.—*Participle*. Poël.

Job 12: 5. He that is ready *to slip* (lit. *to those that slip*) *with* (his) feet

* HIPHIL.—*Imperative*. *

Ps. 69:23(24). *make* their loins continually *to shake*.

4574 **מַעֲדָן** [*mah-^{n}gădāhn'*], m.

Gen49:20. he shall yield royal *dainties*.
1Sa.15:32. And Agag came unto him *delicately*.
Pro.29:17. he shall give *delight* unto thy soul.
Lam. 4: 5. They that did feed *delicately* are desolate

4575 **מַעֲדַנּוֹת** *mah-^{n}gădan-nōhth'*, f. pl.

Job 38:31. thou bind *the sweet influences of* Pleiades,

4576 **מַעְדֵּר** *mag̃-^{n}dēhr'*, m.

Isa. 7:25. shall be digged *with the mattock*,

4579 **מֵעָה** [*māh-^{n}gāh'*], f.

Isa. 48:19. the offspring of thy bowels *like the gravel thereof;*

4580 **מָעוֹג** *māh-^{n}gōhg'*, m.

1K. 17:12. I have not *a cake*, but an handful of meal
Ps. 35:16. With hypocritical mockers in *feasts*,

4581 **מָעוֹז** *māh-^{n}gōhz'*, m.

Jud. 6:26. build an altar...upon the top of this *rock*,
2Sa.22:33. God (is) *my strength* (and) power:
Neh. 8:10. the joy of the Lord is *your strength*.
Ps. 27: 1. the Lord (is) *the strength of* my life;
28: 8. *and* he (is) *the* saving *strength of* his anointed.
Ps. 31: 2(3). be thou my *strong* rock, (lit. to me a rock of *strength*)
4(5). thou (art) *my strength*.
37:39. (he is) *their strength* in the time of trouble,
43: 2. thou (art) the God of *my strength:*
52: 7(9). man (that) made not God *his strength;*
60: 7(9). Ephraim also (is) *the strength of* mine
108: 8(9). Ephraim also (is) *the strength of* mine
Pro.10:29. The way of the Lord (is) *strength* to the
Isa. 17: 9. In that day shall *his strong* cities (lit. the cities of *his strength*)
10. hast not been mindful of the rock of *thy strength*,
23: 4. (even) *the strength of* the sea,
11. to destroy *the strong holds* (marg. *strengths*) *thereof*.
14. *your strength* is laid waste.
25: 4. thou hast been *a strength* to the poor, *a strength* to the needy
27: 5. let him take hold *of my strength*,
30: 2. to strengthen themselves *in the strength of* Pharaoh,
3. Therefore shall *the strength of* Pharaoh
Jer. 16:19. O Lord, my strength, *and my fortress*,
Eze.24:25. when I take from them *their strength*,
30:15. will pour my fury upon Sin, *the strength of*
Dan11: 1. to confirm *and to strengthen* him.
7. shall enter *into the fortress of* the king
10. and be stirred up, (even) to *his fortress*.
19. he shall turn his face *toward the fort of*
31. they shall pollute the sanctuary of *strength*,
38. shall he honour the God of *forces:* (marg. *Mauzzim;* or, *munitions*)
39. in the *most strong* holds (marg. fortresses of *munitions*)
Joel 3:16(4:16). *and the strength of* the children of
Nah. 1: 7. *a strong hold* (marg. *strength*) in the day of trouble;
3 :11. thou also shalt seek *strength*

מָעוֹן *māh-^{n}gōhn'*, m. 4583

Deu 26:15. Look down *from* thy holy *habitation*,
1Sa. 2:29. I have commanded (in my) *habitation*,
32. shalt see an enemy (in my) *habitation*,
1Ch 4:41. *the habitations* that were found there,
2Ch 30:27. prayer came (up) *to* his holy *dwelling place*, (marg. *the habitation of* his holiness)
36:15. his people, and on *his dwelling place:*
Ps. 26: 8. I have loved *the habitation of* thy house,
68: 5(6). God *in* his holy *habitation*.
71: 3. Be thou my strong *habitation*,
90: 1. Lord, thou hast been our *dwelling place*
91: 9. (even) the most high, *thy habitation;*
Jer. 9:11(10). heaps, (and) *a den of* dragons;
10:22. desolate, (and) *a den of* dragons.
25:30. *and* utter his voice *from* his holy *habitation*,
49:33. Hazor shall be *a dwelling for* dragons,
51:37. heaps, *a dwellingplace for* dragons,
Nah. 2:11(12). Where (is) *the dwelling of* the lions,
Zep. 3: 7. *their dwelling* should not be cut off,
Zec. 2:13(17). is raised up *out of* his holy *habitation*. (marg. *the habitation of* his holiness)

מְעוֹנָה *m'^{n}gōh-nāh'*, f. 4585

Deu33:27. The eternal God (is thy) *refuge*,
Job 37: 8. into dens, *and* remain *in their places*.
38:40. When they couch *in* (their) *dens*,
Ps. 76: 2(3). *and his dwelling place* in Zion.
104:22. and lay them down in *their dens*.
Cant.4: 8. *from* the lions' *dens*,
Jer. 21:13. who shall enter *into our habitations?*
Am. 3: 4. will a young lion cry *out of his den*,
Nah. 2:12(13). his holes with prey, *and his dens* with ravin.

מָעוּף [*māh-^{n}gooph'*], m. 4588

Isa. 8:22. darkness, *dimness of* anguish;

מָעוֹר [*māh-^{n}gōhr'*], m. 4589

Hab. 2:15. that thou mayest look on *their nakedness*

4591 ## מָעַט [māh-^{n}gat'].

* KAL.—*Infinitive.* *

Lev.25:16. according to *the fewness of* years

KAL.—*Future.*

Ex. 12: 4. if the houshold *be too little*
Neh 9:32. *let* not all the trouble *seem little*
Ps.107:39. *Again, they are minished* and brought
Pro.13:11. Wealth (gotten) by vanity *shall be diminished:*
Isa. 21:17. of Kedar, *shall be diminished:*
Jer. 29: 6. increased there, and not *diminished.*
30:19. and *they shall* not *be few;*

* PIEL.—*Preterite.* *

Ecc.12: 3. the grinders cease because *they are few,*

* HIPHIL.—*Preterite.* *

Lev.26:22. *and make* you *few in number;*
Eze.29:15. *for I will diminish them,* that they shall

HIPHIL.—*Future.*

Ex. 30:15. the poor *shall* not *give less* (marg. *diminish*) than
Lev.25:16. *thou shalt diminish* the price
Nu. 26:54. to few *thou shalt give the less* (marg. *diminish*)
33:54. to the fewer *ye shall give the less* (marg. *id.*)
35: 8. from (them that have) few *ye shall give few:*
2K. 4: 3. *borrow* not *a few.* (marg. or, *scant* not)
Ps.107:38. *suffereth* not their cattle *to decrease.*
Jer. 10:24. lest *thou bring me to nothing.* (marg. *diminish me*)

HIPHIL.—*Participle.*

Ex. 16:17. and gathered, some more, *some less.*
18. *and he that gathered little* had no lack;
Nu. 11:32. *he that gathered least* gathered ten homers:

4592 ## מְעַט *m'^{n}gat* & מְעָט *m'^{n}gāht*, m.

Gen18: 4. Let *a little* water,...be fetched,
24:17. Let me, I pray thee, drink *a little* water
43. Give me, I pray thee, *a little* water
26:10. one of the people might *lightly* have lien
30:15. (Is it) *a small matter* that thou hast taken
30. (it was) *little* which thou hadst
43: 2. Go again, buy us *a little* food.
11. carry down the man a present, *a little* balm, *and a little* honey,
44:25. Go again, (and) buy us *a little* food.
47: 9. *few* and evil have the days...been,
Ex. 17: 4. they be *almost* ready to stone me. (lit. yet *a little* and they will stone me)
23:30. *By little and little* I will drive them out
Lev.25:52. if there remain but *few* years
Nu. 13:18. strong or weak, *few* or many;
16: 9. (Seemeth it but) *a small thing* unto you,
13. (Is it) *a small thing* that thou hast brought us up
26:54. *and to few* thou shalt give the less
56. between many *and few.*
33:54. *and to the fewer* ye shall give the less
35: 8. but from (them that have) *few*
Deu 7: 7. ye (were) *the fewest* of all people:
22. put out those nations before thee by *little and little:*
26: 5. and sojourned there with *a few,*
28:38. *and* shalt gather (but) *little*
62. ye shall be left *few* in number,
Jos. 7: 3. for they (are but) *few.*
22:17. (Is) the iniquity of Peor *too little* for us,
Jud. 4:19. Give me, I pray thee, *a little* water
Ru. 2: 7. she tarried *a little in* the house.
1Sa.14: 6. to save by many or *by few.*
29. because I tasted *a little* of this honey.
43. I did but taste *a little* honey
17:28. with whom hast thou left those *few* sheep
2Sa.12: 8. if (that had been) *too little,*
16: 1. when David was *a little* past the top
19:36(37). Thy servant will go *a little* way over Jordan
1K. 17:10. Fetch me, I pray thee, *a little* water
12. *and a little* oil in a cruse:
2K. 10:18. Ahab served Baal *a little;*
1Ch 16:19. *even a few,* and strangers in it.
2Ch 12: 7. I will grant them *some* (marg. or, *a little while*) deliverance;
29:34. But the priests were *too few,*
Ezr. 9: 8. And now *for a little* space
— give us *a little* reviving in our bondage.
Neh 2:12. I and *some few* men with me;
7: 4. the people (were) *few* therein,
Job 10:20. (Are) not my days *few?*
— that I may take comfort *a little,*
15:11. (Are) the consolations of God *small* with thee?
24:24. They are exalted *for a little while,*
32:22. my maker would *soon* take me away.
Ps. 2:12. his wrath is kindled *but a little.*
8: 5(6). thou hast made him *a little* lower
37:10. For yet *a little while,*
16. *A little* that a righteous man hath
73: 2. my feet were *almost* gone;
81:14(15). I should *soon* have subdued their enemies,
94:17. my soul had *almost* (marg. or, *quickly*) dwelt in silence.
105:12. *yea, very few,* and strangers in it.
109: 8. Let his days be *few;*
119:87. They had *almost* consumed me upon earth;
Pro. 5:14. I was *almost* in all evil
6:10. (Yet) *a little* sleep, *a little* slumber, *a little* folding of the hands to sleep:
10:20. the heart of the wicked (is) *little* worth.
15:16. Better (is) *little* with the fear of the Lord
16: 8. Better (is) *a little* with righteousness
24:33. (Yet) *a little* sleep, *a little* slumber, *a little* folding of the hands to sleep:
Ecc. 5: 2(1). therefore let thy words be *few.*
12(11). whether he eat *little* or much:
9:14. a little city, and *few* men within it;
10: 1. (so doth) *a little* folly
Cant.3: 4. *but a little* that I passed from them,
Isa. 1: 9. a *very small* remnant,
7:13. (Is it) *a small thing* for you to weary men,
10: 7. cut off nations not *a few.*
25. For yet a very *little* while,
16:14. the remnant (shall be) *very* small (lit. *little* small)
26:20. hide thyself *as it were for a little* moment,
29:17. (Is) it not yet a *very* little while,
Jer. 42: 2. we are left (but) *a few* of many,
51:33. yet a *little* while,
Eze. 5: 3. take thereof *a few* in number,
11:16. yet will I be to them as *a little* sanctuary
16:20. (Is this) of thy whoredoms *a small matter,*
47. *as* (if that were) *a* very *little* (thing),
34:18. (Seemeth it) *a small thing* unto you
Dan 11:23. shall become strong *with a small* people.
34. they shall be holpen with *a little* help:
Hos. 1: 4. for yet *a little* (while),
8:10. they shall sorrow *a little*
Hag. 1: 6. Ye have sown much, and bring in *little;*
9. Ye looked for much, and, lo, (it came) *to little;*
2: 6. Yet once, it (is) *a little while,*
Zec. 1:15. I was but *a little* displeased

מְעֹט [māh-^{n}gōht'], adj. 4593

Eze.21:15(20). (it is) *wrapped up* (marg. or, *sharpened*) for the slaughter.

מַעֲטֶה [mah-^{n}găteh'], m. 4594

Isa. 61: 3. *the garment of* praise for the spirit of heaviness;

מַעֲטָפוֹת *mah-^{n}gătāh-phōhth'*, f. pl. 4595

Isa. 3:22. *and the mantles,* and the wimples,

4596 ## מְעִי m'gee, m.

Isa. 17: 1. it shall be *a* ruinous *heap.*

4598 ## מְעִיל m'geel, m.

Ex. 28: 4. *and a robe,* and a broidered coat,
31. thou shalt make *the robe of* the ephod
34. the hem of *the robe* round about.
29: 5. and *the robe of* the ephod,
39:22. he made *the robe of* the ephod
23. (there was) an hole in the midst of *the robe,*
24. they made upon the hems of *the robe*
25. upon the hem of *the robe,*
26. round about the hem of *the robe*
Lev. 8: 7. clothed him with *the robe,*
1Sa. 2:19. *Moreover* his mother made him *a* little *coat,*
15:27. he laid hold upon the skirt of *his mantle,*
18: 4. Jonathan stripped himself of *the robe*
24: 4(5). cut off the skirt of Saul's *robe* privily.
11(12). see the skirt of *thy robe* in my hand: for in that I cut off the skirt of *thy robe,*
28:14. he (is) covered with *a mantle.*
2Sa.13:18. with such *robes* were the king's daughters
1Ch 15:27. David (was) clothed *with a robe of* fine linen,
Ezr. 9: 3. I rent my garment *and my mantle,*
5. having rent my garment *and my mantle,*
Job 1:20. Then Job arose, and rent *his mantle,* (marg. or, *robe*)
2:12. they rent every one *his mantle,*
29:14. my judgment (was) *as a robe*
Ps.109:29. their own confusion, *as* with *a mantle.*
Isa. 59:17. was clad with zeal *as a cloke.*
61:10. he hath covered me with *the robe of* righteousness,
Eze.26:16. and lay away *their robes,*

4599 ## מַעְיָן mag-yāhn', m.

Gen 7:11. all *the fountains of* the great deep
8: 2. *The fountains* also of the deep
Lev.11:36. Nevertheless *a fountain* or pit,
Jos. 15: 9. *the fountain of* the water of Nephtoah,
18:15. *the well of* waters of Nephtoah
1K. 18: 5. unto all *fountains of* water
2K. 3:19. and stop all *wells of* water,
25. they stopped all *the wells of* water,
2Ch 32: 4. stopped all *the fountains,*
Ps. 74:15. Thou didst cleave *the fountain*
84: 6(7). the valley of Baca make it *a well;*
87: 7. all *my springs* (are) in thee.
104:10. He sendeth *the springs* into the valleys,
114: 8. the flint *into a fountain of* waters.
Pro. 5:16. Let *thy fountains* be dispersed abroad,
8:24. when (there were) no *fountains*
25:26. *a* troubled *fountain,*
Cant.4:12. *a fountain* sealed.
15. *A fountain of* gardens,
Isa. 12: 3. draw water *out of the wells of* salvation.
41:18. and *fountains* in the midst of the valleys:
Hos.13:15. *his fountain* shall be dried up:
Joel 3:18(4:18). *and a fountain* shall come forth

4578 ## מֵעִים [mēh-geem'], m. pl.

Gen15: 4. come forth *out of thine own bowels*
25:23. shall be separated *from thy bowels;*
Nu. 5:22. this water...shall go *into thy bowels,*
Ru. 1:11. (are) there yet (any more) sons *in my womb.*
2Sa. 7:12. which shall proceed *out of thy bowels,*
16:11. which came forth *of my bowels,*
20:10. and shed out *his bowels* to the ground,
2Ch 21:15. of *thy bowels,* until *thy bowels* fall out
18. the Lord smote him *in his bowels*
19. *his bowels* fell out
32:21. they that came forth of *his own bowels*
Job 20:14. his meat *in his bowels* is turned,
Job 30:27. *My bowels* boiled,
Ps. 22:14(15). in the midst of *my bowels.*
40: 8(9). thy law (is) within *my heart.* (marg. in the midst of *my bowels*)
71: 6. *out of* my mother's *bowels:*
Cant.5: 4. *and my bowels* were moved
14. *his belly* (is as) bright ivory
Isa. 16:11. *my bowels* shall sound
48:19. the offspring of *thy bowels*
49: 1. *from the bowels of* my mother
63:15. the sounding of *thy bowels*
Jer. 4:19. *My bowels, my bowels!* I am pained
31:20. *my bowels* are troubled
Lam.1:20. *my bowels* are troubled; mine heart
2:11. *my bowels* are troubled, my liver
Eze. 3: 3. *and* fill *thy bowels* with this roll
7:19. *neither* fill *their bowels:*
Jon. 1:17(2:1). *in the belly* (marg. *bowels*) *of* the fish
2: 1(2). Jonah prayed unto the Lord...*out of* the fish's *belly,*

מְעִין [m'geen], Ch. m. pl. 4577

Dan. 2:32. *his belly* and his thighs of brass,.

מָעַךְ [māh-gach']. 4600

* KAL.—*Participle.* Paül. *

Lev.22:24. Ye shall not offer unto the Lord *that which is bruised,*
1Sa.26: 7. his spear *stuck* in the ground

* PUAL.—*Preterite.* *

Eze.23: 3. there *were* their breasts *pressed,*

מָעַל māh-gal'. 4603

* KAL.—*Preterite.* *

Lev. 6: 2(5:21). If a soul sin, *and commit* a trespass
26:40. which *they trespassed* against me,
Nu. 5:12. *and commit* a trespass against him,
Deu32:51. Because *ye trespassed* against me
Jos. 22:16. trespass (is) this that *ye have committed*
20. *Did* not Achan the son of Zerah *commit* a trespass
31. *ye have* not *committed* this trespass
1Ch 2: 7. who *transgressed* in the thing accursed.
10:13. So Saul died for his transgression which *he committed* (marg. *transgressed*)
2Ch 12: 2. *they had transgressed* against the Lord,
26:18. for *thou hast trespassed;*
29: 6. For our fathers *have trespassed,*
30: 7. which *trespassed* against the Lord
Ezr.10: 2. We *have trespassed* against our God,
10. Ye *have transgressed,* and have taken strange wives,
Eze.15: 8. *they have committed* (marg. *trespassed*) a trespass,
17:20. *he hath trespassed* against me.
18:24. in his trespass that *he hath trespassed,*
39:23. because *they trespassed* against me,
26. *they have trespassed* against me,
Dan. 9: 7. *they have trespassed* against thee.

KAL.—*Infinitive.*

Nu. 5: 6. *to do* a trespass against the Lord, (lit. *to trespass* a trespass)
2Ch 28:19. *transgressed* sore against the Lord.
22. did he *trespass* yet more (lit. did he add *to trespass*)
36:14. *transgressed* very much (lit. multiplied *to transgress* transgression)
Neh 13:27. *to transgress* against our God
Eze.14:13. the land sinneth against me *by trespassing*
20:27. *in that they have committed* (marg. *trespassed*) a trespass

KAL.—*Future.*

Lev. 5:15. If a soul *commit* a trespass,
Nu. 5:27. *and have done* trespass against her husband, (lit. *and have trespassed* trespass)

Jos. 7: 1. *But* the children of Israel *committed* a
1Ch 5:25. *And they transgressed* against the God of
2Ch 26:16. *for he transgressed* against the Lord
Neh. 1: 8. (If) ye *transgress*, I will scatter you
Pro. 16:10. his mouth *transgresseth* not in judgment.

4604 מַעַל *mah'-ğal*, m.

Lev. 5:15. If a soul commit *a trespass*,
6: 2(5:21). commit *a trespass* against the Lord,
26:40. *with their trespass* which they
Nu. 5: 6. to do *a trespass* against the Lord,
12. commit *a trespass* against him,
27. have done *trespass* against her husband,
31:16. to commit *trespass* against the Lord
Jos. 7: 1. children of Israel committed *a trespass*
22:16. *trespass* (is) this that ye have committed
20. Achan the son of Zerah commit *a trespass*
22. if *in transgression* against the Lord,
31. ye have not committed this *trespass*
1Ch 9: 1. away to Babylon *for their transgression.*
10:13. So Saul died *for his transgression*
2Ch 28:19. transgressed *sore* (lit. transgressed *a transgression*)
29:19. did cast away *in his transgression*,
33:19. all his sins, *and his trespass*,
36:14. the people, transgressed *very* much (lit. multiplied to transgress *transgression*)
Ezr. 9: 2. and rulers hath been chief *in* this *trespass.*
4. *the transgression of* those that had been
10: 6. he mourned because of *the transgression of*
Job 21:34. in your answers there remaineth *falsehood?* (marg. *transgression*)
Eze. 14:13. the land sinneth...by trespassing *grievously*, (lit. *a trespass*)
15: 8. they have committed *a trespass*,
17:20. will plead with him there for *his trespass*
18:24. *in his trespass* that he hath trespassed,
20:27. in that they have committed *a trespass* against me.
39:26. and all *their trespasses*
Dan. 9: 7. *because of their trespass* that they

4605 מַעַל *mah'-ğal.*

מִמַּעַל³, מִלְמַעְלָה², לְמַעְלָה¹

Gen 6:16. in a cubit shalt thou finish it *above*[2];
7:20. Fifteen cubits *upward*[2] did the waters
22: 9. on the altar *upon*[3] the wood.
Ex. 20: 4. (of any thing) that (is) in heaven *above*[3],
25:20. stretch forth (their) wings *on high*[1],
21. mercy seat *above*[2] upon the ark;
26:14. a covering *above*[2] (of) badgers' skins.
28:27. *above*[3] the curious girdle of the ephod.
30:14. from twenty years old *and above*,
36:19. covering (of) badgers' skins *above*[2]
37: 9. spread out (their) wings *on high*[1],
38:26. from twenty years old *and upward*,
39:20. *above*[3] the curious girdle of the
31. fasten (it) *on high*[2] upon the mitre;
40:19. covering of the tent *above*[2] upon it;
20. the mercy seat *above*[2] upon the ark:
Lev. 11:21. which have legs *above*[3] their feet,
27: 7. from sixty years old *and above*;
Nu. 1: 3, 18, 20, 22, 24, 26, 28, 30, 32, 34, 36, 38, 40, 42, 45. From twenty years old *and upward*,
3:15, 22, 28, 34, 39, 40, 43. from a month old *and upward*
4: 3, 23, 30, 35, 39, 43, 47. From thirty years old *and upward*
6. shall spread *over*[2] (it) a cloth
25. that (is) *above*[2] upon it,
8:24. from twenty and five years old *and upward*
14:29 & 26:2, 4. twenty years old *and upward*,
26:62. from a month old *and upward:*
32:11. from twenty years old *and upward*,
Deu. 4:39. he (is) God in heaven *above*[3],
5: 8. that (is) in heaven *above*[3],
28:13. thou shalt be *above*[1] only,
43. up above thee *very high*; (lit. *above above*)
Jos. 2:11. he (is) God in heaven *above*[3],
3:13. waters that come down *from above*[2];
Jos. 3:16. waters which came down *from above*[2]
Jud. 1:36. from the rock, *and upward.*
7:13. and overturned it, (lit. overturned it *upward*[1])
1Sa. 9: 2. from his shoulders *and upward*
10:23. from his shoulders *and upward.*
16:13. upon David from that day *forward.*
30:25. from that day *forward*, (marg. *and forward*)
1K. 7: 3. covered with cedar *above*[3]
11. *And above*[2] (were) costly stones,
20. (had pomegranates) also *above*[3],
25. the sea (was set) *above*[2] upon them,
29. (there was) a base *above*[3]:
31. within the chapiter *and above*
8: 7. and the staves thereof *above*[2].
23. no God like thee, in heaven *above*[3],
2K. 3:21. able to put on armour, *and upward*,
19:30. and bear fruit *upward*[1].
1Ch 14: 2. his kingdom was lifted up *on high*[1],
22: 5. (must be) *exceeding*[1] magnifical,
23: 3. from the age of thirty years *and upward.*
17. the sons of Rehabiah were *very*[1] many, (marg. *highly* multiplied)
24. from the age of twenty years *and upward.*
27. from twenty years old *and above:*
29: 3. *over*[1] and above all that I have
25. magnified Solomon *exceedingly*[1]
2Ch 1: 1. and magnified him *exceedingly*[1].
4: 4. the sea (was set) *above*[2] upon them,
5: 8. the staves thereof *above*[2].
16:12. until his disease (was) *exceeding*[1] (great):
17:12. waxed great *exceedingly*[1];
20:19. with a loud voice *on high*[1].
25: 5. from twenty years old *and above*,
26: 8. he strengthened (himself) *exceedingly*[1].
31:16. from three years old *and upward*[1],
17. from twenty years old *and upward*[1],
34: 4. the images, that (were) *on high*[1]
Ezr. 3: 8. from twenty years old *and upward*,
9: 6. iniquities are increased *over*[1] (our) head,
Job 3: 4. let not God regard it *from above*[3],
18:16. *and above*[3] shall his branch be cut off.
31: 2. what portion of God (is there) *from above*[3]?
28. denied the God (that is) *above*[3].
Ps. 74: 5. according as he had lifted *up*[1] (lit. bringing *on high*)
78:23. commanded the clouds *from above*[3],
Pro. 8:28. established the clouds *above*[3]:
15:24. The way of life (is) *above*[1]
Ecc. 3:21. the spirit of man that goeth *upward*[1],
Isa. 6: 2. *Above*[3] it stood the seraphims:
7:11. or in the height *above*[1].
8:21. and look *upward*[1].
14:13. *above*[3] the stars of God:
37:31. and bear fruit *upward*[1]:
45: 8. Drop down, ye heavens, *from above*[3],
Jer. 4:28. the heavens *above*[3] be black:
31:37. If heaven *above*[2] can be measured,
35: 4. which (was) *above*[3] the chamber
43:10. will set his throne *upon*[3] these stones
52:32. set his throne *above*[3] the throne
Eze. 1:11. their wings (were) stretched *upward*[2];
22. stretched forth over their heads *above.*
26. *And above*[3] the firmament
— appearance of a man *above*[2] upon it.
27. appearance of his loins *even upward*[1],
8: 2. from his loins *even upward*[1],
10:19 & 11:22. God of Israel (was) over them *above*[2].
37: 8. the skin covered them *above*[2]:
41: 7. winding about *still upward*[1] (lit. *upward upward*)
— went *still upward*[1] (lit. *id.*) round about the house: therefore the breadth of the house (was still) *upward*[1],
43:15. and from the altar *and upward*[1]
Dan 12: 6. (was) *upon*[3] (marg. *from above*) the waters
7. which (was) *upon*[3] the waters of the river,
Am. 2: 9. I destroyed his fruit *from above*[3],
Hag. 2:15. consider from this day *and upward*,
18. Consider now from this day *and upward*,

מֶעָל [*mĕh-ğāhl'*], Ch. m. 4606

Dan. 6:14(15). laboured till *the going down of* the sun

4607 מֹעַל *mōh'-ⁿgal*, m.

Neh. 8: 6. *with lifting up* their hands:

4609 מַעֲלָה *mah-ⁿgălāh'*, f.

Ex. 20:26. Neither shalt thou go up *by steps*
1K. 10:19. The throne had six *steps*,
20. on the other upon *the* six *steps:*
2K. 9:13. on the top of *the stairs*,
20: 9. shall the shadow go forward ten *degrees*, or go back ten *degrees?*
10. a light thing for the shadow to go down ten *degrees:* nay, but let the shadow return backward ten *degrees.*
11. he brought the shadow ten *degrees* backward, *by* which (lit. *by the degrees* which) it had gone down *in the dial* (marg. *degrees*) *of* Ahaz.
1Ch 17:17. to the estate of a man of *high degree*,
2Ch 9:18. (there were) six *steps* to the throne,
19. and on the other upon *the* six *steps.*
Ezr. 7: 9. the first month began *he to go up* (marg. *the going up*)
Neh. 3:15. *the stairs* that go down from the city
12:37. *the stairs of* the city of David,
Ps. 120[title](1). A Song of *degrees.*
121[title](1). A Song of *degrees.*
122[title](1). A Song of *degrees* of David.
123[title](1). A Song of *degrees.*
124[title](1). A Song of *degrees* of David.
125[title](1) & 126[title](1). A Song of *degrees.*
127[title](1). A Song of *degrees* for Solomon.
128[title](1) & 129[title(1) & 130[title](1). A Song of *degrees.*
131[title](1). A Song of *degrees* of David.
132[title](1). A Song of *degrees.*
133[title](1). A Song of *degrees* of David.
134[title](1). A Song of *degrees.*
Isa. 38: 8. I will bring again the shadow of the *degrees*, which is gone down in the sun *dial* (marg. *degrees*) *of* Ahaz, ten *degrees* backward. So the sun returned ten *degrees, by* which *degrees* it was gone
Eze. 11: 5. *for* I know *the things that come into* your
40: 6. and went up *the stairs thereof*,
22. *and* they went up unto it by seven *steps;*
26. *And* (there were) seven *steps* to go up to it,
31. *and* the going up to it (had) eight *steps.*
34, 37. the going up to it (had) eight *steps.*
49. *and* (he brought me) *by the steps* whereby
43:17. *and his stairs* shall look toward the east.
Am. 9: 6. he that buildeth *his stories* in the heaven, (marg. *ascensions*, or, *spheres*)

4608 מַעֲלֶה *mah-ⁿgăleh'*, m.

Nu. 34: 4. *to the ascent of* Akrabbim,
Jos. 10:10. the way *that goeth up to* Beth-horon,
15: 3. the south side *to Maaleh*-acrabbim, (marg. or, *the going up to* Acrabbim)
7. *before the going up to* Adummim,
18:17. over against *the going up of* Adummim,
Jud. 1:36. *from the going up to* Akrabbim, (marg. or, *Maale*-Akrabbim)
8:13. from battle *before* the sun (was up),
1Sa. 9:11. they went up *the hill to* (lit. *in the ascent of*) the city,
2Sa. 15:30. went up *by the ascent of* (mount) Olivet,
2K. 9:27. *at the going up to* Gur, which (is) by
2Ch 20:16. come up *by the cliff* (marg. *ascent*) *of* Ziz;
32:33. they buried him *in the chiefest* (marg. or, *highest*) *of* the sepulchres
Neh. 9: 4. *the stairs*, (marg. or, *scaffold*) *of* the
12:37. *at the going up of* the wall,
Isa. 15: 5. *the mounting up of* Luhith
Jer. 48: 5. in *the going up of* Luhith
Eze. 40:31. *the going up to it* (had) eight steps.
34, 37. and *the going up to it* (had) eight steps.

4611 מַעֲלִיל [*mah-ⁿgăleel'*], m.

Zec. 1: 4. (כתיב) from your evil ways, and (from) your evil *doings:*

מַעֲלָל [*mah-ⁿgălāhl'*], m. 4611

Deu 28:20. because of the wickedness of *thy doings*,
Jud 2:19. they ceased not *from their own doings*,
1Sa. 25: 3. (was) churlish and evil in his *doings;*
Neh 9:35. turned they from *their* wicked *works.*
Ps. 28: 4. to the wickedness of *their endeavours:*
77:11(12). I will remember *the works of* the
78: 7. and not forget *the works of* God,
106:29. they provoked (him) to anger *with their inventions:*
39. went a whoring *with their own inventions.*
Pro. 20:11. a child is known *by his doings*,
Isa. 1:16. put away the evil of *your doings*
3: 8. *and their doings* (are) against the Lord,
10. they shall eat the fruit of *their doings.*
Jer. 4: 4. because of the evil of *your doings.*
18. Thy way *and thy doings* have procured
7: 3. Amend your ways *and your doings*,
5. amend your ways and *your doings;*
11:18. then thou shewedst me *their doings.*
17:10. according to the fruit of *his doings.*
18:11. make your ways *and your doings* good.
21:12. because of the evil of *your doings.*
14. according to the fruit of *your doings*,
23: 2. visit upon you the evil of *your doings*,
22. and from the evil of *their doings.*
25: 5. and from the evil of *your doings*,
26: 3. because of the evil of *their doings.*
13. amend your ways *and your doings*,
32:19. according to the fruit of *his doings:*
35:15. amend *your doings*, and go not after
44:22. because of the evil of *your doings*,
Eze. 36:31. *and your doings* that (were) not good,
Hos. 4: 9. *and* reward them *their doings.*
5: 4. They will not frame *their doings* to turn
7: 2. *their own doings* have beset them about;
9:15. for the wickedness of *their doings* I will
12: 2(3). *according to his doings* will he
Mic. 2: 7. straitened? (are) these *his doings?*
3: 4. behaved themselves ill in *their doings.*
7:13. for the fruit of *their doings.*
Zec. 1: 4. ways, and (from) *your* evil *doings:*
6. *and according to our doings*, so hath he

מַעֲמָד [*mah-ⁿgămāhd'*], m. 4612

1K. 10: 5. *and the attendance* (marg. *standing*) *of* his
1Ch 23:28. *their office* (marg. *station*) (was) to wait
2Ch 9: 4. *and the attendance of* his ministers,
35:15. the sons of Asaph (were) in *their place*, (marg. *station*)
Isa. 22:19. *and from thy state* shall he pull thee

מָעֳמָד *moh-ⁿgŏmāhd'*, m. 4613

Ps. 69: 2(3). where (there is) no *standing:*

מַעֲמָסָה *măh-ⁿgămāh-sāh'*, f. 4614

Zec. 12: 3. in that day will I make Jerusalem a *burdensome* stone (lit. of *burden*)

מַעֲמַקִּים *mah-ⁿgămak-keem'*, m. pl. 4615

Ps. 69: 2(3). *into deep* (marg. *depth of*) waters,
14(15). and *out of the deep* waters.
130: 1. *Out of the depths* have I cried
Isa. 51:10. that hath made *the depths of* the sea
Eze. 27:34. by the seas *in the depths of* the waters

מַעַן *mah'-gan*, part. 4616

[Always occurring with לְ prefixed]

Gen 12:13. *that* it may be well with me for thy sake;
18:24. spare the place *for* the fifty righteous
50:20. *to* bring to pass, as (it is) this day, to
Ex. 8:22(18). *to the end* thou mayest know that I
1K. 8:41. but cometh...*for* thy name's *sake;*
2K. 13:23. the Lord was gracious...*because of* his

Jer. 43: 3. against us, *for to* deliver us
Eze.40: 4. for *to the intent that* I might shew
&c. &c.

לְמַעַן is sometimes combined in translation with another word, as with אֲשֶׁר

Nu. 16:40(17:5). a memorial...*that* no stranger,

With לֹא

Ps. 125: 3. *lest* the righteous put forth their hands

With pronominal suffixes the signification of לְמַעַן remains unchanged.

4618 **מַעֲנָה** *mah-ğănāh'*, f.

1Sa.14:14. as it were an half)(acre (marg. or, half *a furrow* of an acre) of land,
Ps.129: 3. (כתיב) they made long *their furrows.*

4617 **מַעֲנֶה** *mah-ğăneh'*, m.

Job 32: 3. they had found no *answer,*
5. saw that (there was) no *answer*
Pro.15: 1. *A* soft *answer* turneth away wrath:
23. A man hath joy *by the answer of* his
16: 1. *the answer of* the tongue,
4. hath made all (things) *for himself:*
29:19. though he understand he will not *answer.*
Mic. 3: 7. (there is) no *answer of* God.

4618 **מַעֲנִית** [*mah-ğăneeth'*], f.

Ps.129: 3. they made long *their furrows.*

4620 **מַעֲצֵבָה** *mah-ğătzēh-vāh'*, f.

Isa. 50:11. ye shall lie down *in sorrow.*

4621 **מַעֲצָד** *mah-ğătzāhd'*, m.

Isa. 44:12. The smith *with the tongs* (marg. or, *an ax*)
Jer. 10: 3. hands of the workman, *with the ax.*

4622 **מַעְצוֹר** *mağ-tzōhr'*, m.

1Sa.14: 6. (there is) no *restraint* to the Lord

4623 **מַעְצָר** *mağ-tzāhr'*, m.

Pro.25:28. He that (hath) no *rule* over his own

4624 **מַעֲקֶה** *mah-ğăkeh'*, m.

Deu 22: 8. thou shalt make *a battlement*

4625 **מַעֲקַשִּׁים** *mah-ğăkash-sheem'*, m. pl.

Isa. 42:16. before them, *and crooked things* straight.

4626 **מַעַר** *mah'-ğar*, m.

1K. 7:36. *according to the proportion* (marg. *nakedness*) *of* every one,
Nah 3: 5. I will shew the nations *thy nakedness,*

4627 **מַעֲרָב** [*mah-ğărāhv'*], m.

Eze.27: 9. to occupy *thy merchandise.*
13. vessels of brass *in thy market.* (marg. or, *merchandise*)
17. they traded *in thy market*
Eze.27:19. and calamus, were *in thy market.*
25. sing of thee *in thy market:*
27. Thy riches, and thy fairs, *thy merchandise,*
— the occupiers of *thy merchandise,*
33. thy riches *and* of *thy merchandise.*
34. *thy merchandise* and all thy company

מַעֲרָב *mah-ğărāhv'*, m. 4628

1Ch 7:28. *and westward* Gezer,
12:15. toward the east, *and toward the west.*
26:16. (the lot came forth) *westward,*
18. At Parbar *westward,*
30. on this side Jordan *westward*
2Ch 32:30. *to the west side* of the city
33:14. *on the west side* of Gihon,
Ps. 75: 6(7). from the east, *nor from the west,*
103:12. As far as the east is *from the west,*
107: 3. from the east, *and from the west,*
Isa. 43: 5. *and* gather thee *from the west;*
59:19. fear the name of the Lord *from the west,*
Dan 8: 5. an he goat came from *the west*

מַעֲרָבָה *mah-ğărāh-vāh'*, f. 4628

Isa. 45: 6. of the sun, *and from the west,*

מַעֲרֶה [*mah-ğăreh'*], m. 4629

Jud.20:33. *out of the meadows of* Gibeah.

מַעֲרוֹת *mah-ğărōhth'*, f. pl. 4630

1Sa.17:23. (כתיב) *out of the armies of* the

מְעָרָה *m'ğāh-rāh'*, f. 4631

Gen 19:30. and he dwelt *in a cave,*
23: 9. That he may give me *the cave of*
11. the field give I thee, *and the cave*
17. *and the cave* which (was) therein,
19. in *the cave of* the field
20. the field, *and the cave*
25: 9. in *the cave of* Machpelah, in the field
49:29. in *the cave* that (is) in the field
30. *In the cave* that (is) in the field
32. The purchase of the field *and of the cave*
50:13. buried him *in the cave of* the field
Jos. 10:16. hid themselves *in a cave*
17. The five kings are found hid *in a cave*
18. stones upon the mouth of *the cave,*
22. Open the mouth of *the cave,*
— five kings unto me out of *the cave.*
23. five kings unto him out of *the cave,*
27. cast them into *the cave*
— laid great stones in *the cave*'s mouth,
13: 4. *and Mearah* (marg. or, *the cave*) that (is
Jud. 6: 2. in the mountains, and *caves,*
1Sa.13: 6. the people did hide themselves *in caves,*
22: 1. escaped to *the cave* Adullam:
24: 3(4). where (was) *a cave;* and Saul
—(–). in the sides of *the cave.*
7(8). Saul rose up *out of the cave,*
8(9). went out *of the cave,*
10(11). to day into mine hand *in the cave.*
2Sa.23:13. unto *the cave of* Adullam:
1K. 18: 4. hid them by fifty *in a cave,*
13. I hid an hundred men...*in a cave,*
19: 9. he came thither unto *a cave,*
13. in the entering in of *the cave.*
1Ch 11:15. into *the cave of* Adullam;
Ps. 57 [title](1). when he fled from Saul *in the cave.*
142 [title](1). when he was *in the cave.*
Isa. 2:19. *into the holes of* the rocks,
32:14. the forts and towers shall be for *dens*
Jer. 7:11. *a den of* robbers in your eyes?
Eze.33:27. in the forts *and in the caves*

מַעֲרָךְ [*mah-ğărāhch'*], m. 4633

Pro.16: 1. *The preparations* (marg. *disposings*) *of* the

4634 **מַעֲרָכָה** *mah-ⁿgărāh-chāh'*, f.

Ex. 39:37. (with) the lamps to be *set in order*,
Lev.24: 6. thou shalt set them in two *rows*,
Jud. 6:26. *in the ordered place*, and take
1Sa. 4: 2. they slew *of the army* (marg. *the array*)
12. a man of Benjamin *out of the army*,
16. I (am) he that came out of *the army*, and I fled to day out of *the army*.
17: 8. and cried unto *the armies of* Israel,
10. I defy *the armies of* Israel this day;
20. host was going forth to *the fight*, (marg. or, *battle array*, or, *place of fight*)
21. battle in array, *army* against *army*.
22. and ran *into the army*,
23. out of *the armies of* the Philistines,
26. that he should defy *the armies of* the
36. seeing he hath defied *the armies of*
45. the God of *the armies of* Israel,
48. David hasted, and ran *toward the army*
23: 3. *the armies of* the Philistines?
1Ch 12:38. these men of war, that could keep *rank*,

4635 **מַעֲרֶכֶת** *mah-ⁿgăreh'-cheth*, f.

Lev.24: 6. six on *a row*, upon the pure table
7. pure frankincense upon (each) *row*,
1Ch 9:32. the *shew*bread, (marg. bread of *ordering*)
23:29. Both for the *shew*bread, and for
28:16. gold for the tables of *shewbread*,
2Ch 2: 4(3). *and* for *the* continual *shewbread*,
13:11. the *shew*bread *also* (set they in order)
29:18. and the *shewbread* table,
Neh 10:33(34). For the *shew*bread, and for

4636 **מַעֲרֻמִּים** [*mah-ⁿgăroom-meem'*], m. pl.

2Ch 28:15. clothed all *that were naked among them*,

4637 **מַעֲרָצָה** *mah-ⁿgărāh-tzāh'*, f.

Isa. 10:33. of hosts, shall lop the bough *with terror*:

4639 **מַעֲשֶׂה** *mah-ⁿgăseh'*, m.

Gen 5:29. *concerning our work* and toil
20: 9. thou hast done *deeds* unto me
40:17. of bakemeats for Pharaoh; (marg. meat of Pharaoh, *the work of* a baker)
44:15. What *deed* (is) this that ye have done?
46:33 & 47:3. What (is) *your occupation?*
Ex. 5: 4. let the people *from their works?*
13. Fulfil *your works*, (your) daily tasks,
18:20. *the work* that they must do.
23:12. Six days thou shalt do *thy work*,
16. the firstfruits of *thy labours*,
— *thy labours* out of the field.
24. nor do *after their works*:
24:10. *as it were a* paved *work*
26: 1. cherubims of cunning *work* (marg. *the work of* a cunning workman)
31. fine twined linen of cunning *work*:
36. twined linen, wrought with needle*work*.
27: 4. a grate of net*work*
16. twined linen, wrought with needle*work*:
28: 6. with cunning *work*.
8. the same, *according to the work thereof*;
11. *the work of* an engraver
14. (of) wreathen *work* shalt thou make
15. with cunning *work*; *after the work of* the
22. wreathen *work* (of) pure gold.
32. a binding of woven *work*
39. make the girdle (of) needle*work*.
30:25, 35. after *the art of* the apothecary:
32:16. the tables (were) *the work of* God,
34:10. *the work of* the Lord:
36: 8. cherubims of cunning *work*
35. made he it of cunning *work*.
37. fine twined linen, of needle*work*;
37:29. according to *the work of* the apothecary.
38: 4. a brasen grate of net*work*
18. for the gate...(was) needle*work*,
39: 3. the fine linen, (with) cunning *work*.
5. the same, *according to the work thereof*;
Ex. 39: 8. (of) cunning *work*, *like the work of* the
15. wreathen *work* (of) pure gold.
22. the robe of the ephod (of) woven *work*,
27. fine linen (of) woven *work*
29. purple, and scarlet, (of) needle*work*;
Lev.18: 3. *After the doings of* the land of Egypt,
— *and after the doings of* the land of
Nu. 8: 4. And this *work of* the candlestick
16:28. hath sent me to do all these *works*;
31:20. all *work of* goats' (hair),
51. all *wrought* jewels. (lit. jewels of *work*)
Deu 2: 7. in all *the works of* thy hand:
3:24. *according to thy works*, and according
4:28. gods, *the work of* men's hands,
11: 3. *his acts*, which he did in the midst of
7. all *the* great *acts of* the Lord
14:29. in all *the work of* thine hand
15:10. God shall bless thee in all *thy works*,
16:15. all *the works of* thine hands,
24:19. all *the work of* thine hands.
27:15. *the work of* the hands of the craftsman,
28:12. to bless all *the work of* thine hand:
30: 9. in every *work of* thine hand,
31:29. through *the work of* your hands.
Jos. 24:31. all *the works of* the Lord,
Jud. 2: 7. all *the* great *works of* the Lord,
10. *the works* which he had done
13:12. *and* (how) *shall we do unto him?* (lit. *and his work*; marg. (what shall be) *his work*; or, (what) *shall he do*)
19:16. there came an old man from *his work*
1Sa. 8: 8. *the works* which they have done
19: 4. *his works* (have been) to thee-ward very
20:19. when *the business* was (in hand),
25: 2. a man in Maon, *whose possessions* (marg. or, *business*)
1K. 7: 8. was *of the like work*.
17. checker *work*, and wreaths of chain *work*,
19. the chapiters...(were) of lily *work*
22. top of the pillars (was) lily *work*:
26. *wrought like* (lit. *like the work of*) the brim
28. *the work of* the bases
29. certain additions made of thin *work*.
31. *the work of* the base,
33. *And the work of* the wheels (was) *like the work of* a chariot wheel:
13:11. all *the works* that the man of God
16: 7. to anger *with the work of* his hands,
2K. 16:10. to all *the workmanship thereof*.
19:18. *the work of* men's hands,
22:17. all *the works of* their hands;
23:19. all *the acts* that he had done
1Ch 9:31. *the things that were made in* the pans.
23:28. *and the work of* the service of the house
2Ch 3:10. two cherubims of image *work*,
4: 5. *like the work of* the brim of a cup,
6. *such things as they offered for* the burnt offering (marg. *the work of* burnt offering)
16:14. (spices) prepared by the apothecaries' *art*:
17: 4. not *after the doings of* Israel.
20:37. the Lord hath broken *thy works*.
31:21. in every *work* that he began
32:19. *the work of* the hands of man.
30. Hezekiah prospered in all *his works*.
34:25. all *the works of* their hands;
Ezr. 9:13. *for our* evil *deeds*, and for our great
Neh 6:14. *according to* these *their works*,
Est. 10: 2. all *the acts of* his power
Job 1:10. thou hast blessed *the work of* his hands,
14:15. a desire *to the work of* thine hands.
33:17. man (from his) *purpose*, (marg. *work*)
34:19. they all (are) *the work of* his hands.
37: 7. that all men may know *his work*.
Ps. 8: 3(4). thy heavens, *the work of* thy fingers,
6(7). *over the works of* thy hands;
19: 1(2). *and* the firmament sheweth his handy *work*.
28: 4. give them *after the work of* their hands;
5. nor *the operation of* his hands,
33: 4. all *his works* (are done) in truth.
15. he considereth all *their works*.
45: 1(2). *the things which I have made* touching
62:12(13). to every man *according to his work*.
64: 9(10). *for* they shall wisely consider of *his doing*.
66: 3. How terrible (art thou in) *thy works!*

Ps. 86: 8. (are there any works) *like unto thy works.*
90:17. *and* establish thou *the work of* our hands upon us; *yea, the work of* our hands
92: 4(5). I will triumph *in the works of*
5(6). O Lord, how great are *thy works!*
102:25(26). *and* the heavens (are) *the work of* thy
103:22. Bless the Lord, all *his works*
104:13. the fruit of *thy works.*
24. O Lord, how manifold are *thy works!*
31. the Lord shall rejoice *in his works.*
106:13. They soon forgat *his works;*
35. the heathen, and learned *their works.*
39. defiled *with their own works,*
107:22. declare *his works* with rejoicing.
24. These see *the works of* the Lord,
111: 2. *The works of* the Lord (are) great,
6. shewed his people the power of *his works,*
7. *The works of* his hands (are) verity and
115: 4. *the work* of men's hands.
118:17. declare *the works of* the Lord.
135:15. *the work of* men's hands.
138: 8. forsake not *the works of* thine own hands.
139:14. marvellous (are) *thy works;*
143: 5. I muse *on the work of* thy hands.
145: 4. One generation shall praise *thy works*
9. tender mercies (are) over all *his works.*
10. All *thy works* shall praise thee,
17. holy in all *his works.*
Pro.16: 3. Commit *thy works* unto the Lord,
11. the weights of the bag (are) *his work.*
31:31. let *her own works* praise her
Ecc. 1:14. all *the works* that are done under the sun;
2: 4. I made *me* great *works;* (lit. I greatened *my works*)
11. I looked on all *the works*
17. *the work* that is wrought under
3:11. *the work* that God maketh
17. a time...for every *work.*
22. a man should rejoice *in his own works;*
4: 3. *the* evil *work* that is done
4. and every right *work,*
5: 6(5). destroy *the work of* thine hands?
7:13. Consider *the work of* God:
8: 9. applied my heart unto every *work*
11. sentence against *an* evil *work*
14. *according to the work of* the wicked;
— *according to the work of* the righteous:
17. I beheld all *the work of* God, that a man cannot find out *the work*
9: 7. God now accepteth *thy works.*
10. (there is) no *work,*...in the grave,
11: 5. thou knowest not *the works of* God
12:14. God shall bring every *work* into
Cant.7: 1(2). *the work of* the hands of a cunning
Isa. 2: 8. *the work of* their own hands,
3:24. instead of *well* set hair (lit. *the work of* the curling tool) baldness;
5:12. *neither* consider *the operation of* his hands.
19. make speed, (and) hasten *his work,*
10:12. the Lord hath performed *his* whole *work*
17: 8. the altars, *the work of* his hands,
19:14. Egypt to err in every *work thereof,*
15. Neither shall there be (any) *work* for
25. *and* Assyria *the work of* my hands,
26:12. hast wrought all *our works*
28:21. he may do *his work, his* strange *work;*
29:15. *their works* are in the dark,
16. shall *the work* say of him that made it,
23. his children, *the work of* mine hands,
32:17. *the work of* righteousness
37:19. *the work of* men's hands,
41:29. *their works* (are) nothing:
54:16. forth an instrument *for his work;*
57:12. declare thy righteousness, and *thy works;*
59: 6. cover themselves *with their works: their works* (are) *works of* iniquity,
60:21. my planting, *the work of* my hands,
64: 8(7). *and* we all (are) *the work of* thy hand.
65:22. *the work of* their hands.
66:18. I (know) *their works* and their thoughts:
Jer. 1:16. *the works of* their own hands.
7:13. ye have done all these *works,*
10: 3. *the work of* the hands of the workman,
9. *the work of* the workman,
— *the work of* cunning men.
15. vanity, (and) *the work of* errors:
25: 6, 7. *with the works of* your hands;
Jer. 25:14. *and according to the works of* their own
32:30. *with the work of* their hands,
44: 8. ye provoke me...*with the works of*
48: 7. thou hast trusted *in thy works*
51:10. *the work of* the Lord our God.
18. vanity, *the work of* errors:
Lam 3:64. *according to the work of* their hands.
4: 2. *the work of* the hands of the potter!
Eze. 1:16. *and their work* (was) like unto the
— their appearance *and their work*
6: 6. *your works* may be abolished.
16:30. *the work of* an imperious whorish woman
27:16, 18. multitude of *the wares of thy making* (marg. *thy works*)
46: 1. the six *working* days; (lit. days of *work*)
Dan 9:14. our God (is) righteous in all *his works*
Hos 13: 2. *the work of* the craftsmen:
14: 3(4). *to the work of* our hands,
Am. 8: 7. I will never forget any of *their works.*
Jon. 3:10. And God saw *their works,*
Mic. 5:13(12). *the work of* thine hands.
6:16. *the works of* the house of Ahab,
Hab 3:17. *the labour of* the olive shall fail,
Hag. 2:14. every *work of* their hands;
17. in all *the labours of* your hands;

מַעֲשֵׂר *mah-"găsēhr'*, m. 4643

Gen 14:20. And he gave him *tithes* of all.
Lev.27:30. all *the tithe of* the land,
31. redeem (ought) *of his tithes,*
32. concerning *the tithe of* the herd,
Nu. 18:21. the children of Levi all *the tenth*
24. *the tithes of* the children of Israel,
26. ye take of the children of Israel *the tithes*
— (even) *a tenth* (part) *of the tithe.*
28. all *your tithes,* which ye receive
Deu 12: 6. *your tithes,* and heave offerings
11. *your tithes,* and the heave offering
17. *the tithe of* thy corn, or of thy wine,
14:23. *the tithe of* thy corn, of thy wine,
28. all *the tithe of* thine increase
26:12. all *the tithes of* thine increase
— (which is) the year of *tithing,*
2Ch 31: 5. *and the tithe of* all (things)
6. *the tithe of* oxen and sheep, *and the tithe of* holy things
12. *and the tithes* and the dedicated (things)
Neh 10:37(38). *and the tithes of* our ground
38(39). the Levites shall bring up *the tithe of the tithes*
12:44. for the firstfruits, *and for the tithes,*
13: 5. *and the tithes of* the corn,
12. Then brought all Judah *the tithe of*
Eze.45:11. *the tenth part of* an homer:
14. *the tenth part of* a bath
Am. 4: 4. *your tithes* after three years:
Mal. 3: 8. *In tithes* and offerings.
10. Bring ye all *the tithes*

מַעֲשַׁקּוֹת *mah-"găshak-kōhth'*, f. pl. 4642

Pro.28:16. great *oppressor:* (lit. great of *oppressions*)
Isa. 33:15. he that despiseth the gain of *oppressions,* (marg. or, *deceits*)

מִפְגָּע *miph-gāh"g'*, m. 4645

Job 7:20. why hast thou set me *as a mark*

מַפָּח *map-poo'ăgh*, m. 4647

Jer. 6:29. *The bellows* are burned,

מַפָּח *map-pāh'gh*, m. 4646

Job 11:20. *the giving up* of the ghost. (marg. or, *a puff of* breath)

מֵפִיץ *mēh-pheetz'*, m. 4650

Pro.25:18. that beareth false witness...(is) *a maul,*

4651 **מַפָּל** *map-pāhl'*, m.

Job 41:23(15). *The flakes* (marg. *fallings*) of his flesh are joined together:
Am. 8: 6. *and* sell *the refuse of* the wheat?

4652 **מִפְלָאָה** [*miph-lāh-āh'*], f.

Job 37:16. *the wondrous works of* him which is perfect

4653 **מִפְלַגּוֹת** *miph-lag-gōhth'*, f. pl.

2Ch 35:12. *according to the divisions of* the families

4654 **מַפָּלָה** *map-pāh-lāh'*, f.

Isa. 17: 1. Damascus...it shall be a *ruinous* heap. (lit. a heap of *ruin*)

4654 **מַפֵּלָה** *map-pēh-lāh'*, f.

Isa. 23:13. he brought it *to ruin.*
25: 2. a defenced city *a ruin:*

4655 **מִפְלָט** *miph-lāht'*, m.

Ps. 55: 8(9). I would hasten my *escape*

4656 **מִפְלֶצֶת** *miph-leh'-tzeth*, f.

1K. 15:13. she had made *an idol* in a grove; and Asa destroyed *her idol,*
2Ch 15:16. she had made *an idol* (marg. *horror*) in a grove: and Asa cut down *her idol,*

4657 **מִפְלָשׂ** [*miph-lāhs'*], m.

Job 37:16. thou know *the balancings of* the clouds,

4658 **מַפֶּלֶת** *map-peh'-leth*, f.

Jud. 14: 8. aside to see *the carcase of* the lion:
Pro. 29:16. the righteous shall see *their fall.*
Eze. 26:15. the isles shake at the sound of *thy fall,*
18. the isles tremble in the day of *thy fall;*
27:27. in the day of *thy ruin.*
31:13. Upon *his ruin* shall all the fowls...remain,
16. I made the nations to shake at the sound of *his fall,*
32:10. his own life, in the day of *thy fall.*

4659 **מִפְעָל** [*miph-gāhl'*], m.

Pro. 8:22. before *his works* of old.

4659 **מִפְעָלָה** [*miph-gāh-lāh'*], f.

Ps. 46: 8(9). behold *the works of* the Lord,
66: 5. Come and see *the works of* God:

4660 **מַפָּץ** [*map-pāhtz'*], m.

Eze. 9: 2. every man a *slaughter* weapon (marg. a weapon of *his breaking in pieces*)

4661 **מַפֵּץ** *map-pēhtz'*, m.

Jer. 51:20. Thou (art) my *battle ax* (and) weapons

4662 **מִפְקָד** *miph-kāhd'*, m.

2Sa. 24: 9. Joab gave up the sum of *the number of* the
1Ch 21: 5. Joab gave the sum of *the number of* the
2Ch 31:13. *at the commandment of* Hezekiah
Neh. 3:31. over against the gate *Miphkad*, (lit. or, of *command*)
Eze. 43:21. he shall burn it *in the appointed place of* the house,

---

מִפְרָץ [*miph-rāhtz'*], m. 4664

Jud. 5:17. Asher...abode *in his breaches.* (marg. or, *creeks*)

מַפְרֶקֶת [*maph-reh'-keth*], f. 4665

1Sa. 4:18. and *his neck* brake, and he died:

מִפְרָשׂ *miph-rāhs'*, m. 4666

Job 36:29. *the spreadings of* the clouds,
Eze. 27: 7. *that which thou spreadest forth*

מִפְשָׂעָה *miph-sāh-gāh'*, f. 4667

1Ch 19: 4. off their garments...hard by *their buttocks*

מַפְתֵּחַ *maph-tēh'ăgh*, m. 4668

Jud. 3:25. therefore they took *a key,*
1Ch 9:27. *the opening* thereof every morning
Isa. 22:22. *the key of* the house of David

מִפְתָּח [*miph-tāhgh'*], m. 4669

Pro. 8: 6. *and the opening of* my lips

מִפְתָּן *miph-tāhn'*, m. 4670

1Sa. 5: 4. hands (were) cut off upon *the threshold;*
5. tread on *the threshold of* Dagon
Eze. 9: 3. he was, to *the threshold of* the house.
10: 4. over *the threshold of* the house;
18. off *the threshold of* the house,
46: 2. at *the threshold of* the gate:
47: 1. under *the threshold of* the house
Zep. 1: 9. those that leap on *the threshold,*

מֹץ *mōhtz*, m. 4671

Job 21:18. *and as chaff* that the storm carrieth away.
Ps. 1: 4. *like the chaff* which the wind driveth
35: 5. Let them be *as chaff* before the wind:
Isa. 17:13. chased *as the chaff of* the mountains
29: 5. *and* the multitude...(shall be) *as chaff*
41:15. and shalt make the hills *as chaff.*
Hos 13: 3. *as the chaff* (that) is driven with the
Zep. 2: 2. (before) the day pass *as the chaff,*

מָצָא *māh-tzāh'*. 4672

* KAL.—*Preterite.* *

Gen 2:20. for Adam there *was* not *found* an help
6: 8. Noah *found* grace in the eyes
8: 9. dove *found* no rest for the sole of her foot,
18: 3. if now *I have found* favour
19:19. thy servant *hath found* grace
26:32. *We have found* water.
30:27. if *I have found* favour
31:33. *he found* (them) not.
34. but *found* (them) not.
35. but *found* not the images.
37. what *hast thou found* of all
33:10. if now *I have found* grace
36:24. Anah that *found* the mules
37:32. This *have we found:* know now
38:20. but *he found her* not.

Gen38:22. *I cannot find her;*
23. *thou hast* not *found her.*
44: 8. the money, which *we found*
16. God *hath found out* the iniquity
47:29. If now *I have found* grace in thy sight,
50: 4. If now *I have found* grace in your eyes,
Ex. 15:22. they went three days...and *found* no water.
16:27. and *they found* none.
18: 8. the travail that *had come upon them* (marg. *found them*)
22: 6(5). If fire break out, *and catch in* thorns,
33:12. *thou hast* also *found* grace
13. if *I have found* grace
16. *have found* grace in thy sight?
17. *thou hast found* grace in my sight,
34: 9. If now *I have found* grace
Lev. 6: 3(5:22). *have found* that which was lost,
4(-:23). the lost thing which *he found,*
25:26. himself be able (marg. his hand hath attained *and found* sufficiency) to redeem
28. if he be not able (lit. if his hand *hath* not *found* a sufficiency) to restore
Nu. 11:11. *have I* not *found* favour
15. if *I have found* favour
22. Shall the flocks...be slain...*to suffice* them? (lit. *and find*)
— shall all the fish...be gathered...*to suffice* them? (lit. *id.*)
20:14. the travel that *hath befallen us:* (marg. *found us*)
31:50. what every man *hath gotten,* (marg. *found*)
32: 5. if *we have found* grace
35:27. *And* the revenger of blood *find* him
Deu 4:29. *But* if...*thou shalt find* (him), if thou seek
30. *and* all these things *are come upon thee,*
19: 5. *and lighteth upon* (marg. *findeth*) his neighbour,
22: 3. hath lost, *and thou hast found,*
14. *I found* her not a maid:
17. *I found* not thy daughter a maid;
23. *and* a man *find her* in the city,
27. *he found her* in the field,
24: 1. *he hath found* some uncleanness
31:17. *and* many evils and troubles *shall befall* (marg. *find*) *them;*
— *Are* not these evils *come upon us,*
Jos. 2:22. pursuers sought...but *found* (them) not.
Jud. 6:13. why then *is* all this *befallen us?*
17. If now *I have found* grace
14:12. *and find* (it) *out,* then I will give
18. *ye had* not *found out* my riddle.
21:14. yet so *they sufficed* them not. (lit. *they found* so not for them)
Ru. 2:10. Why *have I found* grace in thine eyes,
1Sa. 9: 4,4. but *they found* (them) not:
11. *they found* young maidens
10: 2. *then thou shalt find* two men
3. *and there shall meet thee* three men
12: 5. *ye have* not *found* ought
14:30. spoil of their enemies which *they found?*
16:22. *he hath found* favour in my sight.
20: 3. *I have found* grace in thine eyes;
29. if *I have found* favour
27: 5. If *I have* now *found* grace
29: 3. *I have found* no fault in him
6. *I have* not *found* evil in thee
8. what *hast thou found* in thy servant
2Sa. 7:27. *hath* thy servant *found* in his heart
14:22. *I have found* grace
17:20. they had sought and *could* not *find*
20: 6. lest *he get* him fenced cities,
1K. 21:20. *Hast thou found me,* O mine enemy?
— *I have found* (thee): because thou
2K. 2:17. they sought three days, but *found him* not.
7: 9. some mischief *will come upon us:* (marg. *we shall find* punishment)
9:35. *they found* no more of her
10:13. Jehu *met with* (marg. *found*) the brethren
22: 8. *I have found* the book
23:24. the book that Hilkiah the priest *found*
1Ch 17:25. thy servant *hath found* (in his heart)
2Ch 20:16. *and ye shall find* them at the end
29:16. *they found* in the temple
32: 4. *and find* much water?
34:14. Hilkiah the priest *found* a book
15. *I have found* the book
Ezr. 8:15. *found* there none of the sons of Levi.
Neh. 5: 8. and *found* nothing (to answer).
9: 8. *And foundest* his heart faithful
32. the trouble...that *hath come upon us,*
Est. 5: 8. If *I have found* favour in the sight of
7: 3. If *I have found* favour in thy sight,
8: 5. if *I have found* favour in his sight,
Job 31:25. mine hand *had gotten* much;
29. when evil *found him:*
32: 3. *they had found* no answer,
13. *We have found* out wisdom:
33:24. *I have found* a ransom.
37:23. *we cannot find him out:*
Ps. 69:20(21). I looked (for)...comforters, but *found* none.
76: 5(6). *have found* their hands.
84: 3(4). the sparrow *hath found* an house,
89:20(21). *I have found* David my servant;
107: 4. *they found* no city to dwell in.
116: 3. the pains of hell *gat hold upon me:* (marg. *found me*)
119:143. Trouble and anguish *have taken hold on me:* (marg *found me*)
132: 6. *we found it* in the fields
Pro. 3:13. the man (that) *findeth* wisdom,
8:35. whoso findeth me *findeth* life,
18:22. (Whoso) *findeth* a wife *findeth* a good (thing),
24:14. when *thou hast found* (it),
25:16. *Hast thou found* honey?
Ecc. 7:27. this *have I found,*
28. Which yet my soul seeketh, but *I find* not: one man among a thousand *have I found;* but a woman among all those *have I* not *found.*
29. this only *have I found,*
9:15. *Now there was found* in it
Cant 3: 1,2. I sought him, but *I found him* not.
3. The watchmen...*found me:*
4. *but I found* him whom my soul loveth:
5: 6. *I could* not *find him;*
7. The watchmen...*found me,*
Isa. 10:10. As my hand *hath found* the kingdoms of
34:14. *and find* for herself a place of rest.
57:10. *thou hast found* the life of thine hand;
Jer. 2: 5. What iniquity *have* your fathers *found*
34. *I have* not *found it* by secret search,
14: 3. (and) *found* no water;
23:11. *have I found* their wickedness,
29:13. ye shall seek me, *and find* (me),
31: 2. The people...*found* grace
45: 3. *I find* no rest.
Lam 1: 3. *she findeth* no rest:
6. like harts (that) *find* no pasture,
2: 9. her prophets also *find* no vision
16. *we have found,* we have seen (it).
Eze. 22:30. but *I found* none.
Hos. 9:10. *I found* Israel like grapes
12: 8(9). *I have found* me out substance:

KAL.—*Infinitive.*

Gen19:11. they wearied themselves *to find* the door.
27:20. How (is it) that thou hast *found* (it) so quickly, (lit. hasted *to find*)
32: 5(6). *that I may find* grace in thy sight.
19(20). speak unto Esau, *when ye find* him.
33: 8. *to find* grace in the sight of
Ps. 32: 6. in a time when *thou mayest be found:* (marg. of *finding*)
36: 2(3). *until* his iniquity *be found* (marg. *to find* his iniquity)
Pro. 19: 8. that keepeth understanding *shall find* good.
Ecc. 7:27. *to find out* the account:
8:17. a man cannot *find out* the work
— shall he not be able *to find* (it).
12:10. *to find out* acceptable words:
Isa. 58:13. *nor finding* thine own pleasure,

KAL.—*Imperative.*

Ru. 1: 9. *that ye may find* rest,
1Sa. 20:21. Go, *find out* the arrows.
36. Run, *find out* now the arrows
Pro. 3: 4. *So shalt thou find* favour
Jer. 6:16. *and ye shall find* rest for your souls.

KAL.—*Future.*

Gen11: 2. *that they found* a plain
16: 7. *And* the angel of the Lord *found her*
18:26. If *I find* in Sodom

Gen18:28. If *I find* there forty and five,
30. if *I find* thirty there.
26:12. *and received* in the same year
19. *and found* there a well
30:14. *and found* mandrakes in the field,
31:32. With whomsoever *thou findest*
33:15. *let me find* grace in the sight
34:11. *Let me find* grace in your eyes,
37:15. *And* a certain man *found him*,
17. *and found them* in Dothan.
39: 4. *And* Joseph *found* grace in his sight,
41:38. *Can we find* (such a one) as this (is),
44:34. the evil that *shall come on* (marg. *find*) my father.
47:25. *let us find* grace in the sight of my lord,
Ex. 5:11. get you straw where *ye can find* it:
16:25. *ye shall* not *find it* in the field.
33:13. that *I may find* grace in thy sight:
Lev.12: 8. if she be not able *to bring* (marg. her hand *find* not sufficiency of) a lamb,
Nu. 15:32. *And* while...*they found* a man that gathered
32:23. be sure your sin *will find* you *out*.
Deu22:25. if a man *find* a betrothed damsel
28. If a man *find* a damsel
24: 1. *she find* no favour in his eyes,
31:21. when many evils and troubles *are befallen*
32:10. *He found him* in a desert land,
Jud. 1: 5. *And they found* Adoni-bezek
5:30. *Have they* not *sped?*
9:33. as thou *shalt find occasion*. (marg. thine hand *shall find*)
15:15. *And he found* a new jawbone
17: 8. to sojourn where *he could find* (a place):
9. I go to sojourn where *I may find* (a place).
21:12. *And they found* among the inhabitants
Ru. 2: 2. in whose sight *I shall find* grace.
13. *Let me find* favour in thy sight,
1Sa. 1:18. *Let* thine handmaid *find* grace
9:13. *ye shall* straightway *find* him,
— about this time *ye shall find* him.
10: 7. do as *occasion serve* thee; (marg. thine hand *shall find*)
23:17. the hand of Saul...*shall* not *find thee;*
24:19(20). if a man *find* his enemy,
25: 8. *Wherefore let* the young men *find* favour
— whatsoever *cometh to* thine hand (lit. thy hand *shall find*)
30:11. *And they found* an Egyptian
31: 3. *and* the archers *hit* (marg. *found*) *him*,
8. *that they found* Saul and his three sons
2Sa.15:25. if *I shall find* favour
16: 4. (that) *I may find* grace
1K. 1: 3. *and found* Abishag a Shunammite,
11:19. *And* Hadad *found* great favour
29. *that* the prophet...*found* him in the way;
13:14. *and found him* sitting under an oak:
24. *And* when...a lion *met him* by the way,
28. he went *and found* his carcase
18: 5. peradventure *we may find* grass
10. that *they found thee* not.
12. *he* cannot *find thee*,
19:19. *and found* Elisha the son of Shaphat,
20:36. *And* as soon as he...a lion *found him*, and slew him.
37. *Then he found* another man,
2K. 4:29. if *thou meet* any man,
39. *and found* a wild vine,
9:21. *and met him* in the portion of Naboth
10:15. *And* when he was...*he lighted on* (marg. *found*) Jehonadab the son of Rechab
17: 4. *And* the king of Assyria *found* conspiracy
19: 8. *and found* the king of Assyria
1Ch. 4:40. *And they found* fat pasture
10: 3. *and* the archers *hit* (marg. *found*) *him*,
8. *that they found* Saul and his sons
20: 2. *and found it* to weigh a talent of gold,
2Ch 20:25. *And* when...*they found* among them in
22: 8. *and found* the princes of Judah,
25: 5. *and found them* three hundred thousand
Neh. 7: 5. *And I found* a register of the genealogy
— *and found* written therein,
8:14. *And they found* written in the law
Est. 8: 6. the evil that *shall come unto* my people?
Job 3:22. glad, when *they can find* the grave?
11: 7. *Canst thou* by searching *find out* God? *canst thou find out* the Almighty
17:10. *I cannot find* (one) wise (man)
Job 20: 8. and *shall* not *be found:* (lit. *they shall* not *find him*)
23: 3. Oh that I knew *where I might find him!*
33:10. *he findeth* occasions against me,
Ps. 10:15. out his wickedness (till) *thou find* none.
17: 3. hast tried me, (and) *shalt find* nothing;
21: 8(9). Thine hand *shall find out* all thine enemies: thy right hand *shall find out*
116: 3. *I found* trouble and sorrow.
132: 5. Until *I find* out a place for the Lord,
Pro. 1:13. *We shall find* all precious substance,
28. *they shall* not *find me:*
2: 5. and *find* the knowledge of God.
6:33. A wound and dishonour *shall he get;*
7:15. to seek thy face, *and I have found thee.*
8:12. *find out* knowledge of witty inventions.
17. those that seek me early *shall find me.*
16:20. a matter wisely *shall find* good:
17:20. froward heart *findeth* no good:
20: 6. a faithful man who *can find?*
21:21. He that followeth after righteousness... *findeth*
28:23. *shall find* more favour than
31:10. Who *can find* a virtuous woman?
Ecc. 3:11. no man *can find out* the work
7:14. that man *should find* nothing
24. who *can find it out?*
8:17. yet *he shall* not *find* (it);
9:10. Whatsoever thy hand *findeth*
11: 1. *thou shalt find it* after many days.
Cant 5: 8. if *ye find* my beloved,
8: 1. (when) *I should find thee* without,
Isa. 10:14. *And* my hand *hath found*...the riches of
37: 8. *and found* the king of Assyria
41:12. and *shalt* not *find* them,
58: 3. in the day of your fast *ye find* pleasure,
Jer. 2:24. in her month *they shall find her.*
5: 1. if *ye can find* a man,
10:18. *that they may find* (it so).
41:12. *and found* him by the great waters
Eze. 3: 1. Son of man, eat that *thou findest;*
Dan. 1:20. *he found them* ten times better than
Hos. 2: 6(8). *she shall* not *find* her paths.
7(9). she shall seek them, but *shall* not *find* (them):
5: 6. *they shall* not *find* (him);
12: 4(5). *he found him* (in) Beth-el,
8(9). *they shall find* none iniquity
Am. 8:12. and *shall* not *find* (it).
Jon. 1: 3. *and he found* a ship going to Tarshish:

KAL.—*Participle.* Poel.

Gen. 4:14. every one *that findeth me*
15. lest any *finding him* should kill him.
Nu. 15:33. *they that found* him gathering
Jos. 2:23. told him all (things) *that befell* them: (lit. *that found* them)
2Sa.18:22. thou hast no tidings *ready?* (marg. or, *convenient*)
Ps.119:162. *as one that findeth* great spoil.
Pro. 4:22. life *unto those that find them*,
8: 9. *to them that find* knowledge.
35. *whoso findeth* me
— (כתיב) *findeth* life,
Ecc. 7:26. *And I find* more bitter than death
Cant 8:10. *as one that found* favour.
Jer. 50: 7. All *that found them* have devoured

* NIPHAL.—*Preterite.* *

Gen44:16. with whom the cup *is found.*
17. in whose hand the cup *is found*,
Ex. 21:16. *or* if *he be found* in his hand,
35:23. with whom *was found* blue, and
24. with whom *was found* shittim wood
Deu22:20. virginity *be* not *found*
28. with her, *and they be found;*
Jos. 10:17. The five kings *are found* hid
1Sa. 9: 8. I *have here* at hand (marg. *there is found* in my hand) the fourth part of a
20. as for thine asses...*they are found.*
10: 2. The asses...*are found:*
16. told us plainly that the asses *were found.*
21. *he could* not *be found.*
13:22. *there was* neither sword nor spear *found*
2Sa.17:12. where *he shall be found*,
13. until *there be* not one small stone *found*
1K. 14:13. in him *there is found* (some) good

2K. 20:13. all *that was found* in his treasures:
25:19. which *were found* in the city,
1Ch 4:41. the habitations that *were found* there,
29:17. people, *which are present* (marg. or, *found*)
2Ch 19: 3. *there are* good things *found* in thee,
34:21. the book that *is found*:
Ezr. 2:62. by genealogy, but *they were* not *found*:
Neh 7:64. by genealogy, but *it was* not *found*:
13: 1. *and* therein *was found* written,
Job 19:28. the root of the matter *is found*
42:15. *were* no women *found* (so) fair as
Ps. 37:36. but *he could* not *be found*.
46: 1(2). a very *present* (lit. much *found*) help
Pro. 6:31. *But* (if) *he be found*,
Isa. 39: 2. all that *was found* in his treasures:
65: 1. *I am found* of (them that) sought me not:
Jer. 2:34. in thy skirts *is found* the blood of
5:26. among my people *are found* wicked
11: 9. A conspiracy *is found* among the men of
15:16. Thy words *were found*,
29:14. *And I will be found* of you,
41: 3. the Chaldeans that *were found* there,
8. ten men *were found* among
48:27. *was he found* among thieves?
50:24. *thou art found*, and also caught,
52:25. which *were found* in the city;
Eze. 28:15. till iniquity *was found* in thee.
Dan 1:19. *was found* none like Daniel,
Hos. 14: 8(9). From me *is* thy fruit *found*.
Mic. 1:13. the transgressions of Israel *were found*
Mal. 2: 6. iniquity *was* not *found* in his lips:

NIPHAL.—*Infinitive*.

Ex. 22: 4(3). the theft be *certainly* found (lit. *being found* be found)
Isa. 55: 6. the Lord *while he may be found*,

NIPHAL.—*Future*.

Gen18:29. Peradventure *there shall be* forty *found*
30. Peradventure *there shall* thirty *be found*
31. Peradventure *there shall be* twenty *found*
32. Peradventure ten *shall be found* there.
44: 9. With whomsoever...*it be found*,
10. *he* with whom it *is found*
12. *and* the cup *was found* in Benjamin's
Ex. 9:19. man and beast which *shall be found*
12:19. *shall there be* no leaven *found*
22: 2(1). If a thief *be found* breaking up,
4(3). If the theft *be* certainly *found*
7(6). if the thief *be found*,
8(7). If the thief *be* not *found*,
Deu 17: 2. If *there be found* among you,
18:10. *There shall* not *be found*
21: 1. If (one) *be found* slain
17. that he *hath*: (marg. *is found* with him)
22:22. If a man *be found* lying with a woman
24: 7. If a man *be found* stealing
Jos. 17:16. The hill *is* not *enough* for us:
1Sa. 13:19. there *was* no smith *found*
22. *but* with Saul...*was there found*.
25:28. evil *hath* not *been found*
1K. 1:52. if wickedness *shall be found* in him,
2K. 12: 5(6). wheresoever any breach *shall be found*.
1Ch 24: 4. *And there were* more chief men *found*
26:31. *and there were found* among them
28: 9. *he will be found* of thee;
2Ch 2:17(16). *and they were found* 153,600.
15: 2. *he will be found* of you;
4. *But* when they...*he was found* of them.
15. *and he was found* of them:
Ezr. 10:18. *there were found* that had taken strange
Est. 2:23. the matter, *it was found out*;
6: 2. *And it was found* written,
Job 28:12. where *shall* wisdom *be found*?
13. neither *is it found* in the land of the
Pro. 10:13. wisdom *is found*:
16:31. (if) *it be found* in the way of
Isa. 30:14. *there shall* not *be found*
35: 9. *it shall* not *be found* there;
51: 3. joy and gladness *shall be found*
65: 8. As the new wine *is found*
Jer. 2:26. As the thief is ashamed when *he is found*,
50:20. *they shall* not *be found*:
Eze. 26:21. *shalt thou* never *be found*
Dan 11:19. he shall stumble...and not *be found*.
Zep. 3:13. neither shall a deceitful tongue *be found*
Zec. 10:10. (place) *shall* not *be found*

NIPHAL.—*Participle*.

Gen19:15. thy two daughters, *which are here*; (marg *are found*)
47:14. the money *that was found*
Deu 20:11. the people *that is found*
Jud. 20:48. all *that came to hand*: (marg. *was found*)
— all the cities *that they came to*. (marg. *were found*)
1Sa. 13:15. people *that were present* (marg. *found*)
16. and the people *that were present* with
21: 3(4). or *what there is present*. (marg. *found*)
2K. 12:10(11). the money *that was found*
18(19). all the gold *that was found*
14:14. the vessels *that were found*
16: 8. the silver and gold *that was found*
18:15. the silver *that was found*
19: 4. the remnant *that are left*. (marg. *found*)
22: 9. the money *that was found*
13. this book *that is found*:
23: 2. the book of the covenant *which was found*
25:19. *that were found* in the city:
1Ch 29: 8. *And* they with whom (precious) stones *were found*
2Ch 5:11. priests *that were present* (marg. *found*)
21:17. the substance *that was found*
25:24. all the vessels *that were found*
29:29. all *that were present* (marg. *found*)
30:21. of Israel *that were present* (marg. *found*)
31: 1. all Israel *that were present* (marg. *found*)
34:17. the money *that was found*
30. the book...*that was found*
32, 33. all *that were present* (marg. *found*)
35: 7. for all *that were present*,
17. of Israel *that were present* (marg. *found*)
18. and Israel *that were present*,
36: 8. *and that which was found* in him,
Ezr. 8:25. all Israel (there) *present*,
Est. 1: 5. all the people *that were present* (marg. *found*)
4:16. all the Jews *that are present* (marg. *id.*)
Isa. 13:15. Every one *that is found*
22: 3. all *that are found in thee*
37: 4. the remnant *that is left*. (marg. *found*)
Jer. 52:25. *that were found* in the midst
Dan 12: 1. every one *that shall be found*

* HIPHIL.—*Preterite*. *

Lev. 9:13. *they presented* the burnt offering
2Sa. 3: 8. and *have* not *delivered thee* into

HIPHIL.—*Future*.

Lev. 9:12, 18. *and* Aaron's sons *presented*
Job 34:11. and *cause* every man *to find* according to
37:13. *He causeth it to come*,

HIPHIL.—*Participle*.

Zec. 11: 6. I *will deliver* (marg. *make to be found*) the

מַצָּב [*matz-tzāhv'*], m. 4673

Jos. 4: 3. *out of the place where* the priests' feet *stood*
9. *the place where* the feet of the priests... *stood*:
1Sa. 13:23. *the garrison* (marg. or, *standing camp*) *of*
14: 1. let us go over to the Philistines' *garrison*,
4. to go over unto the Philistines' *garrison*.
6. let us go over unto *the garrison*
11. *the garrison of* the Philistines:
15. *the garrison*, and the spoilers,
2Sa. 23:14. *and the garrison of* the Philistines (was) then (in)
Isa. 22:19. I will drive thee *from thy station*,

מֻצָּב *mootz-tzāhv'*, m. 4674

Isa. 29: 3. lay siege against thee with *a mount*,

מַצָּבָה *matz-tzāh-vāh'*, f. 4675

1Sa. 14:12. the men of *the garrison* answered

מִצָּבָה *mitz-tzāh-vāh'*, f. 4675

Zec. 9: 8. encamp about mine house because of *the army*,

4676 **מַצֵּבָה** *matz-tzēh-vāh'*, f.

Gen 28:18. set it up (for) *a pillar,*
22. this stone, which I have set (for) *a pillar,*
31:13. thou anointedst *the pillar,*
45. took a stone, and set it up (for) *a pillar.*
51. this heap, and behold (this) *pillar,*
52. (this) *pillar* (be) witness,
— thou shalt not pass over...this *pillar*
35:14. Jacob set up *a pillar*
20. Jacob set *a pillar*
Ex. 23:24. quite break down *their images.*
24: 4. an altar under the hill, and twelve *pillars,*
34:13. break *their images,* (marg. *statues*)
Lev. 26: 1. *neither* rear you up *a standing image,*
Deu 7: 5. *and* break down *their images,* (marg. *statues,* or, *pillars*)
12: 3. break *their pillars,*
16:22. Neither shalt thou set thee up (any) *image;* (marg. *statue,* or, *pillar*)
1K. 14:23. they also built them high places, *and images,* (marg. *standing images,* or, *statues*)
2K. 3: 2. he put away *the image* (marg. *statue*) *of* Baal
10:26. they brought forth *the images*
27. And they brake down *the image of* Baal,
17:10. they set them up *images* (marg. *statues*)
18: 4. brake *the images,* (marg. *id.*) and cut down
23:14. he brake in pieces *the images,* (marg. *id.*)
2Ch 14:3(2). brake down *the images,* (marg. *id.*)
31: 1. brake *the images* (marg. *id.*) in pieces,
Isa. 19:19. *and a pillar* at the border thereof
Jer. 43:13. He shall break also *the images of* (marg. *statues,* or, *standing images*)
Eze. 26:11. *and* thy strong *garrisons* shall go down
Hos. 3: 4. without *an image* (marg. *a standing,* or, *statue*), and without an ephod,
10: 1. they have made goodly *images.* (marg. *statues,* or, *standing images*)
2. he shall spoil *their images.*
Mic. 5:13(12). *and thy standing images* (marg. or, *statues*) out of the midst

---

4678 **מַצֶּבֶת** *matz-tzeh'-veth*, f.

Gen 35:14. (even) *a pillar* of stone:
20. that (is) *the pillar* of Rachel's grave
2Sa. 18:18. Absalom...reared up for himself *a pillar,*
— he called *the pillar* after his own name:
Isa. 6:13. whose *substance* (marg. or, *stock,* or, *stem*)
— the holy seed (shall be) *the substance thereof.*

4679 **מְצָד** *m'tzāhd* & **מְצַד** *m'tzad*, m.

Jud. 6: 2. in the mountains,...and *strong holds.*
1Sa. 23:14. in the wilderness *in strong holds,*
19. hide himself with us *in strong holds*
29(24:1). dwelt *in strong holds at* En-gedi.
1Ch 11: 7. David dwelt *in the castle;*
12: 8. *into the hold* to the wilderness
16. there came...*to the hold*
Isa. 33:16. *the munitions of* rocks:
Jer. 48:41. *and the strong holds* are surprised,
51:30. they have remained *in* (their) *holds:*
Eze. 33:27. they that (be) *in the forts*

4680 **מָצָה** [*māh-tzāh'*].

* KAL.—*Preterite.* *

Isa. 51:17. (and) *wrung* (them) *out.*
Eze. 23:34. Thou shalt even drink it *and suck* (it) *out,*

KAL.—*Future.*

Jud. 6:38. *and wringed* the dew out of the fleece,
Ps. 75: 8(9). the wicked...*shall wring* (them) *out,*

* NIPHAL.—*Preterite.* *

Lev. 1:15. *and* the blood thereof *shall be wrung* out

NIPHAL.—*Future.*

Lev. 5: 9. the blood *shall be wrung out*
Ps. 73:10. waters...*are wrung out* to them.

מַצָּה *matz-tzah'*, f. 4682

Gen 19: 3. *and* did bake *unleavened bread,*
Ex. 12: 8. roast with fire, *and unleavened bread;*
15. Seven days shall ye eat *unleavened bread*
17. (the feast of) *unleavened bread;*
18. ye shall eat *unleavened bread,*
20. shall ye eat *unleavened bread.*
39. they baked *unleavened* cakes
13: 6. thou shalt eat *unleavened bread,*
7. *Unleavened bread* shall be eaten
23:15. the feast of *unleavened bread:* thou shalt eat *unleavened bread*
29: 2. And *unleavened* bread, and cakes *unleavened* tempered with oil, and wafers *unleavened* anointed
23. basket of *the unleavened bread*
34:18. The feast of *unleavened bread* shalt thou keep. Seven days thou shalt eat *unleavened bread,*
Lev. 2: 4. *unleavened* cakes of fine flour mingled with oil, or *unleavened* wafers anointed
5. fine flour *unleavened,*
6:16(9). with *unleavened bread*
7:12. *unleavened* cakes mingled with oil, and *unleavened* wafers anointed
8: 2. a basket of *unleavened bread;*
26. the basket of *unleavened bread,*
— he took one *unleavened* cake,
10:12. eat it *without leaven*
23: 6. the feast of *unleavened bread* unto the Lord: seven days ye must eat *unleavened bread.*
Nu. 6:15. a basket of *unleavened bread,*
— wafers of *unleavened bread*
17. the basket of *unleavened bread:*
19. one *unleavened* cake out of the basket, and one *unleavened* wafer,
9:11. eat it with *unleavened bread*
28:17. shall *unleavened bread* be eaten.
Deu 16: 3. shalt thou eat *unleavened bread*
8. thou shalt eat *unleavened bread:*
16. the feast of *unleavened bread,*
Jos. 5:11. *unleavened cakes,* and parched (corn)
Jud. 6:19. *unleavened cakes* of an ephah of flour:
20, 21. the flesh *and the unleavened cakes,*
21. the flesh *and the unleavened cakes.*
1Sa. 28:24. did bake *unleavened bread*
2K. 23: 9. they did eat of *the unleavened bread*
1Ch 23:29. for *the unleavened cakes,*
2Ch 8:13. in the feast of *unleavened bread,*
30:13, 21. the feast of *unleavened bread*
35:17. the feast of *unleavened bread* seven days.
Ezr. 6:22. the feast of *unleavened bread*
Eze. 45:21. *unleavened bread* shall be eaten.

מַצָּה *matz-tzāh'*, f. 4683

Pro. 13:10. by pride cometh *contention:*
17:19. He loveth transgression that loveth *strife:*
Isa. 58: 4. ye fast for strife *and debate,*

מִצְהָלוֹת *mitz-hălōhth'*, f. pl. 4684

Jer. 8:16. at the sound of *the neighing of* his strong
13:27. thine adulteries, and *thy neighings,*

מָצוֹד [*māh-tzōhd'*], m. 4685

Pro. 12:12. The wicked desireth *the net* (marg. or, *fortress*) *of* evil (men):
Ecc. 7:26. the woman, whose heart (is) *snares* and
9:14. and built great *bulwarks*

מָצוּד [*māh-tzood'*], m. 4686

Job 19: 6. *and* hath compassed me with *his net.*

מְצוֹדָה *m'tzōh-dāh'*, f. 4685

Ecc. 9:12. the fishes that are taken *in an evil net,*
Isa. 29: 7. against her *and her munition,*
Eze. 19: 9. they brought him *into holds,*

4686 ## מְצוּדָה *m'tzoo-dāh'*, f.

1Sa.22: 4. all the while that David was *in the hold.*
5. Abide not *in the hold;*
24:22(23). David and his men gat them up *unto the hold.*
2Sa. 5: 7. David took *the strong hold of* Zion:
9. David dwelt *in the fort,*
17. and went down to *the hold.*
22: 2. The Lord (is) my rock, *and my fortress,*
23:14. David (was) then *in an hold,*
1Ch 11: 5. David took *the castle of* Zion,
16. David (was) then *in the hold,*
Job 39:28. of the rock, *and the strong place.*
Ps. 18: 2(3). The Lord (is) my rock, *and my fortress,*
31: 2(3). for an house of *defence*
3(4). my rock *and my fortress;*
66:11. Thou broughtest us *into the net;*
71: 3. my rock *and my fortress.*
91: 2. my refuge *and my fortress:*
144: 2. My goodness, *and my fortress;*
Eze.12:13. he shall be taken *in my snare:*
13:21. be no more in your hand *to be hunted*
17:20. he shall be taken *in my snare,*

4687 ## מִצְוָה *mitz-vāh'*, f.

Gen26: 5. *my commandments,* my statutes,
Ex. 15:26. give ear *to his commandments,*
16:28. to keep *my commandments*
20: 6. and keep *my commandments.*
24:12. a law, *and commandments*
Lev. 4: 2, 13, 22. any of *the commandments of* the Lord
27. any *of the commandments of* the Lord
5:17. *the commandments of* the Lord;
22:31. Therefore shall ye keep *my commandments,*
26: 3. and keep *my commandments,*
14. do all these *commandments;*
15. do all *my commandments,*
27:34. These (are) *the commandments,*
Nu. 15:22. all these *commandments,*
31. hath broken *his commandment,*
39. *the commandments of* the Lord,
40. do all *my commandments,*
36:13. These (are) *the commandments*
Deu 4: 2. *the commandments of* the Lord
40. his statutes, and *his commandments,*
5:10. and keep *my commandments.*
29(26). keep all *my commandments*
31(28). all *the commandments,*
6: 1. these (are) *the commandments,*
2. his statutes *and his commandments,*
17. *the commandments of* the Lord
25. to do all these *commandments*
7: 9. keep *his commandments*
11. keep *the commandments,*
8: 1. All *the commandments* which
2. wouldest keep *his commandments,*
6. *the commandments of* the Lord
11. keeping *his commandments,*
10:13. *the commandments of* the Lord,
11: 1. his judgments, *and his commandments,*
8. keep all *the commandments*
13. *my commandments* which I command
22. all these *commandments*
27, 28. *the commandments of* the Lord
13: 4(5). keep *his commandments,*
18(19). keep all *his commandments*
15: 5. to do all these *commandments*
17:20. turn not aside from *the commandment,*
19: 9. keep all these *commandments*
26:13. all *thy commandments*
— I have not transgressed *thy commandments,*
17. *and his commandments,* and his judgments,
18. keep all *his commandments;*
27: 1. Keep all *the commandments*
10. and do *his commandments*
28: 1. to do all *his commandments*
9, 13. *the commandments of* the Lord
15. to do all *his commandments*
45. to keep *his commandments,*
30: 8. do all *his commandments*
10. thy God, to keep *his commandments*
11. this *commandment* which I command thee
16. and to keep *his commandments*
Deu31: 5. all *the commandments*
Jos. 22: 3. the charge of *the commandment of*
5. to do *the commandment*
— to keep *his commandments,*
Jud. 2:17 & 3:4. *the commandments of* the Lord;
1Sa. 13:13. thou hast not kept *the commandment of*
1K. 2: 3. his statutes, and *his commandments,*
43. *the commandment* that I have charged
3:14. to keep my statutes *and my commandments,*
6:12. keep all *my commandments*
8:58, 61. to keep *his commandments,*
9: 6. keep *my commandments*
11:34. he kept *my commandments*
38. my statutes *and my commandments,*
13:21. hast not kept *the commandment*
14: 8. David, who kept *my commandments,*
18:18. *the commandments of* the Lord,
2K. 17:13. keep *my commandments*
16. *the commandments of* the Lord
19. Judah kept not *the commandments of*
34. or after the law *and commandment*
37. the law, *and the commandment,*
18: 6. kept *his commandments,*
36. the king's *commandment* was,
23: 3. to keep *his commandments*
1Ch 28: 7. to do *my commandments*
8. *the commandments of* the Lord
29:19. to keep *thy commandments,*
2Ch 7:19. my statutes *and my commandments,*
8:13. *according to the commandment of* Moses,
14. had David the man of God *commanded.* (marg. (was) *the commandment of* David)
15. *the commandment of* the king
14: 4(3). the law *and the commandment.*
17: 4. *and* walked *in his commandments,*
19:10. between law *and commandment,*
24:20. *the commandments of* the Lord,
21. *at the commandment of* the king
29:15. *according to the commandment of* the king,
25. *according to the commandment of* David,
— *the commandment* of the Lord
30: 6. *and according to the commandment of*
12. *the commandment of* the king
31:21. *and in the commandments,*
34:31. to keep *his commandments,*
35:10. *according to* the king's *commandment.*
15. *according to the commandment of* David,
16. *according to the commandment of* king
Ezr. 7:11. *the commandments of* the Lord,
9:10. we have forsaken *thy commandments,*
14. break *thy commandments,*
10: 3. *at the commandment of* our God;
Neh 1: 5. observe *his commandments:*
7. have not kept *the commandments,*
9. and keep *my commandments,*
9:13. good statutes *and commandments:*
14. *and* commandedst them *precepts,*
16. hearkened not to *thy commandments,*
29. hearkened not *unto thy commandments,*
34. nor hearkened unto *thy commandments*
10:29(30). *the commandments of* the Lord
32(33). we made *ordinances* for us,
11:23. the king's *commandment*
12:24, 45. *according to the commandment of* David
13: 5. *which was commanded* (to be given) *to* the Levites, (marg. *the commandment of* the Levites)
Est. 3: 3. the king's *commandment?*
Job 23:12. *the commandment of* his lips;
Ps. 19: 8(9). *the commandment of* the Lord
78: 7. *but* keep *his commandments:*
89:31(32). and keep not *my commandments;*
112: 1. delighteth greatly *in his commandments.*
119: 6. have respect unto all *thy commandments.*
10. wander *from thy commandments.*
19. hide not *thy commandments*
21. do err *from thy commandments.*
32. the way of *thy commandments,*
35. the path of *thy commandments;*
47. *in thy commandments,* which I
48. unto *thy commandments,* which I
60. to keep *thy commandments.*
66. I have believed *thy commandments.*
73. that I may learn *thy commandments.*
86. All *thy commandments* (are) faithful:
96. *thy commandment* (is) exceeding broad.
98. through *thy commandments*

Ps119:115. *the commandments of* my God.
127. I love *thy commandments*
131. I longed *for thy commandments.*
143. *thy commandments* (are) my delights.
151. all *thy commandments* (are) truth.
166. *and* done *thy commandments.*
172. all *thy commandments* (are) righteousness.
176. I do not forget *thy commandments.*
Pro. 2: 1. *and* hide *my commandments* with thee;
3: 1. *but* let thine heart keep *my commandments:*
4: 4. keep *my commandments,* and live.
6:20. keep thy father's *commandment,*
23. *the commandment* (is) a lamp;
7: 1. *and* lay up *my commandments*
2. Keep *my commandments,* and live;
10: 8. wise in heart will receive *commandments:*
13:13. he that feareth *the commandment*
19:16. He that keepeth *the commandment*
Ecc. 8: 5. Whoso keepeth *the commandment*
12:13. Fear God, and keep *his commandments:*
Isa. 29:13. *by the precept of* men:
36:21. the king's *commandment*
48:18. hearkened *to my commandments!*
Jer. 32:11. (according) to *the law* and custom,
35:14. obey their father's *commandment:*
16. *the commandment of* their father,
18. *the commandment of* Jonadab your father, and kept all *his precepts,*
Dan 9: 4. them that keep *his commandments;*
5. departing *from thy precepts*
Mal. 2: 1. O ye priests, this *commandment* (is) for
4. I have sent this *commandment*

4688 מְצוֹלָה [*m'tzōh-lāh'*], f.

Ex. 15: 5. they sank *into the bottom*
Neh 9:11. thou threwest *into the deeps,*
Ps. 88: 6(7). in darkness, *in the deeps.*

4688 מְצוּלָה *m'tzoo-lāh'*, f.

Job 41:31(23). He maketh *the deep* to boil
Ps. 68:22(23). *from the depths of* the sea:
69: 2(3). I sink in *deep* mire, (marg. the mire of *depth*)
15(16). neither let *the deep* swallow me up,
107:24. and his wonders *in the deep.*
Jon. 2: 3(4). thou hadst cast me into *the deep,*
Mic. 7:19. *into the depths of* the sea.
Zec.10:11. *the deeps of* the river shall dry up:

4689 מָצוֹק *māh-tzōhk'*, m.

Deu28:53, 55. in the siege, *and in the straitness,*
57. in the siege *and straitness,*
1Sa.22: 2. every one (that was) in *distress,*
Ps.119:143. Trouble *and anguish* have taken hold
Jer. 19: 9. in the siege *and straitness,*

4690 מָצוּק *māh-tzook'*, m.

1Sa. 2: 8. *the pillars of* the earth (are) the Lord's,
14: 5. The forefront of the one (was) *situate*

4691 מְצוּקָה *m'tzoo-kāh'*, f.

Job 15:24. Trouble *and anguish* shall make him
Ps. 25:17. (O) bring thou me *out of my distresses.*
107: 6. he delivered them *out of their distresses.*
13. he saved them *out of their distresses.*
19. he saveth them *out of their distresses.*
28. *and* he bringeth them *out of their distresses.*
Zep. 1:15. a day of trouble *and distress,*

4692 מָצוֹר *māh-tzōhr'*, m.

Deu20:19. to employ (them) *in the siege:*
20. thou shalt build *bulwarks*
28:53, 55. *in the siege,* and in the straitness,
57. *in the siege* and straitness,

2K. 19:24. the rivers of *besieged* (marg. or, *fenced*) *places.*
24:10 & 25:2. the city was *besieged.* (marg. came *into siege*)
2Ch 8: 5. *fenced* cities, with walls, gates, and bars;
11: 5. Rehoboam...built cities *for defence*
32:10. *in the siege* (marg. or, *strong hold*) in
Ps. 31:21(22). kindness in a *strong* (marg. or, *fenced*) city.
60: 9(11). (into) the *strong* city? (marg. city of *strength*)
Isa. 19: 6. the brooks of *defence* shall be emptied
37:25. *the besieged places.* (marg. or, *fenced and closed*)
Jer. 10:17. O inhabitant *of the fortress.*
19: 9. *in the siege* and straitness,
52: 5. city was *besieged* (lit. came *into siege*)
Eze. 4: 2. And lay *siege* against it,
3. it shall be *besieged,* (lit. *in a siege*)
7. *the siege of* Jerusalem,
8. the days *of thy siege.*
5: 2. when the days of *the siege* are fulfilled:
Mic. 5: 1(4:14). he hath laid *siege* against us:
7:12. (from) the *fortified* cities, and from *the fortress* even to the river,
Nah 3:14. Draw thee waters for *the siege,*
Hab 2: 1. me upon *the tower,* (marg. *fenced place*)
Zec. 9: 3. Tyrus did build herself *a strong hold,*
12: 2. they shall be *in the siege*

מְצוּרָה *m'tzoo-rāh'*, f. 4694

2Ch 11:10. in Judah and in Benjamin *fenced* cities.
11. he fortified *the strong holds,*
23. unto every *fenced* city:
12: 4. he took the *fenced* cities
14: 6(5). he built *fenced* cities
21: 3. *fenced* cities in Judah:
Isa. 29: 3. I will raise *forts* against thee.
Nah 2: 1(2). keep *the munition,* watch the way,

מַצּוּת [*matz-tzooth'*], f. 4695

Isa. 41:12. them that *contended with thee:* (marg. the men of *thy contention*)

מֵצַח *mēh'-tzagh*, com. 4696

Ex. 28:38. it shall be upon Aaron's *forehead,*
— it shall be always upon *his forehead,*
1Sa.17:49. smote the Philistine in *his forehead,* that the stone sunk *into his forehead;*
2Ch 26:19. the leprosy even rose up *in his forehead*
20. he (was) leprous *in his forehead,*
Isa. 48: 4. *and thy brow* brass;
Jer. 3: 3. *and* thou hadst a whore's *forehead,*
Eze. 3: 7. the house of Israel (are) impudent (marg. stiff of *forehead*)
8. *thy forehead* strong against *their foreheads.*
9. than flint have I made *thy forehead:*
9: 4. set a mark upon *the foreheads*

מִצְחָה [*mitz-ghāh'*], f. 4697

1Sa.17: 6. (he had) *greaves of* brass upon his legs,

מְצִלָּה *m'tzool-lāh'*, f. 4699

Zec. 1: 8. that (were) *in the bottom;*

מְצִלּוֹת *m'tzil-lōhth'*, f. pl. 4698

Zec.14:20. upon *the bells* (marg. or, *bridles*) *of* the

מְצִלְתַּיִם *m'tzil-tah'-yim*, dual. 4700

1Ch 13: 8. with timbrels, *and with cymbals,*
15:16. psalteries and harps *and cymbals,*
19. to sound *with cymbals* of brass;
28. with trumpets, *and with cymbals,*

1Ch 16: 5. Asaph made a sound *with cymbals;*
42. with trumpets *and cymbals*
25: 1. with psalteries, *and with cymbals:*
6. *with cymbals*, psalteries, and harps,
2Ch 5:12. *cymbals* and psalteries and harps,
13. with the trumpets *and cymbals*
29:25. *with cymbals*, with psalteries,
Ezr. 3:10. the sons of Asaph *with cymbals*,
Neh 12:27. (with) *cymbals*, psalteries, and with

4701 **מִצְנֶפֶת** *mitz-neh'-pheth*, f.

Ex. 28: 4. *a mitre*, and a girdle:
37. may be upon *the mitre;* upon the forefront of *the mitre* it shall be.
39. make *the mitre* (of) fine linen,
29: 6. put *the mitre* upon his head, and put the holy crown upon *the mitre.*
39:28. And *a mitre* (of) fine linen,
31. on high upon *the mitre;*
Lev. 8: 9. he put *the mitre* upon his head; also upon *the mitre*,
16: 4. and *with the* linen *mitre*
Eze. 21:26(31). Remove *the diadem*,

4702 **מַצָּע** *matz-tzāh^{n}g'*, m.

Isa. 28:20. For *the bed* is shorter

4703 **מִצְעָד** [*mitz-^{n}gāhd'*], m.

Ps. 37:23. *The steps of* a (good) man
Pro. 20:24. Man's *goings* (are) of the Lord;
Dan 11:43. the Ethiopians (shall be) *at his steps.*

4704 **מִצְעִירָה** *mitz-^{n}gee-rāh'*, adj. f.

Dan 8: 9. of one of them came forth a *little* horn,

4705 **מִצְעָר** *mitz-^{n}gāhr'*, m.

Gen 19:20. and it (is) *a little one:*
— (is) it not *a little one?*
2Ch 24:24. *with a small company of* men,
Job 8: 7. Though thy beginning was *small*,
Ps. 42: 6(7). hill *Mizar.* (marg. or, the *little* hill)
Isa. 63:18. possessed (it) *but a little while:*

4707 **מִצְפֶּה** *mitz-peh'*, m.

2Ch 20:24. when Judah came toward *the watch tower*
Isa. 21: 8. I stand continually upon *the watch-tower*

4710 **מַצְפֻּנִים** [*matz-poo-neem'*], m. pl.

Obad 6. (how) are *his hidden things* sought up!

4711 **מָצַץ** [*māh-tzatz'*].

* KAL.—*Future.* *

Isa. 66:11. that *ye may milk out*, and be delighted

4712 **מֵצַר** *mēh-tzar'*, m.

Ps. 116: 3. *and the pains of* hell gat hold upon me:
118: 5. I called upon the Lord in *distress:*
Lam. 1: 3. overtook her between *the straits.*

4715 **מַצְרֵף** *matz-rēhph'*, m.

Pro. 17: 3. *The fining pot* (is) for silver,
27:21. *the fining pot* for silver,

4716 **מַק** *mak*, m.

Isa. 3:24. of sweet smell there shall be *stink;*
5:24. their root shall be *as rottenness*,

מַקָּבָה [*mak-kāh-vāh'*], f. 4717

1K. 6: 7. *neither hammer* nor ax (nor) any tool
Isa. 44:12. *and* fashioneth it *with hammers*,
Jer. 10: 4. they fasten it with nails *and with hammers*,

מַקֶּבֶת *mak-keh'-veth*, f. 4718

Jud. 4:21. took *an hammer* in her hand,
Isa. 51: 1. *the hole of* the pit (whence) ye are

מִקְדָּשׁ *mik-dāhsh'*, m. 4720

Ex. 15:17. (in) *the Sanctuary*, O Lord, which thy
25: 8. let them make me *a sanctuary;*
Lev. 12: 4. nor come into *the sanctuary*,
16:33. make an atonement for *the* holy *sanctuary*,
19:30. *and* reverence *my sanctuary:*
20: 3. to defile *my sanctuary*,
21:12. Neither shall he go out of *the sanctuary*, nor profane *the sanctuary of* his God;
23. profane not *my sanctuaries:*
26: 2. *and* reverence *my sanctuary:*
31. *your sanctuaries* unto desolation,
Nu. 3:38. keeping the charge of *the sanctuary*
10:21. bearing *the sanctuary:*
18: 1. shall bear the iniquity of *the sanctuary:*
29. *the hallowed part thereof* out of it.
19:20. he hath defiled *the sanctuary of* the Lord:
Jos. 24:26. that (was) *by the sanctuary of* the Lord.
1Ch 22:19. build ye *the sanctuary of* the Lord God,
28:10. to build an house *for the sanctuary:*
2Ch 20: 8. have built thee *a sanctuary*
26:18. go out of *the sanctuary;*
29:21. for *the sanctuary*, and for Judah.
30: 8. enter *into his sanctuary*,
36:17. the house of *their sanctuary*,
Neh 10:39(40). (are) the vessels of *the sanctuary*,
Ps. 68:35(36). O God, (thou art) terrible *out of thy holy places:*
73:17. Until I went into *the sanctuary of* God;
74: 7. They have cast fire into *thy sanctuary*,
78:69. he built *his sanctuary* like high (palaces),
96: 6. strength and beauty (are) *in his sanctuary.*
Isa. 8:14. he shall be *for a sanctuary;*
16:12. he shall come to *his sanctuary* to pray;
60:13. to beautify the place of *my sanctuary;*
63:18. our adversaries have trodden down *thy sanctuary.*
Jer. 17:12. the place of *our sanctuary.*
51:51. strangers are come into *the sanctuaries of*
Lam. 1:10. the heathen entered into *her sanctuary*,
2: 7. he hath abhorred *his sanctuary*,
20. the prophet be slain *in the sanctuary of*
Eze. 5:11. because thou hast defiled *my sanctuary*
8: 6. I should go far off from *my sanctuary?*
9: 6. *and* begin *at my sanctuary.*
11:16. yet will I be to them *as a* little *sanctuary*
21: 2(7). drop (thy word) toward *the holy places*,
23:38. they have defiled *my sanctuary*
39. they came the same day into *my sanctuary*
24:21. I will profane *my sanctuary*,
25: 3. Because thou saidst, Aha, against *my sanctuary*,
28:18. Thou hast defiled *thy sanctuaries*
37:26. will set *my sanctuary* in the midst of them
28. *my sanctuary* shall be in the midst of them
43:21. without *the sanctuary.*
44: 1. the gate of *the* outward *sanctuary*
5. with every going forth of *the sanctuary.*
7. to be *in my sanctuary*,
8. keepers of my charge *in my sanctuary*
9. shall enter into *my sanctuary*,
11. they shall be ministers *in my sanctuary*,
15. kept the charge of *my sanctuary*
16. They shall enter into *my sanctuary*,
45: 3. in it shall be *the sanctuary*
4. the ministers of *the sanctuary*,
— *and an holy place for the sanctuary.*
18. cleanse *the sanctuary:*
47:12. they issued out of *the sanctuary:*
48: 8. *the sanctuary* shall be in the midst
10. *the sanctuary of* the Lord shall be in the
21. *and the sanctuary of* the house

Dan. 8:11. the place of *his sanctuary* was cast down.
9:17. cause thy face to shine upon *thy sanctuary*
11:31. they shall pollute *the sanctuary*
Am. 7: 9. *and the sanctuaries of* Israel
13. it (is) the king's *chapel*,

4721 מַקְהֵלוֹת *mak-hēh-lōhth'*, f. pl.

Ps. 68:26(27). Bless ye God *in the congregations*,

4721 מַקְהֵלִים *mak-hēh-leem'*, m. pl.

Ps. 26:12. *in the congregations* will I bless the Lord.

4723 מִקְוֵא *mik-vēh'*, m.

1K. 10:28. Solomon had horses brought out of Egypt, *and linen yarn:* the king's merchants received *the linen yarn* at a price.
2Ch 1:16. Solomon had horses brought out of Egypt, *and linen yarn:* the king's merchants received *the linen yarn* at a price.

4723 מִקְוֶה *mik-veh'*, m.

Gen. 1:10. *and the gathering together of* the waters called he Seas:
Ex. 7:19. upon all their *pools of* water, (marg. *gathering of* their waters)
Lev.11:36. a fountain or pit, (wherein there is) *plenty of* water,
1Ch 29:15. (there is) none *abiding*. (marg. *expectation*)
Ezr.10: 2. yet now there is *hope* in Israel concerning this thing.
Jer. 14: 8. *O the hope of* Israel, the saviour thereof
17:13. O Lord, *the hope of* Israel,
50: 7. *even* the Lord, *the hope of* their fathers.

4724 מִקְוָה *mik-vāh'*, f.

Isa. 22:11. Ye made *also a ditch* between the two walls

4725 מָקוֹם *māh-kōhm'*, com.

Gen. 1: 9. be gathered together unto one *place*,
12: 6. the land unto *the place of* Sichem,
13: 3. *the place* where his tent had been
4. Unto *the place of* the altar,
14. look from *the place* where thou art
18:24. spare *the place* for the fifty righteous
26. I will spare all *the place* for their sakes.
33. Abraham returned *unto his place*.
19:12. bring (them) out of *this place:*
13. For we will destroy this *place*,
14. Up, get you out of this *place;*
27. Abraham gat up early...to *the place*
20:11. the fear of God (is) not *in* this *place;*
13. at every *place* whither we shall come,
21:31. he called that *place* Beer-sheba;
22: 3. *the place* of which God had told him.
4. saw *the place* afar off.
9. *the place* which God had told him of;
14. the name of that *place* Jehovah-jireh:
24:23. is there *room* (in) thy father's house for us to lodge in?
25. provender enough, and *room* to lodge in.
31. the house, *and room* for the camels.
26: 7. the men of *the place* asked (him)
— lest, (said he), the men of *the place* should
28:11. he lighted *upon a* certain *place*,
— he took of the stones of that *place*,
— and lay down *in* that *place* to sleep.
16. Surely the Lord is *in* this *place;*
17. How dreadful (is) this *place!*
19. he called the name of that *place*
29: 3. again upon the well's mouth *in his place*.
22. gathered together all the men of *the place*,
26. It must not be so done *in our country*, (marg. *place*)
30:25. that I may go unto *mine own place*,

Gen31:55(32:1). Laban departed, and returned *unto his place*.
32: 2(3). called the name of that *place* Mahanaim.
30(31). called the name of *the place* Peniel:
33:17. the name of *the place* is called Succoth.
35: 7. and called *the place* El-beth-el:
13. *in the place* where he talked with him.
14. Jacob set up a pillar *in the place*
15. Jacob called the name of *the place*
36:40. *after their places*, by their names;
38:21. he asked the men of *that place*,
22. also the men of *the place* said,
39:20. *a place* where the king's prisoners
40: 3. *the place* where Joseph (was) bound.
Ex. 3: 5. *the place* whereon thou standest
8. unto *the place of* the Canaanites,
16:29. let no man go out *of his place*
17: 7. he called the name of *the place* Massah, and Meribah,
18:23. people shall also go to *their place* in peace.
20:24. in all *places* where I record my name
21:13. appoint thee *a place* whither he shall flee.
23:20. into *the place* which I have prepared.
29:31. seethe his flesh *in the* holy *place*.
33:21. Behold, (there is) *a place* by me,
Lev. 1:16. east part, by *the place of* the ashes:
4:12. without the camp unto *a* clean *place*,
24, 33. *in the place* where they kill the burnt
29. *in the place of* the burnt offering.
6:11(4). forth the ashes...unto *a* clean *place*.
16(9). shall it be eaten *in the* holy *place;*
25(18). *the place* where the burnt offering is
26(19). *in the* holy *place* shall it be eaten,
27(20). it was sprinkled *in the* holy *place*.
7: 2. *In the place* where they kill the burnt
6. it shall be eaten *in the* holy *place:*
10:13. ye shall eat it *in the* holy *place*,
14. shall ye eat *in a* clean *place;*
17. eaten the sin offering *in the* holy *place*,
13:19. *in the place of* the boil there be
14:13. *in the place* where he shall kill the sin offering and the burnt offering, *in the* holy *place:*
28. upon *the place of* the blood of the trespass offering:
40. shall cast them into *an* unclean *place*
41. without the city into *an* unclean *place:*
45. out of the city into *an* unclean *place*.
16:24. his flesh with water *in the* holy *place*,
24: 9. they shall eat it *in the* holy *place:*
Nu. 9:17. *and in the place* where the cloud abode,
10:29. We are journeying unto *the place*
11: 3. he called the name of *the place* Taberah:
34. he called the name of that *place*
13:24. *The place* was called the brook Eshcol,
14:40. will go up unto *the place*
18:31. ye shall eat it in every *place*,
19: 9. without the camp *in a* clean *place*,
20: 5. to bring us in unto this evil *place?* it (is) no *place of* seed, or of figs,
21: 3. he called the name of *the place* Hormah.
22:26. and stood *in a* narrow *place*,
23:13. Come,...with me unto another *place*,
27. I will bring thee unto another *place;*
24:11. Therefore now flee thou to *thy place:*
25. went and returned *to his place:*
32: 1. that, behold, *the place* (was) *a place for* cattle;
17. we have brought them unto *their place:*
Deu 1:31. until ye came into this *place*.
33. search you out *a place* to pitch your tents
9: 7. until ye came unto this *place*,
11: 5. until ye came into this *place;*
24. Every *place* whereon the soles of your feet
12: 2. Ye shall utterly destroy all *the places*,
3. destroy the names of them out of that *place*.
5. *the place* which the Lord your God shall
11. *a place* which the Lord your God
13. offer not thy burnt offerings in every *place*
14. But *in the place* which the Lord shall choose
18. *in the place* which the Lord thy God
21. *the place* which the Lord thy God hath
26. go unto *the place* which the Lord
14:23. *in the place* which he shall choose
24. if *the place* be too far from thee,
25. go unto *the place* which the Lord
15:20 & 16:2. *in the place* which the Lord shall

Deu 16: 6. at *the place* which the Lord thy God
7. thou shalt roast and eat (it) *in the place*
11. *in the place* which the Lord thy God hath
15. *in the place* which the Lord shall choose:
16. *in the place* which he shall choose;
17: 8. get thee up into *the place* which the Lord
10. the sentence, which they of that *place*
18: 6. *the place* which the Lord shall choose;
21:19. unto the gate of *his place;*
23:16(17). *in that place* which he shall choose
26: 2. shalt go unto *the place* which the Lord
9. he hath brought us into this *place*,
29: 7(6). when ye came unto this *place*,
31:11. *in the place* which he shall choose,
Jos. 1: 3. Every *place* that the sole of your foot
3: 3. then ye shall remove *from your place*,
4:18. waters of Jordan returned *unto their place*,
5: 9. the name of *the place* is called Gilgal
15. *the place* whereon thou standest (is) holy.
7:26. the name of that *place* was called,
8:19. the ambush arose quickly *out of their place*,
9:27. in *the place* which he should choose.
20: 4. give him *a place*, that he may dwell
Jud. 2: 5. they called the name of that *place*
7: 7. go every man *unto his place.*
9:55. they departed every man *unto his place.*
11:19. through thy land into *my place.*
15:17. and called that *place* Ramath-lehi.
18:10. *a place* where (there is) no want of any
12. they called that *place* Mahaneh-dan
19:13. let us draw near to one of these *places*
16. the men of *the place* (were) Benjamites.
28. gat him *unto his place.*
20:22. *in the place* where they put themselves in
33. the men of Israel rose up *out of their place*,
— came forth *out of their places*,
36. men of Israel gave *place* to the Benjamites,
Ru. 1: 7. went forth out of *the place* where she was,
3: 4. shalt mark *the place* where he shall lie,
4:10. and from the gate of *his place:*
1Sa. 2:20. they went *unto their own home.*
3: 2. Eli (was) laid down *in his place*,
9. Samuel went and lay down *in his place.*
5: 3. Dagon, and set him *in his place* again.
11. let it go again *to his own place*,
6: 2. wherewith we shall send it *to his place.*
7:16. judged Israel in all those *places.*
9:22. made them sit in *the* chiefest *place*
12: 8. made them dwell *in* this *place.*
14:46. the Philistines went *to their own place.*
20:19. to *the place* where thou didst hide thyself
25, 27. David's *place* was empty.
37. was come to *the place of* the arrow
21: 2(3). (my) servants to such and such *a place.*
23:22. see *his place* where his haunt is,
28. they called that *place* Sela-hammahlekoth.
26: 5. came to *the place* where Saul had pitched:
and David beheld *the place* where Saul
13. *a* great *space* (being) between them:
25. Saul returned *to his place.*
27: 5. let them give me *a place* in some town
29: 4. that he may go again to *his place*
30:31. *the places* where David himself
2Sa. 2:16. that *place* was called Helkath-hazzurim,
23. as many as came to *the place*
5:20. called the name of that *place*
6: 8. called the name of *the place* Perez-uzzah
17. the ark of the Lord, and set it *in his place*,
7:10. I will appoint *a place* for my people
11:16. he assigned Uriah unto *a place*
15:19. return *to thy place*, and abide with the
21. *in* what *place* my lord the king shall be,
17: 9. (other) *place:* (lit. in one of *the places*)
12. come upon him in some *place* (lit. *id.*)
19:39(40). he returned *unto his own place.*
1K. 4:28(5:8). brought they unto *the place*
5: 9(23). *the place* that thou shalt appoint me,
8: 6. brought in the ark...unto *his place*,
7. (their) two wings over *the place of* the
21. I have set there *a place* for the ark,
29. toward *the place* of which thou hast said,
— thy servant shall make toward this *place.*
30. they shall pray toward this *place:* and hear
thou in heaven thy dwelling *place:*
35. if they pray toward this *place*,
10:19. on *the place of* the seat,
13: 8. nor drink water *in* this *place.*

1K. 13:16. nor drink water with thee *in* this *place:*
22. eaten bread and drunk water *in the place*,
20:24. every man *out of his place*,
21:19. *In the place* where dogs licked the blood
2K. 5:11. strike his hand over *the place*,
6: 1. *the place* where we dwell
2. let us make us *a place* there,
6. he shewed him *the place.*
8. In such and such *a place* (shall be) my
9. pass not such *a place;*
10. the king of Israel sent to *the place*
18:25. against this *place* to destroy it?
22:16. I will bring evil upon this *place*,
17. wrath shall be kindled *against* this *place*,
19. I spake against this *place*,
20. I will bring upon this *place.*
23:14. filled *their places* with the bones of men.
1Ch 13:11. that *place* is called Perez-uzza
14:11. the name of that *place* Baal-perazim.
15: 1. prepared *a place* for the ark
3. the ark of the Lord unto *his place*,
16:27. strength and gladness (are) *in his place.*
17: 9. I will ordain *a place* for my people
21:22. Grant me *the place of* (this)
25. David gave to Ornan *for the place*
2Ch 3: 1. *the place* that David had prepared
5: 7. unto *his place*, to the oracle
8. (their) wings over *the place of*
6:20. upon *the place* whereof thou hast said
— prayeth toward this *place.*
21. toward this *place:* hear thou *from* thy
dwelling *place*,
26. if they pray toward this *place*,
40. the prayer (that is made) in this *place.*
7:12. have chosen this *place*
15. the prayer (that is made) in this *place.*
9:18. stays on each side of *the* sitting *place*,
20:26. *the* same *place* was called, The valley of
24:11. carried it to *his place* again.
25:10. to go *home* (marg. *to their place*) again:
— they returned *home* in great anger.
33:19. his trespass, *and the places* wherein
34:24. I will bring evil upon this *place*,
25. shall be poured out *upon* this *place*,
27. heardest his words against this *place*,
28. the evil that I will bring upon this *place.*
Ezr. 1: 4. whosoever remaineth in any *place* where
he sojourneth, let the men of *his place*
8:17. Iddo the chief at *the place* Casiphia,
— the Nethinims, at *the place* Casiphia,
9: 8. to give us a nail *in* his holy *place*,
Neh 1: 9. will bring them unto *the place*
2:14. (there was) no *place* for the beast
4:12(6). From all *places* whence ye shall
13(7). in the lower *places* (lit. from the lower
parts *of the place*)
20(14). *In* what *place* (therefore) ye hear the
12:27. sought the Levites out of all *their places*,
Est. 4: 3. *whither*soever (lit. *the place* which) the
14. arise to the Jews *from* another *place;*
8:17. *whither*soever (lit. *the place* which) the
Job 2:11. every one *from his own place;*
6:17. they are consumed *out of their place.*
7:10. neither shall *his place* know him any
8:18. If he destroy him *from his place*,
9: 6. Which shaketh the earth *out of her place*,
14:18. the rock is removed *out of his place.*
16:18. let my cry have no *place.*
18: 4. shall the rock be removed *out of his place?*
21. this (is) *the place* (of him)
20: 9. neither shall *his place* any more behold
27:21. hurleth him *out of his place.*
23. shall hiss him *out of his place.*
28: 1. *and a place* for gold (where) they fine
6. The stones of it (are) *the place of*
12, 20. where (is) *the place of* understanding?
23. he knoweth *the place thereof.*
34:26. in the open sight of others; (marg. *in the
place of* beholders)
37: 1. moved *out of his place.*
38:12. the dayspring to know *his place;*
19. where (is) *the place thereof*,
Ps. 24: 3. who shall stand *in* his holy *place?*
26: 8. *and the place where* thine honour dwelleth.
37:10. diligently consider *his place*,
44:19(20). sore broken us *in the place of*
103:16. *the place thereof* shall know it no more.

Ps. 103:22. in all *places of* his dominion:
104: 8. by the valleys unto *the place*
132: 5. Until I find out *a place* for the Lord,
Pro. 15: 3. The eyes of the Lord (are) in every *place*,
25: 6. *and* stand not *in the place of* great (men):
27: 8. a man that wandereth *from his place*.
Ecc. 1: 5. hasteth to *his place*
7. unto *the place* from whence the rivers
3:16. *the place of* judgment, (that) wickedness (was) there; *and the place of*
20. All go unto one *place;*
6: 6. do not all go to one *place?*
8:10. gone *from the place of* the holy,
10: 4. leave not *thy place;*
11: 3. *in the place* where the tree falleth,
Isa. 5: 8. (that) lay field to field, till (there be) no *place*,
7:23. (that) every *place* shall be,
13:13. the earth shall remove *out of her place*,
14: 2. bring them to *their place:*
18: 7. to *the place of* the name of the Lord
22:23. fasten him (as) a nail *in a* sure *place;*
25. the nail that is fastened *in the* sure *place*
26:21. the Lord cometh *out of his place*
28: 8. (there is) no *place* (clean).
33:21. *a place of* broad rivers (and) streams;
45:19. *in a* dark *place of* the earth:
46: 7. they carry him, and set him *in his place*,
49:20. *The place* (is) too strait for me:
54: 2. Enlarge *the place of* thy tent,
60:13. to beautify *the place of* my sanctuary; *and* I will make *the place of* my feet
66: 1. where (is) *the place of* my rest?
Jer. 4: 7. he is gone forth *from his place*
7: 3. I will cause you to dwell *in* this *place*.
6. shed not innocent blood *in* this *place*,
7. cause you to dwell *in* this *place*,
12. go ye now unto *my place*
14. *and unto the place* which I gave to you
20. shall be poured out upon this *place*,
32. bury in Tophet, till there be no *place*.
8: 3. which remain in all *the places*
13: 7. took the girdle from *the place*
14:13. give you assured peace *in* this *place*.
16: 2. sons or daughters *in* this *place*.
3. the daughters that are born *in* this *place*,
9. I will cause to cease out of this *place*
17:12. *the place of* our sanctuary.
19: 3. I will bring evil upon this *place*,
4. have estranged this *place*,
— have filled this *place* with the blood
6. this *place* shall no more be called Tophet,
7. of Judah and Jerusalem *in* this *place;*
11. till (there be) no *place* to bury.
12. Thus will I do *unto* this *place*,
13. *as the place of* Tophet,
22: 3. neither shed innocent blood *in* this *place*.
11. went forth out of this *place;*
12. he shall die *in the place*
24: 5. whom I have sent out of this *place*
9. in all *places* whither I shall drive them.
27:22. restore them to this *place*.
28: 3. will I bring again into this *place*
— took away from this *place*,
4. I will bring again to this *place*
6. from Babylon into this *place*.
29:10. causing you to return to this *place*.
14. from all *the places* whither I have driven
— I will bring you again into *the place*
32:37. I will bring them again unto this *place*,
33:10. there shall be heard *in* this *place*,
12. Again *in* this *place*, which is desolate
40: 2. pronounced this evil upon this *place*.
12. the Jews returned out of all *places*
42:18. ye shall see this *place* no more.
22. *in the place* whither ye desire to go
44:29. I will punish you *in* this *place*,
45: 5. in all *places* whither thou goest.
51:62. thou hast spoken against this *place*,
Eze. 3:12. the glory of the Lord *from his place*.
6:13. *the place* where they did offer sweet
10:11. to *the place* whither the head looked
12: 3. shalt remove *from thy place* to another *place*
17:16. *in the place* (where) the king (dwelleth)
21:30(35). I will judge thee *in the place*
34:12. deliver them out of all *places*
Eze. 38:15. thou shalt come *from thy place*
39:11. I will give unto Gog *a place*
41:11. and the breadth of *the place*
42:13. *the place* (is) holy.
43: 7. *the place of* my throne, and *the place of* the soles of my feet,
45: 4. it shall be *a place* for their houses,
46:19. there (was) *a place* on the two sides
20. This (is) *the place* where the priests
Hos. 1:10(2:1). *in the place* where it was said
5:15. I will go (and) return to *my place*,
Joel 3: 7(4:7). I will raise them out of *the place*
Am. 4: 6. want of bread in all *your places:*
8: 3. many dead bodies in every *place;*
Mic. 1: 3. the Lord cometh forth *out of his place*,
Nah 1: 8. an utter end of *the place thereof*,
3:17. *their place* is not known
Zep 1: 4. the remnant of Baal from this *place*,
2:11. every one *from his place*,
Hag 2: 9. *and in* this *place* will I give peace,
Zec. 14:10. from Benjamin's gate unto *the place of*
Mal 1:11. in every *place* incense (shall be) offered

מָקוֹר *māh-kōhr'*, m. 4726

Lev. 12: 7. she shall be cleansed *from the issue of*
20:18. he hath discovered *her fountain*, and she hath uncovered *the fountain of* her
Ps. 36: 9(10). with thee (is) *the fountain of* life:
68:26(27). the Lord, *from the fountain of* Israel.
Pro. 5:18. Let *thy fountain* be blessed:
10:11. mouth of a righteous (man is) *a well of*
13:14. law of the wise (is) *a fountain of* life,
14:27. fear of the Lord (is) *a fountain of* life,
16:22. Understanding (is) *a wellspring of* life
18: 4. *the wellspring of* wisdom (as) a flowing
25:26. *and a* corrupt *spring*.
Jer. 2:13. forsaken me *the fountain of* living waters,
9: 1(8:23). mine eyes *a fountain of* tears,
17:13. forsaken the Lord, *the fountain of* living
51:36. dry up her sea, and make *her springs* dry.
Hos 13:15. *his spring* shall become dry.
Zec. 13: 1. that day there shall be *a fountain* opened

מִקָּח *mik-kagh'*, m. 4727

2Ch 19: 7. respect of persons, *nor taking of* gifts.

מַקָּחוֹת *mak-kāh-ghōhth'*, f. pl. 4728

Neh 10:31(32). (if) the people of the land bring *ware*

מִקְטָר *mik-tar'*, m. 4729

Ex. 30: 1. an altar *to burn* incense *upon:*

מְקַטְּרוֹת *m'kat-t'rōhth'*, f. pl. 6999

2Ch 30:14. all *the altars for incense* took they away,

מִקְטֶרֶת *mik-teh'-reth*, f. 4730

2Ch 26:19. (had) *a censer* in his hand
Eze. 8:11. every man *his censer* in his hand;

מַקֵּל *mak-kēhl'*, m. 4731

Gen 30:37. Jacob took him *rods of* green poplar,
— which (was) in *the rods*.
38. And he set *the rods*
39. the flocks conceived before *the rods*,
41. Jacob laid *the rods*
— might conceive *among the rods*.
32:10(11). *with my staff* I passed over
Ex. 12:11. *and your staff* in your hand;
Nu. 22:27. he smote the ass *with a staff*.
1Sa. 17:40. he took *his staff* in his hand,
43. that thou comest to me *with staves?*
Jer. 1:11. I see *a rod of* an almond tree.
48:17. staff broken, (and) *the* beautiful *rod!*

Eze. 39: 9. *and the* hand*staves* (marg. or, *javelins*), and the spears,
Hos. 4: 12. *and their staff* declareth unto them:
Zec. 11: 7. I took unto me two *staves;*
10. And I took *my staff,*
14. I cut asunder *mine* other *staff,*

4733 **מִקְלָט** *mik-lāht'*, m.

Nu. 35: 6. (there shall be) six cities for *refuge,*
11. to be cities of *refuge* for you;
12. they shall be unto you cities *for refuge*
13. six cities shall ye have for *refuge.*
14. (which) shall be cities of *refuge.*
15. These six cities shall be *a refuge,*
25. restore him to the city of *his refuge,*
26. the border of the city of *his refuge,*
27. the borders of the city of *his refuge,*
28. he should have remained in the city of *his refuge*
32. him that is fled to the city of *his refuge,*
Jos. 20: 2. Appoint out for you cities *of refuge,*
3. they shall be your *refuge* from the avenger of blood.
21: 13, 21, 27, 32, 38(36). (to be) a city of *refuge for* the slayer;
1 Ch. 6: 57(42). Hebron, (the city) of *refuge,*
67(52). they gave unto them, (of) the cities of *refuge,*

4734 **מִקְלַעַת** *mik-lah'-ğath*, f.

1 K. 6: 18. the house within (was) *carved* (lit. *the carving*)
29. carved *figures of* cherubims
32. *carvings of* cherubims
7: 31. upon the mouth of it (were) *gravings*

4735 **מִקְנֶה** *mik-neh'*, m.

Gen. 4: 20. *and* (of such as have) *cattle.*
13: 2. very rich in *cattle,* in silver,
7. herdmen of Abram's *cattle* and the herdmen of Lot's *cattle:*
26: 14. For he had *possession of* flocks, *and possession of* herds,
29: 7. neither (is it) time that *the cattle*
30: 29. how *thy cattle* was with me.
31: 9. *the cattle of* your father,
18. carried away all *his cattle,*
— *the cattle of* his getting, which he had gotten
33: 17. *and* made booths *for his cattle:*
34: 5. his sons were with *his cattle*
23. (Shall) not *their cattle* and their
36: 6. *his cattle,* and all his beasts,
7. bear them because of *their cattle.*
46: 6. And they took *their cattle,*
32. their trade hath been to feed *cattle;* (lit. they are men of *cattle*)
34. trade hath been about *cattle*
47: 6. make them rulers over *my cattle.*
16. Joseph said, Give *your cattle;* and I will give you *for your cattle,*
17. they brought *their cattle* unto
— for horses, *and for* the flocks (lit. *cattle of* sheep), *and for the cattle of* the herds,
— for all *their cattle* for that year.
18. *also* hath our *herds of* cattle;
49: 32. *The purchase of* the field
Ex. 9: 3. hand of the Lord is upon *thy cattle*
4. sever between *the cattle of* Israel and *the cattle of* Egypt:
6. all *the cattle of* Egypt died: *but of the cattle of* the children
7. *of the cattle of* the Israelites
19. now, (and) gather *thy cattle,*
20. his servants and *his cattle*
21. and *his cattle* in the field.
10: 26. *Our cattle* also shall go with
12: 38. herds, (even) very much *cattle.*
17: 3. our children and *our cattle*
34: 19. firstling among *thy cattle,*
Nu. 20: 19. I *and my cattle* drink of thy

Nu. 31: 9. and all *their flocks,*
32: 1. *Now*...had a very great multitude of *cattle:*
— the place (was) a place for *cattle;*
4. Israel, (is) a land for *cattle,* and thy servants have *cattle:*
16. sheepfolds here *for our cattle,*
26. Our little ones, our wives, *our flocks,*
Deu. 3: 19. your little ones, *and your cattle,* (for) I know that ye have much *cattle,*
Jos. 1: 14. your little ones, *and your cattle,*
14: 4. suburbs *for their cattle*
22: 8. *and with* very much *cattle,*
Jud. 6: 5. came up *with their cattle*
18: 21. the little ones and *the cattle*
1Sa. 23: 5. and brought away *their cattle,*
30: 20. before those (other) *cattle,*
2 K. 3: 17. *and your cattle,* and your beasts.
1 Ch 5: 9. because *their cattle* were multiplied
21. they took away *their cattle;*
7: 21. down to take away *their cattle.*
28: 1. *and possession* of the king,
2Ch 14: 15(14). also the tents of *cattle,*
26: 10. for he had much *cattle,*
32: 29. provided him cities, *and possessions of*
Job 1: 3. *His substance* (marg. or, *cattle*) also was seven thousand
10. *and his substance* (marg. *id.*) is increased
36: 33. *the cattle* also concerning the vapour.
Ps. 78: 48. *and their flocks* to hot thunderbolts.
Ecc. 2: 7. *possessions of* great and small
Isa. 30: 23. *thy cattle* feed in large pastures.
Jer. 9: 10(9). hear the voice of *the cattle;*
49: 32. multitude of *their cattle* a spoil:
Eze. 38: 12. which have gotten *cattle* and
13. to take away *cattle* and goods,

מִקְנָה *mik-nāh'*, f. 4736

Gen 17: 12. *or bought with* money of any
13. *and he that is bought with* thy money,
23. all *that were bought with* his money,
27. *and bought with* money of the stranger,
23: 18. Unto Abraham *for a possession*
Ex. 12: 44. servant *that is bought for* money,
Lev. 25: 16. shalt increase *the price thereof,*
— diminish *the price of it:*
51. money *that he was bought* for.
27: 22. field which *he hath bought,*
Jer. 32: 11, 12, 16. the evidence of *the purchase,*
12. the book of *the purchase,*
14. this evidence of *the purchase,*

מִקְסָם *mik-sam'*, m. 4738

Eze. 12: 24. vain vision *nor* flattering *divination*
13: 7. *and* have ye not spoken *a* lying *divination,*

מִקְצוֹעַ *mik-tzōh'-ăğ*, m. 4740

Ex. 26: 24. they shall be for *the* two *corners.*
36: 29. he did to both of them in both *the corners.*
2Ch 26: 9. at *the turning* (of the wall),
Neh 3: 19, 20, 24, 25. *the turning* (of the wall).
Eze. 41: 22. *and the corners thereof,* and the length thereof,
46: 21. by *the* four *corners of* the court; and, behold, *in every corner* of the court (there was) a court. (marg. a court *in a corner of* a court, and a court *in a corner of* a court)
22. In *the* four *corners of* the court

מַקְצֻעוֹת *mak-tzoo-ğōhth'*, f. pl. 4741

Isa. 44: 13. he fitteth it *with planes,*

מְקֻצְעֹת *m'koo-tz'ğōhth'*, f. pl. 4742

Ex. 26: 23. make *for the corners of* the tabernacle
36: 28. made he *for the corners of* the tabernacle

מָקַק [māh-kak'].

✻ NIPHAL.—*Preterite.* ✻

Ps. 38: 5(6). My wounds stink (and) *are corrupt*
Isa. 34: 4. *And* all the host of heaven *shall be dissolved,*
Eze. 4:17. *and consume away* for their iniquity.
24:23. *but ye shall pine away* for your iniquities,

NIPHAL.—*Future.*

Lev. 26:39. they that are left of you *shall pine away*
— *shall they pine away* with them.
Zec. 14:12. their eyes *shall consume away* their holes, and their tongue *shall consume away*

NIPHAL.—*Participle.*

Eze. 33:10. we *pine away* in them,

✻ HIPHIL.—*Infinitive.* ✻

Zec. 14:12. Their flesh *shall consume away*

4744
מִקְרָא *mik-rāh'*, m.

Ex. 12:16, 16. *an* holy *convocation,*
Lev. 23: 2, 4, 37. holy *convocations,*
3, 7, 8, 21, 24, 27, 35, 36. *an* holy *convocation;*
Nu. 10: 2. *for the calling of* the assembly,
28:18, 25, 26 & 29: 1, 7, 12. *an* holy *convocation;*
Neh 8: 8. caused (them) to understand *the reading.*
Isa. 1:13. the calling of *assemblies,*
4: 5. upon *her assemblies,*

4745
מִקְרֶה *mik-reh'*, m.

Ru. 2: 3. *her hap* was to light on a part of the field
1Sa. 6: 9. *a chance* (that) happened to us.
20:26. *Something hath befallen* him,
Ecc. 2:14. *that* one *event* happeneth to them all.
15. *As it happeneth* to the fool,
3:19. *that which befalleth* the sons of men *befalleth* beasts; even one thing *befalleth* them:
9: 2. one *event* to the righteous,
3. one *event* unto all:

4746
מְקָרֶה *m'kāh-reh'*, m.

Ecc. 10:18. By much slothfulness *the building*

4747
מְקֵרָה *m'kēh-rāh'*, f.

Jud. 3:20. he was sitting in a *summer* parlour, (marg. a parlour of *cooling*)
24. covereth his feet in his *summer* chamber.

4749
מִקְשָׁה *mik-shāh'*, f.

Ex. 25:18. (of) *beaten work* shalt thou make them,
31. (of) *beaten work* shall the candlestick be made:
36. one *beaten work* (of) pure gold.
37: 7. two cherubims...*beaten out of one piece*
17. (of) *beaten work* made he the candlestick;
22. one *beaten work* (of) pure gold.
Nu. 8: 4. the candlestick (was of) *beaten* gold,
— unto the flowers thereof, (was) *beaten work:*
10: 2. of *a whole piece* shalt thou make
Jer. 10: 5. They (are) *upright* as the palm tree,

4750
מִקְשָׁה *mik-shāh'*, f.

Isa. 1: 8. as a lodge *in a garden of cucumbers,*

4748
מִקְשֶׁה *mik-sheh'*, m.

Isa. 3:24. instead of *well set hair* (lit. the work of *curling*) baldness;

מַר *mar*, adj. 4751

Gen 27:34. a great *and* exceeding *bitter* cry,
Ex. 15:23. waters of Marah, for they (were) *bitter:*
Nu. 5:18. the *bitter* water that causeth the curse:
19. be thou free from this *bitter* water
23. blot (them) out with the *bitter* water:
24. to drink the *bitter* water
—, 27. enter into her, (and become) *bitter.*
Jud. 18:25. lest *angry* (marg. *bitter of* soul) fellows run upon thee,
Ru. 1:20. not Naomi, call me *Mara:* (marg. *Bitter*)
1Sa. 1:10. she (was) *in bitterness* (lit. *bitter*) of soul,
15:32. Surely the *bitterness of* death is past.
22: 2. every one (that was) *discontented,* (marg *bitter of* soul)
2Sa. 2:26. it will be *bitterness* in the latter end?
17: 8. *and* they (be) *chafed in* their minds, (marg. *and bitter of* soul)
Est. 4: 1. cried with a loud *and* a *bitter* cry;
Job 3:20. life *unto the bitter* (in) soul;
7:11. I will complain *in the bitterness of* my soul.
10: 1. I will speak *in the bitterness of* my soul.
21:25. another dieth in *the bitterness* of his soul,
Ps. 64: 3(4). (to shoot) their arrows, (even) *bitter*
Pro. 5: 4. her end is *bitter* as wormwood,
27: 7. the hungry soul every *bitter* thing is sweet.
31: 6. *unto those that be of heavy* hearts. (marg *bitter of* soul)
Ecc. 7:26. more *bitter* than death the woman,
Isa. 5:20. put *bitter* for sweet, and sweet *for bitter!*
33: 7. ambassadors of peace shall weep *bitterly*
38:15. *in the bitterness of* my soul.
17. for peace I had *great* bitterness:
Jer. 2:19. (it is) an evil (thing) *and bitter,*
4:18. thy wickedness, because it is *bitter,*
Eze. 3:14. I went *in bitterness,* (marg. *bitter*)
27:30. and shall cry *bitterly,*
31. they shall weep for thee *with bitterness of* heart (and) *bitter* wailing.
Am. 8:10. the end thereof as a *bitter* day.
Hab. 1: 6. Chaldeans, (that) *bitter* and hasty nation,
Zep. 1:14. the mighty man shall cry there *bitterly.*

מַר *mar*, m. 4752

Isa. 40:15. *as a drop* of a bucket,

מֹר *mōhr*, m. 4753

Ex. 30:23. of pure *myrrh* five hundred (shekels),
Est. 2:12. six months with oil of *myrrh,*
Ps. 45: 8(9). All thy garments (smell) of *myrrh,*
Pro. 7:17. I have perfumed my bed with *myrrh,*
Cant. 1:13. A bundle of *myrrh*
3: 6. perfumed with *myrrh* and frankincense,
4: 6. I will get me to the mountain of *myrrh,*
14. *myrrh* and aloes, with all the chief spices:
5: 1. I have gathered *my myrrh*
5. my hands dropped (with) *myrrh,* and my fingers (with) sweet smelling *myrrh,*
13. dropping sweet smelling *myrrh.*

מָרָא [māh-rāh']. 4754

✻ KAL.—*Participle.* Poel. ✻

Zep. 3: 1. Woe to *her that is filthy* and polluted,

✻ HIPHIL.—*Future.* ✻

Job 39:18. *she lifteth up herself* on high,

מָרֵא *māh-rēh'*, Ch. m. 4756

Dan. 2:47. *and a Lord of* kings,
4:19(16). *My lord,* the dream (be) to them
24(21). which is come upon *my lord*
5:23. thyself against *the Lord* of heaven;

4759 **מַרְאָה** *mar-āh'*, f.

Gen46: 2. God spake unto Israel *in the visions of* the
Ex. 38: 8. *of the lookingglasses* (marg. or, *brasen glasses*) of (the women)
Nu. 12: 6. make myself known...*in a vision,*
1Sa. 3:15. Samuel feared to shew Eli *the vision.*
Eze. 1: 1. I saw *visions of* God.
8: 3. brought me *in the visions of* God
40: 2. *In the visions of* God brought he me
43: 3. *and the visions* (were) like the vision
Dan10: 7. I Daniel alone saw *the vision:* for the men...saw not *the vision;*
8. saw this great *vision,*
16. *by the vision* my sorrows are turned

4758 **מַרְאֶה** *mar-eh'*, m.

Gen 2: 9. pleasant *to the sight* and good for food;
12:11. a fair woman *to look upon:*
24:16. the damsel (was) very fair *to look upon,* (marg. good of *countenance*)
26: 7. she (was) fair *to look upon.*
29:17. Rachel was beautiful and well *favoured.*
39: 6. (a) goodly (person), and well *favoured.*
41: 2. seven well *favoured* kine
3. seven other kine...ill *favoured*
4. the ill *favoured* and leanfleshed kine did eat up the seven well *favoured*
21. *but they* (were) still ill *favoured,* (lit. *and their appearance* was bad)
Ex. 3: 3. see this great *sight,*
24:17. *And the sight of* the glory of the Lord
Lev.13: 3. *and* the plague *in sight* (be) deeper than
4. *in sight* (be) not deeper
12. wheresoever the priest *look*eth; (lit. to all *the sight of* the eyes of the priest)
20. *in sight* lower than the skin,
25. *and* it (be in) *sight* deeper than the skin;
30. *in sight* deeper than the skin;
31. not *in sight* deeper than the skin,
32. *and* the scall (be) not *in sight* deeper than the skin;
34. *nor* (be) in *sight* deeper than the skin;
43. *as* the leprosy *appeareth*
14:37. *which in sight* (are) lower than
Nu. 8: 4. *according unto the pattern* which
9:15. *as it were the appearance of* fire,
16. *and the appearance of* fire by night.
12: 8. speak mouth to mouth, *even apparently,*
Deu28:34. *for the sight of* thine eyes
67. *and for the sight of* thine eyes which thou
Jos. 22:10. a great altar *to see to.*
Jud.13: 6. A man of God came unto me, *and his countenance* (was) *like the countenance of* an angel
1Sa.16: 7. Look not on *his countenance,*
17:42. ruddy, and of *a* fair *countenance.*
2Sa.11: 2. very beautiful *to look upon.*
14:27. a woman of *a* fair *countenance.*
23:21. an Egyptian, a *goodly* man: (marg. a man of *countenance,* or, *sight*)
Est. 1:11. she (was) fair *to look on.* (marg. good of *countenance*)
2: 2. Let there be *fair* (lit. good of *countenance*) young virgins sought for
3. all the *fair* (lit. *id.*) young virgins
7. the maid (was) fair and *beautiful;* (marg. and good of *countenance*)
Job 4:16. I could not discern *the form thereof:*
41: 9(1). cast down even at *the sight of him?*
Ecc. 6: 9. *the sight of* the eyes
11: 9. *in the sight of* thine eyes:
Cant.2:14. let me see *thy countenance,*
— *thy countenance* (is) comely.
5:15. *his countenance* (is) as Lebanon,
Isa. 11: 3. shall not judge *after the sight of* his eyes,
52:14. *his visage* was so marred
53: 2. no *beauty* that we should desire
Eze. 1: 5. this (was) *their appearance;*
13. *their appearance* (was) like burning coals of fire, (and) *like the appearance of* lamps:
14. *as the appearance of* a flash of lightning.
16. *The appearance of* the wheels
— *and their appearance* and their work
26. *as the appearance of* a sapphire
Eze. 1:26. *as the appearance of* a man
27. *as the appearance of* fire round about within it, *from the appearance of* his loins even upward, *and from the appearance of* his
— *as it were the appearance of* fire,
28. *As the appearance of* the bow
— *the appearance of* the brightness round about. This (was) *the appearance of* the
8: 2. a likeness *as the appearance of* fire: *from the appearance of* his loins
— *as the appearance of* brightness,
4. *according to the vision* that I saw
10: 1. *as the appearance of* the likeness of a throne.
9. *and the appearance of* the wheels
10. *And* (as for) *their appearances,*
22. *their appearances* and themselves:
11:24. brought me *in a vision* by the Spirit
— *the vision* that I had seen
23:15. all of them princes *to look to,*
16. *as soon as* she saw them (marg. *at the sight of* her eyes)
40: 3. a man, *whose appearance* (was) *like the appearance of* brass,
41:21. *the appearance* (of the one) *as the appearance* (of the other).
42:11. *like the appearance of* the chambers
43: 3. *And* (it was) *according to the appearance of the vision* which I saw, (even) *according to the vision* that I saw
— *like the vision* that I saw
Dan. 1: 4. Children...well *favoured* (lit. good of *countenance*)
13. let *our countenances* be looked upon before thee, *and the countenance of* the children
15. *their countenances* appeared fairer
8:15. *as the appearance of* a man.
16. make this (man) to understand *the vision.*
26. *And the vision of* the evening and the
27. I was astonished at *the vision,*
9:23. consider *the vision.*
10: 1. had understanding *of the vision.*
6. *as the appearance of* lightning,
18. *like the appearance of* a man,
Joel 2: 4. *The appearance of them* (is) *as the appearance of* horses;
Nah. 2: 4(5). *they shall seem* (marg. *their show*) like torches,

---

מֻרְאָה [*moor-āh*], f. 4760

Lev. 1:16. he shall pluck away *his crop*

מְרַאֲשֹׁת *m'rah-ăshōhth'*, f. pl. 4763

Gen28:11. he took of the stones...and put (them for) *his pillows,*
18. the stone that he had put (for) *his pillows,*
1Sa.19:13. a pillow of goats' (hair) *for his bolster,*
16. a pillow of goats' (hair) *for his bolster.*
26: 7. spear stuck in the ground *at his bolster:*
11. the spear that (is) *at his bolster,*
16. the cruse of water that (was) *at his bolster.*
1K. 19: 6. cruse of water *at his head.* (marg. *bolster*)

מַרְאָשׁוֹת *mar-āh-shōhth'*, f. pl. 4761

Jer. 13:18. *your principalities* (marg. or, *head tires*) shall come down,

---

מַרְבַדִּים *mar-vad-deem'*, m. pl. 4765

Pro. 7:16. decked my bed with *coverings of tapestry,*
31:22. She maketh herself *coverings of tapestry;*

מַרְבֶּה *mar-beh'*, m. 4766

Isa. 9: 7(6). *Of the increase of* (his) government
33:23. the prey of a *great* spoil divided;

4767 **מִרְבָּה** *mir-bāh'*, f.

Eze.23:32. and had in derision; it containeth *much.*

4768 **מַרְבִּית** *mar-beeth'*, f.

Lev.25:37. *nor* lend him thy victuals *for increase.*
1Sa. 2:33. all *the increase of* thine house shall die
1Ch 12:29. *the greatest part of them* had kept the ward
2Ch 9: 6. *the greatness of* thy wisdom
30:18. *a multitude of* the people,

4769 **מַרְבֵּץ** *mar-bēhtz'*, m.

Zep. 2:15. *a place* for beasts *to lie down in!*

4769 **מִרְבַּץ** *mir-batz'*, m.

Eze.25: 5. *a couchingplace* for flocks:

4770 **מַרְבֵּק** *mar-bēhk'*, m.

1Sa.28:24. woman had a *fat* calf (lit. calf of *the stall*)
Jer. 46:21. her hired men (are)...like *fatted* bullocks; (marg. bullocks of *the stall*)
Am. 6: 4. out of the midst of *the stall;*
Mal. 4: 2(3:20). grow up as calves of *the stall.*

4771 **מַרְגּוֹעַ** *mar-gōh'ăg*, m.

Jer. 6:16. ye shall find *rest* for your souls.

4772 **מַרְגְּלוֹת** *mar-g'lōhth'*, f. pl.

Ru. 3: 4. uncover *his feet*, and lay thee down;
7. she came softly, and uncovered *his feet*,
8. a woman lay at *his feet.*
14. she lay at *his feet* until the morning:
Dan10: 6. his arms *and his feet* like in colour to polished brass,

---

4773 **מַרְגֵּמָה** *mar-gēh-māh'*, f.

Pro.26: 8. he that bindeth a stone *in a sling*, (marg. or, putteth a (precious) stone *in an heap of stones*)

4774 **מַרְגֵּעָה** *mar-gēh-gāh'*, f.

Isa. 28:12. this (is) *the refreshing:*

4775 **מָרַד** [*māh-rad'*].

* KAL.—*Preterite.* *

Gen14: 4. in the thirteenth year *they rebelled.*
2K. 18:20. *thou rebellest* against me?
2Ch 36:13. *he* also *rebelled* against king
Isa. 36: 5. *thou rebellest* against me?
Eze. 2: 3. nation that *hath rebelled* against me:
Dan. 9: 5. done wickedly, *and have rebelled*,
9. though *we have rebelled* against him;

KAL.—*Infinitive.*

Jos. 22:16. *that ye might rebel* this day
29. God forbid *that* we should *rebel*
Neh. 6: 6. thou and the Jews think *to rebel:*

KAL.—*Future.*

Nu. 14: 9. *rebel* not *ye* against the Lord,
Jos. 22:18. *ye rebel* to day against the Lord,
19. *rebel* not against the Lord, nor *rebel* against
2K. 18: 7. *and he rebelled* against the king of Assyria,
24: 1. he turned *and rebelled*
20. *that* Zedekiah *rebelled* against
2Ch 13: 6. and *hath rebelled* against his lord.
Neh. 9:26. *and rebelled* against thee,
Jer. 52: 3. *that* Zedekiah *rebelled*
Eze.17:15. *But he rebelled* against him

KAL.—*Participle.* Poel.

Neh. 2:19. *will* ye *rebel* against the king?
Job 24:13. *of those that rebel against* the light;
Eze. 2: 3. a *rebellious* nation that hath rebelled
20:38. will purge out from among you *the rebels*,

מְרַד *m'rad*, Ch. m. 4776

Ezr. 4:19. *and* (that) *rebellion* and sedition have been

מֶרֶד *meh'-red*, m. 4777

Jos. 22:22. if (it be) *in rebellion*, or if in transgression

---

מָרָד [*māh-rāhd'*], Ch. adj. 4779

Ezr. 4:12. building the *rebellious* and the bad city,
15. and know that this city (is) a *rebellious* city,

מַרְדּוּת *mar-dooth'*, f. 4780

1Sa.20:30. Thou son of the perverse *rebellious* (marg. perverse *rebellion*) woman,

---

מֻרְדָּף *moor-dāhph'*, m. 4783

Isa. 14: 6. ruled the nations in anger, *is persecuted*,

מָרָה *māh-rāh'*. 4784

* KAL.—*Preterite.* *

Nu. 20:24. *ye rebelled* against my word
27:14. *ye rebelled* against my commandment
1Sa.12:15. *but rebel* against the commandment
1K. 13:21. *thou hast disobeyed* the mouth of the Lord,
26. the man of God, who *was disobedient*
Ps. 5:10(11). *they have rebelled* against thee.
105:28. *they rebelled* not against his word.
Isa. 1:20. if ye refuse *and rebel*,
50: 5. *I was* not *rebellious*,
63:10. *they rebelled*, and vexed his holy Spirit:
Jer. 4:17. *she hath been rebellious* against me,
Lam.1:18. *I have rebelled* against his commandment:
20. *I have* grievously *rebelled:*
3:42. We have transgressed *and have rebelled:*
Hos.13:16(14:1). *she hath rebelled* against her God:

KAL.—*Infinitive.*

Lam.1:20. I have *grievously* rebelled: (lit. *rebelling* I have rebelled)

KAL.—*Participle.* Poel.

Nu. 20:10. Hear now, *ye rebels;*
Deu 21:18. a man have a stubborn *and rebellious* son,
20. This our son (is) stubborn *and rebellious*,
2K. 14:26. the affliction of Israel, (that it was) very *bitter:*
Ps. 78: 8. a stubborn *and rebellious* generation;
Jer. 5:23. a revolting *and a rebellious* heart;

* HIPHIL.—*Preterite.* *

Ps.106:33. *they provoked* his spirit,
107:11. *they rebelled against* the words of God,

HIPHIL.—*Infinitive.*

Job 17: 2. and doth not mine eye continue *in their provocation?*
Ps. 78:17. *by provoking* the most high in the
Isa. 3: 8. *to provoke* the eyes of his glory.

HIPHIL.—*Future.*

Deu 1:26, 43. *but rebelled* against the commandment
9:23. *then ye rebelled* against the commandment
Jos. 1:18. Whosoever (he be) that *doth rebel*
1Sa.12:14. not *rebel* against the commandment
Neh. 9:26. were disobedient, *and rebelled* against thee,

Ps. 78:40. How oft *did they provoke* (marg. or, *rebel against*) *him*
56. tempted *and provoked* the most high God,
106: 7. *but provoked* (him) at the sea,
43. *they provoked* (him) with their counsel,
Eze. 5: 6. *And she hath changed* my judgments
20: 8. *But they rebelled* against me,
13. *But* the house of Israel *rebelled* against me
21. *Notwithstanding* the children *rebelled*

HIPHIL.—*Participle.*

Deu 9: 7, 24 & 31:27. ye have been *rebellious*

4787 מָרָּה [*mor-rāh'*], f.

Pro. 14:10. The heart knoweth his own *bitterness*; (marg. *the bitterness of* his soul)

4786 מֹרָה [*mōh-rāh'*], f.

Gen26:35. *a grief of* mind (marg. *bitterness of* spirit) unto Isaac

---

4788 מָרוּד [*māh-rood'*], m.

Isa. 58: 7. poor that *are cast out* (marg. or, *afflicted*)
Lam 1: 7. days of her affliction *and of her miseries*
3:19. mine affliction *and my misery*,

4790 מְרוֹחַ *m'rō'ăgh*, adj. m. const.

Lev. 21:20. or hath his stones *broken*;

4791 מָרוֹם *māh-rōhm'*, m.

Jud. 5:18. in *the high places of* the field.
2Sa. 22:17. He sent *from above*,
2K. 19:22. lifted up thine eyes *on high?*
23. *the height of* the mountains,
Job 5:11. To set up *on high* those that be low;
16:19. my record (is) *on high*. (marg. *in the high places*)
25: 2. he maketh peace *in his high places*.
31: 2. inheritance of the Almighty *from on high?*
39:18. lifteth up herself *on high*,
Ps. 7: 7(8). return thou *on high*.
10: 5. judgments (are) *far above* out of his sight:
18:16(17). He sent *from above*,
56: 2(3). that fight against me, *O thou most high*.
68:18(19). Thou hast ascended *on high*,
71:19. Thy righteousness also, O God, (is) very *high*,
73: 8. they speak *loftily*.
75: 5(6). Lift not up your horn *on high*:
92: 8(9). thou, Lord, (art most) *high*
93: 4. The Lord *on high* (is) mightier than
102:19(20). down *from the height of* his sanctuary;
144: 7. Send thine hand *from above*,
148: 1. praise him *in the heights*.
Pro. 8: 2. in the top of *high places*,
9: 3. *the highest places of* the city,
14. on a seat in *the high places*
Ecc. 10: 6. Folly is set *in great dignity*, (marg. *heights*)
Isa. 22:16. heweth him out a sepulchre *on high*,
24: 4. the *haughty* people of the earth
18. the windows *from on high*
21. the host of *the high ones* (that are) *on high*,
26: 5. them that dwell *on high*;
32:15. the spirit be poured upon us *from on high*,
33: 5. he dwelleth *on high*:
16. He shall dwell *on high*: (marg. *heights*, or, *high places*)
37:23. lifted up thine eyes *on high?*
24. *the height of* the mountains,
— *the height of* his border,
38:14. mine eyes fail (with looking) *upward*:
40:26. Lift up your eyes *on high*,
57:15. I dwell in the *high* and holy (place),
58: 4. to make your voice to be heard *on high*.
Jer. 17:12. A glorious *high* throne
25:30. The Lord shall roar *from on high*,
31:12. sing *in the height of* Zion,
49:16. that holdest *the height of* the hill:
51:53. she should fortify *the height of* her strength,
Lam 1:13. *From above* hath he sent fire
Eze. 17:23 & 20:40. In the mountain of *the height of*
34:14. *the high* mountains of Israel
Obad. 3. whose habitation (is) *high*;
Mic. 6: 6. bow myself before the *high* God?
Hab. 2: 9. that he may set his nest *on high*,

מֵרוֹץ *mēh-rōhtz'*, m. 4793

Ecc. 9:11. *the race* (is) not to the swift,

מְרוּצָה [*m'roo-tzāh'*], f. 4794, 4835

2Sa. 18:27. *the running of* the foremost is like *the running of* Ahimaaz
Jer. 8: 6. every one turned *to his course*,
22:17. for oppression, and *for violence*, (marg. or, *incursion*)
23:10. *their course* (marg. or, *violence*) is evil,

מְרוּקִים [*m'roo-keem'*], m. pl. 4795

Est. 2:12. the days of *their purifications*

מַרְזֵחַ *mar-zēh'ăgh*, m. 4798

Jer. 16: 5. Enter not into the house of *mourning*, (marg. or, *mourning feast*)

מִרְזַח *mir-zagh'*, m. 4797

Am. 6: 7. *the banquet of* them that stretched

מָרַח [*māh-ragh'*]. 4799

* KAL.—*Future.* *

Isa. 38:21. lump of figs, *and lay* (it) *for a plaister*

מֶרְחָב *mer-ghāhv'*, m. 4800

2Sa. 22:20. brought me forth also *into a large place*:
Ps. 18:19(20). me forth also *into a large place*;
31: 8(9). hast set my feet *in a large room*.
118: 5. (set me) *in a large place*.
Hos. 4:16. feed them as a lamb *in a large place*.
Hab. 1: 6. *through the breadth* (marg. *breadths*) *of*

מֶרְחָק *mer-ghāhk'*, m. 4801

2Sa. 15:17. in a place *that was far off*.
Ps. 138: 6. the proud he knoweth *afar off*.
Pro. 25:25. good news from a *far* country.
31:14. she bringeth her food *from afar*.
Isa. 8: 9. all ye of *far* countries:
10: 3. desolation (which) shall come *from far?*
13: 5. They come from a *far* country,
17:13. they shall flee *far off*,
30:27. the name of the Lord cometh *from far*,
33:17. the land *that is very far off*. (marg. of *far distances*)
46:11. my counsel from a *far* country:
Jer. 4:16. watchers come from a *far* country,
5:15. bring a nation upon you *from far*,
6:20. the sweet cane from a *far* country?
8:19. them *that dwell in a far* country: (marg. the country of *them that are far off*)
31:10. in the isles *afar off*,
Eze. 23:40. sent for men to come *from far*,
Zec 10: 9. remember me *in far countries*;

4802 **מַרְחֶשֶׁת** *mar-gheh'-sheth*, f.

Lev. 2: 7. a meat offering (baken) *in the fryingpan,*
7: 9. all that is dressed *in the fryingpan,*

4803 **מָרַט** [*māh-rat'*].

* KAL.—*Infinitive.* *

Eze.21:11(16). he hath given it *to be furbished,*

KAL.—*Future.*

Ezr. 9: 3. *and plucked off* the hair of my head
Neh 13:25. *and plucked off their hair,*

KAL.—*Participle.* Poel.

Isa. 50: 6. my cheeks *to them that plucked off the hair:*

KAL.—*Participle.* Paül.

Eze.21. 9(14). is sharpened, and also *furbished:*
28(33). for the slaughter (it is) *furbished,*
29:18. every shoulder (was) *peeled:*

* NIPHAL.—*Future.* *

Lev.13:40. whose *hair is fallen off* (marg. head *is pilled*)
41. he that *hath his hair fallen off*

* PUAL.—*Participle.* *

1K. 7:45. (of) *bright* brass. (marg. brass *made bright,* or, *scoured*)
Isa. 18: 2. a nation scattered and *peeled,*
7. a people scattered *and peeled,*
Eze.21:10(15). it *is furbished* that it may glitter:
11(16). and it *is furbished,*

4804 **מְרַט** [*m'rat*], Ch.

* P'IL.—*Preterite.* *

Dan 7: 4. till the wings thereof *were plucked,*

4805 **מְרִי** *m'ree*, m.

Nu. 17:10(25). a token against *the rebels;* (marg. children of *rebellion*)
Deu 31:27. I know *thy rebellion,*
1Sa.15:23. *rebellion* (is as) the sin of witchcraft,
Neh 9:17. *in their rebellion* appointed a captain
Job 23: 2. Even to day (is) my complaint *bitter:*
Pro.17:11. evil (man) seeketh only *rebellion:*
Isa. 30: 9. this (is) a *rebellious* people,
Eze. 2: 5. they (are) a *rebellious* house,
6. though they (be) a *rebellious* house.
7. they (are) *most rebellious.* (marg. *rebellion*)
8. thou *rebellious* like that *rebellious* house:
3: 9. though they (be) a *rebellious* house.
26, 27. they (are) a *rebellious* house.
12: 2. in the midst of a *rebellious* house,
— they (are) a *rebellious* house.
3. though they (be) a *rebellious* house.
9. the house of Israel, the *rebellious* house,
25. for in your days, O *rebellious* house,
17:12. Say now to the *rebellious* house,
24: 3. utter a parable unto the *rebellious* house,
44: 6. thou shalt say to *the rebellious,*

4806 **מְרִיא** *m'ree*, m.

2Sa. 6:13. he sacrificed oxen *and fatlings.*
1K. 1: 9. sheep and oxen *and fat cattle*
19, 25. hath slain oxen *and fat cattle*
Isa. 1:11. the fat of *fed beasts;*
11: 6. the young lion *and the fatling*
Eze.39:18. all of them *fatlings of* Bashan.
Am. 5:22. the peace offerings *of your fat beasts.*

4808 **מְרִיבָה** *m'ree-vāh'*, f.

Gen13: 8. Let there be no *strife,*
Ex. 17: 7. called the name of the place Massah, *and Meribah,* (marg. *Chiding,* or, *Strife*)
Nu. 20:13. This (is) the water of *Meribah;* (marg. *Strife*)
24. at the water of *Meribah.*
Nu. 27:14. *in the strife of* the congregation,
— that (is) the water of *Meribah in* Kadesh
Deu32:51. the waters of *Meribah*-Kadesh, (marg. or, *strife* at Kadesh)
33: 8. at the waters of *Meribah;*
Ps. 81: 7(8). waters of *Meribah.* (marg. *strife*)
95: 8. your heart, *as in the provocation,* (marg. *contention*)
106:32. (him) also at the waters of *strife,*
Eze.47:19. to the waters of *strife* (marg. or, *Meribah*)
48:28. the waters of *strife* (in) Kadesh, (marg. *Meribah*-kadesh)

מְרִירוּת *m'ree-rooth'*, f. 4814

Eze.21: 6(11). *and with bitterness* sigh before their

מְרִירִי *m'ree-ree'*, adj. 4815

Deu32:24. and with *bitter* destruction:

מֹרֶךְ *mōh'-rech*, m. 4816

Lev.26:36. I will send *a faintness* into their hearts

מֶרְכָּב [*mer-kāhv'*], m. 4817

Lev.15: 9. what *saddle* soever he rideth upon
1K. 4:26(5:6). stalls of horses *for his chariots,*
Cant.3:10. *the covering of it* (of) purple,

מֶרְכָּבָה *mer-kāh-vāh'*, f. 4818

Gen41:43. he made him to ride in *the* second *chariot*
46:29. Joseph made ready *his chariot,*
Ex. 14:25. took off *their chariot* wheels,
15: 4. Pharaoh's *chariots* and his host
Jos. 11: 6. burn *their chariots* with fire.
9. burnt *their chariots* with fire.
Jud. 4:15. Sisera lighted down off (his) *chariot,*
5:28. why tarry the wheels of *his chariots?*
1Sa. 8:11. will take your sons,...*for his chariots,*
— (some) shall run before *his chariots.*
2Sa.15: 1. Absalom prepared him *chariots* and
1K. 7:33. like the work of a *chariot* wheel:
10:29. *a chariot* came up and went out of
12:18. made speed to get him up *to his chariot,*
20:33. caused him to come up into *the chariot.*
22:35. the king was stayed up *in* his *chariot*
2K. 5:21. he lighted down from *the chariot*
26. the man turned again from *his chariot*
9:27. Smite him also in *the chariot.*
10:15. took him up to him into *the chariot.*
23:11. burned *the chariots of* the sun
1Ch 28:18. *the chariot* of the cherubims,
2Ch 1:17. brought forth out of Egypt *a chariot*
9:25. thousand stalls for horses *and chariots,*
10:18. made speed to get him up *to* (his) *chariot,*
14: 9(8). *and* three hundred *chariots;*
18:34. the king of Israel stayed (himself) up *in* (his) *chariot*
35:24. took him out of *that chariot,*
Cant.6:12. (like) *the chariots of* Amminadib.
Isa. 2: 7. neither (is there any) end *of their chariots:*
22:18. *the chariots of* thy glory
66:15. with *his chariots* like a whirlwind,
Jer. 4:13. *his chariots* (shall be) as a whirlwind:
Joel 2: 5. Like the noise of *chariots*
Mic. 1:13. bind *the chariot* to the swift beast:
5:10(9). I will destroy *thy chariots:*
Nah 3: 2. the pransing horses, *and* of *the* jumping *chariots.*
Hab 3: 8. *thy chariots* of salvation?
Hag 2:22. I will overthrow *the chariots,*
Zec. 6: 1. there came four *chariots*
2. *In the* first *chariot* (were) red horses; *and in the* second *chariot* black horses;
3. *in the* third *chariot* white horses; *and in the* fourth *chariot* grisled and bay

4819 מַרְכֹּלֶת [*mar-kōh'-leth*], f.

Eze.27:24. of cedar, *among thy merchandise.*

4820 מִרְמָה *mir-māh'*, f.

Gen27:35. Thy brother came *with subtilty,*
34:13. the sons of Jacob answered...*deceitfully,*
2K. 9:23. (There is) *treachery,* O Ahaziah.
Job 15:35. their belly prepareth *deceit.*
31: 5. if my foot hath hasted to *deceit;*
Ps. 5: 6(7). the bloody *and deceitful* man. (marg. man of bloods *and deceit*)
10: 7. His mouth is full of cursing *and deceit* (marg. *deceits*)
17: 1. my prayer, (that goeth) not out of *feigned* lips.
24: 4. unto vanity, nor sworn *deceitfully.*
34:13(14). and thy lips from speaking *guile.*
35:20. they devise *deceitful* matters
36: 3(4). The words of his mouth (are) iniquity *and deceit:*
38:12(13). *and* imagine *deceits* all the day long.
43: 1. me from the *deceitful* and unjust man. (marg. a man of *deceit* and iniquity)
50:19. thy tongue frameth *deceit.*
52: 4(6). O (thou) *deceitful* tongue.
55:11(12). deceit *and guile* depart not
23(24). bloody and *deceitful* men (marg. men of bloods *and deceit*)
109: 2. and the mouth of *the deceitful* (marg. *deceit*) are opened
Pro.11: 1. A *false* balance (marg. Balances of *deceit*) (is) abomination to the Lord:
12: 5. the counsels of the wicked (are) *deceit.*
17. a false witness *deceit.*
20. *Deceit* (is) in the heart of them that imagine evil:
14: 8. the folly of fools (is) *deceit.*
25. a *deceitful* (witness) speaketh lies.
20:23. and a *false* balance (marg. balances of *deceit*) (is) not good.
26:24. layeth up *deceit* within him;
Isa. 53: 9. neither (was any) *deceit* in his mouth.
Jer. 5:27. their houses full of *deceit:*
9: 6(5). Thine habitation (is) in the midst of *deceit; through deceit* they refuse to know me,
8(7). it speaketh *deceit:*
Dan 8:25. he shall cause *craft* to prosper
11:23. he shall work *deceitfully:*
Hos11:12(12:1). *and* the house of Israel *with deceit:*
12: 7(8). the balances of *deceit* (are) in his hand:
Am. 8: 5. falsifying the balances by *deceit?*
Mic. 6:11. the bag of *deceitful* weights?
Zep. 1: 9. houses with violence *and deceit.*

4823 מִרְמָס *mir-māhs'*, m.

Isa. 5: 5. it shall be *trodden down:* (marg. *for a treading*)
7:25. *for the treading of* lesser cattle.
10: 6. *to tread them down* (marg. to lay them *a treading*) like the mire
28:18. ye shall be *trodden down* (marg. *a treading down* to it)
Eze.34:19. *that which ye have trodden with* your feet;
Dan. 8:13. the host *to be trodden under foot?*
Mic. 7:10. now shall she be *trodden down*

4828 מֵרֵעַ [*mēh-rēh'ăg*], m.

Gen26:26. Ahuzzath *one of his friends,*
Jud.14:11. they brought thirty *companions*
20. wife was (given) *to his companion,*
15: 2. I gave her *to thy companion:*
6. given her *to his companion.*
2Sa. 3: 8. to his brethren, *and to his friends,*
Pro.19: 7. do *his friends* go far from him?

4829 מִרְעֶה *mir-geh'*, m.

Gen47: 4. thy servants have no *pasture*
1Ch 4:39. to seek *pasture* for their flocks.
40. they found fat *pasture*
41. *pasture* there for their flocks.
Job 39: 8. range of the mountains (is) *his pasture,*
Isa. 32:14. *a pasture of* flocks;
Lam. 1: 6. like harts (that) find no *pasture,*
Eze.34:14. I will feed them *in a* good *pasture,*
— *and* (in) *a* fat *pasture* shall they feed
18. eaten up *the* good *pasture,*
— the residue of *your pastures?*
Joel 1:18. are perplexed, because they have no *pasture;*
Nah. 2:11(12). *and the feedingplace* of the young lions,

מַרְעִית *mar-geeth'*, f. 4830

Ps. 74: 1. the sheep of *thy pasture?*
79:13. thy people and sheep of *thy pasture*
95: 7. we (are) the people of *his pasture,*
100: 3. his people, and the sheep of *his pasture.*
Isa. 49: 9. *their pastures* (shall be) in all high places.
Jer. 10:21. all *their flocks* shall be scattered.
23: 1. the sheep of *my pasture!*
25:36. the Lord hath spoiled *their pasture.*
Eze.34:31. the flock of *my pasture,*
Hos13: 6. *According to their pasture,* so were they

מַרְפֵּא *mar-pēh'*, m. 4832

2Ch 21:18. the Lord smote him...with an *incurable* (lit. no *curing*) disease.
36:16. the wrath of the Lord arose...till (there was) no *remedy.* (marg. *healing*)
Pro. 4:22. *health* (marg. *medicine*) to all their flesh.
6:15. shall he be broken without *remedy.*
12:18. the tongue of the wise (is) *health.*
13:17. a faithful ambassador (is) *health.*
16:24. *and health* to the bones.
29: 1. be destroyed, and that without *remedy.*
Jer. 8:15. We looked...for a time of *health,*
14:19. (there is) no *healing* for us?
— and for the time of *healing,*
33: 6. I will bring it health *and cure,*
Mal. 4: 2(3:20). the Sun of righteousness arise *with healing*

מַרְפֵּא *mar-pēh'*, m. 4832

Pro.14:30. A *sound* heart (is) the life of the flesh:
15: 4. A *wholesome* tongue (marg. *The healing of* the tongue) (is) a tree of life:
Ecc.10: 4. *yielding* pacifieth great offences.

מִרְפָּשׂ *mir-pas'*, m. 4833

Eze.34:19. *and* they drink *that which ye have fouled with* your feet.

מָרַץ [*māh-ratz'*]. 4834

* NIPHAL.—*Preterite.* *

Job 6:25. How *forcible are* right words!

NIPHAL.—*Participle.*

1K. 2: 8. cursed me with a *grievous* (marg. *strong*) curse
Mic. 2:10. even with a *sore* destruction.

* HIPHIL.—*Future.* *

Job 16: 3. what *emboldeneth thee* that thou answerest?

מַרְצֵעַ *mar-tzēh'ăg*, m. 4836

Ex. 21: 6. shall bore his ear through *with an aul;*
Deu15:17. Then thou shalt take *an aul,*

מַרְצֶפֶת *mar-tzeh'-pheth*, f. 4837

2K. 16:17. put it upon *a pavement of* stones.

4838 מָרַק [*māh-rāk'*].

✻ KAL.—*Imperative.* ✻

Jer. 46: 4. *furbish* the spears, (and) put on

KAL.—*Participle.* Paül.

2Ch 4:16. for the house of the Lord of *bright* (marg. *made bright*, or, *scoured*) brass.

✻ PUAL.—*Preterite.* ✻

Lev. 6:28(21). *it shall be both scoured*, and rinsed

4839, 6564 מָרָק *māh-rak'*, m.

Jud. 6:19. *and* he put *the broth* in a pot,
20. pour out *the broth.*
Isa. 65: 4. *and broth* (marg. *pieces*) *of* abominable (things)

4841 מֶרְקָחָה *mer-kāh-ghāh'*, f.

Job 41:31(23). maketh the sea *like a pot of ointment.*
Eze.24:10. consume the flesh, and spice it *well*, (lit. season it with *a seasoning of spices*)

4840 מֶרְקָחִים *mer-kāh-gheem'*, m. pl.

Cant.5:13. cheeks (are) as a bed of spices, (as) *sweet* flowers: (marg. or, towers of *perfumes*)

4842 מִרְקַחַת *mir-kah'-ghath*, f.

Ex. 30:25. an ointment *compound* (lit. an ointment of *ointment*)
1Ch 9:30. sons of the priests made *the ointment*
2Ch 16:14. (spices) *prepared by the apothecaries' art:*

4843 מָרַר [*māh-rar'*].

✻ KAL.—*Preterite.* ✻

Ru. 1:13. for *it grieveth* me much (marg. I *have* much *bitterness*)
1Sa.30: 6. the soul of all the people *was grieved*, (marg. *bitter*)
2K. 4:27. her soul *is vexed* (marg. *bitter*)
Isa. 38:17. I *had* great *bitterness:*
Lam. 1: 4. she *is in bitterness.* (lit. *is bitter* to her)

KAL.—*Future.*

Isa. 24: 9. strong drink *shall be bitter*

✻ PIEL.—*Future.* ✻

Gen49:23. The archers *have sorely grieved him*,
Ex. 1:14. *And they made* their lives *bitter*
Isa. 22: 4. *I will* weep *bitterly*, (marg. *I will be bitter* in weeping)

✻ HIPHIL.—*Preterite.* ✻

Ru. 1:20. the Almighty *hath dealt* very *bitterly*
Job 27: 2. the Almighty, (who) *hath vexed* my soul; (marg. *made* my soul *bitter*)

HIPHIL.—*Infinitive.*

Zec.12:10. *and shall be in bitterness* for him, *as one that is in bitterness* for

HIPHIL.—*Future.*

Ex. 23:21. *provoke* him not;

✻ HITHPALPEL.—*Future.* ✻

Dan. 8: 7. *and he was moved with choler*
11:11. *And* the king of the south *shall be moved with choler*,

4845 מְרֵרָה [*m'rēh-rāh'*], f.

Job 16:13. he poureth out *my gall*

4846 מְרֹרָה [*m'rōh-rāh'*], f.

Deu32:32. their clusters (are) *bitter:*
Job 13:26. thou writest *bitter things* against me,
20:14. *the gall of* asps within him.
25. the glittering sword cometh *out of his gall:*

מְרוֹרִים *m'rōh-reem'*, m. pl. 4844

Ex. 12: 8. with *bitter* (herbs) they shall eat it.
Nu. 9:11. unleavened bread *and bitter* (herbs).
Lam 3:15. me *with bitterness*, (marg. *bitternesses*)

מִרְשַׁעַת *mir-shah'-gath*, f. 4849

2Ch 24: 7. Athaliah, *that wicked woman*,

מְרָתַיִם *m'rāh-thah'-yim*, f. dual. 4850

Jer. 50:21. up against the land of *Merathaim*, (marg. or, *the rebels.* lit. *double rebellion*)

מַשָּׂא *mas-sāh'*, m. 4853

Ex. 23: 5. the ass...lying under *his burden*,
Nu. 4:15. *the burden of* the sons of Kohath
19. every one to his service and to *his burden:*
24. to serve, *and for burdens:*
27. the Gershonites, in all *their burdens*,
— unto them in charge all *their burdens.*
31. the charge of *their burden*,
32. instruments of the charge of *their burden.*
47. the service of *the burden* in the tabernacle
49. according to *his burden:*
11:11. *the burden of* all this people
17. they shall bear *the burden of* the people
Deu 1:12. *your burden*, and your strife?
2Sa.15:33. thou shalt be *a burden* unto me:
19:35(36). should thy servant be yet *a burden*
2K. 5:17. two mules' *burden* of earth?
8: 9. forty camels' *burden*,
9:25. the Lord laid this *burden* upon
1Ch 15:22. Chenaniah,...(was) *for song* (marg. *lifting up*): he instructed *about the song*, (marg. or, (was) *for the carriage:* he instructed *about the carriage*)
27. the master of *the song* (marg. or, *carriage*)
2Ch 17:11. presents, and *tribute* silver;
20:25. jewels,...more than *they could carry away:*
24:27. the greatness of *the burdens* (laid) upon
35: 3. *a burden* upon (your) shoulders:
Neh 10:31(32). *and the exaction of* every debt.
13:15. all (manner of) *burdens*,
19. (that) there should no *burden* be brought
Job 7:20. I am *a burden* to myself?
Ps. 38: 4(5). *as an* heavy *burden* they are too
Pro.30: 1. the son of Jakeh, (even) *the prophecy:*
31: 1. king Lemuel, *the prophecy* that his mother taught him.
Isa. 13: 1. *The burden of* Babylon,
14:28. that king Ahaz died was this *burden.*
15: 1. *The burden of* Moab.
17: 1. *The burden of* Damascus.
19: 1. *The burden of* Egypt.
21: 1. *The burden of* the desert of the sea.
11. *The burden of* Dumah.
13. *The burden* upon Arabia.
22: 1. *The burden of* the valley of vision.
25. *the burden* that (was) upon it
23: 1. *The burden of* Tyre.
30: 6. *The burden of* the beasts of the south:
46: 1. *a burden* to the weary (beast).
2. they could not deliver *the burden*,
Jer. 17:21. bear no *burden* on the sabbath day,
22. Neither carry forth *a burden*
24. to bring in no *burden*
27. not to bear *a burden*,
23:33. What (is) *the burden of* the Lord?
— shalt then say unto them, What *burden?*
34. that shall say, *The burden of* the Lord,
36. *And the burden of* the Lord
— every man's word shall be his *burden;*
38. ye say, *The burden of* the Lord;
— this word, *The burden of* the Lord,
— not say, *The burden of* the Lord;
Eze.12:10. This *burden* (concerneth) the prince
24:25. *that whereupon they set* their minds, (marg. *the lifting up of* their soul)
Hos. 8:10. *for the burden of* the king
Nah 1: 1. *The burden of* Nineveh.
Hab 1: 1. *The burden* which Habakkuk the prophet
Zec. 9: 1 & 12:1. *The burden of* the word of the
Mal. 1: 1. *The burden of* the word of the Lord

4856 **מַשֹּׂא** *mas-sōh*, m.

2Ch 19: 7. with the Lord...*nor respect of* persons,

4858 **מַשָּׂאָה** *mas-sāh-āh'*, f.

Isa. 30.27. *the burden* (marg. or, *grievousness of flame*) (thereof is) heavy:

4864 **מַשְׂאֵת** *mas-ēhth'*, f.

Gen 43:34. he took (and sent) *messes* unto them
— but Benjamin's *mess* was five times so much *as* any of their's. (lit. *than the messes of* all)
Jud.20:38. make *a great flame* (marg. *elevation*)
40. *But when the flame* began to arise
2Sa.11: 8. followed him *a mess* (of meat) *from*
2Ch 24: 6. bring in out of Judah...*the collection*,
9. to bring in to the Lord *the collection*
Est. 2:18. he made a release...and gave *gifts*,
Ps.141: 2. *the lifting up of* my hands
Jer. 6: 1. set up *a sign of fire*
40: 5. the guard gave him victuals *and a reward*,
Lam.2:14. false *burdens* and causes of banishment.
Eze.20:40. the firstfruits of *your oblations*,
Am. 5:11. *and* ye take from him *burdens of* wheat:
Zep. 3:18. the reproach of it (was) *a burden*.

4869 **מִשְׂגָּב** *mis-gāhv'*, m.

2Sa.22: 3. *my high tower*, and my refuge,
Ps. 9: 9(10). be *a refuge* (marg. *an high place*) for the oppressed, *a refuge* in times of
18: 2(3). my salvation, (and) *my high tower*.
46: 7(8), 11(12). God of Jacob (is) our *refuge*. (marg. *an high place* for us)
48: 3(4). known in her palaces *for a refuge*.
59: 9(10), 17(18). God (is) *my defence*. (marg. *high place*)
16(17). thou hast been my *defence*
62: 2(3), 6(7). (he is) *my defence*; (marg. *high place*)
94:22. the Lord is my *defence*;
144: 2. my fortress; *my high tower*,
Isa. 25:12. the fortress of *the high fort of*
33:16. *his place of defence* (shall be) the
Jer. 48: 1. *Misgab* (marg. or, *the high place*) is

4881 **מְשׂוּכָה** [*m'soo-chāh'*], f.

Pro.15:19. slothful (man is) *as an hedge of* thorns:
Isa. 5: 5. I will take away *the hedge thereof*,

4883 **מַשּׂוֹר** *mas-sōhr'*, m.

Isa. 10:15. shall *the saw* magnify itself

4884 **מְשׂוּרָה** *m'soo-rāh'*, f.

Lev.19:35. in meteyard, in weight, *or in measure*.
1Ch 23:29. all manner of *measure* and size;
Eze. 4:11. Thou shalt drink also water *by measure*,
16. they shall drink water *by measure*,

4885 **מָשׂוֹשׂ** *māh-sōhs'*, m.

Job 8:19. *the joy of* his way,
Ps. 48: 2(3). *the joy of* the whole earth,
Isa. 8: 6. *and rejoice* in Rezin and Remaliah's son;
24: 8. *The mirth of* tabrets ceaseth,
— *the joy of* the harp ceaseth.
11. *the mirth of* the land is gone.
32:13. all the houses of *joy*
14. *a joy of* wild asses,
60:15. *a joy of* many generations.
62: 5. *and* (as) the bridegroom *rejoiceth*
65:18. Jerusalem a rejoicing, and her people *a joy*.
66:10. rejoice for *joy* with her,
Jer. 49:25. the city of *my joy*!
Lam. 2:15. *The joy of* the whole earth?
5:15. *The joy of* our heart is ceased;
Eze. 24:25. *the joy of* their glory,
Hos. 2:11(13). I will also cause all *her mirth* to cease,

מִשְׂחָק *mis-ghāhk'*, m. 4890

Hab. 1:10. the princes shall be *a scorn*

מַשְׂטֵמָה *mas-tēh'-māh'*, f. 4895

Hos. 9: 7. for the multitude of thine iniquity, and *the* great *hatred*.
8. *hatred* in the house of his God.

מַשְׂכִּית *mas-keeth'*, f. 4906

Lev.26: 1. (any) *image* of stone (marg. a stone of *picture*, or, *figured* stone) in your land.
Nu. 33:52. destroy all *their pictures*,
Ps. 73: 7. they have more than heart *could wish*. (marg. pass *the thoughts of* the heart)
Pro.18:11. as an high wall *in his own conceit*.
25:11. apples of gold *in pictures of* silver.
Eze. 8:12. in the chambers of *his imagery*?

מַשְׂכֹּרֶת *mas-kōh'-reth*, f. 4909

Gen 29:15. tell me, what (shall) *thy wages* (be)?
31: 7. changed *my wages* ten times;
41. thou hast changed *my wages*
Ru. 2:12. *a* full *reward* be given thee of the Lord (lit. let *thy reward* be full)

מַשְׂמְרוֹת *mas-m'rōhth'*, f. pl. 4930

Ecc.12:11. *and as nails* fastened (by) the masters of

מִשְׂפָּח *mis-pāh'gh'*, m. 4939

Isa. 5: 7. he looked for judgment, but behold *oppression*;

מִשְׂרָה *mis-rāh'*, f. 4951

Isa. 9: 6(5). *the government* shall be upon his
7(6). Of the increase of (his) *government*

מִשְׂרְפוֹת [*mis-rāh-phōhth'*], f. pl. 4955-56

Jos. 11: 8. Zidon, and unto *Misrephoth*-maim, (marg. *burnings*, or, *salt pits*)
13: 6. from Lebanon unto *Misrephoth*-maim,
Isa. 33:12. the people shall be (as) *the burnings of* lime:
Jer. 34: 5. *and with the burnings of* thy fathers,

מַשְׂרֵת *mas-rēhth'*, f. 4958

2Sa.13: 9. she took *a pan*, and poured

מַשָּׁא *mash-shāh'*, m. 4855

Neh 5: 7. Ye exact *usury*,
10. let us leave off this *usury*.

מַשְׁאַבִּים *mash-ab-beem'*, m. pl. 4857

Jud. 5:11. the noise of archers in *the places of drawing water*,

מַשָּׁאָה [*mash-shāh-āh'*], f. 4859

Deu 24:10. When thou dost lend thy brother any *thing*, (marg. *the loan of* any thing)
Pro.22:26. them that are sureties *for debts*.

מַשָּׁאוֹן *mash-shāh -ōhn'*, m. 4860

Pro.26:26 (Whose) hatred is covered *by deceit*,

4862 **מִשְׁאָלָה** [*mish-āh-lāh'*], f.

Ps. 20: 5(6). the Lord fulfil all *thy petitions.*
37: 4. *the desires of* thine heart.

4863 **מִשְׁאֶרֶת** [*mish-eh'-reth*], f.

Ex. 8: 3(7:28). into thine ovens, and *into thy kneadingtroughs:* (marg. or, *dough*)
12:34. *their kneadingtroughs* (marg. or, *dough*) being bound up
Deu 28: 5. Blessed (shall be) thy basket *and thy store.*
17. Cursed (shall be) thy basket *and thy store.*

4865 **מִשְׁבְּצוֹת** *mish-b'tzōhth'*, f. pl.

Ex. 28:11. set *in ouches of* gold.
13. thou shalt make *ouches* (of) gold;
14. fasten the wreathen chains to *the ouches.*
25. thou shalt fasten in *the* two *ouches,*
39: 6. onyx stones inclosed in *ouches of* gold,
13. (they were) inclosed in *ouches of* gold
16. they made two *ouches* (of) gold,
18. they fastened in *the* two *ouches,*
Ps. 45:13(14). her clothing (is) *of wrought* gold.

4866 **מַשְׁבֵּר** *mash-bēhr'*, m.

2K. 19: 3. the children are come to *the birth,*
Isa. 37: 3. the children are come to *the birth,*
Hos 13:13. *in* (the place of) *the breaking forth of* children.

4867 **מִשְׁבָּר** *mish-bāhr'*, m.

2Sa. 22: 5. When *the waves* (marg. or, *pangs*) *of* death compassed me,
Ps. 42: 7(8). all *thy waves* and thy billows are gone over me.
88: 7(8). afflicted (me) with all *thy waves.*
93: 4. *the* mighty *waves of* the sea.
Jon. 2: 3(4). all *thy billows* and thy waves passed over me.

4868 **מִשְׁבַּתִּים** [*mish-bat-teem'*], m. pl.

Lam. 1: 7. the adversaries saw her, (and) did mock *at her sabbaths.* (perhaps lit. *destructions*)

4870' **מִשְׁגֶּה** *mish-geh'*, m.

Gen 43:12. peradventure it (was) *an oversight:*

4871 **מָשָׁה** [*māh-shāh'*].

* KAL.—*Preterite.* *

Ex. 2:10. *I drew him* out of the water.

* HIPHIL.—*Future.* *

2Sa. 22:17. *he drew me* out of many waters;
Ps. 18:16(17). *he drew me* out of many waters.

4874 **מַשֶּׁה** [*mash-sheh'*], m.

Deu 15: 2. Every creditor (marg. master of *the lending of* his hand) that lendeth

---

4875 **מְשׁוֹאָה** *m'shōh-āh'*, f.

Job 30: 3. in former time desolate *and waste.*
38:27. satisfy the desolate *and waste* (ground);
Zep 1:15. a day of wasteness *and desolation,*

4876 **מַשּׁוּאוֹת** *mash-shoo-ōhth'*, f. pl.

Ps. 73:18. castedst them down *into destruction.*
74: 3. *unto the* perpetual *desolations;*

מְשׁוּבָה *m'shoo-vāh'*, f. 4878

Pro. 1:32. *the turning away of* the simple
Jer. 2:19. *and thy backslidings* shall reprove thee:
3: 6. (that) which *backsliding* Israel hath done?
8. *backsliding* Israel committed adultery
11. The *backsliding* Israel hath justified herself
12. Return, thou *backsliding* Israel,
22. I will heal *your backslidings.*
5: 6. *their backslidings* are increased.
8: 5. slidden back by *a* perpetual *backsliding?*
14: 7. *our backslidings* are many;
Hos 11: 7. my people are bent *to backsliding from me:*
14: 4(5). I will heal *their backsliding,*

מְשׁוּגָה [*m'shoo-gāh'*], f. 4879

Job 19: 4. *mine error* remaineth with myself.

מָשׁוֹט *māh-shōht'*, m. 4880

Eze. 27:29. all that handle *the oar,*

מִשּׁוֹט [*mish-shōht'*], m. 4880

Eze. 27: 6. (Of) the oaks of Bashan have they made *thine oars;*

מְשׁוּסָּה *m'shoos-sāh'*, f. 4882

Isa. 42:24. (כתיב) Who gave Jacob *for a spoil,*

מָשַׁח *māh-shagh'*. 4886

* KAL.—*Preterite.* *

Gen 31:13. where *thou anointedst* the pillar,
Ex. 28:41. *and shalt anoint them,* and consecrate them,
29: 7. pour (it) upon his head, *and anoint* him.
36. *and thou shalt anoint* it, to sanctify it.
30:26. *And thou shalt anoint* the tabernacle
40: 9. *and anoint* the tabernacle,
10. *And thou shalt anoint* the altar
11. *And thou shalt anoint* the laver
13. the holy garments, *and anoint* him,
15. *And thou shalt anoint* them, as *thou didst anoint* their father,
Nu. 35:25. the high priest, which *was anointed*
1Sa. 9:16. *and thou shalt anoint him* (to be) captain
10: 1. the Lord *hath anointed thee*
16: 3. *and thou shalt anoint* unto me (him)
2Sa. 2: 7. the house of Judah *have anointed* me king
5:17. *they had anointed* David
12: 7. *I anointed thee* king
19:10(11). Absalom, whom *we anointed*
1K. 1:34. *And let* Zadok the priest and Nathan the prophet *anoint* him
5: 1(15). *they had anointed* him king
19:15. *and* when thou comest, *anoint* Hazael
2K. 9: 3, 6, 12. *I have anointed thee* king
2Ch 22: 7. whom the Lord *had anointed* (lit. *anointed him*)
Ps. 45: 7(8). thy God, *hath anointed thee*
89:20(21). with my holy oil *have I anointed him:*
Isa. 61: 1. the Lord *hath anointed* me to preach

KAL.—*Infinitive.*

Lev. 7:36. in the day *that he anointed* them,
Jud. 9: 8. The trees went forth (on a time) *to anoint* a king
1Sa. 15: 1. The Lord sent me *to anoint thee*
Jer. 22:14. with cedar, *and painted* with vermilion.
Dan. 9:24. *and to anoint* the most Holy.

KAL.—*Imperative.*

1Sa. 16:12. the Lord said, Arise, *anoint him:*
Isa. 21: 5. arise, ye princes, (and) *anoint* the shield

KAL.—*Future.*

Ex. 30:30. *thou shalt anoint* Aaron
Lev. 8:10. *and anointed* the tabernacle
11. *and anointed* the altar

Lev. 8:12. *and anointed* him, to sanctify him.
16:32. And the priest, whom *he shall anoint*,
Nu. 7: 1. set up the tabernacle, *and had anointed* it,
— the vessels thereof, *and had anointed them*,
1Sa. 15:17. *and* the Lord *anointed thee* king
16:13. *and anointed* him in the midst of his
2Sa. 2: 4. *and* there *they anointed* David king
5: 3. *and they anointed* David king
1K. 1:39. *and anointed* Solomon.
45. *And* Zadok the priest and Nathan...*have anointed* him king
19:16. Jehu the son of Nimshi *shalt thou anoint*
— Elisha...*shalt thou anoint*
2K. 11:12. they made him king, *and anointed him*;
23:30. *and anointed* him, and made him king
1Ch 11: 3. *and they anointed* David king
29:22. *and anointed* (him) unto the Lord
2Ch 23:11. *And* Jehoiada and his sons *anointed him*,
Am. 6: 6. *anoint themselves* with the chief

KAL.—*Participle*. Poel.

Jud. 9:15. If in truth ye *anoint* me king

KAL.—*Participle*. Paül.

Ex. 29: 2. wafers unleavened *anointed* with oil:
Lev. 2: 4 & 7:12. unleavened wafers *anointed* with
Nu. 3: 3. the priests *which were anointed*,
6:15. wafers of unleavened bread *anointed*
2Sa. 3:39. (am) this day weak, *though anointed* king;

* NIPHAL.—*Preterite*. *

1Ch 14: 8. David *was anointed* king

NIPHAL.—*Infinitive*.

Lev. 6:20(13). in the day *when* he *is anointed*;
Nu. 7:10. in the day *that* it *was anointed*,
84. in the day *when* it *was anointed*,
88. after *that* it *was anointed*.

4887 **מְשַׁח** *m'shagh'*, Ch. m.

Ezr. 6: 9. wheat, salt, wine, *and oil*,
7:22. and to an hundred baths of *oil*,

4888 **מִשְׁחָה** *mish-'ghāh'*, f.

Ex. 25: 6. spices for *anointing* oil,
29: 7. Then shalt thou take the *anointing* oil,
21. and of the *anointing* oil,
30:25. an oil of holy *ointment*,
— it shall be an holy *anointing* oil.
31. This shall be *an* holy *anointing* oil
31:11. And the *anointing* oil,
35: 8. and spices for *anointing* oil,
15. and the *anointing* oil,
28. and for the *anointing* oil,
37:29. he made the holy *anointing* oil,
39:38. and the *anointing* oil,
40: 9. thou shalt take the *anointing* oil,
Lev. 7:35. (the portion) of *the anointing of* Aaron, *and of the anointing of* his sons,
8: 2. and the *anointing* oil,
10. Moses took the *anointing* oil,
12. he poured of the *anointing* oil
30. Moses took of the *anointing* oil,
10: 7. the *anointing* oil *of* the Lord
21:10. whose head the *anointing* oil was poured,
12. the crown of the *anointing* oil
Nu. 4:16. and the *anointing* oil,

4888 **מָשְׁחָה** *mosh-'ghāh'*, f.

Ex. 29:29. *to be anointed* therein,
40:15. *their anointing* shall surely be
Nu. 18: 8. given them *by reason of the anointing*,

4889 **מַשְׁחִית** *mash-'gheeth'*, f.

Ex. 12:13. be upon you *to destroy* (you), (marg. *for a destruction*)
2K. 23:13. the right hand of the mount of *corruption*,
2Ch 20:23. every one helped *to destroy* (marg. *for the destruction*) another.
22: 4. death of his father *to* his *destruction*.
Jer. 5:26. they set *a trap*, they catch men.
Jer. 51:25. against thee, O *destroying* mountain,
Eze. 5:16. which shall be *for* (their) *destruction*,
9: 6. Slay *utterly* (marg. *to destruction*) old (and) young,
21:31(36). skilful *to destroy*.
25:15. *to destroy* (it) for the old hatred;
Dan 10: 8. was turned in me *into corruption*,

מִשְׁחָר *mish-'ghāhr'*, m. 4891

Ps. 110: 3. the womb of *the morning*:

מַשְׁחֵת *mash-'ghēhth'*, f. 4892

Eze. 9: 1. *his destroying* weapon in his hand.

מִשְׁחַת *mish-'ghath'*, m. 4893

Isa. 52:14. his visage was so *marred*

מָשְׁחָת *mosh-'ghāhth'*, m. 4893

Lev. 22:25. *their corruption* (is) in them,

מִשְׁטוֹחַ *mish-tōh'ăgh*, m. 4894

Eze. 47:10. *a* (place) *to spread forth* nets;

מִשְׁטַח *mish-tagh'*, m. 4894

Eze. 26: 5. (a place for) *the spreading of* nets
14. (a place) *to spread* nets *upon*;

מִשְׁטָר *mish-tāhr'*, m. 4896

Job 38:33. canst thou set *the dominion thereof* in

מֶשִׁי *meh'-shee*, m. 4897

Eze. 16:10. I covered thee *with silk*.
13. thy raiment (was of) fine linen, *and silk*,

מָשִׁיחַ *mah-shee'ăgh*, adj. m. 4899

Lev. 4: 3, 5, 16. the priest *that is anointed*
6:22(15). the priest of his sons *that is anointed*
1Sa. 2:10. and exalt the horn of *his anointed*.
35. he shall walk before *mine anointed*
12: 3. before the Lord, and before *his anointed*:
5. *his anointed* (is) witness this day,
16: 6. the Lord's *anointed* (is) before him. (lit. before the Lord (is) *his anointed*)
24: 6(7). unto my master, the Lord's *anointed*,
—(–). he (is) *the anointed of* the Lord.
10(11). he (is) the Lord's *anointed*.
26: 9. his hand *against* the Lord's *anointed*,
11. mine hand *against* the Lord's *anointed*:
16. your master, the Lord's *anointed*.
23. *against* the Lord's *anointed*.
2Sa. 1:14. to destroy the Lord's *anointed*?
16. I have slain the Lord's *anointed*.
21. (as though he had) not (been) *anointed*
19:21(22). he cursed the Lord's *anointed*?
22:51. sheweth mercy *to his anointed*,
23: 1. *the anointed of* the God of Jacob,
1Ch 16:22. Touch not *mine anointed*,
2Ch 6:42. turn not away the face of *thine anointed*:
Ps. 2: 2. against the Lord, and against *his anointed*,
18:50(51). sheweth mercy *to his anointed*,
20: 6(7). the Lord saveth *his anointed*;
28: 8. the saving strength of *his anointed*.
84: 9(10). look upon the face of *thine anointed*.
89:38(39). hast been wroth with *thine anointed*.
51(52). the footsteps of *thine anointed*.
105:15. Touch not *mine anointed*,
132:10. turn not away the face of *thine anointed*.

Ps.132:17. I have ordained a lamp *for mine anointed.*
Isa. 45: 1. Thus saith the Lord *to his anointed,*
Lam. 4:20. *the anointed of* the Lord, was taken in their
Dan 9:25. unto *the Messiah* the Prince
26. shall *Messiah* be cut off,
Hab 3:13. for salvation with *thine anointed;*

4900 **מָשַׁךְ** *māh-shach'.*

* KAL.—*Preterite.* *

Deu 21: 3. which *hath* not *drawn* in the yoke;
Jud. 4: 6. *and draw* toward mount Tabor,
7. *And I will draw* unto thee to the river
1K. 22:34. a (certain) man *drew* a bow
2Ch 18:33. a (certain) man *drew* a bow
Job 24:22. *He draweth also* the mighty
Jer. 31: 3. with lovingkindness *have I drawn thee.*
Hos. 7: 5. *he stretched out* his hand with

KAL.—*Infinitive.*

Ex. 19:13. *when* the trumpet *soundeth long,*
Jos. 6: 5. *when they make a long* (blast)
Ps. 10: 9. *when he draweth him* into his net.
Ecc. 2: 3. *to give* myself unto wine, (marg. *to draw* my flesh with wine)

KAL.—*Imperative.*

Ex. 12:21. *Draw out* and take you a lamb
Ps. 36:10(11). O *continue* (marg. *draw out at length*)
Cant. 1: 4. *Draw me,* we will run after thee:
Eze. 32:20. *draw* her and all her multitudes.

KAL.—*Future.*

Gen 37:28. *and they drew* and lifted up Joseph
Jud. 20:37. *and* the liers in wait *drew* (themselves) *along,*
Neh 9:30. *Yet* many years *didst thou forbear* (marg. *protract over*)
Job 21:33. every man *shall draw* after him,
41: 1(40:25). *Canst thou draw out* leviathan
Ps. 28: 3. *Draw me* not away with the wicked,
85: 5(6). *wilt thou draw out* thine anger
Jer. 38:13. *So they drew* up Jeremiah
Hos 11: 4. *I drew them* with cords

KAL.—*Participle.* Poel.

Jud. 5:14. *they that handle* (marg. *draw with*) the pen of the writer.
Ps. 109:12. Let there be none *to extend* mercy
Isa. 5:18. *them that draw* iniquity with cords of vanity,
66:19. *that draw* the bow,
Am. 9:13. *him that soweth* (marg. *draweth forth*) seed;

* NIPHAL.—*Future.* *

Isa. 13:22. her days *shall* not *be prolonged.*
Eze. 12:25. *it shall be* no more *prolonged:*
28. There *shall* none of my words *be prolonged*

* PUAL.—*Participle.* *

Pro. 13:12. Hope *deferred* maketh the heart sick:
Isa. 18: 2. a nation *scattered* and peeled,
7. a people *scattered* and peeled,

4901 **מֶשֶׁךְ** *meh'-shech,* m.

Job 28:18. *for the price of* wisdom (is) above rubies.
Ps. 126: 6. He that goeth forth and weepeth, bearing *precious* seed, (marg. or, seed *basket*)

4904 **מִשְׁכָּב** *mish-kāhv',* m.

Gen 49: 4. thou wentest up to thy father's *bed;*
Ex. 8: 3(7:28). *bed*chamber, and upon thy bed,
21:18. but keepeth (his) *bed:*
Lev. 15: 4. Every *bed,* whereon he lieth
5. whosoever toucheth *his bed*
21. whosoever toucheth *her bed*
23. if it (be) on (her) *bed,*
24. all *the bed* whereon he lieth
26. Every *bed* whereon she lieth
— unto her *as the bed of* her separation:
18:22. not lie with mankind, *as with* womankind: (lit. *the lying of* a woman)
Lev. 20:13. *as he lieth with* a woman, (lit. *the lying of* a woman)
Nu. 31:17. woman that hath known man *by lying with* him.
18. known a man *by lying with* him, (lit. known *the lying of* a man)
35. known man *by lying with* him.
Jud. 21:11. that hath *lain by* man. (marg. knoweth *the lying* (with) man)
12. known no man *by lying with* any male:
2Sa. 4: 5. who lay on *a bed* at noon.
7. he lay on his bed in *his bed*chamber.
11. in his own house upon *his bed?*
11: 2. David arose from off *his bed,*
13. he went out to lie *on his bed*
13: 5. Lay thee down on *thy bed,*
17:28. Brought *beds,* and basons,
1K. 1:47. the king bowed himself upon *the bed.*
2K. 6:12. words that thou speakest in *thy bed*-chamber.
2Ch 16:14. laid him *in the bed*
Job 7:13. *my couch* shall ease my complaint;
33:15. in slumberings upon *the bed;*
19. chastened also with pain upon *his bed,*
Ps. 4: 4(5). commune with your own heart upon *your bed,*
36: 4(5). He deviseth mischief upon *his bed;*
41: 3(4). wilt make all *his bed* in his sickness.
149: 5. let them sing aloud upon *their beds.*
Pro. 7:17. I have perfumed *my bed*
22:27. why should he take away *thy bed*
Ecc. 10:20. curse not the rich in *thy bed*chamber:
Cant 3: 1. By night on *my bed* I sought him
Isa. 57: 2. they shall rest in *their beds,*
7. high mountain hast thou set *thy bed:*
8. thou hast enlarged *thy bed,*
— lovedst *their bed* where thou sawest
Eze. 23:17. came to her *into the bed of* love,
32:25. They have set her *a bed*
Hos. 7:14. they howled upon *their beds:*
Mic 2: 1. work evil upon *their beds!*

מִשְׁכַּב [*mish-kav'*], Ch. m. 4903

Dan 2:28. the visions of thy head upon *thy bed,*
29. came (into thy mind) upon *thy bed,*
4: 5(2). and the thoughts upon *my bed*
10(7). the visions of mine head in *my bed;*
13(10). the visions of my head upon *my bed,*
7: 1. and visions of his head upon *his bed:*

מִשְׁכָּן *mish-kāhn',* m. 4908

Ex. 25: 9. the pattern of *the tabernacle,*
26: 1. thou shalt make *the tabernacle*
6. it shall be one *tabernacle.*
7. to be a covering upon *the tabernacle:*
12. hang over the backside of *the tabernacle.*
13. hang over the sides of *the tabernacle*
15. shalt make boards *for the tabernacle*
17. for all the boards of *the tabernacle.*
18. make the boards *for the tabernacle,*
20. the second side of *the tabernacle*
22. for the sides of *the tabernacle*
23. make for the corners of *the tabernacle*
26. the boards of the one side of *the tabernacle,*
27. the other side of *the tabernacle,*
— the boards of the side of *the tabernacle,*
30. thou shalt rear up *the tabernacle*
35. the table on the side of *the tabernacle*
27: 9. shalt make the court of *the tabernacle:*
19. All the vessels of *the tabernacle*
35:11. *The tabernacle,* his tent,
15. at the entering in of *the tabernacle,*
18. The pins of *the tabernacle,*
36: 8. wrought the work of *the tabernacle*
13. so it became one *tabernacle.*
14. for the tent over *the tabernacle:*
20, 23. he made boards *for the tabernacle*
22. for all the boards of *the tabernacle.*
25. for the other side of *the tabernacle,*
27. for the sides of *the tabernacle*
28. for the corners of *the tabernacle*
31. boards of the one side of *the tabernacle,*

Ex. 36:32. the other side of *the tabernacle*,
— bars for the boards of *the tabernacle*
38:20. all the pins *of the tabernacle*,
21. This is the sum of *the tabernacle*, (even) of *the tabernacle of* testimony,
31. and all the pins of *the tabernacle*,
39:32. Thus was all the work of *the tabernacle of*
33. they brought *the tabernacle*
40. the vessels of the service of *the tabernacle*,
40: 2. set up *the tabernacle of* the tent
5. hanging of the door *to the tabernacle*.
6. the door of *the tabernacle of*
9. anoint *the tabernacle*,
17. *the tabernacle* was reared up.
18. Moses reared up *the tabernacle*,
19. spread abroad the tent over *the tabernacle*,
21. brought the ark into *the tabernacle*,
22. the side of *the tabernacle* northward,
24. on the side of *the tabernacle*
28. hanging (at) the door *of the tabernacle*.
29. the door of *the tabernacle of* the tent
33. the court round about *the tabernacle*
34, 35. glory of the Lord filled *the tabernacle*.
36. taken up from over *the tabernacle*,
38. of the Lord (was) upon *the tabernacle*
Lev. 8:10. anointed *the tabernacle* and all
15:31. when they defile *my tabernacle*
17: 4. before *the tabernacle of* the Lord;
26:11. I will set *my tabernacle* among
Nu. 1:50. Levites over *the tabernacle of* testimony,
— they shall bear *the tabernacle*,
— shall encamp round about *the tabernacle*.
51. when *the tabernacle* setteth forward,
— and when *the tabernacle* is to be pitched,
53. pitch round about *the tabernacle of*
— shall keep the charge *of the tabernacle of*
3: 7, 8. to do the service of *the tabernacle*.
23. pitch behind *the tabernacle*
25. *the tabernacle*, and the tent,
26. which (is) by *the tabernacle*,
29. pitch on the side of *the tabernacle*
35. pitch on the side of *the tabernacle*
36. the boards of *the tabernacle*,
38. those that encamp before *the tabernacle*
4:16. the oversight of all *the tabernacle*,
25. shall bear the curtains of *the tabernacle*,
26. which (is) by *the tabernacle*
31. the boards of *the tabernacle*,
5:17. that is in the floor of *the tabernacle*
7: 1. had fully set up *the tabernacle*,
3. brought them before *the tabernacle*.
9:15. day that *the tabernacle* was reared up the cloud covered *the tabernacle*,
— even there was upon *the tabernacle*
18. the cloud abode upon *the tabernacle*
19. cloud tarried long upon *the tabernacle*
20. cloud was a few days upon *the tabernacle*;
22. the cloud tarried upon *the tabernacle*,
10:11. taken up from off *the tabernacle of*
17. *the tabernacle* was taken down;
— bearing *the tabernacle*.
21. did set up *the tabernacle*
16: 9. to do the service of *the tabernacle of*
24. from about *the tabernacle of* Korah,
27. they gat up from *the tabernacle of* Korah,
17:13(28). near unto *the tabernacle of* the Lord
19:13. defileth *the tabernacle of* the Lord;
24: 5. *thy tabernacles*, O Israel!
31:30, 47. the charge of *the tabernacle of* the Lord.
Jos. 22:19. wherein the Lord's *tabernacle* dwelleth,
29. that (is) before *his tabernacle*.
2Sa. 7: 6. walked in a tent *and in a tabernacle*.
1Ch. 6:32(17). ministered before *the dwelling place of*
48(33). manner of service of *the tabernacle of*
16:39. the priests, before *the tabernacle of*
17: 5. *and from* (one) *tabernacle*
21:29. *For the tabernacle of* the Lord,
23:26. shall no (more) carry *the tabernacle*,
2Ch 1: 5. had made, he put before *the tabernacle of*
29: 6. *from the habitation of* the Lord,
Job 18:21. such (are) *the dwellings of* the wicked,
21:28. (are) the *dwelling* places *of* the wicked? (marg. the tent of *the tabernacles*)
39: 6. and the barren land *his dwellings*.
Ps. 26: 8. the place where thine honour *dwelleth*. (marg. of *the tabernacle of* thy honour)
43: 3. thy holy hill, and to *thy tabernacles*.
Ps. 46: 4(5). *the tabernacles of* the most high.
49:11(12). *their dwelling places* to all generations,
74: 7. *the dwelling place of* thy name
78:28. round about *their habitations*.
60. he forsook *the tabernacle of* Shiloh,
84: 1(2). How amiable (are) *thy tabernacles*,
87: 2. Zion more than all *the dwellings of* Jacob.
132: 5. *an habitation* (marg. *habitations*) for the mighty (God)
7. We will go *into his tabernacles*:
Cant. 1: 8. feed thy kids beside the shepherds' *tents*.
Isa. 22:16. graveth *an habitation* for himself
32:18. *and in* sure *dwellings*,
54: 2. forth the curtains of *thine habitations*:
Jer. 9:19(18). *our dwellings* have cast (us) out.
30:18. *and* have mercy on *his dwellingplaces*;
51:30. they have burned *her dwellingplaces*;
Eze. 25: 4. make *their dwellings* in thee:
37:27. *My tabernacle* also shall be
Hab. 1: 6. to possess *the dwellingplaces*

מִשְׁכַּן [*mish-kan'*], Ch. m. 4907

Ezr. 7:15. whose (lit. who *his*) *habitation* (is) in Jerusalem,

---

מָשַׁל *māh-shal'*. 4910

* KAL.—*Preterite.* *

Deu 15: 6. *and thou shalt reign* over many nations,
Ps. 103:19. his kingdom *ruleth* over all.
Isa. 3:12. women *rule* over them.
63:19. *thou* never *barest rule* over them;
Lam. 5: 8. Servants *have ruled* over us:
Dan 11: 3. *that shall rule* with great dominion,
4. his dominion which *he ruled*:
5. he shall be strong above him, *and have dominion*;
43. *But he shall have power* over the treasures
Zec. 6:13. and shall sit *and rule* upon his throne;

KAL.—*Infinitive.*

Gen 1:18. *And to rule* over the day and over the night,
37: 8. shalt thou *indeed* have dominion (lit. *having dominion* shalt thou have dominion) over us?
Jud. 9: 2. *either* that...threescore and ten persons, *reign* over you, or *that* one *reign* over you?
Pro. 19:10. for a servant *to have rule* over princes.
29: 2. *but when* the wicked *beareth rule*,
Eze. 19:14. no strong rod (to be) a sceptre *to rule*.
Joel 2:17. *that* the heathen *should rule* over (marg. or, *use a byword* against) them:

KAL.—*Imperative.*

Jud. 8:22. *Rule thou* over us, both thou,

KAL.—*Future.*

Gen. 3:16. and he *shall rule* over thee.
4: 7. and *thou shalt rule* over him.
37: 8. *shalt thou* indeed *have dominion*
Ex. 21: 8. a strange nation *he shall have* no *power*,
Deu 15: 6. *they shall* not *reign* over thee.
Jud. 8:23. I *will* not *rule* over you, neither *shall* my son *rule* over you: the Lord *shall rule* over you.
Ps. 19:13(14). *let them* not *have dominion* over me:
106:41. *and* they that hated them *ruled* over them.
Pro. 12:24. The hand of the diligent *shall bear rule*:
17: 2. A wise servant *shall have rule*
22: 7. The rich *ruleth* over the poor,
Isa. 3: 4. babes *shall rule* over them.
19: 4. a fierce king *shall rule* over them,

KAL.—*Participle.* Poel.

Gen 24: 2. his eldest servant of his house, *that ruled*
45: 8. *and a ruler* throughout all the land
26. he (is) *governor* over all the land
Jos. 12: 2. (and) *ruled* (lit. *ruling*) from Aroer,
5. *And reigned* in mount Hermon,
Jud. 14: 4. the Philistines *had dominion*
15:11. the Philistines (are) *rulers* over us?
2Sa. 23: 3. *He that ruleth* (marg. or, *Be thou ruler*, &c.) over men (must be) just, *ruling* in the fear of God.

1K. 4:21(5:1). Solomon *reigned* (lit. was *ruler*) over all kingdoms
1Ch 29:12. and thou *reignest* over all;
2Ch 7:18. shall not fail thee a man (to be) *ruler*
9:26. *reign*ed (lit. was *ruler*) over all the kings
20: 6. *rulest* (not) thou over all the kingdoms
23:20. *the governors* of the people,
Neh. 9:37. *they have dominion* over our bodies,
Ps. 22:28(29). *and* he (is) *the governor* among the
59:13(14). them know that God *ruleth* in Jacob
66: 7. He *ruleth* by his power for ever;
89: 9(10). Thou *rulest* the raging of the sea:
105:20. *the ruler of* the people,
21. *and ruler* of all his substance:
Pro. 6: 7. no guide, overseer, *or ruler*,
16:32. *and he that ruleth* his spirit
23: 1. When thou sittest to eat with *a ruler*,
28:15. *a* wicked *ruler* over the poor people.
29:12. If *a ruler* hearken to lies,
26. Many seek *the ruler*'s favour;
Ecc. 9:17. the cry of *him that ruleth* among fools.
10: 4. If the spirit of *the ruler* rise
Isa. 14: 5. the sceptre of *the rulers*.
16: 1. Send ye the lamb to *the ruler of* the land
28:14. ye scornful men, *that rule* this people
40:10. his arm *shall rule* for him:
49: 7. a servant of *rulers*,
52: 5. *they that rule over them* make them
Jer. 22:30. *and ruling* any more in Judah.
30:21. *and their governor* shall proceed from
33:26. *rulers* over the seed of Abraham,
51:46. violence in the land, *ruler* against *ruler*.
Eze.19:11. the sceptres of *them that bare rule*,
Mic. 5: 2(1). to be *ruler* in Israel;
Hab. 1:14. (that have) no *ruler* over them?

* HIPHIL.—*Preterite*. *

Dan11:39. *and he shall cause them to rule* over many,

HIPHIL.—*Infinitive*.

Job 25: 2. *Dominion* and fear (are) with him,

HIPHIL.—*Future*.

Ps. 8: 6(7). *Thou madest him to have dominion* over

4911 מָשַׁל [*māh-shal'*].

* KAL.—*Infinitive*. *

Eze.18: 3. *to use* this proverb in Israel.

KAL.—*Imperative*.

Eze.17: 2. *and speak* a parable unto the house of
24: 3. *And utter* a parable unto the rebellious

KAL.—*Future*.

Eze.12:23. *they shall* no more *use it as a proverb*
16:44. *shall use* (this) *proverb*

KAL.—*Participle*. Poel.

Nu. 21:27. *they that speak in proverbs* say,
Eze.16:44. every one *that useth proverbs*
18: 2. that ye *use* this proverb

* NIPHAL.—*Preterite*. *

Ps. 28: 1. *I become like* them that go down
49:12(13). *he is like* the beasts
20(21). *is like* the beasts (that) perish.
143: 7. *lest I be like* unto them that
Isa. 14:10. *art thou become like* unto us?

* PIEL.—*Participle*. *

Eze.20:49(21:5). *Doth he* not *speak* parables?

* HIPHIL.—*Future*. *

Isa. 46: 5. *and compare me*, that we may be like?

* HITHPAEL.—*Future*. *

Job 30:19. *and I am become like* dust

4912 מָשָׁל *māh-shāhl'*, m.

Nu. 23: 7, 18 & 24:3, 15, 20, 21, 23. took up *his parable*, and said,
Deu28:37. *a proverb*, and a byword,
1Sa.10:12. Therefore it became *a proverb*,
24:13(14). As saith *the proverb of* the ancients,
1K. 4:32(5:12). he spake three thousand *proverbs*:
9: 7. Israel shall be *a proverb*
2Ch 7:20. *a proverb* and a byword
Job 13:12. Your remembrances (are) *like* unto ashes,
27: 1 & 29:1. Job continued *his parable*,
Ps. 44:14(15). Thou makest us *a byword*
49: 4(5). I will incline mine ear *to a parable*:
69:11(12). I became *a proverb* to them.
78: 2. I will open my mouth *in a parable*:
Pro. 1: 1. *The proverbs of* Solomon
6. To understand *a proverb*,
10: 1. *The proverbs of* Solomon.
25: 1. also *proverbs of* Solomon,
26: 7, 9. *so* (is) *a parable* in the mouth of fools.
Ecc.12: 9. set in order many *proverbs*.
Isa. 14: 4. take up this *proverb* (marg. or, *taunting speech*)
Jer. 24: 9. a reproach *and a proverb*,
Eze.12:22. that *proverb* (that) ye have in the land
23. I will make this *proverb* to cease,
14: 8. will make him a sign *and a proverb*,
17: 2. speak *a parable* unto the house
18: 2. that ye use this *proverb*
3. to use this *proverb*
20:49(21:5). Doth he not speak *parables*?
24: 3. utter *a parable* unto the rebellious house,
Mic. 2: 4. take up *a parable* against you,
Hab. 2: 6. Shall not all these take up *a parable*

מֹשֶׁל [*mōh'-shel*], m. 4915

Job 41:33(25). Upon earth there is not *his like*,
Dan11: 4. *according to his dominion*
Zec. 9:10. *and his dominion* (shall be) from sea (even) to sea,

מְשֹׁל *m'shōhl*, m. 4914

Job 17: 6. He hath made me also *a byword*

מִשְׁלוֹחַ *mish-lōh'ăgh*, m. 4916

Est. 9:19. *and of sending* portions one to another.
22. feasting and joy, *and of sending*
Isa. 11:14. they *shall lay* their hand (marg. *the laying on of* their hand)

מִשְׁלָח *mish-lagh'*, m. 4916

Deu12: 7. rejoice in all *that* ye *put* (lit. in all *putting of*) your hand unto,
18. in all *that* thou *puttest* thine hands
15:10. in all *that* thou *puttest* thine hand
23:20(21) & 28:8, 20. in all *that* thou *settest* thine hand
Isa. 7:25. be *for the sending forth of* oxen,

מִשְׁלַחַת *mish-lah'-ghath'*, f. 4917

Ps. 78:49. by *sending* evil angels
Ecc. 8: 8. (there is) no *discharge* (marg. or, *casting off* (weapons)) in (that) war;

מְשַׁמָּה *m'sham-māh'*, f. 4923

Isa. 15: 6. Nimrim shall be *desolate*: (marg. *desolations*)
Jer. 48:34. Nimrim shall be *desolate*. (marg. *id.*)
Eze. 5:15. instruction *and an astonishment*
6:14. *yea*, more *desolate* than the wilderness
33:28. lay the land most *desolate*, (marg. desolation *and desolation*)
29. laid the land most *desolate* (lit. desolation *and desolation*)
35: 3. and I will make thee most *desolate*. (marg. desolation *and desolation*)

מִשְׁמָן *mish-man'*, m 4924

Gen27:28. *and the fatness of* the earth,

Gen 27:39. thy dwelling shall be *the fatness* (marg. or, *of the fatness*) *of* the earth,
Ps. 78:31. slew *the fattest of them,*
Isa. 10:16. the Lord of hosts, send *among his fat ones* leanness;
17: 4. *and the fatness of* his flesh
Dan 11:24. *even upon the fattest places of* the province;

4924 **מַשְׁמַנִּים** *mash-man-neem′*, m. pl.

Neh 8:10. eat *the fat,* and drink the sweet,

4926 **מִשְׁמַע** *mish-ma^{n}g′*, m.

Isa. 11: 3. reprove *after the hearing of* his ears:

4928 **מִשְׁמַעַת** [*mish-mah′-^{n}gath*], f.

1 Sa. 22:14. king's son in law, and goeth at *thy bidding,*
2 Sa. 23:23. David set him over *his guard.* (marg. at *his command,* or, *council*)
1 Ch 11:25. David set him over *his guard.*
Isa. 11:14. the children of Ammon *shall obey them.* (marg. *their obedience*)

4929 **מִשְׁמָר** *mish-māhr′*, m.

Gen 40: 3. he put them *in ward in* the house
4. they continued a season *in ward.*
7. officers that (were) with him *in the ward of*
41:10. put me *in ward in* the
42:17. he put them all together into *ward*
19. be bound in the house of *your prison:*
Lev. 24:12. they put him *in ward,*
Nu. 15:34. they put him *in ward,*
1 Ch 26:16. going up, *ward* against *ward.*
Neh 4: 9(3). set *a watch* against them day and night,
22(16). in the night they may be *a guard*
23(17). nor the men of *the guard*
7: 3. the inhabitants of Jerusalem, every one *in his watch,*
12:24. *ward* over against *ward.*
25. porters keeping *the ward*
13:14. *and* for *the offices* (marg. or, *observations*) *thereof.*
Job 7:12. that thou settest *a watch*
Pro. 4:23. Keep thy heart with all *diligence;* (marg. above all *keeping*)
Jer. 51:12. make *the watch* strong,
Eze. 38: 7. be thou *a guard* unto them.

4931 **מִשְׁמֶרֶת** *mish-meh′-reth*, f.

Gen 26: 5. obeyed my voice, and kept *my charge,*
Ex. 12: 6. And ye shall *keep* it (lit. and it shall be to you *for keeping*)
16:23. for you *to be kept* until the morning.
32. omer of it *to be kept* for your generations;
33. lay it up before the Lord, *to be kept*
34. before the Testimony, *to be kept.*
Lev. 8:35. keep *the charge of* the Lord,
18:30. shall ye keep *mine ordinance,*
22: 9. They shall therefore keep *mine ordinance,*
Nu. 1:53. the Levites shall keep *the charge of*
3: 7. they shall keep *his charge,* and *the charge of* the whole congregation
8. *the charge of* the children of Israel,
25. *And the charge of* the sons of Gershon
28. keeping *the charge of* the sanctuary.
31. *And their charge* (shall be) the ark,
32. keep *the charge of* the sanctuary.
36. the custody and *charge of*
38. keeping *the charge of* the sanctuary *for the charge* of the children of Israel;
4:27. appoint unto them *in charge* all
28. *and their charge* (shall be) under
31. this (is) *the charge of* their burden,
32. instruments of *the charge of* their burden
8:26. congregation, to keep *the charge,*
— the Levites *touching their charge.*

Nu. 9:19. the children of Israel kept *the charge of*
23. they kept *the charge of* the Lord,
17:10(25). *to be kept* for a token
18: 3. shall keep *thy charge, and the charge of*
4. keep *the charge of* the tabernacle
5. keep *the charge of* the sanctuary, and *the charge of* the altar:
8. I also have given thee *the charge of* mine
19: 9. it shall be *kept* for the congregation (lit. it shall be *for keeping* to)
31:30. which keep *the charge of* the tabernacle
47. which kept *the charge of* the tabernacle
Deu 11: 1. keep *his charge,* and his statutes,
Jos. 22: 3. but have kept *the charge of* the
1 Sa. 22:23. but with me thou (shalt be) in *safeguard.*
2 Sa. 20: 3. put them in *ward* (lit. a house of *ward*), and fed them,
1 K. 2: 3. keep *the charge of* the Lord
2 K. 11: 5. shall even be keepers of *the watch of*
6. so shall ye keep *the watch of*
7. even they shall keep *the watch of*
1 Ch 9:23. house of the tabernacle, *by wards.*
27. because *the charge* (was) upon them,
12:29. part of them had kept *the ward of*
23:32. *the charge of* the tabernacle of the congregation, *and the charge of* the holy (place), and *the charge of* the sons of
25: 8. they cast lots, *ward* against (ward),
26:12. *wards* one against another,
2 Ch 7: 6. priests waited on *their offices:*
8:14. the Levites to *their charges,*
13:11. for we keep *the charge of* the Lord
23: 6. all the people shall keep *the watch of*
31:16. for their service *in their charges*
17. upward, *in their charges*
35: 2. set the priests in *their charges,*
Neh 7: 3. appoint *watches of* the inhabitants
12: 9. over against them *in the watches.*
45. porters kept *the ward of* their God, *and the ward of* the purification,
13:30. appointed *the wards* of the priests
Isa. 21: 8. I am set in *my ward* whole nights:
Eze. 40:45. the keepers of *the charge* (marg. or, *ward,* or, *ordinance*) *of* the house.
46. the keepers of *the charge of* the altar:
44: 8. ye have not kept *the charge of*
— ye have set keepers of *my charge* (marg. or, *ward,* or, *ordinance*)
14. make them keepers of *the charge of*
15. kept *the charge of* my sanctuary
16. they shall keep *my charge.*
48:11. which have kept *my charge,* (marg. or, *ward,* or, *ordinance*)
Hab. 2: 1. I will stand upon *my watch,*
Zec. 3: 7. keep *my charge,* (marg. or, *ordinance*)
Mal 3:14. that we have kept *his ordinance,* (marg. *observation*)

מִשְׁנֶה *mish-neh′*, m. 4932

Gen 41:43. he made him to ride in the *second* chariot
43:12. take *double* money in your hand;
15. *and* they took *double* money
Ex. 16: 5. *twice as much* as they gather
22. they gathered *twice as much*
Deu 15:18. worth a *double* hired servant
17:18. he shall write him *a copy of* this law
Jos. 8:32. *a copy of* the law of Moses,
1 Sa. 8: 2. the name of *his second,*
15: 9. *and of the fatlings,* (marg. or, *second sort*)
17:13. *and next unto him* Abinadab,
23:17. I shall be *next* unto thee;
2 Sa. 3: 3. *And his second,* Chileab,
2 K. 22:14. now she dwelt in Jerusalem in *the college;* (marg. or, *in the second part*)
23: 4. the priests of *the second order,*
25:18. Zephaniah *the second* priest,
1 Ch 5:12. Shapham *the next,*
15:18. their brethren of *the second* (degree),
16: 5. *and next to him* Zechariah,
2 Ch 28: 7. Elkanah *that* (was) *next* (marg. *the second*) *to* the king.
31:12. Shimei his brother (was) *the next.*
34:22. now she dwelt in Jerusalem *in the college:* (marg. *school,* or, *second part*)
35:24. put him in the *second* chariot

Ezr. 1:10. silver basons of *a second* (sort)
Neh 11: 9. of Senuah (was) *second* over the city.
17. Bakbukiah *the second* among
Est. 10: 3. Mordecai the Jew (was) *next* unto
Job 42:10. gave Job *twice as much* (marg. *double*)
Isa. 61: 7. (ye shall have) *double;*
— they shall possess *the double:*
Jer. 16:18. their sin *double;*
17:18. *and* destroy them with *double* destruction.
52:24. Zephaniah the *second* priest,
Zep. 1:10. an howling from *the second,*
Zec. 9:12. (that) I will render *double* unto thee;

4933 **מִשְׁסָּה** *m'shis-sāh'*, f.

2K. 21:14. *and a spoil* to all their enemies;
Isa. 42:22. delivereth; for *a spoil,* (marg. *treading*)
24. Who gave Jacob *for a spoil,*
Jer. 30:16. they that spoil thee shall be *a spoil,*
Hab 2: 7. thou shalt be *for booties*
Zep 1:13. their goods shall become *a booty,*

4934 **מִשְׁעוֹל** *mish-ġōhl'*, m.

Nu. 22:24. of the Lord stood *in a path of*

4935 **מִשְׁעִי** *mish-ġee'*, m.

Eze. 16: 4. wast thou washed in water to *supple* (thee); (marg. or, *when I looked* (upon thee))

4937 **מִשְׁעָן** *mish-ġāhn'*, m.

2Sa. 22:19. but the Lord was my *stay.*
Ps. 18:18(19). but the Lord was my *stay.*
Isa. 3: 1. *the* whole *stay of* bread, and the whole *stay of* water,

4937 **מַשְׁעֵן** *mash-ġehn'*, m.

Isa. 3: 1. from Judah *the stay* and the staff,

4938 **מַשְׁעֵנָה** *mash-ġeh-nāh'*, f.

Isa. 3: 1. from Judah the stay *and the staff,*

4938 **מִשְׁעֶנֶת** *mish-ġeh'-neth*, f.

Ex. 21:19. walk abroad upon *his staff,*
Nu. 21:18. (of) the lawgiver, *with their staves.*
Jud. 6:21. put forth the end of *the staff*
2K. 4:29. take *my staff* in thine hand,
— lay *my staff* upon the face of the child.
31. laid *the staff* upon the face of the child;
18:21. thou trustest upon *the staff of*
Ps. 23: 4. thy rod *and thy staff* they comfort me.
Isa. 36: 6. thou trustest in *the staff of*
Eze. 29: 6. they have been *a staff of* reed
Zec. 8: 4. every man with *his staff* in his hand

4940 **מִשְׁפָּחָה** *mish-pāh-ghāh'*, f.

Gen 8:19. upon the earth, *after their kinds,* (marg. *families*)
10: 5. *after their families,* in their nations.
18. afterward were *the families of*
20. *after their families,* after their tongues,
31. sons of Shem, *after their families,*
32. *the families of* the sons of Noah,
12: 3. shall all *families of* the earth
24:38. father's house, and to *my kindred,*
40. take a wife for my son *of my kindred,*
41. when thou comest to *my kindred;*
28:14. shall all *the families of* the earth
36:40. *according to their families,* after their
Ex. 6:14. these (be) *the families of* Reuben.
15. these (are) *the families of* Simeon.
Ex. 6:17. Shimi, *according to their families.*
19. these (are) *the families of* Levi
24. *the families of* the Korhites.
25. the Levites *according to their families.*
12:21. *according to your families,*
Lev. 20: 5. that man, *and against his family,*
25:10. every man unto *his family.*
41. return unto *his own family,*
45. *and of their families* that (are)
47. stock of the stranger's *family:*
49. nigh of kin unto him *of his family*
Nu. 1: 2. Israel, *after their families,*
18. pedigrees after *their families,*
20, 22, 24, 26, 28, 30, 32, 34, 36, 38, 40, 42. generations, *after their families,*
2:34. every one *after their families,*
3:15. *by their families:* every male
18. Gershon *by their families;*
19. Kohath *by their families;*
20. Merari *by their families;*
— These (are) *the families of* the Levites
21. Gershon was *the family of* the Libnites, *and the family of* the Shimites:
—, 23. *the families of* the Gershonites.
27. Kohath (was) *the family of* the Amramites, *and the family of* the Izeharites, *and the family of* the Hebronites, *and the family of* the Uzzielites: these (are) *the families of* the Kohathites.
29. *The families of* the sons of Kohath
30. the father *of the families of*
33. Merari (was) *the family of* the Mahlites, *and the family of* the Mushites: these (are) *the families of* Merari.
35. *of the families of* Merari
39. *throughout their families,* all the males
4: 2. Levi, *after their families,*
18. tribe of *the families of* the Kohathites
22. their fathers, *by their families;*
24. This (is) the service of *the families of*
28. *the families of* the sons of Gershon
29. number them *after their families,*
33, 42, 45. *the families of* the sons of
34. Kohathites *after their families,*
36. numbered of them *by their families*
37. numbered of *the families of* the
38. Gershon, *throughout their families,*
40, 42. *throughout their families,* by the house
41. were numbered of *the families of*
44. numbered of them *after their families,*
46. *after their families,* and after
11:10. heard the people weep *throughout their families,*
26: 5. *the family of* the Hanochites: of Pallu, *the family of* the Palluites:
6. *the family of* the Hezronites: of Carmi, *the family of* the Carmites.
7. *the families of* the Reubenites:
12. The sons of Simeon *after their families:* of Nemuel, *the family of* the Nemuelites: of Jamin, *the family of* the Jaminites: of Jachin, *the family of* the Jachinites:
13. *the family of* the Zarhites: of Shaul, *the family of* the Shaulites.
14. *the families of* the Simeonites,
15. The children of Gad *after their families:* of Zephon, *the family of* the Zephonites: of Haggi, *the family of* the Haggites: of Shuni, *the family of* the Shunites:
16. *the family of* the Oznites: of Eri, *the family of* the Erites:
17. *the family of* the Arodites: of Areli, *the family of* the Arelites.
18. *the families of* the children of Gad
20. the sons of Judah *after their families* were; of Shelah, *the family of* the Shelanites: of Pharez, *the family of* the Pharzites: of Zerah, *the family of* the Zarhites.
21. *the family of* the Hezronites: of Hamul, *the family of* the Hamulites.
22. These (are) *the families of* Judah
23. the sons of Issachar *after their families:* (of) Tola, *the family of* the Tolaites: of Pua, *the family of* the Punites:
24. *the family of* the Jashubites: of Shimron, *the family of* the Shimronites.
25. These (are) *the families of* Issachar

Nu. 26:26. the sons of Zebulun *after their families:* of Sered, *the family of* the Sardites: of Elon, *the family of* the Elonites: of Jahleel, *the family of* the Jahleelites.
27. *the families of* the Zebulunites
28, 37. Joseph *after their families*
29. *the family of* the Machirites:
— *the family of* the Gileadites.
30. *the family of* the Jeezerites: (of) Helek, *the family of* the Helekites:
31. *the family of* the Asrielites: and (of) Shechem, *the family of* the Shechemites:
32. *the family of* the Shemidaites: and (of) Hepher, *the family of* the Hepherites.
34. *the families of* Manasseh,
35. These (are) the sons of Ephraim *after their families:* of Shuthelah, *the family of* the Shuthalhites: of Becher, *the family of* the Bachrites: of Tahan, *the family of*
36. *the family of* the Eranites.
37. *the families of* the sons of Ephraim
38. The sons of Benjamin *after their families:* of Bela, *the family of* the Belaites: of Ashbel, *the family of* the Ashbelites: of Ahiram, *the family of* the Ahiramites:
39. *the family of* the Shuphamites: of Hupham, *the family of* the Huphamites.
40. *the family of* the Ardites: (and) of Naaman, *the family of* the Naamites.
41. Benjamin *after their families:*
42. Dan *after their families:* of Shuham, *the family of* the Shuhamites. These (are) *the families of* Dan *after their families.*
43. *the families of* the Shuhamites,
44. the children of Asher *after their families:* of Jimna, *the family of* the Jimnites: of Jesui, *the family of* the Jesuites: of Beriah, *the family of* the Beriites.
45. *the family of* the Heberites: of Malchiel, *the family of* the Malchielites.
47. *the families of* the sons of Asher
48. Naphtali *after their families:* of Jahzeel, *the family of* the Jahzeelites: of Guni, *the family of* the Gunites:
49. *the family of* the Jezerites: of Shillem, *the family of* the Shillemites.
50. *the families of* Naphtali *according to their families:*
57. Levites *after their families:* of Gershon, *the family of* the Gershonites: of Kohath, *the family of* the Kohathites: of Merari, *the family of* the Merarites.
58. *the families of* the Levites: *the family of* the Libnites, *the family of* the Hebronites, *the family of* the Mahlites, *the family of* the Mushites, *the family of* the
27: 1. *of the families of* Manasseh
4. done away from among *his family,*
11. that is next to him *of his family,*
33:54. inheritance *among your families:*
36: 1. chief fathers *of the families of*
— Manasseh, *of the families of*
6. only *to the family of* the tribe
8. shall be wife unto one *of the family of*
12. were married *into the families of*
— remained in the tribe of *the family of*
Deu 29:18(17). or *family,* or tribe,
Jos. 6:23. brought out all *her kindred,*
7:14. *according to the families* (thereof); *and the family* which the Lord shall take
17. he brought *the family of* Judah; and he took *the family of* the Zarhites: and he brought *the family of* the Zarhites
13:15. (inheritance) *according to their families*
23. Reuben *after their families,*
24. Gad *according to their families.*
28. Gad *after their families,*
29. Manasseh *by their families.*
31. Machir *by their families.*
15: 1. Judah *by their families;*
12. round about *according to their families.*
20. Judah *according to their families.*
16: 5. Ephraim *according to their families*
8. Ephraim *by their families.*
17: 2. Manasseh *by their families;*
— Joseph *by their families.*
18:11. came up *according to their families:*
Jos. 18:20. round about, *according to their families.*
21, 28. Benjamin *according to their families*
19: 1, 8. Simeon *according to their families:*
10, 16. Zebulun *according to their families:*
17, 23. Issachar *according to their families.*
24, 31. Asher *according to their families.*
32, 39. Naphtali *according to their families.*
40, 48. Dan *according to their families.*
21: 4. *for the families of* the Kohathites:
5. by lot *out of the families of*
6. *of the families of* the tribe of Issachar,
7. Merari *by their families*
10. *of the families of* the Kohathites,
20. *And the families of* the children
26. *for the families of* the children of
27. *of the families of* the Levites,
33. *according to their families* (were)
34. *And unto the families of* the children of
40(38). Merari *by their families,* which were remaining *of the families of*
Jud. 1:25. let go the man and all *his family.*
9: 1. with all *the family of* the house
13: 2. *of the family of* the Danites,
17: 7. *of the family of* Judah,
18: 2. Dan sent *of their family* five men
11. from thence *of the family of* the Danites,
19. a tribe *and a family* in Israel?
21:24. to his tribe *and to his family,*
Ru. 2: 1. *of the family of* Elimelech;
3. who (was) *of the kindred of* Elimelech.
1Sa. 9:21. *and my family* the least of all *the families of*
10:21. *by their families, the family of* Matri was
18:18. my father's *family* in Israel,
20: 6. yearly sacrifice there for all *the family.*
29. for our *family* hath a sacrifice
2Sa. 14: 7. *the* whole *family* is risen against
16: 5. *a man of the family of* the house of Saul,
1Ch 2:53. *And the families of* Kirjath-jearim;
55. *And the families of* the scribes
4: 2. *the families of* the Zorathites.
8. *and the families of* Aharhel
21. *and the families of* the house
27. neither did all *their family* multiply,
38. princes *in their families:*
5: 7. his brethren *by their families,*
6:19(4). these (are) *the families of* the Levites
54(39). *of the families of* the Kohathites:
60(45). cities *throughout their families*
61(46). left *of the family of* that tribe,
62(47). the sons of Gershom *throughout their families*
63(48). by lot, *throughout their families,*
66(51). *And* (the residue) *of the families of*
70(55). *for the family of* the remnant
71(56). *out of the family of* the half tribe
7: 5. among all *the families of* Issachar
16:28. *ye kindreds of* the people,
Neh 4:13(7). *after their families* with their swords,
Est. 9:28. *every family* (lit. *family and family*), every province, and every city;
Job 31:34. or did the contempt of *families*
32: 2. *of the kindred of* Ram:
Ps. 22:27(28). all *the kindreds of* the nations
96: 7. *O ye kindreds of* the people,
107:41. maketh (him) *families* like a flock.
Jer. 1:15. all *the families of* the kingdoms
2: 4. all *the families of* the house
3:14. one of a city, and two *of a family,*
8: 3. that remain of this evil *family,*
10:25. *the families* that call not on thy name:
15: 3. over them four *kinds,* (marg. *families*)
25: 9. take all *the families of* the north,
31: 1. all *the families of* Israel,
33:24. *The* two *families* which the Lord
Eze. 20:32. *as the families of* the countries,
Am. 3: 1. against *the* whole *family*
2. have I known of all *the families of* the
Mic. 2: 3. against this *family* do I devise
Nah 3: 4. *and families* through her witchcrafts.
Zec. 12:12. shall mourn, *every family* apart (marg. *families, families*); *the family of* the house of David apart,
— *the family of* the house of Nathan
13. *The family of* the house of Levi
— *the family of* Shimei apart,
14. All *the families* that remain, *every family* (lit. *families, families*) apart,

Zec.14:17. will not come up of (all) *the families of*
18. if *the family of* Egypt go not up,

4941 **מִשְׁפָּט** ***mish-pāht'*, m.**

Gen18:19. to do justice *and judgment;*
25. the Judge of all the earth do *right?*
40:13. *after the* former *manner*
Ex. 15:25. a statute *and an ordinance,*
21: 1. these (are) *the judgments*
9. *after the manner of* daughters.
31. *according to* this *judgment*
23: 6. Thou shalt not wrest *the judgment of*
24: 3. all *the judgments:*
26:30. *according to the fashion thereof* which was
28:15. make the breastplate of *judgment*
29. the breastplate of *judgment* upon his heart,
30. put in the breastplate of *judgment*
— Aaron shall bear *the judgment of*
Lev. 5:10 & 9:16. *according to the manner:* (marg. *ordinance*)
18: 4. Ye shall do *my judgments,*
5. keep my statutes, and *my judgments:*
26. keep my statutes and *my judgments,*
19:15, 35. no unrighteousness *in judgment:*
37 & 20:22. statutes, and all *my judgments,*
24:22. Ye shall have one *manner of law,*
25:18. statutes, and keep *my judgments,*
26:15. if your soul abhor *my judgments,*
43. because they despised *my judgments,*
46. the statutes *and judgments*
Nu. 9: 3. all *the ceremonies thereof,*
14. *and according to the manner thereof,*
15:16. One law *and* one *manner*
24. *according to the manner,* (marg. *ordinance*)
27: 5. Moses brought *their cause*
11. of Israel a statute of *judgment,*
21. *after the judgment of* Urim
29: 6. *according unto their manner,*
18, 21, 24, 27, 30, 37. their number, *after the manner:*
33. to their number, *after the manner:* (lit. *their manner*)
35:12. before the congregation *in judgment.*
24. according to these *judgments:*
29. for a statute of *judgment*
36:13. commandments *and the judgments,*
Deu. 1:17. respect persons *in judgment;*
— for *the judgment* (is) God's:
4: 1. statutes and unto *the judgments,*
5. taught you statutes *and judgments,*
8. that hath statutes *and judgments*
14. teach you statutes *and judgments,*
45. the statutes, *and the judgments,*
5: 1. the statutes and *judgments*
31(28) & 6:1, 20. statutes, *and the judgments,*
7:11. the statutes, and *the judgments,*
12. if ye hearken to these *judgments,*
8:11. *and his judgments,* and his statutes,
10:18. He doth execute *the judgment of*
11: 1. his statutes, *and his judgments,*
32. to do all the statutes and *judgments*
12: 1. These (are) the statutes *and judgments,*
16:18. the people with just *judgment.*
19. Thou shalt not wrest *judgment;*
17: 8. matter too hard for thee *in judgment,*
9. shew thee the sentence of *judgment:*
11. according to *the judgment*
18: 3. this shall be the priests' *due*
19: 6. whereas he (was) not *worthy of* death, (lit. to him was not *judgment of* death)
21:17. *the right of* the firstborn (is) his.
22. committed a sin *worthy of* death, (lit. the *judgment of* death)
24:17. pervert *the judgment of* the stranger,
25: 1. they come unto *judgment,*
26:16. to do these statutes and *judgments:*
17. commandments, *and his judgments,*
27:19. he that perverteth *the judgment of*
30:16. his statutes *and his judgments,*
32: 4. for all his ways (are) *judgment:*
41. mine hand take hold *on judgment;*
33:10. They shall teach Jacob *thy judgments,*
21. *and his judgments* with Israel.
Jos. 6:15. *after the* same *manner*
20: 6. the congregation *for judgment,*
24:25. a statute *and an ordinance*

Jud. 4: 5. Israel came up to her *for judgment.*
13:12. How shall we *order* (marg. What shall be *the manner of*) the child,
18: 7. *after the manner of* the Zidonians,
1Sa. 2:13. *And* the priests' *custom*
8: 3. took bribes, and perverted *judgment.*
9. shew them *the manner of* the king
11. This will be *the manner of*
10:25. told the people *the manner of*
27:11. so (will be) *his manner*
30:25. *and an ordinance* for Israel
2Sa. 8:15. David executed *judgment* and justice
15: 2. came to the king *for judgment,*
4. which hath any suit *or cause*
6. that came to the king *for judgment:*
22:23. all *his judgments* (were) before me:
1K 2: 3. commandments, *and his judgments,*
3:11. understanding to discern *judgment;*
28. all Israel heard of *the judgment*
— God (was) in him, to do *judgment.*
4:28(5:8). every man *according to his charge.*
6:12. and execute *my judgments,*
38. according to all *the fashion of it.*
7: 7. the porch of *judgment:*
8:45, 49. maintain *their cause.* (marg. or, *right*)
58. his statutes, *and his judgments,*
59. that he maintain *the cause of* his servant, *and the cause of* his people Israel
9: 4. keep my statutes *and my judgments:*
10: 9. to do *judgment* and justice.
11:33. my statutes *and my judgments,*
18:28. cut themselves *after their manner*
20:40. So (shall) *thy judgment* (be);
2K. 1: 7. What *manner of* man (was he)
11:14. by a pillar, *as the manner* (was),
17:26. know not *the manner of* the God
— know not *the manner of* the God
27. teach them *the manner of* the God
33. *after the manner of* the nations
34. they do *after the* former *manners:*
— *or after their ordinances,*
37. the statutes, and *the ordinances,*
40. they did *after their* former *manner.*
25: 6. they gave *judgment* upon him.
1Ch 6:32(17). *according to their order.*
15:13. sought him not *after the due order.*
16:12. *and the judgments of* his mouth;
14. *his judgments* (are) in all the earth.
18:14. executed *judgment* and justice
22:13. to fulfil the statutes and *judgments*
23:31. *according to the order* commanded
24:19. of the Lord, *according to their manner,*
28: 7. my commandments *and my judgments,*
2Ch 4: 7. gold *according to their form,*
20. they should burn *after the manner*
6:35, 39. maintain *their cause.* (marg. or, *right*)
7:17. observe my statutes *and my judgments;*
8:14. *according to the order of* David
9: 8. to do *judgment* and justice.
19: 6. who (is) with you in the *judgment.* (marg. matter of *judgment*)
8. *for the judgment of* the Lord,
10. commandment, statutes *and judgments,*
30:16. stood in their place *after their manner,*
33: 8. the statutes *and the ordinances*
35:13. with fire *according to the ordinance:*
Ezr. 3: 4. *according to the custom,* as the duty
7:10. teach in Israel statutes *and judgments.*
Neh. 1: 7. *the judgments,* which thou commandedst
8:18. *according unto the manner.*
9:13. gavest them right *judgments,*
29. *but* sinned *against thy judgments,*
10:29(30). *and his judgments* and his statutes;
Job 8: 3. Doth God pervert *judgment?*
9:19. and if *of judgment,*
32. we should come together *in judgment.*
13:18. I have ordered (my) *cause;*
14: 3. bringest me *into judgment*
19: 7. but (there is) no *judgment.*
22: 4. will he enter with thee *into judgment?*
23: 4. I would order (my) *cause*
27: 2. hath taken away *my judgment;*
29:14. *my judgment* (was) as a robe
31:13. despise *the cause of* my manservant
32: 9. do the aged understand *judgment.*
34: 4. Let us choose to us *judgment:*
5. God hath taken away *my judgment.*

Job 34: 6. Should I lie against *my right?*
12. neither will the Almighty pervert *judgment.*
17. Shall even he that hateth *right* govern?
23. he should enter *into judgment* with God.
35: 2. Thinkest thou this *to be right,*
36: 6. *but* giveth *right to* the poor.
17. judgment *and justice* take hold
37:23. excellent in power, *and in judgment,*
40: 8. Wilt thou also disannul *my judgment?*
Ps 1: 5. shall not stand *in the judgment,*
7: 6(7). awake for me (to) *the judgment*
9: 4(5). For thou hast maintained *my right*
7(8). prepared his throne *for judgment.*
16(17). *the judgment* (which) he executeth:
10: 5. *thy judgments* (are) far above
17: 2. Let *my sentence* come forth
18:22(23). all *his judgments* (were) before me,
19: 9(10). *the judgments of* the Lord
25: 9. The meek will he guide *in judgment:*
33: 5. He loveth righteousness *and judgment:*
35:23. awake *to my judgment,*
36: 6(7). *thy judgments* (are) a great deep:
37: 6. *and thy judgment* as the noonday.
28. For the Lord loveth *judgment,*
30. his tongue talketh of *judgment.*
48:11(12). because of *thy judgments.*
72: 1. Give the king *thy judgments,*
2. thy poor *with judgment.*
76: 9(10). When God arose *to judgment,*
81: 4(5). *a law* of the God of Jacob.
89:14(15). Justice *and judgment*
30(31). *and* walk not *in my judgments;*
94:15. But *judgment* shall return
97: 2. righteousness *and judgment*
8. Judah rejoiced because of *thy judgments,*
99: 4. strength also loveth *judgment;*
— thou executest *judgment*
101: 1. I will sing of mercy *and judgment:*
103: 6. *and judgment* for all that are oppressed.
105: 5. *and the judgments of* his mouth;
7. *his judgments* (are) in all the earth.
106: 3. Blessed (are) they that keep *judgment,*
111: 7. of his hands (are) verity *and judgment;*
112: 5. he will guide his affairs *with discretion.* (marg. *judgment*)
119: 7. have learned thy righteous *judgments.*
13. declared all *the judgments of*
20. unto *thy judgments* at all times.
30. *thy judgments* have I laid
39. for *thy judgments* (are) good.
43. for I have hoped *in thy judgments.*
52. I remembered *thy judgments*
62. because of thy righteous *judgments.*
75. that *thy judgments* (are) right,
84. when wilt thou execute *judgment*
91. this day *according to thine ordinances:*
102. I have not departed *from thy judgments.*
106. I will keep thy righteous *judgments.*
108. *and* teach me *thy judgments.*
120. *and* I am afraid *of thy judgments.*
121. I have done *judgment* and justice:
132. *as thou usest to do* unto (marg. *according to the custom* towards) those
137. upright (are) *thy judgments.*
149. quicken me *according to thy judgment.*
156. quicken me *according to thy judgments.*
160. every one of thy righteous *judgments*
164. because of thy righteous *judgments.*
175. *and* let *thy judgments* help me.
122: 5. there are set thrones *of judgment,*
140:12(13). *the right of* the poor.
143: 2. enter not *into judgment* with thy servant:
146: 7. executeth *judgment* for the oppressed:
147:19. *and his judgments* unto Israel.
20. *and* (as for his) *judgments,* they have not
149: 9. To execute upon them *the judgment*
Pro. 1: 3. justice, *and judgment,* and equity;
2: 8. He keepeth the paths of *judgment,*
9. understand righteousness, *and judgment,*
8:20. in the midst of the paths of *judgment:*
12: 5. The thoughts of the righteous (are) *right:*
13:23. destroyed for want of *judgment.*
16: 8. than great revenues without *right.*
10. his mouth transgresseth not *in judgment.*
11. A *just* weight (lit. weight of *judgment*) and balance (are) the Lord's:
33. *the* whole *disposing thereof*

Pro.17:23. to pervert the ways of *judgment.*
18: 5. to overthrow the righteous *in judgment.*
19:28. ungodly witness scorneth *judgment:*
21: 3. To do justice *and judgment*
7. because they refuse to do *judgment.*
15. joy to the just to do *judgment:*
24:23. to have respect of persons *in judgment.*
28: 5. Evil men understand not *judgment:*
29: 4. The king *by judgment* establisheth
26. man's *judgment* (cometh) from the Lord
Ecc. 3:16. I saw under the sun the place of *judgment,*
5: 8(7). violent perverting of *judgment*
8: 5. discerneth both time *and judgment.*
6. every purpose there is time *and judgment,*
11: 9. God will bring thee *into judgment.*
12:14. God shall bring every work *into judgment,*
Isa. 1:17. Learn to do well; seek *judgment,*
21. it was full of *judgment;*
27. Zion shall be redeemed *with judgment,*
3:14. The Lord will enter *into judgment*
4: 4. by the spirit of *judgment,*
5: 7. he looked *for judgment,*
16. shall be exalted *in judgment,*
9: 7(6). to establish it *with judgment*
10: 2. to take away *the right from*
16: 5. judging, and seeking *judgment,*
26: 8. in the way of *thy judgments,*
9. when *thy judgments* (are) in the earth,
28: 6. of *judgment* to him that sitteth in *judgment,*
17. *Judgment* also will I lay to the line,
26. his God doth instruct him *to discretion,*
30:18. the Lord (is) a God of *judgment:*
32: 1. princes shall rule *in judgment.*
7. when the needy speaketh *right.*
16. *judgment* shall dwell in the wilderness,
33: 5. he hath filled Zion with *judgment*
34: 5. people of my curse, *to judgment.*
40:14. taught him in the path of *judgment,*
27. *my judgment* is passed over
41: 1. let us come near together *to judgment.*
42: 1. bring forth *judgment* to the Gentiles.
3. bring forth *judgment* unto truth.
4. till he have set *judgment* in the earth:
49: 4. *my judgment* (is) with the Lord,
50: 8. who (is) mine adversary? (marg. master of *my cause*)
51: 4. *and* I will make *my judgment*
53: 8. taken from prison *and from judgment:*
54:17. shall rise against thee *in judgment*
56: 1. Keep ye *judgment* (marg. or, *equity*), and do justice:
58: 2. and forsook not *the ordinance of* their God: they ask of me *the ordinances* of
59: 8. no *judgment* (marg. *right*) in their goings:
9. Therefore is *judgment* far from us,
11. we look *for judgment,*
14. *judgment* is turned away
15. that (there was) no *judgment.*
61: 8. For I the Lord love *judgment,*
Jer. 1:16. I will utter *my judgments*
4: 2. *in judgment,* and in righteousness;
12. now also will I give *sentence*
5: 1. that executeth *judgment,*
4, 5. *the judgment of* their God.
28. *and the right of* the needy
7: 5. if ye throughly execute *judgment*
8: 7. know not *the judgment of* the Lord.
9:24(23). *judgment,* and righteousness,
10:24. correct me, but *with judgment;*
12: 1. let me talk with thee of (thy) *judgments:*
17:11. not *by right,* shall leave them
21:12. Execute *judgment* in the morning,
22: 3. Execute ye *judgment*
13. his chambers by wrong; (lit. without *judgment*)
15. do *judgment* and justice,
23: 5. shall execute *judgment*
26:11. This man (is) *worthy to* die; (marg. *The judgment of* death (is) for this man
16. This man (is) not *worthy to* die:
30:11. I will correct thee *in measure,*
18. after *the manner thereof.*
32: 7. *the right of* redemption (is) thine
8. *the right of* inheritance (is) thine,
33:15. he shall execute *judgment*
39: 5. where he gave *judgment* upon him. (marg. spake with him *judgments*)

Jer. 46:28. correct thee *in measure;*
48:21. *And judgment* is come upon the
47. Thus far (is) *the judgment of* Moab.
49:12. whose (lit. who *their*) *judgment* (was) not
51: 9. *her judgment* reacheth unto heaven,
52: 9. where he gave *judgment*
Lam. 3:35. To turn aside *the right of* a man
59. judge thou *my cause.*
Eze. 5: 6. she hath changed *my judgments*
— they have refused *my judgments*
7. *neither* have kept *my judgments, neither* have done *according to the judgments of*
8. execute *judgments* in the midst
7:23. for the land is full of bloody *crimes,* (lit. *the judgment of* bloods)
27. *and according to their deserts* (marg. *with their judgments*)
11:12. *neither* executed *my judgments, but* have done *after the manners of*
20. keep *mine ordinances,*
16:38. *as* women that break wedlock and shed blood *are judged;* (marg. *with judgments of*)
18: 5. do that which *is lawful* and right,
8. hath executed true *judgment*
9. *and* hath kept my *judgments,*
17. hath executed *my judgments,*
19. hath done that which *is lawful*
21. do that which *is lawful*
27. doeth that which *is lawful*
20:11. shewed them *my judgments,*
13. and they despised *my judgments,*
16. Because they despised *my judgments,*
18. neither observe *their judgments,*
19. keep *my judgments,*
21. neither kept *my judgments*
24. they had not executed *my judgments,*
25. *and judgments* whereby they
21:27(32). until he come whose *right* it is;
22:29. they have oppressed the stranger wrongfully. (marg. without *right*)
23:24. set *judgment* before them, and they shall judge thee *according to their judgments.*
45. judge them *after the manner of* adulteresses, *and after the manner of* women
33:14, 19. do *that which is lawful* (marg. *judgment*) and right;
16. hath done *that which is lawful*
34:16. I will feed them *with judgment.*
36:27. *and* ye shall keep *my judgments,*
37:24. they shall *also* walk *in my judgments,*
39:21. the heathen shall see *my judgment*
42:11. *both according to their fashions,*
44:24. they shall stand *in judgment;* (and) they shall judge it *according to my judgments.*
45: 9. *and* execute *judgment* and justice,
Dan. 9: 5. *and from thy judgments:*
Hos. 2:19(21). *and in judgment,* and in lovingkindness,
5: 1. *judgment* (is) toward you, because ye have
11. oppressed (and) broken in *judgment,*
6: 5. *and thy judgments* (are as) the light
10: 4. thus *judgment* springeth up
12: 6(7). keep mercy *and judgment,* and wait on
Am. 5: 7. Ye who turn *judgment* to wormwood,
15. establish *judgment* in the gate:
24. let *judgment* run down as waters,
6:12. ye have turned *judgment* into gall,
Mic. 3: 1. not for you to know *judgment?*
8. *and* of *judgment,* and of might,
9. house of Israel, that abhor *judgment,*
6: 8. but to do *justly,*
7: 9. and execute *judgment for me:*
Hab. 1: 4. *judgment* doth never go forth:
— therefore wrong *judgment* proceedeth.
7. *their judgment* and their dignity
12. thou hast ordained them *for judgment;*
Zep. 2: 3. which have wrought *his judgment;*
3: 5. doth he bring *his judgment*
8. for *my determination* (is) to gather
15. The Lord hath taken away *thy judgments,*
Zec. 7: 9. Execute true *judgment,*
8:16. *the judgment of* truth and peace (lit. truth *and the judgment of* peace)
Mal. 2:17. Where (is) the God of *judgment?*
3: 5. I will come near to you *to judgment;*
4: 4(3:22). the statutes *and judgments.*

מִשְׁפְּתַיִם *mish-p'thah'-yim*, dual. 4942

Gen49:14. couching down between *two burdens:*
Jud. 5:16. Why abodest thou among *the sheepfolds,*

מֶשֶׁק *meh'-shek*, m. 4943

Gen15: 2. the steward (lit. son of *possession*) *of* my house (is) this Eliezer

מַשַּׁק *mash-shak'*, m. 4944

Isa. 33: 4. *as the running to and fro of* locusts

מַשְׁקֶה *mash-keh'*, m. 4945

Gen13:10. that it (was) *well watered* every where,
40:21. the chief butler unto *his butlership*
Lev.11:34. all *drink* that may be drunk
1K. 10:21. king Solomon's *drinking* vessels
2Ch 9:20. the *drinking* vessels *of* king Solomon
Isa. 32: 6. *and* he will cause *the drink of* the thirsty
Eze.45:15. *out of the fat pastures of* Israel;

מִשְׁקוֹל *mish-kōhl'*, m. 4946

Eze. 4:10. thou shalt eat (shall be) *by weight,*

מַשְׁקוֹף *mash-kōhph'*, m. 4947

Ex. 12: 7. on *the upper door post of* the houses,
22. strike *the lintel* and the two side posts
23. seeth the blood upon *the lintel,*

מִשְׁקָל *mish-kāhl'*, m. 4948

Gen24:22. golden earring of half a shekel *weight,*
— bracelets for her hands of ten (shekels) *weight*
43:21. money *in full weight:* (lit. *in its weight*)
Lev.19:35. *in weight,* or in measure.
26:26. deliver (you) your bread again *by weight:*
Nu. 7:13. *the weight thereof* (was) an hundred and
19, 25, 37, 49, 61, 67, 73, 79. *the weight whereof* (was) an hundred and thirty
31, 43, 55. *of the weight* of an hundred and
Jos. 7:21. a wedge of gold of fifty shekels *weight,*
Jud. 8:26. *the weight of* the golden earrings
1Sa.17: 5. *and the weight of* the coat
2Sa.12:30. *the weight whereof* (was) a talent
21:16. *the weight of* whose spear (weighed) three hundred (shekels) of brass in *weight,*
1K. 7:47. neither was *the weight of* the brass found
10:14. *the weight of* gold that came
2K. 25:16. of all these vessels was without *weight.*
1Ch 20: 2. found it *to weigh* (marg. *the weight of*) a
21:25. six hundred shekels of gold by *weight.*
22: 3. brass in abundance without *weight;*
14. of brass and iron without *weight;*
28:14. of gold *by weight* for (things) of gold,
— all instruments of silver *by weight,*
15. *Even the weight* for the candlesticks
— *by weight for* every candlestick,
— candlesticks of silver *by weight,*
16. And by *weight* (he gave) gold
17. *by weight* for every bason; and (likewise silver) *by weight*
18. incense refined gold *by weight;*
2Ch 3: 9. *And the weight* of the nails
4:18. for *the weight of* the brass could not
9:13. *the weight of* gold that came
Ezr. 8:30. Levites *the weight of* the silver,
34. By number (and) *by weight* of every one: and all *the weight* was written
Job 28:25. To make *the weight* for the winds;
Jer. 52:20. of all these vessels was without *weight.*
Eze. 4:16. they shall eat bread *by weight,*
5: 1. then take thee balances *to weigh,*

מִשְׁקֶלֶת [*mish-keh'-leth*], f. 4949

Isa. 28:17. righteousness *to the plummet:*

4949 **מִשְׁקֹלֶת** *mish-kōh'-leth*, f.

2K. 21:13. *the plummet of* the house of Ahab:

4950 **מִשְׁקָע** *mish-kag'*, m.

Eze.34:18. *and* to have drunk of the *deep* waters,

4952 **מִשְׁרָה** [*mish-rāh'*], f.

Nu. 6: 3. neither shall he drink any *liquor of*

4953 **מַשְׁרוֹקִיתָא** *mash-rōh-kee-thāh'*, Ch. f.

Dan 3: 5. ye hear the sound of the cornet, *flute*,
7. heard the sound of the cornet, *flute*,
10. shall hear the sound of the cornet, *flute*,
15. ye hear the sound of the cornet, *flute*,

4959 **מָשַׁשׁ** [*mah-shash'*].

* KAL.—*Future.* *

Gen27:12. My father peradventure *will feel me*,
22. *and he felt him*, and said, The voice

* PIEL.—*Preterite.* *

Gen31:37. *thou hast searched* all my stuff,

PIEL.—*Future.*

Gen31:34. *And* Laban *searched* (marg. *felt*) all the
Deu28:29. as the blind *gropeth*
Job 5:14. and *grope* in the noonday
12:25. *They grope* in the dark

PIEL.—*Participle.*

Deu28:29. *thou shalt grope* at noonday,

* HIPHIL.—*Future.* *

Ex. 10:21. *even* darkness (which) *may be felt.* (marg. *that* (one) *may feel* darkness)

4960 **מִשְׁתֶּה** *mish-teh'*, m.

Gen19: 3. he made them *a feast*,
21: 8. Abraham made *a* great *feast*
26:30. he made them *a feast*,
29:22. the men of the place, and made *a feast.*
40:20. he made *a feast* unto all his servants:
Jud.14:10. Samson made there *a feast;*
12. within the seven days of *the feast*,
17. seven days, while their *feast* lasted:
1Sa.25:36. he held *a feast* in his house, *like the feast of* a king;
2Sa. 3:20. the men that (were) with him *a feast.*
1K. 3:15. and made *a feast* to all his servants.
Ezr. 3: 7. meat, *and drink*, and oil,
Est. 1: 3. he made *a feast* unto all his princes
5. the king made *a feast* unto all the people
9. Vashti the queen made *a feast for* the
2:18. Then the king made *a* great *feast* unto all his princes and his servants, (even) Esther's *feast;*
5: 4. Haman come this day unto *the banquet*
5. the king and Haman came *to the banquet*
6. said unto Esther *at the banquet of* wine,
8. the king and Haman come *to the banquet*
12. come in with the king unto *the banquet*
14. merrily with the king unto *the banquet.*
6:14. hasted to bring Haman unto *the banquet*
7: 2. the second day *at the banquet of* wine,
7. the king arising *from the banquet of* wine
8. into the place of *the banquet of* wine;
8:17. *a feast* and a good day.
9:17, 18. made it a day of *feasting*
19. Adar (a day of) gladness *and feasting*,
22. they should make them days of *feasting*
Job 1: 4. his sons went and *feast*ed (lit. made *a feast*)
5. when the days of (their) *feasting* were
Pro.15:15. of a merry heart (hath) *a* continual *feast.*
Ecc. 7: 2. than to go to the house of *feasting:*
Isa. 5:12. and wine, are in *their feasts*
Isa. 25: 6. make unto all people *a feast of* fat things, *a feast of* wines on the lees,
Jer. 16: 8. not also go into the house of *feasting*,
51:39. In their heat I will make *their feasts*,
Dan 1: 5. wine which *he drank:* (marg. of *his drink*)
8. nor with the wine which *he drank:*
10. appointed your meat and *your drink:*
16. the wine that *they should drink;*

מִשְׁתֵּה [*mish-teh'*], Ch. m. 4961

Dan 5:10. came into the *banquet* house:

מַתְבֵּן *math-bēhn'*, m. 4963

Isa. 25:10. even as *straw* is trodden down

מֶתֶג *meh'-theg*, m. 4964-65

2Sa. 8: 1. David took *Metheg*-ammah (marg. or, *the bridle of* Ammah)
2K. 19:28. *and my bridle* in thy lips,
Ps. 32: 9. must be held in *with bit* and bridle,
Pro.26: 3. *a bridle* for the ass,
Isa. 37:29. *and my bridle* in thy lips,

מָתוֹק *māh-thōhk'*, adj. 4966

Jud.14:14. out of the strong came forth *sweetness.*
18. What (is) *sweet*er than honey?
Ps. 19:10(11). *sweet*er also than honey
Pro.16:24. (as) an honeycomb, *sweet* to the soul,
24:13. the honeycomb, (which is) *sweet*
27: 7. hungry soul every bitter thing is *sweet.*
Ecc. 5:12(11). sleep of a labouring man (is) *sweet*,
11: 7. *Truly* the light (is) *sweet*,
Cant.2: 3. his fruit (was) *sweet* to my taste.
Isa. 5:20. that put bitter *for sweet, and sweet* for
Eze. 3: 3. in my mouth as honey *for sweetness.*

מָתַח [*māh-thagh'*]. 4969

* KAL.—*Future.* *

Isa. 40:22. *and spreadeth them out* as a tent

מָתַי *māh-thah'y*, part. adv. 4970

Gen30:30. *when* shall I provide for mine own
Ex. 10: 3. How *long* wilt thou refuse to humble &c. &c.

With prefix לְמָתַי

Ex. 8: 9(5). *when* (marg. or, *against when*) shall I intreat for thee,

מְתִים *m'theem*, m. pl. 4962

Gen34:30. I (being) *few in* number,
Deu 2:34. utterly destroyed *the men*,
3: 6. utterly destroying *the men*,
4:27. ye shall be left *few in* number
26: 5. sojourned there *with* a few, (lit. *with* a few *men*)
28:62. ye shall be left few in number, (lit. *with* few *men*)
33: 6. let (not) *his men* be few.
1Ch 16:19. were but few, (marg. *men of* number)
Job 11: 3. make *men* hold their peace?
11. he knoweth vain *men:*
19:19. All my inward friends (marg. *the men of* my secret)
22:15. the old way which wicked *men* have
24:12. *Men* groan from out of the city,
31:31. *the men of* my tabernacle
Ps. 17:14. *From men* (which are) thy hand, O Lord, *from men* of the world,
26: 4. I have not sat with vain *persons*,
105:12. *a few men in* number;
Isa. 3:25. *Thy men* shall fall by the sword,
5:13. their honourable *men* (are) famished, (marg. glory (are) *men of* famine)
41:14. *ye men* (marg. or, *few men*) *of* Israel;
Jer. 44:28. Yet a *small* number (lit. *men of* number)

4971 **מַתְכֹּנֶת** *math-kōh'-nĕth*, f.

Ex. 5: 8. *the tale of* the bricks,
30:32. *neither* shall ye make (any other) like it, *after the composition of it:*
37. *according to the composition thereof:*
2Ch 24:13. set the house of God in *his state*,
Eze.45:11. *the measure thereof* shall be after

4972 **מַתְּלָאָה** *mat-t'lāh-āh*.

[Contracted from מַה־תְּלָאָה]

Mal. 1:13. Behold, *what a weariness* (is it)!

4973 **מְתַלְּעוֹת** *m'thal-l'^{n}gōhth'*, f. pl.

Job 29:17. I brake *the jaws* (marg. *jawteeth*, or, *the grinders*) *of* the wicked,
Pro.30:14. *their jaw teeth* (as) knives,
Joel 1: 6. *and* he hath *the cheek teeth of*

4974 **מְתֹם** *m'thōhm*, m.

Jud.20:48. *as well the men* of (every) city,
Ps. 38: 3(4), 7(8). no *soundness* in my flesh
Isa. 1: 6. the head (there is) no *soundness* in it;

4976 **מַתָּן** *mat-tāhn'*, m.

Gen34:12. Ask me never so much dowry *and gift*,
Nu. 18:11. the heave offering of *their gift*,
Pro.18:16. A man's *gift* maketh room for him,
19: 6. every man (is) a friend to him that *giveth gifts.* (marg. a man of *gifts*)
21:14. *A gift* in secret pacifieth anger:

4978 **מַתְּנָא** [*mat-t'nāh'*], Ch. f.

Dan. 2: 6. shall receive of me *gifts* and rewards
48. *and* gave him many great *gifts*,
5:17. Let *thy gifts* be to thyself,

4979 **מַתָּנָה** *mat-tāh-nāh'*, f.

Gen25: 6. Abraham gave *gifts*,
Ex. 28:38. all their holy *gifts;*
Lev.23:38. beside *your gifts*,
Nu. 18: 6. *a gift* for the Lord,
7. a service of *gift:*
29. Out of all *your gifts* ye shall offer
Deu16:17. Every man (shall give) as he is able, (marg. *according to the gift of* his hand)
2Ch21: 3. their father gave them great *gifts*
Est. 9:22. sending portions one to another, *and gifts*
Ps. 68:18(19). thou hast received *gifts* for men;
Pro.15:27. he that hateth *gifts* shall live.
Ecc. 7: 7. *a gift* destroyeth the heart.
Eze.20:26. I polluted them *in their own gifts*,
31. when ye offer *your gifts*,
39. my holy name no more *with your gifts*,
46:16. the prince give *a gift* unto any of his sons,
17. if he give *a gift* of his inheritance

4975 **מָתְנַיִם** *moth-nah'-yim*, dual, m.

Gen37:34. put sackcloth *upon his loins*,
Ex. 12:11. (with) *your loins* girded,
28:42. *from the loins* even unto the thighs
Deu33:11. smite through *the loins*
2Sa.20: 8. a sword fastened *upon his loins*
1K. 2: 5. his girdle that (was) *about his loins*,
12:10. shall be thicker *than* my father's *loins*.
18:46. and he girded up *his loins*,
1K. 20:31. put sackcloth *on our loins*,
32. they girded sackcloth *on their loins*,
2K. 1: 8. a girdle of leather *about his loins*.
4:29 & 9:1. Gird up *thy loins*, and take
2Ch 10:10. thicker *than* my father's *loins*.
Neh. 4:18(12). his sword girded by *his side*, (marg. on *his loins*)
Job 12:18. girdeth *their loins* with a girdle. (lit. a girdle *upon their loins*)
40:16. his strength (is) *in his loins*,
Ps. 66:11. laidst affliction *upon our loins*.
69:23(24). *and* make *their loins* continually to
Pro.30:31. A greyhound (marg. girt in *the loins*, or, horse); an he goat also;
31:17. She girdeth *her loins* with strength,
Isa. 11: 5. righteousness shall be the girdle of *his loins*,
20: 2. loose the sackcloth from off *thy loins*,
21: 3. are *my loins* filled with pain:
45: 1. *and* I will loose *the loins of* kings,
Jer. 1:17. gird up *thy loins*,
13: 1. put it upon *thy loins*,
2. and put (it) on *my loins*.
4. the girdle...which (is) upon *thy loins*,
11. as the girdle cleaveth to *the loins of*
48:37. upon *the loins* sackcloth.
Eze. 1:27. the appearance of *his loins* even upward, and from the appearance of *his loins*
8: 2. from the appearance of *his loins* even downward, fire; *and from his loins* even
9: 2. a writer's inkhorn *by his side:* (marg. *upon his loins*)
3. the writer's inkhorn *by his side;*
11. the inkhorn *by his side*,
21: 6(11). the breaking of (thy) *loins;*
23:15. Girded with girdles *upon their loins*,
29: 7. madest all *their loins* to be at a stand.
44:18. linen breeches upon *their loins;*
47: 4. the waters (were) to *the loins*.
Dan10: 5. *whose loins* (were) girded
Am. 8:10. I will bring up sackcloth upon all *loins*,
Nah. 2: 1(2). make (thy) *loins* strong,
10(11). much pain (is) in all *loins*,

מָתַק [*māh-thak'*] 4985

* KAL.—*Preterite.* * 4988

Job 21:33. The clods of the valley *shall be sweet*
24:20. the worm *shall feed sweetly on him;*

KAL.—*Future.*

Ex. 15:25. the waters *were made sweet:*
Pro. 9:17. Stolen waters *are sweet*,

* HIPHIL.—*Future.* *

Job 20:12. Though wickedness *be sweet*
Ps. 55:14(15). We *took sweet* counsel (marg. Who *sweetened* counsel)

מֶתֶק *meh'-thek*, m. 4986

Pro.16:21. *and the sweetness of* the lips
27: 9. *so* (doth) *the sweetness of* a man's friend

מֹתֶק [*mōh'-thek*], m. 4987

Jud. 9:11. Should I forsake *my sweetness*,

מַתַּת *mat-tath'*, f. 4991

1K. 13: 7. thyself, and I will give thee *a reward*.
Pro.25:14. Whoso boasteth himself *of a false gift*
Ecc. 3:13. of all his labour, it (is) *the gift of* God.
5:19(18). in his labour; this (is) *the gift of* God.
Eze.46: 5. as he shall be able *to give*, (marg. *the gift of* his hand)
11. as he is able *to give*, (lit. *id.*)

נ *nun.*

The fourteenth letter of the Alphabet.

4995 **נָא** *nāh*, adj.

Ex. 12: 9. Eat not of it *raw*,

4994 **נָא** *nāh*, part.

Gen12:11. Behold *now*, I know that thou (art)
13. Say, *I pray thee*, thou (art) my sister:
18: 4. water, *I pray you*, be fetched,
30. *Oh* let not the Lord be angry,
Ex. 33:18. *I beseech thee*, shew me thy glory.
Nu. 12:12. Let (lit. Let, *I pray thee*) her not be as one dead,
Jud. 7: 3. *go to*, proclaim in the ears of
9:38. go out, *I pray* now, and fight
13: 8. let) (the man of God which thou didst send
&c. &c.

4997 **נֹאד** *nōhd*, m.

Jos. 9: 4. *and* wine *bottles*, old, and rent,
13. these *bottles of* wine,
Jud. 4:19. she opened *a bottle of* milk,
1Sa.16:20. *and a bottle of* wine, and a kid,
Ps. 56: 8(9). put thou my tears *into thy bottle:*
119:83. I am become *like a bottle* in the smoke;

4998 **נָאָה** [*nāh-āh'*].

* PILEL.—*Preterite.* *

Ps. 93: 5. holiness *becometh* thine house,
Cant.1:10. Thy cheeks *are comely* with rows
Isa. 52: 7. How *beautiful* upon the mountains *are*

4999 **נָאָה** [*nāh-āh'*], f.

Ps. 23: 2. He maketh me to lie down *in* green *pastures:*
65:12(13). *the pastures of* the wilderness:
74:20. full of *the habitations of* cruelty.
83:12(13). Let us take to ourselves *the houses of* God in possession.
Jer. 9:10(9). *the habitations* (marg. or, *pastures*) *of* the wilderness
23:10. *the pleasant places of* the wilderness are dried up,
25:37. *the* peaceable *habitations* are cut down
Lam. 2: 2. swallowed up all *the habitations of* Jacob,
Joel 1:19, 20. devoured *the pastures* (marg. or, *habitations*) *of* the wilderness,
2:22. *the pastures of* the wilderness do spring,
Am. 1: 2. *the habitations of* the shepherds shall mourn,

5000 **נָאוֶה** *nāh-veh'*, adj.

Ps. 33: 1. praise is *comely* for the upright.
147: 1. praise is *comely.*
Pro.17: 7. Excellent speech *becometh* not a fool:
19:10. Delight is not *seemly* for a fool;
26: 1. so honour is not *seemly* for a fool.
Cant.1: 5. I (am) black, *but comely,*
2:14. thy countenance (is) *comely.*
4: 3. thy speech (is) *comely:*
6: 4. as Tirzah, *comely* as Jerusalem,

נָאַם [*nāh-am'*]. 5001-02

* KAL.—*Future.* *

Jer. 23:31. use their tongues, *and say*, He saith.

KAL.—*Participle.* Paül.

Gen22:16. *saith* the Lord,
Nu. 14:28. *saith* the Lord,
24: 3, 15. Balaam the son of Beor *hath said, and* the man whose eyes are open *hath said:*
4, 16. *hath said*, which heard the words of God,
1Sa. 2:30. the Lord God of Israel *saith*,
— but now the Lord *saith*,
2Sa.23: 1. David the son of Jesse *said, and* the man who was raised up on high,...*said*,
2K. 9:26, 26 & 19:33 & 22:19. *saith* the Lord;
2Ch 34:27. *saith* the Lord.
Ps. 36: 1(2). The transgression of the wicked *saith*
110: 1. The Lord *said* unto my Lord,
Pro.30: 1. the man *spake* unto Ithiel,
Isa. 1:24. *saith* the Lord, the Lord of hosts,
3:15. *saith* the Lord God of hosts.
14:22, 22, 23 & 17:3, 6. *saith* the Lord
19: 4. *saith* the Lord, the Lord of hosts.
22:25 & 30:1 & 31:9 & 37:34 & 41:14 & 43:10, 12 & 49:18 & 52:5, 5 & 54:17 & 55:8. *saith* the Lord
56: 8. gathereth the outcasts of Israel *saith*,
59:20 & 66:2, 17, 22. *saith* the Lord.
Jer. 1: 8, 15, 19 & 2:3, 9, 12. *saith* the Lord.
2:19, 22. *saith* the Lord God
29. *saith* the Lord.
3: 1, 10, 12, 12, 13, 14, 16, 20 & 4:1, 9, 17 & 5:9, 11, 15, 18, 22, 29 & 6:12 & 7:11, 13, 19, 30, 32 & 8:1, 3, 13, 17 & 9:3(2), 6(5), 9(8), 22(21), 24(23), 25(24) & 12:17 & 13:11, 14, 25 & 15:3, 6, 9, 20 & 16:5, 11, 14, 16 & 17:24 & 18:6 & 19:6, 12 & 21:7, 10, 13, 14 & 22:5, 16, 24 & 23:1, 2, 4, 5, 7, 11, 12, 23, 24, 24, 28, 29, 30, 31. *saith* the Lord.
23:31. use their tongues, and say, *He saith.*
32, 32, 33 & 25:7, 9, 12, 29, 31 & 27:8, 11, 15, 22 & 28:4 & 29:9, 11, 14, 14, 19, 19, 23, 32 & 30:3, 8, 10, 11, 17, 21 & 31:1, 14, 16, 17, 20, 27, 28, 31, 32, 33, 34, 36, 37, 38 & 32:5, 30, 44 & 33:14 & 34:5, 17, 22 & 35:13 & 39:17, 18 & 42:11 & 44:29 & 45:5 & 46:5. *saith* the Lord,
46:18. (As) I live, *saith* the king,
23, 26, 28 & 48:12. *saith* the Lord,
48:15. *saith* the king, whose name (is) the Lord of hosts.
25, 30, 35, 38, 43, 44, 47 & 49:2. *saith* the Lord.
49: 5. *saith* the Lord God
6, 13, 16, 26, 30, 31, 32, 37, 38, 39 & 50:4, 10, 20, 21, 30. *saith* the Lord.
50:31. *saith* the Lord God
35, 40 & 51:24, 25, 26, 39, 48, 52, 53. *saith* the Lord,
51:57. *saith* the king, whose name (is) the Lord of hosts.
Eze. 5:11 & 11:8, 21 & 12:25, 28. *saith* the Lord God;
13: 6, 7. The Lord *saith:*
8, 16 & 14:11, 14, 16, 18, 20, 23 & 15:8 & 16:8, 14, 19, 23, 30, 43, 48. *saith* the Lord God;
16:58. *saith* the Lord.
63 & 17:16 & 18:3, 9, 23, 30, 32 & 20:3, 31, 33, 36, 40, 44 & 21:7(12), 13(18) & 22:12, 31 & 23:34 & 24:14 & 25:14 & 26:5, 14, 21 & 28:10 & 29:20 & 30:6 & 31:18 & 32:8, 14, 16, 31, 32 & 33:11 & 34:8, 15, 30, 31 & 35:6, 11 & 36:14, 15, 23, 32. *saith* the Lord God.
37:14. *saith* the Lord.
38:18, 21 & 39:5, 8, 10, 13, 20, 29 & 43:19, 27 & 44:12, 15, 27 & 45:9, 15 & 47:23 & 48:29. *saith* the Lord God:
Hos. 2:13(15), 16(18), 21(23) & 11:11. *saith* the Lord.
Joel 2:12. *saith* the Lord,
Am. 2:11, 16 & 3:10. *saith* the Lord.

Am. 3:13. *saith* the Lord God,
15 & 4:3. *saith* the Lord.
4: 5. *saith* the Lord God.
6, 8, 9, 10, 11 & 6:8, 14. *saith* the Lord.
8: 3, 9, 11. *saith* the Lord God:
9: 7, 8, 12, 13. *saith* the Lord.
Obad 4, 8. *saith* the Lord,
Mic. 4: 6 & 5:10(9). *saith* the Lord,
Nah. 2:13(14) & 3:5. *saith* the Lord
Zep. 1: 2, 3, 10 & 2:9 & 3:8. *saith* the Lord.
Hag. 1: 9, 13 & 2:4, 4, 4, 8, 9, 14, 17, 23, 23, 23. *saith* the Lord
Zec. 1: 3, 4, 16 & 2:5(9), 6(10), 6(10), 10(14) & 3:9, 10 & 5:4 & 8:6, 11, 17 & 10:12 & 11:6 & 12:1, 4 & 13:2, 7, 8. *saith* the Lord
Mal. 1: 2. *saith* the Lord:

5003 **נָאַף** [*nāh-aph'*].

* KAL.—*Infinitive.* *

Jer. 7: 9. Will ye steal, murder, *and commit adultery,*
23:14. *they commit adultery,* and walk in lies:
Hos. 4: 2. stealing, *and committing adultery,*

KAL.—*Future.*

Ex. 20:14. *Thou shalt* not *commit adultery.*
Lev. 20:10. the man that *committeth adultery*
— (he) that *committeth adultery*
Deu. 5:18(17). Neither *shalt thou commit adultery.*
Jer. 3: 9. *and committed adultery* with stones
5: 7. *they then committed adultery,* and assembled

KAL.—*Participle.* Poël.

Lev. 20:10. *the adulterer and the adulteress* shall surely
Job 24:15. the eye also of *the adulterer*
Pro. 6:32. *whoso committeth adultery* with a woman
Eze. 16:38. *women that break wedlock* and shed blood
23:45. after the manner of *adulteresses,*
— because they (are) *adulteresses,*

* PIEL.—*Preterite.* *

Jer. 3: 8. backsliding Israel *committed adultery*
Eze. 23:37. *they have committed adultery,* and blood
— their idols *have they committed adultery,*

PIEL.—*Future.*

Jer. 29:23. in Israel, *and have committed adultery*
Hos. 4:13. your spouses *shall commit adultery.*
14. when *they commit adultery:*

PIEL.—*Participle.*

Ps. 50:18. hast been partaker with *adulterers.*
Pro. 30:20. the way of an *adulterous* woman;
Isa. 57: 3. the seed of *the adulterer*
Jer. 9: 2(1). they (be) all *adulterers,*
23:10. the land is full of *adulterers;*
Eze. 16:32. a wife *that committeth adultery,*
Hos. 3: 1. a woman beloved...*yet an adulteress,*
7: 4. They (are) all *adulterers,*
Mal. 3: 5. the sorcerers, *and against the adulterers,*

5005 **נַאֲפוּפִים** [*nah-ăphoo-pheem'*], m. pl.

Hos. 2: 2(4). out of her sight, *and her adulteries*

5004 **נִאֻפִים** *nee-oo-pheem'*, m. pl.

Jer. 13:27. I have seen *thine adulteries,*
Eze. 23:43. (her that was) old *in adulteries,*

5006 **נָאַץ** *nāh-atz'*.

* KAL.—*Preterite.* *

Ps. 107:11. *contemned* the counsel of the most High:
Pro. 1:30. *they despised* all my reproof.
5:12. my heart *despised* reproof;

KAL.—*Future.*

Deu 32:19. when the Lord saw (it), *he abhorred* (them),
Pro. 15: 5. A fool *despiseth* his father's instruction:
Jer. 14:21. *Do* not *abhor* (us),
33:24. *they have despised* my people,
Lam. 2: 6. *and hath despised* in the indignation of

* PIEL.—*Preterite.* *

Nu. 16:30. these men *have provoked* the Lord.
Deu 31:20. and serve them, *and provoke me,*
1 Sa. 2:17. men *abhorred* the offering of the Lord.
2 Sa. 12:14. *thou hast given* great *occasion...to blaspheme,*
Ps. 10: 3. the covetous, (whom) the Lord *abhorreth.*
13. Wherefore *doth* the wicked *contemn* God?
74:18. the foolish people *have blasphemed*
Isa. 1: 4. *they have provoked...unto anger;*
5:24. *despised* the word of the Holy One

PIEL.—*Infinitive.*

2 Sa. 12:14. thou hast given *great* occasion to the enemies of the Lord to blaspheme, (lit. *giving occasion to blaspheme* thou hast given occasion to blaspheme)

PIEL.—*Future.*

Nu. 14:11. How long *will* this people *provoke me?*
Ps. 74:10. *shall* the enemy *blaspheme* thy name

PIEL.—*Participle.*

Nu. 14:23. any of them *that provoked me*
Isa. 60:14. all *they that despised thee* shall bow
Jer. 23:17. They say still *unto them that despise me,*

* HIPHIL.—*Future.* *

Ecc. 12: 5. *and* the almond tree *shall flourish,*

* HITHPOLEL.—*Participle.* *

Isa. 52: 5. my name continually every day (is) *blasphemed.*

נְאָצָה *n'āh-tzāh'*, f. 5007

2 K. 19: 3. a day of trouble, and of rebuke, *and blasphemy:* (marg. or, *provocation*)
Isa. 37: 3. a day of trouble, and of rebuke, *and of blasphemy:* (marg. or, *provocation*)

נֶאָצוֹת *neh-āh-tzōhth'*, f. pl. 5007

Neh. 9:18. and had wrought great *provocations;*
26. they wrought great *provocations.*
Eze. 35:12. I have heard all *thy blasphemies*

נָאַק *nāh-ak'*. 5008

* KAL.—*Preterite.* *

Eze. 30:24. *and he shall groan* before him

KAL.—*Future.*

Job 24:12. Men *groan* from out of the city,

נְאָקָה [*n'āh-kāh'*], f. 5009

Ex. 2:24. God heard *their groaning,*
6: 5. I have also heard *the groaning of*
Jud. 2:18. *because of their groanings* by reason
Eze. 30:24. *with the groanings of* a deadly wounded (man).

נָאַר [*nāh-ar'*]. 5010

* PIEL.—*Preterite.* *

Ps. 89:39(40). *Thou hast made void* the covenant
Lam. 2: 7. *he hath abhorred* his sanctuary,

נָבָא [*nāh-vāh'*]. 5012

* NIPHAL.—*Preterite.* *

1 Sa. 10:11. *he prophesied* among the prophets,
1 Ch 25: 2. *which prophesied* according to the order
3. *who prophesied* with a harp,
Jer. 2: 8. the prophets *prophesied* by Baal,
5:31. prophets *prophesy* falsely, and the priests
20: 1. Jeremiah *prophesied* these things.
6. *thou hast prophesied* lies.
23:21. yet *they prophesied.*
25:13. Jeremiah *hath prophesied*
26: 9. Why *hast thou prophesied*

Jer. 26:11. *he hath prophesied* against this city,
28: 6. words which *thou hast prophesied*,
29:31. Shemaiah *hath prophesied*
37:19. your prophets which *prophesied*
Eze. 4: 7. *and thou shalt prophesy* against it.
12:27. *he prophesieth* of the times
37: 7. *So I prophesied* as I was commanded:
Joel 2:28(3:1). *and* your sons and your daughters *shall prophesy*,

NIPHAL.—*Infinitive.*

Jer. 19:14. the Lord had sent him *to prophesy;*
26:12. The Lord sent me *to prophesy*
Eze.11:13. it came to pass, *when I prophesied*,
37: 7. and *as I prophesied*,
Am. 7:13. *prophesy* not again any more
Zec.13: 3. thrust him through *when he prophesieth.*
4. of his vision, *when he hath prophesied;*

NIPHAL.—*Imperative.*

Eze. 6: 2. *and prophesy* against them,
11: 4. *prophesy* against them, *prophesy*, O son of man.
13: 2. *prophesy* against the prophets
17. *and prophesy thou* against them,
20:46(21:2). *and prophesy* against the forest
21: 2(7). *and prophesy* against the land of Israel,
9(14), 28(33). Son of man, *prophesy*, and say,
14(19). son of man, *prophesy*,
25: 2. *and prophesy* against them;
28:21. against Zidon, *and prophesy* against it,
29: 2. *and prophesy* against him,
30: 2. Son of man, *prophesy* and say,
34: 2. *prophesy* against the shepherds of Israel, *prophesy*,
35: 2. against mount Seir, *and prophesy*
36: 1. *prophesy* unto the mountains of Israel,
3. Therefore *prophesy* and say,
6. *Prophesy* therefore concerning the land
37: 4. *Prophesy* upon these bones,
9. *Prophesy* unto the wind, *prophesy*,
12. Therefore *prophesy* and say unto them,
38: 2. *and prophesy* against him,
14. *prophesy* and say unto Gog,
39: 1. *prophesy* against Gog,
Am. 7:15. *prophesy* unto my people Israel.

NIPHAL.—*Future.*

Jer. 11:21. *Prophesy* not in the name of the Lord,
25:30. *prophesy* thou against them
26:20. *who prophesied* against this city
28: 8. The prophets...of old *prophesied both*
9. The prophet which *prophesieth*
Am. 2:12. the prophets, saying, *Prophesy* not.
3: 8. who *can* but *prophesy?*
7:12. and *prophesy* there:
16. *Prophesy* not against Israel,
Zec.13: 3. when any *shall* yet *prophesy*,

NIPHAL.—*Participle.*

1Sa.19:20. the prophets *prophesying*,
1K. 22:12. all the prophets *prophesied*
1Ch 25: 1. *who should prophesy* with harps,
2Ch 18:11. all the prophets *prophesied*
Jer. 14:14. The prophets *prophesy* lies in my name:
15. the prophets *that prophesy* in my
16. the people to whom *they prophesy*
23:16. words of the prophets *that prophesy*
25. what the prophets said, *that prophesy*
26. the heart of the prophets *that prophesy*
32. them *that prophesy* false dreams,
26:18. Micah the Morasthite *prophesied* (lit. was *prophesying*)
27:10, 14. *they prophesy* a lie unto you,
15. yet *they prophesy* a lie in my name;
— the prophets *that prophesy* unto you.
16. your prophets *that prophesy*
— *they prophesy* a lie
29: 9. *they prophesy* falsely unto you
21. *which prophesy* a lie unto you
32: 3. Wherefore *dost* thou *prophesy*,
Eze.13: 2. the prophets of Israel *that prophesy*,
16. the prophets of Israel *which prophesy*
38:17. the prophets of Israel, *which prophesied*

* HITHPAEL.—*Preterite.* *

1Sa.10: 6. *and thou shalt prophesy* with them,
Jer. 23:13. *they prophesied* in Baal,
Eze.37:10. *So I prophesied* as he commanded

HITHPAEL.—*Infinitive.*

1Sa.10:13. when he had made an end *of prophesying.*

HITHPAEL.—*Future.*

Nu. 11:25. *that*, when...*they prophesied*, and did not
26. *and they prophesied* in the camp.
1Sa.10:10. *and he prophesied* among them.
18:10. *and he prophesied* in the midst
19:20. *and they* also *prophesied.*
21. *and they prophesied* likewise.
— *and they prophesied* also.
23. he went on, *and prophesied*,
24. *and prophesied* before Samuel
1K. 18:29. *and they prophesied* until the (time) of
22: 8. *he doth* not *prophesy* good
18. *he would prophesy* no good
2Ch 18:17. *he would* not *prophesy* good
20:37. *Then* Eliezer the son of Dodavah...*prophesied*

HITHPAEL.—*Participle.*

Nu. 11:27. Eldad and Medad *do prophesy*
1Sa.10: 5. and they *shall prophesy:*
1K. 22:10. all the prophets *prophesied*
2Ch 18: 7. he never *prophesied* good
9. all the prophets *prophesied*
Jer. 14:14. *they prophesy* unto you a false vision
26:20. a man *that prophesied* in the name of
29:26. mad, *and maketh himself a prophet*,
27. *which maketh himself a prophet* to you?
Eze.13:17. daughters of thy people, *which prophesy*

נְבָא [*n'vāh*], Ch. 5013

* ITHPAEL.—*Preterite.* *

Ezr. 5: 1. *Then* the prophets,...*prophesied*

נָבַב [*nāh-vav'*]. 5014

* KAL.—*Participle.* Paül. *

Ex. 27: 8. *Hollow* with boards shalt thou make
38: 7. he made the altar *hollow*
Job 11:12. *vain* (marg. *empty*) man would be wise,
Jer. 52:21. the thickness thereof (was) four fingers: (it was) *hollow.*

נְבוּאָה *n'voo-āh'*, f. 5016

2Ch 9:29. in *the prophecy of* Ahijah
15: 8. *and the prophecy* of Oded
Neh. 6:12. he pronounced *this prophecy*

נְבוּאָה [*n'voo-āh'*], Ch. f. 5017

Ezr. 6:14. *through the prophesying of* Haggai

נְבִזְבָּה *n'viz-bāh'*, Ch. f. 5023

Dan 2: 6. ye shall receive of me gifts *and rewards* (marg. or, *fee*)
5:17. *and* give *thy rewards* (marg. or, *fee*) to another;

נָבַח [*nāh-vagh'*]. 5024

* KAL.—*Infinitive.* *

Isa. 56:10. all dumb dogs, they cannot *bark;*

נָבַט [*nāh-vat'*]. 5027

* PIEL.—*Preterite.* *

Isa. 5:30. *and* if (one) *look* unto the land,

* HIPHIL.—*Preterite.* *

Ex. 33: 8. *and looked* after Moses,
Nu. 21: 9. *when he beheld* the serpent of brass,
23:21. *He hath* not *beheld* iniquity in Jacob,
1Sa. 2:32. *And thou shalt see* an enemy

Job 6:19. The troops of Tema *looked*,
Ps. 33:13. The Lord *looketh* from heaven ;
34: 5(6). *They looked* (marg. or, *flowed*) unto him,
102:19(20). from heaven *did* the Lord *behold*
Isa. 22:11. *ye have* not *looked* unto the maker
Zec.12:10. *and they shall look* upon me

HIPHIL.—*Infinitive.*

Ex. 3: 6. he was afraid *to look*
Ps.119: 6. *when I have respect* unto all thy
Lam.4:16. he will no more *regard them:*
Jon. 2: 4(5). will *look* again toward thy holy temple.
Hab. 1:13. *and* canst not *look* on iniquity:
2:15. *that thou mayest look* on their nakedness !

HIPHIL.—*Imperative.*

Gen15: 5. *Look* now toward heaven,
1K. 18:43. *look* toward the sea.
Job 35: 5. *Look* unto the heavens,
Ps. 13: 3(4). *Consider* (and) hear me, O Lord
74:20. *Have respect* unto the covenant:
80:14(15). *look down* from heaven,
84: 9(10). *and look upon* the face of thine anointed.
142: 4(5). *I looked* (marg. or, *Look*) on (my) right hand,
Isa. 42:18. *look*, ye blind, that ye may see.
51: 1. *look* unto the rock (whence) ye are hewn,
2. *Look* unto Abraham your father,
6. *and look* upon the earth beneath:
63:15. *Look* down from heaven,
64: 9(8). behold, *see*, we beseech
Lam. 1:11. see, O Lord, *and consider;*
12. *behold*, and see if there be any sorrow
2:20. Behold, O Lord, *and consider* to whom
3:63. *Behold* their sitting down,
5: 1. *consider*, and behold our reproach.
Hab. 1: 5. Behold ye among the heathen, *and regard*,

HIPHIL.—*Future.*

Gen19:17. *look* not behind thee,
26. *But* his wife *looked* back
Nu. 12: 8. the similitude of the Lord *shall he behold:*
1Sa.16: 7. *Look* not on his countenance,
17:42. *And when* the Philistine *looked about*,
24: 8(9). *And when* Saul *looked* behind him,
1K. 18:43. And he went up, *and looked*,
19: 6. *And he looked*, and, behold,
2K. 3:14. *I would* not *look* toward thee,
1Ch 21:21. *And* as David came to Ornan, Ornan *looked*
Job 28:24. *he looketh* to the ends of the earth,
36:25. man *may behold* (it) afar off.
39:29. her eyes *behold* afar off.
Ps. 10:14. *thou beholdest* mischief and spite,
22:17(18). *they look* (and) stare upon me.
91: 8. with thine eyes *shalt thou behold*
92:11(12). Mine eye *also shall see* (my desire)
94: 9. he that formed the eye, *shall he* not *see?*
119:15. *and have respect* unto thy ways.
18. *that I may behold* wondrous things
Pro. 4:25. *Let* thine eyes *look* right on,
Isa. 5:12. *they regard* not the work of the Lord,
8:22. *they shall look* unto the earth ;
18: 4. *and I will consider* in my dwelling (marg. or, *regard* my set dwelling) place
22: 8. *and thou didst look* in that day
38:11. *I shall behold* man no more
63: 5. *And I looked*, and (there was) none to help;
66: 2. to this (man) *will I look*,
Am. 5:22. neither *will I regard*
Hab. 1: 3. Why dost thou...and *cause* (me) *to behold* grievance?
13. wherefore *lookest thou* upon them

HIPHIL.—*Participle.*

Ps.104:32. *He looketh* on the earth,

5030 **נָבִיא** *nāh-vee'*, m.

Gen20: 7. he (is) *a prophet*, and he shall pray
Ex. 7: 1. Aaron thy brother shall be *thy prophet.*
Nu. 11:29. the Lord's people were *prophets*,
12: 6. If there be *a prophet among you*,
Deu 13: 1(2). If there arise among you *a prophet*,
3(4). the words of that *prophet*,
5(6). *And* that *prophet*, or that dreamer
Deu18:15. will raise up unto thee *a Prophet*
18. I will raise them up *a Prophet*
20. But *the prophet*, which shall presume
— even that *prophet* shall die.
22. When *a prophet* speaketh
— *the prophet* hath spoken it presumptuously:
34:10. there arose not *a prophet*
Jud. 6: 8. the Lord sent *a prophet*
1Sa. 3:20. *a prophet* of the Lord.
9: 9. (he that is) now (called) *a Prophet*
10: 5. meet a company of *prophets*
10. a company of *prophets* met him ;
11. he prophesied among *the prophets*,
—, 12. (Is) Saul also *among the prophets?*
19:20. the company of *the prophets*
24. (Is) Saul also *among the prophets?*
22: 5. *the prophet* Gad said unto David,
28: 6. neither by dreams, nor by Urim, nor *by prophets.*
15. neither *by prophets*, nor by dreams:
2Sa. 7: 2. the king said unto Nathan *the prophet*,
12:25. the hand of Nathan *the prophet;*
24:11. came unto *the prophet* Gad,
1K. 1: 8. and Nathan *the prophet*, and Shimei,
10. But Nathan *the prophet*,
22. Nathan *the prophet* also came in.
23. Behold Nathan *the prophet.*
32. the priest, and Nathan *the prophet*,
34. and Nathan *the prophet* anoint
38. and Nathan *the prophet*, and Benaiah
44. and Nathan *the prophet*, and Benaiah
45. and Nathan *the prophet* have anointed
11:29. that *the prophet* Ahijah
13:11. *Now* there dwelt an old *prophet* in Beth-el;
18. I (am) *a prophet* also
20, 26. *the prophet* that brought him back:
23. *the prophet* whom he had brought back.
25. where the old *prophet* dwelt.
29. *the prophet* took up the carcase
— *the* old *prophet* came to the city,
14: 2. there (is) Ahijah *the prophet*,
18. his servant Ahijah *the prophet.*
16: 7. by the hand of *the prophet* Jehu
12. by Jehu *the prophet*,
18: 4. *the prophets of* the Lord, that Obadiah took an hundred *prophets*,
13. when Jezebel slew *the prophets of*
— an hundred men *of* the Lord's *prophets*
19. *the prophets of* Baal four hundred and fifty, *and the prophets of* the groves
20. gathered *the prophets* together
22. I only, remain *a prophet* of the Lord ; *but* Baal's *prophets* (are) four hundred
25. Elijah said *unto the prophets of* Baal,
36. Elijah *the prophet* came near,
40. Take *the prophets of* Baal ;
19: 1. had slain all *the prophets*
10, 14. slain *thy prophets* with the sword ;
16. shalt thou anoint (to be) *prophet*
20:13. there came a *prophet* unto Ahab
22. *the prophet* came to the king of Israel,
35. the sons of *the prophets*
38. So *the prophet* departed,
41. he (was) *of the prophets.*
22: 6. the king of Israel gathered *the prophets*
7. *a prophet* of the Lord
10. all *the prophets* prophesied before them.
12. all *the prophets* prophesied so,
13. the words of *the prophets*
22. the mouth of all *his prophets.*
23. the mouth of all these *thy prophets*,
2K. 2: 3. the sons of *the prophets* that (were) at Beth-el
5. sons of *the prophets* that (were) at Jericho
7. fifty men of the sons of *the prophets*
15. And when the sons of *the prophets*
3:11. (Is there) not here *a prophet*
13. get thee to *the prophets of* thy father, and to *the prophets of* thy mother.
4: 1. of the wives of the sons of *the prophets*
38. the sons of *the prophets* (were) sitting before him:
— seethe pottage for the sons of *the prophets.*
5: 3. *the prophet* that (is) in Samaria !
8. there is *a prophet* in Israel.
13. (if) *the prophet* had bid thee

2K. 5:22. young men of the sons of *the prophets:*
6: 1. the sons of *the prophets* said unto Elisha,
12. *the prophet* that (is) in Israel,
9: 1. Elisha *the prophet* called one of the children of *the prophets*,
4. the young man *the prophet*,
7. the blood of my servants *the prophets*,
10:19. all *the prophets of* Baal,
14:25. the son of Amittai, *the prophet*,
17:13. by all *the prophets*,
— by my servants *the prophets.*
23. by all his servants *the prophets.*
19: 2. Isaiah *the prophet* the son of Amoz.
20: 1. And *the prophet* Isaiah
11. And Isaiah *the prophet* cried
14. Then came Isaiah *the prophet*
21:10. his servants *the prophets*,
23: 2. the priests, *and the prophets*,
18. *the prophet* that came out of Samaria.
24: 2. by his servants *the prophets.*
1Ch 16:22. *and* do *my prophets* no harm.
17: 1. David said to Nathan *the prophet*,
25: 1. (כתיב) *who should prophesy* with harps,
29:29. the book of Nathan *the prophet*,
2Ch 9:29. the book of Nathan *the prophet*,
12: 5. Then came Shemaiah *the prophet*
15. the book of Shemaiah *the prophet*,
13:22. the story of *the prophet* Iddo.
15: 8. the prophecy of Oded *the prophet*,
18: 5. of *prophets* four hundred men,
6. *a prophet* of the Lord
9. all *the prophets* prophesied before them.
11. all *the prophets* prophesied so,
12. the words of *the prophets* (declare) good
21. the mouth of all *his prophets.*
22. the mouth of these *thy prophets*,
20:20. believe *his prophets*,
21:12. from Elijah *the prophet*,
24:19. Yet he sent *prophets* to them,
25:15. he sent unto him *a prophet*,
16. Then *the prophet* forbare,
26:22. did Isaiah *the prophet*,
28: 9. *a prophet* of the Lord was there,
29:25. and Nathan *the prophet:*
— by *his prophets.*
32:20. *the prophet* Isaiah
32. in the vision of Isaiah *the prophet*,
35:18. the days of Samuel *the prophet;*
36:12. before Jeremiah *the prophet*
16. his words, and misused *his prophets*,
Ezr. 9:11. by thy servants *the prophets*,
Neh. 6: 7. thou hast also appointed *prophets*
14. the rest of *the prophets*,
9:26. and slew *thy prophets*
30. by thy spirit in *thy prophets:*
32. on our priests, *and on our prophets*,
Ps. 51 [title](2). Nathan *the prophet* came unto him,
74: 9. (there is) no more any *prophet:*
105:15. *and* do *my prophets* no harm.
Isa. 3: 2. the judge, *and the prophet*,
9:15(14). *and the prophet* that teacheth lies,
28: 7. the priest *and the prophet* have erred
29:10. *the prophets* and your rulers,
37: 2 & 38:1. Isaiah *the prophet* the son of Amoz.
39: 3. Then came Isaiah *the prophet*
Jer. 1: 5. I ordained thee *a prophet*
2: 8. *and the prophets* prophesied by Baal,
26. their priests, *and their prophets*,
30. own sword hath devoured *your prophets*,
4: 9. *and the prophets* shall wonder.
5:13. *And the prophets* shall become wind,
31. *The prophets* prophesy falsely,
6:13. *and from the prophet* even unto the priest
7:25. all my servants *the prophets*,
8: 1. the bones of *the prophets*,
10. *from the prophet* even unto the priest
13:13. the priests, and *the prophets*,
14:13. *the prophets* say unto them,
14. *The prophets* prophesy lies in my name:
15. *the prophets* that prophesy in my name,
— By sword and famine shall those *prophets* be consumed.
18. both *the prophet* and the priest
18:18. nor the word *from the prophet.*
20: 2. Pashur smote Jeremiah *the prophet*,
23: 9. broken *because of the prophets;*
11. both *prophet* and priest are profane;

Jer. 23:13. *And* I have seen folly in *the prophets of*
14. have seen *also in the prophets of* Jerusalem
15. concerning *the prophets;*
— from *the prophets of* Jerusalem
16. Hearken not unto the words of *the prophets*
21. I have not sent these *prophets*,
25. I have heard what *the prophets* said,
26. the heart of *the prophets*
— *yea,* (they are) *prophets of* the deceit
28. *The prophet* that hath a dream,
30, 31. I (am) against *the prophets*, saith the Lord,
33. *the prophet*, or a priest,
34. *And* (as for) *the prophet*,
37. Thus shalt thou say to *the prophet*,
25: 2. Jeremiah *the prophet* spake
4. all his servants *the prophets*,
26: 5. the words of my servants *the prophets*,
7. So the priests *and the prophets*
8. that the priests *and the prophets*
11. Then spake the priests *and the prophets*
16. unto the priests and to *the prophets;*
27: 9. hearken not ye to *your prophets*,
14. the words of *the prophets*
15. *and the prophets* that prophesy unto you.
16. *your prophets* that prophesy unto you,
18. But if they (be) *prophets*,
28: 1. Hananiah the son of Azur *the prophet*,
5. Then *the prophet* Jeremiah said unto *the prophet* Hananiah
6. Even *the prophet* Jeremiah said, Amen:
8. *The prophets* that have been before me
9. *The prophet* which prophesieth
— the word of *the prophet*
— shall *the prophet* be known,
10. Then Hananiah *the prophet* took the yoke from off *the prophet* Jeremiah's neck,
11. *the prophet* Jeremiah went his way.
12. Hananiah *the prophet* had broken the yoke from off the neck of *the prophet* Jeremiah,
15. Then said *the prophet* Jeremiah unto Hananiah *the prophet*,
17. So Hananiah *the prophet* died
29: 1. that Jeremiah *the prophet* sent
— to the priests, and to *the prophets*,
8. Let not *your prophets* and your diviners,
15. The Lord hath raised us up *prophets*
19. by my servants *the prophets*,
29. the ears of Jeremiah *the prophet.*
32: 2. Jeremiah *the prophet* was shut up
32. their priests, *and their prophets*,
34: 6. Then Jeremiah *the prophet* spake
35:15. all my servants *the prophets*,
36: 8. *the prophet* commanded him,
26. Jeremiah *the prophet:*
37: 2. he spake by *the prophet* Jeremiah.
3. to *the prophet* Jeremiah,
6. the word of the Lord unto *the prophet*
13. he took Jeremiah *the prophet*,
19. Where (are) now *your prophets*
38: 9. all that they have done to Jeremiah *the prophet*,
10. take up Jeremiah *the prophet*
14. took Jeremiah *the prophet*
42: 2. said unto Jeremiah *the prophet*,
4. Then Jeremiah *the prophet* said unto them,
43: 6. and Jeremiah *the prophet*,
44: 4. all my servants *the prophets*,
45: 1. The word that Jeremiah *the prophet* spake
46: 1. came to Jeremiah *the prophet*
13. spake to Jeremiah *the prophet*,
47: 1 & 49:34. came to Jeremiah *the prophet*
50: 1. by Jeremiah *the prophet.*
51:59. The word which Jeremiah *the prophet* commanded
Lam. 2: 9. *her prophets* also find no vision
14. *Thy prophets* have seen vain and foolish things
20. shall the priest *and the prophet* be slain
4:13. the sins of *her prophets*,
Eze. 2: 5. there hath been *a prophet* among them.
7:26. a vision of *the prophet;*
13: 2. prophesy against *the prophets of*
— say thou *unto them that prophesy* (marg. are *prophets*) out of their own hearts,
3. Woe unto *the* foolish *prophets*,
4. *thy prophets* are like the foxes

Eze.13: 9. *the prophets* that see vanity,
16. *the prophets of* Israel which prophesy
14: 4. cometh to *the prophet;*
7. cometh to *a prophet*
9. *And* if *the prophet* be deceived
— I the Lord have deceived *that prophet,*
10. the punishment of *the prophet*
22:25. (There is) a conspiracy of *her prophets*
28. *her prophets* have daubed them
33:33. *a prophet* hath been among them.
38:17. my servants *the prophets of* Israel,
Dan. 9: 2. came to Jeremiah *the prophet,*
6. thy servants *the prophets,*
10. his servants *the prophets.*
24. to seal up the vision *and prophecy,* (marg. *prophet*)
Hos. 4: 5. *the prophet* also shall fall
6: 5. I hewed (them) *by the prophets;*
9: 7. *the prophet* (is) a fool,
8. *the prophet* (is) a snare
12:10(11). I have also spoken by *the prophets,*
—(—). by the ministry of *the prophets.*
13(14). *And by a prophet* the Lord brought
—(—). *and by a prophet* was he preserved.
Am. 2:11. I raised up of your sons *for prophets,*
12. and commanded *the prophets,* saying,
3: 7. his servants *the prophets.*
7:14. I (was) no *prophet,* neither (was) I *a prophet*'s son;
Mic. 3: 5. *the prophets* that make my people err,
6. the sun shall go down over *the prophets,*
11. *and the prophets thereof* divine for money:
Hab. 1: 1. which Habakkuk *the prophet* did see.
3: 1. A prayer of Habakkuk *the prophet*
Zep. 3: 4. *Her prophets* (are) light (and) treacherous
Hag. 1: 1, 3. the word of the Lord by Haggai *the prophet*
12. the words of Haggai *the prophet,*
2: 1. by *the prophet* Haggai,
10. by Haggai *the prophet,*
Zec. 1: 1, 7. the son of Iddo *the prophet,*
4. unto whom *the* former *prophets* have cried,
5. *and the prophets,* do they live for ever?
6. my servants *the prophets,*
7: 3. speak unto the priests...and to *the prophets,*
7. cried by *the* former *prophets,*
12. sent in his spirit by *the* former *prophets:*
8: 9. by the mouth of *the prophets,*
13: 2. *the prophets* and the unclean spirit
4. *the prophets* shall be ashamed
5. I (am) no *prophet,*
Mal. 4: 5(3:23). Behold, I will send you Elijah *the prophet*

5029 **נְבִיא** [*n'vee*], Ch. m.

Ezr. 5: 1. Then *the prophets,* Haggai *the prophet,* and Zechariah the son of Iddo, prophesied
2. and with them (were) *the prophets* of God
6:14. through the prophesying of Haggai *the prophet*

5031 **נְבִיאָה** *n'vee-āh',* f.

Ex. 15:20. Miriam *the prophetess,*
Jud. 4: 4. Deborah, a *prophetess,* (lit. a woman *a prophetess*)
2K. 22:14. Huldah *the prophetess,*
2Ch 34:22. Huldah *the prophetess,*
Neh. 6:14. *the prophetess* Noadiah,
Isa. 8: 3. I went unto *the prophetess;*

5033 **נֵבֶךְ** [*nĕh'-vĕch*], m.

Job 38:16. entered into *the springs of* the sea?

5034 **נָבֵל** *nāh-vĕhl'.*

* KAL.—*Preterite.* *

Pro.30:32. If *thou hast done foolishly*
Isa. 24: 4. The earth mourneth (and) *fadeth away,* the world languisheth (and) *fadeth away,*
40: 7, 8. The grass withereth, the flower *fadeth:*
Jer. 8:13. and the leaf *shall fade;*

KAL.—*Infinitive.*

Ex. 18:18. Thou wilt *surely* wear away, (marg. *Fading* thou wilt fade)
Isa. 34: 4. *as* the leaf *falleth off*

KAL.—*Future.*

Ex. 18:18. *Thou wilt* surely *wear away,* (marg. Fading *thou wilt fade*)
2Sa.22:46. Strangers *shall fade away,*
Job 14:18. the mountain falling *cometh to nought,* (marg. *fadeth*)
Ps. 1: 3. his leaf also *shall* not *wither;* (marg. *fade*)
18:45(46). strangers *shall fade away,*
37: 2. and *wither* as the green herb.
Isa. 34: 4. all their host *shall fall down,*
64: 6(5). *and we* all *do fade* as a leaf;
Eze.47:12. whose leaf *shall* not *fade,*

KAL.—*Participle.* Poel.

Isa. 1:30. as an oak whose leaf *fadeth,*
28: 1. whose glorious beauty (is) a *fading* flower,
4. glorious beauty,...shall be a *fading* flower,
34: 4. *as a falling* (fig) from

* PIEL.—*Preterite.* *

Nah. 3: 6. I will cast abominable filth upon thee, *and make thee vile,*

PIEL.—*Future.*

Deu32:15. *and lightly esteemed* the Rock of his salvation.
Jer. 14:21. *do* not *disgrace* the throne of thy glory:

PIEL.—*Participle.*

Mic. 7: 6. the son *dishonoureth* the father,

נָבָל *nāh-vāhl',* adj. 5036

Deu32: 6. O *foolish* people and unwise?
21. I will provoke them to anger with a *foolish* nation.
2Sa. 3:33. Died Abner as *a fool* dieth?
13:13. thou shalt be as one of *the fools* in Israel.
Job 2:10. Thou speakest as one of *the foolish women*
30: 8. (They were) children of *fools,*
Ps. 14: 1. *The fool* hath said in his heart,
39: 8(9). make me not the reproach of *the foolish.*
53: 1(2). *The fool* hath said in his heart,
74:18. the *foolish* people have blasphemed
22. *the foolish man* reproacheth thee
Pro.17: 7. Excellent speech becometh not *a fool:*
21. the father of *a fool* hath no joy.
30:22. *and a fool* when he is filled with meat;
Isa. 32: 5. *The vile person* shall be no more called liberal,
6. *the vile person* will speak villany,
Jer. 17:11. at his end shall be *a fool.*
Eze.13: 3. Woe unto the *foolish* prophets,

נֵבֶל & נֶבֶל *nĕh'-vel,* m. 5035

1Sa. 1:24. one ephah of flour, *and a bottle of* wine,
10: 3. another carrying *a bottle of* wine:
25:18. two *bottles of* wine,
2Sa.16: 1. *and a bottle of* wine.
Job 38:37. *or* who can stay *the bottles of* heaven,
Isa. 30:14. as the breaking of the potters' *vessel* (marg *bottle of* potters)
Jer. 13:12, 12. Every *bottle* shall be filled with wine:
48:12. empty his vessels, and break *their bottles.*
Lam.4: 2. esteemed *as* earthen *pitchers,*

נֵבֶל & נֶבֶל *nĕh'-vel,* m. 5035

1Sa.10: 5. with *a psaltery,* and a tabret,
2Sa. 6: 5. on harps, *and on psalteries,*
1K. 10:12. harps also *and psalteries*
1Ch 13: 8. with harps, *and with psalteries,*
15:16. *psalteries* and harps and cymbals,
20. *with psalteries* on Alamoth;
28. making a noise *with psalteries*
16: 5. with *psalteries* and with harps;
25: 1. with harps, *with psalteries,* and with cymbals:

1Ch 25: 6. with cymbals, *psalteries*, and harps,
2Ch 5:12. cymbals *and psalteries* and harps,
9:11. harps *and psalteries* for singers:
20:28. came to Jerusalem *with psalteries*
29:25. *with psalteries*, and with harps,
Neh 12:27. (with) cymbals, *psalteries*, and with harps.
Ps. 33: 2. sing unto him *with the psaltery*
57: 8(9). awake, *psaltery* and harp:
71:22. I will also praise thee with the *psaltery*, (marg. instrument of *psaltery*)
81: 2(3). the pleasant harp *with the psaltery*.
92: 3(4). and upon *the psaltery*;
108: 2(3). Awake, *psaltery* and harp:
144: 9. *upon a psaltery* (and) an instrument of
150: 3. praise him *with the psaltery* and harp.
Isa. 5:12. the harp, *and the viol*, the tabret,
14:11. the noise of *thy viols*:
22:24. all the vessels of *flagons*. (marg. or, instruments of *viols*)
Am. 5:23. I will not hear the melody of *thy viols*.
6: 5. That chant to the sound of *the viol*,

5039 נְבָלָה *n'vāh-lāh'*, f.

Gen34: 7. he had wrought *folly*
Deu22:21. she hath wrought *folly* in Israel,
Jos. 7:15. hath wrought *folly* (marg. or, *wickedness*)
Jud.19:23. do not this *folly*.
24. do not *so vile* a thing. (marg. the matter of this *folly*)
20: 6. committed lewdness *and folly* in Israel.
10. *the folly* that they have wrought
1Sa.25:25. Nabal (is) his name, *and folly* (is) with him:
2Sa.13:12. do not thou this *folly*.
Job 42: 8. lest I deal with you (after your) *folly*,
Isa. 9:17(16). and every mouth speaketh *folly*. (marg. or, *villany*)
32: 6. the vile person will speak *villany*,
Jer. 29:23. they have committed *villany*

5038 נְבֵלָה *n'vēh-lāh'*, f.

Lev. 5: 2. *a carcase of* an unclean beast, or *a carcase of* unclean cattle, or *the carcase of* unclean creeping things,
7:24. the fat of *the beast that dieth of itself*, (marg. *carcase*)
11: 8. *and their carcase* shall ye not touch;
11. have *their carcases* in abomination.
24. whosoever toucheth *the carcase of them*
25. whosoever beareth (ought) *of the carcase of them*
27. whoso toucheth *their carcase*
28. he that beareth *the carcase*
35. (any part) *of their carcase* falleth
36. that which toucheth *their carcase*
37. if (any part) *of their carcase* fall
38. and (any part) *of their carcase* fall
39. he that toucheth *the carcase thereof*
40. he that eateth *of the carcase of it*
— he also that beareth *the carcase of it*
17:15. that eateth *that which died* (marg. *a carcase*) (of itself),
22: 8. *That which dieth of itself*, or is torn
Deu14: 8. *nor* touch *their dead carcase*.
21. any thing *that dieth of itself*:
21:23. *His body* shall not remain
28:26. *thy carcase* shall be meat
Jos. 8:29. they should take *his carcase* down
1K. 13:22. *thy carcase* shall not come unto
24. *his carcase* was cast in the way,
— the lion also stood by *the carcase*.
25. and saw *the carcase* cast in the way, and the lion standing by *the carcase*:
28. he went and found *his carcase* cast in the way, and the ass and the lion standing by *the carcase*: the lion had not eaten *the carcase*,
29. the prophet took up *the carcase of*
30. he laid *his carcase* in his own grave;
2K. 9:37. *the carcase of* Jezebel shall be as dung
Ps. 79: 2. *The dead bodies of* thy servants
Isa. 5:25. *their carcases* (were) torn in the midst
26:19. (with) *my dead body* shall they arise.
Jer. 7:33. *the carcases of* this people
9:22(21). *the carcases of* men shall fall
16: 4. *their carcases* shall be meat
18. *with the carcases of* their detestable
19: 7. *their carcases* will I give to be meat
26:23. and cast *his dead body* into
34:20. *their dead bodies* shall be for meat
36:30. *and his dead body* shall be cast out
Eze. 4:14. *for*...have I not eaten of *that which dieth of itself*,
44:31. any thing *that is dead of itself*,

נַבְלוּת [*nav-looth'*], f. 5040

Hos. 2:10(12). now will I discover *her lewdness* (marg. *folly*, or, *villany*)

נָבַע [*nāh-vag'*]. 5042

*** KAL.**—*Participle.* Poel. *****

Pro.18: 4. wellspring of wisdom (as) a *flowing* brook.

*** HIPHIL.**—*Future.* *****

Ps. 19: 2(3). Day unto day *uttereth* speech,
59: 7(8). *they belch out* with their mouth:
78: 2. *I will utter* dark sayings
94: 4. *shall they utter* (and) speak hard things?
119:171. My lips *shall utter* praise,
145: 7. *They shall abundantly utter* the memory
Pro. 1:23. *I will pour out* my spirit unto you,
15: 2. the mouth of fools *poureth out* (marg. *belcheth*, or, *bubbleth*) foolishness.
28. mouth of the wicked *poureth out* evil things.
Ecc.10: 1. Dead flies cause the ointment...*to send forth* a stinking savour:

נֶבְרַשְׁתָּה *nev-rash-tāh'*, Ch. f. 5043

Dan. 5: 5. and wrote over against *the candlestick*

נֶגֶב *neh'-gev*, m. 5045

Gen12: 9. going on still *toward the south*.
13: 1. and Lot with him, *into the south*.
3. *from the south* even to Beth-el,
14. northward, *and southward*, and eastward, and westward:
20: 1. toward the *south* country,
24:62. he dwelt in the *south* country.
28:14. to the north, *and to the south*:
Ex. 26:18. *on* the *south* side southward.
27: 9. the *south* side southward
36:23. twenty boards for the *south* side
38: 9. on the *south* side southward
40:24. on the side of the tabernacle *southward*.
Nu. 13:17. Get you up this (way) *southward*,
22. they ascended *by the south*,
29. in the land of *the south*:
21: 1. king Arad...which dwelt in *the south*,
33:40. king Arad...which dwelt *in the south*
34: 3. your *south* quarter shall be
— your *south* border shall be
4. your border shall turn *from the south*
— *from the south* to Kadesh-barnea,
35: 5. on the *south* side two thousand cubits,
Deu. 1: 7. in the vale, *and in the south*,
34: 3. *the south*, and the plain of the valley of
Jos. 10:40. the country of the hills, *and of the south*,
11: 2. the plains *south of* Chinneroth,
16. all *the south country*,
12: 8. *and in the south country*;
15: 1. the wilderness of Zin *southward*
2. their *south* border was from the shore
— the bay that looketh *southward*:
3. *to the south side* to Maaleh-acrabbim,
— *on the south side* unto Kadesh-barnea,
4. this shall be your *south* coast.
7. *on the south side* of the river:
8. unto the *south* side of the Jebusite;
19. thou hast given me a *south* land;
21. toward the coast of Edom *southward*
17: 9. *southward* of the river:

Jos. 17:10. *Southward* (it was) Ephraim's,
18: 5. Judah shall abide in their coast *on the south*,
13. to the side of Luz,...*southward;*
— *on the south side* of the nether Beth-horon.
14. compassed the corner of the sea *southward*,
— before Beth-horon *southward;*
15. the *south* quarter (was) from
16. to the side of Jebusi *on the south*,
19. *at* the *south* end of Jordan: this (was) the *south* coast.
19: 8. Ramath of *the south*.
34. reacheth to Zebulun *on the south side*,
Jud. 1: 9. *and* in *the south*, and in the valley.
15. thou hast given me a *south* land;
16. *in the south of* Arad;
21:19. *and on the south* of Lebonah.
1 Sa.14: 5. *southward* over against Gibeah.
20:41. out of (a place) toward *the south*,
27:10. Against *the south of* Judah, and against *the south of* the Jerahmeelites, and against *the south of* the Kenites.
30: 1. the Amalekites had invaded *the south*,
14. We made an invasion (upon) *the south*
— upon *the south of* Caleb;
27. (them) which (were) in *south* Ramoth,
2Sa.24: 7. they went out to *the south*
1K. 7:25. three looking *toward the south*,
39. over against *the south*.
1Ch 9:24. toward the east, west, north, *and south*.
26:15. To Obed-edom *southward;*
17. *southward* four a day,
2Ch 4: 4. three looking *toward the south*,
10. over against *the south*.
28:18. *and of the south* of Judah,
Ps.126: 4. as the streams *in the south*.
Isa. 21: 1. As whirlwinds *in the south*
30: 6. The burden of the beasts of *the south:*
Jer. 13:19. The cities of *the south* shall be shut up,
17:26. from the mountains, and from *the south*,
32:44 & 33:13. in the cities of *the south:*
Eze.20:46(21:2). the forest of the *south* field;
47(—:3). say to the forest of *the south*,
—(—:-). *from the south* to the north
21: 4(9). *from the south* to the north:
40: 2. as the frame of a city *on the south*.
46: 9. go out by the way of the *south* gate;
— entereth by the way of the *south* gate
47: 1. *at the south* (side) of the altar.
19. And the *south* side southward, from Tamar
— And (this is) the south side *southward*.
48:10. *and toward the south* five and twenty thousand
16. the *south* side four thousand and five hundred,
17. *and toward the south* two hundred and fifty,
28. at the *south* side southward,
33. at the *south* side four thousand
Dan. 8: 4. pushing westward, and northward, *and southward;*
9. toward *the south*, and toward the east,
11: 5. the king of *the south* shall be strong,
6. the king's daughter of *the south*
9. the king of *the south* shall come
11. the king of *the south* shall be moved
14. against the king of *the south:*
15. the arms of *the south* shall not withstand,
25. against the king of *the south*
— the king of *the south* shall be stirred
29. and come *toward the south;*
40. shall the king of *the south* push
Obad. 19. (they of) *the south* shall possess
20. the cities of *the south*.
Zec. 7: 7. *when* (men) inhabited *the south*
14: 4. half of it *toward the south*.
10. to Rimmon *south of* Jerusalem:

5046 ## נָגַד [*nāh-gad'*].

* HIPHIL.—*Preterite.* *

Gen 3:11. Who *told* thee that thou (wast) naked?
12:18. why *didst thou* not *tell* me
21:26. neither *didst thou tell* me,
31:20. *he told* him not that he fled.
27. and *didst* not *tell* me,
41:25. God *hath shewed* Pharaoh
Gen45:13. *And ye shall tell* my father
Ex. 13: 8. *And thou shalt shew* thy son in that day,
Lev.14:35. shall come *and tell* the priest,
Nu. 23: 3. *and* whatsoever he sheweth me *I will tell* thee.
Deu17: 9. *and they shall shew* thee the sentence
26: 3. I *profess* this day unto the Lord
30:18. *I denounce* unto you this day,
Jud 13: 6. neither *told he* me his name:
14: 6. *he told* not his father
9. *he told* not them that he had taken
16. *hast* not *told* (it) me.
— *I have* not *told* (it) my father
16:15. *hast* not *told* me wherein
18. *he had told* her all his heart,
— *he hath shewed* me all his heart.
1Sa. 3:13. *For I have told* (marg. or, *And I will tell*) him that I will judge
8: 9. *and shew* them the manner of the king
9: 8. give to the man of God, *to tell* (lit. *and he will tell*) us
10:16. *He told* us plainly that the asses were found.
— matter of the kingdom,...*he told* him not.
14: 1. *he told* not his father.
19: 3. what I see, *that I will tell* thee.
24:18(19). thou *hast shewed* this day
25:14. one of the young men *told* Abigail,
19. *she told* not her husband
36. *she told* him nothing,
2Sa. 7:11. *Also* the Lord *telleth* thee
15:31. And (one) *told* David,
17:17. a wench went *and told* them; and they went *and told* king David.
19: 6(7). *thou hast declared* this day,
8(9). *they told* unto all the people,
1K. 10: 3. there was not (any) thing hid...which *he told* her not.
2K. 4:27. the Lord...*hath* not *told* me.
2Ch 9: 2. was nothing hid...which *he told* her not.
Neh. 2:12. neither *told I* (any) man
16. neither *had I* as yet *told*
Est. 2:10. Esther *had* not *shewed*
3: 4. *he had told* them that he (was) a Jew.
6. *they had shewed* him the people
6: 2. Mordecai *had told* of Bigthana
8: 1. Esther *had told* what he (was)
Job 26: 4. To whom *hast thou uttered* words?
42: 3. *have I uttered* that I understood not;
Ps. 97: 6. The heavens *declare* his righteousness,
111: 6. *He hath shewed* his people the power of
Isa. 3: 9. *they declare* their sin as Sodom,
21:10. *have I declared* unto you.
41:26. Who *hath declared* from the beginning,
43:12. *I have declared*, and have saved,
44: 8. told thee from that time, *and have declared*
45:21. (who) *hath told it* from that time?
48: 3. *I have declared* the former things
14. among them *hath declared*
66:19. *and they shall declare* my glory
Jon. 1:10. because *he had told* them.
Mic. 6: 8. *He hath shewed* thee, O man,

HIPHIL.—*Infinitive.*

Gen32: 5(6). I have sent *to tell* my lord,
43: 6. *to tell* the man whether ye had
Deu. 5: 5. *to shew* you the word of the Lord:
Jud.14:12. if ye can *certainly* declare (lit. *declaring* ye can declare)
13. if ye cannot *declare* (it) me,
14. they could not in three days *expound*
1Sa. 3:15. Samuel feared *to shew* Eli the vision.
4:13. the man came into the city, *and told* (lit. *to tell*)
10:16. He told us *plainly* (lit. *telling* he told us) that the asses were found.
22:22. he would *surely* tell (lit. *telling* tell)
2Sa.12:18. the servants of David feared *to tell* him
15:28. there come word from you *to certify*
1K. 1:20. *that thou shouldest tell* them
18:12. when I come *and tell* Ahab,
2K. 9:15. to go *to tell* (it) in Jezreel.
Ezr. 2:59. they could not *shew* their father's house,
Neh. 7:61. they could not *shew* their fathers' house,
Est. 4: 8. *and to declare* (it) unto her,
Job 1:15,16,17,19. only am escaped alone *to tell* thee.
33:23. *to shew* unto man his uprightness:
Ps. 92: 2(3). *To shew forth* thy lovingkindness

Ps. 92:15(16). *To shew* that the Lord (is) upright:
Jer. 36:16. will *surely* tell (lit. *telling* tell) the king
50:28. *to declare* in Zion the vengeance of
51:31. *to shew* the king of Babylon that
Dan. 2: 2. *to shew* the king his dreams.
9:23. I am come *to shew* (thee);
Mic. 3: 8. *to declare* unto Jacob his transgression,

HIPHIL.—*Imperative.*

Gen24:23. *tell* me, I pray thee:
49. if ye will deal kindly...*tell* me: and if not, *tell* me;
29:15. *tell* me, what (shall) thy wages (be)?
32:29(30). *Tell* (me), I pray thee, thy name.
37:16. *tell* me, I pray thee, where they feed
Jos. 7:19. *and tell* me now what thou hast done;
Jud. 16: 6, 10. *Tell* me, I pray thee,
13. *tell* me wherewith thou mightest be bound.
Ru. 4: 4. *tell* me, that I may know:
1Sa. 9:18. *Tell* me, I pray thee, where
10:15. *Tell* me, I pray thee, what
14:43. *Tell* me what thou hast done.
23:11. I beseech thee, *tell* thy servant.
2Sa. 1: 4. How went the matter? I pray thee, *tell*
17:16. send quickly, *and tell* David,
18:21. Go *tell* the king what thou hast seen.
2K. 4: 2. *tell* me, what hast thou in the house?
9:12. they said, (It is) false; *tell* us
Job 38: 4. *declare*, if thou hast understanding.
18. *declare* if thou knowest it all.
Ps. 9:11(12). *declare* among the people
Cant. 1: 7. *Tell* me, O thou whom my soul loveth,
Isa. 41:22. *let them shew* the former things,
23. *Shew* the things that are to come
45:21. *Tell ye*, and bring (them) near;
48:20. with a voice of singing *declare ye*,
58: 1. *and shew* my people their transgression,
Jer. 4: 5. *Declare ye* in Judah,
5:20. *Declare* this in the house of Jacob,
20:10. *Report*, (say they), and we will
31:10. *and declare* (it) in the isles afar off,
36:17. *Tell* us now, How didst thou write
38:25. *Declare* unto us now
42:20. *declare* unto us, and we will do (it).
46:14. *Declare ye* in Egypt,
48:20. *tell ye* it in Arnon,
50: 2. *Declare ye* among the nations,
Eze. 23:36. *yea, declare* unto them their abominations;
40: 4. *declare* all that thou seest to the house of
43:10. *shew* the house to the house of Israel,
Jon. 1: 8. *Tell* us, we pray thee, for whose cause

HIPHIL.—*Future.*

Gen 9:22. *and told* his two brethren
14:13. *and told* Abram the Hebrew;
24:28. the damsel ran, *and told* (them)
26:32. *and told* him concerning the well
29:12. *And* Jacob *told* Rachel
— she ran *and told* her father.
37: 5. *and he told* (it) his brethren:
42:29. *and told* him all that befell unto them;
43: 7. *and we told* him according to
44:24. *we told* him the words
45:26. *And told* him, saying,
46:31. I will go up, *and shew* Pharaoh,
47: 1. Joseph came *and told* Pharaoh,
48: 2. *And* (one) *told* Jacob,
49: 1. *that I may tell* you (that) which shall befall you
Ex. 4:28. *And* Moses *told* Aaron
16:22. rulers of the congregation came *and told*
19: 3. *and tell* the children of Israel;
9. *And* Moses *told* the words
Lev. 5: 1. if *he do* not *utter* (it),
Nu. 11:27. there ran a young man, *and told* Moses,
Deu 4:13. *And he declared* unto you
17:10. *they* of that place...*shall shew* thee;
11. *they shall shew* thee,
32: 7. ask thy father, *and he will shew thee;*
Jos. 2:14. if *ye utter* not this our business.
20. if *thou utter* this our business,
Jud. 4:12. *And they shewed* Sisera that
9: 7. *when they told* (it) to Jotham,
42. *and they told* Abimelech.
13:10. haste, and ran, *and shewed* her husband,
14: 2. *and told* his father and his mother,
12. if *ye can* certainly *declare*
Jud. 14:15. *that he may declare* unto us
16. *shall I tell* (it) thee?
17. on the seventh day, *that he told* her,
— *and she told* the riddle
16:17. *That he told* her all his heart,
Ru. 2:19. *And she shewed* her mother in law
3: 4. *he will tell* thee what thou shalt do.
16. *And she told* her all that the man had done
1Sa. 3:18. *And* Samuel *told* him every whit,
4:14. the man came in hastily, *and told* Eli.
9: 6. peradventure *he can shew* us
19. *will tell* thee all that (is) in thine heart.
11: 9. the messengers came *and shewed*
14:33. *Then they told* Saul,
43. *And* Jonathan *told* him, and said,
15:16. *and I will tell* thee what the Lord hath said
17:31. *And* when the words...*they rehearsed* (them) before Saul:
18:20. *and they told* Saul,
24. *And* the servants of Saul *told* him,
26. *when* his servants *told* David
19: 2. *and* Jonathan *told* David,
7. *and* Jonathan *shewed* him all those things.
11. *and* Michal David's wife *told* him,
18. *and told* him all that Saul had done
21. *when it was told* Saul,
20: 9. then *would* not *I tell* it thee?
10. Who *shall tell* me?
22:21. *And* Abiathar *shewed* David
22. that *he would* surely *tell* Saul:
23: 1. *Then they told* David,
25. *And they told* David:
24: 1(2). *that it was told* him,
25: 8. Ask thy young men, *and they will shew*
12. and came *and told* him all those sayings.
37. *and* his wife *had told* him
27:11. Lest *they should tell* on us,
2Sa. 1:20. *Tell* (it) not in Gath,
2: 4. *And they told* David,
3:23. *they* (lit. *and they*) *told* Joab, saying,
10: 5. *When they told* (it) unto David,
11: 5. and sent *and told* David,
10. *when they had told* David,
18. Joab sent *and told* David
22. *and shewed* David all that Joab had sent
13: 4. *wilt thou* not *tell* me?
14:33. Joab came to the king, *and told*
15:35. *thou shalt tell* (it) to Zadok
17:18. a lad saw them, *and told*
21. and went *and told* king David,
18:10. a certain man saw (it), *and told* Joab,
25. the watchman cried, *and told* the king.
24:13. Gad came to David, *and told* him,
1K. 1:23. *And they told* the king, saying,
2:39. *And they told* Shimei,
10: 3. *And* Solomon *told* her all her questions:
14: 3. *he shall tell thee* what
18:16. Obadiah went to meet Ahab, *and told*
19: 1. *And* Ahab *told* Jezebel
20:17. Ben-hadad sent out, *and they told* him,
2K. 4: 7. she came *and told* the man of God.
31. to meet him, *and told* him, saying,
5: 4. (one) went in, *and told* his lord,
6:11. *Will ye* not *shew* me which
12. *telleth* the king of Israel
7: 9. that we may go *and tell*
10. *and they told* them, saying,
11. *and they told* (it) to the king's house
12. *I will* now *shew* you what
15. the messengers returned, *and told*
9:18, 20. *And* the watchman *told*,
36. they came again, *and told* him.
10: 8. there came a messenger, *and told*
18:37. *and told* him the words of Rab-shakeh.
22:10. *And* Shaphan the scribe *shewed*
1Ch 17:10. *Furthermore I tell* thee
19: 5. there went (certain), *and told*
2Ch 9: 2. *And* Solomon *told* her all her questions:
20: 2. there came some *that told* Jehoshaphat,
34:18. *Then* Shaphan the scribe *told*
Neh. 2:18. *Then I told* them of the hand of
Est. 2:10. charged her that *she should* not *shew*
22. Mordecai, *who told* (it) unto Esther
3: 4. *that they told* Haman,
4: 4. Esther's maids...came *and told*
7. *And* Mordecai *told* him of all that had
9. Hatach came *and told* Esther

Est. 4:12. *And they told* to Mordecai Esther's words.
Job 11: 6. *And that he would shew* thee the secrets of
12: 7. *and they shall tell* thee:
15:18. wise men *have told* from their fathers,
17: 5. *He that speaketh* flattery
21:31. Who *shall declare* his way
31:37. *I would declare unto him* the number
36: 9. *Then he sheweth* them their work,
33. The noise thereof *sheweth*
Ps. 22:31(32). *and shall declare* his righteousness
30: 9(10). *shall it declare* thy truth?
38:18(19). *I will declare* mine iniquity;
40: 5(6). (if) *I would declare* and speak
50: 6. *And* the heavens *shall declare* his
51:15(17). my mouth *shall shew forth* thy praise.
52[title](2). when Doeg the Edomite came *and told* Saul,
64: 9(10). *and shall declare* the work of God;
71:17. *have I declared* thy wondrous works.
18. until *I have shewed* thy strength
75: 9(10). *I will declare* for ever;
142: 2(3). *I shewed* before him my trouble.
145: 4. and *shall declare* thy mighty acts.
Pro.12:17. (He that) speaketh truth *sheweth forth* righteousness:
29:24. heareth cursing, and *bewrayeth* (it) not.
Ecc. 6:12. who *can tell* a man what shall be after
8: 7. who *can tell* him when it shall be?
10:14. what shall be after him, who *can tell*
20. that which hath wings *shall tell*
Cant.5: 8. if ye find my beloved, that *ye tell* him,
Isa. 19:12. *and let them tell* thee now,
21: 6. *let him declare* what he seeth.
36:22. *and told* him the words of Rabshakeh.
41:22. *and shew* us what shall happen:
42:12. glory unto the Lord, and *declare* his praise
43: 9. who among them *can declare* this,
44: 7. who, as I, shall call, *and shall declare it*,
— *let them shew* unto them.
48: 5. *I have even* from the beginning *declared*
6. *will* not *ye declare*
57:12. *I will declare* thy righteousness,
Jer. 9:12(11). *that he may declare it*, for what
16:10. when *thou shalt shew* this people
20:10. Report, (say they), *and we will report it*.
33: 3. I will answer thee, *and shew thee*
36:13. *Then* Michaiah *declared* unto them
16. *We will* surely *tell* the king
20. *and told* all the words
38:15. If *I declare* (it) unto thee,
27. *and he told* them according to
42: 3. *That* the Lord thy God *may shew*
4. *I will declare* (it) unto you;
21. *And* (now) *I have* this day *declared* (it)
Eze.24:19. *Wilt thou* not *tell* us what
37:18. *Wilt thou* not *shew* us what thou (meanest)
Dan 10:21. *I will shew* thee that which is noted in the
11: 2. now *will I shew* thee the truth.
Hos. 4:12. their staff *declareth* unto them:
Mic. 1:10. *Declare ye* (it) not at Gath,

HIPHIL.—*Participle.*

Gen41:24. (there was) none *that could declare*
Jud.14:19. *unto them which expounded* the riddle.
2Sa. 1: 5, 6, 13. the young man *that told* him,
4:10. When *one told* me,
15:13. there came *a messenger* to David,
18:11. the man *that told* him,
Est. 2:20. Esther *had* not (yet) *shewed* her kindred
Ps. 19: 1(2). the firmament *sheweth* his handywork.
147:19. *He sheweth* his word unto Jacob,
Isa. 41:26. (there is) none *that sheweth*,
42: 9. new things *do I declare:*
45:19. I *declare* things that are right.
46:10. *Declaring* the end from the beginning,
Jer. 4:15. a voice *declareth* from Dan,
51:31. *and one messenger* to meet *another*, (lit. *and messenger* to meet *messenger*)
Am. 4:13. *and declareth* unto man what (is) his thought,
Zec. 9:12. even to day do *I declare*

* HOPHAL.—*Preterite.* *

Deu17: 4. *And it be told* thee, and thou hast
Jos. 9:24. *it was* certainly *told* thy servants,
Ru. 2:11. *It hath* fully *been shewed* me,
1Sa.23:13. *it was told* Saul
1K. 10: 7. the half *was* not *told* me:
1K. 18:13. *Was it* not *told* my lord
2Ch 9: 6. the one half...*was* not *told* me:
Isa. 21: 2. A grievous vision *is declared*
40:21. *hath it* not *been told* you

HOPHAL.—*Infinitive.*

Jos. 9:24. it was *certainly* told (lit. *being told* it was told) thy servants,
Ru. 2:11. It hath *fully* been shewed me, (lit. *being shewed* it hath been shewed me)

HOPHAL.—*Future.*

Gen22:20. *that it was told* Abraham,
27:42. *And* these words...*were told* to Rebekah:
31:22. *And it was told* Laban on the third day
38:13. *And it was told* Tamar, saying,
24. *that it was told* Judah,
Ex. 14: 5. *And it was told* the king of Egypt
Jos. 10:17. *And it was told* Joshua,
Jud. 9:25, 47. *and it was told* Abimelech.
1Sa.15:12. *And* when Samuel...*it was told* Samuel,
19:19. *And it was told* Saul, saying,
23: 7. *And it was told* Saul that David
27: 4. *And it was told* Saul that David
2Sa. 6:12. *And it was told* king David,
10:17. *when it was told* David,
19: 1(2). *And it was told* Joab, Behold,
21:11. *And it was told* David what Rizpah
1K. 1:51. *And it was told* Solomon, saying,
2:29. *And it was told* king Solomon that Joab
41. *And it was told* Solomon that Shimei
2K. 6:13 & 8:7. *And it was told* him, saying,
1Ch 19:17. *And it was told* David;
Isa. 7: 2. *And it was told* the house of David,

נְגַד [*n'gad*], Ch. 5047

* PAEL.—*Participle.* *

Dan 7:10. A fiery stream *issued* and came forth

נֶגֶד *neh'-ged*, part. prep. 5048

Gen31:32. *before* our brethren discern
Nu. 25: 4. before the Lord *against* the sun,
1K. 8:22. *in the presence of* all the congregation
1Ch 8:32. in Jerusalem, *over against* them.
Neh 13:21. Why lodge ye *about* the wall?
Ps. 78:12. did he *in the sight of* their fathers,
Eze.41:16. *over against* the door, cieled with wood
&c.

With prefixes: as, לְנֶגֶד

2Sa.22:25. according to my cleanness *in* (marg. *before*) his eye sight.
2K. 1:13. fell on his knees *before* Elijah,
Neh. 3:28. every one *over against* his house.
11:22. *over* the business of the house of God.
&c.

מִנֶּגֶד

Gen21:16. and sat her down *over against* (him)
Nu. 2: 2. *far off* (marg. *over against*) about the tabernacle
Deu28:66. life shall hang in doubt *before* thee;
Jud. 9:17. and adventured his life *far*,
20:34. And there came *against* Gibeah
2K. 2: 7. and stood *to view* (marg. *in sight*, or, *over against*) afar off:
3:22. saw the water *on the other side* (as) red
Ps. 31:22(23). cut off *from before* thine eyes:
38:11(12). friends stand *aloof from* my sore;
Pro.14: 7. Go *from the presence of* a foolish man,
Isa. 1:16. of your doings *from before* mine eyes;
Jer. 16:17. their iniquity hid *from* mine eyes.
&c.

The signification of נֶגֶד is not changed by combination with pronominal suffixes.

נֶגֶד *neh'-ged*, Ch. part. prep. 5049

Dan.6:10(11). in his chamber *toward* Jerusalem,

5050 **נָגַהּ** *nāh-gah'.*

* KAL.—*Preterite.* *

Job 22:28. the light *shall shine* upon thy ways.
Isa. 9: 2(1). upon them *hath* the light *shined.*

KAL.—*Future.*

Job 18: 5. the spark of his fire *shall* not *shine.*

* HIPHIL.—*Future.* *

2Sa.22:29. the Lord *will lighten* my darkness.
Ps. 18:28(29). the Lord my God *will enlighten* my darkness.
Isa. 13:10. the moon *shall* not *cause* her light *to shine.*

5051 **נֹגַהּ** *nōh'-gah,* f.

2Sa.22:13. *Through the brightness* before him
23: 4. *by clear shining* after rain.
Ps. 18:12(13). *At the brightness* (that was) before him
Pro. 4:18. the path of the just(is) as the *shining* light,
Isa. 4: 5. *and the shining of* a flaming fire
50:10. walketh (in) darkness, and hath no *light?*
60: 3. kings *to the brightness of* thy rising.
19. *neither for brightness* shall the moon give light
62: 1. until the righteousness thereof go forth *as brightness,*
Eze. 1: 4. *and a brightness* (was) about it,
13. *and* the fire *was bright,*
27. *and* it had *brightness* round about.
28. the appearance of *the brightness*
10: 4. the court was full *of the brightness of*
Joel 2:10 & 3:15(4:15). the stars shall withdraw *their shining:*
Am. 5:20. and no *brightness* in it?
Hab. 3: 4. *And* (his) *brightness* was as the light;
11. *at the shining of* thy glittering spear.

5053 **נֹגַהּ** [*nōh'-gah*], Ch. f.

Dan. 6:19(20). king arose very early *in the morning,*

5054 **נְגֹהוֹת** *n'gōh-hōhth',* f. pl.

Isa. 59: 9. *for brightness,* (but) we walk in darkness.

5055 **נָגַח** [*nāh-gagh'*].

* KAL.—*Future.* *

Ex. 21:28. If an ox *gore* a man
31. Whether *he have gored* a son, or *have gored* a daughter,
32. If the ox *shall push*

* PIEL.—*Future.* *

Deu33:17. *he shall push* the people
1K. 22:11. *shalt thou push* the Syrians,
2Ch 18:10. *thou shalt push* Syria
Ps. 44: 5(6). *will we push down* our enemies:
Eze.34:21. and *pushed* all the diseased

PIEL.—*Participle.*

Dan. 8: 4. I saw the ram *pushing*

* HITHPAEL.—*Future.* *

Dan11:40. *shall* the king of the south *push*

5056 **נַגָּח** *nag-gahgh',* adj.

Ex. 21:29. if the ox *were wont to push*
36. that the ox *hath used to push*

5057 **נָגִיד** *nāh-geed',* m.

1Sa. 9:16. (to be) *captain* over my people
10: 1. (to be) *captain* over his inheritance?
13:14. (to be) *captain* over his people,
25:30. appointed thee *ruler* over Israel;
2Sa. 5: 2. thou shalt be *a captain* over Israel.
6:21. to appoint me *ruler*
2Sa. 7: 8. *to be ruler* over my people,
1K. 1:35. I have appointed him *to be ruler*
14: 7 & 16:2. made thee *prince* over my people
2K. 20: 5. Hezekiah *the captain of* my people,
1Ch. 5: 2. *and* of him (came) *the chief ruler;* (marg. or, *prince*)
9:11. *the ruler of* the house of God;
20. of Eleazar was *the ruler*
11: 2. thou shalt be *ruler*
12:27. Jehoiada (was) *the leader*
13: 1. of thousands and hundreds, (and) with every *leader.*
17: 7. that thou shouldest be *ruler*
26:24. *ruler of* the treasures.
27: 4. Mikloth also *the ruler:*
16. *the ruler* of the Reubenites
28: 4. he hath chosen Judah (to be) *the ruler;*
29:22. anointed (him)...(to be) *the chief governor,*
2Ch. 6: 5. *to be a ruler* over my people
11:11. fortified the strong holds, and put *captains* in them,
22. (to be) *ruler* among his brethren:
19:11. *the ruler* of the house of Judah,
28: 7. Azrikam *the governor of* the house,
31:12. Cononiah the Levite (was) *ruler,*
13. Azariah *the ruler of* the house of God.
32:21. *and the leaders* and captains in the camp
35: 8. *rulers of* the house of God,
Neh11:11. *the ruler of* the house of God.
Job 29:10. *The nobles* held their peace,
31:37. as *a prince* would I go near
Ps. 76:12(13). He shall cut off the spirit of *princes:*
Pro. 8: 6. I will speak of *excellent things;*
28:16. *The prince* that wanteth understanding
Isa. 55: 4. *a leader* and commander to the people.
Jer. 20: 1. *chief* governor in the house of the Lord,
Eze.28: 2. say *unto the prince of* Tyrus,
Dan. 9:25. unto the Messiah *the Prince* (shall be) seven weeks,
26. the people of *the prince* that shall come
11:22. *the prince of* the covenant.

נְגִינָה [*n'gee-nāh'*], f. 5058

Job 30: 9. And now am I *their song,*
Ps. 4[title] (1) & 6[title] (1) & 54[title] (1) & 55[title] (1). To the chief Musician *on Neginoth,*
61[title](1). To the chief Musician upon *Neginah,*
67[title](1). To the chief Musician *on Neginoth,*
69:12(13). *and* I (was) *the song of* the drunkards.
76[title](1). To the chief Musician *on Neginoth,*
77: 6(7). I call to remembrance *my song*
Isa. 38:20. *therefore* we will sing *my songs*
Lam. 3:14. (and) *their song* all the day.
5:14. the young men *from their musick.*
Hab. 3:19. *on my stringed instruments.* (marg. *neginoth,*)

נָגַן [*nāh-gan'*] 5059

* KAL.—*Participle.* Poel. *

Ps. 68:25(26). *the players on instruments* (followed) after;

* PIEL.—*Preterite.* *

1Sa.16:16. *that he shall play* with his hand,
23. David took an harp, *and played*

PIEL.—*Infinitive.*

1Sa.16:17. Provide me now a man that can *play* well, (lit. good *for playing*)
18. son of Jesse...(that is) cunning *in playing,*
2K. 3:15. *when* the minstrel *played,*
Ps. 33: 3. *play* skilfully (lit. be good *to play*) with a loud noise.
Isa. 23:16. make sweet *melody,* (lit. *id.*) sing many
Eze.33:32. can *play* well on an instrument:

PIEL.—*Future.*

Isa. 38:20. *therefore we will sing* my songs *to the stringed instruments*

PIEL.—*Participle.*

1Sa.16:16. a man, (who is) *a cunning player*
18:10. David *played* with his hand,
19: 9. David *played* with (his) hand.
2K. 3:15. bring me *a minstrel.* And it came to pass, when *the minstrel* played,

5060 **נָגַע** *nāh-gag'.*

*** KAL.—*Preterite.* ***

Gen26:29. as *we have* not *touched thee,*
32:32(33). *he touched* the hollow of Jacob's thigh
Jud.20:41. they saw that evil *was come* (marg. *touched*)
1Sa. 6: 9. not his hand (that) *smote* us;
10:26. whose hearts God *had touched.*
Job 19:21. the hand of God *hath touched* me.
Isa. 6: 7. this *hath touched* thy lips;
16: 8. *they are come* (even) unto Jazer,
Jer. 4:10. *whereas* the sword *reacheth*
18. *it reacheth* unto thine heart.
48:32. *they reach* (even) to the sea of Jazer:
51: 9. her judgment *reacheth* unto heaven,
Dan10:10. an hand *touched* me,
Hos. 4: 2. and blood *toucheth* blood.
Mic. 1: 9. *he is come* unto the gate of my people,
Hag. 2:12. *and* with his skirt *do touch* bread,

KAL.—*Infinitive.*

Gen20: 6. suffered I thee not *to touch* her.
Ex. 19:12. *or touch* the border of it:
Lev.15:23. *when he toucheth* it, he shall be
Jos. 9:19. we may not *touch* them.
Ru. 2: 9. charged the young men that they *shall* not *touch thee?*
2Sa.14:10. he shall not *touch* thee any more.
Job 6: 7. my soul refused *to touch*
Eze.17:10. *when* the east wind *toucheth* it?

KAL.—*Imperative.*

Job 1:11. *and touch* all that he hath,
2: 5. *and touch* his bone and his flesh,
Ps.144: 5. *touch* the mountains,

KAL.—*Future.*

Gen 3: 3. neither *shall ye touch* it,
32:25(26). *And* when he saw...*he touched* the hollow of his thigh;
Ex. 19:13. There *shall* not an hand *touch* it,
Lev. 5: 2. if a soul *touch* any unclean thing,
3. if *he touch* the uncleanness of man,
6:18(11). every one that *toucheth* them
27(20). Whatsoever *shall touch* the flesh
7:19. the flesh that *toucheth* any unclean (thing)
21. soul that *shall touch* any unclean (thing),
11: 8. their carcase *shall ye* not *touch;*
12: 4. *she shall touch* no hallowed thing,
15: 5. whosoever *toucheth* his bed
11. whomsoever *he toucheth*
12. the vessel of earth, that *he toucheth*
22: 5. whosoever *toucheth* any creeping thing,
6. The soul which *hath touched*
Nu. 4:15. *they shall* not *touch* (any) holy thing,
16:26. *touch* nothing of their's,
19:16. whosoever *toucheth* one that is slain
22. whatsoever the unclean (person) *toucheth*
Deu14: 8. *nor touch* their dead carcase.
Jud. 6:21. *and touched* the flesh
2Sa. 5: 8. Whosoever *getteth up* to the gutter,
23: 7. the man (that) *shall touch* them
1K. 6:27. *so that* the wing of the one *touched*
19: 7. angel of the Lord came...*and touched* him,
2K. 13:21. *and touched* the bones of Elisha,
1Ch 16:22. *Touch* not mine anointed,
Ezr. 3: 1. *when* the seventh month *was come,*
Neh. 7:73. *when* the seventh month *came,*
Est. 5: 2. *and touched* the top of the sceptre.
Job 1:19. *and smote* the four corners of the house,
4: 5. *it toucheth* thee, and thou art troubled.
5:19. there *shall* no evil *touch* thee.
Ps.104:32. *he toucheth* the hills, and they smoke.
105:15. *Touch* not mine anointed,
Isa. 52:11. *touch* no unclean (thing);
Lam.4:14. men could not *touch*
15. depart, depart, *touch* not:
Dan. 8:18. *but he touched* me, and set me upright.
10:18. there came again *and touched* me
Jon. 3: 6. *For* word *came* unto the king
Hag. 2:13. If (one that is) unclean...*touch*

KAL.—*Participle.* Poel.

Gen26:11. *He that toucheth* this man
Ex. 19:12. whosoever *toucheth* the mount
29:37. whatsoever *toucheth* the altar
30:29. whatsoever *toucheth* them shall be holy.
Lev.11:24. whosoever *toucheth* the carcase
Lev.11:26. every one *that toucheth* them
27. whoso *toucheth* their carcase
31. whosoever *doth touch* them,
36. *but that which toucheth* their carcase
39. *he that toucheth* the carcase
15: 7. *And he that toucheth* the flesh of
10. whosoever *toucheth* any thing that
19. whosoever *toucheth* her
21. whosoever *toucheth* her bed
22. whosoever *toucheth* any thing that
27. whosoever *toucheth* those things
22: 4. *And whoso toucheth* any thing (that)
Nu. 19:11. *He that toucheth* the dead body
13. Whosoever *toucheth* the dead body
18. him *that touched* a bone,
21. *and he that toucheth* the water of
22. the soul *that toucheth* (it) shall
31:19. whosoever *hath touched* any slain,
Jud.20:34. they knew not that evil (was) *near* them.
1K. 6:27. the wing of the other cherub *touched* the other wall; and their wings *touched*
19: 5. then an angel *touched him,*
Pro. 6:29. *toucheth* her shall not be innocent.
Jer. 12:14. *that touch* the inheritance
Dan. 8: 5. and *touched* not the ground:
9:21. *touched* me about the time
10:16. (one) like the similitude of the sons of men *touched*
Am. 9: 5. *he that toucheth* the land,
Zec. 2: 8(12). *he that toucheth* you *toucheth* the apple

KAL.—*Participle.* Paül.

Ps. 73:14. all the day long have I been *plagued,*
Isa. 53: 4. yet we did esteem him *stricken,*

*** NIPHAL.—*Future.* ***

Jos. 8:15. *made as if they were beaten* before them,

*** PIEL.—*Preterite.* ***

2Ch 26:20. the Lord *had smitten him.*

PIEL.—*Future.*

Gen12:17. *And* the Lord *plagued* Pharaoh
2K. 15: 5. *And* the Lord *smote* the king,

*** PUAL.—*Future.* ***

Ps. 73: 5. neither *are they plagued* like (other) men.

*** HIPHIL.—*Preterite.* ***

Ex. 12:22. *and strike* the lintel and the two side posts
2Ch 28: 9. a rage (that) *reacheth up* unto heaven.
Est. 4:14. *thou art come* to the kingdom
6:14. *came* the king's chamberlains,
9: 1. his decree *drew near*
26. which *had come* unto them,
Ps. 88: 3(4). my life *draweth nigh* unto the grave.
Ecc.12: 1. *nor* the years *draw nigh,*
Cant.2:12. the singing (of birds) *is come,*
Isa. 25:12. lay low, (and) *bring* to the ground,
Lam.2: 2. *he hath brought* (them) *down* (marg. *made to touch*) to the ground:
Eze. 7:12. the day *draweth near:*
13:14. *and bring it down* to the ground,

HIPHIL.—*Infinitive.*

1Sa.14: 9. Tarry until *we come*
Est. 2:12. *Now when* every maid's turn *was come*
15. *Now when* the turn of Esther,...*was come*

HIPHIL.—*Future.*

Ex. 4:25. *and cast* (marg. *made* (it) *touch*) (it) at his
Lev. 5: 7. if *he be* not *able to bring* (marg. his hand cannot *reach*) a lamb,
Job 20: 6. his head *reach* unto the clouds;
Ps. 32: 6. *they shall* not *come nigh* unto him.
107:18. *and they draw near* unto the gates of death.
Isa. 6: 7. *And he laid* (it) (marg. *caused* (it) *to touch*) upon my mouth,
8: 8. *he shall reach* (even) to the neck;
26: 5. *he bringeth it* (even) to the dust.
30: 4. his ambassadors *came* to Hanes.
Jer. 1: 9. *and touched* my mouth.
Dan12:12. he that waiteth, *and cometh*
Zec.14: 5. the valley of the mountains *shall reach*

HIPHIL.—*Participle.*

Gen28:12. the top of it *reached* to heaven:
2Ch 3:11. *reaching* to the wall of the house:
— *reaching* to the wing of the other
12. *reaching* to the wall of the house:

Est. 4: 3 & 8:17. whithersoever the king's commandment...*came*,
Ecc. 8:14. just (men), unto whom *it happeneth*
— wicked (men), to *whom it happeneth* (lit. *whom*...unto them)
Isa. 5: 8. Woe *unto them that join* house to house,
Dan. 8: 7. I saw him *come* close unto the ram,

5061 נֶגַע *neh'-gag*, m.

Gen12:17. Lord plagued Pharaoh...with great *plagues*
Ex. 11: 1. Yet will I bring one *plague*
Lev.13: 2. of his flesh (like) *the plague of* leprosy;
3. the priest shall look on *the plague*
— the hair *in the plague* is turned white, and *the plague* in sight (be) deeper than the skin of his flesh, it (is) *a plague of* leprosy:
4. (him that hath) *the plague*
5. *the plague* in his sight be at a stay, (and) *the plague* spread not
6. (if) *the plague* (be) somewhat dark, (and) *the plague* spread not
9. *the plague of* leprosy is in a man,
12. (him that hath) *the plague*
13. clean (that hath) *the plague:*
17. (if) *the plague* be turned into white;
— (that hath) *the plague:*
20. it (is) *a plague of* leprosy
22. it (is) *a plague.*
25, 27. it (is) *the plague of* leprosy.
29. If a man or woman have *a plague*
30. the priest shall see *the plague:*
31. *the plague of* the scall,
— (him that hath) *the plague of*
32. the priest shall look on *the plague:*
42. *a* white reddish *sore;*
43. the rising of *the sore*
44. *his plague* (is) in his head.
45. the leper in whom *the plague* (is),
46. *the plague* (shall be) in him
47. *the plague of* leprosy
49. if *the plague* be greenish
— it (is) *a plague of* leprosy,
50. the priest shall look upon *the plague*, and shut up (it that hath) *the plague*
51. he shall look on *the plague* on the seventh day: if *the plague* be spread
— *the plague* (is) a fretting leprosy;
52. wherein *the plague* is:
53. *the plague* be not spread
54. (the thing) wherein *the plague* (is),
55. the priest shall look on *the plague*,
— (if) *the plague* have not changed his colour, *and the plague* be not spread;
56. *the plague* (be) somewhat dark
57. that wherein *the plague* (is)
58. if *the plague* be departed
59. the law of *the plague of* leprosy
14: 3. (if) *the plague of* leprosy be healed
32. in whom (is) *the plague of* leprosy,
34. I put *the plague of* leprosy in a house
35. *as it were a plague* in the house:
36. the priest go (into it) to see *the plague*,
37. he shall look on *the plague*, and, behold, (if) *the plague* (be)
39. (if) *the plague* be spread
40. the stones in which *the plague* (is),
43. if *the plague* come again,
44. (if) *the plague* be spread in the house,
48. *the plague* hath not spread
— *the plague* is healed.
54. the law for all manner of *plague of* leprosy,
Deu17: 8. between *stroke and stroke*,
21: 5. every controversy and every *stroke*
24: 8. Take heed *in the plague of* leprosy,
2Sa. 7:14. *and with the stripes of* the children of men:
1K. 8:37. whatsoever *plague*, whatsoever sickness
38. *the plague of* his own heart,
2Ch 6:28. whatsoever *sore* or whatsoever sickness
29. every one shall know *his own sore*
Ps. 38:11(12). aloof from *my sore;* (marg. *stroke*)
39:10(11). Remove *thy stroke* away from me:
89:32(33). their iniquity *with stripes.*
91:10. *neither* shall *any plague* come nigh
Pro. 6:33. *A wound* and dishonour shall he get;
Isa. 53: 8. for the transgression of my people was he *stricken.* (marg. *the stroke* upon him)

נָגַף *nāh-gaph'.* 5062

* KAL.—*Preterite.* *

Ex. 21:22. and *hurt* a woman with child,
1Sa. 4: 3. Wherefore *hath* the Lord *smitten us*
2Ch 13:15. God *smote* Jeroboam and all Israel
21:18. after all this the Lord *smote him*
Isa. 19:22. *And* the Lord *shall smite* Egypt:

KAL.—*Infinitive.*

Ex. 12:23. *to smite* the Egyptians;
— to come in unto your houses *to smite* (you)
27. *when he smote* the Egyptians,
Isa. 19:22. *he shall smite* (lit. *smiting*) and heal (it):

KAL.—*Future.*

Ex. 21:35. if one man's ox *hurt* another's,
32:35. *And* the Lord *plagued* the people,
Jos. 24: 5. *and I plagued* Egypt,
Jud.20:35. *And* the Lord *smote* Benjamin
1Sa.25:38. *that* the Lord *smote* Nabal,
26:10. the Lord *shall smite him;*
2Sa.12:15. *And* the Lord *struck* the child
2Ch 13:20. *and* the Lord *struck him*, and he died.
14:12(11). *So* the Lord *smote* the Ethiopians
Ps. 89:23(24). *plague* them that hate him.
91:12. lest *thou dash* thy foot against a stone.
Pro. 3:23. thy foot *shall* not *stumble.*
Zec 14:12, 18. plague wherewith the Lord *will smite*

KAL.—*Participle.* Poel.

Ex. 8: 2(7:27). I *will smite* all thy borders
2Ch 21:14. *will* the Lord *smite* thy people,

* NIPHAL.—*Preterite.* *

Lev.26:17. *and ye shall be slain* before your enemies:
Jud.20:36. the children of Benjamin saw that *they were smitten:*
2Sa.10:15. *they were smitten* before Israel,
19. *they were smitten* before Israel,
1Ch 19:16, 19. *they were put to the worse* before Israel,

NIPHAL.—*Infinitive.*

Jud.20:39. *Surely* they are smitten (lit. *being smitten* they are smitten)
1K. 8:33. *When* thy people Israel *be smitten down*

NIPHAL.—*Future.*

Nu. 14:42. that *ye be* not *smitten*
Deu. 1:42. lest *ye be smitten* before
1Sa. 4: 2. *and* when...Israel *was smitten* before
10. *and* Israel *was smitten*,
7:10. *and they were smitten* before Israel.
2Sa. 2:17. *and* Abner *was beaten*,
18: 7. Where (lit. *And* there) the people of Israel *were slain*
2K. 14:12. *And* Judah *was put to the worse*
2Ch 6:24. if thy people Israel *be put to the worse* (marg. or, *smitten*)
20:22. *and they were smitten.* (marg. or, *smote one another*)
25:22. *And* Judah *was put to the worse* (marg. *smitten*)

NIPHAL.—*Participle.*

Deu28: 7. *to be smitten* before thy face:
25. The Lord shall cause thee *to be smitten*
Jud.20:32. They *are smitten down* before us,
39. they *are smitten down* before us,

* HITHPAEL.—*Future.* *

Jer. 13:16. before your feet *stumble*

נֶגֶף *neh'-geph*, m. 5063

Ex. 12:13. *the plague* shall not be upon you
30:12. that there be no *plague*
Nu. 8:19. that there be no *plague*
16:46(17:11). *the plague* is begun.
47(—:12). *the plague* was begun
Jos. 22:17. there was *a plague* in the congregation
Isa. 8:14. a stone of *stumbling*

נָגַר [*nāh-gar'*]. 5064

* NIPHAL.—*Preterite.* *

Ps. 77: 2(3). my sore *ran* in the night,
Lam.3:49. Mine eye *trickleth down*,

NIPHAL.—*Participle.*

2Sa.14:14. and (are) as water *spilt* on the ground,
Job 20:28. (his goods) *shall flow away*

* HIPHIL.—*Preterite.* *

Mic. 1: 6. *and I will pour down* the stones

HIPHIL.—*Imperative.*

Jer. 18:21. *and pour out their* (blood) (marg. *pour them out*)

HIPHIL.—*Future.*

Ps. 63:10(11). *They shall fall* by the sword: (marg. They *shall make him run out* (like water) by the hands of the sword)
75: 8(9). *and he poureth out* of the same:
Eze.35: 5. *and hast shed* (marg. *poured out*) (the blood of)

* HOPHAL.—*Participle.* *

Mic. 1: 4. the waters (that are) *poured down*

5065 **נָגַשׂ** *nāh-gas'.*

* KAL.—*Preterite.* *

2K. 23:35. *he exacted* the silver and the gold

KAL.—*Future.*

Deu15: 2. *he shall* not *exact* (it) of his neighbour,
3. Of a foreigner *thou mayest exact*
Isa. 58: 3. and *exact* all your labours.

KAL.—*Participle.* Poel.

Ex. 3: 7. by reason of *their taskmasters;*
5: 6. *the taskmasters* of the people,
10. *the taskmasters of* the people
13. *And the taskmasters* hasted (them),
14. Pharaoh's *taskmasters*
Job 3:18. the voice of *the oppressor.*
39: 7. the crying of *the driver.* (marg. *exactor*)
Isa. 3:12. children (are) *their oppressors,*
9: 4(3). the rod of his *oppressor,*
14: 2. they shall rule *over their oppressors.*
4. How hath *the oppressor* ceased!
60:17. *and thine exactors* righteousness.
Dan 11:20. There shall stand up in his estate a raiser of taxes (marg. one that causeth *an exacter* to pass over)
Zec. 9: 8. no *oppressor* shall pass through
10: 4. out of him every *oppressor*

* NIPHAL.—*Preterite.* *

1Sa.13: 6. the people *were distressed,*
14:24. the men of Israel *were distressed*
Isa. 3: 5. *And* the people *shall be oppressed,*
53: 7. *He was oppressed,* and he was afflicted,

5066 **נָגַשׁ** [*nāh-gash'*].

* KAL.—*Infinitive.* *

Gen33: 3. until *he came near* to his brother.
Ex. 28:43. *when they come near* unto the altar
30:20. *when they come near* to the altar
34:30. they were afraid *to come nigh* him.
Nu. 4:19. *when they approach* unto the most
8:19. *when* the children of Israel *come nigh*
Jud 20:23. Shall I *go up* again to battle
Jer. 30:21. engaged his heart *to approach*
Eze.44:13. *nor to come near* to any

KAL.—*Imperative.*

Gen19: 9. And they said, *Stand* back.
27:21. *Come near,* I pray thee,
26. *Come near* now, and kiss me,
45: 4. *Come near* to me, I pray you.
Jos. 3: 9. *Come hither,* and hear the words
Ru. 2:14. At mealtime *come thou* hither,
1Sa.14:38. *Draw ye near* hither,
2Sa. 1:15. *Go near,* (and) fall upon him.
1K. 18:30. *Come near* unto me.
2Ch 29:31. *come near* and bring sacrifices
Isa. 49:20. *give place* to me that I may dwell.
Jer. 46: 3. *and draw near* to battle.

KAL.—*Future.*

Gen18:23. *And* Abraham *drew near,*
19: 9. *and came near* to break the door.
27:22. *And* Jacob *went near*
27:27. *And he came near,* and kissed him:
29:10. *that* Jacob *went near,*
33: 6. *Then* the handmaidens *came near,*
7. *And* Leah also with her children *came near,*
43:19. *And they came near* to the steward
44:18. *Then* Judah *came near*
45: 4. *And they came near.* And he said,
Ex. 19:15. *come* not at (your) wives.
24: 2. *they shall* not *come nigh;*
14. *let him come* unto them.
Lev.21:21. *shall come nigh* to offer
— *he shall* not *come nigh* to offer
23. nor *come nigh* unto the altar,
Nu. 32:16. *And they came near* unto him,
Jos. 8:11. went up, *and drew nigh,*
14: 6. *Then* the children of Judah *came*
21: 1. *Then came near* the heads of the fathers
Jud. 9:52. *and went hard* unto the door of the tower
1Sa. 9:18. *Then* Saul *drew near*
17:16. *And* the Philistine *drew near*
40. *and he drew near* to the Philistine.
30:21. *when* David *came near* to the people,
2Sa.10:13. *And* Joab *drew nigh,* and the people
1K. 18:21. *And* Elijah *came* unto all the people,
30. *And* all the people *came near* unto him.
36. *that* Elijah the prophet *came near,*
20:22. *And* the prophet *came* to the king of Israel,
28. *And there came* a man of God,
22:24. *But* Zedekiah the son of Chenaanah *went near,*
2K. 2: 5. *And* the sons of the prophets...*came* to Elisha,
4:27. *but* Gehazi *came near* to thrust her away.
5:13. *And* his servants *came near,*
1Ch 19:14. *So* Joab and the people...*drew nigh*
2Ch 18:23. *Then* Zedekiah the son of Chenaanah *came near,*
Ezr. 4: 2. *Then they came* to Zerubbabel,
Job 41:16(8). One *is so near* to another,
Ps. 91: 7. *it shall* not *come nigh* thee.
Isa. 41: 1. *let them come near;* then let them speak:
50: 8. *let him come near* to me.
65: 5. *come* not *near* to me;
Jer. 42: 1. *Then* all the captains...*came near,*
Eze. 9: 6. *come* not *near* any man
44:13. *they shall* not *come near* unto me,
Joel 3: 9(4:9). *let* all the men of war *draw near;*

* NIPHAL.—*Preterite.* *

Gen33: 7. and after *came* Joseph *near* and Rachel,
Ex. 20:21. Moses *drew near* unto the thick darkness
24: 2. *And* Moses alone *shall come near*
34:32. all the children of Israel *came nigh:*
Deu20: 2. *that* the priest *shall approach*
21: 5. *And* the priests...*shall come near;*
25: 1. *and they come* unto judgment,
9. *Then shall* his brother's wife *come*
1Sa. 7:10. the Philistines *drew near* to battle
2Sa.11:20. Wherefore *approached ye so nigh*
21. why *went ye nigh* the wall?
1K. 20:13. *there came* (marg. *approached*) a prophet unto Ahab
Ezr. 9: 1. the princes *came* to me,
Isa. 29:13. this people *draw near*
Jer. 30:21. *and he shall approach* unto me:
Am. 9:13. *that* the plowman *shall overtake* the reaper,

NIPHAL.—*Participle.*

Ex. 19:22. the priests also, *which come near*

* HIPHIL.—*Preterite.* *

Ex. 21: 6. *Then* his master *shall bring him* unto the judges; *he shall also bring him*
Lev. 2: 8. *he shall bring it* unto the altar.
2Sa. 17:28(29). *Brought* beds, and basons,
Am. 5:25. *Have ye offered* unto me sacrifices

HIPHIL.—*Imperative.*

Gen27:25. *Bring* (it) *near* to me,
1Sa.13: 9. *Bring hither* a burnt offering
14:18. *Bring hither* the ark of God.
34. *Bring* me *hither* every man his ox,
15:32. *Bring ye hither* to me Agag
23: 9. *Bring hither* the ephod.
30: 7. *bring* me *hither* the ephod.
2K. 4: 6. *Bring* me yet a vessel.
Isa. 41:21. *bring forth* your strong (reasons),
45:21. Tell ye, *and bring* (them) *near;*

HIPHIL.—*Future.*

Gen27:25. *And he brought* (it) *near* to him,
48:10. *And he brought them near* unto him;
13. *and brought* (them) *near* unto him.
Ex. 32: 6. *and brought* peace offerings;
Lev. 8:14. *And he brought* the bullock
Jud. 6:19. brought (it) out...*and presented* (it).
1Sa.14:34. *And* all the people *brought* every man
28:25. *And she brought* (it) before Saul,
30: 7. *And* Abiathar *brought* thither the ephod
2Sa.13:11. *when she had brought* (them)
2Ch 29:23. *And they brought forth* (marg. *near*) the he goats
Job 40:19. *can make* his sword *to approach*
Isa. 41:22. *Let them bring* (them) *forth*, and shew
Am. 6: 3. *and cause* the seat of violence *to come near;*
9:10. The evil *shall* not *overtake*
Mal. 1: 8. if *ye offer* the blind for sacrifice,
— if *ye offer* the lame and sick,

HIPHIL.—*Participle.*

1K. 4:21(5:1). *they brought* presents,
2K. 4: 5. *who brought* (the vessels) to her;
Mal. 1: 7. *Ye offer* (marg. or, *Bring unto*) polluted
2:12. *and him that offereth* an offering
3: 3. that *they may offer*

* HOPHAL.—*Preterite.* *

2Sa. 3:34. nor thy feet *put* into fetters:

HOPHAL.—*Participle.*

Mal. 1:11. in every place incense (shall be) *offered*

*HITHPAEL.—*Imperative.**

Isa. 45:20. *draw near* together,

5067 **נֵד** *nehd*, m.

Ex. 15: 8. the floods stood upright as *an heap*,
Jos. 3:13. they shall stand upon an *heap*.
16. the waters...rose up upon an *heap*
Ps. 33: 7. He gathereth the waters...as *an heap:*
78:13. he made the waters to stand as *an heap*.
Isa. 17:11. the harvest (shall be) *a heap* (marg. or, *removed*)

5077 **נָדָא** [*nāh-dāh'*].

* HIPHIL.—*Future.* *

2K. 17:21. (כתיב) *and* Jeroboam *drave* Israel

5068 **נָדַב** *nāh-dav'*.

* KAL.—*Preterite.* *

Ex. 35:21. every one whom his spirit *made willing*,
29. whose heart *made* them *willing*

KAL.—*Future.*

Ex. 25: 2. every man that *giveth it willingly*

* HITHPAEL.—*Preterite.* *

1Ch 29: 9. with perfect heart *they offered willingly*
17. *I have willingly offered* all these
Ezr. 2:68. *offered freely* for the house of God

HITHPAEL.—*Infinitive.*

Jud. 5: 2. *when* the people *willingly offered themselves*.
1Ch 29: 9. for that *they offered willingly*,
14. that we should be able *to offer* so *willingly*
17. *to offer willingly* unto thee.
Ezr. 1: 6. all (that) *was willingly offered*.

HITHPAEL.—*Future.*

1Ch 29: 6. *Then*...the rulers of the king's work, *offered willingly*,

HITHPAEL.—*Participle.*

Jud. 5: 9. the governors of Israel, *that offered themselves willingly*
1Ch 29: 5. who (then) *is willing* to consecrate
2Ch 17:16. *who willingly offered himself* unto the Lord;
Ezr. 3: 5. every one *that willingly offered*
Neh 11: 2. the men, *that willingly offered themselves*

נְדַב [*n'dav*], Ch. 5069

* ITHPAEL.—*Preterite.* *

Ezr. 7:15. counsellors *have freely offered*

ITHPAEL.—*Infinitive.*

Ezr. 7:16. with *the freewill offering of* the people,

ITHPAEL.—*Participle.*

Ezr. 7:13. *which are minded of their own freewill* to go
16. *offering willingly* for the house

נְדָבָה *n'dāh-vāh'*, f. 5071

Ex. 35:29. The children of Israel brought *a willing offering*
36: 3. they brought yet unto him *free offerings*
Lev. 7:16. a vow, or *a voluntary offering*,
22:18. all *his freewill offerings*,
21. *a freewill offering* in beeves
23. mayest thou offer (for) *a freewill offering;*
23:38. all *your freewill offerings*,
Nu. 15: 3. a vow, or *in a freewill offering*,
29:39. your vows, *and your freewill offerings*,
Deu12: 6. your vows, *and your freewill offerings*,
17. *nor thy freewill offerings* or heave offering
16:10. a tribute of *a freewill offering of* thine hand,
23:23(24). *a freewill offering*, according
2Ch 31:14. *the freewill offerings of* God,
35: 8. his princes gave *willingly*
Ezr. 1: 4. *the freewill offering* for the house
3: 5 & 8:28. *a freewill offering* unto the Lord.
Ps. 54: 6(8). I will *freely* sacrifice
68: 9(10). Thou, O God, didst send a *plentiful* rain,
110: 3. Thy people (shall be) *willing*
119:108. *the freewill offerings of* my mouth,
Eze.46:12. the prince shall prepare a *voluntary* burnt offering or peace offerings *voluntarily*
Hos 14: 4(5). I will love them *freely:*
Am. 4: 5. publish *the free offerings:*

נִדְבָּךְ *nid-bāhch'*, Ch. m. 5073

Ezr. 6: 4. (With) three *rows* of great stones, *and a row* of new timber:

נָדַד [*nāh-dad'*]. 5074

* KAL.—*Preterite.* *

Est. 6: 1. On that night *could not* the king sleep, (marg. the king's sleep *fled away*)
Ps. 31:11(12). they that did see me without *fled*
Isa. 10:31. Madmenah *is removed;*
21:15. *they fled* from the swords,
22: 3. All thy rulers *are fled*
33: 3. At the noise of the tumult the people *fled;*
Jer. 4:25. all the birds of the heavens *were fled*.
9:10(9). the fowl...and the beast *are fled;*
Hos. 7:13. *they have fled* from me:

KAL.—*Infinitive.*

Ps. 55: 7(8). (then) would I *wander* far off,

KAL.—*Future.*

Gen31:40. *and* my sleep *departed* from mine eyes.
Ps. 68:12(13). Kings of armies *did flee apace:* (marg. *did flee, did flee*)
Nah. 3: 7. all they that look upon thee *shall flee*

KAL.—*Participle.* Poel.

Job 15:23. He *wandereth abroad* for bread,
Pro.27: 8. As a bird *that wandereth* from her nest, so (is) a man *that wandereth* from his place.
Isa. 10:14. none *that moved* the wing,
16: 2. as a *wandering* bird
3. bewray not him *that wandereth*.
21:14. they prevented with their bread *him that fled*.
Jer. 49: 5. none shall gather up *him that wandereth*.
Hos. 9:17. they shall be *wanderers*

*POAL.—*Preterite.* *

Nah. 3:17. when the sun ariseth *they flee away*,

*HIPHIL.—*Future**

Job 18:18. and *chased* out of the world

* HOPHAL.—*Future.* *

Job 20: 8. *yea, he shall be chased away* as a vision

HOPHAL.—*Participle.*

2Sa.23: 6. all of them as thorns *thrust away,*

* HITHPOLEL.—*Future.* *

Ps. 64: 8(9). all that see them *shall flee away.*

5075 נְדַד [*n'dad*], Ch.

* P'AL.—*Preterite.* *

Dan. 6:18(19). and his sleep *went from him.*

5076 נְדֻדִים *n'doo-deem'*, m. pl.

Job 7: 4. I am full of *tossings to and fro*

5077 נָדָה [*nāh-dāh'*].

* PIEL.—*Participle.* *

Isa. 66: 5. *that cast you out* for my name's sake,
Am. 6: 3. *Ye that put far away* the evil day,

5078 נֵדֶה *nēh'-deh*, m.

Eze.16:33. They give *gifts* to all whores:

5079 נִדָּה *nid-dāh'*, f.

Lev.12: 2. according to the days of *the separation for*
5. two weeks, *as in her separation:*
15:19. she shall be *put apart* (marg. *in her separation*)
20. lieth upon *in her separation*
24. and *her flowers* be upon him,
25. out of the time of *her separation,*
— beyond *the time of her separation;*
— the days of *her separation:*
26. the bed of *her separation:*
— the uncleanness of *her separation.*
33. her that is sick of *her flowers,*
18:19. *as long as she is put apart* for her
20:21. it (is) *an unclean thing:* (marg. *a separation*)
Nu. 19: 9. a water of *separation:*
13, 20. the water of *separation*
21, 21. the water of *separation*
31:23. the water of *separation:*
2Ch 29: 5. carry forth *the filthiness*
Ezr. 9:11. an *unclean* land *with the filthiness of* the
Lam.1:17. Jerusalem is *as a menstruous woman*
Eze. 7:19. their gold shall be *removed:* (marg. *for a separation,* or, *uncleanness*)
20. I set it *far* from them. (marg. or, made it unto them *an unclean thing*)
18: 6. come near to a *menstruous* woman,
22:10. they humbled her that was *set apart*
36:17. the uncleanness of *a removed woman.*
Zec.13: 1. for sin *and for uncleanness.* (marg. *separation for uncleanness*)

5080 נָדַח [*nāh-dagh'*].

* KAL.—*Infinitive.* *

Deu20:19. destroy the trees thereof *by forcing* an ax against

KAL.—*Future.*

2Sa.14:14. that his banished *be not expelled*

* NIPHAL.—*Preterite.* *

Deu. 4:19. *and* when...*shouldest be driven* to worship
19: 5. *and* his hand *fetcheth a stroke*
30:17. *but shalt be drawn away,* and worship
Job 6:13. is wisdom *driven quite* from me?
Jer. 40:12. all places whither *they were driven,*
43: 5. whither *they had been driven,*
49: 5. *and ye shall be driven out* every man

NIPHAL.—*Participle.*

Deu22: 1. shalt not see thy brother's ox...*go astray,*
Deu30: 4. If (any) *of thine be driven out*
2Sa.14:13. doth not fetch home again *his banished.*
14. that his *banished* be not expelled
Neh. 1: 9. there were *of you cast out*
Isa. 16: 3. hide *the outcasts;*
4. Let *mine outcasts* dwell with thee,
27:13. *the outcasts* in the land of Egypt,
Jer. 30:17. they called thee *an Outcast,*
49:36. *the outcasts of* Elam
Eze.34: 4. brought again *that which was driven away*
16. bring again *that which was driven away,*
Mic. 4: 6. *and* I will gather *her that is driven out,*
Zep. 3:19. *and* gather *her that was driven out;*

* PUAL.—*Participle.* *

Isa. 8:22. (they shall be) *driven* to darkness.

* HIPHIL.—*Preterite.* *

Deu30: 1. whither the Lord thy God *hath driven thee,*
2Sa.15:14. *and bring* (marg. *thrust*) evil upon us,
2Ch 13: 9. *Have ye* not *cast out* the priests
Jer. 8: 3. the places whither *I have driven them,*
16:15. the lands whither *he had driven them:*
23: 3. all countries whither *I have driven* them,
8. all countries whither *I had driven them;*
27:10. *that I should drive* you out,
29:14. all the places whither *I have driven* you,
18. the nations whither *I have driven them:*
32:37. all countries, whither *I have driven them*
46:28. the nations whither *I have driven thee:*
50:17. the lions *have driven* (him) *away:*
Dan. 9: 7. the countries whither *thou hast driven them,*
Joel 2:20. *and will drive him* into a land barren

HIPHIL.—*Infinitive.*

Deu13: 5(6). *to thrust thee* out of the way
10(11). *to thrust thee away* from the Lord
Ps. 62: 4(5). They only consult *to cast* (him) *down*
Jer. 27:15. *that I might drive* you out,

HIPHIL.—*Imperative.*

Ps. 5:10(11). *cast them out* in the multitude of

HIPHIL.—*Future.*

Deu13:13(14). *and have withdrawn* the inhabitants
2K. 17:21. *and* Jeroboam *drave* Israel from
2Ch 21:11. *and compelled* Judah (thereto).
Pro. 7:21. the flattering of her lips *she forced him.*
Jer. 23: 2. scattered my flock, *and driven them away,*
24: 9. all places whither *I shall drive them.*
Eze. 4:13. whither *I will drive them.*

* HOPHAL.—*Participle.* *

Isa. 13:14. it shall be as the *chased* roe,

נָדִיב *nāh-deev',* adj. 5081

Ex. 35: 5. whosoever (is) *of a willing* heart,
22. as many as were *willing* hearted,
Nu. 21:18. *the nobles of* the people
1Sa. 2: 8. to set (them) among *princes,*
1Ch 28:21. every *willing* skilful man,
2Ch 29:31. as many as were *of a free* heart
Job 12:21. He poureth contempt upon *princes,*
21:28. Where (is) the house of *the prince?*
34:18. to say...to *princes,* (Ye are) ungodly?
Ps. 47: 9(10). *The princes of* (marg. or, *The voluntary of*) the people are gathered
51:12(14). uphold me (with thy) *free* spirit.
83:11(12). Make *their nobles* like Oreb,
107:40. He poureth contempt upon *princes,*
113: 8. That he may set (him) with *princes,* (even) with *the princes of* his people.
118: 9. to put confidence *in princes.*
146: 3. Put not your trust *in princes,*
Pro. 8:16. By me princes rule, *and nobles,*
17: 7. much less do lying lips *a prince.*
26. to strike *princes* for equity.
19: 6. Many will intreat the favour of *the prince:*
25: 7. in the presence of *the prince*
Cant.6:12. the chariots of Amminadib. (marg. or, my *willing* people)
7: 1(2). O *prince*'s daughter!
Isa. 13: 2. go into the gates of *the nobles.*
32: 5. vile person shall be no more called *liberal,*
8. *But the liberal* deviseth *liberal things;* and by *liberal things* shall he stand.

5082 ## נְדִיבָה [*n'dee-vāh'*], f.

Job 30:15. they pursue *my soul* (marg. *principal one*) as the wind:

5083 ## נָדָן [*nāh-dāhn'*], m.

Eze.16:33. thou givest *thy gifts*

5084 ## נָדָן [*nāh-dāhn'*].

1Ch 21:27. he put up his sword again into *the sheath thereof.*

5085 ## נִדְנֶה *nid-neh'*, Ch. m.

Dan. 7:15. in my spirit in the midst of (my) *body*, (marg. *sheath*)

5086 ## נָדַף [*nāh-daph'*].

* KAL.—*Future.* *

Job 32:13. God *thrusteth him down*,
Ps. 1: 4. *which* the wind *driveth away.*
68: 2(3). (so) *drive* (them) *away:*

* NIPHAL.—*Preterite.* *

Isa. 19: 7. every thing sown by the brooks, shall wither, *be driven away*,

NIPHAL.—*Infinitive.*

Ps. 68: 2(3). *As* smoke *is driven away*,

NIPHAL.—*Participle.*

Lev.26:36. the sound of a *shaken* (marg. *driven*) leaf
Job 13:25. a leaf *driven to and fro?*
Pro.21: 6. a vanity *tossed to and fro*
Isa. 41: 2. as *driven* stubble to his bow.

5087 ## נָדַר *nāh-dar'.*

* KAL.—*Preterite.* *

Gen31:13. where *thou vowedst* a vow
Nu. 30:10(11). if *she vowed* in her husband's house,
Deu23:23(24). *thou hast vowed* unto the Lord
Jud.11:39. his vow which *he had vowed:*
2Sa.15: 7. *I have vowed* unto the Lord,
8. thy servant *vowed* a vow
Ps.132: 2. *vowed* unto the mighty (God)
Isa. 19:21. *yea, they shall vow* a vow
Jer. 44:25. our vows that *we have vowed*,
Jon. 2: 9(10). I will pay (that) that *I have vowed.*

KAL.—*Infinitive.*

Nu. 6: 2. *to vow* a vow of a Nazarite,
Deu23:22(23). if thou shalt forbear *to vow*,

KAL.—*Imperative.*

Ps. 76:11(12). *Vow*, and pay unto the Lord

KAL.—*Future.*

Gen28:20. *And* Jacob *vowed* a vow,
Nu. 6:21. the Nazarite who *hath vowed*,
— according to the vow which *he vowed*,
21: 2. *And* Israel *vowed* a vow
30: 2(3). If a man *vow* a vow
3(4). If a woman also *vow* a vow
Deu12:11. which *ye vow* unto the Lord:
17. any of thy vows which *thou vowest*,
23:21(22). When *thou shalt vow* a vow
Jud 11:30. *And* Jephthah *vowed* a vow
1Sa. 1:11. *And she vowed* a vow,
Ecc. 5: 4(3). When *thou vowest* a vow
—(–). pay that which *thou hast vowed.*
5(4). Better...that *thou shouldest* not *vow*, *than that thou shouldest vow* and not pay.
Jon. 1:16. offered a sacrifice...*and made* (marg. *vowed*) vows.

KAL.—*Participle.* Poel.

Lev.27: 8. according to his ability *that vowed*
Mal. 1:14. *and voweth*, and sacrificeth unto the Lord

5088 ## נֵדֶר *nēh'-der* & נֶדֶר *neh'-der*, m.

Gen28:20. And Jacob vowed *a vow*,
Gen31:13. vowedst *a vow* unto me:
Lev. 7:16. if the sacrifice of his offering (be) *a vow*,
22:18. for all *his vows*,
21. to accomplish (his) *vow*,
23. *but for a vow* it shall not be accepted.
23:38. and beside all *your vows*,
27: 2. a man shall make *a* singular *vow*,
Nu. 6: 2. separate (themselves) to vow *a vow*
5. the days of *the vow of* his separation
21. according to *the vow* which he vowed,
15: 3, 8. a sacrifice in performing *a vow*,
21: 2. Israel vowed *a vow* unto the Lord,
29:39. *beside your vows*, and your freewill
30: 2(3). If a man vow *a vow*
3(4). If a woman also vow *a vow*
4(5). her father hear *her vow*,
—(–). then all *her vows* shall stand,
5(6). not any of *her vows*,
6(7). *when she* vowed, (lit. *and her vows* were upon her)
7(8). then *her vows* shall stand,
8(9). he shall make *her vow*
9(10). *But every vow of* a widow,
11(12). then all *her vows* shall stand,
12(13). out of her lips *concerning her vows*,
13(14). Every *vow*, and every binding
14(15). establisheth all *her vows*,
Deu12: 6. *and your vows*, and your freewill offerings,
11. all *your* choice *vows*
17. nor any of *thy vows*
26. *and thy vows*, thou shalt take,
23:18(19). Thou shalt not bring the hire of a whore,...for any *vow:*
21(22). When thou shalt vow *a vow*
Jud.11:30. And Jephthah vowed *a vow*
39. (according) to *his vow*
1Sa. 1:11. And she vowed *a vow*,
21. the yearly sacrifice, and *his vow.*
2Sa.15: 7. let me go and pay *my vow*,
8. For thy servant vowed *a vow*
Job 22:27. *and* thou shalt pay *thy vows.*
Ps. 22:25(26). I will pay *my vows*
50:14. pay *thy vows* unto the most high:
56:12(13). *Thy vows* (are) upon me,
61: 5(6). hast heard *my vows:*
8(9). that I may daily perform *my vows.*
65: 1(2). unto thee shall *the vow* be performed.
66:13. I will pay thee *my vows*,
116:14, 18. I will pay *my vows*
Pro. 7:14. this day have I payed *my vows.*
20:25. after *vows* to make enquiry.
31: 2. the son of *my vows?*
Ecc. 5: 4(3). When thou vowest *a vow*
Isa. 19:21. they shall vow *a vow*
Jer. 44:25. We will surely perform *our vows*
— ye will surely accomplish *your vows*, and surely perform *your vows.*
Jon. 1:16. offered a sacrifice...and made *vows.*
Nah. 1:15(2:1). perform *thy vows:*

נֹהַּ *nōh'ăh*, m. 5089

Eze. 7:11. neither (shall there be) *wailing*

נָהַג *nāh-hag'.* 5090

* KAL.—*Preterite.* *

1Sa.30:20. the flocks and the herds, (which) *they drave*
Lam.3: 2. *He hath led* me, and brought (me into)

KAL.—*Imperative.*

2K. 4:24. *Drive*, and go forward;

KAL.—*Future.*

Gen31:18. *And he carried away* all his cattle,
Ex. 3: 1. *and he led* the flock to the backside of the desert,
1Sa.23: 5. *and brought away* their cattle,
30: 2. *but carried* (them) *away*,
22. *that they may lead* (them) *away*,
2K. 9:20. *he driveth* furiously.
1Ch 20: 1. *that*...Joab *led forth* the power of the army,
2Ch 25:11. *and led forth* his people,
Job 24: 3. *They drive away* the ass of the fatherless,

Cant.8: 2. *I would lead thee*, (and) bring thee
Isa. 20: 4. shall the king of Assyria *lead away*

KAL.—*Participle.* Poel.

2Sa. 6: 3. Uzzah and Ahio,...*drave* the new cart.
1Ch 13: 7. Uzza and Ahio *drave* the cart.
Ps. 80: 1(2). *thou that leadest* Joseph like a flock;
Ecc. 2: 3. *acquainting* mine heart with wisdom;
Isa. 11: 6. a little child *shall lead* them.

KAL.—*Participle.* Paül.

Isa. 60:11. (that) their kings (may be) *brought*.

* PIEL.—*Preterite.* *

Ex. 10:13. the Lord *brought* an east wind
Isa. 63:14. so *didst thou lead* thy people,

PIEL.—*Future.*

Gen31:26. *and carried away* my daughters,
Ex. 14:25. *that they drave them* (marg. or, *and made them to go*) heavily:
Deu 4:27. whither the Lord *shall lead* you.
28:37. whither the Lord *shall lead thee.*
Ps. 48:14(15). *he will be our guide* (even) unto death.
78:26. *and* by his power *he brought* in the south wind.
52. *and guided them* in the wilderness
Isa. 49:10. he that hath mercy on them *shall lead them,*

5090 נָהַג [*nāh-hag'*].

* PIEL.—*Participle.* *

Nah. 2: 7(8). her maids *shall lead* (her)

5091 נָהָה *nāh-hāh'*.

* KAL.—*Preterite.* *

Mic. 2: 4. *and lament* with a doleful lamentation,

KAL.—*Imperative.*

Eze.32:18. *wail* for the multitude of Egypt,

* NIPHAL.—*Future.* *

1Sa. 7: 2. *and* all the house of Israel *lamented*

5094 נְהוֹר [*n'hōhr*], Ch. m.

Dan. 2:22. *and the light* dwelleth with him.

5092 נְהִי *n'hee*, m.

Jer. 9:10(9). will I take up a weeping *and wailing,*
18(17). take up *a wailing* for us,
19(18). a voice of *wailing* is heard
20(19). teach your daughters *wailing,*
31:15. A voice was heard in Ramah, *lamentation,*
Am. 5:16. skilful of *lamentation* to wailing..
Mic. 2: 4. lament with *a* doleful *lamentation,*

5093 נִהְיָה *neeh-yāh'*, f.

Mic. 2: 4. lament with a *doleful* lamentation, (marg. a lamentation of *lamentations*)

5094 נְהִיר [*n'heer*], Ch. m.

Dan. 2:22. (כתיב) *and the light* dwelleth with him.

5094 נַהִירוּ *nah-hee-roo'*, Ch. f.

Dan. 5:11. of thy father *light* and understanding
14. *and* (that) *light* and understanding

5095 נָהַל [*nāh-hal'*].

* PIEL.—*Preterite.* *

Ex. 15:13. *thou hast guided* (them) in thy strength

PIEL.—*Future.*

Gen47:17. *and he fed* (marg. *led*) *them* with bread
2Ch 28:15. *and carried* all the feeble *of them*
32:22. *and guided them* on every side.
Ps. 23: 2. *he leadeth me* beside the still waters.
31: 3(4). thy name's sake lead me, *and guide me.*

Isa. 40:11. *shall gently lead* those that are with young.
49:10. by the springs of water *shall he guide them.*

PIEL.—*Participle.*

Isa. 51:18. (There is) none *to guide* her

* HITHPAEL.—*Future.* *

Gen33:14. *I will lead on* softly,

נַהֲלֹלִים *nah-hălōh-leem'*, m. pl. 5097

Isa. 7:19. upon all *bushes.* (marg. *commendable trees*)

נָהַם [*nāh-ham'*]. 5098

* KAL.—*Preterite.* *

Pro. 5:11. *And thou mourn* at the last,
Eze.24:23. ye shall pine away...*and mourn*

KAL.—*Future.*

Isa. 5:29. *yea, they shall roar,* and lay hold
30. *And* in that day *they shall roar*

KAL.—*Participle.* Poel.

Pro.28:15. a *roaring* lion, and a ranging bear;

נַהַם *nah'-ham*, m. 5099

Pro.19:12. king's wrath (is) as *the roaring of* a lion;
20: 2. The fear of a king (is) as *the roaring of*

נְהָמָה [*n'hāh-māh'*], f. 5100

Ps. 38: 8(9). I have roared *by reason of the disquietness of*
Isa. 5:30. *like the roaring of* the sea:

נָהַק [*nāh-hak'*]. 5101

* KAL.—*Future.* *

Job 6: 5. *Doth* the wild ass *bray* when he hath grass?
30: 7. Among the bushes *they brayed;*

נָהַר [*nāh-har'*]. 5102

* KAL.—*Preterite.* *

Ps. 34: 5(6). looked unto him, *and were lightened:*
Isa. 2: 2. *and* all nations *shall flow* unto it.
60: 5. Then thou shalt see, *and flow together,*
Jer. 31:12. *and shall flow together* to the goodness
Mic. 4: 1. *and* people *shall flow* unto it.

KAL.—*Future.*

Jer. 51:44. and the nations shall not *flow together*

נָהָר *nāh-hāhr'*, m. 5104

Gen 2:10. *And a river* went out of Eden
13. the name of *the* second *river*
14. the name of *the* third *river*
— *And the* fourth *river* (is) Euphrates.
15:18. *from the river of* Egypt unto *the* great *river, the river* Euphrates:
24:10. went to Mesopotamia, (lit. Syria of *the two rivers*)
31:21. passed over *the river,*
36:37. Saul of Rehoboth (by) *the river*
Ex. 7:19. upon *their streams,* upon their rivers,
8: 5(1). over *the streams,* over the rivers,
23:31. from the desert unto *the river:*
Nu. 22: 5. which (is) by *the river*
24: 6. as gardens by *the river's* side,
Deu. 1: 7. unto *the* great *river, the river* Euphrates.
11:24. from *the river, the river* Euphrates,
23: 4(5). of Pethor of Mesopotamia, (lit. Syria of *the two rivers*)
Jos. 1: 4. unto *the* great *river, the river* Euphrates,
24: 2. Your fathers dwelt on the other side of *the flood*
3. from the other side of *the flood,*
14. served on the other side of *the flood,*
15. that (were) on the other side of *the flood,*
Jud. 3: 8. king of Mesopotamia: (marg. Aram *naharaim* lit. of *the two rivers*)

2Sa. 8: 3. *at the river* Euphrates.
10:16. that (were) beyond *the river:*
1K. 4:21(5:1). from *the river* unto the land
24(-:4). (the region) on this side *the river,*
—(-:-). all the kings on this side *the river:*
14:15. shall scatter them beyond *the river,*
2K. 5:12. Abana and Pharpar, *rivers of* Damascus,
17: 6 & 18:11. *the river of* Gozan, and in the cities
23:29. to *the river* Euphrates:
24: 7. from the river of Egypt unto *the river* Euphrates
1Ch 1:48. Shaul of Rehoboth by *the river*
5: 9. from *the river* Euphrates:
26. *and* to *the river* Gozan,
18: 3. his dominion *by the river* Euphrates.
19:16. that (were) beyond *the river:*
2Ch 9:26. from *the river* even unto the land
Ezr. 8:15. I gathered them together to *the river*
21. at *the river* of Ahava,
31. *from the river of* Ahava
36. the governors on this side *the river:*
Neh. 2: 7, 9. the governors beyond *the river,*
3: 7. on this side *the river.*
Job 14:11. *and the flood* decayeth and drieth up:
20:17. He shall not see the rivers, *the floods*, the brooks (marg. or, *streaming* brooks)
22:16. was overflown with *a flood:*
28:11. He bindeth *the floods*
40:23. he drinketh up *a river,*
Ps. 24: 2. established it upon *the floods.*
46: 4(5). (There is) *a river,*
60[title](2). when he strove with Aram-*naharaim*
66: 6. they went *through the flood*
72: 8. *and from the river* unto the ends of the earth.
74:15. thou driedst up mighty *rivers.*
78:16. caused waters to run down *like rivers.*
80:11(12). her branches unto *the river.*
89:25(26). *and* his right hand *in the rivers.*
93: 3. *The floods* have lifted up, O Lord, *the floods* have lifted up their voice; *the floods* lift up their waves.
98: 8. Let *the floods* clap (their) hands:
105:41. they ran in the dry places (like) *a river.*
107:33. He turneth *rivers* into a wilderness,
137: 1. *the rivers of* Babylon, there we sat down,
Cant. 8: 7. *neither* can *the floods* drown it:
Isa. 7:20. by them beyond *the river,*
8: 7. the waters of *the river,*
11:15. shake his hand over *the river,*
18: 1. which (is) beyond *the rivers of*
2, 7. whose land *the rivers* have spoiled!
19: 5. *and the river* shall be wasted and dried up.
6. they shall turn *the rivers* far away;
27:12. the channel of *the river*
33:21. a place of broad *rivers*
41:18. I will open *rivers* in high places,
42:15. I will make *the rivers* islands,
43: 2. *and through the rivers,* they shall not
19. *rivers* in the desert.
20. *rivers* in the desert, to give drink
44:27. *and* I will dry up *thy rivers:*
47: 2. pass over *the rivers.*
48:18. then had thy peace been *as a river,*
50: 2. I make *the rivers* a wilderness:
59:19. When the enemy shall come in *like a flood,*
66:12. I will extend peace to her *like a river,*
Jer. 2:18. to drink the waters of *the river?*
46: 2. which was by *the river* Euphrates
6. the north by *the river* Euphrates.
7. whose waters are moved *as the rivers?*
8. *and* (his) waters are moved *like the rivers;*
10. north country by *the river* Euphrates.
Eze. 1: 1. the captives by *the river of* Chebar,
3. of the Chaldeans by *the river* Chebar;
3:15. that dwelt by *the river of* Chebar,
23. I saw by *the river of* Chebar:
10:15. I saw *by the river of* Chebar.
20. of Israel *by the river of* Chebar;
22. I saw by *the river of* Chebar,
31: 4. with *her rivers* running round about
15. I restrained *the floods thereof,*
32: 2. thou camest forth *with thy rivers,*
— and fouledst *their rivers.*
14. *and* cause *their rivers* to run
43: 3. I saw by *the river* Chebar;
Dan 10: 4. the side of *the* great *river,*
Jon. 2: 3(4). *and the floods* compassed me about:
Mic. 7:12. from the fortress even to *the river,*
Nah. 1: 4. and drieth up all *the rivers:*
2: 6(7). The gates of *the rivers*
Hab. 3: 8. Was the Lord displeased *against the rivers?* (was) thine anger *against the rivers?*
9. Thou didst cleave the earth with *rivers.*
Zep. 3:10. From beyond *the rivers of* Ethiopia
Zec. 9:10. *and from the river* (even) to the ends of the earth.

נְהַר *n'har*, Ch. m. 5103

Ezr. 4:10. (that are) on this side *the river,*
11. Thy servants the men on this side *the river,*
16. have no portion on this side *the river.*
17. and (unto) the rest beyond *the river,*
20. over all (countries) beyond *the river;*
5: 3, 6. Tatnai, governor on this side *the river,*
6. Apharsachites, which (were) on this side *the river,*
6: 6. Tatnai, governor beyond *the river,*
— Apharsachites, which (are) beyond *the river,*
8. (even) of the tribute beyond *the river,*
13. governor on this side *the river,*
7:21. treasurers which (are) beyond *the river,*
25. the people that (are) beyond *the river,*
Dan. 7:10. *A* fiery *stream* issued and came forth

נְהָרָה *n'hāh-rāh'*, f. 5105

Job 3: 4. neither let *the light* shine upon it.

נוֹא [*nōh*]. 5106

* KAL.—*Future.* *

Nu. 32: 7. (כתיב) wherefore *discourage* (marg. *break*) *ye* the heart

* HIPHIL.—*Preterite.* *

Nu. 30: 5(6). if her father *disallow* her
—(-). because her father *disallowed* her.
11(12). (and) *disallowed* her not:
Ps. 33:10. *he maketh* the devices of the people *of none effect.*

HIPHIL.—*Future.*

Nu. 30: 8(9). if her husband *disallowed her*
32: 7. wherefore *discourage* (marg. *break*) *ye* the heart of
9. *they discouraged* the heart of
Ps. 141: 5. *shall* not *break* my head:

נוּב [*noov*]. 5107

* KAL.—*Future.* *

Ps. 62:10(11). if riches *increase,*
92:14(15). *They shall* still *bring forth fruit*
Pro. 10:31. mouth of the just *bringeth forth* wisdom:

* PILEL.—*Future.* *

Zec. 9:17. corn *shall make* the young men *chearful,* (marg. or, *grow,* or, *speak*)

נוֹב *nōhv*, m. 5108

Isa. 57:19. (כתיב) I create *the fruit of* the lips;

נוּד [*nood*]. 5110

* KAL.—*Preterite.* *

Jer. 50: 3. *they shall remove,* they shall depart,

KAL.—*Infinitive.*

Job 2:11. *to mourn* with him
Ps. 69:20(21). I looked (for some) *to take pity,* (marg. *to lament* (with me))
Pro. 26: 2. As the bird *by wandering,*

KAL.—*Imperative.*

Ps. 11: 1. *Flee* (as) a bird to your mountain?
Jer. 48:17. All ye that are about him, *bemoan*
49:30. *get you* far off, (marg. *flit* greatly)
50: 8. *Remove* out of the midst of Babylon,

KAL.—*Future.*

1K. 14:15. as a reed *is shaken* in the water,
Job 42:11. *and they bemoaned* him, and comforted him
Isa. 51:19. who *shall be sorry* for thee?
Jer. 4: 1. then *shalt thou* not *remove.*
15: 5. who *shall bemoan* thee?
16: 5. neither go to lament nor *bemoan* them:
22:10. Weep ye not for the dead, neither *bemoan* him:
Nah. 3: 7. who *will bemoan* her?

KAL.—*Participle.* Poel.

Gen. 4:12. *and a vagabond* shalt thou be
14. I shall be a fugitive *and a vagabond*

* HIPHIL.—*Infinitive.* *

2K. 21: 8. Neither will I *make* the feet of Israel *move*

HIPHIL.—*Future.*

Ps. 36:11(12). *let* not the hand of the wicked *remove me.*
Jer. 18:16. shall be astonished, *and wag* his head.

* HITHPOLEL.—*Preterite.* *

Isa. 24:20. *and shall be removed* like a cottage;

HITHPOLEL.—*Future.*

Jer. 48:27. *thou skippedst for joy.* (marg. or, *movedst thyself*)

HITHPOLEL.—*Participle.*

Jer. 31:18. heard Ephraim *bemoaning himself*

5111 **נוּד** *[nood]*, Ch.

* P'AL.—*Future.* *

Dan. 4:14(11). *let* the beasts *get away* from under it,

5112-13 **נוֹד** *nōhd*, m.

Gen. 4:16. And Cain...dwelt in the land of *Nod,* (lit. *wandering*)
Ps. 56: 8(9). Thou tellest *my wanderings:*

5115 **נָוָה** *[nāh-vāh']*.

* KAL.—*Future.* *

Hab. 2: 5. neither *keepeth at home,*

* HIPHIL.—*Future.* *

Ex. 15: 2. *and I will prepare him an habitation;*

5116 **נָוֶה** *nāh-veh'*, m.

Ex. 15:13. in thy strength unto thy holy *habitation.*
2Sa. 7: 8. I took thee from *the sheepcote,*
15:25. shew me (both) it, and *his habitation:*
1Ch 17: 7. I took thee from *the sheepcote,*
Job 5: 3. suddenly I cursed *his habitation.*
24. thou shalt visit *thy habitation,*
18:15. brimstone shall be scattered upon *his habitation.*
Ps. 79: 7. and laid waste *his dwelling place.*
Pro. 3:33. *but* he blesseth *the habitation of* the just.
21:20. *in the dwelling of* the wise;
24:15. *against the dwelling of* the righteous;
Isa. 27:10. *the habitation* forsaken,
32:18. *in a* peaceable *habitation,*
33:20. see Jerusalem *a* quiet *habitation,*
34:13. *an habitation of* dragons,
35: 7. *in the habitation of* dragons,
65:10. Sharon shall be *a fold of* flocks,
Jer. 10:25. have made *his habitation* desolate.
23: 3. will bring them again to *their folds;*
25:30. he shall mightily roar upon *his habitation;*
31:23. *O habitation of* justice,
33:12. *an habitation of* shepherds
49:19. *the habitation of* the strong:
20. he shall make *their habitations* desolate
50: 7. *the habitation of* justice,
19. I will bring Israel again to *his habitation,*
Jer. 50:44. *the habitation of* the strong:
45. he shall make (their) *habitation* desolate
Eze.25: 5. I will make Rabbah *a stable for*
34:14. upon the high mountains of Israel shall *their fold* be: there shall they lie *in a* good *fold,*
Hos. 9:13. Ephraim,...(is) planted *in a pleasant place:*

נָוָה *nāh-vāh'*, f. 5116

Job 8: 6. *the habitation of* thy righteousness
Ps. 68:12(13). *and she that tarried* at home
Jer. 6: 2. to a *comely* (marg. or, (woman) *dwelling at home*) and delicate (woman).
Zep. 2: 6. the sea coast shall be *dwellings*

נוּחַ *[noo'ăgh]*. 5117

* KAL.—*Preterite.* *

2K. 2:15. The spirit of Elijah *doth rest* on Elisha.
Est. 9:22. the days wherein the Jews *rested*
Job 3:26. neither *was I quiet;* yet trouble came.
Isa. 7: 2. Syria *is confederate* with Ephraim.
19. *and shall rest* all of them
11: 2. *And* the spirit of the Lord *shall rest* upon him,
14: 7. The whole earth *is at rest,*

KAL.—*Infinitive.*

Nu. 10:36. *And when it rested,*
11:25. *when* the spirit *rested*
Jos. 3:13. *as soon as* the soles...of the priests...*shall rest*
2Sa.21:10. suffered neither the birds of the air *to rest*
Neh. 9:28. *But after they had rest,* they did

KAL.—*Future.*

Gen 8: 4. *And* the ark *rested* in the seventh month,
Ex. 10:14. *and rested* in all the coasts of Egypt:
20:11. *and rested* the seventh day:
23:12. that thine ox and thine ass *may rest,*
Nu. 11:26. *and* the spirit *rested* upon them;
Deu 5:14. that thy manservant...*may rest*
Jos. 21:44(42). *And* the Lord *gave* them *rest*
1Sa.25: 9. in the name of David, *and ceased.* (marg. *rested*)
2Ch 14: 7(6). *because...he hath given* us *rest*
15:15. *and* the Lord *gave* them *rest*
20:30. *for* his God *gave* him *rest*
Job 3:13. then *had* I *been at rest,* (lit. *it had rested* to me)
17. there the weary *be at rest.*
Ps.125: 3. the rod of the wicked *shall* not *rest*
Pro.14:33. Wisdom *resteth* in the heart
21:16. *shall remain* in the congregation of
Ecc. 7: 9. anger *resteth* in the bosom of fools.
Isa. 23:12. *shalt* thou *have* no *rest.* (lit. *shall rest be* to thee)
25:10. *shall* the hand of the Lord *rest,*
57: 2. *they shall rest* in their beds,
Dan 12:13. *for* (marg. or, *and*) *thou shalt rest,* and
Hab. 3:16. *I might rest* in the day of trouble:

* HIPHIL.—*Preterite.* *

Ex. 33:14. *and I will give* thee *rest.*
Deu12:10. *and* (when) *he giveth* you *rest* from all
Jos.22: 4. the Lord your God *hath given rest*
23: 1. the Lord *had given rest*
2Sa. 7: 1. the Lord *had given* him *rest*
11. *and have caused* thee *to rest*
1K. 5: 4(18). the Lord my God *hath given* me *rest*
1Ch 22: 9. *and I will give* him *rest*
18. *and hath he* (not) *given* you *rest*
23:25. The Lord God of Israel *hath given rest*
2Ch 14: 6(5). the Lord *had given* him *rest.*
Eze. 5:13. *and I will cause* my fury *to rest*
16:42. *So will I make* my fury...*to rest,*
21:17(22). *and I will cause* my fury *to rest:*
Zec. 6: 8. these that go toward the north country *have quieted*

HIPHIL.—*Infinitive.*

Deu25:19. *when* the Lord thy God *hath given* thee *rest*
Isa. 14: 3. *that* the Lord *shall give* thee *rest*
Eze.24:13. till *I have caused* my fury *to rest*
44:30. *that he may cause* the blessing *to rest*

HIPHIL.—*Imperative.*

Isa. 28:12. *ye may cause* the weary *to rest;*

HIPHIL.—*Future.*

Ex. 17:11. when *he let down* his hand,
Deu. 3:20. Until the Lord *have given rest*
Jos. 1:15. Until the Lord *have given* your brethren *rest,*
Pro.29:17. Correct thy son, *and he shall give thee rest;*
Isa. 30:32. the Lord *shall lay* upon him,
63:14. the Spirit of the Lord *caused him to rest:*
Eze.37: 1. *and set me down* in the midst of the valley
40: 2. *and set me* upon a very high mountain,

HIPHIL.—*Participle.*

Jos. 1:13. The Lord your God *hath given* you *rest,*

* HOPHAL.—*Preterite.* *

Lam.5: 5. we labour, (and) *have no rest.*

5118 נוֹחַ *nōh'ăgh*, m.

2Ch 6:41. arise, O Lord God, *into thy resting place,*
Est. 9:16. *and* had *rest* from their enemies,
17. *and* on the fourteenth day...*rested they,* (lit. *and rest*)
18. *and* on the fifteenth (day)...*they rested,*

5120 נוט [*noot*].

* KAL.—*Future.* *

Ps. 99: 1. *let* the earth *be moved.*

5122 נְוָלוּ *n'vāh-loo'*, Ch. f.

Ezr. 6:11. be made *a dunghill* for this.

5122 נְוָלִי *n'vāh-lee'*, Ch. f.

Dan. 2: 5. your houses shall be made *a dunghill.*
3:29. their houses shall be made *a dunghill:*

5123 נוּם [*noom*].

* KAL.—*Preterite.* *

Ps. 76: 5(6). *they have slept* their sleep:
Nah. 3:18. Thy shepherds *slumber,*

KAL.—*Infinitive.*

Isa. 56:10. loving *to slumber.*

KAL.—*Future.*

Ps.121: 3. he that keepeth thee *will* not *slumber.*
4. *shall* neither *slumber* nor sleep.
Isa. 5:27. none *shall slumber* nor sleep;

5124 נוּמָה *noo-māh'*, f.

Pro.23:21. *drowsiness* shall clothe (a man) with rags.

5125 נוּן [*noon*].

* NIPHAL.—*Future.* *

Ps. 72:17. his name *shall be continued*

* HIPHIL.—*Future.* *

Ps. 72:17. (כתיב) his name *shall be continued*

5127 נוּס [*noos*].

* KAL.—*Preterite.* *

Gen14:10. they that remained *fled* to the mountain.
Lev.26:17. *and ye shall flee* when none pursueth
36. *and they shall flee,* as fleeing from a sword;
Nu. 16:34. Israel that (were) round about them *fled*
35:11. *that* the slayer *may flee*
25. refuge, whither *he was fled:*
Deu. 4:42. *and that fleeing* unto one of these cities
19:11. *and fleeth* into one of these cities:
34: 7. nor his natural force *abated.* (marg. moisture *fled*)
Jos. 8: 5. *that we will flee* before them,
6. *therefore we will flee* before them.
20: 4. *when he that doth flee* unto one
6. the city from whence *he fled.*
Jud. 4:17. Sisera *fled away* on his feet
1Sa. 4:16. *I fled* to day out of the army.
17. Israel *is fled* before the Philistines,
14:22. they heard that the Philistines *fled,*
19:10. and David *fled,* and escaped
31: 7. the men of Israel *fled,*
2Sa. 1: 4. the people *are fled*
10:14. saw that the Syrians *were fled,*
17: 2. *and* all the people that (are) with him *shall flee;*
18:17. all Israel *fled* every one
19: 8(9). Israel *had fled* every man
23:11. the people *fled* from the Philistines.
1K. 2:29. told king Solomon that Joab *was fled*
20:30. And Ben-hadad *fled,*
2K. 9: 3. Then open the door, *and flee,*
1Ch 10: 7. the men of Israel...saw that *they fled,*
11:13. the people *fled* from before the Philistines.
19:15. saw that the Syrians *were fled,*
Pro.28: 1. The wicked *flee*
Cant.2:17 & 4:6. *and* the shadows *flee away,*
Isa. 10:29. Gibeah of Saul *is fled.*
17:13. *and they shall flee* far off,
20: 6. whither *we flee* for help
31: 8. *but he shall flee* from the sword,
35:10. *and* sorrow and sighing *shall flee away.*
51:11. sorrow and mourning *shall flee away.*
Jer. 46: 5. their mighty ones are beaten down, and *are fled* apace,
21. are turned back, (and) *are fled away*
Zec.14: 5. *And ye shall flee* (to) the valley
— yea, *ye shall flee,* like as *ye fled* from before the earthquake

KAL.—*Infinitive.*

Gen19:20. this city (is) near *to flee* unto,
Nu. 35: 6. that he may *flee* (lit. shall be *for fleeing*) thither:
15. *that* every one that killeth...unawares *may flee*
32. *for him that is fled* (lit. *for fleeing*) to the city
Deu. 4:42. *That* the slayer *might flee*
19: 3. *that* every slayer *may flee*
Jos. 8:20. they had no power *to flee*
10:11. *as they fled* from before Israel,
20: 3. *That* the slayer...*may flee*
9. *that* whosoever killeth...unawares *might flee*
2Sa. 4: 4. as she made haste *to flee,*
18: 3. for if we flee *away,* (lit. *fleeing* we flee) they will not care for us;
19: 3(4). *when they flee* in battle.
24:13. *wilt thou flee* three months
1K. 12:18. *to flee* to Jerusalem.
2Ch 10:18. *to flee* to Jerusalem.
Jer. 49:24. turneth herself *to flee,*

KAL.—*Imperative.*

Jer. 48: 6. *Flee,* save your lives,
49: 8. *Flee ye,* turn back,
30. *Flee,* get you far off,
51: 6. *Flee* out of the midst of Babylon,
Zec. 2: 6(10). *and flee* from the land of the north,

KAL.—*Future.*

Gen14:10. *and* the kings of Sodom and Gomorrah *fled,*
39:12. he left his garment in her hand, *and fled,*
13. he had left his garment...*and was fled*
15, 18. he left his garment with me, *and fled,*
Ex. 4: 3. *and* Moses *fled* from before it.
14:25. *Let us flee* from the face of Israel;
21:13. a place whither *he shall flee.*
Nu. 10:35. *and let them* that hate thee *flee*
35:26. the city...whither *he was fled;*
Deu19: 4. the slayer, which *shall flee*
5. *he shall flee* unto one of those cities,
28: 7. and *flee* before thee seven ways.
25. and *flee* seven ways before them:
Jos. 7: 4. *and they fled* before the men of Ai.
8:15. *and fled* by the way of the wilderness.
10:16. *But* these five kings *fled,*
Jud. 1: 6. *But* Adoni-bezek *fled;*
4:15. *and fled* away on his feet.

Jud. 7:21. all the host ran, and cried, *and fled.*
22. *and* the host *fled* to Beth-shittah
8:12. And *when* Zebah and Zalmunna *fled,*
9:21. *and* Jotham *ran away,* and fled,
40. *and he fled* before him,
51. *and* thither *fled* all the men and women,
20:32. *Let us flee,* and draw them from
45. they turned *and fled*
47. six hundred men turned *and fled*
1Sa. 4:10. *and they fled* every man into his tent:
17:24. *fled* from him, and were sore afraid.
51. *And* when the Philistines saw their champion was dead, *they fled.*
19: 8. *and they fled* from him.
30:17. rode upon camels, *and fled.*
31: 1. *and* the men of Israel *fled*
7. they forsook the cities, *and fled;*
2Sa. 4: 4. his nurse took him up, *and fled:*
10:13. *and they fled* before him.
14. *then fled they* also before Abishai,
18. *And* the Syrians *fled* before Israel;
13:29. every man gat him up...*and fled.*
18: 3. if *we flee* away, they will not care for us;
1K. 2:28. *And* Joab *fled* unto the tabernacle
20:20. *and* the Syrians *fled;* and Israel
30. *But* the rest *fled* to Aphek,
2K. 3:24. *so that they fled* before them:
7: 7. they arose *and fled* in the twilight,
— *and fled* for their life.
8:21. *and* the people *fled* into their tents.
9:10. he opened the door, *and fled.*
23. Joram turned his hands, *and fled,*
27. *But* when...*he fled* by the way of the garden house.
— *And he fled* to Megiddo,
14:12. *and they fled* every man to their tents.
19. *and he fled* to Lachish;
1Ch 10: 1. *and* the men of Israel *fled*
7. they forsook their cities, *and fled.*
19:14. *and they fled* before him.
15. *And* when...*they* likewise *fled* before Abishai
18. *But* the Syrians *fled* before Israel;
2Ch 13:16. *And* the children of Israel *fled* before
14:12(11). Judah; *and* the Ethiopians *fled.*
25:22. *and they fled* every man to his tent.
27. *and he fled* to Lachish:
Ps. 68: 1(2). *let* them *also* that hate him *flee* before
104: 7. At thy rebuke *they fled;*
114: 3. The sea saw (it), *and fled:*
5. What (ailed) thee, O thou sea, *that thou fleddest?*
Pro. 28:17. *shall flee* to the pit;
Isa. 10: 3. to whom *will ye flee* for help?
13:14. *flee* every one into his own land.
30:16. *we will flee* upon horses; therefore *shall ye flee:*
17. at the rebuke of five *shall ye flee:*
Jer. 46: 6. *Let* not the swift *flee away,*
50:16. *they shall flee* every one to his own land.
Am. 2:16. the mighty *shall flee away*
5:19. As if a man *did flee* from a lion,
9: 1. of them *shall* not *flee away,*

KAL.—*Participle.*

Ex. 14:27. the Egyptians *fled*
Jos. 8: 6. *They flee* before us,
20. the people *that fled*
Isa. 24:18. *he who fleeth* from the noise of
Jer. 48:19. ask *him that fleeth,*
44. *He that fleeth* from the fear
45. *They that fled* stood under the shadow
50:28. The voice of *them that flee*
Am. 9: 1. *he that fleeth* of them
Nah. 2: 8(9). yet they *shall flee away.*

* POLEL.—*Preterite.* *

Isa. 59:19. Spirit of the Lord *shall lift up a standard* (marg. *put* him *to flight*)

* HIPHIL.—*Preterite.* *

Ex. 9:20. *made* his servants and his cattle *flee*

HIPHIL.—*Infinitive.*

Jud. 6:11. *to hide* (marg. *cause* (it) *to flee*) (it) from the Midianites.

HIPHIL.—*Future.*

Deu32:30. two *put* ten thousand *to flight,*
Jud. 7:21. (כתיב) all the host ran, and cried *and fled.*

* HITHPOLEL.—*Infinitive.* *

Ps. 60: 4(6). *that it may be displayed*

נוּעַ noo'ăg. 5128

* KAL.—*Preterite.* *

Job 28: 4. *they are gone away* from men.
Pro. 5: 6. her ways *are moveable,*
Isa. 19: 1. *and* the idols of Egypt *shall be moved*
29: 9. *they stagger,* but not with strong drink.
Lam. 4:14. *They have wandered* (as) blind (men)
15. they fled away and *wandered,*
Am. 4: 8. *So* two (or) three cities *wandered* unto
8:12. *And they shall wander* from sea to sea,

KAL.—*Infinitive.*

Jud. 9: 9, 11, 13. go *to be promoted* (marg. *up and down*) over the trees?
Ps. 109:10. his children be *continually* vagabonds, (lit. *and wandering* let his children wander)
Isa. 7: 2. *as* the trees of the wood *are moved*
24:20. The earth shall reel *to and fro* (lit. *reeling* it shall reel)
Jer. 14:10. Thus have they loved *to wander,*

KAL.—*Future.*

Ex. 20:18. *and* when...*they removed,* and stood afar off.
2Sa. 15:20. (כתיב) *should I...make thee go up and down* (marg. *should I make thee wander* in going)
Ps. 59:15(16). (כתיב) *Let* them *wander up and down*
107:27. They reel to and fro, *and stagger*
109:10. *Let* his children *be* continually *vagabonds,*
Isa. 6: 4. *And* the posts of the door *moved*
7: 2. *And* his heart *was moved,*
24:20. The earth *shall reel* to and fro

KAL.—*Participle.*

Gen. 4:12. *a fugitive* and a vagabond shalt thou be
14. I shall be *a fugitive* and a vagabond
1Sa. 1:13. only her lips *moved,*

* NIPHAL.—*Future.* *

Am. 9: 9. like as (corn) *is sifted*
Nah. 3:12. if *they be shaken,* they shall even fall

* HIPHIL.—*Preterite.* *

2K. 19:21. the daughter of Jerusalem *hath shaken* her head
Isa. 37:22. daughter of Jerusalem *hath shaken* her head
Am. 9: 9. *and I will sift* (marg. *cause to move*) the house of Israel

HIPHIL.—*Imperative.*

Ps. 59:11(12). *scatter them* by thy power;

HIPHIL.—*Future.*

Nu. 32:13. *and he made them wander* in the wilderness
2Sa. 15:20. *should I...make thee* go *up and down* (marg. *should I make thee wander* in going)
2K. 23:18. *let* no man *move* his bones.
Job 16: 4. could heap up words...*and shake* mine head
Ps. 22: 7(8). *they shake* the head,
59:15(16). *Let* them *wander up and down*
109:25. *they shaked* their heads.
Lam. 2:15. they hiss *and wag* their head
Dan 10:10. an hand touched me, *which set me* upon
Zep. 2:15. by her shall hiss, (and) *wag* his hand.

נוּף [nooph]. 5130

* KAL.—*Preterite.* *

Pro. 7:17. *I have perfumed* my bed with myrrh,

* POLEL.—*Future.* *

Isa. 10:32. *he shall shake* his hand

* HIPHIL.—*Preterite.* *

Ex. 20:25. if *thou lift up* thy tool upon it,
29:24. *and shalt wave* (marg. *shake to and fro*)
26. *and wave* it (for) a wave offering
35:22. every man that *offered*
Lev. 9:21. Aaron *waved* (for) a wave offering
14:12. *and wave* them (for) a wave offering
24. *and* the priest *shall wave* them
23:11. *And he shall wave* the sheaf
20. *And* the priest *shall wave* them
Nu. 5:25. *and shall wave* the offering before the Lord,
6:20. *And* the priest *shall wave* them

Nu. 8:11. *And* Aaron *shall offer* (marg. *wave*) the
13, 15. *and offer* them (for) an offering
Jos. 8:31. over which no man *hath lift up* (any) iron:
2K. 5:11. *and strike* (marg. *move up and down*) his hand over the place,
Job 31:21. If *I have lifted up* my hand against
Isa. 11:15. *and* with his mighty wind *shall he shake* his

HIPHIL.—*Infinitive.*

Lev. 7:30. *that* the breast *may be waved*
10:15. *to wave* (it for) a wave offering
23:12. *when ye wave* the sheaf
Isa. 10:15. *as if* the rod *should shake* (itself)
30:28. *to sift* the nations with the sieve of vanity:

HIPHIL.—*Imperative.*

Isa. 13: 2. *shake* the hand, that they may go

HIPHIL.—*Future.*

Lev. 8:27. *and waved* them (for) a wave offering
29. Moses took the breast, *and waved it*
23:11. on the morrow after the sabbath the priest *shall wave it.*
Nu. 8:21. *and* Aaron *offered* them
Deu23:25(26). *thou shalt* not *move* a sickle
27: 5. *thou shalt* not *lift up* (any) iron (tool)
Ps. 68: 9(10). *Thou,* O God, *didst send* (marg. *shake out*) a plentiful rain,

HIPHIL.—*Participle.*

Isa. 10:15. shall the saw magnify itself against *him that shaketh it?*
19:16. the hand of the Lord of hosts, which he *shaketh*
Zec. 2: 9(13). I *will shake* mine hand upon them,

* HOPHAL.—*Preterite.* *

Ex. 29:27. the shoulder...which *is waved,*

5131 נוֹף *nōhph,* m.

Ps. 48: 2(3). Beautiful for *situation,*...(is) mount Zion,

5132 נוּץ [*nootz*].

* KAL.—*Preterite.* *

Lam.4:15. when *they fled away* and wandered,

* HIPHIL.—*Preterite.* *

Cant.6:11. the pomegranates *budded.*
7:12(13). the pomegranates *bud forth:*

5133 נוֹצָה *nōh-tzāh',* f.

Job 39:13. or wings and feathers unto *the ostrich?* (marg. or, feathers of the stork *and ostrich*)
Eze.17: 3. A great eagle...full of *feathers,*
7. another great eagle with...many *feathers:*

5134 נוּק [*nook*].

* HIPHIL.—*Future.* *

Ex. 2: 9. the woman took the child, *and nursed it.*

5135 נוּר *noor,* Ch. m.

Dan. 3: 6, 11, 15. midst of a burning *fiery* furnace.
17. us from the burning *fiery* furnace,
20. cast (them) into the burning *fiery*
21. midst of the burning *fiery*
22. the flame of *the fire* slew those men
23. into the midst of the burning *fiery*
24. bound into the midst of *the fire?*
25. loose, walking in the midst of *the fire,*
26. mouth of the burning *fiery* furnace,
— came forth of the midst of *the fire.*
27. upon whose bodies *the fire* had no power,
— nor the smell of *fire* had passed on them.
7: 9. his throne (was like) the *fiery* flame, (and) his wheels (as) burning *fire.*
10. A *fiery* stream issued and came

נוּשׁ [*noosh*]. 5136

* KAL.—*Future.* *

Ps. 69:20(21). *and I am full of heaviness:* and I looked

נָזָה [*nāh-zāh'*], m. 5137

* KAL.—*Future.* *

Lev. 6:27(20). when there *is sprinkled* of the blood
—(—). that whereon *it was sprinkled*
2K. 9:33. *and* (some) of her blood *was sprinkled*
Isa. 63: 3. *and* their blood *shall be sprinkled*

* HIPHIL.—*Preterite.* *

Ex. 29:21. thou shalt take of the blood...*and sprinkle*
Lev. 4: 6. *and sprinkle* of the blood seven times
17. his finger (in some) of the blood, *and sprinkle*
5: 9. *And he shall sprinkle* of the blood
14: 7. *And he shall sprinkle* upon him
16. *and shall sprinkle* of the oil
27. *And* the priest *shall sprinkle*
51. *and sprinkle* the house seven times:
16:14. he shall take of the blood...*and sprinkle*
15. *and sprinkle* it upon the mercy seat,
19. *And he shall sprinkle* of the blood
Nu. 19: 4. *and sprinkle* of her blood directly
18. *and sprinkle* (it) upon the tent,
19. *And* the clean (person) *shall sprinkle* upon the unclean

HIPHIL.—*Imperative.*

Nu. 8: 7. *Sprinkle* water of purifying

HIPHIL.—*Future.*

Lev. 8:11. *And he sprinkled* thereof upon the altar
30. *and sprinkled* (it) upon Aaron,
16:14. *shall he sprinkle* of the blood
Isa. 52:15. So *shall he sprinkle* many nations;

HIPHIL.—*Participle.*

Nu. 19:21. *that he that sprinkleth* the water

נָזִיד *nāh-zeed',* m. 5138

Gen25:29. And Jacob sod *pottage:*
34. Jacob gave Esau bread *and pottage of* lentiles;
2K. 4:38. seethe *pottage* for the sons of the prophets.
39. into the pot of *pottage:*
40. as they were eating *of the pottage,*
Hag. 2:12. with his skirt do touch bread, or *pottage,*

נָזִיר *nāh-zeer',* m. 5139

Gen49:26. *him that was separate from* his brethren.
Lev.25: 5. the grapes of *thy vine undressed:* (marg. *separation*)
11. (the grapes) in it *of thy vine undressed.*
Nu. 6: 2. to vow a vow of *a Nazarite,*
13, 21. the law of *the Nazarite,*
18. *the Nazarite* shall shave the head of
19. the hands of *the Nazarite,*
20. *the Nazarite* may drink wine.
Deu33:16. *him that was separated from* his brethren.
Jud 13: 5. the child shall be *a Nazarite unto* God
7. the child shall be *a Nazarite to* God
16:17. I (have been) *a Nazarite unto* God
Lam.4: 7. *Her Nazarites* were purer than snow,
Am. 2:11. I raised up...of your young men *for Nazarites.*
12. ye gave *the Nazarites* wine

נָזַל [*nāh-zal'*]. 5140

* KAL.—*Preterite.* *

Jud. 5: 5. The mountains *melted* (marg. *flowed*) from before the Lord,

KAL.—*Future.*

Nu. 24: 7. *He shall pour* the water out of
Deu32: 2. my speech *shall distil* as the dew,
Job 36:28. the clouds *do drop* (and) distil
Ps.147:18. his wind to blow, (and) the waters *flow.*

Cant.4:16. (that) the spices...*may flow out.*
Isa. 45: 8. *let* the skies *pour down* righteousness:
Jer. 9:18(17). our eyelids *gush out* with waters.

KAL.—*Participle.* Poel.

Ex. 15: 8. *the floods* stood upright
Ps. 78:16. He brought *streams* also out of
44. their rivers into blood; *and their floods,*
Pro. 5:15. *and running waters* out of thine own well.
Cant.4:15. *and streams* from Lebanon.
Isa. 44: 3. *and floods* upon the dry ground:
Jer. 18:14. the cold *flowing* waters

* HIPHIL.—*Preterite.* *

Isa. 48:21. *he caused* the waters *to flow*

5141 נֶזֶם *neh'-zem.*

Gen24:22. the man took *a* golden *earring* (marg. or, *jewel for the forehead*)
30. when he saw *the earring*
47. I put *the earring* upon her face,
35: 4. (all their) *earrings* which (were) in their
Ex. 32: 2. Break off *the* golden *earrings,*
3. the people brake off *the* golden *earrings*
35:22. *earrings,* and rings, and tablets,
Jud. 8:24. *the earrings of* his prey. For they had golden *earrings,*
25. did cast therein every man *the earrings of*
26. the weight of *the* golden *earrings*
Job 42:11. every one *an earring of* gold.
Pro.11:22. *a jewel of* gold in a swine's snout,
25:12. *an earring of* gold,
Isa. 3:21. The rings, *and* nose *jewels,*
Eze.16:12. I put *a jewel* on thy forehead,
Hos. 2:13(15). she decked herself *with her earrings*

5142 נְזַק [*n'zak'*], Ch.

* P'AL.—*Participle.* Passive. *

Dan. 6: 2(3). and the king *should have* no *damage.*

* APHEL.—*Infinitive.* *

Ezr. 4:22. why should damage grow *to the hurt of* the kings?

APHEL.—*Future.*

Ezr. 4:13. (so) *thou shalt endamage* the revenue of the kings.

APHEL.—*Participle.*

Ezr. 4:15. a rebellious city, *and hurtful* unto kings

5143 נֵזֶק *nēh'-zek,* m.

Est. 7: 4. could not countervail the king's *damage.*

5144 נָזַר [*nāh-zar'*].

* NIPHAL.—*Infinitive.* *

Zec. 7: 3. *separating myself,* as I have done

NIPHAL.—*Future.*

Lev.22: 2. *that they separate themselves* from the holy
Eze.14: 7. *which separateth himself* from me,
Hos. 9:10. they went to Baal-peor, *and separated themselves*

* HIPHIL.—*Preterite.* *

Lev.15:31. *Thus shall ye separate* the children
Nu. 6:12. *And he shall consecrate* unto the Lord

HIPHIL.—*Infinitive.*

Nu. 6: 2. *to separate* (themselves) unto the Lord:
6. All the days *that he separateth* (himself)

HIPHIL.—*Future.*

Nu. 6: 3. *He shall separate* (himself) from
5. in the which *he separateth* (himself)

5145 נֵזֶר *neh'-zer,* m.

Ex. 29: 6. put *the* holy *crown* upon the mitre.
39:30. the plate of *the* holy *crown*
Lev. 8: 9. the golden plate, *the* holy *crown;*
21:12. *the crown of* the anointing oil
Nu. 6: 4, 8. All the days of *his separation* (marg. or, *Nazariteship*)
5. the vow of *his separation*
7. *the consecration* (marg. *separation*) *of* his God
9. the head of *his consecration;*
12. unto the Lord the days of *his separation,*
— *his separation* was defiled.
13. when the days of *his separation*
18. shave the head of *his separation*
— the hair of the head of *his separation,*
19. (the hair of) *his separation*
21. his offering...for *his separation,*
— the law of *his separation.*
2Sa. 1:10. *the crown* that (was) upon his head,
2K. 11:12. and put *the crown* upon him,
2Ch 23:11. and put upon him *the crown,*
Ps. 89:39(40). thou hast profaned *his crown*
132:18. upon himself shall *his crown* flourish.
Pro.27:24. doth *the crown* (endure)
Jer. 7:29. Cut off *thine hair,* (O Jerusalem),
Zec. 9:16. (they shall be as) the stones of *a crown,*

נָחָה [*nāh-ghāh'*]. 5148

* KAL.—*Preterite.* *

Gen24:27. the Lord *led me* to the house
Ex. 13:17. God *led them* not (through) the way of
15:13. *Thou* in thy mercy *hast led forth* the people
Ps. 60: 9(11). who *will lead me* into Edom?
77:20(21). *Thou leddest* thy people like a flock
108:10(11). who *will lead me* into Edom?
Isa. 58:11. *And* the Lord *shall guide thee*

KAL.—*Imperative.*

Ex. 32:34. *lead* the people unto (the place)
Ps. 5: 8(9). *Lead me,* O Lord, in thy righteousness
27:11. *and lead me* in a plain path,
139:24. *lead me* in the way everlasting.

* HIPHIL.—*Preterite.* *

Gen24:48. God of my master Abraham, which *had led me*
Neh. 9:12. *thou leddest them* in the day

HIPHIL.—*Infinitive.*

Ex. 13:21. *to lead them* the way;
Neh. 9:19. *to lead them* in the way;

HIPHIL.—*Future.*

Nu. 23: 7. Balak the king of Moab *hath brought me*
Deu32:12. the Lord alone *did lead him,*
1Sa.22: 4. *And he brought them* before the king of Moab:
1K. 10:26. horsemen, *whom he bestowed* in the cities
2K. 18:11. *and put them* in Halah and in Habor
Job 12:23. he enlargeth the nations, *and straiteneth* (marg. *leadeth in*) *them*
31:18. *I have guided her* from
38:32. *canst thou guide* (marg. *guide them*)
Ps. 23: 3. *he leadeth me* in the paths of righteousness
31: 3(4). *lead me,* and guide me.
43: 3. *let them lead me;* let them bring me
61: 2(3). *lead me* to the rock (that) is higher than I.
67: 4(5). and *govern* (marg. *lead*) the nations upon earth.
73:24. *Thou shalt guide me* with thy counsel,
78:14. In the daytime *also he led them*
53. *And he led them* on safely,
72. *guided them* by the skilfulness of
107:30. *so he bringeth them* unto their desired haven
139:10. there *shall* thy hand *lead me,*
143:10. *lead me* into the land of uprightness.
Pro. 6:22. When thou goest, *it shall lead* thee;
11: 3. integrity of the upright *shall guide them:*
18:16. *bringeth him* before great men.
Isa. 57:18. *I will lead him also,* and restore

נִחוּמִים [*nee-ghoo-meem'*], m. pl. 5150

Isa. 57:18. and restore *comforts* unto him
Hos11: 8. *my repentings* are kindled together.
Zec. 1:13. good words (and) *comfortable* words.

5153 **נָחוּשׁ** *nāh-ghoosh'*, adj.

Job 6:12. or (is) my flesh *of brass?* (marg. *brasen*)

5154 **נְחוּשָׁה** *n'ghoo-shāh'*, f.

Lev.26:19. heaven as iron, and your earth *as brass:*
2Sa.22:35. a bow of *steel* is broken by mine arms.
Job 20:24. the bow of *steel* shall strike him
28: 2. *brass* (is) molten (out of) the stone.
40:18. His bones (are as) strong pieces of *brass;*
41:27(19). He esteemeth...*brass* as rotten wood.
Ps. 18:34(35). bow of *steel* is broken by mine arms.
Isa. 45: 2. I will break in pieces the gates of *brass,*
48: 4. thy brow *brass;*
Mic. 4:13. I will make thy hoofs *brass:*

5155 **נְחִילָה** [*n'ghee-lāh'*], f.

Ps. 5[title](1). To the chief Musician upon *Nehiloth,*

5156 **נְחִירִים** [*n'ghee-reem'*], m. pl.

Job 41:20(12). *Out of his nostrils* goeth smoke,

5157 **נָחַל** *nāh-ghal'.*

* KAL.—*Preterite.* *

Ex. 23:30. until thou be increased, *and inherit*
32:13. *and they shall inherit* (it) for ever.
34: 9. *and take us for thine inheritance.*
Jos. 14: 1. which the children of Israel *inherited*
17: 6. of Manasseh *had* (lit. *inherited*) an inheritance
Ps.119:111. testimonies *have I taken as an heritage*
Pro.14:18. The simple *inherit* folly: but the prudent
Jer. 16:19. our fathers *have inherited* lies,
Eze.47:14. *And ye shall inherit* it,
Zec. 2:12(16). *And* the Lord *shall inherit* Judah

KAL.—*Infinitive.*

Nu. 34:18. *to divide* the land *by inheritance.*
Jos. 19:49. *of dividing* the land *for inheritance*

KAL.—*Future.*

Nu. 18:20. *Thou shalt have* no *inheritance*
23. the Levites...*they have* (lit. *inherit*) no inheritance.
24. *they shall have* (lit. *shall inherit*) no inheritance.
26:55. of their fathers *they shall inherit.*
32:19. *we will* not *inherit* with them
34:17. which *shall divide* the land
35: 8. his inheritance which *he inheriteth.* (marg. *they inherit*)
Deu19:14. which *thou shalt inherit* in the land
Jos. 16: 4. *So* the children of Joseph,...*took their inheritance.*
19: 9. *therefore* the children of Simeon *had their inheritance*
Jud.11: 2. *Thou shalt* not *inherit* in our
Ps. 69:36(37). The seed also of his servants *shall inherit it:*
82: 8. *thou shalt inherit* all nations.
Pro. 3:35. The wise *shall inherit* glory:
11:29. He that troubleth...*shall inherit* the wind:
28:10. *shall have* good (things) *in possession.*
Isa. 57:13. *shall possess* the land,
Zep. 2: 9. my people *shall possess them.*

* PIEL.—*Preterite.* *

Jos 13:32. Moses *did distribute for inheritance*
14: 1. *distributed for inheritance* to them.
19:51. *divided for an inheritance*
Eze. 7:24. *and* their holy places *shall be defiled.* (marg. or, *they shall inherit.*—see חָלַל)
22:16. *And thou shalt take thine inheritance* (marg. or, *be profaned:*—see also חָלַל) in thyself

PIEL.—*Infinitive.*

Nu 34:29. Lord commanded *to divide the inheritance*

* HIPHIL.—*Preterite.* *

1Ch 28: 8. *and leave* (it) *for an inheritance* for your
Jer. 3:18. that I *have given for an inheritance* unto your fathers. (marg. or, *caused* your fathers *to possess*)
12:14. *I have caused* my people Israel *to inherit;*
Zec. 8:12. *and I will cause* the remnant...*to possess*

HIPHIL.—*Infinitive.*

Deu21:16. when *he maketh* his sons *to inherit*
32: 8. *When* the Most High *divided...their inheritance,*
Pro. 8:21. *That I may cause* those that love me *to inherit*
Isa. 49: 8. *to cause to inherit* the desolate heritages;

HIPHIL.—*Future.*

Deu. 1:38. *he shall cause* Israel *to inherit it.*
3:28. he *shall cause* them *to inherit*
19: 3. thy God *giveth thee to inherit,*
31: 7. *thou shalt cause* them *to inherit it.*
Jos. 1: 6. *shalt* thou *divide for an inheritance*
1Sa. 2: 8. *to make them inherit* the throne
Pro.13:22. A good (man) *leaveth an inheritance to*
Eze.46:18. *he shall give* his sons *inheritance*

HIPHIL.—*Participle.*

Deu12:10. the Lord your God *giveth* you *to inherit,*

* HOPHAL.—*Preterite.* *

Job 7: 3. *So am I made to possess* months of vanity,

* HITHPAEL.—*Preterite.* *

Lev.25:46. *And ye shall take them as an inheritance* for your children
Nu. 33:54. *And ye shall divide* the land...*for an inheritance*
Isa. 14: 2. *and* the house of Israel *shall possess them*

HITHPAEL.—*Infinitive.*

Nu. 32:18. until the children of Israel *have inherited*

HITHPAEL.—*Future.*

Nu. 33:54. the tribes of your fathers *ye shall inherit.*
34:13. the land which *ye shall inherit*
Eze.47:13. whereby *ye shall inherit* the land

נַחַל *nah'-ghal*, m. 5158

Gen26:17. pitched his tent *in the valley of* Gerar,
19. Isaac's servants digged *in the valley,*
32:23(24). and sent them over *the brook,*
Lev.11: 9. *and in the rivers,* them shall ye eat.
10. in the seas, *and in the rivers,*
23:40. willows of *the brook;*
Nu. 13:23. they came unto *the brook* (marg. o. *valley*) *of* Eshcol,
24. The place was called *the brook* (marg. *id.* Eshcol,
21:12. and pitched *in the valley of* Zared.
14. in *the brooks* of Arnon,
15. the stream of *the brooks*
24: 6. *As the valleys* are they spread
32: 9. went up unto *the valley of* Eshcol,
34: 5. *unto the river* of Egypt,
Deu. 1:24. came unto *the valley of* Eshcol,
2:13. you over *the brook* (marg. or, *valley*) Zered. And we went over *the brook* Zered.
14. until we were come over *the brook*
24. pass over *the river* Arnon:
36. by the brink of *the river* of Arnon, and (from) the city that (is) *by the river,*
37. any place of *the river* Jabbok,
3: 8. *from the river of* Arnon
12. which (is) *by the river* Arnon,
16. unto *the river* Arnon half *the valley,* and the border even unto *the river* Jabbok,
4:48. by the bank of *the river* Arnon,
8: 7. a land of *brooks of* water,
9:21. I cast the dust thereof into *the brook*
10: 7. a land of *rivers of* waters.
21: 4. bring down the heifer unto *a* rough *valley,* — off the heifer's neck there *in the valley:*
6. the heifer that is beheaded *in the valley:*
Jos. 12: 1. *from the river* Arnon unto mount
2. upon the bank of *the river* Arnon, and from the middle of *the river,* and from half Gilead, even unto *the river* Jabbok,
13: 9, 16. the bank of *the river* Arnon, and the city that (is) in the midst of *the river*

Jos. 15: 4. unto *the river of* Egypt;
7. on the south side *of the river:*
47. unto *the river of* Egypt,
16: 8. westward unto *the river* Kanah;
17: 9. *the river* Kanah, southward *of the river:*
— on the north side *of the river,*
19:11. *the river* that (is) before Jokneam;
Jud. 4: 7. I will draw unto thee to *the river* Kishon
13. unto *the river of* Kishon.
5:21. *The river of* Kishon swept them away, that ancient *river, the river* Kishon.
16: 4. he loved a woman *in the valley* (marg. or, *by the brook*) *of* Sorek,
1 Sa.15: 5. and laid wait *in the valley.*
17:40. five smooth stones out of *the brook,* (marg. or, *valley*)
30: 9. and came to *the brook* Besor,
10. they could not go over *the brook* Besor.
21. to abide at *the brook* Besor:
2Sa.15:23. the king...passed over *the brook*
17:13. we will draw it into *the river,*
22: 5. *the floods of* ungodly men
23:30. Hiddai *of the brooks* (marg. or, *valleys*) *of*
24: 5. midst of *the river* (marg. or, *valley*) *of* Gad,
1K. 2:37. and passest over *the brook* Kidron,
8:65. unto *the river of* Egypt,
15:13. *by the brook* Kidron.
17: 3. hide thyself *by the brook* Cherith,
4. thou shalt drink *of the brook;*
5. and dwelt *by the brook* Cherith,
6. and he drank of *the brook.*
7. *the brook* dried up,
18: 5. and unto all *brooks:*
40. brought them down to *the brook* Kishon,
2K. 3:16. Make this *valley* full of ditches.
17. *yet* that *valley* shall be filled with water,
10:33. *by the river* Arnon,
23: 6. unto *the brook* Kidron, and burned it *at the brook* Kidron,
12. cast the dust of them into *the brook* Kidron.
24: 7. *from the river of* Egypt
1 Ch 11:32. Hurai *of the brooks of* Gaash,
2Ch 7: 8. unto *the river of* Egypt.
15:16. burnt (it) *at the brook* Kidron.
20:16. at the end of *the brook,* (marg. or, *valley*)
29:16. *into the brook* Kidron.
30:14. cast (them) *into the brook* Kidron.
32: 4. *the brook* that ran through
33:14. on the west side of Gihon, *in the valley,*
Neh. 2:15. went I up in the night *by the brook,*
Job 6:15. brethren have dealt deceitfully as *a brook,* (and) as the stream of *brooks*
20:17. *the brooks of* honey and butter.
21:33. The clods of *the valley* shall be sweet
22:24. as the stones of *the brooks.*
28: 4. *The flood* breaketh out
30: 6. To dwell in the cliffs of *the valleys,*
40:22. the willows of *the brook* compass him
Ps. 18: 4(5). *and the floods of* ungodly men
36: 8(9). *and* thou shalt make them drink *of the river*
74:15. didst cleave the fountain *and the flood:*
78:20. *and the streams* overflowed;
83: 9(10). *at the brook of* Kison:
104:10. He sendeth the springs *into the valleys,*
110: 7. He shall drink *of the brook*
Pro.18: 4. wellspring of wisdom (as) *a flowing brook.*
30:17. the ravens of *the valley* (marg. or, *brook*)
Ecc. 1: 7. All *the rivers* run into the sea;
— the place from *whence the rivers* come,
Cant.6:11. to see the fruits of *the valley,*
Isa. 7:19. *in the* desolate *valleys,*
11:15. in *the* seven *streams,*
15: 7. *the brook of* the willows. (marg. or, *valley of* the Arabians)
27:12. the channel of the river unto *the stream of*
30:28. his breath, *as an* overflowing *stream,*
33. *like a stream of* brimstone,
34: 9. *the streams thereof* shall be turned
35: 6. *and streams* in the desert.
57: 5. *in the valleys* under the clifts
6. the smooth (stones) of *the stream*
66:12. *and* the glory of the Gentiles *like a* flowing *stream:*
Jer. 31: 9. to walk *by the rivers of* waters
40. all the fields unto *the brook of* Kidron,
47: 2. and shall be *an* overflowing *flood,*
Lam.2:18. let tears run down *like a river*
Eze.47: 5. *a river* that I could not pass over:
— *a river* that could not be passed
6. to return to the brink of *the river.*
7. at the bank of *the river*
9. *the rivers* (marg. *two rivers*) snall come,
— whither *the river* cometh.
12. by *the river* upon the bank
Joel 3:18(4:18). shall water *the valley of* Shittim.
Am. 5:24. righteousness *as a* mighty *stream.*
6:14. *the river* (marg. *valley*) *of* the wilderness.
Mic. 6: 7. ten thousands of *rivers of* oil?

נַחְלָה *nag̣h'-lāh,* m. 5158

Ps.124: 4. *the stream* had gone over our soul:

נַחֲלָה *nah-g̣hălāh',* f. 5159

Gen31:14. any portion or *inheritance* for us
48: 6. their brethren *in their inheritance.*
Ex. 15:17. the mountain of *thine inheritance,*
Nu. 16:14. *inheritance of* fields and vineyards:
18:20. thy part *and thine inheritance*
21. the tenth in Israel *for an inheritance,*
23. they have no *inheritance.*
24. I have given to the Levites *to inherit:*
— they shall have no *inheritance.*
26. from them *for your inheritance,*
26:53. the land shall be divided *for an inheritance*
54. thou shalt give *the* more *inheritance,* and to few thou shalt give *the* less *inheritance:* to every one shall *his inheritance* be given
56. According to the lot shall *the possession thereof* be
62. because there was no *inheritance*
27: 7. a possession of *an inheritance*
— *the inheritance of* their father
8. cause *his inheritance* to pass
9, 10, 11. then ye shall give *his inheritance*
32:18. every man *his inheritance.*
19. because *our inheritance* is fallen
32. the possession of *our inheritance*
33:54. shall give the more *inheritance,* and to the fewer ye shall give the less *inheritance:*
34: 2. the land...*for an inheritance,*
14, 15. have received *their inheritance:*
35: 2. *the inheritance of* their possession
8. according to *his inheritance*
36: 2. to give the land *for an inheritance*
— *the inheritance of* Zelophehad
3. then shall *their inheritance* be taken *from the inheritance of* our fathers, and shall be put to *the inheritance of*
— taken from the lot of *our inheritance.*
4. shall *their inheritance* be put unto *the inheritance of* the tribe whereunto they are received: *so* shall *their inheritance* be taken away *from the inheritance of* the tribe of our fathers.
7. *the inheritance* of the children of Israel
— *to the inheritance of* the tribe
8. daughter, that possesseth *an inheritance*
— enjoy every man *the inheritance of*
9. Neither shall *the inheritance* remove
— keep himself *to his own inheritance.*
12. and *their inheritance* remained
Deu. 4:20. to be unto him a people of *inheritance,*
21. giveth thee (for) *an inheritance:*
38. to give thee their land (for) *an inheritance,*
9:26, 29. thy people *and thine inheritance,*
10: 9. no part *nor inheritance* with his brethren, the Lord (is) *his inheritance,*
12: 9. to the rest and to *the inheritance,*
12 & 14:27, 29. he hath no part *nor inheritance*
15: 4. giveth thee (for) *an inheritance*
18: 1. no part *nor inheritance*
— made by fire, *and his inheritance.*
2. *Therefore* shall they have no *inheritance* among their brethren: the Lord (is) *their inheritance,*
19:10. giveth thee (for) *an inheritance,*
14. have set *in thine inheritance,*
20:16. give thee (for) *an inheritance,*

Deu21:23 & 24:4 & 25:19 & 26:1. giveth thee (for) *an inheritance.*
29: 8(7). for *an inheritance* unto the Reubenites,
32: 9. Jacob (is) the lot of *his inheritance.*
Jos. 11:23. Joshua gave it *for an inheritance*
13: 6. unto the Israelites *for an inheritance,*
7. *for an inheritance* unto the nine tribes,
8. the Gadites have received *their inheritance,*
14. he gave none *inheritance;* the sacrifices... (are) *their inheritance,*
23. This (was) *the inheritance of* the children
28. *the inheritance of* the children of Gad
33. Moses gave not (any) *inheritance:* the Lord God of Israel (was) *their inheritance,*
14: 2. By lot (was) *their inheritance,*
3. Moses had given *the inheritance of*
— unto the Levites he gave none *inheritance*
9. the land whereon thy feet have trodden shall be thine *inheritance,*
13. Hebron *for an inheritance.*
14. became *the inheritance of* Caleb (lit. was *for an inheritance* to Caleb)
15:20. *the inheritance of* the tribe of
16: 5. the border of *their inheritance*
8. *the inheritance of* the tribe of
9. *the inheritance of* the children of Manasseh,
17: 4. to give us *an inheritance*
— he gave them *an inheritance*
6. the daughters of Manasseh had *an inheritance*
14. one portion *to inherit,*
18: 2. had not yet received *their inheritance.*
4. according to *the inheritance of them;*
7. the Lord (is) *their inheritance:*
— have received *their inheritance*
20. This (was) *the inheritance of*
28. This (is) *the inheritance of*
19: 1. *their inheritance* was within *the inheritance of*
2. they had *in their inheritance*
8. *the inheritance of* the tribe
9. *the inheritance of* the children of Simeon:
— within *the inheritance of them.*
10. the border of *their inheritance*
16. *the inheritance of* the children of Zebulun
23, 31, 39. *the inheritance of* the tribe
41. the coast of *their inheritance*
48. *the inheritance of* the tribe of
49. the children of Israel gave *an inheritance*
51. These (are) *the inheritances,*
21: 3. *out of their inheritance,* at the
23: 4. *to be an inheritance* for your tribes,
24:28. every man *unto his inheritance.*
30. the border of *his inheritance*
32. became *the inheritance* of (lit. was *for an inheritance* to) the children of Joseph.
Jud. 2: 6. every man *unto his inheritance*
9. the border of *his inheritance*
18: 1. the Danites sought them *an inheritance*
— (all their) *inheritance* had not fallen
20: 6. *the inheritance of* Israel:
21:23. returned unto *their inheritance,*
24. every man *to his inheritance.*
Ru. 4: 5. upon *his inheritance.*
6. lest I mar *mine own inheritance:*
10. of the dead upon *his inheritance,*
1Sa.10: 1. captain over *his inheritance?*
26:19. *in the inheritance of* the Lord,
2Sa.14:16. together *out of the inheritance of* God.
20: 1. neither have we *inheritance*
19 & 21:3. *the inheritance of* the Lord?
1K. 8:36. thy people *for an inheritance.*
51. thy people, *and thine inheritance,*
53. (to be) thine *inheritance,*
12:16. neither (have we) *inheritance*
21: 3. I should give *the inheritance of*
4. I will not give thee *the inheritance of*
2K. 21:14. forsake the remnant of *mine inheritance,*
1Ch 16:18. the lot of *your inheritance;*
2Ch 6:27. thy land, which thou hast given...*for an inheritance.*
10:16. (we have) none *inheritance*
Neh 11:20. every one *in his inheritance.*
Job 20:29. *and the heritage* appointed unto him
27:13. *and the heritage of* oppressors,
31: 2. *and* (what) *inheritance of* the Almighty
42:15. their father gave them *inheritance*

Ps. 2: 8. the heathen (for) *thine inheritance,*
28: 9. thy people, and bless *thine inheritance:*
33:12. chosen *for* his own *inheritance.*
37:18. *and their inheritance* shall be for ever.
47: 4(5). He shall choose *our inheritance*
68: 9(10). thou didst confirm *thine inheritance,*
74: 2. the rod of *thine inheritance,*
78:55. divided them *an inheritance*
62. *and* was wroth *with his inheritance.*
71. his people, and Israel *his inheritance.*
79: 1. heathen are come *into thine inheritance;*
94: 5. *and* afflict *thine heritage.*
14. *neither* will he forsake *his inheritance.*
105:11. the lot of *your inheritance:*
106: 5. that I may glory with *thine inheritance.*
40. he abhorred *his own inheritance.*
111: 6. *the heritage of* the heathen.
127: 3. children (are) *an heritage of*
135:12. gave their land (for) *an heritage, an heritage* unto Israel
136:21. gave their land *for an heritage:*
22. (Even) *an heritage* unto Israel
Pro. 17: 2. part of *the inheritance*
19:14. *the inheritance of* fathers:
20:21. *An inheritance* (may be) gotten
Ecc. 7:11. Wisdom (is) good *with an inheritance:*
Isa. 19:25. Israel *mine inheritance.*
47: 6. I have polluted *mine inheritance,*
49: 8. to inherit *the* desolate *heritages;*
54:17. *the heritage of* the servants
58:14. *the heritage of* Jacob thy father:
63:17. the tribes of *thine inheritance.*
Jer. 2: 7. *and* made *mine heritage* an abomination.
3:19. *a* goodly *heritage of* the hosts of nations?
10:16. the rod of *his inheritance:*
12: 7. I have left *mine heritage;*
8. *Mine heritage* is unto me as a lion
9. *Mine heritage* (is) unto me (as) a speckled bird,
14. touch *the inheritance*
15. every man *to his heritage,*
16:18. they have filled *mine inheritance*
17: 4. *from thine heritage* that I gave thee;
50:11. O ye destroyers of *mine heritage,*
51:19. the rod of *his inheritance:*
Lam. 5: 2. *Our inheritance* is turned to strangers,
Eze. 35:15. *at the inheritance of* the house of Israel,
36:12. thou shalt be their *inheritance,* (lit. *for an inheritance* to them)
44:28. it shall be unto them *for an inheritance:* I (am) *their inheritance:*
45: 1. the land *for inheritance,*
46:16. *the inheritance thereof* shall be his sons'; it (shall be) their possession *by inheritance.*
17. a gift *of his inheritance*
— *his inheritance* shall be his sons'
18. shall not take *of* the people's *inheritance*
47:14. this land shall fall unto you *for inheritance.*
19. *the river* (marg. or, *valley*) to the great sea.
22. by lot *for an inheritance* unto you,
— they shall have *inheritance*
23. there shall ye give (him) *his inheritance,*
48:28. *the river* toward the great sea.
29. the tribes of Israel *for inheritance,*
Joel 2:17. give not *thine heritage* to reproach,
3: 2(4:2). *and* (for) *my heritage* Israel,
Mic. 2: 2. a man *and his heritage.*
7:14. the flock of *thine heritage,*
18. the remnant of *his heritage?*
Mal. 1: 3. laid his mountains and *his heritage* waste

נֶחֱלָמִי *neh-g̣hĕlāh-mee',* adj. 5161

Jer. 29:24. speak to Shemaiah *the Nehelamite,* (marg. or, *dreamer*)
31. concerning Shemaiah *the Nehelamite;*
32. I will punish Shemaiah *the Nehelamite,*

נַחֲלָת *nah-g̣hălāhth',* f. 5159

Ps. 16: 6. I have *a* goodly *heritage.*

נָחַם [*nāh-ġham'*].

* NIPHAL.—*Preterite.* *

Gen. 6: 7. *it repenteth me* that I have made them.
1Sa.15:11. *It repenteth me* that I have set up Saul
35. Lord *repented* that he had made Saul king
2Sa.13:39. *he was comforted* concerning Amnon,
Job 42: 6. I abhor (myself), *and repent*
Jer. 4:28. I have purposed (it), and *will* not *repent*,
18: 8. *I will repent* of the evil
10. *then I will repent* of the good,
20:16. the cities which the Lord overthrew, and *repented* not:
26: 3. *that I may repent me* of the evil,
31:19. after that I was turned, *I repented;*
42:10. *I repent me* of the evil
Eze.14:22. *and ye shall be comforted* concerning
32:31. shall see them, *and shall be comforted*
Joel 2:14. he will return *and repent*,
Am. 7: 3, 6. The Lord *repented* for this:
Jon. 3: 9. (if) God will turn *and repent*,
Zec. 8:14. and *I repented* not:

NIPHAL.—*Infinitive.*

1Sa.15:29. he (is) not a man, *that he should repent*.
Ps. 77: 2(3). my soul refused *to be comforted*.
Jer. 15: 6. I am weary with *repenting*.
31:15. refused *to be comforted* for her children,

NIPHAL.—*Imperative.*

Ex. 32:12. *and repent* of this evil against thy people.
Ps. 90:13. *and let it repent thee* concerning thy servants.

NIPHAL.—*Future.*

Gen. 6: 6. *And it repented* the Lord
24:67. *and* Isaac *was comforted* after his mother's (death).
38:12. *and* Judah *was comforted*,
Ex. 13:17. Lest peradventure the people *repent*
32:14. *And* the Lord *repented*
Jud. 2:18. *it repented* the Lord because of
21: 6. *And* the children of Israel *repented them*
1Sa.15:29. Strength of Israel will not lie nor *repent:*
2Sa.24:16. *And* when...the Lord *repented* him of the
1Ch 21:15. *and he repented him* of the evil,
Ps.106:45. *and repented* according to the multitude
110: 4. The Lord hath sworn, and *will* not *repent*,
Isa. 1:24. *I will ease me* of mine adversaries,
57: 6. *Should I receive comfort* in these?
Jer. 26:13. *and* the Lord *will repent him* of the evil
19. *and* the Lord *repented him* of the evil
Eze.24:14. neither *will I repent;*
31:16. all that drink water, *shall be comforted*
Jon. 3:10. *and* God *repented* of the evil,

NIPHAL.—*Participle.*

Jud.21:15. the people *repented them* for Benjamin,
Jer. 8: 6. no man *repented him* of his wickedness,
Joel 2:13. *and repenteth him* of the evil.
Jon. 4: 2. *and repentest thee* of the evil.

* PIEL.—*Preterite.* *

Ru. 2:13. for that *thou hast comforted me*,
Ps. 86:17. thou, Lord, hast holpen me, *and comforted me*.
Isa. 49:13. the Lord *hath comforted* his people,
51: 3. the Lord *shall comfort* Zion: *he will comfort* all her waste places;
52: 9. the Lord *hath comforted* his people,
Jer. 31:13. turn their mourning into joy, *and will comfort them*,
Eze.14:23. *And they shall comfort* you, when ye
Zec. 1:17. *and* the Lord *shall* yet *comfort* Zion,

PIEL.—*Infinitive.*

Gen37:35. all his daughters rose up *to comfort him;*
2Sa.10: 2. David sent *to comfort him*
1Ch 7:22. his brethren came *to comfort him*.
19: 2. David sent messengers *to comfort him*
— servants of David came...*to comfort him*.
Job 2:11. to mourn with him *and to comfort him*.
Ps.119:76. thy merciful kindness be *for my comfort*, (marg. *to comfort me*)
Isa. 22: 4. labour not *to comfort me*,
61: 2. *to comfort* all that mourn;
Jer. 16: 7. *to comfort them* for the dead;
Eze.16:54. *in that thou art a comfort* unto them.

PIEL.—*Imperative.*

Isa. 40: 1. *Comfort ye, comfort ye* my people, saith your God.

PIEL.—*Future.*

Gen. 5:29. This (same) *shall comfort us*
50:21. *And he comforted* them, and spake
2Sa.12:24. *And* David *comforted* Bath-sheba his wife,
Job 7:13. My bed *shall comfort me*,
21:34. How then *comfort ye me*
29:25. as one (that) *comforteth* the mourners.
42:11. they bemoaned him, *and comforted* him
Ps. 23: 4. thy rod and thy staff *they comfort me*.
71:21. and *comfort me* on every side.
119:82. When *wilt thou comfort me?*
Isa. 12: 1. turned away, *and thou comfortedst me*.
51:19. by whom *shall I comfort thee?*
66:13. As one *whom* his mother *comforteth, so* will *I comfort you;*
Lam.2:13. *that I may comfort thee*, O virgin
Zec.10: 2. *they comfort* in vain:

PIEL.—*Participle.*

2Sa.10: 3. he hath sent *comforters* unto thee?
1Ch 19: 3. he hath sent *comforters* unto thee?
Job 16: 2. miserable *comforters* (are) ye all.
Ps. 69:20(21). *and for comforters*, but I found none.
Ecc. 4: 1, 1. they had no *comforter;*
Isa. 51:12. he *that comforteth you:*
Lam.1: 2. she hath none *to comfort* (her):
9. she had no *comforter*.
16. *the comforter* that should relieve
17. (there is) none *to comfort* her:
21. that I sigh: (there is) none *to comfort* me:
Nah. 3: 7. whence shall I seek *comforters*

* PUAL.—*Future.* *

Isa. 66:13. *ye shall be comforted* in Jerusalem.

PUAL.—*Participle.*

Isa. 54:11. tossed with tempest, (and) not *comforted*.

* HITHPAEL.—*Preterite.* *

Eze. 5:13. upon them, *and I will be comforted:*

HITHPAEL.—*Infinitive.*

Gen37:35. he refused *to be comforted;*

HITHPAEL.—*Future.*

Nu. 23:19. the son of man, *that he should repent:*
Deu32:36. and *repent himself* for his servants,
Ps.119:52. of old, O Lord; *and have comforted myself*.
135:14. *he will repent himself* concerning

HITHPAEL.—*Participle.*

Gen27:42. thy brother Esau,...*doth comfort himself*,

נֹחַם *nōh'-ġham*, m. 5164

Hos.13:14. *repentance* shall be hid from mine eyes.

נֶחָמָה [*neh-ġhāh-māh'*], f. 5165

Job 6:10. Then should *I* yet have *comfort;* (lit. *my comfort* yet would be)
Ps.119:50. *my comfort* in my affliction:

נַחְנוּ *naġh'-noo*, pron. 5168

[i. q. אֲנַחְנוּ]

Gen42:11. *We* (are) all one man's sons;
Ex. 16: 7, 8. *and* what (are) *we*,
Nu. 32:32. *We* will pass over armed
2Sa.17:12. *and we* will light upon him
Lam.3:42. *We* have transgressed

נָחַץ [*nāh-ġhatz'*]. 5169

* KAL.—*Participle.* Paül. *

1Sa.21: 8(9). the king's business *required haste*.

נַחַר [*nah'-ġhar*], m. 5170

Job 39:20. the glory of *his nostrils* (is) terrible.

5170 **נַחֲרָה** [*nah-ghărāh'*], f.

Jer. 8:16. *The snorting of* his horses

5172 **נָחַשׁ** [*nāh-ghash'*].

* PIEL.—*Preterite.* *

Gen30:27. *I have learned by experience* that the Lord
2K. 21: 6. observed times, *and used enchantments,*
2Ch 33: 6. observed times, *and used enchantments,*

PIEL.—*Infinitive.*

Gen44: 5. whereby *indeed* he divineth? (lit. *divining* he divineth)
15. wot ye not that such a man as I can *certainly* divine? (lit. *divining* can divine)

PIEL.—*Future.*

Gen44: 5. whereby indeed *he divineth?*
15. wot ye not that such a man as I *can* certainly *divine?*
Lev.19:26. neither *shall ye use enchantment,*
1K. 20:33. the men *did diligently observe*
2K. 17:17. used divination *and enchantments,* (lit. *and used enchantments*)

PIEL.—*Participle.*

Deu18:10. *or an enchanter,* or a witch,

5173 **נַחַשׁ** *nah'-ghash*, m.

Nu. 23:23. (there is) no *enchantment* against Jacob,
24: 1. to seek for *enchantments,*

5175 **נָחָשׁ** *nāh-ghāhsh'*, m.

Gen. 3: 1. *Now the serpent* was more subtil than
2. the woman said unto *the serpent,*
4. *the serpent* said unto the woman,
13. *The serpent* beguiled me,
14. the Lord God said unto *the serpent,*
49:17. Dan shall be *a serpent* by the way,
Ex. 4: 3. and it became *a serpent;*
7:15. the rod which was turned *to a serpent*
Nu. 21: 6. the Lord sent fiery *serpents*
7. that he take away *the serpents*
9. Moses made *a serpent of* brass,
— if *a serpent* had bitten any man, when he beheld *the serpent of* brass,
Deu. 8:15. fiery *serpents,* and scorpions,
2K. 18: 4. *the* brasen *serpent* that Moses had made:
Job 26:13. his hand hath formed *the* crooked *serpent.*
Ps. 58: 4(5). Their poison (is) like the poison of *a serpent:*
140: 3(4). They have sharpened their tongues *like a serpent;*
Pro.23:32. At the last it biteth *like a serpent,*
30:19. the way of *a serpent* upon a rock;
Ecc.10: 8. *a serpent* shall bite him.
11. *the serpent* will bite without enchantment;
Isa. 14:29. out of *the serpent*'s root shall come forth
27: 1. leviathan *the* piercing *serpent,* even leviathan that crooked *serpent;*
65:25. *and* dust (shall be) *the serpent*'s meat.
Jer. 8:17. I will send *serpents,*
46:22. The voice thereof shall go *like a serpent;*
Am. 5:19. and *a serpent* bit him.
9: 3. thence will I command *the serpent,*
Mic. 7:17. They shall lick the dust *like a serpent,*

5174 **נְחָשׁ** *n'ghāhsh*, Ch. m.

Dan. 2:32. his belly and his thighs of *brass,*
35. the clay, *the brass,* the silver,
39. another third kingdom of *brass,*
45. the iron, *the brass,* the clay,
4:15(12). with a band of iron *and brass,*
23(20). even with a band of iron *and brass,*
5: 4. the gods of gold, and of silver, of *brass,*
23. the gods of silver, and gold, of *brass,*
7:19. and his nails (of) *brass;*

נְחֹשֶׁת *n'ghōh'-sheth*, com. 5178

Gen. 4:22. an instructer of every artificer in *brass*
Ex. 25: 3. gold, and silver, *and brass,*
26:11. thou shalt make fifty taches of *brass,*
37. cast five sockets of *brass*
27: 2. thou shalt overlay it *with brass.*
3. all the vessels...thou shalt make (of) *brass.*
4. a grate of network (of) *brass;*
— make four *brasen* rings
6. and overlay them with *brass.*
10. their twenty sockets (shall be of) *brass;*
11. their twenty sockets (of) *brass;*
17, 18. and their sockets (of) *brass.*
19. the pins of the court, (shall be of) *brass.*
30:18. Thou shalt also make a laver (of) *brass,* and his foot (also of) *brass,*
31: 4. to work in gold, and in silver, *and in brass,*
35: 5. an offering of the Lord; gold, and silver, *and brass,*
16. The altar...with his *brasen* grate,
24. an offering of silver *and brass*
32. to work in gold, and in silver, *and in brass,*
36:18. he made fifty taches (of) *brass*
38. their five sockets (were of) *brass.*
38: 2. he overlaid it with *brass.*
3. all the vessels thereof made he (of) *brass.*
4. he made for the altar a *brasen* grate
5. for the four ends of the grate of *brass,*
6. made the staves...and overlaid them with *brass.*
8. he made the laver (of) *brass,* and the foot of it (of) *brass,*
10. their *brasen* sockets twenty;
11. their sockets of *brass* twenty;
17. the sockets for the pillars (were of) *brass;*
19. their sockets (of) *brass* four;
20. pins of the tabernacle,...(were of) *brass.*
29. *And the brass of* the offering
30. and the *brasen* altar, and the *brasen* grate
39:39. The *brasen* altar, and his grate of *brass,*
Lev. 6:28(21). sodden in a *brasen* pot,
Nu. 16:39(17:4). Eleazar the priest took the *brasen* censers,
21: 9. Moses made a serpent of *brass,*
— when he beheld the serpent of *brass,*
31:22. the gold, and the silver, *the brass,*
Deu. 8: 9. out of whose hills thou mayest dig *brass.*
28:23. thy heaven...shall be *brass,*
33:25. Thy shoes (shall be) iron *and brass;*
Jos. 6:19. vessels of *brass* and iron,
24. the vessels of *brass* and of iron,
22: 8. with gold, *and with brass,*
Jud.16:21. bound him *with fetters of brass;*
1Sa.17: 5. (he had) an helmet of *brass*
— five thousand shekels of *brass.*
6. (he had) greaves of *brass* upon his legs, and a target of *brass*
38. he put an helmet of *brass* upon his head;
2Sa. 3:34. nor thy feet put *into fetters*
8: 8. David took exceeding much *brass.*
10. vessels of gold, and vessels of *brass:*
21:16. three hundred (shekels) of *brass*
1K. 4:13. cities with walls and *brasen* bars:
7:14. a worker in *brass:*
— to work all works *in brass.*
15. he cast two pillars of *brass,*
16. two chapiters (of) molten *brass,*
27. he made ten bases of *brass;*
30. every base had four *brasen* wheels, and plates of *brass:*
38. Then made he ten lavers of *brass:*
45. all these vessels,...(were of) bright *brass.*
47. neither was the weight of *the brass* found
8:64. the *brasen* altar that (was) before the Lord
14:27. king Rehoboam made...*brasen* shields,
2K. 16:14. he brought also the *brasen* altar,
15. the *brasen* altar shall be for me
17. took down the sea from off the *brasen* oxen
18: 4. and brake in pieces the *brasen* serpent
25: 7. bound him *with fetters of brass,*
13. pillars of *brass* that (were) in the house
— and the *brasen* sea
— and carried *the brass of them* to Babylon.
14. all the vessels of *brass*
16. *the brass of* all these vessels
17. the chapiter upon it (was) *brass:*

2K. 25:17. the chapiter round about, all of *brass:*
1Ch 15:19. to sound with cymbals of *brass;*
18: 8. brought David very much *brass*, wherewith Solomon made the *brasen* sea, and the pillars, and the vessels of *brass.*
10. gold and silver *and brass.*
22: 3. *and brass* in abundance without weight;
14. *and of brass* and iron without weight;
16. the gold, the silver, *and the brass,*
29: 2. *and the brass for* (things) *of brass,*
7. *and of brass* eighteen thousand talents,
2Ch 1: 5. Moreover the *brasen* altar,
6. the *brasen* altar before the Lord,
2: 7(6). in silver, *and in brass*, and in iron,
14(13). work in gold, and in silver, *in brass,*
4: 1. he made an altar of *brass,*
9. overlaid the doors of them *with brass.*
16. all their instruments,...of bright *brass.*
18. the weight of *the brass* could not be found
6:13. Solomon had made a *brasen* scaffold,
7: 7. the *brasen* altar which Solomon had made
12:10. king Rehoboam made shields of *brass,*
24:12. also such as wrought iron *and brass*
33:11. bound him *with fetters*, (marg. or, *chains*)
36: 6. and bound him *in fetters*, (marg. *id.*)
Ezr. 8:27. two vessels of fine *copper*, (marg. yellow, or, shining *brass*)
Ps.107:16. he hath broken the gates of *brass,*
Isa. 60:17. For *brass* I will bring gold,
— and for wood *brass,*
Jer. 1:18. an iron pillar, and *brasen* walls
6:28. (they are) *brass* and iron;
15:12. the northern iron *and the steel?*
20. a fenced *brasen* wall:
39: 7. and bound him *with chains*, (marg. *two brasen chains*, or, *fetters*)
52:11. the king of Babylon bound him *in chains*, (marg. or, *fetters*)
17. Also the pillars of *brass*
— the *brasen* sea that (was) in the house
— and carried all *the brass of them* to
18. vessels of *brass* wherewith they ministered,
20. twelve *brasen* bulls
— *the brass of* all these vessels
22. a chapiter of *brass* (was) upon it;
— the chapiters round about, all (of) *brass.*
Lam.3: 7. he hath made *my chain* heavy.
Eze. 1: 7. like the colour of burnished *brass.*
9: 2. and stood beside the *brasen* altar.
16:36. Because *thy filthiness* was poured out,
22:18. all they (are) *brass*, and tin, and iron, and lead,
20. they gather silver, *and brass,*
24:11. that *the brass of it* may be hot,
27:13. persons of men and vessels of *brass*
40: 3. like the appearance of *brass,*
Dan10: 6. his feet like in colour to polished *brass,*
Zec. 6: 1. the mountains (were) mountains of *brass.*

5180 **נְחֻשְׁתָּן** *n'ghoosh-tāhn'*, adj.

2K. 18: 4. and he called it *Nehushtan.*

5181 **נָחַת** [*nāh-ghath'*].

* KAL.—*Future.* *

Job 21:13. in a moment *go down* (see also חָתַת)
Ps. 38: 2(3). *and* thy hand *presseth* me *sore.*
Pro.17:10. A reproof *entereth* (marg. *aweth*) more into a wise man
Jer. 21:13. Who *shall come down* against us?

* NIPHAL.—*Preterite.* *

Ps. 38: 2(3). thine arrows *stick fast* in me,

* PIEL.—*Preterite.* *

2Sa.22:35. *so that* a bow of steel *is broken*
Ps. 18:34(35). *so that* a bow of steel *is broken*

PIEL.—*Infinitive.*

Ps. 65:10(11). *thou settlest* (marg. or, *causest* (rain) *to descend* (into)) the furrows thereof:

* HIPHIL.—*Imperative.* *

Joel 3:11(4.11). *cause* thy mighty ones *to come down*, O Lord. (marg. or, the Lord *shall bring down*)

נְחַת [*n'ghath*], Ch. 5182

* P'AL.—*Participle.* *

Dan. 4:13(10). an holy one *came down* from heaven;
23(20). saw a watcher and an holy one *coming down*

* APHEL.—*Imperative.* *

Ezr. 5:15. go, *carry* them into the temple that (is) in Jerusalem,

APHEL.—*Future.*

Ezr. 6: 5. *and place* (them) in the house of God.

APHEL.—*Participle.*

Ezr. 6: 1. where the treasures were *laid up* (marg. *made to descend*) in Babylon.

* HOPHAL.—*Preterite.* *

Dan. 5:20. *he was deposed* (lit. *caused to descend*) from his kingly throne,

---

נַחַת *nah'-ghath*, m. 5183

Job 17:16. when (our) *rest* together (is) in the dust.
36:16. *and that which should be set on* (marg. *the rest of*) thy table
Pro.29: 9. (there is) no *rest.*
Ecc. 4: 6. an handful (with) *quietness,*
6: 5. this hath more *rest* than the other.
9:17. words of wise (men are) heard *in quiet*
Isa. 30:15. In returning *and rest* shall ye be saved;
30. *and* shall shew *the lighting down* of his arm,

נָחֵת [*nāh-ghēhth'*], adj. 5185

2K. 6: 9. the Syrians *are come down.*

נָטָה *nāh-tāh'.* 5186

* KAL.—*Preterite.* *

Gen33:19. where *he had spread* his tent,
Ex. 15:12. *Thou stretchedst out* thy right hand,
33: 7. Moses took the tabernacle, *and pitched* it
Nu. 21:15. the stream...*that goeth down* to
22:33. unless *she had turned* from me,
Jos. 8:26. *he stretched out* the spear,
2Sa. 2:19. in going *he turned* not
6:17. the tabernacle that David *had pitched* (marg. *stretched*)
1K. 2:28. Joab *had turned* after Adonijah, though *he turned* not after Absalom.
11: 9. his heart *was turned* from the Lord God
2K. 21:13. *And I will stretch* over Jerusalem the line
1Ch 16: 1. the tent that David *had pitched*
2Ch 1: 4. *he had pitched* a tent for it
Job 15:25. *he stretcheth out* his hand against God,
38: 5. who *hath stretched* the line
Ps. 21:11(12). *they intended* evil against thee:
73: 2. my feet *were* almost *gone;*
119:51. (yet) *have I* not *declined* from thy law.
112. *I have inclined* mine heart to perform
157. (yet) *do I* not *decline* from thy testimonies.
Pro. 1:24. *I have stretched out* my hand,
Isa. 23:11. *He stretched out* his hand over the sea,
34:11. *and he shall stretch out* upon it the line
44:13. The carpenter *stretcheth out* (his) rule;
45:12. my hands, *have stretched out* the heavens,
Jer. 10:12. *hath stretched out* the heavens
14: 8. as a wayfaring man (that) *turneth aside*
43:10. *and he shall spread* his royal pavilion
51:15. *hath stretched out* the heaven
25. *and I will stretch out* mine hand
Lam.2: 8. *he hath stretched out* a line,
Eze. 6:14. *So will I stretch out* my hand
14: 9. *and I will stretch out* my hand
13. *then will I stretch out* mine hand
16:27. *I have stretched out* my hand
25: 7. *I will stretch out* mine hand
13. *I will also stretch out* mine hand
30:25. *and he shall stretch* it *out* upon
35: 3. *and I will stretch out* mine hand
Zep. 1: 4. *I will also stretch out* mine hand

KAL.—*Infinitive.*

Ex. 7: 5. *when I stretch forth* mine hand
23: 2. *to decline* after many
Nu. 22:26. where (was) no way *to turn*
Jos. 8:19. *as soon as he had stretched out* his hand:
Jud 19: 8. they tarried until afternoon, (marg. till the day *declined*)
2K. 20:10. for the shadow *to go down* ten degrees:
Ps. 17:11. they have set their eyes *bowing down* (lit. *to bend*)
109:23. am gone like the shadow *when it declineth:*

KAL.—*Imperative.*

Ex. 7:19. *and stretch out* thine hand upon the waters
8: 5(1). *Stretch forth* thine hand
16(12). *Stretch out* thy rod,
9:22. *Stretch forth* thine hand toward heaven,
10:12. *Stretch out* thine hand over the land
21. *Stretch out* thine hand toward heaven,
14:16. *and stretch out* thine hand over the sea,
26. *Stretch out* thine hand over the sea,
Jos. 8:18. *Stretch out* the spear that (is) in thy hand
1Sa.14: 7. *turn thee;* behold, I (am) with thee
2Sa. 2:21. *Turn thee aside* to thy right hand or

KAL.—*Future.*

Gen12: 8. east of Beth-el, *and pitched* his tent,
26:25. *and pitched* his tent there:
35:21. Israel journeyed, *and spread* his tent
38: 1. *and turned* in to a certain Adullamite,
16. *And he turned* unto her by the way,
39:21. the Lord was with Joseph, *and shewed* him mercy,
49:15. *and bowed* his shoulder to bear,
Ex. 8: 6(2). *And* Aaron *stretched out* his hand
17(13). *for* Aaron *stretched out* his hand
9:23. *And* Moses *stretched forth* his rod toward
10:13. *And* Moses *stretched forth* his rod over
22. *And* Moses *stretched forth* his hand toward
14:21. *And* Moses *stretched out* his hand over
27. *And* Moses *stretched forth* his hand
Nu. 20:17. *we will* not *turn* to the right hand nor
21. *wherefore* Israel *turned* away
21:22. *we will* not *turn* into the fields,
22:23. *and* the ass *turned aside*
33. the ass saw me, *and turned* from me
Jos. 8:18. *And* Joshua *stretched out* the spear
Jud. 4:11. *and pitched* his tent unto the plain
9: 3. *and* their hearts *inclined* to follow
16:30. *And he bowed himself* with (all his) might;
1Sa. 8: 3. *but turned aside* after lucre,
2Sa.22:10. *He bowed* the heavens *also,*
1Ch 15: 1. *and pitched* for it a tent.
Job 15:29. neither *shall he prolong* the perfection
31: 7. If my step *hath turned* out of the way,
Ps. 18: 9(10). *He bowed* the heavens *also,*
40: 1(2). *and he inclined* unto me, and heard
44:18(19). *neither have* our steps *declined*
Pro. 4: 5. neither *decline* from the words of
27. *Turn* not to the right hand nor
Isa. 5:25. *and he hath stretched forth* his hand
Zep. 2:13. *And he will stretch out* his hand

KAL.—*Participle.* Poel.

1Ch 21:10. I *offer* (marg. *stretch out*) thee three (things):
Job 9: 8. *Which* alone *spreadeth out* the heavens,
26: 7. *He stretcheth out* the north
Ps.104: 2. who *stretchest out* the heavens
Isa. 40:22. *that stretcheth out* the heavens
42: 5. created the heavens, *and stretched them out;*
44:24. *that stretcheth forth* the heavens
51:13. *that hath stretched forth* the heavens,
66:12. I *will extend* peace to her
Jer. 10:20. (there is) none *to stretch forth* my tent
Eze.25:16. I *will stretch out* mine hand
Zec.12: 1. the Lord, *which stretcheth forth* the heavens,

KAL.—*Participle.* Paül.

Ex. 6: 6. I will redeem you with a *stretched out* arm,
Deu. 4:34 & 5:15. a mighty hand, and by a *stretched out* arm,
7:19. mighty hand, and the *stretched out* arm,
9:29. power and by thy *stretched out* arm.
11: 2. hand, and his *stretched out* arm,
26: 8. and with an *outstretched* arm,
1K. 8:42. and of thy *stretched out* arm;
2K. 17:36. power and a *stretched out* arm,
1Ch 21:16. a drawn sword in his hand *stretched out*
2Ch 6:32. and thy *stretched out* arm;
Ps. 62: 3(4). as a *bowing* wall (shall ye be),
73: 2. (כתיב) my feet *were* almost *gone;*
102:11(12). My days (are) like a shadow *that declineth;*
136:12. and with a *stretched out* arm:
Isa. 3:16. and walk with *stretched forth* necks
5:25 & 9:12(11), 17(16), 21(20) & 10:4, his hand (is) *stretched out* still.
14:26. the hand that is *stretched out*
27. his hand (is) *stretched out,*
Jer. 21: 5. with an *outstretched* hand
27: 5. by my *outstretched* arm,
32:17. thy great power and *stretched out* arm,
21. and with a *stretched out* arm,
Eze. 1:22. *stretched forth* over their heads
20:33, 34. a mighty hand, and with a *stretched out* arm,

* NIPHAL.—*Preterite.* *

Nu. 24: 6. As the valleys *are they spread forth,*

NIPHAL.—*Future.*

Jer. 6: 4. shadows of the evening *are stretched out.*
Zec. 1:16. a line *shall be stretched forth*

* HIPHIL.—*Preterite.* *

1K. 11: 4. his wives *turned away* his heart
Ezr. 7:28. *hath extended* mercy unto me
Ps.116: 2. *he hath inclined* his ear unto me,
Pro. 5:13. nor *inclined* mine ear
7:21. With her much fair speech *she caused him to yield,*
Isa. 44:20. a deceived heart *hath turned him aside,*
Jer. 5:25. Your iniquities *have turned away*
7:24. hearkened not, nor *inclined* their ear,
26. unto me, nor *inclined* their ear,
11: 8. obeyed not, nor *inclined* their ear,
17:23. obeyed not, neither *inclined* their ear,
25: 4. nor *inclined* your ear to hear.
34:14. neither *inclined* their ear.
35:15. *ye have* not *inclined* your ear,
44: 5. nor *inclined* their ear to turn
Am. 5:12. *they turn aside* the poor

HIPHIL.—*Infinitive.*

Ex. 23: 2. to decline after many *to wrest* (judgment):
Nu. 22:23. Balaam smote the ass, *to turn her*
1K. 8:58. *That he may incline* our hearts
Pro.17:23. *to pervert* the ways of judgment.
18: 5. *to overthrow* the righteous in judgment.
Isa. 10: 2. *To turn aside* the needy from judgment,
Lam.3:35. *To turn aside* the right of a man

HIPHIL.—*Imperative.*

Gen24:14. *Let down* thy pitcher,
Jos. 24:23. *and incline* your heart unto the Lord God
2K. 19:16. Lord, *bow down* thine ear, and hear:
Ps. 17: 6. *incline* thine ear unto me,
31: 2(3). *Bow down* thine ear to me;
45:10(11). *and incline* thine ear;
71: 2. *incline* thine ear unto me,
78: 1. *incline* your ears to the words of my mouth.
86: 1. *Bow down* thine ear, O Lord,
88: 2(3). *incline* thine ear unto my cry;
102: 2(3). *incline* thine ear unto me:
119:36. *Incline* my heart unto thy testimonies,
144: 5. *Bow* thy heavens, O Lord, and come down:
Pro. 4:20. *incline* thine ear unto my sayings.
5: 1. *bow* thine ear to my understanding:
22:17. *Bow down* thine ear,
Isa. 30:11. *turn aside* out of the path,
37:17. *Incline* thine ear, O Lord,
55: 3. *Incline* your ear, and come unto me:
Dan. 9:18. O my God, *incline* thine ear,

HIPHIL.—*Future.*

Ex. 23: 6. *Thou shalt* not *wrest* the judgment of
Deu16:19. *Thou shalt* not *wrest* judgment;
24:17. *Thou shalt* not *pervert* the judgment of
1Sa. 8: 3. took bribes, *and perverted* judgment.
2Sa. 3:27. *And* when...Joab *took him aside* in the gate
6:10. *but* David *carried it aside*
16:22. *So they spread* Absalom a tent
19:14(15). *And he bowed* the heart of all the men
21:10. Rizpah...took sackcloth, *and spread it*
1K. 11: 2. *they will turn away* your heart

1K. 11: 3. *and* his wives *turned away* his heart.
1Ch 13:13. *but carried it aside* into the house of Obed-edom
Ezr. 9: 9. *but hath extended* mercy unto us
Job 23:11. his way have I kept, and not *declined.*
24: 4. *They turn* the needy out of the way:
36:18. a great ransom *cannot deliver thee.*
Ps. 27: 9. *put* not thy servant *away*
49: 4(5). *I will incline* mine ear
141: 4. *Incline* not my heart to (any) evil thing,
Pro. 2: 2. *apply* thine heart to understanding;
21: 1. *he turneth it* whithersoever he will.
Isa. 29:21. *and turn aside* the just for a thing of
31: 3. When the Lord *shall stretch out* his hand,
54: 2. *let them stretch forth* the curtains
Jer. 6:12. *I will stretch out* my hand
15: 6. *therefore will I stretch out* my hand
Hos 11: 4. *and I laid* meat unto them.
Am. 2: 7. and *turn aside* the way of the meek:
8. *they lay* (themselves) *down* upon clothes

HIPHIL.—*Participle.*

Deu27:19. *he that perverteth* the judgment of
Ps.125: 5. *As for such as turn aside* unto their crooked ways,
Mal. 3: 5. *and that turn aside* the stranger

5187 **נָטִיל** [*nāh-teel'*], adj.

Zep. 1:11. *they that bear* silver are cut off.

5188 **נְטִיפוֹת** *n'tee-phōhth'*, f. pl.

Jud. 8:26. beside ornaments, *and collars,* (marg. or, *sweet jewels*)
Isa. 3:19. *The chains,* (marg. or, *sweet balls*) and the bracelets,

---

5189 **נְטִישׁוֹת** *n'tee-shōhth'*, f. pl.

Isa. 18: 5. take away (and) cut down *the branches.*
Jer. 5:10. take away *her battlements;*
48:32. *thy plants* are gone over the sea,

5190 **נָטַל** *nāh-tal'.*

* KAL.—*Preterite.* *

Lam.3:28. *he hath borne* (it) upon him.

KAL.—*Future.*

Isa. 40:15. *he taketh up* the isles as a very little thing.

KAL.—*Participle.* Poel.

2Sa.24:12. I *offer* thee three (things);

* PIEL.—*Future.* *

Isa. 63: 9. *and he bare them,* and carried them

5191 **נְטַל** [*n'tal'*], Ch.

* P'AL.—*Preterite.* *

Dan. 4:34(31). I Nebuchadnezzar *lifted up* mine eyes unto heaven,

* P'IL.—*Preterite.* *

Dan. 7: 4. *and it was lifted up* from the earth,

5192 **נֵטֶל** *nĕh'-tel*, m.

Pro.27: 3. A stone (is) heavy, *and* the sand *weighty;*

5193 **נָטַע** *nāh-tag'.*

* KAL.—*Preterite.* *

Lev.19:23. *and shall have planted* all manner of trees
Nu. 24: 6. the Lord *hath planted,*
Deu. 6:11. olive trees, which *thou plantedst* not;
20: 6. (he) that *hath planted* a vineyard,
Jos. 24:13. oliveyards which *ye planted* not
2Sa. 7:10. a place for my people Israel, *and will plant them,*
1Ch 17: 9. a place for my people Israel, *and will plant them,*
Ps. 80:15(16). the vineyard which thy right hand *hath planted,*
104:16. cedars of Lebanon, which *he hath planted;*
Pro.31:16. *she planteth* a vineyard.
Ecc. 2: 4. *I planted* me vineyards:
5. *and I planted* trees
Isa. 44:14. *he planteth* an ash, and the rain doth
65:21. *and they shall plant* vineyards,
Jer. 2:21. *I had planted thee* a noble vine,
12: 2. *Thou hast planted them,* yea, they have
24: 6. *and I will plant them,* and not pluck
31: 5. the planters *shall plant,*
32:41. *and I will plant them* in this land
42:10. *and I will plant* you, and not pluck
45: 4. that which *I have planted*
Eze.28:26. build houses, *and plant* vineyards;
36:36. *plant* that that was desolate:
Am. 5:11. *ye have planted* pleasant vineyards,
9:14. *and they shall plant* vineyards,
15. *and I will plant them* upon their land,
Zep. 1:13. *and they shall plant* vineyards,

KAL.—*Infinitive.*

Ecc. 3: 2. a time *to plant,*
Isa. 51:16. *that I may plant* the heavens,
Jer. 1:10. to throw down, to build, *and to plant.*
18: 9. a kingdom, to build *and to plant* (it);
31:28. watch over them, to build, *and to plant,*

KAL.—*Imperative.*

2K. 19:29. sow ye, and reap, *and plant* vineyards,
Isa. 37:30. sow ye, and reap, *and plant* vineyards,
Jer. 29: 5. *and plant* gardens, and eat the fruit of them;
28. *and plant* gardens, and eat the fruit of them.

KAL.—*Future.*

Gen. 2: 8. *And* the Lord God *planted* a garden
9:20. husbandman, *and he planted* a vineyard:
21:33. *And* (Abraham) *planted* a grove
Ex. 15:17. Thou shalt bring them in, *and plant them*
Deu16:21. *Thou shalt* not *plant* thee a grove
28:30. *thou shalt plant* a vineyard,
39. *Thou shalt plant* vineyards,
Ps. 44: 2(3). thou didst drive out the heathen...*and plantedst them;*
80: 8(9). thou hast cast out the heathen, *and planted it.*
107:37. sow the fields, *and plant* vineyards,
Isa. 5: 2. *and planted it* with the choicest vine,
17:10. *shalt thou plant* pleasant plants,
65:22. *they shall* not *plant,* and another eat:
Jer. 31: 5. *Thou shalt* yet *plant* vines
35: 7. nor sow seed, nor *plant* vineyard,
Dan11:45. *And he shall plant* the tabernacles

KAL.—*Participle.* Poel.

Ps. 94: 9. *He that planted* the ear,
Jer. 11:17. the Lord of hosts, *that planted* thee,
31: 5. *the planters* shall plant,

KAL.—*Participle.* Paül.

Ecc. 3: 2. time to pluck up (that which is) *planted;*
12:11. as nails *fastened* (by) the masters of

* NIPHAL.—*Preterite.* *

Isa. 40:24. *they shall* not *be planted;*

נֶטַע [*nĕh'-tag*], m. 5194

1Ch 4:23. those that dwelt among *plants*
Job 14: 9. bring forth boughs like *a plant.*
Isa. 5: 7. the men of Judah his pleasant *plant:*
17:10. shalt thou plant pleasant *plants,*
11. the day shalt thou make *thy plant* to grow,

נְטִעִים *n'tee-geem'*, m. pl. 5195

Ps.144:12. That our sons (may be) *as plants*

נָטַף [*nāh-taph'*]. 5197

* KAL.—*Preterite.* *

Jud. 5: 4. the heavens *dropped,* the clouds also *dropped* water.

Ps. 68: 8(9). heavens also *dropped* at the presence
Cant.5: 5. my hands *dropped* (with) myrrh,

KAL.—*Future.*

Job 29:22. my speech *dropped* upon them.
Pro. 5: 3. *drop* (as) an honeycomb,
Cant.4:11. *drop* (as) the honeycomb:
Joel 3:18(4:18). the mountains *shall drop* down new wine,

KAL.—*Participle.* Poel.

Cant.5:13. *dropping* sweet smelling myrrh.

* HIPHIL.—*Preterite.* *

Am. 9:13. *and* the mountains *shall drop* sweet wine,

HIPHIL.—*Imperative.*

Eze.20:46(21:2). *and drop* (thy word) toward the south,
21: 2(7). *and drop* (thy word) toward the holy places,

HIPHIL.—*Future.*

Am. 7:16. *drop* not (thy word)
Mic. 2: 6. *Prophesy* (marg. *Drop*) ye not, (say they to them that) *prophesy: they shall* not *prophesy* to them,
11. *I will prophesy* unto thee of wine

HIPHIL.—*Participle.*

Mic. 2:11. he shall even be *the prophet*

5198 **נָטָף** *nāh-tāhph'*, m.

Ex. 30:34. Take unto thee sweet spices, *stacte*,
Job 36:27. he maketh small *the drops of* water:

5201 **נָטַר** [*nāh-tar'*].

* KAL.—*Preterite.* *

Cant.1: 6. mine own vineyard *have I* not *kept*.

KAL.—*Future.*

Lev.19:18. *bear any grudge* against the children
Ps.103: 9. neither *will he keep* (his anger)
Jer. 3: 5. *Will he reserve* (his anger) for ever?
12. *I will* not *keep* (anger)

KAL.—*Participle.* Poel.

Cant.1: 6. they made me *keeper* of the vineyards;
8:11. he let out the vineyard *unto keepers;*
12. *those that keep* the fruit
Nah 1: 2. *and* he *reserveth* (wrath) for his enemies.

5202 **נְטַר** [*n'tar*], Ch.

* P'AL.—*Preterite.* *

Dan. 7:28. but *I kept* the matter in my heart.

5203 **נָטַשׁ** *nāh-tash'*.

* KAL.—*Preterite.* *

Gen31:28. *hast* not *suffered me* to kiss
Ex. 23:11. shalt let it rest *and lie still;*
Jud. 6:13. the Lord *hath forsaken us*,
1Sa.10: 2. thy father *hath left* the care of the asses,
17:28. with whom *hast thou left* those few sheep
2K. 21:14. *And I will forsake* the remnant
Isa. 2: 6. *thou hast forsaken* thy people
Jer. 12: 7. *I have left* mine heritage;
15: 6. *Thou hast forsaken* me, saith the Lord,
23:33. *I will even forsake* you, saith the Lord.
39. *and I will forsake* you, and the city
Eze.29: 5. *And I will leave thee* (thrown) into
32: 4. *Then will I leave thee* upon the land,

KAL.—*Infinitive.*

Pro.17:14. therefore *leave off* contention,

KAL.—*Future.*

Nu. 11:31. *and let* (them) *fall* by the camp,
Deu32:15. *then he forsook* God (which) made him,
1 Sa. 4: 2. and *when they joined* battle, (marg. the battle *was spread*)
12:22. the Lord *will* not *forsake* his people

1Sa.17:20. *and left* the sheep with a keeper,
22. *And* David *left* his carriage in the hand of the keeper
1K. 8:57. let him not leave us, nor *forsake us:*
Neh 10:31(32). *and* (that) *we would leave* the seventh year,
Ps. 27: 9. *leave me* not, neither forsake me,
78:60. *So that he forsook* the tabernacle
94:14. the Lord *will not cast off* his people,
Pro. 1: 8 & 6:20. *forsake* not the law of thy mother:
Jer. 7:29. *and forsaken* the generation of his wrath.
Eze.31:12. have cut him off, *and have left him:*
— are gone down from his shadow, *and have left him.*
Hos 12:14(15). therefore *shall he leave* his blood

KAL.—*Participle.* Paül.

1Sa.30:16. (they were) *spread abroad* upon all the earth,
Isa. 21:15. from the *drawn* sword,

* NIPHAL.—*Preterite.* *

Isa. 16: 8. her branches *are stretched out*, (marg. or, *plucked up*)
33:23. Thy tacklings *are loosed;* (marg. or, *They have forsaken* thy tacklings)
Am. 5: 2. *she is forsaken* upon her land;

NIPHAL.—*Future.*

Jud.15: 9. *and spread themselves* in Lehi.
2Sa. 5:18, 22. *and spread themselves* in the valley

* PUAL.—*Preterite.* *

Isa. 32:14. the palaces *shall be forsaken;*

נִי *nee*, m. 5204

Eze.27:32. *in their wailing* they shall take up

נִיב *neev*, m. 5108

Isa. 57:19. I create *the fruit of* the lips;
Mal. 1:12. *and the fruit thereof*, (even) his meat,

נִיד *need*, m. 5205

Job 16: 5. *and the moving of* my lips

נִידָה *nee-dāh'*, f. 5206

Lam.1: 8. therefore she is *removed:* (marg. become *a removing*, or, *wandering*)

נִיחוֹחַ *nee-ġhōh'ăġh*, m. 5207

Gen. 8:21. the Lord smelled a *sweet* savour; (lit. a savour of *rest*)
Ex. 29:18. it (is) a *sweet* savour,
25. for a *sweet* savour before the Lord:
41. offering thereof, for a *sweet* savour,
Lev. 1: 9, 13, 17 & 2:2, 9. of a *sweet* savour unto the Lord.
2:12. on the altar for a *sweet* savour.
3: 5. of a *sweet* savour unto the Lord.
16. made by fire for a *sweet* savour:
4:31. for a *sweet* savour unto the Lord;
6:15(8). upon the altar (for) a *sweet* savour,
21(14). (for) a *sweet* savour unto the Lord.
8:21. burnt sacrifice for a *sweet* savour,
28. consecrations for a *sweet* savour:
17: 6. for a *sweet* savour unto the Lord.
23:13. unto the Lord (for) a *sweet* savour:
18. of *sweet* savour unto the Lord.
26:31. the savour of *your sweet odours.*
Nu. 15: 3, 7, 10, 13, 14, 24 & 18:17. a *sweet* savour unto the Lord, (lit. a savour of *rest*)
28: 2. a *sweet* savour *unto me*, (marg. a savour of *my rest*)
6. Sinai for a *sweet* savour,
8, 24, 27. a *sweet* savour unto the Lord.
13. burnt offering of a *sweet* savour,
29: 2, 13, 36. a *sweet* savour unto the Lord;

Nu. 29: 6. unto their manner, for a *sweet* savour,
8. unto the Lord (for) a *sweet* savour;
Eze. 6:13. offer *sweet* savour to all their idols.
16:19. before them for a *sweet* savour:
20:28. they made *their sweet* savour,
41. accept you with your *sweet* savour, (marg. savour of *rest*)

5208 נִיחוֹחַ [*nee-ghōh'ăgh*], Ch. m.

Ezr. 6:10. offer sacrifices of *sweet savours* (marg. of *rest*)
Dan. 2:46. *and sweet odours* unto him.

5209 נִין *neen*, m.

Gen21:23. *nor with my son*, nor with my son's son:
Job 18:19. He shall neither have *son* nor nephew
Isa. 14:22. *and son*, and nephew,

5211 נִיס *nees*, m.

Jer. 48:44. (כתיב) *He that fleeth* from the fear

5212 נִיסָן *nee-sāhn'*, m.

Neh. 2: 1. it came to pass in the month *Nisan*,
Est. 3: 7. In the first month, that (is), the month *Nisan*,

5213 נִיצוֹץ *nee-tzōhtz'*, m.

Isa. 1:31. the maker of it *as a spark*,

5216 נֵיר *nēhr*, m.

2Sa.22:29. For thou (art) *my lamp*, (marg. or, *candle*)

5214 נִיר [*neer*].

* KAL.—*Imperative.* *

Jer. 4: 3. *Break up* your fallow ground,
Hos 10:12. *break up* your fallow ground:

5215 נִיר *neer*, m.

Pro.13:23. Much food (is in) *the tillage of* the poor:
Jer. 4: 3. Break up your *fallow ground*,
Hos 10:12. break up your *fallow ground:*

5216 נִיר *neer*, m.

1K. 11:36. *a light* (marg. *lamp*, or, *candle*) alway before me
15: 4. give him *a lamp* (marg. or, *candle*) in Jerusalem,
2K. 8:19. to give him alway *a light*, (marg. *candle*, or, *lamp*)
2Ch 21: 7. promised to give *a light* (marg. *id.*) to him

5218 נָכֵא [*nāh-chēh'*], adj.

Pro.15:13. by sorrow of the heart the spirit is *broken*.
17:22. a *broken* spirit drieth the bones.
18:14. a *wounded* spirit who can bear?

5218 נָכָא [*nāh-chāh'*], adj.

Isa. 16: 7. surely (they are) *stricken*.

5219 נְכֹאת *n'chōhth*, f.

Gen37:25. bearing *spicery* and balm and myrrh,
43:11. *spices*, and myrrh, nuts, and almonds:

נֶכֶד *neh'-ched*, m. 5220

Gen21:23. nor with my son, *nor with my son's son:*
Job 18:19. He shall neither have son nor *nephew*
Isa. 14:22. and son, *and nephew*,

נָכָה [*nāh-chāh'*]. 5221

* NIPHAL.—*Preterite.*

2Sa.11:15. retire ye from him, *that he may be smitten*,

* PUAL.—*Preterite.* *

Ex. 9:31. the flax and the barley *was smitten:*
32. the wheat and the rie *were* not *smitten:*

* HIPHIL.—*Preterite.* *

Gen19:11. And *they smote* the men
32: 8(9). If Esau come...*and smite it*,
11(12). lest he will come *and smite me*,
34:30. gather themselves together against me, *and slay me;*
Ex. 3:20. will stretch out my hand, *and smite* Egypt
9:25. the hail *smote* every herb of the field,
12:12. *and will smite* all the firstborn
29. the Lord *smote* all the firstborn
17: 5. wherewith *thou smotest* the river,
6. *and thou shalt smite* the rock,
21:18. *and* one *smite* another with a stone,
Lev.26:24. *and will punish* you yet seven times
Nu. 22:28. that *thou hast smitten me* these three times?
32. Wherefore *hast thou smitten* thine ass
25:17. Vex the Midianites, *and smite* them:
32: 4. the country which the Lord *smote*
33: 4. which the Lord *had smitten*
35:16. And if *he smite him* with an instrument
17. if *he smite him* with throwing a stone,
18. (if) *he smite him* with an hand weapon
21. in enmity *smite him* with his hand,
Deu. 4:46. the children of Israel *smote*,
7: 2. *And* when...*thou shalt smite them*,
19: 6. overtake him,...*and slay him;*
11. *and smite him* mortally
20:13. *thou shalt smite* every male thereof
21: 1. it be not known who *hath slain him:*
25: 2. *and to be beaten* before his face,
Jos. 9:18. the children of Israel *smote* them not,
11:10. *smote* the king thereof
14. every man *they smote*
12: 1. which the children of Israel *smote*,
6. *Them did* Moses...*smite:*
7. the children of Israel *smote*
13:21. whom Moses *smote* with the princes
20: 5. *he smote* his neighbour unwittingly,
Jud. 6:16. *and thou shalt smite* the Midianites
15:16. *have I slain* a thousand men.
21:10. Go *and smite* the inhabitants of
1Sa. 2:14. *And he struck* (it) into the pan,
6:19. the Lord *had smitten* (many)
13: 4. Saul *had smitten* a garrison
14:14. slaughter, which Jonathan and his armourbearer *made*,
15: 3. Now go *and smite* Amalek,
17: 9. he be able to fight with me, *and to kill me*,
— if I prevail against him, *and kill him*,
35. I went out after him, *and smote him*,
— caught (him) by his beard, *and smote him*,
36. Thy servant *slew* both the lion
46. *and I will smite thee*, and take thine head
18: 7. Saul *hath slain* his thousands,
21: 9(10). whom *thou slewest* in the valley
11(12). Saul *hath slain* his thousands,
22:19. *smote he* with the edge of the sword,
23: 2. Shall I go *and smite* these Philistines?
— Go *and smite* the Philistines,
27: 9. David *smote* the land,
29: 5. Saul *slew* his thousands,
2Sa. 2:31. *had smitten* of Benjamin,
8: 9. David *had smitten* all the host
10:18. and *smote* Shobach the captain
11:21. *smote* Abimelech the son of Jerubbesheth?
12: 9. *thou hast killed* Uriah the Hittite
13:30. Absalom *hath slain* all the king's sons,
15:14. *and smite* the city with the edge of
17: 2. *and I will smite* the king only:
18:11. why *didst thou* not *smite him* there
21:18. Sibbechai the Hushathite *slew* Saph,

2 Sa.23:20. he *slew* two lionlike men
— he went down also *and slew* a lion
21. he *slew* an Egyptian,
1 K. 14:15. *For* the Lord *shall smite* Israel,
15:29. *he smote* all the house of Jeroboam;
16: 7. because *he killed* him.
11. *he slew* all the house of Baasha:
16. and *hath* also *slain* the king:
20:21. *and slew* the Syrians with a great slaughter
36. a lion *shall slay thee.*
2 K. 3:19. *And ye shall smite* every fenced city,
9: 7. *And thou shalt smite* the house of Ahab
10: 9. but who *slew* all these?
12:21(22). his servants, *smote him,*
13:17. *for thou shalt smite* the Syrians
19. then *hadst thou smitten* Syria till thou hadst consumed
25. Three times *did* Joash *beat him,*
14: 7. He *slew* of Edom...ten thousand,
10. *Thou hast* indeed *smitten* Edom,
18: 8. He *smote* the Philistines,
19:37. his sons *smote him* with the sword:
1 Ch 11:22. he *slew* two lionlike men
— *and slew* a lion in a pit
23. And he *slew* an Egyptian,
18: 9. David *had smitten* all the host
12. Abishai...*slew* of the Edomites
20: 4. Sibbechai the Hushathite *slew* Sippai,
2 Ch 14:15(14). *They smote* also the tents of cattle,
22: 6. the wounds which *were given him* (marg. wherewith *they wounded him*)
25:19. *thou hast smitten* the Edomites;
Job 1:15. *they have slain* the servants
17. and *slain* the servants with the edge of the sword;
16:10. *they have smitten* me upon the cheek
Ps. 3: 7(8). *thou hast smitten* all mine enemies
69:26(27). (him) whom thou *hast smitten;*
78:20. *he smote* the rock, that the waters
135: 8. *Who smote* the firstborn of Egypt,
10. *Who smote* great nations, and slew
Pro.23:35. *They have stricken me,* (shalt thou say),
Cant.5: 7. *they smote me,* they wounded me;
Isa. 11: 4. *and he shall smite* the earth
15. *and shall smite it* in the seven streams,
27: 7. *Hath he smitten him,* as he smote
37:38. his sons *smote him* with the sword;
60:10. in my wrath *I smote thee,*
Jer. 2:30. In vain *have I smitten* your children;
5: 3. *thou hast stricken* them, but they
6. a lion out of the forest *shall slay them,*
14:19. why *hast thou smitten us,* and (there is)
20: 4. *and shall slay them* with the sword.
21: 6. *And I will smite* the inhabitants
7. *and he shall smite them* with the edge
29:21. *and he shall slay them* before your eyes;
30:14. *I have wounded thee* with the wound
33: 5. men, whom *I have slain*
37:10. though *ye had smitten* the whole army
15. wroth with Jeremiah, *and smote* him,
41: 3. Ishmael also *slew* all the Jews
9. the men, whom *he had slain*
16. after (that) *he had slain* Gedaliah
18. Ishmael the son of Nethaniah *had slain* Gedaliah
43:11. *And* when...*he shall smite* the land of
46: 2. Nebuchadrezzar king of Babylon *smote*
49:28. Nebuchadrezzar king of Babylon *shall smite,*
Eze. 9: 7. they went forth, *and slew* in the city.
22:13. *I have smitten* mine hand
39: 3. *And I will smite* thy bow
Am. 3:15. *And I will smite* the winter house
4: 9. *I have smitten* you with blasting
6:11. *and he will smite* the great house
Hag. 2:17. *I smote* you with blasting
Zec. 9: 4. *and he will smite* her power
10:11. *and shall smite* the waves in the sea,
Mal. 4: 6(3:24). lest I come *and smite* the earth

HIPHIL.—*Infinitive.*

Gen. 4:15. lest any finding him *should kill* him.
8:21. neither will I again *smite* any more
14:17. after his return *from the slaughter*
Ex. 7:25. after that the Lord *had smitten* the river.
12:13. *when I smite* the land of Egypt.
Nu. 3:13. the day *that I smote* all the firstborn
Nu. 8:17. the day *that I smote* every firstborn
22:25. he *smote her* again. (lit. he added *to smite her*)
Deu. 1: 4. After *he had slain* Sihon
13:15(16). Thou shalt *surely* smite (lit. *smiting* thou shalt smite)
25: 2. the wicked man (be) worthy *to be beaten,*
3. *and* (lit. *to*) *beat him* above these with many stripes,
27:25. he that taketh reward *to slay* an innocent
Jos. 10:20. when Joshua...had made an end *of slaying them*
Jud.20:31. they began *to smite* of the people,
39. began *to smite* (and) kill of the men
1 Sa.17:57. David returned *from the slaughter*
18: 6. David was returned *from the slaughter*
19:10. Saul sought *to smite* David
20:33. Saul cast a javelin at him *to smite him:*
2 Sa. 1: 1. David was returned *from the slaughter*
5:24. *to smite* the host of the Philistines.
8:13. when he returned *from smiting* (marg. *from his smiting*)
21: 2. Saul sought *to slay them*
12. when the Philistines *had slain* Saul
16. thought *to have slain* David.
1 K. 20:35. the man refused *to smite him.*
37. *in smiting* he wounded (him).
2 K. 3:24. they went forward *smiting*
13:19. *Thou shouldest have smitten* five or six
14:10. Thou hast *indeed* smitten (lit. *smiting* thou hast smitten) Edom,
1 Ch 14:15. *to smite* the host of the Philistines.
2 Ch 25:14. come *from the slaughter* of the Edomites,
Pro.17:10. *than* an hundred *stripes* into a fool.
26. *to strike* princes for equity.
Isa. 58: 4. *and to smite* with the fist of wickedness:
Jer. 40:14. hath sent Ishmael...*to slay thee?* (lit. *to smite thee* in soul)
46:13. *smite* the land of Egypt.
Eze. 9: 8. *while they were slaying* them,
32:15. *when I shall smite* all them that
Mic. 6:13. make (thee) sick *in smiting thee,*

HIPHIL.—*Imperative.*

Ex. 8:16(12). *and smite* the dust of the land,
2 Sa.13:28. when I say unto you, *Smite* Amnon;
1 K. 20:35, 37. *Smite me,* I pray thee.
2 K. 6:18. *Smite* this people, I pray thee,
9:27. *Smite him* also in the chariot.
10:25. Go in, (and) *slay them;* let none
13:18. *Smite* upon the ground.
Eze. 6:11. *Smite* with thine hand,
9: 5. ye after him through the city, *and smite:*
21:14(19). *and smite* (thine) hands together,
Am. 9: 1. *Smite* the lintel of the door,
Zec.13: 7. *smite* the shepherd, and the sheep

HIPHIL.—*Future.*

Gen 14: 5. *and smote* the Rephaims
7. *and smote* all the country of the
15. *and smote them,* and pursued them
37:21. *Let us* not *kill him.* (lit. *smite him* in soul)
Ex. 2:12. *and* when he saw...*he slew* the Egyptian, and hid him
13. Wherefore *smitest thou* thy fellow?
7:20. *and smote* the waters
8:17(13). *and smote* the dust of the earth,
9:15. *that I may smite* thee and thy people
25. *And* the hail *smote* throughout all the
21:20. if a man *smite* his servant,
26. if a man *smite* the eye of his servant,
Lev.24:17. he that *killeth* any man (marg. *smiteth* the life of a man)
Nu. 11:33. *and* the Lord *smote* the people
14:12. *I will smite them* with the pestilence,
45. *and smote them,* and discomfited them,
20:11. *and* with his rod *he smote* the rock twice:
21:24. *And* Israel *smote him*
35. *So they smote* him, and his sons,
22: 6. (that) *we may smite* them,
23. *and* Balaam *smote* the ass,
27. *and he smote* the ass
Deu. 2:33. *and we smote* him, and his sons,
3: 3. *and we smote him* until none was left
13:15(16). *Thou shalt* surely *smite*
19: 4. Whoso *killeth* his neighbour ignorantly,
25: 3. Forty *stripes he may give him,*

Deu28:22, 28, 35. The Lord *shall smite thee*
27. The Lord *will smite thee*
29: 7(6). unto battle, *and we smote them:*
Jos. 7: 3. go up *and smite* Ai;
5. *And* the men of Ai *smote* of them
— *and smote them* in the going down:
8:21. they turned again, *and slew*
22. *and they smote* them, so that they let
24. *and smote* it with the edge of the sword.
10: 4. *that we may smite* Gibeon: for it hath
10. *and slew them* with a great slaughter
— *and smote them* to Azekah,
26. *And* afterward Joshua *smote them,*
28. Joshua took Makkedah, *and smote it*
30. *and he smote it* with the edge of the sword,
32. *and smote it* with the edge of the sword,
33. *and* Joshua *smote him* and his people,
35, 37. *and smote it* with the edge of the sword,
39. *and they smote them* with the edge of the sword,
40. *So* Joshua *smote* all the country
41. *And* Joshua *smote them* from Kadesh-barnea
11: 8. Israel, *who smote them,*
— *and they smote them,* until they left them
11. *And they smote* all the souls
12. *and smote them* with the edge of the sword,
17. *and smote them,* and slew them.
13:12. *for* these *did* Moses *smite,*
15:16. He that *smiteth* Kirjath-sepher,
19:47. *and smote* it with the edge of the sword,
Jud. 1: 4. *and they slew of them* in Bezek ten thousand
5. *and they slew* the Canaanites
8. had taken it, *and smitten it*
10. *and they slew* Sheshai, and Ahiman, and Talmai.
12. He that *smiteth* Kirjath-sepher,
17. *and they slew* the Canaanites
25. *And* when...*they smote* the city
3:13. went *and smote* Israel,
29. *And they slew* of Moab...ten thousand men,
31. Shamgar the son of Anath, *which slew*... six hundred men
7:13. came unto a tent, *and smote it*
8:11. Gideon went up...*and smote* the host:
9:43. he rose up against them, *and smote them.*
44. ran upon all (the people)...*and slew them.*
11:21. *and they smote them:* so Israel
33. *And he smote them* from Aroer,
12: 4. *and* the men of Gilead *smote* Ephraim,
14:19. *and slew* thirty men of them,
15: 8. *And he smote* them hip and thigh
15. *and slew* a thousand men
18:27. *and they smote* them with the edge of the sword,
20:37. *and smote* all the city
45. *and slew* two thousand men
48. *and smote them* with the edge of the sword,
1Sa. 4: 2. *and they slew* of the army...four thousand
5: 6. *and smote* them with emerods,
9. *and he smote* the men of the city,
6:19. *And he smote* the men of Beth-shemesh,
— *even he smote* of the people fifty thousand
7:11. pursued the Philistines, *and smote them,*
11:11. *and slew* the Ammonites until the heat of the day:
13: 3. *And* Jonathan *smote* the garrison
14:31. *And they smote* the Philistines
48. gathered an host, *and smote* the Amalekites,
15: 7. *And* Saul *smote* the Amalekites
17:25. the man who *killeth him,*
26. the man that *killeth* this Philistine,
27. the man that *killeth him.*
49. *and smote* the Philistine in his forehead,
50. *and smote* the Philistine, and slew him;
18:11. *I will smite* David even to the wall
27. *and slew* of the Philistines two hundred
19: 5. his life in his hand, *and slew* the Philistine,
8. fought with the Philistines, *and slew* them
10. *and he smote* the javelin into the wall:
23: 5. *and smote* them with a great slaughter.
24: 5(6). afterward, *that* David's heart *smote* him,
26: 8. *let me smite him,* I pray thee,
30: 1. invaded the south,...*and smitten* Ziklag,
17. *And* David *smote them* from the twilight even unto
31: 2. *and* the Philistines *slew* Jonathan,
2Sa. 1:15. *And he smote him* that he died.
2Sa. 2:22. wherefore *should I smite thee*
23. *wherefore* Abner with the hinder end of the spear *smote him*
3:27. *and smote him* there under the fifth (rib):
4: 6. *and they smote him* under the fifth (rib),
7. *and they smote him,* and slew him,
5:20. *and* David *smote them* there,
25. *and smote* the Philistines
6: 7. *and* God *smote him* there
8: 1. *that* David *smote* the Philistines,
2. *And he smote* Moab,
3. David *smote also* Hadadezer,
5. *And* when...David *slew* of the Syrians
10. fought against Hadadezer, *and smitten him*
14: 6. *but* the one *smote* the other,
18:15. *and smote* Absalom, and slew him.
20:10. *so he smote him* therewith
21:17. *and smote* the Philistine, and killed him.
19. *where* Elhanan...*slew* (the brother of) Goliath
21. *And* when...the brother of David *slew him.*
23:10. He arose, *and smote* the Philistines
12. defended it, *and slew* the Philistines:
24:10. *And* David's heart *smote* him
1K. 11:15. *after he had smitten* every male
15:20. *and smote* Ijon, and Dan, and
27. *and* Baasha *smote him* at Gibbethon,
16:10. Zimri went in *and smote him,*
20:20. *And they slew* every one his man:
21. *and smote* the horses and chariots,
29. *and* the children of Israel *slew* of the
36. a lion found him, *and slew him.*
37. *And* the man *smote him,*
22:24. *and smote* Micaiah on the cheek,
34. *and smote* the king of Israel
2K. 2: 8. Elijah took his mantle,...*and smote* the
14. he took the mantle...*and smote* the waters,
— when *he also had smitten* the waters,
3:23. *and they have smitten* one another:
24. Israelites rose up *and smote* the Moabites,
— *but they went forward* smiting (lit. *and they smote* in it even smiting)
25. the slingers went about (it), *and smote it.*
6:18. *And he smote them* with blindness
21. My father, *shall I smite* (them)? *shall I smite* (them)?
22. *Thou shalt* not *smite* (them):
8:21. he rose by night, *and smote* the Edomites
28. *and* the Syrians *wounded* Joram.
29 & 9:15. the wounds which the Syrians *had given him*
9:24. Jehu drew a bow...*and smote* Jehoram
10:11. *So* Jehu *slew* all that remained
17. *And* when he came...*he slew* all that
25. *And they smote them* with the edge
32. *and* Hazael *smote them* in all the coasts
11:12. *and they clapped* their hands, and said,
12:20(21). *and slew* Joash in the house of Millo,
13:18. *And he smote* thrice, and stayed.
19. *thou shalt smite* Syria (but) thrice.
14: 5. *that he slew* his servants
15:10. *and smote him* before the people,
14. came to Samaria, *and smote* Shallum
16. Then Menahem *smote* Tiphsah,
— opened not (to him), *therefore he smote* (it);
25. conspired against him, *and smote him*
30. *and smote him,* and slew him,
19:35. *and smote* in the camp of the Assyrians
21:24. *And* the people of the land *slew*
25:21. *And* the king of Babylon *smote* them,
25. and ten men with him, *and smote* Gedaliah,
1Ch 4:41. *and smote* their tents,
43. *And they smote* the rest of the Amalekites
10: 2. *and* the Philistines *slew* Jonathan,
11:14. *and slew* the Philistines;
13:10. kindled against Uzza, *and he smote him,*
14:11. *and* David *smote them* there.
16. *and they smote* the host of the Philistines
18: 1. *that* David *smote* the Philistines,
2. *And he smote* Moab; and the Moabites
3. *And* David *smote* Hadarezer
5. *And* when the Syrians...David *slew* of the
10. he had fought against Hadarezer, *and smitten him;*
20: 1. *And* Joab *smote* Rabbah,
5. *and* Elhanan...*slew* Lahmi the brother of Goliath

1Ch 20: 7. *But* when he defied...Jonathan...*slew him.*
21: 7. *therefore he smote* Israel.
2Ch 13:17. *And* Abijah and his people *slew* them
14:14(13). *And they smote* all the cities
16: 4. *and they smote* Ijon, and Dan, and
18:23. *and smote* Micaiah upon the cheek,
33. *and smote* the king of Israel
21: 9. *and smote* the Edomites which compassed
22: 5. *and* the Syrians *smote* Joram.
25:11. *and smote* of the children of Seir
13. *and smote* three thousand of them,
16. why *shouldest thou be smitten?* (lit. *shall* (one) *smite thee*)
28: 5. *and they smote* him, and carried away
— *who smote* him with a great slaughter.
17. the Edomites had come *and smitten* Judah,
33:25. *But* the people of the land *slew*
Neh 13:25. *and smote* certain of them,
Est. 9: 5. *Thus* the Jews *smote* all their enemies
Job 2: 7. *and smote* Job with sore boils
Ps. 60[title](2). Joab returned, *and smote* of Edom
78:51. *And smote* all the firstborn in Egypt;
66. *And he smote* his enemies in the hinder part:
105:33. *He smote* their vines *also*
36. *He smote also* all the firstborn
121: 6. The sun *shall* not *smite thee* by day,
Pro.19:25. *Smite* a scorner,
23:13. (if) *thou beatest him* with the rod,
14. Thou *shalt beat him* with the rod,
Isa. 5:25. against them, *and hath smitten them:*
10:24. *he shall smite thee* with a rod,
30:31. the Assyrian...(which) *smote* with a rod.
37:36. angel of the Lord went forth, *and smote*
49:10. neither *shall* the heat nor sun *smite them:*
57:17. was I wroth, *and smote him:*
Jer. 18:18. *and let us smite him* with the tongue,
20: 2. *Then* Pashur *smote* Jeremiah
26:23. the king; *who slew him* (lit. *and he slew him*)
40:15. *and I will slay* Ishmael
— wherefore *should he slay thee,*
41: 2. *and smote* Gedaliah the son of Ahikam
47: 1. before that Pharaoh *smote* Gaza.
52:27. *And* the king of Babylon *smote* them,
Eze. 5: 2. *smite* about it with a knife:
21:17(22). I *will* also *smite* mine hands together,
Dan. 8: 7. *and smote* the ram, and brake his two horns:
Hos. 6: 1. *he hath smitten,* and he will bind us up.
14: 5(6). *and cast forth* his roots as Lebanon.
Jon. 4: 7. *and it smote* the gourd that it withered.
8. *and* the sun *beat* upon the head of Jonah,
Mic. 5: 1(4:14). *they shall smite* the judge of Israel
Zec.12: 4. *I will smite* every horse
— *will smite* every horse of the people

HIPHIL.—*Participle.*

Gen36:35. Hadad...*who smote* Midian
Ex. 2:11. he spied an Egyptian *smiting* an Hebrew,
7:17. I *will smite* with the rod
21:12. *He that smiteth* a man,
15. *And he that smiteth* his father,
19. shall *he that smote* (him) be quit:
Lev.24:18. *he that killeth* (lit. *smiteth* the soul of) a beast
21. *And he that killeth* a beast,
— *and he that killeth* a man,
Nu. 35:11. the slayer...*which killeth* any person
15. every one *that killeth* any person
21. *he that smote* (him) shall surely
24. *the slayer* and the revenger of blood
30. Whoso *killeth* any person,
Deu25:11. out of the hand of *him that smiteth him,*
27:24. *he that smiteth* his neighbour secretly.
Jos. 20: 3. the slayer *that killeth* (any) person
9. whosoever *killeth* (any) person
1Sa. 4: 8. the Gods *that smote* the Egyptians
2Sa. 5: 8. Whosoever getteth up...and *smiteth* the
14: 7. Deliver him *that smote* his brother,
24:17. the angel *that smote* the people,
2K. 6:22. *wouldest* thou *smite* those whom thou hast taken
14: 5. his servants *which had slain* the king
6. the children of *the murderers*
1Ch 1:46. Hadad...*which smote* Midian
11: 6. Whosoever *smiteth* the Jebusites
2Ch 25: 3. his servants *that had killed* the king
2Ch 28:23. the gods of Damascus, *which smote him:*
Ps.136:10. *To him that smote* Egypt
17. *To him which smote* great kings:
Isa. 9:13(12). *him that smiteth them,*
10:20. *him that smote them;*
14: 6. *He who smote* the people
29. the rod of *him that smote thee*
27: 7. as he smote *those that smote him?*
50: 6. I gave my back *to the smiters,*
66: 3. (as if) *he slew* a man;
Lam.3:30. giveth (his) cheek *to him that smiteth him:*
Eze. 7: 9. I (am) the Lord *that smiteth.*

* HOPHAL.—*Preterite.* *

Ex. 22: 2(1). *and be smitten* that he die,
Nu. 25:14. that *was slain* with the Midianitish woman,
1Sa. 5:12. the men that died not *were smitten*
Ps.102: 4(5). My heart *is smitten,*
Eze.33:21. The city *is smitten.*
40: 1. after that the city *was smitten,*
Hos. 9:16. Ephraim *is smitten,*
Zec.13: 6. *I was wounded* (in) the house of my friends.

HOPHAL.—*Future.*

Ex. 5:14. *And* the officers...*were beaten,*
Isa. 1: 5. Why *should ye be stricken* any more?

HOPHAL.—*Participle.*

Ex. 5:16. thy servants (are) *beaten;*
Nu. 25:14. the Israelite *that was slain,*
15. the Midianitish woman *that was slain*
18. Cozbi,...*which was slain*
Isa. 53: 4. *smitten of* God, and afflicted.
Jer. 18:21. (let) their young men (be) *slain by* the sword

נָכֶה [*nāh-ċheh′*], adj. 5223

2Sa. 4: 4. Jonathan,...had a son (that was) *lame of* (his) feet.
9: 3. Jonathan hath yet a son, (which is) *lame on* (his) feet.
Isa. 66: 2. (him that is) poor *and of* a *contrite* spirit,

נֵכֶה [*nēh-ċheh′*], adj. 5222

Ps. 35:15. *the abjects* gathered themselves together

נָכוֹחַ [*nāh-ċhōh′ăgh*], adj. 5228-29

2Sa.15: 3. thy matters (are) good *and right;*
Pro. 8: 9. They (are) all *plain* to him that
24:26. that giveth a *right* answer.
Isa. 26:10. in the land of *uprightness*
30:10. Prophesy not unto us *right things,*
57: 2. (each one) walketh (in) *his uprightness.* (marg. or, *before him*)
59:14. *and equity* cannot enter.
Am. 3:10. they know not to do *right,*

נֹכַח *nōh′-ċhagh*, m. 5227

[Used as a preposition and adverb.]

Gen25:21. Isaac intreated the Lord *for* his wife,
30:38. he set the rods...*before* the flocks
Ex. 26:35. the candlestick *over against* the table
40:24. put the candlestick...*over against* the table,
Nu. 19: 4. *directly* before the tabernacle
Jos. 15: 7. *before* the going up to Adummim,
18:17. *over against* the going up of Adummim,
Jud.18: 6. *before* the Lord (is) your way
19:10. came *over against* Jebus,
20:43. *over against* Gibeah
1K. 20:29. they pitched one *over against* the other
22:35. king was stayed up...*against* the Syrians,
2Ch 18:34. stayed (himself) up...*against* the Syrians
Est. 5: 1. *over against* the king's house:
— *over against* the gate of the house.
Pro. 4:25. Let thine eyes look *right on,*
5:21. the ways of man (are) *before* the eyes of the Lord,
Jer. 17:16. that which came out of my lips was *right* before thee.

Lam.2:19. *before* the face of the Lord:
Eze.14: 3. put the stumblingblock...*before* their face:
4, 7. putteth the stumblingblock...*before* his
47:20. *over against* Hamath.

5226 **נֶכַח** [*nĕh'-chagh*], m.

Ex. 14: 2. *before it* shall ye encamp
Eze.46: 9. shall go forth *over against it*.

5230 **נָכַל** [*nāh-chal'*].

* KAL.—*Participle.* Poel. *

Mal. 1:14. cursed (be) *the deceiver*,

* PIEL.—*Preterite.* *

Nu. 25:18. *they have beguiled* you in the matter of Peor,

* HITHPAEL.—*Infinitive.* *

Ps.105:25. *to deal subtilly* with his servants.

HITHPAEL.—*Future.*

Gen37:18. *And* when they saw...*they conspired* against

5231 **נֵכֶל** [*nĕh'-chel*], m.

Nu. 25:18. they vex you *with their wiles*,

5233 **נְכָסִים** *n'chāh-seem'*, m. pl.

Jos. 22: 8. Return *with* much *riches*
2Ch 1:11. hast not asked riches, *wealth*, or honour,
12. I will give thee riches, *and wealth*,
Ecc. 5:19(18). to whom God hath given riches *and wealth*,
6: 2. to whom God hath given riches, *wealth*, and honour,

5232 **נִכְסִין** *nich-seen'*, Ch. m. pl.

Ezr. 6: 8. *that of* the king's *goods*,
7:26. or to confiscation of *goods*,

5234 **נָכַר** [*nāh-char'*].

* NIPHAL.—*Preterite.* *

Lam.4: 8. *they are* not *known* in the streets:

NIPHAL.—*Future.*

Pro.26:24. He that hateth *dissembleth* (marg. or, *is known*) with his lips,

* PIEL.—*Preterite.* *

1Sa.23: 7. God *hath delivered* him into mine hand;
Job 34:19. nor *regardeth* the rich

PIEL.—*Future.*

Deu32:27. lest their adversaries *should behave themselves strangely*,
Job 21:29. *do ye* not *know* their tokens,
Jer. 19: 4. *and have estranged* this place,

* HIPHIL.—*Preterite.* *

Gen27:23. *he discerned him* not, because
42: 8. but *they knew* not *him*.
Deu33: 9. neither *did he acknowledge* his brethren,
Jud.18: 3. they *knew* the voice of the young man
2Sa. 3:36. all the people *took notice*
Job 2:12. and *knew him* not,
24:13. *they know* not the ways thereof,
Dan 11:39. (כתיב) god, whom *he shall acknowledge*

HIPHIL.—*Infinitive.*

Ru. 2:10. *that thou shouldest take knowledge of me*,
Pro.24:23. (It is) not good *to have respect* of persons
28:21. *To have respect* of persons (is) not good:

HIPHIL.—*Imperative.*

Gen31:32. before our brethren *discern thou*
37:32. *know* now whether it (be) thy son's coat
38:25. *Discern*, I pray thee, whose (are) these,

HIPHIL.—*Future.*

Gen37:33. *And he knew it*, and said,
38:26. *And* Judah *acknowledged* (them),
42: 7. Joseph saw his brethren, *and he knew them*,
8. *And* Joseph *knew* his brethren,
Deu 1:17. *Ye shall* not *respect* persons (marg. *acknowledge* faces)
16:19. *thou shalt* not *respect* persons,
21:17. *he shall acknowledge* the son
Ru. 3:14. before one *could know* another.
1Sa.26:17. *And* Saul *knew* David's voice,
1K. 18: 7. Elijah met him: *and he knew him*,
20:41. *and* the king of Israel *discerned* him
Neh. 6:12. *And*, lo, *I perceived* that God had not sent him;
Job 4:16. *I could* not *discern* the form thereof:
7:10. neither *shall* his place *know him*
24:17. (one) *know* (them, they are in) the terrors
34:25. *he knoweth* their works,
Ps.103:16. the place thereof *shall know it* no more.
Isa. 61: 9. all that see them *shall acknowledge them*,
63:16. Israel *acknowledge us* not:
Jer. 24: 5. so *will I acknowledge* them
Dan 11:39. a strange god, whom *he shall acknowledge*'

HIPHIL.—*Participle.*

Ru. 2:19. he *that did take knowledge of thee*.
Ezr. 3:13. the people *could* not *discern*
Neh13:24. *could* not speak (lit. *discerned* not to speak) in the Jews' language,
Ps.142: 4(5). (there was) no man *that would know me*.

* HITHPAEL.—*Future.* *

Gen42: 7. *but made himself strange* unto them,
Pro.20:11. Even a child *is known* by his doings,

HITHPAEL.—*Participle.*

1K. 14: 5. *shall feign herself* (to be) *another* (woman).
6. why *feignest* thou *thyself* (to be) *another?*

נֵכָר *nĕh-chāhr'*, m. 5236

Gen17:12. bought with money of any *stranger*, (lit. son of *a stranger*)
27. bought with money of the *stranger*, (lit. *id.*)
35: 2. Put away the *strange* gods
4. all the *strange* gods
Ex. 12:43. There shall no *stranger* (lit. son of *a stranger*) eat
Lev.22:25. Neither from *a stranger*'s (lit. *id.*) hand shall ye offer
Deu31:16. the gods of *the strangers*
32:12. (there was) no *strange* god with him.
Jos. 24:20. forsake the Lord, and serve *strange* gods,
23. put away,...the *strange* gods
Jud.10:16. they put away the *strange* gods (marg. gods of *strangers*)
1Sa. 7: 3. put away the *strange* gods
2Sa.22:45. *Strangers* (marg. Sons of *the stranger*) shall submit themselves
46. *Strangers* (lit. *id.*) shall fade away,
2Ch 14: 3(2). the altars of *the strange* (gods),
33:15. he took away the *strange* gods,
Neh. 9: 2. separated themselves from all *strangers*, (lit. sons of *the stranger*: marg. *strange* children)
13:30. cleansed I them from all *strangers*,
Ps. 18:44(45). the *strangers* (marg. sons of *the stranger*) shall submit themselves
45(46). The *strangers* (lit. sons of *the stranger*) shall fade away,
81: 9(10). shalt thou worship any *strange* god.
137: 4. the Lord's song in a *strange* land?
144: 7, 11. from the hand of *strange* children;
Isa. 56: 3. Neither let the son of *the stranger*,...speak,
6. the sons of *the stranger*, that join
60:10. the sons of *strangers* shall build
61: 5. and the sons of *the alien* (shall be) your
62: 8. the sons of *the stranger* shall not drink
Jer. 5:19. and served *strange* gods in your land,
8:19. provoked me...with *strange* vanities?
Eze.44: 7. brought (into my sanctuary) *strangers*, (marg. children of *a stranger*)
9. No *stranger*, (lit. son of *a stranger*)...shall enter into my sanctuary, of any *stranger* (lit. *id.*) that (is) among

Dan 11:39. the most strong holds with a *strange* god,
Mal. 2:11. married the daughter of a *strange* god.

5235 **נֵכֶר** *neh'-cher*, m.

Job 31: 3. *a strange* (punishment) to the workers of iniquity ?

5235 **נֹכֶר** [*nōh'-cher*], m.

Obad. 12. in the day *that he became a stranger;*

5237 **נָכְרִי** *noch-ree'*, adj.

Gen31:15. Are we not counted of him *strangers?*
Ex. 2:22. I have been a stranger in a *strange* land.
18: 3. I have been an alien in a *strange* land:
21: 8. to sell her unto a *strange* nation
Deu14:21. thou mayest sell it *unto an alien:*
15: 3. Of *a foreigner* thou mayest exact
17:15. thou mayest not set a *stranger* (lit. a *strange* man) over thee,
23:20(21). *Unto a stranger* thou mayest lend
29:22(21). *and the stranger* that shall come
Jud.19:12. into the city of *a stranger,*
Ru. 2:10. seeing I (am) *a stranger?*
2Sa.15:19. thou (art) *a stranger,*
1K. 8:41. concerning *a stranger,*
43. all that *the stranger* calleth to thee
11: 1. king Solomon loved many *strange* women,
8. all his *strange* wives,
2Ch 6:32. Moreover concerning *the stranger,*
33. all that *the stranger* calleth to thee for ;
Ezr.10: 2. have taken *strange* wives
10. have taken *strange* wives,
11. from the *strange* wives.
14. which have taken *strange* wives
17. the men that had taken *strange* wives
18. found that had taken *strange* wives:
44. All these had taken *strange* wives:
Neh 13:26. him did *outlandish* women cause to sin.
27. to transgress against our God in marrying *strange* wives ?
Job 19:15. I am *an alien* in their sight.
Ps. 69: 8(9). *an alien* unto my mother's children.
Pro. 2:16. *from the stranger* (which) flattereth
5:10. labours (be) in the house of *a stranger;*
20. embrace the bosom of *a stranger?*
6:24. the tongue of *a strange woman.*
7: 5. *from the stranger* (which) flattereth
20:16. take a pledge of him for *a strange woman.*
23:27. *a strange woman* (is) a narrow pit.
27: 2. *a stranger,* and not thine own lips.
13. take a pledge of him for *a strange woman.*
Ecc. 6: 2. a *stranger* (lit. a *strange* man) eateth it:
Isa. 2: 6. the children of *strangers.*
28:21. bring to pass his act, his *strange* act.
Jer. 2:21. degenerate plant of a *strange* vine
Lam.5: 2. our houses *to aliens.*
Obad. 11. *and foreigners* entered into his gates,
Zep. 1: 8. such as are clothed with *strange* apparel.

5238 **נְכֹת** *n'chōhth*, m.

2K. 20:13. the house of *his precious things,* (marg. or, *spicery*)
Isa. 39: 2. the house of *his precious things,* (marg. or, *spicery*)

5239 **נָלָה** [*nāh-lāh'*].

* HIPHIL.—*Infinitive.* *

Isa. 33: 1. *when thou shalt make an end* to deal

5240 **נְמִבְזָה** *n'miv-zāh'*, adj. f.

1Sa.15: 9. (that was) *vile* and refuse, that they destroyed utterly.

נָמַל [*nāh-mal'*]. 5243

* KAL.—*Preterite.* *

Gen17:11. *And ye shall circumcise* the flesh of your foreskin ;

KAL.—*Future.*

Job 14: 2. He cometh forth like a flower, *and is cut down:*
18:16. above *shall his branch be cut off.*
24:24. *cut off* as the tops of the ears of corn.
Ps. 37: 2. *they shall* soon *be cut down*

נְמָלָה *n'māh-lāh'*, f. 5244

Pro. 6: 6. Go to *the ant,* thou sluggard ;
30:25. *The ants* (are) a people not strong,

נָמֵר *nāh-mēhr'*, m. 5246

Cant.4: 8. the mountains of *the leopards.*
Isa. 11: 6. *and the leopard* shall lie down with the kid;
Jer. 5: 6. *a leopard* shall watch over their cities:
13:23. change his skin, *or the leopard* his spots?
Hos 13: 7. *as a leopard* by the way
Hab. 1: 8. horses also are swifter *than the leopards,*

נְמַר *n'mar*, Ch. m. 5245

Dan. 7: 6. and lo another, *like a leopard,*

נֵס *nēhs*, m. 5251

Ex. 17:15. called the name of it Jehovah-*nissi:* (marg. i. e. The Lord *my banner*)
Nu. 21: 8. a fiery serpent, and set it upon *a pole:*
9. a serpent of brass, and put it upon *a pole,*
26:10. and they became *a sign.*
Ps. 60: 4(6). Thou hast given *a banner*
Isa. 5:26. he will lift up *an ensign*
11:10. shall stand for *an ensign of* the people ;
12. he shall set up *an ensign*
13: 2. Lift ye up *a banner*
18: 3. when he lifteth up *an ensign*
30:17. *and as an ensign* on an hill.
31: 9. his princes shall be afraid *of the ensign.*
33:23. they could not spread *the sail:*
49:22. and set up *my standard* to the people:
62:10. lift up *a standard* for the people.
Jer. 4: 6. Set up *the standard* toward Zion:
21. How long shall I see *the standard,*
50: 2. publish, and set up *a standard;*
51:12. Set up *the standard* upon the walls
27. Set ye up *a standard* in the land,
Eze.27: 7. spreadest forth to be thy *sail;*

נְסִבָּה *n'sib-bāh'*, f. 5252

2Ch 10:15. for *the cause* was of God,

נָסַג [*nāh-sag'*]. 5253

* KAL.—*Infinitive.* *

Isa. 59:13. *departing away* from our God,

KAL.—*Future.*

Mic. 2: 6. *they shall* not *take* shame.

* HIPHIL.—*Future.* *

Deu19:14. *Thou shalt* not *remove* thy neighbour's landmark,
Pro.22:28. *Remove* not the ancient landmark,
23:10. *Remove* not the old landmark ;
Mic. 6:14. *and thou shalt take hold,* but shalt not

HIPHIL.—*Participle.*

Deu27:17. *he that removeth* his neighbour's landmark.
Hos. 5:10. *like them that remove* the bound;

* HOPHAL.—*Preterite.* *

Isa. 59:14. *And* judgment *is turned away*

5254 נָסָה [*nāh-sāh'*].

* PIEL.—*Preterite.* *

Gen22: 1. God *did tempt* Abraham,
Ex. 15:25. and there *he proved them,*
Deu 4:34. Or *hath* God *assayed* to go
6:16. *ye tempted* (him) in Massah.
28:56. *would* not *adventure* to set the sole of her
33: 8. whom *thou didst prove* at Massah,
1Sa.17:39. *he had* not *proved* (it).
— *I have* not *proved* (them).
Job 4: 2. (If) *we assay* to commune with thee,
Ps. 95: 9. When your fathers *tempted me,*
Ecc. 7:23. All this *have I proved*

PIEL.—*Infinitive.*

Ex. 17: 7. because *they tempted* the Lord,
20:20. God is come *to prove* you,
Deu 8: 2. to humble thee, (and) *to prove thee,*
16. that *he might prove thee,*
Jud. 2:22. That through them *I may prove*
3: 1. *to prove* Israel by them,
4. they were *to prove* Israel
1K. 10: 1. she came *to prove him*
2Ch 9: 1. she came to *prove* Solomon
32:31. God left him, *to try him,*

PIEL.—*Imperative.*

Ps. 26: 2. Examine me, O Lord, *and prove me;*
Dan. 1:12. *Prove* thy servants, I beseech thee,

PIEL.—*Future.*

Ex. 16: 4. that *I may prove them,*
17: 2. wherefore *do ye tempt* the Lord?
Nu. 14:22. *have tempted* me *now*
Deu 6:16. *Ye shall* not *tempt* the Lord
Jud. 6:39. *let me prove,* I pray thee,
Ps. 78:18. *And they tempted* God
41. they turned back *and tempted* God,
56. *Yet they tempted* and provoked the most high God,
106:14. *and tempted* God in the desert.
Ecc. 2: 1. *I will prove thee* with mirth,
Isa. 7:12. neither *will I tempt* the Lord.
Dan 1:14. *and proved them* ten days.

PIEL.—*Participle.*

Deu13: 3(4). the Lord your God *proveth* you,

5254 נָסָה (Ps. 4:6(7).) see נָשָׂא

5255 נָסַח [*nāh-sagh'*].

* KAL.—*Future.* *

Ps. 52: 5(7). he shall take thee away, and *pluck thee*
Pro. 2:22. the transgressors *shall be rooted* out of it. (marg. or, *plucked up*)
15:25. Lord *will destroy* the house of the proud:

* NIPHAL.—*Preterite.* *

Deu28:63. *and ye shall be plucked* from off the land

5256 נְסַח [*n'sagh*], Ch.

* ITHP'AL.—*Future.* *

Ezr. 6:11. *let* timber *be pulled down* from

5257 נָסִיךְ [*nāh-seech'*], m.

Deu32:38. the wine of *their drink offerings?*
Jos. 13:21. *dukes of* Sihon, dwelling in the country.
Ps. 83:11(12). all *their princes* as Zebah, and as
Eze.32:30. There (be) *the princes of* the north,
Dan11: 8. with *their princes,* (and) with their precious vessels
Mic. 5: 5(4). eight *principal* (marg. *princes of*) men.

5258 נָסַךְ *nāh-sach'*.

* KAL.—*Preterite.* *

Ps. 2: 6. Yet *have I set* (marg. *anointed*) my king upon my holy hill
Isa. 29:10. Lord *hath poured out* upon you the spirit
40:19. The workman *melteth* a graven image,
44:10. Who hath formed a god, or *molten* a graven image

KAL.—*Infinitive.*

Isa. 30: 1. Woe to the rebellious children,...*that cover*

KAL.—*Future.*

Ex. 30: 9. neither *shall ye pour* drink offering
Hos. 9: 4. *They shall* not *offer* wine (offerings)

* NIPHAL.—*Preterite.* *

Pro. 8:23. *I was set up* from everlasting,

* PIEL.—*Future.* *

1Ch 11:18. *but poured* it *out* to the Lord,

* HIPHIL.—*Preterite.* *

Jer. 32:29. *and poured out* drink offerings

HIPHIL.—*Infinitive.*

Jer. 7:18. *to pour out* drink offerings
19:13. *and have poured out* drink offerings
44:17, 18. *to pour out* drink offerings
19. *and poured out* drink offerings
— *and pour out* drink offerings unto her,
25. *and to pour out* drink offerings

HIPHIL.—*Imperative.*

Nu. 28: 7. *shalt thou cause* the strong wine *to be poured*

HIPHIL.—*Future.*

Gen35:14. *and he poured* a drink offering thereon,
2Sa.23:16. *but poured* it *out* unto the Lord.
2K. 16:13. *and poured* his drink offering,
Ps. 16: 4. drink offerings of blood *will I* not *offer,*
Eze.20:28. *and poured out* there their drink offerings.

* HOPHAL.—*Future.* *

Ex. 25:29. *to cover* withal: (marg. or, *to pour out* withal)
37:16. his covers *to cover withal,* (marg. *id.*)

נָסַךְ [*nāh-sach'*]. 5259

* KAL.—*Participle.* Paül. *

Isa. 25: 7. the vail *that is spread* over all nations.

נְסַךְ [*n'sach*], Ch. 5260

* PAEL.—*Infinitive.* *

Dan. 2:46. *that they should offer* an oblation and

נֶסֶךְ *neh'-sech* & נֵסֶךְ *neh'-sech,* m. 5262

Gen35:14. he poured *a drink offering* thereon,
Ex. 29:40. *and* the fourth part of an hin of wine (for) *a drink offering.*
41. *and according to the drink offering thereof,*
30: 9. *neither* shall ye pour *drink offering* thereon.
Lev.23:13. *and the drink offering thereof*
18. *and their drink offerings,* (even) an offering
37. a sacrifice, *and drink offerings,*
Nu. 4: 7. and the bowls, and covers *to cover withal:* (marg. or, *pour out*)
6:15. *and their drink offerings.*
17. and *his drink offering.*
15: 5, 7, 10. *for a drink offering*
24. *and his drink offering,*
28: 7, 9. *And the drink offering thereof*
— the strong wine...(for) *a drink offering.*
8. *and as the drink offering thereof,*
10. *and his drink offering.*
14, 31. *And their drink offerings*
15, 24. *and his drink offering.*
29: 6, 11, 18, 19, 21, 24, 27, 30, 33, 37. *and their drink offerings,*
16, 22, 25, 28, 34, 38. *and his drink offering.*
31. his meat offering, *and his drink offering.*
39. *and for your drink offerings,*
2K. 16:13. and poured *his drink offering,*
15. *and their drink offerings;*
1Ch 29:21. thousand lambs, *with their drink offerings,*
2Ch 29:35. *and the drink offerings* for (every) burnt offering.
Ps. 16: 4. *their drink offerings* of blood will I not
Isa. 41:29. *their molten images* (are) wind and
48: 5. *and my molten image,* hath commanded
57: 6. hast thou poured *a drink offering,*
Jer. 7:18. *drink offerings* unto other gods,

Jer. 10:14. *his molten image* (is) falsehood,
19:13 & 32:29. *drink offerings* unto other gods.
44:17, 18. to pour out *drink offerings* unto her,
19. and poured out *drink offerings* unto her,
— and pour out *drink offerings* unto her,
25. to pour out *drink offerings* unto her:
51:17. *his molten image* (is) falsehood,
Eze. 20:28. and poured out there *their drink offerings.*
45:17. meat offerings, *and drink offerings,*
Joel 1: 9. *the drink offering* is cut off
13. *and the drink offering* is withholden
2:14. *a drink offering* unto the Lord

5261 ## נְסַךְ [*n'sach*], Ch. m.

Ezr. 7:17. *and their drink offerings,* and offer

5263 ## נָסַס [*nāh-sas'*].

* KAL.—*Participle.* Poel. *

Isa. 10:18. as when *a standardbearer* fainteth.

5264 ## נָסַס [*nāh-sas'*].

* HITHPOEL.—*Participle.* *

Zec. 9:16. *lifted up as an ensign* upon his land.

5265 ## נָסַע *nāh-sag'*.

* KAL.—*Preterite.* *

Gen33:17. Jacob *journeyed* to Succoth,
37:17. *They are departed* hence;
Nu. 2:17. *Then* the tabernacle of the congregation *shall set forward*
34. so *they set forward,*
9:21. cloud was taken up...*then they journeyed:*
— that the cloud was taken up, *they journeyed.*
10: 5. *then* the camps...*shall go forward.*
6. *then* the camps...*shall take their journey:*
17. *and* the sons of Gershon...*set forward,*
18. *And* the standard of the camp of Reuben *set forward*
21. *And* the Kohathites *set forward,*
22. *And* the standard of the camp of the children of Ephraim *set forward*
25. *And* the standard of the camp of the children of Dan *set forward,*
11:31. there *went forth* a wind from the Lord,
35. people *journeyed* from Kibroth-hattaavah
12:15. the people *journeyed* not till Miriam was brought in
16. afterward the people *removed*
21:12, 13. From thence *they removed,*
Deu10: 6. the children of Israel *took their journey*
7. From thence *they journeyed*
2K. 19: 8. *he was departed* from Lachish.
Isa. 37: 8. *he was departed* from Lachish.
Jer. 4: 7. the destroyer of the Gentiles *is on his way;*
31:24. *and they* (that) *go forth* with flocks.
Zec.10: 2. *they went their way* as a flock,

KAL.—*Infinitive.*

Gen11: 2. And it came to pass, *as they journeyed*
12: 9. And Abram journeyed, going *on still* (marg. in going *and journeying*) toward the south.
Nu. 1:51. *And when* the tabernacle *setteth forward,*
4: 5. *And when* the camp *setteth forward,*
15. *as* the camp *is to set forward;*
10:34. *when they went out* of the camp.
35. *when* the ark *set forward,*
Jos. 3:14. *when* the people *removed* from their tents,

KAL.—*Imperative.*

Nu. 14:25. *and get you* into the wilderness
Deu 1: 7. Turn you, *and take your journey,*
40. turn you, *and take your journey*
2:24. Rise ye up, *take your journey,*

KAL.—*Future.*

Gen12: 9. *And* Abram *journeyed,*
13:11. *and* Lot *journeyed* east:
20: 1. *And* Abraham *journeyed* from thence
33:12. *Let us take our journey,* and let us go,
35: 5. *And they journeyed:* and the terror of God
Gen35:16. *And they journeyed* from Beth-el;
21. *And* Israel *journeyed,* and spread
46: 1. *And* Israel *took his journey*
Ex. 12:37. *And* the children of Israel *journeyed* from Rameses
13:20. *And they took their journey* from Succoth,
14:15. children of Israel, *that they go forward:*
19. *And* the angel of God,...*removed*
— *and* the pillar of the cloud *went* from before
16: 1. *And they took their journey* from Elim,
17: 1. *And* all the congregation of the children of Israel *journeyed*
19: 2. *For they were departed* from Rephidim,
40:36. the children of Israel *went onward* (marg. *journeyed*) in all their journeys:
37. *they journeyed* not till the day that
Nu. 2: 9. *These shall* first *set forth.*
16. *they shall set forth* in the second rank.
17. so *shall they set forward,*
24. *they shall go forward* in the third rank.
31. *They shall go* hindmost
9:17. after that the children of Israel *journeyed:*
18. of the Lord the children of Israel *journeyed,*
19. the charge of the Lord, and *journeyed* not.
20. according to the commandment...*they journeyed.*
22. the children of Israel...*journeyed* not: but when it was taken up, *they journeyed.*
23. at the commandment of the Lord *they journeyed:*
10:12. *And* the children of Israel *took* their journeys
13. *And* they first *took their journey*
14. In (lit. *And* in) the first (place) *went* the standard of
28. their armies, *when they set forward.*
33. *And they departed* from the mount of the
20:22. *And* the children of Israel,...*journeyed* from Kadesh,
21: 4. *And they journeyed* from mount Hor
10. *And* the children of Israel *set forward,*
11. *And they journeyed* from Oboth, and
22: 1. *And* the children of Israel *set forward,*
33: 3. *And they departed* from Rameses in the
5. *And* the children of Israel *removed* from
6. *And they departed* from Succoth,
7. *And they removed* from Etham,
8. *And they departed* from before Pi-hahiroth,
9. *And they removed* from Marah,
10. *And they removed* from Elim,
11. *And they removed* from the Red sea,
12. *And they took their journey* out of the wilderness of Sin,
13. *And they departed* from Dophkah,
14. *And they removed* from Alush,
15. *And they departed* from Rephidim,
16. *And they removed* from the desert of Sinai,
17. *And they departed* from Kibroth-hattaavah,
18. *And they departed* from Hazeroth,
19. *And they departed* from Rithmah,
20. *And they departed* from Rimmon-parez,
21. *And they removed* from Libnah,
22. *And they journeyed* from Rissah,
23. *And they went* from Kehelathah,
24. *And they removed* from mount Shapher,
25. *And they removed* from Haradah,
26. *And they removed* from Makheloth,
27. *And they departed* from Tahath,
28. *And they removed* from Tarah,
29. *And they went* from Mithcah,
30. *And they departed* from Hashmonah,
31. *And they departed* from Moseroth,
32. *And they removed* from Benejaakan,
33. *And they went* from Hor-hagidgad,
34. *And they removed* from Jotbathah,
35. *And they departed* from Ebronah,
36. *And they removed* from Ezion-gaber,
37. *And they removed* from Kadesh,
41. *And they departed* from mount Hor,
42. *And they departed* from Zalmonah,
43. *And they departed* from Punon,
44. *And they departed* from Oboth,
45. *And they departed* from Iim,
46. *And they removed* from Dibongad,
47. *And they removed* from Almondiblathaim,
48. *And they departed* from the mountains of
Deu 1:19. *when we departed* from Horeb,
2: 1. Then we turned, *and took our journey*

Jos. 3: 1. *and they removed* from Shittim,
3. *ye shall remove* from your place,
9:17. *And* the children of Israel *journeyed,*
Jud.16: 3. the two posts, *and went away with them,*
14. *and went away* with the pin of the beam,
18:11. *And there went* from thence of the family
2K. 3:27. *and they departed* from him, and returned
19:36. *So* Sennacherib king of Assyria *departed,*
Ezr. 8:31. *Then we departed* from the river
Isa. 33:20. not one of the stakes thereof *shall* ever *be removed,*
37:37. *So* Sennacherib king of Assyria *departed,*

KAL.—*Participle.* Poel.

Ex. 14:10. the Egyptians *marched* after them;
Nu. 10:29. We *are journeying* unto the place of
33. the ark of the covenant...*went* before them

* NIPHAL.—*Preterite.* *

Job 4:21. *Doth* not their excellency...*go away?*
Isa. 38:12. Mine age *is departed,* and is removed

* HIPHIL.—*Future.* *

Ex. 15:22. *So* Moses *brought* Israel from the Red sea,
1K. 5:17(31). *and they brought* great stones,
2K. 4: 4. *thou shalt set aside* that which is full.
Job 19:10. *and* mine hope *hath he removed*
Ps. 78:26. *He caused* an east wind *to blow* (marg. *go*)
52. *But made* his own people *to go forth*
80: 8(9). *Thou hast brought* a vine out of Egypt.

HIPHIL.—*Participle.*

Ecc.10: 9. *Whoso removeth* stones shall be hurt

5266 **נָסַק** [*nāh-sak'*].

* KAL.—*Future.* *

Ps.139: 8. If *I ascend up* into heaven,

5267 **נְסַק** [*n'sak*], Ch.

* APHEL.—*Preterite* *

Dan. 3:22. the fire slew those men that *took up*

APHEL.—*Infinitive.*

Dan. 6:23(24). *that they should take* Daniel *up*

* HOPHAL.—*Preterite.* *

Dan. 6:23(24). *So* Daniel *was taken up*

5271 **נְעוּרוֹת** [*n'goo-rōhth'*], f. pl.

Jer. 32:30. done evil before me *from their youth:*

5271 **נְעוּרִים** *n'goo-reem'*, m. pl.

Gen 8:21. the imagination of man's heart (is) evil *from his youth;*
46:34. *from our youth* even until now,
Lev.22:13. her father's house, *as in her youth,*
Nu. 30: 3(4). (being) in her father's house *in her youth;*
16(17). (being yet) *in her youth*
1Sa.12: 2. *from my childhood* unto this day.
17:33. a man of war *from his youth.*
2Sa.19: 7(8). *from thy youth* until now.
1K. 18:12. I thy servant fear the Lord *from my youth.*
Job 13:26. the iniquities of *my youth.*
31:18. *from my youth* he was brought up
Ps. 25: 7. Remember not the sins of *my youth,*
71: 5. (thou art) my trust *from my youth.*
17. thou hast taught me *from my youth:*
103: 5. *thy youth* is renewed like the eagle's.
127: 4. children of *the youth.*
129: 1, 2. they afflicted me *from my youth,*
144:12. as plants grown up *in their youth;*
Pro. 2:17. forsaketh the guide of *her youth,*
5:18. rejoice with the wife of *thy youth.*
Isa. 47:12. thou hast laboured *from thy youth;*
15. thy merchants, *from thy youth:*
54: 6. a wife of *youth,*
Jer. 2: 2. the kindness of *thy youth,*
3: 4. the guide of *my youth?*
24. the labour of our fathers *from our youth;*
25. *from our youth* even unto this day,
22:21. thy manner *from thy youth,*
31:19. I did bear the reproach of *my youth.*
48:11. Moab hath been at ease *from his youth,*
Lam.3:27. that he bear the yoke *in his youth.*
Eze. 4:14. *from my youth* up even till now
16:22, 43. not remembered the days of *thy youth,*
60. in the days of *thy youth,*
23: 3. committed whoredoms *in their youth:*
8. *in her youth* they lay with her,
19. the days of *her youth,*
21. the lewdness of *thy youth,*
— by the Egyptians for the paps of *thy youth.*
Hos. 2:15(17). in the days of *her youth,*
Joel 1: 8. the husband of *her youth.*
Zec.13: 5. taught me to keep cattle *from my youth.*
Mal. 2:14. between thee and the wife *of thy youth,*
15. let none deal treacherously against the wife of *his youth.*

נָעִים *nāh-geem'*, adj. 5273

2Sa. 1:23. lovely *and pleasant* (marg. or, *sweet*) in their lives,
23: 1. *and* the *sweet* psalmist of Israel,
Job 36:11. they shall spend...their years *in pleasures.*
Ps. 16: 6. The lines are fallen unto me *in pleasant* (places);
11. at thy right hand (there are) *pleasures*
81: 2(3). the *pleasant* harp with the psaltery.
133: 1. how *pleasant* (it is) for brethren to dwell ...in unity!
135: 3. sing praises unto his name; for (it is) *pleasant.*
147: 1. to sing praises unto our God; for (it is) *pleasant;*
Pro.22:18. *a pleasant thing* if thou keep them
23: 8. lose thy *sweet* words.
24: 4. all precious *and pleasant* riches.
Cant.1:16. thou (art) fair, my beloved, yea, *pleasant:*

נָעַל *nāh-gal'*. 5274

* KAL.—*Preterite.* *

Jud. 3:23. shut the doors of the parlour...*and locked*
2Sa.13:18. *and bolted* the door after her.

KAL.—*Imperative.*

2Sa.13:17. Put now this (woman) out from me, *and bolt* the door

KAL.—*Future.*

Eze.16:10. *and shod thee* with badgers' skin,

KAL.—*Participle.* Paül.

Jud. 3:24. the doors of the parlour (were) *locked,*
Cant.4:12. A garden *inclosed* (marg. *barred*) (is) my sister, (my) spouse; a spring *shut up,* a fountain sealed.

* HIPHIL.—*Future.* *

2Ch 28:15. arrayed them, *and shod them,*

נַעַל *nah'-gal*, f. 5275

Gen14:23. from a thread even to a *shoe*latchet,
Ex. 3: 5. put off *thy shoes* from off thy feet,
12:11. *your shoes* on your feet,
Deu25: 9. loose *his shoe* from off his foot,
10. The house of him that hath *his shoe* loosed.
29: 5(4). *and thy shoe* is not waxen old
Jos. 5:15. Loose *thy shoe* from off thy foot;
9: 5. old *shoes* and clouted upon their feet,
13. *and our shoes* are become old
Ru. 4: 7. a man plucked off *his shoe,*
8. So he drew off *his shoe.*
1K. 2: 5. *and in his shoes* that (were) on his feet.
Ps. 60: 8(10). over Edom will I cast out *my shoe:*
108: 9(10). over Edom will I cast out *my shoe;*
Cant.7: 1(2). How beautiful are thy feet *with shoes,*
Isa. 5:27. nor the latchet of *their shoes* be broken:
11:15. make (men) go over *dryshod.* (marg. *in shoes*)
20: 2. put off *thy shoe* from thy foot.
Eze.24:17. *and* put on *thy shoes* upon thy feet,
23. *and your shoes* upon your feet:
Am. 2: 6. sold...the poor for *a pair of shoes;*
8: 6. buy...the needy for *a pair of shoes;*

5276 **נָעֵם** [*nāh-ğehm'*].

* KAL.—*Preterite.* *

Gen49:15. saw...the land that *it was pleasant;*
2Sa. 1:26. very *pleasant hast thou been* unto me:
Ps.141: 6. hear my words; for *they are sweet.*
Cant.7: 6(7). How fair and how *pleasant art thou,*
Eze.32:19. Whom *dost thou pass in beauty?*

KAL.—*Future.*

Pro. 2:10. knowledge *is pleasant* unto thy soul;
9:17. bread (eaten) in secret *is pleasant.*
24:25. to them that rebuke (him) *shall be delight,*

5278 **נֹעַם** *nōh'-ğam,* m.

Ps. 27: 4. to behold *the beauty* (marg. or, *the delight*) *of* the Lord,
90:17. let *the beauty of* the Lord
Pro. 3:17. Her ways (are) ways of *pleasantness,*
15:26. (the words) of the pure (are) *pleasant*
16:24. *Pleasant* words (are as) an honeycomb,
Zec.11: 7. the one I called *Beauty,*
10. I took my staff, (even) *Beauty,*

5282 **נַעֲמָנִים** *nah-ğămāh-neem',* m. pl.

Isa. 17:10. therefore shalt thou plant *pleasant* plants,

5285 **נַעֲצוּץ** *nah-ğătzootz',* m.

Isa. 7:19. upon all *thorns,* and upon all bushes.
55:13. of *the thorn* shall come up the fir tree,

5286-87 **נָעַר** [*nāh-ğar'*].

* KAL.—*Preterite.* *

Neh. 5:13. Also *I shook* my lap, and said,
Jer. 51:38. *they shall yell* (marg. or, *shake themselves*) as lions' whelps.

KAL.—*Participle.* Poel.

Isa. 33: 9. Bashan and Carmel *shake off* (their fruits).
15. *that shaketh* his hands from holding of

KAL.—*Participle.* Paül.

Neh. 5:13. even thus be he *shaken out,*

* NIPHAL.—*Preterite.* *

Ps.109:23. *I am tossed up and down* as the locust.

NIPHAL.—*Future.*

Jud.16:20. I will go out...*and shake myself.*
Job 38:13. *that* the wicked *might be shaken*

* PIEL.—*Preterite.* *

Ps.136:15. *But overthrew* (marg. *shaked off*) Pharaoh and his host

PIEL.—*Future.*

Ex. 14:27. *and* the Lord *overthrew* (marg. *shook off*) the Egyptians
Neh. 5:13. So God *shake* out every man

* HITHPAEL.—*Imperative.* *

Isa. 52: 2. *Shake thyself* from the dust;

5288-89 **נַעַר** *nah'-ğar,* m.

Gen14:24. that which *the young men* have eaten,
18: 7. gave (it) unto *a young man;*
19: 4. compassed the house round, *both* old and *young,* (lit. *from the youth* and to the old man)
21:12. Let it not be grievous...because of *the lad,*
17. God heard the voice of *the lad;*
— God hath heard the voice of *the lad*
18. Arise, lift up *the lad,*
19. gave *the lad* drink.
20. God was with *the lad;*
22: 3. took two of *his young men*
5. Abraham said unto *his young men,*
— I *and the lad* will go yonder and worship,
12. Lay not thine hand upon *the lad,*
19. Abraham returned unto *his young men,*
25:27. And *the boys* grew:
34:19. *the young man* deferred not to do the thing,
37: 2. *the lad* (was) with the sons of Bilhah,
41:12. (there was) there with us *a young man,*
43: 8. Send *the lad* with me,
44:22. *The lad* cannot leave his father:
30. *and the lad* (be) not with us;
31. he seeth that *the lad* (is) not (with us),
32. thy servant became surety for *the lad*
33. let thy servant abide instead of *the lad*
— *and* let *the lad* go up with his brethren.
34. *and the lad* (be) not with me?
48:16. The Angel which redeemed me...bless *the lads;*
Ex. 2: 6. behold, *the babe* wept.
10: 9. will go *with our young* and with our old,
24: 5. *young men of* the children of Israel,
33:11. Joshua, the son of Nun, *a young man,*
Nu. 11:27. there ran *a young man,* and told Moses,
22:22. *his* two *servants* (were) with him.
Deu28:50. *nor* shew favour to *the young:*
Jos. 6:21. both man and woman, *young* and old, (lit. *from the youth* and to the old man)
23. *the young men* that were spies
Jud. 7:10. go thou with Phurah *thy servant*
11. went he down with Phurah *his servant*
8:14. *a young man* of the men of Succoth,
20. *the youth* drew not his sword: for he feared, because he (was) yet *a youth.*
9:54. *the young man* his armourbearer,
— *his young man* thrust him through,
13: 5, 7. *the child* shall be a Nazarite
8. *unto the child* that shall be born.
12. How shall we order *the child,*
24. and *the child* grew,
16:26. Samson said unto *the lad*
17: 7. *a young man* out of Beth-lehem-judah
11. *the young man* was unto him as one of his sons.
12. *the young man* became his priest,
18: 3. they knew the voice of *the young man*
15. came to the house of *the young man*
19: 3. *having his servant* with him,
9. he, and his concubine, *and his servant,*
11. *the servant* said unto his master,
13. he said *unto his servant,*
19. *and for the young man* (which is) with thy servants:
Ru. 2: 5. Then said Boaz *unto his servant*
6. And *the servant* that was set
9. have I not charged *the young men*
— (that) which *the young men* have drawn.
15. Boaz commanded *his young men,*
21. keep fast by *my young men,*
1Sa. 1:22. (I will not go up) until *the child* be weaned,
24. *and the child* (was) *young.* (lit. *and the child* (was) *a child*)
25. brought *the child* to Eli.
27. For this *child* I prayed;
2:11. *And the child* did minister unto the Lord
13, 15. the priest's *servant* came,
17. the sin of *the young men* was very great
18. ministered before the Lord, (being) *a child,*
21. *the child* Samuel grew before the Lord.
26. *And the child* Samuel grew on,
3: 1. *And the child* Samuel ministered unto the Lord
8. the Lord had called *the child.*
4:21. she named *the child* I-chabod,
9: 3. Take now one *of the servants*
5. Saul said *to his servant*
7, 10. Then said Saul *to his servant,*
8. *the servant* answered Saul
22. Samuel took Saul *and his servant,*
27. Bid *the servant* pass on
10:14. said unto him and to *his servant,*
14: 1. Jonathan...said unto *the young man*
6. Jonathan said to *the young man*
16:11. Are here all (thy) *children?*
18. Then answered one *of the servants,*
17:33. thou (art but) *a youth,*
42. he was (but) *a youth,*
55. whose son (is) *this youth?*
58. Whose son (art) thou, (thou) *young man?*
20:21. I will send *a lad,*
— If I expressly say *unto the lad,*
35. *and a* little *lad* with him.
36. he said *unto his lad,*
— as *the lad* ran, he shot an arrow

1Sa.20:37. when *the lad* was come to the place of
—, 38. Jonathan cried after *the lad*,
38. Jonathan's *lad* gathered up the arrows,
39. *But the lad* knew not any thing:
40. Jonathan gave his artillery unto his *lad*,
41. as soon as *the lad* was gone,
21: 2(3). I have appointed (my) *servants*
4(5). if *the young men* have kept themselves
5(6). the vessels of *the young men* are holy,
25: 5. David sent out ten *young men*, and David said *unto the young men*,
8. Ask *thy young men*, and they will shew thee. Wherefore let *the young men* find
9. when David's *young men* came,
12. David's *young men* turned their way,
14. one of *the young men* (lit. one *young man of the young men*)
19. she said *unto her servants*,
25. I thine handmaid saw not *the young men of*
27. *unto the young men* that follow my lord.
26:22. let one *of the young men* come over
30:13. *a young man of* Egypt,
17. four hundred *young* men, which rode
2Sa. 1: 5, 6, 13. *the young man* that told him,
15. David called one *of the young men*,
2:14. Let *the young men* now arise,
21. lay thee hold on one *of the young men*,
4:12. David commanded *his young men*,
9: 9. the king called to Ziba, Saul's *servant*,
12:16. David therefore besought God for *the child*;
13:17. Then he called *his servant*
28. Absalom had commanded *his servants*,
29. *the servants of* Absalom did
32. slain all *the young men*
34. *the young man* that kept the watch
14:21. bring *the young man* Absalom
16: 1. Ziba *the servant of* Mephibosheth
2. the bread...for *the young men* to eat;
17:18. Nevertheless *a lad* saw them,
18: 5. (Deal) gently for my sake *with the young man*,
12. Beware that none (touch) *the young man*
15. ten *young men* that bare Joab's armour
29. Is *the young man* Absalom safe?
32. (Is) *the young man* Absalom safe?
— The enemies of my lord...be *as* (that) *young man* (is).
19:17(18). Ziba *the servant of* the house of Saul,
20:11. one of Joab's men (lit. a man *of the young men of* Joab) stood by him,
1K. 3: 7. I (am but) *a little child*:
11:17. Hadad (being) yet *a* little *child*.
28. Solomon seeing *the young man*
14: 3. what shall become *of the child*.
17. *and* when she came to the threshold...*the child* died;
18:43. And said to *his servant*,
19: 3. and left *his servant* there.
20:14. *by the young men of* the princes
15. he numbered *the young men of*
17. *the young men of* the princes
19. these *young men of* the princes
2K. 2:23. *and* as he...there came forth little *children*
4:12. he said to Gehazi *his servant*,
19. he said to *a lad*, Carry him to his mother.
22. Send me,...one *of the young men*,
24. said to *her servant*, Drive,
25. he said to Gehazi *his servant*,
29. lay my staff upon the face of *the child*.
30. the mother of *the child* said,
31. laid the staff upon the face of *the child*;
— *The child* is not awaked.
32. *the child* was dead,
35. *the child* sneezed seven times, and *the child* opened his eyes.
38. he said *unto his servant*,
5:14. like unto the flesh of *a* little *child*,
20. Gehazi, *the servant of* Elisha
22. two *young men* of the sons of the prophets:
23. laid (them) upon two of *his servants*;
6:15. And *his servant* said unto him,
17. the Lord opened the eyes of *the young man*;
8: 4. *the servant of* the man of God,
9: 4. *the young man*, (even) *the young man* the prophet,
19: 6. *the servants of* the king of Assyria
1Ch 12:28. Zadok, *a young man* mighty of valour,
1Ch 22: 5. Solomon my son (is) *young* and tender,
29: 1. Solomon my son,...(is yet) *young* and
2Ch 13: 7. Rehoboam was *young* and tenderhearted,
34: 3. while he was yet *young*,
Neh. 4:16(10). the half of *my servants* wrought
22(16). Let every one *with his servant* lodge
23(17). nor my brethren, *nor my servants*,
5:10. my brethren, *and my servants*,
15. even *their servants* bare rule
16. all *my servants* (were) gathered thither
6: 5. Then sent Sanballat *his servant*
13:19. *and* (some) *of my servants* set I at the gates,
Est. 2: 2. Then said the king's *servants*
3:13. *both young* and old, (lit. *from the youth* and to the old man)
6: 3. Then said the king's *servants*
5. And the king's *servants* said
Job 1:15, 17. slain *the servants* with the edge of the sword;
16. burned up the sheep, *and the servants*,
19. it fell upon *the young men*,
24: 5. food for them (and) *for* (their) *children*.
29: 5. *my children* (were) about me;
8. *The young men* saw me, and hid
Ps. 37:25. I have been *young*, and (now) am old;
119: 9. Wherewithal shall *a young man* cleanse his way?
148:12. old men, and *children*:
Pro. 1: 4. *to the young man* knowledge and discretion.
7: 7. *a young man* void of understanding,
20:11. *a child* is known by his doings,
22: 6. Train up *a child* in the way he should go:
15. Foolishness (is) bound in the heart of *a child*;
23:13. Withhold not correction *from the child*:
29:15. *but a child* left (to himself)
Ecc.10:16. Woe to thee, O land, when thy king (is) *a child*,
Isa. 3: 4. And I will give *children*
5. *the child* shall behave himself proudly
7:16. before *the child* shall know to refuse
8: 4. *the child* shall have knowledge to cry,
10:19. few, *that a child* may write them.
11: 6. *and a* little *child* shall lead them.
13:18. (Their) bows also shall dash *the young men* to pieces;
20: 4. *young* and old, naked and barefoot,
37: 6. *the servants of* the king of Assyria
40:30. *the young men* shall utterly fall:
65:20. *the child* shall die an hundred years old;
Jer. 1: 6. I cannot speak: for I (am) *a child*.
7. Say not, I (am) *a child*:
51:22. break in pieces old *and young*;
Lam.2:21. *The young* and the old lie
5:13. *and the children* fell under the wood.
Hos 11: 1. When Israel (was) *a child*,
Zec. 2: 4(8). Run, speak to this *young man*, saying,
11:16. neither shall seek *the young one*, (perhaps lit. *the wandering*)

Note.—In the Pentateuch (with the exception of Deut. 22:19), in every occurrence of נַעֲרָה in the singular, there is found נַעַר (כתיב). The textual reading is of course נַעֲרָ, which must have been at first applied to both genders. For the occurrences of this נַעֲרָ (כתיב), see below under נַעֲרָה.

נֹעַר nōh′-^{n}gar, m. 5290

Job 33:25. His flesh shall be fresher *than a child's*: (marg. *childhood*)
36:14. They die *in youth*,
Ps. 88:15(16). ready to die *from* (my) *youth* up:
Pro.29:21. his servant *from a child*

נַעֲרָה nah-^{n}gărāh′, f. 5291

Gen24:14. *the damsel* to whom I shall say,
16. *And the damsel* (was) very fair
28. And *the damsel* ran, and told
55. Let *the damsel* abide with us

Gen24:57. We will call *the damsel*,
61. Rebekah arose, *and her damsels*,
34: 3. he loved *the damsel*, and spake kindly unto *the damsel*.
12. give me *the damsel* to wife.
Ex. 2: 5. *and her maidens* walked along
Deu22:15. the father of *the damsel*, and her
— bring forth (the tokens of) *the damsel*'s virginity
16. And *the damsel*'s father shall say
19. unto the father of *the damsel*,
20. be not found *for the damsel:*
21. they shall bring out *the damsel*
23. *a damsel* (that is) a virgin
24. *the damsel*, because she cried not,
25. if a man find *a* betrothed *damsel*
26. *But unto the damsel* thou shalt do nothing; (there is) *in the damsel* no sin
27. *the* betrothed *damsel* cried,
28. If a man find *a damsel*
29. shall give unto *the damsel*'s father
Jud.19: 3. the father of *the damsel* saw him,
4. *the damsel*'s father, retained him;
5. *the damsel*'s father said unto his son in law,
6. *the damsel*'s father had said unto the man,
8. and *the damsel*'s father said, Comfort
9. his father in law, *the damsel*'s father,
21:12. four hundred *young* virgins,
Ru. 2: 5. Whose *damsel* (is) this?
6. It (is) *the* Moabitish *damsel*
8. abide here fast by *my maidens:*
22. go out with *his maidens*,
23. she kept fast *by the maidens*
3: 2. with whose (lit. who with *his*) *maidens* thou wast?
4:12. of this *young woman*.
1Sa. 9:11. they found *young maidens* going out
25:42. with five *damsels of her's*
1K. 1: 2. Let there be sought...a *young* virgin:
3. So they sought for *a* fair *damsel*
4. *And the damsel* (was) very fair,
2K. 5: 2. had brought away captive...*a* little *maid;*
4. Thus and thus said *the maid*
Est. 2: 2. Let there be fair *young* virgins sought
3. all the fair *young* virgins
4. *And* let *the maiden* which pleaseth the king
7. *and the maid* (was) fair and beautiful;
8. many *maidens* were gathered together
9. And *the maiden* pleased him,
— belonged to her, and seven *maidens*,
— he preferred her and *her maids*
12. when *every maid*'s turn (lit. the turn of *a maid and a maid*)
13. thus came (every) *maiden*
4: 4. So Esther's *maids*...came
16. I also *and my maidens* will fast
Job 41: 5(40:29). wilt thou bind him *for thy maidens?*
Pro. 9: 3. She hath sent forth *her maidens:*
27:27. the maintenance *for thy maidens*.
31:15. a portion *to her maidens*.
Am. 2: 7. a man and his father will go in unto *the* (same) *maid*, (marg. or, *young woman*)

5296 **נְעֹרֶת** *n'gōh'-reth*, f.

Jud.16: 9. as a thread of *tow* is broken
Isa. 1:31. the strong shall be *as tow*,

5299 **נָפָה** [*nāh-phāh'*], f.

Jos. 11: 2. *and in the borders of* Dor
12:23. *in the coast of* Dor,
1K. 4:11. in all *the region of* Dor;
Isa. 30:28. *with the sieve of* vanity:

5301 **נָפַח** [*nāh-phagh'*].

* KAL.—*Preterite.* *

Jer. 15: 9. *she hath given up* the ghost;
Eze.22:21. I will gather you, *and blow* upon you
Hag. 1: 9. *I did blow* upon it.

KAL.—*Infinitive.*

Eze.22:20. *to blow* the fire upon it,

KAL.—*Imperative.*

Eze.37: 9. *and breathe* upon these slain,

KAL.—*Future.*

Gen 2: 7. *and breathed* into his nostrils the breath of life;

KAL.—*Participle.* Poel.

Isa. 54:16. the smith *that bloweth* the coals

KAL.—*Participle.* Paül.

Job 41:20(12). a *seething* pot or caldron.
Jer. 1:13. I see a *seething* pot;

* PUAL.—*Preterite.* *

Job 20:26. a fire not *blown* shall consume him;

* HIPHIL.—*Preterite.* *

Job 31:39. *have caused* the owners thereof *to lose* their life: (marg. the soul of the owners thereof *to expire*, or, *breathe out*)
Mal. 1:13. *and ye have snuffed* at it,

נְפִילִים *n'phee-leem'*, m. pl. 5303

Gen 6: 4. There were *giants* in the earth
Nu. 13:33. And there we saw *the giants*, the sons of Anak, (which come) of *the giants:*

נֹפֶךְ *nōh'-phech*, m. 5306

Ex. 28:18 & 39:11. *an emerald*, a sapphire, and a diamond.
Eze.27:16. occupied in thy fairs *with emeralds*,
28:13. the sapphire, *the emerald*, (marg. or, *chrysoprase*)

נָפַל *nāh-phal'*. 5307

* KAL.—*Preterite.* *

Gen 4: 6. why *is* thy countenance *fallen?*
15:12. a deep sleep *fell* upon Abram;
25:18. *he died* (marg. *fell*) in the presence of all his brethren.
Ex. 19:21. *and* many of them *perish*.
21:18. he die not, *but keepeth* (his) bed:
33. *and* an ox or an ass *fall* therein;
Lev.11:38. *and* (any part) of their carcase *fall*
26: 7. *and they shall fall* before you
8. *and* your enemies *shall fall* before you
36. *and they shall fall* when none pursueth.
Nu. 5:27. *and* her thigh *shall rot:*
14:43. *and ye shall fall* by the sword:
Jos. 2: 9. your terror *is fallen* upon us,
6: 5. *and* the wall of the city *shall fall down*
21:45(43). *There failed* not ought of any good thing
23:14. not one thing *hath failed* of all
— not one thing *hath failed* thereof.
Jud. 5:27. At her feet he bowed, *he fell*, he lay down: at her feet he bowed, *he fell:* where he bowed, there *he fell down* dead.
7:13. *that* the tent *lay along*.
15:18. *and fall* into the hand of the uncircumcised?
18: 1. (their) inheritance *had* not *fallen* unto
1Sa.26:12. a deep sleep...*was fallen* upon them.
2Sa. 1: 4. many of the people also *are fallen*
12. because *they were fallen* by the sword.
19, 25, 27. how *are* the mighty *fallen!*
2:23. Asahel *fell down* and died
3:34. before wicked men, (so) *fellest thou*.
38. *there is* a prince and a great man *fallen* this
19:18(19). Shimei the son of Gera *fell down*
1K. 8:56. *there hath* not *failed* (marg. *fallen*) one word
2K. 2:13, 14. the mantle of Elijah that *fell* from him,
6: 5. the ax head *fell* into the water:
6. Where *fell it?*
14:10. *that thou shouldest fall*, (even) thou, and Judah
25:11. the fugitives that *fell away*
1Ch 5:22. *there fell down* many slain,
12:19. *there fell* (some) of Manasseh to David,

1Ch 12:20. *there fell* to him of Manasseh,
2Ch 15: 9. *they fell* to him out of Israel
20:18. the inhabitants of Jerusalem *fell*
25:19. *that thou shouldest fall*, (even) thou, and Judah
29: 9. our fathers *have fallen* by the sword,
Est. 8:17. the Jews *fell* upon them.
9: 2. the fear of them *fell* upon all people.
3. the fear of Mordecai *fell* upon them.
Job 1:16. The fire of God *is fallen* from heaven,
Ps. 10:10. *that* the poor *may fall*
16: 6. The lines *are fallen* unto me
20: 8(9). They are brought down *and fallen*:
27: 2. they stumbled *and fell*.
36:12(13). *are* the workers of iniquity *fallen*:
55: 4(5). the terrors of death *are fallen* upon me.
57: 6(7). *they are fallen* (themselves).
69: 9(10). the reproaches...*are fallen* upon me.
78:64. Their priests *fell* by the sword;
105:38. the fear of them *fell* upon them.
Isa. 3: 8. and Judah *is fallen*:
8:15. many among them shall stumble, *and fall*,
9: 8(7). *and it hath lighted* upon Israel.
10(9). The bricks *are fallen down*,
14:12. *How art thou fallen* from heaven,
16: 9. thy harvest *is fallen*.
21: 9. Babylon *is fallen*, *is fallen*;
22:25. be cut down, *and fall*;
24:20. *and it shall fall*, and not rise again.
31: 3. *and* he that is holpen *shall fall down*,
8. *Then shall* the Assyrian *fall*
Jer. 9:22(21). *Even* the carcases of men *shall fall*
20: 4. *and they shall fall* by the sword
21: 9. *and falleth* to the Chaldeans
23:12. they shall be driven on, *and fall* therein:
25:34. *and ye shall fall* like a pleasant vessel.
38:19. the Jews that *are fallen* to the Chaldeans,
39: 9. those that fell away, that *fell* to him,
46: 6. shall stumble, *and fall* toward the north
12. *they are fallen* both together.
16. one *fell* upon another:
48:32. the spoiler *is fallen* upon thy summer fruits
50:15. her foundations *are fallen*,
32. the most proud shall stumble *and fall*,
51: 4. *Thus* the slain *shall fall*
8. Babylon *is* suddenly *fallen*
44. the wall of Babylon *shall fall*.
49. at Babylon *shall fall* the slain
52:15. that *fell* to the king of Babylon,
Lam. 2:21. my young men *are fallen* by the sword;
5:16. The crown *is fallen* (from) our head:
Eze. 6: 7. *And* the slain *shall fall* in the midst of you,
13:12. when the wall *is fallen*,
14. *and it shall fall*, and ye shall
24: 6. *let* no lot *fall* upon it.
27:34. all thy company...*shall fall*.
30: 6. *They also* that uphold Egypt *shall fall*;
31:12. in all the valleys his branches *are fallen*,
38:20. *and* the steep places *shall fall*,
47:14. *and* this land *shall fall* unto you
Dan 10: 7. a great quaking *fell* upon them,
11:19. he shall stumble *and fall*,
26. *and* many *shall fall down* slain.
Hos. 7: 7. all their kings *are fallen*:
Am. 3:14. *and fall* to the ground.
5: 2. The virgin of Israel *is fallen*;
8:14. *even they shall fall*, and never
Mic. 7: 8. when *I fall*, I shall arise;
Nah. 3:12. *they shall even fall* into the mouth
Zec. 11: 2. for the cedar *is fallen*;

KAL.—*Infinitive.*

Nu. 14: 3. *to fall* by the sword,
1Sa. 29: 3. found no fault in him since *he fell*
2Sa. 1:10. after that *he was fallen*:
3:34. *as a man falleth* before wicked men,
17: 9. *when* some of them *be overthrown* (marg. *fallen*)
Est. 6:13. before whom thou hast begun *to fall*,
— shalt *surely* fall (lit. *falling* shalt fall)
Job 4:13. *when* deep sleep *falleth* on men,
33:15. *when* deep sleep *falleth* upon men,
Ps. 118:13. Thou hast thrust sore at me *that I might fall*:
Pro. 24:17. Rejoice not *when* thine enemy *falleth*,
Isa. 30:25. *when* the towers *fall*.
Jer. 49:21. the noise of *their fall*,
Jer. 51:49. (caused) the slain of Israel *to fall*,
Lam. 1: 7. *when* her people *fell* into the hand of
Eze. 30: 4. *when* the slain *shall fall*

KAL.—*Imperative.*

Jer. 25:27. be drunken, and spue, *and fall*,
Hos 10: 8. shall say to the mountains,...*Fall* on us.

KAL.—*Future.*

Gen 4: 5. Cain was very wroth, *and* his countenance *fell*.
14:10. the kings of Sodom and Gomorrah fled, *and fell*
17: 3. *And* Abram *fell* on his face:
17. *Then* Abraham *fell* upon his face,
24:64. *and* when she saw Isaac, *she lighted*
33: 4. *and fell* on his neck, and kissed him:
44:14. *and they fell* before him on the ground.
45:14. *And he fell* upon his brother
46:29. *and he fell* on his neck,
49:17. *so that* his rider *shall fall* backward.
50: 1. *And* Joseph *fell* upon his father's face,
18. And his brethren also went *and fell down* before his face;
Ex. 15:16. Fear and dread *shall fall* upon them;
32:28. *and there fell* of the people that day
Lev. 9:24. they shouted, *and fell* on their faces.
11:32. whatsoever (any) of them,...*doth fall*,
33. vessel, whereinto (any) of them *falleth*,
35. (any part) of their carcase *falleth*
37. and (any part) of their carcase *fall*
Nu. 6:12. the days that were before *shall be lost*, (marg. *fall*)
14: 5. *Then* Moses and Aaron *fell* on their faces
29. Your carcases *shall fall* in this wilderness;
32. your carcases, *they shall fall*
16: 4. *And* when...*he fell* upon his face:
22. *And they fell* upon their faces,
45(17:10). *And they fell* upon their faces.
20: 6. *and they fell* upon their faces:
34: 2. the land that *shall fall* unto you
Deu 22: 8. if any man *fall* from thence.
Jos. 5:14. *And* Joshua *fell* on his face to the earth,
6:20. *that* the wall *fell down* flat,
7: 6. *and fell* to the earth upon his face
8:24. *and when they were* all *fallen* on the edge of the sword,
11: 7. *and they fell* upon them.
17: 5. *And there fell* ten portions to Manasseh,
Jud. 4:16. *and* all the host of Sisera *fell* upon
7:13. came unto a tent, and smote it *that it fell*,
9:40. *and* many *were overthrown* (and) wounded,
12: 6. *and there fell* at that time of the
13:20. *and fell* on their faces to the ground.
16:30. *and* the house *fell* upon the lords,
19:26. *and fell down* at the door
20:44. *And there fell* of Benjamin
Ru. 2:10. *Then she fell* on her face,
3:18. until thou know how the matter *will fall*:
1Sa. 4:10. *for there fell* of Israel thirty thousand
18. *that he fell* from off the seat
11: 7. *And* the fear of the Lord *fell* on the people,
14:13. *and they fell* before Jonathan;
45. *there shall* not one hair of his head *fall*
17:32. *Let* no man's heart *fail*
49. *and he fell* upon his face to the earth.
52. *And* the wounded of the Philistines *fell down*
19:24. *and lay down* (marg. *fell*) naked all that day
20:41. *and fell* on his face to the ground,
25:23. *and fell* before David on her face,
24. *And fell* at his feet, and said,
26:20. *let* not my blood *fall* to the earth
28:20. Then Saul *fell* (marg. made haste, *and fell*) straightway
31: 1. *and fell down* slain in mount Gilboa.
4. Therefore Saul took a sword, *and fell* upon
5. *he fell likewise* upon his sword,
2Sa. 1: 2. *that he fell* to the earth,
2:16. *so they fell down* together:
23. *and he fell down* there,
4: 4. as she made haste to flee, *that he fell*,
9: 6. *Now* when...*he fell* on his face, and did reverence.
11:17. *and there fell* (some) of the people
14: 4. *And* when the woman...*she fell* on her face
11. *there shall* not one hair of thy son *fall*

2Sa.14:22. *And* Joab *fell* to the ground
17:12. as the dew *falleth* on the ground
20: 8. *and* as he went forth *it fell* out.
21: 9. *and they fell* (all) seven together,
22. *and fell* by the hand of David,
22:39. *yea, they are fallen* under my feet.
24:14. *let us fall* now into the hand of the Lord;
— *let me* not *fall* into the hand of man.
1K. 1:52. *there shall* not an hair of him *fall*
18: 7. he knew him, *and fell* on his face,
38. *Then* the fire of the Lord *fell*,
39. *And* when all...*they fell* on their faces:
20:30. *and* (there) a wall *fell* upon twenty and seven thousand
22:20. that he may go up *and fall* at
2K. 1: 2. *And* Ahaziah *fell down* through a lattice
4:37. she went in, *and fell* at his feet,
5:21. *And* when Naaman...*he lighted down* from
7: 4. *and let us fall* unto the host of the Syrians:
10:10. *there shall fall* unto the earth nothing
1Ch 5:10. the Hagarites, *who fell* by their hand:
10: 1. *and fell down* slain in mount Gilboa.
4. Saul took a sword, *and fell* upon it.
5. *And* when...he *fell* likewise on the sword,
12:19. *He will fall* to his master Saul
20: 8. *and they fell* by the hand of David,
21:13. *let me fall* now into the hand of the Lord;
— *let me* not *fall* into the hand of man.
14. *and there fell* of Israel seventy thousand
16. *Then* David and the elders...*fell* upon their
26:14. *And* the lot eastward *fell* to Shelemiah.
2Ch 13:17. *so there fell down* slain of Israel
14:13(12). *and* the Ethiopians *were overthrown*,
18:19. that he may go up *and fall*
Neh. 6:16. *they were* much *cast down*
Est. 6:13. but *shalt* surely *fall* before him.
8: 3. *and fell down* at his feet,
Job 1:15. *And* the Sabeans *fell* (upon them),
19. *and it fell* upon the young men,
20. *and fell down* upon the ground,
13:11. his dread *fall* upon you?
31:22. *let* mine arm *fall* from my shoulder blade,
Ps. 5:10 (11). *let them fall* by their own counsels;
7:15(16). *and is fallen* into the ditch
18:38(39). *they are fallen* under my feet.
35: 8. into that very destruction *let him fall.*
37:24. Though *he fall*, he shall not be utterly cast
45: 5(6). the people *fall* under thee.
82: 7. *and fall* like one of the princes.
91: 7. A thousand *shall fall* at thy side,
141:10. *Let* the wicked *fall* into their own nets,
Pro.11: 5. the wicked *shall fall*
14. Where no counsel (is), the people *fall:*
28. He that trusteth in his riches *shall fall:*
13:17. A wicked messenger *falleth*
17:20. he that hath a perverse tongue *falleth*
22:14. he that is abhorred of the Lord *shall fall*
24:16. For a just man *falleth* seven times,
26:27. Whoso diggeth a pit *shall fall* therein:
28:10. *he shall fall* himself
14. he that hardeneth his heart *shall fall*
18. (he that is) perverse...*shall fall*
Ecc. 4:10. if *they fall*, the one will lift up his fellow: but woe to him (that is) alone *when he falleth;*
9:12. *when it falleth* suddenly
10: 8. that diggeth a pit *shall fall* into it;
11: 3. if the tree *fall* toward the south,
— in the place *where* the tree *falleth*,
Isa. 3:25. Thy men *shall fall* by the sword,
10: 4. *they shall fall* under the slain.
34. Lebanon *shall fall* by a mighty one.
13:15. *shall fall* by the sword.
24:18. *shall fall* into the pit;
26:18. *have* the inhabitants of the world *fallen.*
47:11. *and* mischief *shall fall* upon thee;
54:15. whosoever shall gather together...*shall fall*
Jer. 6:15. *they shall fall* among them that fall:
8: 4. *Shall they fall*, and not arise?
12. therefore *shall they fall*
36: 7. they *will present* their supplication (marg. their supplication *shall fall*)
37:20. *let* my supplication,...*be accepted* (marg. *fall*)
39:18. *thou shalt* not *fall* by the sword,
42: 2. *Let*,...our supplication *be accepted* (marg. *fall*)

Jer. 44:12. *they shall...fall* in the land of Egypt;
48:44. He that fleeth...*shall fall*
49:26. her young men *shall fall*
50:30. Therefore *shall* her young men *fall*
51:47. all her slain *shall fall*
Eze. 1:28. *And* when I saw (it), *I fell* upon my face,
3:23. *and I fell* on my face.
5:12. a third part *shall fall* by the sword
6:11. *they shall fall* by the sword,
12. he that is near *shall fall* by the sword;
8: 1. *that* the hand of the Lord God *fell* there upon me.
9: 8. *that I fell* upon my face,
11: 5. *And* the Spirit of the Lord *fell* upon me,
10. *Ye shall fall* by the sword;
13. *Then fell I down* upon my face,
13:11. Say unto them which daub...*that it shall fall:*
— ye, O great hailstones, *shall fall;*
17:21. all his fugitives...*shall fall*
23:25. thy remnant *shall fall*
24:21. your sons and your daughters...*shall fall*
25:13. *they* of Dedan *shall fall*
27:27. thy company...*shall fall*
29: 5. *thou shalt fall* upon the open fields;
30: 5. the men of the land...*shall fall*
6. *shall they fall* in it by the sword,
17. The young men of Aven...*shall fall*
25. the arms of Pharaoh *shall fall down;*
32:20. *They shall fall* in the midst
33:27. *shall fall* by the sword,
35: 8. *shall they fall* that are slain
38:20. and every wall *shall fall*
39: 4. *Thou shalt fall* upon the mountains
5. *Thou shalt fall* upon the open field:
23. *so fell they* all by the sword.
43: 3 & 44:4. *and I fell* upon my face.
47:22. *they shall have* inheritance (lit. *they shall fall* into an inheritance)
Dan. 8:17. *and fell* upon my face:
Hos. 7:16. their princes *shall fall*
13:16(14:1). *they shall fall* by the sword:
Joel 2: 8. (when) *they fall* upon the sword,
Am. 3: 5. *Can* a bird *fall* in a snare upon the earth,
7:17. thy sons and thy daughters *shall fall*
9: 9. yet *shall* not the least grain *fall*
Jon. 1: 7. *and* the lot *fell* upon Jonah.

KAL.—*Participle.* Poel.

Gen15:12. an horror of great darkness *fell* upon
Nu. 5:21. make thy thigh *to rot*, (marg. *fall*)
24: 4, 16. saw the vision of the Almighty, *falling* (into a trance),
Deu21: 1. *lying* in the field,
22: 4. thy brother's ass or his ox *fall down*
8. any man fall (lit. (one) *falling* shall fall)
Jos. 7:10. wherefore *liest* thou thus upon thy face?
8:25. all *that fell* that day,
Jud. 3:25. their lord (was) *fallen down*
4:22. behold, Sisera *lay* dead,
7:12. the children of the east *lay along*
8:10. *for there fell* an hundred and twenty thousand
19:27. his concubine *was fallen down*
20:46. So *that* all *which fell* that day
1Sa. 5: 3, 4. Dagon (was) *fallen* upon his face
31: 8. they found Saul and his three sons *fallen*
2Sa. 3:29. *or that falleth* on the sword,
1K. 20:25. the army *that thou hast lost*, (marg. *was fallen*)
2K. 25:11. *the fugitives* (marg. *fallen away*) that fell away
1Ch 10: 8. they found Saul and his sons *fallen*
2Ch 20:24. they (were) dead bodies *fallen*
Est. 7: 8. Haman *was fallen* upon the bed
Job 12: 3. I (am) not *inferior* to you: (marg. *fall* not lower than you)
13: 2. I (am) not *inferior* unto you. (lit. *id.*)
14:18. the mountain *falling* cometh to nought,
Ps.145:14. The Lord upholdeth all *that fall*,
Isa. 30:13. as a breach *ready to fall*,
Jer. 6:15. they shall fall *among them that fall:*
8:12. shall they fall *among them that fall:*
37:13. Thou *fallest away* to the Chaldeans.
14. I *fall* not *away* to the Chaldeans.
39: 9. *those that fell away*, that fell
52:15. *those that fell away*, that fell to the king

Eze.32:22, 23, 24. slain, *fallen* by the sword:
27. the mighty (that are) *fallen*
Am. 9:11. the tabernacle of David *that is fallen*,

* HIPHIL.—*Preterite.* *

Deu25: 2. *that* the judge *shall cause him to lie down*,
Jos. 23: 4. *I have divided* unto you *by lot*
Jud. 2:19. they ceased not from (marg. *let* nothing *fall* of) their own doings,
1Sa. 3:19. *did let* none of his words *fall*
2K. 19: 7. *and I will cause him to fall* by the sword
1Ch 26:14. Then for Zechariah...*they cast* lots;
2Ch 32:21. they that came forth of his own bowels *slew him* (marg. *made him fall*)
Neh 10:34(35). *we cast* the lots among the priests,
11: 1. the rest of the people also *cast* lots,
Est. 3: 7. *they cast* Pur, that (is), the lot,
9:24. *and had cast* Pur, that (is), the lot,
Ps. 73:18. *thou castedst them down* into destruction.
Pro. 7:26. *she hath cast down* many wounded:
Isa. 34:17. he *hath cast* the lot for them,
37: 7. *and I will cause him to fall* by the sword
Jer. 15: 8. *I have caused* (him) *to fall* upon it
19: 7. *and I will cause them to fall*
22: 7. *and cast* (them) into the fire.
Eze. 6: 4. *and I will cast down* your slain (men)
30:22. *and I will cause* the sword *to fall*
Dan 11:12. *and he shall cast down* (many) ten thousands:

HIPHIL.—*Infinitive.*

Nu. 5:22. to make (thy) belly to swell, *and* (thy) thigh *to rot:*
1Sa.18:25. Saul thought *to make* David *fall*
2Sa.20:15. Joab battered the wall, *to throw* it *down*.
Ps. 37:14. *to cast down* the poor
106:26. *to overthrow* them in the wilderness.
27. *To overthrow* their seed *also*
Jer. 42: 9. *to present* your supplication
Eze.45: 1. *Moreover, when ye shall divide by lot* the land (marg. *cause* the land *to fall*)

HIPHIL.—*Imperative.*

Jos. 13: 6. *divide thou it by lot* unto
1Sa.14:42. *Cast* (lots) between me and Jonathan

HIPHIL.—*Future.*

Gen 2:21. *And* the Lord God *caused* a deep sleep *to fall*
Ex. 21:27. if *he smite out* his manservant's tooth,
Nu. 35:23. *and cast* (it) upon him, that he die,
2K. 3:19. and *shall fell* every good tree,
25. and *felled* all the good trees:
1Ch 24:31. These *likewise cast* lots
25: 8. *And they cast* lots, ward against (ward),
26:13. *And they cast* lots, as well the small
Est. 6:10. *let* nothing *fail* (marg. *suffer* not a whit *to fall*) of all that thou hast spoken.
Job 6:27. Yea, *ye overwhelm* (marg. *cause to fall upon*) the fatherless,
29:24. the light of my countenance *they cast* not *down*.
Ps. 22:18(19). and *cast* lots upon my vesture.
78:28. *And he let* (it) *fall* in the midst of their
55. *and divided them* an inheritance
140:10(11). *let them be cast* into the fire;
Pro. 1:14. *Cast in* thy lot among us;
19:15. Slothfulness *casteth* into a deep sleep;
Isa. 26:19. the earth *shall cast out* the dead.
Jer. 3:12. *I will* not *cause* mine anger *to fall*
Eze.32:12. *will I cause* thy multitude *to fall*,
39: 3. and *will cause* thine arrows *to fall*
47:22. *ye shall divide* it *by lot* for an inheritance
48:29. *ye shall divide by lot* unto the tribes
Dan. 8:10. *and it cast down* (some) of the host
Jon. 1: 7. Come, and *let us cast* lots,
— *So they cast* lots,

HIPHIL.—*Participle.*

2K. 6: 5. as one *was felling* a beam,
Jer. 38:26. I *presented* my supplication
Dan. 9:18. we *do* not *present* (marg. *cause to fall*) our supplications
20. *and presenting* my supplication before the

* HITHPAEL.—*Preterite.* *

Deu 9:25. as *I fell down* (at the first);

HITHPAEL.—*Infinitive.*

Gen43:18. he may seek occasion...*and fall* upon us,

HITHPAEL.—*Future.*

Deu 9:18. *And I fell down* before the Lord,
25. *Thus I fell down* before the Lord

HITHPAEL.—*Participle.*

Ezr. 10: 1. *and casting himself down* before the house

* PILEL.—*Preterite.* *

Eze.28:23. *and* the wounded *shall be judged* (or, *fall*;—see also פָּלַל)

נְפַל *n'phal*, Ch. 5308

* P'AL.—*Preterite.* *

Dan. 2:46. the king Nebuchadnezzar *fell* upon his face,
3:23. *fell down* bound into the midst of
4:31(28). *there fell* a voice from heaven,
7:20. *and* before whom three *fell*;

P'AL.—*Future.*

Ezr. 7:20. *thou shalt have occasion* to bestow,
Dan. 3: 5. *ye fall down* and worship the
6. And whoso *falleth* not *down* and
10. *shall fall down* and worship the golden
11. And whoso *falleth* not *down* and
15. *ye fall down* and worship the

P'AL.—*Participle.*

Dan. 3: 7. *fell down* (and) worshipped the

נֵפֶל *nēh'-phel* & נֶפֶל *neh'-phel*, m. 5309

Job 3:16. *as an* hidden *untimely birth*
Ps. 58: 8(9). (like) *the untimely birth of* a woman,
Ecc. 6: 3. *an untimely birth* (is) better than

נָפַץ *nāh-phatz'*. 5310

* KAL.—*Preterite.* *

Gen 9:19. *was* the whole earth *overspread*.
1Sa.13:11. the people *were scattered* from me,
Isa. 33: 3. the nations *were scattered*.

KAL.—*Infinitive.*

Jud. 7:19. blew the trumpets, *and brake* the pitchers

KAL.—*Participle.* Paül.

Isa. 11:12. *and* gather together *the dispersed of* Judah
Jer. 22:28. (Is) this man Coniah a despised *broken* idol?

* PIEL.—*Preterite.* *

1K. 5: 9(23). *and will cause them to be discharged*
Ps. 137: 9. (he be), that taketh *and dasheth* thy little
Jer. 13:14. *And I will dash them* one against another,
51:20. *for* with thee *will I break in pieces* the
21. *And* with thee *will I break in pieces* the horse and his rider; *and* with thee *will I break in pieces* the chariot
22. With thee *also will I break in pieces* man and woman; *and* with thee *will I break in pieces* old and young; *and* with thee *will I break in pieces* the young man and the maid;
23. *I will also break in pieces*...the shepherd
— *and* with thee *will I break in pieces* the husbandman
— *and* with thee *will I break in pieces*

PIEL.—*Infinitive.*

Dan 12: 7. *to scatter* the power of the holy people,

PIEL.—*Future.*

Ps. 2: 9. *thou shalt dash them in pieces*
Jer. 48:12. empty his vessels, and *break* their bottles.

* PUAL.—*Participle.* *

Isa. 27: 9. as chalkstones *that are beaten in sunder*,

נֶפֶץ *neh'-phetz*, m. 5311

Isa. 30:30. *scattering*, and tempest, and hailstones.

נְפַק *n'phak*, Ch. 5312

* P'AL.—*Preterite.* *

Dan. 2:13. And the decree *went forth* that

Dan. 2:14. which *was gone forth* to slay the wise
5: 5. In the same hour *came forth* fingers

P'AL.—*Imperative.*

Dan. 3:26. *come forth*, and come (hither).

P'AL.—*Participle.*

Dan. 3:26. *came forth* of the midst of the fire.
7:10. A fiery stream issued *and came forth*

* APHEL.—*Preterite.* *

Ezr. 5:14. Nebuchadnezzar *took out* of the temple
— *did* Cyrus the king *take out* of the temple
6: 5. which Nebuchadnezzar *took forth* out of
Dan. 5: 2. Nebuchadnezzar *had taken out* (marg. *brought forth*) of the temple
3. that *were taken out* of the temple

5313 **נִפְקָא** [*niph-kāh'*], Ch. f.

Ezr 6: 4. *and* let *the expences* be given out
8. forthwith *expences* be given unto

5314 **נָפַשׁ** [*nāh-phash'*].

* NIPHAL.—*Future.* *

Ex. 23:12. *and* the stranger, *may be refreshed.*
31:17. seventh day he rested, *and was refreshed.*
2Sa.16:14. *and refreshed themselves* there.

5315 **נֶפֶשׁ** *neh'-phesh*, com.

Gen 1:20. the moving creature *that hath* (marg. *soul*) life,
21. every living *creature* (lit. living *soul*) that moveth,
24. the earth bring forth *the* living *creature*
30. every thing...wherein (there is) *life*, (marg. living *soul*)
2: 7. man became *a* living *soul.*
19. called every living *creature*,
9: 4. flesh *with the life thereof*,
5. your blood *of your lives*
— will I require *the life of* man.
10. every living *creature* that (is) with you,
12. me and you and every living *creature*
15, 16. every living *creature* of all flesh;
12: 5. *the souls* that they had gotten
13. *my soul* shall live because of thee.
14:21. Give me *the persons*, (marg. *souls*)
17:14. that *soul* shall be cut off
19:17. Escape for *thy life;*
19. magnified thy mercy,...in saving *my life;*
20. and *my soul* shall live.
23: 8. If it be *your mind* that I should bury
27: 4. that *my soul* may bless thee
19, 31. that *thy soul* may bless me.
25. that *my soul* may bless thee.
32:30(31). and *my life* is preserved.
34: 3. *his soul* clave unto Dinah
8. *The soul* of my son Shechem (lit. my son Shechem *his soul*)
35:18. as *her soul* was in departing,
36: 6. all *the persons* (marg. *souls*) *of* his house,
37:21. Let us not kill him. (lit. smite him *the soul*)
42:21. we saw the anguish of *his soul*,
44:30. *seeing that his life* is bound up *in the lad's life;* (lit. *in his soul*)
46:15. all *the souls of* his sons and his daughters
18. these she bare...(even) sixteen *souls.*
22. all *the souls* (were) fourteen
25. all *the souls* (were) seven.
26. All *the souls* that came with Jacob
— all *the souls* (were) threescore and six;
27. the sons of Joseph,...(were) two *souls:* all *the souls of* the house of Jacob,
49: 6. *O my soul*, come not thou into their secret;
Ex. 1: 5. all *the souls* that came out of the loins of Jacob were seventy *souls:*
4:19. all the men are dead which sought *thy life.*
12: 4. according to the number of *the souls;*
15. that *soul* shall be cut off from Israel.
16. (that) which every *man* (marg. *soul*) must eat,
19. that *soul* shall be cut off from
15: 9. *my lust* shall be satisfied upon them;

Ex. 16:16. (according to) the number of *your persons;* (marg. *souls*)
21:23. thou shalt give *life* for *life*,
30. for the ransom of *his life*
23: 9. *the heart* (marg. *soul*) *of* a stranger,
30:12. a ransom for *his soul*
15, 16. to make an atonement for *your souls.*
31:14. that *soul* shall be cut off
Lev. 2: 1. *And* when *any* (lit. *And a soul* when he) will offer a meat offering
4: 2. If *a soul* shall sin through ignorance
27. if any *one* (marg. any *soul*) of the common people sin
5: 1. *And* if *a soul* sin, and hear
2. if *a soul* touch any unclean thing,
4. if *a soul* swear, pronouncing
15. If *a soul* commit a trespass,
17. And if *a soul* sin, and commit any
6: 2(5:21). If *a soul* sin, and commit a trespass
7:18. *and the soul* that eateth of it
20. *But the soul* that eateth (of) the flesh
— that *soul* shall be cut off
21. Moreover *the soul* that shall touch
— that *soul* shall be cut off
25. *the soul* that eateth (it)
27. Whatsoever *soul* (it be) that eateth any manner of blood, even that *soul* shall be
11:10. any living *thing* (lit. living *soul*)
43. Ye shall not make *your selves* (marg. *your souls*) abominable
44. neither shall ye defile *yourselves*
46. every living *creature* that moveth
— *creature* that creepeth upon the earth:
16:29. ye shall afflict *your souls*,
31. ye shall afflict *your souls*,
17:10. I will even set my face *against that soul*
11. For *the life of* the flesh (is) in the blood:
— an atonement for *your souls:*
— an atonement *for the soul.*
12. No *soul* of you shall eat blood,
14. *the life of* all flesh; the blood of it (is) *for the life thereof:*
— *the life of* all flesh (is) the blood
15. every *soul* that eateth that which died
18:29. *the souls* that commit (them)
19: 8. that *soul* shall be cut off
28. any cuttings in your flesh *for the dead*,
20: 6. *And the soul* that turneth after
— I will even set my face *against* that *soul*,
25. ye shall not make *your souls* abominable
21: 1. There shall none be defiled *for the dead*
11. any dead *body*, (lit. *souls of* the dead)
22: 3. that *soul* shall be cut off
4. any thing (that is) unclean (by) *the dead*,
6. *The soul* which hath touched
11. if the priest buy (any) *soul*
23:27, 32. ye shall afflict *your souls*,
29. *soul* (it be) that shall not be afflicted
30. whatsoever *soul* (it be) that doeth any work in that same day, *the* same *soul* will I destroy
24:17. he that killeth any)(man (marg. smiteth *the life of* a man)
18. he that killeth)(a beast (lit. smiteth *the life of* a beast) shall make it good; *beast for beast.* (marg. *life* for *life*)
26:11. *my soul* shall not abhor you.
15. if *your soul* abhor my judgments,
16. and cause sorrow of *heart:*
30. *my soul* shall abhor you.
43. *their soul* abhorred my statutes.
27: 2. *the persons* (shall be) for the Lord
Nu. 5: 2. whosoever is defiled *by the dead:*
6. and that *person* be guilty;
6: 6. shall come at no dead *body.* (lit. dead *soul*)
11. he sinned by *the dead*,
9: 6, 7. defiled *by the dead body of* a man,
10. unclean *by reason of a dead body*,
13. *the* same *soul* shall be cut off
11: 6. *our soul* (is) dried away:
15:27. if any *soul* sin through ignorance,
28. make an atonement for *the soul*
30. *But the soul* that doeth (ought)
— that *soul* shall be cut off
31. that *soul* shall utterly be cut off;
16:38(17:3). The censers of these sinners *against their own souls*,

Nu. 19:11. that toucheth the dead body of *any* man
13. Whosoever toucheth *the* dead *body of* any (lit. the dead, *the soul of*) man
— that *soul* shall be cut off
18. *the persons* that were there,
20. that *soul* shall be cut off
22. *and the soul* that toucheth (it)
21: 4. *the soul of* the people was much
5. *and our soul* loatheth this light bread.
23:10. Let *me* (marg. *my soul*, or, *my life*) die the death of the righteous,
29: 7. ye shall afflict *your souls:*
30: 2(3). to bind *his soul* with a bond;
4(5), 4(5), 5(6). she hath bound *her soul*,
6(7), 7(8), 8(9), 11(12). wherewith she bound *her soul;*
9(10). they have bound *their souls*,
10(11). bound *her soul* by a bond
12(13). concerning the bond of *her soul*,
13(14). every binding oath to afflict *the soul*,
31:19. whosoever hath killed *any person*,
28. one *soul* of five hundred,
35. *And* thirty and two thousand *persons in all*, (lit. *and the soul of* man...were thirty two thousand *souls*)
40. *And the persons* (lit. and *the soul of* man) (were) sixteen thousand;
— the Lord's tribute (was) thirty and two *persons*.
46. *And* sixteen thousand *persons;*
50. to make an atonement for *our souls*
35:11. the slayer...which killeth *any person*
15. every one that killeth *any person*
30. Whoso killeth *any person*,
— one witness shall not testify *against any person*
31. no satisfaction *for the life of* a murderer,
Deu 4: 9. keep *thy soul* diligently,
15. ye therefore good heed *unto yourselves;*
29. seek him with all...*thy soul*.
6: 5. with all *thy soul*, and with all thy might.
10:12. with all thy heart and with all *thy soul*,
22. threescore and ten *persons;*
11:13. with all your heart and with all *your soul*,
18. in your heart and in *your soul*,
12:15, 20, 21. whatsoever *thy soul* lusteth after,
20. *thy soul* longeth to eat flesh;
23. the blood (is) *the life;* and thou mayest not eat *the life*
13: 3(4). with all your heart and with all *your soul*.
6(7). thy friend, which (is) *as thine own soul*,
14:26. whatsoever *thy soul* lusteth after,
— whatsoever *thy soul* desireth:
18: 6. with all the desire of *his mind*
19: 6. Lest the avenger of the blood...slay him; (marg. smite him in *life*)
11. if any man hate his neighbour,...and smite him *mortally* (marg. in *life*)
21. *life* (shall go) *for life*,
21:14. if thou have no delight in her, then thou shalt let her go *whither she will;* (lit. *to her soul*)
22:26. against his neighbour, and slayeth him, (lit. smiteth him *the soul*)
23:24(25). eat grapes thy fill *at thine own pleasure;*
24: 6. he taketh (a man's) *life* to pledge.
7. a man be found stealing *any* (lit. *a soul*)
15. setteth *his heart* (marg. *his soul*) upon it:
26:16. with all thine heart, and with all *thy soul*.
27:25. to slay *an* innocent *person*.
28:65. and sorrow of *mind:*
30: 2, 6, 10. all thine heart, and with all *thy soul;*
Jos. 2:13. deliver *our lives* from death.
14. *Our life* for your's,
9:24. we were sore afraid *of our lives*
10:28, 30, 32, 35, 37, 37, 39. all *the souls* that (were) therein;
11:11. they smote all *the souls*
20: 3. that killeth (any) *person*
9. whosoever killeth (any) *person*
22: 5. with all your heart and with all *your soul*.
23:11. Take good heed therefore *unto yourselves*, (marg. *your souls*)
14. in all your hearts and in all *your souls*,
Jud. 5:18. a people (that) jeoparded *their lives*
21. *O my soul*, thou hast trodden down strength.

Jud. 9:17. my father...adventured *his life* far,
10:16. *his soul* was grieved for the misery
12: 3. I put *my life* in my hands,
16:16. *his soul* was vexed unto death;
30. Let *me* (marg. *my soul*) die with the Philistines.
18:25. lest angry (marg. bitter of *soul*) fellows run upon thee, and thou lose *thy life*, *with the lives of* thy houshold.
Ru. 4:15. a restorer of (thy) *life*,
1Sa. 1:10. she (was) in bitterness of *soul*,
15. but have poured out *my soul*
26. (as) *thy soul* liveth, my lord,
2:16. take (as much) as *thy soul* desireth;
33. to grieve *thine heart:*
35. in mine heart *and in my mind:*
17:55. (As) *thy soul* liveth, O king,
18: 1. *that the soul of* Jonathan was knit *with the soul of* David, and Jonathan loved him *as his own soul*.
3. he loved him *as his own soul*.
19: 5. he did put *his life* in his hand,
11. If thou save not *thy life* to night,
20: 1. thy father, that he seeketh *my life?*
3. (as) *thy soul* liveth,
4. Whatsoever *thy soul* desireth,
17. he loved him as he loved *his own soul*.
22: 2. every one (that was) dis*contented*, (marg. bitter of *soul*)
22. all *the persons of* thy father's house.
23. he that seeketh *my life* seeketh *thy life;*
23:15. Saul was come out to seek *his life:*
20. all the desire of *thy soul*
24:11(12). yet thou huntest *my soul* to take it.
25:26. and (as) *thy soul* liveth,
29. and to seek *thy soul:* but *the soul of* my lord shall be bound
— and *the souls of* thine enemies,
26:21. *my soul* was precious in thine eyes
24. as *thy life* was much set by this day in mine eyes, so let *my life* be much set by
28: 9. wherefore then layest thou a snare for *my life*,
21. I have put *my life* in my hand,
30: 6. *the soul of* all the people was grieved,
2Sa. 1: 9. *my life* (is) yet whole in me.
3:21. all that *thine heart* desireth.
4: 8. which sought *thy life;*
9. who hath redeemed *my soul*
5: 8. (that are) hated of David'*s soul*,
11:11. (as) *thy soul* liveth,
14: 7. *for the life of* his brother
14. neither doth God respect (any) *person:*
19. (As) *thy soul* liveth,
16:11. seeketh *my life:*
17: 8. they (be) chafed in their *minds*, (marg. bitter of *soul*)
18:13. I should have wrought falshood *against mine own life:*
19: 5(6). which this day have saved *thy life*, and *the lives of* thy sons...*and the lives of* thy wives, *and the lives of* thy concubines;
23:17. the blood of the men that went *in jeopardy of their lives?* (lit. *with their souls*)
1K. 1:12. that thou mayest save *thine own life*, and *the life of* thy son Solomon.
29. that hath redeemed *my soul*
2: 4. with all their heart and with all *their soul*,
23. this word *against his own life*.
3:11. nor hast asked *the life of* thine enemies;
8:48. with all *their soul*,
11:37. according to all that *thy soul* desireth,
17:21. let this child'*s soul* come into him again.
22. *the soul of* the child came into him again,
19: 2. if I make not *thy life as the life of* one of them
3. arose, and went for *his life*,
4. requested for *himself* (lit. *his soul*)
— O Lord, take away *my life;*
10, 14. they seek *my life*, to take it away.
20:31. peradventure he will save *thy life*.
32. I pray thee, let *me* (lit. *my soul*) live.
39. then shall *thy life* be for *his life*,
42. therefore *thy life* shall go for *his life*,
2K. 1:13. let *my life, and the life of* these fifty thy servants, be precious in thy sight.
14. let *my life* now be precious

2K. 2: 2, 4, 6. (as) *thy soul* liveth,
4:27. *her soul* (is) vexed within her:
30. (as) *thy soul* liveth,
7: 7. fled for *their life.*
9:15. If it be *your minds,* (then) let none go
10:24. *his life* (shall be) for *the life of him.*
12: 4(5). the money *that every man* is set at, (marg. of *the souls of* his estimation)
23: 3. with all (their) heart and all (their) *soul,*
25. with all his heart, and with all *his soul,*
1Ch 5:21. *and* of men (marg. *and souls of* men) an hundred thousand.
11:19. these men *that have put their lives in jeopardy* (marg. *with their lives*)? for *with* (the jeopardy of) *their lives* they brought it.
22:19. set your heart *and your soul* to seek
28: 9. *and with a* willing *mind:*
2Ch 1:11. nor *the life of* thine enemies,
6:38. with all their heart and with all *their soul*
15:12. to seek the Lord...with all *their soul;*
34:31. to keep his commandments,...with all *his soul,*
Est. 4:13. Think not *with thyself* that thou shalt escape
7: 3. let *my life* be given me at my petition,
7. Haman stood up to make request for *his life*
8:11. to stand for *their life,*
9:16. stood for *their lives,*
31. as they had decreed for *themselves* (marg. *their souls*)
Job 2: 4. will he give for *his life.*
6. but save *his life.*
3:20. life unto the bitter (in) *soul;*
6: 7. The things (that) *my soul* refused to touch
11. that I should prolong *my life?*
7:11. I will complain in the bitterness of *my soul.*
15. *my soul* chooseth strangling,
9:21. (yet) would I not know *my soul:*
10: 1. *My soul* is weary of my life;
— I will speak in the bitterness of *my soul.*
11:20. the giving up of *the ghost.* (marg. or, a puff *of breath*)
12:10. *the soul* (marg. or, *life*) *of* every living
13:14. *and* put *my life* in mine hand?
14:22. *and his soul* within him shall mourn.
16: 4. if *your soul* were in *my soul*'s stead,
18: 4. He teareth *himself* (marg. *his soul*) in his anger:
19: 2. How long will ye vex *my soul,*
21:25. another dieth *in* the bitterness of his *soul,* (lit. *in a* bitter *soul*)
23:13. *and* (what) *his soul* desireth, even (that) he doeth.
24:12. *and the soul of* the wounded crieth out:
27: 2. (who) hath vexed *my soul;*
8. when God taketh away *his soul?*
30:16. *my soul* is poured out
25. was (not) *my soul* grieved for the poor?
31:30. wishing a curse to *his soul.*
39. *or* have caused the owners thereof to lose their *life:* (marg. *the soul of* the owners thereof to expire)
32: 2. he justified *himself* (marg. *his soul*)
33:18. He keepeth back *his soul* from the pit,
20. *and his soul* dainty meat.
22. *his soul* draweth near unto the grave,
28. He will deliver *his soul*
30. To bring back *his soul* from the pit,
36:14. *They* die (marg. *Their soul* dieth) in youth,
41:21(13). *His breath* kindleth coals,
Ps. 3: 2(3). which say *of my soul,*
6: 3(4). *My soul* is *also* sore vexed:
4(5). deliver *my soul:*
7: 2(3). Lest he tear *my soul* like a lion,
5(6). Let the enemy persecute *my soul,*
10: 3. the wicked boasteth of *his heart*'s (marg. *soul*'s) desire,
11: 1. how say ye *to my soul,*
5. him that loveth violence *his soul* hateth.
13: 2(3) shall I take counsel *in my soul,*
16:10. thou wilt not leave *my soul* in hell;
17: 9. my *deadly* enemies, (marg. my enemies *against the soul*)
13. deliver *my soul* from the wicked,
19: 7(8). converting *the soul:*
22:20(21). Deliver *my soul* from the sword;

Ps. 22:29(30). *and* none can keep alive *his own soul.*
23: 3. He restoreth *my soul:* he leadeth me
24: 4. hath not lifted up *his soul*
25: 1. do I lift up *my soul.*
13. *His soul* shall dwell at ease;
20. O keep *my soul,* and deliver me:
26: 9. Gather not *my soul* with sinners,
27:12. *unto the will of* mine enemies:
30: 3(4). thou hast brought up *my soul*
31: 7(8). thou hast known *my soul* in adversities;
9(10). *my soul* and my belly.
13(14). they devised to take away *my life.*
33:19. To deliver *their soul* from death,
20. *Our soul* waiteth for the Lord:
34: 2(3). *My soul* shall make her boast
22(23). The Lord redeemeth *the soul*
35: 3. say *unto my soul,* I (am) thy salvation.
4. that seek after *my soul:*
7. they have digged *for my soul.*
9. *And my soul* shall be joyful
12. the spoiling *of my soul.*
13. I humbled *my soul* with fasting;
17. rescue *my soul* from their destructions,
25. Ah, *so would we have it:* (marg. *our soul*)
38:12(13). They also that seek after *my life*
40:14(15). that seek after *my soul*
41: 2(3). *unto the will of* his enemies.
4(5). heal *my soul;*
42: 1(2). so panteth *my soul* after thee,
2(3). *My soul* thirsteth for God,
4(5). I pour out *my soul* in me:
5(6), 11(12). Why art thou cast down, *O my soul?*
6(7). *my soul* is cast down within me:
43: 5. Why art thou cast down, *O my soul?*
44:25(26). *our soul* is bowed down
49: 8(9). the redemption of *their soul*
15(16). God will redeem *my soul*
18(19). he blessed *his soul:*
54: 3(5). oppressors seek after *my soul:*
4(6). them that uphold *my soul.*
55:18(19). He hath delivered *my soul* in peace
56: 6(7). when they wait for *my soul.*
13(14). thou hast delivered *my soul*
57: 1(2). *my soul* trusteth in thee:
4(5). *My soul* (is) among lions:
6(7). *my soul* is bowed down:
59: 3(4). they lie in wait *for my soul:*
62: 1(2). *my soul* waiteth upon God:
5(6). *My soul,* wait thou only upon God;
63: 1(2). *my soul* thirsteth for thee,
5(6). *My soul* shall be satisfied
8(9). *My soul* followeth hard after thee:
9(10). those (that) seek *my soul,*
66: 9. Which holdeth *our soul* in life,
16. will declare what he hath done *for my soul.*
69: 1(2). the waters are come in unto (my) *soul.*
10(11). (chastened) *my soul* with fasting,
18(19). Draw nigh unto *my soul,*
70: 2(3). that seek after *my soul:*
71:10. they that lay wait for *my soul*
13. that are adversaries to *my soul;*
23. *and my soul,* which thou hast redeemed.
72:13. *and* shall save *the souls of* the needy.
14. He shall redeem *their soul*
74:19. O deliver not *the soul of*
77: 2(3). *my soul* refused to be comforted.
78:18. by asking meat *for their lust.*
50. he spared not *their soul* from death,
84: 2(3). *My soul* longeth,...for the courts
86: 2. Preserve *my soul;* for I (am) holy:
4. Rejoice *the soul of* thy servant: for unto thee, O Lord, do I lift up *my soul.*
13. thou hast delivered *my soul*
14. have sought after *my soul;*
88: 3(4). *my soul* is full of troubles:
14(15). why castest thou off *my soul?*
89:48(49). shall he deliver *his soul*
94:17. *my soul* had almost dwelt in silence.
19. thy comforts delight *my soul.*
21. against *the soul of* the righteous,
97:10. he preserveth *the souls of* his saints;
103: 1, 2, 22 & 104: 1. Bless the Lord, *O my soul:*
104:35. Bless thou the Lord, *O my soul.*
105:18. *he* (marg. *his soul*) was laid in iron:
22. To bind his princes *at his pleasure;*
106:15. sent leanness *into their soul.*

Ps. 107: 5. *their soul* fainted in them.
9. he satisfieth *the* longing *soul, and* filleth *the* hungry *soul*
18. *Their soul* abhorreth all manner of meat;
26. *their soul* is melted because of trouble.
109:20. them that speak evil against *my soul.*
31. from those that condemn *his soul.*
116: 4. O Lord, I beseech thee, deliver *my soul.*
7. Return unto thy rest, *O my soul;*
8. thou hast delivered *my soul* from death,
119:20. *My soul* breaketh for the longing
25. *My soul* cleaveth unto the dust:
28. *My soul* melteth for heaviness:
81. *My soul* fainteth for thy salvation:
109. *My soul* (is) continually in my hand:
129. therefore doth *my soul* keep them.
167. *My soul* hath kept thy testimonies;
175. Let *my soul* live,
120: 2. Deliver *my soul*, O Lord,
6. *My soul* hath long dwelt with him that
121: 7. he shall preserve *thy soul.*
123: 4. *Our soul* is exceedingly filled
124: 4. the stream had gone over *our soul:*
5. Then the proud waters had gone over *our soul.*
7. *Our soul* is escaped as a bird
130: 5. *my soul* doth wait,
6. *My soul* (waiteth) for the Lord
131: 2. I have behaved and quieted *myself*, (marg. *my soul*)
— *my soul* (is) even as a weaned child.
138: 3. strengthenedst me (with) strength *in my soul.*
139:14. *and* (that) *my soul* knoweth right well.
141: 8. leave not *my soul* destitute.
142: 4(5). no man cared *for my soul.*
7(8). Bring *my soul* out of prison.
143: 3. the enemy hath persecuted *my soul;*
6. *my soul* (thirsteth) after thee,
8. I lift up *my soul* unto thee.
11. bring *my soul* out of trouble.
12. destroy all them that afflict *my soul:*
146: 1. Praise the Lord, *O my soul.*
Pro. 1:18. they lurk privily *for their* (own) *lives.*
19. taketh away *the life of* the owners
2:10. knowledge is pleasant *unto thy soul;*
3:22. So shall they be life *unto thy soul,*
6:16. seven (are) an abomination unto *him:* (marg. of *his soul*)
26. adulteress will hunt for *the* precious *life.*
30. a thief, if he steal to satisfy *his soul*
32. he (that) doeth it destroyeth *his own soul.*
7:23. knoweth not that it (is) *for his life.*
8:36. against me wrongeth *his own soul:*
10: 3. suffer *the soul of* the righteous to famish:
11:17. merciful man doeth good to *his own soul:*
25. *The* liberal *soul* shall be made fat:
30. he that winneth *souls* (is) wise.
12:10. regardeth *the life of* his beast:
13: 2. *but the soul of* the transgressors
3. He that keepeth his mouth keepeth *his life:*
4. *The soul of* the sluggard desireth,
— *but the soul of* the diligent shall be
8. The ransom of a man's *life*
19. desire accomplished is sweet *to the soul:*
25. eateth to the satisfying of *his soul:*
14:10. The heart knoweth *his own* bitterness; (marg. the bitterness of *his soul*)
25. A true witness delivereth *souls:*
15:32. He that refuseth instruction despiseth *his own soul:*
16:17. he that keepeth his way preserveth *his soul.*
24. an honeycomb, sweet *to the soul,*
26. *He* that laboureth (marg. *The soul of* him that laboureth)
18: 7. his lips (are) the snare of *his soul.*
19: 2. (that) *the soul* (be) without knowledge,
8. getteth wisdom loveth *his own soul:*
15. *and an* idle *soul* shall suffer hunger.
16. that keepeth the commandment keepeth *his own soul;*
18. let not *thy soul* spare
20: 2. sinneth (against) *his own soul.*
21:10. *The soul of* the wicked desireth evil:
23. keepeth *his soul* from troubles.
22: 5. he that doth keep *his soul*
23. spoil *the soul* of those that spoiled

Pro. 22:25. and get a snare *to thy soul.*
23: 2. if thou (be) a man given to *appetite.*
7. as he thinketh *in his heart,*
14. *and* shalt deliver *his soul* from hell.
24:12. he that keepeth *thy soul,*
14. knowledge of wisdom (be) *unto thy soul:*
25:13. *for* he refresheth *the soul of* his masters.
25. cold waters to *a* thirsty *soul,*
27: 7. *The* full *soul* loatheth an honeycomb; *but* to *the* hungry *soul* every bitter thing is sweet.
9. of a man's friend by *hearty* counsel. (marg. from the counsel of *the soul*)
28:17. doeth violence to the blood of (any) *person*
25. He that is of *a* proud *heart*
29:10. the just seek *his soul.*
17. he shall give delight *unto thy soul.*
24. with a thief hateth *his own soul:*
31: 6. those that be of heavy *hearts.*
Ecc. 2:24. should make *his soul* enjoy good (marg. or, delight *his senses*)
4: 8. bereave *my soul* of good?
6: 2. he wanteth nothing *for his soul*
3. *and his soul* be not filled with good,
7. *the appetite* (marg. *soul*) is not filled.
9. the wandering of *the desire:* (marg. walking of *the soul*)
7:28. Which yet *my soul* seeketh,
Cant. 1: 7. O thou whom *my soul* loveth.
3: 1. I sought him whom *my soul* loveth:
2. seek him whom *my soul* loveth:
3. Saw ye him whom *my soul* loveth?
4. I found him whom *my soul* loveth:
5: 6. *my soul* failed when he spake:
6:12. *my soul* made me (like) the chariots
Isa. 1:14. your appointed feasts *my soul* hateth:
3: 9. Woe *unto their soul!* for they have
20. the tablets, (marg. houses of *the soul*) and the earrings,
5:14. hell hath enlarged *herself,*
10:18. shall consume...*both soul* and body: (marg. *from the soul*, and even to the flesh)
15: 4. *his life* shall be grievous unto him.
19:10. all that make sluices (and) ponds for *fish.* (marg. of *living things*)
26: 8. the desire of (our) *soul*
9. With *my soul* have I desired thee
29: 8. and *his soul* is empty:
— *and his soul* hath appetite:
32: 6. to make empty *the soul of* the hungry,
38:15. in the bitterness of *my soul.*
17. in love to *my soul* (delivered it)
42: 1. (in whom) *my soul* delighteth;
43: 4. will I give...people for *thy life.* (marg. or, *person*)
44:20. he cannot deliver *his soul,*
46: 2. *but themselves* (marg. *their soul*) are gone into captivity.
47:14. they shall not deliver *themselves* (marg. *their souls*)
49: 7. to him whom *man* despiseth, (marg. or, despised in *soul*)
51:23. which have said *to thy soul,* Bow down,
53:10. when thou shalt make *his soul* an offering
11. He shall see of the travail of *his soul,*
12. he hath poured out *his soul*
55: 2. let *your soul* delight itself
3. hear, and *your soul* shall live;
56:11. (they are) greedy (lit. strong of *soul*) dogs
58: 3. (wherefore) have we afflicted *our soul,*
5. a day for a man to afflict *his soul?*
10. (if) thou draw out *thy soul* to the hungry, *and* satisfy *the* afflicted *soul;*
11. satisfy *thy soul* in drought,
61:10. *my soul* shall be joyful in my God;
66: 3. *their soul* delighteth in their abominations.
Jer. 2:24. snuffeth up the wind at *her* pleasure; (marg. the desire of *her heart*)
34. the blood of *the souls of* the poor
3:11. The backsliding Israel hath justified *herself*
4:10. the sword reacheth unto *the soul.*
19. *O my soul,* the sound of the trumpet,
30. they will seek *thy life.*
31. *my soul* is wearied
5: 9, 29. shall not *my soul* be avenged
6: 8. lest *my soul* depart from thee;
16. ye shall find rest *for your souls.*

Jer. 9: 9(8). shall not *my soul* be avenged
11:21. the men of Anathoth, that seek *thy life,*
12: 7. the dearly beloved of *my soul*
13:17. *my soul* shall weep
14:19. hath *thy soul* lothed Zion?
15: 1. *my mind* (could) not (be) toward this people:
9. she hath given up *the ghost;*
17:21. Take heed *to yourselves,*
18:20. they have digged a pit *for my soul.*
19: 7. them that seek *their lives:*
9. they that seek *their lives,*
20:13. he hath delivered *the soul of* the poor
21: 7. those that seek *their life:*
9. *his life* shall be unto him for a prey.
22:25. them that seek *thy life,*
27. they desire (marg. lift up *their mind*)
26:19. we procure great evil against *our souls.*
31:12. *their soul* shall be as a watered garden;
14. I will satiate *the soul of* the priests
25. I have satiated *the* weary *soul,* and I have replenished every sorrowful *soul.*
32:41. with my whole heart and with *my* whole *soul.*
34:16. set at liberty *at their pleasure,*
20, 21. them that seek *their life:*
37: 9. Deceive not *yourselves,* (marg. *your souls*)
38: 2. he shall have *his life* for a prey,
16. the Lord liveth, that made us this *soul,*
— these men that seek *thy life.*
17. then *thy soul* shall live,
20. *thy soul* shall live.
39:18. *thy life* shall be for a prey
40:14. to slay thee? (marg. strike thee in *soul*)
15. wherefore should he slay thee, (lit. *id.*)
42:20. ye dissembled *in your hearts,* (marg. or, have used deceit against *your souls*)
43: 6. every *person* that Nebuzar-adan...had left
44: 7. ye (this) great evil against *your souls,*
14. to the which they have a desire (marg. lift up *their soul*) to return
30. them that seek *his life;*
— his enemy, and that sought *his life.*
45: 5. *thy life* will I give unto thee for a prey
46:26. those that seek *their lives,*
48: 6. Flee, save *your lives,*
49:37. them that seek *their life:*
50:19. *his soul* shall be satisfied
51: 6. deliver every man *his soul:*
14. The Lord of hosts hath sworn *by himself,* (marg. *his soul*)
45. deliver ye every man *his soul*
52:29. eight hundred thirty and two *persons:* (marg. *souls*)
30. seven hundred forty and five *persons:* all the *persons* (were) four thousand and six hundred.
Lam. 1:11. meat to relieve *the soul:*
16. the comforter that should relieve *my soul*
19. sought their meat to relieve *their souls.*
2:12. when *their soul* was poured out
19. for *the life of* thy young children,
3:17. thou hast removed *my soul*
20. *My soul* hath (them) still in remembrance,
24. The Lord (is) my portion, saith *my soul;*
25. *to the soul* (that) seeketh him.
51. Mine eye affecteth *mine heart* (marg. *my soul*)
58. thou hast pleaded the causes of *my soul;*
5: 9. gat our bread *with* (the peril of) *our lives*
Eze. 3:19, 21. thou hast delivered *thy soul.*
4:14. *my soul* hath not been polluted:
7:19. they shall not satisfy *their souls,*
13:18. to hunt *souls!* Will ye hunt *the souls of* my people, and will ye save *the souls* alive
19. to slay *the souls* that should not die, and to save *the souls* alive that should not live,
20. wherewith ye there hunt *the souls*
— and will let *the souls* go, (even) *the souls* that ye hunt
14:14. they should deliver (but) *their own souls*
20. they shall (but) deliver *their own souls*
16: 5. to the lothing of *thy person,*
27. delivered thee *unto the will* of them that
17:17. to cut off many *persons:*
18: 4. all *souls* are mine; *as the soul of* the father, *so also the soul of* the son is mine:
Eze.18: 4, 20. *the soul* that sinneth, it shall die.
27. he shall save *his soul* alive.
22:25. they have devoured *souls;*
27. to shed blood, (and) to destroy *souls,*
23:17. *her mind* was alienated
18. *my mind* was alienated from her, like as *my mind* was alienated from her sister.
22, 28. from whom *thy mind* is alienated,
24:21. that which *your soul* pitieth;
25. that whereupon they set *their minds,* (marg. the lifting up of *their soul*)
25: 6. rejoiced *in heart* (marg. *soul*) with all thy despite
15. taken vengeance *with a* despiteful *heart,*
27:13. they traded *the persons of* men
31. shall weep for thee with bitterness of *heart*
32:10. every man *for his own life,*
33: 5. that taketh warning shall deliver *his soul.*
6. take (any) *person* from among them,
9. thou hast delivered *thy soul.*
36: 5. with despiteful *minds,*
47: 9. every *thing that* liveth, (lit. every *soul of* life)
Hos. 4: 8. they set *their heart* on (marg. lift up *their soul* to) their iniquity.
9: 4. their bread *for their soul*
Am. 2:14. neither shall the mighty deliver *himself:* (marg. *his soul*)
15. shall he that rideth...deliver *himself.*
6: 8. The Lord God hath sworn *by himself,*
Jon. 1:14. let us not perish *for* this man's *life,*
2: 5(6). The waters compassed me about, (even) to *the soul:*
7(8). When *my soul* fainted
4: 3. take, I beseech thee, *my life*
8. wished in *himself* to die,
Mic. 6: 7. the sin of *my soul?*
7: 1. *my soul* desired the firstripe fruit.
3. he uttereth *his* mischievous *desire:* (marg. the mischief of *his soul*)
Hab. 2: 4. *his soul* (which) is lifted up
5. who enlargeth *his desire* as hell,
10. hast sinned (against) *thy soul.*
Hag. 2:13. unclean by *a* dead *body*
Zec.11: 8. *my soul* lothed them, *and their soul* also abhorred me.

נֶפֶת [*neh'-pheth*], f. 5316

Jos. 17:11. (even) three *countries.*

נֹפֶת *nōh'-pheth*, f. 5317

Ps. 19:10(11). *and*)(the honeycomb. (marg. *the dropping of* honeycombs)
Pro. 5: 3. drop (as) *an honeycomb,*
24:13. *and the honeycomb,* (which is) sweet
27: 7. The full soul loatheth *an honeycomb;*
Cant. 4:11. drop (as) *the honeycomb:*

נַפְתּוּלִים [*naph-too-leem'*], m. pl. 5319

Gen30: 8. With great *wrestlings* have I wrestled

נֵץ *nehtz*, m. 5322

Gen40:10. *her blossoms* shot forth;
Lev.11:16. *the hawk* after his kind,
Deu14:15. *the hawk* after his kind,
Job 39:26. Doth *the hawk* fly by thy wisdom,

נָצָא [*nāh-tzāh'*]. 5323

* KAL.—*Infinitive.* *

Jer. 48: 9. Moab, that it may *flee* and get away: (lit. that *fleeing* it may go out)

נָצַב [*nāh-tzav'*]. 5324

* NIPHAL.—*Preterite.* *

Gen37: 7. my sheaf arose, and also *stood upright;*
Ex. 7:15. *and thou shalt stand* by the river's brink
15: 8. the floods *stood upright* as an heap,
33: 8. the people rose up, *and stood*

Ex. 33:21. *and thou shalt stand* upon a rock:
34: 2. *and present* thyself there to me
Ps. 45: 9(10). thy right hand *did stand* the queen
Pro. 8: 2. *She standeth* in the top of high places,

NIPHAL.—*Participle.*

Gen18: 2. three men *stood* by him:
24:13. I *stand* (here) by the well of water;
43. I *stand* by the well of water;
28:13. the Lord *stood* above it,
45: 1. all them *that stood* by him;
Ex. 5:20. *who stood* in the way,
17: 9. I *will stand* on the top of the hill
18:14. all the people *stand* by thee
Nu. 16:27. *stood* in the door of their tents,
22:23, 31. of the Lord *standing* in the way,
34. I knew not that thou *stoodest* in the way
23: 6. he *stood* by his burnt sacrifice,
17. he *stood* by his burnt offering,
Deu29:10(9). Ye *stand* this day all of you
Jud.18:16. the six hundred men...*stood*
17. the priest *stood* in the entering of the gate
Ru. 2: 5. his servant *that was set over* the reapers,
6. the servant *that was set over* the reapers
1Sa. 1:26. the woman *that stood* by thee
4:20. the women *that stood* by her
19:20. Samuel standing (as) *appointed* over them,
22: 6. all his servants (were) *standing* about him;
7. his servants *that stood* about him,
9. *was set over* the servants of Saul,
17. the footmen *that stood* about him,
2Sa.13:31. all his servants *stood* by
1K. 4: 5. Azariah...(was) over *the officers*:
7. Solomon had twelve *officers*
27(5:7). those *officers* provided victual
5:16(30). the chief of Solomon's *officers*
9:23. These (were) the chief of *the officers*
22:47(48). *a deputy* (was) king.
2Ch 8:10. these (were) the chief of king Solomon's *officers*,
Ps. 39: 5(6). man *at his best state* (marg. *settled*) (is) altogether vanity.
82: 1. God *standeth* in the congregation
119:89. thy word *is settled* in heaven.
Isa. 3:13. The Lord *standeth up* to plead,
21: 8. and I *am set* in my ward
Lam.2: 4. *he stood* with his right hand as an adversary,
Am. 7: 7. the Lord *stood* upon a wall
9: 1. I saw the Lord *standing* upon the altar:
Zec.11:16. feed *that that standeth still*:

* HIPHIL.—*Preterite.* *

Gen21:29. which *thou hast set* by themselves?
1K. 16:34. *set up* the gates thereof
Ps. 74:17. *Thou hast set* all the borders of the earth.
Jer. 5:26. *they set* a trap, they catch men.

HIPHIL.—*Infinitive.*

1Sa.13:21. *and to sharpen* (marg. *set*) the goads.
1Ch 18: 3. *to stablish* his dominion by the river

HIPHIL.—*Imperative.*

Jer. 31:21. *Set* thee *up* waymarks,

HIPHIL.—*Future.*

Gen21:28. *And* Abraham *set* seven ewe lambs
33:20. *And he erected* there an altar,
35:14. *And* Jacob *set up* a pillar in the place
20. *And* Jacob *set* a pillar upon her grave:
Deu32: 8. *he set* the bounds of the people
Jos. 6:26. his youngest (son) *shall he set up* the gates
2Sa.18:17. *and laid* a very great heap of stones
18. *and reared up* for himself a pillar,
2K. 17:10. *And they set* them *up* images
Ps. 41:12(13). *and settest me* before thy face
78:13. *and he made* the waters *to stand*
Pro.15:25. *but he will establish* the border of the widow.
Lam.3:12. *and set* me as a mark for the arrow.

HIPHIL.—*Participle.*

1Sa.15:12. he *set* him *up* a place,

* HOPHAL.—*Preterite.* *

Nah. 2: 7(8). And *Huzzab* (marg. or, *that which was established*; or, *there was a stand made*) shall be led away captive,

HOPHAL.—*Participle.*

Gen28:12. a ladder *set up* on the earth,
Jud. 9: 6. the plain of *the pillar* that (was) in

נִצָּב *nitz-tzāhv'*, m. 5325

Jud. 3:22. *the haft* also went in after the blade;

נִצְבָּה [*nitz-bāh'*], Ch. f. 5326

Dan. 2:41. be in it of *the strength* of the iron,

נָצָה [*nāh-tzāh'*]. 5327

* NIPHAL.—*Future.* *

Ex. 21:22. men *strive*, and hurt a woman with child,
Lev.24:10. *and* this son...and a man of Israel *strove together* in the camp;
Deu25:11. When men *strive* together
2Sa.14: 6. *and they* two *strove together* in the field,

NIPHAL.—*Participle.*

Ex. 2:13. two men of the Hebrews *strove together*:

* HIPHIL.—*Preterite.* *

Nu. 26: 9. *strove* against Moses and against Aaron

HIPHIL.—*Infinitive.*

Nu. 26: 9. *when they strove* against the Lord:
Ps. 60[title](2). *when he strove* with Aram-naharaim

נָצָה [*nāh-tzāh'*]. 5327

* KAL.—*Future.* *

Jer. 4: 7. thy cities *shall be laid waste*,

* NIPHAL.—*Participle.* *

2K. 19:25. waste fenced cities (into) *ruinous* heaps.
Isa. 37:26. waste defenced cities (into) *ruinous* heaps.

נִצָּה *nitz-tzāh'*, f. 5328

Job 15:33. shall cast off *his flower*
Isa. 18: 5. the sour grape is ripening in *the flower*,

נֹצָה see נוֹצָה See 5133

נֹצָה [*nōh-tzāh'*], f. 5133

Lev. 1:16. he shall pluck away his crop *with his feathers*, (marg. or, *the filth thereof*)

נָצַח [*nāh-tzagh'*]. 5329

* NIPHAL.—*Participle.* *

Jer. 8: 5. slidden back by a *perpetual* backsliding?

* PIEL.—*Infinitive.* *

1Ch 15:21. with harps on the Sheminith *to excel*. (marg. or, *to oversee*)
23: 4. *to set forward* (marg. or, *oversee*) the work
2Ch 34:12. *to set* (it) *forward*;
Ezr. 3: 8. *to set forward* the work
9. *to set forward* the workmen

* PIEL.—*Participle.* *

2Ch 2: 2(1). *and* three thousand and six hundred *to oversee* them.
18(17). three thousand and six hundred *overseers*
34:13. *and* (were) *overseers* of all that wrought
Ps. 4:[title](1) & 5[title](1) & 6[title](1) & 8[title](1) & 9[title](1) & 11[title](1) & 12[title](1) & 13[title](1) & 14[title](1) & 18[title](1) & 19[title](1) & 20[title](1) & 21[title](1) & 22[title](1) & 31[title](1) & 36[title](1) & 39[title](1) & 40[title](1) & 41[title](1) & 42[title](1) & 44[title](1) & 45[title](1) & 46[title](1) & 47[title](1) & 49[title](1) & 51[title](1) & 52[title](1) & 53[title](1) & 54[title](1) & 55[title](1) & 56[title](1) & 57[title](1) & 58[title](1) & 59[title](1) & 60[title](1) & 61[title](1) & 62[title](1) & 64[title](1) & 65[title](1) & 66[title](1) & 67[title](1) & 68[title](1) & 69[title](1) & 70[title](1) & 75[title](1) & 76[title](1) & 77[title](1) & 80[title](1) & 81[title](1) & 84[title](1) & 85[title](1) & 88[title](1) & 109[title](1) & 139[title](1) & 140[title](1). *To the chief Musician* (marg. or, *overseer*)

Hab. 3:19. *To the chief singer* on my stringed instruments.

5330 ## נְצַח [*n'tzagh*], Ch.

∗ ITHPAEL.—*Participle.* ∗

Dan. 6: 3(4). Then this Daniel was *preferred* above

5331 ## נֵצַח *nēh'-tzagh* & נֶצַח *neh'-tzagh*, m.

1Sa.15:29. *the Strength* (marg. or, *Eternity*, or, *victory*) *of* Israel will not lie
2Sa. 2:26. Shall the sword devour *for ever?*
1Ch 29:11. the power, and the glory, and *the victory*,
Job 4:20. they perish *for ever*
14:20. Thou prevailest *for ever* against him,
20: 7. he shall perish *for ever*
23: 7. so should I be delivered *for ever*
34:36. (that) Job may be tried unto *the end*
36: 7. he doth establish them *for ever*,
Ps. 9: 6(7). destructions are come *to a perpetual* end: (lit. completed *for ever*)
18(19). the needy shall not *alway* be forgotten:
10:11. he will *never* (lit. not *for ever*) see (it).
13: 1(2). wilt thou forget me, O Lord? *for ever?*
16:11. at thy right hand (there are) pleasures for *evermore*.
44:23(24). cast (us) not off *for ever*.
49: 9(10). That he should still live *for ever*,
19(20). shall *never* (lit. for *ever* not) see light.
52: 5(7). God shall likewise destroy thee *for ever*,
68:16(17). the Lord will dwell (in it) *for ever*.
74: 1. why hast thou cast (us) off *for ever?*
3. up thy feet unto the *perpetual* desolations;
10. shall the enemy blaspheme...*for ever?*
19. forget not the congregation of thy poor *for ever*.
77: 8(9). Is his mercy clean gone *for ever?*
79: 5. wilt thou be angry *for ever?*
89:46(47). wilt thou hide thyself *for ever?*
103: 9. He will not *always* chide:
Pro.21:28. the man that heareth speaketh *constantly*.
Isa. 13:20. shall *never* (lit. not *for ever*) be inhabited,
25: 8. He will swallow up death *in victory*;
28:28. he will not *ever* be threshing it,
33:20. not one of the stakes thereof shall *ever* be removed,
34:10. it shall lie waste; none shall pass through it *for ever and ever*. [לְנֵצַח נְצָחִים]
57:16. neither will I be *always* wroth:
Jer. 3: 5. will he keep (it) to *the end?*
15:18. Why is my pain *perpetual*,
50:39. it shall be no more inhabited *for ever*;
Lam.3:18. *My strength* and my hope is perished
5:20. Wherefore dost thou forget us *for ever*,
Am. 1:11. he kept his wrath *for ever*:
8: 7. Surely I will *never* (lit. not *for ever*) forget any of their works.
Hab. 1: 4. judgment doth *never* go forth:

5332 ## נֵצַח [*nēh'-tzagh*], m.

Isa. 63: 3. *their blood* shall be sprinkled
6. I will bring down *their strength*

5333 ## נְצִיב *n'tzeev*, m.

Gen19:26. she became *a pillar of* salt.
1Sa.10: 5. *the garrison of* the Philistines:
13: 3. Jonathan smote *the garrison*
4. Saul had smitten *a garrison*
2Sa. 8: 6. David put *garrisons* in Syria
14. he put *garrisons* in Edom; throughout all Edom put he *garrisons*,
1K. 4:19. *and* (he was) *the* only *officer* which (was) in the land.
1Ch 11:16. the Philistines' *garrison*
18:13. he put *garrisons* in Edom;
2Ch 8:10. (כתיב) the chief of king Solomon's *officers*,
17: 2. set *garrisons* in the land of Judah,

5336 ## נָצִיר [*nāh-tzeer'*], m.

Isa. 49: 6. (כתיב) *and* to restore *the preserved of* Israel:

נָצַל [*nāh-tzal'*]. 5337

∗ NIPHAL.—*Preterite.* ∗

Jer. 7:10. *We are delivered* to do all these abominations?

NIPHAL.—*Infinitive.*

Isa. 20: 6. *to be delivered* from the king of Assyria:
Hab. 2: 9. *that he may be delivered* from the power

NIPHAL.—*Imperative.*

Pro. 6: 3. Do this now, my son, *and deliver thyself*,
5. *Deliver thyself* as a roe

NIPHAL.—*Future.*

Gen32:30(31). *and* my life *is preserved*.
Deu23:15(16). the servant which *is escaped*
2K. 19:11. and *shalt* thou *be delivered?*
Ps. 33:16. a mighty man *is* not *delivered*
69:14(15). *let me be delivered* from them that hate
Isa. 37:11. and *shalt* thou *be delivered?*
Eze.14:16. they only *shall be delivered*,
18. they only *shall be delivered* themselves.
Am. 3:12. so *shall* the children of Israel *be taken out*
Mic. 4:10. there *shalt thou be delivered*;

∗ PIEL.—*Preterite.* ∗

Ex. 3:22. *and ye shall spoil* the Egyptians.

PIEL.—*Future.*

Ex. 12:36. *And they spoiled* the Egyptians.
2Ch 20:25. *which they stripped off* for themselves,
Eze.14:14. *they should deliver* (but) their own souls

∗ HIPHIL.—*Preterite.* ∗

Gen31:16. the riches which God *hath taken* from our father,
Ex. 2:19. An Egyptian *delivered us*
5:23. neither *hast thou delivered* thy people
6: 6. *and I will rid* you out of their bondage,
12:27. and *delivered* our houses.
18: 9. *whom he had delivered* out of the hand
10. who *hath delivered* you out of the hand
— who *hath delivered* the people
Nu. 35:25. *And* the congregation *shall deliver* the
Jos. 2:13. *and deliver* our lives from death.
22:31. now *ye have delivered* the children of Israel
Jud.11:26. therefore *did ye* not *recover*
1Sa. 7:14. the coasts thereof *did* Israel *deliver*
17:35. *and delivered* (it) out of his mouth:
37. The Lord that *delivered me*
30:18. David *rescued* his two wives.
22. the spoil that *we have recovered*,
2Sa.12: 7. I *delivered thee* out of the hand
19: 9(10). The king *saved us* out of the hand
20: 6. lest he get him fenced cities, *and escape* us. (marg. *deliver himself* from our eyes)
22: 1. the Lord *had delivered* him
2K. 18:33. *Hath* any of the gods of the nations *delivered*
34. *have they delivered* Samaria
35. that *have delivered* their country
19:12. *Have* the gods of the nations *delivered* them
2Ch 25:15. which *could* not *deliver* their own people
32:17. *have* not *delivered* their people
Ps. 18[title](1). the Lord *delivered* him
34: 4(5). *delivered me* from all my fears.
17(18). *delivereth them* out of all their troubles.
54: 7(9). *he hath delivered me* out of all trouble:
56:13(14). *thou hast delivered* my soul from death:
86:13. *and thou hast delivered* my soul
Isa. 19:20. a great one, *and he shall deliver them.*
31: 5. defending *also he will deliver* (it);
36:18. *Hath* any of the gods of the nations *delivered* his land
19. *have they delivered* Samaria
20. that *have delivered* their land
37:12. *Have* the gods of the nations *delivered* them
Jer. 15:21. *And I will deliver thee* out of the hand of the wicked,
20:13. *he hath delivered* the soul of the poor
39:17. *But I will deliver thee* in that day,
Eze. 3:19. but thou *hast delivered* thy soul.
21. also thou *hast delivered* thy soul.
13:21. *and deliver* my people out of your hand,
23. *for I will deliver* my people out of your
33: 9. but *thou hast delivered* thy soul.
34:10. *for I will deliver* my flock from their mouth,

Eze.34:12. *and will deliver* them out of all places
27. *and delivered them* out of the hand
Hos. 2: 9(11). *and will recover* (marg. or, *take away*) my wool and my flax
Mic. 5: 6(5). *thus shall he deliver* (us) from the Assyrian,

HIPHIL.—*Infinitive.*

Gen37:22. *that he might rid him* out of their hands,
Ex. 3: 8. I am come down *to deliver them*
5:23. neither hast thou delivered thy people *at all.* (lit. *and delivering* hast thou not delivered)
Deu23:14(15). *to deliver thee,*
25:11. *to deliver* her husband
1Sa.30: 8. *and without fail* recover (lit. *and recovering* shalt recover)
2Sa.14:16. *to deliver* his handmaid
2K. 18:29. he shall not be able *to deliver* you
30. The Lord will *surely* deliver us, (lit. *delivering* will deliver)
33. Hath any of the gods...delivered *at all* (lit. *delivering* have they delivered)
2Ch 32:13. able *to deliver* their lands
14. that *could deliver* his people
— that your God should be able *to deliver*
15. was able *to deliver* his people
Ps. 33:19. *To deliver* their soul from death,
40:13(14). Be pleased, O Lord, *to deliver me:*
70: 1(2). (Make haste), O God, *to deliver me;*
Pro. 2:12. *To deliver thee* from the way
16. *To deliver thee* from the strange woman,
Isa. 36:14. he shall not be able *to deliver* you.
15. The Lord will *surely* deliver us: (lit *delivering* will deliver)
50: 2. have I no power *to deliver?*
Jer. 1: 8. I (am) with thee *to deliver thee,*
19. I (am) with thee,...*to deliver thee.*
15:20. to save thee *and to deliver thee,*
42:11. *and to deliver* you from his hand.
Eze. 7:19. their gold shall not be able *to deliver them*
Jon. 4: 6. *to deliver* him from his grief.
Zep. 1:18. shall be able *to deliver them*

HIPHIL.—*Imperative.*

Gen32:11(12). *Deliver me,* I pray thee, from the hand of my brother,
Jud.10:15. *deliver us* only, we pray thee, this day.
1Sa.12:10. *deliver us* out of the hand of our enemies,
1Ch 16:35. *and deliver us* from the heathen,
Ps. 7: 1(2). save me...*and deliver me:*
22:20(21). *Deliver* my soul from the sword;
25:20. O keep my soul, *and deliver me:*
31: 2(3). *deliver me* speedily:
15(16). *deliver me* from the hand of mine enemies,
39: 8(9). *Deliver me* from all my transgressions:
51:14(16). *Deliver me* from bloodguiltiness,
59: 1(2). *Deliver me* from mine enemies,
2(3). *Deliver me* from the workers of iniquity,
69:14(15). *Deliver me* out of the mire,
79: 9. *and deliver us,* and purge away our sins,
82: 4. *rid* (them) out of the hand of the wicked.
109:21. thy mercy (is) good, *deliver thou me.*
119:170. *deliver me* according to thy word.
120: 2. *Deliver* my soul, O Lord,
142: 6(7). *deliver me* from my persecutors;
143: 9. *Deliver me,* O Lord, from mine enemies:
144: 7. *and deliver me* out of great waters,
11. *and deliver me* from the hand of strange children,
Pro.24:11. If thou forbear *to deliver* (lit. *deliver*)
Isa. 44:17. *Deliver me;* for thou (art) my god.
Jer. 21:12. *and deliver* (him that is) spoiled
22: 3. *and deliver* the spoiled out of the hand

HIPHIL.—*Future.*

Gen31: 9. *Thus* God *hath taken away* the cattle of
37:21. *and he delivered him* out of their hands;
Ex. 18: 4. *and delivered me* from the sword
8. *and* (how) the Lord *delivered them.*
Jos. 9:26. *and delivered* them out of the hand
24:10. *so I delivered* you out of his hand.
Jud. 6: 9. *And I delivered* you out of the hand
9:17. *and delivered* you out of the hand of Midian:
1Sa. 4: 8. who *shall deliver us* out of the hand
7: 3. *and he will deliver* you out of the hand
1Sa.10:18. *and delivered* you out of the hand
12:11. *and delivered* you out of the hand
21. which cannot profit nor *deliver;*
14:48. *and delivered* Israel out of the hands
17:37. he *will deliver me* out of the hand
26:24. *and let him deliver me* out of all tribulation.
30: 8. and without fail *recover* (all).
18. *And* David *recovered* all
2Sa.22:18. *He delivered me* from my strong enemy,
49. *thou hast delivered me* from the violent man.
23:12. *and defended it,* and slew the Philistines:
2K. 17:39. he *shall deliver* you out of the hand
18:30. The Lord *will* surely *deliver us,*
32. The Lord *will deliver us.*
35. that the Lord *should deliver* Jerusalem
20: 6. *I will deliver thee* and this city
1Ch 11:14. *and delivered it,* and slew the Philistines;
2Ch 32:11. The Lord our God *shall deliver us*
15. how much less *shall* your God *deliver* you out of mine hand?
17. so *shall* not the God of Hezekiah *deliver* his people
Ezr. 8:31. *and he delivered us* from the hand of the
Neh. 9:28. *and* many times *didst thou deliver them*
Job 5:19. *He shall deliver thee* in six troubles:
Ps. 18:17(18). *He delivered* me from my strong enemy,
48(49). *thou hast delivered me* from the violent
22: 8(9). *let him deliver him,* seeing he
34:19(20). Lord *delivereth him* out of them all.
71: 2. *Deliver me* in thy righteousness,
72:12. *he shall deliver* the needy
91: 3. Surely *he shall deliver thee*
97:10. *he delivereth them* out of the hand
106:43. Many times *did he deliver them;*
107: 6. *he delivered them* out of their distresses.
119:43. *take* not the word of truth utterly out of
Pro.10: 2 & 11:4. righteousness *delivereth* from death.
11: 6. The righteousness of the upright *shall deliver them:*
12: 6. mouth of the upright *shall deliver them.*
19:19. if *thou deliver* (him),
23:14. *shalt deliver* his soul from hell.
Isa. 36:15. The Lord *will* surely *deliver us:*
18. The Lord *will deliver us.*
20. that the Lord *should deliver* Jerusalem
38: 6. And *I will deliver thee* and this city
44:20. *he cannot deliver* his soul,
47:14. *they shall* not *deliver* themselves
57:13. *let* thy companies *deliver thee;*
Eze.14:16. *they shall deliver* neither sons nor daughters;
18. *they shall deliver* neither sons nor daughters,
20. *they shall deliver* neither son nor daughter; *they shall* (but) *deliver* their own souls
33:12. The righteousness of the righteous *shall* not *deliver him*
Hos. 2:10(12). none *shall deliver her*
Am. 3:12. As the shepherd *taketh* (marg. *delivereth*) out of the mouth
Zec.11: 6. out of their hand *I will* not *deliver* (them).

HIPHIL.—*Participle.*

Deu32:39. (any) *that can deliver* out of my hand.
Jud. 8:34. the Lord their God, *who had delivered* them
18:28. (there was) no *deliverer,*
2Sa.14: 6. there was none *to part* (marg. no *deliverer* between) them,
Job 5: 4. neither is there *any to deliver* (them).
10: 7. there is none *that can deliver*
Ps. 7: 2(3). while there is none *to deliver.* (marg. not *a deliverer*)
35:10. *which deliverest* the poor
50:22. lest I tear (you) in pieces, and there be none *to deliver.*
71:11. there is none *to deliver* (him).
Pro.14:25. A true witness *delivereth* souls:
Isa. 5:29. none *shall deliver*
42:22. for a prey, and none *delivereth;*
43:13. there is none *that can deliver*
Dan. 8: 4. neither was there any *that could deliver*
7. there was none *that could deliver*
Hos. 5:14. none *shall rescue* (him).
Mic. 5: 8(7). none *can deliver.*

* HOPHAL.—*Participle.* *

Am. 4:11. ye were as a firebrand *plucked*
Zec. 3: 2. a brand *plucked* out of the fire?

* HITHPAEL.—*Future.* *

Ex. 33: 6. *And* the children of Israel *stripped themselves*

5338 ## נְצַל [*n'tzal*], Ch.

* APHEL.—*Infinitive.* *

Dan. 3:29. that can *deliver* after this sort.
6:14(15). going down of the sun *to deliver him.*

APHEL.—*Participle.*

Dan. 6:27(28). He delivereth *and rescueth*,

5339 ## נִצָּן [*nitz-tzāhn'*], m.

Cant.2:12. *The flowers* appear on the earth;

See 3331 ## נָצַע see יָצַע

5340 ## נָצַץ [*nāh-tzatz'*].

* KAL.—*Participle.* Poel. *

Eze. 1: 7. *and they sparkled* like...burnished brass.

5341 ## נָצַר [*nāh-tzar'*].

* KAL.—*Preterite.* *

Ps.119:22. *I have kept* thy testimonies.
56. because *I kept* thy precepts.
100. because *I keep* thy precepts.
129. therefore *doth* my soul *keep them.*
Pro.22:12. The eyes of the Lord *preserve* knowledge,

KAL.—*Infinitive.*

Pro. 2: 8. *He keepeth* (lit. *to keep*) the paths of judgment,
Nah. 2: 1(2). *keep* the munition,

KAL.—*Imperative.*

Ps. 34:13(14). *Keep* thy tongue from evil,
141: 3. *keep* the door of my lips.
Pro. 3:21. *keep* sound wisdom and discretion:
4:13. Take fast hold of instruction;...*keep her;*
23. *Keep* thy heart with all diligence;
6:20. *keep* thy father's commandment,

KAL.—*Future.*

Deu32:10. *he kept him* as the apple of his eye.
33: 9. thy word, and *kept* thy covenant.
Ps. 12: 7(8). *thou shalt preserve them* (marg. *him*) from this
25:21. *Let* integrity and uprightness *preserve me:*
32: 7. *thou shalt preserve me* from trouble;
40:11(12). *let* thy lovingkindness and thy truth continually *preserve me.*
61: 7(8). mercy and truth, (which) *may preserve him.*
64: 1(2). *preserve* my life from fear of the enemy.
78: 7. *keep* his commandments:
105:45. observe his statutes, and *keep* his laws.
119:33. *and I shall keep it* (unto) the end.
34. *and I shall keep* thy law;
69. *I will keep* thy precepts
115. *for I will keep* the commandments
145. *I will keep* thy statutes.
140: 1(2), 4(5). *preserve me* from the violent man;
Pro. 2:11. understanding *shall keep thee:*
3: 1. *let* thine heart *keep* my commandments:
4: 6. love her, *and she shall keep thee.*
5: 2. thy lips *may keep* knowledge.
13: 6. Righteousness *keepeth* (him that is) upright
20:28. Mercy and truth *preserve* the king:
23:26. *let* thine eyes *observe* my ways.
Isa. 26: 3. *Thou wilt keep* (him) in perfect peace,
27: 3. *I will keep it* night and day.
42: 6. *and will keep thee*, and give thee
49: 8. *and I will preserve thee*, and give thee

KAL.—*Participle.* Poel.

Ex. 34: 7. *Keeping* mercy for thousands,
2K. 17: 9 & 18:8. from the tower of *the watchmen*
Job 7:20. do unto thee, *O thou preserver of* men?
27:18. as a booth (that) *the keeper* maketh.
Ps. 25:10. *unto such as keep* his covenant
31:23(24). the Lord *preserveth* the faithful,
119: 2. Blessed (are) *they that keep* his testimonies,
Pro.13: 3. *He that keepeth* his mouth
16:17. *he that keepeth* his way
24:12. *and he that keepeth* thy soul,
27:18. *Whoso keepeth* the fig tree
28: 7. *Whoso keepeth* the law
Isa. 27: 3. I the Lord *do keep it;* I will water it
Jer. 4:16. *watchers* come from a far country,
31: 6. *the watchmen* upon the mount Ephraim

KAL.—*Participle.* Paül.

Pro. 7:10. (with) the attire of an harlot, *and subtil of* heart.
Isa. 1: 8. as a *besieged* city.
48: 6. I have shewed thee new things...*even hidden things,*
49: 6. to restore *the preserved* (marg. or, *desolations*) *of* Israel:
65: 4. *and* lodge *in the monuments,*
Eze. 6:12. he that remaineth *and is besieged*

נֵצֶר *nēh'-tzer*, m. 5342

Isa. 11: 1. *and a Branch* shall grow out of his roots:
14:19. *like an* abominable *branch,*
60:21. *the branch of* my planting,
Dan11: 7. *out of a branch of* her roots

נָצַת see יָצַת See 3341

נְקֵא *n'kēh*, Ch. adj. 5343

Dan. 7: 9. the hair of his head like the *pure* wool:

נָקַב [*nāh-kav'*]. 5344

* KAL.—*Preterite.* *

2K. 18:21. it will go into his hand, *and pierce it:*
Isa. 36: 6. will go into his hand, *and pierce it:*
Hab. 3:14. *Thou didst strike through* with his staves

KAL.—*Infinitive.*

Lev.24:16. *when he blasphemeth* the name (of the Lord).

KAL.—*Imperative.*

Gen30:28. *Appoint* me thy wages,

KAL.—*Future.*

Lev.24:11. *And* the Israelitish woman's son *blasphemed*
Nu. 23: 8. How *shall I curse,*
25. Neither *curse them* at all,
2K. 12: 9(10). took a chest, *and bored* a hole
Job 3: 8. *Let them curse it* that curse
5: 3. *but* suddenly *I cursed* his habitation.
40:24. (his) nose *pierceth* through snares.
41: 2(40:26). Canst thou...*bore* his jaw through
Pro.11:26. withholdeth corn, the people *shall curse him:*
24:24. *him shall* the people *curse,*
Isa. 62: 2. the mouth of the Lord *shall name.*

KAL.—*Participle.* Poel.

Lev.24:16. *And he that blasphemeth* the name of the Lord,

KAL.—*Participle.* Paül.

Am. 6: 1. (which are) *named* chief of the nations,
Hag. 1: 6. (to put it) into a bag *with holes.* (marg. *pierced*)

* NIPHAL.—*Preterite.* *

Nu. 1:17. these men which *are expressed* by (their) names:
1Ch 12:31. which *were expressed* by name,
16:41. who *were expressed* by name,
2Ch 28:15. the men which *were expressed* by name
31:19. the men that *were expressed* by name,
Ezr. 8:20. all of them *were expressed* by name.

נֶקֶב [*neh'-kev*], m. 5345

Eze.28:13. the workmanship of thy tabrets *and of thy pipes*

5347 נְקֵבָה *n'kēh-vāh'*, f.

Gen. 1:27. male *and female* created he them.
5: 2. Male *and female* created he them;
6:19. they shall be male *and female.*
7: 3. the male *and the female;*
9. the male *and the female,*
16. went in male *and female*
Lev. 3: 1. whether (it be) a male or *female,*
6. male or *female,* he shall offer it
4:28. *a female* without blemish,
32. *a female* without blemish.
5: 6. *a female* from the flock,
12: 5. if she bear *a maid child,*
7. her that hath born a male or *a female.*
15:33. of the man, *and of the woman,*
27: 4. if it (be) *a female,*
5, 7. *and for the female* ten shekels.
6. *and for the female* thy estimation
Nu. 5: 3. Both male and *female* shall ye put out,
31:15. Have ye saved all *the women* alive?
Deu 4:16. the likeness of male or *female,*
Jer. 31:22. *A woman* shall compass a man.

5348 נָקֹד *nāh-kōhd'*, adj.

Gen30:32. all the *speckled* and spotted cattle,
— the spotted *and speckled* among the goats.
33. every one that (is) not *speckled* and spotted
35. all the she goats that were *speckled*
39. cattle ringstraked, *speckled,* and spotted.
31: 8. *The speckled* shall be thy wages; then all the cattle bare *speckled:*
10, 12. ringstraked, *speckled,* and grisled.

5349 נֹקֵד *nōh-kēhd'*, m.

2K. 3: 4. Mesha king of Moab was *a sheepmaster,*
Am. 1: 1. Amos, who was *among the herdmen of* Tekoa,

5351 נְקֻדּוֹת *n'kood-dōhth'*, f. pl.

Cant.1:11. borders of gold with *studs* of silver.

5350 נִקֻּדִים *nik-kood-deem'*, m. pl.

Jos. 9: 5. all the bread...was dry (and) *mouldy.*
12. This our bread...it is dry, and it is *mouldy:*
1K. 14: 3. take with thee ten loaves, *and cracknels,* (marg. or, *cakes*)

5352 נָקָה [*nāh-kāh'*].

* KAL.—*Infinitive.*

Jer. 49:12. he (that) shall *altogether* go unpunished? (lit. *in being clear* shall be clear)

* NIPHAL.—*Preterite.* *

Gen24: 8. *then thou shalt be clear* from this my oath:
Ex. 21:19. *then shall he* that smote (him) *be quit:*
Nu. 5:28. *then she shall be free,*
31. *Then shall* the man *be guiltless*
Jud 15: 3. Now *shall I be* more *blameless* than
1Sa.26: 9. who can stretch forth his hand...*and be guiltless?*
Ps. 19:13(14). *and I shall be innocent* from the great transgression.
Isa. 3:26. *and she* (being) *desolate* (marg. *cleansed,* or, *emptied*) shall sit upon the ground.
Jer. 2:35. Yet thou sayest, Because *I am innocent,*
Zec. 5: 3. every one that stealeth *shall be cut off* (marg. *holdeth* (himself) *guiltless*)
— every one that sweareth *shall be cut off*

NIPHAL.—*Infinitive.*

Jer. 25:29. should ye be *utterly* unpunished? (lit. *being unpunished* should be unpunished)

NIPHAL.—*Imperative.*

Nu. 5:19. *be thou free* from this bitter water

NIPHAL.—*Future.*

Gen24:41. Then *shalt thou be clear* from (this) my oath,
Pro. 6:29. whosoever toucheth her *shall* not *be innocent.*
Pro.11:21. the wicked *shall* not *be unpunished:*
16: 5. *he shall* not *be unpunished.* (marg. *held innocent*)
17: 5. he that is glad at calamities *shall* not *be unpunished.* (marg. *id.*)
19: 5, 9. A false witness *shall* not *be unpunished.* (marg. *id.*)
28:20. he that maketh haste to be rich *shall* not *be innocent.* (marg. or, *unpunished*)
Jer. 25:29. *should* ye *be* utterly *unpunished? Ye shall* not *be unpunished:*
49:12. (art) thou he (that) *shall* altogether *go unpunished? thou shalt* not *go unpunished,*

* PIEL.—*Preterite.* *

Joel 3:21(4:21). *For I will cleanse* their blood (that) *I have* not *cleansed:*

PIEL.—*Infinitive.*

Ex. 34: 7. *and* that will *by no means* clear (lit. *and clearing* will not clear) (the guilty);
Nu. 14:18. *and by no means* clearing (the guilty),
Jer. 30:11. *and* will not leave thee *altogether* unpunished.
46:28. *yet* will I not leave thee *wholly* unpunished. (marg. *utterly* cut thee off)
Nah. 1: 3. *and* will not *at all* acquit

PIEL.—*Imperative.*

Ps. 19:12(13). *cleanse thou me* from secret (faults).

PIEL.—*Future.*

Ex. 20: 7. the Lord *will* not *hold him guiltless*
34: 7. *will* by no means *clear* (the guilty);
Nu. 14:18. by no means *clearing* (the guilty),
Deu 5:11. the Lord *will* not *hold* (him) *guiltless*
1K. 2: 9. *hold him* not *guiltless:*
Job 9:28. I know that *thou wilt* not *hold me innocent.*
10:14. *thou wilt* not *acquit me*
Jer. 30:11. *will* not *leave thee* altogether *unpunished.*
46:28. *will I* not *leave thee* wholly *unpunished.* (marg. or, *utterly* cut thee off)
Nah 1: 3. *will* not at all *acquit* (the wicked):

נָקַט [*nāh-kat'*]. 5354

* KAL.—*Preterite.* *

Job 10: 1. My soul is *weary* of my life; (marg. or, *cut off* while I live)

נָקִי *nāh-kee'*, adj. 5355

Gen24:41. thou shalt be *clear* from my oath.
44:10. ye shall be *blameless.*
Ex. 21:28. the owner of the ox (shall be) *quit.*
23: 7. *and the innocent* and righteous slay thou not:
Nu. 32:22. be *guiltless* before the Lord,
Deu19:10. That *innocent* blood be not shed
13. put away (the guilt of) *innocent* blood
21: 8. lay not *innocent* blood unto thy people
9. put away the (guilt of) *innocent* blood
24: 5. he shall be *free* at home one year,
27:25. taketh reward to slay an *innocent* person.
Jos. 2:17. We (will be) *blameless*
19. we (will be) *guiltless:*
20. then we will be *quit*
1Sa.19: 5. wilt thou sin against *innocent* blood,
2Sa. 3:28. I and my kingdom (are) *guiltless*
14: 9. the king and his throne (be) *guiltless.*
1K. 15:22. none (was) *exempted:* (marg. *free*)
2K. 21:16. Manasseh shed *innocent* blood
24: 4. the *innocent* blood that he shed: for he filled Jerusalem with *innocent* blood;
Job 4: 7. who (ever) perished, being *innocent?*
9:23. he will laugh at the trial of *the innocent.*
17: 8. *the innocent* shall stir up himself
22:19. *and the innocent* laugh them to scorn.
30. He shall deliver the island of *the innocent:*
27:17. *the innocent* shall divide the silver.
Ps. 10: 8. doth he murder *the innocent:*
15: 5. nor taketh reward against *the innocent.*
24: 4. He that hath *clean* hands, (marg. *The clean of* hands)
94:21. and condemn the *innocent* blood.
106:38. And shed *innocent* blood,
Pro. 1:11. let us lurk privily *for the innocent*
6:17. and hands that shed *innocent* blood,
Isa. 59: 7. they make haste to shed *innocent* blood:

Jer. 2:34. the souls of *the* poor *innocents:*
7: 6. shed not *innocent* blood
19: 4. filled this place with the blood of *innocents;*
22: 3. neither shed *innocent* blood
17. for to shed *innocent* blood,
26:15. ye shall surely bring *innocent* blood upon
Jon. 1:14. lay not upon us *innocent* blood:

5355 **נָקִיא** *nāh-kee'*, adj.

Joel 3:19(4:19). they have shed *innocent* blood
Jon. 1:14. (כתיב) lay not upon us *innocent* blood:

5356 **נִקָּיוֹן** *nik-kāh-yōhn'*, m.

Gen20: 5. *and innocency of* my hands
Ps. 26: 6. I will wash mine hands *in innocency:*
73:13. washed my hands *in innocency.*
Hos. 8: 5. how long (will it be) ere they attain to *innocency?*
Am. 4: 6. I also have given you *cleanness of* teeth

5357 **נְקִיק** *n'keek*, m.

Isa. 7:19. *and in the holes of* the rocks,
Jer. 13: 4. *in a hole of* the rock.
16:16. *and out of the holes of* the rocks.

5358 **נָקַם** [*nāh-kam'*].

* KAL.—*Preterite.* *

1Sa.24:12(13). *and* the Lord *avenge me* of thee:

KAL.—*Infinitive.*

Ex. 21:20. he shall be *surely* punished. (lit. *avenging* he shall be avenged)
Eze.24: 8. cause fury to come up *to take* vengeance;
25:12. the house of Judah *by taking* vengeance,

KAL.—*Imperative.*

Nu. 31: 2. *Avenge* (lit. *avenge* the vengeance of) the children of Israel

KAL.—*Future.*

Lev.19:18. *Thou shalt* not *avenge*,
Deu32:43. *he will avenge* the blood of his servants,
Jos. 10:13. until the people *had avenged themselves*

KAL.—*Participle.* Poel.

Lev.26:25. a sword...*that shall avenge*
Ps. 99: 8. *though thou tookest vengeance*
Nah. 1: 2. *and* the Lord *revengeth;* the Lord *revengeth*, and (is) furious; the Lord *will take vengeance*

* NIPHAL.—*Preterite.* *

Jud.15: 7. yet *will I be avenged* of you,
1Sa.14:24. *that I may be avenged* on mine enemies.
Eze.25:12. *and revenged himself* upon them;

NIPHAL.—*Infinitive.*

1Sa.18:25. *to be avenged* of the king's enemies.
Est. 8:13. *to avenge themselves* on their enemies.
Jer. 46:10. *that he may avenge him* of his adversaries:

NIPHAL —*Imperative.*

Jer. 15:15. *and revenge me* of my persecutors;
50:15. *take vengeance* upon her;

NIPHAL.—*Future.*

Ex. 21:20. *he shall be* surely *punished.* (marg. *avenged*)
Jud.16:28. *that I may be* at once *avenged*
Isa. 1:24. *and avenge me* of mine enemies:
Eze.25:15. *and have taken* vengeance with a despiteful

* PIEL.—*Preterite.* *

2K. 9: 7. *that I may avenge* the blood of my servants
Jer. 51:36. *and take* vengeance for thee;

* HOPHAL.—*Future.* *

Gen 4:15. *vengeance shall be taken on him* sevenfold.
24. If Cain *shall be avenged* sevenfold,
Ex. 21:21. *he shall* not *be punished:*

* HITHPAEL.—*Future.* *

Jer. 5: 9, 29 & 9:9(8). *shall* not my soul *be avenged*

HITHPAEL.—*Participle.*

Ps. 8: 2(3). still the enemy *and the avenger.*
44:16(17). by reason of the enemy *and avenger.*

נָקָם *nāh-kāhm'*, m. 5359

Lev.26:25. a sword...that shall avenge *the quarrel of*
Deu32:35. To me (belongeth) *vengeance,*
41. I will render *vengeance* to mine enemies,
43. *and* will render *vengeance* to his
Jud.16:28. that I may be at once avenged (lit. may be avenged *the vengeance*)
Ps. 58:10(11). shall rejoice when he seeth *the vengeance:*
Pro. 6:34. in the day of *vengeance.*
Isa. 34: 8. the day of the Lord's *vengeance,*
35: 4. your God will come (with) *vengeance,*
47: 3. I will take *vengeance,*
59:17. he put on the garments of *vengeance*
61: 2. the day of *vengeance* of our God;
63: 4. the day of *vengeance* (is) in mine heart,
Eze.24: 8. cause fury to come up to take *vengeance;*
25:12. dealt against the house of Judah by taking *vengeance,*
15. the Philistines...have taken *vengeance*
Mic. 5:15(14). I will execute *vengeance*

נְקָמָה *n'kāh-māh'*, f. 5360

Nu. 31: 2. *Avenge* (lit. avenge *the vengeance of*) the children of Israel
3. *avenge* (lit. give *the vengeance of*) the Lord of Midian.
Jud.11:36. the Lord hath taken *vengeance*
2Sa. 4: 8. the Lord hath *aveng*ed (lit. hath given *avengements* to) my lord
22:48. (It is) God that *aveng*eth me, (marg. giveth *avengement* for me)
Ps. 18:47(48). (It is) God that *aveng*eth me, (marg. *id.*)
79:10. *the revenging* (marg. *vengeance*) *of* the blood of thy servants
94: 1. O Lord God, to whom *vengeance* belongeth (marg. God of *revenges*); O God, to whom *vengeance* belongeth,
149: 7. To execute *vengeance* upon the heathen,
Jer. 11:20. let me see *thy vengeance*
20:10. we shall take *our revenge*
12. let me see *thy vengeance*
46:10. a day of *vengeance,*
50:15. *the vengeance of* the Lord:
28. declare in Zion *the vengeance of* the Lord our God, *the vengeance of* his temple.
51: 6. the time of the Lord's *vengeance;*
11. *the vengeance of* the Lord, *the vengeance of* his temple.
36. I will...take *vengeance for thee;*
Lam.3:60. Thou hast seen all *their vengeance*
Eze.25:14. I will lay *my vengeance* upon Edom
— they shall know *my vengeance,*
15. the Philistines have dealt *by revenge,*
17. I will execute *great vengeance* (marg. *vengeances*)
— when I shall lay *my vengeance* upon them.

נָקַע [*nāh-kag'*]. 5361

* KAL.—*Preterite.* *

Eze.23:18. like as my mind *was alienated*
22, 28. from whom thy mind *is alienated,*

נָקַף [*nāh-kaph'*]. 5362

* KAL.—*Future.* *

Isa. 29: 1. *let them kill* sacrifices. (marg. *cut off* the heads)

* PIEL.—*Preterite.* *

Job 19:26. (though) after my skin (worms) *destroy* this (body),
Isa. 10:34. *And he shall cut down* the thickets

* HIPHIL.—*Preterite.* *

2K. 11: 8. *And ye shall compass* the king round about,
2Ch 23: 7. *And* the Levites *shall compass* the king
Job 1: 5. the days of (their) feasting *were gone about,*
19: 6. *hath compassed* me with his net.
Ps. 22:16(17). the wicked *have inclosed me:*

Ps. 88:17(18). *they compassed* me *about* together.
Isa. 15: 8. the cry *is gone round about*

HIPHIL.—*Infinitive.*

Jos. 6: 3. *go round* about the city once.
11. *going about* (it) once:

HIPHIL.—*Imperative.*

Ps. 48:12(13). Walk about Zion, *and go round about* her:

HIPHIL.—*Future.*

Lev 19:27. *Ye shall* not *round* the corners of your heads,
2K. 6:14. *and compassed* the city *about.*
Ps. 17: 9. (who) *compass* me *about.*
Lam.3: 5. *compassed* (me) with gall and travel.

HIPHIL.—*Participle.*

1K. 7:24. *compassing* the sea round about:
2Ch 4: 3. *compassing* the sea round about.

5363 **נֹקֶף** *nōh'-keph'*, m.

Isa. 17: 6. in it, *as the shaking of* an olive tree,
24:13. (shall be) *as the shaking of* an olive tree,

5364 **נִקְפָּה** *nik-pāh'*, f.

Isa. 3:24. instead of a girdle *a rent;* (perhaps lit. *a rope*)

5365 **נָקַר** [*nāh-kar'*].

* KAL.—*Infinitive.* *

1Sa.11: 2. *that I may thrust out* all your right eyes,

KAL.—*Future.*

Pro.30:17. the ravens of the valley *shall pick it out,*

* PIEL.—*Preterite.* *

Job 30:17. My bones *are pierced* in me

PIEL.—*Future.*

Nu. 16:14. *wilt thou put out* (marg. *bore out*) the eyes of these men?
Jud.16:21. took him, *and put out* (marg. *bored out*) his eyes,

* PUAL.—*Preterite.* *

Isa. 51: 1. the pit (whence) *ye are digged.*

5366 **נְקָרָה** [*n'kāh-rāh'*], f.

Ex. 33:22. I will put thee *in a clift of* the rock,
Isa. 2:21. To go *into the clefts of* the rocks,

5367 **נָקַשׁ** [*nāh-kash'*].

* KAL.—*Preterite.* *

Ps. 9:16(17). the wicked *is snared*

* NIPHAL.—*Future.* *

Deu12:30. Take heed...that *thou be not snared*

* PIEL.—*Future.* *

Ps. 38:12(13). They *also* that seek after my life *lay snares*
109:11. *Let* the extortioner *catch* all that he hath;

* HITHPAEL.—*Participle.* *

1Sa.28: 9. wherefore then *layest* thou *a snare* for my life,

---

5368 **נְקַשׁ** [*n'kash*], Ch.

* P'AL.—*Participle.* *

Dan.5: 6. and his knees *smote* one against another.

5216 **נֵר** *nēhr*, m.

Ex. 25:37. *the* seven *lamps thereof:* and they shall light *the lamps thereof,*
27:20. to cause *the lamp* to burn
Ex. 30: 7. when he dresseth *the lamps,*
8. when Aaron lighteth *the lamps*
35:14. his furniture, and *his lamps,*
37:23. he made *his* seven *lamps,*
39:37. *the lamps thereof,* (even with) *the lamps* to be set in order,
40: 4. and light *the lamps thereof.*
25. he lighted *the lamps* before the Lord,
Lev.24: 2. to cause *the lamps* to burn
4. *the lamps* upon the pure candlestick
Nu. 4: 9. *his lamps,* and his tongs,
8: 2. When thou lightest *the lamps, the* seven *lamps* shall give light
3. he lighted *the lamps thereof*
1Sa. 3: 3. *And* ere *the lamp of* God went out
2Sa.21:17. quench not *the light* (marg. *candle,* or, *lamp*) *of* Israel.
1K. 7:49. *and the lamps,* and the tongs (of) gold,
1Ch28:15. *and for their lamps* of gold,
— *and for the lamps thereof:*
— *and* (also) *for the lamps thereof,*
2Ch. 4:20. the candlesticks *with their lamps,*
21. the flowers, *and the lamps,*
13:11. the candlestick...*with the lamps thereof,*
29: 7. and put out *the lamps,*
Job 18: 6. *his candle* (marg. or, *lamp*) shall be put out
21:17. is *the candle* (marg. *id.*) *of* the wicked put out?
29: 3. When *his candle* (marg. *id.*) shined
Ps. 18:28(29). For thou wilt light *my candle:* (marg. *id.*)
119:105. *a lamp* (marg. *candle*) unto my feet,
132:17. I have ordained *a lamp* (marg. or, *candle*)
Pro. 6:23. the commandment (is) *a lamp;* (marg. or, *candle*)
13: 9. *but the lamp* (marg. *id.*) *of* the wicked shall be put out.
20:20. *his lamp* (marg. *id.*) shall be put out
27. *the candle* (marg. or, *lamp*) *of* the Lord,
24:20. *the candle* (marg. *id.*) *of* the wicked shall be put out.
31:18. *her candle* goeth not out
Jer. 25:10. the light of *the candle.*
Zep. 1:12. I will search Jerusalem *with candles,*
Zec. 4: 2. *his* seven *lamps* thereon, and seven pipes to *the* seven *lamps,*

נִר *neer*, m. 5215

Pro.21: 4. *the plowing* (marg. or, *light*) *of* the wicked,

---

נִרְגָּן *neer-gāhn'*, m. 5372

Pro.16:28. *and a whisperer* separateth chief friends.
18: 8. The words of *a talebearer* (marg. or, *whisperer*)
26:20. where (there is) no *talebearer,* (marg. *id.*)
22. The words of *a talebearer* (are) as wounds,

נֵרְדְּ *nēhrd*, m. 5373

Cant.1:12. *my spikenard* sendeth forth the smell
4:13. camphire, *with spikenard,*
14. *Spikenard* and saffron;

נָשָׂא *nāh-sāh'*. 5375

* KAL.—*Preterite.* *

Gen13: 6. the land *was* not *able to bear* them,
18:26. *then I will spare* all the place
19:21. *I have accepted* thee concerning this
45:19. *and bring* your father, and come.
47:30. *and thou shalt carry me* out of Egypt,
Ex. 6: 8. *I did* swear (marg. *I did lift* up my hand) to give it to Abraham,
10:13. the east wind *brought* the locusts.
18:22. *and they shall bear* (the burden) with thee.
28:12. *and* Aaron *shall bear* their names
29. *And* Aaron *shall bear* the names
30. *and* Aaron *shall bear* the judgment
38. *that* Aaron *may bear* the iniquity
35:21. every one whose heart *stirred him up,*
26. all the women whose heart *stirred* them *up*
36: 2. every one whose heart *stirred him up*

Lev. 5: 1. *then he shall bear* his iniquity.
17. *and shall bear* his iniquity.
16:22. *And* the goat *shall bear*...their iniquities
17:16. *then he shall bear* his iniquity.
24:15. Whosoever curseth his God *shall bear* his sin.
Nu. 4:25. *And they shall bear* the curtains
11:17. *and they shall bear* the burden of
14:19. *thou hast forgiven* this people,
30. which *I sware* (marg. *lifted up* my hand) to make you dwell
33. *and bear* your whoredoms,
16:15. *I have* not *taken* one ass
30:15(16). *then he shall bear* her iniquity.
31:49. Thy servants *have taken* the sum
Deu. 1:31. how that the Lord thy God *bare thee*,
1Sa.17:34. *and took* a lamb out of the flock:
2Sa.18:28. the men that *lifted up* their hand
20:21. Sheba...*hath lifted up* his hand
1K. 2:26. because *thou barest* the ark
8:31. *and* an oath *be laid* upon him (marg. *he require* an oath of him)
10:11. *brought* gold from Ophir,
2K. 2:16. *hath taken him up*, and cast him
9:25. the Lord *laid* this burden upon
14:10. *and* thine heart *hath lifted thee up*:
19: 4. *wherefore lift up* (thy) prayer for the remnant
23: 4. *and carried* the ashes of them
25:27. *did lift up* the head of Jehoiachin
1Ch 18:11. the silver and the gold that *he brought*
27:23. David *took* not the number
2Ch 6:22. *and* an oath *be laid* upon him (marg. *he require* an oath of him)
11:21. *he took* eighteen wives,
12:11. the guard came *and fetched them*,
25:19. *and* thine heart *lifteth thee up*
Ezr. 9: 2. *they have taken* of their daughters
10:44. All these *had taken* strange wives:
Neh. 9:15. the land which *thou hadst* sworn (marg. *lift up* thine hand) to give
Est. 5: 2. *she obtained* favour in his sight:
Job 24:10. *they take away* the sheaf
34:19. (him) that *accepteth* not the persons of
31. *I have borne* (chastisement),
Ps. 15: 3. nor *taketh up* a reproach against
24: 4. who *hath* not *lifted up* his soul unto vanity,
32: 5. *thou forgavest* the iniquity of my sin.
69: 7(8). *I have borne* reproach;
83: 2(3). that hate thee *have lifted up* the head.
85: 2(3). *Thou hast forgiven* the iniquity
88:15(16). *I suffer* thy terrors
93: 3. The floods *have lifted up*, O Lord, the floods *have lifted up* their voice;
102:10(11). *thou hast lifted me up*, and cast
123: 1. Unto thee *lift I up* mine eyes,
139:20. thine enemies *take* (thy name) in vain.
143: 8. *I lift up* my soul unto thee.
Cant.5: 7. the keepers of the walls *took away* my veil
Isa. 5:26. *And he will lift up* an ensign
10:26. *so shall he lift it up* after the manner
11:12. *And he shall set up* an ensign for the
14: 4. *That thou shalt take up* this proverb
22: 6. Elam *bare* the quiver
37: 4. *wherefore lift up* (thy) prayer
52: 8. Thy watchmen *shall lift up* the voice;
53: 4. Surely he *hath borne* our griefs,
12. *he bare* the sin of many,
Jer. 31:19. *I did bear* the reproach of my youth.
52:31. *lifted up* the head of Jehoiachin
Lam. 4:16. *they respected* not the persons of the priests,
5:13. *They took* the young men to grind,
Eze. 3:14. the spirit *lifted me up*,
4: 5. *so shalt thou bear* the iniquity
6. *and thou shalt bear* the iniquity
11:24. Afterwards the spirit *took me up*,
12: 7. *I bare* (it) upon (my) shoulder
14:10. *And they shall bear* the punishment
16:58. *Thou hast borne* (marg. *them*) thy lewdness
17:23. *and it shall bring forth* boughs, and bear
18: 6, 15. neither *hath lifted up* his eyes
12. *hath lifted up* his eyes to the idols,
19. *doth* not the son *bear* the iniquity
20: 6. *I lifted up* mine hand unto them,
15. Yet also I *lifted up* my hand
23. I *lifted up* mine hand unto them
28. *I lifted up* mine hand to give
Eze.20:42. (for) the which *I lifted up* mine hand
26:17. *And they shall take up* a lamentation
27:32. *And* in their wailing *they shall take up* a lamentation
29:19. *and he shall take* her multitude,
36: 6. *ye have borne* the shame
7. *I have lifted up* mine hand,
39:26. *After that they have borne* their shame,
44:10. *they shall even bear* their iniquity.
12. therefore *have I lifted up* mine hand
— *and they shall bear* their iniquity.
13. *but they shall bear* their shame,
47:14. (concerning) the which *I lifted up* mine hand (marg. or, *swore*)
Hos 13: 1. When Ephraim spake trembling, *he exalted* himself
Joel 2:22. for the tree *beareth* her fruit,
Am. 5:26. *But ye have borne* the tabernacle
6:10. *And* a man's uncle *shall take him up*,
Mic. 2: 2. and houses, *and take* (them) *away*:
Hab. 3:10. the deep...*lifted up* his hands
Hag. 2:19. the olive tree, *hath* not *brought forth*:
Zec. 1:21(2:4). that no man *did lift up* his head:
Mal. 2: 3. *and* (one) *shall take* you away

KAL.—*Infinitive.*

Gen 4:13. My punishment (is) greater *than I can bear*. (marg. or, *than* (that it may) *be forgiven*)
36: 7. the land...could not *bear* them
44: 1. as much as they can *carry*,
45:27. Joseph had sent *to carry* him,
46: 5. Pharaoh had sent *to carry* him.
Ex. 25:14. *that* the ark *may be borne*
27. staves *to bear* the table.
27: 7. upon the two sides of the altar, *to bear* it. (lit. *in bearing* it)
30: 4. staves *to bear* it withal.
37: 5. staves...*to bear* the ark.
14. staves *to bear* the table.
15. he made the staves...*to bear* the table.
27. the staves *to bear* it withal.
38: 7. the staves...*to bear* it withal;
Lev.10:17. *to bear* the iniquity of the congregation, to make atonement
Nu. 4: 2. *Take* the sum of the sons of Kohath
15. the sons of Kohath shall come *to bear*
22. *Take* also the sum of the sons of Gershon,
11:14. I am not able *to bear* all this people
18:22. *lest they bear* sin, and die.
Deu. 1: 9. I am not able *to bear* you myself
10: 8. *to bear* the ark of the covenant
14:24. thou art not able *to carry it*;
Jud. 8:28. they *lifted up* their heads no more. (lit. added not *to lift up*)
1Sa. 2:28. *to wear* an ephod before me?
1Ch 15: 2, 2. *to carry* the ark of God
23:26. they shall no (more) *carry* the tabernacle, nor any vessels
Job 27: 1 & 29:1. Moreover Job continued (marg. added *to take up*) his parable,
Ps. 28: 2. *when I lift up* my hands toward
89: 9(10). *when* the waves thereof *arise*,
50(51). *I do bear* (lit. *my bearing*) in my
Pro.18: 5. not good *to accept* the person of
30:21. four (which) it cannot *bear*:
Ecc. 5:19(18). *and to take* his portion,
Isa. 1:14. I am weary *to bear*
18: 3. *when he lifteth up* an ensign
Jer. 10: 5. they must *needs* be borne, (lit. *bearing* they must be borne)
15:15. *I have suffered* rebuke.
17:27. not *to bear* a burden,...on the sabbath day;
44:22. the Lord could no longer *bear*,
Eze.10:16. *and when* the cherubims *lifted up*
17: 8. *and that it might bear* fruit,
9. *to pluck* it *up* by the roots
20:31. *For when ye offer* your gifts,
38:13. *to carry away* silver and gold,
45:11. *that* the bath *may contain* the tenth part
Hos. 1: 6. I will *utterly* take them away. (lit. *taking* I will take them away)

KAL.—*Imperative.*

Gen13:14. *Lift up* now thine eyes, and look
21:18. *lift up* the lad,
27: 3. *take*, I pray thee, thy weapons,

Gen31:12. *Lift up* now thine eyes, and see,
50:17. *Forgive*, I pray thee
— *forgive* the trespass of the servants
Ex. 10:17. Now therefore *forgive*,
Lev.10: 4. *carry* your brethren from before the sanctuary
Nu. 1: 2. *Take ye* the sum of all the congregation
3:40. *and take* the number of their names.
11:12. *Carry them* in thy bosom,
26: 2. *Take* the sum of all the congregation
31:26. *Take* the sum of the prey
Deu. 3:27. *lift up* thine eyes westward, and
Jos. 3: 6. *Take up* the ark of the covenant,
4: 3. *Take* you hence...twelve stones,
6: 6. *Take up* the ark of the covenant,
1Sa.15:25. I pray thee, *pardon* my sin,
25:28. *forgive* the trespass of thine handmaid:
2K. 4:19. *Carry him* to his mother.
36. *Take up* thy son.
9:25. *Take up*, (and) cast him in
26. *take* (and) cast him into the plat
1Ch 16:29. *bring* an offering,
Job 21: 3. *Suffer me* that I may speak;
Ps. 4: 6(7). Lord, *lift thou up* the light of thy countenance
10:12. Arise, O Lord; O God, *lift up* thine hand:
24: 7. *Lift up* your heads, O ye gates;
9. *Lift up* your heads, O ye gates; *even lift* (them) *up*, ye everlasting doors;
25:18. *and forgive* all my sins.
81: 2(3). *Take* a psalm, and bring hither
96: 8. *bring* an offering, and come
134: 2. *Lift up* your hands (in) the sanctuary,
Isa. 13: 2. *Lift ye up* a banner upon the high
40:26. *Lift up* your eyes on high,
49:18. *Lift up* thine eyes round about,
51: 6. *Lift up* your eyes to the heavens,
60: 4. *Lift up* thine eyes round about,
Jer. 3: 2. *Lift up* thine eyes unto the high places,
4: 6. *Set up* the standard toward Zion:
6: 1. *set up* a sign of fire
7:29. *and take up* a lamentation
13:20. *Lift up* your eyes,
50: 2. and *set up* (marg. *lift up*) a standard;
51:12. *Set up* the standard
27. *Set ye up* a standard in the land,
Lam.2:19. *lift up* thy hands toward him
Eze. 8: 5. Son of man, *lift up* thine eyes
16:52. *bear* thine own shame
— *and bear* thy shame,
19: 1. *take thou up* a lamentation
23:35. *bear thou* also thy lewdness
27: 2. *take up* a lamentation for Tyrus;
28:12. *take up* a lamentation upon the king
32: 2. *take up* a lamentation for Pharaoh
Jon. 1:12. *Take me up*, and cast me forth
Zec. 5: 5. *Lift up* now thine eyes, and see

KAL.—*Future.*

Gen 7:17. the waters increased, *and bare up* the ark,
13:10. *And* Lot *lifted up* his eyes,
18: 2. *And he lift up* his eyes and looked,
24. wilt thou also destroy and not *spare*
21:16. *and lift up* her voice, and wept.
22: 4. *Then* on the third day Abraham *lifted up* his eyes,
13. *And* Abraham *lifted up* his eyes.
24:63. *and he lifted up* his eyes, and saw,
64. *And* Rebekah *lifted up* her eyes.
27:38. *And* Esau *lifted up* his voice,
29: 1. *Then* Jacob *went on* his journey, (marg. *lift up* his feet)
11. *and lifted up* his voice, and wept.
31:10. *that I lifted up* mine eyes,
17. *and set* his sons and his wives upon camels;
32:20(21). peradventure *he will accept* of me.
33: 1. *And* Jacob *lifted up* his eyes,
5. *And he lifted up* his eyes,
37:25. *and they lifted up* their eyes
39: 7. *that* his master's wife *cast* her eyes upon Joseph;
40:13, 19. Yet within three days *shall* Pharaoh *lift up*
20. *and he lifted up* the head of the chief butler
42:26. *And they laded* their asses
43:29. *And he lifted up* his eyes,
34. *And he took* (and sent) messes

Gen46: 5. *and* the sons of Israel *carried* Jacob
50:13. *For* his sons *carried* him into the land
Ex. 10:19. *which took away* the locusts,
12:34. *And* the people *took* their dough
14:10. *And* when...the children of Israel *lifted up* their eyes,
19: 4. *and* (how) *I bare* you on eagles' wings,
20: 7. *Thou shalt* not *take* the name of the Lord thy God in vain;
— that *taketh* his name in vain.
23: 1. *Thou shalt* not *raise* (marg. or, *receive*) a false report:
21. *he will* not *pardon* your transgressions:
28:43. that *they bear* not iniquity, and die:
30:12. When *thou takest* the sum of
32:32. if *thou wilt forgive* their sin—;
Lev. 7:18. the soul...*shall bear* his iniquity.
9:22. *And* Aaron *lifted up* his hand
10: 5. *and carried them* in their coats
19: 8. *shall bear* his iniquity,
15. *thou shalt* not *respect* the person of
17. and not *suffer* sin upon him.
20:17. *he shall bear* his iniquity.
19. *they shall bear* their iniquity.
20. *they shall bear* their sin;
22: 9. lest *they bear* sin for it,
Nu. 1:49. neither *take* the sum of them among the children
50. *they shall bear* the tabernacle,
5:31. this woman *shall bear* her iniquity.
6:26. The Lord *lift up* his countenance
7: 9. *they should bear* upon their shoulders.
9:13. that man *shall bear* his sin.
11:12. as a nursing father *beareth* the sucking
17. that thou *bear* (it) not thyself alone.
13:23. *and they bare it* between two
14: 1. *And* all the congregation *lifted up* their voice,
34. *shall ye bear* your iniquities,
18: 1. *shall bear* the iniquity of the sanctuary:
— *shall bear* the iniquity of your priesthood.
23. *they shall bear* their iniquity:
32. *ye shall bear* no sin by reason of it,
23: 7, 18. *And he took up* his parable, and said,
24: 2. *And* Balaam *lifted up* his eyes,
3, 15, 23. *And he took up* his parable, and said,
20. *And* when...*he took up* his parable,
21. *and took up* his parable,
Deu. 1:12. *can I* myself alone *bear* your cumbrance,
31. as a man *doth bear* his son,
4:19. lest *thou lift up* thine eyes
5:11. *Thou shalt* not *take* the name of the Lord thy God in vain:
— that *taketh* his name in vain.
10:17. which *regardeth* not persons,
12:26. thy vows, *thou shalt take*,
28:49. The Lord *shall bring* a nation against thee
50. *shall* not *regard* the person of the old,
32:11. *beareth them* on her wings:
40. *I lift up* my hand to heaven,
33: 3. (every one) *shall receive* of thy words.
Jos. 3: 6. *And they took up* the ark
4: 8. *and took up* twelve stones
5:13. *that he lifted up* his eyes and looked,
6: 4. seven priests *shall bear*
6. *let* seven priests *bear* seven trumpets
12. *and* the priests *took up* the ark
24:19. *he will* not *forgive* your transgressions
Jud. 2: 4. *that* the people *lifted up* their voice,
9: 7. *and lifted up* his voice, and cried,
48. cut down a bough...*and took it*,
16:31. came down, *and took* him,
19:17. *when he had lifted up* his eyes,
21: 2. *and lifted up* their voices, and wept
23. *and took* (them) wives,
Ru. 1: 4. *And they took* them wives
9, 14. *and they lifted up* their voice,
2:18. *And she took* (it) *up*, and went
1Sa. 4: 4. *that they might bring* from thence the ark
6:13. *and they lifted up* their eyes, and saw the ark,
11: 4. *and* all the people *lifted up* their voices,
17:20. *and took*, and went, as Jesse
24:16(17). *And* Saul *lifted up* his voice,
25:35. *and have accepted* thy person.
30: 4. *Then* David and the people...*lifted up* their voice

2Sa. 2:22. how then *should I hold up* my face
32. *And they took up* Asahel,
3:32. *and* the king *lifted up* his voice,
4: 4. *and* his nurse *took him up*,
5:21. *and* David and his men *burned them.* (marg. or, *took them away*)
6: 3. *and brought it* out of the house
4. *And they brought it* out of the house
13:34. *And* the young man that kept the watch *lifted up* his eyes,
36. king's sons came, *and lifted up* their voice
14:14. neither *doth* God *respect* (any) person: (marg. or, because God *hath* not *taken away* (his) life)
18:24. *and lifted up* his eyes, and looked,
23:16. drew water out of the well...*and took* (it),
1K. 5: 9(23). and thou *shalt receive* (them):
8: 3. *and* the priests *took up* the ark.
13:29. *And* the prophet *took up* the carcase
14:28. the guard *bare them*,
15:22. *and they took away* the stones of Ramah,
18:12. the Spirit of the Lord *shall carry thee*
2K. 4:20. *when he had taken him*, and brought
37. *and took up* her son,
5:23. *and they bare* (them) before him.
7: 8. *and carried* thence silver, and gold,
— *and carried* thence (also),
9:32. *And he lifted up* his face to the window,
14:20. *And they brought* him on horses:
18:14. that which thou puttest on me *will I bear*.
19:22. *and lifted up* thine eyes on high?
25:13. *and carried* the brass of them
1Ch 10: 9. *they took* his head, and his armour,
12. *and took away* the body of Saul,
11:18. drew water out of the well...*and took* (it),
15:15. *And* the children of the Levites *bare* the ark
21:16. *And* David *lifted up* his eyes,
24. *I will* not *take* (that) which (is) thine
23:22. *and* their brethren the sons of Kish *took them.*
2Ch 5: 4. *and* the Levites *took up* the ark.
13:21. *and married* (lit. *took* to him) fourteen wives,
14:13(12). *and they carried away* very much spoil.
16: 6. *and they carried away* the stones
24: 3. *And* Jehoiada *took* for him two wives;
11. came and emptied the chest, *and took it*,
25:28. *And they brought him* upon horses,
Ezr. 9:12. neither *take* their daughters unto your sons,
Neh. 2: 1. *and I took up* the wine,
13:25. nor *take* their daughters unto your sons,
Est. 2: 9. *and she obtained* kindness of him;
17. *and she obtained* grace and favour
Job 2:12. And *when they lifted up* their eyes
— *And* when...*they lifted up* their voice,
6: 2. *laid* (marg. *lifted up*) in the balances
7:13. my couch *shall ease* my complaint;
21. why *dost thou* not *pardon* my transgression,
10:15. *will I* not *lift up* my head.
11:15. then *shalt thou lift up* thy face
13: 8. *Will ye accept* his person?
10. if *ye do* secretly *accept* persons.
14. Wherefore *do I take* my flesh in my teeth,
21:12. *They take* the timbrel and harp,
22:26. *and shalt lift up* thy face unto God.
27:21. The east wind *carrieth him away*,
30:22. *Thou liftest me up* to the wind;
31:36. *I would take it* upon my shoulder,
32:21. *Let me* not,...*accept* any man's person,
22. my maker *would* soon *take me away*.
36: 3. *I will fetch* my knowledge from afar,
40:20. the mountains *bring* him *forth* food,
42: 8. for him *will I accept*:
9. the Lord *also accepted* Job.
Ps. 16: 4. *take up* their names into my lips.
24: 5. *He shall receive* the blessing
25: 1. Unto thee, O Lord, *do I lift up* my soul.
50:16. *or* (that) *thou shouldest take* my covenant
55:12(13). *then I could have borne* (it):
63: 4(5). *I will lift up* my hands in thy name.
72: 3. The mountains *shall bring* peace
82: 2. and *accept* the persons of the wicked?
86: 4. unto thee, O Lord, *do I lift up* my soul.
91:12. *They shall bear thee up* in (their) hands,
93: 3. the floods *lift up* their waves.
106:26. *Therefore he lifted up* his hand against them,

Ps.116:13. *I will take* the cup of salvation,
119:48. My hands *also will I lift up*
121: 1. *I will lift up* mine eyes
139: 9. (If) *I take* the wings of the morning,
Pro. 6:35. *He will* not *regard* (marg. *accept* the face of) any ransom;
9:12. *thou* alone *shalt bear* (it).
18:14. a wounded spirit who *can bear?*
19:18. *let* not thy soul *spare* (lit. *lift* not *up* thy soul)
Ecc. 5:15(14). and *shall take* nothing of his labour,
Isa. 2: 4. nation *shall* not *lift up* sword against nation,
9. therefore *forgive* them not.
3: 7. In that day *shall he swear*, (marg. *lift up* (the hand))
8: 4. the spoil of Samaria *shall be taken away*
10:24. *shall lift up* his staff against thee,
15: 7. laid up, *shall they carry away*
24:14. They *shall lift up* their voice,
30: 6. *they will carry* their riches
37:23. *and lifted up* thine eyes on high?
38:21. *Let them take* a lump of figs,
40:11. shall gather the lambs...and *carry* (them)
24. the whirlwind *shall take them away*
41:16. the wind *shall carry them away*,
42: 2. He shall not cry, nor *lift up*, nor cause
11. *Let* the wilderness and the cities thereof *lift up* (their voice),
46: 4. I have made, and I *will bear;*
7. *They bear him* upon the shoulder,
49:22. *I will lift up* mine hand to the Gentiles,
57:13. the wind *shall carry* them all *away;*
60: 6. *they shall bring* gold and incense;
64: 6(5). our iniquities,...*have taken us away*.
Jer. 7:16. neither *lift up* cry nor prayer
9:10(9). For the mountains *will I take up* a weeping
18(17). *and take up* a wailing for us,
10:19. this (is) a grief, *and I must bear it.*
11:14. neither *lift up* a cry or prayer
17:21. *bear* no burden on the sabbath day,
49:29. *they shall take* to themselves
52:17. *and carried* all the brass...to Babylon.
Lam.3:27. good for a man that *he bear* the yoke
41. *Let us lift up* our heart
Eze. 3:12. *Then* the spirit *took me up*,
4: 4. *thou shalt bear* their iniquity.
8: 3. *and* the spirit *lifted* me *up*
5. *So I lifted up* mine eyes
10: 7. (one) cherub stretched forth his hand... *and took*
19. *And* the cherubims *lifted up* their wings,
11: 1. *Moreover* the spirit *lifted me up*,
22. *Then did* the cherubims *lift up* their wings,
12: 6. In their sight *shalt thou bear*
12. the prince...*shall bear*
16:54. *That thou mayest bear* thine own shame,
18:20. The son *shall* not *bear*
— neither *shall* the father *bear*
20: 5. *and lifted up* mine hand (marg. or, *sware*) unto the seed of
— *when I lifted up* mine hand
23:27. *thou shalt* not *lift up* thine eyes
49. *ye shall bear* the sins of your idols:
32:24, 25. *yet have they borne* their shame
30. *and bear* their shame with them that go down
33:25. eat with the blood, and *lift up* your eyes
34:29. neither *bear* the shame of the heathen
36: 7. *they shall bear* their shame.
8. ye shall shoot forth...and *yield* your fruit
15. neither *shalt thou bear* the reproach
39:10. *they shall take* no wood
43: 5. *So* the spirit *took me up*,
Dan. 8: 3 & 10:5. *Then I lifted up* mine eyes,
Hos. 1: 6. *I will* utterly *take* them *away*. (marg. or, that *I should* altogether *pardon* them)
4: 8. *they set* their heart on (marg. *lift up* their soul to) their iniquity.
5:14. *I will take away*, and none
14: 2(3). *Take away* all iniquity,
Jon. 1:15. *So they took up* Jonah,
Mic. 2: 4. *shall* (one) *take up* a parable
4: 3. nation *shall* not *lift up* a sword against nation,
6:16. *ye shall bear* the reproach

Mic. 7: 9. *I will bear* the indignation of the Lord,
Nah. 1: 5. *and* the earth *is burned* at his presence,
Hab. 1: 3. *raise up* strife and contention.
2: 6. *Shall* not all these *take up* a parable
Hag. 2:12. If one *bear* holy flesh in the skirt
Zec. 1:18(2:1). *Then lifted I up* mine eyes,
2: 1(5). *I lifted up* mine eyes *again*,
5: 1. Then I turned, *and lifted up* mine eyes,
9. *Then lifted I up* mine eyes,
— *and they lifted up* the ephah
6: 1. I turned, *and lifted up* mine eyes,
13. he *shall bear* the glory,
Mal. 1: 8. will he be pleased with thee, or *accept* thy person ?
9. *will he regard* your persons ?

KAL.—*Participle.* Poel.

Gen37:25. *bearing* spicery and balm
45:23. ten asses *laden with* (marg. *carrying*) the good
— ten she asses *laden* with corn and bread
Ex. 34: 7. *forgiving* iniquity and transgression
Lev.11:25. whosoever *beareth* (ought)
28. *he that beareth* the carcase
40. *he also that beareth* the carcase
15:10. *and he that beareth* (any of) those things
Nu. 10:17. the sons of Merari...*bearing* the tabernacle.
21. the Kohathites...*bearing* the sanctuary:
14:18. *forgiving* iniquity and transgression,
Deu24:15. *setteth* his heart upon it:
31: 9. the sons of Levi, *which bare* the ark
25. the Levites, *which bare* the ark
Jos. 3: 3. the priests the Levites *bearing*
8, 13. the priests *that bear* the ark
14. the priests *bearing* the ark
15. they *that bare* the ark
—, 17. the priests *that bare* the ark
4: 9, 10. the priests *which bare* the ark
16. the priests *that bear* the ark
18. the priests *that bare* the ark
6: 8. seven priests *bearing* the seven trumpets
13. seven priests *bearing* seven trumpets
8:33. the Levites, *which bare* the ark
Jud. 3:18. the people *that bare* the present.
9:54. he called hastily unto...his armour*bearer*,
1Sa.10: 3. three men...one *carrying* three kids, and another *carrying* three loaves of bread, and another *carrying* a bottle of wine:
14: 1. the young man *that bare* his armour,
3. the Lord's priest in Shiloh, *wearing* an ephod.
6. the young man *that bare* his armour,
7. his armour*bearer* said unto him,
12. Jonathan and his armour*bearer*,
— Jonathan said unto his armour*bearer*,
13. *and* his armour*bearer* after him:
— *and* his armour*bearer* slew after him.
14. Jonathan *and* his armour*bearer* made,
17. Jonathan *and* his armour*bearer* (were) not (there).
16:21. he became his armour*bearer*.
17: 7. one *bearing* a shield went before
41. the man *that bare* the shield
22:18. fourscore and five persons *that did wear* a linen ephod.
31: 4. Then said Saul *unto* his armour*bearer*,
— his armour*bearer* would not;
5. when his armour*bearer* saw that Saul was dead,
6. Saul died,...*and* his armour*bearer*,
2Sa. 6:13. they *that bare* the ark of the Lord
8: 2. the Moabites became David's servants, (and) *brought* gifts.
6. the Syrians became servants ... (and) *brought* gifts.
15:24. *bearing* the ark of the covenant
18:15. ten young men *that bare* Joab's armour
23:37. armour*bearer* to Joab the son of
1K. 5:15(29). threescore and ten thousand *that bare* burdens,
10: 2. camels *that bare* spices,
22. *bringing* gold, and silver, ivory, and
2K. 3:14. I *regard* the presence of Jehoshaphat
1Ch. 5:18. men *able to bear* buckler and sword,
10: 4. Then said Saul to his armour*bearer*,
— his armour*bearer* would not;
5. his armour*bearer* saw that Saul was dead,
1Ch 11:39. the armour*bearer* of Joab
12:24. The children of Judah *that bare* shield and spear
15:26. the Levites *that bare* the ark
27. the Levites *that bare* the ark,
18: 2. the Moabites...*brought* gifts.
6. the Syrians...*brought* gifts.
2Ch 9: 1. camels *that bare* spices,
21. ships of Tarshish *bringing* gold, and silver,
14: 8(7). an army (of men) *that bare* targets
—(-). and out of Benjamin, *that bare* shields
Ezr.10:44. (כתיב) All these *had taken* strange wives:
Neh 4:17(11). *and they that bare* burdens, with those
5: 7. (כתיב) *Ye exact* usury, every one
Est. 2:15. Esther *obtained* favour
Ps. 99: 8. thou wast a God *that forgavest* them,
126: 6. *bearing* precious seed,
— *bringing* his sheaves (with him).
Pro.19:19. A man of great wrath *shall suffer* punishment:
Isa. 45:20. *that set up* the wood of their graven image,
52:11. be ye clean, *that bear* the vessels
Dan. 1:16. Melzar *took away* the portion
Am. 5: 1. this word which I *take up*
Mic. 7:18. (is) a God like unto thee, *that pardoneth*
Zec. 1:21(2:4). Gentiles, *which lifted up* (their) horn
Mal. 2: 9. *but have been* partial (marg. *accepted* faces, or, *lifted up* the face against) in the law.

KAL.—*Participle.* Paül.

2K. 5: 1. a great man with his master, *and honourable*, (marg. *lifted up*, or, *accepted in* countenance)
Job 22: 8. *and the honourable man* (marg. or, *accepted for* countenance)
Ps. 32: 1. (he whose) transgression (is) *forgiven*,
Isa. 3: 3. *and the honourable* man, (marg. man *eminent in* countenance)
9:15(14). The ancient *and honourable*, (lit. *and accepted of* countenance)
33:24. the people...(shall be) *forgiven* (their) iniquity.
46: 3. *are carried* from the womb:

* NIPHAL.—*Preterite.* *

Ex. 25:28. *that* the table *may be borne*
2K. 20:17. *and* that which thy fathers have laid up... *shall be carried* into
1Ch 14: 2. his kingdom *was lifted up*
Isa. 39: 6. *and* (that) which thy fathers have laid up ...*shall be carried*
52:13. he shall be exalted *and extolled*,
Jer. 51: 9. *and is lifted up* (even) to the skies.
Dan11:12. *when he hath taken away* the multitude,
Zec. 5: 7. *there was lifted up* a talent of lead:

NIPHAL.—*Infinitive.*

Eze. 1:19. *and when* the living creatures *were lifted up*
21. *and when those were lifted up*

NIPHAL.—*Imperative.*

Ps. 7: 6(7). *lift up thyself* because of the rage
24: 7. *and be ye lift up*, ye everlasting doors;
94: 2. *Lift up thyself*, thou judge of the earth:

NIPHAL.—*Future.*

2Ch 32:23. *so that he was magnified* in the sight
Pro.30:13. their eyelids *are lifted up*.
Isa. 33:10. now *will I lift up myself*.
40: 4. Every valley *shall be exalted*,
49:22. thy daughters *shall be carried* upon
66:12. *ye shall be borne* upon
Jer. 10: 5. *they must* needs *be borne*,
Eze. 1:19. from the earth, the wheels *were lifted up*.
20. and the wheels *were lifted up* over against
21. the wheels *were lifted up* over against

NIPHAL.—*Participle.*

Isa. 2: 2. *and shall be exalted* above the hills;
12. every (one that is) *lifted up*;
13. the cedars of Lebanon, (that are) high *and lifted up*,
14. all the hills (that are) *lifted up*,
6: 1. I saw also the Lord...high *and lifted up*,
30:25. upon every *high* (marg. *lifted up*) hill,
57: 7. Upon a lofty *and high* mountain
15. the high *and lofty* One
Mic. 4: 1. *and* it *shall be exalted* above the hills;

* PIEL.—*Preterite.* *

2Sa. 5:12. *he had exalted* his kingdom
19:42(43). *hath he given* us any gift?
1K. 9:11. Hiram the king of Tyre *had furnished*
Ezr. 8:36. *and they furthered* the people,
Est. 5:11. *he had advanced him* above the princes
Am. 4: 2. *that he will take* you *away*

PIEL.—*Imperative.*

Ps. 28: 9. *and lift them up* for ever.

PIEL.—*Future.*

Ezr. 1: 4. *let* the men of his place *help him* (marg. *lift him up*)
Est. 3: 1. *and advanced him*, and set his seat
Isa. 63: 9. *and carried them* all the days of old.

PIEL.—*Participle.*

Est. 9: 3. and officers of the king, *helped*
Jer. 22:27. the land whereunto they desire (marg. *lift up* their mind) to return,
44:14. the land of Judah, to the which they have a desire (marg. *lift up* their soul) to return

* HIPHIL.—*Preterite.* *

Lev.22:16. *Or suffer them to bear* (marg. or, *lade themselves with*) the iniquity
2Sa.17:13. *then shall* all Israel *bring* ropes

* HITHPAEL.—*Infinitive.* *

Pro.30:32. done foolishly *in lifting up thyself*,
Eze.17:14. that *it might* not *lift itself up*,

HITHPAEL.—*Future.*

Nu. 16: 3. wherefore then *lift ye up yourselves*
23:24. and *lift up himself* as a young lion:
24: 7. *and* his kingdom *shall be exalted.*
Eze.29:15. neither *shall it exalt itself* any more
Dan11:14. robbers of thy people *shall exalt themselves*

HITHPAEL.—*Participle.*

1K. 1: 5. Adonijah the son of Haggith *exalted himself*,
1Ch 29:11. *and thou art exalted* as head above all.

5376 **נְשָׂא** *n'sāh*, Ch.

* P'AL.—*Preterite.* *

Dan. 2:35. *and* the wind *carried* them *away*,

P'AL.—*Imperative.*

Ezr. 5:15. *Take* these vessels, go, carry them

* ITHPAEL.—*Participle.* *

Ezr. 4:19. *hath made insurrection* (marg. *hath lifted up itself*) against kings,

---

5379 **נִשֵּׂאת** *nis-sēhth'*, f.

2Sa.19:42(43). hath he given us *any gift?*

5381 **נָשַׂג** [*nāh-sag'*].

* HIPHIL.—*Preterite.* *

Gen44: 4. *when thou dost overtake them*,
47: 9. *have* not *attained* unto the days of
Lev.25:26. *and* himself *be able* (marg. his hand *hath attained*) to redeem
49. if he *be able* (lit. his hand *hath attained*), he may redeem
26: 5. *And* your threshing *shall reach*
Deu19: 6. *and overtake him*, because the way
28: 2. all these blessings shall come on thee, *and overtake thee*,
15. come upon thee, *and overtake thee:*
45. shall come upon thee, *and...overtake thee*,
2Sa.15:14. lest *he overtake us* suddenly, (lit. lest he hasten *and overtake us*)
Ps. 40:12(13). iniquities *have taken hold upon me*,
Lam.1: 3. all her persecutors *overtook her*
Zec. 1: 6. *did they* not *take hold of* (marg. *overtake*) your fathers?

HIPHIL.—*Infinitive.*

1Sa.30: 8. thou shalt *surely* overtake (lit. *overtaking* thou shalt overtake) (them),

HIPHIL.—*Future.*

Gen31:25. *Then* Laban *overtook* Jacob.
44: 6. *And he overtook them*, and he spake
Ex. 14: 9. *and overtook* them encamping by the sea,
15: 9. I will pursue, *I will overtake*,
Lev. 5:11. if *he be* not *able to bring* (lit. his hand *shall* not *attain*)
14:22, 31. such as he (lit. his hand) *is able to get;*
30. such as he (lit. id.) *can get;*
32. whose hand *is* not *able to get*
25:47. if a sojourner or stranger *wax rich* (marg. his hand *obtain*)
26: 5. the vintage *shall reach*
27: 8. according to his *ability* (lit. his hand *attains*) that vowed
Nu. 6:21. (that) that his hand *shall get:*
Jos. 2: 5. for *ye shall overtake them.*
1Sa.30: 8. *shall I overtake them?*
— *thou shalt* surely *overtake* (them),
2K. 25: 5. *and overtook* him in the plains
Job 24: 2. (Some) *remove* the landmarks;
27:20. Terrors *take hold on him*
Ps. 7: 5(6). Let the enemy persecute my soul, *and take* (it);
18:37(38). I have pursued mine enemies, *and overtaken them:*
69:24(25). *let* thy wrathful anger *take hold of them.*
Pro. 2:19. neither *take they hold*
Isa. 35:10. *they shall obtain* joy and gladness,
51:11. *they shall obtain* gladness and joy;
59: 9. neither *doth* justice *overtake us:*
Jer. 39: 5. *and overtook* Zedekiah in the plains
42:16. the sword,...*shall overtake* you
52: 8. *and overtook* Zedekiah in the plains of Jericho;
Eze.46: 7. as his hand *shall attain unto*,
Hos. 2: 7(9). *she shall* not *overtake* them;
10: 9. the battle in Gibeah against the children of iniquity *did* not *overtake them.*

HIPHIL.—*Participle.*

Lev.14:21. if he (be) poor, and *cannot get* (marg. his hand *reach* not)
1Sa.14:26. no man *put* his hand to his mouth:
1Ch 21:12. the sword of thine enemies *overtaketh*
Job 41:26(18). The sword of him *that layeth at him*

נְשׂוּאָה [*n'soo-āh'*], f. 5385

Isa. 46: 1. *your carriages* (were) heavy loaden;

נָשִׂיא *nāh-see'*, m. 5387

Gen17:20. twelve *princes* shall he beget,
23: 6. thou (art) *a* mighty *prince* among us:
25:16. twelve *princes* according to their nations.
34: 2. Shechem the son of Hamor the Hivite, *prince of* the country,
Ex. 16:22. *the rulers of* the congregation
22:28(27). nor curse *the ruler* of thy people.
34:31. *the rulers* of the congregation
35:27. *And the rulers* brought onyx stones,
Lev. 4:22. When *a ruler* hath sinned,
Nu. 1:16. *princes of* the tribes of their fathers,
44. *and the princes of* Israel,
2: 3. *and...captain* of the children of Judah.
5. *and...captain* of the children of Issachar.
7. *and...captain* of the children of Zebulun.
10. *and the captain* of the children of Reuben
12. *and the captain* of the children of Simeon
14. *and the captain* of the sons of Gad
18. *and the captain* of the sons of Ephraim
20. *and the captain* of the children of Manasseh
22. *and the captain* of the sons of Benjamin
25. *and the captain* of the children of Dan
27. *and the captain* of the children of Asher
29. *and the captain* of the children of Naphtali
3:24, 30. *And the chief of* the house of
32. *chief over the chief of* the Levites,
35. *the chief of* the house of
4:34. *and the chief of* the congregation
46. *and the chief of* Israel
7: 2. *the princes of* Israel,
— *the princes of* the tribes,
3. a wagon for two of *the princes*,
10. *the princes* offered

Nu. 7:10. even *the princes* offered
11. *each prince* on his day, (lit. *a prince* on his day, *a prince* on his day)
18. Nethaneel...*prince of* Issachar,
24. *prince* of the children of Zebulun,
30. *prince* of the children of Reuben,
36. *prince* of the children of Simeon,
42. *prince* of the children of Gad,
48. *prince* of the children of Ephraim,
54. *prince* of the children of Manasseh:
60. *prince* of the children of Benjamin,
66. *prince* of the children of Dan,
72. *prince* of the children of Asher,
78. *prince* of the children of Naphtali,
84. anointed, by *the princes of* Israel:
10: 4. *the princes*, (which are) heads of
13: 2. every one *a ruler* among them.
16: 2. two hundred and fifty *princes of* the assembly,
17: 2(17). a rod...of all *their princes*
6(21). every one of *their princes* gave him a rod apiece, *for each prince* one, (marg. a rod *for one prince*, a rod *for one prince*)
25:14. *a prince of* a chief house
18. the daughter of *a prince of* Midian,
27: 2. *the princes* and all the congregation,
31:13. all *the princes of* the congregation,
32: 2. unto *the princes of* the congregation,
34:18. *And* ye shall take one *prince* of every tribe, (lit. one *prince*, one *prince*)
22. *the prince* of the tribe of the children of Dan,
23. *The prince* of the children of Joseph,
24. *the prince* of the tribe of the children of Ephraim,
25. *the prince* of the tribe of the children of Zebulun,
26. *the prince* of the tribe of the children of Issachar,
27. *the prince* of the tribe of the children of Asher,
28. *the prince* of the tribe of the children of Naphtali,
36: 1. before Moses, and before *the princes*,
Jos. 9:15. *the princes of* the congregation sware
18. *the princes of* the congregation had sworn
— the congregation murmured against *the princes*.
19. *the princes* said unto all the congregation,
21. *the princes* said unto them,
— as *the princes* had promised them.
13:21. *the princes of* Midian,
17: 4. before Joshua ...and before *the princes*,
22:14. And with him ten *princes*, of *each* chief house a *prince* (lit. one *prince*, one *prince*)
30. *and the princes of* the congregation
32. Phinehas the son of Eleazar the priest, *and the princes*,
1K. 8: 1. *the chief* (marg. *princes*) *of* the fathers
11:34. I will make him *prince*
1Ch 2:10. *prince of* the children of Judah;
4:38. These mentioned by (their) names (were) *princes*
5: 6. *prince* of the Reubenites.
7:40. chief of *the princes*.
2Ch 1: 2. every *governor* in all Israel,
5: 2. *the chief of* the fathers
Ezr. 1: 8. *the prince* of Judah.
Ps. 135: 7. He causeth *the vapours* to ascend
Pro. 25:14. *clouds* and wind without rain.
Jer. 10:13. he causeth *the vapours* to ascend
51:16. he causeth *the vapours* to ascend
Eze. 7:27. *and the prince* shall be clothed with desolation,
12:10. This burden (concerneth) *the prince*
12. *the prince* that (is) among them
19: 1. take thou up a lamentation for *the princes of* Israel,
21:12(17). all *the princes of* Israel:
25(30). profane wicked *prince of* Israel,
22: 6. Behold, *the princes of* Israel,
26:16. all *the princes of* the sea
27:21. all *the princes of* Kedar,
30:13. *and* there shall be no more *a prince*
32:29. Edom, her kings, and all *her princes*,
34:24. my servant David *a prince*
37:25. my servant David (shall be) *their prince*

Eze. 38: 2, 3 & 39: 1. *the* chief *prince* of Meshech
39:18. *the princes of* the earth,
44: 3. (It is) for *the prince*; *the prince*, he shall sit in it
45: 7. *And* (a portion shall be) *for the prince*
8. *my princes* shall no more oppress my people;
9. Let it suffice you, *O princes of* Israel:
16. this oblation *for the prince*
17. *the prince*'s part (to give) burnt offerings,
22. shall *the prince* prepare
46: 2. *the prince* shall enter
4. the burnt offering that *the prince* shall offer
8. when *the prince* shall enter,
10. *the prince* in the midst of them,
12. when *the prince* shall prepare
16. If *the prince* give a gift
17. it shall return *to the prince*:
18. *the prince* shall not take of
48:21. the residue (shall be) *for the prince*,
— the portions *for the prince*:
22. (that) which is *the prince*'s,
— the border of Benjamin, shall be *for the prince*.

נָשַׂק [*nāh-sak'*]. 5400

* NIPHAL.—*Preterite.* *

Ps. 78:21. a fire *was kindled* against Jacob,

* HIPHIL.—*Preterite.* *

Eze. 39: 9. shall set on fire *and burn*

HIPHIL.—*Future.*

Isa. 44:15. *he kindleth* (it), and baketh bread;

נָשָׁא [*nāh-shāh'*]. 5377

* KAL.—*Infinitive.* *

Jer. 23:39. *even* I, will *utterly* forget you,

* NIPHAL.—*Preterite.* *

Isa. 19:13. the princes of Noph *are deceived*;

* HIPHIL.—*Preterite.* *

Gen 3:13. The serpent *beguiled me*,
Jer. 4:10. *thou hast* greatly *deceived* this people
49:16. Thy terribleness *hath deceived* thee,
Obad. 3. The pride of thine heart *hath deceived thee*,
7. the men...*have deceived thee*,

HIPHIL.—*Infinitive.*

Jer. 4:10. thou hast *greatly* deceived (lit. *deceiving* thou hast deceived)

HIPHIL.—*Future.*

2K. 18:29. *Let* not Hezekiah *deceive* you:
19:10. *Let* not thy God...*deceive thee*,
2Ch 32:15. *let* not Hezekiah *deceive* you,
Ps. 55:15(16). *Let* death *seize* upon them,
Isa. 36:14. *Let* not Hezekiah *deceive* you:
37:10. *Let* not thy God,...*deceive thee*,
Jer. 29: 8. *Let* not your prophets...*deceive you*,
37: 9. *Deceive* not yourselves,

נָשָׁא [*nāh-shāh'*]. 5378

* KAL.—*Participle.* *

1Sa. 22: 2. every one that (was) in *debt*, (marg. had *a creditor*)
Neh. 5: 7. Ye *exact* usury, every one
Isa. 24: 2. so with *the giver of usury*

* HIPHIL.—*Future.* *

Ps. 89:22(23). The enemy *shall* not *exact*

נָשַׁב [*nāh-shav'*]. 5380

* KAL.—*Preterite.* *

Isa. 40: 7. the spirit of the Lord *bloweth*

* HIPHIL.—*Future.* *

Gen 15:11. *And* when the fowls...Abram *drove* them *away*.
Ps. 147:18. *he causeth* his wind *to blow*,

5382 **נָשָׁה** [*nāh-shāh'*]

∗ KAL.—*Preterite.* ∗

Jer. 23:39. I, *even I, will* utterly *forget* you,
Lam 3:17. *I forgat* prosperity.

∗ NIPHAL.—*Future.* ∗

Isa. 44:21. *thou shalt* not *be forgotten of me.*

∗ PIEL.—*Preterite.* ∗

Gen41:51. God,...*hath made me forget* all my toil,

∗ HIPHIL.—*Preterite.* ∗

Job 39:17. God *hath deprived her* of wisdom,

HIPHIL.—*Future.*

Job 11: 6. God *exacteth* of thee (less) than

5383 **נָשָׁה** [*nāh-shāh'*].

∗ KAL.—*Preterite.* ∗

Jer. 15:10. *I have* neither *lent on usury,* nor men *have lent* to me *on usury;*

KAL.—*Participle.* Poel.

Ex. 22:25(24). thou shalt not be to him *as an usurer*
Deu 24:11. the man to whom thou *dost lend*
2K. 4: 1. *and the creditor* is come to take
Neh. 5: 7. Ye *exact* usury, every one of his brother.
10. likewise, (and) my brethren,...*might exact*
11. the corn,...that ye *exact* of them.
Ps. 109:11. Let *the extortioner* catch all that he hath;
Isa. 24: 2. *as with the taker of usury,*
50: 1. which *of my creditors*

∗ HIPHIL.—*Future.* ∗

Deu 15: 2. Every creditor that *lendeth*
24:10. When *thou dost lend* thy brother any thing,

5384 **נָשֶׁה** *nāh-sheh'*, adj.

Gen32:32(33). the sinew *which shrank,*
—(—). in the sinew *that shrank.*

5386 **נְשִׁי** [*n'shee*], m.

2K. 4: 7. sell the oil, and pay *thy debt,* (marg. or, *creditor*)

5388 **נְשִׁיָּה** *n'sheey-yāh'*, f.

Ps. 88:12(13). in the land of *forgetfulness?*

---

802 **נָשִׁים** *nāh-sheem'*, f. pl.

Gen 4:19. Lamech took unto him two *wives:*
23. Lamech said *unto his wives,...*hear my voice; *ye wives of* Lamech,
6: 2. they took them *wives* of all which
18. *and* thy sons' *wives* with thee.
7: 7. *and* his sons' *wives* with him,
13. *the* three *wives of* his sons.
8:16. thy sons, *and* thy sons' *wives* with thee.
18. *and* his sons' *wives* with him:
11:29. Abram and Nahor took them *wives:*
14:16. *the women* also, and the people.
18:11. *after* the manner of *women.* (lit. the way as of *women*)
28: 9. unto *the wives which he had*
30:26. Give (me) *my wives* and my children,
31:17. set his sons and *his wives* upon camels;
35. for the custom of *women* (is) upon me.
50. if thou shalt take (other) *wives*
32:22(23). took *his* two *wives,*
33: 5. saw *the women* and the children;
34:21. take their daughters to us *for wives,*
29. and *their wives* took they captive,
36: 2. Esau took *his wives* of the daughters
6. Esau took *his wives,* and his sons,
37: 2. his father's *wives:*
45:19. for your little ones, *and for your wives,*
46: 5. their little ones, and *their wives,*
26. besides Jacob's sons' *wives,*
Ex. 1:19. (are) not *as the* Egyptian *women;*
Ex. 15:20. all *the women* went out after her
22:24(23). *your wives* shall be widows,
32: 2. which (are) in the ears of *your wives,*
35:22. they came, both men and *women,*
26. And all *the women* whose heart
Lev. 26:26. ten *women* shall bake your bread
Nu. 14: 3. that *our wives* and our children
16:27. *and their wives,* and their sons,
31: 9. *the women of* Midian captives,
18. But all the *women* children, (lit. the children *among women*)
35. *women* that had not known man
32:26. Our little ones, *our wives,*
36: 3. if they be *married* (lit. be *for wives*)
6. Let them *marry* (marg. be *wives*)
— shall they *marry.* (lit. be *for wives*)
11. were *married* unto (lit. were *for wives*)
12. they were *married* (lit. were *for wives*)
Deu 2:34. the men, *and the women,* and the little ones,
3: 6. destroying the men, *women,*
19. But *your wives,* and your little ones,
17:17. Neither shall he multiply *wives*
20:14. But *the women,* and the little ones,
21:15. If a man have two *wives,*
29:11(10). Your little ones, *your wives,*
31:12. men, *and women,* and children,
Jos. 1:14. *Your wives,* your little ones,
8:35. *with the women,* and the little ones,
Jud 3: 6. to be their *wives,* (lit. to them *for wives*)
5:24. Blessed *above women* shall Jael
— blessed shall she be *above women*
8:30. for he had many *wives.*
9:51. thither fled all the men *and women,*
16:27. the house was full of men *and women;*
21: 7. How shall we do *for wives*
— give them of our daughters *to wives?*
10. *with the women* and the children.
14. they gave them *wives* which they had saved alive *of the women of*
16. How shall we do *for wives* for them
18. we may not give them *wives*
23. and took (them) *wives,*
Ru 1: 4. they took them *wives* of the women
4:14. *the women* said unto Naomi,
1Sa. 1: 2. he had two *wives;*
2:22. how they lay with *the women*
15:33. As thy sword hath made *women* childless, so shall thy mother be childless *among women.*
18: 6. that *the women* came out
7. *the women* answered (one another)
25:43. they were also both of them his *wives.* (lit. to him *for wives*)
27: 3. David with *his* two *wives,*
30: 2. had taken *the women* captives,
3. *and their wives,* and their sons,
5. David's two *wives* were taken
18. David rescued *his* two *wives.*
2Sa. 1:26. passing the love of *women.*
2: 2. *his* two *wives* also,
5:13. *and wives* out of Jerusalem,
12: 8. thy master's *wives* into thy bosom,
11. I will take *thy wives* before thine eyes,
— and he shall lie with *thy wives*
15:16. the king left ten *women,*
19: 5(6). the lives of *thy wives,*
20: 3. the king took *the* ten *women*
1K. 3:16. Then came there two *women,*
11: 1. Solomon loved many strange *women,*
3. he had seven hundred *wives,*
— *his wives* turned away his heart.
4. *his wives* turned away his heart
8. did he for all *his* strange *wives,*
20: 3. *thy wives also* and thy children,
5. *and thy wives,* and thy children
7. he sent unto me *for my wives,*
2K. 4: 1. *of the wives of* the sons of the
23: 7. where *the women* wove hangings
24:15. the king's *wives,* and his officers,
1Ch. 4: 5. Ashur the father of Tekoa had two *wives,*
7: 4. for they had many *wives*
8: 8. Hushim and Baara (were) *his wives.*
14: 3. David took more *wives*
2Ch. 11:21. the daughter of Absalom above all *his wives*
— for he took eighteen *wives,*
23. he desired many *wives.*

2Ch 13:21. married fourteen *wives*,
20:13. *their wives*, and their children.
21:14. thy children, *and thy wives*,
17. his sons also, *and his wives;*
24: 3. Jehoiada took for him two *wives;*
28: 8. *women*, sons, and daughters,
29: 9. *and our wives* (are) in captivity for this.
31:18. *their wives*, and their sons, and their daughters,
Ezr. 10: 1. a very great congregation of men *and women*
2. have taken strange *wives*
3. to put away all *the wives*,
10. have taken strange *wives*,
11. from *the* strange *wives*.
14. which have taken strange *wives*
17. that had taken strange *wives*
18. found that had taken strange *wives:*
19. they would put away *their wives;*
44. All these had taken strange *wives:* and (some) of them had *wives* by whom they had children.
Neh. 4:14(8). *your wives*, and your houses.
5: 1. of the people *and* of *their wives*
8: 3. before the men *and the women*,
10:28(29). *their wives*, their sons, and their daughters,
12:43. *the wives* also and the children rejoiced:
13:23. had married *wives* of Ashdod,
26. did outlandish *women* cause to sin.
27. in marrying strange *wives?*
Est. 1: 9. the queen made a feast for *the women*
17. shall come abroad unto all *women*,
20. all *the wives* shall give
2: 3, 9. the house of *the women*,
—, 8, 15. keeper of *the women;*
11. before the court of *the women*'s house,
12. according to the manner of *the women*,
— for the purifying of *the women;*
13. *the women* unto the king's house.
14. into the second house of *the women*,
17. the king loved Esther above all *the women*,
3:13. little children *and women*,
8:11. little ones *and women*,
Job 42:15. in all the land were no *women* found
Pro 14: 1. Every wise *woman* buildeth her house: (lit. the wise of *women*)
31: 3. Give not thy strength *unto women*,
Cant 1: 8 & 5:9 & 6:1. O thou fairest *among women*,
Isa. 3:12. *and women* rule over them.
4: 1. in that day seven *women*
13:16. *and their wives* ravished.
19:16. shall Egypt be *like unto women:*
27:11. *the women* come, (and) set them on fire:
32: 9. Rise up, *ye women* that are at ease;
Jer. 6:12. (with their) fields *and wives* together:
7:18. *the women* knead (their) dough,
8:10. Therefore will I give *their wives*
9:20(19). hear the word of the Lord, *O ye women*,
14:16. *their wives*, nor their sons,
18:21. let *their wives* be bereaved
29: 6. Take ye *wives*, and beget sons and daughters; and take *wives* for your sons,
23. adultery with their neighbours' *wives*,
35: 8. *our wives*, our sons, nor our daughters;
38:22. all *the women* that are left
23. they shall bring out all *thy wives*
40: 7. unto him men, *and women*,
41:16. *and the women*, and the children,
43: 6. men, and *women*, and children,
44: 9. the wickedness of *their wives*,
— the wickedness of *your wives*,
15. *their wives* had burned incense unto other gods, and all *the women* that stood by,
20. to the men, and to *the women*,
24. and to all *the women*,
25. Ye *and your wives* have both spoken with
50:37. they shall become *as women:*
51:30. they became *as women:*
Lam. 2:20. Shall *the women* eat their fruit,
4:10. The hands of *the* pitiful *women*
5:11. They ravished *the women* in Zion,
Eze. 8:14. there sat *women* weeping for
9: 6. little children, *and women:*
16:34. from (other) *women* in thy whoredoms,
41. in the sight of many *women:*
23: 2. there were two *women*,
Eze. 23:10. she became famous *among women*.
48. that all *women* may be taught
44:22. Neither shall they take *for* their *wives* (lit. to them *for wives*)
Dan 11:17. give him the daughter of *women*,
37. nor the desire of *women*,
Mic. 2: 9. *The women* (marg. or, *wives*) *of* my people
Nah. 3:13. thy people in the midst of thee (are) *women:*
Zec. 5: 9. there came out two *women*,
12:12, 12, 13, 13, 14. *and their wives* apart;
14: 2. *and the women* ravished;

נְשִׁין [*nāh-sheen'*], Ch.f. pl. 5389

Dan. 6:24(25). them, their children, *and their wives;*

נְשִׁיקָה [*n'shee-kāh'*], f. 5390

Pro. 27: 6. *the kisses of* an enemy (are) deceitful.
Cant 1: 2. Let him kiss me *with the kisses of* his mouth:

נָשַׁךְ *nāh-shach'*. 5391

* KAL.—*Preterite.* *

Nu. 21: 9. if a serpent *had bitten* any man,
Am. 5:19. *and* a serpent *bit him.*
9: 3. the serpent, *and he shall bite them:*

KAL.—*Future.*

Deu 23:19(20). any thing that *is lent upon usury:*
Pro 23:32. *it biteth* like a serpent,
Ecc. 10: 8. a serpent *shall bite him.*
11. the serpent *will bite* without enchantment;

KAL.—*Participle.* Poel.

Gen 49:17. an adder...*that biteth* the horse heels,
Mic. 3: 5. the prophets...*that bite* with their teeth,
Hab. 2: 7. they...*that shall bite thee,*

KAL.—*Participle.* Paül.

Nu. 21: 8. every one *that is bitten*,

* PIEL.—*Preterite.* *

Jer. 8:17. serpents,...*and they shall bite* you,

PIEL.—*Future.*

Nu. 21: 6. fiery serpents...*and they bit* the people;

* HIPHIL.—*Future.* *

Deu 23:19(20). *Thou shalt* not *lend upon usury*
20(21). *thou mayest lend upon usury;* but unto thy brother *thou shalt* not *lend upon usury:*

נֶשֶׁךְ *neh'-shech*, m. 5392

Ex. 22:25(24). neither shalt thou lay upon him *usury*.
Lev 25:36. Take thou no *usury* of him,
37. Thou shalt not give him thy money *upon usury*,
Deu 23:19(20). *usury of* money, *usury of* victuals, *usury of* any thing that is lent
Ps. 15: 5. (He that) putteth not out his money *to usury*,
Pro 28: 8. He that *by usury*...increaseth
Eze. 18: 8. hath not given forth *upon usury*,
13. Hath given forth *upon usury*,
17. hath not received *usury*
22:12. thou hast taken *usury*

נִשְׁכָּה *nish-kāh'*, f. 5393

Neh. 3:30. over against *his chamber*.
12:44. *the chambers* for the treasures,
13: 7. *a chamber* in the courts of the house

נָשַׁל *nāh-shal'*. 5394

* KAL.—*Preterite.* *

Deu 7: 1. *and hath cast out* many nations

Deu 7:22. *And* the Lord thy God *will put out* (marg. *pluck off*) those nations
19: 5. *and* the head *slippeth* from the helve,

KAL.—*Imperative.*

Ex. 3: 5. *put off* thy shoes from off thy feet,
Jos. 5:15. *Loose* thy shoe from off thy foot;

KAL.—*Future.*

Deu 28:40. thine olive *shall cast* (his fruit).

* PIEL.—*Future.* *

2K. 16: 6. *and drave* the Jews from Elath:

5395 נָשַׁם [*nāh-sham'*].

* KAL.—*Future.* *

Isa. 42:14. *I will destroy* and devour at once.

5397 נְשָׁמָה *n'shāh-māh'*, f.

Gen. 2: 7. breathed into his nostrils *the breath of* life;
7:22. All in whose nostrils (was) *the breath of* life, (marg. *the breath of* the spirit of life)
Deu 20:16. save alive nothing *that breatheth:*
Jos. 10:40. utterly destroyed all *that breathed,*
11:11. there was not any left *to breathe:* (marg. *breath*)
14. neither left they any *to breathe.*
2Sa.22:16. *at the blast of* the breath of his nostrils.
1K. 15:29. left not to Jeroboam any *that breathed,*
17:17. there was no *breath* left in him.
Job 4: 9. *By the blast of* God they perish,
26: 4. *and* whose *spirit* came from thee?
27: 3. while *my breath* (is) in me,
32: 8. *the inspiration of* the Almighty
33: 4. *and the breath of* the Almighty
34:14. (if) he gather unto himself his spirit and *his breath;*
37:10. *By the breath of* God frost is given:
Ps. 18:15(16). *at the blast of* the breath of thy nostrils.
150: 6. every *thing that hath breath*
Pro. 20:27. *The spirit of* man (is) the candle
Isa. 2:22. man, whose *breath* (is) in his nostrils:
30:33. *the breath of* the Lord,
42: 5. he that giveth *breath*
57:16. *and the souls* (which) I have made.
Dan 10:17. *neither* is there *breath* left in me.

5396 נִשְׁמָא [*nish-māh'*], Ch. f.

Dan 5:23. and the God in whose hand *thy breath* (is),

5398 נָשַׁף *nāh-shaph'*.

* KAL.—*Preterite.* *

Ex. 15:10. *Thou didst blow* with thy wind,
Isa. 40:24. *he shall* also *blow* upon them,

5399 נֶשֶׁף *neh'-sheph*, m.

1Sa.30:17. David smote them *from the twilight*
2K. 7: 5. they rose up *in the twilight,*
7. they arose and fled *in the twilight,*
Job 3: 9. the stars of *the twilight*
7: 4. unto *the dawning of the day.*
24:15. the adulterer waiteth for *the twilight,*
Ps. 119:147. I prevented *the dawning of the morning,*
Pro. 7: 9. *In the twilight,* in the evening,
Isa. 5:11. that continue *until night,*
21: 4. *the night of* my pleasure
59:10. we stumble at noon day *as in the night;*
Jer. 13:16. before your feet stumble upon the *dark* mountains,

---

5401 נָשַׁק *nāh-shak'*.

* KAL.—*Preterite.* *

2 Sa 15: 5. he put forth his hand,...*and kissed* him.
1K. 19:18. every mouth which *hath* not *kissed*
Ps. 85:10(11). righteousness and peace *have kissed* (each other).
Pro. 7:13. she caught him, *and kissed* him,

KAL.—*Infinitive.*

2Sa.20: 9. Joab took Amasa by the beard...*to kiss* him.

KAL.—*Imperative.*

Gen27:26. Come near now, *and kiss* me, my son.

KAL.—*Future.*

Gen27:27. he came near, *and kissed* him:
29:11. *And* Jacob *kissed* Rachel,
33: 4. Esau ran to meet him,...*and kissed him:*
41:40. according unto thy word *shall* all my people *be ruled:* (marg. *be armed,* or, *kiss*)
48:10. *and he kissed* them, and embraced them.
50: 1. Joseph fell upon his father's face,...*and kissed* him.
Ex. 4:27. he went, and met him...*and kissed* him.
18: 7. and did obeisance, *and kissed* him;
Ru. 1: 9. *Then she kissed* them;
14. *and* Orpah *kissed* her mother in law;
1Sa.10: 1. poured (it) upon his head, *and kissed him,*
20:41. *and they kissed* one another,
2Sa.14:33. *and* the king *kissed* Absalom.
19:39(40). *And* when the king...the king *kissed* Barzillai,
1K. 19:20. *Let me,* I pray thee, *kiss* my father
Job 31:27. *or* my mouth *hath kissed* my hand:
Pro.24:26. (Every man) *shall kiss* (his) lips
Cant.1: 2. *Let him kiss me* with the kisses of his mouth:
8: 1. *I would kiss thee;* yea, I should
Hos 13: 2. *Let* the men that sacrifice *kiss* the calves.

KAL.—*Participle.* Poel.

1Ch 12: 2. (They were) *armed* with bows,
2 Ch17:17. *armed men* with bow and shield
Ps. 78: 9. The children of Ephraim, (being) *armed,*

* PIEL.—*Infinitive.* *

Gen31:28. *to kiss* my sons and my daughters?

PIEL.—*Imperative.*

Ps. 2:12. *Kiss* the Son, lest he be angry,

PIEL.—*Future.*

Gen29:13. embraced him, *and kissed* him,
31:55(32:1). Laban rose up, *and kissed* his sons
45:15. *Moreover he kissed* all his brethren,

* HIPHIL.—*Participle.* *

Eze. 3:13. the wings of the living creatures *that touched* (marg. *kissed*)

נֵשֶׁק *nēh'-shek,* & נֶשֶׁק *neh'-shek,* m. 5402

1K. 10:25. garments, *and armour,*
2K. 10: 2. a fenced city also, *and armour;*
2Ch 9:24. raiment, *harness,* and spices,
Neh. 3:19. the going up *to the armoury*
Job 20:24. He shall flee from *the iron weapon,*
39:21. he goeth on to meet *the armed men.* (marg. *armour*)
Ps.140: 7(8). in the day of *battle.*
Isa. 22: 8. *the armour of* the house of the forest.
Eze.39: 9. set on fire and burn *the weapons,*
10. they shall burn *the weapons*

נֶשֶׁר *neh'-sher,* m. 5404

Ex. 19: 4. I bare you on *eagles'* wings,
Lev.11:13. *the eagle,* and the ossifrage,
Deu 14:12. *the eagle,* and the ossifrage,
28:49. (as swift) as *the eagle* flieth;
32:11. *As an eagle* stirreth up her nest,
2Sa. 1:23. they were swifter *than eagles,*
Job 9:26. *as the eagle* (that) hasteth to the prey.
39:27. Doth *the eagle* mount up
Ps.103: 5. thy youth is renewed *like the eagle's.*
Pro 23: 5. they fly away *as an eagle* toward heaven.
30:17. *the* young *eagles* (lit. sons of *the eagle*) shall eat it.
19. The way of *an eagle* in the air;
Isa. 40:31. mount up with wings *as eagles;*
Jer. 4:13. his horses are swifter *than eagles.*
48:40. he shall fly *as an eagle,*
49:16. as high *as the eagle,*
22. and fly *as the eagle,*

Lam. 4:19. swifter *than the eagles of* the heaven:
Eze. 1:10. the face of *an eagle.*
10:14. the fourth the face of *an eagle.*
17: 3. *A* great *eagle* with great wings,
7. There was also another great *eagle*
Hos. 8: 1. (He shall come) *as an eagle*
Obad. 4. Though thou exalt (thyself) *as the eagle,*
Mic. 1:16. enlarge thy baldness *as the eagle;*
Hab. 1: 8. they shall fly *as the eagle*

5403 נְשַׁר *n'shar*, Ch. m.

Dan 4:33(30). his hairs were grown *like eagles'* (feathers),
7: 4. and had *eagle's* wings:

5405 נָשַׁת [*nāh-shath'*].

* KAL.—*Preterite.* *

Isa. 41:17. their tongue *faileth* for thirst,
Jer 51:30. their might *hath failed;*

* NIPHAL.—*Preterite.* *

Isa. 19: 5. *And* the waters *shall fail*

5406 נִשְׁתְּוָן *nish-t'vāhn'*, m.

Ezr. 4: 7. the writing of *the letter*
7:11. the copy of *the letter*

5407 נִשְׁתְּוָן [*nish-t'vāhn'*], Ch. m.

Ezr. 4:18. *The letter* which ye sent unto us
23. the copy of king Artaxerxes' *letter*
5: 5. returned answer *by letter*

5411 נְתוּנִים *n'thoo-neem'*, m. pl.

Ezr. 8:17. (כתיב) to his brethren *the Nethinims,*

5408 נָתַח [*nāh-thagh'*].

* PIEL.—*Preterite.* *

Lev. 1: 6. *and cut* it into his pieces.
12. *And he shall cut* it into his pieces,
8:20. *And he cut* the ram into pieces;

PIEL.—*Future.*

Ex. 29:17. *thou shalt cut* the ram
Jud 19:29. *and divided her,* (together) with her bones,
20: 6. *and cut her in pieces,* and sent her
1Sa. 11: 7. *and hewed them in pieces,* and sent
1K. 18:23. *and cut it in pieces,* and lay
33. *and cut* the bullock *in pieces,*

5409 נֵתַח *neh'-thagh'*, m.

Ex. 29:17. thou shalt cut the ram *in pieces,*
— put (them) unto *his pieces,*
Lev. 1: 6. cut it *into his pieces.*
8. shall lay *the parts,*
12. he shall cut it *into his pieces,*
8:20. he cut the ram *into pieces;*
— *the pieces,* and the fat.
9:13. *with the pieces thereof,* and the head:
Jud. 19:29. divided her,...into twelve *pieces,*
Eze. 24: 4. Gather *the pieces thereof* into it, (even) every good *piece,*
6. bring it out *piece by piece;*

5410 נָתִיב *nāh-theev'*, m.

Job 18:10. a trap for him in *the way.*
28: 7. (There is) *a path* which no fowl knoweth,
41:32(24). He maketh *a path* to shine
Ps. 78:50. He made *a way* (marg. weighed *a path*) to his anger;
119:35. Make me to go *in the path*

נְתִיבָה *n'thee-vāh'*, f. 5410

Jud. 5: 6. the *travellers* (marg. walkers of *paths*) walked through byways.
Job 19: 8. he hath set darkness in *my paths.*
24:13. nor abide *in the paths thereof.*
30:13. They mar *my path,*
38:20. that thou shouldest know *the paths*
Ps 119:105. a light *unto my path.*
142: 3(4). then thou knewest *my path.*
Pro. 1:15. refrain thy foot *from their path:*
3:17. all *her paths* (are) peace.
7:25. go not astray *in her paths.*
8: 2. in the places of *the paths.*
20. the midst of *the paths of* judgment:
12:28. (in) the *path*way (thereof there is) no death.
Isa. 42:16. *in paths* (that) they have not known:
43:16. *a path* in the mighty waters;
58:12. The restorer of *paths* to dwell in.
59: 8. they have made them crooked *paths:* (lit. *their paths* they have made crooked for them)
Jer. 6:16. ask *for the* old *paths,*
18:15. to walk in *paths,*
Lam 3: 9. he hath made *my paths* crooked.
Hos. 2: 6(8). she shall not find *her paths.*

נְתִינִים *n'thee-neem'*, m. pl. 5411

1Ch 9: 2. priests, Levites, *and the Nethinims*
Ezr. 2:43. *The Nethinims:* the children of Ziha,
58. *the Nethinims,* and the children of Solomon's servants,
70. *and the Nethinims,* dwelt in their cities,
7: 7. the porters, *and the Nethinims,*
8:17. to his brethren *the Nethinims,*
20. Also of *the Nethinims,* whom David
— two hundred and twenty *Nethinims:*
Neh. 3:26. *Moreover the Nethinims* dwelt in Ophel,
31. unto the place of *the Nethinims,*
7:46. *The Nethinims:* the children of Ziha,
60. *the Nethinims,* and the children of Solomon's servants,
73. *and the Nethinims,* and all Israel,
10:28(29). porters, the singers, *the Nethinims,*
11: 3. and the Levites, *and the Nethinims,*
21. *But the Nethinims* dwelt in Ophel: and Ziha and Gispa (were) over *the Nethinims.*

נְתִינִין [*n'thee-neen'*], Ch. m. pl. 5412

Ezr. 7:24. porters, *Nethinims,* or ministers

נָתַךְ [*nāh-thach'*]. 5413

* KAL.—*Future.* *

2Ch 12: 7. my wrath *shall* not *be poured out*
34:25. *therefore* my wrath *shall be poured out*
Job 3:24. *and* my roarings *are poured out*
Jer. 42:18. so *shall* my fury *be poured forth*
44: 6. *Wherefore* my fury...*was poured forth,*
Dan. 9:11. *therefore* the curse *is poured* upon us,
27. that determined *shall be poured* upon the desolate.

* NIPHAL.—*Preterite.* *

Ex. 9:33. the rain *was* not *poured* upon the earth.
2Sa. 21:10. until water *dropped* upon them
2Ch 34:21. the wrath of the Lord that *is poured out*
Jer. 42:18. my fury *hath been poured forth*
Eze. 22:21. *and ye shall be melted* in the midst
24:11. *and* (that) the filthiness of it *may be molten*
Nah. 1: 6. his fury *is poured out*

NIPHAL.—*Participle.*

Jer. 7:20. my fury *shall be poured out*

* HIPHIL.—*Preterite.* *

2K. 22: 9. Thy servants *have gathered* (marg. *melted*) the money
Eze. 22:20. I will leave (you there), *and melt you.*

HIPHIL.—*Infinitive.*

Eze. 22:20. blow the fire upon it, *to melt* (it);

HIPHIL.—*Future.*

2Ch 34:17. *And they have gathered together* (marg. *poured out*, or, *melted*) the money
Job 10:10. *Hast thou* not *poured me out* as milk,

* HOPHAL.—*Future.* *

Eze.22:22. so *shall ye be melted*

5414 נָתַן *nāh-than'.*

* KAL.—*Preterite.* *

Gen. 1:29. *I have given* you every herb
3:12. The woman whom *thou gavest* (to be) with me, she *gave* me of the tree,
9: 3. as the green herb *have I given*
13. *I do set* my bow in the cloud,
15: 3. to me *thou hast given* no seed:
18. Unto thy seed *have I given* this land,
16: 5. I *have given* my maid into thy bosom;
17: 5. a father of many nations *have I made thee.*
6. *and I will make* nations *of thee,*
8. *And I will give unto thee,*...the land
16. I will bless her, and *give* thee a son
20. *and I will make him* a great nation.
20: 6. *suffered I thee* not to touch her.
16. *I have given* thy brother a thousand (pieces) of silver:
23:11. the field *give I* thee, and the cave...*I give it* thee; in the presence of the sons...*give I it* thee:
13. *I will give* thee money for the field;
24:53. *he gave* also to her brother
25: 6. Abraham *gave* gifts,
34. Jacob *gave* Esau bread and pottage
26: 4. *and will give* unto thy seed all these countries;
27:37. all his brethren *have I given* to him
28: 4. God *gave* unto Abraham.
20. *and will give* me bread to eat,
30:18. God *hath given* me my hire, because *I have given* my maiden
31: 7. God *suffered him* not to hurt me.
34:16. *Then will we give* our daughters
35:12. the land which *I gave* Abraham
38:26. *I gave her* not to Shelah
39: 4. all (that) he had *he put* into his hand.
8. *he hath committed* all that he hath
40:13. *and thou shalt deliver* Pharaoh's cup into
41:41. *I have set* thee over all the land
48. the food...*laid he up* in the same.
43:23. the God of your father, *hath given* you treasure
45:22. *he gave* each man changes of raiment; but to Benjamin *he gave*
46:18. Zilpah, whom Laban *gave* to Leah
25. Bilhah, which Laban *gave* unto Rachel
47:22. their portion which Pharaoh *gave*
24. *that ye shall give* the fifth
48: 4. *and I will make of thee* a multitude of people; *and will give* this land
9. my sons, whom God *hath given* me
22. *I have given* to thee one portion above
Ex. 3:21. *And I will give* this people favour
6: 8. *and I will give* it you for an heritage:
7: 1. *I have made thee* a god to Pharaoh:
4. *that I may lay* my hand upon Egypt,
9:23. the Lord *sent* thunder and hail,
12: 7. *and strike* (it) on the two side posts
36. the Lord *gave* the people favour
13:11. to thy fathers, *and shall give it* thee,
16:15. the bread which the Lord *hath given* you
29. the Lord *hath given* you the sabbath.
21:22. *and he shall pay* as the judges (determine).
23. *then thou shalt give* life for life,
30. *then he shall give* for the ransom
23:27. *and I will make* all thine enemies turn
25:12. *and put* (them) in the four corners
16. *And thou shalt put* into the ark
21. *And thou shalt put* the mercy seat above
26. *and put* the rings in the four corners
30. *And thou shalt set* upon the table shewbread
26:32. *And thou shalt hang* it upon four pillars
33. *And thou shalt hang up* the vail
34. *And thou shalt put* the mercy seat upon
27: 5. *And thou shalt put* it under the compass
28:14. *and fasten* the wreathen chains

Ex. 28:23. *and shalt put* the two rings on
24. *And thou shalt put* the two wreathen (chains)
25. *and put* (them) on the shoulderpieces
27. *and shalt put* them on the two
30. *And thou shalt put* in the breastplate
29: 3. *And thou shalt put* them into one basket,
6. *and put* the holy crown upon the mitre.
12. thou shalt take of the blood...*and put* (it) upon
17. *and put* (them) unto his pieces,
20. take of his blood, *and put* (it) upon the tip
30: 6. *And thou shalt put* it before the vail
12. *then shall they give* every man a ransom
16. *and shalt appoint* it for the service
18. *and thou shalt put* it between
— *and thou shalt put* water therein.
36. *and put* of it before the testimony
31: 6. I *have given* with him Aholiab,
— in the hearts...*I have put* wisdom,
35:34. *he hath put* in his heart
36: 1. in whom the Lord *put* wisdom
2. in whose heart the Lord *had put* wisdom,
39:18. *they fastened* in the two ouches,
40: 5. *And thou shalt set* the altar...before the ark
6. *And thou shalt set* the altar...before the door
7. *And thou shalt set* the laver between
— *and shalt put* water therein.
8. *and hang up* the hanging
Lev. 1: 7. *And* the sons of Aaron the priest *shall put* fire
2: 1. *and put* frankincense thereon:
15. *And thou shalt put* oil upon it,
4: 7. *And* the priest *shall put* (some) of the blood upon
25, 30, 34. *and put* (it) upon the horns of the altar
5:16. *and give* it unto the priest:
6:17(10). *I have given* it (unto them for)
10:17. (God) *hath given* it you
14:14. *and* the priest shall *put* (it) upon
25. *and put* (it) upon the tip
28. *And* the priest *shall put* of the oil
34. *and I put* the plague of leprosy in a house
15:14. *and give them* unto the priest:
16: 8. *And* Aaron *shall cast* lots
13. *And he shall put* the incense upon
18. *and put* (it) upon the horns
21. *putting* (lit. *and he shall put*) them upon the head of the goat,
17:10. *I will even set* my face against
11. *I have given it* to you
20: 3. *he hath given* of his seed unto Molech,
6. *I will even set* my face against
22:14. *and shall give* (it) unto the priest
24: 7. *And thou shalt put* pure frankincense upon
25:19. *And* the land *shall yield* her fruit,
26: 4. *Then I will give* you rain in due season, *and* the land *shall yield* her increase,
6. *And I will give* peace
11. *And I will set* my tabernacle among you:
17. *And I will set* my face against you,
19. *and I will make* your heaven as iron,
30. *and cast* your carcases upon the carcases
31. *And I will make* your cities waste,
46. the statutes...which the Lord *made*
27:23. *and he shall give* thine estimation
Nu. 3: 9. *And thou shalt give* the Levites unto Aaron
48. *And thou shalt give* the money,
4: 6. *And shall put* thereon the covering
7. *and put* thereon the dishes,
10. *And they shall put* it...within a covering
— *and shall put* (it) upon a bar.
12. *and put* (them) in a cloth of blue,
— *and shall put* (them) on a bar:
14. *And they shall put* upon it all the vessels
5: 7. *and give* (it) unto (him) against
17. *and put* (it) into the water:
18. *and put* the offering of memorial in her hands,
6:18. *and put* (it) in the fire
19. *and shall put* (them) upon the hands of
7: 5. *and thou shalt give* them unto the Levites,
7. *he gave* unto the sons of Gershon,
8. *he gave* unto the sons of Merari,
9. unto the sons of Kohath *he gave* none:
11:18. *therefore* the Lord *will give* you flesh,

Nu. 14: 8. bring us into this land, *and give it* us;
15:38. *that they put* upon the fringe...a ribband
16:17. take every man his censer, *and put* incense
18: 8. I also *have given* thee the charge
— unto thee *have I given them*
11. *I have given them* unto thee,
12. *them have I given* thee.
19. the heave offerings...*have I given* thee,
21. *I have given* the children of Levi
24. the tithes...*I have given* to the Levites
26. the tithes which *I have given* you
28. *and ye shall give* thereof
19: 3. *And ye shall give* her unto Eleazar
17. *and* running water *shall be put* (marg. *given*) thereto
20: 8. *and it shall give forth* his water,
12. the land which *I have given* them.
19. *then I will pay* for it:
24. the land which *I have given*
21:23. Sihon *would* not *suffer* Israel to pass
29. *he hath given* his sons that escaped,
34. *I have delivered* him into thy hand,
27: 9, 10, 11. *then ye shall give* his inheritance
12. the land which *I have given*
20. *And thou shalt put* (some) of thine honour upon
31:29. *and give* (it) unto Eleazar
30. *and give* them unto the Levites,
32: 7. the land which the Lord *hath given*
9. the land which the Lord *had given* them.
29. *then ye shall give* them the land of Gilead
33:53. *I have given* you the land
35: 2. *that they give* unto the Levites
Deu. 1: 8. *I have set* (marg. *given*) the land before you:
21. the Lord thy God *hath set* the land
2: 5. *I have given* mount Seir unto Esau
9. *I have given* Ar unto the children of Lot
12. his possession, which the Lord *gave*
19. *I have given it* unto the children of Lot
24. *I have given* into thine hand Sihon
36. the Lord our God *delivered* all unto us:
3: 2. *I will deliver* him, and all his people,
12. the cities thereof, *gave I* unto
13. the kingdom of Og, *gave I* unto
15. And *I gave* Gilead unto Machir.
16. *I gave* from Gilead even unto the river
18. The Lord your God *hath given*
19. your cities which *I have given*
20. his possession, which *I have given* you.
7: 2. And *when* the Lord thy God *shall deliver them*
15. *but will lay them* upon all (them) that hate
23. *But* the Lord thy God *shall deliver them*
24. *And he shall deliver* their kings
8:10. the good land which *he hath given* thee.
9:11. the Lord *gave* me the two tables
23. the land which *I have given* you;
11:14. *I will give* (you) the rain
15. *And I will send* (marg. *give*) grass in thy fields
29. *that thou shalt put* the blessing upon mount
12: 1. the land, which the Lord God...*giveth* thee
15. the blessing...which *he hath given* thee:
21. thy flock, which the Lord *hath given* thee,
13: 1(2). *and giveth* thee a sign or a wonder,
17(18). *and shew* thee mercy, and have compassion
14:25. *Then shalt thou turn* (it) into money,
26. *And thou shalt bestow* that money
15:17. take an aul, *and thrust* (it) through his ear
16:17. the blessing...which *he hath given*
18: 3. *and they shall give* unto the priest the shoulder,
14. the Lord thy God *hath* not *suffered* thee
18. *and will put* my words in his mouth;
19: 8. *and give* thee all the land
12. *and deliver* him into the hand of
20:13. *And when* the Lord thy God *hath delivered it*
14. the Lord thy God *hath given* thee.
21:10. the Lord thy God *hath delivered them*
22:16. *I gave* my daughter unto this man
19. *and give* (them) unto the father of the damsel,
29. *Then* the man...*shall give* unto the damsel's father
24: 1. her a bill of divorcement, *and give* (it)
Deu24: 3. her a bill of divorcement, *and giveth* (it)
26:10. *thou*, O Lord, *hast given* me.
11. the Lord thy God *hath given* unto thee,
12. *and hast given* (it) unto the Levite,
13. and also *have given them* unto the Levite,
14. nor *given* (ought) thereof for the dead:
15. the land which *thou hast given*
28: 1. *that* the Lord thy God *will set thee* on high
13. *And* the Lord *shall make thee* the head,
48. *and he shall put* a yoke of iron upon thy neck,
52. which the Lord thy God *hath given* thee.
53. the Lord thy God *hath given* thee,
65. *but* the Lord *shall give* thee there
29: 4(3). the Lord *hath* not *given* you an heart
30: 1. the blessing and the curse, which *I have set*
7. *And* the Lord thy God *will put*
15. *I have set* before thee...life and good,
19. *I have set* before you life and death,
31: 5. *And* the Lord *shall give them up*
Jos. 1: 3. *that have I given* unto you,
13. *and hath given* you this land.
14. the land which Moses *gave* you
15. Moses the Lord's servant *gave* you
2: 9. the Lord *hath given* you the land,
12. *and give* me a true token:
24. the Lord *hath delivered*
6: 2. *I have given* into thine hand Jericho,
16. the Lord *hath given* you the city.
24. vessels of brass and of iron, *they put* into
8: 1. *I have given* into thy hand the king of Ai,
7. *for* the Lord your God *will deliver it*
10: 8. *I have delivered them* into thine hand;
19. the Lord your God *hath delivered them*
13: 8. their inheritance, which Moses *gave* them,
— Moses the servant of the Lord *gave* them;
14. the tribe of Levi *he gave* none inheritance;
33. Moses *gave* not (any) inheritance:
14: 3. Moses *had given* the inheritance
— unto the Levites *he gave* none inheritance
4. *they gave* no part unto the Levites
15:13. unto Caleb...*he gave* a part
16. *will I give* Achsah my daughter
19. *thou hast given me* a south land; *give* me *also* springs of water.
17:14. Why *hast thou given* me (but) one lot
18: 3. the land, which the Lord God...*hath given*
7. which Moses the servant of the Lord *gave* them.
19:50. *they gave* him the city
20: 4. *and give* him a place,
8. *they assigned* Bezer in the wilderness
21:12. the villages thereof, *gave they*
13. *they gave* to the children of Aaron
44(42). the Lord *delivered* all their enemies
22: 4. Moses the servant of the Lord *gave*
7. Moses *had given* (possession)
— *gave* Joshua among their brethren
25. the Lord *hath made* Jordan a border
23:13. land which the Lord your God *hath given*
15. good land which the Lord...*hath given*
16. the good land which *he hath given*
Jud. 1: 2. *I have delivered* the land into his hand.
12. to him *will I give* Achsah my daughter
15. *thou hast given me* a south land; *give* me *also* springs of water.
34. *they would* not *suffer them* to come down
2:23. neither *delivered he them*
3: 6. *gave* their daughters to their sons,
28. the Lord *hath delivered* your enemies
— *suffered* not a man to pass
4: 7. *and I will deliver him* into thine hand.
14. the Lord *hath delivered* Sisera
5:25. *she gave* (him) milk;
7: 7. will I save you, *and deliver* the Midianites
9. *I have delivered it* into thine hand.
14. into his hand *hath* God *delivered*
15. the Lord *hath delivered* into your hand
8: 3. God *hath delivered* into your hands
11: 9. *and* the Lord *deliver* them
14:12. *then I will give* you thirty sheets
13. *then shall ye give* me thirty sheets
15: 1. her father *would* not *suffer him* to go in.
13. *and deliver thee* into their hand:
18. Thou *hast given* this great deliverance
16:23,24. Our god *hath delivered*
18:10. God *hath given it* into your hands;
21:22. ye *did* not *give* unto them

Ru. 3:17. These six (measures) of barley *gave he* me;
4: 7. plucked off his shoe, *and gave* (it) to his neighbour:
1Sa. 1: 4. *he gave* to Peninnah his wife,
11. *but wilt give* unto thine handmaid a man child, *then I will give him* unto the Lord
6: 5. *and ye shall give* glory unto the God of Israel:
8. take the ark...*and lay* it upon the cart;
8:14. *and give* (them) to his servants.
15. he will take the tenth...*and give* to
9: 8. *will I give* to the man of God,
23. Bring the portion which *I gave* thee,
10: 4. *and give* thee two (loaves) of bread;
12:13. the Lord *hath set* a king over you.
14:10. the Lord *hath delivered them* into our
12. the Lord *hath delivered them* into the
15:28. *and hath given it* to a neighbour
17:38. *and he put* an helmet of brass upon his head;
46. *and I will give* the carcases of
47. *and he will give* you into our hands.
18: 2. *would let him* go no more home
8. *They have ascribed* unto David
— to me *they have ascribed*
22:10. *gave* him victuals, and *gave* him the sword of Goliath
23:14. God *delivered him* not into
24: 7(8). *suffered them* not to rise
10(11). the Lord *had delivered thee*
25:11. Shall I then take my bread,...*and give* (it)
44. But Saul *had given* Michal
26:23. the Lord *delivered thee* into (my) hand
30:23. that which the Lord *hath given*
2Sa. 9: 9. *I have given* unto thy master's son
10:10. the rest of the people *he delivered*
12:11. I will take thy wives...*and give* (them)
21:10. *suffered* neither the birds...to rest...by day,
22:41. *Thou hast* also *given* me the necks of
24:23. All these (things) *did* Araunah, (as) a king, *give*
1K. 1:48. *hath given* (one) to sit on my throne
2:35. Zadok the priest *did* the king *put*
3: 9. *Give therefore* thy servant
12. *I have given* thee a wise...heart;
13. *I have also given* thee that
5: 7(21). the Lord...which *hath given* unto David
11(25). And Solomon *gave* Hiram
12(26). the Lord *gave* Solomon wisdom,
6: 6. *he made* narrowed rests
7:39. *he set* the sea on the right side
51. and the vessels, *did he put* among
8:34. unto the land which *thou gavest*
36. and *give* rain upon thy land, which *thou hast given*
39. *and give* to every man according to
40. in the land which *thou gavest*
46. *and deliver them* to the enemy,
48. their land, which *thou gavest*
50. *and give them* compassion before them
56. the Lord, that *hath given* rest
9: 6. my statutes which *I have set* before
7. the land which *I have given*
12. the cities which Solomon *had given*
13. cities (are) these which *thou hast given*
22. *did* Solomon *make* no bondmen:
10:10. the queen of Sheba *gave* to king Solomon.
13. king Solomon *gave* unto the queen
— (that) which Solomon *gave* her
24. wisdom, which God *had put* in his heart.
27. cedars *made he* (to be) as the sycomore
11:11. *and will give it* to thy servant.
18. appointed him victuals, and *gave* him land.
31. *and will give* ten tribes to thee:
35. *and will give it* unto thee,
38. *and will give* Israel unto thee.
12: 4. his heavy yoke which *he put* upon us,
9. the yoke which thy father *did put*
29. the other *put he* in Dan.
13: 3. *And he gave* a sign the same day,
5. the sign which the man of God *had given*
14:15. this good land, which *he gave*
15: 4. *did* the Lord his God *give* him a lamp
16: 3. *and will make* thy house like
18:23. I will dress the other bullock, *and lay* (it)
26. the bullock which *was given* (lit. *he gave*) them,

1K. 20:28. *therefore will I deliver* all this
21:22. *And will make* thine house like
22:12, 15. *for* the Lord *shall deliver*
23. the Lord *hath put* a lying spirit in
2K. 3:18. *he will deliver* the Moabites *also* into
5: 1. the Lord *had given* deliverance
9: 9. *And I will make* the house of Ahab like
12: 9(10). *and* the priests...*put* therein all the money
11(12). *And they gave* the money,
19:18. *And have cast* (marg. *given*) their gods into the fire:
21: 8. the land which *I gave*
14. *and deliver them* into the hand of
22:10. Hilkiah the priest *hath delivered* me a book.
23: 5. the kings of Judah *had ordained*
11. the kings of Judah *had given* to the sun,
35. Jehoiakim *gave* the silver and the gold
1Ch 6:56(41). the fields...*they gave* to Caleb
57(42). to the sons of Aaron *they gave* the cities of Judah,
14:10. *and wilt thou deliver them* into mine hand?
— *for I will deliver them* into thine hand.
17. the Lord *brought* the fear of him upon all
16: 7. David *delivered* first (this psalm)
19:11. the rest of the people *he delivered* unto
21:23. *I give* (thee) the oxen (also)
— *I give* it all.
22:18. for *he hath given* the inhabitants...into
28: 5. the Lord *hath given* me many sons,
29: 3. gold and silver, (which) *I have given*
8. *they* with whom (precious) stones were found *gave*
14. of thine own *have we given* thee.
24. sub*mitted* themselves (marg. *gave* the hand under) unto Solomon the king.
2Ch 1:15. cedar trees *made he* as the sycomore trees
2:10(9). *I will give* to thy servants,
11(10). *he hath made* thee king
12(11). *hath given* to David...a wise son,
4:10. *he set* the sea on the right side
5: 1. *put he* among the treasures
10. the two tables which Moses *put* (therein)
6:25. the land which *thou gavest* to them
27. *and send* rain upon thy land, which *thou hast given*
30. *and render* unto every man according
31. land which *thou gavest* unto our fathers.
36. thou be angry...*and deliver them* over
38. their land, which *thou gavest*
7:19. commandments, which *I have set* before
20. my land which *I have given*
8: 2. the cities which Huram *had restored*
9. children of Israel *did* Solomon *make*
9: 9. as the queen of Sheba *gave* king Solomon.
12. king Solomon *gave* to the queen of Sheba
23. his wisdom, that God *had put* in his heart.
27. and cedar trees *made he*
10: 4. his heavy yoke that *he put* upon us,
9. the yoke that thy father *did put*
12: 7. *but I will grant* them some deliverance;
13: 5. the Lord God of Israel *gave* the kingdom
16: 8. *he delivered them* into thine hand.
17:19. (those) whom the king *put* in the fenced cities
18:11. *for* the Lord *shall deliver* (it) into the hand of
22. the Lord *hath put* a lying spirit in
20:10. *thou wouldest* not *let* Israel invade,
22. the Lord *set* ambushments
21: 3. but the kingdom *gave he* to Jehoram;
24:24. the Lord *delivered* a very great host into
25: 9. the hundred talents which *I have given*
16. *Art thou made* (lit. *have we given thee* to be) of the king's counsel?
28: 9. *he hath delivered them* into your hand,
32:24. *he gave* him a sign.
29. God *had given* him substance
34:18. Hilkiah the priest *hath given* me a book.
35: 8. God, *gave* unto the priests
36:17. *he gave* (them) all into his hand.
23. *hath* the Lord God of heaven *given* me;
Ezr. 1: 2. The Lord God of heaven *hath given* me
2:69. *They gave* after their ability
7: 6. which the Lord God of Israel *had given*:
11. that the king Artaxerxes *gave*
27. Lord God of our fathers, which *hath put*
8:20. *whom* David and the princes *had appointed*

Ezr. 9:13. *and hast given* us (such) deliverance as this;
Neh. 7:70. the chief of the fathers *gave* unto the work.
The Tirshatha *gave* to the treasure
71. the chief of the fathers *gave*
72. the rest of the people *gave*
9:15. *gavest* them bread from heaven
20. *Thou gavest* also thy good spirit
— *gavest* them water for their thirst.
35. thy great goodness that *thou gavest* them, and in the large and fat land which *thou gavest*
36. the land that *thou gavest*
37. the kings whom *thou hast set* over
Est. 4: 8. *he gave* him the copy of the writing
8: 1. On that day *did* the king...*give*
7. *I have given* Esther the house of Haman,
11. the king *granted* the Jews
Job 1:21. the Lord *gave*, and the Lord hath taken
22. nor *charged* God foolishly. (marg. or, *attributed* folly to God)
31:30. Neither *have I suffered* my mouth to sin
38:36. who *hath given* understanding
Ps. 4: 7(8). *Thou hast put* gladness in my heart,
15: 5. (He that) *putteth* not out his money to usury,
18:40(41). *Thou hast* also *given* me the necks of
21: 2(3). *Thou hast given* him his heart's desire,
4(5). He asked life of thee, (and) *thou gavest* (it) him,
39: 5(6). *thou hast made* my days (as) an handbreadth;
46: 6(7). *he uttered* his voice, the earth melted.
60: 4(6). *Thou hast given* a banner to them that
61: 5(6). *thou hast given* (me) the heritage of
66: 9. *suffereth* not our feet to be moved.
67: 6(7). (Then) *shall* the earth *yield* her increase;
77:17(18). the skies *sent out* a sound:
78:24. *had given* them of the corn of heaven.
66. *he put* them to a perpetual reproach.
79: 2. The dead bodies of thy servants *have they given*
99: 7. the ordinance (that) *he gave* them.
105:32. *He gave* them hail for rain,
111: 5. *He hath given* meat unto them that fear him:
112: 9. *he hath given* to the poor;
115:16. the earth *hath he given*
118:18. *he hath* not *given me over* unto death.
119:110. The wicked *have laid* a snare for me:
124: 6. *hath* not *given us* (as) a prey
135:12. *And gave* their land (for) an heritage,
136:21. *And gave* their land for an heritage:
148: 6. *he hath made* a decree which shall
Pro. 4: 2. *I give* you good doctrine,
22: 9. *he giveth* of his bread to the poor.
31:24. *delivereth* girdles unto the merchant.
Ecc. 1:13. *And I gave* my heart to seek and search out
— this sore travail *hath* God *given*
2:26. For (God) *giveth*...wisdom,
— to the sinner *he giveth* travail,
3:10. the travail, which God *hath given*
11. *he hath set* the world in their heart,
5:18(17). his life, which God *giveth* him:
19(18). to whom God *hath given* riches
8:15. his life, which God *giveth* him
16. *I applied* mine heart to know wisdom,
9: 1. *I considered* (marg. *gave*, or, *set*) in my heart
9. the life of thy vanity, which *he hath given* thee
12: 7. spirit shall return unto God who *gave it.*
Cant 1:12. spikenard *sendeth forth* the smell thereof.
2:13. the vines...*give* a (good) smell.
7:13(14). The mandrakes *give* a smell,
8:11. *he let out* the vineyard
Isa. 3: 4. *And I will give* children (to be) their princes,
8:18. the children whom the Lord *hath given* me
22:22. *And* the key of the house of David *will I lay*
30:20. *And* (though) the Lord *give* you the bread of adversity,
23. *Then shall he give* the rain of thy seed,
34: 2. *he hath delivered them* to the slaughter.
42: 1. *I have put* my spirit upon him:
24. Who *gave* Jacob for a spoil,
43: 3. *I gave* Egypt (for) thy ransom,
Isa. 43:20. *I give* waters in the wilderness,
45: 3. *And I will give* thee the treasures of
46:13. *and I will place* salvation in Zion
49: 6. *I will also give thee* for a light
50: 4. The Lord God *hath given* me the tongue
6. *I gave* my back to the smiters,
55: 4. *I have given him* (for) a witness
10. *that it may give* seed to the sower,
56: 5. *Even* unto them *will I give*...a place
61: 8. *and I will direct* their work in truth,
Jer. 1: 5. *I ordained* (marg. *gave*) *thee* a prophet
9. *I have put* my words in thy mouth.
15. *and they shall set* every one his throne
18. I *have made* thee...a defenced city,
2:15. The young lions roared...(and) yelled, (marg. *gave* out their voice)
3:15. *And I will give* you pastors
6:27. *I have set thee* (for) a tower
7: 7. the land that *I gave* to your fathers,
14. the place which *I gave* to you
9:11(10). *And I will make* Jerusalem heaps,
13(12). my law which *I set* before them,
12: 7. *I have given* the dearly beloved
8. Mine heritage...*it* crieth out (marg. *giveth out* his voice)
10. *they have made* my pleasant portion a desolate wilderness.
15: 4. *And I will cause them* (marg. *give them*) to be removed
20. *And I will make thee*...a fenced brasen wall:
16:15. their land that *I gave* unto their fathers.
17: 4. thine heritage that *I gave* thee;
19: 7. *and* their carcases *will I give* to be meat
20: 5. *Moreover I will deliver* all the strength
22:25. *And I will give thee* into the hand of
23:39. the city that *I gave* you
40. *And I will bring* an everlasting reproach
24: 7. *And I will give* them an heart to know me,
9. *And I will deliver them* to be removed
10. the land that *I gave* unto them
25: 5. the land that the Lord *hath given*
31. *he will give them*...to the sword,
26: 4. my law, which *I have set* before you,
6. *Then will I make* this house like Shiloh,
27: 2. yokes, *and put them* upon thy neck,
5. *and have given it* unto whom it seemed
6. now *have* I *given* all these lands
— the beasts...*have I given* him
28:14. *I have put* a yoke of iron upon
— *I have given* him the beasts
29:17. *and will make* them like vile figs,
18. *and will deliver them* to be removed
26. The Lord *hath made thee* priest
— *that thou shouldest put* him in prison,
30: 3. the land that *I gave* to their fathers,
31:33. *I will put* my law in their inward parts,
32:14. *and put them* in an earthen vessel,
39. *And I will give* them one heart,
34:17. *and I will make* you to be removed
18. *And I will give* the men that have transgressed
20. *I will even give* them into
35:15. the land which *I have given* to you
37: 4. *they had* not *put* him into prison.
15. *and put* him in prison
18. *ye have put* me in prison?
38: 7. *they had put* Jeremiah in the dungeon;
40:11. the king of Babylon *had left* a remnant
44:10. my statutes, that *I set* before you
30. as *I gave* Zedekiah king of Judah
45: 5. *but* thy life *will I give*...for a prey
46:26. *And I will deliver them* into the hand of
48:34. *have they uttered* their voice,
49:15. *I will make thee* small
50:15. *she hath given* her hand:
51:25. *and will make thee* a burnt mountain.
Lam. 1:11. *they have given* their pleasant things
13. *he hath made me* desolate
14. the Lord *hath delivered* me
2: 7. *they have made* a noise
5: 6. *We have given* the hand
Eze. 3: 8. *I have made* thy face strong
9. harder than flint *have I made* thy forehead:
17. *I have made thee* a watchman
20. *and I lay* a stumblingblock
25. *they shall put* bands upon thee.
4: 1. take thee a tile, *and lay* it before thee,

Eze. 4: 2. *And lay* siege against it.
— *set* the camp *also* against it,
3. *and set* it (for) a wall of iron
5. I *have laid* upon thee the years
6. *I have appointed* (lit. *given it*) thee each day for
8. *I will lay* bands upon thee,
9. *and put* them in one vessel,
15. *I have given* thee cow's dung for
6: 5. *And I will lay* the dead carcases...before
13. the place where *they did offer*
14. *and make* the land desolate,
7: 3. *and will recompense* (marg. *give*) upon thee
8. *and will recompense* thee for
20. *have I set it* far from them.
21. *And I will give it* into the hands of
9: 10. *I will recompense* their way
11: 9. *and deliver* you into the hands of
17. *and I will give* you the land of Israel.
19. *And I will give* them one heart,
— *and will give them* an heart of flesh:
21. *I will recompense* their way
12: 6. *I have set thee* (for) a sign
14: 3. *put* the stumblingblock of their iniquity
8. *And I will set* my face against
15: 6. which *I have given* (lit. *it*) to the fire for fuel, so *will I give* the inhabitants of
7. *And I will set* my face against them;
8. *And I will make* the land desolate,
16: 7. *I have caused thee* to multiply
17. my silver, which *I had given* thee,
18. *thou hast set* mine oil...before them.
19. My meat also which *I gave* thee,
— *thou hast even set it* before them
33. *thou givest* thy gifts to all thy lovers,
36. thy children, which *thou didst give*
38. *and I will give thee* blood
39. *I will also give* thee into their hand,
43. *I* also *will recompense* thy way
61. *and I will give* them unto thee
17: 18. *he had given* his hand,
19. *even it will I recompense* upon his own head.
22. I will also take of the highest branch... *and will set*
18: 13. *Hath given* forth upon usury,
16. *hath given* his bread to the hungry,
20: 12. *I gave* them my sabbaths,
15. the land which *I had given*
25. *I gave* them also statutes
21: 15(20). *I have set* the point of the sword against
27(32). *and I will give it* (him).
31(36). *and deliver thee* into the hand of
22: 4. *therefore have I made thee* a reproach
31. *I recompensed* upon their heads,
23: 9. *I have delivered her* into the hand
24. *and I will set* judgment before them,
25. *And I will set* my jealousy against thee,
31. *therefore will I give* her cup into thine hand.
49. *And they shall recompense* your lewdness
24: 8. *I have set* her blood upon the top of a rock,
25: 4. *and make* their dwellings in thee:
5. *And I will make* Rabbah a stable
7. *and will deliver thee* for a spoil
10. *and will give them* in possession,
13. *and I will make it* desolate
14. *And I will lay* my vengeance upon Edom
26: 4. *and make* her like the top of a rock.
8. *and he shall make* a fort against thee,
14. *And I will make thee* like the top of a rock:
17. her inhabitants, which *cause* their terror
20. *and* I *shall set* glory in the land
27: 10. *they set forth* thy comeliness.
12. *they traded* in thy fairs.
13. *they traded* the persons of men
14. *They* of the house of Togarmah...*traded*
16, 22. *they occupied* in thy fairs
17. *they traded* in thy market
19. *occupied* in thy fairs: bright iron,
28: 14. *and I have set thee* (so): thou wast
17. *I will lay thee* before kings,
25. their land that *I have given*
29: 4. *But I will put* hooks in thy jaws,
5. *I have given thee* for meat
10. *and I will make* the land of Egypt...waste
12. *And I will make* the land of Egypt desolate
20. *I have given* him the land of Egypt

Eze. 30: 12. *And I will make* the rivers dry,
13. *and I will put* a fear in the land of Egypt.
14. *and will set* fire in Zoan,
16. *And I will set* fire in Egypt:
24. *and put* my sword in his hand:
32: 5. *And I will lay* thy flesh upon the mountains,
8. *and set* darkness upon thy land,
23. *caused* terror in the land
24. which *caused* their terror in the land of
25. *They have set* her a bed
26. *they caused* their terror in the land
32. *I have caused* my terror
33: 2. *and set* him for their watchman:
7. *I have set thee* a watchman
27. and *him...will I give* to the beasts
28. *For I will lay* the land most desolate,
34: 26. *And I will make* them...a blessing;
27. *And* the tree of the field *shall yield*
35: 3. *and I will make thee* most desolate.
7. *Thus will I make* mount Seir most desolate,
36: 5. *have appointed* my land
26. A new heart *also will I give* you,
— *and I will give* you an heart of flesh.
28. the land that *I gave* to your fathers;
37: 6. *And I will lay* sinews upon you,
— *and put* breath in you,
14. *And shall put* my spirit in you,
19. *and will put* them with him,
25. the land that *I have given* unto Jacob
26. *and I will place them*, and multiply them, *and will set* my sanctuary
38: 4. *and put* hooks into thy jaws,
39: 4. *I will give thee* unto the ravenous birds
21. *And I will set* my glory among
43: 19. *And thou shalt give* to the priests the Levites
20. take of the blood thereof, *and put* (it) on
44: 14. *But I will make* them keepers
45: 19. *and put* (it) upon the posts of the house,
Dan. 1: 17. God *gave* them knowledge
9: 10. his laws, which *he set* before us
10: 12. *thou didst set* thine heart to
15. *I set* my face toward the ground,
11: 21. *they shall* not *give* the honour
31. *and they shall place* the abomination
Hos. 2: 8(10). I *gave* her corn, and wine,
12(14). rewards that my lovers *have given* me:
15(17). *And I will give* her her vineyards
Joel 2: 11. the Lord *shall utter* his voice
22. the fig tree and the vine *do yield*
23. *he hath given* you the former rain
30(3:3). *And I will shew* wonders
Am. 4: 6. I also *have given* you cleanness of teeth
9: 15. their land which *I have given* them,
Obad. 2. *I have made thee* small
Hab. 3: 10. the deep *uttered* his voice,
Zec. 3: 7. *and I will give* thee places to walk
9. behold the stone that *I have laid*
Mal. 2: 9. *have* I also *made* you contemptible

KAL.—*Infinitive.*

Gen. 4: 12. it shall not henceforth *yield*
15: 7. *to give* thee this land
29: 19. better *that I give* her to thee, *than that I should give* her to another man:
26. *to give* (marg. *place*) the younger before the firstborn.
34: 14. *to give* our sister to one that is uncircumcised;
38: 9. lest that he *should give* seed
41: 43. *and he made* him (ruler) over all the land
42: 25. *and to give* them provision for the way:
27. *to give* his ass provender
Ex. 5: 7. Ye shall no more *give* the people straw
21. *to put* a sword in their hand to slay us.
6: 4. *to give* them the land of Canaan,
8. *to give* it to Abraham, to Isaac, and to Jacob;
13: 5. he sware unto thy fathers *to give* thee,
16: 8. *when* the Lord *shall give*...flesh to eat,
22: 17(16). utterly refuse *to give her* unto him.
30: 15. *when* (they) *give* an offering
32: 29. *that he may bestow* upon you
39: 31. *to fasten* (it) on high
Lev. 7: 36. the Lord commanded *to be given*
20: 4. *when he giveth* of his seed unto Molech,
25: 38. *to give* you the land of Canaan,
Nu. 5: 21. *when* the Lord *doth make* thy thigh to rot,

Nu. 11:13. flesh *to give* unto all this people ?
20:21. Edom refused *to give* Israel passage
21: 2. If thou wilt *indeed* deliver (lit. *delivering* thou wilt deliver)
22:13. the Lord refuseth *to give me leave*
27: 7. thou shalt *surely* give (lit. *giving* thou shalt give) them a possession
31: 3. *and avenge* (lit. *to give* revenge) the Lord of Midian.
34:13. *to give* unto the nine tribes,
36: 2. *to give* the land for an inheritance
— *to give* the inheritance of Zelophehad
Deu. 1: 8. *to give* unto them and to their seed
27. *to deliver* us into the hand of the Amorites,
35. I sware *to give* unto your fathers,
2:25. *to put* the dread of thee and the fear
30. that *he might deliver him* into
31. Behold, I have begun *to give* Sihon
4:38. *to give* thee their land
6:10. *to give* thee great and goodly cities,
23. *to give* us the land which he sware
7:13. the land which he sware...*to give*
10:11. the land, which I sware...*to give*
18. *in giving* him food and raiment.
11: 9. *to give* unto them and to their seed,
21. the land which the Lord sware...*to give*
15:10. Thou shalt *surely* give (lit. *giving* thou shalt give)
— *when thou givest* unto him:
17:15. thou mayest not *set* a stranger over thee,
19: 8. the land which he promised *to give*
21:17. *by giving* him a double portion
23:14(15). *and to give up* thine enemies
26: 3. which the Lord sware...*for to give*
19. *And to make thee* high above all
28:11. the land which the Lord sware...*to give*
12. *to give* the rain unto thy land
55. *So that he will not give* to any
30:20. the land which the Lord sware...*to give*
31: 7. the land which the Lord hath sworn...*to give*
Jos. 1: 6. the land, which I sware...*to give*
2:14. *when* the Lord *hath given* us the land,
5: 6. which the Lord sware...*that he would give*
7: 7. *to deliver* us into the hand of the Amorites,
9:24. *to give* you all the land,
10:12. the Lord *delivered up* the Amorites
17: 4. *to give* us an inheritance
21: 2. *to give* us cities to dwell in,
43(41). the land which he sware *to give*
Jud. 7: 2. *for me to give* the Midianites into
8: 7. *when* the Lord *hath delivered* Zebah
25. We will *willingly* give (lit. *giving* we will give)
11:30. If thou shalt *without fail* deliver (lit. *delivering* thou shalt deliver)
15:12. *that we may deliver thee* into the hand of
21: 7. *we will* not *give* them of our daughters
18. we may not *give* them wives
Ru. 1: 6. visited his people *in giving* them bread.
1Sa. 18:19. at the time when Merab...*should have been given* (lit. at the time of *giving* Merab)
22:13. *in that thou hast given* him bread,
2Sa. 4:10. that *I would have given* him a reward
5:19. I will *doubtless* deliver (lit. *delivering* I will deliver) the Philistines into
18:11. I would *have given* (lit. upon me *to give*) thee ten (shekels)
1K. 5: 3(17). the Lord *put* them under the soles of his feet.
9(23). *in giving* food for my houshold.
6:19. *to set* there the ark of the covenant
7:16. *to set* upon the tops of the pillars:
8:32. *to bring* his way upon his head;
— *to give* him according to his righteousness.
10: 9. *to set thee* on the throne of Israel:
15:17. that *he might* not *suffer* any
17:14. the day (that) the Lord *sendeth* (marg. *giveth*) rain
21: 3. *that I should give* the inheritance of
15. refused *to give* thee for money:
2K. 3:10, 13. *to deliver* them into the hand of Moab!
8:19. *to give* him alway a light,
12:15(16). the money *to be bestowed* on workmen:
15:20. *to give* to the king of Assyria.
18:23. if thou be able...*to set* riders upon
23:35. *to give* the money according to
2K. 23:35. *to give* (it) unto Pharaoh-nechoh.
2Ch 6:23. requiting the wicked, *by recompensing* his way
— *by giving* him according to
9: 8. *to set thee* on his throne,
16: 1. that he *might let* none go out
21: 7. *to give* a light to him and to his sons
25: 9. The Lord is able *to give* thee
20. that *he might deliver them* into
30:12. *to give* them one heart
31: 4. *to give* the portion of the priests
14. *to distribute* the oblations
15. *to give* to their brethren by courses,
19. *to give* portions to all the males
32:11. *to give over* yourselves to die
35:12. *that they might give* according
Ezr. 9: 8. *and to give us* a nail in his holy place,
— *and give* us a little reviving
9. *to give* us a reviving, to set up
— *and to give* us a wall in Judah
Neh. 9: 8. *to give* the land of the Canaanites,
— *to give* (it, I say), to his seed,
15. land which thou hadst sworn *to give* them.
10:32(33). *to charge* ourselves yearly
Est. 2: 3. *and let* their things for purification *be given*
9. he speedily *gave* her her things
— seven maidens, (which were) meet *to be given* her,
5: 8. if it please the king *to grant* my petition,
6: 9. *let* this apparel and horse *be delivered*
Ps. 10:14. *to requite* (it) with thy hand:
78:20. can he *give* bread also?
104:27. *that thou mayest give* (them) their meat
111: 6. *that he may give* them the heritage of
Pro. 1: 4. *To give* subtilty to the simple,
Ecc. 2:26. *that he may give* to (him that is) good
5: 1(4:17). more ready to hear, *than to give* the sacrifice of
8: 9. *and applied* my heart unto every work
Isa. 36: 8. if thou be able...*to set* riders upon
37:19. *And have cast* (marg. *given*) their gods into the fire:
61: 3. *to give* unto them beauty for ashes,
Jer. 10:13. When *he uttereth* his voice,
11: 5. *to give* them a land flowing with milk and honey,
17:10. *even to give* every man according to
19:12. *and* (even) *make* this city as Tophet:
25:18. *to make* them a desolation,
26:24. that they *should* not *give* him into
29:11. *to give* you an expected end.
32:16. *when I had delivered* the evidence
19. *to give* every one according to his ways,
22. *to give* them, a land flowing with milk
37:21. *that they should give* him daily a piece of bread
43: 3. *to deliver* us into the hand of
51:16. *When he uttereth* (his) voice,
Eze. 16:34. *in that thou givest* a reward,
17:15. *that they might give* him horses
20:28, 42. I lifted up mine hand *to give* it
21:11(16). *to give* it into the hand of the slayer.
29(34). *to bring* thee upon the necks of
23:46. *and will give them* to be removed
25:17. *when I shall lay* my vengeance upon
26:19. *When I shall make* thee a desolate city,
28: 6. *thou hast set* thine heart as the heart of God;
30: 8. *when I have set* a fire in Egypt,
21. bound up *to be* healed, (lit. *to give* healings)
25. *when I shall put* my sword into the hand
32:15. *When I shall make* the land of Egypt desolate,
33:29. *when I have laid* the land most desolate
43: 8. *In their setting* of their threshold by
47:14. *to give it* unto your fathers:
Dan. 8:13. *to give* both the sanctuary and the host
12:11. *and* the abomination that maketh desolate *set up*,
Mic. 6:16. that *I should make* thee a desolation,
Mal. 2: 2. *to give* glory unto my name,

KAL.—*Imperative.*

Gen 14:21. *Give* me the persons,
23: 4. *give* me a possession
30:14. *Give* me, I pray thee, of thy son's mandrakes.

Gen30:26. *Give* (me) my wives
34: 8. *give* her him to wife.
12. *but give* me the damsel to wife.
42:37. *deliver* him into my hand,
47:19. *and give* (us) seed,
Ex. 7: 9. *Shew* a miracle for you:
16:33. *and put* an omer full of manna
17: 2. *Give* us water that we may drink.
Nu. 11:13. *Give* us flesh, that we may eat.
16: 7. *And put* fire therein,
46(17:11). Take a censer, *and put* fire therein
27: 4. *Give* unto us (therefore) a possession
Jos. 7:19. *and make* confession unto him;
14:12. *give* me this mountain,
15:19. *Give* me a blessing;
20: 2. *Appoint* out for you cities
Jud. 8: 5. *Give*, I pray you, loaves of bread
24. *that ye would give* me every man the ear-rings of
20:13. *deliver* (us) the men,
1Sa. 2:15. *Give* flesh to roast for the priest;
8: 6. *Give* us a king to judge us.
9:23. *Bring* the portion which I gave thee,
11:12. *bring* the men, that we may put them to death.
17:10. *give* me a man, that we may fight
21: 3(4). *give* (me) five (loaves of) bread
9(10). (There is) none like that; *give it* me.
25: 8. *give*, I pray thee, whatsoever cometh
2Sa. 3:14. *Deliver* (me) my wife Michal,
14: 7. *Deliver* him that smote his brother,
20:21. *deliver* him only,
1K. 3:25. *and give* half to the one,
26, 27. *give* her the living child,
17:19. *Give* me thy son.
21: 2. *Give* me thy vineyard, that I may
6. *Give* me thy vineyard for money;
2K. 4:42. *Give* unto the people,
43. *Give* the people, that they may eat:
5:22. *give* them, I pray thee, a talent of silver,
6:28, 29. *Give* thy son, that we may eat him
10:15. *give* (me) thine hand.
14: 9. *Give* thy daughter to my son to wife:
1Ch 21:22. *Grant* (marg. *Give*) me the place of (this) threshingfloor,
— *thou shalt grant it* me for the full price:
22:19. Now *set* your heart and your soul
29:19. *give* unto Solomon my son a perfect heart,
2Ch 1:10. *Give* me now wisdom
25:18. *Give* thy daughter to my son to wife.
30: 8. *yield* yourselves unto the Lord,
35: 3. *Put* the holy ark in the house
Ezr. 10:11. *make* confession unto the Lord God
Neh. 1:11. *and grant him* mercy in the sight of this
4: 4(3:36). *and give* them for a prey
Ps. 8: 1(2). *hast set* thy glory above the heavens.
28: 4. *Give* them according to their deeds,
— *give* them after the work of their hands;
68:34(35). *Ascribe ye* strength unto God:
69:27(28). *Add* iniquity unto their iniquity:
72: 1. *Give* the king thy judgments,
81: 2(3). *and bring hither* the timbrel,
86:16. *give* thy strength unto thy servant,
115: 1. unto thy name *give* glory,
Pro. 9: 9. *Give* (instruction) to a wise (man),
23:26. My son, *give* me thine heart,
31: 6. *Give* strong drink unto him that
31. *Give her* of the fruit of her hands;
Ecc. 11: 2. *Give* a portion to seven,
Isa. 43: 6. I will say to the north, *Give up;*
Jer. 13:16. *Give* glory to the Lord your God,
18:21. *deliver up* their children to the famine,
22:20. *lift up* thy voice in Bashan,
29: 6. *give* your daughters to husbands,
48: 9. *Give* wings unto Moab,
Hos. 9:14. *Give* them, O Lord: what wilt thou give? *give* them a miscarrying womb
13:10. *Give* me a king and princes?

KAL.—*Future.*

Gen 1:17. *And* God *set* them in the firmament
3: 6. *and gave* also unto her husband
12: 7. Unto thy seed *will I give* this land:
13:15. to thee *will I give it,*
17. *I will give it* unto thee.
14:20. *And he gave* him tithes of all.
15: 2. what *wilt thou give* me,
Gen15:10. *and laid* each piece one against another:
16: 3. *and gave* her to her husband Abram
17: 2. *And I will make* my covenant
18: 7. *and gave* (it) unto a young man;
8. *and set* (it) before them;
20:14. *and gave* (them) unto Abraham,
21:14. took bread,...*and gave* (it) unto Hagar,
27. *and gave* them unto Abimelech;
23: 9. *That he may give* me the cave
— *he shall give it* me
24: 7. Unto thy seed *will I give* this land;
32. *and gave* straw and provender for the
35. *and he hath given* him flocks,
36. *and* unto him *hath he given*
41. if *they give* not thee (one),
53. *and gave* (them) to Rebekah:
25: 5. *And* Abraham *gave* all that he had unto
26: 3. *I will give* all these countries,
27:17. *And she gave* the savoury meat
28. *Therefore* God *give thee* of the dew of
28: 4. *And give* thee the blessing of Abraham,
13. to thee *will I give it,*
22. and of all that *thou shalt give* me
29:24. *And* Laban *gave* unto his daughter Leah
27. *and we will give* thee this also
28. *and he gave* him Rachel
29. *And* Laban *gave* to Rachel his daughter
33. *he hath therefore given* me this (son)
30: 4. *And she gave* him Bilhah
6. *and hath given* me a son:
9. *and gave* her Jacob to wife.
28. *and I will give* (it).
31. What *shall I give* thee? And Jacob said, *Thou shalt* not *give* me any thing:
35. *and gave* (them) into the hand of his sons
40. *and set* the faces of the flocks toward
31: 9. the cattle of your father, *and given* (them)
32:16(17). *And he delivered* (them) into the hand
34: 9. *give* your daughters unto us,
11. what ye shall say unto me *I will give.*
12. *and I will give* according as ye shall say
21. *let us give* them our daughters.
35: 4. *And they gave* unto Jacob all the strange
12. to thee *I will give it,* and to thy seed after thee *will I give*
38:16. What *wilt thou give* me,
17. *Wilt thou give* (me) a pledge,
18. What pledge *shall I give* thee?
— *And he gave* (it) her, and came in unto her,
28. *that* (the one) *put* out (his) hand:
39:20. *and put him* into the prison,
21. *and gave* him favour in the sight of
22. *And* the keeper of the prison *committed* to
40: 3. *And he put* them in ward
11. *and I gave* the cup into Pharaoh's hand.
21. *and he gave* the cup into Pharaoh's hand:
41:10. *and put* me in ward
42. Pharaoh took off his ring...*and put* it
45. *and he gave* him to wife Asenath
48. *and laid up* the food in the cities:
42:30. *and took* us for spies
34. *will I deliver* you your brother,
43:14. God Almighty *give you* mercy
24. *and gave* (them) water, and they washed their feet; *and he gave* their asses
45: 2. *And he* wept aloud: (marg. *and he gave forth* his voice in weeping)
18. *and I will give* you the good of the land
21. *and* Joseph *gave* them wagons,
— *and gave* them provision for the way.
47:11. *and gave* them a possession
16. *and I will give* you for your cattle,
17. *and* Joseph *gave* them bread
49:20. he *shall yield* royal dainties.
Ex. 2: 9. I *will give* (thee) thy wages.
21. *and he gave* Moses Zipporah his daughter.
3:19. the king of Egypt *will* not *let* you go,
5:18. yet *shall ye deliver* the tale of bricks.
10:25. Thou *must give* us also sacrifices
11: 3. *And* the Lord *gave* the people favour
12:23. *will* not *suffer* the destroyer to come in
25. the land which the Lord *will give* you,
16: 3. Would to God (lit. who *will give*) we had
18:25. *and made* them heads over the people,
21: 4. If his master *have given* him a wife,
19. only *he shall pay*
32. *he shall give* unto their master

Ex. 22: 7(6). If a man *shall deliver*
10(9). If a man *deliver* unto his neighbour
29(28). *shalt thou give* unto me.
30(29). on the eighth day *thou shalt give it* me.
23:31. *I will deliver* the inhabitants
24:12. *and I will give* thee tables of stone,
25:16. which *I shall give* thee.
21. and in the ark *thou shalt put* the testimony that *I shall give* thee.
26:35. *thou shalt put* the table on the north side.
28:25. *thou shalt fasten* in the two ouches,
30:13. This *they shall give*,
14. *shall give* an offering
33. whosoever *putteth* (any) of it
31:18. *And he gave* unto Moses,
32:13. *will I give* unto your seed,
24. *So they gave* (it) me:
33: 1. Unto thy seed *will I give it:*
34:33. *he* (lit. *and he*) *put* a vail on his face.
37:13. *and put* the rings upon the four corners
39:16. *and put* the two rings in the two ends of
17. *And they put* the two wreathen chains
18. *and put them* on the shoulderpieces
20. *and put them* on the two sides
25. *and put* the bells between the pomegranates
31. *And they tied* unto it a lace of blue,
40:18. *and fastened* his sockets,
— *and put* in the bars thereof,
20. *and put* the testimony into the ark,
— *and put* the mercy seat above upon the ark:
22. *And he put* the table in the tent
30. *and put* water there,
33. *and set* up the hanging of the court gate.
Lev. 4:18. *he shall put* (some) of the blood
5:11. neither *shall he put* (any) frankincense
6: 5 (5:24). *give it* unto him
7:32. *shall ye give* unto the priest
34. *and have given* them unto Aaron
8: 7. *And he put* upon him the coat,
— *and put* the ephod upon him,
8. *also he put* in the breastplate
15. *put* (it) upon the horns of the altar
23. *and put* (it) upon the tip of Aaron's right
24. *and* Moses *put* of the blood
27. *And he put* all upon Aaron's hands,
9: 9. *and put* (it) upon the horns of the altar,
10: 1. *and put* fire therein,
14:17. *shall* the priest *put*
18. *he shall pour* upon the head
29. *he shall put* upon the head
18:20. *thou shalt* not lie carnally (lit. *thou shalt* not *give* thy lying for seed)
21. *thou shalt* not *let* any of thy seed
23. Neither *shalt thou* lie with (lit. *thou shalt* not *give* thy lying to) any beast
19:14. nor *put* a stumblingblock before the blind,
28. *Ye shall* not *make* any cuttings
— nor *print* any marks
20: 2. *that giveth* (any) of his seed
3. I *will set* my face against that man,
15. if a man lie with (lit. *give* his lying to) a beast,
24. I *will give it* unto you
22:22. nor *make* an offering by fire
23:38. which *ye give* unto the Lord.
24:19. if a man *cause* a blemish
20. as *he hath caused* a blemish
25:24. *ye shall grant* a redemption
37. *Thou shalt* not *give* him thy money
— nor *lend* him thy victuals
26: 1. neither *shall ye set* up (any) image
4. the trees of the field *shall yield* their fruit.
20. your land *shall* not *yield*
— neither *shall* the trees...*yield*
27: 9. all that (any man) *giveth*
Nu. 3:51. *And* Moses *gave* the money of them
5:10. whatsoever any man *giveth*
15. nor *put* frankincense thereon;
20. some man *have* lain (lit. *hath given* his lying)
21. The Lord *make* thee a curse
7: 6. *and gave* them unto the Levites.
8:19. *And I have given* the Levites
10:29. *I will give* it you:
11:21. *I will give* them flesh,
25. *and gave* (it) unto the seventy elders.
29. would God (lit. who *will give*) that all the

Nu. 11:29. that the Lord *would put* his spirit upon
14: 1. lifted up their voice, and cried; (lit. lifted *and gave* their voices)
4. *Let us make* a captain,
15:21. Of the first of your dough *ye shall give*
16:14. *or given* us inheritance of fields
18. took every man his censer, *and put* fire in
47(17:12). *and he put* on incense,
17: 6(21). *and* every one of their princes *gave* him a rod
18: 7. *I have given* your priest's office
12. which *they shall offer* unto the Lord,
21: 2. If *thou wilt* indeed *deliver*
3. *and delivered up* the Canaanites;
16. *and I will give* them water.
22:18 & 24:13. If Balak *would give* me his house
27: 7. *thou shalt* surely *give* them a possession
31:41. *And* Moses *gave* the tribute,
47. *and gave* them unto the Levites,
32:33. *And* Moses *gave* unto them,
40. *And* Moses *gave* Gilead
35: 2. and *ye shall give* (also) unto the Levites
4, 6. *ye shall give* unto the Levites,
6. *ye shall appoint* for the manslayer,
— *ye shall add* forty and two cities.
7. all the cities which *ye shall give* to the Levites
8. the cities which *ye shall give*
— every one *shall give* of his cities
13. these cities which *ye shall give*
14. *Ye shall give* three cities
— three cities *shall ye give*
Deu 1:15. *and made* (marg. *gave*) them heads over
36. to him *will I give* the land
39. unto them *will I give it*,
2: 5. *I will* not *give* you of their land,
9. *I will* not *give* thee of their land
19. *I will* not *give* thee of the land of
28. *give* me water for money,
33. *And* the Lord our God *delivered him*
3: 3. *So* the Lord our God *delivered*
5:22(19). *and delivered them* unto me.
29(26). O that (lit. who *will give*) there were such an heart in them,
6:22. *And* the Lord *shewed* signs and wonders,
7: 3. thy daughter *thou shalt* not *give*
9:10. *And* the Lord *delivered* unto me
10: 4. *and* the Lord *gave them* unto me.
11:17. that the land *yield* not her fruit;
25. your God *shall lay* the fear of you
14:21. *thou shalt give it* unto the stranger
15: 9. *thou givest* him nought;
10. *Thou shalt* surely *give* him,
14. *thou shalt give* unto him.
16:10. *thou shalt give* (unto the Lord thy God),
18. Judges and officers *shalt thou make*
18: 4. the fleece of thy sheep, *shalt thou give*.
21: 8. *lay* not innocent blood unto thy people of Israel's *charge*.
23:24(25). *thou shalt* not *put* (any) in thy vessel.
24:15. *thou shalt give* (him) his hire,
26: 6. *and laid* upon us hard bondage:
9. *and hath given* us this land,
28: 7. The Lord *shall cause* thine enemies...to be
24. The Lord *shall make* the rain of thy land powder and dust:
25. The Lord *shall cause thee* to be smitten
67, 67. Would God (lit. who *will give*) it were
29: 8(7). *and gave it* for an inheritance
31: 9. *and delivered it* unto the priests
34: 4. *I will give it* unto thy seed:
Jos. 8:18. *I will give it* into thine hand.
9:27. *And* Joshua *made them* that day hewers of
10:19. *suffer them* not to enter
30. *And* the Lord *delivered* it also,
32. *And* the Lord *delivered* Lachish
11: 8. *And* the Lord *delivered them* into
23. *and* Joshua *gave it* for an inheritance
12: 6. *and* Moses the servant of the Lord *gave it*
7. *which* Joshua *gave* unto the tribes of Israel
13:15. *And* Moses *gave* unto the tribe of
24. *And* Moses *gave* (inheritance) unto the tribe
29. *And* Moses *gave* (inheritance) unto the half
14:13. *and gave* unto Caleb...Hebron
15:17. *and he gave* him Achsah...to wife.
19. *And he gave* her the upper springs,
17: 4. *Therefore...he gave* them an inheritance

Jos. 17:13. *that they put* the Canaanites to tribute;
19:49. the children of Israel *gave* an inheritance
21: 3. *And* the children of Israel *gave* unto the Levites
8. *And* the children of Israel *gave* by lot
9. *And they gave* out of the tribe
11. *And they gave* them the city of Arba
21. *For they gave* them Shechem
43(41). *And* the Lord *gave* unto Israel
24: 3. multiplied his seed, *and gave* him Isaac.
4. *And I gave* unto Isaac Jacob and Esau: *and I gave* unto Esau mount Seir,
8. *and I gave* them into your hand,
11. *and I delivered* them into your hand.
13. *And I have given* you a land
Jud. 1: 4. *and* the Lord *delivered* the Canaanites
13. *and he gave* him Achsah his daughter
15. *And* Caleb *gave* her the upper springs
20. *And they gave* Hebron unto Caleb,
2:14. *and he delivered them* into the hands of
3:10. *and* the Lord *delivered* Chushan-rishathaim
6: 1. *and* the Lord *delivered them* into
9. *and gave* you their land;
13. *and delivered* us into the hands of the
7:16. *and he put* a trumpet in every man's hand,
8: 6. that *we should give* bread unto thine
15. that *we should give* bread unto thy men
25. *We will* willingly *give* (them).
9: 4. *And they gave* him threescore and ten
29. would to God (lit. who *will give*) this people were
11:21. *And* the Lord God of Israel *delivered* Sihon
30. If *thou shalt* without fail *deliver*
32. *and* the Lord *delivered them* into
12: 3. *and* the Lord *delivered them* into my
13: 1. *and* the Lord *delivered them* into
14: 9. *and he gave* them, and they did eat.
19. *and gave* change of garments unto them
15: 2. *therefore I gave her* to thy companion:
6. taken his wife, *and given her* to his
16: 5. *we will give* thee...eleven hundred (pieces)
17: 4. *and gave them* to the founder,
10. *I will give thee* ten (shekels)
20:28. *I will deliver them* into thine hand.
36. *for* the men of Israel *gave* place
21: 1. *There shall* not any of us *give* his daughter
14. *and they gave* them wives
Ru. 1: 9. The Lord *grant* you that ye may find rest,
2:18. *and gave* to her that she had reserved
4:11. The Lord *make* the woman that is come
12. the seed which the Lord *shall give* thee
13. *and* when...the Lord *gave* her conception,
1Sa. 1: 5. unto Hannah *he gave* a worthy portion;
16. *Count* not thine handmaid for
17. the God of Israel *grant* (thee) thy petition
27. *and* the Lord *hath given* me my petition
2:10. *and he shall give* strength unto his king,
16. *thou shalt give* (it me) now:
28. *and did I give* unto the house of thy father
9:22. *and made* them sit in the chiefest place (lit. *and gave* them a place in chief)
12:17. *and he shall send* thunder and rain;
18. *and* the Lord *sent* thunder and rain
14:37. *wilt thou deliver them* into
17:25. *will give* him his daughter,
44. *and I will give* thy flesh unto the fowls
18: 4. stripped himself of the robe...*and gave it*
17. her *will I give* thee to wife:
21. *I will give* him *her*,
27. *And* Saul *gave* him Michal
20:40. *And* Jonathan *gave* his artillery
21: 6(7). *So* the priest *gave* him hallowed (bread):
22: 7. *will* the son of Jesse *give*...fields
27: 5. *let them give* me a place
6. *Then* Achish *gave* him Ziklag
28:17. *and given it* to thy neighbour,
19. *Moreover* the Lord *will* also *deliver* Israel
— the Lord also *shall deliver* the host
30:11. *and gave* him bread, and he did eat;
12. *And they gave* him a piece of a cake of figs,
22. *we will* not *give* them (ought)
23. *and delivered* the company
2Sa. 4: 8. *and* the Lord *hath* avenged (lit. *and hath given* revenges) my lord
5:19. *wilt thou deliver them* into
— *I will* doubtless *deliver*
11:16. *that he assigned* Uriah unto a place

2Sa. 12: 8. *And I gave* thee thy master's house,
— *and gave thee* the house of Israel
16: 8. *and* the Lord *hath delivered* the kingdom
18:33(19:1). would God (lit. who *will give*) I had died for thee,
20: 3. the king took the ten women...*and put them* in ward,
21: 6. the king said, I *will give*
9. *And he delivered them* into
22:14. the most High *uttered* his voice.
36. *Thou hast also given* me the shield of
24: 9. *And* Joab *gave up* the sum
15. *So* the Lord *sent* a pestilence
1K. 2: 5. *and put* the blood of war upon his girdle
17. *that he give* me Abishag
35. *And* the king *put* Benaiah
3: 5. Ask what *I shall give* thee.
6. *that thou hast given* him a son
4:29(5:9). *And* God *gave* Solomon wisdom
5: 5(19). Thy son, whom *I will set* upon
6(20). unto thee *will I give* hire
11(25). thus *gave* Solomon to Hiram
6:27. *And he set* the cherubims within
7:39. *And he put* five bases on the right side
9:11. king Solomon *gave* Hiram twenty cities
16. *and given it* (for) a present
10:10. *And she gave* the king an hundred and twenty talents
17. *and* the king *put them* in the house of
27. *And* the king *made* silver...as stones,
11:13. *will give* one tribe to thy son
18. *which gave* him an house,
19. *that he gave* him to wife
36. unto his son *will I give* one tribe,
13: 7. *and I will give* thee a reward.
8. If *thou wilt give* me half thine house,
26. *therefore* the Lord *hath delivered him* unto
14: 7. *and made thee* prince
8. rent the kingdom...*and gave it* thee:
16. *And he shall give* Israel up
15:18. *and delivered them* into the hand of
16: 2. *and made thee* prince over my people
17:23. *and delivered him* unto his mother:
18: 1. *and I will send* rain
23. *Let them therefore give* us two bullocks;
19:21. *and gave* unto the people,
20: 5. *Thou shalt deliver* me thy silver,
21: 2. *and I will give* thee for it
— *I will give* thee the worth
4. *I will* not *give* thee the inheritance of
6. *I will give* thee (another) vineyard
— *I will* not *give* thee my vineyard.
7. I *will give* thee the vineyard
22: 6. *for* the Lord *shall deliver*
2K. 4:43. *should I set* this before
44. *So he set* (it) before them,
5:23. *and laid* (them) upon two
8: 6. *So* the king *appointed* unto her
10:15. *And he gave* (him) his hand;
11:10. *And* to the captains...*did* the priest *give*
12. *and put* the crown upon him,
12: 7(8). *deliver it* for the breaches
9(10). *and set* it beside the altar,
14(15). *But they gave* that to the workmen,
15(16). *they delivered* the money
13: 3. *and he delivered them* into the hand of
5. *And* the Lord *gave* Israel a saviour,
15:19. *and* Menahem *gave* Pul a thousand talents
16:14. *and put* it on the north side
17. *and put* it upon a pavement of stones.
17:20. *and delivered them* into the hand of spoilers,
18:14. that which *thou puttest* on me will I bear.
15. *And* Hezekiah *gave* (him) all the silver
16. *and gave it* to the king of Assyria.
23. *and I will deliver* thee two thousand horses,
22: 5. *And let them deliver it* into the hand
— *and let them give* it to the doers
8. *And* Hilkiah *gave* the book to Shaphan,
9. *and have delivered it* into the hand of
23:33. *and put* the land to a tribute
25:28. *and set* his throne above
1Ch 2:35. *And* Sheshan *gave* his daughter to Jarha
6:55(40). *And they gave* them Hebron
64(49). *And* the children of Israel *gave* to the
65(50). *And they gave* by lot
67(52). *And they gave* unto them, (of) the
12:18. *and made them* captains of the band.

1Ch 16: 4. *And he appointed* (certain) of the Levites
18. Unto thee *will I give* the land of Canaan,
17:22. *For* thy people Israel *didst thou make* thine
21: 5. *And* Joab *gave* the sum
14. *So* the Lord *sent* pestilence
25. *So* David *gave* to Ornan
22: 9. and *I will give* peace and quietness
12. the Lord *give* thee wisdom
25: 5. *And* God *gave* to Heman fourteen sons
28:11. *Then* David *gave* to Solomon his son the
29: 7. *And gave* for the service of the house
25. *and bestowed* upon him (such) royal majesty
2Ch 1: 7. Ask what *I shall give* thee.
12. *I will give* thee riches,
15. *And* the king *made* (marg. *gave*) silver and gold
3:16. he made chains,...*and put* (them) on the heads of
— made an hundred pomegranates, *and put* (them) on the chains.
4: 6. made also ten lavers, *and put* five on the right hand,
7. ten candlesticks...*and set* (them) in the temple,
6:13. *and had set it* in the midst of the court:
7:20. *and will make it* (to be) a proverb
9: 8. *therefore made he thee* king
9. *And she gave* the king an hundred and twenty talents
16. *And* the king *put them* in the house of
27. *And* the king *made* silver...as stones,
11:11. fortified the strong holds, *and put* captains
23. *and he gave* them victual in abundance.
13:16. *and* God *delivered them* into their hand.
16:10. *and put him* in a prison house;
17: 2. *And he placed* forces in all the fenced cities
— *and set* garrisons in the land
5. *and* all Judah *brought* (marg. *gave*) to Jehoshaphat presents;
18: 5. *for* God *will deliver* (it) into
20: 3. *and set* himself to seek the Lord,
7. *and gavest it* to the seed of Abraham
21: 3. *And* their father *gave them* great gifts
22:11. *and put* him and his nurse in a bedchamber.
23: 9. *Moreover* Jehoiada the priest *delivered*
11. *and put* upon him the crown,
24: 8. *and set it* without at the gate
9. *And they made* a proclamation
12. *And* the king and Jehoiada *gave it*
26: 8. *And* the Ammonites *gave* gifts
27: 5. *And* the children of Ammon *gave* him
28: 5. *Wherefore* the Lord his God *delivered him*
21. *and gave* (it) unto the king of Assyria:
29: 6. *and turned* (marg. *given*) (their) backs.
8. *and he hath delivered them* to trouble,
30: 7. (who) *therefore gave them up* to desolation,
31: 6. *and laid* (them) by heaps.
32: 6. *And he set* captains of war over the people,
34: 9. *And* when...*they delivered* the money
10. *And they put* (it) in the hand of the
— *and they gave* it to the workmen
11. *Even* to the...builders *gave they* (it),
15. *And* Hilkiah *delivered* the book
17. *and have delivered it* into the hand of
35:25. *and made them* an ordinance in Israel:
36: 7. *and put them* in his temple
Ezr. 1: 7. *and had put them* in the house of
3: 7. *They gave* money *also*
7: 6. *and* the king *granted* him all his request,
8:36. *And they delivered* the king's commissions
9:12. *give* not your daughters unto their sons,
10:19. *And they gave* their hands
Neh 2: 1. I took up the wine, *and gave* (it)
6. *and I set* him a time.
7. *let* letters *be given* me
8. that *he may give* me timber
— *And* the king *granted* me,
9. I came to the governors...*and gave*
5: 7. *And I set* a great assembly against
7: 5. *And* my God *put* into mine heart
9:10. *And shewedst* signs and wonders
13. *and gavest* them right judgments,
17. *and* in their rebellion *appointed* a captain
22. *Moreover thou gavest* them kingdoms
24. *and gavest them* into their hands,
27. *Therefore thou deliveredst them*
— *thou gavest* them saviours,

Neh 9:29. *and* withdrew the shoulder, (marg. *gave* a withdrawing shoulder)
30. *therefore gavest thou them*
10:30(31). that *we would* not *give* our daughters
13:25. *Ye shall* not *give* your daughters
26. *and* God *made him* king
Est. 1:19. *and let* the king *give* her royal estate
20. all the wives *shall give* to their
2:18. *and gave* gifts, according to the state
3:10. the king took his ring,...*and gave it* unto Haman
8: 2. the king took off his ring,...*and gave it* unto Mordecai.
Job 2: 4. all that a man hath *will he give* for his life.
3:20. Wherefore is light *given* to him that is in
6: 8. Oh that (lit. who *will give*) I might have my request; and that God *would grant* (me) the thing that
9:18. *He will* not *suffer me* to take my breath,
11: 5. But oh that (lit. who *will give*) God would
13: 5. O that (lit. *id.*) ye would altogether hold your peace!
14: 4. Who *can bring* (marg. *will give*) a clean (thing) out of an unclean?
13. O that (lit. who *will give*) thou wouldest hide me in the grave,
19:23. Oh that (marg. Who *will give*) my words were now written! oh that (lit. *id.*) they were printed in a book!
23: 3. Oh that (lit. *id.*) I knew where I might find him!
24:23. (Though) *it be given* him (to be) in safety,
29: 2. Oh that *I were* (lit. who *will give me*) as (in) months past,
31:31. Oh that (lit. who *will give*) we had of his flesh!
35. Oh that (lit. *id.*) one would hear me!
35: 7. what *givest thou* him?
36: 3. *will ascribe* righteousness to my Maker,
6. *giveth* right to the poor.
31. *he giveth* meat in abundance.
37:10. By the breath of God frost *is given:*
39:19. *Hast thou given* the horse strength?
42:11. every man *also gave* him a piece of money,
15. their father *gave them* inheritance
Ps. 1: 3. *bringeth forth* his fruit in his season;
2: 8. *and I shall give* (thee) the heathen (for) thine inheritance,
14: 7. Oh that (marg. Who *will give*) the salvation of Israel
16:10. neither *wilt thou suffer* thine Holy One to see corruption.
18:13(14). the Highest *gave* his voice;
32(33). *and maketh* my way perfect.
35(36). *Thou hast also given* me the shield
20: 4(5). *Grant* thee according to thine own
27:12. *Deliver me* not over
29:11. The Lord *will give* strength
37: 4. *and he shall give* thee the desires of thine
40: 3(4). *And he hath put* a new song in my
41: 2(3). *thou wilt* not *deliver him*
44:11(12). *Thou hast given us* like sheep
49: 7(8). nor *give* to God a ransom
50:20. *thou* slanderest (lit. *thou givest* slander against) thine own mother's son.
51:16(18). not sacrifice; *else would I give* (it):
53: 6(7). Oh that (marg. Who *will give*) the salvation of Israel (were come)
55: 6(7). Oh that (lit. who *will give*) I had wings like a dove!
22(23). *he shall* never *suffer* the righteous to
68:11(12). The Lord *gave* the word:
33(34). *he doth send out* (marg. *give*) his voice,
69:11(12). *I made* sackcloth *also* my garment;
21(22). *They gave* me *also* gall for my meat;
72:15. *and* to him *shall be given* (marg. (one) *shall give*) of the gold
74:14. *gavest him* (to be) meat to the people
19. O *deliver* not the soul of thy turtledove
78:46. *He gave also* their increase unto the
61. *And delivered* his strength into captivity,
84:11(12). the Lord *will give* grace and glory:
85: 7(8). O Lord, and *grant* us thy salvation.
12(13). the Lord *shall give* (that which is) good; and our land *shall yield* her increase.
89:27(28). *I will make him* (my) firstborn,

Ps.104:12. the fowls of the heaven...(which) sing (marg. *give* a voice)
28. (That) *thou givest* them they gather:
105:11. Unto thee *will I give* the land of Canaan,
44. *gave them* the lands of the heathen:
106:15. *And he gave them* their request;
41. *And he gave them* into the hand of the heathen;
46. *He made* them *also* to be pitied
120: 3. What *shall be given* unto thee?
121: 3. *He will* not *suffer* thy foot to be moved:
127: 2. *he giveth* his beloved sleep.
132: 4. *I will* not *give* sleep to mine eyes,
140: 8(9). *Grant* not, O Lord, the desires
Pro. 1:20. *she uttereth* her voice in the streets:
2: 3. *liftest up* (marg. *givest*) thy voice for understanding;
6. the Lord *giveth* wisdom:
3:28. to morrow *I will give;*
34. *he giveth* grace unto the lowly.
4: 9. *She shall give* to thine head an ornament
5: 9. Lest *thou give* thine honour
6: 4. *Give* not sleep to thine eyes,
31. *he shall give* all the substance
8: 1. understanding *put forth* her voice?
10:10. He that winketh with the eye *causeth* sorrow:
24. the desire of the righteous *shall be granted.*
12:12. the root of the righteous *yieldeth* (fruit).
13:10. by pride *cometh* contention:
15. Good understanding *giveth* favour:
21:26. the righteous *giveth*
23:31. when *it giveth* his colour in the cup,
29:15. The rod and reproof *give* wisdom:
17. *yea, he shall give* delight
25. The fear of man *bringeth* a snare:
30: 8. *give* me neither poverty nor riches;
31: 3. *Give* not thy strength unto women,
15. *and giveth* meat to her houshold,
Ecc. 1:17. *And I gave* my heart to know wisdom,
2:21. *shall he leave it* (for) his portion.
5: 6(5). *Suffer* not thy mouth to cause thy flesh to sin;
6: 2. God *giveth* him not power
7: 2. the living *will lay* (it) to his heart.
21. *take* no heed (lit. *give* not thy heart) unto
Cant.7:12(13). there *will I give* thee my loves.
8: 1. O that *thou* (*wert*) (lit. who *would give thee*) as my brother,
7. if a man *would give* all the substance
Isa. 7:14. the Lord himself *shall give* you a sign;
22:21. *I will commit* thy government into
27: 4. who *would set* the briers (and) thorns *against me*
29:11. (men) *deliver* to one that is learned,
36: 8. *and I will give* thee two thousand horses,
41: 2. *gave* the nations before him,
— *he gave* (them) as the dust
19. *I will plant* in the wilderness the cedar,
27. *I will give* to Jerusalem one that bringeth
42: 6. *and give thee* for a covenant
8. my glory *will I* not *give* to another,
43: 4. *therefore will I give* men for thee,
9. *let them bring forth* their witnesses,
28. *and have given* Jacob to the curse,
47: 6. *and given them* into thine hand:
48:11. *I will* not *give* my glory unto another.
49: 8. *and give thee* for a covenant
53: 9. *And he made* his grave with the wicked,
56: 5. *I will give* them an everlasting name,
62: 7. *give* him no rest, till he establish,
8. *I will* no more *give* thy corn
Jer. 3: 8. *and given* her a bill of divorce;
19. *and give* thee a pleasant land,
4:16. *and give* out their voice against
8:10. Therefore *will I give* their wives unto
13. *and* (the things that) *I have given* them
9: 1(8:23). Oh that (marg. Who *will give*) my head were waters,
2(1). Oh that *I had* (lit. who *will give me*) in the wilderness a lodging place
11(10). *I will make* the cities of Judah desolate,
14:13. *I will give* you assured peace
22. or *can* the heavens *give* showers?
15: 9. the residue...*will I deliver* to the sword
13. thy treasures *will I give*
16:13. *I will* not *shew* you favour.

Jer. 17: 3. *I will give* thy substance
20: 2. smote Jeremiah...*and put* him in the stocks
4. *I will give* all Judah into the hand
5. the kings of Judah *will I give*
21: 7. *I will deliver* Zedekiah king of Judah,
22:13. *giveth* him not for his work;
24: 8. So *will I give* Zedekiah the king
25:30. The Lord shall roar...and *utter* his voice
26: 6. *will make* this city a curse
27: 8. *will* not *put* their neck under the yoke
30:16. that prey upon thee *will I give* for a prey.
32:12. *And I gave* the evidence of the purchase
22. *And hast given* them this land,
40. *I will put* my fear in their hearts,
34:21. Zedekiah...and his princes *will I give* into
22. *I will make* the cities of Judah a desolation
35: 5. *And I set* before the sons of the...Rechabites
36:32. *and gave it* to Baruch the scribe,
38:16. neither *will I give thee* into
19. lest *they deliver* me into
20. *They shall* not *deliver* (thee).
39:10. *and gave* them vineyards and fields
14. *and committed* him unto Gedaliah
40: 5. *So* the captain of the guard *gave him*
42:12. *And I will shew* mercies unto you,
52:11. *and put him* in prison till the day of his
32. *and set* his throne above the throne of
Lam.2:18. *give* thyself no rest;
3:29. *He putteth* his mouth in the dust;
30. *He giveth* (his) cheek to him that smiteth
65. *Give* them sorrow of heart,
Eze. 5:14. *Moreover I will make thee* waste,
7: 4. *I will recompense* thy ways
9. *I will recompense* thee
10: 7. *and put* (it) into the hands of (him that)
11:19. *I will put* a new spirit within you;
16:11. *and I put* bracelets upon thy hands,
12. *And I put* a jewel on thy forehead,
21. *and delivered them* to cause them to pass
27. *and delivered thee* unto the will of
33. *They give* gifts to all whores:
41. *thou* also *shalt give* no hire
17: 5. *and planted it* in a fruitful field;
18: 7. *hath given* his bread to the hungry,
8. *hath* not *given* forth upon usury,
19: 8. *Then* the nations *set* against him
9. *And they put* him in ward
20:11. *And I gave* them my statutes,
28. *and* there *they presented* the provocation of
21:11(16). *And he hath given* it to be furbished,
23: 7. *Thus she committed* (marg. *bestowed*) her
42. *which put* bracelets upon their hands,
26: 9. *he shall set* engines of war against
21. *I will make thee* a terror,
28: 2. *though thou set* thine heart as the heart
18. *and I will bring thee* to ashes
29:21. *I will give* thee the opening of the mouth
31:10. *and he hath shot up* his top
11. *I have therefore delivered him* into
14. neither *shoot up* their top among the
32:27. *and they have laid* their swords under
34:27. and the earth *shall yield* her increase,
35: 9. *I will make thee* perpetual desolations,
36: 8. *ye shall shoot forth* your branches,
26. a new spirit *will I put* within you:
27. *I will put* my spirit within you,
29. and *lay* no famine upon you.
39:11. *I will give* unto Gog a place
23. *gave them* into the hand of their enemies:
44:28. *ye shall give* them no possession
30. *ye shall* also *give* unto the priest the first
45: 6. *ye shall appoint* the possession of
8. (the rest of) the land *shall they give*
46:16. If the prince *give* a gift
17. if *he give* a gift of his inheritance
47:23. there *shall ye give* (him) his inheritance,
Dan 1: 2. *And* the Lord *gave* Jehoiakim
9. *Now* God *had brought* Daniel into favour
12. *let them give* us pulse
9: 3. *And I set* my face unto the Lord God,
11:17. *he shall give* him the daughter of women,
Hos. 5: 4. *They will* not *frame* (marg. *give*) their
9:14. Give them, O Lord: what *wilt thou give?*
11: 8. How *shall I give thee up,*
— how *shall I make thee* as Admah?
13:11. *I gave* thee a king in mine anger,
Joel 2:17. *give* not thine heritage to reproach,

Joel 2:19. *I will* no more *make* you a reproach
3: 3(4:3). *and have given* a boy for an harlot,
16(-:16). and *utter* his voice from Jerusalem;
Am. 1: 2. and *utter* his voice from Jerusalem;
3: 4. *will* a young lion *cry* (marg. *give forth* his voice) out of his den,
Jon. 1: 3. *so he paid* the fare
14. *lay* not upon us innocent blood:
Mic. 1:14. *shalt thou give* presents
3: 5. he that *putteth* not into their mouths,
5: 3(2). Therefore *will he give them up*,
6: 7. *shall I give* my firstborn (for) my
14. (that) which thou deliverest *will I give up*
7:20. *Thou wilt perform* the truth to Jacob,
Zep. 3: 5. *doth he bring* his judgment to light,
20. *I will make* you a name
Hag. 2: 9. in this place *will I give* peace,
Zec. 7:11. *and pulled* away the shoulder, (marg. *gave* a backsliding shoulder)
8:12. the vine *shall give* her fruit, and the ground *shall give* her increase, and the heavens *shall give* their dew;
10: 1. and *give* them showers of rain,
Mal. 2: 5. *and I gave them* to him

KAL.—*Participle.* Poel.

Gen 9:12. the covenant which I *make*
49:21. Naphtali (is) a hind let loose: *he giveth* goodly words.
Ex. 5:10. I *will* not *give* you straw.
16:29. therefore he *giveth* you on the sixth day
20:12. the land which the Lord thy God *giveth*
Lev.14:34. the land of Canaan, which I *give* to you
23:10. the land which I *give* unto you,
25: 2. the land which I *give* you,
Nu.13: 2. the land of Canaan, which I *give*
15: 2. the land...which I *give* unto you,
25:12. I *give* unto him my covenant
Deu. 1:20, 25. the Lord our God *doth give*
2:29. the land which the Lord our God *giveth* us.
3:20. the Lord your God *hath given*
4: 1. which the Lord God of your fathers *giveth*
8. this law, which I *set* before you
21, 40 & 5:16. which the Lord thy God *giveth*
5:31(28). the land which I *give* them
7:16. the Lord thy God *shall deliver*
8:18. (it is) he *that giveth* thee power
9: 6. the Lord thy God *giveth* thee not
11:17. the good land which the Lord *giveth* you.
26. I *set* before you...a blessing and a curse;
31. the land which the Lord your God *giveth*
32. judgments which I *set* before you
12: 9. which the Lord your God *giveth* you.
13:12(13). thy cities, which...thy God *hath given*
15: 4, 7 & 16:5, 18, 20 & 17:2, 14 & 18:9. which the Lord thy God *giveth* thee
19: 1. land the Lord thy God *giveth* thee,
2, 10, 14. the Lord thy God *giveth* thee
20:16. which the Lord thy God *doth give* thee
21: 1, 23 & 24:4 & 25:15, 19 & 26:1, 2 & 27:2, 3 & 28:8. the Lord thy God *giveth* thee
32:49. the land of Canaan, which I *give*
52. land which I *give* the children of Israel.
Jos. 1: 2. the land which I *do give*
11, 15. which the Lord your God *giveth*
11: 6. to morrow about this time *will* I *deliver*
Jud.21:18. Cursed (be) *he that giveth* a wife
1Sa.23: 4. *will deliver* the Philistines into thine hand.
24: 4(5). *will deliver* thine enemy into thine hand,
2Sa.22:48. It (is) God that avengeth (marg. *giveth* avengement for) me,
1K. 5:10(24). Hiram *gave* (lit. was *giving*) Solomon cedar trees
18: 9. that thou *wouldest deliver* thy servant into
20:13. I *will deliver it* into thine hand
2K. 19: 7. I *will send* a blast upon him,
2Ch 11:16. *such as set* their hearts to seek
Neh 2:12. what my God *had put* in my heart to do
12:47. *gave* the portions of the singers
13: 5. where...they laid (lit. were *placing*) the meat offerings,
Job 5:10. *Who giveth* rain upon the earth,
35:10. *who giveth* songs in the night;
Ps. 18:47(48). (It is) God that avengeth (marg. *giveth* avengements for) me,
33: 7. *he layeth up* the depth
37:21. the righteous sheweth mercy, *and giveth*.
Ps. 68:35(36). he *that giveth* strength and power
136:25. *Who giveth* food to all flesh:
144:10. (he) *that giveth* salvation unto kings:
145:15. thou *givest* them their meat
146: 7. *which giveth* food to the hungry.
147: 9. *He giveth* to the beast his food,
16. *He giveth* snow like wool:
Pro.22:16. *he that giveth* to the rich,
26: 8. *he that giveth* honour to a fool.
28:27. *He that giveth* unto the poor
Isa. 37: 7. I *will send* a blast upon him,
40:23. *That bringeth* the princes to nothing;
29. He *giveth* power to the faint;
42: 5. he *that giveth* breath unto the people
43:16. the Lord, *which maketh* a way in the sea,
Jer. 5:14. I *will make* my words...fire,
24. the Lord our God, *that giveth* rain,
6:21. I *will lay* stumbling blocks before
20: 4. I *will make thee* a terror
21: 8. I *set* before you the way of life,
26:15. ye *shall* surely *bring* innocent blood upon
29:21. I *will deliver* them into the hand
31:35. the Lord, *which giveth* the sun
32: 3, 28 & 34:2. I *will give* this city into the hand
44:30. I *will give* Pharaoh-hophra
Eze. 2: 8. eat that I *give* thee.
3: 3. this roll that I *give* thee.
23:28. I *will deliver thee* into the hand (of)
25: 4. I *will deliver thee* to the men of the east
29:19. I *will give* the land of Egypt
Dan. 1:16. should drink; *and gave* them pulse.
Hos. 2: 5(7). my lovers, *that give* (me) my bread

KAL.—*Participle.* Paül.

Nu. 3: 9. the Levites...they (are) *wholly given* (lit. *given, given*)
8:16. For they (are) *wholly given* (lit. *id.*) unto
19. I have given the Levites (as) *a gift* (marg. *given*)
18: 6. (they are) *given* (as) a gift
Deu28:31. thy sheep (shall be) *given* unto thine enemies,
32. Thy sons and thy daughters (shall be) *given*
1Ch 6:48(33). the Levites (were) *appointed*
2Ch 1:12. Wisdom and knowledge (is) *granted* unto thee;
Neh13: 4. Eliashib the priest, *having* the oversight (marg. *being set* over)
Est. 3:11. The silver (is) *given* to thee,

* NIPHAL.—*Preterite.* *

Gen. 9: 2. into your hand *are they delivered.*
38:14. *she was* not *given* unto him to wife.
Lev.10:14. *are given* out of the sacrifices
19:20. not at all redeemed, nor freedom *given*
26:25. *and ye shall be delivered* into the hand of the enemy.
Nu. 26:62. there *was* no inheritance *given*
Jos. 24:33. a hill...which *was given* him
1Sa.18:19. *she was given* unto Adriel
25:27. *let it even be given* unto the young men
2K. 25:30. a continual allowance *given* him
1Ch 5: 1. his birthright *was given* unto the sons of
2Ch 34:16. All that *was committed*
Ezr. 9: 7. *have we*, our kings, (and) our priests, *been delivered*
Neh 10:29(30). God's law, *which was given*
13:10. the portions of the Levites *had* not *been given*
Est. 3:15. the decree *was given* in Shushan
4: 8. the decree that *was given*
6: 8. the crown royal which *is set*
8:14. the decree *was given* at Shushan
Job 9:24. The earth *is given* into the hand of
15:19. Unto whom alone the earth *was given*,
Ecc.10: 6. Folly *is set* in great dignity,
12:11. *are given* from one shepherd.
Isa. 9: 6(5). unto us a son *is given*:
29:12. *And* the book *is delivered* to
35: 2. the glory of Lebanon *shall be given*
Jer. 13:20. the flock (that) *was given* thee,
32:24, 25. the city *is given* into the hand of
36. *It shall be delivered* into the hand of
43. *it is given* into the hand of
38:18. *then shall* this city *be given*
46:24. *she shall be delivered* into the hand

Jer. 51:55. a noise of their voice *is uttered:*
52:34. continual diet *given* him
Eze. 11:15. *is* this land *given* in possession.
15: 4. *it is cast* into the fire for fuel;
16:34. no reward *is given* unto thee,
31:14. they *are* all *delivered* unto death,
32:20. *she is delivered* to the sword:
23. Whose graves *are set* in the sides
25. *he is put* in the midst
29. *are laid* (marg. *given;* or, *put*) by (them that were) slain
33:24. the land *is given* us for inheritance.
35:12. *they are given* us to consume.
47:11. *they shall be given* to salt.
Dan 11:11. *but* the multitude *shall be given*

NIPHAL.—*Infinitive.*

Est. 3:14 & 8:13. a commandment *to be given*
Jer. 32: 4. Zedekiah...shall *surely* be delivered (lit. *being delivered* shall be delivered)
38: 3. This city shall *surely* be given

NIPHAL.—*Future.*

Ex. 5:18. *there shall* no straw *be given*
Lev. 24:20. so *shall it be done*
2K. 18:30. this city *shall* not *be delivered*
19:10. Jerusalem *shall* not *be delivered*
1Ch 5:20. *and* the Hagarites *were delivered*
2Ch 2:14(13). every device which *shall be put* to him,
18:14. *and they shall be delivered* into
Est. 2:13. whatsoever she desired *was given* her
5: 3. *it shall be even given* thee to
6. *and it shall be granted* thee:
7: 2. *and it shall be granted* thee:
3. *let* my life *be given* me
9:12. *and it shall be granted* thee:
13. *let it be granted* to the Jews
14. *and* the decree *was given* at Shushan;
Isa. 36:15. this city *shall* not *be delivered* into
37:10. Jerusalem *shall* not *be given*
51:12. the son of man (which) *shall be made*
Jer. 21:10. *it shall be given* into the hand of
32: 4. *shall* surely *be delivered*
34: 3. shalt surely be taken, and *delivered*
37:17. *thou shalt be delivered* into the hand of
38: 3. This city *shall* surely *be given*
39:17. *thou shalt* not *be given* into
Dan 8:12. an host *was given* (him)
11: 6. *but* she *shall be given up*, and they that

NIPHAL.—*Participle.*

Ex. 5:16. There is no straw *given* unto thy servants,
2K. 22: 7. the money *that was delivered*
2Ch 28: 5. *he was* also *delivered* into the hand of
Isa. 33:16. bread *shall be given* him;
Eze. 32:25. though their terror *was caused*

* HOPHAL.—*Future.* *

Lev. 11:38. if (any) water *be put* upon the seed,
Nu. 26:54. to every one shall his inheritance *be given*
32: 5. let this land *be given* unto thy servants
2Sa. 18: 9. *and he was taken up* between
21: 6. *Let* seven men of his sons *be delivered*
1K. 2:21. *Let* Abishag the Shunammite *be given*
2K. 5:17. *Shall* there not...*be given* to thy servant
Job 28:15. *It cannot be gotten* for gold, (marg. Fine gold *shall* not *be given* for it)

5415

נְתַן [n'than], Ch.

* P'AL.—*Infinitive.* *

Ezr. 7:20. which thou shalt have occasion *to bestow*,

P'AL.—*Future.*

Ezr. 4:13. (then) *will they* not *pay* (marg. *give*) toll,
7:20. *bestow* (it) out of the king's treasure
Dan 2:16. desired of the king that *he would give* him
4:17(14), 25(22), 32(29). and *giveth it* to whomsoever he will,

---

5420

נָתַס [nāh-thas'].

* KAL.—*Preterite.* *

Job 30:13. *They mar* my path,

נָתַע [nāh-thag'']. 5421

* NIPHAL.—*Preterite.* *

Job 4:10. the teeth of the young lions, *are broken.*

נָתַץ nāh-thatz'. 5422

* KAL.—*Preterite.* *

Lev. 14:45. *And he shall break down* the house,
Jud. 6:30. *he hath cast down* the altar of Baal,
31. because (one) *hath cast down* his altar.
32. *he hath thrown down* his altar.
8:17. *he beat down* the tower of Penuel,
2K. 23: 8. *and brake down* the high places
12. *did* the king *beat down*,
15. the high place *he brake down*,
25:10. *brake down* the walls of Jerusalem
Jer. 39: 8. and *brake down* the walls of Jerusalem.
52:14. *brake down* all the walls of Jerusalem

KAL.—*Infinitive.*

Ps. 58: 6(7). *break out* the great teeth of the
Jer. 1:10 & 18:7. *and to pull down*, and to destroy,
31:28. to pluck up, *and to break down*,

KAL.—*Future.*

Ex. 34:13. But *ye shall destroy* their altars,
Deu. 7: 5. *ye shall destroy* their altars,
Jud. 2: 2. *ye shall throw down* their altars:
8: 9. *I will break down* this tower.
9:45. *and beat down* the city,
2K. 10:27. *And they brake down* the image of Baal, *and brake down* the house of Baal,
11:18. into the house of Baal, *and brake it down*;
23: 7. *And he brake down* the houses of the
2Ch 23:17. to the house of Baal, *and brake it down*,
Job 19:10. *He hath destroyed me* on every side,
Ps. 52: 5(7). God *shall* likewise *destroy thee* (marg *beat thee down*)
Isa. 22:10. *and* the houses *have ye broken down*
Eze. 26: 9. *he shall break down* thy towers.
12. *and destroy* thy pleasant houses:

KAL.—*Participle.* Paül.

Jer. 33: 4. the houses...*which are thrown down*

* NIPHAL.—*Preterite.* *

Jer. 4:26. all the cities...*were broken down*
Nah. 1: 6. the rocks *are thrown down* by him.

* PIEL.—*Preterite.* *

Deu 12: 3. *And ye shall overthrow* (marg. *break down* their altars,
2Ch 33: 3. his father *had broken down*,
Eze. 16:39. *and shall break down* thy high places:

PIEL.—*Future.*

2Ch 31: 1. *and threw down* the high places
34: 4. *And they brake down* the altars of Baalim.
7. *when he had broken down* the altars
36:19. *and brake down* the wall of Jerusalem,

* PUAL.—*Preterite.* *

Jud. 6:28. the altar of Baal *was cast down*,

* HOPHAL.—*Future.* *

Lev. 11:35. *they shall be broken down:* (for) they

נָתַק [nāh-thak']. 5423

* KAL.—*Preterite.* *

Jud. 20:32. *and draw them* from the city

KAL.—*Future.*

Jer. 22:24. yet *would I pluck thee* thence;

KAL.—*Participle.* Paül.

Lev. 22:24. that which is bruised, or crushed, *or broken*,

* NIPHAL.—*Preterite.* *

Jos. 4:18. the soles of the priests' feet *were lifted up* (marg. *plucked up*)
Job 17:11. my purposes *are broken off*,
Isa. 5:27. nor the latchet of their shoes *be broken:*
Jer. 6:29. the wicked *are* not *plucked away.*
10:20. all my cords *are broken:*

NIPHAL.—*Future.*

Jos. 8:16. *and were drawn away* from the city.
Jud.16: 9. as a thread of tow *is broken*
Job 18:14. His confidence *shall be rooted out*
Ecc. 4:12. a threefold cord *is* not quickly *broken.*
Isa. 33:20. neither *shall* any of the cords thereof *be broken.*

* PIEL.—*Preterite.* *

Jer. 2:20. I have broken thy yoke, (and) *burst* thy bands;
5: 5. broken the yoke, (and) *burst* the bonds.

PIEL.—*Future.*

Jud.16: 9. *And he brake* the withs,
12. *And he brake them* from off his arms
Ps. 2: 3. *Let us break* their bands *asunder,*
107:14. and *brake* their bands *in sunder.*
Isa. 58: 6. that *ye break* every yoke?
Jer. 30: 8. and *will burst* thy bonds,
Eze.17: 9. *shall he* not *pull* up the roots
23:34. *pluck off* thine own breasts:
Nah. 1:13. and *will burst* thy bonds *in sunder.*

* HIPHIL.—*Infinitive.* *

Jos. 8: 6. till *we have drawn* (marg. *pulled*) them from the city;

HIPHIL.—*Imperative.*

Jer. 12: 3. *pull them out* like sheep for the slaughter,

* HOPHAL.—*Preterite.* *

Jud.20:31. *were drawn away* from the city;

5424 **נֶתֶק** *neh'-thek,* m.

Lev.13:30. *a dry scall,* (even) a leprosy
31. if the priest look on the plague of *the scall,*
— (him that hath) the plague of *the scall*
32. (if) *the scall* spread not,
— *the scall* (be) not in sight deeper than the skin;
33. *the scall* shall he not shave; and the priest shall shut up (him that hath) *the scall*
34. the priest shall look on *the scall:* and, behold, (if) *the scall* be not spread
35. if *the scall* spread much
36. if *the scall* be spread
37. if *the scall* be in his sight at a stay,
— *the scall* is healed,
14:54. all manner of plague of leprosy, *and scall,*

5425 **נָתַר** [*nāh-thar'*].

* KAL.—*Future.* *

Job 37: 1. *and is moved* out of his place.

* PIEL.—*Infinitive.* *

Lev.11:21. *to leap* withal upon the earth;

* HIPHIL.—*Infinitive.* *

Isa. 58: 6. *to undo* the heavy burdens,

HIPHIL.—*Future.*

2Sa.22:33. *and he maketh* (marg. *riddeth,* or, *looseth*) my way perfect.
Job 6: 9. that *he would let loose* his hand,
Ps.105:20. The king sent *and loosed him;*
Hab. 3: 6. *and drove asunder* the nations;

HIPHIL.—*Participle.*

Ps.146: 7. The Lord *looseth* the prisoners:

5426 **נְתַר** [*n'thar*], Ch.

* APHEL.—*Imperative.* *

Dan. 4:14(11). *shake off* his leaves,

5427 **נֶתֶר** *neh'-ther,* m.

Pro.25:20. (as) vinegar upon *nitre,*
Jer. 2:22. though thou wash thee *with nitre,*

נָתַשׁ *nāh-thash'.* 5428

* KAL.—*Preterite.* *

1K. 14:15. *and he shall root up* Israel
2Ch 7:20. *Then will I pluck them up by the roots*
Ps. 9: 6(7). *thou hast destroyed* cities;
Jer. 12:17. *I will* (lit. *and I will*) utterly *pluck up*
Mic. 5:14(13). *And I will pluck up* thy groves

KAL.—*Infinitive.*

Jer. 1:10. *to root out,* and to pull down,
12:15. *I have plucked* them *out*
17. I will *utterly* pluck up (lit. *in plucking* up I will pluck up)
18: 7. *to pluck up,* and to pull down,
31:28. *to pluck up,* and to break down,

KAL.—*Future.*

Deu29:28(27). *And* the Lord *rooted them out*
Jer. 12:14. *and pluck out* the house of Judah
24: 6. I will plant them, and not *pluck* (them) *up.*
42:10. I will plant you, and not *pluck* (you) *up:*

KAL.—*Participle.* Poël.

Jer. 12:14. I *will pluck them* out
45: 4. I *will pluck up,* even this whole land.

* NIPHAL.—*Future.* *

Jer. 18:14. *shall* the cold flowing waters...*be forsaken?*
31:40. *it shall* not *be plucked up,*
Dan11: 4. his kingdom *shall be plucked up,*
Am. 9:15. *they shall* no more *be pulled up*

* HOPHAL.—*Future.* *

Eze.19:12. *But she was plucked up* in fury,

ס *sāh'-mech.*

The Fifteenth Letter of the Alphabet.

סְאָה *s'āh,* f. 5429

Gen18: 6. three *measures* of fine meal,
1Sa.25:18. five *measures* of parched (corn),
1K. 18:32. contain *two measures* of seed.
2K. 7: 1. *a measure* of fine flour (be sold) for a shekel, and *two measures* of barley for a
16. *a measure* of fine flour was (sold) for a shekel, and *two measures* of barley for a
18. *Two measures* of barley for a shekel, *and a measure* of fine flour for a shekel,

---

סְאוֹן *s'ōhn,* m. 5430

Isa. 9: 5(4). For every *battle* [perhaps lit. *greave*] *of* the warrior

---

סָאַן [*sāh-an'*]. 5431

* KAL.—*Participle.* Poel. *

Isa. 9: 5(4). every battle of *the warrior* (is) with confused noise,

---

סַאסְּאָה *sas-s'āh',* f. 5432

[With Prefix בְּ, for בְּסְאָה־סְאָה].

Isa. 27: 8. *In measure,* when it shooteth forth,

סָבָא [*sāh-vāh'*]. 5433

* KAL.—*Future.* *

Isa. 56:12. *and we will fill ourselves* with strong drink;

KAL.—*Participle.* Poel.

Deu21:20. (he is) a glutton, *and a drunkard.*
Pro.23:20. Be not *among* wine*bibbers;*
21. *the drunkard* and the glutton shall come to
Eze.23:42. (כתיב) (were) brought *Sabeans* (marg. or, *drunkards*)

KAL.—*Participle.* Paül.

Nah 1:10. while they are drunken (as) *drunkards,*

5433 **סָבָא** [*sāh-vāh'*], m.

Eze.23:42. (were) brought *Sabeans* (marg. or, *drunkards*) from the wilderness,

5435 **סֹבֶא** [*sōh'-veh*], m.

Isa. 1:22. *thy wine* mixed with water:
Hos. 4:18. *Their drink* is sour:
Nah 1:10. and *while they are drunken* (as) drunkards,

5437 **סָבַב** *sāh-vav'*.

* KAL.—*Preterite.* *

Jos. 6: 3. *And ye shall compass* the city, all (ye) men
15. only on that day *they compassed* the city
1Sa. 7:16. he went from year to year *in circuit* (marg. *and he circuited*)
22:22. I *have occasioned* (the death) of all the
2Sa.22: 6. The sorrows of hell *compassed me about;*
1K. 5: 3(17). for the wars which *were about him on every side,*
2Ch.33:14. *and compassed* about Ophel,
Ps. 17:11. *They have* now *compassed us* in our steps:
18: 5(6). The sorrows of hell *compassed me about:*
22:12(13). Many bulls *have compassed me:*
16(17). For dogs *have compassed me:*
88:17(18). *They came round about me* daily like
109: 3. *They compassed me about* also with words
118:10. All nations *compassed me about:*
11. *They compassed me about;* yea, *they compassed me about:*
12. *They compassed me about* like bees;
Ecc. 2:20. *Therefore I went about* to cause
7:25. I *applied* mine heart (marg. I and mine heart *compassed*) to know, and to search,
9:14. *and besieged* it, and built great bulwarks
12: 5. *and* the mourners *go about* the streets:
Eze.42:19. *He turned about* to the west side,
Hos 7: 2. their own doings *have beset them about;*
11:12(12:1). Ephraim *compasseth me about* with

KAL.—*Infinitive.*

Nu. 21: 4. *to compass* the land of Edom:
Deu 2: 3. *Ye have compassed* this mountain long

KAL.—*Imperative.*

Jos. 6: 7. Pass on, *and compass* the city,
1Sa.22:17. *Turn,* and slay the priests of the Lord;
18. *Turn thou,* and fall upon the priests.
2Sa.18:30. *Turn aside,* (and) stand here.
2K. 9:18, 19. *turn thee* behind me.
Ps. 48:12(13). *Walk about* Zion,
Cant 2:17. *turn,* my beloved, and be thou like a roe
Isa. 23:16. Take an harp, *go about* the city,

KAL.—*Future.*

Gen37: 7. *stood round about,* and made obeisance
Deu 2: 1. *and we compassed* mount Seir many days.
Jos. 6: 4. *ye shall compass* the city seven times,
14. *And* the second day *they compassed* the city
15. *and compassed* the city after the same
Jud.11:18. *and compassed* the land of Edom,
16: 2. *And they compassed* (him) *in,* and laid wait
20: 5. *and beset* the house round about upon me
1Sa.16:11. for *we will* not *sit down* (marg. *round*) till he come hither.
2Sa.18:15. *And* ten young men...*compassed about*
1K. 7:15. a line of twelve cubits *did compass* either
23. a line of thirty cubits *did compass* it
2K. 3: 9. *and they fetched a compass* of seven days'
25. *howbeit* the slingers *went about* (it),
2Ch 4: 2. a line of thirty cubits *did compass* it
17: 9. *and went about* throughout all the cities
18:31. *Therefore they compassed* about him
23: 2. *And they went about* in Judah,
Job 16:13. His archers *compass* me *round about,*
40:22. willows of the brook *compass him about.*
Ps. 49: 5(6). the iniquity of my heels *shall compass me about?*
Jer. 41:14. *So* all the people...*cast about* and returned,
52:21. a fillet of twelve cubits *did compass it;*

KAL.—*Participle.* Poel.

Gen 2:11. *which compasseth* the whole land of
13. *compasseth* the whole land of Ethiopia.
1K. 7:24. knops *compassing* it,
2K. 6:15. an host *compassed* the city
8:21. smote the Edomites *which compassed* him
2Ch 4: 3. *which did compass* it round about:
21: 9. smote the Edomites *which compassed* him
Ecc. 1: 6. *and turneth about* unto the north; it *whirleth about* (lit. *turning about turning about*)
Cant 3: 3. The watchmen *that go about* the city
5: 7. The watchmen *that went about* the city

* NIPHAL.—*Preterite.* *

Gen19: 4. *compassed* the house *round,* both old
Nu. 34: 4. *And* your border *shall turn* from the south
5. *And* the border *shall fetch a compass*
Jos. 7: 9. *and shall environ* us round, and cut off
15: 3. *and fetched a compass to* Karkaa:
10. *And* the border *compassed* from Baalah
16: 6. *and* the border *went about* eastward
18:14. *and compassed* the corner of the sea
19:14. *And* the border *compasseth* it on the north
Jud.19:22. of Belial, *beset* the house *round about,*
Jer. 6:12. *And* their houses *shall be turned* unto
31:39. *and shall compass about* to Goath.
Eze.26: 2. *she is turned* unto me:
41: 7. *and a winding about* (marg. *went round*)

NIPHAL.—*Future.*

Gen42:24. *And he turned himself about* from them,
Nu. 36: 7. *shall* not the inheritance...*remove*
9. Neither *shall* the inheritance *remove*
1Sa. 5: 8. *Let* the ark...*be carried about* unto Gath.
15:12. he set him up a place, *and is gone about,*
27. *And* as Samuel *turned about* to go away,
17:30. *And he turned* from him toward another,
18:11. *And* David *avoided* out of his presence
22:18. *And* Doeg the Edomite *turned,* and he fell
2Sa.14:24. *Let him turn* to his own house,
— *So* Absalom *returned* to his own house,
18:30. *And he turned aside,* and stood still.
1K. 2:15. *howbeit* the kingdom *is turned about,*
1Ch 16:43. *and* David *returned* to bless his house.
Ps. 71:21. *and* comfort me *on every side.* (lit. *and shalt go about* and comfort me)
114: 3. Jordan *was driven* back.
5. thou Jordan, (that) *thou wast driven* back?
Pro.26:14. As the door *turneth* upon his hinges,
Eze. 1: 9, 12, 17. *they turned* not when they went;
10:11, 11. *they turned* not as they went,
16. the same wheels also *turned* not
Hab 2:16. the cup of the Lord's right hand *shall be turned*
Zec.14:10. All the land *shall be turned* (marg. or, *compassed*) as a plain

* PIEL.—*Infinitive.* *

2Sa.14:20. To *fetch about* this form of speech

* POEL.—*Future.* *

Deu32:10. *he led him about,* (marg. or, *compassed*)
Ps. 7: 7(8). So *shall* the congregation of the people *compass thee about:*
26: 6. *so will I compass* thine altar,
32: 7. *thou shalt compass me about* with songs
10. mercy *shall compass him about.*
55:10(11). Day and night *they go about it*
59: 6(7), 14(15). *and go round about* the city.
Cant.3: 2. I will rise now, *and go about* the city
Jer. 31:22. A woman *shall compass* a man.
Jon. 2: 3(4). the floods *compassed me about:*
5(6). the depth *closed me round about,*

* HIPHIL.—*Preterite.* *

1Sa. 5: 9. that, after *they had carried* it *about,*
10. *They have brought about* the ark of the God
1K. 18:37. *thou hast turned* their heart back again.
2K. 16:18. *turned he* from the house of the Lord
2Ch 13:13. Jeroboam *caused* an ambushment *to come about*
35:22. Josiah *would* not *turn* his face from him,
Ezr. 6:22. *and turned* the heart of the king of Assyria
Eze. 7:22. My face *will I turn also* from them,

HIPHIL.—*Infinitive.*

2Sa. 3:12. *to bring about* all Israel unto thee.
1Ch 12:23. *to turn* the kingdom of Saul to him,

HIPHIL.—*Imperative.*

2Sa. 5:23. (but) *fetch a compass* behind them,
1Ch 14:14. *turn away* from them, and come
Cant.6: 5. *Turn away* thine eyes from me,

HIPHIL.—*Future.*

Ex. 13:18. *But* God *led* the people *about,*

Jos. 6:11. *So* the ark of the Lord *compassed* the city,
Jud.18:23. *And they turned* their faces, and said
1Sa. 5: 8. *And they carried* the ark of the God of Israel
2Sa.20:12. *And* when...*he removed* Amasa out of the
1K. 8:14. *And* the king *turned* his face about,
21: 4. *and turned away* his face, and would eat no
2K. 20: 2. *Then he turned* his face to the wall,
23:34. *and turned* his name to Jehoiakim,
24:17. *and changed* his name to Zedekiah.
1Ch 10:14. *and turned* the kingdom unto David
13: 3. *And let us bring again* the ark of our God
2Ch 6: 3. *And* the king *turned* his face, and blessed
14: 7(6). *and make about* (them) walls, and
29: 6. *and have turned away* their faces
36: 4. *and turned* his name to Jehoiakim.
Isa. 38: 2. *Then* Hezekiah *turned* his face toward the
Eze.47: 2. *and led me about* the way without

HIPHIL.—*Participle.*

Jer. 21: 4. I *will turn back* the weapons of war

* HOPHAL.—*Future.* *

Isa. 28:27. neither *is* a cart wheel *turned about*

HOPHAL.—*Participle.*

Ex. 28:11. *to be set* in ouches of gold.
39: 6. onyx stones *inclosed* in ouches of gold,
13. (they were) *inclosed* in ouches of gold
Nu. 32:38. their names *being changed*,
Eze.41:24. two *turning* leaves;

5438 סִבָּה *sib-bāh'*, f.

1K. 12:15. *the cause* was from the Lord,

5439 סָבִיב *sāh-veev'*, m.

Gen23:17. that (were) in all the borders *round about*,
35: 5. the cities that (were) *round about them*,
41:48. which (was) *round about* every city,
Ex. 7:24. the Egyptians digged *round about* the river
16:13. in the morning the dew lay *round about*
19:12. set bounds unto the people *round about*,
25:11, 24. a crown of gold *round about*.
25. a border of an hand breadth *round about*, and thou shalt make a golden crown to the border thereof *round about*.
27:17. All the pillars *round about* the court
28:32. a binding of woven work *round about*
33. *round about* the hem thereof; and bells of gold between them *round about*:
34. upon the hem of the robe *round about*.
29:16. sprinkle (it) *round about* upon the altar.
20. the blood upon the altar *round about*.
30: 3. the sides thereof *round about*,
— make unto it a crown of gold *round about*.
37: 2. made a crown of gold to it *round about*.
11. thereunto a crown of gold *round about*.
12. a border of an handbreadth *round about*:
— for the border thereof *round about*.
26. the sides thereof *round about*,
— made unto it a crown of gold *round about*.
38:16. the hangings of the court *round about*
20. tabernacle, and of the court *round about*,
31. the sockets of the court *round about*,
— all the pins of the court *round about*.
39:23. (with) a band *round about* the hole,
25. *round about* between the pomegranates;
26. *round about* the hem of the robe
40: 8. thou shalt set up the court *round about*,
33. he reared up the court *round about*
Lev. 1: 5. sprinkle the blood *round about* upon the
11. sprinkle his blood *round about* upon the
3: 2. sprinkle the blood upon the altar *round about*.
8. sprinkle the blood thereof *round about* upon
13. sprinkle the blood thereof upon the altar *round about*.
7: 2. sprinkle *round about* upon the altar.
8:15. (it) upon the horns of the altar *round about*
19, 24. sprinkled the blood upon the altar *round about*.
9:12. he sprinkled *round about* upon the altar.
18. he sprinkled upon the altar *round about*,
14:41. scraped within *round about*,
16:18. put (it) upon the horns of the altar *round about*.

Lev.25:31. which have no wall *round about* them
44. of the heathen that are *round about you*;
Nu. 1:50. *and* shall encamp *round about* the
53. the Levites shall pitch *round about*
2: 2. far off *about* the tabernacle
3:26. by the altar *round about*,
37. the pillars of the court *round about*,
4:26. by the altar *round about*,
32. the pillars of the court *round about*,
11:24. set them *round about* the tabernacle.
31. the other side, *round about* the camp,
32. for themselves *round about* the camp.
16:24. Get you up *from about* the tabernacle of
27. from the tabernacle of Korah,...*on every side*:
34. all Israel that (were) *round about them*
22: 4. lick up all (that are) *round about us*,
32:33. the cities of the country *round about*.
34:12. with the coasts thereof *round about*.
35: 2. suburbs for the cities *round about them*.
4. a thousand cubits *round about*.
Deu 6:14. of the people which (are) *round about you*;
12:10. rest from all your enemies *round about*,
13: 7(8). of the people which (are) *round about you*,
17:14. like as all the nations that (are) *about me*;
21: 2. *round about* him that is slain:
25:19. rest from all thine enemies *round about*,
Jos. 15:12. the coast of the children of Judah *round about*
18:20. by the coasts thereof *round about*,
19: 8. *round about* these cities
21:11. the suburbs thereof *round about it*.
42(40). every one with their suburbs *round about them*:
44(42). the Lord gave them rest *round about*,
23: 1. from all their enemies *round about*,
Jud. 2:12. gods of the people that (were) *round about them*,
14. into the hands of their enemies *round about*,
7:18. *on every side* of all the camp,
21. every man in his place *round about* the camp:
8:34. out of the hands of all their enemies *on every side*:
20:29. Israel set liers in wait *round about* Gibeah.
1Sa.12:11. your enemies *on every side*,
14:21. (from the country) *round about*,
47. fought against all his enemies *on every side*,
26: 5. and the people pitched *round about him*.
7. Abner and the people lay *round about him*.
31: 9. sent into the land of the Philistines *round about*,
2Sa. 5: 9. David built *round about* from Millo
7: 1. the Lord had given him rest *round about*
22:12. made darkness pavilions *round about him*,
24: 6. came to Dan-jaan, *and about* to Zidon,
1K. 3: 1. the wall of Jerusalem *round about*.
4:24(5:4). he had peace on all sides *round about* him.
31(5:11). his fame was in all nations *round about*.
5: 4(18). hath given me rest *on every side*,
6: 5. he built chambers *round about*, (against) the walls of the house *round about*,
— he made chambers *round about*:
6. he made narrowed rests *round about*,
7:12. the great court *round about*
18. two rows *round about* upon the one net-work,
20. two hundred in rows *round about*
23. (it was) round *all about*,
— thirty cubits did compass it *round about*.
24. under the brim of it *round about*
— compassing the sea *round about*:
35. a round *compass* of half a cubit high:
36. and additions *round about*.
18:32. he made a trench *about* the altar,
35. the water ran *round about* the altar;
2K 6:17. horses and chariots of fire *round about*
11: 8. ye shall compass the king *round about*,
11. in his hand, *round about* the king,
17:15. went after the heathen that (were) *round about them*,
25: 1. they built forts against it *round about*.
4. the Chaldees (were) against the city *round about*:

2K. 25:10. brake down the walls of Jerusalem *round about.*
17. pomegranates upon the chapiter *round about,*
1Ch 4:33. villages that (were) *round about*
6:55(40). the suburbs thereof *round about it.*
9:27. *And* they lodged *round about* the house
10: 9. the land of the Philistines *round about.*
11: 8. he built the city *round about,* even from Millo *round about:*
22: 9. rest from all his enemies *round about:*
18. hath he (not) given you rest *on every side?*
28:12. of all the chambers *round about,*
2Ch 4: 2. from brim to brim, round *in compass,*
— thirty cubits did compass it *round about.*
3. which did compass it *round about* (lit. *around, around*): ten in a cubit, compassing the sea *round about.*
14: 7(6). he hath given us rest *on every side.*
14(13). smote all the cities *round about*
15:15. the Lord gave them rest *round about.*
17:10. lands that (were) *round about* Judah,
20:30. God gave him rest *round about.*
23: 7. shall compass the king *round about,*
10. the temple, by the king *round about.*
32:22. and guided them *on every side.*
34: 6. with their mattocks *round about.*
Ezr. 1: 6. they *that* (were) *about them* strengthened
Neh. 5:17. among the heathen that (are) *about us.*
6:16. and all the heathen that (were) *about us*
12:28. the plain country *round about* Jerusalem,
29. builded them villages *round about*
Job 1:10. about all that he hath *on every side?*
10: 8. and fashioned me together *round about;*
18:11. Terrors shall make him afraid *on every side,*
19:10. He hath destroyed me *on every side,*
12. and encamp *round about* my tabernacle.
22:10. Therefore snares (are) *round about thee,*
29: 5. (when) my children (were) *about me;*
41:14(6). his teeth (are) terrible *round about.*
Ps. 3: 6(7). set (themselves) against me *round about.*
12: 8(9). The wicked walk *on every side,*
18:11(12). his pavilion *round about him*
27: 6. above mine enemies *round about me:*
31:13(14). fear (was) *on every side:*
34: 7(8). encampeth *round about* them that fear
44:13(14). a derision to them that are *round about us.*
50: 3. *and* it shall be very tempestuous *round about him.*
76:11(12). let all *that be round about him* bring
78:28. *round about* their habitations.
79: 3. shed like water *round about* Jerusalem;
4. derision to them that are *round about us.*
89: 7(8). in reverence of all (them that are) *about him.*
8(9). to thy faithfulness *round about thee?*
97: 2. and darkness (are) *round about him:*
3. and burneth up his enemies *round about.*
125: 2. (As) the mountains (are) *round about* Jerusalem, so the Lord (is) *round about* his people
128: 3. like olive plants *round about* thy table.
Ecc. 1: 6. the wind returneth again according to *his circuits.*
Cant. 3: 7. threescore valiant men (are) *about* it,
Isa. 42:25. it hath set him on fire *round about,*
49:18 & 60:4. Lift up thine eyes *round about,*
Jer. 1:15. against all the walls thereof *round about,*
4:17. are they against her *round about;*
6: 3. pitch (their) tents against her *round about;*
25. (and) fear (is) *on every side.*
12: 9. the birds *round about* (are) against her;
17:26. *and from the places about* Jerusalem,
20: 3. called thy name Pashur, but Magor-*missabib.* (marg. Fear *round about*)
10. fear *on every side.*
21:14. it shall devour all things *round about it.*
25: 9. against all these nations *round about,*
32:44 & 33:13. *and in the places about* Jerusalem,
46: 5. fear (was) *round about,*
14. the sword shall devour *round about thee.*
48:17. All *ye that are about him,*
39. a dismaying to all them *about him.*
49: 5. from all those that be *about thee;*
29. Fear (is) *on every side.*
Jer. 50:14. in array against Babylon *round about:*
15. Shout against her *round about:*
29. camp against it *round about;*
32. and it shall devour all *round about him.*
51: 2. they shall be against her *round about.*
52: 4. built forts against it *round about.*
7. Chaldeans (were) by the city *round about:*
14. all the walls of Jerusalem *round about.*
22. pomegranates upon the chapiters *round about,*
23. (were) an hundred *round about.*
Lam. 1:17. (that) his adversaries (should be) *round about him:*
2: 3. (which) devoureth *round about.*
22. as in a solemn day my terrors *round about,*
Eze. 1: 4. a brightness (was) *about* it,
18. their rings (were) full of eyes *round about*
27. as the appearance of fire *round about*
— it had brightness *round about.*
28. appearance of the brightness *round about.*
4: 2. set (battering) rams against it *round about.*
5: 2. (and) smite *about it* with a knife:
5. *and* countries (that are) *round about her.*
6. more than the countries that (are) *round about her:*
7. more than the nations that (are) *round about you,*
— judgments of the nations that (are) *round about you;*
12. shall fall by the sword *round about thee;*
14. a reproach among the nations that (are) *round about thee,*
15. unto the nations that (are) *round about thee,*
6: 5. scatter your bones *round about* your altars.
13. among their idols *round about*
8:10. pourtrayed upon the wall *round about.* (lit. *round about, round about*)
10:12. full of eyes *round about,*
11:12. the heathen that (are) *round about you.*
12:14. all that (are) *about him*
16:33. that they may come unto thee *on every side*
37. I will even gather them *round about*
57. the daughters of Syria, and all (that are) *round about her,*
— which despise thee *round about.*
19: 8. the nations set against him *on every side*
23:22. I will bring them against thee *on every side;*
24. buckler and shield and helmet *round about:*
27:11. (were) upon thy walls *round about,*
— their shields upon thy walls *round about;*
28:23. by the sword upon her *on every side;*
24. all (that are) *round about them,*
26. despise them *round about them;*
31: 4. rivers running *round about* his plants,
32:22. his graves (are) *about him:*
23. her company is *round about* her grave:
24. all her multitude *round about* her grave,
25. her graves (are) *round about him:*
26. her graves (are) *round about him:*
34:26. *and the places round about* my hill
36: 3. swallowed you up *on every side,*
4. residue of the heathen that (are) *round about;*
7. Surely the heathen that (are) *about* you,
36. heathen that are left *round about you*
37: 2. caused me to pass by them *round about.* (lit. *round about, round about*)
21. and will gather them *on every side,*
39:17. gather yourselves *on every side*
40: 5. a wall on the outside of the house *round about,* (lit. *round about, round about*)
14. even unto the post of the court *round about* (lit. *id.*)
16. to their posts within the gate *round about,* (lit. *id.*)
— and windows (were) *round about* (lit. *id.*) inward:
17. a pavement made for the court *round about:* (lit. *id.*)
25, 29, 33. in the arches thereof *round about,* (lit. *id.*)
30. the arches *round about* (lit. *id.*) (were) five and twenty cubits
36. the windows to it *round about:* (lit. *id.*)
43. hand broad, fastened *round about:* (lit. *id.*)
41: 5. *round about* (lit. *id.*) the house *on every side.*

Eze.41: 6. for the side chambers *round about*, (lit. *round about, round about*)
7. upward *round about* the house: (lit. *id.*)
8. the height of the house *round about:* (lit. *id.*)
10. the wideness of twenty cubits *round about* the house *on every side.* (lit. *id.*)
11. five cubits *round about.* (lit. *id.*)
12. five cubits thick *round about*, (lit. *id.*)
16. galleries *round about* on their three stories,
— cieled with wood *round about*, (lit. *round about, round about*)
17. by all the wall *round about* (lit. *id.*)
19. through all the house *round about.* (lit. *id.*)
42:15. and measured it *round about.* (lit. *id.*)
16, 17. with the measuring reed *round about.*
20. it had a wall *round about*, (lit. *round about, round about*)
43:12. the whole limit thereof *round about* (lit. *id.*)
13. by the edge thereof *round about*
17. the border *about* it (shall be) half a cubit; and the bottom thereof (shall be) a cubit *about;*
20. and upon the border *round about:*
45: 1. in all the borders thereof *round about.*
2. five hundred (in breadth), square *round about;* and fifty cubits *round about*
46:23. (there was) a row (of building) *round about* in them, *round about* them four,
— under the rows *round about.*
48:35. (It was) *round about* eighteen thousand (measures):
Dan 9:16. a reproach to all (that are) *about us.*
Joel 3:11(4:11). gather yourselves together *round about:*
12(—:12). there will I sit to judge all the heathen *round about.*
Am. 3:11. *even round about* the land;
Nah 3: 8. (that had) the waters *round about* it,
Zec. 2: 5(9). be unto her a wall of fire *round about*,
7: 7. cities thereof *round about her*,
12: 2. a cup of trembling unto all the people *round about*,
6. they shall devour all the people *round about*,
14:14. the wealth of all the heathen *round about*

5440 סָבַךְ [*sāh-vaćh'*].

* KAL.—*Participle.* Paül. *

Nah. 1:10. (they be) *folden together* (as) thorns,

* PUAL.—*Future.* *

Job 8:17. His roots *are wrapped* about the heap,

5442 סְבָךְ *s'vāhćh*, m.

Gen22:13. a ram caught *in a thicket*
Ps. 74: 5. lifted up axes *upon* the *thick* trees.
Isa. 9:18(17). shall kindle *in the thickets of* the forest,
10:34. he shall cut down *the thickets*

5441 סֹבֶךְ [*sōh'-većh*], m.

Jer. 4: 7. The lion is come up *from his thicket*,

5443 סַבְּכָא *sab-b'ćhāh'*, Ch. f.

Dan. 3: 5. harp, *sackbut*, psaltery, dulcimer,

5445 סָבַל [*sāh-val'*].

* KAL.—*Preterite.* *

Isa. 53: 4. and *carried* our sorrows: (lit. *carried them*)
Lam.5: 7. *we have borne* their iniquities.

KAL.—*Infinitive.*

Gen49:15. and bowed his shoulder *to bear*,

KAL.—*Future.*

Isa. 46: 4. to hoar hairs *will I carry* (you):
— *I will carry*, and will deliver (you).
7. *they carry him*, and set him in his place,
53:11. *he shall bear* their iniquities.

* PUAL.—*Participle.* *

Ps. 144:14. (That) our oxen (may be) *strong to labour*

* HITHPAEL.—*Future.* *

Ecc.12: 5. *and* the grasshopper *shall be a burden*,

סְבַל [*s'val*], Ch. 5446

* POAL.—*Participle.* *

Ezr. 6: 3. foundations thereof be *strongly laid;*

סַבָּל *sab-bāhl'*, m. 5449

1K. 5:15(29). threescore and ten thousand that bare *burdens*,
2Ch 2: 2(1). ten thousand men *to bear burdens*,
18(17). (to be) *bearers of burdens*,
34:13. over *the bearers of burdens*,
Neh. 4:10(4). The strength of *the bearers of burdens* is decayed,

---

סֵבֶל *sēh'-vel*, m. 5447

1K. 11:28. *the charge* (marg. *burden*) *of* the house of Joseph.
Neh. 4:17(11). and they that bare *burdens*,
Ps. 81: 6(7). removed his shoulder *from the burden:*

סֹבֶל [*sōh'-vel*], m. 5448

Isa. 9: 4(3). broken the yoke of *his burden*,
10:27. *his burden* shall be taken away
14:25. *and his burden* depart from off their shoulders.

סִבְלָה [*s'vāh-lāh'*], f. 5450

Ex. 1:11. to afflict them *with their burdens.*
2:11. and looked *on their burdens:*
5: 4. get you *unto your burdens.*
5. rest *from their burdens.*
6: 6, 7. from under *the burdens of* the Egyptians,

סִבֹּלֶת *sib-bōh'-leth*, f. 5451

Jud.12: 6. and he said *Sibboleth:*

סְבַר [*s'var*], Ch. 5452

* P'AL.—*Future.* *

Dan 7:25. *and think* to change times and laws:

סָגַד [*sāh-gad'*]. 5456

* KAL.—*Future.* *

Isa. 44:15. *and falleth down* thereto.
17. *he falleth down* unto it,
19. *shall I fall down* to the stock of a tree?
46: 6. *they fall down*, yea, they worship.

סְגִד *s'geed*, Ch. 5457

* P'AL.—*Preterite.* *

Dan 2:46. and *worshipped* Daniel,

P'AL.—*Future.*

Dan 3: 5. ye fall down *and worship* the golden
6. whoso falleth not down *and worshippeth*
10. shall fall down *and worship* the
11. whoso falleth not down *and worshippeth*,
15. ye fall down *and worship* the image which I have made; (well): but *if ye worship* not,
18. nor *worship* the golden image which thou
28. nor *worship* any god, except their own

P'AL.—*Participle.*

Dan 3: 7. fell down (and) *worshipped* the golden
12. nor *worship* the golden image
14. do not ye serve my gods, nor *worship*

5458 ## סְגוֹר *s'gōhr*, m.

Job 28:15. It cannot be gotten for *gold*,
Hos 13: 8. and will rend *the caul of* their heart,

5459 ## סְגֻלָּה *s'gool-lāh'*, f.

Ex. 19: 5. ye shall be *a peculiar treasure* unto me
Deu 7: 6. a *special* people unto himself,
14: 2. a *peculiar* people unto himself,
26:18. to be his *peculiar* people,
1 Ch 29: 3. I have of *mine own proper good*,
Ps. 135: 4. Israel *for his peculiar treasure*.
Ecc. 2: 8. *and the peculiar treasure of* kings
Mal. 3:17. when I make up *my jewels*; (marg. or, *special treasure*)

5461 ## סְגָנִים *s'gāh-neem'*, m. pl.

Ezr. 9: 2. *and rulers* hath been chief in this trespass.
Neh. 2:16. *And the rulers* knew not whither I went,
— nor to the nobles, *nor to the rulers*,
4:14(8), 19(13). the nobles, and to *the rulers*,
5: 7. the nobles, and *the rulers*,
17. hundred and fifty of the Jews *and rulers*,
7: 5. and *the rulers*, and the people,
12:40. the half of *the rulers* with me:
13:11. Then contended I with *the rulers*,
Isa. 41:25. he shall come upon *princes*
Jer. 51:23. break in pieces captains *and rulers*.
28. all *the rulers thereof*, and all the land
57. her captains, *and her rulers*,
Eze. 23: 6. captains *and rulers*, all of them
12. captains *and rulers* clothed most
23. captains *and rulers*, great lords

5460 ## סִגְנִין *sig-neen'*, Ch. m. pl.

Dan 2:48. and chief of *the governors* over all the
3: 2. gather together the princes, *the governors*,
3. Then the princes, *the governors*, and
27. And the princes, *governors*, and
6: 7(8). *the governors*, and the princes, the

5462 ## סָגַר *sāh-gar'*.

* KAL.—*Preterite.* *

Gen 19: 6. and *shut* the door after him,
10. and *shut to* the door.
Ex. 14: 3. the wilderness *hath shut* them in.
Jos. 2: 7. *they shut* the gate.
1 Sa. 1: 5. the Lord *had shut up* her womb.
6. the Lord *had shut* up her womb.
1 K. 11:27. *repaired* (marg. *closed*) the breaches of
2 K. 4: 4. *And* when...*thou shalt shut* the door upon
2 Ch 29: 7. *they have shut up* the doors of the porch,
Job 3:10. *it shut* not up the doors
Ps. 17:10. *They are inclosed* in their own fat:
Isa. 22:22. *and he shall shut*, and none shall open.
Eze. 46:12. *and* after his going forth (one) *shall shut*

KAL.—*Infinitive.*

Jos. 2: 5. (about the time) *of shutting* of the gate,

KAL.—*Imperative.*

2 K. 6:32. *shut* the door, and hold him fast
Ps. 35: 3. *and stop* (the way) against them that
Isa. 26:20. *and shut* thy doors about thee:

KAL.—*Future.*

Gen 2:21. *and closed up* the flesh instead thereof;
7:16. *and* the Lord *shut* him in.
Jud. 3:22. *and* the fat *closed* upon the blade,
23. *and shut* the doors of the parlour upon
9:51. *and shut* (it) to them,
2 K. 4: 5. *and shut* the door upon her
21. *and shut* (the door) upon him,
33. *and shut* the door upon them twain,
2 Ch 28:24. *and shut up* the doors of the house of the
Neh. 6:10. *and let us shut* the doors of the temple:
Job 12:14. *he shutteth* up a man,
Mal. 1:10. *that would shut* the doors (for nought)?

KAL.—*Participle.* Poel.

Jos. 6: 1. Jericho was *straitly* shut up (marg. *did shut up*, and was shut up)
Isa. 22:22. he shall open, and none *shall shut*;

KAL.—*Participle.* Paül.

1 K. 6:20. overlaid it with *pure* (marg. *shut up*) gold;
21. overlaid the house within with *pure* gold:
7:49. And the candlesticks of *pure* gold,
50. and the censers (of) *pure* gold;
10:21. forest of Lebanon (were of) *pure* gold;
2 Ch 4:20. before the oracle, of *pure* gold;
22. the spoons, and the censers, (of) *pure*
9:20. of the forest of Lebanon (were of) *pure* (marg. *shut up*) gold:
Job 41:15(7). *shut up together* (as with) a close seal.
Eze. 44: 1. and it (was) *shut*.
2. This gate shall be *shut*,
— therefore it shall be *shut*.
46: 1. shall be *shut* the six working days;

* NIPHAL.—*Preterite.* *

1 Sa. 23: 7. for *he is shut in*, by entering

NIPHAL.—*Imperative.*

Eze. 3:24. *shut thyself* within thine house.

NIPHAL.—*Future.*

Nu. 12:14. *let her be shut out* from the camp
15. *And* Miriam *was shut out* from the camp
Neh 13:19. commanded *that* the gates *should be shut*,
Isa. 45: 1. and the gates *shall* not *be shut*;
60:11. *they shall* not *be shut* day nor night;
Eze. 46: 2. the gate *shall* not *be shut*

* PIEL.—*Preterite.* *

1 Sa. 24:18(19). the Lord *had delivered* (marg. *shut up*) *me* into thine hand,
26: 8. God *hath delivered* (marg. *id.*) thine enemy into thine hand
2 Sa. 18:28. which *hath delivered* (marg. *id.*) *up* the men

PIEL.—*Future.*

1 Sa. 17:46. This day *will* the Lord *deliver thee* (marg. *shut thee up*) into mine hand;

* PUAL.—*Preterite.* *

Ecc. 12: 4. *And* the doors *shall be shut* in the streets,
Isa. 24:10. every house *is shut up*,
22. *and shall be shut up* in the prison,
Jer. 13:19. The cities of the south *shall be shut up*,

PUAL.—*Participle.*

Jos. 6: 1. Jericho *was* straitly *shut up*

* HIPHIL.—*Preterite.* *

Lev. 13: 4, 31. *then* the priest *shall shut up* (him that hath)
5, 21, 26. *then* the priest *shall shut him up*
33. *and* the priest *shall shut up*
50. *and shut up* (it that hath) the plague
54. *and he shall shut it up* seven days more:
14:38. *and shut up* the house seven days:
46. all the while that it *is shut up*
Deu 32:30. the Lord *had shut them up*?
Ps. 31: 8(9). *hast* not *shut me up* into the hand of the
78:50. *gave* their life *over* to the pestilence;
Lam. 2: 7. *he hath given up* (marg. *shut up*) into the hand of
Am. 6: 8. *therefore will I deliver up* the city

HIPHIL.—*Infinitive.*

1 Sa. 23:20. *to deliver him* into the king's hand.
Am. 1: 6. *to deliver* (them) *up* to Edom:
9. *they delivered up* the whole captivity

HIPHIL.—*Future.*

Lev. 13:11. *shall* not *shut him up*: for he (is) unclean.
Deu 23:15(16). *Thou shalt* not *deliver* unto his master
Jos. 20: 5. *they shall* not *deliver* the slayer up
1 Sa. 23:11. *Will* the men of Keilah *deliver me up*
12. *Will* the men of Keilah *deliver* (marg. *shut up*) me
— *They will deliver* (thee) *up*.
30:15. nor *deliver me* into the hands
Job 11:10. If he cut off, *and shut up*, or gather together,
16:11. God *hath delivered me* (marg. *shut me up*) to the ungodly,
Ps. 78:48. *He gave up* (marg. *shut up*) their cattle *also*

Ps. 78:62. *He gave* his people *over also* unto the sword;
Obad. 14. neither *shouldest thou have delivered up* (marg. *shut up*)

5463 **סְגַר** *s'gar*, Ch.

* P'AL.—*Preterite.* *

Dan 6:22(23). *and hath shut* the lions' mouths,

5464 **סַגְרִיר** *sag-reer'*, m.

Pro.27:15. continual dropping in a *very rainy* day

5465 **סַד** *sad*, m.

Job 13:27. Thou puttest my feet also *in the stocks*,
33:11. He putteth my feet *in the stocks*,

5466 **סָדִין** *sāh-deen'*, m.

Jud.14:12. will give you thirty *sheets* (marg. or, *shirts*)
13. then shall ye give me thirty *sheets*
Pro.31:24. She maketh *fine linen*,
Isa. 3:23. The glasses, *and the fine linen*,

5468 **סְדָרִים** *s'dāh-reem'*, m. pl.

Job 10:22. without any *order*, and (where) the light

5469 **סַהַר** *sah'-har*, m.

Cant.7: 2(3). Thy navel (is like) a *round* goblet,

5470 **סֹהַר** [*sōh'-har*], m.

Gen39:20. put him into the *prison*, (lit. the house of *the tower*)
— and he was there in the *prison*. (lit. *id.*)
21, 22, 23. the keeper of the *prison*. (lit. *id.*)
22. prisoners that (were) in the *prison*; (lit. *id.*)
40: 3. into the *prison*, (lit. *id.*) the place
5. which (were) bound in the *prison*. (lit. *id.*)

5472 **סוּג** [*soog*].

* KAL.—*Preterite.* *

Ps. 53:3(4). Every one of them *is gone back*:

KAL.—*Future.*

Ps. 80:18(19). *will* not *we go back* from thee:

KAL.—*Participle.* Paül.

Pro.14:14. *The backslider in* heart shall be filled

* NIPHAL.—*Preterite.* *

Ps. 44:18(19). Our heart *is* not *turned* back,
Isa. 42:17. *They shall be turned* back, they shall
50: 5. I was not rebellious, neither *turned away*
Jer. 38:22. *they are turned away* back.

NIPHAL.—*Future.*

Ps. 35: 4. *let them be turned* back and brought
40:14(15). *let them be driven* backward
70: 2(3). *let them be turned* backward,
78:57. *But turned back*, and dealt unfaithfully
129: 5. *and turned* back that hate Zion.

NIPHAL.—*Participle.*

Jer. 46: 5. dismayed (and) *turned away* back?
Zep. 1: 6. them *that are turned back* from the Lord;

5473 **סוּג** [*soog*].

* KAL.—*Participle.* Paül. *

Cant.7: 2(3). an heap of wheat *set about* with lilies.

5509 **סוּג** *soog*, m.

Eze.22:18. (כתיב) the house of Israel is to me become *dross*:

סוּגַר *soo'-gar*, m. 5474

Eze.19: 9. they put him *in ward*

סוֹד *sōhd*, m. 5475

Gen49: 6. come not thou *into their secret*;
Job 15: 8. Hast thou heard *the secret of* God?
19:19. All *my inward* friends (marg. the men of *my secret*) abhorred me:
29: 4. *when the secret of* God (was) upon my tabernacle;
Ps. 25:14. *The secret of* the Lord (is) with them that
55:14(15). We took sweet *counsel* together,
64: 2(3). Hide me *from the secret counsel of* the
83: 3(4). taken crafty *counsel* against thy people,
89: 7(8). to be feared *in the assembly of* the saints,
111: 1. *in the assembly of* the upright,
Pro. 3:32. *his secret* (is) with the righteous.
11:13. A talebearer revealeth *secrets*:
15:22. Without *counsel* purposes are disappointed:
20:19. a talebearer revealeth *secrets*:
25: 9. *and* discover not *a secret* to another: (marg. *the secret of* another)
Jer. 6:11. upon *the assembly of* young men together:
15:17. I sat not *in the assembly of* the mockers,
23:18. who hath stood *in the counsel of* the Lord,
22. if they had stood *in my counsel*,
Eze.13: 9. they shall not be *in the assembly of* my
Am. 3: 7. he revealeth *his secret* unto his servants

סוּחָה *soo-ghāh'*, f. 5478

Isa. 5:25. their carcases (were) *torn* (marg. or, *as dung*) in the midst of the streets.

סוּךְ [*sooch*]. 5480

* KAL.—*Preterite.* *

Ru. 3: 3. Wash thyself therefore, *and anoint thee*,
Dan10: 3. neither *did I anoint myself* at all,

KAL.—*Infinitive.*

Dan10: 3. *neither* did I anoint myself *at all*, (lit. *and anointing* I did not, &c.)

KAL.—*Future.*

Deu28:40. *thou shalt* not *anoint* (thyself) with the oil;
2Sa.14: 2. *anoint* not *thyself* with oil,
2Ch28:15. gave them to eat and to drink, *and anointed them*,
Eze.16: 9. *and I anointed thee* with oil.
Mic. 6:15. *thou shalt* not *anoint thee* with oil;

* HIPHIL.—*Future.* *

2Sa.12:20. and washed, *and anointed* (himself),

סוּמְפּוֹנְיָה *soom-pōh-n'yāh'*, Ch. f. 5481

Dan.3: 5. psaltery, *dulcimer*, (marg. *symphony*, or, *singing*) and all kinds of
10, 15. psaltery, *and dulcimer*, and all kinds

סוּס *soos*, m. 5483

Gen47:17. gave them bread (in exchange) *for horses*,
49:17. an adder in the path, that biteth the *horse* heels,
Ex. 9: 3. *upon the horses*, upon the asses,
14: 9. all *the horses* (and) chariots of Pharaoh,
23. (even) all Pharaoh's *horses*, his chariots, and his horsemen.
15: 1, 21. *the horse* and his rider hath he thrown into the sea.
19. For *the horse of* Pharaoh went in
Deu11: 4. *unto their horses*, and to their chariots;
17:16. he shall not multiply *horses* to himself,
— to the end that he should multiply *horses*:
20: 1. and seest *horses*, and chariots,
Jos. 11: 4. *with horses* and chariots very many.
6. thou shalt hough *their horses*,
9. he houghed *their horses*,
Jud. 5:22. Then were the *horse*hoofs broken

2Sa.15: 1. Absalom prepared him chariots *and horses*,
1K. 4:26(5:6). forty thousand stalls of *horses*
28(-:8). Barley also and straw *for the horses*
10:25. and armour, and spices, *horses*, and mules,
28. Solomon had *horses* brought out of Egypt,
29. *and an horse* for an hundred and fifty:
18: 5. find grass to save *the horses* and mules alive,
20: 1. *and horses*, and chariots:
20. the king of Syria escaped on *an horse*
21. and smote *the horses* and chariots,
25. thou hast lost, *horse for horse*,
22: 4. my people as thy people, *my horses as thy horses*.
2K. 2:11. a chariot of fire, *and horses of* fire,
3: 7. my people as thy people, (and) *my horses as thy horses*.
5: 9. Naaman came *with his horses* and with his chariot,
6:14. sent he thither *horses*, and chariots,
15. compassed the city both *with horses* and chariots.
17. and, behold, the mountain (was) full of *horses*
7: 6. a noise of chariots, and a noise of *horses*,
7. left their tents, and *their horses*,
10. *horses* tied, and asses tied,
13. five of *the horses* that remain,
14. They took therefore two chariot *horses*;
9:18. there went one on *horse*back to meet him,
19. he sent out a second on *horse*back,
33. sprinkled on the wall, and on *the horses*:
10: 2. (there are) with you chariots *and horses*,
11:16. by the way by the which *the horses* came
14:20. And they brought him on *horses*:
18:23. I will deliver thee two thousand *horses*,
23:11. he took away *the horses*
2Ch 1:16. Solomon had *horses* brought out of Egypt,
17. *and an horse* for an hundred and fifty:
9:24. and spices, *horses*, and mules,
25. Solomon had four thousand stalls for *horses*
28. brought unto Solomon *horses* out of Egypt,
23:15. come to the entering of the *horse* gate
25:28. they brought him upon *horses*,
Ezr. 2:66. *Their horses* (were) seven hundred thirty and six;
Neh. 3:28. From above the *horse* gate repaired the priests,
7:68. *Their horses*, seven hundred thirty and six:
Est. 6: 8. *and the horse* that the king rideth upon,
9. let this apparel *and horse* be delivered
— bring him *on horse*back through the street
10. take the apparel and *the horse*, as thou hast
11. Then took Haman the apparel and *the horse*,
8:10. sent letters by posts *on horse*back,
Job 39:18. she scorneth *the horse* and his rider.
19. Hast thou given *the horse* strength?
Ps. 20: 7(8). Some (trust) in chariots, and some *in horses*:
32: 9. Be ye not *as the horse*, (or) as the mule,
33:17. *An horse* (is) a vain thing for safety:
76: 6(7). both the chariot *and horse* are cast into
147:10. He delighteth not in the strength of *the horse*:
Pro.21:31. *The horse* (is) prepared against the day
26: 3. A whip *for the horse*,
Ecc.10: 7. I have seen servants upon *horses*,
Isa. 2: 7. their land is also full of *horses*,
5:28. *their horses'* hoofs shall be counted like flint,
30:16. we will flee upon *horses*;
31: 1. stay on *horses*, and trust in chariots,
3. *and their horses* flesh, and not spirit.
36: 8. I will give thee two thousand *horses*,
38:14. *Like a crane* (or) a swallow, so did I chatter:
43:17. bringeth forth the chariot *and horse*,
63:13. *as an horse* in the wilderness,
66:20. out of all nations *upon horses*,
Jer. 4:13. *his horses* are swifter than eagles.
5: 8. They were (as) fed *horses* in the morning:
6:23. they ride upon *horses*,
8: 6. *as the horse* rusheth into the battle.
7. (כתיב) *and the crane* and the swallow observe the time
16. The snorting of *his horses* was heard from Dan:
12: 5. how canst thou contend with *horses*?
17:25 & 22:4. riding in chariots *and on horses*,
31:40. unto the corner of the *horse* gate

Jer. 46: 4. Harness *the horses*; and get up, ye horsemen,
9. Come up, ye *horses*; and rage, ye chariots;
50:37. A sword (is) upon *their horses*,
42. they shall ride upon *horses*,
51:21. break in pieces *the horse* and his rider;
27. cause *the horses* to come up
Eze.17:15. that they might give him *horses*
23: 6, 12. horsemen riding upon *horses*.
20. whose issue (is like) the issue of *horses*.
23. all of them riding upon *horses*.
26: 7. *with horses*, and with chariots,
10. By reason of the abundance of *his horses*
11. With the hoofs of *his horses* shall he tread
27:14. with *horses* and horsemen and mules.
38: 4. all thine army, *horses* and horsemen,
15. all of them riding upon *horses*,
39:20. *horses* and chariots, with mighty men,
Hos. 1: 7. nor by battle, *by horses*, nor by horsemen.
14: 3(4). we will not ride upon *horses*:
Joel 2: 4. as the appearance of *horses*;
Am. 2:15. neither shall he that rideth *the horse*
4:10. and have taken away *your horses*;
6:12. Shall *horses* run upon the rock?
Mic. 5:10(9). I will cut off *thy horses*
Nah. 3: 2. *and of the* pransing *horses*,
Hab. 1: 8. *Their horses* also are swifter than the
3: 8. that thou didst ride upon *thine horses*
15. walk through the sea with *thine horses*,
Hag. 2:22. *the horses* and their riders shall come
Zec. 1: 8. behold a man riding upon *a* red *horse*,
— and behind him (were there) red *horses*,
6: 2. In the first chariot (were) red *horses*; and in the second chariot black *horses*;
3. And in the third chariot white *horses*; and in the fourth chariot grisled and bay *horses*.
6. *The* black *horses* which (are) therein go
9:10. the chariot from Ephraim, *and the horse*
10: 3. made them *as* his goodly *horse*
5. the riders on *horses* shall be confounded.
12: 4. will smite every *horse* with astonishment,
— smite every *horse of* the people with
14:15. so shall be the plague of *the horse*,
20. that day shall there be upon the bells of *the horses*,

סוּסָה [*soo-sāh'*], f. 5484

Cant.1: 9. *to a company of horses* in Pharaoh's

סוֹף *sōhph*, m. 5490

2Ch 20:16. ye shall find them *at the end of* the brook,
Ecc. 3:11. maketh from the beginning to *the end*.
7: 2. that (is) *the end of* all men;
12:13. Let us hear *the conclusion of* the whole
Joel 2:20. *and his hinder part* toward the utmost sea,

סוֹף *sōhph*, Ch. m. 5491

Dan 4:11(8). sight thereof *to the end of* all the earth:
22(19). and thy dominion *to the end of* the
6:26(27). his dominion (shall be even) unto *the end*.
7:26. consume and to destroy (it) unto *the end*.
28. Hitherto (is) *the end* of the matter.

סוּף [*sooph*]. 5486

* KAL.—*Preterite.* *

Ps. 73:19. *they are utterly* consumed (lit. *they are at an end* they are consumed) with terrors.
Am. 3:15. *and* the great houses *shall have an end*,

KAL.—*Future.*

Est. 9:28. nor the memorial of them *perish* (marg. *be ended*) from their seed.
Isa. 66:17. *shall be consumed* together, saith the Lord.

* HIPHIL.—*Future.* *

Jer. 8:13. *I will* surely *consume them*, saith the Lord:
Zep. 1: 2. *I will* utterly *consume* all (things) (marg. By taking away *I will make an end*)
3. *I will consume* man and beast; *I will consume* the fowls of the heaven,

5487 ## סוּף [sooph], Ch.

* P'AL.—*Preterite.* *

Dan 4:33(30). The same hour *was* the thing *fulfilled*

* APHEL.—*Future.* *

Dan 2:44. *and consume* all these kingdoms,

5488 ## סוּף *sooph*, m.

Ex. 2: 3. laid (it) *in the flags* by the river's brink.
5. she saw the ark among *the flags*,
10:19. cast them into the *Red* sea; (lit. sea of *Suph*, or, of *weeds*)
13:18. the wilderness of the *Red* sea:
15: 4. are drowned in the *Red* sea.
22. Moses brought Israel from the *Red* sea,
23:31. set thy bounds from the *Red* sea
Nu. 14:25. by the way of the *Red* sea.
21: 4. Hor by the way of the *Red* sea,
33:10. encamped by the *Red* sea.
11. removed from the *Red* sea,
Deu 1: 1. over against the *Red* (sea), (marg. *Zuph*)
40 & 2:1. by the way of the *Red* sea.
11: 4. the water of the *Red* sea to overflow
Jos. 2:10. dried up the water of the *Red* sea
4:23. your God did to the *Red* sea,
24: 6. chariots and horsemen unto the *Red* sea.
Jud. 11:16. through the wilderness unto the *Red* sea,
1K. 9:26. on the shore of the *Red* sea,
Neh. 9: 9. heardest their cry by the *Red* sea;
Ps. 106: 7. provoked (him) at the sea, (even) at the *Red* sea.
9. He rebuked the *Red* sea also,
22. terrible things by the *Red* sea.
136:13. him which divided the *Red* sea
15. Pharaoh and his host in the *Red* sea:
Isa. 19: 6. the reeds and *flags* shall wither.
Jer. 49:21. noise thereof was heard in the *Red* sea.
Jon. 2: 5(6). *the weeds* were wrapped about my

5492 ## סוּפָה *soo-phāh'*, f.

Job 21:18. as chaff that *the storm* carrieth away.
27:20. *a tempest* stealeth him away
37: 9. Out of the south cometh *the whirlwind:*
Ps. 83:15(16). *and* make them afraid *with thy storm.*
Pro. 1:27. your destruction cometh *as a whirlwind;*
10:25. As *the whirlwind* passeth,
Isa. 5:28. their wheels *like a whirlwind:*
17:13. like a rolling thing before *the whirlwind.*
21: 1. *As whirlwinds* in the south
29: 6. with *storm* and tempest,
66:15. *and* with his chariots *like a whirlwind,*
Jer. 4:13. *and* his chariots (shall be) *as a whirlwind:*
Hos. 8: 7. *and* they shall reap *the whirlwind:*
Am. 1:14. a tempest in the day of *the whirlwind:*
Nah. 1: 3. the Lord (hath) his way *in the whirlwind*

5493 ## סוּר *soor.*

* KAL.—*Preterite.* *

Ex. 3: 4. when the Lord saw that *he turned aside*
8:11(7). *And* the frogs *shall depart* from thee,
29(25). *that* the swarms (of flies) *may depart*
32: 8. *They have turned aside* quickly
Lev. 13:58. *if* the plague *be departed* from them,
Nu. 12:10. the cloud *departed* from off the tabernacle;
14: 9. their defence *is departed* from them,
Deu 9:12. *they are* quickly *turned aside* out of the way
16. *ye had turned aside* quickly out of the way
11:16. *and ye turn aside*, and serve other gods,
28. *but turn aside* out of the way
31:29. utterly corrupt (yourselves), *and turn aside*
Jud. 2:17. *they turned* quickly out of the way
16:17. *then* my strength *will go* from me,
20. he wist not that the Lord *was departed*
1Sa. 6:12. *turned* not *aside* (to) the right hand
15:32. Surely the bitterness of death *is past.* (lit. *turned aside*)
16:14. the Spirit of the Lord *departed* from Saul,
23. *and* the evil spirit *departed* from him.
18:12. was with him, and *was departed* from Saul.
22:14. the king's son in law, *and goeth* at thy
28:15. God *is departed* from me,
1Sa. 28:16. seeing the Lord *is departed* from thee,
1K. 15: 5. *turned* not *aside* from any (thing)
14. the high places *were* not *removed:*
20:39. behold, a man *turned aside*,
22:43. *he turned* not *aside* from it,
—(44). the high places *were* not *taken away;*
2K. 3: 3. *he departed* not therefrom.
10:29. Jehu *departed* not from after them,
31. *he departed* not from the sins of Jeroboam,
12: 3(4). the high places *were* not *taken away:*
13: 2. *he departed* not therefrom.
6. *they departed* not from the sins of
11. *he departed* not from all the sins of Jeroboam
14: 4. the high places *were* not *taken away:*
24. *he departed* not from all the sins of Jeroboam
15: 4, 35. the high places *were* not *removed:*
9, 24, 28. *he departed* not from the sins of Jeroboam
18. *he departed* not all his days from
17:22. *they departed* not from them;
18: 6. he clave to the Lord, (and) *departed* not
22: 2. *turned* not *aside* to the right hand or to the
2Ch 8:15. *they departed* not from the commandment
15:17. the high places *were* not *taken away*
20:10. *they turned* from them, and destroyed them not;
32. and *departed* not from it,
33. the high places *were* not *taken away:*
25:27. time that Amaziah *did turn away* from
34: 2. *declined* (neither) to the right hand, nor
33. *they departed* not from following the Lord,
Neh 9:19. the pillar of the cloud *departed* not from
Job 34:27. *they turned back* from him, and would not
Ps. 14: 3. *They are* all *gone aside*,
119:102. *I have* not *departed* from thy judgments:
Isa. 6: 7. *and* thine iniquity *is taken away*,
11:13. The envy *also* of Ephraim *shall depart*,
14:25. *then shall* his yoke *depart* from off them,
59:15. *and he* (that) *departeth* from evil maketh
Jer. 5:23. *they are revolted* and gone.
Eze. 6: 9. their whorish heart, which *hath departed*
16:42. *and* my jealousy *shall depart* from thee,
Hos. 4:18. Their drink *is sour:* (marg. *gone*)
Am. 6: 7. *and* the banquet of them that stretched themselves *shall be removed.*
Mal. 2: 8. *ye are departed* out of the way;
3: 7. *ye are gone away* from mine ordinances.

KAL.—*Infinitive.*

Deu 17:20. *that he turn* not *aside* from the commandment.
Jos. 23: 6. *that ye turn* not *aside* therefrom
2Sa. 2:21. But Asahel would not *turn aside*
23. Howbeit he refused *to turn aside:*
2Ch 35:15. they might not *depart* from their service;
Job 28:28. *and to depart* from evil (is) understanding.
Pro. 13:14. *to depart* from the snares of death.
19. abomination to fools *to depart* from evil.
14:27. *to depart* from the snares of death.
15:24. that *he may depart* from hell beneath.
16: 6. by the fear of the Lord (men) *depart* from
17. The highway of the upright (is) *to depart* from evil:
Isa. 7:17. from the day that Ephraim *departed*
Jer. 32:40. that *they shall* not *depart* from me.
Dan 9: 5. *even by departing* from thy precepts
11. transgressed thy law, *even by departing*,

KAL.—*Imperative.*

Gen 19: 2. my lords, *turn in*, I pray you,
Nu. 16:26. *Depart*, I pray you, from the tents of
Jud. 4:18. *Turn in*, my lord, *turn in* to me; fear not.
Ru. 4: 1. Ho, such a one! *turn aside*, sit down here.
1Sa. 15: 6. *depart*, get you down from among the Amalekites,
2Sa. 2:22. *Turn thee aside* from following me:
Job 21:14. they say unto God, *Depart* from us;
22:17. Which said unto God, *Depart* from us:
Ps. 6: 8(9). *Depart* from me, all ye workers of
34:14(15) & 37:27. *Depart* from evil, and do good;
119:115. *Depart* from me, ye evildoers:
139:19. *depart* from me therefore, ye bloody men.
Pro. 3: 7. fear the Lord, *and depart* from evil.
Isa. 30:11. *Get you* out of the way,
52:11. *Depart ye, depart ye*, go ye out from
Lam. 4:15. They cried unto them, *Depart ye;* (it is) unclean; *depart, depart*, touch not:

KAL.—*Future.*

Gen19: 3. *and they turned in* unto him,
49:10. The sceptre *shall* not *depart* from Judah,
Ex. 3: 3. *I will* now *turn aside*, and see this great
25:15. *they shall* not *be taken* from it.
Deu 2:27. *I will* neither *turn* unto the right hand
4: 9. lest *they depart* from thy heart all the
5:32(29). *ye shall* not *turn aside* to the right
17:11. *thou shalt* not *decline* from the sentence
17. that his heart *turn* not *away:*
28:14. *thou shalt* not *go aside* from any of the
Jos. 1: 7. *turn* not from it (to) the right hand or
Jud. 4:18. *when he had turned in* unto her
14: 8. *and he turned aside* to see the carcase
16:19. *and* his strength *went* from him.
18: 3. *and they turned in* thither, and said unto
15. *And they turned* thitherward, and came
19:11. *and let us turn in* into this city of the
12. *We will* not *turn aside* hither into the city
15. *And they turned aside* thither, to go in
20: 8. neither *will we* any (of us) *turn* into his
Ru. 4: 1. *And he turned aside*, and sat down.
1Sa. 6: 3. why his hand *is* not *removed* from you.
12:20. *turn* not *aside* from following the Lord,
21. *turn ye* not *aside:* for (then)
15: 6. *So* the Kenites *departed* from among
2Sa. 7:15. my mercy *shall* not *depart away* from
12:10. the sword *shall* never *depart* from thine
22:23. his statutes, *I did* not *depart* from them.
1K. 22:32. *And they turned aside* to fight against
2K. 4: 8. *he turned in* thither to eat bread.
10. *he shall turn in* thither.
11. *and he turned* into the chamber,
Job 15:30. *He shall* not *depart* out of darkness;
— *and* by the breath of his mouth *shall he go away.*
Ps. 101: 4. A froward heart *shall depart* from me:
Pro. 5: 7. *depart* not from the words of my mouth.
9: 4, 16. Whoso (is) simple, *let him turn in*
22: 6. when he is old, *he will* not *depart* from it.
27:22. *will* not his foolishness *depart* from him.
Isa. 10:27. his burden *shall be taken away*
14:25. burden *depart* from off their shoulders.
Jer. 15: 5. who *shall go aside* to ask how thou doest?
17: 5. and whose heart *departeth* from the Lord.
Hos. 7:14. *they rebel* against me.
Zec.10:11. the sceptre of Egypt *shall depart away.*

KAL.—*Participle.* Poel.

Job 1: 1. one that feared God, *and eschewed* (lit. *turned* from) evil.
8. one that feareth God, *and escheweth* evil?
2: 3. one that feareth God, *and escheweth* evil?
Pro.11:22. (so is) a fair woman *which is without* (marg. *departeth from*) discretion.
14:16. A wise (man) feareth, *and departeth* from
Jer. 6:28. They (are) all *grievous* revolters,

KAL.—*Participle.* Paül.

Isa. 49:21. a captive, *and removing to and fro?*
Jer. 17:13. *and they that depart from me* shall be

* POLEL.—*Preterite.* *

Lam.3:11. *He hath turned aside* my ways,

* HIPHIL.—*Preterite.* *

Ex. 23:25. *and I will take* sickness *away*
33:23. *And I will take away* mine hand,
Lev. 1:16. *And he shall pluck away* his crop
Deu 7:15. *And* the Lord *will take away*
21:13. *And she shall put* (lit. *remove*) the raiment of her captivity from off her,
Jos. 11:15. *he left* nothing *undone* (marg. *removed*) of all that the Lord commanded
1Sa.17:26. *and taketh away* the reproach from Israel?
46. I will smite thee, *and take* thine head
28: 3. Saul *had put away* those that had familiar
2Sa. 7:15. as *I took* (it) from Saul, whom *I put away*
1K. 2:31. *that thou mayest take away* the innocent
2K. 17:23. the Lord *removed* Israel out of his sight,
18: 4. He *removed* the high places,
22. whose altars Hezekiah *hath taken away*,
23:19. Josiah *took away*, and did to them
27. as *I have removed* Israel,
1Ch 13:13. David *brought* (marg. *removed*) not the ark (home) to himself
17:13. as *I took* (it) from (him) that was before
2Ch 15:16. *he removed her* from (being) queen,
2Ch 17: 6. moreover he *took away* the high places
30:14. *and* all the altars for incense *took they away*,
32:12. *Hath* not the same Hezekiah *taken away*
Job 27: 2. (who) *hath taken away* my judgment;
34: 5. God *hath taken away* my judgment.
Ps. 66:20. which *hath* not *turned away* my prayer,
81: 6(7). *I removed* his shoulder from the
Isa. 18: 5. and *take away* (and) cut down the
31: 2. *will* not *call back* (marg. *remove*) his
36: 7. whose altars Hezekiah *hath taken away*,
Eze.11:18. *and they shall take away* all the detestable
19. *and I will take* the stony heart out of
26:16. *and lay away* their robes,
36:26. *and I will take away* the stony heart
Dan11:31. *and shall take away* the daily (sacrifice)
Hos. 2:17(19). *For I will take away* the names of
Zep. 3:15. The Lord *hath taken away* thy judgments,
Zec. 9: 7. *And I will take away* his blood out of his

HIPHIL.—*Infinitive.*

Gen30:32. all thy flock to day, *removing* from thence
48:17. he held up his father's hand, *to remove* it
Jos. 7:13. until *ye take away* the accursed thing
2Sa. 5: 6. Except *thou take away* the blind and the lame,
6:10. David would not *remove* the ark
2K. 6:32. hath sent *to take away* mine head?
24: 3. *to remove* (them) out of his sight,
2Ch 33: 8. will I any more *remove* the foot of Israel
Est. 4: 4. *and to take away* his sackcloth from him:
Job 33:17. *That he may withdraw* man (from his) purpose,
Isa. 5: 5. *I will* (lit. *to*) *take away* the hedge thereof,
27: 9. this (is) all the fruit *to take away* his sin;
Jer. 32:31. *that I should remove it* from before my face,

HIPHIL.—*Imperative.*

Gen35: 2. *Put away* the strange gods that (are) among you,
Jos. 24:14. and *put away* the gods which your fathers served
23. *put away*, (said he), the strange gods
1Sa. 1:14. *put away* thy wine from thee.
7: 3. *put away* the strange gods
1K. 20:24. *Take* the kings *away*,
Ps. 39:10(11). *Remove* thy stroke *away* from me:
119:29. *Remove* from me the way of lying:
Pro. 4:24. *Put away* from thee a froward mouth,
27. *remove* thy foot from evil.
Ecc.11:10. *Therefore remove* sorrow from thy heart,
Isa. 1:16. *put away* the evil of your doings
Jer. 4: 4. *and take away* the foreskins of your heart,
5:10. *take away* her battlements; for they (are) not the Lord's.
Eze.21:26(31). *Remove* the diadem, and take off the crown:
45: 9. *remove* violence and spoil,
Am. 5:23. *Take thou away* from me the noise of thy songs;
Zec. 3: 4. *Take away* the filthy garments from him.

HIPHIL.—*Future.*

Gen 8:13. *and* Noah *removed* the covering of the ark,
30:35. *And he removed* that day the he goats
38:14. *And she put* her widow's garments *off* from her,
19. *and laid by* her vail from her,
41:42. *And* Pharaoh *took off* his ring from his
Ex. 8: 8(4). Intreat the Lord, *that he may take away*
31(27). *and he removed* the swarms (of flies)
10:17. intreat the Lord your God, *that he may take away*
14:25. *And took off* their chariot wheels,
34:34. *he took* the vail *off*, until he came out.
Lev. 3: 4, 10, 15. with the kidneys, *it shall he take away.*
9. *it shall he take off* hard by the backbone;
4: 9. with the kidneys, *it shall he take away*,
31, 35. *he shall take away* all the fat thereof,
7: 4. with the kidneys, *it shall he take away:*
Nu. 21: 7. *that he take away* the serpents
Deu 7: 4. *they will turn away* thy son from following
Jud. 9:29. *then would I remove* Abimelech.
10:16. *And they put away* the strange gods
1Sa. 7: 4. *Then* the children of Israel *did put away*
17:39. *And* David *put them* off him.
18:13. *Therefore* Saul *removed him* from him,

2Sa. 4: 7. *and beheaded him*, (lit. *and removed* his head)
16: 9. let me go over, I pray thee, and *take off* his head.
1K. 15:12. *and removed* all the idols that his fathers
13. Maachah his mother, *even her he removed*
20:41. *and took* the ashes *away* from his face;
2K. 3: 2. *for he put away* the image of Baal
16:17. *and removed* the laver from off them;
17:18. angry with Israel, *and removed them*
23:27. *I will remove* Judah also out of my sight,
1Ch 17:13. *I will* not *take* my mercy *away* from him,
2Ch 14: 3(2). *For he took away* the altars of the strange (gods),
5(4). *Also he took away* out of all the cities
30: 9. *will* not *turn away* (his) face from you,
14. they arose *and took away* the altars
33:15. *And he took away* the strange gods,
34:33. *And* Josiah *took away* all the abominations
35:12. *And they removed* the burnt offerings,
36: 3. *And* the king of Egypt *put him down* (marg. *removed him*) at Jerusalem,
Est. 3:10. *And* the king *took* his ring from his hand,
8: 2. *And* the king *took off* his ring,
Job 9:34. *Let him take* his rod *away* from me,
19: 9. *and taken* the crown (from) my head.
27: 5. *I will* not *remove* mine integrity from me.
34:20. *and* the mighty *shall be taken away*
Ps. 18:22(23). *I did* not *put away* his statutes from me.
Isa. 1:25. *and take away* all thy tin:
3:18. In that day the Lord *will take away*
5:23. *take away* the righteousness of the righteous
10:13. *and I have removed* the bounds of the people,
25: 8. the rebuke of his people *shall he take away*
58: 9. If *thou take away* from the midst of thee
Jer. 4: 1. if *thou wilt put away* thine abominations
Eze. 16:50. *therefore I took* them *away* as I saw (good).
23:25. *they shall take away* thy nose and thine ears;
Hos. 2: 2(4). *let her therefore put away* her whoredoms
Zep. 3:11. *I will take away* out of the midst of thee

* HIPHIL.—*Participle.* *

Job 12:20. *He removeth away* the speech of the trusty,
24. *He taketh away* the heart of the chief of
Pro. 28: 9. *He that turneth away* his ear from hearing
Isa. 3: 1. *doth take away* from Jerusalem

* HOPHAL.—*Preterite.* *

Lev. 4:31. as the fat *is taken away*
Dan 12:11. the daily (sacrifice) *shall be taken away*,

HOPHAL.—*Future.*

Lev. 4:35. as the fat of the lamb *is taken away*

HOPHAL.—*Participle.*

1Sa. 21: 6(7). but the shewbread, *that was taken from* before
Isa. 17: 1. Damascus *is taken away* from (being) a city,

5494 סוּר [*soor*], m.

Jer. 2:21. how then art thou turned into the *degenerate* plant

---

5496 סוּת [*sooth*].

* HIPHIL.—*Preterite.* *

1Sa. 26:19. If the Lord *have stirred thee up* against me,
1K. 21:25. whom Jezebel his wife *stirred up*. (marg. or, *incited*)
Job 36:16. Even so *would he have removed thee*
Jer. 38:22. Thy friends *have set thee on*,

HIPHIL.—*Future.*

Deu 13: 6(7). *entice thee* secretly,
Jos. 15:18. *that she moved him* to ask of her father a
Jud. 1:14. *that she moved him* to ask of her father a
2Sa. 24: 1. *and he moved* David against them
2K. 18:32. Hezekiah, when *he persuadeth* (marg. or, *deceiveth*) you,
1Ch 21: 1. *and provoked* David to number Israel.
2Ch 18: 2. *and persuaded him* to go up (with him)
31. *and* God *moved them* (to depart) from him.
32:15. Hezekiah deceive you, nor *persuade* you
Job 2: 3. *although thou movedst me* against him,
Job 36:18. (beware) lest *he take thee away*
Isa. 36:18. (Beware) lest Hezekiah *persuade* you,

HIPHIL.—*Participle.*

2Ch 32:11. Doth not Hezekiah *persuade* you
Jer. 43: 3. Baruch the son of Neriah *setteth* thee *on*

סוּת [*sooth*], m. 5497

Gen 49:11. washed his garments in wine, and *his clothes* in

סָחַב [*sāh-ghav'*]. 5498

* KAL.—*Preterite.* *

2Sa. 17:13. *and we will draw* it into the river,

KAL.—*Infinitive.*

Jer. 15: 3. the sword to slay, and the dogs *to tear*,
22:19. the burial of an ass, *drawn* and cast forth

KAL.—*Future.*

Jer. 49:20 & 50:45. Surely the least of the flock *shall draw them out*:

סְחָבוֹת *s'ghāh-vōhth'*, f. pl. 5499

Jer. 38:11. took thence old *cast clouts* and old rotten
12. Put now (these) old *cast clouts*

סָחָה [*sāh-ghāh'*]. 5500

* PIEL.—*Preterite.* *

Eze. 26: 4. *I will also scrape* her dust from her,

סְחִי *s'ghee*, m. 5501

Lam. 3:45. Thou hast made us (as) *the offscouring*

סָחִישׁ *sāh-gheesh'*, m. 7823

2K. 19:29. the second year *that which springeth of the same*;

סָחַף [*sāh-ghaph'*]. 5502

* KAL.—*Participle.* Poel. *

Pro. 28: 3. A poor man that oppresseth the poor (is like) a *sweeping* rain

* NIPHAL.—*Preterite.* *

Jer. 46:15. Why *are* thy valiant (men) *swept away*?

סָחַר [*sāh-ghar'*]. 5503

* KAL.—*Preterite.* *

Gen 34:10. dwell *and trade ye therein*,
Jer. 14:18. both the prophet and the priest *go about* (marg. or, *make merchandise*) into a land

KAL.—*Future.*

Gen 34:21. let them dwell in the land, *and trade*
42:34. and *ye shall traffick* in the land.

KAL.—*Participle.* Poel.

Gen 23:16. current (money) *with the merchant*.
37:28. there passed by Midianites *merchantmen*;
1K. 10:28. the king's *merchants* received the linen yarn
2Ch 1:16. the king's *merchants* received the linen yarn
9:14. Beside (that which) chapmen *and merchants* brought.
Pro. 31:14. She is like *the merchants'* ships;
Isa. 23: 2. thou whom *the merchants of* Zidon
8. the crowning (city), *whose merchants* (are) princes,
47:15. *thy merchants*, from thy youth:
Eze. 27:12. Tarshish (was) *thy merchant*
16. Syria (was) *thy merchant*
18. Damascus (was) *thy merchant*

Eze.27:21. they *occupied with* thee (marg. (were) *the merchants of* thy hand) in lambs, and rams, and goats: in these (were they) *thy merchants.*
36. *The merchants* among the people shall hiss
38:13. *and the merchants of* Tarshish,

* PILPEL.—*Preterite.* *

Ps. 38:10(11). My heart *panteth*, my strength faileth

5505 סָחָר [*sāh-ghāhr'*], m.

Pro. 3:14. *than the merchandise of* silver,
Isa. 23: 3. she is *a mart of* nations.
45:14. *and merchandise of* Ethiopia and of the Sabeans,

5504 סַחַר [*sah'-ghar*], m.

Pro. 3:14. *the merchandise of it* (is) better
31:18. She perceiveth that *her merchandise* (is) good:
Isa. 23:18. *her merchandise* and her hire shall be
— *her merchandise* shall be for them that

5506 סְחֹרָה [*s'ghōh-rāh'*], f.

Eze.27:15. many isles (were) *the merchandise of* thine

5507 סֹחֵרָה *sōh-ghēh-rāh'*, f.

Ps. 91: 4. his truth (shall be thy) shield *and buckler.*

5508 סֹחֶרֶת [*sōh-gheh'-reth*], f.

Est. 1: 6. a pavement of red, and blue, and white, *and black, marble.*

7750 סֵטִים *sēh-teem'*, m. pl.

Ps.101: 3. I hate the work of *them that turn aside;*

5509 סִיג *seeg*, m.

Ps.119:119. puttest away all the wicked of the earth (like) *dross:*
Pro.25: 4. Take away *the dross* from the silver,
26:23. a potsherd covered with silver *dross.*
Isa. 1:22. Thy silver is become *dross,*
25. purely purge away *thy dross,*
Eze.22:18. the house of Israel is to me become *dross:*
— they are (even) *the dross* (marg. *drosses*) of silver.
19. ye are all become *dross,*

5510 סִיוָן *see-vāhn'*, m.

Est. 8: 9. that (is), the month *Sivan,*

5483 סִיס *sees*, m.

Jer. 8: 7. *and the crane* and the swallow observe the

5481 סִיפֹּנְיָה *see-phōh-n'yāh'*, Ch. f.

Dan. 3:10. (כתיב) psaltery, *and dulcimer*, and all kinds

5518 סִיר *seer*, com.

Ex. 16: 3. when we sat by *the* flesh *pots,*
27: 3. thou shalt make *his pans* to receive his
38: 3. *the pots*, and the shovels, and the basons,
1K. 7:45. *the pots*, and the shovels, and the basons:
2K. 4:38. said unto his servant, Set on *the* great *pot,*
39. shred (them) into *the pot of* pottage:
40. (there is) death *in the pot.*
41. bring meal. And he cast (it) into *the pot;*
— there was no harm *in the pot.*
25:14. *the pots*, and the shovels, and the snuffers,
2Ch 4:11. Huram made *the pots*, and the shovels,
2Ch 4:16. *The pots* also, and the shovels,
35:13. holy (offerings) sod they *in pots,*
Job 41:31(23). He maketh the deep to boil *like a pot:*
Ps. 58: 9(10). Before *your pots* can feel the thorns,
60: 8(10) & 108:9(10). Moab (is) my wash*pot;*
Ecc. 7: 6. the crackling of thorns under *a pot,*
Jer. 1:13. I said, I see *a* seething *pot;*
52:18. *The caldrons* also, and the shovels,
19. *the caldrons*, and the candlesticks,
Eze.11: 3, 7. this (city is) *the caldron,*
11. This (city) shall not be *your caldron*, (lit. be *for a caldron* to you)
24: 3. Thus saith the Lord God; Set on *a pot,*
6. city, to *the pot* whose scum (is) therein,
Mic. 3: 3. chop them in pieces, as *for the pot,*
Zec.14:20. *the pots* in the Lord's house shall be like
21. every *pot* in Jerusalem and in Judah shall be holiness

סִיר [*seer*], com. 5518

Ecc. 7: 6. as the crackling of *thorns* under a pot,
Isa. 34:13. *thorns* shall come up in her palaces,
Hos. 2: 6(8). I will hedge up thy way *with thorns,*
Am. 4: 2. your posterity *with* fish*hooks.*
Nah. 1:10. (they be) folden together (as) *thorns,*

סָךְ *sāhch*, m. 5519

Ps. 42: 4(5). for I had gone *with the multitude,*

סֹךְ [*sōhch*], m. 5520

Ps. 10: 9. lieth in wait secretly as a lion *in his den:*
27: 5. he shall hide me *in his pavilion:*
76: 2(3). In Salem also is *his tabernacle,*
Jer. 25:38. He hath forsaken *his covert,*

סֻכָּה *sook-kāh'*, f. 5521

Gen33:17. made *booths* for his cattle:
— place is called *Succoth.* (marg. i. e. *Booths*)
Lev.23:34. (shall be) the feast of *tabernacles*
42. Ye shall dwell *in booths* seven days; all that are Israelites born shall dwell *in booths:*
43. the children of Israel to dwell *in booths,*
Deu16:13. Thou shalt observe the feast of *tabernacles*
16. and in the feast of *tabernacles:*
31:10. of release, in the feast of *tabernacles,*
2Sa.11:11. ark, and Israel, and Judah, abide *in tents,*
22:12. he made darkness *pavilions* round about
1K. 20:12. the kings *in the pavilions*, (marg. *tents*)
16. drinking himself drunk *in the pavilions,*
2Ch 8:13. and in the feast of *tabernacles.*
Ezr. 3: 4. They kept also the feast of *tabernacles,*
Neh. 8:14. children of Israel should dwell *in booths*
15. branches of thick trees, to make *booths,*
16. made themselves *booths,*
17. that were come again out of the captivity made *booths*, and sat *under the booths:*
Job 27:18. *and as a booth* (that) the keeper maketh.
36:29. (or) the noise of *his tabernacle?*
38:40. they couch in (their) dens, (and) abide *in the covert*
Ps. 18:11(12). *his pavilion* round about him (were)
31:20(21). shalt keep them secretly *in a pavilion*
Isa. 1: 8. the daughter of Zion is left *as a cottage*
4: 6. *And* there shall be *a tabernacle* for a
Am. 9:11. will I raise up *the tabernacle of* David
Jon. 4: 5. and there made him *a booth*, and sat
Zec.14:16, 18, 19. to keep the feast of *tabernacles.*

סִכּוּת *sik-kooth'*, f. 5522

Am. 5:26. ye have borne *the tabernacle of* your Moloch (marg. or, *Siccuth* your king)

סָכַךְ [*sāh-chach'*]. 5526

* KAL.—*Preterite.* *

Ex. 40: 3. *and cover* the ark with the vail.
Ps.140: 7(8). *thou hast covered* my head in the day

Lam.3:43. *Thou hast covered* with anger, and
44. *Thou hast covered* thyself with a cloud,

KAL.—*Future.*

1K. 8: 7. *and* the cherubims *covered* the ark
Job 40:22. The shady trees *cover him*
Ps.139:13. *thou hast covered me* in my mother's

KAL.—*Participle.* Poel.

Ex. 25:20. *covering* the mercy seat with their wings,
37: 9. (and) *covered* with their wings over the
1Ch28:18. *and covered* the ark of the covenant
Eze.28:14. (art) the anointed cherub *that covereth;*
16. I will destroy thee, O *covering* cherub,
Nah. 2: 5(6). *the defence* (marg. *covering*) shall be prepared.

* HIPHIL.—*Infinitive.* *

1Sa.24: 3(4). Saul went in *to cover* his feet:

HIPHIL.—*Future.*

Ex. 40:21. *and covered* the ark of the testimony;
Job 3:23. *and* whom God *hath hedged in?*
38: 8. *Or* (who) *shut up* the sea with doors,
Ps. 5:11(12). *because thou defendest* them: (marg. *coverest over*, or, *protectest*)
91: 4. *He shall cover* thee with his feathers,

HIPHIL.—*Participle.*

Jud. 3:24. he *covereth* his feet in his summer

* PILPEL.—*Preterite.* *

Isa. 19: 2. *And I will set* (marg. *mingle*) the Egyptians against the Egyptians:

PILPEL.—*Future.*

Isa. 9:11(10). and *join* his enemies *together;* (marg. *mingle*)

5528 סָכַל [*sāh-chal'*].

* NIPHAL.—*Preterite.* *

1Sa.13:13. Samuel said to Saul, *Thou hast done foolishly:*
2Sa.24:10. *I have done* very *foolishly.*
1Ch 21: 8. *I have done* very *foolishly.*
2Ch 16: 9. Herein *thou hast done foolishly:*

* PIEL.—*Imperative.* *

2Sa.15:31. *turn* the counsel of Ahithophel *into foolishness.*

PIEL.—*Future.*

Isa. 44:25. and *maketh* their knowledge *foolish;*

* HIPHIL.—*Preterite.* *

Gen31:28. *thou hast* now *done foolishly* in (so)
1Sa.26:21. *I have played the fool*, and have erred

5530 סָכָל *sāh-chāhl'*, m.

Ecc. 2:19. who knoweth whether he shall be a wise (man) or *a fool?*
7:17. neither be thou *foolish:*
10: 3. *when he that is a fool* walketh by the way,
— he saith to every one (that) *he* (is) *a fool.*
14. *A fool also* is full of words:
Jer. 4:22. they (are) *sottish* children,
5:21. Hear now this, O *foolish* people,

5529 סֶכֶל *seh'-chel*, m.

Ecc. 10: 6. *Folly* is set in great dignity,

5531 סִכְלוּת *sich-looth'*, f.

Ecc. 2: 3. to lay hold on *folly*,
12. I turned myself to behold wisdom, and madness, and *folly:*
13. I saw that wisdom excelleth *folly*,
7:25. *even of foolishness* (and) madness:
10: 1. (so doth) *a little folly*
13. the words of his mouth (is) *foolishness:*

סָכַן [*sāh-chan'*]. 5532

* KAL.—*Future.* *

Job 15: 3. Should he reason with un*profitable* talk? (lit. talk which *profiteth* not)
22: 2. *Can* a man *be profitable* unto God, as he that is wise *may be profitable* unto
34: 9. he hath said, *It profiteth* a man nothing
35: 3. thou saidst, What *advantage will it be* unto thee?

KAL.—*Participle.* Poel.

1K. 1: 2. let her *cherish* him, (lit. be *a cherisher* to him)
4. the damsel (was) very fair, and *cherish*ed the king, (lit. was *a cherisher* to the king)
Isa. 22:15. get thee unto this *treasurer*,

* HIPHIL.—*Preterite.* *

Nu. 22:30. *was I* ever *wont* to do so unto thee?
Ps.139: 3. and *art acquainted* (with) all my ways.

HIPHIL.—*Infinitive.*

Nu. 22:30. was I *ever* wont (lit. *being wont* was I wont) to do so unto thee?

HIPHIL.—*Imperative.*

Job 22:21. *Acquaint* now *thyself* with him,

סָכַן [*sāh-chan'*]. 5533

* NIPHAL.—*Future.* *

Ecc.10: 9. he that cleaveth wood *shall be endangered thereby.*

* PUAL.—*Participle.* *

Isa. 40:20. *He that* (is) so *impoverished that he hath no* oblation (marg. (is) *poor of* oblation)

סָכַר [*sāh-char'*]. 5534

* NIPHAL.—*Future.* *

Gen 8: 2. fountains *also* of the deep and the windows of heaven *were stopped*,
Ps. 63:11(12). the mouth of them that speak lies *shall be stopped.*

* PIEL.—*Preterite.* *

Isa. 19: 4. *And* the Egyptians *will I give over* into the hand of a cruel lord;

סָכַר [*sāh-char'*]. 7936

* KAL.—*Participle.* Poel. *

Ezr. 4: 5. *And hired* counsellors against them,

סָכַת [*sāh-chath'*]. 5535

* HIPHIL.—*Imperative.* *

Deu.27: 9. *Take heed*, and hearken, O Israel;

סַל *sal*, m. 5536

Gen40:16. (I had) three white *baskets* on my head:
17. *And in the* uppermost *basket*
— birds did eat them out of *the basket*
18. *The* three *baskets* (are) three days:
Ex. 29: 3. thou shalt put them into one *basket*, and bring them *in the basket*,
23. one wafer *out of the basket*
32. and the bread that (is) *in the basket*,
Lev. 8: 2. and *a basket of* unleavened bread;
26. *And out of the basket of* unleavened bread,
31. with the bread that (is) *in the basket of*
Nu. 6:15. *And a basket of* unleavened bread,
17. with *the basket of* unleavened bread:
19. one unleavened cake *out of the basket*,
Jud. 6:19. the flesh he put *in a basket*,

סָלָא [*sāh-lāh'*]. 5537

* PUAL.—*Participle.* *

Lam.4: 2. The precious sons of Zion, *comparable* to fine gold,

5539 סָלַד [*sāh-lad'*].

* PIEL.—*Future.* *

Job 6:10. *yea, I would harden myself* in sorrow:

5541 סָלָה [*sāh-lāh'*].

* KAL.—*Preterite.* *

Ps. 119:118. *Thou hast trodden down* all them that

* PIEL.—*Preterite.* *

Lam. 1:15. The Lord *hath trodden under foot* all my

* PUAL.—*Future.* *

Job 28:16. *It cannot be valued* with the gold of Ophir,
19. neither *shall it be valued* with pure gold.

5542 סֶלָה *seh'-lāh.*

Ps. 3: 2(3). no help for him in God. *Selah.*
4(5). heard me out of his holy hill. *Selah.*
8(9). blessing (is) upon thy people. *Selah.*
4: 2(3). (and) seek after leasing? *Selah.*
4(5). upon your bed, and be still. *Selah.*
7: 5(6). lay mine honour in the dust. *Selah.*
9: 16(17). of his own hands. Higgaion. *Selah.*
20(21). themselves (to be but) men. *Selah.*
20: 3(4). accept thy burnt sacrifice. *Selah.*
21: 2(3). the request of his lips. *Selah.*
24: 6. that seek thy face, O Jacob. *Selah.*
10. he (is) the King of glory. *Selah.*
32: 4. into the drought of summer. *Selah.*
5. forgavest the iniquity of my sin. *Selah.*
7. with songs of deliverance. *Selah.*
39: 5(6). best state (is) altogether vanity. *Selah.*
11(12). surely every man (is) vanity. *Selah.*
44: 8(9). praise thy name for ever. *Selah.*
46: 3(4). shake with the swelling thereof. *Selah.*
7(8), 11(12). God of Jacob (is) our refuge. *Selah.*
47: 4(5). of Jacob whom he loved. *Selah.*
48: 8(9). God will establish it for ever. *Selah.*
49: 13(14). approve their sayings. *Selah.*
15(16). for he shall receive me. *Selah.*
50: 6. for God (is) judge himself. *Selah.*
52: 3(5). to speak righteousness. *Selah.*
5(7). of the land of the living. *Selah.*
54: 3(5). not set God before them. *Selah.*
55: 7(8). remain in the wilderness. *Selah.*
19(20). he that abideth of old. *Selah.*
57: 3(4). that would swallow me up. *Selah.*
6(7). they are fallen (themselves). *Selah.*
59: 5(6). to any wicked transgressors. *Selah.*
13(14). unto the ends of the earth. *Selah.*
60: 4(6). displayed because of the truth. *Selah.*
61: 4(5). trust in the covert of thy wings. *Selah.*
62: 4(5). but they curse inwardly. *Selah.*
8(9). God (is) a refuge for us. *Selah.*
66: 4. they shall sing (to) thy name. *Selah.*
7. rebellious exalt themselves. *Selah.*
15. I will offer bullocks with goats. *Selah.*
67: 1(2). his face to shine upon us. *Selah.*
4(5). govern the nations upon earth. *Selah.*
68: 7(8). march through the wilderness; *Selah:*
19(20). the God of our salvation. *Selah.*
32(33). O sing praises unto the Lord; *Selah:*
75: 3(4). I bear up the pillars of it. *Selah.*
76: 3(4). the sword, and the battle. *Selah.*
9(10). save all the meek of the earth. *Selah.*
77: 3(4). my spirit was overwhelmed. *Selah.*
9(10). shut up his tender mercies? *Selah.*
15(16). sons of Jacob and Joseph. *Selah.*
81: 7(8). at the waters of Meribah. *Selah.*
82: 2. accept the persons of the wicked? *Selah.*
83: 8(9). holpen the children of Lot. *Selah.*
84: 4(5). they will be still praising thee. *Selah.*
8(9). give ear, O God of Jacob. *Selah.*
85: 2(3). thou hast covered all their sin. *Selah.*
87: 3. O city of God. *Selah.*
6. this (man) was born there. *Selah.*
88: 7(8). afflicted (me) with all thy waves. *Selah.*
10(11). dead arise (and) praise thee? *Selah.*
89: 4(5). thy throne to all generations. *Selah.*
37(38). a faithful witness in heaven. *Selah.*
45(46). hast covered him with shame. *Selah.*
Ps. 89: 48(49). from the hand of the grave? *Selah.*
140: 3(4). poison (is) under their lips. *Selah.*
5(6). they have set gins for me. *Selah.*
8(9). (lest) they exalt themselves. *Selah.*
143: 6. as a thirsty land. *Selah.*
Hab. 3: 3. the Holy One from mount Paran. *Selah.*
9. of the tribes, (even thy) word. *Selah.*
13. foundation unto the neck. *Selah.*

סִלּוֹן *sil-lōhn'*, m. 5544

Eze. 28:24. there shall be no more *a* pricking *brier*

סַלּוֹנִים *sal-lōh-neem'*, m. pl. 5544

Eze. 2: 6. though briers *and thorns* (be) with thee,

סָלַח [*sāh-lagh'*]. 5545

* KAL.—*Preterite.* *

Ex. 34: 9. *and pardon* our iniquity and our sin,
Nu. 14:20. the Lord said, *I have pardoned*
1K. 8:30. *and* when thou hearest, *forgive.*
34. *and forgive* the sin of thy people
36. *and forgive* the sin of thy servants,
39. in heaven thy dwelling place, *and forgive,*
50. *And forgive* thy people that have sinned
2Ch 6:21. *and* when thou hearest, *forgive.*
25. hear thou from the heavens, *and forgive*
27. hear thou from heaven, *and forgive*
30. heaven thy dwelling place, *and forgive,*
39. *and forgive* thy people which have sinned
Ps. 25:11. O Lord, *pardon* mine iniquity;
Jer. 33: 8. *and I will pardon* all their iniquities,
36: 3. *that I may forgive* their iniquity and their
Lam. 3:42. *thou hast* not *pardoned.*

KAL.—*Infinitive.*

Deu 29:20(19). The Lord will not *spare* him,
2K. 24: 4. which the Lord would not *pardon.*
Isa. 55: 7. our God, for he will abundantly *pardon.* (marg. multiply *to pardon*)

KAL.—*Imperative.*

Nu. 14:19. *Pardon*, I beseech thee, the iniquity of this people
Dan. 9:19. O Lord, hear; O Lord, *forgive;*
Am. 7: 2. O Lord God, *forgive,* I beseech thee:

KAL.—*Future.*

Nu. 30: 5(6), 8(9), 12(13). the Lord *shall forgive* her,
2K. 5:18. In this thing the Lord *pardon* thy servant,
— the Lord *pardon* thy servant in this thing.
2Ch 7:14. *and will forgive* their sin,
Jer. 5: 1. *and I will pardon* it.
7. How *shall I pardon* thee for this?
31:34. *I will forgive* their iniquity,
50:20. *I will pardon* them whom I reserve.

KAL.—*Participle.* Poel.

Ps. 103: 3. *Who forgiveth* all thine iniquities;

* NIPHAL.—*Preterite.* *

Lev. 4:20. *and it shall be forgiven* them.
26, 31, 35, & 5:10, 13, 16, 18, & 6:7(5:26). *and it shall be forgiven* him.
19:22. *and* the sin which he hath done *shall be forgiven* him.
Nu. 15:25. *and it shall be forgiven* them;
26. *And it shall be forgiven* all the
28. *and it shall be forgiven* him.

סַלָּח *sal-lāhgh'*, m. 5546

Ps. 86: 5. thou, Lord, (art) good, *and ready to forgive;*

סְלִיחָה *s'lee-ghāh'*, f. 5547

Neh. 9:17. thou (art) a God ready to *pardon*, (marg. a God of *pardons*)
Ps. 130: 4. (there is) *forgiveness* with thee,
Dan. 9: 9. God (belong) mercies *and forgivenesses,*

5549 ## סָלַל [*sāh-lal'*].

* KAL.—*Imperative.* *

Ps. 68: 4(5). *extol* him that rideth upon the
Isa. 57:14. *Cast ye up, cast ye up,* prepare the way,
62:10. *cast up, cast up* the highway;
Jer. 50:26. *cast her up* (marg. *tread*) as heaps,

KAL.—*Future.*

Job 19:12. His troops come together, *and raise up* their way against me,
30:12. *and they raise up* against me the ways of

KAL.—*Participle.* Paül.

Pro.15:19. the way of the righteous (is) *made plain.* (marg. *raised up as a causey*)
Jer. 18:15. (in) a way not *cast up;*

* PILPEL.—*Imperative.* *

Pro. 4: 8. *Exalt her,* and she shall promote thee:

* HITHPOEL.—*Participle.* *

Ex. 9:17. As yet *exaltest thou* thyself against my

5550 ## סֹלְלָה *sōh-l'lāh',* f.

2Sa.20:15. they cast up *a bank* against the city,
2K. 19:32. nor cast *a bank* against it.
Isa. 37:33. nor cast *a bank* against it.
Jer. 6: 6. cast *a mount* against Jerusalem: (marg. or, pour out *the engine of shot*)
32:24. Behold *the mounts* (marg. or, *engines of shot*), they are come unto the city
33: 4. which are thrown down by *the mounts,*
Eze. 4: 2. cast *a mount* against it;
17:17. by casting up *mounts,* and building forts,
21:22(27). to cast *a mount,* (and) to build a fort.
26: 8. cast *a mount* against thee, (marg. or, pour out *the engine of shot*)
Dan11:15. the king of the north shall come, and cast up *a mount,*

5551 ## סֻלָּם *sool-lāhm',* m.

Gen28:12. he dreamed, and behold *a ladder* set up

5552 ## סַלְסִלּוֹת *sal-sil-lōhth',* f. pl.

Jer. 6: 9. turn back thine hand as a grapegatherer *into the baskets.*

5553, 5555 ## סֶלַע *seh'-lag̃,* m.

Nu. 20: 8. speak ye unto *the rock* before their eyes;
— bring forth to them water out of *the rock:*
10. the congregation together before *the rock,*
— must we fetch you water out of *this rock?*
11. with his rod he smote *the rock* twice:
24:21. thou puttest thy nest *in a rock.*
Deu32:13. he made him to suck honey *out of the rock,*
Jud. 1:36. *from the rock,* and upward.
6:20. lay (them) upon this *rock,*
15: 8. he went down and dwelt in the top of *the rock* Etam.
11. went to the top of *the rock* Etam,
13. and brought him up from *the rock.*
20:45. fled toward the wilderness unto *the rock of* Rimmon:
47. unto *the rock* Rimmon, and abode *in the rock* Rimmon four months.
21:13. that (were) *in the rock* Rimmon,
1Sa.13: 6. in caves, and in thickets, *and in rocks,*
14: 4. (there was) *a* sharp *rock* on the one side, and *a* sharp *rock* on the other side:
23:25. wherefore he came down into *a rock,*
28. they called that place *Sela*-hammahlekoth. (marg. i. e. *The rock of* divisions)
2Sa.22: 2. The Lord (is) *my rock,*
1K. 19:11. brake in pieces *the rocks* before the Lord;
2K. 14: 7. and took *Selah* (marg. or, *the rock*) by war,
2Ch 25:12. brought them unto the top of *the rock,* and cast them down from the top of *the rock,*
Neh. 9:15. broughtest forth water for them *out of the rock*
Job 39: 1. when the wild goats of *the rock* bring forth?
28. She dwelleth and abideth on *the rock,* upon the crag of *the rock,* and the strong place.
Ps. 18: 2(3). The Lord (is) *my rock,*
31: 3(4). thou (art) *my rock* and my fortress;
40: 2(3). set my feet upon *a rock,*
42: 9(10). I will say unto God *my rock,*
71: 3. thou (art) *my rock* and my fortress.
78:16. He brought streams also *out of the rock,*
104:18. *the rocks* for the conies.
137: 9. dasheth thy little ones against *the stones.*
141: 6. their judges are overthrown in *stony* places, (lit. by the sides of *the rock*)
Pro.30:26. yet make they their houses *in the rocks;*
Cant.2:14. O my dove, (that art) in the clefts of *the rock,*
Isa. 2:21. and into the tops of *the ragged rocks,*
7:19. and in the holes of *the rocks,*
16: 1. *from Sela* (marg. *a rock,* or, *Petra*) to the wilderness,
22:16. that graveth an habitation for himself *in a rock?*
31: 9. *And* he shall pass over to *his strong hold*
32: 2. the shadow of *a* great *rock* in a weary land.
33:16. his place of defence (shall be) the munitions of *rocks:*
42:11. let the inhabitants of *the rock* sing,
57: 5. the valleys under the clifts of *the rocks?*
Jer. 5: 3. they have made their faces harder *than a rock;*
13: 4. hide it there in a hole of *the rock.*
16:16. out of the holes of *the rocks.*
23:29. like a hammer (that) breaketh *the rock* in pieces?
48:28. leave the cities, and dwell *in the rock,*
49:16. thou that dwellest in the clefts of *the rock,*
51:25. and roll thee down from *the rocks,*
Eze.24: 7. she set it upon the top of *a rock;*
8. have set her blood upon the top of *a rock,*
26: 4. make her like the top of *a rock.*
14. I will make thee like the top of *a rock:*
Am. 6:12. Shall horses run *upon the rock?*
Obad. 3. thou that dwellest in the clefts of *the rock,*

סָלְעָם *sol-g̃āhm',* m. 5556

Lev.11:22. *the bald locust* after his kind,

סָלַף [*sāh-laph'*]. 5557

* PIEL.—*Future.* *

Ex. 23: 8. *and perverteth* the words of the righteous.
Deu16:19. *and pervert* the words of the righteous.
Job 12:19. away spoiled, and *overthroweth* the mighty.
Pro.13: 6. wickedness *overthroweth* the sinner.
19: 3. The foolishness of man *perverteth* his way:
22:12. *and he overthroweth* the words of the transgressor.

PIEL.—*Participle.*

Pro.21:12. (God) *overthroweth* the wicked

סֶלֶף *seh'-leph,* m. 5558

Pro.11: 3. *but the perverseness of* transgressors shall destroy them.
15: 4. *but perverseness* therein (is) a breach in the spirit.

סְלִק [*s'lak*], Ch. 5559

* P'AL.—*Preterite.* *

Dan. 7: 8. *there came up* among them another little horn,
20. and (of) the other which *came up,*

P'AL.—*Participle.* Active.

Dan. 7: 3. four great beasts *came up* from the sea,

* P'IL.—*Preterite.* *

Ezr. 4:12. the Jews which *came up* from thee
Dan. 2:29. O king, thy thoughts *came* (into thy mind)

5560 **סֹלֶת** *sōh'-leth*, com.

Gen18: 6. quickly three measures of fine *meal*,
Ex. 29: 2. (of) wheaten *flour* shalt thou make them.
40. tenth deal of *flour* mingled with the fourth
Lev. 2: 1. his offering shall be (of) *fine flour;*
2. thereout his handful *of the flour thereof,*
4. unleavened cakes of *fine flour*
5. it shall be (of) *fine flour* unleavened,
7. it shall be made (of) *fine flour* with oil.
5:11. the tenth part of an ephah of *fine flour*
6:15(8). he shall take of it his handful, *of the flour*
20(13). the tenth part of an ephah of *fine flour*
7:12. and cakes mingled with oil, *of fine flour,*
14:10. three tenth deals of *fine flour*
21. one tenth deal of *fine flour*
23:13. two tenth deals of *fine flour*
17. of two tenth deals: they shall be of *fine flour;*
24: 5. thou shalt take *fine flour,*
Nu. 6:15. cakes of *fine flour* mingled with oil,
7:13, 19, 25, 31, 37, 43, 49, 55, 61, 67, 73, 79. full of *fine flour* mingled with oil
8: 8. (even) *fine flour* mingled with oil,
15: 4. a meat offering of a tenth deal of *flour*
6. a meat offering two tenth deals of *flour*
9. meat offering of three tenth deals of *flour*
28: 5. a tenth (part) of an ephah of *flour* for a meat offering,
9, 12. two tenth deals of *flour* (for) a
12. three tenth deals of *flour* (for) a
13. a several tenth deal of *flour*
20. (of) *flour* mingled with oil:
28. their meat offering of *flour* mingled with
29: 3, 9, 14. their meat offering (shall be of) *flour* mingled with oil,
1K. 4:22(5:2). thirty measures of *fine flour,*
2K. 7: 1. about this time (shall) a measure of *fine flour* (be sold) for a shekel,
16. So a measure of *fine flour* was (sold) for
18. a measure of *fine flour* for a shekel,
1Ch 9:29. *the fine flour*, and the wine, and the oil,
23:29. *and for the fine flour* for meat offering,
Eze.16:13. thou didst eat *fine flour*, and honey,
19. *fine flour*, and oil, and honey,
46:14. to temper with *the fine flour;*

5563 **סְמָדַר** *s'māh-dar'*, m.

Cant.2:13. the vines (with) *the tender grape* give a
15. our vines (have) *tender grapes.*
7:12(13). (whether) *the tender grape* appear,

5561 **סַמִּים** *sam-meem'*, m. pl.

Ex. 25: 6. for anointing oil, and for *sweet* incense, (lit. incense of *sweet spices*)
30: 7. Aaron shall burn thereon *sweet* incense (marg. incense of *spices*) every morning:
34. Take unto thee *sweet spices,*
— *sweet spices* with pure frankincense:
31:11. *sweet* incense (lit. incense of *spices*) for
35: 8. spices for anointing oil, and for the *sweet* incense, (lit. *id.*)
15. the *sweet* incense, (lit. *id.*) and the
28. anointing oil, and for the *sweet* incense. (lit. *id.*)
37:29. pure incense of *sweet* spices,
39:38. the *sweet* incense, (marg. the incense of *sweet spices*)
40:27. he burnt *sweet* incense (lit. *id.*)
Lev. 4: 7. the altar of *sweet* incense (lit. *id.*) before
16:12. his hands full of *sweet* incense (lit. *id.*)
Nu. 4:16. the light, and the *sweet* incense, (lit. *id.*)
2Ch 2: 4(3). to burn before him *sweet* incense, (marg. incense of *spices*)
13:11. burnt sacrifices and *sweet* incense: (lit. *id.*)

5564 **סָמַךְ** *sāh-mach'*.

* KAL.—*Preterite.* *

Gen27:37. with corn and wine *have I sustained him:* (marg. or, *supported*)
Ex. 29:10, 19. *and* Aaron and his sons *shall put* their hands
Ex. 29:15. *and* Aaron and his sons *shall put* their
Lev. 1: 4. *And he shall put* his hand upon the head
3: 2, 8, 13. *And he shall lay* his hand upon the
4: 4. *and shall lay* his hand upon the bullock's
15. *And* the elders of the congregation *shall lay* their hands
24, 29, 33. *And he shall lay* his hand upon
16:21. *And* Aaron *shall lay* both his hands upon
24:14. *and let* all that heard (him) *lay* their
Nu. 8:10. *and* the children of Israel *shall put* their
27:18. *and lay* thine hand upon him;
Deu34: 9. Moses *had laid* his hands upon him:
Ps. 88: 7(8). Thy wrath *lieth hard* upon me,
Isa. 59:16. his righteousness, it *sustained him.*
63: 5. my fury, it *upheld me.*
Eze.24: 2. the king of Babylon *set himself* against
Am. 5:19. *and leaned* his hand on the wall,

KAL.—*Imperative.*

Ps.119:116. *Uphold me* according unto thy word,

KAL.—*Future.*

Lev. 8:14. *and* Aaron and his sons *laid* their hands
18, 22. *and* Aaron and his sons *laid* their
Nu. 8:12. And the Levites *shall lay* their hands
27:23. *And he laid* his hands upon him,
2Ch 29:23. *and they laid* their hands upon them:
Ps. 3: 5(6). for the Lord *sustained me.*
51:12(14). *uphold me* (with thy) free spirit.

KAL.—*Participle.* Poel.

Ps. 37:17. *but* the Lord *upholdeth* the righteous.
24. the Lord *upholdeth* (him with) his hand.
54: 4(6). the Lord (is) *with them that uphold* my
145:14. The Lord *upholdeth* all that fall,
Isa. 63: 5. I wondered that (there was) none *to uphold:*
Eze.30: 6. *They* also *that uphold* Egypt shall fall;

KAL.—*Participle.* Paül.

Ps.111: 8. *They stand fast* (marg. (are) *established*) for ever and ever,
112: 8. His heart (is) *established,*
Isa. 26: 3. in perfect peace, (whose) mind (is) *stayed*

* NIPHAL.—*Preterite.* *

Ps. 71: 6. By thee *have I been holden up* from the
Isa. 48: 2. and *stay themselves* upon the God of Israel;

NIPHAL.—*Future.*

Jud.16:29. *and* on which *it was borne up*, (marg. or, *he leaned* on them)
2K. 18:21. if a man *lean*, it will go into his hand,
2Ch 32: 8. *And* the people *rested themselves* (marg. *leaned*) upon the words
Isa. 36: 6. whereon if a man *lean*, it will go into his hand,

* PIEL.—*Imperative.* *

Cant.2: 5. *Stay me* with flagons,

סֶמֶל *seh'-mel* & **סֵמֶל** *seh'-mel*, m. 5566

Deu. 4:16. the similitude of any *figure,*
2Ch 33: 7. *the idol* which he had made,
15. *the idol* out of the house of the Lord,
Eze. 8: 3. (was) the seat of *the image of* jealousy,
5. this *image of* jealousy in the entry.

סָמַן [*sāh-man'*]. 5567

* NIPHAL.—*Participle.* *

Isa. 28:25. cast in the principal wheat and the *appointed* barley

---

סָמַר *sāh-mar'*. 5568

* KAL.—*Preterite.* *

Ps.119:120. My flesh *trembleth* for fear of thee;

* PIEL.—*Future.* *

Job 4:15. the hair of my flesh *stood up:*

סָמָר *sāh-māhr'*, adj. 5569

Jer. 51:27. as the *rough* caterpillers.

5572 סְנֶה *s'neh*, m.

Ex. 3: 2. in a flame of fire out of the midst of *a bush:* and he looked, and, behold, *the bush* burned with fire, *and the bush* (was) not consumed.
3. why *the bush* is not burnt.
4. God called unto him out of the midst of *the bush,*
Deu33:16. (for) the good will of him that dwelt in *the bush:*

5575 סַנְוֵרִים *san-vēh-reem'*, m. pl.

Gen19:11. they smote the men...*with blindness,*
2K. 6:18. Smite this people, I pray thee, *with blindness.* And he smote them *with blindness*

5577 סַנְסִנִּים [*san-sin-neem'*], m. pl.

Cant.7: 8(9). I will take hold of *the boughs thereof:*

5579 סְנַפִּיר *s'nap-peer'*, m.

Lev.11: 9. whatsoever hath *fins* and scales
10. all that have not *fins* and scales
12. Whatsoever hath no *fins* nor scales
Deu14: 9. all that have *fins* and scales shall ye eat:
10. whatsoever hath not *fins* and scales ye may not eat;

5580 סָס *sāhs*, m.

Isa. 51: 8. *the worm* shall eat them like wool:

5582 סָעַד *sāh-ğad'*.

* KAL.—*Preterite.* *

Pro.20:28. *and* his throne *is upholden* by mercy.

KAL.—*Infinitive.*

Isa. 9: 7(6). *and to establish it* with judgment and with justice

KAL.—*Imperative.*

Gen18: 5. *and comfort* (marg. *stay*) *ye* your hearts;
Jud.19: 5. *Comfort* (marg. *Strengthen*) thine heart with a morsel of bread,
8. *Comfort* thine heart, I pray thee.
1K. 13: 7. Come home with me, *and refresh thyself,*
Ps.119:117. *Hold thou me up*, and I shall be safe:

KAL.—*Future.*

Ps. 18:35(36). thy right hand *hath holden me up,*
20: 2(3). and *strengthen* (marg. *support*) *thee* out of Zion.
41: 3(4). The Lord *will strengthen him*
94:18. thy mercy, O Lord, *held me up.*
104:15. bread (which) *strengtheneth* man's heart.

5583 סְעַד [*s'ğad*], Ch.

* APHEL.—*Participle.* *

Ezr. 5: 2. the prophets of God *helping* them.

5584 סָעָה [*sāh-ğāh'*].

* KAL.—*Participle.* *

Ps. 55: 8(9). I would hasten my escape from *the* windy *storm* (lit. *storming* wind)

5585 סְעִיף *s'ğeeph*, m.

Jud.15: 8. he went down and dwelt *in the top of* the rock Etam.
11. went to *the top of* the rock Etam,
Isa. 2:21. *and into the tops of* the ragged rocks,
17: 6. *in the outmost* fruitful *branches thereof,*
27:10. and consume *the branches thereof.*
57: 5. under *the clifts of* the rocks?

סֵעֵף [*sāh-ğaph'*]. 5586

* PIEL.—*Participle.* *

Isa. 10:33. *shall lop* the bough with terror:

סְעַפָּה [*s'ğap-pāh'*], f. 5589

Eze.31: 6. the fowls of heaven made their nests *in his boughs,*
8. the fir-trees were not like *his boughs,*

סֵעֲפִים *sēh-ğăpheem'*, m. pl. 5588

Ps. 119:113. I hate (vain) *thoughts:*

סְעִפִּים *s'ğip-peem'*, f. pl. 5587

1K. 18:21. How long halt ye between two *opinions?* (marg. or, *thoughts*)

סָעַר [*sāh-ğar'*]. 5590

* KAL.—*Future.* *

Hab. 3:14. *they came out as a whirlwind* (marg. *were tempestuous*)

KAL.—*Participle.* Poel.

Isa. 54:11. O thou afflicted, *tossed with tempest,*
Jon. 1:11, 13. the sea wrought, *and was tempestuous.*

* NIPHAL.—*Future.* *

2K. 6:11. *Therefore* the heart of the king of Syria *was sore troubled*

* PIEL.—*Future.* *

Zec. 7:14. *But I scattered them with a whirlwind* among

* PUAL.—*Future.* *

Hos.13: 3. as the chaff (that) *is driven with the whirlwind*

סַעַר *sah'-ğar*, m. 5591

Ps. 55: 8(9). escape from the windy storm (and) *tempest.*
83:15(16). persecute them *with thy tempest,*
Jer. 23:19. *even a* grievous *whirlwind:*
25:32. *and a* great *whirlwind* shall be raised
30:23. *a* continuing *whirlwind:*
Am. 1:14. *with a tempest* in the day of the whirlwind:
Jon. 1: 4. there was *a* mighty *tempest* in the sea,
12. my sake this great *tempest* (is) upon you.

סְעָרָה *s'ğāh-rāh'*, f. 5591

2K. 2: 1. take up Elijah into heaven *by a whirlwind,*
11. Elijah went up *by a whirlwind* into heaven.
Job 38: 1. Lord answered Job out of *the whirlwind,*
40: 6. the Lord unto Job out of *the whirlwind,*
Ps. 107:25. commandeth, and raiseth the *stormy* wind,
29. He maketh *the storm* a calm,
148: 8. *stormy* wind fulfilling his word:
Isa. 29: 6. with storm *and tempest,*
40:24. *and the whirlwind* shall take them away
41:16. *and the whirlwind* shall scatter them:
Jer. 23:19. *a whirlwind of* the Lord is gone forth
30:23. *the whirlwind of* the Lord goeth forth
Eze. 1: 4. I looked, and, behold, a *whirl*wind (lit. a wind of *storm*)
13:11. a *stormy* wind shall rend (it).
13. I will even rend (it) with a *stormy* wind
Zec. 9:14. shall go *with whirlwinds of* the south.

סַף *saph*, m. 5592

Ex. 12:22. in the blood that (is) *in the bason,*
— with the blood that (is) *in the bason;*
Jud.19:27. her hands (were) upon *the threshold.*
2Sa.17:28. beds, *and basons,* (marg. or, *cups*) and earthen vessels,

1K. 7:50. *And the bowls*, and the snuffers,
14:17. when she came *to the threshold of* the door,
2K. 12: 9(10). that kept *the door* (marg. *threshold*)
13(14). for the house of the Lord *bowls of*
22: 4. keepers of *the door* (marg. *threshold*) have
23: 4. the keepers of *the door*, to bring forth
25:18. keepers of *the door* : (marg. *threshold*)
1Ch 9:19. keepers of *the gates* (marg. *thresholds*)
22. these (which were) chosen to be porters *in the gates*
2Ch 3: 7. the beams, *the posts*, and the walls thereof,
23: 4. the Levites, (shall be) porters of *the doors* ; (marg. *thresholds*)
34: 9. the Levites that kept *the doors*
Est. 2:21. those which kept *the door*, (marg. *threshold*)
6: 2. the keepers of *the door*, (marg. *id.*)
Isa. 6: 4. posts of *the door* moved (marg. *thresholds*)
Jer. 35: 4. the keeper of *the door* : (marg. *threshold*)
52:19. *the basons*, and the firepans, and the bowls,
24. three keepers of *the door*: (marg. *threshold*)
Eze. 40: 6. measured *the threshold of* the gate, (which was) one reed broad; and *the* other *threshold* (of the gate),
7. *and the threshold of* the gate by the porch
41:16. *The door posts*, and the narrow
— over against *the door*,
43: 8. In their setting of *their threshold* by *my thresholds*,
Am. 9: 1. Smite the lintel of the door, that *the posts* may shake:
Zep. 2:14. desolation (shall be) *in the thresholds* :
Zec. 12: 2. I will make Jerusalem *a cup of* trembling

5594 ## סָפַד [*sāh-phad'*].

* KAL. — *Preterite*. *

1K. 14:13. *And* all Israel *shall mourn* for him,
Zec. 12:10. *and they shall mourn* for him,
12. *And* the land *shall mourn*,

KAL. — *Infinitive*.

Gen 23: 2. Abraham came *to mourn* for Sarah,
1K. 13:29. *to mourn* and to bury him.
Ecc. 3: 4. a time *to mourn*, and a time to dance ;
Jer. 16: 5. neither go *to lament* nor bemoan them:
Zec. 7: 5. When ye fasted *and mourned*

KAL. — *Imperative*.

2Sa. 3:31. gird you with sackcloth, and *mourn* before
Jer. 4: 8. gird you with sackcloth, *lament* and howl:
49: 3. *lament*, and run to and fro
Joel 1:13. Gird yourselves, and *lament*, ye priests:

KAL. — *Future*.

Gen 50:10. *and* there *they mourned*
1Sa. 25: 1. *and lamented* him,
28: 3. *and* all Israel *had lamented* him,
2Sa. 1:12. *And they mourned*, and wept, and fasted
11:26. *And* when the wife...*she mourned* for her
1K. 13:30. *and they mourned* over him,
14:18. *and* all Israel *mourned* for him,
Jer. 16: 6. neither *shall* (men) *lament* for them,
22:18, 18. *They shall* not *lament* for him,
34: 5. *they will lament* thee,
Eze. 24:16. neither *shalt thou mourn* nor weep,
23. *ye shall* not *mourn* nor weep ;
Mic. 1: 8. *I will wail* and howl,

KAL. — *Participle*. Poel.

Ecc. 12: 5. *the mourners* go about the streets:
Isa. 32:12. *They shall lament* for the teats,

* NIPHAL. — *Future*. *

Jer. 16: 4. *they shall* not *be lamented* ; neither shall
25:33. *they shall* not *be lamented*, neither gathered,

5595 ## סָפָה [*sāh-phāh'*].

* KAL. — *Preterite*. *

Jer. 12: 4. the beasts *are consumed*,

KAL. — *Infinitive*.

Ps. 40:14(15). that seek after my soul *to destroy it* ;

KAL. — *Future*.

Gen 18:23. *Wilt thou* also *destroy* the righteous with
24. *wilt thou* also *destroy* and not spare
Isa. 7:20. *it shall* also *consume* the beard.

* NIPHAL. — *Preterite*. *

1Sa. 26:10. he shall descend into battle, *and perish*

NIPHAL. — *Future*.

Gen 19:15. lest *thou be consumed* in the iniquity of
17. to the mountain, lest *thou be consumed*.
Nu. 16:26. lest *ye be consumed* in all their sins.
1Sa. 12:25. *ye shall be consumed*, both ye and your
27: 1. *I shall* now *perish* (marg. *be consumed*)

NIPHAL. — *Participle*.

1Ch 21:12. or three months *to be destroyed* before thy
Pro. 13:23. there is (that is) *destroyed* for want of

* HIPHIL. — *Future*. *

Deu 32:23. *I will heap* mischiefs upon them ;

סָפָה [*sāh-phāh'*]. 5595

* KAL. — *Infinitive*. *

Nu. 32:14. *to augment* yet the fierce anger of the
Deu 29:19(18). *to add* drunkenness to thirst:
Isa. 30: 1. that they *may add* sin to sin:

KAL. — *Imperative*.

Isa. 29: 1. *add ye* year to year ;
Jer. 7:21. *Put* your burnt offerings unto your

* NIPHAL. — *Participle*. *

Isa. 13:15. every one *that is joined* (unto them) shall

סָפַח [*sāh-phagh'*]. 5596

* KAL. — *Imperative*. *

1Sa. 2:36. *Put* (marg. *Join*) me, I pray thee, into

* NIPHAL. — *Preterite*. *

Isa. 14: 1. *and they shall cleave* to the house of

* PIEL. — *Participle*. *

Hab. 2:15. *that puttest* thy bottle to (him),

* PUAL. — *Future*. *

Job 30: 7. the nettles *they were gathered together*.

* HITHPAEL. — *Infinitive*. *

1Sa. 26:19. they have driven me out this day *from abiding* (marg. *cleaving*)

סַפַּחַת *sap-pah'-ghath*, f. 5597

Lev. 13: 2. *a scab*, or bright spot,
14:56. *and for a scab*, and for a bright spot:

סָפִיחַ *sāh-phee'ăgh*, m. 5599

Lev. 25: 5. *That which groweth of its own accord of* thy harvest
11. *that which groweth of itself in it*,
2K. 19:29. *such things as grow of themselves*,
Job 14:19. thou washest away *the things which grow*
Isa. 37:30. eat (this) year *such as groweth of itself* ;

סְפִינָה *s'phee-nāh'*, f. 5600

Jon. 1: 5. was gone down into the sides of *the ship* ;

סַפִּיר *sap-peer'*, m. 5601

Ex. 24:10. a paved work of a *sapphire* stone,
28:18 & 39:11. an emerald, *a sapphire*, and a
Job 28: 6. stones of it (are) the place of *sapphires* :
16. with the precious onyx, *or the sapphire*.
Cant. 5:14. bright ivory overlaid (with) *sapphires*.
Isa. 54:11. and lay thy foundations *with sapphires*.
Lam. 4: 7. their polishing (was) of *sapphire* :
Eze. 1:26. as the appearance of a *sapphire* stone:
10: 1. over them as it were a *sapphire* stone,
28:13. the jasper, *the sapphire*, the emerald,

סֵפֶל *sēh'-phel*, m. 5602

Jud. 5:25. brought forth butter *in a* lordly *dish*.
6:38. out of the fleece, *a bowl* full of water.

סָפַן [*sāh-phan'*]. 5603

* KAL. — *Future*. *

1K. 6: 9. *and covered* the house with beams and

KAL.—*Participle.* Paül.

Deu33:21.(in) a portion of the lawgiver, (was he) *seated;* (marg. *cieled*)
1K. 7: 3. *And* (it was) *covered* with cedar above
7. *and* (it was) *covered* with cedar from
Jer. 22:14. *and* (it is) *cieled* with cedar,
Hag. 1: 4. to dwell in your *cieled* houses,

5604 סִפֻּן *sip-poon'*, m.

1K. 6:15. the house, and the walls of *the ceiling:*

5605 סָפַף [*sāh-phaph'*].

* HITHPOEL.—*Infinitive.* *

Ps. 84:10(11). I had rather *be a doorkeeper* (marg. *to sit at the threshold*)

5606 סָפַק [*sāh-phak'*].

* KAL.—*Preterite.* *

Job 34:26. *He striketh them* as wicked men
Jer. 31:19. *I smote* upon (my) thigh:
48:26. Moab *also shall wallow* in his vomit,
Lam. 2:15. All that pass by *clap* (their) hands at thee;

KAL.—*Imperative.*

Eze.21:12(17). *smite* therefore upon (thy) thigh

KAL.—*Future.*

Nu. 24:10. *and he smote* his hands together:
Job 34:37. *he clappeth* (his hands) among us,

5607 סֵפֶק [*sēh'-phek*], m.

Job 20:22. In the fulness of *his sufficiency* he shall be in straits:

5608 סָפַר *sāh-phar'*.

* KAL.—*Preterite.* *

Lev.15:13. *then he shall number* to himself seven days
28. *then she shall number* to herself seven days,
23:15. *And ye shall count* unto you
25: 8. *And thou shalt number* seven sabbaths
2Sa.24:10. after that *he had numbered* the people.
2Ch 2:17(16). David his father *had numbered them;*
Ps. 56: 8(9). *Thou tellest* my wanderings:
Isa. 22:10. *ye have numbered* the houses of Jerusalem,

KAL.—*Infinitive.*

Gen15: 5. if thou be able *to number* them:
41:49. until he left *numbering;*
Deu 16: 9. begin *to number* the seven weeks

KAL.—*Imperative.*

Gen15: 5. Look now toward heaven, *and tell* the stars,
1Ch21: 2. Go, *number* Israel from Beer-sheba even to Dan;
Ps. 48:12(13). *tell* the towers thereof.

KAL.—*Future.*

Lev.23:16. after the seventh sabbath *shall ye number*
Deu16: 9. Seven weeks *shalt thou number* unto thee:
2Ch 2: 2(1). *And* Solomon *told out* threescore and
17(16). *And* Solomon *numbered* all the
Ezr. 1: 8. *and numbered them* unto Sheshbazzar,
Job 14:16. For now *thou numberest* my steps:
31: 4. Doth not he see my ways, *and count* all my
39: 2. *Canst thou number* the months (that) they
Ps. 87: 6. The Lord *shall count,*
139:18. (If) *I should count them,* they are more
Eze.44:26. *they shall reckon* unto him seven days.

KAL.—*Participle.* Poel.

Jud. 5:14. they that handle the pen of *the writer.*
2Sa. 8:17. and Seraiah (was) *the scribe;* (marg. or, *secretary*)
20:25. And Sheva (was) *scribe:*
1K. 4: 3. Elihoreph and Ahiah, the sons of Shisha, *scribes;* (marg. or, *secretaries*)
2K. 12:10(11). the king's *scribe* (marg. or, *secretary*)
18:18, 37. Shebna *the scribe,* (marg. *id.*) and Joah
19: 2. Shebna *the scribe,* and the elders
22: 3. the son of Meshullam, *the scribe,*
8. said unto Shaphan *the scribe,*
2K. 22: 9. And Shaphan *the scribe* came to the king,
10. And Shaphan *the scribe* shewed the king,
12. Shaphan *the scribe,* and Asahiah
25:19. and *the* principal *scribe* of the host,
1Ch 2:55. And the families of *the scribes*
18:16. and Shavsha was *scribe;*
24: 6. Shemaiah the son of Nethaneel *the scribe,*
27:32. a counsellor, a wise man, *and a scribe:* (marg. or, *secretary*)
2Ch 24:11. the king's *scribe* and the high priest's officer
26:11. Jeiel *the scribe* and Maaseiah the ruler,
34:13. of the Levites (there were) *scribes,* and
15. and said to Shaphan *the scribe,*
18. Then Shaphan *the scribe* told the king,
20. Shaphan *the scribe,* and Asaiah
Ezr. 7: 6. he (was) *a* ready *scribe* in the law of
11. Artaxerxes gave unto Ezra the priest, *the scribe,* (even) *a scribe of* the words of
Neh 8: 1. they spake unto Ezra *the scribe*
4. Ezra *the scribe* stood upon a pulpit of wood,
9. Ezra the priest *the scribe,*
13. and the Levites, unto Ezra *the scribe,*
12:26. Ezra the priest, *the scribe.*
36. and Ezra *the scribe* before them.
13:13. and Zadok *the scribe,*
Est. 3:12 & 8:9. Then were the king's *scribes* (marg. or, *secretaries*) called
Ps. 45: 1(2). tongue (is) the pen of *a* ready *writer.*
Isa. 33:18. Where (is) *the scribe?* where (is) the receiver? where (is) *he that counted* the
36: 3, 22. Shebna *the scribe,* (marg. or, *secretary*)
37: 2. Shebna *the scribe,* and the elders
Jer. 8: 8. the pen of *the scribes* (is) in vain.
36:10. the son of Shaphan *the scribe,*
12. into *the scribe*'s chamber:
— Elishama *the scribe,* and Delaiah
20. roll in the chamber of Elishama *the scribe,*
21. took it out of Elishama *the scribe*'s chamber.
23. with the penknife, (lit. knife of *a writer*)
26. Baruch *the scribe* and Jeremiah the
32. gave it to Baruch *the scribe,*
37:15. in the house of Jonathan *the scribe:*
20. return to the house of Jonathan *the scribe,*
52:25. and *the* principal *scribe of* the host,
Eze. 9: 2. with *a writer*'s inkhorn by his side:
3. (had) *the writer*'s inkhorn by his side;

* NIPHAL.—*Future.* *

Gen16:10. *it shall* not *be numbered* for multitude.
32:12(13). *cannot be numbered* for multitude.
1K. 3: 8. nor *counted* for multitude.
8: 5. sheep and oxen, that *could* not *be told*
1Ch 23: 3. *Now* the Levites *were numbered* from the
2Ch 5: 6. sheep and oxen, which *could* not *be told*
Jer. 33:22. As the host of heaven *cannot be numbered,*
Hos. 1:10(2:1). cannot be measured nor *numbered;*

* PIEL.—*Preterite.* *

Jud. 6:13. his miracles which our fathers *told* us *of,*
Ps. 44: 1(2). our fathers *have told* us, (what) work
75: 1(2). thy wondrous works *declare.*
78: 3. and known, and our fathers *have told* us.
119:13. With my lips *have I declared*
26. *I have declared* my ways,

PIEL.—*Infinitive.*

Ex. 9:16. that my name *may be declared*
Ps. 26: 7. *and tell* of all thy wondrous works.
40: 5(6). they are more *than can be numbered.*
50:16. What hast thou to do *to declare* my statutes,
73:28. *that I may declare* all thy works.
102:21(22). *To declare* the name of the Lord

PIEL.—*Imperative.*

Gen40: 8. *tell* me (them), I pray you.
2K. 8: 4. *Tell me,* I pray thee, all the great things
1Ch 16:24. *Declare* his glory among the heathen;
Ps. 96: 3. *Declare* his glory among the heathen,
Isa. 43:26. *declare* thou, that thou mayest be justified.
Joel 1: 3. *Tell ye* your children of it,

PIEL.—*Future.*

Gen24:66. *And* the servant *told* Isaac all
29:13. *And he told* Laban all these things.
37: 9. *and told* it his brethren,
10. *And he told* (it) to his father,
40: 9. *And* the chief butler *told* his dream
41: 8. *and* Pharaoh *told* them his dream;
12. *and we told* him, and he interpreted

Ex. 10: 2. that *thou mayest tell* in the ears of thy son,
18: 8. *And* Moses *told* his father in law all
24: 3. And Moses came *and told* the people
Nu. 13:27. *And they told* him, and said,
Jos. 2:23. *and told* him all (things) that befell them:
1Sa. 11: 5. *And they told* him the tidings of the men
1K. 13:11. his sons came *and told* him
— *them they told also* to their father.
2K. 8: 6. *And* when the king...*she told*
Est. 5:11. *And* Haman *told* them of the glory of his
6:13. *And* Haman *told* Zeresh his wife and all
Job 12: 8. and the fishes of the sea *shall declare* unto
15:17. that (which) I have seen *I will declare;*
28:27. see it, *and declare* (marg. *number*) *it;*
38:37. Who *can number* the clouds in wisdom?
Ps. 2: 7. *I will declare* the decree:
9: 1(2). *I will shew forth* all thy marvellous
14(15). *That I may shew forth* all thy praise
22:17(18). *I may tell* all my bones:
22(23). *I will declare* thy name unto my
48:13(14). that *ye may tell* (it) to the generation
59:12(13). cursing and lying (which) *they speak.*
64: 5(6). *they commune* of laying snares privily;
66:16. and *I will declare* what he hath done for
69:26(27). *they talk* to the grief of those whom
71:15. mouth *shall shew forth* thy righteousness
73:15. If I say, *I will speak* thus; behold, I
78: 6. should arise *and declare* (them) to their
79:13. *we will shew forth* thy praise to all
107:22. *and declare* his works with rejoicing.
118:17. not die, but live, *and declare* the works
145: 6. *I will declare* thy greatness.
Isa. 43:21. *they shall shew forth* my praise.
Jer. 23:27. *they tell* every man to his neighbour.
28. The prophet that hath a dream, *let him tell*
32. dreams, saith the Lord, *and do tell them,*
51:10. *and let us declare* in Zion the work
Eze. 12:16. *they may declare* all their abominations

PIEL.—*Participle.*

Jud. 7:13. (there was) a man *that told* a dream
2K. 8: 5. as he *was telling* the king
Ps. 19: 1(2). The heavens *declare* the glory of God;
78: 4. *shewing* to the generation to come

* PUAL.—*Preterite.* *

Isa. 52:15. (that) which *had* not *been told* them

PUAL.—*Future.*

Job 37:20. *Shall it be told* him that I speak?
Ps. 22:30(31). *it shall be accounted* to the Lord
88:11(12). *Shall* thy lovingkindness *be declared*
Hab. 1: 5. ye will not believe, though *it be told* (you).

5613 סָפֵר [*sāh-phēhr'*], Ch. m.

Ezr. 4: 8. Shimshai *the scribe* (marg. or, *secretary*)
9. and Shimshai *the scribe*, and the rest
17. and (to) Shimshai *the scribe*, and (to) the
23. and Shimshai *the scribe*, and their
7:12. *a scribe of* the law of the God of
21. *the scribe of* the law of the God of

5612 סֵפֶר *sēh'-pher*, m.

Gen 5: 1. This (is) *the book of* the generations of
Ex. 17:14. Write this (for) a memorial *in a book,*
24: 7. he took *the book of* the covenant,
32:32. blot me, I pray thee, *out of thy book*
33. him will I blot *out of my book.*
Nu. 5:23. priest shall write these curses *in a book,*
21:14. it is said *in the book of* the wars of the
Deu 17:18. write him a copy of this law *in a book*
24: 1. let him write her *a bill of* divorcement,
3. and write her *a bill of* divorcement,
28:58. of this law that are written *in* this *book,*
61. (is) not written *in the book of* this law,
29:20(19). curses that are written *in* this *book*
21(20). that are written *in* this *book*
27(26). curses that are written *in* this *book:*
30:10. statutes which are written *in* this *book*
31:24. writing the words of this law in *a book,*
26. Take this *book of* the law,
Jos 1: 8. This *book of* the law shall not depart
8:31. written *in the book of* the law of Moses,
34. all that is written *in the book of* the law.
10:13. (Is) not this written in *the book of* Jasher?
18: 9. by cities into seven parts in *a book,*
Jos. 23: 6. all that is written *in the book of* the law
24:26. wrote these words *in the book of* the law
1Sa. 10:25. wrote (it) *in a book,* and laid (it) up
2Sa. 1:18. behold, (it is) written in *the book of* Jasher
11:14. David wrote *a letter* to Joab,
15. And he wrote *in the letter,*
1K. 11:41. written in *the book of* the acts of Solomon.
14:19. (are) written in *the book of* the chronicles
29. (are) they not written in *the book of* the
15: 7, 31. (are) they not written in *the book of*
23. (are) they not written in *the book of* the
16: 5, 14, 20, 27. (are) they not written in *the book of* the chronicles
21: 8. So she wrote *letters* in Ahab's name,
— and sent *the letters* unto the elders
9. And she wrote *in the letters,*
11. as it (was) written *in the letters*
22:39, 45(46). they not written in *the book of*
2K. 1:18. written in *the book of* the chronicles
5: 5. I will send *a letter* unto the king of Israel.
6. brought *the letter* to the king
— when this *letter* is come unto thee,
7. the king of Israel had read *the letter,*
8:23. written in *the book of* the chronicles
10: 1. Jehu wrote *letters,* and sent to Samaria,
2. as soon as this *letter* cometh to you,
6. he wrote *a letter* the second time to them,
7. when *the letter* came to them,
34 & 12:19(20) & 13:8, 12. they not written in *the book of* the chronicles
14: 6. that which is written *in the book*
15, 18, 28. (are) they not written in *the book of*
15: 6, 21, 36. written in *the book of* the chronicles
11, 15, 26, 31. they (are) written in *the book of*
16:19. written in *the book of* the chronicles
19:14. And Hezekiah received *the letter*
20:12. sent *letters* and a present unto Hezekiah:
20 & 21:17, 25. (are) they not written in *the book of* the chronicles
22: 8. I have found *the book of* the law
— And Hilkiah gave *the book* to Shaphan,
10. the priest hath delivered me *a book.*
11. the king had heard the words of *the book*
13. concerning the words of this *book* that
— not hearkened unto the words of this *book,*
16. all the words of *the book* which the king
23: 2. all the words of *the book of* the covenant
3. covenant that were written in this *book.*
21. (it is) written in *the book of* this covenant.
24. the law which were written in *the book*
28 & 24:5. written in *the book of* the chronicles
1Ch 9: 1. (were) written in *the book of* the kings
2Ch 16:11. (are) written in *the book of* the kings
17: 9. (had) *the book of* the law of the Lord
20:34. mentioned in *the book of* the kings of
24:27. in the story of *the book of* the kings.
25: 4. written in the law *in the book of* Moses,
26. written in *the book of* the kings of Judah
27: 7 & 28:26. they (are) written in *the book of*
32:17. He wrote *also letters* to rail on the Lord
32. in *the book of* the kings of Judah and
34:14. Hilkiah the priest found *a book of* the law
15. I have found *the book of* the law
— And Hilkiah delivered *the book* to Shaphan.
16. Shaphan carried *the book* to the king,
18. Hilkiah the priest hath given me *a book.*
21. concerning the words of *the book* that is
— do after all that is written in *this book.*
24. the curses that are written in *the book*
30. all the words of *the book of* the covenant
31. covenant which are written in *this book.*
35:12. as (it is) written *in the book of* Moses.
27 & 36:8. written in *the book of* the kings
Neh. 7: 5. I found *a register of* the genealogy of
8: 1. to bring *the book of* the law of Moses,
3. people (were attentive) unto *the book of*
5. And Ezra opened *the book*
8. they read *in the book* in the law of God
18. he read *in the book of* the law of God.
9: 3. read *in the book of* the law of the Lord
12:23. written in *the book of* the chronicles,
13: 1. they read *in the book of* Moses
Est. 1:22. sent *letters* into all the king's provinces,
2:23. was written *in the book of* the chronicles
3:13. *the letters* were sent by posts into all
6: 1. he commanded to bring *the book of*
8: 5. let it be written to reverse *the letters*

Est. 8:10. sent *letters* by posts on horseback,
9:20. sent *letters* unto all the Jews
25. he commanded by *letters*
30. sent *the letters* unto all the Jews,
32. it was written *in the book.*
10: 2. written in *the book of* the chronicles
Job 19:23. oh that they were printed *in a book!*
31:35. *and* (that) mine adversary...*a book.*
Ps. 40: 7(8). in the volume of *the book* (it is)
69:28(29). Let them be blotted *out of the book of*
139:16. in *thy book* all (my members) were
Ecc.12:12. making many *books* (there is) no end
Isa. 29:11. the words of *a book* (marg. or, *letter*) that is sealed, which (men) deliver to one that is *learned*, (lit. that knoweth *a book*)
12. And *the book* is delivered to him that is not *learned*, (lit. that knoweth not *a book*)
— I am not *learned*. (lit. I know not *a book*)
18. shall the deaf hear the words of *the book*,
30: 8. and note it in *a book*,
34: 4. shall be rolled together *as a scroll:*
16. Seek ye out of *the book of* the Lord,
37:14. And Hezekiah received *the letter*
39: 1. sent *letters* and a present to Hezekiah:
50: 1. Where (is) *the bill of* your mother's
Jer. 3: 8. and given her *a bill of* divorce;
25:13. (even) all that is written *in this book*,
29: 1. Now these (are) the words of *the letter*
25. thou hast sent *letters* in thy name
29. And Zephaniah the priest read this *letter*
30: 2. that I have spoken unto thee in *a book.*
32:10. And I subscribed *the evidence*, (marg. wrote *in the book*)
11. So I took *the evidence of* the purchase,
12. And I gave *the evidence of* the purchase
— that subscribed *the book of* the purchase,
14. Take these *evidences*, this *evidence of* the purchase,...*evidence* which is open;
16. had delivered *the evidence of* the purchase
44. and subscribe *evidences*,
36: 2. Take thee a roll of *a book*,
4. upon a roll of *a book.*
8. reading *in the book* the words of the Lord,
10. Then read Baruch *in the book*
11. out of *the book* all the words of the Lord
13. Baruch read *the book* in the ears of the
18. I wrote (them) with ink in *the book.*
32. all the words of *the book*
45: 1. he had written these words in *a book*
51:60. Jeremiah wrote in *a book* all the evil
63. hast made an end of reading this *book*,
Eze. 2: 9. and, lo, a roll of *a book* (was) therein;
Dan. 1: 4. *the learning* and the tongue of the
17. them knowledge and skill in all *learning*
9: 2. I Daniel understood *by books*
12: 1. that shall be found written *in the book.*
4. shut up the words, and seal *the book*,
Nah. 1: 1. *The book of* the vision of Nahum
Mal. 3:16. and *a book of* remembrance was written

5609 **סְפַר** *s'phar*, Ch. m.

Ezr. 4:15. That search may be made *in the book of*
— so shalt thou find *in the book of*
6: 1. in the house *of the rolls*, (marg. *books*)
18. as it is written *in the book of* Moses.
Dan. 7:10. *and the books* were opened.

5610 **סְפָר** *s'phāhr*, m.

2Ch 2:17(16). after *the numbering* wherewith David

5615 **סְפֹרָה** [*s'phōh-rāh'*], f.

Ps. 71:15. I know not *the numbers* (thereof).

5612 **סִפְרָה** [*siph-rāh'*], f.

Ps. 56: 8(9). (are they) not *in thy book?*

5619 **סָקַל** [*sāh-kal'*].

* KAL.—*Preterite.* *

Ex. 17: 4. *they be* almost ready *to stone me.* (lit. yet a little *and they will stone me*)
Deu13:10(11). *And thou shalt stone him* with stones,
17: 5. *and shalt stone them* with stones,
22:21. *and* the men of her city *shall stone her*
24. *and ye shall stone* them with stones

KAL.—*Infinitive.*

Ex. 19:13. he shall *surely* be stoned, (lit. *stoning* he shall be stoned)
21:28. the ox shall be *surely* stoned,
1Sa.30: 6. for the people spake *of stoning him*,

KAL.—*Imperative.*

1K. 21:10. (then) carry him out, *and stone him*,

KAL.—*Future.*

Ex. 8:26(22). and *will they* not *stone us?*
Jos. 7:25. *after they had stoned* them with stones.
1K. 21:13. *and stoned him* with stones,

* NIPHAL.—*Future.* *

Ex. 19:13. *he shall* surely *be stoned*,
21:28. the ox *shall be* surely *stoned*,
29, 32. the ox *shall be stoned*,

* PIEL.—*Imperative.* *

Isa. 62:10. *gather out* the stones;

PIEL.—*Future.*

2Sa.16: 6. *And he cast* stones at David,
13. cursed as he went, *and threw* stones
Isa. 5: 2. it, *and gathered out the stones thereof*,

* PUAL.—*Preterite.* *

1K. 21:14. Naboth *is stoned*, and is dead.
15. Jezebel heard that Naboth *was stoned*,

סַר *sar*, adj. 5620

1K. 20:43. the king of Israel went to his house *heavy*
21: 4. Ahab came into his house *heavy* and
5. Why (is) thy spirit so *sad*,

סָרָבִים *sāh-rāh-veem'*, m. pl. 5621

Eze. 2: 6. *briers* (marg. or, *rebels*) and thorns (be)

סַרְבָּלִין [*sar-bāh-leen'*], Ch. m. pl. 5622

Dan. 3:21. bound *in their coats*, (marg. or, *mantles*)
27. *neither* were *their coats* changed,

סָרָה *sāh-rāh'*, f. 5627

Deu 13: 5(6). spoken *to turn* (you) *away* (marg. *revolt*)
19:16. to testify against him (that which is) *wrong;* (marg. or, *falling away*)
Isa. 1: 5. ye will *revolt* more and more: (marg. increase *revolt*)
14: 6. in wrath with a continual stroke, (marg. a stroke without *removing*)
31: 6. deeply *revolted*. (lit. deepened *revolt*)
59:13. speaking oppression *and revolt*,
Jer. 28:16. thou hast taught *rebellion* (marg. *revolt*)
29:32. because he hath taught *rebellion* (marg. *id.*)

סָרַח [*sāh-ragh'*]. 5628

* KAL.—*Future.* *

Ex. 26:12. *shall hang* over the backside of the

KAL.—*Participle.* Poel.

Eze.17: 6. it grew, and became a *spreading* vine

KAL.—*Participle.* Paül.

Ex. 26:13. it shall *hang* over (lit. shall be *hung* over)
Eze.23:15. *exceeding in* dyed attire upon their heads,
Am. 6: 4. *and stretch themselves* upon their couches, (marg. or, *abound* with superfluities)
7. banquet of *them that stretched themselves*

* NIPHAL.—*Preterite.* *

Jer. 49: 7. *is* their wisdom *vanished?*

סֶרַח *seh'-ragh*, m. 5629

Ex. 26:12. *And the remnant* that remaineth

5630 סִרְיֹן [*sir-yōhn'*], m.

Jer. 46: 4. spears, (and) put on *the brigandines.*
51: 3. and against (him that) lifteth himself up *in his brigandine:*

5631 סָרִיס *sāh-rees'*, m.

Gen37:36. into Egypt unto Potiphar, *an officer* (lit. *eunuch*) *of* Pharaoh's,
39: 1. Potiphar, *an officer of* Pharaoh,
40: 2. was wroth against two (of) *his officers*,
7. asked Pharaoh's *officers* that (were) with
1Sa. 8:15. and give *to his officers*, (marg. *eunuchs*)
1K. 22: 9. called *an officer*, (marg. or, *eunuch*)
2K. 8: 6. the king appointed unto her *a* certain *officer*, (marg. *eunuch*)
9:32. three *eunuchs*. (marg. or, *chamberlains*)
18:17. Tartan and Rab*saris* [perhaps lit. chief *eunuch*]
20:18. they shall be *eunuchs* in the palace of the
23:11. by the chamber of Nathan-melech *the chamberlain*, (marg.or, *eunuch*, or, *officer*)
24:12. and his princes, *and his officers:* (marg. or, *eunuchs*)
15. king's wives, and *his officers*, (marg. *id.*)
25:19. he took *an officer* (marg. or, *eunuch*)
1Ch 28: 1. with *the officers*, (marg. or, *eunuchs*) and
2Ch 18: 8. And the king of Israel called for one (of his) *officers*, (marg. *id.*)
Est. 1:10. the seven *chamberlains* (marg. *id.*) that
12. by (his) *chamberlains:* (marg. *id.*)
15. Ahasuerus by *the chamberlains?*
2: 3. custody of Hege the king's *chamberlain*,
14. of Shaashgaz, the king's *chamberlain*,
15. Hegai the king's *chamberlain*, the keeper
21. two of the king's *chamberlains*,
4: 4. maids *and her chamberlains* (marg. *eunuchs*)
5. Hatach, (one) *of* the king's *chamberlains*,
6: 2. two of the king's *chamberlains*,
14. *And* while...came the king's *chamberlains*,
7: 9. Harbonah, one of *the chamberlains*,
Isa. 39: 7. shall be *eunuchs* in the palace of the king
56: 3. neither let *the eunuch* say, Behold, I
4. *unto the eunuchs* that keep my sabbaths,
Jer. 29: 2. the king, and the queen, *and the eunuchs*, (marg. or, *chamberlains*)
34:19. the princes of Jerusalem, *the eunuchs*, and
38: 7. Ebed-melech the Ethiopian, one of *the eunuchs*
39: 3. Sarsechim, Rab-*saris*, [perhaps lit. chief *eunuch*]
13. Nebushasban, Rab-*saris*, (*id.*)
41:16. women, and the children, *and the eunuchs*,
52:25. He took also out of the city *an eunuch*,
Dan. 1: 3. unto Ashpenaz the master of *his eunuchs*,
7. Unto whom the prince of *the eunuchs* gave
8. he requested of the prince of *the eunuchs*
9. with the prince of *the eunuchs*.
10. the prince of *the eunuchs* said unto Daniel,
11. Melzar, whom the prince of *the eunuchs* had
18. the prince of *the eunuchs* brought them in

5632 סָרְכִין *sāh-r'cheen'*, Ch. m. pl.

Dan. 6: 2(3). And over these three *presidents;*
3(4). above *the presidents* and princes,
4(5). Then *the presidents* and princes sought
6(7). these *presidents* and princes assembled
7(8). All *the presidents of* the kingdom,

5633 סֶרֶן [*seh'-ren*], m.

Jos. 13: 3. five *lords of* the Philistines;
Jud. 3: 3. five *lords of* the Philistines,
16: 5. *the lords of* the Philistines came up unto
8. *the lords of* the Philistines brought up to
18. she sent and called *for the lords of* the
— Then *the lords of* the Philistines came up unto her,
23. *Then the lords of* the Philistines gathered
27. *the lords of* the Philistines (were) there;
30. the house fell upon *the lords*,
1Sa. 5: 8. and gathered all *the lords of* the Philistines
11. and gathered together all *the lords of* the
1Sa. 6: 4. the number of *the lords of* the Philistines:
— plague (was) on you all, *and on your lords*.
12. *and the lords of* the Philistines went after
16. *the* five *lords of* the Philistines had seen
18. cities of the Philistines (belonging) to *the* five *lords*,
7: 7. *the lords of* the Philistines went up against
29: 2. *And the lords of* the Philistines passed on
6. nevertheless *the lords* favour thee not.
7. displease not *the lords of* the Philistines.
1K. 7:30. four brasen wheels, *and plates of* brass:
1Ch 12:19. *the lords of* the Philistines upon advisement

סַרְעַפָּה [*sar-ğap-pāh'*], f. 5634

Eze.31: 5. *his boughs* were multiplied,

סָרַף [*sāh-raph'*]. 5635

* PIEL.—*Participle.* *

Am. 6:10. *and he that burneth him*, to bring out

סִרְפָּד *sir-pāhd'*, m. 5636

Isa. 55:13. instead of *the brier* shall come up the

סָרַר *sāh-rar'*. 5637

* KAL.—*Preterite.* *

Hos. 4:16. Israel *slideth back* as a backsliding

KAL.—*Participle.* Poel.

Deu21:18. a man have a *stubborn* and rebellious son,
20. This our son (is) *stubborn* and rebellious,
Neh 9:29. and *withdrew* the shoulder, (marg. they gave a *withdrawing* shoulder)
Ps. 66: 7. let not *the rebellious* exalt themselves.
68: 6(7). *the rebellious* dwell in a dry (land).
18(19). gifts for men; yea, (for) *the rebellious*
78: 8. a *stubborn* and rebellious generation;
Pro. 7:11. She (is) loud *and stubborn;*
Isa. 1:23. Thy princes (are) *rebellious*,
30: 1. Woe to the *rebellious* children,
65: 2. all the day unto a *rebellious* people,
Jer. 5:23. this people hath a *revolting* and a rebellious
6:28. They (are) all grievous *revolters*,
Hos. 4:16. as a *backsliding* heifer:
9:15. all their princes (are) *revolters*.
Zec. 7:11. and pulled *away* the shoulder, (marg. gave a *backsliding* shoulder)

סְתָיו (קרי) *s'thāh'yv*, or סְתָו (כתיב) *s'thāhv*, m. 5638

Cant.2:11. *the winter* is past, the rain is over (and)

סָתַם *sāh-tham'*. 5640

* KAL.—*Preterite.* *

2Ch 32:30. This same Hezekiah also *stopped* the

KAL.—*Infinitive.*

2Ch 32: 3. *to stop* the waters of the fountains

KAL.—*Imperative.*

Dan 8:26. wherefore *shut* thou *up* the vision;
12: 4. But thou, O Daniel, *shut up* the words,

KAL.—*Future.*

2K. 3:19. every good tree, and *stop* all wells
25. and *they stopped* all the wells of water,
2Ch 32: 4. much people together, who *stopped* all the

KAL.—*Participle.* Paül.

Ps. 51: 6(8). *and in the hidden* (part) thou shalt
Eze.28: 3. there is no *secret* that they can hide from
Dan 12: 9. the words (are) *closed up* and sealed

* NIPHAL.—*Infinitive.* *

Neh. 4: 7(1). the breaches began *to be stopped*,

* PIEL.—*Preterite.* *

Gen26:15. the Philistines *had stopped them*,

PIEL.—*Future.*

Gen26:18. *for* the Philistines *had stopped them*

5641 ## סָתַר [*sāh-thar'*].

* KAL.—*Future.* *

Pro.22: 3. (כתיב) A prudent man foreseeth the evil, *and hideth himself:*

* NIPHAL.—*Preterite.* *

Nu. 5:13. the eyes of her husband, *and be kept close,*
1Sa.20: 5. let me go, *that I may hide myself*
19. to the place where *thou didst hide thyself*
1K. 17: 3. *and hide thyself* by the brook Cherith,
Job 3:23. (Why is light given) to a man whose way *is hid,*
28:21. and *kept close* from the fowls of the air.
Ps. 38: 9(10). my groaning *is* not *hid* from thee.
Pro.22: 3. foreseeth the evil, *and hideth himself:*
27:12. foreseeth the evil, (and) *hideth himself;*
Isa. 28:15. under falsehood *have we hid ourselves:*
40:27. My way *is hid* from the Lord,
65:16. because *they are hid* from mine eyes.
Jer. 16:17. *they are* not *hid* from my face,

NIPHAL.—*Infinitive.*

Job 34:22. workers of iniquity *may hide themselves.*

NIPHAL.—*Imperative.*

Jer. 36:19. the princes unto Baruch, Go, *hide thee,*

NIPHAL.—*Future.*

Gen 4:14. and from thy face *shall I be hid;*
31:49. when *we are absent* one from another.
1Sa.20:24. *So* David *hid himself* in the field:
Job 13:20. then *will I* not *hide myself* from thee.
Ps. 55:12(13). *then I would have hid myself* from
89:46(47). How long, Lord? *wilt thou hide thyself*
Pro.28:28. the wicked rise, men *hide themselves:*
Jer. 23:24. *Can* any *hide himself* in secret places
Hos 13:14. repentance *shall be hid* from mine eyes.
Am. 9: 3. though *they be hid* from my sight
Zep. 2: 3. it may be *ye shall be hid* in the day of

NIPHAL.—*Participle.*

Deu 7:20. are left, *and hide themselves* from thee,
29:29(28). *The secret* (things belong) unto the
Ps. 19: 6(7). there is nothing *hid* from the heat
12(13). cleanse thou me *from secret* (faults).

* PIEL.—*Imperative.* *

Isa. 16: 3. *hide* the outcasts; bewray not him that

* PUAL.—*Participle.* *

Pro.27: 5. Open rebuke (is) better than *secret* love.

* HIPHIL.—*Preterite.* *

Deu31:17. *and I will hide* my face from them,
Ps. 10:11. *he hideth* his face; he will never see (it).
22:24(25). neither *hath he hid* his face from
30: 7(8). *thou didst hide* thy face, (and) I was
Isa. 49: 2. in his quiver *hath he hid me;*
50: 6. *I hid* not my face from shame and
54: 8. In a little wrath *I hid* my face from
59: 2. your sins *have hid* (marg. or, *made* (him) *hide*) (his) face from you,
64: 7(6). for *thou hast hid* thy face from us,
Jer. 33: 5. *I have hid* my face from this city.

HIPHIL.—*Infinitive.*

Deu 31:18. I will *surely* hide (lit. *hiding* I will hide)
Pro 25: 2. (It is) the glory of God *to conceal* a thing:
Isa. 29:15. that seek deep *to hide* their counsel
57:17. *I hid me,* and was wroth,

HIPHIL.—*Imperative.*

Ps. 51: 9(11). *Hide* thy face from my sins,

HIPHIL.—*Future.*

Ex. 3: 6. *And* Moses *hid* his face; for he was
Deu31:18. *I will* surely *hide* my face in that day
32:20. *I will hide* my face from them,
1Sa.20: 2. why *should* my father *hide* this thing
2K. 11: 2. *and they hid* him, (even) him and his
2Ch 22:11. *So* Jehoshabeath,...*hid* him from
Job 3:10. *nor hid* sorrow from mine eyes.
13:24. Wherefore *hidest thou* thy face,
14:13. *that thou wouldest keep me secret,*
34:29. *and when he hideth* (his) face, who then
Ps. 13: 1(2). how long *wilt thou hide* thy face from
17: 8. *hide me* under the shadow of thy wings,
27: 5. secret of his tabernacle *shall he hide me;*
9. *Hide* not thy face (far) from me;
Ps. 31:20(21). *Thou shalt hide them* in the secret of
44:24(25). Wherefore *hidest thou* thy face,
64: 2(3). *Hide me* from the secret counsel of
69:17(18). *hide* not thy face from thy servant;
88:14(15). (why) *hidest thou* thy face from me?
102: 2(3). *Hide* not thy face from me
104:29. *Thou hidest* thy face, they are troubled:
119:19. *hide* not thy commandments from me.
143: 7. *hide* not thy face from me,
Jer. 36:26. *but* the Lord *hid them.*
Eze.39:23. *therefore hid I* my face from them,
24. *and hid* my face from them.
29. Neither *will I hide* my face any more
Mic. 3: 4. *he will even hide* his face from them

HIPHIL.—*Participle.*

Isa. 8:17. *that hideth* his face from the house of
53: 3. *and we hid as it were* (our) faces from him; (marg. *as an hiding of* faces from him)

* HITHPAEL.—*Future.* *

Isa. 29:14. the understanding of their prudent (men) *shall be hid.*

HITHPAEL.—*Participle.*

1Sa.23:19. *Doth* not David *hide himself* with us
26: 1. *Doth* not David *hide himself* in the hill
Ps. 54[title](2). *Doth* not David *hide himself* with
Isa. 45:15. Verily thou (art) a God *that hidest thyself,*

סְתַר [*s'thar*], Ch. 5642

* P'AL.—*Preterite.* *

Ezr. 5:12. who *destroyed* this house,

* PAEL.—*Participle.* *

Dan 2:22. He revealeth the deep *and secret things:*

סֵתֶר *sēh'-ther*, m. 5643

Deu13: 6(7). or thy friend,...entice thee *secretly,*
27:15. and putteth (it) *in a secret place.*
24. he that smiteth his neighbour *secretly.*
28:57. eat them for want of all (things) *secretly*
Jud. 3:19. a *secret* errand (lit. errand of *secrecy*)
1Sa.19: 2. abide *in a secret place,* and hide thyself:
25:20. she came down *by the covert of* the hill,
2Sa.12:12. For thou didst (it) *secretly:*
Job 13:10. surely reprove you, if ye do *secretly*
22:14. Thick clouds (are) *a covering* to him,
24:15. *and disguiseth* (his) face. (marg. setteth (his) face *in secret*)
31:27. my heart hath been *secretly* enticed,
40:21. *in the covert of* the reed, and fens.
Ps. 18:11(12). He made darkness *his secret place;*
27: 5. *in the secret of* his tabernacle shall he
31:20(21). Thou shalt hide them *in the secret of*
32: 7. Thou (art) my *hiding place;*
61: 4(5). I will trust *in the covert of* thy wings.
81: 7(8). I answered thee *in the secret place of*
91: 1. He that dwelleth *in the secret place*
101: 5. Whoso *privily* slandereth his neighbour,
119:114. Thou (art) *my hiding place*
139:15. when I was made *in secret,*
Pro. 9:17. bread (eaten) in *secret* (marg. of *secrecies*) is pleasant.
21:14. A gift *in secret* pacifieth anger:
25:23. angry countenance a *backbiting* tongue.
Cant.2:14. *in the secret places of* the stairs,
Isa. 16: 4. be thou *a covert* to them from the face of
28:17. *and* the waters shall overflow *the hiding place.*
32: 2. *and a covert* from the tempest;
45:19. I have not spoken *in secret,*
48:16. I have not spoken *in secret*
Jer. 37:17. the king asked him *secretly*
38:16. Zedekiah the king sware *secretly*
40:15. spake to Gedaliah in Mizpah *secretly,*

סִתְרָה *sith-rāh'*, f. 5643

Deu32:38. rise up and help you, (and) be your *protection.* (marg. *an hiding* for you)

ע *gah'-yin.*

The Sixteenth Letter of the Alphabet.

5646 עָב *gāhv*, m.

1K. 7: 6. the (other) pillars *and the thick beam*
Eze.41:25. *and* (there were) *thick* planks upon the

5645 עָב *gāhv*,com.

Ex. 19: 9. I come unto thee *in a thick* cloud, (lit. *in the thickness of* a cloud)
Jud. 5: 4. *the clouds* also dropped water.
2Sa.22:12. dark waters, (and) *thick clouds of* the
23: 4. (even) a morning without *clouds;*
1K. 18:44. there ariseth *a* little *cloud*
45. the heaven was black with *clouds*
2Ch 4:17. cast them, *in the clay* ground (marg. *in the thicknesses of* the ground)
Job 20: 6. reach *unto the clouds;* (marg. *cloud*)
22:14. *Thick clouds* (are) a covering to him,
26: 8. bindeth up the waters *in his thick clouds;*
30:15. *and* my welfare passeth away *as a cloud.*
36:29. can (any) understand the spreadings of *the clouds,*
37:11. by watering he wearieth *the thick cloud:*
16. thou know the balancings of *the clouds,*
38:34. Canst thou lift up thy voice *to the clouds,*
Ps. 18:11(12). dark waters (and) *thick clouds of* the
12(13). before him *his thick clouds* passed,
77:17(18). *The clouds* poured out water:
104: 3. who maketh *the clouds* his chariot:
147: 8. Who covereth the heaven *with clouds,*
Pro.16:15. his favour (is) *as a cloud of* the latter
Ecc.11: 3. If *the clouds* be full of rain,
4. he that regardeth *the clouds*
12: 2. nor *the clouds* return after the rain:
Isa. 5: 6. I will also command *the clouds*
14:14. ascend above the heights of *the clouds;*
18: 4. *like a cloud of* dew in the heat of
19: 1. the Lord rideth upon *a* swift *cloud,*
25: 5. the heat with the shadow of *a cloud:*
44:22. I have blotted out, *as a thick cloud,*
60: 8. Who (are) these (that) fly *as a cloud,*
Jer. 4:29. they shall go *into thickets,*

5646 עֹב [*gōhv*], m.

Eze.41:26. of the house, *and thick planks.*

5647 עָבַד *gāh-vad'.*

* KAL.—*Preterite.* *

Gen14: 4. Twelve years *they served* Chedorlaomer,
15:13. *and shall serve them;* and they shall
29:15. *shouldest thou therefore serve me* for
25. *did* not *I serve* with thee for Rachel?
30:26. for whom *I have served* thee,
— my service which *I have done thee.*
29. Thou knowest how *I have served thee,*
31: 6. with all my power *I have served* your
41. *I served thee* fourteen years for thy two
Ex. 1:14. service, wherein *they made* them *serve,*
13: 5. *that thou shalt keep* this service in this
21: 6. *and he shall serve him* for ever.
23:25. *And ye shall serve* the Lord your God,
Nu. 4:26. that is made for them: *so shall they serve.*
18: 7. within the vail; *and ye shall serve:*
23. *But* the Levites *shall do the service*
Deu 4:19. driven to worship them, *and serve them,*
28. *And* there *ye shall serve* gods,
7: 4. *that they may serve* other gods:
8:19. walk after other gods, *and serve them,*
11:16. turn aside, *and serve* other gods,
12: 2. the nations which ye shall possess *served*
15:12. be sold unto thee, *and serve thee*
18. *in serving thee* (lit. *he hath served thee*)
20:11. unto thee, *and they shall serve thee.*
28:36. *and* there *shalt thou serve* other gods,
39. shalt plant vineyards, *and dress* (them),
47. Because *thou servedst* not the Lord thy
48. *Therefore shalt thou serve* thine enemies
64. *and* there *thou shalt serve* other gods.

Deu30:17. worship other gods, *and serve them;*
31:20. turn unto other gods, *and serve them,*
Jos.23:16. and have gone *and served* other gods,
24:14. away the gods which your fathers *served*
15. whether the gods which your fathers *served*
20. *and serve* strange gods,
Jud.10: 6. forsook the Lord, and *served* not *him.*
1Sa. 4: 9. unto the Hebrews, as *they have been* to you: (lit. *they have served* you)
12:14. If ye will fear the Lord, *and serve* him,
20. *but serve* the Lord with all your heart;
24. Only fear the Lord, *and serve* him
17: 9. then shall ye be our servants, *and serve*
2Sa. 9:10. Thou *therefore*, and thy sons, and thy servants, *shall till*
15: 8. *then I will serve* the Lord.
16:19. *I have served* in thy father's presence,
1K. 9: 6. go *and serve* other gods, and worship
12: 7. *and wilt serve them,* and answer them,
2K. 10:18. Ahab *served* Baal a little;
18: 7. the king of Assyria, and *served him* not.
21:21. the idols that his father *served,*
2Ch 7:19. shall go *and serve* other gods,
Neh 9:35. they *have* not *served thee* in their
Isa. 19:21. *and shall do* sacrifice and oblation;
23. *and* the Egyptians *shall serve* with the
Jer. 8: 2. and whom *they have served,*
16:13. *and* there *shall ye serve* other gods
25:11. *and* these nations *shall serve*
14. and great kings *shall serve themselves*
27: 7. *And* all nations *shall serve* him,
— *and* great kings *shall serve* themselves
11. under the yoke of the king of Babylon, *and serve him,*
— *and they shall till it,* and dwell therein.
28:14. *and they shall serve him:* and I have
30: 9. *But they shall serve* the Lord their God,
34:14. and *when he hath served thee* six years,
Eze.29:18. for the service that *he had served*
20. his labour wherewith *he served*
Mal. 3:18. and him that *serveth him* not.

KAL.—*Infinitive.*

Gen 2: 5. (there was) not a man *to till* the ground.
15. *to dress it* and to keep it.
3:23. *to till* the ground from whence he was
Ex. 10:26. thereof must we take *to serve* the Lord
14: 5. we have let Israel go *from serving us?*
12. (it had been) better for us *to serve* the
Nu. 3: 7, 8. *to do* the service of the tabernacle.
4:23. *to do* the work in the tabernacle
24. *to serve,* and for burdens:
30. *to do* the work of the tabernacle
47. *to do* the service of the ministry,
7: 5. *to do* the service of the tabernacle
8:11. that they may *execute* (marg. be *to execute*)
15. *to do the service* of the tabernacle
19. *to do* the service of the children of Israel
22. *to do* their service in the tabernacle
16: 9. *to do* the service of the tabernacle
18: 6. *to do* the service of the tabernacle
Deu10:12. *and to serve* the Lord thy God
11:13. *and to serve him* with all your heart
28:14. to go after other gods *to serve them.*
29:18(17). to go (and) *serve* the gods of these
Jos. 22: 5. *and to serve him* with all your heart
27. *that we might do* the service of the Lord
24:15. if it seem evil unto you *to serve* the Lord,
16. forsake the Lord, *to serve* other gods;
19. Ye cannot *serve* the Lord:
22. have chosen you the Lord, *to serve* him.
Jud. 2:19. following other gods *to serve them,*
2Ch33:16. commanded Judah *to serve* the Lord
34:33. (even) *to serve* the Lord their God.
Job 39: 9. Will the unicorn be willing *to serve thee,*
Ps.102:22(23). and the kingdoms, *to serve* the Lord.
Isa. 28:21. *and bring to pass* his act, his strange act.
Jer. 11:10. went after other gods *to serve them:*
13:10. and walk after other gods, *to serve them,*
25: 6. go not after other gods *to serve them,*
27: 6. have I given him also *to serve him.*
28:14. *that they may serve* Nebuchadnezzar
34: 9. that none *should serve himself* of them,
10. that none *should serve themselves*
35:15. go not after other gods *to serve them,*
40: 9. Fear not *to serve* the Chaldeans:
44: 3. to burn incense, (and) *to serve* other

Zep. 3: 9. call upon the name of the Lord, *to serve him*
Mal. 3:14. Ye have said, It (is) vain *to serve* God:

KAL.—*Imperative.*

Ex. 5:18. Go therefore now, (and) *work;*
10: 8. Go, *serve* the Lord your God:
11. ye (that are) men, *and serve* the Lord;
24. Go ye, *serve* the Lord; only let
12:31. go, *serve* the Lord, as ye have said.
Jos. 24:14. fear the Lord, *and serve* him
— *and serve ye* the Lord.
Jud. 9:28. Zebul his officer? *serve* the men of
1Sa. 7: 3. *and serve him* only: and he will deliver
26:19. saying, Go, *serve* other gods.
2K. 25:24. dwell in the land, *and serve* the king
1Ch 28: 9. the God of thy father, *and serve him*
2Ch 30: 8. *and serve* the Lord your God,
35: 3. *serve* now the Lord your God,
Ps. 2:11. *Serve* the Lord with fear,
100: 2. *Serve* the Lord with gladness:
Jer. 27:12. *and serve* him and his people,
17. *serve* the king of Babylon,
40: 9. dwell in the land, *and serve* the king
Eze. 20:39. Go ye, *serve ye* every one his idols,

KAL.—*Future.*

Gen 4:12. When *thou tillest* the ground,
15:14. whom *they shall serve*, will I judge:
25:23. the elder *shall serve* the younger.
27:29. *Let* people *serve thee*, and nations bow
40. shalt thou live, and *shalt serve* thy
29:18. *I will serve thee* seven years for Rachel
20. *And* Jacob *served* seven years for Rachel;
27. the service which *thou shalt serve* with
30. *and served* with him yet seven other
Ex. 3:12. *ye shall serve* God upon this mountain.
4:23. Let my son go, *that he may serve me:*
7:16 & 8:1(7:26). Let my people go, *that they may serve me*
8:20(16). my people go, *that they may serve me.*
9: 1, 13. my people go, *that they may serve me.*
10: 3. let my people go, *that they may serve me.*
7. let the men go, *that they may serve*
26. we know not with what *we must serve* the
14:12. Let us alone, *that we may serve* the
20: 9. Six days *shalt thou labour,*
21: 2. Hebrew servant, six years *he shall serve:*
23:33. if *thou serve* their gods, it will surely
34:21. Six days *thou shalt work,*
Lev. 25:39. *thou shalt* not *compel* him to serve (marg. *serve thyself* with him with the service)
40. (and) *shall serve* thee unto the year of
46. *they shall be your bondmen* (marg. *ye shall serve yourselves* with them) for ever:
Nu. 8:25. and *shall serve* no more:
26. and *shall do* no service.
Deu 5:13. Six days *thou shalt labour,*
6:13. fear the Lord thy God, and *serve* him,
7:16. neither *shalt thou serve* their gods;
10:20. him *shalt thou serve*, and to him
12:30. How *did* these nations *serve* their gods?
13: 4(5). and *ye shall serve* him, and cleave
6(7), 13(14). Let us go *and serve* other
15:19. *thou shalt* do no *work* with the firstling
17: 3. And hath gone *and served* other gods,
29:26(25). For they went *and served* other gods,
Jos. 23: 7. neither *serve them*, nor bow yourselves
24: 2. *and they served* other gods.
15. choose you this day whom *ye will serve;*
— as for me and my house, *we will serve* the
18. (therefore) *will we* also *serve* the Lord;
21. Nay; but *we will serve* the Lord.
24. The Lord our God *will we serve,*
31. *And* Israel *served* the Lord
Jud. 2: 7. *And* the people *served* the Lord
11. *and served* Baalim:
13. *and served* Baal and Ashtaroth.
3: 6. *and served* their gods.
7. *and served* Baalim and the groves.
8. *and* the children of Israel *served*
14. *So* the children of Israel *served* Eglon
9:28. who (is) Shechem, that *we should serve him?*
— for why *should we serve him?*
38. (is) Abimelech, that *we should serve him?*
10: 6. *and served* Baalim, and Ashtaroth,
10. forsaken our God, *and* also *served* Baalim.
Jud. 10:13. ye have forsaken me, *and served* other
16. *and served* the Lord:
1Sa. 4: 9. that *ye be* not *servants* unto the Hebrews,
7: 4. *and served* the Lord only.
8: 8. they have forsaken me, *and served* other
11: 1. covenant with us, *and we will serve thee.*
12:10. forsaken the Lord, *and have served*
— *and we will serve thee.*
2Sa. 10:19. made peace with Israel, *and served them.*
16:19. whom *should* I *serve?*
22:44. people (which) I knew not *shall serve me.*
1K. 9: 9. worshipped them, *and served them:*
12: 4. upon us, lighter, *and we will serve thee.*
16:31. and went *and served* Baal,
22:53(54). *For he served* Baal, and worshipped
2K. 10:18. Jehu *shall serve him* much.
17:12. *For they served* idols,
16. *and served* Baal.
35. nor *serve them*, nor sacrifice
21: 3. the host of heaven, *and served* them.
21. *and served* the idols that his father served,
1Ch 19:19. with David, *and became his servants:*
2Ch 7:22. worshipped them, *and served them:*
10: 4. put upon us, *and we will serve thee.*
24:18. *and served* groves and idols:
33: 3. the host of heaven, *and served* them.
22. had made, *and served them;*
Job 21:15. the Almighty, that *we should serve him?*
36:11. If they obey *and serve* (him),
Ps. 18:43(44). a people (whom) I have not known *shall serve me.*
22:30(31). A seed *shall serve him;*
72:11. all nations *shall serve him.*
106:36. *And they served* their idols:
Isa. 60:12. and kingdom that *will* not *serve thee*
Jer. 2:20. (כתיב) thou saidst, *I will* not *transgress;*
5:19. *and served* strange gods in your land, so *shall ye serve* strangers in a land
16:11. after other gods, *and have served them,*
22: 9. worshipped other gods, *and served them.*
13. *useth* his neighbour's *service* without
27: 8. nation and kingdom which *will* not *serve*
9, 14. *Ye shall* not *serve* the king of
13. the nation that *will* not *serve* the king of
30: 8. strangers *shall* no more *serve themselves*
Eze. 20:40. *shall* all the house of Israel, all of them in the land, *serve me:*
48:19. *shall serve it* out of all the tribes of
Hos 12:12(13). *and* Israel *served* for a wife,

KAL.—*Participle.* Poel.

Gen 4: 2. Cain was *a tiller of* the ground.
49:15. and became *a servant* unto tribute.
Nu. 4:37, 41. *that might do service* in the tabernacle
18:21. for their service which they *serve,*
Jos. 16:10. and *serve* (lit. were *serving*) under tribute.
1K. 4:21(5:1). they brought presents, *and served*
9:21. upon those did Solomon levy a tribute of *bondservice* (lit. *servile* tribute)
2K. 10:19. Baal, all *his servants*, and all his priests;
— that he might destroy *the worshippers of*
21. all *the worshippers of* Baal came,
22. vestments for all *the worshippers of* Baal.
23. and said *unto the worshippers of* Baal,
— but *the worshippers of* Baal only.
17:33. and served (lit. were *serving*) their own
41. and served (lit. were *serving*) their graven
Ps. 97: 7. Confounded be all *they that serve* graven
Pro. 12:11. *He that tilleth* his land shall be satisfied
28:19. *He that tilleth* his land shall have plenty
Ecc. 5:12(11). The sleep of *a labouring man* (is)
Isa. 19: 9. *they that work in* fine flax,
30:24. the young asses *that ear* the ground
Eze. 34:27. the hand of those *that served themselves*
48:18. for food *unto them that serve* the city.
19. And *they that serve* the city
Zec. 2: 9(13). they shall be a spoil *to their servants:*
13: 5. I (am) an husbandman; (lit. a man *a tiller of* the ground)
Mal. 3:17. as a man spareth his own son *that serveth*
18. between *him that serveth* God

* NIPHAL.—*Preterite.* *

Ecc. 5: 9(8). the king (himself) *is served* by the
Eze. 36: 9. *and ye shall be tilled* and sown:

NIPHAL.—*Future.*

Deu 21: 4. which *is* neither *eared* nor sown,

Eze.36:34. And the desolate land *shall be tilled,*

* PUAL.—*Preterite* *

Deu 21: 3. an heifer, which *hath* not *been wrought*
Isa. 14: 3. thou *wast made to serve,* (lit. which *was served* on thee)

* HIPHIL.—*Preterite.* *

Isa. 43:23. *I have* not *caused thee to serve* with an
24. *thou hast made me to serve* with thy sins,
Jer. 17: 4. *and I will cause thee to serve* thine
Eze.29:18. king of Babylon *caused* his army *to serve*

HIPHIL.—*Infinitive.*

2Ch 2:18(17). overseers *to set* the people *a work.*

HIPHIL.—*Future.*

Ex. 1:13. *And* the Egyptians *made* the children of Israel *to serve*
2Ch 34:33. *and made* all that were present in Israel *to serve,*

HIPHIL.—*Participle.*

Ex. 6: 5. whom the Egyptians *keep in bondage;*

* HOPHAL.—*Future.* *

Ex. 20: 5. bow down thyself to them, nor *serve them:*
23:24. bow down to their gods, nor *serve them,*
Deu 5: 9. down thyself unto them, nor *serve them:*
13: 2(3). not known, *and let us serve them;*

5648 **עֲבַד** *ğăvad,* Ch.

* P'AL.—*Preterite.* *

Ezr. 6:13. so *they did* speedily.
16. *and*...the children of the captivity, *kept*
Jer. 10:11. gods that *have* not *made* the heavens
Dan. 3: 1. Nebuchadnezzar the king *made* an image
15. the image which *I have made;*
4: 2(3:32). high God *hath wrought* toward me.
35(32). or say unto him, What *doest thou?*
5: 1. Belshazzar the king *made* a great feast
6:22(23). before thee, O king, *have I done* no

P'AL.—*Infinitive.*

Ezr. 4:22. Take heed now that ye fail not *to do* this:
7:18. *to do* with the rest of the silver and the

P'AL.—*Future.*

Ezr. 6: 8. I make a decree what *ye shall do*
7:18. gold, *that do* after the will of your God.

P'AL.—*Participle.* Active.

Ezr. 4:15. and that *they have moved* (marg. *made*) sedition
7:26. whosoever will not *do* (lit. will not be *doing*) the law of thy God,
Dan. 4:35(32). and *he doeth* according to his will
6:10(11). as he *did* aforetime.
27(28). *and he worketh* signs and wonders
7:21. the same horn *made* war with the saints,

* ITHP'AL.—*Future.* *

Ezr. 6:11. and *let* his house *be made* a dunghill
12. *let it be done* with speed.
7:21. shall require of you, *it be done* speedily,
23. *let it be* diligently *done* for the house
Dan. 2: 5. *ye shall be cut* (marg. *made*) in pieces, and
3:29. *shall be cut* (marg. *made*) in pieces, and

ITHP'AL.—*Participle.*

Ezr. 4:19. sedition *have been made* therein.
5: 8. and this work *goeth* fast *on,*
7:26. let judgment be *executed* speedily

5650 **עֶבֶד** *ğeh'-ved,* m.

Gen 9:25. Cursed (be) Canaan; *a servant of servants*
26, 27. Canaan shall be his *servant.*
12:16. and oxen, and he asses, *and menservants,*
14:15. he *and his servants,* by night,
18: 3. not away, I pray thee, from *thy servant:*
5. for therefore are ye come to *your servant.*
19: 2. in, I pray you, into *your servant*'s house,
19. *thy servant* hath found grace in thy sight,
20: 8. and called all *his servants,*
14. took sheep, and oxen, *and menservants,*
21:25. Abimelech's *servants* had violently taken
24: 2. Abraham said unto *his* eldest *servant*
5. And *the servant* said unto him,
Gen24: 9. *the servant* put his hand under the thigh
10. And *the servant* took ten camels
14. thou hast appointed *for thy servant*
17. And *the servant* ran to meet her,
34. I (am) Abraham's *servant.*
35. hath given him flocks,...*and menservants,*
52. when Abraham's *servant* heard their words,
53. *the servant* brought forth jewels of silver,
59. and Abraham's *servant,* and his men.
61. and *the servant* took Rebekah,
65. she (had) said unto *the servant,*
— And *the servant* (had) said,
66. And *the servant* told Isaac
26:15. wells which his father's *servants* had digged
19. And Isaac's *servants* digged in the valley,
24. for *my servant* Abraham's sake.
25. there Isaac's *servants* digged a well.
32. Isaac's *servants* came, and told him
27:37. have I given to him *for servants;*
30:43. *and menservants,* and camels, and asses.
32: 4(5). *Thy servant* Jacob saith thus,
5(6). and asses, flocks, *and menservants,*
10(11). thou hast shewed unto *thy servant;*
16(17). he delivered (them) into the hand of *his servants,*
—(—). and said unto *his servants,*
18(19). (They be) *thy servant* Jacob's;
20(21). Behold, *thy servant* Jacob (is) behind
33: 5. God hath graciously given *thy servant.*
14. pass over before *his servant:*
39:17. *The* Hebrew *servant,* which thou hast
19. After this manner did *thy servant*
40:20. he made a feast unto all *his servants:*
— among *his servants.*
41:10. Pharaoh was wroth with *his servants,*
12. *servant* to the captain of the guard;
37. in the eyes of all *his servants.*
38. And Pharaoh said unto *his servants,*
42:10. *but* to buy food are *thy servants* come.
11. *thy servants* are no spies.
13. *Thy servants* (are) twelve brethren,
43:18. and take us *for bondmen,* and our asses.
28. *Thy servant* our father (is) in good health, (lit. good health (is) *to thy servant*)
44: 7. God forbid *that thy servants* should
9. whomsoever *of thy servants* it be found,
— my lord's *bondmen.* (lit. *for bondmen* to my lord)
10. whom it is found shall be my *servant;*
16. found out the iniquity of *thy servants:* behold, we (are) my lord's *servants,*
17. he shall be my *servant;*
18. let *thy servant,* I pray thee, speak a word
— not thine anger burn *against thy servant:*
19. My lord asked *his servants,*
21, 23. thou saidst unto *thy servants,*
24. we came up unto *thy servant* my father,
27. *thy servant* my father said unto us,
30. when I come to *thy servant* my father,
31. and *thy servants* shall bring down the gray hairs of *thy servant* our father
32. For *thy servant* became surety for the lad
33. let *thy servant* abide instead of the lad a *bondman* to my lord;
45:16. it pleased Pharaoh well, and *his servants.*
46:34. *Thy servants*' trade hath been about cattle
47: 3. *Thy servants* (are) shepherds,
4. *thy servants have* no pasture for their flocks;
— *thy servants* dwell in the land of Goshen.
19. and we and our land will be *servants*
25. and we will be Pharaoh's *servants.*
50: 2. And Joseph commanded *his servants*
7. him went up all *the servants of* Pharaoh,
17. forgive the trespass of *the servants of*
18. Behold, we (be) thy *servants.* (lit. *for servants* to thee)
Ex. 4:10. since thou hast spoken unto *thy servant:*
5:15. dealest thou thus *with thy servants?*
16. There is no straw given *unto thy servants,*
— and, behold, *thy servants* (are) beaten;
21. and in the eyes of *his servants,*
7:10. before Pharaoh, and before *his servants,*
20. Pharaoh, and in the sight of *his servants;*
8: 3(7:28). and into the house of *thy servants,*
4(—:29). people, and upon all *thy servants.*
9(5). I intreat for thee, *and for thy servants,*
11(7). from thy houses, *and from thy servants,*

Ex. 8:21(17). swarms (of flies) upon thee, *and upon thy servants*,
24(20). of Pharaoh, and (into) *his servants'*
29(25). depart from Pharaoh, *from his servants*,
31(27). from Pharaoh, *from his servants*, and
9:14. *and upon thy servants*, and upon thy people;
20. *among the servants of* Pharaoh made *his servants* and his cattle flee into the houses:
21. left *his servants* and his cattle in the field.
30. But as for thee *and thy servants*,
34. and hardened his heart, he *and his servants*.
10: 1. and the heart of *his servants*,
6. the houses of all *thy servants*,
7. And Pharaoh's *servants* said unto him,
11: 3. in the sight of Pharaoh's *servants*,
8. all these *thy servants* shall come down
12:30. he, and all *his servants*,
44. every man's *servant* that is bought
13: 3. out of the house of *bondage*;
14. from the house of *bondage*:
14: 5. the heart of Pharaoh *and of his servants*
31. believed the Lord, and *his servant* Moses.
20: 2. the house of *bondage*. (marg. *servants*)
10. *thy manservant*, nor thy maidservant,
17. *nor his manservant*, nor his
21: 2. If thou buy *an* Hebrew *servant*,
5. if *the servant* shall plainly say,
7. she shall not go out as *the menservants* do.
20. if a man smite *his servant*,
26. if a man smite the eye of *his servant*,
27. if he smite out *his manservant*'s tooth,
32. If the ox shall push *a manservant*
32:13. Abraham, Isaac, and Israel, *thy servants*,
Lev.25: 6. for thee, *and for thy servant*,
39. not compel him to serve as *a* bond*servant*:
42. they (are) *my servants*,
— they shall not be sold as *bondmen*. (marg. with the sale of *a bondman*)
44. *Both thy bondmen*, and thy bondmaids,
— of them shall ye buy *bondmen*
55. unto me the children of Israel (are) *servants*; they (are) *my servants*
26:13. that ye should not be their *bondmen*;
Nu. 11:11. Wherefore hast thou afflicted *thy servant*?
12: 7. *My servant* Moses (is) not so,
8. ye not afraid to speak *against my servant*
14:24. *But my servant* Caleb, because
22:18. and said unto *the servants of* Balak,
31:49. *Thy servants* have taken the sum of the
32: 4. *and thy servants have* cattle:
5. let this land be given *unto thy servants*
25. *Thy servants* will do as my lord
27. *But thy servants* will pass over,
31. As the Lord hath said unto *thy servants*,
Deu 3:24. thou hast begun to shew *thy servant* thy
5: 6. the house of *bondage*. (marg. *servants*)
14. *nor thy manservant*, nor thy maidservant,
— that *thy manservant* and thy maidservant
15. And remember that thou wast *a servant*
21(18). *or his manservant*, or his maidservant,
6:12. from the house of *bondage*. (marg. *bondmen*, or, *servants*)
21. We were Pharaoh's *bondmen* in Egypt;
7: 8. redeemed you out of the house of *bondmen*,
8:14. from the house of *bondage*;
9:27. Remember *thy servants*, Abraham,
12:12. *your menservants*, and your maidservants,
18. *and thy manservant*, and thy maidservant,
13: 5(6). you out of the house of *bondage*,
10(11). house of *bondage*. (marg. *bondmen*)
15:15. remember that thou wast *a bondman*
17. he shall be thy *servant* for ever.
16:11, 14. *and thy manservant*, and thy
12. remember that thou wast *a bondman*
23:15(16). not deliver unto his master *the servant*
24:18, 22. remember that thou wast *a bondman*
28:68. be sold unto your enemies *for bondmen*
29: 2(1). unto Pharaoh, and unto all *his servants*,
32:36. and repent himself for *his servants*,
43. he will avenge the blood of *his servants*,
34: 5. So Moses *the servant of* the Lord died
11. to Pharaoh, and to all *his servants*,
Jos. 1: 1. the death of Moses *the servant of* the Lord
2. Moses *my servant* is dead;
7. which Moses *my servant* commanded thee:
13. which Moses *the servant of* the Lord
15. which Moses the Lord's *servant* gave you

Jos. 5:14. What saith my lord unto *his servant*?
8:31, 33. Moses *the servant of* the Lord
9: 8. We (are) *thy servants*.
9. From a very far country *thy servants* are
11. say unto them, We (are) *your servants*:
23. none of you be freed from being *bondmen*,
24. Because it was certainly told *thy servants*,
— the Lord thy God commanded *his servant*
10: 6. Slack not thy hand *from thy servants*;
11:12. Moses *the servant of* the Lord commanded.
15. As the Lord commanded Moses *his servant*,
12: 6. Them did Moses *the servant of* the Lord
— Moses *the servant of* the Lord gave it
13: 8. Moses *the servant of* the Lord gave them;
14: 7. Moses *the servant of* the Lord sent me
18: 7. Moses *the servant of* the Lord gave them.
22: 2. Moses *the servant of* the Lord commanded
4. Moses *the servant of* the Lord gave you
5. Moses *the servant of* the Lord charged you,
24:17. from the house of *bondage*,
29. Joshua the son of Nun, *the servant of* the
Jud. 2: 8. Joshua the son of Nun, *the servant of* the
3:24. When he was gone out, *his servants* came;
6: 8. out of the house of *bondage*;
27. Then Gideon took ten men *of his servants*,
15:18. into the hand of *thy servant*:
19:19. young man (which is) with *thy servants*:
1Sa. 3: 9. Speak, Lord; for *thy servant* heareth.
10. Speak; for *thy servant* heareth.
8:14. and give (them) *to his servants*.
15. to his officers, *and to his servants*.
16. And he will take *your menservants*,
17. and ye shall be his *servants*.
12:19. Pray for *thy servants* unto the Lord
16:15. And Saul's *servants* said unto him,
16. Let our lord now command *thy servants*,
17. And Saul said unto *his servants*,
17: 8. (am) not I a Philistine, and ye *servants* to
9. then will we be your *servants*:
— then shall ye be our *servants*,
32. *thy servant* will go and fight with this
34. *Thy servant* kept his father's sheep,
36. *Thy servant* slew both the lion and the
58. (I am) the son of *thy servant* Jesse
18: 5. and also in the sight of Saul's *servants*.
22. And Saul commanded *his servants*,
— and all *his servants* love thee:
23. And Saul's *servants* spake those words
24. And *the servants of* Saul told him,
26. And when *his servants* told David
30. all *the servants of* Saul;
19: 1. Jonathan his son, and to all *his servants*,
4. Let not the king sin *against his servant*,
20: 7. *thy servant shall have* peace:
8. shalt deal kindly with *thy servant*; for thou hast brought *thy servant* into a covenant
21: 7(8). a certain man *of the servants of* Saul
11(12). And *the servants of* Achish said unto
14(15). Then said Achish unto *his servants*,
22: 6. *his servants* (were) standing about him;
7. Then Saul said *unto his servants*
8. my son hath stirred up *my servant* against
9. which was set over *the servants of* Saul,
14. who (is so) faithful among all *thy servants*
15. king impute (any)thing *unto his servant*,
— for *thy servant* knew nothing of all this,
17. But *the servants of* the king would not
23:10. *thy servant* hath certainly heard
11. come down, as *thy servant* hath heard?
— I beseech thee, tell *thy servant*.
25: 8. *unto thy servants*, and to thy son David.
10. And Nabal answered David's *servants*,
— there be many *servants* now a days
39. and hath kept *his servant* from evil:
40. when *the servants of* David were come to
41. to wash the feet of *the servants of* my
26:18. my lord thus pursue after *his servant*?
19. the king hear the words of *his servant*.
27: 5. why should *thy servant* dwell in the
12. shall be my *servant* (lit. to me *for a servant*)
28: 2. thou shalt know what *thy servant* can do.
7. Then said Saul *unto his servants*,
— And *his servants* said to him,
23. *his servants*, together with the woman,
25. before Saul, and before *his servants*;
29: 3. (Is) not this David, *the servant of* Saul
8. what hast thou found *in thy servant*

1Sa.29:10. in the morning *with* thy master's *servants*
30:13. man of Egypt, *servant* to an Amalekite;
2Sa. 2:12. *and the servants of* Ish-bosheth the son of
13. *and the servants of* David, went out,
15. and twelve *of the servants of* David.
17. before *the servants of* David.
30. there lacked *of* David's *servants* nineteen
31. *But the servants of* David
3:18. By the hand of *my servant* David
22. *the servants of* David and Joab came
38. And the king said unto *his servants*,
6:20. eyes of the handmaids of *his servants*,
7: 5. Go and tell *my servant* David,
8. so shalt thou say *unto my servant* David,
19. thou hast spoken also of *thy servant's*
20. for thou, Lord God, knowest *thy servant*.
21. to make *thy servant* know (them).
25. thou hast spoken concerning *thy servant*,
26. let the house of *thy servant* David be
27. hast revealed to *thy servant*,
— therefore hath *thy servant* found in his
28. promised this goodness unto *thy servant*:
29. to bless the house of *thy servant*,
— house of *thy servant* be blessed for ever.
8: 2. (so) the Moabites became David's *servants*, (lit. *for servants* to David)
6. the Syrians became *servants* to David,
7. shields of gold that were on *the servants of*
14. they of Edom became David's *servants*.
9: 2. (there was) of the house of Saul *a servant*
— And he said, *Thy servant* (is he).
6. And he answered, Behold *thy servant!*
8. What (is) *thy servant*,
10. therefore, and thy sons, *and thy servants*,
— had fifteen sons and twenty *servants*.
11. commanded *his servant*, so shall *thy servant*
12. in the house of Ziba (were) *servants* unto
10: 2. comfort him by the hand of *his servants*
— David's *servants* came into the land
3. hath not David (rather) sent *his servants*
4. Hanun took David's *servants*,
19. kings (that were) *servants to* Hadarezer
11: 1. David sent Joab, and *his servants*
9. with all *the servants of* his lord,
11. Joab, *and the servants of* my lord,
13. to lie on his bed with *the servants of*
17. (some) of the people *of the servants of*
21. *Thy servant* Uriah the Hittite is dead
24. upon *thy servants*; and (some) *of* the king's *servants* be dead, and *thy servant* Uriah
12:18. *the servants of* David feared to tell him
19. when David saw that *his servants*
— therefore David said unto *his servants*,
21. Then said *his servants* unto him,
13:24. *thy servant hath* sheepshearers;
— *and his servants* go with *thy servant*.
31. and all *his servants* stood by
35. as *thy servant* said, so it is.
36. the king also and all *his servants* wept
14:19. *thy servant* Joab, he bade me,
20. *thy servant* Joab done this thing:
22. To day *thy servant* knoweth that I have
— hath fulfilled the request of *his servant*. [marg. or, *thy servant* (so קרי)]
30. Therefore he said unto *his servants*,
— Absalom's *servants* set the field on fire.
31. Wherefore have *thy servants* set my field
15: 2. *Thy servant* (is) of one of the tribes of
8. For *thy servant* vowed a vow
14. And David said unto all *his servants*
15. the king's *servants* said unto the king, Behold, *thy servants* (are ready)
18. And all *his servants* passed on beside him;
21. even there also will *thy servant* be.
34. I will be *thy servant*, O king; (as) I (have been) thy father's *servant* hitherto, so (will) I now also (be) *thy servant*:
16: 6. and at all *the servants of* king David:
11. said to Abishai, and *to all his servants*,
17:20. when Absalom's *servants* came to the
18: 7. of Israel were slain before *the servants of*
9. Absalom met *the servants of* David.
29. the king's *servant*, and (me) *thy servant*,
19: 5(6). this day the faces of all *thy servants*,
6(7). regardest neither princes *nor servants*:
7(8). speak comfortably unto *thy servants*:
14(15). Return thou, and all *thy servants*.

2Sa.19:17(18). fifteen sons and *his* twenty *servants*
19(20). remember that which *thy servant* did
20(21). *thy servant* doth know that I have
26(27). My lord, O king, *my servant* deceived me: for *thy servant* said, I will saddle
—(—). because *thy servant* (is) lame.
27(28). And he hath slandered *thy servant*
28(29). yet didst thou set *thy servant* among
35(36). can *thy servant* taste what I eat or
—(—). wherefore then should *thy servant* be
36(37). *Thy servant* will go a little way
37(38). Let *thy servant*, I pray thee, turn
—(—). But behold *thy servant* Chimham;
20: 6. take thou thy lord's *servants*,
21:15. and David went down, *and his servants*
22. David, and by the hand of *his servants*.
24:10. take away the iniquity of *thy servant*;
20. looked, and saw the king and *his servants*
21. my lord the king come to *his servant?*
1K. 1: 2. Wherefore *his servants* said unto him,
9. the men of Judah the king's *servants*:
19. but Solomon *thy servant* hath he not
26. But me, (even) me *thy servant*,
— *thy servant* Solomon, hath he not
27. hast not shewed (it) unto *thy servant*,
33. Take with you *the servants of* your lord,
47. the king's *servants* came to bless our
51. that he will not slay *his servant*
2:38. the king hath said, so will *thy servant* do.
39. two of *the servants* of Shimei ran away
— Behold, *thy servants* (be) in Gath.
40. to Achish to seek *his servants*:
— brought *his servants* from Gath.
3: 6. Thou hast shewed unto *thy servant* David
7. thou hast made *thy servant* king
8. *And thy servant* (is) in the midst of thy
9. Give therefore *thy servant* an
15. and made a feast to all *his servants*.
4:24(5:4). peace on all *sides* round about *him*. [Some copies read עֲבָדָיו; see עֵבֶר].
5: 1(15). Hiram king of Tyre sent *his servants*
6(20). *my servants* shall be with *thy servants*:
—(—). will I give hire for *thy servants*
9(23). *My servants* shall bring (them) down
8:23. covenant and mercy *with thy servants*
24. Who hast kept *with thy servant* David
25. Lord God of Israel, keep *with thy servant*
26. which thou spakest *unto thy servant*
28. thou respect unto the prayer of *thy servant*,
— to the prayer, which *thy servant* prayeth
29. the prayer which *thy servant* shall make
30. to the supplication of *thy servant*,
32. heaven, and do, and judge *thy servants*,
36. and forgive the sin of *thy servants*,
52. the supplication of *thy servant*,
53. spakest by the hand of Moses *thy servant*,
56. promised by the hand of Moses *his servant*.
59. that he maintain the cause of *his servant*,
66. the Lord had done for David *his servant*,
9:22. did Solomon make no *bondmen*: but they (were) men of war, *and his servants*.
27. And Hiram sent in the navy *his servants*,
— with *the servants of* Solomon.
10: 5. his table, and the sitting of *his servants*,
8. happy (are) these *thy servants*,
13. she *and her servants*.
11:11. from thee, and will give it *to thy servant*.
13. to thy son for David *my servant's* sake,
17. certain Edomites *of* his father's *servants*
26. Ephrathite of Zereda, Solomon's *servant*,
32. one tribe for *my servant* David's sake,
34. of his life for David *my servant's* sake,
36. that David *my servant* may have a light
38. as David *my servant* did;
12: 7. If thou wilt be *a servant* unto this
— then they will be thy *servants* for ever.
14: 8. thou hast not been *as my servant* David,
18. which he spake by the hand of *his servant*
15:18. them into the hand of *his servants*:
29. which he spake by *his servant* Ahijah
16: 9. And *his servant* Zimri,
18: 9. that thou wouldest deliver *thy servant*
12. *but* I *thy servant* fear the Lord
36. and (that) I (am) *thy servant*,
20: 6. Yet I will send *my servants* unto thee
— and the houses of *thy servants*;

1K. 20: 9. that thou didst send for to *thy servant*
12. he said unto *his servants*,
23. *And the servants of* the king of Syria said
31. And *his servants* said unto him,
32. *Thy servant* Ben-hadad saith,
39. *Thy servant* went out into the midst of the
40. And as *thy servant* was busy here and there,
22: 3. the king of Israel said unto *his servants*,
49(50). Let *my servants* go with *thy servants*
2K. 1:13. the life of these fifty *thy servants*,
2:16. there be with *thy servants* fifty strong men;
3:11. And one of the king of Israel's *servants*
4: 1. *Thy servant* my husband is dead; and thou knowest that *thy servant* did fear the Lord:
— to take unto him my two sons to be *bondmen*.
5: 6. I have (therewith) sent Naaman *my servant*
13. And *his servants* came near, and spake
15. take a blessing of *thy servant*.
17. be given *to thy servant* two mules' burden of earth? for *thy servant* will
18. In this thing the Lord pardon *thy servant*,
— the Lord pardon *thy servant* in this thing.
25. he said, *Thy servant* went no whither.
26. sheep, and oxen, *and menservants*,
6: 3. I pray thee, and go with *thy servants*.
8. and took counsel with *his servants*,
11. he called *his servants*, and said unto them,
12. And one *of his servants* said,
7:12. in the night, and said unto *his servants*,
13. And one *of his servants* answered and said,
8:13. and Hazael said, But what, (is) *thy servant*
19. destroy Judah for David *his servant*'s sake,
9: 7. that I may avenge the blood of *my servants* the prophets, and the blood of all *the servants of* the Lord,
11. came forth to *the servants of* his lord:
28. And *his servants* carried him in a chariot
36. which he spake by *his servant* Elijah
10: 5. to Jehu, saying, We (are) *thy servants*,
10. which he spake by *his servant* Elijah.
23. here with you none *of the servants of*
12:20(21). And *his servants* arose, and made a conspiracy,
21(22). *his servants*, smote him, and he died;
14: 5. slew *his servants* which had slain the king
25. he spake by the hand of *his servant* Jonah,
16: 7. Ahaz sent messengers...saying, I (am) *thy servant*
17: 3. and Hoshea became his *servant*,
13. I sent to you by *my servants* the prophets.
23. as he had said by all *his servants*
18:12. all that Moses *the servant of* the Lord
24. of the least of my master's *servants*,
26. Speak, I pray thee, to *thy servants*
19: 5. So *the servants of* king Hezekiah came to Isaiah.
34 & 20:6. and for *my servant* David's sake.
21: 8. all the law that *my servant* Moses
10. Lord spake by *his servants* the prophets,
23. And *the servants of* Amon conspired against him,
22: 9. *Thy servants* have gathered the money
12. Asahiah *a servant of* the king's,
23:30. And *his servants* carried him in a chariot
24: 1. Jehoiakim became his *servant*
2. which he spake by *his servants* the prophets.
10. *the servants of* Nebuchadnezzar
11. *and his servants* did besiege it.
12. and his mother, *and his servants*,
25: 8. Nebuzar-adan, captain of the guard, *a servant of*
24. Fear not *to be the servants of* the Chaldees:
1Ch 2:34. And Sheshan had *a servant*, an Egyptian,
35. gave his daughter to Jarha *his servant*
6:49(34). that Moses *the servant of* God had commanded.
16:13. O ye seed of Israel *his servant*,
17: 4. Go and tell David *my servant*,
7. thus shalt thou say *unto my servant* David,
17. thou hast (also) spoken of *thy servant*'s house
18. for the honour of *thy servant?* for thou knowest *thy servant*.
19. O Lord, for *thy servant*'s sake,
23. thou hast spoken concerning *thy servant*

1Ch 17:24. (let) the house of David *thy servant* (be) established
25. For thou, O my God, hast told *thy servant* – therefore *thy servant* hath found (in his heart)
26. hast promised this goodness unto *thy servant:*
27. to bless the house of *thy servant*,
18: 2. and the Moabites became David's *servants*,
6. and the Syrians became David's *servants*,
7. that were on *the servants of* Hadarezer,
13. all the Edomites became David's *servants*.
19: 2. *the servants of* David came into the land
3. are not *his servants* come unto thee
4. Wherefore Hanun took David's *servants*,
19. *the servants of* Hadarezer
20: 8. by the hand of David, and by the hand of *his servants*.
21: 3. (are) they not all my lord's *servants?*
8. do away the iniquity of *thy servant;*
2Ch 1: 3. Moses *the servant of* the Lord
2: 8(7). I know that *thy servants* can skill to cut timber
—(–). and, behold, *my servants* (shall be) with *thy servants*,
10(9). I will give *to thy servants*,
15(14). let him send *unto his servants:*
6:14. and (shewest) mercy *unto thy servants*,
15. Thou which hast kept *with thy servant*
16. O Lord God of Israel, keep *with thy servant*
17. which thou hast spoken *unto thy servant*
19. Have respect therefore to the prayer of *thy servant*,
— the prayer which *thy servant* prayeth
20. unto the prayer which *thy servant* prayeth
21. therefore unto the supplications of *thy servant*,
23. and judge *thy servants*,
27. and forgive the sin of *thy servants*,
42. remember the mercies of David *thy servant*.
8: 9. did Solomon make no *servants*
18. Huram sent him by the hands of *his servants* ships, *and servants* that had knowledge of the sea; and they went with *the servants of* Solomon
9: 4. and the sitting of *his servants*,
7. happy (are) these *thy servants*,
10. And *the servants* also *of* Huram, *and the servants of* Solomon,
12. she *and her servants*.
21. *the servants of* Huram:
10: 7. they will be thy *servants* for ever.
12: 8. they shall be *his servants;*
13: 6. Jeroboam the son of Nebat, *the servant of*
24: 6. Moses *the servant of* the Lord,
9. Moses *the servant of* God
25. *his own servants* conspired against him
25: 3. he slew *his servants* that had killed the
28:10. of Judah and Jerusalem *for bondmen*
32: 9. did Sennacherib...send *his servants*
16. And *his servants* spake yet (more) against the Lord God, and against *his servant*
33:24. And *his servants* conspired against him,
34:16. that was committed to *thy servants*,
20. Asaiah *a servant of* the king's,
35:23. and the king said *to his servants*,
24. *His servants* therefore took him out of
36:20. Babylon; where they *were servants*
Ezr. 2:55, 58. The children of Solomon's *servants:*
65. Beside *their servants* and their maids,
9: 9. For we (were) *bondmen;*
11. thou hast commanded by *thy servants*
Neh. 1: 6. mayest hear the prayer of *thy servant*,
— for the children of Israel *thy servants*,
7. which thou commandedst *thy servant*
8. that thou commandedst *thy servant* Moses,
10. Now these (are) *thy servants* and thy
11. be attentive to the prayer of *thy servant*, and to the prayer of *thy servants*,
— prosper, I pray thee, *thy servant* this day,
2: 5. If it please the king, and if *thy servant*
10, 19. Tobiah *the servant*, the Ammonite,
20. we *his servants* will arise and build:
5: 5. our sons and our daughters *to be servants*,
7:57, 60. The children of Solomon's *servants:*
67. Beside *their manservants* and their

Neh 9:10. upon Pharaoh, and on all *his servants*,
14. by the hand of Moses *thy servant:*
36. Behold, we (are) *servants* this day,
— we (are) *servants* in it:
10:29(30). given by Moses *the servant of* God,
11: 3. the children of Solomon's *servants.*
Est. 1: 3 & 2:18. all his princes *and his servants;*
3: 2. And all the king's *servants,*
3. Then the king's *servants,*
4:11. All the king's *servants,*
5:11. the princes *and servants of* the king.
7: 4. But if we had been sold *for bondmen*
Job 1: 8 & 2:3. Hast thou considered *my servant*
3:19. *and the servant* (is) free from his master.
4:18. Behold, he put no trust *in his servants;*
7: 2. *As a servant* earnestly desireth the
19:16. *my servant*, and he gave (me) no answer;
31:13. I did despise the cause of *my manservant*
41: 4(40:28). wilt thou take him *for a servant* for ever?
42: 7. *as my servant* Job (hath).
8. and go to *my servant* Job,
— and *my servant* Job shall pray for you:
— *like my servant* Job.
Ps. 18[title](1). David, *the servant of* the Lord,
19:11(12). Moreover by them is *thy servant*
13(14). Keep back *thy servant* also from presumptuous (sins);
27: 9. put not *thy servant* away in anger:
31:16(17). thy face to shine upon *thy servant:*
34:22(23). The Lord redeemeth the soul of *his servants:*
35:27. pleasure in the prosperity of *his servant.*
36[title](1). David *the servant of* the Lord.
69:17(18). hide not thy face *from thy servant;*
36(37). The seed also of *his servants* shall
78:70. He chose David also *his servant,*
79: 2. The dead bodies of *thy servants*
10. the revenging of the blood of *thy servants*
86: 2. O thou my God, save *thy servant*
4. Rejoice the soul of *thy servant:*
16. give thy strength *unto thy servant,*
89: 3(4). I have sworn unto David *my servant,*
20(21). I have found David *my servant;*
39(40). made void the covenant of *thy servant:*
50(51). Remember, Lord, the reproach of *thy servants;*
90:13. let it repent thee concerning *thy servants.*
16. Let thy work appear unto *thy servants,*
102:14(15). For *thy servants* take pleasure
28(29). The children of *thy servants* shall
105: 6. O ye seed of Abraham *his servant,*
17. Joseph, (who) was sold *for a servant:*
25. to deal subtilly *with his servants.*
26. He sent Moses *his servant;*
42. (and) Abraham *his servant.*
109:28. be ashamed; *but* let *thy servant* rejoice.
113: 1. Praise, O ye *servants of* the Lord,
116:16. O Lord, truly I (am) *thy servant;* I (am) *thy servant*, (and) the son of thine
119:17. Deal bountifully with *thy servant,*
23. *thy servant* did meditate in thy statutes.
38. Stablish thy word *unto thy servant,*
49. Remember the word *unto thy servant,*
65. Thou hast dealt well with *thy servant,*
76. according to thy word *unto thy servant.*
84. How many (are) the days of *thy servant?*
91. for all (are) *thy servants.*
122. Be surety for *thy servant* for good:
124. with *thy servant* according unto thy mercy,
125. (am) *thy servant;* give me understanding,
135. Make thy face to shine *upon thy servant;*
140. *therefore thy servant* loveth it.
176. like a lost sheep; seek *thy servant;*
123: 2. the eyes of *servants* (look) unto the hand
132:10. For *thy servant* David's sake
134: 1. ye the Lord, all (ye) *servants of* the Lord,
135: 1. praise (him), O ye *servants of* the Lord.
9. upon Pharaoh, and upon all *his servants.*
14. will repent himself concerning *his servants.*
136:22. (Even) an heritage unto Israel *his servant:*
143: 2. enter not into judgment with *thy servant:*
12. for I (am) *thy servant.*
144:10. who delivereth David *his servant*
Pro. 11:29. *and* the fool (shall be) *servant* to the wise of heart.
12: 9. (He that is) despised, *and* hath *a servant,*
Pro. 14:35. king's favour (is) *toward a* wise *servant:*
17: 2. *A* wise *servant* shall have rule
19:10. less *for a servant* to have rule over princes.
22: 7. *and* the borrower (is) *servant* to the lender.
29:19. *A servant* will not be corrected by words:
21. He that delicately bringeth up *his servant*
30:10. Accuse not *a servant* unto his master,
22. For *a servant* when he reigneth;
Ecc. 2: 7. I got (me) *servants* and maidens,
7:21. lest thou hear *thy servant* curse thee:
10: 7. have seen *servants* upon horses, and princes walking *as servants* upon the earth.
Isa. 14: 2. in the land of the Lord *for servants*
20: 3. the Lord said, Like as *my servant* Isaiah
22:20. I will call *my servant* Eliakim
24: 2. *as with the servant*, so with his master;
36: 9. of the least of my master's *servants,*
11. Speak, I pray thee, unto *thy servants*
37: 5. So *the servants of* king Hezekiah
24. *thy servants* hast thou reproached the Lord,
35. and for *my servant* David's sake.
41: 8. But thou, Israel, (art) *my servant,*
9. Thou (art) *my servant;*
42: 1. Behold *my servant*, whom I uphold;
19. Who (is) blind, but *my servant?*
— and blind *as* the Lord's *servant?*
43:10. *and my servant* whom I have chosen:
44: 1. Yet now hear, O Jacob *my servant;*
2. Fear not, O Jacob, *my servant;*
21. for thou (art) *my servant:* I have formed thee; thou (art) my *servant:*
26. That confirmeth the word of *his servant,*
45: 4. For Jacob *my servant*'s sake,
48:20. The Lord hath redeemed *his servant* Jacob.
49: 3. Thou (art) *my servant*, O Israel,
5. that formed me from the womb (to be) his *servant*, (lit. to him *for a servant*)
6. thing that thou shouldest be my *servant*
7. *to a servant of* rulers,
50:10. that obeyeth the voice of *his servant,*
52:13. Behold, *my servant* shall deal prudently,
53:11. shall *my* righteous *servant* justify many;
54:17. the heritage of *the servants of*
56: 6. the name of the Lord, to be his *servants,*
63:17. Return for *thy servants*' sake,
65: 8. so will I do for *my servants*' sakes,
9. *and my servants* shall dwell there.
13. Behold, *my servants* shall eat,
— behold, *my servants* shall drink,
— behold, *my servants* shall rejoice,
14. Behold, *my servants* shall sing
15. *and* call *his servants* by another name:
66:14. Lord shall be known toward *his servants,*
Jer. 2:14. (Is) Israel *a servant?* (is) he a homeborn (slave)?
7:25. I have even sent unto you all *my servants*
21: 7. Zedekiah king of Judah, and *his servants,*
22: 2. the throne of David, thou, *and thy servants,*
4. he, *and his servants*, and his people.
25: 4. Lord hath sent unto you all *his servants*
9. Nebuchadrezzar the king of Babylon, *my servant,*
19. Pharaoh king of Egypt, and *his servants,*
26: 5. To hearken to the words of *my servants*
27: 6. Nebuchadnezzar the king of Babylon, *my servant;*
29:19. I sent unto them by *my servants*
30:10. fear thou not, O *my servant* Jacob,
33:21. be broken with David *my servant,*
22. multiply the seed of David *my servant,*
26. the seed of Jacob, and David *my servant,*
34: 9. That every man should let *his manservant,*
10. that every one should let *his manservant,*
11. they turned, and caused *the servants*
— brought them into subjection *for servants*
13. out of the house of *bondmen,*
16. and caused every man *his servant,*
— to be unto you *for servants*
35:15. I have sent also unto you all *my servants*
36:24. (neither) the king, nor any of *his servants*
31. punish him and his seed and *his servants*
37: 2. But neither he, *nor his servants,*
18. against thee, *or against thy servants,*
43:10. the king of Babylon, *my servant,*
44: 4. I sent unto you all *my servants*
46:26. king of Babylon, and into the hand of *his servants:*

Jer. 46:27. But fear not thou, O *my servant* Jacob,
28. Fear thou not, O Jacob *my servant*,
Lam. 5: 8. *Servants* have ruled over us:
Eze. 28:25. land that I have given *to my servant*
34:23. feed them, (even) *my servant* David;
24. *and my servant* David a prince among
37:24. *And* David *my servant* (shall be) king
25. that I have given *unto* Jacob *my servant*,
— and *my servant* David (shall be) their
38:17. I have spoken in old time by *my servants*
46:17. of his inheritance to one *of his servants*,
Dan 1:12. Prove *thy servants*, I beseech thee,
13. as thou seest, deal with *thy servants*.
9: 6. have we hearkened unto *thy servants*
10. which he set before us by *his servants*
11. the law of Moses *the servant of* God,
17. God, hear the prayer of *thy servant*,
10:17. how can *the servant of* this my lord talk
Joel 2:29(3:2). And also upon *the servants* and upon the handmaids
Am. 3: 7. he revealeth his secret unto *his servants*
Mic. 6: 4. thee out of the house of *servants*;
Hag. 2:23. take thee, O Zerubbabel, *my servant*,
Zec. 1: 6. I commanded *my servants* the prophets,
3: 8. bring forth *my servant* the Branch.
Mal. 1: 6. A son honoureth (his) father, *and a servant*
4: 4(3:22). Remember ye the law of Moses *my servant*,

5649 ## עֲבַד [^{n}găvad], Ch. m.

Ezr. 4:11. *Thy servants* the men on this side
5:11. We are *the servants* of the God of
Dan 2: 4. tell *thy servants* the dream,
7. Let the king tell *his servants*
3:26. ye *servants* of the most high God,
28. and delivered *his servants*
6:20(21). O Daniel, *servant of* the living God,

5652 ## עֲבָד [^{n}găvāhd], m.

Ecc. 9: 1. the wise, *and their works*, (are) in the

5657 ## עֲבֻדָּה ^{n}găvood-dāh', f.

Gen 26:14. possession of herds, *and* great *store of servants*: (marg. or, *husbandry*)
Job 1: 3. and *a* very great *houshold*; (marg. *id.*)

5659 ## עַבְדוּת [^{n}gav-dooth'], f.

Ezr. 9: 8. give us a little reviving *in our bondage*.
9. *yet* our God hath not forsaken us *in our bondage*,
Neh 9:17. a captain to return *to their bondage*:

5666 ## עָבָה ^{n}gāh-vāh'.

* KAL.—*Preterite.* *

Deu 32:15. thou art waxen fat, *thou art grown thick*,
1K. 12:10. (finger) *shall be thicker* than my father's
2Ch 10:10. (finger) *shall be thicker* than my father's

5656 ## עֲבוֹדָה ^{n}găvōh-dāh', f.

Gen 29:27. *for the service* which thou shalt serve
30:26. thou knowest *my service* which I have
Ex. 1:14. their lives bitter *with* hard *bondage*,
— manner of *service* in the field: all *their service*, wherein they made them serve,
2:23. of Israel sighed by reason of *the bondage*,
— up unto God by reason of *the bondage*.
5: 9. Let there more *work* be laid upon the
11. ought *of your work* shall be diminished.
6: 6. I will rid you *out of their bondage*,
9. anguish of spirit, *and for* cruel *bondage*.
12:25. ye shall keep this *service*.
26. What mean ye by this *service*?
13: 5. thou shalt keep this *service* in this month.
27:19. in all *the service thereof*,
30:16. for *the service of* the tabernacle
35:21. *his service*, and for the holy garments.
Ex. 35:24. for any work of *the service*,
36: 1. of work for *the service of* the sanctuary,
3. the work of *the service of* the sanctuary,
5. *the service* of the work, which the Lord
38:21. (for) *the service of* the Levites,
39:32. Thus was all *the work of* the tabernacle
40. the vessels of *the service of* the tabernacle,
42. the children of Israel made all *the work*.
Lev. 23: 7, 8, 21, 25, 35, 36. ye shall do no *servile* work (lit. work of *service*)
25:39. not compel him to serve as a bondservant: (lit. *the service of* a bondservant)
Nu. 3: 7, 8. to do *the service of* the tabernacle.
26. for all *the service thereof*.
31. and all *the service thereof*.
36. and all *that serveth thereto*,
4: 4. This (shall be) *the service of* the sons of
19. appoint them every one to *his service*
23. that enter in to perform *the service*,
24. This (is) *the service of* the families of the Gershonites,
26. and all the instruments of *their service*,
27. *the service of* the sons of the Gershonites, in all their burdens, and in all *their service*:
28. *the service of* the families of the sons
30. to do *the work of* the tabernacle
31. according to all *their service*
32. instruments, and with all *their service*:
33. *the service of* the families of the sons of Merari, according to all *their service*,
35, 39, 43. into the service, *for the work*
47. every one that came to do *the service of the ministry, and the service of* the burden in the tabernacle
49. every one according to *his service*,
7: 5. to do *the service of* the tabernacle
— to every man according to *his service*.
7. of Gershon, according to *their service*:
8. of Merari, according unto *their service*,
9. *the service of* the sanctuary belonging
8:11. may execute *the service of* the Lord.
19. to do *the service of* the children of Israel
22. went the Levites in to do *their service*
24. go in to wait *upon the service of*
25. they shall cease waiting upon *the service*
26. to keep the charge, *and* shall do no *service*
16: 9. near to himself to do *the service of*
18: 4. for all *the service of* the tabernacle:
6. to do *the service of* the tabernacle
7. priest's office (unto you as) *a service of* gift:
21. for *their service* which they serve, (even) *the service of* the tabernacle
23. Levites shall do *the service of* the tabernacle
31. for it (is) your reward for *your service*
28:18. ye shall do no manner of *servile* work (lit. work of *service*)
25, 26 & 29:1, 12, 35. shall do no *servile* work. (lit. work of *service*)
Deu 26: 6. and laid upon us hard *bondage*:
Jos. 22:27. that we might do *the service of* the Lord
1K. 12: 4. make thou *the* grievous *service of* thy father, and his heavy yoke which he put upon us, lighter, (lit. lighten *from the service*)
1Ch 4:21. the house of *them that wrought* (lit. *the work of*) fine linen,
6:32(17). on *their office* according to their order.
48(33). the Levites (were) appointed unto all manner of *service of*
9:13. very able men for the work of *the service*
19. the Korahites, (were) over the work of *the service*,
28. had the charge of the *ministering* vessels, (lit. vessels of *service*)
23:24. did the work *for the service of* the house
26. nor any vessels of it *for the service thereof*.
28. wait on the sons of Aaron *for the service of*
— work of *the service of* the house of God;
32. *in the service of* the house of the Lord.
24: 3. according to their offices *in their service*.
19. These (were) the orderings of them *in their service*
25: 1. of the host separated *to the service*
— the number of the workmen *according to their service*
6. *for the service of* the house of God,

1Ch 26: 8. able men for strength *for the service,*
30. of the Lord, *and in the service of* the king.
27:26. did the work of the field *for tillage of*
28:13. for all the work of *the service of* the house
— and for all the vessels of *service* in the house
14. instruments of *all manner of service;* (lit. *of service and service*)
— instruments of *every kind of service:* (lit. *id.*)
15. *according to the use of* every candlestick.
20. hast finished all the work for *the service of*
21. for all *the service of* the house of God:
— for any manner of *service:*
29: 7. gave *for the service of* the house of God
2Ch 8:14. the courses of the priests to *their service,*
10: 4. ease thou *somewhat the* grievous *servitude*
12: 8. that they may know *my service, and the service of* the kingdoms of the countries.
24:12. such as did the work of *the service of*
29:35. So *the service of* the house of the Lord
31: 2. every man according to *his service,*
16. his daily portion *for their service*
21. *in the service of* the house of God,
34:13. in *any manner of service:* (lit. *of service and service*)
35: 2. encouraged them *to the service of* the
10. So *the service* was prepared,
15. might not depart from *their service;*
16. *the service of* the Lord was prepared
Ezr. 8:20. had appointed *for the service of*
Neh 3: 5. nobles put not their necks *to the work of*
5:18. because *the bondage* was heavy upon this
10:32(33). third part of a shekel *for the service of*
37(38). tithes in all the cities of *our tillage.*
Ps. 104:14. and herb *for the service of* man:
23. forth unto his work *and to his labour*
Isa. 14: 3. *the* hard *bondage* wherein thou wast made
28:21. and bring to pass *his act, his* strange *act.*
32:17. *and the effect of* righteousness quietness
Lam. 1: 3. because of great *servitude:*
Eze. 29:18. caused his army to serve *a* great *service*
— for *the service* that he had served against
44:14. of the house, for all *the service thereof,*

5667 **עֲבוֹט** ^{n}*găvōht*, m.

Deu 24:10. not go into his house to fetch *his pledge.*
11. bring out *the pledge* abroad unto thee.
12. thou shalt not sleep *with his pledge:*
13. thou shalt deliver him *the pledge* again

5668 **עֲבוּר** ^{n}*găvoor*, part.

Used with prefix, בַּעֲבוּר as a preposition and conjunction.

Gen 8:21. curse the ground any more *for* man's *sake;*
21:30. thou take...*that* they may be a witness
Ex. 9:16. raised thee up, *for* to shew (in) thee my
13: 8. *because of* that (which) the Lord did
2Sa. 10: 3. sent his servants...*to* search the city, &c.

The signification of בַּעֲבוּר continues the same with pronominal suffixes.

It occurs with additional prefix, לְבַעֲבוּר three times:—

Ex. 20:20. God is come *to* prove you,
2Sa. 14:20. *To* fetch about this form of speech
17:14. *to the intent that* the Lord might bring

5669 **עָבוּר** ^{n}*găvoor*, m.

Jos. 5:11. they did eat *of the old corn of*
12. after they had eaten *of the old corn of*

5670 **עָבַט** [^{n}*gāh-vat'*].

* KAL.—*Infinitive.* *

Deu 24:10. thou shalt not go into his house *to fetch* his pledge.

KAL.—*Future.*

Deu 15: 6. thou shalt lend unto many nations, but thou *shalt* not *borrow;*

* PIEL.—*Future.* *

Joel 2: 7. and *they shall* not *break* their ranks:

* HIPHIL.—*Preterite.* *

Deu 15: 6. *and thou shalt lend* unto many nations,

HIPHIL.—*Infinitive.*

Deu 15: 8. *and* shalt *surely* lend him (lit. and *lending* thou shalt lend him)

HIPHIL.—*Future.*

Deu 15: 8. and *shalt* surely *lend him*

עַבְטִיט ^{n}*găv-teet'*, m. 5671

Hab 2: 6. him that ladeth himself with *thick clay!*

עֲבִי ^{n}*găvee*, m. 5672

Job 15:26. upon the *thick* bosses of his bucklers:

עֳבִי [^{n}*gŏvee*], m. 5672

1K. 7:26. *And it* (was) an hand breadth *thick,* (lit. *And its thickness* (was) an handbreadth)
2Ch 4: 5. *And the thickness of it* (was) an
Jer. 52:21. and *the thickness thereof* (was) four

עֲבִידָה [^{n}*găvee-dāh'*], Ch. f. 5673

Ezr. 4:24. Then ceased *the work of* the house
5: 8. *and* this *work* goeth fast on,
6: 7. Let *the work of* this house of God alone;
18. for *the service of* God,
Dan 2:49. over *the affairs* of the province
3:12. whom thou hast set over *the affairs of*

עָבַר ^{n}*gāh-var'*. 5674

* KAL.—*Preterite.* *

Gen 15:17. a burning lamp that *passed* between those
18: 5. for therefore *are ye come* to your servant.
32:10(11). with my staff *I passed over* this
31(32). as *he passed over* Penuel the sun rose
33: 3. he *passed over* before them,
Ex. 12:12. *For I will pass* through the land of Egypt
23. *For* the Lord *will pass through* to smite
Nu. 5:14. *And* the spirit of jealousy *come* upon
— or if the spirit of jealousy *come* upon
13:32. The land, through which *we have gone*
14: 7. The land, which *we passed* through
32:21. *And will go* all of you armed over Jordan
34: 4. *and pass on* to Zin:
— *and pass on* to Azmon:
Deu 2:14. until *we were come over* the brook
12:10. *But* (when) *ye go over* Jordan,
26:13. *I have* not *transgressed* thy commandments,
29:16(15). how *we came* through the nations which *ye passed by;*
Jos. 3: 4. for *ye have* not *passed* (this) way
16. and the people *passed over* right against
4:13. forty thousand prepared for war *passed over*
22. Israel *came over* this Jordan
6: 8. *passed on* before the Lord,
7:11. *they have* also *transgressed* my covenant
15. *he hath transgressed* the covenant
15: 3. *and passed along* to Zin,
— *and passed along* to Hezron,
4. (From thence) *it passed* toward Azmon,
6. *and passed along* by the north
7. *and* the border *passed* toward the waters
10. *and passed along* unto the side of mount
— *and passed on* to Timnah:
11. *and passed along* to mount Baalah,
16: 2. *and passeth along* unto the borders of
6. *and passed by* it on the east to Janohah;
18:13. *And* the border *went over* from thence
18. *And passed along* toward the side
19. *And* the border *passed along*
19:13. And from thence *passeth on along*

Jos. 24:17. all the people through whom *we passed:*
Jud. 2:20. Because that this people *hath transgressed*
3:26. and *passed beyond* the quarries,
11:29. from Mizpeh of Gilead *he passed over*
12: 1. Wherefore *passedst thou over* to fight
19:12. *we* (lit. *and we*) *will pass over* to Gibeah.
1Sa.13: 7. (some of) the Hebrews *went over* Jordan
14:23. and the battle *passed over* unto Beth-aven.
15:24. *I have transgressed* the commandment of
2Sa.15:33. If *thou passest on* with me,
16: 1. when David *was* a little *past* the top
17:20. *They be gone over* the brook of water.
22. not one of them that *was* not *gone over*
24. And Absalom *passed over* Jordan,
18: 9. mule that (was) under him *went away.*
19:18(19). *And there went over* a ferry boat
39(40). when the king *was come over*,
40(41). and Chimham *went on* with him:
20:13. all the people *went on* after Joab,
1K. 2:37. day thou goest out, *and passest over*
22:24. Which way *went* the Spirit of the Lord
2K. 4:31. Gehazi *passed on* before them,
1Ch 12:15. These (are) they that *went over* Jordan
29:30. the times that *went over* him,
2Ch 18:23. Which way *went* the Spirit
Job 11:16. remember (it) as waters (that) *pass away:*
15:19. no stranger *passed* among them.
17:11. My days *are past*,
30:15. *passeth away* as a cloud.
37:21. but the wind *passeth*,
Ps. 18:12(13). before him his thick clouds *passed*,
38: 4(5). mine iniquities *are gone over*
42: 7(8). thy billows *are gone* over me.
48: 4(5). kings were assembled, *they passed by*
73: 7. have more than heart could wish. (marg. *they pass* the thoughts of the heart)
88:16(17). Thy fierce wrath *goeth over* me;
103:16. For the wind *passeth* over it,
124: 4. the stream *had gone over* our soul:
5. proud waters *had gone over* our soul.
Pro.22: 3. but the simple *pass on*,
24:30. *I went by* the field of the slothful,
27:12. (but) the simple *pass on*,
Cant 2:11. For, lo, the winter *is past*,
3: 4. but a little *that I passed* from them,
5: 6. had withdrawn himself, (and) *was gone:*
Isa. 8: 8. he shall overflow *and go over*,
21. *And they shall pass* through it, hardly
10:28. *he is passed* to Migron;
29. *They are gone over* the passage:
16: 8. *they are gone over* the sea.
24: 5. *they have transgressed* the laws,
28:15. (כתיב) the overflowing scourge *shall pass through*,
Jer. 2: 6. a land that no man *passed* through,
5:28. *they overpass* the deeds of the wicked:
8:20. The harvest *is past*, the summer is ended,
22: 8. *And* many nations *shall pass by*
23: 9. like a man whom wine *hath overcome*,
48:32. thy plants *are gone over* the sea,
Eze.39:15. *And* the passengers (that) *pass* through
Dan 9:11. Israel *have transgressed* thy law,
11:10. overflow, *and pass through:*
40. shall overflow *and pass over.*
Hos. 6: 7. *have transgressed* the covenant:
8: 1. *they have transgressed* my covenant,
10:11. *I passed over* upon her fair neck:
Jon. 2: 3(4). thy waves *passed* over me.
Mic. 5: 8(7). who, if *he go through*,
Nah. 1:12. cut down, *when he shall pass through.*
3:19. not thy wickedness *passed* continually?
Hab. 3:10. overflowing of the water *passed by:*
Zep. 2: 2. (before) the day *pass* as the chaff,
Zec 10:11. *And he shall pass* through the sea

KAL.—*Infinitive.*

Ex. 33:22. *while* my glory *passeth by*,
— cover thee with my hand while *I pass by:*
Nu. 20:21. Thus Edom refused *to give* Israel *passage*
21:23. Sihon would not suffer Israel *to pass*
22:18. I cannot *go beyond* the word of the Lord
26. And the angel of the Lord *went* further, (lit. added *to pass*)
24:13. *go beyond* the commandment of the Lord,
32: 7. the children of Israel *from going over*
Deu 4:21. and sware that *I should* not *go over* Jordan,
17: 2. *in transgressing* his covenant,
Deu27: 3. *when thou art passed over*, that thou
4. *when ye be gone over* Jordan,
12. *when ye are come over* Jordan;
29:12(11). *That thou shouldest enter* into covenant
Jos. 3:14. removed from their tents, *to pass over*
17. the people were *passed* clean *over* (lit. had finished *to pass over*)
4: 1. the people were clean *passed over* (lit. had finished *to pass over*)
7. *when it passed over* Jordan,
11. the people were clean *passed over*, (lit. had finished *to pass over*)
23. until *ye were passed over*,
— until *we were gone over:*
5: 1. (כתיב) until *we were passed over*, (lit. according to קרי, *they were passed over*)
23:16. *When ye have transgressed* the covenant
Jud. 3:28. and suffered not a man *to pass over.*
11:20. But Sihon trusted not Israel *to pass*
1Sa.14: 4. Jonathan sought *to go over*
30:10. faint *that they could not go over* the brook
2Sa.15:24. the people had done *passing* out of the city.
17:16. *speedily* pass over; (lit. *passing* pass over)
19:18(19). the king, *as he was come over* Jordan;
1K. 18: 6. they divided the land between them *to pass*
29. And it came to pass, *when* midday *was past*,
2K. 2: 9. *when they were gone over*, that Elijah
4: 8. as oft as *he passed by*,
6: 9. Beware *that thou pass not* such a place;
Neh. 2:14. the beast (that was) under me *to pass.*
Job 33:18. *from perishing* (marg. *passing by*) by the
28. deliver his soul *from going* into the pit,
Pro.10:25. *As* the whirlwind *passeth*,
19:11. glory *to pass* over a transgression.
Isa. 28:19. From the time that *it goeth forth*
51:10. a way for the ransomed *to pass over?*
54: 9. *should* no more *go* over the earth;
Jer. 41:10. departed *to go over* to the Ammonites.
Lam.3:44. that (our) prayer *should not pass through.*
Eze.47: 5. a river that could not *be passed over.*
Am. 7: 8 & 8:2. I will not again *pass* by them any more: (lit. I will add *to pass*)
Nah. 1:15(2:1). wicked shall no more *pass* (lit. shall not add *to pass*)

KAL.—*Imperative.*

Gen32:16(17). and said unto his servants, *Pass over*
Ex. 17: 5. *Go on* before the people,
32:27. man his sword by his side, (and) *go in*
Deu. 2:13. *and get you over* the brook Zered.
24. take your journey, *and pass over*
Jos. 1: 2. now therefore arise, *go over* this Jordan,
11. *Pass* through the host,
3: 6. *and pass over* before the people.
4: 5. *Pass over* before the ark of the Lord
6: 7. *Pass on*, and compass the city,
22:19. *pass* ye *over* unto the land of the possession
1Sa.25:19. said unto her servants, *Go on* before me;
2Sa.15:22. David said to Ittai, Go *and pass over.*
17:21. Arise, *and pass* quickly *over* the water:
19:33(34). *Come thou over* with me, and I will feed
Pro. 4:15. turn from it, *and pass away.*
Isa. 23: 6. *Pass ye over* to Tarshish;
10. *Pass through* thy land as a river,
12. arise, *pass over* to Chittim;
47: 2. *pass* over the rivers.
62:10. *Go through, go through* the gates;
Jer. 2:10. For *pass over* the isles of Chittim,
Eze. 9: 4. *Go through* the midst of the city,
5. *Go ye* after him through the city,
Am. 6: 2. *Pass ye* unto Calneh, and see;
Mic. 1:11. *Pass* ye away, thou inhabitant

KAL.—*Future.*

Gen12: 6. *And* Abram *passed* through the land
18: 3. *pass* not *away*, I pray thee, from thy
5. after that *ye shall pass on:*
30:32. *I will pass through* all thy flock to day,
31:21. and he rose up, *and passed over* the river.
52. *I will* not *pass over* this heap to thee, and that *thou shalt* not *pass over* this heap
32:21(22). *So went* the present *over*
22(23). *and passed over* the ford Jabbok.
33:14. *Let* my lord, I pray thee, *pass over*
37:28. *Then there passed by* Midianites
41:46. *and went* throughout all the land
50: 4. *And when* the days of his mourning *were past*,

Ex. 15:16. till thy people *pass over*, O Lord, till the people *pass over*,
34: 6. *And* the Lord *passed by* before him,
Lev. 26: 6. *shall* the sword *go* through your land.
27:32. whatsoever *passeth* under the rod,
Nu. 5:30. the spirit of jealousy *cometh* upon him,
6: 5. *there shall* no rasor *come* upon his head:
20:17. *Let us pass*, I pray thee, through thy country: *we will* not *pass* through the
— until *we have passed* thy borders.
18. *Thou shalt* not *pass* by me,
19. *I will* only, without (doing) any thing (else), *go through*
20. And he said, *Thou shalt* not *go through*.
21:22. *Let me pass* through thy land:
— until *we be past* thy borders.
32:27. But thy servants *will pass over*,
29. *will pass* with you *over* Jordan,
30. But if *they will* not *pass over* with you
32. We *will pass over* armed before the Lord
33: 8. *and passed through* the midst of the sea
Deu. 2: 8. *And when we passed by* from our brethren
— *and passed by* the way of the wilderness
13. *And we went over* the brook Zered.
27. *Let me pass* through thy land:
28. only *I will pass* through on my feet;
29. until *I shall pass over* Jordan
3:18. *ye shall pass over* armed before your
25. I pray thee, *let me go over*,
27. for *thou shalt* not *go over* this Jordan.
28. *he shall go over* before this people,
24: 5. *shall* he be *charged* with any business: (lit. nor any thing *shall pass* upon him)
27: 2. the day when *ye shall pass over* Jordan
30:13. Who *shall go* over the sea for us,
31: 2. *Thou shalt* not *go over* this Jordan.
34: 4. *thou shalt* not *go over* thither.
Jos. 1:14. ye *shall pass* before your brethren armed,
2:23. *and passed over*, and came to Joshua
3: 1. and lodged there before *they passed over*.
2. *that* the officers *went through* the host;
4:10. and the people hasted *and passed over*.
11. *that* the ark of the Lord *passed over*,
12. *And* the children of Reuben,...*passed over*
6: 7. and *let* him that is armed *pass on*
10:29. *Then* Joshua *passed* from Makkedah,
31. *And* Joshua *passed* from Libnah,
34. *And* from Lachish Joshua *passed* unto
18: 9. the men went *and passed through* the land,
24:11. *And ye went over* Jordan,
Jud. 6:33. were gathered together, *and went over*,
9:25. they robbed all *that came* along that way
26. *and went over* to Shechem:
10: 9. *Moreover* the children of Ammon *passed over*
11:17. *Let me*, I pray thee, *pass* through thy land:
19. Israel said unto him, *Let us pass*, we pray
29. *and he passed over* Gilead, and Manasseh, *and passed over* Mizpeh of Gilead,
32. *So* Jephthah *passed over*
12: 1. gathered themselves together, *and went*
3. *and passed over* against the children of
5. which were escaped said, *Let me go over*;
18:13. *And they passed* thence unto mount
19:14. *And they passed on* and went their way;
Ru. 2: 8. in another field, neither *go* from hence,
1Sa. 9: 4. *And he passed* through mount Ephraim, *and passed* through the land of Shalisha,
— *then they passed* through the land of
— *and he passed* through the land of the
27. Bid the servant *pass on* (lit. *and let him pass on*) before us, *and he passed on*,
14: 1. Come, *and let us go over* to the Philistines'
6. Come, *and let us go over* unto the garrison
15:12. and is gone about, *and passed on*,
26:13. *Then* David *went over* to the other side,
22. *and let* one of the young men *come over* and
27: 2. And David arose, *and he passed over*
2Sa. 2:15. there arose *and went over* by number twelve
29. *and passed over* Jordan, and went through
10:17. he gathered all Israel together, *and passed over*
11:27. *And when* the mourning *was past*,
15:22. *And* Ittai the Gittite *passed over*,
16: 9. *let me go over*, I pray thee, and take off his
17:16. but speedily *pass over*;
22. *and they passed over* Jordan:

2Sa. 18:23. *and overran* (lit. *and passed*) Cushi.
19:31(32). *and went over* Jordan with the king,
36(37). Thy servant *will go* a little way *over*
37(38). thy servant Chimham; *let him go over*
38(39). Chimham *shall go over* with me,
39(40). *And* all the people *went over*
40(41). *Then* the king *went on* to Gilgal,
20:14. *And he went through* all the tribes of
24: 5. *And they passed over* Jordan,
1K. 19:19. *and* Elijah *passed by* him,
22:36. *And there went* a proclamation
2K. 2: 8. *so that they* two *went over* on dry ground.
14. *and* Elisha *went over*.
4: 8. on a day, *that* Elisha *passed* to Shunem,
8:21. *So* Joram *went over* to Zair,
14: 9. *and there passed by* a wild beast
18:12. *but transgressed* his covenant,
1Ch 19:17. *and passed over* Jordan, and came upon
2Ch 21: 9. *Then* Jehoram *went forth* with his princes,
25:18. *and there passed by* a wild beast
Neh 2:14. *Then I went on* to the gate of the
9:11. *so that they went* through the midst of the
Est. 1:19. *it be* not *altered*, (marg. *pass not away*)
4:17. *So* Mordecai *went his way*, (marg. *passed*)
9:27. so as it *should* not *fail*,
28. these days of Purim *should* not *fail*
Job 6:15. as the stream of brooks *they pass away*;
9:11. Lo, *he goeth* by me,
13:13. *and let come* on me what (will).
14: 5. appointed his bounds that *he cannot pass*;
19: 8. fenced up my way that *I cannot pass*,
34:20. troubled at midnight, *and pass away*:
36:12. *they shall perish* (marg. *pass away*) by the
Ps. 17: 3. my mouth *shall* not *transgress*.
37:36. *Yet he passed away*, and, lo,
42: 4(5). *I had gone* with the multitude,
57: 1(2). until (these) calamities *be overpast*.
66: 6. *they went* through the flood on foot:
81: 6(7). his hands *were delivered* (marg. *passed away*) from the pots.
90: 4. as yesterday when *it is past*,
104: 9. a bound that they *may* not *pass over*;
141:10. that I withal *escape*. (marg. *pass over*)
148: 6. made a decree which *shall* not *pass*.
Pro. 4:15. Avoid it, *pass* not by it,
8:29. *should* not *pass* his commandment:
Isa. 26:20. until the indignation *be overpast*.
28:15, 18. overflowing scourge *shall pass through*,
19. morning by morning *shall it pass over*,
31: 9. *he shall pass over* to his strong hold
33:21. neither *shall* gallant ship *pass thereby*.
35: 8. the unclean *shall* not *pass over it*;
40:27. my judgment *is passed over* from my
41: 3. He pursued them, (and) *passed* safely;
43: 2. When *thou passest through* the waters,
45:14. *shall come over* unto thee,
— in chains *they shall come over*,
51:23. Bow down, *that we may go over*:
Jer. 2:20. *I will* not *transgress*;
5:22. that *it cannot pass it*:
— yet *can they* not *pass over it*?
8:13. given them *shall pass away from them*.
11:15. the holy flesh *is passed* from thee?
33:13. *shall* the flocks *pass* again
34:18. *and passed* between the parts thereof,
51:43. neither *doth* (any) son of man *pass*
Lam. 4:21. the cup also *shall pass through* unto thee:
Eze. 5:17. *shall pass* through thee;
14:17. Sword, *go* through the land;
16: 6. *when I passed* by thee,
8. *Now when I passed* by thee,
29:11. No foot of man *shall pass* through it, nor foot of beast *shall pass* through it,
48:14. (כתיב) nor *alienate* the firstfruits of the
Joel 3:17(4:17). *shall* no strangers *pass* through
Am. 5: 5. *pass* not to Beer-sheba:
17. *I will pass* through thee, saith the Lord.
8: 5. When *will* the new moon *be gone*,
Mic. 2:13. *and have passed through* the gate,
— *and* their king *shall pass* before them,
Hab 1:11. *and he shall pass over*, and offend,
Zec. 9: 8. no oppressor *shall pass* through them

KAL.—*Participle.* Poel.

Gen 23:16. *current* (money) with the merchant.
Ex. 30:13, 14. every one *that passeth* among them
38:26. every one *that went* to be numbered,

Nu. 14:41. Wherefore now *do* ye *transgress*
33:51. When ye *are passed over* Jordan
35:10. When ye *be come over* Jordan
Deu 2: 4. Ye (are) *to pass through* the coast of
18. Thou *art to pass over* through Ar,
3:21. the kingdoms whither thou *passest.*
4:14. do them in the land whither ye *go over*
22. I *must* not *go over* Jordan: but ye *shall go over,*
26. ye *go over* Jordan to possess it;
6: 1. the land whither ye *go* (marg. *pass over*)
9: 1. O Israel: Thou (art) *to pass over* Jordan
3. he *which goeth over* before thee;
11: 8, 11. whither ye *go* to possess it;
31. ye *shall pass over* Jordan
30:18. upon the land, whither thou *passest over*
31: 3. he *will go over* before thee,
— he *shall go over* before thee,
13. in the land whither ye *go over*
32:47. whither ye *go over* Jordan to possess it.
Jos. 1:11. within three days ye *shall pass over*
3:11. *passeth over* before you
17. the Israelites *passed over* on dry ground,
Jud. 8: 4. Gideon came to Jordan, (and) *passed over,*
19:18. We (are) *passing* from Beth-lehem-judah
Ru. 4: 1. kinsman of whom Boaz spake *came by;*
1Sa.14: 8. we *will pass over* unto (these) men,
29: 2. the lords of the Philistines *passed on*
— David and his men *passed on* in the
2Sa.15:18. all his servants *passed on* beside him;
— *passed on* before the king.
23. the people *passed over:* the king also himself *passed over* the brook Kidron, and all the people *passed over,*
24:20. saw the king and his servants *coming on*
1K. 9: 8. every one *that passeth* by it shall be
13:25. And, behold, men *passed by,*
19:11. behold, the Lord *passed by,*
20:39. as the king *passed by,*
2K. 4: 9. an holy man of God, which *passeth by* us
6:26. as the king of Israel *was passing* by
30. he *passed by* upon the wall,
12: 4(5). the money of every one *that passeth*
2Ch 7:21. astonishment to every one *that passeth* by
24:20. Why *transgress* ye the commandments
30:10. So the posts *passed* from city to city
Est. 3: 3. Why *transgressest* thou the king's
Job 21:29. asked *them that go by* the way?
Ps. 8: 8(9). *passeth through* the paths of the seas.
80:12(13). *they which pass by* the way do pluck
84: 6(7). *passing* through the valley of Baca
89:41(42). All *that pass by* the way spoil him:
129: 8. Neither do *they which go by* say,
144: 4. as a shadow *that passeth away.*
Pro. 7: 8. *Passing* through the street
9:15. To call *passengers* who go right (lit. *those that pass by* the way)
26:10. and rewardeth *transgressors.*
17. *He that passeth by,* (and) meddleth
Cant.5: 5. (with) *sweet smelling* (marg. *passing,* or, *running about*) myrrh,
13. dropping *sweet smelling* myrrh.
Isa. 23: 2. *that pass over* the sea,
29: 5. as chaff *that passeth away:*
33: 8. *the wayfaring man* (lit. *he that passeth* along the road)
34:10. none *shall pass* through it for ever
51:23. as the street, *to them that went over.*
60:15. so that no man *went through*
Jer. 9:10(9). so that none *can pass through*
12(11). that none *passeth through?*
13:24. as the stubble *that passeth away*
18:16 & 19:8. every one *that passeth* thereby
34:18. men *that have transgressed* my covenant,
19. *which passed* between the parts
49:17. every one *that goeth* by it
50:13. every one *that goeth* by Babylon
Lam. 1:12. all ye *that pass by?*
2:15. All *that pass by* clap (their) hands
Eze. 5:14. in the sight of all *that pass by.*
14:15. that no man *may pass through*
16:15. on every one *that passed by;*
25. opened thy feet to every one *that passed by,*
33:28. desolate, that none *shall pass through.*
35: 7. cut off from it *him that passeth out*
36:34. in the sight of all *that passed by.*
39:11. the valley of *the passengers* on the east

Eze.39:11. stop the (noses) of *the passengers:*
14. *passing* through the land to bury with *the passengers* those
15. And *the passengers* (that) pass through
Mic. 2: 8. the garment *from them that pass by*
7:18. *and passeth by* the transgression
Nah 1: 8. an *overrunning* flood he will make
Zep 2:15. every one *that passeth by* her
3: 6. waste, that none *passeth by:*
Zec. 7:14. *that no man passed through* nor returned:
9: 8. *because of him that passeth by,*

* NIPHAL.—*Future.* *

Eze.47: 5. a river that *could* not *be passed over.*

* PIEL.—*Preterite.* *

Job 21:10. Their bull *gendereth,* and faileth not;

PIEL.—*Future.*

1K. 6:21. *and he made a partition* by the chains

* HIPHIL.—*Preterite.* *

Gen47:21. *he removed* them to cities
Ex. 13:12. *That thou shalt set apart* (marg. *cause to pass over*) unto the Lord
Lev.25: 9. *Then shalt thou cause* the trumpet of the jubile *to sound*
Nu. 8: 7. *and let them* shave all their flesh, (marg. *cause* a rasor *to pass over*)
27: 7. *and thou shalt cause* the inheritance...*to pass* unto them.
8. *then ye shall cause* his inheritance *to pass*
Jos. 4: 3. *and ye shall carry* them *over* with you,
7: 7. *hast thou* at all *brought* this people *over*
2Sa.12:13. The Lord also *hath put away* thy sin;
31. and *made* them *pass* through the
19:40(41). *and* all the people of Judah *conducted*
2K. 16: 3. *made* his son *to pass* through the fire,
21: 6. *And he made* his son *pass* through the
2Ch 33: 6. he *caused* his children *to pass* through
Est. 8: 2. which *he had taken* from Haman,
Ps. 136:14. *And made* Israel *to pass* through
Jer. 15:14. *And I will make* (thee) *to pass*
46:17. *he hath passed* the time appointed.
Eze. 5: 1. *and cause* (it) *to pass* upon thine head
20:37. *And I will cause* you *to pass*
23:37. and *have* also *caused* their sons, whom they bare unto me, *to pass* for them *through*
37: 2. *And caused me to pass* by them
Zec. 3: 4. *I have caused* thine iniquity *to pass* from

HIPHIL.—*Infinitive.*

Lev.18:21. *pass through* (the fire) to Molech,
Deu 2:30. would not let *us pass* by him:
Jos. 7: 7. thou *at all* brought this people *over* (lit. hast thou brought over *bringing over*)
1Sa.20:36. an arrow *beyond* (marg. *to pass over*) *him.*
2Sa. 3:10. *To translate* the kingdom from the house
19:15(16). *to conduct* the king *over* Jordan.
18(19). *to carry over* the king's houshold,
2K. 23:10. *might make* his son or his daughter *to pass*
2Ch 30: 5. *to make proclamation* (lit. *to make* the voice *to pass*)
Est. 8: 3. *to put away* the mischief of Haman
Jer. 32:35. *to cause* their sons and their daughters *to pass*
Eze.16:21. *to cause* them *to pass through* (the fire)
20:26. *in that they caused to pass through*
31. *when ye make* your sons *to pass through*

HIPHIL.—*Imperative.*

2Sa.24:10. *take away* the iniquity of thy servant;
1Ch 21: 8. *do away* the iniquity of thy servant;
2Ch 35:23. *Have me away;* for I am sore wounded.
Ps.119:37. *Turn away* mine eyes from beholding
39. *Turn away* my reproach which I fear:
Ecc.11:10. *and put away* evil from thy flesh:

HIPHIL.—*Future.*

Gen 8: 1. *and* God *made* a wind *to pass* over the
32:23(24). *and sent* (marg. *caused to pass*) *them over* the brook, *and sent over* that he
Ex. 33:19. *I will make* all my goodness *pass* before
36: 6. *and they caused it to be proclaimed* (lit. *caused* a voice *to pass through*)
Lev 25: 9. *shall ye make* the trumpet *sound*
Nu. 31:23. *ye shall make* (it) *go* through
— *ye shall make go* through the water.
32: 5. *bring us* not *over* Jordan.

Jos. 4: 8. *and carried them over* with them
1Sa.16: 8. *and made him pass* before Samuel.
9. *Then* Jesse *made* Shammah *to pass by.*
10. *Again,* Jesse *made* seven of his sons *to pass*
2Sa. 2: 8. *and brought him over* to Mahanaim;
19:40(41). (כתיב) *and* all the people...*conducted* the king,
41(42). *and have brought* the king, and his
1K. 15:12. *And he took away* the sodomites
2K. 17:17. *And they caused* their sons and their daughters *to pass*
2Ch 15: 8. *and put away* the abominable idols
35:24. His servants *therefore took him* out of that
36:22. *that he made a proclamation* (lit. *and he made* the voice *to pass*)
Ezr. 1: 1. *that he made a proclamation* (marg. *caused* a voice *to pass*)
10: 7. *And they made proclamation* throughout (lit. *caused* a voice *to pass*)
Neh. 2: 7. that *they may convey me over*
8:15. *and proclaim* (lit. *cause* a voice *to pass*) in all their cities,
Job 7:21. *and take away* mine iniquity?
Ps. 78:13. *and caused them to pass through;*
Eze.14:15. *I cause* noisome beasts *to pass* through
46:21. *and caused me to pass* by
47: 3. *and he brought me* through the waters;
4. *and brought me* through the waters;
— *and brought me through;* the waters
48:14. shall not sell of it, neither exchange, nor *alienate*
Jon. 3: 6. *and he laid* his robe from him,
Zec.13: 2. *I will cause* the prophets and the unclean spirit *to pass*

HIPHIL.—*Participle.*

Deu18:10. *that maketh...to pass* through the fire,
1Sa. 2:24. *ye make* the Lord's people *to transgress.* (marg. or, *cry out*)
Dan11:20. stand up in his estate a raiser of taxes (marg. one *that causeth* an exacter *to pass over*)

* HITHPAEL.—*Preterite.* *

Ps. 78:62. *was wroth* with his inheritance.
89:38(39). *thou hast been wroth* with thine

HITHPAEL.—*Future.*

Deu 3:26. *But* the Lord *was wroth* with me
Ps. 78:21. the Lord heard (this), *and was wroth:*
59. When God heard (this), *he was wroth,*

HITHPAEL.—*Participle.*

Pro. 14:16. but the fool *rageth,* and is confident.
20: 2. (whoso) *provoketh him to anger* sinneth
26:17. *meddleth* (marg. or, *is enraged*) with strife (belonging) not to him,

---

5676 ## עֵבֶר *gēh'-ver,* m.

Gen50:10. Atad, which (is) *beyond* Jordan,
11. called Abel-Mizraim, which (is) *beyond* Jordan.
Ex. 25:37. that they may give light over *against* it. (lit. upon *the side of* its faces)
28:26. which (is) in *the side of* the ephod inward.
32:15. tables (were) written on both *their sides;*
39:19. on *the side of* the ephod inward.
Nu. 21:13. pitched *on the other side of* Arnon,
22: 1. *on this side* Jordan (by) Jericho.
32:19. will not inherit with them *on yonder side*
— our inheritance is fallen to us *on this side*
32. our inheritance *on this side* Jordan
34:15. their inheritance *on this side* Jordan
35:14. give three cities *on this side* Jordan,
Deu. 1: 1. spake unto all Israel *on this side* Jordan
5. *On this side* Jordan, in the land
3: 8. the land that (was) *on this side* Jordan,
20. your God hath given them *beyond* Jordan:
25. see the good land that (is) *beyond* Jordan,
4:41. severed three cities *on this side* Jordan
46. *On this side* Jordan, in the valley
47. which (were) *on this side* Jordan
49. all the plain *on this side* Jordan eastward,
11:30. (Are) they not *on the other side* Jordan,
30:13. Neither (is) it *beyond* the sea,
— Who shall go *over* the sea for us,

Jos. 1:14. Moses gave you *on this side* Jordan;
15. Lord's servant gave you *on this side* Jordan
2:10. that (were) *on the other side* Jordan,
5: 1. which (were) *on the side of* Jordan
7: 7. dwelt *on the other side* Jordan!
9: 1. which (were) *on this side* Jordan,
10. the Amorites, that (were) *beyond* Jordan,
12: 1. possessed their land *on the other side* Jordan
7. Israel smote *on this side* Jordan
13: 8. Moses gave them, *beyond* Jordan
27. *on the other side* Jordan eastward.
32. plains of Moab, *on the other side* Jordan,
14: 3. *on the other side* Jordan:
17: 5. which (were) *on the other side* Jordan;
18: 7. received their inheritance *beyond* Jordan
20: 8. *And on the other side* Jordan
22: 4. gave you *on the other side* Jordan.
7. among their brethren *on this side* Jordan
11. at *the passage* of the children of Israel.
24: 2. Your fathers dwelt *on the other side*
3. Abraham *from the other side of* the flood,
8. which dwelt *on the other side* Jordan;
14. your fathers served *on the other side of* the flood,
15. that (were) *on the other side of* the flood,
Jud. 5:17. Gilead abode *beyond* Jordan:
7:25. to Gideon *on the other side* Jordan.
10: 8. Israel that (were) *on the other side* Jordan
11:18. pitched *on the other side of* Arnon,
1Sa.14: 1. garrison, that (is) *on the* other *side.*
4. (there was) a sharp rock *on the* one *side,* and a sharp rock *on the* other *side:*
40. Be ye *on* one *side,* and I and Jonathan my son will be *on the* other *side.*
26:13. David went over *to the other side,*
31: 7. Israel that (were) *on the other side of* the valley, and (they) that (were) *on the other side* Jordan,
2Sa.10:16. the Syrians that (were) *beyond* the river:
1K. 4:12. (the place that is) *beyond* Jokneam:
24(5:4). all (the region) *on this side* the river,
—(-:-). all the kings *on this side* the river:
—(-:-). he had peace on all *sides* round about *him.* [see עֲבֶד]
7:20. which (was) *by* the network:
30. *at the side of* every addition.
14:15. shall scatter them *beyond* the river,
1Ch. 6:78(63). *And on the other side* Jordan by Jericho,
12:37. *And on the other side* of Jordan,
19:16. the Syrians that (were) *beyond* the river:
26:30. *on this side* Jordan westward
2Ch 20: 2. *from beyond* the sea on this side Syria;
Ezr. 8:36. to the governors *on this side* the river:
Neh. 2: 7. to the governors *beyond* the river,
9. I came to the governors *beyond* the river,
3: 7. the governor *on this side* the river.
Job 1:19. came a great wind *from* (marg. *from aside*) the wilderness,
Isa. 7:20. *by them beyond* the river,
9: 1(8:23). *beyond* Jordan, in Galilee
18: 1. which (is) *beyond* the rivers of Ethiopia:
47:15. shall wander every one *to his quarter;*
Jer. 22:20. cry *from the passages:*
25:22. the isles which (are) *beyond* the sea,
48:28. maketh her nest *in the sides of*
49:32. bring their calamity from all *sides thereof,*
Eze. 1: 9, 12 & 10:22. they went every one *straight* forward. (lit. on *the side of* their face)
Zep. 3:10. *From beyond* the rivers of Ethiopia

עֲבַר *gavar,* Ch. m. 5675

Ezr. 4:10. the rest (that are) *on this side* the river,
11. the men *on this side* the river,
16. no portion *on this side* the river.
17. the rest *beyond* the river,
20. over all (countries) *beyond* the river;
5: 3, 6. governor *on this side* the river,
6. which (were) *on this side* the river,
6: 6. Tatnai, governor *beyond* the river,
— which (are) *beyond* the river,
8. of the tribute *beyond* the river,
13. governor *on this side* the river,
7:21. treasurers which (are) *beyond* the river,
25. the people that (are) *beyond* the river,

5679 **עֲבָרָה** *găvāh-rāh'*, f.

2Sa.15:28. (כתיב) I will tarry *in the plain of* the
17:16. (——) this night *in the plains of* the
19:18(19). And there went over *a ferry boat*

5678 **עֶבְרָה** *gev-rāh'*, f.

Gen49: 7. *and their wrath*, for it was cruel:
Job 21:30. they shall be brought forth to the day of *wrath*. (marg. *wraths*)
40:11. Cast abroad *the rage of* thy wrath:
Ps. 7: 6(7). *because of the rage of* mine enemies:
78:49. the fierceness of his anger, *wrath*,
85: 3(4). Thou hast taken away all *thy wrath*:
90: 9. all our days are passed away *in thy wrath*:
11. according to thy fear, (so is) *thy wrath*.
Pro.11: 4. Riches profit not in the day of *wrath*:
23. the expectation of the wicked (is) *wrath*.
14:35. *but his wrath* is (against) him
21:24. who dealeth *in* proud *wrath*.
22: 8. the rod of *his anger* shall fail.
Isa. 9:19(18). *Through the wrath of* the Lord of hosts
10: 6. against the people of *my wrath* will I give
13: 9. cruel *both with wrath* and fierce anger,
13. *in the wrath of* the Lord of hosts,
14: 6. He who smote the people *in wrath*
16: 6. haughtiness, and his pride, *and his wrath*:
Jer. 7:29. forsaken the generation of *his wrath*.
48:30. I know *his wrath*,
Lam. 2: 2. he hath thrown down *in his wrath*
3: 1. seen affliction by the rod of *his wrath*.
Eze. 7:19. in the day of *the wrath of* the Lord:
21:31(36). against thee in the fire of *my wrath*,
22:21. blow upon you in the fire of *my wrath*,
31. consumed them with the fire of *my wrath*:
38:19. in the fire of *my wrath*
Hos. 5:10. I will pour out *my wrath* upon them
13:11. took (him) away *in my wrath*.
Am. 1:11. *and* he kept *his wrath* for ever:
Hab. 3: 8. (was) *thy wrath* against the sea,
Zep. 1:15. That day (is) a day of *wrath*,
18. in the day of the Lord's *wrath*;

5685 **עָבַשׁ** [*gāh-vash'*].

* KAL.—*Preterite.* *

Joel 1:17. The seed *is rotten* under their clods,

5686 **עָבַת** [*gāh-vath'*].

* PIEL.—*Future.* *

Mic. 7: 3. his mischievous desire: *so they wrap it up.*

5687 **עָבֹת** *gāh-vōhth'*, adj.

Lev.23:40. the boughs of *thick* trees,
Neh. 8:15. branches of *thick* trees, to make booths,
Eze. 6:13. under every *thick* oak,
20:28. saw every high hill, and all the *thick* trees,

5688 **עֲבֹת** *găvōhth*, com.

Ex. 28:14. *wreathen* work shalt thou make them,
— fasten the *wreathen* chains to the ouches.
22. *wreathen* work (of) pure gold.
24. put *the* two *wreathen* (chains) of gold
25. *the* two *wreathen* (chains) thou shalt fasten
39:15. *wreathen* work (of) pure gold.
17. they put *the* two *wreathen chains* of gold
18. *the* two *wreathen chains* they fastened
Jud.15:13. they bound him with two new *cords*,
14. *the cords* that (were) upon his arms
16:11. If they bind me fast *with* new *ropes*
12. Delilah therefore took new *ropes*,
Job 39:10. bind the unicorn with *his band*
Ps. 2: 3. cast away *their cords* from us.
118:27. bind the sacrifice *with cords*,
129: 4. hath cut asunder *the cords of* the wicked.
Isa. 5:18. *and* sin *as it were with a* cart *rope*:
Eze. 3:25. they shall put *bands* upon thee,
Eze. 4: 8. I will lay *bands* upon thee,
19:11. was exalted among *the thick branches*,
31: 3. his top was among *the thick boughs*.
10. hath shot up his top among *the thick boughs*,
14. shoot up their top among *the thick boughs*
Hos 11: 4. *with bands of* love:

עָגַב [*gāh-gav'*]. 5689

* KAL.—*Preterite.* *

Eze.23: 7. with all on whom *she doted*:
9. the Assyrians, upon whom *she doted*.
12. *She doted* upon the Assyrians

KAL.—*Future.*

Eze.23: 5. *and she doted* on her lovers,
16. *And* as soon as she saw them with her eyes, *she doted*
20. *For she doted* upon their paramours,

KAL.—*Participle.* Poel.

Jer. 4:30. (thy) *lovers* will despise thee,

עֲגָבָה [*găgāh-vāh'*], f. 5691

Eze.23:11. she was more corrupt in *her inordinate love*

עֲגָבִים *găgāh-veem'*, m. pl. 5690

Eze.33:31. with their mouth they shew *much love*, (marg. make *loves*, or, *jests*)
32. thou (art) unto them as a *very lovely* song

עֻגָה *goo-gāh'* & **עֻגָּה** *goog-gāh'*, f. 5692

Gen18: 6. knead (it), and make *cakes upon the hearth*.
Ex. 12:39. And they baked unleavened *cakes*
Nu. 11: 8. baked (it) in pans, and made *cakes* of it:
1K. 17:13. make me thereof *a* little *cake*
19: 6. (there was) *a cake* baken on the coals,
Eze. 4:12. *And* thou shalt eat it (as) barley *cakes*,
Hos. 7: 8. Ephraim is *a cake* not turned.

עָגוּר *gāh-goor'*, m. 5693

Isa. 38:14. Like a crane (or) *a swallow*,
Jer. 8: 7. the crane *and the swallow* observe the time

עָגִיל *gāh-geel'*, m. 5694

Nu. 31:50. chains, and bracelets, rings, *earrings*,
Eze.16:12. *and earrings* in thine ears,

עָגֹל *gāh-gōhl'*, adj. 5696

1K. 7:23. (it was) *round* all about,
31. the mouth thereof (was) *round*
— with their borders, foursquare, not *round*.
35. (was there) a *round* compass of half
10:19. the top of the throne (was) *round*
2Ch 4: 2. from brim to brim, *round* in compass,

עֵגֶל *geh'-gel*, com. 5695

Ex. 32: 4. after he had made it *a* molten *calf*:
8. they have made them *a* molten *calf*,
19. that he saw *the calf*, and the dancing:
20. he took *the calf* which they had made,
24. there came out *this calf*.
35. they made *the calf*, which Aaron made.
Lev. 9: 2. Take thee *a* young *calf* for a sin offering,
3. *and a calf* and a lamb,
8. slew *the calf of* the sin offering,
Deu 9:16. had made you *a* molten *calf*:
21. *the calf* which ye had made,
1Sa.28:24. the woman had *a* fat *calf* in the house;
1K. 12:28. made two *calves* (of) gold,

1K. 12:32. sacrificing *unto the calves* that he had made:
2K. 10:29. *the* golden *calves* that (were) in Beth-el,
17:16. them molten images, (even) two *calves*,
2Ch 11:15. *and for the calves* which he had made.
13: 8. (there are) with you golden *calves*,
Neh. 9:18. when they had made them *a* molten *calf*,
Ps. 29: 6. He maketh them also to skip like *a calf*;
68:30(31). *with the calves of* the people,
106:19. They made *a calf* in Horeb,
Isa. 11: 6. *and the calf* and the young lion
27:10. there shall *the calf* feed,
Jer. 31:18. *as a bullock* unaccustomed (to the yoke):
34:18. when they cut *the calf* in twain,
19. which passed between the parts of *the calf*;
46:21. in the midst of her *like* fatted *bullocks*;
Eze. 1: 7. feet (was) like the sole of *a calf*'s foot:
Hos. 8: 5. *Thy calf*, O Samaria, hath cast (thee) off;
6. *the calf of* Samaria shall be broken
13: 2. Let the men that sacrifice kiss *the calves*.
Am. 6: 4. *and the calves* out of the midst of the stall;
Mic. 6: 6. *with calves of* a year old?
Mal. 4: 2(3:20). grow up *as calves* of the stall.

5697 עֶגְלָה *ⁿgeg-lāh'*, f.

Gen15: 9. Take me *an heifer of* three years old,
Deu21: 3. the elders of that city shall take *an heifer*, (lit. *a heifer of* the herd)
4. bring down *the heifer* unto a rough valley,
— shall strike off *the heifer*'s neck
6. shall wash their hands over *the heifer*
Jud.14:18. If ye had not plowed *with my heifer*,
1Sa.16: 2. Take *an heifer* (lit. *an heifer of* the herd) with thee,
Isa. 7:21. a man shall nourish *a young cow*, (lit. *heifer of* the herd)
15: 5. *an heifer* of three years old:
Jer. 46:20. Egypt (is like) *a* very fair *heifer*,
48:34. (as) *an heifer* of three years old:
50:11. ye are grown fat *as the heifer* at grass,
Hos10: 5. Samaria shall fear *because of the calves of*
11. Ephraim (is as) *an heifer* (that is) taught,

5699 עֲגָלָה *ⁿgăgāh-lāh'*, f.

Gen45:19. take you *wagons* out of the land of Egypt
21. Joseph gave them *wagons*,
27. when he saw *the wagons*
46: 5. *in the wagons* which Pharaoh had sent
Nu. 7: 3. their offering before the Lord, six covered *wagons*,
— *a wagon* for two of the princes,
6. Moses took *the wagons* and the oxen,
7. Two *wagons* and four oxen
8. four *wagons* and eight oxen
1Sa. 6: 7. Now therefore make *a* new *cart*,
— tie the kine *to the cart*,
8. ark of the Lord, and lay it upon *the cart*;
10. two milch kine, and tied them *to the cart*,
11. laid the ark of the Lord upon *the cart*,
14. *And the cart* came into the field of Joshua,
— they clave the wood of *the cart*,
2Sa. 6: 3. they set the ark of God upon *a* new *cart*,
— the sons of Abinadab, drave *the* new *cart*.
1Ch 13: 7. they carried the ark of God *in a* new *cart*
— Uzza and Ahio drave *the cart*.
Ps. 46: 9(10). he burneth *the chariot* in the fire.
Isa. 5:18. and sin as it were with a *cart* rope:
28:27. neither is a *cart* wheel turned about
28. nor break (it with) the wheel of *his cart*,
Am. 2:13. *a cart* is pressed (that is) full of sheaves.

5701 עָגַם [*ⁿgāh-gam'*].

* KAL.—*Preterite.* *

Job 30:25. *was* (not) my soul *grieved* for the poor?

5702 עָגַן [*ⁿgāh-gan'*].

* NIPHAL.—*Future.* *

Ru. 1:13. *would ye stay* for them from having

עַד *ⁿgad*, m. 5703

Ex. 15:18. The Lord shall reign for ever *and ever*.
Nu. 24:20. latter end (shall be) that he perish *for ever*.
24. afflict Eber, and he also shall perish *for ever*.
1Ch 28: 9. he will cast thee off *for ever*.
Job 19:24. an iron pen and lead in the rock *for ever!*
20: 4. Knowest thou (not) this of *old*,
Ps. 9: 5(6). put out their name for ever *and ever*.
18(19). of the poor shall (not) perish *for ever*.
10:16. The Lord (is) King for ever *and ever*:
19: 9(10). fear of the Lord (is) clean, enduring *for ever*:
21: 4(5). (even) length of days for ever *and ever*.
6(7). hast made him most blessed *for ever*:
22:26(27). your heart shall live *for ever*.
37:29. dwell therein *for ever*.
45: 6(7). throne, O God, (is) for ever *and ever*:
17(18). people praise thee for ever *and ever*.
48:14(15). God (is) our God for ever *and ever*:
52: 8(10). in the mercy of God for ever *and ever*.
61: 8(9). I sing praise unto thy name *for ever*,
83:17(18). be confounded and troubled *for ever*;
89:29(30). also will I make (to endure) *for ever*,
92: 7(8). that they shall be destroyed *for ever*:
104: 5. (that) it should not be removed *for ever*. (lit. for ever *and ever*)
111: 3. his righteousness endureth *for ever*.
8. They stand fast *for ever* and ever,
10. his praise endureth *for ever*.
112: 3, 9. his righteousness endureth *for ever*.
119:44. keep thy law continually for ever *and ever*.
132:12. shall also sit upon thy throne *for evermore*.
14. This (is) my rest *for ever*:
145: 1. I will bless thy name for ever *and ever*.
2. I will praise thy name for ever *and ever*.
21. bless his holy name for ever *and ever*.
148: 6. He hath also stablished them *for ever*
Pro.12:19. lip of truth shall be established *for ever*:
29:14. his throne shall be established *for ever*.
Isa. 9: 6(5). The *everlasting* Father, The Prince of Peace.
26: 4. Trust ye in the Lord *for ever*:
30: 8. for the time to come *for ever* and ever:
45:17. nor confounded world without end. (lit. unto the ages of *perpetuity*)
57:15. and lofty One that inhabiteth *eternity*,
64: 9(8). neither remember iniquity *for ever*:
65:18. But be ye glad and rejoice *for ever*
Dan 12: 3. as the stars for ever *and ever*.
Am. 1:11. and his anger did tear *perpetually*,
Mic. 4: 5. the Lord our God for ever *and ever*.
7:18. he retaineth not his anger *for ever*,
Hab. 3: 6. the *everlasting* mountains were scattered,

עַד *ⁿgad*, m. 5706

Gen49:27. in the morning he shall devour *the prey*,
Isa. 33:23. then is *the prey of* a great spoil divided;
Zep. 3: 8. until the day that I rise up *to the prey*:

עַד *ⁿgad*, part. prep. & adv. 5704

Gen 3:19. *till* thou return unto the ground;
6: 7. both man, *and* beast, (marg. from man *unto* beast)
8: 5. *until* the tenth month:
13:12. and pitched (his) tent *toward* Sodom.
15. to thee...and to thy seed *for* ever.
31:24. speak not to Jacob either good *or* bad. (marg. from good *to* bad)
43:25. ready the present *against* Joseph came
48: 5. born unto thee...*before* I came
Ex. 14:28. remained not *so much as* one of them.
22:26(25). deliver it...*by that* the sun goeth down:
27: 5. that the net may be *even to* the midst
33:22. with my hand *while* I pass by:
Lev.23:14. the selfsame day *that* ye have brought
16. *Even* unto the morrow after the seventh
26:18. if ye will not *yet* for all this hearken
Jos. 8:22. they smote them, *so that* they let none
17:14. I (am) a great people, *forasmuch as* the
Jud.11:19. pass,...through thy land *into* my place.
20:48. as well the men of (every) city, *as* the beast, *and* all that came to hand:

1Sa.25:22. if I leave of all...*by* the morning light
2K. 9:22. What peace, *so long as* the whoredoms
Neh 6: 1. though *at* that time I had not set up
Job 38:11. Hither*to* shalt thou come,
Ps. 71:18. also *when* I am old (marg. *unto* old age)
&c. &c.

Several of the combinations of עַד have been noticed under other words; see אֲשֶׁר; מָתַי ; מְאֹד פֶּן ; כִּי ; כֹּה ; הֵנָּה.

The following have also to be noticed :—

עַד אָנָה or עַד אָן

Job 8: 2. *How long* wilt thou speak these (things)?
18: 2. *How long* (will it be ere) ye make an end
&c.

עַד מָה or עַד מֶה

Ps. 4: 2(3). *how long* (will ye turn) my glory
74: 9. neither...any that knoweth *how long.*
&c.

עַד עַתָּה

2K. 13:23. cast he them from his presence *as yet.*
&c.

The signification of עַד is the same when combined with pronominal suffixes.

5705 עַד *gad*, Ch. part.

Ezr. 4:21. *until* (another) commandment shall be
24. *unto* the second year of the reign of
5: 5. *till* the matter came to Darius:
16. since that time *even until* now
6:15. house was finished *on* the third day of
7:22. *Unto* an hundred talents of silver, *and to* an hundred measures of wheat, *and to* an hundred baths of wine, *and to* an hundred baths of oil,
Dan 2: 9. *till* the time be changed:
20. Blessed be the name of God for ever *and* (lit. *and until*) ever:
34. *till* that a stone was cut out without
4: 8(5). *But at* the last Daniel came
17(14). *to* the intent that the living may
23(20). *till* seven times pass over him ;
25(22). *till* thou know that the most High
32(29). *until* thou know that the most High
33(30). *till* his hairs were grown like eagles'
5:21. *till* he knew that the most high God
6: 7(8). a petition of any God or man *for* thirty
12(13). of any God or man *within* thirty days,
14(15). *and* he laboured *till* the going down
24(25). the lions had the mastery of them, and brake all their bones in pieces or ever they came at the bottom of the den. (lit. nor did they come to the bottom *until* the lions had the mastery of them)
26(27). his dominion (shall be even) *unto* the
7: 4. I beheld *till* the wings thereof were
9. I beheld *till* the thrones were cast down,
11. I beheld (even) *till* the beast was slain,
12. their lives were prolonged *for* a season
13. *and* came *to* the Ancient of days,
18. and possess the kingdom *for* ever, *even for* ever and ever.
22. *Until* the Ancient of days came,
25. *until* a time and times and the dividing of
26. to destroy (it) *unto* the end.
28. Hither*to* (is) the end of the matter.

5707 עֵד *gehd*, m.

Gen31:44. let it be *for a witness* between me and
48. And Laban said, This heap (is) *a witness*
50. God (is) *witness* betwixt me and thee.
52. This heap (be) *witness*,
Ex. 20:16. Thou shalt not bear false *witness*
22:13(12). let him bring it (for) *witness*,
23: 1. the wicked to be an unrighteous *witness.*
Lev. 5: 1. the voice of swearing, and (is) *a witness*,
Nu. 5:13. *and* (there be) no *witness* against her,
35:30. put to death by the mouth of *witnesses: but* one *witness* shall not testify
Deu 5:20(17). Neither shalt thou bear false *witness*
17: 6. At the mouth of two *witnesses*, or three *witnesses*, shall he that is worthy of death be put to death ; (but) at the mouth of one *witness* he shall not be put to death.
7. The hands of *the witnesses* shall be first
19:15. One *witness* shall not rise up against a
— at the mouth of two *witnesses*, or at the mouth of three *witnesses*,
16. If *a* false *witness* rise up against any man
18. and, behold, (if) *the witness* (be) *a* false *witness*,
31:19. that this song may be *a witness* for me
21. this song shall testify against them *as a witness* ;
26. that it may be there *for a witness* against
Jos. 22:27. it (may be) *a witness* between us, and you,
28. it (is) *a witness* between us and you.
34. it (shall be) *a witness* between us
24:22. Ye (are) *witnesses* against yourselves
— And they said, (We are) *witnesses.*
Ru. 4: 9, 10. Ye (are) *witnesses* this day,
11. and the elders, said, (We are) *witnesses.*
1Sa.12: 5. The Lord (is) *witness* against you, *and* his anointed (is) *witness* this day,
— And they answered, (He is) *witness.*
Job 10:17. Thou renewest *thy witnesses* against me,
16: 8. filled me with wrinkles, (which) is *a witness*
19. *my witness* (is) in heaven, and my record
Ps. 27:12. false *witnesses* are risen up against me,
35:11. False *witnesses* did rise up ;
89:37(38). *and* (as) *a* faithful *witness* in heaven.
Pro. 6:19. *A* false *witness* (that) speaketh lies,
12:17. righteousness: *but a* false *witness* deceit.
14: 5. *A* faithful *witness* will not lie: but *a* false *witness* will utter lies.
25. *A* true *witness* delivereth souls:
19: 5, 9. *A* false *witness* shall not be unpunished,
28. *An* ungodly *witness* scorneth judgment:
21:28. *A* false *witness* shall perish:
24:28. Be not *a witness* against thy neighbour
25:18. A man that beareth false *witness*
Isa. 8: 2. I took unto me faithful *witnesses*
19:20. And it shall be for a sign *and for a witness*
43: 9. let them bring forth *their witnesses*,
10, 12. Ye (are) *my witnesses*, saith the Lord,
44: 8. ye (are) even *my witnesses.*
9. *and* they (are) *their own witnesses ;*
55: 4. given him (for) *a witness* to the people,
Jer. 29:23. know, *and* (am) *a witness*, saith the Lord.
32:10. and took *witnesses*, and weighed (him) the money
12. in the presence of *the witnesses*
25. the field for money, and take *witnesses ;*
44. take *witnesses* in the land of Benjamin,
42: 5. The Lord be *a* true and faithful *witness*
Mic. 1: 2. let the Lord God be *witness* against you,
Mal. 3: 5. be *a* swift *witness* against the sorcerers,

עָדָה *gāh-dāh'*. 5710

* KAL.—*Preterite.* *

Job 28: 8. nor the fierce lion *passed by* it.
Eze.23:40. *and deckedst thyself* with ornaments,

KAL.—*Imperative.*

Job 40:10. *Deck thyself* now (with) majesty

* KAL.—*Future.* *

Isa. 61:10. a bride *adorneth* (herself) with her jewels.
Jer. 4:30. though *thou deckest thee* with ornaments
31: 4. *thou shalt* again *be adorned* with thy tabrets,
Eze.16:11. *I decked thee also* with ornaments,
13. *Thus wast thou decked* with gold and silver;
Hos. 2:13(15). *and she decked herself* with her earrings

* HIPHIL.—*Participle.* *

Pro.25:20. (As) *he that taketh away* a garment

עֲדָה & עֲדָא [*gădāh*], Ch. 5709

* P'AL.—*Preterite.* *

Dan 3:27. nor the smell of fire *had passed* on them
4:31(28). The kingdom *is departed* from thee.

P'AL.—*Future.*

Dan 6: 8(9), 12 (13). and Persians, which *altereth* (marg. *passeth*) not.
7:14. dominion, which *shall* not *pass away*,

* APHEL.—*Preterite.* *

Dan 5:20. and *they took* his glory from him:
7:12. *they had* their dominion *taken away* :

APHEL.—*Future.*

Dan 7:26. and *they shall take away* his dominion,

APHEL.—*Participle.*

Dan 2:21. *he removeth* kings, and setteth up

5712 עֵדָה *g[n]ēh-dāh'*, f.

Ex. 12: 3. Speak ye unto all *the congregation of* Israel,
6. the whole assembly of *the congregation of*
19. cut off *from the congregation of* Israel,
47. All *the congregation of* Israel shall keep it.
16: 1. *the congregation of* the children of Israel
2. *the* whole *congregation of* the children
9. Say unto all *the congregation of*
10. Aaron spake unto *the* whole *congregation of*
22. all the rulers of *the congregation* came
17: 1. *the congregation of* the children of Israel
34:31. the rulers *of the congregation*
35: 1. Moses gathered all *the congregation of*
4, 20. all *the congregation of* the children of
38:25. that were numbered of *the congregation*
Lev. 4:13. if *the* whole *congregation of* Israel sin
15. the elders of *the congregation*
8: 3. gather thou all *the congregation*
4. *the assembly* was gathered together
5. Moses said unto *the congregation*,
9: 5. and all *the congregation* drew near
10: 6. lest wrath come upon all *the people* :
17. the iniquity of *the congregation*,
16: 5. he shall take of *the congregation of*
19: 2. Speak unto all *the congregation of*
24:14. let all *the congregation* stone him.
16. *the congregation* shall certainly stone him:
Nu. 1: 2. Take ye the sum of all *the congregation of*
16. the renowned of *the congregation*,
18. they assembled all *the congregation*
53. there be no wrath upon *the congregation of*
3: 7. the charge of *the* whole *congregation*
4:34. the chief of *the congregation*
8: 9. thou shalt gather *the* whole *assembly of*
20. all *the congregation of* the children
10: 2. the calling of *the assembly*,
3. all *the assembly* shall assemble
13:26. all *the congregation of* the children
— all *the congregation*, and shewed
14: 1. *the congregation* lifted up their voice,
2. *the* whole *congregation* said unto them,
5. *the congregation of* the children of Israel.
7. they spake unto all *the company of*
10. all *the congregation* bade stone them
27. *with* this evil *congregation*, which murmur
35. all this evil *congregation*, that are
36. made all *the congregation* to murmur
15:24. without the knowledge of *the congregation*, that all *the congregation* shall offer one
25. *the congregation of* the children of Israel,
26. be forgiven all *the congregation of*
33. unto all *the congregation*.
35. all *the congregation* shall stone him
36. *the congregation* brought him without the
16: 2. princes of *the assembly*,
3. all *the congregation* (are) holy,
5. unto all *his company*,
6. Korah, and all *his company* ;
9. *from the congregation of* Israel,
— to stand before *the congregation*
11. thou and all *thy company* (are) gathered
16. Be thou and all *thy company* before the
19. Korah gathered all *the congregation* against them unto the door of the tabernacle of *the congregation* :
21. yourselves from among this *congregation*,
22. thou be wroth with all *the congregation?*
24. Speak unto *the congregation*,
26. he spake unto *the congregation*,
40(17:5). as Korah, *and as his company* :
41(—:6). *the congregation of* the children of
42(—:7). when *the congregation* was gathered
Nu. 16:45(17:10). Get you up from among this *congregation*,
46(—:11). go quickly unto *the congregation*,
19: 9. *for the congregation of* the children of
20: 1. (even) *the* whole *congregation*,
2. there was no water *for the congregation* :
8. gather thou *the assembly* together,
— thou shalt give *the congregation*
11. *the congregation* drank, and their beasts
22. (even) *the* whole *congregation*,
27. in the sight of all *the congregation*.
29. And when all *the congregation* saw
25: 6. in the sight of all *the congregation of*
7. he rose up from among *the congregation*,
26: 2. Take the sum of all *the congregation of*
9. (which were) famous in *the congregation*,
— *in the company of* Korah,
10. when that *company* died,
27: 2. the princes and all *the congregation*,
3. in *the company* of them
— *in the company of* Korah ;
14. the strife of *the congregation*,
16. set a man over *the congregation*,
17. *the congregation of* the Lord
19. before all *the congregation* ;
20. *the congregation of* the children of Israel
21. with him, even all *the congregation*.
22. before all *the congregation* :
31:12. *the congregation of* the children of Israel,
13. all the princes of *the congregation*,
16. *among the congregation of* the Lord.
26. the chief fathers of *the congregation* :
27. between all *the congregation* :
43. (that pertained unto) *the congregation*
32: 2. the princes of *the congregation*,
4. before *the congregation of* Israel,
35:12. stand before *the congregation*
24. *the congregation* shall judge
25. *the congregation* shall deliver
— *the congregation* shall restore him
Jos. 9:15. the princes of *the congregation* sware
18. the princes of *the congregation* had sworn
— all *the congregation* murmured
19. the princes said unto all *the congregation*,
21. drawers of water unto all *the congregation* ;
27. drawers of water *for the congregation*,
18: 1. *the* whole *congregation of* the children of Israel
20: 6. stand before *the congregation*
9. until he stood before *the congregation*.
22:12. *the* whole *congregation of* the children of
16. Thus saith *the* whole *congregation of*
17. *in the congregation of* the Lord,
18. *the* whole *congregation of* Israel.
20. *the congregation of* Israel ?
30. the princes of *the congregation*
Jud.14: 8. (there was) *a swarm of* bees and honey
20: 1. *the congregation* was gathered together
21:10. *the congregation* sent thither twelve
13. *the* whole *congregation* sent
16. the elders of *the congregation*
1K. 8: 5. all *the congregation of* Israel,
12:20. they sent and called him unto *the congregation*,
2Ch 5: 6. all *the congregation of* Israel
Job 15:34. *the congregation of* hypocrites (shall be)
16: 7. thou hast made desolate all *my company*.
Ps. 1: 5. *in the congregation of* the righteous.
7: 7(8). *So* shall *the congregation of* the people
22:16(17). *the assembly of* the wicked have
68:30(31). *the multitude of* the bulls,
74: 2. Remember *thy congregation*, (which)
82: 1. God standeth *in the congregation of* the
86:14. *and the assemblies of* violent (men)
106:17. covered *the company of* Abiram.
18. a fire was kindled *in their company* ;
111: 1. the upright, *and* (in) *the congregation*.
Pro. 5:14. in the midst of the congregation *and assembly*.
Jer. 6:18. know, *O congregation*, what (is)
30:20. *and their congregation* shall be established
Hos. 7:12. as *their congregation* hath heard.

עֵדָה *g[n]ēh-dāh'*, f. 5713

Gen21:30. that they may be *a witness* unto me,
31:52. *and* (this) pillar (be) *witness*, that I will

Deu 4:45. These (are) *the testimonies*, and the statutes,
6:17. of the Lord your God, *and his testimonies*,
20. (mean) *the testimonies*, and the statutes,
Jos. 24:27. this stone shall be *a witness* unto us;
— it shall be therefore *a witness* unto you,
Ps. 25:10. as keep his covenant *and his testimonies*.
78:56. *and* kept not *his testimonies*:
93: 5. *Thy testimonies* are very sure:
99: 7. they kept *his testimonies*, and the ordinance
119: 2. (are) they that keep *his testimonies*,
22. I have kept *thy testimonies*.
24. *Thy testimonies* also (are) my delight
46. I will speak *of thy testimonies*
59. and turned my feet unto *thy testimonies*.
79. those that have known *thy testimonies*.
95. I will consider *thy testimonies*.
119. therefore I love *thy testimonies*.
125. that I may know *thy testimonies*.
138. *Thy testimonies* (that) thou hast
146. I shall keep *thy testimonies*.
152. *Concerning thy testimonies*, I have known
167. My soul hath kept *thy testimonies*;
168. have kept thy precepts *and thy testimonies*:
132:12. will keep my covenant *and my testimony*

5715 עֵדוּת ^{n}*geh-dooth'*, f.

Ex. 16:34. Aaron laid it up before *the Testimony*,
25:16. thou shalt put into the ark *the testimony*
21. in the ark thou shalt put *the testimony*
22. which (are) upon the ark of *the testimony*,
26:33. within the vail the ark of *the testimony*:
34. mercy seat upon the ark of *the testimony*
27:21. which (is) before *the testimony*,
30: 6. the vail that (is) by the ark of *the testimony*, before the mercy seat that (is) over *the testimony*,
26. and the ark of *the testimony*,
36. before *the testimony* in the tabernacle
31: 7. the ark *of the testimony*,
18. two tables of *testimony*,
32:15. two tables of *the testimony*
34:29. two tables of *testimony*
38:21. (even) of the tabernacle of *testimony*,
39:35. The ark of *the testimony*, and the staves
40: 3. the ark of *the testimony*, and cover
5. the ark of *the testimony*, and put
20. he took and put *the testimony* into the ark,
21. and covered the ark of *the testimony*;
Lev. 16:13. the mercy seat that (is) upon *the testimony*,
24: 3. Without the vail of *the testimony*,
Nu. 1:50. Levites over the tabernacle of *testimony*,
53. round about the tabernacle of *testimony*,
— the charge of the tabernacle of *testimony*.
4: 5. and cover the ark of *testimony*
7:89. the mercy seat that (was) upon the ark of *testimony*,
9:15. the tent of *the testimony*:
10:11. the tabernacle of *the testimony*.
17: 4(19). the congregation before *the testimony*,
7(22). in the tabernacle of *witness*.
8(23). went into the tabernacle of *witness*;
10(25). Aaron's rod again before *the testimony*,
18: 2. (shall minister) before the tabernacle of *witness*.
Jos. 4:16. priests that bear the ark of *the testimony*,
1K. 2: 3. his judgments, *and his testimonies*,
2K. 11:12. upon him, and (gave him) *the testimony*;
17:15. *his testimonies* which he testified against
23: 3. keep his commandments and *his testimonies*
1Ch 29:19. keep thy commandments, *thy testimonies*,
2Ch 23:11. the crown, and (gave him) *the testimony*,
24: 6. for the tabernacle of *witness*?
34:31. his commandments, *and his testimonies*,
Neh. 9:34. thy commandments *and thy testimonies*,
Ps. 19: 7(8). *the testimony of* the Lord (is) sure,
60[title](1). To the chief Musician upon Shushan-*eduth*,
78: 5. he established *a testimony* in Jacob,
80[title](1). To the chief Musician upon Shoshannim-*Eduth*,
81: 5(6). ordained in Joseph (for) *a testimony*,
119:14. have rejoiced in the way of *thy testimonies*,
31. I have stuck *unto thy testimonies*:
36. Incline my heart unto *thy testimonies*,
88. so shall I keep *the testimony* of thy mouth.
99. *thy testimonies* (are) my meditation.
Ps. 119:111. *Thy testimonies* have I taken as an
129. *Thy testimonies* (are) wonderful:
144. The righteousness of *thy testimonies* (is) everlasting:
157. (yet) do I not decline *from thy testimonies*.
122: 4. unto *the testimony* of Israel,
Jer. 44:23. nor in his statutes, *nor in his testimonies*;

עֲדִי ^{n}*gădee*, m. 5716

Ex. 33: 4. no man did put on him *his ornaments*.
5. put off *thy ornaments* from thee,
6. stripped themselves of *their ornaments*
2Sa. 1:24. who put on *ornaments of* gold upon your apparel.
Ps. 32: 9. *whose mouth* must be held
103: 5. satisfieth *thy mouth* with good (things);
Isa. 49:18. thee with them all, *as with an ornament*,
Jer. 2:32. Can a maid forget *her ornaments*,
4:30. thou deckest thee with *ornaments of* gold,
Eze. 7:20. As for the beauty of *his ornament*,
16: 7. thou art come *to excellent* (marg. *ornament of*) *ornaments*:
11. I decked thee also with *ornaments*,
23:40. deckedst thyself with *ornaments*,

עִדִּים ^{n}*gid-deem'*, m. pl. 5708

Isa. 64: 6(5). our righteousnesses (are) as *filthy* rags;

עָדִין [^{n}*gāh-deen'*], adj. 5719

Isa. 47: 8. (thou that art) *given to pleasures*,

עָדַן [^{n}*gāh-dan'*]. 5727

* HITHPAEL.—*Future*. *

Neh. 9:25. *and delighted themselves* in thy great

עֵדֶן [^{n}*gēh'-den*], m. 5730

2Sa. 1:24. weep over Saul, who clothed you in scarlet, with (other) *delights*,
Ps. 36: 8(9). drink of the river of *thy pleasures*.
Jer. 51:34. filled his belly *with my delicates*,

עֶדֶן ^{n}*gäden* & עֲדֶנָה ^{n}*gäden'-nāh*, adv. 5728

Ecc. 4: 2. the living which are *yet* alive.
3. both they, which hath not *yet* been,

עֶדְנָה ^{n}*ged-nāh'*, f. 5730

Gen 18:12. I am waxed old shall I have *pleasure*,

עִדָּן ^{n}*gid-dāhn'*, Ch. m. 5732

Dan 2: 8. that ye would gain *the time*,
9. till *the time* be changed:
21. And he changeth *the times*
3: 5, 15. *at* what *time* ye hear the
4:16(13), 23(20). seven *times* pass over him.
25(22), 32(29). seven *times* shall pass over
7:12. for a season *and time*.
25. until *a time and times* and the dividing of *time*.

עָדַף [^{n}*gāh-daph'*]. 5736

* KAL.—*Participle*. Poel. *

Ex. 16:23. *that which remaineth* over lay up for you
26:12. the remnant *that remaineth* of the curtains
— the half curtain *that remaineth*,
13. *of that which remaineth* in the length
Lev. 25:27. restore *the overplus* unto the man to whom

Nu. 3:46. *which are more* than the Levites;
48. *the odd number* of them is to be redeemed,
49. money of *them that were over and above*

* HIPHIL.—*Preterite.* *

Ex. 16:18. he that gathered much *had* nothing *over,*

5737 עָדַר [^{n}*gāh-dar'*].

* NIPHAL.—*Preterite.* *

1Sa.30:19. And *there was* nothing *lacking* to them,
2Sa.17:22. morning light *there lacked* not one of them
Isa. 34:16. no one of these *shall fail,*
40:26. (he is) strong in power; not one *faileth.*
Zep. 3: 5. his judgment to light, *he faileth* not;

NIPHAL.—*Participle.*

Isa. 59:15. Yea, truth *fail*eth;

* PIEL.—*Future.* *

1K. 4:27(5:7). *they lacked* nothing. (lit. *suffered* nothing *to be wanting*)

5737 עָדַר [^{n}*gāh-dar'*].

* KAL.—*Infinitive.* *

1Ch 12:33. fifty thousand, *which could keep rank:* (marg. or, *set the battle in array*)

KAL.—*Participle.* Poel.

1Ch 12:38. All these men of war, *that could keep* rank,

* NIPHAL.—*Future.* *

Isa. 5: 6. it shall not be pruned, nor *digged;*
7:25. (on) all hills that *shall be digged*

5739 עֵדֶר ^{n}*geh'-der,* m.

Gen29: 2. there (were) three *flocks of* sheep lying by it; for out of that well they watered *the flocks:*
3. And thither were all *the flocks* gathered:
8. until all *the flocks* be gathered together,
30:40. and he put his own *flocks* by themselves,
32:16(17). *every drove* (lit. *drove, drove*) by
—(—). put a space betwixt *drove* and *drove.*
19(20). all that followed *the droves,*
Jud. 5:16. to hear the bleatings of *the flocks?*
1Sa.17:34. and took a lamb *out of the flock:*
2Ch 32:28. all manner of beasts, and cotes for *flocks.*
Job 24: 2. they violently take away *flocks,*
Ps. 78:52. guided them in the wilderness *like a flock.*
Pro.27:23. look well *to* (thy) *herds.*
Cant.1: 7. as one that turneth aside by *the flocks*
4: 1. thy hair (is) *as a flock of* goats,
2. Thy teeth (are) *like a flock* (of sheep)
6: 5. thy hair (is) *as a flock of* goats
6. Thy teeth (are) *as a flock of* sheep
Isa. 17: 2. they shall be *for flocks,*
32:14. a joy of wild asses, a pasture of *flocks;*
40:11. He shall feed *his flock* like a shepherd:
Jer. 6: 3. The shepherds *with their flocks* shall come
13:17. the Lord's *flock* is carried away captive.
20. where (is) *the flock* (that) was given thee,
31:10. keep him, as a shepherd (doth) *his flock.*
24. they (that) go forth *with flocks.*
51:23. pieces with thee the shepherd *and his flock;*
Eze.34:12. As a shepherd seeketh out *his flock*
Joel 1:18. *the herds of* cattle are perplexed,
— *the flocks of* sheep are made desolate.
Mic. 2:12. *as the flock* in the midst of their fold:
4: 8. And thou, O tower of *the flock,*
5: 8(7). as a young lion *among the flocks of*
Zep. 2:14. And *flocks* shall lie down in the midst
Zec.10: 3. the Lord of hosts hath visited *his flock*
Mal. 1:14. deceiver, which hath *in his flock* a male,

5742 עֲדָשִׁים ^{n}*gădāh-sheem',* m. pl.

Gen25:34. Jacob gave Esau bread and pottage of *lentiles;*
2Sa.17:28. parched (corn), and beans, *and lentiles,*
23:11. was a piece of ground full of *lentiles:*
Eze. 4: 9. beans, *and lentiles,* and millet,

עוּב [^{n}*goov*]. 5743

* HIPHIL.—*Future.* *

Lam.2: 1. *hath* the Lord *covered* the daughter of Zion *with a cloud*

עוּג [^{n}*goog*]. 5746

* KAL.—*Future.* *

Eze. 4:12. *thou shalt bake it* with dung

עוּגָב ^{n}*goo-gāhv'* & עֻגָּב ^{n}*goog-gāhv',* m. 5748

Gen. 4:21. all such as handle the harp *and organ.*
Job 21:12. rejoice at the sound of *the organ.*
30:31. *and my organ* into the voice of them that
Ps.150: 4. him with stringed instruments *and organs.*

עוֹד ^{n}*gōhd,* part. adv. 5750

Gen 4:25. And Adam knew his wife *again;*
7: 4. For *yet* seven days, and I will cause
8:12. returned not again unto him *any more.*
9:15. the waters shall no *more* become a flood
35:16. was *but* a little way to come to Ephrath:
46:29. and wept on his neck *a good while.*
Ex. 2: 3. when she could not *longer* hide him,
3:15. And God said *moreover* unto Moses,
4: 6. And the Lord said *furthermore* unto him,
Lev.13:57. And if it appear *still* in the garment,
Nu. 18:22. must the children of Israel *henceforth*
Deu 4:35. he (is) God; there is none *else* beside him.
34:10. there arose not a prophet *since* in Israel
Jud. 2:14. they could not *any longer* stand
1K. 22: 7. not here a prophet of the Lord *besides,*
2K. 14: 4. *as yet* the people did sacrifice
Est. 9:12. what (is) thy request *further?*
Job 27: 3. All *the while* my breath (is) in me,
Jer. 13:27. when (shall it) *once* (be)? (marg. after when *yet*)
Eze.37:22. neither shall they be divided...*at all:*
&c. &c.

With Prefix בְּעוֹד;—

Gen40:13. *Yet within* three days shall Pharaoh
48: 7. *when* yet (there was) but a little way
2Sa. 3:35. to eat meat *while* it was *yet* day,
&c. &c.

עוֹד is used in combination with various Pronominal suffixes עוֹדֶנִּי, עוֹדִי &c.

Gen18:22. but Abraham stood *yet* before the Lord.
29: 9. *And while he yet* spake with them,
46:30. *because thou* (art) *yet* alive.
48:15. the God which fed me *all my life long* (מֵעוֹדִי)
Ex. 4:18. and see *whether they* (be) *yet* alive.
Ps.104:33. praise to my God *while I have my being.*
139:18. *when* I awake, *I am still* with thee.
&c. &c.

עוֹד ^{n}*gōhd,* Ch. part. adv. 5751

Dan. 4:31(28). *While* the word (was) in the king's

עוּד [^{n}*good*]. 5749

* KAL.—*Future.* *

Lam.2:13. (כתיב) What thing *shall I take to witness for thee?*

* PIEL.—*Preterite.* *

Ps.119:61. The bands of the wicked *have robbed me:*

* HIPHIL.—*Preterite.* *

Gen43: 3. The man *did* solemnly *protest* unto us,
Ex. 19:23. thou *chargedst* us, saying, Set bounds
Deu 4:26. *I call* heaven and earth *to witness* against
8:19. *I testify* against you this day
30:19. *I call* heaven and earth *to record* this day
2K. 17:15. his testimonies which *he testified* against
Neh. 9:26. and slew thy prophets which *testified*
34. *thou didst testify* against them.
Jer. 11: 7. *I* earnestly *protested* unto your fathers
42:19. know certainly that *I have admonished* you
Mal. 2:14. Because the Lord *hath been witness* between

HIPHIL.—*Infinitive.*

Gen43: 3. The man did *solemnly* protest (marg. *protesting* protested)
1Sa. 8: 9. yet protest *solemnly* (lit. *protesting* protest)
Jer. 11: 7. I *earnestly* protested (lit. *protesting* I protested) unto your fathers
— rising early *and protesting*, saying, Obey my voice.
32:44. *and take* witnesses in the land of Benjamin,

HIPHIL.—*Imperative.*

Ex. 19:21. *charge* (marg. *contest*) the people, lest they break through
Jer. 32:25. Buy thee the field for money, *and take*
Am. 3:13. Hear ye, *and testify* in the house of Jacob,

HIPHIL.—*Future.*

Deu31:28. *and call* heaven and earth *to record* against
1Sa. 8: 9. yet *protest* solemnly unto them,
1K. 2:42. to swear by the Lord, *and protested* unto
21:10. before him, *to bear witness against him*,
13. *and* the men of Belial *witnessed against him*,
2K. 17:13. *Yet* the Lord *testified* against Israel,
2Ch 24:19. *and they testified* against them:
Neh. 9:29. *And testifiedst* against them, that thou
30. *and testifiedst* against them by thy spirit
13:15. *and I testified* (against them) in the day
21. *Then I testified* against them,
Job 29:11. *and* when the eye saw (me), *it gave witness to me:*
Ps. 50: 7. O Israel, *and I will testify* against thee:
81: 8(9). my people, *and I will testify* unto thee:
Isa. 8: 2. *And I took* unto me faithful witnesses *to record*,
Jer. 6:10. To whom shall I speak, *and give warning*,
32:10. the evidence, and sealed (it), *and took*
Lam.2:13. What thing *shall I take to witness for thee?*
Zec. 3: 6. *And* the angel of the Lord *protested* unto

HIPHIL.—*Participle.*

Deu32:46. Set your hearts unto all the words which I *testify*

* HOPHAL.—*Preterite.* *

Ex. 21:29. *and it hath been testified* to his owner,

* PILEL.—*Future.* *

Ps.146: 9. *he relieveth* the fatherless and widow:

PILEL.—*Participle.*

Ps.147: 6. The Lord *lifteth up* the meek:

* HITHPALEL.—*Future.* *

Ps. 20: 8(9). but we are risen, *and stand upright.*

5753 **עָוָה** [*gāh-vāh'*].

* KAL.—*Preterite.* *

Est. 1:16. the queen *hath* not *done wrong* to the king
Dan 9: 5. have sinned, *and have committed iniquity*,

* NIPHAL.—*Preterite.* *

Ps. 38: 6(7). *I am troubled;* I am bowed down
Isa. 21: 3. I *was bowed down* at the hearing (of it);

NIPHAL.—*Participle.*

1Sa.20:30. Thou son of the *perverse* rebellious
Pro.12: 8. *but he that is of a perverse* heart (marg. *perverse of* heart) shall be despised.

* PIEL.—*Preterite.* *

Isa. 24: 1. *and turneth* it upside down, (marg. *perverteth* the face thereof)
Lam.3: 9. *he hath made* my paths *crooked.*

* HIPHIL.—*Preterite.* *

2Sa.19:19(20). that which thy servant *did perversely*
24:17. I have sinned, and I *have done wickedly:*
1K. 8:47. We have sinned, *and have done perversely*,
2Ch 6:37. We have sinned, *we have done amiss*,
Job 33:27. I have sinned, *and perverted* (that which was) right,
Ps.106: 6. *we have committed iniquity*, we have
Jer. 3:21. *they have perverted* their way,

HIPHIL.—*Infinitive.*

2Sa. 7:14. *If he commit iniquity*, I will chasten him
Jer. 9: 5(4). weary themselves *to commit iniquity.*

עַוָּה *gav-vāh'*, f. 5754

Eze.21:27(32). I will *overturn, overturn, overturn*, it: (lit. *Perverted, perverted, perverted* will I make it)

עָוֹן see **עָוֹן** See 5771

עוֹז see **עֹז** See 5797

עוּז [*gooz*]. 5756

* HIPHIL.—*Preterite.* *

Isa. 10:31. the inhabitants of Gebim *gather themselves to flee.*

HIPHIL.—*Imperative.*

Ex. 9:19. Send therefore now, (and) *gather* thy
Jer. 4: 6. Set up the standard toward Zion: *retire*, (marg. or, *strengthen*)
6: 1. ye children of Benjamin, *gather yourselves*

עִוְיָא [*giv-yāh'*], Ch. f. 5758

Dan 4:27(24). *and thine iniquities* by shewing mercy

עֲוִיל *găveel*, m. 5760

Job 16:11. God hath delivered me to *the ungodly*,

עֲוִיל [*găveel*], m. 5759

Job 19:18. *young children* (marg. or, *the wicked*) despised me;
21:11. They send forth *their little ones*

עוֹל see **עֹל** See 5923

עוּל [*gool*]. 5763

* KAL.—*Participle.* Poel. *

Gen33:13. the flocks and herds *with young* (are) with
1Sa. 6: 7. take two *milch* kine,
10. and took two *milch* kine,
Ps. 78:71. From following *the ewes great with young*
Isa. 40:11. gently lead *those that are with young.* (marg. or, *that give suck*)

עוּל *gool*, m. 5764

Isa. 49:15. Can a woman forget *her sucking child*,
65:20. shall be no more thence *an infant of* days,

עָוַל [*gāh-val'*]. 5765

* PIEL.—*Future.* *

Isa. 26:10. land of uprightness *will he deal unjustly*,

PIEL.—*Participle.*

Ps. 71: 4. out of the hand of *the unrighteous* and

עַוָּל *gav-vāhl'*, m. 5767

Job 18:21. such (are) the dwellings of *the wicked*,
27: 7. riseth up against me *as the unrighteous.*
29:17. I brake the jaws of *the wicked*,
31: 3. (Is) not destruction *to the wicked?*
Zep. 3: 5. *the unjust* knoweth no shame.

עָוֶל *gāh'-vel* & **עֶוֶל** [*geh'-vel*], m. 5766

Lev.19:15, 35. Ye shall do no *unrighteousness* in
Deu25:16. do *unrighteously*, (are) an abomination
32: 4. a God of truth and without *iniquity*,

Job.34:10. and (from) the Almighty, (that he should commit) *iniquity*.
32. if I have done *iniquity*, I will do no more.
Ps. 7: 3(4). if there be *iniquity* in my hands;
53: 1(2). and have done abominable *iniquity*:
82: 2. How long will ye judge *unjustly*,
Pro.29:27. An *unjust* man (is) an abomination
Jer. 2: 5. What *iniquity* have your fathers found in
Eze. 3:20. turn from his righteousness, and commit *iniquity*,
18: 8. hath withdrawn his hand *from iniquity*,
24. and committeth *iniquity*,
26. committeth *iniquity*, and dieth in them; *for his iniquity* that he hath done shall
28:18. *by the iniquity of* thy traffick;
33:13. own righteousness, and commit *iniquity*, — *but for his iniquity* that he hath committed,
15. of life, without committing *iniquity*;
18. his righteousness, and committeth *iniquity*,

5766 **עַוְלָה** *gav-lāh'*, f.

2Sa. 3:34. as a man falleth before *wicked* men, (marg. children of *iniquity*)
7:10. neither shall the children of *wickedness*
1Ch 17: 9. neither shall the children of *wickedness*
2Ch 19: 7. no *iniquity* with the Lord our God,
Job 6:29. Return, I pray you, let it not be *iniquity*;
30. Is there *iniquity* in my tongue?
11:14. let not *wickedness* dwell in thy tabernacles.
13: 7. Will ye speak *wickedly* for God?
15:16. which drinketh *iniquity* like water?
22:23. thou shalt put away *iniquity* far from
24:20. *wickedness* shall be broken as a tree.
27: 4. My lips shall not speak *wickedness*,
36:23. Thou hast wrought *iniquity*?
Ps. 37: 1. neither be thou envious against the workers of *iniquity*.
43: 1. from the deceitful *and unjust* man. (marg. a man of deceit *and iniquity*)
89:22(23). nor the son of *wickedness* afflict him.
92:15(16). (there is) no *unrighteousness* in him.
107:42. all *iniquity* shall stop her mouth.
119: 3. They also do no *iniquity*:
125: 3. put forth their hands *unto iniquity*.
Pro.22: 8. He that soweth *iniquity* shall reap vanity:
Isa. 59: 3. your tongue hath muttered *perverseness*.
Eze.28:15. till *iniquity* was found in thee.
Hos 10:13. ye have reaped *iniquity*;
Mic. 3:10. Zion with blood, and Jerusalem *with iniquity*.
Hab. 2:12. and stablisheth a city *by iniquity*!
Zep. 3: 5. he will not do *iniquity*:
13. remnant of Israel shall not do *iniquity*,
Mal. 2: 6. *and iniquity* was not found in his lips:

5766 **עוֹלָה** [*gōh-lāh'*], f.

Job 5:16. *and iniquity* stoppeth her mouth.
Ps. 58: 2(3). Yea, in heart ye work *wickedness*;
64: 6(7). They search out *iniquities*;
92:15(16). (כתיב) (there is) no *unrighteousness* in him.

See 5930 **עוֹלָה** see **עֹלָה**

5768 **עוֹלֵל** *gōh-lēhl'* & **עֹלָל** *gōh-lāhl'*, m.

1Sa.15: 3. slay both man and woman, *infant* (lit. *from infant*) and suckling,
22:19. men and women, *children* (lit. *from children*) and sucklings,
2K. 8:12. *and* wilt dash *their children*, and rip up
Job 3:16. *as infants* (which) never saw light.
Ps. 8: 2(3). Out of the mouth of *babes* and
17:14. rest of their (substance) *to their babes*.
137: 9. that taketh and dasheth *thy little ones*
Isa. 13:16. *Their children also* shall be dashed to
Jer. 6:11. pour it out upon *the children* abroad,
9:21(20). to cut off *the children* from without,
44: 7. cut off from you man and woman, *child* and suckling,
Lam. 1: 5. *her children* are gone into captivity
2:11. *the children* and the sucklings swoon
19. for the life of *thy young children*,
20. women eat their fruit, (and) *children*
4: 4. *the young children* ask bread,
Hos 13:16(14:1). *their infants* shall be dashed in
Joel 2:16. gather *the children*, and those that suck
Mic. 2: 9. from *their children* have ye taken away
Nah. 3:10. *her young children also* were dashed in

עֹלֵלוֹת see **עוֹלֵלוֹת** See 5955

עוֹלָם *gōh-lāhm'*, m. 5769

Gen. 3:22. and eat, and live *for ever*:
6: 3. My spirit shall not *always* strive with man,
4. mighty men which (were) *of old*,
9:12. for *perpetual* generations:
16. I may remember the *everlasting* covenant
13:15. will I give it, and to thy seed for *ever*.
17: 7. an *everlasting* covenant, to be a God
8. for an *everlasting* possession;
13. your flesh for an *everlasting* covenant.
19. with him for an *everlasting* covenant,
21:33. name of the Lord, the *everlasting* God.
48: 4. after thee (for) an *everlasting* possession.
49:26. the utmost bound of the *everlasting* hills:
Ex. 3:15. this (is) my name *for ever*,
12:14. a feast by an ordinance *for ever*.
17. generations by an ordinance *for ever*.
24. to thee and to thy sons for *ever*.
14:13. ye shall see them again no more *for ever*.
15:18. The Lord shall reign *for ever* and ever.
19: 9. and believe thee *for ever*.
21: 6. he shall serve him *for ever*.
27:21 & 28:43. (it shall be) a statute for *ever*
29: 9. shall be their's for a *perpetual* statute:
28. by a statute for *ever*
30:21. it shall be a statute for *ever*
31:16. (for) a *perpetual* covenant.
17. between me and the children of Israel *for ever*:
32:13. they shall inherit (it) *for ever*.
40:15. an *everlasting* priesthood
Lev. 3:17. a *perpetual* statute for your generations
6:18(11). a statute for *ever* in your generations
22(15). a statute for *ever* unto the Lord;
7:34. by a statute for *ever*
36. a statute for *ever* throughout their
10: 9. a statute for *ever* throughout your
15. by a statute for *ever*;
16:29. a statute for *ever* unto you:
31. by a statute for *ever*.
34. this shall be an *everlasting* statute
17: 7. This shall be a statute for *ever*
23:14, 31. a statute for *ever* throughout your
21. a statute for *ever* in all your dwellings
41 & 24:3. statute for *ever* in your generations:
24: 8. by an *everlasting* covenant.
9. made by fire by a *perpetual* statute.
25:32. may the Levites redeem *at any time*.
34. it (is) their *perpetual* possession.
46. they shall be your bondmen *for ever*:
Nu. 10: 8. an ordinance for *ever* throughout your
15:15. ordinance for *ever* in your generations:
18: 8. by an ordinance for *ever*.
11. by a statute for *ever*:
19. by a statute for *ever*: it (is) a covenant of salt *for ever* before the Lord
23. a statute for *ever* throughout your generations,
19:10. among them, for a statute for *ever*.
21. it shall be a *perpetual* statute
25:13. the covenant of an *everlasting* priesthood;
Deu 5:29(26). and with their children *for ever*!
12:28. with thy children after thee for *ever*,
13:16(17). it shall be an heap for *ever*;
15:17. he shall be thy servant *for ever*.
23: 3(4). the congregation of the Lord for *ever*.
6(7). all thy days *for ever*.
28:46. and upon thy seed for *ever*.
29:29(28). and to our children for *ever*,
32: 7. Remember the days of *old*,

Deu32:40. and say, I live *for ever.*
33:15. the precious things of the *lasting* hills,
27. underneath (are) the *everlasting* arms:
Jos. 4: 7. unto the children of Israel for *ever.*
8:28. burnt Ai, and made it an heap for *ever,*
14: 9. inheritance, and thy children's for *ever,*
24: 2. on the other side of the flood *in old time,*
Jud. 2: 1. I will *never* (lit. not *for ever*) break my covenant
1Sa. 1:22. and there abide for *ever.*
2:30. should walk before me for *ever:*
3:13. I will judge his house for *ever*
14. with sacrifice nor offering for *ever.*
13:13. thy kingdom upon Israel for *ever.*
20:15. off thy kindness from my house for *ever:*
23. between thee and me for *ever.*
42. between my seed and thy seed for *ever.*
27: 8. those (nations were) *of old* the inhabitants
12. he shall be my servant for *ever.*
2Sa. 3:28. guiltless before the Lord for *ever*
7:13. stablish the throne of his kingdom for *ever.*
16. established for *ever* before thee: thy throne shall be established for *ever.*
24. Israel (to be) a people unto thee for *ever:*
25. his house, establish (it) for *ever,*
26. let thy name be magnified for *ever,*
29. thy servant, that it may continue *for ever*
— house of thy servant be blessed *for ever.*
12:10. sword shall *never* (lit. not for *ever*) depart
22:51. unto David, and to his seed for *evermore.*
23: 5. hath made with me an *everlasting* covenant,
1K. 1:31. Let my lord king David live *for ever.*
2:33. and upon the head of his seed *for ever:*
— there be peace for *ever* from the Lord.
45. established before the Lord for *ever.*
8:13. a settled place for thee to abide in for *ever.*
9: 3. to put my name there for *ever;*
5. throne of thy kingdom upon Israel *for ever,*
10: 9. because the Lord loved Israel *for ever,*
2K. 5:27. unto thee, and unto thy seed *for ever.*
21: 7. will I put my name *for ever:*
1Ch 15: 2. and to minister unto him for *ever.*
16:15. Be ye mindful *always* of his covenant;
17. to Israel (for) an *everlasting* covenant,
34. for his mercy (endureth) *for ever.*
36. Blessed (be) the Lord God of Israel for *ever* and *ever.*
41. because his mercy (endureth) *for ever;*
17:12. I will stablish his throne for *ever.*
14. in mine house and in my kingdom for *ever:* and his throne shall be established for *evermore.*
22. didst thou make thine own people for *ever;*
23. be established for *ever,*
24. that thy name may be magnified for *ever,*
27. that it may be before thee *for ever:*
— and (it shall be) blessed *for ever.*
22:10. throne of his kingdom over Israel for *ever.*
23:13. he and his sons for *ever,*
— to bless in his name for *ever.*
25. they may dwell in Jerusalem *for ever:*
28: 4. to be king over Israel *for ever:*
7. I will establish his kingdom *for ever,* (lit. unto *for ever*)
8. your children after you for *ever.*
29:10. Blessed (be) thou, Lord God of Israel our father, *for* (lit. *from*) *ever* and *ever.*
18. keep this *for ever* in the imagination of
2Ch. 2: 4(3). (is an ordinance) *for ever* to Israel.
5:13. for his mercy (endureth) *for ever:*
6: 2. a place for thy dwelling for *ever.*
7: 3. for his mercy (endureth) *for ever.*
6. because his mercy (endureth) *for ever,*
16. that my name may be there for *ever:*
9: 8. loved Israel, to establish them *for ever,*
13: 5. the kingdom over Israel to David *for ever,*
20: 7. the seed of Abraham thy friend *for ever?*
21. Lord; for his mercy (endureth) *for ever.*
30: 8. sanctuary, which he hath sanctified *for ever:*
33: 4. In Jerusalem shall my name be *for ever.*
Ezr. 3:11. for his mercy (endureth) *for ever* toward
9:12. seek their peace or their wealth for *ever:*
— an inheritance to your children for *ever.*
Neh. 2: 3. Let the king live *for ever:*
9: 5. bless the Lord your God for *ever* and *ever:*
13: 1. into the congregation of God for *ever;*
Job 7:16. I would not live *alway:*
Job 22:15. Hast thou marked the *old* way
41: 4(40:28). take him for a servant for *ever?*
Ps. 5:11(12). let them *ever* shout for joy,
9: 5(6). put out their name *for ever* and **ever.**
7(8). the Lord shall endure *for ever*
10:16. The Lord (is) King for *ever* and ever:
12: 7(8). them from this generation *for ever.*
15: 5. these (things) shall *never* (lit. not *for ever*)
18:50(51). David, and to his seed for *evermore.*
21: 4(5). length of days for *ever* and ever.
24: 7. be ye lift up, ye *everlasting* doors;
9. even lift (them) up, ye *everlasting* doors;
25: 6. for they (have been) *ever of old.*
28: 9. and lift them up for *ever.*
29:10. the Lord sitteth King *for ever.*
30: 6(7). I shall *never* (lit. not *for ever*) be moved.
12(13). I will give thanks unto thee *for ever.*
31: 1(2). let me *never* (lit. not *for ever*) be
33:11. The counsel of the Lord standeth *for ever,*
37:18. their inheritance shall be *for ever.*
27. and do good; and dwell *for evermore.*
28. his saints; they are preserved *for ever:*
41:12(13). settest me before thy face *for ever.*
13(14). Blessed (be) the Lord God of Israel *from everlasting,* and to *everlasting.*
44: 8(9). and praise thy name *for ever.*
45: 2(3). God hath blessed thee *for ever.*
6(7). Thy throne, O God, (is) for *ever*
17(18). the people praise thee *for ever* and ever.
48: 8(9). God will establish it for *ever.*
14(15). God (is) our God for *ever* and ever:
49: 8(9). and it ceaseth *for ever:*
11(12). their houses (shall continue) *for ever,*
52: 8(10). I trust in the mercy of God for *ever*
9(11). I will praise thee *for ever,*
55:22(23). he shall *never* (lit. not *for ever*) suffer
61: 4(5). I will abide in thy tabernacle for *ever:*
7(8). He shall abide before God for *ever:*
66: 7. He ruleth by his power for *ever;*
71: 1. let me *never* (lit. not *for ever*) be put to confusion.
72:17. His name shall endure *for ever:*
19. blessed (be) his glorious name *for ever:*
73:12. the ungodly, who prosper in *the world;*
26. of my heart, and my portion *for ever.*
75: 9(10). But I will declare *for ever;*
77: 5(6). the years of *ancient times.*
7(8). Will the Lord cast off *for ever?*
78:66. he put them to a *perpetual* reproach.
69. earth which he hath established *for ever.*
79:13. will give thee thanks *for ever:*
81:15(16). time should have endured *for ever.*
85: 5(6). Wilt thou be angry with us *for ever?*
86:12. I will glorify thy name *for evermore.*
89: 1(2). sing of the mercies of the Lord for *ever:*
2(3). Mercy shall be built up for *ever:*
4(5). Thy seed will I establish for *ever,*
28(29). My mercy will I keep for him *for evermore,*
36(37). His seed shall endure *for ever,*
37(38). It shall be established for *ever*
52(53). Blessed (be) the Lord *for evermore.*
90: 2. *even from everlasting* to *everlasting,* thou (art) God.
92: 8(9). Lord, (art most) high *for evermore.*
93: 2. thou (art) *from everlasting.*
100: 5. Lord (is) good; his mercy (is) *everlasting,*
102:12(13). thou, O Lord, shalt endure *for ever;*
103: 9. neither will he keep (his anger) *for ever.*
17. the Lord (is) *from everlasting* to *everlasting*
104: 5. (that) it should not be removed for *ever.* (lit. *ever* and ever)
31. glory of the Lord shall endure *for ever:*
105: 8. hath remembered his covenant *for ever,*
10. to Israel (for) an *everlasting* covenant:
106: 1. for his mercy (endureth) *for ever.*
31. unto all generations for *evermore.*
48. Blessed (be) the Lord God of Israel from *everlasting* to *everlasting:*
107: 1. for his mercy (endureth) *for ever.*
110: 4. Thou (art) a priest *for ever* after the
111: 5. he will *ever* be mindful of his covenant.
8. They stand fast for ever *and ever,*
9. he hath commanded his covenant *for ever:*
112: 6. not be moved *for ever:* the righteous shall be in *everlasting* remembrance.
113: 2 & 115:18. this time forth and for *evermore.*

Ps.117: 2. the truth of the Lord (endureth) *for ever.*
118: 1. because his mercy (endureth) *for ever.*
2, 3, 4. that his mercy (endureth) *for ever.*
29. for his mercy (endureth) *for ever.*
119:44. thy law continually *for ever* and ever.
52. I remembered thy judgments *of old,*
89. *For ever,* O Lord, thy word is settled in
93. I will never (lit. not *for ever*) forget thy
98. mine enemies: for they (are) *ever* with
111. have I taken as an heritage *for ever:*
112. mine heart to perform thy statutes *alway,*
142. Thy righteousness (is) an *everlasting*
144. The righteousness of thy testimonies (is) *everlasting:*
152. that thou hast founded them *for ever.*
160. *and* every one of thy righteous judgments (endureth) *for ever.*
121: 8. this time forth, and even for *evermore.*
125: 1. be removed, (but) abideth *for ever.*
2. from henceforth even for *ever.*
131: 3. from henceforth and for *ever.*
133: 3. the Lord commanded the blessing, (even) life for *evermore.*
135:13. Thy name, O Lord, (endureth) *for ever;*
136: 1, 2, 3, 4, 5, 6, 7, 8, 9, 10, 11, 12, 13, 14, 15, 16, 17, 18, 19, 20, 21, 22, 23, 24, 25, 26. for his mercy (endureth) *for ever.*
138: 8. thy mercy, O Lord, (endureth) *for ever:*
139:24. lead me in the way *everlasting.*
143: 3. as those that have been *long* dead.
145: 1. I will bless thy name *for ever* and ever.
2. I will praise thy name *for ever* and ever.
13. Thy kingdom (is) an *everlasting* kingdom, (marg. kingdom of all *ages*)
21. let all flesh bless his holy name *for ever*
146: 6. which keepeth truth *for ever:*
10. The Lord shall reign *for ever,*
148: 6. also stablished them for ever *and ever:*
Pro. 8:23. I was set up *from everlasting,*
10:25. the righteous (is) an *everlasting*
30. The righteous shall never (lit. not *for ever*) be removed:
22:28. Remove not the *ancient* landmark,
23:10. Remove not the *old* landmark;
27:24. riches (are) not *for ever:*
Ecc. 1: 4. but the earth abideth *for ever.*
10. it hath been already *of old time,*
2:16. of the wise more than of the fool *for ever;*
3:11. he hath set *the world* in their heart,
14. God doeth, it shall be *for ever:*
9: 6. have they any more a portion *for ever*
12: 5. because man goeth to *his long* home,
Isa. 9: 7(6). from henceforth even for *ever.*
14:20. the seed of evildoers shall never (lit. not *for ever*) be renowned.
24: 5. broken the *everlasting* covenant.
25: 2. it shall never (lit. not *for ever*) be built.
26: 4. Lord Jehovah (is) *everlasting* strength:
30: 8. for the time to come for ever and *ever:*
32:14. forts and towers shall be for dens for *ever,*
17. quietness and assurance for *ever.*
33:14. shall dwell with *everlasting* burnings?
34:10. the smoke thereof shall go up *for ever:*
17. they shall possess it for *ever,*
35:10. and *everlasting* joy upon their heads:
40: 8. the word of our God shall stand *for ever.*
28. the *everlasting* God, the Lord,
42:14. I have *long time* holden my peace;
44: 7. since I appointed the *ancient* people?
45:17. with an *everlasting* salvation: ye shall not be ashamed nor confounded *world without end.* (lit. to *the ages of* perpetuity)
46: 9. Remember the former things *of old:*
47: 7. thou saidst, I shall be a lady *for ever:*
51: 6. my salvation shall be *for ever,*
8. my righteousness shall be *for ever,*
9. in the generations *of old.*
11. *everlasting* joy (shall be) upon their head:
54: 8. with *everlasting* kindness will I have
55: 3. I will make an *everlasting* covenant
13. an *everlasting* sign (that) shall not be cut
56: 5. I will give them an *everlasting* name,
57:11. have not I held my peace *even of old,*
16. I will not contend *for ever,*
58:12. shall build the *old* waste places:
59:21. from henceforth and for *ever.*
60:15. I will make thee an *eternal* excellency,
Isa. 60:19. the Lord shall be unto thee an *everlasting*
20. the Lord shall be thine *everlasting* light,
21. they shall inherit the land *for ever,*
61: 4. they shall build the *old* wastes,
7. *everlasting* joy shall be unto them.
8. I will make an *everlasting* covenant
63: 9. carried them all the days *of old.*
11. Then he remembered the days of *old,*
12. to make himself an *everlasting* name?
16. thy name (is) *from everlasting.*
19. We are (thine): thou never barest rule
64: 4(3). *For since the beginning of the world*
5(4). in those is *continuance,*
Jer. 2:20. *of old* time I have broken thy yoke,
3: 5. Will he reserve (his anger) *for ever?*
12. I will not keep (anger) *for ever.*
5:15. it (is) an *ancient* nation,
22. bound of the sea by a *perpetual* decree,
6:16. ask for the *old* paths,
7: 7. the land that I gave to your fathers, for *ever* and *ever.*
10:10. the living God, and an *everlasting* king: (marg. king of *eternity*)
17: 4. mine anger, (which) shall burn for *ever.*
25. this city shall remain *for ever.*
18:15. in their ways (from) the *ancient* paths,
16. land desolate, (and) a *perpetual* hissing;
20:11. (their) *everlasting* confusion shall never
17. and her womb (to be) *always* great
23:40. I will bring an *everlasting* reproach upon you, and a *perpetual* shame,
25: 5. you and to your fathers for *ever* and *ever:*
9. and *perpetual* desolations.
12. will make it *perpetual* desolations.
28: 8. been before me and before thee of *old*
31: 3. loved thee with an *everlasting* love:
40. nor thrown down any more *for ever.*
32:40. I will make an *everlasting* covenant
33:11. his mercy (endureth) *for ever:*
35: 6. (neither) ye, nor your sons for *ever:*
49:13. the cities thereof shall be *perpetual* wastes.
33. a desolation for *ever:*
36. (כתיב) the outcasts of *Elam* [according to 'כ, *everlasting* outcasts]
50: 5. a *perpetual* covenant (that) shall not be
51:26. thou shalt be desolate for *ever,*
39. and sleep a *perpetual* sleep,
57. they shall sleep a *perpetual* sleep,
62. it shall be desolate for *ever.*
Lam. 3: 6. as (they that be) dead of *old.*
31. the Lord will not cast off *for ever:*
5:19. Thou, O Lord, remainest *for ever;*
Eze. 16:60. establish unto thee an *everlasting* covenant.
25:15. to destroy (it) for the *old* hatred;
26:20. with the people of *old time,*
— in places desolate *of old,*
21. yet shalt thou never (lit. not *for ever*)
27:36. never (shalt be) *any more.* (lit. for *ever*)
28:19. never (shalt) thou (be) *any more.* (lit. for *ever*)
35: 5. thou hast had a *perpetual* hatred,
9. I will make thee *perpetual* desolations,
36: 2. the *ancient* high places are our's
37:25. and their children's children for *ever:* and my servant David (shall be) their prince *for ever.*
26. it shall be an *everlasting* covenant
— sanctuary in the midst of them *for evermore.*
28. be in the midst of them *for evermore.*
43: 7. midst of the children of Israel *for ever,*
9. dwell in the midst of them *for ever.*
46:14. a *perpetual* ordinance unto the Lord.
Dan 9:24. to bring in *everlasting* righteousness,
12: 2. some to *everlasting* life, and some to shame (and) *everlasting* contempt.
3. as the stars *for ever* and ever.
7. and sware by him that liveth for *ever*
Hos. 2:19(21). I will betroth thee unto me *for ever;*
Joel 2: 2. there hath not been *ever* (lit. from of *old*)
26, 27. my people shall never (lit. not *for ever*) be ashamed.
3:20(4:20). But Judah shall dwell *for ever,*
Am. 9:11. I will build it as in the days of *old:*
Obad. 10. and thou shalt be cut off *for ever.*
Jon. 2: 6(7). with her bars (was) about me *for ever:*
Mic. 2: 9. have ye taken away my glory *for ever.*
4: 5. name of the Lord our God *for ever* and

Mic. 4: 7. from henceforth, even for *ever.*
5: 2(1). goings forth (have been) from of old, *from everlasting.* (marg. from the days of *eternity*)
7:14. as in the days of *old.*
Hab. 3: 6. the *perpetual* hills did bow: his ways (are) *everlasting.*
Zep. 2: 9. a *perpetual* desolation:
Zec. 1: 5. the prophets, do they live *for ever?*
Mal. 1: 4. the Lord hath indignation for *ever.*
3: 4. as in the days of *old,*

5771 עָוֹן *gāh-vōhn',* m.

Gen 4:13. *My punishment* (marg. *My iniquity*) (is) greater than I can bear.
15:16. *the iniquity of* the Amorites (is) not yet
19:15. lest thou be consumed *in the iniquity* (marg. or, *punishment*) *of*
44:16. hath found out *the iniquity of* thy servants:
Ex. 20: 5. God, visiting *the iniquity of* the fathers
28:38. that Aaron may bear *the iniquity of*
43. that they bear not *iniquity,*
34: 7. forgiving *iniquity* and transgression
— visiting *the iniquity of* the fathers
9. pardon *our iniquity* and our sin,
Lev. 5: 1. he shall bear *his iniquity.*
17. and shall bear *his iniquity.*
7:18. that eateth of it shall bear *his iniquity.*
10:17. hath given it you to bear *the iniquity of*
16:21. all *the iniquities of* the children of Israel,
22. shall bear upon him all *their iniquities*
17:16. he shall bear *his iniquity.*
18:25. I do visit *the iniquity thereof* upon it,
19: 8. that eateth it shall bear *his iniquity,*
20:17. he shall bear *his iniquity.*
19. they shall bear *their iniquity.*
22:16. Or suffer them to bear *the iniquity of*
26:39. shall pine away *in their iniquity*
— *in the iniquities of* their fathers shall they
40. If they shall confess *their iniquity,* and *the iniquity of* their fathers,
41. accept of *the punishment of their iniquity:*
43. they shall accept of *the punishment of their iniquity:*
Nu. 5:15. bringing *iniquity* to remembrance.
31. Then shall the man be guiltless *from iniquity,* and this woman shall bear *her iniquity.*
14:18. forgiving *iniquity* and transgression,
— visiting *the iniquity of* the fathers
19. I beseech thee, *the iniquity of* this people
34. for a year, shall ye bear *your iniquities,*
15:31. *his iniquity* (shall be) upon him.
18: 1. shall bear *the iniquity of* the sanctuary:
— shall bear *the iniquity of* your priesthood.
23. they shall bear *their iniquity:*
30:15(16). he shall bear *her iniquity.*
Deu 5: 9. God, visiting *the iniquity of* the fathers
19:15. against a man for any *iniquity,*
Jos. 22:17. (Is) *the iniquity of* Peor too little for us,
20. that man perished not alone *in his iniquity.*
1Sa. 3:13. *for the iniquity* which he knoweth;
14. *the iniquity of* Eli's house shall not be
20: 1. what (is) *mine iniquity?*
8. if there be in me *iniquity,* slay me thyself;
25:24. (upon) me (let this) *iniquity* (be):
28:10. there shall no *punishment* happen to thee
2Sa. 3: 8. chargest me to day *with a fault concerning*
14: 9. My lord, O king, *the iniquity* (be) on me,
32. if there be (any) *iniquity* in me, let him
19:19(20). Let not my lord impute *iniquity*
22:24. and have kept myself *from mine iniquity.*
24:10. O Lord, take away *the iniquity of* thy
1K. 17:18. art thou come unto me to call *my sin*
2K. 7: 9. *some mischief* will come upon us: (marg. we shall find *punishment*)
1Ch 21: 8. do away *the iniquity of* thy servant;
Ezr. 9: 6. *our iniquities* are increased over (our)
7. *and for our iniquities* have we,
13. hast punished us less *than our iniquities*
Neh. 4: 5(3:37). And cover not *their iniquity,*
9: 2. confessed their sins, *and the iniquities of*
Job 7:21. take away *mine iniquity?*
10: 6. thou enquirest *after mine iniquity,*
14. *and* thou wilt not acquit me *from mine iniquity.*
Job 11: 6. exacteth of thee (less) *than thine iniquity*
13:23. How many (are) *mine iniquities* and sins?
26. me to possess *the iniquities of* my youth.
14:17. thou sewest up *mine iniquity.*
15: 5. thy mouth uttereth *thine iniquity,*
19:29. wrath (bringeth) *the punishments of* the
20:27. The heaven shall reveal *his iniquity;*
22: 5. thy wickedness great? and *thine iniquities*
31:11. it (is) *an iniquity* (to be punished by)
28. also (were) *an iniquity* (to be punished)
33. by hiding *mine iniquity* in my bosom:
33: 9. neither (is there) *iniquity* in me.
Ps. 18:23(24). I kept myself *from mine iniquity.*
25:11. O Lord, pardon *mine iniquity;*
31:10(11). my strength faileth *because of mine iniquity,*
32: 2. unto whom the Lord imputeth not *iniquity,*
5. *and mine iniquity* have I not hid.
— thou forgavest *the iniquity of* my sin.
36: 2(3). *his iniquity* be found to be hateful.
38: 4(5). *mine iniquities* are gone over mine
18(19). I will declare *mine iniquity;*
39:11(12). rebukes dost correct man for *iniquity,*
40:12(13). *mine iniquities* have taken hold
49: 5(6). *the iniquity of* my heels shall compass
51: 2(4). Wash me throughly *from mine iniquity,*
5(7). I was shapen *in iniquity;*
9(11). blot out all *mine iniquities.*
59: 4(5). prepare themselves without (my) *fault:*
65: 3(4). *Iniquities* (marg. Words, or, Matters of *iniquities*) prevail against me:
69:27(28). Add *iniquity* (marg. or, *punishment of iniquity*) unto *their iniquity:*
78:38. of compassion, forgave (their) *iniquity,*
79: 8. remember not against us former *iniquities:*
85: 2(3). Thou hast forgiven *the iniquity of* thy
89:32(33). and *their iniquity* with stripes.
90: 8. Thou hast set *our iniquities* before thee,
103: 3. Who forgiveth all *thine iniquities;*
10. rewarded us *according to our iniquities.*
106:43. and were brought low *for their iniquity.*
107:17. *and because of their iniquities,* are afflicted.
109:14. *the iniquity of* his fathers be remembered
130: 3. If thou, Lord, shouldest mark *iniquities,*
8. shall redeem Israel from all *his iniquities.*
Pro. 5:22. *His own iniquities* shall take the wicked
16: 6. By mercy and truth *iniquity* is purged:
Isa. 1: 4. a people laden with *iniquity,*
5:18. them that draw *iniquity* with cords of
6: 7. *thine iniquity* is taken away,
13:11. and the wicked for *their iniquity;*
14:21. *for the iniquity of* their fathers;
22:14. Surely this *iniquity* shall not be purged
26:21. inhabitants of the earth for their *iniquity:*
27: 9. therefore shall *the iniquity of* Jacob be
30:13. this *iniquity* shall be to you as a breach
33:24. (shall be) forgiven (their) *iniquity.*
40: 2. *her iniquity* is pardoned:
43:24. thou hast wearied me *with thine iniquities.*
50: 1. *for your iniquities* have ye sold yourselves,
53: 5. (he was) bruised *for our iniquities:*
6. the Lord hath laid on him *the iniquity of*
11. *for* he shall bear *their iniquities.*
57:17. *For the iniquity of* his covetousness was
59: 2. *your iniquities* have separated between
3. and your fingers *with iniquity;*
12. *and* (as for) *our iniquities,* we know them;
64: 6(5). *and our iniquities,* like the wind, have
7(6). consumed us, because of *our iniquities.*
9(8). O Lord, neither remember *iniquity*
65: 7. *Your iniquities, and the iniquities of* your
Jer. 2:22. *thine iniquity* is marked before me,
3:13. Only acknowledge *thine iniquity,*
5:25. *Your iniquities* have turned away these
11:10. They are turned back to *the iniquities of*
13:22. For the greatness of *thine iniquity*
14: 7. though *our iniquities* testify against us,
10. he will now remember *their iniquity,*
20. (and) *the iniquity of* our fathers:
16:10. what (is) *our iniquity?*
17. neither is *their iniquity* hid from mine eyes.
18. I will recompense *their iniquity*
18:23. forgive not *their iniquity,*
25:12. nation, saith the Lord, for *their iniquity,*
30:14, 15. for the multitude of *thine iniquity;*
31:30. one shall die *for his own iniquity:*
34. for I will forgive *their iniquity,* and I will

Jer. 32:18. *the iniquity of* the fathers into the bosom
33: 8. I will cleanse them from all *their iniquity*,
— I will pardon all *their iniquities*,
36: 3. that I may forgive *their iniquity* and their
31. his seed and his servants for *their iniquity*;
50:20. *the iniquity of* Israel shall be sought for,
51: 6. be not cut off *in her iniquity*;
Lam. 2:14. they have not discovered *thine iniquity*,
4: 6. *the punishment of the iniquity* (marg. or, *iniquity*) *of* the daughter
13. *the iniquities of* her priests,
22. *The punishment of thine iniquity* (marg. or, *Thine iniquity*) is accomplished,
— he will visit *thine iniquity*,
5: 7. we have borne *their iniquities*.
Eze. 3:18. wicked (man) shall die *in his iniquity*;
19. he shall die *in his iniquity*;
4: 4. lay *the iniquity of* the house of Israel
— thou shalt bear *their iniquity*.
5. laid upon thee the years of *their iniquity*,
— so shalt thou bear *the iniquity of* the house
6. thou shalt bear *the iniquity of* the house
17. and consume away *for their iniquity*.
7:13. shall any strengthen himself *in the iniquity* (marg. *his iniquity*)
16. them mourning, every one *for his iniquity*.
19. the stumblingblock of *their iniquity*.
9: 9. *The iniquity of* the house of Israel
14: 3. the stumblingblock of *their iniquity*
4, 7. the stumblingblock of *his iniquity*
10. they shall bear *the punishment of their iniquity: the punishment of* the prophet shall be even *as the punishment of*
16:49. this was *the iniquity of* thy sister Sodom,
18:17. *for the iniquity of* his father, he shall
18. he shall die in *his iniquity*.
19. Why? doth not the son bear *the iniquity of*
20. The son shall not bear *the iniquity of* the father, neither shall the father bear *the iniquity of* the son:
30. so *iniquity* shall not be your ruin.
21:23(28). will call to remembrance *the iniquity*,
24(29). ye have made *your iniquity* to be
25(30). when *iniquity* (shall have) an end,
29(34). when (their) *iniquity* (shall have)
24:23. ye shall pine away *for your iniquities*,
28:18. by the multitude of *thine iniquities*,
29:16. which bringeth (their) *iniquity* to
32:27. *their iniquities* shall be upon their bones,
33: 6. he is taken away *in his iniquity*;
8. wicked (man) shall die *in his iniquity*;
9. he shall die *in his iniquity*;
35: 5. in the time (that their) *iniquity* (had)
36:31. in your own sight for *your iniquities*
33. cleansed you from all *your iniquities*
39:23. went into captivity *for their iniquity*:
43:10. they may be ashamed *of their iniquities*:
44:10. they shall even bear *their iniquity*.
12. the house of Israel to fall into *iniquity*;
— and they shall bear *their iniquity*.
Dan. 9:13. that we might turn *from our iniquities*,
16. *and for the iniquities of* our fathers,
24. to make reconciliation for *iniquity*,
Hos. 4: 8. they set their heart on *their iniquity*.
5: 5. Israel and Ephraim fall *in their iniquity*;
7: 1. *the iniquity of* Ephraim was discovered,
8:13. now will he remember *their iniquity*,
9: 7. for the multitude of *thine iniquity*,
9. he will remember *their iniquity*,
12: 8(9). they shall find none *iniquity* in me
13:12. *The iniquity of* Ephraim (is) bound up;
14: 1(2). thou hast fallen *by thine iniquity*.
2(3). Take away all *iniquity*,
Am. 3: 2. I will punish you for all *your iniquities*.
Mic. 7:18. like unto thee, that pardoneth *iniquity*,
19. he will subdue *our iniquities*;
Zec. 3: 4. I have caused *thine iniquity* to pass
9. I will remove *the iniquity of* that land
Mal. 2: 6. did turn many away *from iniquity*.

5770 **עָוַן** [*ⁿgāh-van'*].

* KAL.—*Participle.* Poel. *

1Sa.18: 9. (כתיב) And Saul *eyed* (lit. was *eycing*) David

עוֹנָה [*ⁿgōh-nāh'*], **f.** 5772, 5869

Ex. 21:10. *and her duty of marriage*, shall he not diminish.
Hos 10:10. they shall bind themselves in *their two furrows*.

עִוְעִים *ⁿgiv-ⁿgeem'*, **m. pl.** 5773

Isa. 19:14. The Lord hath mingled a *perverse* spirit (marg. a spirit of *perversities*) in the midst thereof:

עוּף *ⁿgooph.* 5774

* KAL.—*Preterite.* *

Isa. 11:14. *But they shall fly* upon the shoulders of

KAL.—*Infinitive.*

Job 5: 7. sparks *fly* upward. (marg. lift up *to fly*)
Pro.26: 2. as the swallow *by flying*,

KAL.—*Future.*

Deu 4:17. likeness of any winged fowl that *flieth*
Jud. 4:21. he was fast asleep *and weary*.
1Sa.14:28. *And* the people *were faint*. (marg. or, *weary*)
31. *and* the people *were* very *faint*.
2Sa. 21:15. and David *waxed faint*.
22:11. he rode upon a cherub, *and did fly*:
Job 11:17. *thou shalt shine forth*,
20: 8. *He shall fly away* as a dream,
Ps. 18:10(11). he rode upon a cherub, *and did fly*:
55: 6(7). (then) *would I fly away*, and be at
90:10. it is soon cut off, *and we fly away*.
91: 5. (nor) for the arrow (that) *flieth* by day;
Pro 23: 5. (כתיב) *Wilt thou set* thine eyes (marg. *cause* thine eyes *to fly*)
— *they fly away* as an eagle
Isa. 6: 6. *Then flew* one of the seraphims unto me,
60: 8. Who (are) these (that) *fly* as a cloud,
Nah 3:16. cankerworm spoileth, and *fleeth away*.
Hab 1: 8. *they shall fly* as the eagle

KAL.—*Participle.* Poel.

Isa. 31: 5. As birds *flying*, so will the Lord of hosts
Zec. 5: 1. and behold a *flying* roll.
2. I see a *flying* roll;

* POLEL.—*Infinitive.* *

Eze.32:10. *when I shall brandish* my sword before

POLEL.—*Future.*

Gen 1:20. and fowl (that) *may fly* (lit. *let* fowl *fly*) above the earth
Isa. 6: 2. and with twain *he did fly*.

POLEL.—*Participle.*

Isa. 14:29. his fruit (shall be) a fiery *flying* serpent.
30: 6. the viper and fiery *flying* serpent,

* HIPHIL.—*Infinitive.* *

Pro.23: 5. (כתיב) *they fly away* as an eagle

HIPHIL.—*Future.*

Pro.23: 5. *Wilt thou set* thine eyes (marg. *cause* thine eyes *to fly*) upon that which

* HITHPOLEL.—*Future.* *

Hos. 9:11. their glory *shall fly away*

עוֹף *ⁿgōhph*, **m.** 5775

Gen 1:20. *and fowl* (that) may fly above the earth
21. and every winged *fowl* after his kind:
22. *and* let *fowl* multiply in the earth.
26, 28. *and over the fowl of* the air,
30. and to every *fowl of* the air,
2:19. and every *fowl of* the air;
20. *and to the fowl of* the air,
6: 7. and *the fowls of* the air;
20. *Of fowls* after their kind,
7: 3. *Of fowls* also *of* the air
8. and *of fowls*, and of every thing that
14. every *fowl* after his kind,
21. *both of fowl*, and of cattle,
23. and *the fowl of* the heaven;
8:17. (both) *of fowl*, and of cattle,

Gen 8:19. every creeping thing, and every *fowl*,
20. clean beast, and of every clean *fowl*,
9: 2. and upon every *fowl of* the air,
10. creature that (is) with you, *of the fowl*,
40:17. *and the birds* did eat them out of the
19. *the birds* shall eat thy flesh from off thee.
Lev. 1:14. his offering to the Lord (be) of *fowls*,
7:26. manner of blood, (whether it be) *of fowl*
11:13. have in abomination among *the fowls*;
20. All *fowls* that creep, going
21. ye eat of every *flying* creeping thing
23. all (other) *flying* creeping things,
46. the law of the beasts, *and of the fowl*,
17:13. hunteth and catcheth any beast or *fowl*
20:25. between unclean *fowls* and clean: and ye shall not make your souls abominable by beast, *or by fowl*,
Deu14:19. every creeping thing *that flieth*
20. (of) all clean *fowls* ye may eat.
28:26. thy carcase shall be meat unto all *fowls of*
1Sa.17:44. I will give thy flesh *unto the fowls of*
46. the Philistines this day *unto the fowls of*
2Sa.21:10. suffered neither *the birds of* the air
1K. 4:33(5:13). he spake also of beasts, and of *fowl*,
14:11 & 16:4 & 21:24. *the fowls of* the air eat:
Job 12: 7. *and the fowls of* the air, and they shall
28:21. *and* kept close *from the fowls of* the air.
35:11. *and* maketh us wiser *than the fowls of*
Ps. 50:11. I know all *the fowls of* the mountains:
78:27. and feathered *fowls* like as the sand
79: 2. given (to be) meat *unto the fowls of*
104:12. By them shall *the fowls of* the heaven
Ecc.10:20. *a bird of* the air shall carry the voice,
Isa. 16: 2. *as a* wandering *bird* cast out of the nest,
Jer. 4:25. all *the birds of* the heavens were fled.
5:27. As a cage is full of *birds*,
7:33. this people shall be meat *for the fowls*
9:10(9). *both the fowl* (marg. *from the fowl*) *of* the heavens and the beast
12: 4. the beasts are consumed, *and the birds*;
15: 3. *the fowls of* the heaven, and the beasts of
16: 4. shall be meat *for the fowls of* heaven,
19: 7. their carcases will I give to be meat *for the fowls of*
34:20. bodies shall be for meat *unto the fowls*
Eze.29: 5. *and to the fowls of* the heaven.
31: 6. *the fowls of* heaven made their nests
13. shall all *the fowls of* the heaven remain,
32: 4. cause all *the fowls of* the heaven to
38:20. *and the fowls of* the heaven,
44:31. whether it be *fowl* or beast.
Hos. 2:18(20). with *the fowls of* heaven,
4: 3. *and with the fowls of* heaven;
7:12. I will bring them down *as the fowls of*
9:11. their glory shall fly away *like a bird*,
Zep. 1: 3. I will consume *the fowls of* the heaven,

5776 **עוֹף** *ᵑgōhph*, Ch. m.

Dan 2:38. *and the fowls of* the heaven
7: 6. four wings of *a fowl*;

5777 **עוֹפֶּרֶת** *ᵑgōh-pheh'-reth*, f.

Ex. 15:10. they sank *as lead* in the mighty waters.
Nu. 31:22. the iron, the tin, and *the lead*,
Job 19:24. graven with an iron pen *and lead*
Jer. 6:29. *the lead* is consumed of the fire;
Eze.22:18. tin, and iron, *and lead*,
20. brass, and iron, *and lead*,
27:12. with silver, iron, tin, *and lead*,
Zec. 5: 7. there was lifted up a talent of *lead*:
8. he cast the weight of *lead* upon

5779 **עוּץ** [*ᵑgootz*].

* KAL.—*Imperative.* *

Jud.19:30. consider of it, *take advice*,
Isa. 8:10. *Take* counsel *together*, and it shall come to

5781 **עוּק** [*ᵑgook*].

* HIPHIL.—*Future.* *

Am. 2:13. *is pressed* (that is) full of sheaves. (marg. or, as a cart full of sheaves *presseth*)

HIPHIL.—*Participle.*

Am. 2:13. Behold, I *am pressed* under you, (marg. or, I *will press* your place)

עִוֵּר [*ᵑgāh-var'*]. 5786

* PIEL.—*Preterite.* *

2K. 25: 7. and *put out* (marg. *made blind*) the eyes of Zedekiah,
Jer. 39: 7. Moreover *he put out* Zedekiah's eyes,
52:11. Then *he put out* the eyes of Zedekiah;

PIEL.—*Future.*

Ex. 23: 8. the gift *blindeth* the wise,
Deu 16:19. a gift *doth blind* the eyes of the wise,

עוֹר *ᵑgōhr*, m. 5785

Gen 3:21. did the Lord God make coats of *skins*,
27:16. put *the skins of* the kids of the goats upon
Ex. 22:27(26). his raiment *for his skin*:
25: 5. *And* rams' *skins* dyed red, *and* badgers' *skins*,
26:14. rams' *skins* dyed red, and a covering above (of) badgers' *skins*.
29:14. the flesh of the bullock, and *his skin*,
34:29, 30. *the skin of* his face shone
35. *the skin of* Moses' face shone:
35: 7. *And* rams' *skins* dyed red, *and* badgers' *skins*,
23. *and* red *skins of* rams, *and* badgers' *skins*,
36:19. rams' *skins* dyed red, and a covering (of) badgers' *skins*
39:34. covering of rams' *skins* dyed red, and the covering of badgers' *skins*,
Lev. 4:11. *the skin of* the bullock,
7: 8. the priest shall have to himself *the skin*
8:17. the bullock, and *his hide*,
9:11. the flesh and *the hide* he burnt
11:32. any vessel of wood, or raiment, or *skin*,
13: 2. When a man shall have *in the skin of* his flesh a rising, a scab, or bright spot, and it be *in the skin of* his flesh
3. look on the plague *in the skin of* the flesh:
— plague in sight (be) deeper *than the skin*
4. the bright spot (be) white *in the skin of* his flesh, and in sight (be) not deeper than *the skin*,
5, 6. the plague spread not *in the skin*;
7. the scab spread much abroad *in the skin*,
8. the scab spreadeth *in the skin*,
10. (if) the rising (be) white *in the skin*,
11. (is) an old leprosy *in the skin of* his flesh,
12. break out abroad *in the skin*, and the leprosy cover all *the skin of*
18. (even) *in the skin thereof*, was a boil,
20. it (be) in sight lower than *the skin*,
21. and (if) it (be) not lower than *the skin*,
22. if it spread much abroad *in the skin*,
24. *in the skin whereof* (there is) a hot burning,
25. and it (be in) sight deeper than *the skin*;
26. it (be) no lower than *the* (other) *skin*,
27. if it be spread much abroad *in the skin*,
28. in his place, (and) spread not *in the skin*,
30. if it (be) in sight deeper than *the skin*;
31. it (be) not in sight deeper than *the skin*,
32. (be) not in sight deeper than *the skin*;
34. (if) the scall be not spread *in the skin*, nor (be) in sight deeper than *the skin*;
35. if the scall spread much *in the skin*
36. if the scall be spread *in the skin*,
38. have *in the skin of* their flesh bright spots,
39. spots *in the skin of* their flesh (be) darkish
— a freckled spot (that) groweth *in the skin*;
43. leprosy appeareth *in the skin of* the flesh;
48. *in a skin*, or in any thing made of *skin*;
49. or *in the skin*, either in the warp, or in the woof, or in any thing of *skin*;
51. in the woof, or *in a skin*, (or) in any work that is made of *skin*;
52. any thing of *skin*, wherein the plague is:
53, 57. or in the woof, or in any thing of *skin*;
56. of the garment, or out of *the skin*,
58. or whatsoever thing of *skin* (it be),
59. in the warp, or woof, or any thing of *skins*,

Lev.15:17. every garment, and every *skin*,
16:27. shall burn in the fire *their skins*,
Nu. 4: 6. the covering of badgers' *skins*,
8, 11, 12. with a covering of badgers' *skins*,
10. within a covering of badgers' *skins*,
14. upon it a covering of badgers' *skins*,
19: 5. shall burn the heifer in his sight; *her skin*,
31:20. all that is made of *skins*,
2K. 1: 8. hairy man, and girt with a girdle of *leather*
Job 2: 4. Satan answered the Lord, and said, *Skin* for *skin*,
7: 5. *my skin* is broken, and become loathsome.
10:11. Thou hast clothed me with *skin* and flesh,
18:13. It shall devour the strength of *his skin:*
19:20. My bone cleaveth *to my skin*...and I am escaped *with the skin of* my teeth.
26. (though) after *my skin* (worms) destroy this (body), (marg. or, After *I shall awake.*—as if Inf. of עוּר)
30:30. *My skin* is black upon me,
41: 7(40:31). thou fill *his skin* with barbed irons?
Jer. 13:23. Can the Ethiopian change *his skin*,
Lam.3: 4. My flesh *and my skin* hath he made old;
4: 8. *their skin* cleaveth to their bones;
5:10. *Our skin* was black like an oven
Eze.37: 6. flesh upon you, and cover you *with skin*,
8. and *the skin* covered them above:
Mic. 3: 2. who pluck off *their skin* from off them,
3. *and* flay *their skin* from off them;

5782 עוּר [*goor*].

*** KAL.—*Imperative.* ***

Jud. 5:12. *Awake, awake*, Deborah: *awake, awake*, utter a song:
Ps. 7: 6(7). *and awake* for me (to) the judgment
44:23(24). *Awake*, why sleepest thou,
57: 8(9). *Awake up*, my glory; *awake*, psaltery and harp:
59: 4(5). *awake* to help me and behold.
108: 2(3). *Awake*, psaltery and harp:
Cant.4:16. *Awake*, O north wind;
Isa. 51: 9. *Awake, awake*, put on strength, O arm of the Lord; *awake*, as in the ancient days,
52: 1. *Awake, awake;* put on thy strength,
Hab. 2:19. Awake; to the dumb stone, *Arise;*
Zec.13: 7. *Awake*, O sword, against my shepherd,

KAL.—*Future.*

Job 41:10(2). None (is so) fierce that *dare stir him up:*

KAL.—*Participle.* Poel.

Cant 5: 2. I sleep, but my heart *waketh:*
Mal. 2:12. *the master* (marg. or, *him that waketh*) and the scholar,

*** NIPHAL.—*Preterite.* ***

Zec. 2:13(17). *he is raised up* out of his holy habitation.

NIPHAL.—*Future.*

Job 14:12. they shall not awake, nor *be raised*
Jer. 6:22. a great nation *shall be raised*
25:32. a great whirlwind *shall be raised up*
50:41. many kings *shall be raised up*
Joel 3:12(4:12). *Let* the heathen *be wakened*,
Zec. 4: 1. as a man that *is wakened* out of his sleep,

*** POLEL.—*Preterite.* ***

2Sa.23:18. he *lifted up* his spear against three hundred
1Ch.11:11. he *lifted up* his spear against three hundred
20. *lifting up* his spear against three hundred,
Cant. 8: 5. *I raised thee up* under the apple tree:
Isa. 10:26. *And* the Lord of hosts *shall stir up*
14: 9. *it stirreth up* the dead for thee,
Zec. 9:13. *and raised up* thy sons, O Zion,

POLEL.—*Infinitive.*

Job 3: 8. who are ready *to raise up* their mourning.

POLEL.—*Imperative.*

Ps. 80: 2(3). *stir up* thy strength, and come

POLEL.—*Future.*

Pro 10:12. Hatred *stirreth up* strifes:
Cant.2: 7 & 3:5. stir not up, nor *awake* (my) love,
8: 4. that ye stir not up, nor *awake* (my) love,
Isa. 15: 5. *they shall raise up* a cry of destruction.

*** HIPHIL.—*Preterite.* ***

2Ch.36:22. the Lord *stirred up* the spirit of Cyrus
Ezr. 1: 1. the Lord *stirred up* the spirit of Cyrus
5. whose spirit God *had raised*,
Isa. 41: 2. Who *raised up* the righteous (man)
25. *I have raised up* (one) from the north,
45:13. I *have raised him up* in righteousness,
Jer. 51:11. Lord *hath raised up* the spirit of the kings

HIPHIL.—*Imperative.*

Ps. 35:23. *Stir up thyself*, and awake to my judgment.
Joel 3: 9(4:9). *wake up* the mighty men,

HIPHIL.—*Future.*

Deu32:11. As an eagle *stirreth up* her nest,
1Ch 5:26. *And* the God of Israel *stirred up*
2Ch 21:16. *Moreover* the Lord *stirred up*
Job 8: 6. surely now *he would awake* for thee,
41:10(2). (כתיב) fierce that *dare stir him up*
Ps. 57: 8(9). *I* (myself) *will awake* early.
78:38. and *did* not *stir up* all his wrath.
108: 2(3). *I* (myself) *will awake* early.
Cant.2: 7 & 3:5. *ye stir* not *up*, nor awake (my) love,
8: 4. that *ye stir* not *up*, nor awake (my) love.
Isa. 42:13. *he shall stir up* jealousy like a man of war:
50: 4. *he wakeneth* morning by morning, *he wakeneth* mine ear to hear as the learned
Dan 11: 2. *he shall stir up* all against the realm of Grecia.
25. *And he shall stir up* his power and his courage
Hag 1:14. *And* the Lord *stirred up* the spirit of
Zec. 4: 1. talked with me came again, *and waked me*

HIPHIL.—*Participle.*

Isa. 13:17. I *will stir up* the Medes against them,
Jer. 50: 9. I *will raise* and cause to come up
51: 1. I *will raise up* against Babylon,
Eze.23:22. I *will raise up* thy lovers against thee,
Joel 3: 7(4:7). I *will raise them* out of the place

*** HITHPOLEL.—*Preterite.* ***

Job 31:29. *or lifted up myself* when evil found him:

HITHPOLEL.—*Imperative.*

Isa. 51:17. *Awake, awake*, stand up, O Jerusalem,

HITHPOLEL.—*Future.*

Job 17: 8. the innocent *shall stir up himself*

HITHPOLEL.—*Participle.*

Isa. 64: 7(6). *that stirreth up himself* to take hold of

עוּר [*goor*]. 5783

*** NIPHAL.—*Future.* ***

Hab.3: 9. Thy bow *was made* quite *naked*,

עוּר *goor*, Ch. m. 5784

Dan 2:35. *like the chaff* of the summer threshing-floors;

עִוֵּר *giv-vēhr'*, adj. 5787

Ex. 4:11. or deaf, or the seeing, or *the blind?*
Lev.19:14. nor put a stumblingblock before *the blind*,
21:18. a *blind* man, or a lame, or he that hath
Deu 15:21. (if it be) lame, or *blind*, (or have) any
27:18. Cursed (be) he that maketh *the blind* to
28:29. as *the blind* gropeth in darkness,
2Sa. 5: 6. Except thou take away *the blind* and the
8. the lame and *the blind*, (that are) hated of David's soul,
— *The blind* and the lame shall not come
Job 29:15. I was eyes *to the blind*,
Ps.146: 8. The Lord openeth (the eyes of) *the blind:*
Isa. 29:18. the eyes of *the blind* shall see
35: 5. Then the eyes of *the blind* shall be
42: 7. To open the *blind* eyes,
16. I will bring *the blind* by a way
18. Hear, ye deaf; *and* look, *ye blind*,
19. Who (is) *blind*, but my servant?
— who (is) *blind* as (he that is) perfect, and *blind* as the Lord's servant?
43: 8. Bring forth *the blind people*

Isa. 56:10. His watchmen (are) *blind:*
59:10. We grope for the wall *like the blind,*
Jer. 31: 8. with them *the blind* and the lame,
Lam.4:14. They have wandered (as) *blind* (men)
Zep. 1:17. they shall walk *like blind men,*
Mal 1: 8. if ye offer *the blind* for sacrifice,

5788 **עִוָּרוֹן** *^{n}giv-vāh-rōhn′*, m.

Deu28:28. The Lord shall smite thee with madness, *and blindness,*
Zec.12: 4. will smite every horse of the people *with blindness.*

5895 **עֲוָרִים** *^{n}găvāh-reem′*, m. pl.

Isa. 30: 6. (כתיב) upon the shoulders of *young asses,*

5788 **עַוֶּרֶת** *^{n}gav-veh′-reth*, f.

Lev.22:22. *Blind,* or broken, or maimed,

5789 **עוּשׁ** [*^{n}goosh*].

* KAL.—*Imperative.* *

Joel 3:11(4:11). *Assemble yourselves,* and come,

5790 **עוּת** *^{n}gooth.*

* KAL.—*Infinitive.* *

Isa. 50: 4. know how *to speak* a word *in season*

5791 **עָוַת** [*^{n}gāh-vath′*].

* PIEL.—*Preterite.* *

Job 19: 6. God *hath overthrown me,*
Ps.119:78. for *they dealt perversely with me*
Ecc. 7:13. straight, which *he hath made crooked?*

PIEL.—*Infinitive.*

Lam.3:36. *To subvert* a man in his cause,
Am. 8: 5. *and falsifying* (marg. *perverting*) the balances by deceit?

PIEL.—*Future.*

Job 8: 3. *Doth* God *pervert* judgment? or *doth* the Almighty *pervert* justice?
34:12. neither *will* the Almighty *pervert*
Ps.146: 9. way of the wicked *he turneth upside down.*

* PUAL.—*Participle.* *

Ecc. 1:15. (That which is) *crooked* cannot be made

* HITHPAEL.—*Preterite.* *

Ecc.12: 3. *and* the strong men *shall bow themselves,*

5792 **עַוָּתָה** [*^{n}gav-vāh-thāh′*], f.

Lam.3:59. O Lord, thou hast seen *my wrong:*

5794 **עַז** *^{n}gaz*, adj.

Gen49: 3. and the excellency of *power:*
7. Cursed (be) their anger, for (it was) *fierce;*
Ex. 14:21. the sea to go (back) by a *strong* east wind
Nu. 13:28. people (be) *strong* that dwell in the land,
21:24. of the children of Ammon (was) *strong.*
Deu28:50. A nation of *fierce* countenance, (marg. *strong of* face)
Jud.14:14. *and out of the strong* came forth sweetness.
18. What (is) sweeter than honey? and what (is) *stronger* than
2Sa.22:18. He delivered me from my *strong* enemy,
Neh. 9:11. as a stone into the *mighty* waters.
Ps. 18:17(18). delivered me from my *strong* enemy,
59: 3(4). *the mighty* are gathered against me;
Pro.18:23. the rich answereth *roughly.*
21:14. and a reward in the bosom *strong* wrath.
30:25. The ants (are) a people not *strong,*
Cant.8: 6. for love (is) *strong* as death;
Isa. 19: 4. a *fierce* king shall rule over them,
25: 3. Therefore shall the *strong* people glorify
43:16. the sea, and a path in the *mighty* waters;
Isa. 56:11. (they are) greedy (marg. *strong* of appetite) dogs
Eze. 7:24. make the pomp of *the strong* to cease;
Dan 8:23. a king of *fierce* countenance,
Am. 5: 9. the spoiled against *the strong,*

עֵז *^{n}gēhz*, f. 5795

Gen15: 9. *and a she goat* of three years old,
27: 9. from thence two good kids of *the goats;*
16. she put the skins of the kids of *the goats*
30:32. the spotted and speckled *among the goats:*
33. speckled and spotted *among the goats,*
35. *the she goats* that were speckled and
31:38. thy ewes *and thy she goats* have not cast
32:14(15). Two hundred *she goats,*
37:31. and killed a kid of *the goats,*
38:17. send (thee) a kid (marg. a kid of *the goats*)
20. And Judah sent the kid (lit. the kid of *the goats*)
Ex. 12: 5. out from the sheep, or from *the goats:*
25: 4. fine linen, *and goats'* (hair),
26: 7. shalt make curtains (of) *goats'* (hair)
35: 6, 23. fine linen, *and goats'* (hair),
26. in wisdom spun *goats'* (hair).
36:14. And he made curtains (of) *goats'* (hair)
Lev. 1:10. of the sheep, or of *the goats,*
3:12. if his offering (be) *a goat,*
4:23. bring his offering, a kid of *the goats,*
28. bring his offering, a kid of *the goats,*
5: 6. a lamb or a kid of *the goats,*
7:23. fat, of ox, or of sheep, *or of goat.*
9: 3. Take ye a kid of *the goats* for a sin
16: 5. two kids of *the goats* for a sin offering,
17: 3. that killeth an ox, or lamb, or *goat,*
22:19. of the sheep, *or of the goats.*
27. When a bullock, or a sheep, or *a goat,*
23:19. one kid of *the goats* for a sin offering,
Nu. 7:16, 22, 28, 34, 40, 46, 52, 58, 64, 70, 76, 82. One kid of *the goats* for a sin offering:
87. the kids of *the goats* for sin offering
15:11. or for a lamb, or a kid. (lit. or for a lamb, in the sheep or *in the goats*)
24. one kid of *the goats* for a sin offering.
27. he shall bring *a she goat* of the first year
18:17. or the firstling of *a goat,*
28:15. one kid of *the goats* for a sin offering
30. kid of *the goats,* to make an atonement
29: 5, 11, 16, 19, 25. one kid of *the goats* (for) a sin offering,
31:20. all work of *goats'* (hair),
Deu14: 4. ye shall eat: the ox, the sheep, and *the goat,* (lit. and the kid of *the goats*)
Jud. 6:19. went in, and made ready a kid, (lit. *id.*)
13:15. made ready a kid (lit. *id.*)
19. Manoah took a kid (lit. *id.*)
15: 1. visited his wife with a kid; (lit. *id.*)
1Sa.16:20. a bottle of wine, and a kid, (lit. *id.*)
19:13. a pillow of *goats'* (hair) for his bolster,
16. an image in the bed, with a pillow of *goats'*
25: 2. had three thousand sheep, and a thousand *goats:*
1K. 20:27. before them like two little flocks of *kids;*
2Ch 29:21. seven lambs, and seven he *goats,* (lit. he goats of *the goats*)
35: 7. flock, lambs and kids, (lit. sons of *goats*)
Pro.27:27. (thou shalt have) *goats'* milk enough
Cant.4: 1 & 6:5. thy hair (is) as a flock of *goats,*
Eze.43:22. thou shalt offer a kid of *the goats*
45:23. a kid of *the goats* daily (for) a sin
Dan 8: 5. behold, an he *goat* (lit. he goat of *the goats*)
8. the he *goat* (lit. he goat of *the goats*)

עֵז [*^{n}gēhz*], Ch. f. 5796

Ezr. 6:17. twelve he *goats,* (lit. he goats of *the goats*)

עֹז *^{n}gōhz*, m. 5797

Ex. 15: 2. The Lord (is) *my strength* and song,
13. thou hast guided (them) *in thy strength*
Lev.26:19. I will break the pride of *your power;*
Jud. 5:21. my soul, thou hast trodden down *strength.*
9:51. there was a *strong* (lit. of *strength*) tower
1Sa. 2:10. he shall give *strength* unto his king,
2Sa. 6:14. before the Lord with all (his) *might;*

1Ch 13: 8. played before God with all (their) *might,*
16:11. Seek the Lord *and his strength,*
27. *strength* and gladness (are) in his place.
28. give unto the Lord glory *and strength.*
2Ch. 6:41. thou, and the ark of *thy strength :*
30:21. (singing) with *loud* instruments (marg. instruments of *strength*)
Ezr. 8:22. *but his power* and his wrath (is) against all
Job 12:16. With him (is) *strength* and wisdom:
26: 2. (how) savest thou the arm (that hath) no *strength?*
37: 6. the great rain of *his strength.*
41:22(14). In his neck remaineth *strength,*
Ps. 8: 2(3). hast thou ordained *strength*
21: 1(2). The king shall joy in *thy strength,*
13(14). Be thou exalted, Lord, *in thine own strength :*
28: 7. The Lord (is) *my strength* and my shield;
8. The Lord (is) their *strength,*
29: 1. give unto the Lord glory *and strength.*
11. The Lord will give *strength* unto his
30: 7(8). made my mountain to stand *strong :*
46: 1(2). God (is) our refuge *and strength,*
59: 9(10). (Because of) *his strength* will I wait
16(17). But I will sing of *thy power ;*
17(18). Unto thee, O *my strength,* will I sing:
61: 3(4). a *strong* tower (lit. of *strength*) from the enemy.
62: 7(8). the rock of *my strength,*
11(12). *power* (marg. or, *strength*) (belongeth) unto God.
63: 2(3). To see *thy power* and thy glory,
66: 3. through the greatness of *thy power*
68:28(29). God hath commanded *thy strength :*
33(34). he doth send out his voice, (and that) a *mighty* voice. (lit. of *strength*)
34(35). Ascribe ye *strength* unto God:
—(—). *and his strength* (is) in the clouds.
35(36). he that giveth *strength* and power
71: 7. thou (art) my *strong* refuge.
74:13. Thou didst divide the sea by *thy strength :*
77:14(15). thou hast declared *thy strength*
78:26. *by his power* he brought in the south wind.
61. And delivered *his strength* into captivity,
81: 1(2). Sing aloud unto God *our strength :*
84: 5(6). Blessed (is) the man whose *strength*
86:16. give *thy strength* unto thy servant,
89:10(11). hast scattered thine enemies with *thy strong* arm. (marg. the arm of *thy strength*)
17(18). thou (art) the glory of *their strength:*
90:11. Who knoweth *the power of* thine anger?
93: 1. the Lord is clothed with *strength,*
96: 6. *strength* and beauty (are) in his sanctuary.
7. give unto the Lord glory *and strength.*
99: 4. The king's *strength also* loveth judgment;
105: 4. Seek the Lord, *and his strength :*
110: 2. The Lord shall send the rod of *thy strength*
118:14. The Lord (is) *my strength* and song,
132: 8. thou, and the ark of *thy strength.*
138: 3. (and) strengthenedst me (with) *strength*
140: 7(8). *the strength of* my salvation,
150: 1. praise him in the firmament of *his power.*
Pro.10:15. The rich man's wealth (is) *his strong* city: (lit. city of *his strength*)
14:26. Lord (is) *strong* confidence: (lit. of *strength*)
18:10. The name of the Lord (is) a *strong* tower: (lit. of *strength*)
11. The rich man's wealth (is) *his strong* city, (lit. city of *his strength*)
19. A brother offended (is harder to be won) than a *strong* city: (lit. of *strength*)
21:22. and casteth down *the strength of* the
24: 5. A wise man (is) *strong ;* (marg. *in strength*)
31:17. She girdeth her loins *with strength,*
25. *Strength* and honour (are) her clothing;
Ecc. 8: 1. *and the boldness* (marg. *strength*) *of* his face shall be changed.
Isa 12: 2. the Lord Jehovah (is) *my strength*
26: 1. have a *strong* city; (lit. a city of *strength*)
45:24. Lord have I righteousness *and strength :*
49: 5. my God shall be *my strength.*
51: 9. Awake, awake, put on *strength,*
52: 1. Awake, awake; put on *thy strength,*
62: 8. by the arm of *his strength,*
Jer. 16:19. O Lord, *my strength,* and my fortress,
48:17. How is the *strong* (lit. of *strength*) staff broken,

Jer. 51:53. fortify the height of *her strength,*
Eze.19:11. she had *strong* rods (lit. of *strength*) for the sceptres
12. *her strong* rods (lit. the rods of *her strength*) were broken
14. she hath no *strong* rod (lit. of *strength*)
24:21. the excellency of *your strength,*
26:11. *thy strong* garrisons (lit. the garrisons of *thy strength*) shall go down
30: 6. the pride of *her power* shall come down:
18. the pomp of *her strength* shall cease
33:28. the pomp of *her strength* shall cease;
Am. 3:11. he shall bring down *thy strength*
Mic. 5: 4(3). shall stand and feed *in the strength of*
Hab. 3: 4. there (was) the hiding of *his power.*

עֲזָאזֵל *găzāh-zēhl',* m. 5799

Lev.16: 8. and the other lot *for the scapegoat.* (marg. *Azazel*)
10. on which the lot fell *to be the scapegoat,*
— let him go *for a scapegoat* into the
26. he that let go the goat *for the scapegoat*

עָזַב *gāh-zav'.* 5800

*** KAL.—*Preterite.* ***

Gen24:27. *hath* not *left destitute* my master
39:13. when she saw that *he had left* his garment
44:22. *for* (if) *he should leave* his father,
50: 8. their herds, *they left* in the land of Goshen.
Ex. 2:20. why (is) it (that) *ye have left* the man?
Deu 28:20. whereby *thou hast forsaken me.*
29:25(24). Because *they have forsaken* the covenant
31:16. *and will forsake me.* and break my covenant
17. *and I will forsake them,* and I will hide
Jos. 22: 3. *Ye have* not *left* your brethren these many
Jud. 2:21. the nations which Joshua *left*
10:10. *we have forsaken* our God,
13. *have forsaken* me, and served other gods
Ru. 2:16. *and leave* (them), that she may glean
20. *hath* not *left off* his kindness to the living
1 Sa.12:10. *we have forsaken* the Lord,
1 K. 9: 9. *they forsook* the Lord their God,
11:33. *they have forsaken me,* and have worshipped
19:10, 14. the children of Israel *have forsaken* thy
2 K.22:17. Because *they have forsaken me :*
2 Ch 7:19. if ye turn away, *and forsake* my statutes
22. *they forsook* the Lord God of their fathers,
11:14. the Levites *left* their suburbs and their
12: 1. *he forsook* the law of the Lord,
5. Thus saith the Lord, *Ye have forsaken* me, and therefore *have I* also *left* you
13:10. the Lord (is) our God, and *we have* not *forsaken him ;*
11. but ye *have forsaken* him.
21:10. *he had forsaken* the Lord God of his fathers.
24:20. *ye have forsaken* the Lord,
24. because *they had forsaken* the Lord
25. *they left* him in great diseases,
32:31. God *left him,* to try him,
34:25. *they have forsaken me,* and have burned
Ezr. 9: 9. our God *hath* not *forsaken us*
10. *we have forsaken* thy commandments.
Neh. 9:17. of great kindness, and *forsookest them* not.
19. in thy manifold mercies *forsookest them* not
31. thou didst not utterly consume them, nor *forsake them ;*
Job 20:19. oppressed (and) *hath forsaken* the poor;
Ps. 9:10(11). *hast* not *forsaken* them that seek thee.
22: 1(2). my God, why *hast thou forsaken me?*
27:10. my father and my mother *forsake me,*
38:10(11). heart panteth, my strength *faileth me :*
40:12(13). therefore my heart *faileth* (marg. *forsaketh*) *me.*
49:10(11). *and leave* their wealth to others.
71:11. God *hath forsaken him :*
119:87. *I forsook* not thy precepts.
Isa. 1: 4. *they have forsaken* the Lord,
17: 9. *they left* because of the children of Israel:
42:16. These things will I do unto them, and not *forsake them.*
49:14. Zion said, The Lord *hath forsaken me,*
54: 7. For a small moment *have I forsaken thee;*
58: 2. and *forsook* not the ordinance of their God:

Jer. 1:16. who *have forsaken me*,
2:13. *they have forsaken* me the fountain of
5: 7. thy children *have forsaken me*,
19. Like as *ye have forsaken* me,
9:19(18). *we have forsaken* the land,
12: 7. *I have forsaken* mine house,
16:11. your fathers *have forsaken* me,
— and *have forsaken* me, and have not kept
17:13. *they have forsaken* the Lord,
19: 4. *they have forsaken me*, and have estranged
22: 9. *they have forsaken* the covenant
25:38. *He hath forsaken* his covert,
Eze. 8:12 & 9:9. the Lord *hath forsaken* the earth.
20: 8. neither *did they forsake* the idols of Egypt:
23: 8. Neither *left she* her whoredoms
29. *and shall leave thee* naked and bare:
24:21. your sons and your daughters whom *ye have left*
Hos. 4:10. *they have left off* to take heed to the Lord.

KAL.—*Infinitive.*

Gen44:22. The lad cannot *leave* his father:
Ex. 23: 5. and wouldest forbear *to help* him, thou shalt *surely* help with him.
Jos. 24:16. God forbid *that we should forsake* the Lord,
Ru. 1:16. Ruth said, Intreat me not *to leave thee*,
1K. 18:18. *in that ye have forsaken* the commandments of the Lord,
2K. 8: 6. since the day *that she left* the land,
2Ch 28: 6. *because they had forsaken* the Lord
Jer. 2:17. *in that thou hast forsaken* the Lord
19. *that thou hast forsaken* the Lord
9:13(12). *they have forsaken* my law
14: 5. the hind also calved in the field, *and forsook* (it),

KAL.—*Imperative.*

Ps. 37: 8. Cease from anger, *and forsake* wrath:
Pro. 9: 6. *Forsake* the foolish, and live;
Jer. 48:28. O ye that dwell in Moab, *leave* the cities,
49:11. *Leave* thy fatherless children,
51: 9. but she is not healed: *forsake her*,

KAL.—*Future.*

Gen 2:24. Therefore *shall* a man *leave* his father and his mother,
28:15. *I will* not *leave thee*, until I have done
39: 6. *And he left* all that he had in Joseph's
12. *and he left* his garment in her hand,
15, 18. *that he left* his garment with me,
Ex. 9:21. *left* his servants and his cattle in the field.
23: 5. *thou shalt* surely *help* with him.
Lev.19:10. *thou shalt leave* them for the poor and
23:22. *thou shalt leave* them unto the poor,
Nu. 10:31. And he said, *Leave* us not, I pray thee;
Deu 12:19. Take heed to thyself *that thou forsake* not
14:27. *thou shalt* not *forsake him;*
31: 6. he will not fail thee, nor *forsake thee.*
8. he will not fail thee, neither *forsake thee:*
Jos. 1: 5. I will not fail thee, nor *forsake thee.*
8:17. *and they left* the city open, and pursued
24:20. If *ye forsake* the Lord, and serve strange
Jud. 2:12. *And they forsook* the Lord God of their
13. *And they forsook* the Lord, and served
10: 6. *and forsook* the Lord, and served not him.
Ru. 2:11. *and* (how) *thou hast left* thy father and thy mother,
1Sa. 8: 8. *wherewith they have forsaken me*, and
30:13. *and* my master *left me*,
31: 7. *And* when...*they forsook* the cities, and fled;
2Sa. 5:21. *And* there *they left* their images,
15:16. *And* the king *left* ten women,
1K. 6:13. and *will* not *forsake* my people Israel.
8:57. *let him* not *leave us*, nor forsake us:
12: 8. *But he forsook* the counsel of the old men,
13. *and forsook* the old men's counsel
19:20. *And he left* the oxen, and ran after Elijah,
2K. 2: 2, 4, 6 & 4:30. (as) thy soul liveth, *I will* not *leave thee.*
7: 7. fled in the twilight, *and left* their tents,
17:16. *And they left* all the commandments of
21:22. *And he forsook* the Lord God of his
1Ch 10: 7. *then they forsook* their cities, and fled:
14:12. *And when they had left* their gods there,
16:37. *So he left* there before the ark
28: 9. if *thou forsake him*, he will cast thee off
20. he will not fail thee, nor *forsake thee*,
2Ch 10: 8. *But he forsook* the counsel which the old
2Ch 10:13. *and* king Rehoboam *forsook* the counsel
15: 2. if *ye forsake him, he will forsake* you.
24:18. *And they left* the house of the Lord God
20. *he hath also forsaken* you.
28:14. *So* the armed men *left* the captives
29: 6. *and have forsaken him*, and have turned
Neh 3: 8. *and they fortified* Jerusalem
4: 2(3:34). What do these feeble Jews? *will they fortify* (marg. *leave*)
5:10. I pray you, *let us leave off* this usury.
9:28. *therefore leftest thou them* in the hand of
10:39(40). *we will* not *forsake* the house of our
Job 6:14. *he forsaketh* the fear of the Almighty.
9:27. *I will leave off* my heaviness,
10: 1. *I will leave* my complaint upon myself;
20:13. (Though) he spare it, and *forsake it* not;
39:11. *or wilt thou leave* thy labour to him?
14. Which *leaveth* her eggs in the earth,
Ps. 10:14. the poor *committeth himself* (marg. *leaveth*) unto thee;
16:10. *thou wilt* not *leave* my soul in hell;
27: 9. leave me not, neither *forsake me*,
37:28. the Lord loveth judgment, and *forsaketh*
33. The Lord *will* not *leave him* in his hand,
38:21(22). *Forsake me* not, O Lord:
71: 9. *forsake me* not when my strength faileth.
18. O God, *forsake me* not;
89:30(31). If his children *forsake* my law,
94:14. neither *will he forsake* his inheritance.
119: 8. I will keep thy statutes: O *forsake me* not
Pro. 3: 3. *Let* not mercy and truth *forsake thee:*
4: 2. *forsake ye* not my law.
6. *Forsake her* not, and she shall preserve
27:10. friend, and thy father's friend, *forsake*
Isa. 10: 3. where *will ye leave* your glory?
41:17. (I) the God of Israel *will* not *forsake them.*
55: 7. *Let* the wicked *forsake* his way,
Jer. 9: 2(1). *that I might leave* my people,
17:11. he that getteth riches, and not by right, *shall leave them*
18:14. *Will* (a man) *leave* the snow of Lebanon
Lam. 5:20. thou forget us for ever, (and) *forsake us*
Jon. 2: 8(9). observe lying vanities *forsake* their own
Mal. 4: 1(3:19). *it shall leave* them neither root nor

KAL.—*Participle.* Poel.

Ezr. 8:22. wrath (is) against all *them that forsake him.*
Ps.119:53. because of the wicked *that forsake* thy
Pro. 2:13. *Who leave* the paths of uprightness,
17. *Which forsaketh* the guide of her youth,
10:17. *but he that refuseth* reproof erreth.
15:10. Correction (is) grievous *unto him that forsaketh*
28: 4. *They that forsake* the law praise the
13. whoso confesseth *and forsaketh* (them)
Isa. 1:28. *and they that forsake* the Lord shall be
65:11. But ye (are) *they that forsake* the Lord,
Jer. 17:13. all *that forsake thee* shall be ashamed,
Dan 11:30. them *that forsake* the holy covenant.
Zec.11:17. Woe to the idol shepherd *that leaveth* the

KAL.—*Participle.* Paül.

Deu 32:36. (there is) none shut up, *or left.*
1K. 14:10 & 21:21. that is shut up *and left* in Israel,
2K. 9: 8. him that is shut up *and left* in Israel:
14:26. (there was) not any shut up, nor any *left*,
Isa. 10:14. as one gathereth eggs (that are) *left*,
17: 2. The cities of Aroer (are) *forsaken:*
9. his strong cities be *as a forsaken* bough,
54: 6. hath called thee as a woman *forsaken*
60:15. thou hast been *forsaken* and hated,
62: 4. Thou shalt no more be termed *Forsaken;*
Jer. 4:29. every city (shall be) *forsaken*,
Zep. 2: 4. For Gaza shall be *forsaken*,

* NIPHAL.—*Preterite.* *

Neh13:11. Why *is* the house of God *forsaken?*

NIPHAL.—*Future.*

Lev.26:43. The land also *shall be left* of them,
Job 18: 4. *shall* the earth *be forsaken* for thee?
Isa. 7:16. land that thou abhorrest *shall be forsaken*
18: 6. *They shall be left* together unto the fowls

NIPHAL.—*Participle.*

Ps. 37:25. have I not seen the righteous *forsaken*,
Isa. 27:10. habitation forsaken, *and left* like a
62:12. Sought out, A city not *forsaken.*
Eze.36: 4. to the cities *that are forsaken*,

* PUAL.—*Preterite.* *

Isa. 32:14. the multitude of the city *shall be left;*
Jer. 49:25. How *is* the city of praise not *left,*

5801 עִזָּבוֹן [^{n}*giz-zāh-vōhn′*], m.

Eze.27:12. they traded *in thy fairs.*
14. the house of Togarmah traded *in thy fairs*
16, 22. they occupied *in thy fairs*
19. going to and fro occupied *in thy fairs:*
27. Thy riches, *and thy fairs,*
33. When *thy wares* went forth out of the

5805 עֲזוּבָה ^{n}*găzoo-vāh′*, f.

Isa. 6:12. and (there be) *a* great *forsaking* in the

5808 עִזּוּז ^{n}*giz-zooz′*, adj.

Ps. 24: 8. The Lord *strong* and mighty,
Isa. 43:17. bringeth forth the chariot and horse, the army *and the power;*

5807 עֱזוּז ^{n}*gĕzooz*, m.

Ps. 78: 4. the praises of the Lord, *and his strength,*
145: 6. (men) shall speak *of the might of* thy
Isa. 42:25. of his anger, *and the strength of* battle:

5810 עָזַז [^{n}*gāh-zaz′*].

* KAL.—*Infinitive.* *

Pro. 8:28. *when he strengthened* the fountains of the
Isa. 30: 2. *to strengthen themselves* in the strength of

KAL.—*Imperative.*

Ps. 68:28(29). *strengthen,* O God, that which thou

KAL.—*Future.*

Jud. 3:10. *and* his hand *prevailed* against Chushan-rishathaim.
6: 2. *And* the hand of Midian *prevailed* (marg. *was strong*) against Israel:
Ps. 9:19(20). Arise, O Lord; *let* not man *prevail:*
52: 7(9). (and) *strengthened himself* in his
89:13(14). *strong is* thy hand, (and) high is thy
Ecc. 7:19. Wisdom *strengtheneth* the wise
Dan 11:12. but *he shall* not *be strengthened* (by it).

* HIPHIL.—*Preterite.* *

Pro. 7:13. *with* an *impudent* face (marg. *she strengthened* her face, and) said unto him,
21:29. A wicked man *hardeneth* his face:

5822 עָזְנִיָּה ^{n}*goz-neey-yāh′*, f.

Lev.11:13. eagle, and the ossifrage, and *the ospray,*
Deu14:12. eagle, and the ossifrage, and *the ospray,*

5823 עָזַק [^{n}*gāh-zak′*].

* PIEL.—*Future.* *

Isa. 5: 2. *And he fenced it,* (marg. or, *made a wall about it*) and gathered out the stones

5824 עִזְקָא [^{n}*giz-kāh′*], Ch. f.

Dan 6:17(18). and the king sealed it *with his own signet, and with the signet of* his lords;

5826 עָזַר [^{n}*gāh-zar′*].

* KAL.—*Preterite.* *

Jos. 1:14. the mighty men of valour, *and help* them;
1Sa. 7:12. Hitherto *hath* the Lord *helped us.*
1Ch 12:18. for thy God *helpeth thee.*
19. but *they helped them* not:
21. And they *helped* David against the band
2Ch 18:31. Jehoshaphat cried out, and the Lord *helped him;*
20:23. every one *helped* to destroy another.
Ezr.10:15. and Shabbethai the Levite *helped them.*
Job 26: 2. How *hast thou helped* (him that is)
Ps. 86:17. *thou,* Lord, *hast holpen me,*
118:13. that I might fall: but the Lord *helped me.*
Isa. 41:10. yea, *I will help thee;*
13. Fear not; *I will help thee.*
14. *I will help thee,* saith the Lord,
49: 8. in a day of salvation *have I helped thee:*
Zec. 1:15. and *they helped* forward the affliction.

KAL.—*Infinitive.*

Jos. 10:33. king of Gezer came up *to help* Lachish;
2Sa. 8: 5. the Syrians of Damascus came *to succour*
18: 3. (it is) better that thou *succour* us (marg. be *to succour*)
1Ch 12:17. ye be come peaceably unto me *to help me,*
22. by day there came to David *to help him,*
15:26. *when* God *helped* the Levites
18: 5. the Syrians of Damascus came *to help*
22:17. all the princes of Israel *to help* Solomon
2Ch 14:11(10). Lord, (it is) nothing with thee *to help,*
19: 2. *Shouldest thou help* the ungodly,
25: 8. God hath power *to help,*
26:13. *to help* the king against the enemy.
28:16. send unto the kings of Assyria *to help*
32: 8. with us (is) the Lord our God *to help us,*
Ezr. 8:22. a band of soldiers and horsemen *to help us*
Ps.119:173. thine hand *help me;* (lit. be *to help me*)
Dan 10:13. one of the chief princes, came *to help me;*

KAL.—*Imperative.*

Jos. 10: 4. Come up unto me, *and help me,*
6. to us quickly, and save us, *and help us:*
2Ch 14:11(10). *help us,* O Lord our God;
Ps. 79: 9. *Help us,* O God of our salvation,
109:26. *Help me,* O Lord my God:
119:86. persecute me wrongfully; *help thou me.*

KAL.—*Future.*

Gen49:25. the God of thy father, *who* (lit. *and he*) *shall help thee;*
Deu32:38. let them rise up *and help you,*
2Sa.21:17. *But* Abishai the son of Zeruiah *succoured*
1K. 1: 7. *and they* following Adonijah *helped* (him).
2Ch 26: 7. *And* God *helped him* against the Philistines,
28:23. I sacrifice to them, *that they may help me.*
32: 3. without the city: *and they did help him.*
Ps. 37:40. *And* the Lord *shall help them,*
46: 5(6). God *shall help her,* (and that) right
119:175. *let* thy judgments *help me.*
Isa. 30: 7. the Egyptians *shall help* in vain,
41: 6. *They helped* every one his neighbour;
44: 2. and formed thee from the womb, (which) *will help thee;*
50: 7, 9. the Lord God *will help* me;

KAL.—*Participle.* Poel.

1K. 20:16. the thirty and two kings *that helped* him.
2K. 14:26. nor any *helper* for Israel.
1Ch 12: 1. they (were) among the mighty men, *helpers of* the war.
18. peace (be) *to thine helpers;*
Job 9:13. *the* proud *helpers* do stoop under him.
29:12. (him that had) none *to help* him. (lit. no *helper* to him)
30:13. forward my calamity, they have no *helper.*
Ps. 10:14. thou art *the helper* of the fatherless.
22:11(12). (there is) none *to help.* (marg. not *a helper*)
30:10(11). Lord, be thou my *helper.*
54: 4(6). Behold, God (is) mine *helper:*
72:12. poor also, and (him) that hath no *helper.*
107:12. they fell down, and (there was) none *to help.* (lit. no *helper*)
118: 7. taketh my part *with them that help me:*
Isa. 31: 3. both he *that helpeth* shall fall,
63: 5. I looked, and (there was) none *to help;* (lit. no *helper*)
Jer. 47: 4. Tyrus, and Zidon every *helper* that
Lam. 1: 7. none *did help* her: (lit. no *helper* to her)
Eze.30: 8. (when) all *her helpers* shall be destroyed.
32:21. the midst of hell with *them that help him:*
Dan 11:45. none *shall help* him. (lit. no *helper* to him)

KAL.—*Participle.* Paül.

Isa. 31: 3. *he that is holpen* shall fall

* NIPHAL.—*Preterite.* *

Ps. 28: 7. my heart trusted in him, *and I am helped:*

NIPHAL.—*Infinitive.*

2Ch 26:15. he was marvellously *helped,* (lit. he marvelled *to be helped*)

NIPHAL.—*Future.*

1Ch 5:20. *And they were helped* against them,
Dan 11:34. *they shall be holpen* with a little help:

* HIPHIL.—*Infinitive.* *

2Sa.18: 3. (כתיב) better that thou *succour* (marg. be *to succour*) us

HIPHIL.—*Participle.*

2Ch 28:23. the gods of the kings of Syria *help* them,

5828 עֵזֶר *gēh'-zer,* m.

Gen 2:18. I will make him *an help* meet for him.
20. for Adam there was not found *an help*
Ex. 18: 4. God of my father, (said he, was) *mine help,*
Deu33: 7. *and* be thou *an help* (to him) from his
26. rideth upon the heaven *in thy help,*
29. the shield of *thy help,*
Ps. 20: 2(3). Send *thee help* from the sanctuary,
33:20. the Lord: he (is) *our help* and our shield.
70: 5(6). O God: thou (art) *my help* and my
89:19(20). I have laid *help* upon (one that is)
115: 9, 10, 11. he (is) *their help* and their shield.
121: 1. from whence cometh *my help.*
2. *My help* (cometh) from the Lord,
124: 8. *Our help* (is) in the name of the Lord,
146: 5. that (hath) the God of Jacob *for his help,*
Isa. 30: 5. *nor be an help* nor profit, but a shame,
Eze.12:14. all that (are) about him to *help him,*
Dan11:34. they shall be holpen with *a* little *help:*
Hos13: 9. but in me (is) (marg. *in*) *thine help.*

5833 עֶזְרָה *gez-rāh'* & עֶזְרַת *gez-rāhth',* f.

Jud. 5:23. they came not *to the help of* the Lord, *to the help of* the Lord against the mighty.
2Ch 28:21. but he *helped* him not. (lit. was not *for a help* to him)
Job 6:13. (Is) not *my help* in me?
31:21. when I saw *my help* in the gate:
Ps. 22:19(20). O my strength, haste thee *to help me.*
27: 9. thou hast been *my help;* leave me not,
35: 2. stand up *for mine help.*
38:22(23). Make haste *to help me,* O Lord
40:13(14). O Lord, make haste *to help me.*
17(18). thou (art) *my help* and my deliverer;
44:26(27). Arise for our *help,* (marg. *a help* for us)
46: 1(2). *a* very present *help* in trouble.
60:11(13). Give us *help* from trouble:
63: 7(8). thou hast been my *help,*
70: 1(2). make haste *to help me,* (marg. *my help*)
71:12. O my God, make haste *for my help.*
94:17. Unless the Lord (had been) my *help,*
108:12(13). Give us *help* from trouble:
Isa. 10: 3. to whom will ye flee *for help?*
20: 6. whither we flee *for help*
31: 1. to them that go down to Egypt *for help;*
2. against *the help of* them that work iniquity.
Jer. 37: 7. army, which is come forth *to help* you, (lit. *for help* to you)
Lam. 4:17. our eyes as yet failed *for our* vain *help:*
Nah. 3: 9. Put and Lubim were *thy helpers.*

5835 עֲזָרָה *găzāh-rāh',* f.

2Ch 4: 9. he made the court of the priests, *and the* great *court,* and doors *for the court,*
6:13. and had set it in the midst of *the court:*
Eze.43:14. (even) to *the* lower *settle*
— *and from the* lesser *settle* (even) to *the* greater *settle*
17. *And the settle* (shall be) fourteen (cubits)
20. on the four corners of *the settle,*
45:19. upon the four corners of *the settle*

5842 עֵט *gēht,* m.

Job 19:24. That they were graven *with an* iron *pen*
Ps. 45: 1(2). my tongue (is) *the pen of* a ready writer.
Jer. 8: 8. *the pen of* the scribes (is) in vain.
17: 1. sin of Judah (is) written *with a pen of* iron,

עֵטָא *gēh-tāh',* Ch. f. 5843

Dan 2:14. Daniel answered with *counsel* and wisdom

עָטָה *gāh-tāh'.* 5844

* KAL.—*Preterite.* *

Jer. 43:12. *and he shall array himself* with the land of Egypt,
Mic. 3: 7. *yea, they shall* all *cover* their lips;

KAL.—*Infinitive.*

Isa. 22:17. and will *surely* cover thee. (lit. *covering* will cover thee)

KAL.—*Future.*

Lev.13:45. *he shall put a covering* upon his upper lip,
Ps. 71:13. *let them be covered* (with) reproach
84: 6(7). the rain also *filleth* (marg. *covereth*) the pools.
109:19. as the garment (which) *covereth* him,
29. *and let them cover themselves* with
Isa. 59:17. *and was clad* with zeal as a cloke.
Jer. 43:12. as a shepherd *putteth on* his garment;
Eze.24:17. *cover* not (thy) lips, and eat not the bread
22. *ye shall* not *cover* (your) lips,

KAL.—*Participle.* Poel.

1Sa.28:14. and he (is) *covered* with a mantle.
Ps.104: 2. *Who coverest* (thyself) with light
Cant.1: 7. why should I be *as one that turneth aside* (marg. or, *is veiled*)
Isa. 22:17. *and will* surely *cover thee.*

* HIPHIL.—*Preterite.* *

Ps. 89:45(46). *thou hast covered* him with shame.

עֲטִין [*gäteen*], m. 5845

Job 21:24. *His breasts* (marg. or, *milk pails*) are full of milk,

עֲטִישָׁה [*gätee-shāh'*], f. 5846

Job 41;18(10). By *his neesings* a light doth shine,

עֲטַלֵּף *gătal-lēhph',* m. 5847

Lev.11:19. and the lapwing, and *the bat.*
Deu14:18. the lapwing, *and the bat.*
Isa. 2:20. to the moles *and to the bats;*

עָטַף [*gāh-taph'*]. 5848

* KAL.—*Infinitive.* *

Ps. 61: 2(3). *when* my heart *is overwhelmed:*

KAL.—*Future.*

Job 23: 9. *he hideth himself* on the right hand,
Ps. 65:13(14). the valleys also *are covered over* with
73: 6. violence *covereth* them (as) a garment.
102: [title](1). afflicted, when *he is overwhelmed,*
Isa. 57:16. the spirit *should fail* before me,

KAL.—*Participle.* Paül.

Gen 30:42. so *the feebler* were Laban's, and the stronger Jacob's.
Lam 2:19. thy young children, *that faint* for hunger

* NIPHAL.—*Infinitive.* *

Lam 2:11. *because* the children and the sucklings *swoon* (marg. or, *faint*)

* HIPHIL.—*Infinitive.* *

Gen30:42. *But when* the cattle *were feeble,*

* HITHPAEL.—*Infinitive.* *

Ps.142: 3(4). *When* my spirit *was overwhelmed*
Lam 2:12. *when they swooned* as the wounded
Jon. 2: 7(8). *When* my soul *fainted* within me

HITHPAEL.—*Future.*

Ps. 77: 3(4). *and* my spirit *was overwhelmed.*
107: 5. their soul *fainted* in them.
143: 4. *Therefore is* my spirit *overwhelmed*

5849 **עָטַר** [*gāh-tar′*].

* KAL.—*Future.* *

Ps. 5:12(13). with favour *wilt thou compass him*

KAL.—*Participle.* Poel.

1Sa.23:26. Saul and his men *compassed* David

* PIEL.—*Preterite.* *

Ps. 65:11(12). *Thou crownest* the year with thy goodness;
Cant.3:11. *wherewith* his mother *crowned him*

PIEL.—*Future.*

Ps. 8: 5(6). and *hast crowned him* with glory

PIEL.—*Participle.*

Ps.103: 4. *who crowneth thee* with lovingkindness

* HIPHIL.—*Participle.* *

Isa. 23: 8. counsel against Tyre, *the crowning* (city),

5850 **עֲטָרָה** *gătāh-rāh′*, f.

2Sa.12:30. And he took their king's *crown*
1Ch 20: 2. David took *the crown of* their king
Est. 8:15. *and with a* great *crown of* gold,
Job 19: 9. and taken *the crown* (from) my head.
31:36. (and) bind it (as) *a crown* to me.
Ps. 21: 3(4). thou settest *a crown of* pure gold on his head.
Pro. 4: 9. *a crown of* glory shall she deliver to thee.
12: 4. A virtuous woman (is) *a crown to* her husband:
14:24. *The crown of* the wise (is) their riches:
16:31. The hoary head (is) *a crown of* glory,
17: 6. Children's children (are) *the crown of* old
Cant.3:11. behold king Solomon *with the crown*
Isa. 28: 1. *the crown of* pride, to the drunkards
3. *The crown of* pride, the drunkards
5. the Lord of hosts be *for a crown of* glory,
62: 3. Thou shalt also be *a crown of* glory
Jer. 13:18. (even) *the crown of* your glory.
Lam 5:16. *The crown* is fallen (from) our head:
Eze. 16:12. *and a* beautiful *crown* upon thine head.
21:26(31). Remove the diadem, and take off *the crown:*
23:42. *and* beautiful *crowns* upon their heads.
Zec. 6:11. take silver and gold, and make *crowns,*
14. *And the crowns* shall be to Helem,

5856 **עִי** *gee*, m.

Nu. 21:11. and pitched *at Ije*-abarim, (marg. or, *heaps of* Abarim)
33:44. and pitched *in Ije*-abarim,
45. they departed *from Iim,* [or, *the heaps*]
Ps. 79: 1. they have laid Jerusalem *on heaps.*
Jer. 26:18. Jerusalem shall become *heaps,*
Mic. 1: 6. I will make Samaria *as an heap of* the field,
3:12. Jerusalem shall become *heaps,*

5860 **עִיט** [*geet*].

* KAL.—*Future.* *

1Sa.14:32. *And* the people *flew* upon the spoil,
15:19. *but didst fly* upon the spoil,
25:14. *and he railed* (marg. *flew* upon) on them.

5861 **עַיִט** *gah′-yit*, m.

Gen15:11. And when *the fowls* came down
Job 28: 7. (There is) a path which no *fowl* knoweth,
Isa. 18: 6. They shall be left together *unto the fowls of* — *the fowls* shall summer upon them,
46:11. *a ravenous bird* from the east,
Jer. 12: 9. Mine heritage (is) unto me (as) *a* speckled *bird, the birds* round about (are) against
Eze.39: 4. I will give thee *unto* the *ravenous* birds

5865 **עֵילוֹם** *gēh-lōhm′*, m.

2Ch.33: 7. I put my name *for ever:*

עְיָם [*găyāhm*], m. 5868

Isa. 11:15. *with* his *mighty* wind (lit. *with the strength of* his wind)

עַיִן *gah′-yin*, com. 5869

Gen 3: 5. then *your eyes* shall be opened,
6. and that it (was) pleasant *to the eyes,*
7. And *the eyes of* them both were opened,
6: 8. Noah found grace *in the eyes of* the Lord.
13:10. And Lot lifted up *his eyes,*
14. Lift up now *thine eyes,*
16: 4. her mistress was despised *in her eyes.*
5. I was despised *in her eyes:*
6. do to her as it pleaseth *thee.* (marg. (that which is) good *in thine eyes*)
7. the angel of the Lord found her by *a fountain of* water in the wilderness, by *the fountain* in the way to Shur.
18: 2. And he lift up *his eyes* and looked,
3. if now I have found favour *in thy sight,*
19: 8. do ye to them as (is) good *in your eyes:*
14. But he seemed as one that mocked *unto* (lit. was *in the eyes of*) his sons in law.
19. thy servant hath found grace *in thy sight,*
20:15. dwell where it pleaseth *thee.* (marg. as (is) good *in thine eyes*)
16. he (is) to thee a covering of *the eyes,*
21:11. And the thing was very grievous in Abraham's *sight*
12. Let it not be grievous *in thy sight*
19. And God opened *her eyes,*
22: 4, 13. Abraham lifted up *his eyes,*
23:11. *in the presence of* the sons of my people
18. *in the presence of* the children of Heth,
24:13. Behold, I stand (here) by *the well of* water;
16. and she went down *to the well,*
29. Laban ran out unto the man, unto *the well.*
30. he stood by the camels at *the well.*
42. I came this day unto *the well,*
43. Behold, I stand by *the well of* water;
45. and she went down *unto the well,*
63. and he lifted up *his eyes,*
64. And Rebekah lifted up *her eyes,*
27: 1. when Isaac was old, and *his eyes* were dim,
12. I shall seem *to him* (lit. be *in his eyes*) as a deceiver;
28: 8. the daughters of Canaan pleased not (marg. (were) evil *in the eyes*) Isaac
29:17. Leah (was) tender *eyed;* (lit. *and the eyes of* Leah were tender)
20. they seemed *unto him* (lit. were *in his eyes*) (but) a few days,
30:27. if I have found favour *in thine eyes,*
41. laid the rods *before the eyes of* the cattle
31:10. I lifted up *mine eyes,*
12. Lift up now *thine eyes,*
35. Let it not displease (lit. Let it not be displeasing *in the eyes of*) my lord
40. my sleep departed *from mine eyes.*
32: 5(6). that I may find grace *in thy sight.*
33: 1. And Jacob lifted up *his eyes,*
5. And he lifted up *his eyes,*
8. (These are) to find grace *in the sight of* my
10. if now I have found grace *in thy sight,*
15. let me find grace *in the sight of* my lord.
34:11. Let me find grace *in your eyes,*
18. their words pleased Hamor, and Shechem (lit. were good *in the eyes of* Hamor, *and in the eyes of* Shechem)
37:25. and they lifted up *their eyes* and looked,
38: 7. was wicked *in the sight of* the Lord;
10. the thing which he did displeased (marg. was evil *in the eyes of*) the Lord:
14. and sat in an *open* place, (marg. in the door of *eyes,* or, of *Enajim*)
21. that (was) *openly* by the way side? (lit. *in the eyes,* marg. or, in *Enajim*)
39: 4. Joseph found grace *in his sight,*
7. his master's wife cast *her eyes* upon
21. gave him favour *in the sight of* the keeper
41:37. And the thing was good *in the eyes of* Pharaoh, *and in the eyes of* all his
42:24. Simeon, and bound him *before their eyes.*
43:29. And he lifted up *his eyes,*
44:21. that I may set *mine eyes* upon him.

Gen 45: 5. be not grieved, nor angry *with yourselves*, (marg. neither let there be anger *in your eyes*)
12. And, behold, *your eyes* see, *and the eyes of*
16. it pleased Pharaoh well (marg. was good *in the eyes of* Pharaoh), and his servants. (lit. *and in the eyes of* his servants)
20. *Also* regard not (lit. & marg. *And* let not *your eye* spare) your stuff;
46: 4. Joseph shall put his hand upon *thine eyes.*
47:19. Wherefore shall we die *before thine eyes,*
25. let us find grace *in the sight of* my lord,
29. If now I have found grace *in thy sight,*
48:10. *Now the eyes of* Israel were dim for age,
17. displeased him: (lit. was evil *in his eyes*)
49:12. *His eyes* (shall be) red with wine,
22. (even) a fruitful bough by *a well;*
50: 4. If now I have found grace *in your eyes,*
Ex. 3:21. give this people favour *in the sight of* the
4:30. did the signs *in the sight of* the people.
5:21. to be abhorred *in the eyes of* Pharaoh, *and in the eyes of* his servants,
7:20. smote the waters that (were) in the river, *in the sight of* Pharaoh, *and in the sight of* his servants;
8:26(22). abomination of the Egyptians *before their eyes,*
9: 8. it toward the heaven *in the sight of*
10: 5. cover *the face* (marg. *eye*) *of* the earth.
15. they covered *the face of* the whole earth,
11: 3. gave the people favour *in the sight of*
— *in the sight of* Pharaoh's servants, *and in the sight of* the people.
12:36. gave the people favour *in the sight of*
13: 9. for a memorial between *thine eyes,*
16. for frontlets between *thine eyes:*
14:10. children of Israel lifted up *their eyes,*
15:26. wilt do that which is right *in his sight,*
27. Elim, where (were) twelve *wells of*
17: 6. Moses did so *in the sight of* the elders of
19:11. the Lord will come down *in the sight of*
21: 8. If she please not (marg. be evil *in the eyes of*) her master,
24. *Eye* for *eye*, tooth for tooth,
26. if a man smite *the eye of* his servant, or *the eye of* his maid, that it perish; he shall let him go free for *his eye's* sake.
24:17. *in the eyes of* the children of Israel.
33:12. thou hast also found grace *in my sight.*
13. if I have found grace *in thy sight,*
— that I may find grace *in thy sight:*
16. thy people have found grace *in thy sight?*
17. thou hast found grace *in my sight,*
34: 9. If now I have found grace *in thy sight,*
40:38. *in the sight of* all the house of Israel,
Lev. 4:13. and the thing be hid *from the eyes of* the
10:19. been accepted *in the sight of* the Lord?
20. when Moses heard (that), he was content. (lit. it was good *in his eyes*)
13: 5. (if) the plague *in his sight* be at a stay,
12. wheresoever the priest looketh; (lit. to all *the sight of* the eyes of the priest)
37. if the scall be *in his sight* at a stay,
55. the plague have not changed *his colour,*
14: 9. shave all his hair off...and *his eye*brows,
20: 4. of the land do any ways hide *their eyes*
17. shall be cut off *in the sight of* their people:
21:20. or that hath a blemish *in his eye,*
24:20. *eye* for *eye*, tooth for tooth:
25:53. not rule with rigour over him *in thy sight.*
26:16. burning ague, that shall consume *the eyes,*
45. *in the sight of* the heathen,
Nu. 5:13. it be hid *from the eyes of* her husband,
10:31. thou mayest be to us *instead of* eyes.
11: 6. this manna, (before) *our eyes.*
7. *and the colour thereof as the colour* (marg. *eye of it as the eye*) *of* bdellium.
10. Moses also was displeased. (lit. *and in the eyes of* Moses it was evil)
11. have I not found favour *in thy sight,*
15. if I have found favour *in thy sight;*
13:33. we were *in our own sight* as grasshoppers, and so we were *in their sight.*
14:14. that thou Lord art seen *face to face,*
15:24. *without the knowledge* (marg. *from the eyes*) *of* the congregation,
39. not after your own heart and *your own eyes,*

Nu. 16:14. wilt thou put out *the eyes of* these men?
19: 5. (one) shall burn the heifer *in his sight;*
20: 8. speak ye unto the rock *before their eyes;*
12. to sanctify me *in the eyes of* the children
27. *in the sight of* all the congregation.
22: 5. they cover *the face* (marg. *eye*) *of* the earth,
11. which covereth *the face of* the earth:
31. the Lord opened *the eyes of* Balaam,
34. if it displease thee (marg. be evil *in thine eyes*), I will get me back again.
23:27. peradventure it will please (lit. it will be right *in the eyes of*) God
24: 1. when Balaam saw that it pleased (lit. was good *in the eyes of*) the Lord
2. And Balaam lifted up *his eyes,*
3, 15. the man whose *eyes* are open hath
4, 16. falling (into a trance), but having his *eyes* open:
25: 6. *in the sight of* Moses, *and in the sight of*
27:14. sanctify me at the water *before their eyes:*
19. and give him a charge *in their sight.*
32: 5. if we have found grace *in thy sight,*
13. the generation, that had done evil *in the sight of*
33: 3. *in the sight of* all the Egyptians.
9. in Elim (were) twelve *fountains of* water,
55. (shall be) pricks *in your eyes,*
36: 6. Let them marry to whom they think best; (lit. to good *in their eyes*)
Deu 1:23. And the saying pleased *me* well: (lit. was good *in mine eyes*)
30. he did for you in Egypt *before your eyes;*
3:21. *Thine eyes* have seen all that the Lord
27. lift up *thine eyes* westward,
— and behold (it) *with thine eyes:*
4: 3. *Your eyes* have seen what the Lord did
6. your understanding *in the sight of* the
9. the things which *thine eyes* have seen,
19. lest thou lift up *thine eyes*
25. and shall do evil *in the sight of* the Lord
34. God did for you in Egypt *before your eyes?*
6: 8. as frontlets between *thine eyes.*
18. do (that which is) right and good *in the sight of* the Lord:
22. upon all his houshold, *before our eyes:*
7:16. *thine eye* shall have no pity upon them:
19. The great temptations which *thine eyes*
8: 7. of *fountains* and depths that spring
9:17. and brake them *before your eyes.*
18. in doing wickedly *in the sight of* the Lord,
10:21. terrible things, which *thine eyes* have seen.
11: 7. *your eyes* have seen all the great acts
12. *the eyes of* the Lord thy God
18. as frontlets between *your eyes.*
12: 8. man whatsoever (is) right *in his own eyes.*
25. do (that which is) right *in the sight of* the
28. (that which is) good and right *in the sight of* the Lord
13: 8(9). neither shall *thine eye* pity him,
18(19). to do (that which is) right *in the eyes of* the Lord
14: 1. nor make any baldness between *your eyes*
15: 9. *thine eye* be evil against thy poor brother,
18. It shall not seem hard *unto thee,*
16:19. a gift doth blind *the eyes of* the wise,
17: 2. wrought wickedness *in the sight of* the Lord
19:13. *Thine eye* shall not pity him,
21. And *thine eye* shall not pity; (but) life (shall go) for life, *eye for eye,*
21: 7. *neither* have *our eyes* seen (it).
9. (that which is) right *in the sight of* the
24: 1. she find no favour *in his eyes,*
25: 3. thy brother should seem vile *unto thee.* (lit. *in thine eyes*)
9. *in the presence of* the elders,
12. *thine eye* shall not pity (her).
28:31. Thine ox (shall be) slain *before thine eyes,*
32. *thine eyes* shall look, and fail (with longing)
34. thou shalt be mad for the sight of *thine eyes*
54. *his eye* shall be evil toward his brother,
56. *her eye* shall be evil toward the husband
65. a trembling heart, and failing of *eyes,*
67. the sight of *thine eyes* which thou shalt see.
29: 2(1). all that the Lord did *before your eyes*
3(2). The great temptations which *thine eyes*
4(3). an heart to perceive, *and eyes* to see,
31: 7. *in the sight of* all Israel,

Deu 31:29. will do evil *in the sight of* the Lord,
32:10. he kept him as the apple of *his eye*.
33:28. *the fountain of* Jacob (shall be) upon a
34: 4. caused thee to see (it) *with thine eyes*,
7. *his eye* was not dim,
12. Moses shewed *in the sight of* all Israel.
Jos. 3: 7. I begin to magnify thee *in the sight of*
4:14. the Lord magnified Joshua *in the sight of*
5:13. he lifted up *his eyes* and looked,
9:25. as it seemeth good and right *unto thee* (lit. *in thine eyes*)
10:12. and he said *in the sight of* Israel,
22:30. it pleased *them*. (marg. was good *in their eyes*)
33. thing pleased (lit. was good *in the eyes of*)
23:13. and thorns *in your eyes*,
24: 7. *your eyes* have seen what I have done
15. if it seem evil *unto you* (lit. *in your eyes*)
17. which did those great signs *in our sight*,
Jud. 2:11 & 3:7. Israel did evil *in the sight of* the
3:12. did evil again *in the sight of* the Lord:
— had done evil *in the sight of* the Lord.
4: 1. again did evil *in the sight of* the Lord,
6: 1. of Israel did evil *in the sight of* the Lord:
17. If now I have found grace *in thy sight*,
21. of the Lord departed *out of his sight*.
10: 6. did evil again *in the sight of* the Lord,
15. good *unto thee*; (marg. *in thine eyes*)
13: 1. did evil again *in the sight of* the Lord;
14: 3. she pleaseth *me* well. (marg. right *in mine eyes*)
7. and she pleased Samson well. (lit. was right *in the eyes of* Samson)
15:19. he called the name thereof *En*-hakkore, (marg. *The well of* him that called)
16:21. Philistines took him, and put out *his eyes*,
28. avenged of the Philistines for *my* two *eyes*.
17: 6. (that which was) right *in his own eyes*.
19:17. when he had lifted up *his eyes*,
24. seemeth good *unto you*: (lit. *in your eyes*)
21:25. (that which was) right *in his own eyes*.
Ru. 2: 2. *in whose* (lit. who *in his*) *sight* I shall find
9. (Let) *thine eyes* (be) on the field
10. Why have I found grace *in thine eyes*,
13. Let me find favour *in thy sight*,
1Sa. 1:18. thine handmaid find grace *in thy sight*.
23. seemeth *thee* good; (lit. good *in thine eyes*)
2:33. (shall be) to consume *thine eyes*,
3: 2. *and his eyes* began to wax dim,
18. let him do what seemeth *him* good. (lit. is good *in his eyes*)
4:15. *and his eyes* were dim,
6:13. and they lifted up *their eyes*,
8: 6. But the thing displeased Samuel, (marg. was evil *in the eyes of* Samuel)
11: 2. that I may thrust out all your right *eyes*,
10. seemeth good *unto you*. (lit. *in your eyes*)
12: 3. (any) bribe to blind *mine eyes* therewith?
16. the Lord will do *before your eyes*.
17. ye have done *in the sight of* the Lord,
14:27. and *his eyes* were enlightened.
29. how *mine eyes* have been enlightened,
36. seemeth good *unto thee*. (lit. *in thine eyes*)
40. seemeth good *unto thee*. (lit. *in thine eyes*)
15:17. thou (wast) little *in thine own sight*,
19. and didst evil *in the sight of* the Lord?
16: 7. man looketh *on the outward appearance*, (marg. *eyes*)
12. (and) withal of a beautiful *countenance*, (marg. fair of *eyes*)
22. he hath found favour *in my sight*.
18: 5. was accepted *in the sight of* all the people, and also *in the sight of* Saul's servants
8. and the saying displeased *him*; (marg. was evil *in his eyes*)
20. and the thing pleased *him*. (marg. was right *in his eyes*)
23. Seemeth it *to you* (lit. *in your eyes*) (a) light (thing) to be a king's son in law,
26. it pleased David well (lit. was right *in the eyes of* David)
20: 3. I have found grace *in thine eyes*;
29. if I have found favour *in thine eyes*,
21:13(14). he changed his behaviour *before them*,
24: 4(5). as it shall seem good *unto thee*. (lit. *in thine eyes*)
10(11). *thine eyes* have seen how that the Lord

1Sa.25: 8. let the young men find favour *in thine eyes*:
26:21. my soul was precious *in thine eyes*
24. thy life was much set by this day *in mine eyes*, so let my life be much set by *in the eyes of* the Lord,
27: 5. If I have now found grace *in thine eyes*,
29: 1. the Israelites pitched *by a fountain*
6. and thy coming in with me in the host (is) good *in my sight*:
— the lords favour thee not. (lit. *and in the eyes of* the lords thou art not good)
7. that thou displease not (marg. do not evil *in the eyes of*) the lords
9. I know that thou (art) good *in my sight*,
2Sa. 3:19. all that seemed good *to* Israel (lit. *in the eyes of*), *and* that seemed good *to* the whole house (lit. *and in the eyes of*)
36. the people took notice (of it), and it pleased *them* (marg. was good *in their eyes*): as whatsoever the king did pleased (lit. was good *in the eyes of*) all the people.
4:10. thinking to have brought (marg. he was *in his own eyes* as a bringer)
6:20. uncovered himself to day *in the eyes of*
22. and will be base *in mine own sight*:
7:19. this was yet a small thing *in thy sight*,
10: 3. *Thinkest thou* that David doth (marg. *In thine eyes* doth David) honour thy father,
12. the Lord do that which seemeth *him* good. (lit. is good *in his eyes*)
11:25. Let not this thing displease *thee*, (marg. be evil *in thine eyes*)
27. the thing that David had done displeased (marg. was evil *in the eyes of*) the Lord.
12: 9. the Lord, to do evil *in his sight*?
11. I will take thy wives *before thine eyes*,
— he shall lie with thy wives *in the sight of* this sun.
13: 2. Amnon thought it hard (marg. it was marvellous *in the eyes of* Amnon)
5. and dress the meat *in my sight*,
6. make me a couple of cakes *in my sight*,
8. and made cakes *in his sight*,
34. that kept the watch lifted up *his eyes*,
14:22. I have found grace *in thy sight*, my lord,
15:25. if I shall find favour *in the eyes of* the Lord
26. let him do to me as seemeth good *unto him*. (lit. *in his eyes*)
16: 4. (that) I may find grace *in thy sight*,
12. that the Lord will look *on mine affliction*, (marg. *eye*, or, *tears*)
22. unto his father's concubines *in the sight of* all Israel.
17: 4. the saying pleased Absalom well (marg. was right *in the eyes of* Absalom), *and* all the elders (lit. *and in the eyes of* all the elders) of Israel.
18: 4. What seemeth *you* best (lit. what seemeth good *in your eyes*) I will do.
24. and lifted up *his eyes*,
19: 6(7). it had pleased *thee* well. (lit. it had been right *in thine eyes*)
18(19). to do what *he* thought good. (marg. the good *in his eyes*)
27(28). therefore (what is) good *in thine eyes*.
37(38). what shall seem good *unto thee*. (lit. *in thine eyes*)
38(39). that which shall seem good *unto thee*: (lit. *in thine eyes*)
20: 6. lest he get him fenced cities, and escape *us*. (marg. deliver himself from *our eyes*)
22:25. according to my cleanness in *his eye sight*.
28. *but thine eyes* (are) upon the haughty,
24: 3. *that the eyes of* my lord the king may see
22. offer up what (seemeth) good *unto him*: (lit. *in his eyes*)
1K. 1:20. O king, *the eyes of* all Israel (are) upon thee,
48. *mine eyes even* seeing (it).
3:10. And the speech pleased (lit. was good *in the eyes of*) the Lord,
8:29. That *thine eyes* may be open toward this
52. That *thine eyes* may be open unto the
9: 3. *mine eyes* and mine heart shall be there
12. and they pleased *him* not. (marg. were not right *in his eyes*)

1K. 10: 7. and *mine eyes* had seen (it):
11: 6. And Solomon did evil *in the sight of* the
19. found great favour *in the sight of* Pharaoh,
33. to do (that which is) right *in mine eyes,*
38. and do (that is) right *in my sight,*
14: 4. Ahijah could not see; for *his eyes* were set
8. to do (that) only (which was) right *in mine eyes;*
22. Judah did evil *in the sight of* the Lord,
15: 5, 11. (that which was) right *in the eyes of*
26, 34. he did evil *in the sight of* the Lord,
16: 7. the evil that he did *in the sight of* the Lord,
19. doing evil *in the sight of* the Lord,
25. Omri wrought evil *in the eyes of* the Lord,
30. of Omri did evil *in the sight of* the Lord
20: 6. whatsoever is pleasant in *thine eyes,*
38. disguised himself with ashes upon *his face.*
41. took the ashes away from *his face;*
21: 2. seem good *to thee,* (marg. *in thine eyes*)
20. sold thyself to work evil *in the sight of*
25. to work wickedness *in the sight of* the
22:43. (that which was) right *in the eyes of* the
52(53). he did evil *in the sight of* the Lord,
2K. 1:13. thy servants, be precious *in thy sight.*
14. my life now be precious *in thy sight.*
3: 2. he wrought evil *in the sight of* the Lord;
18. a light thing *in the sight of* the Lord:
4:34. *and his eyes* upon *his eyes,*
35. and the child opened *his eyes.*
6:17. Lord, I pray thee, open *his eyes,*
— Lord opened *the eyes of* the young man;
20. Lord, open *the eyes of* these (men), that they may see. And the Lord opened *their eyes,*
7: 2. thou shalt see (it) *with thine eyes,*
19. thou shalt see it *with thine eyes,*
8:18. he did evil *in the sight of* the Lord.
27. and did evil *in the sight of* the Lord,
9:30. she painted *her face,* (marg. put *her eyes* in painting)
10: 5. do thou (that which is) good *in thine eyes.*
30. (that which is) right *in mine eyes,*
12: 2(3). (that which was) right *in the sight of*
13: 2, 11. (that which was) evil *in the sight of*
14: 3. (that which was) right *in the sight of* the
24. (that which was) evil *in the sight of* the
15: 3, 34. (that which was) right *in the sight of*
9, 18, 24, 28. (that which was) evil *in the sight of* the Lord,
16: 2. not (that which was) right *in the sight of*
17: 2. (that which was) evil *in the sight of* the
17. sold themselves to do evil *in the sight of*
18: 3. (that which was) right *in the sight of* the
19:16. open, Lord, *thine eyes,* and see:
22. and lifted up *thine eyes* on high?
20: 3. done (that which is) good *in thy sight.*
21: 2, 16, 20. (that which was) evil *in the sight of*
6. much wickedness *in the sight of* the Lord,
15. done (that which was) evil *in my sight,*
22: 2. (that which was) right *in the sight of* the
20. *thine eyes* shall not see all the evil
23:32, 37 & 24:9, 19. (that which was) evil *in the sight of* the Lord,
25: 7. slew the sons of Zedekiah before *his eyes,* and put out *the eyes of* Zedekiah,
1Ch 2: 3. of Judah, was evil *in the sight of* the Lord;
13: 4. the thing was right *in the eyes of* all the
17:17. this was a small thing *in thine eyes,*
19: 3. *Thinkest thou* that David doth (marg. *In thine eyes* doth David) honour thy
13. Lord do (that which is) good *in his sight.*
21: 7. And God was displeased (marg. it was evil *in the eyes of* God)
16. And David lifted up *his eyes,*
23. king do (that which is) good *in his eyes:*
28: 8. *in the sight of* all Israel
29:10. David blessed the Lord *before* all the
25. Solomon exceedingly *in the sight of*
2Ch 6:20. That *thine eyes* may be open upon this
40. let, I beseech thee, *thine eyes* be open,
7:15. Now *mine eyes* shall be open,
16. *mine eyes* and mine heart shall be there
9: 6. and *mine eyes* had seen (it):
14: 2(1). did (that which was) good and right *in the eyes of*
16: 9. *the eyes* of the Lord (lit. the Lord *his eyes*) run to and fro throughout
2Ch 20:12. *our eyes* (are) upon thee.
32. (that which was) right *in the sight of* the
21: 6. (that which was) evil *in the eyes of* the
22: 4. he did evil *in the sight of* the Lord
24. 2 & 25:2 & 26:4 & 27:2. (that which was) right *in the sight of* the Lord
28: 1. (that which was) right *in the sight of*
29: 2. did (that which was) right *in the sight of*
6. (that which was) evil *in the eyes of* the
8. as ye see *with your eyes.*
30: 4. And the thing pleased (marg. was right *in the eyes of*) the king and all the congregation. (lit. *and in the eyes of* all the congregation)
32: 3. to stop the waters of *the fountains*
23. was magnified *in the sight of* all nations
33: 2. (that which was) evil *in the sight of* the
6. much evil *in the sight of* the Lord,
22. (that which was) evil *in the sight of*
34: 2. did (that which was) right *in the sight of*
28. neither shall *thine eyes* see all the evil
36: 5, 9, 12. (that which was) evil *in the sight of*
Ezr. 3:12. of this house was laid *before their eyes,*
9: 8. that our God may lighten *our eyes,*
Neh. 1: 6. *and thine eyes* open, that thou
2:13. before *the* dragon *well,*
14. I went on to the gate of *the fountain,*
3:15. But the gate of *the fountain* repaired
6:16. were much cast down *in their own eyes:*
8: 5. Ezra opened the book *in the sight* (marg. *eyes*) *of* all
12:37. And at the *fountain* gate, which was
Est. 1:17. shall despise their husbands *in their eyes,*
21. the saying pleased (marg. was good *in the eyes of*) the king
2: 4. the maiden which pleaseth the king (lit. is good *in the eyes of* the king)
— And the thing pleased the king; (lit. was right *in the eyes of* the king)
9. And the maiden pleased *him,* (lit. was good *in his eyes*)
15. Esther obtained favour *in the sight of* all
3: 6. he thought scorn (lit. he despised *in his eyes*) to lay hands on Mordecai
11. do with them as it seemeth good *to thee.* (lit. *in thine eyes*)
5: 2. she obtained favour *in his sight:*
8. have found favour *in the sight of* the king,
7: 3. I have found favour *in thy sight,* O king,
8: 5. and I (be) pleasing *in his eyes.*
8. Write ye also for the Jews, as it liketh *you,* (lit. is good *in your eyes*)
Job 2:12. they lifted up *their eyes* afar off,
3:10. nor hid sorrow *from mine eyes.*
4:16. an image (was) before *mine eyes,*
7: 7. *mine eye* shall no more see good.
8. *The eye of* him that hath seen me
— *thine eyes* (are) upon me,
10: 4. Hast thou *eyes of* flesh?
18. *and* no *eye* had seen me!
11: 4. I am clean *in thine eyes.*
20. *But the eyes of* the wicked shall fail,
13: 1. *mine eye* hath seen all (this),
14: 3. dost thou open *thine eyes* upon such an one,
15:12. what do *thy eyes* wink at,
15. the heavens are not clean *in his sight.*
16: 9. mine enemy sharpeneth *his eyes* upon me.
20. *mine eye* poureth out (tears) unto God.
17: 2. not *mine eye* continue in their provocation?
5. *even the eyes of* his children shall fail.
7. *Mine eye* also is dim by reason of sorrow,
18: 3. (and) reputed vile *in your sight?*
19:15. I am an alien *in their sight.*
27. *and mine eyes* shall behold,
20: 9. *The eye* also (which) saw him shall (see him) no more;
21: 8. and their offspring *before their eyes.*
20. *His eyes* shall see his destruction,
22:29. he shall save the humble person. (marg. him that hath low *eyes*)
24:15. *The eye also of* the adulterer waiteth for the twilight, saying, No *eye* shall see me:
23. *yet his eyes* (are) upon their ways.
25: 5. the stars are not pure *in his sight.*
27:19. he openeth *his eyes,* and he (is) not.
28: 7. which the vulture's *eye* hath not seen·
10. *his eye* seeth every precious thing.

Job 28:21. it is hid *from the eyes of* all living,
29:11. and *when the eye* saw (me), it gave witness
15. I was *eyes* to the blind,
31: 1. I made a covenant *with mine eyes;*
7. mine heart walked after *mine eyes,*
16. *or* have caused *the eyes of* the widow to fail;
32: 1. because he (was) righteous *in his own eyes.*
34:21. *his eyes* (are) upon the ways of man,
36: 7. He withdraweth not *his eyes* from the
39:29. *her eyes* behold afar off.
40:24. He taketh it *with his eyes:*
41:18(10). *and his eyes* (are) like the eyelids of the morning.
42: 5. but now *mine eye* seeth thee.
Ps. 5: 5(6). The foolish shall not stand in *thy sight:* (marg. before *thine eyes*)
6: 7(8). *Mine eye* is consumed because of grief;
10: 8. *his eyes* are privily set against the poor.
11: 4. *his eyes* behold, his eyelids try,
13: 3(4). lighten *mine eyes,* lest I sleep
15: 4. *In whose eyes* a vile person is contemned;
17: 2. *thine eyes* behold the things that are equal.
8. Keep me as the apple of *the eye,*
11. they have set *their eyes* bowing down
18:24(25). the cleanness of my hands in *his eyesight.* (marg. before *his eyes*)
27(28). *but* wilt bring down high *looks.* (lit. lofty *eyes*)
19: 8(9). the Lord (is) pure, enlightening *the eyes.*
25:15. *Mine eyes* (are) ever toward the Lord;
26: 3. thy lovingkindness (is) before *mine eyes:*
31: 9(10). *mine eye* is consumed with grief,
22(23). I am cut off from before *thine eyes:*
32: 8. I will guide thee with *mine eye.*
33:18. *the eye of* the Lord (is) upon them that fear him,
34:15(16). *The eyes of* the Lord (are) upon the
35:19. (neither) let them wink with *the eye*
21. Aha, aha, *our eye* hath seen (it).
36: 1(2). (there is) no fear of God before *his eyes.*
2(3). he flattereth himself *in his own eyes,*
38:10(11). the light of *mine eyes,* it also is gone from me.
50:21. and set (them) in order *before thine eyes.*
51: 4(6). and done (this) evil *in thy sight:*
54: 7(9). *mine eye* hath seen (his desire)
66: 7. *his eyes* behold the nations:
69: 3(4). *mine eyes* fail while I wait for my God.
23(24). Let *their eyes* be darkened,
72:14. precious shall their blood be *in his sight.*
73: 7. *Their eyes* stand out with fatness:
16. it (was) too painful *for me;* (marg. labour *in mine eyes*)
77: 4(5). Thou holdest *mine eyes* waking:
79:10. let him be known among the heathen *in our sight*
88: 9(10). *Mine eye* mourneth by reason of affliction:
90: 4. a thousand years *in thy sight* (are but) as
91: 8. *with thine eyes* shalt thou behold
92:11(12). *Mine eye* also shall see (my desire)
94: 9. he that formed *the eye,* shall he not see?
98: 2. openly shewed *in the sight of* the heathen.
101: 3. I will set no wicked thing before *mine eyes:*
5. him that hath an high *look* (lit. that is lofty of *eyes*)
6. *Mine eyes* (shall be) upon the faithful
7. that telleth lies shall not tarry in *my sight.*
115: 5. *eyes* have they, but they see not:
116: 8. my soul from death, *mine eyes* from tears,
15. Precious *in the sight of* the Lord
118:23. Lord's doing; it (is) marvellous *in our eyes.*
119:18. Open thou *mine eyes,*
37. away *mine eyes* from beholding vanity;
82. *Mine eyes* fail for thy word,
123. *Mine eyes* fail for thy salvation,
136. Rivers of waters run down *mine eyes,*
148. *Mine eyes* prevent the (night) watches,
121: 1. I will lift up *mine eyes* unto the hills,
123: 1. Unto thee lift I up *mine eyes,*
2. *as the eyes of* servants (look)
— *as the eyes of* a maiden unto the hand of her mistress; so *our eyes* (wait) upon the Lord our God,
131: 1. heart is not haughty, nor *mine eyes* lofty:
132: 4. I will not give sleep *to mine eyes,*
135:16. *eyes* have they, but they see not;

Ps.139:16. *Thine eyes* did see my substance,
141: 8. *mine eyes* (are) unto thee, O God
145:15. *The eyes of* all wait upon thee;
Pro. 1:17. in vain the net is spread *in the sight* (marg. *eyes*) *of* any bird.
3: 4. *in the sight of* God and man.
7. Be not wise *in thine own eyes:*
21. let not them depart from *thine eyes:*
4:21. Let them not depart from *thine eyes;*
25. Let *thine eyes* look right on,
5:21. of man (are) before *the eyes of* the Lord,
6: 4. Give not sleep to *thine eyes,*
13. He winketh *with his eyes,*
17. *A* proud *look* (marg. Haughty *eyes*), a lying tongue,
7: 2. my law as the apple of *thine eye.*
8:28. when he strengthened *the fountains of*
10:10. that winketh with *the eye* causeth sorrow:
26. as smoke *to the eyes,*
12:15. way of a fool (is) right *in his own eyes:*
15: 3. *The eyes of* the Lord (are) in every place,
30. The light of *the eyes* rejoiceth the heart:
16: 2. the ways of a man (are) clean *in his own eyes;*
30. He shutteth *his eyes* to devise froward
17: 8. A gift (is as) a precious stone *in the eyes of*
24. *but the eyes of* a fool (are) in the ends of
20: 8. scattereth away all evil *with his eyes.*
12. The hearing ear, *and the* seeing *eye,*
13. open *thine eyes,* (and) thou shalt be
21: 2. way of a man (is) right *in his own eyes:*
4. An high *look* (marg. Haughtiness of *eyes*), and a proud heart,
10. neighbour findeth no favour *in his eyes.*
22: 9. He that hath *a* bountiful *eye* shall be
12. *The eyes of* the Lord preserve knowledge,
23: 5. Wilt thou set *thine eyes* upon that which
6. the bread of (him that hath) *an* evil *eye,*
26. *and* let *thine eyes* observe my ways.
29. who hath redness of *eyes?*
31. when it giveth *his colour* in the cup,
33. *Thine eyes* shall behold strange women,
24:18. Lest the Lord see (it), and it displease *him,* (marg. be evil *in his eyes*)
25: 7. the prince whom *thine eyes* have seen.
26: 5. he be wise *in his own conceit.* (marg. *eyes*)
12. Seest thou a man wise *in his own conceit?*
16. The sluggard (is) wiser *in his own conceit*
27:20. *so the eyes of* man are never satisfied.
28:11. The rich man (is) wise *in his own conceit;*
22. that hasteth to be rich (hath) *an* evil *eye,*
27. he that hideth *his eyes* shall have many
29:13. the Lord lighteneth both *their eyes.*
30:12. (that are) pure *in their own eyes,*
13. a generation, O how lofty are *their eyes!*
17. *The eye* (that) mocketh at (his) father,
Ecc. 1: 8. *the eye* is not satisfied with seeing,
2:10. whatsoever *mine eyes* desired
14. The wise man's *eyes* (lit. the wise man *his eyes*) (are) in his head;
4: 8. neither is *his eye* satisfied with riches;
5:11 (10). beholding (of them) *with their eyes?*
6: 9. Better (is) the sight of *the eyes* than
8:16. day nor night seeth sleep *with his eyes:*
11: 7. a pleasant (thing it is) *for the eyes* to
9. thine heart, and in the sight of *thine eyes:*
Cant. 1:15 & 4:1. thou (art) fair; *thou* (hast) doves' *eyes.* (lit. *thine eyes* (are of) doves)
4: 9. ravished my heart with one of *thine eyes,*
5:12. *His eyes* (are) as (the eyes) of doves
6: 5. Turn away *thine eyes* from me,
7: 4(5). *thine eyes* (like) the fishpools
8:10. then was I in *his eyes* as one that found favour.
Isa. 1:15. I will hide *mine eyes* from you:
16. evil of your doings from before *mine eyes;*
2:11. *The* lofty *looks of* man shall be humbled,
3: 8. the Lord, to provoke *the eyes of* his glory.
16. stretched forth necks and wanton *eyes,*
5:15. *and the eyes of* the lofty shall be humbled:
21. (them that are) wise *in their own eyes,*
6: 5. *mine eyes* have seen the King,
10. make their ears heavy, and shut *their eyes* lest they see *with their eyes,*
10:12. Assyria, and the glory of *his* high *looks.*
11: 3. shall not judge after the sight of *his eyes,*
13:16. shall be dashed to pieces *before their eyes*

Isa. 13:18. *their eye* shall not spare children.
17: 7. *and his eyes* shall have respect to the Holy
29:10. and hath closed *your eyes:*
18. *the eyes of* the blind shall see out of
30:20. *thine eyes* shall see thy teachers:
32: 3. *the eyes of* them that see shall not be dim,
33:15. and shutteth *his eyes* from seeing evil;
17. *Thine eyes* shall see the king in his beauty:
20. *thine eyes* shall see Jerusalem
35: 5. Then *the eyes of* the blind shall be opened,
37:17. open *thine eyes,* O Lord,
23. and lifted up *thine eyes* on high?
38: 3. done (that which is) good *in thy sight.*
14. *mine eyes* fail (with looking) upward:
40:26. Lift up *your eyes* on high,
42: 7. To open *the* blind *eyes,*
43: 4. thou wast precious *in my sight,*
8. forth the blind people *that* have *eyes,*
44:18. he hath shut *their eyes,*
49: 5. yet shall I be glorious *in the eyes of* the Lord,
18. Lift up *thine eyes* round about,
51: 6. Lift up *your eyes* to the heavens,
52: 8. they shall see *eye to eye,*
10. made bare his holy arm *in the eyes of* all
59:10. we grope as if (we had) no *eyes:*
15. it displeased *him* (marg. was evil *in his eyes*)
60: 4. Lift up *thine eyes* round about,
64: 4(3). neither hath *the eye* seen, O God,
65:12. but did evil *before mine eyes,*
16. they are hid *from mine eyes.*
66: 4. they did evil *before mine eyes,*
Jer. 3: 2. Lift up *thine eyes* unto the high places,
4:30. thou rentest *thy face* (marg. *eyes*) with painting,
5: 3. (are) not *thine eyes* upon the truth?
21. which have *eyes,* and see not;
7:11. become a den of robbers *in your eyes?*
30. of Judah have done evil *in my sight,*
9: 1(8:23). *and mine eyes* a fountain of tears,
18(17). that *our eyes* may run down with tears,
13:17. *mine eye* shall weep sore,
20. Lift up *your eyes,* and behold
14: 6. *their eyes* did fail, because (there was) no
17. Let *mine eyes* run down with tears
16: 9. to cease out of this place *in your eyes,*
17. *mine eyes* (are) upon all their ways:
— is their iniquity hid from *mine eyes.*
18: 4. good *to* (lit. *in the eyes of*) the potter
10. If it do evil *in my sight,*
19:10. break the bottle *in the sight of* the men
20: 4. *and thine eyes* shall behold (it):
22:17. *thine eyes* and thine heart (are) not but
24: 6. I will set *mine eyes* upon them
26:14. as seemeth good and meet *unto you.* (lit. *in your eyes*)
27: 5. given it unto whom it seemed meet *unto me.* (lit. is right *in my eyes*)
28: 1. *in the presence of* the priests and of all the people,
5. *in the presence of* the priests, *and in the presence* of all the people
11. Hananiah spake *in the presence of* all the people,
29:21. he shall slay them *before your eyes;*
31:16. from weeping, *and thine eyes* from tears:
32: 4. *and his eyes* shall behold *his eyes;*
12. *in the sight of* Hanameel mine uncle's (son), *and in the presence of* the witnesses
— *before* all the Jews that sat in the court
13. I charged Baruch *before them,*
19. *thine eyes* (are) open upon all the ways
30. of Judah have only done evil *before me*
34: 3. *and thine eyes* shall behold *the eyes of* the king of Babylon,
15. turned, and had done right *in my sight,*
39: 6. of Zedekiah in Riblah *before his eyes:*
7. Moreover he put out Zedekiah's *eyes,*
12. and look well to him, (marg. *and* set *thine eyes* upon him)
40. 4. If it seem good *unto thee* (lit. *in thine eyes*) to come with me into Babylon, come; and I will look well (marg. set *mine eye* upon) unto thee: but if it seem ill *unto thee* (lit. *in thine eyes*)

Jer. 40: 4. seemeth good and convenient *for thee*
5. go wheresoever it seemeth convenient *unto thee*
42: 2. a few of many, as *thine eyes* do behold
43: 9. *in the sight of* the men of Judah;
51:24. evil that they have done in Zion *in your sight,*
52: 2. he did (that which was) evil *in the eyes of* the Lord,
10. slew the sons of Zedekiah *before his eyes:*
11. Then he put out *the eyes of* Zedekiah;
Lam 1:16. *mine eye, mine eye* runneth down with water,
2: 4. slew all (that were) pleasant to *the eye*
11. *Mine eyes* do fail with tears,
18. let not the apple of *thine eye* cease.
3:48. *Mine eye* runneth down with rivers of
49. *Mine eye* trickleth down,
51. *Mine eye* affecteth mine heart
4:17. *our eyes* as yet failed for our vain help:
5:17. for these (things) *our eyes* are dim.
Eze. 1: 4. out of the midst thereof *as the colour of*
7. sparkled *like the colour of* burnished brass.
16. *like unto the colour of* a beryl:
18. their rings (were) full of *eyes*
22. *as the colour of* the terrible crystal,
27. I saw *as the colour of* amber,
4:12. bake it...*in their sight.*
5: 8. *in the sight of* the nations.
11. neither shall *mine eye* spare,
14. *in the sight of* all that pass by.
6: 9. *their eyes,* which go a whoring after their idols:
7: 4. And *mine eye* shall not spare thee,
9. And *mine eye* shall not spare, neither will
8: 2. *as the colour of* amber.
5. Son of man, lift up *thine eyes* now the way toward the north. So I lifted up *mine eyes*
18. *mine eye* shall not spare,
9: 5. let not *your eye* spare,
10. *mine eye* shall not spare,
10: 2. And he went in *in my sight.*
9. the appearance of the wheels (was) *as the colour of* a beryl
12. full of *eyes* round about,
19. mounted up from the earth *in my sight:*
12: 2. a rebellious house, which have *eyes* to see,
3. remove by day *in their sight;* and thou shalt remove from thy place to another place *in their sight:*
4. bring forth thy stuff by day *in their sight,* as stuff for removing: and thou shalt go forth at even *in their sight,*
5. Dig thou through the wall *in their sight,*
6. *In their sight* shalt thou bear (it)
7. I bare (it) upon (my) shoulder *in their sight.*
12. that he see not the ground *with* (his) *eyes.*
16: 5. None *eye* pitied thee,
41. *in the sight of* many women:
18: 6. *neither* hath lifted up *his eyes* to the idols
12. hath lifted up *his eyes* to the idols,
15. *neither* hath lifted up *his eyes* to the idols
20: 7. Cast ye away every man the abominations of *his eyes,*
8. the abominations of *their eyes,*
9. that it should not be polluted *before* the heathen,
— *in whose* (lit. who *in their*) *sight* I made
14. that it should not be polluted *before* the heathen, *in whose sight* I brought them out.
17. *mine eye* spared them from destroying
22. *in the sight of* the heathen, *in whose sight* I brought them forth.
24. *their eyes* were after their fathers' idols.
41. be sanctified in you *before* the heathen.
21: 6(11). with bitterness sigh *before their eyes.*
23(28). a false divination *in their sight,*
22:16. *in the sight of* the heathen,
26. have hid *their eyes* from my sabbaths,
23:16. as soon as she saw them with *her eyes,*
27. thou shalt not lift up *thine eyes*
40. thou didst wash thyself, paintedst *thy eyes,*
24:16. take away from thee the desire of *thine eyes*
21. the desire of *your eyes,*

Eze 24:25. the desire of *their eyes*,
28:18. *in the sight of* all them that behold thee.
25. *in the sight of* the heathen,
33:25. *and* lift up *your eyes* toward your idols,
36:23. I shall be sanctified in you *before their eyes*.
34. *in the sight of* all that passed by.
37:20. in thine hand *before their eyes*.
38:16. sanctified in thee, O Gog, *before their eyes*.
23. be known *in the eyes of* many nations,
39:27. *in the sight of* many nations;
40: 4. Son of man, behold *with thine eyes*,
43:11. and write (it) *in their sight*,
44: 5. mark well, and behold *with thine eyes*,
Dan 8: 3. Then I lifted up *mine eyes*,
5. goat (had) a notable horn between *his eyes*.
21. the great horn that (is) between *his eyes*
9:18. open *thine eyes*, and behold our desolations,
10: 5. Then I lifted up *mine eyes*,
6. *and his eyes* as lamps of fire, and his arms and his feet *like in colour* to polished
Hos 2:10(12). discover her lewdness *in the sight of* her lovers,
10:10. (כתיב) themselves in *their* two *furrows*.
13:14. repentance shall be hid *from mine eyes*.
Joel 1:16. Is not the meat cut off before *our eyes*,
Am. 9: 3. though they be hid from *my sight*
4. I will set *mine eyes* upon them for evil,
8. *the eyes of* the Lord God (are) upon
Jon. 2: 4(5). I am cast out of *thy sight*;
Mic 4:11. let *our eye* look upon Zion.
7:10. *mine eyes* shall behold her:
Hab 1:13. (Thou art) of purer *eyes* than to behold evil,
Zep 3:20. when I turn back your captivity *before your eyes*,
Hag 2: 3. (is it) not *in your eyes* in comparison of
Zec 1:18(2:1). Then lifted I up *mine eyes*,
2: 1(5). I lifted up *mine eyes* again,
8(12). he that toucheth you toucheth the apple of *his eye*.
3: 9. upon one stone (shall be) seven *eyes*:
4:10. they (are) *the eyes of* the Lord,
5: 1. I turned, and lifted up *mine eyes*,
5. Lift up now *thine eyes*,
6. (is) *their resemblance* through all the earth.
9. Then lifted I up *mine eyes*,
6: 1. I turned, and lifted up *mine eyes*,
8: 6. be marvellous *in the eyes of* the remnant
— should it also be marvellous *in mine eyes*?
9: 1. when *the eyes of* man, as of all the tribes of Israel,
8. for now have I seen *with mine eyes*.
11:12. If *ye think* good (marg. it (be) good *in your eyes*), give (me) my price;
17. upon his arm, and upon his right *eye*:
— *and* his right *eye* shall be utterly darkened.
12: 4. open *mine eyes* upon the house of Judah,
14:12. *their eyes* shall consume away in their holes,
Mal 1: 5. *And your eyes* shall see,
2:17. ye say, Every one that doeth evil (is) good *in the sight of* the Lord,

---

5870 עַיִן [*ⁿgah'-yin*], Ch. f.

Ezr. 5: 5. *But the eye of* their God was upon the
Dan. 4:34(31). I Nebuchadnezzar lifted up *mine eyes*
7: 8. this horn (were) *eyes like the eyes of* man,
20. even (of) that horn *that* had *eyes*, (lit. *and eyes* (were) to it)

5770 עין [*ⁿgeen*].

* KAL.—*Participle*. Poel. *

1Sa. 18: 9. Saul *eyed* (lit. was *eyeing*) David

5888 עָיֵף [*ⁿgāh-yēhph'*].

* KAL.—*Preterite*. *

Jer. 4:31. my soul *is wearied* because of murderers.

5889 עָיֵף *ⁿgāh-yēhph'*, adj.

Gen 25:29. Esau came from the field, and he (was) *faint*:
30. for I (am) *faint*:
Deu 25:18. when thou (wast) *faint* and weary;
Jud. 8: 4. three hundred men that (were) with him, *faint*,
5. unto the people that follow me; for they (be) *faint*,
2Sa. 16:14. all the people that (were) with him, came *weary*,
17:29. The people (is) hungry, *and weary*,
Job 22: 7. Thou hast not given water to *the weary*
Ps. 63: 1(2). my flesh longeth for thee in a dry *and thirsty* land,
143: 6. my soul (thirsteth) after thee, as a *thirsty* land.
Pro. 25:25. (As) cold waters to a *thirsty* soul,
Isa. 5:27. shall be *weary* nor stumble among them;
28:12. ye may cause *the weary* to rest;
29: 8. he awaketh, and, behold, (he is) *faint*,
32: 2. shadow of a great rock in a *weary* land.
46: 1. (they are) a burden *to the weary* (beast).
Jer. 31:25. I have satiated the *weary* soul,

עֵיפָה *ⁿgēh-phāh'*, f. 5890

Job 10:22. A land of *darkness*, as darkness
Am. 4:13. that maketh the morning *darkness*,

עַיִר *ⁿgah'-yir*, m. 5895

Gen 32:15(16). twenty she asses, *and* ten *foals*.
49:11. Binding *his foal* unto the vine,
Jud. 10: 4. thirty sons that rode on thirty *ass colts*,
12:14. threescore and ten *ass colts*:
Job 11:12. *though* man be born (like) a wild ass's *colt*.
Isa. 30: 6. riches upon the shoulders of *young asses*,
24. *and the young asses* that ear the ground
Zec. 9: 9. riding upon an ass, and upon *a colt* the foal of an ass.

עִיר *ⁿgeer*. 5782

* KAL.—*Infinitive*. *

Hos 7: 4. ceaseth *from raising* (marg. or, *waking*) after

עִיר *ⁿgeer*, f. 5892

Gen 4:17. and he builded *a city*, and called the name of *the city*, after
10:11. and *the city* Rehoboth, and Calah,
12. between Nineveh and Calah: the same (is) *a great city*.
11: 4. let us build us *a city* and a tower,
5. the Lord came down to see *the city*
8. and they left off to build *the city*.
13:12. Lot dwelled *in the cities of* the plain,
18:24. there be fifty righteous within *the city*:
26. in Sodom fifty righteous within *the city*,
28. thou destroy all *the city* for (lack of) five?
19: 4. men of *the city*, (even) the men of Sodom,
12. whatsoever thou hast *in the city*,
14. the Lord will destroy *this city*.
15. be consumed in the iniquity of *the city*.
16. and set him without *the city*.
20. *this city* (is) near to flee unto,
21. that I will not overthrow *this city*,
22. the name of *the city* was called Zoar.
25. he overthrew those *cities*, and all the plain, and all the inhabitants of *the cities*,
29. when God destroyed *the cities of* the plain,
— when he overthrew *the cities* in the which
23:10, 18. all that went in at the gate of *his city*,
24:10. to Mesopotamia, unto *the city of* Nahor.
11. his camels to kneel down without *the city*
13. daughters of the men of *the city* come out
26:33. the name of *the city* (is) Beer-sheba
28:19. the name of *that city* (was called) Luz
33:18. Jacob came to Shalem *a city of* Shechem,
— and pitched his tent before *the city*.
34:20. came unto the gate of *their city*, and communed with the men of *their city*,
24, 24. all that went out of the gate of *his city*;
25. came upon *the city* boldly,
27. and spoiled *the city*,
28. and that which (was) *in the city*,
35: 5. the terror of God was upon *the cities*
36:32. the name of *his city* (was) Dinhabah.
35. the name of *his city* (was) Avith.

Gen36:39. the name of *his city* (was) Pau;
41:35. let them keep food *in the cities*.
48. and laid up the food *in the cities:*
— field, which (was) round about every *city*,
44: 4. when they were gone out of *the city*,
13. and returned *to the city*.
47:21. he removed them *to cities*
Ex. 1:11. they built for Pharaoh treasure *cities*,
9:29. As soon as I am gone out of *the city*,
33. And Moses went out of *the city*
Lev.14:40. cast them into an unclean place without *the city:*
41. dust that they scrape off without *the city*
45. he shall carry (them) forth out of *the city*
53. let go the living bird out of *the city*
25:29. man sell a dwelling house in *a* walled *city*,
30. the house that (is) *in the* walled *city*
32. Notwithstanding *the cities of* the Levites, (and) the houses of *the cities of* their
33. the house that was sold, *and the city of*
— the houses of *the cities of* the Levites
34. the field of the suburbs of *their cities*
26:25. ye are gathered together within *your cities*,
31. I will make *your cities* waste,
33. land shall be desolate, *and your cities* waste.
Nu. 13:19. what *cities* (they be) that they dwell in,
28. *and the cities* (are) walled, (and) very
20:16. Kadesh, *a city* in the uttermost of thy
21: 2. I will utterly destroy *their cities*.
3. they utterly destroyed them and *their cities:*
25. Israel took all these *cities:* and Israel dwelt in all *the cities of* the Amorites,
26. Heshbon (was) *the city of* Sihon
27. let *the city of* Sihon be built and prepared:
22:36. went out to meet him unto *a city of* Moab,
24:19. shall destroy him that remaineth *of the city*.
31:10. they burnt all *their cities*
32:16. for our cattle, *and cities* for our little ones:
17. little ones shall dwell *in the* fenced *cities*
24. Build you *cities* for your little ones,
26. shall be there *in the cities of* Gilead:
33. the land, *with the cities thereof* in the coasts, (even) *the cities of* the country round
36. And Beth-nimrah, and Beth-haran, fenced *cities:*
38. gave other names unto *the cities*
35: 2. of their possession *cities* to dwell in;
— unto the Levites suburbs *for the cities*
3. And *the cities* shall they have to dwell in;
4. And the suburbs of *the cities*,
— from the wall of *the city* and outward
5. ye shall measure from without *the city*
— *and the city* (shall be) in the midst:
— the suburbs of *the cities*.
6. among *the cities* which ye shall give
— (there shall be) six *cities* for refuge,
— to them ye shall add forty and two *cities*.
7. all *the cities* which ye shall give to the Levites (shall be) forty and eight *cities:*
8. *And the cities* which ye shall give
— one shall give *of his cities* unto the Levites
11. ye shall appoint you *cities* to be *cities of* refuge for you;
12. they shall be unto you *cities* for refuge
13. *And* of these *cities* which ye shall give six *cities* shall ye have for refuge.
14. Ye shall give three *cities* on this side Jordan, and three *cities* shall ye give in the land of Canaan, (which) shall be *cities of* refuge.
15. These six *cities* shall be a refuge,
25. shall restore him to *the city of*
26. come without the border of *the city of*
27. find him without the borders of *the city of*
28. he should have remained *in the city of*
32. him that is fled to *the city of* his refuge,
Deu 1:22. and into what *cities* we shall come.
28. *the cities* (are) great and walled up to heaven;
2:34. we took all *his cities* at that time,
— and the little ones, of every *city*,
35. the spoil of *the cities* which we took.
36. *and* (from) *the city* that (is) by the river,
37. *nor* unto *the cities in* the mountains,
3: 4. we took all *his cities*
— which we took not from them, threescore *cities*,

Deu 3: 5. All these *cities* (were) fenced
— beside unwalled *towns* a great many.
6. men, women, and children, of every *city*.
7. the spoil of *the cities*, we took for a prey
10. All *the cities of* the plain,
— *cities of* the kingdom of Og
12. half mount Gilead, *and the cities thereof*,
19. abide *in your cities* which I have given
4:41. Then Moses severed three *cities*
42. unto one of these *cities* he might live:
6:10. to give thee great and goodly *cities*,
9: 1. *cities* great and fenced up to heaven,
13:12(13). shalt hear (say) in one of *thy cities*,
13(14). withdrawn the inhabitants of *their city*,
15(16). surely smite the inhabitants of *that city*
16(17). and shalt burn with fire *the city*,
19: 1. and dwellest *in their cities*,
2, 7. Thou shalt separate three *cities* for thee
5. he shall flee unto one of those *cities*,
9. then shalt thou add three *cities* more
11. and fleeth into one of these *cities:*
12. elders of *his city* shall send and fetch him
20:10. When thou comest nigh unto *a city*
14. and all that is *in the city*,
15. Thus shalt thou do unto all *the cities*
— (are) not *of the cities of* these nations.
16. *of the cities of* these people,
19. When thou shalt besiege *a city*
20. thou shalt build bulwarks against *the city*
21: 2. they shall measure unto *the cities*
3. *the city* (which is) next unto the slain man, even the elders of *that city* shall take
4. the elders of *that city* shall bring down
6. And all the elders of *that city*,
19. bring him out unto the elders of *his city*,
20. they shall say unto the elders of *his city*,
21. And all the men of *his city* shall stone him
22:15. the elders of *the city* in the gate:
17. spread the cloth before the elders of *the city*.
18. the elders of *that city* shall take that man
21. the men of *her city* shall stone her
23. and a man find her *in the city*,
24. them both out unto the gate of that *city*,
— because she cried not, (being) *in the city*
25: 8. the elders of *his city* shall call him,
28: 3. Blessed (shalt) thou (be) *in the city*,
16. Cursed (shalt) thou (be) *in the city*,
34: 3. *the city of* palm trees, unto Zoar.
Jos. 3:16. very far from *the city* Adam,
6: 3. And ye shall compass *the city*,
— (and) go round about *the city* once.
4. the seventh day ye shall compass *the city*
5. and the wall of *the city* shall fall down flat,
7. Pass on, and compass *the city*,
11. the ark of the Lord compassed *the city*,
14. the second day they compassed *the city*
15. compassed *the city* after the same manner
— they compassed *the city* seven times.
16. the Lord hath given you *the city*.
17. *the city* shall be accursed,
20. the people went up *into the city*,
— and they took *the city*.
21. destroyed all that (was) *in the city*,
24. *And* they burnt *the city* with fire,
26. riseth up and buildeth this *city* Jericho:
8: 1. the king of Ai, and his people, and *his city*,
2. lay thee an ambush *for the city*
4. lie in wait *against the city*, (even) behind *the city:* go not very far from *the city*,
5. will approach unto *the city:*
6. till we have drawn them from *the city*;
7. and seize upon *the city:*
8. when ye have taken *the city*, (that) ye shall set *the city* on fire:
11. drew nigh, and came before *the city*,
12. (כתיב) on the west side *of the city*.
13. the host that (was) on the north *of the city*, and their liers in wait on the west *of the city*,
14. the men of *the city* went out against Israel
— in ambush against him behind *the city*.
16. (כתיב) all the people that (were) *in Ai* (lit. according to כתיב, *in the city*)
— and were drawn away from *the city*.
17. and they left *the city* open,
18. the spear that (he had) in his hand toward *the city*.

Jos. 8.19. they entered into *the city*, and took it, and hasted and set *the city* on fire.
20. the smoke of *the city* ascended
21. the ambush had taken *the city*, and that the smoke of *the city* ascended
22. issued out of *the city* against them ;
27. the spoil of that *city* Israel took
29. at the entering of the gate of *the city*,
9:17. and came unto *their cities* on the third day. *Now their cities* (were) Gibeon, and Chephirah,
10: 2. Gibeon (was) *a* great *city*, as one of *the* royal *cities*,
19. suffer them not to enter into *their cities :*
20. of them entered into fenced *cities*.
37, 39. king thereof, and all *the cities thereof*,
11:12. all *the cities of* those kings,
13. *the cities* that stood still in their strength,
14. all the spoil of these *cities*,
19. not *a city* that made peace with
21. destroyed them utterly with *their cities*.
13: 9, 16. *and the city* that (is) in the midst
10. all *the cities of* Sihon
17. Heshbon, and all *her cities*
21. all *the cities of* the plain,
23. *the cities* and the villages thereof.
25. all *the cities of* Gilead,
28. *the cities*, and their villages.
30. which (are) in Bashan, threescore *cities :*
31. *cities of* the kingdom of Og in Bashan,
14: 4. *cities* to dwell (in), with their suburbs
12. *and* (that) *the cities* (were) great (and) fenced:
15: 9. *the cities of* mount Ephron ;
21. uttermost *cities* of the tribe of the children
32. all *the cities* (are) twenty and nine,
36. fourteen *cities* with their villages:
41. sixteen *cities* with their villages:
44, 54. nine *cities* with their villages:
51. eleven *cities* with their villages:
57. ten *cities* with their villages:
59, 62. six *cities* with their villages:
60. two *cities* with their villages:
62. *and the city of* Salt,
16: 9. *And the* separate *cities* for the children of
— all *the cities* with their villages.
17: 9. these *cities* of Ephraim (are) among *the cities of* Manasseh:
12. (the inhabitants of) those *cities ;*
18: 9. through the land, and described it *by cities*
14. *a city of* the children of Judah:
21. *the cities* of the tribe of the children of
24. twelve *cities* with their villages:
28. fourteen *cities* with their villages.
19: 6. thirteen *cities* and their villages:
7. four *cities* and their villages:
8. villages that (were) round about these *cities*
15. twelve *cities* with their villages.
16. these *cities* with their villages.
22. sixteen *cities* with their villages.
23. *the cities* and their villages.
29. and to *the* strong *city* Tyre ;
30. twenty and two *cities* with their villages.
31. these *cities* with their villages.
35. *And the* fenced *cities* (are) Ziddim, Zer,
38. nineteen *cities* with their villages.
39. *the cities* and their villages.
48. these *cities* with their villages.
50. they gave him *the city* which he asked,
— and he built *the city*,
20: 2. Appoint out for you *cities of* refuge,
4. flee unto one *of* those *cities* shall stand at the entering of the gate of *the city*,
— in the ears of the elders of *that city*, they shall take him *into the city*
6. he shall dwell *in* that *city*,
— and come unto *his own city*,
— unto *the city* from whence he fled.
9. *the cities* appointed for all the children of
21: 2. The Lord commanded...to give us *cities*
3. these *cities* and their suburbs.
4. of the tribe of Benjamin, thirteen *cities*.
5. of the half tribe of Manasseh, ten *cities*.
6. of Manasseh in Bashan, thirteen *cities*.
7. out of the tribe of Zebulun, twelve *cities*.
8. gave by lot unto the Levites these *cities*
9. these *cities* which are (here) mentioned

Jos. 21:12. the fields of *the city*, and the villages
13, 21, 27, 32, 38(36). *a city of* refuge for the
16. nine *cities* out of those two tribes.
18. Almon with her suburbs; four *cities*.
19. All *the cities of* the children of Aaron, the priests, (were) thirteen *cities* with their suburbs.
20. they had *the cities of* their lot
22. Beth-horon with her suburbs; four *cities*.
24. Gath-rimmon with her suburbs; four *cities*.
25. Gath-rimmon with her suburbs; two *cities*.
26. All *the cities* (were) ten with their suburbs
27. Beesh-terah with her suburbs; two *cities*.
29. En-gannim with her suburbs ; four *cities*.
31. Rehob with her suburbs ; four *cities*.
32. Kartan with her suburbs ; three *cities*.
33. All *the cities of* the Gershonites
— thirteen *cities* with their suburbs.
35. Nahalal with her suburbs ; four *cities*.
39(37). Jazer with her suburbs; four *cities*
40(38). *the cities* for the children of Merari
—(—). were (by) their lot twelve *cities*.
41(39). All *the cities of* the Levites
—(—). forty and eight *cities* with their
42(40). These *cities* were *every one* (lit. *city. city*) with their suburbs round about them: thus (were) all these *cities*.
24:13. *and cities* which ye built not,
Jud. 1: 8. and set *the city* on fire.
16. *out of the city of* palm trees
17. the name of *the city* was called Hormah.
23. the name of *the city* before (was) Luz.
24. spies saw a man come forth out of *the city*,
— Shew us,...the entrance into *the city*,
25. he shewed them the entrance into *the city*, they smote *the city* with the edge of the sword ;
26. the land of the Hittites, and built *a city*,
3:13. and possessed *the city of* palm trees.
6:27. his father's houshold, and the men of *the city*,
28. men of *the city* arose early in the morning,
30. the men of *the city* said unto Joash,
8:16. he took the elders of *the city*,
17. and slew the men of *the city*.
27. an ephod thereof, and put it *in his city*,
9:30. Zebul the ruler of *the city*
31. they fortify *the city* against thee.
33. thou shalt rise early, and set upon *the city :*
35, 44. the entering of the gate of *the city :*
43. people (were) come forth out of *the city ;*
45. Abimelech fought *against the city* all that day; and he took *the city*,
— and beat down *the city*,
51. there was a strong tower within *the city*,
— men and women, and all they of *the city*,
10: 4. and they had thirty *cities*,
11:26. all *the cities* that (be) along by the coasts
33. to Minnith, (even) twenty *cities*,
12: 7. was buried *in* (one of) *the cities of* Gilead.
14:18. the men of *the city* said unto him
16: 2. for him all night in the gate of *the city*,
3. took the doors of the gate of *the city*,
17: 8. the man departed *out of the city*
18:27. and burnt *the city* with fire.
28. they built *a city*, and dwelt therein.
29. they called the name of *the city* Dan,
— name of *the city* (was) Laish at the first.
19:11. us turn in into this *city* of the Jebusites,
12. will not turn aside hither into *the city of*
15. he sat him down in a street of *the city :*
17. a wayfaring man in the street of *the city :*
22. the men of *the city*, certain sons of Belial,
20:11. of Israel were gathered against *the city*,
14. themselves together out of *the cities*
15. numbered at that time *out of the cities*
31. were drawn away from *the city ;*
32. them from *the city* unto the highways.
37. and smote all *the city*
38. flame with smoke rise up out of *the city*.
40. the flame began to arise up out of *the city*
— the flame of *the city* ascended
42. them which (came) *out of the cities* they
48. the men of (every) *city*, as the beast,
— they set on fire all *the cities* that they
21:23. repaired *the cities*, and dwelt in them.
Ru. 1:19. all *the city* was moved about them,

Ru. 2:18. she took (it) up, and went into *the city:*
3:15. and she went into *the city.*
4: 2. he took ten men of the elders of *the city,*
1Sa. 1: 3. this man went up *out of his city*
4:13. when the man came *into the city,* and told (it), all *the city* cried out.
5: 9. hand of the Lord was *against the city*
— he smote the men of *the city,*
11. deadly destruction throughout all *the city;*
12. the cry of *the city* went up to heaven.
6:18. the number of all *the cities of* the
— *of* fenced *cities,* and of country villages,
7:14. *the cities* which the Philistines had taken
8:22. Go ye every man *unto his city.*
9: 6. (there is) *in* this *city* a man of God,
10. they went unto *the city*
11. as they went up the hill to *the city,*
12. he came to day *to the city;*
13. As soon as ye be come into *the city,*
14. they went up into *the city:* (and) when they were come into *the city,*
25. down from the high place into *the city,*
27. were going down to the end of *the city,*
10: 5. when thou art come thither to *the city,*
15: 5. Saul came to *a city of* Amalek,
16: 4. the elders of *the town* trembled at his
18: 6. the women came out of all *cities of* Israel,
20: 6. he might run to Beth-lehem *his city:*
29. our family hath a sacrifice *in the city;*
40. Go, carry (them) to *the city.*
42(21:1). and Jonathan went into *the city.*
22:19. Nob, *the city of* the priests,
23: 7. by entering *into a town* that hath gates
10. to destroy *the city* for my sake.
27: 5. give me a place *in* some *town in* (lit. in one of *the cities of*) the country,
— thy servant dwell *in the* royal *city*
28: 3. him in Ramah, *even in his own city.*
30: 3. David and his men came to *the city,*
29. *in the cities of* the Jerahmeelites, and to (them) which (were) *in the cities of* the Kenites,
31: 7. they forsook *the cities,* and fled;
2Sa. 2: 1. I go up into any of *the cities of* Judah?
3. they dwelt *in the cities of* Hebron.
5: 7. Zion: the same (is) *the city of* David.
9. and called it *the city of* David.
6:10. unto him into *the city of* David:
12. the house of Obed-edom into *the city of*
16. the ark of the Lord came into *the city of*
8: 8. from Bero-thai, *cities of* Hadadezer,
10: 3. to search *the city,* and to spy it out,
12. our people, and for *the cities of* our God:
14. and entered into *the city.*
11:16. when Joab observed *the city,*
17. the men of *the city* went out,
20. approached ye so nigh unto *the city*
25. thy battle more strong against *the city,*
12: 1. There were two men *in one city;*
26. of Ammon, and took *the* royal *city.*
27. and have taken *the city of* waters.
28. encamp against *the city,* and take it: lest I take *the city,*
30. he brought forth the spoil of *the city*
31. all *the cities of* the children of Ammon.
15: 2. Of what *city* (art) thou?
12. David's counsellor, *from his city,*
14. and smite *the city* with the edge of the
24. people had done passing out of *the city.*
25. Carry back the ark of God into *the city:*
27. return into *the city* in peace,
34. if thou return to *the city,*
37. David's friend came into *the city,*
17:13. if he be gotten into *a city,* then shall all Israel bring ropes to that *city,*
17. might not be seen to come *into the city:*
23. gat him home to his house, to *his city,*
18: 3. that thou succour us *out of the city.*
19: 3(4). them by stealth that day into *the city,*
37(38). that I may die *in mine own city,*
20: 6. get him fenced *cities,* and escape us.
15. they cast up a bank against *the city,*
16. Then cried a wise woman out of *the city,*
19. thou seekest to destroy *a city*
21. I will depart from *the city.*
22. and they retired from *the city,*
24: 5. on the right side of *the city*

2Sa.24: 7. all *the cities of* the Hivites, and of
1K. 2:10. and was buried *in the city of* David.
3: 1. and brought her into *the city of* David,
4:13. threescore great *cities* with walls
8: 1. *out of the city of* David,
16. I chose no *city* out of all the tribes
44. pray unto the Lord toward *the city*
48. *the city* which thou hast chosen,
9:11. king Solomon gave Hiram twenty *cities*
12. Hiram came out from Tyre to see *the cities*
13. What *cities* (are) these which thou hast
16. the Canaanites that dwelt *in the city,*
19. *the cities of* store that Solomon had, and *cities for* his chariots, and *cities for* his horsemen,
24. daughter came up *out of the city of* David
10:26. he bestowed *in the cities for* chariots,
11:27. repaired the breaches of *the city of*
32. sake, *the city* which I have chosen
36. Jerusalem, *the city* which I have chosen
43. was buried *in the city of* David
12:17. Israel which dwelt *in the cities of* Judah,
13:25. they came and told (it) *in the city*
29. the old prophet came to *the city,*
32. high places which (are) *in the cities of*
14:11. Him that dieth of Jeroboam *in the city*
12. when thy feet enter *into the city,*
21. *the city* which the Lord did choose
31. buried with his fathers *in the city of*
15: 8. they buried him *in the city of* David:
20. he had against *the cities of* Israel,
23. that he did, *and the cities* which he built,
24. buried with his fathers *in the city of*
16: 4. Him that dieth of Baasha *in the city*
18. when Zimri saw that *the city* was taken,
24. the name of *the city* which he built,
17:10. when he came to the gate of *the city,*
20: 2. to Ahab king of Israel *into the city,*
12. (themselves in array) against *the city.*
19. of the provinces came out of *the city,*
30. the rest fled to Aphek, into *the city;*
— Ben-hadad fled, and came into *the city,*
34. *The cities,* which my father took from
21: 8. to the nobles that (were) *in his city,*
11. the men of *his city,* (even) the elders and the nobles who were the inhabitants *in his city,*
13. they carried him forth out *of the city,*
24. Him that dieth of Ahab *in the city*
22:26. Amon the governor of *the city,*
36. Every man to *his city,*
39. all *the cities* that he built,
50(51). buried with his fathers *in the city of*
2K. 2:19. the men of *the city* said unto Elisha, Behold, I pray thee, the situation of this *city* (is) pleasant,
23. came forth little children out of *the city,*
3:19. ye shall smite every fenced *city,* and every choice *city,*
25. *And* they beat down *the cities,*
6:14. came by night, and compassed *the city*
15. an host compassed *the city*
19. not the way, neither (is) this *the city:*
7: 4. If we say, we will enter into *the city,* then the famine (is) *in the city,*
10. and called unto the porter of *the city:*
12. When they come out of *the city,* we shall catch them alive, and get into *the city.*
8:24. buried with his fathers *in the city of* David:
9:15. none go forth (nor) escape out of *the city*
28. with his fathers *in the city of* David.
10: 2. chariots and horses, *a* fenced *city also,*
5. he that (was) over *the city,*
6. the great men of *the city,*
25. went to *the city of* the house of Baal.
11:20. *and the city* was in quiet:
12:21(22). with his fathers *in the city of* David:
13:25. of Ben-hadad the son of Hazael *the cities,*
— beat him, and recovered *the cities of* Israel.
14:20 & 15:7, 38 & 16:20. with his fathers *in the city of* David.
17: 6. *and* in *the cities of* the Medes.
9. built them high places in all *their cities,* from the tower of the watchmen to *the* fenced *city.*
24. and placed (them) *in the cities of* Samaria
— Samaria, and dwelt *in the cities thereof.*

2K. 17:26. and placed *in the cities of* Samaria,
29. every nation *in their cities* wherein they dwelt.
18: 8. from the tower of the watchmen to *the* fenced *city.*
11. *and* in *the cities of* the Medes:
13. come up against all *the* fenced *cities of*
30. this *city* shall not be delivered into the hand
19:13. the king *of the city of* Sepharvaim,
25. shouldest be to lay waste fenced *cities*
32. of Assyria, He shall not come into this *city*,
33. return, and shall not come into this *city*,
34. I will defend this *city*, to save it,
20: 4. (כתיב) gone out into *the* middle *court*, (marg. or, *city*)
6. I will deliver thee and this *city*
— I will defend this *city* for mine own sake,
20. and brought water *into the city*,
23: 5. in the high places *in the cities of* Judah,
8. he brought all the priests out *of the cities of* Judah,
— Joshua the governor of *the city*,
— on a man's left hand at the gate of *the city.*
17. And the men of *the city* told him,
19. the high places that (were) *in the cities of*
27. and will cast off this *city* Jerusalem
24:10. and *the city* was besieged.
11. of Babylon came against *the city*,
25: 2. *the city* was besieged unto the eleventh
3. the famine prevailed *in the city*,
4. And *the city* was broken up,
— the Chaldees (were) against *the city*
11. of the people (that were) left *in the city*,
19. out of *the city* he took an officer
— which were found *in the city*,
— people of the land (that were) found *in the city:*
1Ch 1:43. the name of *his city* (was) Dinhabah.
46. the name of *his city* (was) Avith.
50. the name of *his city* (was) Pai;
2:22. Segub begat Jair, who had three and twenty *cities*
23. towns thereof, (even) threescore *cities.*
4:31. These (were) *their cities* unto the reign of
32. and Tochen, and Ashan, five *cities:*
33. that (were) round about *the* same *cities*,
6:56(41). the fields of *the city*, and the villages
57(42). to the sons of Aaron they gave *the cities of* Judah,
60(45). All *their cities* throughout their families (were) thirteen *cities.*
61(46). (out of) the half (tribe) of Manasseh, by lot, ten *cities.*
62(47). tribe of Manasseh in Bashan, thirteen *cities.*
63(48). of the tribe of Zebulun, twelve *cities.*
64(49). Israel gave to the Levites (these) *cities*
65(50). these *cities*, which are called by (their)
66(51). the sons of Kohath had *cities of* their
67(52). they gave unto them, (of) *the cities of*
9: 2. (dwelt) in their possessions *in their cities*
10: 7. they forsook *their cities*, and fled:
11: 5. the castle of Zion, which (is) *the city of*
7. they called it *the city of* David.
8. he built *the city* round about,
— Joab repaired the rest of *the city.*
13: 2. *in their cities* (and) suburbs, (marg. *in the cities of* their suburbs)
13. to himself to *the city of* David,
15: 1. (David) made him houses *in the city of*
29. came to *the city of* David,
18: 8. Tibhath, and from Chun, *cities of* Hadarezer,
19: 7. themselves together *from their cities*,
9. before the gate of *the city:*
13. for our people, and for *the cities of* our
15. and entered *into the city.*
20: 2. exceeding much spoil out of *the city.*
3. so dealt David with all *the cities of*
27:25. the fields, *in the cities*, and in the villages,
2Ch 1:14. horsemen, which he placed *in the* chariot *cities*,
5: 2. *out of the city of* David,
6: 5. I chose no *city* among all the tribes
34. they pray unto thee toward this *city*
38. *and...the city* which thou hast chosen,
8: 2. *That the cities* which Huram had restored

2Ch 8: 4. in the wilderness, and all *the* store *cities*,
5. fenced *cities*, with walls, gates, and bars;
6. all *the* store *cities* that Solomon had, and all *the* chariot *cities, and the cities of* the horsemen,
11. *out of the city of* David
9:25. whom he bestowed *in the* chariot *cities*,
31. buried in *the city of* David his father:
10:17. of Israel that dwelt *in the cities of* Judah,
11: 5. in Jerusalem, and built *cities* for defence
10. in Judah and in Benjamin fenced *cities.*
12. in every *several city* (lit. *city and city*)
23. unto every fenced *city:* (lit. into all *the* fenced *cities*)
12: 4. he took *the* fenced *cities* which
13. *the city* which the Lord had chosen
16. buried *in the city of* David:
13:19. and took *cities* from him,
14: 1(13:23). buried him *in the city of* David:
5(4). out of all *the cities of* Judah
6(5). he built fenced *cities* in Judah:
7(6). he said unto Judah, Let us build these *cities*,
14(13). they smote all *the cities* round about
—(—). they spoiled all *the cities;*
15: 6. nation was destroyed of nation, *and city of city:*
8. *the cities* which he had taken
16: 4. captains of his armies against *the cities of*
— all *the* store *cities of* Naphtali.
14. made for himself *in the city of* David,
17: 2. placed forces in all *the* fenced *cities of*
— *and in the cities of* Ephraim,
7. to teach *in the cities of* Judah.
9. went about throughout all *the cities of*
12. in Judah castles, *and cities of* store.
13. had much business *in the cities of* Judah:
19. *in the* fenced *cities* throughout all Judah.
18:25. Amon the governor of *the city*,
19: 5. *the* fenced *cities of* Judah, *city by city*, (lit. *to city and city*)
10. your brethren that dwell *in their cities*,
20: 4. out of all *the cities of* Judah they came
21: 1. buried with his fathers *in the city of* David.
3. with fenced *cities* in Judah:
20. they buried him *in the city of* David,
23: 2. gathered the Levites out of all *the cities of*
21. *and the city* was quiet,
24: 5. Go out *unto the cities of* Judah,
16, 25. they buried him *in the city of* David
25:13. fell *upon the cities of* Judah,
28. with his fathers *in the city of* Judah.
26: 6. and built *cities* about Ashdod,
27: 4. *Moreover* he built *cities* in the mountains
9. they buried him *in the city of* David:
28:15. Jericho, *the city of* palm trees,
18. *the cities of* the low country,
25. in every *several city* (lit. *city and city*) of Judah he made high places
27. they buried him *in the city*,
29:20. and gathered the rulers of *the city*,
30:10. the posts passed *from city to city*
31: 1. present went out *to the cities of* Judah,
— to his possession, *into their own cities.*
6. Israel and Judah, that dwelt *in the cities of*
15. *in the cities of* the priests,
19. the suburbs of *their cities*,
— in every *several city*, (lit. *city and city*) the men that were
32: 1. encamped against *the* fenced *cities*,
3. fountains which (were) without *the city:*
5. repaired Millo (in) *the city of* David,
6. in the street of the gate of *the city*,
18. that they might take *the city.*
29. *Moreover* he provided him *cities*,
30. to the west side *of the city of* David.
33:14. he built a wall without *the city of* David,
— all *the* fenced *cities* of Judah.
15. and cast (them) out *of the city.*
34: 6. *And* (so did he) *in the cities of* Manasseh,
8. Maaseiah the governor of *the city*,
Ezr. 2: 1. every one *unto his city;*
70. the Nethinims, dwelt *in their cities*, and all Israel *in their cities.*
3: 1. the children of Israel (were) *in the cities*,
10:14. them which have taken strange wives *in our cities*

Ezr.10:14. the elders of *every city*, (lit. *city and city*)
Neh 2: 3. *the city*, the place of my fathers'
5. *the city* of my fathers' sepulchres,
8. the wall of *the city*,
3:15. the stairs that go down *from the city of*
7: 4. *the city* (was) large and great:
6. every one *unto his city*;
73. all Israel, dwelt *in their cities*;
— children of Israel (were) *in their cities*.
8:15. publish and proclaim in all *their cities*,
9:25. they took strong *cities*,
10:37(38). the tithes in all *the cities of* our
11: 1. to dwell in Jerusalem *the* holy *city*, and nine parts (to dwell) *in* (other) *cities*.
3. *but in the cities of* Judah dwelt every one in his possession *in their cities*,
9. son of Senuah (was) second over *the city*.
18. the Levites *in the* holy *city*
20. in all *the cities of* Judah,
12:37. the stairs of *the city of* David,
44. out of the fields of *the cities* the portions
13:18. this evil upon us, and upon this *city*?
Est. 3:15. *but the city* Shushan was perplexed.
4: 1. went out into the midst of *the city*, and
6. unto the street of *the city*,
6: 9. horseback through the street of *the city*,
11. horseback through the street of *the city*,
8:11. the Jews which (were) in *every city* (lit. *city and city*) to gather
15. *and the city* of Shushan rejoiced
17. and in *every city*, (lit. *city and city*)
9: 2. themselves together *in their cities*
19. that dwelt *in the* unwalled *towns*,
28. every province, *and every city*; (lit. *and city and city*)
Job 15:28. he dwelleth in desolate *cities*,
24:12. Men groan from *out of the city*,
Ps. 9: 6(7). *and* thou hast destroyed *cities*;
31:21(22). marvellous kindness *in a* strong *city*.
46: 4(5). shall make glad *the city of* God,
48: 1(2). *in the city of* our God,
8(9). so have we seen *in the city of* the Lord of hosts, *in the city of* our God:
55: 9(10). seen violence and strife *in the city*.
59: 6(7),14(15). and go round about *the city*.
60: 9(11). bring me (into) *the* strong *city*?
69:35(36). save Zion, and will build *the cities of*
72:16. (they) *of the city* shall flourish like grass
87: 3. things are spoken of thee, *O city of*
101: 8. wicked doers *from the city of* the Lord.
107: 4. they found no *city* to dwell in.
7. that they might go to *a city of* habitation.
36. they may prepare *a city for* habitation;
108:10(11). bring me into *the* strong *city*?
122: 3. Jerusalem is builded *as a city* that is
127: 1. except the Lord keep *the city*,
Pro. 1:21. *in the city* she uttereth her words,
16:32. he that taketh *a city*.
21:22. A wise (man) scaleth *the city of* the
25:28. (like) *a city* (that is) broken down,
Ecc. 7:19. ten mighty (men) which are *in the city*.
8:10. they were forgotten *in the city*
9:14. *a* little *city*, and few men within it;
15. by his wisdom delivered *the city*;
10:15. he knoweth not how to go to *the city*.
Cant.3: 2. I will rise now, and go about *the city*
3. that go about *the city* found me:
5: 7. that went about *the city* found me,
Isa. 1: 7. *your cities* (are) burned with fire:
8. *as a* besieged *city*.
26. *The city of* righteousness, the faithful
6:11. *the cities* be wasted without inhabitant,
14:17. *and* destroyed *the cities thereof*;
21. nor fill the face of the world with *cities*.
31. Howl, O gate; cry, *O city*;
17: 1. is taken away *from* (being) *a city*,
2. *The cities of* Aroer (are) forsaken:
9. his strong *cities* be as a forsaken bough,
19: 2. against his neighbour; *city against city*,
18. five *cities* in the land of Egypt
— called, *The city of* destruction.
22: 2. that art full of stirs, *a* tumultuous *city*,
9. the breaches of *the city of* David,
23:16. Take an harp, go about *the city*,
24:12. *In the city* is left desolation,
25: 2. thou hast made *of a city* an heap;
— of strangers *to be no city*; (lit. *from a city*)

Isa. 26: 1. We have *a* strong *city*;
27:10. *the* defenced *city* (shall be) desolate,
32:14. the multitude of *the city* shall be left;
19. *the city* shall be low in a low place.
33: 8. he hath despised *the cities*,
36: 1. *the* defenced *cities of* Judah,
15. this *city* shall not be delivered
37:13. the king *of the city of* Sepharvaim,
26. shouldest be to lay waste defenced *cities*
33. He shall not come into this *city*,
34. shall not come into this *city*,
35. I will defend this *city*
38: 6. I will deliver thee and this *city*
— and I will defend this *city*.
40: 9. say *unto the cities of* Judah, Behold your
42:11. Let the wilderness *and the cities thereof*
44:26. *and to the cities of* Judah, Ye shall be
45:13. he shall build *my city*,
48: 2. they call themselves *of the* holy *city*,
52: 1. O Jerusalem, *the* holy *city*:
54: 3. *and* make *the* desolate *cities* to be
60:14. they shall call thee, *The city of* the Lord,
61: 4. they shall repair *the* waste *cities*,
62:12. *A city* not forsaken.
64:10(9). Thy holy *cities* are a wilderness,
66: 6. A voice of noise *from the city*,
Jer. 1:15. against all *the cities of* Judah.
18. have made thee this day *a* defenced *city*,
2:15. *his cities* are burned without inhabitant.
28. the number of *thy cities* are thy gods,
3:14. I will take you one *of a city*,
4: 5. let us go into *the* defenced *cities*.
7. *thy cities* shall be laid waste,
16. their voice against *the cities of* Judah.
26. *the cities thereof* were broken down
29. *The* whole *city* shall flee
— every *city* (shall be) forsaken,
5: 6. a leopard shall watch over *their cities*:
17. they shall impoverish thy fenced *cities*,
6: 6. Jerusalem: this (is) *the city* to be visited;
7:17. what they do *in the cities of* Judah
34. I cause to cease *from the cities of* Judah,
8:14. let us enter into *the* defenced *cities*,
16. *the city*, and those that dwell therein.
9:11(10). will make *the cities of* Judah desolate,
10:22. to make *the cities of* Judah desolate,
11: 6. all these words *in the cities of* Judah,
12. Then shall *the cities of* Judah
13. the number of *thy cities* were thy gods,
13:19. *The cities of* the south shall be shut up,
14:18. if I enter into *the city*,
15: 8. and terrors upon *the city*.
17:24. no burden through the gates of this *city*
25. shall there enter into the gates of this *city*
— and this *city* shall remain for ever.
26. they shall come *from the cities of* Judah,
19: 8. I will make this *city* desolate,
11. so will I break this people and this *city*,
12. and (even) make this *city* as Tophet:
15. upon this *city* and upon all *her towns*
20: 5. I will deliver all the strength of this *city*,
16. *as the cities* which the Lord overthrew,
21: 4. assemble them into the midst of this *city*.
6. I will smite the inhabitants of this *city*,
7. such as are left *in* this *city*
9. He that abideth *in* this *city* shall die
10. I have set my face *against* this *city*
22: 6. *cities* (which) are not inhabited.
8. many nations shall pass by this *city*,
— the Lord done thus *unto* this great *city*?
23:39. forsake you, and *the city* that I gave
25:18. Jerusalem, and *the cities of* Judah,
29. I begin to bring evil *on the city*
26: 2. speak unto all *the cities of* Judah,
6. and will make this *city* a curse
9. *and* this *city* shall be desolate
11. he hath prophesied against this *city*,
12. against this house and against this *city*
15. upon yourselves, and upon this *city*,
20. who prophesied against this *city*
27:17. wherefore should this *city* be laid waste?
19. the vessels that remain *in* this *city*,
29: 7. And seek the peace of *the city*
16. all the people that dwelleth *in* this *city*,
30:18. *the city* shall be builded upon her own heap,
31:21. turn again to these *thy cities*.
23. the land of Judah *and in the cities thereof*,

Jer. 31:24. in Judah itself, and in all *the cities thereof*
38. *the city* shall be built to the Lord
32: 3. give this *city* into the hand of the king
24. the mounts, they are come unto *the city*
— *and the city* is given into the hand of the
25. *the city* is given into the hand of the
28. I will give this *city* into the hand
29. the Chaldeans, that fight against this *city*, shall come and set fire on this *city*,
31. this *city* hath been to me (as) a provocation
36. concerning this *city*, whereof ye say,
44. Jerusalem, *and in the cities of* Judah, *and in the cities of* the mountains, *and in the cities of* the valley, *and in the cities of*
33: 4. concerning the houses of this *city*,
5. I have hid my face *from* this *city*.
10. *in the cities of* Judah, and in
12. in all *the cities thereof*, shall be
13. *In the cities of* the mountains, *in the cities of* the vale, *and in the cities of* the south,
— *and in the cities of* Judah,
34: 1. Jerusalem, and against all *the cities thereof*,
2. I will give this *city* into the hand of
7. Jerusalem, and against all *the cities of* Judah
— and against Azekah: for these defenced *cities* remained *of the cities of* Judah.
22. cause them to return to this *city*;
— I will make *the cities of* Judah a desolation
36: 6. all Judah that come out *of their cities*.
9. *from the cities of* Judah unto Jerusalem.
37: 8. and fight against this *city*,
10. and burn this *city* with fire.
21. until all the bread in *the city* were spent.
38: 2. He that remaineth *in* this *city* shall die
3. This *city* shall surely be given into the
4. the men of war that remain *in* this *city*,
9. (there is) no more bread *in the city*.
17. *and* this *city* shall not be burned with fire;
18. shall this *city* be given into the hand of
23. and thou shalt cause this *city* to be burned
39: 2. the ninth (day) of the month, *the city* was
4. went forth out of *the city* by night,
9. the people that remained *in the city*,
16. I will bring my words upon this *city*
40: 5. made governor over *the cities of* Judah,
10. dwell *in your cities* that ye have taken.
41: 7. when they came into the midst of *the city*,
44: 2. upon all *the cities of* Judah;
6, 17, 21. *in the cities of* Judah and in the
46: 8. destroy *the city* and the inhabitants thereof.
47: 2. *the city*, and them that dwell therein:
48: 8. the spoiler shall come upon every *city*, *and* no *city* shall escape:
9. *for the cities thereof* shall be desolate,
15. spoiled, *and* gone up (out of) *her cities*,
24. all *the cities of* the land of Moab,
28. O ye that dwell in Moab, leave *the cities*,
49: 1. his people dwell *in his cities?*
13. *the cities thereof* shall be perpetual wastes.
25. How is *the city of* praise not left,
50:32. I will kindle a fire *in his cities*,
51:31. shew the king of Babylon that *his city* is
43. *Her cities* are a desolation,
52: 5. *the city* was besieged unto the eleventh year
6. the famine was sore *in the city*,
7. *the city* was broken up,
— went forth *out of the city* by night
— Chaldeans (were) by *the city* round about:
15. the people that remained *in the city*,
25. He took also out of *the city* an eunuch,
— which were found *in the city*;
— that were found in the midst of *the city*.
Lam. 1: 1. How doth *the city* sit solitary,
19. mine elders gave up the ghost *in the city*,
2:12. the wounded in the streets of *the city*,
15. (Is) this *the city* that (men) call
3:51. because of all the daughters of *my city*.
5:11. the maids *in the cities of* Judah.
Eze. 4: 1. and pourtray upon it *the city*,
3. wall of iron between thee and *the city*:
5: 2. a third part in the midst of *the city*,
6: 6. *the cities* shall be laid waste,
7:15. he that (is) *in the city*,
23. *and the city* is full of violence.
9: 1. them that have charge over *the city*
4. Go through the midst of *the city*,
5. Go ye after him *through the city*,

Eze. 9: 7. And they went forth, and slew *in the city*.
9. *and the city* full of perverseness:
10: 2. scatter (them) over *the city*.
11: 2. and give wicked counsel *in* this *city*:
6. Ye have multiplied your slain *in* this *city*,
23. went up from the midst of *the city*,
— which (is) on the east side *of the city*.
12:20. *And the cities* that are inhabited shall be
17: 4. he set it *in a city of* merchants.
19: 7. *and* he laid waste *their cities*;
21:19(24). at the head of the way to *the city*.
22: 2. wilt thou judge *the* bloody *city?*
3. *The city* sheddeth blood in the midst
24: 6, 9. Woe to *the* bloody *city*,
25: 9. I will open the side of Moab *from the cities*, *from his cities* (which are) on his
26:10. as men enter into *a city wherein is made* (lit. *of*) a breach.
17. *the* renowned *city*, which wast strong in
19. When I shall make thee *a* desolate *city*, *like the cities* that are not inhabited;
29:12. countries (that are) desolate, *and her cities* among *the cities* (that are) laid waste
30: 7. *and her cities* shall be in the midst of *the cities* (that are) wasted.
33:21. *The city* is smitten.
35: 4. I will lay *thy cities* waste,
9. *and thy cities* shall not return:
36: 4. *and to the cities* that are forsaken,
10. *the cities* shall be inhabited,
33. also cause (you) to dwell in *the cities*,
35. *and* ruined *cities* (are become) fenced,
38. *the* waste *cities* be filled with flocks
39: 9. they that dwell in *the cities of* Israel
16. the name of *the city* (shall be) Hamonah.
40: 1. the fourteenth year after that *the city* was
2. as the frame of *a city* on the south.
43: 3. when I came to destroy *the city*:
45: 6. possession of *the city* five thousand broad,
7. possession of *the city*, before the oblation
— before the possession of *the city*,
48:15. a profane (place) *for the city*,
— *the city* shall be in the midst thereof.
17. the suburbs *of the city*
18. for food unto them that serve *the city*.
19. they that serve *the city*
20. with the possession of *the city*.
21. and of the possession of *the city*,
22. from the possession of *the city*,
30. the goings out of *the city*
31. the gates of *the city*
35. name of *the city* from (that) day (shall be),
Dan. 9:16. turned away *from thy city* Jerusalem,
18. *and the city* which is called by thy name:
19. *thy city* and thy people are called by thy
24. upon thy people and upon thy holy *city*,
26. *and* the people...shall destroy *the city* and the sanctuary;
11:15. and take *the* most fenced *cities*: (marg. *city of* munitions)
Hos. 8:14. Judah hath multiplied fenced *cities*: but I will send a fire *upon his cities*,
11: 6. the sword shall abide *on his cities*,
9. I will not enter *into the city*.
13:10. that may save thee in all *thy cities?*
Joel 2: 9. They shall run to and fro *in the city*;
Am. 3: 6. Shall a trumpet be blown *in the city*,
— shall there be evil *in a city*,
4: 6. cleanness of teeth in all *your cities*,
7. I caused it to rain upon one *city*, and caused it not to rain upon another *city*:
8. (or) three *cities* wandered unto one *city*,
5: 3. *The city* that went out (by) a thousand
6: 8. will I deliver up *the city* with all
7:17. Thy wife shall be an harlot *in the city*,
9:14. they shall build *the* waste *cities*,
Obad. 20. shall possess *the cities of* the south.
Jon. 1: 2. go to Nineveh, that great *city*,
3: 2. go unto Nineveh, that great *city*,
3. Nineveh was *an* exceeding great *city*
4. Jonah began to enter *into the city*
4: 5. Jonah went out of *the city*, and sat on the east side *of the city*,
— might see what would become *of the city*,
11. should not I spare Nineveh, that great *city*,
Mic. 5:11(10). I will cut off *the cities of* thy land,
14(13). so will I destroy *thy cities*.

Mic. 6: 9. The Lord's voice crieth *unto the city*,
7:12. from Assyria, *and* (from) *the* fortified *cities*,
Nah. 3: 1. Woe to *the* bloody *city!*
Hab. 2:12. that buildeth *a town* with blood,
Zep. 1:16. and alarm against *the* fenced *cities*,
2:15. *the* rejoicing *city* that dwelt carelessly,
3: 1. filthy and polluted, to *the* oppressing *city!*
6. *their cities* are destroyed,
Zec. 1:12. on Jerusalem and on *the cities of* Judah,
17. *My cities* through prosperity shall yet be
7: 7. and in prosperity, *and the cities thereof*
8: 3. Jerusalem shall be called *a city of* truth;
5. of *the city* shall be full of boys and girls
20. the inhabitants of many *cities:*
14: 2. and *the city* shall be taken,
— half of *the city* shall go forth into captivity,
— the people shall not be cut off from *the city.*

5782 עִיר ^{n}ğeer, m.

Ps. 73:20. *when thou awakest*, (lit. probably, *with wrath*) thou shalt despise

Note.—The English Translation has taken this to be an Infinitive;—some place Jer. 15:8 and Hos. 11:9 under this heading.

5894 עִיר ^{n}ğeer, Ch. m.

Dan. 4:13(10). *a watcher* and an holy one came
17(14). This matter (is) by the decree of *the watchers*,
23(20). whereas the king saw *a watcher*

5903 עֵירֹם ^{n}ğēh-rōhm', adj.

Gen. 3: 7. they knew that they (were) *naked;*
10. I was afraid, because I (was) *naked;*
11. Who told thee that thou (wast) *naked?*
Deu 28:48. in hunger, and in thirst, *and in nakedness*,
Eze. 16: 7. thou (wast) *naked* and bare.
22. when thou wast *naked* and bare,
39. and leave thee *naked* and bare.
18: 7. *and* hath covered *the naked* with a garment;
16. *and* hath covered *the naked* with a garment,
23:29. shall leave thee *naked* and bare:

5906 עַיִשׁ ^{n}ğah'-yish, m.

Job 38:32. *or* canst thou guide *Arcturus* with his sons?

5908 עַכָּבִישׁ ^{n}ğak-kāh-veesh', m.

Job 8:14. whose trust (shall be) *a spider's* web.
Isa. 59: 5. and weave *the spider's* web:

5909 עַכְבָּר ^{n}ğac̣h-bāhr', m.

Lev. 11:29. the weasel, *and the mouse*,
1Sa. 6: 4. and five golden *mice*,
5. images of *your mice*
11. the coffer with *the mice*
18. *And the* golden *mice*,
Isa. 66:17. the abomination, *and the mouse*,

5913 עָכַס [^{n}gāh-c̣has'].

* PIEL.—*Future.* *

Isa. 3:16. *making a tinkling* with their feet:

5914 עֶכֶס ^{n}ğeh'-c̣hes, m.

Pro. 7:22. *or as* a fool to the correction of *the stocks;*
Isa. 3:18. the bravery of (their) *tinkling ornaments*

5916 עָכַר ^{n}gāh-c̣har'.

* KAL.—*Preterite.* *

Gen 34:30. *Ye have troubled* me to make me to stink
Jos. 6:18. the camp of Israel a curse, *and trouble* it.
Jos. 7:25. Why *hast thou troubled* us?
1Sa. 14:29. My father *hath troubled* the land:
1K. 18:18. *I have* not *troubled* Israel;

KAL.—*Future.*

Jos. 7:25. the Lord *shall trouble thee* this day.

KAL.—*Participle* Poel.

Jud. 11:35. thou art *one of them that trouble* me:
1K. 18:17. (Art) thou he *that troubleth* Israel?
1Ch. 2: 7. Achar, *the troubler of* Israel,
Pro 11:17. *but* (he that is) cruel *troubleth* his own
29. *He that troubleth* his own house
15:27. greedy of gain *troubleth* his own house;

* NIPHAL.—*Preterite.* *

Ps. 39: 2(3). my sorrow *was stirred.* (marg. *troubled*)

NIPHAL.—*Participle.*

Pro. 15: 6. in the revenues of the wicked *is trouble.*

עַכְשׁוּב ^{n}ğac̣h-shoov', m. 5919

Ps. 140: 3(4). *adders'* poison (is) under their lips.

עַל ^{n}ğal, part. prep. 5921

Gen. 1: 2. darkness (was) *upon* the face of the deep.
20. fly *above* the earth *in* the open firmament
6: 1. to multiply *on* the face of the earth,
8: 1. made a wind to pass *over* the earth,
14: 6. El-paran, which (is) *by* the wilderness.
18: 5. for therefore are ye come *to* your servant.
19:17. Escape *for* thy life;
24: 9. sware to him *concerning* that matter.
30. he stood *by* the camels *at* the well.
27:41. Esau hated Jacob *because of* the blessing
31:20. *in that* he told him not that he fled.
50. take (other) wives *beside* my daughters,
32:11(12). the mother *with* (marg. *upon*) the children.
40: 2. was wroth *against* two (of) his officers,
43: 7. we told him *according to* the tenor
48: 6. shall be called *after* the name of
Ex. 23:13. neither let it be heard *out of* thy mouth.
30:13. passeth *among* them that are numbered,
35:22. came, *both* men *and* (lit. men *on*) women,
Lev. 15:25. *beyond the time of* her separation;
Nu. 3:46. which are more *than* the Levites;
31: 8. *beside the rest of* them that were slain;
Jud. 15: 8. he smote them hip *and* thigh
1K. 18:21. How long halt ye *between* two opinions?
1Ch. 9:28. And (certain) of them *had the charge of* (lit. (were) *over*) the ministering vessels,
2Ch 20: 3. proclaimed a fast *throughout* all Judah.
21:16. the Arabians, that (were) near (lit. *at* the hand of) the Ethiopians:
Job 22:24. shalt thou lay up gold *as* (marg. *on*) dust,
Jer. 1:16. against them *touching* all their wickedness,
8: 6. no man repented him *of* his wickedness,
52: 3. For *through* the anger of the Lord
Eze 28:17. corrupted thy wisdom *by reason of* thy
&c. &c.

It is combined with prefixes; as כְּעַל

2Ch 32:19. God of Jerusalem, *as against* the gods
Ps. 119:14. *as* (much as) *in* all riches.
Isa. 59:18. *According to* (their) deeds, *accordingly* he

מֵעַל

Gen. 1: 7. waters which (were) *above* the firmament:
4:14. driven me out...*from* the face of
7: 4. I destroy *from off* the face of the earth.
24:64. she lighted *off* the camel.
40:17. out of the basket *upon* my head.
Ex. 25:22. with thee *from above* the mercy seat,
40:36. taken up *from over* the tabernacle,
Deu. 9:17. and cast them *out of* my two hands,
2Ch 33: 8. the foot of Israel *from out of* the land
Ecc. 5: 8(7). (he that is) higher *than* the highest
Jer. 36:21. the princes which stood *beside* the king.
Eze 32:13. the beasts thereof *from beside* the great
Am. 7:17. go into captivity *forth of* his land.
&c. &c.

When combined with pronominal suffixes, עַל is used with the same variety of meaning.

5920 עָל gāhl & עַל gal, m.

Gen27:39. and of the dew of heaven *from above;*
49:25. with blessings of heaven *above,*
2Sa.23: 1. the man (who was) raised up *on high,*
Ps. 50: 4. call to the heavens *from above,*
Hos. 7:16. They return, (but) not to *the most High:*
11: 7. though they called them to *the most High,*

5922 עַל gal, Ch. part. prep.

Ezr. 4: 8. wrote a letter *against* Jerusalem
11. that they sent *unto him,* (even) *unto* Artaxerxes the king;
12. Jews which came up from thee *to us*
14. there*fore* have we sent
15. *for* which cause was this city destroyed.
17. *unto* Rehum the chancellor,
18. The letter which ye sent *unto us*
19. made insurrection *against* kings,
20. *over* Jerusalem, which have ruled over
22. that ye fail not to do)(this:
23. to Jerusalem *unto* the Jews,
5: 1. prophesied *unto* the Jews
— (even) *unto them.*
3. At the same time came *to them*
5. the eye of their God was *upon* the elders
— by letter *concerning* this (matter).
6. sent *unto* Darius the king:
7. They sent a letter *unto him,*
15. house of God be builded *in* his place.
17. if (it seem) good *to* the king,
— let the king send his pleasure *to us concerning* this matter.
6: 7. this house of God *in* his place.
11. let him be hanged *thereon;*
— his house be made a dunghill *for* this.
17. for a sin offering *for* all Israel,
18. *for* the service of God,
7:14. to enquire *concerning* Judah
17. and offer them *upon* the altar
18. shall seem good *to thee, and to* thy brethren,
23. why should there be wrath *against* the
24. tribute, or custom, *upon them.*
Dan. 2:10. There is not a man *upon* the earth that
15. Why (lit. *For* what) is the decree (so) hasty
18. *concerning* this secret;
24. Daniel went in *unto* Arioch,
28. visions of thy head *upon* thy bed,
29. (into thy mind) *upon* thy bed,
30. but *for* (their) sakes that shall make
34. which smote the image *upon* his feet
46. Nebuchadnezzar fell *upon* his face,
48. and made him ruler *over* the
— chief of the governors *over* all the
49. and Abed-nego, *over* the affairs of the
3:12. Jews whom thou hast set *over*
— these men, O king, have not regarded (marg. set no regard *upon*) *thee:*
16. to answer thee *in* this matter.
19. was changed *against* Shadrach,
— one seven times *more* than (lit. *above* that) it was wont
28. his servants that trusted *in him,*
29. which speak any thing amiss *against*
4: 5(2). and the thoughts *upon* my bed
8(5). Daniel came *in* before me,
10(7). visions of mine head *in* my bed;
13(10). the visions of my head *upon* my bed,
16(13). and let seven times pass *over him.*
17(14). setteth up *over it* the basest of men.
23(20). till seven times pass *over him;*
24(21). come *upon* my lord the king:
25(22). and seven times shall pass *over thee,*
27(24). let my counsel be acceptable *unto thee,*
28(25). All this came *upon* the king
29(26). he walked *in* (marg. or, *upon*) the palace
32(29). and seven times shall pass *over thee,*
33(30). thing fulfilled *upon* Nebuchadnezzar:
34(31). understanding returned *unto me,*
36(33). my reason returned *unto me;*
—(—). and brightness returned *unto me;*
—(—). *and* I was established *in* my kingdom,
5: 5. the candlestick *upon* the plaister
7. a chain of gold *about* his neck,
Dan. 5: 9. his countenance was changed *in him,*
14. I have even heard *of thee,*
16. I have heard *of thee,* that thou canst
— a chain of gold *about* thy neck,
21. he appointeth *over it* whomsoever he will.
23. *But* hast lifted up thyself *against*
29. (put) a chain of gold *about* his neck, and made a proclamation *concerning him,*
6: 1(2). It pleased Darius to set *over*
3(4). Daniel was preferred *above* the
—(—). the king thought to set him *over*
4(5). any error or fault found *in him.*
5(6). except we find (it) *against him*
6(7). assembled together *to* the king,
10(11). he kneeled *upon* his knees
12(13). *concerning* the king's decree;
13(14). regardeth not (lit. setteth not his mind *upon*) *thee,* O king, *nor* (lit. *nor upon*) the decree that thou hast signed,
14(15). was sore displeased *with himself, and* set (his) heart *on* Daniel
15(16). assembled *unto* the king,
17(18). and laid *upon* the mouth of the den,
18(19). and his sleep went *from him.*
23(24). was the king exceeding glad *for him,*
7: 1. and visions of his head *upon* his bed:
4. *and* made stand *upon* the feet
6. which had *upon* the back of it
16. near *unto* one of them that stood by, and asked him the truth *of* all this.
19. would know the truth *of* the fourth beast,
20. *And of* the ten horns that (were)
28. my countenance changed *in me:*

עֹל gōhl, m. 5923

Gen27:40. thou shalt break *his yoke* from off thy neck.
Lev.26:13. I have broken the bands of *your yoke,*
Nu. 19: 2. upon which never came *yoke:*
Deu21: 3. which hath not drawn *in the yoke,*
28:48. he shall put *a yoke of* iron upon thy neck,
1Sa. 6: 7. on which there hath come no *yoke,*
1K. 12: 4. Thy father made *our yoke* grievous:
— *and his* heavy *yoke* which he put upon us, lighter, (lit. *and* lighten *from his yoke*)
9. *the yoke* which thy father did put upon us
10. Thy father made *our yoke* heavy,
11. my father did lade you with *a* heavy *yoke,* I will add to *your yoke:*
14. My father made *your yoke* heavy, and I will add to *your yoke:*
2Ch 10: 4. Thy father made *our yoke* grievous:
— *and* (lit. *and from*) *his* heavy *yoke* that he put upon us,
9. *the yoke* that thy father did put upon us?
10. Thy father made *our yoke* heavy,
11. my father put *a* heavy *yoke* upon you, I will put more to *your yoke:*
14. My father made *your yoke* heavy,
Isa. 9: 4(3). thou hast broken *the yoke of* his burden,
10:27. *and his yoke* from off thy neck, and *the yoke* shall be destroyed
14:25. then shall *his yoke* depart from off them,
47: 6. hast thou very heavily laid *thy yoke.*
Jer. 2:20. of old time I have broken *thy yoke,*
5: 5. these have altogether broken *the yoke,*
27: 8, 11, 12. *under the yoke of* the king of
28: 2. broken *the yoke of* the king of Babylon.
4. break *the yoke of* the king of Babylon.
11. so will I break *the yoke of* Nebuchadnezzar
14. I have put *a yoke of* iron upon the neck
30: 8. I will break *his yoke* from off thy neck,
Lam. 1:14. *The yoke of* my transgressions is bound
3:27. (It is) good for a man that he bear *the yoke*
Eze.34:27. I have broken the bands of *their yoke,*
Hos11: 4. take off *the yoke* on their jaws,

עֵלָּא gēhl-lāh', Ch. prep. 5924

Dan. 6: 2(3). *And over* these three presidents;

עִלֵּג [gil-lēhg'], adj. 5926

Isa. 32: 4. the tongue of *the stammerers* shall be ready to speak

5927 **עָלָה** *gāh-lāh'.*

*** KAL.—*Preterite.* ***

Gen19:15. when the morning *arose*,
28. the smoke of the country *went up*
32:26(27). Let me go, for the day *breaketh.*
40:10. her blossoms *shot forth ;*
44:24. when *we came up* unto thy servant
49: 4. *thou wentest up* to thy father's bed;
— *he went up* to my couch. (marg. or, my couch *is gone*)
9. my son, *thou art gone up :*
Ex. 1:10. *and* (so) *get them up* out of the land.
8: 3(7:28). *which shall go up* and come into thine house,
12:38. a mixed multitude *went up*
13:18. the children of Israel *went up*
17:10. Moses, Aaron, and Hur *went up*
19: 3. Moses *went up* unto God,
24. *and thou shalt come up*, thou, and Aaron
34: 2. *and come up* in the morning unto mount
Lev.16: 9. the goat upon which the Lord's lot *fell*,
10. the goat, on which the lot *fell*
Nu. 13:17. *and go up* into the mountain:
31. the men that *went up* with him
14:40. *and will go up* unto the place
19: 2. upon which never *came* yoke:
Deu. 5: 5. and *went* not *up* into the mount;
17: 8. *and get thee up* into the place
25: 7. *then let* his brother's wife *go up*
Jos. 2: 8. she *came up* unto them upon the roof;
4:19. the people *came up* out of Jordan
6: 5. *and* the people *shall ascend up*
8:11. (the people) of war that (were) with him, *went up*,
20. the smoke of the city *ascended up*
21. the smoke of the city *ascended*,
10: 9. came unto them suddenly, (and) *went up*
33. king of Gezer *came up* to help Lachish;
14: 8. my brethren that *went up* with me
15: 3. *and ascended up* on the south side
— *and went up* to Adar,
6. *And* the border *went up* to Beth-hogla,
— *and* the border *went up* to the stone of Bohan
7. *And* the border *went up* toward Debir
8. *And* the border *went up* by the valley
— *and* the border *went up* to the top of the mountain
18:12. *and* the border *went up* to the side of
— *and went up* through the mountains
19:11. *And* their border *went up* toward the sea,
12. *and goeth up* to Japhia,
Jud. 1:16. Moses' father in law, *went up* out of the city
4:12. Barak the son of Abinoam *was gone up*
6: 3. *that* the Midianites *came up*,
— *even they came up* against them;
12: 3. *are ye come up* unto me this day,
15:10. Why *are ye come up* against us? And they answered, To bind Samson *are we come up*,
16:17. There *hath* not *come* a razor upon mine head;
18. *Then* the lords of the Philistines *came up*
20: 3. that the children of Israel *were gone up*
40. the flame of the city *ascended up*
21: 5. *came* not *up* with the congregation
— him that *came* not *up* to the Lord
8. *came* not *up* to Mizpeh to the Lord?
Ru. 4: 1. Then *went* Boaz *up* to the gate,
1Sa. 1: 3. *And* this man *went up* out of his city
22. But Hannah *went* not *up ;*
6: 7. on which there *hath come* no yoke,
14:10. Come up unto us; *then we will go up :*
21. *went up* with them into the camp
15:34. Saul *went up* to his house to Gibeah
24:22(23). David and his men *gat them up* unto the hold.
29:11. the Philistines *went up* to Jezreel.
2Sa.15:30. *and they went up*, weeping as they
22: 9. *There went up* a smoke out of his nostrils,
1K. 1:35. *Then ye shall come up* after him,
9:16. Pharaoh king of Egypt *had gone up*,
24. Pharaoh's daughter *came up*
14:25. Shishak king of Egypt *came up* against
1K. 18:42. Elijah *went up* to the top of Carmel;
2K. 1: 4, 6, 16. that bed on which *thou art gone up*,
6. *There came* a man *up* to meet us,
7. What manner of man (was he) which *came up*
3:21. heard that the kings *were come up*
17: 3. Against him *came up* Shalmaneser
18: 9. Shalmaneser king of Assyria *came up*
13. *did* Sennacherib king of Assyria *come up*
25. *Am I* now *come up* without the Lord
19:23. multitude of my chariots I *am come up*
28. thy tumult *is come up* into mine ears,
20: 8. *and that I shall go up* into the house of
23:29. Pharaoh-nechoh king of Egypt *went up*
24: 1. Nebuchadnezzar king of Babylon *came up*,
10. the servants of Nebuchadnezzar...*came up*
1Ch 27:24. *was* the number *put* (marg. *ascended*)
2Ch 12: 2. Shishak king of Egypt *came up*
16: 1. Baasha king of Israel *came up* against
24:23. the host of Syria *came up* against him:
35:20. Necho king of Egypt *came up* to fight
36: 6. Against him *came up* Nebuchadnezzar
Ezr. 7: 6. This Ezra *went up* from Babylon;
Neh. 4: 7(1). the walls of Jerusalem *were* made *up*, (marg. *ascended;* lit. mending *went up* to the walls)
12: 1. the priests and the Levites that *went up*
37. *they went up* by the stairs of the city of
Ps. 18: 8(9). *There went up* a smoke out of his
47: 5(6). God *is gone up* with a shout,
68:18(19). *Thou hast ascended* on high,
78:21. anger also *came up* against Israel;
31. The wrath of God *came* upon them,
122: 4. Whither the tribes *go up*,
Pro.21:22. A wise (man) *scaleth* the city of the
24:31. *it was* all *grown over* with thorns,
26: 9. (As) a thorn *goeth up* into the hand of a drunkard,
30: 4. Who *hath ascended* up into heaven,
31:29. but *thou excellest* them all.
Cant 4: 2. *which came up* from the washing;
6: 6. as a flock of sheep *which go up* from the
Isa. 5: 6. *but there shall come up* briers and thorns:
7: 1. king of Israel, *went up* toward Jerusalem
8: 7. *and he shall come up* over all his channels,
15: 2. *He is gone up* to Bajith, and to Dibon,
22: 1. *that thou art* wholly *gone up* to the housetops?
34:13. *And* thorns *shall come up* in her palaces,
36: 1. Sennacherib king of Assyria *came up*
10. *am I* now *come up* without the Lord
37:24. multitude of my chariots *am* I *come up*
29. thy tumult, *is come up* into mine ears,
57: 7. thither *wentest thou up* to offer sacrifice.
Jer. 4: 7. The lion *is come up* from his thicket,
29. and *climb up* upon the rocks:
7:31. neither *came it* into my heart.
8:22. *is* not the health of the daughter of my people *recovered?*
9:21(20). death *is come up* into our windows,
14: 2. the cry of Jerusalem *is gone up.*
19: 5. neither *came* (it) into my mind:
32:35. neither *came it* into my mind,
48:15. Moab is spoiled, and *gone up* (out of) her
18. the spoiler of Moab *shall come* upon thee,
50: 3. there *cometh up* a nation against her,
51:42. The sea *is come up* upon Babylon:
Lam.1:14. they are wreathed, (and) *come up* upon my neck:
Eze 13: 5. *Ye have* not *gone up* into the gaps,
37: 8. the sinews and the flesh *came up* upon
38: 9. *Thou shalt ascend and* come like a storm,
16. *And thou shalt come up* against my people of Israel,
Dan11:23. *for he shall come up*, and shall become
Hos. 1:11(2:2). *and they shall come up* out of the
8: 9. *they are gone up* to Assyria,
Joel 1: 6. a nation *is come up* upon my land,
2:20. *and* his stink *shall come up*,
Am. 8: 8. *and it shall rise up* wholly as a flood;
9: 5. *and it shall rise up* wholly like a flood;
Obad. 21. *And* saviours *shall come up* on mount
Jon. 1: 2. their wickedness *is come up* before me.
Mic. 2:13. The breaker *is come up* before them:
Nah. 2: 1(2). He that dasheth in pieces *is come up*
Zec.14:13. *and* his hand *shall rise up* against
16. *shall even go up* from year to year to

KAL.—*Infinitive.*

Gen32:24(25). a man with him until *the breaking* (marg. *ascending*) *of*
46: 4. will also *surely* bring thee up (lit. *bringing* I will bring)
Ex. 19:12. (that ye) *go* (not) *up* into the mount,
23. The people cannot *come up* to mount
24. break through *to come up* unto the Lord,
34:24. *when thou shalt go up* to appear
Nu. 13:30. go up *at once*, (lit. *going up* let us go up)
31. We be not able *to go up* against the
14:44. they presumed *to go up* unto the hill top:
Deu 1:26. ye would not *go up*,
41. ye were ready *to go up* into the hill.
9: 9. *When I was gone up* into the mount
Jos. 4:18. *when* the priests...*were come up* out of
6:15. they rose early *about the dawning of* the
8: 3. *to go up* against Ai:
22:12. *to go up* to war against them.
33. did not intend *to go up* against them
Jud.11:13. *when they came up* out of Egypt,
16. *when* Israel *came up* from Egypt,
13:20. *when* the flame *went up* toward heaven
19:25. *when* the day *began to spring*,
30. day that the children of Israel *came up*
20:40. when the flame began *to arise up*
1Sa. 1: 7. when *she went up* to the house of the
2:19. *when she came up* with her husband
28. *to offer* upon mine altar,
9:14. *for to go up* to the high place.
26. *about the spring of* the day,
15: 2. *when he came up* from Egypt.
6. *when they came up* out of Egypt.
2Sa. 5:22. Philistines *came up* yet again, (lit. added *to come up*)
15:30. weeping *as they went up.*
1K. 11:15. was in Edom, and Joab...*was gone up*
12:18. king Rehoboam made speed *to get him up*
28. too much for you *to go up* to Jerusalem.
18:29. they prophesied until the (time) *of the offering* (marg. *ascending*)
36. *at* (the time of) *the offering*
2K. 3:20. *when* the meat offering *was offered,*
12:17(18). Hazael set his face *to go up* to
2Ch 10:18. king Rehoboam made speed *to get him up*
18: 2. persuaded him *to go up* (with him)
36:16. until the wrath of the Lord *arose*
Ezr. 1: 5. *to go up* to build the house
7:28. out of Israel chief men *to go up* with me.
Neh 3:19. over against *the going up* to the armoury
4:21(15). *from the rising of* the morning
Job 5:26. *as* a shock of corn *cometh in* (marg. *ascendeth*)
36:20. *when* people *are cut off* in their place.
Ps. 62: 9(10). *to be laid* in the balance,
Isa. 11:16. in the day *that he came up* out of the
Jer. 35:11. *when* Nebuchadrezzar king of Babylon *came up*
Hos. 2:15(17). *when she came up* out of the land of
Am. 7: 1. in the beginning of *the shooting up of*
Jon. 4: 7. *when* the morning *rose* the next day,
Hab. 3:16. *when* he *cometh up* unto the people,

KAL.—*Imperative.*

Gen35: 1. unto Jacob, Arise, *go up* to Beth-el,
44:17. *get you up* in peace unto your father.
45: 9. Haste ye, *and go up* to my father,
50: 6. Pharaoh said, *Go up*, and bury thy father,
Ex. 24: 1. *Come up* unto the Lord,
12. the Lord said unto Moses, *Come up* to me
33: 1. said unto Moses, Depart, (and) *go up*
Nu. 13:17. *Get you up* this (way) southward,
21:17. Israel sang this song, *Spring up* (marg. *Ascend*), O well;
27:12. *Get thee up* into this mount Abarim,
Deu 1:21. land before thee: *go up* (and) possess (it),
3:27. *Get thee up* into the top of Pisgah,
9:23. *Go up* and possess the land which I
10: 1. *and come up* unto me into the mount,
32:49. *Get thee up* into this mountain
Jos. 4:17. *Come ye up* out of Jordan.
7: 2. *Go up* and view the country.
8: 1. *go up* to Ai: see, I have given into thy
10: 4. *Come up* unto me, and help me,
6. *come up* to us quickly, and save us,
17:15. *get* thee *up* to the wood (country),
Jud. 1: 3. *Come up* with me into my lot,
16:18. *Come up* this once, for he hath shewed me
20:23. And the Lord said, *Go up* against him.
28. And the Lord said, *Go up;*
1Sa. 9:13. Now therefore *get you up;*
19. *go up* before me unto the high place;
14:10. if they say thus, *Come up* unto us;
12. *Come up* to us, and we will shew you a
— *Come up* after me:
25: 5. *Get you up* to Carmel, and go to Nabal,
35. *Go up* in peace to thine house;
2Sa. 2: 1. And the Lord said unto him, *Go up.*
5:19. And the Lord said unto David, *Go up:*
24:18. *Go up*, rear an altar unto the Lord
1K. 18:41. *Get thee up*, eat and drink;
43. *Go up* now, look toward the sea.
44. *Go up*, say unto Ahab, Prepare (thy chariot),
22: 6. *Go up;* for the Lord shall deliver (it) into
12. *Go up* to Ramoth-gilead, and prosper:
15. *Go*, and prosper: for the Lord
2K. 1: 3. *go up* to meet the messengers of the king
2:23. *Go up*, thou bald head; *go up*, thou
16: 7. *come up*, and save me out of the hand of
18:25. The Lord said to me, *Go up* against this
22: 4. *Go up* to Hilkiah the high priest,
1Ch 14:10. And the Lord said unto him, *Go up;*
2Ch 18: 5. *Go up;* for God will deliver (it) into
11. *Go up* to Ramoth-gilead, and prosper:
14. *Go ye up*, and prosper, and they shall be
Pro.25: 7. *Come up* hither; than that thou
Isa. 21: 2. *Go up*, O Elam: besiege, O Media;
36:10. *Go up* against this land, and destroy it.
40: 9. *get thee up* into the high mountain;
Jer. 5:10. *Go ye up* upon her walls,
22:20. *Go up* to Lebanon, and cry;
46: 4. *and get up*, ye horsemen, and stand forth
9. *Come up*, ye horses; and rage, ye chariots;
11. *Go up* into Gilead, and take balm,
49:28. *go up* to Kedar, and spoil the men of the
31. *get you up* unto the wealthy nation,
50:21. *Go up* against the land of Merathaim,
Hag 1: 8. *Go up* to the mountain, and bring wood,

KAL.—*Future.*

Gen 2: 6. there *went up* a mist from the earth,
13: 1. *And* Abram *went up* out of Egypt,
17:22. *and* God *went up* from Abraham.
19:30. *And* Lot *went up* out of Zoar,
24:16. and filled her pitcher, *and came up.*
26:23. *And he went up* from thence to Beer-sheba.
35: 3. let us arise, *and go up* to Beth-el;
13. *And* God *went up* from him
38:12. Judah was comforted, *and went up* unto his sheepshearers
44:33. *let* the lad *go up* with his brethren.
34. For how *shall I go up* to my father,
45:25. *And they went up* out of Egypt,
46:29. *and went up* to meet Israel his father,
31. *I will go up*, and shew Pharaoh,
50: 5. *let me go up*, I pray thee, and bury
7. *And* Joseph *went up* to bury his father: *and* with him *went up* all the servants
9. *And there went up* with him both chariots and horsemen:
Ex. 2:23. *and* their cry *came up* unto God
8: 4(7:29). the frogs *shall come up* both on thee,
6(2). *and* the frogs *came up*,
10:12. the locusts, *that they may come up* upon the land
14. *And* the locusts *went up* over all the land
16:13. *that* at even the quails *came up*,
14. And *when* the dew that lay *was gone up*,
19:13. *they shall come up* to the mount.
18. *and* the smoke thereof *ascended*
20. the top of the mount; *and* Moses *went up.*
20:26. Neither *shalt thou go up* by steps unto mine
24: 2. neither *shall* the people *go up* with him.
9. *Then went up* Moses, and Aaron,
13. *and* Moses *went up* into the mount of God.
15. *And* Moses *went up* into the mount,
18. *and gat him up* into the mount:
32:30. *I will go up* unto the Lord;
33: 3. *I will* not *go up* in the midst of thee;
5. *I will come up* into the midst of thee
34: 3. no man *shall come up* with thee,
4. Moses rose up early in the morning, *and went up*

Lev. 2:12. *they shall* not *be burnt* (marg. *ascend*) on the altar
19:19. neither *shall* a garment mingled of linen and woollen *come* upon thee.
Nu. 13:21. *So they went up*, and searched the land
22. *And they ascended* by the south,
30. *Let us go up* at once, and possess it;
14:40. *and gat them up* into the top of the
42. *Go* not *up*, for the Lord (is) not among you;
16:12. which said, *We will* not *come up*:
14. of these men? *we will* not *come up*.
20:19. *We will go* by the high way:
27. *and they went up* into mount Hor
21:33. they turned *and went up* by the way
32: 9. For *when they went up* unto the valley of
33:38. *And* Aaron the priest *went up* into
Deu 1:22. by what way *we must go up*,
24. turned *and went up* into the mountain,
41. *we will go up* and fight,
42. *Go* not *up*, neither fight;
43. and *went* presumptuously *up* (lit and were presumptuous *and went up*) into the
3: 1. turned, *and went up* the way to Bashan:
10: 3. *and went up* into the mount,
28:43. stranger that (is) within thee *shall get up*
29:23(22). nor any grass *groweth* therein,
30:12. Who *shall go up* for us to heaven,
34: 1. *And* Moses *went up* from the plains of
Jos. 4:16. *that they come up* out of Jordan.
6:20. *so that* the people *went up* into the city,
7: 2. *And* the men *went up* and viewed
3. *Let* not all the people *go up*; but *let* about two or three thousand men *go up*
4. *So there went up* thither of the people
8:10. numbered the people, *and went up*,
10: 5. *and went up*, they and all their hosts,
7. *So* Joshua *ascended* from Gilgal,
36. *And* Joshua *went up* from Eglon,
15:15. *And he went up* thence to the inhabitants
18:11. *And* the lot of the tribe of the children of Benjamin *came up*
19:10. *And* the third lot *came up* for the children
47. *therefore* the children of Dan *went up* to
Jud. 1: 1. Who *shall go up* for us against
2. the Lord said, Judah *shall go up*:
4. *And* Judah *went up*; and the Lord
22. the house of Joseph, *they also went up*
2: 1. *And* an angel of the Lord *came up* from
4: 5. *and* the children of Israel *came up* to her
10. *and he went up* with ten thousand men
— *and* Deborah *went up* with him.
6: 5. they *came up* with their cattle
21. *and there rose up* fire out of the rock,
35. *and they came up* to meet them.
8: 8. *And he went up* thence to Penuel,
11. *And* Gideon *went up* by the way of
9:48. *And* Abimelech *gat him up*
51. *and gat them up* to the top of the tower.
13: 5. no razor *shall come* on his head:
19. *and offered* (it) upon a rock
20. *that* the angel of the Lord *ascended* in the
14: 2. *And he came up*, and told his father
19. *and he went up* to his father's house.
15: 6. *And* the Philistines *came up*, and burnt
9. *Then* the Philistines *went up*,
16: 5. *And* the lords of the Philistines *came up*
31. *and brought* (him) *up*, [or, *went up*] and buried him
18: 9. Arise, *that we may go up* against them:
12. *And they went up*, and pitched in Kirjath-jearim,
17. *And* the five men that went to spy out the land *went up*,
20:18. *and went up* to the house of God,
— Which of us *shall go up* first to the battle
23, 30. *And* the children of Israel *went up*
26. *and* all the people, *went up*,
1Sa. 1:11. there *shall* no razor *come* upon his head.
21. *And* the man Elkanah, and all his house, *went up*
5:12. *and* the cry of the city *went up* to heaven.
6: 9. if *it goeth up* by the way of his own coast
20. to whom *shall he go up* from us?
7: 7. *And* when...the lords of the Philistines *went up*
9:13. before *he go up* to the high place to eat:
14. *And they went up* into the city:

1Sa. 11: 1. *Then* Nahash the Ammonite *came up*,
13: 5. *and they came up*, and pitched in
15. And Samuel arose, *and gat him up*
14: 9. stand still in our place, and *will* not *go up*
13. *And* Jonathan *climbed up* upon his hands
46. *Then* Saul *went up* from following the
23:19. *Then came up* the Ziphites to Saul
29(24:1). *And* David *went up* from thence,
25:13. *and there went up* after David about four hundred men;
27: 8. *And* David and his men *went up*,
29: 9. *He shall* not *go up* with us to the battle.
2Sa. 2: 1. *Shall I go up* into any of the cities of
— And David said, Whither *shall I go up?*
2. *So* David *went up* thither,
5:17. *But*...the Philistines *came up* to seek David;
19. *Shall I go up* to the Philistines?
23. *Thou shalt* not *go up*;
11:20. if so be that the king's wrath *arise*,
15:24. *and* Abiathar *went up*, until all
17:21. *that they came up* out of the well,
18:33(19:1). king was much moved, *and went up*
19:34(35). that *I should go up* with the king
20: 2. *So* every man of Israel *went up*
23: 9. *and* the men of Israel *were gone away*:
24:19. *And* David, according to the saying of Gad, *went up*
1K. 1:40. *And* all the people *came up* after him,
45. *and they are come up* from thence rejoicing,
2:34. *So* Benaiah the son of Jehoiada *went up*,
6: 8. *and they went up* with winding stairs
10: 5. his ascent by which *he went up*
29. *And* a chariot *came up* and went out of
12:24. saith the Lord, *Ye shall* not *go up*,
27. If this people *go up* to do sacrifice
15:17. *And* Baasha king of Israel *went up*
19. Baasha king of Israel, *that he may depart*
16:17. *And* Omri *went up* from Gibbethon,
18:42. *So* Ahab *went up* to eat and to drink.
43. *And he went up*, and looked,
20: 1. *and he went up* and besieged Samaria,
26. *and went up* to Aphek, to fight
22:20. shall persuade Ahab, *that he may go up*
29. *So*...the king of Judah *went up* to
35. *And* the battle *increased* that day:
2K. 1: 9. *And he went up* to him:
13. *And* the third captain of fifty *went up*,
2:11. *and* Elijah *went up* by a whirlwind
23. *And he went up* from thence unto Beth-el:
3: 7. And he said, *I will go up*:
8. Which way *shall we go up?*
4:21. *And she went up*, and laid him on the
34. *And he went up*, and lay upon the child,
35. *and went up*, and stretched himself upon him:
6:24. *and went up*, and besieged Samaria.
12: 4(5). all the money that *cometh* (marg. *ascendeth*) into any man's heart
10(11). *that* the king's scribe and the high priest *came up*,
17(18). Then Hazael king of Syria *went up*,
18(19). *and he went away* (marg. *up*) from Jerusalem.
14:11. *Therefore* Jehoash king of Israel *went up*;
15:14. *For* Menahem the son of Gadi *went up*
16: 5. of Remaliah king of Israel *came up*
9. *for* the king of Assyria *went up*
17: 5. *Then* the king of Assyria *came up*
— *and went up* to Samaria,
18:17. *And they went up* and came to Jerusalem. And *when they were come up*,
19:14. *and* Hezekiah *went up* into the house of the Lord,
20: 5. on the third day *thou shalt go up*
23: 2. *And* the king *went up* into the house of the Lord,
9. the priests of the high places *came* not *up*
1Ch 11: 6. *So* Joab the son of Zeruiah *went* first *up*,
13: 6. *And* David *went up*, and all Israel,
14: 8. *And* when...all the Philistines *went up* to
10. *Shall I go up* against the Philistines?
11. *So they came up* to Baal-perazim;
14. and God said unto him, *Go* not *up* after
21:18. that David *should go up*,
19. *And* David *went up* at the saying of Gad
2Ch 1:17. *And they fetched up*, and brought forth
9: 4. *he went up* into the house of the Lord;

2Ch.11: 4. *Ye shall* not *go up*, nor fight
12: 9. *So* Shishak king of Egypt *came up*
16: 3. Baasha king of Israel, *that he may depart*
18:19. *that he may go up* and fall at Ramoth-gilead?
28. *So*...the king of Judah *went up* to
34. *And* the battle *increased* that day:
21:17. *And they came up* into Judah,
24:13. *and* the work *was* perfected (marg. *and* the healing *went up* upon the work)
25:21. *So* Joash the king of Israel *went up*;
29:20. *and went up* to the house of the Lord.
34:30. *And* the king *went up* into the house of
36:23. his God (be) with him, *and let him go up.*
Ezr. 1: 3. his God be with him, *and let him go up*
7: 7. *And there went up* (some) of the children of Israel,
Neh 4: 3(3:35). if a fox *go up*, he shall even break
Job 6:18. *they go* to nothing, and perish.
7: 9. down to the grave *shall come up* no
20: 6. Though his excellency *mount up*
Ps. 24: 3. Who *shall ascend* into the hill of the
104: 8. *They go up* by the mountains;
107:26. *They mount up* to the heaven,
132: 3. tabernacle of my house, nor *go up*
Ecc.10: 4. If the spirit of the ruler *rise up* against
Cant 7: 8(9). *I will go up* to the palm tree,
Isa. 2: 3. *and let us go up* to the mountain of the
5:24. their blossom *shall go up* as dust:
7: 6. *Let us go up* against Judah,
14: 8. no feller *is come up* against us.
13. *I will ascend* into heaven,
14. *I will ascend* above the heights of the
15: 5. with weeping *shall they go* it *up*;
32:13. Upon the land of my people *shall come up* thorns
34: 3. their stink *shall come up* out of their
10. the smoke thereof *shall go up* for ever:
35: 9. ravenous beast *shall go up thereon*,
37:14. *and* Hezekiah *went up* unto the house of
38:22. What (is) the sign that *I shall go up*
40:31. *they shall mount up* with wings as eagles;
53: 2. *For he shall grow up* before him
55:13. Instead of the thorn *shall come up* the fir tree, and instead of the brier *shall come up* the myrtle
57: 8. (to another) than me, and *art gone up*;
60: 7. *they shall come up* with acceptance on
65:17. shall not be remembered, nor *come*
Jer. 3:16. neither *shall it come* to mind:
4:13. *he shall come up* as clouds,
6: 4. arise, *and let us go up* at noon.
5. Arise, *and let us go* by night,
21: 2. *that he may go up* from us.
26:10. *then they came up* from the king's house
31: 6. Arise ye, *and let us go up* to Zion
44:21. *and came it* (not) into his mind?
46: 7. Who (is) this (that) *cometh up* as a flood,
8. Egypt *riseth up* like a flood,
— and he saith, *I will go up*,
48: 5. continual weeping *shall go up*;
49:19. *he shall come up* like a lion
22. *he shall come up* and fly as the eagle,
50:44. *he shall come up* like a lion
51:50. *let* Jerusalem *come* into your mind.
53. Though Babylon *should mount up* to
Eze.11:23. *And* the glory of the Lord *went up* from
24. *So* the vision that I had seen *went up*
14: 7. *and setteth up* his idols in his heart,
38:10. at the same time *shall* things *come* into thy mind,
11. *I will go up* to the land of unwalled
18. my fury *shall come up* in my face.
40: 6. *and went up* the stairs thereof,
22. and *they went up* unto it by seven steps;
49. the steps whereby *they went up* to it:
41: 7. and so *increased* (from) the lowest
44:17. no wool *shall come* upon them,
47:12. on this side and on that side, *shall grow* (marg. *come up*) all trees
Dan 8: 8. *and* for it *came up* four notable ones
Hos. 4:15. neither *go ye up* to Beth-aven,
10: 8. the thorn and the thistle *shall come up* on their altars;
Joel 2: 7. *they shall climb* the wall like men of war;
9. *they shall climb up* upon the houses;
20. *and* his ill savour *shall come up*,
Joel 3: 9(4:9). of war draw near; *let them come up*:
12(4:12). *and come up* to the valley of
Am. 3: 5. *shall* (one) *take up* a snare from the earth,
9: 2. though *they climb up* to heaven,
Jon. 4: 6. *and made* (it) *to come up* over Jonah,
Mic. 4: 2. *and let us go up* to the mountain of the
Zec 14:17. whoso *will* not *come up* of (all) the
18. if the family of Egypt *go* not *up*,
— the heathen that *come* not *up*
19. all nations that *come* not *up* to keep the feast

KAL.—*Participle.* Poel.

Gen28:12. angels of God *ascending* and descending
31:10. the rams *which leaped* upon the cattle
12. the rams *which leap* upon the cattle
38:13. thy father in law *goeth up* to Timnath
41: 2,18. *there came up* out of the river
3, 19. seven other kine *came up*
5. seven ears of corn *came up*
22. seven ears *came up* in one stalk,
27. ill favoured kine *that came up* after them
50:14. all *that went up* with him
Nu. 32:11. none of the men *that came up* out of
Deu 1:28. Whither *shall* we *go up?*
32:50. die in the mount whither thou *goest up*,
Jos. 11:17. the mount Halak, *that goeth up* to Seir,
12: 7. the mount Halak, *that goeth up* to Seir;
16: 1. wilderness *that goeth up* from Jericho
Jud.20:31. of which one *goeth up* to the house of
21:19. the highway *that goeth up* from Beth-el
1Sa. 9:11. as they *went up* the hill to the city,
10: 3. meet thee three men *going up* to God
17:23. there *came up* the champion,
25. Have ye seen this man *that is come up?* surely to defy Israel *is he come up*:
28:13. I saw gods *ascending* out of the earth.
14. An old man *cometh up*;
2Sa.15:30. David *went up* by the ascent of (mount) Olivet, and wept as he *went up*,
1K. 18:44. *there ariseth* a little cloud
20:22. the king of Syria *will come up*
2K. 2:23. as he *was going up* by the way,
1Ch 26:16. by the causeway of *the going up*,
2Ch 20:16. they *come up* by the cliff of Ziz;
Ezr. 2: 1. the children of the province *that went up*
59. *they which went up* from Tel-melah,
8: 1. them *that went up* with me from Babylon,
Neh 2:15. Then *went* I *up* (lit. was I *going up*)
7: 5. the genealogy of *them which came up*
6. the children of the province, *that went up*
61. *they which went up* (also) from Tel-melah,
Job 36:33. concerning *the vapour*. (marg. *that which goeth up*)
Ps. 74:23. against thee *increaseth* (marg. *ascendeth*)
Ecc. 3:21. knoweth the spirit of man *that goeth*
Cant.3: 6. Who (is) this *that cometh* out of the
8: 5. Who (is) this *that cometh up* from the
Isa. 24:18. *and he that cometh up* out of the midst of
Jer. 34:21. *which are gone up* from you.
47: 2. waters *rise up* out of the north,
48:44. *and he that getteth up* out of the pit
Eze. 8:11. a thick cloud of incense *went up*.
20:32. *And that which cometh* into your mind
40:40. *as one goeth up* (marg. or, *at the step*) to the entry
Dan 8: 3. and the higher *came up* last.
Hos13:15. the wind of the Lord *shall come up*

* NIPHAL.—*Preterite.* *

Nu. 9:21. *and* (that) the cloud *was taken up*
— *that* the cloud *was taken up*,
10:11. *that* the cloud *was taken up*
2Sa. 2:27. the people *had gone up* every one from
Ps. 47: 9(10). unto God: *he is* greatly *exalted*.
97: 9. *thou art exalted* far above all gods.
Eze. 9: 3. glory of the God of Israel *was gone up*

NIPHAL.—*Infinitive.*

Ex. 40:36. *And when* the cloud *was taken up*
37. till the day *that it was taken up*.
Nu. 9:17. when the cloud *was taken up*
22. *but when it was taken up*, they journeyed.
Ezr. 1:11. the captivity *that were brought up*
Jer. 37:11. *when* the army of the Chaldeans *was broken up*

NIPHAL.—*Imperative.*

Nu. 16:24. *Get you up* from about the tabernacle

NIPHAL.—*Future.*

Ex. 40:37. if the cloud *were* not *taken up*,
Nu. 16:27. *So they gat up* from the tabernacle
Jer. 37: 5. *and* when...*they departed* from Jerusalem.
Eze.36: 3. *and ye are taken* (marg. *made to come*) *up* in the lips of talkers,

* HIPHIL.—*Preterite.* *

Gen50:24. *and bring* you out of this land
25. *and ye shall carry up* my bones from
Ex. 13:19. *and ye shall carry up* my bones away
17: 3. *thou hast brought us up* out of Egypt,
25:37. *and they shall light* (marg. *cause to ascend*) the lamps thereof,
32: 1. the man that *brought us up*
4. thy gods, O Israel, which *brought thee up*
7. thy people which *thou broughtest* out
8. O Israel, which *have brought thee up*
23. the man that *brought us up* out of the
33: 1. the people which *thou hast brought up*
40: 4. shalt bring in the candlestick, *and light*
Lev.14:20. *And* the priest *shall offer* the burnt
Nu. 8: 3. *he lighted* the lamps thereof
14:13. *thou broughtest up* this people
16:13. *thou hast brought us up* out of a land
20: 5. wherefore *have ye made us to come up*
21: 5. Wherefore *have ye brought us up*
Deu27: 6. *and thou shalt offer* burnt offerings
Jos. 2: 6. *she had brought them up* to the roof
24:32. the children of Israel *brought up*
Jud. 6: 8. *I brought* you *up* from Egypt,
13. *Did* not the Lord *bring us up*
26. *and offer* a burnt sacrifice
11:31. *and I will offer it up* for a burnt offering.
1Sa. 2:19. *and brought* (it) to him from year to
6:14. *and offered* the kine a burnt offering
15. and the men of Beth-shemesh *offered*
10:18. *I brought up* Israel out of Egypt,
12: 6. that *brought* your fathers up
2Sa. 2: 3. that (were) with him *did* David *bring up*,
1K. 9:15. the levy which king Solomon *raised*;
25. *And* three times in a year *did* Solomon *offer*
12:28. thy gods, O Israel, which *brought thee up*
2K. 17: 4. *brought* no present to the king of
36. the Lord, who *brought* you *up*
1Ch 15:12. *that ye may bring up* the ark
17: 5. since the day that *I brought up* Israel
2Ch 1: 4. the ark of God *had* David *brought up*
5: 5. these *did* the priests (and) the Levites *bring up*.
8:11. Solomon *brought up* the daughter of
12. Solomon *offered* burnt offerings
29: 7. nor *offered* burnt offerings
Ezr. 1:11. All (these) *did* Sheshbazzar *bring up*
Neh. 9:18. This (is) thy God that *brought thee up*
Job 1: 5. *and offered* burnt offerings
42: 8. go to my servant Job, *and offer up* for
Ps. 30: 3(4). *thou hast brought up* my soul
Isa. 57: 6. *thou hast offered* a meat offering.
Jer. 16:14, 15. The Lord liveth, that *brought up* the
23: 7, 8. The Lord liveth, which *brought up*
27:22. *then will I bring them up*, and restore
38:10. *and take up* Jeremiah the prophet
Lam.2:10. *they have cast up* dust upon their heads;
Eze.14: 3. these men *have set up* their idols
16:40. *They shall also bring up* a company
26: 3. *and will cause* many nations *to come up*
29: 4. *and I will bring thee up* out of the midst
32: 3. *and they shall bring thee up* in my net.
37: 6. *and will bring up* flesh upon you,
12. open your graves, *and cause* you *to come up*
39: 2. *and will cause thee to come up*
43:24. *and they shall offer* them *up* (for)
Hos12:13(14). by a prophet the Lord *brought* Israel
Am. 2:10. I *brought* you *up* from the land of Egypt,
3: 1. *I brought up* from the land of Egypt,
8:10. *and I will bring up* sackcloth upon
9: 7. *Have* not *I brought up* Israel
Mic. 6: 4. *I brought thee up* out of the land of Egypt,
Hab. 1:15. *They take up* all of them with the angle,

HIPHIL.—*Infinitive.*

Ex. 3: 8. *and to bring them up* out of that land
27:20. *to cause* the lamp *to burn* (marg. *to ascend up*) always.
30: 8. *And when* Aaron *lighteth* (marg. *causeth to ascend*, or, *setteth up*) the lamps
Lev.24: 2. *to cause* the lamps *to burn* (marg. *to cause to ascend*)
Nu. 8: 2. *When thou lightest* the lamps,
Jos. 22:23. *to offer* thereon burnt offering
Jud.20:38. *that they should make* a great flame...*rise up*
1Sa. 8: 8. the day that *I brought* them *up*
10: 8. I will come down unto thee, *to offer*
13:10. as soon as he had made an end *of offering*
28:15. hast thou disquieted me, *to bring* me *up*?
2Sa. 6: 2. *to bring up* from thence the ark
18. soon as David had made an end *of offering*
7: 6. *that I brought up* the children of Israel
1K. 8: 1. *that they might bring up* the ark
2K. 2: 1. *when* the Lord *would take up* Elijah
1Ch 13: 6. *to bring up* thence the ark
15: 3, 14. *to bring up* the ark of the Lord
25. *to bring up* the ark of the covenant
16: 2. when David had made an end *of offering*
40. *To offer* burnt offerings unto the Lord
21:24. *nor offer* burnt offerings without cost.
23:31. *to offer* all burnt sacrifices unto the Lord
2Ch 5: 2. *to bring up* the ark of the covenant
8:13. *offering* according to the commandment
23:18. *to offer* the burnt offerings of the Lord,
24:14. vessels to minister, *and to offer*
29:21. the priests the sons of Aaron *to offer*
27. Hezekiah commanded *to offer*
29. when they had made an end *of offering*,
35:14. the sons of Aaron (were busied) *in offering*
16. *and to offer* burnt offerings
Ezr. 3: 2. *to offer* burnt offerings thereon,
6. *to offer* burnt offerings unto the Lord.
Jer. 11: 7. your fathers in the day (that) *I brought* them *up*
Eze.23:46. *I will bring up* a company upon them,
24: 8. *That it might cause* fury *to come up*
26: 3. *as* the sea *causeth* his waves *to come up*.
19. *when I shall bring up* the deep upon thee,
37:13. *and brought* you *up* out of your graves,
43:18. *to offer* burnt offerings thereon,

HIPHIL.—*Imperative.*

Gen22: 2. *and offer him* there for a burnt offering
Ex. 8: 5(1). *and cause* frogs *to come up* upon the land
33:12. *Bring up* this people:
Nu. 20:25. *and bring* them *up* unto mount Hor:
1Sa. 6:21. come ye down, (and) *fetch it up* to you.
19:15. *Bring* him *up* to me in the bed,
28: 8. *and bring* me (him) *up*,
11. *Bring* me *up* Samuel.
Jer. 51:27. *cause* the horses *to come up*

HIPHIL.—*Future.*

Gen 8:20. *and offered* burnt offerings
22:13. *and offered him up* for a burnt offering
37:28. *and lifted up* Joseph out of the pit,
46: 4. *I will* also surely *bring thee up*
Ex. 3:17. *I will bring* you *up* out of the affliction
8: 7(3). *and brought up* frogs upon the land
24: 5. *which offered* burnt offerings,
30: 9. *Ye shall offer* no strange incense
32: 6. *and offered* burnt offerings,
33:15. *carry us* not *up* hence.
40:25. *And he lighted* the lamps before the Lord,
29. *and offered* upon it the burnt offering
Lev.17: 8. that *offereth* a burnt offering
Nu. 22:41. *and brought him up* into the high places
23: 2. *and* Balak and Balaam *offered* on (every) altar
4. *and I have offered* upon (every) altar
14, 30. *and offered* a bullock and a ram
Deu12:13. that *thou offer* not thy burnt offerings
14. there *thou shalt offer* thy burnt offerings,
28:61. *them will* the Lord *bring* (marg. *cause to ascend*) upon thee,
Jos. 7: 6. *and put* dust upon their heads.
24. *and they brought* them unto the valley of
8:31. *and they offered* thereon burnt offerings
Jud. 2: 1. *I made* you *to go up* out of Egypt,
13:16. *thou must offer it* unto the Lord.
15:13. *and brought him up* from the rock.
16: 3. *and carried them up* to the top of an
8. *Then* the lords of the Philistines *brought up*
18. *and brought* money in their hand.
20:26 & 21:4. *and offered* burnt offerings
1Sa. 1:24. *And...she took him up* with her,
2: 6. down to the grave, *and bringeth up*.
14. all that the fleshhook *brought up*

1Sa. 7: 1. *and fetched up* the ark of the Lord,
9. Samuel took a sucking lamb, *and offered*
13: 9. *And he offered* the burnt offering.
12. I forced myself therefore, *and offered*
28:11. Whom *shall I bring up* unto thee?
2Sa. 6:12. David went *and brought up* the ark
17. *and* David *offered* burnt offerings
21:13. *And he brought up* from thence the bones
24:22. Let my lord the king take *and offer up*
24. neither *will I offer* burnt offerings
25. *and offered* burnt offerings and peace
1K. 3: 4. a thousand burnt offerings *did* Solomon *offer*
15. *and offered* peace offerings,
5:13(27). *And* king Solomon *raised* a levy
8: 4. *And they brought up* the ark
— *even* those *did* the priests and the Levites *bring up*.
9:21. *upon those did* Solomon *levy*
10:16. six hundred (shekels) of gold *went* to one
17. three pound of gold *went* to one shield:
12:32, 33. *and he offered* (marg. or, *went up* to) upon the altar.
33. *So he offered* (marg. *id.*) upon the altar
17:19. *and carried him up* into a loft,
20:33. *and he caused him to come up* into the
2K. 3:27. *and offered him* (for) a burnt offering
10:15. *and he took him up* to him into the chariot.
16:12. to the altar, *and offered* thereon.
25: 6. they took the king, *and brought* him *up*
1Ch 21:26. *and offered* burnt offerings and
29:21. *and offered* burnt offerings unto the
2Ch 1: 6. *And* Solomon *went up* [or, *offered*] thither
— *and offered* a thousand burnt offerings
2:16(15). and *thou shalt carry* it *up* to Jerusalem.
3: 5. *and set* thereon palm trees and chains.
14. *and wrought* (marg. *caused to ascend*) cherubims thereon.
5: 5. *And they brought up* the ark,
8: 8. *them did* Solomon *make to pay*
9:15. six hundred (shekels) of beaten gold *went*
16. three hundred (shekels) of gold *went* to
32: 5. *and raised* (it) *up* to the towers,
36:17. *Therefore he brought* upon them
Ezr. 3: 3. *and they offered* burnt offerings thereon
Neh 10:38(39). the Levites *shall bring up* the tithe
12:31. *Then I brought up* the princes
Ps. 40: 2(3). *He brought me up also* out of an
51:19(21). then *shall they offer* bullocks upon
66:15. *I will offer* unto thee burnt sacrifices
71:20. *shalt bring me up* again
102:24(25). O my God, *take me* not *away*
137: 6. if *I prefer* not Jerusalem above my chief
Pro.15: 1. grievous words *stir up* anger.
Jer. 10:13. *and he causeth* the vapours *to ascend*
14:12. when *they offer* burnt offering
30:17. *I will restore* health unto thee,
38:13. *and took* him *up* out of the dungeon:
39: 5. *they brought him up* to Nebuchadnezzar
51:16. *and he causeth* the vapours *to ascend*
52: 9. they took the king, *and carried* him *up*
Eze.14: 4. that *setteth up* his idols in his heart,
19: 3. *And she brought up* one of her whelps:
27:30. *and shall cast up* dust upon their heads,
Am. 4:10. *and I have made* the stink of your camps *to come up*
5:22. Though *ye offer* me burnt offerings
Jon. 2: 6(7). *yet hast thou brought up* my life

HIPHIL.—*Participle.*

Lev.11: 3. *cheweth* the cud, (lit. *maketh* the cud *to come up*)
4. *of them that chew* the cud, (lit. *of them that make* the cud *come up*)
—, 5, 6. he *cheweth* the cud (lit. *maketh* the cud *to ascend*)
26. (is) not clovenfooted, nor *cheweth* the cud, (lit. *maketh* the cud *to come up*)
45. I (am) the Lord *that bringeth* you *up*
Deu14: 6. (and) *cheweth* the cud (lit. *maketh* the cud *to come up*)
7. *of them that chew* the cud, (lit. *of them that make the* cud *come up*)
— *chew* the cud, (lit. *make* the cud *to come up*)
20: 1. God (is) with thee, *which brought thee up*
Jos. 24:17. he (it is) *that brought* us *up*
1Sa. 7:10. Samuel was *offering up* the burnt offering,
2Sa. 1:24. *who put on* ornaments of gold
6:15. *brought up* the ark of the Lord
2K. 17: 7. Lord their God, *which had brought* them *up*
1Ch 15:28. Thus all Israel *brought up* the ark
2Ch 24:14. And *they offered* burnt offerings
Ezr. 4: 2. *which brought* us *up* hither.
Ps. 81:10(11). the Lord thy God, *which brought thee*
135: 7. He *causeth* the vapours *to ascend*
Isa. 8: 7. the Lord *bringeth up* upon them
63:11. Where (is) he *that brought them up* out of
66: 3. *he that offereth* an oblation,
Jer. 2: 6. Where (is) the Lord *that brought* us *up*
33: 6. I *will bring* it health and cure,
18. a man before me *to offer* (lit. *offering*)
48:35. *him that offereth* in the high places,
50: 9. I will raise *and cause to come up* against
Nah 3: 3. The horseman *lifteth up* both the bright

* HOPHAL.—*Preterite.* *

Jud. 6:28. the second bullock *was offered*
2Ch 20:34. who *is mentioned* (marg. *was made to ascend*) in the book of the kings
Nah 2: 7(8). *she shall be brought up*, and her maids

* HITHPAEL.—*Future.* *

Jer. 51: 3. against (him that) *lifteth himself up*

עָלֶה *gāh-leh'*, m. 5929

Gen 3: 7. they sewed fig *leaves* together,
8:11. in her mouth (was) *an* olive *leaf*
Lev.26:36. the sound of *a* shaken *leaf* shall chase
Neh 8:15. and fetch olive *branches*, *and* pine *branches*, *and* myrtle *branches*, *and* palm *branches*, *and branches* of thick trees,
Job 13:25. Wilt thou break *a leaf* driven to and fro?
Ps. 1: 3. *his leaf also* shall not wither;
Pro.11:28. *but* the righteous shall flourish *as a branch.*
Isa. 1:30. as an oak *whose leaf* fadeth,
34: 4. as *the leaf* falleth off from the vine,
64: 6(5). we all do fade *as a leaf;*
Jer. 8:13. *and the leaf* shall fade;
17: 8. *her leaf* shall be green;
Eze.47:12. *whose leaf* shall not fade,
— *and the leaf thereof* for medicine.

עִלָּה *gil-lāh'*, Ch. f. 5931

Dan 6: 4(5). sought to find *occasion* against
—(-). but they could find none *occasion*
5(6). We shall not find any *occasion*

עֹלָה *gōh-lāh'*, f. 5930

Gen 8:20. and offered *burnt offerings* on the altar.
22: 2. and offer him there *for a burnt offering*
3. and clave the wood for *the burnt offering*,
6. Abraham took the wood of *the burnt offering*,
7. where (is) the lamb *for a burnt offering?*
8. God will provide himself a lamb *for a burnt offering:*
13. offered him up *for a burnt offering*
Ex. 10:25. sacrifices *and burnt offerings*,
18:12. Moses' father in law, took *a burnt offering*
20:24. sacrifice thereon *thy burnt offerings*,
24: 5. of Israel, which offered *burnt offerings*,
29:18. it (is) *a burnt offering* unto the Lord:
25. burn (them) upon the altar for *a burnt offering*,
42. *a* continual *burnt offering*
30: 9. *nor burnt sacrifice*, nor meat offering;
28 & 31:9. the altar of *burnt offering*
32: 6. and offered *burnt offerings*,
35:16. The altar of *burnt offering*, with his
38: 1. he made the altar of *burnt offering*
40: 6. set the altar of *the burnt offering*
10. anoint the altar of *the burnt offering*,
29. he put the altar of *burnt offering*
— and offered upon it *the burnt offering*
Lev. 1: 3. If his offering (be) *a burnt sacrifice*
4. upon the head of *the burnt offering;*
6. he shall flay *the burnt offering*,
9. on the altar, (to be) *a burnt sacrifice*,
10. of the goats, *for a burnt sacrifice;*
13, 17. it (is) *a burnt sacrifice*, an offering

Lev. 1:14. *the burnt sacrifice* for his offering
3: 5. upon *the burnt sacrifice*,
4: 7, 18. bottom of the altar of *the burnt offering*,
10. upon the altar of *the burnt offering*.
24, 33. where they kill *the burnt offering*
25, 30, 34. horns of the altar of *burnt offering*,
— bottom of the altar of *burnt offering*.
29. in the place of *the burnt offering*.
5: 7. and the other *for a burnt offering*.
10. he shall offer the second (for) *a burnt offering*,
6: 9(2). the law of *the burnt offering*: It (is) *the burnt offering*, because of the burning
10(3). with *the burnt offering* on the altar,
12(5). and lay *the burnt offering* in order
25(18). In the place where *the burnt offering* is
7: 2. where they kill *the burnt offering*
8. that offereth any man's *burnt offering*,
— the skin *of the burnt offering*
37. the law *of the burnt offering*,
8:18. the ram for *the burnt offering*:
21. *a burnt sacrifice* for a sweet savour,
28. on the altar upon *the burnt offering*:
9: 2. a ram *for a burnt offering*,
3. without blemish, *for a burnt offering*;
7. thy sin offering, and *thy burnt offering*,
12. he slew *the burnt offering*;
13. they presented *the burnt offering*
14. upon *the burnt offering* on the altar.
16. he brought *the burnt offering*,
17. *the burnt sacrifice of* the morning.
22. the sin offering, *and the burnt offering*,
24. consumed upon the altar *the burnt offering*
10:19. they offered their sin offering and *their burnt offering*
12: 6. lamb of the first year *for a burnt offering*,
8. the one *for the burnt offering*,
14:13. the sin offering and *the burnt offering*,
19. he shall kill *the burnt offering*:
20. the priest shall offer *the burnt offering*
22. and the other *a burnt offering*.
31. and the other (for) *a burnt offering*,
15:15, 30. the other (for) *a burnt offering*;
16: 3. a ram *for a burnt offering*.
5. one ram *for a burnt offering*.
24. and offer *his burnt offering*, and *the burnt offering of* the people,
17: 8. *a burnt offering* or sacrifice,
22:18. offer unto the Lord *for a burnt offering*;
23:12. *for a burnt offering* unto the Lord.
18. *a burnt offering* unto the Lord,
37. *a burnt offering*, and a meat offering,
Nu. 6:11. the other *for a burnt offering*,
14. one he lamb...*for a burnt offering*,
16. his sin offering, and *his burnt offering*:
7:15, 21, 27, 33, 39, 45, 51, 57, 63, 69, 75, 81. one lamb of the first year, *for a burnt offering*:
87. the oxen *for the burnt offering*
8:12. the other (for) *a burnt offering*,
10:10. over *your burnt offerings*,
15: 3. *a burnt offering*, or a sacrifice
5. with *the burnt offering* or sacrifice,
8. a bullock (for) *a burnt offering*,
24. one young bullock *for a burnt offering*,
23: 3. Stand by *thy burnt offering*,
6. he stood by *his burnt sacrifice*,
15. Stand here by *thy burnt offering*,
17. he stood by *his burnt offering*,
28: 3. day by day, (for) *a* continual *burnt offering*.
6. *a* continual *burnt offering*, which was
10. *the burnt offering of* every sabbath, beside *the* continual *burnt offering*,
11. ye shall offer *a burnt offering*
13. *a burnt offering* of a sweet savour,
14. *the burnt offering of* every month
15, 24, 31. *the* continual *burnt offering*,
19. *a burnt offering* unto the Lord;
23. *the burnt offering* in the morning, which (is) *for a* continual *burnt offering*.
27. ye shall offer *the burnt offering*
29: 2. ye shall offer *a burnt offering*
6. *the burnt offering of* the month,
— *and the* daily *burnt offering*,
8. *a burnt offering* unto the Lord
11. *and the* continual *burnt offering*,
13. ye shall offer *a burnt offering*,

Nu. 29:16. *the* continual *burnt offering*,
19, 22, 25, 28, 31, 34, 38. beside *the* continual *burnt offering*,
36. ye shall offer *a burnt offering*,
39. *for your burnt offerings*, and for your
Deu 12: 6. thither ye shall bring *your burnt offerings*,
11. *your burnt offerings*, and your sacrifices,
13. that thou offer not *thy burnt offerings*
14. thou shalt offer *thy burnt offerings*,
27. thou shalt offer *thy burnt offerings*,
27: 6. shalt offer *burnt offerings* thereon
Jos. 8:31. they offered thereon *burnt offerings*
22:23. to offer thereon *burnt offering*
26. not *for burnt offering*, nor for sacrifice:
27. before him *with our burnt offerings*,
28. not *for burnt offerings*, nor for sacrifices:
29. to build an altar *for burnt offerings*,
Jud. 6:26. and offer *a burnt sacrifice*
11:31. I will offer it up for *a burnt offering*.
13:16. if thou wilt offer *a burnt offering*,
23. would not have received *a burnt offering*
20:26 & 21:4. and offered *burnt offerings* and
1Sa. 6:14. and offered the kine *a burnt offering*
15. the men of Beth-shemesh offered *burnt offerings*
7: 9. and offered (it for) *a burnt offering*
10. Samuel was offering up *the burnt offering*,
10: 8. down unto thee, to offer *burnt offerings*,
13: 9. Bring hither *a burnt offering* to me,
— And he offered *the burnt offering*.
10. an end of offering *the burnt offering*,
12. I forced myself therefore, and offered *a burnt offering*.
15:22. Lord (as great) delight *in burnt offerings*
2Sa. 6:17. and David offered *burnt offerings*
18. an end of offering *burnt offerings*
24:22. (here be) oxen *for burnt sacrifice*,
24. neither will I offer *burnt offerings*
25. and offered *burnt offerings*
1K. 3: 4. a thousand *burnt offerings* did Solomon
15. and offered up *burnt offerings*,
8:64. there he offered *burnt offerings*,
— too little to receive *the burnt offerings*,
9:25. did Solomon offer *burnt offerings*
10: 5. *and his ascent* by which he went up
18:33(34). pour (it) on *the burnt sacrifice*,
38. fell, and consumed *the burnt sacrifice*,
2K. 3:27. and offered him (for) *a burnt offering*
5:17. offer neither *burnt offering* nor sacrifice
10:24. to offer sacrifices *and burnt offerings*,
25. made an end of offering *the burnt offering*,
16:13. And he burnt *his burnt offering*
15. *the* morning *burnt offering*,
— the king's *burnt sacrifice*,
— *the burnt offering of* all the people
— the blood of *the burnt offering*,
1Ch 6:49(34). the altar of *the burnt offering*,
16: 1. they offered *burnt sacrifices*
2. made an end of offering *the burnt offerings*
40. To offer *burnt offerings* unto the Lord upon the altar of *the burnt offering* continually
21:23. I give (thee) the oxen (also) *for burnt offerings*,
24. nor offer *burnt offerings* without cost.
26. and offered *burnt offerings*
— by fire upon the altar of *burnt offering*.
29. the altar of *the burnt offering*,
22: 1. the altar *of the burnt offering*
23:31. to offer all *burnt sacrifices* unto the Lord
29:21. offered *burnt offerings* unto the Lord,
2Ch 1: 6. offered a thousand *burnt offerings*
2: 4(3). *and for the burnt offerings* morning and evening,
4: 6. things as they offered for *the burnt offering*
7: 1. and consumed *the burnt offering*
7. there he offered *burnt offerings*,
— to receive *the burnt offerings*,
8:12. Solomon offered *burnt offerings*
13:11. *burnt sacrifices* and sweet incense:
23:18. *the burnt offerings of* the Lord,
24:14. they offered *burnt offerings*
29: 7. *nor* offered *burnt offerings*
18. the altar of *burnt offering*,
24. *the burnt offering* and the sin offering
27. to offer *the burnt offering* upon the altar. And when *the burnt offering* began,
28. until *the burnt offering* was finished.

2Ch 29:31. as were of a free heart *burnt offerings.*
32. the number of *the burnt offerings,*
— *for a burnt offering* to the Lord.
34. they could not flay all *the burnt offerings:*
35. *the burnt offerings* (were) in abundance,
— drink offerings *for* (every) *burnt offering.*
30:15. brought in *the burnt offerings*
31: 2. the priests and Levites *for burnt offerings*
3. his substance for *the burnt offerings,* (to wit), *for the* morning and evening *burnt offerings, and the burnt offerings for* the sabbaths,
35:12. they removed *the burnt offerings,*
14. in offering of *burnt offerings*
16. to offer *burnt offerings* upon the altar
Ezr. 3: 2. to offer *burnt offerings* thereon,
3. they offered *burnt offerings* thereon unto the Lord, (even) *burnt offerings* morning and evening.
4. *and* (offered) *the* daily *burnt offerings*
5. (offered) *the* continual *burnt offering,*
6. to offer *burnt offerings* unto the Lord.
8:35. offered *burnt offerings* unto the God of
— *a burnt offering* unto the Lord.
Neh 10:33(34). *and for the* continual *burnt offering,*
Job 1: 5. and offered *burnt offerings*
42: 8. offer up for yourselves *a burnt offering;*
Ps. 20: 3(4). *and* accept *thy burnt sacrifice.*
40: 6(7). *burnt offering* and sin offering hast thou not required.
50: 8. thy sacrifices *or thy burnt offerings,*
51:16(18). thou delightest not in *burnt offering.*
19(21). with *burnt offering* and whole burnt offering:
66:13. go into thy house *with burnt offerings:*
15. I will offer unto thee *burnt sacrifices of*
Isa. 1:11. I am full of *the burnt offerings of* rams,
40:16. nor the beasts thereof sufficient for *a burnt offering.*
43:23. the small cattle of *thy burnt offerings;*
56: 7. *their burnt offerings* and their sacrifices
61: 8. I hate robbery *for burnt offering;*
Jer. 6:20. *your burnt offerings* (are) not acceptable,
7:21. Put *your burnt offerings* unto your
22. concerning *burnt offerings,* or sacrifices:
14:12. when they offer *burnt offering*
17:26. bringing *burnt offerings,* and sacrifices,
19: 5. to burn their sons with fire (for) *burnt offerings*
33:18. a man before me to offer *burnt offerings,*
Eze. 40:26. (there were) seven steps *to go up to it,*
38. they washed *the burnt offering.*
39. to slay thereon *the burnt offering*
42. of hewn stone *for the burnt offering,*
— they slew *the burnt offering*
43:18. to offer *burnt offerings* thereon,
24. *a burnt offering* unto the Lord.
27. the priests shall make *your burnt offerings*
44:11. they shall slay *the burnt offering*
45:15. *and for a burnt offering,* and for peace offerings,
17. the prince's part (to give) *burnt offerings,*
— the meat offering, and *the burnt offering,*
23. *a burnt offering* to the Lord,
25. *according to the burnt offering,*
46: 2. the priests shall prepare *his burnt offering*
4. *And the burnt offering* that the prince shall
12. *a* voluntary *burnt offering*
— he shall prepare *his burnt offering*
13. *a burnt offering* unto the Lord
15. *a* continual *burnt offering.*
Hos. 6: 6. the knowledge of God *more than burnt offerings.*
Am. 5:22. ye offer me *burnt offerings*
Mic. 6: 6. I come before him *with burnt offerings,*

5928 **עֲלָה [ⁿgălāh], Ch. f.**

Ezr. 6: 9. *for the burnt offerings* of the God

5932 **עַלְוָה ⁿgal-vāh', f.**

Hos 10: 9. against the children of *iniquity*

עֲלוּמִים [ⁿgăloo-meem'], m. pl. 5934

Job 20:11. bones are full (of the sin) of *his youth,*
33:25. he shall return to the days of *his youth:*
Ps. 89:45(46). The days of *his youth* hast thou
Isa. 54: 4. thou shalt forget the shame of *thy youth,*

עֲלוּקָה ⁿgăloo-kāh', f. 5936

Pro. 30:15. *The horseleach* hath two daughters,

עָלַז [ⁿgāh-laz']. 5937

* KAL.—*Infinitive.* *

Isa. 23:12. Thou shalt no more *rejoice,* (lit. add *to rejoice*) O thou oppressed virgin,

KAL.—*Imperative.*

Ps. 68: 4(5). *and rejoice* before him.
Zep. 3:14. be glad *and rejoice* with all the heart,

KAL.—*Future.*

2Sa. 1:20. lest the daughters of the uncircumcised *triumph.*
Ps. 28: 7. *therefore* my heart *greatly rejoiceth;*
60: 6(8). *I will rejoice,* I will divide Shechem,
94: 3. how long *shall* the wicked *triumph?*
96:12. *Let* the field *be joyful,*
108: 7(8). *I will rejoice,* I will divide Shechem,
149: 5. *Let* the saints *be joyful* in glory:
Pro 23:16. *Yea,* my reins *shall rejoice,*
Jer. 11:15. when thou doest evil, then *thou rejoicest.*
15:17. assembly of the mockers, *nor rejoiced;*
50:11. because *ye rejoiced,* O ye destroyers
51:39. that *they may rejoice,* and sleep
Hab. 3:18. I *will rejoice* in the Lord,

עָלֵז ⁿgāh-lēhz', adj. 5938

Isa. 5:14. *and he that rejoiceth,* shall descend into it.

עֲלָטָה ⁿgălāh-tāh', f. 5939

Gen 15:17. when the sun went down, *and* it was *dark*
Eze. 12: 6. carry (it) forth *in the twilight:*
7. I brought (it) forth *in the twilight,*
12. bear upon (his) shoulder *in the twilight,*

עֱלִי ⁿgĕlee, m. 5940

Pro. 27:22. in a mortar among wheat *with a pestle,*

עִלִּי [ⁿgil-lee'], adj. 5942

Jos. 15:19. And he gave her the *upper* springs,
Jud. 1:15. Caleb gave her the *upper* springs

עִלָּי [ⁿgil lah'y], Ch. adj. 5943

Dan. 3:26. ye servants of the *most high* God,
4: 2(3:32). and wonders that the *high* God hath wrought
17(14). that *the most High* ruleth in the
24(21). this (is) the decree of *the most High,*
25(22), 32(29). thou know that *the most High*
34(31). *and* I blessed *the most High,*
5:18. O thou king, the *most high* God gave
21. till he knew that the *most high* God ruled
7:25. speak (great) words against *the most High,*

עֲלִיָּה ⁿgăleey-yāh', f. 5944

Jud. 3:20. he was sitting *in a* summer *parlour,*
23. shut the doors of *the parlour* upon him,
24. the doors of *the parlour* (were) locked,
25. he opened not the doors of *the parlour;*
2Sa. 18:33(19:1). *the chamber over* the gate,

1K. 17:19. carried him up into *a loft*,
23. brought him down out of *the chamber*
2K. 1: 2. fell down through a lattice *in his upper chamber*
4:10. Let us make *a* little *chamber*,
11. he turned into *the chamber*,
23:12. *the upper chamber of* Ahaz,
1Ch 28:11. *and of the upper chambers thereof*,
2Ch 3: 9. *And* he overlaid *the upper chambers* with
9: 4. *and his ascent* by which he went up
Neh 3:31. to *the going up of* the corner. (marg. or, corner *chamber*)
32. *the going up of* the corner unto the
Ps. 104: 3. Who layeth the beams of *his chambers* in
13. He watereth the hills *from his chambers*:
Jer. 22:13. his house by unrighteousness, *and his chambers* by wrong;
14. a wide house *and* large *chambers*,

5945 עֶלְיוֹן *gel-yōhn'*, adj.

Gen14:18. he (was) the priest of the *most high* God.
19. Blessed (be) Abram of the *most high* God,
20. And blessed (be) the *most high* God,
22. unto the Lord, the *most high* God,
40:17. in the *uppermost* basket
Nu. 24:16. knew the knowledge of *the most High*,
Deu26:19. to make thee *high* above all nations
28: 1. thy God will set thee *on high*
32: 8. When *the Most High* divided to the nations
Jos. 16: 5. unto Beth-horon *the upper*;
2Sa.22:14. *and the most High* uttered his voice.
1K. 9: 8. this house, (which) is *high*,
2K. 15:35. He built the *higher* gate of the house of
18:17. by the conduit of the *upper* pool,
1Ch 7:24. Beth-horon the nether, and *the upper*,
2Ch 7:21. this house, which is *high*,
8: 5. he built Beth-horon *the upper*,
23:20. through the *high* gate
27: 3. He built the *high* gate of the house
32:30. Hezekiah also stopped the *upper* water-course
Neh 3:25. which lieth out from the king's *high* house,
Ps. 7:17(18). the name of the Lord *most high*.
9: 2(3). to thy name, O thou *most High*.
18:13(14). *and the Highest* gave his voice;
21: 7(8). the mercy of *the most High*
46: 4(5). the tabernacles of *the most high*.
47: 2(3). the Lord *most high* (is) terrible;
50:14. pay thy vows *unto the most high*:
57: 2(3). I will cry unto God *most high*;
73:11. is there knowledge *in the most high*?
77:10(11). the years of the right hand of *the most high*.
78:17. provoking *the most high* in the wilderness.
35. the *high* God their redeemer.
56. tempted and provoked the *most high* God,
82: 6. all of you (are) children of *the most high*.
83:18(19). *the most high* over all the earth.
87: 5. *the highest* himself shall establish her.
89:27(28). *higher* than the kings of the earth.
91: 1. He that dwelleth in the secret place of *the most high*
9. (even) *the most high*, thy habitation;
92: 1(2). praises unto thy name, *O most high*:
97: 9. thou, Lord, (art) *high* above all
107:11. the counsel of *the most High*:
Isa. 7: 3. the conduit of the *upper* pool
14:14. I will be like *the most High*.
36: 2. the conduit of the *upper* pool
Jer. 20: 2. the *high* gate of Benjamin,
36:10. in the *higher* court, at the entry of the
Lam 3:35. before the face of *the most High*, (marg. or, *a superior*)
38. Out of the mouth of *the most High*
Eze. 9: 2. six men came from the way of the *higher* gate,
41: 7. (from) the lowest (chamber) to *the highest*
42: 5. the *upper* chambers (were) shorter:

5946 עֶלְיוֹן [*gel-yōhn'*], Ch. adj.

Dan 7:18. But the saints of *the most High* (marg. *high ones*, i. e. *things*, or, *places*)
Dan. 7:22. to the saints of *the most High*; (lit. *id.*)
25. shall wear out the saints of *the most High*, (lit. *id.*)
27. of the saints of *the most High*, (lit. *id.*)

עַלִּיז [*gal-leez'*], adj. 5947

Isa. 13: 3. *them that rejoice in* my highness.
22: 2. a tumultuous city, a *joyous* city:
23: 7. (Is) this your *joyous* (city),
24: 8. the noise of *them that rejoice* endeth,
32:13. the houses of joy (in) the *joyous* city:
Zep 2:15. This (is) the *rejoicing* city
3:11. *them that rejoice in* thy pride,

עֲלִיל *găleel*, m. 5948

Ps. 12: 6(7). (as) silver tried *in a furnace*

עֲלִילָה *gălee-lāh'*, f. 5949

Deu22:14. give *occasions of* speech against her,
17. hath given *occasions of* speech (against her),
1Sa. 2: 3. by him *actions* are weighed.
1Ch 16: 8. make known *his deeds* among the people.
Ps. 9:11(12). declare among the people *his doings*.
14: 1. they have done abominable *works*,
66: 5. (he is) terrible (in his) *doing* toward the children of men.
77:12(13). *and* talk *of thy doings*.
78:11. forgat *his works*, and his wonders
99: 8. thou tookest vengeance of *their inventions*.
103: 7. *his acts* unto the children of Israel.
105: 1. make known *his deeds* among the people.
141: 4. to practise wicked *works* with men
Isa. 12: 4. declare *his doings* among the people,
Eze.14:22. ye shall see their way and *their doings*:
23. when ye see their ways and *their doings*:
20:43. remember your ways, and all *your doings*,
44. *nor according to your* corrupt *doings*,
21:24(29). in all *your doings* your sins do appear,
24:14. thy ways, *and according to thy doings*,
36:17. by their own way *and by their doings*:
19. *and according to their doings* I judged
Zep 3: 7. they rose early, (and) corrupted all *their doings*.
11. not be ashamed for all *thy doings*,

עֲלִילִיָּה *gălee-leey-yāh'*, f. 5950

Jer. 32:19. Great in counsel, and mighty *in work*: (marg. *doing*)

עֲלִיצוּת [*gălee-tzooth'*], f. 5951

Hab. 3:14. *their rejoicing* (was) as to devour the

עִלִּית [*gil-leeth'*], Ch. f. 5952

Dan. 6:10(11). windows being open *in his chamber*

עָלַל [*gāh-lal'*]. 5953

* POEL.—*Preterite.* *

Job 16:15. *and defiled* my horn in the dust.
Lam. 1:22. *thou hast done* unto me for all my transgressions:
2:20. and consider to whom *thou hast done* this.
3:51. Mine eye *affecteth* mine heart

POEL.—*Infinitive.*

Jer. 6: 9. They shall *throughly* glean the remnant (lit. *gleaning* they shall glean)

POEL.—*Imperative.*

Lam. 1:22. *and do* unto them, as thou hast done unto me

POEL.—*Future.*

Lev.19:10. *thou shalt* not *glean* thy vineyard,
Deu24:21. *thou shalt* not *glean* (it) afterward:

Jud.20:45. *and they gleaned of them* in the highways
Jer. 6: 9. *They shall* throughly *glean* the remnant

POEL.—*Participle.*

Isa. 3:12. (As for) my people, *children* (are) their oppressors,

* POAL.—*Preterite.* *

Lam. 1:12. my sorrow, which *is done* unto me,

* HITHPAEL.—*Preterite.* *

Ex. 10: 2. what things *I have wrought* in Egypt,
Nu. 22:29. Because *thou hast mocked* me:
1Sa. 6: 6. *he had wrought wonderfully* (marg. or, *reproachfully*) among them,
31: 4. and thrust me through, *and abuse* (marg. *mock*) me.
1Ch 10: 4. lest these uncircumcised come *and abuse* (marg. *id.*) me.
Jer. 38:19. me into their hand, *and they mock* me.

HITHPAEL.—*Future.*

Jud.19:25. they knew her, *and abused* her

* HITHPOEL.—*Infinitive.* *

Ps. 141: 4. *to practise* wicked works with men

5954 עֲלַל [*ğălal*], Ch.

* P'AL.—*Preterite.* *

Dan 2:16. Daniel *went in*, and desired
24. Therefore Daniel *went in* unto Arioch,
5:10. *came* into the banquet house:
6:10(11). *he went* into his house;

P'AL.—*Participle.*

Dan 4: 7(4). Then *came in* the magicians,
5: 8. Then *came in* all the king's wise

* APHEL.—*Preterite.* *

Dan 2:25. Then Arioch *brought in* Daniel
6:18(19). neither *were* instruments of musick *brought* before him:

APHEL.—*Infinitive.*

Dan 4: 6(3). made I a decree *to bring in* all the
5: 7. The king cried aloud *to bring in*

APHEL.—*Imperative.*

Dan 2:24. *bring me in* before the king,

* HOPHAL.—*Preterite.* *

Dan 5:13. Then *was* Daniel *brought in*
15. *have been brought in* before me,

5955 עֹלֵלוֹת *ğōh-lēh-lōhth'*, f. pl.

Jud. 8: 2. *the gleaning of the grapes of* Ephraim
Isa. 17: 6. *gleaning grapes* shall be left in it,
24:13. *as the gleaning grapes* when the vintage is
Jer. 49: 9. they not leave (some) *gleaning grapes?*
Obad. 5. would they not leave (some) *grapes?* (marg. or, *gleanings*)
Mic. 7: 1. *as the grapegleanings of* the vintage:

5956 עָלַם [*ğāh-lam'*].

* KAL.—*Participle.* Paül. *

Ps. 90: 8. *our secret* (sins) in the light of thy

* NIPHAL.—*Preterite.* *

Lev. 4:13. *and* the thing *be hid* from the eyes
5: 2. *and* (if) *it be hidden* from him;
3, 4. *and it be hid* from him;
Nu. 5:13. *and it be hid* from the eyes of her husband,
2Ch 9: 2. *there was* nothing *hid* from Solomon
Job 28:21. *Seeing it is hid* from the eyes of all living,

NIPHAL.—*Participle.*

1K. 10: 3. there was not (any) thing *hid*
Ps. 26: 4. neither will I go in *with dissemblers.*
Ecc.12:14. judgment, with every *secret thing,*
Nah. 3:11. thou shalt be *hid,*

* HIPHIL.—*Preterite.* *

2K. 4:27. the Lord *hath hid* (it) from me,
Eze.22:26. and *have hid* their eyes from my sabbaths,

HIPHIL.—*Infinitive.*

Lev.20: 4. if the people of the land do *any ways* hide (lit. *hiding* do hide)

HIPHIL.—*Future.*

Lev.20: 4. if the people of the land *do* any ways *hide*
1Sa. 12: 3. have I received (any) bribe *to blind* (marg. or, *that I should hide*) mine eyes
Ps. 10: 1. O Lord? (why) *hidest thou* (thyself)
Isa. 1:15. *I will hide* mine eyes from you:
Lam. 3:56. *hide* not thine ear at my breathing,

HIPHIL.—*Participle.*

Job 42: 3. Who (is) he *that hideth* counsel without knowledge?
Pro.28:27. *but he that hideth* his eyes shall have

* HITHPAEL.—*Preterite.* *

Deu22: 1, 4. *and hide thyself* from them:

HITHPAEL.—*Infinitive.*

Deu22: 3. thou mayest not *hide thyself.*

HITHPAEL.—*Future.*

Job 6:16. wherein the snow *is hid:*
Ps. 55: 1(2). *hide* not *thyself* from my supplication.
Isa. 58: 7. *that thou hide* not *thyself*

עָלַם *ğāh-lam'*, Ch. m. 5957

Ezr. 4:15. sedition within the same of *old* time: (lit. from the days *of age*)
19. this city of *old* time hath made
Dan 2: 4. O king, live *for ever:*
20. be the name of God for *ever* and *ever:*
44. which shall *never* be destroyed:
— and it shall stand *for ever.*
3: 9. O king, live *for ever.*
4: 3(3:33). his kingdom (is) an *everlasting*
34(31). honoured him that liveth *for ever,* whose dominion (is) an *everlasting*
5:10. O king, live *for ever:*
6: 6(7). King Darius, live *for ever.*
21(22). O king, live *for ever.*
26(27). and stedfast *for ever,*
7:14. his dominion (is) an *everlasting* dominion,
18. and possess the kingdom for *ever,* even for *ever* and *ever.*
27. (is) an *everlasting* kingdom,

עֶלֶם *ğeh'-lem*, m. 5958

1Sa.17:56. Enquire thou whose son *the stripling* (is)
20:22. if I say thus *unto the young man,*

עַלְמָה *ğal-māh'*, f. 5959

Gen24:43. *the virgin* cometh forth to draw (water),
Ex. 2: 8. *the maid* went and called the child's
Ps. 68:25(26). *the damsels* playing with timbrels.
Pro.30:19. the way of a man *with a maid.*
Cant.1: 3. therefore do *the virgins* love thee.
6: 8. *and virgins* without number.
Isa. 7:14. Behold, *a virgin* shall conceive,

עֲלָמוֹת *ğălāh-mōhth'*, f. pl. 5961

1Ch 15:20. with psalteries on *Alamoth;*
Ps. 46[title](1). A song upon *Alamoth.*

עַלְמוּת *ğal-mooth'*. 4192

Ps. 9[title](1). To the chief Musician *upon Muth-labben,*

[Perhaps this is to be read thus in one word, (and not עַל מוּת); it may be thus the construct form of the preceding.]

עָלַס [*ğāh-las'*]. 5965

* KAL.—*Future.* *

Job 20:18. *he shall* not *rejoice* (therein).

* NIPHAL.—*Preterite.* *

Job 39:13. (Gavest thou) the goodly wings *unto the peacocks?* [perhaps, *are joyful*]

* HITHPAEL.—*Future.* *

Pro. 7:18. *let us solace ourselves* with loves.

5966 עָלַע [*gāh-lag'*].

* PIEL.—*Future.* *

Job 39:30. Her young ones also *suck up* blood:

5967 עֲלַע [*gălag*], Ch. com.

Dan 7: 5. and (it had) three *ribs* in the mouth

5968 עָלַף [*gāh-laph'*].

* PUAL.—*Preterite.* *

Isa. 51:20. Thy sons *have fainted*, they lie

PUAL.—*Participle.*

Cant.5:14. his belly (is as) bright ivory *overlaid* (with) sapphires.

* HITHPAEL.—*Future.* *

Gen38:14. her with a vail, *and wrapped herself*,
Am. 8:13. In that day *shall* the fair virgins and young men *faint*
Jon. 4: 8. upon the head of Jonah, *that he fainted*,

5969 עֻלְפֶּה *gool-peh'*, m.

Eze.31:15. all the trees of the field *fainted* for him.

5970 עָלַץ *gāh-latz'*.

* KAL.—*Preterite.* *

1Sa. 2: 1. My heart *rejoiceth* in the Lord,

KAL.—*Infinitive.*

Pro.28:12. *When* righteous (men) *do rejoice*,

KAL.—*Future.*

1Ch 16:32. *let* the fields *rejoice*, and all that (is)
Ps. 5:11(12). *let* them also that love thy name *be joyful*
9: 2(3). I will be glad *and rejoice* in thee:
25: 2. *let* not mine enemies *triumph* over me.
68: 3(4). *let them rejoice* before God:
Pro.11:10. When it goeth well with the righteous, the city *rejoiceth*:

5971 עַם *gam* & עָם *gāhm*, com.

Gen11: 6. the Lord said, Behold, *the people* (is)
14:16. the women also, and *the people*.
17:14. soul shall be cut off *from his people*;
16. kings of *people* shall be of her.
19: 4. all *the people* from every quarter:
23: 7. bowed himself *to the people of* the land,
11. in the presence of the sons of *my people*
12. bowed down himself before *the people of*
13. in the audience of *the people of* the land,
25: 8. was gathered to *his people*.
17. was gathered unto *his people*.
26:10. one of *the people* might lightly have
11. Abimelech charged all (his) *people*,
27:29. Let *people* serve thee,
28: 3. thou mayest be a multitude of *people*;
32: 7(8). he divided *the people* that (was) with
33:15. Let me now leave with thee (some) of *the folk*
34:16. we will become one *people*.
22. to be one *people*,
35: 6. he and all *the people* that (were) with
29. was gathered unto *his people*,
41:40. unto thy word shall all *my people*
55. *the people* cried to Pharaoh for bread:
42: 6. he (it was) that sold to all *the people of*
47:21. as for *the people*, he removed them
23. Then Joseph said unto *the people*,
48: 4. make of thee a multitude of *people*;
19. also shall become (lit. be *for*) *a people*,
49:10. the gathering of *the people*

Gen49:16. Dan shall judge *his people*,
29. I am to be gathered unto *my people*:
33. was gathered unto *his people*.
50:20. to save much *people* alive.
Ex. 1: 9. he said unto *his people*, Behold, *the people of* the children of Israel
20. and *the people* multiplied, and waxed
22. Pharaoh charged all *his people*,
3: 7. I have surely seen the affliction of *my people*
10. that thou mayest bring forth *my people*
12. When thou hast brought forth *the people*
21. give this *people* favour in the sight
4:16. shall be thy spokesman unto *the people*:
21. he shall not let *the people* go.
30. did the signs in the sight of *the people*.
31. And *the people* believed: and when
5: 1. Let *my people* go, that they may
4. let *the people* from their works?
5. *the people of* the land now (are) many,
6. the taskmasters *of the people*,
7. Ye shall no more give *the people* straw
10. the taskmasters of *the people*
— they spake to *the people*,
12. *the people* were scattered abroad
16. but the fault (is) in *thine own people*.
22. (so) evil entreated this *people*?
23. he hath done evil *to* this *people*; neither hast thou delivered *thy people*
6: 7. I will take you to me *for a people*,
7: 4. *my people* the children of Israel,
14. he refuseth to let *the people* go.
16 & 8:1(7:26). Let *my people* go, that they may serve me
8: 3(7:28). thy servants, *and upon thy people*,
4(-:29). both on thee, *and upon thy people*,
8(4). from me, *and from my people*; and I will let *the people* go,
9(5). for thy servants, *and for thy people*,
11(7). from thy servants, *and from thy people*;
20(16). Let *my people* go, that they may
21(17). if thou wilt not let *my people* go,
—(—). upon thy servants, *and upon thy people*,
22(18). Goshen, in which *my people* dwell,
23(19). I will put a division between *my people* and *thy people*:
29(25). from his servants, *and from his people*,
—(—). letting *the people* go to sacrifice
31(27). from his servants, *and from his people*;
32(28). neither would he let *the people* go.
9: 1, 13. Let *my people* go, that they may serve
7. he did not let *the people* go.
14. upon thy servants, *and upon thy people*;
15. that I may smite thee and *thy people*
17. exaltest thou thyself *against my people*,
27. I *and my people* (are) wicked.
10: 3. let *my people* go, that they may serve me.
4. if thou refuse to let *my people* go,
11: 2. Speak now in the ears of *the people*,
3. the Lord gave *the people* favour in the
— in the sight of *the people*.
8. all *the people* that follow thee:
12:27. *the people* bowed the head and worshipped.
31. get you forth from among *my people*,
33. Egyptians were urgent upon *the people*,
34. *the people* took their dough before
36. the Lord gave *the people* favour in the
13: 3. Moses said unto *the people*,
17. when Pharaoh had let *the people* go,
— Lest peradventure *the people* repent
18. God led *the people* about,
22. fire by night, (from) before *the people*.
14: 5. told the king of Egypt that *the people* fled:
— was turned against *the people*,
6. and took *his people* with him:
13. Moses said unto *the people*,
31. and *the people* feared the Lord,
15:13. in thy mercy hast led forth *the people*
14. *The people* shall hear, (and) be afraid:
16. till *thy people* pass over, O Lord, till *the people* pass over,
24. And *the people* murmured against Moses,
16: 4. *the people* shall go out and gather
27. there went out (some) of *the people*
30. So *the people* rested on the seventh day.
17: 1. (there was) no water for *the people*
2. *the people* did chide with Moses,

Ex. 17: 3. *the people* thirsted there for water; and *the people* murmured against Moses,
4. What shall I do *unto* this *people?*
5. Go on before *the people*,
6. that *the people* may drink.
13. Joshua discomfited Amalek and *his people*
18: 1. God had done for Moses, and for Israel *his people*,
10. who hath delivered *the people* from
13. Moses sat to judge *the people:* and *the people* stood by Moses
14. he did *to the people*, he said, What (is) this thing that thou doest *to the people?*
— all *the people* stand by thee
15. Because *the people* come unto me
18. thou, and this *people* that (is) with thee:
19. Be thou *for the people* to God-ward,
21. provide out of all *the people* able men,
22. let them judge *the people* at all seasons:
23. this *people* shall also go to their place in
25. made them heads over *the people*,
26. they judged *the people* at all seasons:
19: 5. treasure unto me above all *people:*
7. and called for the elders of *the people*,
8. all *the people* answered together,
— Moses returned the words of *the people*
9. that *the people* may hear when I speak
— Moses told the words of *the people*
10. Go unto *the people*, and sanctify them
11. in the sight of all *the people*
12. set bounds unto *the people* round about,
14. Moses went down from the mount unto *the people*, and sanctified *the people;*
15. And he said unto *the people*,
16. *the people* that (was) in the camp trembled.
17. Moses brought forth *the people*
21. Go down, charge *the people*,
23. *The people* cannot come up
24. let not the priests *and the people* break
25. Moses went down unto *the people*,
20. 18. all *the people* saw the thunderings,
— when *the people* saw (it), they removed,
20. Moses said unto *the people*,
21. *the people* stood afar off,
21: 8. to sell her *unto a* strange *nation*
22: 25(24). If thou lend money to (any of) *my people*
28(27). nor curse the ruler *of thy people*.
23: 11. that the poor of *thy people* may eat:
27. and will destroy all *the people*
24: 2. *neither* shall *the people* go up with him.
3. Moses came and told *the people*
— all *the people* answered with one voice,
7. in the audience of *the people:*
8. blood, and sprinkled (it) on *the people*,
30: 33, 38. even be cut off *from his people*.
31: 14. shall be cut off from among *his people*.
32: 1. when *the people* saw that Moses delayed
— *the people* gathered themselves together
3. *the people* brake off the golden earrings
6. *the people* sat down to eat and to drink,
7. *thy people*, which thou broughtest out
9. I have seen this *people*, and, behold, it (is) *a* stiffnecked *people:*
11. why doth thy wrath wax hot *against thy people*,
12. repent of this evil *against thy people*.
14. which he thought to do *unto his people*.
17. when Joshua heard the noise of *the people*
21. What did this *people* unto thee,
22. thou knowest *the people*,
25. Moses saw that *the people* (were) naked;
28. there fell of *the people* that day
30. Moses said unto *the people*,
31. this *people* have sinned a great sin,
34. lead *the people* unto (the place)
35. the Lord plagued *the people*,
33: 1. *and the people* which thou hast brought up
3. thou (art) *a* stiffnecked *people:*
4. when *the people* heard these evil tidings,
5. Ye (are) *a* stiffnecked *people:*
8. all *the people* rose up, and stood every man
10. all *the people* saw the cloudy pillar
— all *the people* rose up and worshipped,
12. Bring up this *people:* and thou hast
13. consider that this nation (is) *thy people*.
16. I *and thy people* have found grace

Ex 33: 16. so shall we be separated, I *and thy people*, from all *the people* that (are) upon the
34: 9. it (is) *a* stiffnecked *people;*
10. before all *thy people* I will do marvels,
— all *the people* among which thou (art)
36: 5. *The people* bring much more than enough
6. So *the people* were restrained
Lev. 4: 3. according to the sin of *the people;*
27. if any one *of the* common *people* sin
7: 20, 21, 27. that soul shall be cut off *from his people*.
25. eateth (it) shall be cut off *from his people*.
9: 7. for *the people:* and offer the offering of *the people*,
15. he brought *the people*'s offering,
— the sin offering *for the people*,
18. of peace offerings, which (was) *for the people:*
22. lifted up his hand toward *the people*,
23. and blessed *the people:* and the glory of the Lord appeared unto all *the people*.
24. when all *the people* saw, they shouted,
10: 3. before all *the people* I will be glorified.
16: 15. the sin offering, that (is) *for the people*,
24. the burnt offering of *the people*, and make an atonement for himself, and for *the people*.
33. for all *the people of* the congregation.
17: 4. shall be cut off from among *his people:*
9. cut off *from among his people*.
10. cut him off from among *his people*.
18: 29. cut off from among *their people*.
19: 8. shall be cut off *from among his people*.
16. a talebearer *among thy people:*
18. grudge against the children of *thy people*,
20: 2. *the people of* the land shall stone him
3, 6. cut him off from among *his people;*
4. if *the people of* the land do any ways hide
5. from among *their people*.
17. cut off in the sight of *their people:*
18. cut off from among *their people*. (lit. the sons of *their people*)
24. separated you from (other) *people*.
26. severed you from (other) *people*,
21: 1. the dead *among his people:*
4. a chief man *among his people*,
14. a virgin *of his own people*
15. his seed *among his people:*
23: 29. cut off *from among his people*.
30. will I destroy from among *his people*.
26: 12. shall be my *people*. (lit. *for a people* to me)
Nu. 5: 21. a curse and an oath among *thy people*,
27. the woman shall be a curse among *her people*.
9: 13. shall be cut off *from among his people:*
11: 1. (when) *the people* complained, it displeased the Lord:
2. *the people* cried unto Moses;
8. *the people* went about, and gathered (it),
10. Moses heard *the people* weep
11. layest the burden of all this *people* upon
12. Have I conceived all this *people?*
13. flesh to give unto all this *people?*
14. I am not able to bear all this *people*
16. knowest to be the elders of *the people*,
17. they shall bear the burden of *the people*
18. say thou unto *the people*,
21. *The people*, among whom I (am),
24. Moses went out, and told *the people*
— seventy men of the elders of *the people*,
29. would God that all the Lord's *people* were
32. *the people* stood up all that day,
33. wrath of the Lord was kindled *against the people*, and the Lord smote *the people*
34. there they buried *the people* that lusted.
35. *the people* journeyed from Kibroth-hattaavah
12: 15. *and the people* journeyed not till Miriam
16. afterward *the people* removed from
13: 18. *the people* that dwelleth therein,
28. *the people* (be) strong that dwell in the
30. Caleb stilled *the people* before Moses,
31. We be not able to go up against *the people*
32. *the people* that we saw in it
14: 1. *the people* wept that night.
9. neither fear ye *the people of* the land;
11. How long will this *people* provoke me

Nu. 14:13. thou broughtest up this *people*
14. thou Lord (art) among this *people*,
15. (if) thou shalt kill (all) this *people*
16. the Lord was not able to bring this *people*
19. the iniquity of this *people*
— as thou hast forgiven this *people*,
39. *the people* mourned greatly.
15:26. seeing all *the people* (were) in ignorance.
30. cut off from among *his people*.
16:41(17: 6). have killed *the people of* the Lord.
47(—:12). the plague was begun *among the people:*
—(—:—). made an atonement for *the people*.
20: 1. *the people* abode in Kadesh;
3. *the people* chode with Moses,
20. came out against him *with* much *people*,
24. Aaron shall be gathered unto *his people:*
21: 2. If thou wilt indeed deliver this *people*
4. soul of *the people* was much discouraged
5. *the people* spake against God,
6. the Lord sent fiery serpents *among the people*, and they bit *the people;* and much *people of* Israel died.
7. Therefore *the people* came to Moses,
— And Moses prayed for *the people*.
16. Gather *the people* together,
18. the nobles of *the people* digged
23. Sihon gathered all *his people*
29. *O people of* Chemosh:
33. against them, he, and all *his people*,
34. him into thy hand, and all *his people*,
35. him, and his sons, and all *his people*,
22: 3. Moab was sore afraid of *the people*,
5. the land of the children of *his people*,
— there is *a people* come out from Egypt:
6. curse me this *people;* for they
11. *a people* come out of Egypt,
12. thou shalt not curse *the people:*
17. I pray thee, curse me this *people*.
41. might see the utmost (part) of *the people*.
23: 9. *the people* shall dwell alone,
24. *the people* shall rise up as a great lion,
24:14. I go *unto my people:* come (therefore, and) I will advertise thee what this *people* shall do *to thy people* in the latter days.
25: 1. *the people* began to commit whoredom
2. they called *the people* unto the sacrifices of their gods: and *the people* did eat, and bowed down to their gods.
4. Take all the heads of *the people*,
27:13. thou also shalt be gathered unto *thy people*,
31: 2. shalt thou be gathered unto *thy people*.
3. Moses spake unto *the people*,
32. the prey which *the men of* war had caught,
32:15. ye shall destroy all this *people*.
33:14. no water *for the people* to drink.
Deu 1:28. *The people* (is) greater and taller than we;
2: 4. command thou *the people*,
10. *a people* great, and many,
16. consumed and dead from among *the people*,
21. *A people* great, and many, and tall,
25. *the nations* (that are) under the whole
32. against us, he and all *his people*,
33. him, and his sons, and all *his people*.
3: 1. out against us, he and all *his people*,
2. I will deliver him, and all *his people*,
3. the king of Bashan, and all *his people:*
28. he shall go over before this *people*,
4: 6. in the sight of *the nations*,
— *a* wise and understanding *people*.
10. Gather me *the people* together,
19. all *nations* under the whole heaven.
20. to be unto him *a people of* inheritance,
27. shall scatter you *among the nations*.
33. Did (ever) *people* hear the voice of God
5:28(25). the voice of the words of this *people*,
6:14. the gods of *the people* which (are) round
7: 6. thou (art) *an* holy *people*
— to be *a* special *people* unto himself, above all *people* that (are) upon the face of the
7. more in number than any *people;* for ye (were) the fewest of all *people:*
14. Thou shalt be blessed above all *people:*
16. thou shalt consume all *the people*
19. all *the people* of whom thou art afraid.
9: 2. *A people* great and tall,
6. thou (art) *a* stiffnecked *people*.

Deu 9:12. *thy people* which thou hast brought forth
13. I have seen this *people*, and, behold, it (is) *a* stiffnecked *people:*
26. destroy not *thy people* and thine inheritance,
27. not unto the stubbornness of this *people*,
29. they (are) *thy people* and thine inheritance,
10:11. take (thy) journey before *the people*,
15. you above all *people*,
13: 7(8). the gods of *the people*
9(10). the hand of all *the people*.
14: 2, 21. thou (art) *an* holy *people* unto the Lord
— the Lord hath chosen thee to be *a* peculiar *people*
— all *the nations* that (are) upon the earth.
16:18. they shall judge *the people*
17: 7. the hands of all *the people*.
13. all *the people* shall hear,
16. nor cause *the people* to return to Egypt,
18: 3. the priest's due from *the people*,
20: 1. *a people* more than thou,
2. the priest shall approach and speak unto *the people*,
5. the officers shall speak unto *the people*,
8. shall speak further unto *the people*,
9. an end of speaking unto *the people*,
— captains of the armies to lead *the people*.
11. all *the people* (that is) found therein
16. the cities of these *people*,
21: 8. merciful, O Lord, *unto thy people* Israel,
— lay not innocent blood unto *thy people*
26:15. bless *thy people* Israel,
18. thee this day to be his peculiar *people*,
19. that thou mayest be *an* holy *people*
27: 1. the elders of Israel commanded *the people*,
9. thou art become *the people* of the Lord
11. Moses charged *the people*
12. upon mount Gerizim to bless *the people*,
15. all *the people* shall answer and say, Amen.
16, 17, 18, 19, 20, 21, 22, 23, 24, 25, 26. And all *the people* shall say, Amen.
28: 9. shall establish thee *an* holy *people*
10. all *people of* the earth shall see
32. daughters (shall be) given *unto* another *people*,
33. *a nation* which thou knowest not
37. among all *nations* whither the Lord
64. Lord shall scatter thee among all *people*.
29:13(12). establish thee to day *for a people* unto
30: 3. gather thee from all *the nations*,
31: 7. thou must go with this *people*
12. Gather *the people* together,
16. this *people* will rise up,
32: 6. O foolish *people* and unwise?
8. he set the bounds of *the people*
9. the Lord's portion (is) *his people;*
21. (those which are) not *a people;*
36. the Lord shall judge *his people*,
43. Rejoice, O ye nations, (with) *his people:*
— merciful unto his land, (and) to *his people*.
44. in the ears of *the people*,
50. be gathered unto *thy people;*
— was gathered unto *his people:*
33: 3. Yea, he loved *the people;*
5. the heads of *the people*
7. Judah, and bring him unto *his people:*
17. he shall push *the people*
19. They shall call *the people*
21. he came with the heads of *the people*,
29. *O people* saved by the Lord,
Jos. 1: 2. thou, and all this *people*,
6. unto this *people* shalt thou divide
10. commanded the officers of *the people*,
11. the host, and command *the people*,
3: 3. And they commanded *the people*,
5. Joshua said unto *the people*,
6. pass over before *the people*.
— and went before *the people*.
14. when *the people* removed from their tents
— the ark of the covenant before *the people;*
16. *and the people* passed over right against
4: 2. Take you twelve men out of *the people*,
10. Joshua to speak unto *the people*,
— *the people* hasted and passed over.
11. when all *the people* were clean passed
— in the presence of *the people*.
19. *And the people* came up out of Jordan
24. all *the people of* the earth

Jos. 5: 4. All *the people* that came out of Egypt,
5. all *the people* that came out were circumcised: but all *the people* that were born
6: 5. *the people* shall shout with a great shout;
— *the people* shall ascend up
7. he said unto *the people*,
8. when Joshua had spoken unto *the people*,
10. Joshua had commanded *the people*,
16. Joshua said unto *the people*, Shout;
20. *the people* shouted when (the priests)
— when *the people* heard the sound of the trumpet, and *the people* shouted
— *the people* went up into the city,
7: 3. Let not all *the people* go up;
— make not all *the people* to labour thither;
4. there went up thither of *the people*
5. the hearts of *the people* melted,
7. at all brought this *people* over Jordan,
13. Up, sanctify *the people*,
8: 1. take all *the people of* war with thee,
— the king of Ai, and *his people*,
3. Joshua arose, and all *the people of* war,
5. all *the people* that (are) with me,
9. lodged that night among *the people*.
10. and numbered *the people*,
— before *the people* to Ai.
11. *the people*, (even the people) of war
13. when they had set *the people*,
14. he and all *his people*,
16. all *the people* that (were) in Ai
20. *and the people* that fled to the wilderness
33. they should bless *the people* of Israel.
10: 7. he, and all *the people of* war with him,
21. all *the people* returned to the camp
33. Joshua smote him and *his people*,
11: 4. their hosts with them, much *people*,
7. Joshua came, and all *the people of* war
14: 8. made the heart of *the people* melt:
17:14. I (am) *a* great *people*,
15. If thou (be) *a* great *people*,
17. Thou (art) *a* great *people*,
24: 2, 27. Joshua said unto all *the people*,
16. *the people* answered and said,
17. among all *the people* through whom
18. drave out from before us all *the people*,
19, 22. Joshua said unto *the people*,
21. *the people* said unto Joshua,
24. *the people* said unto Joshua,
25. Joshua made a covenant *with the people*
28. Joshua let *the people* depart,
Jud. 1:16. they went and dwelt among *the people*.
2: 4. *the people* lifted up their voice,
6. when Joshua had let *the people* go,
7. *the people* served the Lord
12. the gods of *the people*
3:18. he sent away *the people* that bare
4:13. all *the people* that (were) with him,
5: 2. *the people* willingly offered themselves.
9. offered themselves willingly *among the people*.
11. *the people of* the Lord go down
13. the nobles among *the people*:
14. Benjamin, *among thy people*;
18. Zebulun and Naphtali (were) *a people*
7: 1. all *the people* that (were) with him,
2. *The people* that (are) with thee (are) too
3. proclaim in the ears of *the people*,
— there returned of *the people* twenty and two thousand;
4. *The people* (are) yet (too) many;
5. So he brought down *the people*
6. all the rest of *the people* bowed
7. let all *the* (other) *people* go
8. *the people* took victuals in their hand,
8: 5. of bread *unto the people* that follow me;
9:29. would to God this *people* were under
32. thou *and the people* that (is) with thee,
33. he *and the people* that (is) with him
34. all *the people* that (were) with him,
35. *and the people* that (were) with him,
36. when Gaal saw *the people*,
— there come *people* down from the top of
37. there come *people* down by the middle of
38. not this *the people* that thou hast despised?
42. *the people* went out into the field;
43. he took *the people*, and divided them
— *the people* (were) come forth out of the

Jud. 9:45. he took the city, and slew *the people*
48. he and all *the people* that (were) with
— and said unto *the people*
49. all *the people* likewise cut down
10:18. *the people* (and) princes of Gilead
11:11. *the people* made him head and captain
20. Sihon gathered all *his people* together,
21. Sihon and all *his people* into the hand of Israel,
23. Amorites from before *his people*
12: 2. I *and my people* were at great strife
14: 3. among all *my people*,
16. a riddle unto the children of *my people*,
17. the riddle to the children of *her people*.
16:24. when *the people* saw him,
30. upon the lords, and upon all *the people*
18: 7. saw *the people* that (were) therein,
10. ye shall come unto *a people* secure,
20. went in the midst of *the people*.
27. unto *a people* (that were) at quiet
20: 2. the chief of all *the people*,
— in the assembly of *the people of* God,
8. all *the people* arose as one man,
10. to fetch victual *for the people*,
16. Among all this *people*
22. *the people* the men of Israel encouraged
26. and all *the people*, went up,
31. of Benjamin went out against *the people*,
— they began to smite *of the people*,
21: 2. *the people* came to the house of God,
4. on the morrow, that *the people* rose early,
9. *the people* were numbered,
15. *And the people* repented them for Benjamin,
Ru. 1: 6. the Lord had visited *his people*
10. we will return with thee *unto thy people*.
15. sister in law is gone back unto *her people*,
16. *thy people* (shall be) *my people*,
2:11. unto *a people* which thou knewest not
3:11. all the city of *my people*
4: 4. before the elders of *my people*.
9. unto the elders, and (unto) all *the people*,
11. all *the people* that (were) in the gate,
1 Sa. 2:13. the priest's custom with *the people*
23. your evil dealings by all this *people*.
24. ye make the Lord's *people* to transgress.
29. the offerings of Israel *my people*?
4: 3. when *the people* were come into the camp,
4. So *the people* sent to Shiloh,
17. a great slaughter *among the people*,
5:10. to slay us and *our people*.
11. that it slay us not, and *our people*:
6:19. even he smote *of the people*
— and *the people* lamented, because the Lord had smitten (many) *of the people*
8: 7. Hearken unto the voice of *the people*
10. the words of the Lord unto *the people*
19. *the people* refused to obey the voice of
21. Samuel heard all the words of *the people*,
9: 2. (he was) higher than any of *the people*.
12. a sacrifice *of the people* to day
13. *the people* will not eat until he come,
16. captain over *my people* Israel, that he may save *my people*
— I have looked upon *my people*,
17. this same shall reign *over my people*.
24. I have invited *the people*.
10:11. *the people* said one to another,
17. Samuel called *the people*
23. when he stood among *the people*, he was higher than any of *the people*
24. Samuel said to all *the people*,
— (there is) none like him among all *the people*? And all *the people* shouted,
25. Then Samuel told *the people*
— Samuel sent all *the people* away,
11: 4. told the tidings in the ears of *the people*: and all *the people* lifted up their voices,
5. What (aileth) *the people* that they weep?
7. the fear of the Lord fell on *the people*,
11. Saul put *the people* in three companies;
12. *the people* said unto Samuel,
14. Then said Samuel to *the people*,
15. all *the people* went to Gilgal;
12: 6. Samuel said unto *the people*,
18. *the people* greatly feared the Lord
19. all *the people* said unto Samuel,
20. Samuel said unto *the people*,

1Sa.12:22. the Lord will not forsake *his people*
— pleased the Lord to make you his *people.*
13: 2. the rest of *the people* he sent every man
4. *the people* were called together
5. *and people* as the sand which (is) on
6. for *the people* were distressed, then *the people* did hide themselves in caves,
7. *the people* followed him trembling.
8. *the people* were scattered from him.
11. I saw that *the people* were scattered
14. commanded him (to be) captain over *his people,*
15. numbered *the people* (that were) present
16. *and the people* (that were) present
22. in the hand of any of *the people*
14: 2. *and the people* that (were) with him
3. *And the people* knew not that Jonathan was
15. among all *the people:*
17. Then said Saul *unto the people*
20. Saul and all *the people* that (were) with
24. Saul had adjured *the people,*
— none of *the people* tasted (any) food.
26. when *the people* were come into the wood,
— *the people* feared the oath.
27. not when his father charged *the people*
28. one *of the people,* and said, Thy father straitly charged *the people*
— And *the people* were faint.
30. if haply *the people* had eaten freely
31. *the people* were very faint.
32. *the people* flew upon the spoil,
— *the people* did eat (them) with the blood.
33. Behold, *the people* sin against the Lord,
34. Disperse yourselves *among the people,*
— all *the people* brought every man his ox
38. all the chief of *the people:*
39. not a man among all *the people*
40. And *the people* said unto Saul,
41. *but the people* escaped.
45. *the people* said unto Saul,
— *the people* rescued Jonathan,
15: 1. to anoint thee (to be) king over *his people,*
4. Saul gathered *the people* together,
8. utterly destroyed all *the people*
9. Saul *and the people* spared Agag,
15. *the people* spared the best of the sheep
21. *the people* took of the spoil,
24. because I feared *the people,*
30. before the elders of *my people,*
17:27. *the people* answered him after this manner,
30. *the people* answered him again
18: 5. in the sight of all *the people,*
13. went out and came in before *the people.*
23: 8. Saul called all *the people* together
26: 5. *and the people* pitched round about him.
7. David and Abishai came to *the people*
— Abner *and the people* lay round about
14. David cried to *the people,*
15. there came one of *the people* in to destroy
27:12. He hath made *his people* Israel utterly
30: 4. David *and the people* that (were) with
6. *the people* spake of stoning him, because the soul of all *the people* was grieved,
21. to meet David, and to meet *the people*
— when David came near to *the people,*
31: 9. and among *the people.*
2Sa. 1: 4. *the people* are fled from the battle, and many of *the people* also are fallen
12. for *the people of* the Lord,
2:26. ere thou bid *the people* return
27. in the morning *the people* had gone up
28. all *the people* stood still,
30. when he had gathered all *the people*
3:18. I will save *my people* Israel
31. David said to Joab, and to all *the people*
32. and all *the people* wept.
34. all *the people* wept again
35. when all *the people* came to cause David to eat
36. all *the people* took notice (of it),
— the king did pleased all *the people.*
37. all *the people* and all Israel
5: 2. Thou shalt feed *my people* Israel,
12. his kingdom for *his people* Israel's sake.
6: 2. arose, and went with all *the people*
18. he blessed *the people* in the name of
19. he dealt among all *the people,*

2Sa. 6:19. all *the people* departed every one
21. ruler over *the people of* the Lord,
7: 7. to feed *my people* Israel,
8. to be ruler over *my people,*
10. I will appoint a place *for my people*
11. judges (to be) over *my people* Israel,
23. nation in the earth (is) *like thy people,*
— whom God went to redeem *for a people*
— before *thy people,* which thou redeemedst
24. confirmed to thyself *thy people* Israel (to be) *a people* unto thee for ever:
8:15. judgment and justice unto all *his people.*
10:10. the rest of *the people* he delivered into
12. let us play the men for *our people,*
13. Joab drew nigh, *and the people*
11: 7. how Joab did, and how *the people* did,
17. there fell (some) of *the people*
12:28. gather the rest of *the people* together,
29. David gathered all *the people*
31. he brought forth *the people*
— David and all *the people* returned
13:34. there came much *people* by the way
14:13. such a thing against *the people of* God?
15. *the people* have made me afraid:
15:12. *for the people* increased continually
17. the king went forth, and all *the people*
23, 23. all *the people* passed over:
24. until all *the people* had done passing
30. all *the people* that (was) with him
16: 6. *the people* and all the mighty men
14. *the people* that (were) with him,
15. Absalom, and all *the people*
18. whom the Lord, *and* this *people,...*choose,
17: 2, 16. *the people* that (are) with him
3. I will bring back all *the people*
— all *the people* shall be in peace.
8. will not lodge with *the people.*
9. There is a slaughter *among the people*
22. David arose, and all *the people*
29. for David, *and for the people*
— *The people* (is) hungry, and weary,
18: 1. David numbered *the people*
2. David sent forth a third part of *the people*
— the king said unto *the people,*
3. *the people* answered, Thou shalt not go
4. all *the people* came out by hundreds
5. *the people* heard when the king gave
6. *the people* went out into the field
7. *the people of* Israel were slain
8. the wood devoured more *people*
16. *the people* returned from pursuing after Israel: for Joab held back *the people.*
19: 2(3). unto all *the people:* for *the people* heard say
3(4). *the people* gat them by stealth
—(–). as *people* being ashamed
8(9). they told unto all *the people,*
—(–). *the people* came before the king:
9(10). all *the people* were at strife
39(40). *the people* went over Jordan.
40(41). all *the people of* Judah conducted the king, and also half *the people of* Israel.
20:12. all *the people* stood still,
15. *the people* that (were) with Joab
22. the woman went unto all *the people*
22:28. *the* afflicted *people* thou wilt save:
44. from the strivings of *my people,*
— *a people* (which) I knew not
48. bringeth down *the people* under me,
23:10. *and the people* returned after him
11. *and the people* fled from the Philistines.
24: 2. number ye *the people,* that I may know the number of *the people.*
3. the Lord thy God add unto *the people,*
4. to number *the people* of Israel.
9. the sum of the number of *the people*
10. after that he had numbered *the people.*
15. there died of *the people*
16. the angel that destroyed *the people,*
17. the angel that smote *the people,*
21. plague may be stayed from *the people.*
1K. 1:39. *the people* said, God save king Solomon.
40. all *the people* came up after him, *and the people* piped with pipes,
3: 2. *the people* sacrificed in high places,
8. thy servant (is) in the midst of *thy people* which thou hast chosen, *a* great *people,*

1K. 3: 9. understanding heart to judge *thy people*,
— is able to judge this *thy* so great *a people?*
4:34(5:14). there came of all *people*
5: 7(21). a wise son over this great *people*.
16(30). ruled *over the people* that wrought
6:13. will not forsake *my people* Israel.
8:16. the day that I brought forth *my people*
— David to be over *my people* Israel.
30. *and* of *thy people* Israel,
33. When *thy people* Israel be smitten
34. forgive the sin of *thy people*
36. *and* of *thy people* Israel,
— land, which thou hast given *to thy people*
38. by all *thy people* Israel,
41. a stranger, that (is) not *of thy people*
43. that all *people of* the earth may know
— *as* (do) *thy people* Israel;
44. If *thy people* go out to battle
50. forgive *thy people* that have sinned
51. For they (be) *thy people*,
52. unto the supplication of *thy people*
53. among all *the people of* the earth,
56. that hath given rest unto *his people*
59. the cause of *his people* Isracl
60. That all *the people of* the earth may know
66. On the eighth day he sent *the people* away:
— his servant, and for Israel *his people*.
9: 7. a proverb and a byword among all *people:*
20. all *the people* (that were) left
23. *over the people* that wrought in the work.
12: 5. And *the people* departed.
6. that I may answer this *people?*
7. If thou wilt be a servant *unto* this *people*
9. that we may answer this *people*,
10. Thus shalt thou speak *unto* this *people*
12. Jeroboam and all *the people*
13. the king answered *the people* roughly,
15. the king hearkened not unto *the people;*
16. *the people* answered the king,
23. the remnant of *the people*,
27. If this *people* go up to do sacrifice
— then shall the heart of this *people* turn
30. *the people* went (to worship)
31. made priests of the lowest of *the people*,
13:33. made again of the lowest of *the people*
14: 2. that (I should be) king over this *people*.
7. I exalted thee from among *the people*, and made thee prince over *my people*
16: 2. made thee prince over *my people*
— hast made *my people* Israel to sin,
15. *And the people* (were) encamped against
16. *the people* (that were) encamped
21. Then were *the people* of Israel divided into two parts: half of *the people* followed
22. *the people* that followed Omri prevailed against *the people* that
18:21. Elijah came unto all *the people*,
— *the people* answered him not a word.
22. Then said Elijah unto *the people*,
24. all *the people* answered and said,
30. Elijah said unto all *the people*,
— all *the people* came near unto him.
37. that this *people* may know
39. when all *the people* saw (it),
19:21. gave *unto the people*, and they did eat.
20: 8. all *the people* said unto him,
10. all *the people* that follow me.
15. he numbered all *the people*,
42. thy life shall go for his life, *and thy people* for *his people*.
21: 9, 12. Naboth on high among *the people:*
13. in the presence of *the people*,
22: 4. *my people as thy people*, my horses
28. Hearken, *O people*, every one of you.
43(44). *the people* offered and burnt incense
2K. 3: 7. (am) as thou (art), *my people as thy people*,
4:13. I dwell among *mine own people*.
41. Pour out *for the people*,
42. Give *unto the people*, that they may eat.
43. Give *the people*, that they may eat:
6:30. and *the people* looked, and, behold,
7:16. And *the people* went out,
17. *the people* trode upon him in the gate,
20. *the people* trode upon him in the gate,
8:21. *the people* fled into their tents.
9: 6. anointed thee king over *the people of*
10: 9. and said to all *the people*,
2K. 10:18. Jehu gathered all *the people*
11:13. heard the noise of the guard (and) of *the people*, she came to *the people*
14. all *the people of* the land rejoiced,
17. the king and *the people*, that they should be the Lord's *people;* between the king also and *the people*.
18. all *the people of* the land went
19. the guard, and all *the people of* the land;
20. all *the people of* the land rejoiced,
12: 3(4). *the people* still sacrificed
8(9). receive no (more) money of *the people*,
13: 7. Neither did he leave of *the people*
14: 4. as yet *the people* did sacrifice
21. all *the people of* Judah
15: 4. *the people* sacrificed and burnt incense
5. judging *the people of* the land.
10. and smote him before *the people*,
35. *the people* sacrificed and burned incense
16:15. of all *the people of* the land,
18:26. in the ears of *the people* that (are) on
36. *the people* held their peace,
20: 5. Hezekiah the captain of *my people*,
21:24. *the people of* the land slew all them
— *the people of* the land made Josiah
22: 4. the keepers of the door have gathered of *the people:*
13. for me, and for *the people*,
23: 2. all *the people*, both small and great.
3. all *the people* stood to the covenant.
6. the graves of the children of *the people*.
21. the king commanded all *the people*,
30. *the people of* the land took Jehoahaz
35. the silver and the gold of *the people of*
24:14. the poorest sort of *the people of*
25: 3. there was no bread *for the people of*
11. the rest of *the people* (that were) left
19. mustered *the people of* the land, and threescore men *of the people of*
22. *And* (as for) *the people* that remained in
26. all *the people*, both small and great,
1Ch 5:25. the gods of *the people of* the land,
10: 9. tidings unto their idols, and to *the people*.
11: 2. Thou shalt feed *my people* Israel, and thou shalt be ruler over *my people*
13. *and the people* fled from before the
13: 4. in the eyes of all *the people*.
14: 2. because of *his people* Israel.
16: 2. he blessed *the people* in the name
8. make known his deeds *among the people*.
20. from (one) kingdom to another *people;*
24. his marvellous works among all *nations*.
26. all the gods of *the people* (are) idols:
28. ye kindreds of *the people*,
36. all *the people* said, Amen,
43. all *the people* departed every man
17: 6. whom I commanded to feed *my people*,
7. ruler over *my people* Israel:
9. I will ordain a place *for my people*
10. judges (to be) over *my people* Israel.
21. nation in the earth (is) *like thy people*
— God went to redeem (to be) his own *people*,
— driving out nations from before *thy people*,
22. *thy people* Israel didst thou make thine own *people* for ever;
18:14. judgment and justice among all *his people*.
19: 7. the king of Maachah and *his people;*
11. the rest of *the people* he delivered
13. behave ourselves valiantly for *our people*,
14. Joab *and the people* that (were) with him
20: 3. he brought out *the people* that (were) in it,
— David and all *the people* returned
21: 2. to Joab and to the rulers of *the people*,
3. The Lord make *his people* an hundred
5. the sum of the number of *the people*
17. commanded *the people* to be numbered?
— *but* not *on thy people*, that they should
22. the plague may be stayed from *the people*.
22:18. before the Lord, and before *his people*.
23:25. of Israel hath given rest *unto his people*,
28: 2. Hear me, my brethren, *and my people:*
21. the princes and all *the people*
29: 9. Then *the people* rejoiced,
14. who (am) I, and what (is) *my people*,
17. now have I seen with joy *thy people*.
18. the thoughts of the heart of *thy people*,

2Ch 1: 9. thou hast made me king over *a people*
10. come in before this *people*: for who can judge this *thy people*,
11. that thou mayest judge *my people*,
2:11(10). the Lord hath loved *his people*,
18(17). six hundred overseers to set *the people*
6: 5. the day that I brought forth *my people*
— to be a ruler over *my people* Israel:
6. chosen David to be over *my people*
21. the supplications of thy servant, *and of thy people*
24. if *thy people* Israel be put to the worse
25. forgive the sin of *thy people* Israel,
27. the sin of thy servants, *and* of *thy people*
— which thou hast given *unto thy people*
29. all *thy people* Israel,
32. the stranger, which is not *of thy people*
33. that all *people of* the earth may know
— *as* (doth) *thy people* Israel,
34. If *thy people* go out to war
39. forgive *thy people* which have sinned
7: 4. the king and all *the people* offered
5. the king and all *the people* dedicated the
10. he sent *the people* away
— to Solomon, and to Israel *his people*.
13. if I send pestilence *among my people*;
14. *my people*, which are called by my name,
20. a byword among all *nations*.
8: 7. all *the people* (that were) left
10. that bare rule *over the people*.
10: 5. And *the people* departed.
6. to return answer *to* this *people*?
7. If thou be kind *to* this *people*,
9. that we may return answer to this *people*,
10. Thus shalt thou answer *the people*
12. Jeroboam and all *the people* came
15. the king hearkened not unto *the people*:
16. *the people* answered the king,
12: 3. *the people* (were) without number (lit. no number *to the people*)
13: 9. *after the manner of the nations of* (other) lands?
17. Abijah *and his people* slew them
14:13(12). Asa *and the people* that (were) with him
16:10. Asa oppressed (some) of *the people*
17: 9. and taught *the people*.
18: 2. *and for the people* that (he had) with him,
3. I (am) as thou (art), *and my people as thy people*;
27. Hearken, all ye *people*.
19: 4. he went out again *through the people*
20: 7. before *thy people* Israel,
21. when he had consulted with *the people*,
25. Jehoshaphat *and his people*
33. *the people* had not prepared
21:14. plague will the Lord smite *thy people*,
19. *his people* made no burning for him,
23: 5. all *the people* (shall be) in the courts
6. *the people* shall keep the watch
10. he set all *the people*, every man
12. heard the noise of *the people*
— she came to *the people* into the house
13. all *the people of* the land rejoiced,
16. between all *the people*,
— that they should be the Lord's *people*.
17. *the people* went to the house of Baal,
20. governors *of the people*, and all *the people*
21. all *the people of* the land rejoiced:
24:10. all *the people* rejoiced,
20. which stood above *the people*,
23. destroyed all the princes of *the people from among the people*,
25:11. strengthened himself, and led forth *his people*,
15. the gods of *the people*, which could not deliver *their own people*
26: 1. all *the people of* Judah took Uzziah,
21. judging *the people of* the land.
27: 2. *the people* did yet corruptly.
29:36. Hezekiah rejoiced, and all *the people*, that God had prepared *the people*:
30: 3. neither had *the people* gathered themselves
13. there assembled at Jerusalem much *people*
18. a multitude of *the people*,
20. to Hezekiah, and healed *the people*.
27. the Levites arose and blessed *the people*:
31: 4. *the people* that dwelt in Jerusalem

2Ch 31: 8. blessed the Lord, and *his people*
10. the Lord hath blessed *his people*;
32: 4. there was gathered much *people*
6. he set captains of war over *the people*,
8. *the people* rested themselves upon
13. *the people of* (other) lands?
14. that could deliver *his people* out of mine
15. to deliver *his people* out of mine hand,
17. have not delivered *their people*
— the God of Hezekiah deliver *his people*
18. *the people of* Jerusalem that (were) on the
19. the gods of *the people of* the earth,
33:10. spake to Manasseh, and to *his people*
17. *the people* did sacrifice still
25. *the people of* the land slew all them
— *the people of* the land made Josiah
34:30. the Levites, and all *the people*,
35: 3. the Lord your God, and *his people* Israel,
5. the fathers of your brethren the (marg. sons of *the*) *people*,
7. Josiah gave to the (lit. *id.*) *people*,
8. his princes gave willingly *unto the people*,
12. the families of the (lit. sons of *the*) *people*,
13. (them) speedily among all *the people*.
36: 1. *the people of* the land took Jehoahaz
14. the chief of the priests, *and the people*,
15. he had compassion on *his people*,
16. of the Lord arose *against his people*,
23. (is there) among you of all *his people*?
Ezr. 1: 3. (is there) among you of all *his people*?
2: 2. The number of the men of *the people of*
70. the Levites, and (some) of *the people*,
3: 1. *the people* gathered themselves together
3. *because of the people of* those countries:
11. *the people* shouted with a great shout,
13. *the people* could not discern the noise
— the noise of the weeping of *the people*: for *the people* shouted
4: 4. *the people of* the land weakened the hands of *the people of* Judah,
8:15. I viewed *the people*, and the priests,
36. they furthered *the people*, and the house
9: 1. *The people* of Israel, and the priests,
— *from the people of* the lands,
2. *with the people of* (those) lands:
11. of *the people of* the lands,
14. *with the people of* these abominations?
10: 1. *the people* wept very sore.
2. wives *of the people of* the land:
9. all *the people* sat in the street
11. *from the people of* the land,
13. *the people* (are) many,
Neh 1: 8. scatter you abroad *among the nations*:
10. thy servants *and thy people*,
4: 6(3:38). *the people* had a mind to work.
13(7). I even set *the people* after their families
14(8), 19(13). to the rulers, and to the rest of *the people*,
22(16). said I *unto the people*,
5: 1. there was a great cry of *the people*
13. *the people* did according to this promise.
15. chargeable unto *the people*,
— their servants bare rule over *the people*:
18. the bondage was heavy upon this *people*.
19. that I have done for this *people*.
7: 4. *but the people* (were) few therein,
5. the rulers, and *the people*,
7. the men of *the people of* Israel
72. (that) which the rest of *the people* gave
73. and (some) of *the people*,
8: 1. *the people* gathered themselves together
3. the ears of all *the people* (were attentive)
5. in the sight of all *the people*; for he was above all *the people*;
— all *the people* stood up:
6. all *the people* answered, Amen,
7. caused *the people* to understand the law: *and the people* (stood) in their place.
9. the Levites that taught *the people*, said unto all *the people*,
— For all *the people* wept, when they heard
11. the Levites stilled all *the people*,
12. all *the people* went their way
13. the fathers of all *the people*,
16. So *the people* went forth,
9:10. on all *the people of* his land:
22. thou gavest them kingdoms *and nations*

Neh 9:24. their kings, *and the people of* the land,
30. the hand of *the people of* the lands.
32. on all *thy people*, since the time
10:14(15). The chief of *the people;*
28(29). the rest of *the people*,
—(—). *from the people of* the lands
30(31). *unto the people of* the land,
31(32). *And* (if) *the people of* the land
34(35). the Levites, *and the people*,
11: 1. the rulers of *the people*
— the rest of *the people*
2. *the people* blessed all the men,
24. in all matters *concerning the people.*
12:30. purified *the people*, and the gates,
38. *the people* upon the wall,
13: 1. in the audience of *the people;*
24. the language of *each people.* (marg. *people and people*)
Est. 1: 5. the king made a feast unto all *the people*
11. *the people* and the princes
16. to all the princes, and to all *the people*
22. to *every people* (lit. *people and people*)
— to the language of every *people.*
2:10. Esther had not shewed *her people*
20. shewed her kindred nor *her people;*
3: 6. shewed him *the people of* Mordecai:
— (even) *the people of* Mordecai.
8. There is *a* certain *people* scattered abroad and dispersed among *the people*
— their laws (are) diverse from all *people;*
11. The silver (is) given to thee, *the people also*,
12. to the rulers of *every people* (lit. *people and people*)
— *and* (to) *every people* (lit. *id.*) after their language;
14. published unto all *people*,
4: 8. to make request before him for *her people.*
11. *and the people of* the king's provinces,
7: 3. *and my people* at my request:
4. we are sold, I *and my people*,
8: 6. the evil that shall come unto *my people?*
9. *and* unto *every people* (lit. *people and people*)
11. all the power of *the people*
13. published unto all *people*,
17. many *of the people of* the land
9: 2. the fear of them fell upon all *people.*
10: 3. seeking the wealth *of his people*,
Job 12: 2. No doubt but ye (are) *the people*,
24. the chief of *the people of* the earth,
17: 6. a byword of *the people;*
18:19. son nor nephew *among his people*,
34:20. *the people* shall be troubled at midnight,
30. lest *the people* be ensnared.
36:20. Desire not the night, when *people* are cut
31. by them judgeth he *the people;*
Ps. 3: 6(7). I will not be afraid of ten thousands of *people*,
8(9). thy blessing (is) upon *thy people.*
7: 8(9). The Lord shall judge *the people:*
9:11(12). declare *among the people*
14: 4. eat up *my people* (as) they eat bread,
7. the captivity of *his people*,
18:27(28). thou wilt save *the* afflicted *people;*
43(44). from the strivings of *the people;*
—(—). *a people* (whom) I have not known
47(48). subdueth *the people* unto me.
22: 6(7). a reproach of men, and despised of *the people.*
31(32). declare his righteousness *unto a people*
28: 9. Save *thy people*, and bless thine inheritance:
29:11. The Lord will give strength *unto his people;* the Lord will bless *his people*
33:10. the devices of *the people*
12. *the people* (whom) he hath chosen
35:18. I will praise thee *among* much *people.*
44:12(13). Thou sellest *thy people* for nought,
45: 5(6). *the people* fall under thee.
10(11). forget also *thine own people*,
12(13). the rich among *the people*
17(18). therefore shall *the people* praise thee
47: 1(2). O clap your hands, all ye *people;*
3(4). He shall subdue *the people*
9(10). The princes of *the people* are gathered together, (even) *the people of* the God of
49: 1(2). Hear this, all (ye) *people;*
50: 4. that he may judge *his people.*
7. Hear, *O my people*, and I will speak;

Ps. 53: 4(5). eat up *my people* (as) they eat bread:
6(7). the captivity of *his people*,
56: 7(8). cast down *the people*, O God.
57: 9(10). praise thee, O Lord, *among the people:*
59:11(12). Slay them not, lest *my people* forget:
60: 3(5). hast shewed *thy people* hard things:
62: 8(9). Trust in him at all times; *ye people*,
66: 8. O bless our God, ye *people*,
67: 3(4), 5(6). Let *the people* praise thee, O God; let all *the people* praise thee.
4(5). thou shalt judge *the people* righteously,
68: 7(8). thou wentest forth before *thy people*,
30(31). the calves of *the people*,
—(—). scatter thou *the people*
35(36). he that giveth strength and power *unto* (his) *people.*
72: 2. shall judge *thy people* with righteousness,
3. The mountains shall bring peace *to the people*,
4. He shall judge the poor of *the people*,
73:10. Therefore *his people* return hither:
74:14. gavest him (to be) meat *to the people*
18. *and* (that) *the* foolish *people* have
77:14(15). thou hast declared thy strength *among the people.*
15(16). with (thine) arm redeemed *thy people*,
20(21). Thou leddest *thy people* like a flock
78: 1. Give ear, *O my people*, (to) my law:
20. can he provide flesh *for his people?*
52. made *his own people* to go forth
62. He gave *his people* over
71. he brought him to feed Jacob *his people*,
79:13. we *thy people* and sheep of thy pasture
80: 4(5). angry against the prayer of *thy people?*
81: 8(9). Hear, *O my people*, and I will testify
11(12). *my people* would not hearken
13(14). Oh that *my people* had hearkened
83: 3(4). They have taken crafty counsel against *thy people*,
85: 2(3). hast forgiven the iniquity of *thy people*,
6(7). *that thy people* may rejoice in thee?
8(9). he will speak peace unto *his people*,
87: 6. when he writeth up *the people*,
89:15(16). Blessed (is) *the people* that know
19(20). exalted (one) chosen *out of the people.*
50(51). all *the* mighty *people;*
94: 5. They break in pieces *thy people*,
8. ye brutish *among the people:*
14. the Lord will not cast off *his people*,
95: 7. we (are) *the people of* his pasture,
10. It (is) *a people* that do err in their heart,
96: 3. his wonders among all *people.*
5. the gods of *the nations* (are) idols:
7. O ye kindreds of *the people*,
10. he shall judge *the people* righteously.
13. *and the people* with his truth.
97: 6. all *the people* see his glory.
98: 9. *and the people* with equity.
99: 1. The Lord reigneth; let *the people* tremble:
2. he (is) high above all *the people.*
100: 3. (we are) *his people*, and the sheep of his
102:18(19). *and the people* which shall be created
22(23). When *the people* are gathered together,
105: 1. make known his deeds *among the people.*
13. from (one) kingdom to another *people;*
20. the ruler of *the people*,
24. he increased *his people* greatly;
25. He turned their heart to hate *his people*,
43. he brought forth *his people* with joy,
106: 4. with the favour (that thou bearest unto) *thy people:*
34. They did not destroy *the nations*,
40. of the Lord kindled *against his people*,
48. let all *the people* say, Amen.
107:32. in the congregation of *the people*,
108: 3(4). praises unto thee *among the nations.*
110: 3. *Thy people* (shall be) willing in the day
111: 6. He hath shewed *his people* the power of
9. He sent redemption *unto his people:*
113: 8. with the princes of *his people.*
114: 1. *from a people of* strange language;
116:14, 18. in the presence of all *his people.*
125: 2. the Lord (is) round about *his people*
135:12. an heritage unto Israel *his people.*
14. the Lord will judge *his people*,
136:16. him which led *his people*
144: 2. who subdueth *my people* under me.

Ps. 144:15. Happy (is that) *people*, that is in such a case: (yea), happy (is that) *people*,
148:14. He also exalteth the horn *of his people*,
— *a people* near unto him.
149: 4. the Lord taketh pleasure *in his people:*
Pro. 11:14. Where no counsel (is), *the people* fall:
14:28. In the multitude of *people*
24:24. him shall *the people* curse,
28:15. a wicked ruler over *the* poor *people*.
29: 2. *the people* rejoice: but when the wicked beareth rule, *the people* mourn.
18. Where (there is) no vision, *the people* perish:
30:25. The ants (are) *a people* not strong,
26. The conies (are but) *a* feeble *folk*,
Ecc. 4:16. (There is) no end of all *the people*,
12: 9. he still taught *the people* knowledge;
Isa. 1: 3. not know, *my people* doth not consider.
4. *a people* laden with iniquity,
10. law of our God, *ye people of* Gomorrah.
2: 3. many *people* shall go and say,
4. the nations, and shall rebuke many *people:*
6. Therefore thou hast forsaken *thy people*
3: 5. *the people* shall be oppressed,
7. make me not a ruler of *the people*.
12. (As for) *my people*, children (are) their
— O *my people*, they which lead thee
13. to plead, and standeth to judge *the people*.
14. judgment with the ancients of *his people*,
15. What mean ye (that) ye beat *my people*
5:13. *my people* are gone into captivity,
25. of the Lord kindled *against his people*,
6: 5. *a people of* unclean lips:
9. Go, and tell this *people*, Hear ye indeed,
10. Make the heart of this *people* fat,
7: 2. his heart was moved, and the heart of *his people*,
8. shall Ephraim be broken, *that it be not a* (marg. *from a*) *people*.
17. bring upon thee, and upon *thy people*,
8: 6. Forasmuch as this *people* refuseth
9. Associate yourselves, O ye *people*,
11. I should not walk in the way of this *people*,
12. (to) whom this *people* shall say,
19. should not *a people* seek unto their God?
9: 2(1). *The people* that walked in darkness
9(8). all *the people* shall know,
13(12). *For the people* turneth not unto him
16(15). the leaders of this *people*
19(18). *the people* shall be as the fuel
10: 2. away the right from the poor of *my people*,
6. *the people of* my wrath
13. I have removed the bounds of *the people*,
14. the riches of *the people:*
22. though *thy people* Israel be as the sand
24. *O my people* that dwellest in Zion,
11:10. an ensign of *the people;*
11. to recover the remnant of *his people*,
16. highway for the remnant of *his people*,
12: 4. his doings *among the people*,
13: 4. like as of *a* great *people;*
14. shall every man turn to *his own people*,
14: 2. *the people* shall take them,
6. He who smote *the people*
20. destroyed thy land, (and) slain *thy people:*
32. the poor of *his people* shall trust in it.
17:12. the multitude of many *people*,
18: 2. *a people* terrible from their beginning
7. *a people* scattered and peeled, *and from a people* terrible from their beginning
19:25. Blessed (be) Egypt *my people*,
22: 4. the spoiling of the daughter of *my people*.
23:13. the Chaldeans; this *people* was not,
24: 2. *as with the people*, so with the priest;
4. *the* haughty *people of* the earth do languish.
13. in the midst of the land among *the people*,
25: 3. shall *the* strong *people* glorify thee,
6. make unto all *people* a feast
7. the covering cast over all *people*,
8. the rebuke of *his people* shall he take away
26:11. ashamed for (their) envy at *the people;*
20. *my people*, enter thou into thy chambers,
27:11. *a people of* no understanding:
28: 5. the residue of *his people*,
11. will he speak to this *people*.
14. ye scornful men, that rule this *people*
29:13. *people* draw near (me) with their mouth,

Isa. 29:14. a marvellous work among this *people*,
30: 5. They were all ashamed of *a people*
6. *a people* (that) shall not profit (them).
9. this (is) *a* rebellious *people*,
19. *the people* shall dwell in Zion
26. Lord bindeth up the breach of *his people*,
28. a bridle in the jaws of *the people*,
32:13. Upon the land of *my people*
18. *my people* shall dwell in a peaceable
33: 3. At the noise of the tumult *the people* fled;
12. *the people* shall be (as) the burnings of
19. Thou shalt not see *a* fierce *people*, *a people of* deeper speech than thou
24. *the people* that dwell therein
34: 5. *the people of* my curse, to judgment.
36:11. ears of *the people* that (are) on the wall.
40: 1. comfort ye *my people*,
7. surely *the people* (is) grass.
42: 5. he that giveth breath *unto the people*
6. give thee for a covenant of *the people*,
22. *a people* robbed and spoiled;
43: 8. Bring forth *the* blind *people*
20. in the desert, to give drink to *my people*,
21. This *people* have I formed for myself;
44: 7. I appointed *the* ancient *people?*
47: 6. I was wroth with *my people*,
49: 8. give thee for a covenant of *the people*,
13. the Lord hath comforted *his people*,
22. set up my standard to *the people:*
51: 4. Hearken unto me, *my people;*
— to rest for a light of *the people*.
5. mine arms shall judge *the people;*
7. *the people* in whose heart (is) my law;
16. Zion, Thou (art) *my people*.
22. pleadeth the cause of *his people*,
52: 4. *My people* went down aforetime
5. *my people* is taken away for nought?
6. *my people* shall know my name:
9. the Lord hath comforted *his people*,
53: 8. for the transgression of *my people*
56: 3. utterly separated me from *his people:*
7. an house of prayer for all *people*.
57:14. out of the way of *my people*.
58: 1. and shew *my people* their transgression,
60:21. *Thy people also* (shall be) all righteous:
61: 9. their offspring among *the people:*
62:10. prepare ye the way of *the people;*
— lift up a standard for *the people*.
12. they shall call them, *The* holy *people*,
63: 3. *and of the people* (there was) none with me:
6. I will tread down *the people*
8. they (are) *my people*,
11. the days of old, Moses, (and) *his people*,
14. so didst thou lead *thy people*,
18. *The people of* thy holiness
64: 9(8). we (are) all *thy people*.
65: 2. *a* rebellious *people*, which walketh
3. *A people* that provoketh me
10. *for my people* that have sought me.
18. Jerusalem a rejoicing, *and her people* a joy.
19. rejoice in Jerusalem, and joy *in my people:*
22. of a tree (are) the days of *my people*,
Jer. 1:18. *and against the people of* the land.
2:11. *but my people* have changed their glory
13. *my people* have committed two evils;
31. wherefore say *my people*, We are lords;
32. *yet my people* have forgotten me
4:10. thou hast greatly deceived this *people*
11. shall it be said *to* this *people*
— the daughter of *my people*,
22. For *my people* (is) foolish,
5:14. *and* this *people* wood, and it shall
21. Hear now this, O foolish *people*,
23. *But* this *people* hath (lit. *But* there is *to* this *people*) a revolting and
26. *among my people* are found wicked (men):
31. *and my people* love (to have it) so:
6:14. the daughter of *my people*
19. I will bring evil upon this *people*,
21. lay stumbling blocks before this *people*,
22. *a people* cometh from the north
26. O daughter of *my people*,
27. a fortress *among my people*,
7:12. the wickedness of *my people* Israel.
16. pray not thou for this *people*,
23. be my *people:* (lit. *for a people* to me)
33. the carcases of this *people*

Jer. 8: 5. is this *people* of Jerusalem slidden back
7. *but my people* know not the judgment of
11, 21. the hurt of the daughter of *my people*
19. the cry of the daughter of *my people*
22. the health of the daughter of *my people*
9: 1(8:23). slain of the daughter of *my people!*
2(1). that I might leave *my people*,
7(6). do for the daughter of *my people?*
15(14). feed them, (even) this *people*,
10: 3. the customs of *the people* (are) vain:
11: 4. ye be my *people*, (lit. *for a people* to me)
14. pray not thou for this *people*,
12:14. I have caused *my people* Israel
16. the ways of *my people*,
— they taught *my people* to swear
— in the midst of *my people*.
13:10. This evil *people*, which refuse to hear
11. that they might be unto me *for a people*,
14:10. Thus saith the Lord *unto* this *people*,
11. Pray not for this *people* for (their) good.
16. *And the people* to whom they prophesy
17. the virgin daughter of *my people*
15: 1. my mind (could) not (be) toward this *people:*
7. I will destroy *my people*,
20. I will make thee *unto* this *people*
16: 5. taken away my peace from this *people*,
10. when thou shalt shew this *people*
17:19. the gate of the children of *the people*,
18:15. *my people* hath forgotten me
19: 1. the ancients of *the people*,
11. so will I break this *people*
14. and said to all *the people*,
21: 7. of Judah, and his servants, and *the people*,
8. unto this *people* thou shalt say,
22: 2. *and thy people* that enter in by these
4. he, and his servants, *and his people*.
23: 2. the pastors that feed *my people;*
13. caused *my people* Israel to err.
22. caused *my people* to hear my words,
27. cause *my people* to forget my name
32. cause *my people* to err
— they shall not profit this *people*
33. this *people*, or the prophet,
34. the prophet, and the priest, *and the people*,
24: 7. they shall be my *people*, (lit. *for a people* to me)
25: 1. concerning all *the people of* Judah
2. unto all *the people of* Judah,
19. his princes, and all *his people ;*
26: 7. and all *the people* heard Jeremiah
8. to speak unto all *the people*,
— all *the people* took him,
9. all *the people* were gathered
11. unto the princes and to all *the people*,
12. all the princes and to all *the people*,
16. said the princes and all *the people*
17. all the assembly of *the people*,
18. all *the people of* Judah,
23. the graves of *the* common *people*.
24. into the hand of *the people*
27:12. serve him *and his people*,
13. Why will ye die, thou *and thy people*,
16. priests and to all this *people*,
28: 1. of the priests and of all *the people*,
5, 11. in the presence of all *the people*
7. in the ears of all *the people ;*
15. thou makest this *people* to trust in a lie.
29: 1. all *the people* whom Nebuchadnezzar
16. *the people* that dwelleth in this city,
25. *the people* that (are) at Jerusalem,
32. a man to dwell among this *people ;*
— the good that I will do *for my people*,
30: 3. the captivity of *my people* Israel
22. be my *people*, (lit. *for a people* to me)
31: 1, 33. they shall be my *people*. (lit. *id.*)
2. *The people* (which were) left of the
7. O Lord, save *thy people*,
14. *and my people* shall be satisfied
32:21. hast brought forth *thy people* Israel
38. be my *people*, (lit. *for a people* to me)
42. this great evil upon this *people*,
33:24. what this *people* have spoken,
— they have despised *my people*,
34: 1. all *the people*, fought against Jerusalem,
8. had made a covenant with all *the people*
10. the princes, and all *the people*,

Jer. 34:19. all *the people of* the land,
35:16. *but* this *people* hath not hearkened unto
36: 6. in the ears of *the people*
7. the Lord hath pronounced against this *people*.
9. *the people* in Jerusalem, and to all *the people* that came from the cities
10. in the ears of all *the people*.
13, 14. in the ears of *the people*.
37: 2. *nor the people of* the land,
4. came in and went out among *the people:*
12. in the midst of *the people*.
18. thy servants, *or against* this *people*,
38: 1. Jeremiah had spoken unto all *the people*,
4. the hands of all *the people*,
— man seeketh not the welfare *of* this *people*,
39: 8. house, and the houses of *the people*,
9. the remnant of *the people* that
— the rest of *the people* that remained.
10. the poor of *the people*,
14. he dwelt among *the people*.
40: 5. dwell with him among *the people:*
6. among *the people* that were left
41:10. the residue of *the people*
— all *the people* that remained
13. *the people* which (were) with Ishmael
14. *the people* that Ishmael had carried
16. all the remnant of *the people*
42: 1. *the people* from the least even unto the
8. all *the people* from the least even to the
43: 1. speaking unto all *the people*
4. *the people*, obeyed not the voice
44:15. *the people* that dwelt in the land
20, 24. Jeremiah said unto all *the people*,
— and to all *the people* which had given
21. *and the people of* the land,
46:16. let us go again to *our own people*,
24. the hand of *the people of* the north.
48:42. shall be destroyed *from* (being) *a people*,
46. *the people of* Chemosh perisheth:
49: 1. *and his people* dwell in his cities?
50: 6. *My people* hath been lost sheep:
16. they shall turn every one to *his people*,
41. *a people* shall come from the north,
51:45. *My people*, go ye out of the midst of her,
58. *the people* shall labour in vain,
52: 6. there was no bread *for the people of*
15. the poor of *the people*, and the residue of *the people*
25. *the people of* the land; and threescore men *of the people of* the land,
28. *the people* whom Nebuchadrezzar
Lam 1: 1. the city sit solitary, (that was) full of *people!*
7. *her people* fell into the hand of the enemy,
11. All *her people* sigh, they seek bread;
18. hear, I pray you, all *people*,
2:11. the daughter of *my people ;*
3:14. I was a derision to all *my people ;*
45. in the midst of *the people*.
48. destruction of the daughter of *my people*.
4: 3. the daughter of *my people* (is become)
6. of the daughter of *my people* is greater
10. destruction of the daughter of *my people*.
Eze. 3: 5. *a people* of a strange speech
6. many *people* of a strange speech
11. the children of *thy people*,
7:27. *the people of* the land shall be troubled:
11: 1. princes of *the people*.
17. I will even gather you from *the people*,
20. they shall be my *people*, (lit. *for a people* to me)
12:19. say unto *the people of* the land,
13: 9. the assembly of *my people*,
10. they have seduced *my people*,
17. the daughters of *thy people*,
18. Will ye hunt the souls *of my people*,
19. will ye pollute me among *my people*
— lying *to my people* that hear (your) lies?
21. and deliver *my people* out of your hand,
23. I will deliver *my people* out of your hand:
14: 8. off from the midst of *my people ;*
9. from the midst of *my people* Israel.
11. that they may be my *people*, (lit. *for a people* to me)
17: 9. without great power *or* many *people*
15. give him horses *and* much *people*.
18:18. which (is) not good *among his people*,

Eze.20:34. I will bring you out from *the people*,
35. the wilderness of *the people*,
41. when I bring you out from *the people*,
21:12(17). for it shall be *upon my people*,
—(—). of the sword shall be upon *my people:*
22:29. *The people of* the land have used
23:24. with an assembly of *people*,
24:18. I spake unto *the people* in the morning:
19. And *the people* said unto me,
25: 7. I will cut thee off from *the people*,
14. by the hand of *my people* Israel:
26: 2. (that was) the gates of *the people:*
7. horsemen, and companies, *and* much *people*.
11. he shall slay *thy people* by the sword,
20. the pit, with *the people of* old time,
27: 3. a merchant of *the people*
33. thou filledst many *people;*
36. The merchants *among the people*
28:19. they that know thee *among the people*
25. *the people* among whom they are scattered,
29:13. gather the Egyptians from *the people*
30:11. He *and his people* with him,
31:12. all *the people of* the earth
32: 3. a company of many *people:*
9. vex the hearts of many *people*,
10. I will make many *people* amazed
33: 2. the children of *thy people*,
— if *the people of* the land take a man
3. blow the trumpet, and warn *the people;*
6. *and the people* be not warned;
12. say unto the children of *thy people*,
17. Yet the children of *thy people* say,
30. the children of *thy people* still are talking
31. they come unto thee as *the people* cometh, and they sit before thee (as) *my people*,
34:13. I will bring them out from *the people*,
30. the house of Israel, (are) *my people*,
36: 3. an infamy of *the people:*
8. yield your fruit *to my people*
12. upon you, (even) *my people* Israel;
15. the reproach of *the people*
20. These (are) *the people of* the Lord,
28. be my *people*, (lit. *for a people* to me)
37:12. *O my people*, I will open your graves,
13. I have opened your graves, *O my people*,
18. the children of *thy people*
23. so shall they be my *people*, (lit. *for a people* to me)
27. they shall be my *people*. (lit. *id.*)
38: 6. many *people* with thee.
8. gathered *out of* many *people*,
— brought forth *out of the nations*,
9. *and* many *people* with thee.
12. *the people* (that are) gathered out of the
14. when *my people* of Israel dwelleth
15. *and* many *people* with thee,
16. shalt come up against *my people*
22. *the* many *people* that (are) with him,
39: 4. *and the people* that (is) with thee:
7. in the midst of *my people* Israel;
13. all *the people of* the land
27. When I have brought them again from *the people*,
42:14. (those things) which (are) *for the people*.
44:11. the sacrifice *for the people*,
19. into the utter court to *the people*,
— they shall not sanctify *the people*
23. they shall teach *my people*
45: 8. shall no more oppress *my people;*
9. take away your exactions from *my people*,
16. All *the people* of the land
22. all *the people of* the land
46: 3. *the people of* the land shall worship
9. when *the people of* the land shall come
18. shall not take of *the people*'s inheritance
— that *my people* be not scattered
20. utter court, to sanctify *the people*.
24. shall boil the sacrifice of *the people*.
Dan. 8:24. the mighty *and the* holy *people*. (marg. *people of* the holy ones)
9: 6. and to all *the people of* the land.
15. our God, that hast brought *thy people*
16. Jerusalem *and thy people* (are become) a reproach
19. *thy people* are called by thy name.
20. the sin of *my people* Israel,

Dan. 9:24. weeks are determined upon *thy people*
26. *the people of* the prince that shall
10:14. what shall befall *thy people*
11:14. robbers of *thy people* shall exalt themselves
15. *neither* his chosen *people*, (lit. *and the people of* his choices)
32. *but the people* that do know their God
33. they that understand among *the people*
12: 1. the children of *thy people:*
— *thy people* shall be delivered,
7. the power of *the* holy *people*,
Hos. 1: 9. Call his name Lo-*ammi:* (marg. (That is), Not *my people*) for ye (are) not *my people*,
10(2:1). Ye (are) not *my people*,
2: 1(3). Say ye unto your brethren, *Ammi;* (marg. (That is), *My people*)
23(25). (them which were) not *my people*, Thou (art) *my people;*
4: 4. *for thy people* (are) as they that strive
6. *My people* are destroyed for lack of
8. They eat up the sin of *my people*,
9. there shall be, *like people*, like priest:
12. *My people* ask counsel at their stocks,
14. *therefore the people* (that) doth not
6:11. I returned the captivity of *my people*.
7: 8. hath mixed himself *among the people;*
9: 1. O Israel, for joy, *as* (other) *people:*
10: 5. *the people thereof* shall mourn
10. *the people* shall be gathered against them,
14. shall a tumult arise *among thy people*,
11: 7. *And my people* are bent to backsliding
Joel 2: 2. *a* great *people* and a strong;
5. *as a* strong *people* set in battle array.
6. *the people* shall be much pained:
16. Gather *the people*, sanctify the
17. Spare *thy people*, O Lord,
— should they say *among the people*,
18. jealous for his land, and pity *his people*.
19. will answer and say *unto his people*,
26, 27. *my people* shall never be ashamed.
3: 2(4:2). for *my people* and (for) my heritage
3(-:3). they have cast lots for *my people;*
16(-:16). Lord (will be) the hope *of his people*,
Am. 1: 5. *the people of* Syria shall go into captivity
3: 6. *and the people* not be afraid?
7: 8. in the midst of *my people* Israel:
15. prophesy unto *my people* Israel.
8: 2. The end is come upon *my people* of
9:10. All the sinners of *my people* shall die
14. bring again the captivity of *my people*
Obad. 13. entered into the gate of *my people*
Jon. 1: 8. of what *people* (art) thou?
Mic. 1: 2. Hear, all ye *people;* hearken,
9. he is come unto the gate of *my people*,
2: 4. changed the portion of *my people:*
8. of late *my people* is risen up
9. The women of *my people* have ye cast out
11. shall even be the prophet of this *people*.
3: 3. Who also eat the flesh of *my people*,
5. the prophets that make *my people* err,
4: 1. and *people* shall flow unto it.
3. he shall judge among many *people*,
5. all *people* will walk every one
13. thou shalt beat in pieces many *people:*
5: 7(6), 8(7). in the midst of many *people*
6: 2. Lord hath a controversy with *his people*,
3. *O my people*, what have I done unto
5. *O my people*, remember now what
16. ye shall bear the reproach of *my people*.
7:14. Feed *thy people* with thy rod,
Nah. 3:13. *thy people* in the midst of thee
18. *thy people* is scattered upon the
Hab. 2: 5. heapeth unto him all *people:*
8. the remnant of *the people* shall spoil thee;
10. by cutting off many *people*,
13. *the people* shall labour in the very fire,
3:13. the salvation of *thy people*,
16. when he cometh up unto *the people*,
Zep. 1:11. all *the* merchant *people* are cut down;
2: 8. they have reproached *my people*,
9. the residue of *my people* shall spoil
10. magnified (themselves) against *the people of*
3: 9. then will I turn to *the people*
12. *an* afflicted and poor *people*,
20. among all *people of* the earth,
Hag. 1: 2. This *people* say, The time is not come,

Hag. 1:12. all the remnant of *the people*,
— *the people* did fear before the Lord.
13. in the Lord's message *unto the people*
14. of all the remnant of *the people*;
2: 2. the residue of *the people*,
4. all *ye people of* the land,
14. So (is) this *people*, and so (is) this nation
Zec. 2:11(15). and shall be my *people*: (lit. *for a people* to me)
7: 5. Speak unto all *the people of* the land,
8: 6, 12. the remnant of this *people*
7. I will save *my people*
8. and they shall be my *people*, (lit. *for a people* to me)
11. the residue of this *people*
20. that there shall come *people*,
22. many *people* and strong nations shall
9:16. in that day as the flock of *his people*:
10: 9. I will sow them *among the people*:
11:10. which I had made with all *the people*.
12: 2. unto all *the people* round about,
3. a burdensome stone for all *people*:
4. every horse of *the people*
6. devour all *the people* round about,
13: 9. I will say, It (is) *my people*:
14: 2. the residue of *the people*
12. the Lord will smite all *the people*
Mal. 1: 4. *and, The people* against whom the Lord
2: 9. and base before all *the people*,

5972 ## עַם *gam*, Ch. m.

Ezr. 5:12. *and* carried *the people* away
6:12. destroy all kings *and people*,
7:13. that all they of *the people* of Israel,
16. the freewill offering of *the people*,
25. which may judge all *the people*
Dan. 2:44. shall not be left *to* other *people*,
3: 4. *O people*, nations, and languages,
7. when all *the people* heard the
— all *the people*, the nations,
29. That every *people*, nation,
4: 1(3:31). Nebuchadnezzar the king, unto all *people*,
5:19. all *people*, nations, and languages,
6:25(26). king Darius wrote unto all *people*,
7:14. that all *people*, nations, and
27. shall be given *to the people of*

5973 ## עִם *geem*, part. prep.

Gen18:23. destroy the righteous *with* the wicked?
24:12. shew kindness *unto* my master Abraham.
25:11. Isaac dwelt *by* the well Lahai-roi.
31:24. Take heed that thou speak not *to* Jacob
Deu 8: 5. Thou shalt also consider *in* thine heart,
9: 7. ye have been rebellious *against* the Lord.
Jos. 7: 2. to Ai, which (is) *beside* Beth-aven,
22: 7. gave Joshua *among* their brethren
Jud. 20:38. the men of Israel *and* (marg. *with*) the
1Sa. 2:21. the child Samuel grew *before* the Lord.
16:12. ruddy, (and) *withal* of a beautiful
2Sa. 6: 4. *accompanying* (marg. *with*) the ark of
21: 4. no silver nor gold *of* Saul,
2Ch 21:19. fell out *by reason of* his sickness:
Neh 5:18. *yet for all* this required not I
Job 9:26. They are passed away *as* the swift ships:
Ps. 72: 5. *as long as* the sun and moon endure, (lit. *with* the sun and before the moon)
73: 5. *neither* are they plagued *like* (marg. *with*) (other) men.
Ecc. 2:16. no remembrance of the wise *more than of* &c. &c.

It occurs with prefix מֵעִם, as

Gen24:27. who hath not left destitute)(my master
41:32. the thing (is) established *by* (marg. or, prepared *of*) God,
44:29. if ye take this also *from* me,
32. surety for the lad *unto* my father,
48:12. brought them out *from between* his knees,
Ex. 22:14(13). if a man borrow (ought) *of* his
Ru. 4:10. be not cut off *from among* his brethren, &c.

עִם is combined with the pronominal suffixes, with similar variations of meaning.

עִם *geem*, Ch. part. prep. 5974

Ezr. 5: 2. *and with them* (were) the prophets
6: 8. what ye shall do *to* the elders
7:13. to go up to Jerusalem, go *with thee*.
16. *with* the freewill offering
Dan 2:11. whose dwelling is not *with* flesh.
18. should not perish *with* the rest of
22. and the light dwelleth *with him*.
43. one *to* another (marg. this *with* this), even as iron is not mixed *with* clay.
4: 2(3:32). God hath wrought *toward me*.
3(-:33). his dominion (is) *from* generation
15(12). *and* (let) his portion (be) *with* the
23(20). *and* (let) his portion (be) *with* the
25(22). *and* thy dwelling shall be *with* the
32(29). *and* thy dwelling (shall be) *with*
34(31). his kingdom (is) *from* generation to
5:21. his heart was made *like* the beasts, *and* his dwelling (was) *with* the
6:21(22). Then said Daniel *unto* the king,
7: 2. I saw in my vision *by* night,
13. (one) like the Son of man came *with*
21. the same horn made war *with*

עָמַד *gāh-mad'*. 5975

* KAL.—*Preterite.* *

Gen19:27. *he stood* before the Lord:
30: 9. When Leah saw that *she had left* bearing, (lit. *she stood* from bearing)
45: 1. And *there stood* no man with him,
Ex. 33: 9. the cloudy pillar descended, *and stood*
Lev.13: 5. (if) the plague...*be at a stay*, (lit. *stood*)
37. *be* in his sight *at a stay*, (lit. *stood*)
Deu 4:10. the day that *thou stoodest* before the Lord
10:10. *I stayed* in the mount, according
19:17. *Then* both the men,...*shall stand*
25: 8. *and* (if) *he stand* (to it),
Jos. 10:13. the sun stood still, and the moon *stayed*,
20: 4. *And* when *he* that doth flee...*shall stand*
21:44(42). *there stood* not a man of all their
23: 9. *hath been able to stand* before you
Jud. 6:31. Joash said unto all that *stood*
1Sa.14: 9. *then we will stand still* in our place,
19: 3. And I will go out *and stand*
30: 9. those that were left behind *stayed*.
2Sa.15: 2. Absalom rose up early, *and stood*
20:11. one of Joab's men *stood* by him,
12. saw that all the people *stood still*,
— every one that came by him *stood still*.
1K. 1: 2. *and let her stand* before the king,
17: 1. of Israel liveth, before whom *I stand*,
18:15. of hosts liveth, before whom *I stand*,
19:11. Go forth, *and stand* upon the mount
2K. 2: 7. and *they* two *stood* by Jordan.
3:14. of hosts liveth, before whom *I stand*,
5:11. surely come out to me, *and stand*,
16. the Lord liveth, before whom *I stand*,
10: 4. two kings *stood* not before him:
13: 6. there *remained* the grove also
15:20. turned back, and *stayed* not there in the
2Ch 20:20. Jehoshaphat *stood* and said,
Ezr.10:15. *were employed* (marg. *stood*) about this
Neh 8: 5. all the people *stood up*:
12:39. *and they stood still* in the prison gate.
Est. 7: 7. Haman *stood up* to make request for his
9: 2. and no man *could withstand* them; for
Job 29: 8. the aged arose, (and) *stood up*.
30:20. *I stand up*, and thou regardest me (not).
32:16. they spake not, but *stood still*,
Ps. 1: 1. nor *standeth* in the way of sinners,
26:12. My foot *standeth* in an even place:
38:11(12). my kinsmen *stand* afar off.
106:23. had not Moses his chosen *stood* before
119:91. *They continue* this day according to
Ecc. 2: 9. my wisdom *remained* with me.
Isa. 61: 5. *And* strangers *shall stand* and feed your flocks,
Jer. 7:10. come *and stand* before me
14: 6. the wild asses *did stand*
17:19. Go *and stand* in the gate
23:18. who *hath stood* in the counsel of
22. if *they had stood* in my counsel,
46:15. *they stood* not, because the Lord
21. *they did* not *stand*, because the day

Jer. 48:11. therefore his taste *remained* (marg. *stood*) in him,
45. *They* that fled *stood* under the shadow
52:12. (which) *served* (marg. *stood* before) the
Eze.21:21(26). the king of Babylon *stood*
33:26. *Ye stand* upon your sword,
44:15. *and they shall stand* before me
46: 2. *and shall stand* by the post of the gate,
47:10. the fishers *shall stand* upon it
Dan10:11. unto me, *I stood* trembling.
11: 3. *And* a mighty king *shall stand up*,
7. *But* out of a branch of her roots *shall* (one) *stand up*
20. *Then shall stand up* in his estate
21. *And* in his estate *shall stand up* a vile
Hos10: 9. there *they stood:* the battle in Gibeah
Mic. 5: 4(3). *And he shall stand* and feed
Hab 3: 6. *He stood*, and measured the earth:
11. The sun (and) moon *stood still* in their
Zec.14: 4. *And* his feet *shall stand* in that day

KAL.—*Infinitive.*

Gen41:46. *when he stood* before Pharaoh
Ex. 9:11. the magicians could not *stand*
28. ye shall *stay* no longer. (lit. ye shall not add *to stand*)
18:23. thou shalt be able *to endure*,
Nu. 16: 9. *and to stand* before the congregation
35:12. until *he stand* before the congregation
Deu10: 8. *to stand* before the Lord
18: 5. *to stand* to minister in the name of the
Jos. 20: 6. until *he stand* before the congregation
9. until *he stood* before the congregation.
Jud. 2:14. they could not any longer *stand*
1Sa. 6:20. Who is able *to stand* before this holy
1K. 8:11. the priests could not *stand* to minister
1Ch 23:30. *And to stand* every morning to thank
2Ch 5:14. the priests could not *stand* to minister
29:11. the Lord hath chosen you *to stand*
Ezr. 2:63. till *there stood* up a priest with Urim
9:15. we cannot *stand* before thee
10:13. we are not able *to stand* without,
Neh 7:65. till *there stood* (up) a priest with Urim
Est. 8:11. *and to stand* for their life,
9:16. *and stood* for their lives,
Isa. 10:32. As yet *shall he remain*
Jer. 18:20. Remember *that I stood* before thee
40:10. I will dwell at Mizpah, *to serve* (lit. *to stand* before)
Eze. 1:21. *and when those stood*, (these) stood;
24. *when they stood*, they let down
25. *when they stood*, (and) had let
10:17. *When they stood*, (these) stood;
13: 5. *to stand* in the battle
17:14. *that* by keeping of his covenant *it might stand.*
Dan 1: 4. *to stand* in the king's palace,
8: 7. no power in the ram *to stand*
11: 4. *And when he shall stand up*, his kingdom
15. (shall there be any) strength *to withstand.*
Obad. 11. In the day *that thou stoodest*

KAL.—*Imperative.*

Nu. 9: 8. Moses said unto them, *Stand still*,
Deu 5:31(28). *stand thou* here by me,
Jud. 4:20. *Stand* in the door of the tent,
1Sa. 9:27. *stand* thou *still* a while,
2Sa. 1: 9. *Stand*, I pray thee, upon me,
20: 4. and *be* thou here *present.*
2Ch 20:17. *stand ye* (still), and see the salvation
35: 5. *And stand* in the holy (place)
Job 37:14. Hearken unto this, O Job: *stand still*,
Isa. 47:12. *Stand* now with thine enchantments,
Jer. 6:16. *Stand ye* in the ways, and see,
7: 2. *Stand* in the gate of the Lord's house,
26: 2. *Stand* in the court of the Lord's house,
48:19. O inhabitant of Aroer, *stand* by the way,
Eze. 2: 1. Son of man, *stand* upon thy feet,
Dan10:11. *and stand* upright:
Nah. 2: 8(9). *Stand, stand*, (shall they cry);

KAL.—*Future.*

Gen 19:17. neither *stay thou* in all the plain;
24:31. wherefore *standest thou* without?
29:35. she called his name Judah; *and left* (marg. *stood* from) bearing.
41: 3. *and stood* by the (other) kine

Gen43:15. to Egypt, *and stood* before Joseph.
45: 9. come down unto me, *tarry* not:
Ex. 9:10. *and stood* before Pharaoh;
14:19. from before their face, *and stood* behind
18:13. *and* the people *stood* by Moses
20:18. saw (it), they removed, *and stood* afar off.
21. *And* the people *stood* afar off,
21:21. if *he continue* a day or two,
32:26. *Then* Moses *stood* in the gate
Lev. 9: 5. drew near *and stood* before the Lord.
13:23, 28. if the bright spot *stay* in his place,
18:23. neither *shall* any woman *stand* before
19:16. neither *shalt thou stand* against the blood
Nu. 1: 5. the men that *shall stand* with you:
12: 5. in the pillar of the cloud, *and stood*
16:18. *and stood* in the door of the tabernacle
48(17:13). *And he stood* between the dead and the living;
22:24. *But* the angel of the Lord *stood* in a path
26. of the Lord went further, *and stood*
27: 2. *And they stood* before Moses,
21. *he shall stand* before Eleazar the priest,
Deu 4:11. came near *and stood* under the mountain;
24:11. *Thou shalt stand* abroad, and the man
27:12. These *shall stand* upon mount Gerizim
13. these *shall stand* upon mount Ebal
31:15. *and* the pillar of the cloud *stood* over the
Jos. 3: 8. *ye shall stand still* in Jordan.
13. *and they shall stand* upon an heap.
16. *That* the waters which came down from above *stood*
17. *And* the priests that bare the ark...*stood firm*
10: 8. *there shall* not a man of them *stand*
13. *And* the sun *stood still*, and the moon
19. *stay* ye not, (but) pursue
18: 5. Judah *shall abide* in their coast
— of Joseph *shall abide* in their coasts
Jud. 7:21. *And they stood* every man in his place
9: 7. Jotham, he went *and stood* in the top of
35. Gaal the son of Ebed went out, *and stood*
44. *and stood* in the entering of the gate
Ru. 2: 7. *and hath continued* even from the morning
1Sa. 6:14. cart came into the field...*and stood* there,
16:21. David came to Saul, *and stood* before him:
22. *Let* David, I pray thee, *stand* before me;
17: 8. *And he stood* and cried unto the armies
51. David ran, *and stood* upon the Philistine,
20:38. Make speed, haste, *stay* not.
26:13. went over to the other side, *and stood*
30:10. *for* two hundred *abode behind*,
2Sa. 1:10. *So I stood* upon him,
2:23. as many as came to the place...*stood still.*
25. *and stood* on the top of an hill.
28. *and* all the people *stood still*,
15:17. *and tarried* in a place that was far off.
18: 4. *And* the king *stood* by the gate side,
30. And he turned aside, *and stood still.*
20:15. *and it stood* in the trench:
1K. 1:28. *and stood* before the king.
3:15. he came to Jerusalem, *and stood* before
16. *and stood* before him.
8:22. *And* Solomon *stood* before the altar
55. *And he stood*, and blessed all
19:13. *and stood* in the entering in of the cave.
20:38. the prophet departed, *and waited* for the
22:21. there came forth a spirit, *and stood*
2K. 2: 7. *and stood* to view afar off:
13. *and stood* by the bank of Jordan;
3:21. and upward, *and stood* in the border.
4: 6. a vessel more. *And* the oil *stayed.*
12. *And* when he had called her, *she stood* before him.
15. *And* when he had called her, *she stood* in the door.
5: 9. *and stood* at the door of the house of
15. and came, *and stood* before him:
25. he went in, *and stood* before his master.
6:31. if the head of Elisha...*shall stand* on him
8: 9. came *and stood* before him,
10: 4. how then *shall* we *stand?*
9. he went out, *and stood*,
11:11. *And* the guard *stood*,
13:18. he smote thrice, *and stayed.*
18:17. they came *and stood* by the conduit
28. *Then* Rab-shakeh *stood* and cried
23: 3. *And* the king *stood* by a pillar,

2K. 23: 3. *And* all the people *stood* to the covenant.
1Ch 6:32(17). *and* (then) *they waited* on their office
20: 4. *that there arose* war at Gezer
21: 1. *And* Satan *stood up* against Israel,
2Ch 6:12. *And he stood* before the altar
13. *and* upon it *he stood*, and kneeled
18:20. there came out a spirit, *and stood*
20: 5. *And* Jehoshaphat *stood* in the congregation
9. *we stand* before this house,
23. *For* the children of Ammon and Moab *stood up*
24:20. *which stood* above the people,
26:18. *And they* with*stood* (lit. *and stood* against) Uzziah the king,
29:26. *And* the Levites *stood* with the instruments
30:16. *And they stood* in their place
34:31. *And* the king *stood* in his place,
35:10. *and* the priests *stood* in their place,
Ezr. 3: 9. *Then stood* Jeshua (with) his sons
10:14. *Let* now our rulers of all the congregation *stand*,
Neh 8: 4. *And* Ezra the scribe *stood* upon a pulpit
— *and* beside him *stood* Mattithiah,
9: 2. *and stood* and confessed their sins,
12:40. *So stood* the two (companies)
Est. 3: 4. *whether* Mordecai's matters *would stand:*
4:14. *shall there* enlargement and deliverance *arise*
5: 1. put on (her) royal (apparel), *and stood*
8: 4. Esther arose, *and stood* before the king,
Job 4:16. *It stood still*, but I could not discern
8:15. upon his house, but *it shall* not *stand:*
14: 2. fleeth also as a shadow, and *continueth* not.
Ps. 10: 1. Why *standest thou* afar off, O Lord?
33: 9. he commanded, *and it stood fast.*
11. The counsel of the Lord *standeth*
38:11(12). My lovers and my friends *stand* aloof
76: 7(8). who *may stand* in thy sight
102:26(27). shall perish, but thou *shalt endure:*
104: 6. the waters *stood* above the mountains.
106:30. *Then stood up* Phinehas,
109: 6. *let* Satan *stand* at his right hand.
31. *he shall stand* at the right hand of the poor,
119:90. established the earth, *and it abideth.* (marg. *standeth*)
130: 3. O Lord, who *shall stand?*
147:17. *who can stand* before his cold?
Pro. 12: 7. the house of the righteous *shall stand.*
25: 6. *stand* not in the place of great (men):
27: 4. who *is able to stand* before envy?
Ecc. 4:12. two *shall* with*stand* him;
15. the second child that *shall stand up*
8: 3. *stand* not in an evil thing;
Isa. 36: 2. *And he stood* by the conduit
13. *Then* Rabshakeh *stood*, and cried
44:11. *let them stand up;* (yet) they shall fear,
46: 7. in his place, *and he standeth;*
47:13. *Let* now the astrologers,...*stand up*,
48:13. unto them, *they stand up* together.
50: 8. *let us stand* together: who (is)
59:14. justice *standeth* afar off:
66:22. so *shall* your seed and your name *remain.*
Jer. 4: 6. retire, *stay* not: for I will
15: 1. Moses and Samuel *stood* before me,
19. *thou shalt stand* before me:
19:14. *and he stood* in the court of the Lord's
32:14. that they *may continue* many days.
49:19 & 50:44. (is) that shepherd that *will stand*
51:50. go away, *stand* not *still:*
Eze. 1:21. when those stood, (these) *stood;*
9: 2. went in, *and stood* beside the brasen altar.
10: 6. he went in, *and stood* beside the wheels.
17. When they stood, (these) *stood;*
18. *and stood* over the cherubims.
19. *and* (every one) *stood* at the door of the
11:23. *and stood* upon the mountain
22:14. *Can* thine heart *endure*,
27:29. *they shall stand* upon the land;
31:14. neither their trees *stand up*
37:10. they lived, *and stood up* upon their feet,
44:11. they *shall stand* before them
24. they *shall stand* in judgment;
47:10. (כתיב) come to pass, (that) the fishers *shall stand*
Dan 1: 5. *they might stand* before the king.
19. *therefore stood they* before the king.
2: 2. they came *and stood* before the king.
Dan. 8: 4. no beasts *might stand* before him,
22. *whereas* four *stood up* for it, four kingdoms *shall stand up*
23. a king...*shall stand up.*
25. *he shall* also *stand up* against the Prince
10:17. *there remained* no strength in me,
11: 6. neither *shall he stand*, nor his arm:
8. he *shall continue* (more) years
14. *there shall* many *stand* up
15. the arms of the south *shall* not *withstand*,
16. *and he shall stand* in the glorious land,
17. *she shall* not *stand* (on his side),
25. *he shall* not *stand:* for they
31. arms *shall stand* on his part,
12: 1. at that time *shall* Michael *stand up*,
13. *and stand* in thy lot at the end
Hos 13:13. *he should* not *stay* long
Am. 2:15. Neither *shall he stand* that handleth
Obad. 14. *shouldest thou have stood* in the crossway,
Jon. 1:15. *and* the sea *ceased* from her raging.
Nah 1: 6. Who *can stand* before his indignation?
Hab 2: 1. *I will stand* upon my watch,

KAL.—*Participle.* Poel.

Gen 18: 8. he *stood* by them under the tree,
22. Abraham *stood* yet before the Lord.
24:30. *he stood* by the camels
41: 1. *he stood* by the river.
17. I *stood* upon the bank of the river:
Ex. 3: 5. the place whereon thou *standest*
8:22(18). Goshen, in which my people *dwell*,
17: 6. I *will stand* before thee
26:15. boards for the tabernacle...*standing up.*
33:10. the people saw the cloudy pillar *stand*
36:20. boards for the tabernacle...*standing up.*
Nu. 7: 2. *and were* (marg. *who stood*) over them that were numbered,
14:14. thy cloud *standeth* over them,
Deu 1:38. the son of Nun, *which standeth*
5: 5. I *stood* between the Lord and you
17:12. *that standeth* to minister
18: 7. *which stand* there before the Lord.
29:15(14). (him) *that standeth* here
Jos. 4:10. the priests which bare the ark *stood*
5:13. *there stood* a man over against him
15. the place whereon thou *standest*
8:33. *stood* on this side the ark
11:13. the cities *that stood still* in their strength,
Jud. 3:19. all *that stood* by him went out
20:28. the son of Aaron, *stood* before it
1Sa. 17: 3. the Philistines *stood* on a mountain
— Israel *stood* on a mountain
26. David spake to the men *that stood*
19:20. Samuel *standing* (as) appointed
2Sa. 17:17. Jonathan and Ahimaaz *stayed*
1K. 7:25. *It stood* upon twelve oxen,
8:14. all the congregation of Israel *stood;*
10: 8. happy (are) these thy servants, *which stand*
19. two lions *stood* beside the stays.
20. twelve lions *stood* there
12: 6. the old men, *that stood* before Solomon
8. *which stood* before him:
13: 1. Jeroboam *stood* by the altar
24. the ass *stood* by it, the lion also *stood* by the carcase.
25. the lion *standing* by the carcase:
28. the ass and the lion *standing* by the
22:19. all the host of heaven *standing* by him
2K. 9:17. there *stood* a watchman on the tower
11:14. the king *stood* by a pillar,
1Ch. 6:33(18). they *that waited* (marg. *stood*) with their children.
39(24). his brother Asaph, *who stood* on his
21:15. the angel of the Lord *stood* by
16. saw the angel of the Lord *stand*
2Ch. 3:13. they *stood* on their feet,
4: 4. *It stood* upon twelve oxen,
5:12. *stood* at the east end of the altar,
6: 3. all the congregation of Israel *stood.*
7: 6. the priests *waited* on their offices:
— before them, and all Israel *stood.*
9: 7. thy servants, *which stand* continually
18. two lions *standing* by the stays:
19. twelve lions *stood* there
10: 6. the old men that had *stood* (lit. had been *standing*)
8. *that stood* before him.

2Ch.18:18. all the host of heaven *standing*
20:13. all Judah *stood* before the Lord,
23:13. the king *stood* at his pillar
Neh 7: 3. while they *stand by*, let them shut
12:44. the Levites *that waited*. (marg. *stood*)
Est. 5: 2. the king saw Esther the queen *standing*
6: 5. Haman *standeth* in the court.
7: 9. *standeth* in the house of Haman.
Ps. 19: 9(10). fear of the Lord (is) clean, *enduring*
111: 3. his righteousness *endureth* for ever.
10. his praise *endureth* for ever.
112: 3, 9. his righteousness *endureth* for ever.
122: 2. Our feet *shall stand* within thy gates,
134: 1. servants of the Lord, *which* by night *stand*
135: 2. *Ye that stand* in the house of the Lord,
Ecc. 1: 4. the earth *abideth* for ever.
Cant.2: 9. he *standeth* behind our wall,
Isa. 3:13. *and standeth* to judge the people.
6: 2. Above it *stood* the seraphims:
11:10. *shall stand* for an ensign of the people;
21: 8. I *stand* continually upon the watchtower
66:22. *shall remain* before me,
Jer. 28: 5. all the people *that stood* in the house
35:19. shall not want a man *to stand* before me
36:21. the princes *which stood* beside the king.
44:15. all the women *that stood by*,
Eze. 3:23. the glory of the Lord *stood* there,
8:11. *there stood* before them seventy men
— in the midst of them *stood* Jaazaniah
10: 3. the cherubims *stood* on the right side
22:30. *and stand* in the gap before me
40: 3. *and he stood* in the gate.
43: 6. the man *stood* (lit. was *standing*) by me.
Dan 8: 3. there *stood* before the river a ram
6. I had seen *standing* before the river,
15. there *stood* before me as the appearance
10:13. of the kingdom of Persia with*stood* (lit. *stood* against) me
16. him *that stood* before me.
11: 2. there *shall stand up* yet three kings
16. none *shall stand* before him:
12: 1. the great prince *which standeth*
5. *there stood* other two,
Hag. 2: 5. my spirit *remaineth* among you:
Zec. 1: 8. he *stood* among the myrtle trees
10. man *that stood* among the myrtle trees
11. the angel of the Lord *that stood*
3: 1. Joshua the high priest *standing*
— and Satan *standing* at his right hand
3. *and stood* before the angel.
4. those *that stood* before him,
5. the angel of the Lord *stood by*.
7. among these *that stand by*.
4:14. the two anointed ones, *that stand* by
14:12. while they *stand* upon their feet,
Mal. 3: 2. who *shall stand* when he appeareth?

* HIPHIL.—*Preterite.* *

Ex. 9:16. for this (cause) *have I raised thee up*, (marg. *made thee stand*)
Lev.14:11. *And* the priest...*shall present* the man
16: 7. take the two goats, *and present* them
27: 8. *then he shall present himself* before
11. *then he shall present* the beast
Nu. 3: 6. Bring the tribe of Levi near, *and present*
5:16. *and set her* before the Lord:
18. *And* the priest *shall set* the woman
30. *and shall set* the woman before the Lord,
8:13. *And thou shalt set* the Levites
27:19. *And set* him before Eleazar
1K. 12:32. *and he placed* in Beth-el the priests
1Ch 6:31(16). whom David *set over* the service
17:14. *But I will settle him* in mine house
2Ch 19: 8. *did* Jehoshaphat *set* of the Levites,
33: 8. the land which *I have appointed*
19. *and set up* groves and graven images,
Neh. 6: 1. *I had* not *set up* the doors
7. *thou hast* also *appointed* prophets
10:32(33). *Also we made* ordinances for us,
13:19. (some) of my servants *set I* at the gates,
Est. 4: 5. whom *he had appointed* to attend upon (marg. *set* before) her,
Ps. 30: 7(8). *thou hast made* my mountain *to stand* strong: (marg. *thou hast settled* strength for my mountain)
31: 8(9). *thou hast set* my feet in a large room.
Eze.29: 7. *and madest* all their loins *to be at a stand.*

Dan 11:11. *and he shall set forth* a great multitude;
13. *and shall set forth* a multitude

HIPHIL.—*Infinitive.*

1K. 15: 4. *and to establish* Jerusalem:
1Ch 15:16. the Levites *to appoint* their brethren
2Ch 9: 8. *to establish them* for ever,
Ezr. 2:68. the house of God *to set it up* in his place:
9: 9. *and to repair* (marg. *set up*) the
Neh 7: 3. *and appoint* watches of the inhabitants
Eze.24:11. *Then set it* empty upon the coals
Dan 11:14. people shall exalt themselves *to establish*

HIPHIL.—*Imperative.*

Isa. 21: 6. Go, *set* a watchman,

HIPHIL.—*Future.*

Gen47: 7. *and set him* before Pharaoh:
Nu. 11:24. *and set* them round about the tabernacle.
27:22. took Joshua, *and set him* before Eleazar
Jud.16:25. *and they set* him between the pillars.
2Sa.22:34. *setteth me* upon my high places.
2K. 8:11. *And he settled* his countenance
1Ch 15:17. *So* the Levites *appointed* Heman
16:17. *And hath confirmed the same* to Jacob
22: 2. *and he set* masons to hew wrought stones
2Ch 8:14. *And he appointed*, according to
11:15. *And he ordained* him priests
22. *And* Rehoboam *made* Abijah the son of
19: 5. *And he set* judges in the land
20:21. *And* when he...*he appointed* singers unto the Lord,
23:10. *And he set* all the people,
19. *And he set* the porters at the gates
24:13. *and they set* the house of God in his state,
25: 5. *and made them* captains
14. *and set them up* (to be) his gods,
29:25. *And he set* the Levites in the house
30: 5. *So they established* a decree
31: 2. *And* Hezekiah *appointed* the courses
34:32. *And he caused* all...*to stand* (to it).
35: 2. *And he set* the priests in their charges,
Ezr. 3: 8. *and appointed* the Levites,
10. *And* when...*they set* the priests in
Neh 3: 1. *and set up* the doors of it;
3, 6, 13, 14, 15. *and set up* the doors thereof,
4: 9(3). *and set* a watch against them
13(7). *Therefore set I* in the lower places
—(-). *I even set* the people
7: 1. *and I had set up* the doors,
12:31. *and appointed* two great (companies)
13:11. *and set them* in their place.
30. *and appointed* the wards of the priests
Job 34:24. *and set* others in their stead.
Ps. 18:33(34). *setteth me* upon my high places.
105:10. *And confirmed the same* unto Jacob
107:25. *and raiseth* the stormy wind,
148: 6. *He hath also stablished them*
Pro.29: 4. The king by judgment *establisheth*
Eze. 2: 2 & 3:24. *and set me* upon my feet,
Dan 8:18. he touched me, *and set me* (marg. *made me stand*) upright.

HIPHIL.—*Participle.*

2Ch 18:34. the king of Israel *stayed* (lit. was *staying*) (himself)

* HOPHAL.—*Future.* *

Lev.16:10. the scapegoat, *shall be presented* alive

HOPHAL.—*Participle.*

1K. 22:35. the king was *stayed up* in his chariot

עִמָּד [gim-māhd'], part. prep. 5978

Always combined with suffix of the first person singular, עִמָּדִי

Gen 3:12. The woman whom thou gavest (to be) *with me*,
19:19. thy mercy, which thou hast shewed *unto me*
31: 7. God suffered him not to hurt *me*.
Deu. 5:31(28). as for thee, stand thou here *by me*,
Job 6: 4. arrows of the Almighty (are) *within me*,
10:17. increasest thine indignation *upon me*;
23: 6. Will he plead *against me*
10. he knoweth the way *that I take*: (marg. (is) *with me*)

Job 29:20. My glory (was) fresh *in me*,
Ps. 50:11. the wild beasts of the field (are) *mine*. (marg. *with me*)
&c. &c.

It occurs twice with prefix מֵעִמָּדִי

1Sa 10: 2. When thou art departed *from me*
20:28. David earnestly asked (leave) *of me*

5977 עֹמֶד [*gōh'-med*], m.

2Ch.30:16. they stood in *their place* (marg. *standing*)
34:31. the king stood in *his place*,
35:10. the priests stood in *their place*,
Neh 8: 7. the people (stood) in *their place*.
9: 3. they stood up in *their place*,
13:11. and set them in *their place*. (marg. *standing*)
Dan 8:17. he came near *where I stood*:
18. set me *upright*. (marg. made me stand upon *my standing*)
10:11. stand *upright*: (marg. upon *thy standing*)
11: 1. *I, stood* to confirm and to strengthen

5979 עֶמְדָּה [*gem-dāh'*], f.

Mic. 1:11. he shall receive of you *his standing*.

5980 עֻמָּה [*goom-māh'*], f.

Ex. 25:27. *Over against* the border shall the rings
28:27. *over against* the (other) coupling
37:14. *Over against* the border were the rings,
38:18. *answerable to* the hangings of the court.
39:20. *over against* the (other) coupling
Lev. 3: 9. *hard by* the backbone;
2Sa.16:13. on the hill's side *over against him*,
— threw stones *at him*,
1K. 7:20. *over against* the belly
1Ch 24:31. cast lots *over against* their brethren
— *over against* their younger brethren.
25: 8. they cast lots, ward *against* (ward),
26:12. (having) wards one *against* another,
16. ward *against* ward.
Neh 12:24. ward *over against* ward.
Ecc. 5:16(15). *in all points* as he came,
7:14. God also hath set the one *over against* the
Eze. 1:20. wheels were lifted up *over against them*:
21. wheels were lifted up *over against them*:
3: 8. I have made thy face strong *against* their faces, and thy forehead strong *against* their foreheads.
13. the noise of the wheels *over against them*,
10:19. the wheels also (were) *beside them*,
11:22. and the wheels *beside them*;
40:18. by the side of the gates *over against*
42: 7. *over against* the chambers,
45: 6. *over against* the oblation
7. *over against* one of the portions,
48:13. *over against* the border of the priests
18, 18. *over against* the oblation
21. *over against* the portions for the prince:

5982 עַמּוּד *gam-mood'*, m.

Ex. 13:21. by day *in a pillar of* a cloud,
— by night *in a pillar of* fire,
22. He took not away *the pillar of* the cloud by day, *nor the pillar* of fire by night,
14:19. *the pillar of* the cloud went from before
24. *through the pillar of* fire and of
26:32. thou shalt hang it upon four *pillars of*
37. five *pillars of* shittim (wood),
27:10. *And the* twenty *pillars thereof*
— the hooks of *the pillars*
11. *and his* twenty *pillars*
— the hooks of *the pillars*
12. *their pillars* ten, and their sockets ten.
14, 15. *their pillars* three, and their sockets
16. *their pillars* (shall be) four, and their
17. All *the pillars* round about the court
33: 9. *the* cloudy *pillar* descended,
10. all the people saw *the* cloudy *pillar*
35:11. his bars, *his pillars*, and his sockets,
Ex. 35:17. *his pillars*, and their sockets,
36:36. he made thereunto four *pillars* (of)
38. *the* five *pillars of it* with their
38:10, 11. *Their pillars* (were) twenty,
—, 11, 12. the hooks of *the pillars*
12. *their pillars* ten, and their sockets ten;
14, 15. *their pillars* three, and their sockets three.
17. the sockets *for the pillars* (were of) brass; the hooks of *the pillars*
— all *the pillars of* the court
19. *And their pillars* (were) four,
28. he made hooks *for the pillars*,
39:33. *and his pillars*, and his sockets,
40. *his pillars*, and his sockets,
40:18. and reared up *his pillars*.
Nu. 3:36. *and the pillars thereof*, and the sockets
37. *And the pillars of* the court
4:31. the bars thereof, *and the pillars thereof*,
32. *And the pillars of* the court round about,
12: 5. the Lord came down *in the pillar of*
14:14. by day time *in a pillar of* a cloud, *and in a pillar of* fire by night.
Deu 31:15. the Lord appeared in the tabernacle *in a pillar of* a cloud: and *the pillar of* the
Jud 16:25. they set him between *the pillars*.
26. Suffer me that I may feel *the pillars*
29. Samson took hold of *the* two middle *pillars*
20:40. with *a pillar of* smoke,
1K. 7: 2. four rows of cedar *pillars*, with cedar beams upon *the pillars*.
3. (lay) on forty five *pillars*,
6. he made a porch of *pillars*;
— *and the* (other) *pillars* and the thick beam
15. he cast two *pillars* of brass, of eighteen cubits high *apiece*: (lit. eighteen cubits was the height of one *pillar*)
— twelve cubits did compass either of *them* (lit. *the* second *pillar*)
16. upon the tops of *the pillars*:
17, 19. upon the top of *the pillars*;
18. he made *the pillars*, and two
20. the chapiters upon *the* two *pillars*
21. he set up *the pillars* in the porch
— he set up *the* right *pillar*,
— he set up *the* left *pillar*,
22. upon the top of *the pillars* (was) lily work: so was the work of *the pillars*
41. *The* two *pillars*, and the (two) bowls
— on the top of *the* two *pillars*;
— upon the top of *the pillars*;
42. the chapiters that (were) upon *the pillars*;
2K. 11:14. the king stood by *a pillar*,
23: 3. the king stood by *a pillar*,
25:13. And *the pillars of* brass that (were) in the
16. *The* two *pillars*, one sea, and the bases
17. The height of *the* one *pillar*
— *had the* second *pillar* with wreathen work.
1Ch 18: 8. Solomon made the brasen sea, and *the pillars*,
2Ch 3:15. he made before the house two *pillars*
16. on the heads of *the pillars*;
17. he reared up *the pillars*
4:12. *the* two *pillars*, and the pommels,
— on the top of *the* two *pillars*,
— on the top of *the pillars*;
13. chapiters which (were) upon *the pillars*.
23:13. the king stood at *his pillar*
Neh. 9:12. *Moreover* thou leddest them in the day *by a* cloudy *pillar*; *and* in the night *by a pillar of* fire,
19. *the pillar of* the cloud departed not
— neither *the pillar of* fire by night,
Est. 1: 6. silver rings *and pillars of* marble:
Job 9: 6. *and the pillars thereof* tremble.
26:11. *The pillars of* heaven tremble
Ps. 75: 3(4). I bear up *the pillars of it*.
99: 7. He spake unto them *in the* cloudy *pillar*:
Pro. 9: 1. she hath hewn out *her* seven *pillars*:
Cant.3:10. He made *the pillars thereof*
5:15. His legs (are as) *pillars of* marble,
Jer. 1:18. a defenced city, *and* (lit. *for*) *an* iron *pillar*,
27:19. concerning *the pillars*, and concerning
52:17. *the pillars of* brass that (were) in the
20. *The* two *pillars*, one sea, and twelve

Jer. 52:21. *And* (concerning) *the pillars*, the height of one *pillar*
22. *The* second *pillar* also...(were) like unto these. (lit. and like these was *to the* second *pillar*)
Eze.40:49. *and* (there were) *pillars* by the posts,
42: 6. but had not *pillars as the pillars of* the

5994 **עֲמִיק** [*gămeek*], Ch. adj.

Dan 2:22. revealeth the *deep* and secret things:

5995 **עָמִיר** *gāh-meer'*, m.

Jer. 9:22(21). *and as the handful* after the harvest-man,
Am. 2:13. cart is pressed (that is) full of *sheaves*.
Mic. 4:12. he shall gather them *as the sheaves*
Zec.12: 6. like a torch of fire *in a sheaf*;

5997 **עָמִית** [*gāh-meeth'*], m.

Lev. 6: 2(5:21). and lie *unto his neighbour*
—(-:—). or hath deceived *his neighbour*;
18:20. not lie carnally with *thy neighbour's* wife,
19:11. neither lie one *to another*. (lit. a man *to his neighbour*)
15. shalt thou judge *thy neighbour*.
17. shalt in any wise rebuke *thy neighbour*,
24:19. man cause a blemish *in his neighbour*;
25:14. if thou sell ought *unto thy neighbour*, or buyest (ought) of *thy neighbour's* hand,
15. thou shalt buy of *thy neighbour*,
17. shall not therefore oppress one *another*; (lit. a man *his neighbour*)
Zec.13: 7. the man (that is) *my fellow*,

5998 **עָמַל** *gāh-mal'*.

* KAL.—*Preterite.* *

Ps.127: 1. *they labour* in vain that build
Pro.16:26. He that laboureth *laboureth* for himself;
Ecc. 2:11. the labour *that I had laboured*
19. my labour *wherein I have laboured*,
20. all the labour *which I took*
21. a man that *hath* not *laboured*
Jon. 4:10. for the which *thou hast* not *laboured*,

KAL.—*Future.*

Ecc. 1: 3. What profit hath a man of all his labour *which he taketh*
5:16(15). he *that hath laboured* for the wind?
18(17). good of all his labour *that he taketh*
8:17. though a man *labour*

5999 **עָמָל** *gāh-māhl'*, m.

Gen41:51. God, (said he), hath made me forget all *my toil*,
Nu. 23:21. neither hath he seen *perverseness* in
Deu 26: 7. *our labour*, and our oppression:
Jud.10:16. his soul was grieved *for the misery of*
Job 3:10. nor hid *sorrow* from mine eyes.
4: 8. that plow iniquity, and sow *wickedness*,
5: 6. neither doth *trouble* spring out of the
7. man is born *unto trouble*,
7: 3. *wearisome* (lit. of *trouble*) nights are appointed to me.
11:16. thou shalt forget (thy) *misery*,
15:35. They conceive *mischief*,
16: 2. *miserable* (marg. or, *troublesome*) comforters
Ps. 7:14(15). and hath conceived *mischief*,
16(17). *His mischief* shall return upon
10: 7. under his tongue (is) *mischief*
14. thou beholdest *mischief* and spite,
25:18. Look upon mine affliction *and my pain*;
55:10(11). mischief also *and sorrow* (are) in the
73: 5. They (are) not *in trouble* (as other) (marg. *the trouble of*) men;
16. (was) too *painful* for me; (marg. *labour* in mine eyes)
90:10. yet (is) their strength *labour* and sorrow;
94:20. which frameth *mischief* by a law?

Ps.105:44. *and* they inherited *the labour of*
107:12. brought down their heart *with labour*;
140: 9(10). *the mischief of* their own lips cover
Pro.24: 2. *and* their lips talk of *mischief*.
31: 7. *and* remember *his misery* no more.
Ecc. 1: 3. What profit hath a man of all *his labour*
2:10. my heart rejoiced in all *my labour*: and this was my portion of all *my labour*.
11. *and on the labour* that I had laboured
18. I hated all *my labour*
19. shall he have rule over all *my labour*
20. all *the labour* which I took
21. there is a man *whose labour* (is) in wisdom,
22. what hath man of all *his labour*,
24. make his soul enjoy good *in his labour*.
3:13. enjoy the good of all *his labour*,
4: 4. I considered all *travail*,
6. both the hands full (with) *travail*
8. no end of all *his labour*;
9. they have a good reward *for their labour*.
5:15(14). shall take nothing *of his labour*,
18(17). to enjoy the good of all *his labour*
19(18). to rejoice *in his labour*;
6: 7. All *the labour of* man
8:15. that shall abide with him *of his labour*
9: 9. *and in thy labour* which thou takest
10:15. *The labour of* the foolish
Isa. 10: 1. that write *grievousness*
53:11. He shall see *of the travail of* his soul,
59: 4. they conceive *mischief*,
Jer. 20:18. came I forth out of the womb to see *labour*
Hab. 1: 3. *and* cause (me) to behold *grievance*?
13. not look on *iniquity*: (marg. or, *grievance*)

עָמֵל *gāh-mēhl'*, adj. 6001

Jud. 5:26. her right hand to the *workmen's* hammer;
Job 3:20. light given *to him that is in misery*,
20:22. every hand of *the wicked* (marg. or, *troublesome*)
Pro.16:26. He *that laboureth*
Ecc. 2:18. my labour which I *had taken* (marg. *laboured*) under the sun:
22. wherein *he hath laboured* under the sun?
3: 9. wherein *he laboureth*?
4: 8. For whom *do I labour*,
9: 9. in thy labour which thou *takest*

עָמַם [*gāh-mam'*]. 6004

* KAL.—*Preterite.* *

Eze.28: 3. no secret that *they can hide from thee*:
31: 8. The cedars in the garden of God *could* not *hide him*:

* HOPHAL.—*Future.* *

Lam 4: 1. How *is* the gold *become dim*!

עֲמָמִים see **עַם** See 5971

עֲמְמִין see **עַם** Ch. See 5972

עָמַס [*gāh-mas'*]. 6006

* KAL.—*Future.* *

Gen44:13. *and laded* every man his ass,
Ps. 68:19(20). the Lord, (who) daily *loadeth* us (with benefits),

KAL.—*Participle.* Poel.

Neh 13:15. bringing in sheaves, *and lading* asses;
Zec.12: 3. *that burden themselves with it*

KAL.—*Participle.* Paül.

Isa. 46: 1. your carriages (were) *heavy loaden*;
3. *which are borne* (by me) from the belly,

* HIPHIL.—*Preterite.* *

1K. 12:11. my father *did lade* you with a heavy yoke,
2Ch 10:11. my father *put* (marg. *laded*) a heavy yoke upon you,

6009 עָמַק [*gāh-mak'*].

✱ KAL.—*Preterite.* ✱

Ps. 92: 5(6). thy thoughts *are* very *deep.*

✱ HIPHIL.—*Preterite.* ✱

Isa. 30:33. *he hath made* (it) *deep* (and) large:
31: 6. the children of Israel *have deeply* revolted. (lit. *have deepened* revolt)
Jer. 49: 8. dwell *deep*, O inhabitants of Dedan; (lit. the inhabitants...*have deepened* to dwell)
30. dwell *deep* O ye inhabitants of Hazor, (lit. *id.*)
Hos. 5: 2. the revolters *are profound* to make
9: 9. *They have deeply* corrupted (lit. *they have deepened*, they have corrupted)

HIPHIL.—*Imperative.*

Isa. 7:11. ask it either *in the depth* (lit. *deepen* thy petition), or in the height

HIPHIL.—*Participle.*

Isa. 29:15. Woe unto them *that seek deep*

6012 עָמֵק [*gāh-mēhk'*], adj.

Pro. 9:18. her guests (are) *in the depths of* hell.
Isa. 33:19. a people of *deeper* speech than thou
Eze. 3: 5. a people of a *strange* speech (marg. *deep of* lip)
6. many people of a *strange* speech (marg. *deep of* lip)

6013 עָמֹק *gāh-mōhk'*, adj.

Lev.13: 3. the plague in sight (be) *deeper*
4. *and* in sight (be) not *deeper* than the
25. it (be in) sight *deeper* than the skin;
30. if it (be) in sight *deeper* than the skin;
31. it (be) not in sight *deeper*
32. in sight *deeper* than the skin;
34. nor (be) in sight *deeper* than the skin;
Job 11: 8. *deeper* than hell;
12:22. He discovereth *deep things*
Ps. 64: 6(7). and the heart, (is) *deep.*
Pro. 18: 4. of a man's mouth (are as) *deep* waters,
20: 5. Counsel in the heart of man (is like) *deep*
22:14. The mouth of strange women (is) a *deep*
23:27. a whore (is) a *deep* ditch;
Ecc. 7:24. far off, *and exceeding deep*, (lit. *and deep deep*)
Eze. 23:32. Thou shalt drink of thy sister's cup *deep*

6010 עֵמֶק *gēh'-mek*, m.

Gen 14: 3. in *the vale of* Siddim,
8. joined battle with them *in the vale of*
10. *And the vale of* Siddim (was full of)
17. at *the valley of* Shaveh, which (is) the king's *dale.*
37:14. he sent him *out of the vale of* Hebron,
Nu. 14:25. the Canaanites dwelt *in the valley.*
Jos. 7:24. brought them unto *the valley of* Achor.
26. that place was called, *The valley of* Achor,
8:13. that night into the midst of *the valley.*
10:12. and thou, Moon, *in the valley of* Ajalon.
13:19. in the mount of *the valley*,
27. *And in the valley*, Beth-aram,
15: 7. *from the valley of* Achor,
8. *the valley of* the giants
17:16. in the land of *the valley*
— (they) who (are) *of the valley of* Jezreel.
18:16. *in the valley of* the giants
21. Beth-hoglah, *and the valley of* Keziz,
19:27. the north side of Beth-*emek*, (lit. the house of *the valley*)
Jud. 1:19. the inhabitants of *the valley*,
34. suffer them to come down *to the valley:*
5:15. he was sent on foot *into the valley.*
6:33. pitched *in the valley of* Jezreel.
7: 1. by the hill of Moreh, *in the valley.*
8. beneath him *in the valley.*
12. children of the east lay along *in the valley*
18:28. *in the valley* that (lieth) by Beth-rehob.
1Sa. 6:13. reaping their wheat harvest *in the valley:*
1Sa.17: 2. pitched *by the valley of* Elah,
19. *in the valley of* Elah, fighting
21: 9(10). whom thou slewest *in the valley of*
31: 7. on the other side of *the valley*,
2Sa. 5:18, 22. spread themselves *in the valley of* Rephaim.
18:18. which (is) *in* the king's *dale:*
23:13. pitched *in the valley of* Rephaim.
1K. 20:28. he (is) not God of *the vallies*,
1Ch.10: 7. the men of Israel that (were) *in the valley*
11:15. the Philistines encamped *in the valley of*
12:15. they put to flight all (them) of *the vallies*,
14: 9. spread themselves *in the valley of* Rephaim.
13. spread themselves abroad *in the valley.*
27:29. *in the vallies* (was) Shaphat
2Ch.20:26. *in the valley of* Berachah;
— *The valley of* Berachah,
Job 39:10. will he harrow *the vallies*
21. He paweth *in the valley*,
Ps. 60: 6(8). *and* mete out *the valley of* Succoth.
65:13(14). *the valleys also* are covered over
84: 6(7). passing *through the valley of* Baca
108: 7(8). *and* mete out *the valley of* Succoth.
Cant.2: 1. the lily of *the valleys.*
Isa. 17: 5. ears *in the valley of* Rephaim.
22: 7. *thy* choicest *valleys* shall be
28:21. he shall be wroth *as* (in) *the valley of*
65:10. *and the valley of* Achor a place
Jer.21:13. O inhabitant of *the valley*,
31:40. *the* whole *valley* of the dead bodies,
47: 5. cut off (with) the remnant of *their valley*·
48: 8. *the valley* also shall perish,
49: 4. Wherefore gloriest thou *in the valleys, thy* flowing *valley*,
Hos. 1: 5. *in the valley of* Jezreel.
2:15(17). *the valley of* Achor for a door
Joel 3: 2(4:2). down into *the valley of* Jehoshaphat,
12(-:12). come up to *the valley of*
14(-:14). multitudes *in the valley of* decision:
—(-:—). the Lord (is) near *in the valley of*
Mic. 1: 4. *and the valleys* shall be cleft,

עֹמֶק *gōh'-mek.* 6011

Pro.25: 3. the earth *for depth*,

עָמַר [*gāh-mar'*]. 6014

✱ PIEL.—*Participle.* ✱

Ps.129: 7. nor *he that bindeth sheaves* his bosom.

✱ HITHPAEL.—*Preterite.* ✱

Deu24: 7. *and maketh merchandise* of him,

HITHPAEL.—*Future.*

Deu21:14. *thou shalt* not *make merchandise* of her,

עֹמֶר *gōh'-mer*, m. 6016

Ex. 16:16. *an omer* for every man,
18. they did mete (it) *with an omer*,
22. two *omers* for one (man):
32. Fill *an omer* of it to be kept
33. Take a pot, and put *an omer* full
36. *Now an omer* (is) the tenth (part) of
Lev.23:10. ye shall bring *a sheaf* (marg. *omer*, or, *handful*)
11. he shall wave *the sheaf*
12. when ye wave *the sheaf*
15. *the sheaf of* the wave offering;
Deu24:19. and hast forgot *a sheaf* in the field,
Ru. 2: 7. after the reapers *among the sheaves:*
15. Let her glean even among *the sheaves*,
Job 24:10. they take away *the sheaf*

עֲמַר *gămar*, Ch. m. 6015

Dan 7: 9. the hair of his head *like the* pure *wool:*

עָמַשׂ [*gāh-mas'*]. 6006

✱ KAL.—*Participle.* Poel. ✱

Neh 4:17(11). bare burdens, *with those that laded*,

6025 עֵנָב ^{n}gĕh-nāhv', m.

Gen40:10. the clusters thereof brought forth *ripe grapes:*
11. and I took *the grapes,*
49:11. in the blood of *grapes:*
Lev.25: 5. neither gather *the grapes of* thy vine
Nu. 6: 3. neither shall he drink any liquor of *grapes,* nor eat moist *grapes,*
13:20. the time of *the* firstripe *grapes.*
23. a branch with one cluster of *grapes,*
Deu23:24(25). thou mayest eat *grapes* thy fill
32:14. the pure blood of *the grape.*
32. *their grapes* (are) *grapes of* gall,
Neh13:15. also wine, *grapes,* and figs,
Isa. 5: 2. looked that it should bring forth *grapes,*
4. when I looked that it should bring forth *grapes,*
Jer. 8:13. (there shall be) no *grapes* on the vine,
Hos. 3: 1. and love flagons of *wine.* (marg. *grapes*)
9:10. I found Israel *like grapes* in the
Am. 9:13. and the treader of *grapes*

6026 עָנַג [^{n}găh-nag'].

* PUAL.—*Participle.* *

Jer. 6: 2. a comely *and delicate* (woman).

* HITHPAEL.—*Preterite.* *

Ps. 37:11. *and shall delight themselves* in the
Isa. 66:11. *and be delighted* with the abundance

HITHPAEL.—*Infinitive.*

Deu28:56. to set the sole of her foot upon the ground *for delicateness*

HITHPAEL.—*Imperative.*

Ps. 37: 4. *Delight thyself also* in the Lord;

HITHPAEL.—*Future.*

Job 22:26. then *shalt thou have thy delight* in the
27:10. *Will he delight himself* in the Almighty?
Isa. 55: 2. *and let* your soul *delight itself*
57: 4. Against whom *do ye sport yourselves?*
58:14. Then *shalt thou delight thyself* in the

6028 עָנֹג ^{n}găh-nōhg', adj.

Deu28:54. the man (that is) tender among you, *and* very *delicate,*
56. The tender *and delicate woman*
Isa. 47: 1. shalt no more be called tender *and delicate.*

6027 עֹנֶג ^{n}gōh'-neg, m.

Isa. 13:22. dragons in (their) *pleasant* palaces: (lit. palaces of *pleasure*)
58:13. and call the sabbath *a delight,*

6029 עָנַד [^{n}găh-nad'].

* KAL.—*Imperative.* *

Pro. 6:21. (and) *tie them* about thy neck.

KAL.—*Future.*

Job 31:36. (and) *bind it* (as) a crown to me.

6030 עָנָה ^{n}găh-nāh'.

* KAL.—*Preterite.* *

Gen30:33. *So shall* my righteousness *answer* for me
Deu19:18. *hath testified* falsely against his brother;
21: 7. *And they shall answer* and say,
25: 9. *and shall answer* and say,
26: 5. *And thou shalt speak* and say
27:14. *And* the Levites *shall speak,*
15. *And* all the people *shall answer*
31:21. *that* this song *shall testify* against them
Jud. 8: 8. as the men of Succoth *had answered*
Ru. 1:21. the Lord *hath testified* against me,
1Sa. 4:20. *she answered* not, neither did she regard
9:17. the Lord *said unto him,*
14:37. *he answered him* not that day.
28: 6. the Lord *answered him* not,
1Sa.28:15. and *answereth me* no more,
2Sa. 1:16. thy mouth *hath testified* against thee,
22:42. the Lord, but *he answered them* not.
1K. 2:30. Thus said Joab, and thus *he answered me*
12: 7. and wilt serve them, *and answer them,*
18:21. the people *answered* him not a word.
2K. 18:36. and *answered* him not a word:
1Ch 21:28. the Lord *had answered him*
Job 32:15. *they answered* no more:
16. stood still, (and) *answered* no more;
Ps. 18:41(42). the Lord, but *he answered them* not.
22:21(22). *thou hast heard me* from the horns of
34: 4(5). I sought the Lord, *and he heard me,*
99: 8. Thou *answeredst them,* O Lord
118: 5. the Lord *answered me,*
21. I will praise thee: for *thou hast heard me.*
Cant.2:10. My beloved *spake,* and said
5: 6. I called him, but *he gave me no answer.*
Isa. 3: 9. shew of their countenance *doth witness*
13:22. *And* the wild beasts of the islands *shall cry*
30:19. when he shall hear it, *he will answer thee.*
36:21. they held their peace, and *answered* him
49: 8. In an acceptable time *have I heard thee,*
59:12. our sins *testify* against us:
65:12. when I called, *ye did* not *answer;*
Jer. 7:13. I called you, but *ye answered* not;
14: 7. our iniquities *testify* against us,
23:35. What *hath* the Lord *answered?*
37. What *hath* the Lord *answered thee?*
35:17. I have called unto them, but *they have* not *answered.*
51:14. *and they shall lift up* (marg. *utter*) a shout against thee.
Hos. 2:15(17). *and she shall sing* there, as in the days
5: 5. *And* the pride of Israel *doth testify*
7:10. *And* the pride of Israel *testifieth*
14: 8(9). I *have heard* (him), and observed him:
Mic. 6: 5. what Balaam the son of Beor *answered*

KAL.—*Infinitive.*

Gen45: 3. his brethren could not *answer* him;
Ex. 32:18. the voice of (them that) *shout*
— the voice of (them that) *cry*
Deu19:16. If a false witness rise up...*to testify*
1Sa. 9: 8. the servant *answered* Saul
Job 32: 1. these three men ceased *to answer* (marg. *from answering*)
Pro.15:28. heart of the righteous studieth *to answer:*

KAL.—*Imperative.*

Nu. 21:17. Spring up, O well; *sing* (marg. or, *answer*) ye unto it:
1Sa.12: 3. *witness* against me before the Lord,
1K. 18:26. O Baal, *hear* (marg. or, *answer*) us.
37. *Hear me,* O Lord, *hear me,* that this people may know
Ps. 4: 1(2). *Hear me* when I call, O God
13: 3(4). Consider (and) *hear me,* O Lord
27: 7. have mercy also upon me, *and answer me.*
55: 2(3). Attend unto me, *and hear me:*
60: 5(7). (with) thy right hand, *and hear me.*
69:13(14). the multitude of thy mercy *hear me,*
16(17). *Hear me,* O Lord; for thy
17(18). *hear me* speedily. (marg. make haste to *hear me*)
86: 1. Bow down thine ear, O Lord, *hear me:*
102: 2(3). in the day (when) I call *answer me*
108: 6(7). (with) thy right hand, *and answer me.*
119:145. *hear me,* O Lord: I will keep
143: 1. in thy faithfulness *answer me,*
7. *Hear me* speedily, O Lord:
147: 7. *Sing* unto the Lord with thanksgiving;
Pro.26: 5. *Answer* a fool according to his folly,
Mic. 6: 3. wherein have I wearied thee? *testify*

KAL.—*Future.*

Gen18:27. *And* Abraham *answered* and said,
23: 5. *And* the children of Heth *answered*
10. *and* Ephron the Hittite *answered* Abraham
14. *And* Ephron *answered* Abraham,
24:50. *Then* Laban and Bethuel *answered* and
27:37. *And* Isaac *answered* and said unto Esau,
39. *And* Isaac his father *answered* and said
31:14. *And* Rachel and Leah *answered* and said
31,36. *And* Jacob *answered* and said
43. *And* Laban *answered* and said
34:13. *And* the sons of Jacob *answered* Shechem
40:18. *And* Joseph *answered* and said,

Gen41:16. *And* Joseph *answered* Pharaoh,
— God *shall give* Pharaoh *an answer*
42:22. *And* Reuben *answered* them,
Ex. 4: 1. *And* Moses *answered* and said,
15:21. *And* Miriam *answered* them,
19: 8. *And* all the people *answered* together,
19. *and* God *answered him* by a voice.
20:16. *Thou shalt* not *bear* false witness
23: 2. neither *shalt thou speak* (marg. *answer*) in a cause
24: 3. *and* all the people *answered*
Nu. 11:28. *And* Joshua the son of Nun,...*answered*
22:18. *And* Balaam *answered* and said
23:12. *And he answered* and said,
26. *But* Balaam *answered* and said
32:31. *And* the children of Gad...*answered*,
35:30. one witness *shall* not *testify*
Deu 1:14. *And ye answered* me, and said,
41. *Then ye answered* and said
5:20(17). Neither *shalt thou bear* false witness
20:11. if *it make thee answer of* peace,
Jos. 1:16. *And they answered* Joshua, saying,
7:20. *And* Achan *answered* Joshua,
9:24. *And they answered* Joshua,
22:21. *Then*...the half tribe of Manasseh *answered*,
24:16. *And* the people *answered* and said,
Jud. 5:29. Her wise ladies *answered* her,
7:14. *And* his fellow *answered* and said,
8: 8. *and* the men of Penuel *answered* him
18:14. *Then answered* the five men
20: 4. *And* the Levite,...*answered*
Ru. 2: 6. *And* the servant...*answered* and said,
11. *And* Boaz *answered* and said
1Sa. 1:15. *And* Hannah *answered* and said,
17. *Then* Eli *answered* and said,
4:17. *And* the messenger *answered* and said,
7: 9. for Israel; *and* the Lord *heard him.*
8:18. the Lord *will* not *hear* you
9:12. *And they answered* them, and said,
19. *And* Samuel *answered* Saul, and said,
21. *And* Saul *answered* and said,
10:12. *And* one of the same place *answered*
14:12. *And* the men of the garrison *answered*
28. *Then answered* one of the people,
16:18. *Then answered* one of the servants,
18: 7. *And* the women *answered* (one another)
20:10. (if) thy father *answer thee* roughly?
28, 32. *And* Jonathan *answered* Saul,
21: 4(5). *And* the priest *answered* David,
5(6). *And* David *answered* the priest,
11(12). *did they* not *sing* one to another
22: 9. *Then answered* Doeg the Edomite,
14. *Then* Ahimelech *answered* the king,
23: 4. *And* the Lord *answered him*
25:10. *And* Nabal *answered* David's servants,
26: 6. *Then answered* David and said
14. *Answerest thou* not, Abner? *Then* Abner *answered* and said,
22. *And* David *answered* and said,
29: 5. this David, of whom *they sang*
9. *And* Achish *answered* and said
30:22. *Then answered* all the wicked men
2Sa. 4: 9. *And* David *answered* Rechab
13:32. *And* Jonadab,...David's brother, *answered*
14:18. *Then* the king *answered* and said
19. *And* the woman *answered* and said,
15:21. *And* Ittai *answered* the king,
19:21(22). *But* Abishai the son of Zeruiah *answered*
42(43). *And* all the men of Judah *answered*
43(44). *And* the men of Israel *answered*
20:20. *And* Joab *answered* and said,
1K. 1:28. *Then* king David *answered* and said,
36. *And* Benaiah...*answered* the king,
43. *And* Jonathan *answered* and said
2:22. *And* king Solomon *answered* and said
3:27. *Then* the king *answered* and said,
12:13. *And* the king *answered* the people
13: 6. *And* the king *answered* and said
18:24. the God that *answereth* by fire,
— *And* all the people *answered* and said,
20: 4, 11. *And* the king of Israel *answered* and
2K. 1:10. *And* Elijah *answered* and said
11. *And he answered* and said unto him,
12. *And* Elijah *answered* and said unto them,
3:11. *And* one of the king of Israel's servants *answered*

2K. 4:29. if any salute thee, *answer him* not
7: 2. *Then* a lord...*answered* the man of God,
13. *And* one of his servants *answered*
19. *And* that lord *answered* the man of God,
18:36. *Answer him* not.
1Ch 12:17. David went out...*and answered*
21:26. *and he answered him* from heaven
2Ch 10:13. *And* the king *answered them*
29:31. *Then* Hezekiah *answered* and said,
34:15. *And* Hilkiah *answered* and said
Ezr. 3:11. *And they sang together by course* in praising
10: 2. *And*...(one) of the sons of Elam, *answered*
12. *Then* all the congregation *answered*
Neh 8: 6. *And* all the people *answered*,
Est. 5: 7. *Then answered* Esther,
7: 3. *Then* Esther the queen *answered*
Job 1: 7, 9. *Then* Satan *answered* the Lord,
2: 2, 4. *And* Satan *answered* the Lord,
3: 2. *And* Job *spake*, and said,
4: 1. *Then* Eliphaz the Temanite *answered*
6: 1. *But* Job *answered* and said,
8: 1. *Then answered* Bildad the Shuhite,
9: 1. *Then* Job *answered* and said,
3. *he cannot answer him*
14. How much less *shall* I *answer him*,
15. *would I* not *answer*,
16. called, *and he had answered me;*
32. *I should answer him*, (and) we should
11: 1. *Then answered* Zophar the Naamathite,
12: 1. *And* Job *answered* and said,
4. upon God, *and he answereth him:*
13:22. Then call thou, and I *will answer:*
14:15. Thou shalt call, and I *will answer thee:*
15: 1. *Then answered* Eliphaz the Temanite,
2. *Should* a wise man *utter* vain knowledge,
6. thine own lips *testify* against thee.
16: 1. *Then* Job *answered* and said,
3. emboldeneth thee that *thou answerest?*
8. leanness rising up in me *beareth witness*
18: 1. *Then answered* Bildad the Shuhite,
19: 1. *Then* Job *answered* and said,
16. my servant, and *he gave* (me) no *answer;*
20: 1. *Then answered* Zophar the Naamathite,
3. the spirit of my understanding *causeth me to answer.*
21: 1. *But* Job *answered* and said,
22: 1. *Then* Eliphaz the Temanite *answered*
23: 1. *Then* Job *answered* and said,
5. the words (which) *he would answer me*,
25: 1. *Then answered* Bildad the Shuhite,
26: 1. *But* Job *answered* and said,
30:20. cry unto thee, and *thou dost* not *hear me:*
31:35. (that) the Almighty *would answer me*,
32: 6. *And* Elihu the son of Barachel the Buzite *answered*
17. *I will answer* also my part,
20. I will open my lips *and answer.*
33:12. I *will answer thee*, that God
13. *he giveth* not *account* of any of his
34: 1. *Furthermore* Elihu *answered* and said,
35: 1. Elihu *spake moreover*, and said,
12. There they cry, but none *giveth answer*,
38: 1. *Then* the Lord *answered* Job
40: 1. *Moreover* the Lord *answered* Job,
2. he that reproveth God, *let him answer it.*
3. *Then* Job *answered* the Lord,
5. have I spoken; but *I will* not *answer*
6. *Then answered* the Lord unto Job
42: 1. *Then* Job *answered* the Lord,
Ps. 3: 4(5). *and he heard me* out of his holy hill.
17: 6. *thou wilt hear me*, O God:
20: 1(2). The Lord *hear thee* in the day of
6(7). *he will hear him* from his holy heaven
9(10). *let* the king *hear us* when we call.
22: 2(3). I cry in the daytime, but *thou hearest*
38:15(16). thou *wilt hear*, (marg. or, *answer*)
55:19(20). God shall hear, *and afflict them*,
65: 5(6). *wilt thou answer us*, O God
81: 7(8). *I answered thee* in the secret place
86: 7. upon thee: for *thou wilt answer me.*
91:15. *and I will answer him:*
99: 6. upon the Lord, and he *answered them.*
119:26. declared my ways, *and thou heardest me:*
42. *So shall I have* wherewith *to answer* (marg. *answer*)
172. My tongue *shall speak* of thy word:
120: 1. I cried unto the Lord, *and he heard me.*

Ps.138: 3. when I cried *thou answeredst me*,
Pro. 1:28. upon me, but *I will* not *answer*;
18:23. the rich *answereth* roughly.
26: 4. *Answer* not a fool
Ecc.10:19. money *answereth* all (things).
Isa. 14:10. *they shall speak* and say unto thee,
32. What *shall* (one) then *answer*
21: 9. *And he answered* and said,
25: 5. the terrible ones *shall be brought low*.
36:21. *Answer him* not.
41:17. I the Lord *will hear them*,
46: 7. yet *can he* not *answer*,
58: 9. the Lord *shall answer*;
65:24. before they call, I *will answer*;
Jer. 7:27. *they will* not *answer thee*.
11: 5. *Then answered I*, and said,
25:30. *he shall give* a shout, as they
33: 3. Call unto me, *and I will answer thee*,
42: 4. the Lord *shall answer* you,
44:15. *Then* all the men...*answered* Jeremiah,
Hos. 2:21(23). *I will hear*, saith the Lord, *I will hear* the heavens, and they *shall hear* the
22(24). And the earth *shall hear*
—(—). and they *shall hear* Jezreel.
Joel 2:19. *Yea*, the Lord *will answer* and say
Am. 7:14. *Then answered* Amos, and said
Jon. 2: 2(3). unto the Lord, *and he heard me*;
Mic. 3: 4. *he will* not *hear* them:
Hab. 2: 2. *And* the Lord *answered me*,
11. the beam out of the timber *shall answer* (marg. *witness against*) *it*.
Hag. 2:12, 13. *And* the priests *answered* and said,
14. *Then answered* Haggai, and said,
Zec. 1:10. *And* the man that stood...*answered* and
11. *And they answered* the angel of the Lord
12. *Then* the angel of the Lord *answered*
13. *And* the Lord *answered* the angel
3: 4. *And he answered* and spake
4: 4. *So I answered* and spake
5. *Then* the angel that talked with me *answered*
6. *Then he answered* and spake
11. *Then answered I*, and said
12. *And I answered* again,
6: 4. *Then I answered* and said
5. *And* the angel *answered* and said
10: 6. I (am) the Lord their God, *and will hear them*.
13: 9. *and* I *will hear* them: I will say,

KAL.—*Participle*. Poel.

Gen35: 3. unto God, *who answered* me
Jud.19:28. But none *answered*.
1Sa.14:39. among all the people (that) *answered him*.
1K. 18:26. nor any *that answered*. (marg. or, *heard*)
29. neither voice, nor any *to answer*,
Job 5: 1. if there be any *that will answer thee*;
32:12. (or) *that answered* his words:
Pro.25:18. A man *that beareth* false witness
Isa. 50: 2. I called, (was there) none *to answer*?
66: 4. when I called, none *did answer*;
Jer. 44:20. all the people *which had given him* (that) *answer*,
Mal. 2:12. the master *and the scholar*, (marg. or, him that waketh, *and him that answereth*)

* NIPHAL.—*Preterite*. *

Eze.14: 4. I the Lord *will answer* him

NIPHAL.—*Future*.

Job 11: 2. *Should* not the multitude of words *be answered*?
19: 7. I cry out of wrong, but *I am* not *heard*:
Pro.21:13. cry himself, but *shall* not *be heard*.

NIPHAL.—*Participle*.

Eze.14: 7. I the Lord *will answer* him

6031 עָנָה [*gāh-nāh'*].

* KAL.—*Preterite*. *

Ps.116:10. I *was* greatly *afflicted*:

KAL.—*Infinitive*.

2Sa.22:36. *and thy gentleness* hath made me great. [See עֲנָוָה]
Ecc. 1:13. *to be exercised* therewith. (marg. or, *afflict them*)
3:10. to the sons of men *to be exercised* in it.

KAL.—*Future*.

Ps.119:67. Before *I was afflicted* I went astray:
Isa. 31: 4. (he) will not be afraid...nor *abase himself*
Zec 10: 2. *they were troubled*, because (marg. or, *answered* that)

* NIPHAL.—*Preterite*. *

Ps.119:107. *I am afflicted* very much:

NIPHAL.—*Infinitive*.

Ex. 10: 3. How long wilt thou refuse *to humble thyself*

NIPHAL.—*Participle*.

Isa. 53: 7. He was oppressed, and he *was afflicted*,
58:10. satisfy the *afflicted* soul;

* PIEL.—*Preterite*. *

Gen15:13. *and they shall afflict* them four hundred
Lev.16:31 & 23:27, 32. *and ye shall afflict* your souls,
Nu. 24:24. *and shall afflict* Asshur, *and shall afflict*
29: 7. *and ye shall afflict* your souls:
Deu21:14. because *thou hast humbled her*.
22:24. *he hath humbled* his neighbour's wife:
29. because *he hath humbled* her,
Jud.20: 5. my concubine *have they forced*, (marg. *humbled*)
2Sa.13:22. *he had forced* his sister Tamar.
Ps. 35:13. *I humbled* (marg. or, *afflicted*) my soul with fasting;
88: 7(8). *thou hast afflicted* (me) with all thy
90:15. *thou hast afflicted us*,
102:23(24). *He weakened* (marg. *afflicted*) my strength
105:18. Whose feet *they hurt* with fetters.
119:75. thou in faithfulness *hast afflicted me*.
Isa. 58: 3. (wherefore) *have we afflicted* our soul,
Lam. 3:33. *he doth* not *afflict* willingly
5:11. *They ravished* the women in Zion,
Eze.22:10. in thee *have they humbled* her
11. *hath humbled* his sister,
Nah. 1:12. *Though I have afflicted thee*,

PIEL.—*Infinitive*.

Ex. 1:11. over them taskmasters *to afflict them*
22:23(22). If thou afflict them *in any wise*, (lit. *afflicting* thou afflictest)
32:18. the noise of (them that) *sing* do I hear.
Nu. 30:13(14). every binding oath *to afflict* the soul,
Deu 8: 2. *to humble thee*, (and) to prove thee,
16. that *he might humble thee*,
Jud.16: 5. that we may bind him *to afflict him*:
6. thou mightest be bound *to afflict thee*.
19. and she began *to afflict him*,
2Sa. 7:10. neither *shall* the children of wickedness *afflict* (lit. add *to afflict*) them any
13:32. the day *that he forced* his sister
Ps. 88[title](1). to the chief Musician upon Mahalath *Leannoth*,
Isa. 58: 5. a day for a man *to afflict* his soul?

PIEL.—*Imperative*.

Jud.19:24. *and humble ye* them, and do
Isa. 27: 2. *sing ye* unto her,

PIEL.—*Future*.

Gen16: 6. And *when* Sarai *dealt hardly with her*, (marg. *afflicted her*)
31:50. If *thou shalt afflict* my daughters,
34: 2. lay with her, *and defiled her*. (marg. *humbled her*)
Ex. 1:12. the more *they afflicted* them,
22:22(21). *Ye shall* not *afflict* any widow,
23(22). If *thou afflict* them in any wise,
Lev.16:29. *ye shall afflict* your souls,
Deu 8: 3. *And he humbled thee*, and suffered
26: 6. evil entreated us, *and afflicted us*,
2Sa.13:12. *do* not *force me*; (marg. *humble me*)
14. *but,...forced her*, and lay with her.
1K. 11:39. *And I will* for this *afflict*
2K. 17:20. the seed of Israel, *and afflicted them*,
Job 30:11. he hath loosed my cord, *and afflicted me*,
37:23. in plenty of justice: *he will* not *afflict*.
Ps. 89:22(23). the son of wickedness *afflict him*.
94: 5. and *afflict* thine heritage.
Isa. 64:12(11). *and afflict us* very sore?
Nah 1:12. *I will afflict thee* no more.

PIEL.—*Participle*.

Isa. 60:14. The sons also of *them that afflicted thee*
Zep. 3:19. I will undo *all that afflict thee*:

* PUAL.—*Preterite.* *

Ps. 119:71. good for me that *I have been afflicted;*

PUAL.—*Infinitive.*

Ps. 132: 1. David, (and) all *his afflictions:*

PUAL.—*Future.*

Lev. 23:29. soul (it be) that *shall* not *be afflicted*

PUAL.—*Participle.*

Isa. 53: 4. smitten of God, *and afflicted.*

* HIPHIL.—*Future.* *

1K. 8:35. their sin, when *thou afflictest them:*
2Ch. 6:26. when *thou dost afflict them;*

HIPHIL.—*Participle.*

Ecc. 5:20(19). God *answereth* (him) in the joy of

* HITHPAEL.—*Preterite.* *

1K. 2:26. *thou hast been afflicted* in all wherein my father *was afflicted.*

HITHPAEL.—*Infinitive.*

Ezr. 8:21. *that* we *might afflict ourselves*
Dan 10:12. *and to chasten thyself* before thy God,

HITHPAEL.—*Imperative.*

Gen 16: 9. Return to thy mistress, *and submit thyself*

HITHPAEL.—*Future.*

Ps. 107:17. because of their iniquities, *are afflicted.*

NOTE.—With regard to several passages it is difficult to decide to which division of עָנָה they rightly belong.

6032 **עֲנָה** [*gănāh*], Ch.

* P'AL.—*Preterite.* *

Dan. 2: 7. *They answered* again and said,
10. Chaldeans *answered* before the king,
3: 9. *They spake* and said to the king
16. *answered* and said to the king,
5:10. (and) the queen *spake* and said,
6:13(14). *Then answered* they and said

P'AL.—*Participle.*

Dan. 2: 5, 8, 26. The king *answered* and said
15. He *answered* and said to Arioch
20. Daniel *answered* and said,
27. Daniel *answered* in the presence
47. The king *answered* unto Daniel,
3:14. Nebuchadnezzar *spake* and said unto
19. (therefore) *he spake,* and commanded
24. rose up in haste, (and) *spake,*
— *They answered* and said unto the king,
25. *He answered* and said,
26. *spake,* and said, Shadrach,
28. (Then) Nebuchadnezzar *spake,* and said,
4:19(16), 30(27). The king *spake,* and said,
—(—). Belteshazzar *answered* and said,
5: 7, 13. (And) the king *spake,* and said
17. Then Daniel *answered* and said
6:12(13). The king *answered* and said,
16(17). (Now) the king *spake*
20(21). (and) the king *spake*
7: 2. Daniel *spake* and said,

6033 **עֲנָה** [*gănāh*], Ch.

* P'AL.—*Participle.* *

Dan. 4:27(24). by shewing mercy to *the poor;*

6035 **עָנָו** *gāh-nāhv'*, adj.

Nu. 12: 3. (כתיב) the man Moses (was) very *meek,*
Job 24: 4. (——) *the poor of* the earth hide
Ps. 9:12(13). he forgetteth not the cry of *the humble.* (marg. or, *afflicted*)
18(19). (כתיב) the expectation of *the poor*
10:12. forget not *the humble.* (marg. *id.*)
17. thou hast heard the desire of *the humble:*
22:26(27). *The meek* shall eat and be satisfied:
25: 9. *The meek* will he guide in judgment: and *the meek* will he teach his way.
34: 2(3). *the humble* shall hear (thereof),
37:11. *But the meek* shall inherit the earth;
69:32(33). *The humble* (marg. or, *meek*) shall see
76: 9(10). to save all *the meek of* the earth.
147: 6. The Lord lifteth up *the meek:*
149: 4. he will beautify *the meek*
Pro. 3:34. *but* he giveth grace *unto the lowly.*
14:21. he that hath mercy on *the poor,*
16:19. of an humble spirit with *the lowly,*
Isa. 11: 4. *for the meek of* the earth:
29:19. *The meek* also shall increase (their) joy
32: 7. (כתיב) *the poor* with lying words,
61: 1. to preach good tidings unto *the meek;*
Am. 2: 7. turn aside the way of *the meek:*
8: 4. (כתיב) *the poor of* the land to fail,
Zep. 2: 3. all *ye meek of* the earth,

עֲנָוָה *gănāh-vāh'*, f. 6038

2Sa. 22:36. *and thy gentleness* hath made me great. [See עָנָה Infinitive].
Pro. 15:33 & 18:12. before honour (is) *humility.*
22: 4. By *humility* (and) the fear of the Lord
Zep. 2: 3. seek righteousness, seek *meekness:*

עַנְוָה *gan-vāh'*, f. 6037

Ps. 18:35(36). and *thy gentleness* (marg. *meekness*) hath made me great.
45: 4(5). because of truth *and meekness*

עֱנוּת *gĕnooth*, f. 6039

Ps. 22:24(25). *the affliction of* the afflicted;

עָנִי *gāh-nee'*, adj. 6041

Ex. 22:25(24). (any of) my people (that is) *poor*
Lev. 19:10. thou shalt leave them *for the poor*
23:22. thou shalt leave them *unto the poor,*
Deu 15:11. *to thy poor,* and to thy needy,
24:12. And if the man (be) *poor,*
14. an hired servant (that is) *poor*
15. for he (is) *poor,* and setteth his heart
2Sa. 22:28. the *afflicted* people thou wilt save:
Job 24: 4. *the poor of* the earth hide themselves
9. and take a pledge of *the poor.*
14. The murderer rising...killeth *the poor*
29:12. I delivered *the poor* that cried,
34:28. he heareth the cry of *the afflicted.*
36: 6. but giveth right to *the poor.*
15. He delivereth *the poor* (marg. or, *afflicted*)
Ps. 9:12(13). (כתיב) the cry of *the humble.* (marg. or, *afflicted*)
18(19). the expectation of *the poor*
10: 2. The wicked...doth persecute *the poor:*
9. he lieth in wait to catch *the poor:* he doth catch *the poor,* when he draweth
12. (כתיב) forget not *the humble.* (marg. or, *afflicted*)
12: 5(6). the oppression of *the poor,*
14: 6. Ye have shamed the counsel of *the poor,*
18:27(28). thou wilt save the *afflicted* people;
22:24(25). the affliction of *the afflicted;*
25:16. I (am) desolate *and afflicted.*
34: 6(7). This *poor* man cried, and the Lord
35:10. deliverest *the poor* from him that is too strong for him, *yea, the poor* and the
37:14. to cast down *the poor* and needy,
40:17(18). I (am) *poor* and needy;
68:10(11). prepared of thy goodness *for the poor.*
69:29(30). I (am) *poor* and sorrowful:
70: 5(6). I (am) *poor* and needy:
72: 2. *and thy poor* with judgment.
4. He shall judge *the poor of* the people,
12. deliver the needy when he crieth; *the poor also,*
74:19. forget not the congregation of *thy poor*
21. let *the poor* and needy praise thy name.
82: 3. do justice to *the afflicted* and needy.
86: 1. hear me: for I (am) *poor* and needy.
88:15(16). I (am) *afflicted* and ready to die
102 [title](1). A prayer *of the afflicted,*
109:16. persecuted the *poor* and needy man,
22. For I (am) *poor* and needy,
140:12(13). the Lord will maintain the cause of *the afflicted,*
Pro. 3:34. (כתיב) *but* he giveth grace *unto the lowly*

Pro.14:21.(כתיב) he that hath mercy on *the poor,*
15:15. All the days of *the afflicted*
16:19.(כתיב) an humble spirit with *the lowly,*
22:22. neither oppress *the afflicted*
30:14. to devour *the poor* from off the earth,
31: 9. plead the cause of *the poor*
20. She stretcheth out her hands *to the poor:*
Ecc. 6: 8. what hath *the poor,*
Isa. 3:14. the spoil of *the poor* (is) in your houses.
15. and grind the faces of *the poor?*
10: 2. to take away the right from *the poor of*
30. O *poor* Anathoth.
14:32. *the poor of* his people shall trust
26: 6. (even) the feet of *the poor,*
32: 7. to destroy *the poor* with lying words,
41:17. (When) *the poor* and needy seek water,
49:13. *and* will have mercy *upon his afflicted.*
51:21. hear now this, thou *afflicted,*
54:11. *O thou afflicted,* tossed with tempest,
58: 7. *the poor* that are cast out
66: 2. (him that is) *poor* and of a contrite spirit,
Jer. 22:16. He judged the cause of *the poor*
Eze.16:49. strengthen the hand of *the poor* and needy.
18:12. Hath oppressed *the poor* and needy,
17. hath taken off his hand *from the poor,*
22:29. *and* have vexed *the poor* and needy:
Am. 8: 4. make *the poor of* the land to fail,
Hab 3:14. to devour *the poor* secretly.
Zep. 3:12. an *afflicted* and poor people,
Zec. 7:10. the stranger, *nor the poor;*
9: 9. *lowly,* and riding upon an ass,
11: 7. *O poor of* the flock.
11. *the poor of* the flock that waited

6040 **עֳנִי** *^{n}gŏnee,* m.

Gen16:11. the Lord hath heard *thy affliction.*
29:32. the Lord hath looked *upon my affliction;*
31:42. God hath seen *mine affliction*
41:52. in the land of *my affliction.*
Ex. 3: 7. I have surely seen *the affliction*
17. I will bring you up *out of the affliction of*
4:31. he had looked upon *their affliction,*
Deu16: 3. the bread of *affliction;*
26: 7. and looked on *our affliction,*
1Sa. 1:11. if thou wilt indeed look *on the affliction of*
2Sa.16:12.(כתיב) that the Lord will look *on mine affliction,*
2K. 14:26. the Lord saw *the affliction of*
1Ch 22:14. *in my trouble* (marg. or, *poverty*) I have
Neh 9: 9. *the affliction of* our fathers
Job 10:15. see thou *mine affliction;*
30:16. the days of *affliction* have taken hold
27. the days of *affliction* prevented me.
36: 8. in cords of *affliction;*
15. He delivereth the poor *in his affliction,*
21. hast thou chosen rather *than affliction.*
Ps. 9:13(14). O Lord; consider *my trouble*
25:18. Look upon *mine affliction*
31: 7(8). thou hast considered *my trouble;*
44:24(25). *our affliction* and our oppression?
88: 9(10). Mine eye mourneth by reason of *affliction:*
107:10. bound *in affliction* and iron;
41. setteth he the poor on high *from* (marg. or, *after*) *affliction,*
119:50. my comfort *in my affliction:*
92. then have perished *in mine affliction.*
153. Consider *mine affliction,*
Pro.31: 5. the judgment of any of the *afflicted.* (marg. all the sons of *affliction*)
Isa. 48:10. in the furnace of *affliction.*
Lam 1: 3. gone into captivity *because of affliction,*
7. remembered in the days of *her affliction*
9. O Lord, behold *my affliction:*
3: 1. the man (that) hath seen *affliction*
19. Remembering *mine affliction*

6035 **עָנָיו** *^{n}gāh-nāh'yv,* adj.

Nu. 12: 3. the man Moses (was) very *meek,*

6045 **עִנְיָן** *^{n}gin-yāhn',* m.

Ecc. 1:13. this sore *travail* hath God given
2:23. days (are) sorrows, and *his travail* grief;
26. to the sinner he giveth *travail,*
Ecc. 3:10. I have seen *the travail,*
4: 8. *yea,* it (is) *a* sore *travail.*
5: 3(2). through the multitude of *business;*
14(13). those riches perish *by* evil *travail:*
8:16. *the business* that is done upon the earth:

עָנַן [*^{n}gāh-nan'*]. 6049

* PIEL.—*Infinitive.* *

Gen 9:14. *when I bring* a cloud over the earth,

* POEL.—*Preterite.* *

2K. 21: 6. *and observed times,* and used
2Ch33: 6. *also he observed times,* and used

POEL.—*Future.*

Lev.19:26. neither shall ye use enchantment, nor *observe times.*

POEL.—*Participle.*

Deu18:10. (or) *an observer of times,* or an enchanter,
14. hearkened unto *observers of times,*
Jud. 9:37. by the plain of *Meonenim.* (marg. or, *the regarders of the times*)
Isa. 2: 6. *and* (are) *soothsayers* like the Philistines,
57: 3. ye sons of *the sorceress,*
Jer. 27: 9. *your enchanters,* nor to your sorcerers,
Mic. 5:12(11). shalt have no (more) *soothsayers:*

עָנָן *^{n}gāh-nāhn',* m. 6051

Gen 9:13. I do set my bow *in the cloud,*
14. when I bring *a cloud* over the earth, that the bow shall be seen *in the cloud:*
16. the bow shall be *in the cloud;*
Ex. 13:21. in a pillar of *a cloud,*
22. He took not away the pillar of *the cloud*
14:19. the pillar of *the cloud* went from before
20. it was *a cloud* and darkness
24. the pillar of fire *and of the cloud,*
16:10. glory of the Lord appeared *in the cloud.*
19: 9. I come unto thee in *a* thick *cloud,*
16. *and a* thick *cloud* upon the mount,
24:15. *a cloud* covered the mount.
16. *the cloud* covered it
— out of the midst of *the cloud.*
18. Moses went into the midst of *the cloud,*
33: 9. the *cloudy* pillar (lit. the pillar of *the cloud*) descended,
10. the people saw the *cloudy* pillar (lit. *id.*)
34: 5. And the Lord descended *in the cloud,*
40:34. *a cloud* covered the tent
35. *the cloud* abode thereon,
36. when *the cloud* was taken up
37. if *the cloud* were not taken up,
38. *the cloud of* the Lord (was) upon the
Lev.16: 2. I will appear *in the cloud*
13. that *the cloud of* the incense may cover
Nu. 9:15. *the cloud* covered the tabernacle,
16. *the cloud* covered it (by day),
17. when *the cloud* was taken up
— in the place where *the cloud* abode,
18. as long as *the cloud* abode
19. when *the cloud* tarried long
20. when *the cloud* was a few days upon
21. when *the cloud* abode
— *the cloud* was taken up
— by night that *the cloud* was taken up,
22. *the cloud* tarried upon the tabernacle,
10:11. *the cloud* was taken up
12. *the cloud* rested in the wilderness
34. *And the cloud of* the Lord (was) upon
11:25. the Lord came down *in a cloud,*
12: 5. Lord came down in the pillar of *the cloud,*
10. *And the cloud* departed from off the
14:14. *and* (that) *thy cloud* standeth over them,
— by day time in a pillar of *a cloud,*
16:42(17:7). behold, *the cloud* covered it,
Deu 1:33. ye should go, *and in a cloud* by day.
4:11. darkness, *clouds,* and thick darkness.
5:22(19). of *the cloud,* and of the thick
31:15. the Lord appeared in the tabernacle in a pillar of *a cloud:* and the pillar of *the cloud* stood over the door
1K. 8:10. *that the cloud* filled the house
11. not stand to minister because of *the cloud:*
2Ch 5:13. the house was filled with *a cloud,*
14. stand to minister by reason of *the cloud:*

Neh. 9:12. thou leddest them in the day by a *cloudy*
19. the pillar of *the cloud* departed not
Job 7: 9. (As) *the cloud* is consumed and
26: 8. *the cloud* is not rent under them.
9. (and) spreadeth *his cloud* upon it.
37:11. he scattereth his bright *cloud:*
15. caused the light of *his cloud* to shine?
38: 9. When I made *the cloud* the garment
Ps. 78:14. the daytime also he led them *with a cloud,*
97: 2. *Clouds* and darkness (are) round about
99: 7. He spake unto them in the *cloudy* pillar:
105:39. He spread *a cloud* for a covering;
Isa. 4: 5. *a cloud* and smoke by day,
44:22. *and, as a cloud,* thy sins:
Jer. 4:13. he shall come up *as clouds,*
Lam. 3:44. Thou hast covered thyself *with a cloud,*
Eze. 1: 4. *a* great *cloud,* and a fire infolding itself,
28. the bow that is *in the cloud*
8:11. *a* thick *cloud of* incense went up.
10: 3. *and the cloud* filled the inner court.
4. the house was filled with *the cloud,*
30: 3. the day of the Lord (is) near, a *cloudy* day; (lit. a day of *cloud*)
18. *a cloud* shall cover her,
32: 7. I will cover the sun *with a cloud,*
34:12. in the *cloudy* and dark day.
38: 9. thou shalt be *like a cloud* to cover
16. *as a cloud* to cover the land;
Hos. 6: 4. your goodness (is) *as a* morning *cloud,*
13: 3. they shall be *as the* morning *cloud,*
Joel 2: 2. a day of *clouds* and of thick darkness,
Nah. 1: 3. *and the clouds* (are) the dust of his feet.
Zep. 1:15. a day of *clouds* and thick darkness,

6050 **עֲנַן** [*gănan*], Ch. m.

Dan. 7:13. the Son of man came with *the clouds of*

6053 **עֲנָנָה** *gănāh-nāh'*, f.

Job 3: 5. let *a cloud* dwell upon it;

6057 **עָנָף** *gāh-nāhph'*, m.

Lev. 23:40. *and the boughs of* thick trees,
Ps. 80:10(11). *and the boughs thereof* (were like)
Eze. 17: 8. that it might bring forth *branches,*
23. it shall bring forth *boughs,*
31: 3. a cedar in Lebanon with fair *branches,*
36: 8. ye shall shoot forth *your branches,*
Mal. 4: 1(3:19). it shall leave them neither root *nor branch.*

6056 **עֲנַף** [*gănaph*], Ch. m.

Dan. 4:12(9). *and the* fowls...*in the boughs thereof,*
14(11). and cut off *his branches,*
—(—). and the fowls from *his branches:*
21(18). *and upon whose branches* the fowls

6058 **עָנֵף** [*gāh-nēhph'*], adj.

Eze. 19:10. fruitful *and full of branches*

6059 **עָנַק** [*gāh-nak'*].

* KAL.—*Preterite.* *

Ps. 73: 6. pride *compasseth them about as a chain;*

* HIPHIL.—*Infinitive.* *

Deu 15:14. Thou shalt furnish him *liberally*

HIPHIL.—*Future.*

Deu 15:14. *Thou shalt furnish him* liberally

6060 **עֲנָק** *gănāhk*, m.

Jud. 8:26. *the chains* that (were) about their camels'
Pro. 1: 9. *and chains* about thy neck.
Cant. 4: 9. with one *chain* of thy neck.

6064 **עָנַשׁ** [*gāh-nash'*].

* KAL.—*Preterite.* *

Deu 22:19. *And they shall amerce* him in

KAL.—*Infinitive.*

Ex. 21:22. he shall be *surely* punished, (lit. *fining* he shall be fined)
Pro. 17:26. *to punish* the just (is) not good,
21:11. *When* the scorner *is punished,*

KAL.—*Future.*

2Ch. 36: 3. *and condemned* (marg. *mulcted*) the land

KAL.—*Participle.* Paül.

Am. 2: 8. drink the wine of *the condemned* (marg. or, *such as have fined,* or, *mulcted*)

* NIPHAL.—*Preterite.* *

Pro. 22: 3. the simple pass on, *and are punished.*
27:12. the simple pass on, (and) *are punished.*

NIPHAL.—*Future.*

Ex. 21:22. *he shall be* surely *punished,*

עֹנֶשׁ *gōh'-nesh*, m. 6066

2K. 23:33. and put the land to *a tribute* (marg. *a mulct*)
Pro. 19:19. of great wrath shall suffer *punishment:*

עֲנָשׁ *gănāhsh*, Ch. m. 6065

Ezr. 7:26. or *to confiscation of* goods,

עֶנֶת see **כְּעֶנֶת** See 3706

עָסִיס *gāh-sees'*, m. 6071

Cant. 8: 2. *of the juice of* my pomegranate.
Isa. 49:26. blood, *as with sweet* (marg. or, *new*) *wine.*
Joel 1: 5. because of *the new wine;*
3:18(4:18). shall drop down *new wine,*
Am. 9:13. shall drop *sweet* (marg. *new*) *wine,*

עָסַס [*gāh-sas'*]. 6072

* KAL.—*Preterite.* *

Mal. 4: 3(3:21). *And ye shall tread down* the

עֳפָאִים *gŏphāh-yeem'*, m. pl. 6073

Ps. 104:12. (which) sing among *the branches.*

עֵפָה see **עֵיפָה** See 5890

עֳפִי [*gŏphee*], Ch. m. 6074

Dan 4:12(9). *The leaves thereof* (were) fair,
14(11). shake off *his leaves,*
21(18). *Whose leaves* (were) fair,

עָפַל [*gāh-phal'*]. 6075

* PUAL.—*Preterite.* *

Hab. 2: 4. his soul (which) *is lifted up*

* HIPHIL.—*Future.* *

Nu. 14:44. *But they presumed* to go up

עֹפֶל *gōh'-phel*, m. 6076

Deu 28:27. (כתיב) of Egypt, *and with the emerods,*
1Sa. 5: 6. (——) and smote them *with emerods,*
9. (——) they had *emerods* in their secret
12. (——) were smitten *with the emerods:*
6: 4. (——) Five golden *emerods,*
5. (——) shall make images of *your emerods,*
2K. 5:24. came to *the tower,* (marg. or, *secret place*)
2Ch. 27: 3. the wall of *Ophel* (marg. or, *the tower*)
33:14. and compassed *about Ophel,* (marg. *id.*)
Neh. 3:26. the Nethinims dwelt *in Ophel,* (marg. *id.*)
27. unto the wall of *Ophel.*
11:21. dwelt *in Ophel:* (marg. or, *the tower*)
Isa. 32:14. *the forts* (marg. or, *clifts*) and towers shall be for dens
Mic. 4: 8. *the strong hold of* the daughter of Zion,

6079 עַפְעַפִּים [gaph-gap-peem'], m. pl.

Job 3: 9. neither let it see *the dawning* (marg. *eyelids*) *of* the day:
16:16. on *my eyelids* (is) the shadow of death;
41:18(10). his eyes (are) *like the eyelids of* the
Ps. 11: 4. *his eyelids* try, the children of men.
132: 4. (or) slumber *to mine eyelids*,
Pro. 4:25. *and* let *thine eyelids* look straight
6: 4. nor slumber *to thine eyelids*.
25. neither let her take thee *with her eyelids*.
30:13. *and their eyelids* are lifted up.
Jer. 9:18(17). *and our eyelids* gush out with waters.

6080 עָפַר [gāh-phar'].

* PIEL.—*Preterite.* *

2Sa. 16:13. threw stones at him, *and cast* dust. (marg. *dusted* (him) with dust)

6083 עָפָר gāh-phāhr', m.

Gen. 2: 7. the Lord God formed man (of) *the dust*
3:14. *and dust* shalt thou eat all the days of
19. for *dust* thou (art), and unto *dust* shalt thou return.
13:16. *as the dust of* the earth: so that if a man can number *the dust of*
18:27. which (am but) *dust* and ashes:
26:15. and filled them *with earth*.
28:14. thy seed shall be *as the dust of*
Ex. 8:16(12). smite *the dust of* the land,
17(13). and smote *the dust of* the earth,
—(—). all *the dust of* the land
Lev. 14:41. they shall pour out *the dust*
42. *and* he shall take other *morter*,
45. all *the morter of* the house;
17:13. thereof, and cover it *with dust*.
Nu. 5:17. *the dust* that is in the floor
19:17. they shall take *of the ashes* (marg. *dust*) *of* the burnt heifer
23:10. Who can count *the dust of* Jacob,
Deu. 9:21. until it was as small *as dust*: and I cast *the dust thereof* into the brook
28:24. the rain of thy land powder *and dust*:
32:24. the poison of serpents of *the dust*.
Jos. 7: 6. and put *dust* upon their heads.
1Sa. 2: 8. He raiseth up the poor *out of the dust*,
2Sa. 16:13. threw stones at him, and cast *dust*.
22:43. I beat them as small *as the dust of*
1K. 16: 2. I exalted thee out of *the dust*,
18:38. the wood, and the stones, and *the dust*,
20:10. if *the dust of* Samaria shall suffice
2K. 13: 7. had made them *like the dust*
23: 4. carried *the ashes of them* unto Beth-el.
6. stamped (it) small *to powder*, and cast *the powder thereof*
12. cast *the dust of them* into the brook Kidron.
15. stamped (it) small *to powder*,
2Ch. 1: 9. a people *like the dust of* the earth
Neh. 4: 2(3:34). the heaps of *the rubbish*
10(4). *and* (there is) much *rubbish*;
Job 2:12. sprinkled *dust* upon their heads
4:19. whose foundation (is) *in the dust*,
5: 6. affliction cometh not forth *of the dust*,
7: 5. clothed with worms and clods of *dust*;
21. now shall I sleep *in the dust*;
8:19. *and out of the earth* shall others grow.
10: 9. wilt thou bring me into *dust* again?
14: 8. *and* the stock thereof die *in the ground*;
19. of *the dust of* the earth;
16:15. and defiled my horn *in the dust*.
17:16. rest together (is) in *the dust*.
19:25. stand at the latter (day) upon *the earth*:
20:11. shall lie down with him in *the dust*.
21:26. They shall lie down alike in *the dust*,
22:24. Then shalt thou lay up gold as *dust*,
27:16. Though he heap up silver as *the dust*,
28: 2. Iron is taken *out of the earth*, (marg. or, *dust*)
6. *and* it hath *dust of* gold. (marg. or, gold **ore**)
30: 6 (in) caves of *the earth*,
19. I am become *like dust*
34:15. man shall turn again unto *dust*.
Job 38:38. When *the dust* groweth into hardness,
39:14. and warmeth them in *dust*,
40:13. Hide them *in the dust* together;
41:33(25). Upon *earth* there is not his like,
42: 6. and repent in *dust* and ashes.
Ps. 7: 5(6). lay mine honour *in the dust*.
18:42(43). I beat them small *as the dust*
22:15(16). *and* thou hast brought me into *the dust of* death.
29(30). they that go down to *the dust*
30: 9(10). Shall *the dust* praise thee?
44:25(26). our soul is bowed down *to the dust*:
72: 9. his enemies shall lick *the dust*.
78:27. rained flesh also upon them *as dust*,
102:14(15). and favour *the dust thereof*.
103:14. he remembereth that we (are) *dust*.
104:29. they die, and return to *their dust*.
113: 7. He raiseth up the poor *out of the dust*,
119:25. My soul cleaveth *unto the dust*:
Pro. 8:26. the highest part of *the dust of* the world.
Ecc. 3:20. all are of *the dust*, and all turn to *dust*
12: 7. Then shall *the dust* return to the earth
Isa. 2:10. hide thee *in the dust*,
19. into the caves of *the earth*, (marg. *dust*)
25:12. bring to the ground, (even) to *the dust*.
26: 5. he bringeth it (even) to *the dust*.
19. ye that dwell in *dust*:
29: 4. *and* thy speech shall be low *out of the dust*,
— *and* thy speech shall whisper *out of the dust*.
34: 7. *and their dust* made fat with fatness.
9. *and the dust thereof* into brimstone,
40:12. comprehended *the dust of* the earth
41: 2. gave (them) *as the dust* to his sword,
47: 1. Come down, and sit in *the dust*,
49:23. *and* lick up *the dust of* thy feet;
52: 2. Shake thyself *from the dust*;
65:25. *dust* (shall be) the serpent's meat.
Lam. 2:10. they have cast up *dust*
3:29. He putteth his mouth *in the dust*;
Eze 24: 7. to cover it with *dust*;
26: 4. I will also scrape *her dust*
12. thy timber *and thy dust*
27:30. and shall cast up *dust* upon their heads,
Dan 12: 2. them that sleep in the dust of *the earth*
Am. 2: 7. That pant after *the dust of* the earth
Mic. 1:10. roll thyself in *the dust*.
7:17. They shall lick *the dust*
Hab. 1:10. they shall heap *dust*,
Zep. 1:17. their blood shall be poured out *as dust*,
Zec. 9: 3. heaped up silver *as the dust*,

עֹפֶר gōh'-pher, m. 6082

Cant. 2: 9. My beloved is like a roe or a *young* hart:
17. be thou like a roe or a *young* hart
4: 5. like two *young* roes (that are) twins,
7: 3(4). like two *young* roes (that are) twins.
8:14. be thou like to a roe or *to a young* hart

עֹפֶרֶת see עוֹפֶרֶת See 5777

עֵץ gēhtz, m. 6086

Gen 1:11. *the* fruit *tree* yielding fruit
12. *and the tree* yielding fruit,
29. and every *tree*, in the which (is) the fruit of *a tree*
2: 9. every *tree* that is pleasant to the sight and good for food; *the tree of* life *also* in the midst of the garden, *and the tree of* knowledge of good and evil.
16. Of every *tree of* the garden
17. *But of the tree of* the knowledge of good
3: 1. Ye shall not eat of every *tree*
2. We may eat of the fruit of *the trees of*
3. of the fruit of *the tree* which (is) in the
6. the woman saw that *the tree* (was) good
— and *a tree* to be desired
8. amongst *the trees of* the garden.
11. Hast thou eaten of *the tree*,
12. she gave me of *the tree*,
17. and hast eaten of *the tree*,
22. and take also *of the tree of* life,

Gen 3:24. to keep the way of *the tree of* life.
6:14. Make thee an ark of gopher *wood;*
18: 4. rest yourselves under *the tree:*
8. he stood by them under *the tree,*
22: 3. clave *the wood for* the burnt offering,
6. Abraham took *the wood of*
7. Behold the fire *and the wood:*
9. and laid *the wood* in order,
— laid him on the altar upon *the wood.*
23:17. all *the trees* that (were) in the field,
40:19. shall hang thee on *a tree;*
Ex. 7:19. *both in* (vessels of) *wood,* and in
9:25. brake every *tree of* the field.
10: 5. shall eat every *tree*
15. all the fruit of *the trees*
— remained not any green thing *in the trees,*
15:25. the Lord shewed him *a tree,*
25: 5. and badgers' skins, *and* shittim *wood,*
10. they shall make an ark (of) shittim *wood:*
13. thou shalt make staves (of) shittim *wood,*
23. Thou shalt also make a table (of) shittim *wood:*
28. shalt make the staves (of) shittim *wood,*
26:15. boards for the tabernacle (of) shittim *wood*
26. thou shalt make bars (of) shittim *wood;*
27: 1. shalt make an altar (of) shittim *wood,*
6. staves (of) shittim *wood,* and overlay
30: 1. an altar to burn incense upon: (of) shittim *wood*
5. shalt make the staves (of) shittim *wood,*
31: 5. and in carving of *timber,*
35: 7. and badgers' skins, *and* shittim *wood,*
24. with whom was found shittim *wood*
33. and in carving of *wood,*
36:20. boards for the tabernacle (of) shittim *wood,*
31. he made bars of shittim *wood;*
37: 1. the ark (of) shittim *wood:*
4. he made staves (of) shittim *wood,*
10. he made the table (of) shittim *wood:*
15, 28. he made the staves (of) shittim *wood,*
25. made the incense altar (of) shittim *wood:*
38: 1. altar of burnt offering (of) shittim *wood:*
6. he made the staves (of) shittim *wood,*
Lev. 1: 7. lay *the wood* in order upon the fire:
8. upon *the wood* that (is) on the fire
12. lay them in order on *the wood*
17. upon *the wood* that (is) upon the fire:
3: 5. upon *the wood* that (is) on the fire:
4:12. burn him on *the wood*
6:12(5). the priest shall burn *wood*
11:32. any vessel of *wood,*
14: 4, 49. *and* cedar *wood,* and scarlet, and
6. he shall take it, and *the* cedar *wood,*
45. the stones of it, and *the timber thereof,*
51. he shall take *the* cedar *wood,*
52. *and with the* cedar *wood,*
15:12. every vessel of *wood*
19:23. all manner of *trees for* food,
23:40. the boughs of goodly *trees,*
— and the boughs of thick *trees,*
26: 4. *and the trees of* the field shall yield their
20. *neither* shall *the trees of* the land
27:30. the fruit of *the tree,*
Nu. 13:20. whether there be *wood* therein,
15:32. they found a man that gathered *sticks*
33. they that found him gathering *sticks*
19: 6. the priest shall take cedar *wood,*
31:20. all things made of *wood.*
35:18. with an hand weapon of *wood,*
Deu 4:28. the work of men's hands, *wood* and stone,
10: 1. make thee an ark of *wood.*
3. made an ark (of) shittim *wood,*
12: 2. under every green *tree:*
16:21. plant thee a grove of any *trees*
19: 5. when a man goeth...to hew *wood,*
— to cut down *the tree,* and the head slippeth from *the helve,* (marg. *wood*)
20:19. thou shalt not destroy *the trees thereof*
— *the tree of* the field (is) man's (life)
20. *the trees* which thou knowest that they (be) not *trees for* meat,
21:22. thou hang him on *a tree:*
23. shall not remain all night upon *the tree,*
22: 6. before thee in the way in any *tree,*
28:36. thou serve other gods, *wood* and stone.
42. All *thy trees* and fruit of thy land
64. (even) *wood* and stone.

Deu29:11(10). the hewer of *thy wood*
17(16). their idols, *wood* and stone,
Jos. 2: 6. hid them with *the stalks* of flax,
8:29. the king of Ai he hanged on *a tree*
— take his carcase down from *the tree,*
9:21. let them be hewers of *wood*
23. bondmen, and hewers of *wood*
27. made them that day hewers of *wood*
10:26. hanged them on five *trees:* and they were hanging upon *the trees*
27. they took them down off *the trees,*
Jud. 6:26. *with the wood of* the grove
9: 8. *The trees* went forth (on a time)
9, 11, 13. to be promoted over *the trees?*
10. And *the trees* said to the fig tree,
12. Then said *the trees* unto the vine,
14. Then said all *the trees*
15. the bramble said unto *the trees,*
48. cut down a bough from *the trees,*
1Sa. 6:14. they clave *the wood of* the cart,
17: 7. *And the staff of* his spear (was) like
2Sa. 5:11. *and* cedar *trees, and* carpenters, (lit. workers of *wood*)
6: 5. (instruments made of) fir *wood,*
21:19. *the staff of* whose spear
23: 7. *and the staff of* a spear;
24:22. instruments of the oxen *for wood.*
1K. 4:33(5:13). he spake of *trees,*
5: 6(20). that can skill to hew *timber*
8(22). *concerning timber of* cedar, *and concerning timber of* fir.
10(24). Hiram gave Solomon cedar *trees and* fir *trees* (acccording to) all his desire.
18(32). so they prepared *timber*
6:10. *with timber of* cedar.
15. covered(them) on the inside with *wood,*
23. two cherubims (of) olive *tree,*
31. he made doors (of) olive *tree:*
32. The two doors also (were of) olive *tree;*
33. for the door of the temple posts (of) olive *tree,*
34. the two doors (were of) fir *tree:*
9:11. Hiram...furnished Solomon *with* cedar *trees and* fir *trees,* and with gold,
10:11. plenty of almug *trees,*
12. the king made of *the* almug *trees* pillars
— there came no such almug *trees,*
14:23. under every green *tree.*
15:22. stones of Ramah, and *the timber thereof,*
17:10. the widow woman (was) there gathering of *sticks:*
12. behold, I (am) gathering two *sticks,*
18:23. and lay (it) on *wood,*
— the other bullock, and lay (it) on *wood,*
33. he put *the wood* in order, and cut the bullock...and laid (him) on *the wood,*
—(34). the burnt sacrifice, and on *the wood.*
38. consumed the burnt sacrifice, and *the wood,*
2K. 3:19. and shall fell every good *tree,*
25. and felled all *the* good *trees:*
6: 4. they came to Jordan, they cut down *wood.*
6. And he cut down *a stick,*
12:11(12). they laid it out to the carpenters (lit. workers of *wood*)
12(13). to buy *timber* and hewed stone
16: 4 & 17:10. under every green *tree.*
19:18. the work of men's hands, *wood* and stone:
22: 6. to buy *timber* and hewn stone
1Ch 14: 1. sent messengers to David, *and timber of* cedars, with masons and carpenters (lit. workers of *trees*), to build him an house.
16:33. Then shall *the trees of* the wood sing
20: 5. *whose* spear *staff* (was) like a weaver's beam.
21:23. the threshing instruments *for wood,*
22: 4. *Also* cedar *trees* in abundance:
— they of Tyre brought much cedar *wood*
14. *timber also* and stone have I prepared;
15. workers of stone *and timber,*
29: 2. *and wood for* (things) *of wood;*
2Ch 2: 8(7). Send me also cedar *trees,*
—(-). thy servants can skill to cut *timber in*
9(8). Even to prepare me *timber*
10(9). servants, the hewers that cut *timber,*
14(13). in iron, in stone, *and in timber,*
16(15). we will cut *wood* out of Lebanon,
3: 5. the greater house he cieled with fir *tree,*
9:10. algum *trees* and precious stones.

2Ch 9:11. the king made (of) *the* algum *trees* terraces
16: 6. stones of Ramah, and *the timber thereof*,
28: 4. under every green *tree*.
34:11. to buy hewn stone, *and timber*
Ezr. 3: 7. to bring cedar *trees* from Lebanon
Neh 2: 8. *timber* to make beams
8: 4. Ezra the scribe stood upon a pulpit of *wood*,
15. fetch olive branches, and pine branches, (lit. branches of oil *trees*)
— branches of thick *trees*,
9:25. *and* fruit *trees* in abundance:
10:34(35). the people, for the *wood* offering,
35(36). the firstfruits of all fruit of all *trees*,
37(38). the fruit of all manner of *trees*,
13:31. And for the *wood* offering,
Est. 2:23. they were both hanged on *a tree*:
5:14. Let *a gallows* (marg. *tree*) be made
— he caused *the gallows* to be made.
6: 4. to hang Mordecai on *the gallows*
7: 9. *the gallows* (marg. *tree*) fifty cubits high,
10. So they hanged Haman on *the gallows*
8: 7. they have hanged upon *the gallows*,
9:13. let Haman's ten sons be hanged upon *the gallows*.
25. his sons should be hanged on *the gallows*.
Job 14: 7. there is hope *of a tree*, if it be cut down,
19:10. mine hope hath he removed like *a tree*.
24:20. wickedness shall be broken *as a tree*.
41:27(19). iron as straw, (and) brass *as rotten wood*.
Ps. 1: 3. he shall be *like a tree* planted by
74: 5. lifted up axes upon *the* thick *trees*.
96:12. then shall all *the trees of* the wood rejoice
104:16. *The trees of* the Lord are full (of sap);
105:33. and brake *the trees of* their coasts.
148: 9. fruitful *trees*, and all cedars:
Pro. 3:18. She (is) *a tree of* life to them that
11:30. The fruit of the righteous (is) *a tree of* life;
13:12. *but* (when) the desire cometh, (it is) *a tree of* life.
15: 4. A wholesome tongue (is) *a tree of* life:
26:20. Where no *wood* is, (there) the fire goeth
21. (As) coals (are) to burning coals, *and wood* to fire;
Ecc. 2: 5. I planted *trees* in them of all (kind of)
6. the wood that bringeth forth *trees*:
10: 9. he that cleaveth *wood* shall be endangered
11: 3. if *the tree* fall toward the south,
— in the place where *the tree* falleth,
Cant. 2: 3. As the apple tree *among the trees of*
3: 9. a chariot *of the wood of* Lebanon.
4:14. all *trees of* frankincense;
Isa. 7: 2. as *the trees of* the wood are moved
10:15. the staff...(as if it were) no *wood*.
19. the rest of *the trees of* his forest
30:33. the pile thereof (is) fire *and* much *wood*;
37:19. the work of men's hands, *wood* and stone:
40:20. He that (is) so impoverished...chooseth *a tree*
41:19. the myrtle, *and the* oil *tree*;
44:13. The carpenter (lit. worker of *trees*) stretcheth out (his) rule;
14. *among the trees of* the forest:
19. shall I fall down to the stock of *a tree*?
23. O forest, and every *tree* therein:
45:20. that set up *the wood of* their graven image,
55:12. all *the trees of* the field shall clap
56: 3. eunuch say, Behold, I (am) *a* dry *tree*.
57: 5. under every green *tree*,
60:17. for *wood* brass, and for stones iron:
65:22. as the days of *a tree*
Jer. 2:20. under every green *tree*
27. Saying *to a stock*, Thou (art) my father;
3: 6, 13. under every green *tree*,
9. adultery with stones and with *stocks*.
5:14. in thy mouth fire, and this people *wood*,
7:18. The children gather *wood*,
20. upon *the trees of* the field,
10: 3. (one) cutteth *a tree* out of the forest,
8. *the stock* (is) a doctrine of vanities.
11:19. Let us destroy *the tree* with the fruit
17: 2. their groves by *the* green *trees*
8. he shall be *as a tree* planted
28:13. Thou hast broken the yokes of *wood*;
46:22. with axes, as hewers of *wood*.
Lam 4: 8. it is become *like a stick*.
5: 4. *our wood* is sold unto us.
Lam. 5:13. the children fell *under the wood*.
Eze. 6:13. under every green *tree*,
15: 2. Son of man, What is *the* vine *tree* more than any *tree*, (or than) a branch which is among *the trees of* the forest?
3. Shall *wood* be taken thereof
6. saith the Lord God; As *the* vine *tree among the trees of* the forest,
17:24. all *the trees of* the field shall know that I the Lord have brought down *the* high *tree*, have exalted *the* low *tree*, have dried up *the* green *tree*, and have made *the* dry *tree* to flourish:
20:28. all *the* thick *trees*,
32. to serve *wood* and stone.
47(21:3). every green *tree* in thee, and every dry *tree*:
21:10(15). contemneth the rod of my son, (as) every *tree*.
24:10. Heap on *wood*, kindle the fire,
26:12. thy stones *and thy timber* and thy dust
31: 4. rivers unto all *the trees of* the field.
5. above all *the trees of* the field,
8. any *tree* in the garden of God
9. so that all *the trees of* Eden,
14. all *the trees by* the waters
15. all *the trees of* the field fainted
16. and all *the trees of* Eden,
18. *among the trees of* Eden?
— with *the trees of* Eden
34:27. *the tree of* the field shall yield her fruit,
36:30. I will multiply the fruit of *the tree*,
37:16. son of man, take thee one *stick*,
— then take another *stick*,
— *the stick of* Ephraim,
17. join them one to another *into* one *stick*;
19. I will take *the stick of* Joseph,
— and will put them...with *the stick of* Judah, and make them one *stick*,
20. *the sticks* whereon thou writest
39:10. they shall take no *wood*
41:16. cieled with *wood* round about,
22. The altar of *wood* (was) three cubits high,
— and the walls thereof, (were) of *wood*:
25. thick *planks* upon the face of the porch
47: 7. bank of the river (were) very many *trees*
12. all *trees for* meat, whose leaf
Hos. 4:12. My people ask counsel *at their stocks*,
Joel 1:12. all *the trees of* the field,
19. the flame hath burned all *the trees of*
2:22. for *the tree* beareth her fruit,
Hab 2:11. the beam *out of the timber*
19. unto him that saith *to the wood*, Awake;
Hag. 1: 8. Go up to the mountain, and bring *wood*,
2:19. the pomegranate, *and the* olive *tree*,
Zec. 5: 4. *the timber thereof* and the stones thereof.
12: 6. an hearth of fire *among the wood*,

עָצַב [*gāh-tzav'*]. 6087

*** KAL.—*Preterite.* ***

1K. 1: 6. his father *had* not *displeased him*

KAL.—*Infinitive.*

1Ch 4:10. (me) from evil, that *it may* not *grieve me*!

KAL.—*Participle.* Paül.

Isa. 54: 6. a woman forsaken *and grieved*

*** NIPHAL.—*Preterite.* ***

1Sa. 20:34. *he was grieved* for David,
2Sa. 19: 2(3). the king *was grieved* for his son.

NIPHAL.—*Future.*

Gen 45: 5. *be* not *grieved*, nor angry
1Sa. 20: 3. not Jonathan know this, lest *he be grieved*:
Neh 8:10. neither *be ye sorry*; for the joy
11. the day (is) holy; neither *be ye grieved*.
Ecc. 10: 9. Whoso removeth stones *shall be hurt*

*** PIEL.—*Preterite.* ***

Job 10: 8. Thine hands *have made me* (marg. *took pains about me*)
Isa. 63:10. they rebelled, *and vexed* his holy Spirit:

PIEL.—*Future.*

Ps. 56: 5(6). Every day *they wrest* my words:

*** HIPHIL.—*Infinitive.* ***

Jer. 44:19. did we make her cakes *to worship her*,

HIPHIL.—*Future.*

Ps. 78:40. How oft did they provoke...(and) *grieve him*

* HITHPAEL.—*Future.* *

Gen 6: 6. *and it grieved him* at his heart.
34: 7. *and* the men *were grieved,*

6088 עֲצַב [*ğătzav*], Ch.

* P'AL.—*Participle.* *

Dan. 6:20(21). he cried with a *lamentable* voice

6091 עָצָב [*ğāh-tzāhv'*], m.

1Sa.31: 9. to publish (it in) the house of *their idols,*
2Sa. 5:21. And there they left *their images,*
1Ch 10: 9. to carry tidings unto *their idols,*
2Ch 24:18. and served groves and *idols:*
Ps.106:36. And they served *their idols:*
38. they sacrificed *unto the idols of*
115: 4. *Their idols* (are) silver and gold,
135:15. *The idols of* the heathen
Isa. 10:11. so do to Jerusalem *and her idols?*
46: 1. *their idols* were upon the beasts,
Jer. 50: 2. *her idols* are confounded, her images
Hos. 4:17. Ephraim (is) joined to *idols:*
8: 4. have they made them *idols,*
13: 2. made them...*idols* according to
14: 8(9). What have I to do any more *with idols?*
Mic. 1: 7. all *the idols thereof* will I lay desolate:
Zec.13: 2. I will cut off the names of *the idols*

6092 עָצֵב [*ğāh-tzēhv'*], m.

Isa. 58: 3. and exact all *your labours.* (marg. *griefs,* or, *things wherewith ye grieve others*)

6089 עֶצֶב *ğeh'-tzev*, m.

Gen 3:16. *in sorrow* thou shalt bring forth children;
Ps.127: 2. to eat the bread of *sorrows:*
Pro. 5:10. and *thy labours* (be) in the house of
10:22. he addeth no *sorrow* with it.
14:23. In all *labour* there is profit:
15: 1. *grievous* words stir up anger.
Jer. 22:28. this man Coniah *a* despised broken *idol?*

6090 עֹצֶב *ğōh'-tzev*, m.

1Ch 4: 9. Because I bare him *with sorrow.*
Ps.139:24. if (there be any) *wicked* way (marg. way of *pain,* or, *grief*) in me,
Isa. 14: 3. Lord shall give thee rest *from thy sorrow,*
48: 5. *Mine idol* hath done them,

6093 עִצָּבוֹן *ğitz-tzāh-vōhn'*, m.

Gen 3:16. I will greatly multiply *thy sorrow*
17. *in sorrow* shalt thou eat (of) it
5:29. our work *and toil of* our hands,

6094 עַצֶּבֶת [*ğatz-tzeh'-veth*], f.

Job 9:28. I am afraid of all *my sorrows,*
Ps. 16: 4. *Their sorrows* shall be multiplied
147: 3. bindeth up *their wounds.* (marg. *griefs*)
Pro.10:10. that winketh with the eye causeth *sorrow:*
15:13. *but by sorrow of* the heart

6095 עָצָה [*ğāh-tzāh'*].

* KAL.—*Participle.* Poel. *

Pro.16:30. *He shutteth* his eyes to devise

6096 עָצֶה *ğāh-tzeh'*, m.

Lev. 3: 9. hard by *the backbone;*

6097 עֵצָה *ğēh-tzāh'*, f.

Jer. 6: 6. Hew ye down *trees,*

עֵצָה *ğēh-tzāh'*, f. 6098

Deu32:28. they (are) a nation void of *counsel,*
Jud.20: 7. give here your advice *and counsel.*
2Sa.15:31. turn *the counsel of* Ahithophel into
34. defeat *the counsel of* Ahithophel.
16:20. Give *counsel* among you what we shall do.
23. And *the counsel of* Ahithophel,
— so (was) all *the counsel of* Ahithophel
17: 7. *The counsel* that Ahithophel hath given
14. *The counsel of* Hushai...(is) better *than the counsel of* Ahithophel. For the Lord had appointed to defeat *the* good *counsel of* Ahithophel,
23. *his counsel* was not followed,
1K. 1:12. let me, I pray thee, give thee *counsel,*
12: 8. he forsook *the counsel of* the old men,
13. forsook the old men's *counsel*
14. spake to them after *the counsel of* the
2K. 18:20. (I have) *counsel* and strength for the war.
1Ch 12:19. the lords...*upon advisement* sent him
2Ch 10: 8. he forsook *the counsel* which the old men gave him,
13. forsook *the counsel of* the old men,
14. answered them after *the advice of* the
22: 5. He walked also after *their counsel,*
25:16. hast not hearkened unto *my counsel.*
Ezr. 4: 5. to frustrate *their purpose,*
10: 3. *according to the counsel of* my lord,
8. *according to the counsel of* the princes
Neh 4:15(9). God had brought *their counsel* to
Job 5:13. *and the counsel of* the froward is carried
10: 3. shine upon *the counsel of* the wicked?
12:13. he hath *counsel* and understanding.
18: 7. *his own counsel* shall cast him down.
21:16. *the counsel of* the wicked is far from me.
22:18. *but the counsel of* the wicked is far from
29:21. kept silence at *my counsel.*
38: 2. Who (is) this that darkeneth *counsel*
42: 3. Who (is) he that hideth *counsel*
Ps. 1: 1. walketh not *in the counsel of* the ungodly,
13: 2(3). How long shall I take *counsel*
14: 6. Ye have shamed *the counsel of* the poor,
20: 4(5). fulfil all *thy counsel.*
33:10. The Lord bringeth *the counsel of* the
11. *The counsel of* the Lord standeth for ever,
73:24. guide me *with thy counsel,*
106:13. they waited not *for his counsel:*
43. they provoked (him) *with their counsel,*
107:11. *and* contemned *the counsel of* the most
119:24. *my counsel*lors. (marg. men of *my counsel*)
Pro. 1:25. ye have set at nought all *my counsel,*
30. They would none *of my counsel:*
8:14. *Counsel* (is) mine, and sound wisdom:
12:15. he that hearkeneth *unto counsel* (is) wise.
19:20. Hear *counsel,* and receive instruction,
21. *nevertheless the counsel of* the Lord, that
20: 5. *Counsel* in the heart of man (is like) deep
18. (Every) purpose is established *by counsel:*
21:30. understanding nor *counsel*
27: 9. the sweetness of a man's friend *by* hearty *counsel.*
Isa. 5:19. let *the counsel of* the Holy One
8:10. Take *counsel* together, and it shall come
11: 2. the spirit of *counsel* and might,
14:26. This (is) *the purpose* that is purposed
16: 3. Take *counsel,* execute judgment;
19: 3. *and* I will destroy *the counsel thereof:*
11. *the counsel of* the wise counsellors
17. because of *the counsel of* the Lord
25: 1. (thy) *counsels* of old (are) faithfulness
28:29. (which) is wonderful in *counsel,*
29:15. hide their *counsel* from the Lord,
30: 1. that take *counsel,* but not of me;
36: 5. (I have) *counsel* and strength for war:
40:13. *his counsel*lor (marg. man of *his counsel*)
44:26. *and* performeth *the counsel of* his
46:10. *My counsel* shall stand,
11. the man that executeth *my counsel*
47:13. the multitude of *thy counsels.*
Jer. 18:18. *nor counsel* from the wise,
23. thou knowest all *their counsel*
19: 7. I will make void *the counsel of* Judah
32:19. Great *in counsel,* and mighty in work:
49: 7. is *counsel* perished from the prudent?
20. hear *the counsel of* the Lord,
30. hath taken *counsel* against you,

Jer. 50:45. hear ye *the counsel of* the Lord,
Eze. 7:26. *and counsel* from the ancients.
11: 2. give wicked *counsel* in this city:
Hos.10: 6. shall be ashamed *of his own counsel.*
Mic. 4:12. neither understand they *his counsel:*
Zec. 6:13. *and the counsel of* peace shall be between them both.

6099 **עָצוּם** *gāh-tzoom'*, adj.

Gen18:18. a great *and mighty* nation,
Ex. 1: 9. the children of Israel (are) more *and mightier*
Nu. 14:12. a greater nation *and mightier* than they.
22: 6. this people; for they (are) too *mighty*
32: 1. the children of Gad had a very *great*
Deu 4:38. nations...greater *and mightier*
7: 1. nations greater *and mightier* than thou;
9: 1. nations greater *and mightier* than thyself,
14. a nation *mightier* and greater than they.
11:23. greater nations *and mightier* than
26: 5. a nation, great, *mighty*, and populous:
Jos. 23: 9. great nations *and strong:*
Ps. 10:10. that the poor may fall *by his strong ones.* (marg. or, *into his strong parts*)
35:18. I will praise thee among *much* (marg. *strong*) people.
135:10. and slew *mighty* kings;
Pro. 7:26. *yea*, many *strong* (men) have been slain
18:18. parteth between *the mighty.*
30:26. The conies (are but) a feeble (lit. not *mighty*) folk,
Isa. 8: 7. the waters of the river, *strong* and many,
53:12. he shall divide the spoil with *the strong;*
60:22. and a small one a *strong* nation:
Dan 8:24. the *mighty* and the holy people.
11:25. a very great *and mighty* army;
Joel 1: 6. a nation is come up upon my land, *strong*,
2: 2. a great people *and a strong;*
5. a *strong* people set in battle
11. (he is) *strong* that executeth his word:
Am. 5:12. *and* your *mighty* sins:
Mic. 4: 3. and rebuke *strong* nations afar off;
7. I will make her... a *strong* nation:
Zec. 8:22. many people *and strong* nations

6101 **עָצַל** [*gāh-tzal'*].

* NIPHAL.—*Future.* *

Jud.18: 9. *be* not *slothful* to go,

6102 **עָצֵל** *gāh-tzēhl'*, adj.

Pro. 6: 6. Go to the ant, thou *sluggard;*
9. How long wilt thou sleep, *O sluggard?*
10:26. vinegar to the teeth,...so (is) *the sluggard*
13: 4. The soul of *the sluggard* desireth,
15:19. The way of *the slothful* (man)
19:24. *A slothful* (man) hideth his hand
20: 4. *The sluggard* will not plow by reason
21:25. The desire of *the slothful*
22:13. *The slothful* (man) saith,
24:30. I went by the field of *the slothful*, (lit. *slothful* man)
26:13. *The slothful* (man) saith,
14. *so* (doth) *the slothful* upon his bed.
15. *The slothful* hideth his hand
16. *The sluggard* (is) wiser in his own conceit

6103 **עַצְלָה** *gatz-lāh'*, f.

Pro.19:15. *Slothfulness* casteth into a deep sleep;
Ecc.10:18. *By much slothfulness* the building

6104 **עַצְלוּת** *gatz-looth'*, f.

Pro.31:27. eateth not the bread of *idleness.*

6105 **עָצַם** *gāh-tzam'*.

* KAL.—*Preterite.* *

Gen26:16. *thou art* much *mightier* than we.
Ps. 38:19(20). mine enemies...*they are strong:*
40: 5(6). *they are more* than can be numbered.
12(13). *they are more* than the hairs of mine
69: 4(5). they that would destroy me,.....*are mighty:*
139:17. O God! how *great is* the sum of them!
Isa. 31: 1. because *they are* very *strong;*
Jer. 5: 6. their backslidings *are increased.* (marg. *strong*)
15: 8. Their widows *are increased* to me
30:14, 15. thy sins *were increased.*
Dan 8:24. *And* his power *shall be mighty,*
11:23. he shall come up, *and shall become strong*

KAL.—*Infinitive.*

Dan 8: 8. *and when he was strong*, the great horn

KAL.—*Future.*

Ex. 1: 7. *and waxed* exceeding *mighty;*
20. people multiplied, *and waxed* very *mighty.*

KAL.—*Participle.* Poel.

Isa. 33:15. *and shutteth* his eyes from seeing evil;

* PIEL.—*Preterite.* *

Jer. 50:17. king of Babylon *hath broken his bones.*

PIEL.—*Future.*

Isa. 29:10. *and hath closed* your eyes:

* HIPHIL.—*Future.* *

Ps.105:24. *and made them stronger* than their enemies.

עֶצֶם *geh'-tzem*, f. 6106

Gen. 2:23. This (is) now *bone of my bones,*
7:13. *In* the *selfsame* day entered Noah,
17:23. *in* the *selfsame* day, as God had
26. *In* the *selfsame* day was Abraham
29:14. Surely thou (art) *my bone* and my flesh.
50:25. ye shall carry up *my bones*
Ex. 12:17. *in* this *selfsame* day have I
41. even the *selfsame* day it came to pass,
46. *neither* shall ye break *a bone* thereof.
51. the *selfsame* day, (that) the Lord
13:19. Moses took *the bones of* Joseph
— ye shall carry up *my bones*
24:10. *and as it were the body of* heaven
Lev.23:14. until the *selfsame* day that ye
21. ye shall proclaim *on* the *selfsame* day,
28. do no work *in* that *same* day:
29. *in* that *same* day, he shall be
30. doeth any work *in* that *same* day,
Nu. 9:12. *nor* break *any bone* of it:
19:16. a dead body, or *a bone of* a man,
18. him that touched *a bone,*
24: 8. and shall break *their bones,*
Deu32:48. spake unto Moses that *selfsame* day,
Jos. 5:11. parched (corn) *in* the *selfsame* day.
10:27. (which remain) until this *very* day.
24:32. And *the bones of* Joseph,
Jud. 9: 2. I (am) *your bone* and your flesh.
19:29. divided her, (together) *with her bones,*
1Sa.31:13. And they took *their bones*
2Sa. 5: 1. we (are) *thy bone* and thy flesh.
19:12(13). ye (are) *my bones* and my flesh:
13(14). (Art) thou not of *my bone,*
21:12. David went and took *the bones of* Saul and *the bones of* Jonathan
13. *the bones of* Saul and *the bones of* Jonathan his son; and they gathered *the bones of* them that were hanged.
14. *the bones of* Saul and Jonathan
1K. 13: 2. *and* men's *bones* shall be burnt upon thee.
31. lay *my bones* beside *his bones:*
2K. 13:21. and touched *the bones of* Elisha,
23:14. with *the bones of* men.
16. took *the bones* out of the sepulchres,
18. let no man move *his bones.* So they let *his bones* alone, with *the bones of* the
20. and burned men's *bones*
1Ch10:12. buried *their bones* under the oak
11: 1. we (are) *thy bone* and thy flesh.
2Ch 34: 5. *And* he burnt *the bones of* the priests
Job 2: 5. touch *his bone* and his flesh,
4:14. made all *my bones* to shake.
7:15. my soul chooseth...death *rather than my life.* (marg. *bones*)
10:11. *and* hast fenced me *with bones*
19:20. *My bone* cleaveth to my skin

Job 20:11. *His bones* are full (of the sin) of
21:23. One dieth *in* his full *strength*,
24. *his bones* are moistened
30:17. *My bones* are pierced in me
30. *and my bones* are burned with heat.
33:19. the multitude of *his bones*
21. *his bones* (that) were not seen
40:18. *His bones* (are as) strong pieces of brass;
Ps. 6: 2(3). O Lord, heal me; for *my bones* are vexed.
22:14(15). all *my bones* are out of joint:
17(18). I may tell all *my bones:*
31:10(11). *and my bones* are consumed.
32: 3. *my bones* waxed old through my roaring
34:20(21). He keepeth all *his bones:*
35:10. All *my bones* shall say,
38: 3(4). neither (is there any) rest *in my bones*
42:10(11). with a sword *in my bones*,
51: 8(10). *the bones* (which) thou hast broken
53: 5(6). God hath scattered *the bones of*
102: 3(4). *and my bones* are burned as an hearth.
5(6). *my bones* cleave to my skin.
109:18. like oil *into his bones*.
141: 7. *Our bones* are scattered at the grave's
Pro. 3: 8. and marrow *to thy bones*.
12: 4. as rottenness *in his bones*.
14:30. *but* envy the rottenness of *the bones*.
15:30. a good report maketh *the bones* fat.
16:24. and health *to the bones*.
Ecc. 11: 5. how *the bones* (do grow) in the womb
Isa. 38:13. so will he break all *my bones:*
58:11. *and* make fat *thy bones:*
66:14. *and your bones* shall flourish
Jer. 8: 1. *the bones of* the kings of Judah, and *the bones of* his princes, and *the bones of* the priests, and *the bones of* the prophets, and *the bones of* the inhabitants
20: 9. as a burning fire shut up *in my bones*,
23: 9. all *my bones* shake; I am like
Lam. 1:13. he sent fire *into my bones*,
3: 4. he hath broken *my bones*.
4: 7. more ruddy in *body* than rubies,
8. their skin cleaveth to *their bones;*
Eze. 2: 3. unto this *very* day.
6: 5. I will scatter *your bones*
24: 2. (even) of this *same* day: the king of Babylon set himself against Jerusalem this *same* day.
4. fill (it) with the choice *bones*.
5. burn also *the bones* under it,
— let them seethe *the bones of it*
10. *and* let *the bones* be burned.
32:27. their iniquities shall be upon *their bones*,
37: 1. the valley which (was) full of *bones*,
3. Son of man, can these *bones* live?
4. Prophesy upon these *bones*, and say unto them, O ye dry *bones*, hear the word
5. Thus saith the Lord God *unto* these *bones;*
7. *the bones* came together, *bone* to *his bone*.
11. these *bones* are the whole house of
— *Our bones* are dried,
39:15. when (any) seeth a man's *bone*,
40: 1. *in* the *selfsame* day the hand of the Lord
Am. 2: 1. he burned *the bones of* the king of Edom
6:10. to bring out *the bones* out of the house,
Mic. 3: 2. their flesh from off *their bones;*
3. they break *their bones*,
Hab. 3:16. rottenness entered *into my bones*,

6108 **עֹצֶם** *gōh'-tzem*, m.

Deu 8:17. *and the might of* mine hand
Job 30:21. *with* thy *strong* hand (marg. *with the strength of* thy hand)
Ps. 139:15. *My substance* (marg. or, *strength*, or, *body*) was not hid from thee,

---

6109 **עָצְמָה** *gotz-māh'*, f.

Isa. 40:29. he increaseth *strength*.
47: 9. *for the* great *abundance of* thine
Nah 3: 9. Ethiopia and Egypt (were) her *strength*,

6110 **עֲצֻמוֹת** *gatz-tzoo-mōhth'*, f.pl.

Isa. 41:21. bring forth *your strong* (reasons),

עָצַר *gāh-tzar'*. 6113

* KAL.—*Preterite.* *

Gen16: 2. the Lord *hath restrained me* from bearing:
20:18. the Lord *had* fast *closed up* all the
Deu11:17. *and he shut up* the heaven,
2Ch 13:20. Neither *did* Jeroboam *recover* strength
20:37. *they were* not *able* to go to Tarshish.
Job 29: 9. The princes *refrained* talking,
Isa. 66: 9. shall I cause to bring forth, *and shut* (the womb)?
Dan10: 8. *I retained* no strength.
16. *I have retained* no strength.

KAL.—*Infinitive.*

Gen20:18. the Lord had *fast* closed up (lit. *closing up* had closed) all the wombs
2Ch 22: 9. had no power *to keep still* the kingdom.
Job 4: 2. *but* who can *withhold himself* from

KAL.—*Future.*

Jud. 13:15. I pray thee, *let us detain* thee,
16. Though *thou detain me*, I will not
1Sa. 9:17. this same *shall reign* over (marg. *restrain* in) my people.
1K. 18:44. that the rain *stop thee* not.
2K. 4:24. *slack* (marg. *restrain*) not (thy) riding
17: 4. *therefore* the king of Assyria *shut him up*,
1Ch 29:14. that *we should be* able (marg. *retain*, or, *obtain* strength) to offer
2Ch 2: 6(5). *who is* able (marg. *hath retained*, or, *obtained* strength) to build him an
7:13. If *I shut up* heaven
14:11(10). *let* not man *prevail* against thee.
Job 12:15. *he withholdeth* the waters,
Dan 11: 6. *she shall* not *retain* the power of

KAL.—*Participle.* Paül.

Deu32:36. (there is) none *shut up*, or left.
1Sa. 21: 5(6). women (have been) *kept* from us
1K. 14:10. him that is *shut up* and left in Israel,
21:21. *and* him that is *shut up* and left in Israel,
2K. 9: 8. *and* him that is *shut up* and left in Israel:
14:26. (there was) not any *shut up*,
1Ch 12: 1. came to David...while he yet *kept himself close* (marg. (being) yet *shut up*)
Neh 6:10. son of Mehetabeel, who (was) *shut up;*
Jer. 20: 9. as a burning fire *shut up* in my bones,
33: 1. Jeremiah...while he *was* yet *shut up*
36: 5. I (am) *shut up;* I cannot go into
39:15. Jeremiah, while he *was shut up*

* NIPHAL.—*Preterite.* *

Nu. 16:50(17:15). and the plague *was stayed*.

NIPHAL.—*Infinitive.*

1K. 8:35. *When* heaven *is shut up*,
2Ch 6:26. *When* the heaven *is shut up*,

NIPHAL.—*Future.*

Nu. 16:48(17:13). *and* the plague *was stayed*.
25: 8. *So* the plague *was stayed*
2Sa. 24:21. *that* the plague *may be stayed*
25. *and* the plague *was stayed*
1Ch 21:22. *that* the plague *may be stayed* from
Ps. 106:30. *and* (so) the plague *was stayed*.

NIPHAL.—*Participle.*

1Sa. 21: 7(8). *detained* before the Lord;

עֹצֶר *gōh'-tzer*, m. 6115

Ps. 107:39. brought low *through oppression*,
Pro. 30:16. The grave; *and the barren* womb;
Isa. 53: 8. taken *from prison* (marg. or, *by distress*)

עֶצֶר *geh'-tzer*, m. 6114

Jud. 18: 7. (there was) no magistrate (marg. possessor of *restraint*) in the land,

---

עֲצָרָה *gătzāh-rāh'*, f. 6116

2K. 10:20. Proclaim *a solemn assembly*
Isa. 1:13. iniquity, *even the solemn meeting*.
Joel 1:14 & 2:15. call *a solemn assembly*, (marg. or, (day of) *restraint*)

6116 **עֲצֶרֶת** *^{n}gătzeh'-reth*, f.

Lev.23:36. it (is) *a solemn assembly;* (marg. (day of) *restraint*)
Nu. 29:35. ye shall have *a solemn assembly:*
Deu16: 8. *a solemn assembly* (marg. *restraint*) to the
2Ch 7: 9. they made *a solemn assembly:* (marg. *id.*)
Neh 8:18. day (was) *a solemn assembly,* (marg. *id.*)
Jer. 9: 2(1). *an assembly of* treacherous men.
Am. 5:21. I will not smell *in your solemn assemblies.* (marg. or, *your holy days*)

6117 **עָקַב** *^{n}gāh-kav'.*

* KAL.—*Preterite.* *

Hos 12: 3(4). *He took* his brother *by the heel*

KAL.—*Infinitive.*

Jer. 9: 4(3). every brother will *utterly* supplant, (lit. in *supplanting* will supplant)

KAL.—*Future.*

Gen27:36. *for he hath supplanted me* these two times:
Jer. 9: 4(3). every brother *will* utterly *supplant,*

* PIEL.—*Future.* *

Job 37: 4. and *he will* not *stay them* when his voice

6119-20 **עָקֵב** *^{n}gāh-kēhv'*, m.

Gen 3:15. thou shalt bruise his *heel.*
25:26. his hand took hold *on* Esau's *heel;*
49:17. that biteth *the* horse *heels,*
19. he shall overcome *at the last.*
Jos. 8:13. *their liers in wait* (marg. *lying in wait*) on
Jud. 5:22. Then were *the* horse*hoofs* broken
Job 18: 9. The gin shall take (him) *by the heel,*
Ps. 41: 9(10). hath lifted up (his) *heel*
49: 5(6). the iniquity *of my heels*
56: 6(7). they mark *my steps,*
77:19(20). *and thy footsteps* are not known.
89:51(52). reproached *the footsteps of* thine
Cant.1: 8. *by the footsteps of* the flock,
Jer. 13:22. thy skirts discovered, (and) *thy heels*

6121 **עָקֹב** *^{n}gāh-kōhv'*, adj.

Isa. 40: 4. *the crooked* shall be made straight,
Jer. 17: 9. The heart (is) *deceitful* above all (things),
Hos. 6: 8. Gilead...(is) *polluted* with (marg. or, *cunning* for) blood.

6118 **עֵקֶב** *^{n}gēh'-kev*, m.

עֵקֶב[3] כִּי עֵקֶב[2] אֲשֶׁר

Gen22:18. *because*[2] thou hast obeyed my voice.
26: 5. *Because* that[2] Abraham obeyed my voice,
Nu. 14:24. *because* he had another spirit
Deu 7:12. *if* (marg. *because*) ye hearken to these judgments,
8:20. *because* ye would not be obedient
2Sa. 12: 6. *because*[2] he did this thing,
10. *because*[3] thou hast despised me,
Ps. 19:11(12). in keeping of them (there is) great *reward.*
40:15(16). Let them be desolate for *a reward of*
70: 3(4). them be turned back for *a reward of*
119:33. I shall keep it (unto) *the end.*
112. thy statutes alway, (even unto) *the end.*
Pro.22: 4. *By* (marg. or, *The reward of*) humility (and) the fear of the Lord
Isa. 5:23. justify the wicked *for* reward,
Am. 4:12. *because*[3] I will do this unto thee,

6122 **עָקְבָה** *^{n}gok-bāh'*, f.

2K. 10:19. But Jehu did (it) *in subtilty,*

6123 **עָקַד** [*^{n}gāh-kad'*].

* KAL.—*Future.* *

Gen22: 9. *and bound* Isaac his son,

עָקֹד *^{n}gāh-kōhd'*, adj. 6124

Gen30:35. the he goats *that were ringstraked*
39. brought forth cattle *ringstraked,*
40. the flocks toward *the ringstraked,*
31: 8. *The ringstraked* shall be thy hire; then bare all the cattle *ringstraked.*
10. the rams...(were) *ringstraked,*
12. the rams...(are) *ringstraked,*

עָקָה [*^{n}gāh-kāh'*], f. 6125

Ps. 55: 3(4). because of *the oppression of* the

עָקַל [*^{n}gāh-kal'*]. 6127

* PUAL.—*Participle.* *

Hab. 1: 4. *wrong* (marg. or, *wrested*) judgment proceedeth.

עֲקַלְקַל [*^{n}găkal-kal'*], adj. 6128

Jud. 5: 6. the travellers walked through *by*ways. (marg. *crooked* ways)
Ps.125: 5. turn aside unto *their crooked ways,*

עֲקַלָּתוֹן *^{n}găkal-lāh-thōhn'*, adj. 6129

Isa. 27: 1. leviathan that *crooked* serpent;

עָקַר [*^{n}gāh-kar'*]. 6131

* KAL.—*Infinitive.* *

Ecc. 3: 2. a time *to pluck up*

* NIPHAL.—*Future.* *

Zep. 2: 4. Ekron *shall be rooted up.*

* PIEL.—*Preterite.* *

Gen49: 6. in their selfwill *they digged down* a wall. (marg. or, *houghed* oxen)
Jos.11: 9. *he houghed* their horses, and burnt

PIEL.—*Future.*

Jos. 11: 6. *thou shalt hough* their horses,
2Sa. 8: 4. *and* David *houghed* all the chariot (horses),
1Ch.18: 4. David *also houghed* all the chariot (horses),

עֲקַר [*^{n}găkar*], Ch. 6132

* ITHP'AL.—*Future.* *

Dan 7: 8. before whom there *were* three of the first horns *plucked up by the roots:*

עֵקֶר *^{n}gēh'-ker*, m. 6133

Lev.25:47. *to the stock of* the stranger's family:

עָקָר *^{n}gāh-kāhr'*, adj. 6135

Gen11:30. But Sarai was *barren;*
25:21. for his wife, because she (was) *barren:*
29:31. but Rachel (was) *barren.*
Ex. 23:26. nothing cast their young, *nor* be *barren,*
Deu 7:14. there shall not be *male or female barren* among you,
Jud.13: 2. his wife (was) *barren,*
3. Behold now, thou (art) *barren,*
1Sa. 2: 5. so that *the barren* hath born seven;
Job 24:21. He evil entreateth *the barren*
Ps.113: 9. He maketh *the barren woman* to
Isa. 54: 1. Sing, *O barren,* thou (that) didst not

עִקַּר *^{n}gik-kar'*, Ch. m. 6136

Dan 4:15(12). Nevertheless leave *the stump of*
23(20). yet leave *the stump of* the roots
26(23). they commanded to leave *the stump of*

6137 **עַקְרָב** [n]*găk-rāhv'*, m.

Deu 8:15. fiery serpents, *and scorpions*,
1K. 12:11, 14. I will chastise you *with scorpions*.
2Ch 10:11, 14. I (will chastise you) *with scorpions*.
Eze. 2: 6. thou dost dwell among *scorpions*:

6140 **עָקַשׁ** [[n]*gāh-kash'*].

* KAL.—*Future*. *

Job 9:20. I (am) perfect, *it shall also prove me perverse*.

* NIPHAL.—*Participle*. *

Pro. 28:18. *but he that is perverse* (in his) ways

* PIEL.—*Preterite*. *

Isa. 59: 8. *they have made* them *crooked* paths:

PIEL.—*Future*.

Mic. 3: 9. abhor judgment, and *pervert* all equity.

PIEL.—*Participle*.

Pro. 10: 9. *but he that perverteth* his ways

6141 **עִקֵּשׁ** [n]*gik-kēhsh'*, adj.

Deu 32: 5. a *perverse* and crooked generation.
2Sa. 22:27. with *the froward* thou wilt shew thyself
Ps. 18:26(27). with *the froward* thou wilt shew thyself
101: 4. A *froward* heart shall depart from me:
Pro. 2:15. Whose ways (are) *crooked*,
8: 8. nothing froward *or perverse*
11:20. *They that are of a froward* heart
17:20. He that hath a *froward* heart (marg. *The froward of* heart)
19: 1. *than* (he that is) *perverse in* his lips,
22: 5. Thorns (and) snares (are) in the way of *the froward*:
28: 6. *than* (he that is) *perverse* (in his) ways,

6143 **עִקְּשׁוּת** [n]*gik-k'shooth'*, f.

Pro. 4:24. Put away from thee a *froward* mouth, (marg. *frowardness of* mouth)
6:12. a wicked man, walketh with a *froward* mouth. (lit. *frowardness of* mouth)

5892, 6145 **עָר** [[n]*gāhr*], m.

[See also עִיר]

1Sa. 28:16. and is become *thine enemy*?
Ps. 9: 6(7). *and* thou hast destroyed *cities*;
139:20. *thine enemies* take (thy name) in vain.
Isa. 14:21. nor fill the face of the world *with cities*.
Mic. 5:11(10). I will cut off *the cities of* thy land,
14(13). destroy *thy cities*. (marg. or, *enemies*)

6146 **עָר** [[n]*gāhr*], Ch. m.

Dan 4:19(16). and the interpretation thereof *to thine enemies*.

6148-49 **עָרַב** [n]*gāh-rav'*.

* KAL.—*Preterite*. *

Gen 44:32. thy servant *became surety for* the lad
Pro. 3:24. *and* thy sleep *shall be sweet*.
6: 1. *if thou be surety for* thy friend,
11:15. He *that is surety for* a stranger
20:16. his garment *that is surety* (for) a stranger:
27:13. Take his garment *that is surety*
Jer. 6:20. nor your sacrifices *sweet* unto me.
30:21. who (is) this that *engaged* his heart
31:26. my sleep *was sweet* unto me.
Eze. 16:37. with whom *thou hast taken pleasure*,
Mal. 3: 4. *Then shall* the offering of Judah and Jerusalem *be pleasant*

KAL.—*Infinitive*.

Eze. 27: 9. their mariners were in thee *to occupy*

KAL.—*Imperative*.

Job 17: 3. *put me in a surety* with thee;
Ps. 119:122. *Be surety* for thy servant for good:
Isa. 38:14. I am oppressed; *undertake for me*. (marg. or, *ease me*)

KAL.—*Future*.

Gen 43: 9. I *will be surety for him*; of my hand
Ps. 104:34. My meditation of him *shall be sweet*:
Pro. 13:19. desire accomplished *is sweet*
Hos 9: 4. neither *shall they be pleasing* unto him:

KAL.—*Participle*. Poel.

Neh 5: 3. We *have mortgaged* our lands,
Pro. 17:18. *becometh* surety in the presence
22:26. *of them that are sureties* for debts.
Eze. 27:27. *and the occupiers* of thy merchandise,

* HITHPAEL.—*Preterite*. *

Ezr. 9: 2. *that* the holy seed *have mingled themselves*

HITHPAEL.—*Imperative*.

2K. 18:23. *give pledges* (marg. or, *hostages*) to my lord the king of
Isa. 36: 8. *give pledges* (marg. or, *hostages*), I pray thee, to my master

HITHPAEL.—*Future*.

Ps. 106:35. *But were mingled* among the heathen,
Pro. 14:10. a stranger *doth* not *intermeddle* with
20:19. *meddle* not *with* him that flattereth
24:21. *meddle* not *with* them that are given to

עָרַב [[n]*gāh-rav'*]. 6150

* KAL.—*Preterite*. *

Isa. 24:11. all joy *is darkened*, the mirth

KAL.—*Infinitive*.

Jud. 19: 9. the day draweth *toward evening*,

* HIPHIL.—*Infinitive*. *

1Sa. 17:16. Philistine drew near morning *and evening*,

עֲרַב [[n]*gărav*], Ch. 6151

* PAEL.—*Participle*. *

Dan 2:41. sawest the iron *mixed* with miry clay.
43. sawest iron *mixed* with miry clay,

* ITHPAEL.—*Participle*. *

Dan 2:43. they shall *mingle themselves*
— even as iron *is* not *mixed* with clay.

עָרֵב [n]*gāh-rēhv'*, adj. 6156

Pro. 20:17. Bread of deceit (is) *sweet*
Cant. 2:14. for *sweet* (is) thy voice,

עָרֹב [n]*gāh-rōhv'*, m. 6157

Ex. 8:21(17). I will send *swarms* (of flies) upon thee, (marg. or, *a mixture* (of noisome beasts, &c.))
—(—). the Egyptians shall be full of *swarms* (of flies),
22(18). no *swarms* (of flies) shall be there;
24(20). there came *a* grievous *swarm* (of flies)
—(—). land was corrupted by reason of *the swarm* (of flies).
29(25). that *the swarms* (of flies) may depart
31(27). he removed *the swarms* (of flies)
Ps. 78:45. He sent *divers sorts of flies*
105:31. there came *divers sorts of flies*,

עֵרֶב [n]*geh'-rev*, m. 6154

Ex. 12:38. a *mixed* multitude (marg. *a* great *mixture*) went up
Lev. 13:48. in the warp, or *woof*;
49, 51, 53, 57. in the warp, or *in the woof*,
52. whether warp or *woof*,
56. out of the warp, or out of *the woof*:
58. either warp, or *woof*,
59. either in the warp, or *woof*,
Neh 13: 3. from Israel all *the mixed multitude*.

עֶרֶב [n]*geh'-rev*, m. 6153

Gen 1: 5, 8, 13, 19, 23, 31. *the evening* and the morning were the

Gen 8:11. the dove came in to him in *the evening;* (lit. at the time of *the evening*)
19: 1. there came two angels to Sodom *at even;*
24:11. at the time of *the evening,*
63. Isaac went out...at the *even*tide:
29:23. it came to pass *in the evening,*
30:16. Jacob came out of the field *in the evening,*
49:27. *and at night* he shall divide the spoil.
Ex. 12: 6. shall kill it in *the evening.* (marg. between *the two evenings*)
18. the fourteenth day of the month *at even,*
— one and twentieth day of the month *at even.*
16: 6. *At even,* then ye shall know
8. *in the evening* flesh to eat,
12. At *even* (lit. between *the two evenings*) ye shall eat flesh,
13. *at even* the quails came up,
18:13. from the morning unto *the evening.*
14. from morning unto *even?*
27:21. *from evening* to morning
29:39, 41. thou shalt offer at *even:* (lit. between *the two evenings*)
30: 8. when Aaron lighteth the lamps at *even,* (marg. between *the two evens*)
Lev. 6:20(13). half thereof *at night.*
11:24, 27, 31, 39. shall be unclean until *the even.*
25, 28, 32, 40, 40. be unclean until *the even.*
14:46. shall be unclean until *the even.*
15: 5, 6, 7, 8, 10, 11, 16, 17, 21, 22, 27. and be unclean until *the even.*
10, 19, 23. shall be unclean until *the even:*
18. and be unclean until *the even.*
17:15. and be unclean until *the even:*
22: 6. shall be unclean until *even,*
23: 5. the fourteenth (day) of the first month at *even* (lit. between *the two evenings*)
32. the ninth (day) of the month *at even, from even* unto *even,*
24: 3. *from the evening* unto the morning
Nu. 9: 3. the fourteenth day of this month, at *even,* (marg. between *the two evenings*)
5. the fourteenth day of the first month at *even* (lit. between *the two evenings*)
11. The fourteenth day of the second month at *even* (lit. between *the two evenings*)
15. *and at even* there was upon the tabernacle
21. cloud abode *from even* unto the morning,
19: 7. the priest shall be unclean until *the even.*
8, 10. be unclean until *the even.*
19. shall be clean *at even.*
21. shall be unclean until *even.*
22. (it) shall be unclean until *even.*
28: 4, 8. the other lamb shalt thou offer at *even;* (marg. between *the two evenings*)
Deu16: 4. the first day *at even,*
6. sacrifice the passover *at even,*
23:11(12). when *evening* cometh on,
28:67. Would God it were *even!* *and at even* thou shalt say,
Jos. 5:10. the fourteenth day of the month *at even*
7: 6. of the Lord until *the eventide,*
8:29. of Ai he hanged on a tree until *even*tide:
10:26. they were hanging...until *the evening.*
Jud.19:16. there came an old man...*at even,*
20:23. wept before the Lord until *even,*
26. fasted that day until *even,*
21: 2. abode there till *even* before God,
Ru. 2:17. she gleaned in the field until *even,*
1Sa.14:24. eateth (any) food until *evening,*
20: 5. the third (day) *at even.*
30:17. unto *the evening* of the next day:
2Sa. 1:12. and fasted until *even,*
11: 2. it came to pass in *an evening*tide,
13. *at even* he went out
1K. 10:15. the kings of *Arabia,* [perhaps lit. of *the mingled people*]
17: 6. and bread and flesh *in the evening;*
22:35. the king was stayed up...and died *at even:*
2K. 16:15. the *evening* meat offering,
1Ch 16:40. continually morning *and evening,*
23:30. to stand every morning...and likewise *at even;*
2Ch 2: 4(3). burnt offerings morning *and evening,*
13:11. every morning *and every evening* (lit. *and in evening in evening*)
— to burn *every evening:* (lit. *in evening in evening*)
2Ch18:34. until *the even:*
31: 3. the morning *and evening* burnt offerings,
Ezr. 3: 3. burnt offerings morning *and evening.*
9: 4. until the *evening* sacrifice.
5. at the *evening* sacrifice
Est. 2:14. *In the evening* she went,
Job 4:20. are destroyed from morning *to evening:*
7: 4. and *the night* (marg. *evening*) be gone?
Ps. 30: 5(6). weeping may endure *for a night,* (marg. *in the evening*)
55:17(18). *Evening,* and morning, and at noon,
59: 6(7). They return *at evening:*
14(15). *at evening* let them return;
65: 8(9). the morning *and evening*
90: 6. *in the evening* it is cut down,
104:23. Man goeth forth unto his work...until *the evening.*
141: 2. of my hands (as) the *evening* sacrifice.
Pro. 7: 9. *in the evening* (marg. *in the evening* of the day), in the black and dark night:
Ecc.11: 6. *and in the evening* withhold not thine
Isa. 17:14. at *evening*tide trouble;
Jer. 6: 4. the shadows of *the evening*
25:20. all *the mingled people,*
24. the kings of *the mingled people*
50:37. upon all *the mingled people*
Eze.12: 4. thou shalt go forth *at even*
7. *and in the even* I digged through the wall
24:18. *at even* my wife died;
30: 5. all *the mingled people,*
33:22. the hand of the Lord was upon me *in the evening,*
46: 2. gate shall not be shut until *the evening.*
Dan 8:14. two thousand and three hundred days; (marg. *evening* morning)
26. the vision of *the evening* and the morning
9:21. about the time of the *evening* oblation.
Hab 1: 8. more fierce than the *evening* wolves:
Zep. 2: 7. they lie down *in the evening:*
3: 3. her judges (are) *evening* wolves;
Zec.14: 7. at *evening* time it shall be light.

עֶרֶב [*geh'-rev*], m. 6155

Lev.23:40. *and willows of* the brook;
Job 40:22. *the willows of* the brook compass
Ps 137: 2. We hanged our harps upon *the willows*
Isa. 15: 7. away to the brook of *the willows.*
44: 4. *as willows* by the water courses.

עֹרֵב *gōh-rēhv'*, m. 6158

Gen. 8: 7. he sent forth *a raven,*
Lev.11:15. Every *raven* after his kind;
Deu14:14. every *raven* after his kind,
1K. 17: 4. I have commanded *the ravens* to feed thee
6. *And the ravens* brought him bread
Job 38:41. Who provideth *for the raven* his food?
Ps.147: 9. *the* young *ravens* which cry.
Pro.30:17. *the ravens of* the valley
Cant.5:11. his locks (are) bushy, (and) black *as a raven.*
Isa. 34:11. *and the raven* shall dwell in it:

עֲרָבָה *gărāh-vāh'*, f. 6160

Nu. 22: 1. pitched *in the plains of* Moab
26: 3. with them *in the plains of* Moab
63. of Israel *in the plains of* Moab
31:12. unto the camp at *the plains of* Moab,
33:48. and pitched *in the plains of* Moab
49. Abel-shittim *in the plains of* Moab.
50. unto Moses *in the plains of* Moab
35: 1. spake unto Moses *in the plains of* Moab
36:13. of Israel *in the plains of* Moab
Deu 1: 1. *in the plain* over against the Red (sea),
7. *in the plain,* in the hills, and in the vale,
2: 8. through the way of *the plain*
3:17. *The plain also,* and Jordan,
— even unto the sea of *the plain,*
4:49. all *the plain* on this side Jordan eastward, even unto the sea of *the plain,*
11:30. *in the champaign* over against Gilgal,

Deu34: 1. Moses went up *from the plains of* Moab
8. wept for Moses *in the plains of* Moab
Jos. 3:16. toward the sea of *the plain,*
4:13. unto battle, to *the plains of* Jericho.
5:10. at even *in the plains of* Jericho.
8:14. at a time appointed, before *the plain;*
11: 2. *and of the plains* south of Chinneroth,
16. the valley, and *the plain,*
12: 1. all *the plain* on the east:
3. *And* from *the plain* to the sea of Chinneroth on the east, and unto the sea of *the plain,*
8. *and in the plains,* and in the springs,
13:32. for inheritance *in the plains of* Moab,
15: 6. by the north of Beth-*arabah;*
18:18. over against *Arabah* (marg. or, *the plain*) northward, and went down unto *Arabah:*
1 Sa. 23:24. *in the plain* on the south of Jeshimon.
2Sa. 2:29. walked all that night *through the plain,*
4: 7. gat them away through *the plain*
15:28. I will tarry *in the plain of* the wilderness,
17:16. Lodge not this night *in the plains of*
2K. 14:25. unto the sea of *the plain,*
25: 4. went the way toward *the plain.*
5. *in the plains of* Jericho:
Job 24: 5. *the wilderness* (yieldeth) food for them
39: 6. Whose house I have made *the wilderness,*
Ps. 68: 4(5). him that rideth *upon the heavens*
Isa. 33: 9. Sharon is *like a wilderness;*
35: 1. *the desert* shall rejoice,
6. and streams *in the desert.*
40: 3. make straight *in the desert* a highway
41:19. I will set *in the desert* the fir tree,
51: 3. *and her desert* like the garden of the
Jer. 2: 6. a land of *deserts* and of pits,
5: 6. a wolf of *the evenings* (marg. or, *deserts*)
17: 6. like the heath *in the desert,*
39: 4. he went out the way of *the plain.*
5. *in the plains of* Jericho:
50:12. a dry land, *and a desert.*
51:43. a dry land, *and a wilderness,*
52: 7. they went by the way of *the plain.*
8. *in the plains of* Jericho;
Eze. 47: 8. go down into *the desert,* (marg. or, *plain*)
Am. 6:14. unto the river of *the wilderness.*
Zec 14:10. All the land shall be turned *as a plain*

6161 ## עֲרֻבָּה *ğăroob-bāh'*, f.

1 Sa. 17:18. look how thy brethren fare, and take *their pledge.*
Pro 17:18. becometh *surety* in the presence

6162 ## עֵרָבוֹן *gēh-rāh-vōhn'*, m.

Gen38:17. Wilt thou give (me) *a pledge,*
18. What *pledge* shall I give thee?
20. to receive (his) *pledge*

6165 ## עָרַג [*gāh-rag'*].

* KAL.—*Future.* *

Ps. 42: 1(2). As the hart *panteth* (marg. *brayeth*) after the water brooks, so *panteth* my soul after thee, O God.
Joel 1:20. The beasts of the field *cry*

6167 ## עֲרָד [*gărāhd*], Ch. m.

Dan 5:21. his dwelling (was) with *the wild asses:*

6168 ## עָרָה [*gāh-rāh'*].

* NIPHAL.—*Future.* *

Isa. 32:15. Until the spirit *be poured* upon us

* PIEL.—*Preterite.* *

Isa. 22: 6. Kir *uncovered* (marg. *made naked*) the
Zep. 2:14. for *he shall uncover* (marg. or, when *he hath uncovered*) the cedar work.

PIEL.—*Infinitive.*

Hab. 3:13. *by discovering* (marg. *making naked*) the foundation unto the neck.

PIEL.—*Imperative.*

Ps. 137: 7. *Rase* (marg. *Make bare*) (it), *rase* (it), (even) to the foundation

PIEL.—*Future.*

Gen 24:20. she hasted, *and emptied* her pitcher
2Ch 24:11. officer came *and emptied* the chest,
Ps. 141: 8. *leave* not my soul *destitute.* (marg. *bare*)
Isa. 3:17. the Lord *will discover* (marg. *make naked*) their secret parts.

* HIPHIL.—*Preterite.* *

Lev. 20:18. *he hath discovered* (marg. *made naked*) her
19. *he uncovereth* his near kin:
Isa. 53:12. *he hath poured out* his soul unto death:

* HITHPAEL.—*Future.* *

Lam. 4:21. *and shalt make thyself naked.*

HITHPAEL.—*Participle.*

Ps. 37:35. *and spreading himself* like a green bay tree.

עֲרוּגָה [*găroo-gāh'*], f. 6170

Cant. 5:13. His cheeks (are) *as a bed of* spices,
6: 2. *to the beds of* spices,
Eze. 17: 7. *by the furrows of* her plantation.
10. it shall wither in *the furrows*

עָרוֹד *gāh-rōhd'*, m. 6171

Job 39: 5. who hath loosed the bands of *the wild ass?*

עֶרְוָה *ger-vāh'*, f. 6172

Gen 9:22. saw *the nakedness of* his father,
23. covered *the nakedness of* their father;
— *and* they saw not their father's *nakedness.*
42: 9. to see *the nakedness of* the land ye are
12. to see *the nakedness of* the land
Ex. 20:26. that *thy nakedness* be not discovered
28:42. linen breeches to cover their *nakedness;* (marg. flesh of their *nakedness*)
Lev. 18: 6. to uncover (their) *nakedness:*
7. *The nakedness of* thy father, *or the nakedness of* thy mother,
—, 11, 15. thou shalt not uncover *her nakedness.*
8. *The nakedness of* thy father's wife
— thy father's *nakedness.*
9. *The nakedness of* thy sister,
— *their nakedness* thou shalt not uncover.
10. *The nakedness of* thy son's daughter,
— *their nakedness* thou shalt not uncover: for their's (is) *thine own nakedness.*
11. *The nakedness of* thy father's wife's
12. *the nakedness of* thy father's sister:
13. *the nakedness of* thy mother's sister:
14. *the nakedness of* thy father's brother,
15. *the nakedness of* thy daughter in law:
16. *the nakedness of* thy brother's wife: it (is) thy brother's *nakedness.*
17. *the nakedness of* a woman
—, 18, 19. to uncover *her nakedness;*
20:11. hath uncovered his father's *nakedness:*
17. and see *her nakedness,* and she see *his nakedness;*
— he hath uncovered his sister's *nakedness;*
18. shall uncover *her nakedness;*
19. *And* thou shalt not uncover *the nakedness of* thy mother's sister,
20. uncovered his uncle's *nakedness:*
21. uncovered his brother's *nakedness;*
Deu 23:14(15). that he see no *unclean* thing (marg. *nakedness of* any thing) in thee,
24: 1. he hath found some *uncleanness* (marg. matter of *nakedness*) in her:
1 Sa. 20:30. the confusion of thy mother's *nakedness?*
Isa. 20: 4. to *the shame* (marg. *nakedness*) *of* Egypt.
47: 3. *Thy nakedness* shall be uncovered,
Lam. 1: 8. they have seen *her nakedness:*
Eze. 16: 8. and covered *thy nakedness:*
36. *thy nakedness* discovered
37. and will discover *thy nakedness* unto them, that they may see all *thy nakedness.*

Eze.22:10. they discovered their father's *nakedness:*
23:10. These discovered *her nakedness:*
18. and discovered *her nakedness:*
29. *the nakedness of* thy whoredoms
Hos. 2: 9(11). my flax (given) to cover *her nakedness.*

6173 עַרְוָה [*ğar-vāh'*], Ch. f.

Ezr. 4:14. *and* it was not meet for us to see the king's *dishonour,*

6174 עָרֹום *ğāh-rōhm'*, adj.

Gen 2:25. And they were both *naked,*
1Sa.19:24. lay down *naked* all that day
Job 1:21. *Naked* came I out of my mother's womb, *and naked* shall I return thither:
22: 6. and stripped *the naked* of their clothing.
24: 7. They cause *the naked* to lodge without
10. They cause (him) to go *naked*
26: 6. Hell (is) *naked* before him,
Ecc. 5:15(14). *naked* shall he return
Isa. 20: 2. walking *naked* and barefoot.
3. my servant Isaiah hath walked *naked*
4. young and old, *naked* and barefoot,
58: 7. when thou seest *the naked,*
Hos. 2: 3(5). Lest I strip her *naked,*
Am. 2:16. the mighty shall flee away *naked*
Mic. 1: 8. I will go stripped *and naked:*

6175 עָרוּם *ğāh-room'*, adj.

Gen 3: 1. the serpent was more *subtil* than any
Job 5:12. the devices of *the crafty,*
15: 5. thou choosest the tongue of *the crafty.*
Pro.12:16. *a prudent* (man) covereth shame.
23. A *prudent* man concealeth knowledge:
13:16. Every *prudent* (man) dealeth with
14: 8. The wisdom of *the prudent*
15. *but the prudent* (man) looketh well to his going.
18. *but the prudent* are crowned with
22: 3 & 27:12. *A prudent* (man) foreseeth the

6176 עֲרוֹעֵר *ğărōh-ğēhr'*, m.

Jer. 48: 6. be *like the heath* (marg. or, *a naked tree*) in the wilderness.

6178 עָרוּץ *ğărootz*, m.

Job 30: 6. *in the cliffs of* the valleys,

6169 עָרוֹת *ğāh-rōhth'*, f. pl.

Isa. 19: 7. *The paper reeds* by the brooks,

6181 עֶרְיָה *ğer-yāh'*, f.

Eze.16: 7. whereas thou (wast) naked *and bare.*
22. when thou wast naked *and bare,*
39. and leave thee naked and *bare.*
23:29. shall leave thee naked *and bare:*
Mic. 1:11. having thy shame *naked:*
Hab. 3: 9. Thy bow was made *quite* naked, (lit. was made naked (with) *nakedness*)

6182 עֲרִיסָה [*ğăree-sāh'*], f.

Nu. 15:20. a cake of the first of *your dough*
21. Of the first of *your dough*
Neh 10:37(38). the firstfruits of *our dough,*
Eze.44:30. the first of *your dough,*

6183 עֲרִיפִים [*ğăree-pheem'*], m. pl.

Isa. 5:30. the light is darkened *in the heavens thereof.* (marg. *in the destructions thereof*)

6184 עָרִיץ *ğāh-reetz'*, adj.

Job 6:23. Redeem me from the hand of *the mighty?*
15:20. number of years is hidden *to the oppressor.*
27:13. the heritage of *oppressors,*
Ps. 37:35. I have seen the wicked *in great power,*
54: 3(5). *and oppressors* seek after my soul:
86:14. the assemblies of *violent* (men)
Pro.11:16. *and strong* (men) retain riches.
Isa. 13:11. the haughtiness of *the terrible.*
25: 3. the city of the *terrible* nations
4. the blast of *the terrible ones*
5. the branch of *the terrible ones*
29: 5. the multitude of *the terrible ones*
20. *the terrible one* is brought to nought,
49:25. the prey of *the terrible* shall be delivered:
Jer. 15:21. out of the hand of *the terrible.*
20:11. the Lord (is) with me as *a* mighty *terrible one:*
Eze.28: 7. upon thee, *the terrible of* the nations:
30:11. with him, *the terrible of* the nations,
31:12. strangers, *the terrible of* the nations,
32:12. *the terrible of* the nations, all of them:

עֲרִירִי *ğăree-ree'*, adj. 6185

Gen15: 2. seeing I go *childless,*
Lev.20:20. they shall die *childless.*
21. they shall be *childless.*
Jer. 22:30. Write ye this man *childless,*

עָרַךְ *ğāh-rach'*. 6186

* KAL.—*Preterite.* *

Ex. 40: 4. *and set in order* the things
Lev. 1: 7. *lay* the wood *in order*
8. *And* the priests,...*shall lay* the parts,...*in order*
12. *and* the priest *shall lay* them *in order*
6:12(5). *and lay* the burnt offering *in order*
Nu. 23: 4. *I have prepared* seven altars,
Jud.20:22. where *they put themselves in array*
2Ch 13: 3. Jeroboam also *set* the battle *in array*
Job 13:18. *I have ordered* (my) cause;
32:14. *he hath* not *directed* (marg. or, *ordered*) (his)
Ps.132:17. *I have ordained* a lamp for mine
Pro. 9: 2. *she hath* also *furnished* her table.
Jer. 50: 9. *and they shall set themselves in array*

KAL.—*Infinitive.*

Jud.20:22. *set* their battle again *in array* (lit. added to *set...in array*)
1Sa.17: 8. Why are ye come out *to set* (your) battle *in array?*
1Ch 12:36. *expert in* war (lit. *to set* the battle *in array*), forty thousand.
Ps. 40: 5(6). *they cannot be reckoned up in order* (marg. or, none *can order*)
78:19. Can God *furnish* (marg. *order*) a table in
Isa. 21: 5. *Prepare* the table, watch in

KAL.—*Imperative.*

Job 33: 5. *set* (thy words) *in order* before me,
Jer. 46: 3. *Order ye* the buckler and shield,
50:14. *Put yourselves in array* against Babylon

KAL.—*Future.*

Gen14: 8. *and they joined* battle with them
22: 9. *and laid* the wood *in order,*
Ex. 27:21. Aaron and his sons *shall order* it
40:23. *And he set* the bread *in order*
Lev.24: 3. *shall* Aaron *order* it from the evening
4. *He shall order* the lamps
8. *he shall set it in order* before the Lord
Jud.20:20. *and* the men of Israel *put themselves in array*
30. *and put themselves in array* against
33. *and put themselves in array* at
1Sa. 4: 2. *And* the Philistines *put themselves in array*
17: 2. *and set* the battle *in array* (marg. *ranged* the battle)
21. *For* Israel and the Philistines *had put the battle in array,*
2Sa.10: 8. *and put* the battle *in array* at the entering
9. *and put* (them) *in array* against the
10. *that he might put* (them) *in array*
17. *And* the Syrians *set themselves in array*
1K. 18:33. *And he put* the wood *in order,*
1Ch 19: 9. *and put* the battle *in array*
10. *and put* (them) *in array* against the

1Ch 19:11. *and they set* (themselves) *in array* against
17. *and set* (the battle) *in array* against them. So *when* David *had put* the battle *in array*
2Ch 14:10(9). *and they set* the battle *in array* in the
Job 6: 4. the terrors of God *do set themselves in array against me.*
23: 4. *I would order* (my) cause before him,
28:17. The gold and the crystal *cannot equal it:*
19. The topaz of Ethiopia *shall* not *equal it,*
36:19. *Will he esteem* thy riches?
37:19. *we cannot order* (our speech)
Ps. 5: 3(4). in the morning *will I direct*(my prayer)
23: 5. *Thou preparest* a table before me
50:21. *and set* (them) *in order* before thine eyes.
89: 6(7). who in the heaven *can be compared*
Isa. 40:18. what likeness *will ye compare* unto him?
44: 7. *and set it in order* for me,

KAL.—*Participle.* Poel.

1Ch 12: 8. *that could handle* shield and buckler,
33. *expert in* war(marg. or, *rangers of* battle, or, *ranged in* battle), with all instruments
35. of the Danites *expert in* war
Isa. 65:11. *that prepare* a table for that troop,

KAL.—*Participle.* Paül.

Jos. 2: 6. stalks of flax, *which* she had *laid in order*
2Sa.23: 5. an everlasting covenant, *ordered* in all
Isa. 30:33. Tophet (is) *ordained* of old;
Jer. 6:23. they ride upon horses, *set in array*
50:42. (every one) *put in array,* like a man
Eze.23:41. a table *prepared* before it,
Joel 2: 5. a strong people *set in* battle *array.*

* HIPHIL.—*Preterite.* *

Lev.27: 8. *and* the priest *shall value* him;
12. *And* the priest *shall value* it,
14. *then* the priest *shall estimate it,*
2K. 23:35. *he taxed* the land to give the money

HIPHIL.—*Future.*

Lev.27: 8. *shall* the priest *value him.*
14. as the priest *shall estimate* it,

6187 **עֵרֶךְ** *[n]geh'-rech,* m.

Ex. 40: 4. *the things that are to be set in order upon it;* (marg. *the order thereof*)
23. he set the bread in order (lit. he set in order *the order of* the bread)
Lev. 5:15. *with thy estimation* by shekels of silver,
18 & 6:6(5:25). *with thy estimation,* for a
27: 2. for the Lord *by thy estimation.*
3, 5, 6. *thy estimation* shall be of the male
— *thy estimation* shall be fifty shekels
4. *thy estimation* shall be thirty shekels.
6. for the female *thy estimation* (shall be)
7. *thy estimation* shall be fifteen shekels,
8. be poorer *than thy estimation,*
12. good or bad: *as thou valuest it,*
13. thereof unto *thy estimation.*
15, 19. the money of *thy estimation* unto it,
16. *thy estimation* shall be according
17. of jubile, *according to thy estimation*
18. shall be abated *from thy estimation.*
23. the worth of *thy estimation,*
— he shall give *thine estimation*
25. all *thy estimations* shall be according
27. redeem (it) *according to thine estimation,*
— sold *according to thy estimation.*
Nu. 18:16. *according to thine estimation,*
Jud.17:10. *and a suit of* apparel, (marg. *an order of* garments)
2K. 12: 4(5). the money that every man is *set at,* (marg. of the souls of *his estimation*)
23:35. of every one *according to his taxation,*
Job 28:13. Man knoweth not *the price thereof;*
41:12(4). nor *his* comely *proportion.*
Ps. 55:13(14). (it was) thou, a man *mine equal,* (marg. *according to my rank*)

6188 **עָרֵל** [*[n]gāh-rēhl'*].

* KAL.—*Preterite.* *

Lev.19:23. *then ye shall count* the fruit thereof *as uncircumcised:*

* NIPHAL.—*Imperative.* *

Hab 2:16. *and let thy foreskin be uncovered:*

עָרֵל *[n]gāh-rēhl',* adj. 6189

Gen17:14. *And* the *uncircumcised* man child
Ex. 6:12. who (am) of *uncircumcised* lips?
30. I (am) of *uncircumcised* lips,
12:48. no *uncircumcised person* shall eat
Lev.19:23. three years shall it be as *uncircumcised*
26:41. their *uncircumcised* hearts
Jos. 5: 7. them Joshua circumcised: for they were *uncircumcised,*
Jud 14: 3. a wife of the *uncircumcised* Philistines?
15:18. into the hand of *the uncircumcised?*
1Sa. 14: 6. the garrison of these *uncircumcised:*
17:26. who (is) this *uncircumcised* Philistine,
36. this *uncircumcised* Philistine shall be
31: 4. lest these *uncircumcised* come and thrust
2Sa. 1:20. lest the daughters of *the uncircumcised*
1Ch 10: 4. lest these *uncircumcised* come and abuse
Isa. 52: 1. *the uncircumcised* and the unclean.
Jer. 6:10. their ear (is) *uncircumcised,*
9:26(25). (these) nations (are) *uncircumcised,* and all the house of Israel (are) *uncircumcised in*
Eze.28:10. the deaths of *the uncircumcised*
31:18. in the midst of *the uncircumcised*
32:19. be thou laid with *the uncircumcised.*
21. they lie *uncircumcised,* slain
24. are gone down *uncircumcised*
25, 26. all of them *uncircumcised,*
27. (that are) fallen *of the uncircumcised,*
28. broken in the midst of *the uncircumcised,*
29. they shall lie with *the uncircumcised,*
30. they lie *uncircumcised* with (them)
32. laid in the midst of *the uncircumcised*
44: 7. strangers, *uncircumcised in* heart, *and uncircumcised in* flesh,
9. No stranger, *uncircumcised in* heart, *nor uncircumcised in* flesh,

---

עָרְלָה *[n]gor-lāh',* f. 6190

Gen17:11. circumcise the flesh of *your foreskin;*
14. whose flesh of *his foreskin* is not
23. circumcised the flesh of *their foreskin*
24. in the flesh of *his foreskin.*
25. in the flesh of *his foreskin.*
34:14. one that is *uncircumcised;* (lit. one that hath *a foreskin*)
Ex. 4:25. cut off *the foreskin of* her son,
Lev.12: 3. the flesh of *his foreskin* shall be
19:23. ye shall count the fruit thereof as uncircumcised: (lit. ye shall count as uncircumcised *the uncircumcision thereof,* the fruit thereof)
Deu 10:16. Circumcise therefore *the foreskin of* your
Jos. 5: 3. at the hill of *the foreskins.*
1Sa.18:25. an hundred *foreskins of* the Philistines,
27. David brought *their foreskins,*
2Sa. 3:14. an hundred *foreskins of* the Philistines.
Jer. 4: 4. take away *the foreskins of* your heart,
9:25(24). circumcised *with the uncircumcised;*

עָרַם [*[n]gāh-ram'*]. 6191

* KAL.—*Infinitive.* *

1Sa.23:22. he dealeth *very* subtilly. (lit. *dealing subtilly* he dealeth subtilly)

* HIPHIL.—*Future.* *

1Sa.23:22. *he dealeth* very *subtilly.*
Ps. 83: 3(4). *They have taken crafty* counsel
Pro.15: 5. he that regardeth reproof *is prudent.*
19:25. Smite a scorner, and the simple *will beware:* (marg. *be cunning*)

עָרַם [*[n]gāh-ram'*]. 6192

* NIPHAL.—*Preterite.* *

Ex. 15: 8. the waters *were gathered together,*

6193 **עֹרֶם** [^{n}gōh'-rem], m.

Job 5:13. taketh the wise *in their own craftiness:*

6195 **עָרְמָה** ^{n}gor-māh', f.

Ex. 21:14. to slay him *with guile;*
Jos. 9: 4. They did work *wilily,*
Pro. 1: 4. To give *subtilty* to the simple,
8: 5. O ye simple, understand *wisdom:*
12. I wisdom dwell with *prudence,* (marg. or, *subtilty*)

6194 **עֲרֵמָה** ^{n}gărēh-māh', f.

Ru. 3: 7. lie down at the end of *the heap of corn:*
2Ch 31: 6. and laid (them) *by heaps.* (marg. *heaps, heaps*)
7. began to lay the foundation of *the heaps,*
8. the princes came and saw *the heaps,*
9. concerning *the heaps.*
Neh. 4: 2(3:34). will they revive the stones *out of the heaps of*
13:15. and bringing in *sheaves,*
Cant. 7: 2(3). thy belly (is like) *an heap of* wheat
Jer. 50:26. cast her up as *heaps,*
Hag. 2:16. *an heap of* twenty (measures),

6196 **עַרְמוֹן** ^{n}gar-mōhn', m.

Gen30:37. of the hazel and *chesnut tree;*
Eze.31: 8. and *the chesnut trees* were not like his

6199 **עַרְעָר** ^{n}gar-^{n}gāhr', adj.

Ps. 102:17(18). will regard the prayer of *the destitute,*
Jer. 17: 6. he shall be *like the heath*

6201 **עָרַף** [^{n}gāh-raph'].

* KAL.—*Future.* *

Deu32: 2. My doctrine *shall drop* as the rain,
33:28. his heavens *shall drop down* dew.

6202 **עָרַף** [^{n}gāh-raph'].

* KAL.—*Preterite.* *

Ex. 13:13. *then thou shalt break his neck:*
34:20. *then shalt thou break his neck.*
Deu21: 4. and *shall strike off* the heifer's *neck*

KAL.—*Future.*

Hos10: 2. *he shall break down* (marg. *behead*) their altars,

KAL.—*Participle.* Poel.

Isa. 66: 3. he that sacrificeth a lamb, (as if) *he cut off a dog's neck;*

KAL.—*Participle.* Paül.

Deu21: 6. the heifer *that is beheaded*

6203 **עֹרֶף** ^{n}gōh'-reph, m.

Gen49: 8. thy hand (shall be) *in the neck of* thine
Ex. 23:27. all thine enemies turn (their) *backs* (marg. *neck*)
32: 9. it (is) a stiff*necked* (lit. stiff of *neck*) people:
33: 3. thou (art) a stiff*necked* (lit. *id.*) people:
5. Ye (are) a stiff*necked* (lit. *id.*) people:
34: 9. it (is) a stiff*necked* (lit. *id.*) people;
Lev. 5: 8. and wring off his head from *his neck,*
Deu 9: 6. thou (art) a stiff*necked* (lit. stiff of *neck*) people.
13. it (is) a stiff*necked* (lit. *id.*) people:
10:16. *and* be no more stiff*necked.* (lit. *and* harden not *your neck*)
31:27. thy rebellion, and *thy* stiff *neck:*
Jos. 7: 8. when Israel turneth (their) *backs* (marg. *necks*) before their enemies!
12. turned (their) *backs* before their enemies,
2Sa. 22:41. Thou hast also given me *the necks* of
2K. 17:14. would not hear, but hardened *their necks, like to the neck of* their fathers,
2Ch 29: 6. and turned (their) *backs.* (marg. given *the neck*)
30: 8. be ye not stiff*necked,* (marg. harden not *your necks*)
36:13. but he stiffened *his neck,*
Neh 9:16, 17. hardened *their necks,*
29. the shoulder, *and* hardened *their neck,*
Job 16:12. he hath also taken (me) *by my neck,*
Ps. 18:40(41). Thou hast also given me *the necks* of
Pro. 29: 1. being often reproved hardeneth (his) *neck,*
Isa. 48: 4. *thy neck* (is) an iron sinew,
Jer. 2:27. they have turned (their) *back* (marg. *the hinder part of the neck*) unto me,
7:26. but hardened *their neck:*
17:23. but made *their neck* stiff,
18:17. I will shew them *the back,*
19:15. they have hardened *their necks,*
32:33. they have turned unto me *the back,* (marg. *neck*)
48:39. how hath Moab turned *the back* (marg. *id.*)

עֲרָפֶל ^{n}gărāh-phel', m. 6205

Ex. 20:21. Moses drew near unto *the thick darkness*
Deu 4:11. darkness, clouds, *and thick darkness.*
5:22(19). the cloud, *and of the thick darkness,*
2Sa. 22:10. *and darkness* (was) under his feet.
1K. 8:12. that he would dwell *in the thick darkness.*
2Ch 6: 1. he would dwell *in the thick darkness.*
Job 22:13. can he judge through *the dark cloud?*
38: 9. *and thick darkness* a swaddlingband
Ps. 18: 9(10). *and darkness* (was) under his feet.
97: 2. Clouds *and darkness* (are) round about
Isa. 60: 2. *and gross darkness* the people:
Jer. 13:16. (and) make (it) *gross darkness.*
Eze. 34:12. in the cloudy *and dark* day.
Joel 2: 2. a day of clouds *and of thick darkness,*
Zep 1:15. a day of clouds *and thick darkness,*

עָרַץ [^{n}gāh-ratz']. 6206

* KAL.—*Infinitive.* *

Ps. 10:18. *that* the man of the earth *may* no more *oppress.* (marg. or, *terrify*)
Isa. 2:19, 21. when he ariseth *to shake terribly* the

KAL.—*Future.*

Deu 1:29. *Dread* not, neither be afraid
7:21. *Thou shalt* not *be affrighted*
20: 3. neither *be ye terrified* because
31: 6. fear not, nor *be afraid* of them:
Jos. 1: 9. *be* not *afraid,* neither be thou dismayed:
Job 13:25. *Wilt thou break* a leaf driven to and fro?
31:34. *Did I fear* a great multitude,
Isa. 47:12. if so be *thou mayest prevail.*

* NIPHAL.—*Participle.* *

Ps. 89: 7(8). God *is* greatly *to be feared*

* HIPHIL.—*Future.* *

Isa. 8:12. neither fear ye their fear, nor *be afraid.*
29:23. and *shall fear* the God of Israel.

HIPHIL.—*Participle.*

Isa. 8:13. and (let) him (be) *your dread.*

עָרַק [^{n}gāh-rak']. 6207

* KAL.—*Participle.* Poel. *

Job 30: 3. *fleeing* into the wilderness
17. *and my sinews* take no rest.

עָרַר [^{n}gāh-rar']. 6209

* KAL.—*Imperative.* *

Isa. 32:11. strip you, *and make you bare,*

* POEL.—*Preterite.* *

Isa. 23:13. *they raised up* the palaces thereof;

* PILPEL.—*Infinitive.* *

Jer. 51:58. The broad walls of Babylon shall be *utterly* broken, (lit. *being broken* shall be broken)

* HITHPALPEL.—*Future.* *

Jer. 51:58. The broad walls of Babylon *shall be* utterly *broken*, (marg. or, *made naked*)

6210 **עֶרֶשׂ** *geh'-res*, m.

Deu 3:11. Og king of Bashan...*his bedstead* (was) *a bedstead of* iron;
Job 7:13. *My bed* shall comfort me,
Ps. 6: 6(7). I water *my couch* with my tears.
41: 3(4). will strengthen him upon *the bed of*
132: 3. nor go up into my bed; (lit. *the bedstead of* my beds)
Pro. 7:16. I have decked *my bed* with coverings
Cant. 1:16. also *our bed* (is) green.
Am. 3:12. and in Damascus (in) *a couch*.
6: 4. stretch themselves upon *their couches*,

6212 **עֵשֶׂב** *geh'-sev*, m.

Gen 1:11. *the herb* yielding seed,
12. *herb* yielding seed after his kind,
29. I have given you every *herb*
30. every green *herb* for meat:
2: 5. every *herb of* the field
3:18. thou shalt eat *the herb of* the field;
9: 3. even as *the* green *herb* have I given
Ex. 9:22. upon every *herb of* the field,
25. the hail smote every *herb of* the field,
10:12. eat every *herb of* the land,
15. they did eat every *herb of* the land,
— *or in the herbs of* the field,
Deu 11:15. I will send *grass* in thy fields
29:23(22). nor any *grass* groweth therein,
32: 2. as the showers upon *the grass*:
2K. 19:26. they were (as) *the grass of* the field,
Job 5:25. thine offspring *as the grass of* the earth.
Ps. 72:16. (they) of the city shall flourish *like grass of*
92: 7(8). When the wicked spring as *the grass*,
102: 4(5). is smitten, and withered *like grass*;
11(12). I am withered *like grass*.
104:14. *and herb* for the service of man:
105:35. did eat up all *the herbs* in their land,
106:20. the similitude of an ox that eateth *grass*.
Pro. 19:12. as dew upon *the grass*.
27:25. *herbs of* the mountains are gathered.
Isa. 37:27. they were (as) *the grass of* the field,
42:15. and dry up all *their herbs*;
Jer. 12: 4. *and the herbs of* every field wither,
14: 6. their eyes did fail, because (there was) no *grass*.
Am. 7: 2. made an end of eating *the grass of*
Mic. 5: 7(6). as the showers upon *the grass*,
Zec. 10: 1. to every one *grass* in the field.

6211' **עֲשַׂב** *găsav*, Ch. m.

Dan 4:15(12). beasts *in the grass of* the earth:
25(22). *and* they shall make thee to eat *grass*
32(29). they shall make thee to eat *grass*
33(30). *and* did eat *grass* as oxen,
5:21. they fed him with *grass* like oxen,

6213 **עָשָׂה** *gāh-sāh'*.

* KAL.—*Preterite.* *

Gen 1:31. God saw every thing that *he had made*,
2: 2. God ended his work which *he had made*;
— all his work which *he had made*.
3: 1. any beast...which the Lord God *had made*.
13. What (is) this (that) *thou hast done?*
14. Because *thou hast done* this,
4:10. What *hast thou done?*
5: 1. in the likeness of God *made he* him;
6: 6. it repented the Lord that *he had made* man
7. it repenteth me that *I have made* them.
22. all that God commanded him, so *did he*.
7: 4. every living substance that *I have made*
8: 6. the window of the ark which *he had made*:
21. neither will I again smite...as *I have done*.
9: 6. in the image of God *made he* man.
24. knew what his younger son *had done*
12: 5. the souls that *they had gotten*
18. What (is) this (that) *thou hast done*
Gen 13: 4. the altar, which *he had made*
14: 2. *made* war with Bera king of Sodom,
18: 8. the calf which *he had dressed*,
21. whether *they have done* altogether
19:19. thy mercy, which *thou hast shewed*
20: 5. integrity of my heart...*have I done* this.
6. I know that *thou didst* this
9. What *hast thou done* unto us?
— *thou hast done* deeds unto me
10. that *thou hast done* this thing?
21: 6. God *hath made* me to laugh,
23. the kindness that *I have done* unto thee,
26. I wot not who *hath done* this thing:
22:16. because *thou hast done* this thing,
24:14. *thou hast shewed* kindness unto my master
66. the servant told Isaac all things that *he had done*.
26:10. What (is) this *thou hast done*
29. as *we have done* unto thee
27:17. the bread, which *she had prepared*,
19. *I have done* according as thou badest me:
45. (that) which *thou hast done*
28:15. I will not leave thee, until *I have done*
29:25. What (is) this *thou hast done* unto me?
31: 1. *hath he gotten* all this glory.
26. What *hast thou done*,
32:10(11). all the truth, which *thou hast shewed*
33:17. and *made* booths for his cattle:
34: 7. because *he had wrought* folly in Israel
37: 3. *and he made* him a coat of (many) colours.
38:10. the thing which *he did* displeased the
39:19. After this manner *did* thy servant
40:14. *and shew* kindness, I pray thee, unto me,
15. here also *have I done* nothing
42:28. What (is) this (that) God *hath done*
44: 5. ye have done evil in so *doing*.
15. What deed (is) this that *ye have done?*
47:29. *and deal* kindly and truly with me;
Ex. 1:17. the midwives feared God, and *did* not as
18. Why *have ye done* this thing,
4:21. see *that thou do* (lit. *them*) all those
7: 6. as the Lord commanded them, so *did they*.
10:25. *that we may sacrifice* unto the Lord
11:10. Moses and Aaron *did* all these wonders
12:28. as the Lord had commanded...so *did they*.
35. the children of Israel *did* according
39. neither *had they prepared* for themselves
48. *and will keep* the passover to the Lord,
50. as the Lord commanded...so *did they*.
13: 8. the Lord *did* unto me when I came forth
14: 5. Why *have we done* this,
11. wherefore *hast thou dealt* thus
31. that great work which the Lord *did*
18: 1. all that God *had done* for Moses,
8. all that the Lord *had done* unto Pharaoh
9. all the goodness which the Lord *had done*
19: 4. Ye have seen what *I did* unto the
20: 9. shalt thou labour, *and do* all thy work:
11. (in) six days the Lord *made* heaven and
23:22. *and do* all that I speak;
25: 8. *And let them make* me a sanctuary;
10. *And they shall make* an ark
11. *and shalt make* upon it a crown
13. *And thou shalt make* staves
17. *And thou shalt make* a mercy seat
18. *And thou shalt make* two cherubims
23. *Thou shalt also make* a table
24. *and make* thereto a crown
25. *And thou shalt make* unto it a border
— *and thou shalt make* a golden crown
26. *And thou shalt make* for it four rings
28. *And thou shalt make* the staves
29. *And thou shalt make* the dishes
31. *And thou shalt make* a candlestick
37. *And thou shalt make* the seven lamps
26: 4. *And thou shalt make* loops of blue
6. *And thou shalt make* fifty taches
7. *And thou shalt make* curtains
10. *And thou shalt make* fifty loops
11. *And thou shalt make* fifty taches
14. *And thou shalt make* a covering for
15. *And thou shalt make* boards for the
18. *And thou shalt make* the boards for
26. *And thou shalt make* bars (of) shittim wood;
31. *And thou shalt make* a vail
36. *And thou shalt make* an hanging
37. *And thou shalt make* for the hanging

Ex. 27: 1. *And thou shalt make* an altar
2. *And thou shalt make* the horns
3. *And thou shalt make* his pans
4. *And thou shalt make* for it a grate
— *and* upon the net *shalt thou make* four brasen rings
6. *And thou shalt make* staves for the altar,
9. *And thou shalt make* the court
28: 2. *And thou shalt make* holy garments
3. *that they may make* Aaron's garments
4. *and they shall make* holy garments
6. *And they shall make* the ephod
13. *And thou shalt make* ouches (of) gold;
15. *And thou shalt make* the breastplate
22, 23. *And thou shalt make* upon the breastplate
26. *And thou shalt make* two rings of gold,
27. *And* two (other) rings of gold *thou shalt make,*
31. *And thou shalt make* the robe of the ephod
33. *And...thou shalt make* pomegranates
36. *And thou shalt make* a plate (of) pure gold,
39. *and thou shalt make* the mitre
40. *and thou shalt make* for them girdles,
29:35. *And* thus *shalt thou do* unto Aaron,
30: 1. *And thou shalt make* an altar
3. *and thou shalt make* unto it a crown
5. *And thou shalt make* the staves
18. *Thou shalt also make* a laver
25. *And thou shalt make* it an oil
35. *And thou shalt make* it a perfume,
31: 6. *that they may make* all that I have
17. (in) six days the Lord *made* heaven and
32: 8. *they have made* them a molten calf,
20. the calf which *they had made,*
21. What *did* this people unto thee,
35. plagued the people, because *they made* the calf, which Aaron *made.*
36: 1. *Then wrought* Bezaleel and Aholiab,
8. of cunning work *made he* them.
11. likewise *he made* in the uttermost side
12. Fifty loops *made he* in one curtain, and fifty loops *made he* in the edge
14. eleven curtains *he made* them.
17. and fifty loops *made he*
22. thus *did he make* for all the boards
24. forty sockets of silver *he made*
25. *he made* twenty boards,
27. *he made* six boards.
28. two boards *made he* for the corners
29. thus *he did* to both of them
34. and *made* their rings (of) gold
35. cherubims *made he* it of cunning work.
37: 7. out of one piece *made he* them,
8. out of the mercy seat *made he* the
17. (of) beaten work *made he* the candlestick;
24. (Of) a talent of pure gold *made he* it,
27. *he made* two rings of gold
38: 3. the vessels thereof *made he* (of) brass.
7. *he made* the altar hollow with boards.
22. Bezaleel the son of Uri,...*made* all
28. *he made* hooks for the pillars,
39: 1. *they made* cloths of service,
4. *They made* shoulderpieces for it,
9. *they made* the breastplate double:
32. all that the Lord commanded Moses, so *did they.*
42. the children of Israel *made* all the work.
43. *they had done* it as the Lord had commanded, even so *had they done* it:
40:16. that the Lord commanded him, so *did he.*
Lev. 4: 2. *and shall do* against any of them:
13. *and they have done* (somewhat against)
20. *And he shall do* with the bullock as *he did* with the bullock for a sin offering,
22. a ruler hath sinned, *and done* (somewhat)
5:17. *and commit* any of these things
8:34. As *he hath done* this day,
14:19. *And* the priest *shall offer* the sin offering,
30. *And he shall offer* the one of the
15:15. *And* the priest *shall offer* them,
30. *And* the priest *shall offer* the one
16: 9. Aaron shall bring the goat...*and offer him*
15. *and do* with that blood as *he did* with the blood of the bullock,
24. *and offer* his burnt offering,
18:27. these abominations *have* the men of the land *done,*

Lev.19:37. all my judgments, *and do* them:
20: 8. ye shall keep my statutes, *and do* them:
12. *they have wrought* confusion;
13. both of them *have committed* an
22. all my judgments, *and do* them:
23. *they committed* all these things,
22:31. keep my commandments, *and do* them:
23:12. *And ye shall offer* that day...an he lamb
19. *Then ye shall sacrifice* one kid of the goats
24:19. as *he hath done,* so shall it be done
23. the children of Israel *did* as the Lord
25:18. *Wherefore ye shall do* my statutes, and keep my judgments, *and do* them;
21. *and it shall bring forth* fruit for
26: 3. keep my commandments, *and do* them;
Nu. 1:54. the Lord commanded Moses, so *did they.*
5: 4. so *did* the children of Israel.
7. confess their sin which *they have done:*
30. *and* the priest *shall execute* upon her
6:11. *And* the priest *shall offer* the one
16. *and shall offer* his sin offering,
17. the priest *shall offer also* his meat offering,
8: 4. so *he made* the candlestick.
20. so *did* the children of Israel
22. concerning the Levites, so *did* they
9: 5. so *did* the children of Israel.
10. *yet he shall keep* the passover unto the
14. if a stranger shall sojourn...*and will keep*
11: 8. baked (it) in pans, *and made* cakes of it:
14:11. all the signs which *I have shewed*
22. my miracles, which *I did* in Egypt
15: 3. *And will make* an offering by fire
14. if a stranger sojourn...*and will offer*
24. all the congregation *shall offer*
38. *that they make* them fringes
39. commandments of the Lord, *and do* them;
40. That ye may remember, *and do* all
16:38(17:3). *let them make* them broad plates
17:11(26). the Lord commanded him, so *did he.*
21:34. *and thou shalt do* to him as *thou didst* unto Sihon
22: 2. all that Israel *had done* to the Amorites.
28. What *have I done* unto thee,
23:11. What *hast thou done* unto me?
29: 2. *And ye shall offer* a burnt offering
32: 8. Thus *did* your fathers, when I sent them
33: 4. upon their gods also the Lord *executed*
36:10. so *did* the daughters of Zelophehad:
Deu 1:30. all that *he did* for you in Egypt
2:12. as Israel *did* unto the land of his
22. As *he did* to the children of Esau,
29. Moabites which dwell in Ar, *did*
3: 2. *and thou shalt do* unto him as *thou didst* unto Sihon
6. as *we did* unto Sihon king of Heshbon,
21. all that the Lord your God *hath done*
4: 3. Your eyes have seen what the Lord *did*
6. Keep therefore *and do* (them);
16. Lest ye corrupt (yourselves), *and make*
23. the covenant of the Lord...*and make* you
25. shall corrupt (yourselves), *and make*
— *and shall do* evil in the sight of the
34. all that the Lord your God *did* for you
5:13. Six days thou shalt labour, *and do* all
27(24). we will hear (it), *and do* (it).
31(28). *that they may do* (them) in the land
6:18. *And thou shalt do* (that which is) right
7:12. to these judgments, and keep, *and do*
18. what the Lord thy God *did* unto Pharaoh,
8:17. My power...*hath gotten* me this
9:12. *they have made* them a molten image.
16. *had made* you a molten calf:
21. the calf which *ye had made,*
10: 1. *and make* thee an ark of wood.
5. the ark which *I had made;*
21. *hath done* for thee these great and terrible
11: 3. his acts, which *he did* in the midst of
4. what *he did* unto the army of Egypt,
5. what *he did* unto you in the wilderness,
6. what *he did* unto Dathan and Abiram,
7. the great acts of the Lord which *he did.*
12:27. *And thou shalt offer* thy burnt offerings,
31. every abomination...*have they done*
16: 1. *and keep* the passover unto the Lord
10. *And thou shalt keep* the feast of weeks
12. and thou shalt observe *and do* these
17: 5. man or that woman, which *have committed*

Deu 17:10. *And thou shalt do* according to the
19:19. *Then shall ye do* unto him, as he had
20:12. no peace with thee, *but will make* war
18. their abominations, which *they have done*
21:12. she shall shave her head, *and pare* (marg. *make, dress*, or, *suffer to grow*) her nails;
22: 8. *then thou shalt make* a battlement for thy
21. *she hath wrought* folly in Israel,
23:23(24). thou shalt keep *and perform;*
24: 9. Remember what the Lord thy God *did*
25:17. Remember what Amalek *did*
26:14. *have done* according to all that thou hast
16. thou shalt therefore keep *and do* them
19. which *he hath made*, in praise,
27:10. obey the voice of the Lord...*and do* his
29: 2(1). all that the Lord *did*
9(8). the words of this covenant, *and do*
24(23). Wherefore *hath* the Lord *done* thus
30: 8. *and do* all his commandments
31: 4. *And* the Lord *shall do* unto them as *he did* to Sihon and to Og,
5. *that ye may do* unto them according
18. evils which *they shall have wrought*,
32: 6. *hath he* not *made thee*,
15. he forsook God (which) *made him*,
33:21. *he executed* the justice of the Lord,
34:12. the great terror which Moses *shewed*
Jos. 2:10. what *ye did* unto the two kings
12. since *I have shewed* you kindness, *that* ye *will* also *shew* kindness unto my
14. *that we will deal* kindly and truly with
4:23. as the Lord your God *did*
6:14. into the camp: so *they did* six days.
7:15. because *he hath wrought* folly in Israel.
19. tell me now what *thou hast done;*
20. and thus and thus *have I done:*
8: 2. *And thou shalt do* to Ai and her king as *thou didst* unto Jericho, and her king:
9: 3. what Joshua had *done* unto Jericho
9. and all that *he did* in Egypt,
10. all that *he did* to the two kings
10: 1. as *he had done* to Jericho and her king, so *he had done* to Ai and her king;
28. he did to the king of Makkedah as *he did* unto the king of Jericho.
30. did unto the king thereof as *he did*
32. all that *he had done* to Libnah.
35. all that *he had done* to Lachish.
37. all that *he had done* to Eglon;
39. as *he had done* to Hebron, so *he did* to Debir, and to the king thereof; as *he had done* also to Libnah,
11:15. and so *did* Joshua; he left
18. Joshua *made* war a long time
14: 5. so the children of Israel *did*,
22:24. if *we have* not (rather) *done* it
28. the altar of the Lord, which our fathers *made*,
23: 3. all that the Lord your God *hath done*
8. as *ye have done* unto this day.
24: 5. according to that which *I did*
7. what *I have done* in Egypt:
17. which *did* those great signs in our sight,
31. works of the Lord, that *he had done*
Jud. 1: 7. as *I have done*, so God hath requited me.
24. *and we will shew* thee mercy.
2: 2. why *have ye done* this?
7. the great works of the Lord, that *he did*
10. the works which *he had done* for Israel.
17. of the Lord; (but) *they did* not so.
3:12. *they had done* evil in the sight of the
6: 2. the children of Israel *made* them the
17. *then shew* me a sign that thou talkest
29. Who *hath done* this thing?
— Gideon the son of Joash *hath done* this
8: 1. Why *hast thou served* us thus, (marg. What thing (is) this *thou hast done* unto us)
2. What *have I done* now in comparison
35. Neither *shewed they* kindness
— all the goodness which *he had shewed*
9:16. if *ye have done* truly and sincerely,
— and if *ye have dealt* well with Jerubbaal
— and *have done* unto him according to
19. If *ye* then *have dealt* truly and sincerely
33. *then mayest thou do* to them
48. ye have seen *me do*, (marg. *I have done*)
56. wickedness of Abimelech, which *he did*

Jud. 11:36. Lord *hath taken* (lit. *hath done*) vengeance
14: 6. he told not...what *he had done*.
15: 6. Who *hath done* this?
10. to do to him as he *hath done* to us.
11. what (is) this (that) *thou hast done* unto us? And he said unto them, As *they did* unto me, so *have I done* unto them.
18: 4. *dealeth* Micah with me, (lit. *did* Micah unto me)
24. have taken away my gods which *I made*,
27. (the things) which Micah *had made*,
31. Micah's graven image, which *he made*,
20: 6. *they have committed* lewdness
10. the folly that *they have wrought* in Israel.
21:15. the Lord *had made* a breach
Ru. 1: 8. as *ye have dealt* with the dead,
2:11. all that *thou hast done*
19. where *wroughtest thou?*
— with whom she *had wrought*, and said, The man's name with whom *I wrought*
3:16. all that the man *had done*
1Sa. 6: 5. *Wherefore ye shall make* images of your
9. he *hath done* us this great evil:
8: 8. all the works which *they have done*
16. your asses, *and put* (them) to his work.
11:10. *and ye shall do* with us all that seemeth
13. to day the Lord *hath wrought* salvation
12: 6. Lord that *advanced* (marg. or, *made*) Moses
7. acts of the Lord, which *he did* to you
17. wickedness (is) great, which *ye have done*
20. *ye have done* all this wickedness:
13:11. What *hast thou done?*
14:43. Tell me what *thou hast done.*
45. *hath wrought* this great salvation
— *he hath wrought* with God this day.
15: 2. I remember (that) which Amalek *did*
6. *ye shewed* kindness to all the
17:29. What *have I* now *done?*
19:18. all that Saul *had done* to him.
20: 1. said before Jonathan, What *have I done?*
2. (כתיב) my father *will do* nothing
8. *Therefore thou shalt deal* kindly with thy
32. what *hath he done?*
24: 4(5). *that thou mayest do* to him as it shall
18(19). *thou hast dealt* well with me:
19(20). that *thou hast done* unto me
26:16. thing (is) not good that *thou hast done.*
18. for what *have I done?* or what evil
27:11. So *did* David, and so
28: 9. thou knowest what Saul *hath done*,
18. nor *executedst* his fierce wrath
— *hath* the Lord *done* this thing unto thee
29: 8. But what *have I done?*
31:11. that which the Philistines *had done*
2Sa. 2: 5. *ye have shewed* this kindness
6. because *ye have done* this thing.
3:24. What *hast thou done?*
36. whatsoever the king *did*
7: 9. *and have made* thee a great name,
21. *hast thou done* all these great things,
10: 2. his father *shewed* kindness unto me.
11:27. the thing that David *had done*
12: 6. because *he did* this thing,
12. For thou *didst* (it) secretly:
18. *how will he then* vex (marg. *do* hurt) *himself*,
21. What thing (is) this that *thou hast done?*
13: 5. *and dress* the meat in my sight,
10. took the cakes which *she had made*,
16. the other that *thou didst* unto me.
14:20. *hath* thy servant Joab *done* this thing:
21. *I have done* this thing:
22. the king *hath fulfilled* the request
16:10. Wherefore *hast thou done* so?
18:13. *I* should *have wrought* falshood
19:24(25). *had* neither *dressed* his feet, nor *trimmed* his beard,
21:11. the concubine of Saul, *had done*.
23:17. These things *did* these three mighty men.
22. These (things) *did* Benaiah
24:10. I have sinned greatly in that *I have done:*
17. but these sheep, what *have they done?*
1K. 1: 6. Why *hast thou done* so?
2: 5. what Joab the son of Zeruiah *did* to me, (and) what *he did* to the two captains
6. *Do therefore* according to thy wisdom,
24. who *hath made* me an house,

1K. 2:44. that *thou didst* to David my father:
3: 6. *Thou hast shewed* unto thy servant
12. *I have done* according to thy words:
6:31. *he made* doors (of) olive tree:
33. *made he* for the door of the temple
7: 6. *he made* a porch of pillars;
7. *he made* a porch for the throne
16. *he made* two chapiters
18. and so *did he* for the other
37. *he made* the ten bases:
40. all the work that *he made* king Solomon
45. these vessels, which Hiram *made*
51. the work that king Solomon *made*
8:32. hear thou in heaven, *and do*,
39. hear thou in heaven...*and do*,
43. Hear thou in heaven thy dwelling...*and do*
45,49. *and maintain* their cause.
64. there *he offered* burnt offerings,
66. the goodness that the Lord *had done*
9: 8. Why *hath* the Lord *done* thus
26. king Solomon *made* a navy
11: 8. likewise *did he* for all his strange wives,
38. *and do* (that is) right in my sight,
— as David my servant *did;*
41. the acts of Solomon, and all that *he did*,
12:32. So *did he* in Beth-el, sacrificing unto the calves that *he had made:*
— the high places which *he had made.*
33. the altar which *he had made*
13:11. the works that the man of God *had done*
14:15. because *they have made* their groves,
22. all that their fathers *had done.*
24. *they did* according to all the abominations
26. shields of gold which Solomon *had made.*
29. the acts of Rehoboam, and all that *he did*,
15: 3. the sins of his father, which *he had done*
5. David *did* (that which was) right
7. the acts of Abijam, and all that *he did*,
12. the idols that his fathers *had made.*
13. *she had made* an idol in a grove;
23. the acts of Asa,...and all *that he did*,
31. the acts of Nadab, and all that *he did*,
16: 5. the acts of Baasha, and what *he did*,
7. for all the evil that *he did*
14. the acts of Elah, and all that *he did*,
19. his sin which *he did*,
27. the acts of Omri which *he did*, and his might that *he shewed*,
17:12. that I may go in *and dress it*
18:13. Was it not told my lord what *I did*
26. leaped upon the altar which *was made.*
36. *I have done* all these things
19: 1. all that Elijah *had done*,
20. Go back again: for what *have I done* to
21:26. according to all (things) as *did* the
22:39. the acts of Ahab, and all that *he did*,
45(46). of Jehoshaphat, and his might that *he shewed*,
48(49). Jehoshaphat *made* ships
53(54). all that his father *had done.*
2K. 1:18. the acts of Ahaziah which *he did*,
3: 2. of Baal that his father *had made.*
7:12. what the Syrians *have done*
8: 4. the great things that Elisha *hath done.*
18. as *did* the house of Ahab:
23. the acts of Joram, and all that *he did*,
10:10. the Lord *hath done* (that) which he spake
19. But Jehu *did* (it) in subtilty,
30. (and) *hast done* unto the house of Ahab
34. the acts of Jehu, and all that *he did*,
12:19(20). the acts of Joash, and all that *he did*,
13: 8. the acts of Jehoahaz, and all that *he did*,
12. the acts of Joash, and all that *he did*,
14: 3. *he did* according to all things as Joash his father *did.*
15. the acts of Jehoash which *he did*,
28. the acts of Jeroboam, and all that *he did*,
15: 3. that his father Amaziah *had done;*
6. the acts of Azariah, and all that *he did*,
9. as his fathers *had done:*
21. the acts of Menahem, and all that *he did*,
26. the acts of Pekahiah, and all that *he did*,
31. the acts of Pekah, and all that *he did*,
34. *he did* according to all that his father Uzziah *had done.*
36. the acts of Jotham, and all that *he did*,
16: 2. *did* not (that which was) right

2K. 16:11. Urijah the priest *made* (it)
19. the acts of Ahaz which *he did*,
17: 8. the kings of Israel, which *they had made.*
19. the statutes of Israel which *they made.*
22. the sins of Jeroboam which *he did;*
29. which the Samaritans *had made*,
30. the men of Babylon *made* Succoth-benoth, and the men of Cuth *made* Nergal, and the men of Hamath *made* Ashima,
31. the Avites *made* Nibhaz
41. as *did* their fathers, so do they
18: 3. according to all that David his father *did.*
4. the brasen serpent that Moses *had made:*
12. would not hear (them), nor *do* (them).
19:11. what the kings of Assyria *have done*
15. thou *hast made* heaven and earth.
25. Hast thou not heard...*I have done* it,
30. root downward, *and bear* fruit upward.
20: 3. *have done* (that which is) good
20. and how *he made* a pool,
21: 3. as *did* Ahab king of Israel;
6. *and dealt with* familiar spirits
7. of the grove that *he had made* in the house,
11. of Judah *hath done* these abominations,
— above all that the Amorites *did*,
15. *they have done* (that which was) evil
17. the acts of Manasseh, and all that *he did*,
20. as his father Manasseh *did.*
25. the acts of Amon which *he did*,
23:12. which the kings of Judah *had made*,
— the altars which Manasseh *had made*
15. the high place which Jeroboam...*had made*,
17. these things that *thou hast done*
19. which the kings of Israel *had made*
— all the acts that *he had done*
28. the acts of Josiah, and all that *he did*,
32. according to all that his fathers *had done.*
37. according to all that his fathers *had done.*
24: 3. Manasseh, according to all that *he did;*
5. the acts of Jehoiakim, and all that *he did*,
9. according to all that his father *had done.*
13. vessels of gold which Solomon...*had made*
19. according to all that Jehoiakim *had done.*
25:16. the bases which Solomon *had made*
1Ch 4:10. *that thou wouldest keep* (marg. *do*) (me) from evil,
5:10. *they made* war with the Hagarites,
10:11. all that the Philistines *had done*
11:19. These things *did* these three mightiest.
24. These (things) *did* Benaiah
16:12. his marvellous works that *he hath done*,
26. the Lord *made* the heavens.
17: 8. *and have made* thee a name
19. *hast thou done* all this greatness,
18: 8. Solomon *made* the brasen sea,
19: 2. because his father *shewed* kindness to me.
21: 8. because *I have done* this thing:
17. (as for) these sheep, what *have they done?*
29. tabernacle of the Lord, which Moses *made*
22: 8. and *hast made* great wars:
23: 5. instruments which *I made*, (said David),
2Ch 1: 3. Moses the servant of the Lord *had made*
5. the brasen altar, that Bezaleel...*had made*,
8. Thou *hast shewed* great mercy
2: 3(2). *thou didst deal* with David my father,
12(11). Lord God of Israel, that *made* heaven
4:11. the work that *he was to make* for
14. *He made* also bases, and lavers *made he* upon the bases;
16. *did* Huram his father *make* to king
5: 1. all the work that Solomon *made*
6:13. Solomon *had made* a brasen scaffold,
23. hear thou from heaven, *and do*,
33. *and do* according to all that the stranger
35,39. *and maintain* their cause.
7: 6. instruments...which David the king *had made*
7. there *he offered* burnt offerings,
— the brasen altar which Solomon *had made*
9. for *they kept* the dedication of the altar
10. the goodness that the Lord *had shewed*
21. Why *hath* the Lord *done* thus
11:15. the calves which *he had made.*
12: 9. shields of gold which Solomon *had made.*
13: 8. golden calves, which Jeroboam *made* you
15:16. *she had made* an idol in a grove:
21: 6. like as *did* the house of Ahab:

2Ch 21:11. *he made* high places in the mountains
19. his people *made* no burning for him,
24: 7. the dedicated things...*did they bestow*
11. Thus *they did* day by day,
16. because *he had done* good in Israel,
22. the kindness which Jehoiada his father *had done*
24. *they executed* judgment against Joash.
25:16. destroy thee, because *thou hast done* this,
26: 4. to all that his father Amaziah *did*.
27: 2. according to all that his father Uzziah *did:*
28: 1. *he did* not (that which was) right
2. *made* also molten images
25. *he made* high places
29: 2. all that David his father *had done*.
6. *and done* (that which was) evil
30: 5. *they had* not *done* (it) of a long (time)
31:21. *he did* (it) with all his heart,
32:13. what I and my fathers *have done*
27. *he made* himself treasuries
29. *he provided* him cities, and possessions
33. inhabitants of Jerusalem *did* him honour
33: 6. *and dealt with* a familiar spirit,
7. the idol which *he had made*,
22. as *did* Manasseh his father:
— which Manasseh his father *had made*,
35:18. neither *did* all the kings of Israel *keep* such a passover as Josiah *kept*,
36: 8. his abominations which *he did*,
Neh. 1: 9. keep my commandments, *and do* them;
5:15. but so *did* not I, because of the fear of God.
19. all that *I have done* for this people.
8: 4. a pulpit of wood, which *they had made*
17. *had* not the children of Israel *done* so.
9: 6. thou *hast made* heaven, the heaven
17. thy wonders that *thou didst*
18. when *they had made* them a molten calf,
31. *didst* not utterly consume *them*, (lit. *didst* not *make them* a consumption)
33. *thou hast done* right,
34. Neither *have* our kings,...*kept* thy law,
13: 7. the evil that Eliashib *did* for Tobiah,
14. my good deeds that *I have done*
18. *Did* not your fathers thus,
Est. 1: 3. *he made* a feast unto all his princes
5. the king *made* a feast unto all the people
9. Vashti the queen *made* a feast
15. because *she hath* not *performed*
2: 1. remembered Vashti, and what *she had done*,
18. and *he made* a release to the provinces,
5: 4. the banquet that *I have prepared*
5. the banquet that Esther *had prepared*.
12. the banquet that *she had prepared*
6:14. the banquet that Esther *had prepared*.
7: 9. the gallows...which Haman *had made*
9:12. what *have they done* in the rest of
Job 1: 4. his sons went *and* feasted (lit. *made* a feast)
10: 9. *thou hast made me* as the clay;
12. *Thou hast granted* me life
12: 9. the hand of the Lord *hath wrought* this?
14: 5. *thou hast appointed* his bounds
9. will bud, *and bring forth* boughs
21:31. who shall repay him (what) he *hath done?*
27:18. as a booth (that) the keeper *maketh*.
31:15. *Did* not he that made me in the womb *make him?*
33: 4. The Spirit of God *hath made me*,
40:15. behemoth, which *I made* with thee;
Ps. 7: 3(4). O Lord my God, if *I have done* this;
9: 4(5). *thou hast maintained* (marg. *made*) my right
15(16). the pit (that) *they made:*
16(17). The Lord is known (by) the judgment (which) *he executeth:*
15: 3. nor *doeth* evil to his neighbour,
22:31(32). shall declare...that *he hath done*
39: 9(10). because thou *didst* (it).
40: 5(6). works (which) thou *hast done*,
50:21. These (things) *hast thou done*,
51: 4(6). and *done* (this) evil in thy sight:
52: 9(11). because *thou hast done* (it):
66:16. I will declare what *he hath done*
71:19. who *hast done* great things:
78: 4. his wonderful works that *he hath done*.
12. Marvellous things *did he*

Ps. 86: 9. All nations whom *thou hast made*
95: 5. The sea (is) his, and he *made it:*
96: 5. the Lord *made* the heavens.
98: 1. *he hath done* marvellous things:
99: 4. thou *executest* judgment
100: 3. (it is) *he* (that) *hath made us*,
103:10. *He hath* not *dealt* with us after our sins;
104:19. *He appointed* the moon
24. in wisdom *hast thou made* them all:
105: 5. his marvellous works that *he hath done*,
109:27. (that) thou, Lord, *hast done* it.
111: 4. *He hath made* his wonderful works
115: 3. *he hath done* whatsoever he hath pleased.
118:24. the day (which) the Lord *hath made;*
119:65. *Thou hast dealt* well with thy servant,
73. Thy hands *have made* me
121. *I have done* judgment and justice:
166. and *done* thy commandments.
135: 6. Whatsoever the Lord pleased, (that) *did he*
7. *he maketh* lightnings for the rain;
147:20. *He hath* not *dealt* so with any nation:
Pro. 8:26. While as yet *he had* not *made* the earth,
20:12. the Lord *hath made* even both
22:28. landmark, which thy fathers *have set*.
24:29. I will do so to him as *he hath done*
31:22. *She maketh* herself coverings
24. *She maketh* fine linen,
29. Many daughters *have done* virtuously,
Ecc. 2: 5. *I made* me gardens and orchards,
6. *I made* me pools of water,
8. *I gat* me men singers and women singers,
11. all the works *that* my hands *had wrought*,
12. that which *hath been* already *done*.
3:11. *He hath made* every (thing) beautiful
— the work that God *maketh*
14. and God *doeth* (it),
7:14. God also *hath set* (marg. *made*) the one over against
29. God *hath made* man upright;
8:10. in the city where *they had* so *done:*
Cant. 3: 9. King Solomon *made* himself a chariot
10. *He made* the pillars thereof (of) silver,
Isa. 2: 8. that which their own fingers *have made:*
20. idols of gold, which *they made*
5: 4. that *I have* not *done* in it?
10:11. as *I have done* unto Samaria
13. the strength of my hand *I have done* (it),
12: 5. the Lord; for *he hath done* excellent
15: 7. the abundance *they have gotten*,
17: 8. (that) which his fingers *have made*,
22:11. *Ye made* also a ditch between the two
25: 1. *thou hast done* wonderful (things);
6. *And* in this mountain *shall* the Lord of hosts *make*
28:15. with hell *are we at* agreement; (lit. *made we* agreement)
29:16. say of him that made it, *He made me* not?
31: 7. of gold, which your own hands *have made*
33:13. Hear, ye...what *I have done;*
37:11. what the kings of Assyria *have done*
16. *thou hast made* heaven and earth.
26. Hast thou not heard...*I have done* it;
31. take root downward, *and bear* fruit upward:
38: 3. *have done* (that which is) good
15. and himself *hath done* (it):
40:23. *he maketh* the judges of the earth as
41: 4. Who hath wrought *and done* (it),
20. the hand of the Lord *hath done* this,
42:16. These things *will I do* unto them,
43: 7. I have formed him; yea, *I have made him*.
44:15. *he maketh it* a graven image,
17. the residue thereof *he maketh* a god,
23. O ye heavens; for the Lord *hath done* (it):
45:12. *I have made* the earth,
46: 4. I *have made*, and I will bear;
48: 3. *I did* (them) suddenly,
5. Mine idol *hath done them*,
53: 9. because *he had done* no violence,
55:11. *it shall accomplish* that which I please,
57:16. the souls (which) I *have made*.
58: 2. a nation that *did* righteousness,
66: 2. all those (things) *hath* mine hand *made*,
Jer. 2:13. my people *have committed* two evils;
23. know what *thou hast done:*
28. where (are) thy gods that *thou hast made*
3: 6. (that) which backsliding Israel *hath done?*

Jer. 4:18. Thy way and thy doings *have procured*
5:19. Wherefore *doeth* the Lord our God all
6:15. when *they had committed* abomination?
7:12. and see what *I did* to it
14. *Therefore will I do* unto (this) house,
— as *I have done* to Shiloh.
30. the children of Judah *have done* evil
8: 6. What *have I done?*
8. Lo, certainly in vain *made he* (it);
12. *they had committed* abomination?
10:13. *he maketh* lightnings with rain,
11: 4. Obey my voice, *and do* them,
6. the words of this covenant, *and do* them.
8. but *they did* (them) not.
17. the house of Israel...which *they have done*
12: 2. they grow, yea, *they bring forth*
14:22. *thou hast made* all these (things).
15: 4. (that) which *he did* in Jerusalem.
18:10. *If it do* evil in my sight,
13. the virgin of Israel *hath done*
22: 8. Wherefore *hath* the Lord *done* thus
15. *and do* judgment and justice,
23: 5. a King shall reign and prosper, *and shall execute*
27: 5. I *have made* the earth,
28:13. *but thou shalt make* for them yokes of
29:23. *they have committed* villany
30:15. *I have done* these things unto thee.
31:37. Israel for all that *they have done*,
32:17. thou *hast made* the heaven and the earth
23. *they have done* nothing of all that thou
32. *they have done* to provoke me
33:15. *and he shall execute* judgment and
37:15. *they had made* that the prison.
38: 9. have done evil in all that *they have done*
16. (As) the Lord liveth, that *made* us this
41: 9. which Asa the king *had made*
11. the evil that Ishmael...*had done*,
42:10. I repent me of the evil that *I have done*
20. so declare unto us, *and we will do* (it).
44: 3. wickedness which *they have committed*
9. of your wives, which *they have committed*
17. as *we have done*, we, and our fathers,
19. *did we make* her cakes to worship her,
22. the abominations which *ye have committed;*
48:30. his lies *shall* not so *effect* (it).
36. the riches (that) *he hath gotten*
50:15. as *she hath done*, do unto her.
29. according to all that *she hath done*,
51:12. the Lord hath both devised and *done*
16. *he maketh* lightnings with rain,
24. their evil that *they have done*
52: 2. according to all that Jehoiakim *had done*.
20. brasen bulls...which king Solomon *had made*
Lam. 1:21. they are glad that thou *hast done* (it):
2:17. The Lord *hath done* (that) which he had
Eze. 3:20. turn from his righteousness, *and commit*
— his righteousness which *he hath done*
4: 9. *and make* thee bread thereof,
15. *and thou shalt prepare* thy bread
5: 7. neither *have kept* my judgments, neither *have done* according to
8. *and will execute* judgments in the midst
9. *And I will do* in thee that which *I have* not *done*,
10. *and I will execute* judgments in thee,
6: 9. the evils which *they have committed*
7:20. *they made* the images of their
8:17. the abominations which *they commit*
9:11. *I have done* as thou hast commanded
11: 9. *and will execute* judgments
12. neither *executed* my judgments, but *have done* after the manners of the heathen
20. keep mine ordinances, *and do* them:
12:11. like as *I have done*,
25. I say the word, *and will perform it*,
14:23. ye shall know that *I have* not *done* without cause all that *I have done*
16:31. *makest* thine high place in every street;
41. *and execute* judgments upon thee
43. *thou shalt* not *commit* this lewdness
47. nor *done* after their abominations:
48. Sodom thy sister *hath* not *done*, she nor her daughters, as *thou hast done*,
51. thine abominations which *thou hast done*.
54. confounded in all that *thou hast done*,

Eze. 16:59. *I will even deal* with thee as *thou hast done*,
63. all that *thou hast done*,
17:18. and *hath done* all these (things),
23. bring forth boughs, *and bear* fruit,
24. the Lord have spoken *and have done* (it).
18: 5. if a man be just, *and do* that which is
10. *and* (that) *doeth* the like to (any) one of
11. that *doeth* not any of those (duties),
12. *hath committed* abomination,
13. *he hath done* all these
14. sins which *he hath done*,
17. *hath executed* my judgments,
18. *did* (that) which (is) not good
19. the son *hath done* that which is lawful
21. from all his sins that *he hath committed*,
— *and do* that which is lawful and right,
22. his transgressions that *he hath committed*,
— his righteousness that *he hath done*
24. *and committeth* iniquity,
— the abominations that the wicked (man) *doeth*,
— his righteousness that *he hath done*
26. *and committeth* iniquity,
— his iniquity that *he hath done*
27. his wickedness that *he hath committed*,
28. his transgressions that *he hath committed*,
20:17. neither *did I make* an end of them
24. *they had* not *executed* my judgments,
43. your evils that *ye have committed*.
22: 3. *and maketh* idols against herself
4. thine idols which *thou hast made;*
7. *they dealt* by oppression
9. in the midst of thee *they commit* lewdness.
11. one *hath committed* abomination
13. gain which *thou hast made*,
14. I the Lord have spoken (it), *and will do* (it).
23:10. *they had executed* judgment
25. *and they shall deal* furiously with thee:
29. *And they shall deal* with thee hatefully,
38. this *they have done* unto me:
39. thus *have they done* in the midst
24:14. come to pass, *and I will do* (it);
22. *And ye shall do* as *I have done:*
24. all that *he hath done* shall ye do:
25:14. *and they shall do* in Edom according to
17. *And I will execute* great vengeance
27: 6. (Of) the oaks of Bashan *have they made*
— *have made* thy benches (of) ivory,
28: 4. *thou hast gotten* thee riches,
29: 3. river (is) mine own, and I *have made* (it)
9. The river (is) mine, and I *have made* (it)
20. because *they wrought* for me,
30:14. *and will execute* judgments in No.
19. Thus *will I execute* judgments
31: 9. *I have made him* fair
33:13. *and commit* iniquity,
— his iniquity that *he hath committed*,
14, 19. *and do* that which is lawful and right,
16. *hath done* that which is lawful
18. *and committeth* iniquity, he shall
26. *ye work* abomination,
29. abominations which *they have committed*.
35:11. *I will even do* according to thine anger,
— which *thou hast used* out of thy hatred
36:27. *and cause* you to walk in my statutes,
— keep my judgments, *and do* (them).
36. Lord have spoken (it), *and I will do* (it).
37:14. have spoken (it), *and performed* (it),
19. *and make them* one stick,
22. *And I will make* them one nation
24. observe my statutes, *and do* them.
39:21. my judgment that *I have executed*,
24. *have I done* unto them,
43: 8. abominations that *they have committed:*
11. ashamed of all that *they have done*,
— all the ordinances thereof, *and do* them.
44:13. abominations which *they have committed*.
45:22. *And* upon that day *shall* the prince *prepare* for himself
46: 2. *and* the priests *shall prepare* his burnt
12. *and he shall prepare* his burnt offering
15. (כתיב) *Thus shall they prepare* the lamb,
Dan. 8: 4. *but he did* according to his will,
12. *and it practised*, and prospered.
24. shall prosper, *and practise*,
9:14. in all his works which *he doeth:*

Dan 11: 3. *and do* according to his will.
7. *and shall deal* against them,
17. *thus shall he do:* and he shall
24. *and he shall do* (that) which his fathers *have* not *done*,
28. *and he shall do* (exploits),
30. *so shall he do;* he shall even
32. shall be strong, *and do* (exploits).
36. *And* the king *shall do* according to his
39. *Thus shall he do* in the most strong holds
Hos. 2: 8(10). silver and gold, (which) *they prepared* for (marg. or, (wherewith) *they made*) Baal.
6: 9. for *they commit* lewdness.
8: 4. their gold *have they made* them idols,
6. the workman *made it;*
10:15. So *shall* Beth-el *do* unto you
Joel 2:26. your God, that *hath dealt* wondrously
Am. 3: 6. and the Lord *hath* not *done* (it)? (marg. or, and *shall* not the Lord *do* (somewhat))
5:26. your images,...which *ye made*
9:14. *they shall also make* gardens,
Obad. 15. as *thou hast done*, it shall be
Jon. 1: 9. which *hath made* the sea and the dry land.
10. Why *hast thou done* this?
14. thou, O Lord, *hast done* as it pleased thee.
3:10. and *he did* (it) not.
Mic. 5:15(14). *And I will execute* vengeance
6: 3. O my people, what *have I done*
7: 9. *and execute* judgment for me:
Hab. 3:17. the fields *shall yield* no meat;
Zec. 1: 6. so *hath he dealt* with us.
6:11. take silver and gold, *and make* crowns,
7: 3. as *I have done* these so many years?
Mal. 2:15. And *did* not *he make* one?

KAL.—*Infinitive.*

Gen 2: 3. his work which God created *and made.* (marg. *to make*)
4. that the Lord God *made* the earth
11: 6. this they begin *to do:*
— they have imagined *to do.*
18: 7. he hasted *to dress* it.
19. *to do* justice and judgment;
25. That be far from thee *to do*
19:22. I cannot *do* (lit. not able *to do*) any thing till thou be come thither.
31:28. hast now done foolishly *in* (so) *doing.*
29. It is in the power of my hand *to do*
34:14. We cannot *do* (lit. are not able *to do*)
19. the young man deferred not *to do* the
39:11. (Joseph) went into the house *to do*
41:32. God will shortly *bring it to pass.*
44: 7. God forbid *that* thy servants *should do*
17. God forbid *that* I *should do* so:
50:20. to *bring to pass*, as (it is) this day,
Ex. 8:26(22). It is not meet so *to do;*
12:48. let him come near *and keep it;*
18:18. thou art not able *to perform it*
31: 4. *to work* in gold,
5. *to work* in all manner of workmanship.
16. *to observe* the sabbath
32:14. the evil which he thought *to do*
35: 1. commanded, *that* (ye) *should do* them.
29. *to be made* by the hand of Moses.
32. *to work* in gold, and in silver,
33. *to make* any manner of cunning work.
35. *to work* all manner of work,
36: 1. *to work* all manner of work
2. to come unto the work *to do* it:
3. the service of the sanctuary, *to make* it
5. the work, which the Lord commanded *to make.*
7. all the work *to make* it,
39: 3. *to work* (it) in the blue,
Lev. 4:27. *while he doeth* (somewhat against) any
8: 5. the Lord commanded *to be done.*
34. the Lord hath commanded *to do,*
9:22. came down *from offering*
17: 9. *to offer* it unto the Lord;
18:30. *that* (ye) *commit* not (any one) of these
26:15. *so that ye will* not *do* all my
Nu. 4: 3. *to do* the work in the tabernacle
9: 4. *that they should keep* the passover.
6. *that they could* not *keep* the passover
13. forbeareth *to keep* the passover,
15: 3. *to make* a sweet savour

Nu. 16:28. that the Lord hath sent me *to do*
22:18. *to do* less or more.
30. was I ever wont *to do* so
24:13. *to do* (either) good or bad
33:56. as I thought *to do* unto them.
Deu 1:14. thou hast spoken (is) good (for us) *to do.*
4: 1. judgments, which I teach you, *for to do*
5. *that ye should do* so in the land
13. he commanded you *to perform,*
14. *that ye might do* them in the land
5: 1. them, and keep, *and* (marg. *to*) *do them.*
15. Lord thy God commanded thee *to keep*
32(29). Ye shall observe *to do*
6: 1. *that ye might do* (them) in the land
3. Hear therefore, O Israel, and observe *to do*
24. the Lord commanded us *to do*
25. if we observe *to do* all these
7:11. I command thee this day, *to do them.*
8: 1. commandments...shall ye observe *to do,*
18. he that giveth thee power *to get* wealth.
9:18. *in doing* wickedly in the sight of
11:22. all these commandments...*to do them,*
32. ye shall observe *to do* all the statutes
12: 1. ye shall observe *to do* in the land,
32(13:1). What thing soever I command you, observe *to do*
13:11(12). shall *do* no more (lit. shall not add *to do*)
18(19). *to do* (that which is) right
15: 5. to observe *to do* all these commandments
17:10. thou shalt observe *to do* according
19. these statutes, *to do them:*
18: 9. thou shalt not learn *to do* after
19: 9. all these commandments *to do them,*
19. as he had thought *to have done*
20. henceforth *commit* (lit. add *to commit*) no more any such evil
20:18. That they teach you not *to do* after
24: 8. *and do* according to all that the priests
— them, (so) ye shall observe *to do.*
18, 22. I command thee *to do* this thing.
26:16. thy God hath commanded thee *to do*
27:26. the words of this law *to do* them.
28: 1, 15. *to do* all his commandments
13. to observe *and to do* (them):
58. If thou wilt not observe *to do*
29:29(28). *that* (we) *may do* all the words
30:14. in thy heart, *that thou mayest do it.*
31:12. and observe *to do* all the words
32:46. to observe *to do,* all the words
34:11. wonders, which the Lord sent him *to do*
Jos. 1: 7. that thou mayest observe *to do*
8. that thou mayest observe *to do*
9:25. seemeth good and right unto thee *to do*
22: 5. take diligent heed *to do*
23. *to offer* peace offerings thereon,
23: 6. to keep *and to do* all that is written
Jud. 3:12. the children of Israel *did* evil again (lit. added *to do* evil)
4: 1. the children of Israel again *did* evil (lit. added *to do* evil)
6:27. *that he could* not *do* (it) by day,
8: 3. what was I able *to do*
10: 6 & 13:1. the children of Israel *did* evil again (lit. added *to do* evil)
13:19. (the angel) *did* wonderously; (lit. acted wonderfully *in doing*)
15:10. *to do* to him as he hath done
17: 3. *to make* a graven image
8. as he journeyed. (marg. *in making* his way)
20:10. *that they may do,* when they come
1Sa. 8:12. *and to make* his instruments of war,
12:22. pleased the Lord *to make* you his people.
25:28. the Lord will *certainly* make (lit. *making* will make)
26:25. thou shalt both do *great* (things), (lit. *doing* thou shalt do)
2Sa. 7:23. *to do* for you great things
9: 7. I will *surely* shew (lit. *shewing* I will shew)
12: 4. *to dress* for the wayfaring man
9. *to do* evil in his sight?
13: 2. Amnon thought it hard for him *to do*
19:18(19). *and to do* what he thought good.
23:17. O Lord, *that I should do* this:
1K. 3:28. in him, *to do* judgment.
7:14. *to work* all works in brass.
40. Hiram made an end *of doing*

1K. 8:59. *that he maintain* the cause of
9: 1. Solomon's desire which he was pleased *to do*,
4. *to do* according to all that I have
10: 9. *to do* judgment and justice.
11:33. *to do* (that which is) right in mine eyes,
12:27. If this people go up *to do* sacrifice
14: 8. *to do* (that) only (which was) right
9. hast *done* evil (lit. hast been evil *to do*) above all
16:19. *in doing* evil in the sight of the Lord,
33. Ahab *did* more (lit. added *to do*) to provoke the Lord
20: 9. but this thing I may not *do*.
21:20. thou hast sold thyself *to work* evil
25. Ahab, which did sell himself *to work*
22:43. *doing* (that which was) right
2K. 3:16. *Make* this valley full of ditches.
4:13. what (is) *to be done* (lit. *to do*) for thee?
14. What then (is) *to be done* (lit. *to do*) for
10:24. when they went in *to offer*
25. as soon as he had made an end *of offering*
30. thou hast done well *in executing*
17:15. *that they should* not do like them.
17. sold themselves *to do* evil
37. ye shall observe *to do* for evermore;
21: 6. he *wrought* much (lit. he multiplied *to work*) wickedness
8. if they will observe *to do*
9. Manasseh seduced them *to do* more evil
16. *in doing* (that which was) evil
22:13. *to do* according unto all
1Ch 11:19. God forbid it me, *that* I *should do* this
13: 4. the congregation said *that they would do*
22:13. if thou takest heed *to fulfil* the statutes
28: 7. if he be constant *to do* my commandments
29:19. *and to do* all (these things),
2Ch 2: 7(6). a man cunning *to work* in gold,
14(13). skilful *to work* in gold,
4:11. Huram finished (marg. finished *to make*) the work
7:11. that came into Solomon's heart *to make*
17. *and do* according to all that I have
9: 8. *to do* judgment and justice.
14: 4(3). *and to do* the law and the
20:32. *doing* (that which was) right
35. did *very* wickedly: (lit. did wickedly *in doing*)
36. he joined himself with him *to make* ships
25: 9. what *shall we do* for the hundred talents
30: 1, 5. *to keep* the passover unto the Lord
2. *to keep* the passover in the second
3. they could not *keep it* at that time,
12. *to do* the commandment of the king
13. *to keep* the feast of unleavened bread
23. *to keep* other seven days:
33: 6. he *wrought* much (lit. he multiplied *to work*) evil
8. they will take heed *to do*
9. *to do* worse than the heathen,
34:21. *to do* after all that is written
31. *to perform* the words of the covenant
35: 6. *that* (they) *may do* according to the word
16. *to keep* the passover,
Ezr. 7:10. to seek the law of the Lord, *and to do* (it),
10: 5. *that they should do* according to
12. As thou hast said, so *must we do*.
Neh. 2:12. what my God had put in my heart *to do*
4: 6(3:38). the people had a mind *to work*.
8(2). fight against Jerusalem, and to hinder it. (lit. *and to make* an error to it)
5:12. *that they should do* according to
6: 2. they thought *to do* me mischief.
8:12. *and to make* great mirth,
15. branches of thick trees, *to make* booths,
9:24. *that they might do* with them
28. they *did* evil again (marg. returned *to do* evil) before thee:
10:29(30). observe *and do* all the commandments
12:27. *to keep* the dedication with gladness,
13: 7. *in preparing* him a chamber
27. Shall we then hearken unto you *to do*
Est. 1: 8. *that they should do* according to
15. What *shall we do* (marg. What *to do*) unto the queen
3:11. *to do* with them as it seemeth good
5: 5. *that he may do* as Esther hath said.
Est. 5: 8. *and to perform* (marg. *do*) my request,
6: 6. What *shall be done* (lit. *to do*) unto the
— To whom would the king delight *to do*
7: 5. that durst presume in his heart *to do* so?
9:13. *to do* to morrow also according
17, 18. *and made* it a day of feasting
22. *that they should make* them days of
23. the Jews undertook *to do*
Job 23: 9. On the left hand, *where he doth work*,
28:25. *To make* the weight for the winds;
26. *When he made* a decree for the rain,
42: 8. lest *I deal* (lit. that not *to do*) with you (after your) folly,
Ps. 40: 8(9). I delight *to do* thy will, O my God:
101: 3. I hate *the work* of them that turn aside;
103:18. remember his commandments *to do them*.
109:16. he remembered not *to shew* mercy,
119:112. *to perform* (marg. *do*) thy statutes alway,
126. (It is) time for (thee), Lord, *to work*:
126: 2. The Lord hath *done* great things (lit. magnified *to do*)
3. The Lord hath *done* great things (lit. *id.*)
143:10. Teach me *to do* thy will;
149: 7. *To execute* vengeance upon the heathen,
9. *To execute* upon them the judgment
Pro. 2:14. Who rejoice *to do* evil,
3:27. when it is in the power of thine hand *to do*
10:23. (It is) as sport to a fool *to do* mischief:
16:12. to kings *to commit* wickedness:
21: 3. *To do* justice and judgment
7. they refuse *to do* judgment.
15. joy to the just *to do* judgment:
25. his hands refuse *to labour*.
23: 5. (riches) *certainly* make (lit. *making* make) themselves wings;
Ecc. 2:11. the labour that I had laboured *to do*:
3:12. for (a man) to rejoice, *and to do* good
5: 1(4:17). they consider not *that they do* evil.
8:11. of the sons of men is fully set...*to do* evil
9:10. Whatsoever thy hand findeth *to do*,
12:12. of *making* many books
Isa. 5: 2. he looked *that it should bring forth*
4. What *could have been done* more
— when I looked *that it should bring forth*
7:22. the abundance of milk (that) *they shall give*
28:21. *that he may do* his work,
30: 1. *that take* counsel, but not of me;
32: 6. *to practise* hypocrisy,
56: 2. keepeth his hand *from doing*
58:13. (from) *doing* thy pleasure on my holy day;
— *not doing* thine own ways,
63:12. *to make* himself an everlasting name?
14. *to make* thyself a glorious name.
64: 3(2). *When thou didst* terrible things
Jer. 1:12. I will hasten my word *to perform it*.
3: 7. after *she had done* all these (things),
7: 5. if ye *throughly* execute (lit. *executing* execute) judgment
10. We are delivered *to do* all these
13. *ye have done* all these works,
18. *to make* cakes to the queen of heaven,
11: 8. which I commanded (them) *to do*;
15. (seeing) *she hath wrought* lewdness
16:12. ye have *done* worse (lit. ye have done ill *in doing*) than your fathers;
17: 8. neither shall cease *from yielding*
24. *to do* no work therein;
18: 4. seemed good to the potter *to make*
6. O house of Israel, cannot I *do*
8. the evil that I thought *to do*
22: 4. if ye do this thing *indeed*, (lit. *doing* ye do)
17. and for violence, *to do* (it).
23:20. until *he have executed*,
26: 3. the evil, which I purpose *to do*
30:24. until *he have done* (it),
32:23. all that thou commandedst them *to do*:
35. *that they should do* this abomination,
36: 3. the evil which I purpose *to do*
44:17. we will *certainly* do (lit. *doing* will do)
25. We will *surely* perform (lit. *performing* will perform)
— and *surely* perform (lit. *performing* perform) your vows.
Eze. 5:15. *when I shall execute* judgments
6:10. *that I would do* this evil
8:17. *that they commit* the abominations
15: 3. wood be taken thereof *to do* any work?

Eze.16: 5. *to do* any of these unto thee,
30. *seeing thou doest* all these (things),
17: 8. *that it might bring forth* branches,
18: 9. kept my judgments, *to deal* truly;
20:21. neither kept my judgments *to do* them,
44. *when I have wrought* with you
23:21. *in bruising* thy teats by the Egyptians
30. *I will do* these (things) unto thee,
25:12. *hath dealt* against the house of Judah
15. the Philistines *have dealt* by revenge,
27: 5. taken cedars from Lebanon *to make* masts
28:22. *when I shall have executed* judgments
26. *when I have executed* judgments
31:11. shall *surely* deal (marg. *doing* he shall do)
33:15. without *committing* iniquity;
36:37. be enquired of by the house of Israel, *to do* (it)
Dan11: 6. *to make* an agreement:
Joel 2:20. *hath done* great things. (marg. magnified *to do*)
21. the Lord will *do* great things. (lit. magnified *to do*)
Am. 3:10. they know not *to do* right,
Jon. 3:10. the evil, that he had said *that he would do*
Mic. 6: 8. *to do* justly, and to love mercy,
Hab. 2:18. trusteth therein, *to make* dumb idols?
Zec. 1: 6. Like as the Lord of hosts thought *to do*
21(2:4). What come these *to do?*

KAL.—*Imperative.*

Gen 6:14. *Make* thee an ark of gopher wood;
16: 6. *do* to her as it pleaseth thee.
18: 6. *and make* cakes upon the hearth.
19: 8. *and do ye* to them as (is) good in your
24:12. *and shew* kindness unto my master
27: 4, 7. *And make* me savoury meat,
31:16. whatsoever God hath said unto thee, *do.*
35: 1. *and make* there an altar unto God,
42:18. This *do*, and live;
43:11. If (it must be) so now, *do* this;
45:17. Say unto thy brethren, This *do ye;*
19. Now thou art commanded, this *do ye;*
Ex. 5:16. they say to us, *Make* brick:
25:19. *And make* one cherub on the one end,
40. look *that thou make* (them) after
28:42. *And thou shalt make* them linen breeches
32: 1. *make* us gods, which shall go before us;
23. they said unto me, *Make* us gods,
Lev. 9: 7. *and offer* thy sin offering,
— *and offer* the offering of the people,
Nu. 4:19. But thus *do* unto them,
8:12. *and thou shalt offer* the one (for) a sin offering,
10: 2. *Make* thee two trumpets of silver;
16: 6. This *do;* Take you censers,
21: 8. *Make* thee a fiery serpent,
Jos. 5: 2. *Make* thee sharp knives,
9:25. as it seemeth good...to do unto us, *do.*
Jud. 9:48. (and) *do* as I (have done).
10:15. *do* thou unto us whatsoever seemeth good
11:36. *do* to me according to that which
19:24. *and do* with them what seemeth good
Ru. 4:11. *and do thou* worthily in Ephratah,
1Sa. 1:23. *Do* what seemeth thee good;
6: 7. *therefore make* a new cart,
10: 7. *do* as occasion serve thee;
14: 7. *Do* all that (is) in thine heart:
36. *Do* whatsoever seemeth good
40. *Do* what seemeth good
2Sa. 3:18. Now then *do* (it):
7: 3. *do* all that (is) in thine heart;
25. *and do* as thou hast said.
13: 7. *and dress* him meat.
19:27(28). *do therefore* (what is) good
37(38). *and do* to him what shall seem good
1K. 2:31. *Do* as he hath said,
17:13. *do* as thou hast said: but *make* me thereof
18:25. Choose you one bullock...*and dress* (it)
20:24. And *do* this thing,
22:22. go forth, *and do* so.
2K. 10: 5. *do* thou (that which is) good
18:31. *Make* (an agreement) with me
23:21. *Keep* the passover unto the Lord
1Ch 17: 2. *Do* all that (is) in thine heart;
23. *and do* as thou hast said.
22:16. Arise (therefore), *and be doing,*
28:10. be strong, *and do* (it).
1Ch 28:20. strong and of good courage, *and do* (it):
2Ch 18:21. go out, *and do* (even) so.
19: 7. take heed *and do* (it):
11. *Deal* courageously, (marg. Take courage *and do*)
25: 8. But if thou wilt go, *do* (it),
Ezr. 10: 4. be of good courage, *and do* (it).
11. *and do* his pleasure:
Est. 6:10. *and do* even so to Mordecai the Jew,
Ps. 34:14(15). Depart from evil, *and do* good;
37: 3. Trust in the Lord, *and do* good;
27. Depart from evil, *and do* good;
83: 9(10). *Do* unto them as (unto) the
86:17. *Shew* me a token for good;
109:21. *do* thou for me, O God
119:124. *Deal* with thy servant according unto
Pro. 6: 3. *Do* this now, my son,
20:18. with good advice *make* war.
Ecc. 9:10. Whatsoever thy hand findeth to do, *do* (it)
Isa. 16: 3. Take counsel, *execute* judgment;
36:16. *Make* (an agreement) with me
56: 1. Keep ye judgment, *and do* justice:
Jer. 6:26. *make* thee mourning, (as for) an only
14: 7. *do thou* (it) for thy name's sake:
18:23. *deal* (thus) with them in the time of
22: 3. *Execute ye* judgment and righteousness,
26:14. *do* with me as seemeth good
27: 2. *Make* thee bonds and yokes,
39:12. but *do* unto him even as he shall say
46:19. *furnish* thyself to go into captivity:
50:15. as she hath done, *do* unto her.
21. *and do* according to all that I have
29. according to all that she hath done, *do*
Eze. 7:23. *Make* a chain: for the land
12: 3. son of man, *prepare* thee stuff
18:31. *and make you* a new heart
20:19. keep my judgments, *and do* them;
45: 9. *execute* judgment and justice,
Dan 1:13. as thou seest, *deal* with thy servants.
9:19. O Lord, hearken *and do;*
Hag 2: 4. be strong, all ye people...*and work*·
Zec. 7: 9. and *shew* mercy and compassions

KAL.—*Future.*

Gen 1: 7. *And* God *made* the firmament,
16. *And* God *made* two great lights;
25. *And* God *made* the beast of the earth
26. God said, *Let us make* man
2:18. *I will make* him an help
3: 7. *and made* themselves aprons.
21. *also...did* the Lord God *make* coats
6:14. rooms *shalt thou make*
15. (the fashion) which *thou shalt make* it
16. A window *shalt thou make* to the ark,
— (with) lower, second, and third (stories) *shalt thou make it.*
22. *Thus did* Noah; according to all that
7: 5. *And* Noah *did* according unto all
11: 4. *and let us make* us a name,
12: 2. *And I will make of thee* a great nation,
18: 5. So *do*, as thou hast said.
25. *Shall* not the Judge of all the earth *do*
29. *I will* not *do* (it) for forty's sake.
30. *I will* not *do* (it), if I find thirty there.
19: 3. *and he made* them a feast,
8. only unto these men *do* nothing;
20:13. thy kindness which *thou shalt shew*
21: 1. *and* the Lord *did* unto Sarah as he had
8. *and* Abraham *made* a great feast
23. *thou shalt do* unto me,
22:12. neither *do thou* any thing unto him:
26:29. That *thou wilt do* us no hurt,
30. *And he made* them a feast,
27: 9. *and I will make* them savoury meat
14. *and* his mother *made* savoury meat,
31. *he also had made* savoury meat,
37. and what *shall I do* now unto thee, my son?
29:22. the men of the place, *and made* a feast.
28. *And* Jacob *did* so,
30:30. when *shall* I *provide* for mine own house
31. if *thou wilt do* this thing for me,
31:43. what *can I do* this day
46. they took stones, *and made* an heap:
34:31. *Should he deal with* our sister as with
35: 3. *and I will make* there an altar
39: 9. how then *can I do* this great wickedness,

Gen40:20. *that he made* a feast unto all his servants :
41:34. *Let* Pharaoh *do* (this),
47. *And*...the earth *brought forth* by handfuls.
55. Joseph ; what he saith to you, *do*.
42:20. *And they did* so.
25. *and* thus *did he* unto them.
43:17. *And* the man *did* as Joseph bade ;
44: 2. *And he did* according to the word
45:21. *And* the children of Israel *did* so:
47:30. I *will do* as thou hast said.
50:10. *and he made* a mourning for his father
12. *And* his sons *did* unto him according
Ex. 1:21. *that he made* them houses.
3:20. my wonders which *I will do*
4:15. will teach you what *ye shall do.*
17. wherewith *thou shalt do* signs.
30. *and did* the signs in the sight of the
5: 9. *that they may labour* therein ;
15. Wherefore *dealest thou* thus with
6: 1. Now shalt thou see what *I will do*
7: 6. *And* Moses and Aaron *did* as the Lord commanded
10. *and they did* so as the Lord had
11. *now* the magicians...they also *did*
20. *And* Moses and Aaron *did* so,
22. *And* the magicians of Egypt *did* so
8: 7(3). *And* the magicians *did* so
13(9), 31(27). *And* the Lord *did* according to
17(13). *And they did* so ; for Aaron
18(14). *And* the magicians *did* so
24(20). *And* the Lord *did* so ;
9: 5. To morrow the Lord *shall do* this
6. *And* the Lord *did* that thing
12:12. *I will execute* judgment:
28. *and did* as the Lord had commanded
47. All the congregation of Israel *shall keep* (marg. *do*) it.
50. *Thus did* all the children of Israel;
14: 4. I (am) the Lord. *And they did* so.
13. salvation of the Lord, which *he will shew*
15:26. and *wilt do* that which is right
16:17. *And* the children of Israel *did* so,
17: 4. What *shall I do* unto this people?
6. *And* Moses *did* so in the sight of the
10. *So* Joshua *did* as Moses had said
18:20. the work that *they must do.*
23. If *thou shalt do* this thing,
24. *and did* all that he had said.
19: 8. All that the Lord hath spoken *we will do.*
20: 4. *Thou shalt* not *make* unto thee
10. (in it) *thou shalt* not *do* any work,
23. *Ye shall* not *make* with me gods
— neither *shall ye make* unto you
24. An altar of earth *thou shalt make*
25. if *thou wilt make* me an altar
21: 9. *he shall deal* with her after the manner
11. if *he do* not these three unto her,
22:30(29). Likewise *shalt thou do* with thine
23:11. *thou shalt deal* with thy vineyard,
12. Six days *thou shalt do* thy work,
24. nor *do* after their works:
24: 3. which the Lord hath said *will we do.*
7. All that the Lord hath said *will we do,*
25: 9. even so *shall ye make* (it).
18. (of) beaten work *shalt thou make* them,
19. *shall ye make* the cherubims
29. (of) pure gold *shalt thou make* them.
39. (Of) a talent of pure gold *shall he make* it,
26: 1. *thou shalt make* the tabernacle
— of cunning work *shalt thou make*
4. likewise *shalt thou make* in the uttermost
5. Fifty loops *shalt thou make* in the one curtain, and fifty loops *shalt thou make*
7. eleven curtains *shalt thou make.*
17. thus *shalt thou make* for all the boards
19. *thou shalt make* forty sockets
22. *thou shalt make* six boards.
23. two boards *shalt thou make*
29. and *make* their rings (of) gold
31. with cherubims *shall* it *be made:* (lit. *shall he make* it)
27: 3. all the vessels thereof *thou shalt make*
8. with boards *shalt thou make* it: as it was shewed...so *shall they make* (it).
28: 4. the garments which *they shall make;*
11. *thou shalt make* them to be set in ouches
14. (of) wreathen work *shalt thou make* them,

Ex. 28:15. the work of the ephod *thou shalt make it:*
— (of) fine twined linen, *shalt thou make* it.
39. *thou shalt make* the girdle (of)
40. *thou shalt make* coats,
— and bonnets *shalt thou make* for them,
29: 1. *thou shalt do* unto them
2. (of) wheaten flour *shalt thou make* them.
36. *thou shalt offer* every day a bullock
38. *thou shalt offer* upon the altar;
39. The one lamb *thou shalt offer*
—, 41. the other lamb *thou shalt offer*
41. *shalt do* thereto according
30: 1. (of) shittim wood *shalt thou make* it.
4. two golden rings *shalt thou make*
— upon the two sides of it *shalt thou make*
32. neither *shall ye make* (any other) like it,
37. the perfume which *thou shalt make, ye shall* not *make* to yourselves
38. Whosoever *shall make* like unto that
31:11. that I have commanded thee *shall they do.*
32: 4. *after he had made it* a molten calf:
10. *and I will make* of thee a great nation.
28. *And* the children of Levi *did* according
31. *and have made* them gods of gold.
33: 5. that I may know what *to do* unto thee.
17. *I will do* this thing also
34:10. before all thy people *I will do* marvels,
17. *Thou shalt make* thee no molten gods.
22. *thou shalt observe* the feast of weeks,
35:10. *and make* all that the Lord hath
36: 6. *Let* neither man nor woman *make* any
8. *And...made* ten curtains (of) fine twined
11. *And he made* loops of blue on the edge
13. *And he made* fifty taches of gold,
14. *And he made* curtains (of) goats' (hair)
17. *And he made* fifty loops upon
18. *And he made* fifty taches (of) brass
19. *And he made* a covering for the tent
20, 23. *And he made* boards for the tabernacle
31. *And he made* bars of shittim wood ;
33. *And he made* the middle bar
35. *And he made* a vail (of) blue,
36. *And he made* thereunto four pillars
37. *And he made* an hanging for the
37: 1. *And* Bezaleel *made* the ark
2. *and made* a crown of gold to it
4. *And he made* staves (of) shittim wood,
6. *And he made* the mercy seat
7. *And he made* two cherubims
10. *And he made* the table (of) shittim wood:
11. *and made* thereunto a crown
12. *Also he made* thereunto a border
— *and made* a crown of gold for the border
15, 28. *And he made* the staves (of) shittim
16. *And he made* the vessels
17. *And he made* the candlestick
23. *And he made* his seven lamps,
25. *And he made* the incense altar
26. *also he made* unto it a crown
29. *And he made* the holy anointing oil,
38: 1. *And he made* the altar of burnt offering
2. *And he made* the horns thereof
3. *And he made* all the vessels of the altar,
4. *And he made* for the altar a brasen grate
6. *And he made* the staves (of) shittim wood,
8. *And he made* the laver (of) brass,
9. *And he made* the court:
30. *And* therewith *he made* the sockets to the door
39: 1. *and made* the holy garments for Aaron ;
2. *And he made* the ephod
6. *And they wrought* onyx stones
8. *And he made* the breastplate
15. *And they made* upon the breastplate
16. *And they made* two ouches (of) gold,
19. *And they made* two rings of gold,
20. *And they made* two (other) golden rings,
22. *And he made* the robe
24. *And they made* upon the hems
25. *And they made* bells (of) pure gold,
27. *And they made* coats (of) fine linen
30. *And they made* the plate of the holy
32. *and* the children of Israel *did*
40:16. *Thus did* Moses: according to all that
Lev. 4:20. so *shall he do* with this:
5:10. *he shall offer* the second (for) a burnt
6: 3(5:22). any of all these that a man *doeth,*

Lev. 6. 7(5:26). any thing of all that *he hath done*
22(15). priest of his sons...*shall offer* it:
8: 4. *And* Moses *did* as the Lord commanded
36. *So* Aaron and his sons *did* all things
9: 6. the Lord commanded that *ye should do:*
16. *and offered it* according to the manner.
10: 7. *And they did* according to the word
16:16. so *shall he do* for the tabernacle
29. afflict your souls, and *do* no work
34. *And he did* as the Lord commanded
18: 3. After the doings of the land...*shall ye* not *do:*
— whither I bring you, *shall ye* not *do:*
4. *Ye shall do* my judgments,
5. which if a man *do*, he shall live in them:
26. and *shall* not *commit* (any) of these
29. whosoever *shall commit* any of these
19: 4. nor *make* to yourselves molten gods:
15, 35. *Ye shall do* no unrighteousness
22:23. that *mayest thou offer*
24. neither *shall ye make* (any offering)
23: 3. *ye shall do* no work (therein):
7, 8, 21, 25, 35, 36. *ye shall do* no servile work
28. *ye shall do* no work in that same day:
30. whatsoever soul (it be) *that doeth* any
31. *Ye shall do* no manner of work:
26: 1. *Ye shall make* you no idols
14. and *will* not *do* all these commandments;
16. I also *will do* this unto you;
Nu. 1:54 & 2:34. *And* the children of Israel *did*
5: 4. *And* the children of Israel *did* so,
6. When a man or woman *shall commit*
6:17. And *he shall offer* the ram
21. *he must do* after the law
8: 3. *And* Aaron *did so;*
7. thus *shalt thou do* unto them,
20. *And* Moses, and Aaron,...*did* to the
26. Thus *shalt thou do* unto the Levites
9: 2. *Let* the children of Israel *also keep*
3. *ye shall keep* it in his appointed season:
— to all the ceremonies thereof, *shall ye keep*
5. *And they kept* the passover
11. at even *they shall keep* it,
12. of the passover *they shall keep* it.
14. the manner thereof, so *shall he do:*
10: 2. of a whole piece *shalt thou make* them:
14:12. *and will make* of thee a greater nation
28. as ye have spoken...so *will I do*
35. *I will* surely *do* it
15: 5. a drink offering *shalt thou prepare*
6. a ram, *thou shalt prepare*
8. when *thou preparest* a bullock
12. the number that *ye shall prepare*, so *shall ye do* to every one
13. *shall do* these things after this manner,
14. as *ye do*, so *he shall do.*
22. if ye have erred, and not *observed*
30. the soul *that doeth* (ought)
17:11(26). *And* Moses *did* (so): as the Lord
20:27. *And* Moses *did* as the Lord commanded:
21: 9. *And* Moses *made* a serpent of brass,
22:17. *I will do* whatsoever thou sayest
20. the word which I shall say....that *shalt thou do.*
23: 2. *And* Balak *did* as Balaam had spoken;
19. hath he said, and *shall he* not *do* (it)?
26. All that the Lord speaketh, that *I must do?*
30. *And* Balak *did* as Balaam had said,
24:14. advertise thee what this people *shall do*
27:22. *And* Moses *did* as the Lord commanded
28: 4. The one lamb *shalt thou offer* in the morning, and the other lamb *shalt thou offer*
8. the other lamb *shalt thou offer*
— *thou shalt offer* (it), a sacrifice
18. *ye shall do* no manner of servile work
20. three tenth deals *shall ye offer*
21. A several tenth deal *shalt thou offer*
23. *Ye shall offer* these beside
24. After this manner *ye shall offer*
25, 26. *ye shall do* no servile work.
31. *Ye shall offer* (them) beside
29: 1, 12, 35. *ye shall do* no servile work:
7. *ye shall* not *do* any work (therein):
39. These (things) *ye shall do* (marg. or, *offer*)
30: 2(3). *he shall do* according to all
31:31. *And* Moses and Eleazar the priest *did*
32:20. If *ye will do* this thing,
Nu. 32:23. if *ye will* not *do* so,
24. *do* that which hath proceeded
25. Thy servants *will do* as my lord
31. As the Lord hath said...so *will we do.*
33:56. *I shall do* unto you, as I thought to do
Deu 1:18. all the things which *ye should do.*
44. chased you, as bees *do,*
3:21. so *shall* the Lord *do* unto all the kingdoms
24. that *can do* according to thy works,
5: 8. *Thou shalt* not *make* thee (any) graven
14. *thou shalt* not *do* any work,
7: 5. thus *shall ye deal* with them;
19. so *shall* the Lord thy God *do*
9:14. *and I will make* of thee a nation mightier
10: 3. *And I made* an ark (of) shittim wood,
12: 4. *Ye shall* not *do* so unto the Lord
8. *Ye shall* not *do* after all (the things)
14. there *thou shalt do* all that I command
25. *thou shalt do* (that which is) right
28. when *thou doest* (that which is) good
30. *even* so *will I do* likewise.
31. *Thou shalt* not *do* so unto the Lord
14:29. the work of thine hand which *thou doest.*
15: 1. *thou shalt make* a release.
17. *thou shalt do* likewise.
18. shall bless thee in all that *thou doest.*
16: 8. *thou shalt do* no work
13. *Thou shalt observe* the feast of tabernacles
21. which *thou shalt make* thee.
17: 2. or woman, that *hath wrought* wickedness
11. which they shall tell thee, *thou shalt do:*
12. the man that *will do* presumptuously,
20:15. Thus *shalt thou do* unto all the cities
21: 9. *thou shalt do* (that which is) right
22: 3. In like manner *shalt thou do* with his ass; and so *shalt thou do* with his raiment;
— hast found, *shalt thou do* likewise:
12. *Thou shalt make* thee fringes
26. unto the damsel *thou shalt do* nothing;
27:15. the man *that maketh* (any) graven...image,
28:20. that thou settest thine hand unto for *to do,* (marg. which *thou wouldest do*)
29: 9(8). that ye may prosper in all that *ye do.*
30:12, 13. that we may hear it, *and do* it?
31:29. *ye will do* evil in the sight of the Lord,
34: 9. *and did* as the Lord commanded Moses.
Jos. 1:16. All that thou commandest us *we will do,*
3: 5. to morrow the Lord *will do* wonders
4: 8. *And* the children of Israel *did* so
5: 3. *And* Joshua *made* him sharp knives,
10. *and kept* the passover
15. *And* Joshua *did* so.
6: 3. Thus *shalt thou do* six days.
7: 9. what *wilt thou do* unto thy great name?
8: 8. the commandment of the Lord *shall ye do.*
9: 4. *They did work* wilily, and went
15. *And* Joshua *made* peace with them,
20. This *we will do* to them;
24. *and have done* this thing.
26. *And* so *did he* unto them,
10:23. *And they did* so,
25. thus *shall* the Lord *do*
28. *and he did* to the king of Makkedah
30. *but did* unto the king thereof
11: 9. *And* Joshua *did* unto them as the Lord
22:26. *Let us* now *prepare* to build
Jud. 2:11 & 3:7. *And* the children of Israel *did* evil
3:16. *But* Ehud *made* him a dagger
6: 1. *And* the children of Israel *did* evil
19. Gideon went in, *and made ready* a kid,
20. pour out the broth. *And he did* so.
27. *and did* as the Lord had said
— *that he did* (it) by night.
40. *And* God *did so* that night:
7:17. Look on me, and *do* likewise:
— as *I do*, so *shall ye do.*
8:27. *And* Gideon *made* an ephod
9:27. *and made* merry, and went into the house
11:10. if *we do* not so according
39. her father, *who* (lit. *and he*) *did* with her (according) to
13: 8. teach us what *we shall do*
15. *until we shall have made ready* a kid
16. if *thou wilt offer* a burnt offering,
14:10. *and* Samson *made* there a feast; for so *used* the young men *to do.*
15: 7. Though *ye have done* this,

Jud.17: 4. *who made thereof* a graven image
5. *and made* an ephod,
6. (but) every man *did* (that which was) right
18:14. consider what *ye have to do.*
19:23. *do* not this folly.
24. unto this man *do* not so vile a thing.
20: 9. the thing which *we will do*
21: 7. How *shall we do* for wives for them
11. the thing that *ye shall do,*
16. How *shall we do* for wives for them
23. *And* the children of Benjamin *did* so,
25. every man *did* (that which was) right
Ru. 1: 8. the Lord *deal* kindly with you,
17. the Lord *do so* to me,
3: 4. he will tell thee what *thou shalt do.*
5. All that thou sayest unto me *I will do.*
6. *and did* according to all that her mother in law bade
11. *I will do* to thee all that thou requirest:
1Sa. 1: 7. And (as) *he did* so year by year,
2:14. So *they did* in Shiloh
19. his mother *made* him a little coat,
22. heard all that his sons *did*
23. Why *do ye* such things?
35. (that) *shall do* according to (that)
3:17. God *do* so to thee, and more also,
18. *let him do* what seemeth him good.
5: 8. What *shall we do* with the ark
6: 2. What *shall we do* to the ark
10. *And* the men *did* so;
10: 2. What *shall I do* for my son?
8. and shew thee what *thou shalt do.*
13:19. Lest the Hebrews *make* (them) swords
14: 6. it may be that the Lord *will work* for us:
32. (כתיב) *And* the people *flew* upon the spoil,
44. God *do so* and more also:
48. *And he gathered* an host, (marg. or, *wrought* mightily)
15:19. *and didst* evil in the sight of the Lord?
16: 3. I will shew thee what *thou shalt do:*
4. *And* Samuel *did* that which the Lord
17:25. and *make* his father's house free
19: 5. *and* the Lord *wrought* a great salvation
20: 2. my father *will do* nothing
4. *I will even do* (it) for thee.
13. The Lord *do* so and much more
14. *thou shalt* not only while yet I live *shew* me
22: 3. till I know what God *will do* for me.
24: 6(7). The Lord forbid that *I should do* this
25:17. know and consider what *thou wilt do;*
22. and more also *do* God unto the enemies of
28. the Lord *will* certainly *make*
30. when the Lord *shall have done* to my lord
26:25. *thou shalt* both *do* great (things),
28: 2. thou shalt know what thy servant *can do.*
15. make known unto me what *I shall do.*
17. *And* the Lord *hath done* to him,
29: 7. that thou displease not (marg. *thou do* not evil in the eyes of) the lords
30:23. *Ye shall* not *do* so,
2Sa. 2: 6. the Lord *shew* kindness and truth
— I also *will requite* you this kindness,
3: 8. *do shew* kindness this day unto the house of Saul
9. So *do* God to Abner,
— even so *I do* to him;
20. *And* David *made* Abner and the men... a feast.
35. So *do* God to me, and more also,
5:25. *And* David *did* so, as the Lord had
7:11. *he will make* thee an house.
8:13. *And* David *gat* (him) a name
9: 1. *that I may shew* him kindness for Jonathan's sake?
3. *that I may shew* the kindness of God
7. *I will* surely *shew* thee kindness
11. so *shall* thy servant *do.*
10: 2. *I will shew* kindness unto Hanun
12. the Lord *do* that which seemeth him good.
11:11. *I will* not *do* this thing.
12: 4. *and dressed it* for the man that was come
12. I *will do* this thing before all Israel
31. thus *did he* unto all the cities
13:12. *do* not *thou* this folly.
29. *And* the servants of Absalom *did*
14:15. it may be that the king *will perform*

2Sa.15: 1. *that* Absalom *prepared* him chariots
6. *And* on this manner *did* Absalom
26. *let him do* to me as seemeth good
16:20. Give counsel among you what *we shall do.*
17: 6. *shall we do* (after) his saying?
18: 4. What seemeth you best *I will do.*
19:13(14). God *do* so to me, and more also,
38(39). I *will do* to him that which shall
—(—). require of me, (that) *will I do* for
21: 3. What *shall I do* for you?
4. (that) *will I do* for you.
14. *and they performed* all that the king
23:10, 12. *and* the Lord *wrought* a great victory
24:12. *that I may do* (it) unto thee.
1K. 1: 5. *and he prepared* him chariots and horsemen,
30. so *will I* certainly *do* this day.
2: 3. mayest prosper in all that *thou doest,*
7. *shew* kindness unto the sons of Barzillai
9. what *thou oughtest to do* unto him;
23. God *do* so to me, and more also,
38. so *will* thy servant *do.*
3:15. *and offered* peace offerings, *and made* a feast to all his servants.
5: 8(22). I *will do* all thy desire
9(23). thou *shalt accomplish* my desire,
6: 4. *And* for the house *he made* windows
5. *and he made* chambers round about:
12. and *execute* my judgments, and keep all
23. *And* within the oracle *he made* two
7: 8. Solomon *made* also an house for Pharaoh's
14. *and wrought* all his work.
18. *And he made* the pillars,
23. *And he made* a molten sea,
27. *And he made* ten bases
38. *Then made he* ten lavers
40. *And* Hiram *made* the lavers, and the
48. *And* Solomon *made* all the vessels
8:65. *And* at that time Solomon *held* a feast,
10:12. *And* the king *made* of the almug trees pillars
16. *And* king Solomon *made* two hundred
18. *Moreover* the king *made* a great throne
11: 6. *And* Solomon *did* evil in the sight of the
12. in thy days *I will* not *do* it
12:28. *and made* two calves (of) gold,
31. *And he made* an house of high places, *and made* priests of the lowest
32. *And* Jeroboam *ordained* a feast
33. *and ordained* a feast unto the children of
13:33. *but made* again of the lowest of the people
14: 4. *And* Jeroboam's wife *did* so,
9. *and made thee* other gods,
22. *And* Judah *did* evil in the sight of the
27. *And* king Rehoboam *made* in their stead
15:11. *And* Asa *did* (that which was) right
26, 34. *And he did* evil in the sight of the
16:25. *But* Omri *wrought* evil
30. *And* Ahab the son of Omri *did* evil
33. *And* Ahab *made* a grove;
17: 5. he went *and did* according unto
13. after *make* for thee and for thy son.
15. she went *and did* according to the saying
18:23. I *will dress* the other bullock,
26. took the bullock...*and they dressed* (it),
32. *and he made* a trench about the altar,
19: 2. So *let* the gods *do* (to me),
20: 9. didst send for to thy servant at the first *I will do:*
10. The gods *do* so unto me,
22. and see what *thou doest:*
25. he hearkened unto their voice, *and did* so.
21: 7. *Dost* thou now *govern* the kingdom
11. *And* the men of his city,...*did* as Jezebel
22:11. *And* Zedekiah...*made* him horns
52(53). *And he did* evil in the sight of the
2K. 2: 9. Ask what *I shall do* for thee,
3: 2. *And he wrought* evil in the sight of the
4: 2. What *shall I do* for thee?
10. *Let us make* a little chamber,
5:13. *wouldest thou* not *have done* (it)?
17. thy servant *will* henceforth *offer*
6: 2. *and let us make* us a place there,
15. Alas, my master! how *shall we do?*
31. God *do* so and more also to me,
8: 2. the woman arose, *and did* after the saying
12. I know the evil that *thou wilt do*
13. (is) thy servant a dog, that *he should do*

2K. 8:18. *and he did* evil in the sight of the Lord.
27. *and did* evil in the sight of the Lord,
10: 5. *will do* all that thou shalt bid us;
11: 5. This (is) the thing that *ye shall do;*
9. *And* the captains over the hundreds *did*
12: 2(3). *And* Jehoash *did* (that which was) right
13: 2, 11. *And he did* (that which was) evil in
14: 3. *And he did* (that which was) right
24. *And he did* (that which was) evil
15: 3, 34. *And he did* (that which was) right
9, 18, 24, 28. *And he did* (that which was)
16:16. *Thus did* Urijah the priest,
17: 2. *And he did* (that which was) evil
11. *and wrought* wicked things
12. *Ye shall* not *do* this thing.
16. *and made* them molten images, (even) two calves, *and made* a grove,
32. *and made* unto themselves of the lowest
18: 3. *And he did* (that which was) right
19:31. the zeal of the Lord (of hosts) *shall do*
20: 9. the Lord *will do* the thing that
21: 2, 20. *And he did* (that which was) evil
3. he reared up altars for Baal, *and made* a
22: 2. *And he did* (that which was) right
23:19. *and did* to them according to
32, 37 & 24:9, 19. *And he did* (that which was) evil
1Ch 5:19. *And they made* war with the Hagarites,
12:32. to know what Israel *ought to do;*
14:16. David *therefore did* as God commanded
15: 1. *And* (David) *made* him houses
19: 2. *I will shew* kindness unto Hanun
13. *let* the Lord *do* (that which is) good
20: 3. so *dealt* David with all the cities
21:10. *that I may do* (it) unto thee.
23. *and let* my lord the king *do*
2Ch 2:18(17). *And he set* threescore and ten
3: 8. *And he made* the most holy house,
10. *And* in the most holy house *he made* two
14. *And he made* the vail (of) blue, and
15. *Also he made* before the house two pillars
16. *And he made* chains,
— *and made* an hundred pomegranates,
4: 1. *Moreover he made* an altar of brass,
2. *Also he made* a molten sea
6. *He made also* ten lavers,
7. *And he made* ten candlesticks
8. *He made also* ten tables,
— *And he made* an hundred basons of gold.
9. *Furthermore he made* the court
11. *And* Huram *made* the pots,
18. *Thus* Solomon *made* all these vessels
19. *And* Solomon *made* all the vessels
7: 8. *Also*...Solomon *kept* the feast seven days,
9. *And* in the eighth day *they made* a solemn
9:11. *And* the king *made* (of) the algum trees
15. *And* king Solomon *made* two hundred targets
17. *Moreover* the king *made* a great throne of
12:10. Instead of which (lit. *And* instead of them) king Rehoboam *made* shields
14. *And he did* evil, because he prepared not
13: 9. *and have made you* priests after the manner
14: 2(1). *And* Asa *did* (that which was) good
18:10. *And* Zedekiah...*had made* him horns
19: 9. Thus *shall ye do* in the fear of the Lord,
10. this *do*, and ye shall not trespass.
20:12. know we what *to do:* (lit. *we shall do*)
36. *and they made* the ships in Ezion-gaber.
21: 6. *and he wrought* (that which was) evil
22: 4. *Wherefore he did* evil in the sight of the
23: 4. This (is) the thing that *ye shall do;*
8. *So* the Levites and all Judah *did*
24: 2. *And* Joash *did* (that which was) right
8. *And*...*they made* a chest,
13. *So* the workmen *wrought,*
14. *whereof were made* (lit. *and they made it*) vessels
25: 2 & 26:4. *And he did* (that which was) right
26:15. *And he made* in Jerusalem engines,
27: 2. *And he did* (that which was) right
28:24. *and he made* him altars in every
29: 2. *And he did* (that which was) right
30:21. *And* the children of Israel...*kept* the feast
23. *and they kept* (other) seven days
31:20. *And* thus *did* Hezekiah throughout all Judah, *and wrought* (that which was)

2Ch 32: 5. *and made* darts and shields in abundance.
33: 2. *But did* (that which was) evil
3. altars for Baalim, *and made* groves,
22. *But he did* (that which was) evil
34: 2. *And he did* (that which was) right
32. *And* the inhabitants of Jerusalem *did*
35: 1. *Moreover* Josiah *kept* a passover
17. *And* the children of Israel...*kept* the
36: 5, 9, 12. *and he did* (that which was) evil
Ezr. 3: 4. *They kept also* the feast of tabernacles,
6:19. *And* the children of the captivity *kept*
22. *And kept* the feast of unleavened bread
10:16. *And* the children of the captivity *did* so.
Neh. 5:12. so *will we do* as thou sayest.
13. *And* the people *did* according to this
6:13. I should be afraid, *and do* so,
8:16. *and made* themselves booths,
17. *And* all the congregation...*made* booths,
18. *And they kept* the feast seven days;
9:10. *So didst thou get* thee a name,
18. *and had wrought* great provocations;
26. *and they wrought* great provocations.
29. which if a man *do*, he shall live
13: 5. *And he had prepared* for him
Est. 1:20. the king's decree which *he shall make*
21. *and* the king *did* according to the word
2: 4. the thing pleased the king; *and he did* so.
18. *Then* the king *made* a great feast
4:17. *and did* according to all
5: 8. the banquet that *I shall prepare* for them, and *I will do* to morrow as the king hath
14. *Let* a gallows *be made*
— *and he caused* the gallows *to be made.*
9: 5. *and did* what they would unto those that
Job 1: 5. Thus *did* Job continually.
5:12. their hands *cannot perform*
9:12. say unto him, What *doest thou?*
10: 8. hands have made me *and fashioned me*
13:20. Only *do* not two (things) unto me:
15:27. *and maketh* collops of fat on (his) flanks.
23:13. (what) his soul desireth, *even* (that) *he doeth.*
31:14. What then *shall I do* when God riseth up?
35: 6. what *doest thou* unto him?
42: 9. *and did* according as the Lord commanded
Ps. 1: 3. whatsoever *he doeth* shall prosper.
37: 5. and he *shall bring* (it) *to pass.*
56: 4(5). I will not fear what flesh *can do*
11(12). I will not be afraid what man *can do*
60:12(14). Through God *we shall do* valiantly:
66:15. *I will offer* bullocks
88:10(11). *Wilt thou shew* wonders to the dead?
106:19. *They made* a calf in Horeb,
107:37. *which may yield* fruits of increase.
108:13(14). Through God *we shall do* valiantly:
118: 6. what *can* man *do* unto me?
119:84. when *wilt thou execute* judgment
140:12(13). the Lord *will maintain* the cause of
145:19. He *will fulfil* the desire
Pro. 6:32. he (that) *doeth it* destroyeth his own
13:16. prudent (man) *dealeth* with knowledge:
14:17. (He that is) soon angry *dealeth* foolishly:
23: 5. (riches) certainly *make* themselves wings;
24: 6. by wise counsel *thou shalt make* thy war:
29. *I will do* so to him as he hath done
25: 8. lest (thou know not) what *to do* (lit. *thou shalt do*)
26:28. a flattering mouth *worketh* ruin.
31:13. *and worketh* willingly with her hands.
Ecc. 2: 3. the sons of men, which *they should do*
3:14. whatsoever God *doeth,*
6:12. the days of his vain life *which he spendeth*
7:20. that *doeth* good, and sinneth not.
8: 3. *he doeth* whatsoever pleaseth him.
4. may say unto him, *What doest thou?*
11: 5. the works of God *who maketh* all.
Cant. 1:11. *We will make* thee borders of gold
8: 8. what *shall we do* for our sister
Isa. 5: 2. *and it brought forth* wild grapes.
4. *brought it forth* wild grapes?
10. ten acres of vineyard *shall yield* one bath, and the seed of an homer *shall yield*
9: 7(6). the Lord of hosts *will perform* this.
10: 3. what *will ye do* in the day of visitation,
11. *Shall I* not, as I have done...so *do* to
19:15. which the head or tail, branch or rush, *may do.*

Isa. 20: 2. *And he did* so, walking naked
26:18. *we have* not *wrought* any deliverance
27: 5. *he may make* peace with me; (and) *he shall make* peace with me.
32: 6. his heart *will work* iniquity,
37:32. the Lord of hosts *shall do* this.
38: 7. the Lord *will do* this thing
44:13. *he fitteth it* with planes,
— *and maketh it* after the figure of a man,
19. *shall I make* the residue thereof
45: 9. What *makest thou?* or thy work,
46: 6. *and he maketh it* a god: they fall
10. *I will do* all my pleasure:
11. *I will* also *do it*.
48:11. for mine own sake, *will I do* (it):
14. *he will do* his pleasure on Babylon,
56: 2. Blessed (is) the man (that) *doeth* this,
64: 4(3). (what) *he hath prepared* for him
65: 8. so *will I do* for my servants' sakes,
12. *but did* evil before mine eyes,
66: 4. *but they did* evil before mine eyes,
Jer. 2:17. *Hast thou* not *procured* this
3: 5. thou hast spoken *and done* evil things
4:27. yet *will I* not *make* a full end.
30. what *wilt thou do?*
5:10. *but make* not a full end:
18. *I will* not *make* a full end
31. what *will ye do* in the end thereof?
7: 5. if *ye* throughly *execute* judgment
9: 7(6). how *shall I do* for the daughter of
12: 5. how *wilt thou do* in the swelling of
16:20. *Shall* a man *make* gods unto himself,
17:22. neither *do ye* any work,
18: 4. so *he made it* again (marg. returned *and made*)
12. *we will* every one *do* the imagination of
19:12. Thus *will I do* unto this place,
21: 2. the Lord *will deal* with us
22: 4. if *ye do* this thing indeed,
28: 6. the Lord *do* so: the Lord perform
30:11. though *I make* a full end
— yet *will I* not *make* a full end
32:20. *and hast made* thee a name,
34:15. *and had done* right in my sight,
35:10. have obeyed, *and done* according
18. *and done* according unto all
36: 8. *And* Baruch the son of Neriah *did*
38:12. *And* Jeremiah *did* so.
39:12. and *do* him no harm;
40: 3. the Lord hath brought (it), *and done*
16. *Thou shalt* not *do* this thing:
42: 3. the thing that *we may do*.
5. if *we do* not even according to all
44: 4. *do* not this abominable thing
17. *we will* certainly *do*
25. *We will* surely *perform* our vows
— and surely *perform* your vows.
46:28. *I will make* a full end
— *I will* not *make* a full end
52: 2. *And he did* (that which was) evil
Eze. 5: 9. *I will* not *do* any more the like,
7:27. *I will do* unto them after their way,
8:18. Therefore *will* I also *deal* in fury:
12: 7. *And I did* so as I was commanded:
16:16. garments thou didst take, *and deckedst*
17. *and madest* to thyself images
24. *and hast made* thee an high place
50. *and committed* abomination before me:
17: 6. became a vine, *and brought forth*
17. Neither *shall* Pharaoh...*make* for him
18: 8. *hath executed* true judgment
14. and *doeth* not such like,
19. *and hath done* them, he shall surely live.
24. *doeth* according to all the abominations
27. *and doeth* that which is lawful and right,
20: 9. *But I wrought* for my name's sake,
11. my judgments, which (if) a man *do*,
13. my judgments, which (if) a man *do*,
14. *But I wrought* for my name's sake,
21. my judgments...which (if) a man *do*,
22. *and wrought* for my name's sake,
23:48. that all women may be taught not *to do* (lit. *they shall* not *do*)
24:17. *make* no mourning for the dead,
18. *and I did* in the morning as I was
24. all that he hath done *shall ye do*:
25:11. *I will execute* judgments upon Moab;

Eze.28: 4. *and hast gotten* gold and silver
31:11. *he shall* surely *deal* with him:
33:31. they hear thy words, but *they will* not *do* them:
35: 6. *I will prepare thee* unto blood,
14. *I will make* thee desolate.
15. so *will I do* unto thee:
40:14. *He made also* posts of threescore cubits,
43:25. *shalt thou prepare* every day a goat
— *they shall* also *prepare* a young bullock,
27. the priests *shall make* your burnt
45:17. he *shall prepare* the sin offering,
20. so *thou shalt do* the seventh (day)
23. *he shall prepare* a burnt offering
24. *he shall prepare* a meat offering
25. *shall he do* the like
46: 7. *he shall prepare* a meat offering,
12. the prince *shall prepare* a...burnt offering
— as *he did* on the sabbath day:
13. *Thou shalt* daily *prepare* a burnt offering
— *thou shalt prepare* it every morning.
14. *thou shalt prepare* a meat offering
15. Thus *shall they prepare* the lamb,
Dan 8:27. I rose up, *and did* the king's business;
9:15. *and hast gotten* thee renown, (marg. *made* thee a name)
11:16. *But* he...*shall do* according to his own
23. *he shall work* deceitfully:
Hos. 6: 4. O Ephraim, what *shall I do* unto thee? O Judah, what *shall I do* unto thee?
8: 7. the bud *shall yield* no meal: if so be it *yield*,
9: 5. What *will ye do* in the solemn day,
16. *they shall bear* no fruit:
10: 3. what then *should* a king *do* to us?
11: 9. *I will* not *execute* the fierceness of
13: 2. *and have made* them molten images
Am. 3: 7. Surely the Lord God *will do* nothing,
4:12. thus *will I do* unto thee,
— *I will do* this unto thee,
Jon. 1:11. What *shall we do* unto thee, that the sea
4: 5. *and* there *made* him a booth, and sat
Mic. 1: 8. *I will make* a wailing like the dragons,
2: 1. the morning is light, *they practise it*,
Nah. 1: 8. *he will make* an utter end
Hab. 1:14. *And makest* men as the fishes of the sea,
Zep. 1:18. *he shall make* even a speedy riddance
3: 5. *he will* not *do* iniquity:
13. remnant of Israel *shall* not *do* iniquity,
Hag. 1:14. they came *and did* work in the house
Zec. 8:16. These (are) the things that *ye shall do*;
Mal. 2:12. The Lord will cut off the man *that doeth this*,
13. this *have ye done* again, covering

KAL.—*Participle.* Poel.

Gen 1:11. the fruit tree *yielding* fruit
12. and the tree *yielding* fruit,
18:17. that thing which I *do*;
21:22. God (is) with thee in all that thou *doest*:
24:49. if ye will *deal* kindly and truly
31:12. all that Laban *doeth* unto thee.
39: 3. the Lord made all that he *did* to prosper
22. whatsoever *they did* there, he was *the doer* (of it).
23. (that) which he *did*, the Lord made
41:25. shewed Pharaoh what he (is) *about to do*.
28. What God (is) *about to do* he sheweth
Ex. 5: 8. the bricks, which they *did make*
15:11. fearful (in) praises, *doing* wonders?
18:14. all that he *did* to the people,
— this thing that thou *doest*
17. The thing that thou *doest*
20: 6. *And shewing* mercy unto thousands
31:14. *whosoever doeth* (any) work therein,
15. *whosoever doeth* (any) work in the
34:10. a terrible thing that I *will do* with thee.
35: 2. *whosoever doeth* work therein
35. *them that do* any work,
36: 4. all the wise men, *that wrought*
— man from his work which *they made*,
8. *among them that wrought* the work
Lev. 18:29. the souls *that commit* (them)
Nu. 11:15. if thou *deal* thus with me,
15:29. *for him that sinneth* (marg. *doeth*) through ignorance,
24:18. Israel *shall do* valiantly.

Nu. 32:13. the generation, *that had done* evil
Deu 5:10. *And shewing* mercy unto thousands
10:18. *He doth execute* the judgment of
12: 8. all (the things) that we *do*
18:12. all *that do* these things
20:20. the city *that maketh* war with thee,
22: 5. all *that do* so (are) abomination
25:16. all *that do* such things, (and) all *that do*
31:21. their imagination which they *go about*, (marg. *do*)
Jud. 11:27. thou *doest* me wrong to war against me:
15: 3. the Philistines, though I *do* them a
18: 3. what *makest* thou in this (place)?
18. said the priest unto them, What *do* ye?
1Sa. 3:11. I *will do* a thing in Israel,
8: 8. so *do* they also unto thee.
12:16. this great thing, which the Lord *will do*
2Sa. 3:25. to know all that thou *doest*.
39. the Lord shall reward *the doer of* evil
8:15. David *executed* judgment and justice
12: 5. the man *that hath done* this (thing)
22:51. *and sheweth* mercy to his anointed,
1K. 5:16(30) & 9:23. the people *that wrought* in the
11:28. Solomon seeing the young man that he was industrious, (marg. *did* work)
12:21. chosen men, which *were* warr*iors*, (lit. *making* war)
20:40. as thy servant *was busy*
2K. 7: 2. (if) the Lord *would make* windows
9. We *do* not well: this day (is) a day
19. (if) the Lord *should make* windows
12:11(12). them *that did* the work,
—(—). *that wrought* upon the house
14(15). they gave that *to the* work*men*, (lit. *doers of* the work)
15(16). hand they delivered the money to be bestowed *on* work*men* (lit. *id.*): for they *dealt* faithfully.
17:29. every nation *made* (lit. were *making*) gods
32. priests of the high places, which *sacrificed*
34. they *do* after the former manners:
— neither *do* they after their statutes,
40. but they *did* after their former manner.
41. so *do* they unto this day.
22: 5. *the doers of* the work,
— give it *to the doers of* the work
7. because they *dealt* faithfully.
9. *them that do* the work,
24:16. all (that were) strong (and) *apt for* war,
1Ch 18:14. *execut*ed judgment and justice
22:15. (there are) work*men* (lit. *doers of* work) with thee in abundance,
23:24. *that did* the work for the service
27:26. *them that did* the work
2Ch 11: 1. chosen (men), *which were* warr*iors*, (lit. *making* war)
19: 6. Take heed what ye *do*:
24:12. *such as did* the work of the service
13. So *the* work*men* (lit. *doers of* the work) wrought, and the work
26:11. Uzziah had an host of fight*ing men*, (lit. *making* war)
13. *that made* war with mighty power,
34:10. the hand of *the* work*men* (lit. *the doers of* the work)
— *the* work*men* that *wrought*
12. the men *did* the work
13. all *that wrought* the work
16. committed to thy servants, they *do*
17. the hand of *the* work*men*.
Ezr. 3: 9. *the* work*men* (lit. *the doers of* the work) in the house
Neh. 2:16. whither I went, or what I *did*;
— the rest *that did* the work.
19. What (is) this thing that ye *do*?
4: 2(3:34). What *do* these feeble Jews?
16(10). half of my servants *wrought*
17(11). with one of his hands *wrought* in
21(15). So we *laboured* in the work:
5: 9. It (is) not good that ye *do*:
6: 3. I (am) *doing* a great work,
11:12. their brethren *that did* the work
13:10. and the singers, *that did* the work,
17. What evil thing (is) this that ye *do*,
Est. 2:20. Esther *did* the commandment
3: 8. neither *keep* they the king's laws:
9. *those that have the charge* of the business,

Est. 9: 3. *and* officers (marg. *those which did* the business) of the king,
19. *made* the fourteenth day...(a day of) gladness
21. that they should *keep* the fourteenth day
27. that they would *keep* these two days
Job 4:17. shall a man be more pure *than his maker?*
5: 9. *Which doeth* great things
9: 9. *Which maketh* Arcturus,
10. *Which doeth* great things
25: 2. he *maketh* peace in his high places.
31:15. *he that made me* in the womb
32:22. *my maker* would soon take me away.
35:10. Where (is) God *my maker*,
37: 5. great things *doeth* he,
40:19. *he that made him* can make his sword
Ps. 14: 1, 3. (there is) none *that doeth* good.
15: 5. He *that doeth* these (things)
18:50(51). *and sheweth* mercy to his anointed,
31:23(24). plentifully rewardeth *the* proud *doer*.
34:16(17). the Lord (is) *against them that do* evil,
37: 1. be thou envious *against the workers of*
7. man *who bringeth* wicked devices *to pass*.
52: 2(4). a sharp razor, *working* deceitfully.
53: 1(2), 3(4). (there is) none *that doeth* good.
72:18. who only *doeth* wondrous things.
77:14(15). the God *that doest* wonders:
86:10. *and doest* wondrous things:
95: 6. let us kneel before the Lord *our maker*.
101: 7. He *that worketh* deceit
103: 6. The Lord *executeth* righteousness
20. *that do* his commandments,
21. (ye) ministers of his, *that do* his pleasure.
104: 4. *Who maketh* his angels spirits;
106: 3. *he that doeth* righteousness
21. God...*which had done* great things
107:23. *that do* business in great waters;
111:10. all *they that do* (his commandments):
115: 8. *They that make them* are like
15. the Lord *which made* heaven and earth.
118:15, 16. right hand of the Lord *doeth* valiantly.
121: 2. the Lord, *which made* heaven and earth.
124: 8. the Lord, *who made* heaven and earth.
134: 3. The Lord *that made* heaven and earth
135:18. *They that make them* are like unto them.
136: 4. him who alone *doeth* great wonders:
5. him that by wisdom *made* the heavens:
7. him *that made* great lights:
146: 6. *Which made* heaven, and earth,
7. *Which executeth* judgment
148: 8. stormy wind *fulfilling* his word:
149: 2. Let Israel rejoice *in him that made him*
Pro. 10: 4. *He* becometh poor *that dealeth* (with)
11:18. The wicked *worketh* a deceitful work:
12:22. *but they that deal* truly (are) his delight.
14:31. oppresseth the poor reproacheth *his Maker*
17: 5. mocketh the poor reproacheth *his Maker:*
21:24. *who dealeth* in proud wrath.
22: 2. the Lord (is) *the maker of* them all.
Ecc. 2: 2. and of mirth, What *doeth* it?
3: 9. What profit hath *he that worketh*
8:12. Though a sinner *do* evil
10:19. A feast *is made* (lit. (men) *make*) for
Isa. 5: 5. I will tell you what I *will do*
10:23. God of hosts *shall make* a consumption,
17: 7. shall a man look to *his Maker*,
19:10. all *that make* sluices (and) ponds
22:11. ye have not looked unto *the maker thereof*,
27:11. *he that made them* will not have mercy
29:16. shall the work say *of him that made it*,
43:19. I *will do* a new thing;
44: 2. the Lord *that made thee*,
24. I (am) the Lord *that maketh* all (things);
45: 7. I *make* peace, and create evil: I the Lord *do* all these (things).
18. God himself that formed the earth *and made it*;
51:13. forgettest the Lord *thy maker*,
54: 5. *thy Maker* (is) thine husband;
64: 5(4). rejoiceth *and worketh* righteousness,
66:22. the new earth, which I *will make*,
Jer. 5: 1. (any) that *executeth* judgment,
6:13. unto the priest every one *dealeth* falsely.
7:17. Seest thou not what they *do*
8:10. every one *dealeth* falsely.
9:24(23). I (am) the Lord *which exercise* loving-kindness,

Jer. 10:12. He *hath made* the earth
17:11. *he that getteth* riches,
18: 3. behold, he *wrought* a work on the wheels.
4. the vessel *that he made* of clay
26:19. Thus *might* we *procure* great evil
29:32. the good that I *will do*
32:18. Thou *shewest* lovingkindness
30. the children of Judah *have* only *done* evil
33: 2. saith the Lord *the maker thereof*,
9. the good that I *do* unto them:
— the prosperity *that* I *procure*
18. *and to do* sacrifice continually.
44: 7. Wherefore *commit* ye (this) great evil
48:10. he *that doeth* the work of the Lord
51:15. He *hath made* the earth
Eze. 8: 6. seest thou what they *do?*
— the house of Israel *committeth*
9. wicked abominations that they *do*
12. the ancients of the house of Israel *do*
13. greater abominations that they *do.*
11:13. Ah Lord God! wilt thou *make* a full end
12: 9. said unto thee, What *doest* thou?
13:18. *and make* kerchiefs upon the head
17:15. shall he escape *that doeth* such (things)?
22:14. in the days that I *shall deal* with thee?
24:19. what these (things are) to us, that thou *doest*
33:31. with their mouth they *shew* (marg. *make*)
32. hear thy words, *but* they *do* them not.
36:22. I *do* not (this) for your sakes,
32. Not for your sakes *do* I (this),
38:12. which have *gotten* cattle and goods,
Hos. 8:14. Israel hath forgotten *his Maker*,
Joel 2:11. (he is) strong that *executeth* his word:
Am. 4:13. that *maketh* the morning darkness,
5: 8. (him) that *maketh* the seven stars
9:12. the Lord that *doeth* this.
Nah 1: 9. he *will make* an utter end:
Zep. 3:19. I *will undo* all that afflict thee:
Zec.10: 1. the Lord shall *make* bright clouds,
Mal. 2:17. Every one *that doeth* evil
3:15. they *that work* wickedness
17. in that day when I *make up* my jewels;
4: 1(3:19). all *that do* wickedly,
3(-:21). in the day that I *shall do* (this),

KAL.—*Participle.* Paül.

Ex. 3:16. (seen) *that which is done* to you
38:24. All the gold *that was occupied*
Nu.28: 6. *which was ordained* in mount Sinai
1Sa.25:18. and five sheep *ready dressed*,
2K. 23: 4. the vessels *that were made* for Baal,
Neh 3:16. the pool *that was made*,
Job 41:33(25). there is not his like, *who is made*
Ps.111: 8. *done* in truth and uprightness.
Eze.21:15(20). ah! (it is) *made* bright,
40:17. a pavement *made* for the court
41:18. *And* (it was) *made* with cherubims
19. (it was) *made* through all the house
20. cherubims and palm trees *made*,
25. *And* (there were) *made* on them,
— like as (were) *made* upon the walls;
46:23. (it was) *made* with boiling places

* NIPHAL.—*Preterite.* *

Lev. 7: 9. all that *is dressed* in the fryingpan,
18:30. abominable customs, which *were committed*
Nu. 15:24. if (ought) *be committed*
Deu13:14(15). such abomination *is wrought* among
17: 4. such abomination *is wrought* in Israel:
Jud.16:11. new ropes that never *were occupied*, (marg. wherewith work *hath* not *been done*)
2Sa.17:23. his counsel *was* not *followed*, (marg. *done*)
1K. 10:20. *there was* not the like *made*
2K. 23:22. *there was* not *holden* such a passover
23. this passover *was holden* to the Lord
2Ch 9:19. *There was* not the like *made*
35:18. *there was* no passover like to that *kept*
19. of Josiah *was* this passover *kept*.
Neh 5:18. also fowls *were prepared* for me,
6:16. this work *was wrought* of our God.
Est. 4: 1. Mordecai perceived all that *was done*,
6: 3. What honour and dignity *hath been done*
— *There is* nothing *done* for him.
Ps. 33: 6. By the word of the Lord *were* the heavens *made;*
Ecc. 1: 9. *that which is done* (is) that which shall be
13. all (things) that *are done*
Ecc. 1:14. I have seen all the works *that are done* under the sun;
2:17. the work *that is wrought*
4: 3. the evil work that *is done*
8: 9. every work that *is done*
11. Because sentence...*is* not *executed*
14. There is a vanity which *is done*
16. the business that *is done*
17. the work that *is done* under the sun:
9: 3. among all (things) that *are done*
6. any (thing) that *is done*
Isa. 46:10. (things) that *are* not (yet) *done*,
Eze.15: 5. *shall it be meet* yet for (any) work,
Dan. 9:12. *hath* not *been done* as *hath been done* upon
11:36. that that is determined *shall be done.*
Mal. 2:11. an abomination *is committed*

NIPHAL.—*Infinitive.*

Est. 9: 1. his decree drew near *to be put in execution*,
14. the king commanded it so *to be done:*
Eze.43:18. altar in the day *when they shall make it*,

NIPHAL.—*Future.*

Gen20: 9. done deeds unto me that *ought* not *to be done.*
29:26. *It must* not *be* so *done*
34: 7. which thing *ought* not *to be done.*
Ex. 2: 4. to wit what *would be done* to him.
12:16. no manner of work *shall be done*
— that only *may be done* of you.
21:31. according to this judgment *shall it be done*
25:31. beaten work *shall* the candlestick *be made:*
31:15. Six days *may* work *be done;*
35: 2. Six days *shall* work *be done*,
Lev. 2: 7. *it shall be made* (of) fine flour
8. the meat offering that *is made*
11. No meat offering,...*shall be made* with
4: 2, 27. (things) which *ought* not *to be done*,
13, 22. (things) which *should* not *be done*,
5:17. things which *are* forbidden *to be done* (lit. *are* not *to be done*)
6:21(14). In a pan *it shall be made*
7:24. the fat...*may be used* in any other use:
11:32. wherein (any) work *is done*,
13:51. any work that *is made* of skin;
23: 3. Six days *shall* work *be done:*
24:19. so *shall* it *be done* to him;
Nu. 4:26. the instruments...and all that *is made*
6: 4. eat nothing that *is made* of the vine tree,
15:11. Thus *shall* it *be done* for one bullock,
34. what *should be done* to him.
28:15. one kid...*shall be offered*,
24. *it shall be offered* beside
Deu25: 9. So *shall it be done* unto that man
Jud.11:37. *Let* this thing *be done* for me:
1Sa.11: 7. so *shall it be done* unto his oxen.
17:26. What *shall be done* to the man
27. So *shall it be done* to the man
2Sa.13:12. no such thing *ought to be done*
2K. 12:13(14). *there were* not *made* for the house
Ezr.10: 3. *let it be done* according to the law.
Neh. 6: 9. the work, that *it be* not *done.*
Est. 2:11. what *should become* of her.
5: 6. even to the half of the kingdom *it shall be performed.*
6: 9. Thus *shall it be done* to the man
11. Thus *shall it be done* unto the man
7: 2. thy request? *and it shall be performed*,
9:12. request further? *and it shall be done.*
Ecc. 1: 9. that which is done (is) that *which shall be done:*
Isa. 3:11. the reward of his hands *shall be given*
Jer. 3:16. neither *shall* (that) *be done* any more.
5:13. thus *shall* it *be done* unto them.
Eze.12:11. so *shall it be done* unto them:
25. *and* the word that I shall speak *shall come to pass;*
28. *but* the word which I have spoken *shall be done*,
15: 5. *it was meet* (marg. *made* (fit)) for no work:
44:14. all that *shall be done* therein.
Obad. 15. *it shall be done* unto thee:

NIPHAL.—*Participle.*

Neh 5:18. (that) which was *prepared* (for me) daily
Est. 9:28. days (should be) remembered *and kept*
Ecc. 4: 1. all the oppressions *that are done*
Eze. 9: 4. the abominations *that be done*

* PIEL.—*Preterite.* *

Eze.23: 3. there *they bruised* the teats
8. *they bruised* the breasts

* PUAL.—*Preterite.* *

Ps.139:15. when *I was made* in secret,

6218 עָשׂוֹר *gāh-sōhr*, m.

Gen24:55. (a few) days, at the least *ten;*
Ex. 12: 3. *In the tenth* (day) of this month
Lev.16:29. *on the tenth* (day) of the month,
23:27. *on the tenth* (day) of this seventh month
25: 9. *on the tenth* (day) of the seventh month,
Nu. 29: 7. *And...on the tenth* (day) of this seventh
Jos. 4:19. *on the tenth* (day) of the first month,
2K. 25: 1. *in the tenth* (day) of the month,
Ps. 33: 2. (and) *an instrument of ten strings.*
92: 3(4). Upon *an instrument of ten strings,*
144: 9. *an instrument of ten strings*
Jer. 52: 4, 12. *in the tenth* (day) of the month,
Eze.20: 1 & 24:1 & 40:1. *the tenth* (day) of the

6224 עֲשִׂירִי *găsee-ree'*, adj. num.

Gen 8: 5. waters decreased...until the *tenth* month: *in the tenth* (month),
Ex. 16:36. an omer (is) *the tenth part of* an ephah.
Lev. 5:11 & 6:20(13). *the tenth part of* an ephah of fine flour
27:32. *the tenth* shall be holy unto the Lord.
Nu. 5:15. *the tenth part of* an ephah
7:66. On the *tenth* day Ahiezer...(offered):
28: 5. *And a tenth part of* an ephah
Deu23: 2(3). even to his *tenth* generation
3(4). even to their *tenth* generation
2K. 25: 1. in the *tenth* month,
1Ch 12:13. Jeremiah *the tenth,*
24:11. *the tenth* to Shecaniah,
25:17. *The tenth* to Shimei,
27:13. *The tenth* (captain) for the *tenth* month
Ezr.10:16. the first day of the *tenth* month
Est. 2:16. in the *tenth* month, which (is)
Isa. 6:13. But yet in it (shall be) *a tenth,*
Jer. 32: 1. in the *tenth* year of Zedekiah
39: 1. in the *tenth* month, came Nebuchadrezzar
52: 4. in the *tenth* month,...(that) Nebuchadrezzar
Eze.24: 1. in the *tenth* month, in the tenth
29: 1. In the *tenth* year, *in the tenth* (month), in the twelfth
33:21. *in the tenth* (month), in the fifth
45:11. *the tenth part of* an homer,
Zec. 8:19. and the fast of *the tenth,*

6229 עָשַׂק [*gāh-sak'*].

* HITHPAEL.—*Preterite.* *

Gen26:20. because *they strove* with him.

6230 עֵשֶׂק *gēh'-sek*, m.

Gen26:20. he called the name of the well *Esek;* (marg. i. e. *Contention*)

6235 עֶשֶׂר *geh'-ser*, f. & עֲשָׂרָה *găsāh-rāh'*, m. adj. num.

Gen 5:14. all the days of Cainan were nine hundred and *ten* years:
16: 3. after Abram had dwelt *ten* years in
18:32. Peradventure *ten* shall be found there.
— I will not destroy (it) for *ten*'s sake.
24:10. the servant took *ten* camels
22. two bracelets for her hands of *ten* (shekels)
31: 7. changed my wages *ten* times;
41. thou hast changed my wages *ten* times.
32:15(16). forty kine, and *ten* bulls, twenty she asses, and *ten* foals.
42: 3. Joseph's *ten* brethren went down
45:23. *ten* asses laden with the good things of
— *ten* she asses laden with corn and bread
50:22. Joseph lived an hundred *and ten* years.
26. Joseph died, (being) an hundred *and ten*
Ex. 18:21, 25. rulers of fifties, and rulers of *tens:*
Ex. 26: 1. make the tabernacle (with) *ten* curtains
16. *Ten* cubits (shall be) the length of a board,
27:12. hangings of fifty cubits: their pillars *ten,* and their sockets *ten.*
34:28. the *ten* commandments.
36: 8. *ten* curtains (of) fine twined linen,
21. The length of a board (was) *ten* cubits,
38:12. hangings of fifty cubits, their pillars *ten,* and their sockets *ten;*
Lev.26:26. *ten* women shall bake your bread
27: 5. and for the female *ten* shekels.
7. for the female *ten* shekels.
Nu. 7:14. One spoon of *ten* (shekels) of gold,
20. One spoon of gold of *ten* (shekels),
26, 32, 38, 44, 50, 56, 62, 68, 74, 80. One golden spoon of *ten* (shekels),
86. (weighing) *ten* (shekels) *apiece,* (lit. *ten, ten*)
11:19. neither *ten* days, nor twenty days;
32. he that gathered least gathered *ten*
14:22. tempted me now these *ten* times,
29:23. on the fourth day *ten* bullocks,
Deu 1:15. over fifties, and captains over *tens,*
4:13. (even) *ten* commandments;
10: 4. the *ten* commandments,
Jos. 15:57. *ten* cities with their villages:
17: 5. there fell *ten* portions to Manasseh,
21: 5. out of the half tribe of Manasseh, *ten*
26. All the cities (were) *ten*
22:14. *And* with him *ten* princes,
24:29. Joshua...died, (being) an hundred *and ten*
Jud. 1: 4. they slew...in Bezek *ten* thousand men.
2: 8. Joshua...died, (being) an hundred *and ten*
3:29. they slew of Moab...*about ten* thousand
4: 6. take with thee *ten* thousand men
10. he went up with *ten* thousand men
14. *and ten* thousand men after him.
6:27. Gideon took *ten* men of his servants,
7: 3. *and* there remained *ten* thousand.
12:11. he judged Israel *ten* years.
17:10. I will give thee *ten* (shekels) of silver
20:10. we will take *ten* men of an hundred
34. there came against Gibeah *ten* thousand
Ru. 1: 4. they dwelled there *about ten* years.
4: 2. he took *ten* men of the elders
1Sa. 1: 8. (am) not I better to thee *than ten* sons?
15: 4. *and ten* thousand men of Judah.
17:17. *and* these *ten* loaves,
18. carry these *ten* cheeses unto the captain,
25: 5. David sent out *ten* young men,
38. it came to pass *about ten* days (after),
2Sa.15:16. the king left *ten* women,
18: 3. (thou art) worth *ten* thousand of us:
11. I would have given thee *ten* (shekels)
15. *ten* young men that bare Joab's armour
19:43(44). We have *ten* parts in the king,
20: 3. the king took the *ten* women
1K. 4:23(5:3). *Ten* fat oxen, and twenty oxen
5:14(28). *ten* thousand a month
6: 3. *ten* cubits (was) the breadth thereof
23. two cherubims...*ten* cubits high.
24. the uttermost part of the other (were) *ten* cubits.
25. *And* the other cherub (was) *ten* cubits:
26. The height of the one cherub (was) *ten*
7:10. stones of *ten* cubits,
23. he made a molten sea, *ten* cubits
24. knops compassing it, *ten* in a cubit,
27. he made *ten* bases of brass;
37. he made the *ten* bases:
38. Then made he *ten* lavers
— upon every one *of* the *ten* bases
43. *ten* bases, and *ten* lavers
11:31. Take thee *ten* pieces:
— and will give *ten* tribes to thee:
35. will give it unto thee, (even) *ten* tribes.
14: 3. take with thee *ten* loaves,
2K. 5: 5. and took with him *ten* talents of silver,
— *and ten* changes of raiment.
13: 7. fifty horsemen, *and ten* chariots, *and ten* thousand footmen;
14: 7. He slew of Edom...*ten* thousand,
15:17. (and reigned) *ten* years in Samaria.
20: 9. shall the shadow go forward *ten* degrees, or go back *ten* degrees?
10. the shadow to go down *ten* degrees: nay, but let the shadow return backward *ten*

2K. 20:11. he brought the shadow *ten* degrees
24:14. he carried away...(even) *ten* thousand
25:25. Ishmael...came, *and ten* men
1Ch 6:61(46). (out of) the half (tribe) of Manasseh, by lot, *ten* cities.
29: 7. of silver *ten* thousand talents,
2Ch 4: 1. *and ten* cubits the height thereof.
2. a molten sea of *ten* cubits
3. the similitude of oxen,...*ten* in a cubit,
6. he made also *ten* lavers,
7. he made *ten* candlesticks
8. He made also *ten* tables,
14. 1(13:23). the land was quiet *ten* years.
25:11. smote of the children of Seir *ten* thousand.
12. *And* (other) *ten* thousand (left) alive
27: 5. *and ten* thousand measures of wheat, and *ten* thousand of barley.
30:24. a thousand bullocks and *ten* thousand
36: 9. he reigned three months *and ten* days
Ezr. 1:10. silver basons...four hundred *and ten*,
8:12. an hundred *and ten* males.
24. *ten* of their brethren with them,
Neh 4:12(6). they said unto us *ten* times,
5:18. once in *ten* days store of all sorts of wine:
11: 1. to bring one of *ten* to dwell in Jerusalem
Est. 3: 9. *and* I will pay *ten* thousand talents
9:10, 12. the *ten* sons of Haman
13. let Haman's *ten* sons be hanged
14. and they hanged Haman's *ten* sons.
Job 19: 3. *ten* times have ye reproached me:
Ecc. 7:19. strengtheneth the wise *more than ten*
Isa. 5:10. *ten* acres of vineyard shall yield one bath,
38: 8. the shadow...*ten* degrees backward. So the sun returned *ten* degrees,
Jer. 32: 9. seven*teen* (lit. seven *and ten*) shekels of silver. (marg. or, seven shekels *and ten* (pieces) of silver)
41: 1. *even ten* men with him,
2. Then arose Ishmael...*and* the *ten* men
8. *But ten* men were found among them
42: 7. And it came to pass after *ten* days,
Eze.40:11. the breadth of the entry...*ten* cubits;
41: 2. the breadth of the door (was) *ten* cubits;
42: 4. before the chambers (was) a walk of *ten*
45: 1. the breadth (shall be) *ten* thousand.
3. the breadth of *ten* thousand:
5. *and* the *ten* thousand of breadth,
12. fif*teen* (lit. *ten* and five) shekels, shall be your maneh.
14. an homer of *ten* baths; for *ten* baths (are)
48: 9. of *ten* thousand in breadth.
10. toward the west *ten* thousand in breadth, and toward the east *ten* thousand in
13. and *ten* thousand in breadth:
— and the breadth *ten* thousand.
18. *ten* thousand eastward, *and ten* thousand
Dan. 1:12. Prove thy servants, I beseech thee, *ten*
14. and proved them *ten* days.
15. at the end of *ten* days
20. he found them *ten* times better
Am 5: 3. went forth (by) an hundred shall leave *ten*
6: 9. if there remain *ten* men
Hag 2:16. to an heap of twenty (measures), there there were (but) *ten*:
Zec. 5: 2. the breadth thereof *ten* cubits.
8:23. *ten* men shall take hold

6240 עָשָׂר *gāh-sāhr'*, adj. num.

Gen. 5: 8. all the days of Seth were nine hundred and twelve (lit. two *ten*) years:
10. after he begat Cainan eight hundred and fif*teen* (lit. five *ten*) years,
7:11. the seven*teenth* (lit. seven *ten*) day of the month,
20. Fif*teen* cubits upward did the waters
8: 4. on the seven*teenth* day of the month,
11:25. Nahor lived after he begat Terah an hundred and nine*teen* (lit. nine *ten*)
14: 4. Twelve (lit. two *ten*) years they served Chedorlaomer, and in the thir*teenth* (lit. three *ten*) year they rebelled.
5. And in the four*teenth* (lit. four *ten*) year came Chedorlaomer,
14. three hundred and eigh*teen*, (lit. eight *ten*)

Gen17:20. twelve (lit. two *ten*) princes shall he beget,
25. Ishmael his son (was) thir*teen* years old,
25:16. twelve (lit. two *ten*) princes according to
31:41. thee four*teen* years for thy two daughters,
32:22(23). took...his eleven (lit. one *ten*) sons, and passed over the ford Jabbok.
35:22. Now the sons of Jacob were twelve: (lit. two *ten*)
37: 2. Joseph, (being) seven*teen* years old,
9. the sun and the moon and the eleven (lit. one *ten*) stars
42:13. Thy servants (are) twelve (lit. two *ten*) brethren,
32. We (be) twelve (lit. two *ten*) brethren,
46:18. sons of Zilpah,...six*teen* (lit. six *ten*) souls.
22. the sons of Rachel,...all the souls (were) four*teen*.
47:28. Jacob lived in the land of Egypt seven*teen*
49:28. All these (are) the twelve (lit. two *ten*) tribes of Israel:
Ex. 12: 6. keep it up until the four*teenth*
18. on the four*teenth* day of the month
15:27. Elim, where (were) twelve (lit. two *ten*)
16: 1. on the fif*teenth* day of the second month
24: 4. the hill, and twelve (lit. two *ten*) pillars, according to the twelve (lit. two *ten*)
26: 7. eleven (lit. one *ten*) curtains shalt thou
8. the eleven (lit. *id.*) curtains (shall be all)
25. their sockets (of) silver, six*teen* sockets;
27:14. The hangings of one side (of the gate shall be) fif*teen* cubits:
15. on the other side (shall be) hangings fif*teen* (cubits):
28:21. the stones shall be...twelve, (lit. two *ten*)
— to the twelve (lit. two *ten*) tribes.
36:14. eleven (lit. one *ten*) curtains he made
15. the eleven (lit. *id.*) curtains (were) of one
30. their sockets (were) six*teen*
38:14. one side (of the gate were) fif*teen* cubits;
15. the other side of the court gate,...(were) hangings of fif*teen* cubits;
39:14. the stones (were)...twelve, (lit. two *ten*)
— his name, according to the twelve (lit. two *ten*) tribes.
Lev.23: 5. In the four*teenth* (day) of the first month
6. on the fif*teenth* day of the same month
34. The fif*teenth* day of this seventh month
39. in the fif*teenth* day of the seventh month,
24: 5. flour, and bake twelve (lit. two *ten*) cakes
27: 7. then thy estimation shall be fif*teen* shekels,
Nu. 1:44. the princes of Israel, (being) twelve (lit. two *ten*) men:
7: 3. six covered wagons, and twelve (lit. two *ten*) oxen;
72. On the eleventh (lit. one *ten*) day Pagiel
78. On the twelfth (lit. two *ten*) day Ahira
84. twelve (lit. two *ten*) chargers of silver, twelve (lit. two *ten*) silver bowls, twelve (lit. two *ten*) spoons of gold:
86. The golden spoons (were) twelve (lit. two *ten*), full of incense,
87. All the oxen for the burnt offering (were) twelve (lit. *id.*) bullocks, the rams twelve (lit. *id.*), the lambs of the first year twelve (lit. *id.*), with their meat offering: and the kids of the goats for sin offering twelve. (lit. *id.*)
9: 3. In the four*teenth* day of this month,
5. kept the passover on the four*teenth* day
11. The four*teenth* day of the second month
16:49(17:14). died in the plague were four*teen* thousand and 700,
17: 2(17). according to the house of their fathers twelve (lit. two *ten*) rods:
6(21). according to their fathers' houses, (even) twelve (lit. two *ten*) rods:
28:16. in the four*teenth* day of the first month
17. in the fif*teenth* day of this month
29:12. on the fif*teenth* day of the seventh month
13. thir*teen* young bullocks, two rams,
—, 17, 20, 23, 26, 29, 32. four*teen* lambs of the first year;
14. every bullock of the thir*teen* bullocks,
15. to each lamb of the four*teen* lambs:
17. twelve (lit. two *ten*) young bullocks,
20. on the third day eleven (lit. one *ten*) bullocks,

Nu. 31: 5. a thousand of (every) tribe, twelve (lit. two *ten*) thousand
40. And the persons (were) six*teen* thousand;
46. And six*teen* thousand persons;
52. the captains of hundreds, was six*teen* thousand seven hundred and fifty shekels.
33: 3. on the fif*teenth* day of the first month;
9. and in Elim (were) twelve (lit. two *ten*) fountains of water,
Deu 1: 2. (There are) eleven (lit. one *ten*) days' (journey) from Horeb
3. in the fortieth year, in the eleventh (lit. one *ten*) month,
23. I took twelve (lit. two *ten*) men of you,
Jos. 3:12. take you twelve (lit. two *ten*) men out of
4: 2. Take you twelve (lit. two *ten*) men out of
3. out of the midst of Jordan,...twelve (lit. two *ten*) stones,
4. Then Joshua called the twelve (lit. two *ten*) men,
8. and took up twelve (lit. two *ten*) stones
9. And Joshua set up twelve (lit. two *ten*) stones
20. those twelve (lit. two *ten*) stones, which
5:10. kept the passover on the four*teenth* day
8:25. all that fell that day,...(were) twelve (lit. two *ten*) thousand,
15:36. four*teen* cities with their villages:
41. six*teen* cities with their villages:
51. eleven (lit. one *ten*) cities with their
18:24. twelve (lit. two *ten*) cities with their
28. four*teen* cities with their
19: 6. thir*teen* cities and their
15. twelve (lit. two *ten*) cities with their
22. six*teen* cities with their
38. nine*teen* cities with their villages.
21: 4. of the tribe of Benjamin, thir*teen* cities.
6. of Manasseh in Bashan, thir*teen* cities.
7. out of the tribe of Zebulun, twelve (lit. two *ten*) cities.
19. thir*teen* cities with their suburbs.
33. thir*teen* cities with their suburbs.
40(38). were (by) their lot twelve (lit. two *ten*) cities.
Jud. 3:14. Eglon the king of Moab eigh*teen* years.
8:10. about fif*teen* thousand (men), all that
10: 8. oppressed the children of Israel eigh*teen* years,
19:29. divided her,...into twelve (lit. two *ten*) pieces,
20:25. destroyed down to the ground...eigh*teen* thousand
44. there fell of Benjamin eigh*teen* thousand
21:10. sent thither twelve (lit. two *ten*) thousand
2Sa. 2:15. there arose and went over by number twelve (lit. two *ten*) of Benjamin,
— and twelve (lit. two *ten*) of the servants
30. there lacked of David's servants nine*teen* (lit. nine *ten*) men
8:13. valley of salt, (being) eigh*teen* thousand
9:10. Ziba had fif*teen* sons and twenty servants.
10: 6. of Ish-tob twelve (lit. two *ten*) thousand
17: 1. Let me now choose out twelve (lit. two *ten*)
19:17(18). Ziba...and his fif*teen* sons
1K. 4: 7. Solomon had twelve (lit. two *ten*) officers
26(5:6). and twelve (lit. two *ten*) thousand
6:38. in the eleventh (lit. one *ten*) year,
7: 1. building his own house thir*teen* years,
3. on forty five pillars, fif*teen* (in) a row.
15. two pillars of brass, of eigh*teen* cubits high apiece: and a line of twelve (lit. two *ten*) cubits did compass
25. It stood upon twelve (lit. two *ten*) oxen,
44. one sea, and twelve (lit. two *ten*) oxen
8:65. seven days and seven days, (even) four*teen* days.
10:20. And twelve (lit. two *ten*) lions stood there
26. twelve (lit. two *ten*) thousand horsemen,
11:30. Ahijah caught the new garment...and rent it (in) twelve (lit. two *ten*) pieces:
12:32. in the eighth month, on the fif*teenth* day
33. the fif*teenth* day of the eighth month,
14:21. and he reigned seven*teen* years
15: 1. in the eigh*teenth* year of king Jeroboam
16:23. Omri to reign over Israel, twelve (lit. two *ten*) years:
18:31. Elijah took twelve (lit. two *ten*) stones,

1K. 19:19. plowing (with) twelve (lit. two *ten*) yoke (of oxen) before him, and he with the twelfth: (lit. the two *tenth*)
22:48(49). (כתיב) Jehoshaphat *made* ships (marg. or, (had) *ten* ships [so 'כ])
51(52). the seven*teenth* year of Jehoshaphat
2K. 3: 1. the eigh*teenth* year of Jehoshaphat
— and reigned twelve (lit. two *ten*) years.
8:25. In the twelfth (lit. two *ten*) year of Joram
9:29. in the eleventh (lit. one *ten*) year of Joram
13: 1. Jehoahaz the son of Jehu...(and reigned) seven*teen* years.
10. Jehoash the son of Jehoahaz...(and reigned) six*teen* years.
14:17. after the death of Jehoash...fif*teen* years.
21. took Azariah, which (was) six*teen* years
23. In the fif*teenth* year of Amaziah...king of
15: 2. Six*teen* years old was he when he began
33. he reigned six*teen* years
16: 1. In the seven*teenth* year of Pekah
2. and reigned six*teen* years in Jerusalem,
17: 1. In the twelfth (lit. two *ten*) year of Ahaz
18:13. in the four*teenth* year of king Hezekiah
20: 6. I will add unto thy days fif*teen* years;
21: 1. Manasseh (was) twelve (lit. two *ten*) years old when
22: 3 & 23:23. in the eigh*teenth* year of king
23:36. he reigned eleven (lit. one *ten*) years in
24: 8. Jehoiachin (was) eigh*teen* years old
18. he reigned eleven (lit. one *ten*) years in
25: 2. the city was besieged unto the eleventh (lit. one *ten*) year
8. the nine*teenth* year of king Nebuchadnezzar
17. The height of the one pillar (was) eigh*teen* cubits,
27. in the seven and thirtieth year...in the twelfth (lit. two *ten*) month,
1Ch 4:27. Shimei had six*teen* sons
6:60(45). All their cities...(were) thir*teen* cities.
62(47). the tribe of Manasseh...thir*teen* cities.
63(48). out of the tribe of Zebulun, twelve (lit. two *ten*) cities.
7:11. seven*teen* thousand and two hundred (soldiers),
9:22. porters... two hundred and twelve. (lit. two *ten*)
12:13. Jeremiah the tenth, Machbanai the eleventh. (lit. one *ten*)
31. of the half tribe of Manasseh eigh*teen* (lit. eight *ten*) thousand,
15:10. his brethren an hundred and twelve. (lit. two *ten*)
18:12. slew of the Edomites...eigh*teen* thousand.
24: 4. the sons of Eleazar (there were) six*teen*
12. The eleventh (lit. one *ten*) to Eliashib, the twelfth (lit. two *ten*) to Jakim,
13. The thir*teenth* to Huppah, the four*teenth* to Jeshebeab,
14. The fif*teenth* to Bilgah, the six*teenth* to Immer,
15. The seven*teenth* to Hezir, the eigh*teenth* to Aphses,
16. The nine*teenth* to Pethahiah,
25: 5. And God gave to Heman four*teen* sons
9. who with his brethren and sons (were) twelve: (lit. two *ten*)
10, 11, 12, 13, 14, 15, 16, 17, 18, 19, 20, 21, 22, 23, 24, 25, 26, 27, 28, 29, 30, 31. his sons, and his brethren, (were) twelve: (lit. two *ten*)
18. The eleventh (lit. one *ten*) to Azareel,
19. The twelfth (lit. two *ten*) to Hashabiah,
20. The thir*teenth* to Shubael,
21. The four*teenth* to Mattithiah,
22. The fif*teenth* to Jeremoth.
23. The six*teenth* to Hananiah,
24. The seven*teenth* to Joshbekashah,
25. The eigh*teenth* to Hanani,
26. The nine*teenth* to Mallothi,
26: 9. sons and brethren, strong men, eigh*teen*.
11. all the sons and brethren of Hosah (were) thir*teen*.
27:14. The eleventh (lit. one *ten*) (captain) for the eleventh (lit. *id.*) month
15. The twelfth (lit. two *ten*) (captain) for the twelfth (lit. *id.*) month
2Ch 1:14. twelve (lit. two *ten*) thousand horsemen,

2Ch 4: 4. It stood upon twelve (lit. two *ten*) oxen,
15. One sea, and twelve (lit. two *ten*) oxen
9:19. And twelve (lit. two *ten*) lions stood
25. twelve (lit. two *ten*) thousand horsemen;
11:21. he took eigh*teen* wives,
12:13. he reigned seven*teen* years in Jerusalem,
13: 1. in the eigh*teenth* year of
21. Abijah waxed mighty, and married four*teen* wives, and begat twenty and two sons, and six*teen* daughters.
15:10. in the fif*teenth* year of the reign of Asa.
25:25. lived after the death of Joash...fif*teen*
26: 1. Uzziah, who (was) six*teen* years old,
3. Six*teen* years old (was) Uzziah when
27: 1. he reigned six*teen* years in Jerusalem.
8. and reigned six*teen* years
28: 1. he reigned six*teen* years in
29:17. in the six*teenth* day of the first month
30:15. they killed the passover on the four*teenth*
33: 1. Manasseh (was) twelve (lit. two *ten*)
34: 3. in the twelfth (lit. *id.*) year he began to
8. Now in the eigh*teenth* year of his reign,
35: 1. they killed the passover on the four*teenth*
19. In the eigh*teenth* year of the reign of
36: 5, 11. reigned eleven (lit. one *ten*) years in Jerusalem:
Ezr. 2: 6. The children of Pahath-moab,...2800 and twelve. (lit. two *ten*)
18. The children of Jorah, an hundred and twelve. (lit. two *ten*)
39. The children of Harim, a thousand and seven*teen*.
6:19. the passover upon the four*teenth* (day)
8: 9. with him two hundred and eigh*teen* males.
18. with his sons and his brethren, eigh*teen*;
24. I separated twelve (lit. two *ten*) of the
31. from the river of Ahava on the twelfth (lit. two *ten*) (day)
35. twelve (lit. two *ten*) bullocks for all
— twelve (lit. two *ten*) he goats (for) a sin
Neh 5:14. (that is), twelve (lit. two *ten*) years,
7:11. The children of Pahath-moab, ... 2800 (and) eigh*teen*.
24. The children of Hariph, an hundred and twelve. (lit. two *ten*)
42. The children of Harim, a thousand and seven*teen*.
Est. 2:12. that she had been twelve (lit. two *ten*)
3: 7. in the twelfth (lit. two *ten*) year of king
— (to) the twelfth (lit. *id.*) month, that
12. the king's scribes called on the thir*teenth*
13. one day, (even) upon the thir*teenth* (day) of the twelfth (lit. two *ten*) month,
8:12. upon the thir*teenth* (day) of the twelfth (lit. two *ten*) month,
9: 1. in the twelfth (lit. two *ten*) month, that (is), the month Adar, on the thir*teenth*
15. on the four*teenth* day also of the month
17. On the thir*teenth* day of the month Adar; and on the four*teenth* (lit. four *ten*) day
18. the thir*teenth* (day) thereof, and on the four*teenth* thereof; and on the fif*teenth* (day) of the same they rested,
19. the four*teenth* day of the month Adar
21. that they should keep the four*teenth* day of the month Adar, and the fif*teenth* day
Job 42:12. he had four*teen* thousand sheep,
Ps. 60[title](2). smote of Edom in the valley of salt twelve (lit. two *ten*) thousand.
Isa. 36: 1. in the four*teenth* year of king Hezekiah,
38: 5. I will add unto thy days fif*teen* years.
Jer. 1: 2. of Josiah...in the thir*teenth* year of his
3. the eleventh (lit. one *ten*) year of
25: 3. From the thir*teenth* year of Josiah
32: 1. the eigh*teenth* year of
39: 2. in the eleventh (lit. one *ten*) year of
52: 1. he reigned eleven (lit. one *ten*) years
5. the city was besieged unto the eleventh (lit. *id.*) year
12. the nine*teenth* year of
20. twelve (lit. two *ten*) brasen bulls
21. the height of one pillar (was) eigh*teen* cubits; and a fillet of twelve (lit. two *ten*) cubits did compass
29. In the eigh*teenth* year of Nebuchadrezzar
31. in the twelfth (lit. two *ten*) month, in the five and twentieth (day)

Eze.26: 1. it came to pass in the eleventh (lit. one *ten*) year,
29: 1. in the tenth (month), in the twelfth (lit. two *ten*) (day) of the month,
30:20. in the eleventh (lit. one *ten*) year, in the first (month),
31: 1. in the eleventh (lit. one *ten*) year, in the third (month),
32: 1. And it came to pass in the twelfth (lit. two *ten*) year, in the twelfth (lit. two *ten*) month,
17. It came to pass also in the twelfth (lit. two *ten*) year, in the fif*teenth* (day)
33:21. in the twelfth (lit. two *ten*) year of our
40: 1. in the four*teenth* year after that the city
11. the length of the gate, thir*teen* cubits.
49. the breadth eleven (lit. one *ten*) cubits;
43:16. the altar (shall be) twelve (lit. two *ten*) (cubits) long, twelve (lit. two *ten*) broad, square in the four
17. the settle (shall be) four*teen* (cubits) long and four*teen* broad
45:21. In the first (month), in the four*teenth* day
25. In the seventh (month), in the fif*teenth*
47:13. according to the twelve (lit. two *ten*)
48:35. (It was) round about eigh*teen* thousand
Hos. 3: 2. I bought her to me for fif*teen* (pieces) of
Jon. 4:11. sixscore thousand (lit. two *ten*[i.e. twelve] myriads) persons
Zec. 1: 7. Upon the four and twentieth day of the eleventh (lit. one *ten*) month,

---

עֲשַׂר *găsar*, f. & עַשְׂרָה *gas-rāh'*, m. 6236
Ch. adj. num.

Ezr. 6:17. twelve (lit. two *ten*) he goats,
Dan 4:29(26). At the end of twelve (lit. *id.*) months
7: 7. and it had *ten* horns.
20. And of the *ten* horns
24. And the *ten* horns out of this kingdom (are) *ten* kings

---

עָשַׂר [*gāh-sar'*]. 6237

* KAL.—*Future.* *

1Sa. 8:15. *he will take the tenth* of your seed,
17. *He will take the tenth* of your sheep:

* PIEL.—*Infinitive.* *

Gen28:22. I will *surely* give the tenth (lit. *giving the tenth* I will give the tenth)
Deu14:22. Thou shalt *truly* tithe (lit. *tithing* thou shalt tithe)

PIEL.—*Future.*

Gen28:22. *I will* surely *give the tenth*
Deu14:22. *Thou shalt* truly *tithe*

PIEL.—*Participle.*

Neh10:37(38). *that* the same Levites *might have the tithes*

* HIPHIL.—*Infinitive.* *

Deu26:12. When thou hast made an end *of tithing*
Neh 10:38(39). *when* the Levites *take tithes:*

עִשָּׂרוֹן *gis-sāh-rōhn'*, m. 6241

Ex. 29:40. *And...a tenth deal* of flour
Lev.14:10. three *tenth deals* of fine flour
21. *and* one *tenth deal* of fine flour
23:13. two *tenth deals* of fine flour
17. two wave loaves of two *tenth deals:*
24: 5. two *tenth deals* shall be in one cake.
Nu. 15: 4. *a tenth deal* of flour
6. two *tenth deals* of flour
9. three *tenth deals* of flour
28: 9, 12. two *tenth deals* of flour
12. three *tenth deals* of flour
13. *And a several tenth deal* (lit. *And a tenth deal a tenth deal*) of flour
20. three *tenth deals* shall ye offer

Nu. 28:20. two *tenth deals* for a ram ;
21. *A several tenth deal* (lit. *a tenth deal a tenth deal*) shalt thou offer
28. three *tenth deals* unto one bullock, two *tenth deals* unto one ram,
29. *A several tenth deal* (lit. *a tenth deal a tenth deal*) unto one lamb,
29: 3. three *tenth deals* for a bullock, (and) two *tenth deals* for a ram,
4. *And* one *tenth deal* for one lamb,
9. three *tenth deals* to a bullock, (and) two *tenth deals* to one ram,
10. *A several tenth deal* (lit. *a tenth deal a tenth deal*) for one lamb,
14. three *tenth deals* unto every bullock
— two *tenth deals* to each ram
15. *And a several tenth deal* (lit. *And a tenth deal a tenth deal*)

6242 עֶשְׂרִים *ges-reem'*, pl. adj. num.

Gen 6: 3. yet his days shall be an hundred *and twenty* years.
8:14. on the seven *and twentieth* day
11:24. Nahor lived nine *and twenty* years,
18:31. Peradventure there shall be *twenty* found there.
— I will not destroy (it) for *twenty*'s sake.
23: 1. Sarah was an hundred and seven *and twenty*
31:38. This *twenty* years (have) I (been) with
41. Thus have I been *twenty* years in thy
32:14(15). Two hundred she goats, and *twenty* he goats, two hundred ewes, and *twenty* rams,
15(16). *twenty* she asses, and ten foals.
37:28. sold Joseph...*for twenty* (pieces) of silver:
Ex. 12:18. the one *and twentieth* day of the month
26: 2. one curtain (shall be) eight *and twenty*
18. *twenty* boards on the south side
19. forty sockets...under the *twenty* boards;
20. (there shall be) *twenty* boards:
27:10. And the *twenty* pillars thereof and their *twenty* sockets
11. his *twenty* pillars and their *twenty* sockets (of) brass;
16. an hanging of *twenty* cubits,
30:13. a shekel (is) *twenty* gerahs:
14. from *twenty* years old and above,
36: 9. The length of one curtain (was) *twenty and* eight cubits,
23. *twenty* boards for the south side
24. under the *twenty* boards;
25. he made *twenty* boards,
38:10, 11. Their pillars (were) *twenty*,
— their brasen sockets *twenty*
11. and their sockets of brass *twenty* ;
18. *and twenty* cubits (was) the length,
24. the offering, was *twenty and* nine talents,
26. from *twenty* years old and upward,
Lev.27: 3. the male from *twenty* years old
5. from five years...unto *twenty* years old,
— of the male *twenty* shekels,
25. *twenty* gerahs shall be the shekel.
Nu. 1: 3, 18, 20, 22, 24, 26, 28, 30, 32, 34, 36, 38, 40, 42, 45. From *twenty* years old and
3:39. all the males...(were) *twenty and* two thousand.
43. those that were numbered...were *twenty and* two thousand 273.
47. the shekel (is) *twenty* gerahs:
7:86. an hundred and *twenty* (shekels).
88. *twenty* and four bullocks,
8:24. from *twenty and* five years old
10:11. *on the twentieth* (day) of the second
11:19. neither ten days, nor *twenty* days;
14:29. from *twenty* years old and upward,
18:16. the shekel of the sanctuary, which (is) *twenty* gerahs.
25: 9. that died...were *twenty and* four thousand.
26: 2, 4. from *twenty* years old and upward,
14. of the Simeonites, *twenty and* two thousand and 200.
62. those that were numbered...were *twenty and* three thousand,

Nu. 32:11. from *twenty* years old and upward,
33:39. Aaron (was) an hundred *and twenty* and three years old
Deu31: 2. I (am) an hundred *and twenty* years old
34: 7. Moses (was) an hundred *and twenty* years old when he died:
Jos. 15:32. all the cities (are) *twenty* and nine,
19:30. *twenty* and two cities with their villages.
Jud. 4: 3. *twenty* years he mightily oppressed the children of Israel.
7: 3. there returned of the people *twenty* and two thousand;
8:10. there fell an hundred *and twenty* thousand
10: 2. he judged Israel *twenty* and three years,
3. judged Israel *twenty* and two years.
11:33. he smote...(even) *twenty* cities,
15:20. judged Israel...*twenty* years.
16:31. he judged Israel *twenty* years.
20:15. *twenty* and six thousand men
21. *twenty and* two thousand men.
35. that day *twenty* and five thousand and an hundred men:
46. *twenty* and five thousand men
1Sa. 7: 2. while the ark abode...it was *twenty* years:
14:14. first slaughter,...was *about twenty* men,
2Sa. 3:20. Abner came to David...and *twenty* men
8: 4. seven hundred horsemen, *and twenty* thousand footmen:
5. David slew of the Syrians two and *twenty* thousand men.
9:10. Ziba had fifteen sons *and twenty* servants.
10: 6. hired the Syrians of Beth-rehob,...*twenty* thousand
18: 7. a great slaughter that day of *twenty* thousand
19:17(18). Ziba...*and* his *twenty* servants
21:20. fingers, and... toes, four and *twenty* in number;
24: 8. nine months *and twenty* days.
1K. 4:23(5:3). *and twenty* oxen out of the pastures,
5:11(25). gave Hiram *twenty* thousand
—(—). *and twenty* measures of pure oil:
6: 2. *and* the breadth thereof *twenty* (cubits),
3. *twenty* cubits (was) the length thereof,
16. he built *twenty* cubits on the sides of
20. the oracle in the forepart (was) *twenty* cubits in length, *and twenty* cubits in breadth, *and twenty* cubits in the height thereof:
8:63. two and *twenty* thousand oxen, and an hundred *and twenty* thousand sheep.
9:10. at the end of *twenty* years,
11. Solomon gave Hiram *twenty* cities
14. Hiram sent to the king six*score* (lit. an hundred *and twenty*) talents
28. gold, four hundred *and twenty* talents,
10:10. she gave the king an hundred *and twenty*
14:20. which Jeroboam reigned (were) two and *twenty* years:
15: 9. in the *twentieth* year of Jeroboam
33. in Tirzah, *twenty* and four years.
16: 8. In the *twenty* and sixth year of Asa
10. in the *twenty* and seventh year of Asa
15. In the *twenty* and seventh year of Asa
29. Ahab...reigned over Israel in Samaria *twenty* and two years.
20:30. a wall fell upon *twenty* and seven thousand
22:42. *and* he reigned *twenty* and five years
2K. 4:42. *twenty* loaves of barley,
8:26. Two and *twenty* years old (was) Ahaziah
10:36. the time that Jehu reigned...(was) *twenty* and eight years.
12: 6(7). in the three and *twentieth* year of king Jehoash the priests
13: 1. In the three and *twentieth* year of Joash
14: 2. He was *twenty* and five years old
— *and* reigned *twenty* and nine years
15: 1. In the *twenty* and seventh year of
27. Pekah the son of Remaliah...(reigned *twenty* years.
30. in the *twentieth* year of Jotham
33. Five and *twenty* years old was he
16: 2. *Twenty* years old (was) Ahaz
18: 2. *Twenty and* five years old was he
— he reigned *twenty* and nine years
21:19. Amon (was) *twenty* and two years old
23:31. Jehoahaz (was) *twenty* and three years

2K. 23:36. Jehoiakim (was) *twenty* and five years
24:18. Zedekiah (was) *twenty* and one years old
25:27. on the seven *and twentieth* (day) of the month, (that) Evil-merodach
1Ch. 2:22. had three and *twenty* cities in the land of Gilead.
7: 2. two and *twenty* thousand and six hundred.
7. *twenty* and two thousand and thirty and four.
9. *twenty* thousand and two hundred.
40. *twenty* and six thousand men.
12:28. *twenty* and two captains.
30. of Ephraim *twenty* thousand and 800,
35. the Danites...*twenty* and eight thousand and 600.
37. of war for the battle, an hundred *and twenty* thousand.
15: 5. and his brethren an hundred *and twenty*:
6. and his brethren two hundred *and twenty*:
18: 4. *and twenty* thousand footmen:
5. slew of the Syrians two and *twenty* thousand men.
20: 6. a man...whose fingers and toes (were) four and *twenty*,
23: 4. *twenty* and four thousand
24. from the age of *twenty* years
27. the Levites (were) numbered from *twenty* years old and above:
24:16. *the twentieth* to Jehezekel,
17. The one *and twentieth* to Jachin, the two *and twentieth* to Gamul,
18. The three *and twentieth* to Delaiah, the four *and twentieth* to Maaziah.
25:27. *The twentieth* to Eliathah,
28. The one *and twentieth* to Hothir,
29. The two *and twentieth* to Giddalti,
30. The three *and twentieth* to Mahazioth,
31. The four *and twentieth* to Romamti-ezer,
27: 1. of every course (were) *twenty* and four thousand.
2, 5, 7, 8, 9, 10, 11, 12, 13, 14, 15. in his course (were) *twenty* and four thousand.
4. in his course likewise (were) *twenty* and four thousand.
23. from *twenty* years old and under:
2Ch 2:10(9). *twenty* thousand measures of beaten wheat, and *twenty* thousand measures of barley, and *twenty* thousand baths of wine, and *twenty* thousand baths of oil.
3: 3. the breadth *twenty* cubits.
4. breadth of the house, *twenty* cubits, and the height (was) an hundred *and twenty*:
8. the breadth of the house, *twenty* cubits, and the breadth thereof *twenty* cubits:
11. the wings of the cherubims (were) *twenty* cubits long:
13. spread themselves forth *twenty* cubits:
4: 1. he made an altar...*twenty* cubits the length thereof, *and twenty* cubits the breadth
5:12. an hundred *and twenty* priests
7: 5. *twenty* and two thousand oxen, and an hundred *and twenty* thousand sheep:
10. on the three and *twentieth* day
8: 1. at the end of *twenty* years,
9: 9. an hundred *and twenty* talents
11:21. and begat *twenty* and eight sons, and threescore daughters.
13:21. and begat *twenty* and two sons, and sixteen daughters.
20:31. *and* he reigned *twenty* and five years
25: 1. Amaziah (was) *twenty* and five years old
— *and* he reigned *twenty* and nine years
5. from *twenty* years old and above,
27: 1. Jotham (was) *twenty* and five years old
8. He was five and *twenty* years old
28: 1. Ahaz (was) *twenty* years old
6. slew in Judah an hundred *and twenty* thousand in one day,
29: 1. Hezekiah...(was) five and *twenty* years old, *and* he reigned nine and *twenty* years in Jerusalem.
31:17. from *twenty* years old and upward,
33:21. Amon (was) two and *twenty* years old
36: 2. Jehoahaz (was) *twenty* and three years
5. Jehoiakim (was) *twenty* and five years old
11. Zedekiah (was) one and *twenty* years old
Ezr. 1: 9. nine *and twenty* knives,

Ezr. 2:11. The children of Bebai, six hundred *twenty* and three.
12. The children of Azgad, 1200 *twenty* and two.
17. The children of Bezai, three hundred *twenty* and three.
19. The children of Hashum, two hundred *twenty* and three.
21. the children of Beth-lehem, an hundred *twenty* and three.
23. The men of Anathoth, an hundred *twenty* and eight.
26. of Ramah and Gaba, six hundred *twenty* and one.
27. The men of Michmas, an hundred *twenty* and two.
28. The men of Beth-el and Ai, two hundred *twenty* and three.
32. The children of Harim, three hundred *and twenty*.
33. and Ono, seven hundred *twenty* and five.
41. the children of Asaph, an hundred *twenty* and eight.
67. six thousand seven hundred *and twenty*.
3: 8. from *twenty* years old and upward,
8:11. *twenty* and eight males.
19. his brethren and their sons, *twenty*;
20. two hundred *and twenty* Nethinims:
27. *twenty* basons of gold,
10: 9. *the twentieth* (day) of the month;
Neh 1: 1. in the *twentieth* year,
2: 1. in the *twentieth* year of Artaxerxes
5:14. from the *twentieth* year
6:15. *in* the *twenty* and fifth (day) of (the month)
7:16. The children of Bebai, 600 *twenty* and eight.
17. children of Azgad, 2300 *twenty* and two.
22. children of Hashum, 300 *twenty* and eight.
23. The children of Bezai, three hundred *twenty* and four.
27. The men of Anathoth, an hundred *twenty* and eight.
30. The men of Ramah and Gaba, six hundred *twenty* and one.
31. The men of Michmas, 100 *and twenty* and two.
32. The men of Beth-el and Ai, an hundred *twenty* and three.
35. The children of Harim, three hundred *and twenty*.
37. and Ono, seven hundred *twenty* and one.
69. six thousand seven hundred *and twenty* asses.
9: 1. in the *twenty* and fourth day
11: 8. nine hundred *twenty* and eight.
12. their brethren...eight hundred *twenty* and two:
14. their brethren,...an hundred *twenty* and eight:
Est. 1: 1. (over) an hundred and seven *and twenty* provinces:
8: 9. on the three *and twentieth* (day)
— an hundred *twenty and* seven provinces,
9:30. the hundred *twenty and* seven provinces
Jer. 25: 3. the three *and twentieth* year,
52: 1. Zedekiah (was) one and *twenty* years old
28. three thousand Jews and three *and twenty*
30. In the three *and twentieth* year
31. in the five *and twentieth* (day)
Eze. 4:10. *twenty* shekels a day:
8:16. *about* five and *twenty* men,
11: 1. of the gate five and *twenty* men;
29:17. *in* the seven and *twentieth* year,
40: 1. *In* the five and *twentieth* year
13. the breadth (was) five and *twenty* cubits,
21. the breadth five *and twenty* cubits.
25. the breadth five *and twenty* cubits.
29. five and *twenty* cubits broad.
30. five *and twenty* cubits long,
33. five *and twenty* cubits broad.
36. the breadth five *and twenty* cubits.
49. The length of the porch (was) *twenty* cubits, and the breadth
41: 2. the breadth, *twenty* cubits.
4. the length thereof, *twenty* cubits; and the breadth, *twenty* cubits,

Eze.41:10. wideness of *twenty* cubits
42: 3. Over against the *twenty* (cubits)
45: 1. five *and twenty* thousand (reeds),
3. the length of five *and twenty* thousand,
5. the five *and twenty* thousand
— a possession for *twenty* chambers.
6. five *and twenty* thousand long,
12. the shekel (shall be) *twenty* gerahs: *twenty* shekels, five *and twenty* shekels,
48: 8. five *and twenty* thousand (reeds in)
9. five *and twenty* thousand in length,
10. toward the north five *and twenty* thousand
— toward the south five *and twenty* thousand
13. five *and twenty* thousand in length,
— the length (shall be) five *and twenty*
15. the five *and twenty* thousand,
20. the oblation (shall be) five *and twenty* thousand by five *and twenty* thousand:
21. over against the five *and twenty* thousand of the oblation
— over against the five *and twenty* thousand toward the west
Dan10: 4. in the four and *twentieth* day
13. the prince...of Persia withstood me one and *twenty* days:
Hag 1:15. In the four and *twentieth* day
2: 1. *in* the one and *twentieth* (day)
10. *In* the four and *twentieth* (day)
16. when (one) came to an heap of *twenty*
— there were (but) *twenty*.
18. from the four and *twentieth* day
20. *in* the four and *twentieth* (day)
Zec. 1: 7. Upon the four and *twentieth* day
5: 2. a flying roll; the length thereof (is) *twenty* cubits,

---

6243 **עֶשְׂרִין** *^{n}ges-reen'*, Ch. pl adj num.

Dan 6: 1(2). to set over the kingdom an hundred *and twenty* princes,

---

6211 **עָשׁ** *^{n}gāhsh*, m.

Job 4:19. are crushed before *the moth?*
13:28. as a garment that is *moth* eaten.
27:18. He buildeth his house *as a moth*,
Ps. 39:11(12). thou makest his beauty to consume away *like a moth:*
Isa. 50: 9. *the moth* shall eat them up.
51: 8. *the moth* shall eat them up
Hos. 5:12. I (be) unto Ephraim *as a moth*,

5906 **עָשׁ** *^{n}gāhsh*, m.

Job 9: 9. Which maketh *Arcturus* (marg. *Ash*), Orion, and Pleiades,

---

6216 **עָשׁוֹק** *^{n}gāh-shōhk'*, m.

Jer. 22: 3. deliver the spoiled out of the hand of *the oppressor:*

6217 **עֲשׁוּקִים** *^{n}găshoo-keem'*, m. pl.

Job 35: 9. By reason of the multitude of *oppressions* they make
Ecc. 4: 1. all *the oppressions* that are done
Am. 3: 9. *and the oppressed* (marg. or, *oppressions*) in the midst thereof.

6219 **עָשׁוּת** *^{n}gāh-shooth'*, adj.

Eze.27:19. *bright* iron, cassia, and calamus, were in thy market.

עָשִׁיר *^{n}gāh-sheer'*, m. 6223

Ex. 30:15. *The rich* shall not give more,
Ru. 3:10. thou followedst not young men, whether poor or *rich*.
2Sa.12: 1. There were two men....the one *rich*, and the other poor.
2. *The rich man had* exceeding many flocks and herds:
4. there came a traveller unto the *rich* man,
Job 27:19. *The rich man* shall lie down,
Ps. 45:12(13). *the rich among* the people
49: 2(3). low and high, *rich* and poor,
Pro.10:15. *The rich man*'s wealth (is) his strong
14:20. *the rich* (hath) many friends.
18:11. *The rich man*'s wealth (is) his strong
23. *but the rich* answereth roughly.
22: 2. *The rich* and poor meet together:
7. *The rich* ruleth over the poor,
16. he that giveth *to the rich*,
28: 6. though he (be) *rich*.
11. The *rich* man (is) wise in his own
Ecc. 5:12(11). the abundance *of the rich*
10: 6. *and the rich* sit in low place.
20. curse not *the rich* in thy bedchamber:
Isa. 53: 9. with *the rich* in his death;
Jer. 9:23(22). let not *the rich man* glory in his
Mic. 6:12. For *the rich men thereof* are full of violence, and the inhabitants

---

עָשַׁן *^{n}gāh-shan'*. 6225

* KAL.—*Preterite.* *

Ex. 19:18. And mount Sinai *was* altogether *on a smoke*, because the Lord
Ps. 80: 4(5). how long *wilt thou be angry* (marg. *smoke*)

KAL.—*Future.*

Deu29:20(19). and his jealousy *shall smoke* against that man,
Ps. 74: 1. (why) *doth* thine anger *smoke*
104:32. he toucheth the hills, *and they smoke.*
144: 5. touch the mountains, *and they shall smoke.*

עָשֵׁן *^{n}gāh-shēhn*, adj. 6226

Ex. 20:18. all the people saw the thunderings,...and the mountain *smoking:*
Isa. 7: 4. the two tails of these *smoking* firebrands,

עָשָׁן *^{n}gāh-shāhn*, m. 6227

Gen15:17. behold a *smoking* furnace, and a burning lamp that passed
Ex. 19:18. *the smoke thereof* ascended *as the smoke of* a furnace,
Jos. 8:20, 21. *the smoke of* the city ascended
Jud.20:38. a great flame with *smoke*
40. a pillar of *smoke*,
2Sa.22: 9. There went up *a smoke* out of his nostrils, and fire
Job 41:20(12). Out of his nostrils goeth *smoke*,
Ps. 18: 8(9). There went up *a smoke* out of his nostrils, and fire
37:20. *into smoke* shall they consume away.
68: 2(3). As *smoke* is driven away, (so) drive (them) away:
102: 3(4). my days are consumed *like smoke*,
Pro.10:26. *and as smoke* to the eyes,
Cant.3: 6. like pillars of *smoke*,
Isa. 4: 5. a cloud *and smoke* by day,
6: 4. the house was filled with *smoke*.
9:18(17). they shall mount up (like) the lifting up of *smoke*.
14:31. there shall come from the north *a smoke*,
34:10. *the smoke thereof* shall go up
51: 6. the heavens shall vanish away *like smoke*,
65: 5. These (are) *a smoke* in my nose, a fire that burneth all the day.
Hos13: 3. *and as the smoke* out of the chimney.
Joel 2:30(3:3). blood, and fire, and pillars of *smoke*
Nah. 2:13(14). I will burn her chariots *in the smoke*,

6231 **עָשַׁק** *gāh-shak'.*

* KAL.—*Preterite.* *

Lev. 6: 2(5:21). taken away by violence, or *hath deceived* his neighbour;
4(–:23). the thing which *he hath deceitfully gotten,*
1Sa.12: 3. whom *have I defrauded?*
4. *Thou hast* not *defrauded us,*
Isa. 52: 4. the Assyrian *oppressed them*
Eze.18:18. because *he* cruelly *oppressed,*
22:29. people of the land *have used* oppression,
— *they have oppressed* the stranger
Mic. 2: 2. *so they oppress* (marg. or, *defraud*) a man and his house,

KAL.—*Infinitive.*

1Ch 16:21. He suffered no man *to do them wrong:*
Ps. 105:14. He suffered no man *to do them wrong:*
Hos.12: 7(8). he loveth *to oppress.* (marg. or, *deceive*)

KAL.—*Future.*

Lev.19:13. *Thou shalt* not *defraud* thy neighbour,
Deu24:14. *Thou shalt* not *oppress* an hired servant (that is) poor and needy,
Job 10: 3. (Is it) good unto thee that *thou shouldest oppress,*
40:23. Behold, *he drinketh up* (marg. *oppresseth*) a river,
Ps.119:122. *let* not the proud *oppress me.*
Jer. 7: 6. (If) *ye oppress* not the stranger,
Zec. 7:10. And *oppress* not the widow,

KAL.—*Participle.* Poel.

Ps. 72: 4. shall break in pieces *the oppressor.*
119:121. leave me not *to mine oppressors.*
Pro.14:31. *He that oppresseth* the poor reproacheth his Maker:
22:16. *He that oppresseth* the poor to increase his (riches),
28: 3. A poor man *that oppresseth*
Ecc. 4: 1. on the side of *their oppressors*
Jer. 21:12. out of the hand of *the oppressor,*
Am. 4: 1. ye kine of Bashan,...*which oppress*
Mal. 3: 5. and *against those that oppress* (marg. or, *defraud*) the hireling

KAL.—*Participle.* Paül.

Deu28:29. thou shalt be only *oppressed*
33. thou shalt be only *oppressed*
Ps. 103: 6. all that are *oppressed.*
146: 7. executeth judgment *for the oppressed:*
Pro.28:17. A man *that doeth violence* to the blood of (any) person
Ecc. 4: 1. the tears of (such as were) *oppressed,*
Jer. 50:33. The children of Israel...(were) *oppressed*
Hos. 5:11. Ephraim (is) *oppressed* (and) broken

* PUAL.—*Participle.* *

Isa. 23:12. Thou shalt no more rejoice, O thou *oppressed* virgin,

---

6233 **עֹשֶׁק** *gōh'-shek,* m.

Lev. 6: 4(5:23). *the thing* which he hath deceitfully gotten,
Ps. 62:10(11). Trust not *in oppression,*
73: 8. speak wickedly (concerning) *oppression:*
119:134. Deliver me *from the oppression of* man:
Ecc. 5: 8(7). *the oppression of* the poor,
7: 7. *oppression* maketh a wise man mad;
Isa. 30:12. and trust *in oppression* (marg. or, *fraud*) and perverseness,
54:14. thou shalt be far *from oppression;*
59:13. speaking *oppression* and revolt,
Jer. 6: 6. she (is) wholly *oppression* in the midst of her.
22:17. for *oppression,* and for violence,
Eze.18:18. he *cruelly* oppressed, (lit. he oppressed *an oppression*)
22: 7. in the midst of thee have they dealt *by oppression* (marg. or, *deceit*)
12. thou hast greedily gained of thy neighbours *by extortion,*
29. The people of the land have used *oppression,* (marg. or, *deceit*)

עָשְׁקָה *gosh-kāh',* f. 6234

Isa. 38:14. O Lord, I am *oppressed;* (lit. *oppression* to me)

עָשַׁר [*gāh-shar'*]. 6238

* KAL.—*Preterite.* *

Hos 12: 8(9). Ephraim said, Yet *I am become rich,* I have found me out

KAL.—*Future.*

Job 15:29. *He shall* not *be rich,* neither shall his substance continue,

* HIPHIL.—*Preterite.* *

Gen 14:23. lest thou shouldest say, *I have made* Abram *rich:*
Eze.27:33. *thou didst enrich* the kings of the earth

HIPHIL.—*Infinitive.*

Pro.23: 4. Labour not *to be rich:*
28:20. he that maketh haste *to be rich*

HIPHIL.—*Future.*

1Sa.17:25. the king *will enrich him* with great riches, and will give
Ps. 49:16(17). when one *is made rich,*
65: 9(10). *thou* greatly *enrichest it* with the river of God,
Pro.10: 4. the hand of the diligent *maketh rich.*
22. The blessing of the Lord, it *maketh rich,*
21:17. he that loveth wine and oil *shall* not *be rich.*
Jer. 5:27. they are become great, *and waxen rich.*
Dan11: 2. the fourth *shall be* far *richer*
Zec.11: 5. Blessed (be) the Lord; *for I am rich:*

HIPHIL.—*Participle.*

1Sa. 2: 7. The Lord maketh poor, *and maketh rich:* he bringeth

* HITHPAEL.—*Participle.* *

Pro.13: 7. There is *that maketh himself rich,* yet (hath) nothing:

עֹשֶׁר *gōh'-sher,* m. 6239

Gen31:16. all *the riches* which God hath taken
1Sa.17:25. the king will enrich him with great *riches,*
1K. 3:11. neither hast asked *riches* for thyself,
13. both *riches,* and honour:
10:23. Solomon exceeded all the kings of the earth *for riches* and for wisdom.
1Ch 29:12. *Both riches* and honour (come) of thee,
28. full of days, *riches,* and honour:
2Ch 1:11. thou hast not asked *riches,*
12. *and* I will give thee *riches,*
9:22. king Solomon passed all the kings of the earth *in riches* and wisdom.
17: 5. he had *riches* and honour in abundance.
18: 1. Jehoshaphat had *riches* and honour in abundance,
32:27. Hezekiah had exceeding much *riches*
Est. 1: 4. he shewed *the riches of* his glorious kingdom and the honour
5:11. Haman told them of the glory of *his riches,*
Ps. 49: 6(7). the multitude of *their riches;*
52: 7(9). trusted in the abundance of *his riches,* (and) strengthened himself
112: 3. Wealth *and riches* (shall be) in his house:
Pro. 3:16. in her left hand *riches* and honour.
8:18. *Riches* and honour (are) with me;
11:16. strong (men) retain *riches.*
28. He that trusteth *in his riches* shall fall: but the righteous
13: 8. ransom of a man's life (are) *his riches:*
14:24. The crown of the wise (is) *their riches:*
22: 1. A (good) name (is) rather to be chosen *than* great *riches,*
4. By humility (and) the fear of the Lord (are) *riches,*
30: 8. give me neither poverty *nor riches;* feed me with food convenient

Ecc. 4: 8. neither is his eye satisfied with *riches;*
5:13(12). *riches* kept for the owners thereof to their hurt.
14(13). those *riches* perish
19(18). to whom God hath given *riches* and wealth, and hath given
6: 2. A man to whom God hath given *riches*, wealth, and honour,
9:11. nor yet *riches* to men of understanding,
Jer. 9:23(22). let not the rich (man) glory *in his riches:*
17:11. he that getteth *riches*, and not by right,
Dan11: 2. the fourth shall be *far* richer (lit. shall be rich *in riches*)
— by his strength *through his riches*

6244 **עָשֵׁשׁ** [*ⁿgāh-shēhsh'*].

* KAL.—*Preterite.* *

Ps. 6: 7(8). Mine eye *is consumed* because of grief;
31: 9(10). mine eye *is consumed* with grief,
10(11). faileth because of mine iniquity, and my bones *are consumed.*

6245 **עָשַׁת** [*ⁿgāh-shath'*].

* KAL.—*Preterite.* *

Jer. 5:28. They are waxen fat, *they shine:* yea, they overpass

* HITHPAEL.—*Future.* *

Jon. 1: 6. if so be that God *will think* upon us, that we perish not.

6246 **עֲשִׁת** *ⁿgăsheeth*, Ch.

* P'AL.—*Preterite.* *

Dan 6: 3(4). and the king *thought* to set him over the whole realm.

6247 **עֶשֶׁת** *ⁿgeh'-sheth*, m.

Cant.5:14. his belly (is as) *bright* ivory overlaid (with) sapphires.

6248 **עַשְׁתּוּת** *ⁿgash-tōhth'*, f. pl.

Job 12: 5. a lamp despised *in the thought of* him that is at ease.

6249 **עַשְׁתֵּי** *ⁿgash-tēh'*, adj. num.

[Always combined with the numeral עָשָׂר].

Ex. 26: 7. eleven (lit. *one* ten) curtains shalt thou make.
8. the eleven (lit. *id.*) curtains (shall be all) of one
36:14. eleven (lit. *id.*) curtains he made them.
15. the eleven (lit. *id.*) curtains (were) of one size.
Nu. 7:72. On the eleventh (lit. *id.*) day Pagiel... (offered):
29:20. on the third day eleven (lit. *id.*) bullocks,
Deu 1: 3. *in* the eleventh (lit. *id.*) month, on the first (day) of the month,
2K. 25: 2. the eleventh (lit. *id.*) year of king Zedekiah.
1Ch 12:13. Machbanai the eleventh. (lit. *id.*)
24:12. The eleventh (lit. *id.*) to Eliashib,
25:18. The eleventh (lit. *id.*) to Azareel,
27:14. The eleventh (lit. *id.*) (captain) *for* the eleventh (lit. *id.*) month (was) Benaiah
Jer. 1: 3. the eleventh (lit. *id.*) year of Zedekiah
39: 2. *in* the eleventh (lit. *id.*) year of Zedekiah,
52: 5. unto the eleventh (lit. *id.*) year of king Zedekiah.
Eze.26: 1. *in* the eleventh (lit. *id.*) year, in the first (day) of the month,
40:49. and the breadth eleven (lit. *id.*) cubits;
Zec. 1: 7. four and twentieth day *of* the eleventh (lit. *id.*) month,

---

עֶשְׁתֹּנֹת *ⁿgesh-tōh-nōhth'*, f. pl. 6250

Ps.146: 4. returneth to his earth; in that very day *his thoughts* perish.

עַשְׁתְּרוֹת *ⁿgash-t'rōhth'*, f. pl. 6251

Deu 7:13. *and the flocks of* thy sheep, in the land which he sware
28: 4, 18. thy kine, *and the flocks of* thy sheep.
51. of thy kine, *or flocks of* thy sheep,

עֵת *ⁿgēhth*, com. 6256

Gen 8:11. the dove came in to him *in the* evening; (lit. *in the time of* the evening)
18:10, 14. *according to the time of* life;
21:22. it came to pass *at* that *time*,
24:11. *at the time of* the evening, (even) *the time* that women
29: 7. neither (is it) *time* that the cattle should be gathered
31:10. *at the time* that the cattle conceived,
38: 1. it came to pass *at* that *time*,
27. *in the time of* her travail,
Ex. 9:18. to morrow *about this time*
18:22. let them judge the people at all *seasons:*
26. they judged the people at all *seasons:*
Lev.15:25. *the time of* her separation,
16: 2. that he come not at all *times* into the holy (place) within the vail
26: 4. I will give you rain *in due season*,
Nu. 22: 4. And Balak the son of Zippor (was) king of the Moabites *at* that *time*.
23:23. *according to this time* it shall be said
Deu. 1: 9. I spake unto you *at* that *time*,
16. I charged your judges *at* that *time*,
18. I commanded you *at* that *time*
2:34 & 3:4. we took all his cities *at* that *time*,
3: 8. we took *at* that *time* out of the hand of the two kings of the Amorites
12. And this land, (which) we possessed *at* that *time*,
18. I commanded you *at* that *time*,
21. I commanded Joshua *at* that *time*,
23. I besought the Lord *at* that *time*,
4:14. the Lord commanded me *at* that *time*
5: 5. between the Lord and you *at* that *time*,
9:20. I prayed for Aaron also *the* same *time*.
10: 1. *At* that *time* the Lord said unto me,
8. *At* that *time* the Lord separated the tribe of Levi,
11:14. the rain of your land *in his due season*,
28:12. the rain unto thy land *in his season*,
32:35. their foot shall slide *in* (due) *time:*
Jos. 5: 2. *At* that *time* the Lord said unto Joshua,
6:26. Joshua adjured (them) *at* that *time*,
8:29. the king of Ai he hanged on a tree until even*tide:*
10:27. it came to pass *at the time of* the going down of the sun,
11: 6. to morrow *about* this *time*
10. Joshua *at* that *time* turned back,
21. *at* that *time* came Joshua, and cut off
Jud. 3:29. they slew of Moab *at* that *time*
4: 4. she judged Israel *at* that *time*.
10:14. *in the time of* your tribulation.
11:26. recover (them) *within* that *time?*
12: 6. there fell *at* that *time*
13:23. *nor* would *as at* this *time*
14: 4. *for at* that *time* the Philistines had
21:14. Benjamin came again *at* that *time;*
22. ye did not give unto them *at* this *time*,
24. departed thence *at* that *time*,
Ru. 2:14. *At* meal*time* come thou hither,

1Sa. 4:20. *And about the time of* her death
9:16. To morrow *about this time* I will send
18:19. it came to pass *at the time when*
20:12. *about* to morrow any *time*,
2Sa. 11: 1. *at the time* when kings go forth (to battle),
2. it came to pass *in an eveningtide*,
24:15. even to *the time* appointed:
1K. 8:65. *at* that *time* Solomon held a feast,
11: 4. For it came to pass, *when* Solomon was old, (that) his wives
29. it came to pass *at* that *time* when Jeroboam went out
14: 1. *At* that *time* Abijah...fell sick.
15:23. *in the time of* his old age
19: 2. of them by to morrow *about* this *time*.
20: 6. unto thee to morrow *about* this *time*,
2K. 4:16. season, *according to the time of* life,
17. unto her, *according to the time of* life.
5:26. (Is it) *a time* to receive money,
7: 1, 18. To morrow *about* this *time*
8:22. Libnah revolted *at the* same *time*.
10: 6. *by* to morrow *this time*.
16: 6. *At* that *time* Rezin king of Syria
18:16. *At* that *time* did Hezekiah cut off
20:12. *At* that *time* Berodach-baladan,...king of Babylon, sent
24:10. *At* that *time* the servants of Nebuchadnezzar king of Babylon
1Ch. 9:25. (were) to come after seven days *from time* to *time* with them.
12:22. *at* (that) *time* day by day
32. (men) that had understanding *of the times*,
20: 1. *after* the year was expired, *at* the *time* that kings go out (to battle),
21:28. *At* that *time* when David saw
29. *at* that *season* in the high place
29:30. *and the times* that went over him,
2Ch. 7: 8. *at the* same *time* Solomon kept
13:18. the children of Israel were brought under *at* that *time*.
15: 5. *And in* those *times* (there was) no peace
16: 7. *And at* that *time* Hanani the seer came
10. Asa oppressed...*the* same *time*.
18:34. *about the time of* the sun going down
20:22. *And when* (marg. *in the time that*) they began to sing
21:10. *The* same *time* (also) did Libnah revolt
19. after (lit. *and as the period of* the going out of) the end of two years,
24:11. *at what time* the chest was brought
25:27. *Now after the time* that Amaziah did turn away from following the Lord
28:16. *At* that *time* did king Ahaz send
22. *And in the time of* his distress
29:27. *And when* (marg. *in the time*) the burnt offering began,
30: 3. they could not keep it *at* that *time*,
35:17. kept the passover *at* that *time*,
Ezr. 8:34. all the weight was written *at* that *time*.
10:13. *and* (it is) *a time* of much rain,
14. come *at* appointed *times*,
Neh. 4:22(16). *at the* same *time* said I
6: 1. *at* that *time* I had not set up the doors
9:27. *and in the time of* their trouble,
28. many *times* didst thou deliver them
10:34(35). *at times* appointed year by year,
13:21. From that *time* forth came they no (more) on the sabbath.
31. wood offering, *at times* appointed,
Est. 1:13. the wise men, which knew *the times*,
4:14. holdest thy peace *at* this *time*,
— the kingdom *for* (such) *a time* as this?
5:13. *so* long *as* (lit. all *the time* that) I see Mordecai the Jew
8: 9. *at* that *time* in the third month,
Job 5:26. as a shock of corn cometh in *in his season*.
6:17. *What time* they wax warm,
22:16. were cut down out of *time*,
24: 1. seeing *times* are not hidden from the Almighty, do they
27:10. will he al*ways* (lit. in all *time*) call upon God?
38:23. reserved *against the time of* trouble,
32. Canst thou bring forth Mazzaroth *in his season?*
39: 1. *the time* when the wild goats
2. *the time* when they bring forth?

Job 39:18. *What time* she lifteth up
Ps. 1: 3. bringeth forth his fruit *in his season;*
4: 7(8). *more than in the time* (that) their corn and their wine
9: 9(10). a refuge *in times of* trouble.
10: 1. (thyself) *in times of* trouble?
5. His ways are al*ways* (lit. in all *time*) grievous;
21: 9(10). *in the time of* thine anger:
31:15(16). *My times* (are) in thy hand:
32: 6. godly pray unto thee *in a time* when thou mayest be found:
34: 1(2). I will bless the Lord at all *times:*
37:19. They shall not be ashamed *in the* evil *time:*
39. of the Lord: (he is) their strength *in the time of* trouble.
62: 8(9). Trust in him at all *times;*
69:13(14). (in) *an* acceptable *time:*
71: 9. Cast me not off *in the time of* old age;
81:15(16). *their time* should have endured for
102:13(14). *the time* to favour her, yea, the set time, is come.
104:27. give (them) their meat *in due season*.
105:19. Until *the time* that his word came:
106: 3. doeth righteousness at all *times*.
119:20. unto thy judgments at all *times*.
126. (It is) *time* for (thee), Lord, to work: (for) they have made void
145:15. thou givest them their meat *in due season*.
Pro. 5:19. satisfy thee at all *times;*
6:14. he deviseth mischief continually; (lit. in all *time*)
8:30. rejoicing al*ways* (lit. in all *time*) before him;
15:23. a word (spoken) *in due season*, (marg. *his season*)
17:17. A friend loveth at all *times*,
Ecc. 3: 1. *and a time* to every purpose under the heaven:
2. *A time* to be born, *and a time* to die; *a time* to plant, *and a time* to pluck up (that which is) planted;
3. *A time* to kill, *and a time* to heal; *a time* to break down, *and a time* to build up;
4. *A time* to weep, *and a time* to laugh; *a time to* mourn, *and a time to* dance;
5. *A time* to cast away stones, *and a time to* gather stones together; *a time* to embrace, *and a time* to refrain from embracing;
6. *A time* to get, *and a time* to lose; *a time* to keep, *and a time* to cast away;
7. *A time* to rend, *and a time* to sew; *a time* to keep silence, *and a time* to speak;
8. *A time* to love, *and a time* to hate; *a time of* war, *and a time of* peace.
11. He hath made every (thing) beautiful *in his time:*
17. (there is) *a time* there for every purpose and for every work.
7:17. why shouldest thou die before *thy time?*
8: 5. a wise man's heart discerneth *both time* and judgment.
6. to every purpose there is *time*
9. *a time* wherein one man ruleth
9: 8. Let thy garments be al*ways* (lit. in all *time*) white;
11. *time* and chance happeneth to them all
12. man also knoweth not *his time:*
— so (are) the sons of men snared *in an* evil *time*, when it falleth
10:17. thy princes eat *in due season*,
Cant. 2:12. *the time of* the singing (of birds)
Isa. 9: 1(8:23). in her vexation, *when* at the first he lightly afflicted
13:22. *her time* (is) near to come,
17:14. *at eveningtide* trouble;
18: 7. *In* that *time* shall the present be brought unto the Lord of hosts
20: 2. *At the* same *time* spake the Lord
33: 2. *in the time of* trouble.
6. the stability of *thy times*,
39: 1. *At* that *time* Merodach-baladan,...king of Babylon, sent
48:16. from the beginning; *from the time* that it was, there (am) I:

Isa. 49: 8. *In an* acceptable *time* have I heard thee,
60:22. I the Lord will hasten it *in his time.*
Jer. 2:17. forsaken the Lord thy God, *when* he led thee by the way?
27. *but in the time of* their trouble
28. *in the time of* thy trouble:
3:17. *At* that *time* they shall call Jerusalem the throne
4:11. *At* that *time* shall it be said
5:24. that giveth rain, both the former and the latter, *in his season:*
6:15. *at the time* (that) I visit them
8: 1. *At* that *time*, saith the Lord,
7. the crane and the swallow observe *the time of*
12. *in the time of* their visitation
15. (and) *for a time of* health, and behold trouble!
10:15. *in the time of* their visitation
11:12. *in the time of* their trouble.
14. *in the time that* they cry unto me
14: 8. the saviour thereof *in time of* trouble,
19. *and for the time of* healing,
15:11. *in the time of* evil *and in the time of* affliction.
18:23. *in the time of* thine anger.
20:16. the shouting *at noontide;*
27: 7. until *the* very *time of* his land come:
30: 7. *even the time of* Jacob's trouble;
31: 1. *At the* same *time*, saith the Lord,
33:15. *and at* that *time*, will I cause the Branch
20. should not be day and night *in their season;*
46:21. *the time of* their visitation.
49: 8. *the time* (that) I will visit him.
50: 4, 20. *and in* that *time*, saith the Lord,
16. *in the time of* harvest:
27. *the time of* their visitation.
31. thy day is come, *the time* (that) I will visit thee.
51: 6. *the time of* the Lord's vengeance;
18. *in the time of* their visitation
33. (it is) *time* to thresh her:
— *the time of* her harvest
Eze. 4:10. *from time* to *time* shalt thou eat it.
11. *from time* to *time* shalt thou drink.
7: 7. *the time* is come, the day of trouble
12. *The time* is come, the day draweth
12:27. *and* he prophesieth *of the times* (that are) far off.
16: 8. *thy time* (was) *the time of* love;
57. *the time of* (thy) reproach
21:25(30). whose day is come, *when* iniquity (shall have) an end,
29(34). *when* their iniquity (shall have) an end.
22: 3. sheddeth blood in the midst of it, that *her time* may come,
27:34. *In the time* (when) thou shalt be broken
30: 3. *the time of* the heathen.
34:26. will cause the shower to come down *in his season;*
35: 5. *in the time of* their calamity, *in the time* (that their) iniquity
Dan. 8:17. Understand, O son of man: for *at the time of* the end (shall be) the vision.
9:21. *about the time of* the evening oblation.
25. even in troublous *times.*
11: 6. he that strengthened her *in* (these) *times.*
13. certainly come after *certain* years (marg. at the end of *times*, even years)
14. *And in* those *times* there shall many stand up against the king
24. strong holds, even for *a time.*
35. to *the time of* the end:
40. *And at the time of* the end
12: 1. *And at* that *time* shall Michael stand up,
— there shall be *a time of* trouble,
— to that same *time: and at* that *time* thy people shall be delivered,
4. shut up the words, and seal the book, (even) to *the time of* the end:
9. the words (are) closed up and sealed till *the time of* the end.
11. *And from the time* (that) the daily (sacrifice)
Hos. 2: 9(11) my corn *in the time thereof,*
10:12. *for* (it is) *time* to seek the Lord,
13:13. for he should not stay *long* (marg. *a time*) in (the place)
Joel 3: 1(4:1). *and in* that *time*, when I shall bring again
Am. 5:13. the prudent shall keep silence *in* that *time;* for it (is) *an* evil *time.*
Mic. 2: 3. for this *time* (is) evil
3: 4. he will even hide his face from them *at* that *time*,
5: 3(2). *the time* (that) she which travaileth
Zep. 1:12. it shall come to pass *at* that *time*,
3:19. *at* that *time* I will undo all that afflict
20. *At* that *time* will I bring you (again), *even in* the *time* that I gather you:
Hag. 1: 2. *The time* is not come, *the time that* the Lord's house should be built.
4. (Is it) *time* for you, O ye, to dwell
Zec. 10: 1. Ask ye of the Lord rain *in the time of* the latter rain;
14: 7. *at* evening *time* it shall be light.

עֵת Ch. see כְּעֶת — See 3706

עָתַד [*gāh-thad'*]. — 6257

* PIEL.—*Imperative.* *

Pro. 24:27. Prepare thy work without, *and make it fit* for thyself in the field;

* HITHPAEL.—*Preterite.* *

Job 15:28. in houses which no man inhabiteth, which *are ready to become* heaps.

עַתָּה *gat-tāh'*, part. adv. — 6258

Gen 22:12. for *now* I know that thou fearest God,
26:22. For *now* the Lord hath made room for us,
29. thou (art) *now* the blessed of the Lord.
2Ch 10:11. *For whereas* my father put a heavy yoke &c. &c.

For the combination of this word with עַד see עַד,

It occurs with prefix מֵעַתָּה

2Ch 16: 9. *from henceforth* thou shalt have wars.
Ps. 113: 2. *from this time forth* and for evermore.
Isa. 48: 6. shewed thee new things *from this time,*
Dan 10:17. for as for me, *straightway* there remained no strength
Hos. 2: 7(9). then (was it) better with me *than now.* &c.

עַתּוּד [*gat-tood'*], m. — 6260

Gen 31:10. *the rams* (marg. or, *he goats*) which leaped upon the cattle
12. *the rams* which leap upon the cattle (are) ringstraked, speckled, and grisled:
Nu. 7:17, 23, 29, 35, 41, 47, 53, 59, 65, 71, 77, 83. five rams, five *he goats*,
88. the rams sixty, *the he goats* sixty,
Deu 32:14. and rams of the breed of Bashan, *and goats*,
Ps. 50: 9. I will take no bullock out of thy house, (nor) *he goats*
13. or drink the blood of *goats?*
66:15. I will offer bullocks with *goats.*
Pro. 27:26. for thy clothing, and *the goats* (are) the price of the field.
Isa. 1:11. I delight not in the blood of bullocks,...*or of he goats.* (marg. *great he goats*)
14: 9. *the chief ones* (marg. *leaders*, or, *great goats*) *of* the earth;
34: 6. the blood of lambs *and goats*,
Jer. 50: 8. *as the he goats* before the flocks.
51:40. like rams with *he goats.*
Eze. 27:21. lambs, and rams, *and goats:*
34:17. the rams *and the he goats.* (marg. *great he goats*)
39:18. the blood...of rams, of lambs, *and* of *goats*, (marg. *great goats*)
Zec. 10: 3. I punished *the goats:*

6259, 6264 **עָתוּד** [*"gāh-thood'*], adj.

Est. 8:13. (כתיב) that the Jews should be *ready*
Isa. 10:13. removed the bounds of the people, *and* have robbed *their treasures*,

---

6261 **עִתִּי** *"git-tee'*, adj.

Lev.16:21. by the hand of a *fit* man (marg. a man of *opportunity*)

6264 **עָתִיד** *"gāh-theed'*, adj.

Deu32:35. at hand, and *the things that shall come* upon them make haste.
Est. 3:14. that they should be *ready*
8:13. that the Jews should be *ready*
Job 3: 8. curse the day, *who are ready* to raise up their mourning.
15:24. as a king *ready* to the battle.
Isa. 10:13. (כתיב) *and* have robbed *their treasures*,

6263 **עֲתִיד** [*"gătheed*], Ch. adj.

Dan 3:15. Now if ye *be ready* that at what time ye hear the sound

---

6266 **עָתִיק** *"gāh-theek'*, adj.

Isa. 23:18. to eat sufficiently, and for *durable* (marg. *old*) clothing.

6267 **עַתִּיק** [*"gat-teek'*], adj.

1Ch 4:22. And (these are) *ancient* things.
Isa. 28: 9. (them that are) weaned from the milk, (and) *drawn from* the breasts.

6268 **עַתִּיק** *"gat-teek'*, Ch.

Dan 7: 9. *and the Ancient of* days did sit,
13. and came to *the Ancient of* days,
22. Until *the Ancient of* days came,

6272 **עָתַם** [*"gāh-tham'*].

* NIPHAL.—*Preterite.* *

Isa. 9:19(18). Through the wrath of the Lord...*is* the land *darkened*,

---

6275 **עָתַק** [*"gāh-thak'*].

* KAL.—*Preterite.* *

Job 21: 7. Wherefore do the wicked live, *become old*, yea, are mighty
Ps. 6: 7(8). Mine eye is consumed because of grief; *it waxeth old*

KAL.—*Future.*

Job 14:18. the rock *is removed* out of his place.
18: 4. and *shall* the rock *be removed* out of his place?

* HIPHIL.—*Preterite.* *

Job 32:15. *they left off* speaking. (marg. *removed* speeches from themselves)
Pro.25: 1. proverbs of Solomon, which the men of Hezekiah...*copied out.*

HIPHIL.—*Future.*

Gen12: 8. *And he removed* from thence unto a mountain on the east
26:22. *And he removed* from thence, and digged

HIPHIL.—*Participle.*

Job 9: 5. *Which removeth* the mountains, and they know not:

עָתָק *"gāh-thāhk'*, adj. 6277

1Sa. 2: 3. let (not) *arrogancy* (marg. *hard*) come out of your mouth:
Ps. 31:18(19). the lying lips...which speak *grievous things* (marg. *a hard thing*)
75: 5(6). your horn on high: speak (not with) a *stiff* neck.
94: 4. (How long) shall they utter (and) speak *hard things?*

עָתֵק *"gāh-thēhk'*, adj. 6276

Pro. 8:18. (are) with me; (yea), *durable* riches and righteousness.

עָתַר [*"gāh-thar'*]. 6279

* KAL.—*Future.* *

Gen25:21. *And* Isaac *intreated* the Lord
Ex. 8:30(26). And Moses went out from Pharaoh, *and intreated* the Lord.
10:18. he went out from Pharaoh, *and intreated* the Lord.
Jud.13: 8. *Then* Manoah *intreated* the Lord,
Job 33:26. *He shall pray* unto God, and he will be favourable

* NIPHAL.—*Preterite.* *

Isa. 19:22. *and he shall be intreated* of them, and shall heal them.

NIPHAL.—*Infinitive.*

1Ch 5:20. *and he was intreated* of them;
2Ch 33:19. *and* (how God) *was intreated* of him,

NIPHAL.—*Future.*

Gen25:21. *and* the Lord *was intreated* of him,
2Sa.21:14. *And* after that God *was intreated* for the land.
24:25. *So* the Lord *was intreated* for the land,
2Ch 33:13. *and* he *was intreated* of him,
Ezr. 8:23. *and he was intreated* of us.

* HIPHIL.—*Preterite.* *

Ex. 8:29(25). I go out from thee, *and I will intreat* the Lord

HIPHIL.—*Imperative.*

Ex. 8: 8(4). *Intreat* the Lord, that he may take
28(24). only ye shall not go very far away: *intreat* for me.
9:28. *Intreat* the Lord for (it is) enough
10:17. *and intreat* the Lord your God,

HIPHIL.—*Future.*

Ex. 8: 9(5). when *shall I intreat* for thee,
Job 22:27. *Thou shalt make thy prayer* unto him,

עָתַר [*"gāh-thar'*]. 6280

* NIPHAL.—*Participle.* *

Pro.27: 6. *but* the kisses of an enemy (are) *deceitful.* (marg. or, *earnest*, or, *frequent*)

* HIPHIL.—*Preterite.* *

Eze.35:13. ye have boasted against me, *and have multiplied* your words

---

עָתָר [*"gāh-thāhr'*], m. 6282

Eze. 8:11. *and* a *thick* cloud of incense went up.
Zep. 3:10. From beyond the rivers of Ethiopia *my suppliants*,

---

עֲתֶרֶת *"gătheh'-reth*, f. 6283

Jer. 33: 6. reveal unto them *the abundance of* peace and truth.

פ pēh.

The Seventeenth Letter of the Alphabet.

6311 **פֹּא** *pōh*, part. adv.

Job 38:11. *and here* shall thy proud waves be stayed?

6284 **פָּאָה** [*pāh-āh'*].

* HIPHIL.—*Future.* *

Deu32:26. *I would scatter them into corners,*

6285 **פֵּאָה** *pēh-āh'*, f.

Ex. 25:26. put the rings in *the* four *corners*
26:18. twenty boards *on the* south *side*
20. *on the* north *side* (there shall be)
27: 9. *for the* south *side*
— hangings...*for* one *side:*
11. likewise *for the* north *side*
12. *on the* west *side* (shall be) hangings
13. *on the* east *side* eastward
36:23. twenty boards *for the* south *side*
25. *toward the* north *corner,*
37:13. put the rings upon *the* four *corners*
38: 9. *on the* south *side* southward
11. *for the* north *side* (the hangings were)
12. *And for the* west *side* (were) hangings
13. *And for the* east *side* eastward
Lev.13:41. *from the part of* his head
19: 9. *the corners of* thy field,
27. Ye shall not round *the corners of* your heads, neither shalt thou mar *the corners of* thy beard.
21: 5. *neither* shall they shave off *the corner of* their beard,
23:22. riddance of *the corners of* thy field
Nu. 24:17. shall smite *the corners* (marg. or, through *the princes*) of Moab,
34: 3. your south *quarter* shall be
35: 5. *the* east *side* two thousand cubits, and on *the* south *side* two thousand cubits, and on *the* west *side* two thousand cubits, and on *the* north *side* two thousand cubits;
Jos. 15: 5. And (their) border *in the* north *quarter*
18:12. their border *on the* north *side*
14. compassed *the corner of* the sea
— of Judah: this (was) *the* west *quarter.*
15. *And the* south *quarter* (was) from
20. the border of it *on the* east *side.*
Neh. 9:22. didst divide them *into corners:*
Jer. 9:26(25) & 25:23. all (that are) in *the* utmost *corners,*
48:45. shall devour *the corner of* Moab,
49:32. them (that are) in *the* utmost *corners;*
Eze.41:12. *at the end* toward the west
45: 7. *from the* west *side* westward, *and from the* east *side* eastward:
47:15. *toward the* north *side,*
17. And (this is) *the* north *side.*
18. *And the* east *side* ye shall measure
— And (this is) *the* east *side.*
19. *And the* south *side* southward,
— And (this is) *the* south *side*
20. *The* west *side also* (shall be) the great sea
— This (is) *the* west *side.*
48: 1. these are his *sides* east (and) west;
2, 8. *from the* east *side* unto *the* west *side,*
3. *from the* east *side* even unto *the* west *side,*
4, 5, 8. *from the* east *side* unto *the* west *side,*
6. *from the* east *side* even unto *the* west *side,*
7. *from the* east *side* unto *the* west *side,*
16. *the* north *side* four thousand and five hundred, *and the* south *side* four thousand and five hundred, *and on the* east *side* 4500, *and the* west *side* 4500.
23, 24, 25, 26, 27. *from the* east *side* unto *the* west *side*
28. at *the* south *side* southward,
30. goings out of the city *on the* north *side,*
32. at *the* east *side* four thousand and five hundred:
33. *And* at *the* south *side*
Eze.48:34. At *the* west *side* four thousand and five hundred,
Am. 3:12. in Samaria *in the corner of* a bed,

פָּאַר [*pāh-ar'*]. 6286

* PIEL.—*Preterite.* *

Isa. 55: 5. the Holy One of Israel; for *he hath glorified thee.*
60: 9. because *he hath glorified thee.*

PIEL.—*Infinitive.*

Ezr. 7:27. *to beautify* the house of the Lord
Isa. 60:13. *to beautify* the place of my sanctuary;

PIEL.—*Future.*

Deu24:20. *thou shalt* not *go over the boughs* again: (marg. *bough* (it) after thee)
Ps.149: 4. *he will beautify* the meek
Isa. 60: 7. *I will glorify* the house of my glory.

* HITHPAEL.—*Infinitive.* *

Isa. 60:21. of my hands, *that I may be glorified.*
61: 3. of the Lord, *that he might be glorified.*

HITHPAEL.—*Imperative.*

Ex. 8: 9(5). Moses said unto Pharaoh, *Glory* (marg. or, *Have* (this) *honour*) over me:

HITHPAEL.—*Future.*

Jud. 7: 2. lest Israel *vaunt themselves*
Isa. 10:15. *Shall* the ax *boast itself*
44:23. and *glorified himself* in Israel.
49: 3. O Israel, in whom *I will be glorified.*

פְּאֵר *p'ēhr*, m. 6287

Ex. 39:28. and *goodly* bonnets (lit. *ornaments of* bonnets) (of) fine linen,
Isa. 3:20. *The bonnets,* and the ornaments of the
61: 3. to give unto them *beauty* for ashes,
10. as a bridegroom decketh (himself) with *ornaments,*
Eze.24:17. bind *the tire of thine head*
23. *And your tires* (shall be) upon your heads,
44:18. They shall have linen *bonnets*

פֹּארָה [*p'ōh-rāh'*], f. 6288

Eze.17: 6. and shot forth *sprigs.*
31: 5. *his branches* became long
6. under *his branches*
8. chesnut trees were not *like his branches;*
12. *his boughs* are broken
13. the beasts...shall be upon *his branches:*

פֻּארָה *poo-rāh'*, f. 6288

Isa. 10:33. the Lord of hosts, shall lop *the bough*

פָּארוּר *pāh-roor'*, m. 6289

Joel 2: 6. faces shall gather *blackness.* (marg. *pot*)
Nah 2:10(11). the faces of them all gather *blackness.*

פַּג [*pag*], m. 6291

Cant.2:13. The fig tree putteth forth *her green figs,*

פִּגּוּל *pig-gool'*, m. 6292

Lev. 7:18. it shall be *an abomination,*
19: 7. it (is) *abominable;*
Isa. 65: 4. broth of *abominable things*
Eze. 4:14. neither came there *abominable* flesh into

פָּגַע *pāh-gāg'*. 6293

* KAL.—*Preterite.* *

Jos. 16: 7. *and came* to Jericho,
19:11. *and reached* to Dabbasheth, *and reached* to the river
22. *And* the coast *reacheth* to Tabor,
26. *and reacheth* to Carmel westward,

Jos. 19:27. to Beth-dagon, *and reacheth* to Zebulun,
34. *and reacheth* to Zebulun on the south side, and *reacheth* to Asher
1Sa.10: 5. *that thou shalt meet* a company
1K. 2:32. who *fell upon* two men
Isa. 64: 5(4). *Thou meetest* him that rejoiceth
Am. 5:19. *and* a bear *met him;*

KAL.—*Infinitive.*

Nu. 35:19. *when he meeteth him,* he shall slay him.
21. slay the murderer, *when he meeteth him.*
1Sa.22:17. would not put forth their hand *to fall*

KAL.—*Imperative.*

Gen23: 8. *and intreat* for me to Ephron
Jud. 8:21. Rise thou, *and fall* upon us:
1Sa.22:18. *and fall* upon the priests.
2Sa. 1:15. Go near, (and) *fall* upon him.
1K. 2:29. Go, *fall* upon him.
31. Do as he hath said, *and fall* upon him,

KAL.—*Future.*

Gen28:11. *And he lighted* upon a certain place,
32: 1(2). *and* the angels of God *met* him.
Ex. 5: 3. lest *he fall upon us* with pestilence,
20. *And they met* Moses and Aaron,
23: 4. If *thou meet* thine enemy's ox
Jos. 2:16. lest the pursuers *meet* you;
17:10. *they met together* in Asher
Jud.15:12. that *ye will* not *fall* upon me
18:25. lest angry fellows *run* upon thee,
Ru. 1:16. *Intreat* (marg. *Be* not *against*) me not to
2:22. that *they meet* thee not
1Sa.22:18. *and he fell* upon the priests,
1K. 2:25. *and he fell* upon him that he died.
34. *and fell* upon him, and slew him:
46. *and fell* upon him, that he died.
Job 21:15. what profit...if *we pray* unto him?
Isa. 47: 3. and *I will* not *meet* (thee as) a man.
Jer. 7:16. neither *make intercession*
27:18. *let them* now *make intercession*

* HIPHIL.—*Preterite.* *

Isa. 53: 6. the Lord *hath laid* (marg. *hath made...to meet*) on him the iniquity
Jer. 15:11. *I will cause* the enemy *to entreat* thee (well)
36:25. Gemariah *had made intercession*

HIPHIL.—*Future.*

Isa. 53:12. and *made intercession* for the transgressors.

HIPHIL.—*Participle.*

Job 36:32. *by* (the cloud) *that cometh betwixt.*
Isa. 59:16. wondered that there was no *intercessor:*

6294 **פֶּגַע** *peh'-gag*, m.

1K. 5: 4(18). neither adversary nor evil *occurrent.*
Ecc. 9:11. time *and chance* happeneth to them all.

6296 **פָּגַר** [*pāh-gar'*].

* PIEL.—*Preterite.* *

1Sa.30:10. *were so faint* that they could not go
21. two hundred men, which *were so faint*

6297 **פֶּגֶר** *peh'-ger*, m.

Gen15:11. the fowls came down upon *the carcases,*
Lev.26:30. and cast *your carcases* upon *the carcases of* your idols,
Nu. 14:29. *Your carcases* shall fall
32. *But* (as for) you, *your carcases,* they shall
33. until *your carcases* be wasted
1Sa.17:46. *the carcases of* the host of the Philistines
2K. 19:35. they (were) all dead *corpses.*
2Ch 20:24. they (were) *dead bodies* fallen
25. riches *with the dead bodies,*
Isa. 14:19. *as a carcase* trodden under feet.
34: 3. *and* their stink shall come up out of *their carcases,*
37:36. they (were) all dead *corpses.*
66:24. *upon the carcases of* the men that
Jer. 31:40. the whole valley of *the dead bodies,*
33: 5. *the dead bodies of* men,
41: 9. *the dead bodies of* the men,
Eze. 6: 5. *the dead carcases of* the children of Israel
43: 7. *nor by the carcases of* their kings
9. *and the carcases of* their kings,
Am. 8: 3. (there shall be) many *dead bodies*
Nah 3: 3. a great number of *carcases;*

פָּגַשׁ [*pāh-gash'*]. 6298

* KAL.—*Preterite.* *

Gen33: 8. this drove which *I met?*
Isa. 34:14. The wild beasts of the desert *shall also meet*

KAL.—*Infinitive.*

Pro.17:12. *Let* a bear robbed of her whelps *meet* a
Jer. 41: 6. *as he met* them, he said unto them,

KAL.—*Future.*

Gen32:17(18). When Esau my brother *meeteth thee,*
Ex. 4:24. *that* the Lord *met him,*
27. *and met him* in the mount of God,
1Sa.25:20. David and his men came down...*and she met* them.
2Sa. 2:13. the servants of David, went out, *and met together* (marg. *them together*)
Hos13: 8. *I will meet them* as a bear

* NIPHAL.—*Preterite.* *

Ps. 85:10(11). Mercy and truth *are met* together;
Pro.22: 2. The rich and poor *meet* together:
29:13. The poor and the deceitful man *meet together:*

* PIEL.—*Future.* *

Job 5:14. *They meet with* (marg. or, *run into*) darkness

פָּדָה *pāh-dāh'*. 6299

* KAL.—*Preterite.* *

Lev.27:27. *then he shall redeem* (it) according
Deu 9:26. thine inheritance, which *thou hast redeemed*
21: 8. Israel, whom *thou hast redeemed,*
2Sa. 4: 9. the Lord liveth, who *hath redeemed*
7:23. thy people, which *thou redeemedst*
1K. 1:29. (As) the Lord liveth, that *hath redeemed*
1Ch.17:21. thy people, whom *thou hast redeemed*
Neh 1:10. thy people, whom *thou hast redeemed*
Job 5:20. In famine *he shall redeem thee*
33:28. *He will deliver* his soul
Ps. 31: 5(6). *thou hast redeemed* me, O Lord God
55:18(19). *He hath delivered* my soul
71:23. my soul, which *thou hast redeemed.*
78:42. *he delivered them* from the enemy
Isa. 29:22. the Lord, who *redeemed* Abraham,
Jer. 15:21. *and I will redeem thee* out of the hand of
31:11. the Lord *hath redeemed* Jacob,
Mic. 6: 4. and *redeemed thee* out of the house of
Zec 10: 8. *I have redeemed them:* and they

KAL.—*Infinitive.*

Nu. 18:15. the firstborn of man shalt thou *surely* redeem, (lit. *redeeming* thou shalt redeem)
2Sa. 7:23. whom God went *to redeem*
1Ch 17:21. whom God went *to redeem*
Ps. 49: 7(8). None (of them) can *by any means* redeem (lit. *redeeming* can redeem) his brother,

KAL.—*Imperative.*

Ps. 25:22. *Redeem* Israel, O God,
26:11. *redeem me,* and be merciful unto me.
44:26(27). *and redeem us* for thy mercies' sake
69:18(19). *deliver me* because of mine enemies.
119:134. *Deliver me* from the oppression

KAL.—*Future.*

Ex. 13:13. every firstling of an ass *thou shalt redeem*
— if *thou wilt* not *redeem* it,
— all the firstborn of man...*shalt thou redeem*
15. all the firstborn of my children *I redeem.*
34:20. the firstling of an ass *thou shalt redeem*
— if *thou redeem* (him) not,
— the firstborn of thy sons *thou shalt redeem.*
Nu. 18:15. the firstborn of man *shalt thou* surely *redeem,* and the firstling of unclean beasts *shalt thou redeem.*

Nu. 18:16. from a month old *shalt thou redeem*,
17. firstling of a goat, *thou shalt* not *redeem;*
Deu 7: 8. *and redeemed you* out of the house of
15:15 & 24:18. *and* the Lord thy God *redeemed thee:*
1 Sa. 14:45. *So* the people *rescued* Jonathan,
Job 6:23. *Redeem me* from the hand of the mighty?
Ps. 49: 7(8). None (of them) *can* by any means *redeem*
15(16). God *will redeem* my soul
130: 8. *he shall redeem* Israel
Hos. 7:13. though I *have redeemed them*,
13:14. *I will ransom them* from the power

KAL.—*Participle.* Poel.

Deu 13: 5(6). *and redeemed you* out of the house of
Ps. 34:22(23). The Lord *redeemeth* the soul of his

KAL.—*Participle.* Paül.

Nu. 18:16. *And those that are to be redeemed*
Isa. 35:10. *And the ransomed of* the Lord shall return,
51:11. *Therefore the redeemed of* the Lord

* NIPHAL.—*Preterite.* *

Lev. 19:20. and not at all *redeemed*,

NIPHAL.—*Future.*

Lev. 27:29. None devoted,...*shall be redeemed;*
Isa. 1:27. Zion *shall be redeemed* with judgment,

* HIPHIL.—*Preterite.* *

Ex. 21: 8. *then shall he let her be redeemed:* to sell

* HOPHAL.—*Infinitive.* *

Lev. 19:20. a woman, that (is) a bondmaid,...*and* not *at all* redeemed, (lit. *and being redeemed* not redeemed)

6302 פְּדוּיִם [*p'doo-yeem'*], m. pl.

Nu. 3:46. *those that are to be redeemed*
48. *wherewith* the odd number of them is *to be redeemed*,
49. above them *that were redeemed*
51. money of *them that were redeemed*

6304 פְּדוּת *p'dooth*, f.

Ex. 8:23(19). I will put *a division* (marg. *a redemption*) between my people
Ps. 111: 9. He sent *redemption* unto his people:
130: 7. with him (is) plenteous *redemption*.
Isa. 50: 2. shortened at all, *that it cannot redeem?*

6306 פִּדְיוֹם *pid-yōhm'*, m.

Nu. 3:49. Moses took the *redemption* money
51. (כתיב) money of *them that were redeemed*

6306 פִּדְיוֹן *pid-yōhn'*, m.

Ex. 21:30. *for the ransom of* his life
Ps. 49: 8(9). *the redemption of* their soul

6308 פָּדַע [*pāh-dag'*].

* KAL.—*Imperative.* *

Job 33:24. *Deliver him* from going down

6309 פֶּדֶר [*peh'-der*], m.

Lev. 1: 8. the head, and *the fat*,
12. with his head and *his fat:*
8:20. the pieces, and *the fat*.

6310 פֶּה *peh*, m.

Gen 4:11. the earth, which hath opened *her mouth*
8:11. *in her mouth* (was) an olive leaf
24:57. the damsel, and enquire at *her mouth*.
25:28. he *did eat* of (his) venison: (marg. venison (was) *in his mouth*)
29: 2. stone (was) upon the well's *mouth*.
3. rolled the stone from the well's *mouth*,
— upon the well's *mouth* in his place.
8. roll the stone from the well's *mouth;*
10. rolled the stone from the well's *mouth*,
Gen 34:26. *with the edge* (marg. *mouth*) *of* the sword,
41:40. according unto *thy word*
42:27. for, behold, it (was) *in* his sack's *mouth*.
43: 7. *according to the tenor* (marg. *mouth*) *of*
12. *in the mouth of* your sacks,
21. *in the mouth of* his sack,
44: 1. money *in* his sack's *mouth*.
2. *in* the sack's *mouth* of the youngest,
8. found *in* our sacks' *mouths*,
45:12. (it is) *my mouth* that speaketh
21. according to *the commandment* (marg *mouth*) *of* Pharaoh,
47:12. *according to* (their) families.
Ex. 4:10. I (am) slow of *speech*,
11. Who hath made man's *mouth?*
12. I will be with *thy mouth*,
15. and put words *in his mouth:* and I will be with *thy mouth*, and with *his mouth*,
16. he shall be to thee *instead of a mouth*,
12: 4. every man *according to* his eating
13: 9. that the Lord's law may be *in thy mouth:*
16:16, 18, 21. every man *according to* his eating,
17: 1. according to *the commandment of*
13. his people *with the edge of* the sword.
23:13. neither let it be heard out of *thy mouth*.
28:32. there shall be *an hole in* the top...round *about the hole of it, as it were the hole of* an habergeon,
34:27. after *the tenor of* these words
38:21. according to *the commandment of*
39:23. *And* (there was) *an hole* in the midst of the robe, *as the hole of* an habergeon, (with) a band round *about the hole*,
Lev. 24:12. that *the mind of* the Lord might be
25:16. *According to* the multitude of years...*and according to* the fewness of years
51. *according unto them* he shall give
52. *according unto* his years shall he give
27: 8. *according to* his ability that vowed
16. thy estimation shall be *according to*
18. *according to* the years that remain,
Nu. 3:16. according to *the word* (marg. *mouth*) *of* the Lord,
39. at *the commandment of* the Lord,
51. according to *the word of* the Lord,
4:27. At *the appointment* (marg. *mouth*) *of*
37, 41, 49. according to *the commandment of*
45. according to *the word of* the Lord
6:21. *according to* the vow which he vowed,
7: 5. every man *according to* his service.
7. *according to* their service:
8. *according unto* their service,
9:17. *And when* the cloud was taken up
18, 18, 23, 23, 23. At *the commandment of* the
20, 20. according to *the commandment of*
10:13. according to *the commandment of*
12: 8. With him will I speak *mouth* to *mouth*,
13: 3. by *the commandment of* the Lord
14:41. transgress *the commandment of* the Lord?
16:30. and the earth open *her mouth*,
32. And the earth opened *her mouth*,
20:24. ye rebelled against *my word* (marg. *mouth*)
21:24. *with the edge of* the sword,
22:18. go beyond *the word of* the Lord
28. the Lord opened *the mouth of* the ass,
38. the word that God putteth *in my mouth*,
23: 5. the Lord put a word *in* Balaam's *mouth*,
12. the Lord hath put *in my mouth?*
16. and put a word *in his mouth*,
24:13. *the commandment of* the Lord,
26:10. the earth opened *her mouth*,
54. *according to* those that were numbered
56. *According to* the lot shall
27:14. rebelled against *my commandment*
21. at *his word* shall they go out, and at *his word* they shall come in,
30: 2(3). all that proceedeth *out of his mouth*.
32:24. hath proceeded *out of your mouth*.
33: 2. by *the commandment of* the Lord:
38. at *the commandment of* the Lord,
35: 8. *according to* his inheritance
30. *by the mouth of* witnesses:
36: 5. according to *the word of* the Lord,
Deu 1:26, 43. rebelled against *the commandment of*
8: 3. proceedeth out of *the mouth of* the Lord
9:23. *the commandment of* the Lord
11: 6. the earth opened *her mouth*,

Deu 13:15(16), 15(16). *with the edge of* the sword,
17: 6. At *the mouth of* two witnesses,
— at *the mouth of* one witness
10. thou shalt do *according to* the sentence,
11. According to *the sentence of* the law
18:18. will put my words *in his mouth;*
19:15. at *the mouth of* two witnesses, or at *the mouth of* three witnesses,
20:13. *with the edge of* the sword:
21: 5. by *their word* (marg. *mouth*) shall every
17. *a* double *portion of* all
23:23(24). hast promised *with thy mouth.*
30:14. the word (is) very nigh unto thee, *in thy mouth,*
31:19. put it *in their mouths,* that this song
21. *out of the mouths of* their seed:
32: 1. the words of *my mouth.*
34: 5. according to *the word of* the Lord.
Jos. 1: 8. shall not depart *out of thy mouth;*
18. doth rebel against *thy commandment,*
6:10. (any) word proceed *out of your mouth,*
21. *with the edge of* the sword.
8:24. fallen *on the edge of* the sword,
— smote it *with the edge of* the sword.
9: 2. with Joshua and with Israel, with one *accord.* (marg. *mouth*)
14. at *the mouth of* the Lord.
10:18. upon *the mouth of* the cave,
22. Open *the mouth of* the cave,
27. laid great stones in the cave's *mouth,*
28, 30, 32. smote it *with the edge of* the sword,
35, 37. and smote it *with the edge of* the
39. smote them *with the edge of* the sword,
11:11. therein *with the edge of* the sword,
12. smote them *with the edge of* the sword,
14. they smote *with the edge of* the sword,
15:13 & 17:4. according to *the commandment of*
18: 4. *according to* the inheritance
19:47. smote it *with the edge of* the sword,
50. According to *the word of* the Lord
21: 3. at *the commandment of* the Lord,
22: 9. according to *the word of* the Lord
Jud. 1: 8. smitten it *with the edge of* the sword,
25. they smote the city *with the edge of* the
4:15. all (his) host, *with the edge of* the sword
16. fell *upon the edge of* the sword;
7: 6. lapped, (putting) their hand to *their mouth,*
9:38. Where (is) now *thy mouth,*
11:35. I have opened *my mouth* unto the Lord,
36. (if) thou hast opened *thy mouth*
— which hath proceeded *out of thy mouth;*
18:19. lay thine hand upon *thy mouth,*
27. smote them *with the edge of* the sword,
20:37. the city *with the edge of* the sword.
48. smote them *with the edge of* the sword,
21:10. Jabesh-gilead *with the edge of* the sword,
1Sa. 1:12. Eli marked *her mouth.*
2: 1. *my mouth* is enlarged
3. (not) arrogancy come *out of your mouth:*
12:14. *the commandment* (marg. *mouth*) *of* the
15. rebel against *the commandment of* the
13:21. they had a file (marg. a file *with mouths*) for the mattocks,
14:26. no man put his hand to *his mouth:*
27. and put his hand to *his mouth;*
15: 8. the people *with the edge of* the sword.
24. *the commandment of* the Lord,
17:35. delivered (it) *out of his mouth:*
22:19. smote he *with the edge of* the sword,
— sheep, *with the edge of* the sword.
2Sa. 1:16. *thy mouth* hath testified
13:32. by *the appointment* (marg. *mouth*) *of* Absalom
14: 3. Joab put the words *in her mouth.*
19. *in the mouth of* thine handmaid:
15:14. the city *with the edge of* the sword.
17: 5. what *he saith.* (marg. what (is) *in his mouth*)
18:25. (there is) tidings *in his mouth.*
22: 9. fire *out of his mouth* devoured:
1K. 7:31. *And the mouth of it* within
— *but the mouth thereof* (was) round
— upon *the mouth of it* (were) gravings
8:15. spake *with his mouth* unto David
24. thou spakest also *with thy mouth,*
13:21. disobeyed *the mouth of* the Lord,
26. disobedient unto *the word of* the Lord;

1K. 17: 1. *according* to my *word.*
24. the word of the Lord *in thy mouth*
19:18. every *mouth* which hath not kissed him.
22:13. (declare) good unto the king with one *mouth:*
22. *in the mouth of* all his prophets.
23. *in the mouth of* all these thy prophets,
2K. 2: 9. *a* double *portion of* thy spirit
4:34. and put *his mouth* upon *his mouth,*
10:21. the house of Baal was full *from one end to another.* (lit. *mouth to mouth*)
25. *with the edge* (marg. *mouth*) *of* the sword;
21:16. Jerusalem *from one end to another;* (marg. from *mouth to mouth*)
23:35. according to *the commandment of*
24: 3. at *the commandment of* the Lord
1Ch 12:23. *according to the word of* the Lord.
32. brethren (were) at *their commandment.*
16:12. the judgments of *his mouth;*
2Ch 6: 4. spake *with his mouth* to my father David,
15. and spakest *with thy mouth,*
18:12. (declare) good to the king with one *assent;* (marg. *mouth*)
21. *in the mouth of* all his prophets.
22. *in the mouth of* these thy prophets,
31: 2. every man *according to* his service,
35:22. *from the mouth of* God,
36:12. *from the mouth of* the Lord.
21, 22. *by the mouth of* Jeremiah,
Ezr. 1: 1. *by the mouth of* Jeremiah
8:17. I told them what they should say (marg. I put words *in their mouth*)
9:11. filled it *from one end to another* (marg. *mouth* to *mouth*)
Neh 9:20. not thy manna *from their mouth,*
Est. 7: 8. As the word went *out of* the king's *mouth,*
Job 1:15, 17. *with the edge of* the sword;
3: 1. opened Job *his mouth,*
5:15. *from their mouth,* and from the hand
16. iniquity stoppeth *her mouth.*
7:11. I will not refrain *my mouth;*
8: 2. the words of *thy mouth*
21. Till he fill *thy mouth*
9:20. *mine own mouth* shall condemn me:
15: 5. *thy mouth* uttereth thine iniquity,
6. *Thine own mouth* condemneth thee,
13. lettest (such) words go *out of thy mouth?*
30. by the breath of *his mouth*
16: 5. I would strengthen you with *my mouth,*
10. gaped upon me *with their mouth;*
19:16. I intreated him with *my mouth.*
20:12. Though wickedness be sweet in *his mouth,*
21: 5. lay (your) hand upon (your) *mouth.*
22:22. the law *from his mouth,*
23: 4. *and* fill *my mouth* with arguments.
12. the words of *his mouth*
29: 9. laid (their) hand *on their mouth.*
23. *and* they opened *their mouth* wide
30:18. *as the collar of* my coat.
31:27. *my mouth* hath kissed my hand:
32: 5. no answer *in the mouth of*
33: 2. now I have opened *my mouth,*
6. I (am) *according to thy wish* (marg. *mouth*)
35:16. Therefore doth Job open *his mouth*
36:16. would he have removed thee *out of* the
37: 2. the sound (that) goeth out *of his mouth.*
39:27. Doth the eagle mount up at *thy command,* (marg. by *thy mouth*)
40: 4. I will lay mine hand upon *my mouth.*
23. he can draw up Jordan into *his mouth.*
41:19(11). *Out of his mouth* go burning lamps,
21(13). a flame goeth *out of his mouth.*
Ps. 5: 9(10). no faithfulness *in their* (marg. *his*) *mouth;*
8: 2(3). *Out of the mouth of* babes and
10: 7. *His mouth* is full of cursing
17: 3. *my mouth* shall not transgress.
10. with *their mouth* they speak proudly.
18: 8(9). fire *out of his mouth* devoured:
19:14(15). Let the words of *my mouth,*
22:13(14). gaped upon me (with) *their mouths,*
21(22). Save me *from* the lion's *mouth:*
33: 6. by the breath of *his mouth.*
34: 1(2). his praise (shall) continually (be) *in my mouth.*
35:21. they opened *their mouth* wide
36: 3(4). The words of *his mouth* (are) iniquity

Ps. 37:30. *The mouth of* the righteous speaketh
38:13(14). openeth not *his mouth.*
14(15). *in whose mouth* (are) no reproofs.
39: 1(2). I will keep *my mouth* with a bridle, (marg. a bridle *for my mouth*)
9(10). I opened not *my mouth;*
40: 3(4). he hath put a new song *in my mouth,*
49: 3(4). *My mouth* shall speak of wisdom;
13(14). their posterity approve *their sayings.* (marg. delight *in their mouth*)
50:16. take my covenant in *thy mouth?*
19. Thou givest *thy mouth* to evil,
51:15(17). open thou my lips; *and my mouth*
54: 2(4). the words of *my mouth.*
55:21(22). (The words) of *his mouth* were
58: 6(7). Break their teeth, O God, *in their mouth:*
59: 7(8). they belch out *with their mouth:*
12(13). the sin of *their mouth* (and) the
62: 4(5). they bless *with their mouth,*
63: 5(6). *my mouth* shall praise (thee) with
11(12). *the mouth of* them that speak lies
66:14. *my mouth* hath spoken, when I
17. I cried unto him with *my mouth,*
69:15(16). let not the pit shut *her mouth* upon
71: 8. Let *my mouth* be filled (with) thy praise
15. *My mouth* shall shew forth thy
73: 9. They set *their mouth* against the heavens,
78: 1. your ears to the words of *my mouth.*
2. I will open *my mouth*
30. while their meat (was) yet *in their mouths,*
36. they did flatter him *with their mouth,*
81:10(11). open *thy mouth* wide, and I will fill
89: 1(2). *with my mouth* will I make known
105: 5. the judgments of *his mouth;*
107:42. iniquity shall stop *her mouth.*
109: 2. *the mouth of* the wicked *and the mouth of*
30. praise the Lord *with my mouth;*
115: 5. They have *mouths,* but they speak not:
119:13. the judgments of *thy mouth.*
43. take not the word...*out of my mouth;*
72. The law of *thy mouth*
88. the testimony of *thy mouth.*
103. (sweeter) than honey *to my mouth!*
108. the freewill offerings of *my mouth,*
131. I opened *my mouth,* and panted:
126: 2. Then was *our mouth* filled with laughter,
133: 2. went down to *the skirts of* his garments;
135:16. They have *mouths,* but they speak not;
17. neither is there (any) breath *in their mouths.*
138: 4. the words of *thy mouth.*
141: 3. Set a watch, O Lord, *before my mouth;*
7. Our bones are scattered at the grave's *mouth,*
144: 8, 11. *Whose mouth* speaketh vanity,
145:21. *My mouth* shall speak the praise of
Pro. 2: 6. *out of his mouth* (cometh) knowledge
4: 5. the words of *my mouth.*
24. Put away from thee *a* froward *mouth,*
5: 4. sharp as a *twoedged* sword. (lit. a sword of *edges*)
7. depart not from the words of *my mouth.*
6: 2. snared with the words of *thy mouth,* thou art taken with the words of *thy mouth.*
12. man, walketh with *a* froward *mouth.*
7:24. attend to the words of *my mouth.*
8: 3. *at the entry of* the city,
8. All the words of *my mouth*
13. *and the* froward *mouth,* do I hate.
29. waters should not pass *his commandment:*
10: 6, 11. *but* violence covereth *the mouth of* the
11. *The mouth of* a righteous (man)
14. *but the mouth of* the foolish (is) near
31. *The mouth of* the just bringeth
32. *but the mouth of* the wicked (speaketh)
11: 9. An hypocrite *with* (his) *mouth* destroyeth
11. *by the mouth of* the wicked.
12: 6. *but the mouth of* the upright
8. *according to* his wisdom:
14. satisfied with good by the fruit of (his) *mouth:*
13: 2. shall eat good by the fruit of (his) *mouth:*
3. He that keepeth *his mouth*
14: 3. *In the mouth of* the foolish
15: 2. *but the mouth of* fools poureth out
14. *but the mouth of* fools feedeth on
23. man hath joy by the answer of *his mouth:*
28. *but the mouth of* the wicked poureth out

Pro.16:10. *his mouth* transgresseth not in judgment.
23. The heart of the wise teacheth *his mouth,*
26. *his mouth* craveth it of him.
18: 4. The words of a man's *mouth*
6. *and his mouth* calleth for strokes.
7. A fool's *mouth* (is) his destruction,
20. satisfied with the fruit of his *mouth;*
19:24. bring it to *his mouth* again.
28. *and the mouth of* the wicked
20:17. *his mouth* shall be filled with gravel.
21:23. Whoso keepeth *his mouth*
22: 6. Train up a child *in* the way
14. *The mouth of* strange women
24: 7. he openeth not *his mouth* in the gate.
26: 7, 9. a parable *in the mouth of* fools.
15. to bring it again to *his mouth.*
28. and *a* flattering *mouth* worketh ruin.
27: 2. praise thee, and not *thine own mouth;*
21. so (is) a man *to* his praise.
30:20. she eateth, and wipeth *her mouth,*
32. (lay) thine hand *upon* thy *mouth.* (lit. hand *to mouth*)
31: 8. Open *thy mouth* for the dumb
9. Open *thy mouth,* judge righteously,
26. She openeth *her mouth* with wisdom;
Ecc. 5: 2(1). Be not rash with *thy mouth,*
6(5). Suffer not *thy mouth* to cause
6: 7. All the labour of man (is) *for his mouth,*
8: 2. to keep the king's *commandment,*
10:12. The words of a wise man's *mouth*
13. The beginning of the words of *his mouth* (is) foolishness: and the end of *his talk* (marg. *mouth*) (is) mischievous
Cant. 1: 2. Let him kiss me with the kisses of *his mouth:*
Isa. 1:20. *the mouth of* the Lord hath spoken (it).
5:14. opened *her mouth* without measure:
6: 7. he laid (it) upon *my mouth,*
9:12(11). shall devour Israel with open *mouth.*
17(16). and every *mouth* speaketh folly.
10:14. or opened *the mouth,* or peeped.
11: 4. the earth with the rod of *his mouth,*
19: 7. by *the mouth of* the brooks,
29:13. people draw near (me) *with their mouth,*
30: 2. *and* have not asked at *my mouth;*
34:16. *my mouth* it hath commanded,
40: 5. *the mouth of* the Lord hath spoken (it).
45:23. the word is gone out *of my mouth*
48: 3. *and* they went forth *out of my mouth,*
49: 2. he hath made *my mouth*
51:16. I have put my words *in thy mouth,*
52:15. the kings shall shut *their mouths*
53: 7. he opened not *his mouth:*
— so he openeth not *his mouth.*
9. neither (was any) deceit *in his mouth.*
55:11. my word be that goeth forth *out of my mouth:*
57: 4. against whom make ye *a* wide *mouth,*
58:14. *the mouth of* the Lord hath spoken (it).
59:21. my words which I have put *in thy mouth,* shall not depart *out of thy mouth, nor out of the mouth of* thy seed, *nor out of the mouth of* thy seed's seed,
62: 2. which *the mouth of* the Lord shall name.
Jer. 1: 9. the Lord...touched *my mouth.*
— I have put my words *in thy mouth.*
5:14. I will make my words *in thy mouth* fire,
7:28. truth is perished,...*from their mouth.*
9: 8(7). (one) speaketh peaceably...*with his mouth,*
12(11). *the mouth of* the Lord hath spoken,
20(19). receive the word of *his mouth,*
12: 2. thou (art) near *in their mouth,*
15:19. thou shalt be *as my mouth:*
21: 7. *with the edge of* the sword;
23:16. *out of the mouth of* the Lord.
29:10. That *after* seventy years be accomplished
32: 4. shall speak with him *mouth* to *mouth,* (lit. *his mouth* with *his mouth*)
34: 3. *and* he shall speak with thee *mouth* to *mouth,* (marg. *his mouth* shall speak *to thy mouth*)
36: 4. Baruch wrote *from the mouth of* Jeremiah
6. which thou hast written *from my mouth,*
17. write all these words *at his mouth?*
18. He pronounced all these words...*with his mouth,*

Jer. 36:27. Baruch wrote *at the mouth of* Jeremiah,
32. wrote therein *from the mouth of* Jeremiah
44:17. *out of our own mouth*,
25. have both spoken *with your mouths*,
26. *in the mouth of* any man of Judah
45: 1. in a book *at the mouth of* Jeremiah,
48:28. in the sides of the hole's *mouth*.
51:44. I will bring forth *out of his mouth*
Lam. 1:18. rebelled against *his commandment*: (marg. *mouth*)
2:16. thine enemies have opened *their mouth*
3:29. He putteth *his mouth* in the dust;
38. *Out of the mouth of* the most High
46. our enemies have opened *their mouths*
Eze. 2: 8. open *thy mouth*, and eat that I give thee.
3: 2. So I opened *my mouth*, and he caused
3. it was *in my mouth* as honey
17. hear the word *at my mouth*,
27. I will open *thy mouth*, and thou
4:14. neither came there abominable flesh *into my mouth*.
16:56. Sodom was not mentioned *by thy mouth*
63. never open thy *mouth*
21:22(27). to open *the mouth* in the slaughter,
24:27. shall *thy mouth* be opened
29:21. I will give thee the opening of *the mouth*
33: 7. thou shalt hear the word *at my mouth*,
22. and had opened *my mouth*,
— and *my mouth* was opened, and I was no
31. *with their mouth* they shew much love,
34:10. I will deliver my flock *from their mouth*,
35:13. *with your mouth* ye have boasted
Dan 10: 3. neither came flesh nor wine in *my mouth*,
16. then I opened *my mouth*,
Hos. 2:17(19). take away the names of Baalim *out of her mouth*,
6: 5. slain them by the words of *my mouth*:
10:12. Sow to yourselves in righteousness, reap *in* mercy;
Joel 1: 5. it is cut off *from your mouth*.
Am. 3:12. *out of the mouth of* the lion
6: 5. That chant to *the sound of* the viol,
Obad. 12. shouldest thou have *spoken* proudly (marg. magnified *thy mouth*)
Mic. 3: 5. he that putteth not into *their mouths*,
4: 4. *the mouth of* the Lord of hosts
6:12. their tongue (is) deceitful *in their mouth*.
7: 5. keep the doors of *thy mouth*
16. shall lay (their) hand upon (their) *mouth*,
Nah. 3:12. fall into *the mouth of* the eater.
Zep. 3:13. neither shall a deceitful tongue be found *in their mouth*:
Zec. 1:21(2:4). *so that* no man did lift up his head:
5: 8. of lead upon *the mouth thereof*.
8: 9. *by the mouth of* the prophets,
9: 7. take away his blood *out of his mouth*,
13: 8. two *parts* therein shall be cut off
14:12. tongue shall consume away *in their mouth*.
Mal. 2: 6. The law of truth was *in his mouth*,
7. they should seek the law *at his mouth*:
9. *according as* ye have not kept

6311 פֹּה & פּוֹ *pōh*, part. adv.

Gen19:12. Hast thou *here* any besides?
1Sa.16:11. we will not sit down till he come *hither*.
Isa. 22:16. hast thou *here*? and whom hast thou *here*, &c.

With prefix מִפּוֹ, מִפֹּה only in Ezekiel.

Eze.40:10. three *on this side*, and three *on that side*;
41: 1. six cubits broad *on the one side*, and six cubits broad *on the other side*.
&c.

6313 פּוּג [*poog*].

∗ KAL.—*Future*. ∗

Gen45:26. *And* Jacob's heart *fainted*,
Ps. 77: 2(3). my sore ran in the night, and *ceased*
Hab. 1: 4. Therefore the law *is slacked*,

∗ NIPHAL.—*Preterite*. ∗

Ps. 38: 8(9). *I am feeble* and sore broken:

פּוּגָה [*poo-gāh'*], f. 6314

Lam. 2:18. give thyself no *rest*;

פּוּחַ [*poo'ăgh*]. 6315

∗ KAL.—*Future*. ∗

Cant. 2:17 & 4:6. Until the day *break*, (marg. *breathe*)

∗ HIPHIL.—*Imperative*. ∗

Cant. 4:16. *blow upon* my garden,

HIPHIL.—*Future*.

Ps. 10: 5. his enemies, *he puffeth* at them.
12: 5(6). (from him that) *puffeth* at him. (marg. or, *would ensnare* him)
Pro. 6:19. A false witness (that) *speaketh* lies,
12:17. (He that) *speaketh* truth
14: 5. *but* a false witness *will utter* lies.
25. *but* a deceitful (witness) *speaketh* lies.
19: 5. *and* (he that) *speaketh* lies shall not
9. *and* (he that) *speaketh* lies shall perish.
29: 8. Scornful men *bring* a city *into a snare*:
Eze. 21:31(36). *I will blow* against thee
Hab. 2: 3. *but* at the end *it shall speak*,

פּוּךְ *pooch*, m. 6320

2K. 9:30. and she *painted* her face, (marg. put her eyes *in painting*)
1Ch 29: 2. *glistering* stones, and of divers colours,
Isa. 54:11. I will lay thy stones *with fair colours*,
Jer. 4:30. thou rentest thy face *with painting*,

פּוֹל *pōhl*, m. 6321

2Sa. 17:28. flour, and parched (corn), *and beans*,
Eze. 4: 9. barley, *and beans*, and lentiles,

פּוּן [*poon*]. 6323

∗ KAL.—*Future*. ∗

Ps. 88:15(16). I suffer thy terrors *I am distracted*.

פּוּץ [*pootz*]. 6327

∗ KAL.—*Imperative*. ∗

1Sa. 14:34. *Disperse yourselves* among the people,

KAL.—*Future*.

Gen11: 4. lest *we be scattered* abroad
Nu. 10:35. *and let* thine enemies *be scattered*;
1Sa. 11:11. *that they* which remained *were scattered*,
2Sa. 20:22. *and they retired* (marg. *were scattered*) from the city,
Ps. 68:1(2). *let* his enemies *be scattered*:
Pro. 5:16. *Let* thy fountains *be dispersed*
Eze. 34: 5. *And they were scattered*, because
— of the field, *when they were scattered*.
46:18. *that* my people *be* not *scattered*
Zec. 1:17. My cities...*shall* yet *be spread abroad*;
13: 7. *and* the sheep *shall be scattered*:

KAL.—*Participle*. Paül.

Zep. 3:10. the daughter of *my dispersed*,

∗ NIPHAL.—*Preterite*. ∗

Gen10:18. *were* the families of the Canaanites *spread abroad*.
2K. 25: 5. all his army *were scattered* from him.
Jer. 10:21. and all their flocks *shall be scattered*.
40:15. *that* all the Jews...*should be scattered*,
52: 8. all his army *was scattered*
Eze. 11:17. countries where *ye have been scattered*,
20:34. the countries wherein *ye are scattered*,
41. countries wherein *ye have been scattered*;
28:25. people among whom *they are scattered*,
29:13. the people whither *they were scattered*:
34: 6. my flock *was scattered* upon all
12. places where *they have been scattered*

NIPHAL.—*Participle*.

2Sa. 18: 8. For the battle was there *scattered*
1K. 22:17. I saw all Israel *scattered*
2Ch 18:16. I did see all Israel *scattered*

* POLEL.—*Future.* *

Jer. 23:29. like a hammer (that) *breaketh...in pieces?*

* PILPEL.—*Future.* *

Job 16:12. *and shaken me to pieces,* and set

* HIPHIL.—*Preterite.* *

Gen11: 9. from thence *did* the Lord *scatter them*
Deu 4:27. *And* the Lord *shall scatter* you
28:64. *And* the Lord *shall scatter thee*
30: 3. the Lord thy God *hath scattered thee.*
Job 18:11. *and shall drive* (marg. *scatter*) *him* to his
Isa. 24: 1. *and scattereth abroad* the inhabitants
28:25. *doth he* not *cast abroad* the fitches,
Jer. 9:16(15). *I will scatter them also*
23: 2. *Ye have scattered* my flock,
30:11. whither *I have scattered thee,*
Eze.11:16. although *I have scattered them*
22:15. *And I will scatter* thee among
29:12 & 30:23,26. *and I will scatter* the Egyptians
34:21. *ye have scattered* them abroad ;

HIPHIL.—*Infinitive.*

Eze.12:15. *when I shall scatter* them
20:23. *that I would scatter* them among
Hab. 3:14. came out as a whirlwind *to scatter me :*

HIPHIL.—*Imperative.*

Job 40:11. *Cast abroad* the rage of thy wrath:

HIPHIL.—*Future.*

Gen11: 8. *So* the Lord *scattered* them
49: 7. *and scatter them* in Israel.
Ex. 5:12. *So* the people *were scattered abroad*
1Sa.13: 8. *and* the people *were scattered* from him.
2Sa.22:15. he sent out arrows, *and scattered them;*
Neh 1: 8. I *will scatter* you abroad
Job 37:11. *he scattereth* his bright cloud:
38:24. *scattereth* the east wind
Ps. 18:14(15). he sent out his arrows, *and scattered them;*
144: 6. Cast forth lightning, *and scatter them:*
Isa. 41:16. the whirlwind *shall scatter* them:
Jer. 13:24. *Therefore will I scatter them* as
18:17. *I will scatter them* as with
Eze.36:19. *And I scattered* them among the heathen,

HIPHIL.—*Participle.*

Jer. 23: 1. Woe be unto the pastors that destroy *and scatter* the sheep
Nah 2: 1(2). *He that dasheth in pieces* (marg. or, *The disperser,* or, *hammer*) is come

* HITHPAEL.—*Future.* *

Hab 3: 6. *and* the everlasting mountains *were scattered,*

6328 פּוּק [*pook*].

* KAL.—*Preterite.* *

Isa. 28: 7. *they stumble* (in) judgment.

* HIPHIL.—*Future.* *

Jer. 10: 4. fasten it with nails and with hammers, that *it move* not.

6329 פּוּק [*pook*].

* HIPHIL.—*Future.* *

Ps.140: 8(9). *further* not his wicked device;
Pro. 3:13. the man (that) *getteth* understanding.
8:35. *and shall obtain* (marg. *bring forth*) favour of the Lord.
12: 2. A good (man) *obtaineth* favour of the
18:22. *and obtaineth* favour of the Lord.
Isa. 58:10. *And* (if) *thou draw out* thy soul to the

HIPHIL.—*Participle.*

Ps.144:13. (That) our garners (may be) full, *affording* all

6330 פּוּקָה *poo-kāh',* f.

1Sa.25:31. this shall be no *grief* (marg. *staggering,* or, *stumbling*)

פּוּר [*poor*]. 6331

* HIPHIL.—*Preterite.* *

Ps. 33:10. The Lord *bringeth* the counsel of the heathen *to nought:* (marg. *maketh frustrate*)
Eze.17:19. and my covenant that *he hath broken,*

HIPHIL.—*Future.*

Ps. 89:33(34). my lovingkindness *will I* not *utterly take* (marg. *I will* not *make void*)

פּוּר *poor,* m. 6332

Est. 3: 7. they cast *Pur,* that (is), the lot,
9:24. and had cast *Pur,* that (is), the lot,
26. they called these days *Purim* after the name of *Pur.* (marg. (That is), *lot*)
28. these days of *Purim* should not fail
29. this second letter of *Purim.*
31. To confirm these days of *Purim*
32. Esther confirmed these matters of *Purim;*

פּוּרָה *poo-rāh',* f. 6333

Isa. 63: 3. I have trodden *the winepress* alone;
Hag 2:16. to draw out fifty (vessels) out of *the press,*

פּוּשׁ [*poosh*]. 6335

* KAL.—*Preterite.* *

Hab 1: 8. *and* their horsemen *shall spread themselves,*
Mal 4: 2(3:20). *and grow up* as calves of the stall.

KAL.—*Future.*

Jer. 50:11. *ye are grown fat* (marg. *big,* or, *corpulent*) as the heifer

* NIPHAL.—*Preterite.* *

Nah 3:18. thy people *is scattered*

פָּז *pāhz',* m. 6337

Job 28:17. jewels of *fine gold.*
Ps. 19:10(11). *yea, than* much *fine gold:*
21: 3(4). thou settest a crown of *pure gold*
119:127. above gold; *yea, above fine gold.*
Pro. 8:19. than gold, *yea, than fine gold;*
Cant.5:11. *the* most *fine gold,*
15. sockets of *fine gold:*
Isa. 13:12. a man more precious *than fine gold;*
Lam 4: 2. sons of Zion, comparable *to fine gold,*

פָּזַז [*pāh-zaz'*]. 6338

* HOPHAL.—*Participle.* *

1K. 10:18. overlaid it with the *best* (lit. *purified*) gold.

פָּזַז [*pāh-zaz'*]. 6339

* KAL.—*Future.* *

Gen49:24. *and* the arms of his hands *were made strong*

* PIEL.—*Participle.* *

2Sa. 6:16. king David *leaping* and dancing before the Lord;

פָּזַר [*pāh-zar'*]. 6340

* KAL.—*Participle.* *

Jer. 50:17. Israel (is) a *scattered* sheep;

* NIPHAL.—*Preterite.* *

Ps.141: 7. Our bones *are scattered*

* PIEL.—*Preterite.* *

Ps. 53: 5(6). God *hath scattered* the bones of
89:10(11). *thou hast scattered* thine enemies
112: 9. *He hath dispersed,* he hath given
Joel 3: 2(4:2). *they have scattered* among the nations,

PIEL.—*Future.*

Ps.147:16. *he scattereth* the hoarfrost
Jer. 3:13. *and hast scattered* thy ways

PIEL.—*Participle.*

Pro. 11:24. There is *that scattereth*,

∗ PUAL.—*Participle.* ∗

Est. 3: 8. There is a certain people *scattered abroad*

6341 פַּח *pagh*, m.

Ex. 39: 3. they did beat the gold into *thin plates*,
Nu. 16:38(17:3). let them make them broad *plates*
Jos. 23:13. they shall be *snares* and traps unto you,
Job 18: 9. *The gin* shall take (him) by the heel,
22:10. *snares* (are) round about thee,
Ps. 11: 6. Upon the wicked he shall rain *snares*,
69:22(23). Let their table become *a snare*
91: 3. *from the snare of* the fowler,
119:110. The wicked have laid *a snare* for me:
124: 7. *out of the snare* of the fowlers: *the snare* is broken, and we are escaped.
140: 5(6). The proud have hid *a snare* for me,
141: 9. Keep me from *the snares*
142: 3(4). they privily laid *a snare* for me.
Pro. 7:23. as a bird hasteth to *the snare*,
22: 5. Thorns (and) *snares* (are) in the way of
Ecc. 9:12. as the birds that are caught *in the snare;*
Isa. 8:14. *for a gin* and for a snare to
24:17. Fear, and the pit, *and the snare*,
18. shall be taken *in the snare:*
Jer. 18:22. *and* hid *snares* for my feet.
48:43. Fear, and the pit, *and the snare*,
44. shall be taken *in the snare:*
Hos 5: 1. ye have been *a snare*
9: 8. the prophet (is) *a snare of* a fowler
Am. 3: 5. Can a bird fall in *a snare upon* the earth,
— shall (one) take up *a snare*

6342 פָּחַד *pāh-ghad'*.

∗ KAL.—*Preterite.* ∗

Deu28:66. *and thou shalt fear* day and night,
Job 3:25. the thing which *I* greatly *feared*
Ps. 14: 5 & 53:5(6). There *were they in* great *fear:* (marg. *they feared* a fear)
78:53. so that *they feared* not:
119:161. my heart *standeth in awe*
Isa. 19:16. *and fear* because of the shaking of the
33:14. The sinners in Zion *are afraid;*
60: 5. *and* thine heart *shall fear*,
Jer. 33: 9. *and they shall fear* and tremble
36:16. when they had heard all the words, *they were afraid*
24. Yet *they were* not *afraid*,
Hos. 3: 5. *and shall fear* the Lord and his goodness

KAL.—*Future.*

Deu28:67. of thine heart wherewith *thou shalt fear*,
Job 23:15. *when* I consider, *I am afraid* of him.
Ps. 27: 1. of whom *shall I be afraid?*
Pro. 3:24. *thou shalt* not *be afraid:*
Isa. 12: 2. I will trust, and not *be afraid:*
19:17. every one that maketh mention thereof *shall be afraid*
44: 8. *Fear ye* not, neither be afraid:
11. *they shall fear*, (and) they shall be
Mic. 7:17. *they shall be afraid* of the Lord

∗ PIEL.—*Future.* ∗

Isa. 51:13. *and hast feared* continually

PIEL.—*Participle.*

Pro. 28:14. Happy (is) the man *that feareth* alway:

∗ HIPHIL.—*Preterite.* ∗

Job 4:14. *made* all my bones *to shake.* (lit. *affrighted*)

6343 פַּחַד *pah'-ghad*, m.

Gen31:42. *and the fear of* Isaac,
53. Jacob sware *by the fear of* his father
Ex. 15:16. Fear *and dread* shall fall upon them;
Deu 2:25. *the dread of thee* and the fear of thee
11:25. *the fear of you* and the dread of you
28:67. *for the fear of* thine heart
1Sa. 11: 7. And *the fear of* the Lord fell on the people,
1Ch 14:17. the Lord brought *the fear of him* upon
2Ch 14:14(13). *the fear of* the Lord came upon them;
17:10. *the fear of* the Lord fell upon all
19: 7. let *the fear of* the Lord be upon you;
20:29. *the fear of* God was on all
Est. 8:17. *the fear of* the Jews fell upon them.
9: 2. *the fear of them* fell upon all people.
3. *the fear of* Mordecai fell upon them.
Job 3:25. *the thing which* I *greatly* feared (marg. I feared *a fear*)
4:14. *Fear* came upon me, and trembling,
13:11. *and his dread* fall upon you?
15:21. A *dreadful* sound (marg. A sound *of fears*) (is) in his ears:
21: 9. Their houses (are) safe *from fear*,
22:10. sudden *fear* troubleth thee;
25: 2. Dominion *and fear* (are) with him,
31:23. destruction (from) God (was) *a terror* to
39:16. her labour is in vain without *fear;*
22. He mocketh *at fear*,
Ps. 14: 5. There were they in *great* fear: (marg. they feared *a fear*)
31:11(12). *and a fear* to mine acquaintance:
36: 1(2). (there is) no *fear of* God before his
53: 5(6). There were they in *great* fear, (marg. they feared *a fear*) (where) no *fear* was:
64: 1(2). preserve my life *from fear of* the
91: 5. not be afraid *for the terror* by night;
105:38. *the fear of them* fell upon them.
119:120. My flesh trembleth for *fear of thee;*
Pro. 1:26. I will mock when *your fear* cometh;
27. When *your fear* cometh as desolation,
33. shall be quiet *from fear of* evil.
3:25. Be not afraid *of* sudden *fear*,
Cant. 3: 8. *because of fear* in the night.
Isa. 2:10, 19, 21. for *fear of* the Lord, and for the
24:17. *Fear*, and the pit, and the snare,
18. fleeth from the noise of *the fear*
Jer. 30: 5. a voice of trembling, of *fear*,
48:43. *Fear*, and the pit, and the snare,
44. He that fleeth from *the fear*
49: 5. Behold, I will bring *a fear* upon thee,
Lam. 3:47. *Fear* and a snare is come upon us,

פַּחַד [*pah'-ghad*], m. 6344

Job 40:17. the sinews of *his stones*

פַּחְדָּה [*pagh-dāh'*], f. 6345

Jer. 2:19. *my fear* (is) not in thee,

פֶּחָה *peh-ghāh'*, m. 6346

1K. 10:15. *and of the governors* (marg. or, *captains*) *of*
20:24. Take the kings away,...and put *captains*
2K. 18:24. one *captain* of the least of my master's
2Ch 9:14. *and governors* (marg. or, *captains*) *of* the
Ezr. 8:36. *and to the governors* on this side the river:
Neh. 2: 7. to *the governors* beyond the river,
9. Then I came to *the governors*
3: 7. unto the throne of *the governor on* this
5:14. I was appointed to be *their governor*
— eaten the bread of *the governor*.
15. *But the* former *governors*
18. required not I the bread of *the governor*,
12:26. in the days of Nehemiah *the governor*,
Est. 3:12. to *the governors* that (were) over every
8: 9. *and the deputies* and rulers
9: 3. *and the deputies*, and officers
Isa. 36: 9. one *captain* of the least of my master's
Jer. 51:23. with thee will I break in pieces *captains*
28. the Medes, *the captains thereof*,
57. *her captains*, and her rulers,
Eze 23: 6. *captains* and rulers, all of them desirable
12. *captains* and rulers clothed most
23. desirable young men, *captains* and
Hag. 1: 1, 14 & 2:2. Zerubbabel the son of Shealtiel, *governor* (marg. or, *captain*) *of* Judah,
2:21. Zerubbabel, *governor of* Judah,
Mal. 1: 8. offer it now *unto thy governor;*

פֶּחָה [*peh-ghāh'*], Ch. m. 6347

Ezr. 5: 3, 6. Tatnai, *governor* on this side the river,
14. he had made *governor;* (marg. or, *deputy*)

Ezr. 6: 6. Tatnai, *governor* beyond the river,
7. let *the governor of* the Jews
13. Tatnai, *governor* on this side the river,
Dan 3: 2. *and the captains*, the judges,
3. the governors, *and captains*,
27. *and captains*, and the king's counsellors,
6: 7(8). the counsellors, *and the captains*,

6348 **פָּחַז** [*pāh-ghaz'*].

* KAL.—*Participle.* Poel. *

Jud. 9: 4. Abimelech hired vain *and light* persons,
Zep. 3: 4. Her prophets (are) *light* (and)

6349 **פַּחַז** *pah'-ghaz*, m.

Gen49: 4. *Unstable* as water, thou shalt not excel;

6350 **פַּחֲזוּת** [*pah-ghăzooth'*], f.

Jer. 23:32. by their lies, *and by their lightness;*

6351 **פָּחַח** [*pāh-ghagh'*].

* HIPHIL.—*Infinitive.* *

Isa. 42:22. (they are) all of them *snared*

6352 **פֶּחָם** *peh-ghāhm'*, m.

Pro.26:21. (As) *coals* (are) to burning coals,
Isa. 44:12. The smith...both worketh *in the coals*,
54:16. the smith that bloweth *the coals*

6353 **פֶּחָר** *peh-ghāhr'*, Ch. m.

Dan 2:41. part of *potter*'s clay, and part of iron,

6354 **פַּחַת** *pah'-ghath*, m.

2Sa. 17: 9. he is hid now in some *pit*, (lit. in one of *the pits*)
18:17. cast him into *a* great *pit*
Isa. 24:17. Fear, *and the pit*, and the snare,
18. he who fleeth...shall fall into *the pit;* and he that cometh up out of the midst of *the pit*
Jer. 48:28. in the sides of *the hole*'s mouth.
43. Fear, *and the pit*, and the snare,
44. He that fleeth...shall fall into *the pit;* and he that getteth up out of *the pit*
Lam. 3:47. *and a snare* is come upon us,

6356 **פְּחֶתֶת** *p'gheh'-theth*, f.

Lev.13:55. thou shalt burn it in the fire; it (is) *fret inward*,

---

6357 **פִּטְדָה** *pit-dāh'*, f.

Ex. 28:17 & 39:10. a sardius, *a topaz*, and a
Job 28:19. *The topaz of* Ethiopia shall not equal
Eze.28:13. the sardius, *topaz*, and the diamond,

6359 **פָּטִיר** [*pāh-teer'*], adj.

1Ch 9:33. (כתיב) (who remaining) in the chambers (were) *free:*

6360 **פַּטִּישׁ** *pat-teesh'*, m.

Isa. 41: 7. he that smootheth (with) *the hammer*
Jer. 23:29. *and like a hammer* (that) breaketh the
50:23. *the hammer of* the whole earth

6361 **פַּטִּישׁ** [*pat-teesh'*], Ch. m.

Dan 3:21. (כתיב) bound in their coats, *their hosen*,

פָּטַר *pāh-tar'*. 6362

* KAL.—*Preterite.* *

2Ch 23: 8. Jehoiada the priest *dismissed* not the

KAL.—*Future.*

1Sa.19:10. *but he slipped away* out of Saul's

KAL.—*Participle.* Poel.

Pro.17:14. *when one letteth out* water:

KAL.—*Participle.* Paül.

1K. 6:18. carved with knops *and open* (marg. *openings of*) flowers:
29, 32, 35. palm trees *and open* (marg. *id.*) flowers,
1Ch 9:33. (remaining) in the chambers (were) *free:*

* HIPHIL.—*Future.* *

Ps. 22: 7(8). *they shoot out* (marg. *open*) the lip,

פֶּטֶר *peh'-ter*, m. 6363

Ex. 13: 2. whatsoever *openeth* the womb (lit. *the opening of* every womb)
12. all *that openeth* the matrix (lit. every *opening of* the womb), and every *firstling* that cometh of a beast
13. every *firstling of* an ass
15. all *that openeth* the matrix, (lit. every *opening of* the womb)
34:19. All *that openeth* the matrix (is) mine; and every *firstling* among thy cattle,
20. *But the firstling of* an ass
Nu. 3:12. *that openeth* the matrix (lit. *the opening of* the womb)
18:15. Every thing *that openeth* the matrix (lit. every *opening of* the womb)
Eze.20:26. all *that openeth* the womb, (lit. every *opening of* the womb)

פִּטְרָה [*pit-rāh'*], f. 6363

Nu. 8:16. *such as open* every womb,

פַּטֵּשׁ [*peh'-tesh*], Ch. m. 6361

Dan 3:21. were bound in their coats, *their hosen*, and

פִּיד *peed*, m. 6365

Job 30:24. they cry *in his destruction.*
31:29. If I rejoiced *at the destruction of*
Pro.24:22. *and who knoweth the ruin of* them both?

פֵּיָה [*pēh-yāh'*], f. 6366

Jud. 3:16. a dagger which had two *edges*,

פִּיחַ *pee'ăgh*, m. 6368

Ex. 9: 8. Take to you handfuls of *ashes of*
10. And they took *ashes of* the furnace,

פִּילֶגֶשׁ *pee-leh'-gesh*, f. 6370

Gen22:24. *And his concubine*, whose name (was)
25: 6. the sons of *the concubines*,
35:22. Bilhah his father's *concubine:*
36:12. Timna was *concubine* to Eliphaz
Jud. 8:31. *And his concubine* that (was) in Shechem,
19: 1. *a concubine* out of Beth-lehem-judah.
2. *his concubine* played the whore
9. *and his concubine*, and his servant,
10. *his concubine also* (was) with him.
24. my daughter...*and his concubine;*
25. so the man took *his concubine*,
27. the woman *his concubine*
29. laid hold *on his concubine.*
20: 4. I *and my concubine*, to lodge.
5. *my concubine* have they forced,
6. And I took *my concubine*,
2Sa. 3: 7. And Saul had *a concubine*,
— gone in unto my father's *concubine?*

2Sa. 5:13. David took (him) more *concubines*
15:16. ten women, (which were) *concubines*,
16:21. Go in unto thy father's *concubines*,
22. Absalom went in unto his father's *concubines*
19: 5(6). the lives of *thy concubines*;
20: 3. the ten women (his) *concubines*,
21:11. Rizpah...*the concubine of* Saul,
1K. 11: 3. *and* three hundred *concubines*:
1Ch 1:32. Keturah, Abraham's *concubine*:
2:46. Ephah, Caleb's *concubine*,
48. Maachah, Caleb's *concubine*,
3: 9. beside the sons of *the concubines*,
7:14. *his concubine* the Aramitess
2Ch 11:21. above all his wives *and his concubines*:
— and threescore *concubines*;
Est. 2:14. Shaashgaz,...which kept *the concubines*:
Cant.6: 8. and fourscore *concubines*,
9. the queens *and the concubines*,
Eze.23:20. she doted upon *their paramours*,

6371 פִּימָה *pee-māh'*, f.

Job 15:27. maketh *collops of fat* on (his) flanks.

6374 פִּיפִיּוֹת *pee-pheey-yōhth'*, f. pl.

Ps.149: 6. a *twoedged* sword (lit. a sword of *edges*) in their hand;
Isa. 41:15. sharp threshing instrument having *teeth*:

6375 פִּיק *peek*, m.

Nah 2:10(11). *and* the knees *smite together*, (lit. *the smiting together of* the knees,)

6378 פַּךְ *pach*, m.

1Sa.10: 1. Samuel took *a vial of* oil,
2K. 9: 1. take this *box of* oil in thine hand,
3. Then take *the box of* oil, and pour

6379 פָּכָה [*pāh-chāh'*].

* PIEL.—*Participle.* *

Eze.47: 2. *there ran out* waters on the right side.

6381 פָּלָא [*pāh-lāh'*].

* NIPHAL.—*Preterite.* *

2Sa. 1:26. thy love to me *was wonderful*,
Ps.118:23. the Lord's doing; it *is marvellous*
Pro.30:18. three (things which) *are* too *wonderful*

NIPHAL.—*Future.*

Gen18:14. *Is* any thing *too hard* for the Lord?
Deu17: 8. If *there arise* a matter *too hard* for thee
2Sa.13: 2. *and* Amnon thought *it hard* (marg. *and it was marvellous*, or, *hidden* in the eyes of)
Jer. 32:17. *there is* nothing *too hard* for (marg. or, *hid* from) thee:
27. *is there* any thing *too hard* for me?
Zec. 8: 6. *it be marvellous* (marg. or, *hard*, or, *difficult*) in the eyes
— *should it* also *be marvellous* in mine eyes?

NIPHAL.—*Participle.*

Ex. 3:20. and smite Egypt with all *my wonders*
34:10. before all thy people I will do *marvels*,
Deu30:11. it (is) not *hidden* from thee, neither (is)
Jos. 3: 5. the Lord will do *wonders*
Jud. 6:13. where (be) all *his miracles*
1Ch 16: 9. talk ye of all *his wondrous works*.
12. Remember *his marvellous works*
24. *his marvellous works* among all
Neh 9:17. neither were mindful of *thy wonders*
Job 5: 9. *marvellous things* without number:
9:10. yea, *and wonders* without number.
37: 5. God thundereth *marvellously*
14. consider *the wondrous works of* God.
42: 3. *things* too *wonderful* for me,
Ps. 9: 1(2). all *thy marvellous works*.
26: 7. and tell of all *thy wondrous works*.
Ps. 40: 5(6). Many, O Lord my God, (are) *thy wonderful works*
71:17. I declared *thy wondrous works*.
72:18. who only doeth *wondrous things*.
75: 1(2). *thy wondrous works* declare.
78: 4. *and his wonderful works* that he hath done.
11. forgat his works, *and his wonders*
32. believed not *for his wondrous works*.
86:10. (art) great, and doest *wondrous things*:
96: 3. *his wonders* among all people.
98: 1. he hath done *marvellous things*:
105: 2. talk ye of all *his wondrous works*.
5. Remember *his marvellous works*
106: 7. Our fathers understood not *thy wonders*
22. *Wondrous works* in the land of Ham,
107: 8,15,21,31. *and* (for) *his wonderful works* to the children of men!
24. *and his wonders* in the deep.
111: 4. He hath made *his wonderful works*
119:18. that I may behold *wondrous things*
27. so shall I talk *of thy wondrous works*.
131: 1. in great matters, *or in things too high* (marg. *wonderful*)
136: 4. who alone doeth great *wonders*:
139:14. *marvellous* (are) thy works;
145: 5. thy majesty, and of *thy wondrous* works. (lit. words of *thy wonders*.)
Jer. 21: 2. according to all *his wondrous works*,
Dan 8:24. *and* he shall destroy *wonderfully*,
11:36. and shall speak *marvellous things*
Mic. 7:15. will I shew unto him *marvellous things*.

* PIEL.—*Infinitive.* *

Lev.22:21. *to accomplish* (his) vow,
Nu. 15: 3, 8. a sacrifice *in performing* (marg. *separating*) a vow,

* HIPHIL.—*Preterite.* *

Deu28:59. *Then* the Lord *will make* thy plagues *wonderful*,
2Ch 26:15. *he was marvellously* helped, (lit. *he did marvellously* to help)
Ps. 31:21(22). *he hath shewed* me his *marvellous* kindness (lit. *he hath marvellously shewed* his kindness)
Isa. 28:29. (which) *is wonderful* in counsel,

HIPHIL.—*Infinitive.*

2Ch 2: 9(8). the house...(shall be) *wonderful* great. (marg. great *and wonderful*)
Isa. 29:14. I will proceed *to do a marvellous work* among this people, (even) *a marvellous work* and a wonder:
Joel 2:26. God, that hath dealt *wondrously*

HIPHIL.—*Future.*

Lev.27: 2. When a man *shall make a singular* vow, (lit. *shall separate* a vow)
Nu. 6: 2. or woman *shall separate* (themselves)

HIPHIL.—*Participle.*

Jud.13:19. *and* (the angel) did *wonderously*;

* HITHPAEL.—*Future.* *

Job 10:16. *thou shewest thyself marvellous* upon me.

פֶּלֶא *peh'-leh*, m. 6382

Ex. 15:11. fearful (in) praises, doing *wonders*?
Ps. 77:11(12). I will remember *thy wonders* of old.
14(15). the God that doest *wonders*:
78:12. *Marvellous things* did he
88:10(11). Wilt thou shew *wonders* to the dead?
12(13). Shall *thy wonders* be known in the
89: 5(6). the heavens shall praise *thy wonders*,
119:129. Thy testimonies (are) *wonderful*:
Isa. 9: 6(5). his name shall be called *Wonderful*,
25: 1. thou hast done *wonderful* (things);
29:14. a marvellous work *and a wonder*:
Lam 1: 9. she came down *wonderfully*:
Dan12: 6. the end of *these wonders*?

פִּלְאִי *pil-ee'*, adj. 6383

Jud.13:18. (כתיב) my name, seeing it (is) *secret*? (marg. or, *wonderful*)
Ps.139: 6. (——) (Such) knowledge (is) too *wonderful* for me;

6385 פָּלַג [*pāh-lag'*].

* NIPHAL.—*Preterite.* *

Gen10:25. in his days *was* the earth *divided;*
1Ch 1:19. in his days the earth *was divided:*

* PIEL.—*Preterite.* *

Job 38:25. Who *hath divided* a watercourse

PIEL.—*Imperative.*

Ps. 55: 9(10). Destroy, O Lord, (and) *divide* their

6386 פְּלַג [*p'lag*], Ch.

* P'AL.—*Participle.* Passive. *

Dan 2:41. the kingdom shall be *divided;*

6388 פֶּלֶג *peh'-leg*, m.

Job 29: 6. the rock poured me out *rivers of* oil;
Ps. 1: 3. like a tree planted by *the rivers of*
46: 4(5). a river, *the streams whereof* shall make
65: 9(10). enrichest it with *the river of* God,
119:136. *Rivers of* waters run down mine eyes,
Pro. 5:16. (and) *rivers of* waters in the streets.
21: 1. (as) *the rivers of* water: he turneth it
Isa. 30:25. *rivers* (and) streams of waters
32: 2. *as rivers of* water in a dry place,
Lam 3:48. Mine eye runneth down with *rivers of*

6387 פְּלַג *p'lag*, Ch. m.

Dan 7:25. a time and times *and the dividing of* time.

6390 פְּלַגָּה [*p'lag-gāh'*], f.

Jud. 5:15. *For* (marg. or, *In*) *the divisions of* Reuben
16. *For* (marg. or, *In*) *the divisions of* Reuben
Job 20:17. He shall not see *the rivers,*

6391 פְּלֻגָּה [*p'loog-gāh'*], f.

2Ch 35: 5. *according to the divisions of* the families

6392 פְּלֻגָּה [*p'loog-gāh'*], Ch. f.

Ezr. 6:18. they set the priests *in their divisions,*

See 6370 פִּילֶגֶשׁ see פִּלֶגֶשׁ

6393 פְּלָדָה [*p'lāh-dāh'*], f.

Nah. 2: 3(4). the chariots (shall be) with flaming *torches*

6395 פָּלָה [*pāh-lāh'*].

* NIPHAL.—*Preterite.* *

Ex. 33:16. *so shall we be separated,* I and thy
Ps.139:14. *I am* fearfully (and) *wonderfully made:*

* HIPHIL.—*Preterite.* *

Ex. 8:22(18). *And I will sever* in that day
9: 4. *And* the Lord *shall sever* between
Ps. 4: 3(4). the Lord *hath set apart* him that is

HIPHIL.—*Imperative.*

Ps. 17: 7. *Shew* thy *marvellous* lovingkindness,

HIPHIL.—*Future.*

Ex. 11: 7. the Lord *doth put a difference* between

6398 פָּלַח [*pāh-lagh'*].

* KAL.—*Participle* Poel. *

Ps.141: 7. as when *one cutteth* and cleaveth (wood)

* PIEL.—*Future.* *

2K. 4:39. *and shred* (them) into the pot of pottage:
Job 16:13. *he cleaveth* my reins asunder,
39: 3. They bow themselves, *they bring forth*
Pro. 7:23. Till a dart *strike through* his liver;

פְּלַח [*p'lagh*], Ch. 6399

* P'AL.—*Future.* *

Dan 3:28. that *they might* not *serve* nor worship
7:14. and languages, *should serve* him:
27. dominions *shall serve* and obey him.

P'AL.—*Participle.*

Ezr. 7:24. Nethinims, *or ministers of* this house
Dan 3:12. *they serve* not thy gods, nor
14. do not ye *serve* my gods,
17. our God whom we *serve* is able
18. we *will* not *serve* thy gods,
6:16(17). Thy God whom thou *servest*
20(21). is thy God, whom thou *servest*

פֶּלַח *peh'-lagh*, m. 6400

Jud. 9:53. a certain woman cast *a piece of* a millstone
1Sa.30:12. they gave him *a piece of* a cake
2Sa.11:21. did not a woman cast *a piece of* a millstone
Job 41:24(16). *as a piece of* the nether (millstone).
Cant.4: 3. thy temples (are) *like a piece of* a
6: 7. *As a piece of* a pomegranate (are) thy temples

פָּלְחָן *pol-ghan'*, Ch. m. 6402

Ezr. 7:19. *for the service of* the house

פָּלַט [*pāh-lat'*]. 6403

* KAL.—*Preterite.* *

Eze. 7:16. *But* they that escape of them *shall escape,*

* PIEL.—*Imperative.* *

Ps. 17:13. *deliver* my soul from the wicked,
31: 1(2). *deliver me* in thy righteousness.
71: 4. *Deliver me,* O my God,
82: 4. *Deliver* the poor and needy:

PIEL.—*Future.*

2Sa.22:44. *Thou also hast delivered me* from
Job 21:10. their cow *calveth,* and casteth not her calf.
23: 7. *so should I be delivered* for ever
Ps. 18:43(44). *Thou hast delivered me* from
22: 4(5). they trusted, *and thou didst deliver them.*
8(9). He trusted on the Lord (that) *he would deliver him:*
37:40. the Lord shall help them, *and deliver them: he shall deliver them* from the
43: 1. *O deliver me* from the deceitful
71: 2. *and cause me to escape:* incline
91:14. *therefore will I deliver him:* I will
Mic. 6:14. (that) which *thou deliverest* will I give

PIEL.—*Participle.*

2Sa.22: 2. and my fortress, *and my deliverer;*
Ps. 18: 2(3). and my fortress, *and my deliverer;*
48(49). *He delivereth me* from mine enemies:
40:17(18) & 70:5(6). thou (art) my help *and my deliverer;*
144: 2. my high tower, *and my deliverer;*

* HIPHIL.—*Future.* *

Isa. 5:29. the prey, *and shall carry* (it) *away safe,*
Mic. 6:14. shalt take hold, but *shalt* not *deliver;*

פָּלֵט [*pāh-lēht*], m. 6412

Jer. 44:14. none shall return but *such as shall escape.*
50:28. The voice of them that flee *and escape*
51:50. *Ye that have escaped* the sword,

פַּלֵּט *pal-lēht'*, m. 6405

Ps. 32: 7. me about with songs of *deliverance.*
56: 7(8). Shall they *escape* (lit. shall *deliverance* be to them) by iniquity?

6383 **פְּלִי** *p'lee*, adj.

Jud.13:18. after my name, seeing it (is) *secret?* (marg. or, *wonderful*)

6383 **פָּלִיא** [*pāh-lee'*], adj.

Ps.139: 6. (Such) knowledge (is) too *wonderful*

6412 **פָּלִיט** *pāh-leet'*, m.

Gen14:13. there came *one that had escaped,*
Jos 8:22. let none of them remain *or escape.* (lit. a remainder *or escaper*)
Jud.12: 4. Ye Gileadites (are) *fugitives of* Ephraim
5. *those* Ephraimites *which were escaped*
2K. 9:15. let none go forth (nor) *escape* (lit. let no *escaper* go forth)
Isa. 45:20. *ye that are escaped* of the nations:
Jer. 42:17. none of them shall remain *or escape* (lit. a remainder *or escaper*)
44:14. none of the remnant...shall *escape* (lit. there shall be no *escaper*)
28. *Yet* a small number *that escape* the sword
Lam. 2:22. none *escaped* (lit. there was no *escaper*)
Eze. 6: 8. ye may have (some) *that shall escape*
9. *they that escape of you* shall remember
7:16. *they that escape of them* shall escape,
24:26. *he that escapeth* in that day
27. to *him which is escaped,*
33:21. *one that had escaped* out of Jerusalem
22. afore *he that was escaped* came;
Am. 9: 1. *he that escapeth* of them
Obad. 14. to cut off *those of his that did escape;*

6412 **פָּלֵיט** [*pāh-lēht'*], m.

Nu. 21:29. he hath given his sons *that escaped,*
Isa. 66:19. I will send *those that escape* of them

6413 **פְּלֵיטָה** *p'lēh-tāh'*, f.

Gen32: 8(9). the other company which is left shall *escape.* (lit. shall be *for an escaping*)
45: 7. to save your lives by *a* great *deliverance.*
Ex. 10: 5. the residue of *that which is escaped,*
Jud.21:17. *them that be escaped* of Benjamin,
2Sa.15:14. we shall not (else) *escape* (lit. there shall not be *an escape* to us)
2K. 19:30. the remnant *that is escaped of* the house of Judah (marg. *the escaping of* the house of Judah that remaineth)
31. *and they that escape* (marg. *the escaping*) out of mount Zion:
1Ch. 4:43. rest of the Amalekites *that were escaped,*
2Ch 12: 7. I will grant them some *deliverance;*
20:24. and none *escaped.* (marg. (there was) not *an escaping*)
30: 6. the remnant of you, *that are escaped*
Ezr. 9: 8. to leave us a remnant *to escape,*
13. hast given us (such) *deliverance*
14. (should be) no remnant *nor escaping?*
15. we remain yet *escaped,*
Neh. 1: 2. the Jews *that had escaped,*
Isa. 4: 2. *for them that are escaped of* Israel. (marg. *the escaping of* Israel)
10:20. the remnant of Israel, *and such as are escaped of*
15: 9. lions *upon him that escapeth*
37:31. the remnant *that is escaped* (marg. *the escaping*) *of* the house of Judah
32. *and they that escape* (marg. *the escaping*) out of mount Zion:
Jer. 25:35. *nor* the principal of the flock *to escape.* (lit. *and escaping* (shall perish) from the principal of the flock)
50:29. let none thereof *escape:* (lit. let there be no *escaping*)
Eze.14:22. therein shall be left *a remnant*
Dan11:42. the land of Egypt shall not *escape.* (lit. shall not be *for an escaping*)
Joel 2: 3. nothing shall *escape* (lit. there shall be no *escape*)
Joel 2:32(3:5). in Jerusalem shall be *deliverance,*
Obad. 17. upon mount Zion shall be *deliverance,* (marg. or, *they that escape*)

פָּלִיל [*pāh-leel'*], m. 6414

Ex. 21:22. he shall pay *as the judges* (determine).
Deu32:31. our enemies themselves (being) *judges.*
Job 31:11. an iniquity (to be punished by) *the judges.*

פְּלִילָה *p'lee-lāh'*, f. 6415

Isa. 16: 3. Take counsel, execute *judgment;*

פְּלִילִי *p'lee-lee'*, adj. 6416-17

Job 31:28. an iniquity (to be punished by) *the judge:*
Isa. 28: 7. they stumble (in) *judgment.*

פֶּלֶךְ *peh'-lech*, m. 6418

2Sa. 3:29. or that leaneth *on a staff,*
Neh. 3: 9, 12. the ruler of the half *part of* Jerusalem.
14. the ruler of *part of* Beth-haccerem;
15. the ruler of *part of* Mizpah;
16. the ruler of the half *part of* Beth-zur,
17. the ruler of the half *part of* Keilah, *in his part.*
18. the ruler of the half *part of* Keilah.
Pro.31:19. and her hands hold *the distaff.*

פָּלַל [*pāh-lal'*]. 6419

* PIEL.—*Preterite.* *

Gen48:11. *I had* not *thought* to see thy face:
1Sa. 2:25. If one man sin against another, the judge *shall judge him:*
Eze.16:52. Thou also, which *hast judged* thy sisters,

PIEL.—*Future.*

Ps.106:30. stood up Phinehas, *and executed judgment:*

* HITHPAEL.—*Preterite.* *

1Sa. 1:27. For this child *I prayed;*
1K. 8:33. confess thy name, *and pray,*
35. *if they pray* toward this place,
42. when he shall come *and pray*
44. *and shall pray* unto the Lord
48. *and pray* unto thee toward their land,
2K. 19:20. (That) which *thou hast prayed* to me
2Ch 6:24. *and pray* and make supplication
26. *if they pray* toward this place,
32. if they come *and pray*
34. *and they pray* unto thee
38. *and pray* toward their land,
30:18. But Hezekiah *prayed* for them,
Isa. 37:21. *thou hast prayed* to me against
Jer. 29:12. ye shall go *and pray* unto me,

HITHPAEL.—*Infinitive.*

1Sa. 1:12. she continued *praying* (marg. multiplied *to pray*)
26. woman that stood by thee here, *praying*
12:23. in ceasing *to pray* for you:
2Sa. 7:27. thy servant found in his heart *to pray*
1K. 8:54. Solomon had made an end *of praying*
1Ch17:25. servant hath found (in his heart) *to pray*
2Ch 7: 1. Solomon had made an end *of praying,*
Ezr.10: 1. *Now when* Ezra *had prayed,*
Job 42:10. *when he prayed* for his friends:
Isa. 16:12. he shall come to his sanctuary *to pray;*

HITHPAEL.—*Imperative.*

Nu.21: 7. *pray* unto the Lord,
1Sa.12:19. *Pray* for thy servants unto the Lord
1K. 13: 6. *and pray* for me, that my hand may
Jer. 29: 7. *and pray* unto the Lord
37: 3. *Pray* now unto the Lord
42: 2. *and pray* for us unto the Lord
20. *Pray* for us unto the Lord

HITHPAEL.—*Future.*

Gen20: 7. *and he shall pray* for thee,
17. So Abraham *prayed* unto God:

Nu. 11: 2. and *when* Moses *prayed* unto the Lord,
21: 7. *And* Moses *prayed* for the people.
Deu 9:20. *and I prayed* for Aaron
26. *I prayed therefore* unto the Lord,
1Sa. 1:10. *and prayed* unto the Lord,
2: 1. *And* Hannah *prayed*, and said,
25. if a man sin against the Lord, who *shall intreat*
7: 5. *and I will pray* for you unto the Lord.
8: 6. *And* Samuel *prayed* unto the Lord.
1K. 8:29. the prayer which thy servant *shall make*
30. thy people Israel, when *they shall pray*
2K. 4:33. *and prayed* unto the Lord.
6:17. *And* Elisha *prayed*, and said,
18. *And* when...Elisha *prayed* unto the Lord,
19:15. *And* Hezekiah *prayed* before the Lord,
20: 2. *and prayed* unto the Lord,
2Ch 6:20. the prayer which thy servant *prayeth*
21. the supplications...which *they shall make* (marg. *pray*)
7:14. If my people,...shall humble themselves, *and pray*,
32:20. *And...prayed* and cried to heaven.
24. sick to the death, *and prayed* unto the
33:13. *And prayed* unto him: and he was
Neh 2: 4. *So I prayed* to the God of heaven.
4: 9(3). *Nevertheless we made our prayer*
Job 42: 8. my servant Job *shall pray* for you:
Ps. 5: 2(3). unto thee *will I pray*.
32: 6. *shall* every one that is godly *pray* unto
72:15. *prayer also shall be made* for him
Isa. 37:15. *And* Hezekiah *prayed* unto the Lord,
38: 2. his face toward the wall, *and prayed* unto
44:17. *and prayeth* unto it, and saith, Deliver
45:14. *they shall make supplication* unto thee,
Jer. 7:16 & 11:14. *pray* not thou for this people,
14:11. *Pray* not for this people
32:16. *Now...I prayed* unto the Lord,
Dan 9: 4. *And I prayed* unto the Lord
Jon. 2: 1(2). *Then* Jonah *prayed* unto the Lord
4: 2. *And he prayed* unto the Lord,

HITHPAEL.—*Participle.*

1K. 8:28. thy servant *prayeth* before thee
2Ch 6:19. thy servant *prayeth* before thee:
Neh 1: 4. *and prayed* before the God of heaven,
6. I *pray* before thee
Isa. 45:20. *and pray* unto a god (that) cannot save.
Jer. 42: 4. I *will pray* unto the Lord
Dan 9:20. whiles I was speaking, *and praying*,

6422 **פַּלְמוֹנִי** *pal-mōh-nee'*, m.

Dan 8:13. another saint said *unto that certain* (saint) (marg. *Palmoni*, or, *the numberer of secrets*, or, *the wonderful numberer*)

6423 **פְּלֹנִי** *p'lōh-nee'*, m.

[Always followed by אַלְמֹנִי].

Ru. 4: 1. *Ho, such* a one! turn aside,
1Sa.21: 2(3). appointed (my) servants to *such* and such a place.
2K. 6: 8. In *such* and such a place (shall be) my

6424 **פָּלַס** [*pāh-las'*].

* PIEL.—*Imperative.* *

Pro. 4:26. *Ponder* the path of thy feet,

PIEL.—*Future.*

Ps. 58: 2(3). *ye weigh* the violence of your hands
78:50. *He made* (marg. *weighed*) a way to his
Pro. 5: 6. Lest *thou shouldest ponder* the path
Isa. 26: 7. *thou,...dost weigh* the path of the just.

PIEL.—*Participle.*

Pro. 5:21. *he pondereth* all his goings.

6425 **פֶּלֶס** *peh'-les*, m.

Pro.16:11. *A* just *weight* and balance
Isa. 40:12. weighed the mountains *in scales*,

פָּלַץ [*pāh-latz'*]. 6426

* HITHPAEL.—*Future.* *

Job 9: 6. and the pillars thereof *tremble*.

פַּלָּצוּת *pal-lāh-tzooth'*, f. 6427

Job 21: 6. *trembling* taketh hold on my flesh.
Ps. 55: 5(6). *horror* hath overwhelmed me.
Isa. 21: 4. *fearfulness* affrighted me:
Eze. 7:18. *horror* shall cover them;

פָּלַשׁ [*pāh-lash'*]. 6428

* HITHPAEL.—*Preterite.* *

Mic. 1:10. (כתיב) *roll thyself* (lit. [according to 'כ] *I have rolled myself*) in the dust.

HITHPAEL.—*Imperative.*

Jer. 6:26. *and wallow thyself* in ashes:
25:34. *and wallow yourselves* (in the ashes),
Mic. 1:10. *roll thyself* in the dust.

HITHPAEL.—*Future.*

Eze.27:30. *they shall wallow themselves* in the ashes:

פְּלֵתִי *p'lēh-thee'*, m. 6432

2Sa. 8:18. the Cherethites *and the Pelethites;*
15:18. and all *the Pelethites*,
20: 7. the Cherethites, *and the Pelethites*,
23. the Cherethites and over *the Pelethites:*
1K. 1:38, 44. the Cherethites, *and the Pelethites*,
1Ch 18:17. over the Cherethites *and the Pelethites;*

פֻּם *poom*, Ch. m. 6433

Dan 4:31(28). the word (was) *in* the king's *mouth*,
6:17(18). and laid upon *the mouth of* the den;
22(23). and hath shut the lions' *mouths*,
7: 5. (it had) three ribs *in the mouth of it*
8. *and a mouth* speaking great things.
20. *and a mouth* that spake very great

פֵּן [*pēhn*], m. 6434

Pro. 7: 8. Passing through the street near *her corner;*
Zec.14:10. unto the *corner* gate,

פֶּן *pen*, part. conj. 6435

Gen 3: 3. neither shall ye touch it, *lest* ye die.
24: 6. Beware thou *that* thou bring *not* my son
31:31. *Peradventure* thou wouldest take by force
42: 4. *Lest peradventure* mischief befall him.
&c. &c.

פַּנַּג *pan-nag'*, m. 6436

Eze.27:17. wheat of Minnith, *and Pannag*, [Perhaps lit. *a kind of spice*]

פָּנָה *pāh-nāh'*. 6437

*KAL.—*Preterite.* *

Lev.26: 9. *For I will have respect* unto you,
Deu16: 7. *and thou shalt turn* in the morning,
31:18. *they are turned* unto other gods.
20. *then will they turn* unto other gods,
2Sa. 9: 8. that *thou shouldest look* upon such
1K. 8:28. *Yet have thou respect* unto the prayer
17: 3. Get thee hence, *and turn* thee eastward,
2Ch 6:19. *Have respect therefore* to the prayer
Ps. 40: 4(5). *and respecteth* not the proud,
90: 9. our days *are passed away* (marg. *turned*)
102:17(18). *He will regard* the prayer of
Ecc. 2:11. *Then* I *looked* on all the works
12. *And I turned* myself to behold
Cant.6: 1. whither *is* thy beloved *turned aside?*
Isa. 8:21. curse their king and their God, *and look*
53: 6. *we have turned* every one to his own way;

Isa. 56:11. *they* all *look* to their own way,
Jer. 2:27. *they have turned* (their) back
6: 4. the day *goeth away*,
Eze.36: 9. *and I will turn* unto you,

KAL.—*Infinitive.*

Gen24:63. *at* the eventide:
Ex. 14:27. *when* the morning *appeared;*
Deu23:11(12). *when* evening *cometh* on, (marg. *turneth* toward)
Jud.19:26. Then came the woman *in the dawning of*
Ps. 46: 5(6). shall help her, (and that) *right* early. (marg. when the morning *appeareth*)
Eze.17: 6. whose branches *turned* toward him,
29:16. *when they shall look* after them:
43:17. his stairs *shall look* toward the east.
Hag. 1: 9. *Ye looked* for much, and, lo, (it came) to
Mal. 2:13. *he regardeth* not the offering any more,

KAL.—*Imperative.*

Nu. 14:25. To morrow *turn you*, and get you
Deu. 1: 7. *Turn you*, and take your journey,
40. *turn* you, and take your journey
2: 3. *turn* you northward.
Jos. 22: 4. *return ye*, and get you unto your tents,
Job 6:28. Now therefore be content, *look* upon me;
21: 5. *Mark* (marg. *Look* unto) me, and be
Ps. 25:16. *Turn thee* unto me, and have mercy
69:16(17). *turn* unto me according to the
86:16. *O turn* unto me, and have mercy upon me;
119:132. *Look thou* upon me, and be merciful
Isa. 45:22. *Look* unto me, and be ye saved,

KAL.—*Future.*

Gen18:22. *And* the men *turned their faces*
24:49. *that I may turn* to the right hand,
Ex. 2:12. *And he looked* this way and that way,
7:23. *And* Pharaoh *turned* and went into
10: 6. *And he turned* himself,
16:10. *that they looked* toward the wilderness,
32:15. *And* Moses *turned*, and went down
Lev.19: 4. *Turn ye* not unto idols,
31. *Regard* not them that have
20: 6. the soul that *turneth* after such
Nu. 12:10. *and* Aaron *looked* upon Miriam,
16:15. *Respect* not *thou* their offering:
42(17:7). *that they looked* toward the tabernacle
21:33. *And they turned* and went up
Deu. 1:24. *And they turned* and went up
2: 1. *Then we turned*, and took our journey
8. *And* when we passed...*we turned* and
3: 1. *Then we turned*, and went up the way
9:15. *So I turned* and came down
27. *look* not unto the stubbornness of
10: 5. *And I turned* myself and came down
30:17. if thine heart *turn away*,
Jos. 7:12. *turned* (their) backs before their enemies,
8:20. And *when* the men of Ai *looked*
Jud. 6:14. *And* the Lord *looked* upon him,
18:21. *So they turned* and departed,
26. *and* when Micah...*he turned* and went back
20:40. *But* when...the Benjamites *looked* behind
42. *Therefore they turned* (their backs)
45. *And they turned* and fled
47. *But* six hundred men *turned*
1Sa.13:17. one company *turned* unto the way
18. another company *turned* the way (to) Beth-horon: and another company *turned*
14:47. whithersoever *he turned himself*,
2Sa. 1: 7. And *when he looked* behind him,
2:20. *Then* Abner *looked* behind him,
1K. 2: 3. whithersoever *thou turnest thyself:*
10:13. *So she turned* and went to her own country,
2K. 2:24. *And he turned* back, and looked on them,
5:12. *So he turned* and went away
13:23. *and had respect* unto them,
23:16. *And* as Josiah *turned himself*,
2Ch 13:14. And *when* Judah *looked* back,
20:24. *And* when Judah...*they looked* unto the
26:20. *And* Azariah...and all the priests, *looked*
Job 5: 1. to which of the saints *wilt thou turn?* (marg. or, *look*)
24:18. *he beholdeth* not the way of
36:21. Take heed, *regard* not iniquity:
Pro.17: 8. whithersoever *it turneth*, it prospereth.
Isa. 13:14. *they shall* every man *turn*
Jer. 32:33. *And they have turned* unto me the back,
50:16. *they shall turn* every one to his people,
Eze.10:11. whither the head *looked*

KAL.—*Participle.* Poel.

Deu29:18(17). whose heart *turneth away*
Jos. 15: 2. the bay *that looketh* southward:
7. *looking* toward Gilgal,
1K. 7:25. three *looking* toward the north, and three *looking* toward the west, and three *looking* toward the south, and three *looking* toward the east:
2Ch 4: 4. three *looking* toward the north, and three *looking* toward the west, and three *looking* toward the south, and three *looking* toward the east:
25:23. from the gate of Ephraim to the *corner* (marg. gate of it *that looketh*)
Eze. 8: 3. inner gate *that looketh* toward the north;
11: 1. gate of the Lord's house, which *looketh* eastward:
43: 1. the gate that *looketh* toward the east:
44: 1. *which looketh* toward the east;
46: 1. The gate of the inner court *that looketh* toward the east
12. the gate *that looketh* toward the east,
19. *which looked* toward the north:
47: 2. the utter gate by the way *that looketh*
Hos. 3: 1. the children of Israel, *who look* to other

* PIEL.—*Preterite.* *

Gen24:31. I *have prepared* the house,
Lev.14:36. *that they empty* (marg. or, *prepare*) the house,
Ps. 80: 9(10). *Thou preparedst* (room) before it,
Zep. 3:15. *he hath cast out* thine enemy:
Mal. 3: 1. and *he shall prepare* the way

PIEL.—*Imperative.*

Isa. 40: 3. *Prepare ye* the way of the Lord,
57:14. *prepare* the way, take up
62:10. *prepare ye* the way of the people;

* HIPHIL.—*Preterite.* *

Jer. 46: 5. are fled apace, and *look* not *back:*
21. *they* also *are turned back*,
47: 3. the fathers *shall* not *look back*
48:39. how *hath* Moab *turned* the back
49:24. Damascus is waxed feeble, (and) *turneth herself* to flee,

HIPHIL.—*Infinitive.*

1Sa.10: 9. *when he had turned* his back

HIPHIL.—*Future.*

Jud.15: 4. *and turned* tail to tail,

HIPHIL.—*Participle.*

Nah 2: 8(9). but none *shall look back.* (marg. or, *cause* (them) *to turn*)

* HOPHAL.—*Preterite.* *

Jer. 49: 8. Flee ye, *turn back* (marg. or, *they are turned back*), dwell deep,

HOPHAL.—*Participle.*

Eze. 9: 2. the higher gate, which *lieth* (marg. *is turned*) toward the north,

---

פִּנָּה *pin-nāh'*, f. 6438

Ex. 27: 2. upon *the* four *corners thereof:*
38: 2. the horns thereof on *the* four *corners of it;*
Jud.20: 2. *the chief of* all the people,
1Sa.14:38. all *the chief* (marg. *corners*) *of* the people:
1K. 7:34. *the* four *corners of* one base:
2K. 14:13. the gate of Ephraim unto the *corner* gate,
2Ch 26: 9. in Jerusalem at the *corner* gate,
15. on the towers and upon *the bulwarks*,
28:24. he made him altars in every *corner*
Neh 3:24. even unto *the corner.*
31. to the going up of *the corner.*
32. between the going up of *the corner*
Job 1:19. *the* four *corners of* the house,
38: 6. who laid the *corner* stone *thereof;*
Ps.118:22. the head (stone) of *the corner.*
Pro. 7:12. lieth in wait at every *corner.*
21: 9. to dwell in *a corner of* the housetop,
25:24. to dwell in *the corner of* the housetop,
Isa. 19:13. *the stay* (marg. *corners*, or, *governors*) *of* the tribes thereof.
28:16. *a* precious *corner* (stone),
Jer. 31:38. the gate of *the corner.*

Jer. 31:40. unto *the corner of* the horse gate
51:26. a stone *for a corner,*
Eze.43:20. on *the* four *corners of* the settle,
45:19. upon *the* four *corners of* the settle
Zep. 1:16. against *the* high *towers.*
3: 6. *their towers* (marg. or, *corners*) are desolate;
Zec.10: 4. Out of him came forth *the corner,*

6443 **פְּנִיִּים** *p'neey-yeem',* m. pl.

Pro. 3:15. (כתיב) She (is) more precious *than rubies:*

6440 **פָּנִים** *pāh-neem',* m. pl.

Gen 1: 2. darkness (was) upon *the face of* the deep. And the Spirit of God moved upon *the face of*
20. in the *open* firmament (marg. *the face of* the firmament)
29. upon *the face of* all the earth,
2: 6. *the* whole *face of* the ground.
3: 8. hid themselves *from the presence of* the
4: 5. Cain was very wroth, and *his countenance*
6. why is *thy countenance* fallen?
14. driven me out this day from *the face of* the earth; *and from thy face*
16. Cain went out *from the presence of* the
6: 1. on *the face of* the earth,
7. from *the face of* the earth;
11. The earth also was corrupt *before* God,
13. of all flesh is come *before me;* for the earth is filled with violence *through them;*
7: 1. thee have I seen righteous *before me*
3. upon *the face of* all the earth.
4. from off *the face of* the earth.
7. *because of* the waters of the flood.
18. upon *the face of* the waters.
23. upon *the face of* the ground,
8: 8. from off *the face of* the ground;
9. on *the face of* the whole earth:
13. *the face of* the ground was dry.
9:23. *and their faces* (were) backward,
10: 9. a mighty hunter *before* the Lord:
— Nimrod the mighty hunter *before* the
11: 4. upon *the face of* the whole earth.
8, 9. upon *the face of* all the earth:
28. Haran died *before* (lit. upon *the face of*) his father Terah
13: 9. (Is) not the whole land *before thee?*
10. *before* the Lord destroyed Sodom
16: 6. she fled *from her face.*
8. I flee *from the face of* my mistress
12. he shall dwell in *the presence of* all his
17: 1. walk *before me,* and be thou perfect.
3. And Abram fell on *his face:*
17. Then Abraham fell upon *his face,*
18. O that Ishmael might live *before thee!*
18: 8. and set (it) *before them;*
16. the men...looked toward (lit. on *the face of*) Sodom:
22. Abraham stood yet *before* the Lord.
19:13. before *the face of* the Lord;
21. I have accepted *thee* (marg. *thy face*)
27. he stood *before* the Lord:
28. And he looked toward (lit. toward *the face of*) Sodom
— and toward (lit. toward *the face of*) all the land
20:15. my land (is) *before thee:*
23: 3. Abraham stood up from *before* his dead,
4. that I may bury my dead *out of my sight.*
8. I should bury my dead *out of my sight;*
12. Abraham bowed down himself *before* the
17. Machpelah, which (was) *before* Mamre,
19. the field of Machpelah *before* Mamre:
24: 7. he shall send his angel *before thee,*
12. send *me* good speed (lit. bring to pass *before me*) this day,
33. there was set (meat) *before him*
40. The Lord, *before whom* I walk,
51. Rebekah (is) *before thee,*
25: 9. the field of Ephron...which (is) *before*
18. Shur, that (is) *before* Egypt,...toward Assyria: (and) he died in *the presence of* all

Gen 27: 7. bless thee *before* the Lord *before* my
10. that he may bless thee *before* his death.
20. the Lord thy God brought (it) *to me.* (marg. *before me*)
30. from *the presence of* Isaac
46. *because of* the daughters of Heth:
29:26. to give the younger *before* the firstborn.
30:30. little which thou hadst *before I* (came),
33. for my hire *before thy face:*
40. *the faces of* the flocks
31: 2. Jacob beheld *the countenance of* Laban,
5. I see your father's *countenance,* that it (is)
21. set *his face* (toward) the mount Gilead.
35. I cannot rise up *before thee;*
32: 3(4). Jacob sent messengers *before him*
16(17). Pass over *before me,*
17(18). whose (are) these *before thee?*
20(21). I will appease *him* with the present that goeth *before me,* and afterward I will see *his face;* peradventure he will accept *of me.* (marg. *my face*)
21(22). So went the present over before *him:* (lit. upon *his face*)
30(31). I have seen God *face* to *face,*
33: 3. he passed over *before them,*
10. I have seen *thy face,* as though I had seen *the face of* God,
14. pass over *before* his servant:
— the cattle that goeth *before me*
18. pitched his tent *before* the city.
34:10. the land shall be *before you;*
21. the land,...(is) large enough *for them;*
35: 1. thou fleddest *from the face of* Esau
7. when he fled *from the face of* his brother.
36: 6. *from the face of* his brother Jacob.
7. *because of* their cattle.
31. *before* there reigned any king
38:15. she had covered *her face.*
40: 7. Wherefore look *ye* (so) sadly (marg. (are) *your faces* evil)
9. a vine (was) *before me;*
41:31. *by reason of* that famine
43. they cried *before him,* Bow the knee:
46. when he stood *before* Pharaoh
— Joseph went out *from the presence of*
56. all *the face of* the earth:
43: 3, 5. Ye shall not see *my face,*
9. and set him *before thee,*
14. God Almighty give you mercy *before* the
15. and stood *before* Joseph.
31. And he washed *his face,*
33. And they sat *before him,*
34. (sent) messes unto them from *before him:* (lit. *his face*)
44:14. they fell *before him*
23. ye shall see *my face* no more.
26. we may not see the man's *face,*
29. if ye take this also from *me,* (lit. from *my face*)
45: 3. they were troubled *at his presence.*
5. God did send me *before you*
7. God sent me *before you*
46:28. he sent Judah *before him* unto Joseph, to direct *his face*
30. since I have seen *thy face,*
47: 2. and presented them *unto* Pharaoh.
6. The land of Egypt (is) *before thee;*
7. and set him *before* Pharaoh:
10. Jacob...went out *from before* Pharaoh.
13. *by reason of* the famine.
18. there is not ought left *in the sight of*
48:11. I had not thought to see *thy face:*
15. God, *before whom* (lit. who *before him*) my fathers...did walk,
20. he set Ephraim *before* Manasseh.
49:30. the field of Machpelah, which (is) *before*
50: 1. Joseph fell upon his father's *face,*
13. buryingplace of Ephron the Hittite, *before* Mamre.
16. Thy father did command *before* he died,
18. and fell down *before his face;*
Ex. 1:12. *because of* the children of Israel.
2:15. *from the face of* Pharaoh,
3: 6. And Moses hid *his face;*
7. *by reason of* their taskmasters;
4: 3. and Moses fled *from before it.*
21. do all those wonders *before* Pharaoh,

Ex. 6:12. Moses spake *before* the Lord,
30. Moses said *before* the Lord,
7: 9. Take thy rod, and cast (it) *before* Pharaoh,
10. Aaron cast down his rod *before* Pharaoh, *and before* his servants,
8:20(16). and stand *before* Pharaoh;
24(20). *by reason of* the swarm (of flies).
9:10. and stood *before* Pharaoh;
11. the magicians could not stand *before* Moses *because of* the boils;
13. and stand *before* Pharaoh,
30. ye will not yet fear the Lord (lit. fear *before* the Lord) God.
10: 3. to humble thyself *before me?*
10. for evil (is) before *you.* (lit. *your faces*)
11. were driven out from Pharaoh's *presence.*
14. *before them* there were no such locusts
28. see *my face* no more; for in (that) day thou seest *my face*
29. I will see *thy face* again no more.
11:10. all these wonders *before* Pharaoh:
13:21. the Lord went *before them*
22. (from) *before* the people.
14: 2. encamp *before* Pi-hahiroth,
— *over against* Baal-zephon:
9. *before* Baal-zephon.
19. the angel of God, which went *before* the
— the pillar of the cloud went *from before their face,*
25. Let us flee *from the face of* Israel;
16: 9. Come near *before* the Lord:
14. upon *the face of* the wilderness
33. lay it up *before* the Lord,
34. laid it up *before* the Testimony,
17: 5. Go on *before* the people,
6. I will stand *before thee* there
18:12. to eat bread...*before* God.
19: 7. laid *before their faces* all these words
18. *because* (lit. *because* that) the Lord
20: 3. Thou shalt have no other gods before *me.* (lit. before *my face*)
20. that his fear may be before *your faces,*
21: 1. the judgments which thou shalt set *before them.*
23:15. none shall appear *before me* empty:
17. thy males shall appear *before* the Lord
20. I send an Angel *before thee,*
21. Beware *of him,* and obey his voice,
23. mine Angel shall go *before thee,*
27. I will send my fear *before thee,*
28. I will send hornets *before thee,* which shall drive out the Hivite, the Canaanite, and the Hittite, *from before thee.*
29. not drive them out *from before thee*
30. I will drive them out *from before thee,*
31. thou shalt drive them out *before thee.*
25:20. *and their faces* (shall look) one to another; toward the mercy seat shall *the faces of* the cherubims be.
30. thou shalt set upon the table *shewbread* (lit. bread of *faces*) *before me* alway.
37. that they may give light over against *it.* (marg. *the face of it*)
26: 9. in the fore*front* (lit. over against *the face*) *of* the tabernacle.
27:21. evening to morning *before* the Lord:
28:12. bear their names *before* the Lord
25. the shoulderpieces of the ephod before *it.* (lit. *his face*)
27. toward *the forepart thereof,*
29. for a memorial *before* the Lord
30. when he goeth in *before* the Lord:
— *before* the Lord continually.
35. the holy (place) *before* the Lord,
37. upon the fore*front* (lit. over against *the face*) *of* the mitre
38. that they may be accepted *before* the Lord.
29:10. *before* the tabernacle
11. kill the bullock *before* the Lord,
23. the unleavened bread that (is) *before* the
24, 26. a wave offering *before* the Lord.
25. a sweet savour *before* the Lord:
42. the congregation *before* the Lord:
30: 6. *before* the vail that (is) by the ark of the testimony, *before* the mercy seat
8. incense *before* the Lord
16. of Israel *before* the Lord,

Ex. 30:36. *before* the testimony
32: 1, 23. make us gods, which shall go *before us;*
5. he built an altar *before it;*
11. And Moses besought the Lord (marg. *the face of* the Lord)
12. to consume them from *the face of* the
20. strawed (it) upon (lit. upon *the face of*) the water,
34. mine Angel shall go *before thee:*
33: 2. I will send an angel *before thee;*
11. And the Lord spake unto Moses *face* to *face,* as a man speaketh
14. *My presence* shall go (with thee),
15. If *thy presence* go not (with me),
16. upon *the face of* the earth.
19. my goodness pass *before thee,* and I will proclaim the name of the Lord *before thee;*
20. Thou canst not see *my face:*
23. *but my face* shall not be seen.
34: 6. the Lord passed by before *him,* (lit. *his face*)
11. I drive out *before thee* the Amorite,
20. none shall appear *before me* empty.
23. your menchildren appear *before*
24. I will cast out the nations *before thee,*
— go up to appear *before* the Lord
29. wist not that the skin of *his face* shone
30. behold, the skin of *his face* shone;
33. he put a vail on *his face.*
34. when Moses went in *before* the Lord
35. saw *the face of* Moses, that the skin of Moses' *face* shone: and Moses put the vail upon *his face*
35:13. and the *shewbread,* (lit. bread of *faces*)
20. *from the presence of* Moses.
36: 3. And they received *of* Moses
37: 9. *with their faces* one to another; (even) to the mercy seatward were *the faces of* the cherubims.
39:18. the shoulderpieces of the ephod, before *it.* (lit. *his face*)
20. toward *the forepart of it,*
36. and the *shewbread,* (lit. bread of *faces*)
40: 5. *before* the ark of the testimony,
6. *before* the door of the tabernacle
23. upon it *before* the Lord;
25. he lighted the lamps *before* the Lord,
26. *before* the vail:
Lev. 1: 3. at the door...*before* the Lord.
5. the bullock *before* the Lord:
11. northward *before* the Lord:
3: 1. without blemish *before* the Lord.
7. shall he offer it *before* the Lord.
8, 13. kill it *before* the tabernacle
12. offer it *before* the Lord.
4: 4. the congregation *before* the Lord;
— kill the bullock *before* the Lord.
6. *before* the Lord, *before* the vail of the
7. incense *before* the Lord,
14. bring him *before* the tabernacle
15. the bullock *before* the Lord:
— killed *before* the Lord.
17. seven times *before* the Lord, (even) *before* the vail.
18. the altar which (is) *before* the Lord,
24. burnt offering *before* the Lord:
6: 7(5:26). an atonement for him *before* the
14(7). offer it *before* the Lord, *before* (lit. to *the face of*) the altar.
25(18). killed *before* the Lord:
7:30. a wave offering *before* the Lord.
8: 9. upon his fore*front,* did he put the golden
26. that (was) *before* the Lord,
27, 29. a wave offering *before* the Lord.
9: 2. offer (them) *before* the Lord.
4. to sacrifice *before* the Lord;
5. *before* the tabernacle of the congregation:
— and stood *before* the Lord.
21. a wave offering *before* the Lord;
24. there came a fire out *from before* the
— they shouted, and fell on *their faces.*
10: 1. offered strange fire *before* the Lord,
2. there went out fire *from* the Lord, and devoured them, and they died *before* the
3. *before* all the people I will be glorified.
4. carry your brethren from *before* the

Lev.10:15. a wave offering *before* the Lord;
17. atonement for them *before* the Lord?
19. burnt offering *before* the Lord;
12: 7. Who shall offer it *before* the Lord,
13:41. from the part of his head toward *his face*,
14: 7. let the living bird loose into the *open* field. (marg. upon *the face of* the field)
11. those things, *before* the Lord,
12, 24. a wave offering *before* the Lord:
16, 27. seven times *before* the Lord:
18. an atonement for him *before* the Lord.
23. the congregation, *before* the Lord.
29. an atonement for him *before* the Lord.
31. cleansed *before* the Lord.
53. let go the living bird...into the *open* fields, (lit. upon *the face of* the fields)
15:14. and come *before* the Lord
15. for him *before* the Lord
30. an atonement for her *before* the Lord
16: 1. they offered *before* the Lord,
2. the vail *before* (lit. at *the face of*) the
7. present them *before* the Lord
10. presented alive *before* the Lord,
12. the altar *before* the Lord,
13. incense upon the fire *before* the Lord,
14. upon (lit. on *the face of*) the mercy seat eastward; *and before* the mercy seat
15. *and before* the mercy seat:
18. that (is) *before* the Lord,
30. your sins *before* the Lord.
17: 4. *before* the tabernacle
5. sacrifices, which they offer in the *open* field, (lit. *upon the face of* the field)
10. I will even set *my face* against
18:23. neither shall any woman stand *before*
24. nations...which I cast out *before you:*
27. the men of the land...which (were) *before you,*
28. the nations that (were) *before you.*
30. customs, which were committed *before you,*
19:14. *nor* put a stumblingblock *before* the
15. thou shalt not respect *the person of* the poor, nor honour *the person of* the
22. trespass offering *before* the Lord
32. Thou shalt rise up *before* the hoary head, and honour *the face of* the old man,
20: 3. I will set *my face* against that man,
5. I will set *my face* against
6. I will even set *my face* against
23. the nation, which I cast out *before you* ·
22: 3. soul shall be cut off *from my presence:*
23:11. wave the sheaf *before* the Lord,
20. a wave offering *before* the Lord,
28. for you *before* the Lord your God.
40. rejoice *before* the Lord
24: 3, 4, 8. *before* the Lord continually:
6. upon the pure table *before* the Lord.
26: 7. they shall fall *before you*
8. your enemies shall fall *before you*
10. bring forth the old *because of* the new.
17. I will set *my face* against you, and ye shall be slain *before* your enemies:
37. *as it were before* a sword,
— no power to stand *before* your enemies.
27: 8. present himself *before* the priest,
11. present the beast *before* the priest:
Nu. 3: 4. died *before* the Lord, when they offered strange fire *before* the Lord,
— in *the sight of* Aaron their father.
6. present them *before* Aaron
7. *before* the tabernacle of the congregation,
38. *before* the tabernacle toward the east, (even) *before* the tabernacle of the
4: 7. the table of *shewbread* (lit. table of *faces*)
5:16. set her *before* the Lord:
18. set the woman *before* the Lord,
25. wave the offering *before* the Lord,
30. the woman *before* the Lord,
6:16. priest shall bring (them) *before* the Lord,
20. a wave offering *before* the Lord:
25. The Lord make *his face* shine
26. The Lord lift up *his countenance*
7: 3. brought their offering *before* the Lord,
— brought them *before* the tabernacle.
10. their offering *before* the altar
8: 2, 3. over against (lit. over against *the face of*) the candlestick.

Nu. 8: 9. *before* the tabernacle of the congregation.
10. bring the Levites *before* the Lord:
11. offer the Levites *before* the Lord
13. set the Levites *before* Aaron, *and before*
21. an offering *before* the Lord;
22. went the Levites in...*before* Aaron, *and before* his sons:
9: 6. they came *before* Moses *and before* Aaron
10: 9. *before* the Lord your God,
10. a memorial *before* your God:
33. of the Lord went *before them*
35. let them that hate thee flee *before thee.*
11:20. and have wept *before him,*
31. upon *the face of* the earth.
12: 3. upon *the face of* the earth.
14. If her father had but spit *in her face,*
13:22. Hebron was built seven years *before* Zoan
14: 5. Moses and Aaron fell on *their faces before* all the assembly
14. thou goest *before them,* by day time
37. the plague *before* the Lord.
42. smitten *before* your enemies.
43. the Canaanites (are) there *before you,*
15:15. the stranger be *before* the Lord.
25. their sin offering *before* the Lord,
28. by ignorance *before* the Lord,
16: 2. they rose up *before* Moses,
4. when Moses heard (it), he fell upon *his face:*
7. *before* the Lord to morrow:
9. *before* the congregation
16. *before* the Lord, thou, and they,
17. bring ye *before* the Lord every
22. they fell upon *their faces,*
38(17:3). offered them *before* the Lord,
40(—:5). to offer incense *before* the Lord;
43(—:8). Moses and Aaron came *before* the
45(—:10). they fell upon *their faces.*
46(—:11). there is wrath gone out *from* the
17: 4(19). *before* the testimony, where I
7(22). the rods *before* the Lord
9(24). the rods *from before* the Lord
10(25). *before* the testimony, to be kept
18: 2. *before* the tabernacle of witness.
19. for ever *before* the Lord
19: 3. slay her *before* his face:
4. directly *before* the tabernacle
16. that is slain with a sword in the *open* fields,
20: 3. died *before* the Lord!
6. *from the presence of* the assembly
— they fell upon *their faces:*
9. Moses took the rod *from before* the Lord,
10. the congregation together *before* the rock,
21:11. the wilderness which (is) *before* Moab,
20. Pisgah, which looketh toward (lit. upon *the face of*) Jeshimon.
22: 3. Moab was sore afraid *of* the people,
— *because of* the children of Israel.
33. the ass saw me, and turned *from me* these three times: unless she had turned *from me,*
23:28. Peor, that looketh *toward* (lit. upon the *face of*) Jeshimon.
24: 1. he set *his face* toward the wilderness.
26:61. offered strange fire *before* the Lord.
27: 2. And they stood *before* Moses, *and before* Eleazar the priest, *and before* the princes
5. brought their cause *before* the Lord.
17. Which may go out *before them,* and which may go in *before them,*
19, 22. *before* Eleazar the priest, *and before* all
21. *And* he shall stand *before* Eleazar the
— of Urim *before* the Lord:
31:50. for our souls *before* the Lord.
54. of Israel *before* the Lord.
32: 4. *before* the congregation of Israel,
17. *before* the children of Israel,
— *because of* the inhabitants
20. armed *before* the Lord
21. over Jordan *before* the Lord, until he hath driven out his enemies *from before him,*
22. and be guiltless *before* the Lord,
— your possession *before* the Lord.
27. *before* the Lord to battle,
29. to battle, *before* the Lord, and the land shall be subdued *before you;*
32. pass over armed *before* the Lord

Nu. 33: 7. *before* (lit. upon *the face of*) Baal-zephon: and they pitched *before* Migdol.
8. they departed *from before* Pi-hahiroth,
47. in the mountains of Abarim, *before* Nebo.
52, 55. inhabitants of the land *from before you,*
35:12. he stand *before* the congregation
36: 1. and spake *before* Moses, *and before* the
Deu. 1: 8. I have set the land *before you:*
17. Ye shall not respect *persons* (marg. *faces*)
— ye shall not be afraid *of the face of* man;
21. thy God hath set the land *before thee:*
22. We will send men *before us,*
30. your God which goeth *before you,*
33. Who went in the way *before you,*
38. son of Nun, which standeth *before thee,*
42. lest ye be smitten *before* your enemies.
45. and wept *before* the Lord;
2:10. The Emims dwelt therein *in times past,*
12. The Horims also dwelt in Seir *beforetime;*
— destroyed them *from before them,*
20. giants dwelt therein *in old time;*
21. the Lord destroyed them *before them;*
22. he destroyed the Horims *from before them;*
25. the fear of thee upon (lit. upon *the face of*) the nations
— and be in anguish *because of thee.*
31. to give Sihon and his land *before thee:*
33. the Lord our God delivered him *before us;*
36. our God delivered all *unto us:*
3:18. pass over armed *before* your brethren
28. he shall go over *before* this people,
4: 8. this law, which I set *before you*
10. thou stoodest *before* the Lord thy God
32. the days...which were *before thee,*
37. brought thee out *in his sight*
38. To drive out nations *from before thee*
44. *before* the children of Israel:
5: 4. The Lord talked with you *face to face* in the mount
5. afraid *by reason of* the fire,
7. Thou shalt have none other gods *before me.*
6:15. from off *the face of* the earth.
19. To cast out all thine enemies *from before thee,*
25. *before* the Lord our God,
7: 1. cast out many nations *before thee,*
2. the Lord thy God shall deliver them *before thee;*
6. upon *the face of* the earth.
10. repayeth them that hate him to *their face,*
— he will repay him to *his face.*
19. the people *of whom* thou art afraid.
20. and hide themselves *from thee,*
21. Thou shalt not be affrighted *at them*·
22. put out those nations *before thee*
23. thy God shall deliver them *unto thee,* (marg. *before thy face*)
24. no man be able to stand *before thee,*
8:20. the Lord destroyeth *before your face,*
9: 2. Who can stand *before* the children of
3. he which goeth over *before thee;*
— bring them down *before thy face:*
4. cast them out *from before thee,*
—, 5. doth drive them out *from before thee.*
18, 25. I fell down *before* the Lord,
19. I was afraid *of* the anger
10: 8. to stand *before* the Lord
11. take (thy) journey *before* the people,
17. which regardeth not *persons,*
11: 4. he made the water of the Red sea to overflow *them* (lit. upon *their faces*)
23. all these nations *from before you,*
25. There shall no man be able to stand *before you:*
— the dread of you upon (lit. upon *the face of*) all the land
26. I set *before you* this day a blessing
32. which I set *before you* this day.
12: 7. there ye shall eat *before* the Lord
12. ye shall rejoice *before* the Lord
18. thou must eat them *before* the Lord
— thou shalt rejoice *before* the Lord
29. cut off the nations *from before thee,*
30. that they be destroyed *from before thee;*
14: 2. nations that (are) upon (lit. upon *the face of*) the earth.
23. thou shalt eat *before* the Lord

Deu 14:26. thou shalt eat there *before* the Lord
15:20. Thou shalt eat (it) *before* the Lord
16:11. thou shalt rejoice *before* the Lord
16. all thy males appear *before* the Lord
— shall not appear *before* the Lord empty:
19. thou shalt not respect *persons,*
17:18. (that which is) *before* the priests
18: 7. the Levites (do), which stand there *before* the Lord.
12. drive them out *from before thee.*
19:17. *before* the Lord, *before* the priests
20: 3. neither be ye terrified *because of them;*
19. to employ (them) (marg. to go *from before thee*) in the siege:
21:16. *before* the son of the hated,
22: 6. If a bird's nest chance to be *before thee*
17. *before* the elders of the city.
23:14(15). to give up thine enemies *before thee;*
24: 4. abomination *before* the Lord:
13. unto thee *before* the Lord thy God.
25: 2. to be beaten *before his face,*
9. and spit *in his face,*
26: 4. *before* the altar of the Lord
5. thou shalt speak and say *before* the Lord
10. set it *before* the Lord thy God, and worship *before* the Lord thy God:
13. shalt say *before* the Lord thy God,
27: 7. rejoice *before* the Lord thy God.
28: 7. enemies...to be smitten *before thy face.*
— and flee *before thee* seven ways.
20. *because of* the wickedness of thy doings,
25. smitten *before* thine enemies:
— and flee seven ways *before them:*
31. taken away *from before thy face,*
50. A nation of fierce *countenance* (marg. strong of *face*), which shall not regard *the person* of
60. the diseases of Egypt, which thou wast afraid *of;* (lit. which thou wast afraid *before them*)
29:10(9). all of you *before* the Lord your God;
15(14). this day *before* the Lord our God,
30: 1. the curse, which I have set *before thee,*
15. I have set *before thee* this day
19. I have set *before you* life and death,
31: 3. he will go over *before thee,* (and) he will destroy these nations *from before thee,*
— Joshua, he shall go over *before thee,*
5. shall give them up *before your face,*
6. nor be afraid *of them:*
8. he (it is) that doth go *before thee;*
11. Israel is come to appear *before* the Lord
17. I will hide *my face* from them,
18. I will surely hide *my face*
21. this song shall testify *against them*
32:20. I will hide *my face* from them,
49. over *against* (lit. upon *the face of*) Jericho;
33: 1. the children of Israel *before* his death.
27. thrust out the enemy *from before thee;*
34: 1. over *against* Jericho.
10. whom the Lord knew *face* to *face,*
Jos. 1: 5. not any man be able to stand *before thee*
14. ye shall pass *before* your brethren
2: 9. the land faint *because of you.*
10. the Lord dried up the water...*for you.*
11. more courage in any man, *because of you:*
24. the country do faint *because of us.*
3: 6. pass over *before* the people.
— and went *before* the people.
10. without fail drive out *from before you*
11. the ark...passeth over *before you*
14. bearing the ark...*before* the people;
4: 5. Pass over *before* the ark
7. *before* the ark of the covenant
11. *in the presence of* the people.
12. *before* the children of Israel,
13. passed over *before* the Lord
23. dried up the waters of Jordan *from before you,*
— which he dried up *from before us,*
5: 1. *from before* the children of Israel,
— *because of* the children of Israel.
14. Joshua fell on *his face*
6: 1. *because of* the children of Israel:
4. And seven priests shall bear *before* the ark
6. rams' horns *before* the ark of the Lord.
7. pass on *before* the ark of the Lord.

Jos. 6: 8. passed on *before* the Lord,
9. the armed men went *before* the priests
13. rams' horns *before* the ark of the Lord
— the armed men went *before them;*
26. the man *before* the Lord,
7: 4. they fled *before* the men of Ai.
5. *before* the gate (even) unto Shebarim,
6. fell to the earth upon *his face before* the
8. turneth their backs *before* their enemies!
10. wherefore liest thou thus upon *thy face?*
12. could not stand *before* their enemies, (but) turned (their) backs *before* their
13. thou canst not stand *before* thine enemies,
23. laid them out *before* the Lord.
8: 5. we will flee *before them,*
6. They flee *before us,* as at the first: therefore we will flee *before them.*
10. went up,...*before* the people to Ai.
14. appointed, *before* the plain;
15. made as if they were beaten *before them,*
32. he wrote *in the presence of* the children of
9.24. to destroy all the inhabitants...*from before you,*
— sore afraid of our lives *because of you,*
10: 8. not a man of them stand *before thee.*
10. the Lord discomfited them *before* Israel,
11. as they fled *from before* Israel,
12. *before* the children of Israel,
14. no day like that *before it*
11: 6. Be not afraid *because of them:*
— deliver them up all slain *before* Israel:
10. Hazor *beforetime* was the head
13: 3. Sihor, which (is) *before* Egypt,
6. I drive out *from before* the children
25. Aroer that (is) *before* Rabbah;
14:15. the name of Hebron *before*
15: 8. the mountain that (lieth) *before* the valley
15. the name of Debir *before*
17: 4. they came near *before* Eleazar the priest, *and before* Joshua the son of Nun, *and before* the princes,
7. Michmethah, that (lieth) *before* Shechem;
18: 1. the land was subdued *before them.*
6. cast lots for you here *before* the Lord
8. *before* the Lord in Shiloh.
10. Joshua cast lots...*before* the Lord:
14. the hill that (lieth) *before* Beth-horon
16. *before* the valley of the son of Hinnom,
19:11. the river that (is) *before* Jokneam;
51. in Shiloh *before* the Lord,
20: 6. he stand *before* the congregation
9. he stood *before* the congregation.
21:44(42). there stood not a man...*before them,*
22:27. do the service of the Lord *before him*
29. the altar of the Lord...*before* his
23: 3. all that the Lord your God hath done... *because of you;*
5. he shall expel them *from before you,* and drive them *from out of your sight;*
9. the Lord hath driven out *from before you*
— no man hath been able to stand *before you*
13. these nations *from before you;*
24: 1. they presented themselves *before* God.
8. I destroyed them *from before you.*
12. I sent the hornet *before you,* which drave them out *from before you,*
18. the Lord drave out *from before us*
Jud. 1:10. the name of Hebron *before*
11. the name of Debir *before*
23. the name of the city *before*
2: 3. I will not drive them out *from before you;*
14. could not...stand *before* their enemies.
18. *because of* their groanings
21. drive out any *from before them*
3: 2. such as *before* knew nothing
27. from the mount, and he *before them.*
4:14. is not the Lord gone out *before thee?*
15. with the edge of the sword *before* Barak;
23. *before* the children of Israel.
5: 5. The mountains melted *from before* the Lord, (even) that Sinai *from before* the Lord God
6: 2. against Israel: (and) *because of* the
6. impoverished *because of* the Midianites;
9. drave them out *from before you,*
11. to hide (it) *from* the Midianites.
18. my present, and set (it) *before thee.*

Jud. 6:22. I have seen an angel of the Lord *face to face.*
8:28. Thus was Midian subdued *before* the
9:21. *for fear of* Abimelech his brother.
39. Gaal went out *before* the men
40. and he fled *before him,*
11: 3. Jephthah fled from (marg. from *the face*) his brethren,
9. the Lord deliver them *before me,*
11. Jephthah uttered all his words *before* the
23. *from before* his people Israel,
24. our God shall drive out *from before us,*
33. *before* the children of Israel.
13:15. we shall have made ready a kid *for thee.*
20. and fell on *their faces* to the ground.
16: 3. an hill that (is) *before* Hebron.
25. he made *them* (lit. *before them*) sport:
18:21. the cattle and the carriage *before them.*
23. And they turned *their faces,*
20:23. the children of Israel...wept *before* the
26. and sat there *before* the Lord,
— offered burnt offerings...*before* the Lord.
28. Phinehas,...stood *before it* in those days,
32. They (are) smitten down *before us,*
35. the Lord smote Benjamin *before* Israel:
39. they are smitten down *before us,*
42. turned (their backs) *before* the men of
21: 2. abode there till even *before* God,
Ru. 2:10. Then she fell on *her face,* and bowed
4: 7. (the manner) *in former time*
1Sa. 1:12. as she continued praying *before* the Lord,
15. poured out my soul *before* the Lord.
16. Count not thine handmaid *for* a daughter
18. *and her countenance* was no more (sad).
19. and worshipped *before* the Lord,
22. that he may appear *before* the Lord,
2:11. *before* Eli the priest.
17. the sin of the young men was very great *before* the Lord:
18. Samuel ministered *before* the Lord,
28. to wear an ephod *before me?*
30. the house...should walk *before me*
35. he shall walk *before* mine anointed
3: 1. Samuel ministered unto the Lord *before*
4: 2. Israel was smitten *before* the Philistines:
3. smitten us to day *before* the Philistines?
17. Israel is fled *before* the Philistines,
5: 3, 4. Dagon (was) fallen *upon his face*
—, 4. *before* the ark of the Lord.
6:20. Who is able to stand *before* this holy Lord
7: 6. drew water, and poured (it) out *before*
7. they were afraid *of* the Philistines.
10. they were smitten *before* Israel.
8:11. (some) shall run *before* his chariots.
18. *because of* your king
20. that our king may judge us, and go out *before us,*
9: 9. *Beforetime* in Israel,
— *beforetime* called a Seer.
12. (he is) *before you:*
15. a day *before* Saul came,
19. go up *before me* unto the high place;
24. the cook took up the shoulder,...and set (it) *before* Saul.
— set (it) *before thee,* (and) eat:
27. Bid the servant pass on *before us,*
10: 5. *with* a psaltery, and a tabret,...*before them;*
8. thou shalt go down *before me*
19. present yourselves *before* the Lord
25. laid (it) up *before* the Lord.
11:15. they made Saul king *before* the Lord
— they sacrificed...*before* the Lord;
12: 2. the king walketh *before you:*
— I have walked *before you*
7. that I may reason with you *before* the
13:12. *and* I have not made supplication *unto* (marg. intreated *the face*) the Lord:
14:13. they fell *before* Jonathan;
25. there was honey upon (lit. upon *the face of*) the ground.
15: 7. Shur, that (is) over *against* (lit. upon *the face of*) Egypt.
33. hewed Agag in pieces *before* the Lord
16: 8. made him pass *before* Samuel.
10. made seven of his sons to pass *before*
16. thy servants, (which are) *before thee,*

1Sa.16:21. came to Saul, and stood *before him:*
22. Let David, I pray thee, stand *before me;*
17: 7. went *before him.*
24. fled *from him,* (marg. *his face*)
31. rehearsed (them) *before* Saul:
41. that bare the shield (went) *before him.*
49. he fell upon *his face* to the earth.
57. and brought him *before* Saul
18:11. David avoided *out of his presence*
12. Saul was afraid *of* David,
13. he went out and came in *before* the
15. he was afraid *of him.*
16. he went out and came in *before them.*
29. Saul was yet the more afraid *of* David;
19: 7. and he was *in his presence,*
8. and they fled *from him.* (marg. *his face*)
10. he slipped away *out of* Saul's *presence,*
24. prophesied *before* Samuel
20: 1. and came and said *before* Jonathan,
— what (is) my sin *before* thy father,
15. from *the face of* the earth.
21: 6(7). the *shew*bread (lit. bread of *faces*), that was taken *from before* the Lord,
7(8). detained *before* the Lord;
10(11). *for fear of* Saul,
12(13). was sore afraid *of* Achish
22: 4. he brought them *before* the king
23:18. they two made a covenant *before* the
24. and went to Ziph *before* Saul:
26. *for fear of* Saul;
24: 2(3). upon (lit. upon *the face of*) the rocks
25:10. break away every man *from* his master.
19. Go on *before me;*
23. fell before David on *her face,*
35. and have accepted *thy person.*
26: 1. of Hachilah, (which is) *before* Jeshimon?
3. of Hachilah, which (is) *before* Jeshimon,
19. cursed (be) they *before* the Lord;
20. before *the face of* the Lord:
28:22. let me set a morsel of bread *before thee;*
25. And she brought (it) *before* Saul, *and before* his servants;
29: 8. so long as I have been *with* (marg. *before*) *thee*
30:16. upon (lit. upon *the face of*) all the earth,
20. they drave *before* those (other) cattle,
31: 1. of Israel fled *from before* the Philistines,
2Sa. 2:14. Let the young men now arise, and play *before us.*
17. *before* the servants of David.
22. how then should I hold up *my face*
24. the hill of Ammah, that (lieth) *before*
3:13. Thou shalt not see *my face,* except thou *first* bring Michal Saul's daughter, when thou comest to see *my face.*
31. mourn *before* Abner.
34. as a man falleth *before* wicked men,
35. if I taste bread,...*till* the sun be down.
5: 3. in Hebron *before* the Lord:
20. upon mine enemies *before me,*
24. the Lord go out *before thee,*
6: 4. Ahio went *before* the ark.
5. David...played *before* the Lord
14. David danced *before* the Lord
16. leaping and dancing *before* the Lord;
17. offered burnt offerings...*before* the Lord.
21. (It was) *before* the Lord,
— therefore will I play *before* the Lord.
7: 9. cut off all thine enemies *out of thy sight,* (marg. *from thy face*)
15. Saul, whom I put away *before thee.*
16. established for ever *before thee:*
18. and sat *before* the Lord,
23. for thy land, *before* thy people,
26. be established *before thee.*
29. may continue for ever *before thee:*
9: 6. he fell on *his face,* and did reverence.
10: 9. Joab saw that *the front of* the battle was against him *before*
13. and they fled *before him.*
14. fled they also *before* Abishai,
15. were smitten *before* Israel,
16. the host of Hadarezer (went) *before them.*
18. the Syrians fled *before* Israel;
19. they were smitten *before* Israel,
11:11. are encamped in the *open* fields; (lit. upon *the face of* the fields)

2Sa.11:13. he did eat and drink *before him;*
15. Set ye Uriah in the *fore*front of (lit. over against *the face of*) the hottest battle,
13: 9. and poured (them) out *before him;*
14: 7. upon (marg. *the face of*) the earth.
20. To fetch about *this form of* speech
22. Joab fell to the ground on *his face,*
24. *and* let him not see *my face.*
—, 28. *and* saw not the king's *face.*
32. let me see the king's *face;*
33. bowed himself...*before* the king:
15: 1. and fifty men to run *before him.*
14. we shall not (else) escape *from* Absalom:
18. passed on *before* the king.
23. toward (lit. upon *the face of*) the way of
16:19. *in the presence of* his son? as I have served in thy father's *presence,* so will I be *in thy presence.*
17:11. *and* that thou go to battle in *thine own person.* (marg. *thy face,* or, *presence* go)
19. over the well's *mouth,*
18: 7. the people of Israel were slain *before*
8. *the face of* all the country:
9. Absalom met the servants (lit. met *before* the servants)
14. I may not tarry thus *with* (marg. *before*) *thee.*
19: 4(5). But the king covered *his face,*
5(6). *the faces of* all thy servants,
8(9). all the people came *before* the king:
13(14). captain of the host *before me*
17(18). went over Jordan *before* the king.
18(19). Shimei...fell down *before* the king,
20: 8. Amasa went *before them.*
21: 1. and David enquired (marg. sought *the face*) *of* the Lord.
9. they hanged them...*before* the Lord:
23:11. the people fled *from* the Philistines.
24: 4. Joab...went out *from the presence of*
13. wilt thou flee three months *before* thine
1K. 1: 2. let her stand *before* the king,
5. and fifty men to run *before him.*
23. when he was come in *before* the king,
25. they eat and drink *before him,*
28. she came *into* the king's *presence* (marg. *before* the king), and stood *before* the
32. And they came *before* the king.
50. Adonijah feared *because of* Solomon,
2: 4. thy children take heed...to walk *before me*
7. *because of* Absalom thy brother.
15. all Israel set *their faces* on me,
16. I ask one petition of thee, deny *me* not. (marg. turn not away *my face*)
17. he will not say *thee* nay, (lit. will not turn away *thy face*)
20. (I pray thee), say *me* not nay. (lit. turn not away *my face*)
— I will not say *thee* nay. (lit. will not turn away *thy face*)
26. barest the ark...*before* David
45. of David shall be established *before* the
3: 6. according as he walked *before thee*
12. there was none like thee *before thee,*
15. and stood *before* the ark
16. unto the king, and stood *before him.*
22. Thus they spake *before* the king.
24. they brought a sword *before* the king.
28. they feared the king: (lit. feared *before* the king)
5: 3(17). *for* the wars which were about him
6: 3. the porch *before* the temple of the house, twenty cubits (was) the length thereof, according *to* (lit. upon *the face of*) the breadth of the house; (and) ten cubits (was) the breadth thereof *before* the
20. *And* the oracle *in the forepart*
21. he made a partition...*before* the oracle;
7: 6. the porch (was) *before* (marg. or, according *to*) *them:* and the (other) pillars and the thick beam (were) *before* (marg. *id.*) *them.*
42. upon (marg. upon *the face of*) the pillars;
48. whereupon the *shew*bread
49. *before* the oracle, with the flowers,
8: 5. *before* the ark, sacrificing sheep
8. in the holy (place) *before* the oracle,
11. to minister *because of* the cloud:

1K. 8:14. the king turned *his face* about,
22. Solomon stood *before* the altar
23. thy servants that walk *before thee*
25. There shall not fail thee a man *in my sight*
— that they walk *before me* as thou hast walked *before me*.
28. thy servant prayeth *before thee*
31. *before* thine altar
33. thy people Israel be smitten down *before*
40. that they live in the land (lit. upon *the face of* the land)
46. and deliver them *to* the enemy,
50. *before them* who carried them captive,
54. he arose *from before* the altar
59. made supplication *before* the Lord,
62. the king,...offered sacrifice *before*
64. *before* the house of the Lord:
— the brasen altar...*before* the Lord
65. *before* the Lord our God,
9: 3. supplication, that thou hast made *before me*:
4. if thou wilt walk *before me*,
6. my statutes which I have set *before you*,
7. Then will I cut off Israel out of the land (lit. from *the face of* the land)
— this house,...will I cast out of *my sight*;
25. the altar that (was) *before* the Lord.
10: 8. thy servants, which stand...*before thee*,
24. all the earth sought *to* (marg. *the face of*) Solomon,
11: 7. in the hill that (is) *before* Jerusalem,
36. a light alway *before me* in Jerusalem,
12: 2. *from the presence of* king Solomon,
6. the old men, that stood *before* Solomon
8. young men...which stood *before him*:
30. the people went (to worship) *before*
13: 6. Intreat now *the face of* the Lord
— the man of God besought (marg. *the face of*) the Lord,
34. from off *the face of* the earth.
14: 9. all that were *before thee*:
24. *before* the children of Israel.
15: 3. which he had done *before him*:
16:25. than all that (were) *before him*.
30. above all that (were) *before him*.
33. the kings of Israel that were *before him*.
17: 1. the Lord God...*before whom* I stand,
3, 5. brook Cherith, that (is) *before* Jordan.
14. sendeth rain upon (lit. upon *the face of*) the earth.
18: 1. send rain upon (lit. upon *the face of*) the
7. and fell on *his face*,
15. liveth, *before whom* I stand, (lit. who *before him*)
39. they fell on *their faces*:
42. put *his face* between his knees,
46. and ran *before* Ahab to the entrance
19:11. stand upon the mount *before* the Lord.
— brake in pieces the rocks *before* the Lord;
13. he wrapped *his face* in his mantle,
19. (with) twelve yoke (of oxen) *before him*,
21: 4. and turned away *his face*,
26. *before* the children of Israel.
29. how Ahab humbleth himself *before me*? because he humbleth himself *before me*,
22:10. the prophets prophesied *before them*.
21. there came forth a spirit, and stood *before*
2K. 1:15. be not afraid *of him*.
3:14. *before whom* (lit. who *before him*) I stand, surely, were it not that I regard *the presence of* Jehoshaphat
24. they fled *before them*:
4:12. she stood *before him*.
29. lay my staff upon *the face of* the child.
31. Gehazi passed on *before them*, and laid the staff upon *the face of* the child;
38. the sons of the prophets...*before him*:
43. should I set this *before* an hundred men?
44. So he set (it) *before them*,
5: 1. great man *with* (marg. *before*) his master, and honourable, (marg. accepted in *countenance*)
2. waited *on* (marg. was *before*) Naaman's
3. Would God my lord (were) *with* (marg. *before*) the prophet
15. and came, and stood *before him*:
16. the Lord liveth, *before whom* I stand,

2K. 5:23. and they bare (them) *before him*.
27. he went out *from his presence*
6: 1. the place where we dwell *with thee*
22. set bread and water *before them*,
32. (the king) sent a man *from before him*:
8: 9. and came and stood *before him*,
11. he settled *his countenance*
15. and spread (it) on *his face*,
9:14. *because of* Hazael king of Syria.
32. he lifted up *his face* to the window,
37. upon *the face of* the field
10: 4. two kings stood not *before him*:
11: 2. *from* Athaliah, so that he was not
18. slew Mattan the priest of Baal *before* the
12:17(18). Hazael set *his face* to go up to
13: 4. Jehoahaz besought the Lord, (lit. *the face of* the Lord)
14. and wept over *his face*,
23. he them from *his presence* (marg. *face*)
14: 8. let us look one another in *the face*.
11. looked one another in *the face*
12. Judah was put to the worse *before* Israel;
16: 3. *from before* the children of Israel.
14. the brasen altar,...*before* the Lord, from *the forefront of* the house,
18. *from* the house of the Lord *for* the king
17: 2. the kings of Israel that were *before him*.
8. *from before* the children of Israel,
11. carried away *before them*;
18. removed them out of *his sight*:
20. had cast them *out of his sight*.
23. the Lord removed Israel out of *his sight*,
18: 5. (any) that were *before him*.
22. Ye shall worship *before* this altar
24. *the face of* one captain of
19: 6. Be not afraid *of* the words
14. spread it *before* the Lord.
15. Hezekiah prayed *before* the Lord,
26. (as corn) blasted *before* it be grown up.
20: 2. he turned *his face* to the wall,
3. I have walked *before thee* in truth
21: 2. cast out *before* the children of Israel.
9. destroyed *before* the children of Israel.
11. Amorites did, which (were) *before him*,
13. as (a man) wipeth a dish,...turning (it) *upside down*. (lit. upon *its face*)
22:10. Shaphan read it *before* the king.
19. hast humbled thyself *before* the Lord,
— rent thy clothes, and wept *before me*;
23: 3. made a covenant *before* the Lord,
13. the high places that (were) *before*
25. was there no king *before him*,
27. I will remove Judah also out of *my sight*,
24: 3. to remove (them) out of *his sight*,
20. cast them out from *his presence*,
25:19. them that were in the king's *presence*, (marg. saw the king's *face*)
26. they were afraid *of* the Chaldees.
29. he did eat bread continually *before him*
1Ch 1:43. *before* (any) king reigned over the
4:40. (they) of Ham had dwelt there *of old*.
5:10. throughout (lit. upon *the face of*) all the
25. God destroyed *before them*.
6:32(17). they ministered *before* the dwelling
9:20. ruler over them *in time past*,
10: 1. fled *from before* the Philistines,
11: 3. David made a covenant...*before* the Lord;
13. the people fled *from before* the Philistines.
12: 1. *because of* Saul the son of Kish:
8. *whose faces* (were like) *the faces of* lions,
17. went out *to meet them*, (marg. *before them*)
13: 8. David and all Israel played *before* God
10. and there he died *before* God.
14: 8. heard (of it), and went out *against them*.
15. God is gone forth *before thee*
15:24. trumpets *before* the ark of God:
16: 1. they offered burnt sacrifices...*before* God.
4. *before* the ark of the Lord,
6. *before* the ark of the covenant
11. seek *his face* continually.
27. Glory and honour (are) *in his presence*;
29. bring an offering, and come *before him*:
30. Fear *before him*, all the earth:
33. *at the presence of* the Lord,
37. *before* the ark of the covenant
— Asaph and his brethren, to minister *before* the ark continually,

1Ch 16:39. *before* the tabernacle of the Lord
17: 8. cut off all thine enemies *from before thee,*
13. (him) that was *before thee:*
16. the king came and sat *before* the Lord,
21. driving out nations *from before* thy people,
24. (let) the house of David...(be) established *before thee.*
25. found (in his heart) to pray *before thee.*
27. that it may be *before thee* for ever:
19: 7. came and pitched *before* Medeba.
10. when Joab saw that the battle (marg. *the face of* the battle) was set against him *before* and behind,
14. *before* the Syrians unto the battle; and they fled *before him.*
15. fled *before* Abishai
16, 19. put to the worse *before* Israel,
— Shophach the captain of the host...(went) *before them.*
18. the Syrians fled *before* Israel;
21:12. to be destroyed *before* thy foes,
16. elders (of Israel),... fell upon *their faces.*
30. David could not go *before it* to enquire of God: for he was afraid *because of* the sword of the angel
22: 5. David prepared abundantly *before*
8. hast shed much blood...*in my sight.*
18. the land is subdued *before* the Lord, *and before* his people.
23:13. to burn incense *before* the Lord,
31. continually *before* the Lord:
24: 2. Nadab and Abihu died *before* their father,
6. Shemaiah...wrote them *before* the king,
31. *in the presence of* David the king,
29:12. riches and honour (come) *of thee,*
15. we (are) strangers *before thee,*
22. did eat and drink *before* the Lord
25. on any king *before him* in Israel.
2Ch 1: 5. *before* the tabernacle of the Lord:
6. the brasen altar *before* the Lord,
10. come in *before* this people:
12. the kings...that (have been) *before thee,*
13. *from before* the tabernacle
2: 4(3). to burn *before him* sweet incense,
6(5). to burn sacrifice *before him?*
3: 4. the porch that (was) in *the front* (of the house), the length (of it was) according *to* (lit. upon *the face of*) the breadth of
8. according *to* (lit. upon *the face of*) the breadth of the house,
13. *and their faces* (were) inward.
15. he made *before* the house two pillars
17. the pillars *before* the temple,
4:13. upon (lit. upon *the face of*) the pillars.
19. the tables whereon the *shew*bread (was set);
20. after the manner *before* the oracle,
5: 6. assembled unto him *before* the ark,
9. the ark *before* the oracle;
14. *by reason of* the cloud:
6: 3. And the king turned *his face,*
12. he stood *before* the altar
14. thy servants, that walk *before thee*
16. shall not fail thee a man *in my sight*
— as thou hast walked *before me.*
19. thy servant prayeth *before thee:*
22. *before* thine altar in this house;
24. be put to the worse *before* the enemy,
— pray and make supplication *before thee*
31. so long as they live in (marg. upon *the face of*) the land
36. deliver them over *before* (their) enemies,
42. turn not away *the face of* thine anointed:
7: 4. sacrifices *before* the Lord.
7. *before* the house of the Lord:
14. and pray, and seek *my face,*
17. if thou wilt walk *before me,*
19. my commandments, which I have set *be-fore you,*
20. will I cast out of *my sight,*
8:12. built *before* the porch,
9: 7. thy servants, which stand...*before thee,*
11. there were none such seen *before*
23. all the kings of the earth sought *the presence of* Solomon,
10: 2. *from the presence of* Solomon
6. the old men that had stood *before* Solomon

2Ch 10: 8. the young men...that stood *before him.*
12: 5. to Jerusalem *because of* Shishak,
13: 7. Rehoboam...could not withstand *them.* (lit. strengthen himself *before them*)
8. ye think to withstand the kingdom (lit. strengthen yourselves *before* the kingdom)
13. they were *before* Judah,
14. the battle (was) *before* and behind:
15. God smote Jeroboam...*before* Abijah
16. the children of Israel fled *before* Judah:
14: 5(4). the kingdom was quiet *before him.*
7(6). (while) the land (is) yet *before us;*
10(9). Then Asa went out *against him,*
12(11). the Lord smote the Ethiopians *before* Asa, *and before* Judah;
13(12). they were destroyed *before* the Lord, *and before* his host;
15: 2. he went out *to meet* (marg. *before*) Asa,
8. that (was) *before* the porch of the Lord.
18: 9. all the prophets prophesied *before them.*
20. and stood *before* the Lord,
19: 2. Jehu...went out *to meet him,* (lit. *to his face*)
— upon thee *from before* the Lord.
7. no iniquity with the Lord...nor respect of *persons,*
11. the Levites (shall be) officers *before you.*
20: 3. and set *himself* (marg. *his face*) to seek the
5. *before* the new court,
7. *before* thy people Israel,
9. we stand *before* this house, *and in thy presence,*
12. *against* this great company
13. all Judah stood *before* the Lord,
15. *by reason of* this great multitude;
16. *before* the wilderness of Jeruel.
17. to morrow go out *against them:*
18. all Judah...fell *before* the Lord,
21. as they went out *before* the army,
22:11. hid him *from* Athaliah,
23:17. slew Mattan the priest of Baal *before* the
24:14. brought the rest of the money *before* the
25: 8. God shall make thee fall *before*
14. *and* bowed down himself *before them,*
17. let us see one another in *the face.*
21. they saw one another in *the face,*
22. Judah was put to the worse *before* Israel,
26:19. *before* the priests in the house
27: 6. he prepared his ways *before* the Lord
28: 3. cast out *before* the children of Israel.
9. he went out *before* the host
14. *before* the princes and all the congregation.
29: 6. have turned away *their faces*
11. the Lord hath chosen you to stand *before him,*
19. *before* the altar of the Lord.
23. *before* the king and the congregation;
30: 9. *before* them that lead them captive,
— will not turn away (his) *face* from you,
31:20. *before* the Lord his God.
32: 2. *and that he was purposed* (lit. *and his face* (was)) to fight
7. *for* the king of Assyria, *nor for* all the
12. Ye shall worship *before* one altar,
21. he returned with shame of *face*
33: 2. cast out *before* the children of Israel.
9. destroyed *before* the children of Israel.
12. he besought (lit. besought *the face of*) the Lord his God, and humbled himself greatly *before* the God of his fathers,
19. *before* he was humbled:
23. humbled not himself *before* the Lord,
34: 4. down the altars of Baalim in *his presence;*
— and strowed (it) upon (marg. upon *the face of*) the graves of them
18. Shaphan read it *before* the king.
24. *before* the king of Judah:
27. thou didst humble thyself *before* God,
— humbledst thyself *before me,* and didst rend thy clothes, and weep *before me;*
31. made a covenant *before* the Lord,
35:22. Josiah would not turn *his face*
36:12. humbled not himself *before* Jeremiah
Ezr. 7:28. extended mercy unto me *before* the king
8:21. afflict ourselves *before* our God,
29. *before* the chief of the priests

Ezr. 9: 6. blush to lift up *my face* to thee,
7. and to confusion of *face*,
9. *in the sight of* the kings of Persia,
15. we (are) *before thee* in our trespasses: for we cannot stand *before thee*
10: 1. down *before* the house of God,
6. Ezra rose up *from before* the house of
Neh 1: 4. prayed *before* the God of heaven,
6. I pray *before thee* now,
11. grant him mercy *in the sight of*
2: 1. Artaxerxes the king, (that) wine (was) *before him:*
— not been (beforetime) sad *in his presence.*
2. Why (is) *thy countenance* sad,
3. why should not *my countenance* be sad,
5. servant have found favour *in thy sight*,
6. it pleased the king (lit. was good *before* the king) to send me;
13. even *before* the dragon well,
4: 2(3:34). he spake *before* his brethren
5(-:37). blotted out *from before thee:*
9(3). set a watch...*because of them.*
14(8). Be not ye afraid *of them:*
5:15. governors that (had been) *before me*
— *because of* the fear of God.
6:19. they reported his good deeds *before me*,
8: 1. street that (was) *before* the water gate;
2. *before* the congregation both of men
3. he read therein *before* the street that (was) *before* the water gate
9: 8. foundest his heart faithful *before thee*,
11. didst divide the sea *before them*,
24. thou subduedst *before them*
28. they did evil again *before thee:*
32. all the trouble seem little *before thee*,
35. land which thou gavest *before them*,
12:36. and Ezra the scribe *before them.*
13: 4. *And before* this, Eliashib the priest,
5. where *aforetime* they laid the meat
19. dark *before* the sabbath,
Est. 1: 3. and princes of the provinces, (being) *before him:*
10. in *the presence of* Ahasuerus
11. To bring Vashti the queen *before* the
13. the king's manner *toward* all that knew
14. which saw the king's *face*,
16. Memucan answered *before* the king
17. the queen to be brought in *before him*,
19. a royal commandment *from him*, (marg. *from before him*)
— That Vashti come no more *before* king
2: 9. she obtained kindness *of him;*
11. walked every day *before* the court
17. she obtained grace and favour *in his sight* (marg. *before him*)
23. it was written...*before* the king.
3: 7. *before* Haman from day to day,
4: 2. came even *before* the king's gate:
5. appointed to attend *upon her*,
6. which (was) *before* the king's gate.
8. to make request *before him*
5:14. And the thing pleased Haman; (lit. was good *before* Haman)
6: 1. they were read *before* the king.
9. and proclaim *before him*,
11. and proclaimed *before him*,
13. *before whom* (lit. who *before him*) thou hast begun to fall, thou shalt not prevail against him, but shalt surely fall *before him.*
7: 6. *before* the king and the queen.
8. *As* the word...they covered Haman's *face.*
9. Harbonah,...said *before* the king,
8: 1. Mordecai came *before* the king;
3. Esther spake yet again *before* the king, and fell down *at* his feet,
4. Esther...stood *before* the king,
5. if I have found favour *in his sight*, and the thing (seem) right *before* the king,
15. went out *from the presence of* the king
9: 2. no man could *withstand them;* (lit. stand *before them*)
11. the number...was brought *before* the
25. when (Esther) came *before* the king,
Job 1:11. he will curse thee to *thy face.*
12. *the presence of* the Lord.
2: 5. he will curse thee to *thy face.*

Job 2: 7. from *the presence of* the Lord,
3:24. my sighing cometh *before* I eat,
4:15. a spirit passed before *my face;*
19. are crushed *before* the moth?
5:10. upon (lit. upon *the face of*) the earth,
— upon (lit. upon *the face of*) the fields:
6:28. (it is) evident *unto you* (marg. before *your face*) if I lie.
8:12. *Whilst*...it withereth *before* any (other)
16. He (is) green *before* the sun,
9:24. he covereth *the faces of* the judges
27. I will leave off *my heaviness*,
11:15. shalt thou lift up *thy face*
19. many shall make suit unto *thee.* (marg. intreat *thy face*)
13: 8. Will ye accept *his person?*
10. if ye do secretly accept *persons.*
15. maintain mine own ways *before him.*
16. an hypocrite shall not come *before him.*
20. will I not hide myself *from thee.*
24. Wherefore hidest thou *thy face*,
14:20. thou changest *his countenance*,
15: 4. restrainest prayer *before* God.
7. *or* wast thou made *before* the hills?
27. he covereth *his face* with his fatness,
16: 8. beareth witness *to my face.*
14. breach upon (lit. upon *the face of*) breach,
16. *My face* is foul with weeping,
17: 6. *aforetime* I was as a tabret.
12. the light (is) short *because of* darkness.
18:17. he shall have no name in the street. (lit. upon *the face of* the street)
19:29. Be ye afraid *of* the sword:
21: 8. established *in their sight* with them,
18. They are as stubble *before* the wind,
31. Who shall declare his way to *his face?*
33. *as* (there are) innumerable *before him.*
22: 8. the honourable man (marg. accepted for *countenance*)
26. shall lift up *thy face* unto God.
23: 4. I would order (my) cause *before him*,
15. Therefore am I troubled *at his presence:*
17. I was not cut off *before* the darkness, (neither) hath he covered the darkness *from my face.*
24:15. and disguiseth (his) *face.*
18. He (is) swift *as* the waters; (lit. he is light upon *the face of* the waters)
26: 9. He holdeth back *the face of* his throne,
10. He hath compassed the waters (lit. *the face of* the waters)
29:24. the light of *my countenance*
30:10. *and* spare not to spit in *my face.* (lit. *and from my face* spare not)
11. let loose the bridle *before me.*
32:21. Let me not,...accept any man's *person*,
33: 5. set (thy words) in order *before me*,
26. he shall see *his face* with joy:
34:19. accepteth not *the persons of* princes, nor regardeth the rich *more than* the poor?
29. when he hideth (his) *face*,
35:12. *because of* the pride of evil men.
14. judgment (is) *before him;*
37:12. upon *the face of* the world
19. *by reason of* darkness.
38:30. *and the face of* the deep is frozen.
39:22. neither turneth he back *from* the sword.
40:13. bind *their faces* in secret.
41:10(2). who then is able to stand *before me?*
13(5). Who can discover *the face of* his
14(6). Who can open the doors of *his face?*
22(14). *and* sorrow is turned into joy *before him.*
42: 8. for *him* (marg. *his face*, or, *person*) will I accept:
9. the Lord also accepted Job. (marg. accepted *the face of* Job)
11. had been of his acquaintance *before*,
Ps. 3 [title](1). David, when he fled *from* Absalom
4: 6(7). lift thou up the light of *thy countenance*
5: 8(9). make thy way straight *before my face.*
9: 3(4). shall fall and perish *at thy presence.*
19(20). the heathen be judged in *thy sight.*
10:11. he hideth *his face*
11: 7. *his countenance* doth behold the upright.
13: 1(2). how long wilt thou hide *thy face*
16:11. in *thy presence* (is) fulness of joy;

Ps. 17: 2. Let my sentence come forth *from thy presence;*
9. *From* the wicked that oppress
13. Arise, O Lord, disappoint *him* (marg. prevent *his face*), cast him down:
15. I will behold *thy face*
18: 6(7). and my cry came *before him,*
42(43). as the dust *before* the wind:
19:14(15). be acceptable *in thy sight,* O Lord,
21: 6(7). exceeding glad with *thy countenance.*
9(10). in the time of *thine anger:*
12(13). against *the face of them.*
22:24(25). neither hath he hid *his face*
27(28). the nations shall worship *before thee.*
29(30). shall bow *before him:*
23: 5. Thou preparest a table *before me*
24: 6. that seek *thy face,* O Jacob.
27: 8. Seek ye *my face;*
— *Thy face,* Lord, will I seek.
9. Hide not *thy face* (far) from me;
30: 7(8). thou didst hide *thy face,*
31:16(17). Make *thy face* to shine
20(21). in the secret of *thy presence*
34 [title](1). David, when he changed his behaviour *before* Abimelech;
5(6). *and their faces* were not ashamed.
16(17). *The face of* the Lord
35: 5. as chaff *before* the wind:
38: 3(4). *because of* thine anger; neither (is there any) rest in my bones *because of* my sin.
5(6). *because of* my foolishness.
41:12(13). settest me *before thy face*
42: 2(3). when shall I come and appear *before* God?
5(6). the help of *his countenance.*
11(12) & 43:5. the health of *my countenance,* and my God.
44: 3(4). and the light of *thy countenance,*
15(16). the shame of *my face* hath covered
16(17). *by reason of* the enemy
24(25). Wherefore hidest thou *thy face,*
45:12(13). the people shall intreat *thy favour.* (marg. *face*)
50: 3. a fire shall devour *before him,*
51: 9(11). Hide *thy face* from my sins,
11(13). Cast me not away *from thy presence;*
55: 3(4). *because of* the oppression of the
56:13(14). that I may walk *before* God
57 [title](1). David, when he fled *from* Saul
6(7). they have digged a pit *before me,*
60: 4(6). *because of* the truth.
61: 3(4). a strong tower *from* the enemy.
7(8). He shall abide *before* God
62: 8(9). pour out your heart *before him:*
67: 1(2). cause *his face* to shine upon us.
68: 1(2). that hate him flee *before him.* (marg. *from his face*)
2(3). as wax melteth *before* the fire, (so) let the wicked perish *at the presence of*
3(4). let them rejoice *before* God:
4(5). and rejoice *before him.*
7(8). thou wentest forth *before* thy people,
8(9). the heavens also dropped *at the presence of* God:
—(—). *at the presence of* God, the God of
69: 7(8). shame hath covered *my face.*
17(18). hide not *thy face* from thy servant;
22(23). Let their table become a snare *before them:*
72: 5. as long as the sun and moon *endure,*
9. They...shall bow *before him;*
17. shall be continued *as long as* the sun:
76: 7(8). who may stand *in thy sight*
78:55. cast out the heathen also *before them,*
79:11. sighing of the prisoner come *before thee;*
80: 2(3). *Before* Ephraim and Benjamin and
3(4), 7(8), 19(20). cause *thy face* to shine; and we shall be saved.
9(10). Thou preparedst (room) *before it,*
16(17). the rebuke of *thy countenance.*
82: 2. *and* accept *the persons of* the wicked?
83:13(14). as the stubble *before* the wind.
16(17). Fill *their faces* with shame;
84: 9(10). look upon *the face of* thine anointed.
85:13(14). Righteousness shall go *before him;*
86: 9. worship *before thee,* O Lord;
88: 2(3). Let my prayer come *before thee:*

Ps. 88:14(15). (why) hidest thou *thy face*
89:14(15). and truth shall go before *thy face.*
15(16). in the light of *thy countenance.*
23(24). will beat down his foes *before his face,*
90: 8. in the light of *thy countenance.*
95: 2. Let us come before *his presence* (marg. prevent *his face*)
6. let us kneel *before* the Lord our maker.
96: 6. Honour and majesty (are) *before him:*
9. fear *before* him, all the earth.
13. *Before* the Lord: for he cometh,
97: 3. A fire goeth *before him,*
5. *at the presence of* the Lord, *at the presence of* the Lord of the whole earth.
98: 6. make a joyful noise *before* the Lord,
9. *Before* the Lord; for he cometh
100: 2. come *before* his presence with singing.
102 [title](1). *and* poureth out his complaint *before* the Lord.
2(3). Hide not *thy face* from me
10(11). *Because of* thine indignation
25(26). *Of old* hast thou laid the foundation
28(29). seed shall be established *before thee.*
104:15. oil to make (his) *face* to shine,
29. Thou hidest *thy face,*
30. thou renewest *the face of* the earth.
105: 4. seek *his face* evermore.
17. He sent a man *before them,*
106:23. Moses his chosen stood *before him*
46. *of* all those that carried them captives.
114: 7. *at the presence of* the Lord, *at the presence of* the God of Jacob;
116: 9. I will walk *before* the Lord
119:58. I intreated *thy favour* (marg. *face*)
135. Make *thy face* to shine upon thy servant;
169. Let my cry come near *before thee,*
170. Let my supplication come *before thee:*
132:10. *the face of* thine anointed.
139: 7. whither shall I flee *from thy presence?*
140:13(14). upright shall dwell in *thy presence.*
141: 2. Let my prayer be set forth *before thee*
142: 2(3). I poured out my complaint *before him;* I shewed *before him* my trouble.
143: 2. *in thy sight* shall no man living be
7. hide not *thy face* from me,
147:17. who can stand *before* his cold?
Pro. 4: 3. (beloved) *in the sight of* my mother.
6:35. He will not regard (marg. He will not accept *the face of*) any ransom;
7:13. with an impudent *face* (marg. she strengthened *her face*) said unto him,
15. diligently to seek *thy face,*
8:25. *before* the hills was I brought forth:
27. he set a compass upon *the face of* the
30. rejoicing always *before him;*
14:12. a way which seemeth right *unto* a man,
19. The evil bow *before* the good;
15:13. heart maketh *a* cheerful *countenance:*
14. (כתיב) *but the mouth of* fools feedeth on
33. *and before* honour (is) humility.
16:15. the light of the king's *countenance*
18. Pride (goeth) *before* destruction, *and* an haughty spirit *before* a fall.
25. a way that seemeth right *unto* a man,
17:14. *therefore* leave off contention, *before* it
18. *in the presence of* his friend.
24. Wisdom (is) *before* him that hath
18: 5. to accept *the person of* the wicked,
12. *Before* destruction the heart of man is haughty, *and before* honour (is) humility.
16. *and* bringeth him *before* great men.
19: 6. Many will intreat *the favour of*
21:29. A wicked man hardeneth *his face:*
22:29. he shall stand *before* kings; he shall not stand *before* mean (men).
23: 1. consider diligently what (is) *before thee:*
24:23. (It is) not good to have respect of *persons*
31. nettles had covered *the face thereof,*
25: 5. Take away the wicked (from) *before* the
6. *in the presence of* the king,
7. *in the presence of* the prince
23. *so* (doth) *an* angry *countenance*
26. falling down *before* the wicked
27: 4. who (is) able to stand *before* envy?
17. *the countenance of* his friend.
19. As in water *face* (answereth) *to face,* so the heart of man to man.

Pro.27:23. to know *the state of* thy flocks,
28:21. To have respect of *persons* (is) not good:
29:26. Many seek the ruler's *favour;* (marg. *face of* a ruler)
30:30. turneth not away *for* any;
Ecc. 1:10. which was *before us.*
16. all (they) that have been *before me*
2: 7. all that were in Jerusalem *before me:*
9. increased more than all that were *before me*
26. a man that (is) good *in his sight* (marg. *before him*)
— (him that is) good *before* God.
3:14. that (men) should fear *before him.*
4:16. all that have been *before them:*
5: 2(1). to utter (any) thing *before* God:
6(5). neither say thou *before* the angel,
7: 3. by the sadness of *the countenance*
26. whoso pleaseth God (marg. (is) good *before* God)
8: 1. a man's wisdom maketh *his face* to shine, and the boldness of *his face*
3. Be not hasty to go *out of his sight:*
12. which fear *before him:*
13. he feareth not *before* God.
9: 1. all (that is) *before them.*
10: 5. an error (which) proceedeth *from* (marg. *from before*) the ruler:
10. he do not whet *the edge,*
11: 1. upon (marg. upon *the face of*) the waters:
Cant.7: 4(5). of Lebanon which looketh *toward*
8:12. vineyard, which (is) mine, (is) *before me:*
Isa. 1:12. When ye come to appear *before me,*
2:10, 19, 21. *for* fear of the Lord, and for
3: 3. the honourable man, (marg. a man eminent in *countenance*)
9. The shew of *their countenance*
15. *and* grind *the faces of* the poor?
5:21. and prudent in *their own sight!* (marg. before *their face*)
6: 2. with twain he covered *his face,*
7: 2. as the trees...are moved *with* the wind.
16. the land...shall be forsaken *of* both
8: 4. shall be taken away *before* the king of
17. hideth *his face* from the house of Jacob,
9: 3(2). they joy *before thee*
15(14). The ancient and honourable, (lit. acceptable of *countenance*)
10:27. destroyed *because of* the anointing.
13: 8. *their faces* (shall be as) flames. (marg. *faces of* the flames)
14:21. nor fill *the face of* the world
16: 4. *from the face of* the spoiler:
17: 9. *because of* the children of Israel:
13. as the chaff of the mountains *before* the wind, and like a rolling thing *before* the
18: 2. upon (lit. upon *the face of*) the waters,
5. *afore* the harvest,
19: 1. the idols...shall be moved *at his presence,*
8. upon (lit. upon *the face of*) the waters
16. *because of* the shaking of the hand
17. *because of* the counsel of the Lord
20. *because of* the oppressors,
20: 6. delivered *from* the king of Assyria:
21:15. they fled *from* (marg. *from the face*) the swords, *from* the drawn sword, *and from* the bent bow, *and from* the grievousness
23:17. upon *the face of* the earth.
18. them that dwell *before* the Lord,
24: 1. turneth *it upside* down, (marg. perverteth *the face thereof*)
25: 7. *the face of* the covering cast over
8. wipe away tears from off all *faces;*
26:17. have we been *in thy sight,* O Lord.
27: 6. fill *the face of* the world with fruit.
28:25. he hath made plain *the face thereof,*
29:22. neither shall *his face* now wax pale.
30:11. the Holy One of Israel to cease *from before us.*
17. *at* the rebuke of one; *at* the rebuke of five
31: 8. he shall flee *from* the sword,
36: 7. Ye shall worship *before* this altar?
9. *the face of* one captain
37: 6. Be not afraid *of* the words
14. and spread it *before* the Lord.
27. (as corn) blasted *before* it be grown up.
38: 2. Hezekiah turned *his face* toward the wall,
3. I have walked *before thee* in truth

Isa. 40:10. and his work *before him.*
41: 2. gave the nations *before him,*
26. and *beforetime,* that we may say,
42:16. I will make darkness light *before them,*
43:10. *before me* there was no God
45: 1. to subdue nations *before him;* and I will loose the loins of kings, to open *before him* the two leaved gates;
2. I will go *before thee,* and make
48: 7. *even before* the day when thou heardest
19. destroyed *from before me.*
50: 6. I hid not *my face* from shame and spitting.
7. I set *my face* like a flint,
51:13. *because of* the fury of the oppressor,
52:12. the Lord will go *before you;*
53: 2. he shall grow up *before him*
3. we hid as it were (our) *faces*
7. as a sheep *before* her shearers
54: 8. I hid *my face* from thee
55:12. the hills shall break forth *before you*
57: 1. the righteous is taken away *from* the evil
16. the spirit should fail *before me,*
58: 8. thy righteousness shall go *before thee;*
59: 2. your sins have hid (his) *face*
62:11. and his work *before him.*
63: 9. the angel of *his presence* saved them:
12. dividing the water *before them,*
64: 1(63:19). the mountains might flow down *at thy presence,*
2(1). nations may tremble *at thy presence!*
3(2). the mountains flowed down *at thy presence.*
7(6). thou hast hid *thy face* from us,
65: 3. provoketh me to anger...to *my face;*
6. (it is) written *before me:*
66:22. shall remain *before me,*
23. all flesh come to worship *before me,*
Jer. 1: 8. Be not afraid *of their faces:*
13. *and the face thereof* (is) *toward* (marg. *from the face of*) the north.
17. be not dismayed *at their faces,* lest I confound thee *before* them.
2:22. thine iniquity is marked *before me,*
27. turned (their) back...and not (their) *face.*
3:12. I will not cause *mine anger* to fall
4: 1. away thine abominations *out of my sight,*
4. *because of* the evil of your doings.
26. *at the presence of* the Lord, (and) *by* his
5: 3. they have made *their faces* harder than a
22. will ye not tremble *at my presence,*
6: 7. *before me* continually (is) grief and
7:10. come and stand *before me*
12. *for* the wickedness of my people
15. I will cast you out of *my sight,*
19. the confusion of *their own faces?*
24. went backward, and not *forward.*
8: 2. upon *the face of* the earth.
9: 7(6). *for* the daughter of my people?
13(12). my law which I set *before them,*
22(21). as dung upon the *open* field, (lit. upon *the face of* the field)
13:17. my soul shall weep...*for* (your) pride;
26. discover thy skirts upon *thy face,*
14:16. *because of* the famine and the sword;
15: 1. Moses and Samuel stood *before me,*
— cast (them) out of *my sight,*
9. deliver to the sword *before* their enemies,
17. I sat alone *because of* thy hand:
19. thou shalt stand *before me:*
16: 4. upon *the face of* the earth:
17. they are not hid *from my face,*
17:16. which came out of my lips was (right) *before thee.*
18:17. scatter them...*before* the enemy; I will shew them the back, and not *the face,*
20. I stood *before thee* to speak good
23. neither blot out their sin *from thy sight,* but let them be overthrown *before thee,*
19: 7. to fall by the sword *before* their enemies,
21: 8. I set *before you* the way of life,
10. I have set *my face* against this city
12. *because of* the evil of your doings.
22:25. *whose* (lit. who *their*) *face* thou fearest,
23: 9. *because of* the Lord, *and because of* the
10. *because of* swearing the land mourneth;
39. (cast you) out of *my presence:*
24: 1. two baskets of figs (were) set *before* the

Jer. 25:16. *because of* the sword that I will
26. upon *the face of* the earth:
27. *because of* the sword which I will send
33. they shall be dung upon (lit. upon *the face of*) the ground.
37. *because of* the fierce anger of the Lord.
38. *because of* the fierceness of the oppressor, *and because of* his fierce anger.
26: 3. *because of* the evil of their doings.
4. my law, which I have set *before you,*
19. and besought the Lord, (marg. besought *the face of* the Lord)
27: 5. upon (lit. upon *the face of*) the ground,
28: 8. The prophets that have been *before me and before thee* of old prophesied
16. from off *the face of* the earth:
30: 6. all *faces* are turned into paleness?
20. congregation shall be established *before me,*
31:36. If those ordinances depart *from before me,*
— being a nation *before me* for ever.
32:24. against it, *because of* the sword,
31. remove it from before *my face,*
33. turned...the back, and not *the face:*
33: 5. I have hid *my face* from this city.
18. Neither shall the priests...want a man *before me*
24. should be no more a nation *before them.*
34: 5. the former kings which were *before thee,*
15. ye had made a covenant *before me*
18. covenant which they had made *before me,*
35: 5. I set *before* the sons of the house
7. that ye may live many days in the land (lit. upon *the face of* the land)
11. *for fear of* the army of the Chaldeans, *and for fear of* the army of the Syrians:
19. shall not want a man to stand *before me*
36: 7. present their supplication *before* the Lord,
9. proclaimed a fast *before* the Lord
22. (a fire) on the hearth burning *before him.*
37:11. *for fear of* Pharaoh's army,
20. my supplication,...be accepted *before thee;*
38: 9. he is like to die *for* hunger
26. I presented my supplication *before* the
39:16. be (accomplished) in that day *before thee.*
17. the men *of whom* (lit. who *before them*) thou (art) afraid.
40: 4. all the land (is) *before thee:*
10. to serve (lit. to stand *before*) the Chaldeans,
41: 9. *for fear of* Baasha king of Israel:
15. Ishmael...escaped *from* Johanan
18. *Because of* the Chaldeans: for they were afraid *of them,*
42: 2. our supplication be accepted *before thee,*
9. to present your supplication *before him;*
11. Be not afraid *of* the king of Babylon, *of whom* (lit. who *of him*) ye are afraid;
15. If ye wholly set *your faces*
17. all the men that set *their faces*
— escape *from* the evil that I will bring
44: 3. *Because of* their wickedness
10. my statutes, that I set *before you and before*
11. I will set *my face* against you
12. have set *their faces* to go into the land
22. *because of* the evil of your doings, (and) *because of* the abominations
23. *Because* (lit. *because* that) ye have burned
46:16. *from* the oppressing sword.
48:44. He that fleeth *from* the fear
49: 5. shall be driven out every man *right forth;*
19. that shepherd that will stand *before me?*
37. Elam to be dismayed *before* their enemies, *and before* them that seek their life:
50: 5. Zion with *their faces* thitherward,
8. be as the he goats *before* the flocks.
16. *for fear of* the oppressing sword
44. that shepherd that will stand *before me?*
51:51. shame hath covered *our faces:*
64. *from* the evil that I will bring
52: 3. cast them out from *his presence,*
12. served (marg. stood *before*) the king of Babylon,
25. them that were near the king's *person,* (marg. saw *the face of* the king)
33. he did continually eat bread *before him*
Lam. 1: 5. gone into captivity *before* the enemy.
6. without strength *before* the pursuer.
Lam. 1:22. Let all their wickedness come *before thee;*
2: 3. *from before* the enemy,
19. before *the face of* the Lord:
3:35. before *the face of* the most High,
4:16. *The anger* (marg. or, *face*) *of* the Lord
— they respected not *the persons of*
5: 9. *because of* the sword
10. *because of* the terrible famine.
12. *the faces of* elders were not honoured.
Eze. 1: 6. every one had four *faces,*
8. *and* they four had *their faces*
9. they went...*straight* forward. (lit. on the side of *their face*)
10. the likeness of *their faces,* they four had *the face of* a man, *and the face of* a lion, on the right side: *and* they four had *the face of* an ox on the left side; they four *also* had the *face of* an eagle.
11. *Thus* (were) *their faces:*
12. they went...*straight* forward: (lit. on the side of *their face*)
15. one wheel...with *his* four *faces.*
28. I fell upon *my face,*
2: 4. (they are) impudent (marg. hard of *face*) children and stiffhearted.
6. *nor* be dismayed *at their looks,*
10. And he spread it *before me:* and it (was) written *within* and without:
3: 8. I have made *thy face* strong against *their faces,*
9. neither be dismayed *at their looks,*
20. I lay a stumblingblock *before him,*
23. and I fell on *my face.*
4: 1. take thee a tile, and lay it *before thee,*
3. and set *thy face* against it,
7. thou shalt set *thy face* toward the siege
6: 2. set *thy face* toward the mountains
4. I will cast down your slain (men) *before*
5. the children of Israel *before* their idols;
9. they shall lothe *themselves* (lit. shall be lothesome *before their faces*)
7:18. shame (shall be) upon all *faces*
22. *My face* will I turn also
8: 1. the elders of Judah sat *before me,*
11. there stood *before them* seventy men
16. *and their faces* toward the east;
9: 6. the ancient men which (were) *before* the
8. I fell upon *my face,*
10:14. every one had four *faces:* the first *face* (was) *the face of* a cherub, *and the* second *face* (was) *the face of* a man, and the third *the face of* a lion, and the fourth *the face of* an eagle.
21. Every one had four *faces* apiece,
22. the likeness of *their faces* (was) *the* same *faces* which I saw
— they went every one *straight* forward. (lit. on the side of *their face*)
11:13. Then fell I down upon *my face,*
12: 6. thou shalt cover *thy face,*
12. he shall cover *his face,*
13:17. set *thy face* against the daughters of
14: 1. certain of the elders...and sat *before me.*
3. their iniquity before *their face:*
4, 7. his iniquity before *his face,*
6. turn away *your faces* from all your
8. I will set *my face* against that man,
15. may pass through *because of* the beasts:
15: 7. I will set *my face* against them;
— when I set *my face* against them.
16: 5. thou wast cast out in the *open* field, (lit. upon *the face of* the field)
18. set mine oil and mine incense *before them,*
19. thou hast even set it *before them*
50. committed abomination *before me:*
63. *because of* thy shame,
20: 1. certain of the elders...sat *before me.*
35. there will I plead with you *face* to *face.*
43. lothe yourselves *in your own sight*
46(21:2). set *thy face* toward the south,
47(—:3). all *faces*...shall be burned
21: 2(7). set *thy face* toward Jerusalem,
16(21). whithersoever *thy face* (is) set.
22:30. and stand in the gap *before me*
23:24. I will set judgment *before them,*
41. stately bed, and a table prepared *before it,*
25: 2. set *thy face* against the Ammonites

Eze.27:35. shall be troubled in (their) *countenance.*
28: 9. *before* him that slayeth
17. I will lay thee *before* kings,
21. set *thy face* against Zidon,
29: 2. set *thy face* against Pharaoh
5. thou shalt fall upon the *open* fields; (marg. upon *the face of* the field)
30: 9. shall messengers go forth *from me*
24. he shall groan *before him*
32: 4. cast thee forth upon the *open* field, (lit. upon *the face of* the field)
10. I shall brandish my sword *before them;*
33:22. *afore* he that was escaped came;
27. him that (is) in the *open* field (lit. upon *the face of* the field)
31. they sit *before thee* (as) my people,
34: 6. all *the face of* the earth,
35: 2. set *thy face* against mount Seir,
36:17. their way was *before me*
31. lothe yourselves *in your own sight*
37: 2. in the *open* valley; (lit. upon *the face of* the valley)
38: 2. set *thy face* against Gog,
20. upon *the face of* the earth, shall shake *at my presence,*
39: 5. Thou shalt fall upon the *open* field: (marg. upon *the face of* the field)
14. upon *the face of* the earth,
23. therefore hid I *my face*
24. and hid *my face* from them.
29. Neither will I hide *my face*
40: 6. the gate *which look*eth (lit. who *its face* (is)) toward the east,
12. The space also *before* the little chambers
15. And from *the face of* the gate of the entrance unto *the face of* the porch
19. *from the forefront of* the lower gate *unto the forefront of* the inner court
20. the gate...*that look*ed (lit. who *its face* (was)) toward the north,
22. the gate *that look*eth (lit. *id.*) toward the
—, 26. the arches thereof (were) *before them.*
44. *and their prospect* (was) toward the south:
— *the prospect* toward the north.
45. This chamber, *whose prospect* (is) toward
46. the chamber *whose prospect*
47. the altar (that was) *before* the house.
41: 4. the breadth,...*before* the temple:
12. *before* the separate place
14. the breadth of *the face of* the house,
15. over *against* (lit. upon *the face of*) the
18. (every) cherub had two *faces;*
19. *So* that *the face of* a man (was) toward the palm tree on the one side, *and the face of* a young lion toward
21. (and) *the face of* the sanctuary;
22. the table that (is) *before* the Lord.
25. upon *the face of* the porch
42: 2. *Before* the length of an hundred cubits
3. gallery *against* (lit. gallery to *the face of*) gallery
4. *And before* the chambers (was) a walk
7. on *the forepart of* the chambers,
8. *before* the temple (were) an hundred
10. over *against* (lit. upon *the face of*) the separate place, and over *against* (lit. upon *the face of*) the building.
11. the way *before them* (was) like
12. *before* the wall toward the east,
13. *before* the separate place,
15. the gate *whose prospect* (is) toward
43: 3. I fell upon *my face.*
4. the gate *whose* (lit. who *its*) *prospect* (is)
24. thou shalt offer them *before* the Lord,
44: 3. to eat bread *before* the Lord;
4. the north gate *before* the house:
— and I fell upon *my face.*
11. they shall stand *before them* to minister
12. they ministered unto them *before* their
15. they shall stand *before me*
45: 7. *before* the oblation of the holy (portion), and *before* the possession of the city,
46: 3. *before* the Lord in the sabbaths
9. shall come *before* the Lord
47: 1. *the forefront of* the house
48:15, 21. over *against* (lit. upon *the face of*) the
21. over *against* the five and twenty thousand

Dan 1: 5. they might stand *before* the king.
9. *with* the prince of the eunuchs.
10. why should he see *your faces* worse
13. let our countenances be looked upon *before thee,*
18. brought them in *before* Nebuchadnezzar.
19. therefore stood they *before* the king.
2: 2. they came and stood *before* the king.
8: 3. there stood *before* the river
4. no beasts might stand *before him,*
5. on *the face of* the whole earth,
6. the ram...standing *before* the river,
7. no power in the ram to stand *before him,*
17. and fell upon *my face:*
18. I was in a deep sleep on *my face*
23. a king of fierce *countenance,*
9: 3. I set *my face* unto the Lord
7. unto us confusion of *faces,*
8. to us (belongeth) confusion of *face,*
10. his laws, which he set *before us*
13. *before* the Lord our God,
17. cause *thy face* to shine
18. we do not present our supplications *before thee*
20. *before* the Lord my God
10: 6. *and his face* as the appearance of
9. in a deep sleep on *my face, and my face* toward the ground.
12. to chasten thyself *before* thy God,
15. I set *my face* toward the ground,
11:16. none shall stand *before him:*
17. He shall also set *his face* to enter
18. shall he turn *his face* unto the isles,
19. he shall turn *his face* toward the fort
22. shall they be overflown *from before him,*
Hos. 2: 2(4). away her whoredoms *out of her sight,*
5: 5. the pride of Israel doth testify *to his face:*
15. acknowledge their offence, and seek *my face:*
6: 2. we shall live *in his sight.*
7: 2. they are before *my face.*
10. the pride of Israel testifieth *to his face:*
10: 7. as the foam upon (lit. upon *the face of*) the water.
15. *because of* your great wickedness:
11: 2. so they went *from them:*
Joel 2: 3. A fire devoureth *before them;*
— as the garden of Eden *before them,*
6. *Before their face* the people
— all *faces* shall gather blackness.
10. The earth shall quake *before them;*
11. the Lord shall utter his voice *before* his
20. with *his face* toward the east sea,
31(3:4). *before* the great and the terrible day
Am. 1: 1. two years *before* the earthquake.
2: 9. destroyed I the Amorite *before them,*
5: 8. upon *the face of* the earth:
19. As if a man did flee *from* a lion,
9: 4. they go into captivity *before* their enemies,
6. upon *the face of* the earth:
8. from off *the face of* the earth;
Jon. 1: 2. their wickedness is come up *before me.*
3, 3. unto Tarshish *from the presence of* the
10. he fled *from the presence of* the Lord,
Mic. 1: 4. as wax *before* the fire,
2:13. The breaker is come up *before them:*
— their king shall pass *before them,*
3: 4. he will even hide *his face*
6: 4. I sent *before thee* Moses, Aaron, and
Nah 1: 5. the earth is burned *at his presence,*
6. Who can stand *before* his indignation?
2: 1(2). come up before *thy face:*
10(11). *and the faces of* them all gather
3: 5. discover thy skirts upon *thy face,*
Hab 1: 9. *their faces* shall sup up (as) the east
2:20. let all the earth keep silence *before him.*
3: 5. *Before him* went the pestilence,
Zep. 1: 2. consume all (things) from *off* the land, (marg. from *the face of* the land)
3. cut off man from *off* the land, (lit. *id.*)
7. *at the presence of* the Lord God:
Hag. 1:12. the people did fear *before* the Lord.
2:14. so (is) this nation *before me,* saith the
Zec. 2:13(17). Be silent, O all flesh, *before* the Lord:
3: 1. *before* the angel of the Lord,
3. and stood *before* the angel.
4. those that stood *before him,*

Zec. 3: 8. thy fellows that sit *before thee:*
9. the stone that I have laid *before* Joshua;
4: 7. *before* Zerubbabel (thou shalt become) a
5: 3. over *the face of* the whole earth:
7: 2. to pray *before* (marg. intreat *the face of*) the Lord,
8: 10. *before* these days there was no hire
21, 22. to pray *before* (marg. intreat *the face of*) the Lord,
12: 8. the angel of the Lord *before them.*
14: 4. the mount of Olives, which (is) *before*
5. like as ye fled from *before* the earthquake
20. like the bowls *before* the altar.
Mal. 1: 8. be pleased with thee, or accept *thy person?*
9. beseech God (marg. *the face of* God)
— will he regard *your persons?*
2: 3. and spread dung upon *your faces,*
5. *and* was afraid *before* my name.
9. have been partial in (marg. accepted *faces,* or, lifted up *the face* against) the law.
3: 1. he shall prepare the way *before me:*
14. *before* the Lord of hosts?
16. a book of remembrance was written *before him*
4: 5(3:23). *before* the coming of the great and

6441 **פְּנִים** *p'neem,* adv.

Lev. 10: 18. *within* the holy (place):
1K. 6: 18. the cedar of the house *within*
19. prepared in the house *within,*
21. Solomon overlaid the house *within*
29. open flowers, *within* and without.
30. the floor of the house...*within*
2K. 7: 11. the king's house *within.*
2Ch 3: 4. he overlaid it *within* with pure gold.
29: 16. the priests went *into the inner part*
18. Then they went *in* to Hezekiah
Ps. 45: 13(14). The king's daughter (is) all glorious *within:*
Eze. 40: 16. *within* the gate round about,
— windows (were) round about *inward:* (marg. or, *within*)
41: 3. Then went he *inward,*

6442 **פְּנִימִי** *p'nee-mee',* adj.

1K. 6: 27. the cherubims within the *inner* house:
36. he built the *inner* court
7: 12. the *inner* court of the house
50. the doors of the *inner* house,
1Ch 28: 11. the *inner* parlours thereof,
2Ch 4: 22. the *inner* doors thereof
Est. 4: 11. into the *inner* court,
5: 1. in the *inner* court
Eze. 8: 3. the door of the *inner* gate that looketh
16. he brought me into the *inner* court
10: 3. the cloud filled the *inner* court.
40: 15. the porch of the *inner* gate
19. the forefront of the *inner* court
23. the gate of the *inner* court
27. a gate in the *inner* court
28. And he brought me to the *inner* court
32. And he brought me into the *inner* court
44. without the *inner* gate
— of the singers in the *inner* court,
41: 15. with the *inner* temple,
17. unto the *inner* house,
— the wall round about *within*
42: 3. for the *inner* court,
4. a walk of ten cubits breadth *inward,*
15. made an end of measuring the *inner*
43: 5. brought me into the *inner* court;
44: 17. at the gates of the *inner* court,
— in the gates of the *inner* court,
21. when they enter into the *inner* court.
27. goeth...unto the *inner* court,
45: 19. posts of the gate of the *inner* court.
46: 1. The gate of the *inner* court that

6443 **פְּנִינִים** *p'nee-neem',* m. pl.

Job 28: 18. the price of wisdom (is) *above rubies.*
Pro. 3: 15. She (is) more precious *than rubies:*
8: 11. wisdom (is) better *than rubies;*
20: 15. a multitude of *rubies:*
Pro. 31: 10. her price (is) far *above rubies.*
Lam. 4: 7. more ruddy in body *than rubies,*

פָּנַק [*pāh-nak'*]. 6445

* PIEL.—*Participle.* *

Pro. 29: 21. *He that delicately bringeth up* his servant

פַּס *pas,* Ch. m. 6447

Dan 5: 5. the king saw *the part of* the hand
24. Then was *the part* of the hand

פָּסַג [*pāh-sag'*]. 6448

* PIEL.—*Imperative.* *

Ps. 48: 13(14). *consider* (marg. or, *raise up*) her

פִּסָּה [*pis-sāh'*], f. 6451

Ps. 72: 16. There shall be *an handful of* corn

פָּסַח *pāh-sagh'.* 6452

* KAL.—*Preterite.* *

Ex. 12: 13. *and* when I see the blood, *I will pass over*
23. *and* when he seeth...the Lord *will pass over*
27. who *passed over* the houses of the

KAL.—*Infinitive.*

Isa. 31: 5. *passing over* he will preserve (it).

KAL.—*Participle.* Poel.

1K. 18: 21. How long *halt* ye between two opinions?

* NIPHAL.—*Future.* *

2Sa. 4: 4. he fell, *and became lame.*

* PIEL.—*Future.* *

1K. 18: 26. *And they leaped* upon the altar

פֶּסַח *peh'-sagh,* m. 6453

Ex. 12: 11. it (is) the Lord's *passover.*
21. and kill *the passover.*
27. the sacrifice of the Lord's *passover,*
43. the ordinance of *the passover:*
48. *the passover* to the Lord,
34: 25. the feast of *the passover*
Lev. 23: 5. at even (is) the Lord's *passover.*
Nu. 9: 2. keep *the passover* at his appointed season.
4. they should keep *the passover.*
5. they kept *the passover*
6. they could not keep *the passover*
10. he shall keep *the passover*
12. the ordinances of *the passover*
13. forbeareth to keep *the passover,*
14. will keep *the passover*
— the ordinance of *the passover,*
28: 16. *the passover* of the Lord.
33: 3. on the morrow after *the passover*
Deu 16: 1. keep *the passover* unto the Lord
2. therefore sacrifice *the passover*
5. Thou mayest not sacrifice *the passover*
6. thou shalt sacrifice *the passover*
Jos. 5: 10. kept *the passover* on the fourteenth day
11. on the morrow after *the passover,*
2K. 23: 21. Keep *the passover* unto the Lord
22. there was not holden *such a passover*
23. *this passover* was holden
2Ch 30: 1, 5. to keep *the passover* unto the Lord
2. to keep *the passover* in the second month.
15. they killed *the passover*
17. the killing of *the passovers*
18. yet did they eat *the passover*
35: 1. Josiah kept *a passover*
— they killed *the passover* on the
6. So kill *the passover,* and sanctify
7. all *for the passover offerings,*
8. the priests *for the passover offerings*
9. the Levites *for passover offerings*
11. And they killed *the passover,*
13. they roasted *the passover*
16. to keep *the passover,*

2Ch 35:17. the children of Israel...kept *the passover*
18. there was no *passover* like to that
— *such a passover* as Josiah kept,
19. In the eighteenth year...was this *passover*
Ezr. 6:19. children of the captivity kept *the passover*
20. and killed *the passover*
Eze.45:21. ye shall have *the passover*,

6455 פִּסֵּחַ *pis-sēh'ăgh*, adj.

Lev.21:18. a blind man, or *a lame*,
Deu 15:21. (if it be) *lame*, or blind,
2Sa. 5: 6. thou take away the blind *and the lame*,
8. smiteth the Jebusites, and *the lame*
— The blind and *the lame* shall not come
9:13. and was *lame* on both his feet.
19:26(27). because thy servant (is) *lame*.
Job 29:15. and feet (was) I *to the lame*.
Pro.26: 7. The legs *of the lame* are not equal:
Isa. 33:23. *the lame* take the prey.
35: 6. Then shall *the lame* (man) leap
Jer. 31: 8. with them the blind *and the lame*,
Mal. 1: 8. if ye offer *the lame* and sick,
13. and *the lame*, and the sick;

6456 פְּסִילִים *p'see-leem'*, m. pl.

Deu 7: 5. *and* burn *their graven images*
25. *The graven images of* their gods
12: 3. *and* ye shall hew down *the graven images of*
Jud. 3:19. turned again from *the quarries* (marg. or, *graven images*)
26. and passed beyond *the quarries*,
2K. 17:41. and served *their graven images*,
2Ch 33:19. set up groves *and graven images*,
22. sacrificed unto all *the carved images*
34: 3, 4. the groves, *and the carved images*,
7. *and* had beaten *the graven images* into
Ps. 78:58. *and* moved him to jealousy *with their graven images*.
Isa. 10:10. *and whose graven images* did excel
21: 9. all *the graven images of* her gods
30:22. the covering of thy *graven images of*
42: 8. neither my praise *to graven images*.
Jer. 8:19. provoked me to anger *with their graven images*,
50:38. the land of *graven images*,
51:47. *the graven images of* Babylon:
52. do judgment upon *her graven images*.
Hos.11: 2. *and* burned incense *to graven images*.
Mic. 1: 7. all *the graven images thereof*
5:13(12). *Thy graven images* also will I cut off,

6446 פַּסִּים *pas-seem'*, m. pl.

Gen37: 3. he made him a coat of (many) *colours*. (marg. or, *pieces*)
23. (his) coat of (many) *colours* (marg. *id.*)
32. they sent the coat of (many) *colours*,
2Sa.13:18. (she had) a garment of *divers colours*
19. rent her garment of *divers colours*

6458 פָּסַל [*pāh-sal'*].

* KAL.—*Preterite.* *

Hab 2:18. the maker thereof *hath graven it*;

KAL.—*Imperative.*

Ex. 34: 1. *Hew* thee two tables of stone
Deu10: 1. *Hew* thee two tables of stone

KAL.—*Future.*

Ex. 34: 4. *And he hewed* two tables of stone
Deu10: 3. *and hewed* two tables of stone
1K. 5:18(32). *And* Solomon's builders and Hiram's builders *did hew* (them),

6459 פֶּסֶל *peh'-sel*, m.

Ex. 20: 4. shalt not make unto thee any *graven image*,
Lev.26: 1. make you no idols *nor graven image*,
Deu 4:16, 23. and make you *a graven image*,
25. and make *a graven image*,
Deu 5: 8. shalt not make thee (any) *graven image*
27:15. that maketh (any) *graven* or molten
Jud.17: 3. to make *a graven image*
4. who made thereof *a graven image*
18:14. and teraphim, *and a graven image*,
17. (and) took *the graven image*,
18. and fetched *the carved image*,
20. the teraphim, and *the graven image*,
30. children of Dan set up *the graven image*
31. they set them up Micah's *graven image*,
2K. 21: 7. he set *a graven image of*
2Ch 33: 7. he set *a carved image*,
Ps. 97: 7. they that serve *graven images*,
Isa. 40:19. The workman melteth *a graven image*,
20. to prepare *a graven image*,
42:17. that trust *in graven images*,
44: 9. They that make *a graven image*
10. *or* molten *a graven image*
15. he maketh it *a graven image*,
17. (even) *his graven image*:
45:20. the wood of *their graven image*,
48: 5. done them, *and my graven image*,
Jer. 10:14 & 51:17. confounded *by the graven image*:
Nah 1:14. will I cut off *the graven image*
Hab 2:18. What profiteth *the graven image*

פְּסַנְטֵרִין *p'san-tēh-reen'*, Ch. m. pl. 6460

Dan 3: 7. *psaltery*, and all kinds of musick,

פְּסַנְתֵּרִין *p'san-tēh-reen'*, Ch. m. pl. 6460

Dan 3: 5. *psaltery*, dulcimer, and all kinds of
10, 15. sackbut, *psaltery*, and dulcimer,

פָּסַס [*pāh-sas'*]. 6461

* KAL.—*Preterite.* *

Ps. 12: 1(2). the faithful *fail* from among

פָּעָה [*pāh-gāh'*]. 6463

* KAL.—*Future.* *

Isa. 42:14. (now) *will I cry* like a travailing woman

פָּעַל *pāh-gal'*. 6466

* KAL.—*Preterite.* *

Ex. 15:17. the place, O Lord, (which) *thou hast made*
Nu. 23:23. What *hath* God *wrought!*
Deu32:27. the Lord *hath* not *done* all this.
Job 34:32. if *I have done* iniquity,
36:23. *Thou hast wrought* iniquity?
Ps. 11: 3. what *can* the righteous *do?*
31:19(20). *thou hast wrought* for them
44: 1(2). (what) work *thou didst*
68:28(29). *thou hast wrought* for us.
119: 3. *They* also *do* no iniquity:
Pro.16: 4. The Lord *hath made* all (things)
30:20. *I have done* no wickedness.
Isa. 26:12. *thou* also *hast wrought* all our works
41: 4. Who *hath wrought* and done (it),
44:12. The smith with the tongs *both worketh*
Hos. 7: 1. *they commit* falsehood;
Zep. 2: 3. which *have wrought* his judgment;

KAL.—*Future.*

Job 7:20. what *shall I do* unto thee,
11: 8. what *canst thou do?*
22:17. what *can* the Almighty *do*
33:29. all these (things) *worketh* God
35: 6. sinnest, what *doest thou* against him?
Ps. 7:13(14). *he ordaineth* his arrows
15(16). into the ditch (which) *he made*.
58: 2(3). *ye work* wickedness;
Isa. 43:13. *I will work*, and who shall let it?
44:12. *and worketh it* with the strength of his
15. yea, *he maketh* a god,

KAL.—*Participle.* Poel.

Job 31: 3. (punishment) *to the workers of* iniquity?
34: 8. in company with *the workers of* iniquity,
22. where *the workers of* iniquity may hide

Job 36: 3. *and* will ascribe righteousness *to my Maker.*
Ps. 5: 5(6). thou hatest all *workers of* iniquity.
6: 8(9), all ye *workers of* iniquity;
14: 4. all *the workers of* iniquity
15: 2. *and worketh* righteousness,
28: 3. with *the workers of* iniquity,
36:12(13). There are *the workers of* iniquity
53: 4(5). Have *the workers of* iniquity no
59: 2(3). Deliver me *from the workers of* iniquity,
64: 2(3). from the insurrection of *the workers of*
74:12. *working* salvation in the midst
92: 7(8). when all *the workers of* iniquity do
9(10). all *the workers of* iniquity shall be
94: 4. all *the workers of* iniquity boast
16. against *the workers of* iniquity?
101: 8. that I may cut off all wicked *doers* from
125: 5. lead them forth with *the workers of*
141: 4. men *that work* iniquity:
9. the gins of *the workers of* iniquity.
Pro. 10:29 & 21:15. destruction (shall be) *to the workers of* iniquity.
Isa. 31: 2. arise against the house of *the evildoers,*
Hos. 6: 8. a city of *them that work* iniquity,
Mic. 2: 1. *and work* evil upon their beds!
Hab. 1: 5. (I) *will work* a work in your days,

6467 פֹּעַל *pōh'-^{n}gal*, m.

Deu 32: 4. *his work* (is) perfect:
33:11. *and* accept *the work of* his hands:
Ru. 2:12. The Lord recompense *thy work,*
2Sa. 23:20. who had done many *acts,*
1Ch 11:22. who had done many *acts;*
Job 7: 2. an hireling looketh for (the reward of) *his work:*
24: 5. go they forth *to their work;*
34:11. *the work of* a man shall he render
36: 9. Then he sheweth them *their work,*
24. Remember that thou magnify *his work,*
37:12. *that they may do* whatsoever he
Ps. 9:16(17). the wicked is snared *in the work of*
28: 4. Give them *according to their deeds,*
44: 1(2). (what) *work* thou didst in their days,
64: 9(10). and shall declare *the work of* God;
77:12(13). I will meditate also of all *thy work,*
90:16. Let *thy work* appear unto thy servants,
92: 4(5). made me glad *through thy work:*
95: 9. proved me, and saw *my work.*
104:23. Man goeth forth *unto his work*
111: 3. *His work* (is) honourable and glorious:
143: 5. I meditate on all *thy works;*
Pro. 20:11. whether *his work* (be) pure,
21: 6. *The getting of* treasures by a lying tongue
8. (as for) the pure, *his work* (is) right.
24:12. (every) man *according to his works?*
29. the man *according to his work.*
Isa. 1:31. *and the maker of it* as a spark,
5:12. they regard not *the work of* the Lord,
41:24. *and your work* of nought:
45: 9. What makest thou? *or thy work,*
11. concerning *the work of* my hands
59: 6. *and the act of* violence (is) in their hands.
Jer. 22:13. *and* giveth him not *for his work;*
25:14. recompense them *according to their deeds,*
50:29. recompense her *according to her work;*
Hab. 1: 5. (I) will work *a work* in your days,
3: 2. O Lord, revive *thy work*

6468 פְּעֻלָּה [*p'^{n}gool-lāh'*], f.

Lev. 19:13. *the wages of* him that is hired
2Ch 15: 7. for *your work* shall be rewarded.
Ps. 17: 4. *Concerning the works of* men,
28: 5. they regard not *the works of* the Lord,
109:20. *the reward of* mine adversaries
Pro. 10:16. *The labour of* the righteous
11:18. The wicked worketh *a* deceitful *work:*
Isa. 40:10. *and his work* (marg. or, *recompence for his work*) before him.
49: 4. *and my work* (marg. or, *reward*) with my
61: 8. I will direct *their work* in truth,
62:11. *and his work* (marg. or, *recompence*) before
Isa. 65: 7. therefore will I measure *their* former *work*
Jer. 31:16. *thy work* shall be rewarded,
Eze. 29:20. *his labour* (marg. or, *hire*) wherewith he

פָּעַם [*pāh-^{n}gam'*]. 6470

* KAL.—*Infinitive.* *

Jud. 13:25. the Spirit of the Lord began *to move him*

* NIPHAL.—*Preterite.* *

Ps. 77: 4(5). *I am* so *troubled* that I cannot speak.

NIPHAL.—*Future.*

Gen 41: 8. *that* his spirit *was troubled;*
Dan 2: 3. *and* my spirit *was troubled* to know

* HITHPAEL.—*Future.* *

Dan 2: 1. *wherewith* his spirit *was troubled,*

פַּעַם *pah'-^{n}gam*, com. 6471

Gen 2:23. This (is) *now* bone of my bones,
18:32. I will speak yet but *this once:*
27:36. supplanted me these *two times:*
29:34. Now *this time* will my husband be joined
35. *Now* will I praise the Lord:
30:20. *now* will my husband dwell with me,
33: 3. bowed himself to the ground seven *times,*
41:32. dream was doubled unto Pharaoh *twice;*
43:10. we had returned this *second time.* (marg. or, *twice* by this)
46:30. *Now* let me die,
Ex. 8:32(28). hardened his heart *at* this *time*
9:14. I will *at* this *time* send all my plagues
27. I have sinned *this time:*
10:17. forgive,...my sin only *this once,*
23:17. Three *times* in the year
25:12. in *the* four *corners thereof;*
34:23. Thrice (lit. three *times*) in the year shall
24. go up to appear before the Lord thy God thrice (lit. *id.*)
37: 3. *the* four *corners of it;*
Lev. 4: 6. sprinkle of the blood seven *times*
17. sprinkle (it) seven *times* before the Lord,
8:11. he sprinkled thereof...seven *times,*
14: 7. cleansed from the leprosy seven *times,*
16. sprinkle of the oil...seven *times*
27. seven *times* before the Lord:
51. sprinkle the house seven *times:*
16:14. sprinkle of the blood...seven *times.*
19. sprinkle of the blood...seven *times,*
25: 8. seven *times* seven years;
Nu. 14:22. tempted me now these ten *times,*
19: 4. sprinkle of her blood...seven *times:*
20:11. he smote the rock *twice:*
24: 1. *as at other times,* (lit. *as a time, in a time*).
10. blessed (them) these three *times.*
Deu 1:11. a thousand *times* so many more
9:19 & 10:10. the Lord hearkened unto me *at* that *time*
16:16. Three *times* in a year
Jos. 6: 3. round about the city once. (lit. one *time*)
4. compass the city seven *times,*
11. going about (it) once: (lit. one *time*)
14. they compassed the city once, (lit. *id.*)
15. after the same manner seven *times:*
— compassed the city seven *times.*
16. *at the* seventh *time,*
10:42. did Joshua take at one *time,*
Jud. 5:28. why tarry *the wheels of* his chariots?
6:39. I will speak but *this once:* let me prove,... but *this once*
15: 3. *Now* shall I be more blameless
16:15. hast mocked me these three *times,*
18. Come up *this once,*
20. I will go out *as at other times before,* (lit. *as a time in a time*)
28. strengthen me,...only this *once,* O God,
20:30. against Gibeah, *as at other times.* (lit. *as a time in a time*)
31. kill, *as at other times,* (lit. *id.*)
1Sa. 3:10. and called *as at other times,* (lit. *id.*)
18:11. David avoided out of his presence *twice.*
20:25. the king sat upon his seat, *as at other times,* (lit. *as a time in a time*)
41. bowed himself three *times* ·

1 Sa.26: 8. let me smite him,...at once, (lit. one *time*)
2Sa.17: 7. The counsel...(is) not good *at* this *time*.
23: 8. eight hundred, whom he slew *at* one *time*.
24: 3. the Lord thy God add unto the people,... an hundred*fold*,
1K. 7: 4,5. (was) against light (in) three *ranks*.
30. *the* four *corners thereof*
9:25. three *times* in a year
11: 9. had appeared unto him *twice*,
17:21. himself upon the child three *times*,
18:43. Go again seven *times*.
22:16. How many *times* shall I adjure thee
2K. 4:35. the child sneezed seven *times*,
5:10. Go and wash in Jordan seven *times*,
14. dipped himself seven *times*
13:18. And he smote thrice, (lit. three *times*) and stayed.
19. shouldest have smitten five or six *times;*
— now thou shalt smite Syria (but) thrice. (lit. three *times*)
25. Three *times* did Joash beat him,
19:24. with the sole of *my feet* have I dried up
1Ch 11:11. three hundred slain (by him) *at* one *time*.
21: 3. Lord make his people an hundred *times*
2Ch 8:13. three *times* in the year,
18:15. How many *times* shall I adjure thee
Neh 4:12(6). they said unto us ten *times*,
6: 4. they sent unto me four *times*
5. Then sent Sanballat...*the* fifth *time*
13:20. lodged without Jerusalem *once* or twice.
Job 19: 3. These ten *times* have ye reproached me:
33:29. worketh God often*times* (marg. *twice* (and) thrice) with man,
Ps. 17: 5. (that) *my footsteps* slip not.
57: 6(7). prepared a net *for my steps;*
58:10(11). he shall wash *his feet* in the blood of
74: 3. Lift up *thy feet* unto
85:13(14). shall set (us) in the way of *his steps*.
106:43. Many *times* did he deliver them;
119:133. Order *my steps* in thy word:
140: 4(5). have purposed to overthrow *my goings*.
Pro. 7:12. *Now* (is she) without, *now* in the streets,
29: 5. spreadeth a net for *his feet*.
Ecc. 6: 6. he live a thousand years *twice* (told),
7:22. often*times* also thine own heart knoweth
Cant.7: 1(2). How beautiful are *thy feet*
Isa. 26: 6. *the steps of* the needy.
37:25. with the sole of *my feet* have I dried up
41: 7. him that smote *the anvil*,
66: 8. shall a nation be born at once? (lit. at one *time*)
Jer. 10:18. sling out the inhabitants...*at* this *once*,
16:21. I will this *once* cause them to know,
Eze.41: 6. and thirty *in order;* (marg. or, *times*, or, *foot*)
Nah 1: 9. affliction shall not rise up *the second time*.

6472 **פַּעֲמוֹן** *pah-^{n}gămōhn'*, m.

Ex. 28:33. *and bells of* gold between them
34. *A* golden *bell* and a pomegranate, *a* golden *bell* and a pomegranate,
39:25. they made *bells of* pure gold, and put *the bells* between the pomegranates
26. *A bell* and a pomegranate, *a bell* and a pomegranate,

6473 **פָּעַר** [*pāh-^{n}gar'*].

* KAL.—*Preterite.* *

Job 16:10. *They have gaped* upon me
29:23. *they opened* their mouth *wide*
Ps.119:131. *I opened* my mouth, and panted:
Isa. 5:14. hell hath enlarged herself, *and opened* her mouth without measure:

6475 **פָּצָה** [*pāh-tzāh'*].

* KAL.—*Preterite.* *

Gen 4:11. the earth, which *hath opened* her mouth
Nu. 16:30. and the earth *open* her mouth,
Deu11: 6. how the earth *opened* her mouth,
Jud.11:35. I *have opened* my mouth unto the Lord,
Jud.11:36. (if) *thou hast opened* thy mouth unto the
Ps. 22:13(14). *They gaped* upon me
66:14. Which my lips *have uttered*, (marg. *opened*)
Lam.2:16. thine enemies *have opened* their mouth
3:46. our enemies *have opened* their mouths

KAL.—*Imperative.*

Ps.144: 7. *rid me*, and deliver me out of
11. *Rid me*, and deliver me from
Eze. 2: 8. *open* thy mouth, and eat that I give thee.

KAL.—*Future.*

Job 35:16. *doth* Job *open* his mouth in vain;

KAL.—*Participle.* Poel.

Ps.144:10. *who delivereth* David
Isa. 10:14. moved the wing, *or opened* the mouth,

פָּצַח [*pāh-tzagh'*]. 6476

* KAL.—*Preterite.* *

Isa. 14: 7. *they break forth* into singing.

KAL.—*Imperative.*

Ps. 98: 4. *make a loud noise*, and rejoice,
Isa. 44:23. *break forth* into singing ye mountains,
49:13. *and break forth* into singing, O mountains:
52: 9. *Break forth into joy*, sing together,
54: 1. *break forth* into singing, and cry aloud,

KAL.—*Future.*

Isa. 55:12. mountains and the hills *shall break forth*

* PIEL.—*Preterite.* *

Mic. 3: 3. *they break* their bones,

פְּצִירָה *p'tzee-rāh'*, f. 6477

1Sa.13:21. they had *a file* (marg. *a file* with mouths) for the mattocks,

---

פָּצַל [*pāh-tzal'*]. 6478

* PIEL.—*Preterite.* *

Gen30:38. the rods which *he had pilled*

PIEL.—*Future.*

Gen30:37. *and pilled* white strakes in them,

פְּצָלוֹת *p'tzāh-lōhth'*, f. pl. 6479

Gen30:37. and pilled white *strakes* in them,

פָּצַם [*pāh-tzam'*]. 6480

* KAL.—*Preterite.* *

Ps. 60: 2(4). earth to tremble; *thou hast broken* it:

פָּצַע [*pāh-tza^{n}g'*]. 6481

* KAL.—*Preterite.* *

Cant.5: 7. they smote me, *they wounded me;*

KAL.—*Infinitive.*

1K. 20:37. so that in smiting *he wounded* (marg. smiting *and wounding*)

KAL.—*Participle.* Paül.

Deu 23: 1(2). *He that is wounded in* the stones,

פֶּצַע *peh'-tza^{n}g*, com. 6482

Gen 4:23. I have slain a man *to my wounding*,
Ex. 21:25. *wound* for *wound*, stripe for stripe.
Job 9:17. and multiplieth *my wounds*
Pro.20:30. The blueness of *a wound*
23:29. who hath *wounds* without cause?
27: 6. Faithful (are) *the wounds of* a friend;
Isa. 1: 6. *wounds*, and bruises, and putrifying sores:

פָּצַר [*pāh-tzar'*]. 6484

* KAL.—*Future.* *

Gen19: 3. *And he pressed* upon them greatly;
9. *And they pressed* sore upon the man,

Gen33:11. *And he urged* him, and he took (it).
Jud.19: 7. *And* when the man...his father in law *urged* him:
2K. 2:17. And *when they urged* him
5:16. *And he urged* him to take (it);

* HIPHIL.—*Infinitive.* *

1Sa.15:23. *stubbornness* (is as) iniquity and idolatry.

6485 פָּקַד *pāh-kad'.*

* KAL.—*Preterite.* *

Gen21: 1. the Lord *visited* Sarah
Ex. 3:16. *I have* surely *visited* you,
4:31. heard that the Lord *had visited*
32:34. *I will visit* their sin upon them.
Nu. 1:44 & 3:39. which Moses and Aaron *numbered,*
4:27. *and ye shall appoint* unto them
37. which Moses and Aaron *did number*
41. whom Moses and Aaron *did number*
45. whom Moses and Aaron *numbered*
46. the chief of Israel *numbered,*
49. of the Lord *they were numbered*
26:63. who *numbered* the children of Israel
64. when *they numbered* the children
Deu20: 9. *that they shall make* captains
Ru. 1: 6. the Lord *had visited* his people
1Sa. 2:21. the Lord *visited* Hannah,
15: 2. *I remember* (that) which Amalek did
25:15. neither *missed we* any thing,
1K. 20:15. after them *he numbered* all the people,
1Ch21: 6. Levi and Benjamin *counted he* not
2Ch36:23. he *hath charged* me to build
Ezr. 1: 2. he *hath charged* me to build
Job 5:24. *and thou shalt visit* thy habitation,
34:13. Who *hath given him a charge*
35:15. *he hath visited* in his anger;
36:23. Who *hath enjoined* him his way?
Ps. 17: 3. *thou hast visited* (me) in the night;
65: 9(10). *Thou visitest* the earth, and waterest
89:32(33). *Then will I visit* their transgression
Isa. 13:11. *And I will punish* the world
26:14. *hast thou visited* and destroyed them,
16. in trouble *have they visited thee,*
34:16. none *shall want* her mate:
Jer. 6:15. at the time (that) *I visit them*
9:25(24). the days come,...*that I will punish* (marg. *visit* upon)
15: 3. *And I will appoint* over them
21:14. *But I will punish* (marg. *visit* upon) you
23: 2. Ye have scattered...*and have* not *visited*
34. *I will even punish* (marg. *visit* upon) that
30:20. *and I will punish* (lit. *id.*) all that oppress
36:31. *And I will punish* (marg. *id.*) him and his
44:13. *For I will punish* (lit. *id.*) them that
— as *I have punished* (lit. *id.*) Jerusalem,
49: 8. the time (that) *I will visit him.*
50:18. *I have punished* the king of Assyria.
31. thy day is come, the time (that) *I will visit thee.*
51:44. *And I will punish* (lit. *visit* upon) Bel
47. the days come, *that I will do judgment* (marg. *visit*) upon
52. the days come,...*that I will do judgment* (lit. *id.*)
Lam 4:22. *he will visit* thine iniquity,
Hos. 1: 4. *and I will avenge* the blood of Jezreel
2:13(15). *And I will visit* upon her
4: 9. *and I will punish* (marg. *visit* upon) them
Am. 3:14. *I will also visit* the altars of Beth-el:
Zep. 1: 8. *that I will punish* (marg. *visit* upon) the
9. In the same day *also will I punish* (lit. *id.*)
12. *and punish* (lit. *id.*) the men that are
3: 7. howsoever *I punished* (lit. *id.*) them:
Zec.10: 3. the Lord of hosts *hath visited*

KAL.—*Infinitive.*

Gen50:24. God will *surely* visit (lit. *visiting* will visit)
25. God will *surely* visit (lit. *id.*) you,
Ex. 3:16. I have *surely* visited you,
13:19. God will *surely* visit you;
30:12,12. *when* (thou) *numberest* them;
32:34. in the day *when I visit*
1Sa.20: 6. If thy father *at all* miss me, (lit. *missing* shall miss me)
2Sa.24: 4. *to number* the people of Israel.
Ps. 59: 5(6). awake *to visit* all the heathen:
Isa. 26:21. the Lord cometh...*to punish*
Jer. 27:22. the day *that I visit* them,
32: 5. there shall he be until *I visit* him,
Hos 12: 2(3). *and will punish* (marg. *visit* upon) Jacob according to
Am. 3:14. in the day *that I shall visit*

KAL.—*Imperative.*

Nu. 3:15. *Number* the children of Levi
40. *Number* all the firstborn
1Sa.14:17. *Number* now, and see who is gone
2Sa.24: 2. *and number ye* the people,
2K. 9:34. *Go, see* now this cursed (woman),
Ps. 80:14(15). behold, *and visit* this vine;
106: 4. *O visit me* with thy salvation;
Jer. 15:15. remember me, *and visit me,*
51:27. *appoint* a captain against her;

KAL.—*Future.*

Gen40: 4. *And* the captain of the guard *charged*
50:24. God *will* surely *visit* you,
25. God *will* surely *visit* you,
Ex. 13:19. God *will* surely *visit* you;
Lev.18:25. *therefore I do visit* the iniquity
Nu. 1: 3. thou and Aaron *shall number*
19. *so he numbered them* in the wilderness
49. *thou shalt* not *number* the tribe of Levi,
3:10. And *thou shalt appoint* Aaron
15. from a month old and upward *shalt thou number them.*
16. *And* Moses *numbered* them
42. *And* Moses *numbered,*
4:23. until fifty years old *shalt thou number* them;
29. *thou shalt number* them after their
30. unto fifty years old *shalt thou number them,*
32. *ye shall reckon* the instruments
34. *And* Moses and Aaron...*numbered*
27:16. *Let* the Lord,...*set* a man over
Jos. 8:10. *and numbered* the people, and went up,
Jud.15: 1. *that* Samson *visited* his wife
1Sa.11: 8. And *when he numbered them*
13:15. *And* Saul *numbered* the people
14:17. And *when they had numbered,*
15: 4. gathered the people together, *and numbered them*
17:18. *look* how thy brethren fare,
20: 6. If thy father at all *miss me,*
2Sa. 3: 8. *that thou chargest* me to day
18: 1. *And* David *numbered* the people
1K. 20:15. *Then he numbered* the young men
26. *that* Ben-hadad *numbered* the Syrians,
2K. 3: 6. went out of Samaria...*and numbered* all
5:24. *and bestowed* (them) in the house:
2Ch 25: 5. *and he numbered them* from twenty
Job 7:18. *And* (that) *thou shouldest visit him*
31:14. when *he visiteth,* what shall I answer
Ps. 8: 4(5). son of man, that *thou visitest him?*
Isa. 10:12. *I will punish* (marg. *visit* upon) the fruit
23:17. the Lord *will visit* Tyre,
24:21. the Lord *shall punish* (marg. *visit* upon)
27: 1. the Lord...*shall punish* (lit. *id.*) leviathan
3. lest (any) *hurt* (lit. *id.*) it, I will keep it
Jer. 3:16. neither *shall they visit* (it);
5: 9, 29. *Shall I* not *visit* for these (things)?
9: 9(8). *Shall I* not *visit* them for these
13:21. when *he shall punish* (marg. *visit* upon)
14:10. *and visit* their sins.
25:12. *I will punish* (marg. *visit* upon) the king
27: 8. that nation *will I punish,* (lit. *id.*)
29:10. *I will visit* you, and perform
49:19 & 50:44. (that) *I may appoint* over her?
Eze.23:21. *Thus thou calledst to remembrance*
Hos. 4:14. *I will* not (marg. *Shall I* not) *punish* (lit. *visit* upon) your daughters
8:13. *and visit* their sins:
9: 9. *he will visit* their sins.
Am. 3: 2. *I will punish* (marg. *visit* upon) you for
Zep. 2: 7. the Lord their God *shall visit them,*
Zec.10: 3. *I punished* (marg. *visited* upon) the goats:
11:16. *shall* not *visit* those that be cut off,

KAL.—*Participle.* Poel.

Ex. 20: 5 & 34:7. *visiting* the iniquity of the fathers
Nu. 14:18. *visiting* the iniquity of the fathers
Deu 5: 9. *visiting* the iniquity of the fathers
Jer. 11:22. I *will punish* (marg. *visit* upon) them:
23: 2. I *will visit* upon you

Jer. 29:32. I *will punish* Shemaiah
44:29. I *will punish* you in this place,
46:25. I *will punish* the multitude of No,
50:18. I *will punish* the king of Babylon

KAL.—*Participle.* Paŭl.

Ex. 30:12. of the children of Israel *after their number,*
13, 14. among *them that are numbered,*
38:21. *the sum of* the tabernacle,
25. the silver of *them that were numbered of*
26. every one that went to *be numbered,*
Nu. 1:21, 23, 25, 27, 29, 31, 33, 35, 37, 39, 41, 43. *Those that were numbered of them,* (even)
22. *those that were numbered of them,*
44. These (are) *those that were numbered,*
45. were all *those that were numbered of*
46. all *they that were numbered*
2: 4, 13, 15, 19, 21, 23, 26, 28, 30. *and those that were numbered of them,*
6, 8, 11. *and those that were numbered thereof,*
9, 16, 24. All *that were numbered*
31. All *they that were numbered*
32. *those which were numbered of*
— *those that were numbered of*
3:22, 22. *Those that were numbered of them,*
34. *And those that were numbered of them,*
39. All *that were numbered of*
43. *of those that were numbered of them,*
4:36, 40, 44, 48. *those that were numbered of them*
37, 41. *they that were numbered of* the families
38. *And those that were numbered of* the sons
42. *And those that were numbered of* the
45. *those that were numbered of*
46. *those that were numbered*
49. *thus were they numbered of him,* (lit. and *the numbered of him*)
7: 2. over *them that were numbered,*
14:29. all *that were numbered of you,*
26: 7. *they that were numbered of them*
18, 22, 25, 27, 37, 43, 47. *according to those that were numbered of them,*
34. *and those that were numbered of them,*
41, 50. *and they that were numbered of them*
51. *the numbered of* the children of Israel,
54. *those that were numbered of him.*
57. *they that were numbered of*
62. *those that were numbered of them*
63. *they that were numbered by*
64. *of them whom* Moses and Aaron...*numbered,*
31:14. Moses was wroth with *the officers of*
48. And *the officers* which (were) over
2K. 11:15. *the officers of* the host, and said unto
18. the priest appointed *officers* (marg. *offices*)
12:11(12). (כתיב) *that had the oversight* of the
1Ch 23:24. *as they were counted* by number
2Ch 23:14. captains of hundreds *that were set over*

* NIPHAL.—*Preterite.* *

Nu. 31:49. *there lacketh* not one man of us.
1Sa. 20:18. *and thou shalt be missed,*
25: 7. neither *was there* ought *missing*
21. nothing *was missed* of all that (pertained)

NIPHAL.—*Infinitive.*

Jud. 21: 3. *that there should be*...one tribe *lacking*
1K. 20:39. if *by any means* he be missing, (lit. if *missing* he be missed)

NIPHAL.—*Future.*

Nu. 16:29. if *they be visited* after the visitation of
1Sa. 20:18. thy seat *will be empty.* (marg. *missed*)
25. *and* David's place *was empty.*
27. *that* David's place *was empty:*
2Sa. 2:30. *there lacked* of David's servants
1K. 20:39. if by any means *he be missing,*
2K. 10:19. *let* none *be wanting:*
— whosoever *shall be wanting,*
Neh 7: 1. *and* the Levites *were appointed,*
12:44. *And* at that time *were* some *appointed*
Pro. 19:23. *he shall* not *be visited* with evil.
Isa. 24:22. after many days *shall they be visited.* (marg. or, *found wanting*)
29: 6. *Thou shalt be visited* of the Lord
Jer. 23: 4. neither *shall they be lacking,*
Eze. 38: 8. After many days *thou shalt be visited.*

* PIEL.—*Participle.* *

Isa. 13: 4. the Lord of hosts *mustereth* the host

* PUAL.—*Preterite.* *

Ex. 38:21. as *it was counted,* according to the
Isa. 38:10. *I am deprived* of the residue of my years.

* HIPHIL.—*Preterite.* *

Gen 39: 5. *he had made* him *overseer*
Lev. 26:16. *I will even appoint* over you terror,
1Sa. 29: 4. his place which *thou hast appointed him,*
1K. 14:27. *and committed* (them) unto the hands of
2K. 7:17. king *appointed* the lord...*to have the charge*
25:23. *had made* Gedaliah *governor,*
2Ch 12:10. *and committed* (them) to the hands of the
Isa. 62: 6. *I have set* watchmen upon thy walls,
Jer. 1:10. *I have* this day *set thee* over the nations
36:20. *they laid up* the roll in the chamber
40: 5. the king of Babylon *hath made governor*
7. of Babylon *had made* Gedaliah...*governor*
— and *had committed* unto him men,
11. *he had set* over them Gedaliah
41: 2. the king of Babylon *had made governor*
10. the captain of the guard *had committed* to
18. whom the king of Babylon *made governor*

HIPHIL.—*Imperative.*

Nu. 1:50. thou *shalt appoint* the Levites
Jos. 10:18. *and set* men by it for to keep them:
Ps. 109: 6. *Set thou* a wicked man over him:

HIPHIL.—*Future.*

Gen 39: 4. *and he made him overseer* over his house,
41:34. *and let him appoint* officers
1K. 11:28. *he made* him *ruler* over all the charge
2K. 25:22. *even* over them *he made* Gedaliah *ruler.*
1Ch 26:32. *whom* king David *made rulers*
Est. 2: 3. *And let* the king *appoint* officers
Ps. 31: 5(6). Into thine hand *I commit* my spirit:
Isa. 10:28. *he hath laid up* his carriages:
Jer. 37:21. *that they should commit* Jeremiah

* HOPHAL.—*Preterite.* *

Lev. 6: 4(5:23). which *was delivered* him *to keep,*
Jer. 6: 6. this *is* the city *to be visited;*

HOPHAL.—*Participle.*

2K. 12:11(12). them...*that had the oversight* of the
22: 5. doers of the work, *that have the oversight*
9. *that have the oversight* of the house
2Ch 34:10. the workmen *that had the oversight*
12. and *the overseers* of them
17. into the hand of *the overseers,*

* HITHPAEL.—*Preterite.* *

Jud. 20:15. of Gibeah, which *were numbered*
17. of Israel, beside Benjamin, *were numbered*

HITHPAEL.—*Future.*

Jud. 20:15. *And* the children of Benjamin *were numbered*
21: 9. *For* the people *were numbered,*

* HOTHPAEL.—*Preterite.* *

Nu. 1:47. the Levites...*were* not *numbered*
2:33. the Levites *were* not *numbered*
26:62. *they were* not *numbered* among
1K. 20:27. the children of Israel *were numbered,*

פְּקֻדָּה *p'kood-dāh'*, f. 6486

Nu. 3:32. *the oversight of* them that keep the charge
36. And (under) *the custody and* (marg. *the office of* the) charge of
4:16. *And* to *the office of* Eleazar
— *the oversight of* all the tabernacle,
16:29. *or* if they be visited *after the visitation of*
2K. 11:18. the priest appointed *officers* (marg. *offices*)
1Ch 23:11. they were *in* one *reckoning,*
24: 3. *according to their offices*
19. *the orderings of them* in their service
26:30. *officers* (marg. over *the charge*) among them
2Ch 17:14. *the numbers of them* according
23:18. *the offices of* the house of the Lord
24:11. brought unto the king's *office*
26:11. the number of *their account*
Job 10:12. *and thy visitation* hath preserved my
Ps. 109: 8. another take *his office.* (marg. or, *charge*)
Isa. 10: 3. what will ye do in the day of *visitation,*
15: 7. *and that which they have laid up,*
60:17. I will also make *thy officers* peace,
Jer. 8:12. in the time of *their visitation* they shall be
10:15. in the time of *their visitation* they shall

Jer. 11:23. (even) the year of *their visitation.*
23:12. them, (even) the year of *their visitation,*
46:21. them, (and) the time of *their visitation.*
48:44. upon Moab, the year of *their visitation,*
50:27. is come, the time of *their visitation.*
51:18. in the time of *their visitation* they shall
52:11. and put him in prison (marg. house of *the wards*) till the day of his death.
Eze. 9: 1. *them that have charge* over the city
44:11. (having) *charge* at the gates of the house.
Hos. 9: 7. The days of *visitation*
Mic. 7: 4. *thy visitation* cometh;

6487 פִּקָּדוֹן *pik-kāh-dōhn'*, m.

Gen41:36. that food shall be *for store*
Lev. 6: 2(5:21). *in that which was delivered him to keep,*
4(-:23). *that* which was delivered him to keep, (lit. *the deposit* which was deposited with him)

6488 פְּקִדֻת *p'kee-dooth'*, f.

Jer. 37:13. a captain of *the ward* (was) there,

6489 פְּקוֹד *p'kōhd*, m.

Jer. 50:21. inhabitants of *Pekod:* (marg. or, *visitation*)
Eze.23:23. the Chaldeans, *Pekod*, and Shoa,

6490 פִּקּוּדִים [*pik-koo-deem'*], m. pl.

Ps. 19: 8(9). *The statutes of* the Lord (are) right,
103:18. remember *his commandments*
111: 7. all *his commandments* (are) sure.
119: 4. commanded (us) to keep *thy precepts*
15. I will meditate *in thy precepts,*
27. the way of *thy precepts:*
40. I have longed *after thy precepts:*
45. I seek *thy precepts.*
56. because I kept *thy precepts.*
63. them that keep *thy precepts.*
69. I will keep *thy precepts*
78. I will meditate *in thy precepts.*
87. I forsook not *thy precepts.*
93. I will never forget *thy precepts:*
94. I have sought *thy precepts.*
100. because I keep *thy precepts.*
104. *Through thy precepts* I get understanding:
110. *yet* I erred not *from thy precepts.*
128. I esteem all (thy) *precepts*
134. so will I keep *thy precepts.*
141. (yet) do not I forget *thy precepts.*
159. how I love *thy precepts:*
168. I have kept *thy precepts*
173. I have chosen *thy precepts.*

6491 פָּקַח *pāh-kagh'.*

* KAL.—*Preterite.* *

Job 14: 3. *dost thou open* thine eyes
27:19. *he openeth* his eyes,

KAL.—*Infinitive.*

Isa. 42: 7. *To open* the blind eyes,
20. *opening* the ears, but he heareth not.

KAL.—*Imperative.*

2K. 6:17. Lord, I pray thee, *open* his eyes,
20. Lord, *open* the eyes of these (men),
19:16. *open*, Lord, thine eyes, and see:
Pro.20:13. *open* thine eyes, (and) thou shalt be
Isa. 37:17. *open* thine eyes, O Lord, and see:
Dan 9:18. *open* thine eyes, and behold

KAL.—*Future.*

Gen21:19. *And* God *opened* her eyes,
2K. 4:35. *and* the child *opened* his eyes.
6:17. *And* the Lord *opened* the eyes of the young
20. *And* the Lord *opened* their eyes,
Zec.12: 4. *I will open* mine eyes

KAL.—*Participle.* Poel.

Ps.146: 8. The Lord *openeth* (the eyes of) the blind:

KAL.—*Participle.* Paül.

Jer. 32:19. thine eyes (are) *open* upon all

* NIPHAL.—*Preterite.* *

Gen 3: 5. *then* your eyes *shall be opened,*

NIPHAL.—*Future.*

Gen 3: 7. *And* the eyes of them both *were opened,*
Isa. 35: 5. Then the eyes of the blind *shall be opened,*

פִּקֵּחַ *pik-kēh'ăgh*, adj. 6493

Ex. 4:11. maketh the dumb, or deaf, or *the seeing,*
23: 8. gift blindeth *the wise,* (marg. *the seeing*)

פְּקַח־קוֹחַ *p'kagh-kōh'ăgh*, m. 6495

Isa. 61: 1. *the opening of the prison* to (them that are)

פָּקִיד *pāh-keed'*, m. 6496

Gen41:34. let him appoint *officers*
Jud. 9:28. and Zebul *his officer?*
2K. 25:19. an officer that *was set* over the men of
2Ch24:11. *and* the high priest's *officer* came
31:13. *overseers* under the hand of Cononiah
Neh11: 9. Joel the son of Zichri (was) their *overseer:*
14. *and* their *overseer* (was) Zabdiel,
22. *The overseer also* of the Levites
12:42. Jezrahiah (their) *overseer.*
Est. 2: 3. let the king appoint *officers*
Jer. 20: 1. chief *governor* in the house of the Lord,
29:26. *officers* in the house of the Lord,
52:25. an eunuch, *which had the charge* of

פְּקָעִים *p'kāh-geem'*, m. pl. 6497

1K. 6:18. carved with *knops* (marg. or, *gourds*) and
7:24. *And* under the brim...(were) *knops*
— *the knops* (were) cast in two rows,

פַּקֻּעֹת *pak-koo-gōhth'*, f. pl. 6498

2K. 4:39. gathered thereof wild *gourds*

פַּר *par* & פָּר *pāhr*, m. 6499

2 פַּר בֶּן בָּקָר

Gen32:15(16). forty kine, *and* ten *bulls,*
Ex. 24: 5. sacrificed peace offerings of *oxen*
29: 1. Take one young bullock,[2] (lit. one *steer* the son of a bull)
3. *the bullock* and the two rams.
10. thou shalt cause *a bullock* to be brought
— upon the head of *the bullock.*
11. thou shalt kill *the bullock*
12. take of the blood of *the bullock,*
14. the flesh of *the bullock,*
36. *And* thou shalt offer...*a bullock*
Lev. 4: 3. a young bullock[2] (lit. *a steer* the son of a bull) without blemish
4. he shall bring *the bullock*
— upon *the bullock*'s head, and kill *the bullock*
5. the priest...shall take of *the bullock*'s blood,
7. the blood of *the bullock*
8. the fat of *the bullock*
11. the skin of *the bullock,*
12. Even *the* whole *bullock*
14. congregation shall offer a young bullock[2] (lit. *a steer* the son of a bull)
15. upon the head of *the bullock* before the Lord: and *the bullock* shall be killed
16. the priest...shall bring of *the bullock's*
20. And he shall do *with the bullock* as he did *with the bullock for*
21. he shall carry forth *the bullock*
— as he burned *the first bullock:*
8: 2. *a bullock for* the sin offering,
14. he brought *the bullock for* the sin offering:
— hands upon the head of *the bullock for*
17. *the bullock*, and his hide,
16: 3. with a young bullock[2] (lit. *with a steer* the son of a bull) for a
6. Aaron shall offer *his bullock of* the
11. Aaron shall bring *the bullock of* the

Lev.16:11. and shall kill *the bullock of*
14, 18. take of the blood of *the bullock*,
15. with the blood of *the bullock*,
27. *the bullock* (for) the sin offering,
23:18. *and* one young bullock,[2] (lit. *and* one *steer* the son of a bull)
Nu. 7:15, 21, 27, 33, 39, 45, 51, 57, 63, 69, 75, 81. One young bullock[2] (lit. one *steer* the son of a bull), one ram,
87. All the oxen...(were) twelve *bullocks*,
88. oxen...(were) twenty and four *bullocks*,
8: 8. let them take a young bullock[2] (lit. *a steer* the son of a bull)
— *and* another young bullock[2] (lit. *and* another *steer* the son of a bull)
12. upon the heads of *the bullocks:*
15:24. the congregation shall offer one young bullock[2] (lit. one *steer* the son of a bull)
23: 1. prepare me here seven *oxen*
2. offered on (every) altar *a bullock*
4. offered upon (every) altar *a bullock*
14, 30. offered *a bullock* and a ram
29. prepare me here seven *bullocks*
28:11, 19. two young bullocks (lit. *steers* sons of a bull), and one ram,
12. three tenth deals...*for* one *bullock;*
14. half an hin of wine *unto a bullock*,
20. three tenth deals shall ye offer *for a bullock*,
27. two young bullocks (lit. *steers* sons of a bull), one ram,
28. three tenth deals *unto* one *bullock*,
29: 2, 8. one young bullock[2] (lit. one *steer* the son of a bull), one ram,
3. three tenth deals *for a bullock*,
9. three tenth deals *to a bullock*,
13. thirteen young bullocks[2] (lit. *steers* sons of a bull), two rams,
14. three tenth deals *unto* every *bullock* of *the* thirteen *bullocks*,
17. twelve young bullocks[2] (lit. *steers* sons of a bull), two rams,
18, 21, 24, 27, 30, 33. their drink offerings *for the bullocks*,
20. on the third day eleven *bullocks*,
23. on the fourth day ten *bullocks*,
26. on the fifth day nine *bullocks*,
29. on the sixth day eight *bullocks*,
32. on the seventh day seven *bullocks*,
36. one *bullock*, one ram,
37. *for the bullock*, for the ram,
Jud. 6:25. Take thy father's *young* bullock, *even the* second *bullock*
26. and take *the* second *bullock*,
28. *the* second *bullock* was offered
1Sa. 1:24. she took him up...*with* three *bullocks*,
25. And they slew *a bullock*,
1K. 18:23. Let them therefore give us two *bullocks;* and let them choose one *bullock*
— I will dress *the* other *bullock*,
25. Choose you one *bullock*
26. And they took *the bullock*
33. and cut *the bullock* in pieces,
1Ch 15:26. they offered seven *bullocks*
29:21. a thousand *bullocks*, a thousand rams,
2Ch 13: 9. with a young bullock[2] (lit. *with a steer* the son of a bull)
29:21. they brought seven *bullocks*,
30:24. a thousand *bullocks*
— a thousand *bullocks*
Ezr. 8:35. twelve *bullocks* for all Israel,
Job 42: 8. take unto you now seven *bullocks*
Ps. 22:12(13). Many *bulls* have compassed me:
50: 9. I will take no *bullock* out of thy house,
51:19(21). then shall they offer *bullocks*
69:31(32). (or) *bullock* that hath horns and
Isa. 1:11. I delight not in the blood of *bullocks*,
34: 7. *and the bullocks* with the bulls;
Jer. 50:27. Slay all *her bullocks;*
Eze.39:18. of lambs, and of goats, of *bullocks*,
43:19. a young bullock[2] (lit. *a steer* the son of a bull) for a sin offering.
21. Thou shalt take *the bullock* also of
22. as they did cleanse (it) *with the bullock.*
23. thou shalt offer a young bullock[2] (lit. *a steer* the son of a bull)
25. they shall *also* prepare a young bullock,[2] (lit. *and a steer* the son of a bull)
Eze.45:18. thou shalt take a young bullock[2] (lit. *a steer* the son of a bull)
22. the prince prepare for himself...*a bullock*
23. seven *bullocks* and seven rams
24. an ephah *for a bullock*,
46: 6. a young bullock[2] (lit. *a steer* the son of a bull) without blemish,
7. an ephah *for a bullock*,
11. an ephah *to a bullock*,
Hos 14: 2(3). so will we render *the calves* of our

פָּרָא [*pāh-rāh'*]. 6500

∗ HIPHIL.—*Future.* ∗

Hos.13:15. Though *he be fruitful* among

פֶּרֶא *peh'-reh*, com. 6501

Gen16:12. he will be a *wild* man;
Job 6: 5. Doth *the wild ass* bray
11:12. though man be born (like) *a wild ass's*
24: 5. (as) *wild asses* in the desert,
39: 5. Who hath sent out *the wild ass* free?
Ps.104:11. *the wild asses* quench their thirst.
Isa. 32:14. a joy of *wild asses*,
Jer. 2:24. *A wild ass* used to the wilderness,
14: 6. *And the wild asses* did stand in the high
Hos. 8: 9. *a wild ass* alone by himself:

פַּרְבָּר *par-bāhr'*, m. 6503

1Ch 26:18. *At Parbar* [probably lit. *at the suburb*] westward,
— (and) two *at Parbar.* [probably lit. *id.*]

פָּרַד [*pāh-rad'*]. 6504

∗ KAL.—*Participle.* Paül. ∗

Eze. 1:11. their wings (were) *stretched* upward; (marg. or, *divided* above)

∗ NIPHAL.—*Preterite.* ∗

Gen10: 5. *were* the isles of the Gentiles *divided*
32. by these *were* the nations *divided*
2Sa. 1:23. in their death *they were* not *divided:*

NIPHAL.—*Infinitive.*

Gen13:14. after that Lot *was separated*

NIPHAL.—*Imperative.*

Gen13: 9. *separate thyself*, I pray thee,

NIPHAL.—*Future.*

Gen 2:10. from thence *it was parted*, and became
13:11. *and they separated themselves* the one from
25:23. two manner of people *shall be separated*
Pro.19: 4. the poor *is separated* from his neighbour.

NIPHAL.—*Participle.*

Jud. 4:11. *had severed himself* from the Kenites,
Neh 4:19(13). we *are separated* upon the wall,
Pro.18: 1. Through desire a man, *having separated himself*,

∗ PIEL.—*Future.* ∗

Hos. 4:14. themselves *are separated*

∗ PUAL.—*Participle.* ∗

Est. 3: 8. *and dispersed* among the people

∗ HIPHIL.—*Preterite.* ∗

Gen30:40. Jacob *did separate* the lambs,

HIPHIL.—*Infinitive.*

Deu32: 8. *when he separated* the sons of Adam,

HIPHIL.—*Future.*

Ru. 1:17. (if ought) but death *part* thee and me.
2K. 2:11. *and parted* them both asunder;
Pro.18:18. and *parteth* between the mighty.

HIPHIL.—*Participle.*

Pro.16:28. a whisperer *separateth* chief friends.
17: 9. he that repeateth a matter *separateth* (very) friends.

∗ HITHPAEL.—*Preterite.* ∗

Ps. 22:14(15). *and* all my bones *are out of joint* (marg. or, *sundered*)

HITHPAEL.—*Future.*

Job 4:11. the stout lion's whelps *are scattered abroad.*
41:17(9). *they cannot be sundered.*
Ps. 92: 9(10). all the workers of iniquity *shall be scattered.*

6505 ## פֶּרֶד *peh'-red*, m.

2Sa. 13:29. gat him up upon *his mule*,
18: 9. Absalom rode upon *a mule*, and *the mule*
— *and the mule* that (was) under him
1K. 10:25. horses, and *mules*,
18: 5. to save the horses *and mules* alive,
2K. 5:17. two *mules'* burden of earth?
1Ch 12:40. on camels, *and on mules*,
2Ch 9:24. horses, *and mules*,
Ezr. 2:66. *their mules*, two hundred forty and five;
Neh 7:68. *their mules*, two hundred forty and five:
Ps. 32: 9. Be ye not as the horse, (or) *as the mule*,
Isa. 66:20. in litters, *and upon mules*,
Eze. 27:14. horsemen *and mules*.
Zec. 14:15. the plague of the horse, of *the mule*,

6506 ## פִּרְדָּה *pir-dāh'*, f.

1K. 1:33. to ride upon mine own *mule*,
38. upon king David's *mule*,
44. upon the king's *mule*:

6507 ## פְּרֻדוֹת *p'roo-dōhth'*, f. pl.

Joel 1:17. *The seed* (marg. *grains*) is rotten under

6508 ## פַּרְדֵּס *par-dēhs'*, m.

Neh 2: 8. Asaph the keeper of the king's *forest*,
Ecc. 2: 5. I made me gardens *and orchards*,
Cant. 4:13. *an orchard of* pomegranates,

6509 ## פָּרָה [*pāh-rāh'*].

* KAL.—*Preterite.* *

Gen 8:17. *and be fruitful*, and multiply
26:22. *and we shall be fruitful* in the land.
Ex. 1: 7. the children of Israel *were fruitful*,
Jer. 3:16. when ye be multiplied *and increased*
23: 3. *and they shall be fruitful* and increase.
Eze. 36:11. they shall increase *and bring fruit*:

KAL.—*Imperative.*

Gen 1:22, 28 & 9:1. *Be fruitful*, and multiply,
9: 7. *be ye fruitful*, and multiply;
35:11. *be fruitful* and multiply;

KAL.—*Future.*

Gen 47:27. they had possessions therein, *and grew*,
Ex. 23:30. until *thou be increased*,
Isa. 11: 1. a Branch *shall grow* out of his roots:
45: 8. *and let them bring forth* salvation,

KAL.—*Participle.* Poel.

Gen 49:22. Joseph (is) a *fruitful* bough, (even) a *fruitful* bough
Deu 29:18(17). a root that *beareth* gall
Ps. 128: 3. Thy wife (shall be) as a *fruitful* vine
Isa. 17: 6. *fruitful* branches thereof,
32:12. the pleasant fields, for the *fruitful* vine.
Eze. 19:10. she was *fruitful* and full of branches

* HIPHIL.—*Preterite.* *

Gen 17: 6. *And I will make* thee exceeding *fruitful*,
20. *and will make* him *fruitful*,
41:52. God *hath caused me to be fruitful*
Lev. 26: 9. I will have respect unto you, *and make* you *fruitful*,

HIPHIL.—*Future.*

Gen 28: 3. God Almighty bless thee, *and make thee fruitful*,
Ps. 105:24. *And he increased* his people

HIPHIL.—*Participle.*

Gen 48: 4. Behold, I *will make thee fruitful*,

פָּרָה [*pāh-rāh'*], f. 6510

Gen 32:15(16). forty *kine*, and ten bulls,
41: 2. seven well favoured *kine*
3. seven other *kine* came up
— *the* (other) *kine* upon the brink
4. ill favoured and leanfleshed *kine*
— well favoured and fat *kine*.
18. came up out of the river seven *kine*,
19. seven other *kine* came up
20. *the* lean and *the* ill favoured *kine* did eat up *the* first seven fat *kine*:
26. *The* seven good *kine*
27. *the* seven thin and ill favoured *kine*
Nu. 19: 2. they bring thee *a* red *heifer*
5. (one) shall burn *the heifer*
6. the burning of *the heifer*.
9, 10. the ashes of *the heifer*,
1Sa. 6: 7. take two milch *kine*,
— tie *the kine* to the cart,
10. and took two milch *kine*,
12. *the kine* took the straight way
14. and offered *the kine* a burnt offering
Job 21:10. *their cow* calveth, and casteth not her
Isa. 11: 7. *And the cow* and the bear shall feed;
Hos 4:16. Israel slideth back *as a* backsliding *heifer*:
Am. 4: 1. Hear this word, ye *kine of* Bashan,

פֶּרֶה see פֶּרֶא See 6501

פְּרוֹזִים *p'rōh-zeem'*, m. pl. 6521

Est. 9:19. (כתיב) Therefore the Jews *of the villages*,

פַּרְוָר [*par-vāhr'*], m. 6503

2K. 23:11. which (was) *in the suburbs*,

פָּרוּר *pāh-roor'*, m. 6517

Nu. 11: 8. and baked (it) *in pans*,
Jud. 6:19. he put the broth *in a pot*,
1Sa. 2:14. he struck (it) into the pan,...or *pot*;

פֵּרוֹת *pēh-rōhth'*, f. pl. 6512

Isa. 2:20. to the moles (lit. to the dig-*holes*)

פָּרָז [*pāh-rāhz'*], m. 6518

Hab. 3:14. the head of *his villages*: [perhaps *leaders*]

פְּרָזוֹן *p'rāh-zōhn'*, m. 6520

Jud. 5: 7. (The inhabitants of) *the villages* ceased,
11. (the inhabitants) *of his villages* in Israel:

פְּרָזוֹת *p'rāh-zōhth'*, f. pl. 6519

Est. 9:19. the Jews...that dwelt in *the unwalled towns*,
Eze. 38:11. the land of *unwalled villages*;
Zec. 2: 4(8). (as) *towns without walls*

פְּרָזִי *p'rāh-zee'*, m. 6521

Deu. 3: 5. *unwalled* towns a great many.
1Sa. 6:18. of fenced cities, and of *country* villages,
Est. 9:19. the Jews of *the villages*,

פַּרְזֶל *par-zel'*, Ch. m. 6523

Dan. 2:33. His legs of *iron*, his feet part of *iron* and part of clay.
34. his feet (that were) of *iron*
35. Then was *the iron*, the clay,
40. kingdom shall be strong *as iron*: forasmuch as *iron* breaketh in pieces and subdueth all (things): *and as iron*

Dan. 2:41. and part of *iron*,
-- of the strength of *the iron*, forasmuch as thou sawest *the iron*
42. the toes of the feet (were) part of *iron*,
43. whereas thou sawest *iron* mixed with
— even as *iron* is not mixed with clay.
45. it brake in pieces *the iron*, the brass,
4:15(12), 23(20). with a band of *iron* and brass,
5: 4. and praised the gods of gold,...of *iron*,
23. thou hast praised the gods of...*iron*,
7: 7. and it had great *iron* teeth:
19. whose teeth (were of) *iron*,

6524 פָּרַח *pāh-ragh'*.

* KAL.—*Preterite.* *

Lev.13:20. a plague of leprosy *broken out*
25. a leprosy *broken out* of the burning:
39. a freckled spot (that) *groweth* in the skin ;
14:43. *and break out* in the house,
Nu. 17: 8(23). the rod of Aaron for the house of Levi *was budded*,
Cant.6:11. to see *whether* the vine *flourished*,
7:12(13). let us see if the vine *flourish*,
Isa. 27: 6. Israel shall blossom *and bud*,
Eze. 7:10. hath blossomed, pride *hath budded*.
Hos10: 4. *thus* judgment *springeth up* as hemlock

KAL.—*Infinitive.*

Lev.13:12. if a leprosy break out *abroad* (lit. *breaking out* break out)
Ps. 92: 7(8). *When* the wicked *spring* as the grass,
Isa. 35: 2. It shall blossom *abundantly*, (lit. *blossoming* it shall blossom)

KAL.—*Future.*

Lev.13:12. if a leprosy *break out* abroad
Nu. 17: 5(20). the man's rod, whom I shall choose, *shall blossom*:
Ps. 72: 7. In his days *shall* the righteous *flourish*;
92:12(13). The righteous *shall flourish*
Pro.11:28. the righteous *shall flourish*
Isa. 35: 1. the desert shall rejoice, *and blossom*
2. *It shall blossom* abundantly,
66:14. your bones *shall flourish*
Hos14: 5(6). *he shall grow* (marg. or, *blossom*) as the lily,
7(8). *and grow* (marg. *id.*) as the vine:
Hab. 3:17. Although the fig tree *shall* not *blossom*,

KAL.—*Participle.* Poël.

Gen40:10. it (was) *as though it budded*,
Ex. 9: 9. a boil *breaking forth* (with) blains
10. it became a boil *breaking forth*
Lev.13:42. a leprosy *sprung up* in his bald head,
57. it (is) a *spreading* (plague):
Eze.13:20. hunt the souls *to make* (them) *fly*, (marg. or, *into gardens*)
— the souls that ye hunt *to make* (them) *fly*.

* HIPHIL.—*Preterite.* *

Eze.17:24. *and have made* the dry tree *to flourish*:

HIPHIL.—*Future.*

Job 14: 9. through the scent of water *it will bud*,
Ps. 92:13(14). *shall flourish* in the courts of our God.
Pro.14:11. the tabernacle of the upright *shall flourish*.
Isa. 17:11. *shalt thou make* thy seed *to flourish*:

6525 פֶּרַח *peh'-ragh*, m.

Ex. 25:31. his knops, *and his flowers*,
33. a knop *and a flower* in one branch ;
— in the other branch, (with) a knop *and a flower*:
34. their knops *and their flowers*.
37:17, 20. his knops, *and his flowers*,
19. in one branch, a knop *and a flower*;
— in another branch, a knop *and a flower*:
Nu. 8: 4. unto *the flowers thereof*,
17: 8(23). budded, and brought forth *buds*,
1K. 7:26. a cup, with *flowers* of lilies:
49. *with the flowers*, and the lamps, and the
2Ch 4: 5. the brim of a cup, with *flowers* of lilies ;
21. *And the flowers*, and the lamps,
Isa. 5:24. *and their blossom* shall go up as dust:
18: 5. when *the bud* is perfect,
Nah. 1: 4. *and the flower of* Lebanon languisheth.

פִּרְחָה *pir-ghāh'*, f. 6526

Job 30:12. Upon (my) right (hand) rise *the youth*;

פָּרַט [*pāh-rat'*]. 6527

* KAL.—*Participle.* Poel. *

Am. 6: 5. *That chant* (marg. or, *quaver*) to the sound of the viol,

פֶּרֶט *peh'-ret*, m. 6528

Lev.19:10. *neither* shalt thou gather (every) *grape of*

פְּרִי *p'ree*, m. 6529

Gen 1:11. (and) the *fruit* tree yielding *fruit* after his
12. and the tree yielding *fruit*,
29. *the fruit of* a tree yielding seed ;
3: 2. *of the fruit of* the trees of the garden:
3. *But of the fruit of* the tree
6. she took *of the fruit thereof*,
4: 3. Cain brought *of the fruit of* the ground
30: 2. from thee *the fruit of* the womb?
Ex. 10:15. all *the fruit of* the trees
Lev.19:23. ye shall count *the fruit thereof*
24. all *the fruit thereof*
25. eat of *the fruit thereof*,
23:40. *the boughs* (marg. *fruit*) *of* goodly trees,
25:19. the land shall yield *her fruit*,
26: 4. the trees...shall yield *their fruit*.
20. neither shall the trees...yield *their fruits*
27:30. *of the fruit of* the tree,
Nu. 13:20. bring *of the fruit of* the land.
26. shewed them *the fruit of* the land.
27. and this (is) *the fruit of it*.
Deu 1:25. they took *of the fruit of* the land
7:13. *the fruit of* thy womb, *and the fruit of* thy
26: 2. the first of all *the fruit of*
10. I have brought *the* first*fruits of*
28: 4. *the fruit of* thy body, *and the fruit of* thy ground, *and the fruit of* thy cattle,
11. *in the fruit of* thy body, *and in the fruit of* thy cattle, *and in the fruit of* thy ground,
18. *the fruit of* thy body, *and the fruit of* thy
33. *The fruit of* thy land, and all thy
42. All thy trees *and fruit of* thy land
51. *the fruit of* thy cattle, *and the fruit of* thy
53. *the fruit of* thine own body,
30: 9. *in the fruit of* thy body, *and in the fruit of* thy cattle, *and in the fruit of* thy land,
2K. 19:29. vineyards, and eat *the fruits thereof*.
30. and bear *fruit* upward.
Neh. 9:36. to eat *the fruit thereof*
10:35(36). all *fruit of* all trees,
37(38). *and the fruit of* all manner of trees,
Ps. 1: 3. bringeth forth *his fruit* in his season ;
21:10(11). *Their fruit* shalt thou destroy
58:11(12). Verily (there is) *a reward for* (marg *fruit of*) the righteous:
72:16. *the fruit thereof* shall shake
104:13. satisfied *with the fruit of* thy works.
105:35. devoured *the fruit of* their ground.
107:34. A *fruit*ful land (lit. a land of *fruit*)
37. vineyards, which may yield *fruits*
127: 3. *the fruit of* the womb
132:11. *Of the fruit of* thy body
148: 9. *fruit*ful trees, (lit. trees of *fruit*)
Pro. 1:31. they eat *of the fruit of* their own way,
8:19. *My fruit* (is) better than gold,
11:30. *The fruit of* the righteous
12:14. satisfied with good *by the fruit of*
13: 2. A man shall eat good *by the fruit of*
18:20. satisfied *with the fruit of* his mouth ;
21 & 27:18. shall eat *the fruit thereof*.
31:16. *with the fruit of* her hands
31. Give her *of the fruit of* her hands ;
Ecc. 2: 5. of all (kind of) *fruits*:
Cant.2: 3. *and his fruit* (was) sweet to my taste.
4:13. with pleasant *fruits*;
16. and eat his pleasant *fruits*.
8:11. every one *for the fruit thereof*
12. those that keep *the fruit thereof*
Isa. 3:10. they shall eat *the fruit of* their doings
4: 2. *and the fruit of* the earth

Isa. 10:12. *the fruit of* the stout heart of
13:18. *and* they shall have no pity on *the fruit of* the womb;
14:29. *and his fruit* (shall be) a fiery flying
27: 9. all *the fruit* to take away his sin;
37:30. plant vineyards, and eat *the fruit thereof.*
31. and bear *fruit* upward:
65:21. plant vineyards, and eat *the fruit of them.*
Jer. 2: 7. to eat *the fruit thereof*
6:19. *the fruit of* their thoughts,
7:20. and upon *the fruit of* the ground;
11:16. A green olive tree,...of goodly *fruit:*
12: 2. they bring forth *fruit:*
17: 8. neither shall cease from yielding *fruit.*
10. *according to the fruit of* his doings.
21:14. *according to the fruit of* your doings,
29: 5. plant gardens, and eat *the fruit of them;*
28. plant gardens, and eat *the fruit of them.*
32:19. *and according to the fruit of* his doings:
Lam. 2:20. Shall the women eat *their fruit,*
Eze. 17: 8. and that it might bear *fruit,*
9. cut off *the fruit thereof,*
23. bring forth boughs, and bear *fruit,*
19:12. the east wind dried up *her fruit:*
14. hath devoured *her fruit,*
25: 4. they shall eat *thy fruit,*
34:27. the tree...shall yield *her fruit,*
36: 8. *and* yield *your fruit* to my people
30. I will multiply *the fruit of* the tree,
47:12. *the fruit thereof* be consumed:
— and *the fruit thereof* shall be for meat,
Hos. 9:16. they shall bear no *fruit:*
10: 1. Israel...bringeth forth *fruit* unto himself: according to the multitude *of his fruit*
13. ye have eaten *the fruit of* lies:
14: 8(9). From me is *thy fruit* found.
Joel 2:22. the tree beareth *her fruit,*
Am. 2: 9. I destroyed *his fruit* from above,
6:12. *and the fruit of* righteousness
9:14. make gardens, and eat *the fruit of them.*
Mic. 6: 7. *the fruit of* my body (for) the sin of my
7:13. *for the fruit of* their doings.
Zec. 8:12. the vine shall give *her fruit,*
Mal. 3:11. *the fruits of* your ground;

6530 פָּרִיץ *pāh-reetz'*, m.

Ps. 17: 4. (from) the paths of *the destroyer.*
Isa. 35: 9. *nor* (any) *ravenous* beast shall go up
Jer. 7:11. Is this house,...become a den of *robbers*
Eze. 7:22. *the robbers* (marg. or, *burglars*) shall enter
18:10. If he beget a son (that is) *a robber,* (marg. or, *breaker up of an house*)
Dan 11:14. *the robbers* (marg. children of *robbers*) *of* thy people

---

6531 פֶּרֶךְ *peh'-rech*, m.

Ex. 1:13. the children of Israel to serve *with rigour:*
14. all their service,...(was) *with rigour.*
Lev.25:43. Thou shalt not rule over him *with rigour;*
46. ye shall not rule...*with rigour.*
53. shall not rule *with rigour*
Eze.34: 4. *and with cruelty* have ye ruled them.

6532 פָּרֹכֶת *pāh-rōh'-cheth*, f.

Ex. 26:31. thou shalt make *a vail*
33. thou shalt hang up *the vail*
— bring in thither within *the vail*
— *the vail* shall divide unto you
35. thou shalt set the table without *the vail,*
27:21. In the tabernacle...without *the vail,*
30: 6. *the vail* that (is) by the ark
35:12. and *the vail of* the covering,
36:35. And he made *a vail*
38:27. the sockets of *the vail;*
39:34. *the vail of* the covering,
40: 3. cover the ark with *the vail.*
21. set up *the vail of* the covering,
22. he put the table...without *the vail.*
26. he put the golden altar...before *the vail:*
Lev. 4: 6. before *the vail of* the sanctuary.
17. (even) before *the vail.*
16: 2. the holy (place) within *the vail*
Lev.16:12. censer full...and bring (it) within *the vail:*
15. bring his blood within *the vail,*
21:23. he shall not go in unto *the vail,*
24: 3. Without *the vail of* the testimony,
Nu. 4: 5. they shall take down *the* covering *vail,*
18: 7. within *the vail;*
2Ch 3:14. And he made *the vail*

פָּרַם [*pāh-ram'*]. 6533

* KAL.—*Future.* *

Lev.10: 6. neither *rend* your clothes;
21:10. shall not uncover his head, nor *rend* his

KAL.—*Participle.* Paül.

Lev.13:45. his clothes shall be *rent,*

פָּרַס [*pāh-ras'*]. 6536

* KAL.—*Infinitive.* *

Isa. 58: 7. *to deal* thy bread to the hungry,

KAL.—*Future.*

Jer. 16: 7. Neither *shall* (men) *tear* (themselves)

* HIPHIL.—*Preterite.* *

Lev.11: 6. but *divideth* not the hoof;
Deu14: 7. but *divide* not the hoof;

HIPHIL.—*Future.*

Lev.11: 5. but *divideth* not the hoof;

HIPHIL.—*Participle.*

Lev.11: 3. Whatsoever *parteth* the hoof,
4. *or of them that divide* the hoof:
— but *divideth* not the hoof;
7. the swine, though *he divide* the hoof,
26. every beast which *divideth* the hoof,
Deu14: 6. every beast that *parteth* the hoof,
7. *or of them that divide* the cloven hoof;
8. the swine, because it *divideth* the hoof,
Ps. 69:31(32). bullock that hath horns and *hoofs.*

פְּרַס [*p'ras*], Ch. 6537

* P'AL.—*Participle.* Active. *

Dan 5:25. Mene, Mene, Tekel, *Upharsin.*

P'AL.—*Participle.* Passive.

Dan 5:28. *Peres;* Thy kingdom *is divided,*

פֶּרֶס *peh'-res*, m. 6538

Lev.11:13. the eagle, and *the ossifrage,*
Deu14:12. the eagle, *and the ossifrage,*

פַּרְסָה *par-sāh'*, f. 6541

Ex. 10:26. there shall not *an hoof* be left behind;
Lev.11: 3. Whatsoever parteth *the hoof,* and is cloven-*footed,* (lit. cleaveth the cleft of *the hoofs*)
4. of them that divide *the hoof:*
— *but* divideth not *the hoof;*
5. *but* divideth not *the hoof;*
6. *but* divideth not *the hoof;*
7. And the swine, though he divide *the hoof,* and be cloven*footed,* (lit. cleaveth the cleft of *the hoof*)
26. every beast which divideth *the hoof,*
Deu14: 6. And every beast that parteth *the hoof,* and cleaveth the cleft into two *claws,*
7. them that divide *the* cloven *hoof;*
— *but* divide not *the hoof;*
8. the swine, because it divideth *the hoof,*
Isa. 5:28. their horses' *hoofs* shall be counted like
Jer. 47: 3. the noise of the stamping of *the hoofs*
Eze.26:11. *With the hoofs of* his horses
32:13. *nor the hoofs of* beasts trouble them.
Mic. 4:13. *and* I will make *thy hoofs* brass:
Zec.11:16. *and* tear *their claws* in pieces.

פָּרַע *pāh-rag'*. 6544

* KAL.—*Preterite.* *

Ex. 32:25. Aaron *had made them naked*
Nu. 5:18. *and uncover* the woman's head,

KAL.—*Infinitive.*

Jud. 5: 2. Praise ye the Lord *for the avenging* (lit. *avenging* the avenges) of Israel,

KAL.—*Imperative.*

Pro. 4:15. *Avoid it*, pass not by it,

KAL.—*Future.*

Lev.10: 6. *Uncover* not your heads,
21:10. the high priest...*shall* not *uncover*
Pro. 1:25. *But ye have set at nought* all my counsel,
8:33. Hear instruction, and be wise, and *refuse* it not.
Eze.24:14. *I will* not *go back*,

KAL.—*Participle.* Poel.

Pro.13:18. him *that refuseth* instruction:
15:32. He *that refuseth* instruction

KAL.—*Participle.* Paül.

Ex. 32:25. Moses saw that the people (were) *naked;*
Lev.13:45. and his head *bare*,

* NIPHAL.—*Future.* *

Pro.29:18. people *perish:* (marg. or, *is made naked*)

* HIPHIL.—*Preterite.* *

2Ch 28:19. *he made* Judah *naked*,

HIPHIL.—*Future.*

Ex. 5: 4. Wherefore *do ye*, Moses and Aaron, *let* the people from their works?

6545 **פֶּרַע** *peh'-rag*, m.

Nu. 6: 5. shall let *the locks of* the hair of his head
Eze.44:20. *nor* suffer *their locks* to grow

6546 **פְּרָעוֹת** *p'rāh-gōhth'*, f. pl.

Deu32:42. the beginning of *revenges*
Jud. 5: 2. Praise ye the Lord for the avenging (lit. for avenging *the avenges*) of Israel,

---

6550 **פַּרְעֹשׁ** *par-gōhsh'*, m.

1Sa.24:14(15). after a dead dog, after *a flea.*
26:20. king of Israel is come out to seek *a flea*,

6555 **פָּרַץ** *pāh-ratz'.*

* KAL.—*Preterite.* *

Gen28:14. *and thou shalt spread abroad* (marg. *break forth*) to the west,
38:29. How *hast thou broken forth?*
2Sa. 5:20. The Lord *hath broken forth* upon
6: 8. the Lord *had made* (marg. *broken*) a
1Ch 4:38. the house of their fathers *increased*
13:11. the Lord *had made* a breach
14:11. God *hath broken in* upon
15:13. the Lord our God *made* a breach
2Ch 20:37. the Lord *hath broken* thy works.
24: 7. the sons of Athaliah,...*had broken up*
Neh. 4: 3(3:35). *he shall even break down* their
Job 1:10. his substance *is increased*
28: 4. The flood *breaketh out*
Ps. 60: 1(3). O God,...*thou hast scattered* (marg. *broken*) *us*,
80:12(13). Why *hast thou* (then) *broken down* her
89:40(41). *Thou hast broken down* all his hedges;
Hos. 4: 2. *they break out*, and blood toucheth blood.
Mic. 2:13. *they have broken up*, and have passed

KAL.—*Infinitive.*

2Ch 31: 5. *And as soon as* the commandment *came abroad*, (marg. *brake forth*)
Ecc. 3: 3. a time *to break down*,
Isa. 5: 5. (and) *break down* the wall thereof,

KAL.—*Future.*

Gen30:30. *and it is* (now) *increased* (marg. *broken forth*) unto a multitude;
43. *And* the man *increased* exceedingly,
Ex. 1:12. the more they multiplied and *grew.*
19:22. lest the Lord *break forth*
24. lest *he break forth* upon them.
1Sa.28:23. *But* his servants,...*compelled* him;
2Sa.13:25. *And he pressed* him: howbeit
27. *But* Absalom *pressed* him,
2K. 5:23. *And he urged* him, and bound two talents
14:13. *and brake down* the wall of Jerusalem
1Ch 13: 2. *let us* send *abroad* (marg. *let us break forth* (and) send) unto our brethren
2Ch 11:23. *and dispersed* of all his children
25:23. *and brake down* the wall of Jerusalem
26: 6. *and brake down* the wall of Gath,
Job 16:14. *He breaketh me* with breach upon breach,
Ps.106:29. and the plague *brake in* upon them.
Pro. 3:10. thy presses *shall burst out*
Isa. 54: 3. *thou shalt break forth* on the right
Hos. 4:10. shall commit whoredom, and *shall* not *increase:*

KAL.—*Participle.* Poel.

Ecc.10: 8. *and whoso breaketh* an hedge,
Mic. 2:13. *The breaker* is come up

KAL.—*Participle.* Paül.

2Ch 32: 5. all the wall *that was broken*,
Neh. 2:13. of Jerusalem, which *were broken down*,
4: 7(1). *the breaches* began to be stopped,
Pro.25:28. a city (that is) *broken down*,

* NIPHAL.—*Participle.* *

1Sa. 3: 1. (there was) no *open* vision.

* PUAL.—*Participle.* *

Neh. 1: 3. wall of Jerusalem also (is) *broken down*,

* HITHPAEL.—*Participle.* *

1Sa.25:10. servants now a days *that break away*

פֶּרֶץ *peh'-retz*, m. 6556

Gen38:29. How hast thou broken forth? (this) *breach* (be) upon thee.
Jud.21:15. the Lord had made *a breach*
2Sa. 5:20. David came to Baal-*perazim*,
— *as the breach of* waters.
— the name of that place Baal-*perazim.* (marg. i. e. The plain of *breaches*)
6: 8. the Lord had made *a breach*
— he called the name of the place *Perez*-uzzah (marg. *The breach of* Uzzah)
1K. 11:27. repaired *the breaches of* the city of David
1Ch 13:11. the Lord had made *a breach*
— that place is called *Perez*-uzza (marg. *The breach of* Uzzah)
14:11. they came up to Baal-*perazim;*
— *like the breaking forth of* waters:
— the name of that place Baal-*perazim.* (marg. i. e. A place *of breaches*)
Neh. 6: 1. there was no *breach* left
Job 16:14. He breaketh me with *breach* upon *breach*,
30:14. *as a* wide *breaking in* (of waters):
Ps.106:23. his chosen stood before him *in the breach*,
144:14. (that there be) no *breaking in*,
Isa. 28:21. the Lord shall rise up as (in) mount *Perazim*,
30:13. *as a breach* ready to fall,
58:12. The repairer of *the breach*,
Eze.13: 5. Ye have not gone up *into the gaps*, (marg. or, *breaches*)
22:30. and stand *in the gap* before me
Am. 4: 3. *And* ye shall go out *at the breaches*,
9:11. and close up *the breaches thereof;*

פָּרַק [*pāh-rak'*]. 6561

* KAL.—*Preterite.* *

Gen27:40. *that thou shalt break* his yoke

KAL.—*Future.*

Ps.136:24. *And hath redeemed us* from our enemies:

KAL.—*Participle.* Poel.

Ps. 7: 2(3). tear my soul...*rending* (it) *in pieces*,
Lam.5: 8. (there is) none *that doth deliver*

* PIEL.—*Imperative.* *

Ex. 32: 2. *Break off* the golden earrings,

PIEL.—*Future.*

Zec.11:16. and *tear* their claws *in pieces.*

PIEL.—*Participle.*

1K. 19:11. a great and strong wind *rent* the

* HITHPAEL.—*Preterite.* *

Eze.19:12. her strong rods *were broken*

HITHPAEL.—*Imperative.*

Ex. 32:24. Whosoever hath any gold, *let them break* (it) *off.*

HITHPAEL.—*Future.*

Ex. 32: 3. *And* all the people *brake off* the golden earrings

---

6562 פְּרַק [*p'rak*], Ch.

* P'AL.—*Imperative.* *

Dan 4:27(24). and *break off* thy sins by

6564 פָּרָק [*pāh-rāhk'*], m.

Isa. 65: 4. (כתיב) *and broth* (marg. or, *pieces*) of abominable (things)

6563 פֶּרֶק *peh'-rek*, m.

Obad. 14. shouldest thou have stood in *the crossway,*
Nah 3: 1. all full of lies (and) *robbery;*

6565 פָּרַר [*pāh-rar'*].

* KAL.—*Infinitive.* *

Isa. 24:19. the earth is *clean* dissolved, (lit. *dissolving* is dissolved)

* POEL.—*Preterite.* *

Ps. 74:13. Thou *didst divide* (marg. *break*) the sea

* PILPEL.—*Future.* *

Job 16:12. *but he hath broken me asunder:* he hath

* HIPHIL.—*Preterite.* *

Gen17:14. *he hath broken* my covenant.
Nu. 15:31. and *hath broken* his commandment,
30: 8(9). *then he shall make* her vow...*of none effect:*
12(13). her husband *hath made them void;*
Deu31:16. *and break* my covenant which I have made
20. provoke me, *and break* my covenant
2Sa.15:34. *then mayest thou* for me *defeat* the counsel
Ps.119:126. *they have made void* thy law.
Isa. 24: 5. they have transgressed...*broken* the everlasting covenant.
33: 8. *he hath broken* the covenant,
Jer. 11:10. the house of Israel and the house of Judah *have broken* my covenant
31:32. my covenant they *brake,*
Eze.17:15. *or shall he break* the covenant,
16. whose covenant *he brake,*

HIPHIL.—*Infinitive.*

Lev.26:15. *that ye break* my covenant:
44. *to break* my covenant with them:
Nu. 30:12(13). if her husband hath *utterly* made them void (lit. *making void* hath made void)
15(16). if he shall *any ways* make them void (lit. *making void* shall make void)
2Sa.17:14. *to defeat* the good counsel of Ahithophel,
Ezr. 4: 5. *to frustrate* their purpose,
9:14. Should we again *break* (lit. should we turn *to break*) thy commandments,
Pro.15:22. Without counsel purposes *are disappointed:*
Eze.16:59. *in breaking* the covenant.
17:18. *by breaking* the covenant,
Zec.11:10. *that I might break* my covenant
14. *that I might break* the brotherhood

HIPHIL.—*Imperative.*

1K. 15:19. and *break* thy league with Baasha
2Ch 16: 3. go, *break* thy league with Baasha
Ps. 85: 4(5). *and cause* thine anger toward us *to cease.*

HIPHIL.—*Future.*

Nu. 30:12(13). husband *hath* utterly *made* them *void*
13(14). her husband *may make it void.*
15(16). if he *shall* any ways *make* them *void*
Jud. 2: 1. *I will* never *break* my covenant
Neh 4:15(9). *and* God *had brought* their counsel *to nought,*
Job 15: 4. Yea, thou *castest off* (marg. *makest void*) fear,
40: 8. *Wilt thou* also *disannul* my judgment?
Ecc.12: 5. *and* desire *shall fail:*
Isa. 14:27. and who *shall disannul* (it)?
Jer. 14:21. *break* not thy covenant with us.
33:20. If *ye can break* my covenant
Eze.44: 7. *and they have broken* my covenant

HIPHIL.—*Participle.*

Job 5:12. *He disappointeth* the devices of the crafty,
Isa. 44:25. *That frustrateth* the tokens of the liars,

* HOPHAL.—*Future.* *

Isa. 8:10. Take counsel together, *and it shall come to nought;*
Jer. 33:21. (Then) *may* also my covenant *be broken*
Zec.11:11. *And it was broken* in that day:

* HITHPOEL.—*Preterite.* *

Isa. 24:19. the earth *is* clean *dissolved,*

פָּרַשׂ *pāh-ras'.* 6566

* KAL.—*Preterite.* *

Nu. 4: 6. *and shall spread* over (it) a cloth
8. *And they shall spread* upon them a cloth
13. *and spread* a purple cloth thereon:
14. *and they shall spread* upon it a covering
Deu22:17. *And they shall spread* the cloth
Ru. 3: 9. *spread therefore* thy skirt over
1K. 8:38. *and spread forth* his hands toward this
2Ch. 6:29. *and shall spread forth* his hands in this
Job 11:13. *and stretch out* thine hands toward him;
36:30. *he spreadeth* his light upon it,
Ps.105:39. *He spread* a cloud for a covering;
140: 5(6). *they have spread* a net
Pro.31:20. *She stretcheth* (marg. *spreadeth*) out her
Isa. 33:23. *they could* not *spread* the sail:
Jer. 48:40. *and shall spread* his wings over Moab.
Lam. 1:10. The adversary *hath spread* out his hand
13. *he hath spread* a net for my feet,
Eze.12:13. My net *also will I spread*
17:20. *And I will spread* my net
32: 3. *I will therefore spread out* my net
Mic. 3: 3. break their bones, *and chop them in pieces*

KAL.—*Future.*

Ex. 9:29. *I will spread abroad* my hands
33. *and spread abroad* his hands
40:19. *And he spread abroad* the tent
Nu. 4: 7, 11. *they shall spread* a cloth of blue,
Deu32:11. As an eagle...*spreadeth abroad* her wings,
Jud. 8:25. *And they spread* a garment,
2Sa.17:19. the woman took *and spread* a covering
1K. 6:27. *and they stretched forth* the wings
8:22. And Solomon stood...*and spread forth* his
2K. 8:15. he took a thick cloth,...*and spread* (it) on his face,
19:14. *and spread it* before the Lord.
2Ch. 6:12, 13. *and spread forth* his hands:
Ezr. 9: 5. *and spread out* my hands unto the Lord
Job 39:26. Doth the hawk fly by thy wisdom, (and) *stretch* her wings
Ps. 44:20(21). *or stretched out* our hands to a strange
Pro.13:16. a fool *layeth open* (marg. *spreadeth*) (his)
Isa. 37:14. *and spread it* before the Lord.
Jer. 49:22. *and spread* his wings over Bozrah:
Eze. 2:10. *And he spread* it before me:
16: 8. *and I spread* my skirt over thee,
19: 8. *and spread* their net over him:
Hos. 7:12. *I will spread* my net upon them;

KAL.—*Participle.* Poel.

Ex. 25:20. the cherubims shall *stretch forth* (their)
37: 9. the cherubims *spread* (lit. were *spreading*) *out* (their) wings
1K. 8: 7. the cherubims *spread* forth (their) two
1Ch28:18. cherubims, *that spread out* (their wings),
2Ch. 3:13. these cherubims *spread themselves forth*
5: 8. the cherubims *spread forth* (their) wings
Pro 29: 5. flattereth his neighbour *spreadeth* a net
Isa. 19: 8. *and they that spread* nets upon the waters
Lam.4: 4. no man *breaketh* (it) unto them.

KAL.—*Participle.* Paül.

1K. 8:54. his hands *spread* up to heaven.
Hos. 5: 1. and a net *spread* upon Tabor.
Joel 2: 2. the morning *spread* upon the mountains:

* NIPHAL.—*Future.* *

Eze. 17:21. they that remain *shall be scattered*

* PIEL.—*Preterite.* *

Ps. 143: 6. *I stretch forth* my hands unto thee:
Isa. 25:11. *And he shall spread forth* his hands
65: 2. *I have spread out* my hands
Lam. 1:17. Zion *spreadeth forth* her hands,
Zec. 2: 6(10). *I have spread* you abroad

PIEL.—*Infinitive.*

Ps. 68:14(15). *When* the Almighty *scattered* kings
Isa. 1:15. *And when ye spread forth* your hands,

PIEL.—*Future.*

Isa. 25:11. that swimmeth *spreadeth forth* (his hands)
Jer. 4:31. the daughter of Zion, (that) bewaileth herself, (that) *spreadeth* her hands,

---

6567 פָּרַשׁ [*pāh-rash'*].

* KAL.—*Infinitive.* *

Lev. 24:12. *that* the mind of the Lord *might be shewed*

* NIPHAL.—*Participle.* *

Eze. 34:12. his sheep (that are) *scattered;*

* PUAL.—*Preterite.* *

Nu. 15:34. *it was* not *declared* what should be done

PUAL.—*Participle.*

Neh. 8: 8. in the book in the law of God *distinctly,*

* HIPHIL.—*Future.* *

Pro. 23:32. and *stingeth* like an adder.

6568 פְּרַשׁ [*p'rash*], Ch.

* PAEL.—*Participle.* Passive. *

Ezr. 4:18. hath been *plainly* read before me.

6571 פָּרָשׁ *pāh-rāhsh'*, m.

Gen50: 9. there went up with him both chariots and *horsemen:*
Ex. 14: 9. chariots of Pharaoh, *and his horsemen,*
17, 18. his chariots, *and upon his horsemen.*
23. his chariots, *and his horsemen.*
26. their chariots, and upon *their horsemen.*
28. the chariots, and *the horsemen,*
15:19. with his chariots *and with his horsemen*
Jos. 24: 6. with chariots *and horsemen*
1Sa. 8:11. for his chariots, *and* (to be) *his horsemen;*
13: 5. and six thousand *horsemen,*
2Sa. 1: 6. *horsemen* (lit. masters of *the horsemen*) followed hard after him.
8: 4. and seven hundred *horsemen,*
10:18. and forty thousand *horsemen,*
1K. 1: 5. he prepared him chariots *and horsemen,*
4:26 (5:6). and twelve thousand *horsemen.*
9:19. and cities for his *horsemen,*
22. rulers of his chariots, *and his horsemen.*
10:26. Solomon gathered together chariots *and horsemen:*
— and twelve thousand *horsemen,*
20:20. the king of Syria escaped on an horse *with the horsemen.*
2K. 2:12. chariot of Israel, *and the horsemen thereof.*
13: 7. he leave of the people...but fifty *horsemen,*
14. chariot of Israel, *and the horsemen thereof.*
18:24. trust on Egypt for chariots *and for horsemen?*
1Ch 18: 4. David took ... a thousand chariots, and seven thousand *horsemen,*
19: 6. to hire them chariots *and horsemen*
2Ch 1:14. Solomon gathered chariots *and horsemen:*
— and twelve thousand *horsemen,*
8: 6. the cities of *the horsemen,*
9. captains of his chariots *and horsemen.*
9:25. and twelve thousand *horsemen;*
12: 3. and threescore thousand *horsemen:*
16: 8. very many chariots *and horsemen?*
Ezr. 8:22. a band of soldiers *and horsemen*
Neh 2: 9. the king had sent captains...*and horsemen*
Isa. 21: 7. a chariot (with) a couple of *horsemen,*
9. a chariot...(with) a couple of *horsemen.*
22: 6. chariots of men (and) *horsemen,*
Isa. 22: 7. *and the horsemen* shall set themselves in
28:28. *nor* bruise it (with) *his horsemen.*
31: 1. in *horsemen,* because they are very strong;
36: 9. trust on Egypt for chariots *and for horsemen?*
Jer. 4:29. the noise of *the horsemen*
46: 4. get up, ye *horsemen,*
Eze. 23: 6, 12. *horsemen* riding upon horses.
26: 7. with chariots, *and with horsemen,*
10. at the noise of *the horsemen,*
27:14. with horses *and horsemen*
38: 4. thine army, horses *and horsemen,*
Dan 11:40. with chariots, *and with horsemen,*
Hos 1: 7. nor by battle, by horses, *nor by horsemen.*
Joel 2: 4. *and as horsemen,* so shall they run.
Nah. 3: 3. *The horseman* lifteth up both the bright
Hab 1: 8. and *their horsemen* shall spread themselves, *and their horsemen* shall come

---

פֶּרֶשׁ *peh'-resh,* m. 6569

Ex. 29:14. the flesh of the bullock,...*and his dung,*
Lev. 4:11. the skin of the bullock,...*and his dung*
8:17. the bullock,...his flesh, *and his dung,*
16:27. their skins, and their flesh, and *their dung.*
Nu. 19: 5. shall burn the heifer...with *her dung,*
Mal. 2: 3. spread *dung* upon your faces, (even) *the dung of* your solemn feasts;

פָּרָשָׁה [*pāh-rāh-shāh'*], f. 6575

Est. 4: 7. *the sum of* the money that Haman had
10: 2. and *the declaration of* the greatness of

פַּרְשֶׁגֶן *par-sheh'-gen,* m. 6572

Ezr. 7:11. Now this (is) *the copy of* the letter

פַּרְשֶׁגֶן *par-sheh'-gen,* Ch. m. 6573

Ezr. 4:11. This (is) *the copy of* the letter
23. Now when *the copy of* king Artaxerxes'
5: 6. *The copy of* the letter that Tatnai,

פַּרְשְׁדֹנָה *par-sh'dōh'-nāh,* m. 6574

Jud. 3:22. and *the dirt* came out. (marg. or, it came out *at the fundament*)

פַּרְשֵׁז *par-shēhz'.* 6576

* *Preterite.* *

Job 26: 9. (and) *spreadeth* his cloud upon it.

פַּרְתְּמִים *par-t'meem',* m. pl. 6579

Est. 1: 3. *the nobles* and princes of the provinces,
6: 9. one of the king's *most noble* princes,
Dan. 1: 3. of the king's seed, and of *the princes;*

פָּשָׂה *pāh-sāh'.* 6581

* KAL.—*Preterite.* *

Lev. 13: 5, 6. the plague *spread* not in the skin;
8. the scab *spreadeth* in the skin,
23, 28. if the bright spot stay in his place, (and) *spread* not,
32. (if) the scall *spread* not,
34. (if) the scall *be* not *spread*
36. if the scall *be spread*
51. if the plague *be spread*
53. the plague *be* not *spread*
55. and the plague *be* not *spread;*
14:39. (if) the plague *be spread* in the walls
44. (if) the plague *be spread* in the house,
48. the plague *hath* not *spread*

KAL.—*Infinitive.*

Lev. 13: 7. if the scab spread *much abroad* (lit. *spreading* spread)
22. if it spread *much abroad* (lit. *id.*)
27. if it be spread *much abroad* (lit. *id.*)
35. if the scall spread *much* (lit. *id.*)

KAL.—*Future.*

Lev.13: 7. if the scab *spread* much abroad
22. if *it spread* much abroad
27. if *it be spread* much abroad
35. if the scall *spread* much

6585 **פָּשַׂע** [*pāh-sag′*].

* KAL.—*Future.* *

Isa 27: 4. *I would go* through (marg. or, *march* against) them,

---

6587 **פֶּשַׂע** *peh′-sag*, m.

1Sa.20: 3. (there is) *but a step* between me and death.

6589 **פָּשַׂק** [*pāh-sak′*].

* KAL.—*Participle.* Poel. *

Pro.13: 3. *he that openeth wide* his lips

* PIEL.—*Future.* *

Eze.16:25. and *hast opened* thy feet to every one

6580 **פַּשׁ** *pash*, m.

Job 35:15. he knoweth (it) not *in* great *extremity:*

6582 **פָּשַׁח** [*pāh-shagh′*].

* PIEL.—*Future.* *

Lam. 3:11. turned aside my ways, *and pulled me in pieces:*

6584 **פָּשַׁט** *pāh-shat′*.

* KAL.—*Preterite.* *

Lev. 6:11(4). *And he shall put off* his garments,
16:23. *and shall put off* the linen garments,
Jud. 9:33. shalt rise early, *and set* upon the city:
44. *rushed* forward, and stood in the entering of the gate of the city: and the two (other) companies *ran upon*
1Sa.23:27. the Philistines *have invaded* the land.
27:10. Whither *have ye made a road* to day?
30: 1. the Amalekites *had invaded*
14. *We made an invasion* (upon) the south
2Ch 28:18. The Philistines also *had invaded*
Cant.5: 3. *I have put off* my coat;
Hos. 7: 1. troop of robbers *spoileth* (marg. *strippeth*)
Nah 3:16. cankerworm *spoileth*, (marg. or, *spreadeth himself*)

KAL.—*Infinitive.*

Isa. 32:11. *strip you*, and make you bare,

KAL.—*Future.*

Jud.20:37. the liers in wait hasted, *and rushed* upon
1Sa.19:24. *And* he *stripped* off his clothes
27: 8. David and his men went up, *and invaded*
1Ch 14: 9. the Philistines came *and spread themselves*
13. *And* the Philistines yet again *spread themselves abroad*
2Ch 25:13. *fell upon* the cities of Judah,
Job 1:17. The Chaldeans made out three bands, *and fell upon* the camels,
Eze.26:16. and *put off* their broidered garments:
44:19. *they shall put off* their garments

KAL.—*Participle.* Poel.

Neh. 4:23(17). none of us *put off* our clothes,

* PIEL.—*Infinitive.* *

1Sa.31: 8. when the Philistines came *to strip* the
2Sa.23:10. people returned after him only *to spoil.*
1Ch 10: 8. when the Philistines came *to strip* the

* HIPHIL.—*Preterite.* *

Lev. 1: 6. *And he shall flay* the burnt offering,
Job 19: 9. *He hath stripped* me of my glory,
Eze.16:39. *they shall strip* thee *also* of thy clothes,
23:26. *They shall also strip thee*
Mic. 3: 3. and *flay* their skin from off them;

HIPHIL.—*Infinitive.*

2Ch 29:34. they could not *flay* all the burnt

HIPHIL.—*Imperative.*

Nu. 20:26. *And strip* Aaron of his garments,

HIPHIL.—*Future.*

Gen37:23. *that they stript* Joseph out of his coat,
Nu. 20:28. *And* Moses *stripped* Aaron of
1Sa.31: 9. *and stripped off* his armour,
1Ch 10: 9. And *when they had stripped him*,
Job 22: 6. and *stripped* the naked of their clothing.
Hos. 2: 3(5). Lest *I strip her* naked,
Mic. 2: 8. *ye pull off* the robe with the garment

HIPHIL.—*Participle.*

2Ch 35:11. and the Levites *flayed* (them).

* HITHPAEL.—*Future.* *

1Sa.18: 4. *And* Jonathan *stripped himself*

פָּשַׁע *pāh-shag′*. 6586

* KAL.—*Preterite.* *

1K. 8:50. *they have transgressed* against thee,
2K. 3: 7. The king of Moab *hath rebelled*
8:20. In his days Edom *revolted*
2Ch 21: 8. In his days the Edomites *revolted*
Isa. 1: 2. *they have rebelled* against me.
43:27. thy teachers *have transgressed*
Jer. 2: 8. the pastors also *transgressed*
29. *ye* all *have transgressed*
3:13. *thou hast transgressed* against the Lord
33: 8. *they have transgressed* against me.
Lam.3:42. We *have transgressed* and have
Eze. 2: 3. they and their fathers *have transgressed*
18:31. whereby *ye have transgressed;*
Hos. 7:13. *they have transgressed* against me:
8: 1. and *trespassed* against my law.
Zep. 3:11. *thou hast transgressed* against me:

KAL.—*Infinitive.*

Ezr.10:13. we are many *that have transgressed*
Isa. 59:13. *In transgressing* and lying
Am. 4: 4. at Gilgal multiply *transgression;*

KAL.—*Imperative.*

Am. 4: 4. Come to Beth-el, *and transgress;*

KAL.—*Future.*

1K. 12:19. *So* Israel *rebelled* (marg. or, *fell away*) against the house of David
2K. 1: 1. *Then* Moab *rebelled* against Israel
3: 5. *that* the king of Moab *rebelled*
8:22. *Yet* Edom *revolted*
— *Then* Libnah *revolted*
2Ch 10:19. *And* Israel *rebelled* against
21:10. *So* the Edomites *revolted*
— The same time (also) *did* Libnah *revolt*
Pro.28:21. piece of bread (that) man *will transgress.*

KAL.—*Participle.* Poel.

Ps. 37:38. *But the transgressors* shall be destroyed
51:13(15). (Then) will I teach *transgressors*
Isa. 1:28. And the destruction of *the transgressors*
46: 8. (it) again to mind, *O ye transgressors.*
48: 8. *and* wast called *a transgressor*
53:12. was numbered with *the transgressors;*
— *and* made intercession *for the transgressors.*
66:24. the men *that have transgressed*
Eze.20:38. *and them that transgress* against me:
Dan. 8:23. when *the transgressors* are come
Hos14: 9(10). *but the transgressors* shall fall therein.

* NIPHAL.—*Participle.* *

Pro.18:19. A brother *offended*

פֶּשַׁע *peh′-shag*, m. 6588

Gen31:36. What (is) *my trespass?* what (is) my sin,
50:17. Forgive,...*the trespass of* thy brethren,
— forgive *the trespass of* the servants of
Ex. 22: 9(8). all manner of *trespass*,
23:21. he will not pardon *your transgressions:*
34: 7. forgiving iniquity *and transgression*
Lev.16:16. *and because of their transgressions*
21. and all *their transgressions*
Nu. 14:18. forgiving iniquity *and transgression*,

Jos. 24:19. he will not forgive *your transgressions*
1Sa. 24:11(12). neither evil *nor transgression*
25:28. forgive *the trespass of* thine handmaid:
1K. 8:50. all *their transgressions*
Job 7:21. pardon *my transgression*,
8: 4. cast them away for *their transgression*;
13:23. make me to know *my transgression*
14:17. *My transgression* (is) sealed up
31:33. If I covered *my transgressions*
33: 9. I am clean without *transgression*,
34: 6. my wound (is) incurable without *transgression*.
37. he addeth *rebellion* unto his sin,
35: 6. or (if) *thy transgressions* be multiplied,
36: 9. *and their transgressions* that they have
Ps. 5:10(11). the multitude of *their transgressions*;
19:13(14). *from the* great *transgression*.
25: 7. Remember not the sins...*nor my transgressions*:
32: 1. (he whose) *transgression* (is) forgiven,
5. I will confess *my transgressions*
36: 1(2). *The transgression of* the wicked
39: 8(9). Deliver me from all *my transgressions*:
51: 1(3). blot out *my transgressions*.
3(5). I acknowledge *my transgressions*:
59: 3(4). not (for) *my transgression*,
65: 3(4). (as for) *our transgressions*,
89:32(33). Then will I visit *their transgression*
103:12. he removed *our transgressions*
107:17. Fools because of *their transgression*,
Pro. 10:12. love covereth all *sins*.
19. there wanteth not *sin*:
12:13. The wicked is snared *by the transgression*
17: 9. He that covereth *a transgression*
19. He loveth *transgression*
19:11. his glory to pass over *a transgression*.
28: 2. *For the transgression of* a land
13. He that covereth *his sins*
24. It is no *transgression*;
29: 6. *In the transgression of* an evil man
16. *transgression* increaseth:
22. a furious man aboundeth *in transgression*.
Isa. 24:20. *the transgression thereof* shall be heavy
43:25. he that blotteth out *thy transgressions*
44:22. I have blotted out,...*thy transgressions*,
50: 1. *and for your transgressions* is your mother put away.
53: 5. he (was) wounded *for our transgressions*,
8. *for the transgression of* my people
57: 4. (are) ye not children of *transgression*,
58: 1. shew my people *their transgression*,
59:12. For *our transgressions* are multiplied
— *our transgressions* (are) with us;
20. them that turn from *transgression*
Jer. 5: 6. because *their transgressions* are many,
Lam. 1: 5. the multitude of *her transgressions*:
14. The yoke of *my transgressions*
22. all *my transgressions*:
Eze. 14:11. all *their transgressions*;
18:22. All *his transgressions* that he
28. turneth away from all *his transgressions*
30. turn...from all *your transgressions*;
31. away from you all *your transgressions*,
21:24(29). *your transgressions* are discovered,
33:10. If *our transgressions*...(be) upon us,
12. in the day of *his transgression*:
37:23. any of *their transgressions*:
39:24. *and according to their transgressions*
Dan. 8:12. *by reason of transgression*,
13. *and the transgression of* desolation,
9:24. to finish *the transgression*,
Am. 1: 3. For three *transgressions of* Damascus,
6. For three *transgressions of* Gaza,
9. For three *transgressions of* Tyrus,
11. For three *transgressions of* Edom,
13. For three *transgressions of*...Ammon,
2: 1. For three *transgressions of* Moab,
4. For three *transgressions of* Judah,
6. For three *transgressions of* Israel,
3:14. I shall visit *the transgressions of*
5:12. I know *your* manifold *transgressions*
Mic. 1: 5. *For the transgression of* Jacob
— What (is) *the transgression of* Jacob?
13. for *the transgressions of* Israel
3: 8. to declare unto Jacob *his transgression*,
6: 7. give my firstborn (for) *my transgression*,
7:18. passeth by *the transgression*

פְּשַׁר [*p'shar*], Ch. 6590

* P'AL.—*Infinitive*. *

Dan. 5:16. that thou canst *make* (marg. *interpret*) interpretations,

* PAEL.—*Participle*. *

Dan. 5:12. understanding, *interpreting* (marg. or, of *an interpreter*) of dreams,

פְּשַׁר [*p'shar*], Ch. m. 6591

Dan. 2: 4. *and* we will shew *the interpretation*.
5. the dream, *with the interpretation thereof*,
6. *and the interpretation thereof*,
— the dream, *and the interpretation thereof*.
7. and we will shew *the interpretation*
9. shew me *the interpretation thereof*.
16. *and* that he would shew...*the interpretation*.
24. *and* I will shew unto the king *the interpretation*.
25. unto the king *the interpretation*.
26. seen, *and the interpretation thereof?*
30. known *the interpretation* to the king,
36. *and* we will tell *the interpretation thereof*
45. and *the interpretation thereof* sure.
4: 6(3). *the interpretation of* the dream.
7(4). unto me *the interpretation thereof*.
9(6). have seen, *and the interpretation thereof*.
18(15). declare *the interpretation thereof*,
—(—). known unto me *the interpretation*:
19(16). *or the interpretation thereof*,
—(—). *and the interpretation thereof* to thine
24(21). This (is) *the interpretation*,
5: 7. *and* shew me *the interpretation thereof*,
8. *nor* make known to the king *the interpretation thereof*.
12. *and* he will shew *the interpretation*.
15. *and* make known unto me *the interpretation thereof*: but they could not shew *the interpretation of*
16. that thou canst make *interpretations*,
— *and* make known to me *the interpretation thereof*,
17. *and* make known to him *the interpretation*.
26. This (is) *the interpretation of*
7:16. *and* made me know *the interpretation of*

פֵּשֶׁר *pēh'-sher*, m. 6592

Ecc. 8: 1. who knoweth *the interpretation of*

פִּשְׁתָּה *pish-tāh'*, f. 6594

Ex. 9:31. *And the flax* and the barley was
— *and the flax* (was) bolled.
Isa. 42: 3. *and the* smoking *flax* shall he not quench:
43:17. they are quenched *as tow*.

פִּשְׁתֶּה *pish-teh'*, m. 6593

Lev. 13:47. a woollen...or a *linen* garment;
48. *of linen*, or of woollen;
52. in woollen or *in linen*,
59. a garment of woollen or *linen*,
Deu 22:11. a garment...of woollen *and linen*
Jos. 2: 6. *with* the stalks *of flax*, (lit. *with flax of* stalks)
Jud. 15:14. the cords...became *as flax*
Pro. 31:13. She seeketh wool, *and flax*,
Isa. 19: 9. they that work in fine *flax*,
Jer. 13: 1. Go and get thee a *linen* girdle,
Eze. 40: 3. a line of *flax* in his hand,
44:17. they shall be clothed with *linen* garments;
18. They shall have *linen* bonnets upon their heads, and shall have *linen* breeches
Hos. 2: 5(7), 9(11). my wool *and my flax*,

פַּת *path*, f. 6595

Gen 18: 5. I will fetch *a morsel of* bread,
Lev. 2: 6. Thou shalt part it *in pieces*,

Lev. 6:21(14). *the* baken *pieces* of the meat offering
Jud. 19: 5. Comfort thine heart with *a morsel of*
Ru. 2:14. dip *thy morsel* in the vinegar.
1Sa. 2:36. that I may eat *a piece of* bread.
28:22. let me set *a morsel of* bread
2Sa. 12: 3. it did eat *of his own meat*, (marg. *morsel*)
1K. 17:11. Bring me, I pray thee, *a morsel of*
Job 31:17. Or have eaten *my morsel* myself
Ps. 147:17. He casteth forth his ice *like morsels:*
Pro. 17: 1. Better (is) *a dry morsel*,
23: 8. *The morsel* (which) thou hast eaten
28:21. for *a piece of* bread

6596 **פֹּת** [*pōhth*], m.

1K. 7:50. *and the hinges* (of) gold,
Isa. 3:17. the Lord will discover *their secret parts.*

6597 **פִּתְאוֹם** *pith-ōhm'*, adv.

Nu. 6: 9. if any man die very *suddenly*
12: 4. the Lord spake *suddenly*
Jos. 10: 9. Joshua therefore came unto them *suddenly*,
11: 7. Joshua came,...against them...*suddenly*;
2Ch 29:36. the thing was (done) *suddenly.*
Job 5: 3. but *suddenly* I cursed his habitation.
9:23. If the scourge slay *suddenly*,
22:10. *sudden* fear troubleth thee;
Ps. 64: 4(5). *suddenly* do they shoot at him,
7(8). *suddenly* shall they be wounded.
Pro. 3:25. Be not afraid of *sudden* fear,
6:15. shall his calamity come *suddenly*;
7:22. He goeth after her *straightway*, (marg. *suddenly*)
24:22. their calamity shall rise *suddenly*;
Ecc. 9:12. it falleth *suddenly* upon them.
Isa. 29: 5. it shall be at an instant *suddenly.*
30:13. whose breaking cometh *suddenly*
47:11. desolation shall come upon thee *suddenly*,
48: 3. I did (them) *suddenly*,
Jer. 4:20. *suddenly* are my tents spoiled,
6:26. the spoiler shall *suddenly* come
15: 8. to fall upon it *suddenly*,
18:22. thou shalt bring a troop *suddenly*
51: 8. Babylon is *suddenly* fallen
Mal. 3: 1. *and* the Lord,...shall *suddenly* come

See 6612 **פְּתָאִים** see **פְּתִי**

6598 **פַּתְבַּג** *path-bag'*, m.

Dan 1: 5. a daily provision of the king's *meat*,
8. *with the portion of* the king's *meat*,
13. *the portion of* the king's *meat:*
15. which did eat *the portion of* the king's *meat.*
16. Melzar took away *the portion of their meat*,
11:26. they that feed *of the portion of his meat*

6599 **פִּתְגָּם** *pith-gāhm'*, m.

Est. 1:20. the king's *decree* which he shall make
Ecc. 8:11. *sentence* against an evil work

6600 **פִּתְגָם** *pith-gāhm'*, Ch. m.

Ezr. 4:17. (Then) sent the king *an answer*
5: 7. They sent *a letter* unto him,
11. And thus they returned us *answer*,
6:11. that whosoever shall alter this *word*,
Dan 3:16. to answer thee in this *matter.*
4:17(14). *This matter* (is) by the decree

6601 **פָּתָה** [*pāh-thāh'*].

* KAL.—*Future.* *

Deu 11:16. that your heart *be* not *deceived*,
Job 31:27. *And* my heart *hath been* secretly *enticed*,

KAL.—*Participle.* Poel.

Job 5: 2. *and* envy slayeth *the silly one.*
Pro. 20:19. *therefore* meddle not *with him that flattereth* (marg. or, *enticeth*)
Hos. 7:11. Ephraim also is like a *silly* dove

* NIPHAL.—*Preterite.* *

Job 31: 9. If mine heart *have been deceived*

NIPHAL.—*Future.*

Jer. 20: 7. O Lord, thou hast deceived me, *and I was deceived:* (marg. or, *enticed*)

* PIEL.—*Preterite.* *

Pro. 24:28. *and deceive* (not) with thy lips.
Jer. 20: 7. O Lord, *thou hast deceived me*,
Eze. 14: 9. I the Lord *have deceived* that prophet,

PIEL.—*Infinitive.*

2Sa. 3:25. that he came *to deceive thee*,

PIEL.—*Imperative.*

Jud. 14:15. *Entice* thy husband,
16: 5. *Entice* him, and see wherein

PIEL.—*Future.*

Ex. 22:16(15). if a man *entice* a maid
1K. 22:20. Who *shall persuade* (marg. or, *deceive*)
21. and said, I *will persuade him.*
22. And he said, *Thou shalt persuade* (him),
2Ch 18:19. Who *shall entice* Ahab
20. and said, I *will entice him.*
21. *Thou shalt entice* (him), and thou shalt
Ps. 78:36. *Nevertheless they did flatter him*
Pro. 1:10. My son, if sinners *entice thee*,
16:29. A violent man *enticeth* his neighbour,

PIEL.—*Participle.*

Hos. 2:14(16). I will *allure her*

* PUAL.—*Future.* *

Pro. 25:15. By long forbearing *is* a prince *persuaded*,
Jer. 20:10. Peradventure *he will be enticed*,
Eze. 14: 9. if the prophet *be deceived*

* HIPHIL.—*Future.* *

Gen 9:27. God *shall enlarge* (marg. or, *persuade*)

פִּתּוּחַ *pit-too'ăgh*, m. 6603

Ex. 28:11, 21, 36. (like) *the engravings of* a signet,
39: 6. as signets *are graven*, (lit. *as the engravings of* signets)
14. (like) *the engravings of* a signet,
30. (like to) *the engravings of* a signet,
1K. 6:29. *carved* figures (lit. *the engravings of* figures) of cherubims
2Ch 2: 7(6). to grave (marg. to grave *gravings*) with the cunning men
14(13). any manner of *graving*,
Ps. 74: 6. they break down *the carved work thereof*
Zec. 3: 9. I will engrave *the graving thereof*,

פְּתוֹת [*p'thōhth*], m. 6595

Eze. 13:19. handfuls of barley *and for pieces of* bread,

פָּתַח *pāh-thăgh'*. 6605

* KAL.—*Preterite.* *

Deu 20:11. if it make thee answer of peace, *and open* unto thee,
2K. 9: 3. *Then open* the door, and flee,
15:16. because *they opened* not (to him),
2Ch 29: 3. He...*opened* the doors of the house of the
Job 3: 1. After this *opened* Job his mouth,
33: 2. *I have opened* my mouth,
Ps. 37:14. The wicked *have drawn out* the sword,
78:23. and *opened* the doors of heaven,
105:41. *He opened* the rock,
109: 2. and the mouth of the deceitful *are opened* (marg. *have opened* (themselves))
Pro. 31:26. *She openeth* her mouth with wisdom;
Cant. 5: 6. I *opened* to my beloved;
Isa. 14:17. *opened* not the house of his prisoners? (marg. or, *did* not *let* his prisoners *loose* homeward)
22:22. *so he shall open*, and none shall shut;
50: 5. The Lord God *hath opened* mine ear,
Jer. 50:25. The Lord *hath opened* his armoury,
Eze. 46:12. (one) *shall then open* him the gate

KAL.—*Infinitive.*

Deu15: 8, 11. thou shalt open thine hand *wide* (lit. *opening* thou shalt open)
Neh 8: 5. *and when he opened* it,
Cant.5: 5. I rose up *to open* to my beloved;
Isa. 45: 1. *to open* before him the two leaved gates;
Eze.21:22(27). *to open* the mouth in the slaughter,
37:13. *when I have opened* your graves,
Nah 3:13. the gates of thy land shall be set *wide* open (lit. *opening* shall be opened)

KAL.—*Imperative.*

Jos. 10:22. *Open* the mouth of the cave,
2K. 13:17. *Open* the window eastward.
Ps.118:19. *Open* to me the gates of righteousness:
Pro.31: 8. *Open* thy mouth for the dumb
9. *Open* thy mouth, judge righteously,
Cant.5: 2. *Open* to me, my sister,
Isa. 26: 2. *Open ye* the gates,
Jer. 50:26. *open* her storehouses:
Zec.11: 1. *Open* thy doors, O Lebanon,

KAL.—*Future.*

Gen 8: 6. *that* Noah *opened* the window
29:31. *And* when...that Leah (was) hated, *he opened* her womb:
30:22. *and opened* her womb.
41:56. *And* Joseph *opened* all the storehouses,
42:27. *And* as one of them *opened* his sack
43:21. *that we opened* our sacks,
44:11. *and opened* every man his sack.
Ex. 2: 6. *And when she had opened* (it),
21:33. if a man *shall open* a pit,
Nu. 16:32. *And* the earth *opened* her mouth,
22:28. *And* the Lord *opened* the mouth of the ass,
26:10. *And* the earth *opened* her mouth,
Deu 15: 8, 11. *thou shalt open* thine hand wide
28:12. The Lord *shall open* unto thee
Jud. 3:25. they took a key, *and opened* (them):
4:19. *And she opened* a bottle of milk,
19:27. *and opened* the doors of the house,
1Sa. 3:15. *and opened* the doors of the house
2K. 9:10. *And he opened* the door, and fled.
13:17. *And he opened* (it).
Neh 8: 5. *And* Ezra *opened* the book
13:19. that *they should* not *be opened*
Job 11: 5. *and open* his lips against thee;
31:32. *I opened* my doors to the traveller.
32:20. *I will open* my lips and answer.
Ps. 38:13(14). a dumb man (that) *openeth* not his
39: 9(10). *I opened* not my mouth;
49: 4(5). *I will open* my dark saying
51:15(17). O Lord, *open thou* my lips;
78: 2. *I will open* my mouth in a parable:
104:28. *thou openest* thine hand,
106:17. The earth *opened* and swallowed up
Pro.24: 7. *he openeth* not his mouth
Isa. 41:18. *I will open* rivers in high places,
45: 8. *let* the earth *open*,
53: 7. *he opened* not his mouth:
— so *he openeth* not his mouth.
Eze. 3: 2. *So I opened* my mouth,
27. *I will open* thy mouth,
33:22. *and had opened* my mouth,
Dan10:16. *then I opened* my mouth, and spake,
Am. 8: 5. *that we may set forth* (marg. *open*) wheat,
Mal 3:10. *I will* not *open* you the windows

KAL.—*Participle.* Poel.

Jud. 3:25. he *opened* not the doors
Ps.145:16. *Thou openest* thine hand,
Isa. 22:22. and none *shall open*.
Jer. 13:19. and none *shall open* (them):
Eze.25: 9. I *will open* the side of Moab
37:12. I *will open* your graves,

KAL.—*Participle.* Paül.

Nu. 19:15. And every *open* vessel,
Jos. 8:17. they left the city *open*,
1K. 8:29, 52. That thine eyes may be *open*
2Ch 6:20. That thine eyes may be *open*
40. let, I beseech thee, thine eyes be *open*,
7:15. Now mine eyes shall be *open*,
Neh 1: 6. and thine eyes *open*,
6: 5. with an *open* letter in his hand;
Job 29:19. My root (was) *spread out*
Ps. 5: 9(10). their throat (is) an *open* sepulchre;
Jer. 5:16. Their quiver (is) as an *open* sepulchre,
Eze.21:28(33). The sword, the sword (is) *drawn*:

* NIPHAL.—*Preterite.* *

Gen 7:11. the windows of heaven *were opened.*
Isa. 5:27. neither *shall* the girdle of their loins *be loosed*,
24:18. the windows from on high *are open*,
Eze. 1: 1. the heavens *were opened*,
Nah 2: 6(7). The gates of the rivers *shall be opened*,
3:13. the gates of thy land *shall be set* wide *open*

NIPHAL.—*Infinitive.*

Isa. 51:14. exile hasteneth *that he may be loosed*,

NIPHAL.—*Future.*

Neh. 7: 3. *Let* not the gates of Jerusalem *be opened*
Job 12:14. *there can be* no *opening.*
32:19. as wine (which) *hath* no *vent;* (marg. *is* not *opened*)
Isa. 35: 5. the ears of the deaf *shall be unstopped.*
Jer. 1:14. an evil *shall break forth* (marg. *be opened*)
Eze.24:27. *shall* thy mouth *be opened*
33:22. *and* my mouth *was opened*,
44: 2. *it shall* not *be opened*,
46: 1. on the sabbath *it shall be opened*,
— the day of the new moon *it shall be opened.*

NIPHAL.—*Participle.*

Zec.13: 1. there shall be a fountain *opened*

* PIEL.—*Preterite.* *

Ex. 28: 9. *and grave* on them the names of
36. *and grave* upon it,
2Ch 3: 7. *and graved* cherubims on the walls.
Job 12:18. *He looseth* the bond of kings,
30:11. *he hath loosed* my cord,
39: 5. who *hath loosed* the bands of the wild ass?
41:14(6). Who *can open* the doors of his face?
Ps. 30:11(12). *thou hast put off* my sackcloth,
116:16. *thou hast loosed* my bonds.
Cant.7:12(13). (whether) the tender grape *appear*, (marg. *open*)
Isa. 20: 2. *and loose* the sackcloth from off
48: 8. thine ear *was* not *opened:*
60:11. *Therefore* thy gates *shall be open*
Jer. 40: 4. And now, behold, *I loose thee*

PIEL.—*Infinitive.*

2Ch 2: 7(6). *to grave* with the cunning men
14(13). *also to grave* any manner of graving,
Ps.102:20(21). *to loose* those that are appointed to death;
Isa. 58: 6. *to loose* the bands of wickedness,

PIEL.—*Future.*

Gen24:32. *and he ungirded* his camels,
Ex. 28:11. *shalt thou engrave* the two stones
1K. 7:36. *For* on the plates...*he graved*
Job 38:31. or *loose* the bands of Orion?
Ps.105:20. the ruler of the people, *and let him go free.*
Isa. 28:24. *doth he open* and break the clods
45: 1. *I will loose* the loins of kings,

PIEL.—*Participle.*

1K. 20:11. *as he that putteth it off.*
Zec. 3: 9. I *will engrave* the graving thereof,

* PUAL.—*Participle.* *

Ex. 39: 6. *graven*, as signets are graven,

* HITHPAEL.—*Imperative.* *

Isa. 52: 2. *loose thyself* from the bands of thy neck,

פתח פְּתַח [*p'thagh*], Ch. 6606

* P'IL.—*Preterite.* *

Dan 7:10. and the books *were opened.*

P'IL.—*Participle.*

Dan 6:10(11). his windows *being open*

פתח פֶּתַח *peh'-thagh*, m. 6607

Gen 4: 7. sin lieth *at the door.*
6:16. *and the door of* the ark
18: 1. he sat in *the* tent *door*
2. ran to meet them *from the* tent *door*,
10. Sarah heard (it) in *the* tent *door*,
19: 6. Lot went out *at the door*
11. the men that (were) at *the door*
they wearied themselves to find *the door.*

Gen 38:14. and sat *in an* open *place*, (marg. *in the door of* eyes, or, of Enajim)
43:19. at *the door of* the house,
Ex. 12:22. go out *at the door of* his house
23. the Lord will pass over *the door*,
26:36. thou shalt make an hanging *for the door*
29: 4. unto *the door of* the tabernacle
11, 32. (by) *the door of* the tabernacle
42. (at) *the door of* the tabernacle
33: 8. every man (at) his tent *door*,
9. (at) *the door of* the tabernacle,
10. (at) *the* tabernacle *door :*
— every man (in) his tent *door*.
35:15. the hanging for *the door at the entering in of* the tabernacle,
36:37. an hanging *for the* tabernacle *door*
38: 8. (at) *the door of* the tabernacle
30. to *the door of* the tabernacle
39:38. the hanging for *the* tabernacle *door*,
40: 5. the hanging of *the door*
6. before *the door of* the tabernacle
12. unto *the door of* the tabernacle
28. the hanging (at) *the door*
29. (by) *the door of* the tabernacle
Lev. 1: 3. at *the door of* the tabernacle
5. (by) *the door of* the tabernacle
3: 2. (at) *the door of* the tabernacle
4: 4. unto *the door of* the tabernacle
7, 18. (at) *the door of* the tabernacle
8: 3, 4. unto *the door of* the tabernacle
31. (at) *the door of* the tabernacle
33. *And* ye shall not go *out of the door*
35. *Therefore* shall ye abide (at) *the door*
10: 7. *And* ye shall not go out *from the door of*
12: 6. unto *the door of* the tabernacle
14:11. (at) *the door of* the tabernacle
23. unto *the door of* the tabernacle
38. to *the door of* the house,
15:14. unto *the door of* the tabernacle
29. to *the door of* the tabernacle
16: 7. (at) *the door of* the tabernacle
17: 4, 5, 9. unto *the door of* the tabernacle
6. (at) *the door of* the tabernacle
19:21. unto *the door of* the tabernacle
Nu. 3:25. the hanging for *the door of*
26. the curtain for *the door of*
4:25. for *the door of* the tabernacle
26. the hanging for *the door of*
6:10. to *the door of* the tabernacle
13. unto *the door of* the tabernacle
18. (at) *the door of* the tabernacle
10: 3. at *the door of* the tabernacle
11:10. every man *in the door of* his tent:
12: 5. (in) *the door of* the tabernacle,
16:18. in *the door of* the tabernacle
19. unto *the door of* the tabernacle
27. in *the door of* their tents,
50(17:15) & 20:6. unto *the door of* the tabernacle
25: 6. (before) *the door of* the tabernacle
27: 2. (by) *the door of* the tabernacle
Deu 22:21. to *the door of* her father's house,
31:15. over *the door of* the tabernacle.
Jos. 8:29. at *the entering of* the gate
19:51. at *the door of* the tabernacle
20: 4. at *the entering of* the gate
Jud. 4:20. Stand in *the door of* the tent,
9:35. stood in *the entering of* the gate
40. unto *the entering of* the gate.
44. stood in *the entering of* the gate
52. unto *the door of* the tower
18:16. by *the entering of* the gate.
17. the priest stood in *the entering of*
19:26. at *the door of* the man's house
27. (at) *the door of* the house,
1 Sa. 2:22. (at) *the door of* the tabernacle
2Sa. 10: 8. at *the entering in of* the gate:
11: 9. Uriah slept at *the door of* the king's house
23. unto *the entering of* the gate.
1K. 6: 8. *The door* for the middle chamber
31. *the entering of* the oracle
33. *for the door of* the temple
7: 5. all *the doors* and posts
14: 6. as she came in *at the door*,
27. *the door of* the king's house.
17:10. he came to *the gate of* the city,
19:13. in *the entering in of* the cave.
1K. 22:10. in *the entrance of* the gate of Samaria;
2K. 4:15. she stood *in the door*.
5: 9. at *the door of* the house of Elisha.
7: 3 & 10:8. at *the entering in of* the gate:
23: 8. in *the entering in of* the gate
1Ch 9:21. porter of *the door of* the tabernacle
19: 9. before *the gate of* the city:
2Ch 4:22. *and the entry of* the house,
12:10. *the entrance of* the king's house.
18: 9. at *the entering in of* the gate
Neh. 3:20. *the door of* the house of Eliashib
21. *from the door of* the house
Est. 5: 1. over against *the gate of* the house.
Job 31: 9. laid wait at my neighbour's *door*;
34. went not out of *the door?*
Ps. 24: 7. be ye lift up, ye everlasting *doors*;
9. lift (them) up, ye everlasting *doors*;
Pro. 1:21. *in the openings of* the gates:
5: 8. come not nigh *the door of* her house:
8: 3. the coming in at *the doors*.
34. waiting at the posts of *my doors*.
9:14. For she sitteth *at the door of*
17:19. he that exalteth *his gate*
Cant. 7:13(14). at *our gates* (are) all manner of
Isa. 3:26. *her gates* shall lament and mourn;
13: 2. *the gates of* the nobles.
Jer. 1:15. at *the entering of* the gates of Jerusalem,
19: 2. by *the entry of* the east gate,
26:10. *in the entry* (marg. or, *door*) *of* the new gate
36:10. *at the entry of* the new gate
43: 9. *at the entry of* Pharaoh's house
Eze. 8: 3. to *the door of* the inner gate
7. to *the door of* the court;
8. when I had digged...behold a *door*.
14. he brought me to *the door of*
16. at *the door of* the temple
10:19. at *the door of* the east gate
11: 1. *at the door of* the gate
33:30. *and in the doors of* the houses,
40:11. the breadth of *the entry of*
13. *door* against *door*.
38. the chambers and *the entries thereof*
40. *to the entry of* the north gate,
41: 2. the breadth of *the door* (was) ten cubits; and the sides of *the door*
3. and measured the post of *the door*, two cubits; *and the door*, six cubits; and the breadth of *the door*,
11. *And the doors of* the side chambers
— one *door* toward the north, *and* another *door* toward the south:
17. To that above *the door*,
20. From the ground unto above *the door*
42: 2. an hundred cubits (was) *the* north *door*,
4. *and their doors* toward the north.
11. *and according to their doors*.
12. *And according to the doors of*
— *a door* in the head of the way,
46: 3. at *the door of* this gate
47: 1. unto *the door of* the house;
Hos. 2:15(17). the valley of Achor *for a door of* hope:
Mic. 5: 6(5). *in the entrances thereof*: (marg. or, *with her own naked swords*)
7: 5. keep *the doors of* thy mouth

פֶּתַח *pēh'-thagh*, m 6608

Ps. 119:130. *The entrance of* thy words giveth light:

פִּתְחוֹן *pith-ghōhn'*, m. 6610

Eze. 16:63. and never *open* thy mouth (lit. *opening of* the mouth may not be to thee) any more
29:21. I will give thee *the opening of* the mouth

פְּתִחוֹת *p'thee-ghōhth'*, f. pl. 6609

Ps. 55:21(22). yet (were) they *drawn swords*.

פְּתִי [*p'thee*], adj. 6612

Ps. 19: 7(8). making wise *the simple*.
116: 6. The Lord preserveth *the simple*:
119:130. it giveth understanding *unto the simple*.

Pro. 1: 4. To give subtilty *to the simple*,
22. How long, *ye simple ones*, will ye love *simplicity?*
32. the turning away of *the simple*
7: 7. beheld *among the simple ones*,
8: 5. *O ye simple*, understand wisdom:
9: 4, 16. (is) *simple*, let him turn in hither:
6. Forsake *the foolish*, and live;
14:15. *The simple* believeth every word:
18. *The simple* inherit folly:
19:25. *and the simple* will beware:
21:11. *the simple* is made wise:
22: 3. *but the simple* pass on, and are
27:12. *the simple* pass on, (and) are punished.
Eze.45:20. *and for* (him that is) *simple*:

6613 **פְּתָי** *[p'thāh'y]*, Ch. m.

Ezr. 6: 3. *the breadth thereof* threescore cubits;
Dan. 3: 1. *the breadth thereof* six cubits:

6614 **פְּתִיגִיל** *p'thee-geel'*, m.

Isa. 3:24. of *a stomacher* a girding of sackcloth;

6615 **פְּתַיּוּת** *p'thahy-yooth'*, f.

Pro. 9:13. (she is) *simple*, and knoweth nothing.

6616 **פָּתִיל** *pāh-theel'*, m.

Gen38:18. Thy signet, *and thy bracelets*,
25. the signet, *and bracelets*, and staff.
Ex. 28:28. *with a lace of* blue,
37. thou shalt put it on *a* blue *lace*,
39: 3. did beat the gold...and cut (it into) *wires*,
21. bind the breastplate...*with a lace of*
31. they tied unto it *a lace of* blue,
Nu. 15:38. put upon the fringe...*a ribband of* blue:
19:15. open vessel, which hath no covering *bound*
Jud.16: 9. he brake the withs, as *a thread of* tow
Eze.40: 3. *with a line of* flax in his hand,

6617 **פָּתַל** *[pāh-thal']*.

* NIPHAL.—*Preterite.* *

Gen30: 8. *have I wrestled* with my sister,

NIPHAL.—*Participle.*

Job 5:13. the counsel of *the froward*
Pro. 8: 8. nothing *froward* (marg. *wreathed*) or perverse in them.

* HITHPAEL.—*Future.* *

2Sa. 22:27. *thou wilt shew thyself unsavoury.* (marg. or, *wrestle*)
Ps. 18:26(27). *thou wilt shew thyself froward.* (marg. or, *wrestle*)

6618 **פְּתַלְתֹּל** *p'thal-tōhl'*, adj.

Deu32: 5. a perverse and *crooked* generation.

6620 **פֶּתֶן** *peh'-then*, m.

Deu32:33. and the cruel venom of *asps*.
Job 20:14. the gall of *asps* within him.
16. He shall suck the poison of *asps*:
Ps. 58: 4(5). the deaf *adder* (marg. or, *asp*) (that) stoppeth her ear;
91:13. Thou shalt tread upon the lion *and adder*: (marg. or, *asp*)
Isa. 11: 8. on the hole of *the asp*,

6621 **פֶּתַע** *peh'-thag*, m.

Nu. 6: 9. if any man die *very* suddenly (lit. *in a moment* suddenly)
35:22. if he thrust him *suddenly*
Pro. 6:15. *suddenly* shall he be broken
29: 1. shall *suddenly* be destroyed,
Isa. 29: 5. it shall be *at an instant* suddenly.
30:13. whose breaking cometh suddenly *at an instant*.
Hab 2: 7. Shall they not rise up *suddenly*

פָּתַר *pāh-thar'*. 6622

* KAL.—*Preterite.* *

Gen40:16. that *the interpretation* was good, (lit. that *he had given a* good *interpretation*)
22. as Joseph *had interpreted*
41:12. according to his dream *he did interpret.*
13. as *he interpreted* to us,

KAL.—*Infinitive.*

Gen41:15. understand a dream *to interpret* it.

KAL.—*Future.*

Gen41:12. *and he interpreted* to us our dreams;

KAL.—*Participle.* Poel.

Gen40: 8. *and* (there is) no *interpreter* of it.
41: 8. there was none *that could interpret*
15. *and* (there is) none *that can interpret*

פִּתְרוֹן *pith-rōhn'*, m. 6623

Gen40: 5. *according to the interpretation of* his dream,
8. (Do) not *interpretations* (belong) to God?
12. This (is) *the interpretation of it*:
18. This (is) *the interpretation thereof*:
41:11. *according to the interpretation of*

פַּתְשֶׁגֶן *path-sheh'-gen*, m. 6572

Est. 3:14. *The copy of* the writing
4: 8. *the copy of* the writing
8:13. *The copy of* the writing

פָּתַת *[pāh-thath']*. 6626

* KAL.—*Infinitive.* *

Lev. 2: 6. *Thou shalt part* it in pieces,

צ *tzāh-dēh'*.

The Eighteenth Letter of the Alphabet.

צֵאָה *[tzēh-āh']*, f. 6627

Deu23:13(14). and cover *that which cometh from thee*:
Eze. 4:12. with dung *that cometh out of* man,

צֹאָה see **צוֹאָה** See 6675

צְאוֹן *[tz'ōhn]*, com. 6629

Ps.144:13. (כתיב) *our sheep* may bring forth thousands

צֶאֱלִים *tzeh-ĕleem'*, m. pl. 6628

Job 40:21. He lieth under *the shady trees*,
22. *The shady trees* cover him

צֹאן *tzōhn*, com. 6629

Gen 4: 2. Abel was a keeper of *sheep*,
4. the firstlings of *his flock*
12:16. he had *sheep*, and oxen,
13: 5. *flocks*, and herds, and tents.
20:14. Abimelech took *sheep*,
21:27. Abraham took *sheep* and oxen,
28. seven ewe lambs of *the flock*
24:35. he hath given him *flocks*,
26:14. he had possession of *flocks*,
27: 9. Go now to *the flock*,
29: 2. three flocks of *sheep* lying by it;
3. and watered *the sheep*,
6. Rachel...cometh with *the sheep*.
7. water ye *the sheep*,
8. then we water *the sheep*.
9. Rachel came with her father's *sheep*:
10. *the sheep of* Laban
— and watered *the flock of* Laban
30:31. I will again feed (and) keep *thy flock*:
32. I will pass through all *thy flock* to day,

Gen30:36. Jacob fed the rest of Laban's *flocks.*
38. he set the rods...before *the flocks*
— when *the flocks* came to drink,
39. *the flocks* conceived before the rods, and brought forth *cattle* ringstraked,
40. and set the faces of *the flocks* toward the ringstraked, and all the brown *in the flock of* Laban;
— and put them not unto Laban's *cattle.*
41. *the* stronger *cattle* did conceive,
— before the eyes of *the cattle*
42. when *the cattle* were feeble,
43. and had much *cattle,*
31: 4. to the field unto *his flock,*
8. all *the cattle* bare speckled:
— then bare all *the cattle* ringstraked.
10. the time that *the cattle* conceived,
— the rams which leaped upon *the cattle*
12. the rams which leap upon *the cattle*
19. Laban went to shear *his sheep:*
38. the rams of *thy flock*
41. and six years *for thy cattle:*
43. *and* (these) *cattle* (are) *my cattle,*
32: 5(6). I have oxen, and asses, *flocks,* and
7(8). *the flocks,* and herds, and the camels,
33:13. *and the flocks* and herds
— all *the flock* will die.
34:28. They took *their sheep,*
37: 2. Joseph,...was feeding *the flock*
12. brethren went to feed their father's *flock*
14. well with thy brethren, and well with *the flocks;*
38:12. went up unto *his sheep*shearers
13. to shear *his sheep.*
17. a kid from *the flock.*
45:10. *and thy flocks,* and thy herds,
46:32. And the men (are) *sh*epherds, (lit. feeders of *sheep*)
— *and* they have brought *their flocks,*
34. every *sh*epherd (is) an abomination unto
47: 1. my brethren, *and their flocks,*
3. Thy servants (are) *sh*epherds,
4. have no pasture *for* their *flocks;*
17. for horses, and for the flocks, (lit. cattle of *sheep*)
50: 8. their little ones, *and their flocks,*
Ex. 2:16. to water their father's *flock.*
17. Moses stood up...and watered *their flock.*
19. and watered *the flock.*
3: 1. Moses kept *the flock of* Jethro
— he led *the flock* to the backside of the
9: 3. upon the oxen, *and upon the sheep:*
10: 9. *with our flocks* and with our herds
24. let *your flocks* and your herds be stayed:
12:21. Draw out and take you *a lamb*
32. Also take *your flocks*
38. *and flocks,* and herds,
20:24. *thy sheep,* and thine oxen:
22: 1(21:37). and four *sheep* for a sheep.
30(29). with thine oxen, (and) *with thy sheep:*
34: 3. neither let *the flocks* nor herds feed
Lev. 1: 2. of the herd, and of *the flock.*
10. if his offering (be) of *the flocks,*
3: 6. if his offering...(be) of *the flock;*
5: 6. a female from *the flock,*
15. a ram without blemish out of *the flocks,*
18 & 6:6(5:25). a ram without blemish out of *the flock,*
22:21. a freewill offering in beeves or *sheep,* (marg. or, *goats*)
27:32. of the herd, *or* of *the flock,*
Nu. 11:22. Shall *the flocks* and the herds be slain
15: 3. of the herd, or of *the flock:*
22:40. Balak offered oxen *and sheep,*
27:17. *as sheep* which have no shepherd.
31:28. of the asses, and of *the sheep:*
30. of the asses, and of *the flocks,* (marg. or, *goats*)
32. six hundred thousand and seventy thousand and five thousand *sheep,*
36. three hundred thousand and seven and thirty thousand and five hundred *sheep:*
37. the Lord's tribute of *the sheep*
43. was 337500 *sheep,*
32:16. We will build *sheep*folds
36. and folds for *sheep.*
Deu 7:13. and the flocks of *thy sheep,*
Deu. 8:13. thy herds *and thy flocks*
12: 6. firstlings of your herds *and of your flocks*
17. the firstlings of thy herds *or of thy flock,*
21. of thy herd *and of thy flock,*
14:23. the firstlings of thy herds *and of thy flocks*
26. for oxen, *or for sheep,*
15:14. *out of thy flock,* and out of thy floor,
19. of thy herd and *of thy flock*
— the firstling of *thy sheep.*
16: 2. of *the flock* and the herd,
18: 4. the first of the fleece of *thy sheep,*
28: 4, 18, 51. flocks of *thy sheep.*
31. *thy sheep* (shall be) given unto
32:14. Butter of kine, and milk of *sheep,*
Jos. 7:24. his asses, and *his sheep,*
1Sa. 8:17. the tenth of *your sheep:*
14:32. *sheep,* and oxen, and calves,
15: 9. and the best of *the sheep,*
14. this bleating of *the sheep* in mine ears,
15. spared the best of *the sheep*
21. the people took...*sheep* and oxen,
16:11. behold, he keepeth *the sheep.*
19. David...which (is) *with the sheep.*
17:15. David went...to feed his father's *sheep*
20. and left *the sheep* with a keeper,
28. with whom hast thou left those few *sheep*
34. Thy servant kept his father's *sheep,*
24: 3(4). he came to the *sheep*cotes
25: 2. he had three thousand *sheep,*
— he was shearing *his sheep* in Carmel.
4. Nabal did shear *his sheep.*
16. we were with them keeping *the sheep.*
18. five *sheep* ready dressed,
27: 9. and took away *the sheep,*
30:20. David took all *the flocks*
2Sa. 7: 8. from following *the sheep,*
12: 2. exceeding many *flocks* and herds:
4. he spared to take *of his own flock*
17:29. honey, and butter, *and sheep,*
24:17. these *sheep,* what have they done?
1K. 1: 9. Adonijah slew *sheep*
19, 25. *and sheep* in abundance,
4:23(5:3). and an hundred *sheep,* beside harts,
8: 5. sacrificing *sheep* and oxen,
63. *and* an hundred and twenty thousand *sheep.*
22:17. *as sheep* that have not a shepherd:
2K. 5:26. and vineyards, *and sheep,*
1Ch. 4:39. to seek pasture *for their flocks.*
41. pasture there *for their flocks.*
5:21. of *sheep* two hundred and fifty thousand,
12:40. and oxen, *and sheep* abundantly:
17: 7. from following *the sheep,*
21:17. these *sheep,* what have they done?
27:31. over *the flocks* (was) Jaziz
2Ch. 5: 6. king Solomon,...sacrificed *sheep*
7: 5. *and* an hundred and twenty thousand *sheep:*
14:15(14). carried away *sheep* and camels
15:11. *and* seven thousand *sheep.*
17:11. the Arabians brought him *flocks,*
18: 2. Ahab killed *sheep* and oxen
16. *as sheep* that have no shepherd:
29:33. *and* three thousand *sheep.*
30:24. and seven thousand *sheep;*
— *and* ten thousand *sheep:*
31: 6. the tithe of oxen *and sheep,*
32:29. possessions of *flocks* and herds
35: 7. Josiah gave to the people, of *the flock,*
Ezr. 10:19. (they offered) a ram of *the flock*
Neh 3: 1. they builded the *sheep* gate;
32. unto the *sheep* gate
5:18. one ox (and) six choice *sheep;*
10:36(37). firstlings of our herds *and of our flocks,*
12:39. unto the *sheep* gate:
Job 1: 3. seven thousand *sheep,*
16. The fire of God...hath burned *up the sheep,*
21:11. their little ones *like a flock,*
30: 1. the dogs of *my flock.*
42:12. he had fourteen thousand *sheep,*
Ps. 44:11(12). Thou hast given us *like sheep* (appointed) *for* meat; (marg. *as sheep of* meat)
22(23). we are counted *as sheep for* the
49:14(15). *Like sheep* they are laid in the grave:
65:13(14). The pastures are clothed with *flocks;*

Ps. 74: 1. *against the sheep of* thy pasture?
77:20(21). Thou leddest thy people *like a flock*
78:52. his own people to go forth *like sheep*,
70. and took him from the *sheep*folds:
79:13. we thy people *and sheep of* thy pasture
80: 1(2). thou that leadest Joseph *like a flock*;
95: 7. *and the sheep of* his hand.
100: 3. *and the sheep of* his pasture.
107:41. maketh (him) families *like a flock*.
114: 4. the little hills like lambs. (lit. sons of *sheep*)
6. ye little hills, like lambs? (lit. sons of *sheep*)
144:13. (that) *our sheep* may bring forth thousands
Pro. 27:23. know the state of *thy flocks*,
Ecc. 2: 7. possessions of great *and small cattle*
Cant. 1: 8. by the footsteps of *the flock*,
Isa. 7:21. shall nourish a young cow, and two *sheep*;
13:14. *and as a sheep* that no man taketh up:
22:13. slaying oxen, and killing *sheep*,
53: 6. All we *like sheep* have gone astray;
60: 7. All *the flocks of* Kedar
61: 5. strangers shall stand and feed *your flocks*,
63:11. the shepherd of *his flock*?
65:10. Sharon shall be a fold of *flocks*,
Jer. 3:24. *their flocks* and their herds,
5:17. *thy flocks* and thine herds:
12: 3. pull them out *like sheep* for the slaughter,
13:20. thy beautiful *flock*?
23: 1. pastors that destroy and scatter *the sheep*
2. Ye have scattered *my flock*,
3. I will gather the remnant of *my flock*
25:34. ye principal of *the flock*:
35. nor the principal of *the flock*
36. an howling of the principal of *the flock*,
31:12. the young of *the flock*
33:12. shepherds causing (their) *flocks* to lie
13. the cities of Judah, shall *the flocks* pass
49:20. the least of *the flock* shall draw them out:
29. Their tents *and their flocks*
50: 6. My people hath been lost *sheep*:
8. as the he goats before *the flocks*.
45. the least of *the flock* shall draw
Eze. 24: 5. Take the choice of *the flock*,
25: 5. a couchingplace for *flocks*:
34: 2. should not the shepherds feed *the flocks*?
3. ye feed not *the flock*.
6. *My sheep* wandered through
— *my flock* was scattered
8. *my flock* became a prey, and *my flock* became meat
— search for *my flock*,
— and fed not *my flock*;
10. I will require *my flock*
— to cease from feeding *the flock*;
— I will deliver *my flock*
11. I, will both search *my sheep*, and
12. in the day that he is among *his sheep*
— so will I seek out *my sheep*,
15. I will feed *my flock*,
17. (as for) you, *O my flock*,
19. *And* (as for) *my flock*,
22. Therefore will I save *my flock*,
31. And ye *my flock*, *the flock of* my pasture,
36:37. I will increase them...*like a flock*.
38. *As the* holy *flock*, *as the flock of* Jerusalem
— the waste cities be filled with *flocks of*
43:23. a ram out of *the flock* without blemish.
25. and a ram out of *the flock*, without
45:15. And one lamb out of *the flock*,
Hos. 5: 6. They shall go *with their flocks*
Joel 1:18. the flocks of *sheep* are made desolate.
Am. 6: 4. the lambs *out of the flock*,
7:15. as I followed *the flock*,
Jon. 3: 7. herd *nor flock*, taste any thing:
Mic. 2:12. together *as the sheep of* Bozrah,
5: 8(7). young lion among the flocks of *sheep*: (marg. or, *goats*)
7:14. *the flock of* thine heritage,
Hab. 3:17. *the flock* shall be cut off
Zep. 2: 6. and folds for *flocks*.
Zec. 9:16. *as the flock of* his people:
10: 2. they went their way as *a flock*,
11: 4. Feed *the flock of* the slaughter;
7. I will feed *the flock of* slaughter,
— O poor of *the flock*.
— and I fed *the flock*.
Zec. 11:11. the poor of *the flock*
17. shepherd that leaveth *the flock*?
13: 7. *the sheep* shall be scattered:

צֶאֱצָאִים *tzeh-ĕtzāh-eem'*, m. pl. 6631

Job 5:25. *and thine offspring* as the grass
21: 8. *and their offspring* before their eyes.
27:14. *and his offspring* shall not be satisfied
31: 8. *yea, let my offspring* be rooted out.
Isa. 22:24. *the offspring* and the issue,
34: 1. all things *that come forth of it*.
42: 5. *and that which cometh out* of it;
44: 3. my blessing upon *thine offspring*:
48:19. *and the offspring of* thy bowels
61: 9. *and their offspring* among the people:
65:23. *and their offspring* with them.

צָב *tzāhv*, m. 6632

Lev. 11:29. *and the tortoise* after his kind,
Nu. 7: 3. six *covered* wagons,
Isa. 66:20. chariots, *and in litters*, (marg. or, *coaches*)

צָבָא [*tzāh-vāh'*]. 6633

* KAL.—*Preterite.* *

Ex. 38: 8. *assembled* (at) the door of the tabernacle
Zec. 14:12. the people that *have fought*

KAL.—*Infinitive.*

Nu. 4:23. *to perform* the service, (marg. *war* the warfare)
8:24. *to wait upon* (marg. *war*) the service
Isa. 31: 4. *to fight* for mount Zion,

KAL.—*Future.*

Nu. 31: 7. *And they warred* against the Midianites,

KAL.—*Participle.* Poel.

Ex. 38: 8. the lookingglasses of (the women) *assembling*, (marg. *assembling by troops*)
Nu. 31:42. the men *that warred*,
1Sa. 2:22. the women *that assembled* (marg. *assembled by troops*)
Isa. 29: 7. the nations *that fight* against Ariel,
8. nations be, *that fight* against mount Zion.

* HIPHIL.—*Participle.* *

2K. 25:19. the principal scribe of the host, *which mustered*
Jer. 52:25. principal scribe of the host, *who mustered*

צָבָא *tzāh-vāh'*, m. 6635

Gen 2: 1. and all *the host of them*.
21:22, 32. Phichol the chief captain of *his host*
26:26. the chief captain of *his army*.
Ex. 6:26. from...Egypt according to *their armies*.
7: 4. and bring forth *mine armies*,
12:17. brought *your armies* out of the land of
41. *the hosts of* the Lord went out
51. out of the land of Egypt by *their armies*.
Nu. 1: 3. all that are able to go forth *to war*
— number them *by their armies*.
20, 22, 24, 26, 28, 30, 32, 34, 36, 38, 40, 42, 45. all that were able to go forth *to war*;
52. standard, *throughout their hosts*.
2: 3. pitch *throughout their armies*:
4, 13, 15, 19, 21, 23, 26, 28, 30. *And his host*, and those that were numbered
6, 8, 11. *And his host*, and those that were numbered
9. *throughout their armies*. These shall first
10. of Reuben *according to their armies*:
16. *throughout their armies*. And they shall
18. of Ephraim *according to their armies*:
24. *throughout their armies*. And they shall
25. on the north side *by their armies*:
32. the camps *throughout their hosts*
4: 3. all that enter *into the host*,
23. all that enter in to perform *the service*, (marg. war *the warfare*)
30, 35, 39, 43. every one that entereth *into the service*, (marg. *warfare*)

Nu. 8:24. *the service* (marg. *warfare*) of the tabernacle
25. they shall cease *waiting upon* (marg. return *from the warfare of*) the service
10:14. *according to their armies:* and over *his host* (was) Nahshon
15, 16, 19, 20, 23, 24, 26, 27. over *the host of* the
18. *according to their armies:* and over *his host*
22. *according to their armies* and over *his host*
25. *throughout their hosts:* and over *his host*
28. of Israel *according to their armies,*
26: 2. all that are able to go *to war*
31: 3. Arm some of yourselves *unto the war,*
4. shall ye send *to the war.*
5. twelve thousand armed *for war.*
6. Moses sent them *to the war,*
— *to the war,* with the holy instruments,
14. the captains...which came *from* the battle. (marg. *from the host of* war)
21. the men of *war* which went to the battle,
27. who went out *to battle,*
28. the men of war which went out *to battle:*
32. the prey which the men of *war* had caught,
36. them that went out *to war,*
48. thousands of *the host,*
53. the men of *war* had taken spoil,
32:27. every man armed *for war,*
33: 1. *with their armies* under the hand
Deu 4:19. all *the host of* heaven,
17: 3. any of *the host of* heaven,
20: 9. make captains of *the armies*
24: 5. he shall not go out *to war,*
Jos. 4:13. About forty thousand prepared for *war*
5:14. captain of *the host of* the Lord
15. the captain of the Lord's *host*
22:12. to go up *to war* against them.
33. to go up against them *in battle,*
Jud. 4: 2. the captain of *whose host*
7. Sisera, the captain of Jabin's *army,*
8: 6. that we should give bread *unto thine army?*
9:29. Increase *thine army,*
1Sa. 1: 3. sacrifice unto the Lord of *hosts* in Shiloh.
11. and said, O Lord of *hosts,* if thou
4: 4. of the covenant of the Lord of *hosts,*
12: 9. captain of *the host of* Hazor,
14:50. the captain of *his host* (was) Abner,
15: 2. Thus saith the Lord of *hosts,*
17:45. to thee in the name of the Lord of *hosts,*
55. Abner, the captain of *the host,*
26: 5. the son of Ner, the captain of *his host:*
28: 1. gathered their armies...*for warfare,*
2Sa. 2: 8. Abner...captain of Saul's *host,*
3:23. Joab and all *the host*
5:10. and the Lord God of *hosts* (was) with
6: 2. called by the name of the Lord of *hosts*
18. in the name of the Lord of *hosts.*
7: 8. Thus saith the Lord of *hosts,*
26. The Lord of *hosts* (is) the God over
27. For thou, O Lord of *hosts,* God of Israel,
8:16. Joab...(was) over *the host;*
10: 7. all *the host* of the mighty men.
16. Shobach the captain of *the host of*
18. Shobach the captain of *their host,*
17:25. Amasa captain of *the host*
19:13(14). captain of *the host* before me
20:23. Joab (was) over all *the host*
1K. 1:19. Joab the captain of *the host:*
25. the captains of *the host,*
2: 5. captains of *the hosts of* Israel,
32. captain of *the host of* Israel,
— captain of *the host of* Judah.
35. the king put Benaiah...over *the host:*
4: 4. Benaiah...(was) over *the host:*
11:15, 21. Joab the captain of *the host*
16:16. Omri, the captain of *the host,*
18:15. (As) the Lord of *hosts* liveth,
19:10, 14. jealous for the Lord God of *hosts.*
22:19. all *the host of* heaven
2K. 3:14. (As) the Lord of *hosts* liveth,
4:13. or to the captain of *the host?*
5: 1. Naaman, captain of *the host of*
17:16. worshipped all *the host of* heaven,
19:31. (קרי ולא כתיב) the Lord (of *hosts*) shall do this.
21: 3. worshipped all *the host of* heaven,
5. built altars for all *the host of*
23: 4. for all *the host of* heaven:
2K. 23: 5. and to all *the host of* heaven.
25:19. the principal scribe of *the host,*
1Ch 5:18. that went out *to the war.*
7: 4. bands of *soldiers for* war,
11. fit to go out for *war*
40. them that were apt *to the war*
11: 9. for the Lord of *hosts* (was) with him.
12: 8. men of *war* (fit) for the battle,
14. captains of *the host:*
21. captains *in the host.*
23. the bands that were ready armed *to the war,*
24. 6800, ready armed to *the war.*
25. mighty men of valour *for the war,*
33, 36. such as went forth *to battle,*
37. all manner of instruments of *war*
17: 7. Thus saith the Lord of *hosts,*
24. The Lord of *hosts* (is) the God of Israel,
18:15. Joab...(was) over *the host;*
19: 8. all *the host* of the mighty men.
16. Shophach the captain of *the host of*
18. Shophach the captain of *the host.*
20: 1. Joab led forth the power of *the army,*
25: 1. David and the captains of *the host*
26:26. hundreds, and the captains of *the host,*
27: 3. the captains of *the host*
5. The third captain of *the host*
34. the general of the king's *army*
2Ch 17:18. ready prepared *for the war.*
18:18. all *the host of* heaven
25: 5. choice (men, able) to go forth *to war,*
7. let not *the army of* Israel go
26:11. fighting men, that went out *to war*
13. under their hand (was) *an army,* (marg. the power of *an army*)
14. throughout all *the host*
28: 9. *the host* that came to Samaria,
12. them that came from *the war,*
33: 3. worshipped all *the host of* heaven,
5. altars for all *the host of* heaven
11. captains of *the host*
Neh. 9: 6. the heaven of heavens, with all *their host,*
— *and the host of* heaven
Job 7: 1. *an appointed time* to man
10:17. changes *and war* (are) against me.
14:14. the days of *my appointed time*
Ps. 24:10. The Lord of *hosts,* he (is) the King of
33: 6. heavens made; and all *the host of them*
44: 9(10). goest not forth *with our armies.*
46: 7(8), 11(12). The Lord of *hosts* (is) with us;
48: 8(9). seen in the city of the Lord of *hosts,*
59: 5(6). Thou therefore, O Lord God of *hosts,*
60:10(12). didst not go out *with our armies?*
68:11(12). *the company* (marg. *army*) of those that published (it).
12(13). Kings of *armies* did flee
69: 6(7). wait on thee, O Lord God of *hosts,*
80: 4(5). O Lord God of *hosts,* how long wilt
7(8). Turn us again, O God of *hosts,*
14(15). we beseech thee, O God of *hosts:*
19(20). Turn us again, O Lord God of *hosts,*
84: 1(2). (are) thy tabernacles, O Lord of *hosts!*
3(4). (even) thine altars, O Lord of *hosts,*
8(9). O Lord God of *hosts,* hear my prayer:
12(13). O Lord of *hosts,* blessed (is) the
89: 8(9). Lord God of *hosts,* who (is) a strong
103:21. ye the Lord, all (ye) *his hosts;*
108:11(12). O God, go forth *with our hosts?*
148: 2. praise ye him, all *his hosts.*
Isa. 1: 9. Except the Lord of *hosts* had left unto
24. Therefore saith the Lord, the Lord of *hosts,*
2:12. For the day of the Lord of *hosts*
3: 1. the Lord of *hosts,* doth take away from
15. saith the Lord God of *hosts.*
5: 7. For the vineyard of the Lord of *hosts*
9. In mine ears (said) the Lord of *hosts,*
16. But the Lord of *hosts* shall be exalted
24. cast away the law of the Lord of *hosts,*
6: 3. Holy, holy, holy, (is) the Lord of *hosts:*
5. seen the King, the Lord of *hosts.*
8:13. Sanctify the Lord of *hosts* himself;
18. wonders in Israel from the Lord of *hosts,*
9: 7(6). The zeal of the Lord of *hosts* will
13(12). neither do they seek the Lord of *hosts.*
19(18). Through the wrath of the Lord of *hosts*
10:16. shall the Lord, the Lord of *hosts,*
23. For the Lord God of *hosts* shall make
24. thus saith the Lord God of *hosts,*

Isa. 10:26. And the Lord of *hosts* shall stir up
33. Behold, the Lord, the Lord of *hosts*,
13: 4. the Lord of *hosts* mustereth *the host of*
13. in the wrath of the Lord of *hosts*,
14:22. against them, saith the Lord of *hosts*,
23. of destruction, saith the Lord of *hosts*.
24. The Lord of *hosts* hath sworn,
27. For the Lord of *hosts* hath purposed,
17: 3. of Israel, saith the Lord of *hosts*.
18: 7. be brought unto the Lord of *hosts*
— of the name of the Lord of *hosts*,
19: 4. saith the Lord, the Lord of *hosts*.
12. what the Lord of *hosts* hath purposed
16. the hand of the Lord of *hosts*,
17. the counsel of the Lord of *hosts*,
18. and swear to the Lord of *hosts*;
20. for a witness unto the Lord of *hosts*
25. Whom the Lord of *hosts* shall bless,
21:10. I have heard of the Lord of *hosts*,
22: 5. perplexity by the Lord God of *hosts*
12. in that day did the Lord God of *hosts*
14. in mine ears by the Lord of *hosts*,
— saith the Lord God of *hosts*.
15. Thus saith the Lord God of *hosts*,
25. In that day, saith the Lord of *hosts*,
23: 9. The Lord of *hosts* hath purposed it,
24:21. the Lord shall punish *the host of*
23. when the Lord of *hosts* shall reign
25: 6. this mountain shall the Lord of *hosts*
28: 5. In that day shall the Lord of *hosts*
22. I have heard from the Lord God of *hosts*
29. cometh forth from the Lord of *hosts*,
29: 6. shalt be visited of the Lord of *hosts*
31: 4. so shall the Lord of *hosts* come down
5. will the Lord of *hosts* defend Jerusalem;
34: 2. upon all *their armies*:
4. all *the host of* heaven
— all *their host* shall fall down,
37:16. O Lord of *hosts*, God of Israel,
32. zeal of the Lord of *hosts* shall do this.
39: 5. Hear the word of the Lord of *hosts*:
40: 2. *her warfare* is accomplished,
26. that bringeth out *their host*
44: 6. and his redeemer the Lord of *hosts*;
45:12. all *their host* have I commanded.
13. nor reward, saith the Lord of *hosts*.
47: 4 & 48:2 & 51:15 & 54:5. the Lord of *hosts* (is) his name,
Jer. 2:19. saith the Lord God of *hosts*.
3:19. a goodly heritage of *the hosts of*
5:14. saith the Lord God of *hosts*,
6: 6. thus hath the Lord of *hosts* said,
9 & 7:3, 21. Thus saith the Lord of *hosts*,
8: 2. the moon, and all *the host of* heaven,
3. have driven them, saith the Lord of *hosts*.
9: 7(6), 15(14). thus saith the Lord of *hosts*,
17(16). Thus saith the Lord of *hosts*, Consider
10:16. The Lord of *hosts* (is) his name.
11:17. the Lord of *hosts*, that planted thee,
20. But, O Lord of *hosts*, that judgest
22. Therefore thus saith the Lord of *hosts*,
15:16. by thy name, O Lord God of *hosts*.
16: 9. For thus saith the Lord of *hosts*,
19: 3, 11, 15. Thus saith the Lord of *hosts*,
13. incense unto all *the host of* heaven,
20:12. But, O Lord of *hosts*, that triest
23:15. Therefore thus saith the Lord of *hosts*
16. Thus saith the Lord of *hosts*,
36. of the Lord of *hosts* our God.
25: 8. Therefore thus saith the Lord of *hosts*;
27, 28. Thus saith the Lord of *hosts*,
29. of the earth, saith the Lord of *hosts*.
32 & 26:18 & 27:4. saith the Lord of *hosts*,
27:18. make intercession to the Lord of *hosts*,
19. For thus saith the Lord of *hosts*
21. Yea, thus saith the Lord of *hosts*,
28: 2. Thus speaketh the Lord of *hosts*,
14. For thus saith the Lord of *hosts*,
29: 4. Thus saith the Lord of *hosts*,
8. For thus saith the Lord of *hosts*,
17, 21. Thus saith the Lord of *hosts*;
25. Thus speaketh the Lord of *hosts*,
30: 8. in that day, saith the Lord of *hosts*,
31:23. Thus saith the Lord of *hosts*,
35. The Lord of *hosts* (is) his name:
32:14. Thus saith the Lord of *hosts*,
15. For thus saith the Lord of *hosts*,

Jer. 32:18. the Lord of *hosts*, (is) his name,
33:11. shall say, Praise the Lord of *hosts*:
12. Thus saith the Lord of *hosts*;
22. As *the host of* heaven cannot be numbered,
35:13. Thus saith the Lord of *hosts*,
17. Therefore thus saith the Lord God of *hosts*,
18. Thus saith the Lord of *hosts*,
19. Therefore thus saith the Lord of *hosts*,
38:17. Thus saith the Lord, the God of *hosts*,
39:16 & 42:15. Thus saith the Lord of *hosts*,
42:18. For thus saith the Lord of *hosts*,
43:10 & 44:2. Thus saith the Lord of *hosts*,
44: 7. thus saith the Lord, the God of *hosts*,
11. Therefore thus saith the Lord of *hosts*,
25. Thus saith the Lord of *hosts*,
46:10. the day of the Lord God of *hosts*,
— for the Lord God of *hosts* hath
18. whose name (is) the Lord of *hosts*,
25 & 48:1. The Lord of *hosts*, the God of
48:15. whose name (is) the Lord of *hosts*.
49: 5. saith the Lord God of *hosts*,
7. thus saith the Lord of *hosts*;
26. in that day, saith the Lord of *hosts*.
35. Thus saith the Lord of *hosts*;
50:18. Therefore thus saith the Lord of *hosts*,
25. the work of the Lord God of *hosts*
31. saith the Lord God of *hosts*:
33. Thus saith the Lord of *hosts*;
34. the Lord of *hosts* (is) his name:
51: 3. destroy ye utterly all *her host*.
5. of his God, of the Lord of *hosts*;
14. The Lord of *hosts* hath sworn by
19. the Lord of *hosts* (is) his name.
33. For thus saith the Lord of *hosts*,
57. whose name (is) the Lord of *hosts*.
58. Thus saith the Lord of *hosts*;
52:25. the principal scribe of *the host*,
Dan. 8:10. (even) to *the host of* heaven; and it cast down (some) *of the host*
11. the prince of *the host*,
12. *And an host* was given (him)
13. the sanctuary *and the host*
10: 1. *but the time appointed* (was) long:
Hos.12: 5(6). Even the Lord God of *hosts*;
Am. 3:13. the God of *hosts*,
4:13. The Lord, The God of *hosts*,
5:14. the God of *hosts*, shall be with you,
15. it may be that the Lord God of *hosts*
16. Therefore the Lord, the God of *hosts*,
27. whose name (is) The God of *hosts*.
6: 8. saith the Lord the God of *hosts*,
14. the Lord the God of *hosts*;
9: 5. the Lord God of *hosts* (is) he
Mic. 4: 4. the Lord of *hosts* hath spoken (it).
Nah 2:13(14) & 3:5. saith the Lord of *hosts*,
Hab 2:13. (is it) not of the Lord of *hosts*
Zep. 1: 5. them that worship *the host of*
2: 9. (as) I live, saith the Lord of *hosts*,
10. against the people of the Lord of *hosts*.
Hag 1: 2. Thus speaketh the Lord of *hosts*,
5. therefore thus saith the Lord of *hosts*;
7. Thus saith the Lord of *hosts*;
9. Why? saith the Lord of *hosts*.
14. in the house of the Lord of *hosts*,
2: 4. I (am) with you, saith the Lord of *hosts*:
6. For thus saith the Lord of *hosts*;
7. with glory, saith the Lord of *hosts*.
8. gold (is) mine, saith the Lord of *hosts*.
9. saith the Lord of *hosts*: and in this place will I give peace, saith the Lord of *hosts*.
11. Thus saith the Lord of *hosts*;
23. In that day, saith the Lord of *hosts*,
— I have chosen thee, saith the Lord of *hosts*.
Zec. 1: 3. Thus saith the Lord of *hosts*; Turn ye unto me, saith the Lord of *hosts*, and I will turn unto you, saith the Lord of *hosts*.
4. Thus saith the Lord of *hosts*;
6. Like as the Lord of *hosts* thought to do
12. O Lord of *hosts*, how long wilt thou
14. Thus saith the Lord of *hosts*;
16. built in it, saith the Lord of *hosts*,
17. Thus saith the Lord of *hosts*;
2: 8(12). For thus saith the Lord of *hosts*;
9(13), 11(15). that the Lord of *hosts* hath
3: 7. Thus saith the Lord of *hosts*;
9. graving thereof, saith the Lord of *hosts*,
10. In that day, saith the Lord of *hosts*,

Zec. 4: 6. by my spirit, saith the Lord of *hosts*.
9. that the Lord of *hosts* hath sent me
5: 4. bring it forth, saith the Lord of *hosts*,
6:12. Thus speaketh the Lord of *hosts*,
15. that the Lord of *hosts* hath sent me
7: 3. in the house of the Lord of *hosts*,
4. came the word of the Lord of *hosts*
9. Thus speaketh the Lord of *hosts*,
12. the words which the Lord of *hosts*
— great wrath from the Lord of *hosts*.
13. would not hear, saith the Lord of *hosts* :
8: 1. the word of the Lord of *hosts* came
2. Thus saith the Lord of *hosts*,
3. the mountain of the Lord of *hosts*
4, 6. Thus saith the Lord of *hosts*;
6. in mine eyes? saith the Lord of *hosts*.
7, 9. Thus saith the Lord of *hosts*;
9. the house of the Lord of *hosts*
11. former days, saith the Lord of *hosts*.
14. For thus saith the Lord of *hosts*;
— saith the Lord of *hosts*, and I repented not:
18. And the word of the Lord of *hosts*
19, 20. Thus saith the Lord of *hosts*;
21. and to seek the Lord of *hosts*:
22. shall come to seek the Lord of *hosts*
23. Thus saith the Lord of *hosts*;
9:15. The Lord of *hosts* shall defend them;
10: 3. for the Lord of *hosts* hath visited
12: 5. my strength in the Lord of *hosts*
13: 2. in that day, saith the Lord of *hosts*,
7. my fellow, saith the Lord of *hosts* :
14:16, 17. worship the King, the Lord of *hosts*,
21. be holiness unto the Lord of *hosts* :
— in the house of the Lord of *hosts*.
Mal 1: 4. thus saith the Lord of *hosts*,
6. saith the Lord of *hosts* unto you,
8. thy person? saith the Lord of *hosts*.
9. your persons? saith the Lord of *hosts*.
10. pleasure in you, saith the Lord of *hosts*,
11. among the heathen, saith the Lord of *hosts*.
13. at it, saith the Lord of *hosts*;
14. a great King, saith the Lord of *hosts*,
2: 2. unto my name, saith the Lord of *hosts*,
4. with Levi, saith the Lord of *hosts*.
7. the messenger of the Lord of *hosts*.
8. of Levi, saith the Lord of *hosts*.
12. an offering unto the Lord of *hosts*.
16. his garment, saith the Lord of *hosts* :
3: 1. shall come, saith the Lord of *hosts*.
5. and fear not me, saith the Lord of *hosts*.
7. return unto you, saith the Lord of *hosts*.
10. herewith, saith the Lord of *hosts*,
11. in the field, saith the Lord of *hosts*.
12. delightsome land, saith the Lord of *hosts*.
14. mournfully before the Lord of *hosts* ?
17. shall be mine, saith the Lord of *hosts*,
4: 1(3:19). burn them up, saith the Lord of *hosts*,
3(–:21). do (this), saith the Lord of *hosts*.

6634 צְבָא [*tz'vāh*], Ch.

* P'AL.—*Preterite*. *

Dan. 7:19. Then *I would* know the truth

P'AL.—*Infinitive*.

Dan. 4:35(32). *and* he doeth *according to his will*

P'AL.—*Future*.

Dan. 4:17(14), 25(22), 32(29). giveth it to whomsoever *he will*,
5:21. over it whomsoever *he will*.

P'AL.—*Participle*.

Dan. 5:19. whom *he would* he slew; and whom *he would* he kept alive; and whom *he would* he set up; and whom *he would* he put down.

See 6643 צְבָאוֹת & צְבָאִים see צְבִי

6638 צָבָה [*tzāh-vāh'*].

* KAL.—*Preterite*. *

Nu. 5:27. *and* her belly *shall swell*,

KAL.—*Participle*. Poel.

Isa. 29: 7. even all *that fight against her*

* HIPHIL.—*Infinitive*. *

Nu. 5:22. *to make* (thy) belly *to swell*,

צָבֶה [*tzāh-veh'*], adj. 6639

Nu. 5:21. and thy belly *to swell*;

צְבוּ *tz'voo*, Ch. f. 6640

Dan 6:17(18). that *the purpose* might not be

צָבוּעַ *tzāh-voo'ăg*, m. 6641

Jer. 12: 9. unto me (as) a *speckled* bird,

צָבַט [*tzāh-vat'*]. 6642

* KAL.—*Future*. *

Ru. 2:14. *and he reached* her parched (corn),

צְבִי *tz'vee*, m. 6643

Deu 12:15. *as of the roebuck*, and as of the hart.
22. as *the roebuck* and the hart
14: 5. The hart, *and the roebuck*,
15:22. *as the roebuck*, and as the hart.
2Sa. 1:19. *The beauty* of Israel is slain
2:18. Asahel (was as) light of foot as *a wild roe* (marg. one of *the roes* that (is) in the field)
1K. 4:23(5:3). *and roebucks*, and fallowdeer,
1Ch 12: 8. *and* (were) as swift *as the roes*
Pro. 6: 5. Deliver thyself *as a roe*
Cant. 2: 7. *by the roes*, and by the hinds
9. My beloved is *like a roe*
17. be thou *like a roe*
3: 5. *by the roes*, and by the hinds
8:14. and be thou *like to a roe*
Isa. 4: 2. shall the branch of the Lord be *beautiful* (marg. *beauty*)
13:14. it shall be *as the* chased *roe*,
19. Babylon, *the glory of* kingdoms,
23: 9. to stain the pride of all *glory*,
24:16. *glory* to the righteous.
28: 1. whose *glorious* beauty (is) a fading
4. And the *glorious* beauty,
5. the Lord of hosts be for a crown of *glory*,
Jer. 3:19. a *goodly* heritage of the hosts
Eze. 7:20. *As for the beauty of* his ornament,
20: 6, 15. which (is) *the glory of* all lands:
25: 9. on his frontiers, *the glory of* the country,
26:20. I shall set *glory* in the land of
Dan. 8: 9. toward *the pleasant* (land).
11:16. he shall stand in the *glorious* land, (marg. the land of *ornament*, or, *goodly* land)
41. He shall enter also into the *glorious* land, (marg. land of *delight*, or, *ornament*, or, *goodly* land)
45. the *glorious* (marg. or, *goodly*) holy

צְבִיָּה *tz'veey-yāh'*, f. 6646

Cant. 4: 5 & 7:3(4). like two young *roes* that are twins, (lit. twins of *a roe*)

צְבַע [*tz'vag*], Ch. 6647

* PAEL.—*Participle*. *

Dan. 4:25(22). and *they shall wet thee* with the dew

* ITHPAEL.—*Future*. *

Dan. 4:15(12), 23(20). and *let it be wet* with the dew
33(30) & 5:21. and his body *was wet* with the

צֶבַע *tzeh'-vag*, m. 6648

Jud. 5:30. to Sisera a prey of *divers colours*, a prey of *divers colours* of needlework, of *divers colours* of needlework

6651 **צָבַר** [*tzāh-var'*].

✱ KAL.—*Future.* ✱

Gen 41:35. *and lay up* corn under the hand of
49. *And* Joseph *gathered* corn
Ex. 8:14(10). *And they gathered* them *together*
Job 27:16. Though *he heap up* silver as
Ps. 39: 6(7). *he heapeth up* (riches),
Hab. 1:10. *for they shall heap* dust,
Zec. 9: 3. *and heaped up* silver as the dust,

6652 **צִבֻּרִים** *tzib-boo-reem'*, m. pl.

2K. 10: 8. Lay ye them in two *heaps*

6653 **צְבָתִים** *tz'vāh-theem'*, m. pl.

Ru. 2:16. let fall also (some) of *the handfuls*

6654 **צַד** *tzad*, m.

Gen 6:16. the door of the ark shalt thou set *in the side thereof;*
Ex. 25:32. six branches shall come *out of the sides of it;* three branches...*out of* the one *side,* and three branches...*out of the* other *side:*
26:13. over *the sides of* the tabernacle
30: 4. upon the two *sides of it*
37:18. six branches going *out of the sides thereof;* three branches...*out of the* one *side thereof,* and three branches ...*out of the* other *side thereof:*
27. upon the two *sides thereof,*
Nu. 33:55. and thorns *in your sides,*
Deu 31:26. *in the side of* the ark
Jos. 3:16. the city Adam, that (is) *beside* Zaretan:
12: 9. the king of Ai, which (is) *beside* Beth-el,
23:13. and scourges *in your sides,*
Jud. 2: 3. they shall be (as thorns) *in* your *sides,*
Ru. 2:14. she sat *beside* the reapers:
1Sa. 6: 8. in a coffer *by the side thereof;*
20:20. I will shoot three arrows *on the side*
25. and Abner sat *by* Saul's *side,*
23:26. went *on* this *side of* the mountain, and David and his men *on* that *side of*
2Sa. 2:16. (thrust) his sword *in* his fellow's *side;*
13:34. by the way *of the* hill *side*
Ps. 91: 7. A thousand shall fall *at thy side,*
Isa. 60: 4. daughters shall be nursed at (thy) *side.*
66:12. ye shall be borne upon (her) *sides,*
Eze. 4: 4. Lie thou also upon *thy* left *side,*
6. lie again on *thy* right *side,* and thou shalt
8. thou shalt not turn thee *from one side* to *another,* (marg. *from thy side* to *thy side*)
9. number of the days that thou shalt lie upon *thy side,*
34:21. ye have thrust *with side*

6655 **צַד** *tzad*, Ch. m.

Dan 6: 4(5). against Daniel *concerning* the
7:25. he shall speak (great) words *against*

6656 **צְדָא** *tz'dāh*, Ch. m.

Dan 3:14. and said unto them, (Is it) *true,* (marg. or, *of purpose*) O Shadrach,

---

6658 **צָדָה** *tzāh-dāh'*.

✱ KAL.—*Preterite.* ✱

Ex. 21:13. if a man *lie* not *in wait,*

KAL.—*Participle.* Poel.

1Sa.24:11(12). yet thou *huntest* my soul to take it.

✱ NIPHAL.—*Preterite.* ✱

Zep. 3: 6. their cities *are destroyed,*

6660 **צְדִיָּה** *tz'deey-yāh'*, f.

Nu. 35:20. or hurl at him *by laying of wait,*
22. without *laying of wait,*

צַדִּיק *tzad-deek'*, adj. 6662

Gen 6: 9. Noah was a *just* man
7: 1. thee have I seen *righteous*
18:23. Wilt thou also destroy *the righteous*
24. Peradventure there be fifty *righteous*
— *the* fifty *righteous* that (are) therein?
25. to slay *the righteous* with the wicked: and that *the righteous* should be as the wicked, (lit. that it should be *like righteous* like wicked)
26. If I find in Sodom fifty *righteous*
28. there shall lack five of the fifty *righteous:*
20: 4. wilt thou slay also a *righteous* nation?
Ex. 9:27. the Lord (is) *righteous,* and I
23: 7. the innocent *and righteous*
8. perverteth the words of *the righteous.*
Deu 4: 8. and judgments (so) *righteous*
16:19. and pervert the words of *the righteous.*
25: 1. they shall justify *the righteous,*
32: 4. *just* and right (is) he.
1Sa.24:17(18). Thou (art) more *righteous* than I:
2Sa. 4:11. when wicked men have slain a *righteous*
23: 3. He that ruleth over men (must be) *just,*
1K. 2:32. two men more *righteous* and better than
8:32. and justifying *the righteous,*
2K. 10: 9. Ye (be) *righteous:* behold, I conspired
2Ch 6:23. and by justifying *the righteous,*
12: 6. they said, The Lord (is) *righteous.*
Ezr. 9:15. Lord God of Israel, thou (art) *righteous:*
Neh 9: 8. for thou (art) *righteous:*
33. thou (art) *just* in all that is brought upon
Job 12: 4. the *just* upright (man is) laughed
17: 9. *The righteous* also shall hold on his way,
22:19. *The righteous* see (it), and are glad:
27:17. *but the just* shall put (it) on,
32: 1. because he (was) *righteous* in his own
34:17. wilt thou condemn him that is most *just?*
36: 7. He withdraweth not his eyes *from the righteous:*
Ps. 1: 5. in the congregation of *the righteous.*
6. Lord knoweth the way of *the righteous*
5:12(13). thou, Lord, wilt bless *the righteous;*
7: 9(10). but establish *the just:* for the *righteous* God trieth the hearts
11(12). God judgeth *the righteous,* (marg. or, (is) a *righteous* judge)
11: 3. what can *the righteous* do?
5. The Lord trieth *the righteous:*
7. the *righteous* Lord loveth righteousness;
14: 5. the generation of *the righteous.*
31:18(19). proudly and contemptuously against *the righteous.*
32:11. rejoice, *ye righteous:*
33: 1. Rejoice in the Lord, O *ye righteous:*
34:15(16). of the Lord (are) upon *the righteous,*
19(20). the afflictions of *the righteous:*
21(22). they that hate *the righteous*
37:12. The wicked plotteth *against the just,*
16. A little that *a righteous man hath*
17. the Lord upholdeth *the righteous.*
21. *but the righteous* sheweth mercy,
25. yet have I not seen *the righteous* forsaken,
29. *The righteous* shall inherit the land,
30. The mouth of *the righteous*
32. The wicked watcheth *the righteous,*
39. the salvation of *the righteous*
52: 6(8). *The righteous* also shall see,
55:22(23). he shall never suffer *the righteous* to
58:10(11). *The righteous* shall rejoice
11(12). a reward *for the righteous:*
64:10(11). *The righteous* shall be glad
68: 3(4). *But* let *the righteous* be glad;
69:28(29). and not be written with *the righteous.*
72: 7. In his days shall *the righteous* flourish;
75:10(11). the horns of *the righteous*
92:12(13). *The righteous* shall flourish
94:21. against the soul of *the righteous,*
97:11. Light is sown *for the righteous,*
12. Rejoice in the Lord, *ye righteous;*
112: 4. full of compassion, *and righteous.*
6. *the righteous* shall be in everlasting
116: 5. Gracious (is) the Lord, *and righteous;*
118:15. in the tabernacles of *the righteous:*
20. into which *the righteous* shall enter.
119:137. *Righteous* (art) thou, O Lord,
125: 3. the lot of *the righteous;* lest *the righteous*

Ps.129: 4. The Lord (is) *righteous:* he hath cut
140:13(14). *the righteous* shall give thanks
141: 5. Let *the righteous* smite me;
142: 7(8). *the righteous* shall compass me about;
145:17. The Lord (is) *righteous*
146: 8. the Lord loveth *the righteous:*
Pro. 2:20. keep the paths of *the righteous.*
3:33. the habitation of *the just.*
4:18. the path of *the just*
9: 9. teach *a just* (man),
10: 3. The Lord will not suffer the soul of *the righteous* to famish:
6. Blessings (are) upon the head of *the just:*
7. The memory of *the just*
11. The mouth of *a righteous* (man)
16. The labour of *the righteous*
20. The tongue of *the just*
21. The lips of *the righteous* feed many:
24. the desire of *the righteous*
25. *but the righteous* (is) an everlasting
28. The hope of *the righteous*
30. *The righteous* shall never be removed:
31. The mouth of *the just*
32. The lips of *the righteous* know what
11: 8. *The righteous* is delivered out of trouble,
9. shall *the just* be delivered.
10. When it goeth well with *the righteous,*
21. the seed of *the righteous*
23. The desire of *the righteous*
28. *the righteous* shall flourish
30. The fruit of *the righteous*
31. *the righteous* shall be recompensed
12: 3. the root of *the righteous* shall not
5. The thoughts of *the righteous* (are) right:
7. the house of *the righteous*
10. *A righteous* (man) regardeth the life of
12. the root of *the righteous*
13. *the just* shall come out of trouble.
21. There shall no evil happen *to the just:*
26. *The righteous* (is) more excellent than
13: 5. *A righteous* (man) hateth lying:
9. The light of *the righteous*
21. to *the righteous* good shall be repayed.
22. the wealth of the sinner (is) laid up *for the just.*
25. *The righteous* eateth to the satisfying of
14:19. the wicked at the gates of *the righteous.*
32. *the righteous* hath hope in his death.
15: 6. In the house of *the righteous*
28. The heart of *the righteous* studieth to
29. the prayer of *the righteous.*
17:15. he that condemneth *the just,*
26. to punish *the just* (is) not good,
18: 5. to overthrow *the righteous*
10. *the righteous* runneth into it,
17. (He that is) first in his own cause (seemeth) *just;*
20: 7. *The just* (man) walketh in his integrity:
21:12. *The righteous* (man) wisely considereth
15. joy *to the just* to do judgment:
18. a ransom *for the righteous,*
26. *but the righteous* giveth and spareth not.
23:24. The father of *the righteous*
24:15. the dwelling of *the righteous;*
16. *a just* (man) falleth seven times,
24. unto the wicked, Thou (art) *righteous;*
25:26. A *righteous* man falling down
28: 1. *but the righteous* are bold as a lion.
12. When *righteous* (men) do rejoice,
28. *the righteous* increase.
29: 2. When *the righteous* are in authority,
6. *but the righteous* doth sing
7. *The righteous* considereth
16. *but the righteous* shall see their fall.
27. an abomination to *the just:*
Ecc. 3:17. God shall judge *the righteous*
7:15. there is *a just* (man) that perisheth
16. Be not *righteous* over much;
20. (there is) not a *just* man upon earth,
8:14. that there be *just* (men),
— the work of *the righteous:*
9: 1. *the righteous,* and the wise,
2. (there is) one event *to the righteous,*
Isa. 3:10. Say ye to *the righteous,*
5:23. the righteousness of *the righteous*
24:16. glory *to the righteous*
26: 2. the *righteous* nation

Isa. 26: 7. The way *of the just* (is) uprightness: thou, ...dost weigh the path of *the just.*
29:21. turn aside *the just*
41:26. that we may say, (He is) *righteous?*
45:21. a *just* God and a Saviour;
49:24. or the *lawful* captive (marg. the captivity of *the just*) delivered?
53:11. shall my *righteous* servant justify many;
57: 1. *The righteous* perisheth, and no man
— *the righteous* is taken away from
60:21. Thy people also (shall be) all *righteous:*
Jer. 12: 1. *Righteous* (art) thou, O Lord,
20:12. O Lord of hosts, that triest *the righteous,*
23: 5. will raise unto David a *righteous* Branch,
Lam. 1:18. The Lord is *righteous;*
4:13. that have shed the blood of *the just*
Eze. 3:20. When a *righteous* (man) doth turn
21. if thou warn *the righteous* (man), that *the righteous* sin not,
13:22. made the heart of *the righteous* sad,
18: 5. if a man be *just,*
9. he (is) *just,* he shall surely live,
20. the righteousness of *the righteous*
24. when *the righteous* turneth away
26. When a *righteous* (man) turneth away
21: 3(8), 4(9). will cut off from thee *the righteous*
23:45. And the *righteous* men, they shall
33:12. The righteousness of *the righteous*
— *neither* shall *the righteous* be able to live
13. When I shall say to *the righteous,*
18. When *the righteous* turneth from
Dan. 9:14. the Lord our God (is) *righteous*
Hos 14: 9(10). *and the just* shall walk in them:
Am. 2: 6. they sold *the righteous* for silver,
5:12. they afflict *the just,*
Hab. 1: 4. wicked doth compass about *the righteous;*
13. (the man that is) more *righteous*
2: 4. *but the just* shall live by his faith.
Zep. 3: 5. The *just* Lord (is) in the midst
Zec. 9: 9. he (is) *just,* and having salvation;
Mal. 3:18. discern between *the righteous* and

צָדַק [*tzāh-dak'*]. 6663

* KAL.—*Preterite.* *

Gen38:26. *She hath been* more *righteous* than I;
Job 9:15. though *I were righteous,*
10:15. *and* (if) *I be righteous,*
33:12. (in) this *thou art* not *just:*
34: 5. Job hath said, *I am righteous:*
35: 7. If *thou be righteous,* what
Ps. 19: 9(10). the judgments of the Lord *are* true (and) *righteous*

KAL.—*Future.*

Job 4:17. *Shall* mortal man *be* more *just* than God?
9: 2. how *should* man *be just* with God?
20. If *I justify myself,* mine own
11: 2. *should* a man full of talk *be justified?*
13:18. I know that *I shall be justified.*
15:14. that *he should be righteous?*
22: 3. that *thou art righteous?*
25: 4. How then *can* man *be justified*
40: 8. *that thou mayest be righteous?*
Ps. 51: 4(6). that *thou mightest be justified*
143: 2. in thy sight *shall* no man living *be justified.*
Isa. 43: 9. witnesses, *that they may be justified:*
26. declare thou, that *thou mayest be justified.*
45:25. *shall* all the seed of Israel *be justified,*
Eze.16:52. *they are more righteous* than thou:

* NIPHAL.—*Preterite.* *

Dan 8:14. *then shall* the sanctuary *be cleansed.* (marg. *justified*)

* PIEL.—*Preterite.* *

Jer. 3:11. The backsliding Israel *hath justified* herself

PIEL.—*Infinitive.*

Job 32: 2. *he justified* himself rather than God.
33:32. for I desire *to justify thee.*
Eze.16:52. *in that thou hast justified* thy sisters.

PIEL.—*Future.*

Eze.16:51. *and hast justified* thy sisters

* HIPHIL.—*Preterite.* *

Deu25: 1. *then they shall justify* the righteous,
2Sa.15: 4. unto me, *and I would do him justice!*

HIPHIL.—*Infinitive.*

1K. 8:32. *and justifying* the righteous,
2Ch 6:23. *and by justifying* the righteous,

HIPHIL.—*Imperative.*

Ps. 82: 3. *do justice to* the afflicted

HIPHIL.—*Future.*

Ex. 23: 7. *I will* not *justify* the wicked.
Job 27: 5. God forbid that *I should justify* you:
Isa. 53:11. *shall* my righteous servant *justify*

HIPHIL.—*Participle.*

Pro.17:15. *He that justifieth* the wicked,
Isa. 5:23. *Which justify* the wicked for reward,
50: 8. (He is) near *that justifieth me;*
Dan12: 3. *and they that turn* many *to righteousness*

* HITHPAEL.—*Future.* *

Gen44:16. how *shall we clear ourselves?*

6664 **צֶדֶק** *tzeh'-dek*, m.

Lev.19:15. *in righteousness* shalt thou judge
36. *Just* balances (lit. balances of *righteousness*), *just* weights, a *just* ephah, and a *just* hin, shall ye have:
Deu 1:16. judge *righteously* between (every) man
16:18. they shall judge...with *just* judgment. (lit. judgment of *righteousness*)
20. *That which is altogether just* (marg. *Justice, justice*) shalt thou follow,
25:15. a perfect *and just* weight, a perfect *and just* measure
33:19. they shall offer sacrifices of *righteousness:*
Job 6:29. *my righteousness* (is) in it.
8: 3. doth the Almighty pervert *justice?*
6. the habitation of *thy righteousness*
29:14. I put on *righteousness,*
31: 6. Let me be weighed in an *even* balance, (lit. balance of *righteousness*)
35: 2. *My righteousness* (is) more than God's?
36: 3. and will ascribe *righteousness* to my
Ps. 4: 1(2). O God of *my righteousness:*
5(6). Offer the sacrifices of *righteousness,*
7: 8(9). *according to my righteousness,*
17(18). *according to his righteousness:*
9: 4(5). thou satest in the throne judging *right.* (marg. in *righteousness*)
8(9). he shall judge the world *in righteousness,*
15: 2. and worketh *righteousness,*
17: 1. Hear *the right* (marg. *justice*), O Lord,
15. I will behold thy face *in righteousness:*
18:20(21). rewarded me *according to my righteousness;*
24(25). me *according to my righteousness,*
23: 3. leadeth me in the paths of *righteousness*
35:24. *according to thy righteousness;*
27. that favour *my righteous cause:* (marg. *my righteousness*)
28. my tongue shall speak of *thy righteousness*
37: 6. he shall bring forth *thy righteousness*
40: 9(10). I have preached *righteousness*
45: 4(5). because of truth and meekness (and) *righteousness;*
7(8). Thou lovest *righteousness,*
48:10(11). thy right hand is full of *righteousness.*
50: 6. the heavens shall declare *his righteousness:*
51:19(21). the sacrifices of *righteousness,*
52: 3(5). to speak *righteousness.*
58: 1(2). Do ye indeed speak *righteousness,*
65: 5(6). *in righteousness* wilt thou answer us,
72: 2. shall judge thy people *with righteousness,*
85:10(11). *righteousness* and peace have kissed
11(12). *and righteousness* shall look down
13(14). *Righteousness* shall go before him;
89:14(15). *Justice* and judgment (are) the
94:15. judgment shall return unto *righteousness:*
96:13. he shall judge the world *with righteousness,*
97: 2. *righteousness* and judgment (are) the
6. The heavens declare *his righteousness,*
98: 9. *with righteousness* shall he judge
118:19. Open to me the gates of *righteousness:*
119: 7. learned *thy righteous* judgments. (marg. judgments of *thy righteousness*)
62. because of *thy righteous* judgments. (lit. *id.*)
Ps.119:75. thy judgments (are) *right,* (marg. *righteousness*)
106. I will keep *thy righteous* judgments.
121. I have done judgment *and justice:*
123. the word of *thy righteousness.*
138. Thy testimonies...(are) *righteous* (marg. *righteousness*)
142. Thy righteousness (is) *an* everlasting *righteousness,*
144. *The righteousness of* thy testimonies
160. every one of *thy righteous* judgments
164. praise thee because of *thy righteous*
172. thy commandments (are) *righteousness.*
132: 9. thy priests be clothed with *righteousness;*
Pro. 1: 3. *justice*, and judgment, and equity;
2: 9. shalt thou understand *righteousness,*
8: 8. words of my mouth (are) *in righteousness;*
15. reign, and princes decree *justice.*
12:17. (He that) speaketh truth sheweth forth *righteousness:*
16:13. *Righteous* lips (are) the delight of kings;
25: 5. throne shall be established *in righteousness.*
31: 9. Open thy mouth, judge *righteously,*
Ecc. 3:16. the place of *righteousness,*
5: 8(7). perverting of judgment *and justice*
7:15. that perisheth *in his righteousness,*
Isa. 1:21. *righteousness* lodged in it;
26. The city of *righteousness,*
11: 4. *with righteousness* shall he judge
5. *righteousness* shall be the girdle
16: 5. and hasting *righteousness.*
26: 9. the world will learn *righteousness.*
10. will he not learn *righteousness:*
32: 1. a king shall reign *in righteousness,*
41: 2. Who raised up *the righteous* (man) (marg. *righteousness*)
10. the right hand of *my righteousness.*
42: 6. I the Lord have called thee *in righteousness,*
21. for *his righteousness'* sake;
45: 8. the skies pour down *righteousness:*
13. I have raised him up *in righteousness,*
19. I the Lord speak *righteousness,*
51: 1. ye that follow after *righteousness,*
5. *My righteousness* (is) near;
7. ye that know *righteousness,*
58: 2. they ask of me the ordinances of *justice;*
8. *thy righteousness* shall go before thee;
59: 4. None calleth *for justice,*
61: 3. called trees of *righteousness,*
62: 1. *the righteousness thereof* go forth
2. the Gentiles shall see *thy righteousness,*
64: 5(4). him that...worketh *righteousness,*
Jer. 11:20. O Lord of hosts, that judgest *righteously,*
22:13. him that buildeth his house by un*righteousness,* (lit. not *righteousness*)
23: 6. The Lord *our righteousness.*
31:23. O habitation of *justice,*
33:16. The Lord *our righteousness.*
50: 7. the habitation of *justice,*
Eze. 3:20. doth turn *from his righteousness,*
45:10. Ye shall have *just* balances (lit. balances of *righteousness*), and a *just* ephah, and a *just* bath.
Dan. 9:24. to bring in everlasting *righteousness,*
Hos. 2:19(21). I will betroth thee unto me *in righteousness,*
10:12. till he come and rain *righteousness*
Zep. 2: 3. seek *righteousness*, seek meekness:

צְדָקָה *tz'dāh-kāh'*, f. 6666

Gen15: 6. counted it to him *for righteousness.*
18:19. to do *justice* and judgment;
30:33. So shall *my righteousness* answer
Deu 6:25. *And* it shall be our *righteousness,*
9: 4. *For my righteousness* the Lord hath
5. Not *for thy righteousness,* or for the
6. to possess it *for thy righteousness;*
24:13. it shall be *righteousness* unto thee
33:21. he executed *the justice of* the Lord,
Jud. 5:11. *the righteous acts* (marg. *righteousnesses*) *of* the Lord, (even) *the righteous acts*
1Sa.12: 7. all *the righteous acts* (marg. *righteousnesses*, or, *benefits*) *of* the Lord,
26:23. to every man *his righteousness*
2Sa. 8:15. David executed judgment *and justice*

2Sa.19:28(29). What *right* therefore have I yet to
22:21, 25. *according to my righteousness :*
1K. 3: 6. in truth, *and in righteousness,*
8:32. to give him *according to his righteousness.*
10: 9. to do judgment *and justice.*
1Ch 18:14. executed judgment *and justice*
2Ch 6:23. giving him *according to his righteousness.*
9: 8. to do judgment *and justice.*
Neh. 2:20. ye have no portion, *nor right,*
Job 27: 6. *My righteousness* I hold fast,
33:26. render unto man *his righteousness.*
35: 8. *thy righteousness* (may profit)
37:23. in plenty of *justice :*
Ps. 5: 8(9). Lead me, O Lord, *in thy righteousness*
11: 7. the righteous Lord loveth *righteousness ;*
22:31(32). and shall declare *his righteousness*
24: 5. *and righteousness* from the God of
31: 1(2). deliver me *in thy righteousness.*
33: 5. He loveth *righteousness*
36: 6(7). *Thy righteousness* (is) like the great
10(11). *and thy righteousness* to the upright
40:10(11). I have not hid *thy righteousness*
51:14(16). shall sing aloud of *thy righteousness.*
69:27(28). them not come *into thy righteousness.*
71: 2. Deliver me *in thy righteousness,*
15. mouth shall shew forth *thy righteousness*
16. will make mention of *thy righteousness,*
19. *Thy righteousness also,* O God,
24. shall talk of *thy righteousness*
72: 1. *and thy righteousness* unto the king's son.
3. and the little hills, *by righteousness.*
88:12(13). *and thy righteousness* in the land
89:16(17). *and in thy righteousness* shall they be
98: 2. *his righteousness* hath he openly shewed
99: 4. executest judgment *and righteousness*
103: 6. The Lord executeth *righteousness*
17. *and his righteousness* unto children's
106: 3. he that doeth *righteousness*
31. was counted unto him *for righteousness*
111: 3 & 112:3. *and his righteousness* endureth for
112: 9. *his righteousness* endureth for ever;
119:40. quicken me *in thy righteousness.*
142. *Thy righteousness* (is) an everlasting
143: 1. answer me, (and) *in thy righteousness.*
11. *for thy righteousness' sake* bring
145: 7. *and* shall sing of *thy righteousness.*
Pro. 8:18. durable riches *and righteousness.*
20. I lead in the way of *righteousness,*
10: 2 & 11:4. *but righteousness* delivereth from
11: 5. *The righteousness of* the perfect
6. *The righteousness of* the upright
18. him that soweth *righteousness*
19. As *righteousness* (tendeth) to life:
12:28. In the way of *righteousness* (is) life;
13: 6. *Righteousness* keepeth (him that is)
14:34. *Righteousness* exalteth a nation:
15: 9. him that followeth after *righteousness.*
16: 8. a little *with righteousness*
12. the throne is established *by righteousness.*
31. in the way of *righteousness.*
21: 3. To do *justice* and judgment
21. He that followeth after *righteousness*
— *righteousness,* and honour.
Isa. 1:27. her converts *with righteousness.*
5: 7. *for righteousness,* but behold a cry.
16. sanctified *in righteousness.*
23. *and* take away *the righteousness of* the righteous
9: 7(6). with judgment *and with justice*
10:22. shall overflow with *righteousness.*
28:17. *and righteousness* to the plummet:
32:16. *and righteousness* remain in the fruitful
17. the work of *righteousness* shall be peace; and the effect of *righteousness*
33: 5. Zion with judgment *and righteousness.*
15. He that walketh *righteously,* (marg. in *righteousnesses*)
45: 8. *and* let *righteousness* spring up together;
23. the word is gone out...(in) *righteousness,*
24. in the Lord have I *righteousness* (marg. *righteousnesses*)
46:12. that (are) far *from righteousness :*
13. I bring near *my righteousness ;*
48: 1. not in truth, nor *in righteousness.*
18. *and thy righteousness* as the waves
51: 6. *and my righteousness* shall not be
8. *but my righteousness* shall be for ever,

Isa. 54:14. *In righteousness* shalt thou be established,
17. *and their righteousness* (is) of me,
56: 1. Keep ye judgment, and do *justice :*
— *and my righteousness* to be revealed.
57:12. I will declare *thy righteousness,*
58: 2. a nation that did *righteousness,*
59: 9. neither doth *justice* overtake us:
14. *and justice* standeth afar off:
16. *and his righteousness,* it sustained him.
17. For he put on *righteousness*
60:17. and thine exactors *righteousness.*
61:10. covered me with the robe of *righteousness*
11. the Lord God will cause *righteousness*
63: 1. I that speak *in righteousness,*
64: 6(5). all *our righteousnesses* (are) as filthy
Jer. 4: 2. in judgment, *and in righteousness ;*
9:24(23). lovingkindness, judgment, *and righteousness,*
22: 3. Execute ye judgment *and righteousness,*
15. do judgment *and justice,*
23: 5. execute judgment *and justice*
33:15. will I cause the Branch of *righteousness*
— execute judgment *and righteousness*
51:10. Lord hath brought forth *our righteousness*
Eze. 3:20. *his righteousness* which he hath done
14:14. their own souls *by their righteousness,*
20. their own souls *by their righteousness.*
18: 5, 21. and do that which is lawful *and right* (marg. judgment *and justice*)
19. done that which is lawful *and right,*
20. *the righteousness of* the righteous
22. *in his righteousness* that he hath done
24, 26. turneth away *from his righteousness,*
— All *his righteousness* that he hath done
27. and doeth that which is lawful *and right,*
33:12. *The righteousness of* the righteous
13. he trust to *his own righteousness,*
— all *his righteousnesses* shall not be
14, 19. and do that which is lawful *and right,* (marg. judgment *and justice*)
16. hath done that which is lawful *and right ;*
18. turneth *from his righteousness,*
45: 9. execute judgment *and justice,*
Dan 9: 7. *righteousness* (belongeth) unto thee,
16. according to all *thy righteousness,*
18. before thee for *our righteousnesses,*
Hos 10:12. Sow to yourselves *in righteousness,*
Joel 2:23. given you the former rain *moderately* (marg. *according to righteousness*)
Am. 5: 7. *and* leave off *righteousness* in the earth,
24. let judgment run down...*and righteousness*
6:12. the fruit of *righteousness* into hemlock:
Mic. 6: 5. *the righteousness of* the Lord.
7: 9. I shall behold *his righteousness.*
Zec. 8: 8. in truth *and in righteousness.*
Mal 3: 3. an offering *in righteousness.*
4: 2(3:20). shall the Sun of *righteousness* arise

צִדְקָה *tzid-kāh',* Ch. f. 6665

Dan 4:27(24). break off thy sins *by righteousness,*

צָהַב [*tzāh-hav'*]. 6668

* HOPHAL.—*Participle.* *

Ezr. 8:27. two vessels of *fine* copper, (marg. *yellow* or, *shining* brass)

צָהֹב *tzāh-hōhv',* adj. 6669

Lev.13:30. (there be) in it a *yellow* thin hair;
32. there be in it no *yellow* hair,
36. the priest shall not seek for *yellow* hair;

צָהַל [*tzāh-hal'*]. 6670

* KAL.—*Preterite.* *

Est. 8:15. the city of Shushan *rejoiced*
Isa. 24:14. *they shall cry aloud* from the sea.

KAL.—*Future.*

Jer. 5: 8. every one *neighed* after his neighbour's
50:11. *and bellow* as bulls;

* PIEL.—*Imperative.* *

Isa. 10:30. *Lift up* (marg. *Cry shrill* with) thy voice,
12: 6. *Cry out* and shout,
54: 1. break forth into singing, *and cry aloud,*
Jer. 31: 7. *and shout* among the chief of the nations:

* HIPHIL.—*Infinitive.* *

Ps.104:15. oil *to make* (his) face *to shine,*

6671 **צָהַר** [*tzāh-har'*].

* HIPHIL.—*Future.* *

Job 24:11. (Which) *make oil* within their walls,

6672 **צֹהַר** *tzōh'-har,* m.

Gen 6:16. *A window* shalt thou make
43:16. (these) men shall dine with me *at noon.*
25. against Joseph came *at noon:*
Deu28:29. thou shalt grope *at noonday,*
2Sa. 4: 5. who lay on a bed *at noon.*
1K. 18:26. from morning even until *noon,*
27. it came to pass *at noon,*
29. when *midday* was past,
20:16. And they went out *at noon.*
2K. 4:20. he sat on her knees till *noon,*
Job 5:14. and grope in *the noonday*
11:17. *And* (thine) age shall be clearer *than the noonday;*
Ps. 37: 6. thy judgment *as the noonday.*
55:17(18). Evening, and morning, *and at noon,*
91: 6. the destruction (that) wasteth *at noonday.*
Cant. 1: 7. thou makest (thy flock) to rest *at noon:*
Isa. 16: 3. in the midst of *the noonday;*
58:10. thy darkness (be) *as the noon day:*
59:10. we stumble *at noon day*
Jer. 6: 4. let us go up *at noon.*
15: 8. a spoiler *at noonday:*
20:16. the shouting *at noontide;*
Am. 8: 9. the sun to go down *at noon,*
Zep. 2: 4. shall drive out Ashdod *at the noon day,*

6673 **צַו & צָו** *tzav & tzāhv,* m.

Isa. 28:10. *precept* (must be) *upon precept, precept upon precept;*
13. *precept upon precept, precept upon precept;*
Hos. 5:11. willingly walked after *the commandment.*

6674 **צוֹא** [*tzōh*], adj.

Zec. 3: 3. Joshua was clothed with *filthy* garments,
4. Take away the *filthy* garments

6675 **צוֹאָה** [*tzōh-āh'*], f.

2K. 18:27. that they may eat *their own dung,*
Pro. 30:12. *and* (yet) is not washed *from their filthiness.*
Isa. 4: 4. *the filth of* the daughters of Zion,
28: 8. tables are full of vomit (and) *filthiness,*
36:12. that they may eat *their own dung,*

6677 **צַוָּאר** *tzav-vāhr',* m.

Gen27:16. upon the smooth of *his neck:*
40. shalt break his yoke from off *thy neck.*
33: 4. and fell on *his neck,*
41:42. and put a gold chain about *his neck;*
45:14. upon his brother Benjamin's *neck,* and wept; and Benjamin wept upon *his neck.*
46:29. and he fell on *his neck,* and he wept on *his neck*
Deu28:48. shall put a yoke of iron upon *thy neck,*
Jos. 10:24. put your feet upon *the necks of* these
— and put their feet upon *the necks of them.*
Jud. 5:30. *for the necks of* (them that take) the
8:21. *on* their camels' *necks.*
26. *about* their camels' *necks.*
Neh. 3: 5. put not *their necks* to the work
Job 15:26. (even) *on* (his) *neck,*
39:19. hast thou clothed *his neck* with thunder?
41:22(14). *In his neck* remaineth strength,
Ps. 75: 5(6). speak (not) *with a* stiff *neck.*
Cant. 1:10. *thy neck* with chains (of gold).
4: 4. *Thy neck* (is) like the tower of David
7: 4(5). *Thy neck* (is) as a tower of ivory;
Isa. 8: 8. he shall reach (even) to *the neck;*
10:27. his yoke from off *thy neck,*
30:28. shall reach to the midst of *the neck,*
52: 2. the bands of *thy neck,*
Jer. 27: 2. put them upon *thy neck,*
8. that will not put *their neck* under
11. the nations that bring *their neck*
12. Bring *your necks* under the yoke
28:10. the prophet Jeremiah's *neck,*
11. *the neck of* all nations
12. from off *the neck of* the prophet
14. *the neck of* all these nations,
30: 8. break his yoke from off *thy neck,*
Lam. 1:14. come up upon *my neck:*
5: 5. *Our necks* (are) under persecution:
Eze. 21:29(34). *the necks of* (them that are) slain,
Hos 10:11. upon *her* fair *neck:*
Mic. 2: 3. ye shall not remove *your necks;*
Hab. 3:13. the foundation unto *the neck.*

צַוְּאר [*tzav-vāhr'*], Ch. m. 6676

Dan 5: 7, 29. a chain of gold about *his neck,*
16. a chain of gold about *thy neck,*

צוּד *tzood.* 6679

* KAL.—*Preterite.* *

Jer. 16:16. *and they shall hunt them* from every
Lam. 3:52. Mine enemies *chased me* sore,
4:18. *They hunt* our steps, that we cannot

KAL.—*Infinitive.*

Gen27: 5. *to hunt* (for) venison,
Lam. 3:52. Mine enemies chased me *sore,* (lit. *chasing* chased me)

KAL.—*Imperative.*

Gen27: 3. *and take* (marg. *hunt*) *me* (some) venison;

KAL.—*Future.*

Lev. 17:13. which *hunteth* and catcheth any beast
Job 10:16. *Thou huntest me* as a fierce lion:
38:39. *Wilt thou hunt* the prey
Ps. 140:11(12). evil *shall hunt* the violent man
Pro. 6:26. the adulteress *will hunt*
Mic. 7: 2. *they hunt* every man his brother with a

KAL.—*Participle.*

Gen27:33. he *that hath taken* venison,

* POEL.—*Infinitive.* *

Eze. 13:18. *to hunt* souls!

POEL.—*Future.*

Eze. 13:18. *Will ye hunt* the souls of my people,

POEL.—*Participle.*

Eze. 13:20. wherewith *ye* there *hunt* the souls
— the souls that *ye hunt*

* HITHPAEL.—*Preterite.* *

Jos. 9:12. This our bread *we took* hot (for) *our provision*

צָוָה [*tzāh-vāh'*]. 6680

* PIEL.—*Preterite.* *

Gen 3:11. the tree, whereof *I commanded thee*
17. the tree, of which *I commanded thee,*
6:22. all that God *commanded* him,
7: 5. all that the Lord *commanded him.*
9. as God *had commanded* Noah.
16. of all flesh, as God *had commanded* him:
21: 4. days old, as God *had commanded* him.
47:11. as Pharaoh *had commanded.*
50:12. according as *he commanded them:*
16. Thy father *did command*
Ex. 4:28. the signs which *he had commanded him.*
7: 6. as the Lord *commanded* them,
10. as the Lord *had commanded:*
20. did so, as the Lord *commanded;*
12:28. as the Lord *had commanded* Moses

Ex. 12:50. as the Lord *commanded* Moses
16:16. the Lord *hath commanded*,
24. they laid it up...as Moses *bade:*
32. the thing which the Lord *commandeth*,
34. As the Lord *commanded* Moses,
18:23. *and* God *command thee*
19: 7. the Lord *commanded him.*
23:15. as *I commanded thee*, in the time
29:35. which *I have commanded* thee:
31: 6, 11. all that *I have commanded thee;*
32: 8. the way which *I commanded them:*
34: 4. as the Lord *had commanded* him,
18. as *I commanded thee*, in the time
35: 1. words which the Lord *hath commanded*,
4. the thing which the Lord *commanded*,
10. all that the Lord *hath commanded;*
29. which the Lord *had commanded*
36: 1. all that the Lord *had commanded.*
5. the work, which the Lord *commanded*
38:22. all that the Lord *commanded*
39: 1, 5, 7, 21, 26, 29, 31. as the Lord *commanded* Moses.
32, 42. all that the Lord *commanded*
43. as the Lord *had commanded*,
40:16. all that the Lord *commanded* him,
19, 21, 25, 27, 29, 32. as the Lord *commanded* Moses.
23. as the Lord *had commanded*
Lev. 7:36. Which the Lord *commanded* to be given
38. the Lord *commanded* Moses
8: 4. as the Lord *commanded* him;
5. the Lord *commanded* to be done.
9, 13, 17, 21, 29. the Lord *commanded* Moses.
31. as *I commanded*, saying, Aaron
34. the Lord *hath commanded*
36. the Lord *commanded* by
9: 5. (that) which Moses *commanded*
6. which the Lord *commanded* that ye
7. as the Lord *commanded.*
10. as the Lord *commanded* Moses.
21. before the Lord; as Moses *commanded.*
10: 1. *he commanded* them not.
15. as the Lord *hath commanded.*
18. in the holy (place), as *I commanded.*
13:54. *Then* the priest *shall command*
14: 4. *Then shall* the priest *command*
5. *And* the priest *shall command*
36, 40. *Then* the priest *shall command*
16:34. as the Lord *commanded* Moses.
17: 2. the Lord *hath commanded*,
24:23. as the Lord *commanded* Moses.
25:21. *Then I will command* my blessing
27:34. the Lord *commanded* Moses
Nu. 1:19. As the Lord *commanded* Moses,
54. all that the Lord *commanded*
2:33. as the Lord *commanded* Moses.
34. all that the Lord *commanded*
3:42. as the Lord *commanded* him,
51. as the Lord *commanded* Moses.
4:49. as the Lord *commanded* Moses.
8: 3. as the Lord *commanded* Moses.
20. all that the Lord *commanded*
22. as the Lord *had commanded*
9: 5. all that the Lord *commanded*
15:23. all that the Lord *hath commanded*
— the day that the Lord *commanded* (Moses),
36. as the Lord *commanded* Moses.
17:11(26). as the Lord *commanded*
19: 2. the Lord *hath commanded*,
20: 9. before the Lord, as *he commanded him.*
27. did as the Lord *commanded:*
26: 4 & 27:11. as the Lord *commanded* Moses
27:19. *and give* him *a charge* in their sight.
22. Moses did as the Lord *commanded*
29:40(30:1). all that the Lord *commanded*
30: 1(2). which the Lord *hath commanded.*
16(17). which the Lord *commanded* Moses,
31: 7. as the Lord *commanded* Moses;
21. the law which the Lord *commanded*
31, 41, 47. as the Lord *commanded* Moses.
34:13. the Lord *commanded* to give
29. the Lord *commanded* to divide
36: 2. The Lord *commanded* my lord
6. which the Lord *doth command*
10. as the Lord *commanded* Moses, so did the daughters
13. which the Lord *commanded*

Deu 1: 3. the Lord *had given* him *in commandment*
19. as the Lord our God *commanded* us;
41. the Lord our God *commanded us.*
2:37. the Lord our God *forbad* (lit. *commanded*) us.
3:21. *I commanded* Joshua
4: 5. as the Lord my God *commanded me*,
13. which *he commanded* you
14. the Lord *commanded* me
23. the Lord thy God *hath forbidden thee.*
5:12, 16. the Lord thy God *hath commanded thee.*
15. the Lord thy God *commanded thee*
32(29). the Lord your God *hath commanded* you:
33(30). the Lord your God *hath commanded*
6: 1. the Lord your God *commanded*
17. which *he hath commanded thee.*
20. the Lord our God *hath commanded*
25. our God, as *he hath commanded us.*
9:12. the way which *I commanded them;*
16. the way which the Lord *had commanded*
10: 5. as the Lord *commanded me.*
12:21. as *I have commanded thee*,
13: 5(6). the Lord thy God *commanded thee*
17: 3. which *I have* not *commanded;*
18:20. *I have* not *commanded him*
20:17. as the Lord thy God *hath commanded thee:*
24: 8. as *I commanded them*, (so) ye shall
26:13. which *thou hast commanded me:*
14. all that *thou hast commanded me.*
28:45. and his statutes which *he commanded thee:*
29: 1(28:69). the Lord *commanded* Moses
31: 5. which *I have commanded* you.
29. the way which *I have commanded*
33: 4. Moses *commanded* us a law,
34: 9. as the Lord *commanded* Moses.
Jos. 1: 7. Moses my servant *commanded thee:*
9. *Have* not *I commanded thee?*
13. the servant of the Lord *commanded*
16. All that *thou commandest us*
4: 8. as Joshua *commanded*,
10. the Lord *commanded* Joshua
— all that Moses *commanded*
6:10. Joshua *had commanded*
7:11. my covenant which *I commanded*
8: 8. See, *I have commanded* you.
27. which *he commanded* Joshua.
29. Joshua *commanded* that they
31. the servant of the Lord *commanded*
33. the servant of the Lord *had commanded*
35. all that Moses *commanded*,
9:24. the Lord thy God *commanded*
10:27. Joshua *commanded*, and they took
40. the Lord God of Israel *commanded.*
11:12. the servant of the Lord *commanded.*
15. As the Lord *commanded* Moses his servant, so *did* Moses *command*
— all that the Lord *commanded*
20. destroy them, as the Lord *commanded* Moses.
13: 6. inheritance, as *I have commanded thee.*
14: 2. as the Lord *commanded* by the hand
5. As the Lord *commanded* Moses,
17: 4. The Lord *commanded* Moses
21: 2. The Lord *commanded* by the hand
8. as the Lord *commanded* by the
22: 2. the servant of the Lord *commanded*
— in all that *I commanded* you:
5. Moses the servant of the Lord *charged*
23:16. the covenant of the Lord...which *he commanded*
Jud. 2:20. my covenant which *I commanded*
3: 4. *he commanded* their fathers
4: 6. the Lord God of Israel *commanded*,
13:14. all that *I commanded her*
Ru. 2: 9. *have I* not *charged* the young men
3: 6. all that her mother in law *bade her.*
1Sa. 2:29. *I have commanded* (in my) habitation;
13:13. which *he commanded thee:*
14. the Lord *commanded thee.*
17:20. as Jesse *had commanded him;*
20:29. he *hath commanded* me
21: 2(3). The king *hath commanded me*
—(–). what *I have commanded thee:*
25:30. *and shall have appointed thee* ruler
2Sa. 5:25. as the Lord *had commanded him;*
7: 7. whom *I commanded* to feed my people

2Sa. 7:11. the time that *I commanded* judges
13:28. *have* not I *commanded* you?
29. as Absalom *had commanded.*
14:19. thy servant Joab, he *bade me*,
17:14. Lord *had appointed* (marg. *commanded*)
18:12. the king *charged* thee
21:14. all that the king *commanded.*
24:19. went up as the Lord *commanded.*
1K. 1:35. *I have appointed* him to be ruler
2:43. that *I have charged* thee with?
8:58. *he commanded* our fathers.
9: 4. all that *I have commanded thee,*
11:10. *And had commanded* him
— that which the Lord *commanded.*
11. which *I have commanded* thee,
13: 9. For so *was it charged* me
21. the Lord thy God *commanded thee,*
15: 5. any (thing) that *he commanded him*
17: 4. *I have commanded* the ravens
9. *I have commanded* a widow
22:31. the king of Syria *commanded*
2K. 11: 9. Jehoiada the priest *commanded:*
14: 6. wherein the Lord *commanded,*
16:16. all that king Ahaz *commanded.*
17:13. the law which *I commanded*
15. the Lord *had charged* them,
34. which the Lord *commanded*
18: 6. the Lord *commanded* Moses.
12. the servant of the Lord *commanded,*
21: 8. all that *I have commanded them,*
— my servant Moses *commanded* them.
1Ch 6:49(34). the servant of God *had commanded.*
14:16. David therefore did as God *commanded him:*
15:15. thereon, as Moses *commanded*
16:15. *he commanded* to a thousand generations;
40. *he commanded* Israel;
17: 6. *I commanded* to feed my people,
10. *I commanded* judges
22:13. the Lord *charged* Moses
24:19. Lord God of Israel *had commanded him.*
2Ch 7:17. *I have commanded thee,*
18:30. the king of Syria *had commanded*
23: 8. Jehoiada the priest *had commanded,*
25: 4. the Lord *commanded,* saying,
33: 8. to do all that *I have commanded them,*
Ezr. 4: 3. the king of Persia *hath commanded us.*
9:11. Which *thou hast commanded*
Neh 1: 7, 8. *thou commandedst* thy servant Moses.
5:14. I *was appointed* (lit. *he appointed* me) to be their governor
8: 1. the Lord *had commanded* to Israel.
14. the Lord *had commanded* by Moses,
9:14. and *commandedst* them precepts,
Est. 2:10. Mordecai *had charged* her
20. as Mordecai *had charged* her:
3: 2. the king *had* so *commanded*
12. Haman *had commanded*
4:17. all that Esther *had commanded*
8: 9. all that Mordecai *commanded*
Job 38:12. *Hast thou commanded* the morning
Ps. 7: 6(7). judgment (that) *thou hast commanded.*
33: 9. *he commanded,* and it stood fast.
68:28(29). Thy God *hath commanded*
71: 3. *thou hast given commandment* to save
78: 5. *he commanded* our fathers, that they
105: 8. the word (which) *he commanded*
111: 9. *he hath commanded* his covenant
119: 4. Thou *hast commanded* (us) to keep
138. testimonies (that) *thou hast commanded*
133: 3. the Lord *commanded* the blessing,
148: 5. *he commanded,* and they were created.
Isa. 13: 3. I *have commanded* my sanctified
23:11. the Lord *hath given a commandment*
34:16. my mouth it *hath commanded,*
45:12. all their host *have I commanded.*
48: 5. my molten image, *hath commanded them.*
Jer. 7:22. nor *commanded them* in the day
23. But this thing *commanded I* them,
31. *I commanded* (them) not,
11: 4. *I commanded* your fathers
8. *I commanded* (them) to do;
13: 5. as the Lord *commanded me.*
6. *I commanded thee* to hide
14:14. neither have *I commanded them,*
17:22. as *I commanded* your fathers.
19: 5. which *I commanded* not,
23:32. nor *commanded them:*
Jer. 26: 2. the words that *I command thee*
8. the Lord *had commanded*
27: 4. *And command* them to say unto their
29:23. *I have* not *commanded them;*
32:23. all that *thou commandedst*
35. *I commanded them* not, neither
35: 6. our father *commanded* us, saying,
8. *he hath charged us,* to drink no wine
10. our father *commanded us.*
14. *he commanded* his sons not to drink
16. which *he commanded them;*
18. all that *he hath commanded* you:
36: 8. Jeremiah the prophet *commanded him,*
38:27. the king *had commanded.*
47: 7. the Lord *hath given it a charge*
50:21. all that *I have commanded thee.*
51:59. Jeremiah the prophet *commanded*
Lam 1:10. whom *thou didst command*
17. the Lord *hath commanded* concerning
2:17. *he had commanded* in the days
3:37. the Lord *commandeth* (it) not?
Eze. 9:11. as *thou hast commanded me.*
37:10. I prophesied as *he commanded me,*
Am. 2:12. and *commanded* the prophets, saying,
Nah 1:14. *And* the Lord *hath given a commandment*
Zec. 1: 6. *I commanded* my servants
Mal. 4: 4(3:22). which *I commanded* unto him

PIEL.—*Infinitive.*

Gen49:33. Jacob had made an end *of commanding*
Lev. 7:38. in the day *that he commanded*
2Sa. 6:21. *to appoint* me ruler
18: 5. *when* the king *gave* all the captains *charge*
Est. 4: 8. *and to charge* her that she should go in unto the king,
Eze.10: 6. *when he had commanded* the man clothed

PIEL.—*Imperative.*

Lev. 6: 9(2). *Command* Aaron and his sons,
24: 2. *Command* the children of Israel,
Nu. 5: 2 & 28:2 & 34:2 & 35:2. *Command* the children of Israel,
Deu. 2: 4. *command thou* the people,
3:28. *But charge* Joshua, and encourage
Jos. 1:11. *and command* the people, saying,
4: 3. *And command ye* them, saying,
16. *Command* the priests that bear
1K. 5: 6(20). *command thou* that they hew
2K. 20: 1. *Set* thine house *in order;* (marg. *Give charge* concerning thine house)
Ps. 44: 4(5). *command* deliverances for Jacob.
Isa. 38: 1. *Set* thine house *in order:* (marg. *Give charge* concerning thy house)

PIEL.—*Future.*

Gen. 2:16. *And* the Lord God *commanded* the man,
12:20. *And* Pharaoh *commanded* (his) men
18:19. *he will command* his children
26:11. *And* Abimelech *charged* all (his) people,
28: 1. Isaac called Jacob,...*and charged him,*
6. *and* that...*he gave* him *a charge,*
32: 4(5). *And he commanded* them, saying,
17(18). *And he commanded* the foremost,
19(20). *And* so *commanded he* the second,
42:25. *Then* Joseph *commanded* to fill
44: 1. *And he commanded* the steward
49:29. *And he charged* them, and said unto
50: 2. *And* Joseph *commanded* his servants
16. *And they sent a messenger* (marg. *charged*)
Ex. 1:22. *And* Pharaoh *charged* all his people,
5: 6. *And* Pharaoh *commanded* the same day
6:13. *and gave them a charge* unto the children
7: 2. all that *I command thee:*
25:22. *I will give* thee *in commandment*
27:20. thou *shalt command* the children of
34:32. *and he gave them in commandment*
36: 6. *And* Moses *gave commandment,*
Nu. 9: 8. what the Lord *will command*
27:23. *and gave him a charge,* as the Lord
32:28. *So* concerning them Moses *commanded*
34:13 & 36:5. *And* Moses *commanded* the children of Israel,
Deu 1:16. *And I charged* your judges
18. *And I commanded* you at that time
3:18. *And I commanded* you at that time,
6:24. *And* the Lord *commanded us*
18:18. all that *I shall command him.*
27: 1. *And* Moses...*commanded* the people,

Deu27:11. *And* Moses *charged* the people
28: 8. The Lord *shall command* the blessing
31:10. *And* Moses *commanded* them,
14. *that I may give him a charge.*
23. *And he gave* Joshua the son of Nun *a charge,*
25. *That* Moses *commanded* the Levites,
32:46. *ye shall command* your children
Jos. 1:10. *Then* Joshua *commanded*
18. all that *thou commandest him,*
3: 3. *And they commanded* the people,
8. thou *shalt command* the priests
4:17. Joshua *therefore commanded*
8: 4. *And he commanded* them,
18: 8. *and* Joshua *charged* them
Jud.21:10. And the congregation sent...*and commanded* them,
20. *Therefore they commanded* the children of
Ru. 2:15. *And* when...Boaz *commanded* his young
1Sa.13:14. *and* the Lord *hath commanded him*
18:22. *And* Saul *commanded* his servants,
2Sa. 4:12. *And* David *commanded* his young men,
9:11. the king *hath commanded* his servant,
11:19. *And charged* the messenger,
13:28. *Now* Absalom *had commanded*
14: 8. *I will give charge* concerning thee.
17:23. *and put* his houshold *in order,* (marg. *and gave charge* concerning his house)
18: 5. *And* the king *commanded* Joab
1K. 2: 1. *and he charged* Solomon his son,
46. *So* the king *commanded* Benaiah
5:17(31). *And* the king *commanded,* and they
11:38. all that *I command thee,*
2K. 11: 5. *And he commanded them,* saying,
15. *But* Jehoiada the priest *commanded*
16:15. *And* king Ahaz *commanded*
17:27. *Then* the king of Assyria *commanded,*
35. the Lord had made a covenant, *and charged them,*
22:12 & 23:4. *And* the king *commanded* Hilkiah
23:21. *And* the king *commanded* all the people,
1Ch 22: 6. *and charged him* to build an house
12. *and give thee charge* concerning Israel,
17. David *also commanded*
2Ch 7:13. if *I command* the locusts
19: 9. *And he charged* them, saying,
34:20. *And* the king *commanded* Hilkiah,
Ezr. 8:17. *And I sent* them *with commandment*
Neh. 7: 2. *That I gave* my brother...*charge*
Est. 4: 5. *and gave him a commandment* to Mordecai,
10. *and gave him commandment* unto Mordecai;
Job 36:32. *and commandeth* it (not to shine)
37:12. do whatsoever *he commandeth them*
Ps. 42: 8(9). the Lord *will command*
78:23. *Though he had commanded* the clouds from
91:11. *he shall give* his angels *charge*
Isa. 5: 6. *I will* also *command* the clouds
10: 6. of my wrath *will I give him a charge,*
45:11. work of my hands *command ye me.*
Jer. 1: 7. whatsoever *I command thee*
17. all that I *command thee:*
7:23. the ways that *I have commanded* you,
11: 4. all which *I command* you
32:13. *And I charged* Baruch before them,
36: 5. *And* Jeremiah *commanded* Baruch,
26. *But* the king *commanded* Jerahmeel
37:21. *Then* Zedekiah the king *commanded*
38:10. *Then* the king *commanded*
39:11. *Now* Nebuchadrezzar...*gave charge*
Am. 9: 3. thence *will I command* the serpent,
4. thence *will I command* the sword,

PIEL.—*Participle.*

Gen27: 8. according to that which I *command* thee.
Ex. 34:11. that which I *command thee*
Nu. 32:25. as my lord *commandeth.*
Deu 4: 2. the word which I *command* you,
— the commandments...which I *command*
40. I *command thee* this day,
6: 2. commandments, which I *command thee,*
6. these words, which I *command thee*
7:11. I *command thee* this day,
8: 1. the commandments which I *command thee*
11 & 10:13. statutes, which I *command thee*
11: 8. the commandments which I *command you*
13. my commandments which I *command*
22. these commandments which I *command*
Deu11:27. I *command* you this day:
28. the way which I *command* you
12:11. all that I *command* you;
14. all that I *command thee.*
28. all these words which I *command thee,*
32(13:1). What thing soever I *command*
13:18(19). commandments which I *command thee* this day,
15: 5. commandments which I *command thee*
11. therefore I *command thee,*
15. I *command thee* this thing
19: 7. Wherefore I *command thee,*
9. I *command thee* this day,
24:18, 22. I *command thee* to do this
26:16. the Lord thy God *hath commanded thee*
27: 1, 4. I *command* you this day.
10 & 28:1, 13. I *command thee* this day.
28:14. the words which I *command* thee
15. I *command thee* this day;
30: 2. all that I *command thee*
8. his commandments which I *command thee*
11. I *command thee* this day,
16. In that I *command thee*
Isa. 55: 4. a leader *and commander* to the people.
Jer. 34:22. I *will command,* saith the Lord,
Am. 6:11. the Lord *commandeth,*
9: 9. For, lo, I *will command,*

* PUAL.—*Preterite.* *

Gen45:19. Now thou *art commanded,* this do ye;
Lev. 8:35. that ye die not: for so *I am commanded.*
10:13. made by fire: for so *I am commanded.*
Nu. 3:16. of the Lord, as *he was commanded.*
36: 2. and my lord *was commanded*
Eze.12: 7. And I did so as *I was commanded:*
24:18. in the morning as *I was commanded.*
37: 7. I prophesied as *I was commanded:*

PUAL.—*Future.*

Ex. 34:34. (that) which *he was commanded.*

צָוַח [*tzāh-vagh'*]. 6681

* KAL.—*Future.* *

Isa. 42:11. *let them shout* from the top

צְוָחָה *tz'vāh-ghāh'*, f. 6682

Ps.144:14. no *complaining* in our streets.
Isa. 24:11. *a crying* for wine in the streets;
Jer. 14: 2. *and the cry of* Jerusalem is gone up.
46:12. *and thy cry* hath filled the land:

צוּלָה *tzoo-lāh'*, f. 6683

Isa. 44:27. That saith *to the deep,* Be dry,

צוּם [*tzoom*]. 6684

* KAL.—*Preterite.* *

2Sa.12:21. *thou didst fast* and weep for the child,
22. *I fasted* and wept:
Isa. 58: 3. Wherefore *have we fasted,*
Zec. 7: 5. When *ye fasted* and mourned
— *did ye* at all *fast unto me,*

KAL.—*Infinitive.*

Zec. 7: 5. did ye *at all* fast (lit. *fasting* did ye fast) unto me,

KAL.—*Imperative.*

Est. 4:16. *and fast ye* for me,

KAL.—*Future.*

Jud.20:26. *and fasted* that day until even,
1Sa. 7: 6. *and fasted* on that day,
31:13. *and fasted* seven days.
2Sa. 1:12. *and fasted* until even,
12:16. *and* David *fasted,*
1K. 21:27. *and fasted,* and lay in sackcloth,
1Ch 10:12. in Jabesh, *and fasted* seven days.
Ezr. 8:23. *So we fasted* and besought our God
Est. 4:16. I also and my maidens *will fast*
Isa. 58: 4. *ye fast* for strife and debate,
— *ye shall* not *fast* as (ye do this) day,
Jer. 14:12. When *they fast,* I will not hear their cry;

KAL.—*Participle.* Poel.

2Sa.12:23. wherefore *should I fast?* (lit. (be) *fasting*)
Neh 1: 4. and *fast*ed, and prayed before the God of

6685 **צוֹם** *tzōhm*, m.

2Sa.12:16. and David fasted, (marg. fasted *a fast*)
1K. 21: 9. Proclaim *a fast*, and set Naboth
12. They proclaimed *a fast*, and set Naboth
2Ch 20: 3. and proclaimed *a fast*
Ezr. 8:21. Then I proclaimed *a fast*
Neh 9: 1. assembled *with fasting*,
Est. 4: 3. *and fasting*, and weeping, and wailing;
9:31. the matters of *the fastings*
Ps. 35:13. I humbled my soul *with fasting;*
69:10(11). (and chastened) my soul *with fasting*,
109:24. My knees are weak *through fasting;*
Isa. 58: 3. in the day of *your fast*
5. Is it such *a fast* that I have chosen?
— wilt thou call this *a fast*,
6. *the fast* that I have chosen?
Jer. 36: 6. in the Lord's house upon the *fasting* day:
9. they proclaimed *a fast* before the Lord
Dan 9: 3. *with fasting*, and sackcloth,
Joel 1:14. Sanctify ye *a fast*,
2:12. *and with fasting*, and with weeping,
15. sanctify *a fast*, call a solemn assembly:
Jon. 3: 5. and proclaimed *a fast*,
Zec. 8:19. *The fast of* the fourth (month), *and the fast of* the fifth, *and the fast of* the seventh, *and the fast of* the tenth,

6687 **צוּף** [*tzooph*].

* KAL.—*Preterite.* *

Lam.3:54. Waters *flowed* over mine head;

* HIPHIL.—*Preterite.* *

Deu11: 4. *he made* the water of the Red sea *to overflow*

HIPHIL.—*Future.*

2K. 6: 6. *and* the iron *did swim.*

6688 **צוּף** *tzooph*, m.

Ps. 19:10(11). sweeter also than honey and *the honeycomb.* (marg. the dropping of *honeycombs*)
Pro.16:24. Pleasant words (are as) *an* honey*comb*,

6692 **צוּץ** [*tzootz*].

* KAL.—*Preterite.* *

Eze. 7:10. the rod *hath blossomed*,

* HIPHIL.—*Future.* *

Nu. 17: 8(23). *and bloomed* blossoms,
Ps. 72:16. *and* (they) of the city *shall flourish*
90: 6. In the morning *it flourisheth*,
92: 7(8). *and* when all the workers of iniquity *do flourish;*
103:15. as a flower of the field, so *he flourisheth.*
132:18. upon himself *shall* his crown *flourish.*
Isa. 27: 6. Israel *shall blossom* and bud,

HIPHIL.—*Participle.*

Cant.2: 9. *shewing himself* (marg. *flourishing*) through the lattice.

6693 **צוּק** [*tzook*].

* HIPHIL.—*Preterite.* *

Jud.14:17. because *she lay sore upon him:*
16:16. *she pressed* him daily with her words,
Job 32:18. the spirit within me *constraineth me.*
Isa. 29: 2. *Yet I will distress* Ariel,

HIPHIL.—*Future.*

Deu28:53, 55. thine enemies *shall distress* thee:
57. thine enemy *shall distress* thee
Jer. 19: 9. that seek their lives, *shall straiten* them.

HIPHIL.—*Participle.*

Isa. 29: 7. her munition, *and that distress* her,
51:13. because of the fury of *the oppressor*,
— and where (is) the fury of *the oppressor?*

צוּק [*tzook*]. 6694

* KAL.—*Preterite.* *

Isa. 26:16. *they poured out* a prayer

KAL.—*Future.*

Job 28: 2. brass *is molten* (out of) the stone.
29: 6. the rock *poured* me *out* rivers of oil;

צוֹק *tzōhk*, m. 6695

Dan 9:25. *even in troublous* (marg. *strait of*) times.

צוּקָה *tzoo-kāh'*, f. 6695

Pro. 1:27. when distress *and anguish* cometh
Isa. 8:22. dimness of *anguish;*
30: 6. the land of trouble *and anguish*,

צוּר *tzoor*. 6696

* KAL.—*Preterite.* *

Ex. 23:22. *and an adversary* (marg. or, *I will afflict*) unto thine adversaries.
Deu14:25. *and bind up* the money in thine hand,
20:12. against thee, *then thou shalt besiege* it:
Ps.139: 5. *Thou hast beset me* behind and before,
Isa. 29: 3. *and will lay siege* against thee
Eze. 4: 3. *and thou shalt lay siege* against
5: 3. a few in number, *and bind* them in thy skirts.

KAL.—*Infinitive.*

1Sa.23: 8. *to besiege* David and his men.

KAL.—*Imperative.*

Isa. 21: 2. Go up, O Elam: *besiege*, O Media;

KAL.—*Future.*

Ex. 32: 4. *and fashioned* it with a graving tool,
Deu 2: 9. *Distress* not (marg. *Use* no *hostility against*) the Moabites,
19. *distress them* not, nor meddle
20:19. When *thou shalt besiege* a city
2Sa.11: 1. of Ammon, *and besieged* Rabbah.
20:15. And they came *and besieged* him
1K. 7:15. *For he cast* two pillars of brass,
16:17. with him, *and they besieged* Tirzah.
20: 1. he went up *and besieged* Samaria,
2K. 5:23. *and bound* two talents of silver
6:24. and went up, *and besieged* Samaria.
12:10(11). *and they put up in bags*, (marg. *bound up*)
16: 5. *and they besieged* Ahaz, but could not
17: 5. to Samaria, *and besieged* it three years.
18: 9. came up against Samaria, *and besieged* it.
1Ch 20: 1. and came *and besieged* Rabbah.
2Ch 28:20. *and distressed* him, but strengthened him not.
Cant.8: 9. *we will inclose* her with boards of cedar.
Jer. 39: 1. against Jerusalem, *and they besieged* it.
Dan 1: 1. unto Jerusalem, *and besieged* it.

KAL.—*Participle.* Poel.

Jud. 9:31. *they fortify* the city against thee.
1K. 15:27. all Israel *laid siege* to Gibbethon.
2K. 6:25. and, behold, *they besieged* it,
24:11. and his servants *did besiege*
Est. 8:11. the people...*that would assault* them,
Jer. 21: 4. the Chaldeans, *which besiege* you
9. falleth to the Chaldeans *that besiege* you,
32: 2. the king of Babylon's army *besieged*
37: 5. the Chaldeans *that besieged* Jerusalem

צוּר *tzoor*, m. 6697

Ex. 17: 6. stand before thee there *upon the rock* in Horeb; and thou shalt smite *the rock*,
33:21. thou shalt stand *upon a rock:*
22. I will put thee in a clift of *the rock*,
Nu. 23: 9. from the top of *the rocks* I see him,
Deu 8:15. brought thee forth water *out of the rock of*
32: 4. (He is) *the Rock*, his work (is) perfect:

Deu 32:13. oil out of *the* flinty *rock;*
15. esteemed *the Rock of* his salvation.
18. *Of the Rock* (that) begat thee
30. except *their Rock* had sold them,
31. For *their rock* (is) not *as our Rock,*
37. (their) *rock* in whom they trusted,
Jos. 5: 2. Make thee *sharp* knives, (marg. or, knives of *flints*)
3. Joshua made him *sharp* knives,
Jud. 6:21. there rose up fire out of *the rock,*
7:25. they slew Oreb upon *the rock* Oreb,
13:19. offered (it) upon *a rock*
1Sa. 2: 2. neither (is there) any *rock* like our God.
24: 2(3). *the rocks of* the wild goats.
2Sa. 2:16. that place was called Helkath-*hazzurim,* (marg. The field of *strong men*)
21:10. spread it for her upon *the rock,*
22: 3. The God of *my rock;* in him will I
32. and who (is) *a rock,* save our God?
47. blessed (be) *my rock;*
— the God of *the rock of* my salvation.
23: 3. *the Rock of* Israel spake to me,
1Ch 11:15. to *the rock* to David,
Job 14:18. *and the rock* is removed out of his place.
18: 4. shall *the rock* be removed out of
19:24. pen and lead *in the rock* for ever!
22:24. of Ophir *as the stones of* the brooks.
24: 8. embrace *the rock* for want of a shelter.
28:10. He cutteth out rivers *among the rocks;*
29: 6. *and the rock* poured me out rivers of oil;
Ps. 18: 2(3). my God, *my strength,* (marg. *rock*)
31(32). who (is) *a rock* save our God?
46(47). and blessed (be) *my rock;*
19:14(15). O Lord, *my strength* (marg. *rock*), and my redeemer.
27: 5. he shall set me up *upon a rock.*
28: 1. O Lord *my rock;* be not silent
31: 2(3). be thou my strong *rock,*
49:14(15). *and their beauty* (marg. or, *strength*) shall consume
61: 2(3). lead me *to the rock*
62: 2(3), 6(7). He only (is) *my rock*
7(8). *the rock of* my strength,
71: 3. Be thou my *strong* habitation, (marg. Be thou to me *for a rock of* habitation)
73:26. God (is) *the strength* (marg. *rock*) *of* my heart,
78:15. He clave *the rocks* in the wilderness,
20. he smote *the rock,*
35. remembered that God (was) *their rock,*
81:16(17). *and* with honey *out of the rock*
89:26(27). my God, *and the rock of* my
43(44). Thou hast also turned *the edge of* his
92:15(16). (he is) *my rock,* and (there is) no
94:22. my God (is) *the rock of* my refuge.
95: 1. *to the rock of* our salvation.
105:41. He opened *the rock,* and the waters
114: 8. turned *the rock* (into) a standing water,
144: 1. Blessed (be) the Lord *my strength,* (marg. *rock*)
Pro. 30:19. the way of a serpent *upon a rock;*
Isa. 2:10. Enter *into the rock,* and hide thee
19. into the holes of *the rocks,*
21. into the clefts of *the rocks,*
8:14. of stumbling *and for a rock of* offence
10:26. the slaughter of Midian *at the rock of*
17:10. *and* hast not been mindful of *the rock of*
26: 4. in the Lord Jehovah (is) everlasting *strength:* (marg. *the rock of* ages)
30:29. *the mighty One* (marg. *Rock*) *of* Israel.
44: 8. (there is) no *God* (marg. *rock*); I know not (any).
48:21. he caused the waters to flow *out of the rock* for them: he clave *the rock* also,
51: 1. look unto *the rock* (whence) ye are hewn,
Jer. 18:14. *from the rock of* the field?
21:13. of the valley, (and) *rock of* the plain,
Nah 1: 6. *and the rocks* are thrown down
Hab 1:12. *and, O mighty God* (marg. *rock*), thou hast established

---

6699 **צוּרָה** [*tzoo-rāh'*].

Eze. 43:11. *the form of* the house,
— all *the forms thereof,* and all the ordinances thereof, and all *the forms thereof,*
— *the* whole *form thereof,*

צַוְּרֹנִים [*tzav-vāh-rōh-neem'*], m. pl. 6677

Cant. 4: 9. with one chain *of thy neck.*

צוּת [*tzooth*]. 6702

* HIPHIL.—*Future.* *

Isa. 27: 4. *I would burn them* together.

צַח *tzaġh*, adj. 6703

Cant. 5:10. My beloved (is) *white* and ruddy,
Isa. 18: 4. like a *clear* heat upon herbs,
32: 4. ready to speak *plainly.* (marg. or, *elegantly*)
Jer. 4:11. A *dry* wind of the high places

צִחֵה [*tzee-ġheh'*], adj. 6704

Isa. 5:13. their multitude *dried up*

צָחַח [*tzāh-ġhaġh'*]. 6705

* KAL.—*Preterite.* *

Lam. 4: 7. *they were whiter* than milk,

צְחִיחַ *tz'ġhee'ăġh*, m. 6706

Neh 4:13(7). *on the higher places,* I even set
Eze. 24: 7. she set it upon *the top of* a rock;
8. set her blood upon *the top of* a rock,
26: 4. and make her *like the top of* a rock.
14. make thee *like the top of* a rock:

צְחִיחָה *tz'ġhee-ġhāh'*, f. 6707

Ps. 68: 6(7). but the rebellious dwell *in a dry land.*

צְחִיחִי [*tz'ġhee-ġhee'*], adj. 6708

Neh 4:13(7). (כתיב) *on the higher places,* I even set

צַחֲנָה [*tzah-ġhănāh'*], f. 6709

Joel 2:20. and *his ill savour* shall come up,

צַחְצָחוֹת *tzaġh-tzāh-ġhōhth'*, f. pl. 6710

Isa. 58:11. and satisfy thy soul *in drought,* (marg. *droughts*)

צָחַק [*tzāh-ġhak'*]. 6711

* KAL.—*Preterite.* *

Gen 18:13. Wherefore *did* Sarah *laugh,*
15. *I laughed* not; for she was afraid.
— Nay; but *thou didst laugh.*

KAL.—*Future.*

Gen 17:17. Abraham fell upon his face, *and laughed,*
18:12. *Therefore* Sarah *laughed* within
21: 6. all that hear *will laugh* with me.

* PIEL.—*Infinitive.* *

Gen 39:14. brought in an Hebrew unto us *to mock* us;
17. came in unto me *to mock* me:
Ex. 32: 6. and rose up *to play.*

PIEL.—*Future.*

Jud. 16:25. *and he made* them *sport:*

PIEL.—*Participle.*

Gen 19:14. he seemed *as one that mocked*
21: 9. Sarah saw the son of Hagar...*mocking.*
26: 8. Isaac (was) *sporting* with Rebekah

צְחֹק *tz'ġhōhk*, m. 6712

Gen 21: 6. God hath made me to *laugh,* (lit. made *laughter* to me)
Eze. 23:32. thou shalt be *laughed to scorn*

6713 צַחַר [tzah'-ghar], m.

Eze.27:18. in the wine of Helbon, and *white* wool.

6715 צָחֹר [tzāh-ghōhr'], adj.

Jud. 5:10. ye that ride on *white* asses,

6716 צִי tzee, m.

Nu. 24:24. *And ships* (shall come) from the coast of
Isa. 33:21. *neither* shall gallant *ship* pass thereby.
Eze.30: 9. messengers go forth from me *in ships*
Dan11:30. *the ships* of Chittim shall come

See 6679 צוּד see צַיִד

6718 צַיִד tzah'-yid, m.

Gen10: 9. He was a mighty *hunt*er (lit. mighty of *hunting*)
— as Nimrod the mighty *hunt*er (lit. mighty of *hunting*)
25:27. Esau was a cunning *hunt*er (lit. skilful of *hunting*)
28. because he did eat of (his) *venison:*
27: 3. and take me (some) *venison;*
5. Esau went to the field to hunt (for) *venison,*
7. Bring me *venison*, and make me savoury
19. sit and eat *of my venison,*
25. I will eat *of* my son's *venison,*
30. Esau...came in *from his hunting.*
31. and eat *of* his son's *venison,*
33. where (is) he that hath taken *venison,*
Lev.17:13. which hunteth and *catcheth* (lit. hunteth *a hunting*)
Jos. 9: 5. of *their provision* was dry (and) mouldy.
14. the men took *of their victuals,*
Neh13:15. the day wherein they sold *victuals.*
Job 38:41. Who provideth for the raven *his food?*
Ps.132:15. I will abundantly bless *her provision:*
Pro.12:27. roasteth not *that which he took in hunting:*

6719 צַיָּד [tzahy-yāhd'], m.

Jer. 16:16. will I send for many *hunters,*

6720 צֵידָה tzēh-dāh', f.

Gen27: 3. (כתיב) and take me (some) *venison;*
42:25. give them *provision* for the way:
45:21. and gave them *provision* for the way.
Ex. 12:39. prepared for themselves any *victual.*
Jos. 1:11. Prepare you *victuals;* for within
9:11. Take *victuals* with you for the journey,
Jud. 7: 8. the people took *victuals*
20:10. fetch *victual* for the people,
1Sa.22:10. *and* gave him *victuals,*
Ps. 78:25. he sent them *meat* to the full.

6723 צִיָּה tzeey-yāh', f.

Job 24:19. *Drought* and heat consume
30: 3. fleeing *into the wilderness*
Ps. 63: 1(2). in a *dry* and thirsty land,
78:17. provoking the most high *in the wilderness.*
105:41. they ran *in the dry places*
107:35. and *dry* ground (lit. ground of *drought*) into watersprings.
Isa. 35: 1. The wilderness *and the solitary place*
41:18. and the *dry* land (lit. land of *drought*) springs of water.
53: 2. as a root out of a *dry* ground:
Jer. 2: 6. through a land of *drought,*
50:12. *a dry land,* and a desert.
51:43. a *dry* land, and a wilderness,
Eze.19:13. in a *dry* and thirsty ground.
Hos 2: 3(5). and set her like a *dry* land,
Joel 2:20. a land *barren* and desolate,
Zep 2:13. a desolation, (and) *dry* like a wilderness.

צָיוֹן tzāh-yōhn', m. 6724

Isa. 25: 5. as the heat *in a dry place;*
32: 2. of water *in a dry place,*

צִיּוּן tzeey-yoon', m. 6725

2K. 23:17. What *title* (is) that that I see?
Jer. 31:21. Set thee up *waymarks,*
Eze.39:15. then shall he set up *a sign*

צִיִּים tzeey-yeem', m. pl. 6728

Ps. 72: 9. *They that dwell in the wilderness* shall bow
74:14. the people *inhabiting the wilderness.*
Isa. 13:21. *wild beasts of the desert* (marg. *Ziim*) shall
23:13. founded it *for them that dwell in the wilderness:*
34:14. *The wild beasts of the desert* (marg. *Ziim*)
Jer. 50:39. Therefore *the wild beasts of the desert*

צִינֹק tzee-nōhk', m. 6729

Jer. 29:26. put him in prison, and in *the stocks.*

צִיץ tzeetz, m. 6731

Ex. 28:36. thou shalt make *a plate* (of) pure
39:30. And they made *the plate of* the holy
Lev. 8: 9. he put *the* golden *plate,*
Nu. 17: 8(23). and bloomed *blossoms,*
1K. 6:18. knops and open *flowers:*
29, 32, 35. palm trees and open *flowers,*
Job 14: 2. He cometh forth *like a flower,*
Ps 103:15. *as a flower of* the field,
Isa. 28: 1. whose (lit. *and* his) glorious beauty (is) a fading *flower,*
40: 6. *as the flower of* the field:
7. *the flower* fadeth: because the spirit
8. *the flower* fadeth: but the word
Jer. 48: 9. Give *wings* unto Moab,

צִיצָה [tzee-tzāh'], f. 6733

Isa. 28: 4. shall be *a* fading *flower,*

צִיצִת tzee-tzeeth', f. 6734

Nu. 15:38. that they make them *fringes*
— put upon *the fringe of* the borders
39. it shall be unto you *for a fringe,*
Eze. 8: 3. took me *by a lock of* mine head;

צָיַר [tzāh-yar']. 6737

* HITHPAEL.—*Future.* *

Jos. 9: 4. *and made as if they had been ambassadors,*

צִיר [tzeer], m. 6736

Ps. 49:14(15). (כתיב) *and their beauty* (marg. or, *strength*) shall consume
Isa. 45:16. together (that are) makers of *idols.*

צִיר tzeer, m. 6735

1Sa. 4:19. *her pains* came upon her.
Pro.13:17. *but a* faithful *ambassador*
25:13. *a* faithful *messenger* to them that
26:14. the door turneth upon *his hinges,*
Isa. 13: 8. *pangs* and sorrows shall take hold
18: 2. That sendeth *ambassadors* by the sea,
21: 3. *pangs* have taken hold upon me, *as the pangs of* a woman
57: 9. didst send *thy messengers*
Jer. 49:14. *and an ambassador* is sent unto the
Dan10:16. *my sorrows* are turned upon me,
Obad 1. *and an ambassador* is sent among the

צֵל *tzēhl*, m.

Gen19: 8. *under the shadow of* my roof.
Nu. 14: 9. *their defence* (marg. *shadow*) is departed
Jud. 9:15. put your trust *in my shadow:*
36. *the shadow of* the mountains
2K. 20: 9. shall *the shadow* go forward
10. *for the shadow* to go down ten degrees.
— let *the shadow* return backward
11. he brought *the shadow* ten degrees
1Ch 29:15. our days on the earth (are) *as a shadow,*
Job 7: 2. a servant earnestly desireth *the shadow,*
8: 9. our days upon earth (are) *a shadow:*
14: 2. he fleeth also *as a shadow,*
17: 7. all my members (are) *as a shadow.*
Ps. 17: 8. hide me *under the shadow of* thy wings,
36: 7(8). put their trust *under the shadow of* thy
57: 1(2). *yea, in the shadow of* thy wings
63: 7(8). *therefore in the shadow of* thy wings
80:10(11). The hills were covered *with the shadow of it,*
91: 1. *under the shadow of* the Almighty.
102:11(12). My days (are) *like a shadow*
109:23. I am gone *like the shadow*
121: 5. the Lord (is) *thy shade*
144: 4. *as a shadow* that passeth away.
Ecc. 6:12. he spendeth *as a shadow?*
7:12. wisdom (is) *a defence,* (and) money (is) *a defence:*
8:13. (his) days, (which are) *as a shadow;*
Cant. 2: 3. I sat down *under his shadow*
Isa. 4: 6. *for a shadow* in the daytime
16: 3. make *thy shadow* as the night
25: 4. *a shadow* from the heat,
5. *with the shadow of* a cloud:
30: 2. to trust *in the shadow of* Egypt!
3. the trust *in the shadow of* Egypt
32: 2. *as the shadow of* a great rock
34:15. and gather *under her shadow:*
38: 8. *the shadow of* the degrees,
49: 2. *in the shadow of* his hand
51:16. *and* I have covered thee *in the shadow of* mine hand,
Jer. 48:45. stood *under the shadow of* Heshbon
Lam. 4:20. *Under his shadow* we shall live
Eze. 17:23. *in the shadow of* the branches
31: 6. *and under his shadow* dwelt all great
12. gone down *from his shadow,*
17. dwelt *under his shadow* in the midst
Hos. 4:13. *the shadow thereof* (is) good:
14: 7(8). They that dwell *under his shadow*
Jon. 4: 5. sat under it *in the shadow,*
6. that it might be *a shadow*

6739 צְלָא [*tz'lāh*], Ch.

* PAEL.—*Participle.* *

Ezr. 6:10. *and pray* for the life of the king,
Dan. 6:10(11). *and prayed,* and gave thanks

6740 צָלָה [*tzāh-lāh'*].

* KAL.—*Infinitive.* *

1Sa. 2:15. Give flesh *to roast* for the priest;

KAL.—*Future.*

Isa. 44:16. *he roasteth* roast, and is satisfied:
19. *I have roasted* flesh, and eaten

6742 צְלוּל *tz'lool*, m.

Jud. 7:13. (כתיב) *a cake of* barley bread

6743 צָלֵחַ [*tzāh-lēh'ăgh*].

* KAL.—*Preterite.* *

1Sa. 10: 6. the Spirit of the Lord *will come* upon thee,
2Sa. 19:17(18). *and they went over* Jordan
Jer. 12: 1. *doth* the way of the wicked *prosper?*

KAL.—*Imperative.*

Ps. 45: 4(5). ride *prosperously* (marg. *prosper thou,* ride thou.)

KAL.—*Future.*

Nu. 14:41. of the Lord? but it *shall* not *prosper.*
Jud. 14: 6. *And* the Spirit of the Lord *came mightily*
19. *And* the Spirit of the Lord *came* upon him,
15:14. *and* the Spirit of the Lord *came mightily*
1Sa. 10:10. *and* the Spirit of God *came* upon him,
11: 6. *And* the Spirit of God *came* upon Saul
16:13. *and* the Spirit of the Lord *came* upon
18:10. *that* the evil spirit from God *came*
Isa. 53:10. the pleasure of the Lord *shall prosper*
54:17. No weapon that is formed against thee *shall prosper;*
Jer. 13: 7. *it was profitable* for nothing.
10. this girdle, which *is good* for nothing.
22:30. *shall* not *prosper* in his days: for no man of his seed *shall prosper,*
Eze. 15: 4. *Is it meet* (marg. *Will it prosper*) for (any) work?
16:13. *and thou didst prosper* into a kingdom.
17: 9. *Shall it prosper?* shall he not pull
10. (being) planted, *shall it prosper?*
15. *Shall he prosper?* shall he escape
Dan 11:27. *it shall* not *prosper:* for yet the end
Am. 5: 6. lest *he break out* like fire

* HIPHIL.—*Preterite.* *

Gen24:21. *whether* the Lord *had made* his journey *prosperous*
40. *and prosper* thy way;
56. the Lord *hath prospered* my way;
1Ch 22:11. *and prosper thou,* and build the house
2Ch 7:11. in his own house, *he prosperously effected.*
26: 5. sought the Lord, God *made him to prosper.*
31:21. did (it) with all his heart, *and prospered.*
Isa. 48:15. *and he shall make* his way *prosperous.*
55:11. *and it shall prosper* (in the thing)
Dan. 8:12. it practised, *and prospered.*
24. *and shall prosper,* and practise,
25. *also he shall cause* craft *to prosper*
11:36. *and shall prosper* till the indignation

HIPHIL.—*Imperative.*

1K. 22:12. Go up to Ramoth-gilead, *and prosper:*
15. Go, *and prosper:* for the Lord
2Ch 18:11. Go up to Ramoth-gilead, *and prosper:*
14. Go ye up, *and prosper,*
20:20. believe his prophets, *so shall ye prosper.*
Neh 1:11. *and prosper,* I pray thee, thy servant
Ps. 118:25. O Lord,...*send* now *prosperity.*

HIPHIL.—*Future.*

Deu28:29. and *thou shalt* not *prosper* in thy ways:
Jos. 1: 8. *thou shalt make* thy way *prosperous,*
Jud. 18: 5. *whether* our way which we go *shall be prosperous.*
1Ch 22:13. Then *shalt thou prosper,* if thou takest
29:23. on the throne of the Lord...*and prospered,*
2Ch 13:12. for *ye shall* not *prosper.*
14: 7(6). So they built *and prospered.*
24:20. *ye cannot prosper?*
32:30. *And* Hezekiah *prospered*
Neh 2:20. The God of heaven, he *will prosper* us;
Ps. 1: 3. whatsoever he doeth *shall prosper.*
Pro. 28:13. that covereth his sins *shall* not *prosper:*
Jer. 2:37. thy confidences, and *thou shalt* not *prosper* in them.
5:28. cause of the fatherless, *yet they prosper;*
32: 5. with the Chaldeans, *ye shall* not *prosper.*

HIPHIL.—*Participle.*

Gen24:42. if now thou do *prosper* (lit. thou art *prospering*) my way
39: 2. he was a *prosperous* man;
3. the Lord *made* all that he did *to prosper*
23. the Lord *made* (it) *to prosper.*
Ps. 37: 7. *because of him who prospereth* in his way,

צְלַח [*tz'lagh*], Ch. 6744

* APHEL.—*Preterite.* *

Dan 3:30. Then the king *promoted* (marg. *made to prosper*) Shadrach,
6:28(29). So this Daniel *prospered* in the reign

APHEL.—*Participle.*

Ezr. 5: 8. *and prospereth* in their hands.
6:14. *and they prospered* through the

6745 צְלָחָה [*tzēh-lāh-ghāh'*], f.

2Ch 35:13. in caldrons, *and in pans*,

6746 צְלֹחִית *tz'lōh-gheeth'*, f.

2K. 2:20. Bring me *a* new *cruse*, and put

6747 צַלַּחַת *tzal-lah'-ghath*, f.

2K. 21:13. as (a man) wipeth *a dish*,
Pro.19:24. A slothful (man) hideth his hand *in* (his) *bosom*,
26:15. slothful hideth his hand *in* (his) *bosom*;

6748 צָלִי *tzāh-lee'*, adj.

Ex. 12: 8. they shall eat the flesh...*roast* with fire,
9. with water, but *roast* (with) fire;
Isa. 44:16. he roasteth *roast*, and is satisfied:

6742 צְלִיל *tz'leel*, m.

Jud. 7:13. *a cake of* barley bread

6750 צָלַל [*tzāh-lal'*].

* KAL.—*Preterite.* *

Hab. 3:16. my lips *quivered* at the voice:

KAL.—*Future.*

1Sa. 3:11. the ears of every one...*shall tingle.*
2K. 21:12. both his ears *shall tingle.*
Jer. 19: 3. whosoever heareth, his ears *shall tingle.*

6749 צָלַל [*tzāh-lal'*].

* KAL.—*Preterite.* *

Ex. 15:10. *they sank* as lead in the mighty waters.

6751 צָלַל [*tzāh-lal'*].

* KAL.—*Preterite.* *

Neh 13:19. when the gates of Jerusalem *began to be dark*

* HIPHIL.—*Participle.* *

Eze.31: 3. a *shadowing* shroud,

6752 צֵלֶל [*tzēh'-lel*], m.

Job 40:22. cover him (with) *their shadow*;
Cant.2:17 & 4:6. and *the shadows* flee away,
Jer. 6: 4. *the shadows of* the evening are stretched

6754 צֶלֶם *tzeh'-lem*, m.

Gen 1:26. Let us make man *in our image*,
27. God created man *in his* (own) *image*, *in the image of* God created he him;
5: 3. in his own likeness, *after his image*;
9: 6. *in the image of* God made he man.
Nu. 33:52. destroy all their molten *images*,
1Sa. 6: 5. *images of* your emerods, *and images of* your mice
11. *the images of* their emerods.
2K. 11:18. *his images* brake they in pieces
2Ch 23:17. and brake his altars *and his images*
Ps. 39: 6(7). man walketh *in a vain shew*: (marg. *an image*)
73:20. thou shalt despise *their image*.
Eze. 7:20. *but* they made *the images of* their
16:17. madest to thyself *images of* men,
23:14. *the images of* the Chaldeans
Am. 5:26. Moloch and Chiun *your images*,

צֶלֶם *tzeh'-lem* & צְלֵם *tz'lēhm*, Ch. m. 6755

Dan. 2:31. and behold a great *image*. This great *image*, whose brightness
32. This *image's* head (was) of fine gold,
34. which smote *the image* upon his feet
35. and the stone that smote *the image*
3: 1. the king made *an image* of gold,
2. to come to the dedication of *the image*
3. unto the dedication of *the image*
— and they stood before *the image*
5. and worship *the* golden *image*
7. (and) worshipped *the* golden *image*
10. and worship *the* golden *image*:
12. *nor* worship *the* golden *image*
14. *nor* worship *the* golden *image*
15. fall down and worship *the image*
18. *nor* worship *the* golden *image*
19. *and the form of* his visage was changed

צַלְמָוֶת *tzal-māh'-veth*, f. 6757

Job 3: 5. Let darkness *and the shadow of death*
10:21. land of darkness *and the shadow of death*;
22. as darkness (itself; and) of *the shadow of death*,
12:22. bringeth out to light *the shadow of death.*
16:16. on my eyelids (is) *the shadow of death*;
24:17. to them even as *the shadow of death*:
— the terrors of *the shadow of death.*
28: 3. of darkness, *and the shadow of death.*
34:22. no darkness, nor *shadow of death*,
38:17. the doors of *the shadow of death*?
Ps. 23: 4. the valley of *the shadow of death*,
44:19(20). covered us *with the shadow of death.*
107:10. darkness *and* in *the shadow of death*,
14. out of darkness *and the shadow of death*,
Isa. 9: 2(1). the land of *the shadow of death*,
Jer. 2: 6. of drought, *and* of *the shadow of death*,
13:16. he turn it *into the shadow of death*,
Am. 5: 8. turneth *the shadow of death* into the

צָלַע [*tzāh-lag'*]. 6760

* KAL.—*Participle.* Poel. *

Gen32:31(32). he *halted* upon his thigh.
Mic. 4: 6. will I assemble *her that halteth*,
7. I will make *her that halted* a remnant,
Zep. 3:19. I will save *her that halteth*,

צֵלָע *tzēh'-lag*, f. 6763

Gen 2:21. he took one *of his ribs*,
22. *the rib*, which the Lord God had taken
Ex. 25:12. in *the* one *side of it*, and two rings in *the* other *side of it*.
14. by *the sides of* the ark,
26:20. *And for the* second *side of* the
26. *the* one *side of* the tabernacle,
27. *the* other *side of* the tabernacle, and five bars for the boards of *the side of* the
35. on *the side of* the tabernacle toward the south: and thou shalt put the table on *the* north *side*.
27: 7. *the* two *sides of* the altar,
30: 4. by *the* two *corners* (marg. *ribs*) thereof,
36:25. *And for the* other *side of* the
31. *the* one *side of* the tabernacle,
32. *the* other *side of* the tabernacle,
37: 3. two rings upon *the* one *side of it*, and two rings upon *the* other *side of it*.
5. by *the sides of* the ark, to bear the ark.
27. by *the* two *corners of it*,
38: 7. on *the sides of* the altar,
2Sa.16:13. Shimei went along on the hill's *side*
1K. 6: 5. he made *chambers* (marg. *ribs*) round
8. The door for *the* middle *chamber*
15. he built the walls...*with boards of*
— and covered the floor...*with planks of*
16. and the walls *with boards of* cedar:
34. *the* two *leaves of* the one door
7: 3. above upon *the beams*, (marg. *ribs*)
Job 18:12. destruction (shall be) ready *at his side.*
Jer. 20:10. All my familiars watched for *my halting*

[or, at *my side*, (see also צֶלַע)]

Eze.41: 5. the breadth of (every) *side chamber,*
6. *And the side chambers* (were) three, *one* over *another* (lit. *side chamber* over *side chamber*), and 30 in order; and they entered into the wall which (was) of the house *for the side chambers*
7. upward *to the side chambers :*
8. the foundations of *the side chambers*
9. which (was) *for the side chamber* without,
— the place *of the side chambers*
11. the doors of *the side chambers*
26. *and* (upon) *the side chambers of* the house,

6761 **צֶלַע** *tzeh'-la^{n}g*, m.

Ps. 35:15. *But in mine adversity* (marg. *halting*) they rejoiced,
38:17(18). I (am) ready *to halt*, (marg. *for halting*)
Jer. 20:10. All my familiars watched for *my halting*,
(See also צֵלָע)

6767 **צְלָצַל** *tz'lāh-tzāhl'*, m.

Deu 28:42. shall *the locust* consume.
2Sa. 6: 5. on cornets, *and on cymbals.*
Job 41: 7(40:31). *or* his head *with* fish *spears?*
Ps. 150: 5. Praise him *upon the* loud *cymbals:* praise him *upon the* high sounding *cymbals.*
Isa. 18: 1. the land *shadowing with* wings,

6770 **צָמֵא** [*tzāh-mēh'*].

* KAL.—*Preterite.* *

Jud. 4:19. to drink; for *I am thirsty.*
Ru. 2: 9. and *when thou art athirst,* go unto the vessels,
Ps. 42: 2(3). My soul *thirsteth* for God,
63: 1(2). my soul *thirsteth* for thee,
Isa. 48:21. And *they thirsted* not

KAL.—*Future.*

Ex. 17: 3. *And* the people *thirsted*
Jud. 15:18. *And he was* sore *athirst,*
Job 24:11. tread (their) winepresses, *and suffer thirst.*
Isa. 49:10. They shall not hunger nor *thirst;*
65:13. but *ye shall be thirsty:*

6772 **צָמָא** *tzāh-māh'*, m.

Ex. 17: 3. to kill us and our children...*with thirst?*
Deu 28:48. in hunger, *and in thirst,*
Jud. 15:18. and now shall I die *for thirst,*
2Ch 32:11. to die by famine *and by thirst,*
Neh 9:15. broughtest forth water...*for their thirst,*
20. and gavest them water *for their thirst.*
Ps. 69:21(22). *in my thirst* they gave me vinegar
104:11. the wild asses quench *their thirst.*
Isa. 41:17. their tongue faileth *for thirst,*
50: 2. their fish...dieth *for thirst.*
Jer. 48:18. and sit *in thirst;*
Lam. 4: 4. The tongue of the sucking child cleaveth... *for thirst:*
Eze. 19:13. in a dry *and thirsty* ground.
Hos. 2: 3(5). and slay her *with thirst.*
Am. 8:11. nor *a thirst* for water,
13. young men faint *for thirst.*

6771 **צָמֵא** *tzāh-mēh'*, adj.

Deu 29:19(18). to add drunkenness to *thirst:* (marg. the drunken *to the thirsty*)
2Sa. 17:29. people (is) hungry, and weary, *and thirsty,*
Ps. 107: 5. Hungry and *thirsty,* their soul fainted
Pro. 25:21. if he be *thirsty,* give him water
Isa. 21:14. brought water to *him that was thirsty,*
29: 8. when a *thirsty* man dreameth,
32: 6. the drink of *the thirsty* to fail.
44: 3. I will pour water upon *him that is thirsty,*
55: 1. Ho, every one *that thirsteth,*

6773 **צִמְאָה** *tzim-āh'*, f.

Jer. 2:25. Withhold...thy throat *from thirst:*

צִמָּאוֹן *tzim-māh-ōhn'*, m. 6774

Deu 8:15. fiery serpents, and scorpions, *and drought,*
Ps. 107:33. turneth...the watersprings *into dry ground;*
Isa. 35: 7. *and the thirsty land* springs of water:

צָמַד [*tzāh-mad'*]. 6775

* NIPHAL.—*Future.* *

Nu. 25: 3. *And* Israel *joined himself* unto Baal-peor:
Ps. 106:28. *They joined themselves also* unto Baal-peor,

NIPHAL.—*Participle.*

Nu. 25: 5. *that were joined* unto Baal-peor.

* PUAL.—*Participle.* *

2Sa. 20: 8. a sword *fastened* upon his loins

* HIPHIL.—*Future.* *

Ps. 50:19. thy tongue *frameth* deceit

צֶמֶד *tzeh'-med*, m. 6776

Jud. 19: 3. *and a couple of* asses: and she brought
10. (there were) with him *two* asses
1Sa. 11: 7. And he took *a yoke of* oxen,
14:14. (which) *a yoke* (of oxen might plow).
2Sa. 16: 1. *with a couple of* asses saddled,
1K. 19:19. plowing (with) twelve *yoke* (of oxen)
21. and took *a yoke of* oxen,
2K. 5:17. *two* mules' burden of earth?
9:25. when I and thou rode *together*
Job 1: 3. five hundred *yoke of* oxen,
42:12. a thousand *yoke of* oxen,
Isa. 5:10. ten *acres of* vineyard shall yield one bath,
21: 7. a chariot (with) *a couple of* horsemen,
9. a chariot of men, (with) *a couple of* horsemen.
Jer. 51:23. the husbandman *and his yoke of oxen;*

צָמָה *tzāh-māh'*, f. 6772

Isa. 5:13. their multitude dried up *with thirst.*

צַמָּה [*tzam-māh'*], f. 6777

Cant. 4: 1. thou (hast) doves' eyes within *thy locks:*
3. of a pomegranate within *thy locks.*
6: 7. thy temples within *thy locks.*
Isa. 47: 2. grind meal: uncover *thy locks,*

צִמּוּקִים *tzim-moo-keem'*, m. pl. 6778

1Sa. 25:18. an hundred *clusters of raisins,*
30:12. and two *clusters of raisins:*
2Sa. 16: 1. an hundred *bunches of raisins,*
1Ch 12:40. cakes of figs, *and bunches of raisins,*

צָמַח *tzāh-magh'*. 6779

* KAL.—*Preterite.* *

Lev. 13:37. *there is* black hair *grown up*
Isa. 44: 4. *And they shall spring up* (as) among the

KAL.—*Future.*

Gen 2: 5. every herb of the field before *it grew:*
Job 5: 6. neither *doth* trouble *spring* out of the
8:19. out of the earth *shall* others *grow.*
Ps. 85:11(12). Truth *shall spring* out of the earth;
Isa. 42: 9. before *they spring forth* I tell you
43:19. now *it shall spring forth;*
58: 8. thine health *shall spring forth*
Eze. 17: 6. *And it grew,* and became a spreading vine
Zec. 6:12. *he shall grow up* (marg. or, *branch up*) out of his place,

KAL.—*Participle.* Poel.

Gen 41: 6, 23. blasted with the east wind *sprung up*
Ex. 10: 5. every tree *which groweth* for you
Ecc. 2: 6. the wood *that bringeth forth* trees:

* PIEL.—*Preterite.* *

Eze. 16: 7. are fashioned, and thine hair *is grown,*

PIEL.—*Infinitive.*

Jud.16:22. the hair of his head began *to grow again*

PIEL.—*Future.*

2Sa.10: 5. until your beards *be grown,*
1Ch 19: 5. until your beards *be grown,*

* HIPHIL.—*Preterite.* *

Isa. 55:10. maketh it bring forth *and bud,*

HIPHIL.—*Infinitive.*

Job 38:27. *and to cause* the bud...*to spring forth?*

HIPHIL.—*Future.*

Gen 2: 9. *And* out of the ground *made* the Lord God *to grow*
3:18. Thorns also and thistles *shall it bring forth* (marg. *cause to bud*)
Deu 29:23(22). it is not sown, nor *beareth,*
2Sa.23: 5. although *he make* (it) not *to grow.*
Ps. 132:17. *will I make* the horn of David *to bud:*
Isa. 45: 8. *let* righteousness *spring up* together;
61:11. as the garden *causeth* the things...*to spring forth;* so the Lord God *will cause* righteousness...*to spring forth*
Jer. 33:15. *will I cause* the Branch of righteousness *to grow up*
Eze. 29:21. *will I cause* the horn of the house of Israel *to bud forth,*

HIPHIL.—*Participle.*

Ps. 104:14. *He causeth* the grass *to grow*
147: 8. *who maketh* grass *to grow*

6780 **צֶמַח** *tzeh'-magh*, m.

Gen19:25. *and that which grew upon* the ground.
Ps. 65:10(11). thou blessest *the springing thereof.*
Isa. 4: 2. In that day shall *the branch of* the Lord
61:11. the earth bringeth forth *her bud,*
Jer. 23: 5. I will raise unto David *a* righteous *Branch,*
33:15. *the Branch of* righteousness to grow up
Eze. 16: 7. to multiply *as the bud of* the field,
17: 9. all the leaves of *her spring,*
10. in the furrows *where it grew.*
Hos. 8: 7. *the bud* shall yield no meal:
Zec. 3: 8. bring forth my servant *the Branch.*
6:12. the man whose name (is) *The Branch;*

6781 **צָמִיד** *tzāh-meed'*, m.

Gen24:22. two *bracelets* for her hands
30. *bracelets* upon his sister's hands,
47. *the bracelets* upon her hands.
Nu. 19:15. hath no *covering* bound upon it,
31:50. jewels of gold, chains, and *bracelets,*
Eze.16:11. I put *bracelets* upon thy hands,
23:42. *bracelets* upon their hands,

6782 **צַמִּים** *tzam-meem'*, m.

Job 5: 5. *the robber* swalloweth up
18: 9. *the robber* shall prevail against him.

6783 **צְמִיתֻת** *tz'mee-thooth'*, f.

Lev.25:23. The land shall not be sold *for ever:* (marg. *for cutting off,* or, *to be quite cut off*)
30. shall be established *for ever*

6784 **צָמַק** [*tzāh-mak'*].

* KAL.—*Participle.* Poel. *

Hos. 9:14. a miscarrying womb and *dry* breasts.

6785 **צֶמֶר** *tzeh'-mer*, m.

Lev.13:47. (whether it be) a *woollen* garment, (lit. a garment of *wool*)
48. of linen, *or of woollen;*
52. *in woollen* or in linen,
59. in a garment of *woollen* or linen,
Deu22:11. a garment of divers sorts, (as) of *woollen* and linen together.
Jud. 6:37. I will put a fleece of *wool* in the floor;
2K. 3: 4. an hundred thousand rams, *with the wool.*
Ps.147:16. He giveth snow *like wool:*
Pro.31:13. She seeketh *wool,* and flax,
Isa. 1:18. like crimson, they shall be *as wool.*
51: 8. *and* the worm shall eat them *like wool:*
Eze.27:18. in the wine of Helbon, *and* white *wool.*
34: 3. ye clothe you with *the wool,*
44:17. no *wool* shall come upon them,
Hos. 2: 5(7). my water, *my wool* and my flax,
9(11). recover *my wool* and my flax

צַמֶּרֶת *tzam-meh'-reth*, f. 6788

Eze.17: 3. and took *the highest branch of* the cedar:
22. *of the highest branch of* the high cedar,
31: 3. *his top* was among the thick boughs.
10. *his top* among the thick boughs,
14. neither shoot up *their top*

צָמַת [*tzāh-math'*]. 6789

* KAL.—*Preterite.* *

Lam. 3:53. *They have cut off* my life in the dungeon,

* NIPHAL.—*Preterite.* *

Job 6:17. What time they wax warm, *they vanish:*
23:17. *I was* not *cut off* before the darkness,

* PIEL.—*Preterite.* *

Ps.119:139. My zeal *hath consumed me,* (marg. *cut me off*)

* PILEL.—*Preterite.* *

Ps. 88:16(17). thy terrors *have cut me off.*

* HIPHIL.—*Preterite.* *

Ps. 73:27. *thou hast destroyed* all them

HIPHIL.—*Imperative.*

Ps. 54: 5(7). *cut them off* in thy truth.

HIPHIL.—*Future.*

2Sa.22:41. *that I might destroy them* that hate me.
Ps. 18:40(41). that *I might destroy them* that hate
94:23. and *shall cut them off* in their own wickedness; (yea), the Lord our God *shall cut them off.*
101: 5. his neighbour, him *will I cut off:*
8. *I will* early *destroy* all the wicked
143:12. *cut off* mine enemies,

HIPHIL.—*Participle.*

Ps. 69: 4(5). *they that would destroy me,* (being) mine enemies

---

צֵן [*tzēhn*], m. 6791

Job 5: 5. taketh it even *out of the thorns,*
Pro.22: 5. *Thorns* (and) snares (are) in the way of

צֹנֶא & צֹנֶה *tzōh-neh'*, com. 6792

Nu. 32:24. Build you cities...and folds *for your sheep;*
Ps. 8: 7(8). All *sheep* (marg. *Flocks*) and oxen,

צִנָּה [*tzin-nāh'*], f. 6793

Am. 4: 2. he will take you away *with hooks,*

צִנָּה *tzin-nāh'*, f. 6793

1Sa.17: 7. one bearing *a shield* went before him.
41. the man that bare *the shield*
1K. 10:16. Solomon made two hundred *targets*
— six hundred (shekels)...went to one *target.*
1Ch 12: 8. that could handle *shield* and buckler,
24. The children of Judah that bare *shield*
34. them *with shield* and spear
2Ch 9:15. Solomon made two hundred *targets*
— six hundred (shekels)...went to one *target.*
11:12. in every several city (he put) *shields*
14: 8(7). an army (of men) that bare *targets*
25: 5. that could handle spear *and shield.*
Ps. 5:12(13). compass him *as* (with) *a shield.*
35: 2. Take hold of shield and *buckler,*

Ps. 91: 4. his truth (shall be thy) *shield* and buckler.
Jer. 46: 3. Order ye the buckler *and shield*,
Eze.23:24. shall set against thee *buckler* and shield
26: 8. and lift up *the buckler* against thee.
38: 4. a great company (with) *bucklers* and
39: 9. the shields *and the bucklers*,

6793 **צִנָּה** [*tzin-nāh'*].

Pro.25:13. *As the cold of* snow in the time

6797 **צָנוֹף** *tzāh-nōhph'*, m.

Isa. 62: 3. (כתיב) *and a* royal *diadem* in the hand of thy God.

6794 **צִנּוֹר** *tzin-nōhr'*, m.

2Sa. 5: 8. Whosoever getteth up *to the gutter*,
Ps. 42: 7(8). the noise of *thy waterspouts*:

6795 **צָנַח** [*tzāh-nag̣h'*].

* KAL.—*Future.* *

Jos. 15:18. *and she lighted* off (her) ass;
Jud. 1:14. *and she lighted* from off (her) ass;
4:21. *and fastened* it into the ground:

6796 **צְנִינִים** *tz'nee-neem'*, m. pl.

Nu. 33:55. *and thorns* in your sides, and shall vex
Jos. 23:13. *and thorns* in your eyes, until ye perish

6797 **צָנִיף** *tzāh-neeph'*, m.

Job 29:14. my judgment (was) as a robe *and a diadem*.
Isa. 3:23. The glasses, and the fine linen, *and the hoods*,
62: 3. *and a* royal *diadem* in the hand of thy God.
Zec. 3: 5. Let them set *a* fair *mitre* upon his head. So they set *a* fair *mitre* upon his head,

---

6798 **צָנַם** [*tzāh-nam'*].

* KAL.—*Participle.* Paül. *

Gen41:23. seven ears, *withered*, thin, (and) blasted

6800 **צָנַע** [*tzāh-nag'*].

* KAL.—*Participle.* Paül. *

Pro.11: 2. with *the lowly* (is) wisdom.

* HIPHIL.—*Infinitive.* *

Mic. 6: 8. *and to* walk *humbly* (marg. *to humble* (thyself) to walk) with thy God?

6801 **צָנַף** [*tzāh-naph'*].

* KAL.—*Infinitive.* *

Isa. 22:18. He will *surely* violently turn (lit. *violently turning* he will violently turn)

KAL.—*Future.*

Lev.16: 4. with the linen mitre *shall he be attired*:
Isa. 22:18. *He will* surely *violently turn* and toss *thee*

6802 **צְנֵפָה** *tz'nēh-phāh'*, f.

Isa. 22:18. violently turn and *toss* (lit. *with turning*) thee

---

6803 **צִנְצֶנֶת** *tzin-tzeh'-neth*, f.

Ex. 16:33. Take a *pot*, and put an omer full

6804 **צַנְתָּרוֹת** [*tzan-tāh-rōhth'*], f. pl.

Zec. 4:12. two golden *pipes* empty

צָעַד [*tzāh-gad'*]. 6805

* KAL.—*Preterite.* *

Gen49:22. a fruitful bough...(whose) branches *run over*
2Sa. 6:13. when they that bare the ark...*had gone*

KAL.—*Infinitive.*

Jud. 5: 4. *when thou marchedst* out of the field of
Ps. 68: 7(8). *when thou didst march* through

KAL.—*Future.*

Pro. 7: 8. *he went* the way to her house,
Jer. 10: 5. be borne, because *they cannot go*.
Hab 3:12. *Thou didst march through* the land

* HIPHIL.—*Future.* *

Job 18:14. *and it shall bring him* to the king of terrors.

צַעַד [*tzah'-gad*], m. 6806

2Sa. 6:13. they that bare the ark...had gone six *paces*,
22:37. Thou hast enlarged *my steps*
Job 14:16. thou numberest *my steps*:
18: 7. *The steps of* his strength shall be
31: 4. my ways, and count all *my steps*?
37. I would declare...the number of *my steps*;
34:21. he seeth all *his goings*.
Ps. 18:36(37). Thou hast enlarged *my steps*
Pro. 4:12. *thy steps* shall not be straitened;
5: 5. *her steps* take hold on hell.
16: 9. the Lord directeth *his steps*.
30:29. three (things) which *go* well, (lit. which do well in *going*)
Jer. 10:23. to direct *his steps*.
Lam. 4:18. They hunt *our steps*,

צְעָדָה *tz'gāh-dāh'*, f. 6807

2Sa. 5:24. when thou hearest the sound of *a going*
1Ch 14:15. when thou shalt hear a sound of *going*
Isa. 3:20. *and the ornaments of the legs*, and the headbands,

---

צָעָה [*tzāh-gāh'*]. 6808

* KAL.—*Participle.* Poel. *

Isa. 51:14. *The captive exile* hasteneth that he may
63: 1. *travelling* in the greatness of his strength?
Jer. 2:20. under every green tree thou *wanderest*,
48:12. I will send unto him *wanderers*,

* PIEL.—*Preterite.* *

Jer. 48:12. *that shall cause him to wander*, and shall

צָעוֹר [*tzāh-gōhr'*], adj. 6810

Jer. 14: 3. (כתיב) their nobles have sent *their little ones*
48: 4. (——) *her little ones* have caused a cry

צָעִיף *tzāh-geeph'*, m. 6809

Gen24:65. therefore she took *a vail*, and covered
38:14. and covered her *with a vail*,
19. and laid by *her vail* from her,

צָעִיר *tzāh-geer'*, adj. 6810

Gen19:31, 34. the firstborn said unto *the younger*,
35. and *the younger* arose, and lay with him;
38. And *the younger*, she also bare a son,
25:23. the elder shall serve *the younger*.
29:26. to give *the younger* before the firstborn.
43:33. *and the youngest* according to his youth:
48:14. Ephraim's head, who (was) *the younger*,
Jos. 6:26. *and in his youngest* (son) shall he set up
Jud. 6:15. I (am) *the least* in my father's house.
1Sa. 9:21. *the least* of all the families
1K. 16:34. in *his youngest* (son) Segub,
Job 30: 1. (they that are) *younger* (marg. of *fewer* days) than I have me in derision,
32: 6. I (am) *young* (marg. *few* of days), and ye (are) very old;
Ps. 68:27(28). There (is) *little* Benjamin (with) their
119:141. I (am) *small* and despised:

Isa. 60:22. *and a small one* a strong nation:
Jer. 14: 3. their nobles have sent *their little ones*
48: 4. *her little ones* have caused a cry
49:20 & 50:45. *the least of* the flock shall draw
Mic. 5: 2(1). be *little* among the thousands of Judah,

6812 צְעִירָה [*tz'ngee-rāh'*], f.

Gen43:33. the youngest *according to his youth:*

6813 צָעַן [*tzāh-ngan'*].

* KAL.—*Future.* *

Isa. 33:20. a tabernacle (that) *shall* not *be taken down;*

6813 צַעֲצֻעִים *tzah-ngătzoo-ngeem'*, m. pl.

2Ch 3:10. two cherubims of *image* work, (marg. or, (as some think) of *moveable* work)

6817 צָעַק *tzāh-ngak'.*

* KAL.—*Preterite.* *

Deu22:24. the damsel, because *she cried* not,
27. the betrothed damsel *cried*,
1K. 20:39. *he cried* unto the king: and he said,
2K. 4: 1. Now *there cried* a certain woman
40. *they cried out*, and said, O (thou) man of
6:26. *there cried* a woman unto him,
Ps. 34:17(18). (The righteous) *cry*, and the Lord
88: 1(2). *I have cried* day (and) night
Isa. 33: 7. their valiant ones *shall cry*
Lam. 2:18. Their heart *cried* unto the Lord,

KAL.—*Infinitive.*

Ex. 22:23(22). they cry *at all* (lit. *crying* they cry)
2K. 8: 3. she went forth *to cry* unto the king

KAL.—*Imperative.*

Jer. 22:20. Go up to Lebanon, *and cry;* and lift up thy voice in Bashan, *and cry*
49: 3. *cry*, ye daughters of Rabbah,

KAL.—*Future.*

Gen27:34. *And* when...*he cried* with a great...cry,
41:55. *And* when...the people *cried* to Pharaoh
Ex. 5:15. the officers...came *and cried* unto Pharaoh,
8:12(8). *and* Moses *cried* unto the Lord because
14:10. *and* the children of Israel *cried out*
15. Wherefore *criest thou* unto me?
15:25. *And he cried* unto the Lord;
17: 4. *And* Moses *cried* unto the Lord,
22:23(22). and *they cry* at all unto me,
27(26). when *he crieth* unto me,
Nu. 11: 2. *And* the people *cried* unto Moses;
12:13. *And* Moses *cried* unto the Lord,
20:16. And *when we cried* unto the Lord,
Deu26: 7. And *when we cried* unto the Lord
Jos. 24: 7. And *when they cried* unto the Lord,
Jud. 4: 3. *And* the children of Israel *cried* unto the
10:12. *and ye cried* to me, and I delivered
2K. 6: 5. *and he cried*, and said, Alas, master!
2Ch 13:14. *and they cried* unto the Lord,
Neh. 9:27. when *they cried* unto thee,
Job 19: 7. *I cry out* of wrong,
35:12. There *they cry*, but none giveth answer,
Ps. 77: 1(2). *I cried* unto God with my voice,
107: 6. *Then they cried* unto the Lord
28. *Then they cry* unto the Lord
Isa. 19:20. *they shall cry* unto the Lord
42: 2. *He shall* not *cry*, nor lift up,
46: 7. yea, (one) *shall cry* unto him, yet can
65:14. ye *shall cry* for sorrow of heart,

KAL.—*Participle.* Poel.

Gen 4:10. the voice of thy brother's blood *crieth*
Ex. 5: 8. they *cry*, saying, Let us go (and) sacrifice
2K. 8: 5. *cried* to the king for her house

* NIPHAL.—*Future.* *

Jud. 7:23. *And* the men of Israel *gathered themselves together*
24. *Then* all the men of Ephraim *gathered themselves together*,
10:17. *Then* the children of Ammon *were gathered together*, (marg. *cried*)
12: 1. *And* the men of Ephraim *gathered themselves together*, (marg. *were called*)
1Sa. 13: 4. *And* the people *were called together*
2K. 3:21. *And* when...*they gathered* (marg. *were cried together*) all that were able

* PIEL.—*Participle.* *

2K. 2:12. and he *cried*, My father, my father,

* HIPHIL.—*Future.* *

1Sa. 10:17. *And* Samuel *called* the people *together*

צְעָקָה *tz'ngāh-kāh'*, f. 6818

Gen18:21. *whether* they have done...*according to the cry of it*,
19:13. *the cry of them* is waxen great
27:34. *a* great and exceeding bitter *cry*,
Ex. 3: 7. and have heard *their cry*
9. *the cry of* the children of Israel
11: 6. there shall be *a* great *cry*
12:30. there was *a* great *cry* in Egypt;
22:23(22). I will surely hear *their cry;*
1Sa. 4:14. Eli heard the noise of *the crying*,
9:16. *their cry* is come unto me.
Neh. 5: 1. there was *a* great *cry of* the people
Job 27: 9. Will God hear *his cry*
34:28. they cause *the cry of* the poor to come unto him, *and* he heareth *the cry of* the
Ps. 9:12(13). *the cry of* the humble.
Isa. 5: 7. for righteousness, but behold *a cry.*
Jer. 25:36. A voice of *the cry of* the shepherds,
48: 3. A voice of *crying*
5. the enemies have heard *a cry of*
49:21. at *the cry* the noise thereof
Zep. 1:10. the noise of *a cry* from the fish gate,

צָעַר [*tzāh-ngar'*]. 6819

* KAL.—*Future.* *

Job 14:21. *and they are brought low*, but he perceiveth
Jer. 30:19. and *they shall* not *be small.*

KAL.—*Participle.* Poel.

Zec 13: 7. I will turn mine hand upon *the little ones.*

צָפַד *tzāh-phad'.* 6821

* KAL.—*Preterite.* *

Lam. 4: 8. their skin *cleaveth* to their bones;

צָפָה [*tzāh-phāh'*]. 6822-23

* KAL.—*Infinitive.* *

Isa. 21: 5. *watch* in the watchtower,

KAL.—*Future.*

Gen 31:49. The Lord *watch* between me and thee,
Ps. 66: 7. his eyes *behold* the nations:

KAL.—*Participle.* Poel.

Nu. 23:14. he brought him into the field of *Zophim*, [or, of *watchmen*]
1Sa. 1: 1. a certain man of Ramathaim-*zophim*, [or, *id.*]
14:16. *the watchmen* of Saul in Gibeah
2Sa. 13:34. the young man *that kept the watch*
18:24. and *the watchman* went up
25. And *the watchman* cried,
26. *the watchman* saw another man running: and *the watchman* called unto the porter,
27. And *the watchman* said,
2K. 9:17. *And* there stood *a watchman* on the tower
18, 20. And *the watchman* told, saying,
Ps. 37:32. The wicked *watcheth* the righteous
Pro. 15: 3. *beholding* the evil and the good.
31:27. *She looketh well to* the ways of
Cant. 7: 4(5). *which looketh* toward Damascus.
Isa. 52: 8. *Thy watchmen* shall lift up the voice;
56:10. *His watchmen* (are) blind: they are all
Jer. 6:17. I set *watchmen* over you,
Eze. 3:17. I have made thee *a watchman*
33: 2. and set him *for* their *watchman:*
6. *But* if *the watchman* see the sword require at *the watchman*'s hand.

Eze.33: 7. I have set thee *a watchman*
Hos. 9: 8. *The watchman* of Ephraim (was) with my God:

KAL.—*Participle.* Paül.

Job 15:22. *and* he *is waited for* of the sword.

* PIEL.—*Preterite.* *

Ex. 25:11, 24. *And thou shalt overlay* it with pure
13, 28. *and overlay* them with gold.
26:29. *and thou shalt overlay* the bars with gold.
37. *and overlay* them with gold,
27: 2. *and thou shalt overlay* it with brass.
6. *and overlay* them with brass.
30: 3. *And thou shalt overlay* it with pure gold,
5. *and overlay* them with gold.
36:34. And *he overlaid* the boards
38. *and he overlaid* their chapiters
38:28. *and overlaid* their chapiters,
1K. 6:15. *he covered* (them) on the inside
22. the whole house *he overlaid*
— by the oracle *he overlaid* with gold.
30. the floor of the house *he overlaid*
32. *and overlaid* (them) with gold,
35. *and covered* (them) with gold
2K. 18:16. the pillars which Hezekiah...*had overlaid*,
2Ch 4: 9. and *overlaid* the doors of them
Lam. 4:17. *we have watched* for a nation

PIEL.—*Imperative.*

Jer. 48:19. stand by the way, *and espy;*
Nah 2: 1(2). keep the munition, *watch* the way,

PIEL.—*Future.*

Ex. 25:11. and without *shalt thou overlay it*,
26:29. And *thou shalt overlay* the boards
36:34. *and overlaid* the bars with gold.
36. *and overlaid them* with gold:
37: 2. *And he overlaid it* with pure gold
4, 15, 28. *and overlaid* them with gold.
11, 26. *And he overlaid* it with pure gold,
38: 2. *and he overlaid* it with brass.
6. *and overlaid* them with brass.
1K. 6:15. *and covered* the floor of the house
20. *and he overlaid it* with pure gold; *and* (so) *covered* the altar
21. *So* Solomon *overlaid* the house
— *and he overlaid it* with gold.
28. *And he overlaid* the cherubims with gold.
10:18. *and overlaid it* with the best gold.
2Ch 3: 4. *and he overlaid it* within with pure gold.
6. *And he garnished* (marg. *covered*) the house
10. *and overlaid* them with gold.
9:17. *and overlaid it* with pure gold.
Ps. 5: 3(4). in the morning will I direct (my prayer) unto thee, *and will look up.*
Mic. 7: 7. *I will look* unto the Lord;
Hab 2: 1. *and will watch* to see what he will say

PIEL.—*Participle.*

1Sa. 4:13. Eli sat upon a seat...*watching:*
Isa. 21: 6. Go, set *a watchman*, let him declare
Mic. 7: 4. the day of *thy watchmen*

* PUAL.—*Participle.* *

Ex. 26:32. of shittim (wood) *overlaid* with gold:
Pro. 26:23. a potsherd *covered* with silver dross.

6824 צָפָה [*tzāh-phāh'*], f.

Eze.32: 6. the land wherein *thou swimmest*, (marg. of *thy swimming*)

6826 צִפּוּי *tzip-pooy'*, m.

Ex. 38:17, 19. *and the overlaying of* their chapiters
Nu. 16:38(17:3). broad plates (for) *a covering of* the altar:
39(—:4). broad (plates for) *a covering of* the
Isa. 30:22. *the covering of* thy graven images

6828 צָפוֹן *tzāh-phōhn'*, com.

Gen13:14. *northward*, and southward,
28:14. *and to the north*, and to the south:
Ex. 26:20. on the *north* side (there shall be)
35. put the table on the *north* side.
Ex. 27:11. for the *north* side in length
36:25. toward the *north* corner,
38:11. And for the *north* side
40:22. upon the side of the tabernacle *northward*,
Lev. 1:11. on the side of the altar *northward*
Nu. 2:25. of Dan (shall be) *on the north side*
3:35. on the side of the tabernacle *northward*.
34: 7, 9. this shall be your *north* border:
35: 5. and on the *north* side
Deu 2: 3. turn you *northward*.
3:27. *and northward*, and southward,
Jos. 8:11. and pitched *on the north side* of Ai:
13. *on the north* of the city,
11: 2. *on the north* of the mountains,
13: 3. unto the borders of Ekron *northward*,
15: 5. (their) border in the *north* quarter
6. and passed along *by the north*
7. *and so northward*, looking toward Gilgal,
8. the valley of the giants *northward:*
10. which (is) Chesalon, *on the north side*,
11. the side of Ekron *northward:*
16: 6. to Michmethah *on the north side;*
17: 9. *on the north side* of the river,
10. *and northward* (it was) Manasseh's,
— they met together...*on the north*,
18: 5. in their coasts *on the north*.
12. their border on *the north* side
— the side of Jericho *on the north side*,
16. the valley of the giants *on the north*,
17. And was drawn *from the north*,
18. over against Arabah *northward*,
19. to the side of Beth-hoglah *northward:*
— at the *north* bay of the salt sea
19:14. *on the north side* to Hannathon:
27. *toward the north side* of Beth-emek,
24:30. *on the north side* of the hill of Gaash.
Jud. 2: 9. *on the north side* of the hill Gaash.
7: 1. *on the north side* of them,
12: 1. the men of Ephraim...went *northward*,
21:19. *on the north side* of Beth-el,
1Sa. 14: 5. The forefront of the one (was) situate *northward*
1K. 7:25. three looking *toward the north*,
2K. 16:14. on the *north* side of the altar.
1Ch 9:24. toward the east, west, *north*, and south.
26:14. his lot came out *northward*.
17. *northward* four a day,
2Ch 4: 4. three looking *toward the north*,
Job 26: 7. He stretcheth out *the north*
37:22. Fair weather cometh *out of the north:*
Ps. 48: 2(3). mount Zion, (on) the sides of *the north*,
89:12(13). *The north* and the south thou hast
107: 3. *from the north*, and from the south.
Pro. 25:23. The *north* wind driveth away rain:
Ecc. 1: 6. turneth about unto *the north;*
11: 3. toward the south, or *toward the north*,
Cant. 4:16. Awake, *O north wind;*
Isa. 14:13. in the sides of *the north:*
31. shall come *from the north* a smoke,
41:25. I have raised up (one) *from the north*,
43: 6. I will say *to the north*, Give up;
49:12. *from the north* and from the west;
Jer. 1:13. the face thereof (is) toward *the north*.
14. *Out of the north* an evil shall break
15. the kingdoms of *the north*,
3:12. proclaim these words *toward the north*,
18. out of the land of *the north* to the land
4: 6. I will bring evil *from the north*,
6: 1. evil appeareth *out of the north*,
22. a people cometh from the *north* country,
10:22. out of the *north* country,
13:20. them that come *from the north:*
15:12. Shall iron break the *northern* iron
16:15. from the land of *the north*,
23: 8. out of the *north* country,
25: 9. all the families of *the north*,
26. all the kings of *the north*,
31: 8. I will bring them from the *north* country,
46: 6. and fall *toward the north*
10. a sacrifice in the *north* country
20. it cometh *out of the north*.
24. the people of *the north*.
47: 2. waters rise up *out of the north*,
50: 3. *out of the north* there cometh up a nation
9. nations from the *north* country:
41. a people shall come *from the north*,
51:48. the spoilers shall come...*from the north*,

Eze. 1: 4. a whirlwind came *out of the north*,
8: 3. inner gate that looketh *toward the north*;
5. thine eyes now the way *toward the north*.
— the way *toward the north*, and behold *northward* at the gate of the altar
14. which (was) *toward the north*;
9: 2. gate, which lieth *toward the north*,
20:47(21:3). from the south *to the north*
21: 4(9). from the south *to the north*:
26: 7. a king of kings, *from the north*,
32:30. the princes of *the north*,
38: 6. of Togarmah of the *north* quarters,
15. from thy place out of the *north* parts,
39: 2. to come up from the *north* parts, (marg. sides of *the north*)
40:19. eastward *and northward*.
20. that looked *toward the north*,
23. the gate *toward the north*,
35. he brought me to the *north* gate,
40. the entry of the *north* gate,
44. at the side of the *north* gate;
— the prospect toward *the north*.
46. whose prospect (is) *toward the north*
41:11. one door toward *the north*, and another
42: 1. the way toward *the north*:
— before the building toward *the north*.
2. an hundred cubits (was) the *north* door,
4. their doors *toward the north*.
11. chambers which (were) toward *the north*,
13. The *north* chambers (and) the south
17. He measured the *north* side,
44: 4. me the way of the *north* gate
46: 9. by the way of the *north* gate
— by the way of the *north* gate:
19. which looked *toward the north*:
47: 2. the way of the gate *northward*,
15. toward the *north* side,
17. *and the north northward*, and the border of Hamath. And (this is) the *north* side.
48: 1. From the *north* end
— the border of Damascus *northward*,
10. *toward the north*
16. the *north* side four thousand
17. *toward the north* two hundred and fifty,
30. of the city on the *north* side,
31. three gates *northward*; one gate of
Dan 8: 4. *northward*, and southward;
11: 6. shall come to the king of *the north*
7. the fortress of the king of *the north*,
8. years than the king of *the north*.
11. with the king of *the north*:
13. the king of *the north* shall return,
15. So the king of *the north* shall come,
40. and the king of *the north* shall come
44. out of the east *and out of the north*
Am. 8:12. *and from the north* even to the east,
Zep. 2:13. stretch out his hand against *the north*,
Zec. 2: 6(10). from the land of *the north*,
6: 6. into the *north* country;
8. these that go toward the *north* country have quieted my spirit in the *north* country.
14: 4. mountain shall remove *toward the north*,

6830 צְפוֹנִי *tz'phōh-nee'*, adj.

Joel 2:20. I will remove...*the northern* (army),

6832 צְפוּעַ [*tz'phoo'ăg*], m.

Eze. 4:15. (כתיב) I have given thee cow's *dung*

6833 צִפּוֹר *tzip-pōhr'*, com.

Gen. 7:14. every *bird of* every sort.
15:10. *the birds* divided he not.
Lev.14: 4. two *birds* (marg. or, *sparrows*) alive
5. one of *the birds* be killed
6. As for *the* living *bird*,
— *the* living *bird* in the blood of *the bird*
7. and shall let *the* living *bird* loose
49. he shall take...two *birds*,
50. he shall kill the one of *the birds*
51. and *the* living *bird*,
— in the blood of *the* slain *bird*,
52. with the blood of *the bird*,
Lev.14:52. *and with the* living *bird*,
53. he shall let go *the* living *bird*
Deu. 4:17. the likeness of any winged *fowl*
14:11. all clean *birds* ye shall eat.
22: 6. If *a bird*'s nest chance to be before thee
Neh. 5:18. *also fowls* were prepared for me,
Job 41: 5(40:29). play with him *as* (with) *a bird?*
Ps. 8: 8(9). *The fowl of* the air, and the fish
11: 1. Flee (as) *a bird* to your mountain?
84: 3(4). *the sparrow* hath found an house,
102: 7(8). I watch, and am *as a sparrow*
104:17. Where *the birds* make their nests:
124: 7. *as a bird* out of the snare
148:10. creeping things, *and* flying *fowl*: (marg. *birds of* wing)
Pro. 6: 5. *and as a bird* from the hand of the fowler.
7:23. *as a bird* hasteth to the snare,
26: 2. *As the bird* by wandering,
27: 8. *As a bird* that wandereth
Ecc. 9:12. *and as the birds* that are caught
12: 4. the voice of *the bird*,
Isa. 31: 5. *As birds* flying, so will the Lord
Lam.3:52. Mine enemies chased me sore, *like a bird*,
Eze.17:23. all *fowl of* every wing;
39: 4. I will give thee unto *the* ravenous *birds*
17. *unto* every feathered *fowl*,
Hos 11:11. They shall tremble *as a bird*
Am. 3: 5. Can *a bird* fall in a snare

צַפַּחַת *tzap-pah'-ghath*, f. 6835

1Sa.26:11. and *the cruse of* water, and let us go.
12. the spear and *the cruse of* water
16. and *the cruse of* water that (was) at his
1K. 17:12. and a little oil *in a cruse*:
14. *neither* shall *the cruse of* oil fail,
16. *neither* did *the cruse of* oil fail,
19: 6. *and a cruse of* water at his head.

צְפִיָּה [*tz'pheey-yāh'*], f. 6836

Lam.4:17. *in our watching* we have watched

צַפִּיחִת *tz'phee-gheeth'*, f. 6838

Ex. 16:31. the taste of it (was) *like wafers* (made) with honey.

צָפִין [*tzāh-pheen'*], adj. 6840

Ps. 17:14. (כתיב) *and* whose belly thou fillest *with thy hid* (treasure):

צְפִיעַ [*tz'phee'ăg*], m. 6832

Eze. 4:15. I have given thee cow's *dung*

צָפִיר *tzāh-pheer'*, m. 6842

2Ch 29:21. *and* seven *he* goats, (lit. *and he goats of* the goats)
Ezr. 8:35. twelve *he goats* (for) a sin offering:
Dan. 8: 5. *an he* goat (lit. *an he goat of* the goats) came from the west
— *and the goat* (had) a notable horn
8. *Therefore the he* goat (lit. *And he goat of* the goats) waxed very great:
21. *And the* rough *goat* (is) the king of

צְפִיר [*tz'pheer*], Ch. m. 6841

Ezr. 6:17. *and* for a sin offering...twelve *he* goats, (lit. *and he goats of* the goats)

צְפִירָה *tz'phee-rāh'*, f. 6843

Isa. 28: 5. *and for a diadem of* beauty,
Eze. 7: 7. *The morning* is come unto thee, O thou
10. *the morning* is gone forth; the rod hath

צָפִית *tzāh-pheeth'*, f. 6844

Isa. 21: 5. watch *in the watchtower*.

צָפַן tzāh-phan'.

* KAL.—*Preterite.* *

Job 10:13. *hast thou hid* in thine heart:
17: 4. *thou hast hid* their heart
23:12. *I have esteemed* (marg. *hid*, or, *laid up*)
Ps. 31:19(20). thy goodness, which *thou hast laid up*
119:11. Thy word *have I hid* in mine heart,
Pro. 2: 7. (כתיב) *He layeth up* sound wisdom
27:16. *hideth* the wind,
Cant. 7:13(14). *I have laid up* for thee,

KAL.—*Future.*

Ex. 2: 2. *she hid him* three months.
Jos. 2: 4. woman took the two men, *and hid them*,
Job 21:19. God *layeth up* his iniquity
Ps. 10: 8. his eyes *are privily set* (marg. *hide themselves*) against the poor.
27: 5. in the time of trouble *he shall hide me*
31:20(21). *thou shalt keep them secretly* in a
56: 6(7). *they hide themselves*, they mark my
Pro. 1:11. *let us lurk privily* for the innocent
18. *they lurk privily* for their (own) lives.
2: 1. and *hide* my commandments with thee;
7. *He layeth up* sound wisdom for the
7: 1. *lay up* my commandments
10:14. Wise (men) *lay up* knowledge:

KAL.—*Participle.* Poel.

Pro. 27:16. Whosoever *hideth her*

KAL.—*Participle.* Paül.

Job 20:26. darkness (shall be) hid *in his secret places:*
Ps. 17:14. and whose belly thou fillest *with thy hid*
83: 3(4). and consulted against *thy hidden ones.*
Pro. 13:22. *and* the wealth of the sinner (is) *laid up*
Eze. 7:22. and they shall pollute *my secret* (place):
Hos 13:12. bound up; and sin (is) *hid.*

* NIPHAL.—*Preterite.* *

Job 15:20. the number of years *is hidden*
24: 1. times *are* not *hidden* from the Almighty,
Jer. 16:17. neither *is* their iniquity *hid*

* HIPHIL.—*Infinitive.* *

Ex. 2: 3. when she could not longer *hide him*,

HIPHIL.—*Future.*

Job 14:13. O that *thou wouldest hide me*
Ps. 56: 6(7). (כתיב) *they hide themselves*, they mark

6848 ### צֶפַע tzeh'-phag̃, m.

Isa. 14:29. shall come forth *a cockatrice*, (marg. or, *adder*)

6848 ### צִפְעֹנִי tziph-g̃ōh-nee', m.

Pro 23:32. *and* stingeth *like an adder.* (marg. or, *a cockatrice*)
Isa. 11: 8. his hand on *the cockatrice'* (marg. or, *adder's*) den.
59: 5. They hatch *cockatrice'* (marg. *id.*) eggs,
Jer. 8:17. I will send...*cockatrices*, among you,

6849 ### צְפִעוֹת tz'phee-g̃ōhth', f. pl.

Isa. 22:24. the offspring *and the issue*,

6850 ### צָפַף [tzāh-phaph'].

* PILPEL.—*Future.* *

Isa. 29: 4. thy speech *shall whisper* (marg. *peep*, or, *chirp*)
38:14. so *did I chatter:*

PILPEL.—*Participle.*

Isa. 8:19. wizards *that peep*,
10:14. or opened the mouth, *or peeped.*

6851 ### צַפְצָפָה tzaph-tzāh-phāh', f.

Eze. 17: 5. (and) set it (as) *a willow tree.*

צָפַר [tzāh-phar']. 6852

* KAL.—*Future.* *

Jud. 7: 3. let him return *and depart early*

צְפַר [tz'phar], Ch. m. 6853

Dan 4:12(9). *and the fowls of* the heaven dwelt
14(11). *and the fowls* from his branches:
21(18). *the fowls of* the heaven had their
33(30). and his nails *like birds'* (claws).

צְפַרְדֵּעַ tz'phar-dēh'ăg̃, m. 6854

Ex. 8: 2(7:27). smite all thy borders *with frogs:*
3(–:28). the river shall bring forth *frogs*
4(–:29). *the frogs* shall come up
5(1). and cause *frogs* to come up
6(2). and *the frogs* came up,
7(3). and brought up *frogs*
8(4). that he may take away *the frogs*
9(5). to destroy *the frogs*
11(7). And *the frogs* shall depart
12(8). because of *the frogs*
13(9). and *the frogs* died out of the houses,
Ps. 78:45. and *frogs*, which destroyed them.
105:30. Their land brought forth *frogs*

צִפֹּרֶן tzip-pōh'-ren, m. 6856

Deu 21:12. and pare *her nails;*
Jer. 17: 1. (and) *with the point* (marg. *nail*) *of* a diamond:

צֶפֶת tzeh'-pheth, f. 6858

2Ch. 3:15. *and the chapiter* that (was) on the top

צִקְלוֹן [tzik-lōhn'], m. 6861

2K. 4:42. corn *in the husk thereof.* (marg. or, *in his scrip*, or, *garment*)

צַר tzar & צָר tzāhr, m. 6862

Gen 14:20. hath delivered *thine enemies* into thy hand.
Nu. 10: 9. *the enemy* that oppresseth you,
24: 8. he shall eat up the nations *his enemies*,
Deu 4:30. *When* thou art *in tribulation*,
32:27. *their adversaries* should behave themselves
41. I will render vengeance *to mine enemies*,
43. render vengeance *to his adversaries*,
33: 7. an help (to him) *from his enemies.*
Jos. 5:13. (Art) thou for us, or *for our adversaries?*
1Sa. 2:32. *an enemy* (in) (marg. or, *the affliction of*) (my) habitation,
2Sa. 22: 7. *In* my *distress* I called upon the Lord,
24:13. flee three months before *thine enemies*,
2K. 6: 1. the place where we dwell...is too *strait*
1Ch 12:17. to betray me *to mine enemies*,
21:12. to be destroyed before *thy foes*,
2Ch 15: 4. when they *in* their *trouble* did turn
Ezr. 4: 1. *the adversaries of* Judah and Benjamin
Neh 4:11(5). And *our adversaries* said,
9:27. into the hand of *their enemies*,
— out of the hand of *their enemies.*
Est. 7: 4. *the enemy* could not countervail
6. *The adversary* and enemy (is) this wicked Haman.
Job 6:23. Deliver me from *the enemy's* hand?
7:11. I will speak *in the anguish of* my spirit;
15:24. *Trouble* and anguish shall make him
16: 9. *mine enemy* sharpeneth his eyes
19:11. he counteth me...*as* (one of) *his enemies.*
36:16. removed thee out of the *strait*...place,
38:23. against the time of *trouble*,
Ps. 3: 1(2). *they* increased *that trouble me?*
4: 1(2). (when I was) *in distress;*
13: 4(5). *those that trouble me* rejoice when I
18: 6(7). *In* my *distress* I called upon the Lord,
27: 2. *mine enemies* and my foes,

Ps. 27:12. the will of *mine enemies:*
32: 7. thou shalt preserve me *from trouble;*
44: 5(6). Through thee will we push down *our enemies:*
7(8). thou hast saved us *from our enemies,*
10(11). to turn back from *the enemy:*
59:16(17). in the day of my *trouble.*
60:11(13). Give us help *from trouble:*
12(14). shall tread down *our enemies.*
66:14. when I was *in trouble.*
74:10. how long shall *the adversary* reproach?
78:42. he delivered them from *the enemy.* (marg. or, *affliction*)
61. his glory into *the enemy's* hand.
66. he smote *his enemies* in the hinder part:
81:14(15). turned my hand against *their adversaries.*
89:23(24). I will beat down *his foes*
42(43). the right hand of *his adversaries;*
97: 3. burneth up *his enemies* round about.
102: 2(3). in the day (when) I am in *trouble;*
105:24. made them stronger *than their enemies.*
106:11. the waters covered *their enemies:*
44. he regarded their *affliction,*
107: 2. from the hand of *the enemy;*
6, 13. cried unto the Lord *in* their *trouble,*
19, 28. cry unto the Lord *in* their *trouble,*
108:12(13). Give us help *from trouble:* for vain
13(14). shall tread down *our enemies.*
112: 8. (his desire) *upon his enemies.*
119:139. *mine enemies* have forgotten thy words.
143. *Trouble* and anguish have taken hold
157. my persecutors *and mine enemies;*
136:24. redeemed us *from our enemies:*
Pro.24:10. in the day of adversity, thy strength (is) *small.* (marg. *narrow*)
Isa. 1:24. I will ease me *of mine adversaries,*
5:28. their horses' hoofs shall be counted *like flint,*
30. behold darkness (and) *sorrow,* (marg. or, *distress*)
9:11(10). shall set up *the adversaries of* Rezin
25: 4. a strength to the needy *in* his *distress,*
26:11. the fire of *thine enemies* shall devour
16. *in trouble* have they visited thee,
30:20. the bread of *adversity,*
49:20. The place (is) too *strait* for me:
59:18. he will repay, fury *to his adversaries,*
19. *the enemy* shall come in like a flood,
63: 9. In all their affliction he was *afflicted,* (lit. *affliction* was to him)
18. *our adversaries* have trodden down
64: 2(1). thy name known *to thine adversaries,*
Jer. 30:16. devoured; and all *thine adversaries,*
46:10. avenge him *of his adversaries:*
48: 5. *the enemies* have heard a cry
50: 7. *and their adversaries* said,
Lam.1: 5. *Her adversaries* are the chief,
— gone into captivity before *the enemy.*
7. fell into the hand of *the enemy,*
— *the adversaries* saw her,
10. *The adversary* hath spread out his hand
17. *his adversaries* (should be) round about
2: 4. with his right hand *as an adversary,*
17. set up the horn of *thine adversaries.*
4:12. *the adversary* and the enemy
Eze.30:16. Noph (shall have) *distresses* daily.
39:23. into the hand of *their enemies:*
Hos. 5:15. *in* their *affliction* they will seek me
Am. 3:11. *An adversary* (there shall be) even round
Mic. 5: 9(8). lifted up upon *thine adversaries,*
Nah 1: 2. the Lord will take vengeance *on his adversaries,*
Zec. 8:10. or came in because of *the affliction:*

6862 צַר *tzāhr,* adj.

Nu. 22:26. and stood in a *narrow* place,
Job 41:15(7). (as with) a *close* seal.
Pro.23:27. a strange woman (is) a *narrow* pit.

6864 צֹר *tzōhr,* m.

Ex. 4:25. Zipporah took *a sharp stone,* (marg. or, *knife*)
Eze. 3: 9. As an adamant harder *than flint*

צָרַב [*tzāh-rav'*]. 6866

* NIPHAL.—*Preterite.* *

Eze.20:47(21:3). *and* all faces...*shall be burned*

צָרֶבֶת *tzāh-reh'-veth,* f. 6867

Lev.13:23. it (is) a *burning* boil;
28. *an inflammation of* the burning.
Pro.16:27. (there is) as a *burning* fire.

צָרָה *tzāh-rāh',* f. 6869

Gen35: 3. in the day of *my distress,* and was
42:21. we saw *the anguish of* his soul,
— therefore is this *distress* come upon us.
Deu31:17. many evils *and troubles* shall befall them;
21. many evils *and troubles* are befallen
Jud.10:14. in the time of *your tribulation.*
1Sa. 1: 6. *her adversary* also provoked her
10:19. your adversities *and your tribulations;*
26:24. deliver me out of all *tribulation.*
2Sa. 4: 9. redeemed my soul out of all *adversity,*
1K. 1:29. redeemed my soul out of all *distress,*
2K. 19: 3. This day (is) a day of *trouble,* and of
2Ch 15: 6. God did vex them with all *adversity.*
20: 9. and cry unto thee *in our affliction,*
Neh. 9:27. in the time of *their trouble,*
37. *and* we (are) *in* great *distress.*
Job 5:19. He shall deliver thee in six *troubles:*
27: 9. when *trouble* cometh upon him?
Ps. 9: 9(10). a refuge in times *of trouble.*
10: 1. hidest thou (thyself) in times *of trouble?*
20: 1(2). hear thee in the day of *trouble;*
22:11(12). from me; for *trouble* (is) near;
25:17. *The troubles of* my heart are enlarged:
22. Redeem Israel, O God, out of all *his troubles.*
31: 7(8). hast known my soul *in adversities;*
34: 6(7). saved him out of all *his troubles.*
17(18). out of all *their troubles.*
37:39. their strength in the time of *trouble.*
46: 1(2). a very present help *in trouble.*
50:15. call upon me in the day of *trouble:*
54: 7(9). delivered me out of all *trouble:*
71:20. shewed me great and sore *troubles,*
77: 2(3). In the day of *my trouble*
78:49. anger, wrath, and indignation, *and trouble,*
81: 7(8). Thou calledst *in trouble,*
86: 7. In the day of *my trouble*
91:15. I (will be) with him *in trouble;*
116: 3. I found *trouble* and sorrow.
120: 1. *In* my *distress* I cried unto the Lord,
138: 7. Though I walk in the midst of *trouble,*
142: 2(3). I shewed before him *my trouble.*
143:11. bring my soul *out of trouble.*
Pro. 1:27. when *distress* and anguish cometh
11: 8. The righteous is delivered *out of trouble,*
12:13. the just shall come *out of trouble.*
17:17. a brother is born *for adversity.*
21:23. keepeth his soul *from troubles.*
24:10. in the day of *adversity,*
25:19. in time of *trouble*
Isa. 8:22. and behold *trouble* and darkness,
30: 6. the land of *trouble* and anguish,
33: 2. salvation also in the time of *trouble.*
37: 3. This day (is) a day of *trouble,*
46: 7. nor save him *out of his trouble.*
63: 9. In all *their affliction* he was
65:16. *the* former *troubles* are forgotten,
Jer. 4:31. *the anguish* as of her that bringeth forth
6:24. *anguish* hath taken hold of us,
14: 8. the saviour thereof in time of *trouble,*
15:11. of evil and in the time of *affliction.*
16:19. in the day of *affliction,*
30: 7. the time of Jacob's *trouble;*
49:24. *anguish* and sorrows have taken her,
50:43. *anguish* took hold of him,
Dan12: 1. there shall be a time of *trouble,*
Obad. 12. spoken proudly in the day of *distress.*
14. that did remain in the day of *distress.*
Jon. 2: 2(3). *by reason of* mine *affliction*
Nah. 1: 7. in the day of *trouble;*
9. *affliction* shall not rise up
Hab. 3:16. in the day of *trouble:*
Zep. 1:15. a day of *trouble* and distress,
Zec.10:11. shall pass through the sea with *affliction,*

6872 ## צְרוֹר *tz'rōhr*, m.

Gen42:35. every man's *bundle of* money
— they and their father saw *the bundles of*
1Sa.25:29. bound *in the bundle of* life
2Sa.17:13. until there be not *one small stone*
Job 14:17. My transgression (is) sealed up *in a bag*,
Pro. 7:20. He hath taken *a bag of* money
26: 8. *As he that bindeth* a stone [see צָרַר Kal. Inf.]
Cant.1:13. *A bundle of* myrrh (is) my wellbeloved
Am. 9: 9. yet shall not *the least grain* (marg. *stone*)
Hag. 1: 6. into *a bag* with holes.

6873 ## צָרַח [*tzāh-rağh'*].

* KAL.—*Participle.* Poel. *

Zep. 1:14. the mighty man *shall cry*

* HIPHIL.—*Future.* *

Isa. 42:13. he shall cry, yea, *roar*,

6875 ## צֳרִי *tzŏree* & צְרִי *tz'ree*, m.

Gen37:25. spicery *and balm* and myrrh,
43:11. *a* little *balm*, and a little honey,
Jer. 8:22. (Is there) no *balm* in Gilead;
46:11. Go up into Gilead, and take *balm*,
51: 8. take *balm* for her pain,
Eze.27:17. honey, and oil, *and balm.* (marg. or, *rosin*)

6877 ## צְרִיחַ [*tzāh-ree'ăğh*], m.

Jud. 9:46. they entered into *an hold of* the house
49. and put (them) to *the hold*, and set *the hold* on fire
1Sa.13: 6. in rocks, *and in high places*,

6878 ## צֹרֶךְ [*tzōh'-rech*], m.

2Ch 2:16(15). as much as *thou shalt need:* (marg. according to all *thy need*)

6879 ## צָרַע [*tzāh-rağ'*].

* KAL.—*Participle.* Paül. *

Lev.13:44. He is a *leprous* man,
45. *And the leper* in whom the plague (is),
14: 3. leprosy be healed in *the leper*;
22: 4. What man soever of the seed of Aaron (is) *a leper*,
Nu. 5: 2. that they put out of the camp every *leper*,

* PUAL.—*Participle.* *

Ex. 4: 6. his hand (was) *leprous* as snow.
Lev.14: 2. the law of *the leper*
Nu. 12:10. Miriam (became) *leprous*,
— behold, (she was) *leprous*.
2Sa. 3:29. one that hath an issue, *or that is a leper*,
2K. 5: 1. (but he was) *a leper*.
11. and recover *the leper*.
27. he went out from his presence *a leper*
7: 3. there were four *leprous* men
8. when these *lepers* came
15: 5. he was *a leper* unto the day of his death,
2Ch 26:20. he (was) *leprous* in his forehead,
21. Uzziah the king was *a leper*
— dwelt in a several house, (being) *a leper*;
23. they said, He (is) *a leper*:

6880 ## צִרְעָה *tzeer-ğāh'*, f.

Ex. 23:28. I will send *hornets* before thee,
Deu 7:20. the Lord thy God will send *the hornet*
Jos. 24:12. I sent *the hornet* before you,

6883 ## צָרַעַת *tzāh-rah'-ğath*, f.

Lev.13: 2. (like) the plague of *leprosy*;
3. it (is) a plague of *leprosy:* and the
8. unclean: it (is) *a leprosy*.
9. When the plague of *leprosy* is in a man,
11. *an* old *leprosy* in the skin
12. if *a leprosy* break out
— and *the leprosy* cover all the skin
13. (if) *the leprosy* have covered all
15. unclean: it (is) *a leprosy*.
20. a plague of *leprosy* broken out
25. *a leprosy* broken out of the burning:
—, 27. it (is) the plague of *leprosy*.
30. *a leprosy upon* the head
42. *a leprosy* sprung up
43. as *the leprosy* appeareth
47. that the plague of *leprosy* is in,
49. it (is) a plague of *leprosy*, and shall
51. the plague (is) *a* fretting *leprosy*;
52. it (is) *a* fretting *leprosy*;
59. This (is) the law of the plague of *leprosy*
14: 3. (if) the plague of *leprosy* be healed
7. cleansed from *the leprosy*
32. in whom (is) the plague of *leprosy*,
34. I put the plague of *leprosy* in
44. *a* fretting *leprosy* in the house:
54. all manner of plague of *leprosy*,
55. *And for the leprosy of* a garment,
57. this (is) the law of *leprosy*.
Deu24: 8. Take heed in the plague of *leprosy*,
2K. 5: 3. he would recover him *of his leprosy*.
6. mayest recover him *of his leprosy*.
7. to recover a man *of his leprosy?*
27. *The leprosy therefore of* Naaman
2Ch 26:19. *the leprosy even* rose up

צָרַף *tzāh-raph'*. 6884

* KAL.—*Preterite.* *

Ps. 17: 3. *thou hast tried me*, (and) shalt find
66:10. *thou hast tried us*, as silver
105:19. the word of the Lord *tried him*.
Isa. 48:10. *I have refined thee*, but not
Jer. 6:29. the founder *melteth* in vain:
Zec.13: 9. *and will refine them* as silver

KAL.—*Infinitive.*

Ps. 66:10. tried us, *as* silver *is tried*.
Jer. 6:29. *the founder* melteth in vain:
Dan11:35. *to try* them, and to purge,
Zec.13: 9. and will refine them *as* silver *is refined*,

KAL.—*Imperative.*

Ps. 26: 2. *try* my reins and my heart.

KAL.—*Future.*

Jud. 7: 4. *and I will try them* for thee there:
Isa. 1:25. *and* purely *purge away* thy dross,

KAL.—*Participle.* Poel.

Jud.17: 4. and gave them *to the founder*,
Neh 3: 8. Uzziel the son of Harhaiah, of *the goldsmiths*.
32. *the goldsmiths* and the merchants.
Pro.25: 4. come forth a vessel *for the finer*.
Isa. 40:19. *and the goldsmith* spreadeth it over
— and *casteth* silver chains.
41: 7. the carpenter encouraged *the goldsmith*, (marg. or, *founder*)
46: 6. (and) hire *a goldsmith*;
Jer. 9: 7(6). I *will melt them*,
10: 9. of the hands of *the founder*:
14 & 51:17. every *founder* is confounded

KAL.—*Participle.* Paül.

2Sa.22:31. the word of the Lord (is) *tried:* (marg. or, *refined*)
Ps. 12: 6(7). (as) silver *tried* in a furnace
18:30(31). the word of the Lord is *tried:* (marg. or, *refined*)
119:140. Thy word (is) very *pure:* (marg. *tried*, or, *refined*)
Pro.30: 5. Every word of God (is) *pure:* (marg. *purified*)

* NIPHAL.—*Future.* *

Dan12:10. Many shall be purified,...*and tried*;

* PIEL.—*Participle.* *

Mal. 3: 2. he (is) like *a refiner*'s fire,
3. he shall sit (as) *a refiner*

צֹרְפִי *tzōh-r'phee'*, m. 6885

Neh 3:31. Malchiah *the goldsmith*'s son

6887 צָרַר tzāh-rar'.

* KAL.—*Preterite.* *

Nu. 33:55. *and shall vex* you in the land
Jud.11: 7. now when ye *are in distress?*
1Sa.13: 6. men of Israel saw that they *were in a strait,*
28:15. And Saul answered, I *am* sore *distressed;*
2Sa. 1:26. I *am distressed* for thee, my brother
24:14. I *am in a* great *strait:*
1Ch 21:13. I *am in a* great *strait:*
Ps. 31: 9(10). O Lord, for I *am in trouble:*
69:17(18). from thy servant; for I *am in trouble:*
129: 1, 2. Many a time *have they afflicted* me
Pro.30: 4. who *hath bound* the waters
Isa. 28:20. and the covering *narrower*
Lam. 1:20. O Lord; for I *am in distress:*
Hos. 4:19. The wind *hath bound* her up

KAL.—*Infinitive.*

Lev.18:18. Neither shalt thou take a wife...*to vex*
Nu. 25:17. *Vex* the Midianites,
Pro.26: 8. *As he that bindeth* a stone [See also צְרוֹר]

KAL.—*Imperative.*

Isa. 8:16. *Bind up* the testimony,

KAL.—*Future.*

Isa. 11:13. Judah *shall* not *vex* Ephraim.

KAL.—*Participle.* Poel.

Ex. 23:22. an adversary unto *thine adversaries.* (marg. *them that afflict thee*)
Nu. 10: 9. the enemy *that oppresseth* you,
25:18. For they *vex* you with their wiles,
Est. 3:10. Haman...the Jews' *enemy.* (marg. or, *oppressor*)
8: 1. Haman the Jews' *enemy*
9:10. Haman...*the enemy of* the Jews,
24. Haman...*the enemy of* all the Jews,
Job 26: 8. *He bindeth up* the waters
Ps. 6: 7(8). because of all *mine enemies.*
7: 4(5). him that without cause is *mine enemy:*
6(7). the rage of *mine enemies:*
8: 2(3). because of *thine enemies,*
10: 5. all *his enemies,* he puffeth at them.
23: 5. in the presence of *mine enemies:*
31:11(12). reproach among all *mine enemies,*
42:10(11). *mine enemies* reproach me;
69:19(20). *mine adversaries* (are) all before thee.
74: 4. *Thine enemies* roar in the midst
23. Forget not the voice of *thine enemies:*
143:12. *them that afflict* my soul:
Isa. 11:13. *and the adversaries of* Judah
Am. 5:12. *they afflict* the just,

KAL.—*Participle.* Paül.

Ex. 12:34. their kneadingtroughs *being bound up*
1Sa.25:29. the soul of my lord shall be *bound*
2Sa.20: 3. So they were *shut up* (marg. *bound*)
Hos.13:12. The iniquity of Ephraim (is) *bound up;*

* PUAL.—*Participle.* *

Jos. 9: 4. wine bottles, old, and rent, *and bound up;*

* HIPHIL.—*Preterite.* *

Deu 28:52, 52. *And he shall besiege* thee in all thy
Jer. 10:18. *and will distress* them,
Zep. 1:17. *And I will bring distress* upon men,

HIPHIL.—*Infinitive.*

2Ch 28:22. in the time *of* his *distress*
33:12. *And when* he *was in affliction,*

HIPHIL.—*Future.*

1K. 8:37. if their enemy *besiege* them
2Ch 6:28. if their enemies *besiege* them
Neh 9:27. the hand of their enemies, *who vexed* them:

HIPHIL.—*Participle.*

Jer. 48:41 & 49:22. as the heart of a woman *in her pangs.*

ק kooph.

The Nineteenth Letter of the Alphabet.

6892 קֵא [kēh], m.

Pro.26:11. a dog returneth to *his vomit,*

קָאַת kāh-ath', f. 6893

Lev.11:18. And the swan, and *the pelican,*
Deu 14:17. *And the pelican,* and the gier eagle,
Ps.102: 6(7). I am *like a pelican of* the wilderness:
Isa. 34:11. *the cormorant* (marg. or, *pelican*) and the bittern shall possess it;
Zep. 2:14. *the cormorant* (marg. *id.*) and the bittern

קַב kav, m. 6894

2K. 6:25. the fourth part of *a cab of* dove's dung

קָבַב [kāh-vav']. 6895

* KAL.—*Preterite.* *

Nu. 23: 8. How shall I curse, *whom* God *hath* not *cursed?*
27. *that thou mayest curse* me *them*

KAL.—*Infinitive.*

Nu. 23:11. I took thee *to curse* mine enemies,
25. Neither curse them *at all,* (lit. in *cursing* curse)
24:10. I called thee *to curse* mine enemies,

KAL.—*Imperative.*

Nu. 22:11. come now, *curse* me them;
17. *curse* me this people.
23:13. and *curse* me *them* from thence.

קֵבָה kēh-vāh', f. 6896

Deu 18: 3. the two cheeks, *and the maw.*

קֹבָה [kōh-vāh'], f. 6897

Nu. 25: 8. and the woman through *her belly.*

קֻבָּה koob-bāh', f. 6898

Nu. 25: 8. And he went after the man of Israel into *the tent,*

קִבּוּץ [kib-bootz'], m. 6899

Isa. 57:13. When thou criest, let *thy companies* deliver

קְבוּרָה k'voo-rāh', f. 6900

Gen35:20. Jacob set a pillar upon *her grave:* that (is) the pillar of Rachel's *grave*
47:30. bury me *in their buryingplace.*
Deu34: 6. no man knoweth of *his sepulchre*
1Sa.10: 2. find two men by Rachel's *sepulchre*
2K. 9:28. buried him *in his sepulchre* with his fathers
21:26. he was buried *in his sepulchre*
23:30. buried him in *his own sepulchre.*
2Ch 26:23. in the field of *the burial*
Ecc. 6: 3. and also (that) he have no *burial;*
Isa. 14:20. shalt not be joined with them *in burial,*
Jer. 22:19. with *the burial of* an ass,
Eze.32:23. her company is round about *her grave:*
24. all her multitude round about *her grave,*

קָבַל [kāh-val']. 6901

* PIEL.—*Preterite.* *

Ezr. 8:30. *So took* the priests and the Levites
Est. 4: 4. but *he received* (it) not.
9:23. *And* the Jews *undertook* to do as they had
27. The Jews ordained, *and took* upon them,

PIEL.—*Imperative.*

1Ch 21:11. Thus saith the Lord, *Choose* thee (marg. *Take* to thee)
Pro.19:20. *and receive* instruction,

PIEL.—*Future.*

1Ch 12:18. *Then* David *received them,* and made
2Ch 29:16. *And* the Levites *took* (it), to carry
22. *and* the priests *received* the blood,
Job 2:10. *shall we receive* good at the hand of God, and *shall we* not *receive* evil?

* HIPHIL.—*Participle.* *

Ex. 26: 5. *that* the loops *may take hold* one of another.
36:12. the loops *held* one (curtain) to another.

6902 **קְבַל** [*k'val*], Ch.

* PAEL.—*Preterite.* *

Dan 5:31(6:1). And Darius the Median *took* the

PAEL.—*Future.*

Dan 2: 6. *ye shall receive* of me gifts
7:18. *But* the saints of the most High *shall take*

6903 **קְבֵל** *k'vēhl* & **קֳבֵל** *kŏvēhl*, Ch. m.

[Used as a preposition.]

כָּל־קֳבֵל דִּי ², לָקֳבֵל דִּי ¹ or דְּנָה,
כָּל־קֳבֵל דְּנָה ³.

Ezr. 4:14. Now *because*[2] we have maintenance
16. *by this means*[1] thou shalt have no
6:13. *according to*[1] that which Darius
7:14. *Forasmuch as*[2] thou art sent of
17. *That*[3] thou mayest buy speedily
Dan 2: 8. *because*[2] ye see the thing is gone from me.
10. *therefore*[2] (there is) no king, lord, nor
12. *For this cause*[3] the king was angry
24. *Therefore*[3] Daniel went in unto
31. This great image,...stood *before thee;*
40. *forasmuch as*[2] iron breaketh
41, 45. *forasmuch as*[2] thou sawest
3: 3. and they stood *before* the image
7. *Therefore*[3] at that time,
8. *Wherefore*[3] at that time
22. *Therefore*[3] because the king's
29. *because*[2] there is no other God
4:18(15). *forasmuch as*[2] all the wise
5: 1. *and* drank wine *before* the
5. and wrote *over against* the candlestick
10. (Now) the queen *by reason of* the words
12. *Forasmuch as* an excellent spirit,
22. *though*[2] thou knewest all this;
6: 3(4). *because*[2] an excellent spirit (was) in
4(5). *forasmuch as*[2] he (was) faithful,
9(10). *Wherefore*[3] king Darius signed
10(11). *as*[2] he did aforetime.
22(23). *forasmuch as*[2] before him innocency

6905 **קֳבָל** [*ko'-vāhl*], prep.

2K. 15:10. and smote him *before* the people,

6904 **קֹבֶל** [*kōh'-vel*], m.

Eze.26: 9. And he shall set engines of *war* against

6906 **קָבַע** *kāh-vag'.*

* KAL.—*Preterite.* *

Pro.22:23. the Lord will plead their cause, *and spoil*
Mal. 3: 8. But ye say, Wherein *have we robbed thee?*

KAL.—*Future.*

Mal. 3: 8. *Will* a man *rob* God?

KAL.—*Participle.* Poel.

Pro.22:23. spoil the soul of *those that spoiled them.*
Mal. 3: 8. Yet ye *have robbed* me.
9. for ye *have robbed* me,

6907 **קֻבַּעַת** *koob-bah'-gath*, f.

Isa. 51:17. thou hast drunken *the dregs of* the cup
22. (even) *the dregs of* the cup of my fury;

6908 **קָבַץ** *kāh-vatz'.*

* KAL.—*Preterite.* *

1K. 20: 1. king of Syria *gathered* all his host *together:*

KAL.—*Infinitive.*

Zep 3: 8. *that I may assemble* the kingdoms,

KAL.—*Imperative.*

1Sa. 7: 5. *Gather* all Israel to Mizpeh,
1K. 18:19. (and) *gather* to me all Israel unto
2Ch 24: 5. *and gather* of all Israel money
Joel 2:16. Gather the people,...*assemble* the elders,

KAL.—*Future.*

Gen41:35. *And let them gather* all the food
48. *And he gathered up* all the food of the
Deu 13:16(17). *And thou shalt gather* all the spoil of
Jud.12: 4. *Then* Jephthah *gathered together* all the
1Sa.28: 1. *that* the Philistines *gathered* their armies *together*
4. *and* Saul *gathered* all Israel *together,*
29: 1. *Now* the Philistines *gathered together* all their armies
2Sa. 2:30. and *when he had gathered* all the people *together,*
3:21. *and will gather* all Israel unto my lord the
1K. 11:24. *And he gathered* men unto him,
18:20. *and gathered* the prophets *together*
22: 6. *Then* the king of Israel *gathered* the prophets *together,*
2K. 6:24. *that* Ben-hadad king of Syria *gathered* all
10:18. *And* Jehu *gathered* all the people *together,*
2Ch 15: 9. *And he gathered* all Judah and Benjamin,
18: 5. *Therefore* the king of Israel *gathered together*
23: 2. *and gathered* the Levites out of all
24: 5. *And he gathered together* the priests
25: 5. *Moreover* Amaziah *gathered* Judah *together,*
32: 6. *and gathered them together* to him
Ezr. 7:28. *and I gathered together* out of Israel
8:15. *And I gathered them together* to the river
Neh. 7: 5. *to gather together* the nobles, and the
Est. 2: 3. *that they may gather together* all the fair
Ps. 41: 6(7). his heart *gathereth* iniquity to itself;
Eze.22:20. so *will I gather* (you) in mine anger
Hab. 2: 5. *and heapeth* unto him all people:

KAL.—*Participle.* Poel.

Pro.13:11. *but he that gathereth* by labour shall
Eze.22:19. therefore I will *gather* you into the midst of Jerusalem.

KAL.—*Participle.* Paül.

Neh 5:16. all my servants (were) *gathered* thither

* NIPHAL.—*Preterite.* *

Jos. 10: 6. all the kings of the Amorites...*are gathered together*
Ezr.10: 1. *there assembled* unto him...a very great
Isa. 34:15. *there shall* the vultures also *be gathered,*
43: 9. *Let* all the nations *be gathered together,*
49:18. all these *gather themselves together,*
60: 4. all they *gather themselves together,*
Hos. 1:11(2:2). *Then shall* the children of Judah...*be gathered together,*
Joel 3:11(4:11). *and gather yourselves together* round

NIPHAL.—*Infinitive.*

Ezr.10: 7. *that they should gather themselves together*
Est. 2: 8. *and when* many maidens *were gathered together*
19. *And when* the virgins *were gathered together*
Ps. 102:22(23). *When* the people *are gathered together,*

NIPHAL.—*Imperative.*

Gen49: 2. *Gather yourselves together,* and hear, ye sons of Jacob;
Isa. 45:20. *Assemble yourselves* and come;
48:14. All ye, *assemble yourselves,* and hear;
Eze.39:17. *Assemble yourselves,* and come;

NIPHAL.—*Future.*

1Sa. 7: 6. *And they gathered together* to Mizpeh,
25: 1. all the Israelites *were gathered together,*
28: 4. *And* the Philistines *gathered themselves together,*
1Ch 11: 1. *Then* all Israel *gathered themselves* to David
13: 2. *that they may gather themselves* unto us:
2Ch 13: 7. *And there are gathered* unto him vain men,
15:10. *So they gathered themselves together* at
20: 4. *And* Judah *gathered themselves together,*
32: 4. *So there was gathered* much people *together,*
Ezr.10: 9. *Then* all the men of Judah and Benjamin *gathered themselves together*

Neh. 4:20(14). *resort ye* thither unto us:
Isa. 60: 7. All the flocks of Kedar *shall be gathered together*
Eze.29: 5. thou shalt not be brought together, nor *gathered*:

NIPHAL.—*Participle.*

Isa. 56: 8. beside *those that are gathered unto him.*
Jer. 40:15. the Jews *which are gathered* unto thee should be scattered,

* PIEL.—*Preterite.* *

Deu30: 3. return *and gather thee* from all the nations,
Ps.107: 3. And *gathered them* out of the lands,
Isa. 34:16. his spirit it *hath gathered them.*
Jer. 29:14. *and I will gather* you from all the nations,
31: 8. *and gather them* from the coasts of the
Eze.11:17. *I will even gather* you from the people,
16:37. *I will even gather* them round about
20:34. *and will gather* you out of the countries
41. *and gather* you out of the countries wherein ye have been scattered;
34:13. *and gather them* from the countries,
36:24. *and gather* you out of all countries,
37:21. *and will gather* them on every side,
39:27. *and gathered* them out of their enemies'
Joel 2: 6. all faces *shall gather* blackness.
3: 2(4:2). *I will also gather* all nations,
Mic. 1: 7. *she gathered* (it) of the hire of an harlot,
4:12. for *he shall gather them* as the sheaves
Nah. 2:10(11). the faces of them all *gather* blackness.

PIEL.—*Infinitive.*

Isa. 66:18. *that I will gather* all nations and tongues;
Eze.28:25. *When I shall have gathered* the house of
Mic. 2:12. I will *surely* gather (lit. *gathering* I will gather) the remnant of Israel;
Zep. 3:20. even in the time that *I gather* you:

PIEL.—*Imperative.*

1Ch 16:35. *and gather us together*, and deliver us
Ps.106:47. *and gather us* from among the heathen,

PIEL.—*Future.*

Deu30: 4. thence *will* the Lord thy God *gather thee*,
Neh. 1: 9. (yet) *will I gather them* from thence,
13:11. *And I gathered them together*, and set
Pro.28: 8. *he shall gather it* for him that will pity
Isa. 11:12. and *gather together* the dispersed of Judah
22: 9. *and ye gathered together* the waters
40:11. *he shall gather* the lambs
43: 5. and *gather thee* from the west;
54: 7. with great mercies *will I gather thee.*
56: 8. Yet *will I gather* (others) to him,
Jer. 23: 3. I *will gather* the remnant of my flock
31:10. He that scattered Israel *will gather him*,
Eze.29:13. At the end of forty years *will I gather* the
Hos. 8:10. now *will I gather them*,
9: 6. Egypt *shall gather them up*,
Mic. 2:12. *I will* surely *gather* the remnant
4: 6. *I will gather* her that is driven out,
Zep. 3:19. and *gather* her that was driven out;
Zec.10: 8. *and gather them*; for I have
10. and *gather them* out of Assyria;

PIEL.—*Participle.*

Isa. 13:14. as a sheep that no man *taketh up*:
56: 8. *which gathereth* the outcasts of Israel
62: 9. *and they that have brought it together* shall
Jer. 32:37. I *will gather them* out of all countries,
49: 5. none *shall gather up* him that wandereth.
Eze.16:37. I *will gather* all thy lovers,
Nah. 3:18. no man *gathereth* (them).

* PUAL.—*Participle.* *

Eze.38: 8. (and is) *gathered* out of many people,

* HITHPAEL.—*Preterite.* *

Jud. 9:47. the men of the tower of Shechem *were gathered together.*
1Sa. 7: 7. children of Israel *were gathered together*

HITHPAEL.—*Imperative.*

Jer. 49:14. *Gather ye together*, and come against her,

HITHPAEL.—*Future.*

Jos. 9: 2. *That they gathered themselves* together, to
1Sa. 8: 4. *Then* all the elders of Israel *gathered themselves together*,
22: 2. *And* every one...*gathered themselves* unto
2Sa. 2:25. *And* the children of Benjamin *gathered themselves together*
Isa. 44:11. *let* them all *be gathered together*,

קְבֻצָה [*k'voo-tzāh'*], f. 6910

Eze.22:20. (As) *they gather* (marg. (According) to *the gathering*) silver, and brass,

---

קָבַר *kāh-var'*. 6912

* KAL.—*Preterite.* *

Gen 23:19. Abraham *buried* Sarah his wife
47:30. *and bury me* in their buryingplace.
49:31. There *they buried* Abraham and Sarah his wife; there *they buried* Isaac and Rebekah his wife; and there *I buried* Leah.
Nu. 11:34. there *they buried* the people that lusted.
Jos. 24:32. the bones of Joseph,...*buried they* in
2Sa. 2: 4. the men of Jabesh-gilead (were they) that *buried* Saul.
1K. 2:31. and fall upon him, *and bury him*;
13:31. When I am dead, *then bury* me in the
14:13. all Israel shall mourn for him, *and bury*
2Ch 24:25. but *they buried him* not in the
Jer. 7:32. *for they shall bury* in Tophet,
Eze.39:11. *and* there *shall they bury* Gog
12. *And* seven months *shall* the house of Israel *be burying of them*,
13. *Yea*, all the people of the land *shall bury* (them);
15. till the buriers *have buried* it in the valley

KAL.—*Infinitive.*

Gen23: 6. *but that thou mayest bury* thy dead.
8. If it be your mind *that I should bury* my
50: 7. Joseph went up *to bury* his father:
14. all that went up with him *to bury* his father, after *he had buried* his father.
Deu21:23. thou shalt *in any wise* bury (lit. *burying* thou shalt bury) him that day;
1K. 13:29. to mourn *and to bury him.*
31. after *he had buried* him,
2K. 9:35. they went *to bury her*:
Jer. 19:11. till (there be) no place *to bury.*

KAL.—*Imperative.*

Gen23: 6. in the choice of our sepulchres *bury* thy
11. give I it thee: *bury* thy dead.
15. *bury* therefore thy dead.
49:29. *bury* me with my fathers
50: 6. Go up, *and bury* thy father,
2K. 9:34. *and bury her*: for she (is) a king's

KAL.—*Future.*

Gen23: 4. *that I may bury* my dead out of my sight.
13. *and I will bury* my dead there.
25: 9. *And* his sons Isaac and Ishmael *buried*
35:29. *and* his sons Esau and Jacob *buried* him
47:29. *bury me* not, I pray thee, in Egypt:
48: 7. *and I buried her* there in the way of
50: 5. in the land of Canaan, there *shalt thou bury me.*
— *and bury* my father, and I will come again.
13. *and buried* him in the cave of the field
Deu21:23. *thou shalt* in any wise *bury him* that day;
34: 6. *And he buried* him in a valley
Jos.24:30. *And they buried* him in the border of his
33. *and they buried* him in a hill
Jud. 2: 9. *And they buried* him in the border of his
16:31. *and buried* him between Zorah and
1Sa.25: 1. *and buried him* in his house at Ramah.
28: 3. *and buried him* in Ramah,
31:13. *and buried* (them) under a tree
2Sa. 2: 5. unto Saul, *and have buried* him.
32. *and buried him* in the sepulchre of his
3:32. *And they buried* Abner in Hebron:
4:12. they took the head of Ish-bosheth, *and buried* (it)
21:14. *And* the bones of Saul and Jonathan... *buried they*
1K. 14:18. *And they buried* him; and all Israel
15: 8. *and they buried* him in the city of David:
22:37. *and they buried* the king in Samaria.
2K. 9:28. *and buried* him in his sepulchre
10:35. *and they buried* him in Samaria.

2K. 12:21(22). *and they buried* him with his fathers
13: 9. *and they buried him* in Samaria:
20. Elisha died, *and they buried him.*
15: 7. *and they buried* him with his fathers
21:26. *And* he *was buried* (lit. *and* (one) *buried* him) in his sepulchre
23:30. *and buried him* in his own sepulchre.
1Ch 10:12. *and buried* their bones under the oak
2Ch 9:31. *and he was buried* (lit. *and* (one) *buried him*) in the city of David
14: 1(13:23). *and they buried* him in the city of
16:14. *And they buried him* in his own sepulchres,
21:20. *Howbeit they buried him* in the city of
22: 9. *and* when they had slain him, *they buried him:*
24:16, 25. *And they buried him* in the city of
25:28. *and buried* him with his fathers in the city
26:23. *and they buried* him with his fathers
27: 9. *and they buried* him in the city of David:
28:27. *and they buried him* in the city,
32:33. *and they buried him* in the chiefest of the
33:20. *and they buried him* in his own house:
Jer. 19:11. *they shall bury* (them) in Tophet,

KAL.—*Participle.* Poel.

2K. 9:10. and (there shall be) none *to bury* (her).
13:21. as they were *burying* a man,
Ps. 79: 3. (there was) none *to bury* (them).

KAL.—*Participle.* Paül.

1K. 13:31. the sepulchre wherein the man of God (is) *buried;*
Ecc. 8:10. so I saw the wicked *buried,*

* NIPHAL.—*Future.* *

Gen15:15. *thou shalt be buried* in a good old age.
35: 8. Rebekah's nurse died, *and she was buried*
19. Rachel died, *and was buried* in the way
Nu. 20: 1. Miriam died there, *and was buried* there.
Deu 10: 6. Aaron died, *and* there *he was buried;*
Jud. 8:32. Gideon...died in a good old age, *and was buried*
10: 2. died, *and was buried* in Shamir.
5. Jair died, *and was buried* in Camon.
12: 7. Then died Jephthah...*and was buried*
10. died Ibzan, *and was buried* in Beth-lehem.
12. Elon...died, *and was buried* in Aijalon
15. Abdon...died, *and was buried* in Pirathon
Ru. 1:17. and there *will I be buried:*
2Sa.17:23. *and was buried* in the sepulchre
1K. 2:10. slept with his fathers, *and was buried*
34. *and he was buried* in his own house in
11:43. Solomon slept with his fathers, *and was buried*
14:31. slept with his fathers, *and was buried*
15:24. Asa slept with his fathers, *and was buried*
16: 6. slept with his fathers, *and was buried*
28. slept with his fathers, *and was buried*
22:50(51). slept with his fathers, *and was buried*
2K. 8:24. slept with his fathers, *and was buried*
13:13. *and* Joash *was buried* in Samaria
14:16. slept with his fathers, *and was buried*
20. *and he was buried* at Jerusalem
15:38. slept with his fathers, *and was buried*
16:20. slept with his fathers, *and was buried*
21:18. slept with his fathers, *and was buried*
2Ch 12:16. Rehoboam slept with his fathers, *and was buried*
21: 1. slept with his fathers, *and was buried*
35:24. *and was buried* in (one of) the sepulchres
Job 27:15. Those that remain of him *shall be buried*
Jer. 8: 2. they shall not be gathered, nor *be buried;*
16: 4. neither *shall they be buried;*
6. *they shall* not *be buried,*
20: 6. thou shalt die, and *shalt be buried* there,
22:19. *He shall be buried* with the burial of an
25:33. they shall not be lamented,...nor *buried;*

* PIEL.—*Infinitive.* *

1K. 11:15. the host was gone up *to bury* the slain,

PIEL.—*Future.*

Hos. 9: 6. Memphis *shall bury them:*

PIEL.—*Participle.*

Nu. 33: 4. the Egyptians *buried* all (their) firstborn,
Jer. 14:16. they shall have none *to bury* them,
Eze.39:14. *to bury* with the passengers those that
15. till *the buriers* have buried it in the

* PUAL.—*Preterite.* *

Gen25:10. there *was* Abraham *buried.*

קֶבֶר *keh'-ver*, m. 6913

Gen23: 4. give me a possession of *a buryingplace*
6. in the choice of *our sepulchres* bury thy
— us shall withhold from thee *his sepulchre,*
9, 20. for a possession of *a buryingplace*
49:30. for a possession of *a buryingplace.*
50: 5. Lo, I die: *in my grave* which I have
13. for a possession of *a buryingplace*
Ex. 14:11. (there were) no *graves* in Egypt,
Nu. 11:34. he called the name of that place *Kibroth*-hattaavah: (marg. *The graves of* lust)
35. people journeyed *from Kibroth*-hattaavah (lit. *id.*)
19:16. whosoever toucheth...*a grave,* shall be
18. or one dead, or *a grave:*
33:16. pitched *at Kibroth*-hattaavah. (marg. *the graves of* lust)
17. departed *from Kibroth*-hattaavah, (lit. *id.*)
Deu. 9:22. *and at Kibroth*-hattaavah (lit. *id.*), ye provoked the Lord
Jud. 8:32. Gideon...was buried *in the sepulchre of*
16:31. *in the buryingplace of* Manoah
2Sa. 2:32. buried him *in the sepulchre of* his father,
3:32. wept at *the grave of* Abner;
4:12. buried (it) *in the sepulchre of* Abner
17:23. was buried *in the sepulchre of* his father.
19:37(38). (be buried) by *the grave of* my father
21:14. buried they...*in the sepulchre of* Kish
1K. 13:22. carcase shall not come unto *the sepulchre of* thy fathers.
30. he laid his carcase *in his own grave;*
31. then bury me *in the sepulchre*
14:13. only of Jeroboam shall come to *the grave,*
2K. 13:21. cast the man *into the sepulchre of* Elisha:
22:20. thou shalt be gathered into *thy grave*
23: 6. the powder thereof upon *the graves of*
16. he spied *the sepulchres*
— took the bones out of *the sepulchres,*
17. (It is) *the sepulchre of* the man of God,
2Ch 16:14. they buried him *in his own sepulchres,*
21:20. but not *in the sepulchres of* the kings.
24:25. they buried him not *in the sepulchres of*
28:27. brought him not *into the sepulchres of*
32:33. him in the chiefest of *the sepulchres of*
34: 4. strowed (it) upon *the graves* of them
28. shalt be gathered to *thy grave* in peace,
35:24. buried *in* (one of) *the sepulchres of* his
Neh. 2: 3. the place of my fathers' *sepulchres,* (lieth)
5. the city of my fathers' *sepulchres,*
3:16. over against *the sepulchres of* David,
Job 3:22. are glad, when they can find *the grave?*
5:26. Thou shalt come to (thy) *grave* in a full
10:19. I should have been carried from the womb *to the grave.*
17: 1. *the graves* (are ready) for me.
21:32. he be brought *to the grave,* (marg. *graves*)
Ps. 5: 9(10). their throat (is) *an open sepulchre;*
88: 5(6). like the slain that lie in *the grave,*
11(12). Shall thy lovingkindness be declared *in the grave?*
Isa. 14:19. thou art cast *out of thy grave*
22:16. hast hewed thee out *a sepulchre* here, (as) he that heweth *him* out *a sepulchre* on
53: 9. he made *his grave* with the wicked,
65: 4. Which remain *among the graves,*
Jer. 5:16. Their quiver (is) *as an open sepulchre,*
8: 1. bring out the bones...*out of their graves:*
20:17. my mother might have been *my grave,*
26:23. cast his dead body into *the graves of*
Eze.32:22. *his graves* (are) about him:
23. Whose *graves* are set in the sides of the
25, 26. *her graves* (are) round about him:
37:12. I will open *your graves,* and cause you to come up *out of your graves,*
13. when I have opened *your graves,*
— brought you up *out of your graves,*
39:11. will give unto Gog a place there of *graves*
Nah. 1:14. I will make *thy grave;*

קָדַד [*kāh-dad'*]. 6915

* KAL.—*Future.* *

Gen24:26. *And* the man *bowed down his head,* and
48. *And I bowed down my head,* and
43:28. *And they bowed down their heads,* and made

Ex. 4:31. *then they bowed their heads* and worshipped.
12:27. *And* the people *bowed the head* and
34: 8. Moses made haste, *and bowed his head*
Nu. 22:31. *and he bowed down his head*, and fell
1Sa. 24: 8(9). *And*...David *stooped* with his face to
28:14. *and he stooped* with (his) face to the
1K. 1:16. *And* Bath-sheba *bowed*, and did obeisance
31. *Then* Bath-sheba *bowed* with (her) face
1Ch 29:20. *and bowed down their heads*, and
2Ch 20:18. *And* Jehoshaphat *bowed his head*
29:30. *and they bowed their heads* and
Neh. 8: 6. *and they bowed their heads*, and

6916 **קִדָּה** *kid-dāh'*, f.

Ex. 30:24. *And* of *cassia* five hundred (shekels),
Eze. 27:19. bright iron, *cassia*, and calamus,

6917 **קְדוּמִים** *k'doo-meem'*, m. pl.

Jud. 5:21. that *ancient* river, the river Kishon.

6918 **קָדוֹשׁ** *kāh-dōhsh'*, adj.

Ex. 19: 6. of priests, and an *holy* nation.
29:31. seethe his flesh in the *holy* place.
Lev. 6:16(9). shall it be eaten in the *holy* place;
26(19). in the *holy* place shall it be eaten,
27(20). it was sprinkled in the *holy* place.
7: 6. it shall be eaten in the *holy* place:
10:13. ye shall eat it in the *holy* place,
11:44. ye shall be *holy*; for I (am) *holy*:
45. ye shall therefore be *holy*, for I (am) *holy*
16:24. he shall wash his flesh with water in the *holy* place,
19: 2. Ye shall be *holy*: for I the Lord your God (am) *holy*.
20: 7. be ye *holy*: for I (am) the Lord
26. be *holy* unto me: for I the Lord (am) *holy*,
21: 6. They shall be *holy* unto their God,
7. for he (is) *holy* unto his God.
8. he shall be *holy* unto thee: for I the Lord, which sanctify you, (am) *holy*.
24: 9. they shall eat it in the *holy* place:
Nu. 5:17. the priest shall take *holy* water
6: 5. he shall be *holy*,
8. he (is) *holy* unto the Lord.
15:40. be *holy* unto your God.
16: 3. seeing all the congregation (are) *holy*,
5. who (are) his, and (who is) *holy*;
7. doth choose, he (shall be) *holy*:
Deu 7: 6 & 14:2, 21. For thou (art) an *holy* people
23:14(15). therefore shall thy camp be *holy*:
26:19. that thou mayest be an *holy* people
28: 9. The Lord shall establish thee an *holy* people
33: 3. all *his saints* (are) in thy hand:
Jos. 24:19. he (is) an *holy* God;
1Sa. 2: 2. There is none *holy* as the Lord:
6:20. Who is able to stand before this *holy* Lord
2K. 4: 9. I perceive that this (is) an *holy* man
19:22. (even) against *the Holy One of* Israel.
2Ch 35: 3. *which were holy* unto the Lord,
Neh 8: 9. This day (is) *holy* unto the Lord
10. (this) day (is) *holy* unto our Lord:
11. Hold your peace, for the day (is) *holy*;
Job 5: 1. to which *of the saints* wilt thou turn?
6:10. I have not concealed the words of *the Holy One*.
15:15. he putteth no trust *in his saints*;
Ps. 16: 3. *to the saints* that (are) in the earth,
22: 3(4). thou (art) *holy*, (O thou) that
34: 9(10). O fear the Lord, *ye his saints*:
46: 4(5). *the holy* (place) *of* the tabernacles
65: 4(5). thy house, (even) of thy *holy* temple.
71:22. O *thou Holy One of* Israel.
78:41. *and* limited *the Holy One of* Israel.
89: 5(6). thy faithfulness also in the congregation of *the saints*.
7(8). be feared in the assembly of *the saints*,
18(19). *and the Holy One of* Israel (is) our
99: 3. Let them praise thy...name; (for) it (is) *holy*.
5. Exalt ye the Lord our God,...(for) he (is) *holy*.
9. the Lord our God (is) *holy*.
Ps. 106:16. Aaron *the saint of* the Lord.
111: 9. *holy* and reverend (is) his name.
Pro. 9:10. knowledge of *the holy* (is) understanding.
30: 3. nor have the knowledge of *the holy*.
Ecc. 8:10. gone from the place of *the holy*,
Isa. 1: 4. they have provoked *the Holy One of* Israel
4: 3. (he that) remaineth in Jerusalem, shall be called *holy*,
5:16. God *that is holy* shall be sanctified
19. counsel of *the Holy One of* Israel draw
24. despised the word of *the Holy One of* Israel.
6: 3. *Holy, holy, holy*, (is) the Lord of hosts:
10:17. *and his Holy One* for a flame:
20. shall stay upon the Lord, *the Holy One of*
12: 6. great (is) *the Holy One of* Israel
17: 7. eyes shall have respect to *the Holy One of*
29:19. shall rejoice *in the Holy One of* Israel.
23. sanctify *the Holy One of* Jacob,
30:11. cause *the Holy One of* Israel to cease from
12. thus saith *the Holy One of* Israel,
15. the Lord God, *the Holy One of* Israel;
31: 1. they look not unto *the Holy One of* Israel,
37:23. against *the Holy One of* Israel.
40:25. or shall I be equal? saith *the Holy One*.
41:14. thy redeemer, *the Holy One of* Israel.
16. shalt glory *in the Holy One of* Israel.
20. *and the Holy One of* Israel hath created it.
43: 3. the Lord thy God, *the Holy One of* Israel,
14. your redeemer, *the Holy One of* Israel;
15. I (am) the Lord, *your Holy One*,
45:11. saith the Lord, *the Holy One of* Israel,
47: 4. (is) his name, *the Holy One of* Israel.
48:17. thy Redeemer, *the Holy One of* Israel;
49: 7. Redeemer of Israel, (and) *his Holy One*,
— *the Holy One of* Israel, and he shall
54: 5. thy Redeemer *the Holy One of* Israel;
55: 5. *and for the Holy One of* Israel;
57:15. thus saith the high and lofty One...*whose* name (is) *Holy*; I dwell in the high *and holy* (place),
58:13. *the holy of* the Lord, honourable;
60: 9. *and to the Holy One of* Israel,
14. The Zion of *the Holy One of* Israel.
Jer. 50:29. the Lord, against *the Holy One of* Israel.
51: 5. sin *against the Holy One of* Israel.
Eze. 39: 7. the Lord, *the Holy One* in Israel.
42:13. for the place (is) *holy*.
Dan 8:13. I heard one *saint* speaking, and another *saint* said
24. destroy the mighty and the *holy* people. (marg. people of *the holy ones*)
Hos. 11: 9. *the Holy One* in the midst of thee:
12(12:1). and is faithful with *the saints*. (marg. or, *most holy*)
Hab 1:12. O Lord my God, *mine Holy One*?
3: 3. *and the Holy One* from mount Paran.
Zec. 14: 5. (and) all *the saints* with thee.

קָדַח [*kāh-dagh'*]. 6919

* KAL.—*Preterite*. *

Deu 32:22. For a fire *is kindled* in mine anger,
Jer. 15:14. for a fire *is kindled* in mine anger,
17: 4. *ye have kindled* a fire in mine anger,

KAL.—*Infinitive*.

Isa. 64: 2(1). *As* (when) the melting fire *burneth*,

KAL.—*Participle*. Poel.

Isa. 50:11. all ye *that kindle* a fire,

קַדַּחַת *kad-dah'-ghath*, f. 6920

Lev. 26:16. I will even appoint over you terror,...and *the burning ague*,
Deu 28:22. with a consumption, *and with a fever*,

קָדִים *kāh-deem'*, m. 6921

Gen 41: 6. thin ears and blasted with *the east wind*
23. seven ears,...blasted with *the east wind*,
27. seven empty ears blasted with *the east wind*
Ex. 10:13. the Lord brought an *east* wind upon the
— the *east* wind brought the locusts.
14:21. the Lord caused the sea to go (back) by a strong *east* wind

Job 15: 2. and fill his belly with *the east wind?*
27:21. *The east wind* carrieth him away,
38:24. (which) scattereth *the east wind* upon the
Ps. 48: 7(8). breakest the ships of Tarshish with an *east* wind.
78:26. He caused *an east wind* to blow in the
Isa. 27: 8. his rough wind in the day of *the east wind.*
Jer. 18:17. I will scatter them as with an *east* wind
Eze. 11: 1. the east gate of the Lord's house, which looketh *eastward:*
17:10. when the *east* wind toucheth it?
19:12. the *east* wind dried up her fruit:
27:26. the *east* wind hath broken thee
40: 6. the gate which looketh *toward the east,*
10. the little chambers of the gate *east*ward (lit. the way of *the east*)
19. an hundred cubits *eastward*
22. of the gate that looketh toward *the east;*
23. gate toward the north, *and toward the east;*
32. me into the inner court toward *the east:*
44. at the side of the *east* gate
41:14. of the separate place *toward the east,*
42: 9. (was) the entry *on the east side,*
10. the wall of the court toward *the east,*
12. before the wall toward *the east,*
15. gate whose prospect (is) toward *the east,*
16. He measured the *east* side with the
43: 1. the gate that looketh toward *the east:*
2. came from the way of *the east:*
4. gate whose prospect (is) toward *the east.*
17. his stairs shall look toward *the east.*
44: 1. which looketh toward *the east;*
45: 7. from the west side westward, and from the east side *eastward:*
— from the west border unto the *east* border.
46: 1. inner court that looketh toward *the east*
12. the gate that looketh toward *the east,*
47: 1. the threshold of the house *eastward:*
— the house (stood toward) *the east,*
2. the utter gate by the way that looketh *eastward;*
3. the line in his hand went forth *eastward,*
18. the *east* side ye shall measure
— And (this is) the *east* side.
48: 1. for these are his sides *east* (and) west;
2. the border of Dan, from the *east* side
3. the border of Asher, from the *east* side
4. by the border of Naphtali, from the *east*
5. of Manasseh, from the *east* side
6. the border of Ephraim, from the *east* side
7. the border of Reuben, from the *east* side
8. the border of Judah, from the *east* side
— from the *east* side unto the west side:
10. *and toward the east* ten thousand in
16. on the *east* side four thousand and five
17. *and toward the east* two hundred and fifty,
18. the residue...(shall be) ten thousand *eastward,*
21. the oblation *toward* the *east* border,
23. from the *east* side unto
24. from the *east* side unto the west
25. the border of Simeon, from the *east* side
26. the border of Issachar, from the *east* side
27. the border of Zebulun, from the *east* side
32. at the *east* side four thousand and five hundred:
Hos. 12: 1(2). and followeth after *the east wind:*
13:15. an *east* wind shall come,
Jon. 4: 8. God prepared a vehement *east* wind;
Hab 1: 9. their faces shall sup up (as) *the east wind,*

6922 ## קַדִּישׁ *kad-deesh'*, Ch. adj.

Dan 4: 8(5), 9(6). the spirit of the *holy* gods:
13(10). a watcher *and an holy one* came
17(14). by the word of *the holy ones:*
18(15). the spirit of the *holy* gods
23(20). a watcher *and an holy one* coming
5:11. the spirit of the *holy* gods;
7:18. But *the saints of* the most High
21. made war with *the saints,*
22. judgment was given *to the saints of*
— and the time came that *the saints*
25. *and* shall wear out *the saints of*
27. given to the people of *the saints of*

קָדַם [*kāh-dam'*]. 6923

* PIEL.—*Preterite.* *

Deu 23: 4(5). *they met* you not with bread
2Sa. 22: 6. the snares of death *prevented me,*
Neh 13: 2. *they met* not the children of Israel
Job 3:12. Why *did* the knees *prevent me?*
30:27. the days of affliction *prevented me.*
Ps. 18: 5(6). the snares of death *prevented me.*
68:25(26). The singers *went before,*
119:147. *I prevented* the dawning of the morning
148. Mine eyes *prevent* the (night) watches,
Isa. 21:14. *they prevented* with their bread him that
Jon. 4: 2. *I* fled *before* (lit. *I was beforehand* in fleeing) unto Tarshish:

PIEL.—*Imperative.*

Ps. 17:13. *disappoint* him (marg. *prevent* his face), cast him down:

PIEL.—*Future.*

2Sa. 22:19. *They prevented me* in the day of my
2K. 19:32. nor *come before it* with shield,
Ps. 18:18(19). *They prevented me* in the day of my
21: 3(4). *thou preventest him* with the blessings
59:10(11). The God of my mercy *shall prevent me:*
79: 8. *let* thy tender mercies speedily *prevent us:*
88:13(14). in the morning *shall* my prayer *prevent thee.*
89:14(15). mercy and truth *shall go before* thy
95: 2. *Let us come before* his presence (marg. *prevent* his face) with thanksgiving,
Isa. 37:33. nor *come before it* with shields,
Mic. 6: 6. Wherewith *shall I come before* the Lord,
— *shall I come before* him with burnt offerings,

* HIPHIL.—*Preterite.* *

Job 41:11(3). Who *hath prevented me,* that I should repay (him)?

HIPHIL.—*Future.*

Am. 9:10. The evil shall not overtake *nor prevent* us.

קֶדֶם *keh'-dem*, m. 6924

Gen 2: 8. planted a garden *eastward* in Eden;
3:24. he placed *at the east* of the garden of
10:30. their dwelling was...Sephar a mount of *the east.*
11: 2. as they journeyed *from the east,*
12: 8. he removed from thence unto a mountain *on the east* of Beth-el, and pitched his tent, (having)...Hai *on the east:*
13:11. Lot journeyed *east:*
25: 6. unto the *east* country.
29: 1. Jacob...came into the land of the people of *the east.*
Nu. 23: 7. out of the mountains of *the east,*
34:11. to Riblah, *on the east side* of Ain;
Deu 33:15. the chief things of the *ancient* mountains,
27. The *eternal* God (is thy) refuge,
Jos. 7: 2. to Ai,...*on the east side* of Beth-el,
Jud. 6: 3. the children of *the east,*...came up
33. the children of *the east* were gathered
7:12. all the children of *the east* lay along in the
8:10. all the hosts of the children of *the east:*
11. them that dwelt in tents *on the east*
1K. 4:30(5:10). the wisdom of all the children of the *east* country,
2K. 19:25. Hast thou not heard...of *ancient* times
Neh 12:46. in the days of David and Asaph *of old*
Job 1: 3. the greatest of all the men of *the east.*
23: 8. I go *forward*, but he (is) not (there);
29: 2. Oh that I were as (in) months *past,*
Ps. 44: 1(2). in their days, in the times of *old.*
55:19(20). even he that abideth of *old.*
68:33(34). the heavens of heavens, (which were) of *old;*
74: 2. thy congregation, (which) thou hast purchased *of old;*
12. God (is) my King *of old,*
77: 5(6). I have considered the days *of old,*
11(12). I will remember thy wonders *of old.*
78: 2. I will utter dark sayings of *old:*
119:152. I have known of *old* that thou hast
139: 5. Thou hast beset me behind *and before,*

Ps.143: 5. I remember the days *of old;*
Pro. 8:22. The Lord possessed me...*before* his works of old.
23. or *ever* the earth was. (lit. *from the olden times of* the earth)
Isa. 2: 6. they be replenished *from the east,*
9:12(11). The Syrians *before,* and the Philistines
11:14. they shall spoil them of *the east*
19:11. the son of the wise, the son of *ancient*
23: 7. whose antiquity (is) of *ancient* days?
37:26. Hast thou not heard...of *ancient* times,
45:21. who hath declared this *from ancient time?*
46:10. *and from ancient times* (the things) that
51: 9. awake, as in the *ancient* days,
Jer. 30:20. Their children also shall be *as aforetime,*
46:26. inhabited, as in the days of *old,*
49:28. Arise ye,...and spoil the men of *the east.*
Lam. 1: 7. all her pleasant things that she had in the days of *old,*
2:17. that he had commanded in the days of *old:*
5:21. renew our days *as of old.*
Eze. 11:23. the mountain which (is) *on the east side* of
25: 4. I will deliver thee to the men of *the east*
10. Unto the men of *the east*
Jon. 4: 5. and sat *on the east side* of the city,
Mic. 5: 2(1). whose goings forth (have been) *from of old,*
7:20. unto our fathers from the days of *old.*
Hab 1:12. (Art) thou not *from everlasting,*
Zec. 14: 4. which (is) before Jerusalem *on the east,*

6924 קֵדְמָה [*kēh'-dem*], m.

[Only found with ה local, קֵדְמָה.]

Gen 13:14. *and eastward,* and westward:
25: 6. *eastward,* unto the east country.
28:14. thou shalt spread abroad to the west, *and to the east,*
Ex. 27:13. the breadth of the court on the *east* side
38:13. for the *east* side eastward fifty cubits.
Lev. 1:16. cast it beside the altar *on the east part,*
16:14. his finger upon the mercy seat *eastward;*
Nu. 2: 3. *on the east side* toward the rising of the
3:38. before the tabernacle *toward the east,*
10: 5. the camps that lie *on the east parts*
34: 3. the outmost coast of the salt sea *eastward:*
10. ye shall point out your *east* border from
11. side of the sea of Chinnereth *eastward:*
15. *eastward,* toward the sunrising.
35: 5. from without the city on the *east* side
Jos. 15: 5. the *east* border (was) the salt sea,
18:20. the border of it on the *east* side.
19:12. turned from Sarid *eastward* toward the
13. thence passeth on along on *the east* (lit. *eastward* toward the sunrising)
1K. 7:39. on the right side of the house *eastward*
17: 3. Get thee hence, and turn thee *eastward,*
2K. 13:17. Open the window *eastward.* And he opened (it).
2Ch. 4:10. the sea on the right side of *the east end,*
Eze. 8:16. their faces *toward the east;* and they worshipped the sun *toward the east.*
45: 7. from the *east* side eastward:

6925 קֳדָם *kŏdāhm,* Ch. prep.

Ezr. 4:18. hath been plainly read *before me.*
23. (was) read *before* Rehum,
7:14. as thou art sent of (marg. from *before*) the
19. (those) deliver thou *before* the God
Dan. 2: 6. ye shall receive of *me* (lit. from *before me*) gifts
9. corrupt words to speak *before me,*
10. The Chaldeans answered *before* the king,
11. that can shew it *before* the king,
15. Why (is) the decree (so) hasty from (lit. from *before*) the king?
18. desire mercies of (lit. *id.*) the God of
24. bring me in *before* the king,
25. brought in Daniel *before* the king
27. Daniel answered *in the presence of*
36. interpretation thereof *before* the king.
3:13. brought these men *before* the king.
4: 2(3:32). *I thought* it good (marg. It was seemly *before me*) to shew the signs
Dan. 4: 6(3). the wise (men) of Babylon *before me,*
7(4). and I told the dream *before them;*
8(5). at the last Daniel came in *before me,*
—(–). and *before him* I told the dream,
5:13. Daniel brought in *before* the king.
15. have been brought in *before me,*
17. Daniel answered and said *before* the king
19. trembled and feared *before him:*
23. the vessels of his house *before thee,*
24. part of the hand sent *from him;*
6: 1(2). It pleased (lit. It was seemly *before* Darius to set over the kingdom
10(11). and gave thanks *before* his God,
11(12). making supplication *before* his God.
12(13). and spake *before* the king
13(14). and said *before* the king,
18(19). of musick brought *before him:*
22(23). forasmuch as *before him* innocency was found in me; and also *before thee,*
26(27). *I* make (lit. *before me* is made) a
—(–). tremble and fear *before* the God
7: 7. from all the beasts that (were) *before it;*
8. *before whom* there were three
10. and came forth from *before him:*
— times ten thousand stood *before him:*
13. *and* they brought him near *before him.*
20. and *before whom* three fell;

קַדְמָה [*kad-māh'*], f. 6927

Ps. 129: 6. *which* withereth *afore* it groweth up:
Isa. 23: 7. *whose antiquity* (is) of ancient days?
Eze. 16:55, 55. her daughters, shall return *to their former estate,*
— thy daughters shall return *to your former estate.*
36:11. I will settle you after *your old estates,*

קַדְמָה [*kad-māh'*], Ch. f. 6928

Ezr. 5:11. that was builded these many years *ago,*
Dan. 6:10(11). as he did *aforetime.* (lit. *from before* this)

קִדְמָה [*kid-māh'*], f. 6926

Gen 2:14. which goeth *toward the east of* Assyria.
4:16. in the land of Nod, *on the east of* Eden.
1Sa. 13: 5. in Michmash, *eastward from* Beth-aven.
Eze. 39:11. the valley of the passengers *on the east of*

קַדְמוֹן [*kad-mōhn'*], adj. 6930

Eze. 47: 8. These waters issue out toward the *east* country,

קַדְמוֹנִי *kad-mōh-nee',* adj. 6931

1Sa. 24:13(14). As saith the proverb of *the ancients,*
Job 18:20. *as they that went before* were affrighted.
Isa. 43:18. *neither* consider *the things of old.*
Eze. 10:19. (every one) stood at the door of the *east*
11: 1. the spirit...brought me unto the *east* gate
38:17. he of whom I have spoken in *old* time
47:18. from the border unto the *east* sea.
Joel 2:20. with his face toward the *east* sea,
Zec. 14: 8. half of them toward the *former* sea,
Mal. 3: 4. as in the days of old, and as in *former* (marg. or, *ancient*) years.

קַדְמַי [*kad-mah'y*], Ch. adj. 6933

Dan. 7: 4. *The first* (was) like a lion,
8. three of the *first* horns plucked up
24. he shall be diverse from *the first,*

קָדְקֹד *kod-kōhd',* m. 6936

Gen 49:26. *and on the crown of the head of* him that
Deu 28:35. sole of thy foot unto *the top of thy head.*
33:16. *and upon the top of the head of* him (that was) separated
20. the arm with *the crown of the head.*

2Sa.14:25. of his foot even to *the crown of his head*
Job 2: 7. from the sole of his foot unto *his crown.*
Ps. 7:16(17). shall come down upon *his own pate.*
68:21(22). *the* hairy *scalp* of such an one
Isa. 3:17. the Lord will smite with a scab *the crown of the head of*
Jer. 2:16. Tahapanes have broken *the crown of* thy *head.*
48:45. *and the crown of the head of* the

6937 קָדַר *kāh-dar'.*

* KAL.—*Preterite.* *

Jer. 4:28. *and* the heavens above *be black:*
8:21. *I am black;* astonishment hath taken
14: 2. *they are black* unto the ground;
Joel 2:10. the sun and the moon *shall be dark,*
3:15(4:15). sun and the moon *shall be darkened,*
Mic. 3: 6. *and* the day *shall be dark*

KAL.—*Participle.* Poel.

Job 5:11. *that those which mourn* may be exalted
6:16. *Which are blackish* by reason of the ice,
30:28. I went *mourning* without the sun:
Ps. 35:14. I bowed down *heavily,*
38: 6(7). I go *mourning* all the day long.
42: 9(10). why go I *mourning*
43: 2. why go I *mourning* because of

* HIPHIL.—*Preterite.* *

Eze.32: 7. *and make* the stars thereof *dark;*

HIPHIL.—*Future.*

Eze.31:15. *and I caused* Lebanon *to mourn* (marg. *be black*) for him,
32: 8. bright lights of heaven *will I make dark*

* HITHPAEL.—*Preterite.* *

1K. 18:45. the heaven *was black* with clouds

6940 קַדְרוּת *kad-rooth',* f.

Isa. 50: 3. I clothe the heavens with *blackness,*

6941 קְדֹרַנִּית *k'dōh-ran-neeth',* adv.

Mal. 3:14. we have walked *mournfully* (marg. *in black*) before the Lord

---

6942 קָדַשׁ *kāh-dash'* & קָדֵשׁ [*kāh-dēhsh'*].

* KAL.—*Preterite.* *

Ex. 29:21. *and* he *shall be hallowed,* and his garments,
Nu. 16:37(17:2). fire yonder; for *they are hallowed.*
Isa. 65: 5. not near to me; for *I am holier than thou.*

KAL.—*Future.*

Ex. 29:37. whatsoever toucheth the altar *shall be holy.*
30:29. whatsoever toucheth them *shall be holy.*
Lev. 6:18(11). one that toucheth them *shall be holy.*
27(20). touch the flesh thereof *shall be holy:*
Nu. 16:38(17:3). *therefore they are hallowed:*
Deu22: 9. the fruit of thy vineyard, *be defiled.*
1Sa.21: 5(6). though *it were sanctified*
Hag. 2:12. *shall it be holy?* And the priests answered

* NIPHAL.—*Preterite.* *

Ex. 29:43. *and* (the tabernacle) *shall be sanctified* by my glory.
Lev.22:32. *but I will be hallowed* among the children
Isa. 5:16. God that is holy *shall be sanctified*
Eze.20:41. *and I will be sanctified* in you
28:22. *and shall be sanctified* in her.
25. *and shall be sanctified* in them
39:27. *and am sanctified* in them

NIPHAL.—*Infinitive.*

Eze.36:23. *when I shall be sanctified* in you
38:16. *when I shall be sanctified* in thee,

NIPHAL.—*Future.*

Lev.10: 3. *I will be sanctified* in them
Nu. 20:13. *and he was sanctified* in them.

* PIEL.—*Preterite.* *

Ex. 19:10. *and sanctify* them to day and to morrow,
23. bounds about the mount, *and sanctify it.*
28:41. *and sanctify* them, that they may minister
Ex. 29:27. *And thou shalt sanctify* the breast
37. shalt make an atonement for the altar, *and sanctify* it;
44. *And I will sanctify* the tabernacle
30:29. *And thou shalt sanctify* them, that they
30. Aaron and his sons, *and consecrate them,*
40: 9. *and shalt hallow* it, and all the vessels
10. all his vessels, *and sanctify* the altar:
11. the laver and his foot, *and sanctify it.*
13. anoint him, *and sanctify him;*
Lev.16:19. cleanse it, *and hallow it*
21: 8. *Thou shalt sanctify him therefore;* for he
25:10. *And ye shall hallow* the fiftieth year,
Nu. 6:11. *and shall hallow* his head that same day.
Deu32:51. because *ye sanctified* me not
1Sa. 7: 1. *sanctified* Eleazar his son
1K. 8:64. The same day *did* the king *hallow* the
Neh. 3: 1. they *sanctified it,* and set up the doors of it; even unto the tower of Meah *they sanctified it,*
Jer. 17:22. *but hallow ye* the sabbath day,
22: 7. *And I will prepare* destroyers against
Eze.36:23. *And I will sanctify* my great name,
Mic. 3: 5. *they even prepare* war against him:

PIEL.—*Infinitive.*

Ex. 20: 8. the sabbath day, *to keep it holy.*
28: 3. make Aaron's garments *to consecrate him,*
29: 1. *to hallow* them, to minister unto me
33. to consecrate (and) *to sanctify* them:
36. thou shalt anoint it, *to sanctify it.*
Lev. 8:11. the laver and his foot, *to sanctify them.*
12. and anointed him, *to sanctify him.*
Deu. 5:12. Keep the sabbath day *to sanctify it,*
2Ch 29:17. first (day) of the first month *to sanctify,*
Neh 13:22. *to sanctify* the sabbath day.
Jer. 17:24. *but hallow* the sabbath day,
27. *to hallow* the sabbath day,
Eze.46:20. the utter court, *to sanctify* the people.

PIEL.—*Imperative.*

Ex. 13: 2. *Sanctify* unto me all the firstborn,
Jos. 7:13. Up, *sanctify* the people,
2K. 10:20. *Proclaim* (marg. *Sanctify*) a solemn
2Ch 29: 5. *and sanctify* the house of the Lord
Jer. 6: 4. *Prepare ye* war against her;
51:27. *prepare* the nations against her,
28. *Prepare* against her the nations
Eze.20:20. *hallow* my sabbaths; and they shall be a
Joel 1:14. *Sanctify ye* a fast, call a solemn assembly,
2:15. *sanctify* a fast, call a solemn assembly:
16. *sanctify* the congregation, assemble the
3: 9(4:9). *Prepare* (marg. *Sanctify*) war, wake up the mighty men,

PIEL.—*Future.*

Gen. 2: 3. blessed the seventh day, *and sanctified* it:
Ex. 19:14. *and sanctified* the people; and they
20:11. blessed the sabbath day, *and hallowed it.*
29:44. *I will sanctify* also both Aaron and his
Lev. 8:10. all that (was) therein, and *sanctified*
15. *and sanctified it,* to make reconciliation
30. *and sanctified* Aaron, (and) his garments,
Nu. 7: 1. *and sanctified* it, and all the instruments — had anointed them, *and sanctified* them;
1Sa.16: 5. *And he sanctified* Jesse and his sons,
2Ch 7: 7. *Moreover* Solomon *hallowed* the middle of
29:17. *so they sanctified* the house of the Lord
Job 1: 5. Job sent *and sanctified them,*
Eze.44:19. *they shall* not *sanctify* the people
24. *they shall hallow* my sabbaths.

PIEL.—*Participle.*

Ex. 31:13. I (am) the Lord *that doth sanctify you.*
Lev.20: 8. I (am) the Lord *which sanctify you.*
21: 8. I the Lord, *which sanctify you,* (am)
15. I the Lord *do sanctify him.*
23 & 22:9, 16. I the Lord *do sanctify them.*
22:32. the Lord *which hallow you,*
Eze. 7:24. *their holy places* shall be defiled.
20:12. I (am) the Lord *that sanctify them.*
37:28. I the Lord *do sanctify* Israel,

* PUAL.—*Participle.* *

2Ch 26:18. *that are consecrated* to burn incense:
31: 6. *which were consecrated* unto the Lord
Ezr. 3: 5. feasts of the Lord *that were consecrated,*
Isa. 13: 3. I have commanded *my sanctified ones,*
Eze.48:11. the priests *that are sanctified*

* HIPHIL.—*Preterite.* *

Nu. 3:13. *I hallowed* unto me all the firstborn
8:17. *I sanctified* them for myself.
Jud.17: 3. wholly *dedicated* the silver unto the Lord
2Sa. 8:11. Which also king David *did dedicate*
— the silver and gold that *he had dedicated*
1K. 9: 3. *I have hallowed* this house,
7. which *I have hallowed* for my name,
2K. 12:18(19). kings of Judah, *had dedicated*,
1Ch 18:11. Them also king David *dedicated*
26:26. the captains of the host, *had dedicated.*
27. *did they dedicate* to maintain the house
28. all *that* Samuel the seer,...*had dedicated*;
2Ch 7:16. now have I chosen *and sanctified* this
20. which *I have sanctified* for my name,
29:19. all the vessels,...have we prepared *and sanctified*,
30: 8. which *he hath sanctified*
36:14. which *he had hallowed* in Jerusalem.
Isa. 29:23. *and sanctify* the Holy One of Jacob,
Jer. 1: 5. out of the womb *I sanctified thee*,
Zep. 1: 7. *he hath bid* (marg. *sanctified*, or, *prepared*) his guests.

HIPHIL.—*Infinitive.*

Nu. 20:12. *to sanctify me* in the eyes of the children
27:14. *to sanctify me* at the water
Jud.17: 3. I had *wholly* dedicated (lit. *dedicating* I had dedicated) the silver unto the Lord
1Ch 23:13. *that he should sanctify* the most holy
2Ch 2: 4(3). *to dedicate* (it) to him,
30:17. *to sanctify* (them) unto the Lord.

HIPHIL.—*Imperative.*

Jer. 12: 3. *and prepare them* for the day of slaughter.

HIPHIL.—*Future.*

Ex. 28:38. the children of Israel *shall hallow*
Lev.22: 3. which the children of Israel *hallow*
27:14. when a man *shall sanctify* his house
16. if a man *shall sanctify* unto the Lord
17. If *he sanctify* his field from the year
18. if *he sanctify* his field after the
22. if (a man) *sanctify* unto the Lord a field
26. no man *shall sanctify* it;
Deu 15:19. *thou shalt sanctify* unto the Lord
Jos. 20: 7. *And they appointed* (marg. *sanctified*) Kedesh in Galilee
Isa. 8:13. *Sanctify* the Lord of hosts
29:23. *they shall sanctify* my name,

HIPHIL.—*Participle.*

Lev.22: 2. (those things) which they *hallow* unto
27:15. if *he that sanctified* it will redeem his
19. if *he that sanctified* the field
1Ch 26:28. whosoever *had dedicated* (any thing),
Neh 12:47. *and they sanctified* (holy things) unto the Levites; and the Levites *sanctified*

* HITHPAEL.—*Preterite.* *

Lev.11:44. *ye shall therefore sanctify yourselves*,
20: 7. *Sanctify yourselves therefore*, and be ye
2Ch 5:11. the priests (that were) present *were sanctified*,
30: 3. the priests *had* not *sanctified themselves*
17. the congregation that *were* not *sanctified*:
Eze.38:23. I magnify myself, *and sanctify myself*;

HITHPAEL.—*Infinitive.*

2Ch 29:34. the Levites (were) more upright in heart *to sanctify themselves*
Isa. 30:29. a holy solemnity *is kept*;

HITHPAEL.—*Imperative.*

Nu. 11:18. *Sanctify yourselves* against to morrow,
Jos. 3: 5. *Sanctify yourselves*: for to morrow
7:13. *Sanctify yourselves* against to morrow:
1Sa.16: 5. *sanctify yourselves*, and come with me to
1Ch 15:12. *sanctify yourselves*, (both) ye and your
2Ch 29: 5. Hear me, ye Levites, *sanctify* now *yourselves*,
35: 6. kill the passover, *and sanctify yourselves*,

HITHPAEL.—*Future.*

Ex. 19:22. *let* the priests also,...*sanctify themselves*,
1Ch 15:14. *So* the priests and the Levites *sanctified themselves*
2Ch 29:15. they gathered their brethren, *and sanctified themselves*,
2Ch 29:34. (other) priests *had sanctified themselves*:
30:15. were ashamed, *and sanctified themselves*,
24. *and* a great number of priests *sanctified themselves*.
31:18. in their set office *they sanctified themselves*

HITHPAEL.—*Participle.*

2Sa.11: 4. she *was purified* from her uncleanness:
Isa. 66:17. They *that sanctify themselves*,

קָדֵשׁ *kāh-dēhsh'*, m. 6945

Deu 23:17(18). nor *a sodomite* of the sons of Israel.
1K. 14:24. there were also *sodomites* in the land:
15:12. he took away *the sodomites* out of the
22:46(47). the remnant of *the sodomites*,
2K. 23: 7. he brake down the houses of *the sodomites*,
Job 36:14. their life (is) *among the unclean.* (marg. or, *sodomites*)

קֹדֶשׁ *kōh'-desh*, m. 6944

קֹדֶשׁ הַקֳּדָשִׁים [2]

Ex. 3: 5. the place whereon thou standest (is) *holy*
12:16. the first day (there shall be) an *holy*
— there shall be an *holy* convocation to you;
15:11. who (is) like thee, glorious *in holiness*,
13. in thy strength unto *thy holy* habitation.
16:23. the rest of the *holy* sabbath
22:31(30). ye shall be *holy* men unto me:
26:33. the vail shall divide unto you between *the holy* (place) and *the most holy.*[2]
34. testimony in *the most holy*[2] (place).
28: 2. thou shalt make *holy* garments
4. they shall make *holy* garments
29, 35. when he goeth in unto *the holy* (place),
36. *Holiness* to the Lord.
38. the iniquity of *the holy things*,
— shall hallow in all *their holy* gifts;
43. to minister *in the holy* (place);
29: 6. put the *holy* crown upon the mitre.
29. the *holy* garments of Aaron
30. to minister *in the holy* (place).
33. because they (are) *holy.*
34. because it (is) *holy.*
37. it shall be an altar *most holy*:[2]
30:10. it (is) *most holy*[2] unto the Lord.
13, 24. after the shekel of *the sanctuary*:
25. make it an oil of *holy* ointment,
— it shall be an *holy* anointing oil.
29. that they may be *most holy*:[2]
31. This shall be an *holy* anointing oil
32. it (is) *holy*, (and) it shall be *holy* unto
35. a confection...pure (and) *holy*:
36. it shall be unto you *most holy.*[2]
37. it shall be unto thee *holy* for the Lord.
31:10. *the holy* garments for Aaron
11. and sweet incense *for the holy* (place):
14. it (is) *holy* unto you:
15. *holy* (marg. *holiness*) to the Lord:
35: 2. there shall be to you *an holy day*, (marg. *holiness*)
19. to do service *in the holy* (place), the *holy* garments for Aaron
21. and for the *holy* garments.
36: 1. for the service of *the sanctuary*,
3. of the service of *the sanctuary*,
4. the work of *the sanctuary*,
6. the offering of *the sanctuary.*
37:29. he made the *holy* anointing oil,
38:24. in all the work of *the holy* (place),
—, 25, 26. after the skekel of *the sanctuary.*
27. the sockets of *the sanctuary*,
39: 1. to do service *in the holy* (place), and made the *holy* garments for Aaron;
30. the *holy* crown (of) pure gold,
— *Holiness* to the Lord.
41. to do service *in the holy* (place), and the *holy* garments for Aaron
40: 9. it shall be *holy.*
10. it shall be an altar *most holy.*[2] (marg *holiness of holinesses*)
13. thou shalt put upon Aaron the *holy*
Lev. 2: 3, 10. (it is) a thing *most holy*[2] of the
4: 6. before the vail of *the sanctuary.*
5:15. *in the holy things of* the Lord;

Lev. 5:15. after the shekel of *the sanctuary,*
16. that he hath done in *the holy thing,*
6:17(10). it (is) *most holy,*[2] as (is) the
25(18). before the Lord: it (is) *most holy.*[2]
29(22). eat thereof: it (is) *most holy.*[2]
30(23). to reconcile (withal) *in the holy*
7: 1. the trespass offering: it (is) *most holy.*[2]
6. in the holy place: it (is) *most holy.*[2]
8: 9. the *holy* crown; as the Lord commanded
10: 4. your brethren from before *the sanctuary*
10. that ye may put difference between *holy*
12. beside the altar: for it (is) *most holy:*[2]
17. Wherefore have ye not eaten...in the *holy* place, seeing it (is) *most holy,*[2]
18. within *the holy* (place): ye should indeed have eaten it *in the holy* (place),
12: 4. she shall touch no *hallowed thing,*
14:13. the burnt offering, in the *holy* place:
— the trespass offering: it (is) *most holy:*[2]
16: 2. come not at all times into *the holy* (place)
3. Thus shall Aaron come into *the holy*
4. He shall put on the *holy* linen coat,
— these (are) *holy* garments;
16. he shall make an atonement for *the holy* (place),
17. to make an atonement *in the holy* (place),
20. made an end of reconciling *the holy*
23. he went into *the holy* (place),
27. to make atonement *in the holy* (place),
32. (even) the *holy* garments:
33. make an atonement for the *holy* sanctuary,
19: 8. profaned *the hallowed thing of* the Lord:
24. all the fruit thereof shall be *holy* to praise (marg. *holiness of* praises)
20: 3. to profane my *holy* name. (lit. the name of *my holiness*)
21: 6. therefore they shall be *holy.*
22. (both) *of the most holy* (lit. *of the holies of holies*), and of *the holy.*
22: 2. separate themselves *from the holy things of*
— that they profane not *my holy* name
3. that goeth unto *the holy things,*
4. he shall not eat *of the holy things,*
6. shall not eat of *the holy things,*
7. shall afterward eat of *the holy things;*
10. There shall no stranger eat (of) *the holy thing:*
— an hired servant, shall not eat (of) *the holy thing.*
12. she may not eat of an offering of *the holy things.*
14. a man eat (of) *the holy thing* unwittingly,
— shall give (it) unto the priest with *the holy thing.*
15. they shall not profane *the holy things of*
16. when they eat *their holy things:*
32. Neither shall ye profane *my holy* name;
23: 2, 37. which ye shall proclaim (to be) *holy*
3. of rest, an *holy* convocation;
4. (even) *holy* convocations,
7. first day ye shall have an *holy* convocation:
8. the seventh day (is) an *holy* convocation:
20. they shall be *holy* to the Lord
21. it may be an *holy* convocation unto you:
24. of trumpets, an *holy* convocation.
27. it shall be an *holy* convocation unto you;
35. first day (shall be) an *holy* convocation:
36. the eighth day shall be an *holy* convocation
24: 9. it (is) *most holy*[2] unto him
25:12. it shall be *holy* unto you:
27: 3. after the shekel of *the sanctuary.*
9. unto the Lord shall be *holy.*
10. the exchange thereof shall be *holy.*
14. a man shall sanctify his house (to be) *holy*
21. the field,...shall be *holy* unto the Lord,
23. (as) a *holy* thing unto the Lord.
25. according to the shekel of *the sanctuary:*
28. every devoted thing (is) *most holy*[2]
30. (it is) *holy* unto the Lord.
32. the tenth shall be *holy* unto the Lord.
33. the change thereof shall be *holy;*
Nu. 3:28. keeping the charge of *the sanctuary.*
31. the vessels of *the sanctuary*
32. that keep the charge of *the sanctuary.*
47, 50. after the shekel of *the sanctuary*
4: 4. (about) the *most holy things:*[2]
12. wherewith they minister *in the sanctuary,*

Nu. 4:15. made an end of covering *the sanctuary* and all the vessels of *the sanctuary,*
— they shall not touch (any) *holy thing,*
16. *in the sanctuary,* and in the vessels
19. they approach unto *the most holy things:*[2]
20. when *the holy things* are covered,
5: 9. every offering of all *the holy things of*
10. every man's *hallowed things* shall be his:
6:20. this (is) *holy* for the priest,
7: 9. the service of *the sanctuary*
13, 19, 25, 31, 37, 43, 49, 55, 61, 67, 73, 79, 85, 86. after the shekel of *the sanctuary;*
8:19. come nigh unto *the sanctuary.*
18: 3. they shall not come nigh the vessels of *the sanctuary*
5. ye shall keep the charge of *the sanctuary,*
8. all *the hallowed things of* the children
9. This shall be thine *of the most holy things,*[2]
— (shall be) *most holy*[2] for thee
10. *In the most holy*[2] (place) shalt thou eat it;
— it shall be *holy* unto thee.
16. after the shekel of *the sanctuary,*
17. they (are) *holy:*
19. All the heave offerings of *the holy things,*
32. neither shall ye pollute *the holy things of*
28: 7. *in the holy* (place) shalt thou cause
18. first day (shall be) an *holy* convocation;
25, 26, & 29:1. ye shall have an *holy* convocation;
29: 7. an *holy* convocation; and ye shall afflict
12. ye shall have an *holy* convocation;
31: 6. with the *holy* instruments,
35:25. which was anointed with the *holy* oil.
Deu 12:26. Only *thy holy things* which thou hast,
26:13. I have brought away *the hallowed things*
15. Look down from *thy holy* habitation, (lit. the habitation of *thy holiness*)
33: 2. he came with ten thousands of *saints:*
Jos. 5:15. the place whereon thou standest (is) *holy.*
6:19. all...(are) *consecrated* unto the Lord:
1Sa.21: 4(5). there is *hallowed* bread;
5(6). the vessels of the young men are *holy,*
6(7). the priest gave him *hallowed* (bread):
1K. 6:16. (even) *for the most holy*[2] (place).
7:50. the inner house, *the most holy*[2] (place),
51. *things* which David his father *had dedicated;* (marg. *holy things of* David)
8: 4. all the *holy* vessels
6. the house, to *the most holy*[2] (place),
8. in *the holy* (place) before the oracle,
10. when the priests were come out of *the holy* (place),
15:15. *things which* his father *had dedicated, and the things which himself had dedicated,*
2K. 12: 4(5). money of *the dedicated things* (marg. *holinesses,* or, *holy things*)
18(19). *all the hallowed things* that Jehoshaphat,
—(—). and *his own hallowed things,* and all
1Ch. 6:49(34). the work of *the* (place) *most holy,*[2]
9:29. all the instruments of *the sanctuary,*
16:10. Glory ye in *his holy* name:
29. worship the Lord in the beauty of *holiness.*
35. that we may give thanks to *thy holy* name,
22:19. the *holy* vessels of God,
23:13. he should sanctify *the most holy things,*[2]
28. in the purifying of all *holy things,*
32. the charge of *the holy* (place),
24: 5. the governors of *the sanctuary,*
26:20. over the treasures of *the dedicated* (marg. *holy*) *things*
26. all the treasures of *the dedicated things,*
28:12. the treasuries of *the dedicated things:*
29: 3. all that I have prepared for the *holy* house,
16. to build thee an house for *thine holy* name
2Ch. 3: 8. he made the *most holy*[2] house,
10. in the *most holy*[2] house he made two
4:22. the inner doors thereof *for the most holy*[2] (place),
5: 1. *things that* David his father *had dedicated;*
5. all the *holy* vessels
7. into *the most holy*[2] (place),
11. when the priests were come out of *the holy* (place):
8:11. because (the places are) *holy,* (marg. *holiness*)
15:18. the *things that* his father *had dedicated, and that he himself had dedicated,*

2Ch 20:21. that should praise the beauty of *holiness*,
23: 6. go in, for they (are) *holy:*
24: 7. also all *the dedicated things of*
29: 5. forth the filthiness out of *the holy* (place).
7. offered burnt offerings *in the holy* (place)
33. *And the consecrated things* (were)
30:19. the purification of *the sanctuary.*
27. prayer came (up) to *his holy* dwelling
31: 6. the tithe of *holy things*
12. *and the dedicated things* faithfully:
14. *and the most holy things.* (lit. the *holies of holies*)
18. they sanctified themselves *in holiness:*
35: 3. Put the *holy* ark in the house
5. stand *in the holy* (place)
13. *but the* (other) *holy* (offerings) sod they
Ezr. 2:63. they should not eat of *the most holy things*,[2]
8:28. Ye (are) *holy* unto the Lord; the vessels (are) *holy* also;
9: 2. the *holy* seed have mingled themselves
8. to give us a nail in *his holy* place,
Neh 7:65. they should not eat of *the most holy things*,[2]
9:14. madest known unto them *thy holy* sabbath,
10:31(32). the sabbath, or on the *holy* day:
33(34). set feasts, *and for the holy* (things),
11: 1. to dwell in Jerusalem the *holy* city,
18. All the Levites in the *holy* city
Ps. 2: 6. *my holy* hill of Zion. (marg. Zion, the hill of *my holiness*)
3: 4(5). he heard me out of *his holy* hill.
5: 7(8). in thy fear will I worship toward *thy holy* temple. (marg. the temple of *thy holiness*)
11: 4. The Lord (is) in *his holy* temple,
15: 1. who shall dwell in *thy holy* hill?
20: 2(3). Send thee help *from the sanctuary*,
6(7). he will hear him from *his holy* heaven (marg. heaven of *his holiness*)
24: 3. who shall stand in *his holy* place?
28: 2. toward *thy holy* oracle. (marg. or, the oracle of *thy sanctuary*)
29: 2. worship the Lord in the beauty of *holiness*. (marg. or, (his) glorious *sanctuary*)
30: 4(5). at the remembrance of *his holiness*.
33:21. we have trusted in *his holy* name.
43: 3. let them bring me unto *thy holy* hill,
47: 8(9). sitteth upon the throne of *his holiness*.
48: 1(2). the mountain of *his holiness*.
51:11(13). take not *thy holy* spirit from me.
60: 6(8). God hath spoken *in his holiness;*
63: 2(3). (as) I have seen thee *in the sanctuary*.
68: 5(6). God in *his holy* habitation.
17(18). (as in) Sinai, *in the holy* (place).
24(25). my King, *in the sanctuary*.
74: 3. enemy hath done wickedly *in the sanctuary*.
77:13(14). Thy way, O God, (is) *in the sanctuary:*
78:54. them to the border of *his sanctuary*,
79: 1. *thy holy* temple have they defiled;
87: 1. His foundation (is) in the *holy* mountains.
89:20(21). with *my holy* oil have I anointed him:
35(36). Once have I sworn *by my holiness*
93: 5. *holiness* becometh thine house,
96: 9. worship the Lord in the beauty of *holiness:* (marg. or, glorious *sanctuary*)
97:12. thanks at the remembrance of *his holiness*.
98: 1. *his holy* arm, hath gotten him the victory.
99: 9. worship at *his holy* hill;
102:19(20). he hath looked down from the height of *his sanctuary;*
103: 1. within me, (bless) *his holy* name.
105: 3. Glory ye in *his holy* name:
42. he remembered *his holy* promise,
106:47. to give thanks unto *thy holy* name,
108: 7(8). God hath spoken *in his holiness;*
110: 3. in the beauties of *holiness*
114: 2. Judah was *his sanctuary*,
134: 2. Lift up your hands (in) *the sanctuary*, (marg. or, *holiness*)
138: 2. I will worship toward *thy holy* temple,
145:21. let all flesh bless *his holy* name
150: 1. Praise God *in his sanctuary:*
Pro. 20:25. (It is) a snare to the man (who) devoureth (that which is) *holy*,
Isa. 6:13. (so) the *holy* seed (shall be) the substance
11: 9. hurt nor destroy in all *my holy* mountain:
23:18. her hire shall be *holiness* to the Lord:
27:13. worship the Lord in the *holy* mount at

Isa. 35: 8. be called The way of *holiness;*
43:28. profaned the princes of *the sanctuary*,
48: 2. they call themselves of the *holy* city,
52: 1. O Jerusalem, the *holy* city:
10. The Lord hath made bare *his holy* arm
56: 7. them will I bring to *my holy* mountain,
57:13. shall inherit *my holy* mountain;
58:13. (from) doing thy pleasure on *my holy* day;
62: 9. shall drink it in the courts of *my holiness*.
12. they shall call them, The *holy* people,
63:10. they rebelled, and vexed *his holy* Spirit:
11. (is) he that put *his holy* Spirit within him?
15. behold from the habitation of *thy holiness*
18. people of *thy holiness* have possessed (it)
64:10(9). *Thy holy* cities are a wilderness,
11(10). *Our holy* and our beautiful house, (lit. the house of *our holiness* and our beauty)
65:11. that forget *my holy* mountain,
25. nor destroy in all *my holy* mountain,
66:20. to *my holy* mountain Jerusalem,
Jer. 2: 3. Israel (was) *holiness* unto the Lord,
11:15. the *holy* flesh is passed from thee?
23: 9. because of the words of *his holiness*.
25:30. utter his voice from *his holy* habitation;
31:23. mountain of *holiness*.
40. (shall be) *holy* unto the Lord;
Lam 4: 1. the stones of *the sanctuary* are poured out
Eze. 20:39. pollute ye *my holy* name no more
40. in *mine holy* mountain, in the mountain
— with all *your holy things*.
22: 8. Thou hast despised *mine holy things*,
26. and have profaned *mine holy things:* they have put no difference between *the holy* and profane,
28:14. thou wast upon the *holy* mountain *of* God;
36:20. they profaned *my holy* name,
21. I had pity for *mine holy* name,
22. but for *mine holy* name's sake,
38. As the *holy* flock, (marg. flock of *holy things*)
39: 7. So will I make *my holy* name known
— will not (let them) pollute *my holy* name
25. and will be jealous for *my holy* name;
41: 4. This (is) *the most holy*[2] (place).
21. the face of *the sanctuary;*
23. the temple *and the sanctuary* had two
42:13. they (be) *holy* chambers,
— shall eat *the most holy things* (lit. *holies of holies*): there shall they lay *the most holy things*, (lit. *id.*)
14. shall they not go out *of the holy* (place)
— for they (are) *holy;*
20. make a separation between *the sanctuary*
43: 7. and *my holy* name, shall the house of
8. they have even defiled *my holy* name
12. round about (shall be) *most holy*.[2]
44: 8. ye have not kept the charge of *mine holy things:*
13. to come near to any of *my holy things*, in *the most holy* (place): (lit. *holies of holies*)
19. lay them in the *holy* chambers,
23. (the difference) between *the holy* and
27. the day that he goeth into *the sanctuary*,
— to minister *in the sanctuary*,
45: 1. *an holy portion* (marg. *holiness*) of the
— This (shall be) *holy* in all the borders
2. Of this there shall be for *the sanctuary*
3. sanctuary (and) *the most holy*[2] (place).
4. *The holy* (portion) of the land shall be for the priests
6. against the oblation of *the holy* (portion):
7. on the other side of the oblation of *the holy* (portion),
— before the oblation of *the holy* (portion),
46:19. into the *holy* chambers of the priests,
48:10. for them,...shall be (this) *holy* oblation;
12. shall be unto them *a thing most holy*[2]
14. for (it is) *holy* unto the Lord.
18, 18. over against the oblation of *the holy* (portion)
20. ye shall offer the *holy* oblation
21. on the other of the *holy* oblation,
— it shall be the *holy* oblation;
Dan. 8:13. to give *both the sanctuary* and the host
14. then shall *the sanctuary* be cleansed.
9:16. Jerusalem, *thy holy* mountain:

Dan 9:20. the Lord my God for the *holy* mountain *of*
24. upon thy people and upon *thy holy* city,
— to anoint *the most Holy.*[2]
26. destroy the city *and the sanctuary;*
11:28. heart (shall be) against the *holy* covenant;
30. indignation against the *holy* covenant:
— them that forsake the *holy* covenant.
45. the glorious *holy* mountain;
12: 7. to scatter the power of the *holy* people,
Joel 2: 1. sound an alarm in *my holy* mountain:
3:17(4:17). dwelling in Zion, *my holy* mountain: then shall Jerusalem be *holy,* (marg. *holiness*)
Am. 2: 7. to profane *my holy* name:
4: 2. The Lord God hath sworn *by his holiness,*
Obad. 16. as ye have drunk upon *my holy* mountain,
17. there shall be *holiness;* and the house
Jon. 2: 4(5). yet I will look again toward *thy holy* temple.
7(8). unto thee, into *thine holy* temple.
Mic. 1: 2. the Lord from *his holy* temple.
Hab 2:20. the Lord (is) in *his holy* temple:
Zep. 3: 4. her priests have polluted *the sanctuary,*
11. because of *my holy* mountain.
Hag 2:12. If one bear *holy* flesh in the skirt of his
Zec. 2:12(16). his portion in the *holy* land,
13(17). out of *his holy* habitation. (marg. the habitation of *his holiness*)
8: 3. of the Lord of hosts the *holy* mountain.
14:20. of the horses, *Holiness* unto the Lord;
21. Yea, every pot...shall be *holiness* unto the
Mal. 2:11. Judah hath profaned *the holiness of* the

6948 **קְדֵשָׁה** *k'dēh-shāh',* f.

Gen38:21. Where (is) *the harlot,*
— There was no *harlot* in this (place).
22. there was no *harlot* in this (place).
Deu23:17(18). There shall be no *whore* (marg. or, *sodomitess*)
Hos. 4:14. they sacrifice with *harlots:*

6949 **קָהָה** [*kāh-hāh'*].

* KAL.—*Future.* *

Jer. 31:29. the children's teeth *are set on edge.*
30. his teeth *shall be set on edge.*
Eze.18: 2. the children's teeth *are set on edge?*

* PIEL.—*Preterite.* *

Ecc 10:10. If the iron *be blunt,* and he do not whet

6950 **קָהַל** [*kāh-hal'*].

* NIPHAL.—*Preterite.* *

2Ch 20:26. the fourth day *they assembled themselves*
Est. 9: 2. The Jews *gathered themselves together* in
16. *gathered themselves together,* and stood for
18. Jews that (were) at Shushan *assembled together*

NIPHAL.—*Infinitive.*

Nu. 16:42(17:7). *when* the congregation *was gathered*
Est. 8:11. the Jews...*to gather themselves together,*

NIPHAL.—*Future.*

Ex. 32: 1. *And* when...the people *gathered themselves together* unto Aaron,
Lev. 8: 4. *and* the assembly *was gathered together*
Nu. 16: 3 & 20:2. *And they gathered themselves together* against Moses
Jos. 18: 1. *And* the whole congregation...*assembled together* at Shiloh,
22:12. *And* when...the children of Israel *gathered themselves together* at Shiloh,
Jud.20: 1. *and* the congregation *was gathered together*
2Sa.20:14. *and they were gathered together,* and went
1K. 8: 2. *And* all the men of Israel *assembled themselves* unto king Solomon
2Ch 5: 3. *Wherefore* all the men of Israel *assembled themselves*
Est. 9:15. *For* the Jews that (were) in Shushan *gathered themselves together*
Jer. 26: 9. *And* all the people *were gathered* against

NIPHAL.—*Participle.*

Eze.38: 7. all thy company *that are assembled* unto

* HIPHIL.—*Preterite.* *

Nu. 1:18. *they assembled* all the congregation
8: 9. *and thou shalt gather* the whole assembly of the children of Israel *together:*
Eze.38:13. *hast thou gathered* thy company to take a

HIPHIL.—*Infinitive.*

Nu. 10: 7. *But when* the congregation *is to be gathered together,*

HIPHIL.—*Imperative.*

Lev. 8: 3. *gather* thou all the congregation *together*
Nu. 20: 8. Take the rod, *and gather thou* the assembly *together,*
Deu 4:10. *Gather* me the people *together,* and I will
31:12. *Gather* the people *together,* men, and
28. *Gather* unto me all the elders of your

HIPHIL.—*Future.*

Ex. 35: 1. *And* Moses *gathered* all the congregation of the children of Israel *together,*
Nu. 16:19. *And* Korah *gathered* all the congregation
20:10. *And* Moses and Aaron *gathered* the congregation *together* before the rock,
1K. 8: 1. Then Solomon *assembled* the elders of
12:21. *And* when...*he assembled* all the house of
1Ch 13: 5. *So* David *gathered* all Israel *together,*
15: 3. *And* David *gathered* all Israel *together*
28: 1. *And* David *assembled* all the princes of
2Ch 5: 2. Then Solomon *assembled* the elders of
11: 1. *And* when...*he gathered* of the house of
Job 11:10. and shut up, *or gather together,*

קָהָל *kāh-hāhl',* m. 6951

Gen28: 3. that thou mayest be *a multitude* (marg. *assembly*) *of* people;
35:11. a nation *and a company of* nations shall
48: 4. I will make of thee *a multitude of* people;
49: 6. thou into their secret; *unto their assembly,*
Ex. 12: 6. *the* whole *assembly of* the congregation of Israel shall kill it
16: 3. to kill *this* whole *assembly* with hunger.
Lev. 4:13. thing be hid from the eyes of *the assembly,*
14. then *the congregation* shall offer a young
21. it (is) a sin offering for *the congregation.*
16:17. for all *the congregation of* Israel.
33. for all the people of *the congregation.*
Nu. 10: 7. when *the congregation* is to be gathered
14: 5. on their faces before all *the assembly of*
15:15. (shall be both) for you of *the congregation,*
16: 3. ye up yourselves above *the congregation of*
33. perished from among *the congregation.*
47(17:12). the midst of *the congregation;*
19:20. be cut off from among *the congregation,*
20: 4. have ye brought up *the congregation of*
6. Moses and Aaron went from the presence of *the assembly*
10. Moses and Aaron gathered *the congregation*
12. ye shall not bring this *congregation* into
22: 4. Now shall this *company* lick up all
Deu 5:22(19). the Lord spake unto all *your assembly*
9:10 & 10:4. fire in the day of *the assembly.*
18:16. Horeb in the day of *the assembly,*
23: 1(2). shall not enter *into the congregation of*
2(3). A bastard shall not enter *into the congregation of* the Lord;
—(-). he not enter *into the congregation of*
3(4). shall not enter *into the congregation of*
—(-). they not enter *into the congregation of*
8(9). shall enter *into the congregation of* the
31:30. spake in the ears of all *the congregation of*
Jos. 8:35. before all *the congregation of* Israel,
Jud.20: 2. presented themselves *in the assembly of*
21: 5. that came not up *with the congregation*
8. from Jabesh-gilead to *the assembly.*
1Sa.17:47. all this *assembly* shall know
1K. 8:14. blessed all *the congregation of* Israel: and all *the congregation of* Israel stood;
22. in the presence of all *the congregation of*
55. blessed all *the congregation of* Israel
65. all Israel with him, *a great congregation,*
12: 3. Jeroboam and all *the congregation of*
1Ch 13: 2. David said unto all *the congregation of*
4. all *the congregation* said that they would

1Ch 28: 8. sight of all Israel *the congregation of* the
29: 1. the king said unto all *the congregation*,
10. blessed the Lord before all *the congregation:*
20. David said to all *the congregation*,
— all *the congregation* blessed the Lord God
2Ch 1: 3. Solomon, and all *the congregation* with
5. *and the congregation* sought unto it.
6: 3. blessed *the* whole *congregation of* Israel: and all *the congregation of* Israel stood.
12. presence of all *the congregation of* Israel,
13. kneeled down upon his knees before all *the congregation of*
7: 8. Israel with him, *a* very great *congregation*,
20: 5. Jehoshaphat stood *in the congregation of*
14. in the midst of *the congregation;*
23: 3. all *the congregation* made a covenant
24: 6. *and of the congregation* of Israel,
28: 14. the princes and all *the congregation.*
29: 23. before the king *and the congregation;*
28. all *the congregation* worshipped,
31. *the congregation* brought in sacrifices
32. the burnt offerings, which *the congregation*
30: 2. all *the congregation* in Jerusalem,
4. the king and all *the congregation.*
13. second month, *a* very great *congregation.*
17. (there were) many *in the congregation*
23. *the* whole *assembly* took counsel
24. did give *to the congregation* a thousand
— gave *to the congregation* a thousand
25. all *the congregation of* Judah,
— all *the congregation* that came out of
31: 18. through all *the congregation:*
Ezr. 2: 64. *The* whole *congregation* together
10: 1. *a* very great *congregation* of men and
8. himself separated *from the congregation of*
12. Then all *the congregation* answered
14. Let now our rulers of all *the congregation*
Neh. 5: 13. all *the congregation* said, Amen,
7: 66. *The* whole *congregation* together
8: 2. brought the law before *the congregation*
17. all *the congregation* of them that were
13: 1. should not come *into the congregation of*
Job 30: 28. stood up, (and) I cried *in the congregation.*
Ps. 22: 22(23). in the midst of *the congregation* will I
25(26). My praise (shall be) of thee *in the* great *congregation:*
26: 5. have hated *the congregation of* evil doers;
35: 18. give thee thanks *in the* great *congregation:*
40: 9(10). I have preached righteousness *in the* great *congregation:*
10(11). thy truth *from the* great *congregation.*
89: 5(6). faithfulness also *in the congregation of*
107: 32. exalt him also *in the congregation of* the
149: 1. his praise *in the congregation of* saints.
Pro. 5: 14. in the midst of *the congregation*
21: 16. remain *in the congregation of* the dead.
26: 26. be shewed *before the* (whole) *congregation.*
Jer. 26: 17. spake to all *the assembly of* the people,
31: 8. *a* great *company* shall return thither.
44: 15. *a* great *multitude*, even all the people
50: 9. against Babylon *an assembly of* great
Lam. 1: 10. should not enter *into* thy *congregation.*
Eze. 16: 40. They shall also bring up *a company*
17: 17. with (his) mighty army *and* great *company*
23: 24. *and with an assembly of* people,
46. I will bring up *a company* upon them,
47. *the company* shall stone them with stónes,
26: 7. horsemen, *and companies*, and much
27: 27. in all *thy company* which (is) in the midst
34. all *thy company* in the midst of thee shall
32: 3. *with a company of* many people;
22. Asshur (is) there and all *her company:*
23. *her company* is round about her grave:
38: 4. *a* great *company* (with) bucklers and
7. all *thy company* that are assembled unto
13. hast thou gathered *thy company* to take a
15. *a* great *company*, and a mighty army:
Joel 2: 16. the people, sanctify *the congregation*,
Mic. 2: 5. *in the congregation of* the Lord.

6952 **קְהִלָּה** [*k'hil-lāh'*], f.

Deu33: 4. (even) the inheritance of *the congregation of* Jacob.
Neh. 5: 7. And I set *a* great *assembly*

קֹהֶלֶת *kōh-heh'-leth*, m. 6953

Ecc. 1: 1. words of *the Preacher*, the son of David,
2. Vanity of vanities, saith *the Preacher*,
12. I *the Preacher* was king over Israel in
7: 27. this have I found, saith *the preacher*,
12: 8. Vanity of vanities, saith *the preacher;*
9. because *the preacher* was wise, he still taught the people knowledge;
10. *The preacher* sought to find out acceptable

קַו *kāhv* & **קָו** *kav*, m. 6957

1K. 7: 23. *and a line* of thirty cubits did compass it
2K. 21: 13. I will stretch over Jerusalem *the line of*
2Ch 4: 2. *and a line* of thirty cubits did compass it
Job 38: 5. who hath stretched *the line* upon it?
Ps. 19: 4(5). *Their line* (marg. or, *rule*, or, *direction*) is gone out through all the earth,
Isa. 18: 2, 7. a nation *meted out* (lit. a nation of *a line a line*) and trodden
28: 10, 13. *line upon line, line upon line;*
17. Judgment also will I lay *to the line*,
34: 11. stretch out upon it *the line of* confusion,
17. his hand hath divided it unto them *by line:*
44: 13. The carpenter stretcheth out (his) *rule*,
Jer. 31: 39. *the* measuring *line* shall yet go forth over
Lam. 2: 8. he hath stretched out *a line*,
Eze. 47: 3. when the man that had *the line* in his hand went forth eastward,
Zec. 1: 16. *and a line* shall be stretched forth upon

קוֹא [*kōh*]. 6958

* KAL.—*Preterite.* *

Lev. 18: 28. as *it spued* out the nations

* HIPHIL.—*Preterite.* *

Pro. 25: 16. lest thou be filled therewith, *and vomit* it.

HIPHIL.—*Future.*

Lev. 18: 25. *and* the land itself *vomiteth* out her
28. That the land *spue* not you *out*
20: 22. that the land,...*spue* you not *out.*
Job 20: 15. *and he shall vomit them up again:*
Pro. 23: 8. The morsel (which) thou hast eaten *shalt thou vomit up*,
Jon. 2: 10(11). *and it vomited out* Jonah upon the dry

קוֹבַע *kōh'-vag*, m. 6959

1Sa. 17: 38. he put *an helmet of* brass upon his head;
Eze. 23: 24. and shield *and helmet*, round about:

קָוָה [*kāh-vāh'*]. 6960

* KAL.—*Participle.* Poel. *

Ps. 25: 3. let none *that wait on thee* be ashamed:
37: 9. *but those that wait upon* the Lord,
69: 6(7). Let not *them that wait on thee*, O Lord
Isa. 40: 31. *But they that wait upon* the Lord shall
49: 23. *they* shall not be ashamed *that wait for me.*
Lam. 3: 25. The Lord (is) good *unto them that wait for him*,

* NIPHAL.—*Preterite.* *

Jer. 3: 17. *and* all the nations *shall be gathered* unto

NIPHAL.—*Future.*

Gen 1: 9. *Let* the waters under the heaven *be gathered together* unto one place,

* PIEL.—*Preterite.* *

Gen 49: 18. *I have waited* for thy salvation, O Lord.
Job 6: 19. the companies of Sheba *waited* for them.
30: 26. When *I looked* for good, then evil came
Ps. 25: 5. on thee *do I wait* all the day.
21. preserve me; for *I wait on thee.*
39: 7(8). And now, Lord, what *wait I* for? my
40: 1(2). *I waited* patiently for the Lord;
56: 6(7). they mark my steps, when *they wait for* my soul.
119: 95. The wicked *have waited* for me to destroy
130: 5. *I wait* for the Lord, my soul *doth wait*,

Isa. 5: 4. *I looked* that it should bring forth grapes,
8:17. *and I will look* for him.
25: 9. *we have waited* for him, and he will save
— *we have waited* for him, we will be glad
26: 8. in the way of thy judgments, O Lord, *have we waited for thee;*
33: 2. *we have waited* for thee:
Jer. 13:16. *and, while ye look* for light, he turn it
Lam. 2:16. certainly this (is) the day *that we looked for;*

PIEL.—*Infinitive.*

Ps. 40: 1(2). waited *patiently* (marg. *in waiting* I waited) for the Lord;
Jer. 8:15. We *looked* for peace, but no good (came);
14:19. we *looked* for peace, and there is no good;

PIEL.—*Imperative.*

Ps. 27:14. *Wait* on the Lord: be of good courage,
— *wait, I say,* on the Lord.
37:34. *Wait* on the Lord, and keep his way,
Pro. 20:22. *wait* on the Lord, and he shall save thee.
Hos 12: 6(7). *and wait* on thy God continually.

PIEL.—*Future.*

Job 3: 9. *let it look* for light, but (have) none;
7: 2. as an hireling *looketh* for (the reward of)
17:13. If *I wait,* the grave (is) mine house:
Ps. 52: 9(11). *and I will wait on* thy name;
69:20(21). *and I looked* (for some) to take pity,
Isa. 5: 2. *and he looked* that it should bring forth
7. *and he looked* for judgment, but behold
51: 5. the isles *shall wait* upon me,
59: 9. *we wait* for light, but behold obscurity;
11. *we look* for judgment, but there is none;
60: 9. Surely the isles *shall wait* for me,
64: 3(2). thou didst terrible things (which) *we looked* not *for,*
Jer. 14:22. *therefore we will wait* upon thee:
Mic. 5: 7(6). that *tarrieth* not for man, nor waiteth

6961 **קֶוֶה** *keh'-veh*, m.

1K. 7:23. (כתיב) *and a line* of thirty cubits
Jer. 31:39. (——) And *the* measuring *line* shall yet
Zec. 1:16. (——) *and a line* shall be stretched forth

6495 **קוֹחַ** *kōh'ăgh*, m.

Isa. 61: 1. opening of *the prison* [see also פְּקַח־קוֹחַ]

6962 **קוּט** [*koot*].

* KAL.—*Preterite.* *

Eze. 16:47. as (if that were) a *very* little (thing), (marg. or, that *was lothed* as a small (thing))

KAL.—*Future.*

Ps. 95:10. Forty years long *was I grieved* with (this)

* NIPHAL.—*Preterite.* *

Eze. 6: 9. *and they shall lothe themselves*
20:43. *and ye shall lothe yourselves* in your own
36:31. *and shall lothe yourselves* in your own

* HITHPOLEL.—*Future.* *

Ps. 119:158. I beheld the transgressors, *and was grieved;*
139:21. *am* not *I grieved* with those that rise up

6962 **קוּט** [*koot*].

* KAL.—*Future.* *

Job 8:14. Whose hope *shall be cut off,*

6963 **קוֹל** *kōhl*, m.

Gen 3: 8. they heard *the voice of* the Lord God
10. I heard *thy voice* in the garden, and I was
17. Because thou hast hearkened *unto the voice of* thy wife,
4:10. *the voice of* thy brother's blood crieth unto
23. Adah and Zillah, hear *my voice;*
16: 2. Abram hearkened *to the voice of* Sarai.
21:12. hearken *unto her voice;*
16. over against (him), and lift up *her voice,*
Gen 21:17. God heard *the voice of* the lad;
— God hath heard *the voice of* the lad where
22:18. because thou hast obeyed *my voice.*
26: 5. Because that Abraham obeyed *my voice,*
27: 8. Now therefore, my son, obey *my voice*
13. obey *my voice,* and go fetch me (them).
22. *The voice* (is) Jacob's *voice,* but the hands
38. Esau lifted up *his voice,* and wept.
43. Now therefore, my son, obey *my voice;*
29:11. and lifted up *his voice,* and wept.
30: 6. judged me, and hath also heard *my voice,*
39:14. I cried *with a* loud *voice:*
15. he heard that I lifted up *my voice*
18. as I lifted up *my voice* and cried,
45: 2. he wept aloud: (marg. gave forth *his voice* in weeping)
16. *And the fame* thereof was heard in
Ex. 3:18. they shall hearken *to thy voice:*
4: 1. nor hearken *unto my voice:*
8. neither hearken *to the voice of* the first sign, that they will believe *the voice of* the latter sign.
9. neither hearken *unto thy voice,*
5: 2. Who (is) the Lord, that I should obey *his voice*
9:23. the Lord sent *thunder* and hail,
28. there be no (more) mighty *thunderings*
29. *the thunder* shall cease, neither shall there
33. *thunders* and hail ceased, and the rain
34. *and the thunders* were ceased, he sinned
15:26. hearken *to the voice of* the Lord thy God,
18:19. Hearken now *unto my voice,*
24. Moses hearkened *to the voice of* his
19: 5. if ye will obey *my voice* indeed,
16. there were *thunders* and lightnings,
— *and the voice of* the trumpet
19. when *the voice of* the trumpet sounded
— spake, and God answered him *by a voice.*
20:18. all the people saw *the thunderings,*
— *the noise of* the trumpet,
23:21. Beware of him, and obey *his voice,*
22. if thou shalt indeed obey *his voice,*
24: 3. all the people answered with one *voice,*
28:35. *his sound* shall be heard
32:17. Joshua heard *the noise of* the people
— (There is) *a noise of* war in the camp.
18. (It is) not *the voice of* them that shout for mastery, neither (is it) *the voice of* them
— *the noise of* them that sing do I hear.
36: 6. they caused it to be proclaimed (lit. *the voice* to pass)
Lev. 5: 1. hear *the voice of* swearing,
26:36. *the sound of* a shaken leaf shall chase
Nu. 7:89. he heard *the voice* of one speaking unto
14: 1. all the congregation lifted up *their voice,*
22. have not hearkened *to my voice;*
16:34. all Israel...fled *at the cry of them:*
20:16. cried unto the Lord, he heard *our voice,*
21: 3. the Lord hearkened *to the voice of* Israel,
Deu. 1:34. the Lord heard *the voice of* your words,
45. the Lord would not hearken *to your voice,*
4:12. ye heard *the voice of* the words,
— only (ye heard) *a voice.*
30. shalt be obedient *unto his voice;*
33. Did (ever) people hear *the voice of* God
36. Out of heaven he made thee to hear *his voice,*
5:22(19). the thick darkness, with *a* great *voice:*
23(20). when ye heard *the voice* out of the
24(21). we have heard *his voice* out of the
25(22). if we hear *the voice of* the Lord our
26(23). hath heard *the voice of* the living God
28(25). the Lord heard *the voice of* your words,
—(—). I have heard *the voice of* the words
8:20. ye would not be obedient *unto the voice of*
9:23. nor hearkened *to his voice.*
13: 4(5). keep his commandments, *and* obey *his voice,*
18(19). shalt hearken *to the voice of* the Lord
15: 5. if thou carefully hearken *unto the voice of*
18:16. Let me not hear again *the voice of* the Lord
21:18. will not obey *the voice of* his father, *or the voice of* his mother,
20. he will not obey *our voice;*
26: 7. the Lord heard *our voice,*
14. I have hearkened *to the voice of* the Lord
17. to hearken *unto his voice:*

Deu27:10. obey *the voice of* the Lord thy God,
14. unto all the men of Israel with *a* loud *voice*,
28: 1. hearken diligently *unto the voice of* the
2. thou shalt hearken *unto the voice of* the
15. not hearken *unto the voice of* the Lord thy
45. thou hearkenedst not *unto the voice of* the
62. thou wouldest not obey *the voice of* the
30: 2. shalt obey *his voice*
8. obey *the voice of* the Lord,
10. If thou shalt hearken *unto the voice of* the
20. that thou mayest obey *his voice*,
33: 7. Hear, Lord, *the voice of* Judah,
Jos. 5: 6. they obeyed not *the voice of* the Lord:
6: 5. when ye hear *the sound of* the trumpet,
10. nor make any noise with *your voice*,
20. the people heard *the sound of* the trumpet,
10:14. the Lord hearkened *unto the voice of* a
22: 2. have obeyed *my voice*
24:24. *and his voice* will we obey.
Jud. 2: 2. ye have not obeyed *my voice:*
4. the people lifted up *their voice*,
20. have not hearkened *unto my voice;*
5:11. (delivered) *from the noise of* archers
6:10. ye have not obeyed *my voice*.
9: 7. lifted up *his voice*, and cried,
13: 9. God hearkened *to the voice of* Manoah;
18: 3. they knew *the voice of* the young man
25. Let not *thy voice* be heard among us,
20:13. would not hearken *to the voice of* their
21: 2. lifted up *their voices*, and wept sore;
Ru. 1: 9. they lifted up *their voice*, and wept.
14. they lifted up *their voice*, and wept again:
1Sa. 1:13. *but her voice* was not heard:
2:25. they hearkened not *unto the voice of* their
4: 6. the Philistines heard *the noise of* the shout,
— What (meaneth) *the noise of* this great
14. Eli heard *the noise of* the crying,
— What (meaneth) *the noise of* this tumult?
7:10. the Lord thundered *with a* great *thunder*
8: 7. Hearken *unto the voice of* the people
9. Now therefore hearken *unto their voice:*
19. refused to obey *the voice of* Samuel;
22. Hearken *unto their voice*,
11: 4. all the people lifted up *their voices*, and
12: 1. I have hearkened *unto your voice*
14. serve him, and obey *his voice*,
15. if ye will not obey *the voice of* the Lord,
17. he shall send *thunder* and rain;
18. the Lord sent *thunder* and rain that day:
15: 1. hearken thou *unto the voice of* the words
14. What (meaneth) then this *bleating of* the sheep in mine ears, *and the lowing of*
19. Wherefore then didst thou not obey *the voice of* the Lord,
20. Yea, I have obeyed *the voice of* the Lord,
22. in obeying *the voice of* the Lord?
24. I feared the people, and obeyed *their voice*.
19: 6. Saul hearkened *unto the voice of* Jonathan:
24:16(17). (Is) this *thy voice*, my son David? And Saul lifted up *his voice*, and wept.
25:35. see, I have hearkened *to thy voice*,
26:17. Saul knew David's *voice*, and said, (Is) this *thy voice*, my son David? And David said, (It is) *my voice*,
28:12. saw Samuel, she cried *with a* loud *voice:*
18. thou obeyedst not *the voice of* the Lord,
21. thine handmaid hath obeyed *thy voice*,
22. hearken thou also *unto the voice of* thine
23. he hearkened *unto their voice*.
30: 4. David and the people...lifted up *their voice* and wept,
2Sa. 3:32. the king lifted up *his voice*, and wept
5:24. when thou hearest *the sound of* a going in
6:15. *and with the sound of* the trumpet.
12:18. he would not hearken *unto our voice:*
13:14. he would not hearken unto *her voice:*
36. lifted up *their voice* and wept:
15:10. soon as ye hear *the sound of* the trumpet,
23. all the country wept with *a* loud *voice*,
19: 4(5). the king cried with *a* loud *voice*,
35(36). I hear any more *the voice of* singing
22: 7. he did hear *my voice*
14. the most High uttered *his voice*.
1K. 1:40. that the earth rent *with the sound of them*.
41. Joab heard *the sound of* the trumpet, he said, Wherefore (is this) *noise of* the city being in an uproar?

1K. 1:45. This (is) *the noise* that ye have heard.
8:55. blessed all the congregation of Israel with *a* loud *voice*,
14: 6. when Ahijah heard *the sound of* her feet,
17:22. the Lord heard *the voice of* Elijah;
18:26. But (there was) no *voice*, nor any that
27. Cry aloud: (marg. *with a* great *voice*)
28. they cried aloud, (lit. *id.*)
29. that (there was) neither *voice*,
41. (there is) *a sound* (marg. or, *a noise*) *of* abundance of rain.
19:12. after the fire *a* still small *voice*.
13. (there came) *a voice* unto him,
20:25. he hearkened *unto their voice*, and did so.
36. thou hast not obeyed *the voice of* the Lord,
2K. 4:31. (there was) neither *voice*, nor hearing.
6:32. (is) not *the sound of* his master's feet behind him?
7: 6. to hear *a noise of* chariots, *and a noise of* horses, (even) *the noise of* a great host:
10. neither *voice of* man,
10: 6. *and* (if) ye will hearken *unto my voice*,
11:13. when Athaliah heard *the noise of* the guard
18:12. they obeyed not *the voice of* the Lord
28. Rab-shakeh stood and cried *with a* loud *voice*
19:22. whom hast thou exalted (thy) *voice*,
1Ch 14:15. when thou shalt hear *a sound of* going
15:16. lifting up *the voice* with joy.
28. *and with sound of* the cornet,
2Ch 5:13. to make one *sound* to be heard
— when they lifted up (their) *voice*
15:14. they sware unto the Lord *with a* loud *voice*,
20:19. *with a* loud *voice* on high.
23:12. Athaliah heard *the noise of* the people
24: 9. they made *a proclamation* (marg. *voice*)
30: 5. to make *proclamation* throughout all Israel,
27. *their voice* was heard,
32:18. they cried *with a* loud *voice*
36:22. he made *a proclamation* throughout
Ezr. 1: 1. he made *a proclamation* (marg. caused *a voice* to pass) throughout all his
3:12. wept *with a* loud *voice;* and many shouted aloud (lit. lifting up *the voice*) for joy:
13. discern *the noise of* the shout of joy *from the noise*
— *and the noise* was heard afar off.
10: 7. they made *proclamation*
12. said with *a* loud *voice*,
Neh. 4:20(14). ye hear *the sound of* the trumpet,
8:15. they should publish and pro*claim* (lit. cause *the voice* to pass)
9: 4. cried *with a* loud *voice* unto the Lord
Job 2:12. they lifted up *their voice*, and wept;
3:18. they hear not *the voice of* the oppressor.
4:10. The roaring of the lion, *and the voice of*
16. (there was) silence, *and* I heard *a voice*, (saying),
9:16. that he had hearkened unto *my voice*.
15:21. *A* dreadful *sound* (is) in his ears:
21:12. rejoice *at the sound of* the organ.
28:26. a way for the lightning of *the thunder:*
29:10. The nobles held their peace, (marg. *The voice of* the nobles was hid)
30:31. my organ *into the voice of* them that weep.
33: 8. *and* I have heard *the voice of* (thy) words,
34:16. hearken *to the voice of* my words.
37: 2. Hear attentively the noise of *his voice*,
4. After it *a voice* roareth: he thundereth *with the voice of*
— when *his voice* is heard.
5. thundereth marvellously *with his voice;*
38:25. a way for the lightning of *thunder;*
34. Canst thou lift up *thy voice* to the clouds,
39:24. that (it is) *the sound of* the trumpet.
40: 9. *or* canst thou thunder with *a voice* like
Ps. 3: 4(5). cried unto the Lord with *my voice*,
5: 2(3). Hearken *unto the voice of* my cry,
3(4). *My voice* shalt thou hear in the
6: 8(9). the Lord hath heard *the voice of* my
18: 6(7). he heard *my voice*
13(14). the Highest gave *his voice;*
19: 3(4). (where) *their voice* is not heard.
26: 7. *with the voice of* thanksgiving,
27: 7. Hear, O Lord, (when) I cry with *my voice*.
28: 2. Hear *the voice of* my supplications,
6. he hath heard *the voice of* my supplications.

Ps. 29: 3. *The voice of* the Lord (is) upon the waters:
4. *The voice of* the Lord (is) powerful; *the voice of* the Lord (is) full of majesty.
5. *The voice of* the Lord breaketh the cedars;
7. *The voice of* the Lord divideth the flames
8. *The voice of* the Lord shaketh the
9. *The voice of* the Lord maketh the hinds to
31:22(23). heardest *the voice of* my supplications
42: 4(5). *with the voice of* joy and praise,
7(8). *at the noise of* thy waterspouts:
44:16(17). *For the voice of* him that reproacheth
46: 6(7). he uttered *his voice*, the earth melted.
47: 1(2). unto God *with the voice of* triumph.
5(6). the Lord *with the sound of* a trumpet.
55: 3(4). *Because of the voice of* the enemy,
17(18). he shall hear *my voice*.
58: 5(6). not hearken *to the voice of* charmers,
64: 1(2). Hear *my voice*, O God,
66: 8. make *the voice of* his praise to be heard:
19. he hath attended *to the voice of* my prayer.
68:33(34). lo, he doth send out *his voice*, (and that) *a* mighty *voice*.
74:23. Forget not *the voice of* thine enemies:
77: 1(2). cried unto God with *my voice*, (even) unto God with *my voice;*
17(18). the skies sent out *a sound*.
18(19). *The voice of* thy thunder (was) in the
81:11(12). would not hearken *to my voice;*
86: 6. attend *to the voice of* my supplications.
93: 3. the floods have lifted up *their voice;*
4. *than the noise of* many waters,
95: 7. To day if ye will hear *his voice*,
98: 5. with the harp, *and the voice of* a psalm.
6. With trumpets *and sound of* cornet make a joyful
102: 5(6). By reason of *the voice of* my groaning
103:20. hearkening *unto the voice of* his word.
104: 7. at *the voice of* thy thunder they hasted
12. sing (marg. give *a voice*) among the branches.
106:25. hearkened not *unto the voice of* the Lord.
116: 1. because he hath heard *my voice*
118:15. *The voice of* rejoicing and salvation
119:149. Hear *my voice* according unto thy
130: 2. Lord, hear *my voice:*
— be attentive *to the voice of* my
140: 6(7). hear *the voice of* my supplications,
141: 1. give ear unto *my voice*,
142: 1(2). I cried unto the Lord with *my voice;* with *my voice* unto the Lord
Pro. 1:20. she uttereth *her voice* in the streets:
2: 3. liftest up *thy voice* for understanding;
5:13. have not obeyed *the voice of* my teachers,
8: 1. understanding put forth *her voice?*
4. *and my voice* (is) to the sons of man.
26:25. When he *speaketh* fair, (marg. maketh *his voice* gracious)
27:14. that blesseth his friend *with a* loud *voice*,
Ecc. 5: 3(2). *and* a fool's *voice* (is known) by
6(5). should God be angry at *thy voice*,
7: 6. *as the crackling* (marg. *sound*) *of* thorns under a pot,
10:20. a bird of the air shall carry *the voice*,
12: 4. when *the sound of* the grinding is low, and he shall rise up *at the voice of* the bird,
Cant. 2: 8. *The voice of* my beloved!
12. *and the voice of* the turtle is heard in our
14. let me hear *thy voice;* for sweet (is) *thy voice*,
5: 2. (it is) *the voice of* my beloved
8:13. the companions hearken *to thy voice:*
Isa. 6: 4. *at the voice of* him that cried,
8. I heard *the voice of* the Lord,
10:30. Lift up *thy voice*, O daughter of Gallim:
13: 2. exalt *the voice* unto them,
4. *The noise of* a multitude
— *a* tumultuous *noise* of the kingdoms
15: 4. *their voice* shall be heard
24:14. They shall lift up *their voice*,
18. he who fleeth *from the noise of* the fear
28:23. Give ye ear, and hear *my voice;*
29: 4. *thy voice* shall be, as of one that hath a
6. with earthquake, *and* great *noise*,
30:19. he will be very gracious unto thee *at the voice of* thy cry;
30. the Lord shall cause *his* glorious *voice* to
31. *through the voice of* the Lord shall the

Isa. 31: 4. (he) will not be afraid *of their voice*,
32: 9. hear *my voice*, ye careless daughters;
33: 3. *At the noise of* the tumult the people fled;
36:13. Rabshakeh stood, and cried *with a* loud *voice*
37:23. against whom hast thou exalted (thy) *voice*,
40: 3. *The voice of* him that crieth in the
6. *The voice* said, Cry. And he said,
9. lift up *thy voice* with strength;
42: 2. nor cause *his voice* to be heard
48:20. *with a voice of* singing declare
50:10. that obeyeth *the voice of* his servant,
51: 3. thanksgiving, *and the voice of* melody.
52: 8. Thy watchmen shall lift up *the voice;* with *the voice* together shall they sing:
58: 1. lift up *thy voice* like a trumpet, and shew
4. make *your voice* to be heard on high.
65:19. *the voice of* weeping shall be no more heard in her, *nor the voice of* crying.
66: 6. *A voice of* noise from the city, *a voice* from the temple, *a voice of* the Lord that
Jer. 2:15. The young lions roared upon him, (and) yelled, (marg. gave out *their voice*)
3: 9. *through the lightness* (marg. or, *fame*) *of* her whoredom,
13. *and* ye have not obeyed *my voice*, saith
21. *A voice* was heard upon the high
25. have not obeyed *the voice of* the Lord
4:15. *a voice* declareth from Dan,
16. give out *their voice* against the cities
19. *the sound of* the trumpet, the alarm of
21. hear *the sound of* the trumpet?
29. *for the noise of* the horsemen and
31. I have heard *a voice*
— *the voice of* the daughter of Zion,
6:17. Hearken *to the sound of* the trumpet.
23. *their voice* roareth like the sea;
7:23. Obey *my voice*, and I will be your God,
28. that obeyeth not *the voice of* the Lord
34. *the voice of* mirth, *and the voice of* gladness, *the voice of* the bridegroom, *and the voice of* the bride:
8:16. the whole land trembled *at the sound*
19. Behold *the voice of* the cry
9:10(9). neither can (men) hear *the voice of*
13(12). have not obeyed *my voice*,
19(18). *a voice of* wailing is heard out of Zion,
10:13. When he uttereth his *voice*,
22. *the noise of* the bruit is come,
11: 4, 7. saying, Obey *my voice*,
16. *with the noise of* a great tumult
12: 8. it crieth out (marg. giveth out *his voice*) against me:
16: 9. *the voice of* mirth, *and the voice of* gladness, *the voice of* the bridegroom, *and the voice of* the bride.
18:10. that it obey not *my voice*,
19. hearken *to the voice of* them that contend
22:20. lift up *thy voice* in Bashan,
21. that thou obeyedst not *my voice*.
25:10. *the voice of* mirth, *and the voice of* gladness, *the voice of* the bridegroom, *and the voice of* the bride, *the sound of* the
30. utter *his voice* from his holy habitation;
36. *A voice of* the cry of the shepherds,
26:13. obey *the voice of* the Lord your God;
30: 5. We have heard *a voice of* trembling,
19. *and the voice of* them that make merry:
31:15. *A voice* was heard in Ramah,
16. Refrain *thy voice* from weeping,
32:23. they obeyed not *thy voice*,
33:11. *The voice of* joy, *and the voice of* gladness, *the voice of* the bridegroom, *and the voice of* the bride, *the voice of* them that shall
35: 8. Thus have we obeyed *the voice of* Jonadab
38:20. Obey, I beseech thee, *the voice of* the
40: 3. have not obeyed *his voice*,
42: 6. we will obey *the voice of* the Lord
— when we obey *the voice of* the Lord
13. neither obey *the voice of* the Lord your
14. see no war, *nor* hear *the sound of* the
21. ye have not obeyed *the voice of* the Lord
43: 4. the people, obeyed not *the voice of* the
7. for they obeyed not *the voice of* the Lord:
44:23. have not obeyed *the voice of* the Lord,
46:22. *The voice thereof* shall go like a serpent;

Jer. 47: 3. *At the noise of* the stamping of the hoofs
48: 3. *A voice of* crying (shall be) from Horonaim,
34. have they uttered *their voice*,
49:21. The earth is moved *at the noise of* their fall, at the cry *the noise thereof* was
50:22. *A sound of* battle (is) in the land,
28. *The voice of* them that flee
42. *their voice* shall roar like the sea,
46. *At the noise of* the taking of Babylon
51:16. When he uttereth (his) *voice*,
54. *A sound of* a cry (cometh) from Babylon,
55. destroyed out of her *the* great *voice;*
— noise of *their voice* is uttered:
Lam. 2: 7. they have made *a noise* in the house of the Lord,
3:56. Thou hast heard *my voice:*
Eze. 1:24. I heard *the noise of* their wings, *like the noise of* great waters, *as the voice of* the Almighty, *the voice of* speech, *as the noise of* an host:
25. there was *a voice* from the firmament
28. I heard *a voice of* one that spake.
3:12. I heard behind me *a voice of* a great rushing,
13. (I heard) *also the noise of* the wings
— *and the noise of* the wheels over against them, *and a noise of* a great rushing.
8:18. though they cry in mine ears with *a* loud *voice*,
9: 1. cried also in mine ears with *a* loud *voice*,
10: 5. *And the sound of* the cherubims' wings
— *as the voice of* the Almighty God
11:13. and cried with *a* loud *voice*,
19: 7. *by the noise of* his roaring.
9. that *his voice* should no more be heard
21:22(27). to lift up *the voice* with shouting,
23:42. *And a voice of* a multitude
26:10. thy walls shall shake *at the noise of* the
13. *and the sound of* thy harps
15. Shall not the isles shake *at the sound of*
27:28. The suburbs shall shake *at the sound of*
30. shall cause *their voice* to be heard against
31:16. made the nations to shake *at the sound of*
33: 4. whosoever heareth *the sound of* the
5. He heard *the sound of* the trumpet,
32. one that hath *a* pleasant *voice*,
37: 7. as I prophesied, there was *a noise*,
43: 2. *and his voice* (was) *like a noise of* many
Dan 8:16. And I heard a man's *voice*
9:10. Neither have we obeyed *the voice of* the
11. that they might not obey *thy voice;*
14. for we obeyed not *his voice.*
10: 6. *and the voice of* his words *like the voice of*
9. Yet heard I *the voice of* his words: and when I heard *the voice of* his words,
Joel 2: 5. *Like the noise of* chariots
— *like the noise of* a flame of fire
11. the Lord shall utter *his voice*
3:16(4:16). utter *his voice* from Jerusalem;
Am. 1: 2. utter *his voice* from Jerusalem;
2: 2. *with the sound of* the trumpet:
3: 4. will a young lion cry (marg. give forth *his voice*) out of his den,
Jon. 2: 2(3). thou heardest *my voice.*
9(10). *with the voice of* thanksgiving;
Mic. 6: 1. let the hills hear *thy voice.*
9. The Lord's *voice* crieth unto the city,
Nah 2: 7(8). *as with the voice of* doves,
13(14). *the voice of* thy messengers shall no more be heard.
3: 2. *The noise of* a whip, *and the noise of* the
Hab 3:10. the deep uttered *his voice*,
16. my lips quivered *at the voice:*
Zep. 1:10. *the noise of* a cry from the fish gate,
14. *the voice of* the day of the Lord:
2:14. (their) *voice* shall sing in the windows;
3: 2. She obeyed not *the voice;*
Hag. 1:12. obeyed *the voice of* the Lord their God,
Zec. 6:15. diligently obey *the voice of* the Lord
11: 3. (There is) *a voice of* the howling
— *a voice of* the roaring of young lions;

6965 **קוּם** *koom.*

*** KAL.—*Preterite.* ***

Gen37: 7. my sheaf *arose*, and also stood upright;
41:30. *And there shall arise* after them seven years
Ex. 10:23. neither *rose* any from his place for three
33:10. *and* all the people *rose up* and worshipped,
Lev.25:30. *then* the house...*shall be established*
27:19. *and it shall be assured* to him.
Nu. 24:17. *and* a Sceptre *shall rise* out of Israel,
30: 4(5), 11(12). *then* all her vows *shall stand*,
7(8). *then* her vows *shall stand*,
32:14. *ye are risen up* in your fathers' stead,
Deu17: 8. *then shalt thou arise*, and get thee up
19:11. lie in wait for him, *and rise up* against
31:16. *and* this people *will rise up*, and go
34:10. there *arose* not a prophet since in Israel
Jos. 2:11. neither *did there remain* (marg. *rose up*) any more courage in any man,
3:16. the waters...*rose up* upon an heap
8:19. the ambush *arose* quickly out of their
Jud. 5: 7. until *that I* Deborah *arose, that I arose* a mother in Israel.
9:18. ye *are risen up* against my father's house
20:33. all the men of Israel *rose up*
1Sa. 4:15. his eyes *were dim* (marg. *stood*), that he could not see.
17:48. it came to pass, when the Philistine *arose*,
20:41. as soon as the lad was gone, David *arose*
24: 7(8). Saul *rose up* out of the cave,
20(21). *that* the kingdom of Israel *shall be established*
2Sa.12:21. when the child was dead, *thou didst rise*
14: 7. the whole family *is risen* against thine
18:32. all *that rise* against thee to do (thee) hurt,
23:10. He *arose*, and smote the Philistines
1K. 8:54. *he arose* from before the altar of the Lord,
14: 4. his eyes *were set* (marg. *stood*) by reason
2K. 8:21. he *rose* by night, and smote the Edomites
23:25. neither after him *arose* there (any) like
2Ch 21: 9. *he rose up* by night, and smote the
Ezr. 9: 5. *I arose up* from my heaviness;
Est. 5: 9. that *he stood* not *up*, nor moved for him,
7: 7. the king *arising* from the banquet of wine
Job 29: 8. the aged *arose*, (and) stood up.
30:28. *I stood up*, (and) I cried in the
Ps. 20: 8(9). *we are risen*, and stand upright.
27:12. false witnesses *are risen up* against me,
54: 3(5). strangers *are risen up* against me,
86:14. the proud *are risen* against me,
109:28. when *they arise*, let them be ashamed;
Pro.24:16. falleth seven times, *and riseth up again:*
31:28. Her children *arise up*, and call her blessed;
Cant 5: 5. I *rose up* to open to my beloved;
Isa. 14:22. *For I will rise up* against them,
31: 2. *but will arise* against the house of the
49: 7. Kings shall see *and arise*,
Jer. 1:17. gird up thy loins, *and arise*,
51:29. every purpose of the Lord *shall be performed*
Eze. 7:11. Violence *is risen up* into a rod of
Hos.10:14. *Therefore shall* a tumult *arise* among thy
Am. 7: 9. *and I will rise* against the house of
Mic. 7: 8. when I fall, *I shall arise;*

KAL.—*Infinitive.*

Gen19:33, 35. he perceived not when she lay down, *nor when she arose.*
31:35. displease my lord that I cannot *rise up*
Deu 6: 7 & 11:19. when thou liest down, *and when thou risest up.*
Jos. 7:12. children of Israel could not *stand* before
13. thou canst not *stand* before thine enemies,
1Sa.22:13. *that* he *should rise* against me,
24: 7(8). and suffered them not *to rise* against
2K. 6:15. servant of the man of God was *risen* early,
Ps. 18:38(39). I have wounded them that they were not able *to rise:*
36:12(13). shall not be able *to rise.*
41: 8(9). he shall *rise up* no more. (lit. not add *to rise up*)
76: 9(10). *When* God *arose* to judgment,
124: 2. *when* men *rose up* against us:
127: 2. (It is) vain for you *to rise up* early,
139: 2. knowest my downsitting *and mine uprising*,
Pro.28:12. *but when* the wicked *rise*,
28. *When* the wicked *rise*, men hide themselves:
Isa. 2:19, 21. *when he ariseth* to shake terribly the
24:20. it shall fall, and not *rise* again. (lit. add *to rise*)
Jer. 44:29. my words shall *surely* stand (lit. *standing* shall stand)
Lam. 1:14. (from whom) I am not able *to rise up.*

Am. 5: 2. The virgin of Israel is fallen; she shall no more *rise:* (lit. add *to rise*)
Zep. 3: 8. the day *that I rise up* to the prey:

KAL.—*Imperative.*

Gen13:17. *Arise*, walk through the land
19:14. *Up*, get you out of this place;
15. *Arise*, take thy wife, and thy two
21:18. *Arise*, lift up the lad,
27:19. *arise*, I pray thee, sit and eat of my
43. *and arise*, flee thou to Laban
28: 2. *Arise*, go to Padan-aram,
31:13. *arise*, get thee out from this land,
35: 1. *Arise*, go up to Beth-el,
43:13. Take also your brother, *and arise*,
44: 4. *Up*, follow after the men;
Ex. 12:31. *Rise up*, (and) get you forth from among
32: 1. *Up*, make us gods, which shall go before
Nu. 10:35. *Rise up*, Lord, and let thine enemies be
22:20. *rise up*, (and) go with them;
23:18. *Rise up*, Balak, and hear;
Deu 2:13. Now *rise up*, (said I), and get you over
24. *Rise ye up*, take your journey,
9:12. *Arise*, get thee down quickly from hence;
10:11. *Arise*, take (thy) journey before the
Jos. 1: 2. now therefore *arise*, go over this Jordan,
7:10. *Get thee up;* wherefore liest thou thus upon thy face?
13. *Up*, sanctify the people,
8: 1. *and arise*, go up to Ai:
Jud. 4:14. *Up;* for this (is) the day
5:12. *arise*, Barak, and lead thy captivity captive,
7: 9. *Arise*, get thee down unto the host;
15. *Arise;* for the Lord hath delivered into your hand the host of Midian.
8:20. *Up*, (and) slay them.
21. *Rise* thou, and fall upon us:
9:32. Now therefore *up* by night,
18: 9. *Arise*, that we may go up against them:
19:28. *Up*, and let us be going.
1Sa. 9: 3. *and arise*, go seek the asses.
26. *Up*, that I may send thee away.
16:12. *Arise*, anoint him: for this (is) he.
23: 4. *Arise*, go down to Keilah;
2Sa.13:15. Amnon said unto her, *Arise*, be gone.
15:14. *Arise*, and let us flee;
17:21. *Arise*, and pass quickly over the water:
19: 7(8). Now therefore *arise*, go forth,
1K. 14: 2. *Arise*, I pray thee, and disguise thyself,
12. *Arise* thou therefore, get thee to thine
17: 9. *Arise*, get thee to Zarephath,
19: 5. said unto him, *Arise* (and) eat.
7. *Arise* (and) eat; because the journey (is) too great for thee.
21: 7. *arise*, (and) eat bread, and let thine heart
15. *Arise*, take possession of the vineyard
18. *Arise*, go down to meet Ahab
2K. 1: 3. *Arise*, go up to meet the messengers of
8: 1. *Arise*, and go thou and thine houshold,
1Ch22:16. *Arise* (therefore), and be doing,
19. *arise therefore*, and build ye the sanctuary
2Ch 6:41. Now therefore *arise*, O Lord God,
Ezr.10: 4. *Arise;* for (this) matter (belongeth) unto
Neh 9: 5. *Stand up* (and) bless the Lord your God
Ps. 3: 7(8). *Arise*, O Lord; save me, O my God:
7: 6(7). *Arise*, O Lord, in thine anger,
9:19(20). *Arise*, O Lord; let not man prevail:
10:12. *Arise*, O Lord; O God, lift up thine
17:13. *Arise*, O Lord, disappoint him,
35: 2. and buckler, *and stand up* for mine help.
44:26(27). *Arise* for our help,
74:22. *Arise*, O God, plead thine own cause:
82: 8. *Arise*, O God, judge the earth:
132: 8. *Arise*, O Lord, into thy rest;
Cant.2:10. *Rise up*, my love, my fair one,
13. *Arise*, my love, my fair one,
Isa. 21: 5. *arise*, ye princes, (and) anoint the shield.
23:12. *arise*, pass over to Chittim;
32: 9. *Rise up*, ye women that are at ease;
51:17. Awake, awake, *stand up*, O Jerusalem,
52: 2. *arise*, (and) sit down, O Jerusalem:
60: 1. *Arise*, shine; for thy light is come,
Jer. 2:27. *Arise*, and save us.
6: 4. *arise*, and let us go up at noon.
5. *Arise*, and let us go by night,
13: 4. *and arise*, go to Euphrates, and hide it
6. *Arise*, go to Euphrates, and take the girdle from thence,
Jer. 18: 2. *Arise*, and go down to the potter's house,
31: 6. *Arise ye*, and let us go up to Zion
46:16. *Arise*, and let us go again to our own
49:14. Gather ye together,...*and rise up* to the
28. *Arise ye*, go up to Kedar,
31. *Arise*, get you up unto the wealthy nation,
Lam. 2:19. *Arise*, cry out in the night:
Eze. 3:22. *Arise*, go forth into the plain,
Obad. 1. *Arise ye*, and let us rise up against
Jon. 1: 2. *Arise*, go to Nineveh,
6. *arise*, call upon thy God,
3: 2. *Arise*, go unto Nineveh,
Mic. 2:10. *Arise ye*, and depart; for this (is) not (your) rest:
4:13. *Arise* and thresh, O daughter of Zion:
6: 1. *Arise*, contend thou before the mountains,

KAL.—*Future.*

Gen. 4: 8. *that* Cain *rose up* against Abel his
18:16. *And* the men *rose up* from thence,
19: 1. *and* Lot seeing (them) *rose up* to meet
35. *and* the younger *arose*, and lay with him;
21:32. *then* Abimelech *rose up*,
22: 3. *and rose up*, and went unto
19. *and they rose up* and went together to
23: 3. *And* Abraham *stood up* from before his
7. *And* Abraham *stood up*, and bowed
17. *And* the field...and the cave...*were made sure*
20. *And* the field, and the cave...*were made sure*
24:10. *and he arose*, and went to Mesopotamia,
54. *and they rose up* in the morning,
61. *And* Rebekah *arose*, and her damsels,
25:34. *and rose up*, and went his way:
27:31. *Let* my father *arise*, and eat of his son's
31:17. *Then* Jacob *rose up*, and set his
21. *and he rose up*, and passed over the river,
32:22(23). *And he rose up* that night,
35: 3. *And let us arise*, and go up to Beth-el;
37:35. *And* all his sons and all his daughters *rose up* to comfort him;
38:19. *And she arose*, and went away,
43: 8. Send the lad with me, *and we will arise*
15. *and rose up*, and went down to Egypt,
46: 5. *And* Jacob *rose up* from Beer-sheba:
Ex. 1: 8. *Now* there *arose up* a new king over
2:17. *but* Moses *stood up* and helped them,
12:30. *And* Pharaoh *rose up* in the night,
21:19. If *he rise* again, and walk abroad upon
24:13. *And* Moses *rose up*, and his minister
32: 6. to eat and to drink, *and rose up* to play.
33: 8. all the people *rose up*,
Lev.19:32. *Thou shalt rise up* before the hoary head,
27:14. priest shall estimate it, *so shall it stand.*
17. according to thy estimation *it shall stand.*
Nu. 11:32. *And* the people *stood up* all that day,
16: 2. *And they rose up* before Moses,
25. *And* Moses *rose up* and went unto Dathan
22:13, 21. *And* Balaam *rose up* in the morning,
14. *And* the princes of Moab *rose up*,
23:24. the people *shall rise up* as a great lion,
24:25. *And* Balaam *rose up*, and went
25: 7. *And* when...*he rose up* from among the
30: 4(5). every bond wherewith she hath bound her soul *shall stand.*
5(6). she hath bound her soul, *shall stand:*
7(8). she bound her soul *shall stand.*
9(10). every vow...*shall stand* against her.
11(12). then all her vows *shall stand*,
12(13). the bond of her soul, *shall* not *stand:*
Deu 13: 1(2). If *there arise* among you a prophet,
19:15. One witness *shall* not *rise up* against a — *shall* the matter *be established.*
16. If a false witness *rise up* against any man
22:26. as when a man *riseth* against his
25: 6. *shall succeed* in the name of his brother
29:22(21). your children that *shall rise up* after
32:38. let them *rise up* and help you,
33:11. that *they rise* not again.
Jos. 6:26. Cursed (be) the man...that *riseth up*
8: 3. *So* Joshua *arose*, and all the people of
7. Then ye *shall rise up* from the ambush,
18: 4. *and they shall rise*, and go through the
8. *And* the men *arose*, and went away:
24: 9. *Then* Balak...*arose* and warred against
Jud. 2:10. *there arose* another generation after them,
3:20. *And he arose* out of (his) seat.

Jud 4: 9. *And* Deborah *arose*, and went with Barak
8:21. *And* Gideon *arose*, and slew Zebah and
9:34. *And* Abimelech *rose up*, and all the people
35. *and* Abimelech *rose up*, and the people
43. *and he rose up* against them, and smote
10: 1. *And* after Abimelech *there arose* to defend
3. *And* after him *arose* Jair, a Gileadite,
13:11. *And* Manoah *arose*, and went after his
16: 3. Samson lay till midnight, *and arose* at
19: 3. *And* her husband *arose*, and went after
5. *that he rose up* to depart:
7, 9. *when* the man *rose up* to depart,
10. *but he rose up* and departed,
27. *And* her lord *rose up* in the morning,
28. *and* the man *rose up*, and gat him unto
20: 5. *And* the men of Gibeah *rose* against
8. *And* all the people *arose* as one man,
18. *And* the children of Israel *arose*,
19. *And* the children of Israel *rose up* in the
Ru. 1: 6. *Then* she *arose* with her daughters in law,
2:15. *when she was risen up* to glean,
3:14. *and she rose up* before one could know
1Sa. 1: 9. *So* Hannah *rose up* after they had eaten
3: 6. *And* Samuel *arose* and went to Eli,
8. *And he arose* and went to Eli,
9:26. *And* Saul *arose*, and they went out
13:14. now thy kingdom *shall* not *continue:*
15. *And* Samuel *arose*, and gat him up from
16:13. *So* Samuel *rose* up, and went to Ramah.
17:35. *when he arose* against me, I caught (him)
52. *And* the men of Israel and of Judah *arose*,
18:27. *Wherefore* David *arose* and went,
20:25. *and* Jonathan *arose*, and Abner sat by
34. *So* Jonathan *arose* from the table
42(21:1). *And he arose* and departed:
21:10(11). *And* David *arose*, and fled that day
23:13. *Then* David...*arose* and departed out of
16. *And* Jonathan Saul's son *arose*,
24. *And they arose*, and went to Ziph before
24: 4(5). *Then* David *arose*, and cut off the skirt of Saul's robe privily.
8(9). David *also arose* afterward,
25: 1. *And* David *arose*, and went down to the
29. *Yet* a man *is risen* to pursue thee,
41. *And she arose*, and bowed herself
42. Abigail hasted, *and arose*,
26: 2. *Then* Saul *arose*, and went down to the
5. *And* David *arose*, and came to the place
27: 2. *And* David *arose*, and he passed over with the six hundred men
28:23. *So he arose* from the earth,
25. *Then they rose up*, and went away that
31:12. All the valiant men *arose*,
2Sa. 2:14. young men now *arise*, and play before us. *And* Joab said, Let them *arise*.
15. *Then there arose* and went over by number
3:21. Abner said unto David, *I will arise* and
6: 2. *And* David *arose*, and went with all the
11: 2. *that* David *arose* from off his bed,
12:17. *And* the elders of his house *arose*,
20. *Then* David *arose* from the earth,
13:29. *Then* all the king's sons *arose*,
31. *Then* the king *arose*, and tare his garments,
14:23. *So* Joab *arose* and went to Geshur,
31. *Then* Joab *arose*, and came to Absalom
15: 9. *So he arose*, and went to Hebron.
17: 1. *I will arise* and pursue after David
22. *Then* David *arose*, and all the people that (were) with him,
23. he saddled (his) ass, *and arose*,
19: 8(9). *Then* the king *arose*, and sat in the
22:39. wounded them, that *they could* not *arise:*
24:11. For *when* David *was up* in the morning,
1K. 1:49. *and rose up*, and went every man his way.
50. *and arose*, and went, and caught hold on
2:19. *And* the king *rose up* to meet her,
40. *And* Shimei *arose*, and saddled his ass,
3:12. neither after thee *shall* any *arise* like
20. *And she arose* at midnight,
21. *when I rose* in the morning
8:20. *and I am risen up* in the room of David
11:18. *And they arose* out of Midian,
40. *And* Jeroboam *arose*, and fled into Egypt,
14: 4. Jeroboam's wife did so, *and arose*,
17. *And* Jeroboam's wife *arose*, and departed,
17:10. *So he arose* and went to Zarephath.
19: 3. *And* when he saw (that), *he arose*,

1K. 19: 8. *And he arose*, and did eat and drink,
21. *Then he arose*, and went after Elijah,
21:16. *that* Ahab *rose up* to go down to the
2K. 1:15. *And he arose*, and went down with him
3:24. *And* when...the Israelites *rose up* and
4:30. *And he arose*, and followed her.
7: 5. *And they rose up* in the twilight,
7. *Wherefore they arose* and fled in the
12. *And* the king *arose* in the night,
8: 2. *And* the woman *arose*, and did after the
9: 6. *And he arose*, and went into the house;
10:12. *And he arose* and departed,
11: 1. *And* when...*she arose* and destroyed all the
12:20(21). *And* his servants *arose*, and made a
13:21. he revived, *and stood up* on his feet.
25:26. *And*...the captains of the armies, *arose*,
1Ch 10:12. *They arose*, all the valiant men,
28: 2. *Then* David the king *stood up* upon his
2Ch 6:10. *for I am risen up* in the room of David my
13: 4. *And* Abijah *stood up* upon mount
6. *Yet* Jeroboam...*is risen up*,
20:19. *And* the Levites,...*stood up* to praise the
21: 4. *when* Jehoram *was risen up* to the kingdom
22:10. *But* when...*she arose* and destroyed all the
28:12. *Then*...*stood up* against them that came
15. *And* the men which were expressed by name *rose up*,
29:12. *Then* the Levites *arose*,
30:14. *And* they *arose* and took away the altars
27. *Then* the priests the Levites *arose*
Ezr. 1: 5. *Then rose up* the chief of the fathers
3: 2. *Then stood up* Jeshua the son of
10: 5. *Then arose* Ezra, and made
6. *Then* Ezra *rose up* from before the house
10. *And* Ezra the priest *stood up*,
Neh. 2:12. *And I arose* in the night,
18. they said, *Let us rise up* and build.
20. therefore we his servants *will arise* and
3: 1. *Then* Eliashib the high priest *rose up*
4:14(8). I looked, *and rose up*,
9: 3. *And they stood up* in their place,
4. *Then stood up* upon the stairs,
Est. 8: 4. *So* Esther *arose*, and stood before the
Job 1:20. *Then* Job *arose*, and rent his mantle,
7: 4. When *shall I arise*, and the night be gone?
8:15. but *it shall* not *endure*.
11:17. (thine) age *shall be clearer* than (marg. *arise* above) the noonday;
14:12. So man lieth down, and *riseth* not:
15:29. neither *shall* his substance *continue*,
16: 8. *and* my leanness *rising up* in me
19:18. *I arose*, and they spake against me.
25. (that) *he shall stand* at the latter (day) upon the earth:
22:28. *and it shall be established* unto thee:
24:14. The murderer *rising* with the light
22. *he riseth up*, and no (man) is sure of life.
25: 3. upon whom *doth* not his light *arise?*
30:12. Upon (my) right (hand) *rise* the youth;
31:14. What then shall I do when God *riseth up?*
41:26(18). The sword of him that layeth at him *cannot hold:*
Ps. 1: 5. the ungodly *shall* not *stand* in the
12: 5(6). now *will I arise*, saith the Lord;
24: 3. who *shall stand* in his holy place?
27: 3. though war *should rise* against me,
35:11. False witnesses *did rise up;*
68: 1(2). *Let* God *arise*, let his enemies be
78: 6. (who) *should arise* and declare (them) to
88:10(11). *shall* the dead *arise* (and) praise thee?
94:16. Who *will rise up* for me against the
102:13(14). Thou *shalt arise*, (and) have mercy
119:62. At midnight *I will rise* to give thanks
140:10(11). that *they rise* not *up* again.
Pro. 6: 9. when *wilt thou arise* out of thy sleep?
15:22. in the multitude of counsellors *they are established*.
19:21. the counsel of the Lord, that *shall stand*.
24:22. their calamity *shall rise* suddenly;
31:15. *She riseth also* while it is yet night,
Ecc.12: 4. *and he shall rise up* at the voice of the
Cant.3: 2. *I will rise* now, and go about the city in
Isa. 7: 7. *It shall* not *stand*, neither shall it come to
8:10. speak the word, and *it shall* not *stand:*
14:21. that *they do* not *rise*, nor possess the land,
24. as I have purposed, (so) *shall it stand:*
26:14. (they are) deceased, *they shall* not *rise:*

Isa. 26:19. (together with) my dead body *shall they arise.*
27: 9. the groves and images *shall* not *stand up.*
28:18. your agreement with hell *shall* not *stand;*
21. the Lord *shall rise up*
32: 8. by liberal things *shall he stand.* (marg. or, *be established*)
33:10. Now *will I rise*, saith the Lord;
40: 8. the word of our God *shall stand* for ever.
43:17. *they shall* not *rise:* they are extinct,
46:10. My counsel *shall stand*,
54:17. every tongue (that) *shall rise* against
Jer. 2:28. *let them arise*, if they can save thee
8: 4. Shall they fall, and not *arise?*
25:27. fall, and *rise* no more,
26:17. *Then rose up* certain of the elders
37:10. *should they rise up* every man in
41: 2. *Then arose* Ishmael the son of Nethaniah,
44:28. all the remnant...shall know whose words *shall stand*,
29. my words *shall* surely *stand* against
51:64. *shall* not *rise* from the evil
Eze. 3:23. *Then I arose*, and went forth into the
Dan. 8:27. *afterward I rose up*, and did the king's
Am. 7: 2, 5. by whom *shall* Jacob *arise?* for he (is)
8:14. they shall fall, and never *rise up* again.
Obad. 1. *let us rise up* against her in battle.
Jon. 1: 3. *But* Jonah *rose up* to flee unto Tarshish
3: 3. *So* Jonah *arose*, and went unto Nineveh,
6. *and he arose* from his throne,
Nah. 1: 6. who *can abide* (marg. *stand up*) in the
9. affliction *shall* not *rise up* the second time.
Hab. 2: 7. *Shall they* not *rise up* suddenly

KAL.—*Participle.*

Ex. 15: 7. thou hast overthrown *them that rose up against thee:*
32:25. Aaron had made them naked unto (their) shame *among their enemies:* (marg. *those that rose up against them*)
Deu28: 7. thine enemies *that rise up* against thee
33:11. the loins of *them that rise against him*,
2Sa. 18:31. all *them that rose up* against thee.
22:40. *them that rose up against me* hast thou
49. *also...above them that rose up against me:*
2K. 16: 7. *which rise up* against me.
Ps. 3: 1(2). many (are) *they that rise up* against
18:39(40). under me *those that rose up against me.*
48(49). *those that rise up against me:*
44: 5(6). tread *them* under *that rise up against us.*
74:23. tumult of *those that rise up against thee*
92:11(12). the wicked *that rise up* against me.
Jer. 51: 1. the midst of *them that rise up against me*,
Lam. 3:62. The lips of *those that rose up against me*,
Mic. 7: 6. the daughter *riseth up* against her mother,

* PIEL.—*Preterite.* *

Est. 9:27. The Jews *ordained*, and took upon them,
31. and Esther the queen *had enjoined them*, and as *they had decreed* for themselves
32. the decree of Esther *confirmed* these

PIEL.—*Infinitive.*

Ru. 4: 7. *for to confirm* all things;
Est. 9:21. *To stablish* (this) among them,
29. *to confirm* this second letter of Purim.
31. *To confirm* these days of Purim
Eze. 13: 6. *that* they *would confirm* the word.

PIEL.—*Imperative.*

Ps. 119:28. *strengthen* thou me according unto thy

PIEL.—*Future.*

Ps. 119:106. I have sworn, *and I will perform* (it),

* POLEL.—*Future.* *

Isa. 44:26. *I will raise up* the decayed places
58:12. *thou shalt raise up* the foundations
61: 4. *they shall raise up* the former desolations,
Mic. 2: 8. my people *is risen up* as an enemy:

* HIPHIL.—*Preterite.* *

Gen 6:18. *But* with thee *will I establish* my covenant;
9:11. *And I will establish* my covenant
17. the covenant, which *I have established*
17: 7. *And I will establish* my covenant between me and thee
19. *and I will establish* my covenant with
Gen26: 3. *and I will perform* the oath which I sware
Ex. 6: 4. *I have* also *established* my covenant with
26:30. *And thou shalt rear up* the tabernacle
Lev. 26: 9. *and establish* my covenant with you.
Nu. 10:21. *and* (the other) *did set up* the tabernacle
30:14(15). *then he establisheth* all her vows,
— *he confirmeth* them,
Deu27: 2. *that thou shalt set* thee *up* great stones,
Jos. 4: 9. Joshua *set up* twelve stones in the midst
20. those twelve stones,...*did* Joshua *pitch* in
5: 7. their children, (whom) *he raised up* in
Jud. 2:18. when the Lord *raised* them *up* judges,
7:19. *they had* but newly *set* the watch:
1 Sa. 2:35. *And I will raise* me *up* a faithful priest,
15:11. *hath* not *performed* my commandments.
13. *I have performed* the commandment
22: 8. that my son *hath stirred up*
2Sa. 7:12. *And...I will set up* thy seed after thee,
1K. 6:12. *then will I perform* my word with thee,
9: 5. *Then I will establish* the throne of thy
14:14. *Moreover* the Lord *shall raise* him *up* a
2K. 9: 2. *and make him arise up* from among his
1Ch 17:11. *that I will raise up* thy seed after thee,
2Ch 7:18. *Then will I stablish* the throne of thy
Ps. 89:43(44). *hast* not *made him to stand* in the
Pro. 30: 4. who *hath established* all the ends of the
Isa. 14: 9. *it hath raised up* from their thrones all
23:13. *they set up* the towers thereof,
29: 3. *and I will raise* forts against thee.
Jer. 6:17. *Also I set* watchmen over you,
23: 4. *And I will set up* shepherds over them
5. *that I will raise* unto David a righteous
29:10. *and perform* my good word toward you,
15. The Lord *hath raised* us *up* prophets in
33:14. that *I will perform* that good thing which
34:18. which *have* not *performed* the words of
35:16. *have performed* the commandment of their
Eze. 16:60. *and I will establish* unto thee an everlasting covenant.
62. *And* I *will establish* my covenant with
26: 8. *and lift up* the buckler against thee.
34:23. *And I will set up* one shepherd over
29. *And I will raise up* for them a plant of
Mic. 5: 5(4). *then shall we raise* against him seven

HIPHIL.—*Infinitive.*

Nu 7: 1. Moses *had* fully *set up* the tabernacle,
9:15. the day that the tabernacle *was reared up*
Deu 8:18. that he *may establish* his covenant
9: 5. that he *may perform* the word which the
22: 4. thou shalt *surely* help him to lift (them) up again. (lit. *raising up* thou shalt raise up with him)
25: 7. refuseth *to raise up* unto his brother a
29:13(12). That he *may establish* thee to day
Jud. 7:19. they had *but newly* set (lit. *setting* they had set) the watch:
Ru. 4: 5, 10. *to raise up* the name of the dead
2Sa. 3:10. *and to set up* the throne of David over
12:17. (went) to him, *to raise him up* from the
1K. 12:15. that he *might perform* his saying,
15: 4. *to set up* his son after him,
2K. 23: 3. *to perform* the words of this covenant
24. that he *might perform* the words of the
1Ch 21:18. David should go up, *and set up* an altar
2Ch 10:15. *that* the Lord *might perform* his word,
Ecc. 4:10. (he hath) not another *to help him up.*
Isa. 49: 6. *to raise up* the tribes of Jacob,
8. *to establish* the earth,
Jer. 11: 5. That *I may perform* the oath which I have
23:20. till *he have performed* the thoughts of his
30:24. until *he have performed* the intents of his
44:25. ye will *surely* accomplish (lit. *accomplishing* ye will accomplish) your vows,

HIPHIL.—*Imperative.*

Gen38: 8. *and raise up* seed to thy brother.
2Sa. 7:25. *establish* (it) for ever, and do as thou hast
24:18. Go up, *rear* an altar unto the Lord
Ps. 41:10(11). *and raise* me *up*, that I may requite
119:38. *Stablish* thy word unto thy servant,
Jer. 51:12. *set up* the watchmen,

HIPHIL.—*Future.*

Gen17:21. my covenant *will I establish* with Isaac,
49: 9. who *shall rouse him up?*
Ex. 40: 2. On the first day...*shalt thou set up* the tabernacle

Ex. 40:18. *And* Moses *reared up* the tabernacle,
— *and reared up* his pillars.
33. *And he reared up* the court
Lev.26: 1. Ye shall make you no idols...neither *rear you up* a standing image,
Nu. 1:51. the Levites *shall set* it *up:*
23:19. hath he spoken, and *shall he* not *make it good?*
24: 9. as a great lion: who *shall stir him up?*
30:13(14). her husband *may establish it,*
Deu 16:22. Neither *shalt thou set* thee *up* (any) image;
18:15. The Lord thy God *will raise up* unto thee
18. *I will raise* them *up* a Prophet
22: 4. *thou shalt* surely *help* him *to lift* (them) *up again.*
27: 4. *ye shall set up* these stones, which I
26. Cursed (be) he that *confirmeth* not (all)
28: 9. The Lord *shall establish thee* an holy people
36. thy king which *thou shalt set* over thee,
Jos. 7:26. *And they raised* over him a great heap of
8:29. *and raise* thereon a great heap of stones,
24:26. *and set it up* there under an oak,
Jud. 2:16. *Nevertheless* the Lord *raised up* judges,
3: 9. *And* when...the Lord *raised up* a deliverer
15. *But* when...the Lord *raised* them *up* a
18:30. *And* the children of Dan *set up* the graven
1Sa. 1:23. the Lord *establish* his word.
3:12. In that day *I will perform* against Eli all
1K. 2: 4. That the Lord *may continue* his word
7:21. *And he set up* the pillars in the porch of the temple: *and he set up* the right
— *and he set up* the left pillar,
8:20. *And* the Lord *hath performed* his word
11:14. *And* the Lord *stirred up* an adversary unto
23. *And* God *stirred* him *up* (another)
16:32. *And he reared up* an altar for Baal
2K. 21: 3. *and he reared up* altars for Baal,
2Ch 3:17. *And he reared up* the pillars before the
6:10. The Lord *therefore hath performed* his
33: 3. *and he reared up* altars for Baalim,
Neh 5:13. that *performeth* not this promise,
9: 8. *and hast performed* thy words; for thou
Job 4: 4. Thy words *have upholden* him that was
16:12. *and set me up* for his mark.
Ps. 40: 2(3). *and set* my feet upon a rock,
78: 5. *For he established* a testimony in Jacob,
107:29. *He maketh* the storm a calm,
Ecc. 4:10. the one *will lift up* his fellow:
Jer. 28: 6. the Lord *perform* thy words which thou
30: 9. David their king, whom *I will raise up*
44:25. *ye will* surely *accomplish* your vows,
Dan 9:12. *And he hath confirmed* his words,
Hos 6: 2. in the third day *he will raise us up,*
Am. 2:11. *And I raised up* of your sons for prophets,
9:11. In that day *will I raise up* the tabernacle
— *I will raise up* his ruins,

HIPHIL.—*Participle.*

Gen 9: 9. I *establish* my covenant with you,
1Sa. 2: 8. He *raiseth up* the poor out of the dust,
2Sa.12:11. I *will raise up* evil against thee out of
Ps.113: 7. He *raiseth up* the poor out of the dust,
Isa. 44:26. *That confirmeth* the word of his servant,
Jer. 10:20. *and to set up* my curtains.
50:32. none *shall raise* him *up:*
Am. 5: 2. (there is) none *to raise* her *up.*
6:14. behold, I *will raise up* against you a
Hab 1: 6. lo, I *raise up* the Chaldeans,
Zec.11:16. lo, I *will raise up* a shepherd in the land,

* HOPHAL.—*Preterite.* *

Ex. 40:17. the tabernacle *was reared up.*
2Sa.23: 1. the man (who) *was raised up* on high,
Jer. 35:14. The words of Jonadab...*are performed;*

* HITHPAEL.—*Participle.* *

Job 20:27. the earth *shall rise up* against him.
27: 7. *and he that riseth up against me*
Ps. 17: 7. *from those that rise up* (against them).
59: 1(2). defend me *from them that rise up against me.*

6966 קוּם [*koom*], Ch.

* P'AL.—*Preterite.* *

Ezr. 5: 2. Then *rose up* Zerubbabel
Dan. 3:24. *and rose up* in haste,

P'AL.—*Imperative.*

Dan. 7: 5. *Arise,* devour much flesh.

P'AL.—*Future.*

Dan. 2:39. And after thee *shall arise* another
44. and it *shall stand* for ever.
6:19(20). Then the king *arose* very early
7:10. ten thousand times ten thousand *stood* before him:
17. (which) *shall arise* out of the earth.
24. ten kings (that) *shall arise:* and another *shall rise* after them;

P'AL.—*Participle.*

Dan. 2:31. *stood* before thee;
3: 3. *and they stood* before the image
7:16. unto one of *them that stood by,*

* PAEL.—*Infinitive.* *

Dan. 6: 7(8). consulted together *to establish* a

* APHEL.—*Preterite.* *

Ezr. 6:18. *And they set* the priests
Dan. 3: 1. *he set it up* in the plain of Dura,
2, 3, 7. Nebuchadnezzar the king *had set up*
3. Nebuchadnezzar *had set up.*
5. Nebuchadnezzar the king *hath set up:*
12, 18. golden image which *thou hast set up.*
14. which *I have set up?*
5:11. *whom* the king...*made* master
6: 1(2). It pleased Darius *to set* (lit. *and he set*)
7: 5. and it *raised up itself* on one side,

APHEL.—*Infinitive.*

Dan. 6: 3(4). the king thought *to set him* over

APHEL.—*Future.*

Dan. 2:44. *shall* the God of heaven *set up* a
4:17(14). and *setteth up* over it the basest
5:21. *he appointeth* over it whomsoever he will.
6: 8(9). Now, O king, *establish* the decree,
15(16). no decree nor statute which the king *establisheth*

APHEL.—*Participle.*

Dan. 2:21. he removeth kings, *and setteth up* kings:

* HOPHAL.—*Preterite.* *

Dan. 7: 4. and *made stand* upon the feet

קוֹמָה *kōh-māh'*, f. 6967

Gen. 6:15. and *the height of it* thirty cubits.
Ex. 25:10, 23. a cubit and a half *the height thereof.*
27: 1. *the height thereof* (shall be) three cubits.
18. *and the height* five cubits
30: 2. two cubits (shall be) *the height thereof:*
37: 1. a half *the height of it:*
10. a cubit and a half *the height thereof:*
25. two cubits (was) *the height of it;*
38: 1. three cubits *the height thereof.*
18. *and the height* in the breadth (was) five
1Sa.16: 7. Look not on his countenance, or on the height of *his stature;*
28:20. Saul fell straightway all *along* (marg. with the fulness of *his stature*)
1K. 6: 2. *the height thereof* thirty cubits.
10. against all the house, five cubits *high:* (lit. *the height thereof*)
20. twenty cubits in *the height thereof:*
23. (each) ten cubits *high.* (lit. *the height thereof*)
26. *The height of* the one cherub (was) ten
7: 2. *the height thereof* thirty cubits,
15. he cast two pillars of brass, of eighteen cubits *high* (lit. *the height*)
16. *the height of* the one chapiter (was) five cubits, and *the height of* the other chapiter (was) five cubits:
23. *his height* (was) five cubits:
27. three cubits *the height of it.*
32. *and the height of* a wheel (was) a cubit and half
35. half a cubit *high:* (lit. half a cubit *the height*)
2K. 19:23. cut down the *tall* (lit. *tallness of*) cedar

2K. 25:17. *The height of* the one pillar (was)
— *and the height of* the chapiter three cubits;
2Ch 4: 1. ten cubits *the height thereof.*
2. five cubits *the height thereof;*
6:13. three cubits *high*, (lit. *the height thereof*)
Cant.7: 7(8). This *thy stature* is like to a palm tree,
Isa. 10:33. the high ones of *stature* (shall be) hewn
37:24. cut down the *tall* (marg. *tallness of*) cedars
Jer. 52:21. *the height of* one pillar (was) eighteen
22. *and the height of* one chapiter (was) five
Eze.13:18. kerchiefs upon the head of every *stature*
17: 6. became a spreading vine of low *stature*,
19:11. *her stature* was exalted among the thick
31: 3. shadowing shroud, and of *an high stature;*
5. *his height* was exalted above all the trees
10. thou hast lifted up thyself *in height*,
14. exalt themselves *for their height*,
40: 5. *and the height*, one reed.

6968 קוֹמְמִיּוּת *kōh-m'meey-yooth'*, adv.

Lev.26:13. your yoke, and made you go *upright.*

6969 קוּן [*koon*].

* POLEL.—*Preterite.* *

Eze.27:32. *and lament* over thee, (saying), What
32:16. *wherewith they shall lament* her:

POLEL.—*Future.*

2Sa. 1:17. *And* David *lamented* with this lamentation
3:33. *And* the king *lamented* over Abner,
2Ch 35:25. *And* Jeremiah *lamented* for Josiah:
Eze.32:16. the daughters of the nations *shall lament*
her: *they shall lament* for her,

POLEL.—*Participle.*

Jer. 9:17(16). call *for the mourning women*, that they

6970 קוֹעַ *kōh'ăg*, m.

Eze.23:23. and Shoa, *and Koa*, [perhaps this is an appellative, *a prince*]

6971 קוֹף [*kōhph*], m.

1K. 10:22. ivory, *and apes*, and peacocks.
2Ch 9:21. ivory, *and apes*, and peacocks.

6974 קוּץ [*kootz*].

* HIPHIL.—*Preterite.* *

2K. 4:31. The child *is not awaked.*
Ps. 3: 5(6). *I awaked;* for the Lord sustained me.
139:18. when *I awake*, I am still with thee.
Pro. 6:22. *and* (when) *thou awakest*, it shall talk
Isa. 29: 8. *but he awaketh*, and his soul is empty:
— *but he awaketh*, and, behold, (he is) faint,
Jer. 31:26. Upon this *I awaked*, and beheld;
Eze. 7: 6. *it watcheth* (marg. *awaketh*) for thee;

HIPHIL.—*Infinitive.*

Ps. 17:15. I shall be satisfied, *when I awake*, with thy
73:20. As a dream *when* (one) *awaketh;*

HIPHIL.—*Imperative.*

Ps. 35:23. Stir up thyself, *and awake* to my
44:23(24). why sleepest thou, O Lord? *arise*,
59: 5(6). *awake* to visit all the heathen:
Isa. 26:19. *Awake* and sing, ye that dwell in dust:
Joel 1: 5. *Awake*, ye drunkards, and weep;
Hab 2:19. *Awake;* to the dumb stone,

HIPHIL.—*Future.*

Job 14:12. *they shall* not *awake*, nor be raised out of
Pro.23:35. when *shall I awake?* I will seek it yet
Jer. 51:39, 57. sleep a perpetual sleep, and not *wake*,
Dan 12: 2. many of them that sleep in the dust of the earth *shall awake*,

HIPHIL.—*Participle.*

1Sa.26:12. nor knew (it), neither *awaked:*

6972 קוּץ [*kootz*].

* KAL.—*Preterite.* *

Isa. 18: 6. *and* the fowls *shall summer* upon them,

קוּץ [*kootz*]. 6973

* KAL.—*Preterite.* *

Gen27:46. *I am weary* of my life
Nu. 21: 5. our soul *loatheth* this light bread.

KAL.—*Future.*

Ex. 1:12. *And they were grieved* because of the
Lev.20:23. *therefore I abhorred* them.
Nu. 22: 3. *and* Moab *was distressed* because of the
1K. 11:25. *and he abhorred* Israel, and reigned over
Pro. 3:11. neither *be weary* of his correction:

KAL.—*Participle.*

Isa. 7:16. the land that thou *abhorrest* shall be

* HIPHIL.—*Future.* *

Isa. 7: 6. Let us go up against Judah, *and vex* (marg. or, *waken*) *it*,

קוֹץ *kōhtz*, m. 6975

Gen 3:18. *Thorns also* and thistles shall it bring
Ex. 22: 6(5). If fire break out, and catch in *thorns*,
Jud. 8: 7. tear your flesh with *the thorns of* the
16. *thorns of* the wilderness and briers,
2Sa.23: 6. all of them *as thorns* thrust away,
Ps.118:12. they are quenched as the fire of *thorns:*
Isa. 32:13. Upon the land of my people shall come up *thorns* (and) briers;
33:12. (as) *thorns* cut up shall they be burned in
Jer. 4: 3. Break up your fallow ground, and sow not among *thorns.*
12:13. have sown wheat, *but* shall reap *thorns:*
Eze.28:24. *nor* (any) grieving *thorn* of all (that are)
Hos.10: 8. *the thorn* and the thistle shall come up on

קְוֻצּוֹת [*k'vootz-tzōhth'*], f. pl. 6977

Cant.5: 2. *my locks* with the drops of the night.
11. *his locks* (are) bushy, (and) black as a

קוּר [*koor*]. 6979

* KAL.—*Preterite.* *

2K. 19:24. I *have digged* and drunk strange waters,
Isa. 37:25. I *have digged*, and drunk water;

* HIPHIL.—*Preterite.* *

Jer. 6: 7. so *she casteth out* her wickedness:

HIPHIL.—*Infinitive.*

Jer. 6: 7. *As* a fountain *casteth out* her waters,

* PILPEL.—*Preterite.* *

Nu. 24:17. *and destroy* all the children of Sheth.

PILPEL.—*Participle.*

Isa. 22: 5. *breaking down* the walls,

קוֹרָה *koo-rāh'*, f. 6982

Gen19: 8. came they under the shadow of *my roof.*
2K. 6: 2. take thence every man *a beam*,
5. as one was felling *a beam*,
2Ch 3: 7. *the beams*, the posts, and the walls
Cant.1:17. *The beams of* our house (are) cedar,

קוּרִים *koo-reem'*, m. pl. 6980

Isa. 59: 5. *and* weave the spider's *web:*
6. *Their webs* shall not become garments,

קוֹשׁ [*kōhsh*]. 6983

* KAL.—*Future.* *

Isa. 29:21. and *lay a snare* for him that reproveth

קַט *kat*, adv. 6985

Eze.16:47. but, as (if that were) a *very* little (thing
[see also קוּט Pret.]

6986 **קֶטֶב** *keh'-tev*, m.

Deu 32:24. burning heat, *and with* bitter *destruction:*
Ps. 91: 6. *for the destruction* (that) wasteth at
Isa. 28: 2. a *destroying* storm, (lit. a storm of *destruction*)

6987 **קֹטֶב** [*kōh'-tev*], m.

Hos. 13:14. O grave, I will be *thy destruction:*

6988 **קְטוֹרָה** *k'tōh-rāh'*, f.

Deu 33:10. they shall put *incense* before thee,

6990 **קָטַט** Pret. (Eze. 6:9). see **קוט**

6991 **קָטַל** [*kāh-tal'*].

* KAL.—*Future.* *

Job 13:15. Though *he slay me*, yet will I trust in
24:14. The murderer...*killeth* the poor and
Ps. 139:19. Surely *thou wilt slay* the wicked, O God:

6992 **קְטַל** [*k'tal*], Ch.

* P'AL.—*Participle.* Active. *

Dan 5:19. whom he would he *slew*; (lit. he was *slaying*)

P'AL.—*Participle.* Passive.

Dan 5:30. *was* Belshazzar the king of the Chaldeans *slain.*
7:11. I beheld (even) till the beast *was slain*,

* PAEL.—*Preterite.* *

Dan 3:22. the flame of the fire *slew* those men

PAEL.—*Infinitive.*

Dan 2:14. which was gone forth *to slay*

* ITHP'AL.—*Infinitive.* *

Dan 2:13. that the wise (men) *should be slain*;

* ITHPAEL.—*Participle.* *

Dan 2:13. Daniel and his fellows *to be slain.*

6993 **קֶטֶל** [*keh'-tel*], m.

Obad. 9. to the end that every one...may be cut off *by slaughter.*

6994 **קָטֹן** [*kāh-tōhn'*].

* KAL.—*Preterite.* *

Gen 32:10(11). *I am not worthy* of (marg. *less* than) the least of all the mercies,

KAL.—*Future.*

2Sa. 7:19. *And* this *was* yet *a small thing* in thy
1Ch 17:17. *And* (yet) this *was a small thing* in thine eyes,

* HIPHIL.—*Infinitive.* *

Am. 8: 5. *making* the ephah *small*,

6996 **קָטָן** *kāh-tāhn'*, adj.

Gen 9:24. knew what his *younger* son had done unto
27:15. put them upon Jacob her *younger* son:
42. she sent and called Jacob her *younger*
29:16. the name of *the younger* (was) Rachel.
18. seven years for Rachel thy *younger*
44:20. a child of his old age, *a little one;*
Nu. 22:18. to do *less* or more.
Deu 25:13. divers weights, a great *and a small.*
14. divers measures, a great *and a small.*
Jud. 15: 2. (is) not her *younger* sister fairer than she?
1Sa. 9:21. (Am) not I a Benjamite, *of the smallest of* the tribes
14:49. the name of *the younger* Michal:
16:11. There remaineth yet *the youngest*,
17:14. David (was) *the youngest:*
2Sa. 9:12. Mephibosheth had a *young* son,
2Sa. 12: 3. save one *little* ewe lamb.
1K. 2:20. I desire one *small* petition of thee;
11:17. Hadad (being) yet a *little* child.
17:13. make me thereof a *little* cake
18:44. there ariseth a *little* cloud out of the sea,
2K. 2:23. there came forth *little* children out of the city,
4:10. Let us make a *little* chamber,
5: 2. brought away captive out of the land of Israel a *little* maid;
18:24. *the least* of my master's servants,
1Ch 12:14. one of *the least* (was) over an hundred,
24:31. the principal fathers over against their *younger* brethren.
2Ch 31:15. as well to the great *as to the small:*
34:30. all the people, great and *small:*
36:18. all the vessels of the house of God, great *and small*,
Est. 1: 5. both unto great and *small*,
20. both to great and *small.*
Ps. 104:25. both *small* and great beasts.
115:13. (both) *small* and great.
Pro. 30:24. There be four (things which are) *little upon*
Ecc. 9:14. (There was) a *little* city, and few men
Cant. 2:15. Take us the foxes, the *little* foxes,
8: 8. We have a *little* sister, and she hath no
Isa. 22:24. all vessels of *small quantity*,
36: 9. *the least* of my master's servants,
Jer. 6:13. *from the least of them* even unto the greatest
16: 6. Both the great *and the small* shall die in
31:34. *from the least of them* unto the
Eze. 16:46. thy *younger* (marg. *lesser*) sister,...(is) Sodom and her daughters.
61. thine elder and thy *younger:*
43:14. from the *lesser* settle (even) to the
Jon. 3: 5. from the greatest of them even to *the least*
Zec. 4:10. who hath despised the day of *small things?*

קָטֹן *kāh-tōhn'*, adj. 6995-96

Gen 1:16. the *lesser* light to rule the night:
19:11. *both small* and great:
42:13. *the youngest* (is) this day with our father,
15. except your *youngest* brother come
20. bring your *youngest* brother unto me;
32. *and the youngest* (is) this day with our
34. bring your *youngest* brother unto me:
43:29. (Is) this your *younger* brother,
44: 2. put my cup,...in the sack's mouth of *the youngest*,
12. at the eldest, *and* left *at the youngest:*
23. Except your *youngest* brother come down
26. if our *youngest* brother be with us, then
— except our *youngest* brother (be) with us.
48:19. his *younger* brother shall be greater than
Ex. 18:22. every *small* matter they shall judge:
26. every *small* matter they judged
Deu. 1:17. ye shall hear *the small as well* as the
Jud. 1:13. Caleb's *younger* brother, took it:
3: 9. Kenaz, Caleb's *younger* brother.
9: 5. the *youngest* son of Jerubbaal was left;
1Sa. 2:19. his mother made him a *little* coat,
5: 9. smote the men of the city, *both small* and
15:17. When thou (wast) *little* in thine own
20: 2. father will do nothing either great or *small*,
35. a *little* lad with him.
22:15. thy servant knew nothing of all this, *less* (marg. *little*) or more.
25:36. she told him nothing, *less* or more,
30: 2. they slew not any, *either* great or *small*,
19. neither *small* nor great,
1K. 3: 7. I (am but) a *little* child:
8:64. the brasen altar...(was) too *little*
12:10. *My little* (finger) shall be thicker
22:31. Fight neither with *small* nor great,
2K. 5:14. came again like unto the flesh of a *little*
23: 2. all the people, *both small* and great:
25:26. all the people, both *small* and great,
1Ch 25: 8 & 26:13. *as well the small* as the great,
2Ch 10:10. *My little* (finger) shall be thicker
15:13. whether *small* or great,
18:30. Fight ye not with *small* or great,
21:17. Jehoahaz, *the youngest of* his sons.
22: 1. made Ahaziah his *youngest* son king
Job 3:19. *The small* and great are there;
Isa. 11: 6. a *little* child shall lead them.

Isa. 54: 7. For a *small* moment have I forsaken
60:22. *a little one* shall become a thousand,
Jer. 8:10 & 42:1. *from the least* even unto the
42: 8. *from the least* even to the greatest,
44:12. *from the least* even unto the greatest,
49:15. will make thee *small* among the heathen,
Am. 6:11. the *little* house with clefts.
7: 2, 5. shall Jacob arise? for he (is) *small.*
Obad. 2. I have made thee *small* among the

6998 קָטַף [*kāh-taph'*]

* KAL.—*Preterite.* *

Deu23:25(26). *then thou mayest pluck* the ears with thine hand;
Eze.17: 4. *He cropped off* the top of his young twigs,

KAL.—*Future.*

Eze.17:22. *I will crop off* from the top of his young

KAL.—*Participle.*

Job 30: 4. *Who cut up* mallows by the bushes,

* NIPHAL.—*Future.* *

Job 8:12. Whilst it (is) yet in his greenness, (and) not *cut down,*

6999 קָטַר [*kāh-tar'*].

* PIEL.—*Preterite.* *

2K. 23: 8. defiled the high places where the priests *had burned incense,*
Isa. 65: 7. which *have burned incense* upon the
Jer. 19:13. *they have burned incense* unto all the host
32:29. *they have offered incense* unto Baal,
44:21. The incense that *ye burned* in the cities of
23. Because *ye have burned incense,*

PIEL.—*Infinitive.*

1Sa. 2:16. Let them not fail *to burn* (lit. *burning let them burn*)
2Ch 28:25. places *to burn incense* (marg. *offer*) unto
Jer. 7: 9. *and burn incense* unto Baal,
11:13. altars *to burn incense* unto Baal.
17. *in offering incense* unto Baal.
44: 3. in that they went *to burn incense,*
5. *to burn* no *incense* unto other gods.
8. *burning incense* unto other gods
17. *to burn incense* unto the queen of heaven,
18. since we left off *to burn incense* to the
25. *to burn incense* to the queen of heaven,
Am. 4: 5. *And offer a sacrifice* (marg. *by burning*) of

PIEL.—*Future.*

2K. 16: 4. he sacrificed *and burnt incense* in the high
17:11. *And there they burnt incense* in all the
22:17. *and have burned incense* unto other gods,
23: 5. ordained *to burn incense* in the high
2Ch 25:14. *burned incense* unto them.
28: 4. He sacrificed also *and burnt incense*
34:25. *and have burned incense* unto other gods,
Jer. 1:16. *and have burned incense* unto other gods,
18:15. *they have burned incense* to vanity,
19: 4. *and have burned incense* in it unto other
Hos. 4:13. *burn incense* upon the hills,
11: 2. *burned incense* to graven images.
Hab. 1:16. *and burn incense* unto their drag;

PIEL.—*Participle.*

1K. 22:43(44). the people offered *and burnt incense*
2K. 12: 3(4). people still sacrificed *and burnt incense*
14: 4. *and burnt incense* on the high places.
15: 4. people sacrificed *and burnt incense* still
35. *and burned incense* still in the high places.
18: 4. children of Israel did *burn incense* to it:
23: 5. them also *that burned incense* unto Baal,
Isa. 65: 3. *and burneth incense* upon altars of brick;
Jer. 11:12. the gods unto whom they *offer incense:*
44:15. their wives *had burned incense* unto other
19. when we *burned incense* to the queen of

* PUAL.—*Participle.* *

Cant.3: 6. *perfumed* with myrrh and frankincense,

* HIPHIL.—*Preterite.* *

Ex. 29:13. *and burn* (them) upon the altar.
18. *And thou shalt burn* the whole ram
25. *and burn* (them) upon the altar
Ex. 30: 7. *And* Aaron *shall burn* thereon
Lev. 1: 9. *and* the priest *shall burn* all on the altar,
13. *and burn* (it) upon the altar:
15. *and burn* (it) on the altar;
17. *and* the priest *shall burn* it upon the altar.
2: 2, 16. *and* the priest *shall burn* the memorial
9. *and shall burn* (it) upon the altar:
3: 5. *And* Aaron's sons *shall burn* it on the
11. *And* the priest *shall burn* it upon the
16. *And* the priest *shall burn them* upon the
4:10. *and* the priest *shall burn them* upon the
19. *and burn* (it) upon the altar.
31. *and* the priest *shall burn* (it) upon the
35. *and* the priest *shall burn* them upon the
5:12. *and burn* (it) on the altar,
6:12(5). *and he shall burn* thereon the fat
15(8). *and shall burn* (it) upon the altar
7: 5. *And* the priest *shall burn* them upon the
31. *And* the priest *shall burn* the fat upon the
9:10. But the fat,...*he burnt* upon the altar;
17: 6. *and burn* the fat for a sweet savour unto
Nu. 5:26. *and burn* (it) upon the altar,
2Ch 28: 3. *he burnt incense* (marg. or, *offered sacrifice*) in the valley of the son of Hinnom,
29: 7. *have* not *burned* incense

HIPHIL.—*Infinitive.*

Ex 30:20. *to burn* offering made by fire unto the
Nu. 16:40(17:5). come near *to offer* incense before
1Sa. 2:28. *to burn* incense, to wear an ephod before
1K. 9:25. *and he burnt incense* upon the altar
12:33. offered upon the altar, *and burnt incense.*
13: 1. by the altar *to burn incense.* (marg. or, *offer*)
1Ch 23:13. *to burn incense* before the Lord,
2Ch 2: 4(3). *to burn* before him sweet incense,
6(5). save only *to burn sacrifice* before him?
26:16. into the temple of the Lord *to burn incense*
18. *to burn incense* unto the Lord,
— that are consecrated *to burn incense:*
19. (had) a censer in his hand *to burn incense:*

HIPHIL.—*Imperative.*

2K. 16:15. Upon the great altar *burn* the morning

HIPHIL.—*Future.*

Ex. 30: 7. the lamps, *he shall burn incense upon it.*
8. at even, *he shall burn incense upon it,*
40:27. *And he burnt* sweet incense thereon;
Lev. 2:11. *ye shall burn* no leaven, nor any honey,
4:26. *he shall burn* all his fat upon the altar,
8:16. *and* Moses *burned* (it) upon the altar.
20. *and* Moses *burnt* the head, and the pieces,
21. *and* Moses *burnt* the whole ram upon the
28. *and burnt* (them) on the altar
9:13. *and he burnt* (them) upon the altar.
14. *and burnt* (them) upon the burnt
17. *and burnt* (it) upon the altar,
20. *and he burnt* the fat upon the altar:
16:25. the fat...*shall he burn* upon the altar.
Nu. 18:17. *shalt burn* their fat (for) an offering
1Sa. 2:15. before *they burnt* the fat, the priest's
16. *Let them* not fail to *burn* the fat
2K. 16:13. *And he burnt* his burnt offering
2Ch 32:12. worship before one altar, and *burn incense*
34:25. (כתיב) *and have burned incense* unto other
Hos. 2:13(15). wherein *she burned* incense to them,

HIPHIL.—*Participle.*

1K. 3: 3. he sacrificed *and burnt incense* in high
11: 8. *which burnt incense* and sacrificed unto
13: 2. the high places *that burn incense* upon
1Ch. 6:49(34). Aaron and his sons *offered* upon the
2Ch 13:11. *And they burn* unto the Lord every
29:11. ye should minister unto him, *and burn incense.* (marg. or, *offer sacrifice*)
Jer. 33:18. *and* to *kindle* meat offerings, and to do
48:35. *and him that burneth incense* to his gods.

* HOPHAL.—*Future.* *

Lev. 6:22(15). *it shall be* wholly *burnt.*

HOPHAL.—*Participle.*

Mal. 1:11. in every place *incense* (shall be) offered

קָטַר [*kāh-tar'*]. 7000

* KAL.—*Participle.* Paül. *

Eze.46:22. (there were) courts *joined* (marg. or, *made with chimnies*) of forty (cubits)

7001 **קְטַר [*k'tar*], Ch. m.**

Dan. 5: 6. *so that the joints* (marg. *bindings*, or, *knots*, or, *girdles*) *of* his loins
12. and dissolving of *doubts*, (marg. *knots*)
16. *and* dissolve *doubts* :

7002 **קִטֵּר *kit-tēhr'*, m.**

Jer. 44:21. *The incense* that ye burned in the cities of

7004 **קְטֹרֶת *k'tōh'-reth*, f.**

Ex. 25: 6. spices for anointing oil, *and for* sweet *incense*,
30: 1. shalt make an altar to burn *incense* upon:
7. Aaron shall burn thereon sweet *incense*
8. *a* perpetual *incense* before the Lord
9. Ye shall offer no strange *incense* thereon,
27. his vessels, and the altar of *incense*,
35. thou shalt make it *a perfume*,
37. (as for) *the perfume* which thou shalt
31: 8. the altar of *incense*,
11. *sweet incense* for the holy (place):
35: 8. spices for anointing oil, *and for the* sweet *incense*,
15. the *incense* altar, and his staves, and the anointing oil, and *the* sweet *incense*,
28. the anointing oil, *and for the* sweet *incense*.
37:25. made the *incense* altar (of) shittim wood:
29. *the* pure *incense of* sweet spices,
39:38. the anointing oil, and *the* sweet *incense*
40: 5. shalt set the altar of gold *for the incense*
27. burnt sweet *incense* thereon ;
Lev. 4: 7. the altar of *sweet incense*
10: 1. put fire therein, and put *incense* thereon,
16:12. his hands full of sweet *incense*
13. he shall put *the incense* upon the fire before the Lord, that the cloud of *the incense* may cover the mercy seat
Nu. 4:16. *and the* sweet *incense*,
7:14. of ten (shekels) of gold, full of *incense :*
20. of gold of ten (shekels), full of *incense :*
26, 32, 38, 44, 50, 56, 62, 68, 74, 80. One golden spoon of ten (shekels), full of *incense :*
86. The golden spoons (were) twelve, full of *incense*,
16: 7. put *incense* in them before the Lord
17. his censer, and put *incense* in them,
18. put fire in them, and laid *incense* thereon.
35. two hundred and fifty men that offered *incense*.
40(17:5). come near to offer *incense* before
46(—:11). off the altar, and put on *incense*,
47(—:12). he put on *incense*, and made an
1 Sa. 2:28. to burn *incense*, to wear an ephod before
1 Ch 6:49(34). on the altar of *incense*,
28:18. for the altar of *incense* refined gold by
2 Ch 2: 4(3). to burn before him sweet *incense*,
13:11. burnt sacrifices *and* sweet *incense:*
26:16. upon the altar of *incense*.
19. from beside the *incense* altar.
29: 7. *and* have not burned *incense* nor offered
Ps. 66:15. with *the incense of* rams;
141: 2. Let my prayer be set forth before thee (as) *incense;*
Pro. 27: 9. Ointment *and perfume* rejoice the heart:
Isa. 1:13. *incense* is an abomination unto me;
Eze. 8:11. a thick cloud of *incense* went up.
16:18. hast set mine oil *and mine incense* before
23:41. whereupon (lit *and* on it) thou hast set *mine incense* and mine oil.

6892 **קִיא *kee*, m.**

Isa. 19:14. a drunken (man) staggereth *in his vomit*.
28: 8. all tables are full of *vomit*
Jer. 48:26. Moab also shall wallow *in his vomit*,

7006 **קָיָה [*kāh-yāh'*].**

✱ KAL.—*Imperative.* ✱

Jer. 25:27. be drunken, *and spue*, and fall,

קַיִט *kah'-yit*, Ch. m. 7007

Dan. 2:35. the chaff of the *summer* threshingfloors ;

קִיטוֹר *kee-tōhr'*, m. 7008

Gen 19:28. *the smoke of* the country went up *as the smoke of* a furnace.
Ps. 119:83. I am become like a bottle *in the smoke ;*
148: 8. Fire, and hail; snow, *and vapours ;*

קִים [*keem*], m. 7009

Job 22:20. Whereas *our substance* [perhaps lit. *enemies*] is not cut down,

קְיָם *k'yāhm*, Ch. m. 7010

Dan. 6: 7(8). and to make *a* firm *decree*, (marg. or, *interdict*)
15(16). That no decree *nor statute*

קַיָּם *kay-yāhm'*, Ch. adj. 7011

Dan. 4:26(23). thy kingdom shall be *sure* unto thee,
6:26(27). *and stedfast* for ever,

קִימָה [*kee-māh'*], f. 7012

Lam. 3:63. Behold their sitting down, *and their rising up ;*

קִימוֹשׁ see קִמּוֹשׁ See 7057

קַיִן [*kah'-yin*], m. 7013

2 Sa. 21:16. weight of *whose spear* (marg. *staff*, or, *the head*) (weighed) three hundred (shekels)

קִינָה *kee-nāh'*, f. 7015

2 Sa. 1:17. this *lamentation* over Saul
2 Ch 35:25. spake of Josiah *in their lamentations*
— they (are) written *in the lamentations*.
Jer. 7:29. take up *a lamentation* on high places ;
9:10(9). of the wilderness *a lamentation*,
20(19). every one her neighbour *lamentation*.
Eze. 2:10. (there was) written therein *lamentations*,
19: 1. take thou up *a lamentation* for the princes
14. This (is) *a lamentation*, and shall be *for a lamentation*.
26:17. they shall take up *a lamentation* for thee,
27: 2. take up *a lamentation* for Tyrus ;
32. they shall take up *a lamentation* for thee,
28:12. up *a lamentation* upon the king of Tyrus,
32: 2. take up *a lamentation* for Pharaoh
16. This (is) *the lamentation* wherewith
Am. 5: 1. *a lamentation*, O house of Israel.
8:10. all your songs *into lamentation ;*

קַיִץ *kah'-yitz*, m. 7019

Gen 8:22. *and summer* and winter, and day and
2 Sa. 16: 1. an hundred of *summer fruits*, and a bottle
2. the bread *and summer fruit* for the young
Ps. 32: 4. my moisture is turned into the drought of *summer*.
74:17. thou hast made *summer* and winter.
Pro. 6: 8. Provideth her meat *in the summer*,
10: 5. He that gathereth *in summer* (is) a wise
26: 1. As snow *in summer*, and as rain in harvest,
30:25. they prepare their meat *in the summer ;*
Isa. 16: 9. the shouting for *thy summer fruits*...is
28: 4. as the hasty fruit before *the summer ;*
Jer. 8:20. The harvest is past, *the summer* is ended,
40:10. gather ye wine, *and summer fruits*, and
12. gathered wine *and summer fruits* very
48:32. spoiler is fallen upon *thy summer fruits*
Am. 3:15. the winter house with *the summer house ;*
8: 1. behold a basket of *summer fruit*.
2. And I said, A basket of *summer fruit*.
Mic 7: 1. they have gathered *the summer fruits*,
Zec. 14: 8. *in summer* and in winter shall it be.

7020 קִיצוֹן [*kee-tzōhn'*], adj.

Ex. 26: 4. in the *uttermost* edge of (another) curtain,
10. *outmost* in the coupling,
36:11. in the *uttermost* side of (another) curtain,
17. the *uttermost* edge of the curtain

7021 קִיקָיוֹן *kee-kāh-yōhn'*, m.

Jon. 4: 6. the Lord God prepared *a gourd*, (marg. *Kikajon*, or, *palmcrist*)
— Jonah was exceeding glad of *the gourd*.
7. it smote *the gourd*
9. Doest thou well to be angry for *the gourd?*
10. Thou hast had pity on *the gourd*,

7022 קִיקָלוֹן *kee-kāh-lōhn'*, m.

Hab. 2:16. *and shameful spewing* (shall be) on thy

7023 קִיר *keer*, m.

Ex. 30: 3 & 37:26. *the sides* (marg. *walls*) *thereof* round about,
Lev. 1:15. wrung out at *the side of* the altar:
5: 9. shall sprinkle...upon *the side of* the altar;
14:37. (if) the plague (be) *in the walls of* the
— which in sight (are) lower than *the wall;*
39. (if) the plague be spread *in the walls of*
Nu. 22:25. she thrust herself unto *the wall*, and crushed Balaam's foot against *the wall:*
35: 4. (shall reach) *from the wall of* the city
Jos. 2:15. her house (was) *upon* the *town* wall,
1Sa. 18:11. I will smite David *even to the wall*
19:10. Saul sought to smite David *even to the wall*
— he smote the javelin *into the wall:*
20:25. upon a seat by *the wall:*
25:22, 34. *against the wall.*
2Sa. 5:11. carpenters, and masons: (marg. hewers of the stone of the *wall*)
1K. 4:33(5:13). the hyssop that springeth out of *the wall:*
6: 5. against *the wall of* the house
— (against) *the walls of* the house
6. fastened *in the walls of* the house.
15. he built *the walls of* the house
— *the walls of* the ceiling:
16. *the walls* with boards of cedar:
27. one touched *the* (one) *wall*, and the wing of the other cherub touched *the* other *wall;*
29. he carved all *the walls of* the house
14:10. *against the wall*,
16:11. *against a wall*,
21:21. *against the wall*,
2K. 4:10. I pray thee, on *the wall;*
9: 8. *against the wall*,
33. her blood was sprinkled on *the wall*,
20: 2. he turned his face to *the wall*,
1Ch 14: 1. with masons (lit. hewers of *wall* stone)
29: 4. to overlay *the walls of* the houses
2Ch 3: 7. *and the walls thereof*,
— graved cherubims on *the walls*.
11. reaching *to the wall of* the house:
12. reaching *to the wall of* the house:
Ps. 62: 3(4). *as a* bowing *wall* (shall ye be),
Isa. 22: 5. breaking down *the walls*,
25: 4. a storm (against) *the wall*.
38: 2. Hezekiah turned his face toward *the wall*,
59:10. We grope for *the wall* like the blind,
Jer. 4:19. I am pained at my *very* heart; (marg. *the walls of* my heart)
Eze. 4: 3. set it (for) *a wall of* iron between thee
8: 7. behold a hole *in the wall*.
8. dig now *in the wall:* and when I had digged *in the wall*,
10. pourtrayed upon *the wall*
12: 5. Dig thou *through the wall*
7. I digged *through the wall*
12. they shall dig *through the wall*
13:12. when *the wall* is fallen,
14. I break down *the wall*
15. will I accomplish my wrath *upon the wall*,
— *The wall* (is) no (more),
23:14. pourtrayed upon *the wall*,
Eze. 33:30. are talking against thee by *the walls*
41: 5. After he measured *the wall of*
6. they entered *into the wall*
— they had not hold *in the wall of*
9. The thickness of *the wall*,
12. *and the wall of* the building
13. the building, *with the walls thereof*,
17. *the wall* round about
20. *and* (on) *the wall of* the temple.
22. *and the walls thereof*, (were) of wood:
25. like as (were) made *upon the walls;*
43: 8. *and the wall* between me and them,
Am. 5:19. leaned his hand on *the wall*,
Hab. 2:11. the stone shall cry *out of the wall*,

קִיתָרֹס *kee-thāh-rōhs'*, Ch. m. 7030

Dan 3: 5, 7, 10, 15. (כתיב) cornet, flute, *harp*, sackbut,

קַל *kal*, adj. 7031

2Sa. 2:18. Asahel (was as) *light* of foot as a wild roe.
Job 24:18. He (is) *swift* as the waters;
Ecc. 9:11. the race (is) not *to the swift*,
Isa. 5:26. they shall come with speed *swiftly:*
18: 2. Go, ye *swift* messengers,
19: 1. the Lord rideth upon a *swift* cloud,
30:16. We will ride upon *the swift;*
Jer. 2:23. (thou art) a *swift* dromedary traversing
46: 6. Let not the *swift* flee away,
Lam 4:19. Our persecutors are *swifter* than the eagles
Joel 3: 4(4:4). *swiftly* (and) speedily will I return your recompence
Am. 2:14. the flight shall perish *from the swift*,
15. *and* (he that is) *swift* of foot shall not

קָל *kāhl*, Ch. m. 7032

Dan 3: 5, 15. at what time ye hear *the sound of*
7. when all the people heard *the sound of*
10. every man that shall hear *the sound of*
4:31(28). there fell *a voice* from heaven,
6:20(21). *with a* lamentable *voice*
7:11. because of *the voice of* the great words

קָלָה [*kāh-lah'*]. 7035

* NIPHAL.—*Future.* *

2Sa 20:14. (כתיב) *and they were gathered together*, and

קָלָה [*kāh-lāh'*]. 7033

* KAL.—*Preterite.* *

Jer. 29:22. whom the king of Babylon *roasted* (lit. *them*) in the fire;

KAL.—*Participle.* Paül.

Lev. 2:14. green ears of corn *dried* by the fire,
Jos. 5:11. and *parched* (corn) in the selfsame day.

* NIPHAL.—*Participle.* *

Ps. 38: 7(8). my loins are filled with *a loathsome* (disease):

קָלָה [*kāh-lāh'*]. 7034

* NIPHAL.—*Preterite.* *

Deu 25: 3. *then* thy brother *should seem vile* unto thee.
Isa. 16:14. the glory of Moab *shall be contemned*,

NIPHAL.—*Participle.*

1Sa. 18:23. seeing that I (am) a poor man, *and lightly esteemed?*
Pro. 12: 9. *He that is despised*, and hath a servant,
Isa. 3: 5. *and the base* against the honourable.

* HIPHIL.—*Participle.* *

Deu 27:16. Cursed (be) he *that setteth light* by his father or his mother.

קָלוֹן *kāh-lōhn'*, m. 7036

Job 10:15. (I am) full of *confusion;*
Ps. 83:16(17). Fill their faces with *shame;*

Pro. 3:35. *shame* shall be the promotion of fools.
6:33. A wound *and dishonour* shall he get;
9: 7. He that reproveth a scorner getteth to himself *shame:*
11: 2. (When) pride cometh, then cometh *shame:*
12:16. a prudent (man) covereth *shame.*
13:18. Poverty *and shame* (shall be to) him
18: 3. with *ignominy* reproach.
22:10. strife *and reproach* shall cease.
Isa. 22:18. thy glory (shall be) *the shame of* thy lord's
Jer. 13:26. that *thy shame* may appear.
46:12. The nations have heard of *thy shame,*
Hos. 4: 7. change their glory *into shame.*
18. her rulers (with) *shame* do love,
Nah 3: 5. the kingdoms *thy shame.*
Hab 2:16. Thou art filled with *shame* for glory:

7037 קַלַּחַת *kal-lah'-ghath*, f.

1Sa. 2:14. the pan, or kettle, *or caldron,* or pot;
Mic. 3: 3. as flesh within *the caldron.*

7038 קָלַט [*kāh-lat'*].

* KAL.—*Participle.* Paül. *

Lev. 22:23. a lamb that hath any thing superfluous or *lacking in his parts,*

7039 קָלִי & קָלִיא *kāh-lee'*, m.

Lev.23:14. shall eat neither bread, *nor parched corn,*
Ru. 2:14. he reached her *parched corn,*
1Sa.17:17. Take now for thy brethren an ephah of this *parched corn,*
25:18. five measures of *parched corn,*
2Sa.17:28. *and parched corn,* and beans, and lentiles, *and parched* (pulse),

---

7043 קָלַל [*kāh-lal'*].

* KAL.—*Preterite.* *

Gen 8: 8. to see if the waters *were abated*
11. Noah knew that the waters *were abated*
2Sa. 1:23. *they were swifter* than eagles,
Job 7: 6. My days *are swifter* than a weaver's shuttle,
9:25. my days *are swifter* than a post:
40: 4. *I am vile;* what shall I answer thee?
Jer. 4:13. his horses *are swifter* than eagles.
Nah 1:14. I will make thy grave; for *thou art vile.*
Hab 1: 8. Their horses *also are swifter* than the

KAL.—*Future.*

Gen16: 4. *and* when...her mistress *was despised* in her
5. *and* when...*I was despised* in her eyes:
1Sa. 2:30. they that despise me *shall be lightly esteemed.*

* NIPHAL.—*Preterite.* *

1Sa.18:23. *Seemeth it* to you *a light thing* to be a
2Sa. 6:22. *And I will* yet *be more vile* than thus,
1K. 16:31. *as if it had been a light thing* (marg. *was it a light thing*) for him to walk in the
2K. 3:18. *And* this *is* (but) *a light thing* in the sight
20:10. *It is a light thing* for the shadow to go
Pro.14: 6. knowledge *is easy* unto him that
Isa. 49: 6. *It is a light thing* that thou shouldest be
Jer. 6:14. healed also the hurt...*slightly,*
8:11. they have healed the hurt...*slightly,*
Eze. 8:17. *Is it a light thing to* the house of Judah

NIPHAL.—*Future.*

Isa. 30:16. therefore *shall* they that pursue you *be swift.*

* PIEL.—*Preterite.* *

Lev.20: 9. *he hath cursed* his father or his mother;
2Sa.19:21(22). *he cursed* the Lord's anointed?
1K. 2: 8. *cursed* me with a grievous curse
Ecc. 7:22. thou thyself likewise *hast cursed* others.
Isa. 8:21. *and curse* their king and their God,

PIEL.—*Infinitive.*

Gen 8:21. I will not again *curse* (lit. add *to curse*) the ground
Deu23: 4(5). they hired against thee Balaam...*to curse thee.*
Jos. 24: 9. called Balaam the son of Beor *to curse* you:
2Sa.16: 7. thus said Shimei *when he cursed,*
Neh 13: 2. hired Balaam against them, *that he should curse them:*

PIEL.—*Imperative.*

2Sa.16:10. the Lord hath said unto him, *Curse* David.

PIEL.—*Future.*

Ex. 22:28(27). *Thou shalt* not *revile* the gods,
Lev.19:14. *Thou shalt* not *curse* the deaf,
20: 9. every one that *curseth* his father or his
24:11. blasphemed the name (of the Lord), *and cursed.*
15. Whosoever *curseth* his God shall bear his
Jud. 9:27. did eat and drink, *and cursed* Abimelech.
1Sa.17:43. *And* the Philistine *cursed* David by his
2Sa.16: 9. Why *should* this dead dog *curse* my lord
10. so *let him curse,* because the Lord
11. let him alone, *and let him curse;*
13. *and cursed* as he went, and threw stones
2K. 2:24. *and cursed* them in the name of the Lord.
Neh 13:25. I contended with them, *and cursed* (marg. or, *reviled*) *them,*
Job 3: 1. After this opened Job his mouth, *and cursed* his day.
Ps. 62: 4(5). they bless with their mouth, but *they curse* inwardly.
109:28. *Let* them *curse,* but bless thou:
Pro.30:10. lest *he curse thee,* and thou be found guilty.
11. (There is) a generation (that) *curseth* their
Ecc.10:20. *Curse* not the king,
— *curse* not the rich in thy bedchamber:

PIEL.—*Participle.*

Gen12: 3. *and* curse *him that curseth thee:*
Ex. 21:17. *And he that curseth* (marg. or, *revileth*) his father, or his mother,
Lev.24:14. Bring forth *him that hath cursed*
23. bring forth *him that had cursed*
1Sa. 3:13. his sons *made* themselves *vile,* (marg. or, *accursed*)
2Sa.16: 5. he came forth, *and cursed* still as he came.
Pro.20:20. *Whoso curseth* his father or his mother,
Ecc. 7:21. lest thou hear thy servant *curse thee:*
Jer. 15:10. every one of them *doth curse* me.

* PILPEL.—*Preterite.* *

Ecc.10:10. If the iron be blunt, and he *do* not *whet*
Eze.21:21(26). he *made* (his) arrows *bright,*

* PUAL.—*Future.* *

Job 24:18. their portion *is cursed* in the earth:
Isa. 65:20. (being) 100 years old *shall be accursed.*

PUAL.—*Participle.*

Ps. 37:22. *and* (they that be) *cursed of him* shall be cut off.

* HIPHIL.—*Preterite.* *

2Sa.19:43(44). why then *did ye despise us,* (marg. *set us at light*)
Isa. 9: 1(8:23). *he lightly afflicted* the land of
Eze.22: 7. In thee *have they set light* by father and

HIPHIL.—*Infinitive.*

Isa. 23: 9. *to bring into contempt* all the honourable
Jon. 1: 5. cast forth the wares...*to lighten* (it) of

HIPHIL.—*Imperative.*

Ex. 18:22. *so shall it be easier* for thyself,
1K. 12: 4. *make* thou...his heavy yoke which he put upon us, *lighter,*
9. *Make* the yoke which thy father did put upon us *lighter?*
10. *make* thou (it) *lighter* unto us;
2Ch 10: 4. *ease thou* somewhat the grievous servitude
9. *Ease* somewhat the yoke
10. *make* thou (it) *somewhat lighter*

HIPHIL.—*Future.*

1Sa. 6: 5. *he will lighten* his hand from off you,

* HITHPALPEL.—*Preterite.* *

Jer. 4:24. all the hills *moved lightly.*

קָלָל *kāh-lāhl'*, adj. 7044

Eze. 1: 7. sparkled like the colour of *burnished* brass
Dan 10: 6. his feet like in colour to *polished* brass,

7045 **קְלָלָה** *k'lāh-lāh'*, f.

Gen27:12. I shall bring *a curse* upon me,
13. Upon me (be) *thy curse*, my son:
Deu11:26. I set before you this day a blessing *and a curse;*
28. *And a curse*, if ye will not obey the
29. *the curse* upon mount Ebal.
21:23. *accursed of* God; (marg. *the curse of* God)
23: 5(6). the Lord thy God turned *the curse* into
27:13. these shall stand upon mount Ebal to *curse;* (lit. for *the curse*)
28:15, 45. all these *curses* shall come upon thee,
29:27(26). to bring upon it all *the curses*
30: 1. the blessing *and the curse*,
19. I have set before you life and death, blessing *and cursing:*
Jos. 8:34. the blessings *and cursings*,
Jud. 9:57. upon them came *the curse of* Jotham
2Sa.16:12. will requite me good for *his cursing*
1K. 2: 8. with *a* grievous *curse*
2K. 22:19. should become a desolation *and a curse*,
Neh 13: 2. our God turned *the curse* into a blessing.
Ps.109:17. As he loved *cursing*, so let it come unto
18. he clothed himself with *cursing*
Pro.26: 2. *the curse* causeless shall not come.
27:14. it shall be counted *a curse* to him.
Jer. 24: 9. a proverb, a taunt *and a curse*,
25:18. an astonishment, an hissing, *and a curse;*
26: 6. and will make this city *a curse*
29:22. of them shall be taken up *a curse*
42:18. an astonishment, *and a curse*, and a
44: 8. that ye might be *a curse* and a reproach
12. an astonishment, *and a curse*, and a
22. an astonishment, *and a curse*, without
49:13. a reproach, a waste, *and a curse;*
Zec. 8:13. as ye were *a curse* among the heathen,

7046 **קָלַס** [*kāh-las'*].

* PIEL.—*Infinitive.* *

Eze.16:31. *in that thou scornest* hire;

* HITHPAEL.—*Future.* *

2K. 2:23. there came forth little children out of the city, *and mocked him*,
Eze.22: 5. those that be far from thee, *shall mock*
Hab 1:10. they *shall scoff* at the kings,

7047 **קֶלֶס** *keh'-les*, m.

Ps. 44:13(14). a scorn *and a derision* to them that are round about us.
79: 4. a scorn *and derision* to them that are
Jer. 20: 8. the word of the Lord was made a reproach unto me, *and a derision*,

---

7048 **קַלָּסָה** *kal-lāh-sāh'*, f.

Eze.22: 4. *and a mocking* to all countries.

7049 **קָלַע** *kāh-lag'*.

* KAL.—*Preterite.* *

1K. 6:29. *he carved* all the walls of the house round
32. *and he carved* upon them carvings
35. *And he carved* (thereon) cherubims

KAL.—*Participle.* Poel.

Jud.20:16. every one *could sling* stones
Jer. 10:18. I will *sling out* the inhabitants of the

* PIEL.—*Future.* *

1Sa.17:49. took thence a stone, *and slang* (it),
25:29. the souls of thine enemies, them *shall he sling out*,

---

7050 **קֶלַע** *keh'-lag*, m.

1Sa.17:40. *and* his *sling* (was) in his hand:
50. David prevailed over the Philistine *with a sling* and with a stone,
25:29. (as out) of the middle of *a sling*.
2Ch 26:14. and *slings* (to cast) stones.
Job 41:28(20). *sling*stones are turned with him into
Zec. 9:15. shall devour, and subdue with *sling* stones;

קַלָּע [*kal-lāhg'*], m. 7051

2K. 3:25. *the slingers* went about (it), and smote it.

קְלָעִים *k'lāh-geem'*, m. pl 7050

Ex. 27: 9. for the south side southward (there shall be) *hangings*
11. the north side in length (there shall be) *hangings*
12. west side (shall be) *hangings* of fifty
14. *The hangings* of one side
15. on the other side (shall be) *hangings*
35:17. *The hangings of* the court, his pillars,
38: 9. *the hangings of* the court (were of) fine
12. for the west side (were) *hangings*
14. *The hangings* of the one side
15. (were) *hangings* of fifteen cubits;
16. All *the hangings of* the court
18. answerable to *the hangings of* the court.
39:40. *The hangings of* the court, his pillars,
Nu. 3:26. *And the hangings of* the court,
4:26. And *the hangings of* the court,
1K. 6:34. the two *leaves* of the other door (were)

קְלֹקֵל *k'lōh-kēhl'*, adj. 7052

Nu. 21: 5. our soul loatheth this *light* bread.

קִלְשׁוֹן *kil-shōhn'*, m. 7053

1Sa.13:21. the coulters, and for *the forks*,

קָמָה *kāh-māh'*, f. 7054

Ex. 22: 6(5). *the standing corn*, or the field, be
Deu16: 9. from (such time as) thou beginnest (to put) the sickle *to the corn*.
23:25(26). thou comest *into the standing corn of*
—(—). thou shalt not move a sickle unto thy neighbour's *standing corn*.
Jud.15: 5. go *into the standing corn of* the Philistines, and burnt up...*the standing corn*,
2K. 19:26. (as corn) blasted before *it be grown up*.
Isa. 17: 5. when the harvestman gathereth *the corn*,
37:27. (as corn) blasted before *it be grown up*.
Hos. 8: 7. it hath no *stalk:*

קִמּוֹשׁ *kim-mōhsh'*, & **קִימוֹשׁ** *kee-mōhsh'*, m. 7057

Isa. 34:13. *nettles* and brambles in the
Hos. 9: 6. *nettles* shall possess them:

קֶמַח *keh'-magh*, m. 7058

Gen18: 6. Make ready quickly three measures of fine *meal*,
Nu. 5:15. the tenth part of an ephah of barley *meal;*
Jud. 6:19. unleavened cakes of an ephah of *flour:*
1Sa. 1:24. one ephah of *flour*,
28:24. took *flour*, and kneaded (it),
2Sa.17:28. wheat, and barley, *and flour*,
1K. 4:22(5:2). threescore measures of *meal*,
17:12. an handful of *meal* in a barrel,
14. The barrel of *meal* shall not waste,
16. the barrel of *meal* wasted not,
2K. 4:41. But he said, Then bring *meal*.
1Ch 12:40. meat, *meal*, cakes of figs,
Isa. 47: 2. Take the millstones, and grind *meal:*
Hos. 8: 7. the bud shall yield no *meal:*

קָמַט [*kāh-mat'*]. 7059

* KAL.—*Future.* *

Job 16: 8. *And thou hast filled me with wrinkles*,

* PUAL.—*Preterite.* *

Job 22:16. Which *were cut down* out of time,

7060 קָמַל *kāh-mal'.*

* KAL.—*Preterite.* *

Isa. 19: 6. reeds and flags *shall wither.*
33: 9. is ashamed (and) *hewn down:* (marg. or, *withered away*)

7061 קָמַץ *kāh-matz'.*

* KAL.—*Preterite.* *

Lev. 2: 2. *and he shall take* thereout his handful
5:12. *and* the priest *shall take* his handful
Nu. 5:26. *And* the priest *shall take an handful*

7062 קֹמֶץ *kōh'-metz,* m.

Gen41:47. earth brought forth *by handfuls.*
Lev. 2: 2. shall take thereout *his handful*
5:12. shall take *his handful*
6:15(8). take of it *his handful,*

7063 קִמָּשׁוֹן [*kim-māh-shōhn'*], m.

Pro.24:31. all grown over with *thorns,*

7064 קֵן *kēhn,* m.

Gen 6:14. *rooms* (marg. *nests*) shalt thou make in
Nu. 24:21. thou puttest *thy nest* in a rock.
Deu22: 6. If a bird's *nest* chance to be
32:11. eagle stirreth up *her nest,*
Job 29:18. I shall die in *my nest,*
39:27. and make *her nest* on high?
Ps. 84: 3(4). the swallow *a nest* for herself,
Pro.27: 8. bird that wandereth from *her nest,*
Isa. 10:14. found *as a nest* the riches
16: 2. cast out of *the nest,*
Jer. 49:16. make *thy nest* as high as
Obad. 4. set *thy nest* among the stars,
Hab. 2: 9. may set *his nest* on high,

7065 קָנָא [*kāh-nāh'*].

* PIEL.—*Preterite.* *

Nu. 5:14, 14. *and he be jealous* of his wife,
30. *and he be jealous* over his wife,
25:13. *he was zealous* for his God,
Deu32:21. They *have moved me to jealousy*
1K. 19:10, 14. *I have been* very *jealous* for
Ps. 73: 3. For *I was envious* at the foolish,
Eze.39:25. *and will be jealous* for my
Zec. 1:14. *I am jealous* for Jerusalem
8: 2. *I was jealous* for Zion
— *I was jealous* for her with

PIEL.—*Infinitive.*

Nu. 25:11. *while he was zealous* for
2Sa.21: 2. sought to slay them *in his zeal*
1K. 19:10, 14. I have been *very* jealous (lit. *being jealous* I have been jealous)

PIEL.—*Future.*

Gen26:14. *and* the Philistines *envied* him.
30: 1. *And* when...Rachel *envied* her sister;
37:11. *And* his brethren *envied* him;
1K. 14:22. *and they provoked* him *to jealousy*
Ps. 37: 1. neither *be thou envious* against
106:16. *They envied* Moses *also* in the
Pro. 3:31. *Envy thou* not the oppressor,
23:17. *Let* not thine heart *envy*
24: 1. *Be* not *thou envious* against
19. neither *be thou envious* at the
Isa. 11:13. Ephraim *shall* not *envy* Judah,
Eze 31: 9. *so that* all the trees of Eden,...*envied him.*
Joel 2:18. *Then will* the Lord *be jealous*

PIEL.—*Participle.*

Nu. 11:29. *Enviest* thou for my sake?

* HIPHIL.—*Future.* *

Deu32:16. *They provoked him to jealousy*
21. I *will move them to jealousy*
Ps. 78:58. and *moved him to jealousy*

קְנָא [*k'nāh*], Ch. 7066

* P'AL.—*Future.* *

Ezr. 7:17. That *thou mayest buy* speedily

קַנָּא *kan-nāh',* adj. 7067

Ex. 20: 5. Lord thy God (am) a *jealous* God,
34:14. the Lord, whose name (is) *Jealous,* (is) a *jealous* God:
Deu 4:24. fire, (even) a *jealous* God.
5: 9. Lord thy God (am) a *jealous* God,
6:15. Lord thy God (is) a *jealous* God

קִנְאָה *kin-āh',* f. 7068

Nu. 5:14. And the spirit of *jealousy*
— if the spirit of *jealousy* come
15. it (is) an offering of *jealousy,*
18. which (is) the *jealousy* offering:
25. shall take the *jealousy* offering
29. This (is) the law of *jealousies,*
30. when the spirit of *jealousy* cometh upon
25:11. zealous *for my sake* (lit. *with my zeal*)
— consumed not the children of Israel *in my jealousy.*
Deu29:20(19). *and his jealousy* shall smoke
2K. 10:16. see *my zeal* for the Lord.
19:31. *the zeal of* the Lord (of hosts)
Job 5: 2. *and envy* (marg. or, *indignation*) slayeth
Ps. 69: 9(10). *the zeal of* thine house hath eaten
79: 5. shall *thy jealousy* burn like fire?
119:139. *My zeal* hath consumed me,
Pro. 6:34. *jealousy* (is) the rage of a man:
14:30. but *envy* the rottenness of the
27: 4. to stand before *envy?* (marg. or, *jealousy*)
Ecc. 4: 4. for this a man is *envied* of (marg. this (is) *the envy of* a man from) his neighbour
9: 6. their hatred, and *their envy,*
Cant.8: 6. *jealousy* (is) cruel as the grave:
Isa. 9: 7(6). *The zeal of* the Lord of hosts
11:13. *The envy* also *of* Ephraim
26:11. *for* (their) *envy at* the people;
37:32. *the zeal of* the Lord of hosts
42:13. stir up *jealousy* like a man
59:17. clad with *zeal* as a cloke.
63:15. where (is) *thy zeal* and thy strength,
Eze. 5:13. have spoken (it) *in my zeal,*
8: 3. the seat of the image of *jealousy,*
5. this image of *jealousy* in the entry.
16:38. blood in fury *and jealousy.*
42. and *my jealousy* shall depart
23:25. I will set *my jealousy* against
35:11. *and according to thine envy*
36: 5. in the fire of *my jealousy* have I spoken
6. *in my jealousy* and in my fury,
38:19. *For in my jealousy* (and) in the fire
Zep. 1:18. by the fire of *his jealousy:*
3: 8. with the fire of *my jealousy.*
Zec. 1:14. for Zion with *a* great *jealousy.*
8: 2. for Zion with great *jealousy,*

קָנָה *kāh-nāh'.* 7069

* KAL.—*Preterite.* *

Gen. 4: 1. *I have gotten* a man from the Lord.
25:10. Abraham *purchased* of the sons
47:22. land of the priests *bought he* not;
23. Behold, *I have bought* you this day
49:30 & 50:13. which Abraham *bought* with
Ex. 15:16. which *thou hast purchased.*
Lev.27:24. of whom *it was bought,*
Deu32: 6. thy father (that) *hath bought thee?*
Jos. 24:32. which Jacob *bought* of the sons
Ru. 4: 5. *thou must buy* (it) also of Ruth
9. that *I have bought* all that
10. *have I purchased* to be my
2Sa.12: 3. which *he had bought* and nourished
Neh. 5: 8. We after our ability *have redeemed*
16. neither *bought we* any land:
Ps. 74: 2. (which) *thou hast purchased*
78:54. his right hand *had purchased.*
139:13. For thou *hast possessed* my reins:

Pro. 8:22. The Lord *possessed me* in the
Ecc. 2: 7. *I got* (me) servants and maidens,
Isa. 43:24. *Thou hast bought* me no sweet
Jer. 13: 1. Go *and get* thee a linen girdle,
4. the girdle that *thou hast got*,
19: 1. Go *and get* a potter's earthen bottle,

KAL.—*Infinitive.*

Lev.25:14. or *buyest* (ought) of thy neighbour's
Ru. 4: 5. What day *thou buyest* the field
2Sa.24:21. *To buy* the threshingfloor of thee,
24. I will *surely* buy (it) of thee
2K. 12:12(13). *and to buy* timber and hewed stone
22: 6. *and to buy* timber and hewn stone
1Ch 21:24. I will *verily* buy it for the full
2Ch 34:11. *to buy* hewn stone, and timber
Pro. 16:16. better (is it) *to get* wisdom than gold? *and to get* understanding rather to be chosen
17:16. hand of a fool *to get* wisdom,
Isa. 11:11. the second time *to recover* the remnant
Jer. 32: 7. the right of redemption (is) thine *to buy*
Am. 8: 6. *That* we *may buy* the poor

KAL.—*Imperative.*

Gen47:19. *buy* us and our land for bread,
Ru. 4: 4. *Buy* (it) before the inhabitants,
8. said unto Boaz, *Buy* (it) for thee.
Pro. 4: 5. *Get* wisdom, *get* understanding: forget (it) not;
7. (therefore) *get* wisdom: and with all thy getting *get* understanding.
23:23. *Buy* the truth, and sell (it) not;
Jer. 32: 7. *Buy* thee my field that (is)
8. *Buy* my field, I pray thee,
— *buy* (it) for thyself.
25. *Buy* thee the field for money,

KAL.—*Future.*

Gen33:19. *And he bought* a parcel of a field,
39: 1. *and* Potiphar,...*bought him* of the hands
47:20. *And* Joseph *bought* all the land
Ex. 21: 2. If *thou buy* an Hebrew servant,
Lev.22:11. But if the priest *buy* (any) soul
25:15. *thou shalt buy* of thy neighbour,
44. of them *shall* ye *buy* bondmen
45. of them *shall ye buy*, and of their
2Sa.24:24. *I will* surely *buy* (it) of thee
— *So* David *bought* the threshingfloor
1K. 16:24. *And he bought* the hill Samaria
1Ch 21:24. *I will* verily *buy* it for the
Pro. 1: 5. a man of understanding *shall attain*
18:15. the prudent *getteth* knowledge;
Jer. 13: 2. *So I got* a girdle according to
32: 9. *And I bought* the field of
44. Men *shall buy* fields for money,

KAL.—*Participle.* Poel.

Gen14:19. high God, *possessor of* heaven and earth:
22. *the possessor of* heaven and earth,
Lev.25:28. hand of *him that hath bought*
30. *to him that bought* it throughout
50. *him that bought him* from
Deu28:68. and no man *shall buy* (you).
Pro.15:32. heareth reproof *getteth* understanding.
19: 8. He *that getteth* wisdom
20:14. it is naught, saith *the buyer*:
Isa. 1: 3. The ox knoweth *his owner*,
24: 2. as with *the buyer*, so with
Eze. 7:12. let not *the buyer* rejoice,
Zec.11: 5. *Whose possessors* slay them,

* NIPHAL.—*Preterite* *

Jer. 32:43. *And* fields *shall be bought*

NIPHAL.—*Future.*

Jer. 32:15. *shall be possessed* again in

* HIPHIL.—*Preterite.* *

Zec.13: 5. *taught me to keep cattle* from

7069 קָנָה [*kāh-nāh'*].

* HIPHIL.—*Participle.* *

Eze. 8: 3. which *provoketh to jealousy.*

7070 קָנֶה *kāh-neh'*, m.

Gen41: 5. came up *upon* one *stalk*,
22. came up *in* one *stalk*,
Ex. 25:31. his shaft, *and his branches*,
32. six *branches* shall come out of the sides of it; three *branches* of the candlestick
— and three *branches* of the candlestick
33. *in* one *branch*; and three bowls made like almonds *in the* other *branch*,
— so in *the* six *branches*
35. a knop under two *branches* of the same, and a knop under two *branches* of the same, and a knop under two *branches* of the same, according to *the* six *branches*
36. *and their branches* shall be of the same:
30:23. *and* of sweet *calamus* two hundred
37:17. his shaft, *and his branch*,
18. six *branches* going out of the sides
— three *branches* of the candlestick out of
— three *branches* of the candlestick out of
19. after the fashion of almonds *in* one *branch*,
— bowls made like almonds *in* another *branch*,
— so throughout *the* six *branches*
21. a knop under two *branches* of the same, and a knop under two *branches* of the same, and a knop under two *branches* of the same, according to *the* six *branches* going out of it.
22. *and their branches* were of the same:
1K. 14:15. as *a reed* is shaken in the water,
2K. 18:21. the staff of this bruised *reed*,
Job 31:22. be broken *from the bone.* (marg. or, *the chanelbone*)
40:21. in the covert of *the reed*,
Ps. 68:30(31). Rebuke the company of *spearmen*, (marg. or, the beasts of *the reeds*)
Cant.4:14. Spikenard and saffron; *calamus* and cinnamon,
Isa. 19: 6. *the reeds* and flags shall wither.
35: 7. where each lay, (shall be) grass *with reeds*
36: 6. staff of this broken *reed*,
42: 3. *A* bruised *reed* shall he not break,
43:24. Thou hast bought me no sweet *cane*
46: 6. weigh silver *in the balance*,
Jer. 6:20. *and the* sweet *cane* from a
Eze.27:19. cassia, *and calamus*, were in thy market.
29: 6. been a staff of *reed* to the
40: 3. *and a* measuring *reed*; and he stood
5. *a* measuring *reed* of six cubits
— breadth of the building, one *reed*; and the height, one *reed*.
6. threshold of the gate, (which was) one *reed*
— (the gate, which was) one *reed* broad.
7. chamber (was) one *reed* long, *and* one *reed* broad;
— porch of the gate within (was) one *reed*.
8. porch of the gate within, one *reed*.
41: 8. *a* full *reed* of six great cubits.
42:16. measured...*with the* measuring *reed*, five hundred *reeds*, *with the* measuring *reed*
17, 18, 19. five hundred *reeds*, *with the* measuring *reed*

קַנּוֹא *kan-nōh'*, adj. 7072

Jos. 24:19. he (is) a *jealous* God;
Nah 1: 2. God (is) *jealous*, and the Lord

קִנְיָן *kin-yāhn'*, m. 7075

Gen31:18. the cattle of *his getting*,
34:23. (Shall) not their cattle *and their substance*
36: 6. all his beasts, and all *his substance*,
Lev.22:11. buy (any) soul *with*)(his money, (marg. *the purchase of* his money)
Jos. 14: 4. their cattle *and for their substance.*
Ps.104:24. is full of *thy riches.*
105:21. ruler of all *his substance*: (marg. *possession*)
Pro. 4: 7. and with all *thy getting*
Eze.38:12. which have gotten cattle *and goods*,
13. to take away cattle *and goods*,

קִנָּמוֹן *kin-nāh-mōhn'*, m. 7076

Ex. 30:23. *and* of sweet *cinnamon* half so much,
Pro. 7:17. myrrh, aloes, *and cinnamon.*
Cant.4:14. calamus *and cinnamon*,

7077 קָנַן [kāh-nan'].

* PIEL.—*Preterite.* *

Isa. 34:15. *shall* the great owl *make her nest*,
Eze.31: 6. *made their nests* in his boughs,

PIEL.—*Future.*

Ps. 104:17. the birds *make their nests* :
Jer. 48:28. the dove (that) *maketh her nest*

* PUAL.—*Participle.* *

Jer. 22:23. *that makest thy nest* in the

See 7093 קִנְצֵי see קֵץ

7080 קָסַם [kāh-sam'].

* KAL.—*Infinitive.* *

Eze.21:21(26). *to use* divination:
23(28). be unto them *as a false divination*
29(34). *whiles they divine* a lie unto thee,
Mic. 3: 6. *that* ye *shall not divine* ;

KAL.—*Imperative.*

1Sa.28: 8. *divine* unto me by the familiar spirit,

KAL.—*Future.*

2K. 17:17. *and used* divination and enchantments,
Eze.13:23. nor *divine* divinations:
Mic. 3:11. the prophets thereof *divine* for money:

KAL.—*Participle.* Poel.

Deu 18:10. (or) *that useth* divination,
14. hearkened unto observers of times, and unto *diviners* :
Jos. 13:22. Balaam also...*the soothsayer*, (marg. or, *diviner*)
1Sa. 6: 2. the priests *and the diviners*,
Isa. 3: 2. the prophet, *and the prudent*,
44:25. *and* maketh *diviners* mad ;
Jer. 27: 9. nor to *your diviners*,
29: 8. Let not your prophets *and your diviners*,
Eze.13: 9. *and that divine* lies:
22:28. *and divining* lies unto them,
Mic. 3: 7. and *the diviners* confounded:
Zec.10: 2. *and the diviners* have seen a lie,

7081 קֶסֶם keh'-sem, m.

Nu. 22: 7. *with the rewards of divination* in their
23:23. any *divination* against Israel:
Deu 18:10. (or) that useth *divination*,
1Sa.15:23. rebellion (is as) the sin of *witchcraft*, (marg. *divination*)
2K. 17:17. used *divination* and enchantments,
Pro.16:10. *A divine sentence* (marg. *Divination*) (is) in the lips
Jer. 14:14. a false vision *and divination*,
Eze.13: 6. vanity *and* lying *divination*,
23. *nor* divine *divinations* :
21:21(26). to use *divination* :
22(27). *the divination for* Jerusalem,

7082 קָסַס [kāh-sas'].

* POEL.—*Future.* *

Eze.17: 9. and *cut off* the fruit thereof,

7083 קֶסֶת keh'-seth, f.

Eze. 9: 2. *with* a writer's *inkhorn* by his side:
3. the writer's *inkhorn* by his side ;
11. which (had) *the inkhorn* by his side,

7085 קַעֲקַע kah-ⁿgăkaⁿg', m.

Lev.19:28. nor print any *marks* (lit. the inscription of *a mark*)

7086 קְעָרָה k'ⁿgāh-rāh', f.

Ex. 25:29. thou shalt make *the dishes thereof*,
37:16. *his dishes*, and his spoons,
Nu. 4: 7. and put thereon *the dishes*,
7:13. his offering (was) one silver *charger*,
19. his offering one silver *charger*,
25. His offering (was) one silver *charger*,
31, 37, 43, 49, 55, 61, 67, 73, 79. His offering (was) one silver *charger*
84. twelve *chargers* of silver,
85. Each *charger* of silver (weighing)

קָפָא [kāh-phāh']. 7087

* KAL.—*Preterite.* *

Ex. 15: 8. the depths *were congealed* in the heart

KAL.—*Future.*

Zec.14: 6. (כתיב) shall not be clear, (nor) *dark* :

KAL.—*Participle.* Poel.

Zep. 1:12. men *that are settled* (marg. *curded*, or, *thickened*) on their lees:

* HIPHIL.—*Future.* *

Job 10:10. and *curdled me* like cheese?

קִפָּאוֹן kip-pāh-ōhn', m. 7087

Zec.14: 6. the light shall not be clear, *nor dark* :

קָפַד [kāh-phad']. 7088

* PIEL.—*Preterite.* *

Isa. 38:12. *I have cut off* like a weaver my life :

קִפֹּד kip-pōhd', m. 7090

Isa. 14:23. make it a possession for *the bittern*,
34:11. *the bittern* shall possess it;
Zep. 2:14. the cormorant and *the bittern* shall lodge

קְפָדָה k'phāh'-dāh, m. 7089

Eze. 7:25. *Destruction* (marg. *Cutting off*) cometh ;

קִפּוֹז kip-pōhz', m. 7091

Isa. 34:15. There shall *the great owl* make her nest,

קָפַץ kāh-phatz'. 7092

* KAL.—*Preterite.* *

Job 5:16. iniquity *stoppeth* her mouth.
Ps. 77: 9(10). *hath he* in anger *shut up* his tender
107:42. iniquity *shall stop* her mouth.

KAL.—*Future.*

Deu15: 7. nor *shut* thine hand from thy poor
Isa. 52:15. kings *shall shut* their mouths

* NIPHAL.—*Future.* *

Job 24:24. *they are taken out of the way* (marg. *closed up*)

* PIEL.—*Participle.* *

Cant.2: 8. *skipping* upon the hills.

קֵץ kēhtz, m. 7093

Gen. 4: 3. And *in process of* time (marg. *at the end* of days)
6:13. *The end of* all flesh is come
8: 6. *at the end of* forty days,
16: 3. *after* Abram had dwelt
41: 1. *at the end of* two full years,
Ex. 12:41. *at the end of* the four hundred and thirty
Nu. 13:25. of the land *after* forty days.
Deu. 9:11. *at the end of* forty days
15: 1 & 31:10. *At the end of* (every) seven years
Jud.11:39. *at the end of* two months,
2Sa.14:26. *at* every year's *end* that he polled
15: 7. it came to pass *after* forty years,
1K. 2:39. *at the end of* three years,
17: 7. *after* a while, (marg. *at the end of* days)
2K. 19:23. into the lodgings of *his borders*,
2Ch 8: 1. came to pass *at the end of* twenty years,
18: 2. *after* (certain) years (marg. *at the end of* years)

2Ch 21:19. after *the end of* two years,
Neh13: 6. *and after* certain days (marg. *at the end of* days)
Est. 2:12. *after* that she had been
Job 6:11. and what (is) *mine end,*
16: 3. Shall vain words have *an end?*
18: 2. make *an end of* words ?
22: 5. and thine iniquities in*finite?* (lit. no *end* to thine iniquities)
28: 3. He setteth *an end* to darkness,
Ps. 39: 4(5). make me to know *mine end,*
119:96. I have seen *an end* of all
Ecc. 4: 8. no *end* of all his labour;
16. no *end* of all the people,
12:12. making many books there is no *end;*
Isa. 9: 7(6). and peace (there shall be) no *end,*
23:15, 17. *after the end of* seventy years
37:24. into the height of *his border,*
Jer. 13: 6. *after* many days,
34:14. *At the end of* seven years
42: 7. it came to pass *after* ten days, that
50:26. *from the utmost border,* (marg. *end*)
51:13. *thine end* is come,
Lam.4:18. *our end* is near,
— *our end* is come.
Eze. 7: 2. thus saith the Lord...*An end, the end* is
3. Now (is) *the end* (come) upon thee,
6. *An end* is come, *the end* is come:
21:25(30). when iniquity (shall have) *an end,*
29(34). their iniquity (shall have) *an end.*
29:13. *At the end of* forty years
35: 5. iniquity (had) *an end:*
Dan. 8:17. for at the time of *the end*
19. at the time appointed *the end* (shall be).
9:26. *and the end thereof* (shall be) with a flood, and unto *the end of* the war
11: 6. *And in the end of* years
13. come *after* certain years (marg. *at the end of* times, even years)
27. for yet *the end* (shall be) at the time
35. to the time of *the end:*
40. at the time of *the end*
45. he shall come to *his end,*
12: 4. to the time of *the end:*
6. How long (shall it be to) *the end of*
9. sealed till the time of *the end.*
13. go thou thy way *till the end* (be):
— *at the end of* the days.
Am. 8: 2. *The end* is come upon my people
Hab. 2: 3. *at the end* it shall speak,

7094 ## קָצַב [*kāh-tzav'*].

* KAL.—*Future.* *

2K. 6: 6. *And he cut down* a stick,

KAL.—*Participle.* Paül.

Cant.4: 2. a flock (of sheep that are even) *shorn,*

7095 ## קֶצֶב *keh'-tzev,* m.

1K. 6:25. one measure *and* one *size.*
7:37. one measure, (and) one *size.*
Jon. 2: 6(7). I went down *to the bottoms* (marg. *cuttings off*) *of* the mountains;

7096 ## קָצָה [*kāh-tzāh'*].

* KAL.—*Infinitive.* *

Hab. 2:10. *by cutting off* many people

* PIEL.—*Infinitive.* *

2K. 10:32. began *to cut* Israel *short:* (marg. *to cut off the ends*)

PIEL.—*Participle.*

Pro.26: 6. by the hand of a fool *cutteth off* the feet,

* HIPHIL.—*Preterite.* *

Lev.14:41. the dust that *they scrape off*

HIPHIL.—*Infinitive.*

Lev.14:43. after *he hath scraped* (lit. after *scraping*)

7098 ## קָצָה *kāh-tzāh',* f.

Ex. 25:18. in *the* two *ends of* the mercy seat.
19. one cherub *on the* one *end,* and the other cherub *on the* other *end*·
Ex. 25:19. on *the* two *ends thereof.*
26: 4. *from the selvedge* in the coupling;
27: 4. in *the* four *corners thereof.*
28: 7. at *the* two *edges thereof;*
23. on *the* two *ends of* the breastplate.
24. on *the ends of* the breastplate.
25. And *the* (other) two *ends of*
26. upon *the* two *ends of*
36:11. *from the selvedge* in the coupling:
37: 7. *the* two *ends of* the mercy seat;
8. One cherub *on the end* on this side, and another cherub *on the* (other) *end*
— on *the* two *ends thereof.*
39: 4. by *the* two *edges* was it coupled
16. in *the* two *ends of* the breastplate.
17. on *the ends of* the breastplate.
18. *the* two *ends of* the two wreathen chains
19. on *the* two *ends of* the breastplate,
Jud.18: 2. five men *from their coasts,*
1K. 6:24. *from the uttermost part of* the one wing unto *the uttermost part of*
12:31. priests *of the lowest of* the people,
13:33. *of the lowest of* the people priests
2K. 17:32. made...*of the lowest of them* priests
Job 26:14. these (are) *parts of* his ways:
28:24. he looketh *to the ends of* the earth,
Ps. 19: 6(7). his circuit unto *the ends of it:*
Isa. 40:28. the Creator of *the ends of* the earth,
41: 5. *the ends of* the earth were afraid,
9. *from the ends of* the earth,
Jer. 49:36. from *the* four *quarters of* heaven,
Eze. 15: 4. the fire devoureth both *the ends of it,*

קָצֶה *kāh-tzeh',* m. 7097

Gen. 8: 3. *after the end of* the hundred and fifty
19: 4. all the people *from* every *quarter:*
23: 9. *in the end of* his field;
47: 2. *And* he took *some of* his brethren,
21. *from* (one) *end of* the borders of Egypt even to *the* (other) *end thereof.*
Ex. 13:20. *in the edge of* the wilderness.
16:35. *the borders of* the land
19:12. or touch *the border of it:*
26: 5. shalt thou make *in the edge of*
28. the boards shall reach from *end* to *end.*
36:12. *in the edge of* the curtain
33. from *the* one *end* to *the other.* (lit. *from end* to *end*)
Nu. 11: 1. *in the uttermost parts of* the camp.
20:16. *the uttermost of* thy border:
22:36. which (is) *in the utmost* coast.
41. *the utmost part of* the people.
23:13. *the utmost part of* them,
33: 6. Etham, which (is) *in the edge of* the
37. Hor, *in the edge of* the land of Edom.
34: 3. the *outmost coast of* the salt sea
Deu. 4:32. *from the* one *side of* heaven unto *the other,* (lit. unto *side*)
13: 7(8). *from the* (one) *end of* the earth even unto *the* (other) *end of* the earth;
14:28. *At the end of* three years
28:49. *from the end of* the earth,
64. *from the* one *end of* the earth even unto *the other;* (lit. to *the end of* the earth)
30: 4. *unto the utmost* (parts) *of* heaven,
Jos. 3: 2. came to pass *after* three days,
8. When ye are come to *the brink of*
15. were dipped *in the brim of*
4:19. *in the* east *border of* Jericho.
9:16. *at the end of* three days
13:27. unto *the edge of* the sea
15: 1. *the uttermost part of* the south coast.
2. *from the shore of* the salt sea,
5. unto *the end of* Jordan.
— *the uttermost part of* Jordan:
8. *at the end of* the valley
21. *the uttermost* cities of the tribe
18:15. *from the end of* Kirjath-jearim,
16. *the end of* the mountain
19. at *the* south *end of* Jordan:
Jud. 6:21. put forth *the end of* the staff
7:11. *the outside of* the armed men
17. *to the outside of* the camp,
19. *unto the outside of* the camp
Ru. 3: 7. *at the end of* the heap of corn:
1Sa. 9:27. going down *to the end of* the city,

1Sa.14: 2. *in the uttermost part of* Gibeah
27. he put forth *the end of* the rod
43. *with the end of* the rod
2Sa.24: 8. *at the end of* nine months
1K. 9:10. *at the end of* twenty years,
2K. 7: 5, 8. *the uttermost part of* the camp
8: 3. *at the* seven years' *end*,
18:10. *at the end of* three years
Neh. 1: 9. *unto the uttermost part of* the heaven,
Ps. 19: 4(5). *and* their words *to the end of* the world.
6(7). *from the end of* the heaven,
46: 9(10). *the end of* the earth ;
61: 2(3). *From the end of* the earth
135: 7. *from the ends of* the earth ;
Pro.17:24. *in the ends of* the earth.
Isa. 5:26. *from the end of* the earth:
7: 3. at *the end of* the conduit
18. *in the uttermost part of* the
13: 5. *from the end of* heaven,
42:10. *from the end of* the earth,
43: 6. *from the ends of* the earth ;
48:20. to *the end of* the earth ;
49: 6. unto *the end of* the earth.
56:11. every one for his gain, *from his quarter.*
62:11. unto *the end of* the world,
Jer. 10:13. *from the ends of* the earth ;
12:12. *from the* (one) *end of* the land even to *the* (other) *end of* the land:
25:31. to *the ends of* the earth ;
33. *from* (one) *end of* the earth even unto *the* (other) *end of* the earth:
51:16. *from the ends of* the earth:
31. his city is taken *at* (one) *end*,
Eze. 3:16. *at the end of* seven days,
25: 9. cities (which are) *on his frontiers*,
33: 2. take a man *of their coasts*,
39:14. *after the end of* seven months
48: 1. *From the* north *end* to the coast

7097 ## קֵצֶה *kēh'-tzeh*, m.

Isa. 2: 7. neither (is there any) *end* of their treasures ;
— neither (is there any) *end* of their
Nah. 2: 9(10). none *end* of the store
3: 3. none *end* of (their) corpses ;
9. and (it was) in*finite* ; (lit. no *end*)

7099 ## קֶצֶו [*keh'-tzev*], m.

Ps. 48:10(11). unto *the ends of* the earth:
65: 5(6). all *the ends of* the earth,
Isa. 26:15. all *the ends of* the earth.

7099 ## קִצְוָה [*kitz-vāh'*], f.

Ex. 37: 8. (כתיב) cherubims on *the* two *ends thereof.*
38: 5. four rings for *the* four *ends*
Ps. 39: 4. (כתיב) by *the* two *edges* was it coupled
65: 8(9). dwell in *the uttermost parts*

7100 ## קֶצַח *keh'-tzagh*, m.

Isa. 28:25. cast abroad *the fitches*,
27. For *the fitches* are not threshed
— but *the fitches* are beaten

7101 ## קָצִין *kāh-tzeen'*, m.

Jos. 10:24. and said unto *the captains of*
Jud.11: 6. and be our *captain*, (lit. *for captain* to us)
11. made him head *and captain*
Pro. 6: 7. Which having no *guide*,
25:15. By long forbearing is *a prince* persuaded,
Isa. 1:10. *ye rulers of* Sodom ;
3: 6. be thou our *ruler*,
7. *a ruler of* the people.
22: 3. All *thy rulers* are fled
Dan11:18. *a prince* for his own behalf
Mic. 3: 1. *and ye princes of* the house of Israel ;
9. *and princes of* the house of Israel,

7102 ## קְצִיעוֹת *k'tzee-gōhth'*, f. pl.

Ps. 45: 8(9). All thy garments (smell) of myrrh, and aloes, (and) *cassia*,

---

קָצִיר *kāh-tzeer'*, m. 7105

Gen 8:22. seedtime *and harvest*,
30:14. in the days of wheat *harvest*,
45: 6. (there shall) neither (be) earing *nor harvest.*
Ex. 23:16. the feast of *harvest*,
34:21. in earing time *and in harvest*
22. the firstfruits of wheat *harvest*,
Lev.19: 9. when ye reap *the harvest of* your land,
— the gleanings of *thy harvest.*
23:10. shall reap *the harvest thereof*,
— the firstfruits of *your harvest*
22. when ye reap *the harvest of* your land,
— any gleaning of *thy harvest:*
25: 5. That which groweth of its own accord of *thy harvest*
Deu24:19. When thou cuttest down *thine harvest*
Jos. 3:15. all the time of *harvest*,
Jud.15: 1. in the time of wheat *harvest*,
Ru. 1:22. in the beginning of barley *harvest.*
2:21. until they have ended all my *harvest.*
23. unto the end of barley *harvest* and of wheat *harvest ;*
1Sa. 6:13. reaping their wheat *harvest*
8:12. to reap *his harvest*,
12:17. (Is it) not wheat *harvest* to day ?
2Sa.21: 9. were put to death in the days of *harvest*,
— in the beginning of barley *harvest.*
10. from the beginning of *harvest*
23:13. came to David in *the harvest time*
Job 5: 5. Whose (lit. who *his*) *harvest* the hungry eateth
14: 9. will bud, and bring forth *boughs*
18:16. above shall *his branch* be cut off.
29:19. the dew lay all night *upon my branch.*
Ps. 80:11(12). She sent out *her boughs* unto the sea,
Pro. 6: 8. gathereth her food *in the harvest*
10: 5. he that sleepeth *in harvest*
20: 4. (therefore) shall he beg *in harvest*,
25:13. the cold of snow in the time of *harvest*,
26: 1. as rain *in harvest*,
Isa. 9: 3(2). according to the joy *in harvest*,
16: 9. *thy harvest* is fallen.
17: 5. when *the harvestman* gathereth
11. *the harvest* (shall be) a heap
18: 4. like a cloud of dew in the heat of *harvest.*
5. For afore *the harvest*,
23: 3. *the harvest of* the river,
27:11. When *the boughs thereof* are withered,
Jer. 5:17. they shall eat up *thine harvest*,
24. the appointed weeks of *the harvest.*
8:20. *The harvest* is past,
50:16. in the time of *harvest :*
51:33. the time of her *harvest* shall come.
Hos. 6:11. he hath set *an harvest* for thee,
Joel 1:11. *the harvest of* the field is perished.
3:13(4:13). *the harvest* is ripe:
Am. 4: 7. (there were) yet three months *to the harvest:*

קָצַע [*kāh-tzag'*]. 7106

* HIPHIL.—*Future.* *

Lev.14:41. *he shall cause* the house *to be scraped*

* HOPHAL.—*Participle.* *

Eze.46:22. these four *corners* (marg. *cornered*) (were) of one measure.

קָצַף *kāh-tzaph'*. 7107

* KAL.—*Preterite.* *

Gen41:10. Pharaoh *was wroth* with his servants,
Deu 9:19. the Lord *was wroth* against you
Est. 2:21. two of the king's chamberlains,...*were wroth*,
Isa. 47: 6. *I was wroth* with my people,
57:17. For the iniquity of his covetousness *was I wroth*,
64: 5(4). behold, thou *art wroth ;*
Lam. 5:22. *thou art* very *wroth* against us.
Zec. 1: 2. The Lord *hath been* sore *displeased*
15. I *was* but a little *displeased*,

KAL.—*Infinitive.*

Isa. 54: 9. *that I would not be wroth* with thee,

KAL.—*Future.*

Gen40: 2. *And* Pharaoh *was wroth* against
Ex. 16:20. *and* Moses *was wroth* with them.
Lev.10: 6. *lest wrath come* upon all the people:
16. *and he was angry* with Eleazar and
Nu. 16:22. *wilt thou be wroth* with all the congregation?
31:14. *And* Moses *was wroth* with the officers
Deu 1:34. *and was wroth*, and sware, saying,
Jos. 22:18. to morrow *he will be wroth*
1Sa.29: 4. *And* the princes of the Philistines *were wroth*
2K. 5:11. *But* Naaman *was wroth*, and went away,
13:19. *And* the man of God *was wroth*
Est. 1:12. *therefore was* the king very *wroth*,
Ecc. 5: 6(5). wherefore *should* God *be angry* at thy
Isa. 57:16. neither *will I be* always *wroth:*
17. I hid me, *and was wroth*,
64: 9(8). *Be* not *wroth* very sore,
Jer. 37:15. *Wherefore* the princes *were wroth*

KAL.—*Participle.* Poel.

Zec. 1:15. I am very sore *displeased*

* HIPHIL.—*Preterite.* *

Deu 9: 7. *thou provokedst* the Lord thy God *to wrath*
8. *ye provoked* the Lord *to wrath*,

HIPHIL.—*Infinitive.*

Zec. 8:14. *when* your fathers *provoked* me *to wrath*,

HIPHIL.—*Future.*

Ps.106:32. *They angered* (him) *also* at the waters of

HIPHIL.—*Participle.*

Deu 9:22. ye *provoked* (lit. were *provoking*) the Lord to wrath.

* HITHPAEL.—*Preterite.* *

Isa. 8:21. *that* when...*they shall fret themselves*, and

7108 **קְצַף** *k'tzaph*, Ch.

* P'AL.—*Preterite.* *

Dan 2:12. the king was angry *and* very *furious*,

7110 **קֶצֶף** *keh'-tzeph*, m.

Nu. 1:53. that there be no *wrath* upon
16:46(17:11). there is *wrath* gone out from the
18: 5. that there be no *wrath* any more
Deu 29:28(27). in wrath, *and in* great *indignation*,
Jos. 9:20. lest *wrath* be upon us,
22:20. *wrath* fell on all the congregation
2K. 3:27. there was great *indignation* against Israel:
1Ch 27:24. there fell *wrath*...against Israel;
2Ch 19: 2. therefore (is) *wrath* upon thee from
10. and (so) *wrath* come upon you,
24:18. *wrath* came upon Judah
29: 8. *the wrath of* the Lord was upon Judah
32:25. therefore there was *wrath* upon him,
26. *the wrath of* the Lord came not
Est. 1:18. (shall there arise) too much contempt *and wrath*.
Ps. 38: 1(2). O Lord, rebuke me not *in thy wrath:*
102:10(11). Because of thine indignation *and thy wrath:*
Ecc. 5:17(16). (he hath) much sorrow and *wrath*
Isa. 34: 2. *the indignation* of the Lord
54: 8. In *a* little *wrath* I hid my face
60:10. *in my wrath* I smote thee,
Jer. 10:10. *at his wrath* the earth shall tremble,
21: 5. in fury, *and in* great *wrath*.
32:37. in my fury, *and in* great *wrath;*
50:13. *Because of the wrath of* the Lord
Hos.10: 7. *as the foam* upon the water.
Zec. 1: 2. The Lord hath been *sore* (marg. with *displeasure*) displeased
15. I am *very sore* displeased (lit. I am displeased with great *displeasure*)
7:12. therefore came *a* great *wrath* from the

7109 **קְצַף** *k'tzaph*, Ch. m.

Ezr. 7:23. why should there be *wrath* against

קְצָפָה *k'tzāh-phāh'*, f. 7111

Joel 1: 7. He hath laid my vine waste, and *bark*ed my fig tree: (marg. (laid) my fig tree *for a barking*)

קָצַץ [*kāh-tzatz'*]. 7112

* KAL.—*Preterite.* *

Deu25:12. *Then thou shalt cut off* her hand,

KAL.—*Participle.* Paül.

Jer. 9:26(25) & 25:23 & 49:32. (that are) in the *utmost* corners, (marg. *cut off into* corners)

* PIEL.—*Preterite.* *

Ex. 39: 3. *and cut* (it into) wires,
2K. 18:16. *cut off* (the gold from) the doors
Ps. 46: 9(10). breaketh the bow, *and cutteth* the spear *in sunder;*
129: 4. *he hath cut asunder* the cords

PIEL.—*Future.*

Jud. 1: 6. *and cut off* his thumbs
2Sa. 4:12. *and cut off* their hands
2K. 16:17. *And* king Ahaz *cut off* the borders of the
24:13. *and cut in pieces* all the vessels of gold
2Ch 28:24. *and cut in pieces* the vessels

* PUAL.—*Participle.* *

Jud. 1: 7. *having*...their great toes *cut off*,

קְצַץ [*k'tzatz*], Ch. 7113

* PAEL.—*Preterite.* *

Dan. 4:14(11). *and cut off* his branches,

קָצַר *kāh-tzar'*. 7114

* KAL.—*Preterite.* *

Lev.23:10. *and shall reap* the harvest
Isa. 28:20. the bed *is shorter* than
50: 2. *Is* my hand *shortened* at all,
59: 1. the Lord's hand *is* not *shortened*,
Jer. 12:13. have sown wheat, but *shall reap* thorns:
Hos 10:13. *ye have reaped* iniquity;
Mic. 2: 7. *is* the spirit of the Lord *straitened?* (marg. or, *shortened*)

KAL.—*Infinitive.*

Lev.19: 9. *And when ye reap* the harvest of your land, thou shalt not wholly *reap* the corners
23:22. *And when ye reap* the harvest
— thou shalt not make clean riddance...*when thou reapest*,
1Sa. 8:12. *to reap* his harvest,
Isa. 50: 2. Is my hand shortened *at all*, (lit. *shortening* is it shortened)

KAL.—*Imperative.*

2K. 19:29. in the third year sow ye, *and reap*,
Isa. 37:30. in the third year sow ye, *and reap*,
Hos 10:12. *reap* in mercy;

KAL.—*Future.*

Lev.25: 5. That which groweth of its own accord... *thou shalt* not *reap*,
11. neither *reap* that which groweth of itself
Nu. 11:23. *Is* the Lord's hand *waxed short?*
21: 4. *and* the soul of the people *was much discouraged* (marg. *shortened*, or, *grieved*)
Deu24:19. When *thou cuttest down* thine harvest
Jud 10:16. *and* his soul *was grieved* (marg. *shortened*) for the misery of Israel.
16:16. (so) *that* his soul *was vexed* (marg. *id.*) unto death;
Ru. 2: 9. the field that *they do reap*,
Job 4: 8. they that...sow wickedness, *reap the same.*
21: 4. why *should* not my spirit *be troubled?* (marg. *shortened.*)
24: 6. *They reap* (every one) his corn
Ps.126: 5. They that sow in tears *shall reap* in joy.
Pro.10:27. the years of the wicked *shall be shortened.*
22: 8. He that soweth iniquity *shall reap* vanity:
Ecc.11: 4. he that regardeth the clouds *shall* not *reap.*

Isa. 17: 5. *reapeth* the ears with his arm;
Hos. 8: 7. *they shall reap* the whirlwind:
Mic. 6:15. Thou shalt sow, but *thou shalt* not *reap;*
Zec 11: 8. *and* my soul *lothed them,*

KAL.—*Participle.* Poel.

Ru. 2: 3. gleaned in the field after *the reapers:*
4. Boaz...said *unto the reapers,*
5. his servant that was set over *the reapers,*
6. the servant that was set over *the reapers*
7. let me glean and gather after *the reapers*
14. she sat beside *the reapers:*
1Sa. 6:13. *reaping* their wheat harvest
2K. 4:18. he went out to his father to *the reapers.*
Ps. 129: 7. Wherewith *the mower* filleth not his hand;
Jer. 9:22(21). as the handful after *the harvestman,*
Am. 9:13. the plowman shall overtake *the reaper,*

KAL.—*Participle.* Paül.

Eze. 42: 5. the upper chambers (were) *shorter:*

* PIEL.—*Preterite.* *

Ps. 102:23(24). *he shortened* my days.

* HIPHIL.—*Preterite.* *

Ps. 89:45(46). days of his youth *hast thou shortened:*

HIPHIL.—*Future.*

Job 24: 6. (כתיב) *They reap* (every one) his corn

7116 קָצֵר [*kāh-tzēhr'*], adj.

2K 19:26. their inhabitants were of *small* power, (marg. *short of* hand)
Job 14: 1. Man...(is) of *few* days, (marg. *short of* days)
Pro. 14:17. (He that is) *soon* angry (lit. *short of* nostrils) dealeth foolishly:
29. *but* (he that is) *hasty of* (marg. *short of*) spirit
Isa. 37:27. their inhabitants (were) of *small* power, (marg. *id.*)

7115 קֹצֶר *kōh'-tzer*, m.

Ex. 6: 9. they hearkened not...*for anguish of* spirit, (marg. *shortness*, or, *straitness*)

7117 קְצָת *k'tzāhth*, f.

Neh. 7:70. *And some* (marg. *part*) *of* the chief of the
Dan. 1: 2. *with part of* the vessels of the house
5. *that at the end thereof*
15. *And at the end of* ten days
18. *Now at the end of* the days

7118 קְצָת *k'tzāhth*, Ch. f.

Dan. 2:42. (so) the kingdom shall be *part*ly strong,
4:29(26). *At the end of* twelve months
34(31). *And at the end of* the days

7119 קַר *kar*, adj.

Pro. 17:27. (כתיב) is of an *excellent* (marg. or, *cool*) spirit.
25:25. *cold* waters to a thirsty soul,
Jer. 18:14. shall the *cold* flowing waters...be forsaken?

7120 קֹר *kōhr*, m.

Gen 8:22. *and cold* and heat, and summer and winter,

7121 קָרָא *kāh-rāh'*.

* KAL.—*Preterite.* *

Gen 1: 5. the darkness *he called* Night.
10. the gathering together of the waters *called he* Seas:
11: 9. Therefore *is* the name of it *called* Babel;
16:11. *and shalt call* his name Ishmael;
14. the well *was called* Beer-lahai-roi;
17:19. *and thou shalt call* his name Isaac:
19:22. the name of the city *was called* Zoar.
21:31. *he called* that place Beer-sheba;
25:30. therefore *was* his name *called* Edom.
26:18. by which his father *had called* them.
Gen27:36. *Is* not he rightly *named* Jacob?
29:34. therefore *was* his name *called* Levi.
35. *she called* his name Judah;
30: 6. therefore *called she* his name Dan.
31:47. Jacob *called it* Galeed.
48. Therefore *was* the name of it *called*
33:17. the name of the place *is called* Succoth.
35:18. his father *called* him Benjamin.
41:52. the name of the second *called he* Ephraim:
50:11. the name of it *was called* Abel-mizraim,
Ex. 2: 7. Shall I go *and call* to thee a nurse
15:23. the name of it *was called* Marah.
31: 2. *I have called* by name Bezaleel
33: 7. *and called* it the Tabernacle of the
19. *and I will proclaim* the name of the Lord
34:15. *and* (one) *call* thee, and thou eat of his
35:30. the Lord *hath called* by name Bezaleel
Lev. 9: 1. Moses *called* Aaron and his sons,
23:21. *And ye shall proclaim* on the selfsame
25:10. *and proclaim* liberty throughout (all) the
Nu. 13:24. The place *was called* the brook Eshcol,
24:10. *I called thee* to curse mine enemies,
Deu 15: 2. *it is called* the Lord's release.
9. *and he cry* unto the Lord
17:19. *and he shall read* therein all the days of
20:10. *then proclaim* peace unto it.
25: 8. *Then* the elders of his city *shall call* him,
Jos. 7:26. the name of that place *was called*, The valley of Achor,
8:34. *he read* all the words of the law,
35. was not a word...which Joshua *read* not
Jud. 12: 1. *didst* not *call* us to go with thee?
14:15. *have ye called* us to take that we have?
15:19. *he called* the name...En-hakkore,
18:12. *they called* that place Mahaneh-dan
1Sa. 3: 5. for *thou calledst* me. And he said, *I called* not;
6. *thou didst call* me. And he answered, *I called* not, my son;
8. for *thou didst call* me.
9:24. *I have invited* the people.
16: 3. *And call* Jesse to the sacrifice,
23:28. *they called* that place Sela-hammahlekoth.
26:14. Who (art) thou (that) *criest* to the king?
2Sa. 5:20. *he called* the name of that place Baal-perazim.
1K. 1:10. Solomon his brother, *he called* not.
19. Solomon thy servant *hath he* not *called.*
26. thy servant Solomon, *hath he* not *called.*
13: 4. the man of God, which *had cried*
32. For the saying which *he cried*
18:24. *And call ye* on the name of your gods,
21:12. *They proclaimed* a fast,
2K. 3:10, 13. the Lord *hath called* these three kings
5:11. *and call* on the name of the Lord his God,
8: 1. the Lord *hath called* for a famine;
9: 1. Elisha the prophet *called* one of the
22:16. which the king of Judah *hath read:*
23:16. the man of God *proclaimed*, who *proclaimed* these words.
1Ch 4: 9. his mother *called* his name Jabez,
11: 7. *they called* it the city of David.
14:11. *they called* the name of that place
2Ch 20:26. the name of the same place *was called*,
34:24. *they have read* before the king
Est. 6: 9. *and proclaim* before him,
9:26. *they called* these days Purim
Job 1: 4. *and called* for their three sisters
9:16. If *I had called*, and he had
17:14. *I have said* (marg. *cried*, or, *called*) to corruption, Thou (art) my father:
19:16. *I called* my servant, and he gave
Ps. 14: 4. *call* not *upon* the Lord.
17: 6. I *have called upon thee*, for thou
31:17(18). O Lord; for *I have called upon thee:*
34: 6(7). This poor man *cried*, and the Lord
49:11(12). *they call* (their) lands after their own
53: 4(5). *they have* not *called upon* God.
66:17. *I cried* unto him with my mouth,
79: 6. the kingdoms that *have* not *called* upon
81: 7(8). *Thou calledst* in trouble,
88: 9(10). *I have called* daily *upon thee,*
118: 5. *I called upon* the Lord
119:145. *I cried* with (my) whole heart;
146. *I cried unto thee;* save me,
120: 1. In my distress *I cried* unto the Lord,
130: 1. Out of the depths *have I cried unto thee,*

Ps.138: 3. In the day when *I cried*
141: 1. Lord, *I cry unto thee:*
Pro. 1:24. *I have called*, and ye refused;
Cant.5: 6. *I called him*, but he gave me no answer.
Isa. 6: 3. *And* one *cried* unto another,
7:14. *and shall call* his name Immanuel.
13: 3. *I have* also *called* my mighty ones
22:20. *that I will call* my servant Eliakim
30: 7. therefore *have I cried* concerning
41: 9. *called thee* from the chief men
42: 6. I the Lord *have called thee*
43: 1. *I have called* (thee) by thy name;
22. *thou hast* not *called* upon me,
48:15. yea, *I have called him:*
49: 1. The Lord *hath called me* from
50: 2. when *I called*, (was there) none to answer?
51: 2. *I called* him alone,
54: 6. the Lord *hath called thee*
58:13. *and call* the sabbath a delight,
60:14. *and they shall call* thee, The city of the
18. *but thou shalt call* thy walls Salvation,
62:12. *And they shall call* them, The holy people,
65:12. when *I called*, ye did not answer;
66: 4. when *I called*, none did answer;
Jer. 2: 2. Go *and cry* in the ears of Jerusalem,
3: 4. *Wilt thou* not from this time *cry*
12. Go *and proclaim* these words
6:30. Reprobate silver *shall* (men) *call* them,
7: 2. *and proclaim* there this word,
27. *thou shalt also call* unto them;
10:25. the families that *call* not on thy name:
11:16. The Lord *called* thy name,
12: 6. *they have called* a multitude after thee: (marg. or, *cried* after thee fully)
19: 2. *and proclaim* there the words that
20: 3. The Lord *hath* not *called* thy name Pashur,
29:12. *Then shall ye call* upon me,
30:17. *they called* thee an Outcast,
31: 6. the watchmen upon the mount Ephraim *shall cry*,
36: 6. go thou, *and read* in the roll,
9. *they proclaimed* a fast
14. the roll wherein *thou hast read*
46:17. *They did cry* there,
49:29. *and they shall cry* unto them,
51:61. *and shalt read* all these words;
Lam. 1:15. *he hath called* an assembly
19. *I called* for my lovers,
21. thou wilt bring the day (that) *thou hast called*, (marg. or, *proclaimed*)
3:55. *I called upon* thy name, O Lord,
4:15. *They cried* unto them, Depart ye;
Eze. 8:18. *though they cry*...(yet) will I not hear
36:29. *and I will call* for the corn,
38:21. *And I will call* for a sword
39:11. *and they shall call* (it) The valley of
Hos. 7:11. *they call* to Egypt,
11: 1. *called* my son out of Egypt.
2. (As) *they called* them, so they went from
Am. 5:16. *and they shall call* the husbandman to
Jon. 2: 2(3). *I cried* by reason of mine affliction
Mic. 3: 5. that bite with their teeth, *and cry*, Peace;
Zec. 1: 4. unto whom the former prophets *have cried*,
7: 7. the words which the Lord *hath cried*
13. as *he cried*, and they would not hear;
11: 7. took unto me two staves; the one *I called* Beauty, and the other *I called* Bands;
Mal. 1: 4. *and they shall call* them, The border of wickedness,

KAL.—*Infinitive*.

Gen 4:26. then began men *to call* upon the name of
Ex. 10:16. Pharaoh *called*...in haste; (marg. hastened *to call*)
Nu. 16:12. Moses sent *to call* Dathan and Abiram,
22: 5. sent messengers therefore unto Balaam... *to call* him,
20. If the men come *to call* thee,
37. Did I not earnestly send unto thee *to call*
Deu. 4: 7. all (things that) *we call* upon him (for)?
Jud. 8: 1. *that thou calledst* us not,
1Sa. 3: 6. the Lord *called* yet again, (lit. added *to call*) Samuel.
8. the Lord *called* Samuel again (lit. added *to call*) the third time.
22:11. the king sent *to call* Ahimelech
1K. 8:52. in all *that they call for*
1K. 22:13. the messenger that was gone *to call*
2K. 5: 7. *when* the king of Israel *had read* the
2Ch 18:12. the messenger that went *to call* Micaiah
Neh. 6: 7. *to preach* of thee at Jerusalem,
Ps. 4: 1(2). Hear me *when I call*,
3(4). the Lord will hear *when I call*
20: 9(10). let the king hear us *when we call*.
69: 3(4). I am weary of *my crying:*
141: 1. give ear unto my voice, *when I cry*
Pro. 9:15. *To call* passengers who go right
Isa. 1:13. *the calling of* assemblies,
8: 4. before the child shall have knowledge *to cry*,
61: 1. *to proclaim* liberty to the captives,
2. *To proclaim* the acceptable year of the
Jer. 11:14. in the time *that they cry* unto me
34: 8. *to proclaim* liberty unto them;
15. *in proclaiming* liberty every man to
17. *in proclaiming* liberty, every one to
36: 8. *reading* in the book the words
13. *when* Baruch *read* the book
23. *when* Jehudi *had read* three or four leaves,
51:63. when thou hast made an end *of reading*
Dan. 2: 2. the king commanded *to call* the magicians,
Zep. 3: 9. *that* they *may* all *call* upon the name of

KAL.—*Imperative*.

Ex. 2:20. *call* him, that he may eat bread.
Deu 31:14. *call* Joshua, and present yourselves
Jud. 7: 3. *proclaim* in the ears of the people,
16:25. they said, *Call* for Samson,
Ru. 1:20. *call* me Mara:
4:11. do thou worthily in Ephratah, *and be famous* (marg. *proclaim* (thy) name) in Beth-lehem:
2Sa.17: 5. *Call* now Hushai the Archite
1K. 1:28. *Call* me Bath-sheba.
32. *Call* me Zadok the priest,
18:25. *and call* on the name of your gods,
27. *Cry* aloud: for he (is) a god;
21: 9. *Proclaim* a fast, and set Naboth
2K. 4:12. *Call* this Shunammite.
15. And he said, *Call* her.
36. *Call* this Shunammite.
10:19. *call* unto me all the prophets of Baal,
1Ch 16: 8. *call* upon his name,
Job 5: 1. *Call* now, if there be any that will
13:22. *Then call thou*, and I will answer:
Ps. 50:15. *And call upon me* in the day of trouble:
105: 1. *call* upon his name:
Isa. 8: 3. *Call* his name Maher-shalal-hash-baz.
12: 4. Praise the Lord, *call* (marg. or, *proclaim*) upon his name,
29:11,12. *Read* this, I pray thee:
34:16. Seek ye out of the book of the Lord, *and read:*
40: 2. comfortably to Jerusalem, *and cry* unto
6. The voice said, *Cry*.
55: 6. *call ye upon him* while he is near:
58: 1. *Cry* aloud, spare not,
Jer. 4: 5. *cry*, gather together, and say, Assemble
9:17(16). *and call* for the mourning women,
11: 6. *Proclaim* all these words
33: 3. *Call* unto me, and I will answer
36:15. *and read it* in our ears.
Hos. 1: 4. *Call* his name Jezreel;
6. *Call* her name Lo-ruhamah:
9. *Call* his name Lo-ammi:
Joel 1:14 & 2:15. *call* a solemn assembly,
3: 9(4:9). *Proclaim ye* this among the Gentiles;
Am. 4: 5. *and proclaim* (and) publish the free
Jon. 1: 2. go to Nineveh,...*and cry* against it;
6. arise, *call* upon thy God,
3: 2. go unto Nineveh,...*and preach* unto it
Zec. 1:14. the angel that communed with me said... *Cry thou*,
17. *Cry* yet, saying, Thus saith the Lord of

KAL.—*Future*.

Gen. 1: 5. *And* God *called* the light Day,
8. *And* God *called* the firmament Heaven.
10. *And* God *called* the dry (land) Earth;
2:19. to see what *he would call* them: and whatsoever Adam *called*
20. *And* Adam *gave* (marg. *called*) names to all cattle,
3: 9. *And* the Lord God *called* unto Adam,

Gen. 3:20. *And* Adam *called* his wife's name Eve;
4:17. *and called* the name of the city, after
25. *and called* his name Seth:
26. *and he called* his name Enos:
5: 2. *and called* their name Adam,
3. begat (a son)...*and called* his name Seth:
29. *And he called* his name Noah,
12: 8. *and called* upon the name of the Lord.
18. *And* Pharaoh *called* Abram,
13: 4. *and* there Abram *called* on the name of
16:13. *And she called* the name of the Lord
15. *and* Abram *called* his son's name,
17:15. *thou shalt* not *call* her name Sarai,
19: 5. *And they called* unto Lot,
37. *and called* his name Moab:
38. *and called* his name Ben-ammi:
20: 8. *and called* all his servants,
9. *Then* Abimelech *called* Abraham,
21: 3. *And* Abraham *called* the name of his son
17. *and* the angel of God *called* to Hagar
33. *and called* there on the name of the Lord,
22:11. *And* the angel of the Lord *called* unto
14. *And* Abraham *called* the name of that
15. *And* the angel of the Lord *called*
24:57. *We will call* the damsel,
58. *And they called* Rebekah,
25:25. *and they called* his name Esau.
26. *and* his name *was called* Jacob:
26: 9. *And* Abimelech *called* Isaac,
18. *and he called* their names after
20. *and he called* the name of the well Esek;
21. *and he called* the name of it Sitnah.
22. *and he called* the name of it Rehoboth;
25. *and called* upon the name of the Lord,
33. *And he called* it Shebah:
27: 1. *that...he called* Esau his eldest son
42. she sent *and called* Jacob
28: 1. *And* Isaac *called* Jacob,
19. *And he called* the name of that place
29:32. *and she called* his name Reuben:
33. *and she called* his name Simeon.
30: 8. *and she called* his name Naphtali.
11. *and she called* his name Gad.
13. *and she called* his name Asher.
18. *and she called* his name Issachar.
20. *and she called* his name Zebulun.
21. *and called* her name Dinah.
24. *And she called* his name Joseph;
31: 4. Jacob sent *and called* Rachel and Leah
47. *And* Laban *called* it Jegar-sahadutha:
54. *and called* his brethren to eat bread:
32: 2(3). *and he called* the name of that place
30(31). *And* Jacob *called* the name of the
33:20. erected there an altar, *and called* it
35: 7. *and called* the place El-beth-el:
8. *and* the name of it *was called*
10. *and he called* his name Israel.
15. *And* Jacob *called* the name of the place
18. *that she called* his name Ben-oni:
38: 3. *and he called* his name Er.
4. *and she called* his name Onan.
5. *and called* his name Shelah:
29. *therefore* his name *was called* Pharez.
30. *and* his name *was called* Zarah.
39:14. *That she called* unto the men of her house,
— *and I cried* with a loud voice:
15. that I lifted up my voice *and cried*,
18. as I lifted up my voice *and cried*,
41: 8. he sent *and called* for all the magicians
14. Pharaoh sent *and called* Joseph,
43. *and they cried* before him, Bow the knee:
45. *And* Pharaoh *called* Joseph's name
51. *And* Joseph *called* the name of the
45: 1. *and he cried*, Cause every man to go out
46:33. when Pharaoh *shall call* you,
47:29. *and he called* his son Joseph,
49: 1. *And* Jacob *called* unto his sons,
Ex. 1:18. *And* the king of Egypt *called* for the
2: 8. the maid went *and called* the child's
10. *And she called* his name Moses:
22. *and he called* his name Gershom:
3: 4. *And* when...God *called* unto him out of
7:11. *Then* Pharaoh also *called* the wise men
8: 8(4). *Then* Pharaoh *called* for Moses and
25(21). *And* Pharaoh *called* for Moses
9:27. Pharaoh sent, *and called* for Moses
10:24. *And* Pharaoh *called* unto Moses,

Ex. 12:21. *Then* Moses *called* for all the elders
31. *And he called* for Moses and Aaron
16:31. *And* the house of Israel *called* the name
17: 7. *And he called* the name of the place
15. *and called* the name of it Jehovah-nissi:
19: 3. *and* the Lord *called* unto him
7. Moses came *and called* for the elders
20. *and* the Lord *called* Moses (up)
24: 7. *and read* in the audience of the people:
16. *and* the seventh day *he called* unto
32: 5. *and* Aaron *made proclamation*,
34: 5. *and proclaimed* the name of the Lord.
6. Lord passed by before him, *and proclaimed*,
31. *And* Moses *called* unto them;
36: 2. *And* Moses *called* Bezaleel
Lev. 1: 1. *And* the Lord *called* unto Moses,
10: 4. *And* Moses *called* Mishael
13:45. *shall cry*, Unclean, unclean.
23: 2. the feasts...which *ye shall proclaim*
4. *ye shall proclaim* in their seasons.
37. the feasts of the Lord, which *ye shall proclaim*
Nu. 11: 3. *And he called* the name of the place
34. *And he called* the name of that place
12: 5. *and called* Aaron and Miriam:
13:16. *And* Moses *called* Oshea the son of Nun
21: 3. *and he called* the name of the place
25: 2. *And they called* the people unto the
32:38. *and gave* other names (marg. *they called* by names the names)
41. *and called* them Havoth-jair.
42. took Kenath,...*and called* it Nobah,
Deu. 2:11. the Moabites *call* them Emims.
20. the Ammonites *call* them Zamzummims;
3: 9. Hermon the Sidonians *call* Sirion; and the Amorites *call* it Shenir;
14. *and called* them after his own name,
5: 1. *And* Moses *called* all Israel,
24:15. lest *he cry* against thee unto the Lord,
29: 2(1). *And* Moses *called* unto all Israel,
31: 7. *And* Moses *called* unto Joshua,
11. *thou shalt read* this law before
32: 3. *I will publish* the name of the Lord:
33:19. *They shall call* the people unto the
Jos. 4: 4. *Then* Joshua *called* the twelve men,
5: 9. *Wherefore* the name of the place *is called*
6: 6. *And* Joshua the son of Nun *called* the
9:22. *And* Joshua *called* for them,
10:24. *that* Joshua *called* for all the men of
19:47. *and called* Leshem, Dan, after the name
21: 9. these cities which *are* (here) *mentioned*
22: 1. Then Joshua *called* the Reubenites,
34. *and* the children of Gad *called* the
23: 2. *And* Joshua *called* for all Israel,
24: 1. *and called* for the elders of Israel,
9. Balak...sent *and called* Balaam
Jud. 1:17. *And* the name of the city *was called*
26. *and called* the name thereof Luz:
2: 5. *And they called* the name...Bochim
4: 6. she sent *and called* Barak
6:24. *and called* it Jehovah-shalom:
32. *Therefore* on that day *he called* him
7:20. *and they cried*, The sword of the Lord,
9: 7. lifted up his voice, *and cried*,
54. *Then he called* hastily unto the young
10: 4. thirty cities, which *are called*
13:24. *and called* his name Samson:
15:17. *and called* that place Ramath-lehi.
18. *and called* on the Lord,
16:18. she sent *and called* for the lords
19. *and she called* for a man,
25. *And they called* for Samson
28. *And* Samson *called* unto the Lord,
18:23. *And they cried* unto the children of Dan.
29. *And they called* the name of the city Dan,
21:13. *and to call* peaceably unto them. (lit. *and they called*; marg. or, *proclaim* peace)
Ru. 1:20. *Call* me not Naomi,
21. why (then) *call ye* me Naomi,
4:17. *And* the women her neighbours *gave it a name*,
— *and they called* his name Obed:
1Sa. 1:20. she bare a son, *and called* his name
3: 4. *That* the Lord *called* Samuel:
9. if *he call* thee,
10. the Lord came, and stood, *and called*
16. *Then* Eli *called* Samuel,

1Sa. 4:21. *And she named* the child I-chabod,
6: 2. *And* the Philistines *called* for the priests
7:12. *and called* the name of it Eben-ezer,
9:26. *that* Samuel *called* Saul to the top
12:17. *I will call* unto the Lord,
18. *So* Samuel *called* unto the Lord;
16: 5. he sanctified Jesse and his sons, *and called* them to the sacrifice.
8. *Then* Jesse *called* Abinadab,
17: 8. he stood *and cried* unto the armies of
19: 7. *And* Jonathan *called* David,
20:37. *And* when...Jonathan *cried* after the lad,
38. *And* Jonathan *cried* after the lad,
24: 8(9). *and cried* after Saul, saying,
26:14. *And* David *cried* to the people,
28:15. *therefore I have called* thee,
29: 6. *Then* Achish *called* David,
2Sa. 1: 7. he saw me, *and called* unto me.
15. *And* David *called* one of the young men,
2:16. *wherefore* that place *was called* Helkath-hazzurim,
26. *Then* Abner *called* to Joab,
5: 9. *and called* it the city of David.
6: 8. *and he called* the name of the place
9: 2. *when they had called* him unto David,
9. *Then* the king *called* to Ziba,
11:13. *when* David *had called* him,
12:24. *and he called* his name Solomon:
25. *and he called* his name Jedidiah,
13:17. *Then he called* his servant
23. *and* Absalom *invited* all the king's sons.
14:33. *when he had called* for Absalom,
15: 2. *then* Absalom *called* unto him,
18:18. *and he called* the pillar after his own
25. *And* the watchman *cried*, and told the
26. *and* the watchman *called* unto the porter,
28. *And* Ahimaaz *called*, and said unto
20:16. *Then cried* a wise woman
21: 2. *And* the king *called* the Gibeonites,
22: 4. *I will call* on the Lord,
7. In my distress *I called* upon the Lord, and *cried* to my God:
1K. 1: 9. *and called* all his brethren the king's
19. *and hath called* all the sons of the king,
25. *and hath called* all the king's sons,
2:36, 42. the king sent *and called* for Shimei,
7:21. set up the right pillar, *and called* the name
— set up the left pillar, *and called* the name
8:43. all that the stranger *calleth* to thee for:
9:13. *And he called* them the land of Cabul
12: 3. they sent *and called* him.
20. they sent *and called* him
13: 2. *And he cried* against the altar
21. *And he cried* unto the man of God
16:24. *and called* the name of the city...Shemer,
17:10. *and he called* to her, and said, Fetch me,
11. *And* as...*he called* to her, and said, Bring me,...a morsel of bread
20. *And he cried* unto the Lord,
21. *and cried* unto the Lord,
18: 3. *And* Ahab *called* Obadiah,
24. I *will call* on the name of the Lord:
26. *and called* on the name of Baal
28. *And they cried* aloud,
20: 7. *Then* the king of Israel *called* all the
22: 9. *Then* the king of Israel *called* an officer,
2K. 4:12, 15. *when he had called* her, she stood
22. *And she called* unto her husband,
36. *And he called* Gehazi, and said, Call this Shunammite. *So he called her.*
6:11. *and he called* his servants, and said
7:10. they came *and called* unto the porter
11. *And he called* the porters;
10:20. Proclaim a solemn assembly for Baal. *And they proclaimed*
11:14. Athaliah rent her clothes, *and cried*,
12: 7(8). *Then* king Jehoash *called* for Jehoiada
14: 7. *and called* the name of it Joktheel
18: 4. *and he called* it Nehushtan.
18. *when they had called* to the king,
28. Rab-shakeh stood *and cried*
19:14. Hezekiah received the letter...*and read it:*
20:11. *And* Isaiah the prophet *cried* unto the
22: 8. gave the book to Shaphan, *and he read it.*
10. *And* Shaphan *read it* before the king.
23: 2. *and he read* in their ears all the words
17. *and proclaimed* these things that thou

1Ch 4:10. *And* Jabez *called* on the God of Israel,
6:65(50). cities, which *are called* by (their)
7:16. *and she called* his name Peresh;
23. *and he called* his name Beriah,
13:11. *wherefore* that place *is called* Perez-uzza
15:11. *And* David *called* for Zadok
21:26. *and called* upon the Lord;
22: 6. *Then he called* for Solomon
2Ch 3:17. *and called* the name of that on the right
6:33. all that the stranger *calleth* to thee for;
10: 3. they sent *and called* him.
14:11(10). *And* Asa *cried* unto the Lord his
18: 8. *And* the king of Israel *called* for one (of his) officers,
20: 3. *and proclaimed* a fast throughout all Judah.
24: 6. *And* the king *called* for Jehoiada
32:18. *Then they cried* with a loud voice
34:18. *And* Shaphan *read* it before the king.
30. *and he read* in their ears all the words
Ezr. 8:21. *Then I proclaimed* a fast
Neh. 5:12. *Then I called* the priests,
8: 3. *And he read* therein before the street
8. *So they read* in the book in the law
18. *Also...he read* in the book of the law of
9: 3. *and read* in the book of the law of
Est. 4: 5. *Then called* Esther for Hatach,
6:11. *and proclaimed* before him,
Job 14:15. *Thou shalt call*, and I will answer thee:
27:10. *will he* always *call* upon God?
42:14. *And he called* the name of the first,
Ps. 3: 4(5). *I cried* unto the Lord
18: 3(4). *I will call* upon the Lord,
6(7). In my distress *I called* upon the Lord,
22: 2(3). *I cry* in the daytime,
27: 7. Hear, O Lord, (when) *I cry*
28: 1. Unto thee *will I cry*, O Lord
30: 8(9). *I cried* to thee, O Lord;
50: 1. the Lord, hath spoken, *and called* the earth
4. *He shall call* to the heavens
55:16(17). I *will call* upon God;
56: 9(10). When *I cry* (unto thee),
57: 2(3). *I will cry* unto God most high;
61: 2(3). From the end of the earth *will I cry*
80:18(19). *we will call* upon thy name.
86: 3. *I cry* unto thee daily.
7. In the day of my trouble *I will call upon thee:*
89:26(27). *He shall cry unto me*,
91:15. *He shall call upon me*,
102: 2(3). in the day (when) *I call* answer
105:16. *Moreover he called* for a famine
116: 2. therefore *will I call* upon (him)
4. Then *called I* upon the name of the Lord;
13. and *call* upon the name of the Lord.
17. *will call* upon the name of the Lord.
145:18. to all that *call upon him*
147: 4. *he calleth* them all by (their) names.
9. the young ravens which *cry*.
Pro. 1:21. *She crieth* in the chief place of concourse,
28. Then *shall they call upon me*,
2: 3. if *thou criest* after knowledge,
7: 4. *call* understanding (thy) kinswoman:
8: 1. *Doth* not wisdom *cry?*
4. Unto you, O men, *I call;*
9: 3. *she crieth* upon the highest places
12:23. the heart of fools *proclaimeth* foolishness.
18: 6. and his mouth *calleth* for strokes.
20: 6. Most men *will proclaim* every one
21:13. *he* also *shall cry* himself,
24: 8. *shall be called* a mischievous person. (lit. *they shall call*)
27:16. the ointment of his right hand, (which) *bewrayeth* (itself).
Isa. 9: 6(5). *and* his name *shall be called* Wonderful,
21: 8. *And he cried*, A lion: My lord, I stand
22:12. *And...did* the Lord God of hosts *call* to
34:12. *They shall call* the nobles
14. the satyr *shall cry* to his fellow;
36:13. Rabshakeh stood, *and cried*
37:14. Hezekiah received the letter...*and read it:*
40: 6. What *shall I cry?*
26. *he calleth* them all by names by the
41: 2. the righteous (man) from the east, *called him*
25. *shall he call* upon my name:
44: 5. another *shall call* (himself) by the name
7. who, as I, *shall call*,

Isa. 45: 4. *I have even called* thee by thy name:
47: 1. thou *shalt* no more *be called* tender (lit. *they shall* not *call* thee)
5. thou *shalt* no more *be called*, The lady of kingdoms. (lit. *they shall* not *call* thee)
55: 5. *thou shalt call* a nation
58: 5. *wilt thou call* this a fast,
9. Then *shalt thou call*, and the Lord shall
65:15. *call* his servants by another name:
24. before *they call*, I will answer;
Jer. 3:17. *they shall call* Jerusalem the throne
19. *Thou shalt call* me, My father;
7:13. *and I called* you, but ye answered not;
20: 8. *I cried* violence and spoil;
23: 6. *he shall be called*, The Lord our Righteousness. (lit. (one) *shall call him*)
29:29. *And* Zephaniah the priest *read* this letter
33:16. (the name) wherewith she *shall be called*, (lit. (one) *shall call* to her) The Lord our righteousness.
35:17. *and I have called* unto them,
36: 4. *Then* Jeremiah *called* Baruch
6. also *thou shalt read them*
10. *Then read* Baruch in the book
15. *and read* it in our ears.
18. *He pronounced* all these words
21. *And* Jehudi *read it* in the ears of the king,
42: 8. *Then called he* Johanan
Lam. 2:22. *Thou hast called* as in a solemn day
3:57. in the day (that) *I called upon thee:*
Eze. 9: 1. *He cried also* in mine ears
3. *And he called* to the man clothed with
Dan 8:16. I heard a man's voice...*which called*,
Hos. 2:16(18). *thou shalt call* me Ishi; and *shalt call*
11: 7. *though they called them* to the most High,
Joel 1:19. O Lord, to thee *will I cry:*
2:32(3:5). whosoever *shall call* on the name of
Jon. 1:14. *Wherefore they cried* unto the Lord,
3: 4. *and he cried*, and said, Yet forty days,
5. *and proclaimed* a fast, and put on sackcloth,
8. *and cry* mightily unto God:
Mic. 6: 9. The Lord's voice *crieth* unto the city,
Hag. 1:11. *And I called* for a drought
Zec. 3:10. *shall ye call* every man his neighbour
7:13. so *they cried*, and I would not hear,
13: 9. *they shall call* on my name,

KAL.—*Participle.* Poel.

Jud.15:19. called the name thereof En-*hakkore*, (marg. The well of *him that called*, or, *cried*)
1Sa. 3: 8. the Lord *had called* the child.
Job 12: 4. *who calleth* upon God,
Ps. 42: 7(8). Deep *calleth* unto deep
86: 5. all *them that call upon thee.*
99: 6. *among them that call* upon his name; *they called* upon the Lord,
145:18. nigh unto all *them that call upon him*,
Isa. 6: 4. the voice of *him that cried*,
21:11. *He calleth* to me out of Seir,
40: 3. The voice of *him that crieth*
41: 4. *calling* the generations from the
45: 3. I, the Lord, *which call* (thee)
46:11. *Calling* a ravenous bird from the east,
48:13. (when) I *call* unto them,
59: 4. None *calleth* for justice,
64: 7(6). (there is) none *that calleth*
Jer. 1:15. I *will call* all the families
25:29. I *will call* for a sword
34:17. I *proclaim* a liberty for you,
Hos. 7: 7. (there is) none among them *that calleth*
Joel 2:32(3:5). remnant whom the Lord *shall call.*
Am. 5: 8. *that calleth* for the waters of the sea,
7: 4. the Lord God *called* to contend by fire,
9: 6. *he that calleth* for the waters of the sea,
Hab 2: 2. that he may run *that readeth*

KAL.—*Participle.* Paül.

Nu. 1:16. *the renowned of* the congregation,
26: 9. (כתיב) *famous* in the congregation,
1Sa. 9:13. they eat *that be bidden.*
22. among *them that were bidden*,
2Sa. 15:11. men out of Jerusalem, (that were) *called*,
1K. 1:41. Adonijah and all *the guests* that (were)
49. *the guests* that (were) with Adonijah were
Est. 5:12. to morrow am I *invited* unto her also
Pro. 9:18. *her guests* (are) in the depths of hell.
Eze. 23:23. great lords *and renowned*, all of them
Zep. 1: 7. prepared a sacrifice, he hath bid *his guests.*

* NIPHAL.—*Preterite.* *

Deu 25:10. *And* his name *shall be called* in Israel,
28:10. thou *art called by* the name of the Lord; (lit. the name of the Lord *is called* upon thee)
2Sa. 6: 2. whose name *is called* by the name of the
12:28. *and* it *be called* after my name.
1K. 8:43. this house,...*is called* by thy name.
1Ch 13: 6. ark of God...whose name *is called* (on it).
2Ch 6:33. this house...*is called* by thy name.
7:14. my people, which *are called* by my name, (lit. upon whom my name *is called*)
Neh 13: 1. *they read* (marg. *there was read*) in the book of Moses
Est. 2:14. *that she were called* by name.
4:11. *I have* not *been called* to come in
Ecc. 6:10. That which hath been *is named* (lit. its name *is called*) already,
Isa. 48: 2. *they call themselves* of the holy city,
63:19. they *were* not *called* by thy name. (marg. or, thy name *was* not *called* upon them)
Jer. 4:20. Destruction upon destruction *is cried;*
7:10, 11. this house, which *is called* by my name,
14. (this) house, which *is called* by my name,
30. the house which *is called* by my name,
14: 9. we *are called* by thy name; (marg. thy name *is called* upon us)
15:16. I *am called by* thy name, (marg. thy name *is called* upon me)
25:29. the city which *is called* by my name, (marg. upon which my name *is called*)
32:34 & 34:15. house, which *is called* by my name, (marg. whereupon my name *is called*)
Dan 9:18. the city which *is called* by thy name: (marg. whereupon thy name *is called*)
19. thy people *are called* by thy name.
10: 1. unto Daniel, whose name *was called* Belteshazzar;
Am. 9:12. the heathen, which *are called* by my name (marg. upon whom my name *is called*)
Zec. 8: 3. *and* Jerusalem *shall be called* a city of

NIPHAL.—*Future.*

Gen 2:23. she *shall be called* Woman,
17: 5. Neither *shall* thy name any more *be called* Abram,
21:12. in Isaac *shall* thy seed *be called.*
35:10. thy name *shall* not *be called* any more
48: 6. thy issue,...*shall be called* after
16. *and let* my name *be named* on them,
Deu 3:13. which *was called* the land of giants.
Ru. 4:14. *that* his name *may be famous*
1Sa. 9: 9. (he that is) now (called) a Prophet *was* beforetime *called* a Seer.
2Sa. 18:18. *and it is called*...Absalom's place.
1Ch 23:14. his sons *were named* of the tribe of Levi.
Ezr. 2:61. *and was called* after their name.
Neh 7:63. *and was called* after their name.
Est. 3:12. *Then were* the king's scribes *called*
4:11. man or woman...who *is* not *called*,
8: 9. *Then were* the king's scribes *called*
Pro. 16:21. The wise in heart *shall be called* prudent:
Isa. 1:26. thou *shalt be called* (lit. *it shall be called* to thee), The city of righteousness,
4: 1. *let* us *be called* by thy name, (marg. *let* thy name *be called* upon us)
14:20. seed of evildoers *shall* never *be renowned.*
31: 4. a multitude of shepherds *is called forth*
32: 5. vile person *shall be* no more *called* liberal,
35: 8. *it shall be called* The way of holiness;
54: 5. God of the whole earth *shall he be called.*
56: 7. mine house *shall be called* an house of
61: 6. ye *shall be named* the Priests of the Lord:
62: 4. thou *shalt be called* (lit. *it shall be called* to thee) Hephzi-bah,
12. thou *shalt be called*, Sought out,
Jer. 19: 6. this place *shall* no more *be called* Tophet,
Eze. 20:29. *And* the name thereof *is called* Bamah

NIPHAL.—*Participle.*

Est. 6: 1. they were *read* before the king.
Isa. 43: 7. every one *that is called* by my name:
48: 1. *which are called* by the name of Israel,
Jer. 44:26. my name shall no more be *named*

* PUAL.—*Preterite.* *

Isa. 48: 8. *wast called* (lit. *it was called* to thee) a transgressor

Isa. 58:12. *and* thou *shalt be called,* (lit. *and it shall be called* to thee)
61: 3. *that* they *might be called* (lit. *that it might be called* to them)
62: 2. *and* thou *shalt be called* (lit. *it shall be called* to thee)
65: 1. a nation (that) *was* not *called*
Eze.10:13. *it was cried* unto them

PUAL.—*Participle.*

Isa. 48:12. O Jacob and Israel, *my called;*

7122, 7125

קָרָא [*kāh-rāh'*].

✱KAL.—*Preterite.*✱

Gen42:38. if mischief *befall him*
Deu31:29. *and* evil *will befall* you
Job 4:14. Fear *came upon me,* (marg. *met me*)
Jer. 13:22. Wherefore *come* these things *upon me?*
44:23. therefore this evil *is happened* unto you,

KAL.—*Infinitive.*

Gen14:17. the king of Sodom went out *to meet him*
15:10. laid each piece one *against* another:
18: 2. he ran *to meet them*
19: 1. Lot seeing (them) rose up *to meet them;*
24:17. the servant ran *to meet her,*
65. man (is) this that walketh...*to meet us?*
29:13. he ran *to meet him,*
30:16. Leah went out *to meet him,*
32: 6(7). he cometh *to meet thee,*
33: 4. Esau ran *to meet him,*
46:29. Joseph...went up *to meet* Israel
Ex. 4:14. he cometh forth *to meet thee:*
27. Go into the wilderness *to meet* Moses.
5:20. Moses and Aaron, who stood *in the way.*
7:15. stand by the river's brink *against he come;* (lit. *to meet him*)
14:27. the Egyptians fled *against it;*
18: 7. Moses went out *to meet* his father in law,
19:17. Moses brought forth the people...*to meet with* God;
Nu. 20:18. lest I come out *against thee*
20. Edom came out *against him*
21:23. Sihon...went out *against* Israel
33. Og the king of Bashan went out *against them,*
22:34. I knew not that thou stoodest in the way *against me:*
36. he went out *to meet him*
23: 3. the Lord will come *to meet me:*
24: 1. *to seek* for enchantments,
31:13. Moses, and Eleazar...went forth *to meet them*
Deu 1:44. the Amorites,...came out *against you,*
2:32. Sihon came out *against us,*
3: 1. the king of Bashan came out *against us,*
29: 7(6). Og the king of Bashan, came out *against us*
Jos. 8: 5. when they come out *against us,*
14. men of the city went out *against* Israel
22. other issued out of the city *against them;*
9:11. Take victuals...and go *to meet them,*
11:20. that they should come *against* Israel
Jud. 4:18. Jael went out *to meet* Sisera,
22. Jael came out *to meet him,*
6:35. they came up *to meet them.*
7:24. Come down *against* the Midianites.
11:31. whatsoever cometh forth...*to meet me,*
34. his daughter came out *to meet him*
14: 5. a young lion roared *against him.* (marg. *in meeting him*)
15:14. the Philistines shouted *against him:*
19: 3. he rejoiced *to meet him.*
20:25. Benjamin went forth *against them*
31. children of Benjamin went out *against* the
1Sa. 4: 1. Israel went out *against* the Philistines
2. Philistines put themselves in array *against*
9:14. Samuel came out *against them,*
10:10. a company of prophets *met him;*
13:10. Saul went out *to meet him,*
15:12. Samuel rose early *to meet* Saul
16: 4. elders of the town trembled *at his coming,*
17: 2. the battle in array *against* the Philistines.
21. army *against* army.
48. the Philistine...drew nigh *to meet* David,
1Sa.17:48. ran toward the army *to meet* the Philistine.
55. Saul saw David go forth *against* the
18: 6. the women came out...*to meet* king Saul,
21: 1(2). Ahimelech was afraid *at the meeting of*
23:28. Saul...went *against* the Philistines:
25:20. his men came down *against her;*
32. sent thee this day *to meet me:*
34. except thou hadst hasted...*to meet me,*
30:21. they went forth *to meet* David, *and to meet* the people that (were) with him:
2Sa. 6:20. Michal...came out *to meet* David,
10: 5. he sent *to meet them,*
9. put (them) in array *against* the Syrians:
10. put (them) in array *against* the children
17. the Syrians set themselves in array *against*
15:32. Hushai the Archite came *to meet him*
16: 1. Ziba the servant of Mephibosheth *met him,*
18: 6. the people went out into the field *against*
19:15(16). Judah came to Gilgal, to go *to meet*
16(17). the men of Judah *to meet* king David.
20(21). *to meet* my lord the king.
24(25). Mephibosheth...came down *to meet*
25(26). when he was come to Jerusalem *to meet* the king,
1K. 2: 8. he came down *to meet me*
19. the king rose up *to meet her,*
18: 7. behold, Elijah *met him:*
16. Obadiah went *to meet* Ahab,
— Ahab went *to meet* Elijah.
20:27. the children of Israel...went *against them.*
21:18. go down *to meet* Ahab
2K. 1: 3. go up *to meet* the messengers of
6. There came a man up *to meet us,*
7. (he) which came up *to meet you,*
2:15. they came *to meet him,*
4:26. Run now, I pray thee, *to meet her,*
31. he went again *to meet him,*
5:21. he lighted down from the chariot *to meet him,*
26. the man turned again...*to meet thee?*
8: 8. go, *meet* the man of God,
9. Hazael went *to meet him,*
9:17. send *to meet them,*
18. there went one...*to meet him,*
21. they went out *against* Jehu,
10:15. Jehonadab the son of Rechab (coming) *to meet him:*
16:10. Ahaz went...*to meet* Tiglath-pileser
23:29. and king Josiah went *against him;*
1Ch 19: 5. he sent *to meet them:*
10. put (them) in array *against* the Syrians.
11. set (themselves) in array *against* the
17. put the battle in array *against* the Syrians,
2Ch 35:20. Josiah went out *against him.*
Job 39:21. he goeth on *to meet* the armed men.
Ps. 35: 3. stop (the way) *against* them that persecute
59: 4(5). awake *to help* (marg. *meet*) *me,*, and behold.
Pro. 7:10. there *met him* a woman
15. Therefore came I forth *to meet thee,*
Isa. 7: 3. Go forth now *to meet* Ahaz,
14: 9. Hell...is moved for thee *to meet* (thee)
21:14. The inhabitants of the land of Tema brought water *to him* (lit. *to meet him*)
Jer. 41: 6. Ishmael...went forth from Mizpah *to meet them,*
51:31. One post shall run *to meet* another, and one messenger *to meet* another,
Am. 4:12. prepare *to meet* thy God,
Zec. 2: 3(7). another angel went out *to meet him,*

KAL.—*Future.*

Gen42: 4. Lest peradventure mischief *befall him.*
49: 1. (that) which *shall befall* you
Ex. 1:10. when *there falleth out* any war,
Lev.10:19. *and* such things *have befallen* me:

KAL.—*Participle.* Poel.

Isa. 51:19. These two (things) *are come* (marg. *happened*) *unto thee;*

✱NIPHAL.—*Preterite.*✱

Ex. 5: 3. The God of the Hebrews *hath met* with us:
2Sa.20: 1. *there happened to be* there a man of

NIPHAL.—*Infinitive.*

2Sa. 1: 6. I happened *by chance* (lit. *happening* I happened)

NIPHAL.—*Future.*

Deu22: 6. If a bird's nest *chance* to be before thee
2Sa.18: 9. *And* Absalom *met* the servants of David.

* HIPHIL.—*Future.* *

Jer. 32:23. *therefore thou hast caused* all this evil *to come*

7123 קְרָא [*k'rah*], Ch.

* P'AL.—*Infinitive.* *

Dan 5: 8. but they could not *read* the writing,
16. now if thou canst *read* the writing,

P'AL.—*Future.*

Dan 5: 7. The king *cried* aloud
15. that *they should read* this writing,
17. yet *I will read* the writing

P'AL.—*Participle.* Active.

Dan 3: 4. Then an herald *cried* aloud,
4:14(11). *He cried* aloud, and said
5: 7. Whosoever *shall read* this writing,

P'AL.—*Participle.* Passive.

Ezr. 4:18. *hath been* plainly *read* before me.
23. Artaxerxes' letter (was) *read* before

* ITHP'EL.—*Future.* *

Dan 5:12. now *let* Daniel *be called*,

7124 קֹרֵא *kōh-rēh'*, m.

1Sa.26:20. as when one doth hunt *a partridge*
Jer. 17:11. (As) *the partridge* sitteth

7126 קָרַב *kāh-rav'* & קָרֵב [*kāh-rēhv'*].

* KAL.—*Preterite.* *

Gen20: 4. Abimelech *had* not *come near* her:
Ex. 14:20. the one *came* not *near* the other
32:19. as soon as *he came nigh*
Deu 2:19. *And* (when) *thou comest nigh*
37. unto the land of the children of Ammon *thou camest* not,
15: 9. the year of release, *is at hand;*
25:11. *and* the wife of the one *draweth near*
31:14. thy days *approach* that thou must die:
1K. 2: 7. *they came* to me when I fled
Ps.119:150. *They draw nigh* that follow after mischief:
Isa. 41: 5. the ends of the earth were afraid, *drew near*,
Lam.3:57. *Thou drewest near* in the day
4:18. our end *is near*,
Eze. 9: 1. *Cause* them...*to draw near*,
12:23. The days *are at hand*,
42:14. *shall approach* to (those things) which
Zep. 3: 2. *she drew* not *near* to her God.
Mal. 3: 5. *And I will come near* to you to judgment;

KAL.—*Infinitive.*

Ex. 36: 2. *to come* unto the work
40:32. *and when they came near* unto the altar,
Lev.16: 1. *when they offered* before the Lord,
Deu20: 2. *when ye are come nigh* unto the battle,
2Sa.15: 5. *when* any man *came nigh*
Ps. 27: 2. *When* the wicked,...*came* upon (marg. *approached* against) me
32: 9. lest *they come near* unto thee.

KAL.—*Imperative.*

Ex. 16: 9. *Come near* before the Lord:
Lev. 9: 7. *Go* unto the altar,
10: 4. *Come near*, carry your brethren
Deu 5:27(24). *Go* thou *near*, and hear all
Jos. 10:24. *Come near*, put your feet upon
2Sa.20:16. *Come near* hither, that I may speak
Ps. 69:18(19). *Draw nigh* unto my soul,
Isa. 34: 1. *Come near*, ye nations, to hear;
48:16. *Come ye near* unto me,
57: 3. But *draw near* hither, ye sons
65: 5. *Stand by* thyself, come not

KAL.—*Future.*

Gen27:41. The days of mourning for my father *are at hand;*
37:18. before *he came near* unto them,
Gen47:29. *And* the time *drew nigh* that Israel must
Ex. 3: 5. *Draw* not *nigh* hither:
12:48. *let him come near* and keep it;
Lev. 9: 5. *and* all the congregation *drew near*
8. Aaron *therefore went* unto the altar,
10: 5. *So they went near*, and carried
18: 6. None of you *shall approach*
14. *thou shalt* not *approach* to his wife:
19. *thou shalt* not *approach* unto a woman to
20:16. if a woman *approach* unto any beast,
21:17. *let him* not *approach* to offer
18. *he shall* not *approach:*
22: 3. Whosoever (he be)...that *goeth* unto the holy
Nu. 9: 6. *and they came* before Moses and before
16:40(17:5). *come near* to offer incense
18: 3. *they shall* not *come nigh* the vessels
4. a stranger *shall* not *come nigh*
22. Neither *must* the children of Israel...*come nigh*
27: 1. *Then came* the daughters of Zelophehad,
31:48. *And* the officers...*came near* unto Moses:
36: 1. *And* the chief fathers...*came near*,
Deu 1:22. *And ye came near* unto me
4:11. *And ye came near* and stood
5:23(20). *that ye came near* unto me,
20:10. *When thou comest nigh* unto a city
22:14. I took this woman, *and when I came* to
Jos. 3: 4. *come* not *near* unto it,
7:14. the tribe which the Lord taketh *shall come*
— the family which the Lord shall take *shall come*
— the houshold which the Lord shall take *shall come*
8: 5. I, and all the people...*will approach*
10:24. *And they came near*, and put their feet
17: 4. *And they came near* before Eleazar
Jud.19:13. *and let us draw near* to one of these places
20:24. *And* the children of Israel *came near*
1Sa.14:36. *Let us draw near* hither unto God.
17:48. when the Philistine...came *and drew nigh*
2Sa.20:17. *when he was come near* unto her,
1K. 2: 1. *Now* the days of David *drew nigh*
20:29. *that* in the seventh day the battle *was joined:*
2K. 16:12. *and* the king *approached* to the altar,
Est. 5: 2. *So* Esther *drew near*,
Job 33:22. *Yea*, his soul *draweth near* unto the grave,
Ps. 91:10. neither *shall* any plague *come nigh*
119:169. *Let* my cry *come near*
Pro. 5: 8. *come* not *nigh* the door of her house:
Isa. 5:19. *and let* the counsel of the Holy One of Israel *draw nigh*
8: 3. *And I went* (marg. *approached*) unto the
41: 1. *let us come near* together to judgment.
54:14. *it shall* not *come near* thee.
Eze.18: 6. neither *hath come near* to a menstruous
37: 7. *and* the bones *came together*,
44:15. *they shall come near* to me
16. *they shall come near* to my table,
Jon. 1: 6. *So* the shipmaster *came* to him,

* NIPHAL.—*Preterite.* *

Ex. 22: 8(7). *then* the master of the house *shall be brought*
Jos. 7:14. the morning *therefore ye shall be brought*

* PIEL.—*Preterite.* *

Isa. 46:13. *I bring near* my righteousness;
Eze.36: 8. *they are at hand* to come.
Hos. 7: 6. *they have made ready* their heart

PIEL.—*Imperative.*

Isa. 41:21. *Produce* (marg. *Cause to come near*) your cause,
Eze.37:17. *And join* them one to another

PIEL.—*Future.*

Job 31:37. as a prince *would I go near*
Ps. 65: 4(5). (the man whom) thou choosest, *and causest to approach*

* HIPHIL.—*Preterite.* *

Gen12:11. when *he was come near*
Ex. 14:10. when Pharaoh *drew nigh*,
29: 3. *and bring* them in the basket,
10. *And thou shalt cause* a bullock *to be brought*
40:12. *And thou shalt bring* Aaron and his sons

Lev. 1: 5. *and* the priests, Aaron's sons, *shall bring* the blood,
13. *and* the priest *shall bring* (it) all,
14. *then he shall bring* his offering
15. *And* the priest *shall bring it*
2: 8. *when it is presented* unto the priest,
3: 3. *And he shall offer* of the sacrifice
7. *then shall he offer* it before the Lord.
9. *And he shall offer* of the sacrifice
12. *then he shall offer it*
14. *And he shall offer* thereof his offering,
4: 3. *then let him bring*...a young bullock
14. *then* the congregation *shall offer*
5: 8. *who shall offer* (that) which (is) for
7: 8. the skin of the burnt offering which *he hath offered.*
12. *then he shall offer* with the sacrifice
14. *And* of it *he shall offer* one out of
35. *he presented* them to minister
10:19. this day *have they offered*
12: 7. *Who shall offer it* before the Lord,
14:12. *and offer* him for a trespass offering,
16: 6. *And* Aaron *shall offer* his bullock
9. *And* Aaron *shall bring* the goat
11. *And* Aaron *shall bring* the bullock
20. *And* when...*he shall bring* the live goat:
23: 8, 25. *But ye shall offer* an offering
16. *and ye shall offer* a new meat offering
18. *And ye shall offer* with the bread seven
27. *and offer* an offering made by fire
36. *and ye shall offer* an offering made by fire
Nu. 5:16. *And* the priest *shall bring* her *near,*
25. *and offer it* upon the altar:
6:14. *And he shall offer* his offering
16. *And* the priest *shall bring* (them)
7:18. On the second day Nethaneel...*did offer.*
19. *He offered* (for) his offering
8: 9. *And thou shalt bring* the Levites
10. *And thou shalt bring* the Levites
9:13. *he brought* not the offering
15: 4. *Then shall* he that offereth...*bring*
9. *Then shall he bring*...a meat offering
27. *then he shall bring* a she goat
16: 5. *and will cause* (him) *to come near*
17. *and bring ye* before the Lord
38(17:3). *they offered them* before the Lord,
39(—:4). they that were burnt *had offered;*
28:19. *But ye shall offer* a sacrifice made by fire
27. *But ye shall offer* the burnt offering
29: 8, 36. *But ye shall offer* a burnt offering
13. *And ye shall offer* a burnt offering,
Jud. 5:25. *she brought forth* butter in a lordly dish.
Ezr. 8:35. *offered* burnt offerings unto the God of
Jer. 30:21. *and I will cause him to draw near,*
Eze. 43:24. *And thou shalt offer them* before the Lord,

HIPHIL.—*Infinitive.*

Lev. 7:16. the same day *that he offereth*
38. *to offer* their oblations
17: 4. *to offer* an offering
21:17. *to offer* the bread of his God.
21. shall come nigh *to offer*
— he shall not come nigh *to offer*
23:37. *to offer* an offering
Nu. 3: 4. *when they offered* strange fire
9: 7. that *we may* not *offer* an offering
15:13. *in offering* an offering made by fire,
16: 9. *to bring* you *near* to himself
26:61. *when they offered* strange fire
28: 2. observe *to offer* unto me
26. *when ye bring* a new meat offering
Jud. 3:18. when he had made an end *to offer*
2Ch 35:12. *to offer* unto the Lord,
Eze. 44: 7. *when ye offer* my bread,
15. *to offer* unto me the fat and the blood,

HIPHIL.—*Imperative.*

Ex. 28: 1. *take* thou unto thee
Lev. 6:14(7). the sons of Aaron *shall offer*
9: 2. *and offer* (them) before the Lord.
Nu. 3: 6. *Bring* the tribe of Levi *near,*
18: 2. *bring thou* with thee,
Mal. 1: 8. *offer it* now unto thy governor;

HIPHIL.—*Future.*

Ex. 29: 4. Aaron and his sons *thou shalt bring*
8. *thou shalt bring* his sons,
40:14. *thou shalt bring* his sons,

Lev. 1: 2. If any man of you *bring* an offering unto the Lord, *ye shall bring* your offering
3. *let him offer* a male without blemish: *he shall offer* it of his own...will
10. *he shall bring it* a male
2: 1. when any *will offer* a meat offering
4. *if thou bring* an oblation
11. meat offering, which *ye shall bring*
12. *ye shall offer* them unto the Lord:
13. *thou shalt offer* salt.
14. if *thou offer* a meat offering
— *thou shalt offer* for the meat offering
3: 1, 6. *he shall offer it* without blemish
6:20(13). which *they shall offer* unto the Lord
21(14). the meat offering *shalt thou offer*
7: 3. *he shall offer* of it all the fat
11. the sacrifice...which *he shall offer*
12. If *he offer it* for a thanksgiving,
13. *he shall offer* (for) his offering leavened bread
25. *men offer* an offering made by fire
8: 6. *And* Moses *brought* Aaron and his sons,
13. *And* Moses *brought* Aaron's sons,
18. *And he brought* the ram
22. *And he brought* the other ram,
24. *And he brought* Aaron's sons,
9: 9. *And* the sons of Aaron *brought* the blood
15. *And he brought* the people's offering,
16. *And he brought* the burnt offering,
17. *And he brought* the meat offering,
10: 1. *and offered* strange fire before the Lord,
22:18. Whatsoever (he be)...that *will offer*
— *they will offer* unto the Lord
20. whatsoever hath a blemish, (that) *shall ye* not *offer:*
21. whosoever *offereth* a sacrifice
22. *ye shall* not *offer* these
24. *Ye shall* not *offer*...that which is bruised,
25. Neither from a stranger's hand *shall ye offer*
23:36. Seven days *ye shall offer* an offering
27: 9. whereof *men bring* an offering
11. *they do* not *offer* a sacrifice
Nu. 5: 9. which *they bring* unto the priest,
7: 2. *That* the princes...*offered:*
3. *and they brought* them before the
10. *And* the princes *offered*
— *even* the princes *offered*
11. *They shall offer* their offering,
15: 7. *thou shalt offer* the third (part)
10. *thou shalt bring* for a drink offering
33. *And* they that found him...*brought* him
16: 5. *will he cause to come near* unto him.
10. *And he hath brought* thee *near*
18:15. which *they bring* unto the Lord,
25: 6. *and brought* unto his brethren
27: 5. *And* Moses *brought* their cause
28: 3. which *ye shall offer*
11. *ye shall offer* a burnt offering
31:50. *We have therefore brought* an oblation
Deu. 1:17. *bring* (it) unto me,
Jos. 7:16. *and brought* Israel by their tribes;
17. *And he brought* the family of Judah;
— *and he brought* the family of the Zarhites
18. *And he brought* his houshold
8:23. *and brought* him to Joshua.
Jud. 3:17. *And he brought* the present
1Sa. 10:20. *when* Samuel *had caused...to come near,*
21. *When he had caused...to come near*
2K. 16:14. And *he brought also* the brasen altar
1Ch 16: 1. *and they offered* burnt sacrifices
Ps. 72:10. Seba *shall offer* gifts.
Isa. 5: 8. (that) *lay* (lit. *make to be near*) field to
26:17. *draweth near* the time
Eze. 22: 4. *and thou hast caused* thy days *to draw near,*
43:22. *thou shalt offer* a kid
23. *thou shalt offer* a young bullock
44:27. *he shall offer* his sin offering,
46: 4. that the prince *shall offer*
Hag. 2:14. that which *they offer*

HIPHIL.—*Participle.*

Lev. 3: 1. if he *offer* (it) of the herd;
7. If he *offer* a lamb
7: 8. the priest *that offereth* any man's burnt
9. shall be the priest's *that offereth*
18. imputed unto him *that offereth*

Lev. 7:29. *He that offereth* the sacrifice
33. He among the sons of Aaron, *that offereth*
21: 6. the bread of their God, they *do offer:*
8. he *offereth* the bread of thy God:
Nu. 7:12. *he that offered* his offering the first day
15: 4. *he that offereth* his offering unto the Lord
16:35. men *that offered* incense.

7131 קָרֵב *kāh-rēhv'*, adj.

Nu. 1:51 & 3:10, 38. the stranger *that cometh nigh*
17:13(28). Whosoever *cometh any thing near* (lit. *cometh near cometh near*)
18: 7. the stranger *that cometh nigh*
Deu20: 3. ye *approach* this day unto battle
1Sa.17:41. And the Philistine came on *and drew near*
2Sa.18:25. he came apace, *and drew near.*
1K. 4:27(5:7). all *that came* unto king Solomon's
Eze.40:46. the sons of Levi, *which come near*
45: 4. the priests...*which shall come near*

7127 קְרֵב *k'rēhv*, Ch.

* P'AL.—*Preterite.* *

Dan. 3: 8. at that time certain Chaldeans *came near,*
26. Nebuchadnezzar *came near* to the
6:12(13). Then *they came near,* and spake
7:16. *I came near* unto one of them

P'AL.—*Infinitive.*

Dan 6:20(21). *And when he came* to the den,

* PAEL.—*Future.* *

Ezr. 7:17. *and offer* them upon the altar

* APHEL.—*Preterite.* *

Ezr. 6:17. *And offered* at the dedication
Dan. 7:13. *and they brought him near* before

APHEL.—*Participle.*

Ezr. 6:10. That they may *offer* sacrifices (lit. may be *offering*)

7128 קְרָב *k'rāhv*, m.

2Sa.17:11. that thou go *to battle* in thine own person.
Job 38:23. against the day of *battle* and war?
Ps. 55:18(19). delivered my soul in peace *from the battle*
21(22). *but war* (was) in his heart:
68:30(31). scatter thou the people (that) delight *in war.*
78: 9. turned back in the day of *battle.*
144: 1. teacheth my hands *to war,* (marg. *to the war*)
Ecc. 9:18. Wisdom (is) better than weapons of *war:*
Zec.14: 3. he fought in the day of *battle.*

7129 קְרָב *k'rāhv*, Ch. m.

Dan. 7:21. and the same horn made *war*

7130 קֶרֶב *keh'-rev*, m.

Gen18:12. Sarah laughed *within herself,*
24. fifty righteous that (are) *therein?*
24: 3. the daughters of the Canaanites, *among* whom (lit. who *among them*)
25:22. the children struggled together *within her;*
41:21. when they had eaten them up (marg. come to *the inward parts of them*), it could not be known that they had eaten them; (lit. they were come into *their inward parts*)
45: 6. (hath) the famine (been) *in* the land:
48:16. *in the midst of* the earth.
Ex. 3:20. I will do *in the midst thereof*
8:22(18). I (am) the Lord *in the midst of* the
10: 1. might shew these my signs *before him:*
12: 9. with *the purtenance thereof.*
17: 7. Is the Lord *among us,*
23:21. for my name (is) *in him.* (lit. *in the midst of him*)
25. take sickness away *from the midst of thee.*
Ex. 29:13, 22. the fat that covereth *the inwards,*
17. wash *the inwards of him,*
31:14. cut off *from among* his people.
33: 3. I will not go up *in the midst of thee;*
5. I will come up *into the midst of thee*
34: 9. let my Lord,...go *among us;*
10. the people *among which* thou (art)
12. lest it be for a snare *in the midst of thee:*
Lev. 1: 9. *But his inwards* and his legs shall he wash
13. *But* he shall wash *the inwards*
3: 3, 9, 14 & 4:8. the fat that covereth *the inwards,* and all the fat that (is) upon *the inwards,*
4:11. *and his inwards,* and his dung,
7: 3. the fat that covereth *the inwards,*
8:16, 25. the fat that (was) upon *the inwards,*
21. he washed *the inwards* and the legs
9:14. he did wash *the inwards*
17: 4. cut off *from among* his people:
10. cut him off *from among* his people.
18:29. cut off *from among* their people.
20: 3. will cut him off *from among* his people;
5. cut him off,...*from among* their people.
6. cut him off *from among* his people.
18. shall be cut off *from among* their people.
23:30. will I destroy *from among* his people.
Nu. 5:27. a curse *among* her people.
11: 4. mixt multitude that (was) *among them*
20. the Lord which (is) *among you,*
21. The people, *among whom* I (am),
14:11. the signs which I have shewed *among them?*
13. broughtest up this people...from *among them;*
14. thou Lord (art) *among* this people,
42. the Lord (is) not *among you;*
44. Moses, departed not *out of* the camp.
15:30. cut off *from among* his people.
Deu 1:42. I (am) not *among you;*
2:14. wasted out *from among* the host,
15. to destroy them *from among* the host,
16. consumed and dead *from among* the
4: 3. destroyed them *from among you.*
5. that ye should do so *in* the land
34. take him a nation *from the midst of*
6:15. a jealous God *among you*
7:21. the Lord thy God (is) *among you,*
11: 6. *in the midst of* all Israel:
13: 1(2). If there arise *among you* a prophet,
5(6). the evil away *from the midst of thee.*
11(12). such wickedness as this is *among you.*
13(14). (Certain) men,...are gone out *from among you,*
14(15). abomination is wrought *among you;*
15:11. the poor shall never cease *out of* the land:
16:11. and the widow, that (are) *among you,*
17: 2. If there be found *among you,*
7. put the evil away *from among you.*
15. (one) *from among* thy brethren
20. prolong (his) days...*in the midst of* Israel.
18: 2. no inheritance *among* their brethren:
15. a Prophet *from the midst of thee,*
18. a Prophet *from among* their brethren.
19:10. That innocent blood be not shed *in* thy
19. put the evil away *from among you.*
20. commit no more any such evil *among you.* (lit. *among thee*)
21: 8. lay not innocent blood *unto* thy people of Israel's *charge.* (lit. *in the midst of*)
9. put away the (guilt)...*from among you,*
21 & 22:21. put evil away *from among you;*
22:24. put away evil *from among you.*
23:14(15). the Lord thy God walketh *in the midst of* thy camp,
16(17). dwell with thee, (even) *among you,*
24: 7. put evil away *from among you.*
26:11. the stranger that (is) *among you.*
28:43. the stranger that (is) *within thee*
29:11(10). thy stranger that (is) *in* thy camp,
16(15). how we came *through* the nations
31:16. strangers...whither they go (to be) *among them,*
17. our God (is) not *among us?* (lit. *in me*)
Jos. 1:11. Pass *through* the host,
3: 2. the officers went *through* the host;
5. the Lord will do wonders *among you,*
10. the living God (is) *among you,*

Jos. 4: 6. That this may be a sign *among you,*
6:25. she dwelleth *in* Israel
7:12. destroy the accursed *from among you.*
13. (There is) an accursed thing *in the midst of thee,*
— the accursed thing *from among you.*
8:35. strangers that were conversant *among them.*
9: 7. Peradventure ye dwell *among us;*
16. they heard...(that) they dwelt *among them.*
22. when ye dwell *among us?*
10: 1. inhabitants of Gibeon...were *among them;*
13:13. the Maachathites dwell *among* the
16:10. the Canaanites dwell *among* the
18: 7. the Levites have no part *among you;*
24: 5. that which I did *among them:*
17. among all the people *through* whom (lit. who *through them*) we passed:
23. strange gods which (are) *among you,*
Jud. 1:29. Canaanites dwelt in Gezer *among them.*
30. the Canaanites dwelt *among them,*
32. the Asherites dwelt *among* the Canaanites,
33. Naphtali...dwelt *among* the Canaanites,
3: 5. the children of Israel dwelt *among* the
10:16. they put away the strange gods *from among them,*
18: 7. the people that (were) *therein,*
20. went *in the midst of* the people.
1Sa. 4: 3. when it cometh *among us,*
16:13. anointed him *in the midst of* his brethren:
25:37. his heart died *within him,*
1K. 3:28. the wisdom of God (was) *in him,* (lit. *in the midst of him*)
17:21. let this child's soul come into *him* (marg. *his inward parts*)
22. soul of the child came into *him* (lit. *id.*)
20:39. *into the midst of* the battle;
Job 20:14. the gall of asps *within him.*
Ps. 5: 9(10). *their inward part* (is) very
36: 1(2). of the wicked saith *within* my heart,
39: 3(4). My heart was hot *within me,*
46: 5(6). God (is) *in the midst of her;*
48: 9(10). *in the midst of* thy temple.
49:11(12). *Their inward thought* (is, that) their
51:10(12). renew a right spirit *within me.*
55: 4(5). My heart is sore pained *within me:*
10(11). mischief also and sorrow (are) *in the midst of it.*
11(12). Wickedness (is) *in the midst thereof:*
15(16). wickedness (is)...*among them.*
62: 4(5). *but* they curse *inwardly.* (marg. *in their inward parts*)
64: 6(7). *both the inward* (thought)...and the heart,
74: 4. *in the midst of* thy congregations;
11. pluck (it) *out of* thy bosom.
12. *in the midst of* the earth.
78:28. *in the midst of* their camp,
82: 1. he judgeth *among* the gods.
94:19. the multitude of my thoughts *within me*
101: 2. walk *within* my house with a perfect heart.
7. He that worketh deceit shall not dwell *within* my house:
103: 1. all *that is within me,* (bless)
109:18. let it come *into his bowels* like water,
22. my heart is wounded *within me.*
110: 2. rule thou *in the midst of* thine enemies.
138: 7. Though I walk *in the midst of* trouble,
147:13. he hath blessed thy children *within thee.*
Pro.14:33. *but* (that which is) *in the midst of* fools
15:31. heareth the reproof of life abideth *among*
26:24. *and* layeth up deceit *within him;*
Isa. 4: 4. purged the blood of Jerusalem *from the midst thereof*
5: 8. *in the midst of* the earth!
25. *in the midst of* the streets.
6:12. great forsaking *in the midst of* the land.
7:22. every one eat that is left *in* (marg. *in the midst of*) the land.
10:23. *in the midst of* all the land.
12: 6. great (is) the Holy One of Israel *in the midst of thee.*
16:11. *and mine inward parts* for Kir-haresh.
19: 1. heart of Egypt shall melt *in the midst of it.*
3. spirit of Egypt shall fail *in the midst thereof;*
14. a perverse spirit *in the midst thereof:*
24. a blessing *in the midst of* the land:
24:13. *in the midst of* the land among the people,
Isa. 25:11. spread forth his hands *in the midst of them,*
26: 9. with my spirit *within me* will I seek
29:23. of mine hands, *in the midst of him,*
63:11. put his holy Spirit *within him?*
Jer. 4:14. How long shall thy vain thoughts lodge *within thee?*
6: 1. to flee *out of the midst of* Jerusalem,
6. wholly oppression *in the midst of her.*
9: 8(7). *but in heart* (marg. *the midst of him*) he layeth his wait.
14: 9. thou, O Lord, (art) *in the midst of us,*
23: 9. Mine heart *within me* is broken
29: 8. prophets...that (be) *in the midst of you,*
30:21. their governor shall proceed *from the midst of them;*
31:33. I will put my law *in their inward parts,*
46:21. her hired men (are) *in the midst of her* like
Lam. 1:15. my mighty (men) *in the midst of me:*
20. mine heart is turned *within me;*
3:45. made us...refuse *in the midst of* the people.
4:13. the blood of the just *in the midst of her,*
Eze.11:19. I will put a new spirit *within you;*
22:27. Her princes *in the midst thereof* (are) like wolves
36:26. a new spirit will I put *within you:*
27. I will put my spirit *within you,*
Hos. 5: 4. the spirit of whoredoms (is) *in the midst of them,*
11: 9. the Holy One *in the midst of thee:*
Joel 2:27. *in the midst of* Israel,
Am. 2: 3. I will cut off the judge *from the midst thereof,*
3: 9. the oppressed *in the midst thereof.*
5:17. I will pass *through thee,* saith the Lord.
7: 8. I will set a plumbline *in the midst of*
10. *in the midst of* the house of Israel:
Mic. 3:11. (Is) not the Lord *among us?*
5: 7(6), 8(7). *in the midst of* many people
10(9). off thy horses *out of the midst of thee,*
13(12). Thy graven images also will I cut off, ...*out of the midst of thee;*
14(13). I will pluck up thy groves *out of the midst of thee:*
6:14. thy casting down (shall be) *in the midst of thee;*
Nah. 3:13. people *in the midst of thee* (are) women:
Hab. 2:19. no breath at all *in the midst of it.*
3: 2. revive thy work *in the midst of* the years, *in the midst of* the years make known;
Zep. 3: 3. Her princes *within her* (are) roaring lions;
5. The just Lord (is) *in the midst thereof;*
11. I will take away *out of the midst of thee*
12. I will also leave *in the midst of thee*
15. the Lord, (is) *in the midst of thee:*
17. The Lord thy God *in the midst of thee*
Zec.12: 1. formeth the spirit of man *within him.*
14: 1. spoil shall be divided *in the midst of thee.*

קִרְבָה [*k'rāh-vāh'*], f. 7132

Ps. 73:28. (it is) good for me *to draw near to* God:
Isa. 58: 2. they take delight *in approaching to* God.

קָרְבָּן *kor-bāhn'*, m. 7133

Lev. 1: 2. If any man of you bring *an offering*
— ye shall bring *your offering* of the cattle,
3. If *his offering* (be) a burnt sacrifice
10. if *his offering* (be) of the flocks,
14. the burnt sacrifice for *his offering*
— he shall bring *his offering*
2: 1. when any will offer *a meat offering* unto the Lord, *his offering* shall be (of) fine
4. if thou bring *an oblation of* a meat offering
5, 7. if *thy oblation* (be) a meat offering
12. *the oblation of* the firstfruits,
13. every *oblation of* thy meat offering
— with all *thine offerings* thou shalt offer salt.
3: 1. if *his oblation* (be) a sacrifice of
2. lay his hand upon the head of *his offering,*
6. if *his offering*...(be) of the flock;
7. If he offer a lamb for *his offering,*
8. lay his hand upon the head of *his offering,*
12. if *his offering* (be) a goat,
14. he shall offer thereof *his offering,*
4:23. shall bring *his offering,* a kid of the goats,

Lev. 4:28. shall bring *his offering*, a kid of the goats,
32. if he bring a lamb for *a* sin *offering*,
5:11. he that sinned shall bring for *his offering*
6:20(13). *the offering of* Aaron and of his sons,
7:13. he shall offer (for) *his offering* leavened
14. one out of *the* whole *oblation*
15. eaten the same day *that it is offered*;
16. the sacrifice of *his offering*
29. shall bring *his oblation* unto the Lord
38. commanded the children of Israel to offer *their oblations*
9: 7. offer *the offering of* the people,
15. he brought the people's *offering*,
17: 4. to offer *an offering* unto the Lord
22:18. offer *his oblation* for all his vows,
27. *for an offering* made by fire
23:14. the selfsame day that ye have brought *an offering unto*
27: 9. men bring *an offering* unto the Lord,
11. offer *a sacrifice* unto the Lord,
Nu. 5:15. he shall bring *her offering*
6:14. he shall offer *his offering*
21. *his offering* unto the Lord
7: 3. they brought *their offering*
10. the princes offered *their offering*
11. They shall offer *their offering*,
12. And he that offered *his offering*
13. *And his offering* (was) one silver charger,
17. *the offering of* Nahshon
19. *his offering* one silver charger,
23. *the offering of* Nethaneel
25, 31, 37, 43, 49, 55, 61, 67, 73, 79. *His offering* (was) one silver charger,
29. *the offering of* Eliab
35. *the offering of* Elizur
41. *the offering of* Shelumiel
47. *the offering of* Eliasaph
53. *the offering of* Elishama
59. *the offering of* Gamaliel
65. *the offering of* Abidan
71. *the offering of* Ahiezer
77. *the offering of* Pagiel
83. *the offering of* Ahira
9: 7. we may not offer *an offering of*
13. he brought not *the offering of* the Lord
15: 4. he that offereth *his offering*
25. they shall bring *their offering*,
18: 9. every *oblation of their's*,
28: 2. *My offering*, (and) my bread for
31:50. We have therefore brought *an oblation for*
Eze. 20:28. they presented...*their offering*:
40:43. upon the tables (was) the flesh of *the offering*.

7133 קֻרְבָּן *koor-ban'*, m.

Neh 10:34(35). cast the lots...for *the* wood *offering*,
13:31. *And for the* wood *offering*, at times

7134 קַרְדֹּם [*kar-dōhm'*], m.

Jud. 9:48. Abimelech took *an ax*
1Sa. 13:20. to sharpen every man...*his ax*,
21. for the forks, *and for the axes*,
Ps. 74: 5. he had lifted up *axes*
Jer. 46:22. *and* come against her *with axes*,

7135 קָרָה *kāh-rāh'*, f.

Job 24: 7. (they have) no covering *in the cold*.
37: 9. *cold* out of the north.
Ps. 147:17. who can stand before *his cold*?
Pro. 25:20. he that taketh away a garment in *cold* weather,
Nah 3:17. camp in the hedges in the *cold* day,

7136 קָרָה [*kāh-rāh'*], f.

* KAL.—*Preterite.* *

Gen44:29. *and* mischief *befall him*,
Deu 25:18. How *he met thee* by the way,
Est. 4: 7. all that *had happened unto him*,
6:13. every (thing) that *had befallen him*.

KAL.—*Future.*

Nu. 11:23. *whether* my word *shall come to pass unto thee* or not.
Ru. 2: 3. *and* her hap *was* (marg. *happened*) *to* light on
1Sa. 28:10. there *shall* no punishment *happen to thee*
Ecc. 2:14. one event *happeneth* to them all.
15. As it happeneth to the fool, so *it happeneth* even to me;
9:11. time and chance *happeneth*
Isa. 41:22. shew us what *shall happen*.
Dan 10:14. make thee understand what *shall befall* thy people

KAL.—*Participle.* Poel.

Gen42:29. told him all *that befell* unto them;

* NIPHAL.—*Preterite.* *

Ex. 3:18. Lord God of the Hebrews *hath met* with
2Sa. 1: 6. As *I happened* by chance upon mount

NIPHAL.—*Future.*

Nu. 23: 3. the Lord *will come* to meet me:
4. *And* God *met* Balaam:
15. while I *meet* (the Lord) yonder.
16. *And* the Lord *met* Balaam,

* PIEL.—*Preterite.* *

Neh 3: 3. who (also) *laid the beams thereof*,
6. *they laid the beams thereof*, and set up

PIEL.—*Infinitive.*

2Ch 34:11. *to floor* (marg. or, *rafter*) the houses
Neh 2: 8. give me timber *to make beams*

PIEL.—*Participle.*

Ps. 104: 3. *Who layeth the beams* of his chambers

* HIPHIL.—*Preterite.* *

Gen27:20. the Lord thy God *brought* (it) to me.
Nu. 35:11. *Then ye shall appoint you* cities

HIPHIL.—*Imperative.*

Gen24:12. *send* me *good speed* this day,

קָרֶה [*kāh-reh'*], m. 7137

Deu 23:10(11). *by reason of uncleanness that chanceth him by* night,

---

קָרוֹב *kāh-rōhv'*, adj. 7138

Gen19:20. this city (is) *near* to flee unto,
45:10. thou shalt be *near* unto me,
Ex. 12: 4. him and his neighbour *next*
13:17. although that (was) *near*;
32:27. slay every man...*his neighbour*.
Lev. 10: 3. I will be sanctified *in them that come nigh*
21: 2. his kin, *that is near* unto him,
3. his sister...*that is nigh* unto him,
25:25. if any of his kin (lit. his kinsman *that is near* unto him) come to redeem
Nu. 24:17. I shall behold him, but not *nigh*:
27:11. his kinsman *that is next* to him
Deu 4: 7. who (hath) God (so) *nigh* unto them,
13: 7(8). the gods of the people...*nigh* unto thee,
21: 3. the city *which is next*
6. the elders...*that are next*
22: 2. if thy brother (be) not *nigh* unto thee,
30:14. the word (is) very *nigh* unto thee,
32:17. new (gods that) came *newly* (lit. *from near*) up,
35. the day of their calamity (is) *at hand*
Jos. 9:16. heard that they (were) their *neighbours*,
Ru. 2:20. The man (is) *near of kin*
3:12. there is a kinsman *near*er than I.
2Sa. 19:42(43). the king (is) *near of kin* to us:
1K. 8:46. the land of the enemy, far or *near*;
59. be *nigh* unto the Lord our God
21: 2. it (is) *near* unto my house:
1Ch 12:40. *they that were nigh* them,
2Ch 6:36. a land far off or *near*;
Neh 13: 4. *allied* unto Tobiah:
Est. 1:14. *And the next* unto him (was) Carshena,
9:20. the Jews...(both) *nigh* and far,
Job 17:12. the light (is) *short* (marg. *near*) because of darkness.
19:14. *My kinsfolk* have failed,

Job 20: 5. the triumphing of the wicked (is) *short*,
Ps. 15: 3. taketh up a reproach against *his neighbour*.
22:11(12). Be not far from me; for trouble (is) *near*;
34:18(19). The Lord (is) *nigh* unto them that
38:11(12). *and my kinsmen* (marg. or, *my neighbours*) stand afar off.
75: 1(2). *for* (that) thy name *is near*
85: 9(10). his salvation (is) *nigh* them that fear
119:151. Thou (art) *near*, O Lord;
145:18. The Lord (is) *nigh* unto all them that
148:14. a people *near unto him*.
Pro. 10:14. mouth of the foolish (is) *near* destruction.
27:10. a neighbour (that is) *near*
Ecc. 5: 1(4:17). *and be more ready* (lit. *and be near*) to hear, than to give the sacrifice of fools:
Isa. 13: 6. the day of the Lord (is) *at hand*;
22. *and* her time (is) *near* to come,
33:13. ye (that are) *near*, acknowledge
50: 8. (He is) *near* that justifieth me;
51: 5. My righteousness (is) *near*;
55: 6. call ye upon him while he is *near*:
56: 1. my salvation (is) *near*
57:19. him that is far off, *and to him that is near*.
Jer. 12: 2. thou (art) *near* in their mouth,
23:23. (Am) I a God *at hand*,
25:26. all the kings of the north, far and *near*, (lit. *near* and far)
48:16. The calamity of Moab (is) *near*
24. the cities of the land of Moab, far *or near*.
Eze. 6:12. *and he that is near* shall fall
7: 7. the day of trouble (is) *near*,
8. Now will I *shortly* pour out my fury
11: 3. (It is) not *near*;
22: 5. *Those that be near*, and those that be
23: 5. doted on...the Assyrians (her) *neighbours*,
12. doted upon the Assyrians (her) *neighbours*,
30: 3. the day (is) *near*, *even* the day of the Lord (is) *near*,
42:13. the priests that *approach* unto the Lord
43:19. the Levites...*which approach* unto me,
Dan 9: 7. all Israel, *that are near*,
Joel 1:15. the day of the Lord (is) *at hand*,
2: 1. the day of the Lord...(is) *nigh at hand*;
3:14(4:14). the day of the Lord (is) *near*
Obad. 15. the day of the Lord (is) *near*
Zep. 1: 7. the day of the Lord (is) *at hand*:
14. The great day of the Lord (is) *near*, (it is) *near*, and hasteth greatly,

---

7139 **קָרַח** [*kāh-ra'gh'*].

* KAL.—*Imperative*. *

Mic. 1:16. *Make thee bald*, and poll thee

KAL.—*Future*.

Lev.21: 5. *They shall* not *make* baldness

* NIPHAL.—*Future*. *

Jer. 16: 6. nor *make themselves bald*

* HIPHIL.—*Preterite*. *

Eze.27:31. *And they shall make themselves* utterly *bald*

* HOPHAL.—*Participle*. *

Eze.29:18. every head (was) *made bald*,

7140 **קֶרַח** *keh'-ragh*, m.

Gen31:40. *and the frost* by night;
Job 6:16. blackish by reason of *the ice*,
37:10. By the breath of God *frost* is given:
38:29. Out of whose womb came *the ice*?
Jer. 36:30. *and* in the night *to the frost*.
Eze. 1:22. as the colour of *the* terrible *crystal*,

7140 **קֹרַח** *kōh'-ragh*, m.

Ps. 147:17. He casteth forth *his ice* like morsels:
[Some copies read קָרְחוֹ from the preceding word.]

7142 **קֵרֵחַ** *keh-reh'ăgh*, m.

Lev.13:40. man whose hair is fallen...he (is) *bald*;
2K. 2:23. Go up, *thou bald head*; go up, *thou bald head*.

קָרְחָה *kor-ghāh'*, f. 7144

Lev.21: 5. They shall not make *baldness* upon their
Deu14: 1. nor make any *baldness* between your eyes
Isa. 3:24. instead of well set hair *baldness*;
15: 2. on all their heads (shall be) *baldness*,
22:12. to mourning, *and to baldness*,
Jer. 47: 5. *Baldness* is come upon Gaza;
48:37. every head (shall be) *bald*,
Eze. 7:18. *baldness* upon all their heads.
27:31. make themselves *utterly* bald (lit. made bald *baldness*)
Am. 8:10. *baldness* upon every head;
Mic. 1:16. enlarge *thy baldness* as the eagle;

קָרַחַת *kāh-rah'-ghath*, f. 7146

Lev.13:42. if there be *in the bald head*,...a white — sprung up *in his bald head*,
43. white reddish *in his bald head*,
55. (whether) it (be) *bare within* (marg. *bald in the head thereof*) or without.

קְרִי [*k'ree*], m. 7147

Lev.26:21. walk *contrary* (marg. or, *at all adventures*) unto me,
23. but will walk *contrary* unto me;
24. will I also walk *contrary* unto you,
27. but walk *contrary* unto me;
28. I will walk *contrary* unto you
40. they have walked *contrary* unto me;
41. I also have walked *contrary* unto them,

קָרִיא [*kāh-ree'*], m. 7148

Nu. 1:16. (כתיב) These (were) *the renowned of* the
16: 2. *famous in* the congregation,
26: 9. *famous in* the congregation,

קְרִיאָה *k'ree-āh'*, f. 7150

Jon. 3: 2. *the preaching* that I bid thee.

קִרְיָה *kir-yāh'*, f. 7151

Nu. 21:28. a flame *from the city of* Sihon:
Deu 2:36. there was not one *city* too strong for us:
3: 4. not *a city* which we took not
1K. 1:41. *the city* being in an uproar?
45. so that *the city* rang again.
Job 39: 7. the multitude of *the city*,
Ps. 48: 2(3). *the city of* the great King.
Pro. 10:15. The rich man's wealth (is) his strong *city*
11:10. *the city* rejoiceth:
18:11. The rich man's wealth (is) his strong *city*,
19. A brother offended (is harder to be won) *than a* strong *city*:
29: 8. Scornful men bring *a city* into a snare:
Isa. 1:21. How is *the* faithful *city* become an harlot!
26. The city of righteousness, *the* faithful *city*.
22: 2. a tumultuous city, *a* joyous *city*:
24:10. *The city of* confusion is broken down:
25: 2. thou hast made of *a city* an heap;
3. *the city of* the terrible nations shall fear
26: 5. *the* lofty *city*, he layeth it low;
29: 1. *the city* (where) David dwelt!
32:13. all the houses of joy (in) *the* joyous *city*:
33:20. Zion, *the city of* our solemnities:
Jer. 49:25. How is *the city of* praise not left,
Lam. 2:11. in the streets of *the city*.
Hos. 6: 8. Gilead (is) *a city of* them that work
Mic. 4:10. shalt thou go forth *out of the city*,
Hab. 2: 8, 17. the violence of the land, of *the city*,
12. stablisheth *a city* by iniquity!

קִרְיָה & קִרְיָא *kir-yāh'*, Ch. f. 7149

Ezr. 4:10. and set *in the cities* of Samaria,
12. the rebellious and *the* bad *city*,
13. if this *city* be builded, and the walls
15. know that this *city* (is) *a* rebellious *city* — for which cause was this *city* destroyed.

Ezr. 4:16. if this *city* be builded (again),
19. and it is found that this *city*
21. *and* that this *city* be not builded,

7159 קָרַם [*kāh-ram'*].

* KAL.—*Preterite.* *

Eze.37: 6. *and cover* you with skin,

KAL.—*Future.*

Eze.37: 8. *and* the skin *covered* them above:

7160 קָרַן *kāh-ran'*.

* KAL.—*Preterite.* *

Ex. 34:29. Moses wist not that the skin of his face *shone*
30. behold, the skin of his face *shone*
35. the skin of Moses' face *shone:*

* HIPHIL.—*Participle.* *

Ps. 69:31(32). an ox (or) bullock *that hath horns*

7161 קֶרֶן *keh'-ren*, f.

Gen22:13. a ram caught in a thicket *by his horns:*
Ex. 27: 2. thou shalt make *the horns of it*
— *his horns* shall be of the same:
29:12. upon *the horns of* the altar
30: 2. *the horns thereof* (shall be) of the same.
3. the sides thereof...and *the horns thereof;*
10. an atonement upon *the horns of it*
37:25. *the horns thereof* were of the same.
26. round about, and *the horns of it:*
38: 2. he made *the norns thereof*
— *the horns thereof* were of the same:
Lev. 4: 7, 25, 30, 34. upon *the horns of* the altar
18 & 8:15 & 9:9 & 16:18. upon *the horns of* the
Deu33:17. *and his horns* (are like) *the horns of*
Jos. 6: 5. make a long (blast) *with* the ram's *horn*,
1Sa. 2: 1. *mine horn* is exalted in the Lord;
10. exalt *the horn of* his anointed.
16: 1. fill *thine horn* with oil,
13. Samuel took *the horn of* oil,
2Sa.22: 3. *and the horn of* my salvation,
1K. 1:39. Zadok the priest took *an horn of* oil
50. caught hold *on the horns of* the altar.
51. he hath caught hold *on the horns of* the
2:28. and caught hold *on the horns of* the altar.
22:11. Zedekiah...made him *horns of* iron:
1Ch 25: 5. to lift up *the horn.*
2Ch 18:10. Zedekiah...made him *horns of* iron,
Job 16:15. defiled *my horn* in the dust.
Ps. 18: 2(3). *and the horn of* my salvation,
22:21(22). *for* thou hast heard me *from the horns of* the unicorns.
75: 4(5). Lift not up *the horn:*
5(6). Lift not up *your horn* on high:
10(11). All *the horns of* the wicked
—(—). (but) *the horns of* the righteous
89:17(18). *our horn* shall be exalted.
24(25). in my name shall *his horn* be exalted.
92:10(11). *my horn* shalt thou exalt
112: 9. *his horn* shall be exalted with honour.
118:27. unto *the horns of* the altar.
132:17. will I make *the horn* of David to bud:
148:14. He also exalteth *the horn* of his people,
Isa. 5: 1. a vineyard *in a* very fruitful *hill:* (marg. *in the horn of* the son of oil)
Jer. 17: 1. *and upon the horns of* your altars;
48:25. *The horn of* Moab is cut off,
Lam. 2: 3. He hath cut off...all *the horn of* Israel:
17. set up *the horn of* thine adversaries.
Eze.27:15. brought thee (for) a present *horns of*
29:21. will I cause *the horn* of the house of Israel
34:21. *and* pushed all the diseased *with your horns*,
43:15. from the altar and upward (shall be) four *horns.*
20. on *the* four *horns of it*,
Dan 8: 3. a ram which had *two horns: and the two horns* (were) high;
5. the goat (had) *a* notable *horn*
6. the ram that had *two horns*,
7. brake *his two horns:*
8. *the* great *horn* was broken;
9. came forth a little *horn*,
20. The ram...having *two horns*

Dan 8:21. *and the* great *horn* that (is) between his
Am. 3:14. *the horns of* the altar shall be cut off,
6:13. Have we not taken to us *horns*
Mic. 4:13. I will make *thine horn* iron,
Hab. 3: 4. he had *horns* (marg. *bright beams*) (coming) out of his hand:
Zec. 1:18(2:1). saw, and behold four *horns.*
19(-:2). *the horns* which have scattered
21(-:4). These (are) *the horns* which have
—(-:-). to cast out *the horns of* the Gentiles, which lifted up (their) *horn*

קֶרֶן *keh'-ren*, Ch. f. 7162

Dan 3: 5, 7, 10, 15. the sound of *the cornet*, flute,
7: 7. *and* it had ten *horns.*
8. I considered *the horns*,
— among them another little *horn*,
— there were three of *the* first *horns*
— and, behold, *in this horn* (were) eyes
11. great words which *the horn* spake:
20. And of *the* ten *horns* that (were) in
— *even* (of) that *horn* that had eyes,
21. *and the* same *horn* made war
24. *And the* ten *horns* out of this

קָרַס [*kāh-ras'*]. 7164

* KAL.—*Preterite.* *

Isa. 46: 2. *They stoop*, they bow down together;

KAL.—*Participle.* Poel.

Isa. 46: 1. Bel boweth down, Nebo *stoopeth*,

קְרָסִים *k'rāh-seem'*, m. pl. 7165

Ex. 26: 6. thou shalt make fifty *taches of* gold, and couple the curtains...*with the taches:*
11. thou shalt make fifty *taches of* brass, and put *the taches* into the loops,
33. hang up the vail under *the taches*,
35:11. The tabernacle, his tent,...*his taches*,
36:13. he made fifty *taches of* gold, and coupled the curtains...*with the taches:*
18. he made fifty *taches of* brass
39:33. the tabernacle...and all his furniture, *his taches*,

קַרְסֻלַּיִם [*kar-sool-lah'-yim*], dual. 7166

2Sa.22:37. *my feet* (marg. *ankles*) did not slip.
Ps. 18:36(37). *my feet* (marg. *id.*) did not slip.

קָרַע *kāh-rag'*. 7167

* KAL.—*Preterite.* *

Lev.13:56. *then he shall rend* it out of the garment,
Nu. 14: 6. them that searched the land, *rent* their
1Sa.15:28. The Lord *hath rent* the kingdom
2Sa.13:19. Tamar...*rent* her garment of divers
2K. 5: 8. Elisha...heard that the king of Israel *had rent* his clothes,
— Wherefore *hast thou rent* thy clothes?
17:21. *he rent* Israel from the house of David;
Ezr. 9: 3. *I rent* my garment and my mantle,
Ps. 35:15. *they did tear* (me), and ceased not:
Isa. 64: 1(63:19). Oh that *thou wouldest rend* the
Jer. 22:14. *and cutteth* him *out* windows;
36:24. were not afraid, nor *rent* their garments,
Eze.13:20. *and I will tear* them from your arms,
21. Your kerchiefs *also will I tear*,

KAL.—*Infinitive.*

1K. 11:11. I will *surely* rend (lit. *rending* I will rend) the kingdom
Ezr. 9: 5. *and having rent* my garment and my
Ecc. 3: 7. A time *to rend*, and a time to sew;

KAL.—*Imperative.*

2Sa. 3:31. *Rend* your clothes,
Joel 2:13. *And rend* your heart, and not your

KAL.—*Future.*

Gen37:29. *and he rent* his clothes.
34. *And* Jacob *rent* his clothes,

Gen44:13. *Then they rent* their clothes,
Jos. 7: 6. *And* Joshua *rent* his clothes,
Jud.11:35. when he saw her, *that he rent* his clothes,
1Sa.28:17. *for* the Lord *hath rent* the kingdom
2Sa. 1:11. took hold on his clothes, *and rent them;*
13:31. the king arose, *and tare* his garments,
1K. 11:11. *I will* surely *rend* the kingdom
12. *I will rend it* out of the hand of thy son.
13. *I will* not *rend* away all the kingdom;
30. caught the new garment...*and rent it*
14: 8. *And rent* the kingdom away
21:27. when Ahab heard those words, *that he rent*
2K 2:12. hold of his own clothes, *and rent them*
5: 7. the letter, *that he rent* his clothes,
6:30. when the king heard...*that he rent* his
11:14. *and* Athaliah *rent* her clothes,
19: 1. king Hezekiah heard (it), *that he rent* his
22:11. when the king had heard...*that he rent*
19. *and hast rent* thy clothes, and wept
2Ch 23:13. *Then* Athaliah *rent* her clothes,
34:19. king had heard...*that he rent* his clothes.
27. *and didst rend* thy clothes, and weep
Est. 4: 1. Mordecai *rent* his clothes,
Job 1:20. Job arose, *and rent* his mantle,
2:12. *and they rent* every one his mantle,
Isa. 37: 1. when king Hezekiah heard (it), *that he rent*
Jer. 4:30. though *thou rentest* thy face with painting,
36:23. *he cut it* with the penknife,
Hos 13: 8. *and will rend* the caul of their heart,

KAL.—*Participle.* Poel.

1K. 11:31. I *will rend* the kingdom

KAL.—*Participle.* Paül.

1Sa. 4:12. there ran a man...with his clothes *rent*,
2Sa. 1: 2. a man came out of the camp...with his clothes *rent*,
13:31. servants stood by with their clothes *rent*.
15:32. came to meet him with his coat *rent*,
2K. 18:37. to Hezekiah with (their) clothes *rent*,
Isa. 36:22. to Hezekiah with (their) clothes *rent*,
Jer. 41: 5. beards shaven, *and* their clothes *rent*,

* NIPHAL.—*Preterite.* *

1K. 13: 3. the altar *shall be rent*,
5. The altar also *was rent*,

NIPHAL.—*Future.*

Ex. 28:32. that *it be* not *rent*.
39:23. that *it should* not *rend*.
1Sa.15:27. upon the skirt of his mantle, *and it rent*.

7168 קְרָעִים *k'rāh-ⁿgeem'*, m. pl.

1K. 11:30. rent it (in) twelve *pieces:*
31. Take thee ten *pieces:*
2K. 2:12. rent them in two *pieces*.
Pro.23:21. drowsiness shall clothe (a man) *with rags*.

7169 קָרַץ [*kāh-ratz'*].

* KAL.—*Future.* *

Ps. 35:19. (neither) *let them wink* with the eye

KAL.—*Participle.* Poel.

Pro. 6:13. *He winketh* with his eyes,
10:10. *He that winketh* with the eye
16:30. *moving* his lips he bringeth evil to pass.

* PUAL.—*Preterite.* *

Job 33: 6. I also *am formed* (marg. *cut*) out of the

7171 קֶרֶץ *keh'-retz*, m.

Jer. 46:20. *destruction* cometh;

7170 קְרַץ [*k'ratz*], Ch. m.

Dan 3: 8. came near, and accused (lit. ate *the pieces* of) the Jews.
6:24(25). those men which had accused (lit. *id.*)

7172 קַרְקַע *kar-kaⁿg'*, m.

Nu. 5:17. the dust that is *in the floor of*
1K. 6:15. *both the floor of* the house, and
1K. 6:15. covered *the floor of* the house
16. both *the floor* and the walls
30. *the floor of* the house he overlaid
7: 7. covered with cedar *from one side of the floor* to *the other.* (marg. *from floor* to *floor*)
Am. 9: 3. *in the bottom of* the sea,

קֶרֶשׁ *keh'-resh*, m. 7175

Ex. 26:15. thou shalt make *boards* for the tabernacle
16. cubits (shall be) the length of *a board*,
— the breadth of one *board*.
17. Two tenons (shall there be) *in* one *board*,
— all *the boards of* the tabernacle.
18. *the boards* for the tabernacle, twenty *boards* on the south side
19. sockets of silver under *the* twenty *boards;* two sockets under one *board*
— two sockets under another *board*
20. on the north side...twenty *boards:*
21. two sockets under one *board*, and two sockets under another *board*.
22. thou shalt make six *boards*.
23. two *boards* shalt thou make for
25. And they shall be eight *boards*,
— two sockets under one *board*, and two sockets under another *board*.
26. *for the boards of* the one side
27. five bars *for the boards of* the other
— five bars *for the boards of* the side
28. in the midst of *the boards*
29. overlay *the boards* with gold,
35:11. *his boards*, his bars, his pillars,
36:20. he made *boards* for the tabernacle
21. The length of *a board* (was) ten cubits, and the breadth of a *board* one cubit
22. One *board had* two tenons,
— all *the boards of* the tabernacle.
23. he made *boards* for the tabernacle; twenty *boards* for the south side
24. he made under *the* twenty *boards;* two sockets under one *board*...and two sockets under another *board*
25. he made twenty *boards*,
26. two sockets under one *board*, and two sockets under another *board*.
27. he made six *boards*.
28. two *boards* made he for
30. And there were eight *boards;*
— under every *board* two sockets.
31. *for the boards of* the one side
32. *for the boards of* the other side
— five bars *for the boards*
33. middle bar to shoot through *the boards*
34. he overlaid *the boards* with gold,
39:33. his furniture, his taches, *his boards*,
40:18. set up *the boards thereof*,
Nu. 3:36 & 4:31. *the boards of* the tabernacle,
Eze.27: 6. made *thy benches* (of) ivory,

קֶרֶת *keh'-reth*, f. 7176

Job 29: 7. I went out to the gate through *the city*,
Pro. 8: 3. at the entry of *the city*,
9: 3. the highest places of *the city*,
14. in the high places of *the city*,
11:11. By the blessing of the upright *the city* is

קָשָׂה [*kāh-sāh'*] & קַשְׂוָה [*kas-vāh'*], f. 7184

Ex. 25:29. *and covers thereof*, and bowls thereof,
37:16. (his) *covers* to cover withal,
Nu. 4: 7. *covers* to cover withal:
1Ch 28:17. the bowls, *and the cups:*

קְשִׂיטָה *k'see-tāh'*, f. 7192

Gen33:19. hundred *pieces of money*. (marg. or, *lambs*)
Jos. 24:32. an hundred *pieces of silver:* (marg. or, *lambs*)
Job 42:11. man also gave him *a piece of money*,

7193 **קַשְׂקֶשֶׂת** *kas-keh'-seth*, f.

Lev.11: 9. whatsoever hath fins *and scales*
10. all that have not fins *and scales*
12. Whatsoever hath no fins *nor scales*
Deu 14: 9. all that have fins *and scales*
10. whatsoever hath not fins *and scales*
1Sa.17: 5. armed with a coat of *mail;*
Eze.29: 4. to stick *unto thy scales,*
— the fish of thy rivers shall stick *unto thy scales.*

7179 **קַשׁ** *kash*, m.

Ex. 5:12. to gather *stubble* instead of straw.
15: 7. consumed them *as stubble.*
Job 13:25. wilt thou pursue *the dry stubble?*
41:28(20). slingstones are turned...*into stubble.*
29(21). Darts are counted *as stubble:*
Ps. 83:13(14). *as the stubble* before the wind.
Isa. 5:24. as the fire devoureth *the stubble,*
33:11. ye shall bring forth *stubble:*
40:24. take them away *as stubble.*
41: 2. *as* driven *stubble* to his bow.
47:14. they shall be *as stubble;*
Jer. 13:24. will I scatter them *as the stubble*
Joel 2: 5. a flame of fire that devoureth *the stubble,*
Obad. 18. the house of Esau *for stubble,*
Nah. 1:10. they shall be devoured *as stubble*
Mal. 4: 1(3:19). and all that do wickedly, shall be *stubble:*

7180 **קִשֻּׁאִים** *kish-shoo-eem'*, m. pl.

Nu. 11: 5. *the cucumbers,* and the melons,

7181 **קָשַׁב** [*kāh-shav'*].

* KAL.—*Future.* *

Isa. 32: 3. the ears of them that hear *shall hearken.*

* HIPHIL.—*Preterite.* *

2Ch 33:10. *they would* not *hearken.*
Neh 9:34. nor *hearkened* unto thy commandments
Ps. 66:19. *he hath attended* to the voice of my prayer.
Isa. 21: 7. *and he hearkened* diligently
48:18. O *that thou hadst hearkened*
Jer. 6:19. *they have* not *hearkened*
8: 6. *I hearkened* and heard,
23:18. who *hath marked* his word,
Zec. 1: 4. they did not hear, nor *hearken*

HIPHIL.—*Infinitive.*

1Sa.15:22. *to hearken* than the fat of rams.
Pro. 2: 2. *So that thou incline* thine ear
Jer. 6:10. they cannot *hearken:*
Zec. 7:11. they refused *to hearken,*

HIPHIL.—*Imperative.*

2Ch 20:15. *Hearken ye,* all Judah,
Job 13: 6. *hearken* to the pleadings of my lips.
33:31. *Mark well,* O Job, hearken unto me:
Ps. 5: 2(3). *Hearken* unto the voice of my cry,
17: 1. *attend* unto my cry,
55: 2(3). *Attend* unto me, and hear me:
61: 1(2). *attend* unto my prayer.
86: 6. *and attend* to the voice of my supplications.
142: 6(7). *Attend* unto my cry;
Pro. 4: 1. *and attend* to know understanding.
20. My son, *attend* to my words;
5: 1. My son, *attend* unto my wisdom,
7:24. *and attend* to the words of my mouth.
Isa. 10:30. *cause it to be heard* unto Laish,
28:23. *hearken,* and hear my speech.
34: 1. *hearken, ye* people:
49: 1. *and hearken, ye* people, from far;
51: 4. *Hearken* unto me, my people;
Jer. 6:17. *Hearken* to the sound of the trumpet.
18:19. *Give heed* to me, O Lord,
Dan 9:19. O Lord, *hearken* and do;
Hos. 5: 1. *hearken, ye* house of Israel;
Mic. 1: 2. *hearken,* O earth,

HIPHIL.—*Future.*

Ps. 10:17. *thou wilt cause* thine ear *to hear.*
Isa. 42:23. (who) *will hearken* and hear
Jer. 6:17. *We will* not *hearken.*
18:18. *let us* not *give heed*
Mal. 3:16. *and* the Lord *hearkened,* and heard

HIPHIL.—*Participle.*

Pro. 1:24. no man *regarded;*
17: 4. A wicked doer *giveth heed* to false lips;
29:12. If a ruler *hearken* to lies,
Cant.8:13. the companions *hearken* to thy voice:

קֶשֶׁב *keh'-shev*, m. 7182

1K. 18:29. nor any *that regarded.* (marg. *attention*)
2K. 4:31. (there was) neither voice, nor *hearing.* (marg. *id.*)
Isa. 21: 7. he hearkened *diligently with much heed:* (lit. hearkened (with) *attention* (with) much *attention*)

קַשֻּׁב [*kash-shoov'*], adj. 7183

2Ch 6:40. (let) thine ears (be) *attent*
7:15. mine ears *attent* unto the prayer
Ps.130: 2. let thine ears be *attentive*

קַשָּׁב [*kash-shāhv'*], adj. 7183

Neh 1: 6. Let thine ear now be *attentive,*
11. let now thine ear be *attentive*

קָשָׁה [*kāh-shāh'*]. 7185

* KAL.—*Preterite.* *

Gen49: 7. their wrath, for *it was cruel:*
1Sa. 5: 7. his hand *is sore* upon us,

KAL.—*Future.*

Deu 1:17. the cause that *is* too *hard* for you,
15:18. *It shall* not *seem hard* unto thee,
2Sa.19:43(44). *And* the words of the men of Judah *were fiercer*

* NIPHAL.—*Participle.* *

Isa. 8:21. they shall pass through it, *hardly bestead*

* PIEL.—*Future.* *

Gen35:16. Rachel travailed, *and she had hard* labour

* HIPHIL.—*Preterite.* *

Ex. 13:15. Pharaoh *would hardly* let us go, (lit. *hardened* to let us go)
Deu 2:30. the Lord thy God *hardened* his spirit,
1K. 12: 4. Thy father *made* our yoke *grievous:*
2K. 2:10. *Thou hast* asked *a hard thing:* (marg. *done hard* in asking)
2Ch 10: 4. Thy father *made* our yoke *grievous:*
Neh 9:29. *hardened* their neck,
Job 9: 4. who *hath hardened* (himself)
Jer. 19:15. *they have hardened* their necks,

HIPHIL.—*Infinitive.*

Gen35:17. *when she was in hard* labour, (lit. *when she had difficulty* in labour)

HIPHIL.—*Future.*

Ex. 7: 3. I *will harden* Pharaoh's heart,
Deu 10:16. *be* no more *stiff*necked.
2K. 17:14. would not hear, *but hardened* their necks,
2Ch 30: 8. *be ye* not *stiff*necked, (marg. *harden* not your necks)
36:13. *but he stiffened* his neck,
Neh 9:16. *and hardened* their necks,
17. *but hardened* their necks,
Ps. 95: 8. *Harden* not your heart,
Jer. 7:26. *but hardened* their neck:
17:23. *but made* their neck *stiff,*

HIPHIL.—*Participle.*

Pro.28:14. *but he that hardeneth* his heart shall fall
29: 1. He, that...*hardeneth* (his) neck,

קָשֶׁה *kāh-sheh'*, adj. 7186

Gen42: 7. spake *roughly* (marg. *hard things*) unto them;
30. The man,...spake *roughly* (marg. *id.*) to us

Ex. 1:14. made their lives bitter with *hard* bondage,
6: 9. for anguish of spirit, and for *cruel*
18:26. the *hard* causes they brought unto Moses,
32: 9. it (is) a *stiff*necked people:
33: 3. thou (art) a *stiff*necked people:
5. Ye (are) a *stiff*necked people:
34: 9. it (is) a *stiff*necked people;
Deu 9: 6. thou (art) a *stiff*necked people.
13. it (is) a *stiff*necked people:
26: 6. laid upon us *hard* bondage:
31:27. I know thy rebellion, and thy *stiff* neck:
Jud. 2:19. ceased not from...their *stubborn* way.
4:24. the hand of the children of Israel prospered, *and prevailed* (marg. going went *and was hard*)
1Sa. 1:15. a woman of a *sorrowful* spirit: (marg. *hard of* spirit)
20:10. (if) thy father answer thee *roughly?*
25: 3. the man (was) *churlish*
2Sa. 2:17. there was a very *sore* battle
3:39. the sons of Zeruiah (be) *too hard* for me:
1K. 12: 4. the *grievous* service of thy father,
13. the king answered the people *roughly*, (marg. *hardly*)
14: 6. I (am) sent to thee (with) *heavy* (tidings). (marg. *hard*)
2Ch 10: 4. the *grievous* servitude of thy father,
13. the king answered them *roughly;*
Job 30:25. Did not I weep *for him* that was *in trouble?* (marg. *hard of* day)
Ps. 60: 3(5). Thou hast shewed thy people *hard things:*
Cant. 8: 6. jealousy (is) *cruel* (marg. *hard*) as the grave:
Isa. 14: 3. the *hard* bondage wherein thou wast
19: 4. into the hand of a *cruel* lord;
21: 2. A *grievous* (marg. *hard*) vision is declared
27: 1. his *sore* and great and strong sword
8. he stayeth his *rough* wind
48: 4. I knew that thou (art) *obstinate*,
Eze. 2: 4. impudent (marg. *hard of* face) children and stiffhearted.
3: 7. impudent *and hard*hearted. (marg. *hard of* heart)

7187 **קְשׁוֹט** *k'shōht*, Ch. m.

Dan 2:47. Of *a truth* (it is), that your God
4:37(34). all whose works (are) *truth*,

7188 **קָשַׁח** [*kāh-shagh'*].

* HIPHIL.—*Preterite.* *

Job 39:16. *She is hardened* against her young

HIPHIL.—*Future.*

Isa. 63:17. from thy ways, (and) *hardened* our heart

7189 **קֹשְׁטְ** *kōhsht*, m

Pro. 22:21. the *certainty* of the words of truth;

7189 **קֹשֶׁט** *kōh'-shet*, m.

Ps. 60: 4(6). displayed because of *the truth*.

7190 **קְשִׁי** *k'shee*, m.

Deu 9:27. *the stubbornness of* this people,

7194 **קָשַׁר** *kāh-shar'*.

* KAL.—*Preterite.* *

Deu 6: 8. *And thou shalt bind them* for a sign
11:18. *and bind them* for a sign
1Sa. 22: 8. all of you *have conspired* against me,
13. Why *have ye conspired* against me,
1K. 16:16. Zimri *hath conspired*,
20. his treason that *he wrought*, (lit. the conspiracy which *he conspired*)
2K. 10: 9. I *conspired* against my master,
15:15. conspiracy which *he made*, (lit. *conspired*)
Am. 7:10. Amos *hath conspired* against thee

KAL.—*Imperative.*

Pro. 3: 3. *bind them* about thy neck;
6:21. *Bind them* continually upon thine heart,
7: 3. *Bind them* upon thy fingers,

KAL.—*Future.*

Gen 38:28. *and bound* upon his hand a scarlet thread,
Jos. 2:18. *thou shalt bind* this line of scarlet thread
21. *and she bound* the scarlet line
1K. 15:27. *And* Baasha...*conspired* against him;
16: 9. *And* his servant Zimri,...*conspired*
2K. 12:20(21). servants arose, *and made* a conspiracy,
14:19. *Now they made* a conspiracy
15:10. *And* Shallum the son of Jabesh *conspired*
25. *But* Pekah the son of Remaliah,...*conspired*
30. *And* Hoshea the son of Elah *made* a conspiracy
21:23. *And* the servants of Amon *conspired*
2Ch 24:21. *And they conspired* against him,
25:27. *Now...they made* (marg. *conspired*) a
33:24. *And* his servants *conspired* against him,
Neh. 4: 8(2). *And conspired* all of them together
Job 39:10. *Canst thou bind* the unicorn
41: 5(40:29). *or wilt thou bind him* for thy
Jer. 51:63. *thou shalt bind* a stone to it,

KAL.—*Participle.* Poel.

2Sa. 15:31. Ahithophel (is) *among the conspirators*
2K. 21:24. *them that had conspired* against king
2Ch 33:25. *them that had conspired* against king

KAL.—*Participle.* Paül.

Gen 30:42. the feebler were Laban's, *and the stronger*
44:30. his life is *bound up* in the lad's life;
Pro. 22:15. Foolishness (is) *bound* in the heart of a

* NIPHAL.—*Preterite.* *

1Sa. 18: 1. the soul of Jonathan *was knit* with

NIPHAL.—*Future.*

Neh. 4: 6(3:38). *and* all the wall *was joined together*

* PIEL.—*Future.* *

Job 38:31. *Canst thou bind* the sweet influences
Isa. 49:18. *and bind them* (on thee), as a bride (doeth).

* PUAL.—*Participle.* *

Gen 30:41. whensoever the *stronger* cattle did conceive,

* HITHPAEL.—*Preterite.* *

2Ch 24:25. his own servants *conspired*

HITHPAEL.—*Future.*

2K. 9:14. *So* Jehu the son of...*conspired*

HITHPAEL.—*Participle.*

2Ch 24:26. *they that conspired* against him;

קֶשֶׁר *keh'-sher*, m. 7195

2Sa. 15:12. *the conspiracy* was strong;
1K. 16:20. *and his treason* that he wrought,
2K. 11:14. Athaliah rent her clothes, and cried, *Treason*, *Treason*.
12:20(21). servants arose, and made *a conspiracy*,
14:19. Now they made *a conspiracy*
15:15. *and his conspiracy* which he made,
30. Hoshea...made *a conspiracy*
17: 4. the king of Assyria found *conspiracy*
2Ch 23:13. Athaliah rent her clothes, and said, *Treason* (marg. *Conspiracy*), *Treason*.
25:27. they made *a conspiracy*
Isa. 8:12. Say ye not, *A confederacy*,
— this people shall say, *A confederacy;*
Jer. 11: 9. *A conspiracy* is found
Eze. 22:25. *a conspiracy of* her prophets

קִשֻּׁרִים *kish-shoo-reem'*, m. pl. 7196

Isa. 3:20. *and the headbands*, and the tablets,
Jer. 2:32. her ornaments, (or) a bride *her attire?*

קָשַׁשׁ [*kāh-shash'*]. 7197

* KAL.—*Imperative.* *

Zep. 2: 1. *yea, gather together*, O nation

* POEL.—*Preterite.* *

Ex. 5: 7. let them go *and gather* straw

POEL.—*Infinitive.*

Ex. 5:12. *to gather* stubble instead of straw.

POEL.—*Participle.*

Nu. 15:32. they found a man *that gathered* sticks
33. they that found him *gathering* sticks
1K. 17:10. the widow woman...*gathering of* sticks:
12. I (am) *gathering* two sticks,

* HITHPOEL.—*Imperative.* *

Zep. 2: 1. *Gather yourselves together,*

7198 קֶשֶׁת *keh'-sheth,* com.

Gen 9:13. I do set *my bow* in the cloud,
14. *the bow* shall be seen in the cloud:
16. *the bow* shall be in the cloud;
21:16. as it were a *bow*shot:
27: 3. thy weapons, thy quiver *and thy bow,*
48:22. with my sword *and with my bow.*
49:24. *his bow* abode in strength,
Jos. 24:12. not with thy sword, nor *with thy bow.*
1Sa. 2: 4. *The bows of* the mighty men (are) broken,
18: 4. and to *his bow,* and to his girdle.
31: 3. the *arch*ers (marg. shooters, men *with bows*) hit him;
2Sa. 1:18. bade them teach...(the use of) *the bow:*
22. *the bow of* Jonathan turned not back,
22:35. *a bow of* steel is broken by mine arms.
1K. 22:34. a (certain) man drew *a bow*
2K. 6:22. with thy sword *and with thy bow?*
9:24. Jehu drew *a bow*
13:15. Take *bow* and arrows. And he took unto him *bow* and arrows.
16. Put thine hand upon *the bow.*
1Ch 5:18. to shoot with *bow,* and skilful
8:40. mighty men of valour, *archers,*
10: 3. the *arch*ers (marg. shooters *with bows*) hit
12: 2. (They were) armed with *bows,*
— (shooting) arrows *out of a bow,*
2Ch 14: 8(7). bare shields and drew *bows,*
17:17. armed men with *bow* and shield
18:33. a (certain) man drew *a bow*
26:14. helmets, and habergeons, *and bows,*
Neh. 4:13(7). their swords, their spears, *and their bows.*
16(10). the spears, the shields, *and the bows,*
Job 20:24. *the bow of* steel shall strike him
29:20. *and my bow* was renewed in my hand.
41:28(20). The arrow (lit. the son of the *bow*) cannot make him flee:
Ps. 7:12(13). he hath bent *his bow,*
11: 2. the wicked bend (their) *bow,*
18:34(35). *a bow of* steel is broken by mine
37:14. have bent *their bow,*
15. *and their bows* shall be broken.
44: 6(7). I will not trust *in my bow,*
46: 9(10). he breaketh *the bow,*
76: 3(4). brake he the arrows of *the bow,*
78: 9. The children of Ephraim,...carrying *bows,*
57. turned aside *like a* deceitful *bow.*
Isa. 5:28. all *their bows* bent,
7:24. With arrows *and with bows*
13:18. (Their) *bows also* shall dash
21:15. they fled...from *the* bent *bow,*
17. the residue of the number of *archers,* (marg. *bows*)
22: 3. they are bound *by the archers:* (marg. *of the bow*)
41: 2. as driven stubble to *his bow.*
66:19. Tarshish, Pul, and Lud, that draw *the bow,*
Jer. 4:29. the noise of the horsemen and *bow*men; (lit. that cast (with the) *bow*)
6:23. They shall lay hold on *bow* and spear;
9: 3(2). bend their tongues (like) *their bow*
46: 9. Lydians, that handle (and) bend *the bow.*
49:35. I will break *the bow of* Elam,
50:14, 29. all ye that bend *the bow,*
42. They shall hold *the bow* and the lance:
51: 3. let the archer bend *his bow,*
56. every one of *their bows* is broken:
Lam. 2: 4. He hath bent *his bow* like an enemy:
3:12. He hath bent *his bow,* and set me
Eze. 1:28. As the appearance of *the bow*
39: 3. I will smite *thy bow*
9. *the bows* and the arrows,
Hos. 1: 5. I will break *the bow of* Israel
Hos. 1: 7. will not save them *by bow,*
2:18(20). *and* I will break *the bow*
7:16. they are *like a* deceitful *bow:*
Am. 2:15. Neither shall he stand that handleth *the bow;*
Hab. 3: 9. *Thy bow* was made quite naked,
Zec. 9:10. *the* battle *bow* shall be cut off:
13. filled *the bow* with Ephraim,
10: 4. out of him *the* battle *bow,*

קַשָּׁת *kash-shāhth',* m. 7199

Gen21:20. he grew,...and became an *arch*er. (lit. a shooter (with) *a bow*)

קִתְרוֹס *kath-rōhs',* Ch. m. 7030

Dan 3: 5, 7, 10, 15. cornet, flute, *harp,* sackbut,

ר *rēhsh.*

The Twentieth Letter of the Alphabet.

רָאָה *rāh-āh'.* 7200

* KAL.—*Preterite.* *

Gen 7: 1. thee *have I seen* righteous
9:16. *and I will look upon it,* that I may
23. *they saw* not their father's nakedness.
16:13. *Have I* also here *looked*
20:10. said unto Abraham, What *sawest thou,*
26:28. *We saw* certainly that the Lord was with
29:10. when Jacob *saw* Rachel
32. the Lord *hath looked* upon my affliction;
31:12. *I have seen* all that Laban doeth
42. God *hath seen* mine affliction
32: 2(3). when Jacob *saw them,*
30(31). *I have seen* God face to face,
33:10. therefore *I have seen* thy face,
38:14. *she saw* that Shelah was grown,
41:19. such as *I* never *saw* in all the land
42:21. in that *we saw* the anguish of his soul,
44:28. *I saw him* not since:
45:13. all that *ye have seen;*
Ex. 1:16. *and see* (them) upon the stools;
3: 7. *I have* surely *seen* the affliction of my
9. *I have* also *seen* the oppression
4:14. *when he seeth thee,* he will
31. *he had looked upon* their affliction,
10: 6. nor thy fathers' fathers *have seen,*
23. *They saw* not one another,
12:13. *when I see* the blood,
23. *when he seeth* the blood
14:13. the Egyptians whom *ye have seen* to day,
16: 7. *then ye shall see* the glory
19: 4. Ye *have seen* what I did
20:22. Ye *have seen* that I have talked with you
32: 9. *I have seen* this people,
33:10. *And* all the people *saw* the cloudy pillar
23. *and thou shalt see* my back parts:
34:10. *and* all...*shall see* the work of the Lord:
35. *And* the children of Israel *saw* the face
Lev. 5: 1. whether *he hath seen* or known
13: 3. *And* the priest *shall look* on the plague
—, 5. *and* the priest *shall look on him,*
6. *And* the priest *shall look on* him
8. *And* (if) the priest *see* that, behold,
10. *And* the priest *shall see* (him):
13. *Then* the priest *shall consider:*
15. *And* the priest *shall see* the raw flesh,
17. *And* the priest *shall see him:*
20. if, *when* the priest *seeth it,*
25. *Then* the priest *shall look* upon it:
27. *And* the priest *shall look upon him*
30. *Then* the priest *shall see* the plague:
32. *And*...the priest *shall look* on the plague:
34. *And*...the priest *shall look* on the scall:
36. *Then* the priest *shall look on him:*
39. *Then* the priest *shall look:*
43. *Then* the priest *shall look* upon it:
50. *And* the priest *shall look* upon

Lev.13:51. *And he shall look* on the plague
55. *And* the priest *shall look* on the plague,
56. And if the priest *look,*
14: 3. *and* the priest *shall look,*
37. *And he shall look* on the plague,
39. the priest shall come again... *and shall look:*
44. Then the priest shall come *and look,*
48. if the priest shall come in, *and look*
20:17. *and see* her nakedness,
Nu. 13:18. *And see* the land, what it (is);
28. *we saw* the children of Anak
32. the people that *we saw*
33. there *we saw* the giants,
15:39. *that ye may look* upon it,
21: 8. *when he looketh* upon it,
23:21. neither *hath he seen* perverseness
27:13. *when thou hast seen* it,
Deu 1:19. wilderness, which *ye saw*
28. *we have seen* the sons of the Anakims
31. *thou hast seen* how that the Lord thy God
4: 9. the things which thine eyes *have seen,*
15. *ye saw* no manner of similitude
19. *when thou seest* the sun,
5:24(21). *we have seen* this day
7:19. great temptations which thine eyes *saw,*
9:13. *I have seen* this people,
10:21. terrible things, which thine eyes *have seen.*
11: 2. *have* not *seen* the chastisement
20: 1. *and seest* horses, and chariots,
21: 7. neither *have* our eyes *seen*
11. *And seest* among the captives a beautiful
28:10. *And* all people of the earth *shall see*
29: 2(1). Ye *have seen* all that the Lord did
3(2). temptations which thine eyes *have seen,*
22(21). *when they see* the plagues
33: 9. *I have* not *seen him;*
Jos. 8:21. Joshua and all Israel *saw*
23: 3. ye *have seen* all that the Lord your God
Jud. 2: 7. who *had seen* all the great works
6:22. *I have seen* an angel
9:48. What *ye have seen* me do,
13:22. *we have seen* God.
14: 2. *I have seen* a woman in Timnath
18: 9. *we have seen* the land,
20:41. *they saw* that evil was come
21:21. *And see,* and, behold, if the daughters of
1Sa. 6: 9. *And see,* if it goeth up by the way
16. when the five lords...*had seen*
19. *they had looked* into the ark
9:16. *I have looked* upon my people,
17. And when Samuel *saw* Saul,
10:24. *See ye* him whom the Lord hath chosen,
13: 6. When the men of Israel *saw*
11. *I saw* that the people were scattered
14:52. *when* Saul *saw* any strong man,
16: 1. *I have provided* me a king
18. *I have seen* a son of Jesse
17:25. *Have ye seen* this man
19: 3. *and* what *I see,* that I will tell thee.
5. *thou sawest* (it), and didst rejoice:
22: 9. *I saw* the son of Jesse coming to Nob,
23:22. who *hath seen him* there:
24:10(11). thine eyes *have seen*
25:25. I thine handmaid *saw* not the young men
28:13. what *sawest thou?*
— *I saw* gods ascending
2Sa.10:14. when the children of Ammon *saw*
14:24. and *saw* not the king's face.
28. Absalom...*saw* not the king's face.
17:23. *saw* that his counsel was not followed,
18:10. *I saw* Absalom hanged in an oak.
11. behold, *thou sawest* (him),
21. Go tell the king what *thou hast seen.*
29. *I saw* a great tumult,
20:12. when *he saw* that every one
1K. 3:28. *they saw* that the wisdom of God (was) in
20:13. *Hast thou seen* all this great multitude?
21:29. *Seest thou* how Ahab humbleth himself
22:17. *I saw* all Israel scattered
19. *I saw* the Lord sitting on his throne,
2K. 2:12. *he saw* him no more:
6:32. *See ye* how this son of a murderer hath
9:26. *I have seen* yesterday the blood of Naboth,
27. when Ahaziah the king of Judah *saw*
10: 3. *Look even* out the best and meetest
11: 1. *when* Athaliah the mother of Ahaziah *saw*
13: 4. *he saw* the oppression of Israel,

2K. 13:21. *they spied* a band (of men);
14:26. the Lord *saw* the affliction of Israel,
20: 5. *I have seen* thy tears:
15. What *have they seen* in thine house?
— All (the things) that (are) in mine house *have they seen:*
1Ch 17:17. *and hast regarded me* according to
19:15. when the children of Ammon *saw*
21:15. the Lord *beheld,* and he repented
29:17. now *have I seen* with joy thy people,
2Ch 10:16. when all Israel *saw* that the king
18:16. *I did see* all Israel scattered
18. *I saw* the Lord sitting upon his throne,
22:10. when Athaliah the mother of Ahaziah *saw*
Ezr. 3:12. and chief of the fathers,...that *had seen*
Neh 13:15. *saw I* in Judah (some) treading
23. *saw I* Jews (that) had married wives of
Est. 7: 7. *he saw* that there was evil determined
8: 6. how can I endure *to see* (marg. be able *that I may see*) the evil
— or how can I endure *to see* the destruction
9:26. (that) which *they had seen*
Job 2:13. *they saw* that (his) grief was very great.
3:16. as infants (which) never *saw* light.
4: 8. Even as *I have seen,*
5: 3. I *have seen* the foolish taking root:
8:18. *I have* not *seen thee.*
9:25. *they see* no good.
13: 1. mine eye *hath seen* all (this),
19:27. mine eyes *shall behold,*
28:10. his eye *seeth* every precious thing.
27. Then *did he see it,*
29: 8. The young men *saw me,*
11. when the eye *saw* (me),
37:21. (men) *see* not the bright light
42: 5. now mine eye *seeth thee.*
Ps. 10:11. *he will* never *see* (it).
14. *Thou hast seen* (it); for thou
31: 7(8). *thou hast considered* my trouble;
33:13. *he beholdeth* all the sons of men.
35:21. our eye *hath seen* (it).
22. *thou hast seen,* O Lord:
37:13. *he seeth* that his day is coming.
25. yet *have I* not *seen* the righteous forsaken,
35. *I have seen* the wicked in great power,
48: 5(6). They *saw* (it, and) so they marvelled;
8(9). so *have we seen* in the city of the Lord
50:18. When *thou sawest* a thief,
54: 7(9). mine eye *hath seen* (his desire)
55: 9(10). *I have seen* violence and strife
66:18. If *I regard* iniquity in my heart,
68:24(25). *They have seen* thy goings,
69:32(33). The humble *shall see* (this),
74: 9. *We see* not our signs:
77:16(17). The waters *saw thee,* O God, the waters *saw thee;*
90:15. years (wherein) *we have seen* evil.
95: 9. When your fathers...*saw* my work.
97: 4. the earth *saw,* and trembled.
6. *and* all the people *see* his glory.
98: 3. all the ends of the earth *have seen*
107:24. These *see* the works of the Lord,
114: 3. The sea *saw* (it), and fled:
119:96. *I have seen* an end of all perfection:
158. *I beheld* the transgressors,
139:16. Thine eyes *did see* my substance,
Pro. 22: 3. A prudent (man) *foreseeth* the evil,
24:32. *I looked upon* (it, and) received instruction.
25: 7. the prince whom thine eyes *have seen.*
26:12. *Seest thou* a man wise in his own conceit?
27:12. A prudent (man) *foreseeth* the evil,
Ecc. 1:14. *I have seen* all the works that are done
16. *had* great *experience* (marg. *seen* much) of wisdom
2:13. *Then* I *saw* that wisdom excelleth
24. This also I *saw,*
3:10. *I have seen* the travail,
13. *and enjoy* the good of all his labour,
16. *I saw* under the sun the place of
22. *Wherefore I perceive* that there is nothing
4: 3. *who hath* not *seen* the evil work
4. *Again,* I *considered* all travail,
15. *I considered* all the living which walk
5:13(12). a sore evil (which) *I have seen*
18(17). (that) which I *have seen:*
6: 1. an evil which *I have seen*
5. *he hath* not *seen* the sun,

Ecc. 6: 6. yet *hath he seen* no good:
7:15. All (things) *have I seen*
8: 9. All this *have I seen,*
10. *I saw* the wicked buried,
17. *Then I beheld* all the work of God,
9:13. This wisdom *have I seen*
10: 5. an evil (which) *I have seen*
7. *I have seen* servants upon horses,
Cant. 3: 3. *Saw ye* him whom my soul loveth?
6: 9. The daughters *saw her,*
Isa. 5:12. neither *consider* the operation
6: 5. mine eyes *have seen* the King,
9: 2(1). The people...*have seen* a great light:
21: 7. *And he saw* a chariot
22: 9. *Ye have seen* also the breaches
11. neither *had respect* unto him
38: 5. *I have seen* thy tears:
39: 4. What *have they seen*
— that (is) in mine house *have they seen:*
40: 5. *and* all flesh *shall see* (it) together:
41: 5. The isles *saw* (it), and feared;
42:20. (כתיב) *Seeing* many things, but thou
44:16. *I have seen* the fire:
52:10. *and* all the ends of the earth *shall see* the
15. (that) which had not been told them *shall they see;*
57:18. *I have seen* his ways,
58: 3. Wherefore have we fasted,...and *thou seest*
62: 2. *And* the Gentiles *shall see* thy
64: 4(3). neither *hath* the eye *seen,*
66: 8. who *hath seen* such things?
14. *when ye see* (this), your heart
18. they shall come, *and see* my glory.
19. neither *have seen* my glory;
24. they shall go forth, *and look* upon the
Jer. 3: 6. *Hast thou seen* (that) which
4:23. *I beheld* the earth,
24. *I beheld* the mountains,
25. *I beheld,* and, lo, (there was) no man,
26. *I beheld,* and, lo, the fruitful place
7:11. even I *have seen* (it),
13:27. *I have seen* thine adulteries,
22:10. *nor see* his native country.
23:13. *I have seen* folly in the prophets
14. *I have seen* also in the prophets
30: 6. wherefore *do I see* every man
33:24. *Considerest thou* not what this people
39: 4. Zedekiah the king of Judah *saw them,*
44: 2. Ye *have seen* all the evil
17. were well, and *saw* no evil.
46: 5. Wherefore *have I seen* them dismayed
51:61. thou comest to Babylon, *and shalt see,*
Lam. 1: 7. the adversaries *saw her,*
8. *they have seen* her nakedness:
10. *she hath seen* (that) the heathen entered
2:16. we have found, *we have seen* (it).
3: 1. I (am) the man (that) *hath seen*
36. the Lord *approveth* (marg. or, *seeth*) not.
59. O Lord, *thou hast seen* my wrong:
60. *Thou hast seen* all their vengeance
Eze. 1:27. *I saw* as it were the appearance of fire,
3:23. *I saw* by the river Chebar:
8: 4. according to the vision that *I saw* in the
12. *hast thou seen* what the ancients
15, 17. *Hast thou seen* (this), O son of man?
10:15. *I saw* by the river of Chebar.
20. the living creature that *I saw*
22. *I saw* by the river of Chebar,
11:24. the vision that *I had seen*
12: 2. have eyes to see, and *see* not;
13: 3. and *have seen* nothing!
14:22. *and ye shall see* their way
16:37. *that they may see* all thy nakedness.
50. I took them away as *I saw* (good).
20:48(21:4). *And* all flesh *shall see*
21:21(26). *he looked* in the liver.
33: 3. *when he seeth* the sword
37: 8. *when I beheld,* lo, the sinews
39:15. *when* (any) *seeth* a man's bone,
21. *and* all the heathen *shall see* my judgment
41: 8. *I saw also* the height of the house
43: 3. the vision which *I saw,* (even) according to the vision that *I saw*
— the vision that *I saw*
47: 6. *hast thou seen* (this)?
Dan. 8: 4. *I saw* the ram pushing westward,
6. the ram...which *I had seen* standing

Dan. 8: 7. *And I saw him* come close unto the ram,
20. The ram which *thou sawest*
9:21. the man Gabriel, whom *I had seen*
10: 7. *And* I Daniel alone *saw*
— the men that were with me *saw*
12: 5. *Then I* Daniel *looked,*
Hos. 6:10. *I have seen* an horrible thing
9:10. *I saw* your fathers
13. as *I saw* Tyrus,
Am. 9: 1. *I saw* the Lord standing
Hab. 3: 6. *he beheld,* and drove asunder the nations;
7. *I saw* the tents of Cushan
10. The mountains *saw thee,*
Hag. 2: 3. that *saw* this house in her first glory?
Zec. 1: 8. *I saw* by night, and behold
4: 2. *I have looked,* and behold a candlestick
10. *and shall see* the plummet in the hand
9: 8. *have I seen* with mine eyes.
Mal. 3:18. *and discern* between the righteous

KAL.—*Infinitive.*

Gen. 2:19. *to see* what he would call them:
8: 8. *to see* if the waters were abated
11: 5. the Lord came down *to see* the city
24:30. *when he saw* the earring
26:28. We saw *certainly* (marg. *Seeing* we saw) that the Lord was with thee:
27: 1. Isaac was old, and his eyes were dim, *so that he could not see,*
33:10. *as though I had seen* the face of God,
34: 1. Dinah...went out *to see* the daughters
39:13. *when she saw* that he had left his
42: 9. spies; *to see* the nakedness of the land
12. but *to see* the nakedness of the land
44:23. ye shall *see* my face no more. (lit. shall not add *to see*)
26. we may not *see* the man's face,
31. *when he seeth* that the lad (is) not
46:30. since *I have seen* thy face,
48:10. (so that) he could not *see.*
11. I had not thought *to see* thy face:
Ex. 3: 4. he turned aside *to see,*
7. I have *surely* seen (lit. *seeing* I have seen) the affliction
10: 5. one cannot be able *to see* the earth:
28. *see* my face no more; (lit. add not *to see*)
— in (that) day *thou seest* my face
29. I will *see* thy face again no more. (lit. I will not add *to see*)
13:17. the people repent *when they see* war,
14:13. ye shall *see them* again no more (lit. ye shall not add *to see them*)
19:21. lest they break through...*to gaze,*
33:20. Thou canst not *see* my face:
Lev. 14:36. the priest go (into it) *to see* the plague,
— the priest shall go in *to see* the house:
Nu. 4:20. they shall not go in *to see*
32: 8. when I sent them...*to see* the land.
35:23. *seeing* (him) not, and cast (it) upon him,
Deu 28:68. Thou shalt *see it* no more (lit. thou shalt not add *to see it*)
29: 4(3). eyes *to see,* and ears to hear,
Jos. 3: 3. *When ye see* the ark of the covenant
8:14. *when* the king of Ai *saw*
Jud. 11:35. *when he saw* her,
14: 8. he turned aside *to see* the carcase
11. *when they saw* him,
1Sa. 1:11. if thou wilt *indeed* look (lit. *looking* thou wilt look)
3: 2. to wax dim, (that) he *could* not *see;*
4:15. his eyes were dim, that he could not *see.*
6:13. saw the ark, and rejoiced *to see* (it).
15:35. Samuel came no more *to see* Saul
17:24. *when they saw* the man, fled
28. that thou *mightest see* the battle.
55. *And when* Saul *saw* David go forth
19:15. Saul sent the messengers...*to see* David,
2Sa. 3:13. when thou comest *to see* my face.
13: 5. when thy father cometh *to see thee,*
6. when the king was come *to see him,*
24:17. *when he saw* the angel
1K. 9:12. Hiram came out...*to see* the cities
14: 4. Ahijah could not *see;*
16:18. *when* Zimri *saw* that the city was taken,
18:17. *when* Ahab *saw* Elijah,
22:32. *when* the captains...*saw* Jehoshaphat,
33. *when* the captains...*perceived*

2K. 4:25. *when* the man of God *saw* her
6:21. the king of Israel...*when he saw* them,
8:29. Ahaziah...went down *to see* Joram
9:16. Ahaziah...was come down *to see*
22. *when* Joram *saw* Jehu,
12:10(11). *when they saw* that (there was) much
23:29. he slew him...*when he had seen* him.
1Ch 21:28. *when* David *saw* that the Lord had
2Ch 12: 7. *And when* the Lord *saw* that they
15: 9. *when they saw* that the Lord...(was) with
18:31. *when* the captains...*saw* Jehoshaphat,
32. *when* the captains...*perceived*
22: 6. Azariah...went down *to see* Jehoram
24:11. *and when they saw*...much money,
26: 5. had understanding *in the visions of* (marg. *seeing*) God:
Est. 3: 4. *to see* whether Mordecai's matters would
5: 2. *when* the king *saw* Esther
9. *but when* Haman *saw* Mordecai
Job 7: 7. mine eye shall no more *see* good. (lit. shall not return *to see*)
10: 4. seest thou *as* man *seeth?*
Ps. 14: 2. *to see* if there were any that did
16:10. wilt thou suffer thine Holy One *to see*
27:13. *to see* the goodness of the Lord
34:12(13). loveth (many) days, *that he may see*
40:12(13). I am not able *to look up;*
41: 6(7). if he come *to see* (me),
53: 2(3). *to see* if there were (any) that did
63: 2(3). *To see* thy power and thy glory,
69:23(24). Let their eyes be darkened, *that they see* not;
106: 5. *That I may see* the good of thy chosen,
113: 6. *to behold* (the things that are) in heaven,
119:37. Turn away mine eyes *from beholding*
Ecc. 1: 8. the eye is not satisfied *with seeing,*
2:12. I turned myself *to behold* wisdom,
3:18. *and that they might see* that they...are
22. who shall bring him *to see*
5:18(17). *and to enjoy* the good of all his
8:16. *and to see* the business that is done
9:11. I returned, *and saw* under the sun,
11: 7. pleasant...for the eyes *to behold* the sun:
Cant.6:11. *to see* the fruits of the valley, and *to see* whether the vine flourished,
Isa. 6: 9. see ye *indeed,* but perceive not.
21: 3. I was dismayed *at the seeing*
29:23. *when he seeth* his children,
33:15. shutteth his eyes *from seeing* evil;
42:18. look, ye blind, *that ye may see.*
20. *Seeing* many things,
44:18. shut their eyes, *that they cannot see;*
Jer. 1:12. Thou hast well *seen:* (lit. thou hast done well *in seeing*)
20:18. *to see* labour and sorrow,
41:13. *when* all the people...*saw* Johanan
Eze.12: 2. have eyes *to see,* and see not;
28:17. *that they may behold* thee.
Dan 8: 2. *when I saw,* that I (was) at Shushan
15. *when I,* (even) I Daniel, *had seen*
Hab. 1:13. (Thou art) of purer eyes *than to behold*
2: 1. *to see* what he will say unto me,
Zec. 2: 2(6). *to see* what (is) the breadth

KAL.—*Imperative.*

Gen13:14. *and look* from the place where thou art
27:27. *See,* the smell of my son
31:12. *and see,* all the rams which leap
50. *see,* God (is) witness betwixt me and
37:14. *see* whether it be well with thy brethren,
39:14. *See,* he hath brought in an Hebrew
41:41. *See,* I have set thee over all the land
Ex. 4:21. *see* that thou do all those wonders
7: 1. *See,* I have made thee a god
10:10. *look* (to it); for evil (is) before you.
14:13. *and see* the salvation of the Lord,
16:29. *See,* for that the Lord hath given
25:40. *And look* that thou make (them) after
31: 2. *See,* I have called my name Bezaleel
33:12. *See,* thou sayest unto me, Bring up this people:
13. *and consider* that this nation (is) thy
35:30. *See,* the Lord hath called by name
Nu. 27:12. *and see* the land which I have given
Deu 1: 8. *Behold,* I have set the land before you:
21. *Behold,* the Lord thy God hath set
2:24. *behold,* I have given into thine hand

Deu 2:31. *Behold,* I have begun to give Sihon
3:27. *and behold* (it) with thine eyes:
4: 5. *Behold,* I have taught you statutes
11:26. *Behold,* I set before you this day
30:15. *See,* I have set before thee
32:39. *See* now that I, (even) I, (am) he,
49. *and behold* the land of Canaan,
Jos. 2: 1. Go *view* the land, even Jericho.
6: 2. *See,* I have given into thine hand
8: 1. *see,* I have given into thy hand the king
4. *Behold,* ye shall lie in wait
8. *See,* I have commanded you.
22:28. *Behold* the pattern of the altar
23: 4. *Behold,* I have divided unto you
Jud.16: 5. *and see* wherein his great strength (lieth),
1Sa.12:16. stand *and see* this great thing,
17. *and see* that your wickedness (is) great,
24. *consider* how great (things) he hath done
14:17. *and see* who is gone from us.
29. *see,* I pray you, how mine eyes have been
38. *and see* wherein this sin hath been
16:17. *Provide* me now a man
23:22. know *and see* his place
23. *See therefore,* and take knowledge
24:11(12). Moreover, my father, *see,* yea, *see* the skirt of thy robe
—(—). *and see* that (there is) neither evil
25:17. know *and consider* what thou wilt do;
35. *see,* I have hearkened to thy voice,
26:16. *see* where the king's spear (is),
2Sa. 7: 2. *See* now, I dwell in an house of cedar,
13:28. *Mark ye* now when Amnon's heart is
14:30. *See,* Joab's field is near mine,
15: 3. *See,* thy matters (are) good
28. *See,* I will tarry in the plain
24:13. *and see* what answer I shall return
22. *behold,* (here be) oxen
1K. 12:16. *see* to thine own house, David.
17:23. Elijah said, *See,* thy son liveth.
20: 7. *and see* how this (man) seeketh mischief:
22. *and see* what thou doest:
2K. 5: 7. I pray you, *and see* how he seeketh
6:13. Go *and spy* where he (is),
32. *look,* when the messenger cometh,
7:14. the king sent after the host...saying, Go *and see.*
9: 2. *look out* there Jehu the son of
10:16. *and see* my zeal for the Lord.
23. *and look* that there be here with you none
19:16. open, Lord, thine eyes, *and see:*
1Ch 21:12. *advise thyself* what word I shall bring
23. *lo,* I give (thee) the oxen (also)
28:10. *Take heed* now;
2Ch 10:16. David, *see* to thine own house.
19: 6. *Take heed* what ye do:
20:17. *and see* the salvation of the Lord
Job 10:15. *therefore see thou* mine affliction;
22:12. *and behold* the height of the stars,
35: 5. Look unto the heavens, *and see;*
40:11. *and behold* every one (that is) proud,
12. *Look* on every one (that is) proud,
Ps. 9:13(14). *consider* my trouble (which I suffer)
25:18. *Look* upon mine affliction
19. *Consider* mine enemies;
34: 8(9). O taste *and see* that the Lord (is)
37:37. *and behold* the upright:
45:10(11). Hearken, O daughter, *and consider,*
59: 4(5). awake to help me, *and behold.*
66: 5. Come *and see* the works of God:
80:14(15). look down from heaven, *and behold,*
84: 9(10). *Behold,* O God our shield,
119:153. *Consider* mine affliction,
159. *Consider* how I love thy precepts:
128: 5. *and thou shalt see* the good of Jerusalem
6. *Yea, thou shalt see* thy children's children,
139:24. *And see* if (there be any) wicked way in
142: 4(5). *and beheld* (marg. or, *and see*), but (there was) no man
Pro. 6: 6. Go to the ant, thou sluggard; *consider*
Ecc. 1:10. *See,* this (is) new?
2: 1. *therefore enjoy* pleasure:
7:13. *Consider* the work of God:
14. in the day of adversity *consider:*
27. *Behold,* this have I found,
29. *Lo,* this only have I found,
9: 9. Live *joyfully* (marg. *See,* or, *enjoy* life) with the wife whom thou lovest

Cant.3:11. *and behold* king Solomon
Isa. 6: 9. *and see ye* indeed, but perceive not.
37:17. open thine eyes, O Lord, *and see:*
40:26. *and behold* who hath created these
49:18. Lift up thine eyes round about, *and behold:*
60: 4. Lift up thine eyes round about, *and see:*
63:15. Look down from heaven, *and behold*
Jer. 1:10. *See*, I have this day set thee over
2:10. pass over the isles of Chittim, *and see;*
— consider diligently, *and see*
19. know therefore *and see*
23. *see* thy way in the valley, know what thou hast done:
31. *see* ye the word of the Lord.
3: 2. *and see* where thou hast not been lien
5: 1. *and see* now, and know, and seek
6:16. *and see*, and ask for the old paths,
7:12. *and see* what I did to it
13:20. Lift up your eyes, *and behold*
30: 6. *and see* whether a man doth travail
40: 4. *behold*, all the land (is) before thee:
Lam.1: 9. O Lord, *behold* my affliction:
11. *see*, O Lord, and consider;
12. *and see* if there be any sorrow
18. *and behold* my sorrow:
20. *Behold*, O Lord; for I (am) in distress:
2:20. *Behold*, O Lord, and consider
5: 1. *behold* our reproach.
Eze. 4:15. *Lo*, I have given thee cow's dung for
8: 9. *and behold* the wicked abominations
40: 4. Son of man, *behold* with thine eyes,
44: 5. *and behold* with thine eyes,
Dan 9:18. *and behold* our desolations,
Am. 3: 9. *and behold* the great tumults
6: 2. Pass ye unto Calneh, *and see;*
Hab 1: 5. *Behold* ye among the heathen,
Zec. 3: 4. *Behold*, I have caused thine iniquity to
5: 5. Lift up now thine eyes, *and see*
6: 8. *Behold*, these that go toward the north

KAL.—*Future.*

Gen 1: 4. *And* God *saw* the light,
10, 12, 18, 21, 25. *and* God *saw* that (it was) good.
31. *And* God *saw* every thing that he had
3: 6. And *when* the woman *saw*
6: 2. *That* the sons of God *saw* the daughters
5. *And* God *saw* that the wickedness of
12. *And* God *looked* upon the earth,
8:13. Noah removed the covering of the ark, *and looked*,
9:22. *And* Ham,...*saw* the nakedness of his
12:12. when the Egyptians *shall see* thee,
14. *that*, when...the Egyptians *beheld* the
15. The princes *also* of Pharaoh *saw* her,
13:10. *and beheld* all the plain of Jordan,
16: 4, 5. *when she saw* that she had conceived,
18: 2. he lift up his eyes *and looked*,
— *when he saw* (them),
21. I will go down now, *and see*
19: 1. *and* Lot *seeing* (them) rose up
28. *and beheld*, and, lo, the smoke
21: 9. *And* Sarah *saw* the son of Hagar
16. *Let me* not *see* the death of the child.
19. *and she saw* a well of water;
22: 4. *and saw* the place afar off.
8. God *will provide* himself a lamb
13. Abraham lifted up his eyes, *and looked*,
14. called the name of that place Jehovah-*jireh:* (marg. The Lord *will see*, or, *provide*)
24:63. he lifted up his eyes, *and saw*,
64. *when she saw* Isaac,
26: 8. looked out at a window, *and saw*,
28: 6. *When* Esau *saw* that Isaac had blessed
8. *And* Esau *seeing* that the daughters of Canaan pleased not
29: 2. *And he looked*, and behold a well
31. *when* the Lord *saw* that Leah (was)
30: 1. *when* Rachel *saw* that she bare
9. *When* Leah *saw* that she had left bearing,
31: 2. *And* Jacob *beheld* the countenance of
10. I lifted up mine eyes, *and saw*
32:20(21). afterward *I will see* his face;
25(26). *when he saw* that he prevailed not
33: 1. Jacob lifted up his eyes, *and looked*,
5. he lifted up his eyes, *and saw* the women

Gen34: 2. *when* Shechem...*saw* her,
37: 4. *when* his brethren *saw* that their father loved him
18. *when they saw* him afar off,
20. *and we shall see* what will become of his
25. they lifted up their eyes *and looked*,
38: 2. *And* Judah *saw* there a daughter of
15. *When* Judah *saw her*,
39: 3. *And* his master *saw* that the Lord (was)
40: 6. Joseph came in...*and looked* upon them,
16. *When* the chief baker *saw* that
41:22. *And I saw* in my dream,
33. *let* Pharaoh *look out* a man discreet
42: 1. Now *when* Jacob *saw* that there was corn
7. *And* Joseph *saw* his brethren,
27. *And* as one of them opened his sack...*he espied*
35. *when* (both) they and their father *saw*
43: 3, 5. *Ye shall* not *see* my face,
16. *when* Joseph *saw* Benjamin
29. he lifted up his eyes, *and saw* his brother
44:34. lest peradventure *I see* the evil
45:27. *when he saw* the wagons
28. I will go *and see him* before I die.
48: 8. *And* Israel *beheld* Joseph's sons,
17. *when* Joseph *saw* that his father laid
49:15. *And he saw* that rest (was) good,
50:11. *when* the inhabitants...*saw* the mourning
15. *when* Joseph's brethren *saw*
23. *And* Joseph *saw* Ephraim's children
Ex. 2: 2. *when she saw* him
5. *when she saw* the ark
6. *when* she had opened (it), *she saw* the
11. *and looked* on their burdens: *and he spied* an Egyptian smiting
12. *when he saw* that (there was) no man,
25. *And* God *looked* upon the children of
3: 2. *and he looked*, and, behold, the bush
3. I will now turn aside, *and see*
4. *when* the Lord *saw* that he turned aside
4:18. *and see* whether they be yet alive.
5:19. *And* the officers of the children of Israel *did see*
21. The Lord *look* upon you, and judge;
6: 1. Now *shalt thou see* what I will do
8:15(11). *But when* Pharaoh *saw* that there was respite,
9:34. *when* Pharaoh *saw* that the rain...ceased,
14:30. *and* Israel *saw* the Egyptians dead
31. *And* Israel *saw* that great work
16:15. *when* the children of Israel *saw*
32. that *they may see* the bread
18:14. *when* Moses' father in law *saw*
20:18. and *when* the people *saw* (it),
23: 5. If *thou see* the ass of him that hateth
24:10. *And they saw* the God of Israel:
32: 1. *when* the people *saw* that Moses delayed
5. *when* Aaron *saw* (it),
19. *that he saw* the calf,
25. *when* Moses *saw* that the people (were)
33:20. *there shall* no man *see me*, and live.
34:30. *when* Aaron...*saw* Moses,
39:43. *And* Moses *did look* upon all the work,
Lev. 9:24. *when* all the people *saw*,
13:21, 26. if the priest *look on it*,
31. if the priest *look* on the plague
53. if the priest *shall look*,
20:17. *she see* his nakedness;
Nu. 11:15. *let me* not *see* my wretchedness.
23. *thou shalt see* now whether my word
14:23. *they shall* not *see* the land
— neither *shall* any of them...*see it:*
17: 9(24). *and they looked*, and took every man
20:29. *when* all the congregation *saw*
22: 2. *And* Balak the son of Zippor *saw* all
23. *And* the ass *saw* the angel
25, 27. *when* the ass *saw* the angel
31. *and he saw* the angel of the Lord
33. *And* the ass *saw me*, and turned from me
41. *that* thence *he might see* the utmost
23: 9. from the top of the rocks *I see him*,
13. from whence *thou mayest see them: thou shalt see* but the utmost part of them, and *shalt* not *see* them all:
24: 1. *when* Balaam *saw* that it pleased
2. lifted up his eyes, *and he saw* Israel
17. *I shall see him*, but not now:

Nu. 24:20. *when he looked* on Amalek,
21. *And he looked* on the Kenites,
25: 7. *when* Phinehas, the son of Eleazar,...*saw*
32: 1. *when they saw* the land of Jazer,
9. when they went up...*and saw* the land,
11. none of the men...*shall see* the land
Deu 1:35. *there shall* not one...*see* that good land,
36. Save Caleb...he *shall see it,*
3:25. let me go over, *and see* the good land
28. the land which *thou shalt see.*
4:28. gods,...which neither *see,* nor hear,
9:16. *And I looked,* and, behold, ye had sinned
12:13. every place that *thou seest:*
18:16. neither *let me see* this great fire
22: 1. *Thou shalt* not *see* thy brother's ox...go astray,
4. *Thou shalt* not *see* thy brother's ass...fall
23:14(15). that *he see* no unclean thing
26: 7. *and looked* on our affliction,
28:34, 67. the sight of thine eyes which *thou shalt see.*
29:17(16). *And ye have seen* their abominations,
32:19. *when* the Lord *saw* (it), he abhorred
20. *I will see* what their end (shall be):
36. when *he seeth* that (their) power is gone,
52. Yet *thou shalt see* the land
33:21. *And he provided* the first part for himself,
Jos. 5:13. he lifted up his eyes *and looked,*
7:21. *When I saw*...a goodly Babylonish
8:20. *And* when the men of Ai looked...*they saw,*
24: 7. *and* your eyes *have seen* what I have done
Jud. 1:24. *And* the spies *saw* a man come forth
3:24. *when they saw* that, behold, the doors...(were) locked,
6:22. *And* when Gideon *perceived*
7:17. *Look* on me, and do likewise:
9:36. *when* Gaal *saw* the people,
43. laid wait in the field, *and looked,*
55. *when* the men of Israel *saw* that
12: 3. *when I saw* that ye delivered (me) not,
14: 1. *and saw* a woman in Timnath
16: 1. Then went Samson to Gaza, *and saw* there
18. *when* Delilah *saw* that he had told her
24. *when* the people *saw* him,
18: 7. *and saw* the people that (were) therein,
26. *when* Micah *saw* that they (were) too
19: 3. *when* the father of the damsel *saw him,*
17. *And* when...*he saw* a wayfaring man
20:36. *So* the children of Benjamin *saw* that they were smitten:
Ru. 1:18. *When she saw* that she was stedfastly
2:18. *and* her mother in law *saw*
1Sa. 1:11. if *thou wilt* indeed *look* on
5: 7. *when* the men of Ashdod *saw*
6:13. they lifted up their eyes, *and saw* the ark,
10:11. *when* all that knew him...*saw*
14. *when we saw* that (they were) no where,
12:12. *when ye saw* that Nahash...came against
14:16. *And* the watchmen of Saul...*looked;*
16: 6. *that he looked* on Eliab, and said,
7. (the Lord seeth) not as man *seeth;* for man *looketh* on the outward appearance, but the Lord *looketh* on the heart.
17:42. Philistine looked about, *and saw* David,
51. *when* the Philistines *saw*
18:15. *when* Saul *saw* that he behaved
28. *And* Saul *saw* and knew
19:20. *when they saw* the company
20:29. let me get away,...*and see* my brethren.
21:14(15). *ye see* the man is mad:
23:15. *And* David *saw* that Saul was come
24:15(16). *and see,* and plead my cause,
25:23. *when* Abigail *saw* David,
26: 3. *and he saw* that Saul came
5. *and* David *beheld* the place
28: 5. *when* Saul *saw* the host
12. *when* the woman *saw* Samuel,
21. *and saw* that he was sore troubled,
31: 5. *when* his armourbearer *saw* that Saul
7. *when* the men of Israel...*saw*
2Sa. 1: 7. *And* when...*he saw me,* and called unto me.
3:13. *Thou shalt* not *see* my face,
6:16. *and saw* king David leaping
10: 6. *when* the children of Ammon *saw*
9. *When* Joab *saw* that the front
15. *when* the Syrians *saw*
19. *when* all the kings...*saw*

2Sa.11: 2. *and* from the roof *he saw* a woman
12:19. *when* David *saw* that his servants
13: 5. dress the meat...that *I may see* (it),
34. *and looked,* and, behold, there came much
14:24. and *let him* not *see* my face.
32. *let me see* the king's face;
16:12. the Lord *will look* on mine affliction,
17:18. *Nevertheless* a lad *saw them,* and told
18:10. *And* a certain man *saw* (it),
24. the watchman...lifted up his eyes, *and looked,*
26. *And* the watchman *saw* another man
20:12. *when* the man *saw*
24:20. Araunah looked, *and saw* the king
1K. 10: 4. *when* the queen of Sheba *had seen*
7. *and* mine eyes *had seen*
11:28. *and* Solomon *seeing* the young man
12:16. *when* all Israel *saw* that the king hearkened
13:12. *For* his sons *had seen* what way the man
25. men passed by, *and saw* the carcase
18:39. *when* all the people *saw* (it),
19: 3. *when he saw* (that), he arose,
2K. 2:10. if *thou see* me (when I am) taken
15. *when* the sons of the prophets...*saw him,*
24. he turned back, *and looked on them,*
3:14. would not look toward thee, nor *see thee.*
17. *Ye shall* not *see* wind, neither *shall ye see* rain;
22. *and* the Moabites *saw* the water
26. *when* the king of Moab *saw* that the battle
5:21. *when* Naaman *saw* (him) running
6:17. open his eyes, *that he may see.* And the Lord opened the eyes of the young man; *and he saw:*
20. open the eyes of these (men), *that they may see.* And the Lord opened their eyes, *and they saw;*
30. *and* the people *looked,* and, behold,
7:13. let us send *and see.*
9:17. *and he spied* the company of Jehu as he
11:14. *when she looked,* behold, the king stood
16:10. *and saw* an altar that (was) at Damascus:
12. *And* when...the king *saw* the altar:
22:20. thine eyes *shall* not *see* all the evil
23:16. *And* as...*he spied* the sepulchres
1Ch 10: 5. *when* his armourbearer *saw*
7. *when* all the men of Israel...*saw*
12:17. the God of our fathers *look* (thereon),
15:29. that Michal...*saw* king David dancing
19: 6. *when* the children of Ammon *saw*
10. Now *when* Joab *saw*
16. *when* the Syrians *saw* that they were put to the worse
19. *when* the servants of Hadarezer *saw* that they were put to the worse
21:16. David...*and saw* the angel of the Lord
20. Ornan turned back, *and saw* the angel;
21. Ornan looked *and saw* David,
2Ch 9: 3. *when* the queen of Sheba *had seen* the
6. *and* mine eyes *had seen* (it):
23:13. *And she looked,* and, behold, the king
24:22. The Lord *look* upon (it),
31: 8. when Hezekiah and the princes came *and saw* the heaps,
32: 2. *when* Hezekiah *saw* that Sennacherib was
34:28. neither *shall* thine eyes *see* all the evil
Neh 4:11(5). They shall not know, neither *see,*
14(8). *And I looked,* and rose up,
6:16. *and* all the heathen that (were) about us *saw*
9: 9. *And didst see* the affliction of our fathers
Est. 3: 5. *when* Haman *saw* that Mordecai bowed
Job 3: 9. neither *let it see* the dawning of the day:
6:21. *ye see* (my) casting down,
9:11. he goeth by me, and *I see* (him) not:
10: 4. *seest thou* as man seeth?
18. no eye *had seen me!*
11:11. *he seeth* wickedness *also;*
20:17. *He shall* not *see* the rivers,
21:20. His eyes *shall see* his destruction,
22:11. darkness, (that) *thou canst* not *see;*
14. a covering to him, that *he seeth* not;
19. The righteous *see* (it),
23: 9. hideth himself...that *I cannot see* (him):
28:24. (and) *seeth* under the whole heaven;
31: 4. *Doth* not he *see* my ways,
19. If *I have seen* any perish

Job 31:21. when *I saw* my help in the gate:
26. If *I beheld* the sun when it shined,
32: 5. *When* Elihu *saw* that (there was) no
33:26. *and he shall see* his face with joy:
28. his life *shall see* the light.
34:21. *he seeth* all his goings.
37:24. *he respecteth* not any
38:17. *hast thou seen* the doors of the shadow
22. *hast thou seen* the treasures of the hail,
41:34(26). *He beholdeth* all high (things):
42:16. *and saw* his sons, and his sons' sons,
Ps. 8: 3(4). When *I consider* thy heavens,
22:17(18). they look (and) *stare* upon me.
35:17. Lord, how long *wilt thou look on?*
36: 9(10). in thy light *shall we see* light.
37:34. when the wicked are cut off, *thou shalt see*
40: 3(4). many *shall see* (it), and fear,
49: 9(10). live for ever, (and) not *see*
10(11). *he seeth* (that) wise men die,
19(20). *they shall* never *see* light.
52: 6(8). The righteous *also shall see*, and fear,
64: 5(6). they say, Who *shall see* them?
73: 3. (when) *I saw* the prosperity of
86:17. *that* they which hate me *may see*
89:48(49). (that) liveth, and *shall* not *see* death?
91: 8. and *see* the reward of the
94: 7. they say, The Lord *shall* not *see*,
106:44. *Nevertheless he regarded* their affliction,
107:42. The righteous *shall see* (it),
109:25. *they looked* upon me
112: 8. until *he see* (his desire)
10. The wicked *shall see* (it),
115: 5. eyes have they, but *they see* not:
118: 7. therefore *shall* I *see* (my desire)
119:74. will be glad *when they see me;*
135:16. eyes have they, but *they see* not;
138: 6. yet *hath he respect* unto the lowly:
Pro. 7: 7. *And beheld* among the simple ones,
23:31. *Look* not thou upon the wine
33. Thine eyes *shall behold* strange women,
24:18. Lest the Lord *see* (it),
29:16. the righteous *shall see* their fall.
Ecc. 2: 3. till *I might see* what (was) that good
4: 1. I returned, *and considered*
7. *and I saw* vanity under the sun.
5: 8(7). If *thou seest* the oppression of the
Cant. 1: 6. *Look* not *upon me*, because I (am) black,
7:12(13). *let us see* if the vine flourish,
Isa. 5:19. hasten his work, that *we may see* (it):
6: 1. *I saw also* the Lord sitting
10. *lest they see* with their eyes,
17: 7. his eyes *shall have respect* to the Holy One of Israel.
8. neither *shall respect* (that) which
18: 3. *see ye*, when he lifteth up an ensign
21: 6. let him declare what *he seeth.*
26:10. *will* not *behold* the majesty of the Lord.
28: 4. he that looketh upon it *seeth,*
29:18. the eyes of the blind *shall see*
30:10. Which say to the seers, *See* not;
33:17. *they shall behold* the land that is
19. *Thou shalt* not *see* a fierce people,
20. thine eyes *shall see* Jerusalem
35: 2. *they shall see* the glory of the Lord,
38:11. *I shall* not *see* the Lord,
41:20. That *they may see*, and know,
23. that we may be dismayed, *and behold* (it)
28. *For I beheld*, and (there was) no man;
44: 9. *they see* not, nor know;
49: 7. Kings *shall see* and arise,
52: 8. *they shall see* eye to eye,
53: 2. *when we shall see him,*
10. *he shall see* (his) seed,
11. *He shall see* of the travail of his soul,
58: 7. when *thou seest* the naked,
59:15. *and* the Lord *saw* (it),
16. *And he saw* that (there was) no man,
60: 5. Then *thou shalt see*, and flow together,
[see also יָרָא]
Jer. 3: 7. *And* her treacherous sister Judah *saw*
8. *And I saw*, when for all the causes
4:21. How long *shall I see* the standard,
5:12. neither *shall we see* sword
21. O foolish people,...which have eyes, and *see* not;
11:20. *let me see* thy vengeance
12: 3. *thou hast seen me*, and tried mine heart

Jer. 12: 4. *He shall* not *see* our last end.
14:13. *Ye shall* not *see* the sword,
17: 6. *shall* not *see* when good cometh;
8. *shall* not *see* when heat cometh,
18:17. *I will shew them* the back,
20:12. *let me see* thy vengeance
22:12. *shall see* this land no more.
23:18. *and hath perceived* and heard his word?
24. *I shall* not *see him?*
29:32. neither *shall he behold* the good
31:26. I awaked, *and beheld;*
32: 4. his eyes *shall behold* his eyes;
34: 3. thine eyes *shall behold* the eyes of
42:14. where *we shall see* no war,
18. *ye shall see* this place no more.
Lam. 3:50. Till the Lord look down, *and behold*
Eze. 1: 1. *and I saw* visions of God.
4. *And I looked*, and, behold, a whirlwind
15. *Now as I beheld* the living creatures,
27. *And I saw* as the colour of amber,
28. *when I saw* (it), I fell upon my face,
2: 9. *when I looked*, behold, an hand (was)
8: 2. *Then I beheld*, and lo a likeness
6, 13, 15. *thou shalt see* greater abominations.
7. *when I looked*, behold a hole in the wall.
10. So I went in *and saw;*
10: 1. *Then I looked*, and, behold, in the
9. *when I looked*, behold the four wheels
11: 1. *I saw* Jaazaniah the son of Azur,
12: 3. it may be *they will consider*,
6. that *thou see* not the ground:
12. *that he see* not the ground
13. yet *shall he* not *see* it,
14:23. when *ye see* their ways and their doings:
16: 6. *and saw thee* polluted in thine own blood,
8. when I passed by thee, *and looked upon thee*,
18:14. a son, *that seeth* all his father's sins
— *and considereth*, and doeth not such like.
28. *Because he considereth*, and turneth
19: 5. *when she saw* that she had waited,
20:28. *then they saw* every high hill,
23:11. *when* her sister Aholibah *saw* (this),
13. *Then I saw* that she was defiled,
14. *when she saw* men pourtrayed
32:31. Pharaoh *shall see* them,
33: 6. if the watchman *see* the sword
44: 4. *and I looked*, and, behold, the glory of the Lord
Dan 1:10. why *should he see* your faces worse
13. as *thou seest*, deal with thy servants.
8: 2. *And I saw* in a vision; and it came
— *and I saw* in a vision, and I was
3. Then I lifted up mine eyes, *and saw*,
10: 5. Then I lifted up mine eyes, *and looked*,
8. *and saw* this great vision,
Hos. 5:13. *When* Ephraim *saw* his sickness,
Joel 2:28(3:1). your young men *shall see* visions:
Obad. 12, 13. *thou shouldest* not *have looked*
Jon. 3:10. *And* God *saw* their works,
4: 5. till *he might see* what would become
Mic. 6: 9. (the man of) wisdom *shall see* thy name:
7: 9. *I shall behold* his righteousness.
10. *Then* (she that is) mine enemy *shall see*
— mine eyes *shall behold*
16. The nations *shall see*
Zep. 3:15. *thou shalt* not *see* evil any more.
Zec. 1:18(2:1). Then lifted I up mine eyes, *and saw*,
2: 1(5). I lifted up mine eyes again, *and looked*,
5: 1. lifted up mine eyes, *and looked*,
9. Then lifted I up mine eyes, *and looked*,
6: 1. lifted up mine eyes, *and looked*,
9: 5. Ashkelon *shall see* (it),
10: 7. their children *shall see* (it),
Mal. 1: 5. your eyes *shall see*,

KAL.—*Participle.* Poel.

Gen 13:15. all the land which thou *seest*,
31: 5. I *see* your father's countenance,
43. all that thou *seest* (is) mine:
39:23. The keeper of the prison *looked* not to
45:12. behold, your eyes *see*,
Ex. 20:18. all the people *saw* the thunderings,
22:10(9). no man *seeing*
Nu. 14:22. all those men *which have seen*
Deu 3:21. Thine eyes *have seen* all that the Lord... hath done

Deu 4: 3. Your eyes *have seen* what the Lord did
12. *saw* no similitude ;
11: 7. your eyes *have seen* all the great acts
28:32. thine eyes *shall look,*
Jud. 9:36. Thou *seest* the shadow of the mountains
13:19, 20. Manoah and his wife *looked on.*
16:27. thousand men and women, *that beheld*
19:30. that all *that saw* it
1Sa. 9: 9. let us go to *the seer :* for (he that is) now (called) a Prophet was beforetime called *a Seer.*
11. Is *the seer* here?
18. Tell me,...where *the seer's* house (is).
19. Samuel answered...I (am) *the seer :*
26:12. no man *saw* (it),
2Sa. 15:27. (Art not) thou *a seer?*
18:27. Me *thinketh* (marg. I *see*) the running of the foremost is like
24: 3. that the eyes of my lord...*may see*
1K. 1:48. mine eyes even *seeing* (it).
22:25. thou *shalt see* in that day,
2K. 2:12. And Elisha *saw* (it), and he cried,
19. as my lord *seeth :*
7: 2, 19. thou *shalt see* (it) with thine eyes,
9:17. I *see* a company.
23:17. What title (is) that I *see?*
25:19. of *them that were in* the king's presence, (marg. *of them that saw* the king's face)
1Ch 9:22. whom David and Samuel *the seer* did
26:28. all that Samuel *the seer,*...had dedicated;
29:29. the book of Samuel *the seer,*
2Ch 7: 3. when all the children of Israel *saw*
16: 7. Hanani *the seer* came to Asa
10. Asa was wroth with *the seer,*
18:24. thou *shalt see* on that day
29: 8. as ye *see* with your eyes.
30: 7. gave them up to desolation, as ye *see.*
Neh 2:17. Ye *see* the distress that we (are) in,
Est. 1:14. seven princes...*which saw* the king's face,
2:15. all them *that looked upon her.*
5:13. so long as I *see* Mordecai the Jew sitting
Job 20: 7. *they which have seen him* shall say,
34:26. in the open *sight of others ;* (marg. the place of *beholders*)
Ps. 22: 7(8). All they *that see me* laugh
31:11(12). *they that did see me* without
64: 8(9). all *that see* them shall flee away.
Pro. 20:12. The hearing ear, and the *seeing* eye,
Ecc. 7:11. *to them that see* the sun.
8:16. neither day nor night *seeth* sleep
11: 4. *and he that regardeth* the clouds
12: 3. *those that look* out of the windows
Isa. 14:16. *They that see thee* shall narrowly look
28: 4. *he that looketh* upon it
29:15. they say, Who *seeth us?*
30:10. Which say *to the seers,* See not;
20. thine eyes *shall see* thy teachers:
32: 3. the eyes of them *that see*
47:10. thou hast said, None *seeth me.*
61: 9. all *that see them* shall acknowledge
Jer. 1:11. Jeremiah, what *seest* thou?
— I *see* a rod of an almond tree.
13. What *seest* thou?
— I *see* a seething pot;
7:17. *Seest* thou not what they do
20: 4. thine eyes *shall behold*
12. *seest* the reins and the heart,
24: 3. What *seest* thou, Jeremiah?
32:24. behold, thou *seest*
42: 2. as thine eyes *do behold*
52:25. *of them that were near* the king's person, (marg. of them *that saw* the face of the king)
Eze. 8: 6. *seest* thou what they do?
12. The Lord *seeth* us not;
9: 9. the Lord *seeth* not.
28:18. all *them that behold thee.*
40: 4. declare all that thou *seest*
Am. 7: 8 & 8:2. Amos, what *seest* thou?
Nah 3: 7. all *they that look upon thee*
Hag 2: 3. how do ye *see* it now?
Zec. 4: 2. And said unto me, What *seest* thou?
5: 2. What *seest* thou? And I answered, I *see* a flying roll;

KAL.—*Participle.* Paül.

Est. 2: 9. seven maidens, (which were) *meet*

* NIPHAL.—*Preterite.* *

Gen 8: 5. *were* the tops of the mountains *seen.*
9:14. *that* the bow *shall be seen*
48: 3. God Almighty *appeared* (lit. *was seen*)
Ex. 3:16. The Lord God of your fathers,...*appeared*
4: 1. The Lord *hath* not *appeared*
5. the God of Jacob, *hath appeared*
16:10. the glory of the Lord *appeared*
Lev. 9: 4. to day the Lord *will appear* unto you.
13: 7. *he shall be seen* of the priest
19. *and it be shewed* to the priest;
14:35. *It seemeth* to me...a plague
Nu. 14:10. the glory of the Lord *appeared*
14. thou Lord *art seen* face to face.
Jud. 13:10. the man *hath appeared* unto me,
19:30. There was no such deed done nor *seen*
1Sa. 1:22. *that he may appear* before the Lord,
1K. 3: 5. In Gibeon the Lord *appeared*
6:18. there *was* no stone *seen.*
9: 2. as *he had appeared* unto him at Gibeon.
10:12. nor *were seen* unto this day.
11: 9. the Lord God of Israel, *which had appeared*
2K. 23:24. the abominations that *were spied*
2Ch 1: 7. that night *did* God *appear* unto Solomon,
3: 1. where (the Lord) *appeared* unto David (marg. or, which *was seen* of David)
9:11. there *were* none such *seen*
Ps. 102:16(17). *he shall appear* in his glory.
Pro. 27:25. the tender grass *sheweth itself,*
Cant. 2:12. The flowers *appear* on the earth;
Isa. 16:12. when *it is seen* that Moab is weary
Jer. 13:26. *that* thy shame *may appear.*
31: 3. The Lord *hath appeared*
Eze. 10: 1. *there appeared* over them
Dan 1:15. their countenances *appeared* fairer
8: 1. a vision *appeared* unto me,
— after *that which appeared*

NIPHAL.—*Infinitive.*

Ex. 34:24. *to appear* before the Lord
Lev. 13: 7. after that *he hath been seen* of the priest
14. when raw flesh *appeareth*
Deu 31:11. When all Israel is come *to appear*
Jud. 13:21. the angel of the Lord did no more *appear* (lit. added not *to appear*)
1Sa. 3:21. the Lord *appeared* again (lit. added *to appear*)
2Sa. 17:17. they might not *be seen*
1K. 18: 2. Elijah went *to shew himself*
Isa. 1:12. When ye come *to appear* (marg. *be seen*)
Eze. 21:24(29). *so that*...your sins *do appear;*
Mal. 3: 2. who shall stand *when he appeareth?*

NIPHAL.—*Imperative.*

1K. 18: 1. Go, *shew thyself* (lit. *be seen*) unto Ahab;

NIPHAL.—*Future.*

Gen 1: 9. *and let* the dry (land) *appear.*
12: 7. *And* the Lord *appeared* unto Abram,
17: 1. *And* when...the Lord *appeared* to Abram,
18: 1. *And* the Lord *appeared* unto him
22:14. In the mount of the Lord *it shall be seen.*
26: 2, 24. *And* the Lord *appeared* unto him,
35: 9. *And* God *appeared* unto Jacob
46:29. *and presented himself* unto him;
Ex. 3: 2. *And* the angel of the Lord *appeared*
6: 3. *And I appeared* unto Abraham,
13: 7. *there shall* no leavened bread *be seen* with thee, neither *shall there be* leaven *seen*
23:15. none *shall appear* before me empty:
17. all thy males *shall appear*
33:23. but my face *shall* not *be seen.*
34: 3. neither *let* any man *be seen*
20. none *shall appear* before me empty.
23. *shall* all your menchildren *appear* before
Lev. 9: 6. *and* the glory of the Lord *shall appear*
23. *and* the glory of the Lord *appeared*
13:57. if *it appear* still in the garment,
16: 2. *I will appear* in the cloud
Nu. 16:19, 42(17:7) & 20:6. *and* the glory of the Lord *appeared*
Deu 16: 4. *there shall be* no leavened bread *seen*
16. *shall* all thy males *appear* before the Lord thy God
— *they shall* not *appear*...empty:
31:15. *And* the Lord *appeared* in the tabernacle
Jud. 5: 8. *was there* a shield or spear *seen*
6:12 & 13:3. *And* the angel of the Lord *appeared*

2Sa.22:11. *and he was seen* upon the wings of the
16. *And* the channels of the sea *appeared*,
1K. 8: 8. *that* the ends of the staves *were seen*
— *they were* not *seen* without:
9: 2. *That* the Lord *appeared* to Solomon
18:15. *I will* surely *shew myself*
2Ch 5: 9. *that* the ends of the staves *were seen*
— *they were* not *seen* without.
7:12. *And* the Lord *appeared* to Solomon
Ps. 18:15(16). *Then* the channels of waters *were seen*,
42: 2(3). when shall I come *and appear*
84: 7(8). (every one of them) in Zion *appeareth*
90:16. *Let* thy work *appear*
Isa. 47: 3. thy shame *shall be seen :*
60: 2. his glory *shall be seen* upon thee.
Eze.10: 8. *And there appeared* in the cherubims
19:11. *and she appeared* in her height
Dan 1:13. *Then let* our countenances *be looked upon*
Zec. 9:14. the Lord *shall be seen* over them,

NIPHAL.—*Participle.*

Gen12: 7. unto the Lord, who *appeared* unto him.
35: 1. God, *that appeared* unto thee
Isa. 66: 5. *but he shall appear* to your joy, and they

* PUAL.—*Preterite.* *

Job 33:21. his bones (that) *were* not *seen*

* HIPHIL.—*Preterite.* *

Gen41:28. *he sheweth* unto Pharaoh.
48:11. God *hath shewed* me also thy seed.
Ex. 27: 8. as *it was shewed* (marg. *he shewed*) thee in the mount,
Nu. 8: 4. the Lord *had shewed* Moses,
Deu 4:36. *he shewed thee* his great fire ;
5:24(21). the Lord our God *hath shewed us*
34: 4. *I have caused thee to see*
Jud.13:23. neither *would he have shewed us*
2Sa.15:25. *and shew me* (both) it, and his habitation:
2K. 8:10. *howbeit* the Lord *hath shewed me*
13. The Lord *hath shewed me* that thou
20:13. nothing...that Hezekiah *shewed them* not.
15. nothing...that *I have* not *shewed them.*
Ps. 60: 3(5). *Thou hast shewed* thy people hard
71:20. which *hast shewed me* great...troubles,
78:11. his wonders that *he had shewed them.*
Ecc. 2:24. *and* (that) *he should make* his soul *enjoy*
Isa. 39: 2. nothing...that Hezekiah *shewed them* not.
4. nothing...that *I have* not *shewed them.*
Jer. 11:18. then *thou shewedst me* their doings.
24: 1. The Lord *shewed me*,
38:21. the word that the Lord *hath shewed me :*
Eze.11:25. the things that the Lord *had shewed me.*
Am. 7: 1, 4. Thus *hath* the Lord God *shewed unto me ;*
7. Thus *he shewed me :*
8: 1. Thus *hath* the Lord God *shewed unto me :*
Nah. 3: 5. *and I will shew*...thy nakedness,

HIPHIL.—*Infinitive.*

Ex. 9:16. *to shew* (in) *thee* my power ;
Deu 1:33. *to shew you* by what way ye should go,
3:24. *to shew* thy servant thy greatness,
Jos. 5: 6. he *would* not *shew them* the land,
Est. 1: 4. *When he shewed* the riches of his...kingdom
11. *to shew* the people...her beauty:
4: 8. *to shew* (it) unto Esther,
Eze.40: 4. that *I might shew* (them) *unto thee*

HIPHIL.—*Imperative.*

Ex. 33:18. *shew me* thy glory.
Jud. 1:24. *Shew us*,...the entrance
Ps. 85: 7(8). *Shew us* thy mercy, O Lord,
Cant.2:14. *let me see* thy countenance,

HIPHIL.—*Future.*

Gen12: 1. a land that *I will shew thee :*
Nu. 13:26. *and shewed them* the fruit of the land.
23: 3. whatsoever *he sheweth me*
Deu34: 1. *And* the Lord *shewed him* all the land
Jud. 1:25. *when he shewed them* the entrance
4:22. *and I will shew thee* the man
2K. 6: 6. *And he shewed him* the place.
11: 4. *and shewed* them the king's son.
20:13. *and shewed them* all the house of
Ps. 4: 6(7). Who *will shew us* (any) good?
50:23. *will I shew* the salvation of God.
59:10(11). God *shall let me see* (my desire)
91:16. *and shew him* my salvation.

Isa. 30:30. *shall shew* the lighting down of his arm,
39: 2. *and shewed them* the house of
Mic. 7:15. *will I shew unto him* marvellous (things).
Hab. 1: 3. Why *dost thou shew me* iniquity,
Zec. 1: 9. I *will shew thee* what these (be).
20(2:3). *And* the Lord *shewed me* four carpenters.
3: 1. *And he shewed me* Joshua

HIPHIL.—*Participle.*

Ex. 25: 9. According to all that I *shew* thee,
Eze.40: 4. all that I *shall shew thee ;*

* HOPHAL.—*Preterite.* *

Ex. 26:30. the fashion...which *was shewed thee*
Lev.13:49. *and shall be shewed* unto the priest:
Deu 4:35. Unto thee *it was shewed*, (lit. thou *wast caused to see*)

HOPHAL.—*Participle.*

Ex. 25:40. their pattern, which *was shewed* thee (marg. thou *wast caused to see*)

* HITHPAEL.—*Future.* *

Gen42: 1. *Why do ye look one upon another?*
2K. 14: 8. *let us look one another* in the face.
11. *looked one another* in the face
2Ch25:17. *let us see one another* in the face.
21. *and they saw one another* in the face,

רָאָה *rāh-āh'*, f. 7201

Deu14:13. *And the glede*, and the kite,

רָאֶה [*rāh-eh'*], adj. 7202

Job 10:15. *therefore see* thou mine affliction ;

רֹאֶה *rōh'-eh*, m. 7203

Isa. 28: 7. they err *in vision*,

רְאוּת *r'ooth*, f. 7207

Ecc. 5:11(10). *the beholding*...with their eyes?

רְאִי *r'ee*, m. 7209

Job 37:18. *as a* molten *looking glass?*

רֳאִי *rŏee*, m. 7210

Gen16:13. Thou God *seest me:* for she said, Have I also here looked after *him that seeth me?*
1Sa.16:12. goodly *to look to.*
Job 7: 8. The eye of *him that hath seen me*
33:21. His flesh is consumed away, *that it cannot be seen ;*
Nah. 3: 6. will set thee *as a gazingstock.*

רְאֵים see רְאֵם See 7214

רִאישׁוֹן *r'ee-shōhn'*, adj. 7223

Jos.21:10. (כתיב) their's was the *first* lot.
Job 15: 7. (——) (Art) thou the *first* man (that)

רְאִית *r'eeth*, f. 7212

Ecc. 5:11(10). (כתיב) *the beholding*...with their

רָאַם [*rāh-am'*]. 7213

* KAL.—*Preterite.* *

Zec.14:10. *and it shall be lifted up*,

רְאֵם *r'ēhm*, m. 7214

Nu. 23:22 & 24:8. the strength of *an unicorn.*
Deu33:17. (like) the horns of *unicorns:* (lit. *an unicorn*)

Job 39: 9. Will *the unicorn* be willing to serve thee,
10. Canst thou bind *the unicorn*
Ps. 22:21(22). from the horns of *the unicorns*.
29: 6. Lebanon and Sirion like a young *unicorn*. (lit. son of *unicorns*)
92:10(11). *like* (the horn of) *an unicorn*:
Isa. 34: 7. *the unicorns* (marg. or, *rhinocerots*) shall

7215 רָאמוֹת *rāh-mōhth'*, f. pl.

Job 28:18. shall be made of *coral*, (marg. or, *Ramoth*)
Eze.27:16. fine linen, *and coral*, and agate.

See 7326 רָאשׁ see רוּשׁ (Kal. Part.)

7389 רֵאשׁ *rēhsh*, m.

Pro. 6:11. So shall *thy poverty* come as one that
30: 8. give me neither *poverty* nor riches;

7217 רֵאשׁ *rēhsh*, Ch. m.

Ezr. 5:10. the men that (were) *the chief of them*.
Dan 2:28. and the visions of *thy head*
32. This image's *head* (was) of fine gold,
38. Thou (art) this *head* of gold.
3:27. nor was an hair of *their head* singed,
4: 5(2). and the visions of *my head*
10(7). the visions of *mine head* in my
13(10). I saw in the visions of *my head*
7: 1. and visions of *his head* upon his bed:
— (and) told *the sum of* the matters.
6. the beast had also four *heads*;
9. and the hair of *his head* like the pure
15. the visions of *my head* troubled me.
20. that (were) *in his head*,

7218 רֹאשׁ *rōhsh*, m.

Gen. 2:10. a river...became into four *heads*.
3:15. it shall bruise thy *head*,
8: 5. *the tops of* the mountains
11: 4. *whose top* (may reach) unto heaven;
28:12. *and the top of it* reached to heaven:
18. poured oil *upon the top of it*.
40:13. shall Pharaoh lift up *thine head*,
16. (I had) three white baskets on *my head*:
17. the basket upon *my head*.
19. shall Pharaoh lift up *thy head*
20. he lifted up *the head of* the chief butler and *of* the chief baker (lit. and *the head of* the chief baker)
47:31. Israel bowed himself upon the bed's *head*.
48:14. laid (it) upon Ephraim's *head*,
— his left hand upon Manasseh's *head*,
17. upon *the head of* Ephraim,
— to remove it from Ephraim's *head* unto Manasseh's *head*.
18. put thy right hand upon *his head*.
49:26. they shall be *on the head of* Joseph,
Ex. 6:14. *the heads of* their fathers' houses:
25. *the heads of* the fathers of the Levites
12: 2. *the beginning of* months:
9. *his head* with his legs,
17: 9. I will stand on *the top of* the hill
10. and Hur went up to *the top of* the hill.
18:25. *heads* over the people,
19:20. on *the top of* the mount: and the Lord called Moses (up) to *the top*
24:17. devouring fire *on the top of* the mount
26:24. coupled together above *the head of it*
28:32. an hole *in the top of it*,
29: 6. put the mitre upon *his head*,
7. pour (it) upon *his head*,
10. upon *the head of* the bullock.
15. put their hands upon *the head of* the ram.
17. unto his pieces, and unto *his head*.
19. put their hands upon *the head of*
30:12. When thou takest *the sum of*
23. Take thou also unto thee *principal* spices,
34: 2. in *the top of* the mount.
36:29. coupled together at *the head thereof*,
38. he overlaid *their chapiters*

Ex. 38:17, 19. the overlaying of *their chapiters*
28. overlaid *their chapiters*,
Lev. 1: 4. upon *the head of* the burnt offering;
8. the parts, *the head*, and the fat,
12. with *his head* and his fat:
15. wring off *his head*,
3: 2. he shall lay his hand upon *the head of*
8. lay his hand upon *the head of* his offering,
13. lay his hand upon *the head of it*,
4: 4. lay his hand upon the bullock's *head*,
11. with *his head*, and with his legs,
15. lay their hands upon *the head of* the
24. lay his hand upon *the head of* the goat,
29, 33. upon *the head of* the sin offering,
5: 8. wring off *his head* from his neck,
6: 5(5:24). restore it *in the principal*,
8: 9. And he put the mitre upon *his head*;
12. he poured...upon Aaron's *head*,
14. upon *the head of* the bullock
18, 22. upon *the head of* the ram.
20. Moses burnt *the head*,
9:13. the pieces thereof, and *the head*:
10: 6. Uncover not *your heads*,
13:12. *from his head* even to his foot,
29. a plague *upon the head* or
30. a leprosy upon *the head*
40. whose hair is fallen off *his head*,
41. the part of *his head* toward his face,
44. his plague (is) *in his head*.
45. his clothes shall be rent, *and his head*
14: 9. shave all his hair off *his head*
18, 29. *the head of* him that is to be cleansed:
16:21. upon *the head of* the live goat,
— upon *the head of* the goat,
19:27. round the corners of *your heads*,
21: 5. shall not make baldness *upon their head*,
10. upon *whose head* the anointing oil was
— shall not uncover *his head*,
24:14. lay their hands upon *his head*,
Nu. 1: 2. Take ye *the sum of* all the congregation
4. every one *head* of the house
16. *heads of* thousands in Israel.
49. neither take *the sum of them*
4: 2. Take *the sum of* the sons of Kohath
22. Take also *the sum of* the sons of Gershon,
5: 7. his trespass *with the principal thereof*,
18. uncover the woman's *head*,
6: 5. shall no rasor come upon *his head*:
— shall let the locks of the hair of *his head* grow.
7. consecration of his God (is) upon *his head*.
9. *the head of* his consecration; then he shall shave *his head* in the day
11. and shall hallow *his head*
18. shave *the head of* his separation
— the hair of *the head of* his separation,
7: 2. *heads of* the house of their fathers,
8:12. upon *the heads of* the bullocks:
10: 4. *heads of* the thousands of Israel,
10. *and in the beginnings of* your months,
13: 3. *heads of* the children of Israel.
14: 4. Let us make *a captain*,
40. them up into *the top of* the mountain,
44. presumed to go up unto *the* hill *top*:
17: 3(18). *for the head of* the house of their
20:28. Aaron died there *in the top of* the mount:
21:20. to *the top of* Pisgah,
23: 9. *from the top of* the rocks I see him,
14. to *the top of* Pisgah,
28. unto *the top of* Peor,
25: 4. Take all *the heads of* the people,
15. *head* over a people,
26: 2. Take *the sum of* all the congregation
28:11. *in the beginnings of* your months
30: 1(2). *the heads of* the tribes
31:26. Take *the sum of* the prey
— and the *chief* fathers of the congregation:
49. *the sum of* the men of war
32:28. *and* the *chief* fathers of the tribes
36: 1. And the *chief* fathers of the families
— the *chief* fathers of the children of Israel:
Deu 1:13. I will make them *rulers over you*.
15. I took *the chief of* your tribes,
— and made them *heads*
3:27. into *the top of* Pisgah,
5:23(20). all *the heads of* your tribes,
20: 9. captains...*to lead* (marg. *in the head of*)

Deu 21:12. she shall shave *her head,*
28:13. the Lord shall make thee *the head,*
23. thy heaven that (is) over *thy head*
44. he shall be *the head,*
29:10(9). *your captains* of your tribes,
32:42. *from the beginning of* revenges
33: 5. when *the heads of* the people
15. *And for the chief things of* the ancient
16. come *upon the head of* Joseph,
21. came with *the heads of* the people,
34: 1. to *the top of* Pisgah,
Jos. 2:19. his blood (shall be) *upon his head,*
— his blood (shall be) *on our head,*
7: 6. put dust upon *their heads.*
11:10. *the head of* all those kingdoms.
14: 1. *and the heads of* the fathers of the tribes
15: 8. *the top of* the mountain
9. *from the top of* the hill
19:51. *and the heads of* the fathers of the tribes
21: 1. Then came near *the heads of*
— *the heads of* the fathers
22:14. and each one (was) *an head of*
21. *the heads of* the thousands of Israel,
30. *and heads of* the thousands of Israel
23: 2 & 24:1. *and for their heads,* and for their judges, and for their officers,
Jud. 5:26. she smote off *his head,*
30. *to every* man (marg. *to the head of* a man)
6:26. upon *the top* of this rock,
7:16. divided the three hundred men (into) three *companies,*
19. *in the beginning of* the middle watch;
20. *the* three *companies* blew the trumpets,
25. *and* brought *the heads of* Oreb and Zeeb
8:28. they lifted up *their heads* no more.
9: 7. *in the top of* mount Gerizim,
25. in *the top of* the mountains,
34. laid wait...in four *companies.*
36. *from the top of* the mountains.
37. *and* another *company* come along
43. divided them into three *companies,*
44. Abimelech, *and the company*
— the two (other) *companies* ran
53. cast a piece of a millstone upon Abimelech's *head,*
57. did God render *upon their heads:*
10:18. *head* over all the inhabitants of Gilead.
11: 8. be *our head* over all the inhabitants
9. shall I be your *head?*
11. the people made him *head*
13: 5. no razor shall come on *his head:*
16: 3. carried them up to *the top of* an hill
13. weavest the seven locks of *my head*
17. hath not come a razor upon *mine head;*
19. to shave off the seven locks of *his head;*
22. the hair of *his head* began to grow
1Sa. 1:11. there shall no razor come upon *his head.*
4:12. a man...with earth upon *his head.*
5: 4. *and the head of* Dagon
9:22. *in the chiefest place among* them that
10: 1. a vial of oil, and poured (it) upon *his head,*
11:11. Saul put the people in three *companies;*
13:17. the spoilers came out...in three *companies:* one *company* turned unto the way
18. *And* another *company* turned the way (to) Beth-horon: *and* another *company* turned
14:45. there shall not one hair of *his head* fall
15:17. *the head of* the tribes of Israel,
17: 5. (he had) an helmet of brass upon *his head,*
38. put an helmet of brass upon *his head;*
46. take *thine head* from thee;
51. cut off *his head* therewith.
54. David took *the head of* the Philistine,
57. *with the head of* the Philistine in his hand.
25:39. returned the wickedness of Nabal *upon his own head.*
26:13. stood on *the top of* an hill
28: 2. make thee keeper *of mine head* for ever.
29: 4. *with the heads of* these men?
31: 9. they cut off *his head,*
2Sa. 1: 2. earth upon *his head:*
10. took the crown that (was) upon *his head,*
16. Thy blood (be) upon *thy head;*
2:16. caught every one his fellow *by the head,*
25. stood *on the top of* an hill.
3: 8. (Am) I a dog's *head,*
29. Let it rest *on the head of* Joab

2Sa. 4: 7. smote him, and slew him, and be*headed him* (lit. took off *his head*), and took *his head,*
8. they brought *the head of* Ish-bosheth
— Behold *the head of* Ish-bosheth
12. they took *the head of* Ish-bosheth,
5:24. *in the tops of* the mulberry trees,
12:30. took their king's crown from off *his head,*
— and it was (set) on David's *head.*
13:19. Tamar put ashes on *her head,*
— laid her hand on *her head,*
14:26. when he polled *his head,*
— he weighed the hair of *his head*
15:30. *and* had his *head* covered,
— covered every man *his head,*
32. (when) David was come to *the top* (of the mount),
— earth upon *his head:*
16: 1. when David was a little *past the top*
9. let me go over,...and take off *his head.*
18: 9. and *his head* caught hold of the oak,
20:21. *his head* shall be thrown to thee
22. they cut off *the head of* Sheba
22:44. (to be) *head of* the heathen:
23: 8. *chief* among the captains;
13. three of the thirty *chief*
18. *chief* among three.
1K. 2:32. return his blood upon *his own head,*
33. *upon the head of* Joab, *and upon the head of* his seed for ever:
37. thy blood shall be *upon thine own head.*
44. return thy wickedness *upon thine own head;*
7:16. *the tops of* the pillars:
17. upon *the top of* the pillars;
18. the chapiters that (were) upon *the top,*
19. upon *the top of* the pillars
22. upon *the top of* the pillars
35. *And in the top of* the base (was there) a
— and on *the top of* the base the ledges
41. on *the top of* the two pillars;
— upon *the top of* the pillars;
8: 1. *the heads of* the tribes,
8. *the ends* (marg. *heads*) *of* the staves
32. to bring his way *upon his head;*
10:19. *and the top of* the throne (was) round
18:42. Elijah went up to *the top of* Carmel;
20:31. ropes *upon our heads,*
32. (put) ropes *on their heads,*
21: 9. set Naboth *on high among* (marg. *the top of*) the people:
12. They proclaimed a fast, and set Naboth *on high among* (lit. *id.*)
2K. 1: 9. he sat on *the top of* an hill.
2: 3, 5. away thy master from *thy head* to day?
4:19. he said unto his father, *My head, my head.*
6:25. an ass's *head* was (sold) for fourscore
31. *the head of* Elisha
32. hath sent to take away *mine head?*
9: 3. the box of oil, and pour (it) on *his head,*
6. he poured the oil on *his head,*
30. painted her face, and tired *her head,*
10: 6. *the heads of* the men
7. put *their heads* in baskets,
8. *the heads of* the king's sons.
19:21. the daughter of Jerusalem hath shaken *her head*
25:18. Seraiah the *chief* priest,
27. did lift up *the head of* Jehoiachin
1Ch 4:42. having *for their captains*
5: 7. *the chief,* Jeiel, and Zechariah,
12. Joel *the chief,*
15. *chief* of the house of their fathers.
24. *heads of* the house of their fathers,
— *heads* of the house of their fathers.
7: 2. *heads* of their father's house,
3. all of them *chief men.*
7. *heads of* the house of (their) fathers,
9. *heads of* the house of their fathers,
11. *by the heads of* their fathers,
40. *heads* of (their) father's house,
— *chief of* the princes.
8: 6. *the heads of* the fathers
10, 28. *heads of* the fathers.
13. *heads of* the fathers
28. by their generations, *chief* (men).
9: 9. *chief of* the fathers
13. *heads* of the house of their fathers,

1Ch 9:17. Shallum (was) *the chief;*
33. *chief of* the fathers of the Levites,
34. *chief* fathers of the Levites (were) *chief* throughout their generations;
10: 9. they took *his head,* and his armour, and sent into the land of the Philistines
11: 6. Whosoever smiteth the Jebusites **first** shall be *chief* (marg. *head*)
— Joab the son of Zeruiah went first up, and was *chief.*
10. *chief of* the mighty men
11. *the chief of* the captains:
15. three of the thirty *captains*
20. *chief of* the three:
42. *a captain of* the Reubenites,
12: 3. *The chief* (was) Ahiezer,
9. Ezer *the first,* Obadiah the second,
14. *captains of* the host:
18. Amasai, (who was) *chief of* the captains,
— *and* made them *captains of* the band.
19. fall to his master Saul *to* (the jeopardy of) *our heads.*
20. *captains of* the thousands
23. the numbers of *the bands* (marg. *heads,* or, *captains,* or, *men*)
32. *the heads of them* (were) two hundred;
14:15. *in the tops of* the mulberry trees,
15:12. *the chief of* the fathers
16: 5. Asaph *the chief,* and next to him
7. David delivered *first* (this psalm)
20: 2. David took the crown...from off *his head,*
— it was set upon David's *head:*
23: 8. *the chief* (was) Jehiel,
9. *the chief of* the fathers of Laadan.
11. Jahath was *the chief,*
16. Shebuel (was) *the chief.*
17. Rehabiah *the chief.* (marg. or, *first*)
18. Shelomith *the chief.*
19. Jeriah *the first,*
20. Micah *the first,*
24. *the chief of* the fathers, as they were
24: 4. more *chief* (lit. more *among the chief*) men found of the sons of Eleazar
— sixteen *chief men of*
6. *and* (before) *the chief of* the fathers
21. *the first* (was) Isshiah.
31. *and the chief of* the fathers of the priests
— the *principal* fathers
26:10. Simri *the chief,*
— his father made him *the chief;*
12. *among* the *chief* men,
21. *chief* fathers, (even) of Laadan
26. *and* the *chief* fathers,
31. Jerijah *the chief,*
32. two thousand and seven hundred *chief* fathers,
27: 1. the *chief* fathers and captains
3. the chief of all *the captains*
5. Benaiah the son of Jehoiada, a *chief* priest:
29:11. thou art exalted *as head*
2Ch 1: 2. *the chief of* the fathers.
3:15. on *the top of each*
16. on *the heads of* the pillars;
4:12. *on the top of* the two pillars,
— which (were) on *the top of* the pillars;
5: 2. all *the heads of* the tribes,
9. *the ends of* the staves
6:23. recompensing his way *upon his own head;*
11:22. Rehoboam made Abijah...*the chief,*
13:12. God himself (is) with us *for* (our) *captain,*
19: 8. *and of the chief of* the fathers of Israel,
11. Amariah the *chief* priest
20:27. Jehoshaphat *in the forefront* (marg. *head*) *of them,*
23: 2. *and the chief of* the fathers of Israel,
24: 6. the king called for Jehoiada *the chief,*
11. the *high* priest's officer
25:12. brought them *unto the top of* the rock, and cast them down *from the top of* the rock,
26:12. *the chief of* the fathers of the mighty
20. Azariah the *chief* priest,
28:12. *of the heads of* the children of Ephraim,
31:10. Azariah the *chief* priest
Ezr. 1: 5. *the chief of* the fathers
2:68. *And* (some) *of the chief of* the fathers,
3:12. *and chief of* the fathers,
4: 2,3. *the chief of* the fathers,

Ezr. 7: 5. Eleazar, the son of Aaron the *chief* priest;
28. I gathered together...*chief men*
8: 1. *the chief of* their fathers,
16. sent I for Eliezer, for Ariel,...*chief men;*
17. sent them...unto Iddo *the chief*
9: 3. plucked off the hair of *my head*
6. iniquities are increased over (our) *head,*
10:16. *chief of* the fathers,
Neh 4: 4(3:36). turn their reproach upon *their own head,*
7:70, 71. *the chief of* the fathers
8:13. *the chief of* the fathers
9:17. in their rebellion appointed *a captain*
10:14(15). *The chief of* the people;
11: 3. *the chief of* the province
13. his brethren, *chief* of the fathers,
16. *of the chief of* the Levites,
17. *the principal* to begin the thanksgiving
12: 7. *the chief of* the priests
12, 23. *the chief of* the fathers:
22. *chief of* the fathers:
24. *And the chief of* the Levites:
46. *chief of* the singers,
Est. 2:17. he set the royal crown *upon her head,*
5: 2. Esther drew near, and touched *the top of* the sceptre.
6: 8. crown royal which is set *upon his head:*
12. Haman hasted to his house...having *his head* covered.
9:25. should return upon *his own head,*
Job 1:17. The Chaldeans made out three *bands,*
20. Job arose,...and shaved *his head,*
2:12. sprinkled dust upon *their heads*
10:15. (yet) will I not lift up *my head.*
12:24. *the chief of* the people
16: 4. shake *mine head* at you.
19: 9. taken the crown (from) *my head.*
20: 6. *and his head* reach unto the clouds;
22:12. behold *the height* (marg. *head*) *of* the stars,
24:24. *and* cut off *as the tops of* the ears of corn.
29: 3. When his candle shined upon *my head,*
25. I chose out their way, and sat *chief,*
41: 7(40:31). or *his head* with fish spears?
Ps. 3: 3(4). the lifter up of *mine head.*
7:16(17). His mischief shall return *upon his own head,*
18:43(44). thou hast made me *the head of*
21: 3(4). thou settest a crown of pure gold *on his head.*
22: 7(8). they shake *the head,*
23: 5. thou anointest *my head* with oil;
24: 7, 9. Lift up *your heads,* O ye gates;
27: 6. now shall *mine head* be lifted up
38: 4(5). mine iniquities are gone over *mine head:*
40:12(13). more than the hairs of *mine head:*
44:14(15). a shaking of *the head* among the
60: 7(9). Ephraim also (is) the strength of *mine head;*
66:12. caused men to ride *over our heads;*
68:21(22). God shall wound *the head of* his
69: 4(5). more than the hairs of *mine head:*
72:16. *upon the top of* the mountains;
74:13. thou brakest *the heads of* the dragons
14. Thou brakest *the heads of* leviathan
83: 2(3). they that hate thee have lifted up *the head.*
108: 8(9). Ephraim also (is) the strength of *mine head;*
109:25. they shaked *their heads.*
110: 6. he shall wound *the heads*
7. therefore shall he lift up *the head.*
118:22. The stone...refused is become *the head*
119:160. Thy word (is) true (from) *the beginning:*
133: 2. the precious ointment upon *the head,*
137: 6. if I prefer not Jerusalem above my *chief*
139:17. how great is *the sum of them!*
140: 7(8). covered *my head* in the day of battle.
9(10). *the head of* those that compass me
141: 5. (it shall be) an *excellent* oil, (which) shall not break *my head:*
Pro. 1: 9. an ornament of grace *unto thy head,*
21. She crieth *in the chief place*
4: 9. She shall give *to thine head* an ornament
8: 2. She standeth *in the top of* high places,
23. set up...*from the beginning,*
26. *nor the highest part* (marg. *chief*) *of* the

Pro.10: 6. Blessings (are) upon *the head of* the just:
11:26. blessing (shall be) upon *the head of*
13:23. the tillage of *the poor*: [see רוּשׁ]
23:34. as he that lieth *upon the top of* a mast.
25:22. heap coals of fire upon *his head*,
Ecc. 2:14. The wise man's eyes (are) *in his head*;
3:11. work that God maketh *from the beginning*
9: 8. let *thy head* lack no ointment.
Cant.2: 6. His left hand (is) under *my head*,
4: 8. look *from the top of* Amana, *from the top of* Shenir
14. myrrh and aloes, with all the *chief* spices:
5: 2. *for my head* is filled with dew,
11. *His head* (is as) the most fine gold,
7: 5(6). *Thine head* upon thee (is) like Carmel, and the hair of *thine head* like purple;
8: 3. His left hand (should be) under *my head*,
Isa. 1: 5. *the* whole *head* is sick,
6. From the sole of the foot even unto *the head*
2: 2. *in the top of* the mountains,
7: 8. *the head of* Syria (is) Damascus, *and the head of* Damascus (is) Rezin;
9. *And the head of* Ephraim (is) Samaria, *and the head of* Samaria (is) Remaliah's
20. *the head*, and the hair of the feet:
9:14(13). the Lord will cut off...*head* and tail,
15(14). The ancient and honourable, he (is) *the head*;
15: 2. on all *their heads* (shall be) baldness,
17: 6. *in the top of* the uppermost bough,
19:15. *the head* or tail, branch or rush,
28: 1. on *the head of* the fat valleys
4. on *the head of* the fat valley,
29:10. the prophets and *your rulers*, (marg. *heads*)
30:17. upon *the top of* a mountain,
35:10. songs and everlasting joy upon *their heads*:
37:22. the daughter of Jerusalem hath shaken *her head*
40:21. told you *from the beginning*?
41: 4. calling the generations *from the beginning*?
26. Who hath declared *from the beginning*,
42:11. let them shout *from the top of*
48:16. spoken in secret *from the beginning*;
51:11. everlasting joy (shall be) upon *their head*:
20. *at the head of* all the streets,
58: 5. to bow down *his head* as a bulrush,
59:17. an helmet of salvation *upon his head*;
Jer. 2:37. thine hands upon *thine head*:
9: 1(8:23). Oh that *my head* were waters,
13:21. them (to be) captains, (and) *as chief*
14: 3. were ashamed...and covered *their heads*.
4. they covered *their heads*.
18:16. every one that passeth thereby shall... wag *his head*.
22: 6. *the head of* Lebanon:
23:19. grievously upon *the head of* the wicked.
30:23. with pain upon *the head of* the wicked.
31: 7. shout *among the chief of* the nations:
48:37. every *head* (shall be) bald,
52:24. Seraiah the *chief* priest,
31. *the head of* Jehoiachin
Lam.1: 5. Her adversaries are *the chief*,
2:10. cast up dust upon *their heads*;
— the virgins of Jerusalem hang down *their heads*
15. they hiss and wag *their head*
19. *in the beginning of* the watches
— *in the top of* every street.
3:54. Waters flowed over *mine head*;
4: 1. *in the top of* every street.
5:16. The crown is fallen (from) *our head*:
Eze. 1:22. *the heads of* the living creature
— over *their heads* above.
25. a voice from the firmament that (was) over *their heads*,
26. the firmament that (was) over *their heads*
5: 1. upon *thine head* and upon thy beard:
6:13. in all *the tops of* the mountains,
7:18. baldness upon all *their heads*.
8: 3. took me by a lock of *mine head*;
9:10. recompense their way *upon their head*.
10: 1. above *the head of* the cherubims
11. whither *the head* looked
11:21. their way *upon their own heads*,
13:18. upon *the head of* every stature
16:12. a beautiful crown *upon thine head*.
Eze.16:25. at every *head of* the way,
31. *in the head of* every way,
43. recompense thy way *upon* (thine) *head*,
17: 4. *the top of* his young twigs,
19. recompense *upon his own head*.
22. *from the top of* his young twigs
21:19(24). *at the head of* the way
21(26). *at the head of* the two ways,
22:31. their own way have I recompensed *upon their heads*,
23:15. dyed attire *upon their heads*,
42. beautiful crowns upon *their heads*.
24:23. your tires (shall be) upon *your heads*,
27:22. *with chief of* all spices,
30. cast up dust upon *their heads*,
29:18. every *head* (was) made bald,
32:27. laid their swords under *their heads*,
33: 4. his blood shall be *upon his own head*.
38: 2, 3 & 39:1. the *chief* prince *of* Meshech and
40: 1. *in the beginning of* the year,
42:12. *in the head of* the way,
43:12. Upon *the top of* the mountain the whole
44:18. shall have linen bonnets upon *their heads*,
20. Neither shall they shave *their heads*,
— they shall only poll *their heads*.
Dan 1:10. endanger *my head* to the king.
Hos. 1:11(2:2). appoint themselves one *head*,
4:13. upon *the tops of* the mountains,
Joel 2: 5. on *the tops of* mountains
3: 4(4:4), 7(4:7). your recompence *upon your own head*;
Am. 1: 2. *the top of* Carmel shall wither.
2: 7. *on the head of* the poor,
6: 7. *with the first* that go captive,
8:10. baldness upon every *head*;
9: 1. cut them *in the head*,
3. *in the top of* Carmel,
Obad. 15. *upon thine own head*.
Jon. 2: 5(6). the weeds were wrapped *about my head*.
4: 6. a shadow over *his head*,
8. the sun beat upon *the head of*
Mic. 2:13. the Lord *on the head of them*.
3: 1. Hear, I pray you, *O heads of* Jacob,
9. *ye heads of* the house of Jacob,
11. *The heads thereof* judge for reward,
4: 1. *in the top of* the mountains,
Nah 3:10. *at the top of* all the streets:
Hab 3:13. thou woundedst *the head*
14. *the head of* his villages:
Zec. 1:21(2:4). so that no man did lift up *his head*:
3: 5. set a fair mitre upon *his head*. So they set a fair mitre upon *his head*,
4: 2. with a bowl upon *the top of it*,
— seven lamps, which (are) upon *the top thereof*:
6:11. *upon the head of* Joshua

רֹאשׁ *rōhsh*, m. 7219

Deu29:18(17). a root that beareth *gall* (marg. *rosh*, or, *a poisonful herb*)
32:33. *and the* cruel *venom of* asps.
Job 20:16. He shall suck *the poison of* asps:
Ps. 69:21(22). They gave me also *gall* for my meat;
Jer. 8:14. given us water of *gall* to drink,
9:15(14). give them water of *gall* to drink.
23:15. make them drink the water of *gall*:
Lam.3: 5. compassed (me) with *gall* and travel.
19. the wormwood *and the gall*.
Hos.10: 4. judgment springeth up *as hemlock*
Am. 6:12. turned judgment *into gall*,

רֵאשָׁה [*ree-shāh'*], f. 7221

Eze.36:11. will do better...*than at your beginnings*:

רֹאשָׁה *rōh-shāh'*, f. 7222

Zec. 4: 7. he shall bring forth the *head*stone

רִאשׁוֹן *ree-shōhn'*, adj. 7223

Gen 8:13. *in the first* (month),
13: 4. the altar, which he had made...*at the first*.

Gen25:25. *the first* came out red,
26: 1. the *first* famine that was
28:19. (was called) Luz *at the first.*
32:17(18). he commanded *the foremost,*
33: 2. he put the handmaids...*foremost,*
38:28. This came out *first.*
40:13. after the *former* manner
41:20. the *first* seven fat kine:
Ex. 4: 8. hearken to the voice of the *first* sign,
12: 2. the *first* month of the year
15. the *first* day ye shall put away leaven
— from the *first* day until the seventh
16. in the *first* day...an holy convocation,
18. *In the first* (month),
34: 1, 4. two tables...*like unto the first:*
— the words that were in the *first* tables,
40: 2. the first day of the *first* month
17. in the *first* month in the second year,
Lev. 4:21. as he burned the *first* bullock:
5: 8. shall offer...the sin offering *first,*
9:15. offered it for sin, *as the first.*
23: 5. the fourteenth (day) of the *first* month
7. In the *first* day...an holy convocation:
35. On the *first* day...an holy convocation:
39. on the *first* day (shall be) a sabbath,
40. take you on the *first* day the boughs of
26:45. the covenant of their *ancestors,*
Nu. 2: 9. These shall *first* set forth.
6:12. the days *that were before*
7:12. offered his offering the *first* day
9: 1. in the *first* month of the second year
5. the *first* month at even
10:13. they *first* took their journey
14. *In the first* (place) went the standard
20: 1. in the *first* month:
21:26. the *former* king of Moab,
28:16. the fourteenth day of the *first* month
18. In the *first* day...an holy convocation;
33: 3. departed from Rameses in the *first* month, on the fifteenth day of the *first* month;
Deu 4:32. the days *that are past,*
9:18. I fell down...*as at the first,*
10: 1, 3. two tables of stone *like unto the first,*
2. the words that were in the *first* tables
4. according to the *first* writing,
10. stayed in the mount, according to the *first* time, (marg. or, *former* days)
13: 9(10). thine hand shall be *first* upon
16: 4. the *first* day at even,
17: 7. The hands of the witnesses shall be *first*
19:14. *they of old time* have set
24: 4. Her *former* husband,
Jos. 4:19. on the tenth (day) of the *first* month,
8: 5. when they come out...*as at the first,*
6. They flee before us, *as at the first:*
33. had commanded *before,* that they
21:10. their's was the *first* lot.
Jud. 18:29. the name of the city...*first.*
20:22. put themselves in array the *first* day.
32. smitten down before us, *as at the first.*
39. smitten...as (in) the *first* battle.
Ru. 3:10. shewed more kindness in the latter end than at *the beginning,*
1Sa. 14:14. *first* slaughter, which Jonathan...made,
17:30. after the *former* manner.
2Sa. 7:10. afflict them any more, as *beforetime,*
18:27. the running of *the foremost*
19:20(21). I am come *the first* this day
43(44). that our advice should not be *first* had
20:18. They were wont to speak *in old time,* (marg. or, They plainly spake *in the beginning*)
21: 9. in the days of harvest, *in the first* (days),
1K. 13: 6. became *as* (it was) *before.*
17:13. make me...a little cake *first,*
18:25. Choose you one bullock...and dress (it) *first;*
20: 9. All that thou didst...*at the first*
17. the young men...went out *first;*
2K. 1:14. two captains of the *former* fifties
17:34. do after the *former* manners:
40. they did after their *former* manner.
1Ch 9: 2. the *first* inhabitants that (dwelt)
11: 6. Whosoever smiteth...*first*
— Joab the son of Zeruiah went *first* up,
12:15. in the *first* month,
15:13. ye (did it) not *at the first,*

1Ch 17: 9. as *at the beginning,*
18:17. the sons of David (were) *chief*
24: 7. the *first* lot came forth to Jehoiarib,
25: 9. the *first* lot came forth for Asaph
27: 2. the *first* course for the *first* month
3. the captains...for the *first* month.
29:29. the acts of David the king, *first* and last,
2Ch 3: 3. the *first* measure (was) threescore cubits,
9:29. the acts of Solomon, *first* and last,
12:15. the acts of Rehoboam, *first* and last,
16:11. the acts of Asa, *first* and last,
17: 3. in the *first* ways of his father David,
20:34. the acts of Jehoshaphat, *first* and last,
22: 1. the band of men...had slain all *the eldest.*
25:26. the acts of Amaziah, *first* and last,
26:22. the acts of Uzziah, *first* and last,
28:26. his acts...*first* and last,
29: 3. in the *first* year of his reign, in the *first* month,
17. the first (day) of *the first* month
— the sixteenth day of the *first* month
35: 1. the fourteenth (day) of the *first* month.
27. his deeds, *first* and last, behold,
Ezr. 3:12. had seen the *first* house,
6:19. the fourteenth (day) of the *first* month.
7: 9. the first (day) of the *first* month
8:31. the twelfth (day) of the *first* month,
9: 2. the hand of the princes and rulers hath been *chief*
10:17. by the first day of the *first* month.
Neh. 5:15. the *former* governors
7: 5. them which came up *at the first,*
8:18. from the *first* day unto the last day,
Est. 1:14. sat *the first* in the kingdom;
3: 7. In the *first* month,
12. on the thirteenth day of the *first* month,
Job 8: 8. enquire, I pray thee, of the *former* age,
15: 7. the *first* man (that) was born?
Ps. 79: 8. O remember not...*former* iniquities:
89:49(50). thy *former* lovingkindnesses,
Pro. 18:17. (He that is) *first* in his own cause
20:21. gotten hastily *at the beginning;*
Ecc. 1:11. no remembrance *of former* (things);
7:10. the *former* days were better than these?
Isa. 1:26. I will restore thy judges *as at the first,*
9: 1(8:23). at the *first* (lit. at the *first* time) he lightly afflicted
41: 4. I the Lord, *the first,*
22. let them shew *the former things,*
27. *The first* (shall say) to Zion,
42: 9. the *former things* are come to pass,
43: 9. *and* shew us *former things?*
18. Remember ye not *the former things,*
27. Thy *first* father hath sinned,
44: 6. I (am) *the first,* and I (am) the last;
46: 9. Remember *the former things*
48: 3. I have declared *the former things*
12. I (am) *the first,* I also (am) the last.
52: 4. My people went down *aforetime*
60: 9. the ships of Tarshish *first,*
61: 4. raise up the *former* desolations,
65: 7. therefore will I measure their *former* work
16. the *former* troubles are forgotten,
17. *the former* shall not be remembered,
Jer. 7:12. where I set my name *at the first,*
11:10. iniquities of their *fore*fathers, (lit. *former* fathers)
16:18. And *first* I will recompense their iniquity and their sin double;
17:12. A glorious high throne *from the beginning*
33: 7. will build them, *as at the first.*
11. I will cause to return...*as at the first,*
34: 5. the *former* kings
36:28. all the *former* words that were in the *first* roll,
50:17. *first* the king of Assyria hath devoured
Eze. 29:17. *in the first* (month), in the first (day)
30:20. *in the first* (month), in the seventh (day
40:21. the measure of the *first* gate:
45:18. *in the first* (day) of the month,
21. *In the first* (month),
Dan 8:21. the great horn...(is) the *first* king.
10: 4. four and twentieth day of the *first* month,
12. from the *first* day
13. Michael, one of the *chief* princes,
11:13. a multitude greater than *the former*
29. it shall not be *as the former,*

Hos. 2: 7(9). I will go and return to my *first*
Joel 2:23. the latter rain *in the first* (month).
Mic. 4: 8. even the *first* dominion;
Hag. 2: 3. saw this house in her *first* glory?
9. The glory of this latter house shall be greater than of *the former*,
Zec. 1: 4. unto whom the *former* prophets have cried,
6: 2. In the *first* chariot (were) red horses;
7: 7. the Lord hath cried by the *former* prophets,
12. sent in his spirit by the *former* prophets:
8:11. as in the *former* days,
12: 7. The Lord also shall save the tents of Judah *first*,
14:10. unto the place of the *first* gate,

7224 רִאשֹׁנִי [*ree-shōh-nee'*], adj.

Jer. 25: 1. the *first* year of Nebuchadrezzar

7225 רֵאשִׁית *rēh-sheeth'*, f.

Gen. 1: 1. *In the beginning* God created
10:10. *the beginning of* his kingdom
49: 3. *and the beginning of* my strength,
Ex. 23:19. *The first of* the firstfruits of thy land
34:26. *The first of* the firstfruits of
Lev. 2:12. the oblation of *the firstfruits*,
23:10. a sheaf of *the firstfruits*
Nu. 15:20. a cake of *the first of* your dough
21. *Of the first of* your dough
18:12. *the firstfruits of them* which they shall
24:20. Amalek (was) *the first of* the nations;
Deu 11:12. *from the beginning of* the year
18: 4. *The firstfruit* (also) *of* thy corn,
— *and the first of* the fleece of thy sheep,
21:17. *the beginning of* his strength;
26: 2. *of the first of* all the fruit
10. the *first*fruits of the land,
33:21. he provided *the first part* for himself,
1 Sa. 2:29. *with the chiefest of* all the offerings
15:21. *the chief of* the things
2 Ch 31: 5. *the firstfruits of* corn, wine,
Neh 10:37(38). *the firstfruits of* our dough,
12:44. *for the firstfruits*, and for the tithes,
Job 8: 7. Though *thy beginning* was small,
40:19. *the chief of* the ways of God:
42:12. the Lord blessed the latter end of Job *more than his beginning:*
Ps. 78:51. *the chief of* (their) strength
105:36. *the chief of* all their strength.
111:10. *the beginning of* wisdom:
Pro. 1: 7. *the beginning of* knowledge:
3: 9. *and with the firstfruits of* all thine
4: 7. Wisdom (is) *the principal thing;*
8:22. possessed me in *the beginning of* his
17:14. *The beginning of* strife
Ecc. 7: 8. Better (is) the end of a thing *than the beginning thereof:*
Isa. 46:10. Declaring the end *from the beginning*,
Jer. 2: 3. *the firstfruits of* his increase:
26: 1 & 27:1. *In the beginning of* the reign of
28: 1 & 49:34. *in the beginning of* the reign of Zedekiah king of Judah,
49:35. *the chief of* their might.
Eze. 20:40. *the firstfruits* (marg. or, *chief*) *of* your
44:30. *And the first* (marg. or, *chief*) *of* all the
— *also...the first of* your dough,
48:14. *the firstfruits of* the land:
Dan 11:41. *and the chief of* the children of Ammon.
Hos 9:10. firstripe in the fig tree *at her first time:*
Am. 6: 1. *chief* (marg. or, *firstfruits*) *of* the nations,
6. *and* anoint themselves *with the chief*
Mic. 1:13. *the beginning of* the sin

7226 רַאֲשֹׁת [*rah-ăshōhth'*], m.

1 Sa. 26:12. and the cruse of water *from Saul's bolster;*

7227 רַב *rav*, adj.

Gen. 6: 5. the wickedness of man (was) *great*
7:11. the fountains of the *great* deep
13: 6. their substance was *great*,
18:20. the cry of Sodom and Gomorrah is *great*,
Gen 21:34. Abraham sojourned...*many* days.
24:25. have both straw and provender *enough*,
25:23. *and the elder* shall serve the younger.
26:14. he had...*great* store of servants:
30:43. *much* cattle, and maidservants,
33: 9. Esau said, I have *enough*,
36: 7. their riches were *more* than that
37:34. mourned for his son *many* days.
45:28. Israel said, (It is) *enough;*
50:20. to save *much* people alive.
Ex. 1: 9. the children of Israel (are) *more*
2:23. in *process* of time (lit. in those *many* days), that the king of Egypt died:
5: 5. the people of the land now (are) *many*,
9:28. Intreat the Lord *for* (it is) *enough*
12:38. a mixed *multitude* (marg. a *great* mixture
19:21. *many* of them perish.
23: 2. Thou shalt not follow *a multitude* to (do)
— to decline after *many*
29. the beast of the field *multiply*
34: 6. *and abundant* in goodness and truth,
Lev. 15:25. an issue of her blood *many* days
25:51. If (there be) yet *many* years (behind),
Nu. 9:19. when the cloud tarried...*many* days,
11:33. smote the people with a very *great* plague.
13:18. strong or weak, few or *many;*
14:18. longsuffering, *and of great* mercy,
16: 3, 7. (Ye take) *too much* upon you,
20:11. the water came out *abundantly*,
15. in Egypt *a long time;* (lit. *many* days)
21: 6. *much* people of Israel died.
22: 3. of the people, because they (were) *many*
15. Balak sent yet again princes, *more*,
24: 7. his seed (shall be) in *many* waters,
26:54. *To many* thou shalt give the more
56. divided between *many* and few.
32: 1. a very *great multitude* of cattle:
33:54. *to the more* ye shall give the more
35: 8. (them that have) *many* ye shall
Deu. 1: 6. Ye have dwelt *long enough*
46. ye abode in Kadesh *many* days,
2: 1. we compassed mount Seir *many* days.
3. compassed this mountain *long enough:*
10, 21. a people great, *and many*,
3:19. I know that ye have *much* cattle,
26. *Let it suffice* thee;
7: 1. cast out *many* nations
— nations *greater* and mightier than thou;
17. These nations (are) *more* than I;
9:14. a nation mightier *and greater*
15: 6. thou shalt lend unto *many* nations,
— thou shalt reign over *many* nations,
20: 1. a people *more* than thou,
19. When thou shalt besiege a city a *long* time, (lit. *many* days)
25: 3. beat him above these with *many* stripes,
26: 5. a nation, great, mighty, *and populous:*
28:12. thou shalt lend unto *many* nations,
38. Thou shalt carry *much* seed
31:17. *many* evils and troubles shall befall them;
21. when *many* evils and troubles are
33: 7. let his hands be *sufficient*
Jos. 10:11. *more* which died with hailstones
11: 4. *much* people, even as the sand
— horses and chariots very *many*.
8. chased them unto *great* Zidon,
18. made war a *long* time (lit. *many* days)
17:14. I (am) a *great* people,
15. If thou (be) a *great* people,
17. Thou (art) a *great* people,
19: 9. the part of the children of Judah was *too much*
28. and Kanah, (even) unto *great* Zidon:
22: 3. not left your brethren these *many* days
8. Return with *much* riches
— very *much* cattle,
23: 1. a *long* time after that the Lord had given
24: 7. ye dwelt in the wilderness a *long* season.
Jud. 7: 2. The people...(are) too *many*
4. The people (are) yet (too) *many;*
8:30. for he had *many* wives.
9:40. *many* were overthrown
16:30. the dead which he slew...were *more*
1 Sa. 2: 5. *and she that hath many* children
12:17. see that your wickedness (is) *great*,
14: 6. no restraint to the Lord to save *by many*
9. the Philistines went on *and increased:*

1Sa.26:13. a *great* space (being) between
2Sa. 3:22. brought in a *great* spoil
13:34. there came *much* people by the way
14: 2. as a woman that had a *long* time mourned
15:12. the people *increased* continually
22:17. he drew me out of *many* (marg. or, *great*) waters;
23:20. *had done many* (lit. *mighty of*) acts,
24:14. his mercies (are) *great*: (marg. or, *many*)
16. It is *enough*: stay now thine hand.
1K. 2:38. Shimei dwelt in Jerusalem *many* days.
3: 8. a *great* people, that cannot be numbered
11. for thyself *long* life; (marg. *many* days)
4:20. Judah and Israel (were) *many*,
5: 7(21). unto David a wise son over this *great*
10: 2. very *much* gold, and precious stones:
11: 1. Solomon loved *many* strange women,
12:28. *too much* for you to go up to Jerusalem:
18: 1. (after) *many* days,
25. dress (it) first; for ye (are) *many*;
19: 4. It is *enough*; now, O Lord,
7. the journey (is) *too great* for thee.
2K. 6:16. they that (be) with us (are) *more*
9:22. the whoredoms of thy mother Jezebel... (are so) *many*?
12:10(11). *much* money in the chest,
18:17. Tartan, and *Rabsaris* [or, *the chief* eunuch]
25: 8, 20. *captain of* the guard, (marg. or, *chief* marshal)
10, 11, 12, 15, 18. *the captain of* the guard,
1Ch 4:27. his brethren had not *many* children,
5:22. there fell down *many* slain,
7:22. Ephraim...mourned *many* days,
11:22. Benaiah...*who had done many* acts; (marg. *great of* deeds)
18: 8. brought David very *much* brass,
21:13. very *great* (marg. or, *many*) (are) his mercies:
15. It is *enough*, stay now thine hand.
22: 8. thou hast shed *much* blood
24: 4. *more* chief men found
28: 5. the Lord hath given me *many* sons,
2Ch 1: 9. a people like the dust...in *multitude*. (marg. *much* as the dust)
11. neither yet hast asked *long* life; (lit. *many* days)
13: 8. ye (be) a *great* multitude,
17. slew them with a *great* slaughter:
14:11(10). whether with *many*, or with
14(13). there was exceeding *much* spoil
15: 3. for a *long* season Israel (hath been)
5. *great* vexations (were) upon all
17:13. *much* business in the cities of Judah:
20: 2. There cometh a *great* multitude
12. this *great* company that cometh
15. by reason of this *great* multitude;
25. the spoil, it was so *much*.
21: 3. their father gave them *great* gifts
15. thou (shalt have) *great* sickness
24:11. (there was) *much* money,
25. they left him in *great* diseases,
25:13. smote three thousand...and took *much*
26:10. digged *many* wells: for he had *much* cattle,
28: 8. took also away *much* spoil
13. our trespass is *great*,
30:13. assembled at Jerusalem *much* people
17. *many* in the congregation
18. *many of* Ephraim, and Manasseh,
32: 4. there was gathered *much* people
— and find *much* water?
7. *more* with us than with him:
23. *And many* brought gifts
29. God had given him substance *very much*.
Ezr. 3:12. *But many* of the priests and Levites
— *and many* shouted aloud for joy:
10: 1. a very *great* congregation
13. the people (are) *many*,
Neh 5: 2. our sons, and our daughters, (are) *many*:
6:18. (there were) *many* in Judah sworn unto
7: 2. feared God *above many*.
9:17. slow to anger, *and of great* kindness,
19. Yet thou in thy *manifold* mercies
27. according to thy *manifold* mercies
28. *many* times didst thou deliver them
30. *many* years didst thou forbear
Neh 9:31. for thy *great* mercies' sake
35. in thy *great* goodness
13:26. among *many* nations
Est. 1: 4. shewed the riches of his glorious kingdom...*many* days,
7. royal wine *in abundance*,
8. all *the officers of* his house,
20. his empire, for it is *great*,
2: 8. when *many* maidens were gathered
4: 3. *many* lay in sackcloth and ashes.
8:17. *many* of the people of the land
Job 1: 3. a very *great* houshold;
4: 3. thou hast instructed *many*,
5:25. thy seed (shall be) *great*,
11:19. *many* shall make suit unto thee.
16: 2. I have heard *many* such things:
22: 5. (Is) not thy wickedness *great*?
23:14. *many* such (things are) with him.
31:25. rejoiced because my wealth (was) *great*,
34. Did I fear a *great* multitude,
32: 9. *Great men* are not (always) wise:
35: 9. by reason of the arm of *the mighty*.
36:28. distil upon man *abundantly*.
38:21. the number of thy days (is) *great*?
39:11. because his strength (is) *great*?
Ps. 3: 1(2). *many* (are) they that rise up against
2(3). *Many* (there be) which say of my
4: 6(7). *many* that say, Who will shew us (any)
18:16(17). he drew me out of *many* (marg. or, *great*) waters.
19:10(11). More to be desired...than *much* fine
11(12). in keeping of them (there is) *great* reward.
13(14). innocent from the *great* transgression.
22:12(13). *Many* bulls have compassed me:
25(26). in the *great* congregation:
25:11. pardon mine iniquity; for it (is) *great*.
29: 3. the Lord (is) upon *many* waters.
31:13(14). I have heard the slander of *many*:
19(20). how *great* (is) thy goodness,
32: 6. in the floods of *great* waters
10. *Many* sorrows (shall be) to the wicked:
34:19(20). *Many* (are) the afflictions of the
35:18. I will give thee thanks in the *great*
36: 6(7). thy judgments (are) a *great* deep:
37:16. the riches of *many* wicked.
40: 3(4). *many* shall see (it), and fear,
5(6). *Many*, O Lord my God, (are) thy
9(10). I have preached...in the *great*
10(11). I have not concealed...thy truth from the *great* congregation.
48: 2(3). the city of the *great* King.
55:18(19). there were *many* with me.
56: 2(3). *many* that fight against me,
62: 2(3). I shall not be *greatly* moved.
65: 9(10). thou *greatly* enrichest
68:11(12). *great* (was) the company
71: 7. I am as a wonder *unto many*;
20. shewed me *great* and sore troubles,
77:19(20). thy path in the *great* waters,
78:15. as (out of) the *great* depths.
86: 5. *and plenteous* in mercy unto all
15. *and plenteous* in mercy and truth.
89: 7(8). God is *greatly* to be feared
50(51). (the reproach of) all the *mighty*
93: 4. the noise of *many* waters,
97: 1. let *the multitude* (marg. *many*, or, *great*) of isles be glad
103: 8. *and plenteous* (marg. *great of*) in mercy.
106:43. *Many* times did he deliver them;
107:23. do business in *great* waters;
109:30. I will praise him among *the multitude*.
110: 6. the heads over *many* (marg. or, *great*) countries.
119:156. *Great* (marg. or, *Many*) (are) thy tender mercies,
157. *Many* (are) my persecutors
162. one that findeth *great* spoil.
165. *Great* peace have they which love
120: 6. My soul hath *long* dwelt with
123: 3. we are *exceedingly* filled with contempt.
4. Our soul is *exceedingly* filled with
129: 1, 2. *Many a time* (marg. or, *Much*) have they afflicted me from my youth,
135:10. Who smote *great* nations,
144: 7. deliver me out of *great* waters,
145: 7. the memory of thy *great* goodness,

Ps.147: 5. Great (is) our Lord, and *of great* power:
Pro. 7:26. she hath cast down *many* wounded:
10:21. The lips of the righteous feed *many :*
13: 7. maketh himself poor, yet (hath) *great*
14:20. the rich (hath) *many* friends.
29. of *great* understanding:
15: 6. In the house of the righteous (is) *much* treasure:
16. *great* treasure and trouble therewith.
19: 4. Wealth maketh *many* friends;
6. *Many* will intreat the favour of
21. *many* devices in a man's heart;
22: 1. (A good) name (is) rather to be chosen than *great* riches,
26:10. *The great* (God) that formed all (things)
28: 2. *many* (are) the princes thereof:
12. When righteous (men) do rejoice, (there is) *great* glory:
16. *also* a *great* oppressor:
20. A faithful man *shall abound*
27. he that hideth his eyes shall have *many* a
29:22. a furious man *aboundeth* in transgression.
26. *Many* seek the ruler's favour;
31:29. *Many* daughters have done virtuously,
Ecc. 2:21. vanity and a *great* evil.
6: 1. *and* it (is) *common* among men:
3. If a man...live *many* years, *so* that the days of his years be *many*,
7:22. *often*times also thine own heart knoweth
29. they have sought out *many* inventions.
8: 6. the misery of man (is) *great*
10: 6. Folly is set in *great* dignity,
Cant.7: 4(5). by the gate of Bath-*rabbim :* (lit. the daughter of *many*)
8: 7. *Many* waters cannot quench love,
Isa. 2: 3. *many* people shall go and say,
4. shall rebuke *many* people:
5: 9. *many* houses shall be desolate,
6:12. *and* (there be) a *great* forsaking in the
8: 7. the waters of the river, strong *and many*,
15. *many* among them shall stumble,
13: 4. like as of a *great* people;
16:14. all that *great* multitude;
17:12. the multitude of *many* people,
13. the rushing of *many* waters:
19:20. shall send them a saviour, *and a great one*,
21: 7. he hearkened diligently with *much* heed:
23: 3. by *great* waters the seed of Sihor,
30:25. in the day of the *great* slaughter,
31: 1. trust in chariots, because (they are) *many ;*
42:20. Seeing *many things*,
51:10. the waters of the *great* deep;
52:14. *many* were astonished
15. So shall he sprinkle *many* nations;
53:11. shall my righteous servant justify *many ;*
12. I divide him (a portion) *with the great*,
— he bare the sin of *many*,
54: 1. *more* (are) the children of the desolate
13. *and great* (shall be) the peace of thy
63: 1. I that speak in righteousness, *mighty* to
7. *and* the *great* goodness toward the house
Jer. 3: 1. played the harlot with *many* lovers;
11:15. wrought lewdness with *many*,
12:10. *Many* pastors have destroyed
13: 6. it came to pass after *many* days,
9. the *great* pride of Jerusalem.
16:16. I will send for *many* fishers,
— will I send *for many* hunters,
20:10. I heard the defaming of *many*,
22: 8. *many* nations shall pass by
25:14. *many* nations...shall serve themselves of them also:
27: 7. *many* nations...shall serve themselves of
28: 8. prophesied both against *many* countries,
32:14. that they may continue *many* days.
19. Great in counsel, *and mighty* in work:
35: 7. that ye may live *many* days
36:32. added besides unto them *many* like words.
37:16. Jeremiah had remained there *many* days;
39: 3. Sarsechim, *Rab*-saris [or, the *chief* eunuch], Nergal-sharezer, *Rab*-mag, [or, the *chief* magian]
9, 10, 11, 13. Nebuzar-adan *the captain of* the
13. *Rab*-saris, and Nergal-sharezer, *Rab*-mag, and all the king of Babylon's *princes ;*
40: 1, 2, 5. *the captain of* the guard
41: 1. *and the princes of* the king,
Jer. 41:10. Nebuzar-adan *the captain of* the guard
12. the *great* waters that (are) in Gibeon.
43: 6. Nebuzar-adan *the captain of* the guard
50:41. *many* kings shall be raised up
51:13. O thou that dwellest upon *many* waters, *abundant* in treasures,
55. her waves do roar like *great* waters,
52:12. Nebuzar-adan, *captain of* the guard,
14. that (were) with *the captain of* the guard,
15, 16, 19, 24, 26, 30. *the captain of* the guard
Lam. 1: 1. the city...(that was) *full* of people!
— she (that was) *great* among the nations,
22. my sighs (are) *many*,
3:23. *great* (is) thy faithfulness.
Eze. 1:24. like the noise of *great* waters,
3: 6. *many* people of a strange speech
12:27. for *many* days (to come),
16:41. in the sight of *many* women:
17: 5. he placed (it) by *great* waters,
7. great eagle with great wings *and many* feathers:
8. in a good soil by *great* waters,
9. or *many* people to pluck
15. horses and *much* people.
17. mighty army and *great* company
— to cut off *many* persons:
19:10. full of branches by reason of *many* waters.
22: 5. infamous (and) *much* vexed.
24:12. her *great* scum went not forth
26: 3. will cause *many* nations to come up
7. horsemen, and companies, and *much*
19. *great* waters shall cover thee;
27: 3. a merchant of the people for *many* isles,
15. *many* isles (were) the merchandise of
26. brought thee into *great* waters:
33. thou filledst *many* people;
31: 5. because of *the multitude* of waters,
6. under his shadow dwelt all *great* nations.
7. his root was by *great* waters.
15. the *great* waters were stayed:
32: 3. a company of *many* people;
9. vex the hearts of *many* people,
10. I will make *many* people amazed
13. from beside the *great* waters;
33:24. but we (are) *many ;*
37: 2. very *many* in the open valley;
38: 4. a *great* company (with) bucklers
6. (and) *many* people with thee.
8. After *many* days thou shalt be visited:
— gathered out of *many* people,
9. thy bands, and *many* people with thee.
15. thou, and *many* people with thee,
— a great company, and a *mighty* army:
22. the *many* people that (are) with him.
23. will be known in the eyes of *many* nations,
39:27. in the sight of *many* nations;
43: 2. like a noise of *many* waters:
44: 6. *let it suffice* you of all your abominations,
45: 9. *Let it suffice* you, O princes of Israel:
47: 7. very *many* trees on the one side
9. a very *great* multitude of fish,
10. the fish of the great sea, exceeding *many*.
Dan 1: 3. Ashpenaz *the master of* his eunuchs,
8:25. by peace shall destroy *many :*
26. it (shall be) for *many* days.
9:18. but for thy *great* mercies.
27. confirm the covenant *with many*
11: 3. a mighty king...shall rule with *great* dominion,
5. his dominion (shall be) a *great* dominion.
10. a multitude of *great* forces:
11. he shall set forth a *great* multitude;
13. a multitude *greater* than the former,
— a great army and with *much* riches.
14. there shall *many* stand up
18. turn his face...and shall take *many :*
26. *many* shall fall down slain.
33. that understand...shall instruct *many :*
34. *many* shall cleave to them
39. cause them to rule *over many*,
40. with horsemen, and with *many* ships;
41. *and many* (countries) shall be overthrown:
44. utterly to make away *many*.
12: 2. *And many* of them that sleep...shall awake,
3. they that turn *many* to righteousness
4. *many* shall run to and fro,
10. *Many* shall be purified,

Hos. 3: 3. Thou shalt abide for me *many* days;
4. children of Israel shall abide *many* days
9: 7. the multitude of thine iniquity, *and* the *great* hatred.
Joel 2: 2. a *great* people and a strong;
11. his camp (is) very *great:*
13. slow to anger, *and* of *great* kindness,
3:13(4:13). their wickedness (is) *great.*
Am. 3: 9. the *great* tumults in the midst
15. the *great* houses shall have an end,
5:12. I know your *manifold* transgressions
6: 2. go ye to Hamath *the great:*
— their border *greater* than your border?
7: 4. it devoured the *great* deep,
8: 3. *many* dead bodies in every place;
Jon. 1: 6. the ship*master* came to him,
4: 2. slow to anger, *and* of *great* kindness,
11. and (also) *much* cattle?
Mic. 4: 2. *many* nations shall come,
3. he shall judge among *many* people,
11. also *many* nations are gathered
13. thou shalt beat in pieces *many* people:
5: 7(6), 8(7). in the midst of *many* people
Nah 1:12. Though (they be) quiet, and likewise *many*,
Hab 2: 8. thou hast spoiled *many* nations,
10. by cutting off *many* people,
3:15. (through) the heap of *great* waters.
Zec. 2:11(15). *many* nations shall be joined
8:20. the inhabitants of *many* cities:
22. *many* people...shall come
14:13. a *great* tumult from the Lord
Mal 2: 6. *and* did turn *many* away from iniquity.
8. caused *many* to stumble

7228 **רַב** [*rav*], m.

Job 16:13. *His archers* compass me round about,
Jer. 50:29. Call together *the archers*

7229 **רַב** *rav*, Ch. adj.

Ezr. 4:10. the *great* and noble Asnapper
5: 8. to the house of the *great* God,
11. which a *great* king of Israel builded
Dan 2:10. (there is) no king, *lord*, nor ruler, (that)
14. *the captain* (marg. or, *chief*) *of* the king's guard,
31. This *great* image, whose brightness
35. became a *great* mountain,
45. the *great* God hath made known
48. *and chief of* the governors
4: 9(6). O Belteshazzar, *master of* the
30(27). Is not this *great* Babylon,
5: 1. the king made a *great* feast
11. made *master of* the magicians,
7: 2. strove upon the *great* sea.
20. look (was) more *stout* than his fellows.

7230 **רֹב** *rōhv*, m.

Gen16:10. shall not be numbered *for multitude.*
27:28. *and plenty of* corn and wine:
30:30. increased *unto a multitude;*
32:12(13). cannot be numbered *for multitude.*
48:16. let them grow *into a multitude*
Ex. 15: 7. *And in the greatness of* thine excellency
Lev.25:16. According to *the multitude of* years
Deu 1:10. as the stars of heaven *for multitude.*
7: 7. *because ye were more in number* than
10:22. as the stars of heaven *for multitude.*
28:47. *for the abundance of* all (things);
62. as the stars of heaven *for multitude;*
Jos. 9:13. *by reason of* the very *long* journey.
11: 4. as the sand...*in multitude,*
Jud. 6: 5. as grasshoppers *for multitude;*
7:12. like grasshoppers *for multitude;*
— as the sand by the sea side *for multitude.*
1Sa. 1:16. *out of the abundance of* my complaint
13: 5. as the sand...*in multitude:*
2Sa.17:11. as the sand...*for multitude;*
1K. 1:19, 25. fat cattle and sheep *in abundance,*
3: 8. cannot be numbered...*for multitude.*
4:20. as the sand...by the sea *in multitude,*
1K. 7:47. *because they were* exceeding *many:* (lit. *for the* very great *multitude*)
8: 5. could not be told...*for multitude.*
10:10. there came no more such *abundance*
27. as the sycomore trees...*for abundance.*
2K. 19:23. *With the multitude of* my chariots
1Ch 4:38. house of their fathers increased *greatly.*
12:40. oxen, and sheep *abundantly:*
22: 3. David prepared iron *in abundance*
— brass *in abundance* without weight;
4. brought *much* cedar wood
5. David prepared *abundantly*
8. Thou hast shed blood *abundantly,*
14. iron...for it is *in abundance:*
15. workmen with thee *in abundance,*
29: 2. marble stones *in abundance.*
21. sacrifices *in abundance* for all Israel:
2Ch 1:15. as the sycomore trees...*for abundance.*
2: 9(8). to prepare me timber *in abundance:*
4:18. vessels *in* great *abundance:*
5: 6. sheep and oxen, which could not be told ..*for multitude.*
9: 1. spices, and gold *in abundance,*
9. of spices great *abundance,*
27. as the sycomore trees...*in abundance.*
11:23. gave them victual *in abundance.*
14:15(14). sheep and camels *in abundance,*
15: 9. fell to him out of Israel *in abundance,*
16: 8. Ethiopians and the Lubims a *huge* host,
17: 5. he had riches and honour *in abundance.*
18: 1. had riches and honour *in abundance,*
2. killed sheep and oxen...*in abundance,*
20:25. found among them *in abundance* both
24:11. gathered money *in abundance.*
24. the Lord delivered a very *great* host into
27. (כתיב) *and the greatness of* the burdens
27: 3. on the wall of Ophel he built *much.*
29:35. the burnt offerings (were) *in abundance,*
30: 5. they had not done (it) *of a long* (time)
13. a very *great* congregation.
24. *a great number* of priests sanctified
31: 5. all (things) brought they in *abundantly.*
10. enough to eat, and have left *plenty:*
32: 5. made darts and shields *in abundance.*
29. flocks and herds *in abundance:*
Neh 9:25. fruit trees *in abundance:*
13:22. *according to the greatness* (marg. or, *multitude*) *of* thy mercy.
Est. 5:11. *and the multitude of* his children,
10: 3. accepted *of the multitude of* his brethren,
Job 4:14. *which* made *all* (marg. *the multitude of*) my bones to shake.
11: 2. Should not *the multitude of* words be
23: 6. plead against me *with* (his) *great* power?
26: 3. (how) hast thou *plentifully* declared
30:18. *By* the *great* force (of my disease)
32: 7. *and multitude of* years should teach
33:19. *the multitude of* his bones
35: 9. *By reason of the multitude of* oppressions
36:18. *then* a *great* ransom cannot deliver
37:23. *and in plenty of* justice:
Ps. 5: 7(8). *in the multitude of* thy mercy;
10(11). *in the multitude of* their transgressions;
33:16. no king saved *by the multitude of* an host: a mighty man is not delivered *by much* strength.
17. *neither* shall he deliver (any) *by* his *great*
37:11. delight...in *the abundance of* peace.
49: 6(7). *and* boast...*in the multitude of* their
51: 1(3). *according unto the multitude of* thy
52: 7(9). trusted *in the abundance of* his riches,
66: 3. *through the greatness of* thy power
69:13(14). *in the multitude of* thy mercy
16(17). *according to the multitude of* thy
72: 7. *abundance of* peace
94:19. *In the multitude of* my thoughts
106: 7. *the multitude of* thy mercies;
45. *according to the multitude of* his mercies.
150: 2. *according to* his *excellent* greatness.
Pro. 5:23. *and in the greatness of* his folly
7:21. *With* her *much* fair speech
10:19 *In the multitude of* words
11:14. *in the multitude of* counsellors
13:23. *Much* food (is in) the tillage of the poor:
14: 4. *but much* increase (is) by the strength of
28. *In the multitude of* people
15:22. *but in the multitude of* counsellors

Pro.16: 8. *than great* revenues without right.
20: 6. *Most* men will proclaim every one his
15. *and a multitude of* rubies:
24: 6. *in multitude of* counsellors
Ecc. 1:18. *in much* wisdom (is) *much* grief:
5: 3(2). dream cometh *through the multitude of*
—(-). a fool's voice (is known) *by multitude of* words.
7(6). *in the multitude of* dreams
11: 1. thou shalt find it *after many* days.
Isa. 1:11. *the multitude of* your sacrifices
7:22. *for the abundance of* milk (that) they
24:22. *and after many* days shall they be visited.
37:24. *By the multitude of* my chariots
40:26. *by the greatness of* his might,
47: 9. *for the multitude of* thy sorceries,
12. *with the multitude of* thy sorceries,
13. *in the multitude of* thy counsels.
57:10. wearied *in the greatness of* thy way;
63: 1. travelling *in the greatness of* his strength?
7. *and according to the multitude of* his
Jer. 13:22. *For the greatness of* thine iniquity
30:14,15. for *the multitude of* thine iniquity;
Lam. 1: 3. *and because of great* (marg. *for the greatness of*) servitude:
5. *the multitude of* her transgressions:
3:32. *according to the multitude of* his mercies.
Eze.14: 4. *according to the multitude of* his idols;
19:11. *with the multitude of* her branches.
23:42. the *common sort* (marg. *multitude of* men)
27:12. *by reason of the multitude of* all (kind of)
16. *by reason of the multitude of* the wares
18. *in the multitude of* the wares
— *for the multitude of* all riches;
33. *with the multitude of* thy riches
28: 5. *By* thy *great* (marg. *the greatness of*) wisdom...hast thou increased
16. *By the multitude of* thy merchandise
18. *by the multitude of* thine iniquities,
31: 9. made him fair *by the multitude of* his
Hos. 4: 7. *As they were increased*,
8:12. *the great things of* my law,
9: 7. for *the multitude of* thine iniquity,
10: 1. *according to the multitude* of his fruit
13. *in the multitude of* thy mighty men.
Nah. 3: 3. *and* (there is) *a multitude of* slain,
4. *Because of the multitude of* the whoredoms
Zec. 2: 4(8). *for the multitude of* men and cattle
8: 4. every man with his staff in his hand *for very* age. (marg. *for multitude of* days)
14:14. gold, and silver, and apparel, *in* great *abundance*.

7231 רָבַב [*rāh-vav'*].

✻ KAL.—*Preterite.* ✻

1Sa.25:10. *there be many* servants...that break away
Job 35: 6. *or* (if) thy transgressions *be multiplied*,
Ps. 3: 1(2). how *are they increased* that trouble me?
4: 7(8). their corn and their wine *increased*.
25:19. mine enemies; for *they are many*;
38:19(20). *and* they that hate me...*are multiplied*.
69: 4(5). They that hate me...*are more* than
104:24. O Lord, how *manifold are* thy works!
Ecc. 5:11(10). goods increase, *they are increased*
Isa. 22: 9. Ye have seen also the breaches...that *they are many*:
59:12. our transgressions *are multiplied*
66:16. *and* the slain of the Lord *shall be many*.
Jer. 5: 6. their transgressions *are many*,
14: 7. our backslidings *are many*;
46:23. *they are more* than the grasshoppers,

KAL.—*Infinitive.*

Gen 6: 1. when men began *to multiply*

✻ PUAL.—*Participle.* ✻

Ps.144:13. our sheep may bring forth thousands and *ten thousands*

7232 רָבַב [*rāh-vav'*].

✻ KAL.—*Preterite.* ✻

Gen49:23. *and shot* (at him), and hated him:
Ps. 18:14(15). *he shot out* lightnings,

רְבָבָה *r'vāh-vāh'*, f. 7233

Gen24:60. (the mother) of thousands of *millions*,
Lev.26: 8. an hundred...shall put *ten thousand* to
Nu. 10:36. *many* (marg. *ten thousand*) thousands of
Deu32:30. two put *ten thousand* to flight,
33: 2. he came *with ten thousands of* saints:
17. *the ten thousands of* Ephraim,
Jud.20:10. a thousand *out of ten thousand*,
1Sa.18: 7. David *his ten thousands*.
8. ascribed unto David *ten thousands*,
21:11(12) & 29:5. David *his ten thousands*?
Ps. 3: 6(7). I will not be afraid *of ten thousands of*
91: 7. *and ten thousand* at thy right hand;
Cant.5:10. the chiefest *among ten thousand*.
Eze.16: 7. I have caused thee *to multiply* (marg. made thee *a million*)
Mic. 6: 7. *with ten thousands of* rivers of oil?

רָבַד [*rāh-vad'*]. 7234

✻ KAL.—*Preterite.* ✻

Pro. 7:16. *I have decked* my bed

רָבָה [*rāh-vāh'*]. 7235

✻ KAL.—*Preterite.* ✻

Gen 8:17. be fruitful, *and multiply*
Deu 8: 1. that ye may live, *and multiply*,
30:16. that thou mayest live *and multiply*:
1Sa.14:30. *had there* not *been* now a *much greater* slaughter
1Ch 5: 9. their cattle *were multiplied*
23. *they increased* from Bashan unto Baal-hermon
23:17. the sons of Rehabiah *were* very *many*. (marg. highly *multiplied*)
Ezr. 9: 6. our iniquities *are increased*
Jer. 23: 3. they shall be fruitful *and increase*.
Eze.36:11. and *they shall increase* and bring fruit:
Zec.10: 8. *and they shall increase* as *they have increased*.

KAL.—*Infinitive.*

Ex. 11: 9. that my wonders *may be multiplied*
Pro.29: 2. *When* the righteous *are in authority*, (marg. or, *increased*)
16. *When* the wicked *are multiplied*,
Ecc. 5:11(10). *When* goods *increase*,

KAL.—*Imperative.*

Gen 1:22. Be fruitful, *and multiply*, and fill
28 & 9:1. fruitful, *and multiply*, and replenish
9: 7. be ye fruitful, *and multiply*; bring forth abundantly in the earth, *and multiply*
35:11. be fruitful *and multiply*;
Jer. 29: 6. *that ye may be increased* there, and not

KAL.—*Future.*

Gen 1:22. *let* fowl *multiply* in the earth.
7:17. *and* the waters *increased*,
18. *and were increased* greatly
38:12. *And in process of* time (marg. *and* the days *were multiplied*)
43:34. *but* Benjamin's mess *was* five times *so much* as any
47:27. Israel...grew, *and multiplied*
Ex. 1: 7. the children of Israel were fruitful,...*and multiplied*,
10. lest *they multiply*, and it come
12. the more *they multiplied*
20. *and* the people *multiplied*,
Deu 6: 3. that *ye may increase* mightily,
7:22. lest the beasts of the field *increase*
8:13. (when) thy herds and thy flocks *multiply*, and thy silver and thy gold *is multiplied*, and all that thou hast *is multiplied*;
11:21. That your days *may be multiplied*,
14:24. if the way *be too long*
19: 6. because the way *is long*,
1Sa. 7: 2. while the ark abode in Kirjath-jearim, *that* the time *was long*;
1K. 4:30(5:10). *And* Solomon's wisdom *excelled*
2Ch 24:27. *and the greatness* of the burdens
Job 27:14. If his children *be multiplied*,
33:12. God *is greater* than man.
39: 4. *they grow up* with corn;

Ps. 16: 4. Their sorrows *shall be multiplied*
49:16(17). the glory of his house *is increased;*
107:38. *so that they are multiplied* greatly;
139:18. *they are more in number* than the sand:
Pro. 4:10. *and* the years of thy life *shall be many.*
9:11. thy days *shall be multiplied,*
28:28. the righteous *increase.*
29:16. When the wicked are multiplied, transgression *increaseth:*
Jer. 3:16. when *ye be multiplied*
Eze.16: 7. *and thou hast increased* and waxen great,
31: 5. *and* his boughs *were multiplied,*
Dan 12: 4. *and* knowledge *shall be increased.*

KAL.—*Participle.* Poel.

Gen21:20. the lad;...became an archer. (lit. *shooter* with a bow)

* PIEL.—*Preterite.* *

Ps. 44:12(13). *dost* not *increase* (thy wealth)
Lam 2:22. those that I have swaddled *and brought up*
Eze.19: 2. *she nourished* her whelps

PIEL.—*Imperative.*

Jud. 9:29. *Increase* thine army, and come out.

* HIPHIL.—*Preterite.* *

Gen17:20. *and will multiply* him exceedingly;
26: 4. *And I will make* thy seed *to multiply*
24. *and multiply* thy seed for my servant
48: 4. will make thee fruitful, *and multiply* thee,
Ex. 7: 3. *and multiply* my signs and my wonders
Lev.26: 9. make you fruitful, *and multiply* you,
Deu 1:10. The Lord your God *hath multiplied* you,
7:13. he will...bless thee, *and multiply thee:*
13:17(18). have compassion upon thee, *and multiply thee,*
30: 5. *and multiply thee* above thy fathers.
Jud.16:24. which slew *many* of us. (marg. *multiplied* our slain)
1Sa. 1:12. as *she continued* praying (marg. *multiplied* to pray)
2K. 21: 6. *he* wrought *much* wickedness (lit. *he multiplied* to do evil)
1Ch 4:10. thou wouldest bless...*and enlarge* my
27. neither *did* all their family *multiply,*
7: 4. *they had many* wives and sons.
23:11. Jeush and Beriah *had* not *many* (marg. *did* not *multiply*) sons;
2Ch 31: 5. the children of Israel *brought in abundance*
33: 6. *he* wrought *much* evil (lit. *he multiplied* to do evil)
23. Amon trespassed *more and more.* (marg. *multiplied* trespass)
36:14. the people, transgressed *very much* (lit. *multiplied* to transgress)
Ezr.10:13. *we are many* that have transgressed (marg. or, *have greatly* offended)
Neh 9:23. Their children also *multipliedst thou*
Job 9:17. *and multiplieth* my wounds without cause.
Ps. 78:38. *yea, many a time* turned *he* (lit. *and he multiplied* to turn)
Isa. 9: 3(2). *Thou hast multiplied* the nation,
Jer. 30:19. *and I will multiply them,*
46:11. in vain *shalt thou use many* medicines;
16. *He made many* to fall, (marg. *multiplied* the faller)
Eze.11: 6. *Ye have multiplied* your slain
22:25. *they have made* her *many* widows
28: 5. *hast thou increased* thy riches,
36:10. *And I will multiply* men upon you,
11. *And I will multiply* upon you man and
29. I will call for the corn, *and will increase* it,
30. *And I will multiply* the fruit of the tree,
37:26. I will place them, *and multiply* them,
Hos. 2: 8(10). and *multiplied* her silver and gold,
8:11. Ephraim *hath made many* altars
14. Judah *hath multiplied* fenced cities:
10: 1. *he hath increased* the altars;
12:10(11). *I have multiplied* visions,
Nah. 3:16. *Thou hast multiplied* thy merchants

HIPHIL.—*Infinitive.*

Gen 3:16. I will *greatly* multiply (lit. *multiplying* I will multiply)
15: 1. thy exceeding *great* reward.
16:10. I will multiply thy seed *exceedingly,* (lit. *multiplying* I will multiply)
Gen22:17. *and in multiplying* I will multiply thy seed
41:49. Joseph gathered corn...very *much,*
Deu. 3: 5. unwalled towns a great *many.*
17:16. to the end that he *should multiply* horses.
28:63. to do you good, *and to multiply* you;
Jos. 13: 1. remaineth yet very *much* land
22: 8. very *much* raiment:
1Sa.26:21. have erred *exceedingly.* (lit. very *much*)
2Sa. 1: 4. *many* of the people also are fallen
8: 8. king David took exceeding *much* brass.
12: 2. The rich (man) had exceeding *many* flocks
30. forth the spoil...in great *abundance.*
14:11. that thou wouldest not suffer the revengers of blood to destroy *any more,* (marg. that the revenger of blood *do* not *multiply* to destroy)
1K. 4:29(5:9). God gave Solomon wisdom...exceeding *much,*
10:10. and of spices very great *store,*
11. great *plenty* of almug trees,
2K. 10:18. Jehu shall serve him *much.*
21:16. Manasseh shed innocent blood very *much,*
1Ch 20: 2. brought also exceeding *much* spoil
27:23. the Lord had said *he would increase* Israel
2Ch 11:12. made them *exceeding* strong, (lit. strong *unto* very *much*)
14:13(12). carried away very *much* spoil.
16: 8. with very *many* chariots and horsemen?
25: 9. The Lord is able to give thee *much more*
32:27. Hezekiah had exceeding *much* riches
Ezr. 10: 1. the people wept *very* sore. (marg. a *great* weeping)
Neh. 2: 2. Then I was very *sore* afraid,
4: 1(3:33). took *great* indignation,
10(4). (there is) *much* rubbish;
19(13). The work (is) *great* and large,
5:18. *store* of all sorts of wine:
Ps.130: 7. *and* with him (is) *plenteous* redemption.
Pro.22:16. oppresseth the poor *to increase* his (riches),
25:27. (It is) not good to eat *much* honey:
Ecc. 1:16. my heart had *great* experience (marg. seen *much*)
2: 7. *great* possessions of great and small cattle
5: 7(6). multitude of dreams and *many* words
12(11). whether he eat little or *much:*
17(16). (he hath) *much* sorrow and wrath
20(19). he shall not *much* remember the days
6:11. *many* things that increase vanity,
7:16. Be not righteous *over much;*
17. Be not *over much* wicked,
9:18. one sinner destroyeth *much* good.
11: 8. But if a man live *many* years,
— for they shall be *many.*
12: 9. (and) set in order *many* proverbs.
12. of making *many* books there is no end; and *much* study (is) a weariness of the
Isa. 30:33. the pile thereof (is) fire and *much* wood;
Jer. 40:12. gathered wine and summer fruits very *much.*
42: 2. for we are left (but) a few *of many,*
Eze.21:15(20). *and* (their) ruins *be multiplied:*
Am. 4: 9. *when* your gardens...*increased,* (marg. *the multitude of*)
Jon. 4:11. *more* than sixscore thousand persons
Hag. 1: 6. Ye have sown *much,*
9. Ye looked for *much,*

HIPHIL.—*Imperative.*

Gen34:12. *Ask* me never so *much* (lit. *multiply* upon me very much) dowry and gift,
Jud.20:38. *that they should make* a *great* flame
Ps. 51: 2(4). Wash me *throughly* from mine iniquity,
Isa. 23:16. sing *many* songs, (lit. *multiply* the song)
Eze.24:10. *Heap* on wood, kindle the fire,
Am. 4: 4. at Gilgal *multiply* transgression;

HIPHIL.—*Future.*

Gen 3:16. *I will* greatly *multiply* thy sorrow
16:10. *I will multiply* thy seed exceedingly,
17: 2. *and will multiply* thee exceedingly.
22:17. *I will multiply* thy seed as the stars
28: 3. make thee fruitful, *and multiply thee,*
Ex. 30:15. The rich *shall* not *give more,* (marg. *multiply*)
32:13. *I will multiply* your seed as the stars
Lev.25:16. *thou shalt increase* the price
Nu. 26:54. To many *thou shalt give the more* (marg. *multiply*)

Nu. 33:54. to the more *ye shall give the more* (marg. *multiply*)
35: 8. from (them that have) many *ye shall give many;*
Deu 17:16. *he shall* not *multiply* horses
17. Neither *shall he multiply* wives
— neither *shall he* greatly *multiply*...silver
Jos. 24: 3. took your father Abraham...*and multiplied*
1Sa. 2: 3. Talk no *more* (lit. *multiply* not talk)
2Sa. 18: 8. *and* the wood devoured *more* (marg. *multiplied* to devour)...than the sword
22:36. thy gentleness *hath made me great.* (marg. *multiplied me*)
Job 10:17. *and increasest* thine indignation
29:18. *and I shall multiply* (my) days
34:37. *and multiplieth* his words against God.
41: 3(40:27). *Will he make many* supplications
Ps. 18:35(36). thy gentleness *hath made me great.* (marg. or, *thou hast multiplied me*)
71:21. *Thou shalt increase* my greatness,
Pro. 6:35. though *thou givest many* gifts.
13:11. he that gathereth by labour *shall increase.*
Ecc. 10:14. A fool also *is full of* (marg. *multiplieth*) words:
Isa. 1:15. when *ye make many* (marg. *multiply*) prayers,
40:29. *he increaseth* strength.
51: 2. blessed him, *and increased him.*
55: 7. *he will abundantly* pardon. (marg. *multiply* to pardon)
57: 9. *and didst increase* thy perfumes,
Jer. 2:22. *and take* thee *much* sope,
33:22. so *will I multiply* the seed of David
Lam. 2: 5. *and hath increased* in the daughter of
Eze. 16:25. *and multiplied* thy whoredoms.
26. *and hast increased* thy whoredoms,
29. *Thou hast moreover multiplied*
51. *but thou hast multiplied* thine abominations
23:19. *Yet she multiplied* her whoredoms,
36:37. *I will increase* them with men
Dan 11:39. he shall acknowledge (and) *increase*
Hos. 12: 1(2). *he* daily *increaseth* lies

HIPHIL.—*Participle.*

Ex. 16:17. gathered, *some more,* some less.
18. *he that gathered much* had nothing over,
36: 5. The people bring *much more* (lit. *multiply* in bringing) than enough
Lev. 11:42. whatsoever *hath more* (marg. *doth multiply*) feet
1Ch 8:40. *and had many* sons,
Neh 6:17. the nobles of Judah sent *many* letters (marg. *multiplied* their letters passing)
9:37. *it yieldeth much* increase
Pro. 28: 8. *He that* by usury...*increaseth*
Ecc. 6:11. many things *that increase* vanity,
Hab 2: 6. Woe to *him that increaseth*

7236 **רְבָה** *r'vāh*, Ch.

* P'AL.—*Preterite.* *

Dan 4:11(8). The tree *grew,* and was strong,
20(17). The tree that thou sawest, which *grew,*
22(19). that *art grown* and become strong: for thy greatness *is grown,*
33(30). till his hairs *were grown* like eagles'

* PAEL.—*Preterite.* *

Dan 2:48. the king *made* Daniel *a great man,*

7239 **רִבּוֹ & רִבּוֹא** *rib-bōh'*, f.

1Ch 29: 7. five thousand talents and *ten thousand*
— of brass eigh*teen thousand* (lit. *ten thousand* and eight thousand) talents,
Ezr. 2:64. The whole congregation together (was) forty and two *thousand* (lit. four *ten thousands* two thousand) three hundred (and) threescore,
69. gave...unto the treasure of the work *threescore* (lit. six *ten thousands*) and one thousand drams of gold,
Neh. 7:66. The whole congregation together (was) *forty* (lit. four *ten thousands*) and two thousand three hundred and threescore,
72. twen*ty thousand* (lit. two *ten thousands*) drams of gold,
Dan 11:12. he shall cast down (many) *ten thousands.*
Hos. 8:12. (כתיב) written to him *the great things of*
Jon. 4:11. wherein are more than sixscore *thousand* (lit. twelve *ten thousand*) persons

---

רִבּוֹ *rib-bōh'*, Ch. f. 7240

Dan 7:10. *and ten thousand times ten thousand* stood before him:

רְבוּ *r'voo*, Ch. f. 7238

Dan 4:22(19). *for thy greatness* is grown,
36(33). *and* excellent *majesty* was added
5:18. *and majesty,* and glory, and honour:
19. for *the majesty* that he gave him,
7:27. *and the greatness* of the kingdom

רִבּוֹת *rib-bōhth'*, f. pl. 7239

Neh. 7:71. twen*ty thousand* drams (lit. two *ten thousands*)
Ps. 68:17(18). The chariots of God (are) *twenty thousand,*

רְבִיבִים *r'vee-veem'*, m. pl. 7241

Deu 32: 2. *and as the showers* upon the grass:
Ps. 65:10(11). thou makest it soft *with showers:*
72: 6. *as showers* (that) water the earth.
Jer. 3: 3. *the showers* have been withholden,
14:22. can the heavens give *showers?*
Mic. 5: 7(6). *as the showers* upon the grass,

רָבִיד *rāh-veed'*, m. 7242

Gen 41:42. put *a* gold *chain* about his neck;
Eze. 16:11. *and a chain* on thy neck.

רְבִיעִי *r'vee-ğee'*, adj. num. 7243

Gen 1:19. the evening and the morning were the *fourth* day.
2:14. the *fourth* river (is) Euphrates.
15:16. in the *fourth* generation
Ex. 28:20. the *fourth* row a beryl, and an onyx, and
29:40. and *the fourth part of* an hin of wine
39:13. the *fourth* row, a beryl, an onyx,
Lev. 19:24. in the *fourth* year all the fruit thereof
23:13. wine, *the fourth part of* an hin.
Nu. 7:30. On the *fourth* day Elizur
15: 4. *with the fourth part of* an hin of oil.
5. *the fourth part of* an hin of wine
28: 5. *the fourth part of* an hin of beaten oil.
7. *the fourth part of* an hin for the one
14. *and a fourth part of* an hin unto a lamb:
29:23. on the *fourth* day ten bullocks,
Jos. 19:17. the *fourth* lot came out to Issachar,
Jud. 19: 5. it came to pass on the *fourth* day,
2Sa. 3: 4. *And the fourth,* Adonijah the son of
1K. 6: 1. in the *fourth* year of Solomon's reign
33. *a fourth part* (of the wall). (marg. or, *foursquare*)
37. In the *fourth* year was the foundation
2K. 10:30. thy children of *the fourth* (generation)
15:12. Thy sons shall sit... *unto the fourth*
18: 9. in the *fourth* year of king Hezekiah,
1Ch 2:14. Nethaneel *the fourth,*
3: 2. *the fourth,* Adonijah
15. *the fourth* Shallum.
8: 2. Nohah *the fourth,*
12:10. Mishmannah *the fourth,*
23:19. Jekameam *the fourth.*
24: 8. *the fourth* to Seorim,
23. Jekameam *the fourth.*
25:11. *The fourth* to Izri,
26: 2. Jathniel *the fourth,*
4. Sacar *the fourth,*
11. Zechariah *the fourth:*
27: 7. *The fourth* (captain) for the *fourth* month

2Ch 20.26. on the *fourth* day they assembled
Ezr. 8:33. on the *fourth* day was the silver...weighed
Neh. 9: 3. (one) *fourth part of* the day; *and* (another) *fourth part* they confessed,
Jer. 25: 1 & 28:1 & 36:1. in the *fourth* year
39: 2. in the *fourth* month, the ninth (day) of the month,
45: 1 & 46:2 & 51:59. in the *fourth* year
52: 6. in the *fourth* month, in the ninth
Eze. 1: 1. *in the fourth* (month),
10:14. *and the fourth* the face of an eagle.
48:20. ye shall offer the holy oblation *foursquare*,
Dan11: 2. *and the fourth* shall be far richer than
Zec. 6: 3. in the *fourth* chariot grisled and bay
8:19. The fast of *the fourth* (month),

7244 רְבִיעָי [r'vee-^{n}gah'y], Ch. adj. num.

Dan 2:40. And the *fourth* kingdom
3:25. and the form of *the fourth* is like the
7: 7. and behold a *fourth* beast,
19. I would know the truth of the *fourth*
23. The *fourth* beast shall be the *fourth*

7246 רָבַךְ [rāh-vach'].

* HOPHAL.—*Participle.* *

Lev. 6:21(14). (when it is) *baken*,
7:12. cakes mingled with oil,...*fried*.
1Ch 23:29. *and for that which is fried*,

7250 רָבַע [rāh-va^{n}g'].

* KAL.—*Infinitive.* *

Lev.18:23. stand before a beast *to lie down thereto*:
20:16. *and lie down* thereto,

* HIPHIL.—*Future.* *

Lev.19:19. *Thou shalt* not *let* thy cattle *gender*

7251 רָבַע [rāh-va^{n}g'].

* KAL.—*Participle.* Paül. *

Ex. 27: 1. the altar shall be *foursquare*:
28:16. *Foursquare* it shall be (being) doubled;
30: 2. *foursquare* shall it be: and two
37:25. (it was) *foursquare*; and two cubits (was) the height
38: 1. (it was) *foursquare*; and three cubits the
39: 9. It was *foursquare*; they made
1K. 7: 5. the doors and posts (were) *square*,
Eze.41:21. The posts of the temple (were) *squared*,
43:16. *square* in the four squares thereof.

* PUAL.—*Participle.* *

1K. 7:31. gravings with their borders, *foursquare*,
Eze.40:47. an hundred cubits broad, *foursquare*;
45: 2. *square* round about;

7252 רֶבַע [reh'-va^{n}g], m.

Ps.139: 3. compassest my path *and my lying down*,

7253 רֶבַע reh'-va^{n}g, m.

Ex. 29:40. *the fourth part of* an hin of beaten oil;
1Sa. 9: 8. *the fourth part of* a shekel of silver:
Eze. 1: 8. hands of a man under their wings on *their* four *sides*;
17. When they went, they went upon *their* four *sides*:
10:11. they went upon *their* four *sides*;
43:16. square in *the* four *squares thereof*.
17. broad in *the* four *squares thereof*;

7255 רֹבַע rōh'-va^{n}g, m.

Nu. 23:10. the number of *the fourth part of* Israel?
2K. 6:25. *and the fourth part of* a cab of doves'

רִבֵּעִים rib-bēh-^{n}geem', m. pl. 7256

Ex. 20: 5. unto the third and *fourth* (generation)
34: 7. the third and to *the fourth* (generation).
Nu. 14:18. unto the third and *fourth* (generation).
Deu 5: 9. unto the third and *fourth* (generation) of them that hate me,

---

רָבַץ rāh-vatz'. 7257

* KAL.—*Preterite.* *

Gen49: 9. *he couched* as a lion,
Deu29:20(19). *and* all the curses...*shall lie* upon
Job 11:19. *Also thou shalt lie down*, and none
Isa. 13:21. *But* wild beasts...*shall lie* there;
17: 2. flocks, *which shall lie down*,
Eze.19: 2. *she lay down* among lions,
Zep. 2:14. *And* flocks *shall lie down*
3:13. they shall feed *and lie down*,

KAL.—*Future.*

Nu. 22:27. *And* when the ass...*she fell down* under
Ps. 104:22. *lay them down* in their dens.
Isa. 11: 6. the leopard *shall lie down* with the kid;
7. their young ones *shall lie down*
14:30. the needy *shall lie down* in safety:
27:10. there *shall he lie down*,
Eze.34:14. there *shall they lie* in a good fold,
Zep. 2: 7. *shall they lie down* in the evening:

KAL.—*Participle.* Poel.

Gen. 4: 7. sin *lieth* at the door.
29: 2. three flocks of sheep *lying*
49:14. Issachar (is) a strong ass *couching down*
25. blessings of the deep *that lieth* under,
Ex. 23: 5. the ass...*lying* under his burden,
Deu 22: 6. the dam *sitting* upon the young,
33:13. the deep *that coucheth* beneath,
Eze.29: 3. the great dragon *that lieth*

* HIPHIL.—*Future.* *

Ps. 23: 2. *He maketh me to lie down* in green
Cant.1: 7. where *thou makest* (thy flock) *to rest*
Isa. 13:20. neither *shall* the shepherds *make their fold*
Eze.34:15. I *will cause them to lie down*,

HIPHIL.—*Participle.*

Isa. 54:11. I *will lay* thy stones with fair colours,
Jer. 33:12. *causing* (their) flocks *to lie down*.

רֵבֶץ rēh'-vetz, m. 7258

Pro.24:15. spoil not *his resting place*:
Isa. 35: 7. habitation of dragons, *where each lay*,
65:10. a place for the herds *to lie down in*,
Jer. 50: 6. they have forgotten *their restingplace*. (marg. *place to lie down in*)

רַבְרַב [rav-rav'], Ch. adj. 7260

Dan. 2:48. and gave him many *great* gifts,
4: 3(3:33). How *great* (are) his signs!
7: 3. And four *great* beasts came up
7. and it had *great* iron teeth:
8. and a mouth speaking *great things*.
11. because of the voice of the *great* words
17. These *great* beasts, which are four,
20. a mouth that spake *very great things*,

רַבְרְבָן [rav-r'vāhn'], Ch. m. 7261

Dan. 4:36(33). *and my lords* sought unto me;
5: 1. *to* a thousand of *his lords*,
2. that the king, *and his princes*,
3. and the king, *and his princes*,
9. *and his lords* were astonied.
10. the words of the king *and his lords*
23. and thou, *and thy lords*, thy wives,
6:17(18). and with the signet *of his lords*;

רֶגֶב reh'-gev, m. 7263

Job 21:33. *The clods of* the valley shall be sweet
38:38. *and the clods* cleave fast together?

7264 רָגַז rāh-gaz'.

* KAL.—*Preterite.* *

Deu. 2:25. *and shall tremble*, and be in anguish
Ps. 77:18(19). the earth *trembled* and shook.
Pro.29: 9. a foolish man, *whether he rage* or laugh,
30:21. For three (things) the earth *is disquieted*,
Isa. 14: 9. Hell from beneath *is moved*
Jer. 33: 9. they shall fear *and tremble*
Joel 2:10. The earth *shall quake*

KAL.—*Imperative.*

Ps. 4: 4(5). *Stand in awe*, and sin not:
Isa. 32:11. *be troubled*, ye careless ones:

KAL.—*Future.*

Gen45:24. See that *ye fall* not *out* by the way.
Ex. 15:14. The people shall hear, (and) *be afraid:*
1Sa.14:15. *and* the earth *quaked:*
2Sa. 7:10. that they may dwell...and *move* no more;
18:33(19:1). *And* the king *was much moved*,
22: 8. the foundations of heaven *moved*
1Ch 17: 9. they shall dwell...and *shall be moved* no
Ps. 18: 7(8). the foundations also of the hills *moved*
77:16(17). the depths also *were troubled.*
99: 1. *let* the people *tremble:*
Isa. 5:25. the hills *did tremble*,
28:21. *he shall be wroth* as (in) the valley of
32:10. Many days and years *shall ye be troubled*,
64: 2(1). (that) the nations *may tremble*
Eze.16:43. *but hast fretted me* in all these (things);
Joel 2: 1. *let* all the inhabitants of the land *tremble:*
Am. 8: 8. *Shall* not the land *tremble* for this,
Mic. 7:17. *they shall move* out of their holes
Hab. 3: 7. the curtains of the land of Midian *did tremble.*
16. *When* I heard, my belly *trembled;*
— *I trembled* in myself,

* HIPHIL.—*Preterite.* *

1Sa.28:15. Why *hast thou disquieted me*,
Isa. 23:11. *he shook* the kingdoms:
Jer. 50:34. *and disquiet* the inhabitants of Babylon.

HIPHIL.—*Future.*

Isa. 13:13. *I will shake* the heavens,

HIPHIL.—*Participle.*

Job 9: 6. *Which shaketh* the earth out of her place,
12: 6. *they that provoke* God are secure;
Isa. 14:16. the man *that made* the earth *to tremble*,

* HITHPAEL.—*Infinitive.* *

2K. 19:27. I know thy abode,...and *thy rage* against
28. Because *thy rage* against me...is come up
Isa. 37:28. I know thy abode,...and *thy rage* against
29. Because *thy rage* against me,...is come up

7265 רְגַז [r'gaz], Ch.

* APHEL.—*Preterite.* *

Ezr. 5:12. that our fathers *had provoked* the God of heaven *unto wrath*,

---

7266 רְגַז r'gaz, Ch. m.

Dan. 3:13. Then Nebuchadnezzar *in* (his) *rage* and

7268 רַגָּז rag-gāhz', adj.

Deu28:65. the Lord shall give thee there a *trembling* heart,

---

7267 רֹגֶז rōh'-gez, m.

Job 3:17. There the wicked cease (from) *troubling;*
26. yet *trouble* came.
14: 1. of few days, and full of *trouble.*
37: 2. Hear attentively *the noise of* his voice,
39:24. the ground with fierceness *and rage:*
Isa. 14: 3. rest from thy sorrow, *and* from *thy fear*,
Hab. 3: 2. *in wrath* remember mercy.

7269 רָגְזָה rog-zāh', f.

Eze.12:18. drink thy water *with trembling*

רָגַל rāh-gal'. 7270

* KAL.—*Preterite.* *

Ps. 15: 3. (He that) *backbiteth* not with his tongue,

* PIEL.—*Infinitive.* *

Nu. 21:32. Moses sent *to spy out* Jaazer,
Jos. 6:25. Joshua sent *to spy out* Jericho.
14: 7. sent me from Kadesh-barnea *to espy out* the land;
Jud.18: 2. from Eshtaol, *to spy out* the land,
14. the five men that went *to spy out*
17. the five men that went *to spy out* the land
2Sa.10: 3. to search the city, *and to spy it out*,
1Ch 19: 3. *and to spy out* the land?

PIEL.—*Imperative.*

Jos. 7: 2. Go up *and view* the country.

PIEL.—*Future.*

Deu 1:24. unto the valley of Eshcol, *and searched*
Jos. 7: 2. the men went up *and viewed*
2Sa.19:27(28). *he hath slandered* thy servant

PIEL.—*Participle.*

Gen42: 9. said unto them, Ye (are) *spies;*
11. thy servants are no *spies.*
14. That (is it) that I spake...Ye (are) *spies*
16. by the life of Pharaoh surely ye (are) *spies.*
30. took us *for spies of* the country.
31. We (are) true (men); we are no *spies:*
34. then shall I know that ye (are) no *spies*,
Jos. 2: 1. sent out of Shittim two men *to spy*
6:22. the two men *that had spied*
23. the young men *that were spies*
1Sa.26: 4. David therefore sent out *spies*,
2Sa.15:10. Absalom sent *spies* throughout

* TIPHEL.—*Preterite.* *

Hos 11: 3. I *taught* Ephraim also *to go*,

רֶגֶל reh'-gel, f. 7272

Gen 8: 9. dove found no rest for the sole of *her foot*,
18: 4. wash *your feet*, and rest yourselves
19: 2. tarry all night, and wash *your feet*,
24:32. water to wash *his feet, and* the men's *feet* that (were) with him.
29: 1. Jacob went on his journey, (marg. lift up *his feet*)
30:30. the Lord hath blessed thee *since my coming:* (marg. *at my foot*)
33:14. *according* as the cattle that goeth before me *and* the children *be able to endure*, (marg. *according to the foot of* the work, &c. *and according to the foot of* the children)
41:44. shall no man lift up his hand or (lit. or *his*) *foot*
43:24. they washed *their feet;*
49:10. nor a lawgiver from between *his feet*,
33. he gathered up *his feet*
Ex. 3: 5. put off thy shoes from off *thy feet*,
4:25. cut off the foreskin of her son, and cast (it) *at his feet*,
11: 8. all the people that *follow thee:* (marg. *at thy feet*)
12:11. your shoes on *your feet*,
21:24. hand for hand, *foot* for *foot*,
23:14. Three *times* thou shalt keep a feast
24:10. under *his feet* as it were a paved work
25:26. *the* four *feet thereof.*
29:20. the great toe of *their* right *foot*,
30:19. wash their hands and *their feet*
21. shall wash their hands *and their feet*,
37:13. in *the* four *feet thereof.*
40:31. Moses and Aaron...washed their hands and *their feet*
Lev. 8:23. the great toe of *his* right *foot.*
24. the great toes of *their* right *feet:*
11:21. which have legs above *their feet*,
23. creeping things, which have four *feet*,
42. whatsoever hath more *feet* among all
13:12. from his head even to *his foot*,
14:14, 17, 25, 28. the great toe of *his* right *foot:*
21:19. a man that is broken*footed*,
Nu. 20:19. I will only,...go through *on my feet.*
22:25. crushed Balaam's *foot* against the wall;

Nu. 22:28. smitten me these three *times?*
32. smitten thine ass these three *times?*
33. turned from me these three *times:*
Deu 2: 5. not so much as a *foot* breadth;
28. only I will pass through *on my feet;*
8: 4. *neither* did *thy foot* swell,
11: 6. the substance that (was) *in their possession,* (marg. *at their feet*)
10. wateredst (it) *with thy foot,*
24. whereon the soles of *your feet* shall tread
19:21. hand for hand, *foot* for *foot.*
25: 9. loose his shoe from off *his foot,*
28:35. from the sole of *thy foot* unto the top of
56. set the sole of *her foot* upon the ground
57. her young one that cometh out from between *her feet,*
65. neither shall the sole of *thy foot* have rest:
29: 5(4). shoe is not waxen old upon *thy foot.*
32:35. *their foot* shall slide in (due) time:
33: 3. they sat down *at thy feet;*
24. let him dip *his foot* in oil.
Jos. 1: 3. the sole of *your foot* shall tread upon,
3:13. of *the feet of* the priests that bear
15. *and the feet of* the priests that bare
4: 3. where the priests' *feet* stood
9. *the feet of* the priests which
18. the soles of the priests' *feet* were lifted up
5:15. Loose thy shoe from off *thy foot;*
9: 5. old shoes and clouted *upon their feet,*
10:24. put *your feet* upon the necks of these
— and put *their feet* upon the necks of them.
14: 9. the land whereon *thy feet* have trodden
Jud. 1: 6. cut off his thumbs and his great toes. (lit. thumbs of his hands *and his feet*)
7. Threescore and ten kings, having their thumbs and their great toes (marg. thumbs of their hands *and of their feet*) cut off,
3:24. covereth *his feet* in his summer chamber.
4:10. he went up with ten thousand men *at his feet:*
15. Sisera...fled away *on his feet.*
17. Sisera fled away *on his feet*
5:15. he was sent *on foot* (marg. *on his feet*) into the valley.
27. At *her feet* he bowed, he fell, he lay down: at *her feet* he bowed,
8: 5. the people that *follow me;* (lit. (are) *at my feet*)
19:21. they washed *their feet,*
1Sa. 2: 9. He will keep *the feet of* his saints,
14:13. up upon his hands and upon *his feet,*
17: 6. greaves of brass upon *his legs,*
23:22. his place where *his haunt* (marg. *foot*) is,
24: 3(4). Saul went in to cover *his feet:*
25:24. And fell at *his feet,*
27. the young men that follow (marg. walk *at the feet of*) my lord.
41. to wash *the feet of* the servants of my lord.
42. five damsels...that went *after her;* (marg. at *her feet*)
2Sa. 2:18. Asahel (was as) light *of foot* (lit. *of his feet*) as a wild roe.
3:34. *nor thy feet* put into fetters:
4: 4. had a son (that was) lame of (his) *feet.*
12. cut off their hands and *their feet,*
9: 3. yet a son, (which is) lame on (his) *feet.*
13. was lame on both *his feet.*
11: 8. Go down to thy house, and wash *thy feet.*
14:25. from the sole of *his foot*
15:16. the king went forth, and all his houshold *after him.* (marg. *at his feet*)
17. the king went forth, and all the people *after him,* (lit. *at his feet*)
18. six hundred men which came *after him* (lit. *at his foot*)
19:24(25). had neither dressed *his feet,* nor
21:20. on every *foot* six toes, (lit. the toes of his *feet* six)
22:10. darkness (was) under *his feet.*
34. He maketh *my feet* like hinds' (feet):
39. they are fallen under *my feet.*
1K. 2: 5. his shoes that (were) *on his feet.*
5: 3(17). under the soles of *his feet.*
14: 6. when Ahijah heard the sound of *her feet,*
12. when *thy feet* enter into the city,
15:23. he was diseased in *his feet.*

1K. 20:10. all the people that follow *me.* (marg. (are) *at my feet*)
2K. 3: 9. the cattle that followed *them.* (marg. *at their feet*)
4:27. she caught him *by the* (marg. *his*) *feet.*
37. she went in, and fell at *his feet,*
6:32. the sound of his master's *feet*
9:35. the scull, *and the feet,*
13:21. he revived, and stood up on *his feet.*
18:27. eat their own dung, and drink their own piss (marg. the water of *their feet*)
21: 8. Neither will I make *the feet of* Israel move
1Ch 28: 2. David the king stood up upon *his feet,*
— the *foot*stool (lit. the stool of *the feet*) *of* our God,
2Ch 3:13. they stood on *their feet,*
16:12. Asa...was diseased *in his feet,*
33: 8. Neither will I any more remove *the foot of*
Neh. 9:21. *and their feet* swelled not.
Est. 8: 3. Esther...fell down at *his feet,*
Job 2: 7. from the sole of *his foot* unto his crown.
12: 5. He that is ready to slip with (his) *feet*
13:27. Thou puttest *my feet* also in the stocks,
— settest a print upon the heels of *my feet.*
18: 8. cast into a net *by his own feet,*
11. Terrors...shall drive him *to his feet.*
23:11. *My foot* hath held his steps,
28: 4. (the waters) forgotten of *the foot.*
29:15. *and feet* (was) I to the lame.
30:12. they push away *my feet,*
31: 5. if *my foot* hath hasted to deceit;
33:11. He putteth *my feet* in the stocks,
39:15. forgetteth that *the foot* may crush them,
Ps. 8: 6(7). hast put all (things) under *his feet:*
9:15(16). in the net...is *their own foot* taken.
18: 9(10). darkness (was) under *his feet.*
33(34). He maketh *my feet* like hinds' (feet),
38(39). they are fallen under *my feet.*
22:16(17). they pierced my hands *and my feet.*
25:15. he shall pluck *my feet* out of the net.
26:12. *My foot* standeth in an even place:
31: 8(9). hast set *my feet* in a large room.
36:11(12). Let not *the foot of* pride come against
38:16(17). when *my foot* slippeth,
40: 2(3). set *my feet* upon a rock,
47: 3(4). subdue...the nations under *our feet.*
56:13(14). (wilt) not (thou deliver) *my feet* from falling,
66: 6. they went through the flood *on foot:*
9. suffereth not *our feet* to be moved.
68:23(24). That *thy foot* may be dipped in the blood of
73: 2. *my feet* were almost gone;
91:12. lest thou dash *thy foot* against a stone.
94:18. When I said, *My foot* slippeth;
99: 5. worship at *his foot*stool; (lit. the stool of *his feet*)
105:18. *Whose feet* they hurt with fetters:
110: 1. until I make thine enemies *thy foot*stool. (lit. a stool *for thy feet*)
115: 7. *feet have they,* but they walk not:
116: 8. delivered...*my feet* from falling.
119:59. turned *my feet* unto thy testimonies.
101. I have refrained *my feet* from
105. Thy word (is) a lamp unto *my feet,*
121: 3. He will not suffer *thy foot* to be moved:
122: 2. *Our feet* shall stand within thy gates,
132: 7. we will worship at *his foot*stool. (lit. the stool of *his feet*)
Pro. 1:15. refrain *thy foot* from their path:
16. *their feet* run to evil,
3:23. *and thy foot* shall not stumble.
26. shall keep *thy foot* from being taken.
4:26. Ponder the path of *thy feet,*
27. remove *thy foot* from evil.
5: 5. *Her feet* go down to death;
6:13. he speaketh *with his feet,*
18. *feet* that be swift in running to mischief,
28. *and his feet* not be burned?
7:11. *her feet* abide not in her house:
19: 2. he that hasteth *with* (his) *feet* sinneth.
25:17. Withdraw *thy foot* from thy neighbour's
19. *and a foot* out of joint.
26: 6. He that sendeth a message by the hand of a fool cutteth off *the feet,*
Ecc. 5: 1(4:17). Keep *thy foot* when thou goest to
Cant. 5: 3. I have washed *my feet*

Isa. 1: 6. From the sole of *the foot* even unto the
3:16. *and* making a tinkling *with their feet:*
6: 2. with twain he covered *his feet,*
7:20. the hair of *the feet:*
20: 2. put off thy shoe from *thy foot.*
23: 7. *her own feet* shall carry her afar
26: 6. *The foot* shall tread it down, (even) *the feet of* the poor,
28: 3. the drunkards of Ephraim, shall be trodden *under* (marg. *with*) *feet:*
32:20. *the feet of* the ox and the ass.
36:12. eat their own dung, and drink their own piss (lit. the water of *their feet*)
41: 2. Who raised up the righteous (man)... called him *to his foot,*
3. way (that) he had not gone *with his feet.*
49:23. lick up the dust of *thy feet;*
52: 7. *the feet of* him that bringeth good tidings,
58:13. If thou turn away *thy foot* from the
59: 7. *Their feet* run to evil,
60:13. I will make the place of *my feet* glorious.
14. themselves down at the soles of *thy feet;*
66: 1. the earth (is) *my foot*stool: (lit. the stool of *my feet*)
Jer. 2:25. Withhold *thy foot* from being unshod,
13:16. before *your feet* stumble
14:10. they have not refrained *their feet,*
18:22. hid snares *for my feet.*
38:22. *thy feet* are sunk in the mire,
Lam. 1:13. spread a net *for my feet,*
2: 1. remembered not *his foot*stool (lit. the stool of *his feet*)
3:34. To crush under *his feet* all the prisoners
Eze. 1: 7. *And their feet* (were) straight *feet;* and the sole of *their feet* (was) like the sole of a calf's *foot:*
2: 1. Son of man, stand upon *thy feet,*
2. and set me upon *my feet,*
3:24. the spirit...set me upon *my feet,*
6:11. stamp *with thy foot,*
16:25. opened *thy feet* to every one
24:17. put on thy shoes *upon thy feet,*
23. your shoes *upon your feet:*
25: 6. stamped *with the feet,* (marg. *foot*)
29:11. No *foot of* man shall pass through it, *nor foot* of beast shall pass through
32: 2. troubledst the waters *with thy feet,*
13. neither shall *the foot of* man trouble
34:18. tread down *with your feet* the residue
— foul the residue *with your feet?*
19. that which ye have trodden with *your feet;*
— that which ye have fouled with *your feet.*
37:10. stood up upon *their feet,*
43: 7. the place of the soles of *my feet,*
Am. 2:15. (he that is) swift *of foot*
Nah 1: 3. the clouds (are) the dust of *his feet.*
15(2:1). *the feet of* him that bringeth good
Hab 3: 5. burning coals went forth *at his feet.*
19. he will make *my feet* like
Zec.14: 4. *his feet* shall stand in that day
12. while they stand upon *their feet,*
Mal. 4: 3(3:21). ashes under the soles of *your feet*

7271 **רְגַל** [*r'gal*], Ch. com.

Dan 2:33. *his feet* part of iron and part of clay.
34. smote the image upon *his feet*
41. *the feet* and toes, part of potters' clay,
42. And (as) the toes of *the feet*
7: 4. and made stand upon *the feet* as a man,
7. stamped the residue *with the feet of it:*
19. stamped the residue *with his feet;*

7273 **רַגְלִי** *rag-lee'*, m.

Ex. 12:37. about six hundred thousand *on foot*
Nu. 11:21. six hundred thousand *footmen;*
Jud.20: 2. four hundred thousand *foot*men
1Sa. 4:10. fell of Israel thirty thousand *footmen.*
15: 4. two hundred thousand *footmen,*
2Sa. 8: 4. twenty thousand *footmen:*
10: 6. twenty thousand *footmen,*
1K. 20:29. an hundred thousand *footmen*
2K. 13: 7. ten thousand *footmen*
1Ch 18: 4. twenty thousand *foot*men:
19:18. forty thousand *foot*men,
Jer. 12: 5. If thou hast run with *the footmen,*

רָגַם [*rāh-gam'*]. 7275

* KAL.—*Preterite.* *

Lev.24:14. *and let* all the congregation *stone* him.
Deu21:21. *And* all the men...*shall stone him*
Eze.16:40. *and they shall stone* thee with stones,
23:47. *And* the company *shall stone* them with

KAL.—*Infinitive.*

Lev.24:16. all the congregation shall *certainly* stone *him:* (lit. *stoning* shall stone him)
Nu. 14:10. all the congregation bade *stone* them
15:35. all the congregation *shall stone* him

KAL.—*Future.*

Lev.20: 2. the people of the land *shall stone him*
27. *they shall stone* them with stones:
24:16. all the congregation *shall* certainly *stone*
23. forth him that had cursed...*and stone* him
Nu. 15:36. *and stoned* him with stones, and he died;
Jos. 7:25. *And* all Israel *stoned* him
1K. 12:18. *and* all Israel *stoned* him with stones,
2Ch 10:18. *and* the children of Israel *stoned* him
24:21. *and stoned him* with stones

רִגְמָה [*rig-māh'*], f. 7277

Ps. 68:27(28). princes of Judah (and) *their council,* (marg. or, (with) *their company*)

רָגַן [*rāh-gan'*]. 7279

* KAL.—*Participle.* Paül. *

Isa. 29:24. *and they that murmured* shall learn

* NIPHAL.—*Future.* *

Deu. 1:27. *And ye murmured* in your tents,
Ps.106:25. *But murmured* in their tents,

רָגַע *rāh-gag'*. 7280

* KAL.—*Preterite.* *

Job 7: 5. my skin *is broken,*
26:12. *He divideth* the sea with his power,

KAL.—*Participle.* Poel.

Isa. 51:15. the Lord thy God, *that divided* the sea,
Jer. 31:35. the Lord,...*which divideth* the sea

* NIPHAL.—*Imperative.* *

Jer. 47: 6. *rest,* and be still.

* HIPHIL.—*Preterite.* *

Isa. 34:14. the screech owl also *shall rest* there,
Jer. 50:34. that *he may give rest* to the land,

HIPHIL.—*Infinitive.*

Jer. 31: 2. when I went *to cause him to rest.*

HIPHIL.—*Future.*

Deu28:65. *shalt thou find* no *ease,*
Pro.12:19. a lying tongue *is* but for *a moment.*
Isa. 51: 4. *I will make* my judgment *to rest*
Jer. 49:19. *I will suddenly make* him run away
50:44. *I will make* them *suddenly* run away

רָגֵעַ [*rāh-gēh'ăg*], adj. 7282

Ps. 35:20. *them that are quiet in* the land.

רֶגַע *reh'-gag*, m. 7281

Ex. 33: 5. I will come up...in *a moment,*
Nu. 16:21. that I may consume them *in a moment.*
45(17:10). that I may consume them *as in a moment.*
Ezr. 9: 8. for *a* little *space* grace hath been (shewed)
Job 7:18. try him *every moment?*
20: 5. joy of the hypocrite (but) for *a moment?*
21:13. *and in a moment* go down to the grave.
34:20. In *a moment* shall they die,
Ps. 6:10(11). return (and) be ashamed *suddenly.*

Ps. 30: 5(6). his anger (endureth but) *a moment;*
73:19. into desolation, *as in a moment!*
Isa. 26:20. hide thyself...for *a little moment,*
27: 3. I will water it *every moment:*
47: 9. (things) shall come to thee in *a moment*
54: 7. *For a* small *moment* have I forsaken thee;
8. I hid my face from thee for *a moment;*
Jer. 4:20. are my tents spoiled, (and) my curtains in *a moment.*
18: 7. (At what) *instant* I shall speak
9. *And* (at what) *instant* I shall speak
Lam. 4: 6. overthrown as *in a moment,*
Eze. 26:16. and shall tremble *at* (every) *moment,*
32:10. they shall tremble *at* (every) *moment,*

7283 **רָגַשׁ** [*rāh-gash'*].

* KAL.—*Preterite.* *

Ps. 2: 1. Why *do* the heathen *rage,* (marg. or, *tumultuously assemble*)

7284 **רְגַשׁ** [*r'gash*], Ch.

* APHEL.—*Preterite.* *

Dan 6: 6(7). *assembled together* (marg. or, *came tumultuously*) to the king,
11(12), 15(16). Then these men *assembled,*

7285 **רֶגֶשׁ** [*reh'-gesh*], m.

Ps. 55:14(15). walked unto the house of God *in company.*

7285 **רִגְשָׁה** [*rig-shāh'*], f.

Ps. 64: 2(3). *from the insurrection of* the workers

7286 **רָדַד** [*rāh-dad'*].

* KAL.—*Preterite.* *

Jud. 19:11. the day *was* far *spent;*

KAL.—*Infinitive.*

Isa. 45: 1. *to subdue* nations before him;

KAL.—*Participle.* Poel.

Ps. 144: 2. *who subdueth* my people under me.

* HIPHIL.—*Future.* *

1K. 6:32. *and spread* gold upon the cherubims,

7287 **רָדָה** [*rāh-dāh'*].

* KAL.—*Preterite.* *

Lev. 26:17. they that hate you *shall reign* over you;
Isa. 14: 2. *and they shall rule* over their oppressors.
Eze. 34: 4. with force and with cruelty *have ye ruled*

KAL.—*Infinitive.*

Eze. 29:15. *they shall* no more *rule*

KAL.—*Imperative.*

Gen 1:28. *and have dominion* over the fish of the sea,
Ps. 110: 2. *rule thou* in the midst

KAL.—*Future.*

Gen 1:26. *and let them have dominion* over
Lev. 25:43. *Thou shalt* not *rule*...with rigour;
46. *ye shall* not *rule*...with rigour.
53. *shall* not *rule* with rigour *over him*
Nu. 24:19. Out of Jacob *shall come he that shall have dominion,*
Neh. 9:28. *so that they had the dominion*
Ps. 49:14(15). *and* the upright *shall have dominion*
72: 8. *He shall have dominion also*
Jer. 5:31. the priests *bear rule*
Lam. 1:13. *and it prevaileth against them:*

KAL.—*Participle.* Poel.

1K. 4:24(5:4). he *had dominion* over all
5:16(30). three thousand and three hundred, *which ruled*
9:23. five hundred and fifty, *which bare rule*
2Ch 8:10. two hundred and fifty, *that bare rule*
Ps. 68:27(28). little Benjamin (with) *their ruler,*
Isa. 14: 6. *he that ruled* the nations

* PIEL.—*Future.* *

Jud. 5:13. Then *he made* him that remaineth *have dominion* over the nobles among the people: the Lord *made* me *have dominion* over the mighty.

* HIPHIL.—*Future.* *

Isa. 41: 2. *made* (him) *rule* over kings?

רָדָה *rāh-dāh'*. 7287

* KAL.—*Preterite.* *

Jud. 14: 9. *he had taken* the honey out of the carcase

KAL.—*Future.*

Jud. 14: 9. *And he took thereof* in his hands,

רָדִיד [*rah-deed'*], m. 7289

Cant. 5: 7. the keepers...took away *my veil*
Isa. 3:23. the hoods, and *the vails.*

רָדַם [*rāh-dam'*]. 7290

* NIPHAL.—*Preterite.* *

Jud. 4:21. he *was fast asleep* and weary.
Dan 8:18. *I was in a deep sleep* on my face

NIPHAL.—*Future.*

Jon. 1: 5. and he lay, *and was fast asleep.*

NIPHAL.—*Participle.*

Ps. 76: 6(7). the chariot and horse are *cast into a dead sleep.*
Pro. 10: 5. *he that sleepeth* in harvest
Dan 10: 9. then was I *in a deep sleep*
Jon. 1: 6. What meanest thou, *O sleeper?*

רָדַף *rāh-daph'*. 7291

* KAL.—*Preterite.* *

Gen 35: 5. *they did* not *pursue* after the sons of Jacob.
Ex. 14: 4. *that he shall follow* after them;
Lev. 26: 7. *And ye shall chase* your enemies,
8. *And* five of you *shall chase* an hundred,
36. *and* the sound of a shaken leaf *shall chase*
Deu 28:22. *and they shall pursue thee* until thou
45. *and shall pursue thee,* and overtake thee,
30: 7. them that hate thee, which *persecuted thee.*
Jos. 2: 7. the men *pursued* after them
8:24. the wilderness wherein *they chased them,*
Jud. 4:16. Barak *pursued* after the chariots,
2Sa. 20:10. Joab and Abishai his brother *pursued*
Ps. 69:26(27). *they persecute* (him) whom thou hast
119:86. *they persecute me* wrongfully;
161. Princes *have persecuted me* without a
143: 3. the enemy *hath persecuted* my soul;
Jer. 29:18. *And I will persecute* them with the sword,

KAL.—*Infinitive.*

Deu 11: 4. *as they pursued* after you,
Jos. 8:16. called together *to pursue*
1Sa. 23:28. Wherefore Saul returned *from pursuing*
25:29. a man is risen *to pursue thee,*
2Sa. 18:16. the people returned *from pursuing*
20: 7, 13. *to pursue* after Sheba the son of
Ps. 38:20(21). *I follow* (the thing that) good (is).
Am. 1:11. because *he did pursue* his brother

KAL.—*Imperative.*

Gen 44: 4. Up, *follow* after the men;
Jos. 2: 5. *pursue* after them quickly;
10:19. *pursue* after your enemies,
Jud. 3:28. *Follow* after me:
1Sa. 30: 8. *Pursue:* for thou shalt surely overtake
2Sa. 20: 6. take thou thy lord's servants, *and pursue*
Ps. 34:14(15). seek peace, *and pursue it.*
71:11. *persecute* and take him;

KAL.—*Future.*

Gen 14:14. *and pursued* (them) unto Dan.
15. *and pursued them* unto Hobah,
31:23. *and pursued* after him seven days' journey;

Ex. 14: 8. *and he pursued* after the children of
9. *But* the Egyptians *pursued* after them,
23. *And* the Egyptians *pursued*,
15: 9. The enemy said, *I will pursue*,
Lev.26: 8. *shall put* ten thousand *to flight:* (lit. *pursue*)
Deu 1:44. the Amorites,...came out against you, *and chased* you,
16:20. which is altogether just *shalt thou follow*,
19: 6. Lest the avenger of the blood *pursue*
32:30. How *should* one *chase* a thousand,
Jos. 7: 5. *for they chased them* (from) before the
8:16. *and they pursued* after Joshua,
17. left the city open, *and pursued*
10:10. *and chased them* along the way
11: 8. *and chased them* unto great Zidon,
20: 5. if the avenger of blood *pursue*
23:10. One man of you *shall chase* a thousand:
24: 6. *and* the Egyptians *pursued* after your
Jud. 1: 6. *and they pursued* after him,
7:23. *and pursued* after the Midianites.
25. *and pursued* Midian,
8:12. *And* when...*he pursued* after them,
9:40. *And* Abimelech *chased him*,
1Sa. 7:11. went out of Mizpeh, *and pursued* the
17:52. the men of Israel and of Judah...shouted, *and pursued*
23:25. *And* when Saul heard (that), *he pursued*
26:20. as when one *doth hunt* a partridge
30: 8. *Shall I pursue* after this troop?
10. *But* David *pursued*,
2Sa. 2:19. *And* Asahel *pursued* after Abner;
24. Joab *also* and Abishai *pursued*
28. and *pursued* after Israel no more,
17: 1. I will arise *and pursue* after David
22:38. *I have pursued* mine enemies,
1K. 20:20. *and* Israel *pursued them:*
2K. 5:21. *So* Gehazi *followed* after Naaman.
9:27. *And* Jehu *followed* after him,
25: 5. *And* the army of the Chaldees *pursued*
2Ch 13:19. *And* Abijah *pursued* after Jeroboam,
14:13(12). *And* Asa and the people...*pursued them*
Job 13:25. *wilt thou pursue* the dry stubble?
19:22. Why *do ye persecute me* as God,
28. Why *persecute we* him,
30:15. *they pursue* my soul as the wind:
Ps. 18:37(38). *I have pursued* mine enemies,
23: 6. goodness and mercy *shall follow me*
83:15(16). So *persecute them* with thy tempest,
109:16. *but persecuted* the poor and needy man,
Isa. 5:11. (that) *they may follow* strong drink;
41: 3. *He pursued them*, (and) passed safely;
Jer. 39: 5. *But* the Chaldeans' army *pursued*
52: 8. *But* the army of the Chaldeans *pursued*
Lam. 3:43. hast covered with anger, *and persecuted us:*
66. *Persecute* and destroy them
Eze.35: 6, 6. blood *shall pursue thee:*
Hos. 6: 3. *we follow on* to know the Lord:
8: 3. the enemy *shall pursue him*.

KAL.—*Participle.* Poel.

Lev.26:17. ye shall flee when none *pursueth*
36. they shall fall when none *pursueth*.
37. they shall fall...*when* none *pursueth:*
Jos. 2: 7. *they which pursued* after them
16. lest *the pursuers* meet you;
— until *the pursuers* be returned:
22. until *the pursuers* were returned: and *the pursuers* sought (them)
8:20. turned back upon *the pursuers*.
Jud. 4:22. as Barak *pursued* Sisera,
8: 4. faint, *yet pursuing* (them).
5. I *am pursuing* after Zebah and Zalmunna,
1Sa.24:14(15). after whom *dost* thou *pursue?*
26:18. Wherefore *doth* my lord thus *pursue*
2Sa.24:13. thine enemies, while they *pursue thee?*
Neh 9:11. *their persecutors* thou threwest into the
Ps. 7: 1(2). all *them that persecute me*,
31:15(16). mine enemies, *and from them that persecute me.*
35: 3. (the way) against them *that persecute me:*
6. let the angel of the Lord *persecute them.*
119:84. execute judgment *on them that persecute me?*
150. They draw nigh *that follow after* mischief:
157. Many (are) *my persecutors*
142: 6(7). deliver me *from my persecutors;*

Pro.21:21. *He that followeth after* righteousness
28: 1. The wicked flee when no man *pursueth*.
Isa. 1:23. *and followeth after* rewards:
30:16. shall *they that pursue you* be swift.
51: 1. *ye that follow after* righteousness,
Jer. 15:15. revenge me *of my persecutors;*
17:18. Let them be confounded *that persecute me*,
20:11. *my persecutors* shall stumble,
Lam.1: 3. *her persecutors* overtook her
6. gone without strength before *the pursuer*.
4:19. *Our persecutors* are swifter than the
Hos 12: 1(2). *and followeth after* the east wind:

* NIPHAL.—*Preterite.* *

Lam.5: 5. Our necks (are) *under persecution:* (marg. On our necks *are we persecuted*)

NIPHAL.—*Participle.*

Ecc. 3:15. God requireth *that which is past.* (marg. *driven away*)

* PIEL.—*Preterite.* *

Hos 2: 7(9). *And she shall follow after* her lovers,

PIEL.—*Future.*

Ps. 7: 5(6). *Let* the enemy *persecute* my soul,
Pro.13:21. Evil *pursueth* sinners:
Nah 1: 8. darkness *shall pursue* his enemies.

PIEL.—*Participle.*

Pro.11:19. *so he that pursueth* evil
12:11. *but he that followeth* vain (persons)
15: 9. *but* he loveth *him that followeth after*
19: 7. *he pursueth* (them with) words,
28:19. *but he that followeth after* vain (persons)

* PUAL.—*Preterite.* *

Isa. 17:13. *and shall be chased* as the chaff

* HIPHIL.—*Preterite.* *

Jud.20:43. *chased them*, (and) trode them down

רָהַב [*rah-hav'*]. 7292

* KAL.—*Imperative.* *

Pro. 6: 3. *and make sure* thy friend.

KAL.—*Future.*

Isa. 3: 5. the child *shall behave himself proudly*

* HIPHIL.—*Preterite.* *

Cant.6: 5. *they have overcome me:* (marg. or, *puffed me up*)

HIPHIL.—*Future.*

Ps.138: 3. *strengthenedst me* (with) strength

רָהָב [*rāh-hāhv'*], adj. 7295

Ps. 40: 4(5). man that...respecteth not *the proud*,

רַהַב *rah'-hav*, m. 7293

Job 9:13. the *proud* helpers (marg. helpers of *pride*)
26:12. smiteth through *the proud*. (marg. *pride*)
Ps. 87: 4. will make mention of *Rahab* (lit. *pride*)
89:10. Thou hast broken *Rahab* in pieces,
Isa. 30: 7. Their *strength* (is) to sit still.
51: 9. it that hath cut *Rahab*,

רֹהַב [*rōh'-hav*]. 7296

Ps. 90:10. *yet* (is) *their strength* labour and sorrow;

רָהָה [*rāh-hāh'*]. 7297

* KAL.—*Preterite.* *

Isa. 44: 8. Fear ye not, neither *be afraid:* [See also יָרֵא]

רַהַט [*rah'-hat*], m. 7298

Gen30:38. he set the rods...*in the gutters*
41. Jacob laid the rods...*in the gutters*,
Ex. 2:16. filled *the troughs* to water
Cant.7: 5(6). the king (is) held *in the galleries.*

7351 רָהִיט [*rāh-heet'*], m.

Cant.1:17. *our rafters* (marg. or, *galleries*) of fir.

7299 רֵו [*rēhv*], Ch. m.

Dan 2:31. *and the form thereof* (was) terrible.
3:25. *and the form* of the fourth is

See 7230 רֹב see רוב

See 7378 רִיב see רוב

7300 רוּד [*rood*].

* KAL.—*Preterite.* *

Jer. 2:31. wherefore say my people, *We are lords;* (marg. *have dominion*)
Hos11:12(12:1). Judah yet *ruleth* with God,

* HIPHIL.—*Future.* *

Gen27:40. when *thou shalt have the dominion,*

7300 רוּד [*rood*].

* HIPHIL.—*Future.* *

Ps. 55: 2(3). *I mourn* in my complaint,

7301 רָוָה [*rāh-vah'*].

* KAL.—*Preterite.* *

Jer. 46:10. *and made drunk* with their blood:

KAL.—*Future.*

Ps. 36: 8(9). *They shall be abundantly satisfied* (marg. *watered*)
Pro. 7:18. *let us take our fill* of love

* PIEL.—*Preterite.* *

Isa. 34: 5. my sword *shall be bathed* in heaven:
7. *and* their land *shall be soaked* (marg. or, *drunken*) with blood,
Jer. 31:14. *And I will satiate* the soul of the priests

PIEL.—*Imperative.*

Ps. 65:10(11). *Thou waterest* the ridges...*abundantly:*

PIEL.—*Future.*

Pro. 5:19. *let* her breasts *satisfy* (marg. *water*) *thee*
Isa. 16: 9. *I will water thee* with my tears,

* HIPHIL.—*Preterite.* *

Isa. 43:24. neither *hast thou filled me* (marg. *made me drunk*, or, *abundantly moistened*) with
55:10. as the rain...*watereth* the earth,
Jer. 31:25. *I have satiated* the weary soul,
Lam.3:15. *he hath made me drunken*

HIPHIL.—*Participle.*

Pro.11:25. *and he that watereth* shall be watered

7302 רָוֶה *rāh-veh'*, adj.

Deu29:19(18). to add *drunkenness* to thirst: (marg. *the drunken* to the thirsty)
Isa. 58:11. thou shalt be like a *watered* garden,
Jer. 31:12. their soul shall be as a *watered* garden;

7304 רָוַח *rāh-vaḡh'*.

* KAL.—*Preterite.* *

1Sa.16:23. *so* Saul *was refreshed*, (lit. *and refreshing was* to Saul)

KAL.—*Future.*

Job 32:20. *that I may be refreshed:* (marg. *breathe;* lit. *that refreshing may be* to me)

* PUAL.—*Participle.* *

Jer. 22:14. wide house *and large* (marg. *throughaired*) chambers,

---

רֶוַח *reh'-vaḡh*, m. 7305

Gen32:16(17). *and* put *a space* betwixt drove and
Est. 4:14. shall there *enlargement* (marg. *respiration*) and deliverance arise

---

רוּחַ [*roo'ăḡh*]. 7306

* HIPHIL.—*Infinitive.* *

Ex. 30:38. *to smell* thereto,
Jud.16: 9. as a thread of tow is broken *when it toucheth* (marg. *smelleth*) the fire.
Isa. 11: 3. *And shall make him of quick understanding* (marg. *scent*, or, *smell*)

HIPHIL.—*Future.*

Gen. 8:21. *And* the Lord *smelled* a sweet savour;
27:27. *and he smelled* the smell of his raiment,
Lev.26:31. *I will* not *smell* the savour
Deu 4:28. neither see, nor hear, nor eat, nor *smell.*
1Sa.26:19. If the Lord have stirred thee up against me, *let him accept* (marg. *smell*) an
Job 39:25. *he smelleth* the battle afar off,
Ps.115: 6. noses have they, but *they smell* not:
Am. 5:21. *I will* not *smell* in your solemn assemblies.

רוּחַ *roo'ăḡh*, com. 7307

Gen. 1: 2. *And the Spirit of* God moved
3: 8. walking in the garden *in the cool* (marg. *wind*) *of* the day:
6: 3. *My spirit* shall not always strive with
17 & 7:15. all flesh, wherein (is) *the breath of*
7.22. All in whose nostrils (was) the breath)(*of* life, (marg. the breath of *the spirit of* life)
8: 1. God made *a wind* to pass over
26:35. a grief of *mind* (marg. bitterness of *spirit*) unto Isaac and to Rebekah.
41: 8. *his spirit* was troubled;
38. in whom *the Spirit of* God (is)?
45:27. *the spirit of* Jacob their father revived:
Ex. 6: 9. they hearkened not unto Moses for anguish of *spirit,*
10:13. the Lord brought *an* east *wind*
— *the* east *wind* brought the locusts.
19. *a* mighty strong west *wind,*
14:21. the sea to go (back) *by a* strong east *wind*
15: 8. *And with the blast of* thy nostrils
10. Thou didst blow *with thy wind,*
28: 3. I have filled *with the spirit of* wisdom,
31: 3. I have filled him with *the spirit of* God,
35:21. every one whom *his spirit* made willing,
31. he hath filled him with *the spirit of* God,
Nu. 5:14, 14. *the spirit of* jealousy come
30. *the spirit of* jealousy cometh
11:17. *the spirit* which (is) upon thee,
25. of *the spirit* that (was) upon him
— *the spirit* rested upon them,
26. *the spirit* rested upon them;
29. that the Lord would put *his spirit* upon
31. *And* there went forth *a wind*
14:24. because he had another *spirit*
16:22. the God of *the spirits* of all flesh,
24: 2. and *the spirit of* God came upon him.
27:16. the God of *the spirits* of all flesh,
18. Joshua...a man in whom (is) *the spirit,*
Deu 2:30. the Lord thy God hardened *his spirit,*
34: 9. full of *the spirit of* wisdom;
Jos. 2:11. neither did there remain any more *courage*
5: 1. neither was there *spirit* in them any more,
Jud. 3:10. And *the Spirit of* the Lord came upon him,
6:34. *But the Spirit of* the Lord came upon
8: 3. *their anger* (marg. *spirit*) was abated
9:23. God sent *an* evil *spirit*
11:29 & 13:25 & 14:6, 19 & 15:14. *the Spirit of* the Lord
15:19. *his spirit* came again,
1Sa. 1:15. a woman of *a* sorrowful *spirit:*
10: 6. And *the Spirit of* the Lord
10 & 11:6. *the Spirit of* God
16:13. and *the Spirit of* the Lord came upon
14. *But the Spirit of* the Lord departed from Saul, and *an* evil *spirit* from the Lord
15. *an* evil *spirit from* God
16. *the* evil *spirit from* God

1Sa.16:23. *the* (evil) *spirit from* God
— *the* evil *spirit* departed from him.
18:10. *the* evil *spirit from* God
19: 9. *the* evil *spirit from* the Lord
20, 23. *the Spirit of* God
30:12. *his spirit* came again
2Sa.22:11. he was seen upon the wings of *the wind.*
16. at the blast of *the breath of* his nostrils.
23: 2. *The Spirit of* the Lord spake by me,
1K. 10: 5. there was no more *spirit* in her.
18:12. *that the Spirit of* the Lord shall carry
45. heaven was black with clouds *and wind,*
19:11. *and a* great and strong *wind* rent the
— the Lord (was) not *in the wind:* and after *the wind* an earthquake;
21: 5. Why is *thy spirit* so sad,
22:21. there came forth *a spirit,*
22. I will be *a* lying *spirit*
23. the Lord hath put *a* lying *spirit* in
24. Which way went *the Spirit of* the Lord
2K. 2: 9. let a double portion *of thy spirit* be upon
15. *The spirit of* Elijah doth rest on Elisha.
16. *the Spirit of* the Lord hath taken him
3:17. Ye shall not see *wind,*
19: 7. I will send *a blast* upon him,
1Ch 5:26. *the spirit of* Pul king of Assyria, and *the spirit of* Tilgath-pilneser
9:24. In four *quarters* (lit. *winds*) were the
12:18. *Then the spirit* came upon Amasai,
28:12. the pattern of all that he had *by the spirit,*
2Ch 9: 4. there was no more *spirit* in her.
15: 1. And *the Spirit of* God came upon Azariah
18:20. Then there came out *a spirit,*
21. I will...be *a* lying *spirit*
22. the Lord hath put *a* lying *spirit* in
23. Which way went *the Spirit of* the Lord
20:14. came *the Spirit of* the Lord in the midst
21:16. *the spirit of* the Philistines,
24:20. *And the Spirit of* God came upon
36:22. *the spirit of* Cyrus king of Persia,
Ezr. 1: 1. *the spirit of* Cyrus king of Persia,
5. (them) *whose spirit* God had raised,
Neh. 9:20. Thou gavest *also thy* good *spirit*
30. testifiedst against them *by thy spirit*
Job 1:19. there came *a* great *wind*
4: 9. *and by the breath of* his nostrils...consumed.
15. *Then a spirit* passed before my face;
6: 4. the poison...drinketh up *my spirit:*
26. *and* the speeches of one that is desperate, (which are) *as wind?*
7: 7. O remember that my life (is) *wind:*
11. I will speak in the anguish of *my spirit;*
8: 2. *and...* (like) *a* strong *wind?*
9:18. He will not suffer me to take *my breath,*
10:12. thy visitation hath preserved *my spirit.*
12:10. *and the breath of* all mankind.
15: 2. *vain* knowledge, (m. knowledge of *wind*)
13. turnest *thy spirit* against God,
30. *by the breath of* his mouth shall he go
16: 3. Shall *vain* words (marg. words of *wind*) have an end?
17: 1. *My breath* (marg. or, *spirit*) is corrupt
19:17. *My breath* is strange to my wife,
20: 3. *and the spirit of* my understanding
21: 4. why should not *my spirit* be troubled?
18. as stubble before *the wind,*
26:13. *By his spirit* he hath garnished the
27: 3. *and the spirit of* God (is) in my nostrils;
28:25. To make the weight *for the winds;*
30:15. they pursue my soul *as the wind:*
22. Thou liftest me up to *the wind;*
32: 8. (there is) *a spirit* in man:
18. *the spirit* within me constraineth
33: 4. *The Spirit of* God hath made me,
34:14. (if) he gather unto himself *his spirit*
37:21. *but the wind* passeth,
41:16(8). *that* no *air* can come between them.
Ps. 1: 4. like the chaff which *the wind* driveth
11: 6. *and an* horrible *tempest:*
18:10(11). he did fly upon the wings of *the wind.*
15(16). *the breath of* thy nostrils.
42(43). small as the dust before *the wind:*
31: 5(6). Into thine hand I commit *my spirit:*
32: 2. *in whose spirit* there is no guile.
33: 6. *and* all the host of them *by the breath of* his
34:18(19). such as be of *a* contrite *spirit.*

Ps. 35: 5. as chaff before *the wind:*
48: 7(8). the ships of Tarshish with *an* east *wind.*
51:10(12). *and* renew *a* right *spirit* within me.
11(13). *and* take not *thy* holy *spirit* from me.
12(14). *and* uphold me (with thy) free *spirit.*
17(19). The sacrifices of God (are) *a* broken *spirit:*
55: 8(9). hasten my escape *from* the *windy* storm (lit. *from the wind of* storm)
76:12(13). He shall cut off *the spirit of* princes.
77: 3(4). *my spirit* was overwhelmed.
6(7). *my spirit* made diligent search.
78: 8. *whose spirit* was not stedfast
39. *a wind* that passeth away,
83:13(14). as the stubble before *the wind.*
103:16. *the wind* passeth over it,
104: 3. walketh upon the wings of *the wind*
4. Who maketh his angels *spirits;*
29. thou takest away *their breath,*
30. Thou sendest forth *thy spirit,*
106:33. they provoked *his spirit,*
107:25. raiseth *the* stormy *wind,*
135: 7. he bringeth *the wind* out of his treasuries.
17. neither is there (any) *breath* in their
139: 7. Whither shall I go *from thy spirit?*
142: 3(4). When *my spirit* was overwhelmed
143: 4. Therefore is *my spirit* overwhelmed
7. O Lord: *my spirit* faileth:
10. *thy spirit* (is) good;
146: 4. *His breath* goeth forth,
147:18. he causeth *his wind* to blow,
148: 8. stormy *wind* fulfilling his word:
Pro. 1:23. I will pour out *my spirit* unto you,
11:13. he that is of *a* faithful *spirit*
29. He that troubleth his own house shall inherit *the wind:*
14:29. (he that is) hasty of *spirit*
15: 4. a breach *in the spirit.*
13. by sorrow of the heart *the spirit* is broken.
16: 2. the Lord weigheth *the spirits.*
18. *an* haughty *spirit*
19. (to be) of *an* humble *spirit*
32. he that ruleth *his spirit*
17:22. *but a* broken *spirit* drieth the bones.
27. a man of understanding is of *an* excellent *spirit.*
18:14. *The spirit of* a man will sustain his infirmity; *but a* wounded *spirit* who can
25:14. clouds *and wind* without rain.
23. *The* north *wind* driveth away rain:
28. (hath) no rule *over his own spirit*
27:16. Whosoever hideth her hideth *the wind,*
29:11. A fool uttereth all *his mind:*
23. honour shall uphold the humble in *spirit.*
30: 4. who hath gathered *the wind* in his fists?
Ecc. 1: 6. *The wind* goeth toward the south,
— *the wind* returneth again
14. all (is) vanity and vexation of *spirit.*
17. this also is vexation of *spirit.*
2:11, 17, 26. vanity and vexation of *spirit,*
3:19. *yea,* they have all one *breath;*
21. *the spirit of* man that goeth upward, *and the spirit of* the beast that goeth
4: 4, 16. vanity and vexation of *spirit.*
6. travail and vexation of *spirit.*
5:16(15). he that hath laboured *for the wind?*
6: 9. vanity and vexation of *spirit.*
7: 8. the patient in *spirit*
— the proud in *spirit.*
9. Be not hasty *in thy spirit*
8: 8. power *over the spirit* to retain *the spirit;*
10: 4. If *the spirit of* the ruler rise up
11: 4. He that observeth *the wind*
5. knowest not what (is) the way of *the spirit,*
12: 7. *and the spirit* shall return unto God
Isa. 4: 4. *by the spirit of* judgment, *and by the spirit of* burning.
7: 2. trees of the wood are moved with *the wind.*
11: 2. And *the spirit of* the Lord shall rest upon him, *the spirit of* wisdom and understanding, *the spirit of* counsel and might, *the spirit of* knowledge and
4. *and with the breath of* his lips shall he slay
15. with *his* mighty *wind*
17:13. as the chaff...before *the wind,*
19: 3. *the spirit of* Egypt shall fail
14. mingled *a* perverse *spirit* in the midst

Isa. 25: 4. *the blast of* the terrible ones
26: 9. with *my spirit* within me will I seek
18. we have...brought forth *wind;*
27: 8. he stayeth *his* rough *wind*
28: 6. *And for a spirit of* judgment
29:10. *the spirit of* deep sleep,
24. They also that erred in *spirit*
30: 1. not of *my spirit,*
28. *And his breath,* as an overflowing stream,
31: 3. their horses flesh, and not *spirit.*
32: 2. an hiding place from *the wind,*
15. Until *the spirit* be poured upon us
33:11. *your breath,* (as) fire, shall devour you.
34:16. *and his spirit* it hath gathered them.
37: 7. I will send *a blast* upon him,
38:16. the life of *my spirit:*
40: 7, 13. *the spirit of* the Lord
41:16. *and the wind* shall carry them away,
29. their molten images (are) *wind*
42: 1. I have put *my spirit* upon him:
5. giveth breath...*and spirit* to them that
44: 3. I will pour *my spirit* upon thy seed,
48:16. *and his Spirit,* hath sent me.
54: 6. a woman forsaken and grieved in *spirit,*
57:13. *the wind* shall carry them all away;
15. *a* contrite and humble *spirit,* to revive *the spirit of* the humble,
16. *the spirit* should fail before me,
59:19. *the Spirit of* the Lord shall lift up
21. *My spirit* that (is) upon thee,
61: 1. *The Spirit of* the Lord God (is) upon me;
3. *the spirit of* heaviness;
63:10. vexed his holy *Spirit:*
11. put his holy *Spirit* within him?
14. *the Spirit of* the Lord caused him to rest:
64: 6(5). our iniquities, *like the wind,*
65:14. shall howl for vexation of *spirit.*
66: 2. (him that is) poor and of *a* contrite *spirit,*
Jer. 2:24. A wild ass...(that) snuffeth up *the wind*
4:11. *A* dry *wind* of the high places
12. *a* full *wind* from those (places)
5:13. the prophets shall become *wind,*
10:13. bringeth forth *the wind* out of his treasures.
14. (there is) no *breath* in them.
13:24. *by the wind of* the wilderness.
14: 6. they snuffed up *the wind*
18:17. I will scatter them *as* with *an* east *wind*
22:22. *The wind* shall eat up all thy pastors,
49:32. I will scatter into all *winds* them
36. upon Elam will I bring *the* four *winds*
— will scatter them toward all those *winds;*
51: 1. I will raise up...*a* destroying *wind;*
11. *the spirit of* the kings of the Medes:
16. bringeth forth *the wind* out of his
17. (there is) no *breath* in them.
52:23. ninety and six pomegranates *on a side;* (lit. *wind*)
Lam. 4:20. *The breath of* our nostrils,
Eze. 1: 4. *a* whirl*wind* came out of the north,
12. whither *the spirit* was to go,
20. Whithersoever *the spirit* was to go, they went, thither (was their) *spirit* to go;
—, 21. *the spirit of* the living creature (was) in the wheels.
2: 2. *the spirit* entered into me
3:12. *the spirit* took me up,
14. *So the spirit* lifted me up,
— in the heat of *my spirit;*
24. *the spirit* entered into me,
5: 2. thou shalt scatter *in the wind;*
10. will I scatter into all *the winds.*
12. I will scatter...into all *the winds,*
8: 3. *the spirit* lifted me up
10:17. *the spirit of* the living creature
11: 1. *the spirit* lifted me up,
5. *the Spirit of* the Lord fell upon me,
— know the things that come into *your mind,*
19. *and* I will put *a* new *spirit* within you;
24. *Afterwards the spirit* took me up, and brought me in a vision *by the Spirit of*
12:14. I will scatter toward every *wind*
13: 3. prophets, that follow *their own spirit,*
11. *and a* stormy *wind* shall rend (it).
13. I will even rend (it) with *a* stormy *wind*
17:10. when *the* east *wind* toucheth it?
21. scattered toward all *winds:*
18:31. make you a new heart *and a* new *spirit:*

Eze. 19:12. *and the* east *wind* dried up her fruit:
20:32. that which cometh into *your mind*
21: 7(12). every *spirit* shall faint,
27:26. *the* east *wind* hath broken thee
36:26. *and a* new *spirit* will I put within you:
27. I will put *my spirit* within you,
37: 1. carried me out *in the spirit of* the Lord,
5. I will cause *breath* to enter
6. and put *breath* in you,
8. *but* (there was) no *breath* in them.
9. Prophesy unto *the wind* (marg. or, *breath*), prophesy, son of man, and say to *the wind,*
— Come from *the* four *winds, O breath,*
10. *the breath* came into them,
14. shall put *my spirit* in you,
39:29. I have poured out *my spirit*
42:16. He measured *the* east *side* (marg. *wind*) with the measuring reed,
17. He measured *the* north *side,* (lit. *wind*)
18. He measured *the* south *side* (lit. *wind*), five hundred reeds,
19. He turned about to *the* west *side* (lit *wind*), (and) measured
20. measured it by *the* four *sides:* (lit. *winds*)
43: 5. So *the spirit* took me up,
Dan 2: 1. dreams, wherewith *his spirit* was troubled,
3. *my spirit* was troubled to know the dream.
8: 8 & 11:4. toward *the* four *winds* of heaven.
Hos 4:12. *the spirit of* whoredoms hath caused
19. *The wind* hath bound her up
5: 4. *the spirit of* whoredoms (is) in the midst
8: 7. they have sown *the wind,*
9: 7. the *spirit*ual man (marg. man of *the spirit*) (is) mad,
12: 1(2). Ephraim feedeth on *wind,*
13:15. *the wind of* the Lord shall come up
Joel 2:28(3:1). I will pour out *my spirit* upon all
29(-:2). will I pour out *my spirit.*
Am. 4:13. that...createth *the wind,* (marg. or, *spirit*)
Jon. 1: 4. the Lord sent out *a* great *wind*
4: 8. God prepared *a* vehement east *wind;*
Mic. 2: 7. *the spirit of* the Lord straitened?
11. If a man walking in *the spirit* (marg. or, with *the wind*)
3: 8. full of power by *the spirit of* the Lord,
Hab. 1:11. Then shall (his) *mind* change,
2:19. no *breath* at all in the midst
Hag. 1:14. *the spirit of* Zerubbabel the son of
— *the spirit of* Joshua the son of Josedech, the high priest, and *the spirit of* all the
2: 5. *so my spirit* remaineth
Zec. 2: 6(10). *the* four *winds of* the heaven,
4: 6. Not by might, nor by power, but *by my spirit,*
5: 9. *and the wind* (was) in their wings;
6: 5. *the* four *spirits* (marg. or, *winds*) *of* the heavens,
8. quieted *my spirit* in the north
7:12. the Lord of hosts hath sent *in his spirit*
12: 1. formeth *the spirit of* man
10. *the spirit of* grace and of supplications:
13: 2. I will cause...*the* unclean *spirit* to pass
Mal. 2:15. Yet had he the residue of *the spirit.*
—, 16. Therefore take heed *to your spirit,*

רוּחַ *roo'ăgh,* Ch. com. 7308

Dan 2:35. and *the wind* carried them away,
4: 8(5). and in whom (is) *the spirit of*
9(6). I know that *the spirit of* the holy
18(15). for *the spirit of* the holy gods
5:11. in whom (is) *the spirit of* the holy
12. Forasmuch as *an* excellent *spirit,*
14. that *the spirit of* the gods (is) in thee,
20. *and his mind* hardened in pride,
6: 3(4). because *an* excellent *spirit*
7: 2. and, behold, *the* four *winds of*
15. I Daniel was grieved in *my spirit*

רְוָחָה *r'vāh-ghāh',* f. 7309

Ex. 8:15(11). Pharaoh saw that there was *respite,*
Lam. 3:56. hide not thine ear *at my breathing,*

7310 ## רְוָיָה *r'vāh-yāh'*, f.

Ps. 23: 5. my cup *runneth over.*
66:12. broughtest us out *into a wealthy* (marg. *moist*) (place).

7311 ## רוּם *room.*

* KAL.—*Preterite.* *

Deu 8:14. *Then* thine heart *be lifted up,*
32:27. Our hand *is high,*
1Sa. 2: 1. mine horn *is exalted* in the Lord;
Job 22:12. the stars, how *high they are!*
Ps. 99: 2. *and* he *is high* above all the people.
131: 1. nor mine eyes *lofty:*
Pro.30:13. O how *lofty are* their eyes!
Isa. 26:11. (when) thy hand *is lifted up,*
Eze.31:10. *and* his heart *is lifted up*
Dan 11:12. his heart *shall be lifted up;*

KAL.—*Infinitive.*

Deu17:20. That his heart *be* not *lifted up*
Ps. 12: 8(9). *when* the vilest men *are exalted.*
Eze.10:16. *to mount up* from the earth,
17. *and when they were lifted up,*

KAL.—*Imperative.*

Ps. 21:13(14). *Be thou exalted,* Lord,
57: 5(6), 11(12) & 108:5(6). *Be thou exalted,* O God, above the heavens;

KAL.—*Future.*

Gen. 7:17. *and it was lift up* above the earth.
Ex. 16:20. *and it bred* worms, and stank:
Nu. 24: 7. *and* his king *shall be higher* than Agag,
2Sa.22:47. *and exalted be* the God of...my salvation.
Ps 13: 2(3). how long *shall* mine enemy *be exalted*
18:46(47). *and let* the God of my salvation *be exalted.*
27: 6. now *shall* mine head *be lifted up*
46:10(11). *I will be exalted* among the heathen, *I will be exalted* in the earth.
61: 2(3). the rock (that) *is higher* than I.
66: 7. *let* not the rebellious *exalt themselves.*
89:13(14). *high is* thy right hand.
16(17). righteousness *shall they be exalted.*
17(18). our horn *shall be exalted.*
24(25). *shall* his horn *be exalted.*
112: 9. his horn *shall be exalted* with honour.
140: 8(9). (lest) *they exalt themselves.* (marg. or, *let them* (not) *be exalted*)
Pro.11:11. the city *is exalted:*
Isa. 30:18. therefore *will he be exalted,*
49:11. my highways *shall be exalted.*
52:13. *he shall be exalted* and extolled,
Eze.10: 4. *Then* the glory of the Lord *went up* (marg. *was lifted*)
Dan 11:12. (כתיב) his heart *shall be lifted up*
Hos13: 6. *and* their heart *was exalted;*
Mic. 5: 9(8). Thine hand *shall be lifted up*

KAL.—*Participle.* Poel.

Ex. 14: 8. children of Israel went out with an *high*
Nu. 15:30. the soul that doeth (ought) presumptuously, (marg. with an *high* hand)
33: 3. children of Israel went out with an *high*
Deu 1:28. The people (is) greater *and taller* than
2:10, 21. a people great, and many, *and tall,* as
9: 2. A people great *and tall,*
12: 2. upon the *high* mountains,
27:14. the Levites shall speak,...with a *loud*
2Sa.22:28. thine eyes (are) upon *the haughty,*
Job 21:22. he judgeth *those that are high.*
38:15. the *high* arm shall be broken.
Ps. 18:27(28). wilt bring down *high* looks.
78:69. he built his sanctuary like *high* (palaces),
113: 4. The Lord (is) *high* above all nations,
138: 6. Though the Lord (be) *high,* yet hath he
Pro. 6:17. A *proud* look, (marg. *Haughty* eyes) a
24: 7. Wisdom (is) *too high* for a fool:
Isa. 2:12. every (one that is) proud *and lofty,*
13. the cedars of Lebanon, (that are) *high*
14. upon all the *high* mountains,
6: 1. the Lord sitting upon a throne, *high*
10:33. *and the high ones* of stature (shall be)
57:15. the *high* and lofty One that inhabiteth
Eze. 6:13. upon every *high* hill,
Eze.17:22. the highest branch of the *high* cedar,
20:28. they saw every *high* hill,
34: 6. upon every *high* hill:

* POLEL.—*Preterite.* *

Isa. 1: 2. I have nourished *and brought up* children,
23: 4. neither do I...*bring up* virgins.
Eze.31: 4. the deep *set* (marg. or, *brought*) *him up on high*

POLEL.—*Infinitive.*

Ezr. 9: 9. *to set up* the house of our God,

POLEL.—*Imperative.*

Ps. 99: 5. *Exalt ye* the Lord our God, and worship
9. *Exalt* the Lord our God,

POLEL.—*Future.*

Ex. 15: 2. my father's God, *and I will exalt him.*
2Sa.22:49. *thou* also *hast lifted me up on high*
Job 17: 4. therefore *shalt thou* not *exalt* (them).
Ps. 18:48(49). *thou liftest me up* above those that
27: 5. *he shall set me up* upon a rock.
30: 1(2). *I will extol thee,* O Lord;
34: 3(4). *and let us exalt* his name together.
37:34. *and he shall exalt thee* to inherit the land:
107:25. *which lifteth up* the waves thereof.
32. *Let them exalt him also*
118:28. (thou art) my God, *I will exalt thee.*
145: 1. *I will extol thee,* my God,
Pro. 4: 8. Exalt her, *and she shall promote thee:*
14:34. Righteousness *exalteth* a nation:
Isa. 25: 1. O Lord,...*I will exalt thee,*
Hos11: 7. none at all *would exalt* (him).

POLEL.—*Participle.*

1Sa. 2: 7. he bringeth low, and *lifteth up.*
Ps. 9:13(14). *thou that liftest me up* from

* POLAL.—*Preterite.* *

Ps. 66:17. *and he was extolled* with my tongue. [see also רוֹמָם]

POLAL.—*Future.*

Ps. 75:10(11). the horns of the righteous *shall be exalted.*

POLAL.—*Participle.*

Neh. 9: 5. thy glorious name, *which is exalted*

* HIPHIL.—*Preterite.* *

Gen14:22. *I have lift up* mine hand unto the Lord,
39:15. *I lifted up* my voice and cried,
Lev. 2: 9. *And* the priest *shall take* from the meat
6:10(3). *and take up* the ashes which the fire
15(8). *And he shall take* of it his handful,
Nu. 18:26. *then ye shall offer up* an heave offering
31:28. *And levy* a tribute unto the Lord
52. all the gold...*they offered up*
1K. 11:27. *he lifted up* (his) hand against the king:
14: 7. *I exalted thee* from among the people,
16: 2. *I exalted thee* out of the dust,
2K. 19:22. against whom *hast thou exalted* (thy)
2Ch 30:24. Hezekiah king of Judah *did give* (marg. *lifted up,* or, *offered*)
— the princes *gave* to the congregation
35: 8. his princes *gave* (marg. *offered*)
9. chief of the Levites, *gave* (marg. *id.*)
Ezr. 8:25. *which* the king,...*offered:*
Ps. 89:19(20). *I have exalted* (one) chosen
42(43). *Thou hast set up* the right hand of
Isa. 37:23. against whom *hast thou exalted* (thy)
Lam.2:17. *he hath set up* the horn of thine
Dan 8:11. (כתיב) the daily (sacrifice) *was taken away,* (lit. according to כ׳, *he took away* the daily (sacrifice))

HIPHIL.—*Infinitive.*

Gen39:18. *as I lifted up* my voice and cried,
Nu. 18:30. *When ye have heaved* the best
32. *when ye have heaved* from
1Ch 15:16. *by lifting up* the voice with joy.
25: 5. *to lift up* the horn.
2Ch 5:13. *and when they lifted up* (their) voice
Ezr. 3:12. many shouted aloud for joy: (lit. unto shouting for joy *by lifting up* the voice)
9: 6. *to lift up* my face to thee,
Ps. 75: 6(7). *promotion* (cometh) neither from the
Isa. 10:15. *as if* the staff *should lift up* (itself),
Eze.21:22(27). *to lift up* the voice with shouting

HIPHIL.—*Imperative.*

Ex. 14:16. But *lift* thou *up* thy rod,
Jos. 4: 5. *and take you up* every man...a stone
2K. 6: 7. *Take* (it) *up* to thee.
Ps. 74: 3. *Lift up* thy feet unto the perpetual
Isa. 13: 2. *exalt* the voice unto them,
40: 9. *lift up* thy voice
— *lift* (it) *up*, be not afraid;
57:14. *take up* the stumbling block
58: 1. *lift up* thy voice like a trumpet,
62:10. *lift up* a standard for the people.
Eze. 21:26(31). *and take off* the crown:
45: 9. *take away* your exactions

HIPHIL.—*Future.*

Gen31:45. Jacob took a stone, *and set it up*
41:44. *shall* no man *lift up* his hand or foot
Ex. 7:20. *and he lifted up* the rod, and smote the
17:11. when Moses *held up* his hand,
Lev. 4: 8. *he shall take off*...all the fat
19. *he shall take* all his fat from him,
22:15. the holy things...which *they offer*
Nu. 15:19. *ye shall offer up* an heave offering
20. *Ye shall offer up* a cake
— so *shall ye heave* it.
16:37(17:2). *that he take up* the censers
18:19. the children of Israel *offer*
24. *they offer* (as) an heave offering
28. *ye* also *shall offer* an heave offering
29. Out of all your gifts *ye shall offer*
20:11. *And* Moses *lifted up* his hand,
1Sa. 2: 8. *lifteth up* the beggar from the dunghill,
10. *and exalt* the horn of his anointed.
9:24. *And* the cook *took up* the shoulder,
1K. 11:26. *even he lifted up* (his) hand against
2K. 2:13. *He took up also* the mantle
2Ch 35: 7. *And* Josiah *gave* (marg. *offered*) to the
Job 38:34. *Canst thou lift up* thy voice
39:27. the eagle...and *make* her nest *on high?*
Ps. 66: 7. (כתיב) *let* not the rebellious *exalt*
75: 4(5). *Lift* not *up* the horn:
5(6). *Lift* not *up* your horn on high:
7(8). he putteth down one, and *setteth up*
89:17(18). (כתיב) our horn *shall be exalted.*
92:10(11). *But* my horn *shalt thou exalt*
110: 7. *shall he lift up* the head.
113: 7. *lifteth* the needy out of the dunghill;
148:14. *He also exalteth* the horn of his people,
Isa. 14:13. *I will exalt* my throne above the stars
49:22. *set up* my standard to the people:
Eze. 45: 1. *ye shall offer* an oblation
13. the oblation that *ye shall offer;*
48: 8. the offering which *ye shall offer*
9. The oblation that *ye shall offer*
20. *ye shall offer* the holy oblation
Dan 12: 7. *when he held up* his right hand

HIPHIL.—*Participle.*

Ex. 35:24. Every one *that did offer* an offering
Ps. 3: 3(4). *and the lifter up of* mine head.
Pro. 3:35. shame *shall be the promotion of* fools. (marg. *exalteth* the fools)
14:29. he that is hasty of spirit *exalteth* folly.
Isa. 10:15. against *them that lift it up*,
Hos 11: 4. *as they that take off* (marg. *lift up*) the

* HOPHAL.—*Preterite.* *

Ex. 29:27. the shoulder...which *is heaved up*,
Dan 8:11. the daily (sacrifice) *was taken away*,

HOPHAL.—*Future.*

Lev. 4:10. *it was taken off* from the bullock

* HITHPOLEL.—*Future.* *

Dan 11:36. *and he shall exalt himself*, and magnify

7313 רוּם [*room*], Ch.

* P'AL.—*Participle.* Active. *

Dan 4:37(34). I Nebuchadnezzar praise *and extol*

P'AL.—*Participle.* Passive.

Dan 5:20. But when his heart *was lifted up*,

* APHEL.—*Participle.* *

Dan 5:19. whom he would *he set up;*

* HITHPOLEL.—*Preterite.* *

Dan 5:23. But *hast lifted up thyself*

רוּם *room*, m. 7312

Pro. 21: 4. An *high* look, (marg. *Haughtiness of* eyes)
25: 3. The heaven *for height*,
Isa. 2:11. *the haughtiness of* men shall be bowed
17. *the haughtiness of* men shall be made low:
10:12. of his *high* looks. (lit. *haughtiness of* his eyes)
Jer. 48:29. *and the haughtiness of* his heart.

רוּם [*room*], Ch. m. 7314

Ezr. 6: 3. *the height thereof* threescore cubits,
Dan 3: 1. *whose height* (was) threescore cubits,
4:10(7). *and the height thereof* (was) great.
11(8). *and the height thereof* reached unto
20(17). *whose height* reached unto the heaven,

רוֹם *rōhm*, adv. 7315

Hab 3:10. lifted up his hands *on high.*

רוֹמָה *rōh-māh'*, adv. 7317

Mic. 2: 3. neither shall ye go *haughtily:*

רוֹמָם *rōh-māhm'*, m. 7318-19

Ps. 66:17. *and he was extolled* with my tongue. [Perhaps this is a verb;—see רוּם Polal.]
149: 6. *the high* (praises) of God

רֹמֵמוּת see רוֹמֵמוּת See 7427

רוּן see רָנַן See 7442

רוּעַ [*rooăg*]. 7321

* NIPHAL.—*Future.* *

Pro. 11:15. surety for a stranger *shall smart* (marg. *be* sore *broken*)
13:20. of fools *shall be destroyed.* (marg. *broken*)

* POLAL.—*Future.* *

Isa. 16:10. neither *shall there be shouting:*

* HIPHIL.—*Preterite.* *

Nu. 10: 9. *then ye shall blow an alarm*
Jos. 6:10. the day I bid you shout; *then shall ye shout.*
Jud. 15:14. the Philistines *shouted* against him:
1Sa. 17:20. *and shouted* for the battle.
Ezr. 3:11. all the people *shouted*

HIPHIL.—*Infinitive.*

2Ch 13:12. with sounding trumpets *to cry alarm*
15. *as* the men of Judah *shouted*,

HIPHIL.—*Imperative.*

Jos. 6:10. until the day I bid you *shout;*
16. Joshua said unto the people, *Shout;*
Ps. 47: 1(2). *shout* unto God with the voice of
66: 1. *Make a joyful noise* unto God,
81: 1(2). *make a joyful noise* unto the God of
98: 4. *Make a joyful noise* unto the Lord,
6. *make a joyful noise* before the Lord,
100: 1. *Make a joyful noise* unto the Lord,
Isa. 44:23. *shout, ye* lower parts of the earth:
Jer. 50:15. *Shout* against her round about:
Hos. 5: 8. *cry aloud* (at) Beth-aven,
Joel 2: 1. *and sound an alarm* in my holy mountain:
Zep. 3:14. *shout*, O Israel;
Zec. 9: 9. *shout*, O daughter of Jerusalem:

HIPHIL.—*Future.*

Nu. 10: 7. *ye shall* not *sound an alarm.*
Jos. 6: 5. all the people *shall shout*
10. *Ye shall* not *shout*,
20. *So* the people *shouted*
— *and* the people *shouted* with a great shout,
Jud. 7:21. all the host ran, *and cried*,
1Sa. 4: 5. *And* when...all Israel *shouted*
10:24. *And* all the people *shouted*,
17:52. of Israel and of Judah arose, *and shouted*,
2Ch 13:15. *Then* the men of Judah *gave a shout:*
Job 30: 5. *they cried* after them as (after) a thief;

Job 38: 7. *and* all the sons of God *shouted for joy?*
Ps. 41:11(12). mine enemy *doth* not *triumph*
95: 1. *let us make a joyful noise* to the rock of
2. *Let us...make a joyful noise* unto him
Isa. 15: 4. of Moab *shall cry out;*
42:13. *he shall cry*, yea, roar;
Mic. 4: 9. why *dost thou cry out* aloud?

HIPHIL.—*Participle.*

Ezr. 3:13. the people *shouted* with a loud shout,

* HITHPOLEL.—*Imperative.* *

Ps. 60: 8(10). Philistia, *triumph thou*

HITHPOLEL.—*Future.*

Ps. 65:13(14). *they shout for joy*, they also sing.
108: 9(10). over Philistia *will I triumph.*

7322 ## רוּף [*rooph*].

* POLEL.—*Future.* *

Job 26:11. The pillars of heaven *tremble*

7323 ## רוּץ *rootz.*

* KAL.—*Preterite.* *

Gen 18: 7. Abraham *ran* unto the herd,
1Sa. 8:11. *and* (some) *shall run* before his chariots.
2K. 5:20. *I will run* after him,
Jer. 12: 5. If *thou hast run* with the footmen,
23:21. have not sent these prophets, yet they *ran:*

KAL.—*Infinitive.*

1Sa. 20: 6. *that he might run* to Beth-lehem
Ps. 19: 5(6). rejoiceth as a strong man *to run* a race.
Pro. 6:18. feet that be swift *in running*

KAL.—*Imperative.*

1Sa. 20:36. *Run*, find out now the arrows
2Sa. 18:23. he said unto him, *Run.*
2K. 4:26. *Run* now, I pray thee, to meet her,
Zec. 2: 4(8). *Run*, speak to this young man,

KAL.—*Future.*

Gen 18: 2. *and* when...*he ran* to meet them from the
24:17. *And* the servant *ran* to meet her,
20. *and ran* again unto the well
28. *And* the damsel *ran*,
29. *and* Laban *ran* out unto the man,
29:12. *and she ran* and told her father.
13. when Laban heard...*that he ran* to meet
33: 4. *And* Esau *ran* to meet him,
Nu. 11:27. *And* there *ran* a young man,
16:47(17:12). *and ran* into the midst
Jos. 7:22. *and they ran* unto the tent;
8:19. *and they ran* as soon as he had stretched
Jud. 7:21. *and* all the host *ran*, and cried,
13:10. the woman made haste, *and ran*,
1Sa. 3: 5. *And he ran* unto Eli,
4:12. *And there ran* a man of Benjamin
10:23. *And they ran* and fetched him thence:
17:22. *and ran* into the army,
48. David hasted, *and ran*
51. *Therefore* David *ran*,
2Sa. 18:19. *Let me* now *run*, and bear the king
21. Cushi bowed himself unto Joab, *and ran.*
22. *let me*, I pray thee, also *run*
23. But howsoever, (said he), *let me run.*
— *Then* Ahimaaz *ran* by the way
22:30. by thee *I have run* (marg. or, *broken*) *through* a troop:
1K. 18:46. he girded up his loins, *and ran*
19:20. he left the oxen, *and ran*
2K. 4:22. *that I may run* to the man of God,
23:12. *and brake* (them) *down* (marg. or, *ran*) from thence,
Job 15:26. *He runneth* upon him,
16:14. *he runneth* upon me like a giant.
Ps. 18:29(30). by thee *I have run* (marg. or, *broken*) *through* a troop;
59: 4(5). *They run* and prepare themselves
119:32. *I will run* the way of thy commandments,
147:15. his word *runneth* very swiftly.
Pro. 1:16. their feet *run* to evil,
4:12. when *thou runnest*, thou shalt not stumble.
18:10. the righteous *runneth*
Cant 1: 4. *we will run* after thee:
Isa. 40:31. *they shall run*, and not be weary;
55: 5. nations (that) knew not thee *shall run*
59: 7. Their feet *run* to evil,
Jer. 50:44. (כתיב) *I will make them* suddenly *run away*
51:31. One post *shall run* to meet another,
Dan 8: 6. ram that had two horns,...*and ran* unto him
Joel 2: 4. as horsemen, so *shall they run.*
7. *They shall run* like mighty men;
9. *they shall run* upon the wall,
Am. 6:12. *Shall* horses *run* upon the rock?
Hab. 2: 2. that *he may run* that readeth

KAL.—*Participle.*

1Sa. 20:36. as the lad *ran*, he shot an arrow
22:17. the king said *unto the footmen* (marg. *runners*, or, *guard*)
2Sa. 15: 1. fifty men *to run* before him.
18:22. Wherefore *wilt* thou *run*,
24. a man *running* alone.
26. the watchman saw another man *running:*
— Behold (another) man *running* alone.
1K. 1: 5. fifty men *to run* before him.
14:27. unto the hands of the chief of *the guard*, (marg. *runners*)
28. *the guard* bare them, and brought them back into the *guard* chamber.
2K. 5:21. when Naaman saw (him) *running*
10:25. Jehu said to *the guard*
— *the guard* and the captains cast (them)
11: 4. the captains *and the guard*,
6. a third part at the gate behind *the guard:*
11. And *the guard* stood,
13. when Athaliah heard the noise of *the guard* (lit. *runners*)
19. the captains, and *the guard*,
— the gate of *the guard*
2Ch 12:10. the chief of *the guard*,
11. *the guard* came and fetched them, and brought them again into *the guard*
23:12. the noise of the people *running*
30: 6. *the posts* (lit. *runners*) went with the
10. *the posts* passed from city to city
Est. 3:13. the letters were sent by *posts*
15. *The posts* went out,
8:10. sent letters by *posts* on horseback,
14. *the posts* that rode upon mules
Job 9:25. my days are swifter than *a post:*
Jer. 51:31. One *post* shall run to meet *another*, (lit. *post* shall run to meet *post*)
Hag. 1: 9. *ye run* every man unto his own house.

* POLEL.—*Future.* *

Nah. 2: 4(5). *they shall run* like the lightnings.

* HIPHIL.—*Imperative.* *

1Sa. 17:17. *and run* to the camp to thy brethren;

HIPHIL.—*Future.*

Gen 41:14. *and they brought him hastily* (marg. *made him run*)
2Ch 35:13. *and divided* (them) *speedily* (marg. *made* (them) *run*)
Ps. 68:31(32). Ethiopia *shall soon stretch out* her
Jer. 49:19. *I will* suddenly *make him run away*
50:44. *I will make them* suddenly *run away*

רוּק [*rook*]. 7324

* HIPHIL.—*Preterite.* *

Lev. 26:33. *and will draw out* a sword after you:
Eze. 28: 7 & 30:11. *and they shall draw* their swords
Mal. 3:10. *and pour* you *out* (marg. *empty out*) a blessing,

HIPHIL.—*Infinitive.*

Isa. 32: 6. *to make empty* the soul of the hungry,

HIPHIL.—*Imperative.*

Ps. 35: 3. *Draw out also* the spear,

HIPHIL.—*Future.*

Gen 14:14. *And* when...*he armed* (marg. or, *led forth*) his trained (servants),
Ex. 15: 9. *I will draw* my sword,
Ps. 18:42(43). *I did cast them out* as the dirt
Ecc. 11: 3. *they empty* (themselves) upon the earth:
Jer. 48:12. *shall empty* his vessels,

Eze. 5: 2, 12. *I will draw out* a sword after them.
12:14. *I will draw out* the sword after them.
Hab. 1:17. *Shall they* therefore *empty* their net,

HIPHIL.—*Participle.*

Gen42:35. as they *emptied* their sacks,
Zec. 4:12. *which* through the two golden pipes *empty*

* HOPHAL.—*Preterite.* *

Jer. 48:11. *hath* not *been emptied* from vessel to vessel,

HOPHAL.—*Future.*

Cant.1: 3. thy name is (as) ointment *poured forth,*

7325 **רוּר** [*roor*].

* KAL.—*Preterite.* *

Lev.15: 3. his flesh *run* with his issue,

7219 **רוֹשׁ** *rōhsh*, m.

Deu32:32. their grapes (are) grapes of *gall,*

7326 **רוּשׁ** [*roosh*].

* KAL.—*Preterite.* *

Ps. 34:10(11). The young lions *do lack,*

KAL.—*Participle.* Poel.

1Sa.18:23. seeing that I (am) *a poor man,*
2Sa.12: 1. two men...the one rich, and the other *poor.*
3. *But the poor man had* nothing,
4. took the *poor* man's lamb,
Ps. 82: 3. do justice to the afflicted *and needy.*
Pro.10: 4. He becometh *poor* that dealeth (with) a
13: 8. *but the poor* heareth not rebuke.
23. Much food (is in) the tillage of *the poor:*
14:20. *The poor* is hated even of his own
17: 5. Whoso mocketh *the poor*
18:23. *The poor* useth intreaties;
19: 1. *the poor* that walketh in his integrity,
7. the brethren of *the poor* do hate him:
22. *a poor man* (is) better than a liar.
22: 2. The rich *and poor* meet together:
7. The rich ruleth *over the poor,*
28: 3. A *poor* man that oppresseth
6. *the poor* that walketh in his uprightness,
27. He that giveth *unto the poor*
29:13. *The poor* and the deceitful man
Ecc. 4:14. (he that is) born in his kingdom becometh *poor.*
5: 8(7). the oppression of *the poor,*

* HITHPOLEL.—*Participle.* *

Pro 13: 7. (there is) *that maketh himself poor,*

7328 **רָז** *rāhz*, Ch. m.

Dan 2:18. desire mercies...concerning this *secret;*
19. Then was *the secret* revealed unto Daniel
27. *The secret* which the king hath demanded
28. a God in heaven that revealeth *secrets,*
29. he that revealeth *secrets* maketh known
30. this *secret* is not revealed to me for
47. and a revealer of *secrets,* seeing thou couldest reveal this *secret.*
4: 9(6). and no *secret* troubleth thee,

7329 **רָזָה** *rāh-zāh'*.

* KAL.—*Preterite.* *

Zep. 2:11. *he will famish* (marg. *make lean*) all the

* NIPHAL.—*Future.* *

Isa. 17: 4. the fatness of his flesh *shall wax lean.*

7330 **רָזֶה** [*rāh-zeh'*].

Nu. 13:20. the land (is), whether it (be) fat or *lean,*
Eze.34:20. the fat cattle and between the *lean* cattle.

7332 **רָזוֹן** *rāh-zōhn'*, m.

Ps.106:15. sent *leanness* into their soul.
Isa. 10:16. send among his fat ones *leanness;*
Mic. 6:10. the *scant* measure (marg. the measure of *leanness*)

רָזוֹן *rāh-zōhn'*, m. 7333

Pro.14:28. the destruction of *the prince.*

רָזִי *rāh-zee'*, m. 7334

Isa. 24:16. I said, My *leanness* (marg. *Leanness* to me, or, *My secret* to me), my *leanness,* woe unto me!

רָזַם [*rāh-zam'*]. 7335

* KAL.—*Future.* *

Job 15:12. what *do* thy eyes *wink at,*

רָזַן [*rāh-zan'*]. 7336

* KAL.—*Participle.* Poel. *

Jud. 5: 3. give ear, *O ye princes;*
Ps. 2: 2. *and the rulers* take counsel together,
Pro. 8:15. *and princes* decree justice.
31: 4. *nor for princes* strong drink:
Isa. 40:23. That bringeth *the princes* to nothing;
Hab 1:10. *and the princes* shall be a scorn

רָחַב *rāh-ghav'*. 7337

* KAL.—*Preterite.* *

1Sa. 2: 1. my mouth *is enlarged*
Isa. 60: 5. thine heart shall fear, *and be enlarged;*
Eze.41: 7. *And there was an enlarging* (marg. *it was made broader*), and a winding

* NIPHAL.—*Participle.* *

Isa. 30:23. thy cattle feed in *large* pastures.

* HIPHIL.—*Preterite.* *

Gen26:22. the Lord *hath made room* for us,
Ex. 34:24. *and enlarge* thy borders:
Ps. 4: 1(2). *thou hast enlarged* me
25:17. The troubles of my heart *are enlarged:*
Isa. 5:14. hell *hath enlarged* herself,
30:33. *he hath made* (it) deep (and) *large:*
57: 8. *thou hast enlarged* thy bed,
Hab 2: 5. who *enlargeth* his desire as hell,

HIPHIL.—*Infinitive.*

Am. 1:13. that *they might enlarge* their border:

HIPHIL.—*Imperative.*

Ps. 81:10(11). *open* thy mouth *wide,*
Isa. 54: 2. *Enlarge* the place of thy tent,
Mic. 1:16. *enlarge* thy baldness

HIPHIL.—*Future.*

Deu12:20. When the Lord thy God *shall enlarge*
19: 8. if the Lord thy God *enlarge* thy coast,
2Sa.22:37. *Thou hast enlarged* my steps
Ps. 18:36(37). *Thou hast enlarged* my steps
35:21. *Yea, they opened* their mouth *wide*
119:32. when *thou shalt enlarge* my heart.
Pro.18:16. A man's gift *maketh room* (lit. *enlargeth*) for him,
Isa. 57: 4. against whom *make ye* a *wide* mouth,

HIPHIL.—*Participle.*

Deu33:20. *he that enlargeth* Gad:

רָחָב *rāh-ghāhv'*, adj. 7342

Gen34:21. for the land, behold, (it is) *large* enough
Ex. 3: 8. a good land *and a large,*
Jud.18:10. a *large* (lit. *large of* hands, or, sides) land:
1Ch 4:40. the land (was) *wide* (lit. *id.*), and quiet,
Neh. 3: 8. fortified Jerusalem unto the *broad* wall.
4:19(13). The work (is) great *and large,*
7: 4. city (was) *large* (marg. *broad in* spaces)
9:35. the *large* and fat land
12:38. even unto the *broad* wall;
Job 11: 9. *and broader* than the sea.
30:14. a *wide* breaking in (of waters):
Ps.101: 5. that hath an high look *and a proud* heart

Ps. 104:25. (So is) this great *and wide* sea, (lit. *wide of* spaces)
119:45. I will walk *at liberty*: (marg. *at large*)
96. thy commandment (is) exceeding *broad*.
Pro.21: 4. An high look, *and a proud* heart,
28:25. He that is of a *proud* heart
Isa. 22:18. a *large* country: (marg. *large of* spaces)
33:21. a place of *broad* (marg. *broad of* spaces, or, hands) rivers (and) streams;
Jer. 51:58. The *broad* walls of Babylon
Eze.23:32. drink of thy sister's cup deep *and large*:

7338 **רַחַב** *rah'-ghav*, m.

Job 36:16. out of the strait (into) *a broad place*,
38:18. Hast thou perceived *the breadth of* the

7341 **רֹחַב** *rōh'-ghav*, m.

Gen 6:15. *the breadth of it* fifty cubits,
13:17. the length of it *and in the breadth of it*,
Ex. 25:10. a cubit and a half *the breadth thereof*,
17. a cubit and a half *the breadth thereof*.
23. a cubit *the breadth thereof*,
26: 2, 8. *and the breadth of* one curtain
16. *the breadth of* one board.
27: 1. five cubits long, and five cubits *broad*;
12. *And* (for) *the breadth of* the court
13. *And the breadth of* the court
18. *and the breadth* fifty every where,
28:16. a span (shall be) *the breadth thereof*.
30: 2. a cubit *the breadth thereof*;
36: 9. *and the breadth of* one curtain
15. four cubits (was) *the breadth of* one
21. *the breadth of* a board
37: 1. a cubit and a half *the breadth of it*,
6. one cubit and a half *the breadth thereof*.
10. a cubit *the breadth thereof*,
25. *the breadth of it* a cubit;
38: 1. five cubits *the breadth thereof*;
18. the height *in the breadth*
39: 9. a span *the breadth thereof*,
Deu 3:11. four cubits *the breadth of it*,
1K. 4:29(5:9). understanding...*and largeness of*
6: 2. *the breadth thereof* twenty (cubits),
3. *according to the breadth of* the house;
— *the breadth thereof* before the house.
6. The nethermost chamber (was) five cubits *broad*, and the middle (was) six cubits *broad*, and the third (was) seven cubits *broad*:
20. in length, and twenty cubits in *breadth*,
7: 2. *the breadth thereof* fifty cubits,
6. *the breadth thereof* thirty cubits:
27. four cubits *the breadth thereof*,
2Ch 3: 3. *and the breadth* twenty cubits.
4. *the breadth of* the house, twenty cubits,
8. (was) according *to the breadth of* the house, twenty cubits, *and the breadth thereof*
4: 1. twenty cubits *the breadth thereof*,
6:13. a brasen scaffold,...five cubits *broad*,
Job 37:10. *the breadth of* the waters is straitened.
Isa. 8: 8. shall fill *the breadth of* thy land,
Eze.40: 5. he measured *the breadth of* the building,
6. the threshold of the gate,...one reed *broad*; and the other threshold...one reed *broad*.
7. (every) little chamber (was) one reed long, and one reed *broad*;
11. *the breadth of* the entry of the gate,
13. *the breadth* (was) five and twenty cubits,
19. *the breadth* from the forefront
20. length thereof, *and the breadth thereof*.
21. *and the breadth* five and twenty cubits.
25, 36. *and the breadth* five and twenty cubits.
29, 33. *and* five and twenty cubits *broad*.
30. *and* five cubits *broad*. (marg. *breadth*)
42. *and* a cubit and an half *broad*,
47. *and* an hundred cubits *broad*,
48. *and the breadth of* the gate
49. *and the breadth* eleven cubits;
41: 1. six cubits *broad* on the one side, and six cubits *broad* on the other side, (which was) *the breadth of* the tabernacle.
2, 3. *And the breadth of* the door
—, 4. *and the breadth*, twenty cubits.
5. *and the breadth of* (every) side chamber,
Eze.41: 7. *the breadth* of the house
9. *The thickness of* the wall,
10. *the wideness of* twenty cubits
11. *and the breadth of* the place
12. the west (was) seventy cubits *broad*;
— wall of the building (was) five cubits *thick*
14. *Also the breadth of* the face of the house,
42: 2. *and the breadth* (was) fifty cubits.
4. a walk of ten cubits *breadth*
10. *in the thickness of* the wall
11. as long as they, (and) *as broad as they*: (lit. as the length of them so *the breadth of them*)
20. *and* five hundred *broad*,
43:13. and *the breadth* a cubit,
14. *and the breadth* one cubit;
— *and the breadth* (one) cubit.
16. the altar (shall be)...twelve *broad*,
17. fourteen (cubits) long and fourteen *broad*
45: 1. *and the breadth* (shall be) ten thousand.
3. *and the breadth of* ten thousand:
5. the ten thousand of *breadth*,
6. possession of the city five thousand *broad*,
46:22. forty (cubits) long and thirty *broad*:
48: 8. twenty thousand (reeds in) *breadth*,
9. *and* of ten thousand in *breadth*.
10. toward the west ten thousand *in breadth*, and toward the east ten thousand *in breadth*,
13. *and* ten thousand *in breadth*:
— *and the breadth* ten thousand.
15. *in the breadth* over against
Zec. 2: 2(6). to see what (is) *the breadth thereof*,
5: 2. *and the breadth thereof* ten cubits.

רְחוֹב *r'ghōhv*, f. 7339

Gen19: 2. we will abide *in the street*
Deu13:16(17). the midst of *the street thereof*,
Jud.19:15. sat him down *in a street of* the city:
17. *in the street of* the city:
20. only lodge not *in the street*.
2Sa.21:12. *from the street of* Beth-shan,
2Ch 29: 4. gathered them together *into the* east *street*,
32: 6. in *the street of* the gate of the city,
Ezr.10: 9. *in the street of* the house of God,
Neh 8: 1. *into the street* that (was) before the
3. before *the street* that (was) before
16. *and in the street of* the water gate, *and in the street of* the gate of Ephraim.
Est. 4: 6. went forth...unto *the street of* the city,
6: 9, 11. *through the street of* the city,
Job 29: 7. (when) I prepared my seat *in the street!*
Ps. 55:11(12). and guile depart not *from her streets*.
144:14. no complaining *in our streets*.
Pro. 1:20. she uttereth her voice *in the streets*:
5:16. rivers of waters *in the streets*.
7:12. now *in the streets*,
22:13. I shall be slain in *the streets*.
26:13. a lion (is) in *the streets*.
Cant.3: 2. go about the city in the streets, *and in the broad ways*
Isa. 15: 3. *and in their streets*, every one shall howl,
59:14. truth is fallen *in the street*,
Jer. 5: 1. seek *in the broad places thereof*,
9:21(20). the young men *from the streets*.
48:38. *and in the streets thereof*:
49:26. her young men shall fall *in her streets*,
50:30. shall her young men fall *in the streets*,
Lam.2:11. the sucklings swoon *in the streets of* the
12. they swooned...*in the streets of*
4:18. we cannot go *in our streets*:
Eze.16:24. made thee an high place in every *street*.
31. makest thine high place in every *street*;
Dan 9:25. *the street* shall be built again,
Am. 5:16. Wailing (shall be) in all *streets*;
Nah 2: 4(5). one against another *in the broad ways*:
Zec. 8: 4. men and old women dwell *in the streets of*
5. *And the streets of* the city shall be full
— playing *in the streets thereof*.

רַחוּם *rah-ghoom'*, adj. 7349

Ex. 34: 6. The Lord God, *merciful* and gracious,
Deu 4:31. the Lord thy God (is) a *merciful* God;
2Ch 30: 9. Lord your God (is) gracious *and merciful*,

Neh 9:17. a God...gracious *and merciful*,
31. a gracious *and merciful* God.
Ps. 78:38. he, (being) *full of compassion*, forgave
86:15. a God *full of compassion*,
103: 8. The Lord (is) *merciful* and gracious,
111: 4. Lord (is) gracious *and full of compassion*.
112: 4. (he is) gracious, *and full of compassion*,
145: 8. Lord (is) gracious, *and full of compassion*;
Joel 2:13. he (is) gracious *and merciful*,
Jon. 4: 2. a gracious God, *and merciful*,

7350 **רָחוֹק** *rāh-ǵhōhk'*, adj.

Gen22: 4. Abraham...saw the place *afar off*.
37:18. when they saw him *afar off*,
Ex. 2: 4. his sister stood *afar off*,
20:18. they removed, and stood *afar off*.
21. the people stood *afar off*,
24: 1. worship ye *afar off*.
Nu. 9:10. in a journey *afar off*,
Deu13: 7(8). the gods...*far off* from thee,
20:15. the cities (which are) very *far off*
28:49. The Lord shall bring a nation...*from far*,
29:22(21). the stranger that shall come from a *far* land,
30:11. neither (is) it *far off*.
Jos. 3: 4. there shall be *a space* between you
9: 6. We be come from a *far* country:
9. From a very *far* country
22. We (are) *very far* from you;
Jud.18: 7. *and* they (were) *far* from the Zidonians,
28. it (was) *far* from Zidon,
1Sa.26:13. stood on the top of an hill *afar off*;
2Sa. 7:19. *for a great while to come*.
1K. 8:41. cometh out of a *far* country
46. the land of the enemy, *far* or near;
2K. 2: 7. fifty men...stood to view *afar off*:
19:25. Hast thou not heard *long ago*
20:14. They are come from a *far* country,
1Ch 17:17. spoken of thy servant's house *for a great while to come*,
2Ch 6:32. is come from a *far* country
36. a land *far off* or near;
26:15. his name spread *far abroad*,
Ezr. 3:13. the noise was heard *afar off*.
Neh 4:19(13). one *far* from another.
12:43. the joy...was heard even *afar off*.
Est. 9:20. all the Jews...(both) nigh *and far*,
Job 2:12. when they lifted up their eyes *afar off*,
36: 3. I will fetch my knowledge *from afar*,
25. man may behold (it) *afar off*.
39:25. *and* he smelleth the battle *afar off*,
29. her eyes behold *afar off*.
Ps. 10: 1. Why standest thou *afar off*,
22: 1(2). (why art thou so) *far* from helping me,
38:11(12). my kinsmen stand *afar off*.
56[title](1). To the chief Musician upon Jonath-elem-*rechokim*,
65: 5(6). them *that are afar off*
119:155. Salvation (is) *far* from the wicked:
139: 2. thou understandest my thought *afar off*.
Pro. 7:19. he is gone a *long* journey:
15:29. The Lord (is) *far* from the wicked:
27:10. a brother *far off*.
31:10. *for* her price (is) *far* above rubies.
Ecc. 7:23. it (was) *far* from me.
24. That which is *far off*,
Isa. 5:26. will lift up an ensign...*from far*,
22: 3. have fled *from far*.
11. him that fashioned it *long ago*.
23: 7. her own feet shall carry her *afar off* (marg. *from afar off*)
25: 1. (thy) counsels *of old*
33:13. Hear, ye (that are) *far off*,
37:26. Hast thou not heard *long ago*,
39: 3. They are come from a *far* country
43: 6. bring my sons *from far*,
46:12. ye stouthearted, that (are) *far* from
49: 1. hearken, ye people, *from far*;
12. these shall come *from far*:
57: 9. didst send thy messengers *far off*.
19. Peace, peace *to him that is far off*,
59:14. justice standeth *afar off*:
60: 4. thy sons shall come *from far*,
9. to bring thy sons *from far*,
66:19. the isles *afar off*,
Jer. 12: 2. *and far* from their reins.
23:23. a God at hand,...and not a God *afar off*?
25:26. the kings of the north, *far* and near,
30:10. I will save thee *from afar*,
31: 3. The Lord hath appeared *of old* (marg. *from afar*)
46:27. I will save thee *from afar off*,
48:24. all the cities.. *far* or near.
51:50. remember the Lord *afar off*,
Eze. 6:12. *He that is far off* shall die
12:27. the times (that are) *far off*.
22: 5. *and those that be far* from thee,
Dan 9: 7. all Israel, that are near, *and that are far off*,
Joel 3: 8(4:8). the Sabeans, to a people *far off*:
Mic 4: 3. rebuke strong nations *afar off*;
Hab 1: 8. their horsemen shall come *from far*;
Zec. 6:15. *And they that are far off* shall come

רָהִיט [*rāh-ǵheet'*], m. 7351

Cant.1:17. (כתיב) *our rafters* (marg. or, *galleries*) of fir.

רֵחַיִם *rēh-ǵhah'-yim*, dual. 7347

Ex. 11: 5. the maidservant that (is) behind *the mill*,
Nu. 11: 8. the people...ground (it) *in mills*,
Deu24: 6. the *nether* or the upper millstone
Isa. 47: 2. Take *the millstones*, and grind meal:
Jer. 25:10. the sound of *the millstones*,

רַחִיק [*rah-ǵheek'*], Ch. adj. 7352

Ezr. 6: 6. be ye *far* from thence:

רָחֵל *rāh-ǵhēhl'*, f. 7353

Gen31:38. *thy ewes* and thy she goats
32:14(15). two hundred *ewes*, and twenty rams,
Cant.6: 6. Thy teeth (are) as a flock of *sheep*
Isa. 53: 7. *and as a sheep* before her shearers is

רָחַם [*rāh-ǵham'*]. 7355

* KAL.—*Future*. *

Ps. 18: 1(2). *I will love thee*, O Lord,

* PIEL.—*Preterite*. *

Ex. 33:19. *and will shew mercy* on
Deu13:17(18) & 30:3. *and have compassion upon thee*,
1K. 8:50. *that they may have compassion on them*:
Ps.103:13. the Lord *pitieth* them that fear him.
Isa. 54: 8. *will I have mercy on thee*,
60:10. in my favour *have I had mercy on thee*.
Jer. 12:15. *and have compassion on them*,
33:26. *and have mercy on them*.
42:12. *that he may have mercy*
Lam 3:32. *yet will he have compassion*
Eze.39:25. *and have mercy* upon the whole house of Israel,
Hos 2:23(25). *and I will have mercy upon* her
Zec.10: 6. *for I have mercy upon them*:

PIEL.—*Infinitive*.

Ps.103:13. Like as a father *pitieth* (his) children,
Isa. 30:18. *that he may have mercy upon you*
49:15. *that she should not have compassion* (marg. *from having compassion*)
Jer. 31:20. I will *surely* have mercy (lit. *having mercy* I will have mercy)
Hab 3: 2. in wrath remember *mercy*.

PIEL.—*Future*.

Ex. 33:19. on whom *I will shew mercy*.
2K. 13:23. *and had compassion on them*,
Ps.102:13(14). Thou shalt arise, (and) *have mercy upon* Zion:
Isa. 9:17(16). neither *shall have mercy* on
13:18. *they shall have no pity*
14: 1. the Lord *will have mercy*
27:11. he that made them *will* not *have mercy on them*,
49:13. and *will have mercy upon* his afflicted.
55: 7. *and he will have mercy upon him*;

Jer. 6:23. they (are) cruel, and *have* no *mercy;*
13:14. I will not pity,...nor *have mercy,*
21: 7. he shall not spare...nor *have mercy.*
30:18. *have mercy* on his dwellingplaces;
31:20. *I will* surely *have mercy* upon him,
50:42. they (are) cruel, and *will* not *shew mercy:*
Hos. 1: 6. I will no more *have mercy*
7. *I will have mercy* upon the house of Judah,
2: 4(6). *I will* not *have mercy* upon her children;
Mic 7:19. *he will have compassion upon us;*
Zec. 1:12. how long *wilt* thou not *have mercy*

PIEL.—*Participle.*

Ps.116: 5. our God (is) *merciful.*
Isa. 49:10. *he that hath mercy on them*
54:10. the Lord *that hath mercy on thee.*

* PUAL.—*Preterite.* *

Hos. 1: 6. Call her name Lo-*ruhamah:* (marg. Not *having obtained mercy*)
8. when she had weaned Lo-*ruhamah,*
2: 1(3). your sisters, *Ruhamah.* (marg. *Having obtained mercy*)
23(25). *her that* had not *obtained mercy;*

PUAL.—*Future.*

Pro.28:13. whoso confesseth...*shall have mercy.*
Hos.14: 3(4). in thee the fatherless *findeth mercy.*

7360 רָחָם *rāh-ghāhm'*, m.

Lev.11:18. the pelican, and *the gier eagle,*

7356 רַחַם *rah'-gham*, com.

Gen49:25. blessings of the breasts, *and of the womb:*
Jud. 5:30. to every man a *damsel* (or) two;
Pro.30:16. The grave; and *the* barren *womb;*
Isa. 46: 3. are carried from *the womb:*
Eze.20:26. all that openeth *the womb,*

7358 רֶחֶם *reh'-ghem*, m.

Gen20:18. the Lord had fast closed up all *the wombs*
29:31. he opened *her womb:*
30:22. God...opened *her womb.*
Ex. 13: 2. whatsoever openeth *the womb*
12, 15 & 34:19. all that openeth *the matrix,*
Nu. 3:12. firstborn that openeth *the matrix*
8:16. such as open every *womb,*
12:12. cometh out of his mother's *womb.*
18:15. Every thing that openeth *the matrix*
1Sa. 1: 5. the Lord had shut up *her womb.*
6. the Lord had shut up *her womb.*
Job 3:11. Why died I not *from the womb?*
10:18. brought me forth *out of the womb?*
24:20. *The womb* shall forget him;
31:15. one fashion us *in the womb?*
38: 8. issued *out of the womb?*
Ps. 22:10(11). I was cast upon thee *from the womb:*
58: 3(4). The wicked are estranged *from the womb:*
110: 3. *from the womb of* the morning:
Jer. 1: 5. before thou camest forth *out of the womb*
20:17. he slew me not *from the womb;*
— *and her womb* (to be) always great
18. Wherefore came I forth *out of the womb*
Hos. 9:14. give them *a* miscarrying *womb*

7360 רָחָמָה *rāh-ghāh'-māh*, m.

Deu14:17. the pelican, *and the gier eagle,*

7361 [רַחֲמָה] [*rah-ghămāh'*], f.

Jud. 5:30. to every man a damsel (or) *two;* (lit. *two damsels*)

7356 רַחֲמִים *rah-ghămeem'*, m. pl.

Gen43:14. God Almighty give you *mercy*
30. *his bowels* did yern
Deu13:17(18). and shew thee *mercy,*
2Sa.24:14. *his mercies* (are) great:
1K. 3:26. *her bowels* yearned upon her son,
8:50. give them *compassion* before them
1Ch21:13. very great (are) *his mercies:*
2Ch30: 9. your children (shall find) *compassion*
Neh. 1:11. grant him *mercy* in the sight of
9:19. *in thy* manifold *mercies* forsookest them
27. *and according to thy* manifold *mercies*
28. deliver them *according to thy mercies;*
31. *Nevertheless for thy* great *mercies' sake*
Ps. 25: 6. *thy tender mercies* (marg. *bowels*) and thy
40:11(12). Withhold not thou *thy tender mercies*
51: 1(3) & 69:16(17). the multitude of *thy tender mercies*
77: 9(10). shut up *his tender mercies?*
79: 8. let *thy tender mercies* speedily prevent
103: 4. lovingkindness *and tender mercies;*
106:46. He made them also *to be pitied*
119:77. Let *thy tender mercies* come unto me,
156. Great (are) *thy tender mercies,*
145: 9. *and his tender mercies* (are) over all his
Pro.12:10. *but the tender mercies* (marg. or, *bowels*) *of* the wicked (are) cruel.
Isa. 47: 6. thou didst shew them no *mercy;*
54: 7. *but with* great *mercies* will I gather thee.
63: 7. on them *according to his mercies,*
15. the sounding of thy bowels *and of thy mercies*
Jer. 16: 5. lovingkindness and *mercies.*
42:12. I will shew *mercies* unto you,
Lam. 3:22. *his compassions* fail not.
Dan 1: 9. God had brought Daniel into favour *and tender love*
9: 9. To the Lord our God (belong) *mercies* and
18. but for *thy great mercies.*
Hos. 2:19(21). in lovingkindness, *and in mercies.*
Am. 1:11. did cast off all *pity,* (marg. corrupted *his compassions*)
Zec. 1:16. I am returned to Jerusalem *with mercies:*
7: 9. shew mercy *and compassions*

רַחֲמִין *rah-ghămeen'*, Ch. m. pl. 7359

Dan 2:18. *That* they would desire *mercies*

[רַחְמָנִי] [*ragh-māh-nee'*], adj. 7362

Lam. 4:10. The hands of the *pitiful* women

[רָחַף] [*rāh-ghaph'*]. 7363

* KAL.—*Preterite.* *

Jer. 23: 9. all my bones *shake;*

* PIEL.—*Future.* *

Deu32:11. As an eagle...*fluttereth* over her young,

PIEL.—*Participle.*

Gen 1: 2. the Spirit of God *moved*

רָחַץ *rāh-ghatz'*. 7364

* KAL.—*Preterite.* *

Ex. 29: 4. Aaron and his sons thou shalt bring...*and shalt wash* them
17. cut the ram in pieces, *and wash* the
30:19. *For* Aaron and his sons *shall wash* their
21. *So they shall wash* their hands
40:12. thou shalt bring Aaron and his sons...*and wash* them
31. *And* Moses and Aaron and his sons *washed*
Lev. 8:21. *he washed* the inwards and the legs
14: 8. *and wash himself* in water,
9. *also he shall wash* his flesh in water,
15: 5, 6, 7, 8, 10, 11, 21, 22, 27. *and bathe himself* in water,
13. *and bathe* his flesh in running water,
16. *then he shall wash* all his flesh
18. *they shall* (both) *bathe themselves*
16: 4. *therefore shall he wash* his flesh
24. *And he shall wash* his flesh with water
26. *and bathe* his flesh in water,
28. *and bathe* his flesh in water,
17:15. *and bathe himself* in water,
22: 6. unless *he wash* his flesh with water.

Nu. 19: 7. *he shall bathe* his flesh
8. *and bathe* his flesh in water,
19. wash his clothes, *and bathe himself*
Ru. 3: 3. *Wash thyself therefore*, and anoint
1K. 22:38. *they washed* his armour;
2K. 5:10. Go *and wash* in Jordan seven times,
Cant.5: 3. *I have washed* my feet;
Isa. 4: 4. When the Lord *shall have washed*
Eze.23:40. for whom *thou didst wash thyself*,

KAL.—*Infinitive.*

Gen24:32. straw and provender for the camels, and water *to wash*
Ex. 2: 5. daughter of Pharaoh came down *to wash*
30:18. a laver (of) brass,...*to wash*
40:30. put water there, *to wash*
1Sa.25:41. *to wash* the feet of the servants
2Ch 4: 6. ten lavers,...*to wash* in
— the sea (was) for the priests *to wash* in.
Job 29: 6. *When I washed* my steps with butter,

KAL.—*Imperative.*

Gen18: 4. *and wash* your feet, and rest yourselves
19: 2. tarry all night, *and wash* your feet,
2Sa.11: 8. Go down to thy house, *and wash* thy feet.
2K. 5:13. when he saith to thee, *Wash*,
Isa. 1:16. *Wash you*, make you clean;

KAL.—*Future.*

Gen43:24. *and they washed* their feet;
31. *And he washed* his face, and went out,
Ex. 30:20. *they shall wash* with water,
40:32. when they came near...*they washed*;
Lev. 1: 9. his inwards and his legs *shall he wash*
13. *he shall wash* the inwards and the legs
8: 6. brought Aaron and his sons, *and washed*
9:14. *And he did wash* the inwards and the legs,
17:16. nor *bathe* his flesh;
Deu21: 6. all the elders of that city,...*shall wash* their
23:11(12). *he shall wash himself* with water:
Jud.19:21. *and they washed* their feet,
2Sa.12:20. David arose from the earth, *and washed*,
2K. 5:12. *may I* not *wash* in them,
Ps. 26: 6. *I will wash* mine hands in innocency:
58:10(11). *he shall wash* his feet in the blood
73:13. *and washed* my hands in innocency.
Eze.16: 9. *Then washed I thee* with water;

KAL.—*Participle.*

2Sa.11: 2. he saw a woman *washing herself*;
Cant.5:12. His eyes (are)...*washed* with milk,

* PUAL.—*Preterite.* *

Pro.30:12. a generation...*is* not *washed* from their
Eze.16: 4. neither *wast thou washed* in water

* HITHPAEL.—*Preterite.* *

Job 9:30. *If I wash myself* with snow water,

7366 רַחַץ [*rah'-ghatz*], m.

Ps. 60: 8(10) & 108:9(10). Moab (is) *my washpot*; (lit. the pot of *my washing*)

7365 רְחַץ *r'ghatz*, Ch.

* HITHP'IL.—*Preterite.* *

Dan 3:28. delivered his servants that *trusted*

7367 רַחְצָה *ragh-tzāh'*, f.

Cant 4: 2. a flock (of sheep)...which came up from *the washing*;
6: 6. of sheep which go up from *the washing*,

7368 רָחַק *rāh-ghak'*.

* KAL.—*Preterite.* *

Job 21:16 & 22:18. the counsel of the wicked *is far*
30:10. *they flee far* from me,
Ps.119:150. *they are far* from thy law.
Pro.19: 7. his friends *go far* from him?
Isa. 49:19. *and* they that swallowed thee up *shall be far away*.
59: 9. Therefore *is* judgment *far* from us,
11. salvation, (but) *it is far off* from us.
Jer. 2: 5. *they are gone far* from me,
Lam. 1:16. the comforter...*is far* from me:
Eze.44:10. the Levites that *are gone away far*

KAL.—*Infinitive.*

Ps.103:12. *As far as* the east is from the west,
Ecc. 3: 5. a time *to refrain* (marg. *to be far*) from embracing;
Eze. 8: 6. *that I should go far off* from

KAL.—*Imperative.*

Isa. 54:14. *thou shalt be far* from oppression;
Eze.11:15. *Get you far* from the Lord:

KAL.—*Future.*

Ex. 23: 7. *Keep thee far* from a false matter;
Deu12:21. If the place...*be too far*
14:24. if the place *be too far*
Job 5: 4. His children *are far* from safety,
Ps. 22:11(12). *Be* not *far* from me;
19(20). *be* not thou *far* from me,
35:22. O Lord, *be* not *far* from me.
38:21(22). O my God, *be* not *far* from me.
71:12. O God, *be* not *far* from me:
109:17. *so let it be far* from him.
Pro.22: 5. he that doth keep his soul *shall be far*
Isa. 46:13. *it shall* not *be far off*,
Mic. 7:11. (in) that day *shall* the decree *be far removed*.

* NIPHAL.—*Future.* *

Ecc.12: 6. (כתיב) Or ever the silver cord *be loosed*,

* PIEL.—*Preterite.* *

Isa. 6:12. *And* the Lord *have removed* men *far away*,
26:15. *thou hadst removed* (it) *far*
29:13. *have removed* their heart *far*

PIEL.—*Future.*

Eze.43: 9. *let them put away* their whoredom,...*far*

* HIPHIL.—*Preterite.* *

Gen44: 4. when they were gone out...not (yet) *far off*,
Jud.18:22. when they *were a good way*
Job 19:13. *He hath put* my brethren *far*
Ps. 88: 8(9). *Thou hast put away* mine acquaintance *far*
18(19). Lover and friend *hast thou put far*
103:12. (so) *far hath he removed* our transgressions
Eze.11:16. *I have cast them far off*

HIPHIL.—*Infinitive.*

Gen21:16. sat her down...*a good way off*,
Ex. 8:28(24). ye shall not go *very* far away: (lit. *going far* ye shall not go far away)
33: 7. *afar off* from the camp,
Jos. 3:16. very *far* from the city Adam,
Jer. 27:10. *to remove* you *far* from your land;
Joel 3: 6(4:6). that ye *might remove them far*

HIPHIL.—*Imperative.*

Job 11:14. If iniquity (be) in thine hand, *put it far away*,
13:21. *Withdraw* thine hand *far* from me:
Pro. 4:24. perverse lips *put far* from thee.
5: 8. *Remove* thy way *far* from her,
30: 8. *Remove far* from me vanity

HIPHIL.—*Future.*

Ex. 8:28(24). *ye shall* not *go* very *far away*:
Jos. 8: 4. *go* not very *far* from the city,
Job 22:23. *thou shalt put away* iniquity
Ps. 55: 7(8). Lo, (then) *would I* wander *far off*, (lit. *would I go far off* by wandering)
Pro.22:15. the rod of correction *shall drive it far*
Joel 2:20. *I will remove far off* from you the

רָחֵק [*rāh-ghēhk'*], adj. 7369

Ps. 73:27. *they that are far from thee*

רָחַשׁ *rāh-ghash'*. 7370

* KAL.—*Preterite.* *

Ps. 45: 1(2). My heart *is inditing* (marg. *boileth*, or, *bubbleth up*) a good matter:

7371 **רַהַת** *rah'-ghath*, f.

Isa. 30:24. winnowed *with the shovel*

7372 **רָטַב** [*rāh-tav'*].

* KAL.—*Future*. *

Job 24: 8. *They are wet* with the showers

7373 **רָטֹב** *rāh-tōhv'*, adj.

Job 8:16. He (is) *green* before the sun,

7374 **רֶטֶט** *reh'-tet*, m.

Jer. 49:24. *and fear* hath seized on (her):

7375 **רֻטֲפַשׁ** *roo-tăphash'*.

* *Preterite*. *

Job 33:25. His flesh *shall be fresher* than a child's:

7376 **רָטַשׁ** [*rāh-tash'*].

* PIEL.—*Future*. *

2K. 8:12. *wilt dash* their children,
Isa. 13:18. *shall dash* the young men *to pieces*;

* PUAL.—*Preterite*. *

Hos.10:14. the mother *was dashed in pieces*

PUAL.—*Future*.

Isa. 13:16. Their children also *shall be dashed to pieces*
Hos.13:16(14:1). their infants *shall be dashed in pieces*,
Nah 3:10. her young children also *were dashed in pieces*

7377 **רִי** *ree*, m.

Job 37:11. *by watering* he wearieth the thick cloud:

7378 **רִיב** *reev*.

* KAL.—*Preterite*. *

Gen26:22. another well; and for that *they strove* not:
Nu. 20:13. the children of Israel *strove*
Jud.11:25. Balak the son of Zippor, king of Moab? *did he* ever *strive*
1Sa.25:39. the Lord, that *hath pleaded* the cause
Job 33:13. Why *dost thou strive* against him?
Lam. 3:58. *thou hast pleaded* the causes of my soul;

KAL.—*Infinitive*.

Jud.11:25. did he *ever* strive (lit. *striving* did he strive)
21:22. when their fathers...come unto us *to complain*,
Job 9: 3. If he will *contend* with him,
40: 2. Shall *he that contendeth* (lit. *contending*) with the Almighty
Pro.25: 8. Go not forth hastily *to strive*,
Isa. 3:13. The Lord standeth up *to plead*,
Jer. 50:34. he shall *throughly* plead (lit. *pleading* he shall plead)
Am. 7: 4. the Lord God called *to contend* by fire,

KAL.—*Imperative*.

Ps. 35: 1. *Plead* (my cause), O Lord,
43: 1. Judge me, O God, *and plead* my cause
74:22. O God, *plead* thine own cause:
119:154. *Plead* my cause, and deliver me:
Pro.25: 9. *Debate* thy cause with thy neighbour
Isa. 1:17. *plead* for the widow.
Hos. 2: 2(4). *Plead* with your mother, *plead*:
Mic. 6: 1. *contend thou* before the mountains,

KAL.—*Future*.

Gen26:20. *And* the herdmen of Gerar *did strive*
21. they digged another well, *and strove* for
31:36. Jacob was wroth, *and chode* with Laban:
Ex. 17: 2. *Wherefore* the people *did chide* with
— Why *chide ye* with me?
21:18. if men *strive* together,
Nu. 20: 3. *And* the people *chode* with Moses,
Deu33: 8. (with) *whom thou didst strive*
Jud. 6:31. *Will* ye *plead* for Baal?
— he that *will plead* for him,
— *let him plead* for himself,
32. *Let* Baal *plead* against him,
8: 1. *And they did chide* with him sharply.
1Sa.15: 5. Saul came to a city of Amalek, *and laid wait* (marg. or, *fought*)
24:15(16). and see, *and plead* my cause,
Neh 5: 7. *and I rebuked* the nobles,
13:11. *Then contended I* with the rulers,
17. *Then I contended* with the nobles
25. *And I contended* with them,
Job 10: 2. shew me wherefore *thou contendest with me*.
13: 8. *will ye contend* for God?
19. Who (is) he (that) *will plead* with me?
23: 6. *Will he plead* against me
Ps.103: 9. *He will* not always *chide*:
Pro. 3:30. *Strive* not with a man without cause,
22:23. the Lord *will plead* their cause,
23:11. he *shall plead* their cause
Isa. 27: 8. *thou wilt debate with it*:
49:25. I *will contend* with him that contendeth
50: 8. who *will contend* with me?
51:22. thy God (that) *pleadeth* the cause of
57:16. *I will* not *contend* for ever,
Jer. 2: 9. *I will* yet *plead* with you, saith the Lord, and with your children's children *will I plead*.
29. Wherefore *will ye plead* with me?
12: 1. when *I plead* with thee:
50:34. *he shall* throughly *plead* their cause,
Hos. 4: 4. *let* no man *strive*,
5:13. Ephraim...sent to king *Jareb*: (marg. or, the king (that) *should plead*)
10: 6. a present to king *Jareb*:
Mic. 7: 9. until *he plead* my cause,

KAL.—*Participle*.

Isa. 45: 9. *him that striveth* with his Maker!
Jer. 51:36. I *will plead* thy cause,

* HIPHIL.—*Participle*. *

1Sa. 2:10. *The adversaries* of the Lord
Hos 4: 4. *as they that strive* with the priest.

רִיב *reev*, m. 7379

Gen13: 7. there was *a strife* between the herdmen
Ex. 17: 7. *the chiding of* the children of Israel,
23: 2. neither shalt thou speak in *a cause* to
3. countenance a poor man *in his cause*.
6. wrest the judgment of thy poor *in his cause*.
Deu 1:12. your burden, *and your strife?*
17: 8. If there arise...matters of *controversy*
19:17. between whom *the controversy* (is),
21: 5. by their word shall every *controversy*...be
25: 1. If there be *a controversy* between men,
Jud.12: 2. I and my people were at great *strife*
1Sa.24:15(16). see, and plead *my cause*,
25:39. pleaded *the cause of* my reproach
2Sa.15: 2. any man that had *a controversy*
4. every man which hath any *suit*
22:44. delivered me *from the strivings of*
2Ch 19: 8. of the Lord, *and for controversies*,
10. what *cause* soever shall come to you
Job 13: 6. *and* hearken to *the pleadings of* my lips.
29:16. *and the cause* (which) I knew not
31:13. *when they contended* with me;
35. *mine adversary* (lit. the man of *my strife*)
33:19. (כתיב) *and the multitude of* his bones with
Ps. 18:43(44). delivered me *from the strivings of*
31:20(21). keep them...*from the strife of*
35:23. Stir up thyself,...*unto my cause*,
43: 1. plead *my cause* against an ungodly
55: 9(10). I have seen violence *and strife*
74:22. O God, plead *thine own cause*:
119:154. Plead *my cause*, and deliver me:
Pro.15:18. slow to anger appeaseth *strife*.
17: 1. house full of sacrifices (with) *strife*.
14. leave off *contention*,
18: 6. A fool's lips enter into *contention*,
17. (He that is) first *in his own cause*
20: 3. honour for a man to cease *from strife*:
22:23. the Lord will plead *their cause*,
23:11. he shall plead *their cause*

Pro.25: 9. Debate *thy cause* with thy neighbour
26:17. He that...meddleth with *strife*
21. a contentious man to kindle *strife*.
30:33. the forcing of wrath bringeth forth *strife*.
Isa. 1:23. *neither* doth *the cause of* the widow come
34: 8. year of recompences *for the controversy of*
41:11. they that *strive with thee* (marg. the men of *thy contention*)
21. Produce *your cause*,
58: 4. ye fast *for strife* and debate,
Jer. 11:20. unto thee have I revealed *my cause*.
15:10. a man of *strife* and a man of contention
20:12. unto thee have I opened *my cause*.
25:31. the Lord hath *a controversy* with the
50:34. he shall throughly plead *their cause*,
51:36. I will plead *thy cause*,
Lam. 3:36. To subvert a man *in his cause*,
58. thou hast pleaded *the causes of* my soul;
Eze. 44:24. in *controversy* they shall stand in
Hos 4: 1. the Lord hath *a controversy*
12: 2(3). The Lord hath *also a controversy*
Mic. 6: 2. the Lord's *controversy*,
— the Lord hath *a controversy*
7: 9. until he plead *my cause*,
Hab. 1: 3. there are (that) raise up *strife*

7381 ## רֵיחַ *rēh'ăgh*, m.

Gen. 8:21. the Lord smelled *a sweet savour;*
27:27. he smelled *the smell of* his raiment,
— *the smell of* my son (is) *as the smell of* a
Ex. 5:21. ye have made *our savour* to be abhorred
29:18. *a sweet savour*, an offering made by fire
25. *for a sweet savour* before the Lord:
41. *for a sweet savour*, an offering
Lev. 1: 9. offering made by fire, of *a sweet savour*
13, 17 & 2:2, 9. *a sweet savour* unto the Lord.
2:12. burnt on the altar *for a sweet savour*.
3: 5. an offering...of *a sweet savour*
16. the offering...*for a sweet savour:*
4:31. shall burn (it)...*for a sweet savour*
6:15(8). burn (it) upon the altar (for) *a sweet savour*,
21(14). shalt thou offer (for) *a sweet savour*
8:21. a burnt sacrifice *for a sweet savour*,
28. consecrations *for a sweet savour:*
17: 6. burn the fat *for a sweet savour*
23:13. an offering...(for) *a sweet savour:*
18. an offering...of sweet *savour*
26:31. *the savour of* your sweet odours.
Nu. 15: 3. to make *a sweet savour*
7. the third (part) of an hin of wine, (for) *a sweet savour*
10, 13, 14. made by fire, of *a sweet savour*
24. one young bullock...*for a sweet savour*
18:17. offering made by fire, *for a sweet savour*
28: 2. *a sweet savour* unto me,
6. in mount Sinai *for a sweet savour*,
8, 24. *a sweet savour* unto the Lord.
13. a burnt offering of *a sweet savour*,
27. the burnt offering *for a sweet savour*
29: 2. a burnt offering *for a sweet savour*
6. *for a sweet savour*, a sacrifice
8. a burnt offering...(for) *a sweet savour;*
13, 36. *a sweet savour* unto the Lord;
Job 14: 9. *through the scent of* water
Cant. 1: 3. *Because of the savour of* thy good ointments
12. spikenard sendeth forth *the smell thereof.*
2:13. the vines...give *a* (good) *smell*.
4:10. *and the smell of* thine ointments
11. *and the smell of* thy garments (is) *like the smell of* Lebanon.
7: 8(9). *and the smell of* thy nose like apples;
13(14). The mandrakes give *a smell*,
Jer. 48:11. *and his scent* is not changed.
Eze. 6:13. where they did offer sweet *savour*
16:19. set it before them *for a sweet savour:*
20:28. there also they made their sweet *savour*,
41. I will accept you *with* your sweet *savour*,
Hos 14: 6(7). *and* his *smell* as Lebanon.

7382 ## רֵיחַ *rēh'ăgh*, Ch. m.

Dan 3:27. *nor the smell of* fire had passed on them.

רֵיעַ [*rēh'ăg*], m. 7453

Job 6:27. ye dig (a pit) for *your friend*.

רִיפוֹת *ree-phōhth'*, f. pl. 7383

2Sa. 17:19. spread *ground corn* thereon;
Pro. 27:22. bray a fool in a mortar among *wheat* with a pestle,

---

רִיק *reek*, adj. 7385

Lev. 26:16. ye shall sow your seed *in vain*,
20. your strength shall be spent *in vain:*
Job 39:16. her labour is *in vain* without fear;
Ps. 2: 1. the people imagine *a vain thing?*
4: 2(3). (how long) will ye love *vanity*,
73:13. I have cleansed my heart (in) *vain*,
Isa. 30: 7. the Egyptians shall help in vain, *and to no purpose:*
49: 4. I have laboured *in vain*,
65:23. They shall not labour *in vain*,
Jer. 51:34. he hath made me an *empty* vessel,
58. the people shall labour *in vain*,
Hab. 2:13. shall weary themselves for very *vanity?* (marg. or, *in vain*)

רֵיק & רֵק *rēhk*, adj. 7386

Gen 37:24. the pit (was) *empty*,
41:27. the seven *empty* ears blasted
Deu 32:47. it (is) not a *vain* thing for you;
Jud. 7:16. *empty* pitchers, and lamps
9: 4. Abimelech hired *vain* and light persons,
11: 3. there were gathered *vain men*
2Sa. 6:20. as one of *the vain fellows*
2K. 4: 3. borrow thee vessels...*empty* vessels;
2Ch 13: 7. there are gathered unto him *vain* men,
Neh. 5:13. even thus be he shaken out, *and emptied.* (marg. *empty*, or, *void*)
Pro. 12:11. he that followeth *vain* (persons)
28:19. he that followeth after *vain* (persons)
Isa. 29: 8. and his soul (is) *empty:*
Eze. 24:11. set it *empty* upon the coals

רֵיקָם *rēh-kāhm'*, adv. 7387

Gen 31:42. sent me away now *empty*.
Ex. 3:21. ye shall not go *empty:*
23:15 & 34:20. shall appear before me *empty:*
Deu 15:13. thou shalt not let him go away *empty:*
16:16. they shall not appear...*empty:*
Ru. 1:21. *and* the Lord hath brought me home again *empty:*
3:17. Go not *empty* unto thy mother in law.
1Sa. 6: 3. send it not *empty;*
2Sa. 1:22. the sword of Saul returned not *empty*.
Job 22: 9. Thou hast sent widows away *empty*,
Ps. 7: 4(5). delivered him that *without cause* is
25: 3. them...which transgress *without cause*.
Isa. 55:11. shall not return unto me *void*,
Jer. 14: 3. they returned with their vessels *empty:*
50: 9. none shall return *in vain*.

רִיר *reer*, m. 7388

1Sa. 21:13(14). let *his spittle* fall down upon his
Job 6: 6. is there (any) taste *in the white of* an egg?

רֵישׁ *rēhsh*, m. 7389

Pro. 10:15. destruction of the poor (is) *their poverty*.
13:18. *Poverty* and shame (shall be to) him
24:34. So shall *thy poverty* come

רִישׁ *reesh*, m. 7389

Pro. 28:19. he that followeth after vain (persons) shall have *poverty*
31: 7. Let him drink, and forget *his poverty*,

רִישׁוֹן *ree-shōhn'*, adj. 7223

Job 8: 8. (כתיב) enquire, I pray thee, of the *former*

7390 ## רַךְ *rach*, adj.

Gen18: 7. fetcht a calf *tender* and good,
29:17. Leah (was) *tender* eyed;
33:13. the children (are) *tender*,
Deu20: 8. What man (is there that is) fearful *and faint*hearted?
28:54. the man (that is) *tender* among you,
56. The *tender* and delicate woman
2Sa. 3:39. I (am) this day *weak*, (marg. *tender*) though anointed king;
1Ch 22: 5. Solomon my son (is) young *and tender*,
29: 1. Solomon...(is yet) young *and tender*,
2Ch 13: 7. Rehoboam was young *and tender*hearted,
Job 41: 3(40:27). will he speak *soft* (words) unto
Pro. 4: 3. my father's son, *tender* and only (beloved)
15: 1. A *soft* answer turneth away wrath:
25:15. a *soft* tongue breaketh the bone.
Isa. 47: 1. thou shalt no more be called *tender*
Eze. 17:22. I will crop off...*a tender one*,

7391 ## רֹךְ *rōhch*, m.

Deu 28:56. for delicateness *and tenderness*,

7392 ## רָכַב *rāh-chav'*.

* KAL.—*Preterite.* *

Nu. 22:30. thine ass, upon which *thou hast ridden*
1 Sa.30:17. four hundred young men, which *rode*
Est. 6: 8. the horse that the king *rideth* upon,

KAL.—*Infinitive.*

2Sa.16: 2. The asses (be) for the king's houshold *to ride on*;
2K. 4:24. slack not (thy) *riding* for me,

KAL.—*Imperative.*

Ps. 45: 4(5). in thy majesty *ride* prosperously

KAL.—*Future.*

Gen24:61. *and they rode* upon the camels,
Lev.15: 9. what saddle soever *he rideth* upon
1 Sa.25:42. Abigail hasted,...*and rode* upon an ass,
2Sa.13:29. *and* every man *gat him up* (marg. *rode*)
19:26(27). saddle me an ass, *that I may ride* thereon,
22:11. *And he rode* upon a cherub,
1K. 13:13. saddled him the ass: *and he rode* thereon,
18:45. *And* Ahab *rode*, and went to Jezreel.
2K. 9:16. *So* Jehu *rode in a chariot*,
Ps. 18:10(11). *And he rode* upon a cherub,
Isa. 30:16. *We will ride* upon the swift;
Jer. 6:23. *they ride* upon horses,
50:42. *they shall ride* upon horses,
Hos 14: 3(4). *we will* not *ride* upon horses:
Hab 3: 8. *thou didst ride* upon thine horses

KAL.—*Participle.* Poel.

Gen49:17. *his rider* shall fall backward.
Ex. 15: 1, 21. the horse *and his rider* hath he thrown into the sea.
Nu. 22:22. he was *riding* upon his ass,
Deu33:26. *rideth upon* the heaven
Jud. 5:10. ye *that ride on* white asses,
10: 4. thirty sons *that rode* on thirty ass colts,
12:14. forty sons and thirty nephews, *that rode*
1 Sa.25:20. she *rode* on the ass,
2Sa.18: 9. Absalom *rode* upon a mule,
2K. 9:18. there went one *on* horse*back* (lit. *riding* on a horse)
19. he sent out a second *on* horse*back*,
25. when I and thou *rode* together
18:23. if thou be able...to set *riders* upon
Neh 2:12. the beast *that* I *rode* upon.
Est. 8:10. *riders on* mules, camels, (and) young dromedaries:
14. the posts *that rode upon* mules
Job 39:18. she scorneth the horse *and his rider*.
Ps. 68: 4(5). *him that rideth* upon the heavens
33(34). *To him that rideth* upon the heavens
Isa. 19: 1. the Lord *rideth* upon a swift cloud,
36: 8. if thou be able...to set *riders* upon
Jer. 17:25 & 22:4. *riding* in chariots and on horses,
51:21. with thee will I break in pieces the horse *and his rider*; and with thee will I break in pieces the chariot *and his rider*;
Eze.23: 6, 12. horsemen *riding upon* horses.
23 & 38:15. all of them *riding upon* horses.
Am. 2:15. *neither* shall *he that rideth* the horse
Hag 2:22. the chariots, *and those that ride in them*, and the horses *and their riders*
Zec. 1: 8. a man *riding* upon a red horse,
9: 9. lowly, *and riding* upon an ass,
10: 5. *the riders on* horses shall be confounded.
12: 4. smite every horse...*and his rider*

* HIPHIL.—*Preterite.* *

1K. 1:33. *and cause* Solomon my son *to ride*
Est. 6: 9. *and bring him* (marg. *cause him to ride*) on horseback through the street
Ps. 66:12. *Thou hast caused* men *to ride* over
Isa. 58:14. *and I will cause thee to ride*

HIPHIL.—*Imperative.*

2K. 13:16. *Put* thine hand (marg. *Make* thine hand *to ride*) upon the bow.

HIPHIL.—*Future.*

Gen41:43. *And he made him to ride* in the second
Ex. 4:20. Moses took his wife and his sons, *and set them* (lit. *and made them ride*) upon an
Deu 32:13. *He made him ride* on the high places
2Sa. 6: 3. *And they set* (marg. *made to ride*) the ark of God
1K. 1:38. *and caused* Solomon *to ride*
44. *and they have caused* him *to ride*
2K. 9:28. *And* his servants *carried him* (lit. *and made him to ride*) in a chariot
10:16. *So they made* him *ride*
13:16. *And he put* his hand (upon it):
23:30. *And* his servants *carried him* (lit. *and made him ride*) in a chariot
1Ch 13: 7. *And they carried* the ark (marg. *made* the ark *to ride*) of God
2Ch 35:24. *and put him* (lit. *and made him ride*) in the second chariot
Est. 6:11. *and brought him on horseback*
Job 30:22. *thou causest me to ride*
Hos.10:11. *I will make* Ephraim *to ride*;

רֶכֶב *reh'-chev*, com. 7393

Gen50: 9. there went up with him both *chariots* and
Ex. 14: 6. he made ready *his chariot*,
7. he took six hundred chosen *chariots*, and all the *chariots of* Egypt,
9. horses (and) *chariots of* Pharaoh,
17. I will get me honour...*upon his chariots*.
18. when I have gotten me honour...*upon his chariots*,
23. all Pharaoh's horses, *his chariots*,
26. upon *their chariots*, and upon their
28. waters returned, and covered *the chariots*,
15:19. Pharaoh went in *with his chariots*
Deu 11: 4. unto their horses, *and to their chariots*;
20: 1. When thou goest out to battle...and seest horses, *and chariots*,
24: 6. the nether *or the upper millstone*
Jos. 11: 4. horses *and chariots* very many.
17:16. *and* all the Canaanites...have *chariots of*
18. though they have iron *chariots*,
24: 6. the Egyptians pursued...*with chariots*
Jud. 1:19. they had *chariots of* iron.
4: 3. he had nine hundred *chariots of* iron;
7. draw unto thee...Sisera,...with *his chariots*
13. Sisera gathered together all *his chariots*, (even) nine hundred *chariots of* iron,
15. the Lord discomfited Sisera, and all (his) *chariots*,
16. Barak pursued after *the chariots*,
5:28. Why is *his chariot* (so) long in coming?
9:53. certain woman cast a piece of *a millstone*
1Sa. 8:12. instruments of *his chariots*.
13: 5. thirty thousand *chariots*,
2Sa. 1: 6. *the chariots* and horsemen followed hard
8: 4. David houghed all *the chariot* (horses), but reserved of them (for) an hundred *chariots*.
10:18. seven hundred *chariots of* the Syrians,
11:21. a woman cast a piece of *a millstone*
1K. 1: 5. he prepared him *chariots* and horsemen,
9:19. cities for his *chariots*, and cities for his
22. rulers of *his chariots*,
10:26. Solomon gathered together *chariots*

1K. 10:26. had a thousand and four hundred *chariots*,
— bestowed in the cities for *chariots*,
16: 9. Zimri, captain of half (his) *chariots*,
20: 1. thirty and two kings with him, and horses, *and chariots :*
21. of Israel...smote the horses and *chariots*,
25. horse for horse, *and chariot for chariot :*
22:31. captains that had rule over his *chariots*,
32. when the captains of *the chariots* saw
33. when the captains of *the chariots* perceived
35. ran out...into the midst of *the chariot*.
38. (one) washed *the chariot*
2K. 2:11. (there appeared) *a chariot of* fire,
12. *the chariot of* Israel, and the horsemen
5: 9. Naaman came with his horses *and with his chariot*,
6:14. sent he thither horses, *and chariots*,
15. the city both with horses *and chariots*.
17. mountain (was) full of horses *and chariots*
7: 6. a noise of *chariots*, and a noise of horses,
14. They took therefore two *chariot* horses ;
8:21. went over to Zair, and all *the chariots*
— the captains of *the chariots :*
9:21. *his chariot* was made ready.
— went out, each *in his chariot*,
24. he sunk down *in his chariot*.
10: 2. (there are) with you *chariots* and horses,
16. they made him ride *in his chariot*.
13: 7. fifty horsemen, and ten *chariots*,
14. *the chariot of* Israel, and the horsemen
18:24. put thy trust on Egypt *for chariots*
19:23. (כתיב) *With the multitude of* (lit. according to כ׳ *with the chariot of*)
— With the multitude of *my chariots* I am
1Ch 18: 4. David took...a thousand *chariots*,
— also houghed all *the chariot* (horses), but reserved of them an hundred *chariots*.
19: 6. *chariots* and horsemen out of Mesopotamia,
7. hired thirty and two thousand *chariots*,
18. seven thousand (men which fought in) *chariots*,
2Ch 1:14. Solomon gathered *chariots* and horsemen: and he had a thousand and four hundred *chariots*,
— which he placed in the *chariot* cities ;
8: 6. all the *chariot* cities,
9. captains of *his chariots*
9:25. bestowed in the *chariot* cities,
12: 3. twelve hundred *chariots*,
16: 8. very many *chariots* and horsemen ?
18:30. the captains of *the chariots* that (were)
31. when the captains of *the chariots* saw
32. when the captains of *the chariots* perceived
21: 9. all his *chariots* with him:
— the captains of *the chariots*.
35:24. put him in *the* second *chariot*
Ps. 20: 7(8). Some (trust) *in chariots*,
68:17(18). *The chariots of* God (are) twenty
76: 6(7). *both the chariot* and horse are cast
Cant 1: 9. company of horses in Pharaoh's *chariots*.
Isa. 21: 7. *a chariot* (with) a couple of horsemen, *a chariot of* asses, (and) *a chariot of*
9. here cometh *a chariot of* men,
22: 6. Elam bare the quiver *with chariots*
7. choicest valleys shall be full of *chariots*,
31: 1. Woe to them that...trust in *chariots*,
36: 9. put thy trust on Egypt *for chariots*
37:24. By the multitude of *my chariots* am I
43:17. Which bringeth forth *the chariot* and
66:20. upon horses, *and in chariots*, and in litters, and upon mules,
Jer. 17:25. kings...riding *in chariots*
22: 4. kings...riding *in chariots*
46: 9. rage, *ye chariots ;*
47: 3. the rushing *of his chariots*,
50:37. A sword...upon *their chariots*,
51:21. with thee will I break in pieces *the chariot*
Eze.23:24. come against thee with chariots, *wagons*,
26: 7. with horses, *and with chariots*, and with
10. of the wheels, *and of the chariots*,
39:20. ye shall be filled...with horses *and chariots*,
Dan 11:40. the king of the north shall come...*with chariots*,
Nah. 2: 3(4). *the chariots* (shall be) with flaming
4(5). *The chariots* shall rage
13(14). I will burn *her chariots*
Zec. 9:10. I will cut off *the chariot*

רַכָּב *rak-kāhv'*, m. 7395

1K. 22:34. he said *unto the driver of his chariot*,
2K. 9:17. Joram said, Take *an horseman*,
2Ch 18:33. he said *to* (his) *chariot man*,

רִכְבָּה *rĭch-bāh'*, f. 7396

Eze.27:20. merchant in precious clothes *for chariots*.

רְכוּב *[r'choov]*, m. 7398

Ps.104: 3. who maketh the clouds *his chariot :*

רְכוּשׁ *r'choosh*, m. 7399

Gen12: 5. all *their substance* that they had gathered,
13: 6. *their substance* was great,
14:11. they took all *the goods of* Sodom
12. and *his goods*, and departed.
16. he brought back all *the goods*, and also brought again his brother Lot, *and his goods*,
21. *and* take *the goods* to thyself.
15:14. shall they come out *with* great *substance*.
31:18. all *his goods* which he had gotten
36: 7. *their riches* were more than that they might dwell
46: 6. they took their cattle, and *their goods*.
Nu. 16:32. all the men that (appertained) unto Korah, and all (their) *goods*.
35: 3. for their cattle, *and for their goods*,
1Ch 27:31. the rulers of *the substance*
28: 1. the stewards over all *the substance*
2Ch 20:25. *both riches* with the dead bodies, and precious jewels,
21:14. thy children, and thy wives, and all *thy goods :*
17. all *the substance* that was found
31: 3. the king's portion of *his substance*
32:29. God had given him *substance* very much.
35: 7. *of the* king's *substance*.
Ezr. 1: 4. with silver, and with gold, *and with goods*,
6. with vessels of silver, with gold, *with goods*,
8:21. our little ones, and for all *our substance*.
10: 8. all *his substance* should be forfeited,
Dan 11:13. with a great army *and with* much *riches*.
24. he shall scatter...the prey, and spoil, *and riches :*
28. shall he return into his land *with* great *riches ;*

רָכִיל *rāh-cheel'*, m. 7400

Lev. 19:16. *a talebearer* among thy people:
Pro.11:13. *A talebearer* (marg. He that walketh, (being) *a talebearer*) revealeth secrets:
20:19. He that goeth about (as) *a talebearer*
Jer. 6:28. walking with *slanders :*
9: 4(3). every neighbour will walk with *slanders*.
Eze.22: 9. In thee are men that *carry tales* (marg. of *slanders*)

רָכַךְ *[rāh-chach']*. 7401

* KAL.—*Preterite.* *

2K. 22:19. Because thine heart *was tender*,
2Ch 34:27. Because thine heart *was tender*.
Ps. 55:21(22). his words *were softer* than oil

* NIPHAL.—*Future.* *

Deu 20: 3. *let* not your hearts *faint* (marg. *be tender*), fear not,
Isa. 7: 4. neither *be faint*hearted (marg. *let* not thy heart *be tender*)
Jer. 51:46. lest your heart *faint*,

* PUAL.—*Preterite.* *

Isa. 1: 6. neither *mollified* with ointment.

* HIPHIL.—*Preterite.* *

Job 23:16. God *maketh* my heart *soft*,

7402 רָכַל [*rāh-chal'*].

* KAL.—*Participle.* Poel. *

1K. 10:15. the traffick of *the spice merchants,*
Neh 3:31. the place of the Nethinims, *and of the merchants,*
32. the goldsmiths *and the merchants.*
13:20. *the merchants*...lodged without Jerusalem
Cant. 3: 6. all powders of *the merchant?*
Eze. 17: 4. a city of *merchants.*
27: 3. *a merchant of* the people
13. Javan, Tubal, and Meshech,...*thy merchants:*
15. The men of Dedan (were) *thy merchants;*
17. and the land of Israel,...*thy merchants:*
20. Dedan (was) *thy merchant*
22. *The merchants of* Sheba and Raamah, they (were) *thy merchants:*
23. *the merchants of* Sheba, Asshur, (and) Chilmad, (were) *thy merchants.*
24. *thy merchants* in all sorts
Nah 3:16. Thou hast multiplied *thy merchants*

7404 רְכֻלָּה [*r'chool-lāh'*], f.

Eze. 26:12. make a prey of *thy merchandise:*
28: 5. *by thy traffick* hast thou increased
16. the multitude of *thy merchandise*
18. the iniquity of *thy traffick;*

7405 רָכַס [*rāh-chas'*].

* KAL.—*Future.* *

Ex. 28:28. *And they shall bind* the breastplate
39:21. *And they did bind* the breastplate

7407 רֹכֶס [*rōh'-ches*], m.

Ps. 31:20(21). hide them...*from the pride of* man:

7406 רְכָסִים *r'chāh-seem'*, m. pl.

Isa. 40: 4. *and the rough places* plain:

7408 רָכַשׁ *rāh-chash'*.

* KAL.—*Preterite.* *

Gen12: 5. all their substance that *they had gathered,*
31:18. all his goods which *he had gotten,* the cattle...which *he had gotten*
36: 6. his substance, which *he had got*
46: 6. their goods, which *they had gotten*

7409 רֶכֶשׁ *reh'-chesh*, m.

1K. 4:28(5:8). *and dromedaries* (marg. or, *mules,* or, *swift beasts*) brought they
Est. 8:10. riders *on mules,* camels,
14. the posts that rode *upon mules*
Mic. 1:13. bind the chariot *to the swift beast:*

7411 רָמָה *rāh-māh'*.

* KAL.—*Preterite.* *

Ex. 15: 1, 21. the horse and his rider *hath he thrown*

KAL.—*Participle.* Poel.

Ps. 78: 9. children of Ephraim,...*carrying* (marg. *throwing forth*) bows,
Jer. 4:29. the noise of the horsemen *and bowmen;* (lit. *that cast with* the bow)

* PIEL.—*Preterite.* *

Gen29:25. wherefore then *hast thou beguiled me?*
Jos. 9:22. Wherefore *have ye beguiled* us,
1Sa. 19:17. Why *hast thou deceived me* so,
28:12. Why *hast thou deceived me?*
2Sa. 19:26(27). my servant *deceived me:*
Pro. 26:19. the man (that) *deceiveth* his neighbour,
Lam. 1:19. I called for my lovers, (but) they *deceived me:*

PIEL.—*Infinitive.*

1Ch 12:17. *to betray me* to mine enemies,

רָמָה *rāh-māh'*, f. 7413

Jud. 15:17. called that place *Ramath*-lehi. (marg. *The lifting up of* the jawbone, or, *casting away of* the jawbone)
Eze. 16:24. hast made thee *an high place*
25. Thou hast built *thy high place*
31. *and* makest *thine high place*
39. shall break down *thy high places:*

רְמָה [*r'māh*], Ch. 7412

* P'AL.—*Preterite.* *

Dan 3:24. *Did* not *we cast* three men bound
6:16(17). they brought Daniel, *and cast* (him)
24(25). *they cast* (them) into the den of

P'AL.—*Infinitive.*

Ezr. 7:24. it shall not be lawful *to impose* toll,
Dan 3:20. (and) *to cast* (them) into the burning

P'AL.—*Participle.* Passive.

Dan 3:21. *and were cast* into the midst of the
7: 9. till the thrones *were cast down,*

* ITHP'EL.—*Future.* *

Dan 3: 6. *shall* the same hour *be cast* into the
11. *he should be cast* into the midst
15. *ye shall be cast* the same hour into
6: 7(8). *he shall be cast* into the den of lions.
12(13). *shall be cast* into the den of lions?

רִמָּה *rim-māh'*, f. 7415

Ex. 16:24. *neither* was there *any worm* therein.
Job 7: 5. My flesh is clothed *with worms*
17:14. I have said...*to the worm,*
21:26. *and the worms* shall cover them.
24:20. *the worm* shall feed sweetly
25: 6. man, (that is) *a worm?*
Isa. 14:11. *the worm* is spread under thee,

רִמּוֹן *rim-mōhn'*, m. 7416

Ex. 28:33. upon the hem of it thou shalt make *pomegranates of*
34. A golden bell *and a pomegranate,* a golden bell *and a pomegranate,*
39:24. made upon the hems...*pomegranates of*
25. put the bells between *the pomegranates*
— round about between *the pomegranates;*
26. A bell *and a pomegranate,* a bell *and a pomegranate,*
Nu. 13:23. (they brought) of *the pomegranates,*
20: 5. of vines, *or of pomegranates;*
Deu 8: 8. A land of wheat,...*and pomegranates;*
1Sa. 14: 2. Saul tarried...under *a pomegranate tree*
1K. 7:18. cover the chapiters...with *pomegranates:*
20. *and the pomegranates* (were) two hundred
42. four hundred *pomegranates*
— two rows of *pomegranates*
2K. 25:17. *and pomegranates* upon the chapiter
2Ch 3:16. made an hundred *pomegranates,*
4:13. four hundred *pomegranates*
— two rows of *pomegranates*
Cant. 4: 3. temples (are) like a piece of *a pomegranate*
13. an orchard of *pomegranates,*
6: 7. a piece of *a pomegranate*
11. *the pomegranates* budded.
7:12(13). *the pomegranates* bud forth:
8: 2. the juice of *my pomegranate.*
Jer. 52:22. *and pomegranates* upon the chapiters
— second pillar also *and the pomegranates*
23. ninety and six *pomegranates* on a side; (and) all *the pomegranates* upon the
Joel 1:12. *the pomegranate tree,* the palm tree
Hag. 2:19. *the pomegranate,* and the olive tree,

רָמוּת [*rāh-mooth'*], f. 7419

Eze. 32: 5. fill the valleys with *thy height.*

רֹמַח *rōh'-magh*, m. 7420

Nu. 25: 7. took *a javelin* in his hand;
Jud. 5: 8. was there a shield *or spear* seen

1K. 18:28. cut themselves...with knives *and lancets,*
1Ch 12: 8. that could handle shield *and buckler,*
24. The children of Judah that bare shield *and spear*
2Ch 11:12. every several city... shields *and spears,*
14: 8(7). (of men) that bare targets *and spears,*
25: 5. thousand...that could handle *spear*
26:14. throughout all the host shields, *and spears,*
Neh 4:13(7). with their swords, *their spears,*
16(10). held *both the spears,* the shields,
21(15). half of them held *the spears*
Jer. 46: 4. furbish *the spears,*
Eze.39: 9. the handstaves, *and the spears,*
Joel 3:10(4:10). your pruninghooks into *spears*

7423 רְמִיָּה *r'meey-yāh'*, f.

Job 13: 7. talk *deceitfully* for him?
27: 4. nor my tongue utter *deceit.*
Ps. 32: 2. in whose spirit (there is) no *guile.*
52: 2(4). Thy tongue...like a sharp razor, working *deceitfully.*
78:57. were turned aside like a *deceitful* bow.
101: 7. He that worketh *deceit* shall not dwell
120: 2. Deliver my soul,...from a *deceitful*
3. what shall be done unto thee, thou *false*
Pro. 10: 4. He...that dealeth (with) a *slack* hand:
12:24. *but the slothful* (marg. or, *deceitful*) shall be under tribute.
27. *The slothful* (man) roasteth not
19:15. an *idle* soul shall suffer hunger.
Jer 48:10. doeth the work of the Lord *deceitfully,* (marg. or, *negligently*)
Hos 7:16. they are like a *deceitful* bow:
Mic. 6:12. their tongue (is) *deceitful* in their mouth.

7424 רַמָּךְ [*ram-māch'*], f.

Est. 8:10. mules, camels, (and) young *dromedaries:*

7426 רָמַם [*rāh-mam'*].

* KAL.—*Preterite.* *

Job 24:24. *They are exalted* for a little while,

KAL.—*Participle.* Poel.

Ps.118:16. The right hand of the Lord *is exalted:*

* NIPHAL.—*Imperative.* *

Nu. 16:45(17:10). *Get you up* from among this

NIPHAL.—*Future.*

Isa. 33:10. now *will I be exalted;*
Eze.10:15. *And* the cherubims *were lifted up.*
17. (these) *lifted up themselves* (also):
19. lifted up their wings, *and mounted up*

7427 רֹמֵמוּת *rōh-mēh-mooth'*, f.

Isa. 33: 3. *at the lifting up of thyself*

7429 רָמַס *rāh-mas'*.

* KAL.—*Preterite.* *

Mic. 5: 8(7). *both treadeth down,* and teareth in

KAL.—*Infinitive.*

Isa. 1:12. *to tread* my courts?

KAL.—*Imperative.*

Nah. 3:14. *and tread* the morter,

KAL.—*Future.*

2K. 7:17. *and* the people *trode upon him*
20. *for* the people *trode upon* him
9:33. *and he trode her* under foot.
14: 9. there passed by a wild beast...*and trode down* the thistle.
2Ch 25:18. there passed by a wild beast...*and trode down* the thistle.
Ps. 7: 5(6). *yea, let him tread down* my life
91:13. the dragon *shalt thou trample under feet.*
Isa. 26: 6. The foot *shall tread it down,*
41:25. as the potter *treadeth* clay.
63: 3. *and trample them* in my fury;
Eze.26:11. *shall he tread down* all thy streets:
34:18. *ye must tread down* with your feet
Dan 8: 7. cast him down...*and stamped upon him:*
10. down (some) of the host...*and stamped upon them.*

KAL.—*Participle.* Poel.

Isa. 16: 4. *the oppressors* (marg. *treaders down*) are consumed out of the land.

* NIPHAL.—*Future.* *

Isa. 28: 3. drunkards of Ephraim, *shall be trodden*

רָמַשׂ [*rāh-mas'*]. 7430

* KAL.—*Future.* *

Gen. 9: 2. all that *moveth* (upon) the earth,
Lev. 20:25. thing that *creepeth* (marg. or, *moveth*)
Ps. 104:20. all the beasts of the forest *do creep* (marg. thereof *do trample on* the forest)

KAL.—*Participle.* Poel.

Gen. 1:21. every living creature *that moveth,*
26. every creeping thing *that creepeth*
28. living thing *that moveth* (marg. *creepeth*)
30 & 7:8. every thing *that creepeth* upon the
7:14. every creeping thing *that creepeth*
21. all flesh died *that moved* upon the earth,
8:17. of every creeping thing *that creepeth*
19. whatsoever *creepeth* upon the earth,
Lev.11:44. manner of creeping thing *that creepeth*
46. living creature *that moveth*
Deu 4:18. The likeness of any thing *that creepeth*
Ps. 69:34(35). thing *that moveth* (marg. *creepeth*)
Eze.38:20. all creeping things *that creep*

רֶמֶשׂ *reh'-mes*, m. 7431

Gen. 1:24. cattle, *and creeping thing,*
25. every thing *that creepeth*
26. every *creeping thing* that creepeth
6: 7. *the creeping thing,* and the fowls of the
20. every *creeping thing of* the earth
7:14. every *creeping thing* that creepeth
23. *the creeping things,* and the fowl
8:17. *every creeping thing,* that creepeth
19. Every beast, every *creeping thing,*
9: 3. Every *moving thing* that liveth
1K. 4:33(5:13). he spake also of...*creeping things,*
Ps.104:25. *things creeping* innumerable,
148:10. *creeping things,* and flying fowl:
Eze. 8:10. every form of *creeping things,*
38:20. all *creeping things* that creep
Hos. 2:18(20). *and* (with) *the creeping things of* the ground:
Hab. 1:14. *as the creeping* (marg. or, *moving*) *things,* (that have) no ruler

רֹן [*rōhn*], m. 7438

Ps. 32: 7. shalt compass me about with *songs of*

רָנָה [*rāh-nāh'*]. 7439

* KAL.—*Future.* *

Job 39:23. The quiver *rattleth* against him,

רִנָּה *rin-nāh'*, f. 7440

1K. 8:28. to hearken unto *the cry* and to the prayer,
22:36. there went *a proclamation* throughout the
2Ch 6:19. hearken unto *the cry* and the prayer
20:22. they began *to sing* (marg. *in singing*)
Ps. 17: 1. attend unto *my cry,*
30: 5(6). but *joy* (marg. *singing*) (cometh) in the morning.
42: 4(5). the voice of *joy* and praise,
47: 1(2). unto God with the voice of *triumph.*
61: 1(2). Hear *my cry,* O God;
88: 2(3). incline thine ear *unto my cry;*
105:43. brought forth...his chosen *with gladness:*
106:44. he heard *their cry:*
107:22. his works *with rejoicing.* (marg. *singing*)
118:15. The voice of *rejoicing* and salvation

Ps.119:169. Let *my cry* come near before thee,
126: 2. Then was...our tongue with *singing:*
5. They that sow in tears shall reap *in joy.* (marg. or, *singing*)
6. doubtless come again *with rejoicing,*
142: 6(7). Attend unto *my cry;*
Pro. 11:10. the wicked perish, (there is) *shouting.*
Isa. 14: 7. they break forth into *singing.*
35:10. come to Zion *with songs*
43:14. the Chaldeans, *whose cry* (is) in the ships.
44:23. break forth into *singing,*
48:20. with a voice of *singing* declare
49:13. break forth into *singing,*
51:11. come *with singing* unto Zion;
54: 1. break forth into *singing,* and cry aloud,
55:12. the hills shall break forth...into *singing,*
Jer. 7:16. neither lift up *cry* nor prayer
11:14. neither lift up *a cry* or prayer
14:12. I will not hear *their cry;*
Zep 3:17. he will joy over thee *with singing.*

רָנַן [*rāh-nan'*]. 7442, 7444

* KAL.—*Infinitive.* *

Job 38: 7. *When* the morning stars *sang* together,

KAL.—*Imperative.*

Isa. 12: 6. Cry out *and shout,* thou inhabitant of
44:23. *Sing,* O ye heavens;
49:13. *Sing,* O heavens;
54: 1. *Sing,* O barren,
Jer. 31: 7. *Sing* with gladness for Jacob,
Lam. 2:19. Arise, *cry out* in the night:
Zep 3:14. *Sing,* O daughter of Zion;
Zec. 2:10(14). *Sing* and rejoice, O daughter of Zion:

KAL.—*Future.*

Lev. 9:24. when all the people saw, *they shouted,*
Ps. 35:27. *Let them shout for joy,* and be glad,
Pro. 1:20. Wisdom *crieth* without;
8: 3. *She crieth* at the gates,
29: 6. the righteous *doth sing* and rejoice.
Isa. 24:14. *they shall sing* for the majesty of the Lord,
35: 6. *and* the tongue of the dumb *sing:*
42:11. *let* the inhabitants of the rock *sing,*
61: 7. *they shall rejoice* in their portion:
65:14. my servants *shall sing* for joy of heart,

* PIEL.—*Preterite.* *

Jer. 31:12. they shall come *and sing* in the height of
51:48. *Then* the heaven and the earth,...*shall sing*

PIEL.—*Infinitive.*

Ps.132:16. her saints shall shout *aloud for joy.* (lit. *shouting* shall shout)
Isa. 35: 2. rejoice even with joy *and singing:*

PIEL.—*Imperative.*

Ps. 33: 1. *Rejoice* in the Lord, O ye righteous:
98: 4. *and rejoice,* and sing praise.
Isa. 26:19. Awake *and sing,* ye that dwell in dust:
52: 9. *sing* together, ye waste places

PIEL.—*Future.*

1Ch 16:33. Then *shall* the trees of the wood *sing out*
Ps. 5:11(12). *let them* ever *shout for joy,*
20: 5(6). *We will rejoice* in thy salvation,
51:14(16). my tongue *shall sing aloud*
59:16(17). *yea, I will sing aloud* of thy mercy
63: 7(8). the shadow of thy wings *will I rejoice.*
67: 4(5). let the nations be glad *and sing for joy:*
71:23. My lips *shall greatly rejoice*
84: 2(3). my heart and my flesh *crieth out*
89:12(13). Tabor and Hermon *shall rejoice*
90:14. *that we may rejoice* and be glad
92: 4(5). *I will triumph* in the works
95: 1. *let us sing* unto the Lord:
96:12. then *shall* all the trees of the wood *rejoice*
98: 8. *let* the hills *be joyful* together
132: 9. *let* thy saints *shout for joy.*
16. her saints *shall shout* aloud *for joy.*
145: 7. *shall sing* of thy righteousness.
149: 5. *let them sing aloud* upon their beds.
Isa. 52: 8. with the voice together *shall they sing:*

* PUAL.—*Future.* *

Isa. 16:10. *there shall be* no *singing,*

* HIPHIL.—*Imperative.* *

Deu32:43. *Rejoice* (marg. or, *Sing ye,* or, *Praise*), O ye nations,
Ps. 32:11. *and shout for joy,* all (ye that are) upright
81: 1(2). *Sing aloud* unto God

HIPHIL.—*Future.*

Job 29:13. *I caused* the widow's heart *to sing for joy.*
Ps. 65: 8(9). *thou makest* the outgoings of the morning...*to rejoice.* (marg. or, *sing*)

* HITHPOLEL.—*Participle.* *

Ps. 78:65. like a mighty man *that shouteth*

רְנָנָה *r'nāh-nāh',* f. 7445

Job 3: 7. let no *joyful voice* come therein.
20: 5. *the triumphing of* the wicked (is) short,
Ps. 63: 5(6). my mouth shall praise (thee) with *joyful* lips:
100: 2. come before his presence *with singing.*

רְנָנִים *r'nāh-neem',* m. pl. 7443

Job 39:13. (Gavest thou) the *goodly* wings unto the [prob. lit. *ostriches*]

רְסִיסִים [*r'see-seem'*], m. pl. 7447

Cant. 5: 2. my head is filled with dew, (and) my locks *with the drops of* the night.

רְסִיסִים *r'see-seem',* m. pl. 7447

Am. 6:11. he will smite the great house *with breaches,* (marg. or, *droppings*)

רֶסֶן *reh'-sen,* m. 7448

Job 30:11. they have *also* let loose *the bridle*
41:13(5). who can come (to him) with *his* double *bridle?*
Ps. 32: 9. mouth must be held in with bit *and bridle,*
Isa. 30:28. *and...a bridle* in the jaws of the people,

רָסַס [*rāh-sas'*]. 7450

* KAL.—*Infinitive.* *

Eze. 46:14. the third part of an hin of oil, *to temper* (lit. *moisten*)

רַע *ra'g,* adj. 7451

Gen 2: 9. the tree of knowledge of good *and evil.*
17. the tree of the knowledge of good *and evil,*
3: 5. as gods, knowing good *and evil.*
22. to know good *and evil:*
6: 5. God saw that *the wickedness of* man
— every imagination...of his heart (was) only *evil*
8:21. the imagination of man's heart (is) *evil*
13:13. the men of Sodom (were) *wicked*
19:19. lest *some evil* take me, and I die:
24:50. we cannot speak unto thee *bad* or good.
26:29. That thou wilt do us no *hurt,*
28: 8. the daughters of Canaan pleased not (marg. (were) *evil* in the eyes) Isaac
31:24. speak not to Jacob either good or *bad.*
29. in the power of my hand to do you *hurt*
— speak not to Jacob either good or *bad.*
52. that thou shalt not pass over...*for harm.*
37: 2. brought unto his father their *evil* report.
20. Some *evil* beast hath devoured him:
33. an *evil* beast hath devoured him;
38: 7. Er,...was *wicked* in the sight of the Lord;
39: 9. how then can I do this great *wickedness,*
40: 7. Wherefore look ye (so) *sadly* (marg. (are) your faces *evil*)
41: 3. seven other kine...*ill* favoured
4. the *ill* favoured and leanfleshed kine
19. came up after them, poor *and* very *ill*
20. the lean *and* the *ill favoured* kine
21. they (were) still *ill* favoured,
27. the seven thin *and ill favoured* kine
44: 4. Wherefore have ye rewarded *evil* for good?

Gen 44:29. bring down my gray hairs *with sorrow*
34. lest...I see *the evil* that shall come
47: 9. few *and evil* have the days of the years
48:16. The Angel which redeemed me from all *evil*,
50:15. *the evil* which we did unto him.
17. they did unto thee *evil:*
20. ye thought *evil* against me;
Ex. 5:19. they (were) *in evil* (case),
10:10. *evil* (is) before you.
21: 8. If she please not (marg. be *evil* in the eyes of)
23: 2. Thou shalt not follow a multitude *to* (do) *evil;*
32:12. *For mischief* did he bring them out,
— repent of this *evil*
14. *the evil* which he thought to do
22. they (are set) *on mischief.*
33: 4. when the people heard these *evil* tidings,
Lev. 26: 6. I will rid *evil* beasts out of
27:10. nor change it, a good *for a bad*, or *a bad*
12, 14. whether it be good or *bad:*
33. whether it be good *or bad*,
Nu. 11: 1. it displeased (marg. it was *evil* in the ears of) the Lord:
15. let me not see *my wretchedness.*
13:19. whether it (be) good or *bad;*
14:27. (with) this *evil* congregation,
35. all this *evil* congregation,
37. did bring up the *evil* report
20: 5. to bring us in unto this *evil* place?
24:13. to do (either) good or *bad* of mine own
32:13. the generation, that had done *evil*
35:23. not his enemy, neither sought *his harm*
Deu 1:35. these men of this *evil* generation
39. no knowledge between good *and evil*,
4:25. do *evil* in the sight of the Lord
6:22. signs and wonders, great *and sore*, (marg. *evil*)
7:15. the *evil* diseases of Egypt,
9:18. doing *wickedly* in the sight of
13: 5(6). put *the evil* away
11(12). do no more any such *wickedness* (lit. *wicked* thing)
15:21. (or have) any *ill* blemish,
17: 1. blemish, (or) any *evil*favouredness:
2. hath wrought *wickedness* in the sight of
5. have committed that *wicked* thing,
7. put *the evil* away from among you.
12. put away *the evil* from Israel.
19:19. put *the evil* away from among you.
20. commit no more any such *evil* (lit. *evil* thing)
21:21. so shalt thou put *evil* away
22:14. bring up an *evil* name upon her,
19. brought up an *evil* name
21. put *evil* away from among you.
22. so shalt thou put away *evil*
24. thou shalt put away *evil*
23: 9(10). keep thee from every *wicked* thing.
24: 7. put *evil* away from among you.
28:35. a *sore* botch that cannot be healed,
59. *sore* sicknesses, and of long continuance.
29:21(20). the Lord shall separate him *unto evil*
30:15. life and good, and death and *evil;*
31:17. many *evils* and troubles shall befall them;
— Are not these *evils* come upon us,
18. *the evils* which they shall have wrought,
21. when many *evils* and troubles are befallen
29. *evil* will befall you
— ye will do *evil* in the sight of the Lord,
32:23. I will heap *mischiefs* upon them;
Jos. 23:15. the Lord bring upon you all *evil* things,
Jud. 2:11. the children of Israel did *evil*
15. the hand of the Lord was against them *for evil*,
3: 7. did *evil* in the sight of the Lord,
12. did *evil* again in the sight of the Lord:
— they had done *evil* in the sight of the
4: 1. the children of Israel again did *evil*
6: 1. the children of Israel did *evil*
9:23. God sent an *evil* spirit
56. God rendered *the wickedness of* Abimelech,
57. all *the evil of* the men of Shechem
10: 6. did *evil* again in the sight of the Lord,
11:27. thou doest me *wrong* to war
13: 1. did *evil* again in the sight of the Lord;

Jud. 15: 3. though I do them *a displeasure.*
20: 3. Tell (us), how was this *wickedness?*
12. What *wickedness* (is) this that is done
13. put away *evil* from Israel.
34. they knew not that *evil* (was) near
41. *evil* was come upon them.
1Sa. 2:23. I hear of your *evil* dealings
6: 9. he hath done us this great *evil:*
10;19. saved you out of all *your adversities*
12:17. see that *your wickedness* (is) great,
19. we have added unto all our sins (this) *evil*,
20. ye have done all this *wickedness:*
15:19. didst *evil* in the sight of the Lord?
16:14. an *evil* spirit from the Lord
15. an *evil* spirit from God
16. the *evil* spirit from God
23. and the *evil* spirit departed
18:10. the *evil* spirit from God
19: 9. the *evil* spirit from the Lord
20: 7. *evil* is determined by him.
9. if I knew...that *evil* were determined
13. if it please my father (to do) thee *evil*,
23: 9. Saul secretly practised *mischief*
24: 9(10). David seeketh *thy hurt?*
11(12). neither *evil* nor transgression
17(18). I have rewarded thee *evil.*
25: 3. the man (was) churlish *and evil in*
17. *evil* is determined against our master,
21. he hath requited me *evil* for good.
26. they that seek *evil* to my lord,
28. *and evil* hath not been found
39. hath kept his servant *from evil:* for the Lord hath returned *the wickedness of*
26:18. what *evil* (is) in mine hand?
29: 6. I have not found *evil* in thee
7. that thou displease not (marg. do not *evil* in the eyes of) the lords
30:22. Then answered all the *wicked* men
2Sa. 3:39. reward the doer of *evil according to his wickedness.*
12: 9. to do *evil* in his sight?
11. I will raise up *evil* against thee
18. how will he then *vex* (marg. do *hurt*) himself,
13:16. this *evil* in sending me away
22. Absalom spake...neither good *nor bad:*
14:17. to discern good *and bad:*
15:14. lest he...bring *evil* upon us,
16: 8. thou (art taken) *in thy mischief*,
17:14. that the Lord might bring *evil* upon
18:32. all that rise against thee *to do* (thee) *hurt*,
19: 7(8). than all *the evil* that befell thee
35(36). can I discern between good *and evil?*
24:16. the Lord repented him of *the evil*,
1K. 1:52. if *wickedness* shall be found
2:44. all *the wickedness* which thine heart is
— the Lord shall return *thy wickedness*
3: 9. that I may discern between good *and bad:*
5: 4(18). neither adversary nor *evil* occurrent.
9: 9. the Lord brought upon them all this *evil.*
11: 6. Solomon did *evil* in the sight of the Lord,
25. *the mischief* that Hadad (did):
13:33. Jeroboam returned not from his *evil* way,
14:10. I will bring *evil* upon the house of
22. Judah did *evil* in the sight of the Lord,
15:26, 34. he did *evil* in the sight of the Lord,
16: 7. all *the evil* that he did
19. sinned in doing *evil*
25. Omri wrought *evil* in the eyes of the
30. Ahab the son of Omri did *evil*
20: 7. see how this (man) seeketh *mischief.*
21:20. sold thyself to work *evil*
21. I will bring *evil* upon thee,
25. did sell himself to work *wickedness*
29. I will not bring *the evil*
— in his son's days will I bring *the evil*
22: 8. doth not prophesy good...but *evil.*
18. he would prophesy no good...but *evil?*
23. the Lord hath spoken *evil* concerning
52(53). did *evil* in the sight of the Lord,
2K. 2:19. the water (is) *naught*,
3: 2. wrought *evil* in the sight of the Lord;
4:41. there was no *harm* (marg. *evil* thing) in the pot.
6:33. this *evil* (is) of the Lord;
8:12. I know *the evil* that thou wilt do
18, 27. did *evil* in the sight of the Lord.

2K. 13: 2, 11. did (that which was) *evil* in the sight
14:10. why shouldest thou meddle *to* (thy) *hurt*,
24 & 15:9, 18, 24, 28 & 17:2. he did (that which was) *evil*
17:11. wrought *wicked* things to provoke
13. Turn ye from your *evil* ways,
17. sold themselves to do *evil* in the sight of
21: 2. did (that which was) *evil* in the sight of
6. wrought much *wickedness*
9. seduced them to do more *evil*
12. I (am) bringing (such) *evil* upon
15. done (that which was) *evil*
16. in doing (that which was) *evil*
20. did (that which was) *evil* in the sight of
22:16. I will bring *evil* upon this place,
20. all *the evil* which I will bring
23:32, 37 & 24:9, 19. did (that which was) *evil* in the sight of the Lord,
1Ch 2: 3. Er, the firstborn of Judah, was *evil*
4:10. that thou wouldest keep (me) *from evil*,
7:23. it went *evil* with his house.
21:15. he repented him of *the evil*,
2Ch 7:14. turn from their *wicked* ways;
22. therefore hath he brought all this *evil*
12:14. he did *evil*, because he prepared not his
18: 7. never prophesied good...but always *evil*:
17. he would not prophesy good...but *evil?*
22. the Lord hath spoken *evil*
20: 9. (when) *evil* cometh upon us,
21: 6. wrought (that which was) *evil*
19. he died of *sore* diseases.
22: 4. he did *evil* in the sight of the Lord
25:19. shouldest thou meddle *to* (thine) *hurt*,
29: 6. done (that which was) *evil*
33: 2. But did (that which was) *evil*
6. wrought much *evil* in the sight of the
9. to do *worse* than the heathen,
22. he did (that which was) *evil* in the sight
34:24. I will bring *evil* upon this place,
28. *the evil* that I will bring
36: 5, 9, 12. he did (that which was) *evil* in the
Ezr. 9:13. for our *evil* deeds,
Neh. 1: 3. *in* great *affliction* and reproach:
2: 1. I had not been (beforetime) *sad*
2. Why (is) thy countenance *sad*,
10. it grieved them exceedingly (lit. with great *grief*)
17. *the distress* that we (are) in,
6: 2. they thought to do me *mischief*.
13. have (matter) for an *evil* report,
9:28. they did *evil* again before thee:
35. neither turned they from their *wicked*
13: 7. understood *of the evil* that Eliashib did
17. What *evil* thing (is) this that ye do,
18. did not our God bring all this *evil*
27. to do all this great *evil*,
Est. 7: 6. The adversary and enemy (is) this *wicked*
7. there was *evil* determined against him
8: 3. to put away *the mischief of* Haman
6. *the evil* that shall come unto my people?
9: 2. to lay hand on such as sought *their hurt*:
25. his *wicked* device, which he devised
Job 1: 1. one that feared God, and eschewed *evil*.
8 & 2:3. that feareth God, and escheweth *evil?*
2: 7. Satan...smote Job with *sore* boils
10. shall we not receive *evil?*
11. this *evil* that was come upon him,
5:19. there shall no *evil* touch thee.
20:12. Though *wickedness* be sweet in his mouth,
21:30. *the wicked* is reserved to the day of
22: 5. (Is) not *thy wickedness* great?
28:28. to depart *from evil* (is) understanding.
30:26. then *evil* came (unto me):
31:29. lifted up myself when *evil* found him:
35:12. the pride of *evil men*.
42:11. all *the evil* that the Lord had brought
Ps. 5: 4(5). neither shall *evil* dwell with thee.
7: 4(5). If I have rewarded *evil*
9(10). Oh let *the wickedness of* the wicked
10: 6. (I shall) never (be) *in adversity*.
15. the wicked *and the evil* (man):
15: 3. nor doeth *evil* to his neighbour,
21:11(12). they intended *evil* against thee:
23: 4. I will fear no *evil*:
27: 5. in the time of *trouble* he shall hide me
28: 3. *but mischief* (is) in their hearts.
34:13(14). Keep thy tongue *from evil*,

Ps. 34:14(15). Depart *from evil*, and do good;
16(17). The face of the Lord (is) against them that do *evil*,
19(20). Many (are) *the afflictions of* the
21(22). *Evil* shall slay the wicked:
35: 4. them be turned back...that devise *my hurt*.
12. They rewarded me *evil* for good
26. be ashamed...that rejoice at *mine hurt*:
36: 4(5). he abhorreth not *evil*.
37:19. shall not be ashamed in the *evil* time:
27. Depart *from evil*, and do good;
38:12(13). they that seek *my hurt*
20(21). They also that render *evil* for good
40:12(13). innumerable *evils* have compassed
14(15). let them be driven backward...that wish *me evil*.
41: 1(2). time of *trouble*. (marg. the day of *evil*)
5(6). Mine enemies speak *evil* of me,
7(8). against me do they devise *my hurt*. (marg. *evil* to me)
49: 5(6). should I fear in the days of *evil*,
50:19. Thou givest thy mouth *to evil*,
51: 4(6). *and* done (this) *evil* in thy sight:
52: 1(3). Why boastest thou thyself *in mischief*,
3(5). Thou lovest *evil* more than good;
54: 5(7). shall reward *evil* unto mine enemies:
55:15(16). *wickedness* (is) in their dwellings,
56: 5(6). their thoughts (are) against me *for evil*.
64: 5(6). They encourage themselves (in) an *evil* matter:
70: 2(3). them...that desire *my hurt*.
71:13. them...that seek *my hurt*.
20. shewed me great *and sore* troubles,
24. they...that seek *my hurt*.
73: 8. They are corrupt, and speak *wickedly*
78:49. by sending *evil* angels (among them).
88: 3(4). my soul is full *of troubles*:
90:15. the years (wherein) we have seen *evil*.
91:10. There shall no *evil* befall thee,
94:13. rest from the days of *adversity*,
23. *and* shall cut them off *in their own wickedness*;
97:10. Ye that love the Lord, hate *evil*:
101: 4. I will not know a *wicked* (person).
107:26. their soul is melted *because of trouble*.
34. *for the wickedness of* them that dwell
39. through oppression, *affliction*, and sorrow.
109: 5. rewarded me *evil* for good,
20. them that speak *evil* against
112: 7. He shall not be afraid of *evil* tidings:
119:101. refrained my feet from every *evil* way,
121: 7. Lord shall preserve thee from all *evil*:
140: 1(2). Deliver me, O Lord, from the *evil* man:
2(3). Which imagine *mischiefs* in (their)
11(12). *evil* shall hunt the violent man
141: 4. Incline not my heart to (any) *evil* thing,
5. prayer also (shall be) *in their calamities*.
144:10. delivereth David his servant from the *hurtful* sword.
Pro. 1:16. their feet run *to evil*,
33. quiet from fear of *evil*.
2:12. from the way of *the evil* (man),
14. Who rejoice to do *evil*, (and) delight in the frowardness of *the wicked*;
3: 7. fear the Lord, and depart *from evil*.
29. Devise not *evil* against thy neighbour,
30. if he have done thee no *harm*.
4:14. go not in the way of *evil* (men).
27. remove thy foot *from evil*.
5:14. I was almost in all *evil*
6:14. he deviseth *mischief* continually;
18. feet that be swift in running to *mischief*,
24. To keep thee from the *evil* woman,
8:13. The fear of the Lord (is) to hate *evil*: pride, and arrogancy, and the *evil* way,
11:15. surety for a stranger shall smart (marg. be *sore* broken)
19. he that pursueth *evil*
21. *the wicked* shall not be unpunished:
27. he that seeketh *mischief*,
12:12. the net of *evil* (men):
13. *The wicked* is snared by the transgression
20. them that imagine *evil*:
21. the wicked shall be filled with *mischief*
13:17. A wicked messenger falleth *into mischief*:
19. abomination to fools to depart *from evil*.
21. *Evil* pursueth sinners:

Pro 14:16. A wise (man) feareth, and departeth *from evil:*
19. *The evil* bow before the good;
22. Do they not err that devise *evil?*
32. The wicked is driven away *in his wickedness:*
15: 3. The eyes of the Lord...beholding *the evil*
10. Correction (is) *grievous* unto him that
15. All the days of the afflicted (are) *evil:*
26. The thoughts of *the wicked*
28. the mouth of the wicked poureth out *evil things.*
16: 4. the wicked for the day of *evil.*
6. (men) depart *from evil.*
17. The highway of the upright (is) to depart *from evil:*
27. An ungodly man diggeth up *evil:*
30. he bringeth *evil* to pass.
17:11. An *evil* (man) seeketh only rebellion:
13. Whoso rewardeth *evil* for good, *evil* shall not depart from his house.
20. a perverse tongue falleth *into mischief.*
19:23. he shall not be visited with *evil.*
20: 8. A king...scattereth away all *evil*
14. (It is) *naught,* (it is) *naught,* saith the
22. I will recompense *evil;*
30. blueness of a wound cleanseth away *evil:*
21:10. The soul of the wicked desireth *evil:*
12. (God) overthroweth the wicked *for* (their) *wickedness.*
22: 3. A prudent (man) foreseeth *the evil,*
23: 6. (him that hath) an *evil* eye,
24: 1. Be not thou envious against *evil* men,
16. the wicked shall fall *into mischief.*
20. no reward *to the evil* (man);
25:20. he that singeth songs to an *heavy* heart.
26:23. Burning lips and a *wicked* heart
26. *his wickedness* shall be shewed
27:12. A prudent (man) foreseeth *the evil,*
28: 5. *Evil* men understand not judgment:
10. to go astray in an *evil* way,
14. he that hardeneth his heart shall fall *into mischief.*
22. that hasteth to be rich (hath) an *evil* eye,
29: 6. the transgression of an *evil* man
31:12. She will do him good and not *evil*
Ecc. 1:13. this *sore* travail hath God given
2:17. the work that is wrought...(is) *grievous*
21. vanity *and a* great *evil.*
4: 3. the *evil* work that is done under the sun.
8. yea, it (is) a *sore* travail.
5: 1(4:17). they consider not that they do *evil.*
13(12). *a* sore *evil* (which) I have seen
—(—). riches kept for the owners...*to their hurt.*
14(13). riches perish by *evil* travail:
16(15). this also (is) *a* sore *evil,*
6: 1. *an evil* which I have seen
2. it (is) an *evil* disease.
7:14. in the day of *adversity* consider:
15. prolongeth (his life) *in his wickedness.*
8: 3. stand not in an *evil* thing;
5. Whoso keepeth the commandment shall feel no *evil* thing:
6. *the misery of* man (is) great
9. ruleth over another *to* his own *hurt.*
11. sentence against an *evil* work
— the heart of the sons of men is fully set... to do *evil.*
12. Though a sinner do *evil* an hundred
9: 3. *an evil* among all (things)
— the heart of the sons of men is full of *evil,*
12. the fishes that are taken in an *evil* net,
— the sons of men snared in an *evil* time,
10: 5. *an evil* (which) I have seen
13. end of his talk (is) *mischievous* madness.
11: 2. knowest not what *evil* shall be upon the
10. put away *evil* from thy flesh:
12: 1. while the *evil* days come not,
14. (it be) good, or whether (it be) *evil.*
Isa. 3: 9. they have rewarded *evil* unto themselves.
11. (it shall be) *ill* (with him):
5:20. them that call *evil* good, and good *evil;*
7: 5. taken *evil* counsel against thee,
15. that he may know to refuse *the evil,*
16. shall know to refuse *the evil,*
13:11. I will punish the world *for* (their) *evil,*
31: 2. he also (is) wise, and will bring *evil,*

Isa. 32: 7. instruments also of the churl (are) *evil:*
33:15. shutteth his eyes from seeing *evil;*
45: 7. I make peace, and create *evil:*
47:10. thou hast trusted *in thy wickedness:*
11. Therefore shall *evil* come upon thee;
56: 2. keepeth his hand from doing any *evil.*
57: 1. the righteous is taken away from *the evil*
59: 7. Their feet run *to evil,*
15. he (that) departeth *from evil*
65:12. but did *evil* before mine eyes,
66: 4. they did *evil* before mine eyes,
Jer. 1:14. *an evil* shall break forth
16. touching all *their wickedness,*
2: 3. *evil* shall come upon them,
13. my people have committed two *evils;*
19. *Thine own wickedness* shall correct thee,
— (it is) *an evil* (thing) and bitter,
27. in the time of *their trouble*
28. in the time of *thy trouble:* (marg. *evil*)
33. also taught *the wicked ones*
3: 2. thy whoredoms *and with thy wickedness.*
5. thou hast spoken and done *evil things*
17. the imagination of their *evil* heart.
4: 6. I will bring *evil* from the north,
14. wash thine heart *from wickedness,*
18. this (is) *thy wickedness,*
5:12. neither shall *evil* come upon us;
28. the deeds of *the wicked:*
6: 1. *evil* appeareth out of the north,
7. she casteth out *her wickedness:*
19. I will bring *evil* upon this people,
29. *for the wicked* are not plucked away.
7: 6. neither walk after other gods *to* your *hurt:*
12. *the wickedness of* my people Israel.
24. the imagination of their *evil* heart,
30. have done *evil* in my sight,
8: 3. them that remain of this *evil* family,
6. no man repented him of *his wickedness,*
9: 3(2). they proceed *from evil* to *evil,* and they
11: 8. the imagination of their *evil* heart:
11. I will bring *evil* upon them,
12. in the time of *their trouble.* (marg. *evil*)
14. cry unto me for *their trouble.* (marg. *id.*)
15. when *thou doest* (marg. *thy*) evil,
17. the Lord of hosts,...hath pronounced *evil* against thee, for *the evil of* the house of
23. I will bring *evil* upon the men of
12: 4. *for the wickedness of* them that dwell
14. all mine *evil* neighbours,
13:10. This *evil* people,
14:16. I will pour *their wickedness* upon them.
15:11. to entreat thee (well) in the time of *evil*
21. out of the hand of *the wicked,*
16:10. pronounced all this great *evil* against us?
12. the imagination of his *evil* heart,
17:17. my hope in the day of *evil.*
18. bring upon them the day of *evil,*
18: 8. If that nation,...turn *from their evil,* I will repent of *the evil*
10. If it do *evil* in my sight,
11. I frame *evil* against you,
— return ye now every one from his *evil*
12. the imagination of his *evil* heart.
20. Shall *evil* be recompensed for good?
19: 3. I will bring *evil* upon this place,
15. I will bring upon this city...all *the evil*
21:10. set my face against this city *for evil,*
22:22. confounded for all *thy wickedness.*
23:10. their course is *evil,*
11. have I found *their wickedness,*
12. I will bring *evil* upon them,
14. none doth return *from his wickedness:*
17. No *evil* shall come upon you.
22. turned them from their *evil* way,
24: 2. the other basket (had) very *naughty* figs,
3. *the evil,* very *evil,*
8. the *evil* figs, which cannot be eaten,
9. I will deliver them...*for* (their) *hurt,*
25: 5. Turn...every one from his *evil* way,
7. provoke me to anger...*to* your own *hurt.*
32. *evil* shall go forth from nation to nation,
26: 3. turn every man from his *evil* way, that I may repent me of *the evil,*
13. the Lord will repent him of *the evil*
19. the Lord repented him of *the evil*
— might we procure great *evil* against our
28: 8. of war, *and of evil,* and of pestilence.

Jer. 29:11. thoughts of peace, and not *of evil*,
32:23. caused all this *evil* to come
30. only done *evil* before me
32. *the evil of* the children of Israel
42. I have brought all this great *evil*
33: 5. for all *whose wickedness* I have hid my
35:15. Return ye now every man from his *evil*
17. all *the evil* that I have pronounced
36: 3. all *the evil* which I purpose to do unto them; that they may return every man from his *evil* way;
7. return every one from his *evil* way:
31. all *the evil* that I have pronounced
38: 4. not the welfare of this people, but *the hurt*.
39:12. do him no *harm*;
16. bring my words upon this city *for evil*,
40: 2. thy God hath pronounced this *evil*
41:11. *the evil* that Ishmael...had done,
42: 6. (it be) good, or whether (it be) *evil*,
10. I repent me of *the evil*
17. *the evil* that I will bring
44: 2. all *the evil* that I have brought
3. *their wickedness* which they have
5. nor inclined their ear to turn *from their wickedness*,
7. Wherefore commit ye (this) great *evil*
9. *the wickedness* (marg. *wickednesses*, or, *punishments*) *of* your fathers, and *the wickedness of* the kings of Judah, and *the wickedness of* their wives, and *your own wickedness*, and *the wickedness of*
11. I will set my face against you *for evil*,
17. *and* saw no *evil*.
23. therefore this *evil* is happened unto you,
27. I will watch over them *for evil*,
29. my words shall surely stand...*for evil*:
45: 5. I will bring *evil* upon all flesh,
48: 2. they have devised *evil*
16. *and his affliction* hasteth fast.
49:23. they have heard *evil* tidings:
37. I will bring *evil* upon them,
51: 2. in the day of *trouble*
24. all *their evil* that they have done in Zion
60. *the evil* that should come upon Babylon,
64. *the evil* that I will bring
52: 2. he did (that which was) *evil*
Lam. 1:21. mine enemies have heard of *my trouble*;
22. Let all *their wickedness* come before thee;
3:38. Out of the mouth of the most High proceedeth not *evil* and good?
Eze. 5:16. the *evil* arrows of famine,
17. I send upon you famine and *evil* beasts,
6: 9. *the evils* which they have committed
10. not said in vain that I would do this *evil*
11. all the *evil* abominations of the house of
7: 5. Thus saith the Lord God; *An evil*, *an* only *evil*, behold, is come.
24. *the worst of* the heathen,
8: 9. the *wicked* abominations that they do
11: 2. the men that...give *wicked* counsel
13:22. strengthened the hands of *the wicked*,
14:15. If I cause *noisome* beasts to pass
21. I send my four *sore* judgments
— and the famine, and the *noisome* beast,
22. *the evil* that I have brought upon
16:23. after all *thy wickedness*,
57. Before *thy wickedness* was discovered,
20:43. *your evils* that ye have committed.
44. not according to your *wicked* ways,
30:12. the hand of *the wicked*:
33:11. turn ye from your *evil* ways;
34:25. will cause the *evil* beasts to cease
36:31. remember your own *evil* ways,
38:10. thou shalt think an *evil* thought:
Dan 9:12. by bringing upon us *a* great *evil*:
13. all this *evil* is come upon us:
14. hath the Lord watched upon *the evil*,
11:27. kings' hearts (shall be) *to do mischief*,
Hos 7: 1. *and the wickedness* (marg. *evils*) *of*
2. I remember all *their wickedness*:
3. make the king glad *with their wickedness*,
15. they imagine *mischief* against me.
9:15. All *their wickedness* (is) in Gilgal:
10:15. So shall Beth-el do unto you because of *your great wickedness* (marg. *the evil of your evil*)
Joel 2:13. repenteth him of *the evil*.
Joel 3:13(4:13). *their wickedness* (is) great.
Am. 3: 6. shall there be *evil* in a city,
5:13. for it (is) an *evil* time.
14. Seek good, and not *evil*,
15. Hate *the evil*, and love the good
6: 3. Ye that put far away the *evil* day,
9: 4. I will set mine eyes upon them *for evil*,
10. *The evil* shall not overtake...us.
Obad. 13. not have looked *on their affliction*
Jon. 1: 2. *their wickedness* is come up before me.
7. for whose cause this *evil* (is) upon us.
8. for whose cause this *evil* (is) upon us;
3: 8. turn every one from his *evil* way,
10. they turned from their *evil* way; and God repented of *the evil*,
4: 1. But it displeased Jonah exceedingly, (lit. with great *grief*)
2. repentest thee of *the evil*.
6. to deliver him *from his grief*.
Mic. 1:12. *evil* came down from the Lord
2: 1. work *evil* upon their beds!
3. against this family do I devise *an evil*,
— for this time (is) *evil*.
3: 2. Who hate the good, and love *the evil*;
11. none *evil* can come upon us.
7: 3. That they may do *evil* with both hands
Nah 1:11. imagineth *evil* against the Lord,
3:19. upon whom hath not *thy wickedness*
Hab 1:13. of purer eyes than to behold *evil*,
2: 9. him that coveteth an *evil* covetousness
— delivered from the power of *evil*!
Zep. 3:15. thou shalt not see *evil* any more.
Zec. 1: 4. Turn ye now from your *evil* ways, and (from) your *evil* doings:
15. they helped forward *the affliction*.
7:10. *and* let none of you imagine *evil* against
8:17. let none of you imagine *evil* in your
Mal. 1: 8. if ye offer the blind...(is it) not *evil*? and if ye offer the lame...(is it) not *evil*?
2:17. Every one that doeth *evil*

רֵעַ *rēh'ăg*, m. 7452

Ex. 32:17. the noise of the people *as they shouted*,
Job 36:33. *The noise thereof* sheweth concerning it,
Mic. 4: 9. thou cry out *aloud*? (lit. cry *a crying*)

רֵעַ *rēh'ăg*, m. 7453

Gen 11: 3. said one to *another*, (lit. *his neighbour*)
7. that they may not understand one *another*'s (lit. *his neighbour*'s) speech.
15:10. laid each piece one against *another*: (lit. *his neighbour*)
31:49. when we are absent one *from another*.
38:12. *his friend* Hirah the Adullamite.
20. sent the kid by the hand of *his friend*
43:33. the men marvelled one at *another*. (lit. *his neighbour*)
Ex. 2:13. Wherefore smitest thou *thy fellow*?
11: 2. let every man borrow of *his neighbour*,
18: 7. asked each *other* of (their) welfare;
16. I judge between one and *another*, (lit. *his neighbour*)
20:16. Thou shalt not bear false witness *against thy neighbour*.
17. shalt not covet *thy neighbour*'s house, thou shalt not covet *thy neighbour*'s wife,
— nor any thing that (is) *thy neighbour*'s.
21:14. come presumptuously upon *his neighbour*,
18. if men strive together, and one smite *another* (lit. *his neighbour*)
35. if one man's ox hurt *another*'s, (lit. *his neighbour*'s)
22: 7(6). a man shall deliver unto *his neighbour*
8(7). put his hand unto *his neighbour*'s
9(8). shall pay double unto *his neighbour*.
10(9). If a man deliver unto *his neighbour* an
11(10). not put his hand unto *his neighbour*'s
14(13). man borrow (ought) of *his neighbour*,
26(25). If thou at all take *thy neighbour*'s
32:27. slay every man...*his neighbour*.
33:11. as a man speaketh unto *his friend*.
Lev. 19:13. Thou shalt not defraud *thy neighbour*,
16. stand against the blood of *thy neighbour*:
18. thou shalt love *thy neighbour* as thyself:

Lev.20:10. committeth adultery with *his neighbour's*
Deu 4:42. kill *his neighbour* unawares,
5:20(17). bear false witness *against thy neighbour.*
21(18). Neither shalt thou desire *thy neighbour's* wife, neither shalt thou covet *thy neighbour's* house,
—(—). or any (thing) that (is) *thy neighbour's.*
13: 6(7). the wife of thy bosom, or *thy friend,*
15: 2. lendeth (ought) *unto his neighbour*
— he shall not exact (it) of *his neighbour,*
19: 4. Whoso killeth *his neighbour* ignorantly,
5. goeth into the wood with *his neighbour*
— the head...lighteth upon *his neighbour,*
11. if any man hate *his neighbour,*
14. Thou shalt not remove *thy neighbour's*
22:24. he hath humbled *his neighbour's* wife:
26. when a man riseth against *his neighbour,*
23:24(25). When thou comest into *thy neighbour's*
25(26). the standing corn of *thy neighbour,*
—(—). *thy neighbour's* standing corn.
24:10. When thou dost lend *thy brother* any
27:17. he that removeth *his neighbour's*
24. he that smiteth *his neighbour* secretly.
Jos. 20: 5. he smote *his neighbour* unwittingly,
Jud. 6:29. said one to *another,* (lit. *his neighbour*)
7:13. a man that told a dream *unto his fellow,*
14. *his fellow* answered and said,
22. every man's sword *against his fellow,*
10:18. princes of Gilead said one to *another,* (lit. *his fellow*)
Ru. 3:14. she rose up before one could know *another.* (lit. *his neighbour*)
4: 7. his shoe, and gave (it) to *his neighbour:*
1Sa.10:11. the people said one to *another,* (marg. *his neighbour*)
14:20. every man's sword was *against his fellow,*
15:28. hath given it *to a neighbour of thine,*
20:41. and they kissed one *another,* and wept one with *another,*
28:17. kingdom...and given it to *thy neighbour,*
30:26. sent of the spoil...to *his friends,*
2Sa. 2:16. they caught every one *his fellow*
— and (thrust) his sword in *his fellow's* side;
12:11. and give (them) *unto thy neighbour,*
13: 3. Amnon had *a friend,*
16:17. thy kindness to *thy friend?* why wentest thou not with *thy friend?*
1K. 8:31. If any man trespass *against his neighbour,*
16:11. he left him not...*nor of his friends.*
20:35. a certain man...said unto *his neighbour*
2K. 3:23. they have smitten one *another:* (lit. *his neighbour*)
7: 3. said one to *another,* (lit. *his neighbour*)
9. Then they said one to *another,* (lit. *id.*)
1Ch 27:33. Hushai...(was) the king's *companion:*
2Ch 6:22. If a man sin *against his neighbour,*
20:23. every one helped to destroy *another.* (lit. *against his neighbour* for destruction)
Est. 9:19, 22. sending portions one *to another.*
Job 2:11. when Job's three *friends* heard
6:14. pity (should be shewed) *from his friend;*
12: 4. I am (as) one mocked of *his neighbour,*
16:20. *My friends* scorn me:
21. as a man (pleadeth) *for his neighbour!*
17: 5. He that speaketh flattery to (his) *friends,*
19:21. have pity upon me, O ye *my friends;*
30:29. *and a companion* to owls.
31: 9. (if) I have laid wait at *my neighbour's*
32: 3. against *his* three *friends* was his wrath
35: 4. I will answer thee, and *thy companions*
42: 7. against thee, and against *thy* two *friends:*
10. when he prayed for *his friends:*
Ps. 12: 2(3). They speak vanity every one with *his neighbour:*
15: 3. nor doeth evil *to his neighbour,*
28: 3. which speak peace to *their neighbours,*
35:14. *as though* (he had been) my *friend*
38:11(12). My lovers *and my friends* stand aloof
88:18(19). Lover *and friend* hast thou put far
101: 5. Whoso privily slandereth *his neighbour,*
122: 8. For my brethren *and companions'* sakes,
Pro. 3:28. Say not *unto thy neighbour,* Go, and come
29. Devise not evil *against thy neighbour,*
6: 1. if thou be surety *for thy friend,*
3. come into the hand of *thy friend:*
— make sure *thy friend.* (lit. *friends*)
Pro. 6:29. he that goeth in to *his neighbour's* wife;
11: 9. An hypocrite...destroyeth *his neighbour:*
12. void of wisdom despiseth *his neighbour:*
12:26. (is) more excellent *than his neighbour:*
14:20. poor is hated even of *his own neighbour:*
21. He that despiseth *his neighbour* sinneth:
16:29. A violent man enticeth *his neighbour,*
17:17. *A friend* loveth at all times,
18. in the presence of *his friend.*
18:17. *his neighbour* cometh and searcheth
24. A man (that hath) *friends*
19: 4. Wealth maketh many *friends:* but the poor is separated *from his neighbour.*
6. *a friend* to him that giveth gifts.
21:10. *his neighbour* findeth no favour
22:11. the king (shall be) *his friend.*
24:28. Be not a witness *against thy neighbour*
25: 8. when *thy neighbour* hath put thee to
9. Debate thy cause with *thy neighbour*
17. Withdraw thy foot from *thy neighbour's*
18. beareth false witness *against his neighbour*
26:19. the man (that) deceiveth *his neighbour,*
27: 9. the sweetness of a man's *friend*
10. *Thine own friend, and* thy father's *friend,*
14. He that blesseth *his friend*
17. sharpeneth the countenance of *his friend.*
29: 5. A man that flattereth *his neighbour*
Ecc. 4: 4. a man is envied *of his neighbour.*
Cant 5: 1. eat, *O friends;* drink, yea, drink
16. this (is) *my friend,* O daughters of
Isa. 3: 5. the people shall be oppressed,...every one *by his neighbour:*
13: 8. they shall be amazed one at *another;* (marg. *his neighbour*)
19: 2. and every one *against his neighbour;*
34:14. the satyr shall cry to *his fellow;*
41: 6. They helped every one *his neighbour;*
Jer. 3: 1. played the harlot with many *lovers;*
20. a wife treacherously departeth *from her husband,* (marg. *friend*)
5: 8. every one neighed after *his neighbour's*
6:21. the neighbour *and his friend* shall perish.
7: 5. between a man and *his neighbour;*
9: 4(3). Take ye heed every one of *his neighbour,* (marg. or, *friend*)
—(—). every *neighbour* will walk with
5(4). will deceive every one *his neighbour,*
8(7). speaketh peaceably to *his neighbour*
19: 9. shall eat every one the flesh of *his friend*
22: 8. shall say every man to *his neighbour,*
13. useth *his neighbour's* service without
23:27. they tell every man to *his neighbour,*
30. my words every one from *his neighbour.*
35. shall ye say every one to *his neighbour,*
29:23. adultery with *their neighbours'* wives,
31:34. teach no more every man *his neighbour,*
34:15. liberty every man to *his neighbour;*
17. and every man *to his neighbour:*
36:16. they were afraid both one and *other,* (lit. *his neighbour*)
46:16. yea, one fell upon *another:* (lit. *his neighbour*)
Lam. 1: 2. all *her friends* have dealt treacherously
Eze.18: 6. neither hath defiled *his neighbour's* wife,
11. and defiled *his neighbour's* wife,
15. hath not defiled *his neighbour's* wife,
22:11. abomination with *his neighbour's* wife;
12. greedily gained of *thy neighbours*
33:26. ye defile every one *his neighbour's* wife:
Hos. 3: 1. love a woman beloved of (her) *friend,*
Jon. 1: 7. they said every one to *his fellow,*
Mic. 7: 5. Trust ye not *in a friend,*
Hab. 2:15. Woe unto him that giveth *his neighbour*
Zec. 3: 8. Hear now, O Joshua...*and thy fellows*
10. shall ye call every man *his neighbour*
8:10. I set...every one *against his neighbour.*
16. Speak ye every man the truth to *his neighbour;*
17. let none of you imagine evil...against *his neighbour;*
11: 6. I will deliver...every one into *his neighbour's* hand,
14:13. lay hold every one on...*his neighbour,* and his hand shall rise up against...*his neighbour.*
Mal. 3:16. they that feared the Lord spake often one to *another:* (lit. *his neighbour*)

7454 **רֵעַ** *rēh'ăg*, m.

Ps.139: 2. thou understandest *my thought*
17. How precious also are *thy thoughts* unto

7455 **רֹעַ** *rōh'ăg*, m.

Gen41:19. such as I never saw...*for badness:*
Deu28:20. *the wickedness of* thy doings,
1Sa.17:28. *the naughtiness of* thine heart;
Neh 2: 2. nothing (else) but *sorrow of* heart.
Ps. 28: 4. *and according to the wickedness of* their
Ecc. 7: 3. *by the sadness of* the countenance
Isa. 1:16. put away *the evil of* your doings
Jer. 4: 4 & 21:12. because of *the evil of* your doings.
23: 2. I will visit upon you *the evil of* your
22. *and from the evil of* their doings.
24: 2. could not be eaten, *they were so bad.*
3, 8. cannot be eaten, *they are so evil.*
25: 5. *and from the evil of* your doings,
26: 3. because of *the evil of* their doings.
29:17. cannot be eaten, *they are so evil.*
44:22. because of *the evil of* your doings,
Hos. 9:15. *the wickedness of* their doings

7456 **רָעֵב** [*rāh-gehv'*].

* KAL.—*Preterite.* *

Ps. 34:10(11). The young lions do lack, *and suffer hunger:*

KAL.—*Future.*

Gen41:55. *when* all the land of Egypt *was famished,*
Ps. 50:12. If *I were hungry,* I would not tell thee:
Pro. 6:30. to satisfy his soul when *he is hungry;*
19:15. an idle soul *shall suffer hunger.*
Isa. 8:21. when *they shall be hungry,*
49:10. *They shall* not *hunger* nor thirst;
65:13. eat, but *ye shall be hungry:*
Jer. 42:14. where we shall see no war,...nor *have hunger*

* HIPHIL.—*Future.* *

Deu 8: 3. *and suffered thee to hunger,*
Pro.10: 3. The Lord *will* not *suffer* the soul of the righteous *to famish:*

7458 **רָעָב** *rāh-gāhv'*, m.

Gen12:10. there was *a famine* in the land:
— *the famine* (was) grievous in the land.
26: 1. there was *a famine* in the land, beside *the* first *famine* that was
41:27. the seven empty ears...shall be seven years of *famine.*
30. arise after them seven years of *famine;*
— *the famine* shall consume the land;
31. not be known...by reason of that *famine*
36. the seven years of *famine,*
— that the land perish not *through the famine.*
50. before the years of *famine* came,
54. the seven years of *dearth* began to come,
— *the dearth* was in all lands;
56. *And the famine* was over all...the earth:
— *the famine* waxed sore
57. *the famine* was (so) sore
42: 5. *the famine* was in the land of Canaan.
43: 1. *And the famine* (was) sore in the land.
45: 6. (hath) *the famine* (been) in the land:
11. yet (there are) five years of *famine;*
47: 4. *the famine* (is) sore in the land
13. *the famine* (was) very sore,
— the land of Canaan fainted by reason of *the famine.*
20. *the famine* prevailed over them:
Ex. 16: 3. to kill this whole assembly *with hunger.*
Deu28:48. *in hunger,* and in thirst, and in nakedness,
32:24. (They shall be) burnt with *hunger,*
Ru. 1: 1. there was *a famine* in the land.
2Sa.21: 1. there was *a famine* in the days of David
24:13. Shall seven years of *famine* come
1K. 8:37. If there be in the land *famine,*
18: 2. *And* (there was) *a sore famine* in Samaria.
2K. 4:38. *and* (there was) *a dearth* in the land;
6:25. there was *a* great *famine* in Samaria:
2K. 7: 4. *then the famine* (is) in the city,
8: 1. the Lord hath called *for a famine;*
25: 3. *the famine* prevailed in the city,
1Ch 21:12. Either three years' *famine;* or
2Ch 6:28. If there be *dearth* in the land,
20: 9. the sword, judgment, or pestilence, *or famine,*
32:11. to die *by famine* and by thirst,
Neh 5: 3. buy corn, *because of the dearth.*
9:15. gavest them bread...*for their hunger,*
Job 5:20. *In famine* he shall redeem thee
Ps. 33:19. to keep them alive *in famine.*
105:16. he called for *a famine* upon the land:
Isa. 5:13. their honourable men (are) *famished,* (marg. men of *famine*)
14:30. I will kill thy root *with famine,*
51:19. *and the famine,* and the sword:
Jer. 5:12. neither shall we see sword *nor famine:*
11:22. their sons and their daughters shall die *by famine:*
14:12. *but* I will consume them...*by the famine,*
13. *neither* shall ye have *famine;*
15. *and famine* shall not be in this land; By sword *and famine* shall...be consumed.
16. because of *the famine* and the sword;
18. them that are sick *with famine!*
15: 2. such as (are) *for the famine, to the famine;*
16: 4. consumed by the sword, *and by famine;*
18:21. deliver up their children *to the famine,*
21: 7. from the sword, and from *the famine,*
9. shall die by the sword, *and by the famine,*
24:10. I will send the sword, *the famine,*
27: 8. will I punish,...with the sword, *and with the famine,*
13. Why will ye die,...*by the famine,*
29:17. I will send upon them the sword, *the famine,*
18. I will persecute them...*with the famine,*
32:24. because of the sword, *and of the famine,*
36. by the sword, *and by the famine,*
34:17. to the sword, to the pestilence, and to *the famine;*
38: 2. shall die by the sword, *by the famine,*
9. he is like to die for *hunger*
42:16. *and the famine,* whereof ye were afraid,
17. they shall die...*by the famine,*
22. ye shall die...*by the famine,*
44:12. consumed by the sword (and) *by the famine:*
— by the sword *and by the famine:*
13. I will punish them...*by the famine,*
18. consumed by the sword *and by the famine.*
27. consumed by the sword *and by the famine,*
52: 6. *the famine* was sore in the city,
Lam. 2:19. thy young children, that faint *for hunger*
4: 9. they that be slain with *hunger:*
5:10. because of *the* terrible *famine.*
Eze. 5:12. *and with famine* shall they be consumed
16. the evil arrows of *famine,*
— *and* I will increase *the famine*
17. So will I send upon you *famine*
6:11. they shall fall...*by the famine,*
12. he that remaineth...shall die *by the famine*
7:15. the pestilence *and the famine* within:
— *famine* and pestilence shall devour
12:16. I will leave a few...*from the famine,*
14:13. will send *famine* upon
21. the sword, *and the famine,* and the noisome
34:29. they shall be no more consumed with *hunger*
36:29. and lay no *famine* upon you.
30. shall receive no more reproach of *famine*
Am. 8:11. I will send *a famine* in the land, not *a famine* of bread,

רָעֵב *rāh-gehv'*, adj. 7457

1Sa. 2: 5. *and* (they that were) *hungry* ceased:
2Sa.17:29. The people (is) *hungry,* and weary, and
2K. 7:12. They know that we (be) *hungry;*
Job 5: 5. Whose harvest *the hungry* eateth
18:12. His strength shall be *hungerbitten,*
22: 7. *and* thou hast withholden bread *from the hungry.*
24:10. *and* they take away the sheaf (from) the *hungry;*

Ps.107: 5. *Hungry* and thirsty, their soul fainted
9. filleth the *hungry* soul with goodness.
36. there he maketh *the hungry* to dwell,
146: 7. which giveth food *to the hungry.*
Pro.25:21. If thine enemy be *hungry,*
27: 7. to the *hungry* soul every bitter thing is
Isa. 8:21. hardly bestead *and hungry:*
9:20(19). shall snatch...*and be hungry;*
29: 8. when *an hungry* (man) dreameth,
32: 6. to make empty the soul of *the hungry,*
44:12. he is *hungry,* and his strength faileth:
58: 7. to deal thy bread *to the hungry,*
10. (if) thou draw out thy soul *to the hungry,*
Eze.18: 7. hath given his bread *to the hungry,*
16. hath given his bread *to the hungry,*

7459 רְעָבוֹן *r'^{n}gāh-vōhn'*, m.

Gen42:19. carry corn *for the famine of* your houses:
33. (food for) *the famine of* your housholds,
Ps. 37:19. in the days of *famine* they shall be

7460 רָעַד [*rāh-^{n}gad'*].

* KAL.—*Future.* *

Ps.104:32. He looketh on the earth, *and it trembleth:*

* HIPHIL.—*Participle.* *

Ezr.10: 9. all the people sat...*trembling*
Dan10:11. when he had spoken...I stood *trembling.*

7461 רַעַד *rah'-^{n}gad*, m.

Ex. 15:15. *trembling* shall take hold upon them;
Ps. 55: 5(6). Fearfulness *and trembling* are come

7461 רְעָדָה *r'^{n}gāh-dāh'*, f.

Job 4:14. Fear came upon me, *and trembling,*
Ps. 2:11. rejoice *with trembling*
48: 6(7). *Fear* took hold upon them
Isa. 33:14. *fearfulness* hath surprised the hypocrites.

7462 רָעָה *rāh-^{n}gāh'*.

* KAL.—*Preterite.* *

Isa. 5:17. *Then shall* the lambs *feed*
14:30. *And* the firstborn of the poor *shall feed,*
61: 5. strangers shall stand *and feed* your flocks,
Jer. 3:15. pastors...*which shall feed* you with
6: 3. *they shall feed* every one in his place.
23: 4. shepherds...*which shall feed them:*
50:19. *and he shall feed* on Carmel and Bashan,
Eze.34: 8. the shepherds...*fed* not my flock;
13. *and feed them* upon the mountains of
23. *and he shall feed* them, (even) my servant
Mic. 5: 4(3). *and feed* (marg. or, *rule*) in the strength of the Lord,
6(5). *And they shall waste* (marg. *eat up*) the land

KAL.—*Infinitive.*

Gen36:24. *as he fed* the asses of Zibeon
37:12. his brethren went *to feed* their father's
1Sa.17:15. David went...*to feed* his father's sheep
2Sa. 7: 7. commanded *to feed* my people Israel,
1Ch 17: 6. commanded *to feed* my people,
Ps. 78:71. he brought him *to feed* Jacob his people,
Cant.6: 2. My beloved is gone down...*to feed* in the gardens,
Eze.34:10. cause them to cease *from feeding*

KAL.—*Imperative.*

Gen29: 7. water ye the sheep, and go (and) *feed* (them).
Ps. 28: 9. *feed* (marg. or, *rule*) *them also,* and lift
37: 3. *and* verily *thou shalt be fed.*
Cant.1: 8. *and feed* thy kids beside the shepherds'
Mic. 7:14. *Feed* thy people with thy rod,
Zec.11: 4. *Feed* the flock of the slaughter;

KAL.—*Future.*

Gen30:31. *I will* again *feed* (and) keep thy flock:
41: 2. came up out of the river seven...*and they fed*
Gen41:18. kine,...*and they fed* in a meadow:
Ex. 34: 3. neither *let* the flocks nor herds *feed*
2Sa. 5: 2. Thou *shalt feed* my people Israel,
1Ch 11: 2. Thou *shalt feed* (marg. or, *rule*) my people
Job 24: 2. they violently take away flocks, *and feed*
Ps. 49:14(15). death *shall feed on them;*
80:13(14). wild beast of the field *doth devour it.*
Pro.10:21. The lips of the righteous *feed* many:
15:14. the mouth of fools *feedeth* on foolishness.
Cant.1: 7. Tell me,...where *thou feedest,*
Isa. 11: 7. the cow and the bear *shall feed;*
27:10. there *shall* the calf *feed,*
30:23. *shall* thy cattle *feed* in large pastures.
40:11. *He shall feed* his flock like a shepherd:
49: 9. *They shall feed* in the ways,
65:25. The wolf and the lamb *shall feed* together,
Jer. 2:16. *have broken* (marg. or, *feed on*) the crown of *thy* head.
22:22. The wind *shall eat up* all thy pastors,
Eze.34: 2. *should* not the shepherds *feed* the flocks?
3. *ye feed* not the flock.
8. *but* the shepherds *fed* themselves,
10. neither *shall* the shepherds *feed* themselves
14. *I will feed* them (in) a good pasture,
— (in) a fat pasture *shall they feed*
15. I *will feed* my flock,
16. *I will feed them* with judgment.
18. *to have eaten up* the good pasture,
19. *they eat* that which ye have trodden
23. he *shall feed* them, and he shall be
Hos. 4:16. the Lord *will feed them*
9: 2. flour and the winepress *shall* not *feed them,*
Jon 3: 7. *let them* not *feed,* nor drink water:
Mic. 7:14. *let them feed* (in) Bashan and Gilead,
Zep 2: 7. *they shall feed* thereupon:
3:13. they *shall feed* and lie down,
Zec.11: 7. *And I will feed* the flock of slaughter,
— *and I fed* the flock.
9. *I will* not *feed* you:

KAL.—*Participle.* Poel.

Gen 4: 2. Abel was *a keeper* (marg. *feeder*) *of* sheep,
13: 7. *the herdmen of* Abram's cattle and *the herdmen of* Lot's cattle:
8. between *my herdmen* and *thy herdmen;*
26:20. *the herdmen of* Gerar did strive with Isaac's *herdmen,*
29: 9. Rachel came with her father's sheep: for *she kept* them.
30:36. Jacob *fed* the rest of Laban's flocks.
37: 2. *feeding* the flock with his brethren;
13. Do not thy brethren *feed* (the flock)
16. tell me,...where they *feed* (their flocks).
46:32. the men (are) shep*herds,* (lit. *feeders of* sheep)
34. every shep*herd* (lit. *id.*) (is) an abomination unto the Egyptians.
47: 3. Thy servants (are) shep*herds,* (lit. *id.*)
48:15. the God *which fed* me all my life long
49:24. from thence (is) *the shepherd,*
Ex. 2:17. *the shepherds* came and drove them away:
19. us out of the hand of *the shepherds,*
3: 1. Moses *kept* (lit. was *keeping*) the flock of
Nu. 14:33. your children shall *wander* (marg. or, *feed;* lit. be *feeding*)
27:17. as sheep which have no *shepherd.*
1Sa.16:11. the youngest,...*he keepeth* the sheep.
17:34. Thy servant *kept* (lit. was *keeping*) his father's sheep,
40. *a shepherd*'s bag which he had,
21: 7(8). the chiefest of *the herdmen*
25: 7. *thy shepherds* which were with us,
16. we were with them *keeping* the sheep.
1K. 22:17. sheep that have not *a shepherd:*
2K. 10:12. as he (was) at the shearing house (marg. house of *shepherds* binding (sheep))
1Ch 27:29. the herds *that fed* in Sharon
2Ch 18:16. sheep that have no *shepherd:*
Job 1:14. oxen were plowing, and the asses *feeding*
24:21. *He evil entreateth* the barren
Ps. 23: 1. The Lord (is) *my shepherd;*
80: 1(2). Give ear, *O Shepherd of* Israel,
Pro.13:20. *but a companion of* fools shall be destroyed.
28: 7. *but he that is a companion of* (marg. or *feedeth*) riotous (men)
29: 3. *but he that keepeth company with* harlots
Ecc.12:11. (which) are given *from* one *shepherd.*

Cant. 1: 8. feed thy kids beside *the shepherds'* tents.
2:16. *he feedeth* among the lilies.
4: 5. two young roes...*which feed* among the
6: 3. *he feedeth* among the lilies.
Isa. 13:20. *neither* shall *the shepherds* make their fold
31: 4. a multitude of *shepherds*
40:11. He shall feed his flock *like a shepherd:*
44:20. *He feedeth* on ashes:
28. That saith of Cyrus, (He is) *my shepherd,*
56:11. (they are) *shepherds* (that) cannot
63:11. brought them up out of the sea with *the shepherd of*
Jer. 2: 8. *the pastors also* transgressed
3:15. I will give you *pastors*
6: 3. *The shepherds* with their flocks
10:21. *the pastors* are become brutish,
12:10. Many *pastors* have destroyed my vineyard,
17:16. I have not hastened *from* (being) *a pastor*
22:22. The wind shall eat up all *thy pastors,*
23: 1. Woe be unto *the pastors*
2. *the pastors that feed* my people;
4. I will set up *shepherds* over them
25:34. Howl, ye *shepherds,* and cry;
35. *the shepherds* shall have no way to flee,
36. A voice of the cry of *the shepherds,*
31:10. keep him, *as a shepherd* (doth) his flock.
33:12. an habitation of *shepherds*
43:12. as *a shepherd* putteth on his garment;
49:19. who (is) that *shepherd* that will stand
50: 6. *their shepherds* have caused them to go
44. who (is) that *shepherd* that will stand
51:23. I will also break in pieces...*the shepherd*
Eze.34: 2. prophesy against *the shepherds of* Israel,
— Thus saith the Lord God *unto the shepherds;* Woe (be) to *the shepherds of* Israel that *do feed* themselves! should not *the shepherds* feed the flocks?
5. (there is) no *shepherd:*
7. ye *shepherds,* hear the word of the Lord;
8. because (there was) no *shepherd,* neither did *my shepherds* search for my flock, but *the shepherds* fed themselves,
9. O ye *shepherds,* hear the word of the Lord;
10. I (am) against *the shepherds;*
— neither shall *the shepherds* feed themselves
12. As *a shepherd* seeketh out his flock
23. I will set up one *shepherd*
— he shall be their *shepherd.*
37:24. *and* they all shall have one *shepherd:*
Hos 12: 1(2). Ephraim *feedeth* on wind,
Am. 1: 2. habitations of *the shepherds* shall mourn,
3:12. As *the shepherd* taketh out of the mouth of
Mic. 5: 5(4). raise against him seven *shepherds,*
Nah. 3:18. *Thy shepherds* slumber, O king of
Zep. 2: 6. dwellings (and) cottages for *shepherds,*
Zec.10: 2. (there was) no *shepherd.*
3. Mine anger was kindled against *the shepherds,*
11: 3. a voice of the howling of *the shepherds;*
5. *and their own shepherds* pity them not.
8. Three *shepherds* also I cut off
15. the instruments of *a* foolish *shepherd.*
16. I will raise up *a shepherd*
13: 7. Awake, O sword, against *my shepherd,*
— smite *the shepherd,*

* PIEL.—*Preterite.* *

Jud. 14:20. his companion, whom *he had used as his friend.*

* HIPHIL.—*Future.* *

Ps. 78:72. *So he fed them* according to

* HITHPAEL.—*Future.* *

Pro. 22:24. *Make* no *friendship with* an angry man;

7463 רֵעֶה *rēh-geh',* m.

2Sa. 15:37. Hushai David's *friend* came
16:16. Hushai the Archite, David's *friend,*
1K. 4: 5. principal officer, (and) the king's *friend:*

7464 רֵעָה [*rēh-gāh'*], f.

Jud. 11:37. bewail my virginity, I and *my fellows.*
38. she went *with her companions,*
Ps. 45:14(15). the virgins *her companions*

רֹעָה *rōh-gāh',* f. 7465

Pro. 25:19. a *broken* tooth,

רְעוּת [*r'gooth*], f. 7468

Ex. 11: 2. every woman of *her neighbour,*
Est. 1:19. give her royal estate *unto another* (marg. *her companion*)
Isa. 34:15. gathered, every one with *her mate.*
16. none shall want *her mate:*
Jer. 9:20(19). teach...every one *her neighbour*
Zec.11: 9. eat every one the flesh of *another.* (marg. *his fellow,* or, *neighbour*)

רְעוּת *r'gooth,* f. 7469

Ecc. 1:14. all (is) vanity *and vexation of* spirit.
2:11. all (was) vanity *and vexation of* spirit,
17. all (is) vanity *and vexation of* spirit.
26. This also (is) vanity *and vexation of* spirit.
4: 4. This (is) also vanity *and vexation of* spirit.
6. the hands full (with) travail *and vexation of* spirit.
6: 9. this (is) also vanity *and vexation of* spirit.

רְעוּת *r'gooth,* Ch. f. 7470

Ezr. 5:17. *and* let the king send his *pleasure*
7:18. that do *after the will of* your God.

רְעִי *r'gee,* m. 7471

1K. 4:23(5:3). twenty oxen out *of the pastures,*

רֹעִי *rōh-gee',* m. 7473

Isa. 38:12. Mine age...is removed from me as *a shepherd's* tent:
Zec.11:17. Woe to *the* idol *shepherd*

רַעְיָה [*rag-yāh'*], f. 7474

Jud.11:37. (כתיב) my virginity, I and *my fellows.*
Cant.1: 9. I have compared thee, *O my love,*
15. thou (art) fair, *my love;* (marg. or, *companion*)
2: 2. *my love* among the daughters.
10. Rise up, *my love,* my fair one,
13. Arise, *my love,* my fair one,
4: 1. thou (art) fair, *my love;*
7. Thou (art) all fair, *my love;*
5: 2. Open to me, my sister, *my love,*
6: 4. Thou (art) beautiful, *O my love,*

רַעְיוֹן *rag-yohn',* m. 7475

Ecc. 1:17. I perceived that this also is *vexation* of
2:22. of all his labour, *and of the vexation of* his heart,
4:16. vanity *and vexation of* spirit.

רַעְיוֹן [*rag-yohn'*], Ch. m. 7476

Dan 2:29. king, *thy thoughts* came (into thy mind)
30. *and* that thou mightest know *the thoughts*
4:19(16) & 5:6. *and his thoughts* troubled him.
5:10. let not *thy thoughts* trouble thee,
7:28. *my cogitations* much troubled me,

רָעַל [*rāh-gal'*] 7477

* HOPHAL.—*Preterite.* *

Nah. 2: 3(4). the fir trees *shall be terribly shaken.*

רַעַל *rah'-gal,* m. 7478-79

Isa. 3:19. the bracelets, *and the mufflers,* (marg. or, *spangled ornaments*)
Zec. 12: 2. I will make Jerusalem a cup of *trembling* (marg. or, *slumber,* or, *poison*)

7481 **רָעַם** [*rāh-gam'*].

* KAL.—*Preterite.* *

Eze.27:35. *they shall be troubled* in (their)

KAL.—*Future.*

1Ch 16:32. *Let* the sea *roar*, and the fulness thereof:
Ps 96:11 & 98:7. *let* the sea *roar*, and the fulness thereof.

* HIPHIL.—*Preterite.* *

Ps. 29: 3. the God of glory *thundereth:*

HIPHIL.—*Infinitive.*

1Sa. 1: 6. provoked her sore, for to *make her fret*,

HIPHIL.—*Future.*

1Sa. 2:10. out of heaven *shall he thunder*
7:10. *but* the Lord *thundered*
2Sa.22:14. The Lord *thundered* from heaven,
Job 37: 4. *he thundereth* with the voice of
5. God *thundereth* marvellously
40: 9. *canst thou thunder* with a voice like him?
Ps. 18:13(14). The Lord *also thundered*

7482 **רַעַם** *rah'-gam*, m.

Job 26:14. *but the thunder of* his power
39:25. *the thunder of* the captains,
Ps. 77:18(19). The voice of *thy thunder* (was)
81: 7(8). in the secret place of *thunder:*
104: 7. the voice of *thy thunder*
Isa. 29: 6. visited of the Lord of hosts *with thunder*,

7483 **רַעְמָה** *rag-māh'*, f.

Job 39:19. hast thou clothed his neck *with thunder?*

7488 **רַעֲנָן** *rah-gănāhn'*, adj.

Deu12: 2. under every *green* tree:
1K. 14:23. under every *green* tree.
2K. 16: 4 & 17:10. under every *green* tree.
2Ch 28: 4. under every *green* tree.
Job 15:32. his branch (shall) not (be) *green.*
Ps. 37:35. like a *green* bay tree.
52: 8(10). I (am) like a *green* olive tree
92:10(11). I shall be anointed with *fresh* oil.
14(15). they shall be fat *and flourishing;* (marg. *green*)
Cant.1:16. also our bed (is) *green.*
Isa. 57: 5. under every *green* tree,
Jer. 2:20. under every *green* tree thou wanderest,
3: 6, 13. under every *green* tree,
11:16. A *green* olive tree, fair,
17: 2. the *green* trees upon the high hills.
8. her leaf shall be *green;*
Eze. 6:13. under every *green* tree,
Hos14: 8(9). I (am) like a *green* fir tree.

7487 **רַעֲנַן** *rah-gănan'*, Ch. adj.

Dan 4: 4(1). *and flourishing* in my palace:

7489 **רָעַע** [*rāh-gag'*].

* KAL.—*Preterite.* *

Nu. 11:10. Moses also was displeased. (lit. *was evil* in the eyes of Moses)
22:34. displease thee, (marg. *be evil* in thine eyes)
Deu15: 9. thine eye *be evil* against thy poor brother,
Jos. 24:15. if it seem *evil* unto you to serve the Lord,
2Sa.19: 7(8). *and* that *will be worse* unto thee than
Pro.24:18. Lest the Lord see (it), and it displease him, (marg. *and it be evil* in his eyes)
Jer. 11:16. *and* the branches of it *are broken.*
40: 4. if it seem *ill* unto thee to come

KAL.—*Infinitive.*

Isa. 24:19. The earth is *utterly* broken down, (lit. in *breaking down* is broken down)

KAL.—*Imperative.*

Isa. 8: 9. *Associate yourselves*, O ye people,

KAL.—*Future.*

Job 34:24. *He shall break in pieces* mighty men
Ps. 2: 9. *Thou shalt break them* with a rod of iron;
Jer. 15:12. *Shall* iron *break* the northern iron

* HIPHIL.—*Preterite.* *

Gen43: 6. Wherefore *dealt ye* (so) *ill* with me,
44: 5. *ye have done evil* in so doing.
Ex. 5:22. wherefore *hast thou* (so) *evil entreated*
23. *he hath done evil* to this people;
Nu. 11:11. Wherefore *hast thou afflicted* thy servant?
16:15. neither *have I hurt* one of them.
Jos. 24:20. he will turn *and do you hurt*,
Ru. 1:21. the Almighty *hath afflicted* me?
1K. 17:20. *hast thou* also *brought evil* upon the widow
2K. 21:11. *hath done wickedly* above all
1Ch 21:17. I it is that have sinned *and done evil*
Ps. 74: 3. the enemy *hath done wickedly*
Jer. 7:26. *they did worse* than their fathers.
16:12. ye *have done worse* than your fathers;
38: 9. these men *have done evil*
Mic. 3: 4. *they have behaved themselves ill*
4: 6. her that *I have afflicted;*

HIPHIL.—*Infinitive.*

Gen31: 7. God suffered him not *to hurt* me.
Lev. 5: 4. pronouncing with (his) lips *to do evil*,
1Sa.12:25. shall *still* do wickedly, (lit. *doing wickedly* ye shall do wickedly)
25:34. kept me back *from hurting* thee,
1Ch 21:17. *and* done evil *indeed;* (lit. *doing evil* have done evil)
Ps. 15: 4. (He that) sweareth *to* (his own) *hurt*,
37: 8. fret not thyself in any wise *to do evil.*
Pro.24: 8. He that deviseth *to do evil*
Isa. 1:16. cease *to do evil;*
Jer. 4:22. they (are) wise *to do evil*,
13:23. ye...that are accustomed *to do evil.*
25:29. I begin *to bring evil* on the city
31:28. to destroy, *and to afflict;*
Zec. 8:14. As I thought *to punish* you,

HIPHIL.—*Future.*

Gen19: 7. I pray you, brethren, *do* not so *wickedly.*
9. now *will we deal worse* with thee, than
Nu. 20:15. *and* the Egyptians *vexed* us,
Deu26: 6. *And* the Egyptians *evil entreated* us,
Jud. 19:23. Nay, my brethren,...*do* not (so) *wickedly*
1Sa.12:25. if *ye shall* still *do wickedly*,
26:21. *I will* no more *do thee harm*,
1K. 14: 9. *But hast done evil* above all
16:25. *and did worse* than all that (were) before him.
1Ch 16:22. *do* my prophets no *harm.*
Ps. 44: 2(3). (how) *thou didst afflict* the people,
105:15. *do* my prophets no *harm.*
Pro. 4:16. except *they have done mischief;*
Isa. 11: 9. *They shall* not *hurt* nor destroy
41:23. do good, *or do evil*,
65:25. *They shall* not *hurt* nor destroy
Jer. 10: 5. *they cannot do evil*,
25: 6. *I will do* you no *hurt.*
Zep. 1:12. neither *will he do evil.*

HIPHIL.—*Participle.*

Job 8:20. neither will he help *the evil doers:*
Ps. 22:16(17). the assembly of *the wicked*
26: 5. the congregation of *evil doers;*
27: 2. When *the wicked*,...came upon me
37: 1. Fret not thyself *because of evildoers*,
9. *evildoers* shall be cut off:
64: 2(3). the secret counsel of *the wicked;*
92:11(12). *the wicked* that rise up against me.
94:16. Who will rise up for me against *the evil doers?*
119:115. Depart from me, ye *evildoers:*
Pro.17: 4. *A wicked doer* giveth heed to false lips;
24:19. Fret not thyself *because of evil* (men),
Isa. 1: 4. a seed of *evildoers*,
9:17(16). an hypocrite *and an evildoer*
14:20. the seed of *evildoers*
31: 2. the house of *the evildoers*,
Jer. 20:13. from the hand of *evildoers.*
23:14. the hands of *evildoers*,

* HITHPOLEL.—*Preterite.* *

Isa. 24:19. The earth *is* utterly *broken down,*

HITHPOLEL.—*Infinitive.*

Pro. 18:24. A man (that hath) friends *must shew himself friendly :*

7490 **רְעַע** [*r'găg*], Ch.

* P'AL.—*Future.* *

Dan 2:40. shall it break in pieces *and bruise.*

P'AL.—*Participle.*

Dan 2:40. as iron *that breaketh* all these,

7491 **רָעַף** [*rāh-găph'*].

* KAL.—*Future.* *

Job 36:28. the clouds do drop (and) *distil*
Ps. 65:11(12). thy paths *drop* fatness.
12(13). *They drop* (upon) the pastures
Pro. 3:20. the clouds *drop down* the dew.

* HIPHIL.—*Imperative.* *

Isa. 45: 8. *Drop down,* ye heavens,

7492 **רָעַץ** [*rāh-gatz'*].

* KAL.—*Future.* *

Ex. 15: 6. thy right hand, O Lord, *hath dashed in pieces*
Jud. 10: 8. *And* that year *they vexed* and oppressed

7493 **רָעַשׁ** [*rāh-găsh'*].

* KAL.—*Preterite.* *

Jud. 5: 4. earth *trembled,* and the heavens dropped,
Ps. 68: 8(9). The earth *shook,* the heavens also
Jer. 8:16. the whole land *trembled*
49:21. The earth *is moved* at the noise
Eze. 38:20. *So that* the fishes of the sea,...*shall shake*
Joel 2:10. the heavens *shall tremble :*
3:16(4:16). *and* the heavens and the earth *shall shake :*
Nah 1: 5. The mountains *quake* at him,

KAL.—*Future.*

2Sa. 22: 8. Then the earth shook *and trembled ;*
Ps. 18: 7(8). Then the earth shook *and trembled ;*
46: 3(4). (though) the mountains *shake*
72:16. the fruit thereof *shall shake*
77:18(19). the earth trembled *and shook.*
Isa. 13:13. *and* the earth *shall remove* out of her place,
24:18. *and* the foundations of the earth *do shake.*
Jer. 10:10. the earth *shall tremble,*
51:29. *And* the land *shall tremble* and sorrow:
Eze. 26:10. thy walls *shall shake*
15. *Shall* not the isles *shake*
27:28. The suburbs *shall shake*
Am. 9: 1. *that* the posts *may shake :*

KAL.—*Participle.*

Jer. 4:24. I beheld the mountains, and, lo, *they trembled,*

* NIPHAL.—*Future.* *

Jer. 50:46. the earth *is moved,*

* HIPHIL.—*Preterite.* *

Ps. 60: 2(4). *Thou hast made* the earth *to tremble ;*
Eze. 31:16. *I made* the nations *to shake*
Hag. 2: 7. *And I will shake* all nations,

HIPHIL.—*Future.*

Job 39:20. *Canst thou make him afraid*

HIPHIL.—*Participle.*

Isa. 14:16. the man...*that did shake* kingdoms;
Hag 2: 6. I *will shake* the heavens,
21. I *will shake* the heavens

7494 **רַעַשׁ** *rah'-găsh,* m.

1K. 19:11. after the wind *an earthquake ;* (but) the Lord (was) not *in the earthquake :*
12. after *the earthquake* a fire;
Job 39:24. He swalloweth the ground *with fierceness*
41:29(21). he laugheth *at the shaking of* a
Isa. 9: 5(4). every battle of the warrior (is) *with confused noise,*
29: 6. with thunder, *and with earthquake,*
Jer. 10:22. *and a* great *commotion* out of the north
47: 3. *at the rushing* of his chariots,
Eze. 3:12. a voice of *a* great *rushing,*
13. a noise of *a* great *rushing.*
12:18. eat thy bread *with quaking,*
37: 7. there was a noise, and behold *a shaking,*
38:19. *a* great *shaking* in the land of Israel;
Am. 1: 1. two years before *the earthquake.*
Nah 3: 2. *the rattling of* the wheels,
Zec. 14: 5. *the earthquake* in the days of Uzziah

רָפָא *rāh-phāh'.* 7495

* KAL.—*Preterite.* *

Isa. 6:10. understand with their heart, and convert, *and be healed.* (lit. *healing be* to them)
19:22. he shall be intreated of them, *and shall heal them.*
57:19. *and I will heal him.*
Jer. 33: 6. *and I will cure them,*
Hos. 11: 3. they knew not that *I healed them.*

KAL.—*Infinitive.*

Ecc. 3: 3. A time to kill, and a time *to heal ;*
Isa. 19:22. he shall smite *and heal*
Hos 5:13. yet could he not *heal* you,
7: 1. *When I would have healed* Israel,

KAL.—*Imperative.*

Nu. 12:13. *Heal* her now, O God,
Ps. 6: 2(3). O Lord, *heal me ;* for my bones are
41: 4(5). Lord, be merciful unto me: *heal* my
60: 2(4). *heal* the breaches thereof;
Jer. 17:14. *Heal me,* O Lord, and I shall be healed;

KAL.—*Future.*

Gen 20:17. *and* God *healed* Abimelech,
Deu 32:39. I wound, and I *heal :*
2K. 20: 8. that the Lord *will heal* me,
2Ch 7:14. *and will heal* their land.
30:20. hearkened to Hezekiah, *and healed* the
Job 5:18. he woundeth, and his hands *make whole.*
Ps. 30: 2(3). *and thou hast healed me.*
107:20. He sent his word, *and healed them,*
Isa. 30:26. *healeth* the stroke of their wound.
57:18. *and will heal him :*
Jer. 3:22. *I will heal* your backslidings.
30:17. *I will heal thee* of thy wounds,
Lam 2:13. who *can heal* thee?
Hos. 6: 1. he hath torn, *and he will heal us ;*
14: 4(5). *I will heal* their backsliding,

KAL.—*Participle.* Poel.

Gen 50: 2. Joseph commanded...*the physicians* to
— and *the physicians* embalmed Israel.
Ex. 15:26. I (am) the Lord *that healeth thee.*
2K. 20: 5. I *will heal* thee:
2Ch 16:12. sought not to the Lord, but *to the physicians.*
Job 13: 4. all *physicians of* no value.
Ps. 103: 3. *who healeth* all thy diseases;
147: 3. *He healeth* the broken in heart,
Jer. 8:22. (is there) no *physician* there?

* NIPHAL.—*Preterite.* *

Lev. 13:18. in the skin thereof, was a boil, *and is healed,*
37. the scall *is healed,*
14: 3. (if) the plague of leprosy *be healed*
48. the plague *is healed.*
Isa. 53: 5. with his stripes we *are healed.* (lit. *it is healed* to us)
Jer. 51: 9. *she is* not *healed :*
Eze. 47: 8. the waters *shall be healed.*

NIPHAL.—*Infinitive.*

Deu 28:27. the itch, whereof thou canst not *be healed.*
35. a sore botch that cannot *be healed,*
Jer. 15:18. my wound incurable, (which) refuseth *to be healed ?*

Jer. 19:11. a potter's vessel, that *cannot be made whole* (marg. *healed*)

NIPHAL.—*Future.*

1Sa. 6: 3. then *ye shall be healed,*
2K. 2:22. *So* the waters *were healed*
Jer. 17:14. Heal me, O Lord, *and I shall be healed;*
51: 8. if so be *she may be healed.*
Eze.47: 9. *for they shall be healed;*
11. the marishes thereof *shall* not *be healed;*

* PIEL.—*Preterite.* *

2K. 2:21. Thus saith the Lord, *I have healed* these
Jer. 51: 9. *We would have healed* Babylon,
Eze.34: 4. neither *have ye healed* that which was sick,

PIEL.—*Infinitive.*

Ex. 21:19. shall cause (him) to be *thoroughly* healed.

PIEL.—*Future.*

Ex. 21:19. *shall cause* (him) *to be* thoroughly *healed.*
1K. 18:30. *And he repaired* the altar of the Lord
Jer. 6:14. *They have healed also* the hurt
8:11. *For they have healed* the hurt
Zec.11:16. nor *heal* that that is broken,

* HITHPAEL.—*Infinitive.* *

2K. 8:29. king Joram went back *to be healed*
9:15. king Joram was returned *to be healed*
2Ch 22: 6. he returned *to be healed* in Jezreel

NOTE.—In some instances רָפָא and רָפָה are interchanged in their forms. They are here arranged according to their signification.

7497 רָפָא *rāh-phāh'*, m.

Gen 14: 5. smote *the Rephaims*
15:20. the Perizzites, and *the Rephaims,*
Deu 2:11. also were accounted *giants,*
20. accounted a land of *giants: giants* dwelt therein
3:11. of the remnant of *giants;*
13. called the land of *giants.*
Jos. 12: 4. (was) of the remnant of *the giants,*
13:12. the kingdom of Og...the remnant of *the giants:*
15: 8. the valley of *the giants*
17:15. the land of the Perizzites *and of the giants,* (marg. or, *Rephaims*)
18:16. in the valley of *the giants*
2Sa. 5:18, 22 & 23:13. in the valley of *Rephaim.*
1Ch 11:15. in the valley of *Rephaim.*
14: 9. spread themselves in the valley of *Rephaim.*
20: 4. children of *the giant:* (marg. or, *Rapha*)
6. also was the son *of the giant.*
8. born *unto the giant* in Gath;
Isa. 17: 5. gathereth ears in the valley of *Rephaim.*

7500 רִפְאוּת *riph-ooth'*, f.

Pro. 3: 8. *health* (marg. *medicine*) to thy navel,

7499 רְפֻאוֹת *r'phoo-ōhth'*, f. pl.

Jer. 30:13. thou hast no healing *medicines.*
46:11. in vain shalt thou use many *medicines;*
Eze.30:21. shall not be bound up to be *healed,* (lit. to apply *medicines*)

7496 רְפָאִים *r'phāh-eem'*, m. pl.

Job 26: 5. *Dead* (things) are formed from under
Ps. 88:10(11). shall *the dead* arise (and) praise thee?
Pro. 2:18. and her paths unto *the dead.*
9:18. knoweth not that *the dead* (are) there;
21:16. the congregation of *the dead.*
Isa. 14: 9. it stirreth up *the dead* for thee,
26:14. (they are) *deceased,*
19. the earth shall cast out *the dead.*

רָפַד [*rāh-phad'*] 7502

* KAL.—*Future.* *

Job 41:30(22). *he spreadeth* sharp pointed things

* PIEL.—*Preterite.* *

Job 17:13. *I have made* my bed in the darkness.

PIEL.—*Imperative.*

Cant 2: 5. *comfort* (marg. *straw*) *me* with apples:

רָפָה *rāh-phāh'*. 7503

* KAL.—*Preterite.* *

Jud. 8: 3. their anger *was abated*
19: 9. the day *draweth* (marg. *is weak*) toward evening,
Jer. 6:24. our hands *wax feeble:*
49:24. Damascus *is waxed feeble,*
50:43. *and* his hands *waxed feeble:*
Eze.21: 7(12). *and* all hands *shall be feeble,*

KAL.—*Future.*

Ex. 4:26. *So he let* him *go:* (lit. *loosened* from him)
2Sa. 4: 1. *And* when...his hands *were feeble,*
2Ch 15: 7. *let* not your hands *be weak:*
Neh 6: 9. Their hands *shall be weakened*
Isa. 5:24. the flame *consumeth* the chaff,
13: 7. Therefore *shall* all hands *be faint,* (marg. or, *fall down*)
Eze. 7:17. All hands *shall be feeble,*
Zep. 3:16. *Let* not thine hands *be slack.* (marg. or, *faint*)

* NIPHAL.—*Participle.* *

Ex. 5: 8. for they (be) *idle;*
17. he said, Ye (are) *idle,* (ye are) *idle:*

* PIEL.—*Preterite.* *

Job 12:21. *weakeneth* the strength of the mighty.

PIEL.—*Future.*

Eze. 1:24. *they let down* their wings.
25. *had let down* their wings.

PIEL.—*Participle.*

Ezr. 4: 4. the people of the land *weakened*
Jer. 38: 4. he *weakeneth* the hands of the men of

* HIPHIL.—*Imperative.* *

Deu 9:14. *Let* me *alone,* that I may destroy them,
Jud.11:37. *let* me *alone* two months,
1Sa.11: 3. *Give* us seven days' *respite,* (marg. *Forbear* us)
15:16. Samuel said unto Saul, *Stay,*
2Sa.24:16. *stay* now thine hand.
2K. 4:27. *Let* her *alone;* for her soul
1Ch 21:15. *stay* now thine hand.
Ps. 37: 8. *Cease* from anger,
46:10(11). *Be still,* and know that I (am) God:

HIPHIL.—*Future.*

Deu 4:31. *he will* not *forsake thee,*
31: 6, 8. *he will* not *fail thee,*
Jos. 1: 5. *I will* not *fail thee,*
10: 6. *Slack* not thy hand
1Ch 28:20. *he will* not *fail thee,*
Neh 6: 3. should the work cease, whilst *I leave it,*
Job 7:19. nor *let me alone* till I swallow down my spittle?
27: 6. My righteousness I hold fast, and *will* not *let it go:*
Ps.138: 8. *forsake* not the works of thine own hands.
Pro. 4:13. fast hold of instruction; *let* (her) not *go:*
Cant.3: 4. I held him, and *would* not *let him go,*

* HITHPAEL.—*Preterite.* *

Pro.24:10. (If) *thou faint* in the day of adversity,

HITHPAEL.—*Participle.*

Jos. 18: 3. How long (are) ye *slack* to go to possess
Pro.18: 9. *He* also *that is slothful*

רָפָה *rāh-phāh'*, m. 7497

2Sa.21:16. Ishbi-benob, which (was) of the sons of *the giant,* (marg. or, *Rapha*)
18. Saph, which (was) of the sons of *the giant.* (marg. *id.*)
20. also was born *to the giant.* (marg. *id.*)
22. four were born *to the giant*

7504 **רָפֶה** *rāh-pheh'*, adj.

Nu. 13:18. whether they (be) strong or *weak*,
2Sa. 17: 2. while he (is) weary *and weak* handed,
Job 4: 3. thou hast strengthened the *weak* hands.
Isa. 35: 3. Strengthen ye the *weak* hands,

7507 **רְפִידָה** [*r'phee-dāh'*], f.

Cant. 3:10. *the bottom thereof* (of) gold,

7510 **רִפְיוֹן** *riph-yōhn'*, m.

Jer. 47: 3. the fathers shall not look back...*for feebleness of*

7511 **רָפַס** [*rāh-phas'*].

* HITHPAEL.—*Imperative.* *

Pro. 6: 3. *humble thyself*, and make sure thy friend.

HITHPAEL.—*Participle.*

Ps. 68:30(31). (till every one) *submit himself*

7512 **רְפַס** [*r'phas*], Ch.

* P'AL.—*Participle.* Active. *

Dan 7: 7. and *stamped* the residue with the feet
19. and *stamped* the residue with his feet;

7513 **רַפְסֹדוֹת** *raph-sōh-dōhth'*, f. pl.

2Ch 2:16(15). we will bring it to thee *in flotes*

7514 **רָפַק** [*rāh-phak'*].

* HITHPAEL.—*Participle.* *

Cant. 8: 5. Who (is) this that cometh up...*leaning*

7515 **רָפַשׂ** [*rāh-phās'*].

* KAL.—*Future.* *

Eze. 32: 2. *and fouledst* their rivers.
34:18. *ye must foul* the residue

* NIPHAL.—*Participle.* *

Pro. 25:26. a *troubled* fountain, and a corrupt

7516 **רֶפֶשׁ** *reh'-phesh*, m.

Isa. 57:20. the troubled sea,...whose waters cast up *mire*

7517 **רְפָתִים** *r'phāh-theem'*, m. pl.

Hab 3:17. no herd *in the stalls:*

7518 **רַץ** [*ratz*], m.

Ps. 68:30(31). submit himself *with pieces of* silver:

7519 **רָצָא** [*rāh-tzāh'*].

* KAL.—*Infinitive.* *

Eze. 1:14. the living creatures *ran*

7520 **רָצַד** [*rāh-tzad'*].

* PIEL.—*Future.* *

Ps. 68:16(17). Why *leap ye*, ye high hills?

7521 **רָצָה** *rāh-tzāh'*.

* KAL.—*Preterite.* *

1Ch 28: 4. *he liked* me to make (me) king
2Ch 10: 7. kind to this people, *and please them*,
36:21. until the land *had enjoyed* her sabbaths:
Ps. 44: 3(4). *thou hadst a favour unto them.*
85: 1(2). *thou hast been favourable* unto (marg. *well pleased*) thy land:
102:14(15). servants *take pleasure* in her stones,
Ecc. 9: 7. God now *accepteth* thy works.
Isa. 42: 1. mine elect, (in whom) my soul *delighteth;*
Jer. 14:10. the Lord *doth* not *accept* them ;
Eze. 43:27. *and I will accept* you, saith the Lord
Hos. 8:13. the Lord *accepteth* them not ;

KAL.—*Infinitive.*

1Ch 29: 3. *because I have set my affection* to
Job 34: 9. *that he should delight himself* with God.
Ps. 77: 7(8). will he *be favourable* no more?
Pro. 16: 7. *When* a man's ways *please* the Lord,

KAL.—*Imperative.*

Ps. 40:13(14). *Be pleased*, O Lord, to deliver me.
119:108. *Accept*,...the freewill offerings of my

KAL.—*Future.*

Gen 33:10. *and thou wast pleased with me.*
Lev. 26:34. Then *shall* the land *enjoy* her sabbaths,
41. *they* then *accept* of the punishment
43. *and shall enjoy* her sabbaths,
— they *shall accept* of the punishment
Deu 33:11. *accept* the work of his hands:
2Sa. 24:23. The Lord thy God *accept thee.*
1Ch 29:17. *hast pleasure* in uprightness.
Job 14: 6. till *he shall accomplish*,...his day.
33:26. *and he will be favourable unto him:*
Ps. 49:13(14). their posterity *approve* their sayings. (marg. *delight* in their mouth)
50:18. *then thou consentedst with him,*
51:16(18). *thou delightest* not in burnt offering.
62: 4(5). *they delight* in lies:
147:10. *he taketh* not *pleasure* in the legs of a man.
Pro. 3:12. a father the son (in whom) *he delighteth.*
23:26. (כתיב) and *let* thine eyes *observe* my ways.
Eze. 20:40. there *will I accept them,*
41. *I will accept* you with your sweet savour,
Am. 5:22. your meat offerings, *I will* not *accept*
Mic. 6: 7. *Will* the Lord *be pleased* with thousands of
Hag. 1: 8. *and I will take pleasure* in it,
Mal. 1: 8. *will he be pleased with thee,*
10. neither *will I accept* an offering
13. *should I accept* this of your hand?

KAL.—*Participle.* Poel.

Ps. 147:11. The Lord *taketh pleasure* in them that fear
149: 4. the Lord *taketh pleasure* in his people:
Jer. 14:12. I *will* not *accept them:*

KAL.—*Participle.* Paül.

Deu 33:24. let him be *acceptable* to his brethren,
Est. 10: 3. *and accepted* of the multitude of his

* NIPHAL.—*Preterite.* *

Lev. 1: 4. *and it shall be accepted* for him
Isa. 40: 2. her iniquity *is pardoned:*

NIPHAL.—*Future.*

Lev. 7:18. the third day, *it shall* not *be accepted,*
19: 7. abominable; *it shall* not *be accepted.*
22:23. for a vow *it shall* not *be accepted.*
25. *they shall* not *be accepted* for you.
27. *it shall be accepted* for an offering

* PIEL.—*Future.* *

Job 20:10. His children *shall seek to please* the poor, (marg. or, The poor *shall oppress* his children)

* HIPHIL.—*Preterite.* *

Lev. 26:34. rest, and *enjoy* her sabbaths

* HITHPAEL.—*Future.* *

1Sa. 29: 4. wherewith *should he reconcile himself*

רָצוֹן *rāh-tzōhn'*, m. 7522

Gen 49: 6. *and in their selfwill* they digged down a
Ex. 28:38. *that* they *may be accepted* before the Lord.
Lev. 1: 3. offer it *of his own voluntary will*
19: 5. offer it *at your own will.*
22:19. (Ye shall offer) *at your own will*
20. it shall not be *acceptable* for you.
21. shall be perfect *to be accepted;*
29. offer (it) *at your own will.*
23:11. *to be accepted for you:* (lit. *for your acceptance*)

Deu33:16. *and* (for) *the good will of* him that dwelt
23. O Naphtali, satisfied *with favour*,
2Ch 15:15. sought him with *their* whole *desire;*
Ezr. 10:11. make confession unto the Lord...and do *his pleasure :*
Neh 9:24. they might do with them *as they would.*
37. have dominion over...*at their pleasure*,
Est. 1: 8. *according to* every man's *pleasure.*
9: 5. did *what they would* (marg. *according to their will*) unto
Ps. 5:12(13). *with favour* wilt thou compass
19:14(15). words of my mouth,...*be acceptable*
30: 5(6). *in his favour* (is) life:
7(8). *by thy favour* thou hast made...to
40: 8(9). I delight to do *thy will*, O my God:
51:18(20). Do good *in thy good pleasure*
69:13(14). (in) an *acceptable* time: (lit. a time of *acceptance*)
89:17(18). *and in thy favour* our horn shall be
103:21. (ye) ministers of his, that do *his pleasure.*
106: 4. *with the favour* (that thou bearest unto)
143:10. Teach me to do *thy will;*
145:16. satisfiest *the desire of* every living thing.
19. He will fulfil *the desire of* them that
Pro. 8:35. shall obtain *favour* of the Lord.
10:32. the righteous know *what is acceptable:*
11: 1. a just weight (is) *his delight.*
20. *but* (such as are) upright...(are) *his delight.*
27. diligently seeketh good procureth *favour:*
12: 2. A good (man) obtaineth *favour*
22. they that deal truly (are) *his delight.*
14: 9. among the righteous (there is) *favour.*
35. The king's *favour* (is) toward a wise
15: 8. the prayer of the upright (is) *his delight.*
16:13. Righteous lips (are) *the delight of* kings;
15. *his favour* (is) as a cloud of the latter
18:22. obtaineth *favour* of the Lord.
19:12. *his favour* (is) as dew upon the grass.
Isa. 49: 8. In an *acceptable* time (lit. a time of *acceptance*)
56: 7. their sacrifices (shall be) *accepted* (lit. *unto favour*)
58: 5. an *acceptable* day to the Lord? (lit. a day of *acceptance*)
60: 7. they shall come up with *acceptance*
10. *but in my favour* have I had mercy
61: 2. To proclaim the *acceptable* year
Jer. 6:20. your burnt offerings (are) not *acceptable*,
Dan 8: 4. he did *according to his will*,
11: 3. do *according to his will.*
16. shall do *according to his own will*,
36. the king shall do *according to his will;*
Mal. 2:13. or receiveth (it) *with good will*

7523 **רָצַח** *rāh-tzagh'.*

*** KAL.—*Preterite.* ***

Nu. 35:27. *and* the revenger of blood *kill* the slayer;
Deu22:26. against his neighbour, *and slayeth him*,
1K. 21:19. *Hast thou killed*, and also taken

KAL.—*Infinitive.*

Jer. 7: 9. Will ye steal, *murder*, and commit
Hos. 4: 2. By swearing, and lying, *and killing*,

KAL.—*Future.*

Ex. 20:13. *Thou shalt* not *kill.*
Nu. 35:30. the murderer *shall be put to death*
Deu 4:42. the slayer...which *should kill*
5:17. *Thou shalt* not *kill.*

KAL.—*Participle.* Poel.

Nu. 35: 6. cities for refuge,...for *the manslayer*,
11. that *the slayer* may flee
12. that *the manslayer* die not,
16, 17, 18. he (is) *a murderer: the murderer* shall surely be put to death.
19. shall slay *the murderer:*
21. he (is) *a murderer:* the revenger of blood shall slay *the murderer*,
25. the congregation shall deliver *the slayer*
26. if *the slayer* shall at any time come
27. the revenger of blood kill *the slayer;*
28. *the slayer* shall return
30. *the murderer* shall be put to death
31. satisfaction for the life of *a murderer*,
Deu. 4:42. That *the slayer* might flee thither,
19: 3. that every *slayer* may flee
4. the case of *the slayer*,
6. avenger of the blood pursue *the slayer*,
Jos. 20: 3. That *the slayer*...may flee
5. they shall not deliver *the slayer*
6. then shall *the slayer* return,
21:13, 21, 27, 32, 38(36). city of refuge for *the slayer;*
Job 24:14. *The murderer* rising with the light

*** NIPHAL.—*Future.* ***

Pro.22:13. *I shall be slain* in the streets.

NIPHAL.—*Participle.*

Jud.20: 4. the woman *that was slain*,

*** PIEL.—*Future.* ***

Ps. 94: 6. and *murder* the fatherless.
Hos. 6: 9. the company of priests *murder*

PIEL.—*Participle.*

2K. 6:32. this son of *a murderer* hath sent
Isa. 1:21. lodged in it; but now *murderers.*

*** PUAL.—*Future.* ***

Ps. 62: 3(4). *ye shall be slain* all of you.

רֶצַח *reh'-tzagh*, m. 7524

Ps. 42:10(11). (As) *with a sword* (marg. or, *killing*) in my bones,
Eze.21:22(27). to open the mouth *in the slaughter*,

רָצַע *rāh-tzag'.* 7527

*** KAL.—*Preterite.* ***

Ex. 21: 6. *and* his master *shall bore* his ear through

רָצַף [*rāh-tzaph'*]. 7528

*** KAL.—*Participle.* Paül. ***

Cant 3:10. the midst thereof *being paved* (with)

רֶצֶף [*reh'-tzeph*], m. 7529

1K. 19: 6. a cake *baken on the coals*,

רִצְפָּה *ritz-pāh'*, f. 7531

2Ch 7: 3. bowed themselves...upon *the pavement*,
Est. 1: 6. *a pavement of* red, and blue, and white,
Isa. 6: 6. having *a live coal* in his hand,
Eze.40:17. *and a pavement* made for the court
— thirty chambers (were) upon *the pavement.*
18. *And the pavement* by the side of the gates
— the lower *pavement.*
42: 3. *the pavement* which (was) for the utter

רָצַץ [*rāh-tzatz'*]. 7533

*** KAL.—*Preterite.* ***

1Sa.12: 3. whom *have I oppressed?*
4. hast not defrauded us, nor *oppressed us*,

KAL.—*Future.*

Ecc.12: 6. *or* the golden bowl *be broken*,
Isa. 42: 4. He shall not fail nor *be discouraged*, (marg *broken*)

KAL.—*Participle.* Poel.

Am. 4: 1. ye kine of Bashan,...*which crush*

KAL.—*Participle.* Paül.

Deu 28:33. oppressed *and crushed* alway:
2K. 18:21. the staff of this *bruised* reed,
Isa. 36: 6. the staff of this *broken* reed,
42: 3. A *bruised* reed shall he not break,
58: 6. to let *the oppressed* (marg. *broken*) go free,
Hos. 5:11. Ephraim (is) oppressed (and) *broken*

*** NIPHAL.—*Preterite.* ***

Ecc.12: 6. *or* the wheel *broken* at the cistern.

NIPHAL.—*Future.*

Eze.29: 7. *thou didst break*, and rend

* PIEL.—*Preterite.* *

Job 20:19. *he hath oppressed* (marg. *crushed*) (and) hath forsaken the poor;
Ps. 74:14. Thou *brakest* the heads of leviathan

PIEL.—*Future.*

2Ch 16:10. *And* Asa *oppressed* (marg. *crushed*) (some) of the people

* POEL.—*Future.* *

Jud. 10: 8. they vexed *and oppressed* the children of

* HIPHIL.—*Future.* *

Jud. 9:53. *and all to brake* his scull.

* HITHPOEL.—*Future.* *

Gen 25:22. *And* the children *struggled together*

7534 רַק *rak*, adj.

Gen 41:19. seven other kine...poor...*and lean*fleshed,
20. the *lean* and the ill favoured kine
27. the seven *thin* and ill favoured kine

7535 רַק *rak*, part. conj.

Gen 6: 5. of his heart (was) *only* evil continually.
20:11. *Surely* the fear of God (is) not in this place;
26:29. done unto thee *nothing but* good,
47:26. *except* the land of the priests only,
Ex. 8:29(25). *but* let not Pharaoh deal deceitfully
Jos. 6:18. *And* ye, *in any wise* keep (yourselves)
Jud. 3: 2. *at the least* such as before knew nothing thereof;
19:20. *howsoever* (let) all thy wants (lie) upon
1K. 8: 9. nothing in the ark *save* the two tables
19. *Nevertheless* thou shalt not build
25. *so* that (marg. *only* if) thy children take
11:13. *Howbeit* I will not rend away all
2K. 14: 3. *yet* not like David his father:
2Ch 6: 9. *Notwithstanding* thou shalt not build
16. *yet so* that thy children take heed
28:10. (are there) not with you, *even* with you, &c. &c.

7536 רֹק *rōhk*, m.

Job 7:19. let me alone till I swallow down *my spittle?*
30:10. spare not *to spit* in (marg. withhold not *spittle* from) my face.
Isa. 50: 6. I hid not my face from shame *and spitting.*

7537 רָקַב [*rāh-kav'*].

* KAL.—*Future.* *

Pro. 10: 7. the name of the wicked *shall rot.*
Isa. 40:20. chooseth a tree (that) *will* not *rot;*

7538 רָקָב *rāh-kāhv'*, m.

Job 13:28. he, *as a rotten thing*, consumeth,
Pro. 12: 4. *but* she that maketh ashamed (is) *as rottenness*
14:30. *but* envy *the rottenness of* the bones.
Hos. 5:12. *and* to the house of Judah *as rottenness.* (marg. or, *a worm*)
Hab 3:16. *rottenness* entered into my bones,

7539 רִקָּבוֹן *rik-kāh-vōhn'*, m.

Job 41:27(19). esteemeth...brass as *rotten* wood.

7540 רָקַד [*rāh-kad'*].

* KAL.—*Preterite.* *

Ps. 114: 4. The mountains *skipped* like rams,

KAL.—*Infinitive.*

Ecc. 3: 4. a time to mourn, and a time *to dance;*

KAL.—*Future.*

Ps. 114: 6. Ye mountains, (that) *ye skipped* like

* PIEL.—*Future.* *

Job 21:11. their children *dance.*
Isa. 13:21. satyrs *shall dance* there.
Joel 2: 5. on the tops of mountains *shall they leap,*

PIEL.—*Participle.*

1Ch 15:29. saw king David *dancing*
Nah 3: 2. the noise...of the *jumping* chariots.

* HIPHIL.—*Future.* *

Ps. 29: 6. *He maketh them also to skip*

רַקָּה [*rak-kāh'*], f. 7541

Jud. 4:21. smote the nail *into his temples,*
22. the nail (was) *in his temples.*
5:26. pierced and stricken through *his temples.*
Cant. 4: 3. *thy temples* (are) like a piece of a
6: 7. *thy temples* within thy locks.

רָקַח [*rāh-kagh'*]. 7543

* KAL.—*Future.* *

Ex. 30:33. Whosoever *compoundeth* (any) like it,

KAL.—*Participle.* Poel.

Ex. 30:25, 35. after the art of *the apothecary:*
37:29. according to the work of *the apothecary.*
1Ch 9:30. the sons of the priests *made* the ointment
Ecc. 10: 1. the ointment of *the apothecary*

* PUAL.—*Participle.* *

2Ch 16:14. divers kinds (of spices) *prepared*

* HIPHIL.—*Infinitive.* *

Eze. 24:10. consume the flesh, *and spice* it well,

רֶקַח *reh'-kagh*, m. 7544

Cant. 8: 2. I would cause thee to drink of *spiced* wine

רֹקַח *rōh'-kagh*, m. 7545

Ex. 30:25. *an ointment* compound
35. *a confection* after the art of the apothecary,

רַקָּח [*rak-kāhgh'*], m. 7546

Neh 3: 8. son of (one of) *the apothecaries,*

רַקָּחָה [*rak-kāh-ghāh'*], f. 7548

1Sa. 8:13. take your daughters (to be) *confectionaries,*

רִקֻּחִים [*rik-kŭh-gheem'*], m. pl 7547

Isa. 57: 9. didst increase *thy perfumes,*

רָקִיעַ *rāh-kee'ăg*, m. 7549

Gen 1: 6. Let there be *a firmament* (marg. *expansion*)
7. God made *the firmament,*
— which (were) under *the firmament* from the waters which (were) above *the firmament:*
8. God called *the firmament* Heaven.
14. Let there be lights *in the firmament of*
15. for lights *in the firmament of*
17. God set them *in the firmament of*
20. in *the* open *firmament of* heaven.
Ps. 19: 1(2). *the firmament* sheweth his handywork.
150: 1. praise him *in the firmament of* his power.
Eze. 1:22. the likeness of *the firmament*
23. under *the firmament*
25. a voice from *the firmament*
26. above *the firmament*
10: 1. in *the firmament* that was above
Dan 12: 3. shine as the brightness of *the firmament;*

רָקִיק *rāh-keek'*, m. 7550

Ex. 29: 2. *and wafers* unleavened anointed
23. *and* one *wafer* out of the basket
Lev. 2: 4. *or* unleavened *wafers* anointed

Lev. 7:12. *and* unleavened *wafers* anointed with
8:26. a cake of oiled bread, *and* one *wafer*,
Nu. 6:15. *and wafers of* unleavened bread
19. *and* one unleavened *wafer*,
1Ch 23:29. *and for the* unleavened *cakes*,

7551 רָקַם [*rāh-kam'*].

* KAL.—*Participle.* Poel. *

Ex. 26:36 & 27:16. fine twined linen, wrought with *needle*work.
28:39. make the girdle (of) *needle*work.
35:35. manner of work,...*and of the embroiderer*,
36:37. an hanging...of *needle*work; (marg. the work of *a needleworker*, or, *embroiderer*)
38:18. the hanging for the gate...(was) *needle*-work,
23. *and an embroiderer* in blue, and in purple,
39:29. a girdle (of) fine twined linen,...(of) *needle*work;

* PUAL.—*Preterite.* *

Ps. 139:15. I was made...(and) *curiously wrought* (lit. *embroidered*)

7553 רִקְמָה *rik-māh'*, f.

Jud. 5:30. a prey of divers colours...of *needlework*, of divers colours of *needlework on both sides*,
1Ch 29: 2. glistering stones, *and of divers colours*,
Ps. 45:14(15). brought unto the king *in raiment of needlework*:
Eze. 16:10. I clothed thee also with *broidered work*,
13. fine linen, and silk, *and broidered work*;
18. tookest *thy broidered* garments,
17: 3. feathers, which had *divers colours*, (marg. *embroidering*)
26:16. put off *their broidered* garments:
27: 7. Fine linen *with broidered work*
16. *and broidered work*, and fine linen,
24. blue clothes, *and broidered work*,

7554 רָקַע [*rāh-ka^{n}g'*].

* KAL.—*Infinitive.* *

Eze. 25: 6. clapped (thine) hands, *and stamped* with the

KAL.—*Imperative.*

Eze. 6:11. Smite with thine hand, *and stamp* with thy

KAL.—*Future.*

2Sa. 22:43. *did spread them abroad.*

KAL.—*Participle.* Poel.

Ps. 136: 6. *To him that stretched out* the earth
Isa. 42: 5. *he that spread forth* the earth,
44:24. *that spreadeth abroad* the earth

* PIEL.—*Future.* *

Ex. 39: 3. *And they did beat* the gold into thin plates,
Nu. 16:39(17:4). *and they were made broad* (plates)
Isa. 40:19. the goldsmith *spreadeth it over* with gold,

* PUAL.—*Participle.* *

Jer. 10: 9. Silver *spread into plates*

* HIPHIL.—*Future.* *

Job 37:18. *Hast thou...spread out* the sky,

7555 רִקֻּעִים [*rik-koo-^{n}geem'*], m. pl.

Nu. 16:38(17:3). let them make them *broad* plates

7556 רָקַק [*rāh-kak'*].

* KAL.—*Future.* *

Lev. 15: 8. if he that hath the issue *spit*

רִשְׁיוֹן *rish-yōhn'*, m. 7558

Ezr. 3: 7. *according to the grant* that they had of

רָשַׁם [*rāh-sham'*]. 7559

* KAL.—*Participle.* Paül. *

Dan 10:21. *that which is noted* in the scripture

רְשַׁם *r'sham*, Ch. 7560

* P'AL.—*Preterite.* *

Dan 6: 9(10). king Darius *signed* the writing
12(13). *Hast thou* not *signed* a decree,
13(14). nor the decree that *thou hast signed*,

P'AL.—*Future.*

Dan 6: 8(9). *and sign* the writing,

P'AL.—*Participle.* Passive.

Dan 5:24. and this writing *was written.*
25. this (is) the writing that *was written*,
6:10(11). when Daniel knew that the writing *was signed*,

רָשַׁע [*rāh-sha^{n}g'*]. 7561

* KAL.—*Preterite.* *

2Sa. 22:22. and *have* not *wickedly departed*
1K. 8:47. *we have committed wickedness*;
2Ch 6:37. have done amiss, *and have dealt wickedly*;
Job 10:15. If *I be wicked*, woe unto me;
Ps. 18:21(22). and *have* not *wickedly departed*
Dan 9:15. we have sinned, *we have done wickedly.*

KAL.—*Future.*

Job 9:29. (If) I *be wicked*, why then labour I in
10: 7. Thou knowest that *I am* not *wicked*;
Ecc. 7:17. *Be* not over much *wicked*,

* HIPHIL.—*Preterite.* *

Deu 25: 1. they shall justify the righteous, *and condemn* the wicked.
2Ch 20:35. who *did* very *wickedly*:
Neh 9:33. but *we have done wickedly*:
Ps. 106: 6. iniquity, *we have done wickedly.*
Dan 9: 5. We have sinned,...*and have done wickedly*,
12:10. *but* the wicked *shall do wickedly*:

HIPHIL.—*Infinitive.*

1K. 8:32. *condemning* the wicked,
2Ch 22: 3. mother was his counsellor *to do wickedly.*

HIPHIL.—*Future.*

Ex. 22: 9(8). whom the judges *shall condemn*,
1Sa. 14:47. whithersoever he turned himself, *he vexed*
Job 9:20. mine own mouth *shall condemn me*:
10: 2. *Do* not *condemn me*;
15: 6. Thine own mouth *condemneth thee*,
32: 3. *and* (yet) *had condemned* Job.
34:12. surely God *will* not *do wickedly*,
17. *wilt thou condemn* him that is most just?
29. who then *can make trouble*?
40: 8. *wilt thou condemn me*,
Ps. 37:33. The Lord will not leave...nor *condemn him*
94:21. and *condemn* the innocent blood.
Pro. 12: 2. a man of wicked devices *will he condemn.*
Isa. 50: 9. who (is) he (that) *shall condemn me*?
54:17. every tongue...*thou shalt condemn.*

HIPHIL.—*Participle.*

Pro. 17:15. *and he that condemneth* the just,
Dan 11:32. *And such as do wickedly against* the

רָשָׁע *rāh-shāh^{n}g'*, adj. 7563

Gen 18:23. Wilt thou also destroy the righteous with *the wicked*?
25. the righteous with *the wicked*: and that the righteous should be *as the wicked*,
Ex. 2:13. said *to him that did the wrong*,
9:27. I and my people (are) *wicked.*
23: 1. put not thine hand with *the wicked*
7. I will not justify *the wicked.*

Nu. 16:26. Depart,...from the tents of these *wicked*
35:31. a murderer, which (is) *guilty* of death: (marg. *faulty* to die)
Deu25: 1. the righteous, and condemn *the wicked.*
2. if *the wicked man* (be) worthy to be
1Sa. 2: 9. *and the wicked* shall be silent in darkness;
24:13(14). proceedeth *from the wicked:*
2Sa. 4:11. when *wicked* men have slain a righteous
1K. 8:32. condemning *the wicked,*
2Ch 6:23. by requiting *the wicked,*
19: 2. Shouldest thou help *the ungodly,*
Job 3:17. There *the wicked* cease (from) troubling;
8:22. the dwelling place of *the wicked*
9:22. He destroyeth the perfect *and the wicked.*
24. The earth is given into the hand of *the wicked:*
10: 3. the counsel of *the wicked?*
11:20. the eyes of *the wicked* shall fail,
15:20. *The wicked man* travaileth with pain
16:11. me over into the hands of *the wicked.*
18: 5. the light of *the wicked* shall be put out,
20: 5. the triumphing of *the wicked* (is) short,
29. the portion of *a wicked* man
21: 7. Wherefore do *the wicked* live,
16. the counsel of *the wicked* is far from me.
17. the candle of *the wicked* put out?
28. the dwelling places of *the wicked?*
22:18. the counsel of *the wicked* is far from me.
24: 6. they gather the vintage of *the wicked.*
27: 7. Let mine enemy be *as the wicked,*
13. the portion of a *wicked* man
34:18. to princes, (Ye are) *ungodly?*
26. He striketh them as *wicked men*
36: 6. He preserveth not the life of *the wicked:*
17. fulfilled the judgment of *the wicked:*
38:13. that *the wicked* might be shaken out
15. *from the wicked* their light is withholden,
40:12. tread down *the wicked* in their place.
Ps. 1: 1. walketh not in the counsel of *the ungodly,* (marg. or, *wicked*)
4. *The ungodly* (are) not so:
5. *the ungodly* shall not stand
6. the way of *the ungodly* shall perish.
3: 7(8). broken the teeth of *the ungodly.*
7: 9(10). Oh let the wickedness of *the wicked* come to an end;
9: 5(6). thou hast destroyed *the wicked,*
16(17). *the wicked* is snared in the work
17(18). *The wicked* shall be turned into hell,
10: 2. *The wicked* in (his) pride doth persecute
3. *the wicked* boasteth of his heart's desire,
4. *The wicked,*...will not seek (after God):
13. Wherefore doth *the wicked* contemn God?
15. Break thou the arm of *the wicked*
11: 2. *the wicked* bend (their) bow,
5. *but the wicked* and him that loveth violence
6. Upon *the wicked* he shall rain snares,
12: 8(9). *The wicked* walk on every side,
17: 9. *the wicked* that oppress me,
13. deliver my soul *from the wicked,*
26: 5. will not sit with *the wicked.*
28: 3. Draw me not away with *the wicked,*
31:17(18). let *the wicked* be ashamed,
32:10. Many sorrows (shall be) *to the wicked:*
34:21(22). Evil shall slay *the wicked:*
36: 1(2). The transgression of *the wicked*
11(12). let not the hand of *the wicked* remove
37:10. *the wicked* (shall) not (be):
12. *The wicked* plotteth against the just,
14. *The wicked* have drawn out the sword,
16. the riches of many *wicked.*
17. the arms of *the wicked* shall be broken:
20. *the wicked* shall perish,
21. *The wicked* borroweth, and payeth not
28. the seed of *the wicked* shall be cut off.
32. *The wicked* watcheth the righteous,
34. when *the wicked* are cut off,
35. I have seen *the wicked* in great power,
38. the end of *the wicked* shall be cut off.
40. deliver them *from the wicked,*
39: 1(2). while *the wicked* is before me.
50:16. *But unto the wicked* God saith,
55: 3(4). the oppression of *the wicked:*
58: 3(4). *The wicked* are estranged from the
10(11). wash his feet in the blood of *the wicked.*
68: 2(3). let *the wicked* perish at the presence of

Ps. 71: 4. Deliver me, O my God, out of the hand of *the wicked,*
73: 3. I saw the prosperity of *the wicked.*
12. *the ungodly,* who prosper in the world;
75: 4(5). *and to the wicked,* Lift not up the horn:
8(9). all *the wicked of* the earth
10(11). the horns of *the wicked* also will I cut
82: 2. accept the persons of *the wicked?*
4. rid (them) out of the hand of *the wicked.*
91: 8. see the reward of *the wicked.*
92: 7(8). When *the wicked* spring as the grass.
94: 3. how long shall *the wicked,* how long shall *the wicked* triumph?
13. until the pit be digged *for the wicked.*
97:10. them out of the hand of *the wicked.*
101: 8. I will early destroy all *the wicked of*
104:35. *and* let *the wicked* be no more.
106:18. the flame burned up *the wicked.*
109: 2. the mouth of *the wicked*
6. Set thou *a wicked man* over him:
7. When he shall be judged, let him be *condemned:* (marg. go out *guilty,* or, *wicked*)
112:10. *The wicked* shall see (it),
— the desire of *the wicked* shall perish.
119:53. *because of the wicked* that forsake thy law.
61. The bands of *the wicked* have robbed me:
95. *The wicked* have waited for me
110. *The wicked* have laid a snare for me:
119. Thou puttest away all *the wicked of*
155. Salvation (is) far *from the wicked:*
129: 4. cut asunder the cords of *the wicked.*
139:19. Surely thou wilt slay *the wicked,*
140: 4(5). Keep me, O Lord, from the hands of *the wicked;*
8(9). the desires of *the wicked:*
141:10. Let *the wicked* fall into their own nets,
145:20. all *the wicked* will he destroy.
146: 9. way of *the wicked* he turneth upside down.
147: 6. casteth *the wicked* down to the ground.
Pro. 2:22. *But the wicked* shall be cut off
3:25. the desolation of *the wicked,*
33. in the house of *the wicked:*
4:14. Enter not into the path of *the wicked,*
19. The way of *the wicked* (is) as darkness:
5:22. His own iniquity shall take *the wicked*
9: 7. he that rebuketh *a wicked* (man)
10: 3. casteth away the substance of *the wicked.*
6, 11. violence covereth the mouth of *the wicked.*
7. the name of *the wicked* shall rot.
16. the fruit of *the wicked* to sin.
20. the heart of *the wicked* (is) little worth.
24. The fear of *the wicked,*
25. so (is) *the wicked* no (more):
27. the years of *the wicked* shall be shortened.
28. the expectation of *the wicked* shall perish.
30. *but the wicked* shall not inhabit the earth.
32. mouth of *the wicked* (speaketh) frowardness.
11: 5. *the wicked* shall fall by his own wickedness.
7. When a *wicked* man dieth,
8. *the wicked* cometh in his stead.
10. when *the wicked* perish, (there is) shouting.
11. overthrown by the mouth of *the wicked.*
18. *The wicked* worketh a deceitful work.
23. the expectation of *the wicked* (is) wrath.
31. *the wicked* and the sinner.
12: 5. the counsels of *the wicked* (are) deceit.
6. The words of *the wicked* (are) to lie in
7. *The wicked* are overthrown, and (are) not:
10. tender mercies of *the wicked* (are) cruel.
12. *The wicked* desireth the net of evil
21. *the wicked* shall be filled with mischief.
26. the way of *the wicked* seduceth them.
13: 5. *but a wicked* (man) is loathsome,
9. the lamp of *the wicked* shall be put out.
17. A *wicked* messenger falleth into mischief:
25. the belly of *the wicked* shall want.
14:11. house of *the wicked* shall be overthrown:
19. *and the wicked* at the gates of the
32. *The wicked* is driven away
15: 6. in the revenues of *the wicked* is trouble.
8. The sacrifice of *the wicked* (is) an
9. The way of *the wicked* (is) an abomination
28. the mouth of *the wicked* poureth out evil
29. The Lord (is) far *from the wicked:*
16: 4. *the wicked* for the day of evil.
17:15. He that justifieth *the wicked,*

Pro.17:23. *A wicked* (man) taketh a gift
18: 3. When *the wicked* cometh,
5. good to accept the person of *the wicked*,
19:28. mouth of *the wicked* devoureth iniquity.
20:26. A wise king scattereth *the wicked*,
21: 4. the plowing of *the wicked*, (is) sin.
7. robbery of *the wicked* shall destroy them;
10. The soul of *the wicked* desireth evil:
12. the house of *the wicked*: (but God) overthroweth *the wicked*
18. *The wicked* (shall be) a ransom
27. sacrifice of *the wicked* (is) abomination:
29. A *wicked* man hardeneth his face:
24:15. Lay not wait, *O wicked* (man),
16. *but the wicked* shall fall into mischief.
19. neither be thou envious *at the wicked;*
20. the candle of *the wicked* shall be put out.
24. He that saith *unto the wicked*, Thou (art) righteous;
25: 5. away *the wicked* (from) before the king,
26. A righteous man falling down before *the wicked*
28: 1. *The wicked* flee when no man pursueth:
4. They that forsake the law praise *the wicked:*
12. when *the wicked* rise, a man is hidden.
15. a *wicked* ruler over the poor people.
28. *the wicked* rise, men hide themselves:
29: 2. when *the wicked* beareth rule,
7. *the wicked* regardeth not
12. all his servants (are) *wicked*.
16. When *the wicked* are multiplied,
27. abomination to *the wicked*.
Ecc. 3:17. shall judge the righteous and *the wicked:*
7:15. *a wicked* (man) that prolongeth (his life)
8:10. I saw *the wicked* buried,
13. it shall not be well *with the wicked*,
14. according to the work of *the wicked;* again, there be *wicked* (men),
9: 2. event to the righteous, *and to the wicked;*
Isa. 3:11. Woe *unto the wicked!*
5:23. justify *the wicked* for reward,
11: 4. shall he slay *the wicked*.
13:11. will punish...*the wicked* for their iniquity;
14: 5. Lord hath broken the staff of *the wicked*,
26:10. Let favour be shewed to *the wicked*,
48:22. no peace, saith the Lord, *unto the wicked*.
53: 9. he made his grave with *the wicked*,
55: 7. Let *the wicked* forsake his way,
57:20. *But the wicked* (are) like the troubled sea,
21. no peace, saith my God, *to the wicked*.
Jer. 5:26. my people are found *wicked* (men):
12: 1. doth the way of *the wicked* prosper?
23:19. grievously upon the head of *the wicked*.
25:31. give *them that are wicked* to the sword,
30:23. fall with pain upon the head of *the wicked*.
Eze. 3:18. When I say unto *the wicked*,
— to warn *the wicked* from his *wicked* way,
— *the* same *wicked* (man) shall die
19. if thou warn *the wicked*,
— nor from his *wicked* way,
7:21. *and to the wicked of* the earth
13:22. strengthened the hands of *the wicked*,
18:20. the wickedness of *the wicked*
21. *But* if *the wicked* will turn from
23. that *the wicked* should die?
24. abominations that *the wicked* (man) doeth,
27. when *the wicked* (man) turneth away
21: 3(8), 4(9). cut off from thee the righteous *and the wicked*.
25(30). profane *wicked* prince of Israel,
29(34). *the wicked*, whose day
33: 8. When I say *unto the wicked, O wicked* (man), thou shalt surely die;
— to warn *the wicked* from his way, that *wicked* (man) shall die
9. if thou warn *the wicked*
11. no pleasure in the death of *the wicked;* but that *the wicked* turn
12. the wickedness of *the wicked*,
14. when I say *unto the wicked*,
15. (If) *the wicked* restore the pledge,
19. if *the wicked* turn from his wickedness,
Dan12:10. *the wicked* shall do wickedly: and none of *the wicked* shall understand;
Mic. 6:10. in the house of *the wicked*,
Hab. 1: 4. *the wicked* doth compass about the
13. holdest thy tongue when *the wicked*
Hab. 3:13. out of the house of *the wicked*,
Zep. 1: 3. I will consume...the stumblingblocks with *the wicked;*
Mal. 3:18. discern between the righteous *and the wicked*,
4: 3(3:21). ye shall tread down *the wicked;*

רֶשַׁע *reh'-shag*, m. 7562

Deu. 9:27. look not...to *their wickedness*,
1Sa.24:13(14). *Wickedness* proceedeth from the
Job 34: 8. walketh with *wicked* men. (lit. men of *wickedness*)
10. from God, (that he should do) *wickedness;*
35: 8. *Thy wickedness* (may hurt) a man as
Ps. 5: 4(5). that hath pleasure in *wickedness:*
10:15. seek out *his wickedness* (till) thou find
45: 7(8). righteousness, and hatest *wickedness:*
84:10(11). to dwell in the tents of *wickedness*.
125: 3. the rod of *the wicked* (marg. *wickedness*)
141: 4. to practise *wicked* works (lit. works *in wickedness*)
Pro. 4:17. they eat the bread of *wickedness*,
8: 7. *wickedness* (is) an abomination to my
10: 2. Treasures of *wickedness* profit nothing:
12: 3. shall not be established *by wickedness:*
16:12. to kings to commit *wickedness:*
Ecc. 3:16. I saw under the sun...(that) *wickedness* (was) there; and the place of righteousness, (that) *iniquity* (was) there.
7:25. to know *the wickedness of* folly,
8: 8. neither shall *wickedness* deliver
Isa. 58: 4. to smite with the fist of *wickedness:*
6. to loose the bands of *wickedness*,
Jer. 14:20. We acknowledge, O Lord, *our wickedness*,
Eze. 3:19. he turn not *from his wickedness*,
7:11. is risen up into a rod of *wickedness:*
31:11. driven him out *for his wickedness*.
33:12. day that he turneth *from his wickedness;*
Hos10:13. Ye have plowed *wickedness*,
Mic. 6:10. treasures of *wickedness* in the house of
11. Shall I count (them) pure with the *wicked* balances, (lit. balances of *wickedness*)

רִשְׁעָה *rish-gāh'*, f. 7564

Deu. 9: 4. *but for the wickedness of* these nations
5. *for the wickedness of* these nations
25: 2. beaten...according to *his fault*,
Pro.11: 5. *but* the wicked shall fall *by his own wickedness*.
13: 6. *but wickedness* overthroweth the sinner.
Isa. 9:18(17). *wickedness* burneth as the fire:
Eze. 5: 6. changed my judgments *into wickedness*
18:20. *the wickedness of* the wicked shall be
27. turneth away *from his wickedness*
33:12. *as for the wickedness of* the wicked,
19. if the wicked turn *from his wickedness*,
Zec. 5: 8. This (is) *wickedness*.
Mal. 1: 4. The border of *wickedness*,
3:15. they that work *wickedness*
4: 1(3:19). that do *wickedly*, (lit. do *wickedness*)

רֶשֶׁף *reh'-sheph*, m. 7565

Deu32:24. devoured with *burning heat*, (marg. *coals*)
Job 5: 7. man is born unto trouble, as the sparks (marg. the sons of *the burning coal*) fly
Ps. 76: 3(4). brake he *the arrows of* the bow,
78:48. gave up...their flocks *to hot thunderbolts*. (marg. or, *lightnings*)
Cant. 8: 6. jealousy...*the coals thereof* (are) *coals of*
Hab. 3: 5. *burning coals* (marg. or, *diseases*) went forth at his feet.

רָשַׁשׁ [*rāh-shash'*]. 7567

* POEL.—*Future*. *

Jer. 5:17. *they shall impoverish* thy fenced cities,

* PUAL.—*Preterite*. *

Mal 1: 4. Edom saith, *We are impoverished*,

7568 **רֶשֶׁת** *reh'-sheth*, f.

Ex. 27: 4. a grate of *net*work (of) brass; and upon *the net* shalt thou make
5. that *the net* may be even
38: 4. a brasen grate of *net*work
Job 18: 8. he is cast *into a net*
Ps. 9:15(16). *in the net* which they hid is their own
10: 9. draweth him *into his net*.
25:15. shall pluck my feet *out of the net*.
31: 4(5). Pull me *out of the net*
35: 7. hid for me *their net* (in) a pit,
8. *and* let *his net* that he hath hid
57: 6(7). They have prepared *a net* for my
140: 5(6). they have spread *a net*
Pro. 1:17. in vain *the net* is spread in the sight of
29: 5. spreadeth *a net* for his feet.
Lam. 1:13. he hath spread *a net* for my feet,
Eze. 12:13. *My net* also will I spread
17:20. I will spread *my net* upon
19: 8. spread *their net* over him:
32: 3. I will therefore spread out *my net*
Hos. 5: 1. *and a net* spread upon Tabor.
7:12. I will spread *my net* upon them;

7569 **רַתּוֹק** *rat-tōhk'*, m.

Eze. 7:23. Make *a chain*: for the land is full of

7572 **רַתּוֹקָה** [*rat-tōh-kāh'*], f.

1K. 6:21. made a partition *by the chains*

7570 **רָתַח** [*rāh-thaġh'*].

* PIEL.—*Imperative*. *

Eze. 24: 5. *make it boil* well,

* PUAL.—*Preterite*. *

Job 30:27. My bowels *boiled*,

* HIPHIL.—*Future*. *

Job 41:31(23). *He maketh* the deep *to boil*

7571 **רֶתַח** [*reh'-thaġh*], m.

Eze. 24: 5. make it boil *well*, (lit. make it boil *its boilings*)

7572 **רַתִּיקָה** [*rat-tee-kāh'*], f.

1K. 6:21. (כתיב) made a partition *by the chains*

7573 **רָתַם** [*rāh-tham'*].

* KAL.—*Imperative*. *

Mic. 1:13. *bind* the chariot to the swift beast:

7574 **רֹתֶם** *rōh'-them*, com.

1K. 19: 4. sat down under a *juniper tree*:
5. slept under a *juniper tree*,
Job 30: 4. cut up...*juniper* roots (for) their meat.
Ps. 120: 4. arrows of the mighty, with coals of *juniper*.

7576 **רָתַק** [*rāh-thak'*].

* NIPHAL.—*Future*. *

Ecc. 12: 6. Or ever the silver cord *be loosed*,

* PUAL.—*Preterite*. *

Nah. 3:10. her great men *were bound* in chains.

7577 **רְתֻקוֹת** *r'thoo-kōhth'*, f. pl.

Isa. 40:19. *and* casteth silver *chains*.

7578 **רְתֵת** *r'thēhth*, m.

Hos 13: 1. When Ephraim spake *trembling*,

שׂ *seen*.

(With שׂ) The Twenty-first Letter of the Alphabet.

שְׂאֹר *s'ōhr*, m. 7603

Ex. 12:15. ye shall put away *leaven*
19. shall there be no *leaven* found
13: 7. neither shall there be *leaven* seen
Lev. 2:11. for ye shall burn no *leaven*,
Deu 16: 4. there shall be no *leavened bread*

שְׂאֵת *s'ēhth*, f. 7613

Gen 4: 7. If thou doest well, shalt thou not be *accepted?* (marg. or, have *the excellency*)
49: 3. the excellency of *dignity*, and the
Lev. 13: 2. When a man shall have...*a rising*, (marg. or, *swelling*)
10. (if) *the rising* (be) white in the skin,
— quick raw flesh *in the rising*;
19. in the place of the boil there be *a* white *rising*,
28. *a rising of* the burning,
43. (if) *the rising of* the sore (be) white
14:56. *And for a rising*, and for a scab,
Job 13:11. Shall not *his excellency* make you afraid?
31:23. and by reason of *his highness* I could not endure.
41:25(17). *When he raiseth up himself*,
Ps. 62: 4(5). consult to cast (him) down *from his excellency*:
Hab 1: 7. their judgment *and their dignity* shall

שָׂבָךְ [*sāh-vāh'ch'*], m. 7638

1K. 7:17. *nets* of checker work,

שְׂבָכָה *s'vāh-'chāh'*, f. 7639

1K. 7:17. nets of *checker* work,
18. upon *the* one *network*,
20. the belly which (was) by *the network*:
41. *and the* two *networks*, to cover
42. pomegranates for *the* two *networks*,
— pomegranates *for* one *network*,
2K. 1: 2. Ahaziah fell down through *a lattice*
25:17. *and the wreathen work*, and pomegranates upon the chapiter round about,
— pillar with *wreathen work*.
2Ch 4:12. *and the* two *wreaths* to cover
13. pomegranates on *the* two *wreaths*;
— pomegranates *on* each *wreath*,
Job 18: 8. and he walketh upon *a snare*.
Jer. 52:22. *with network* and pomegranates
23. pomegranates upon *the network*

שַׂבְּכָא *sab-b'chāh'*, Ch. f. 5443

Dan 3: 7, 10, 15. cornet, flute, harp, *sackbut*,

שָׂבַע *sāh-vag'* & **שָׂבֵעַ** [*sāh-veh'ăg*]. 7646

* KAL.—*Preterite*. *

Deu 6:11. when thou shalt have eaten *and be full*;
8:10. When thou hast eaten *and art full*,
12. (when) thou hast eaten *and art full*,
11:15. that thou mayest eat *and be full*.
14:29. shall eat *and be satisfied*;
26:12. that they may eat...*and be filled*;
31:20. shall have eaten *and filled themselves*,
1Ch 23: 1. when David was old *and full of* days,
Job 7: 4. *and I am full of* tossings
Ps. 88: 3(4). my soul *is full of* troubles:
123: 3. *we are* exceedingly *filled with* contempt.
4. Our soul *is* exceedingly *filled with*
Pro. 30:16. the earth (that) *is* not *filled with* water;
Isa. 1:11. *I am full of* the burnt offerings of rams,
9:20(19). *they shall* not *be satisfied*:
66:11. That ye may suck, *and be satisfied*

Jer. 46:10. *and it shall be satiate* and made drunk
Eze.16:28. yet *couldest* not *be satisfied.*
29. yet *thou wast* not *satisfied*
39:20. *Thus ye shall be filled* at my table
Hos.13: 6. *they were filled*, and their heart was
Joel 2:19. *and ye shall be satisfied therewith:*
Hab 2:16. *Thou art filled with* shame

KAL.—*Infinitive.*

Ex. 16: 8. in the morning bread *to the full;*
2Ch 31:10. *we have had enough* to eat,
Lam. 5: 6. *to be satisfied with* bread.
Joel 2:26. eat in plenty, *and be satisfied,*

KAL.—*Imperative.*

Pro.20:13. *thou shalt be satisfied with* bread.

KAL.—*Future.*

Ex. 16:12. *ye shall be filled with* bread;
Lev.26:26. ye shall eat, and not *be satisfied.*
Ru. 2:14. she did eat, *and was sufficed,*
2Ch 24:15. *and was full of* days when he died;
Neh 9:25. they did eat, *and were filled,*
Job 19:22. *are* not *satisfied* with my flesh?
27:14. his offspring *shall* not *be satisfied with*
31:31. *we cannot be satisfied.*
Ps. 17:14. *they are full of* children, (marg. or, their children *are full*)
15. *I shall be satisfied*, when I awake,
22:26(27). The meek shall eat *and be satisfied:*
37:19. in the days of famine *they shall be satisfied.*
59:15(16). grudge if *they be* not *satisfied.*
63: 5(6). My soul *shall be satisfied*
65: 4(5). *we shall be satisfied*
78:29. they did eat, *and were* well *filled:*
104:13. the earth *is satisfied*
16. The trees of the Lord *are full* (of sap);
28. *they are filled with* good.
Pro. 1:31. shall they eat...and *be filled*
5:10. Lest strangers *be filled with* thy wealth;
12:11. He that tilleth his land *shall be satisfied with*
14. A man *shall be satisfied with* good
14:14. The backslider in heart *shall be filled*
18:20. A man's belly *shall be satisfied*
— *with* the increase of his lips *shall he be filled.*
25:16. lest *thou be filled therewith*, and vomit
17. lest *he be weary* (marg. *full*) *of thee*, and (so) hate thee.
27:20. Hell and destruction *are* never *full;* so the eyes of man *are* never *satisfied.*
28:19. He that tilleth his land *shall have plenty of* bread: but he that followeth after vain (persons) *shall have* poverty *enough.*
30: 9. Lest *I be full*, and deny (thee),
15. three (things that) *are* never *satisfied,*
22. a fool when *he is filled with* meat;
Ecc. 1: 8. the eye *is* not *satisfied* with seeing,
4: 8. neither *is* his eye *satisfied with* riches;
5:10(9). He that loveth silver *shall* not *be satisfied*
6: 3. his soul *be* not *filled* with good,
Isa. 44:16. he roasteth roast, *and is satisfied:*
53:11. He shall see of the travail of his soul, (and) *shall be satisfied:*
Jer. 31:14. my people *shall be satisfied*
44:17. *for* (then) *had we plenty of* victuals,
50:10. all that spoil her *shall be satisfied,*
19. his soul *shall be satisfied*
Lam. 3:30. *he is filled full* with reproach.
Hos. 4:10. they shall eat, and not *have enough:*
13: 6. According to their pasture, *so were they filled;*
Am. 4: 8. *they were* not *satisfied:*
Mic. 6:14. Thou shalt eat, but not *be satisfied;*
Hab 2: 5. enlargeth his desire...and cannot *be satisfied,*

* PIEL.—*Imperative.* *

Ps. 90:14. *O satisfy* us early with thy mercy;

PIEL.—*Future.*

Eze. 7:19. *they shall* not *satisfy* their souls,

* HIPHIL.—*Preterite.* *

Ps.107: 9. *he satisfieth* the longing soul,
Isa. 58:11. *and satisfy* thy soul in drought,
Lam. 3:15. *He hath filled me* with bitterness,
Eze.27:33. *thou filledst* many people;
32: 4. *and I will fill* the beasts of the whole

HIPHIL.—*Infinitive.*

Job 38:27. *To satisfy* the desolate and waste

HIPHIL.—*Future.*

Job 9:18. *filleth me* with bitterness.
Ps. 81:16(17). with honey...*should I have satisfied thee.*
91:16. With long life *will I satisfy him,*
105:40. *satisfied them with* the bread of heaven.
132:15. *I will satisfy* her poor *with* bread.
147:14. *filleth thee* with the finest of the wheat.
Isa. 58:10. *satisfy* the afflicted soul;

HIPHIL.—*Participle.*

Ps.103: 5. *Who satisfieth* thy mouth with good
145:16. *and satisfiest* the desire of every living thing.

שָׂבָע *sāh-vāhg'*, m. 7647

Gen41:29. seven years of great *plenty*
30. *the plenty* shall be forgotten
31. *the plenty* shall not be known
34. the seven *plenteous* years.
47. *in* the seven *plenteous* years,
53. the seven years of *plenteousness,*
Pro. 3:10. So shall thy barns be filled with *plenty,*
Ecc. 5:12(11). *but the abundance* of the rich

שָׂבֵעַ *sāh-vēh'ăg*, adj. 7649

Gen25: 8. an old man, *and full* (of years);
35:29. old *and full of* days:
Deu33:23. O Naphtali, *satisfied with* favour,
1Sa. 2: 5. (They that were) *full* have hired out
1Ch 29:28. *full of* days, riches, and honour:
Job 10:15. (I am) *full of* confusion;
14: 1. of few days, *and full of* trouble.
42:17. Job died, (being) old *and full of* days.
Pro.19:23. *and* (he that hath it) shall abide *satisfied;*
27: 7. The *full* soul loatheth an honeycomb;

שֹׂבַע *sōh'-vag*, m. 7648

Ex. 16: 3. when we did eat bread *to the full;*
Lev.25:19. ye shall eat your *fill*, (lit. *to fulness*)
26: 5. eat your bread *to the full,*
Deu23:24(25). thou mayest eat grapes *thy fill*
Ru. 2:18. *after she was sufficed.*
Ps. 16:11. in thy presence (is) *fulness of* joy;
78:25. he sent them meat *to the full.*
Pro.13:25. The righteous eateth *to the satisfying of* his soul:

שָׂבְעָה *sov-găh'*, f. 7654

Isa. 23:18. to eat *sufficiently,*
55: 2. (that which) *satisfieth* not?
56:11. can never have *enough*, (marg. know not *to be satisfied*)
Eze.16:28. because *thou wast* unsatiable; (lit. without *thy satisfaction*)
39:19. ye shall eat fat *till ye be full*, (lit. *unto fulness*)
Hag 1: 6. ye eat, but *ye have* not *enough;*

שִׂבְעָה [*siv-găh'*], f. 7653

Eze.16:49. *fulness of* bread, and abundance of

שָׂבַר [*sāh-var'*]. 7663

* KAL.—*Participle.* Poel. *

Neh 2:13. *viewed* (lit. was *viewing*) the walls of Jerusalem,
15. went I up...and *viewed* (lit. *id.*) the wall,

* PIEL.—*Preterite.* *

Est. 9: 1. the enemies of the Jews *hoped*
Ps.119:166. *I have hoped* for thy salvation,

PIEL.—*Future.*

Ru. 1:13. *Would ye tarry* (marg. *hope*) for them
Ps.104:27. These *wait* all upon thee;
145:15. The eyes of all *wait* upon (marg. or, *look* unto) thee;
Isa. 38:18. they that go down into the pit *cannot hope*

7664 שֵׂבֶר [*sĕh'-ver*], m.

Ps.119:116. let me not be ashamed *of my hope.*
146: 5. *whose hope* (is) in the Lord his God:

7679 שָׂגָא [*sāh-gāh'*].

* HIPHIL.—*Future.* *

Job 36:24. Remember that *thou magnify* his work,

HIPHIL.—*Participle.*

Job 12:23. *He increaseth* the nations,

7680 שְׂגָא [*s'gāh*], Ch.

* P'AL.—*Future.* *

Ezr. 4:22. why *should* damage *grow* to the hurt
Dan 4: 1(3:31) & 6:25(26). Peace *be multiplied* unto you.

7682 שָׂגַב [*sāh-gav'*].

* KAL.—*Preterite.* *

Deu 2:36. not one city *too strong* for us:
Job 5:11. those which mourn *may be exalted*

* NIPHAL.—*Preterite.* *

Ps.139: 6. *it is high,* I cannot (attain) unto it.
Pro.18:10. a strong tower:...*and is safe.* (marg. *set aloft*)
Isa. 2:11,17. *and* the Lord alone *shall be exalted* in

NIPHAL.—*Participle.*

Ps.148:13. his name alone *is excellent;* (marg. *exalted*)
Pro.18:11. as an *high* wall in his own conceit.
Isa. 12: 4. his name *is exalted.*
26: 5. the *lofty* city, he layeth it low;
30:13. a *high* wall, whose breaking cometh
33: 5. The Lord *is exalted;*

* PIEL.—*Future.* *

Ps. 20: 1(2). the name of the God of Jacob *defend thee.* (marg. *set thee on an high place*)
59: 1(2). *defend me* from them that rise up
69:29(30). O God, *set me up on high.*
91:14. *I will set him on high,* because he hath
107:41. *Yet setteth he* the poor *on high*
Isa. 9:11(10). *Therefore* the Lord *shall set up*

* PUAL.—*Future.* *

Pro.29:25. whoso putteth his trust in the Lord *shall be safe.* (marg. *set on high*)

* HIPHIL.—*Future.* *

Job 36:22. God *exalteth* by his power:

7685 שָׂגָה [*sāh-gāh'*].

* KAL.—*Future.* *

Job 8: 7. thy latter end *should* greatly *increase.*
11. *Can* the flag *grow* without water?
Ps. 92:12(13). *he shall grow* like a cedar

* HIPHIL.—*Preterite.* *

Ps. 73:12. *they increase* (in) riches.

7689 שַׂגִּיא *sag-gee'*, adj.

Job 36:26. God (is) *great,* and we know (him) not,
37:23. (he is) *excellent in* power,

7690 שַׂגִּיא *sag-gee'*, Ch. adj.

Ezr. 5:11. that was builded these *many* years ago,
Dan 2: 6. and rewards and *great* honour:
12. the king was angry and *very* furious,
Dan 2:31. and behold a *great* image.
48. and gave him *many* great gifts,
4:10(7). and the height thereof (was) *great.*
12(9), 21(18). and the fruit thereof *much,*
5: 9. was king Belshazzar *greatly* troubled,
6:14(15). was *sore* displeased with himself,
23(24). Then was the king *exceeding* glad
7: 5. Arise, devour *much* flesh.
28. my cogitations *much* troubled me,

שָׂדַד [*sāh-dad'*]. 7702

* PIEL.—*Future.* *

Job 39:10. *will he harrow* the vallies
Isa. 28:24. *and break the clods* of his ground?
Hos.10:11. Jacob *shall break* his *clods.*

שָׂדֶה *sāh-deh'*, m. 7704

Gen 2: 5. every plant of *the field*
— every herb of *the field*
19. the Lord God formed every beast of *the field,*
20. to every beast of *the field;*
3: 1. any beast of *the field* which the Lord God
14. cursed...above every beast of *the field;*
18. thou shalt eat the herb of *the field;*
4: 8. when they were *in the field,*
14: 7. all *the country of* the Amalekites,
23: 9. the cave...in the end of *his field;*
11. *the field* give I thee,
13. I will give thee money for *the field;*
17. *the field of* Ephron,
— *the field,* and the cave which (was) therein, and all the trees that (were) *in the field,*
19. the cave of *the field of* Machpelah
20. *the field,* and the cave
24:63. Isaac went out to meditate *in the field*
65. man (is) this that walketh *in the field*
25: 9. *the field of* Ephron the son of Zohar
10. *The field* which Abraham purchased
27. Esau was...a man of *the field;*
29. and Esau came from *the field,*
27: 3. and go out to *the field*
5. And Esau went to *the field*
27. (is) as the smell of *a field*
29: 2. a well *in the field,*
30:14. found mandrakes *in the field,*
16. Jacob came out of *the field*
31: 4. Jacob sent and called Rachel and Leah to *the field*
32: 3(4). *the country* (marg. *field*) *of* Edom.
33:19. he bought a parcel of *a field,*
34: 5. his sons were with his cattle *in the field:*
7. the sons of Jacob came out of *the field*
28. that which (was) *in the field,*
36:35. smote Midian *in the field of* Moab,
37: 7. binding sheaves in *the field,*
15. wandering *in the field:*
39: 5. that he had in the house, *and in the field.*
41:48. the food of *the field,*
47:20. the Egyptians sold every man *his field,*
24. seed of *the field,*
49:29. *in the field of* Ephron the Hittite,
30. the cave that (is) *in the field of*
— *the field* of Ephron the Hittite
32. The purchase of *the field*
50:13. the cave of *the field of* Machpelah, which Abraham bought with *the field*
Ex. 1:14. in all manner of service *in the field:*
8:13(9). the frogs died...out of *the fields.*
9: 3. thy cattle which (is) *in the field,*
19. all that thou hast *in the field;*
— shall be found *in the field,*
21. left his servants and his cattle *in the field.*
22. upon every herb of *the field,*
25. all that (was) *in the field,*
— the hail smote every herb of *the field,* and brake every tree of *the field.*
10: 5. groweth for you out of *the field:*
15. the herbs of *the field,*
16:25. ye shall not find it *in the field.*
22: 5(4). If a man shall cause *a field*...to be

Ex. 22: 5(4). shall feed *in* another man's *field*; of the best of *his own field*,
6(5). *the field*, be consumed
31(30). torn of beasts *in the field*;
23:11. the beasts of *the field* shall eat.
16. which thou hast sown *in the field*:
— gathered in thy labours out of *the field*.
29. the beast of *the field* multiply
Lev.14: 7. let the living bird loose into *the* open *field*.
53. let go the living bird...into *the* open *fields*,
17: 5. they offer in *the* open *field*,
19: 9. not wholly reap the corners of *thy field*,
19. shalt not sow *thy field* with mingled seed:
23:22. shalt not make clean riddance of the corners of *thy field*
25: 3. Six years thou shalt sow *thy field*,
4. thou shalt neither sow *thy field*,
12. eat the increase thereof out of *the field*.
31. *the fields of* the country:
34. *the field of* the suburbs
26: 4. the trees of *the field* shall yield
22. send *wild* beasts (lit. beasts of *the field*)
27:16. shall sanctify unto the Lord (some part) *of a field of*
17. If he sanctify *his field* from
18. if he sanctify *his field* after
19. he that sanctified *the field*
20. if he will not redeem *the field*, or if he have sold *the field*
21. But *the field*,...shall be holy unto the Lord, *as a field* devoted;
22. if (a man) sanctify...*a field which*
— *of the fields of* his possession;
24. *the field* shall return unto him
28. *and of the field of* his possession,
Nu. 16:14. inheritance of *fields* and vineyards:
19:16. slain with a sword in *the* open *fields*,
20:17. we will not pass *through the fields*,
21:20. *in the country* (marg. *field*) *of* Moab,
22. we will not turn *into the fields*,
22: 4. round about us, as the ox licketh up the grass of *the field*.
23. the ass...went *into the field*:
23:14. *the field of* Zophim,
Deu 5:21(18). thy neighbour's house, *his field*,
7:22. lest the beasts of *the field* increase
11:15. I will send grass *in thy fields*
14:22. that *the field* bringeth forth
20:19. the tree of *the field* (is) man's (life)
21: 1. (one) be found slain...lying *in the field*,
22:25. man find a betrothed damsel *in the field*,
27. he found her *in the field*,
24:19. cuttest down thine harvest *in thy field*, and hast forgot a sheaf *in the field*,
28: 3. blessed (shalt) thou (be) *in the field*.
16. cursed (shalt) thou (be) *in the field*.
38. shalt carry much seed out into *the field*,
Jos. 8:24. all the inhabitants of Ai *in the field*,
15:18. moved him to ask of her father *a field*:
21:12. *the fields of* the city,...gave they to Caleb
24:32. a parcel of *ground* which Jacob bought
Jud. 1:14. moved him to ask of her father *a field*:
5: 4. marchedst *out of the field of* Edom,
18. the high places of *the field*.
9:27. they went out into *the fields*,
32. lie in wait *in the field*:
42. the people went out into *the field*;
43. laid wait *in the field*,
44. (the people) that (were) *in the fields*,
13: 9. as she sat *in the field*:
19:16. came an old man...out of *the field*
20: 6. *the country of* the inheritance of Israel:
31. to Gibeah *in the field*,
Ru. 1: 1. to sojourn *in the country of* Moab,
2. came *into the country of* Moab,
6. might return *from the country* (lit. *fields*) *of* Moab: for she had heard *in the country of* Moab
22. returned *out of the country of* Moab:
2: 2. Let me now go to *the field*,
3. gleaned *in the field* after the reapers:
—a part of *the field* (belonging) unto Boaz,
6. came back...*out of the country of* Moab:
8. Go not to glean *in* another *field*,
9. *on the field* that they do reap,
17. gleaned *in the field* until even,
22. they meet thee not *in* any other *field*.
Ru. 4: 3. *out of the country of* Moab, selleth a parcel of *land*,
5. buyest *the field of* the hand of Naomi,
1Sa. 4: 2. they slew of the army *in the field*
6: 1. *in the country of* the Philistines
14. *the field of* Joshua, a Beth-shemite,
18. (remaineth) unto this day *in the field of*
8:14. he will take *your fields*,
11: 5. Saul came after the herd out of *the field*;
14:14. an half acre of *land*,
15. trembling in the host, *in the field*,
25. there was honey upon *the ground*.
17:44. give thy flesh...to the beasts of *the field*.
19: 3. I will go out and stand...*in the field*
20: 5. that I may hide myself *in the field*
11. let us go out into *the field*. And they went out both of them into *the field*.
24. David hid himself *in the field*:
35. Jonathan went out into *the field*
22: 7. the son of Jesse give every one of you *fields*
25:15. when we were *in the fields*:
27: 5. me a place in some town in *the country*,
7. the time that David dwelt *in the country of*
11. *in the country of* the Philistines.
30:11. found an Egyptian *in the field*,
2Sa. 1:21. rain, upon you, *nor fields of* offerings:
2:18. Asahel (was as) light of foot as a *wild* roe. (marg. as one of the roes that (is) *in the field*)
9: 7. all *the land of* Saul thy father;
10: 8. by themselves *in the field*.
11:11. encamped in *the* open *fields*;
23. came out unto us into *the field*,
14: 6. strove together *in the field*,
17: 8. a bear robbed of her whelps *in the field*:
18: 6. the people went out into *the field*
19:29(30). Thou and Ziba divide *the land*.
20:12. removed Amasa...into *the field*,
21:10. the beasts of *the field*
23:11. a piece of *ground* full of lentiles:
1K. 2:26. Get thee...unto *thine own fields*;
11:29. they two (were) alone *in the field*:
14:11. him that dieth *in the field*
16: 4. him that dieth of his *in the fields*
21:24. him that dieth *in the field*
2K. 4:39. one went out into *the field*
— and found a *wild* vine (lit. vine of *the field*), and gathered thereof *wild* gourds
7:12. to hide themselves *in the field*,
8: 3. for her house and for *her land*.
5. cried to the king for her house and for *her land*.
6. all the fruits of *the field*
9:25. the portion of *the field of* Naboth
37. *the field* in the portion of Jezreel;
14: 9. there passed by a *wild* beast (lit. beast of *the field*)
18:17. the highway of the fuller's *field*.
19:26. (as) the grass of *the field*,
1Ch 1:46. smote Midian *in the field of* Moab,
6:56(41). *the fields of* the city,
8: 8. *in the country of* Moab,
11:13. a parcel of *ground* full of barley;
16:32. let *the fields* rejoice,
19: 9. by themselves *in the field*.
27:25. the storehouses *in the fields*,
26. them that did the work of *the field*
2Ch 25:18. a *wild* beast (lit. beast of *the field*)
26:23. *the field of* the burial
31: 5. all the increase of *the field*;
19. *in the fields of* the suburbs
Neh 5: 3. We have mortgaged *our lands*,
4. *our lands* and vineyards.
5. *for* other men have *our lands*
11. Restore, I pray you,...*their lands*,
16. *neither* bought we any *land*:
11:25. the villages, *with their fields*,
30. Lachish, *and the fields thereof*,
12:29. *and out of the fields of* Geba and Azmaveth:
44. *out of the fields of* the cities
13:10. fled every one *to his field*.
Job 5:23. in league with the stones of *the field*: and the beasts of *the field* shall be at peace
24: 6. reap (every one) his corn *in the field*:
39:15. forgetteth...that the *wild* beast (lit. beast of *the field*) may break them.
40:20. where all the beasts of *the field* play.

Ps 78:12. Egypt, (in) *the field of* Zoan.
43. his wonders *in the field of* Zoan:
103:15. as a flower of *the field*,
107:37. sow *the fields*, and plant vineyards,
132: 6. we found it *in the fields of* the wood.
Pro.23:10. *and* enter not *into the fields of* the
24:27. make it fit for thyself *in the field*;
30. I went by *the field of* the slothful,
27:26. the goats (are) the price of *the field*.
31:16. She considereth *a field*,
Ecc. 5: 9(8). king (himself) is served *by the field*.
Cant 2: 7 & 3:5. the hinds of *the field*,
7:11(12). let us go forth into *the field*;
Isa. 5: 8. Woe unto them...(that) lay *field to field*, till (there be) no place,
7: 3. the highway of the fuller's *field*;
32:12. lament...for *the* pleasant *fields*,
36: 2. the highway of the fuller's *field*.
37:27. (as) the grass of *the field*,
40: 6. the flower of *the field*:
43:20. The beast of *the field* shall honour me,
55:12. all the trees of *the field* shall clap
Jer. 6:12. (their) *fields* and wives
25. Go not forth into *the field*,
7:20. the trees of *the field*,
8:10. give...*their fields* to them that shall inherit
9:22(21). as dung upon *the* open *field*,
12: 4. the herbs of every *field* wither,
9. assemble all the beasts of *the field*,
13:27. thine abominations on the hills *in the fields*.
14: 5. the hind also calved *in the field*,
18. If I go forth into *the field*,
17: 3. O my mountain *in the field*,
26:18. Zion shall be plowed (like) *a field*,
27: 6. the beasts of *the field* have I given
28:14. I have given him the beasts of *the field*
32: 7. Buy thee *my field* that (is)
8. Buy *my field*, I pray thee,
9. I bought *the field* of Hanameel
15. Houses *and fields* and vineyards
25. Buy thee *the field* for money,
43. And *fields* shall be bought in this land,
44. Men shall buy *fields* for money,
35: 9. neither have we vineyard, *nor field*,
40: 7. of the forces which (were) *in the fields*,
13. of the forces that (were) *in the fields*,
41: 8. we have treasures *in the field*,
Eze 7:15. he that (is) *in the field* shall die
16: 5. thou wast cast out in *the* open *field*,
7. thee to multiply as the bud of *the field*,
17: 5. planted it *in a* fruitful *field*;
8. planted in *a* good *soil* by great waters,
24. all the trees of *the field* shall know
20:46(21:2). prophesy against the forest of *the* south *field*,
26: 6. her daughters which (are) *in the field*
8. shall slay...thy daughters *in the field*:
29: 5. thou shalt fall upon *the* open *fields*;
31: 4. rivers unto all the trees of *the field*.
5. exalted above all the trees of *the field*,
6. all the beasts of *the field* bring forth their
13. all the beasts of *the field* shall be upon his
15. all the trees of *the field* fainted
32: 4. I will cast thee forth upon *the* open *field*,
33:27. him that (is) in *the* open *field*
34: 5. became meat to all the beasts of *the field*,
8. became meat to every beast of *the field*,
27. the tree of *the field* shall yield her fruit,
36:30. the increase of *the field*,
38:20. the heaven, and the beasts of *the field*,
39: 4. I will give thee unto...the beasts of *the field*
5. Thou shalt fall upon *the* open *field*:
10. they shall take no wood out of *the field*,
17. every beast of *the field*,
Hos. 2:12(14). the beasts of *the field* shall eat
18(20). covenant...with the beasts of *the field*
4: 3. languish, with the beasts of *the field*,
12:12(13). Jacob fled into *the country of* Syria,
13: 8. the *wild* beast (marg. beast of *the field*)
Joel 1:10. *The field* is wasted,
11. the harvest of *the field* is perished.
12. all the trees of *the field*, are withered:
19. flame hath burned all the trees of *the field*.
20. The beasts of *the field* cry
Obad. 19. *the fields of* Ephraim, and *the fields of*
Mic. 1: 6. make Samaria as an heap of *the field*,
2: 2. covet *fields*, and take (them) by violence;
Mic. 2: 4. he hath divided *our fields*.
3:12. shall Zion...be plowed (as) *a field*,
4:10. thou shalt dwell *in the field*,
Zec.10: 1. give...to every one grass *in the field*.
Mal. 3:11. neither shall your vine cast her fruit...*in the field*,

---

שָׂדַי *sāh-dah'y*, m. 7704

Deu 32:13. that he might eat the increase of *the fields*;
Ps. 8: 7(8). the beasts of *the field*;
50:11. the wild beasts of *the field*
80:13(14). the wild beast of *the field*
96:12. Let *the field* be joyful,
104:11. every beast of *the field*:
Isa. 56: 9. All ye beasts of *the field*,
Jer. 4:17. As keepers of *a field*, are they
18:14. the rock of *the field*?
Lam 4: 9. the fruits of *the field*.
Hos.10: 4. hemlock in the furrows of *the field*.
12:11(12). heaps in the furrows of *the fields*.
Joel 2:22. Be not afraid, ye beasts of *the field*:

שְׂדֵרָה [*s'dēh-rāh'*], f. 7713

1K. 6: 9. covered the house with beams *and boards* (marg. *ceilings*)
2K. 11: 8. he that cometh within *the ranges*,
15. Have her forth without *the ranges*:
2Ch 23:14. Have her forth of *the ranges*:

שֶׂה *seh*, com. 7716

Gen22: 7. where (is) *the lamb* (marg. or, *kid*) for a burnt offering?
8. God will provide himself *a lamb*
30:32. all *the* speckled and spotted *cattle*, and all the brown *cattle*
Ex. 12: 3. they shall take to them every man *a lamb*, (marg. or, *kid*)
— *a lamb* for an house:
4. if the houshold be too little *for the lamb*
— make your count for *the lamb*.
5. Your *lamb* shall be without blemish,
13:13. thou shalt redeem *with a lamb*; (marg. or, *kid*)
22: 1(21:37). If a man shall steal an ox, or *a sheep*, (marg. or, *goat*)
—(—:—). four sheep for *a sheep*.
4(3). ox, or ass, or *sheep*;
9(8). for ox, for ass, for *sheep*,
10(9). an ass, or an ox, or *a sheep*,
34:19. ox *or sheep*, that is male.
20. thou shalt redeem *with a lamb*: (marg. or, *kid*)
Lev. 5: 7. if he be not able to bring *a lamb*,
12: 8. if she be not able to bring *a lamb*,
22:23. Either a bullock *or a lamb* (marg. or, *kid*)
28. cow or *ewe* (marg. or, *she goat*), ye shall not kill it and her young
27:26. whether (it be) ox, or *sheep*: it (is) the
Nu. 15:11. *for a lamb*, or a kid. (lit. *for a lamb of* the sheep or of the goats)
Deu 14: 4. the beasts which ye shall eat: the ox, the sheep (lit. *the lamb of* sheep), and the goat, (lit. *and the kid of* goats)
17: 1. bullock, *or sheep* (marg. or, *goat*), wherein
18: 3. whether (it be) ox or *sheep*;
22: 1. thy brother's ox or *his sheep*
Jos. 6:21. ox, *and sheep*, and ass,
Jud. 6: 4. left...*neither sheep* (marg. or, *goat*), nor ox, nor ass.
1Sa.14:34. Bring me...every man *his sheep*,
15: 3. infant and suckling, ox and *sheep*,
17:34. took *a lamb* (marg. or, *kid*) out of the
22:19. oxen, and asses, *and sheep*,
Ps.119:176. I have gone astray *like a* lost *sheep*;
Isa. 7:25. the treading of *lesser cattle*.
43:23. *the small cattle* (marg. *lambs*, or, *kids*) *of* thy burnt offerings;
53: 7. he is brought *as a lamb* to the slaughter.
66: 3. he that sacrificeth *a lamb*, (marg. or, *kid*)
Jer. 50:17. Israel (is) *a scattered sheep*;
Eze.34:17. I judge between *cattle* (marg. *small cattle of lambs and kids*) *and cattle*,

Eze.34:20. I, will judge between *the* fat *cattle* and between *the* lean *cattle*.
22. I will judge between *cattle and cattle.*
45:15. *And* one *lamb* (marg. or, *kid*) out of the

7717 **שָׂהֵד** [*sāh-hēhd'*], m.

Job 16:19. *and my record* (is) on high.

3026 **שָׂהֲדוּתָא** *sah-hădoo-thāh'*, Ch. f. emph.

Gen31:47. Laban called it Jegar-*sahadutha:* (marg. The heap of *witness*)

7720 **שַׂהֲרֹנִים** *sah-hărōh-neem'*, m.pl.

Jud. 8:21. took away *the ornaments* (marg. *ornaments like* the *moon*)
26. *ornaments*, and collars, and purple
Isa. 3:18. *and* (their) *round tires like the moon*,

See 7867 שׂוּב see שִׂיב

7730 **שׂוֹךְ** *sōh'-vech*, m.

2Sa. 18: 9. *the thick boughs of* a great oak,

7734 **שׂוּג** [*soog*].

* NIPHAL.—*Preterite.* *

2Sa. 1:22. the bow of Jonathan *turned* not *back*,

7735 **שׂוּג** *soog*.

* PILPEL.—*Future.* *

Isa. 17:11. *shalt thou make* thy plant *to grow*,

7742 **שׂוּחַ** *soo'ăgh*.

* KAL.—*Infinitive.* *

Gen24:63. Isaac went out *to meditate* (marg. or, *to pray*) in the field

7750 **שׂוּט** [*soot*].

* KAL.—*Participle.* Poel. *

Ps. 40: 4(5). *nor such as turn aside* to lies.

7753 **שׂוּךְ** [*sooch*].

* KAL.—*Preterite.* *

Job 1:10. *Hast* not thou *made an hedge* about him,

KAL.—*Participle.*

Hos. 2: 6(8). I *will hedge up* thy way with thorns,

* POLEL.—*Future.* *

Job 10:11. *hast fenced* (marg. *hedged*) *me* with bones and sinews.

7754 **שׂוֹךְ** [*sōhch*], m.

Jud. 9:49. cut down every man *his bough*,

7754 **שׂוֹכָה** [*sōh-chāh'*], f.

Jud. 9:48. cut down *a bough from* the trees,

7760 **שׂוּם** *soom* & **שִׂים** *seem*.

* KAL.—*Preterite.* *

Gen13:16. *And I will make* thy seed as the dust
21:14. *putting* (it) on her shoulder,
27:37. *I have made him* thy lord,
28:18. the stone that *he had put* (for) his pillows,
22. this stone, which *I have set* (for) a
30:41. *that* Jacob *laid* the rods before...the cattle
32:12(13). *and make* thy seed as the sand
40:15. that *they should put* me into the dungeon.
43:22. we cannot tell who *put* our money in
Gen45: 9. God *hath made me* lord of all Egypt:
47: 6. *then make them* rulers over my cattle.
Ex. 2:14. Who *made thee* a prince and a judge
3:22. *and ye shall put* (them) upon your sons,
4:11. Who *hath made* man's mouth?
15. *and put* words in his mouth:
21. wonders...which *I have put* in thine hand:
5:14. Pharaoh's taskmasters *had set* over them,
8:12(8). the frogs which *he had brought*
23(19). *And I will put* a division between
9:21. he that regarded not (marg. *set* not his heart unto) the word of the Lord
10: 2. my signs which *I have done*
15:25. *he made* for them a statute
26. diseases...*I have brought* upon the
18:21. *and place* (such) over them,
21:13. *then I will appoint* thee a place
26:35. *And thou shalt set* the table without the
28:12. *And thou shalt put* the two stones upon
26. *and thou shalt put* them upon the two
37. *And thou shalt put* it on a blue lace,
29: 6. *And thou shalt put* the mitre upon
24. *And thou shalt put* all in the hands of
33:22. *that I will put thee* in a clift
40: 3. *And thou shalt put* therein the ark
5. *and put* the hanging of the door
8. *And thou shalt set up* the court
29. And *he put* the altar...(by) the door of
Lev. 2:15. *and lay* frankincense thereon:
6:10(3). *and he shall put them* beside the altar.
20: 5. *Then* I *will set* my face against
24: 6. *And thou shalt set* them in two rows,
Nu. 4: 6. *and shall put in* the staves thereof.
8. *and shall put in* the staves thereof.
11. *and shall put to* the staves thereof:
14. *and put to* the staves of it.
19. *and appoint* them every one to his service
6:27. *And they shall put* my name upon
11:17. *and will put* (it) upon them;
Deu 4:44. the law which Moses *set* before
10: 2. *and thou shalt put them* in the ark.
22. the Lord thy God *hath made thee* as the
11:18. *Therefore shall ye lay up* these my words
22:14. *And give* occasions of speech
17. he *hath given* occasions of speech
26: 2. *and shalt put* (it) in a basket,
27:15. *and putteth* (it) in (a) secret (place).
31:26. *and put* it in the side of the ark
Jos. 6:18. *and make* the camp of Israel a curse,
7:11. *they have put* (it) even among their own
Jud. 6:19. the flesh *he put* in a basket, and *he put* the
20:36. liers in wait which *they had set*
Ru. 3: 3. *and put* thy raiment upon thee,
1Sa. 8:11. *and appoint* (them) for himself,
11: 2. *and lay it* (for) a reproach upon all
15: 2. *he laid* (wait) for him in the way,
17:54. *he put* his armour in his tent.
19:13. *and put* a pillow of goats' (hair)
2Sa. 7:10. *Moreover I will appoint* a place
8:14. throughout all Edom *put he* garrisons,
14:19. he *put* all these words in the mouth
17:25. Absalom *made* Amasa captain
23: 5. he *hath made* with me an everlasting
1K. 2:15. all Israel *set* their faces on me,
20:34. as my father *made* in Samaria.
2K. 4:29. *and lay* my staff upon the face of the
10: 3. *and set* (him) on his father's throne,
24. Jehu *appointed* fourscore men
17:34. the children of Jacob, whom he named Israel; (lit. whose name *he put* Israel)
19:28. *therefore I will put* my hook in thy nose,
1Ch 17: 9. *Also I will ordain* a place
2Ch 1: 5. *he put* before the tabernacle (marg. or, (was) *there* [as if שָׁם])
Neh. 9: 7. *and gavest* him the name of Abraham;
Job 1: 8. *Hast thou* considered (marg. *Hast thou set* thy heart on) my servant Job,
17. The Chaldeans *made out* three bands,
2: 3. *Hast thou* considered (lit. *set* thine heart upon)
7:20. why *hast thou set me* as a mark
28: 3. *He setteth* an end to darkness,
31:24. If *I have made* gold my hope,
34:13. who *hath disposed* the whole world?
38: 5. Who *hath laid* the measures thereof,
39: 6. Whose house *I have made* the wilderness

Job 40: 4. *I will lay* mine hand upon my mouth.
Ps. 19: 4(5). *hath he set* a tabernacle for the sun,
40: 4(5). that man that *maketh* the Lord his
46: 8(9). desolations *he hath made* in the earth.
50:23. him *that ordereth* (his) conversation (marg. *disposeth* (his) way) (aright)
54: 3(5). *they have* not *set* God before them.
66:11. *thou laidst* affliction upon our loins.
74: 4. *they set up* their ensigns (for) signs.
78: 5. *appointed* a law in Israel,
43. *he had wrought* (marg. *set*) his signs in
79: 1. *they have laid* Jerusalem on heaps.
81: 5(6). *This he ordained* in Joseph
86:14. *have* not *set thee* before them.
89:25(26). *I will set* his hand *also* in the sea,
29(30). His seed *also will I make* (to endure)
40(41). *thou hast brought*...to ruin.
91: 9. thou *hast made* the Lord (which is) my refuge,
104: 9. *Thou hast set* a bound
105:21. *He made him* lord of his house,
27. *They shewed* his signs among them,
Pro.23: 2. *And put* a knife to thy throat,
Cant 1: 6. *they made me* keeper of the vineyards;
6:12. my soul *made me* (marg. or, *set me*) (like)
Isa. 14:17. *made* the world as a wilderness,
23. *I will also make it* a possession
21: 4. the night of my pleasure *hath he turned* (marg. *put*)
23:13. *he brought it* to ruin.
25: 2. *thou hast made* of a city an heap;
28:15. *we have made* lies our refuge,
17. Judgment *also will I lay* to the line,
25. *and cast in* the principal wheat
37:29. *therefore will I put* my hook in thy nose,
41:15. *I will make thee* a new sharp threshing
42:15. and *I will make* the rivers islands,
47: 6. *thou didst shew* them no mercy;
7. *thou didst* not *lay*...to thy heart,
49:11. *And I will make* all my mountains a way,
50: 7. therefore *have I set* my face like a flint,
51:10. *that hath made* the depths...a way
23. *But I will put it* into the hand of
54:12. *I will make* thy windows of agates,
57: 7. Upon a lofty and high mountain *hast thou set* thy bed:
8. the doors...*hast thou set up*
11. nor *laid* (it) to thy heart?
59:21. my words which *I have put* in thy mouth,
60:15. *I will make thee* an eternal excellency,
17. *I will also make* thy officers peace,
66:19. *And I will set* a sign among them,
Jer. 2: 7. and *made* mine heritage an abomination.
5:22. *have placed* the sand (for) the bound
7:30. *they have set* their abominations in the
11:13. *have ye set up* altars
12:11. *They have made it* desolate,
13: 1. get thee a linen girdle, *and put it* upon
16. *he turn it* into the shadow of death,
17: 5. *and maketh* flesh his arm,
19: 8. *And I will make* this city desolate,
21:10. *I have set* my face against this city
24: 6. *For I will set* mine eyes upon them
25: 9. *and make them* an astonishment,
12. *and will make* it perpetual desolations.
32:20. *hast set* signs and wonders
33:25. (if) *I have* not *appointed* the ordinances
42:17. the men *that set* their faces to go
43:10. *and will set* his throne upon these stones
44:12. *have set* their faces to go
49:38. *And I will set* my throne in Elam,
Lam.3:11. *he hath made me* desolate.
Eze. 4: 4. *and lay* the iniquity of the house of Israel
5: 5. *I have set it* in the midst of the nations
7:20. *he set it* in majesty:
11: 7. Your slain whom *ye have laid*
16:14. my comeliness, which *I had put* upon
17: 4. *he set it* in a city of merchants.
5. *set it* (as) a willow tree.
19: 5. *made him* a young lion.
23:41. *thou hast set* mine incense
24: 7. *she set it* upon the top of a rock;
39:21. my hand that *I have laid* upon them.
44: 5. *and mark* well (lit. *and set* thine heart to) the entering
Hos. 1:11(2:2). *and appoint* themselves one head,
2: 3(5). *and make her* as a wilderness,
Hos. 2:12(14). *and I will make them* a forest,
Joel 1: 7. *He hath laid* my vine waste,
Am. 8:10. *and I will make it* as the mourning
9: 4. *and I will set* mine eyes upon them
Mic. 1: 6. *Therefore I will make* Samaria as an heap
4: 7. *And I will make* her...a remnant,
5: 1(4:14). *he hath laid* siege
Nah. 3: 6. *and will set thee* as a gazingstock.
Hab. 1:12. *thou hast ordained them*
Zep. 3:19. *and I will get them* (marg. *set them* for a) praise and fame
Hag. 2:23. *and will make thee* as a signet:
Zec. 6:11. *and set* (them) upon the head of Joshua
7:12. *they made* their hearts (as) an adamant
9:13. *and made thee* as the sword of a mighty
10: 3. *and hath made* them as his goodly horse

KAL.—*Infinitive.*

Gen45: 7. *to preserve* you (marg. *to put* for you) a posterity
Nu. 11:11. *that thou layest* the burden...upon me?
24:23. who shall live *when* God *doeth this!*
Deu12: 5. the Lord your God shall choose...*to put* his name there,
21. the Lord thy God hath chosen *to put* his name there
14:24. the Lord thy God shall choose *to set* his name there,
17:15. Thou shalt in *any wise* set (lit. *setting* thou shalt set)
Jud. 9:24. and their blood *be laid* upon Abimelech
1Sa. 8:12. *And he will appoint* him captains
21: 6(7). *to put* hot bread in the day
2Sa. 7:23. *and to make* him a name,
14: 7. *shall* not *leave* to my husband
19:19(20). *that* the king *should take* it to his
1K. 9: 3. *to put* my name there
11:36. the city which I have chosen me *to put* my
14:21. *to put* his name there.
1Ch 17:21. *to make* thee a name of greatness
2Ch 6:20. *that thou wouldest put* thy name there;
12:13. chosen...*to put* his name there.
Neh. 8: 8. they read in the book...*and gave* the sense,
Job 5:11. *To set up* on high those that be low;
20: 4. since man *was placed* upon earth,
37:15. *when* God *disposed* them,
38: 9. *When I made* the cloud the garment
Pro. 8:29. *When he gave* to the sea his decree,
Isa. 10: 6. *and to* tread *them* down (lit. *and to lay them* a treading)
13: 9. *to lay* the land desolate:
27: 9. *when he maketh* all the stones...as chalkstones
44: 7. *since I appointed* the ancient people?
61: 3. *To appoint* unto them that mourn
Jer. 4: 7. *to make* thy land desolate;
10:22. *to make* the cities of Judah desolate,
18:16. *To make* their land desolate,
42:15. If ye *wholly* set (lit. *setting* ye set) your faces to enter
51:29. *to make* the land of Babylon a desolation
Eze.15: 7. *when I set* my face against them.
21:22(27). *to appoint* captains,
—(—). *to appoint* (battering) rams
30:21. *to put* a roller to bind it,
Obad. 4. though thou *set* thy nest among the stars,
Hab. 2: 9. *that he may set* his nest on high,
Hag. 2:15. before a stone *was laid* upon a stone

KAL.—*Imperative.*

Gen24: 2. *Put*,...thy hand under my thigh:
31:37. *set* (it) here before my brethren
43:31. and said, *Set on* bread.
44: 1. *put* every man's money in his sack's
47:29. *put*,...thy hand under my thigh,
48:18. *put* thy right hand upon his head.
Ex. 17:14. *and rehearse* (it) in the ears of Joshua:
32:27. *Put* every man his sword by his side,
Nu. 16: 7. put fire therein, *and put* incense in
46(17:11). *and put on* incense,
21: 8. *and set* it upon a pole:
24:21. *and thou puttest* thy nest in a rock.
Deu31:19. *put* it in their mouths,
32:46. *Set* your hearts unto all the words
Jos. 7:19. *give*,...glory to the Lord God of Israel,
8: 2. *lay* thee an ambush for the city
10:24. *put* your feet upon the necks of these
Jud.18:19. *lay* thine hand upon thy mouth,

Jud.19:30. *consider* of it, (lit. *put* to yourselves upon it)
1Sa. 8: 5. *make* us a king to judge us
9:23. I said unto thee, *Set* it by thee.
24. *set* (it) before thee, (and) eat:
1K. 20:12. *Set* (yourselves in array). (marg. or, *Place* (the engines))
24. *and put* captains in their rooms:
22:27. *Put* this (fellow) in the prison,
2K. 2:20. Bring me a new cruse, *and put* salt
6:22. *set* bread and water before them,
10: 8. *Lay ye* them in two heaps
2Ch 18:26. *Put* this (fellow) in the prison,
Job 17: 3. *Lay down* now,
21: 5. *and lay* (your) hand upon (your) mouth.
22:22. *and lay up* his words in thine heart.
41: 8(40:32). *Lay* thine hand upon him,
Ps. 56: 8(9). *put thou* my tears into thy bottle:
66: 2. *make* his praise glorious.
Cant.8: 6. *Set me* as a seal upon thine heart,
Jer. 31:21. *make* thee high heaps:
38:12. *Put* now (these) old cast clouts...under
39:12. *look* well to (marg. *set* thine eyes upon)
40:10. *and put* (them) in your vessels,
Eze. 4: 2. *and set* (battering) rams against
6: 2. *set* thy face toward the mountains of
13:17. *set* thy face against the daughters
20:46(21:2). *set* thy face toward the south,
21: 2(7). *set* thy face toward Jerusalem,
19(24). *appoint* thee two ways,
25: 2. *set* thy face against the Ammonites,
28:21. *set* thy face against Zidon,
29: 2. *set* thy face against Pharaoh
35: 2. *set* thy face against mount Seir,
38: 2. *set* thy face against Gog,
40: 4. *and set* thine heart upon all
44: 5. of man, *mark* well, (marg. *set* thine heart)
Hag. 1: 5, 7. Consider (marg. *Set* your heart on) your
2:15. consider (lit. *id.*) from this day and
18. Consider (lit. *id.*) now from this day and
— consider (it). (lit. *id.*)

KAL.—*Future.*

Gen. 2: 8. *and* there *he put* the man whom he had
4:15. *And* the Lord *set* a mark upon Cain,
6:16. the door...*shalt thou set* in the side
9:23. *and laid* (it) upon both their shoulders,
21:13. the son of the bondwoman *will I make* a
18. *I will make him* a great nation.
22: 6. *and laid* (it) upon Isaac his son;
9. *and laid* him on the altar
24: 9. *And* the servant *put* his hand under
47. *and I put* the earring upon her face,
28:11. took of the stones...*and put* (them for)
18. *and set it up* (for) a pillar,
30:36. *And he set* three days' journey betwixt
42. *he put* (them) not *in:*
31:21. *and set* his face (toward) the mount
34. *and put them* in the camel's furniture,
32:16(17). *and put* a space betwixt drove and
33: 2. *And he put* the handmaids...foremost,
37:34. *and put* sackcloth upon his loins,
41:42. *and put* a gold chain about his neck;
43:32. *And they set on* for him by himself,
44: 2. *And put* my cup,...in the sack's mouth
21. *that I may set* mine eyes upon him.
45: 8. *and he hath made me* a father to Pharaoh,
46: 3. *I will* there *make of thee* a great nation:
47:26. *And* Joseph *made* it a law
48:20. God *make thee* as Ephraim and as
— *and he set* Ephraim before
Ex. 1:11. *Therefore they did set* over them
2: 3. *and put* the child therein; *and she laid*
4:11. who *maketh* the dumb, or deaf,
5: 8. the tale of the bricks,...*ye shall lay* upon
9: 5. *And* the Lord *appointed* a set time,
14:21. *and made* the sea dry (land),
15:26. *I will put* none of these diseases upon
17:12. they took a stone, *and put* (it) under
19: 7. *and laid* before their faces
21: 1. the judgments which *thou shalt set* before
22:25(24). neither *shalt thou lay* upon him
24: 6. Moses took half of the blood, *and put* (it)
39: 7. *And he put* them on the shoulders of the
19. *and put* (them) on the two ends
40:18. *and set up* the boards thereof,
19. *and put* the covering of the tent above
Ex. 40:20. *and set* the staves on the ark,
21. *and set up* the vail of the covering,
24. *And he put* the candlestick in the tent
26. *And he put* the golden altar in the tent
28. *And he set up* the hanging
30. *And he set* the laver between the tent
Lev. 5:11. *he shall put* no oil upon it,
8: 8. *And he put* the breastplate upon him:
9. *And he put* the mitre upon his head; *also* upon the mitre,...*did he put* the golden
26. *and put* (them) on the fat, and upon
9:20. *And they put* the fat upon the breasts,
10: 1. *and put* incense thereon,
Nu. 6:26. his countenance...*and give* thee peace.
16:18. *and laid* incense thereon,
21: 9. Moses made a serpent of brass, *and put it*
22:38. the word that God *putteth* in my mouth,
23: 5. *And* the Lord *put* a word in Balaam's
12. that which the Lord *hath put* in my
16. *and put* a word in his mouth,
Deu 1:13. *and I will make them* rulers over you.
7:15. *will put* none of the evil diseases...upon
10: 5. *and put* the tables in the ark
14: 1. not cut yourselves, nor *make* any baldness
17:14. *I will set* a king over me,
15. *Thou shalt* in any wise *set* (him) king
— *shalt thou set* king over thee:
22: 8. that *thou bring* not blood upon
33:10. *they shall put* incense before thee,
Jos. 8:12. *and set* them to lie in ambush
13. *when they had set* the people,
28. *and made it* an heap for ever,
10:24. *and put* their feet upon the necks of
27. *and laid* great stones in the cave's mouth,
24: 7. *And* when...*he put* darkness between you
25. *and set* them a statute and an ordinance
Jud. 1:28. *that they put* the Canaanites to tribute,
4:21. *and took* (marg. *put*) an hammer in her
7:22. *and* the Lord *set* every man's sword
8:31. a son, whose name *he called* (marg. *set;* lit. *and he set* his name) Abimelech.
33. *and made* Baal-berith their god.
9:25. *And...set* liers in wait for him
48. *and laid* (it) on his shoulder,
49. *and put* (them) to the hold,
11:11. *and* the people *made* him head and
12: 3. *I put* my life in my hands,
15: 4. *and put* a firebrand in the midst
16: 3. *and put* (them) upon his shoulders,
18:21. *and put* the little ones...before
31. *And they set* them *up* Micah's graven
20:29. *And* Israel *set* liers in wait
1Sa. 2:20. The Lord *give* thee seed of this woman
6: 8. *put* the jewels of gold,...in a coffer
11. *And they laid* the ark...upon the cart,
15. *and put* (them) on the great stone:
7:12. Samuel took a stone, *and set* (it) between
8: 1. *that he made* his sons judges
9:20. *set* not thy mind on them;
24. the cook took up the shoulder,...*and set*
10:19. *set* a king over us.
11:11. *that* Saul *put* the people in three
17:40. *and put* them in a shepherd's bag
18: 5. *and* Saul *set him* over the men of war,
13. *and made him* his captain over a thousand;
19: 5. *For he did put* his life in his hand,
13. took an image, *and laid* (it) in the bed,
21:12(13). *And* David *laid up* these words
22: 7. *make* you all captains of thousands,
15. *let* not the king *impute* (any) thing
25:18. *and laid* (them) on asses.
25. *Let* not my lord....regard (marg. *lay* (it) to his heart) this man of
28: 2. Therefore *will I make thee* keeper
21. *and I have put* my life in my hand,
22. *let me set* a morsel of bread before thee;
30:25. *that he made it* a statute
31:10. *And they put* his armour in the house of
2Sa. 8: 6. *Then* David *put* garrisons in Syria
14. *And he put* garrisons in Edom;
12:20. *they set* bread before him,
31. *and put* (them) under saws, and under
13:19. *and laid* her hand on her head,
33. *let* not my lord the king *take*
14: 3. *So* Joab *put* the words in her mouth.
15: 4. Oh that *I were made* judge (lit. Who *will make me* judge)

2Sa.18: 1. *and set* captains of thousands...over
3. *they will* not *care* (marg. *set* (their) heart) for us; neither...*will they care* for us: (lit. *id.*)
23:23. *And* David *set him* over his guard.
1K. 2: 5. *and shed* the blood of war in peace,
19. *and caused* a seat *to be set* for the king's
5: 9(23). *I will convey them* by sea
8:21. *And I have set* there a place for the ark,
10: 9. *therefore made he thee* king,
12:29. *And he set* the one in Beth-el,
18:23. *and lay* (it) on wood, and *put* no fire (under):
— and *put* no fire (under):
25. but *put* no fire (under).
33. *and laid* (him) on the wood,
42. *and put* his face between his knees,
19: 2. if *I make* not thy life as the life of one of
20: 6. *they shall put* (it) in their hand,
12. *And they set* (themselves in array)
31. *let us*, I pray thee, *put* sackcloth on our
34. *thou shalt make* streets for thee
21:27. *and put* sackcloth upon his flesh,
2K. 4:10. *and let us set* for him there a bed,
31. *and laid* the staff upon the face
34. *and put* his mouth upon his mouth,
8:11. he settled his countenance *stedfastly*, (marg. *and set* (it))
9:13. *and put* (it) under him on the top of the
30. Jezebel heard (of it); *and she* painted her face, (marg. *she put* her eyes in painting)
10: 7. *and put* their heads in baskets,
27. *and made it* a draught house
11:16. *And they laid* hands on her;
18. *And* the priest *appointed* officers
12:17(18). *and* Hazael *set* his face to go up to
13: 7. *and had made them* like the dust
16. *And he put* his hand (upon it):
18:14. *And* the king of Assyria *appointed*
20: 7. they took *and laid* (it) on the boil,
21: 4. In Jerusalem *will I put* my name.
7. *And he set* a graven image...in the house,
— in Jerusalem,...*will I put* my name
1Ch 10:10. *And they put* his armour in the house
11:25. *and* David *set him* over his guard.
18: 6. *Then* David *put* (garrisons) in Syria-damascus;
13. *And he put* garrisons in Edom;
26:10. *yet* his father *made him* the chief;
2Ch 6:11. *And* in it *have I put* the ark,
23:15. *So they laid* hands on her;
18. *Also* Jehoiada *appointed*
33: 7. *And he set* a carved image,...in the house
— in Jerusalem,...*will I put* my name
14. *and put* captains of war in all the fenced
Ezr. 8:17. *and I told them* what they should say (marg. *and I put* words in their mouth)
10:44. *by whom they had* children.
Est. 2:17. *so that he set* the royal crown upon
3: 1. *and set* his seat above all the princes
8: 2. *And* Esther *set* Mordecai over the house
10: 1. *And* the king Ahasuerus *laid* a tribute
Job 4:18. his angels *he charged* with folly:
5: 8. unto God *would I commit* my cause:
7:12. *thou settest* a watch over me?
13:14. *put* my life in mine hand?
27. *Thou puttest* my feet *also* in the stocks,
17:12. *They change* the night into day:
18: 2. (ere) *ye make* an end of words?
19: 8. *he hath set* darkness in my paths.
23: 6. *he would put* (strength) in me.
24:12. God *layeth* not folly (to them).
15. *disguiseth* (his) *face*. (marg. *setteth* (his) face in secret)
25. *and make* my speech nothing worth?
29: 9. *laid* (their) hand on their mouth.
33:11. *He putteth* my feet in the stocks,
34:14. If *he set* his heart upon man,
23. *he will* not *lay* upon man more
36:13. the hypocrites in heart *heap up* wrath:
38:10. *and set* bars and doors,
33. *canst thou set* the dominion thereof
41: 2(40:26). *Canst thou put* an hook into his
31(23). *he maketh* the sea like a pot
Ps. 18:43(44). *thou hast made me* the head of the
39: 8(9). *make me* not the reproach of the
Ps. 44:13(14). *Thou makest us* a reproach
14(15). *Thou makest us* a byword
52: 7(9). the man (that) *made* not God his
78: 7. *That they might set* their hope in God,
80: 6(7). *Thou makest us* a strife unto our
85:13(14). *and shall set* (us) in the way of his
107:33. *He turneth* rivers into a wilderness,
35. *He turneth* the wilderness into a standing
41. *and maketh* (him) families like a flock.
109: 5. *And they have rewarded* me (lit. *and put* upon me) evil for good,
Pro.30:26. *yet make they* their houses in the rocks;
Isa. 3: 7. *make me* not a ruler of the people.
41:15. *shalt make* the hills as chaff.
18. *I will make* the wilderness a pool
19. *I will set* in the desert the fir tree,
20. That they may see, and know, *and consider*,
22. *that we may* consider (marg. *set* our heart (upon)) them,
42: 4. till *he have set* judgment in the earth:
12. *Let them give* glory unto the Lord,
16. *I will make* darkness light
25. *he laid* (it) not to heart.
43:19. *I will* even *make* a way in the wilderness,
49: 2. *And he hath made* my mouth like a sharp
— *and made me* a polished shaft;
50: 2. *I make* the rivers a wilderness:
3. *I make* sackcloth their covering.
51: 3. *and he will make* her wilderness like Eden,
16. *And I have put* my words in thy mouth,
23. *and thou hast laid* thy body as the ground,
53:10. when *thou shalt make* his soul an offering
62: 7. till *he make* Jerusalem a praise
Jer. 6: 8. lest *I make thee* desolate,
9: 8(7). in heart *he layeth* his wait.
13: 2. I got a girdle...*and put* (it) on my loins.
29:22. The Lord *make thee* like Zedekiah
32:34. *But they set* their abominations in
40: 4. *and I will look* well unto (marg. *set* mine eye upon) thee:
42:15. If ye wholly *set* your faces to enter
Lam. 3:45. *Thou hast made us* (as) the offscouring
Eze.14: 4, 7. *putteth* the stumblingblock...before
20:28. *also they made* their sweet savour,
21:20(25). *Appoint* a way,
27(32). *I will* overturn,...it: (marg. perverted, *will I make* it)
23:24. *shall set* against thee buckler and shield
24:17. *put on* thy shoes upon thy feet,
26:12. *they shall lay* thy stones...in the midst
35: 4. *I will lay* thy cities waste,
44: 8. *but ye have set* keepers
Dan 1: 7. the prince of the eunuchs *gave* names: *for he gave* unto Daniel (the name) of
8. *But* Daniel *purposed* in his heart
11:17. *He shall also set* his face to enter
18. *After this shall he turn* his face
Hos 11: 8. (how) *shall I set thee* as Zeboim?
Obad. 7. *have laid* a wound under thee:
Mic. 1: 7. the idols thereof *will I lay* desolate:
2:12. *I will put them* together
4:13. *I will make* thine horn iron, and *I will make* thy hoofs brass:
7:16. *they shall lay* (their) hand upon (their)
Nah. 1:14. *I will make* thy grave;
Hab. 3:19. *and he will make* my feet like hinds' (feet),
Zep. 2:13. *and will make* Nineveh a desolation,
Zec. 3: 5. *Let them set* a fair mitre upon his head. *So they set* a fair mitre upon his head,
7:14. *for they laid* the pleasant land desolate.
12: 3. *will I make* Jerusalem a burdensome stone
6. *will I make* the governors of Judah like
Mal. 1: 3. *and laid* his mountains...waste
2: 2. if *ye will* not *lay* (it) to heart,

KAL.—*Participle*. Poel.

Ps. 66: 9. *Which holdeth* (marg. *putteth*) our soul
104: 3. *who maketh* the clouds his chariot:
147:14. *He maketh* peace (in) thy borders,
Isa. 5:20. *that put* darkness for light,
— *that put* bitter for sweet,
57: 1. no man *layeth* (it) to heart:
63:11. *he that put* his holy Spirit within him?
Jer. 12:11. no man *layeth* (it) to heart.
44:11. I will *set* my face against you
Am. 7: 8. I will *set* a plumbline in the midst of

Zec 12: 2. I will *make* Jerusalem a cup of trembling
Mal. 2: 2. because ye do not *lay* (it) to heart.

KAL.—*Participle.* Paül.

2Sa.13:32. this hath been *determined* (marg. or, *settled*)

* HIPHIL.—*Imperative.* *

Eze.21:16(21). on the right hand, (or) on the left, (marg. *set* thyself, take the left hand)

HIPHIL.—*Participle.*

Job 4:20. they perish for ever without *any regarding*

* HOPHAL.—*Future.* *

Gen 24:33. *And there was set* (meat) before him to

7761 שׂוּם [*soom*], Ch.

* P'AL.—*Preterite.* *

Ezr. 5: 3. Who *hath* command*ed* (lit. *hath set* a decree) you to build
9. Who command*ed* (lit. *id.*) you to build
13. Cyrus *made* a decree to build
14. whom *he had made* governor;
6: 1. Then Darius the king *made* a decree,
3. Cyrus the king *made* a decree
12. Darius *have made* a decree;
Dan 3:10. Thou, O king, *hast made* a decree,
12. O king, *have* not regard*ed* thee: (marg. *set* no regard upon thee)
5:12. whom the king nam*ed* Belteshazzar: (lit. *put* his name)
6:13(14). regard*eth* not thee, O king, (lit. *hath set* no regard upon thee)
14(15). and *set* (his) heart on Daniel

P'AL.—*Imperative.*

Ezr. 4:21. *Give ye* now commandment (marg. *Make* a decree)

P'AL.—*Participle.* Passive.

Ezr. 4:19. And I commanded (marg. by me a decree *is set*), and search hath
5:17. that a decree *was made* of Cyrus
6: 8. I *make* a decree (marg. by me a decree *is made*) what ye shall do
11. Also I *have made* (lit. *id.*) a decree,
7:13. I *make* a decree, that all they of
21. I, (even) I Artaxerxes the king, *do make* (lit. by me *is made*) a decree
Dan 3:29. Therefore I *make* a decree, (marg. a decree *is made* by me)
4: 6(3). Therefore *made* I a decree (lit. *id.*)
6:17(18). *and laid* upon the mouth of the den;
26(27). I *make* a decree, (lit. from before me a decree *is made*)

* ITHP'AL.—*Future.* *

Ezr. 4:21. commandment *shall be given* from me.
Dan 2: 5. and your houses *shall be made*

ITHP'AL.—*Participle.*

Ezr. 5: 8. and timber *is laid* in the walls,

5493 שׂוּר [*soor*].

* KAL.—*Infinitive.* *

Hos. 9:12. woe also to them *when I depart* from

7786 שׂוּר [*soor*].

* KAL.—*Future.* *

Jud. 9:22. *When* Abimelech *had reigned* three years
Hos.12: 4(5). *Yea, he had power* over the angel,

* HIPHIL.—*Preterite.* *

Hos. 8: 4. *they have made princes,* and I

7787 שׂוּר [*soor*].

* KAL.—*Future.* *

1Ch 20: 3. he brought out the people...*and cut* (them) with saws,

---

שׂוֹרָה *sōh-rāh'*, f. 7795

Isa. 28:25. cast in the *principal* wheat (marg. or, the wheat in *the principal* (place))

שׂוֹרֵק see שׂרֵק See 8321

שׂוּשׂ *soos* & שִׂישׂ [*sees*]. 7797

* KAL.—*Preterite.* *

Deu 28:63. as the Lord *rejoiced* over you
30: 9. as *he rejoiced* over thy fathers:
Ps.119:14. *I have rejoiced* in the way of thy
Isa. 65:19. I will rejoice...*and joy* in my people:
66:14. your heart *shall rejoice,*
Jer. 32:41. *Yea, I will rejoice* over them
Lam 1:21. *they are glad* that thou hast done (it):

KAL.—*Infinitive.*

Deu 30: 9. the Lord will again *rejoice* (lit. will return *to rejoice*)
Isa. 61:10. I will *greatly* rejoice (lit. *rejoicing* I will rejoice)

KAL.—*Imperative.*

Isa. 65:18. *be ye glad* and rejoice
66:10. *rejoice* for joy with her,
Lam 4:21. *Rejoice* and be glad, O daughter of

KAL.—*Future.*

Deu 28:63. the Lord *will rejoice* over you
Job 3:22. rejoice exceedingly, (and) *are glad,*
39:21. *and rejoiceth* in (his) strength:
Ps. 19: 5(6). *rejoiceth* as a strong man to run a race.
35: 9. *it shall rejoice* in his salvation.
40:16(17). *Let* all those that seek thee *rejoice*
68: 3(4). *yea, let them* exceedingly *rejoice.*
70: 4(5). *Let* all those that seek thee *rejoice*
Isa. 35: 1. The wilderness and the solitary place *shall be glad for them;*
61:10. *I will* greatly *rejoice* in the Lord,
62: 5. (so) *shall* thy God *rejoice* over thee.
Eze.21:10(15). *should we* then *make mirth?*
Zep. 3:17. *he will rejoice* over thee with joy;

KAL.—*Participle.*

Ps.119:162. I *rejoice* at thy word,
Isa. 64: 5(4). Thou meetest *him that rejoiceth*

שֵׂחַ [*sēh'ăgh*], m. 7808

Am. 4:13. declareth unto man what (is) *his thought,*

שָׂחָה [*sāh-ghāh'*]. 7811

* KAL.—*Infinitive.* *

Isa. 25:11. forth (his hands) *to swim:*

KAL.—*Participle.* Poel.

Isa. 25:11. as *he that swimmeth* spreadeth

* HIPHIL.—*Future.* *

Ps. 6: 6(7). all the night *make I* my bed *to swim;*

שָׂחוּ *sāh'-ghoo.* 7813

Eze.47: 5. waters to *swim in,* (marg. of *swimming*)

שְׂחוֹק *s'ghōhk*, m. 7814

Job 8:21. fill thy mouth with *laughing,*
12: 4. I am (as) one *mocked* of his neighbour,
— the just upright (man is) *laughed to scorn.*
Ps.126: 2. our mouth filled with *laughter,*
Pro.10:23. *as sport* to a fool to do mischief:
14:13. Even *in laughter* the heart is sorrowful;
Ecc. 2: 2. I said *of laughter,* (It is) mad:
7: 3. Sorrow (is) better *than laughter:*
6. *the laughter of* the fool:
10:19. A feast is made *for laughter,*
Jer. 20: 7. I am *in derision* daily
48:26. he also shall be *in derision.*
27. was not Israel *a derision*
39. so shall Moab be *a derision*
Lam.3:14. I was *a derision* to all my people;

7818 שָׂחַט [*sāh-ghat'*].

* KAL.—*Future.* *

Gen40:11. *and pressed* them into Pharaoh's cup,

7832 שָׂחַק *sāh-ghak'*.

* KAL.—*Preterite.* *

Job 30: 1. (they that are) younger than I *have* me *in derision,*
Pro.29: 9. whether he rage *or laugh,*
Lam. 1: 7. *did mock* at her sabbaths.

KAL.—*Infinitive.*

Jud.16:27. beheld while Samson *made sport.*
Ecc. 3: 4. A time to weep, and a time *to laugh;*

KAL.—*Future.*

Job 5:22. At destruction and famine *thou shalt laugh:*
29:24. *I laughed* on them,
39: 7. *He scorneth* the multitude
18. *she scorneth* the horse and his rider.
22. *He mocketh* at fear,
41:29(21). *he laugheth* at the shaking of a spear.
Ps. 2: 4. He that sitteth in the heavens *shall laugh:*
37:13. The Lord *shall laugh* at him:
52: 6(8). The righteous also shall see, and fear, and *shall laugh*
59: 8(9). thou, O Lord, *shalt laugh* at them;
Pro. 1:26. I also *will laugh* at your calamity;
31:25. *and she shall rejoice* in time to come.
Hab 1:10. *they shall deride* every strong hold;

* PIEL.—*Preterite.* *

2Sa. 6:21. *therefore will I play* before the Lord.

PIEL.—*Infinitive.*

Ps.104:26. (whom) thou hast made *to play*

PIEL.—*Future.*

Jud.16:25. *that he may make us sport.*
2Sa. 2:14. Let the young men now arise, *and play*
Job 40:20. where all the beasts of the field *play.*
41: 5(40:29). *Wilt thou play* with him

PIEL.—*Participle.*

1Sa.18: 7. the women answered...*as they played,*
2Sa. 6: 5. all the house of Israel *played*
1Ch 13: 8. all Israel *played* before God
15:29. saw king David dancing *and playing:*
Pro. 8:30. *rejoicing* always before him;
31. *Rejoicing* in the habitable part of his
26:19. Am not I *in sport?*
Jer. 15:17. the assembly of *the mockers,*
30:19. the voice of *them that make merry:*
31: 4. the dances of *them that make merry.*
Zec. 8: 5. boys and girls *playing* in the streets

* HIPHIL.—*Participle.* *

2Ch 30:10. they *laugh*ed them *to scorn,*

7846 שֵׂט [*sēht*], m.

Hos. 5: 2. *the revolters* are profound to make

7847 שָׂטָה [*sāh-tāh'*].

* KAL.—*Preterite.* *

Nu. 5:19. if *thou hast* not *gone aside*
20. if thou *hast gone aside*

KAL.—*Imperative.*

Pro. 4:15. *turn* from it, and pass away.

KAL.—*Future.*

Nu. 5:12. If any man's wife *go aside,*
29. when a wife *goeth aside*
Pro. 7:25. *Let* not thine heart *decline*

7852 שָׂטַם [*sāh-tam'*].

* KAL.—*Future.* *

Gen27:41. *And* Esau *hated* Jacob
49:23. and shot (at him), *and hated him:*
50:15. Joseph *will* peradventure *hate us,*
Job 16: 9. He teareth (me) in his wrath, *who hateth me:*
30:21. *thou opposest thyself against me.*
Ps. 55: 3(4). in wrath *they hate me.*

שָׂטַן *sāh-tan'*. 7853

* KAL.—*Infinitive.* *

Zec. 3: 1. Satan standing at his right hand *to resist him.* (marg. *be his adversary*)

KAL.—*Future.*

Ps. 38:20(21). They also that render evil for good *are mine adversaries;*
109: 4. For my love *they are my adversaries:*

KAL.—*Participle.* Poel.

Ps. 71:13. *adversaries* to my soul;
109:20. the reward of *mine adversaries*
29. Let *mine adversaries* be clothed with

שָׂטָן *sāh-tāhn'*, m. 7854

Nu. 22:22. stood in the way *for an adversary*
32. I went out *to withstand* thee, (marg. *to be an adversary*)
1Sa.29: 4. lest in the battle he be *an adversary*
2Sa.19:22(23). should this day be *adversaries*
1K. 5: 4(18). (there is) neither *adversary* nor evil occurrent.
11:14. the Lord stirred up *an adversary*
23. God stirred him up (another) *adversary,*
25. he was *an adversary* to Israel
1Ch 21: 1. *Satan* stood up against Israel,
Job 1: 6. *Satan* (marg. *the adversary*) came also among them.
7, 8, 12. the Lord said unto *Satan,*
—, 9. Then *Satan* answered the Lord,
12. *Satan* went forth from the presence of the
2: 1. *Satan* came also among them
2, 3, 6. the Lord said unto *Satan,*
—, 4. *Satan* answered the Lord,
7. So went *Satan* forth
Ps.109: 6. *and* let *Satan* (marg. or, *an adversary*) stand at his right hand.
Zec. 3: 1. *and Satan* (marg. *an adversary*) standing at his right hand
2. the Lord said unto *Satan,* The Lord rebuke thee, *O Satan;*

שִׂטְנָה *sit-nāh'*, f. 7855

Ezr. 4: 6. wrote they (unto him) *an accusation*

שִׂיא [*see*], m. 7863

Job 20: 6. Though *his excellency* mount up

שִׂיב [*seev*]. 7867

* KAL.—*Preterite.* *

1Sa.12: 2. I am old *and grayheaded;*

KAL.—*Participle.* Poel.

Job 15:10. the *grayheaded* and very aged men,

שִׂיב [*seev*], Ch. 7868

* P'AL.—*Participle.* *

Ezr. 5: 5. of their God was upon *the elders of*
9. Then asked we those *elders,*
6: 7. *and the elders of* the Jews
8. what ye shall do to *the elders of* these
14. *And the elders of* the Jews

שֵׂיב [*sēhv*], m. 7869

1K. 14: 4. his eyes were set *by reason of his age.*

שֵׂיבָה *sēh-vāh'*, f. 7872

Gen15:15. thou shalt be buried *in a good old age.*
25: 8. Abraham...died *in a good old age,*

Gen42:38. bring down *my gray hairs* with sorrow
44:29. bring down *my gray hairs* with sorrow
31. *the gray hairs of* thy servant our father
Lev.19:32. rise up before *the hoary head*,
Deu32:25. the man of *gray hairs*.
Jud. 8:32. Gideon...died *in a* good *old age*,
Ru. 4:15. a nourisher of *thine old age*: (marg. *thy gray hairs*)
1K. 2: 6. let not *his hoar head* go down...in peace.
9. *his hoar head* bring thou down...with
1Ch 29:28. he died *in a* good *old age*,
Job 41:32(24). would think the deep *to be hoary*.
Ps. 71:18. when I am old *and greyheaded*,
92:14(15). still bring forth fruit *in old age*;
Pro.16:31. *The hoary head* (is) a crown of glory,
20:29. the beauty of old men (is) *the grey head*.
Isa. 46: 4. (even) to *hoar hairs* will I carry (you):
Hos. 7: 9. *gray hairs* are here and there upon him,

7873 **שִׂיג** *seeg*, m.

1K. 18:27. either he is talking, or he is *pursuing*, (marg. hath *a pursuit*)

7874 **שִׂיד** [*seed*].

* KAL.—*Preterite.* *

Deu27: 2. *and plaister* them with plaister:
4. *and thou shalt plaister* them with plaister.

7875 **שִׂיד** *seed*, m.

Deu27: 2. plaister them *with plaister*:
4. thou shalt plaister them *with plaister*.
Isa. 33:12. people shall be (as) the burnings of *lime*:
Am. 2: 1. the bones of the king of Edom *into lime*:

7878 **שִׂיחַ** *see'ăgh*.

* KAL.—*Infinitive.* *

Ps.119:148. *that I might meditate* in thy word.

KAL.—*Imperative.*

Jud. 5:10. *Speak* (marg. or, *Meditate*), ye that ride on white asses,
1Ch 16: 9. *talk ye* of all his wondrous works.
Job 12: 8. *speak* to the earth,
Ps. 105: 2. *talk ye* of all his wondrous works.

KAL.—*Future.*

Job 7:11. *I will complain* in the bitterness of my
Ps. 55:17(18). and morning, and at noon, *will I pray*,
69:12(13). They that sit in the gate *speak*
77: 3(4). *I complained*, and my spirit was
6(7). *I commune* with mine own heart:
12(13). and *talk* of thy doings.
119:15. *I will meditate* in thy precepts,
23. thy servant *did meditate*
27. *so shall I talk* of thy wondrous works.
48. *and I will meditate* in thy statutes.
78. I *will meditate* in thy precepts.
145: 5. *I will speak* of the glorious honour of thy majesty,
Pro. 6:22. thou awakest, *it shall talk with thee*.

* POLEL.—*Future.* *

Ps.143: 5. *I muse* on the work of thy hands.
Isa. 53: 8. who *shall declare* his generation?

7880 **שִׂיחַ** *see'ăgh*, m.

Gen. 2: 5. every *plant of* the field
21:15. cast the child under one of *the shrubs*.
Job 30: 4. Who cut up mallows by *the bushes*,
7. Among *the bushes* they brayed;

7879 **שִׂיחַ** *see'ăgh*, m.

1Sa. 1:16. the abundance of *my complaint* (marg. or, *meditation*)
1K. 18:27. either he is *talking*, (marg. or, *meditateth*)
2K. 9:11. Ye know the man, and *his communication*.
Job 7:13. my couch shall ease *my complaint*;
Job 9:27. I will forget *my complaint*,
10: 1. I will leave *my complaint* upon myself;
21: 4. (is) *my complaint* to man?
23: 2. to day (is) *my complaint* bitter:
Ps 55: 2(3). I mourn *in my complaint*,
64: 1(2). Hear my voice, O God, *in my prayer*.
102[title](1). poureth out *his complaint* before
104:34. *My meditation* of him shall be sweet:
142: 2(3). I poured out *my complaint*
Pro.23:29. who hath *babbling*?

שִׂיחָה *see-ghāh'*, f. 7881

Job 15: 4. restrainest *prayer* (marg. or, *speech*)
Ps.119:97. *my meditation* all the day.
99. thy testimonies (are) my *meditation*.

שִׂים see **שׂוּם** See 7760

שֵׂךְ [*sehch*], m. 7899

Nu. 33:55. *pricks* in your eyes, and thorns in your

שֹׂךְ [*sohch*], m. 7900

Lam.2: 6. violently taken away *his tabernacle*,

שֻׂכָּה [*sook-kāh'*], f. 7905

Job 41: 7(40:31). Canst thou fill his skin *with barbed irons*?

שֶׂכְוִי *sech-vee'*, m. 7907

Job 38:36. given understanding *to the heart*?

שְׂכִיָּה [*s'cheey-yāh'*], f. 7914

Isa. 2:16. upon all pleasant *pictures*.

שַׂכִּין *sak-keen'*, m. 7915

Pro.23: 2. put *a knife* to thy throat, if thou

שָׂכִיר *sāh-cheer'*, m. 7916

Ex. 12:45. A foreigner *and an hired servant*
22:15(14). if it (be) *an hired* (thing), it came
Lev.19:13. the wages of *him that is hired*
22:10. *or an hired servant*, shall not
25: 6. *and for thy hired servant*,
40. *as an hired servant*, (and) as
50. according to the time of *an hired servant*
53. *as a* yearly *hired servant*
Deu15:18. worth a double *hired servant*
24:14. shalt not oppress *an hired servant*
Job 7: 1. days also like the days of *an hireling*?
2. *and as an hireling* looketh for
14: 6. *as an hireling*, his day.
Isa. 16:14. as the years of *an hireling*,
21:16. according to the years of *an hireling*,
Jer. 46:21. *her hired men* (are) in the midst
Mal. 3: 5. those that oppress *the hireling*

שְׂכִירָה *s'chee-rāh'*, f. 7917

Isa. 7:20. with a razor *that is hired*,

שָׂכַךְ [*sāh-chach'*]. 5526

* KAL.—*Preterite.* *

Ex. 33:22. *and will cover* thee with my hand

שָׂכַל *sāh-chal'*. 7919

* KAL.—*Preterite.* *

1Sa.18:30. David *behaved himself* more *wisely*

* PIEL.—*Preterite.* *

Gen48:14. *guiding* his hands *wittingly*;

* HIPHIL.—*Preterite.* *

1Ch 28:19. the Lord *made* me *understand*
Job 34:27. *would* not *consider* any of his ways:
Ps. 64: 9(10). they *shall wisely consider* of his doing.
106: 7. Our fathers *understood* not
119:99. *I have* more *understanding* than
Jer. 10:21. therefore *they shall* not *prosper*,
20:11. for *they shall* not *prosper*:
23: 5. a King shall reign *and prosper*,

HIPHIL.—*Infinitive.*

Gen 3: 6. a tree to be desired *to make* (one) *wise*,
Neh 8:13. *even to understand* the words (marg. or, *that they might instruct in*)
9:20. also thy good spirit *to instruct them*,
Job 34:35. his words (were) *without wisdom.*
Ps. 36: 3(4). he hath left off *to be wise.*
Pro. 1: 3. To receive the instruction of *wisdom*,
21:11. *and when* the wise *is instructed*,
16. out of the way of *understanding*
Isa. 44:18. that they *cannot understand.*
Jer. 3:15. with knowledge *and understanding.*
9:24(23). that he *understandeth* and knoweth
Dan 1:17. God gave them knowledge *and skill*
9:13. *and understand* thy truth.
22. *to give thee skill* and (marg. *to make thee skilful of*) understanding.

HIPHIL.—*Imperative.*

Ps. 2:10. *Be wise* now therefore,

HIPHIL.—*Future.*

Deu29: 9(8). that *ye may prosper* in all that ye do.
32:29. wise, (that) *they understood* this,
Jos. 1: 7. that *thou mayest prosper* (marg. or, *do wisely*)
8. *thou shalt have good success.* (marg. *id.*)
1Sa.18: 5. sent him, (and) *behaved himself wisely:* (marg. or, *prospered*)
1K. 2: 3. *thou mayest prosper* (marg. or, *do wisely*)
2K. 18: 7. *he prospered* whithersoever he went
Ps. 32: 8. *I will instruct thee* and teach thee
94: 8. fools, when *will ye be wise?*
101: 2. *I will behave myself wisely*
Pro.16:23. The heart of the wise *teacheth* (marg. *maketh wise*)
17: 8. whithersoever it turneth, *it prospereth.*
Isa. 41:20. consider, *and understand* together,
52:13. *shall deal prudently*, (marg. or, *prosper*)
Dan 9:25. Know therefore *and understand*,

HIPHIL.—*Participle.*

1Sa.18:14. David *behaved himself wisely* (marg. or, *prospered*)
15. saw that he *behaved himself* very *wisely*,
2Ch 30:22. *that taught* the good knowledge
Job 22: 2. as *he that is wise*
Ps. 14: 2. if there were any *that did understand*,
32: [title](1). (A psalm) of David, *Maschil.* (marg. or, *giving instruction*)
41: 1(2). Blessed (is) *he that considereth* the
42: [title](1). To the chief Musician, *Maschil*, (marg. or, *giving instruction*)
44: [title](1). Musician for the sons of Korah, *Maschil.*
45: [title](1). for the sons of Korah, *Maschil*, (marg. or, of *instruction*)
47: 7(8). sing ye praises with *understanding.* (marg. or, (every one) *that hath understanding*)
52: [title](1). To the chief Musician, *Maschil*,
53: [title](1). Musician upon Mahalath, *Maschil*,
2(3). if there were (any) *that did understand*,
54: [title](1) & 55: [title](1). Musician on Neginoth, *Maschil*,
74: [title](1) & 78: [title](1). *Maschil* (marg or, *to give instruction*) of Asaph.
88: [title](1). *Maschil* (marg. or, *giving instruction*) of Heman
89: [title](1). *Maschil* (marg. or, *to give instruction*) of Ethan
142: [title](1). *Maschil* (marg. or, *giving instruction*) of David;
Pro. 10: 5. gathereth in summer (is) a *wise* son:
19. he that refraineth his lips (is) *wise.*
14:35. king's favour (is) toward a *wise* servant:
15:24. way of life (is) above *to the wise*,
16:20. He that handleth a matter *wisely*
Pro.17: 2. A *wise* servant shall have rule
19:14. a *prudent* wife (is) from the Lord.
21:12. The righteous (man) *wisely considereth* the
Jer. 50: 9. as of a mighty *expert* man;
Dan 1: 4. well favoured, *and skilful*
11:33. *And they that understand among* the people
35. And (some) of *them of understanding* shall
12: 3. *And they that be wise* (marg. or, *teachers*) shall shine
10. *but the wise* shall understand.
Am. 5:13. *the prudent* shall keep silence in that time;

שְׂכַל [*s'chal*], Ch. 7920

* ITHPAEL.—*Participle.* *

Dan 7: 8. I *considered* the horns, (lit. was *considering*)

שֵׂכֶל *sēh'-chel* & שֶׂכֶל *seh'-chel*, m. 7922

1Sa.25: 3. a woman of good *understanding*,
1Ch 22:12. Only the Lord give thee *wisdom*
26:14. a *wise* counsellor, (lit. *in wisdom*)
2Ch 2:12(11). a wise son, endued with *prudence*
30:22. taught *the* good *knowledge of* the Lord:
Ezr. 8:18. brought us a man of *understanding*,
Neh 8: 8. distinctly, and gave *the sense*,
Job 17: 4. hid their heart *from understanding:*
Ps.111:10. *a* good *understanding* have all they
Pro. 3: 4. find favour *and* good *understanding* (marg. or, *success*)
12: 8. commended according to *his wisdom:*
13:15. Good *understanding* giveth favour:
16:22. *Understanding* (is) a wellspring
19:11. *The discretion* (marg. or, *prudence*) *of* a man deferreth
23: 9. he will despise *the wisdom of* thy words.
Dan 8:25. through *his policy* also he shall

שִׂכְלוּת *sich-looth'*, f. 5531

Ecc. 1:17. to know madness and *folly:*

שָׂכְלְתָנוּ *soch-l'thāh-noo'*, Ch. f. 7924

Dan 5:11. light *and understanding* and wisdom,
12. *and understanding*, interpreting of dreams,
14. and (that) light *and understanding*

שָׂכַר [*sāh-char'*]. 7936

* KAL.—*Preterite.* *

Gen30:16. for surely *I have hired thee*
Deu 23: 4(5). *they hired* against thee
2K. 7: 6. the king of Israel *hath hired* against us
Neh 6:12. Tobiah and Sanballat *had hired* him.

KAL.—*Infinitive.*

Gen30:16. for *surely* I have hired thee (lit. *hiring* I have hired)
1Ch 19: 6. *to hire* them chariots and horsemen

KAL.—*Future.*

Jud. 9: 4. *wherewith* Abimelech *hired* vain
18: 4. with me, *and hath hired me*, and I am his
2Sa.10: 6. Ammon sent *and hired* the Syrians
1Ch 19: 7. *So they hired* thirty and two thousand
2Ch 25: 6. *He hired also* an hundred thousand
Neh 13: 2. *but hired* Balaam against them,
Isa. 46: 6. *hire* a goldsmith; and he maketh it

KAL.—*Participle.* Poel.

2Ch 24:12. and *hired* (lit. and were *hiring*) masons and carpenters to repair
Pro.26:10. *both rewardeth* (marg. *hireth*) the fool, *and rewardeth* (marg. *hireth*) transgressors.

KAL.—*Participle.* Paül.

Neh 6:13. Therefore (was) he *hired*,

* NIPHAL.—*Preterite.* *

1Sa. 2: 5. full *have hired out themselves* for bread;

* HITHPAEL.—*Participle.* *

Hag 1: 6. *and he that earneth wages earneth wages* (to put it) into a bag

שָׂכָר sāh-chāhr', m.

Gen15: 1. *thy* exceeding great *reward.*
30:18. God hath given me *my hire,*
28. Appoint me *thy wages,*
32. and (of such) shall be *my hire.*
33. when it shall come for *my hire*
31: 8. The speckled shall be *thy wages;*
— The ringstraked shall be *thy hire;*
Ex. 2: 9. I will give (thee) *thy wages.*
22:15(14). it came *for his hire.*
Nu. 18:31. for it (is) your *reward* for your service
Deu15:18. for he hath been *worth* a double hired servant (lit. for the double of *the hire of* an hired servant)
24:15. At his day thou shalt give (him) *his hire,*
1K. 5: 6(20). *and* unto thee will I give *hire for*
2Ch 15: 7. for your work shall be *rewarded.* (lit. *a reward* shall be to your work)
Ps.127: 3. the fruit of the womb (is his) *reward.*
Ecc. 4: 9. because they have *a* good *reward*
9: 5. neither have they any more *a reward;*
Isa. 40:10 & 62:11. *his reward* (is) with him,
Jer. 31:16. for thy work shall be *rewarded,* (lit. *a reward* shall be to thy work)
Eze.29:18. *yet* had he no *wages,*
19. it shall be *the wages* for his army.
Jon. 1: 3. so he paid *the fare thereof,*
Zec. 8:10. there was no *hire for* man, *nor any hire for* beast;
11:12. give (me) *my price;*
— weighed for *my price* thirty (pieces)
Mal. 3: 5. oppress the hireling in (his) *wages,*

7938 שֶׂכֶר seh'-cher, m.

Pro.11:18. soweth righteousness (shall be) *a* sure *reward.*
Isa. 19:10. all that make *sluices*

7958 שְׂלָו (כתיב) שְׂלָיו (קרי) s'lāhv, m.

Ex. 16:13. at even *the quails* came up,
Nu. 11:31. brought *quails* from the sea,
32. they gathered *the quails:*
Ps.105:40. asked, and he brought *quails,*

8008 שַׂלְמָה sal-māh', f.

Ex. 22: 9(8). for ass, for sheep, for *raiment,*
26(25). at all take thy neighbour's *raiment*
Deu24:13. he may sleep *in his own raiment,*
29: 5(4). *your clothes* are not waxen old
Jos. 9: 5. *and* old *garments* upon them;
13. these *our garments*
22: 8. *and with* very much *raiment:*
1K. 10:25. vessels of gold, *and garments,*
11:29. he had clad himself *with a* new *garment;*
30. Ahijah caught *the* new *garment*
2Ch 9:24. vessels of gold, *and raiment,*
Neh 9:21. *their clothes* waxed not old,
Job 9:31. *mine own clothes* shall abhor me.
Ps.104: 2. coverest (thyself) with light *as* (with) *a garment:*
Cant.4:11. the smell of *thy garments*
Mic. 2: 8. ye pull off the robe with *the garment*

8040 שְׂמֹאול s'mōhl, m.

Gen13: 9. if (thou wilt take) *the left hand,*
14:15. which (is) *on the left hand*
24:49. turn to the right hand, or to *the left.*
48:13. *toward* Israel's *left hand,* and Manasseh *in his left hand*
14. *his left hand* upon Manasseh's head,
Ex. 14:22, 29. on their right hand, *and on their left.*
Nu. 20:17. right hand *nor to the left,*
22:26. the right hand *or to the left.*
Deu 2:27. neither turn unto the right hand *nor to the left.*
5:32(29). to the right hand *or to the left.*
17:11. right hand, *nor* (to) *the left.*
20 & 28:14. the right hand, *or* (to) *the left*
Jos. 1: 7. the right hand *or* (to) *the left,*
19:27. goeth out to Cabul *on the left hand,*
23: 6. the right hand *or* (to) *the left;*
Jud. 3:21. Ehud put forth *his left hand,*
7:20. held the lamps in *their left* hands,
16:29. of the other *with his left.*
1Sa. 6:12. aside (to) the right hand *or* (to) *the left;*
2Sa. 2:19. nor to *the left* from following Abner.
21. to thy right hand or to *thy left,*
16: 6. on his right hand *and on his left.*
1K. 7:39. and five on the *left* side of
49. five *on the left,*
22:19. on his right hand *and on his left.*
2K. 22: 2. to the right hand *or to the left.*
23: 8. which (were) on a man's *left hand*
1Ch 6:44(29). Merari (stood) on *the left hand:*
2Ch 3:17. and the other *on the left;*
4: 6, 8. five *on the left,*
7. five *on the left.*
18:18. on his right hand *and* (on) *his left.*
34: 2. the right hand, *nor to the left.*
Neh 8: 4. *and on his left hand,* Pedaiah,
Job 23: 9. *On the left hand,* where he doth work,
Pro. 3:16. *in her left hand* riches and honour.
4:27. Turn not to the right hand *nor to the left.*
Ecc.10: 2. but a fool's heart *at his left.*
Cant.2: 6. *His left hand* (is) under my head,
8: 3. *His left hand* (should be) under my head,
Isa. 9:20(19). he shall eat on *the left hand,*
54: 3. on the right hand *and on the left;*
Eze. 1:10. the face of an ox *on the left side;*
16:46. she and her daughters that dwell at *thy left hand:*
39: 3. bow out of *thy left* hand,
Dan12: 7. and his *left hand* unto heaven,
Jon. 4:11. their right hand and *their left hand;*
Zec. 4: 3. the other upon *the left* (side) *thereof.*
11. and upon *the left* (side) *thereof?*
12: 6. on the right hand and on *the left:*

שָׂמַאל [sāh-mal']. 8041

* HIPHIL.—*Infinitive.* *

2Sa.14:19. to the right hand *or to the left*

HIPHIL.—*Imperative.*

Eze.21:16(21). Go thee one way or other, (either) on the right hand, (or) *on the left,* (marg. set thyself, *take the left hand*)

HIPHIL.—*Future.*

Gen13: 9. *then I will go to the left.*
Isa. 30:21. when *ye turn to the left.*

HIPHIL.—*Participle.*

1Ch 12: 2. use both the right hand *and the left*

שְׂמָאלִי s'māh-lee', adj. 8042

Lev.14:15, 26. into the palm of his own *left* hand:
16, 27. the oil that (is) in his *left* hand,
1K. 7:21. he set up the *left* pillar,
2K. 11:11. to the *left* corner of the temple,
2Ch 3:17. the name of that on *the left*
23:10. to the *left* side of the temple,
Eze. 4: 4. Lie thou also upon thy *left* side,

שָׂמַח sāh-magh' & שָׂמֵחַ [sāh-meh'ăgh]. 8055

* KAL.—*Preterite.* *

Ex. 4:14. *and* when...*he will be glad* in his heart.
Lev.23:40. *and ye shall rejoice* before the Lord
Deu12: 7. *and ye shall rejoice* in all
12. *And ye shall rejoice* before the Lord
18. *and thou shalt rejoice* before the Lord
14:26. *and thou shalt rejoice,* thou, and
16:11. *And thou shalt rejoice* before the Lord
14. *And thou shalt rejoice* in thy feast,
26:11. *And thou shalt rejoice* in every
27: 7. *and rejoice* before the Lord
1Sa. 2: 1. *I rejoice* in thy salvation.
1Ch 29: 9. also *rejoiced* with great joy
Neh12:43. the children *rejoiced:*

Ps. 16: 9. my heart *is glad*, and my glory rejoiceth:
35:15. But in mine adversity *they rejoiced*,
105:38. Egypt *was glad* when they departed:
122: 1. *I was glad* when they said
Isa. 9: 3(2). *they joy* before thee according
14: 8. the fir trees *rejoice* at thee,
Zec. 4:10. *for they shall rejoice*,
10: 7. *and* their heart *shall rejoice*
— shall see (it), *and be glad;*

KAL.—*Infinitive.*

Ps.106: 5. *that* I *may rejoice* in the gladness
Ecc. 3:12. but for (a man) *to rejoice*,
5:19(18). *and to rejoice* in his labour;
8:15. to drink, *and to be merry:*
Eze.35:14. *When* the whole earth *rejoiceth*,

KAL.—*Imperative.*

Deu 33:18. of Zebulun he said, *Rejoice*,
Jud. 9:19. *rejoice ye* in Abimelech,
Ps. 32:11. *Be glad* in the Lord,
97:12. *Rejoice* in the Lord,
Pro. 5:18. *and rejoice* with the wife of thy youth.
Ecc.11: 9. *Rejoice*, O young man,
Isa. 66:10. *Rejoice ye* with Jerusalem,
Lam.4:21. Rejoice *and be glad*, O daughter
Joel 2:21. Fear not, O land; be glad *and rejoice:*
23. *and rejoice* in the Lord
Zep. 3:14. *be glad* and rejoice with all
Zec. 2:10(14). Sing *and rejoice*, O daughter

KAL.—*Future.*

Jud. 9:19. *and let* him also *rejoice* in you:
19: 3. *and* when the father of the damsel saw him, *he rejoiced*
1Sa. 6:13. *and rejoiced* to see (it).
11: 9. men of Jabesh; *and they were glad.*
15. *and* there Saul and all the men of Israel *rejoiced*
19: 5. thou sawest (it), *and didst rejoice:*
2Sa. 1:20. lest the daughters of the Philistines *rejoice*,
1K. 5: 7(21). *that he rejoiced* greatly,
2K. 11:20. *And* all the people of the land *rejoiced*,
1Ch 16:10. *let* the heart of them *rejoice*
31. *Let* the heavens *be glad*,
29: 9. *Then* the people *rejoiced*,
2Ch 6:41. *let* thy saints *rejoice* in goodness.
15:15. *And* all Judah *rejoiced*
23:21. *And* all the people of the land *rejoiced:*
24:10. *and* all the people *rejoiced*,
29:36. *And* Hezekiah *rejoiced*, and all the people,
30:25. *And* all the congregation...*rejoiced.*
Neh 12:43. offered great sacrifices, *and rejoiced:*
Job 21:12. *and rejoice* at the sound of the organ.
22:19. The righteous see (it), *and are glad:*
31:25. If *I rejoiced* because my wealth
29. If *I rejoiced* at the destruction of him
Ps. 5:11(12). *But let* all those that put their trust in thee *rejoice:*
9: 2(3). *I will be glad* and rejoice
14: 7. Israel *shall be glad.*
21: 1(2). The king *shall joy* in thy strength,
31: 7(8). I will be glad *and rejoice* in
33:21. our heart *shall rejoice* in him,
34: 2(3). the humble shall hear (thereof), *and be glad.*
35:19. *Let* not them that are mine enemies wrongfully *rejoice*
24. *let* them not *rejoice* over me.
27. shout for joy, *and be glad*,
38:16(17). *they should rejoice* over me:
40:16(17). rejoice *and be glad* in thee:
48:11(12). *Let* mount Zion *rejoice*,
53: 6(7). Israel *shall be glad.*
58:10(11). The righteous *shall rejoice*
63:11(12). But the king *shall rejoice* in God;
64:10(11). The righteous *shall be glad*
66: 6. there *did we rejoice* in him.
67: 4(5). O *let* the nations *be glad*
68: 3(4). But *let* the righteous *be glad;*
69:32(33). The humble shall see (this, and) *be glad:*
70: 4(5). seek thee rejoice *and be glad*
85: 6(7). that thy people *may rejoice* in thee?
90:14. that we may rejoice *and be glad* all our
96:11. *Let* the heavens *rejoice*,
97: 1. *let* the multitude of isles *be glad*
Ps. 97: 8. Zion heard, *and was glad;*
104:31. the Lord *shall rejoice* in his works.
34. *I will be glad* in the Lord.
105: 3. *let* the heart of them *rejoice*
107:30. *Then are they glad* because
42. The righteous shall see (it), *and rejoice:*
109:28. but *let* thy servant *rejoice.*
118:24. we will rejoice *and be glad*
119:74. They that fear thee *will be glad*
149: 2. *Let* Israel *rejoice* in him
Pro. 13: 9. The light of the righteous *rejoiceth:*
17:21. the father of a fool *hath* no *joy.*
23:15. if thine heart be wise, my heart *shall rejoice*,
24. begetteth a wise (child) *shall have joy*
25. Thy father and thy mother *shall be glad*,
24:17. *Rejoice* not when thine enemy falleth,
29: 2. in authority, the people *rejoice:*
Ecc. 3:22. man *should rejoice* in his own works;
4:16. that come after *shall* not *rejoice*
11: 8. live many years, (and) *rejoice* in them
Cant 1: 4. will be glad *and rejoice* in thee,
Isa. 9:17(16). the Lord *shall have* no *joy* in their
14:29. *Rejoice* not thou, whole Palestina,
25: 9. be glad *and rejoice* in his salvation.
39: 2. *And* Hezekiah *was glad* of them,
65:13. my servants *shall rejoice*,
Jer. 31:13. Then *shall* the virgin *rejoice*
41:13. with him, *then they were glad.*
50:11. Because *ye were glad*,
Eze. 7:12. *let* not the buyer *rejoice*,
25: 6. *and rejoiced* in heart
Hos. 9: 1. *Rejoice* not, O Israel, for joy,
Obad. 12. neither *shouldest thou have rejoiced*
Jon. 4: 6. *So* Jonah *was* exceeding *glad*
Mic. 7: 8. *Rejoice* not against me,
Hab. 1:15. *they rejoice* and are glad.

* PIEL.—*Preterite.* *

Deu 24: 5. *and shall cheer up* his wife
2Ch 20:27. the Lord *had made them to rejoice*
Ezr. 6:22. the Lord *had made them joyful*,
Neh 12:43. God *had made them rejoice*
Ps. 30: 1(2). *hast* not *made* my foes *to rejoice*
45: 8(9). whereby *they have made thee glad.*
92: 4(5). *thou*, Lord, *hast made me glad*
Isa. 56: 7. *and make them joyful*
Jer. 20:15. *making him* very *glad.*
31:13. *and make them rejoice* from

PIEL.—*Infinitive.*

Jer. 20:15. making him *very* glad. (lit. *making glad* made him glad)

PIEL.—*Imperative.*

Ps. 86: 4. *Rejoice* the soul of thy servant:
90:15. *Make us glad* according to
Pro.27:11. be wise, *and make* my heart *glad*,

PIEL.—*Future.*

Ps. 46: 4(5). *shall make glad* the city of God,
104:15. wine (that) *maketh glad* the heart
Pro. 10: 1. A wise son *maketh* a *glad* father:
12:25. a good word *maketh it glad.*
15:20. A wise son *maketh* a *glad* father:
30. The light of the eyes *rejoiceth* the heart:
27: 9. Ointment and perfume *rejoice* the heart:
29: 3. Whoso loveth wisdom *rejoiceth* his father:
Ecc.10:19. and wine *maketh merry:* (marg. *maketh glad* the life)
Lam.2:17. *and he hath caused* (thine) enemy *to rejoice*
Hos. 7: 3. *They make* the king *glad*

PIEL.—*Participle.*

Jud. 9:13. *which cheereth* God and man,
Ps. 19: 8(9). *rejoicing* the heart:

* HIPHIL.—*Preterite.* *

Ps. 89:42(43). *thou hast made* all his enemies *to rejoice.*

שָׂמֵחַ *sāh-mēh'ăgh*, adj. 8056

Deu 16:15. therefore thou shalt surely *rejoice.* (lit. thou shalt be *joyful*)
1K. 1:40. *and rejoiced* with great joy,
45. are come up from thence *rejoicing*,

1K. 4:20. eating and drinking, *and making merry.*
8:66. went unto their tents *joyful*
2K. 11:14. all the people of the land *rejoiced,*
2Ch 7:10. *glad* and merry in heart
23:13. all the people of the land *rejoiced,*
Est. 5: 9. Then went Haman forth that day *joyful*
14. then go thou in *merrily*
8:15. city of Shushan rejoiced *and was glad.*
Job 3:22. Which *rejoice* exceedingly,
Ps. 35:26. *that rejoice at* mine hurt:
113: 9. a *joyful* mother of children.
126: 3. things for us; (whereof) we are *glad.*
Pro. 2:14. Who *rejoice* to do evil,
15:13. A *merry* heart maketh a chearful
17: 5. *he that is glad* at calamities
22. A *merry* heart doeth good
29: 6. the righteous doth sing *and rejoice.*
Ecc. 2:10. my heart *rejoiced* in all my labour;
Isa. 24: 7. all the *merry*hearted do sigh.
Am. 6:13. Ye *which rejoice* in a thing of nought,

8057 **שִׂמְחָה** *sim-ghāh'*, f.

Gen31:27. have sent thee away *with mirth,*
Nu. 10:10. Also in the day of *your gladness,*
Deu28:47. the Lord thy God *with joyfulness,*
Jud.16:23. Dagon their god, *and to rejoice:*
1Sa.18: 6. to meet king Saul, with tabrets, *with joy,*
2Sa. 6:12. into the city of David *with gladness.*
1K. 1:40. rejoiced with great *joy,*
1Ch 12:40. for (there was) *joy* in Israel.
15:16. lifting up the voice *with joy.*
25. the house of Obed-edom *with joy.*
29: 9. the king also rejoiced with great *joy.*
17. now have I seen *with joy*
22. on that day *with* great *gladness.*
2Ch 20:27. to go again to Jerusalem *with joy;*
23:18. *with rejoicing* and with singing,
29:30. they sang praises *with gladness,*
30:21. seven days *with* great *gladness:*
23. kept (other) seven days with *gladness.*
26. So there was great *joy* in Jerusalem:
Ezr. 3:12. many shouted aloud *for joy:*
13. discern the noise of the shout of *joy*
6:22. seven days with *joy:*
Neh 8:12. to make great *mirth,*
17. there was very great *gladness.*
12:27. keep the dedication *with gladness,*
43. made them rejoice with great *joy:*
— so that *the joy of* Jerusalem
44. Judah *rejoiced* for the priests (lit. *the joy of* Judah)
Est. 8:16. Jews had light, *and gladness,* and joy,
17. the Jews had *joy* and gladness,
9:17, 18. made it a day of feasting *and gladness.*
19. day of the month Adar (a day of) *gladness*
22. from sorrow *to joy,*
— make them days of feasting *and joy,*
Job 20: 5. *and the joy of* the hypocrite
Ps. 4: 7(8). Thou hast put *gladness* in my
16:11. thy presence (is) fulness of *joy;* (lit. *joys*)
21: 6(7). thou hast made him *exceeding* glad (marg. gladded him *with joy*)
30:11(12). girded me with *gladness;*
43: 4. unto God my *exceeding* joy: (marg. the *gladness of* my joy)
45:15(16). *With gladness* and rejoicing shall
51: 8(10). Make me to hear joy *and gladness;*
68: 3(4). let them *exceedingly* rejoice. (marg. rejoice *with gladness*)
97:11. and *gladness* for the upright
100: 2. Serve the Lord *with gladness:*
106: 5. rejoice *in the gladness of* thy nation,
137: 3. wasted us (required of us) *mirth,*
6. Jerusalem above *my* chief *joy.*
Pro 10:28. hope of the righteous (shall be) *gladness:*
12:20. counsellors of peace (is) *joy.*
14:10. *and* a stranger doth not intermeddle *with his joy.*
13. the end of that *mirth* (is) heaviness.
15:21. Folly (is) *joy* to (him that is)
23. A man hath *joy* by the answer
21:15. *joy* to the just to do judgment:
17. He that loveth *pleasure* (marg. or, *sport*)
Ecc. 2: 1. I will prove thee *with mirth,*
2. *and of mirth,* What doeth (it)?
Ecc. 2:10. withheld not my heart from any *joy;*
26. knowledge, *and joy:*
5:20(19). answereth (him) *in the joy of*
7: 4. heart of fools (is) in the house of *mirth.*
8:15. Then I commended *mirth,*
9: 7. eat thy bread *with joy,*
Cant.3:11. in the day of *the gladness of* his heart.
Isa. 9: 3(2). not increased *the joy:*
—(–). *according to the joy* in harvest,
16:10. *gladness* is taken away,
22:13. behold joy *and gladness,*
24:11. all *joy* is darkened,
29:19. The meek also shall increase (their) *joy*
30:29. *and gladness of* heart,
35:10. and everlasting *joy* upon their heads: they shall obtain joy *and gladness,*
51: 3. joy *and gladness* shall be found
11. *and* everlasting *joy* (shall be)
— they shall obtain gladness *and joy;*
55:12. For ye shall go out *with joy,*
61: 7. everlasting *joy* shall be unto them.
66: 5. but he shall appear *to your joy,*
Jer. 7:34. the voice of *gladness,*
15:16. the joy *and rejoicing of* mine heart:
16: 9 & 25:10. the voice of *gladness,*
31: 7. Sing with *gladness* for Jacob,
33:11. voice of joy, and the voice of *gladness,*
48:33. *joy* and gladness is taken from the
Eze.35:15. *As thou didst rejoice* at the inheritance
36: 5. *with the joy of* all (their) heart,
Joel 1:16. *joy* and gladness from the house
Jon. 4: 6. Jonah was exceeding glad (marg. rejoiced with great *joy*) of the gourd.
Zep. 3:17. he will rejoice over thee *with joy;*
Zec. 8:19. to the house of Judah joy *and gladness,*

שְׂמִיכָה *s'mee-chāh'*, f. 8063

Jud. 4:18. she covered him *with a mantle* (marg. or, *rug,* or, *blanket*)

שַׂמַל see **שְׂמָאל** See 8041

שִׂמְלָה *sim-lāh'*, f. 8071

Gen 9:23. Shem and Japheth took *a garment,*
35: 2. change *your garments:*
37:34. Jacob rent *his clothes,*
41:14. changed *his raiment,*
44:13. Then they rent *their clothes,*
45:22. gave each man changes of *raiment;*
— five changes of *raiment.*
Ex. 3:22. jewels of gold, *and raiment:*
12:34. being bound up *in their clothes*
35. jewels of gold, *and raiment:*
19:10. let them wash *their clothes,*
14. they washed *their clothes.*
22:27(26). it (is) *his raiment* for his skin:
Deu 8: 4. *Thy raiment* waxed not old
10:18. in giving him food *and raiment.*
21:13. she shall put *the raiment of*
22: 3. so shalt thou do *with his raiment;*
5. shall a man put on a woman's *garment:*
17. shall spread *the cloth* before the elders
Jos. 7: 6. Joshua rent *his clothes,*
Jud. 8:25. they spread *a garment,*
Ru. 3: 3. anoint thee, and put *thy raiment* upon
1Sa.21: 9(10). it (is here) wrapped in *a cloth*
2Sa.12:20. changed *his apparel,*
Pro.30: 4. hath bound the waters *in a garment?*
Isa. 3: 6. Thou hast *clothing,*
7. neither bread nor *clothing:*
4: 1. *and* wear *our own apparel:*
9: 5(4). *and garments* rolled in blood;

שְׂמָמִית *s'māh-meeth'*, f. 8079

Pro.30:28. *The spider* taketh hold with her hands,

שָׂנֵא *sāh-nēh'*. 8130

* KAL.—*Preterite.* *

Gen26:27. come ye to me, seeing ye *hate* me
Deu12:31. which *he hateth,* have they done

Deu16:22. image; which the Lord thy God *hateth.*
22:13. go in unto her, *and hate her,*
24: 3. *And* (if) the latter husband *hate her,*
Jud.11: 7. *Did* not ye *hate* me,
14:16. *Thou dost* but *hate* me,
15: 2. thought that *thou hadst* utterly *hated her;*
2Sa.13:15. the hatred wherewith *he hated her*
22. for Absalom *hated* Amnon,
1K. 22: 8. but *I hate him;* for he doth not prophesy
2Ch 18: 7. but *I hate him;* for he never
Ps. 5: 5(6). *thou hatest* all workers of iniquity.
11: 5. him that loveth violence his soul *hateth.*
25:19. *they hate me* with cruel hatred.
26: 5. *I have hated* the congregation
31: 6(7). *I have hated* them that regard
50:17. Seeing thou *hatest* instruction,
101: 3. *I hate* the work of them
119:104. therefore *I hate* every false way.
113. *I hate* (vain) thoughts:
128. *I hate* every false way.
163. *I hate* and abhor lying:
139:22. *I hate them* with perfect hatred:
Pro. 1:29. For that *they hated* knowledge,
5:12. How *have I hated* instruction,
6:16. These six (things) *doth* the Lord *hate:*
8:13. the froward mouth, *do I hate.*
19: 7. the brethren of the poor *do hate him:*
25:17. he be weary of thee, *and* (so) *hate thee.*
Ecc. 2:17. *Therefore I hated* life;
18. *Yea,* I *hated* all my labour
Isa. 1:14. your appointed feasts my soul *hateth:*
Jer. 12: 8. therefore *have I hated it.*
44: 4. do not this abominable thing that *I hate.*
Eze.16:37. all (them) that *thou hast hated;*
23:28. the hand (of them) whom *thou hatest,*
35: 6. sith *thou hast* not *hated* blood,
Hos 9:15. for there *I hated them:*
Am. 5:10. *They hate* him that rebuketh
21. *I hate,* I despise your feast days,
6: 8. and *hate* his palaces:
Zec. 8:17. for all these (are things) that *I hate,*
Mal. 1: 3. *I hated* Esau, and laid his mountains
2:16. saith that *he hateth* putting away:

KAL.—*Infinitive.*

Gen37: 5, 8. they *hated* him yet *the more.* (lit. added *to hate*)
Jud.15: 2. thought that thou hadst *utterly* hated her; (lit. *hating* hadst hated)
2Sa.19: 6(7). *and hatest* thy friends.
Ps. 36: 2(3). until his iniquity be found *to be hateful.* (marg. *to hate*)
105:25. turned their heart *to hate* his people,
Pro. 8:13. The fear of the Lord (is) *to hate* evil:
Ecc. 3: 8. A time to love, and a time *to hate;*

KAL.—*Imperative.*

Ps. 97:10. Ye that love the Lord, *hate* evil:
Am. 5:15. *Hate* the evil, and love the good,

KAL.—*Future.*

Gen37: 4. *And* when his brethren saw...*they hated*
Lev.19:17. *Thou shalt* not *hate* thy brother
Deu22:16. unto this man to wife, *and he hateth her;*
2Sa.13:15. *Then* Amnon *hated her* exceedingly;
Ps. 45: 7(8). lovest righteousness, *and hatest*
139:21. *Do* not *I hate* them, O Lord,
Pro. 1:22. fools *hate* knowledge?
9: 8. Reprove not a scorner, lest *he hate thee:*
13: 5. A righteous (man) *hateth* lying:
26:28. A lying tongue *hateth* (those that are)
29:10. The bloodthirsty *hate* the upright:

KAL.—*Participle.* Poel.

Gen24:60. possess the gate of *those which hate them.*
Ex. 1:10. they join also unto *our enemies,*
18:21. men of truth, *hating* covetousness;
20: 5. fourth (generation) *of them that hate me;*
23: 5. see the ass of him *that hateth thee*
Lev.26:17. *they that hate you* shall reign over you;
Deu 4:42. *hated* him not in times past;
5: 9. fourth (generation) *of them that hate me,*
7:10. repayeth them *that hate him*
— will not be slack *to him that hateth him,*
15. all (them) *that hate thee.*
19: 4. whom he *hated* not in time past;
6. inasmuch as he *hated* him not
11. But if any man *hate* his neighbour,

Deu30: 7. on *them that hate thee,*
Jos. 20: 5. *hated* him not beforetime.
2Sa.19: 6(7). In that thou lovest *thine enemies,*
22:18. *from them that hated me:*
2Ch 1:11. nor the life of *thine enemies,*
19: 2. *and* love *them that hate* the Lord?
Est. 9: 1. Jews had rule *over them that hated them;*
5. what they would *unto those that hated them.*
16. slew *of their foes* seventy and five thousand,
Job 8:22. *They that hate thee* shall be
34:17. even *he that hateth* right govern?
Ps. 9:13(14). *of them that hate me,*
18:17(18). *and from them which hated me:*
21: 8(9). shall find out *those that hate thee.*
34:21(22). *and they that hate* the righteous
35:19. *that hate me* without a cause.
38:19(20). *they that hate me* wrongfully
41: 7(8). All *that hate me* whisper together
69: 4(5). *They that hate me* without a cause
14(15). delivered *from them that hate me,*
86:17. that *they which hate me* may see
106:10. from the hand of *him that hated*
41. they *that hated them* ruled
118: 7. see (my desire) *upon them that hate me.*
120: 6. hath long dwelt with *him that hateth* peace.
129: 5. confounded and turned back *that hate* Zion.
Pro.11:15. *and he that hateth* suretiship
12: 1. *but he that hateth* reproof
13:24. He that spareth his rod *hateth* his son:
15:10. *he that hateth* reproof shall die.
27. *but he that hateth* gifts shall live.
25:21. If *thine enemy* be hungry, give him bread
26:24. *He that hateth* dissembleth
27: 6. the kisses of *an enemy* (are) deceitful.
28:16. *he that hateth* covetousness
29:24. partner with a thief *hateth* his own soul:
Isa. 61: 8. I *hate* robbery for burnt offering;
66: 5. Your brethren *that hated you,*
Eze.16:27. unto the will of *them that hate thee,*
Mic. 3: 2. *Who hate* the good, and love the evil;

KAL.—*Participle.* Paül.

Gen29:31. the Lord saw that Leah (was) *hated,*
33. the Lord hath heard that I (was) *hated,*
Deu21:15. one beloved, and another *hated,*
— the beloved *and the hated;*
16. firstborn before the son of *the hated,*
17. acknowledge the son of *the hated*
2Sa. 5: 8. (that are) *hated of* David's soul,
Pro.30:23. For an *odious* (woman) when she is
Isa. 60:15. thou hast been forsaken *and hated,*

* NIPHAL.—*Future.* *

Pro.14:17. a man of wicked devices *is hated.*
20. The poor *is hated* even of his own

* PIEL.—*Participle.* *

Nu. 10:35. let *them that hate thee* flee before thee.
Deu32:41. and will reward *them that hate me.*
33:11. *and of them that hate him,*
2Sa.22:41. that I might destroy *them that hate me.*
Job 31:29. the destruction of *him that hated*
Ps. 18:40(41). *that* I might destroy *them that hate me.*
44: 7(8). *and* hast put *them* to shame *that hated us.*
10(11). *and they which hate us* spoil
55:12(13). neither (was it) *he that hated me*
68: 1(2). let *them* also *that hate him* flee
81:15(16). *The haters of* the Lord should have
83: 2(3). *and they that hate thee* have
89:23(24). *and* plague *them that hate him.*
139:21. I hate *them,* O Lord, *that hate thee?*
Pro. 8:36. all *they that hate me* love death.

שְׂנֵא [*s'nēh*], Ch. 8131

* P'AL.—*Participle.* *

Dan 4:19(16). the dream (be) *to them that hate thee,*

שִׂנְאָה *sin-āh',* f. 8135

Nu. 35:20. But if he thrust him *of hatred,*
Deu 1:27. *Because* the Lord *hated* us,
9:28. *and because he hated* them,
2Sa.13:15. Then Amnon hated her exceedingly (marg. with great *hatred* greatly); so that *the hatred* wherewith he hated her

Ps. 25:19. *and* they hate me with cruel *hatred.*
109: 3. me about also with words of *hatred;*
5. *and hatred* for my love.
139:22. I hate them with perfect *hatred:*
Pro. 10:12. *Hatred* stirreth up strifes:
18. He that hideth *hatred* (with) lying lips,
15:17. than a stalled ox *and hatred* therewith.
26:26. *hatred* is covered by deceit,
Ecc. 9: 1. no man knoweth either love or *hatred*
6. Also their love, and *their hatred,*
Eze. 23:29. they shall deal with thee *hatefully,*
35:11. which thou hast used *out of thy hatred*

8146 **שְׂנִיא** [*sāh-nee'*], adj.

Deu 21:15. firstborn son be her's *that was hated:*

8163 **שָׂעִיר** *sāh-ngeer'*, m.

Gen 27:11. Esau my brother (is) a *hairy* man,
23. because his hands were *hairy,*
37:31. killed *a kid of* the goats,
Lev. 4:23. *a kid of* the goats,
24. lay his hand upon the head of *the goat,*
9: 3. Take ye *a kid of* the goats
15. took *the goat,* which (was) the sin offering
10:16. Moses diligently sought *the goat of*
16: 5. two *kids of* the goats
7. he shall take *the* two *goats,*
8. cast lots upon *the* two *goats;*
9. Aaron shall bring *the goat*
10. *But the goat,* on which the lot fell
15. Then shall he kill *the goat of*
18. of the blood of *the goat,*
20. he shall bring *the* live *goat:*
21. hands upon the head of *the* live *goat,*
— upon the head of *the goat,*
22. *the goat* shall bear upon him
— shall let go *the goat* in the wilderness.
26. he that let go *the goat*
27. *the goat* (for) the sin offering,
17: 7. offer their sacrifices *unto devils,*
23:19. Then ye shall sacrifice one *kid of*
Nu. 7:16, 22, 28, 34, 40, 46, 52, 58, 64, 70, 76, 82. One *kid of* the goats
87. *and the kids of* the goats
15:24 & 28:15. *and* one *kid of* the goats
28:22. *And* one *goat* (for) a sin offering,
30. one *kid of* the goats,
29: 5, 16, 19, 25. *And* one *kid of* the goats
11. One *kid of* the goats (for) a sin offering;
22, 28, 31, 34, 38. *And* one *goat* (for) a sin
2Ch 11:15. *and for the devils,*
29:23. they brought forth *the he goats* (for) the
Isa. 13:21. *and satyrs* shall dance there.
34:14. *and the satyr* shall cry to his fellow;
Eze. 43:22. offer *a kid of* the goats
25. every day *a goat* (for) a sin offering:
45:23. *a kid of* the goats daily
Dan 8:21. the *rough* goat (is) the king of Grecia:

8166 **שְׂעִירָה** [*s'ngee-rāh'*], f.

Lev. 4:28. offering, *a kid of* the goats,
5: 6. a lamb or *a kid of* the goats,

8164 **שְׂעִירִים** *s'ngee-reem'*, m. pl.

Deu 32: 2. *as the small rain* upon the tender herb,

5587 **שְׂעִפִּים** *s'ngip-peem'*, m. pl.

Job 4:13. *In thoughts* from the visions
20: 2. do *my thoughts* cause me to

8175 **שָׂעַר** [*sāh-ngar'*].

* KAL.—*Preterite.* *

Deu 32:17. whom your fathers *feared* not.
Eze. 27:35. their kings *shall be* sore *afraid,*

KAL.—*Imperative.*

Jer. 2:12. *and be horribly afraid,*

KAL.—*Future.*

Ps. 58: 9(10). *he shall take them away as with a whirlwind,*
Eze. 32:10. their kings *shall be* horribly *afraid*

* NIPHAL.—*Preterite.* *

Ps. 50: 3. *it shall be* very *tempestuous*

* PIEL.—*Future.* *

Job 27:21. *and as a storm hurleth him*

* HITHPAEL.—*Future.* *

Dan 11:40. *and* the king...*shall come...like a whirlwind,*

שַׂעַר *sah'-ngar*, m. 8178

Job 18:20. as they that went before were *affrighted.* (marg. laid hold on *horror*)
Isa. 28: 2. as a tempest of hail (and) *a* destroying *storm,*
Eze. 27:35. their kings shall be *sore* afraid, (lit. afraid with *horror*)
32:10. their kings shall be *horribly* afraid (lit. afraid with *horror*)

שַׂעַר *sah'-ngar.* 8181

Isa. 7:20. *and the hair of* the feet:

שֵׂעָר *sēh-ngāhr'*, m. 8181

Gen 25:25. all over like an *hairy* garment;
Lev. 13: 3. *and* (when) *the hair* in the plague
4. *and the hair thereof* be not turned
10. it have turned *the hair* white,
20. *and the hair thereof* be turned
21. no white *hairs* therein,
25. the *hair* in the bright spot
26. no white *hair* in the bright spot,
30. in it *a* yellow thin *hair;*
31. *and* (that there is) no black *hair*
32. there be in it no yellow *hair,*
36. the priest shall not seek *for* yellow *hair;*
37. *and* (that) there is black *hair*
14: 8. shave off all *his hair,*
9. he shall shave all *his hair* off
— even all *his hair* he shall shave
Nu. 6: 5. let the locks of *the hair of* his head grow.
18. shall take *the hair of* the head
Jud. 16:22. *the hair of* his head began to grow
2Sa. 14:26. he weighed *the hair of* his head
2K. 1: 8. they answered him, (He was) an *hairy* man, (lit. owner of *hair*)
Ezr. 9: 3. plucked off *the hair of* my head
Ps. 68:21(22). the *hairy* scalp of such an one
Cant 4: 1. *thy hair* (is) as a flock of goats,
6: 5. *thy hair* (is) as a flock of goats
Eze. 16: 7. *and thine hair* is grown,
Zec. 13: 4. neither shall they wear a *rough* garment (marg. garment of *hair*)

שְׂעַר *s'ngar*, Ch. m. 8177

Dan 3:27. *nor* was *an hair of* their head singed,
4:33(30). till *his hairs* were grown like eagles'
7: 9. *and the hair of* his head like the pure

שְׂעָרָה *s'ngāh-rāh'*, f. 8183

Job 9:17. he breaketh me *with a tempest,*
Nah. 1: 3. in the whirlwind *and in the storm,*

שַׂעֲרָה *sah-ngărāh'*, f. 8185

Jud. 20:16. could sling stones *at an hair*
1Sa. 14:45. there shall not one *hair of* his head fall
2Sa. 14:11. there shall not one *hair of* thy son fall
1K. 1:52. there shall not *an hair of him* fall
Job 4:15. *the hair of* my flesh stood up:
Ps. 40:12(13). they are more *than the hairs of* mine head:
69: 4(5). are more *than the hairs of*

שְׂעֹרָה *s'ngōh-rāh'*, f. 8184

Ex. 9:31. the flax *and the barley*
— for *the barley* (was) in the ear,
Lev. 27:16. an homer of *barley*
Nu. 5:15. tenth (part) of an ephah of *barley* meal;
Deu 8: 8. A land of wheat, *and barley,*
Jud. 7:13. a cake of *barley* bread

Ru. 1:22. in the beginning of *barley* harvest.
2:17. about an ephah of *barley*.
23. to glean unto the end of *barley* harvest
3: 2. he winnoweth *barley* to night
15. he measured six (measures) of *barley*,
17. six (measures) of *barley* gave he me;
2Sa. 14:30. he hath *barley* there;
17:28. wheat, *and barley*,
21: 9. beginning of *barley* harvest.
1K. 4:28(5:8). *Barley also* and straw for
2K. 4:42. twenty loaves of *barley*,
7: 1,16,18. two measures of *barley*
1Ch 11:13. parcel of ground full of *barley*;
2Ch 2:10(9). *and* twenty thousand measures of *barley*,
15(14). *and the barley*, the oil,
27: 5. *and* ten thousand of *barley*.
Job 31:40. cockle instead of *barley*.
Isa. 28:25. *and the* appointed *barley*
Jer. 41: 8. *and* of *barley*, and of oil,
Eze. 4: 9. unto thee wheat, *and barley*,
12. eat it (as) *barley* cakes,
13:19. for handfuls of *barley*
45:13. sixth part of an ephah of an homer of *barley*:
Hos. 3: 2. and (for) an homer of *barley*, and an half homer of *barley*:
Joel 1:11. for the wheat and for *the barley*;

8193 **שָׂפָה** *sāh-phāh'*, f.

Gen 11: 1. earth was of one *language*, (marg. *lip*)
6. *and* they have all one *language*;
7. there confound *their language*, that they may not understand one another's *speech*.
9. did there confound *the language of*
22:17. sand which (is) upon *the* sea *shore*;
41: 3. kine upon *the brink of* the river.
17. I stood upon *the bank of* the river:
Ex. 2: 3. in the flags by the river's *brink*.
6:12. hear me, who (am) of uncircumcised *lips*?
30. I (am) of uncircumcised *lips*,
7:15. stand by the river's *brink*
14:30. Egyptians dead upon *the* sea *shore*.
26: 4. upon *the edge of* the one curtain
— make *in the* uttermost *edge of*
10. make fifty loops on *the edge of*
— fifty loops in *the edge of*
28:26. breastplate in *the border thereof*,
32. it shall have *a binding*
36:11. blue on *the edge of* one curtain
— made *in the* uttermost *side of*
17. fifty loops upon *the* uttermost *edge of*
— fifty loops made he upon *the edge of*
39:19. upon *the border of it*,
23. *a band* round about the hole,
Lev. 5: 4. pronouncing *with* (his) *lips* to do
Nu. 30: 6(7). uttered ought out of *her lips*,
8(9). which she uttered with *her lips*,
12(13). whatsoever proceeded out of *her lips*
Deu 2:36. which (is) by *the brink of*
4:48. which (is) by *the bank of*
23:23(24). That which is gone out of *thy lips*
Jos. 11: 4. that (is) upon *the* sea *shore*
12: 2. which (is) upon *the bank of*
13: 9. that (is) upon *the bank of*
16. that (is) on *the bank of*
Jud. 7:12. as the sand by *the* sea *side*
22. to *the border* (marg. *lip*) *of* Abel-meholah,
1Sa. 1:13. only *her lips* moved,
13: 5. as the sand which (is) on *the* seashore
1K. 4:29(5:9). as the sand that (is) on *the* sea *shore*.
7:23. *from the one brim* to *the other*: (marg. *from his brim* to *his brim*)
24. under *the brim of it*
26. *and the brim thereof* was wrought like *the brim of* a cup,
9:26. on *the shore* (marg. *lip*) *of* the Red sea,
2K. 2:13. stood by *the bank* (marg. *id.*) *of* Jordan;
18:20. but (they are but) *vain* words, (marg. word of *the lips*)
19:28. my bridle *in thy lips*,
2Ch 4: 2. *from brim* to *brim*, (marg. *from his brim* to *his brim*)
5. *and the brim of it* like the work of *the brim of* a cup,
2Ch 8:17. at *the* sea *side* in the land of Edom.
Job 2:10. In all this did not Job sin *with his lips*.
8:21. *and thy lips* with rejoicing.
11: 2. should a man full of *talk* (marg. of *lips*) be justified?
5. and open *his lips* against thee;
12:20. He removeth away *the speech* (marg. *lip*)
13: 6. hearken to the pleadings of *my lips*.
15: 6. *yea, thine own lips* testify against thee.
16: 5. the moving of *my lips*
23:12. from the commandment of *his lips*;
27: 4. *My lips* shall not speak wickedness,
32:20. I will open *my lips* and answer.
33: 3. and *my lips* shall utter knowledge
Ps. 12: 2(3). flattering *lips* (and) with a double
3(4). shall cut off all flattering *lips*,
4(5). *our lips* (are) our own:
16: 4. take up their names into *my lips*.
17: 1. my prayer, (that goeth) not out of feigned *lips*.
4. by the word of *thy lips*
21: 2(3). the request of *his lips*.
22: 7(8). they shoot out *the lip*,
31:18(19). Let *the* lying *lips* be put to silence;
34:13(14). *and thy lips* from speaking guile.
40: 9(10). I have not refrained *my lips*,
45: 2(3). grace is poured *into thy lips*:
51:15(17). O Lord, open thou *my lips*;
59: 7(8). swords (are) *in their lips*:
12(13). the words of *their lips*
63: 3(4). *my lips* shall praise thee.
5(6). *and* my mouth shall praise (thee) *with* joyful *lips*:
66:14. Which *my lips* have uttered,
71:23. *My lips* shall greatly rejoice
81: 5(6). I heard *a language* (that) I understood
89:34(35). the thing that is gone out of *my lips*.
106:33. he spake unadvisedly *with his lips*.
119:13. *With my lips* have I declared
171. *My lips* shall utter praise,
120: 2. Deliver my soul, O Lord, *from* lying *lips*,
140: 3(4). adders' poison (is) under *their lips*.
9(10). the mischief of *their own lips*
141: 3. keep the door of *my lips*.
Pro. 4:24. and perverse *lips* put far from thee.
5: 2. (that) *thy lips* may keep knowledge.
3. For *the lips of* a strange woman
7:21. with the flattering of *her lips*
8: 6. and the opening of *my lips*
7. an abomination to *my lips*.
10: 8, 10. but a *prating* fool shall fall. (marg. a fool of *lips*)
13. *In the lips of* him that
18. that hideth hatred (with) lying *lips*,
19. but he that refraineth *his lips*
21. *The lips of* the righteous feed
32. *The lips of* the righteous know
12:13. the transgression of (his) *lips*:
19. *The lip of* truth shall be established
22. Lying *lips* (are) abomination
13: 3. he that openeth wide *his lips*
14: 3. *but the lips of* the wise
7. (in him) *the lips of* knowledge.
23. talk of *the lips* (tendeth)
15: 7. *The lips of* the wise disperse
16:10. A divine sentence (is) in *the lips of* the
13. Righteous *lips* (are) the delight of kings;
21. and the sweetness of *the lips*
23. and addeth learning to *his lips*.
27. and in *his lips* (there is) as a burning fire.
30. moving *his lips* he bringeth evil to pass.
17: 4. wicked doer giveth heed to false *lips*;
7. Excellent *speech* (marg. *A lip of* excellency) becometh not a fool: much less do lying *lips* (marg. *a lip of* lying) a prince.
28. he that shutteth *his lips*
18: 6. A fool's *lips* enter into contention,
7. *and his lips* (are) the snare of his soul.
20. with the increase of *his lips*
19: 1. (he that is) perverse in *his lips*,
20:15. but *the lips of* knowledge
19. that flattereth with *his lips*.
22:11. the grace of *his lips*
18. be fitted in *thy lips*.
23:16. when *thy lips* speak right things.
24: 2. *their lips* talk of mischief.

Pro.24:26. (Every man) shall kiss (his) *lips*
28. deceive (not) *with thy lips.*
26:23. Burning *lips* and a wicked heart
24. dissembleth *with his lips,*
27: 2. a stranger, and not *thine own lips.*
Ecc.10:12. *but the lips of* a fool
Cant.4: 3. *Thy lips* (are) like a thread of
11. *Thy lips,* O (my) spouse, drop (as)
5:13. *his lips* (like) lilies,
7: 9(10). causing *the lips of* those
Isa. 6: 5. a man of unclean *lips,*
— a people of unclean *lips:*
7. this hath touched *thy lips;*
11: 4. with the breath of *his lips*
19:18. speak *the language* (marg. *lip*) *of* Canaan,
28:11. For with stammering *lips*
29:13. *and with their lips* do honour
30:27. *his lips* are full of indignation,
33:19. a people of deeper *speech*
36: 5. but (they are but) *vain* words (marg. a word of *lips*)
37:29. and my bridle *in thy lips,*
57:19. I create the fruit of *the lips;*
59: 3. *your lips* have spoken lies,
Jer. 17:16. came out of *my lips*
Lam.3:62. *The lips of* those that rose
Eze. 3: 5. sent to a people of *a* strange *speech* (marg. *lip*)
6. Not to many people of *a* strange *speech* (marg. *id.*)
36: 3. in *the lips of* talkers,
43:13. by *the edge thereof* round about
47: 6. return to *the brink of* the river.
7. at *the bank* (marg. *lip*) *of* the river
12. by the river upon *the bank thereof,*
Dan10:16. of the sons of men touched *my lips:*
12: 5. one on this side *of the bank* (marg. *lip*) *of* the river, and the other on that side *of the bank of*
Hos.14: 2(3). render the calves of *our lips.*
Hab. 3:16. *my lips* quivered at the voice:
Zep. 3: 9. turn to the people *a* pure *language,* (marg. *lip*)
Mal. 2: 6. not found *in his lips:*
7. For the priest's *lips* should

5596 **שִׂפַּח [sāh-phag̣h'].**

* PIEL.—*Preterite.* *

Isa. 3:17. *Therefore* the Lord *will smite with a scab*

8222 **שָׂפָם sāh-phāhm', m.**

Lev.13:45. a covering upon (his) *upper lip,*
2Sa.19:24(25). nor trimmed *his beard,*
Eze.24:17. cover not (thy) *lips,* (marg. *upper lip*)
22. ye shall not cover (your) *lips,*
Mic. 3: 7. they shall all cover (their) *lips;* (marg. *upper lip*)

8226 **שָׂפַן [sāh-phan'].**

* KAL.—*Participle.* Paül. *

Deu33:19. *and* (of) *treasures* hid in the sand.

5606 **שָׂפַק [sāh-phak'].**

* KAL.—*Future.* *

Job 27:23. *shall clap* their hands at him,

* HIPHIL.—*Future.* *

Isa. 2: 6. *they please themselves* in (marg. or, *abound* with) the

---

5606 **שָׂפַק sāh-phak'].**

* KAL.—*Future.* *

1K. 20:10. if the dust of Samaria *shall suffice*

5607 **שֶׂפֶק [seh'-phek], m.**

Job 20:22. In the fulness of *his sufficiency* [Some copies read סִפְקוֹ]
36:18. lest he take thee away *with* (his) *stroke:*

שַׂק sak, m. 8242

Gen37:34. put *sackcloth* upon his loins,
42:25. every man's money into *his sack,*
27. as one of them opened *his sack*
35. they emptied *their sacks,*
— every man's bundle of money (was) *in his sack:*
Lev.11:32. or raiment, or skin, or *sack,*
Jos. 9: 4. and took old *sacks*
2Sa. 3:31. gird you with *sackcloth,*
21:10. the daughter of Aiah took *sackcloth,*
1K. 20:31. put *sackcloth* on our loins,
32. So they girded *sackcloth* on their loins,
21:27. put *sackcloth* upon his flesh, and fasted, and lay *in sackcloth,*
2K. 6:30. *sackcloth* within upon his flesh.
19: 1. covered himself *with sackcloth,*
2. covered *with sackcloth*
1Ch 21:16. (who were) clothed *in sackcloth,*
Neh. 9: 1. with fasting, *and with sackclothes,*
Est. 4: 1. put on *sackcloth* with ashes,
2. king's gate clothed with *sackcloth.*
3. many lay in *sackcloth* and ashes.
4. to take away *his sackcloth*
Job 16:15. I have sewed *sackcloth* upon my skin,
Ps. 30:11(12). thou hast put off *my sackcloth,*
35:13. my clothing (was) *sackcloth:*
69:11(12). I made *sackcloth* also my
Isa. 3:24. a girding of *sackcloth;*
15: 3. gird themselves with *sackcloth:*
20: 2. Go and loose *the sackcloth*
22:12. to girding with *sackcloth:*
37: 1. covered himself *with sackcloth,*
2. covered *with sackcloth,*
50: 3. *and* I make *sackcloth* their covering.
58: 5. *and* to spread *sackcloth*
Jer. 4: 8. For this gird you with *sackcloth,*
6:26. gird (thee) with *sackcloth,*
48:37. and upon the loins *sackcloth.*
49: 3. gird you with *sackcloth;*
Lam 2:10. girded themselves with *sackcloth:*
Eze. 7:18. gird (themselves) with *sackcloth,*
27:31. and gird them with *sackcloth,*
Dan 9: 3. with fasting, *and sackcloth,*
Joel 1: 8. like a virgin girded with *sackcloth*
13. lie all night *in sackcloth,*
Am. 8:10. I will bring up *sackcloth*
Jon. 3: 5. put on *sackcloth,*
6. covered (him) with *sackcloth,*
8. man and beast be covered with *sackcloth,*

שָׂקַד [sāh-kad']. 8244

* NIPHAL.—*Preterite.* *

Lam 1:14. yoke of my transgressions *is bound*

שָׂקַר [sāh-kar']. 8265

* PIEL.—*Participle.* *

Isa. 3:16. stretched forth necks *and wanton* eyes,

שַׂר sar, m. 8269

Gen12:15. *The princes* also *of* Pharaoh saw her,
21:22, 32. Phichol *the chief captain of* his host
26:26. Phichol *the chief captain of* his army.
37:36. *captain of* the guard. (marg. or, *chief* marshal)
39: 1. Potiphar,...*captain of* the guard,
21. him favour in the sight of *the keeper of*
22. *the keeper of* the prison committed
23. *The keeper of* the prison looked not
40: 2. *the chief of* the butlers, and against *the chief of* the bakers.
3. the house of *the captain of* the guard,
4. *the captain of* the guard charged Joseph
9. the *chief* butler told his dream
16. When the *chief* baker saw
20. lifted up the head of the *chief* butler and of the *chief* baker
21. he restored the *chief* butler
22. he hanged the *chief* baker:
23. Yet did not the *chief* butler remember

Gen41: 9. Then spake the *chief* butler
10. *the captain of* the guard's house, (both) me and the *chief* baker:
12. servant *to the captain of* the guard;
47: 6. make them *rulers over* my cattle.
Ex. 1:11. they did set over them task*masters*
2:14. Who made thee *a prince*
18:21. place (such) over them, (to be) *rulers of* thousands, (and) *rulers of* hundreds, *rulers of* fifties, *and rulers of* tens:
25. *rulers of* thousands, *rulers of* hundreds, *rulers of* fifties, *and rulers of* tens.
Nu. 21:18. *The princes* digged the well,
22: 8. *the princes of* Moab abode
13. Balaam...said unto *the princes of* Balak,
14. *the princes of* Moab rose up,
15. Balak sent yet again *princes*,
21. Balaam...went with *the princes of* Moab.
35. Balaam went with *the princes of*
40. *and to the princes* that (were) with him.
23: 6. all *the princes of* Moab.
17. *and the princes of* Moab with him.
31:14. *the captains over* thousands, *and captains over* hundreds,
48. *the captains of* thousands, *and captains of* hundreds,
52. of *the captains of* thousands, and of *the captains of* hundreds,
54. *the captains of* thousands and of hundreds,
Deu 1:15. *captains over* thousands, *and captains over* hundreds, *and captains over* fifties, *and captains over* tens,
20: 9. *captains of* the armies to lead
Jos. 5:14. *captain* (marg. or, *prince*) *of* the host of the Lord
15. *the captain of* the Lord's host
Jud. 4: 2. *the captain of* whose host (was) Sisera,
7. *the captain of* Jabin's army,
5:15. *And the princes* of Issachar
7:25. two *princes of* the Midianites,
8: 3. *the princes of* Midian,
6, 14. *the princes of* Succoth
9:30. Zebul *the ruler of* the city
10:18. the people (and) *princes of* Gilead
1Sa. 8:12. *captains over* thousands, *and captains over* fifties;
12: 9. *captain of* the host of Hazor,
14:50. the name of *the captain of* his host
17:18. *unto the captain of* (their) thousand,
55. *the captain of* the host,
18:13. made him his *captain over* a thousand;
30. *the princes of* the Philistines
22: 2. he became *a captain* over them:
7. make you all *captains of* thousands, *and captains of* hundreds;
26: 5. Abner...*the captain of* his host:
29: 3, 3, 4, 4, 9. *the princes of* the Philistines,
2Sa. 2: 8. Abner...*captain of* Saul's host,
3:38. *a prince* and a great man fallen
4: 2. two men (that were) *captains of* bands:
10: 3. *the princes of* the children of Ammon
16. Shobach *the captain of* the host
18. Shobach *the captain of* their host,
18: 1. *captains of* thousands *and captains of*
5. the king gave all *the captains* charge
19: 6(7). regardest neither *princes* nor servants:
13(14). *captain of* the host before me
23:19. therefore he was *their captain:*
24: 2. Joab *the captain of* the host,
4. prevailed...against *the captains of* the host.
— *and the captains of* the host went out
1K. 1:19. Joab *the captain of* the host:
25. *and the captains of* the host,
2: 5. two *captains of* the hosts of Israel,
32. *captain of* the host of Israel,
— *captain of* the host of Judah.
4: 2. *the princes* which he had;
5:16(30). *Beside the chief of* Solomon's officers
9:22. *and his princes*, and his captains, *and rulers of* his chariots,
23. *the chief of* the officers
11:15, 21. Joab *the captain of* the host
24. became *captain over* a band,
14:27. *the chief of* the guard,
15:20. *the captains of* the hosts
16: 9. *captain of* half (his) chariots,
16. Omri, *the captain of* the host,

1K. 20:14, 15, 17, 19. *the princes of* the provinces.
22:26. Amon *the governor of* the city,
31. thirty and two *captains that had rule over*
32, 33. *the captains of* the chariots
2K. 1: 9. *a captain of* fifty with his fifty.
10. said to *the captain of* fifty,
11. another *captain of* fifty
13. *a captain of* the third fifty
— *the* third *captain of* fifty
14. *the* two *captains of* the former fifties
4:13. *the captain of* the host?
5: 1. *captain of* the host of the king of Syria,
8:21. *the captains of* the chariots:
9: 5. *the captains of* the host (were) sitting;
— I have an errand to thee, *O captain.*
— To thee, *O captain.*
10: 1. *the rulers of* Jezreel,
11: 4. *the rulers over* hundreds,
9. *the captains over* the hundreds
10. *to the captains over* hundreds
14. *and the princes* and the trumpeters
15. *the captains of* the hundreds,
19. *the rulers over* hundreds,
23: 8. Joshua *the governor of* the city,
24:12. *and his princes*, and his officers:
14. all *the princes*, and all the mighty men
25:19. the *principal* scribe (marg. or, *scribe of* the captain) of the host,
23. *the captains of* the armies,
26. *and the captains of* the armies,
1Ch 11: 6. Whosoever smiteth the Jebusites first shall be chief *and captain.*
21. he was their *captain:*
12:21. *captains* in the host.
28. twenty and two *captains.*
34. of Naphtali a thousand *captains*,
13: 1. *captains of* thousands and hundreds,
15: 5. Of the sons of Kohath; Uriel *the chief*,
6. Of the sons of Merari; Asaiah *the chief*,
7. Of the sons of Gershom; Joel *the chief*,
8. Of the sons of Elizaphan; Shemaiah *the chief*,
9. Of the sons of Hebron; Eliel *the chief*,
10. Of the sons of Uzziel; Amminadab *the chief*,
16. David spake *to the chief of* the Levites
22. Chenaniah, *chief of* the Levites,
25. *and the captains over* thousands,
27. Chenaniah *the master of* the song
19: 3. *the princes of* the children of Ammon
16, 18. Shophach *the captain of* the host
21: 2. *the rulers of* the people,
22:17 & 23:2. all *the princes of* Israel
24: 5. *the governors of* the sanctuary, *and governors* (of the house) *of* God,
6. the king, *and the princes*,
25: 1. *and the captains of* the host separated
26:26. *the captains over* thousands and hundreds, *and the captains of* the host,
27: 1. *and captains of* thousands and hundreds,
3. the chief of all *the captains of*
5. *The* third *captain of* the host
8. *The* fifth *captain* for the fifth month
22. *the princes of* the tribes of Israel.
31. *the rulers of* the substance
34. *and the general of* the king's army
28: 1. all *the princes of* Israel, *the princes of* the tribes, *and the captains of* the companies
— *and the captains over* the thousands, *and captains over* the hundreds, *and the stewards over* all the substance
21. *also the princes* and all the people
29: 6. *the chief of* the fathers *and princes of* the tribes of Israel, *and the captains of* thousands and of hundreds, *with the rulers of* the king's work,
24. all *the princes*, and the mighty men,
2Ch 1: 2. *to the captains of* thousands
8: 9. *and chief of* his captains, *and captains of* his chariots
10. *chief of* king Solomon's officers,
12: 5. *and* (to) *the princes of* Judah,
6. *the princes of* Israel
10. *the chief of* the guard,
16: 4. *the captains of* his armies
17: 7. he sent *to his princes*,
14. *the captains of* thousands

2Ch 17:14. Adnah *the chief,*
15. Jehohanan *the captain,*
18:25. Amon *the governor of* the city,
30, 31, 32. *the captains of* the chariots
21: 4. slew...*of the princes of* Israel.
9. Jehoram went forth with *his princes,*
— *the captains of* the chariots.
22: 8. *the princes of* Judah,
23: 1, 14, 20. *the captains of* hundreds,
9. *to the captains of* hundreds
13. *and the princes* and the trumpets by the
24:10. all *the princes*...rejoiced,
17. *the princes of* Judah,
23. all *the princes of* the people
25: 5. *captains over* thousands, *and captains over* hundreds,
26:11. Hananiah, (one) *of* the king's *captains.*
28:14. *the princes* and all the congregation.
21. house of the king, *and of the princes,*
29:20. gathered *the rulers of* the city,
30. *and the princes* commanded the Levites
30: 2. king had taken counsel, *and his princes,*
6. the king *and his princes*
12. of the king *and of the princes,*
24. *and the princes* gave to the congregation
31: 8. when Hezekiah *and the princes* came
32: 3. He took counsel with *his princes*
6. he set *captains of* war over
21. the leaders *and captains*
31. the ambassadors of *the princes of*
33:11. *the captains of* the host
14. put *captains of* war in all the fenced
34: 8. Maaseiah *the governor of* the city,
35: 8. *And his princes* gave willingly
9. *chief of* the Levites,
36:14. all *the chief of* the priests,
18. treasures of the king, *and of his princes;*
Ezr. 7:28. before all the king's mighty *princes.*
8:20. whom David *and the princes* had
24. I separated twelve *of the chief of* the
25. king, and his counsellors, *and his lords,*
29. before *the chief of* the priests and the Levites, *and chief of* the fathers of Israel,
9: 1. *the princes* came to me, saying,
2. the hand of *the princes* and rulers
10: 5. Then arose Ezra, and made the *chief*
8. according to the counsel of *the princes*
14. *our rulers* of all the congregation
Neh 2: 9. the king had sent *captains of* the army
3: 9, 12. *the ruler of* the half part of Jerusalem.
14. *the ruler of* part of Beth-haccerem;
15. *the ruler of* part of Mizpah;
16. *the ruler of* the half part of Beth-zur,
17, 18. *the ruler of* the half part of Keilah,
19. *the ruler of* Mizpah,
4:16(10). *and the rulers* (were) behind all the
7: 2. Hananiah *the ruler of* the palace,
9:32. on our kings, *on our princes,*
34. Neither have our kings, *our princes,*
38(10:1). *our princes,* Levites, (and) priests,
11: 1. *the rulers of* the people
12:31. Then I brought up *the princes of*
32. half of *the princes of* Judah,
Est. 1: 3. made a feast unto all *his princes*
— the nobles *and princes of* the provinces,
11. to shew the people *and the princes* her
14. *the* seven *princes of* Persia
16. before the king *and the princes,*
— also to all *the princes,*
18. all the king's *princes,*
21. saying pleased the king *and the princes;*
2:18. made a great feast unto all *his princes*
3: 1. set his seat above all *the princes*
12. *the rulers of* every people
5:11. advanced him above *the princes*
6: 9. one *of* the king's most noble *princes,*
8: 9. *and rulers of* the provinces
9: 3. all *the rulers of* the provinces, and the
Job 3:15. *princes* that had gold,
29: 9. *The princes* refrained talking,
34:19. accepteth not the persons of *princes,*
39:25. the thunder of *the captains,*
Ps. 45:16(17). whom thou mayest make *princes*
68:27(28). *the princes of* Judah (and) their council, *the princes of* Zebulun, (and) *the princes of* Naphtali.
82: 7. fall like one of *the princes.*
Ps. 105:22. To bind *his princes* at his pleasure;
119:23. *Princes* also did sit (and) speak
161. *Princes* have persecuted me without a
148:11. *princes,* and all judges of the earth:
Pro. 8:16. By me *princes* rule,
19:10. for a servant to have rule *over princes.*
28: 2. many (are) *the princes thereof:*
Ecc. 10: 7. *and princes* walking as servants
16. *and thy princes* eat in the morning!
17. *and thy princes* eat in due season,
Isa. 1:23. *Thy princes* (are) rebellious,
3: 3. *The captain of* fifty,
4. I will give children (to be) *their princes,*
14. of his people, *and the princes thereof:*
9: 6(5). *The Prince of* Peace.
10: 8. (Are) not *my princes* altogether kings?
19:11. *the princes of* Zoan (are) fools,
13. *The princes of* Zoan are become fools, *the princes of* Noph are deceived;
21: 5. arise, *ye princes,* (and) anoint the shield.
23: 8. whose merchants (are) *princes,*
30: 4. *his princes* were at Zoan,
31: 9. *his princes* shall be afraid
32: 1. *and princes* shall rule in judgment.
34:12. all *her princes* shall be nothing.
43:28. *the princes of* the sanctuary,
49: 7. *princes* also shall worship,
Jer. 1:18. *against the princes thereof,*
2:26. they, their kings, *their princes,*
4: 9. the heart of *the princes;*
8: 1. the bones of *his princes,*
17:25. kings *and princes* sitting upon the throne
— *and their princes,* the men of Judah,
24: 1. *the princes of* Judah,
8. the king of Judah, and *his princes,*
25:18. the kings thereof, and *the princes thereof,*
19. Pharaoh king of Egypt,...and *his princes,*
26:10. When *the princes of* Judah heard
11. Then spake the priests...unto *the princes*
12. Then spake Jeremiah unto all *the princes*
16. Then said *the princes*
21. Jehoiakim...and all *the princes,*
29: 2. *the princes of* Judah and Jerusalem,
32:32. their kings, *their princes,* their priests,
34:10. when all *the princes*....heard
19. *The princes of* Judah, *and the princes of* Jerusalem,
21. Zedekiah king of Judah and *his princes*
35: 4. the chamber of *the princes,*
36:12. all *the princes* sat there,
— Zedekiah the son of Hananiah, and all *the princes.*
14. all *the princes* sent Jehudi
19. Then said *the princes* unto Baruch,
21. *the princes* which stood beside the king.
37:14. Jeremiah, and brought him to *the princes.*
15. *the princes* were wroth
38: 4. *the princes* said unto the king,
17, 18, 22. the king of Babylon's *princes,*
25. if *the princes* hear that I have talked
27. Then came all *the princes*
39: 3, 3. *the princes of* the king of Babylon
40: 7, 13 & 41:11, 13, 16 & 42:1, 8 & 43:4, 5. *the captains of* the forces
44:17. our fathers, our kings, *and our princes,*
21. your fathers, your kings, *and your princes,*
48: 7 & 49:3. his priests *and his princes* together.
49:38. from thence the king *and the princes,*
50:35. upon the inhabitants of Babylon, and upon *her princes,*
51:57. I will make drunk *her princes,*
59. And (this) Seraiah (was) *a* quiet *prince.* (marg. or, *chief* chamberlain)
52:10. slew also all *the princes of* Judah
25. the *principal* scribe (marg. or, scribe of *the captain*) *of* the host,
Lam 1: 6. *her princes* are become like harts
2: 2. polluted the kingdom *and the princes thereof.*
9. her king *and her princes* (are) among the
5:12. *Princes* are hanged up by their hand:
Eze. 11: 1. *princes of* the people.
17:12. the king thereof, *and the princes thereof,*
22:27. *Her princes* in the midst thereof
Dan 1: 7. *the prince of* the eunuchs gave names:
8. he requested *of the prince of* the eunuchs
9. tender love with *the prince of* the eunuchs.

Dan 1:10. And *the prince of* the eunuchs said
11. Melzar, whom *the prince of* the eunuchs had set over
18. *the prince of* the eunuchs brought them in
8:11. *the prince of* the host,
25. against *the Prince of princes;*
9: 6. our kings, *our princes*, and our fathers,
8. to our kings, *to our princes*, and to our fathers,
10:13. *But the prince of* the kingdom of Persia
— Michael, one of *the* chief *princes*
20. to fight with *the prince of* Persia:
— *the prince of* Grecia shall come.
21. Michael *your prince.*
11: 5. king of the south...and (one) of *his princes;*
12: 1. Michael...*the* great *prince*
Hos. 3: 4. without a king, and without *a prince*,
5:10. *The princes of* Judah
7: 3. They make the king glad...and *the princes*
5. *the princes* have made (him) sick
16. *their princes* shall fall by the sword
8:10. the burden of the king of *princes.*
9:15. all *their princes* (are) revolters.
13:10. Give me a king *and princes?*
Am. 1:15. he *and his princes* together,
2: 3. will slay all *the princes thereof*
Mic. 7: 3. *the prince* asketh,...for a reward;
Zep. 1: 8. I will punish *the princes*,
3: 3. *Her princes* within her (are) roaring lions;

8276 שָׂרַג [*sāh-rag'*].

* PUAL.—*Future.* *

Job 40:17. sinews of his stones *are wrapped together.*

* HITHPAEL.—*Future.* *

Lam 1:14. by his hand: *they are wreathed,*

8277 שָׂרַד [*sāh-rad'*].

* KAL.—*Preterite.* *

Jos. 10:20. the rest (which) *remained* of them

8278 שְׂרָד *s'rāhd*, m.

Ex. 31:10. the cloths of *service*, and the holy
35:19. The cloths of *service*, to do service
39: 1. they made cloths of *service*,
41. The cloths of *service* to do service

8279 שֶׂרֶד *seh'-red*, m.

Isa. 44:13. he marketh it out *with a line;*

8280 שָׂרָה *sāh-rāh'*.

* KAL.—*Preterite.* *

Gen32:28(29). *as a prince hast thou power* with God
Hos.12: 3(4). by his strength *he had power* (marg. *was a prince*) with God:

8282 שָׂרָה [*sāh-rāh'*], f.

Jud. 5:29. *Her* wise *ladies* answered
1K. 11: 3. seven hundred wives, *princesses*,
Est. 1:18. *the ladies of* Persia and Media
Isa. 49:23. *and their queens* (marg. *princesses*) thy nursing mothers:
Lam 1: 1. *princess* among the provinces,

8288 שְׂרוֹךְ *s'rōhch*, m.

Gen14:23. from a thread even to *a* shoe*latchet*,
Isa. 5:27. nor *the latchet of* their shoes

8291 שְׂרוּקִּים [*s'rook-keem'*], m. pl.

Isa. 16: 8. broken down *the principal plants thereof*,

שָׂרַט [*sāh-rat'*]. 8295

* KAL.—*Infinitive.* *

Zec.12: 3. with it shall be cut *in pieces*, (lit. in *cutting* shall be cut)

KAL.—*Future.*

Lev.21: 5. nor *make* any cuttings in their flesh.

* NIPHAL.—*Future.* *

Zec.12: 3. with it *shall be cut in pieces*, (lit. cutting *shall be cut*)

שֶׂרֶט *seh'-ret*, m. 8296

Lev.19:28. Ye shall not make *any cuttings*

שָׂרֶטֶת [*sāh-reh'-teth*], f. 8296

Lev.21: 5. nor make *any cuttings* in their flesh.

שָׂרִיגִים *sāh-ree-geem'*, m. pl. 8299

Gen40:10. in the vine (were) three *branches:*
12. *The* three *branches* (are) three days:
Joel 1: 7. *the branches thereof* are made white.

שָׂרִיד *sāh-reed'*, m. 8300

Nu. 21:35. until there was none left him *alive:* (lit. *remaining*)
24:19. destroy *him that remaineth*
Deu 2:34. we left none *to remain:*
3: 3. until none was left to him *remaining.*
Jos. 8:22. so that they let none of them *remain*
10:20. *that the rest* (which) remained
28. he let none *remain:* and he did
30. he let none *remain* in it;
33. until he had left him none *remaining.*
37, 39. he left none *remaining*,
40. none *remaining*, but utterly destroyed
11: 8. until they left them none *remaining.*
Jud. 5:13. Then he made *him that remaineth*
2K. 10:11. he left him none *remaining.*
Job 18:19. nor any *remaining* in his dwellings.
20:21. There shall none of his meat *be left;*
26. it shall go ill with him that *is left*
27:15. Those that *remain of him*
Isa. 1: 9. had left unto us *a* very small *remnant*,
Jer. 31: 2. The people (which were) *left of* the sword
42:17. none of them shall *remain*
44:14. shall escape *or remain*,
47: 4. Tyrus and Zidon every helper that *remaineth:*
Lam.2:22. none escaped *nor remained:*
Joel 2:32(3:5). *and in the remnant* whom the Lord
Obad. 14. delivered up *those of his that did remain*
18. there shall not be (any) *remaining*

שָׂרִיק [*sāh-reek'*], adj. 8305

Isa. 19: 9. Moreover they that work in *fine* flax,

שָׂרַךְ [*sāh-rach'*]. 8308

* PIEL.—*Participle.* *

Jer. 2:23. a swift dromedary *traversing* her ways;

שָׂרַע [*sāh-rāg'*]. 8311

* KAL.—*Participle.* Paül. *

Lev.21:18. or *any thing superfluous*,
22:23. *that hath any thing superfluous*

* HITHPAEL.—*Infinitive.* *

Isa. 28:20. the bed is shorter *than that* (a man) *can stretch out himself*

8312 שַׂרְעַפִּים [*sar-ğap-peem'*], m. pl.

Ps. 94:19. In the multitude of *my thoughts*
139:23. try me, and know *my thoughts:*

8313 שָׂרַף *sāh-raph'.*

* KAL.—*Preterite.* *

Ex. 29:34. *then thou shalt burn* the remainder
Lev. 4:12. *and burn* him on the wood
21. bullock without the camp, *and burn* him as *he burned* the first bullock:
8:17. *he burnt* with fire without the camp;
9:11. the hide *he burnt* with fire
10: 6. burning which the Lord *hath kindled.* (lit. *burned*)
13:52. *He shall therefore burn* that
16:27. *and they shall burn* in the fire
Nu. 19: 5. *And* (one) *shall burn* the heifer
31:10. *they burnt* all their cities
Deu 13:16(17). *and shalt burn* with fire the city,
Jos. 6:24. *they burnt* the city with fire,
11: 9. *burnt* their chariots with fire.
11. *he burnt* Hazor with fire.
13. Israel *burned* none of *them*, save Hazor only; (that) *did* Joshua *burn.*
Jud. 18:27. *burnt* the city with fire.
1 Sa. 30:14. and *we burned* Ziklag with fire.
2K. 23:11. *burned* the chariots of the sun
15. *and burned* the grove.
25: 9. every great (man's) house *burnt he*
2Ch 34: 5. *he burnt* the bones of the priests
36:19. and *burnt* the palaces thereof
Ps. 74: 8. *they have burned up* all the synagogues
Isa. 44:16. *He burneth* part thereof in the fire;
19. *I have burned* part of it in the fire;
47:14. the fire *shall burn them;*
Jer. 21:10. *and he shall burn it* with fire.
32:29. *and burn it* with the houses,
34: 2. *and he shall burn it* with fire:
22. *and burn it* with fire:
36:28. Jehoiakim the king of Judah *hath burned.*
29. Thou *hast burned* this roll,
32. Jehoiakim king of Judah *had burned*
37: 8. take it, *and burn it* with fire.
10. *and burn* this city with fire.
38:18. *and they shall burn* it with fire,
39: 8. the Chaldeans *burned* the king's house,
43:12. *and he shall burn them,*
51:32. the reeds *they have burned* with fire,
52:13. *burned he* with fire:
Eze. 5: 4. *and burn* them in the fire;
16:41. *And they shall burn* thine houses
43:21. *and he shall burn it* in the appointed place

KAL.—*Infinitive.*

Jud. 9:52. door of the tower *to burn it*
2Sa. 23: 7. they shall be *utterly* burned with fire (lit. *burning* shall be burnt)
Jer. 7:31. *to burn* their sons and their daughters
19: 5. *to burn* their sons with fire
36:25. that he *would* not *burn* the roll:
27. after *that* the king *had burned* the roll,
Am. 2: 1. *he burned* the bones of the king of Edom

KAL.—*Future.*

Gen 11: 3. *and burn* them throughly.
Ex. 12:10. until the morning *ye shall burn*
29:14. his dung, *shalt thou burn*
32:20. *and burnt* (it) in the fire,
Lev. 8:32. the bread *shall ye burn* with fire.
13:55. *thou shalt burn it* in the fire;
57. *thou shalt burn that* wherein
20:14. they *shall be burnt* with fire,
Nu. 19: 5. her dung, *shall he burn:*
Deu 7: 5. *burn* their graven images with fire.
25. graven images of their gods *shall ye burn*
9:21. *and burnt* it with fire,
12: 3. *burn* their groves with fire;
31. their daughters *they have burnt*
Jos. 7:25. *and burned* them with fire,
8:28. *And* Joshua *burnt* Ai,
11: 6. *burn* their chariots with fire.
Jud. 12: 1. *we will burn* thine house
14:15. lest *we burn* thee and thy father's house
15: 6. *and burnt* her and her father
1Sa. 30: 1. *and burned* it with fire;
31:12. *and burnt them* there.
1K. 9:16. Gezer, *and burnt it* with fire,
13: 2. men's bones *shall be burnt* (lit. *they shall burn*)
15:13. idol, *and burnt* (it) by the brook
16:18. *and burnt* the king's house over him
2K. 10:26. house of Baal, *and burned them.*
23: 4. *and he burned them* without Jerusalem
6. *and burned* it at the brook
15. *and burned* the high place,
16. *and burned* (them) upon the altar,
20. *and burned* men's bones upon them,
25: 9. *And he burnt* the house of the Lord,
2Ch 15:16. *and burnt* (it) at the brook
16:14. *and they made* (lit. *burnt*) a very great burning
36:19. *And they burnt* the house of God,
Ps. 46: 9(10). *he burneth* the chariot in the fire.
Jer. 34: 5. so *shall they burn* (odours) for thee;
38:23. *thou shalt cause* this city *to be burned* (marg. *burn*)
43:13. the Egyptians *shall he burn* with fire.
52:13. *And burned* the house of the Lord,
Eze. 23:47. *burn up* their houses with fire.

KAL.—*Participle.* Poel.

Lev. 16:28. *And he that burneth* them
Nu. 19: 8. *And he that burneth* her
2K. 17:31. the Sepharvites *burnt* their children

KAL.—*Participle.* Paül.

Nu. 16:39(17:4). wherewith *they that were burnt*
1 Sa. 30: 3. behold, (it was) *burned* with fire;
Neh. 4: 2(3:34). heaps of the rubbish which *are burned?*
Ps. 80:16(17). *burned* with fire, (it is) cut down:
Isa. 1: 7. your cities (are) *burned* with fire:

* NIPHAL.—*Future.* *

Gen 38:24. Bring her forth, *and let her be burnt.*
Lev. 4:12. ashes are poured out *shall he be burnt.*
6:30(23). *it shall be burnt* in the fire.
7:17. on the third day *shall be burnt*
19. *it shall be burnt* with fire:
13:52. *shall be burnt* in the fire.
19: 6. *it shall be burnt* in the fire.
21: 9. *she shall be burnt* with fire.
Jos. 7:15. the accursed thing *shall be burnt*
2Sa. 23: 7. *they shall be* utterly *burned*
1 Ch 14:12. *and they were burned* with fire.
Pro. 6:27. his clothes not *be burned?*
Jer. 38:17. this city *shall* not *be burned*
Mic. 1: 7. all the hires thereof *shall be burned*

* PUAL.—*Preterite.* *

Lev. 10:16. *it was burnt:* and he was angry

שָׂרָף *sāh-rāhph'*, m. 8314

Nu. 21: 6. the Lord sent *fiery* serpents
8. Make thee *a fiery serpent,*
Deu 8:15. *fiery* serpents, and scorpions,
Isa. 6: 2. Above it stood *the seraphims:*
6. Then flew one of *the seraphims*
14:29. his fruit (shall be) *a fiery* flying *serpent.*
30: 6. the viper and *fiery* flying *serpent,*

שְׂרֵפָה *s'rēh-phāh'*, f. 8316

Gen 11: 3. make brick, and burn them *throughly.* (marg. burn them *to a burning*)
Lev. 10: 6. *the burning* which the Lord hath
Nu. 16:37(17:2). take up the censers out of *the burning,*
19: 6. cast (it) into the midst of *the burning of*
17. take of the ashes of the *burnt* heifer
Deu 29:23(22). brimstone, and salt, (and) *burning,*
2Ch 16:14. they made *a* very great *burning*
21:19. his people made no *burning* for him, *like the burning of* his fathers.
Isa. 9: 5(4). but (this) shall be *with burning*
64:11(10). is *burned* up with fire: (lit. *for burning of* fire)
Jer. 51:25. will make thee a *burnt* mountain.
Am. 4:11. as a firebrand plucked *out of the burning:*

8320 **שָׂרֹק** [*sāh-rōhk'*], adj.

Zec. 1: 8. red horses, *speckled* (marg. or, *bay*), and white.

8321 **שֹׂרֵק** *sōh-rēhk'*, m.

Isa. 5: 2. planted it with *the choicest vine*,
Jer. 2:21. Yet I had planted thee *a noble vine*,

8321 **שֹׂרֵקָה** *sōh-rēh-kāh'*, f.

Gen 49:11. *and* his ass's colt *unto the choice vine*;

8323 **שָׂרַר** [*sāh-rar'*].

* KAL.—*Future.* *

Pro. 8:16. By me princes *rule*,
Isa. 32: 1. princes *shall rule* in judgment.

KAL.—*Participle.* Poel.

Est. 1:22. every man *should bear rule*

* HITHPAEL.—*Infinitive.* *

Nu. 16:13. except thou make thyself *altogether* a prince (lit. *making thyself a prince* thou make thyself a prince)

HITHPAEL.—*Future.*

Nu. 16:13. except *thou make thyself* altogether *a prince*

8342 **שָׂשׂוֹן** *sāh-sōhn'*, m.

Est. 8:16. The Jews had light, and gladness, *and joy*,
17. the Jews had joy *and gladness*,
Ps. 45: 7(8). anointed thee with the oil of *gladness*
51: 8(10). Make me to hear *joy* and gladness;
12(14). Restore unto me *the joy of* thy
105:43. he brought forth his people *with joy*,
119:111. *the rejoicing of* my heart.
Isa. 12: 3. *with joy* shall ye draw water
22:13. *joy* and gladness, slaying oxen,
35:10. they shall obtain *joy* and gladness,
51: 3. *joy* and gladness shall be found
11. they shall obtain *gladness* and joy;
61: 3. the oil of *joy* for mourning,
Jer. 7:34. the voice of *mirth*,
15:16. *the joy* and rejoicing of mine heart:
16: 9. the voice of *mirth*,
25:10. I will take from them the voice of *mirth*,
31:13. I will turn their mourning *into joy*,
33: 9. shall be to me a name of *joy*,
11. The voice of *joy*, and the voice of gladness,
Joel 1:12. *joy* is withered away
Zec. 8:19. shall be to the house of Judah *joy* and gladness,

5640 **שָׂתַם** *sāh-tham'*.

* KAL.—*Preterite.* *

Lam. 3: 8. *he shutteth out* my prayer.

8368 **שָׂתַר** [*sāh-thar'*].

* NIPHAL.—*Future.* *

1Sa. 5: 9. *and* they *had* emerods *in their secret parts*. (lit. *there were* to them, &c.)

שׁ *sheen.*

(With שׂ) the Twenty-first Letter of the Alphabet.

7579 **שָׁאַב** [*shāh-av'*].

* KAL.—*Preterite.* *

Isa. 12: 3. *Therefore* with joy *shall ye draw* water

KAL.—*Infinitive.*

Gen24:13. the daughters...come out *to draw* water:
20. ran again unto the well *to draw* (water),
43. when the virgin cometh forth *to draw*
1Sa. 9:11. young maidens going out *to draw* water,

KAL.—*Imperative.*

Nah. 3:14. *Draw* thee waters for the siege,

KAL.—*Future.*

Gen24:19. *I will draw* (water) for thy camels
20. *and drew* for all his camels.
44. *I will* also *draw* for thy camels:
45. she went down unto the well, *and drew*
Ru. 2: 9. (that) which the young men *have drawn*.
1Sa. 7: 6. gathered together to Mizpeh, *and drew*
2Sa.23:16. *and drew* water out of the well
1Ch 11:18. *and drew* water out of the well

KAL.—*Participle.* Poel.

Gen24:11. the time that *women* go out *to draw*
Deu29:11(10). *the drawer of* thy water:
Jos. 9:21, 23, 27. hewers of wood *and drawers of*

שָׁאַג [*shāh-ag'*]. 7580

* KAL.—*Preterite.* *

Ps. 38: 8(9). *I have roared* by reason of the
74: 4. Thine enemies *roar* in the midst
Isa. 5:29. (כתיב) *they shall roar* like young lions:
Am. 3: 8. The lion *hath roared*,

KAL.—*Infinitive.*

Jer. 25:30. he shall *mightily* roar (lit. *roaring* he shall roar)

KAL.—*Future.*

Job 37: 4. After it a voice *roareth*:
Isa. 5:29. *they shall roar* like young lions:
Jer. 2:15. The young lions *roared*
25:30. The Lord *shall roar* from on high,
— *he shall* mightily *roar*
51:38. *They shall roar* together like lions:
Hos11:10. *he shall roar* like a lion: when he *shall roar*,
Joel 3:16(4:16). The Lord also *shall roar*
Am. 1: 2. The Lord *will roar* from Zion,
3: 4. *Will* a lion *roar* in the forest,

KAL.—*Participle.* Poel.

Jud.14: 5. a young lion *roared* against him.
Ps. 22:13(14). a ravening *and* a *roaring* lion.
104:21. The young lions *roar* after their prey,
Eze.22:25. a *roaring* lion ravening the prey;
Zep. 3: 3. Her princes...(are) *roaring* lions;

שְׁאָגָה *sh'āh-gāh'*, f. 7581

Job 3:24. *my roarings* are poured out
4:10. *The roaring of* the lion,
Ps. 22: 1(2). the words of *my roaring*?
32: 3. my bones waxed old *through my roaring*
Isa. 5:29. Their *roaring* (shall be) like a lion,
Eze.19: 7. the noise of *his roaring*.
Zec.11: 3. *the roaring of* young lions;

שָׁאָה [*shāh-āh'*]. 7582-83

* KAL.—*Preterite.* *

Isa. 6:11. Until the cities *be wasted*

* NIPHAL.—*Future.* *

Isa. 6:11. the land *be* utterly *desolate*,
17:12. *make a rushing* like the rushing
13. The nations *shall rush*

* HIPHIL.—*Infinitive.* *

2K. 19:25. *to lay waste* fenced cities (into) ruinous heaps.
Isa. 37:26. *to lay waste* defenced cities

* HITHPAEL.—*Participle.* *

Gen24:21. the man *wondering* at her

שֹׁאָה see **שׁוֹאָה** See 7722

7584 **שַׁאֲוָה** *shah-ăvāh'*, f.

Pro. 1: 27. (כתיב) your fear cometh *as desolution,*

7585 **שְׁאוֹל** *sh'ōhl*, com.

Gen37:35. I will go down *into the grave*
42:38. my gray hairs with sorrow *to the grave.*
44:29. my gray hairs with sorrow *to the grave.*
31. the gray hairs of thy servant...*to the grave.*
Nu. 16:30. they go down quick *into the pit;*
33. went down alive *into the pit,*
Deu 32:22. shall burn unto *the* lowest *hell,*
1Sa. 2: 6. he bringeth down to *the grave,*
2Sa.22: 6. The sorrows of *hell* compassed me about;
1K. 2: 6. let not his hoar head go down to *the grave* in peace.
9. hoar head bring thou down to *the grave*
Job 7: 9. he that goeth down to *the grave*
11: 8. deeper *than hell;* what canst thou know?
14:13. wouldest hide me *in the grave,*
17:13. *the grave* (is) mine house:
16. They shall go down to the bars of *the pit,*
21:13. in a moment go down to *the grave.*
24:19. (so doth) *the grave* those which have
26: 6. *Hell* (is) naked before him,
Ps. 6: 5(6). *in the grave* who shall give thee
9:17(18). The wicked shall be turned *into hell,*
16:10. thou wilt not leave my soul *in hell;*
18: 5(6). The sorrows of *hell* compassed me
30: 3(4). brought up my soul from *the grave:*
31:17(18). let them be silent *in the grave.*
49:14(15). sheep they are laid *in the grave;*
—(—). their beauty shall consume in *the grave*
15(16). redeem my soul from the power of *the grave:*
55:15(16). let them go down quick into *hell:*
86:13. delivered my soul *from the* lowest *hell.*
88: 3(4). my life draweth nigh *unto the grave.*
89:48(49). his soul from the hand of *the grave?*
116: 3. the pains of *hell* gat hold upon me:
139: 8. if I make my bed in *hell,*
141: 7. bones are scattered at the *grave*'s mouth,
Pro. 1:12. swallow them up alive *as the grave;*
5: 5. her steps take hold on *hell.*
7:27. Her house (is) the way to *hell,*
9:18. her guests (are) in the depths of *hell.*
15:11. *Hell* and destruction (are) before the
24. depart *from hell* beneath.
23:14. deliver his soul *from hell.*
27:20. *Hell* and destruction are never full;
30:16. *The grave;* and the barren womb;
Ecc. 9:10. no work, nor device,...*in the grave,*
Cant.8: 6. jealousy (is) cruel *as the grave:*
Isa. 5:14. *hell* hath enlarged herself,
14: 9. *Hell* (marg. or, *The grave*) from beneath is moved for thee
11. Thy pomp is brought down to *the grave,*
15. thou shalt be brought down to *hell,*
28:15. with *hell* are we at agreement;
18. your agreement with *hell* shall not stand;
38:10. I shall go to the gates of *the grave:*
18. *the grave* cannot praise thee,
57: 9. didst debase (thyself even) unto *hell.*
Eze.31:15. he went down *to the grave*
16. I cast him down *to hell*
17. They also went down *into hell*
32:21. speak to him out of the midst of *hell*
27. gone down to *hell* with their weapons
Hos 13:14. ransom them from the power of *the grave;*
— *O grave,* I will be thy destruction:
Am. 9: 2. Though they dig *into hell,*
Jon. 2: 2(3). out of the belly of *hell* (marg. or, *the grave*) cried I,
Hab. 2: 5. enlargeth his desire *as hell,*

7588 **שָׁאוֹן** *shāh-ōhn'*, m.

Ps. 40: 2(3). brought me up also out of an *horrible* pit, (marg. a pit of *noise*)
65: 7(8). Which stilleth *the noise of* the seas, *the noise of* their waves,
74:23. *the tumult of* those that rise up
Isa. 5:14. their multitude, *and their pomp,*
13: 4. a *tumultuous* noise of the kingdoms
Isa. 17:12. *and to the rushing of* nations, (that) make a rushing *like the rushing of* mighty
13. *like the rushing of* many waters:
24: 8. *the noise of* them that rejoice
25: 5. Thou shalt bring down *the noise of*
66: 6. A voice of *noise* from the city,
Jer. 25:31. *A noise* shall come
46:17. Pharaoh king of Egypt (is but) *a noise;*
48:45. the head of the *tumultuous* ones.
51:55. *a noise of* their voice is uttered:
Hos 10:14. Therefore shall *a tumult* arise
Am. 2: 2. Moab shall die *with tumult,*

שְׁאָט *sh'āht*, m. 7589

Eze.25: 6. rejoiced in heart with all *thy despite*
15. taken vengeance *with* a *despiteful* heart,
36: 5. *with despiteful* minds,

שְׁאִיָּה *sh'eey-yāh'*, f. 7591

Isa. 24:12. *and* the gate is smitten *with destruction.*

שָׁאַל *shāh-al'.* 7592

* KAL.—*Preterite.* *

Gen32:17(18). When Esau my brother meeteth thee, *and asketh thee,*
43: 7. The man *asked* us straitly
44:19. My lord *asked* his servants,
Ex. 3:22. *But* every woman *shall borrow* (lit. *ask*)
Nu. 27:21. *who shall ask* (counsel) for him
Deu 13:14(15). enquire, and make search, *and ask*
18:16. According to all that *thou desiredst*
Jos. 9:14. *asked* not (counsel) at the mouth of the
19:50. gave him the city which *he asked,*
Jud. 4:20. when any man doth come *and enquire of thee,*
5:25. *He asked* water, (and) she gave (him)
8:26. the golden earrings that *he requested*
13: 6. *I asked him* not whence he (was),
1Sa. 1:17. thy petition that *thou hast asked*
20. *I have asked him* of the Lord.
27. my petition which *I asked* of him:
2:20. the loan which *is lent* to the Lord. (marg. or, petition which *she asked*)
10: 4. *And they will* salute thee, (marg. *ask* thee of peace)
12:13. the king...whom *ye have desired!*
25: 5. go to Nabal, *and greet* him (marg. *ask him* ...of peace)
1K. 3:10. Solomon *had asked* this thing.
11. Because *thou hast asked* this thing, and *hast* not *asked* for thyself long life; neither *hast asked* riches for thyself, nor *hast asked* the life of thine enemies; *but hast asked* for thyself understanding
13. given thee that which *thou hast* not *asked,*
10:13. whatsoever *she asked,*
2K. 4:28. *Did I desire* a son of my lord?
1Ch 4:10. God granted him that which *he requested.*
2Ch 1:11. *thou hast* not *asked* riches,
— neither yet *hast asked* long life
9:12. all her desire, whatsoever *she asked,*
Job 21:29. *Have ye* not *asked* them that go by the
Ps. 21: 4(5). *He asked* life of thee,
27: 4. One (thing) *have I desired*
40: 6(7). and sin offering *hast thou* not *required.*
105:40. (The people) *asked,* and he brought
137: 3. they that carried us away captive *required of us* a song;
Pro.20: 4. *therefore shall he beg* in harvest,
30: 7. Two (things) *have I required* of thee;
Ecc. 2:10. whatsoever mine eyes *desired*
7:10. *thou dost* not *enquire* wisely
Isa. 30: 2. *have* not *asked* at my mouth;
65: 1. I am sought of (them that) *asked* not
Jer. 36:17. *they asked* Baruch,
Lam. 4: 4. the young children *ask* bread,
Eze.21:21(26). *he consulted* with images,

KAL.—*Infinitive.*

Gen43: 7. The man asked us *straitly* (marg. *asking* asked us) of our state.
Jos. 15:18. she moved him *to ask* of her father

Jud. 1:14. she moved him *to ask* of her father
1Sa.12:17. *in asking* you a king.
19. we have added unto all our sins (this) evil, *to ask* us a king.
22:13. and *hast enquired* of God for him,
15. Did I then begin *to enquire* of God
23: 4. David *enquired* of the Lord yet again. (lit. added *to enquire*)
2Sa. 8:10. Toi sent Joram his son unto king David, *to salute* (marg. *to ask* him of peace)
20:18. They shall *surely* ask (lit. *asking* they shall ask) (counsel)
2K. 2:10. Thou hast *ask*ed a hard thing: (marg. done hard *in asking*)
1Ch 10:13. *for asking* (counsel) of (one that had) a
18:10. sent Hadoram his son to king David, *to enquire*
Ezr. 8:22. I was ashamed *to require* of the king a
Job 31:30. *by wishing* a curse to his soul.
Ps. 78:18. tempted God in their heart *by asking*
Isa. 7:11. *ask* it either in the depth, or in the height
Jer. 15: 5. who shall go aside *to ask* how thou doest?

KAL.—*Imperative.*

Deu 4:32. *ask* now of the days that are past,
32: 7. *ask* thy father, and he will shew thee;
Jud.18: 5. *Ask counsel*, we pray thee, of God,
1Sa.17:56. *Enquire* thou whose son the stripling (is).
25: 8. *Ask* thy young men,
1K. 2:20. the king said unto her, *Ask on*, my
22. *ask* for him the kingdom *also;*
3: 5. *Ask* what I shall give thee.
2K. 2: 9. *Ask* what I shall do for thee,
4: 3. *borrow* thee vessels abroad
2Ch 1: 7. *Ask* what I shall give thee.
Job 8: 8. *enquire*, I pray thee, of the former age,
12: 7. *ask* now the beasts,
Ps. 2: 8. *Ask* of me, and I shall give (thee) the heathen
122: 6. *Pray* for the peace of Jerusalem:
Isa. 7:11. *Ask* thee a sign of the Lord
45:11. *Ask me* of things to come
Jer. 6:16. *and ask* for the old paths,
18:13. *Ask ye* now among the heathen,
30: 6. *Ask ye* now, and see
48:19. *ask* him that fleeth,
Hag. 2:11. *Ask* now the priests
Zec.10: 1. *Ask ye* of the Lord rain

KAL.—*Future.*

Gen24:47. *And I asked* her, and said,
57. We will call the damsel, *and enquire*
26: 7. *And* the men of the place *asked* (him) of
32:29(30). *And* Jacob *asked* (him),
—(—). *thou dost ask* after my name?
37:15. *and* the man *asked him,*
38:21. *Then he asked* the men of that place,
40: 7. *And he asked* Pharaoh's officers
43:27. *And he asked* them of (their) welfare,
Ex. 11: 2. *and let* every man *borrow* of his neighbour,
12:35. *and they borrowed* of the Egyptians
13:14. when thy son *asketh thee*
18: 7. *and they asked* each other of (their)
22:14(13). if a man *borrow* (ought)
Deu 6:20. when thy son *asketh thee*
14:26. whatsoever thy soul *desireth:* (marg. *asketh* of thee)
Jos. 4: 6. when your children *ask* (their fathers)
21. When your children *shall ask*
Jud. 1: 1. *that* the children of Israel *asked*
8:14. caught a young man...*and enquired of him:*
24. *I would desire* a request of you,
13:18. Why *askest thou* thus after my name,
18:15. came to the house...*and saluted* him. (marg. *asked* him of peace)
20:18. *and asked counsel* of God,
23. *and asked counsel* of the Lord,
27. *And* the children of Israel *enquired*
1Sa.10:22. *Therefore they enquired* of the Lord
14:37. *And* Saul *asked counsel* of God,
17:22. into the army, and came *and saluted* (marg. *asked* his brethren of peace) his brethren.
19:22. *and he asked* and said,
22:10. *And he enquired* of the Lord
23: 2. *Therefore* David *enquired* of the Lord,
28: 6. *when* Saul *enquired* of the Lord,
16. Wherefore then *dost thou ask of me,*

1Sa.30: 8. *And* David *enquired* at the Lord,
21. *and* when...*he saluted* them. (marg. or *asked* them how they did)
2Sa. 2: 1. *that* David *enquired* of the Lord,
5:19. *And* David *enquired* of the Lord,
23. *when* David *enquired* of the Lord,
11: 7. *And* when...David *demanded* (of him)
12:20. *when he required*, they set bread
16:23. as if a man *had enquired* at the oracle
1K. 19: 4. *and he requested* for himself that he might
2K. 8: 6. *when* the king *asked* the woman,
1Ch 14:10. *And* David *enquired* of God,
14. *Therefore* David *enquired* again
2Ch 1:11. *but hast asked* wisdom and knowledge
11:23. *And he desired* many wives.
Neh 1: 2. *and I asked them* concerning the Jews
Job 38: 3. *for I will demand of thee*, and answer
40: 7 & 42:4. *I will demand of thee*, and declare
Ps. 35:11. *they laid to my charge* (marg. *asked me*) (things) that I knew not.
Pro.20: 4. (כתיב) (therefore) *shall he beg* in harvest,
Isa. 7:12. Ahaz said, *I will* not *ask*
41:28. that, *when I asked* of them, could answer
58: 2. *they ask of me* the ordinances of justice;
Jer. 23:33. the prophet, or a priest, *shall ask thee*,
37:17. *and* the king *asked him* secretly in his
38:27. Then came all the princes unto Jeremiah, *and asked*
50: 5. *They shall ask* the way to Zion
Hos. 4:12. My people *ask counsel* at their stocks,
Jon. 4: 8. *and wished* in himself to die,

KAL.—*Participle.* Poel.

Deu 10:12. what *doth* the Lord thy God *require*
18:11. *or a consulter* with familiar spirits,
1Sa. 8:10. the people *that asked* of him a king.
2Sa. 3:13. one thing I *require* of thee,
14:18. Hide not from me, I pray thee, the thing that I *shall ask* thee.
1K. 2:16. I *ask* one petition of thee,
20. I *desire* one small petition
22. why *dost* thou *ask* Abishag
Jer. 38:14. I *will ask* thee a thing;
Mic. 7: 3. the prince *asketh*,...for a reward;

KAL.—*Participle.* Paül.

1Sa. 1:28. he *shall be lent* to the Lord.
2K. 6: 5. Alas, master! for *it was borrowed.*

* NIPHAL.—*Preterite.* *

1Sa.20: 6, 28. David earnestly *asked* (leave)
Neh 13: 6. *obtained I leave* (marg. or, *I earnestly requested*) of the king:

NIPHAL.—*Infinitive.*

1Sa.20: 6, 28. David *earnestly* asked (lit. *asking* asked) (leave)

* PIEL.—*Preterite.* *

Ps.109:10. Let his children be continually vagabonds, *and beg:*

PIEL.—*Future.*

2Sa.20:18. *They shall* surely *ask* (counsel)

* HIPHIL.—*Preterite.* *

1Sa. 1:28. I *have lent him* to the Lord;

HIPHIL.—*Future.*

Ex. 12:36. *so that they lent unto them*

שְׁאֵל *sh'ēhl*, Ch. 7593

* P'AL.—*Preterite.* *

Ezr. 5: 9. Then *asked we* those elders,
10. *We asked* their names also,
Dan 2:10. (that) *asked* such things at any magician,

P'AL.—*Future.*

Ezr. 7:21. *shall require of you*, it be done speedily,

P'AL.—*Participle.* Active.

Dan 2:11. (it is) a rare thing that the king *requireth*,
27. The secret which the king *hath demanded*

שְׁאֵלָא [*sh'ēh-lāh'*], Ch. f. 7595

Dan 4:17(14). and *the demand* by the word of the holy

7596 **שְׁאֵלָה** *sh'ĕh-lāh'*, f.

Jud. 8:24. I would desire *a request* of you,
1Sa. 1:17. the God of Israel grant (thee) *thy petition*
27. the Lord hath given me *my petition*
2:20. *the loan* (marg. or, *petition*) which is lent to the Lord.
1K. 2:16. I ask one *petition* of thee,
20. I desire one small *petition*
Est. 5: 6. What (is) *thy petition?*
7. *My petition* and my request
8. please the king to grant *my petition*,
7: 2. What (is) *thy petition*,
3. let my life be given me *at my petition*,
9:12. now what (is) *thy petition?*
Job 6: 8. Oh that I might have *my request*;
Ps. 106:15. he gave them *their request*;

7599 **שָׁאַן** [*shāh-an'*].

* PILEL.—*Preterite.* *

Job 3:18. (There) the prisoners *rest* together;
Pro. 1:33. *and shall be quiet* from fear of evil.
Jer. 30:10. shall be in rest, *and be quiet*,
46:27. be in rest *and at ease*,
48:11. Moab *hath been at ease*

7600 **שַׁאֲנָן** *shah-ănāhn'*, adj.

2K. 19:28. thy rage against me *and thy tumult*
Job 12: 5. the thought of *him that is at ease*.
Ps. 123: 4. the scorning of *those that are at ease*,
Isa. 32: 9. ye women *that are at ease*;
11. Tremble, ye *women that are at ease*;
18. my people shall dwell...in *quiet* resting places;
33:20. shall see Jerusalem a *quiet* habitation,
37:29. thy rage against me, *and thy tumult*,
Am. 6: 1. Woe to *them that are at ease* (marg. or, *secure*)
Zec. 1:15. the heathen *that are at ease*:

7601 **שָׁאַס** see **שָׁסַס**

7602 **שָׁאַף** *shāh-aph'*.

* KAL.—*Preterite.* *

Job 5: 5. *and* the robber *swalloweth up* their
Ps. 56: 1(2). man *would swallow me up*;
2(3). Mine enemies *would* daily *swallow* (me) *up*:
Jer. 2:24. A wild ass...(that) *snuffeth up* the wind
14: 6. *they snuffed up* the wind like dragons;

KAL.—*Infinitive.*

Eze. 36: 3. *and swallowed* you *up* on every side,

KAL.—*Future.*

Job 7: 2. As a servant *earnestly desireth* (marg. *gapeth after*) the shadow,
36:20. *Desire* not the night,
Ps. 119:131. I opened my mouth, *and panted*:
Isa. 42:14. I will destroy *and devour* (marg. *swallow*, or, *sup up*) at once.

KAL.—*Participle.* Poel.

Ps. 57: 3(4). *him that would swallow me up*.
Ecc. 1: 5. the sun goeth down, and *hasteth* (marg. *panteth*)
Am. 2: 7. *That pant* after the dust
8: 4. *O ye that swallow up* the needy,

7604 **שָׁאַר** *shāh-ar'*.

* KAL.—*Preterite.* *

1Sa. 16:11. *There remaineth* yet the youngest,

* NIPHAL.—*Preterite.* *

Gen 42:38. he *is left* alone:
47:18. *there is* not ought *left* in the sight of
Ex. 8:31(27). *there remained* not one.
10:19. *there remained* not one locust
14:28. *there remained* not so much as one
Lev. 25:52. if *there remain* but few years
Deu 3:11. only Og king of Bashan *remained*
4:27. *and ye shall be left* few in number
28:62. *And ye shall be left* few in number,
Jos. 8:17. *there was* not a man *left*
11:22. and in Ashdod, *there remained*.
13: 1. *there remaineth* yet very much land
12. Og...who *remained* of the remnant
Jud. 4:16. *there was* not a man *left*.
7: 3. *there remained* ten thousand.
1Sa. 5: 4. only (the stump of) Dagon *was left*
11:11. two of them *were* not *left* together.
2Sa. 14: 7. they shall quench my coal which *is left*,
1K. 22:46(47). the sodomites, which *remained*
2K. 7:13. which *are left* in the city, behold, they (are) as all the multitude of Israel that *are left*
10:21. *there was* not a man *left*
17:18. *there was* none *left* but the tribe of Judah
24:14. none *remained*, save the poorest sort
2Ch 21:17. that *there was* never a son *left* him,
Ezr. 9:15. *we remain* yet escaped,
Neh 1: 2. *were left* of the captivity,
3. The remnant *that are left*
Job 21:34. in your answers *there remaineth* falsehood?
Isa. 17: 6. *Yet* gleaning grapes *shall be left*
24: 6. are burned, *and* few men *left*.
12. In the city *is left* desolation,
49:21. I *was left* alone;
Jer. 34: 7. these defenced cities *remained*
37:10. *there remained* (but) wounded men
38:22. all the women that *are left*
42: 2. *we are left* (but) a few
Dan 10: 8. I *was left* alone,
— *there remained* no strength in me:
17. neither *is there* breath *left* in me.
Zec. 9: 7. *but he that remaineth*,

NIPHAL.—*Future.*

Gen 7:23. *and* Noah only *remained*
Ex. 8: 9(5). *they may remain* in the river only?
11(7). *they shall remain* in the river only.
10:26. *there shall* not an hoof *be left*
Nu. 11:26. *But there remained* two (of the) men
Ru. 1: 3. *and she was left*, and her two sons.
5. *and* the woman *was left* of her two sons
Isa. 11:11, 16. the remnant of his people, which *shall be left*,
Eze. 36:36. the heathen that *are left*

NIPHAL.—*Participle.*

Gen 14:10. *and they that remained* fled to the
32: 8(9). the other company *which is left*
Ex. 10: 5. *which remaineth* unto you from the hail,
Lev. 5: 9. *the rest* of the blood shall be wrung out
26:36. *And upon them that are left* (alive)
39. *And they that are left*...shall pine away
Deu 7:20. among them, until *they that are left*,
19:20. *And those which remain* shall hear,
Jos. 13: 2. the land *that yet remaineth*:
23: 4. these nations *that remain*,
7, 12. these *that remain* among you;
1Sa. 9:24. Behold that *which is left!* (marg. or, *reserved*)
11:11. *they which remained* were scattered,
2K. 7:13. five of the horses *that remain*,
10:11. Jehu slew all *that remained*
17. he slew all *that remained*
19:30. *the remnant* that is escaped (marg. the escaping...*that remaineth*)
25:11. the rest of the people *that were left*
22. the people *that remained* in the land
1Ch 13: 2. *left* in all the land of Israel,
2Ch 30: 6. *the remnant* of you, that are escaped
34:21. and for them *that are left* in Israel and in
Ezr. 1: 4. whosoever *remaineth* in any place
Neh 1: 3. *The remnant* that are left
Isa. 4: 3. *he that is left* in Zion,
37:31. *the remnant* that is escaped (marg. the escaping...*that remaineth*)
Jer. 8: 3. *them that remain* of this evil family, *which remain* in all the places
21: 7. such as *are left* in this city
24: 8. the residue of Jerusalem, *that remain*
38: 4. the men of war *that remain*
39: 9. the remnant of the people *that remained*
— the rest of the people *that remained*.
40: 6. the people *that were left* in the land.

Jer. 41:10. all the people *that remained*
52:15. the residue of the people *that remained*
Eze. 6:12. *and he that remaineth* and is besieged shall
9: 8. while they were slaying them, *and I was left*, [וְנֵאשֲׁאַר]
17:21. *they that remain* shall be scattered
Hag 2: 3. Who (is) *left* among you that saw
Zec. 11: 9. *and* let *the rest* eat every one
12:14. All the families *that remain*,

* HIPHIL.—*Preterite*. *

Ex. 10:12. all that the hail *hath left*.
Nu. 21:35. *there was* none *left* him alive:
Deu 2:34. *we left* none to remain:
3: 3. none *was left* to him remaining.
28:55. *hath* nothing *left* him in the siege,
Jos. 8:22. *they let* (lit. *left*) none of them remain
10:28. *he let* (lit. *id.*) none remain:
30. *he let* none remain in it;
33. *he had left* him none remaining.
37, 39, 40. *he left* none remaining,
11: 8. *they left* them none remaining.
14. neither *left they* any to breathe.
1K. 15:29. *he left* not to Jeroboam any that breathed,
16:11. *he left* him not one
19:18. *Yet I have left* (marg. or, *will leave*) (me) seven thousand
2K. 3:25. in Kir-haraseth *left they* the stones
10:11. *he left* him none remaining.
14. neither *left he* any of them.
13: 7. Neither *did he leave* of the people
25:12. the captain of the guard *left*
22. king of Babylon *had left*,
Jer. 39:10 & 52:16. the captain of the guard *left*
Joel 2:14. *and leave* a blessing behind him;
Zep. 3:12. *I will also leave* in the midst

HIPHIL.—*Infinitive*.

Ezr. 9: 8. *to leave* us a remnant

HIPHIL.—*Future*.

Nu. 9:12. *They shall leave* none of it
Deu 28:51. *shall* not *leave* thee (either) corn,
Jud. 6: 4. *left* no sustenance for Israel,
1Sa. 14:36. *let us* not *leave* a man of them.
25:22. if *I leave* of all them that (pertain)
Jer. 49: 9. *would they* not *leave* (some) gleaning
50:20. I will pardon them whom *I reserve*.
Am. 5: 3. a thousand *shall leave* an hundred,
— an hundred *shall leave* ten,
Obad. 5. *would they* not *leave* (some) grapes?

7605 **שְׁאָר** *sh'āhr*, m.

1Ch 11: 8. Joab repaired *the rest of* the city.
16:41. *and the rest* that were chosen,
2Ch 9:29. *Now the rest of* the acts of Solomon,
24:14. they brought *the rest of* the money
Ezr. 3: 8. *and the remnant of* their brethren
4: 3. *and the rest of* the chief of the fathers
7. *and the rest of* their companions,
Neh 10:28(29). *And the rest of* the people, the
11: 1. *the rest of* the people *also* cast lots,
20. *And the residue of* Israel,
Est. 9:12. *in the rest of* the king's provinces?
16. *But the other* Jews that (were) in
Isa. 7: 3. thou, *and Shear*-jashub (marg. *the remnant* shall return) thy son,
10:19. *And the rest of* the trees of his forest
20. *the remnant of* Israel, and such
21. *The remnant* shall return, (even) *the remnant of* Jacob,
22. *a remnant* of them shall return:
11:11. to recover *the remnant of* his people,
16. an highway *for the remnant of*
14:22. the name, *and remnant*, and son,
16:14. *and the remnant* (shall be) very small
17: 3. *and the remnant of* Syria:
21:17. *And the residue of* the number of archers,
28: 5. *unto the residue of* his people,
Zep. 1: 4. I will cut off *the remnant of* Baal
Mal. 2:15. *Yet* had he *the residue* (marg. or, *excellency*)

7606 **שְׁאָר** *sh'āhr*, Ch. m.

Ezr. 4: 9. *and the rest of* their companions;
10. *And the rest of* the nations
— *and the rest* (that are) on this side the
Ezr. 4:17. *and* (to) *the rest of* their companions
— *and* (unto) *the rest* beyond the river,
6:16. *and the rest of* the children
7:18. to do *with the rest of* the silver
20. *And whatsoever more* shall be
Dan 2:18. with *the rest of* the wise (men)
7: 7. *and* stamped *the residue* with the feet
12. *As concerning the rest of* the beasts,
19. *and* stamped *the residue* with his feet;

שְׁאֵר *sh'ēhr*, m. 7607

Ex. 21:10. *her food*, her raiment, and her duty of
Lev. 18: 6. any that is *near of* kin (marg. *remainder of* his flesh)
12. thy father's *near kinswoman*.
13. thy mother's *near kinswoman*.
20:19. uncovereth *his near kin*:
21: 2. *for his kin*, that is near
25:49. (any) *that is nigh of* kin
Nu. 27:11. give his inheritance *unto his kinsman*
Ps. 73:26. *My flesh* and my heart faileth:
78:20. can he provide *flesh* for his people?
27. He rained *flesh* also upon them
Pro. 5:11. when thy flesh *and thy body* are
11:17. (he that is) cruel troubleth *his own flesh*.
Jer. 51:35. violence done to me *and to my flesh* (marg. or, *remainder*)
Mic. 3: 2. *their flesh* from off their bones;
3. Who also eat *the flesh of* my people,

שַׁאֲרָה *shah-ărāh'*, f. 7608

Lev. 18:17. they (are) *her near kinswomen*:

שְׁאֵרִית *sh'ēh-reeth'*, f. 7611

Gen 45: 7. to preserve you *a posterity* (marg. to put for you *a remnant*)
2Sa. 14: 7. shall not leave...(neither) name *nor remainder*
2K. 19: 4. lift up (thy) prayer for *the remnant*
31. out of Jerusalem shall go forth *a remnant*,
21:14. I will forsake *the remnant*
1Ch 4:43. they smote *the rest* of the Amalekites
12:38. *the rest* also *of* Israel (were) of one heart
2Ch 34: 9. and of all *the remnant of* Israel,
36:20. *them that had escaped* (marg. *the remainder*) from the sword carried he
Ezr. 9:14. (there should be) no *remnant*
Neh 7:72. (that) which *the rest of* the people gave
Ps. 76:10(11). *the remainder of* wrath shalt thou
Isa. 14:30. *and* he shall slay *thy remnant*.
15: 9. *and upon the remnant of* the land.
37: 4. lift up (thy) prayer for *the remnant*
32. out of Jerusalem shall go forth *a remnant*,
44:17. *And the residue thereof* he maketh a god,
46: 3. all *the remnant of* the house of Israel,
Jer. 6: 9. shall throughly glean *the remnant of*
8: 3. *the residue of* them that remain
11:23. *And* there shall be no *remnant*
15: 9. *and the residue of them* will I deliver
23: 3. I will gather *the remnant of*
24: 8. *the residue of* Jerusalem
25:20. *the remnant of* Ashdod,
31: 7. thy people, *the remnant of* Israel.
39: 3. all *the residue of* the princes
40:11. the king of Babylon had left *a remnant*
15. *the remnant in* Judah perish?
41:10. all *the residue of* the people
16. all *the remnant of* the people
42: 2. for all this *remnant*;
15. ye *remnant of* Judah;
19. O ye *remnant of* Judah;
43: 5. all *the remnant of* Judah,
44: 7. to leave you none *to remain*; (lit. no *remnant*)
12. I will take *the remnant of* Judah,
14. none *of the remnant of* Judah,...shall
28. all *the remnant of* Judah,
47: 4. *the remnant of* the country of Caphtor.
5. *the remnant of* their valley:
50:26. let nothing of her be *left*. (lit. let no *remnant* be to her)
Eze. 5:10. *the* whole *remnant of thee* will I scatter

Eze. 9: 8. wilt thou destroy all *the residue of*
11:13. make a full end of *the remnant of* Israel?
25:16. destroy *the remnant of* the sea coast.
36: 3. *unto the residue of* the heathen,
4. *to the residue of* the heathen
5. have I spoken against *the residue of* the
Am. 1: 8. *the remnant of* the Philistines shall perish,
5:15. be gracious unto *the remnant of* Joseph.
9:12. possess *the remnant of* Edom,
Mic. 2:12. I will surely gather *the remnant of* Israel;
4: 7. I will make her that halted *a remnant,*
5: 7(6), 8(7). *the remnant of* Jacob shall be
7:18. *the remnant of* his heritage?
Zep. 2: 7. *the remnant of* the house of Judah;
9. *the residue of* my people
3:13. *The remnant of* Israel
Hag. 1:12, 14. all *the remnant of* the people,
2: 2. *the residue of* the people,
Zec. 8: 6. the eyes of *the remnant of* this people
11. *unto the residue of* this people
12. I will cause *the remnant of* this people to possess

7612 ## שְׁאֵת *shēhth*, f.

Lam. 3:47. *desolation* and destruction.

7616 ## שְׁבָבִים *sh'vāh-veem'*, m. pl.

Hos. 8: 6. calf of Samaria shall be *broken in pieces.*

7617 ## שָׁבָה *shāh-vāh'*.

* KAL.—*Preterite.* *

Gen34:29. their wives *took they captive,*
Deu21:10. *and thou hast taken* them captive,
1K. 8:46. *so that* they *carry them away* captives
48. their enemies, which *led* them *away captive,*
2K. 6:22. those whom *thou hast taken captive*
2Ch 6:36. *and* they *carry them away* captives
38. *they have carried* them *captives,*
25:12. *did* the children of Judah *carry away captive,*
28:11. the captives...*ye have taken captive*
Ps. 68:18(19). *thou hast led* captivity *captive:*
Jer. 41:14. Ishmael *had carried away captive*
43:12. *and carry them away captives:*

KAL.—*Infinitive.*

Obad. 11. the strangers *carried away captive*

KAL.—*Imperative.*

Jud. 5:12. *and lead* thy captivity *captive,*

KAL.—*Future.*

Nu. 21: 1. *and took* (some) of them prisoners.
24:22. *shall carry thee away captive.*
31: 9. *And* the children of Israel *took...captives,*
1Sa.30: 2. *And had taken* the women *captives,*
2K. 5: 2. *and had brought away captive*
1Ch 5:21. *And they took away* (marg. *led captive*) their cattle;
2Ch 14:15(14). *and carried away* sheep and camels
21:17. *and carried away* all the substance
28: 5. *and carried away* a great multitude
8. *And* the children of Israel *carried away* captive of their brethren
17. smitten Judah, *and carried away* captives.
Jer. 41:10. *Then* Ishmael *carried away captive*
— *and* Ishmael...*carried them away captive,*

KAL.—*Participle.* Poel.

1K. 8:46. they carry them away captives (lit. *their captors* captivate them)
47. the land of *them that carried them captives,*
50. *who carried them captive,*
2Ch 6:36. they carry them away captives (marg. *they that take them captives* carry them away)
30: 9. *them that lead them captive,*
Ps. 106:46. *those that carried them captives.*
137: 3. *they that carried us away captive*
Isa. 14: 2. they *shall take them captives, whose captives they were;*
Jer. 50:33. all *that took them captives*

KAL.—*Participle.* Paül.

Gen31:26. carried away my daughters, *as captives*
Isa. 61: 1. to proclaim liberty *to the captives,*

* NIPHAL.—*Preterite.* *

Gen14:14. when Abram heard that his brother *was taken captive,*
Ex. 22:10(9). die, or be hurt, or *driven away,*
1Sa.30: 3. and their daughters, *were taken captives.*
5. David's two wives *were taken captives,*
1K. 8:47. whither *they were carried captives,*
2Ch 6:37. whither *they are carried captive,*
Jer. 13:17. the Lord's flock *is carried away captive.*
Eze. 6: 9. *they shall be carried captives,*

שְׁבוֹ *sh'voo*, m. 7618

Ex. 28:19 & 39:12. the third row a ligure, *an agate,*

שְׁבוּל [*sh'vool*], m. 7635

Jer. 18:15. (כתיב) to stumble...(from) *the* ancient *paths,*

שָׁבוּעַ *shāh-voo'ăg*, com. 7620

m. pl.[2],—f. pl.[3]

Gen29:27. Fulfil her *week,*
28. Jacob...fulfilled her *week:*
Ex. 34:22. thou shalt observe the feast of *weeks,*[3]
Lev.12: 5. shall be unclean *two weeks,*
Nu. 28:26. *after your weeks*[3] (be out),
Deu16: 9. Seven *weeks*[3] shalt thou number unto thee: begin to number *the* seven *weeks*[3]
10. thou shalt keep the feast of *weeks*[3]
16. in the feast of *weeks,*[3]
2Ch 8:13. in the feast of *weeks,*[3]
Jer. 5:24. *the* appointed *weeks*[3] of the harvest.
Eze.45:21. a feast of *seven*[3] days;
Dan 9:24. Seventy *weeks*[2] are determined
25. seven *weeks,*[2] and threescore *and* two *weeks:*[2]
26. after threescore and two *weeks*[2]
27. confirm the covenant with many for one *week:* and in the midst of *the week*
10: 2. I Daniel was mourning three full *weeks.*[2] (lit. *weeks* days)
3. till three whole *weeks*[2] (lit. *id.*) were fulfilled.

שְׁבוּעָה *sh'voo-ğāh'*, f. 7621

Gen24: 8. clear *from* this *my oath:*
26: 3. I will perform *the oath* which I sware
Ex. 22:11(10). *an oath of* the Lord
Lev. 5: 4. shall pronounce *with an oath,*
Nu. 5:21. charge the woman *with an oath of*
— The Lord make thee a curse *and an oath*
30: 2(3). swear *an oath* to bind his soul
10(11). bound her soul by a bond *with an oath;*
13(14). every binding *oath* to afflict
Deu 7: 8. he would keep *the oath*
Jos. 2:17. blameless *of* this *thine oath*
20. we will be quit *of thine oath*
9:20. *the oath* which we sware
Jud.21: 5. they had made *a* great *oath*
1Sa.14:26. the people feared *the oath.*
2Sa.21: 7. the Lord's *oath* that (was) between them,
1K. 2:43. not kept *the oath of* the Lord,
1Ch 16:16. and *of his oath* unto Isaac;
2Ch 15:15. all Judah rejoiced at *the oath:*
Neh 6:18. (there were) many in Judah *sworn* (lit. were *oath* masters)
10:29(30). entered into a curse, *and into an oath*
Ps.105: 9. *and his oath* unto Isaac;
Ecc. 8: 2. regard of *the oath of* God.
9: 2. he that feareth *an oath.*
Isa. 65:15. leave your name *for a curse*
Jer. 11: 5. That I may perform *the oath*
Eze.21:23(28). them that have sworn *oaths:*
Dan 9:11. *and the oath* that (is) written in the law of
Hab 3: 9. (according) to *the oaths of* the tribes,
Zec. 8:17. his neighbour; *and* love no false *oath:*

7622 **שְׁבוּת** *sh'vooth*, f.

Deu30: 3. the Lord thy God will turn *thy captivity*,
Job 42:10. the Lord turned *the captivity of* Job,
Ps. 14: 7. when the Lord bringeth back *the captivity of* his people,
53: 6(7). When God bringeth back *the captivity of*
85: 1(2). (כתיב) brought back *the captivity of*
126: 4. (כתיב) Turn again *our captivity*,
Jer. 29:14. I will turn away *your captivity*,
30: 3. I will bring again *the captivity of*
18. bring again *the captivity of* Jacob's tents,
31:23. I shall bring again *their captivity*;
32:44. I will cause *their captivity* to return,
33: 7. I will cause *the captivity of* Judah and *the captivity of* Israel to return,
11. I will cause to return *the captivity of*
26. I will cause *their captivity* to return,
48:47. Yet will I bring again *the captivity of*
49: 6. I will bring again *the captivity of*...Ammon,
39. I will bring again *the captivity of* Elam,
Lam. 2:14. to turn away *thy captivity*;
Eze. 16:53. (כתיב) I shall bring again *their captivity*,
— *the captivity of* Sodom and her daughters, and *the captivity of* Samaria and her
— *the captivity of* thy captives
29:14. I will bring again *the captivity of* Egypt,
39:25. will I bring again *the captivity of* Jacob,
Hos. 6:11. when I returned *the captivity of* my
Joel 3: 1(4:1). when I shall bring again *the captivity of* Judah
Am. 9:14. I will bring again *the captivity of*
Zep. 2: 7. (כתיב) and turn away *their captivity*.
3:20. when I turn back *your captivity*

7623 **שָׁבַח** [*shāh-vagh'*].

* PIEL.—*Preterite*. *

Ecc. 8:15. *Then* I *commended* mirth,

PIEL.—*Imperative*.

Ps. 117: 1. *praise him*, all ye people.
147:12. *Praise* the Lord, O Jerusalem;

PIEL.—*Future*.

Ps. 63: 3(4). my lips *shall praise thee*.
89: 9(10). when the waves thereof arise, thou *stillest them*.
145: 4. One generation *shall praise* thy works
Pro. 29:11. a wise (man) *keepeth it in*

PIEL.—*Participle*.

Ecc. 4: 2. *Wherefore* I *praised* the dead

* HIPHIL.—*Participle*. *

Ps. 65: 7(8). *Which stilleth* the noise of the seas,

* HITHPAEL.—*Infinitive*. *

1 Ch 16:35. *glory* in thy praise.
Ps. 106:47. *to triumph* in thy praise.

7624 **שְׁבַח** [*sh'vagh*], Ch.

* PAEL.—*Preterite*. *

Dan 4:34(31). and I *praised* and honoured him
5: 4. *and praised* the gods of gold,
23. and *thou hast praised* the gods of silver,

PAEL.—*Participle*.

Dan 2:23. I thank thee, *and praise* thee, O thou
4:37(34). Now I Nebuchadnezzar *praise* and

7626 **שֵׁבֶט** *shēh'-vet*, com.

Gen49:10. *The sceptre* shall not depart
16. as one of *the tribes of* Israel.
28. these (are) *the* twelve *tribes of* Israel:
Ex. 21:20. if a man smite his servant,...*with a rod*,
24: 4. according to *the* twelve *tribes of* Israel.
28:21. they be according to *the* twelve *tribes*.
39:14. his name, according to *the* twelve *tribes*.
Lev. 27:32. whatsoever passeth under *the rod*,
Nu. 4:18. *the tribe of* the families of
18: 2. *the tribe of* thy father,
24: 2. abiding...*according to their tribes*;
17. *a Sceptre* shall rise out of Israel,
32:33. and unto half *the tribe of* Manasseh
Nu. 36: 3. *tribes of* the children of Israel,
Deu 1:13. wise men, and understanding, and known *among your tribes*,
15. I took the chief of *your tribes*,
— officers *among your tribes*.
23. I took twelve men of you, one of *a tribe*:
3:13. gave I unto *the* half *tribe of* Manasseh;
5:23(20). all the heads of *your tribes*,
10: 8. the Lord separated *the tribe of* Levi,
12: 5. choose out of all *your tribes*
14. choose in one of *thy tribes*,
16:18. giveth thee, *throughout thy tribes*:
18: 1. (and) all *the tribe of* Levi, shall have no
5. chosen him out of all *thy tribes*,
29: 8(7). and to *the* half *tribe of* Manasseh.
10(9). your captains of *your tribes*,
18(17). man, or woman, or family, or *tribe*,
21(20). him unto evil out of all *the tribes of*
31:28. all the elders of *your tribes*,
33: 5. *the tribes of* Israel were gathered together.
Jos. 1:12. and to half *the tribe of* Manasseh, spake
3:12. twelve men *out of the tribes of* Israel, *out of* every *tribe* a man.
4: 2, 4. *out of* every *tribe* a man,
5, 8. the number of *the tribes of* the children
12. and half *the tribe of* Manasseh, passed
7:14. *according to your tribes*: and it shall be, (that) *the tribe* which the Lord taketh
16. brought Israel *by their tribes*; and *the tribe of* Judah was taken:
11:23. according to their divisions *by their tribes*.
12: 6. and *the* half *tribe of* Manasseh.
7. which Joshua gave *unto the tribes of*
13: 7. an inheritance unto *the* nine *tribes*, and *the* half *tribe* of Manasseh,
14. *unto the tribe of* Levi he gave none
29. (inheritance) unto *the* half *tribe of*
33. *But unto the tribe of* Levi Moses gave not
18: 2. there remained among the children of Israel seven *tribes*,
4. three men *for* (each) *tribe*:
7. and half *the tribe of* Manasseh,
21:16. nine cities out of those two *tribes*.
22: 7. the (one) half of *the tribe of* Manasseh
9, 10, 11, 21. *the* half *tribe of* Manasseh
13, 15. and to *the* half *tribe of* Manasseh,
23: 4. an inheritance *for your tribes*,
24: 1. Joshua gathered all *the tribes of* Israel
Jud. 5:14. they that handle *the pen of* the writer.
18: 1. *the tribe of* the Danites
— had not fallen unto them among *the tribes of* Israel.
19. a priest unto *a tribe*
30. he and his sons were priests *to the tribe of*
20: 2. (even) of all *the tribes of* Israel,
10. throughout all *the tribes of* Israel,
12. And *the tribes of* Israel sent men through all *the tribe of* Benjamin,
21: 3. one *tribe* lacking in Israel?
5. Who (is there) among all *the tribes of*
6. There is one *tribe* cut off
8. What one (is there) *of the tribes of* Israel
15. had made a breach *in the tribes of* Israel.
17. that *a tribe* be not destroyed
24. every man *to his tribe*
1 Sa. 2:28. I choose him out of all *the tribes of* Israel
9:21. of the smallest of *the tribes of* Israel? and my family the least of all the families of *the tribe of* Benjamin?
10:19. *by your tribes*, and by your thousands.
20. Samuel had caused all *the tribes of* Israel to come near, *the tribe of* Benjamin was
21. When he had caused *the tribe of* Benjamin
15:17. (made) the head of *the tribes of* Israel,
2 Sa. 5: 1. Then came all *the tribes* of Israel
7: 7. spake I a word with any of *the tribes* (marg. *judges*) *of* Israel,
14. I will chasten him *with the rod of* men,
15: 2. servant (is) of one of *the tribes of* Israel.
10. spies throughout all *the tribes of* Israel,
18:14. he took three *darts* in his hand,
19: 9(10). strife throughout all *the tribes of* Israel,
20:14. he went through all *the tribes of* Israel
23:21. went down to him *with a staff*,
24: 2. Go now through all *the tribes of* Israel.
1 K. 8:16. chose no city out of all *the tribes of* Israel
11:13. will give one *tribe* to thy son

1K. 11:31. and will give ten *tribes* to thee:
32. *But* he shall have one *tribe*
— chosen out of all *the tribes of* Israel:
35. will give it unto thee, (even) ten *tribes.*
36. unto his son will I give one *tribe,*
12:20. but *the tribe of* Judah only.
21. house of Judah, with *the tribe of* Benjamin,
14:21. did choose out of all *the tribes of* Israel,
18:31. *the tribes of* the sons of Jacob,
2K. 17:18. there was none left but *the tribe of* Judah
21: 7. which I have chosen out of all *tribes of* Israel,
1Ch 5:18. and half *the tribe of* Manasseh,
23. the children of *the* half *tribe of* Manasseh
26. the Gadites, and *the* half *tribe of* Manasseh,
11:23. went down to him *with a staff,*
12:37. and of *the* half *tribe of* Manasseh,
23:14. his sons were named of *the tribe of* Levi.
26:32. Gadites, and *the* half *tribe of* Manasseh,
27:16. Furthermore over *the tribes of* Israel:
20. of *the* half *tribe of* Manasseh, Joel
22. These (were) the princes of *the tribes of* Israel.
28: 1. the princes of *the tribes,*
29: 6. and princes of *the tribes of* Israel,
2Ch 6: 5. chose no city among all *the tribes of* Israel
11:16. out of all *the tribes of* Israel such
12:13. chosen out of all *the tribes of* Israel,
33: 7. chosen before all *the tribes of* Israel,
Job 9:34. Let him take *his rod* away
21: 9. neither (is) *the rod of* God upon them.
37:13. whether *for correction* (marg. *a rod*), or for his land,
Ps. 2: 9. Thou shalt break them *with a rod of* iron;
23: 4. *thy rod* and thy staff they comfort me.
45: 6(7). *the sceptre of* thy kingdom (is) *a* right *sceptre.*
74: 2. *the rod* (marg. or, *tribe*) *of* thine
78:55. made *the tribes of* Israel to dwell
67. *and* chose not *the tribe of* Ephraim:
68. But chose *the tribe of* Judah,
89:32(33). will I visit their transgressions *with the rod,*
105:37. not one feeble (person) *among their tribes.*
122: 4. Whither *the tribes* go up, *the tribes of* the
125: 3. *the rod of* the wicked shall not rest
Pro. 10:13. *but a rod* (is) for the back of him that
13:24. He that spareth *his rod* hateth his son:
22: 8. *and the rod of* his anger shall fail.
15. *the rod of* correction
23:13. beatest him *with the rod,*
14. Thou shalt beat him *with the rod,*
26: 3. *and a rod* for the fool's back.
29:15. *The rod* and reproof give wisdom:
Isa. 9: 4(3). *the rod of* his oppressor, as in the day
10: 5. O Assyrian, *the rod of* mine anger,
15. as if *the rod* should shake (itself)
24. he shall smite thee *with a rod,*
11: 4. he shall smite the earth *with the rod of*
14: 5. *the sceptre of* the rulers.
29. *the rod of* him that smote thee
19:13. the stay of *the tribes*
28:27. the cummin *with a rod.*
30:31. the Assyrian...(which) smote *with a rod.*
49: 6. to raise up *the tribes of* Jacob,
63:17. *the tribes of* thine inheritance.
Jer. 10:16. Israel (is) *the rod of* his inheritance:
51:19. *and* (Israel is) *the rod of* his inheritance:
Lam 3: 1. seen affliction *by the rod of* his wrath.
Eze. 19:11. *the sceptres of* them that bare rule,
14. no strong rod (to be) *a sceptre* to rule.
20:37. I will cause you to pass under *the rod,*
21:10(15). *the rod of* my son,
13(18). if (the sword) contemn even *the rod?*
37:19. *and the tribes of* Israel his fellows,
45: 8. of Israel *according to their tribes.*
47:13. according to *the* twelve *tribes of* Israel:
21. unto you *according to the tribes of* Israel.
22. among *the tribes of* Israel.
23. *in* what *tribe* the stranger sojourneth,
48: 1. the names of *the tribes.*
19. serve it out of all *the tribes of* Israel.
23. the rest of *the tribes,*
29. divide by lot *unto the tribes of* Israel
31. after the names of *the tribes of* Israel:
Hos 5: 9. *among the tribes of* Israel have I made
Am. 1: 5, 8. him that holdeth *the sceptre*
Mic 5: 1(4:14). they shall smite the judge of Israel *with a rod*
7:14. Feed thy people *with thy rod,*
Zec. 9: 1. as of all *the tribes of* Israel,
10:11. *and the sceptre of* Egypt shall depart

שְׁבָט *sh'vāht*, m. 7627

Zec. 1: 7. the month *Sebat,*

שְׁבַט [*sh'vat'*], Ch. com. 7625

Ezr. 6:17. according to the number of *the tribes of*

שְׁבִי *sh'vee*, m. (also adj.) 7628

Ex. 12:29. the firstborn of *the captive*
Nu. 21: 1. took (some) of them *prisoners.*
31:12. they brought *the captives,*
19. purify (both) yourselves *and your captives*
26. the sum of the prey *that was taken,* (marg. of *the captivity*)
Deu 21:10. thou hast taken *them captive,*
13. the raiment of *her captivity*
28:41. they shall go *into captivity.*
Jud. 5:12. lead *thy captivity* captive,
2Ch 6:37, 38. the land of *their captivity,*
28:17. the Edomites....carried away *captives.* (marg. *a captivity*)
29: 9. our wives (are) *in captivity*
Ezr. 2: 1. went up *out of the captivity,*
3: 8. that were come *out of the captivity*
8:35. which were come *out of the captivity,*
9: 7. delivered...to the sword, *to captivity,*
Neh 1: 2. the Jews that had escaped,...left of *the captivity,*
3. The remnant that are left of *the captivity*
7: 6. went up *out of the captivity,*
8:17. that were come again *out of the captivity*
Ps. 68:18(19). thou hast led *captivity* captive:
78:61. delivered his strength *into captivity,*
Isa. 20: 4. lead away the Egyptians *prisoners,*
46: 2. themselves are gone *into captivity.*
49:24. or *the* lawful *captive* delivered?
25. *the captives* (marg. *captivity*) *of* the mighty
52: 2. O *captive* daughter of Zion.
Jer. 15: 2. such as (are) *for the captivity, to the captivity.*
20: 6. Pashur,...shall go *into captivity:*
22:22. thy lovers shall go *into captivity:*
30:10. save...thy seed from the land of *their captivity;*
16. every one of them, shall go *into captivity;*
43:11. such (as are) *for captivity to captivity;*
46:27. will save...thy seed from the land of *their captivity;*
48:46. thy sons are taken *captives,* (marg. *in captivity*)
Lam 1: 5. her children are gone into *captivity*
18. my young men are gone *into captivity.*
Eze. 12:11. they shall remove (and) go *into captivity.*
30:17. these (cities) shall go *into captivity.*
18. her daughters shall go *into captivity.*
Dan 11: 8. shall also carry *captives* (lit. shall bring *into captivity*) into Egypt
33. they shall fall by the sword, and by flame, *by captivity,*
Am. 4:10. and *have taken away* (marg. with *the captivity of*) your horses;
9: 4. though they go *into captivity*
Nah 3:10. she went *into captivity:*
Hab 1: 9. they shall gather *the captivity*

שָׁבִיב [*shāh-veev'*], m. 7632

Job 18: 5. *the spark of* his fire shall not shine.

שְׁבִיב [*sh'veev,*] Ch. m. 7631

Dan 3:22. *the flame* (marg. or, *spark*) of the fire slew
7: 9. his throne (was like) *the* fiery *flame,*

7633 **שִׁבְיָה** *shiv-yāh'*, f.

Deu 21:11. seest *among the captives* a beautiful woman,
32:42. the blood of the slain *and of the captives*,
2Ch 28: 5. carried away a great multitude *of them captives*,
11. deliver *the captives* again,
13. Ye shall not bring in *the captives*
14. the armed men left *the captives*
15. rose up, and took *the captives*,
Neh 4: 4(3:36). for a prey in the land of *captivity:*
Jer. 48:46. thy daughters *captives*. (lit. *into captivity*)

7635 **שְׁבִיל** [*sh'veel*], m.

Ps. 77:19(20). *and thy path* in the great waters,
Jer. 18:15. in their ways (from) *the* ancient *paths*,

7636 **שְׁבִיסִים** *sh'vee-seem'*, m. pl.

Isa. 3:18. (their) tinkling ornaments...and (their) *cauls*, (marg. or, *networks*)

7637 **שְׁבִיעִי** *sh'vee-"gee'*, adj.

Gen 2: 2. on the *seventh* day God ended his work which he had made; and he rested on the *seventh*
3. God blessed the *seventh* day, and sanctified
8: 4. the ark rested in the *seventh* month,
Ex. 12:15. from the first day until the *seventh* day,
16. in the *seventh* day there shall be an holy
13: 6. in the *seventh* day (shall be) a feast
16:26. on the *seventh* day, (which is) the
27. on the *seventh* day for to gather,
29. go out of his place on the *seventh* day.
30. So the people rested on the *seventh* day.
20:10. But the *seventh* day (is) the sabbath
11. and rested the *seventh* day:
21: 2. *and in the seventh* he shall go out free
23:11. *But the seventh* (year) thou shalt let it
12. on the *seventh* day thou shalt rest:
24:16. the *seventh* day he called unto Moses
31:15. in *the seventh* (is) the sabbath of rest,
17. on the *seventh* day he rested,
34:21. on the *seventh* day thou shalt rest:
35: 2. on the *seventh* day there shall be
Lev.13: 5. the priest shall look on him the *seventh* day:
6. the priest shall look on him again the *seventh* day:
27. shall look upon him the *seventh* day:
32. in the *seventh* day the priest shall look
34. in the *seventh* day the priest shall look
51. shall look on the plague on the *seventh* day:
14: 9. But it shall be on the *seventh* day,
39. shall come again the *seventh* day,
16:29. (that) in the *seventh* month,
23: 3. the *seventh* day (is) the sabbath
8. in the *seventh* day (is) an holy
16. after the *seventh* sabbath
24. In the *seventh* month, in the first (day)
27. the tenth (day) of this *seventh* month
34. The fifteenth day of this *seventh* month
39. the fifteenth day of the *seventh* month,
41. ye shall celebrate it in the *seventh* month.
25: 4. in the *seventh* year shall be a sabbath
9. on the tenth (day) of the *seventh* month,
20. What shall we eat the *seventh* year?
Nu. 6: 9. on the *seventh* day shall he shave it.
7:48. On the *seventh* day Elishama
19:12. on the *seventh* day he shall be clean:
— then the *seventh* day he shall not be clean.
19. on the third day, and on the *seventh* day: and on the *seventh* day he shall purify
28:25. on the *seventh* day ye shall have an holy
29: 1. And in the *seventh* month, on the first
7. on the tenth (day) of this *seventh* month
12. on the fifteenth day of the *seventh* month
32. on the *seventh* day seven bullocks,
31:19. on the third day, and on the *seventh* day.
24. wash your clothes on the *seventh* day,
Deu 5:14. But the *seventh* day (is) the sabbath
15:12. in the *seventh* year thou shalt let him go
16: 8. on the *seventh* day (shall be) a solemn
Jos. 6: 4. and the *seventh* day ye shall compass
Jos. 6:15. it came to pass on the *seventh* day,
16. it came to pass at the *seventh* time,
19:40. the *seventh* lot came out for the tribe
Jud.14:15, 17. it came to pass on the *seventh* day,
18. on the *seventh* day before the sun went
2Sa.12:18. it came to pass on the *seventh* day, that the child died.
1K. 8: 2. the month Ethanim, which (is) the *seventh*
18:44. And it came to pass *at the seventh time*,
20:29. in the *seventh* day the battle was joined:
2K. 11: 4. And the *seventh* year Jehoiada sent
18: 9. which (was) the *seventh* year of Hoshea
25:25. to pass in the *seventh* month, that
1Ch 2:15. Ozem the sixth, David *the seventh:*
12:11. Attai the sixth, Eliel *the seventh*,
24:10. *The seventh* to Hakkoz,
25:14. *The seventh* to Jesharelah,
26: 3. Jehohanan the sixth, Elioenai *the seventh*.
5. Ammiel the sixth, Issachar *the seventh*,
27:10. *The seventh* (captain) for the *seventh*
2Ch 5: 3. the feast which (was) in the *seventh*
7:10. the three and twentieth day of the *seventh*
23: 1. the *seventh* year Jehoiada strengthened
31: 7. finished (them) in the *seventh* month.
Ezr. 3: 1. when the *seventh* month was come,
6. From the first day of the *seventh* month
7: 8. which (was) in the *seventh* year of the
Neh 7:73. and when the *seventh* month came,
8: 2. upon the first day of the *seventh* month.
14. in booths in the feast of the *seventh*
10:31(32). we would leave the *seventh* year,
Est. 1:10. On the *seventh* day, when the heart of
Jer. 28:17. died the same year in the *seventh*
41: 1. it came to pass in the *seventh* month,
Eze.20: 1. it came to pass in the *seventh* year,
45:25. *In the seventh* (month), in the fifteenth
Hag 2: 1. *In the seventh* (month), in the
Zec. 7: 5. and mourned in the fifth *and seventh*
8:19. the fast of *the seventh*, and the fast of the

שְׁבִית *sh'veeth*, f. 7622

Nu. 21:29. given his sons...*into captivity*
Job 42:10. (כתיב) the Lord turned *the captivity of*
Ps. 85: 1(2). brought back *the captivity of* Jacob.
126: 4. Turn again *our captivity*,
Jer. 29:14. (כתיב) I will turn away *your captivity*,
49:39. (——) I will bring again *the captivity of*
Lam.2:14. (——) to turn away *thy captivity;*
Eze.16:53. I shall bring again *their captivity*,
— (כתיב) *the captivity of* Sodom and her daughters, *and the captivity of* Samaria
— (כתיב) (bring again) *the captivity of*
— *thy captives* in the midst
39:25. (כתיב) again *the captivity of* Jacob,
Zep. 2: 7. turn away *their captivity*.

שֹׁבֶל *shōh'-vel*, m. 7640

Isa. 47: 2. make bare *the leg*,

שַׁבְּלוּל *shav-lool'*, m. 7642

Ps. 58: 8(9). As *a snail* (which) melteth,

שִׁבֹּלֶת *shib-bōh'-leth*, f. 7641

Gen41: 5. seven *ears of corn* came up
6. seven thin *ears* and blasted
7. *the* seven thin *ears* devoured *the* seven rank and full *ears*.
22. seven *ears* came up in one stalk,
23. seven *ears*, withered, thin,
24. *the* thin *ears* devoured *the* seven good *ears:*
26. *the* seven good *ears* (are) seven years:
27. *the* seven empty *ears*
Jud.12: 6. Say now *Shibboleth:*
Ru. 2: 2. glean *ears of corn*
Job 24:24. the tops of *the ears of corn*.
Ps. 69: 2(3). *where the floods* overflow me.
15(16). Let not *the waterflood* overflow me,
Isa. 17: 5. reapeth *the ears* with his arm; and it shall be as he that gathereth *ears*
27:12. *from the channel of* the river
Zec. 4:12. (these) two olive *branches*

7650 **שָׁבַע** [*shāh-văgⁿ′*].

* KAL.—*Participle.* Paül. *

Eze.21:23(28). *them that have sworn* oaths:

* NIPHAL.—*Preterite.* *

Gen21:31. *they sware* both of them.
22:16. By myself *have I sworn*,
24: 7. The Lord God of heaven,...that *sware*
26: 3. *I sware* unto Abraham
50:24. the land which *he sware* to Abraham,
Ex. 13: 5. *he sware* unto thy fathers to give
11. as *he sware* unto thee and to thy fathers,
32:13. *thou swarest* by thine own self,
33: 1. the land which *I sware* unto Abraham,
Lev. 6: 3(5:22). lieth concerning it, *and sweareth*
Nu. 11:12. the land which *thou swarest*
14:16. the land which *he sware* unto them,
23. the land which *I sware* unto their fathers,
32:11. the land which *I sware* unto Abraham,
Deu 1: 8. the land which the Lord *sware*
35. that good land, which *I sware* to give
2:14. as the Lord *sware*
4:31. covenant of thy fathers which *he sware*
6:10. the land which *he sware*...to give
18. the good land which the Lord *sware*
23. to give us the land which *he sware*
7: 8. the oath which *he had sworn*
12. mercy which *he sware* unto thy fathers:
13. the land which *he sware* unto thy fathers
8: 1. the land which the Lord *sware* unto
18. his covenant which *he sware*
9: 5. the word which the Lord *sware*
10:11. the land, which *I sware*...to give
11: 9, 21. the Lord *sware* unto your fathers
13:17(18) & 19:8. as *he hath sworn* unto thy
26: 3. the Lord *sware* unto our fathers
15. *thou swarest* unto our fathers,
28: 9. as *he hath sworn* unto thee,
11. the land which the Lord *sware* unto
29:13(12). as *he hath sworn* unto thy fathers,
30:20. the land which the Lord *sware* unto
31: 7. the land which the Lord *hath sworn*...to
20. the land which *I sware* unto
21, 23. the land which *I sware*.
34: 4. the land which *I sware* unto Abraham,
Jos. 1: 6. *I sware* unto their fathers
5: 6. unto whom the Lord *sware*
— the land, which the Lord *sware*
6:22. as *ye sware* unto her.
9:18. the princes of the congregation *had sworn*
19. We *have sworn* unto them
20. the oath which *we sware*
21:43(41). the land which *he sware* to give
44(42). according to all that *he sware*
Jud. 2: 1. the land which *I sware* unto
15. as the Lord *had sworn*
21: 1. the men of Israel *had sworn*
7. we *have sworn* by the Lord
18. the children of Israel *have sworn*,
1Sa. 3:14. *I have sworn* unto the house
20:42. *we have sworn* both of us
2Sa. 3: 9. as the Lord *hath sworn* to David,
19: 7(8). *I swear* by the Lord,
21: 2. the children of Israel *had sworn*
17. Then the men of David *sware*
1K. 1:13. *Didst* not thou, my lord, O king, *swear*
17. thou *swarest* by the Lord
30. Even as *I sware* unto thee
2Ch 15:15. *they had sworn* with all their heart,
Ps. 15: 4. (He that) *sweareth* to (his own) hurt,
24: 4. nor *sworn* deceitfully.
89: 3(4). *I have sworn* unto David my servant,
35(36). Once *have I sworn* by my holiness
49(50). *thou swarest* unto David
95:11. Unto whom *I sware* in my wrath
102: 8(9). they that are mad against me *are sworn*
110: 4. The Lord *hath sworn*,
119:106. *I have sworn*, and I will perform (it),
132: 2. *he sware* unto the Lord,
11. The Lord *hath sworn* (in) truth
Isa. 14:24. The Lord of hosts *hath sworn*,
45:23. *I have sworn* by myself,
54: 9. *I have sworn* that the waters of Noah should no more go over the earth; so *have I sworn*
62: 8. The Lord *hath sworn* by his right hand,
Jer. 4: 2. *And thou shalt swear*, The Lord
11: 5. the oath which *I have sworn*
22: 5. *I swear* by myself,
32:22. *thou didst swear* to their fathers
44:26. *I have sworn* by my great name,
49:13. *I have sworn* by myself,
51:14. The Lord of hosts *hath sworn*
Am. 4: 2 & 6:8. The Lord God *hath sworn* by
8: 7. The Lord *hath sworn*
Mic. 7:20. *thou hast sworn* unto our fathers

NIPHAL.—*Infinitive.*

Nu. 30: 2(3). *swear* an oath to bind his soul
Jer. 7: 9. commit adultery, *and swear* falsely,
12:16. *to swear* by my name, The Lord liveth; as they taught my people *to swear*

NIPHAL.—*Imperative.*

Gen21:23. *swear* unto me here by God
25:33. Jacob said, *Swear* to me this day;
47:31. *Swear* unto me.
Jos. 2:12. *swear* unto me by the Lord,
Jud.15:12. Samson said...*Swear* unto me,
1Sa.24:21(22). *Swear* now therefore unto me
30:15. *Swear* unto me by God,

NIPHAL.—*Future.*

Gen21:24. Abraham said, I *will swear*.
24: 9. *and sware* to him concerning
25:33. *and he sware* unto him:
26:31. *and sware* one to another:
31:53. *And* Jacob *sware* by the fear of his father
47:31. *And he sware* unto him.
Lev. 5: 4. if a soul *swear*,
6: 5(5:24). *he hath sworn* falsely;
19:12. *ye shall* not *swear* by my name falsely,
Nu. 32:10. *and he sware*, saying,
Deu 1:34. the Lord...was wroth, *and sware*,
4:21. *and sware* that I should not go over
6:13. *shalt swear* by his name.
10:20. *swear* by his name.
Jos. 9:15. the princes of the congregation *sware*
14: 9. *And* Moses *sware* on that day,
1Sa.19: 6. *and* Saul *sware*, (As) the Lord liveth,
20: 3. *And* David *sware* moreover,
24:22(23). *And* David *sware* unto Saul.
28:10. *And* Saul *sware* to her by the Lord,
2Sa. 3:35. *And* when...David *sware*, saying,
19:23(24). *And* the king *sware* unto him.
1K. 1:29. *And* the king *sware*,
51. *Let* king Solomon *swear*
2: 8. *and I sware* to him by the Lord,
23. *Then* king Solomon *sware*
2K. 25:24. *And* Gedaliah *sware* to them,
2Ch 15:14. *And they sware* unto the Lord
Ezr.10: 5. to this word. *And they sware*.
Isa. 45:23. every knee shall bow, every tongue *shall swear*.
65:16. *shall swear* by the God of truth;
Jer. 5: 2. surely *they swear* falsely.
7. *sworn* by (them that are) no gods:
38:16. *So* Zedekiah the king *sware*
40: 9. *And* Gedaliah the son of Ahikam...*sware*
Eze.16: 8. *yea, I sware* unto thee,
Dan12: 7. *and sware* by him that liveth for ever
Hos. 4:15. neither go ye up to Beth-aven, nor *swear*,

NIPHAL.—*Participle.*

Ps. 63:11(12). every one *that sweareth* by him
Ecc. 9: 2. *he that sweareth*, as (he) that feareth an
Isa. 19:18. *and swear* to the Lord of hosts;
48: 1. *which swear* by the name of the Lord,
65:16. *and he that sweareth* in the earth
Am. 8:14. *They that swear* by the sin of Samaria,
Zep. 1: 5. them that worship (and) *that swear* by the Lord, *and that swear* by Malcham;
Zec. 5: 3. every one *that sweareth* shall be cut off
4. *him that sweareth* falsely
Mal. 3: 5. *and against* false *swearers*,

* HIPHIL.—*Preterite.* *

Gen50: 5. My father *made me swear*,
6. according as *he made thee swear*.
Ex. 13:19. *he had* straitly *sworn* the children of Israel,
Nu. 5:19. *And* the priest *shall charge* her *by an oath*,
21. *Then* the priest *shall charge* the woman *with an oath*
Jos. 2:17. *thou hast made us swear*.
20. *thou hast made us to swear*.

1Sa.14:28. Thy father straitly *charged* the people *with an oath,*
1K. 2:42. *Did I* not *make thee to swear*
18:10. *he took an oath* of the kingdom
2Ch 36:13. *had made him swear* by God:
Cant.2: 7 & 3:5. *I charge* (marg. *adjure*) you, O ye daughters of Jerusalem,
5: 8. *I charge* you, O daughters of Jerusalem,
9. that *thou dost* so *charge us?*
8: 4. *I charge* you, O daughters of Jerusalem,

HIPHIL.—*Infinitive.*

Ex. 13:19. he had *straitly* sworn (lit. *causing to swear* he had caused to swear)
1Sa.14:27. *when* his father *charged* the people *with the oath:*
28. Thy father *straitly* charged the people with an oath,
20:17. Jonathan *caused* David *to swear*

HIPHIL.—*Future.*

Gen24: 3. *And I will make thee swear* by the Lord,
37. *And* my master *made me swear,*
50:25. *And* Joseph *took an oath of* the children
Jos. 6:26. *And* Joshua *adjured* (them) at that time,
23: 7. nor *cause to swear* (by them),
2K. 11: 4. *and took an oath* of them in the house
Ezr.10: 5. *and made* the chief priests,...*to swear*
Neh 5:12. called the priests, *and took an oath of them,*
13:25. *and made them swear* by God, (saying),
Jer. 5: 7. *when I had fed* them *to the full,* [or, *when I adjured* them]

HIPHIL.—*Participle.*

1K. 22:16. How many times *shall* I *adjure thee*
2Ch 18:15. How many times *shall* I *adjure thee*

7651 שֶׁבַע *sheh'-vag*, f. & שִׁבְעָה *shiv-gāh'*, m. adj. num.

Gen 4:24. truly Lamech seventy *and seven*fold.
5: 7. after he begat Enos eight hundred and *seven* years,
25. Methuselah lived an hundred eighty and *seven* years, and begat
26. after he begat Lamech *seven* hundred eighty and two years,
31. all the days of Lamech were *seven* hundred seventy *and seven* years:
7: 2. thou shalt take to thee *by sevens,* (marg. *seven seven*)
3. Of fowls also of the air *by sevens,* (lit. *id.*)
4. For yet *seven* days, and I will cause
10. it came to pass *after seven* days, (marg. or, the *seventh* day)
11. the second month, the *seven*teenth
8: 4. *on* the *seven*teenth day of the month,
10,12. he stayed yet other *seven* days;
14. *on* the *seven* and twentieth day of the
11:21. after he begat Serug two hundred and *seven* years,
21:28. Abraham set *seven* ewe lambs
29. What (mean) these *seven* ewe lambs
30. For (these) *seven* ewe lambs shalt thou
23: 1. And Sarah was an hundred *and seven* and
25:17. these (are) the years of...Ishmael, an hundred and thirty *and seven* years:
26:33. And he called it *Shebah:* (marg. *An oath*)
29:18. I will serve thee *seven* years for Rachel
20. Jacob served *seven* years for Rachel;
27. shalt serve with me yet *seven* other years.
30. and served with him yet *seven* other years.
31:23. pursued after him *seven* days' journey;
33: 3. bowed himself to the ground *seven* times,
37: 2. Joseph, (being) *seven*teen years old,
41: 2. out of the river *seven* well favoured kine
3. *seven* other kine came up after them
4. did eat up the *seven* well favoured
5. *seven* ears of corn came up upon
6. *seven* thin ears and blasted
7. (seven) thin ears devoured the *seven* rank
18. there came up out of the river *seven* kine,
19. *seven* other kine came up after them,
20. did eat up the first *seven* fat kine:
22. *seven* ears came up in one stalk,
23. *seven* ears, withered, thin, (and) blasted
24. the thin ears devoured the *seven* good

Gen41:26. The *seven* good kine (are) *seven* years; *and* the *seven* good ears (are) *seven* years:
27. And the *seven* thin and ill favoured kine that came up after them (are) *seven* years; *and* the *seven* empty ears blasted with the east wind shall be *seven* years
29. there come *seven* years of great plenty
30. there shall arise after them *seven* years
34. of Egypt *in* the *seven* plenteous years.
36. *against* the *seven* years of famine,
47. And *in* the *seven* plenteous years
48. all the food of the *seven* years,
53. And the *seven* years of plenteousness,
54. the *seven* years of dearth began
46:25. all the souls (were) *seven.*
47:28. Jacob lived in the land...*seven*teen years: so the whole age of Jacob was an hundred forty and *seven* years.
50:10. made a mourning for his father *seven* days.
Ex. 2:16. the priest of Midian had *seven* daughters:
6:16. the years of the life of Levi (were) an hundred thirty and *seven* years.
20. an hundred and thirty and *seven*
7:25. And *seven* days were fulfilled,
12:15. *Seven* days shall ye eat unleavened bread;
19. *Seven* days shall there be no leaven
13: 6. *Seven* days thou shalt eat unleavened
7. Unleavened bread shall be eaten *seven*
22:30(29). *seven* days it shall be with his dam;
23:15. shalt eat unleavened bread *seven* days,
25:37. thou shalt make the *seven* lamps
29:30. priest in his stead shall put them on *seven*
35. *seven* days shalt thou consecrate
37. *Seven* days thou shalt make an atonement
34:18. *Seven* days thou shalt eat unleavened
37:23. And he made his *seven* lamps,
38:24. *and seven* hundred and thirty shekels,
25. *and* a thousand *seven* hundred and three-score and fifteen shekels, after the shekel
28. thousand *seven* hundred seventy and five
Lev. 4: 6. and sprinkle of the blood *seven* times
17. and sprinkle (it) *seven* times
8:11. sprinkled thereof upon the altar *seven*
33. of the congregation (in) *seven* days,
— *seven* days shall he consecrate you.
35. day and night *seven* days,
12: 2. she shall be unclean *seven* days;
13: 4. shut up (him that hath) the plague *seven*
5, 21, 26. the priest shall shut him up *seven*
31. the plague of the scall *seven* days:
33. (him that hath) the scall *seven* days more:
50. shut up (it that hath) the plague *seven*
54. he shall shut it up *seven* days more:
14: 7. cleansed from the leprosy *seven* times,
8. tarry abroad out of his tent *seven* days.
16. sprinkle of the oil with his finger *seven*
27. in his left hand *seven* times
38. shut up the house *seven* days:
51. and sprinkle the house *seven* times:
15:13. he shall number to himself *seven* days
19. she shall be put apart *seven* days:
24. he shall be unclean *seven* days;
28. she shall number to herself *seven* days,
16:14. sprinkle of the blood with his finger *seven*
19. upon it with his finger *seven* times,
22:27. it shall be *seven* days under the dam;
23: 6. *seven* days ye must eat unleavened
8. made by fire unto the Lord *seven* days:
15. *seven* sabbaths shall be complete:
18. *seven* lambs without blemish
34. the feast of tabernacles (for) *seven* days
36. *Seven* days ye shall offer an offering
39. a feast unto the Lord *seven* days: on the
40. rejoice before the Lord your God *seven*
41. feast unto the Lord *seven* days in the year.
42. Ye shall dwell in booths *seven* days;
25: 8. thou shalt number *seven* sabbaths of years unto thee, *seven* times *seven* years; and the space of the *seven* sabbaths of years
26:18. *seven times* more for your sins.
21. I will bring *seven times* more plagues
24. yet *seven times* for your sins.
28. chastise you *seven times* for your sins.
Nu. 1:31. of the tribe of Zebulun, (were) fifty and *seven* thousand and four hundred.
39. of the tribe of Dan, (were) threescore and two thousand *and seven* hundred.

Nu. 2: 8. that were numbered thereof, (were) fifty and *seven* thousand and four hundred.
26. those that were numbered of them, (were) threescore and two thousand *and seven* hundred.
31. numbered in the camp of Dan (were) an hundred thousand and fifty *and seven* thousand and 600.
3:22. those that were numbered of them (were) *seven* thousand and five hundred.
4:36. numbered of them by their families were two thousand *seven* hundred and fifty.
8: 2. *seven* lamps shall give light
12:14. be ashamed *seven* days? let her be shut out from the camp *seven* days,
15. was shut out from the camp *seven* days:
13:22. Hebron was built *seven* years before Zoan
16:49(17:14). they that died in the plague were fourteen thousand *and seven* hundred,
19: 4. before the tabernacle of the congregation *seven* times:
11. body of any man shall be unclean *seven*
14. that (is) in the tent, shall be unclean *seven*
16. or a grave, shall be unclean *seven* days.
23: 1. Build me here *seven* altars, and prepare me here *seven* oxen *and seven* rams.
4. I have prepared *seven* altars,
14. and built *seven* altars, and offered
29. Build me here *seven* altars, and prepare me here *seven* bullocks *and seven* rams.
26: 7. that were numbered of them were forty and three thousand *and seven* hundred and 30.
34. those that were numbered of them, fifty and two thousand *and seven* hundred.
51. numbered of the children of Israel, six hundred thousand and a thousand *seven* hundred and 30.
28:11. *seven* lambs of the first year without spot;
17. *seven* days shall unleavened bread be
19. *and seven* lambs of the first year:
21,29. *throughout* the *seven* lambs:
24. offer daily, throughout the *seven* days,
27. *seven* lambs of the first year;
29: 2,36. *seven* lambs of the first year without
4,10. *throughout* the *seven* lambs:
8. *seven* lambs of the first year;
12. keep a feast unto the Lord *seven* days:
32. on the seventh day *seven* bullocks,
31:19. abide without the camp *seven* days:
36. was in number three hundred thousand *and seven* and thirty thousand and 500.
43. (pertained unto) the congregation was three hundred thousand and thirty thousand (and) *seven* thousand and 500.
52. and of the captains of hundreds, was sixteen thousand *seven* hundred and fifty
Deu 7: 1. *seven* nations greater and mightier
15: 1. *seven* years thou shalt make a release.
9. The *seventh* year (lit. the year *seven*), the year of release,
16: 3. *seven* days shalt thou eat unleavened
4. in all thy coast *seven* days;
9. *Seven* weeks shalt thou number unto thee: begin to number the *seven* weeks
13. observe the feast of tabernacles *seven*
15. *Seven* days shalt thou keep a solemn feast
28: 7. *and* flee before thee *seven* ways.
25. *and* flee *seven* ways before them:
31:10. At the end of (every) *seven* years,
Jos. 6: 4. *And seven* priests shall bear before the ark *seven* trumpets of rams' horns: and the seventh day ye shall compass the city *seven* times,
6. *and* let *seven* priests bear *seven* trumpets
8. *that* the *seven* priests bearing the *seven*
13. *And seven* priests bearing *seven* trumpets
15. compassed the city after the same manner *seven* times: only on that day they compassed the city *seven* times.
18: 2. remained among the children of Israel *seven* tribes,
5. they shall divide it *into seven* parts:
6. describe the land (into) *seven* parts,
9. by cities *into seven* parts
Jud. 6: 1. into the hand of Midian *seven* years.
25. the second bullock of *seven* years old,
Jud. 8:14. and the elders thereof, (even) threescore *and seven*teen men.
26. golden earrings that he requested was a thousand *and seven* hundred (shekels)
12: 9. he judged Israel *seven* years.
14:12. declare it me within the *seven* days
17. she wept before him the *seven* days,
16: 7. If they bind me with *seven* green withs
8. brought up to her *seven* green withs
13. If thou weavest the *seven* locks
19. caused him to shave off the *seven* locks
20:15,16. *seven* hundred chosen men.
Ru. 4:15. which is better to thee *than seven* sons,
1Sa. 2: 5. so that the barren hath born *seven;*
6: 1. country of the Philistines *seven* months.
10: 8. *seven* days shalt thou tarry, till I come
11: 3. Give us *seven* days' respite,
13: 8. And he tarried *seven* days, according
16:10. Jesse made *seven of* his sons to pass
31:13. under a tree at Jabesh, and fasted *seven*
2Sa. 2:11. king in Hebron over the house of Judah was *seven* years and six months.
5: 5. In Hebron he reigned over Judah *seven* years and six months:
8: 4. And David took from him a thousand (chariots), *and seven* hundred horsemen,
10:18. and David slew (the men of) *seven* hundred chariots
21: 6. Let *seven* men of his sons be delivered
9. and *they* fell (all) *seven* together, (lit. *the seven of them*)
23:39. Uriah the Hittite: thirty *and seven* in all.
24:13. Shall *seven* years of famine come unto
1K. 2:11. *seven* years reigned he in Hebron,
6: 6. and the third (was) *seven* cubits broad:
38. So was he *seven* years in building it.
7:17. *seven* for the one chapiter, *and seven* for
8:65. *seven* days *and seven* days, (even) fourteen
11: 3. And he had *seven* hundred wives,
14:21. *and* he reigned *seven*teen years in
16:10. killed him, in the twenty *and seventh* year
15. In the twenty *and seventh* year of Asa king of Judah did Zimri reign *seven* days
18:43. And he said, Go again *seven* times.
19:18. Yet I have left (me) *seven* thousand in
20:15. all the children of Israel, (being) *seven* thousand.
29. one over against the other *seven* days.
30. a wall fell upon twenty *and seven* thousand
22:51(52). over Israel in Samaria the *seven*teenth
2K. 3: 9. fetched a compass of *seven* days' journey:
26. took with him *seven* hundred men that
4:35. and the child sneezed *seven* times,
5:10. Go and wash in Jordan *seven* times,
14. and dipped himself *seven* times in Jordan,
8: 1. shall also come upon the land *seven* years.
2. in the land of the Philistines *seven* years.
3. at the *seven* years' end, that the woman
11:21(12:1). *Seven* years old (was) Jehoash when
12: 1(2). *seventh* year of Jehu Jehoash began
13: 1. over Israel in Samaria, (and reigned) *seven*teen years.
10. In the thirty *and seventh* year of Joash
15: 1. In the twenty *and seventh* year of Jeroboam
16: 1. In the *seven*teenth year of Pekah
24:16. the men of might, (even) *seven* thousand,
25: 8. And in the fifth month, *on the seventh*
27. to pass in the *seven and* thirtieth year of
— on the *seven* and twentieth (day) of the
1Ch 3: 4. Hebron; and there he reigned *seven* years
24. And the sons of Elioenai...*seven.*
5:13. their brethren of the house of their fathers ...*seven.*
18. four and forty thousand *seven* hundred and threescore, that went out to the war.
7: 5. reckoned in all by their genealogies fourscore *and seven* thousand.
11. *seven*teen thousand and two hundred (soldiers), fit to go out for war
9:13. heads of the house of their fathers, a thousand *and seven* hundred and threescore;
25. (were) to come *after seven* days
10:12. the oak in Jabesh, and fasted *seven* days.
12:25. mighty men of valour for the war, *seven* thousand and one hundred.
27. leader of the Aaronites, and with him (were) three thousand *and seven* hundred:

1Ch 12:34. and with them with shield and spear thirty *and seven* thousand.
15:26. they offered *seven* bullocks *and seven* rams.
18: 4. *and seven* thousand horsemen, and twenty
19:18. slew of the Syrians *seven* thousand (men)
24:15. *The seven*teenth to Hezir,
25:24. *The seven*teenth to Joshbekashah,
26:30. a thousand *and seven* hundred, (were) officers among them
32. (were) two thousand *and seven* hundred chief fathers,
29: 4. *and seven* thousand talents of refined silver,
27. *seven* years reigned he in Hebron,
2Ch 7: 8. Solomon kept the feast *seven* days,
9. kept the dedication of the altar *seven* days, and the feast *seven* days.
12:13. *and* he reigned *seven*teen years in
13: 9. with a young bullock and *seven* rams,
15:11. of the spoil (which) they had brought, *seven* hundred oxen and *seven* thousand
17:11. *seven* thousand *and seven* hundred rams, and *seven* thousand *and seven* hundred he goats.
24: 1. Joash (was) *seven* years old when he
26:13. under their hand (was) an army, three hundred thousand *and seven* thousand and five hundred,
29:21. they brought *seven* bullocks, and *seven* rams, and *seven* lambs, and *seven*
30:21. the feast of unleavened bread *seven* days
22. did eat throughout the feast *seven* days,
23. took counsel to keep other *seven* days: and they kept (other) *seven* days
24. a thousand bullocks *and seven* thousand sheep;
35:17. the feast of unleavened bread *seven* days.
Ezr. 2: 5. The children of Arah, *seven* hundred seventy and five.
9. The children of Zaccai, *seven* hundred and threescore.
25. The children of Kirjath-arim,...*seven* hundred and forty and three.
33. The children of Lod,...*seven* hundred twenty and five.
38. The children of Pashur, a thousand two hundred forty *and seven.*
39. The children of Harim, a thousand *and seven*teen.
65. and their maids, of whom (there were) *seven* thousand three hundred thirty *and seven:*
66. Their horses (were) *seven* hundred thirty and six;
67. (their) asses, six thousand *seven* hundred and twenty.
6:22. the feast of unleavened bread *seven* days
7: 7. in the *seventh* year (lit. the year *seven*) of
8:35. seventy *and seven* lambs, twelve he goats
Neh 7:14. The children of Zaccai, *seven* hundred and threescore.
18. The children of Adonikam, six hundred threescore *and seven.*
19. The children of Bigvai, two thousand threescore *and seven.*
29. The men of Kirjath-jearim,...*seven* hundred forty and three.
37. The children of Lod,....*seven* hundred twenty and one.
41. The children of Pashur, a thousand two hundred forty *and seven.*
42. The children of Harim, a thousand and *seven*teen.
67. their maidservants, of whom (there were) *seven* thousand three hundred thirty *and seven:*
68. Their horses, *seven* hundred thirty and six:
69. six thousand *seven* hundred and twenty asses.
72. two thousand pound of silver, and threescore *and seven* priests' garments.
8:18. they kept the feast *seven* days;
Est. 1: 1. from India even unto Ethiopia, (over) an hundred and *seven* and twenty provinces:
5. both unto great and small, *seven* days,
10. the *seven* chamberlains that served
14. the *seven* princes of Persia and Media,
2: 9. and *seven* maidens, (which were) meet
Est. 2:16. in the *seventh* year of his reign.
8: 9. from India unto Ethiopia, an hundred twenty and *seven* provinces,
9:30. to the hundred twenty and *seven* provinces
Job 1: 2. there were born unto him *seven* sons
3. substance also was *seven* thousand sheep,
2:13. the ground *seven* days *and seven* nights,
5:19. *yea, in seven* there shall no evil touch thee.
42: 8. take unto you now *seven* bullocks *and seven* rams,
Ps. 119:164. *Seven times* a day do I praise thee
Pro. 6:16. *yea, seven* (are) an abomination unto him:
9: 1. she hath hewn out her *seven* pillars:
24:16. a just (man) falleth *seven times,*
26:16. *than seven* men that can render a reason.
25. (there are) *seven* abominations in his
Ecc. 11: 2. Give a portion *to seven,*
Isa. 4: 1. *seven* women shall take hold of
11:15. and shall smite it *in* the *seven* streams,
30:26. as the light of *seven* days,
Jer. 15: 9. She that hath borne *seven* languisheth:
32: 9. the money, (even) *seven*teen shekels
34:14. At the end of *seven* years let ye go
52:25. *and seven* men of them that were near
28. in the *seventh* year (lit. the year *seven*) three thousand Jews
30. carried away captive of the Jews *seven* hundred forty and five persons:
31. it came to pass in the *seven* and thirtieth
Eze. 3:15. there astonished among them *seven* days.
16. it came to pass at the end of *seven* days,
29:17. it came to pass in the *seven and* twentieth
30:20. *in the seventh* (day) of the month,
39: 9. shall burn them with fire *seven* years:
12. And *seven* months shall the house of
14. after the end of *seven* months
40:22. they went up unto it by *seven* steps;
26. And (there were) *seven* steps to go up to
41: 3. the breadth of the door, *seven* cubits.
43:25. *Seven* days shalt thou prepare
26. *Seven* days shall they purge
44:26. they shall reckon unto him *seven* days.
45:20. And so thou shalt do *the seventh*
23. *And seven* days of the feast he shall
— *seven* bullocks *and seven* rams without blemish daily the *seven* days;
25. shall he do the like in the feast of the *seven*
Dan 9:25. unto the Messiah the Prince (shall be) *seven* weeks,
Mic. 5: 5(4). we raise against him *seven* shepherds,
Zec. 3: 9. upon one stone (shall be) *seven* eyes:
4: 2. *and* his *seven* lamps thereon, *and seven* pipes to the *seven* lamps,
10. hand of Zerubbabel (with) those *seven;*

שִׁבְעָה *shiv-ngāh'*, Ch. adj. num. 7655

Ezr. 7:14. *and* of his *seven* counsellors,
Dan 3:19. heat the furnace one *seven times*
4:16(13). *and* let *seven times* pass over him.
23(20). till *seven times* pass over him;
25(22), 32(29). *and seven times* shall pass

שִׁבְעִים *shiv-ngeem'*, adj. num. 7657

Gen 4:24. truly Lamech *seventy* and sevenfold.
5:12. And Cainan lived *seventy* years,
31. the days of Lamech were seven hundred *seventy* and seven
11:26. Terah lived *seventy* years, and begat
12: 4. Abram (was) *seventy and* five years old
25: 7. of Abraham's life which he lived, an hundred *threescore and* fifteen
46:27. the souls...(were) *threescore and ten.*
50: 3. mourned for him *threescore and ten* days.
Ex. 1: 5. of the loins of Jacob were *seventy* souls:
15:27. *and threescore and ten* palm trees:
24: 1, 9. *and seventy* of the elders of Israel;
38:25. and a thousand seven hundred *and threescore* and fifteen shekels, after the
28. And of the thousand seven hundred *seventy and* five (shekels) he made hooks
29. the brass of the offering (was) *seventy*
Nu. 1:27. of the tribe of Judah, (were) *threescore and* fourteen thousand and six hundred.
2: 4. numbered of them, (were) *threescore and* fourteen thousand and six hundred.

Nu. 3:43. of them, were twenty and two thousand two hundred and *threescore and* thir*teen*.
46. redeemed of the two hundred and *threescore and* thirteen of the firstborn
7:13, 19, 25, 31, 37, 43, 49, 55, 61, 67, 73, 79. *seventy* shekels, after the shekel of the
85. an hundred and thirty (shekels), each bowl *seventy:*
11:16. *seventy* men of the elders of Israel,
24. gathered the *seventy* men of the elders
25. and gave (it) unto the *seventy* elders:
26:22. that were numbered of them, *threescore and* six*teen* thousand and five hundred.
31:32. had caught, was six hundred thousand and *seventy* thousand and five thousand
33. *threescore and* twelve (lit. *seventy* two) thousand beeves,
37. tribute of the sheep was six hundred and *threescore and* fif*teen*.
38. the Lord's tribute (was) *threescore and* twelve. (lit. *seventy* two)
33: 9. twelve fountains of water, *and threescore and ten* palm trees;
Deu10:22. into Egypt *with threescore and ten* persons;
Jud. 1: 7. Adoni-bezek said, *Threescore and ten*
8:14. and the elders thereof, (even) *threescore* and seven*teen* men.
30. Gideon had *threescore and ten* sons of his
9: 2. the sons of Jerubbaal, (which are) *threescore and ten* persons,
4. they gave him *threescore and ten* (pieces)
5. the sons of Jerubbaal, (being) *threescore and ten* persons,
18. slain his sons, *threescore and ten* persons,
24. cruelty (done) to the *threescore and ten*
56. in slaying his *seventy* brethren:
12:14. that rode on *threescore and ten* ass colts:
1Sa. 6:19. he smote of the people fifty thousand and *threescore and ten* men:
2Sa.24:15. even to Beer-sheba *seventy* thousand men.
1K. 5:15(29). Solomon had *threescore and ten* thousand that bare burdens,
2K. 10: 1. And Ahab had *seventy* sons in Samaria.
6. Now the king's sons, (being) *seventy*
7. took the king's sons, and slew *seventy*
1Ch 21: 5. Judah (was) four hundred *threescore and ten* thousand men that drew sword.
14. there fell of Israel *seventy* thousand men.
2Ch 2: 2(1). told out *threescore and ten* thousand
18(17). *threescore and ten* thousand of them
29:32. was *threescore and ten* bullocks,
36:21. she kept sabbath, to fulfil *threescore and ten* years.
Ezr. 2: 3. The children of Parosh, two thousand an hundred *seventy* and two.
4. The children of Shephatiah, three hundred *seventy* and two.
5. The children of Arah, seven hundred *seventy and* five.
36. the children of Jedaiah, of the house of Jeshua, nine hundred *seventy* and three.
40. children of Hodaviah, *seventy* and four.
8: 7. the son of Athaliah, and with him *seventy*
14. Zabbud, and with them *seventy* males.
35. *seventy* and seven lambs, twelve he goats
Neh 7: 8. The children of Parosh, two thousand an hundred *seventy* and two.
9. The children of Shephatiah, three hundred *seventy* and two.
39. of Jedaiah, of the house of Jeshua, nine hundred *seventy* and three.
43. the children of Hodevah, *seventy* and four.
11:19. their brethren that kept the gates, (were) an hundred *seventy* and two.
Est. 9:16. of their foes *seventy and* five thousand,
Ps. 90:10. our years (are) *threescore* years *and ten;*
Isa. 23:15. Tyre shall be forgotten *seventy* years, according to the days of one king: after the end of *seventy* years
17. come to pass after the end of *seventy*
Jer. 25:11. shall serve the king of Babylon *seventy*
12. when *seventy* years are accomplished,
29:10. after *seventy* years be accomplished
Eze. 8:11. *And* there stood before them *seventy* men
41:12. toward the west (was) *seventy* cubits
Dan 9: 2. that he would accomplish *seventy* years
24. *Seventy* weeks are determined

Zec. 1:12. hast had indignation these *threescore and ten* years?
7: 5. even those *seventy* years, did ye at all

שִׁבְעָנָה *shiv-"gāh'-nāh*, adj. num. 7658

Job 42:13. He had also *seven* sons and three

שִׁבְעָתַיִם *shiv-"gāh-thah'-yim*, dual. 7659

Gen 4:15. vengeance shall be taken on him *sevenfold*.
24. If Cain shall be avenged *sevenfold*,
2Sa.21: 9. (כתיב) and they fell (all) *seven* together,
Ps. 12: 6(7). furnace of earth, purified *seven times*.
79:12. render unto our neighbours *sevenfold*
Pro. 6:31. he shall restore *sevenfold;*
Isa. 30:26. the light of the sun shall be *sevenfold*,

שָׁבַץ [*shāh-vatz'*]. 7660

* PIEL.—*Preterite.* *

Ex. 28:39. *And thou shalt embroider* the coat

* PUAL.—*Participle.* *

Ex. 28:20. *they shall be set* in gold

שָׁבָץ *shāh-vāhtz'*, m. 7661

2Sa. 1: 9. *anguish* is come upon me, (marg. or, *my coat of mail*, or, *my embroidered coat* hindereth me)

שְׁבַק [*sh'vak*], Ch. 7662

* P'AL.—*Infinitive.* *

Dan 4:26(23). whereas they commanded *to leave*

P'AL.—*Imperative.*

Ezr. 6: 7. *Let* the work of this house of God *alone;*
Dan 4:15(12). Nevertheless *leave* the stump
23(20). yet *leave* the stump of the roots

* ITHPAEL.—*Future.* *

Dan 2:44. the kingdom *shall* not *be left* to other

שָׁבַר *shāh-var'*. 7665

* KAL.—*Preterite.* *

Lev.26:19. *And I will break* the pride of your power;
1K. 13:28. nor *torn* (marg. *broken*) the ass.
Ps. 69:20(21). Reproach *hath broken* my heart;
105:16. *he brake* the whole staff of bread.
Isa. 14: 5. The Lord *hath broken* the staff
30:14. *And he shall break it* as the breaking
Jer. 2:20. *I have broken* thy yoke,
5: 5. these *have* altogether *broken* the yoke,
19:10. *Then shalt thou break* the bottle
28: 2. *I have broken* the yoke of the king of
13. *Thou hast broken* the yokes of wood;
48:38. *I have broken* Moab
Eze. 5:16. *and will break* your staff of bread:
14:13. *and will break* the staff of the bread
27:26. the east wind *hath broken thee*
30:21. *I have broken* the arm of Pharaoh
22. *and will break* his arms,
24. *but I will break* Pharaoh's arms,
Hos. 1: 5. *that I will break* the bow of Israel
Am. 1: 5. *I will break also* the bar of Damascus,

KAL.—*Infinitive.*

Gen19: 9. came near *to break* the door.
Lev.26:26. *when I have broken* the staff of your bread.
Isa. 14:25. *That I will break* the Assyrian
Jer. 28:12. *had broken* the yoke from off
Lam.1:15. *to crush* my young men:
Eze.30:18. *when I shall break* there the yokes
34:27. *when I have broken* the bands

KAL.—*Imperative.*

Ps. 10:15. *Break thou* the arm of the wicked
Jer. 17:18. *destroy them* (marg. *break them*) with double destruction.

KAL.—*Future.*

Ex. 12:46. neither *shall ye break* a bone
Lev.11:33. every earthen vessel, ..*ye shall break*

Lev.26:13. *and I have broken* the bands of your yoke,
Nu. 9:12. leave none of it unto the morning, nor *break* any
Jud. 7:20. blew the trumpets, *and brake* the pitchers,
1K. 13:26. the lion, *which hath torn him*, (marg. *broken him*)
Job 38:10. *And brake up* for it my decreed (place),
Ps.104:11. the wild asses *quench* (marg. *break*) their thirst.
Pro.25:15. a soft tongue *breaketh* the bone.
Isa. 42: 3. A bruised reed *shall he* not *break*,
Jer. 19:11. Even so *will I break* this people
— as (one) *breaketh* a potter's vessel,
28: 4. *I will break* the yoke of the king of
10. took the yoke...*and brake it*.
11. Even so *will I break* the yoke
30: 8. *I will break* his yoke
Dan11:26. of the portion of his meat *shall destroy him*, (lit. *break him*)
Hos. 2:18(20). *I will break* the bow and the sword
Nah 1:13. now *will I break* his yoke

KAL.—*Participle*. Poel.

Neh 2:13. and *viewed* (lit. was *viewing*) the walls of Jerusalem [see also שָׂבַר]
15. went I up...and *viewed* the wall, [id.]
Ps. 29: 5. The voice of the Lord *breaketh*
Jer. 49:35. I *will break* the bow of Elam,
Eze. 4:16. I *will break* the staff of bread

KAL.—*Participle*. Paül.

Lev.22:22. Blind, or *broken*, or maimed,
Ps.147: 3. He healeth *the broken in* heart,

* NIPHAL.—*Preterite*. *

Ex. 22:10(9). die, *or be hurt*, or driven away,
14(13). if a man borrow (ought)...*and it be hurt*,
1K. 22:48(49). the ships *were broken* at Ezion-geber.
2Ch 14:13(12). *they were destroyed* (marg. *broken*) before the Lord,
Ps. 34:20(21). not one of them *is broken*.
124: 7. the snare *is broken*,
Isa. 8:15. shall stumble, and fall, *and be broken*,
14:29. the rod of him that smote thee *is broken*:
24:10. The city of confusion *is broken down*:
28:13. that they might go, and fall...*and be broken*,
Jer. 14:17. the virgin daughter of my people *is broken*
22:20. all thy lovers *are destroyed*.
23: 9. Mine heart within me *is broken*
48: 4. Moab *is destroyed*;
17. How *is* the strong staff *broken*,
25. his arm *is broken*,
51:30. her bars *are broken*.
Eze. 6: 4. *and* your images *shall be broken*:
6. *and* your idols *may be broken*
9. *I am broken* with their whorish heart,
26: 2. *she is broken* (that was) the gates of the people:
30: 8. *and* (when) all her helpers *shall be destroyed*. (marg. *broken*)
Dan 8: 8. the great horn *was broken*;

NIPHAL.—*Infinitive*.

Jon. 1: 4. the ship was like *to be broken*.

NIPHAL.—*Future*.

Lev. 6:28(21). the earthen vessel...*shall be broken*:
15:12. which hath the issue, *shall be broken*:
1Sa. 4:18. *and* his neck *brake*,
2Ch 20:37. *And* the ships *were broken*,
Job 24:20. *and* wickedness *shall be broken* as a tree.
31:22. let...mine arm *be broken* from the bone.
38:15. the high arm *shall be broken*.
Ps. 37:15. their bows *shall be broken*.
17. the arms of the wicked *shall be broken*:
Pro. 6:15. suddenly *shall he be broken*
29: 1. *shall* suddenly *be destroyed*, and that
Ecc.12: 6. *or* the pitcher *be broken* at the fountain,
Isa. 27:11. *they shall be broken off*:
Jer. 50:23. the hammer of the whole earth cut asunder *and broken!*
51: 8. Babylon is suddenly fallen *and destroyed*:
Eze.29: 7. when they leaned upon thee, *thou brakest*,
31:12. *and* his boughs *are broken*
32:28. *thou shalt be broken* in the midst of
Dan 8:25. *he shall be broken* without hand.
11: 4. his kingdom *shall be broken*,
Dan11:20. within few days *he shall be destroyed*,
22. *and shall be broken*; yea, also

NIPHAL.—*Participle*.

Ps. 34:18(19). nigh *unto them that are* of a *broken*
51:17(19). The sacrifices of God (are) a *broken* spirit: a *broken* and a contrite heart,
Isa. 61: 1. to bind up the *broken*hearted,
Jer. 2:13. *broken* cisterns, that can hold no water.
Eze.27:34. *thou shalt be broken* by the seas
30:22. *that which was broken*;
34: 4. *neither* have ye bound up *that which was broken*,
16. will bind up *that which was broken*,
Dan 8:22. *Now that being broken*, whereas
Zec.11:16. *nor* heal *that that is broken*,

* PIEL.—*Preterite*. *

Ex. 9:25. *brake* every tree of the field.
34: 1. the first tables, which *thou brakest*.
Deu10: 2. the first tables which *thou brakest*,
12: 3. *and break* their pillars,
2K. 11:18. his images *brake they in pieces*
18: 4. *and brake* the images,
23:14. *and he brake*...the images, and cut down the groves,
25:13. *did* the Chaldees *break in pieces*,
2Ch 23:17. and *brake* his altars and his images *in pieces*,
34: 4. the molten images, *he brake in pieces*,
Ps. 3: 7(8). *thou hast broken* the teeth of the
74:13. *thou brakest* the heads of the dragons
76: 3(4). There *brake he* the arrows of the bow,
107:16. *he hath broken* the gates of brass,
Isa. 21: 9. the graven images...*he hath broken*
Jer. 43:13. *He shall break also* the images
52:17. the brasen sea...the Chaldeans *brake*,
Lam. 2: 9. destroyed *and broken* her bars:
3: 4. *he hath broken* my bones.

PIEL.—*Infinitive*.

Ex. 23:24. *and quite* break down (lit. *and breaking down* shalt break down)

PIEL.—*Future*.

Ex. 23:24. quite *break down* their images.
32:19. *and brake* them beneath the mount.
34:13. *break* their images,
Deu 7: 5. *break down* their images,
9:17. *and brake them* before your eyes.
2Ch 14: 3(2). *and brake down* the images,
31: 1. *and brake* the images in pieces,
Job 29:17. *And I brake* the jaws of the wicked,
Ps. 29: 5. *yea*, the Lord *breaketh* the cedars
46: 9(10). *he breaketh* the bow,
48: 7(8). *Thou breakest* the ships of Tarshish
105:33. *and brake* the trees of their coasts.
Isa. 38:13. so *will he break* all my bones:
45: 2. *I will break in pieces* the gates of brass,
Dan 8: 7. *and brake* his two horns:

PIEL.—*Participle*.

1K. 19:11. *and brake in pieces* the rocks

* HIPHIL.—*Future*. *

Isa. 66: 9. *Shall* I *bring to the birth*,

* HOPHAL.—*Preterite*. *

Jer. 8:21. For the hurt of the daughter of my people *am I hurt*;

שָׁבַר [*shāh-var'*]. 7666

* KAL.—*Infinitive*. *

Gen41:57. all countries came...*for to buy* (corn);
42: 3. Joseph's ten brethren went down *to buy*
5. the sons of Israel came *to buy* (corn)
7. From the land of Canaan *to buy* food.
10. *to buy* food are thy servants come.
43:20. we came indeed down...*to buy* food:
22. other money have we brought...*to buy* food:

KAL.—*Imperative*.

Gen42: 2. *and buy* for us from thence;
43: 2. *buy* us a little food.
44:25. *buy* us a little food.
Isa. 55: 1. come ye, *buy*, and eat; yea, come, *buy* wine and milk

KAL.—*Future.*

Gen41:56. *and sold* unto the Egyptians ;
43: 4. we will go down *and buy* thee food:
Deu 2: 6. *Ye shall buy* meat of them

KAL.—*Participle.* Poel.

Gen47:14. for the corn *which* they *bought :*

* HIPHIL.—*Future.* *

Deu 2:28. *Thou shalt sell me* meat
Am. 8: 5. *that we may sell* corn ?
6. and *sell* the refuse of the wheat ?

HIPHIL.—*Participle.*

Gen42: 6. he (it was) *that sold* to all the people
Pro.11:26. upon the head *of him that selleth* (it).

7667 שֵׁבֶר *shĕh'-ver* & שֶׁבֶר *sheh'-ver*, m.

Lev.21:19. Or a man that is *broken*footed, or *broken*handed,
24:20. *Breach* for *breach*,
Jud. 7:15. the dream, and *the interpretation* (marg. *breaking*) *thereof*,
Job 41:25(17). *by reason of breakings* they purify
Ps. 60: 2(4). heal *the breaches thereof ;*
Pro.15: 4. *a breach* in the spirit.
16:18. Pride (goeth) before *destruction*,
17:19. he that exalteth his gate seeketh *destruction.*
18:12. Before *destruction* the heart of man is
Isa. 1:28. *And the destruction* (marg. *breaking*) *of* the
15: 5. a cry of *destruction.* (marg. *id.*)
30:13. *whose breaking* cometh suddenly
14. *as the breaking of* the potters' vessel
26. the Lord bindeth up *the breach of*
51:19. desolation, *and destruction* (marg. *breaking*), and the famine,
59: 7. wasting *and destruction* (marg. *id.*) (are)
60:18. wasting *nor destruction*
65:14. *and* shall howl *for vexation* (marg. *breaking*) *of* spirit.
Jer. 4: 6. evil...*and a* great *destruction.* (marg. *breaking*)
20. *Destruction* upon *destruction* is cried ;
6: 1. evil...*and* great *destruction.*
14. *the hurt* (marg. *bruise*, or, *breach*) *of* the
8:11, 21. *the hurt of* the daughter of my people
10:19. Woe is me for *my hurt !*
14:17. my people is broken with *a* great *breach*,
30:12. *Thy bruise* (is) incurable,
15. Why criest thou for *thine affliction ?*
48: 3. spoiling *and* great *destruction.*
5. enemies have heard a cry of *destruction.*
50:22. A sound of battle...*and* of great *destruction.*
51:54. *and* great *destruction* from the land
Lam.2:11. *the destruction of* the daughter of my
13. *thy breach* (is) great like the sea:
3:47. desolation *and destruction.*
48. *the destruction of* the daughter of my
4:10. *in the destruction of* the daughter
Eze.32: 9. I shall bring *thy destruction*
Am. 6: 6. grieved for *the affliction* (marg. *breach*) *of*
Nah. 3:19. no healing *of thy bruise ;*
Zep. 1:10. *and* a great *crashing* from the hills.

7668 שֶׁבֶר *sheh'-ver*, m.

Gen42: 1. when Jacob saw that there was *corn*
2. I have heard that there is *corn* in Egypt:
19. carry *corn* for the famine
26. laded their asses with *the corn*,
43: 2. when they had eaten up *the corn*
44: 2. and his *corn* money.
47:14. *for the corn* which they bought:
Neh 10:31(32). ware or any *victuals*
Am. 8: 5. new moon be gone, that we may sell *corn ?*

7670 שִׁבָּרוֹן *shib-bāh-rōhn'*, m.

Jer. 17:18. destroy them with double *destruction.* (marg. *breach*)
Eze.21: 6(11). *with the breaking of* (thy) loins :

7672 שְׁבַשׁ [*sh'vash*], Ch.

* ITHPAEL.—*Participle.* *

Dan 5: 9. and his lords *were astonied.*

שָׁבַת *shāh-vath'*. 7673

* KAL.—*Preterite.* *

Gen 2: 3. *he had rested* from all his work
Ex. 31:17. on the seventh day *he rested*,
Lev.25: 2. *then shall* the land *keep* (marg. *rest*)
26:35. because *it did* not *rest*
2Ch 36:21. long as she lay desolate *she kept sabbath*,
Isa. 14: 4. How *hath* the oppressor *ceased !* the golden city *ceased !*
24: 8. The mirth of tabrets *ceaseth*,
— the joy of the harp *ceaseth.*
33: 8. the wayfaring man *ceaseth.*
Lam.5:14. The elders *have ceased* from the gate,
15. The joy of our heart *is ceased ;*

KAL.—*Future.*

Gen 2: 2. *and he rested* on the seventh day
8:22. and day and night *shall* not *cease.*
Ex. 16:30. *So* the people *rested* on the seventh day.
23:12 & 34:21. on the seventh day *thou shalt rest :*
34:21. in earing time and in harvest *thou shalt rest.*
Lev.23:32. from even unto even, *shall ye celebrate* (marg. *rest*) your sabbath.
26:34. then *shall* the land *rest*,
35. as it lieth desolate *it shall rest ;*
Jos. 5:12. *And* the manna *ceased* on the morrow
Neh 6: 3. why *should* the work *cease*,
Job 32: 1. *So* these three men *ceased* to answer
Pro.22:10. *yea*, strife and reproach *shall cease.*
Jer. 31:36. the seed of Israel also *shall cease*
Hos. 7: 4. (who) *ceaseth* from raising after

* NIPHAL.—*Preterite.* *

Isa. 17: 3. The fortress *also shall cease*
Eze. 6: 6. your idols may be broken *and cease*,
30:18 & 33:28. *and* the pomp of her strength *shall cease*

* HIPHIL.—*Preterite.* *

Ex. 5: 5. *and ye make* them *rest* from their burdens
Lev.26: 6. *and I will rid* (marg. *cause to cease*) evil
Jos. 22:25. *so shall* your children *make* our children *cease*
Ru. 4:14. *hath* not *left* thee (marg. *caused to cease* unto thee) this day without a kinsman,
2K. 23: 5. *And he put down* (marg. *caused to cease*) the idolatrous priests,
Neh 4:11(5). *and cause* the work *to cease.*
Ps. 89:44(45). *Thou hast made* his glory *to cease*,
119:119. *Thou puttest away* (marg. *causest to cease*)
Isa. 13:11. *and I will cause* the arrogancy of the proud *to cease*,
16:10. *I have made* (their vintage) shouting *to cease.*
21: 2. all the sighing...*have I made to cease.*
Jer. 7:34. *Then will I cause to cease* from the cities
36:29. *and shall cause to cease* from thence man
48:33. *I have caused* wine *to fail*
35. *Moreover I will cause to cease* in Moab,
Eze. 7:24. *I will also make* the pomp of the strong *to cease ;*
12:23. *I will make* this proverb *to cease*,
16:41. *and I will cause thee to cease*
23:27. *Thus will I make* thy lewdness *to cease*
48. *Thus will I cause* lewdness *to cease*
26:13. *And I will cause* the noise of thy songs *to cease ;*
30:10. *I will also make* the multitude of Egypt *to cease*
13. *and I will cause* (their) images *to cease*
34:10. *and cause them to cease* from feeding
25. *and will cause* the evil beasts *to cease*
Dan11:18. *shall cause* the reproach offered by him *to cease ;*
Hos. 1: 4. *and will cause to cease* the kingdom
2:11(13). *I will also cause* all her mirth *to cease*

HIPHIL.—*Infinitive.*

Ps. 8: 2(3). *that thou mightest still* (lit. *cause to cease*) the enemy
Am. 8: 4. *even to make* the poor of the land *to fail*, (lit. *to cease*)

HIPHIL.—*Imperative.*

Isa. 30:11. *cause* the Holy One of Israel *to cease*

HIPHIL.—*Future.*

Ex. 12:15. *ye shall put away* (lit. *cause to cease*) leaven
Lev. 2:13. neither *shalt thou suffer* the salt...*to be lacking* (lit. *to cease*)
Deu 32:26. *I would make* the remembrance of them *to cease*
2K. 23:11. *And he took away* (lit. *caused to cease*) the
2Ch 16: 5. *and let* his work *cease.*
Pro. 18:18. The lot *causeth* contentions *to cease,*
Dan 9:27. *shall cause* the sacrifice and the oblation *to cease,*

HIPHIL.—*Participle.*

Ps. 46: 9(10). *He maketh* wars *to cease*
Jer. 16: 9. I *will cause to cease*...the voice of mirth,

7674 **שֶׁבֶת** *sheh'-veth*, m.

Ex. 21:19. he shall pay (for) *the loss of his time*, (marg. *his ceasing*)
Pro. 20: 3. an honour for a man *to cease* from strife:
Isa. 30: 7. strength (is) *to sit still.* (lit. *to cease*)

7676 **שַׁבָּת** *shab-bāhth'*, com.

Ex. 16:23. the rest of *the* holy *sabbath*
25. *a sabbath* unto the Lord:
26. the seventh day, (which is) *the sabbath*,
29. the Lord hath given you *the sabbath*,
20: 8. Remember the *sabbath* day,
10. *the sabbath* of the Lord thy God:
11. the Lord blessed the *sabbath* day,
31:13. Verily *my sabbaths* ye shall keep:
14. Ye shall keep *the sabbath*
15. the seventh (is) *the sabbath of* rest,
— whosoever doeth (any) work in *the sabbath*
16. the children of Israel shall keep *the sabbath*, to observe *the sabbath*
35: 2. *a sabbath of* rest to the Lord:
3. kindle no fire...upon the *sabbath* day.
Lev. 16:31. *a sabbath of* rest unto you,
19: 3. and keep *my sabbaths*:
30. Ye shall keep *my sabbaths*,
23: 3. the seventh day (is) *the sabbath of* rest,
— *the sabbath* of the Lord
11. on the morrow after *the sabbath*
15. from the morrow after *the sabbath*,
— seven *sabbaths* shall be complete:
16. the morrow after *the* seventh *sabbath*
32. (be) unto you *a sabbath of* rest,
— shall ye celebrate *your sabbath.*
38. *the sabbaths of* the Lord,
24: 8. *Every sabbath* (lit. on *the sabbath* day, on *the sabbath* day) he shall set it in order
25: 2. *a sabbath* unto the Lord.
4. shall be *a sabbath of* rest
— *a sabbath* for the Lord:
6. *the sabbath of* the land shall be
8. thou shalt number seven *sabbaths*
— the space of *the* seven *sabbaths*
26: 2. Ye shall keep *my sabbaths*,
34. Then shall the land enjoy *her sabbaths*,
— then shall the land...enjoy *her sabbaths.*
35. did not rest *in your sabbaths*,
43. The land...shall enjoy *her sabbaths*,
Nu. 15:32. a man that gathered sticks upon the *sabbath* day.
28: 9. on the *sabbath* day two lambs
10. the burnt offering *of every sabbath*, (lit. *the sabbath in its sabbath*)
Deu 5:12. Keep the *sabbath* day
14. *the sabbath* of the Lord thy God:
15. commanded thee to keep the *sabbath* day.
2K. 4:23. neither new moon, nor *sabbath.*
11: 5. you that enter in on *the sabbath*
7. you that go forth on *the sabbath*,
9. to come in on *the sabbath*, with them that should go out on *the sabbath*,
16:18. the covert for *the sabbath*
1Ch 9:32. over the shewbread, to prepare (it) *every sabbath.* (lit. *the sabbath the sabbath*)
23:31. *in the sabbaths*, in the new moons,
2Ch 2: 4(3) & 8:13. *on the sabbaths*, and on the new
23: 4. third part of you entering on *the sabbath*,
8. that were to come in on *the sabbath*, with them that were to go (out) on *the sabbath*:
2Ch 31: 3. the burnt offerings *for the sabbaths*,
36:21. the land had enjoyed *her sabbaths*:
Neh 9:14. madest known...thy holy *sabbath*,
10:31(32). bring ware or any victuals on the *sabbath* day
—(—). would not buy...on *the sabbath*,
33(34). of *the sabbaths*, of the new moons,
13:15. treading wine presses on *the sabbath*,
— brought into Jerusalem on the *sabbath*
16. sold *on the sabbath* unto the children of
17. profane the *sabbath* day?
18. by profaning *the sabbath.*
19. began to be dark before *the sabbath*,
— not be opened till after *the sabbath*:
— no burden be brought in on *the sabbath*
21. came they no (more) *on the sabbath.*
22. to sanctify the *sabbath* day.
Ps. 92[title](1). A Psalm (or) Song for the *sabbath*
Isa. 1:13. the new moons *and sabbaths*,
56: 2. keepeth *the sabbath* from polluting it,
4. the eunuchs that keep *my sabbaths*,
6. every one that keepeth *the sabbath*
58:13. thou turn away thy foot *from the sabbath*,
— call *the sabbath* a delight,
66:23. *from one sabbath to another*, (lit. from *a sabbath unto his sabbath*)
Jer. 17:21. bear no burden on the *sabbath* day,
22. carry forth a burden...on *the sabbath*
— hallow ye the *sabbath* day,
24. bring in no burden...on the *sabbath* day, but hallow the *sabbath* day,
27. to hallow the *sabbath* day, and not to bear a burden,...on the *sabbath* day;
Lam. 2: 6. the solemn feasts *and sabbaths*
Eze. 20:12. I gave them *my sabbaths*,
13. *my sabbaths* they greatly polluted:
16. but polluted *my sabbaths*:
20. hallow *my sabbaths*;
21. they polluted *my sabbaths*:
24. had polluted *my sabbaths*,
22: 8. hast profaned *my sabbaths.*
26. *and* have hid their eyes *from my sabbaths*,
23:38. have profaned *my sabbaths.*
44:24. they shall hallow *my sabbaths.*
45:17. in the new moons, *and in the sabbaths*,
46: 1. on *the sabbath* it shall be opened,
3. *in the sabbaths* and in the new moons.
4. in the *sabbath* day (shall be) six lambs
12. as he did on the *sabbath* day:
Hos 2:11(13). her new moons, *and her sabbaths*,
Am. 8: 5. *and the sabbath*, that we may set forth

שַׁבָּתוֹן *shab-bāh-thōhn'*, m. 7677

Ex. 16:23. *the rest of* the holy sabbath
31:15. the seventh (is) the sabbath of *rest*,
35: 2. a sabbath of *rest* to the Lord:
Lev. 16:31. a sabbath of *rest* unto you,
23: 3. the seventh day (is) the sabbath of *rest*,
24. shall ye have *a sabbath*,
32. (shall be) unto you a sabbath of *rest*,
39. on the first day (shall be) *a sabbath*, and on the eighth day (shall be) *a sabbath.*
25: 4. a sabbath of *rest* unto the land,
5. a year of *rest* unto the land.

שָׁגַג [*shāh-gag'*]. 7683

* KAL.—*Preterite.* *

Lev. 5:18. his ignorance wherein *he erred*

KAL.—*Infinitive.*

Gen 6: 3. *for that* he *also* (is) flesh: [or, (if taken as a verb,) *in their erring*—see also גַּם]

KAL.—*Participle.* Poel.

Nu. 15:28. the soul *that sinneth ignorantly*,
Job 12:16. *the deceived* and the deceiver
Ps. 119:67. Before I was afflicted I *went astray*:

שְׁגָגָה *sh'gāh-gāh'*, f. 7684

Lev. 4: 2. If a soul shall sin *through ignorance*
22. a ruler hath sinned,...*through ignorance*
27. if any one...sin *through ignorance*,

Lev. 5:15. If a soul...sin *through ignorance*,
18. *his ignorance* wherein he erred
22:14. man eat (of) the holy thing *unwittingly*,
Nu. 15:24. if (ought) be committed *by ignorance*
25. for it (is) *ignorance*:
— their sin offering...for *their ignorance*:
26. all the people (were) *in ignorance*.
27. if any soul sin *through ignorance*,
28. when he sinneth *by ignorance*
29. him that sinneth *through ignorance*,
35:11. killeth any person *at unawares*. (marg. *by error*)
15. killeth any person *unawares*
Jos. 20: 3. slayer that killeth (any) person *unawares*
9. killeth (any) person *at unawares*
Ecc. 5: 6(5). neither say thou...it (was) *an error*:
10: 5. *as an error* (which) proceedeth from the

7686 שָׁגָה [*shāh-gāh'*].

* KAL.—*Preterite*. *

Job 6:24. me to understand wherein *I have erred*.
19: 4. indeed (that) *I have erred*,
Isa. 28: 7. they also *have erred* through wine,
— the priest and the prophet *have erred*
— *they err* in vision,

KAL.—*Infinitive*.

Pro.19:27. the instruction (that causeth) *to err*

KAL.—*Future*.

Lev. 4:13. if the whole congregation...*sin through ignorance*,
Nu. 15:22. if *ye have erred*,
1Sa.26:21. *and have erred* exceedingly.
Pro. 5:19. *be thou ravished* (marg. *err*) always with
20. *why wilt thou*, my son, *be ravished*
23. the greatness of his folly *he shall go astray*.
Eze.34: 6. My sheep *wandered* through all

KAL.—*Participle*. Poel.

Ps.119:21. rebuked the proud...*which do err*
118. trodden down all *them that err*
Pro.20: 1. whosoever *is deceived*
Eze.45:20. every one *that erreth*,

* HIPHIL.—*Future*. *

Ps.119:10. *O let me* not *wander* from thy

HIPHIL.—*Participle*.

Deu27:18. *he that maketh* the blind *to wander*
Job 12:16. the deceived *and the deceiver*
Pro.28:10. *causeth* the righteous *to go astray*

7688 שָׁגַח [*shāh-gaḡh'*].

* HIPHIL.—*Preterite*. *

Ps. 33:14. *he looketh* upon all the inhabitants

HIPHIL.—*Future*.

Isa. 14:16. They that see thee *shall narrowly look*

HIPHIL.—*Participle*.

Cant.2: 9. *he looketh* forth at the windows,

7691 שְׁגִיאוֹת *sh'gee-ōhth'*, f. pl.

Ps. 19:12(13). Who can understand (his) *errors*?

7692 שִׁגָּיוֹן *shig-gāh-yōhn'*, m.

Ps. 7[title](1). *Shiggaion* of David,
Hab 3: 1. A prayer of Habakkuk...upon *Shigionoth*.

7693 שָׁגַל [*shāh-gal'*].

* KAL.—*Future*. *

Deu28:30. (כתיב) another man *shall lie with her*:

* NIPHAL.—*Future*. *

Isa. 13:16. (כתיב) their houses shall be spoiled, and their wives *ravished*.
Zec.14: 2. (כתיב) the city shall be taken,...and the women *ravished*;

* PUAL.—*Preterite*. *

Jer. 3: 2. see where *thou hast* not *been lien with*.

שֵׁגָל *shēh-gāhl'*, f. 7694

Neh 2: 6. *the queen* (marg. *wife*) *also* sitting by him,
Ps. 45: 9(10). thy right hand did stand *the queen*

שֵׁגָל [*shēh-gāhl'*], Ch. f. 7695

Dan 5: 2, 3. *his wives*, and his concubines,
23. *thy wives*, and thy concubines,

שָׁגַע [*shāh-gag'*]. 7696

* PUAL.—*Participle*. *

Deu 28:34. thou shalt be *mad* for the sight of thine
1Sa.21:15(16). Have I need of *mad men*,
2K. 9:11. wherefore came this *mad* (fellow)
Jer. 29:26. every man (that is) *mad*,
Hos. 9: 7. the spiritual man (is) *mad*,

* HITHPAEL.—*Infinitive*. *

1Sa.21:15(16). *to play the mad man* in my presence?

HITHPAEL.—*Participle*.

1Sa.21:14(15). ye see the man *is mad*: (marg. or, *playeth the mad man*)

שִׁגָּעוֹן *shig-gāh-gōhn'*, m. 7697

Deu28:28. The Lord shall smite thee *with madness*,
2K. 9:20. for he driveth *furiously*. (marg. *in madness*)
Zec.12: 4. smite...his rider *with madness*:

שֶׁגֶר *sheh'-ger*, m. 7698

Ex. 13:12. every firstling *that cometh of* a beast
Deu 7:13 & 28:4, 18, 51. *the increase of* thy kine,

שַׁד *shad*, m. 7699

Gen49:25. blessings of *the breasts*, and of the womb:
Job 3:12. *the breasts* that I should suck?
Ps. 22: 9(10). (when I was) upon my mother's *breasts*.
Cant 1:13. he shall lie all night betwixt *my breasts*.
4: 5 & 7:3(4). *Thy* two *breasts* (are) like two young roes
7: 7(8). *and thy breasts* to clusters (of grapes).
8(9). *thy breasts* shall be as clusters of the
8: 1. sucked *the breasts of* my mother!
8. have a little sister, and she hath no *breasts*.
10. *and my breasts* like towers:
Isa. 28: 9. drawn *from the breasts*.
32:12. They shall lament for *the teats*,
Lam 4: 3. the sea monsters draw out *the breast*,
Eze.16: 7. (thy) *breasts* are fashioned,
23: 3. there were *their breasts* pressed,
21. *the paps of* thy youth.
34. *and* pluck off *thine own breasts*:
Hos. 2: 2(4). adulteries from between *her breasts*;
9:14. a miscarrying womb *and* dry *breasts*.
Joel 2:16. those that suck *the breasts*:

שֵׁד [*shēhd*], m. 7700

Deu 32:17. They sacrificed *unto devils*,
Ps. 106:37. sacrificed their sons...*unto devils*,

שֹׁד *shōhd*, m. 7699

Job 24: 9. They pluck the fatherless *from the breast*,
Isa. 60:16. shalt suck *the breast of* kings:
66:11. satisfied *with the breasts of*

שֹׁד *shōhd*, m. 7701

Job 5:21. neither shalt thou be afraid *of destruction*
22. *At destruction* and famine thou shalt laugh
Ps. 12: 5(6). *For the oppression of* the poor,
Pro 21: 7. *The robbery of* the wicked
24: 2. their heart studieth *destruction*,

Isa. 13: 6. *as a destruction* from the Almighty.
16: 4. *the spoiler* ceaseth,
22: 4. *the spoiling of* the daughter of my people.
51:19. *desolation*, and destruction, and the
59: 7. *wasting* and destruction (are) in their
60:18. *wasting* nor destruction within thy borders;
Jer. 6: 7. violence *and spoil* is heard
20: 8. I cried violence *and spoil*;
48: 3. *spoiling* and great destruction.
Eze.45: 9. remove violence *and spoil*,
Hos 7:13. *destruction* (marg. *spoil*) unto them!
9: 6. they are gone *because of destruction*: (marg. *spoil*)
10:14. *as* Shalman *spoiled* Beth-arbel
12: 1(2). increaseth lies *and desolation*;
Joel 1:15. *and as a destruction* from the Almighty
Am. 3:10. who store up violence *and robbery* (marg. or, *spoil*)
5: 9. strengtheneth *the spoiled* (marg. *spoil*) against the strong, *so that the spoiled* shall come
Hab 1: 3. *for spoiling* and violence (are) before me:
2:17. *and the spoil of* beasts,

7703 ## שָׁדַד [*shāh-dad'*].

*** KAL.—*Preterite*. ***

Ps. 17: 9. the wicked that *oppress me*,
Pro.11: 3. (כתיב) of transgressors *shall destroy them*.
Eze.32:12. *and they shall spoil* the pomp of Egypt,

KAL.—*Infinitive*.

Jer. 47: 4. *to spoil* all the Philistines,
Mic. 2: 4. We be *utterly* spoiled: (lit. *destroying* we be destroyed)

KAL.—*Imperative*.

Jer. 49:28. *and spoil* the men of the east.

KAL.—*Future*.

Pro.11: 3. the perverseness of transgressors *shall destroy them*.
Jer. 5: 6. a wolf of the evenings *shall spoil them*,

KAL.—*Participle*. Poel.

Job 12: 6. The tabernacles *of robbers* prosper,
15:21. *the destroyer* shall come upon him.
Isa. 16: 4. a covert...from the face of *the spoiler*:
21: 2. *and the spoiler spoileth*.
33: 1. Woe to thee that *spoilest*,
— thou shalt cease *to spoil*, (lit. *spoiling*)
Jer. 6:26. *the spoiler* shall suddenly come
12:12. *The spoilers* are come upon all high places
15: 8. I have brought upon them...*a spoiler*
25:36. the Lord *hath spoiled* their pasture.
47: 4. the Lord *will spoil* the Philistines,
48: 8. *the spoiler* shall come upon every city,
18. *the spoiler of* Moab shall come
32. *the spoiler* is fallen upon thy summer fruits
51:48. *the spoilers* shall come unto her
53. from me shall *spoilers* come
55. the Lord *hath spoiled* Babylon,
56. *the spoiler* is come upon her,
Obad. 5. If thieves came to thee, if *robbers by* night,

KAL.—*Participle*. Paül.

Jud. 5:27. where he bowed, there he fell down *dead*. (marg. *destroyed*)
Ps.137: 8. O daughter of Babylon, *who art to be destroyed*; (marg. *wasted*)
Isa. 33: 1. thou (wast) not *spoiled*;
Jer. 4:30. (when) thou (art) *spoiled*,

*** NIPHAL.—*Preterite*. ***

Mic. 2: 4. *We be* utterly *spoiled*.

*** PIEL.—*Future*. ***

Pro.24:15. *spoil* not his resting place:

PIEL.—*Participle*.

Pro.19:26. *He that wasteth* (his) father,

*** PUAL.—*Preterite*. ***

Isa. 15: 1. Ar of Moab *is laid waste*,
— Kir of Moab *is laid waste*,
23: 1. for *it is laid waste*, so that
14. your strength *is laid waste*.
Jer. 4:13. Woe unto us! for *we are spoiled*.
20. the whole land *is spoiled*: suddenly *are* my tents *spoiled*,
9:19(18). How *are we spoiled!*
10:20. My tabernacle *is spoiled*,
48: 1. Woe unto Nebo! for *it is spoiled*:
15. Moab *is spoiled*, and gone
20. tell ye it in Arnon, that Moab *is spoiled*,
49: 3. Howl, O Heshbon, for Ai *is spoiled*:
10. his seed *is spoiled*,
Joel 1:10. The field *is wasted*, the land mourneth; for the corn *is wasted*:
Nah 3: 7. Nineveh *is laid waste*:
Zec.11: 2. the mighty *are spoiled*:
3. their glory *is spoiled*:
— the pride of Jordan *is spoiled*.

*** POEL.—*Future*. ***

Hos 10: 2. *he shall spoil* their images.

*** HOPHAL.—*Future*. ***

Isa. 33: 1. *thou shalt be spoiled*;
Hos 10:14. all thy fortresses *shall be spoiled*,

שִׁדָּה *shid-dāh'*, f. 7705

Ecc. 2: 8. *musical instruments, and that of all sorts*. (marg. *instrument and instruments*)

שַׁדַּי *shad-dah'y*, m. 7706

Gen17: 1. said unto him, I (am) the *Almighty* God:
28: 3. And God *Almighty* bless thee,
35:11. God said unto him, I (am) God *Almighty*:
43:14. God *Almighty* give you mercy
48: 3. God *Almighty* appeared unto me
49:25. and by *the Almighty*, who shall bless thee
Ex. 6: 3. by (the name of) God *Almighty*,
Nu. 24: 4. which saw the vision of *the Almighty*,
16. (which) saw the vision of *the Almighty*,
Ru. 1:20. *the Almighty* hath dealt very bitterly
21. *and the Almighty* hath afflicted me?
Job 5:17. despise not thou the chastening of *the Almighty*:
6: 4. the arrows of *the Almighty* (are) within
14. he forsaketh the fear of *the Almighty*.
8: 3. doth *the Almighty* pervert justice?
5. make thy supplication to *the Almighty*;
11: 7. canst thou find out *the Almighty*
13: 3. Surely I would speak to *the Almighty*,
15:25. strengtheneth himself against *the Almighty*.
21:15. What (is) *the Almighty*, that we should
20. he shall drink of the wrath of *the Almighty*.
22: 3. (Is it) any pleasure *to the Almighty*,
17. what can *the Almighty* do for them?
23. If thou return to *the Almighty*,
25. *the Almighty* shall be thy defence,
26. have thy delight in *the Almighty*,
23:16. *and the Almighty* troubleth me:
24: 1. times are not hidden *from the Almighty*,
27: 2. *and the Almighty*, (who) hath vexed my
10. Will he delight himself in *the Almighty*?
11. which (is) with *the Almighty* will I not conceal.
13. they shall receive *of the Almighty*.
29: 5. When *the Almighty* (was) yet with me,
31: 2. inheritance of *the Almighty* from on high?
35. (that) *the Almighty* would answer me,
32: 8. the inspiration of *the Almighty* giveth
33: 4. the breath of *the Almighty* hath given
34:10. *and* (from) *the Almighty*, (that he should)
12. *neither* will *the Almighty* pervert
35:13. *neither* will *the Almighty* regard it.
37:23. *the Almighty*, we cannot find him out:
40: 2. he that contendeth with *the Almighty*
Ps. 68:14(15). When *the Almighty* scattered kings
91: 1. under the shadow of *the Almighty*.
Isa. 13: 6. as a destruction *from the Almighty*.
Eze. 1:24. as the voice of *the Almighty*,
10: 5. the *Almighty* God when he speaketh.
Joel 1:15. as a destruction *from the Almighty*

שִׁדִּין see דִּין See 1777

שְׁדֵמָה *sh'dēh-māh'*, f. 7709

Isa. 37:27. *and* (as corn) *blasted* before it be grown

7709 **שְׁדֵמָה** [*sh'dēh-māh'*], f.

Deu 32:32. *and of the fields of* Gomorrah:
2K. 23: 4. burned them...*in the fields of* Kidron,
Isa. 16: 8. *the fields of* Heshbon languish,
Jer. 31:40. *the fields* unto the brook of Kidron,
Hab 3:17. *and the fields* shall yield no meat;

7710 **שָׁדַף** [*shāh-daph'*].

* KAL.—*Participle.* Paül. *

Gen41: 6. seven thin ears *and blasted*
23. seven ears, withered, thin, (and) *blasted*
27. seven empty ears *blasted*

7711 **שְׁדֵפָה** *sh'dēh-phāh'*, f.

2K. 19:26. *and* (as corn) *blasted* before it be grown

7711 **שִׁדָּפוֹן** *shid-dāh-phōhn'*, m.

Deu28:22. *and with blasting*, and with mildew;
1K. 8:37. If there be in the land...*blasting*,
2Ch 6:28. if there be *blasting*,
Am. 4: 9. I have smitten you *with blasting*
Hag 2:17. I smote you *with blasting*

7712 **שְׁדַר** [*sh'dar*], Ch.

* ITHPAEL.—*Participle.* *

Dan 6:14(15). and he *laboured* till the going down

7718 **שֹׁהַם** *shōh'-ham*, m.

Gen 2:12. bdellium and the *onyx* stone.
Ex. 25: 7. *Onyx* stones, and stones to be set
28: 9. thou shalt take two *onyx* stones,
20. the fourth row a beryl, and *an onyx*,
35: 9. *onyx* stones, and stones to be set
27. the rulers brought *onyx* stones,
39: 6. they wrought *onyx* stones
13. a beryl, *an onyx*, and a jasper:
1Ch 29: 2. *onyx* stones, and (stones) to be set,
Job 28:16. *with the* precious *onyx*, or the sapphire.
Eze.28:13. the beryl, *the onyx*, and the jasper,

7723 **שַׁו** *shav*, m.

Job 15:31. (כתיב) Let not him...trust *in vanity:*

7722 **שׁוֹא** [*shōh*], m.

Ps. 35:17. rescue my soul *from their destructions*,

7723 **שָׁוְא** *shāhv*, m.

Ex. 20: 7. not take the name of the Lord thy God *in vain;* for the Lord will not hold him guiltless that taketh his name *in vain.*
23: 1. Thou shalt not raise a *false* report:
Deu 5:11. not take the name of the Lord thy God *in vain:* for the Lord will not hold (him) guiltless that taketh his name *in vain.*
20(17). Neither shalt thou bear *false* witness
Job 7: 3. made to possess months of *vanity*,
11:11. he knoweth *vain* men:
15:31. trust *in vanity:* for *vanity* shall be his recompence.
31: 5. If I have walked with *vanity*,
35:13. God will not hear *vanity*,
Ps. 12: 2(3). They speak *vanity* every one
24: 4. hath not lifted up his soul *unto vanity*,
26: 4. I have not sat with *vain* persons,
31: 6(7). them that regard *lying* vanities:
41: 6(7). he speaketh *vanity:*
60:11(13). *for vain* (is) the help of man.
89:47(48). wherefore hast thou made all men *in vain?*
108:12(13). *for vain* (is) the help of man.
Ps.119:37. Turn away mine eyes from beholding *vanity;*
127: 1. Except the Lord build the house, they labour *in vain*
— the watchman waketh (but) *in vain.*
2. *vain* for you to rise up early,
139:20. thine enemies take (thy name) *in vain.*
144: 8, 11. Whose mouth speaketh *vanity*,
Pro.30: 8. Remove far from me *vanity* and lies:
Isa. 1:13. Bring no more *vain* oblations;
5:18. draw iniquity with cords of *vanity*,
30:28. sift the nations with the sieve of *vanity:*
59: 4. they trust in vanity, and speak *lies;*
Jer. 2:30. *In vain* have I smitten your children;
4:30. *in vain* shalt thou make thyself fair;
6:29. the founder melteth *in vain:*
18:15. burned incense *to vanity*,
46:11. *in vain* shalt thou use many medicines;
Lam. 2:14. Thy prophets have seen *vain* and foolish things
— have seen for thee *false* burdens
Eze.12:24. shall be no more any *vain* vision
13: 6. They have seen *vanity*
7. Have ye not seen a *vain* vision,
8. ye have spoken *vanity*,
9. the prophets that see *vanity*
23. ye shall see no more *vanity*,
21:23(28). a *false* divination in their sight,
29(34). they see *vanity* unto thee,
22:28. seeing *vanity*, and divining lies
Hos 10: 4. swearing *falsely* in making a covenant:
12:11(12). surely they are *vanity:*
Jon. 2: 8(9). They that observe *lying* vanities
Zec.10: 2. and have told *false* dreams;
Mal. 3:14. It (is) *vain* to serve God:

שׁוֹאָה *shōh-āh'*, f. 7722

Job 30: 3. fleeing into the wilderness...*desolate*
14. in *the desolation* they rolled themselves
38:27. satisfy *the desolate* and waste (ground);
Ps. 35: 8. Let *destruction* come upon him
— *into* that very *destruction* let him fall.
63: 9(10). those (that) seek my soul, *to destroy*
Pro. 1:27. When your fear cometh *as desolation*,
3:25. *neither* of *the desolation of* the wicked,
Isa. 10: 3. *and in the desolation* (which) shall come
47:11. *desolation* shall come upon thee
Eze.38: 9. shalt ascend and come *like a storm*,
Zep. 1:15. a day of *wasteness* and desolation,

שׁוּב *shoov.* 7725

* KAL.—*Preterite.* *

Gen18:33. Abraham *returned* unto his place.
28:21. *So that I come again* to my father's house
43:10. *we had returned* this second time.
Ex. 4: 7. *it was turned* again as his (other) flesh.
13:17. *and they return* to Egypt:
33:11. *And he turned again* into the camp:
Lev.14:39. *And* the priest *shall come again*
22:13. *and is returned* unto her father's house,
25:10. *and ye shall return* every man unto his
27. *that he may return* unto his possession.
28. *and he shall return* unto his possession.
41. *and shall return* unto his own family,
Nu. 14:43. *ye are turned away* from the Lord,
Deu 3:20. *and* (then) *shall ye return* every man
4:30. *if thou turn* to the Lord thy God,
23:13(14). *and shalt turn back* and cover that
14(15). *and turn away* from thee.
30: 2. *And shalt return* unto the Lord thy God,
3. *That then* the Lord thy God *will turn*
— *and will return* and gather thee
Jos. 1:15. *then ye shall return* unto the land of
2:22. the pursuers *were returned*
19:12. *And turned* from Sarid eastward
27. *And turneth* toward the sunrising
29. *And* (then) the coast *turneth* to Ramah,
— *and* the coast *turneth* to Hosah;
34. *And* (then) the coast *turneth* westward
24:20. *then he will turn* and do you hurt,
Jud. 3:19. himself *turned again* from the quarries
11: 8. *we turn again* to thee now,
20:48. the men of Israel *turned again*

Ru. 1:15. thy sister in law *is gone back* (lit. *returned*)
22. *which returned* out of the country of
2: 6. the Moabitish damsel *that came back*
4: 3. Naomi, *that is come again*
1Sa. 15:11. *he is turned back* from following me,
23:23. *and come ye again* to me with the certainty,
24: 1(2). when Saul *was returned*
26:25. Saul *returned* to his place.
2Sa. 1: 1. when David *was returned* from the
2:30. Joab *returned* from following Abner:
10: 5. Tarry at Jericho until your beards be grown, *and* (then) *return*.
11:15. *and retire ye* (lit. *turn* back) from him,
20:22. Joab *returned* to Jerusalem
1K. 2:33. Their blood *shall therefore return*
8:33. *and shall turn* again to thee, and confess
47. shall bethink themselves...*and repent*,
48. *And* (so) *return* unto thee with all their
12:20. when all Israel heard that Jeroboam *was come again*, (lit. *returned*)
27. *then shall* the heart of this people *turn again*
— *and go again* to Rehoboam
13:10. *returned* not by the way that he came
33. Jeroboam *returned* not from his evil way,
2K. 1: 5. Why *are ye* now *turned back?*
2:25. from thence *he returned* to Samaria.
4:38. Elisha *came again* (lit. *returned*) to
9:18. *he cometh* not *again*.
20. even unto them, and *cometh* not *again:*
19: 7. *and shall return* to his own land;
23:25. no king before him, that *turned* to the
26. the Lord *turned* not from the fierceness
1Ch 19: 5. your beards be grown, *and* (then) *return*.
2Ch 6:24. *and shall return* and confess thy name,
37. (if) they bethink themselves...*and turn*
38. *If they return* to thee with all their heart
12:12. the wrath of the Lord *turned* from him,
Neh 1: 9. *But* (if) *ye turn* unto me,
9:35. neither *turned they* from their wicked
Est. 7: 8. the king *returned* out of the palace
Job 39: 4. they go forth, and *return* not
42:10. the Lord *turned* the captivity of Job,
Ps. 78:34. *and they returned* and enquired early
85: 1(2). *thou hast brought back* the captivity of
Pro. 26:11. As a dog *returneth* to his vomit,
Ecc. 1: 6. the wind *returneth again*
3:20. all *turn* to dust *again*.
4: 1. *So* I *returned*, and considered
7. *Then* I *returned*, and I saw
9:11. *I returned*, and saw under the sun,
12: 2. *nor* the clouds *return* after the rain:
Isa. 5:25. his anger *is* not *turned away*,
6:13. (shall be) a tenth, *and* (it) *shall return*,
9:12(11). his anger *is* not *turned away*,
13(12). the people *turneth* not unto him
17(16), 21(20) & 10:4. his anger *is* not *turned away*,
19:22. *and they shall return* (even) to the Lord,
23:17. *and she shall turn* to her hire,
29:17. *and* Lebanon *shall be turned* into a
37: 7. *and return* to his own land;
Jer. 2:35. his anger *shall turn* from me.
3: 7. *she returned* not.
10. treacherous sister Judah *hath* not *turned*
4: 8. anger of the Lord *is* not *turned back*
8: 6. every one *turned* to his course,
11:10. *They are turned back* to the iniquities
14: 3. *they returned* with their vessels
15: 7. *they return* not from their ways.
18: 4. *so he* made it *again* (lit. *and he turned* and made it)
8. *If* that nation,...*turn* from their evil,
23:14. none *doth return* from his wickedness:
29:14. *and I will turn away* your captivity,
30: 3. *that I will bring again* the captivity
10. *and* Jacob *shall return*,
31:16. *and they shall come again* from the land
17. *that* thy children *shall come again*
37: 7. *shall return* to Egypt into their own land.
8. *And* the Chaldeans *shall come again*,
43: 5. the remnant of Judah, that *were returned*
46:27. *and* Jacob *shall return*,
48:47. *Yet will I bring again* the captivity
Eze. 3:19. *he turn* not from his wickedness,
16:53. *When I shall bring again* their captivity,
29:14. *And I will bring again* the captivity of

Eze. 33: 9. if *he do* not *turn* from his way,
14. *if he turn* from his sin,
46:17. *after it shall return* to the prince:
Dan 11: 9. *and shall return* into his own land.
13. *For* the king of the north *shall return*,
28. *Then shall he return* into his land
30. he shall be grieved, *and return*,
— *he shall even return*, and have
Hos. 7:10. *they do* not *return* to the Lord
9: 3. *but* Ephraim *shall return* to Egypt,
14: 4(5). mine anger *is turned away*
Am. 4: 6. I also have given you cleanness of teeth.. yet *have ye* not *returned*
8, 9, 10, 11. yet *have ye* not *returned* unto me,
9:14. *And I will bring again* the captivity
Jon. 3: 9. *and turn away* from his fierce anger,
10. *they turned* from their evil way;
Nah 2: 2(3). the Lord *hath turned away* the
Zep. 2: 7. *and turn away* their captivity.
Zec. 1:16. *I am returned* to Jerusalem
8: 3. *I am returned* unto Zion,
15. *So again* have I thought
10: 9. shall live with their children, *and turn again*.
Mal. 3:18. *Then shall ye return*, and discern

KAL.—*Infinitive*.

Gen 3:19. till *thou return* unto the ground;
8: 3. the waters returned from off the earth continually: (marg. going *and returning*)
7. a raven, which went forth to *and fro*, (marg. in going forth *and returning*)
12. sent forth the dove; which *returned* not again (lit. added not *to return*)
14:17. after *his return* from the slaughter
18:10. I will *certainly* return (lit. *returning* I will return)
27:45. Until thy brother's anger *turn away*
Ex. 4:21. When thou goest *to return* into Egypt,
Nu. 14: 3. were it not better for us *to return*
35:32. *that he should come again* to dwell
Deu 17:16. Ye shall henceforth *return* no more
24: 4. Her former husband,...*may* not take her *again* (lit. may not *return* to take her)
Jos. 2:16. until the pursuers *be returned:*
22:16. *to turn away* this day from...the Lord,
23. *to turn* from following the Lord,
29. *and turn* this day from following the Lord,
23:12. ye do *in any wise* go back, (lit. *going* back ye do go back)
Jud. 6:18. I will tarry until *thou come again*.
8: 9. *When I come again* in peace,
11:31. *when I return* in peace
35. I cannot *go back*.
Ru. 1: 7. *to return* unto the land of Judah.
16. *to return* from following after thee:
1Sa. 17:57. *And as* David *returned* from the slaughter
18: 2. let him *go* no *more home* to his father's
6. *when* David *was returned*
29:11. *to return* into the land of the Philistines.
2Sa. 2:26. ere thou bid the people *return*
8:13. *when he returned* from smiting
17: 3. the man whom thou seekest (is) *as if* all *returned:*
1K. 9: 6. if ye shall *at all* turn (lit. *turning* ye shall turn) from following
13:16. I may not *return* with thee,
22:28. If thou return *at all* (lit. in *returning* thou return) in peace,
2Ch 18:26. until *I return* in peace.
27. If thou *certainly* return (lit. *returning* thou return)
20:27. *to go again* to Jerusalem
30: 9. *if ye turn again* unto the Lord,
— *so that they shall come again*
36:13. hardened his heart *from turning*
Neh 9:17. *to return* to their bondage:
Job 14:13. hide me...until thy wrath *be past*, (lit. *return*)
15:22. believeth not *that he shall return*
Ps. 9: 3(4). *When* mine enemies *are turned back*,
14: 7. *when* the Lord *bringeth back* the captivity
53: 6(7). *When* God *bringeth back* the captivity
126: 1. *When* the Lord *turned again* the captivity
Isa. 52: 8. *when* the Lord *shall bring again* Zion.
Jer. 3: 1. *yet return again* to me,
5: 3. they have refused *to return*.
8: 5. they refuse *to return*.
22:27. the land whereunto they desire *to return*,

Jer. 31:19. after that *I was turned*, I repented;
23. *when I shall bring again* their captivity;
42:10. If ye will *still* abide (lit. *returning* ye will abide) in this land,
44: 5. *to turn* from their wickedness,
14. *that they should return* into the land
— they have a desire *to return*
Eze. 1:14. the living creatures ran *and returned*
3:20. *Again, When* a righteous (man) *doth turn*
13:22. that *he should* not *return* from his wicked
18:23. not *that he should return* from his ways,
24. *But when the* righteous *turneth away*
26. *When* a righteous (man) *turneth away*
27. *Again, when* the wicked (man) *turneth away*
33: 9. if thou warn the wicked...*to turn*
11. but *that* the wicked *turn* from his way
12. in the day *that he turneth*
18. *When* the righteous *turneth* from
19. *But* if the wicked *turn* from
47: 7. *Now when I had returned*,
Dan 9:13. *that we might turn* from our iniquities,
Hos 5: 4. *to turn* unto their God:
6:11. *when I returned* the captivity
11: 5. because they refused *to return*.
Zep 3:20. *when I turn back* your captivity

KAL.—*Imperative.*

Gen16: 9. *Return* to thy mistress,
31: 3. *Return* unto the land of thy fathers,
13. *return* unto the land of thy kindred.
32: 9(10). *Return* unto thy country,
43: 2. *Go again*, buy us a little food.
13. *go again* unto the man:
44:25. *Go again*, (and) buy us a little food.
Ex. 4:19. Go, *return* into Egypt:
32:12. *Turn* from thy fierce wrath,
27. go in *and out* (lit. pass through *and return*) from gate to gate
Nu. 10:36. *Return*, O Lord, unto the many thousands
23: 5. *Return* unto Balak,
16. *Go again* unto Balak,
Deu 5:30(27). *Get you* into your tents *again*.
Jos. 5: 2. *and* circumcise *again* (lit. *and return* and circumcise) the children of Israel
18: 8. Go and walk through the land,...*and come again* to me,
22: 8. *Return* with much riches
Ru. 1: 8. Go, *return* each to her mother's house:
11. Naomi said, *Turn again*, my daughters:
12. *Turn again*, my daughters, go
15. *return thou* after thy sister in law.
1Sa. 3: 5. I called not; lie down *again*. (lit. *return*, lie down)
6. I called not, my son; lie down *again*.
15:25. *and turn again* with me, that I may
30. *and turn again* with me, that I may
26:21. *return*, my son David:
29: 7. Wherefore now *return*, and go in peace,
2Sa. 3:16. Then said Abner...Go, *return*.
15:19. *return* to thy place,
20. *return* thou, and take back thy brethren:
27. *return* into the city in peace,
19:14(15). *Return* thou, and all thy servants.
1K. 12: 5. Depart yet (for) three days, *then come again*
12. *Come* to me *again* the third day.
24. *return* every man to his house;
18:43. *Go again* seven times.
19:15. *return* on thy way to the wilderness
20. Go back *again* (marg. Go *return*): for what have I done
2K. 1: 6. *turn again* unto the king
17:13. *Turn ye* from your evil ways,
18:14. I have offended; *return* from me:
20: 5. *Turn again*, and tell Hezekiah
2Ch 10: 5. *Come again* unto me after three days.
12. *Come again* to me on the third day.
11: 4. *return* every man to his house:
30: 6. *turn again* unto the Lord God of Abraham,
Job 6:29. *Return*, I pray you, let it not be iniquity; yea, *return* again,
Ps. 6: 4(5). *Return*, O Lord, deliver my soul:
7: 7(8). for their sakes *return* thou
80:14(15). *Return*, we beseech thee, O God
85: 4(5). *Turn us*, O God of our salvation,
90: 3. *Return, ye* children of men.
Ps. 90:13. *Return*, O Lord, how long?
116: 7. *Return* unto thy rest, O my soul,
126: 4. *Turn again* our captivity,
Pro. 3:28. Say not unto thy neighbour, Go, *and come again*,
Cant 6:13(7:1). *Return, return*, O Shulamite; *return, return*, that we may look upon thee.
Isa. 21:12. if ye will enquire, enquire ye: *return*,
31: 6. *Turn ye* unto (him)
44:22. *return* unto me; for I have redeemed
63:17. *Return* for thy servants' sake,
Jer. 3:12. *Return*, thou backsliding Israel,
14. *Turn*, O backsliding children,
22. *Return*, ye backsliding children,
18:11. *return ye* now every one from his evil way,
25: 5. *Turn ye again* now every one from
31:21. *turn again*, O virgin of Israel, *turn again* to these thy cities.
35:15. *Return ye* now every man from
36:28. Take thee *again* (lit. *return* take thee) another roll,
40: 5. *Go back also* to Gedaliah
Eze. 14: 6. *Repent*, and turn (yourselves) from your
18:30. *Repent*, and turn (yourselves) from all
33:11. *turn ye, turn ye* from your evil ways;
Hos 14: 1(2). O Israel, *return* unto the Lord
2(3). *and turn* to the Lord:
Joel 2:12. *turn ye* (even) to me
13. *and turn* unto the Lord your God:
Zec. 1: 3. *Turn ye* unto me, saith the Lord
4. *Turn ye* now from your evil ways,
9:12. *Turn you* to the strong hold,
Mal 3: 7. *Return* unto me, and I will return

KAL.—*Future.*

Gen 3:19. unto dust *shalt thou return*.
8: 3. *And* the waters *returned* from off the
9. *and she returned* unto him into the ark,
14: 7. *And they returned*, and came to En-mishpat,
15:16. *they shall come* hither *again*:
18:10. *I will* certainly *return* unto thee
14. At the time appointed *I will return*
21:32. *and they returned* into the land of the
22: 5. go yonder and worship, *and come again*
19. *So* Abraham *returned*
26:18. *And* Isaac digged *again* (lit. *and he returned* and digged) the wells
27:44. until thy brother's fury *turn away*;
30:31. *I will again* feed (lit. *I will return* I will feed) (and) keep thy flock:
31:55(32:1). Laban departed, *and returned*
32: 6(7). *And* the messengers *returned* to Jacob,
33:16. *So* Esau *returned* that day
37:29. *And* Reuben *returned* unto the pit;
30. *And he returned* unto his brethren,
38:22. *And he returned* to Judah,
42:24. *and returned* to them *again*,
44:13. laded every man his ass, *and returned*
50: 5. bury my father, *and I will come again*.
14. *And* Joseph *returned* into Egypt,
Ex. 4:18. Moses went *and returned* to Jethro
— Let me go,...*and return* unto my brethren
20. *and he returned* to the land of Egypt:
5:22. *And* Moses *returned* unto the Lord,
14: 2. the children of Israel, *that they turn*
26. *that* the waters *may come again*
27. *and* the sea *returned* to his strength
28. *And* the waters *returned*,
24:14. until *we come again* unto you:
32:31. *And* Moses *returned* unto the Lord,
34:31. *and* Aaron and all the rulers...*returned*
Lev. 13:16. if the raw flesh *turn again*,
14:43. if the plague *come again*,
25:10. *ye shall return* every man unto his family.
13. *ye shall return* every man unto his
41. of his fathers *shall he return*
27:24. the field *shall return* unto him
Nu. 8:25. *they shall cease* (marg. *return* from) waiting upon the service
11: 4. *and* the children of Israel also wept *again* (marg. *returned* and wept)
13:25. *And they returned* from searching
14: 4. *and let us return* into Egypt.
36. *who returned*, and made all the
16:50(17:15). *And* Aaron *returned* unto Moses
22:34. *I will get* me *back again*.

Nu. 23: 6. *And he returned* unto him,
24:25. Balaam rose up, and went *and returned*
25: 4. *that* the fierce anger of the Lord *may be turned away*
32:15. if *ye turn away* from after him,
18. *We will* not *return* unto our houses,
22. afterward *ye shall return*,
33: 7. *and turned again* unto Pi-hahiroth,
35:28. the slayer *shall return*
Deu 1:45. *And ye returned* and wept before the
13:17(18). that the Lord *may turn* from the
20: 5. let him go *and return* to his house,
6. let him (also) go *and return*
7, 8. let him go *and return* unto his house,
24:19. *thou shalt* not *go again* to fetch
28:31. *shall* not *be restored* (marg. *return*) to
30: 8. *thou shalt return* and obey
9. *will again* rejoice (lit. *will return* to rejoice)
10. if *thou turn* unto the Lord thy God
Jos. 2:23. *So* the two men *returned*,
4:18. *that* the waters of Jordan *returned*
6:14. *and returned* into the camp:
7: 3. *And they returned* to Joshua,
26. *So* the Lord *turned* from the fierceness
8:21. *then they turned again*, and slew
24. *that* all the Israelites *returned*
10:15, 38, 43. *And* Joshua *returned*,
21. *And* all the people *returned* to the camp
11:10. *And* Joshua at that time *turned back*,
20: 6. then *shall* the slayer *return*,
22: 9. *And* the children of Reuben...*returned*,
18. *ye must turn away* this day from following
32. *And* Phinehas the son of Eleazar...*returned*
23:12. if *ye do* in any wise *go back*,
Jud. 2:19. *they returned*, and corrupted (themselves)
7: 3. *let him return* and depart early
— *And* there *returned* of the people
15. *and returned* into the host of Israel,
8:13. *And* Gideon...*returned* from battle
33. *that* the children of Israel *turned again*,
11:39. *that she returned* unto her father,
14: 8. *And* after a time *he returned* to take her,
15:19. *and* when...his spirit *came again*,
18:26. he turned *and went back* unto his house.
19: 7. *therefore he* lodged there *again*. (lit. *and he returned* and lodged)
21:14. *And* Benjamin *came again*
23. *and returned* unto their inheritance,
Ru. 1: 6. *that she might return* from the country of
10. Surely *we will return* with thee
22. *So* Naomi *returned*,
1Sa. 1:19. worshipped before the Lord, *and returned*,
5:11. *and let it go again* to his own place,
6:16. *And* when...*they returned* to Ekron the
7:14. *And* the cities...*were restored* to Israel,
9: 5. Come, *and let us return*;
15:26. *I will* not *return* with thee:
31. *So* Samuel *turned again*
17:53. *And* the children of Israel *returned* from
23:28. *Wherefore* Saul *returned*
25:12. David's young men turned their way, *and went again*,
27: 9. *and returned*, and came to Achish.
29: 4. *that he may go again* to his place
30:12. *and* when...his spirit *came again*
2Sa. 1:22. the sword of Saul *returned* not empty.
3:16. Go, return. *And he returned*.
27. *when* Abner *was returned* to Hebron,
6:20. *Then* David *returned* to bless his
10:14. *So* Joab *returned* from the children of
11: 4. *and she returned* unto her house.
12:23. *he shall* not *return* to me.
31. *So* David and all the people *returned*
15: 8. If the Lord *shall bring me again* indeed
34. if *thou return* to the city,
17:20. *And* when...*they returned* to Jerusalem.
18:16. *and* the people *returned* from pursuing
19:15(16). *So* the king *returned*,
37(38). *Let* thy servant,...*turn back again*,
39(40). *and he returned* unto his own place.
22:38. *and turned* not *again* until I had consumed
23:10. *and* the people *returned* after him
1K. 2:41. Jerusalem to Gath, *and was come again*.
8:35. and *turn* from their sin,
9: 6. if *ye shall* at all *turn*
12:24. *and returned* to depart, according to the
1K. 12:26. Now *shall* the kingdom *return*
13: 6. *that* my hand *may be restored* me *again*.
— *and* the king's hand *was restored* him *again*,
9. nor *turn again* by the same way
17. nor *turn again* to go by the way
19. *So he went back* with him,
22. *But camest back*, and hast eaten
33. *but* made *again* (marg. *returned* and made) ...priests
17:21. *let* this child's soul *come* into him *again*.
22. *and* the soul of the child *came* into him *again*,
19: 6. did eat and drink, *and* laid him down *again*. (lit. *and returned* and laid down)
7. *And* the angel of the Lord *came again*
21. *And he returned back* from him,
20: 5. *And* the messengers *came again*,
22:17. *let them return* every man to his house
28. If *thou return* at all in peace,
33. *that they turned* back from pursuing
2K. 1: 5. *when* the messengers *turned back*
11. *Again also* he sent (lit. *and he returned* and sent) another captain
13. *And he* sent *again* (lit. *and he returned* and sent) a captain
2:13. *and went back*, and stood by the bank of
18. *when they came again* to him,
3:27. *and returned* to (their own) land.
4:22. may run to the man of God, *and come again*.
31. *Wherefore he went again* to meet him,
35. *Then he returned*, and walked in the house
5:10. *and* thy flesh *shall come again* to thee,
14. *and* his flesh *came again*
15. *And he returned* to the man of God,
7: 8. *and came again*, and entered into another
15. *And* the messengers *returned*,
8: 3. it came to pass...*that* the woman *returned*
29. *And* king Joram *went back* to be healed
9:15. *But* king Joram *was returned* to be healed
36. *Wherefore they came again*, and told
13:25. *And* Jehoash the son of Jehoahaz took *again* (marg. *returned* and took)
14:14. took all...*and returned* to Samaria.
15:20. *So* the king of Assyria *turned back*,
19: 8. *So* Rab-shakeh *returned*,
9. *he* sent messengers *again* (lit. *and he returned* and sent)
33. by the same *shall he return*,
36. *So* Sennacherib king of Assyria...*returned*,
20: 9. shall the shadow...*go back*
10. *let* the shadow *return* backward
21: 3. *For he* built up *again* (lit. *and he returned* and built) the high places
23:20. men's bones upon them, *and returned*
24: 1. *then he turned* and rebelled against him.
1Ch 20: 3. *And* David and all the people *returned*
21:20. *And* Ornan *turned back*,
2Ch 6:26. confess thy name, *and turn* from their
7:14. *and turn* from their wicked ways;
19. But if ye *turn away*, and forsake
10: 2. *that* Jeroboam *returned* out of Egypt.
11: 4. *and returned* from going against
14:15(14). *and returned* to Jerusalem.
15: 4. *when they* in their trouble *did turn*
18:16. *let them return*...every man to his house
27. If *thou* certainly *return* in peace,
32. *they turned back again* from pursuing
19: 1. *And* Jehoshaphat the king of Judah *returned*
4. *and he* went out *again* (marg. *returned* and went out)
8. *when they returned* to Jerusalem.
20:27. *Then they returned*, every man
22: 6. *And he returned* to be healed in Jezreel
25:10. *and they returned* home in great anger.
24. (took) all the gold...*and returned* to
28:15. *then they returned* to Samaria.
29:10. *that* his fierce wrath *may turn away*
30: 6. *and he will return* to the remnant
8. *that* the fierceness of his wrath *may turn away*
9. if *ye return* unto him.
31: 1. *Then* all the children of Israel *returned*,
32:21. *So he returned* with shame of face
33: 3. *For he* built *again* (marg. *returned* and built) the high places
34: 7. *And* when he had...*he returned* to

2Ch 34: 9. *and they returned* to Jerusalem.
Ezr. 2: 1. *and came again* unto Jerusalem and Judah,
9:14. *Should we again* break (lit. *shall we return* to break) thy commandments,
Neh 2: 6. when *wilt thou return?*
15. viewed the wall, *and turned back*, and entered by the gate of the valley, *and* (so) *returned*.
4:12(6). From all places whence *ye shall return*
15(9). *that we returned* all of us to the wall,
7: 6. *and came again* to Jerusalem
9:28. *they did* evil *again* (marg. *returned* to do evil)
— yet *when they returned*,...thou heardest
Est. 6:12. *And* Mordecai *came again*
9:25. that his wicked device,...*should return*
Job 1:21. naked *shall I return*
7: 7. mine eye *shall* no *more* see (lit. not *return* to see) good.
10. *He shall return* no more to his house,
10:16. *and again thou* shewest (lit. *and thou returnest* thou shewest) thyself marvellous
21. Before I go (whence) *I shall* not *return*,
16:22. shall go the way (whence) *I shall* not *return*.
17:10. *do ye return*, and come now:
22:23. If *thou return* to the Almighty,
33:25. *he shall return* to the days of his youth:
34:15. man *shall turn again* unto dust.
36:10. commandeth *that they return*
39:12. (כתיב) that *he will bring* home thy seed,
22. neither *turneth he back* from the sword.
Ps. 6:10(11). *let them return* (and) be ashamed
7:12(13). If *he turn* not, he will whet his sword;
16(17). His mischief *shall return*
9:17(18). The wicked *shall be turned* into hell,
18:37(38). neither *did I turn again*
22:27(28). All the ends of the world shall remember *and turn*
35:13. my prayer *returned* into mine own bosom.
51:13(15). sinners *shall be converted*
54: 5(7). (כתיב) *He shall reward* evil unto mine
56: 9(10). *then shall* mine enemies *turn*
59: 6(7). *They return* at evening:
14(15). *And* at evening *let them return;*
60[title](2). *when* Joab *returned*, and smote
70: 3(4). *Let them be turned back* for a reward
71:20. *shalt* quicken me *again* (lit. *shalt return* shalt quicken me), and *shalt* bring me up *again* (lit. *shalt return* shalt bring me up)
73:10. Therefore his people *return*
74:21. O *let* not the oppressed *return* ashamed:
78:39. a wind that passeth away, and *cometh* not *again*.
41. *Yea, they turned back* and tempted God,
85: 6(7). *Wilt* thou not revive us *again:* (lit. *wilt thou* not *return* wilt thou revive us)
8(9). *let them* not *turn again* to folly.
94:15. judgment *shall return* unto righteousness:
104: 9. that *they turn* not *again* to cover
29. they die, and *return* to their dust.
119:79. *Let* those that fear thee *turn* unto me,
132:11. *he will* not *turn* from it;
146: 4. *he returneth* to his earth;
Pro. 1:23. *Turn you* at my reproof:
2:19. None that go unto her *return again*,
12:14. (כתיב) *shall be rendered* unto him.
25:10. thine infamy *turn* not *away*.
26:27. *it will return* upon him.
30:30. A lion...*turneth* not *away* for any;
Ecc. 5:15(14). naked *shall he return*
12: 7. *Then shall* the dust *return* to the earth as it was: and the spirit *shall return* unto
Isa. 7: 3. thou, and Shear-*jashub* (marg. the remnant *shall return*) thy son,
10:21. The remnant *shall return*, (even) the
22. a remnant of them *shall return:*
12: 1. thine anger *is turned away*,
35:10. the ransomed of the Lord *shall return*,
37: 8. *So* Rabshakeh *returned*,
34. by the same *shall he return*,
37. So Sennacherib...departed, and went *and returned*,
38: 8. *So* the sun *returned* ten degrees,
45:23. gone out of my mouth (in) righteousness, *and shall* not *return*,

Isa. 51:11. the redeemed of the Lord *shall return*,
55: 7. *and let him return* unto the Lord,
10. rain cometh down,...and *returneth* not
11. So shall my word be...*it shall* not *return*
Jer. 3: 1. man put away his wife,...*shall he return*
7. *Turn thou* unto me.
19. *shalt* not *turn* away from me.
4: 1. If *thou wilt return*, O Israel, saith the Lord, *return* unto me:
28. neither *will I turn back*
8: 4. *shall he turn* away, and not *return?*
12:15. *I will return*, and have compassion
15:19. If *thou return*, then will I bring thee
— *let* them *return* unto thee; but *return* not thou unto them.
22:10. *he shall return* no more,
11. *He shall* not *return* thither
27. thither *shall they* not *return*.
23:20. anger of the Lord *shall* not *return*,
24: 7. *they shall return* unto me
26: 3. *and turn* every man from his evil way,
30:24. fierce anger of the Lord *shall* not *return*,
31: 8. a great company *shall return*
18. turn thou me, *and I shall be turned;*
32:40. *I will* not *turn away* from them,
33:26. (כתיב) *I will cause* their captivity *to return*,
34:11. *But* afterward *they turned*,
15. *And* ye *were* now *turned*,
16. *But ye turned* and polluted my name,
36: 3. that *they may return* every man
7. *and will return* every one from his evil
40: 5. while *he was* not yet *gone back*,
12. *Even* all the Jews *returned*
41:14. *and returned*, and went unto Johanan
44:14. none *shall return* but such as shall
28. number that escape the sword *shall return*
46:16. *and let us go again* to our own people,
49:39. (כתיב) *I will bring again* the captivity
50: 9. none *shall return* in vain.
Lam. 1: 8. she sigheth, *and turneth backward*.
3: 3. against me *is he turned;*
40. try our ways, *and turn again* to the Lord.
5:21. Turn thou us...*and we shall be turned;*
Eze. 7:13. the seller *shall* not *return*
— the whole multitude...*shall* not *return;*
8: 6, 13, 15. *turn thee* yet *again*, (and) thou
17. *and have returned* to provoke me
16:55. Sodom and her daughters, *shall return* to their former estate, and Samaria and her daughters *shall return* to their former estate, then thou and thy daughters *shall return*
18:21. if the wicked *will turn*
28. *and turneth away from* all his
21: 5(10). my sword....*shall* not *return*
35: 9. thy cities *shall* not *return:*
46: 9. *he shall* not *return* by the way
Dan 9:16. *let* thine anger and thy fury *be turned away*
25. the street *shall* be built *again*, (marg. *return* and be builded)
10:20. now *will I return* to fight
11:10. *then shall he return*, and be stirred up,
28. *Then shall he return* into his land
29. At the time appointed *he shall return*,
Hos. 2: 7(9). I will go *and return* to my first
9(11). Therefore *will I return*,
3: 5. *shall* the children of Israel *return*,
5:15. I will go (and) *return* to my place,
6: 1. Come, *and let us return*
7:16. *They return*, (but) not to the most High.
8:13. *they shall return* to Egypt.
11: 5. *He shall* not *return* into the land of
9. *I will* not *return* to destroy
12: 6(7). *turn* thou to thy God:
14: 7(8). dwell under his shadow *shall return;*
Joel 2:14. Who knoweth (if) *he will return*
3: 1(4:1). (כתיב) *I shall bring again* the captivity
Obad. 15. thy reward *shall return*
Jon. 3: 8. *yea, let them turn* every one
9. Who can tell (if) God *will turn*
Mic. 1: 7. *they shall return* to the hire of an harlot.
5: 3(2). remnant of his brethren *shall return*
7:19. *He will turn again*, he will have
Zec. 1: 3. *and I will turn* unto you,
6. *and they returned* and said,
4: 1. *And* the angel...*came again*,
5: 1. *Then I turned*, and lifted up mine eyes,

Zec. 6: 1. *And I turned*, and lifted up mine eyes,
Mal. 1: 4. *but we will return* and build
3: 7. *and I will return* unto you,
— Wherein *shall we return?*

KAL.—*Participle.* Poel.

Gen43:18. the money *that was returned*
1Sa. 7: 3. If ye *do return* unto the Lord
17:15. David went *and returned* from Saul
Ezr. 6:21. children of Israel, *which were come again*
Neh. 8:17. the congregation...*that were come again*
Est. 2:14. on the morrow she *returned*
Ecc. 1: 7. thither they *return* again.
Isa. 1:27. Zion shall be redeemed with judgment, and *her converts* (marg. or, *they that return of her*)
6:10. understand with their heart, *and convert*,
59:20. *and unto them that turn from*
Jer. 30:18. I *will bring again* the captivity of
Eze.35: 7. that passeth out *and him that returneth.*
Zec. 7:14. no man passed through *nor returned:*
9: 8. *because of him that returneth:*

KAL.—*Participle.* Paül.

Mic. 2: 8. *as men averse* from war.

* POLEL.—*Preterite.* *

Isa. 47:10. thy knowledge, it *hath perverted thee;* (marg. or, *caused thee to turn away*)
Jer. 8: 5. *is* this people of Jerusalem *slidden back*
50: 6. *they have turned them away*
19. *And I will bring* Israel *again*
Eze.38: 4. *And I will turn thee back*,
39: 2. *And I will turn thee back*,

POLEL.—*Infinitive.*

Isa. 49: 5. *to bring* Jacob *again* to him,
Eze.39:27. *When I have brought them again*
Mic. 2: 4. *turning away* (marg. or, *instead of restoring*) he hath divided

POLEL.—*Future.*

Ps. 23: 3. *He restoreth* my soul:
60: 1(3). *O turn thyself* to us *again.*

POLEL.—*Participle.*

Isa. 58:12. *The restorer* of paths to dwell in.

* PULAL.—*Participle.* *

Eze.38: 8. the land *that is brought back*

* HIPHIL.—*Preterite.* *

Gen14:16. *brought again* his brother Lot,
28:15. *and will bring thee again* into this land;
29: 3. *and put* the stone *again* upon the well's
40:13. *and restore thee* unto thy place:
41:13. me *he restored* unto mine office,
44: 8. the money,...*we brought again*
48:21. *and bring you again* unto the land
Ex. 34:35. Moses *put* the vail upon his face *again*,
Lev. 6: 4(5:23). *that he shall restore* that which he
25:27. *and restore* the overplus
26:26. *and they shall deliver* (you) your bread *again*
Nu. 5: 7. *and he shall recompense* his trespass
22: 8. *and I will bring* you word *again*,
25:11. Phinehas,...*hath turned* my wrath *away*
35:25. *and* the congregation *shall restore*
Deu 4:39. Know therefore this day, *and consider* (it) in (lit. *cause to return* to) thine heart,
22: 2. *and thou shalt restore it* to him again.
28:60. *Moreover he will bring* upon thee
68. *And* the Lord *shall bring thee* into Egypt *again*
30: 1. *and thou shalt call* (lit. *cause to return*) (them) to mind
Jos. 8:26. Joshua *drew* not his hand *back*,
Jud. 9:57. all the evil...*did* God *render* upon
Ru. 1:21. the Lord *hath brought me home again*
1Sa. 6: 7. *bring* their calves home from them:
8. the jewels of gold, which *ye return*
17. which the Philistines *returned*
21. The Philistines *have brought again* the ark
25:39. the Lord *hath returned* the wickedness
30:19. David *recovered* all.
2Sa. 9: 7. *and will restore* thee all the land
15:25. *he will bring me again*,
16: 8. The Lord *hath returned*...all the blood
12. *and* that the Lord *will requite* me good
1K. 2:32. *And* the Lord *shall return* his blood
1K. 2:44. *therefore* the Lord *shall return* thy
8:34. *and bring them again* unto the land
47. *if they shall bethink* themselves (marg. *bring back* to their heart)
13:20, 26. the prophet that *brought him back:*
23. the prophet *whom he had brought back.*
14:28. *and brought them back* into the guard
2K. 3: 4. *and rendered* unto the king of Israel
14:25. *He restored* the coast of Israel
28. how *he recovered* Damascus,
16: 6. Rezin king of Syria *recovered* Elath
19:28. *and I will turn thee back* by the way
2Ch 6:25. *and bring them again* unto the land
37. *Yet* (if) *they bethink* themselves (marg. *bring back* to their heart)
12:11. *and brought them again* into the guard
25:13. the soldiers...which Amaziah *sent back*,
27: 5. So much *did* the children of Ammon *pay* (lit. *make to return*)
32:25. Hezekiah *rendered* not *again*
Ps. 85: 3(4). *thou hast turned* (thyself) from
Pro.24:12. *and shall* (not) *he render* to (every) man
18. *and he turn away* his wrath
Isa. 37:29. *and I will turn thee back* by the way
Jer. 12:15. *and will bring them again*,
16:15. *and I will bring them again*
23: 3. *and will bring* them *again*
24: 6. *and I will bring them again*
27:22. *and restore them* to this place.
29:14. *and I will bring* you *again* into the place
30: 3. *and I will cause them to return*
32:37. *and I will bring them again*
33: 7. *And I will cause* the captivity...*to return*,
34:22. *and cause them to return* to this city;
41:16. the remnant...whom *he had recovered*
— eunuchs, whom *he had brought again*
42:12. *and cause* you *to return* to your own land.
Lam. 1:13. *he hath turned me* back:
2: 3. *he hath drawn* back his right hand
8. *he hath* not *withdrawn* his hand
Eze.18:17. *hath taken off* his hand from the poor,
20:22. *Nevertheless I withdrew* mine hand,
27:15. *they brought* thee (for) a present horns
29:14. *and will cause them to return* (into) the
34: 4. neither *have ye brought again*
Joel 3: 7(4:7). *and will return* your recompence
Am. 1: 8. *and I will turn* mine hand against Ekron:
Zec.10:10. *I will bring them again also*
13: 7. *and I will turn* mine hand upon the little
Mal. 2: 6. *did turn* many *away* from iniquity.
4: 6(3:24). *And he shall turn* the heart of the

HIPHIL.—*Infinitive.*

Gen24: 5. must I *needs* bring thy son *again* (lit. *bringing again* must I bring again)
37:22. *to deliver him* to his father *again.*
42:25. *and to restore* every man's money
50:15. *and* will *certainly* requite (lit. and *requiting* will requite)
Ex. 23: 4. thou shalt *surely* bring it back to him again. (lit. *bringing back* thou shalt bring it back)
Lev.25:28. if he be not able *to restore*
Nu. 5: 8. if the man have no kinsman *to recompense*
Deu22: 1. thou shalt *in any case* bring them *again* (lit. *bringing again* thou shalt bring them again)
24:13. *In any case* thou shalt deliver him the pledge again (lit. *delivering* thou shalt &c.)
Jud.19: 3. friendly unto her, (and) *to bring her again*,
1Sa. 6: 3. *in any wise* return (lit. in *returning* return)
2Sa. 3:11. he could not *answer* Abner a word
8: 3. went *to recover* his border
12:23. can I *bring him back again?*
14:13. the king *doth* not *fetch home again*
19:10(11). speak ye not a word *of bringing...back?*
11(12). *to bring* the king *back*
12(13). *to bring back* the king?
43(44). *in bringing back* our king?
1K. 12: 6. *that* I *may* answer (lit. may *return* word to) this people?
21 *to bring* the kingdom *again*
13: 4. he could not *pull it in again*
2Ch 6:23. *by requiting* the wicked,
10: 6. *to return* answer to this people?
11: 1. *that he might bring* the kingdom *again*
24:19. *to bring them again* unto the Lord;

Ezr.10:14. until the fierce wrath...*be turned*
Neh 9:26. *to turn them* to thee,
29. *that thou mightest bring them again*
Est. 4:13. Mordecai commanded *to answer* Esther,
15. Esther bade (them) *return* Mordecai (this answer),
8: 5. *to reverse* the letters devised by Haman
8. *may* no man *reverse.*
Job 9:18. He will not suffer me *to take*
33: 5. If thou canst *answer me,*
30. *To bring back* his soul from the pit,
Ps. 78:38. many a time *turned he* his anger *away,*
106:23. *to turn away* his wrath,
Pro.22:21. *that thou mightest answer* the words of
26:15. *to bring it again* to his mouth.
Isa. 49: 6. *to restore* the preserved of Israel:
66:15. *to render* his anger with fury,
Jer. 18:20. *to turn away* thy wrath from them.
28: 6. *to bring again* the vessels of the Lord's
29:10. *in causing* you *to return* to this place.
38:26. that *he would* not *cause me to return*
Lam. 1:11. meat *to relieve* the soul: (marg. or, *make* the soul *to come again*)
2:14. *to turn away* thy captivity;
Eze.38:12. *to turn* thine hand upon the desolate
Dan 9:25. *to restore* and to build Jerusalem
Jon. 1:13. the men rowed hard *to bring* (lit. *to make to return*)

HIPHIL.—*Imperative.*

Gen20: 7. *restore* the man (his) wife;
37:14. *and bring me* word *again.*
Ex. 4: 7. *Put* thine hand into thy bosom *again.*
Nu. 17:10(25). *Bring* Aaron's rod *again*
Jud 11:13. *restore* those (lands) *again*
1Sa.29: 4. *Make* this fellow *return,*
2Sa.14:21. *bring* the young man Absalom *again.*
15:20. *and take back* thy brethren:
25. *Carry back* the ark of God
1K. 13:18. *Bring him back* with thee
22:26. *and carry him back* unto Amon
2K. 8: 6. *Restore* all that (was) her's,
2Ch 18:25. *and carry him back* to Amon
28:11. *and deliver* the captives *again,*
Neh 4: 4(3:36). *and turn* their reproach upon their own head,
5:11. *Restore,* I pray you,...their lands,
Job 13:22. *and answer thou me.*
33:32. If thou hast any thing to say, *answer me:*
Ps. 28: 4. *render* to them their desert.
35:17. *rescue* my soul from their destructions,
51:12(14). *Restore* unto me the joy
79:12. *And render* unto our neighbours sevenfold
80: 3(4). *Turn us again,* O God, and cause
7(8). *Turn us again,* O God of hosts,
19(20). *Turn us again,* O Lord God of hosts,
94: 2. *render* a reward to the proud.
Isa. 42:22. none saith, *Restore.*
46: 8. *bring* (it) *again* to mind,
Jer. 6: 9. *turn back* thine hand as a grapegatherer
31:18. *turn thou me,* and I shall be turned;
Lam 5:21. *Turn thou us* unto thee, O Lord,
Eze.14: 6. Repent, *and turn* (yourselves)
— *turn away* your faces from all
18:30. *and turn* (yourselves) from all your transgressions;
32. *wherefore turn* (yourselves),
21:30(35). *Shall I cause* (it) (marg. or, *Cause* (it)) *to return*

HIPHIL.—*Future.*

Gen14:16. *And he brought back* all the goods,
20:14. *and restored him* Sarah his wife.
24: 5. *must I* needs *bring* thy son *again*
6. Beware thou that *thou bring* not my son thither *again.*
8. *bring* not my son thither *again.*
40:21. *And he restored* the chief butler
42:37. I *will bring him* to thee *again.*
43:12. *carry* (it) *again* in your hand;
21. *and we have brought* it *again* in our hand.
50:15. Joseph...*will* certainly *requite*
Ex. 4: 7. *And he put* his hand into his bosom *again;*
15:19. *and* the Lord *brought again* the waters
19: 8. *And* Moses *returned* the words of the
21:34. The owner of the pit shall make...(and) *give* money
22:26(25). *thou shalt deliver it* unto him
Ex. 23: 4. *thou shalt* surely *bring it back*
Lev.25:51. *he shall give again* the price
52. according unto his years *shall he give* him *again*
Nu. 13:26. *and brought back* word unto them,
18: 9. *they shall render* unto me,
23:20. *I cannot reverse it.*
Deu 1:22. *and bring* us word *again*
25. *and brought* us word *again,*
17:16. nor *cause* the people *to return*
22: 1. *thou shalt* in any case *bring them again*
24:13. *thou shalt deliver* him the pledge *again*
32:41. *I will render* vengeance
43. *will render* vengeance
Jos. 14: 7. *and I brought* him word *again*
22:32. *and brought* them word *again.*
Jud. 5:29. *she returned* answer to herself,
9:56. *Thus* God *rendered* the wickedness
17: 3. *when he had restored* the eleven hundred
— *I will restore it* unto thee.
4. *Yet he restored* the money
1Sa. 5: 3. *and set* him in his place *again.*
6: 3. *return* him a trespass offering:
4. the trespass offering which *we shall return*
12: 3. *and I will restore* it you.
14:27. *and put* (lit. *returned*) his hand to his mouth;
17:30. *and* the people answer*ed* him *again* (lit. *returned* word)
25:21. *and he hath requited* me evil for good.
26:23. The Lord *render* to every man his
2Sa. 3:26. sent messengers after Abner, *which brought* him *again*
15: 8. (כתיב) If the Lord *shall bring me again* indeed
29. Zadok *therefore* and Abiathar *carried* the ark of God *again*
16: 3. To day *shall* the house of Israel *restore me*
17: 3. *I will bring back* all the people
22:21. *hath he recompensed* me.
25. *Therefore* the Lord *hath recompensed*
24:13. see what answer *I shall return*
1K. 2:16. I ask one petition of thee, *deny* me not. (marg. *turn* not *away* my face)
17. *he will* not *say* thee *nay,* (lit. *he will* not *turn away* thy face)
20. *say* me not *nay.* (lit. *turn* not *away* my face)
— *I will* not *say* thee *nay.* (lit. *I will* not *turn away* thy face)
30. *And* Benaiah *brought* the king word *again,*
12: 9. *that we may* answer (lit. *return* word to) this people,
16. *So*...the people answer*ed* (lit. *returned* word to) the king,
13:29. took up the carcase...*and brought it back:*
20: 9. the messengers departed, *and brought* him word *again.*
34. The cities, which my father took...*I will restore;*
2K. 13:25. *and recovered* the cities of Israel.
14:22. built Elath, *and restored it* to Judah,
17: 3. Hoshea became his servant, *and gave* (marg. *rendered*) him presents.
18:24. How then *wilt thou turn away*
20:11. *and he brought* the shadow ten degrees
22: 9. *and brought* the king word *again,*
20. *And they brought* the king word *again.*
1Ch 21:12. what word *I shall bring again*
27. *and he put up* his sword *again*
2Ch 6:42. *turn* not *away* the face of thine anointed:
10: 9. *that we may return* answer
16. *And* when...the people *answered* the king,
19: 4. *and brought* them *back* unto the Lord
24:11. *and carried it* to his place *again.*
26: 2. built Eloth, *and restored it* to Judah,
33:13. *and brought him again* to Jerusalem
34:16. *and brought* the king word *back again,*
28. *So they brought* the king word *again.*
Neh 2:20. *Then* answered *I* (lit. *then I returned* word)
5:12. Then said they, *We will restore*
6: 4. *and I answered* them after the same
13: 9. *and* thither *brought I again* the vessels
Job 9:12. he taketh away, who *can hinder him?* (marg. *turn him away*)
13. (If) God *will* not *withdraw* his anger,

Job 10: 9. *wilt thou bring me* into dust *again?*
11:10. who *can hinder him?* (marg. *turn him away*)
15:13. *thou turnest* thy spirit against God,
20: 2. do my thoughts *cause me to answer,*
10. his hands *shall restore* their goods.
23:13. who *can turn him?*
30:23. *thou wilt bring me* (to) death,
31:14. what *shall I answer him?*
32:14. neither *will I answer him* with your
33:26. *for he will render* unto man his
35: 4. I *will answer thee* (marg. *return to thee* words), and thy companions
39:12. *he will bring home* thy seed,
40: 4. what *shall I answer thee?*
Ps. 18:20(21). *hath he recompensed* me.
24(25). *Therefore hath* the Lord *recompensed*
44:10(11). *Thou makest us to turn* back
54: 5(7). *He shall reward* evil unto mine
68:22(23). *I will bring again* from Bashan, *I will bring* (my people) *again*
69: 4(5). *I restored* (that) which I took not
72:10. The kings of Tarshish...*shall bring*
73:10. (כתיב) Therefore his people *return* hither:
74:11. Why *withdrawest thou* thy hand,
81:14(15). *and turned* my hand against their
89:43(44). *Thou hast* also *turned* the edge of his
90: 3. *Thou turnest* man to destruction;
94:23. *And he shall bring* upon them their own
116:12. What *shall I render* unto the Lord
119:59. *and turned* my feet unto thy testimonies.
132:10. *turn* not *away* the face of thine anointed.
Pro.12:14. the recompence of a man's hands *shall be rendered*
15: 1. A soft answer *turneth away* wrath:
19:24. *will* not so much as *bring it* to his mouth *again.*
20:26. *and bringeth* the wheel over them.
24:29. *I will render* to the man according
25:13. *he refresheth* the soul of his masters.
27:11. *that I may* answer (lit. *return* word) him
29: 8. wise (men) *turn away* wrath.
Isa. 1:25. *And I will turn* my hand upon thee,
26. *And I will restore* thy judges
14:27. who *shall turn it back?*
36: 9. How then *wilt thou turn away*
41:28. no counsellor, *that,* when I asked of them, *could answer* (marg. *return*)
43:13. I will work, and who *shall let it?* (marg. *turn it back*)
44:19. none *considereth* (marg. *setteth* to) in his
58:13. If *thou turn away* thy foot from the
Jer. 2:24. in her occasion who *can turn her away?* (marg. or, *reverse it*)
15:19. *then will I bring thee again,*
23:22. *then they should have turned them*
32:44. *I will cause* their captivity *to return,*
33:11. *I will cause to return* the captivity
26. *I will cause* their captivity *to return,*
34:11. *and caused* the servants...*to return,*
16. *and caused* every man his servant,...*to return,*
37:20. that *thou cause me* not *to return*
49: 6,39. *I will bring again* the captivity
Lam 1:19. sought their meat *to relieve* their souls.
3:21. This *I recall* (marg. *make to return*) to my
64. *Render* unto them a recompence,
Eze.18: 7. *hath restored* to the debtor his pledge,
8. *hath withdrawn* his hand from iniquity,
12. *hath* not *restored* the pledge,
33:15. (If) the wicked *restore* the pledge,
34:16. and *bring again* that which was driven
39:25. Now *will I bring again* the captivity
44: 1. *Then he brought* me *back* the way
47: 1. *Afterward he brought me again*
6. *and caused me to return* to the brink of the
Dan11:18. (כתיב) *After this shall he turn* his face
— *he shall cause* (it) *to turn*
19. *Then he shall turn* his face
Hos. 4: 9. and *reward* them their doings.
12: 2(3). *will he recompense* him.
14(15). his reproach *shall* his Lord *return*
Joel 3: 1(4:1). *I shall bring again* the captivity
4(-:4). speedily *will I return*
Am. 1: 3,6,9,11,13 & 2:1,4,6. *I will* not *turn away* (marg. or, *convert it,* or, *let it be quiet*) (the punishment) thereof;

Hab. 2: 1. what *I shall answer* when I am reproved.
Zec. 9:12. *I will render* double unto thee;

HIPHIL.—*Participle.*

Gen20: 7. if thou *restore* (her) not,
38:29. *as he drew back* his hand,
Jud.11: 9. If ye *bring me home again* to fight
Ru. 4:15. *a restorer of* (thy) life,
Job 20:18. That which he laboured for *shall he restore.*
Ps. 19: 7(8). The law of the Lord (is) perfect, *converting* the soul:
Pro.17:13. *Whoso rewardeth* evil for good,
18:13. *He that answereth* (marg. *returneth*) a matter before he heareth (it),
24:26. *that giveth a* right *answer.* (marg. *answereth* right words)
26:16. seven men *that can render* a reason.
Isa. 28: 6. *them that turn* the battle
38: 8. I *will bring again* the shadow
44:25. *that turneth* wise (men) backward,
Jer. 28: 3. *will* I *bring again* into this place all the
4. I *will bring again* to this place Jeconiah
Lam 1:16. the comforter *that should relieve* (marg. *bring back*) my soul
Eze. 9:11. the man clothed with linen,...*reported* (marg. *returned*)

* HOPHAL.—*Preterite.* *

Gen42:28. My money *is restored;*

HOPHAL.—*Future.*

Ex. 10: 8. *And* Moses and Aaron *were brought again*

HOPHAL.—*Participle.*

Gen43:12. the money *that was brought again*
Nu. 5: 8. *let* the trespass *be recompensed*
Jer. 27:16. the vessels...*shall* now shortly *be brought again*

שׁוֹבָב *shōh-vāhv',* adj. 7726

Isa. 57:17. went on *frowardly* (marg. *turning away*)
Jer. 3:14. Turn, O *backsliding* children,
22. Return, ye *backsliding* children,
50: 6. (כתיב) *they have turned them away* (lit. according to כ׳, *backsliding*)

שׁוֹבֵב [*shōh-vēhv'*], adj. 7728

Jer. 31:22. O thou *backsliding* daughter?
49: 4. O *backsliding* daughter?

שׁוּבָה *shoo-vāh',* f. 7729

Isa. 30:15. *In returning* and rest shall ye be saved;

שׁוּר see שׁר See 7701

שׁוּד [*shood*]. 7736

* KAL.—*Future.* *

Ps. 91: 6. the destruction (that) *wasteth*

שָׁוָה *shāh-vāh'.* 7737

* KAL.—*Preterite.* *

Job 33:27. perverted...right, *and it profited* me not;

KAL.—*Future.*

Pro. 3:15. all the things thou canst desire *are* not *to be compared*
8:11. that may be desired *are* not *to be compared*
26: 4. lest *thou* also *be like* unto him.
Isa. 40:25. will ye liken me, *or shall I be equal?*

KAL.—*Participle.* Poel.

Est. 3: 8. not for the king's *profit* (marg. *meet,* or *equal*) to suffer
5:13. all this *availeth* me nothing,
7: 4. the enemy *could* not *countervail* the king's

* PIEL.—*Preterite.* *

Ps. 16: 8. *I have set* the Lord always before me:
89:19(20). *I have laid* help upon (one that is)
119:30. thy judgments *have I laid* (before me).
131: 2. *I have behaved* and quieted myself

Isa. 28:25. *he hath made plain* the face thereof,
38:13. *I reckoned* till morning,

PIEL.—*Future.*

Ps. 21: 5(6). honour and majesty *hast thou laid*
Hos 10: 1. *he bringeth forth* fruit unto himself:

PIEL.—*Participle.*

2Sa.22:34. *He maketh* (marg. *equalleth*) my feet *like* hinds' (feet):
Ps. 18:33(34). *He maketh* my feet *like* hinds' (feet),

* HIPHIL.—*Future.* *

Isa. 46: 5. will ye liken me, *and make* (me) *equal,*
Lam.2:13. what *shall I equal* to thee,

* NITHPAEL.—*Preterite.* *

Pro.27:15. A continual dropping...and a contentious woman *are alike.*

7738 ## שָׁוָה [*shāh-vāh'*].

* PIEL.—*Future.* *

Job 30:22. (כתיב) and dissolvest *my substance.* (marg. or, *wisdom;* lit. according to כתיב *thou terrifiest*)

7739 ## שְׁוָה [*sh'vāh*], Ch.

* PAEL.—*Preterite.* *

Dan 5:21. and his heart *was made like* the beasts,

* ITHPAEL.—*Future.* *

Dan 3:29. and their houses *shall be made* a dunghill:

7743 ## שׁוּחַ [*shoo'ăgh*].

* KAL.—*Preterite.* *

Ps. 44:25(26). our soul *is bowed down* to the dust:
Pro. 2:18. her house *inclineth* unto death,

* HIPHIL.—*Future.* *

Lam.3:20. in remembrance, *and is humbled* (marg. *bowed*) in me.

7745 ## שׁוּחָה *shoo-ghāh'*, f.

Pro.22:14. mouth of strange women (is) *a* deep *pit:*
23:27. a whore (is) *a* deep *ditch;*
Jer. 2: 6. a land of deserts *and of pits,*
18:20. they have digged *a pit* for my soul.
22. they have digged *a pit* to take me,

7590 ## שׁוּט [*shoot*].

* KAL.—*Participle.* *

Eze.16:57. daughters of the Philistines, *which despise* (marg. or, *spoil*)
28:24. all...*that despised* them;
26. all *those that despise* (marg. or, *spoil*) them

7751 ## שׁוּט *shoot.*

* KAL.—*Preterite.* *

Nu. 11: 8. the people *went about,*

KAL.—*Infinitive.*

Job 1: 7. *From going to and fro* in the earth,
2: 2. *From going to and fro* in the earth,

KAL.—*Imperative.*

2Sa.24: 2. *Go* now *through* (marg. or, *Compass*) all

KAL.—*Future.*

2Sa.24: 8. *So when they had gone* through

KAL.—*Participle.*

Eze.27: 8. The inhabitants of Zidon and Arvad were thy *mariners:*
26. Thy *rowers* have brought thee

* POLEL.—*Imperative.* *

Jer. 5: 1. *Run ye to and fro*

POLEL.—*Future.*

Dan12: 4. many *shall run to and fro,*
Am. 8:12. *they shall run to and fro*

POLEL.—*Participle.*

2Ch 16: 9. the eyes of the Lord *run to and fro*
Zec. 4:10. the eyes of the Lord, *which run to and fro*

* HITHPOLEL.—*Imperative.* *

Jer. 49: 3. *run to and fro* by the hedges;

שׁוֹט *shōht*, m. 7752

1K. 12:11. my father hath chastised you *with whips,*
14. my father (also) chastised you *with whips,*
2Ch 10:11, 14. my father chastised you *with whips,*
Job 5:21. be hid *from the scourge* (marg. or, *when* the tongue *scourgeth*) *of* the tongue:
9:23. If *the scourge* slay suddenly,
Pro.26: 3. *A whip* for the horse,
Isa. 10:26. the Lord of hosts shall stir up *a scourge*
28:15, 18. when *the* overflowing *scourge* shall
Nah 3: 2. The noise of *a whip,*

שׁוּל [*shool*], m. 7757

Ex. 28:33. upon *the hem* (marg. or, *skirts*) *of it*
— round about *the hem thereof;*
34. upon *the hem of* the robe round about.
39:24. made upon *the hems of* the robe
25. upon *the hem of* the robe,
26. round about *the hem of* the robe
Isa. 6: 1. *and his train* (marg. or, *the skirts thereof*) filled the temple.
Jer. 13:22. are *thy skirts* discovered,
26. Therefore will I discover *thy skirts*
Lam.1: 9. Her filthiness (is) *in her skirts;*
Nah 3: 5. I will discover *thy skirts*

שׁוֹלָל *shōh-lāhl'*, m. 7758

Job 12:17. He leadeth counsellors away *spoiled,*
19. He leadeth princes away *spoiled,*
Mic. 1: 8. I will go *stripped* and naked:

שׁוּלַמִּית *shoo-lam-meeth'*, f. 7759

Cant.6:13(7:1). Return, return, *O Shulamite;*
—(-:-). What will ye see *in the Shulamite?*

שׁוּם [*shoom*], m. 7762

Nu. 11: 5. the leeks, and the onions, *and the garlick:*

שָׁוַע [*shāh-vag'*]. 7768

* PIEL.—*Preterite.* *

Ps. 30: 2(3). O Lord my God, *I cried* unto thee,
88:13(14). unto thee *have I cried,* O Lord;
Jon. 2: 2(3). out of the belly of hell *cried I,*
Hab. 1: 2. O Lord, how long *shall I cry,*

PIEL.—*Infinitive.*

Ps. 22:24(25). *but when he cried* unto him, he heard.
28: 2. *when I cry* unto thee,
31:22(23). *when I cried* unto thee.

PIEL.—*Future.*

Job 19: 7. *I cry aloud,* but (there is) no judgment.
24:12. the soul of the wounded *crieth out:*
30:20. *I cry* unto thee,
28. *I cried* in the congregation.
35: 9. *they cry out* by reason of the arm of the
36:13. *they cry* not when he bindeth them.
38:41. when his young ones *cry*
Ps. 18: 6(7). and *cried* unto my God:
41(42). *They cried,* but (there was) none to
119:147. the dawning of the morning, *and cried:*
Isa. 58: 9. *thou shalt cry,* and he shall
Lam.3: 8. Also when I cry *and shout,*

PIEL.—*Participle.*

Job 29:12. I delivered the poor *that cried,*
Ps. 72:12. he shall deliver the needy *when he crieth;*

7771 שֹׁוַע *shōh'ăg*, m.

Job 34:19. nor regardeth *the rich* more than the
Isa. 22: 5. of *crying* to the mountains.
32: 5. nor the churl said (to be) *bountiful.*
Eze.23:23. and all the Chaldeans, Pekod, *and Shoa,* [perhaps, lit. *riches;* perhaps a proper name.]

7769 שׁוּעַ *shoo'ăg*, m.

Job 30:24. they *cry* (lit. *crying* (is) to them) in his
36:19. Will he esteem *thy riches?*

7773 שֶׁוַע [*sheh'-vag*], m.

Ps. 5: 2(3). Hearken unto the voice of *my cry,*

7775 שַׁוְעָה [*shav-gāh'*], f.

Ex. 2:23. *their cry* came up unto God
1Sa. 5:12. *the cry of* the city went up to heaven.
2Sa.22: 7. *and my cry* (did enter) into his ears.
Ps. 18: 6(7). *and my cry* came before him,
34:15(16). his ears (are open) unto *their cry.*
39:12(13). *and* give ear unto *my cry;*
40: 1(2). inclined unto me, and heard *my cry.*
102: 1(2). *and* let *my cry* come unto thee.
145:19. he also will hear *their cry,*
Jer. 8:19. *the cry of* the daughter of my people
Lam.3:56. hide not thine ear at my breathing, *at my cry.*

7776 שׁוּעָל *shoo-gāhl'*, m.

Jud.15: 4. caught three hundred *foxes,*
Neh 4: 3(3:35). if *a fox* go up, he shall even
Ps. 63:10(11). they shall be a portion for *foxes.*
Cant.2:15. Take us *the foxes, the* little *foxes,* that
Lam. 5:18. *the foxes* walk upon it.
Eze.13: 4. thy prophets are *like the foxes*

7778 שׁוֹעֵר *shōh-gēhr'*, m.

2Sa.18:26. the watchman called unto *the porter,*
2K. 7:10. called unto *the porter of* the city:
11. he called *the porters;*
1Ch 9:17. *And the porters* (were), Shallum,
18. *porters* in the companies
21. *porter of* the door of the tabernacle
22. chosen *to be porters* in the gates
24. In four quarters were *the porters,*
26. *the* four chief *porters,*
15:18. Obed-edom, and Jeiel, *the porters.*
23. and Elkanah (were) *doorkeepers* for the
24. and Jehiah (were) *doorkeepers*
16:38. Jeduthun and Hosah (to be) *porters:*
23: 5. four thousand (were) *porters;*
26: 1. the divisions *of the porters:*
12,19. the divisions of *the porters,*
2Ch 8:14. *the porters also* by their courses
23: 4. the Levites, (shall be) *porters*
19. he set *the porters* at the gates
31:14. *the porter* toward the east,
34:13. scribes, and officers, *and porters.*
35:15. *and the porters* (waited) at every gate;
Ezr. 2:42. The children of *the porters:*
70. the singers, *and the porters,*
7: 7. the singers, *and the porters,*
10:24. of *the porters;* Shallum,
Neh 7: 1. *the porters* and the singers
45. *The porters:* the children of
73. the Levites, *and the porters,*
10:28(29). the Levites, *the porters,*
39(40). *and the porters,* and the singers:
11:19. *Moreover the porters,* Akkub,
12:25. *porters* keeping the ward at the thresholds
45. both the singers *and the porters*
47. of the singers *and the porters,*
13: 5. and the singers, *and the porters;*

שׁוּף [*shooph*]. 7779

* KAL.—*Future.* *

Gen 3:15. it *shall bruise thy* head, and *thou shall bruise his* heel.
Job 9:17. *he breaketh me* with a tempest,
Ps.139:11. the darkness *shall cover me;*

שׁוֹפָר *shōh-phāhr'*, m. 7782

Ex. 19:16. the voice of *the trumpet* exceeding
19. the voice of *the trumpet* sounded
20:18. the noise of *the trumpet,*
Lev.25: 9. cause *the trumpet of*
— make *the trumpet* sound
Jos. 6: 4. before the ark seven *trumpets*
— the priests shall blow *with the trumpets.*
5. hear the sound of *the trumpet,*
6. bear seven *trumpets* of rams' horns
8. priests bearing *the* seven *trumpets*
— blew *with the trumpets:*
9. priests that blew with *the trumpets,*
— blowing *with the trumpets.*
13. priests bearing seven *trumpets*
— and blew *with the trumpets:*
— blowing *with the trumpets.*
16. the priests blew *with the trumpets,*
20. (the priests) blew *with the trumpets:*
— heard the sound of *the trumpet,*
Jud. 3:27. that he blew *a trumpet*
6:34. and he blew *a trumpet;*
7: 8. victuals in their hand, and *their trumpets*
16. he put *a trumpet* in every man's hand, (marg. *trumpets* in the hand of all)
18. When I blow *with a trumpet,*
— then blow ye *the trumpets* also
19. they blew *the trumpets,*
20. three companies blew *the trumpets,*
— *the trumpets* in their right hands
22. the three hundred blew *the trumpets,*
1Sa.13: 3. Saul blew *the trumpet*
2Sa. 2:28. So Joab blew *a trumpet,*
6:15. with the sound of *the trumpet.*
15:10. hear the sound of *the trumpet,*
18:16. And Joab blew *the trumpet,*
20: 1. and he blew *a trumpet,*
22. he blew *a trumpet,* and they
1K. 1:34. blow ye *with the trumpet,*
39. And they blew *the trumpet;*
41. heard the sound of *the trumpet,*
2K. 9:13. blew *with trumpets,*
1Ch 15:28. with sound of *the cornet,* and with
2Ch 15:14. and with trumpets, *and with cornets.*
Neh 4:18(12). he that sounded *the trumpet*
20(14). ye hear the sound of *the trumpet,*
Job 39:24. (it is) the sound of *the trumpet.*
25. He saith among *the trumpets,*
Ps. 47: 5(6). the Lord with the sound of *a trumpet.*
81: 3(4). Blow up *the trumpet* in the new moon,
98: 6. With trumpets and sound of *cornet*
150: 3. Praise him with the sound of *the trumpet:* (marg. or, *cornet*)
Isa. 18: 3. when he bloweth *a trumpet,*
27:13. *the* great *trumpet* shall be
58: 1. lift up thy voice *like a trumpet,*
Jer. 4: 5. Blow ye *the trumpet* in the land:
19. O my soul, the sound of *the trumpet,*
21. hear the sound of *the trumpet?*
6: 1. blow *the trumpet* in Tekoa,
17. Hearken to the sound of *the trumpet.*
42:14. hear the sound of *the trumpet,*
51:27. blow *the trumpet* among the nations,
Eze.33: 3. If when...he blow *the trumpet,*
4. heareth the sound of *the trumpet,*
5. He heard the sound of *the trumpet,*
6. blow not *the trumpet,*
Hos. 5: 8. Blow ye *the cornet* in Gibeah,
8: 1. (Set) *the trumpet* to thy mouth.
Joel 2: 1. Blow ye *the trumpet* (marg. or, *cornet*) in Zion,
15. Blow *the trumpet* in Zion,
Am. 2: 2. with the sound of *the trumpet:*
3: 6. Shall *a trumpet* be blown
Zep. 1:16. A day of *the trumpet* and alarm
Zec. 9:14. the Lord God shall blow *the trumpet,*

7785 **שׁוֹק** *shōhk*, m.

Ex. 29:22. the fat...and *the* right *shoulder;*
27. *the shoulder of* the heave offering,
Lev. 7:32. *the* right *shoulder* shall ye give
33. He...shall have *the* right *shoulder*
34. *the* heave *shoulder* have I taken
8:25. the two kidneys,...and *the* right *shoulder:*
26. upon *the* right *shoulder:*
9:21. the breasts and *the* right *shoulder*
10:14. the wave breast and heave *shoulder*
15. *The* heave *shoulder* and the wave breast
Nu. 6:20. the wave breast and heave *shoulder:*
18:18. as the wave breast *and as the* right *shoulder*
Deu 28:35. The Lord shall smite thee in the knees, and in *the legs*,
Jud. 15: 8. he smote them *hip* and thigh
1 Sa. 9:24. the cook took up *the shoulder*,
Ps. 147:10. he taketh not pleasure *in the legs of* a
Pro. 26: 7. *The legs* of the lame are not equal:
Cant. 5:15. *His legs* (are as) pillars of marble,
Isa. 47: 2. uncover *the thigh*,

7783 **שׁוּק** [*shook*].

* POLEL.—*Future.* *

Ps. 65: 9(10). Thou visitest the earth, *and waterest it:*

* HIPHIL.—*Preterite.* *

Joel 2:24. *and* the fats *shall overflow*
3:13(4:13). the fats *overflow;*

7784 **שׁוּק** *shook*, m.

Pro. 7: 8. Passing *through the street*
Ecc. 12: 4. the doors shall be shut *in the streets*,
5. the mourners go *about the streets:*
Cant. 3: 2. go about the city *in the streets*,

7794 **שׁוֹר** *shōhr*, m.

Gen 32: 5(6). I have *oxen*, and asses, flocks,
49: 6. in their selfwill they digged down *a wall*. (marg. or, houghed *oxen*)
Ex. 20:17. *nor his ox*, nor his ass,
21:28. If *an ox* gore a man
— then *the ox* shall be surely stoned,
— the owner of *the ox* (shall be) quit.
29. if *the ox* were wont to push
— *the ox* shall be stoned,
32. If *the ox* shall push a manservant
— *and the ox* shall be stoned.
33. *an ox* or an ass fall therein;
35. if one man's *ox* hurt another's, (lit. his neighbour's *ox*)
— they shall sell *the* live *ox*,
36. *the ox* hath used to push
— he shall surely pay *ox* for *ox;*
22: 1(21:37). If a man shall steal *an ox*,
—(—:—). he shall restore five oxen for *an ox*,
4(3). *whether it be ox*, or ass, (lit. *from ox* to ass)
9(8). (whether it be) for *ox*, for ass,
10(9). deliver unto his neighbour...*an ox*,
30(29). Likewise shalt thou do with *thine oxen*,
23: 4. If thou meet thine enemy's *ox*
12. that *thine ox* and thine ass may rest,
34:19. every firstling...(whether) *ox* or sheep,
Lev. 4:10. *from the bullock of* the sacrifice
7:23. fat, of *ox*, or of sheep, or of goat.
9: 4. *Also a bullock* and a ram for peace
18. He slew also *the bullock* and the ram
19. the fat of *the bullock* and of the ram,
17: 3. killeth *an ox*, or lamb, or goat,
22:23. *Either a bullock* or a lamb
27. When *a bullock*,...is brought forth,
28. *And* (whether it be) *cow* or ewe,
27:26. whether (it be) *ox*, or sheep:
Nu. 7: 3. *and* for each one *an ox:*
15:11. *for* one *bullock*, or for one ram,
18:17. the firstling of *a cow*,
22: 4. as *the ox* licketh up the grass
Deu 5:14. *nor thine ox*, nor thine ass,
21(18). *his ox*, or his ass,
Deu 14: 4. *the ox*, the sheep, and the goat,
15:19. the firstling of *thy bullock*,
17: 1. (any) *bullock*, or sheep, wherein is
18: 3. a sacrifice, whether (it be) *ox* or sheep;
22: 1. thy brother's *ox* or his sheep
4. thy brother's ass or *his ox*
10. Thou shalt not plow *with an ox* and
25: 4. Thou shalt not muzzle *the ox*
28:31. *Thine ox* (shall be) slain
33:17. (like) the firstling of *his bullock*,
Jos. 6:21. *ox*, and sheep, and ass,
7:24. *his oxen*, and his asses,
Jud. 6: 4. left...neither sheep, *nor ox*,
25. thy father's young *bullock*, (lit. steer *ox*)
1 Sa. 12: 3. whose *ox* have I taken?
14:34. Bring me hither every man *his ox*,
— all the people brought every man *his ox*
15: 3. slay both man and woman,...*ox* and sheep, (lit. *from ox* to sheep)
22:19. *oxen*, and asses, and sheep,
2 Sa. 6:13. he sacrificed *oxen* and fatlings.
1 K. 1:19. he hath slain *oxen* and fat cattle
25. hath slain *oxen* and fat cattle
Neh 5:18. one *ox* (and) six choice sheep;
Job 6: 5. loweth *the ox* over his fodder?
21:10. *Their bull* gendereth, and faileth not;
24: 3. they take the widow's *ox*
Ps. 69:31(32). please the Lord better *than an ox* (or) bullock
106:20. the similitude of *an ox* that eateth grass.
Pro. 7:22. *as an ox* goeth to the slaughter,
14: 4. increase (is) by the strength of *the ox*.
15:17. *than a* stalled *ox* and hatred therewith.
Isa. 1: 3. *The ox* knoweth his owner,
7:25. the sending forth of *oxen*,
32:20. the feet of *the ox* and the ass.
66: 3. He that killeth *an ox* (is as if) he slew a
Eze. 1:10. they four had the face of *an ox*
Hos 12:11(12). they sacrifice *bullocks* in Gilgal;

שׁוּר *shoor*. 7788

* KAL.—*Future.* *

Isa. 57: 9. *thou wentest* (marg. or, *respectedst*) to the

KAL.—*Participle.* Poel.

Eze. 27:25. The ships of Tarshish *did sing of thee*

שׁוּר [*shoor*]. 7789

* KAL.—*Imperative.* *

Job 35: 5. *and behold* the clouds (which) are higher

KAL.—*Future.*

Nu. 23: 9. from the hills *I behold him:*
24:17. *I shall behold him*, but not nigh:
Job 7: 8. *shall see me* no (more):
17:15. as for my hope, who *shall see it?*
20: 9. neither *shall* his place any more *behold him.*
24:15. No eye *shall see me:*
33:14. (man) *perceiveth it* not.
27. *He looketh* (marg. or, *shall look*) upon men,
34:29. who then *can behold him?*
35:13. neither *will* the Almighty *regard it.*
14. thou sayest thou *shalt* not *see him*,
Cant 4: 8. *look* from the top of Amana,
Jer. 5:26. *they lay wait*, as he that setteth snares;
Hos 13: 7. as a leopard by the way *will I observe*
14: 8(9). I have heard (him), *and observed him:*

שׁוּר see **שִׁיר** See 7891

שׁוּר [*shoor*], m. 7790

Ps. 92:11(12). shall see (my desire) *on mine enemies*,

שׁוּר *shoor*, m. 7791

Gen 49:22. (whose) branches run over *the wall:*
2 Sa. 22:30. by my God have I leaped over *a wall*.
Job 24:11. (Which) make oil within *their walls*,
Ps. 18:29(30). by my God have I leaped over *a wall*.

7792 שׂוּר [*shoar*], Ch. m.

Ezr. 4:12. *and* have set up *the walls* (thereof),
13. *and the walls* set up (again),
16. *and the walls* thereof set up,

7799 שׁוֹשַׁן *shōh-shāhn'*, m.

1K. 7:22. top of the pillars (was) *lily* work:
26. the brim of a cup, with flowers *of lilies:*
Ps. 45[title](1). To the chief Musician upon *Shoshannim*,
69[title](1). To the chief Musician upon *Shoshannim*,
80[title](1). To the chief Musician upon *Shoshannim*-Eduth,
Cant 2:16. he feedeth *among the lilies.*
4: 5. young roes...which feed *among the lilies.*
5:13. his lips (like) *lilies*,
6: 2. feed in the gardens, and to gather *lilies.*
3. he feedeth *among the lilies.*
7: 2(3). an heap of wheat set about *with lilies.*

7799 שׁוּשַׁן *shoo-shan'*, m.

1K. 7:19. the chapiters...(were) of *lily* work
Ps. 60[title](1). To the chief Musician upon *Shushan*-eduth,

7799 שׁוֹשַׁנָּה *shōh-shan-nāh'*, f.

2Ch 4: 5. the brim of a cup, with flowers of *lilies;*
Cant 2: 1. *the lily of* the valleys.
2. *As the lily* among thorns,
Hos 14: 5(6). he shall grow *as the lily*,

See 7896 שׁוּת see שִׁית

7804 שְׁזַב [*sh'zav*], Ch.

* PEEL or PEIL.—*Preterite.* *

Dan 3:28. hath sent his angel, *and delivered* his
6:27(28). who *hath delivered* Daniel

PEEL or PEIL.—*Infinitive.*

Dan 3:17. is able *to deliver us* from the burning
6:14(15). set (his) heart on Daniel *to deliver him:*
20(21). able *to deliver thee* from the lions?

PEEL or PEIL.—*Future.*

Dan 3:15. who (is) that God that *shall deliver you*
17. and *he will deliver* (us) out of thine hand,
6:16(17). servest continually, *he will deliver thee.*

PEEL or PEIL.—*Participle.*

Dan 6:27(28). *He delivereth* and rescueth,

7805 שָׁזַף [*shāh-zaph'*].

* KAL.—*Preterite.* *

Job 20: 9. The eye also (which) *saw him*
28: 7. which the vulture's eye *hath* not *seen:*
Cant 1: 6. *because* the sun *hath looked upon* me:

7806 שָׁזַר [*shāh-zar'*].

* HOPHAL.—*Participle.* *

Ex. 26: 1, 31, 36 & 27:9, 16, 18 & 28:6, 8, 15 & 36:8, 35, 37 & 38:9, 16, 18 & 39:2, 5, 8, 28, 29. fine *twined* linen,
39:24. scarlet, (and) *twined* (linen).

7807 שַׁח *shagh*, adj.

Job 22:29. *and* he shall save the *humble* person. (marg. *him that hath low* eyes)

7809 שָׁחַד [*shāh-ghad'*].

* KAL.—*Imperative.* *

Job 6:22. *Give a reward* for me of your substance?

KAL.—*Future.*

Eze.16:33. givest thy gifts to all thy lovers, *and hirest* (marg. *bribest*) them,

שֹׁחַד *shōh'-ghad*, m. 7810

Ex. 23: 8. *And* thou shalt take no *gift:* for *the gift* blindeth the wise,
Deu 10:17. regardeth not persons, nor taketh *reward*
16:19. neither take *a gift:* for *a gift* doth blind
27:25. he that taketh *reward* to slay an innocent
1Sa. 8: 3. turned aside after lucre, and took *bribes*,
1K. 15:19. I have sent unto thee *a present*
2K. 16: 8. *a present* to the king of Assyria.
2Ch 19: 7. respect of persons, nor taking of *gifts.*
Job 15:34. the tabernacles of *bribery.*
Ps. 15: 5. *nor* taketh *reward* against the innocent.
26:10. their right hand is full of *bribes.*
Pro. 6:35. though thou givest many *gifts.*
17: 8. *A gift* (is as) a precious stone
23. A wicked (man) taketh *a gift*
21:14. *and a reward* in the bosom
Isa. 1:23. every one loveth *gifts*,
5:23. Which justify the wicked for *reward*,
33:15. shaketh his hands from holding *of bribes*,
45:13. not for price nor *reward*,
Eze.22:12. taken *gifts* to shed blood;
Mic. 3:11. The heads thereof judge *for reward*,

שָׁחָה [*shāh-ghāh'*]. 7812

* KAL.—*Imperative.* *

Isa. 51:23. *Bow down*, that we may go over:

* HIPHIL.—*Future.* *

Pro.12:25. Heaviness in the heart of man *maketh it stoop:*

* HITHPAEL.—*Preterite.* *

Ex. 11: 8. *and bow down themselves* unto me,
24: 1. *and worship ye* afar off.
33:10. all the people rose up *and worshipped.*
Deu 4:19. shouldest be driven *to worship* (lit. shouldest be driven *and shouldest worship*)
8:19. walk after other gods,...*and worship* them,
11:16. serve other gods, *and worship* them;
26:10. *and worship* before the Lord thy God:
30:17. *and worship* other gods, and serve them;
Jos. 23:16. *and bowed yourselves* to them;
1Sa.15:30. *that I may worship* the Lord thy God.
2Sa.16: 4. *I humbly beseech thee* (marg. *do obeisance*)
1K. 9: 6. serve other gods, *and worship* them:
2K. 5:18. *and I bow myself* in the house of Rimmon:
2Ch 7:19. serve other gods, *and worship* them;
Isa. 27:13. *and shall worship* the Lord
60:14. *and* all they...*shall bow themselves down*
Jer. 8: 2. whom *they have worshipped:*
Eze.46: 2. *and he shall worship* at the threshold of
3. *Likewise* the people of the land *shall worship*

HITHPAEL.—*Infinitive.*

Gen37:10. come *to bow down ourselves* to thee
Lev.26: 1. *to bow down* unto it:
Jud. 2:19. *and to bow down* unto them;
1Sa. 1: 3. went up out of his city...*to worship*
2:36. *crouch* to him for a piece of silver
2Sa.15: 5. came nigh (to him) *to do* him *obeisance*,
2K. 5:18. goeth into the house of Rimmon *to worship* — *when I bow down myself* in the house of
2Ch 20:18. *worshipping* the Lord.
Isa. 2:20. made (each one) for himself *to worship*,
66:23. shall all flesh come *to worship*
Jer. 7: 2. enter in at these gates *to worship*
13:10. walk after other gods, to serve them, *and to worship* them,
25: 6. go not after other gods to serve them *and to worship*
26: 2. come *to worship* in the Lord's house,
Eze.46: 9. he that entereth...*to worship*
Zec.14:16. go up from year to year *to worship*
17. will not come up...*to worship*

HITHPAEL.—*Imperative.*

1Ch 16:29. *worship* the Lord in the beauty of holiness.
Ps. 29: 2. *worship* the Lord in the beauty of holiness.
45:11(12). (is) thy Lord; *and worship thou* him.
96: 9. *O worship* the Lord in the beauty of

Ps. 97: 7. *worship* him, all (ye) gods.
99: 5. *and worship* at his footstool;
9. *and worship* at his holy hill;

HITHPAEL.—*Future.*

Gen18: 2. *and bowed himself* toward the ground,
19: 1. *and he bowed himself*...toward the ground;
22: 5. I and the lad will go yonder *and worship,*
23: 7. Abraham stood up, *and bowed himself* to the people
12. *And* Abraham *bowed down himself* before
24:26. man bowed down his head, *and worshipped*
48. I bowed down my head, *and worshipped*
52. *that,* when...*he worshipped* the Lord,
27:29. *and* nations *bow down* to thee:
— *and let* thy mother's sons *bow down* to thee:
33: 3. *and bowed himself* to the ground
6. came near,...*and they bowed themselves.*
7. Leah also with her children came near, *and bowed themselves:*
— came Joseph near and Rachel, *and they bowed themselves.*
37: 7. *and made obeisance* to my sheaf.
42: 6. *and bowed down themselves* before him
43:26. *and bowed themselves* to him to the earth.
28. *and made obeisance.* (lit. *bowed themselves*)
47:31. *And* Israel *bowed himself*
48:12. *and he bowed himself* with his face
49: 8. thy father's children *shall bow down*
Ex. 4:31. they bowed their heads *and worshipped.*
12:27. the people bowed the head *and worshipped.*
18: 7. Moses went out...*and did obeisance,*
20: 5. *Thou shalt* not *bow down thyself*
23:24. *Thou shalt* not *bow down* to their gods,
32: 8. a molten calf, *and have worshipped* it,
34: 8. Moses made haste, and bowed his head... *and worshipped.*
14. *thou shalt worship* no other god:
Nu. 22:31. and he bowed down his head, *and fell flat* (marg. or, *bowed himself*)
25: 2. *and bowed down* to their gods.
Deu 5: 9. *Thou shalt* not *bow down thyself*
17: 3. served other gods, *and worshipped*
29:26(25). served other gods, *and worshipped*
Jos. 5:14. Joshua fell on his face...*and did worship,*
23: 7. nor *bow yourselves* unto them:
Jud. 2:12, 17. *and bowed themselves* unto them,
7:15. *that he worshipped,* and returned
Ru. 2:10. *and bowed herself* to the ground,
1Sa. 1:19. *and worshipped* before the Lord,
28. *And he worshipped* the Lord
15:25. *that I may worship* the Lord.
31. *and* Saul *worshipped* the Lord,
20:41. *and bowed himself* three times:
24: 8(9). David stooped...*and bowed himself.*
25:23. *and bowed herself* to the ground,
41. *and bowed herself* on (her) face
28:14. he stooped...*and bowed himself.*
2Sa. 1: 2. fell to the earth, *and did obeisance.*
9: 6. fell on his face, *and did reverence.*
8. *And he bowed himself,* and said,
12:20. came into the house of the Lord, *and worshipped:*
14: 4. fell on her face...*and did obeisance,*
22. Joab fell to the ground...*and bowed himself,*
33. *and bowed himself* on his face
15:32. the top (of the mount), where *he worshipped*
18:21. *And* Cushi *bowed himself* unto Joab,
28. *And he fell down* to the earth
24:20. *and bowed himself* before the king
1K. 1:16. Bath-sheba bowed, *and did obeisance*
23. *And* when...*he bowed himself* before the king
31. Bath-sheba bowed...*and did reverence*
47. *And* the king *bowed himself* upon the bed.
53. he came *and bowed himself*
2:19. rose up to meet her, *and bowed himself*
9: 9. taken hold upon other gods, *and have worshipped*
11:33. forsaken me, *and have worshipped*
16:31 & 22:53(54). served Baal, *and worshipped*
2K. 2:15. *and bowed themselves* to the ground
4:37. *and bowed herself* to the ground,
17:16. *and worshipped* all the host of heaven,
35. not fear other gods, nor *bow yourselves*
36. him *shall ye worship,*
2K. 18:22. *Ye shall worship* before this altar
21: 3. *and worshipped* all the host of heaven,
21. served the idols...*and worshipped* them:
1Ch 21:21. *and bowed himself* to David
29:20. *and worshipped* the Lord, and the king.
2Ch 7: 3. bowed themselves...*and worshipped,*
22. laid hold on other gods, *and worshipped*
24:17. *and made obeisance* to the king.
25:14. *bowed down himself* before them,
29:29. bowed themselves, *and worshipped.*
30. bowed their heads *and worshipped.*
32:12. *Ye shall worship* before one altar,
33: 3. *and worshipped* all the host of heaven,
Neh 8: 6. bowed their heads, *and worshipped*
Est. 3: 2. Mordecai bowed not, nor *did* (him) *reverence.*
Job 1:20. Then Job arose,...*and worshipped,*
Ps. 5: 7(8). in thy fear *will I worship*
22:27(28). *and* all the kindreds of the nations *shall worship*
29(30). All (they that be) fat...shall eat *and worship:*
66: 4. All the earth *shall worship* thee,
72:11. *Yea,* all kings *shall fall down*
81: 9(10). neither *shalt thou worship* any strange god.
86: 9. All nations...shall come *and worship*
95: 6. *let us worship* and bow down:
106:19. *and worshipped* the molten image.
132: 7. *we will worship* at his footstool.
138: 2. *I will worship* toward thy holy temple,
Isa. 2: 8. *they worship* the work of their own hands,
36: 7. *Ye shall worship* before this altar?
44:15. maketh a god, *and worshippeth* (it);
17. falleth down unto it, *and worshippeth*
45:14. *they shall fall down* unto thee,
46: 6. they fall down, yea, *they worship.*
49: 7. princes *also shall worship,*
23. *they shall bow down* to thee
Jer. 1:16. *and worshipped* the works of their own
16:11. walked after other gods,...*and have worshipped*
22: 9. *and worshipped* other gods, and served
Mic. 5:13(12). *thou shalt* no more *worship*
Zep 2:11. *and* (men) *shall worship* him, every one

HITHPAEL.—*Participle.*

Gen37: 9. the sun and the moon and the eleven stars *made obeisance*
2K. 19:37. *as he was worshipping* in the house of
2Ch 29:28. all the congregation *worshipped.*
Neh 9: 3. *and worshipped* the Lord their God.
6. the host of heaven *worshippeth* thee.
Est. 3: 2. bowed, *and reverenced* Haman:
5. Mordecai bowed not, *nor did* him *reverence.*
Isa. 37:38. *as he was worshipping* in the house of Nisroch his god,
Eze. 8:16. *they worshipped* the sun
Zep. 1: 5. *them that worship* the host of heaven
— *them that worship*...by the Lord,

שְׁחוֹר *sh'ghōhr,* m. 7815

Lam. 4: 8. Their visage is blacker *than a coal;* (marg. *than blackness*)

שְׁחוּת *sh'ghooth,* f. 7816

Pro. 28:10. shall fall himself *into his own pit:*

שָׁחַח [*shāh-ghagh'*]. 7817

✻ KAL.—*Preterite.* ✻

Job 9:13. the proud helpers *do stoop*
Ps. 35 14. *I bowed down* heavily,
38 6(7). *I am bowed down* greatly;
Pro. 14:19. The evil *bow* before the good;
Isa. 2:11. *and* the haughtiness of men *shall be bowed down,*
17. *And* the loftiness of man *shall be bowed down,*
Hab 3: 6. the perpetual hills *did bow:*

KAL.—*Infinitive.*

Isa. 60:14. shall come *bending* unto thee;

KAL.—*Future.*

Job 38:40. When *they couch* in (their) dens,
Ps. 10:10. He croucheth, (and) *humbleth himself,*
107:39. they are minished *and brought low*

* NIPHAL.—*Future.* *

Ecc. 12: 4. *and* all the daughters of musick *shall be brought low;*
Isa. 2: 9. *And* the mean man *boweth down,*
5:15. *And* the mean man *shall be brought down,*
29: 4. thy speech *shall be low*

* HIPHIL.—*Preterite.* *

Isa. 25:12. the fortress...*shall he bring down,*
26: 5. *he bringeth down* them that dwell on high;

* HITHPOLEL.—*Future.* *

Ps. 42: 5(6). Why *art thou cast down,* (marg. *bowed down*) O my soul?
6(7). my soul *is cast down*
11(12) & 43:5. Why *art thou cast down,* O my soul?

7819-20 **שָׁחַט** *shāh-ghat'.*

* KAL.—*Preterite.* *

Ex. 12: 6. *and* the whole assembly...*shall kill* it
29:11. *And thou shalt kill* the bullock
16. *And thou shalt slay* the ram,
20. *Then shalt thou kill* the ram,
Lev. 1: 5. *And he shall kill* the bullock
11. *And he shall kill* it on the side
3: 2. *and kill it* (at) the door of the tabernacle
8, 13. *and kill* it before the tabernacle
4: 4. *and kill* the bullock before the Lord.
15. *and* the bullock *shall be killed* before the
24. *and kill* it in the place where they kill
29. *and slay* the sin offering
33. *and slay* it for a sin offering
14: 5. *that* one of the birds *be killed*
13. *And he shall slay* the lamb
25. *And he shall kill* the lamb
50. *And he shall kill* the one of the birds
16:11. *and shall kill* the bullock
15. *Then shall he kill* the goat
Nu. 19: 3. *and* (one) *shall slay* her before his face:
1Sa. 14:34. *and slay* (them) here, and eat;
2K. 25: 7. *they slew* the sons of Zedekiah
Jer. 39: 6. also the king of Babylon *slew*
52:10. *he slew* also all the princes

KAL.—*Infinitive.*

Gen 22:10. Abraham...took the knife *to slay* his son.
Isa. 22:13. slaying oxen, *and killing* sheep,
Eze. 23:39. *For when they had slain* their children
40:39. *to slay* thereon the burnt offering
Hos. 5: 2. *And* the revolters are profound *to make slaughter,*

KAL.—*Imperative.*

Ex. 12:21. *and kill* the passover.
2Ch 35: 6. *So kill* the passover,

KAL.—*Future.*

Gen 37:31. *and killed* a kid of the goats,
Ex. 34:25. *Thou shalt* not *offer* the blood
Lev. 4:24, 33. the place where *they kill* the burnt offering
7: 2. In the place where *they kill* the burnt offering *shall they kill* the trespass
8:15. *And he slew* (it); and Moses took the
19. *And he killed* (it); and Moses sprinkled
23. *And he slew* (it); and Moses took of the
9: 8. *and slew* the calf of the sin offering,
12. *And he slew* the burnt offering;
15. took the goat,...*and slew it,*
18. *He slew also* the bullock
14:13. *he shall kill* the sin offering
19. afterward *he shall kill* the burnt offering:
17: 3. What man soever (there be)...*that killeth*
— or *that killeth* (it) out of the camp,
22:28. *ye shall* not *kill* it and her young
Nu. 14:16. *therefore he hath slain them*
Jud. 12: 6. *and slew him* at the passages of Jordan:
1Sa. 1:25. *And they slew* a bullock,
14:32. took sheep, and oxen,...*and slew* (them)
34. brought every man his ox...*and slew*
1K. 18:40. Elijah brought them down...*and slew them*
2K. 10: 7. took the king's sons, *and slew* seventy
2K. 10:14. *and slew them* at the pit of the shearing
2Ch 29:22. *So they killed* the bullocks,
— likewise, *when they had killed* the rams,
— *they killed also* the lambs,
24. *And* the priests *killed them,*
30:15. *Then they killed* the passover
35: 1, 11. *and they killed* the passover
Ezr. 6:20. *and killed* the passover for all the children
Jer. 39: 6. *Then* the king of Babylon *slew*
41: 7. *that* Ishmael the son of Nethaniah *slew them,*
52:10. *And* the king of Babylon *slew*
Eze. 16:21. *That thou hast slain* my children,
40:41. eight tables, whereupon *they slew*
42. instruments wherewith *they slew*
44:11. *they shall slay* the burnt offering

KAL.—*Participle.* Poel.

Isa. 57: 5. *slaying* the children in the valleys
66: 3. *He that killeth* an ox.

KAL.—*Participle.* Paül.

Lev. 14: 6. the blood of the bird *that was killed*
51. the blood of the *slain* bird,
1K. 10:16. two hundred targets (of) *beaten* gold:
17. three hundred shields (of) *beaten* gold;
2Ch 9:15. two hundred targets (of) *beaten* gold: six hundred (shekels) of *beaten* gold
16. three hundred shields...(of) *beaten* gold:
Jer. 9: 8(7). Their tongue (is as) an arrow *shot out*

* NIPHAL.—*Future.* *

Lev. 6:25(18). the place where the burnt offering *is killed shall* the sin offering *be killed*
Nu. 11:22. *Shall* the flocks and the herds *be slain*

שְׁחִיטָה [*sh'ghee-tāh'*], f. 7821

2Ch 30:17. the charge of *the killing of* the passovers

שְׁחִין *sh'gheen,* m. 7822

Ex. 9: 9. *a boil* breaking forth (with) blains
10. *a boil* breaking forth
11. the magicians could not stand...because of *the boils;* for *the boil* was upon the
Lev. 13:18. in the skin thereof, was *a boil,*
19. in the place of *the boil*
20. a plague of leprosy broken *out of the boil.*
23. it (is) *a burning boil;*
Deu 28:27. The Lord will smite thee *with the botch of* Egypt,
35. The Lord shall smite thee...*with a* sore *botch*
2K. 20: 7. they took and laid (it) on *the boil,*
Job 2: 7. smote Job *with* sore *boils*
Isa. 38:21. lay (it) for a plaister upon *the boil,*

שָׁחִיס *shāh-ghees',* m. 7823

Isa. 37:30. *that which springeth of the same:*

שְׁחִיף *sh'gheeph,* m. 7824

Eze. 41:16. *cieled with* (marg. *cieling of*) wood round about,

---

שְׁחִית [*sh'gheeth*], f. 7825

Ps. 107:20. delivered (them) *from their destructions.*
Lam. 4:20. was taken *in their pits,*

שַׁחַל *shah'-ghal,* m. 7826

Job 4:10. the voice of *the fierce lion,*
10:16. huntest me *as a fierce lion:*
28: 8. *the fierce lion* passed by it.
Ps. 91:13. Thou shalt tread upon *the lion*
Pro. 26:13. (There is) *a lion* in the way;
Hos. 5:14. I (will be) unto Ephraim *as a lion,*
13: 7. I will be unto them as *a lion:*

7827 **שְׁחֵלֶת** *sh'ghĕh'-leth*, f.

Ex. 30:34. stacte, and *onycha*, and galbanum;

7828 **שַׁחַף** [*shah'-ghaph*], m.

Lev.11:16. the night hawk, and *the cuckow*,
Deu14:15. the night hawk, and *the cuckow*,

7829 **שַׁחֶפֶת** *shah-ghĕh'-pheth*, f.

Lev.26:16. terror, *consumption*, and the burning
Deu28:22. Lord shall smite thee *with a consumption*,

7830 **שַׁחַץ** [*shah'-ghatz*], m.

Job 28: 8. *The lion's* whelps (lit. sons of *pride*) have
41:34(26). king over all the children *of pride*.

7833 **שָׁחַק** [*shāh-ghak'*].

* KAL.—*Preterite*. *

Ex. 30:36. *And thou shalt beat* (some) of it
Job 14:19. The waters *wear* the stones:

KAL.—*Future*.

2Sa.22:43. *Then did I beat* them as small as the dust
Ps. 18:42(43). *Then did I beat them* small

7834 **שַׁחַק** *shah'-ghak*, m.

Deu33:26. rideth...his excellency *on the sky*.
2Sa.22:12. thick clouds of *the skies*.
Job 35: 5. behold *the clouds*
36:28. *the clouds* do drop
37:18. Hast thou with him spread out *the sky*,
21. the bright light which (is) *in the clouds*:
38:37. Who can number *the clouds*
Ps. 18:11(12). thick clouds of *the skies*.
36: 5(6). faithfulness (reacheth) unto *the clouds*.
57:10(11). thy truth unto *the clouds*.
68:34(35). his strength (is) *in the clouds*. (marg. or, *heavens*)
77:17(18). *the skies* sent out a sound:
78:23. commanded *the clouds* from above,
89: 6(7). who *in the heaven* can be compared
37(38). (as) a faithful witness *in heaven*.
108: 4(5). thy truth (reacheth) unto *the clouds*. (marg. or, *skies*)
Pro. 3:20. *and the clouds* drop down the dew.
8:28. established *the clouds* above:
Isa. 40:15. *and* are counted *as the small dust of* the
45: 8. *and* let *the skies* pour down righteousness:
Jer. 51: 9. is lifted up (even) to *the skies*.

7835 **שָׁחַר** *shāh-ghar'*.

* KAL.—*Preterite*. *

Job 30:30. My skin *is black* upon me,

7836 **שָׁחַר** [*shāh-ghar'*].

* KAL.—*Participle*. Poel. *

Pro.11:27. *He that diligently seeketh* good

* PIEL.—*Preterite*. *

Job 7:21. *and thou shalt seek me in the morning*,
Ps. 78:34. *and enquired early* after God.
Pro.13:24. he that loveth him *chasteneth him betimes*. (lit. *seeketh for him* chastening *betimes*)

PIEL.—*Infinitive*.

Pro. 7:15. *diligently to seek* thy face,

PIEL.—*Future*.

Job 8: 5. If *thou wouldest seek* unto God *betimes*,
Ps. 63: 1(2). *early will I seek thee*:
Pro. 1:28. *they shall seek me early*,
Isa. 26: 9. *will I seek thee early*:
Hos 5:15. *they will seek me early*.

PIEL.—*Participle*.

Job 24: 5. *rising betimes* for a prey:
Pro. 8:17. *and those that seek me early*

שַׁחַר *shah'-ghar*, m. 7837

Gen19:15. when *the morning* arose,
32:24(25). until the breaking of *the day*. (marg. ascending of *the morning*)
26(27). Let me go, for *the day* breaketh. (lit. *the morning* riseth)
Jos. 6:15. the dawning of *the day*, (lit. the rising of *the morning*)
Jud.19:25. when *the day* began to spring,
1Sa. 9:26. about the spring of *the day*,
Neh 4:21(15). from the rising of *the morning*
Job 3: 9. the dawning of *the day*: (marg. the eyelids of *the morning*)
38:12. caused *the dayspring* to know his place;
41:18(10). like the eyelids of *the morning*.
Ps. 22[title](1). To the chief Musician upon Aijeleth *Shahar*, (marg. or, the hind of *the morning*)
57: 8(9) & 108:2(3). (myself) will awake *early*.
139: 9. (If) I take the wings of *the morning*,
Cant.6:10. looketh forth as *the morning*,
Isa. 8:20. because (there is) no *light* (marg. *morning*) in them.
14:12. O Lucifer, son of *the morning*!
47:11. shalt not know *from whence it riseth*: (marg. *the morning thereof*)
58: 8. thy light break forth *as the morning*,
Hos 6: 3. going forth is prepared *as the morning*;
10:15. *in a morning* shall the king...be cut off.
Joel 2: 2. *as the morning* spread upon the
Am. 4:13. maketh *the morning* darkness,
Jon. 4: 7. when *the morning* rose the next day,

שָׁחֹר *shāh-ghōhr'*, adj. 7838

Lev.13:31. no *black* hair in it;
37. *black* hair grown up therein;
Cant.1: 5. I (am) *black*, but comely,
5:11. his locks (are) bushy, (and) *black*
Zec. 6: 2. in the second chariot *black* horses;
6. The *black* horses which (are) therein

שַׁחֲרוּת *shah-ghărooth'*, f. 7839

Ecc.11:10. childhood *and youth* (are) vanity.

שְׁחַרְחֹרֶת *sh'ghar-ghōh'-reth*, adj. f. 7840

Cant.1: 6. Look not upon me, because I (am) *black*,

שָׁחַת [*shāh-ghath'*]. 7843

* NIPHAL.—*Preterite*. *

Gen 6:12. behold, *it was corrupt*;
Jer. 13: 7. the girdle *was marred*,
18: 4. *And* the vessel that he made of clay *was marred*

NIPHAL.—*Future*.

Gen 6:11. The earth *also was corrupt*
Ex. 8:24(20). the land *was corrupted* (marg. or, *destroyed*)

NIPHAL.—*Participle*.

Eze.20:44. nor according to your *corrupt* doings,

* PIEL.—*Preterite*. *

Gen38: 9. *that he spilled* (it) on the ground,
Ex. 21:26. if a man smite the eye...*that it perish*;
32: 7. thy people,...*have corrupted* (themselves):
Nu. 32:15. *and ye shall destroy* all this people.
Deu 9:12. thy people...*have corrupted*
32: 5. *They have corrupted* themselves, (marg. *He hath corrupted* to himself)
2K. 19:12. them which my fathers *have destroyed*;
Pro.23: 8. *and lose* thy sweet words.
Isa. 14:20. *thou hast destroyed* thy land,
Jer. 12:10. Many pastors *have destroyed* my
48:18. *he shall destroy* thy strong holds.
Lam. 2: 5. *he hath destroyed* his strong holds,
6. *he hath destroyed* his places of the
Eze.26: 4. *And they shall destroy* the walls of Tyrus,
28:17. *thou hast corrupted* thy wisdom

Hos 9: 9. *They have* deeply *corrupted*
13: 9. O Israel, *thou hast destroyed thyself;*
Am. 1 11. *and did cast off* all pity, (marg. *corrupted* his compassions)
Nah 2: 2(3). *marred* their vine branches.
Mal. 2: 8. *ye have corrupted* the covenant of Levi,

PIEL.—*Infinitive.*

Gen 6:17. *to destroy* all flesh,
9:11. a flood *to destroy* the earth.
15. a flood *to destroy* all flesh.
13:10. before the Lord *destroyed* Sodom and
19:13. the Lord hath sent us *to destroy it.*
29. *when* God *destroyed* the cities
Jos. 22:33. *to destroy* the land
Jud. 6: 5. entered into the land *to destroy it.*
1Sa.23:10. *to destroy* the city for my sake.
2Sa. 1:14. *to destroy* the Lord's anointed?
14:11. not suffer the revengers...*to destroy*
24:16. stretched out his hand upon Jerusalem *to destroy it,*
Eze. 5:16. I will send *to destroy you:*
20:17. spared them *from destroying them,*
22:30. that I *should* not *destroy it:*
30:11. *to destroy* the land:
43: 3. when I came *to destroy* the city:
Hos 11: 9. I will not return *to destroy*

PIEL.—*Imperative.*

Jer. 5:10. Go ye up upon her walls, *and destroy;*

∗ HIPHIL.—*Preterite.* ∗

Gen 6:12. all flesh *had corrupted* his way
Deu 4:25. *and shall corrupt* (yourselves),
Jud. 2:19. *and corrupted* (marg. or, *were corrupt*) (themselves) more
2Ch 34:11. which the kings of Judah *had destroyed.*
Ps. 14: 1. *They are corrupt,* they have done
53: 1(2). *Corrupt are they,* and have done
Isa. 37:12. them which my fathers *have destroyed,*
Jer. 36:29. certainly come *and destroy* this land,
49: 9. *they will destroy* till they have enough.
51:20. *and* with thee *will I destroy* kingdoms;
Dan 8:24. *and shall destroy* the mighty and the
Zep. 3: 7. *corrupted* all their doings.

HIPHIL.—*Infinitive.*

Deu 10:10. the Lord would not *destroy thee.*
31:29. ye will *utterly* corrupt (lit. *corrupting* ye will corrupt)
1Sa. 26:15. came one of the people in *to destroy*
2K. 8:19. the Lord would not *destroy* Judah
13:23. would not *destroy them,*
18:25. up...against this place *to destroy it?*
1Ch 21:15. God sent an angel unto Jerusalem *to destroy it: and as he was destroying,* the Lord beheld,
2Ch 12:12. he would not *destroy* (him)
21: 7. the Lord would not *destroy*
25:16. God hath determined *to destroy thee,*
26:16. heart was lifted up *to* (his) *destruction:*
36:19. *destroyed* all the goodly vessels
Ps. 106:23. *lest he should destroy* (them).
Isa. 36:10. come up...against this land *to destroy it?*
51:13. as if he were ready *to destroy?*
65: 8. that I *may* not *destroy* them all.
Jer. 13:14. I will not pity,...*but destroy them.* (marg. *from destroying them*)
15: 3. to devour *and destroy.*
51:11. against Babylon, *to destroy it;*
Lam. 2: 8. The Lord hath purposed *to destroy*
Dan 11:17. shall give him the daughter of women, *corrupting* (marg. *to corrupt*) *her:*

HIPHIL.—*Imperative.*

2K. 18:25. Go up against this land, *and destroy it.*
Isa. 36:10. Go up against this land, *and destroy it.*

HIPHIL.—*Future.*

Gen 18:28. *wilt thou destroy* all the city
— *I will* not *destroy* (it).
31. *I will* not *destroy* (it) for twenty's sake.
32. *I will* not *destroy* (it) for ten's sake.
Lev. 19:27. neither *shalt thou mar* the corners
Deu 4:16. Lest *ye corrupt* (yourselves),
31. neither *destroy thee,* nor forget
9:26. *destroy* not thy people
20:19. *thou shalt* not *destroy* the trees
20. *thou shalt destroy* and cut them down
31:29. *ye will* utterly *corrupt* (yourselves),
Jud. 6: 4. *and destroyed* the increase of the earth,
20:21, 25. *and destroyed* down to the ground
35. *and* the children of Israel *destroyed* of the Benjamites
Ru. 4: 6. lest *I mar* mine own inheritance:
1Sa. 26: 9. *Destroy him* not:
2Sa. 11: 1. *and they destroyed* the children of
20:20. that I should swallow up or *destroy.*
1Ch 20: 1. *and wasted* the country of the children of
2Ch 12: 7. *I will* not *destroy them,*
24:23. *and destroyed* all the princes of the
35:21. that *he destroy thee* not.
Ps. 57 & 58 & 59 & 75 [title] (1). To the chief Musician, Al-*taschith,* (marg. or, *Destroy* not)
78:38. *destroyed* (them) not:
45. frogs, *which destroyed them.*
Pro. 11: 9. An hypocrite...*destroyeth* his neighbour:
Isa. 11: 9. They shall not hurt nor *destroy*
65: 8. *Destroy it* not;
25. They shall not hurt nor *destroy*
Jer. 6: 5. *and let us destroy* her palaces.
11:19. *Let us destroy* the tree with the fruit
13: 9. *will I mar* the pride of Judah,
15: 6. stretch out my hand...*and destroy thee;*
Eze. 16:47. *thou wast corrupted* more
23:11. *And* when...*she was* more *corrupt*
Dan 8:24. *he shall destroy* wonderfully,
25. by peace *shall destroy* many:
9:26. *shall destroy* the city and the sanctuary;
Mal. 3:11. *he shall* not *destroy* (marg. *corrupt*) the

HIPHIL.—*Participle.*

Gen 6:13. I *will destroy them* with the earth.
19:13. we *will destroy* this place,
14. the Lord *will destroy* this city.
Ex. 12:23. will not suffer *the destroyer* to come in
Jud. 20:42. the cities *they destroyed*
1Sa. 6: 5. your mice *that mar* the land;
13:17. *the spoilers* came out of the camp
14:15. *and the spoilers,* they also trembled,
2Sa. 20:15. all the people...*battered* (marg. *marred*) the wall, to throw it down.
24:16. the angel *that destroyed* the people,
1Ch 21:12. the angel of the Lord *destroying*
15. the angel *that destroyed,*
2Ch 27: 2. the people *did* yet *corruptly.*
Pro. 6:32. *destroyeth* his own soul.
18: 9. him that is *a* great *waster.*
28:24. the same (is) the companion of a *destroyer.* (lit. a *destroying* man)
Isa. 1: 4. children *that are corrupters:*
54:16. I have created *the waster* to destroy.
Jer. 2:30. like a *destroying* lion.
4: 7. *and the destroyer of* the Gentiles
6:28. they (are) all *corrupters.*
22: 7. I will prepare *destroyers*
51: 1. I will raise up...a *destroying* wind;
25. *which destroyest* all the earth:
Eze. 9: 8. *wilt thou destroy* all the residue

∗ HOPHAL.—*Participle.* ∗

Pro. 25:26. a troubled fountain, and a *corrupt* spring.
Mal. 1:14. sacrificeth unto the Lord *a corrupt thing:*

שְׁחַת [*sh'ghath*], Ch. 7844

∗ P'AL.—*Participle.* Passive. ∗

Dan 2: 9. ye have prepared lying *and corrupt* words
6: 4(5). find none occasion *nor fault;*
—(-). any error *or fault* found in him.

שַׁחַת *shah'-ghath*, f. 7845

Job 9:31. Yet shalt thou plunge me *in the ditch,*
17:14. I have said *to corruption,* Thou (art) my father:
33:18. keepeth back his soul from *the pit,*
22. his soul draweth near *unto the grave,*
24. Deliver him from going down to *the pit:*
28. deliver his soul from going *into the pit,*
30. To bring back his soul from *the pit,*
Ps. 7:15(16). is fallen *into the ditch*
9:15(16). The heathen are sunk down *in the pit*
16:10. neither wilt thou suffer...to see *corruption*
30: 9(10). when I go down *to the pit?*
35: 7. hid for me their net (in) *a pit,*

Ps. 49: 9(10). still live for ever, (and) not see *corruption.*
55:23(24). down into the pit of *destruction :*
94:13. until *the pit* be digged for the wicked.
103: 4. redeemeth thy life *from destruction ;*
Pro.26:27. whoso diggeth *a pit* shall fall
Isa. 38:17. (delivered it) from *the pit of* corruption:
51:14. that he should not die *in the pit,*
Eze.19: 4, 8. he was taken *in their pit,*
28: 8. They shall bring thee down *to the pit,*
Jon. 2: 6(7). brought up my life *from corruption,* (marg. or, *the pit*)

7848 שִׁטָּה *shit-tāh'*, f.

Ex. 25: 5. badgers' skins, and *shittim* wood,
10. make an ark (of) *shittim* wood:
13. thou shalt make staves (of) *shittim* wood,
23. also make a table (of) *shittim* wood:
28. shalt make the staves (of) *shittim* wood,
26:15. boards for the tabernacle (of) *shittim*
26. thou shalt make bars (of) *shittim* wood;
32. it upon four pillars of *shittim* (wood)
37. hanging five pillars of *shittim* (wood),
27: 1. shalt make an altar (of) *shittim* wood,
6. for the altar, staves (of) *shittim* wood,
30: 1. (of) *shittim* wood shalt thou make it.
5. shalt make the staves (of) *shittim* wood,
35: 7. badgers' skins, and *shittim* wood,
24. with whom was found *shittim* wood
36:20. boards for the tabernacle (of) *shittim*
31. And he made bars of *shittim* wood;
36. thereunto four pillars (of) *shittim* (wood),
37: 1. Bezaleel made the ark (of) *shittim* wood:
4. And he made staves (of) *shittim* wood,
10. And he made the table (of) *shittim* wood:
15, 28. he made the staves (of) *shittim* wood,
25. made the incense altar (of) *shittim* wood:
38: 1. the altar of burnt offering (of) *shittim*
6. he made the staves (of) *shittim* wood,
Deu 10: 3. I made an ark (of) *shittim* wood,
Isa. 41:19. the cedar, *the shittah tree,* and the myrtle,

7849 שָׁטַח [*shāh-tagh'*].

* KAL.—*Preterite.* *

Jer. 8: 2. *And they shall spread them* before the sun,

KAL.—*Infinitive.*

Nu. 11:32. they spread (them) *all abroad*

KAL.—*Future.*

Nu. 11:32. *and they spread* (them) all abroad
2Sa.17:19. *and spread* ground corn thereon;

KAL.—*Participle.* Poel.

Job 12:23. *he enlargeth* (lit. *spreadeth out*) the

* PIEL.—*Preterite.* *

Ps. 88: 9(10). *I have stretched out* my hands unto thee.

7850 שֹׁטֵט *shōh-tēht'*, m.

Jos. 23:13. *scourges* in your sides,

7857 שָׁטַף *shāh-taph'.*

* KAL.—*Preterite.* *

Lev.15:11. *hath* not *rinsed* his hands in water,
Ps. 69: 2(3). the floods *overflow me.*
124: 4. the waters *had overwhelmed us,*
Isa. 8: 8. *he shall overflow* and go over,
Dan 11:10. (one) shall certainly come, *and overflow,*
40. *and shall overflow* and pass over.

KAL.—*Future.*

1K. 22:38. *And* (one) *washed* the chariot
Job 14:19. *thou washest away* (marg. *overflowest*) the
Ps. 69:15(16). *Let* not the waterflood *overflow me,*
78:20. the streams *overflowed ;*
Cant 8: 7. neither *can* the floods *drown it :*
Isa. 28:17. the waters *shall overflow*
43: 2. *they shall* not *overflow thee*
Jer. 47: 2. *and shall overflow* the land,
Eze.16: 9. *yea, I throughly washed away* thy blood
Dan 11:26. his army *shall overflow :*

KAL.—*Participle.* Poel.

2Ch 32: 4. the brook *that ran* (marg. *overflowed*)
Isa. 10:22. the consumption decreed *shall overflow*
28: 2. a flood of mighty waters *overflowing,*
15, 18. when the *overflowing* scourge shall
30:28. his breath, as an *overflowing* stream,
66:12. the glory of the Gentiles like a *flowing*
Jer. 8: 6. as the horse *rusheth* into the battle.
47: 2. shall be an *overflowing* flood,
Eze.13:11. there shall be an *overflowing* shower;
13. there shall be an *overflowing* shower
38:22. an *overflowing* rain, and great hailstones,

* NIPHAL.—*Future.* *

Lev.15:12. every vessel of wood *shall be rinsed* in water.
Dan 11:22. *shall they be overflown*

* PUAL.—*Preterite.* *

Lev. 6:28(21). shall be both scoured, *and rinsed*

שֵׁטֶף *shēh'-teph* & שֶׁטֶף *sheh'-teph*, m. 7858

Job 38:25. *for the overflowing of waters,*
Ps. 32: 6. *in the floods of* great waters
Pro.27: 4. *and* anger (is) *outrageous ;* (marg. *an overflowing*)
Dan 9:26. the end thereof (shall be) *with a flood,*
11:22. the arms of *a flood*
Nah 1: 8. *But with an* overrunning *flood*

שָׁטַר [*shāh-tar'*]. 7860

* KAL.—*Participle.* Poel. *

Ex. 5: 6. the taskmasters of the people, and *their officers,*
10. of the people went out, *and their officers,*
14, 15, 19. *the officers of* the children of Israel.
Nu. 11:16. the elders of the people, *and officers over them ;*
Deu 1:15. *and officers* among your tribes.
16:18. Judges *and officers* shalt thou make
20: 5. *the officers* shall speak unto the people,
8. *the officers* shall speak further
9. when *the officers* have made an end
29:10(9). your elders, *and your officers,*
31:28. the elders of your tribes, *and your officers,*
Jos. 1:10. Joshua commanded *the officers of*
3: 2. *the officers* went through the host;
8:33. all Israel, and their elders, *and officers,*
23: 2 & 24:1. their judges, *and for their officers,*
1Ch 23: 4. *and* six thousand (were) *officers*
26:29. *for officers* and judges.
27: 1. *their officers* that served the king
2Ch 19:11. the Levites (shall be) *officers*
26:11. Maaseiah *the ruler,*
34:13. *and officers,* and porters.
Pro. 6: 7. having no guide, *overseer,* or ruler,

שְׁטַר *sh'tar*, Ch. m. 7859

Dan 7: 5. *and* it raised up itself *on one side,*

שַׁי *shah'y*, m. 7862

Ps. 68:29(30). shall kings bring *presents*
76:11(12). bring *presents* unto him that ought to be feared.
Isa. 18: 7. shall *the present* be brought

שִׁיבָה [*shee-vāh'*], f. 7870

Ps.126: 1. When the Lord turned again *the captivity* (marg. returned *the returning*)

שִׁיבָה [*shee-vāh'*], f. 7871

2Sa.19:32(33). *while he lay* at Mahanaim;

7876 **שָׁיָה** [*shāh-yāh'*].

* KAL.—*Future.* *

Deu 32:18. Rock (that) begat thee *thou art unmindful,*

See 7804 **שֵׁיזָב** see **שׁוּב**

7882 **שִׁיחָה** *shee-ghāh'*, f.

Ps. 57: 6(7). they have digged *a pit* before me,
119:85. The proud have digged *pits*
Jer. 18:22. (כתיב) they have digged *a pit* to take me,

7885 **שַׁיִט** *shah'-yit*, m.

Isa. 28:15. (כתיב) when *the* overflowing *scourge* shall
33:21. shall go no galley *with oars,*

7886 **שִׁילֹה** *shee-lōh'*, m.

Gen 49:10. The sceptre shall not depart...until *Shiloh*

7758 **שֵׁילָל** *shēh-lāhl'*, m.

Mic. 1: 8. (כתיב) I will go *stripped* and naked:

7890 **שֵׁינִים** [*shēh-neem'*], m. pl.

2K. 18:27. (כתיב) own dung, and drink *their own piss*
Isa. 36:12. (——) own dung, and drink *their own piss*

See 3319 **שֵׁיצִא** Ch. see **יְצָא**

7891 **שִׁיר** *sheer.*

* KAL.—*Preterite.* *

Ps. 7[title](1). Shiggaion of David, which *he sang*

KAL.—*Infinitive.*

1Sa. 18: 6. women came out...*singing* and dancing,

KAL.—*Imperative.*

Ex. 15:21. *Sing ye* to the Lord,
1Ch 16: 9. *Sing* unto him, sing psalms
23. *Sing* unto the Lord,
Ps. 33: 3. *Sing* unto him a new song;
68: 4(5). *Sing* unto God, sing praises
32(33). *Sing* unto God, ye kingdoms
96: 1. *O sing* unto the Lord a new song: *sing* unto the Lord, all the earth.
2. *Sing* unto the Lord, bless his name;
98: 1. *O sing* unto the Lord a new song;
105: 2. *Sing* unto him, sing psalms
137: 3. *Sing* us (one) of the songs of Zion.
149: 1. *Sing* unto the Lord a new song,
Isa. 42:10. *Sing* unto the Lord a new song,
Jer. 20:13. *Sing* unto the Lord, praise ye

KAL.—*Future.*

Ex. 15: 1. Then *sang* Moses and the children of Israel
— *I will sing* unto the Lord,
Nu. 21:17. Then Israel *sang* this song,
Jud. 5: 1. *Then sang* Deborah and Barak
3. I, (even) I, *will sing* unto the Lord;
Ps. 13: 6. *I will sing* unto the Lord,
21:13(14). (so) *will we sing* and praise
27: 6. *I will sing*, yea, I will
57: 7(8). *I will sing* and give praise.
59:16(17). But I *will sing* of thy power;
65:13(14). they shout for joy, *they* also *sing.*
89: 1(2). *I will sing* of the mercies of the Lord
101: 1. *I will sing* of mercy and judgment:
104:33. *I will sing* unto the Lord
106:12. *they sang* his praise.
108: 1(2). *I will sing* and give praise,
137: 4. How *shall we sing* the Lord's song
138: 5. *Yea, they shall sing* in the ways of the
144: 9. *I will sing* a new song unto thee,
Isa. 5: 1. Now *will I sing* to my wellbeloved

KAL.—*Participle.* Poel.

2Sa. 19:35(36). can I hear any more the voice of *singing men and singing women?*
1K. 10:12. harps also and psalteries *for singers:*
2Ch 9:11. harps and psalteries *for singers:*
35:25. all *the singing men and the singing women*
Ps. 68:25(26). *The singers* went before,
87: 7. *As well the singers* as the players
Pro. 25:20. *so* (is) *he that singeth* songs
Ecc. 2: 8. I gat me *men singers and women singers,*
Eze. 40:44. the chambers of *the singers*

* POLEL.—*Preterite.* *

Job 36:24. magnify his work, which men *behold.*

POLEL.—*Future.*

Zep. 2:14. (their) voice *shall sing* in the windows;

POLEL.—*Participle.*

1Ch 6:33(18). Heman *a singer,*
9:33. *the singers*, chief of the fathers
15:16. *the singers* with instruments of musick,
19. *So the singers*,...(were appointed)
27. all the Levites...*and the singers*, and Chenaniah the master of the song with *the singers:*
2Ch 5:12. the Levites *which were the singers,*
13. the trumpeters *and singers* (were) as one,
20:21. he appointed *singers* unto the Lord,
23:13. *also the singers* with instruments of musick,
29:28. the singers *sang,*
35:15. *And the singers* the sons of Asaph
Ezr. 2:41. *The singers:* the children of Asaph,
65. two hundred *singing men and singing women.*
70. *and the singers*, and the porters,
7: 7. the priests, and the Levites, *and the singers,*
10:24. Of *the singers* also;
Neh 7: 1. the porters *and the singers*
44. *The singers:* the children of Asaph,
67. two hundred forty and five *singing men and singing women.*
73. the porters, *and the singers,*
10:28(29). Levites, the porters, *the singers,*
39(40). the porters, *and the singers:*
11:22. *the singers* (were) over the business
23. a certain portion should be for *the singers,*
12:28. the sons of *the singers*
29. *the singers* had builded them villages
42. *the singers* sang loud,
45. *And* both *the singers* and the porters
46. chief of *the singers,*
47. *the singers* and the porters,
13: 5, 10. the Levites, *and the singers,*

* HOPHAL.—*Future.* *

Isa. 26: 1. In that day *shall* this song *be sung*

שִׁיר *sheer*, m. 7892

Gen 31:27. sent thee away with mirth, *and with songs,*
Jud. 5:12. awake, awake, utter *a song:*
1K. 4:32(5:12). *his songs* were a thousand and five.
1Ch 6:31(16). David set over the service of *song*
32(17). ministered...*with singing,*
13: 8. *and with singing* (marg. *songs*), and with harps,
15:16. the singers with instruments of *musick,*
16:42. *musical* instruments (lit. instruments of *song*)
25: 6. under the hands of their father *for song*
7. instructed *in the songs of* the Lord,
2Ch 5:13. cymbals and instruments of *musick,*
7: 6. instruments of *musick of* the Lord,
23:13. the singers with instruments of *musick,*
18. with rejoicing *and with singing,*
29:27. *the song of* the Lord began
28. *and the singers* sang, (lit. *and the song* was sung)
34:12. could skill of instruments of *musick.*
Neh 12:27. with thanksgivings, *and with singing,*
36. the *musical* instruments (lit. instruments of *song*) *of* David
46. *and songs of* praise and thanksgiving
Ps. 28: 7. *and with my song* will I praise him.
30[title](1). A Psalm (and) *Song* (at) the
33: 3. Sing unto him *a* new *song;*
40: 3(4). he hath put *a* new *song* in my mouth,
42: 8(9). in the night *his song* (shall be) with
45[title](1). *A song of* loves.
46[title](1). *A song* upon Alamoth.

Ps. 48[title](1). *A Song* (and) Psalm for the sons of
65[title](1). A Psalm (and) *Song of* David.
66[title](1). *A Song* (or) Psalm.
67[title](1). A Psalm (or) *Song.*
68[title](1). A Psalm (or) *Song of* David.
69:30(31). praise the name of God *with a song,*
75[title](1) & 76[title](1). A Psalm (or) *Song of* Asaph.
83[title](1). *A Song* (or) Psalm of Asaph.
87[title](1). A Psalm (or) *Song* for the sons of
88[title](1). *A Song* (or) Psalm for the sons of
92[title](1). A Psalm (or) *Song* for the sabbath
96: 1 & 98:1. Sing unto the Lord *a* new *song:*
108[title](1). *A Song* (or) Psalm of David.
120[title](1). *A Song of* degrees.
121[title](1). *A Song* of degrees.
122[title](1) & 123[title](1) & 124[title](1) & 125[title](1) & 126[title](1) & 127[title](1) & 128[title](1) & 129[title](1) & 130[title](1) & 131[title](1) & 132[title](1) & 133[title](1) & 134[title](1). *A Song of* degrees
137: 3. of us *a song;* (marg. the words of *a song*)
— Sing us (one) *of the songs of* Zion.
4. How shall we sing the Lord's *song*
144: 9. I will sing *a* new *song*
149: 1. Sing unto the Lord *a* new *song,*
Pro. 25:20. singeth *songs* to an heavy heart.
Ecc. 7: 5. to hear *the song of* fools.
12: 4. the daughters of *musick*
Cant. 1: 1. *The song of songs,* which (is) Solomon's.
Isa. 23:16. make sweet melody, sing many *songs,*
24: 9. They shall not drink wine with *a song;*
26: 1. In that day shall this *song* be sung
30:29. Ye shall have *a song,*
42:10. Sing unto the Lord *a* new *song,*
Eze. 26:13. will cause the noise of *thy songs* to cease;
33:32. thou (art) unto them *as a* very lovely *song*
Am. 5:23. Take thou away...the noise of *thy songs;*
6: 5. to themselves instruments of *musick,*
8:10. I will turn...*your songs* into lamentation;

7892 שִׁירָה *shee-rāh',* f.

Ex. 15: 1. Then sang Moses...this *song*
Nu. 21:17. Then Israel sang this *song,*
Deu 31:19. write ye this *song* for you,
— that this *song* may be a witness
21. this *song* shall testify
22. Moses therefore wrote this *song*
30. Moses spake...the words of this *song,*
32:44. spake all the words of this *song*
2Sa. 22: 1. unto the Lord the words of this *song*
Ps. 18[title](1). spake unto the Lord the words of this *song*
Isa. 5: 1. *a song of* my beloved
23:15. shall Tyre *sing* as an harlot. (marg. it shall be unto Tyre *as the song of* an harlot)
Am. 8: 3. *the songs of* the temple

7893 שַׁיִשׁ *shah'-yish,* m.

1Ch 29: 2. precious stones, and *marble* stones

7896 שִׁית *sheeth.*

* KAL.—*Preterite.* *

Gen 4:25. God,...*hath appointed* me another
30:40. *put them* not unto Laban's cattle.
Ex. 7:23. neither *did he set* his heart
23:31. *And I will set* thy bounds
33: 4. no man *did put on* him his ornaments.
1Sa. 4:20. neither *did she regard* (marg. *did set* not her heart)
Job 38:36. Who *hath put* wisdom in the inward
Ps. 3: 6(7). *have set* (themselves) against me
8: 6(7). *thou hast put* all (things) under his
73:28. *I have put* my trust in the Lord
84: 3(4). a nest...where *she may lay* her young,
88: 6(7). *Thou hast laid me* in the lowest pit,
8(9). *thou hast made me* an abomination
90: 8. *Thou hast set* our iniquities before thee,
140: 5(6). *they have set* gins for me.
Isa. 22: 7. the horsemen *shall set* themselves
Hos. 2: 3(5). *and set her* like a dry land,
6:11. *he hath set* an harvest for thee,

KAL.—*Infinitive.*

Ex. 10: 1. that *I might shew* these my signs
Job 22:24. *Then shalt thou lay up* gold
30: 1. disdained *to have set* with the dogs
Isa. 22: 7. shall set themselves *in array* (lit. *setting* shall set themselves)

KAL.—*Imperative.*

Job 10:20. *and let* me *alone,* that I may take comfort
Ps. 9:20(21). *Put* them in fear, O Lord:
48:13(14). *Mark* ye well (marg. *Set* your heart to) her bulwarks,
83:11(12). *Make* their nobles like Oreb,
13(14). O my God, *make them* like a wheel;
141: 3. *Set* a watch, O Lord, before my mouth;
Pro. 27:23. *look* well (marg. *set* thy heart) to thy herds.
Isa. 16: 3. *make* thy shadow as the night
Jer. 13:16. *and make* (it) gross darkness.
31:21. *set* thine heart toward the highway,

KAL.—*Future.*

Gen 3:15. *I will put* enmity between
30:40. *he put* his own flocks by themselves,
41:33. *and set him* over the land of Egypt.
46: 4. Joseph *shall put* his hand upon
48:14. *and laid* (it) upon Ephraim's head,
17. *laid* his right hand upon the head of
Ex. 21:22. as the woman's husband *will lay*
23: 1. *put* not thine hand with the wicked
Nu. 12:11. *lay* not the sin upon us,
24: 1. *but he set* his face toward the wilderness.
Ru. 3:15. measured six (measures) of barley, *and laid* (it) on her:
4:16. *and laid it* in her bosom,
1Sa. 2: 8. *and he hath set* the world upon them.
2Sa. 13:20. *regard* not (marg. *set* not thine heart) this thing.
19:28(29). *yet didst thou set* thy servant among
22:12. *And he made* darkness pavilions
1K. 11:34. *I will make him* prince
Job 7:17. that *thou shouldest set*
9:33. *might lay* his hand upon us both.
10:20. (כתיב) (and) *let* me alone, that I may
14:13. that *thou wouldest appoint* me a set time,
38:11. here *shall* thy proud waves *be stayed?*
Ps. 12: 5(6). *I will set* (him) in safety
13: 2(3). How long *shall I take* counsel
17:11. *they have set* their eyes bowing down
18:11(12). *He made* darkness his secret place;
21: 3(4). *thou settest* a crown of pure gold
6(7). *thou hast made him* (marg. *set him*) most blessed
9(10). *Thou shalt make them* as a fiery oven
12(13). *shalt thou make them* (marg. *set them*) turn their back,
45:16(17). children, *whom thou mayest make*
62:10(11). *set* not your heart (upon them).
73:18. *thou didst set* them in slippery places:
84: 6(7). passing through the valley of Baca *make it* a well;
101: 3. *I will set* no wicked thing before mine
104:20. *Thou makest* darkness, and it is night:
110: 1. *I make* thine enemies thy footstool.
132:11. Of the fruit of thy body *will I set* upon
139: 5. *and laid* thine hand upon me.
Pro. 22:17. *apply* thine heart unto my knowledge.
24:32. I saw, (and) *considered* (it) well: (marg. *set* my heart)
26:24. *layeth up* deceit within him;
Isa. 5: 6. *And I will lay it* waste:
15: 9. *I will bring* more upon Dimon,
26: 1. salvation *will* (God) *appoint*
Jer. 2:15. *they made* his land waste:
3:19. How *shall I put thee* among the children,
13:16. (כתיב) (and) *make* (it) gross darkness.
22: 6. *I will make* thee a wilderness,
50: 3. *shall make* her land desolate,
51:39. *I will make* their feasts,

* HOPHAL.—*Future.* *

Ex. 21:30. If *there be laid* on him a sum of money, then he shall give for the ransom of his life whatsoever *is laid* upon him.

7898 שַׁיִת *shah'-yith*, m.

Isa. 5: 6. shall come up briers *and thorns :*
7:23. it shall (even) be for briers *and thorns.*
24. the land shall become briers *and thorns.*
25. the fear of briers *and thorns :*
9:18(17). it shall devour the briers *and thorns,*
10:17. shall burn and devour *his thorns*
27: 4. who would set the briers (and) *thorns*

7897 שִׁית *sheeth*, m.

Ps. 73: 6. violence covereth them (as) *a garment.*
Pro. 7:10. *the attire of* an harlot,

7901 שָׁכַב *shāh-chav'.*

* KAL.—*Preterite.* *

Gen19:34. *I lay* yesternight with my father:
26:10. the people *might* lightly *have lien*
47:30. *But I will lie* with my fathers,
Ex. 22:16(15). not betrothed, *and lie* with her,
Lev.26: 6. *and ye shall lie down*, and none
Nu. 5:13. *And* a man *lie* with her carnally,
19. If no man *have lain* with thee,
24: 9. *he lay down* as a lion,
Deu22:23. find her in the city, *and lie* with her ;
25. force her, *and lie* with her: then the man only that *lay* with her
28. lay hold on her, *and lie* with her,
24:13. *that he may sleep* in his own (lit. *lie down*)
Jud. 5:27. he fell, *he lay down :*
Ru. 3: 4. uncover his feet, *and lay thee down ;*
1Sa.26: 5. the place where Saul *lay*, and Abner
2Sa. 7:12. *and thou shalt sleep* with thy fathers,
12:11. *and he shall lie* with thy wives
16. *and lay* all night upon the earth.
1K. 1: 2. *and let her lie* in thy bosom,
3:19. child died in the night; because *she overlaid* it.
11:21. David *slept* with his fathers,
Job 3:13. For now should *I have lain still*
7: 4. When *I lie down,*
14:12. So man *lieth down,*
Ps. 3: 5(6). I *laid me down* and slept ;
41: 8(9). and (now) that *he lieth*
Pro. 3:24. *yea, thou shalt lie down,*
Ecc. 2:23. his heart *taketh* not *rest*
Isa. 14: 8. Since *thou art laid down,*
18. all of them, *lie* in glory,
51:20. *they lie* at the head of all the streets,
Lam 2:21. The young and the old *lie* on the ground
Eze. 4: 6. *And* when thou hast accomplished them, *lie*
23: 8. in her youth *they lay* with her,
32:21. *they lie* uncircumcised,

KAL.—*Infinitive.*

Gen19:33, 35. perceived not *when she lay down,*
34: 7. *in lying with* Jacob's daughter ;
39:10. *to lie* by her, (or) to be with her.
14. he came in unto me *to lie* with me,
Lev.15:24. any man lie with her *at all*, (lit. *lying* lie)
Deu 6: 7. *and when thou liest down,*
11:19. *when thou liest* down,
Ru. 3: 4. shall be, *when he lieth down,*
7. he went *to lie down*
2Sa.11:11. *and to lie* with my wife?
13. at even he went out *to lie*
1K. 1:21. *when* my lord the king *shall sleep* (lit. *lie*)
2K. 14:22. after that the king *slept* (lit. *laid*)
2Ch 26: 2. after that the king *slept* (lit. *laid*)
Pro. 6:10. folding of the hands *to sleep:* (lit. *for lying down*)
22. *when thou sleepest*, (lit. *liest down*)
24:33. folding of the hands *to sleep:* (lit. *for lying down*)

KAL.—*Imperative.*

Gen19:34. go thou in, (and) *lie* with him,
39: 7. she said, *Lie* with me.
12. saying, *Lie* with me:
Ru. 3:13. *lie down* until the morning.
1Sa. 3: 5. I called not; *lie down* again.
6. my son ; *lie down* again.
9. Go, *lie down :* and it shall be,
2Sa.13: 5. *Lay thee down* on thy bed,
2Sa.13:11. Come *lie* with me, my sister.
Eze. 4: 4. *Lie* thou also upon thy left side,

KAL.—*Future.*

Gen19: 4. before *they lay down,*
32. *and we will lie* with him,
33. went in, *and lay* with her father ;
35. the younger arose, *and lay* with him ;
28:11. *and lay down* in that place *to sleep.*
30:15. *he shall lie* with thee to night
16. *And he lay* with her that night.
34: 2. he took her, *and lay* with her,
35:22. *and lay* with Bilhah
Ex. 22:27(26). wherein *shall he sleep?* (lit. *lie down*)
Lev.15: 4. Every bed, whereon *he lieth*
18. also with whom man *shall lie*
20. every thing that *she lieth* upon
24. if any man *lie* with her at all,
— all the bed whereon *he lieth*
26. Every bed whereon *she lieth*
33. of him that *lieth* with her
18:22. *Thou shalt* not *lie* with mankind,
19:20. whosoever *lieth* carnally with
20:11. the man that *lieth*
12. if a man *lie* with his
13. If a man also *lie* with mankind,
18. if a man *shall lie* with a woman
20. if a man *shall lie* with his uncle's wife,
Nu. 23:24. *shall* not *lie down* until he eat
Deu24:12. *thou shalt* not *sleep* (lit. *lie down*)
28:30. another man *shall lie with her :*
Jos. 2: 1. named Rahab, *and lodged* (marg. *lay*)
8. before they *were laid down,*
Jud.16: 3. *And* Samson *lay* till midnight,
Ru. 3: 4. mark the place where *he shall lie,*
7. uncovered his feet, *and laid her down.*
14. *And she lay* at his feet
1Sa. 2:22. how *they lay* with the women
3: 5. he went *and lay down.*
9. Samuel went *and lay down*
15. *And* Samuel *lay* until the morning,
2Sa.11: 4. *and he lay* with her ;
9. *But* Uriah *slept* at the door (lit. *lay down*)
12: 3. and *lay* in his bosom,
24. went in unto her, *and lay* with her:
13: 6. *So* Amnon *lay down,*
14. forced her, *and lay* with her.
31. *and lay* on the earth ;
1K. 2:10. *So* David *slept* with his fathers,
11:43. *And* Solomon *slept* with his fathers,
14:20. *and he slept* with his fathers,
31. *And* Rehoboam *slept* with his fathers,
15: 8. *And* Abijam *slept* with his fathers ;
24. *And* Asa *slept* with his fathers,
16: 6. *So* Baasha *slept* with his fathers,
28. *So* Omri *slept* with his fathers,
19: 5. *And as he lay* and slept
6. eat and drink, *and laid him down*
21: 4. *And he laid him down* upon
27. fasted, *and lay* in sackcloth,
22:40. *So* Ahab *slept* with his fathers ;
50(51). *And* Jehoshaphat *slept* with
2K. 4:11. into the chamber, *and lay* there.
34. he went up, *and lay* upon the child,
8:24. *And* Joram *slept* with his fathers,
10:35. *And* Jehu *slept* with his fathers:
13: 9. *And* Jehoahaz *slept* with his fathers ;
13. *And* Joash *slept* with his fathers ;
14:16. *And* Jehoash *slept* with his fathers,
29. *And* Jeroboam *slept* with his fathers,
15: 7. *So* Azariah *slept* with his fathers ;
22. *And* Menahem *slept* with his fathers ;
38. *And* Jotham *slept* with his fathers,
16:20. *And* Ahaz *slept* with his fathers,
20:21. *And* Hezekiah *slept* with his fathers:
21:18. *And* Manasseh *slept* with his fathers,
24: 6. *So* Jehoiakim *slept* with his fathers:
2Ch 9:31. *And* Solomon *slept* with his fathers,
12:16. *And* Rehoboam *slept* with his fathers,
14: 1(13:23). *So* Abijah *slept* with his fathers,
16:13. *And* Asa *slept* with his fathers,
21: 1. *Now* Jehoshaphat *slept* with his fathers,
26:23. *So* Uzziah *slept* with his fathers,
27: 9. *And* Jotham *slept* with his fathers,
28:27. *And* Ahaz *slept* with his fathers,
32:33. *And* Hezekiah *slept* with his fathers,
33:20. *So* Manasseh *slept* with his fathers,

Job 7:21. for now *shall I sleep* in the dust; (lit. *lie down*)
11:18. *thou shalt take thy rest* (lit. *lie down*)
20:11. *shall lie down* with him in the dust.
21:26. *They shall lie down* alike
27:19. The rich man *shall lie down*,
30:17. my sinews *take* no *rest*.
40:21. *He lieth* under the shady trees,
Ps. 4: 8(9). *I will* both *lay me down* in peace,
57: 4(5). *I lie* (even among) them that are
68:13(14). Though *ye have lien* among the pots,
Pro. 3:24. When *thou liest down*,
6: 9. How long *wilt thou sleep*, O sluggard? (lit. *lie down*)
Ecc. 4:11. Again, if two *lie* together,
Isa. 43:17. *they shall lie down* together,
50:11. *ye shall lie down* in sorrow.
Jer. 3:25. *We lie down* in our shame,
Eze. 4: 4. that *thou shalt lie* upon it
31:18. *thou shalt lie* in the midst
32:27. *they shall* not *lie* with the mighty
28. *and shalt lie* with (them that are) slain
29. *they shall lie* with the uncircumcised,
30. *and they lie* uncircumcised
Jon. 1: 5. *and he lay*, and was fast asleep.

KAL.—*Participle.* Poel.

Gen28:13. the land whereon thou *liest*,
Ex. 22:19(18). Whosoever *lieth* with a beast
Lev.14:47. *And he that lieth* in the house
Deu22:22. If a man be found *lying* with a woman
— the man *that lay* with the woman,
29. Then the man *that lay* with her
27:20, 21, 22, 23. Cursed (be) *he that lieth*
31:16. thou *shalt sleep* (marg. *lie down*) with thy
Ru. 3: 8. behold, a woman *lay* at his feet.
1Sa. 3: 2. when Eli *was laid down*
3. Samuel *was laid down*
26: 5. Saul *lay* in the trench,
7. Saul *lay* sleeping within
— Abner and the people *lay* round about
2Sa. 4: 5. who *lay* on a bed at noon.
7. he *lay* on his bed in his bedchamber,
13: 8. he *was laid down*.
2K. 9:16. for Joram *lay* there.
Ps. 88: 5(6). like the slain *that lie* in the grave,
Pro.23:34. thou shalt be *as he that lieth down*
— *or as he that lieth* upon the top
Isa. 56:10. sleeping, *lying down*,
Eze. 4: 9. the number of the days that thou *shalt lie*
Am. 6: 4. *That lie* upon beds of ivory,
Mic. 7: 5. *from her that lieth* in thy bosom.

* NIPHAL.—*Future.* *

Isa. 13:16. and their wives *ravished*.
Zec.14: 2. shall be taken,...and the women *ravished*;

* PUAL.—*Preterite.* *

Jer. 3: 2. see where *thou hast* not *been lien with*.

* HIPHIL.—*Preterite.* *

1K. 3:20. and *laid* her dead child in my bosom.
Hos 2:18(20). *and will make them to lie down*

HIPHIL.—*Infinitive.*

2Sa. 8: 2. *casting* them *down* to the ground; (lit. *making* them *to lie down*)

HIPHIL.—*Future.*

1K. 3:20. *and laid it* in her bosom,
17:19. *and laid him* upon his own bed.
2K. 4:21. *and laid him* on the bed
2Ch 16:14. *and laid him* in the bed
Job 38:37. or who *can stay* (marg. *cause to lie down*) the bottles of heaven,

* HOPHAL.—*Preterite.* *

Eze.32:32. *and he shall be laid* in the

HOPHAL.—*Imperative.*

Eze.32:19. *and be thou laid* with the uncircumcised.

HOPHAL.—*Participle.*

2K. 4:32. *laid* upon his bed.

7902 שְׁכָבָה [*sh'chāh-vāh'*], f.

Ex. 16:13. the dew *lay* (lit. *the lying of* the dew was) round about the host.
14. when the dew *that lay* (lit. *the lying of* the dew) was gone

Lev.15:16. if any man's seed of *copulation* (lit. *lying*)
17. whereon is the seed of *copulation*, (lit. *lying*)
18. lie (with) seed of *copulation*, (lit. *lying*)
32. and (of him) whose *seed* goeth from him, (lit. *lying of* seed)
19:20. whosoever lieth *carnally* with a woman, (lit. *the lying of* seed)
22: 4. a man whose seed (lit. *lying of* seed) goeth from him;
Nu. 5:13. a man lie with her *carnally*, (lit. with *the lying of* seed)

שְׁכֹבֶת *sh'chōh'-veth*, f. 7903

Lev.18:20. thou shalt not *lie* carnally (lit. thou shalt not give *thy lying*)
23. Neither shalt thou *lie* with any beast (lit. shalt thou give *thy lying*)
20:15. if a man *lie* with a beast, (lit. give *his lying*)
Nu. 5:20. some man have *lain* with thee beside (lit. hath had *his lying*)

שָׁכָה [*shāh-chāh'*]. 7904

* HIPHIL.—*Participle.* *

Jer. 5: 8. They *were* (as) fed horses *in the morning* [perhaps lit. *wandered*]

שְׁכוֹל *sh'chōhl*, m. 7908

Ps. 35:12. *the spoiling* (marg. *depriving*) *of* my soul.
Isa. 47: 8. neither shall I know *the loss of children*:
9. one day, *the loss of children*,

שַׁכּוּל *shak-kool'*, adj. 7909

2Sa.17: 8. as a bear *robbed of her whelps*
Pro.17:12. Let a bear *robbed of her whelps*
Cant 4: 2. *and* none (is) *barren* among
6: 6. *and* (there is) not one *barren*
Jer. 18:21. let their wives be *bereaved of their children*,
Hos13: 8. meet them as a bear (that is) *bereaved of her whelps*,

---

שִׁכּוֹר *shik-koor'*, adj. 7910

1Sa. 1:13. Eli thought she *had been drunken*.
25:36. for he (was) very *drunken*:
1K. 16: 9 & 20:16. drinking himself *drunk*
Job 12:25. to stagger *like* (a) *drunken* (man).
Ps.107:27. and stagger *like a drunken man*,
Pro.26: 9. goeth up into the hand of *a drunkard*,
Isa. 19:14. as *a drunken* (man) staggereth
24:20. earth shall reel to and fro *like a drunkard*,
28: 1, 3. *the drunkards of* Ephraim,
Jer. 23: 9. I am like a *drunken* man
Joel 1: 5. Awake, ye *drunkards*, and weep;

שָׁכַח *shāh-chagh'*. 7911

* KAL.—*Preterite.* *

Gen27:45. *and he forget* (that) which thou
Deu 8:14. *and thou forget* the Lord
24:19. *and hast forgot* a sheaf
26:13. neither *have I forgotten*
Job 19:14. my familiar friends *have forgotten me*.
Ps. 9:12(13). *he forgetteth* not the cry
10:11. said in his heart, God *hath forgotten*:
42: 9(10). Why *hast thou forgotten me*?
44:17(18). yet *have we* not *forgotten thee*,
20(21). If *we have forgotten* the name
77: 9(10). *Hath* God *forgotten* to be gracious?
102: 4(5). so that I *forget* to eat my bread.
106:13. *They* soon *forgat* his works;
21. *They forgat* God their saviour,
119:61. *I have* not *forgotten* thy law.
83. *do I* not *forget* thy statutes.
109. yet *do I* not *forget* thy law.
139. mine enemies *have forgotten*
141. *do* not *I forget* thy precepts.
153. for *I do* not *forget* thy law.

Ps.119:176. *I do* not *forget* thy commandments.
Pro. 2:17. *forgetteth* the covenant of her God.
Isa. 17:10. Because *thou hast forgotten*
49:14. my Lord *hath forgotten me.*
Jer. 2:32. yet my people *have forgotten me*
3:21. *they have forgotten* the Lord
13:25. because *thou hast forgotten* me,
18:15. my people *hath forgotten me,*
23:27. their fathers *have forgotten* my name
30:14. All thy lovers *have forgotten thee;*
44: 9. *Have ye forgotten* the wickedness
50: 6. *they have forgotten* their restingplace.
Eze.22:12. *hast forgotten* me, saith the Lord
23:35. Because *thou hast forgotten* me,
Hos. 2:13(15). after her lovers, and *forgat* me,
13: 6. therefore *have they forgotten me.*

KAL.—*Infinitive.*

Deu 8:19. thou do *at all* forget (lit. *forgetting* thou do forget)

KAL.—*Imperative.*

Ps. 45:10(11). *forget also* thine own people,

KAL.—*Future.*

Gen40:23. chief butler remember Joseph, *but forgat him.*
Deu 4: 9. lest *thou forget* the things
23. *lest ye forget* the covenant
31. nor *forget* the covenant of thy fathers
6:12. beware lest *thou forget* the Lord,
8:11. Beware that *thou forget* not the Lord
19. if *thou do* at all *forget* the Lord
9: 7. Remember, (and) *forget* not,
25:19. *thou shalt* not *forget*
32:18. *and hast forgotten* God
Jud. 3: 7. *and forgat* the Lord
1Sa. 1:11. remember me, and not *forget*
12: 9. *And when they forgat* the Lord
2K. 17:38. the covenant that I have made with you *ye shall* not *forget;*
Job 9:27. *I will forget* my complaint,
11:16. thou *shalt forget* (thy) misery,
24:20. The womb *shall forget him;*
39:15. *And forgetteth* that the foot may
Ps. 10:12. *forget* not the humble.
13: 1(2). How long *wilt thou forget me,*
44:24(25). *forgettest* our affliction
59:11(12). lest my people *forget:*
74:19. *forget* not the congregation
23. *Forget* not the voice of thine enemies:
78: 7. and not *forget* the works of God,
11. *And forgat* his works,
103: 2. *forget* not all his benefits:
119:16. *I will* not *forget* thy word.
93. *I will* never *forget* thy precepts:
137: 5. If *I forget thee,* O Jerusalem, *let* my right hand *forget*
Pro. 3: 1. My son, *forget* not my law;
4: 5. get understanding: *forget* (it) not;
31: 5. Lest they drink, *and forget* the law,
7. Let him drink, *and forget* his poverty,
Isa. 49:15. *Can* a woman *forget* her sucking child, that she should not have compassion on the son of her womb? yea, they *may forget,* yet *will I* not *forget thee.*
51:13. *And forgettest* the Lord thy maker,
54: 4. *thou shalt forget* the shame of thy youth,
Jer. 2:32. *Can* a maid *forget* her ornaments,
Lam.5:20. Wherefore *dost thou forget us*
Hos. 4: 6. *seeing thou hast forgotten* the law of thy God, I *will* also *forget* thy children.
8:14. *For* Israel *hath forgotten* his Maker,
Am. 8: 7. Surely *I will* never *forget*

KAL.—*Participle.* Poel.

Job 8:13. the paths of all *that forget* God;
Ps. 50:22. *ye that forget* God,

* NIPHAL.—*Preterite.* *

Gen41:30. *and* all the plenty *shall be forgotten*
Ps. 31:12(13). *I am forgotten* as a dead man
Ecc. 2:16. the days to come *shall* all *be forgotten.*
9: 5. the memory of them *is forgotten.*
Isa. 65:16. the former troubles *are forgotten,*

NIPHAL.—*Future.*

Deu31:21. for *it shall* not *be forgotten*
Ps. 9:18(19). the needy *shall* not alway *be forgotten:*
Jer. 20:11. confusion *shall* never *be forgotten.*
23:40. which *shall* not *be forgotten.*
50: 5. covenant (that) *shall* not *be forgotten.*

NIPHAL.—*Participle.*

Job 28: 4. *forgotten* of the foot:
Isa. 23:15. *that* Tyre *shall be forgotten* seventy years,
16. thou harlot *that hast been forgotten;*

* PIEL.—*Preterite.* *

Lam. 2: 6. *hath caused* the solemn feasts and sabbaths *to be forgotten*

* HIPHIL.—*Infinitive.* *

Jer. 23:27. *to cause* my people *to forget*

* HITHPAEL.—*Future.* *

Ecc. 8:10. *and they were forgotten* in the city

שָׁכֵחַ [*shāh-chēh'ăgh*], adj. 7913

Ps. 9:17(18). all the nations *that forget* God.
Isa. 65:11. ye (are) they...*that forget* my holy

שְׁכַח [*sh'chagh*]. Ch. 7912

* ITHP'AL.—*Preterite.* *

Ezr. 6: 2. *And there was found* at Achmetha,
Dan 2:35. that no place *was found* for them:
5:11. wisdom of the gods, *was found* in him;
12. *were found* in the same Daniel,
14. and excellent wisdom *is found* in thee.
27. *and art found* wanting.
6: 4(5). neither *was* there any...*found* in him.
22(23). before him innocency *was found* in
23(24). no manner of hurt *was found* upon

* APHEL.—*Preterite.* *

Ezr. 4:19. *and it is found* that this city
Dan 2:25. *I have found* a man of the captives
6: 5(6). *We shall* not *find* any occasion against
11(12). *and found* Daniel praying

APHEL.—*Infinitive.*

Dan 6: 4(5). sought *to find* occasion against Daniel
—(-). but they could *find* none occasion

APHEL.—*Future.*

Ezr. 4:15. *so shalt thou find* in the book of the
7:16. and gold that *thou canst find* in all the province
Dan 6: 5(6). this Daniel, except *we find* (it) against

שָׁכַךְ [*shāh-chach'*]. 7918

* KAL.—*Preterite.* *

Est. 7:10. Then *was* the king's wrath *pacified.*

KAL.—*Infinitive.*

Est. 2: 1. *when* the wrath of king Ahasuerus *was appeased,*
Jer. 5:26. *as he that setteth* snares;

KAL.—*Future.*

Gen 8: 1. *and* the waters *asswaged.*

* HIPHIL.—*Preterite.* *

Nu. 17: 5(20). *and I will make to cease*

שָׁכֹל [*shāh-chohl'*]. 7921

* KAL.—*Preterite.* *

Gen43:14. If *I be bereaved* (of my children), *I am bereaved.*

KAL.—*Future.*

Gen27:45. why *should I be deprived* also
1Sa.15:33. so *shall* thy mother *be childless*

KAL.—*Participle.* Paül.

Isa. 49:21. seeing I *have lost my children,*

* PIEL.—*Preterite.* *

Gen31:38. *have* not *cast their young,*
42:36. Me *have ye bereaved*
Lev.26:22. *which shall rob* you *of your children,*
1Sa.15:33. thy sword *hath made* women *childless,*

Jer. 15: 7. *I will bereave* (them) *of children*,
Lam. 1:20. abroad the sword *bereaveth*,
Eze. 5:17. *and they shall bereave thee;*
14:15. through the land, *and they spoil* (marg. or, *bereave*) *it*,
Hos. 9:12. *yet will I bereave them*,

PIEL.—*Infinitive.*

Eze.36:12. no more henceforth *bereave them*

PIEL.—*Future.*

Deu32:25. *shall destroy* both the young man
Job 21:10. calveth, and *casteth* not *her calf.*
Eze.36:14. neither *bereave* thy nations
Mal. 3:11. *shall* your vine *cast her fruit before the time*

PIEL.—*Participle.*

Ex. 23:26. There shall nothing *cast their young*,
2K. 2:19. the ground *barren.* (marg. causing to *miscarry*)
21. any more dearth *or barren*
Eze.36:13. *and hast bereaved* thy nations;

* HIPHIL.—*Participle.* *

Jer. 50: 9. as of a mighty *expert* (marg. or, *destroyer*) man; [Some copies read מַשְׂכִּיל]
Hos. 9:14. give them a *miscarrying* (marg. *that casteth the fruit*) womb

---

7923 שִׁכֻּלִים *shik-koo-leem'*, m. pl.

Isa. 49:20. which *thou shalt have, after thou hast lost the other*, (lit. of *thy bereavement*)

7925 שָׁכַם [*shāh-chăm'*].

* HIPHIL.—*Preterite.* *

Gen19: 2. *and ye shall rise up early*, and go
Jud.19: 9. *and* to morrow *get you early*
1Sa.29:10. *and as soon as ye be up early*
2Sa.15: 2. *And* Absalom *rose up early*,
Job 1: 5. *and rose up early* in the morning,
Zep. 3: 7. but *they rose early*,

HIPHIL.—*Infinitive.*

1Sa.17:16. Philistine drew near *morning* and evening,
2Ch 36:15. *rising up betimes*, and sending;
Pro.27:14. *rising early* in the morning,
Jer. 7:13. *rising up early* and speaking,
25. daily *rising up early* and sending
11: 7. *rising early* and protesting,
25: 3. *rising early* and speaking;
4. *rising early* and sending
26: 5. *both rising up early*,
29:19. *rising up early* and sending
32:33. *rising up early* and teaching
35:14. *rising early* and speaking;
15. *rising up early* and sending
44: 4. *rising early* and sending

HIPHIL.—*Imperative.*

Ex. 8:20(16) & 9:13. *Rise up early* in the morning,
1Sa.29:10. Wherefore now *rise up early*

HIPHIL.—*Future.*

Gen19:27. And Abraham *gat up early*
20: 8. *Therefore* Abimelech *rose early*
21:14 & 22:3. *And* Abraham *rose up early*
26:31. *And they rose up betimes*
28:18. *And* Jacob *rose up early*
31:55(32:1). *And early* in the morning Laban *rose up*,
Ex. 24: 4. *and rose up early* in the morning,
32: 6. *And they rose up early*
34: 4. *and* Moses *rose up early* in the morning,
Nu. 14:40. *And they rose up early*
Jos. 3: 1. *And* Joshua *rose early* in the morning;
6:12. *And* Joshua *rose early* in the morning,
15. *that they rose early* about the dawning
7:16. *So* Joshua *rose up early* in the morning,
8:10. *And* Joshua *rose up early*
14. they hasted *and rose up early*,
Jud. 6:28. *And when* the men of the city *arose early*
38. *for he rose up early* on the morrow,
7: 1. *Then* Jerubbaal,...*rose up early*,
9:33. *thou shalt rise early*, and set upon the city:
19: 5. *when they arose early* in the morning,
Jud.19: 8. *And he arose early* in the morning
21: 4. *that* the people *rose early*,
1Sa. 1:19. *And they rose up* in the morning *early*,
5: 3. *And when* they of Ashdod *arose early*
4. *when they arose early* on the morrow
9:26. *And they arose early*: and it came
15:12. And *when* Samuel *rose early*
17:20. *And* David *rose up early*
29:11. *So* David and his men *rose up early*
2K. 3:22. *And they rose up early* in the morning,
6:15. And *when* the servant of the man of God *was risen early*,
19:35. and *when they arose early*
2Ch 20:20. *And they rose early* in the morning,
29:20. *Then* Hezekiah the king *rose early*,
Cant.7:12(13). *Let us get up early* to the vineyards;
Isa. 37:36. and *when they arose early*

HIPHIL.—*Participle.*

Ps.127: 2. vain for you to rise up *early*,
Isa. 5:11. Woe unto them *that rise up early*
Hos. 6: 4. as the *early* dew it goeth away.
13: 3. as the *early* dew that passeth away,

שְׁכֶם *sh'chem*, m. 7926

Gen 9:23. laid (it) upon both their *shoulders*,
21:14. putting (it) on *her shoulder*,
24:15. with her pitcher upon *her shoulder.*
45. with her pitcher on *her shoulder;*
48:22. I have given to thee one *portion*
49:15. bowed *his shoulder* to bear,
Ex. 12:34. their clothes upon *their shoulders.*
Jos. 4: 5. every man of you a stone upon *his shoulder*,
Jud. 9:48. laid (it) on *his shoulder*,
1Sa. 9: 2. *from his shoulders* and upward
10: 9. he had turned *his back* (marg. *shoulder*)
23. any of the people *from his shoulders*
Job 31:36. I would take it upon *my shoulder*,
Ps. 21:12(13). shalt thou make them turn (their) *back*, (marg. *shoulder*)
81: 6(7). I removed *his shoulder* from the
Isa. 9: 4(3). the staff of *his shoulder*,
6(5). government shall be upon *his shoulder:*
10:27. taken away from off *thy shoulder*,
14:25. burden depart from off *their shoulders.*
22:22. of the house of David will I lay upon *his shoulder;*
Hos. 6: 9. murder in the way *by consent:* (marg. *with* (one) *shoulder*, or, *to Shechem*)
Zep. 3: 9. to serve him with one *consent.* (marg. *shoulder*)

שִׁכְמָה *shich-māh'*, f. 7929

Job 31:22. let mine arm fall *from* (my) *shoulder blade*,

שָׁכַן *shāh-chan'* & שָׁכֵן *shāh-chēhn'*. 7931

* KAL.—*Preterite.* *

Ex. 25: 8. *that I may dwell* among them.
29:45. *And I will dwell* among the children of
40:35. because the cloud *abode* thereon,
Deu33:12. *he shall dwell* between his shoulders.
20. *he dwelleth* as a lion,
Jos. 22:19. the Lord's tabernacle *dwelleth*,
Jud. 5:17. Gilead *abode* beyond Jordan:
2Sa. 7:10. *that they may dwell* in a place
1K. 6:13. *And I will dwell* among
1Ch 17: 9. *and they shall dwell* in their place,
Ps. 68: 6(7). the rebellious *dwell* in a dry
74: 2. Zion, wherein *thou hast dwelt.*
94:17. my soul *had* almost *dwelt* in silence.
120: 5. *I dwell* in the tents of Kedar!
6. My soul *hath* long *dwelt* with him
Pro. 8:12. I wisdom *dwell* with prudence,
Isa. 13:21. *and* owls *shall dwell* there,
32:16. *Then* judgment *shall dwell*
Jer. 17: 6. *but shall inhabit* the parched places
51:13. (כתיב) *O thou that dwellest* upon many
Eze.17:23. *and* under it *shall dwell*
43: 9. *and I will dwell* in the midst
Mic. 4:10. *and thou shalt dwell* in the field,

Zec. 2:10(14),11(15). *and I will dwell* in the midst
8: 3. *and will dwell* in the midst
8. *and they shall dwell*

KAL.—*Infinitive.*

Gen35:22. *when* Israel *dwelt* in that land,
Ex. 29:46. *that I may dwell* among
Nu. 9:22. tabernacle, *remaining* thereon,
1K. 8:12. The Lord said *that he would dwell*
2Ch 6: 1. The Lord hath said *that he would dwell*
Job 30: 6. *To dwell* in the cliffs
Ps. 68:18(19). *that* the Lord God *might dwell*
85: 9(10). *that* glory *may dwell* in our land.

KAL.—*Imperative.*

Gen26: 2. *dwell* in the land
Ps. 37: 3. *shalt thou dwell* in the land,
27. *and dwell* for evermore.
Jer. 48:28. *and dwell* in the rock,

KAL.—*Future.*

Gen 9:27. *and he shall dwell* in the tents
16:12. *he shall dwell* in the presence
25:18. *And they dwelt* from Havilah
49:13. Zebulun *shall dwell* at the haven
Ex. 24:16. *And* the glory of the Lord *abode*
Nu. 9:17. the place where the cloud *abode*,
18. as long as the cloud *abode*
10:12. *and* the cloud *rested* in the wilderness
23: 9. the people *shall dwell* alone,
Deu33:12. *shall dwell* in safety by him;
28. Israel *then shall dwell* in safety
Jud. 5:17. and *abode* in his breaches.
1Ch 23:25. *that they may dwell* in Jerusalem
Job 3: 5. *let* a cloud *dwell* upon it;
15:28. *And he dwelleth* in desolate cities,
18:15. *It shall dwell* in his tabernacle,
29:25. *and dwelt* as a king in the army,
37: 8. and *remain* in their places.
38:19. the way (where) light *dwelleth?*
39:28. *She dwelleth* and abideth on the rock,
Ps. 15: 1. who *shall dwell* in thy holy hill?
16: 9. my flesh also *shall rest* (marg. *dwell*)
37:29. *and dwell* therein for ever.
55: 6(7). I fly away, *and be at rest.*
65: 4(5). *he may dwell* in thy courts:
68:16(17). the Lord *will dwell* (in it) for ever.
69:36(37). they that love his name *shall dwell*
102:28(29). children of thy servants *shall continue*,
104:12. *shall* the fowls of the heaven *have their habitation*,
139: 9. *dwell* in the uttermost parts
Pro. 1:33. hearkeneth unto me *shall dwell* safely,
2:21. the upright *shall dwell* in the land,
7:11. her feet *abide* not in her house:
10:30. the wicked *shall* not *inhabit* the earth.
Isa. 13:20. neither *shall it be dwelt in*
33:16. He *shall dwell* on high:
34:11. the raven *shall dwell* in it:
17. *shall they dwell* therein.
57:15. *I dwell* in the high and holy
65: 9. my servants *shall dwell* there.
Jer. 23: 6. Israel *shall dwell* safely:
33:16. Jerusalem *shall dwell* safely:
46:26. afterward *it shall be inhabited*,
49:31. gates nor bars, (which) *dwell* alone.
50:39. neither *shall it be dwelt in*
Eze.17:23. of the branches thereof *shall they dwell.*
31:13. shall all the fowls of the heaven *remain*,
43: 7. *I will dwell* in the midst
Nah. 3:18. thy nobles *shall dwell*

KAL.—*Participle.* Poel.

Gen14:13. for he *dwelt* in the plain
Lev.16:16. the congregation, *that remaineth* (marg. *dwelleth*)
Nu. 5: 3. in the midst whereof I *dwell.*
24: 2. he saw Israel *abiding*
35:34. ye shall inhabit, wherein I *dwell:* for I the Lord *dwell* among the children of
Deu33:16. the good will of *him that dwelt*
Job 4:19. How much less (in) *them that dwell*
26: 5. the waters, *and the inhabitants thereof.*
Ps.135:21. the Lord out of Zion, *which dwelleth* at
Isa. 8:18. *which dwelleth* in mount Zion.
18: 3. of the world, *and dwellers on* the earth,
26:19. *ye that dwell in* dust:
33: 5. for he *dwelleth* on high:
Isa. 57:15. lofty One that *inhabiteth* eternity,
Jer. 25:24. mingled people *that dwell*
49:16. *O thou that dwellest in* the clefts
51:13. *O thou that dwellest* upon many waters,
Joel 3:17(4:17). the Lord your God *dwelling* in
21(-:21). for the Lord *dwelleth* in Zion.
Obad. 3. thou *that dwellest* in the clefts of the rock,
Mic. 7:14. *which dwell* solitarily (in) the wood,

KAL.—*Participle.* Paül.

Jud. 8:11. by the way of *them that dwelt*

* PIEL.—*Preterite.* *

Ps. 78:60. the tent (which) *he placed* among men;
Jer. 7: 7. *Then will I cause* you *to dwell*
12. where *I set* my name at the first,

PIEL.—*Infinitive.*

Nu. 14:30. *to make* you *dwell* therein,
Deu12:11. choose *to cause* his name *to dwell*
14:23. shall choose *to place* his name there,
16: 2. the Lord shall choose *to place* his name
6. the Lord thy God shall choose *to place*
11. hath chosen *to place* his name there.
26: 2. shall choose *to place* his name there.
Neh 1: 9. I have chosen *to set* my name there.

PIEL.—*Future.*

Jer. 7: 3. *and I will cause* you *to dwell*

* HIPHIL.—*Preterite.* *

Eze.32: 4. *and will cause* all the fowls of the heaven *to remain*

HIPHIL.—*Future.*

Gen 3:24. *and he placed* at the east of the garden
Jos. 18: 1. *and set up* the tabernacle
Job 11:14. *let* not wickedness *dwell*
Ps. 7: 5(6). and *lay* mine honour in the dust.
78:55. *and made* the tribes of Israel *to dwell*

שְׁכַן [*sh'chan*], Ch. 7932

* P'AL.—*Future.* *

Dan 4:21(18). fowls of the heaven *had their habitation:*

* PAEL.—*Preterite.* *

Ezr. 6:12. God that *hath caused* his name *to dwell*

שָׁכֵן *shāh-chēhn'*, adj. 7934

Ex. 3:22. woman shall borrow *of her neighbour*,
12: 4. let him *and his neighbour* next unto his
Deu 1: 7. all (the places) *nigh thereunto*, (marg. all *his neighbours*)
Ru. 4:17. the women *her neighbours*
2K. 4: 3. vessels abroad of all *thy neighbours*,
Ps. 31:11(12). *but* especially *among my neighbours*,
44:13(14). us a reproach *to our neighbours*,
79: 4. become a reproach *to our neighbours*,
12. render *unto our neighbours*
80: 6(7). makest us a strife *unto our neighbours*:
89:41(42). he is a reproach *to his neighbours.*
Pro.27:10. better (is) *a neighbour* (that is) near
Isa. 33:24. *the inhabitant* shall not say,
Jer. 6:21. *the neighbour* and his friend
12:14. against all *mine* evil *neighbours*,
49:10. his brethren, *and his neighbours*,
18. *and the neighbour* (cities) *thereof*,
50:40. and *the neighbour* (cities) *thereof*,
Eze.16:26. with the Egyptians *thy neighbours*,
Hos 10: 5. *The inhabitants of* Samaria

שֶׁכֶן [*sheh'-chen*], m. 7933

Deu12: 5. *unto his habitation* shall ye seek,

שָׁכַר [*shāh-char'*]. 7937

* KAL.—*Preterite.* *

Isa. 29: 9. cry: *they are drunken*,

KAL.—*Infinitive.*

Hag 1: 6. but ye *are not filled with drink*;

KAL.—*Imperative.*

Cant 5: 1. drink, *yea, drink abundantly*, (marg. or, *and be drunken*)
Jer. 25:27. Drink ye, *and be drunken*,

KAL.—*Future.*

Gen 9:21. he drank of the wine, *and was drunken;*
43:34. drank, *and were merry* (marg. *drank largely*) with him.
Isa. 49:26. *they shall be drunken* with their own
Lam.4:21. *thou shalt be drunken*,
Nah. 3:11. Thou also *shalt be drunken:*

KAL.—*Participle.* Paül.

Isa. 51:21. thou afflicted, *and drunken*,

* PIEL.—*Infinitive.* *

Hab. 2:15. *makest* (him) *drunken* also,

PIEL.—*Future.*

2Sa.11:13. *and he made him drunk:*
Isa. 63: 6. *and make them drunk* in my fury,

PIEL.—*Participle.*

Jer. 51: 7. *that made* all the earth *drunken:*

* HIPHIL.—*Preterite.* *

Jer. 51:39. *and I will make them drunken*,
57. *And I will make drunk* her princes,

HIPHIL.—*Imperative.*

Jer. 48:26. *Make ye him drunken:*

HIPHIL.—*Future.*

Deu32:42. *I will make* mine arrows *drunk*

* HITHPAEL.—*Future.* *

1Sa. 1:14. How long *wilt thou be drunken?*

7941 **שֵׁכָר** *shēh-chāhr'*, m.

Lev.10: 9. Do not drink wine *nor strong drink*,
Nu. 6: 3. from wine *and strong drink*,
— or vinegar of *strong drink*,
28: 7. cause *the strong wine* to be poured
Deu 14:26. for wine, *or for strong drink*,
29: 6(5). neither have ye drunk wine *or strong drink:*
Jud.13: 4. drink not wine *nor strong drink*,
7. drink no wine *nor strong drink*,
14. drink wine *or strong drink*,
1Sa. 1:15. drunk neither wine *nor strong drink*,
Ps. 69:12(13). I (was) the song of the drunkards. (marg. drinkers of *strong drink*)
Pro.20: 1. *strong drink* (is) raging:
31: 4. nor for princes *strong drink:*
6. Give *strong drink* unto him
Isa. 5:11. they may follow *strong drink;*
22. men of strength to mingle *strong drink:*
24: 9. *strong drink* shall be bitter
28: 7. *and through strong drink*
— have erred *through strong drink*,
— the way through *strong drink;* they err
29: 9. but not with *strong drink*.
56:12. fill ourselves with *strong drink;*
Mic. 2:11. wine *and of strong drink;*

7943 **שִׁכָּרוֹן** *shik-kāh-rōhn'*, m.

Jer. 13:13. all the inhabitants of Jerusalem, with *drunkenness*.
Eze.23:33. Thou shalt be filled with *drunkenness*
39:19. drink blood *till ye be drunken*,

7944 **שַׁל** *shal*, m.

2Sa. 6: 7. God smote him there for (his) *error;* (marg. or, *rashness*)

7945 **שֶׁל** *shel*, part.

Ecc. 8:17. because though (בְּשֶׁל אֲשֶׁר) a man labour to seek (it) out,
Jon. 1: 7. *for whose cause* (בְּשֶׁלְּמִי) this evil (is)
12. *for my sake* (בְּשֶׁלִּי) this great tempest

שַׁלְאֲנָן *shal-ănāhn'*, adj. 7946

Job 21:23. *being* wholly *at ease* and quiet.

שָׁלַב [*shāh-lav'*]. 7947

* PUAL.—*Participle.* *

Ex. 26:17. *set in order* one against another:
36:22. *equally distant* one from another:

שְׁלַבִּים *sh'lab-beem'*, m. pl. 7948

1K. 7:28. the borders (were) between *the ledges:*
29. borders that (were) between *the ledges*
— upon *the ledges* (there was) a base above:

שָׁלַג [*shāh-lag'*]. 7949

* HIPHIL.—*Future.* *

Ps. 68:14(15). it *was* (white) *as snow* in Salmon.

שֶׁלֶג *sheh'-leg*, m. 7950

Ex. 4: 6. his hand (was) leprous *as snow*.
Nu. 12:10. leprous, (white) *as snow:*
2Sa.23:20. lion in the midst of a pit in time of *snow:*
2K. 5:27. from his presence a leper (as white) *as snow*.
1Ch 11:22. slew a lion in a pit in a *snowy* day. (lit. in a day of *snow*)
Job 6:16. wherein *the snow* is hid:
9:30. If I wash myself with *snow* water,
24:19. Drought and heat consume the *snow* waters:
37: 6. For he saith to *the snow*,
38:22. Hast thou entered into the treasures of *the snow?*
Ps. 51: 7(9). wash me, *and* I shall be whiter *than snow*.
147:16. He giveth *snow* like wool:
148: 8. Fire, and hail; *snow*, and vapours
Pro.25:13. As the cold of *snow* in the time
26: 1. *As snow* in summer,
31:21. She is not afraid *of the snow*
Isa. 1:18. they shall be as white *as snow;*
55:10. *and the snow* from heaven,
Jer. 18:14. Will (a man) leave *the snow of* Lebanon
Lam.4: 7. Nazarites were purer *than snow*,

שָׁלָה [*shāh-lāh'*] & **שָׁלַו** [*shāh-lav'*]. 7951

* KAL.—*Preterite.* *

Job 3:26. *I was* not *in safety*,
Jer. 12: 1. *are* all *they happy* that deal
Lam.1: 5. the chief, her enemies *prosper;*

KAL.—*Future.*

Job 12: 6. tabernacles of robbers *prosper*,
Ps.122: 6. *they shall prosper* that love thee.

שָׁלָה [*shāh-lāh'*]. 7952

* NIPHAL.—*Future.* *

2Ch 29:11. My sons, *be* not now *negligent:* (marg. or, *deceived*)

* HIPHIL.—*Future.* *

2K. 4:28. *Do* not *deceive* me?

שָׁלָה [*shāh-lāh'*]. 7953

* KAL.—*Future.* *

Job 27: 8. when God *taketh away* his soul?

שְׁלָה [*sh'lāh*], Ch. 7954

* P'AL.—*Participle.* Passive. *

Dan 4: 4(1). I Nebuchadnezzar was *at rest* in mine house,

7955 **שָׁלָה** *shāh-lāh'*, Ch. f.

Dan 3:29. (כתיב) which speak *any thing amiss* (marg. *error*) against

---

7957 **שַׁלְהֶבֶת** *shal-heh'-veth*, f.

Job 15:30. *the flame* shall dry up his branches,
Cant. 8: 6. (which hath) *a* most vehement *flame*.
Eze. 20:47(21:3). *the flaming flame* shall not be

7960 **שָׁלוּ** *shāh-loo'*, Ch. f.

Ezr. 4:22. Take heed now that *ye fail not* to do this: (lit. to do *error* about this)
6: 9. be given them day by day without *fail*:
Dan 3:29. speak *any thing amiss* (marg. *error*) against the God
6: 4(5). neither was there any *error* or fault

7961 **שָׁלֵו** & **שָׁלֵיו** *shāh-lēhv'*, adj.

1Ch 4:40. wide, and quiet, *and peaceable*;
Job 16:12. I was *at ease*, but he hath
20:20. he shall not feel *quietness* in his belly,
21:23. being wholly at ease *and quiet*.
Ps. 73:12. *who prosper* in the world;
Jer. 49:31. get you up unto the *wealthy* (marg. or, *that is at ease*) nation,
Eze. 23:42. a voice of a multitude *being at ease*
Zec. 7: 7. was inhabited *and in prosperity*,

7959 **שֶׁלֶו** [*sheh'-lev*], m.

Ps. 30: 6(7). *in my prosperity* I said, I shall never be moved.

7962 **שַׁלְוָה** *shal-vāh'*, f.

Ps. 122: 7. *prosperity* within thy palaces.
Pro. 1:32. *and the prosperity* (marg. or, *ease*) *of* fools
17: 1. a dry morsel, *and quietness*
Jer. 22:21. I spake unto thee *in thy prosperity*; (marg. *prosperities*)
Eze. 16:49. *and abundance of* idleness
Dan 8:25. *and by peace* (marg. or, *prosperity*) shall destroy many:
11:21. but he shall come in *peaceably*,
24. He shall enter *peaceably*

7963 **שְׁלֵוָה** [*sh'lēh-vāh'*], Ch. f.

Dan 4:27(24). it may be a lengthening *of thy tranquillity*. (marg. or, an healing *of thine error*)

7964 **שִׁלּוּחִים** *shil-loo-gheem'*, m. pl.

Ex. 18: 2. after *he had sent her back*,
1K. 9:16. *a present* unto his daughter,
Mic. 1:14. Therefore shalt thou give *presents*

7965 **שָׁלוֹם** *shāh-lōhm'*, m.

Gen 15:15. thou shalt go to thy fathers *in peace*;
26:29. have sent thee away *in peace*:
31. they departed from him *in peace*.
28:21. come again to my father's house *in peace*;
29: 6. he said unto them, (Is) he *well* (marg. (Is there) *peace* to him)? And they said, (He is) *well*:
37: 4. could not speak *peaceably*
14. see *whether it be well with* (marg. see *the peace of*) thy brethren, and *well with* the
41:16. give Pharaoh an answer of *peace*.
43:23. *Peace* (be) to you, fear not:
27. he asked them of (their) *welfare*, (marg. *peace*)
Gen 43:27. (Is) your father *well*, (marg. (Is there) *peace* to your father)
28. Thy servant our father (is) *in good health*,
44:17. get you up *in peace* unto your father.
Ex. 4:18. Jethro said to Moses, Go *in peace*.
18: 7. they asked each other of (their) *welfare*; (marg. *peace*)
23. shall also go to their place *in peace*.
Lev. 26: 6. I will give *peace* in the land,
Nu. 6:26. lift up his countenance upon thee, and give thee *peace*.
25:12. I give unto him my covenant of *peace*:
Deu 2:26. king of Heshbon with words of *peace*,
20:10. then proclaim *peace* unto it.
11. if it make thee answer of *peace*,
23: 6(7). Thou shalt not seek *their peace*
29:19(18). I shall have *peace*,
Jos. 9:15. Joshua made *peace* with them,
10:21. returned to the camp to Joshua at Makkedah *in peace*:
Jud. 4:17. *peace* between Jabin...and the house of
6:23. *Peace* (be) unto thee;
24. called it Jehovah-*shalom*: (marg. The Lord (send) *peace*)
8: 9. When I come again *in peace*,
11:13. restore those (lands) again *peaceably*.
31. when I return *in peace*
18: 6. the priest said unto them, Go *in peace*:
15. Micah, and *saluted* him. (lit. asked him *of peace*)
19:20. the old man said, *Peace* (be) with thee;
21:13. to call *peaceably* (marg. or, proclaim *peace*) unto them.
1Sa. 1:17. Go *in peace*: and the God of Israel grant
7:14. *peace* between Israel and the Amorites.
10: 4. they will *salute* thee, (marg. ask thee of *peace*)
16: 4. Comest thou *peaceably*?
5. he said, *Peaceably*: I am come
17:18. look how thy brethren *fare*, (lit. visit thy brethren *for peace*)
22. came and *saluted* his brethren. (marg. asked his brethren *of peace*)
20: 7. thy servant shall have *peace*:
13. that thou mayest go *in peace*:
21. for (there is) *peace* to thee,
42. Jonathan said to David, Go *in peace*,
25: 5. *greet* him in my name: (marg. ask him... *of peace*)
6. *Peace* (be) both to thee, and *peace* (be) to thine house, and *peace* (be) unto all
35. Go up *in peace* to thine house;
29: 7. Wherefore now return, and go *in peace*,
30:21. he *saluted* them. (lit. asked them *of peace*; marg. or, asked them *how they did*)
2Sa. 3:21. sent Abner away; and he went *in peace*.
22. he was gone *in peace*.
23. he is gone *in peace*.
8:10. unto king David, to *salute* him, (marg. ask him *of peace*)
11: 7. David demanded (of him) *how* Joab *did* (marg. *of the peace of* Joab), *and how* the people *did*, *and how* the war *prospered*. (lit. *and of the peace of* the people *and of the peace of* the war)
15: 9. the king said unto him, Go *in peace*.
27. return into the city *in peace*,
17: 3. all the people shall be *in peace*.
18:28. unto the king, *All is well*. (marg. *Peace*)
29. Is the young man Absalom *safe*? (marg. (Is there) *peace*)
32. (Is) the young man Absalom *safe*?
19:24(25). the day he came (again) *in peace*.
30(31). the king is come again *in peace*
20: 9. Joab said to Amasa, (Art) thou *in health*,
1K. 2: 5. shed the blood of war *in peace*,
6. hoar head go down to the grave *in peace*.
13. And she said, Comest thou *peaceably*? And he said, *Peaceably*.
33. upon his throne, shall there be *peace*
4:24(5:4). *and* he had *peace* on all sides
5:12(26). there was *peace* between Hiram and
20:18. Whether they be come out *for peace*,
22:17. return every man to his house *in peace*.
27. until I come *in peace*.
28. If thou return at all *in peace*,
2K. 4:23. she said, (It shall be) *well*. (marg. *peace*)

2K. 4:26. (Is it) *well* with thee? (is it) *well* with thy husband? (is it) *well* with the child? And she answered, (It is) *well*.
5:19. he said unto him, Go *in peace*.
21. to meet him, and said (Is) all *well?*
22. he said, All (is) *well*.
9:11. said unto him, (Is) all *well?*
17. let him say, (Is it) *peace?*
18,19. Thus saith the king, (Is it) *peace?*
—,— What hast thou to do *with peace?* (lit. what to thee *and to peace*)
22. that he said, (Is it) *peace*, Jehu? And he answered, What *peace*,
31. she said, (Had) Zimri *peace*,
10:13. we go down to *salute* (lit. *to the peace of*) the children of the king
20:19. if *peace* and truth be in my days?
22:20. be gathered into thy grave *in peace;*
1Ch 12:17. If ye be come *peaceably* unto me
18. thou son of Jesse: *peace, peace* (be) unto thee, *and peace* (be) to thine helpers;
18:10. to enquire *of* his *welfare*,
22: 9. *and* I will give *peace* and quietness
2Ch 15: 5. in those times (there was) no *peace*
18:16. every man to his house *in peace*.
26. until I return *in peace*.
27. If thou certainly return *in peace*,
19: 1. returned to his house *in peace*
34:28. shalt be gathered to thy grave *in peace*,
Ezr. 9:12. nor seek their *peace* or their wealth
Est. 2:11. the women's house, to know *how* Esther *did*, (marg. *the peace*)
9:30. words of *peace* and truth,
10: 3. speaking *peace* to all his seed.
Job 5:24. thy tabernacle (shall be) in *peace;*
15:21. *in prosperity* the destroyer shall come
21: 9. Their houses (are) *safe* (marg. *peace*)
25: 2. he maketh *peace* in his high places.
Ps. 4: 8(9). I will both lay me down *in peace*,
28: 3. speak *peace* to their neighbours,
29:11. the Lord will bless his people *with peace*.
34:14(15). seek *peace*, and pursue it.
35:20. For they speak not *peace:*
27. hath pleasure in *the prosperity of*
37:11. themselves in the abundance of *peace*.
37. for the end of (that) man (is) *peace*.
38: 3(4). neither (is there any) *rest*
41: 9(10). Yea, *mine own familiar* friend, (marg. the man of *my peace*)
55:18(19). He hath delivered my soul *in peace*
20(21). *against such as be at peace with him:*
69:22(23). *and* (that which should have been) for (their) *welfare*,
72: 3. The mountains shall bring *peace*
7. abundance of *peace* so long
73: 3. I saw *the prosperity of* the wicked.
85: 8(9). he will speak *peace* unto his people,
10(11). righteousness *and peace* have kissed
119:165. Great *peace* have they which love
120: 6. long dwelt with him that hateth *peace*.
7. I (am for) *peace:* but when I speak,
122: 6. Pray for *the peace of* Jerusalem:
7. *Peace* be within thy walls,
8. I will now say, *Peace* (be) within thee.
125: 5. *peace* (shall be) upon Israel.
128: 6. children's children, (and) *peace* upon
147:14. He maketh *peace* (in) thy borders,
Pro. 3: 2. long life, *and peace*, shall they add
17. all her paths (are) *peace*.
12:20. but to the counsellors of *peace* (is) joy.
Ecc. 3: 8. a time of war, and a time of *peace*.
Cant. 8:10. then was I in his eyes as one that found *favour*. (marg. *peace*)
Isa. 9: 6(5). The Prince of *Peace*.
7(6). government *and peace* (there shall be)
26: 3. Thou wilt keep (him) in *perfect peace*, (marg. *peace, peace*)
12. Lord, thou wilt ordain *peace* for us:
27: 5. he may make *peace* with me; (and) he shall make *peace* with me.
32:17. the work of righteousness shall be *peace;*
18. my people shall dwell in a *peaceable*
33: 7. the ambassadors of *peace* shall weep
38:17. *for peace* I had great bitterness:
39: 8. there shall be *peace* and truth
41: 3. He pursued them, (and) passed *safely;* (marg. *in peace*)
Isa. 45: 7. I make *peace*, and create evil:
48:18. then had *thy peace* been as a river,
22. no *peace*, saith the Lord,
52: 7. that publisheth *peace;*
53: 5. chastisement of *our peace* (was)
54:10. the covenant of *my peace*
13. great (shall be) *the peace of*
55:12. out with joy, *and* be led forth *with peace:*
57: 2. He shall enter into *peace:*
19. I create the fruit of the lips; *Peace, peace* to him that is far off,
21. no *peace*, saith my God, to the wicked.
59: 8. The way of *peace* they know not;
— goeth therein shall not know *peace*.
60:17. I will also make thy officers *peace*,
66:12. I will extend *peace* to her
Jer. 4:10. Ye shall have *peace;*
6:14 & 8:11. my people slightly, saying, *Peace, peace;* when (there is) no *peace*.
8:15. We looked *for peace*,
9: 8(7). speaketh *peaceably* to his neighbour
12: 5. in the land of *peace*,
12. no flesh shall have *peace*.
13:19. it shall be *wholly* carried away
14:13. I will give you assured *peace*
19. we looked *for peace*,
15: 5. who shall go aside to ask *how* thou *doest?* (marg. *of* thy *peace*)
16: 5. for I have taken away *my peace*
20:10. All *my familiars* (lit. every man of *my peace*) watched for my halting,
23:17. Ye shall have *peace;*
25:37. the *peaceable* habitations
28: 9. The prophet which prophesieth *of peace*,
29: 7. seek *the peace of* the city
— for *in the peace thereof* shall ye have *peace*.
11. thoughts of *peace*, and not of evil,
30: 5. trembling, of fear, and not of *peace*.
33: 6. the abundance of *peace* and truth.
9. all *the prosperity* that I procure
34: 5. thou shalt die *in peace:*
38: 4. seeketh not *the welfare* (marg. *peace*) of
22. Thy *friends* (marg. Men of *thy peace*) have set thee on,
43:12. he shall go forth from thence *in peace*.
Lam. 3:17. removed my soul far off *from peace:*
Eze. 7:25. they shall seek *peace*,
13:10. have seduced my people, saying, *Peace;* and (there was) no *peace;*
16. which see visions of *peace* for her, and (there is) no *peace*, saith the Lord God.
34:25. make with them a covenant of *peace*,
37:26. I will make a covenant of *peace*
Dan 10:19. *peace* (be) unto thee,
Obad. 7. the men that *were at peace with thee* (marg. of *thy peace*)
Mic. 3: 5. bite with their teeth, and cry, *Peace;*
5: 5(4). this (man) shall be *the peace*,
Nah 1:15(2:1). that publisheth *peace!*
Hag 2: 9. in this place will I give *peace*, saith the
Zec. 6:13. the counsel of *peace* shall be between
8:10. neither (was there any) *peace*
12. For the seed (shall be) *prosperous;* (marg. of *peace*)
16. execute the judgment of truth and *peace*
19. therefore love the truth *and peace*.
9:10. he shall speak *peace* unto the heathen:
Mal 2: 5. covenant was with him of life *and peace;*
6. he walked with me *in peace*

שִׁלּוּם *shil-loom'*, m. 7966

Isa. 34: 8. the year of *recompences*
Hos 9: 7. the days of *recompence* are come;
Mic. 7: 3. the judge (asketh) *for a reward;*

שְׁלוֹשׁ *shāh-lōhsh'*, m. & שְׁלוֹשָׁה *sh'lōh-shāh'*, f. adj. num. 7969

Gen 5:22. Methuselah *three* hundred years,
23. all the days of Enoch were *three* hundred sixty and five years:
6:10. Noah begat *three* sons,
15. the ark (shall be) *three* hundred cubits,

Gen 7:13. *and* the *three* wives of his sons
9:19. These (are) the *three* sons of Noah:
28. Noah lived after the flood *three* hundred and fifty
11:13. after he begat Salah four hundred and *three* years,
15. after he begat Eber four hundred and *three*
14: 4. *and* in the *thir*teenth year they rebelled.
14. *three* hundred *and* eighteen,
17:25. Ishmael his son (was) *thir*teen years old
18: 2. lo, *three* men stood by him:
6. Make ready quickly *three* measures
29: 2. there (were) *three* flocks of sheep
34. I have born him *three* sons:
30:36. he set *three* days' journey
38:24. it came to pass *about three* months after,
40:10. in the vine (were) *three* branches:
12. The *three* branches (are) *three* days:
13,19. Yet within *three* days shall Pharoah
16. *three* white baskets on my head:
18. The *three* baskets (are) *three* days:
42:17. all together into ward *three* days.
45:22. Benjamin he gave *three* hundred
46:15. his daughters (were) thirty and *three*.
Ex. 2: 2. she hid him *three* months.
3:18. *three* days' journey into the wilderness,
5: 3. *three* days' journey into the desert,
6:18. the years of the life of Kohath (were) an hundred thirty and *three*
7: 7. Aaron fourscore and *three* years old,
8:27(23). We will go *three* days' journey
10:22. darkness in all the land of Egypt *three*
23. neither rose any from his place for *three*
15:22. they went *three* days in the wilderness,
19:15. Be ready *against* the *third* day:
21:11. if he do not these *three* unto her,
23:14. *Three* times thou shalt keep a feast
17. *Three* times in the year
25:32. *three* branches of the candlestick
— *and three* branches of the candlestick
33. *Three* bowls made like
— *and three* bowls made like almonds
27: 1. the height thereof (shall be) *three* cubits.
14,15. pillars *three*, and their sockets *three*.
32:28. that day *about three* thousand
34:23,24. *Thrice* (lit. *three* times) in the year
37:18. *three* branches of the candlestick out of the one side thereof, *and three* branches
19. *Three* bowls made after the fashion
— *and three* bowls made like almonds
38: 1. *and three* cubits the height thereof.
14,15. pillars *three*, and their sockets *three*
26. 600 thousand *and three* thousand and 550
Lev. 12: 4. her purifying *three and* thirty days;
14:10. *and three* tenth deals of fine flour
19:23. *three* years shall it be as uncircumcised
25:21. bring forth fruit *for three* years.
27: 6. estimation (shall be) *three* shekels
Nu. 1:23. fifty and nine thousand *and three*
43. fifty and *three* thousand and 400.
46. six hundred thousand *and three* thousand and 550.
2:13. those that were numbered of them, (were) 59 thousand *and three* hundred.
30. those that were numbered of them, (were) fifty and *three* thousand and 400.
32. those that were numbered...(were) 600 thousand *and three* thousand and 550.
3:43. that were numbered of them, were 22,200 and threescore and *thir*teen.
46. that are to be redeemed of the 200 and threescore and *thir*teen
50. a thousand *three* hundred and threescore and five (shekels), after the shekel
4:44. that were numbered of them after their families, were *three* thousand and 200.
10:33. mount of the Lord *three* days' journey:
— before them in the *three* days' journey,
12: 4. Come out *ye three* unto the tabernacle of the congregation. And *they three* came
15: 9. meat offering of *three* tenth deals
22:28. hast smitten me these *three* times?
32. smitten thine ass these *three* times?
33. turned from me these *three* times:
24:10. altogether blessed (them) these *three*
26: 7. they that were numbered of them were forty and *three* thousand and 730.
Nu. 26:25. according to those that were numbered of them, 64 thousand and *three* hundred.
47. those that were numbered of them; (who were) fifty and *three* thousand and 400.
62. were twenty and *three* thousand,
28:12. *And three* tenth deals of flour
20. *three* tenth deals shall ye offer
28. *three* tenth deals unto one bullock,
29: 3. *three* tenth deals for a bullock,
9. *three* tenth deals to a bullock,
13. *thir*teen young bullocks,
14. *three* tenth deals unto every bullock *of the* *thir*teen bullocks,
31:36. was in number *three* hundred thousand and seven and thirty thousand and 500.
43. *three* hundred thousand and thirty thousand (and) seven thousand and five hundred sheep,
33: 8. went *three* days' journey
39. Aaron (was) an hundred and twenty and *three* years old when he died
35:14. Ye shall give *three* cities
— and *three* cities shall ye give
Deu 4:41. Then Moses severed *three* cities
14:28. At the end of *three* years
16:16. *Three* times in a year
17: 6. two witnesses, or *three* witnesses,
19: 2,7. Thou shalt separate *three* cities
9. then shalt thou add *three* cities more for thee, beside these *three*:
15. or at the mouth of *three* witnesses,
Jos. 1:11. within *three* days ye shall pass over
2:16. hide yourselves there *three* days,
22. and abode there *three* days.
3: 2. it came to pass after *three* days,
7: 3. about two or (marg. *about*) *three* thousand
4. *about three* thousand men:
9:16. at the end of *three* days after they
15:14. Caleb drove thence the *three* sons
17:11. her towns, (even) *three* countries.
18: 4. Give out from among you *three* men
19: 6. *thir*teen cities and their villages:
21: 4. out of the tribe of Benjamin, *thir*teen
6. Manasseh in Bashan, *thir*teen cities.
19. *thir*teen cities with their suburbs.
32. and Kartan with her suburbs; *three* cities.
33. to their families (were) *thir*teen cities.
Jud. 1:20. thence the *three* sons of Anak.
7: 6. were *three* hundred men:
7. *By* the *three* hundred men
8. *and* retained those *three* hundred
16. he divided the *three* hundred men (into) *three* companies,
20. the *three* companies blew the trumpets,
22. the *three* hundred blew the trumpets,
8: 4. the *three* hundred men
9:22. Abimelech had reigned *three* years
43. divided them *into three* companies,
10: 2. judged Israel twenty *and three* years,
11:26. coasts of Arnon, *three* hundred years?
14:14. they could not in *three* days expound
15: 4. caught *three* hundred foxes,
11. Then *three* thousand men
16:15. thou hast mocked me these *three* times,
27. *about three* thousand men
19: 4. and he abode with him *three* days:
1 Sa. 1:24. with *three* bullocks, and one ephah
2:13. with a fleshhook of *three* teeth
21. bare *three* sons and two daughters.
9:20. as for thine asses that were lost *three* days
10: 3. there shall meet thee *three* men
— one carrying *three* kids, and another carrying *three* loaves
11: 8. numbered them in Bezek, the children of Israel were *three* hundred thousand,
11. Saul put the people in *three* companies;
13: 2. Saul chose him *three* thousand
17. camp of the Philistines in *three*
21. *and for the* forks, (lit. and *for the triple* forks)
17:13. the *three* eldest sons
— the names of his *three* sons
14. *and* the *three* eldest followed Saul
20:20. I will shoot *three* arrows
41. bowed himself *three* times:
24: 2(3). Saul took *three* thousand
25: 2. he had *three* thousand sheep,
26: 2. having *three* thousand chosen men

1Sa.30:12. nor drunk (any) water, *three* days *and three* nights.
13. because *three* days agone I fell sick.
31: 6. So Saul died, and his *three* sons,
8. they found Saul and his *three* sons
2Sa. 2:18. there were *three* sons of Zeruiah
31. (so that) *three* hundred and threescore
5: 5. he reigned thirty *and three* years
6:11. in the house of Obed-edom...*three* months:
13:38. was there *three* years.
14:27. unto Absalom there were born *three* sons,
18:14. he took *three* darts in his hand,
20: 4. Assemble me the men of Judah within *three* days,
21: 1. famine in the days of David *three* years,
16. whose spear (weighed) *three* hundred
23: 9. Ahohite, (one) *of* the *three* mighty
13. And *three* of the thirty chief went down,
16. the *three* mighty men
17. These things did these *three* mighty men.
18. was chief among *three*. And he lifted up his spear against *three* hundred, (and) slew (them), and had the name *among three*.
19. Was he not most honourable of *three?*
— he attained not unto *the* (first) *three*.
22. had the name *among three* mighty men.
23. He was more honourable than the thirty, but he attained not to *the* (first) *three*.
24:12. Thus saith the Lord, I offer thee *three*
13. or wilt thou flee *three* months
— that there be *three* days' pestilence
1K. 2:11. thirty *and three* years reigned he
39. came to pass at the end of *three* years,
4:32(5:12). he spake *three* thousand
5:16(30). *three* thousand *and three* hundred, which ruled over the people
6:36. with *three* rows of hewed stone,
7: 1. building his own house *thir*teen years,
4. windows (in) *three* rows, and light (was) against light (in) *three* ranks.
5. light (was) against light (in) *three* ranks.
12. with *three* rows of hewed stones,
25. *three* looking toward the north, *and three* looking toward the west, *and three* looking toward the south, *and three*
27. *and three* cubits the height of it.
9:25. *three* times in a year did Solomon
10:17. *And* (he made) *three* hundred shields
— *three* pound of gold went to one shield:
22. once *in three* years came the navy
11: 3. *three* hundred concubines:
12: 5. Depart yet (for) *three* days,
15: 2. *Three* years reigned he in Jerusalem.
28. Even in the *third* year of Asa
33. In the *third* year of Asa
17:21. himself upon the child *three* times,
22: 1. continued *three* years without war
2K. 2:17. and they sought *three* days, but found
3:10, 13. hath called these *three* kings together,
9:32. looked out to him two (or) *three*
12: 6(7). in the *three and* twentieth year of
13: 1. In the *three and* twentieth year of Joash
18. And he smote *thrice*, (lit. *three* times)
19. now thou shalt smite Syria (but) *thrice*. (lit. *id.*)
25. *Three* times did Joash beat him,
17: 5. besieged it *three* years.
18: 1. it came to pass in the *third* year
10. at the end of *three* years
14. *three* hundred talents of silver
23:31. Jehoahaz (was) twenty *and three* years
— *and* he reigned *three* months
24: 1. became his servant *three* years:
8. *and* he reigned in Jerusalem *three* months.
25:17. height of the chapiter *three* cubits;
18. the *three* keepers of the door:
1Ch 2: 3. *three* were born unto him
16. Abishai, and Joab, and Asahel, *three*.
22. who had *three* and twenty cities
3: 4. he reigned thirty *and three* years.
23. Elioenai, and Hezekiah, and Azrikam, *three*.
6:60(45). their families (were) *thir*teen
62(47). Bashan, *thir*teen cities.
7: 6. Bela, and Becher, and Jediael, *three*.
10: 6. Saul died, *and* his *three* sons,

1Ch 11:11. his spear against *three* hundred
12. who (was one) *of* the *three* mighties.
15. Now *three* of the thirty captains
18. *the three* brake through the host
19. These things did these *three*
20. Abishai the brother of Joab, he was chief of *the three:* for lifting up his spear against *three* hundred, he slew (them), and had a name *among the three*.
21. Of *the three*, he was more honourable
— he attained not to *the* (first) *three*.
24. had a name *among the three*
25. but attained not to *the* (first) *three:*
12:27. with him (were) *three* thousand
29. the kindred of Saul, *three* thousand:
39. there they were with David *three* days,
13:14. in his house *three* months.
21:10. I offer thee *three* (things):
12. Either *three* years' famine; or *three* months to be destroyed before thy foes,
— or else *three* days the sword of the Lord,
23: 8. Jehiel, and Zetham, and Joel, *three*.
9. Shelomith, and Haziel, and Haran, *three*.
23. Mahli, and Eder, Jeremoth, *three*.
24:13. The *thir*teenth to Huppah,
18. The *three* and twentieth to Delaiah,
25: 5. Heman fourteen sons and *three* daughters.
20. The *thir*teenth to Shubael,
30. The *three* and twentieth to Mahazioth,
26:11. Tebaliah *the third*,
29: 4. *three* thousand talents of gold,
27. thirty *and three* (years) reigned he
2Ch 2: 2(1). *three* thousand and six hundred to
17(16). and they were found an hundred and fifty thousand and *three* thousand and 600.
18(17). *and three* thousand and six hundred overseers to set the people a work.
4: 4. *three* looking toward the north, *and three* looking toward the west, *and three* looking toward the south, *and three*
5. it received and held *three* thousand baths.
6:13. and *three* cubits high,
7:10. on the *three* and twentieth day
8:13. *three* times in the year,
9:16. *And three* hundred shields (made he of) beaten gold: *three* hundred (shekels)
21. *every three* years once came the ships
10: 5. Come again unto me after *three* days.
11:17. *three* years: for *three* years they walked
13: 2. He reigned *three* years in Jerusalem.
14: 8(7). out of Judah *three* hundred thousand;
9(8). of a thousand thousand, and *three* hundred chariots;
17: 7. Also in the *third* year of his reign
14. men of valour *three* hundred thousand.
20:25. they were *three* days in gathering of the
25: 5. found them *three* hundred thousand
13. smote *three* thousand of them, and took
26:13. (was) an army, *three* hundred thousand and seven thousand and five hundred,
29:33. *three* thousand sheep.
31:16. from *three* years old and upward,
35: 7. *three* thousand bullocks:
8. *three* hundred oxen.
36: 2. Jehoahaz (was) twenty and *three* years
— *and* he reigned *three* months in Jerusalem.
9. *and* he reigned *three* months and ten days
Ezr. 2: 4. of Shephatiah, *three* hundred seventy and two.
11. of Bebai, six hundred twenty *and three*.
17. of Bezai, *three* hundred twenty and *three*.
19. Hashum, two hundred twenty *and three*.
21. of Beth-lehem, an hundred twenty *and three*.
25. and Beeroth, seven hundred and forty *and three*.
28. Beth-el and Ai, two hundred twenty *and three*.
32. Harim, *three* hundred and twenty.
34. Jericho, *three* hundred forty and five.
35. The children of Senaah, *three* thousand and six hundred and thirty.
36. the children of Jedaiah, of the house of Jeshua, nine hundred seventy *and three*.
58. the children of Solomon's servants, (were) *three* hundred ninety and two.

Ezr. 2:64. The whole congregation together (was) forty and two thousand *three* hundred (and) 60,
65. of whom (there were) seven thousand *three* hundred thirty and seven:
8: 5. with him *three* hundred males.
15. there abode we in tents *three* days:
32. and abode there *three* days.
10: 8. would not come *within three* days,
9. unto Jerusalem *within three* days.
Neh 2:11. was there *three* days.
7: 9. Shephatiah, *three* hundred seventy and 2.
17. Azgad, two thousand *three* hundred 22.
22. Hashum, *three* hundred twenty and eight.
23. Bezai, *three* hundred twenty and four.
29. seven hundred forty *and three.*
32. Ai, an hundred twenty *and three.*
35. Harim, *three* hundred and twenty.
36. Jericho, *three* hundred forty and five.
38. The children of Senaah, *three* thousand nine hundred and thirty.
39. nine hundred seventy *and three.*
60. *three* hundred ninety and two.
66. forty and two thousand *three* hundred and threescore,
67. seven thousand *three* hundred thirty and 7:
Est 1: 3. In the *third* year of his reign,
3:12. *on* the *thir*teenth day of the first month,
13. *upon the thir*teenth (day) of the twelfth
4:16. neither eat nor drink *three* days,
8: 9. *on the three* and twentieth
12. *upon the thir*teenth (day) of the twelfth
9: 1. *on* the *thir*teenth day of the same,
15. slew *three* hundred men
17. On the *thir*teenth day of the month
18. *on the thir*teenth (day) thereof,
Job 1: 2. unto him seven sons *and three* daughters.
3. *and three* thousand camels,
4. called *for* their *three* sisters
17. The Chaldeans made out *three* bands,
2:11. when Job's *three* friends heard
32: 1. So these *three* men ceased
3. *Also against* his *three* friends
5. in the mouth of (these) *three* men,
33:29. these (things) worketh God *oftentimes* (marg. twice (and) *thrice*) with man,
42:13. had also seven sons *and three* daughters.
Pro. 30:15. *three* (things that) are never satisfied,
18. There be *three* (things which) are
21. For *three* (things) the earth is disquieted,
29. There be *three* (things) which go well,
Isa. 16:14. Within *three* years, as the years
17: 6. two (or) *three* berries in the top
20: 3. walked naked and barefoot *three* years
Jer. 1: 2. *in the thir*teenth year of his reign.
25: 3. the *thir*teenth year of Josiah
— that (is) the *three* and twentieth year,
36:23. Jehudi had read *three* or four
52:24. the *three* keepers of the door:
28. *three* thousand Jews *and three* and 20:
30. In the *three* and twentieth year
Eze. 4: 5. according to the number of the days, *three* hundred and ninety days:
9. *three* hundred and ninety days
14:14. these *three* men, Noah, Daniel, and Job,
16. (Though) these *three* men (were) in it,
18. *Though* these *three* men (were) in it,
40:10. *three* on this side, *and three* on that side; *they three* (were) of one
11. the length of the gate, *thir*teen cubits.
21. *three* on this side *and three* on that side;
48. *three* cubits on this side, *and three* cubits
41: 6. the side chambers (were) *three,*
16. round about *on their three* stories,
22. The altar of wood (was) *three* cubits
48:31. *three* gates northward;
32. five hundred: and *three* gates;
33. five hundred measures: and *three* gates;
34. their *three* gates;
Dan 1: 1. the *third* year of the reign of Jehoiakim
5. nourishing them *three* years,
8: 1. In the *third* year of the reign of king
14. two thousand *and three* hundred days;
10: 1. In the *third* year of Cyrus
2. Daniel was mourning *three* full weeks.
3. till *three* whole weeks were fulfilled.
11: 2. shall stand up yet *three* kings

Dan 12:12. cometh to the thousand *three* hundred and five and thirty days.
Am. 1: 3, 6, 9, 11, 13 & 2:1, 4, 6. For *three* transgressions
4: 4. your tithes *after three* years:
7. when (there were) yet *three* months
8. So two (or) *three* cities wandered
Jon. 1:17(2:1). the fish *three* days *and three* nights.
3: 3. an exceeding great city of *three* days'
Zec. 11: 8. *Three* shepherds also I cut off

שְׁלוֹשִׁים *sh'lōh-sheem'*, pl.adj. num. 7970

Gen 5: 3. Adam lived an hundred and *thirty*
5. all the days that Adam lived were nine hundred *and thirty* years:
16. he begat Jared eight hundred and *thirty*
6:15. *and* the height of it *thirty* cubits.
11:12. Arphaxad lived five *and thirty* years,
14. Salah lived *thirty* years, and begat
16. Eber lived four *and thirty* years,
17. Eber lived after he begat Peleg four hundred *and thirty* years, and begat
18. Peleg lived *thirty* years, and begat
20. Reu lived two *and thirty* years,
22. Serug lived *thirty* years, and begat
18:30. there shall *thirty* be found there.
— I will not do (it), if I find *thirty* there.
25:17. the life of Ishmael, an hundred *and thirty* and seven years:
32:15(16). *Thirty* milch camels with their colts,
41:46. Joseph (was) *thirty* years old
46:15. his daughters (were) *thirty* and three.
47: 9. the years of my pilgrimage (are) an hundred and *thirty* years:
Ex. 6:16. the years of the life of Levi (were) an hundred *thirty* and seven years.
18. the life of Kohath (were) an hundred *thirty* and three years.
20. the years of the life of Amram (were) an hundred *and thirty* and seven
12:40. Egypt, (was) four hundred and *thirty*
41. end of the four hundred and *thirty* years,
21:32. give unto their master *thirty* shekels
26: 8. one curtain (shall be) *thirty* cubits,
36:15. length of one curtain (was) *thirty* cubits,
38:24. seven hundred *and thirty* shekels,
Lev. 12: 4. *And* she shall then continue...three and *thirty* days;
27: 4. thy estimation shall be *thirty* shekels.
Nu. 1:35. Manasseh, (were) *thirty and* two thousand
37. Benjamin, (were) *thirty and* five thousand
2:21. those that were numbered of them, (were) *thirty and* two thousand and two hundred.
23. those that were numbered of them, (were) *thirty and* five thousand and four hundred.
4: 3, 23, 30, 35, 39, 43, 47. From *thirty* years old and upward
40. by the house of their fathers, were two thousand and six hundred *and thirty.*
7:13, 19, 25, 31, 37, 43, 49, 55, 61, 67, 73, 79, 85. an hundred and *thirty* (shekels),
20:29. they mourned for Aaron *thirty* days,
26: 7. forty and three thousand and seven hundred *and thirty.*
37. those that were numbered of them, *thirty* and two thousand and five hundred.
51. the numbered of the children of Israel, six hundred thousand and a thousand seven hundred *and thirty.*
31:35. And *thirty and* two thousand persons
36. was in number three hundred thousand and seven *and thirty* thousand and five hundred sheep:
38. beeves (were) *thirty and* six thousand;
39. the asses (were) *thirty* thousand and five hundred;
40. the Lord's tribute (was) *thirty and* two
43. (unto) the congregation was three hundred thousand *and thirty* thousand (and) seven thousand and five hundred sheep,
44. And *thirty and* six thousand beeves,
45. *thirty* thousand asses and five hundred,
Deu 2:14. brook Zered, (was) *thirty* and eight years;

Deu34: 8. Moses in the plains of Moab *thirty* days:
Jos. 7: 5. *about thirty* and six men:
8: 3. Joshua chose out *thirty* thousand
12:24. all the kings *thirty* and one.
Jud.10: 4. And he had *thirty* sons that rode on *thirty* ass colts, *and* they had *thirty* cities,
12: 9. he had *thirty* sons, *and thirty* daughters,
— *and* took in *thirty* daughters
14. forty sons *and thirty* nephews,
14:11. they brought *thirty* companions
12. then I will give you *thirty* sheets *and thirty* change of garments:
13. then shall ye give me *thirty* sheets *and thirty* change of garments.
19. slew *thirty* men of them,
20:31. *about thirty* men of Israel.
39. kill of the men of Israel *about thirty*
1Sa. 4:10. there fell of Israel *thirty* thousand
9:22. which (were) *about thirty* persons.
11: 8. the men of Judah *thirty* thousand.
13: 5. *thirty* thousand chariots,
2Sa. 5: 4. David (was) *thirty* years old
5. he reigned *thirty* and three years
6: 1. chosen (men) of Israel, *thirty* thousand.
23:13. (כתיב) *three of the thirty* chief went (lit. according to כתיב, *thirty of the thirty*)
23. more honourable than *the thirty*,
24. brother of Joab (was) one *of the thirty;*
39. *thirty* and seven in all.
1K. 2:11. *thirty* and three years reigned he
4:22(5:2). for one day was *thirty* measures
5:13(27). the levy was *thirty* thousand men.
6: 2&7:2. *and* the height thereof *thirty* cubits.
7: 6. *and* the breadth thereof *thirty* cubits:
23. a line of *thirty* cubits did compass
16:23. In the *thirty* and first year of Asa
29. in the *thirty* and eighth year
20: 1. *and* (there were) *thirty* and two kings
15. the young men of the princes of the provinces, and they were two hundred *and thirty* two:
16. the *thirty* and two kings
22:31. *thirty* and two captains that had rule
42. Jehoshaphat (was) *thirty* and five
2K. 8:17. *Thirty* and two years old
13:10. In the *thirty* and seventh year
15: 8. In the *thirty* and eighth year
13. in the nine and *thirtieth* year of Uzziah
17. In the nine and *thirtieth* year of Azariah
18:14. *and thirty* talents of gold.
22: 1. *and* he reigned *thirty* and one years
25:27. *in* the seven and *thirtieth* year of the
1Ch 3: 4. *and*...he reigned *thirty* and three years.
7: 4. bands of soldiers for war, six *and thirty* thousand (men):
7. were reckoned by their genealogies twenty and two thousand *and thirty* and four.
11:11. (כתיב)chief of *the captains:*
15. Now three of the *thirty* captains
25. he was honourable among *the thirty*,
42. Reubenites, and *thirty* with him,
12: 4. a mighty man *among the thirty*, and over *the thirty;*
18. chief of *the captains*,
34. shield and spear *thirty* and seven thousand.
15: 7. his brethren an hundred *and thirty:*
19: 7. hired *thirty and* two thousand
23: 3. from the age of *thirty* years and upward: and their number by their polls, man by man, was *thirty* and eight thousand.
27: 6. mighty (among) *the thirty*, and above *the thirty:*
29:27. *thirty* and three (years) reigned he in
2Ch 3:15. two pillars of *thirty* and five cubits
4: 2. a line of *thirty* cubits did compass
15:19. no (more) war unto the five and *thirtieth* year of the reign of Asa.
16: 1. In the six and *thirtieth* year of the reign
12. Asa in the *thirty* and ninth year
20:31. *thirty* and five years old when he began
21: 5. Jehoram (was) *thirty* and two
20. *Thirty* and two years old was he when
24:15. an hundred *and thirty* years old (was he) when he died.
34: 1. he reigned in Jerusalem one *and thirty*
35: 7. to the number of *thirty* thousand,
Ezr. 1: 9. *thirty* chargers of gold,
Ezr. 1:10. *Thirty* basons of gold,
2:35. The children of Senaah, three thousand and six hundred *and thirty.*
42. all an hundred *thirty* and nine.
65. their servants and their maids, of whom (there were) seven thousand three hundred *thirty* and seven:
66. Their horses (were) seven hundred *thirty* and six;
67. Their camels, four hundred *thirty* and five;
Neh 5:14. the two and *thirtieth* year of Artaxerxes
7:38. The children of Senaah, three thousand nine hundred *and thirty.*
45. Shobai, an hundred *thirty* and eight.
67. their manservants and their maidservants, of whom (there were) seven thousand three hundred *thirty* and seven:
68. Their horses, seven hundred *thirty* and six:
69. (Their) camels, four hundred *thirty* and five:
70. five hundred and *thirty* priests' garments.
13: 6. two and *thirtieth* year of Artaxerxes
Est. 4:11. come in unto the king these *thirty* days.
Jer. 38:10. Take from hence *thirty* men
52:29. captive from Jerusalem eight hundred *thirty* and two persons:
31. *in* the seven and *thirtieth* year of the
Eze. 1: 1. it came to pass *in* the *thirtieth* year,
40:17. *thirty* chambers (were) upon
41: 6. one over another, *and thirty* in order;
46:22. forty (cubits) long *and thirty* broad:
Dan12:12. the thousand three hundred and five and *thirty* days.
Zec.11:12. weighed for my price *thirty* (pieces) of
13. I took *the thirty* (pieces) of silver,

שָׁלַח *shāh-lăgh'.* 7971

✱ KAL.—*Preterite.* ✱

Gen27:45. *then I will send*, and fetch thee
38:23. behold, *I sent* this kid,
25. she *sent* to her father in law,
42: 4. Jacob *sent* not with his brethren;
45: 5. God *did send me* before you
8. not you (that) *sent* me hither,
23. to his father *he sent* after this
27. the wagons which Joseph *had sent*
46: 5. wagons which Pharaoh *had sent*
28. *he sent* Judah before him
Ex. 3:12. unto thee, that I *have sent thee:*
13. The God of your fathers *hath sent me*
14. I AM *hath sent me* unto you.
15. the God of Jacob, *hath sent me*
20. *And I will stretch out* my hand,
4:28. the Lord who *had sent him*,
5:22. why (is) it (that) *thou hast sent me?*
7:16. God of the Hebrews *hath sent me*
9:15. now *I will stretch* out my hand,
22: 8(7). whether *he have put* his hand
11(10). that *he hath* not *put* his hand
23:28. *And I will send* hornets before thee,
24:11. Israel *he laid* not his hand:
33: 2. *And I will send* an angel before thee;
Nu. 13:16. the men which Moses *sent* to spy
27. We came unto the land whither *thou sentest us*,
14:36. the men, which Moses *sent*
16:28. know that the Lord *hath sent me*
29. the Lord *hath* not *sent me.*
22:10. king of Moab, *hath sent* unto me,
37. *Did I* not earnestly *send* unto thee
24:12. which *thou sentest* unto me,
Deu 19:12. *Then* the elders of his city *shall send*
25:11. *and putteth forth* her hand,
34:11. which the Lord *sent him* to do
Jos. 6:17. she hid the messengers that *we sent.*
25. messengers, which Joshua *sent*
Jud. 6:14. *have* not *I sent thee?*
35. *he sent* messengers throughout
— *he sent* messengers unto Asher,
7:24. Gideon *sent* messengers throughout
11:17. *they sent* unto the king of Moab:
28. words of Jephthah which *he sent*
13: 8. which *thou didst send*
1Sa.15: 1. The Lord *sent* me to anoint thee
20. the way which the Lord *sent me*,

1Sa.25:14. David *sent* messengers out of
25. whom *thou didst send.*
32. which *sent thee* this day
40. David *sent us* unto thee,
26: 9. who *can stretch forth* his hand
2Sa.10: 3. that *he hath sent* comforters
— *hath* not David (rather) *sent* his servants
11:22. David all that Joab *had sent him*
14:32. Behold, *I sent* unto thee,
15: 5. *he put forth* his hand,
36. *and* by them *ye shall send*
19:11(12). king David *sent* to Zadok
1K. 5: 8(22). the things which *thou sentest*
13: 4. which *he put forth* against him,
15:19. *I have sent* unto thee a present
18:10. whither my lord *hath* not *sent*
20: 5. Although *I have sent* unto thee,
7. for *he sent* unto me for my wives,
9. All that *thou didst send* for
21:11. did as Jezebel *had sent* unto them,
— written in the letters which *she had sent*
2K. 1: 6. turn again unto the king that *sent* you,
16. Forasmuch as *thou hast sent*
2: 2,4,6. for the Lord *hath sent me* to
5: 6. *I have* (therewith) *sent* Naaman
22. My master *hath sent me,*
6:32. how this son of a murderer *hath sent*
8: 9. king of Syria *hath sent me* to thee,
11: 4. Jehoiada *sent* and fetched the rulers
14: 8. Amaziah *sent* messengers to Jehoash,
9. The thistle...*sent* to the cedar
16:11. all that king Ahaz *had sent*
17: 4. *he had sent* messengers to So
13. which *I sent* to you by my servants
18:27. *Hath* my master *sent me* to thy master,
19: 4. whom the king of Assyria his master *hath sent* (lit. *him*)
16. which *hath sent him* to reproach
20:12. *sent* letters and a present
22: 3. the king *sent* Shaphan
15. Tell the man that *sent* you
1Ch 13:10. because *he put* his hand to the ark:
19: 3. that *he hath sent* comforters
2Ch 2:13(12). now *I have sent* a cunning man,
16: 3. *I have sent* thee silver and gold;
17: 7. third year of his reign *he sent*
25:18. The thistle...*sent* to the cedar
28:16. At that time *did* king Ahaz *send*
32: 9. *did* Sennacherib king of Assyria *send*
34: 8. *he sent* Shaphan the son of Azaliah,
23. Tell ye the man that *sent* you
36:10. Nebuchadnezzar *sent*, and brought
Neh 6:12. I perceived that God *had* not *sent him;*
19. Tobiah *sent* letters to put me in fear.
Est. 8: 7. because *he laid* his hand upon the Jews.
9:10. but on the spoil *laid they* not their hand.
15. but on the prey *they laid* not their hand.
16. but *they laid* not their hands
Job 1: 4. *and sent* and called for
28: 9. *He putteth forth* his hand
Ps. 50:19. *Thou givest* (marg. *sendest*) thy mouth to evil,
55:20(21). *He hath put forth* his hands
78:25. *he sent* them meat to the full.
105:17. *He sent* a man before them,
20. The king *sent* and loosed him;
26. *He sent* Moses his servant;
28. *He sent* darkness, and made it dark;
111: 9. *He sent* redemption unto his people:
135: 9. *sent* tokens and wonders
Pro. 9: 3. *She hath sent forth* her maidens:
Cant 5: 4. My beloved *put in* his hand
Isa. 9: 8(7). The Lord *sent* a word into Jacob,
36:12. *Hath* my master *sent me* to thy master
37: 4. whom the king of Assyria his master *hath sent* (lit. *him*)
17. which *hath sent* to reproach
39: 1. *sent* letters and a present to Hezekiah:
48:16. his Spirit, *hath sent me.*
55:11. prosper (in the thing) whereto *I sent it.*
61: 1. *he hath sent me* to bind up the
Jer. 14: 3. their nobles *have sent* their little ones
14. *I sent them* not, neither have I
15. *I sent them* not, yet they say,
19:14. whither the Lord *had sent him*
23:21. *I have* not *sent* these prophets,
32. yet I *sent them* not,

Jer. 25: 4. *And* the Lord *hath sent* unto you
17. unto whom the Lord *had sent me:*
26:12. The Lord *sent me* to prophesy
15. the Lord *hath sent me* unto you
27:15. For *I have* not *sent them,*
28: 9. the Lord *hath* truly *sent him.*
15. The Lord *hath* not *sent thee;*
29: 1. the prophet *sent* from Jerusalem
3. king of Judah *sent* unto Babylon
9. *I have* not *sent them,*
19. which *I sent* unto them by my servants
25. Because thou *hast sent* letters
28. therefore *he sent* unto us
31. I *sent him* not, and he caused
40:14. *hath sent* Ishmael the son of
42: 9. unto whom *ye sent* me
20. when ye *sent* me unto the Lord
21. for the which *he hath sent me*
43: 1. which the Lord their God *had sent*
2. Lord our God *hath* not *sent thee*
Lam 1:13. From above *hath he sent* fire
Eze. 3: 6. *had I sent thee* to them,
13: 6. the Lord *hath* not *sent them:*
Hag. 1:12. as the Lord their God *had sent him*
Zec. 1:10. whom the Lord *hath sent*
2: 8(12). After the glory *hath he sent me*
9(13), 11(15) & 4:9 & 6:15. the Lord of hosts *hath sent me.*
7:12. which the Lord of hosts *hath sent*

KAL.—*Infinitive.*

Gen38:17. a pledge, till *thou send* (it)?
Nu. 22:15. Balak *sent* yet again princes, (lit. added *to send*)
37. Did I not *earnestly* send unto thee (lit. *sending* did I not send)
32: 8. *when I sent* them from Kadesh-barnea
Deu 9:23. *Likewise when* the Lord *sent*
Jos. 14: 7. *when* Moses the servant of the Lord *sent*
11. in the day that Moses *sent*
1Sa.22:17. servants of the king would not *put forth*
24: 6(7). *to stretch forth* mine hand
26:11. *that* I *should stretch forth*
23. I would not *stretch forth* mine hand
2Sa. 1:14. wast thou not afraid *to stretch forth*
14:29. *to have sent* him to the king;
18:29. *When* Joab *sent* the king's servant,
2Ch 36:15. rising up betimes, *and sending;*
Est. 2:21. sought *to lay* hand on
3: 6. he thought scorn *to lay* hands
6: 2. who sought *to lay* hand on the king
9: 2. *to lay* hand on such as sought their hurt:
Ps. 59[title](1). *when* Saul *sent*, and they watched
Isa. 20: 1. *when* Sargon the king of Assyria *sent*
58: 9. *the putting forth* of the finger,
Jer. 7:25. daily rising up early *and sending*
21: 1. *when* king Zedekiah *sent* unto him
25: 4. rising early *and sending*
26: 5 & 29:19 & 35:15. rising up early, *and sending*
44: 4. rising early *and sending*
Eze.17:15. rebelled against him *in sending*

KAL.—*Imperative.*

Gen42:16. *Send* one of you, and let him fetch
43: 8. *Send* the lad with me,
Ex. 4: 4. *Put forth* thine hand,
13. *send*, I pray thee, by the hand
9:19. *Send* therefore now,
Nu. 13: 2. *Send* thou men, that they may
1Sa.16:11. *Send* and fetch him:
19. *Send* me David thy son,
20:31. Wherefore now *send* and fetch him
2Sa.11: 6. *Send* me Uriah the Hittite.
13:17. *Put* now this (woman) *out*
17:16. Now therefore *send* quickly,
1K. 18:19. *send*, (and) gather to me all Israel
2K. 2:17. till he was ashamed, he said, *Send.*
4:22. *Send* me, I pray thee,
9:17. Take an horseman, *and send* to meet
2Ch 2: 7(6). *Send* me now therefore a man
8(7). *Send* me *also* cedar trees,
Neh 8:10. *and send* portions unto them
Job 1:11 & 2:5. *put forth* thine hand now,
Ps. 43: 3. *O send out* thy light and thy truth:
144: 6. *shoot out* thine arrows,
7. *Send* thine hand from above;
Isa. 6: 8. Then said I, Here (am) I; *send me.*
16: 1. *Send ye* the lamb to the ruler

Jer. 2:10. *send* unto Kedar,
9:17(16). *send* for cunning (women),
29:31. *Send* to all them of the captivity,
Joel 3:13(4:13). *Put ye in* the sickle,

KAL.—*Future.*

Gen 3:22. lest *he put forth* his hand,
8: 9. *then he put forth* his hand,
19:10. *But* the men *put forth* their hand,
20: 2. *and* Abimelech king of Gerar *sent*,
22:10. *And* Abraham *stretched forth*
12. *Lay* not thine hand upon the lad,
24: 7. he *shall send* his angel
40. *will send* his angel with thee,
27:42. *and she sent* and called Jacob
28: 5. *And* Isaac *sent away* Jacob:
31: 4. *And* Jacob *sent* and called Rachel
32: 3(4). *And* Jacob *sent* messengers
5(6). *and I have sent* to tell my lord,
37:13. *and I will send thee* unto them.
14. *So he sent him* out of the vale
22. *lay* no hand upon him;
38:20. *And* Judah *sent* the kid
41: 8. *and he sent* and called for
14. *Then* Pharaoh *sent*
45: 7. *And* God *sent me* before you
48:14. *And* Israel *stretched out* his right hand,
Ex. 2: 5. *and* when she saw...*she sent*
3:10. *and I will send thee* unto Pharaoh,
4: 4. *And he put forth* his hand,
13. by the hand (of him whom) *thou wilt send.*
9: 7. *And* Pharaoh *sent*, and, behold,
27. *And* Pharaoh *sent*, and called for
24: 5. *And he sent* young men
33:12. let me know whom *thou wilt send*
Nu. 13: 2. of every tribe of their fathers *shall ye send*
3. *And* Moses...*sent* them from the wilderness
17. *And* Moses *sent* them to spy
16:12. *And* Moses *sent* to call Dathan
20:14. *And* Moses *sent* messengers
16. heard our voice, *and sent* an angel,
21:21. *And* Israel *sent* messengers
32. *And* Moses *sent* to spy out
22: 5. *He sent* messengers *therefore*
31: 4. *shall ye send* to the war.
6. *And* Moses *sent* them to the war,
Deu 1:22. *We will send* men before us,
2:26. *And I sent* messengers
Jos. 1:16. whithersoever *thou sendest us*,
2: 1. *And* Joshua the son of Nun *sent*
3. *And* the king of Jericho *sent*
7: 2. *And* Joshua *sent* men
22. *So* Joshua *sent* messengers,
8: 3. *and sent them away* by night.
9. Joshua *therefore sent them forth*:
10: 3. *Wherefore*...king of Jerusalem *sent*
6. *And* the men of Gibeon *sent*
11: 1. *that he sent* to Jobab
18: 4. *and I will send them*,
22:13. *And* the children of Israel *sent*
24: 5. *I sent* Moses *also*
9. *and sent* and called Balaam
12. *And I sent* the hornet before
Jud. 3:15. *and* by him the children of Israel *sent*
21. *And* Ehud *put forth* his left hand,
4: 6. *And she sent* and called Barak
5:26. *She put* her hand to the nail,
6: 8. *That* the Lord *sent* a prophet
21. *Then* the angel of the Lord *put forth* the
9:23. *Then* God *sent* an evil spirit
31. *And he sent* messengers
11:12. *And* Jephthah *sent* messengers
14. *And* Jephthah *sent* messengers again
17. *Then* Israel *sent* messengers
19. *And* Israel *sent* messengers
38. *And he sent* her *away*
15:15. *and put forth* his hand, and took it,
16:18. *she sent* and called for the lords
18: 2. *And* the children of Dan *sent*
20:12. *And* the tribes of Israel *sent*
21:10. *And* the congregation *sent*
13. *And* the whole congregation *sent*
1Sa. 4: 4. *So* the people *sent* to Shiloh,
5: 8. *They sent therefore* and gathered all
11. *So they sent* and gathered together
6:21. *And they sent* messengers

1Sa. 9:16. *I will send* thee a man
11: 3. *that we may send* messengers unto all
12: 8. *then* the Lord *sent* Moses and Aaron,
11. *And* the Lord *sent* Jerubbaal,
14:27. *wherefore he put forth* the end of the rod
15:18. *And* the Lord *sent thee* on a journey,
16: 1. go, *I will send thee* to Jesse
12. *And he sent*, and brought him in.
19. *Wherefore* Saul *sent* messengers unto Jesse,
20. a kid, *and sent* (them) by David
22. *And* Saul *sent* to Jesse,
17:49. *And* David *put* his hand
18: 5. went out whithersoever Saul *sent him*,
19:11. Saul *also sent* messengers
14. *And when* Saul *sent* messengers
15. *And* Saul *sent* the messengers
20. *And* Saul *sent* messengers to take
21. *And* when...*he sent* other messengers,
— *And* Saul *sent* messengers again
20:12. and *I* then *send* not unto thee, and shew
21. behold, *I will send* a lad,
22:11. *Then* the king *sent* to call
24:10(11). *I will* not *put forth* mine hand
25: 5. *And* David *sent* out ten young men,
39. *And* David *sent* and communed
26: 4. David *therefore sent* out spies,
2Sa. 2: 5. *And* David *sent* messengers
3:12. *And* Abner *sent* messengers
14. *And* David *sent* messengers to
15. *And* Ish-bosheth *sent*,
26. *And* when...*he sent* messengers after
5:11. *And* Hiram king of Tyre *sent*
6: 6. *And* when...Uzzah *put forth* (his hand) to the ark
8:10. *Then* Toi *sent* Joram
9: 5. *Then* king David *sent*,
10: 2. *And* David *sent* to comfort him
5. *he sent* to meet them,
6. *And* when...the children of Ammon *sent*
7. *And* when...*he sent* Joab, and all the host
16. *And* Hadarezer *sent*,
11: 1. *that* David *sent* Joab,
3. *And* David *sent* and enquired after
4. *And* David *sent* messengers,
5. *and sent* and told David,
6. *And* David *sent* to Joab,
— *And* Joab *sent* Uriah to David.
14. *and sent* (it) by the hand of
18. *Then* Joab *sent* and told David
27. *And* when...David *sent* and fetched her
12: 1. *And* the Lord *sent* Nathan
25. *And he sent* by the hand
27. *And* Joab *sent* messengers
13: 7. *Then* David *sent* home to Tamar,
27. *that he let* Amnon and all the king's sons *go*
14: 2. *And* Joab *sent* to Tekoah,
29. *Therefore* Absalom *sent* for Joab,
— and *when he sent* again
32. *that I may send* thee to the king,
15:10. *But* Absalom *sent* spies
12. *And* Absalom *sent* for Ahithophel
18:12. *would I* not *put forth* mine hand
19:14(15). *so that they sent* (this word)
22:15. *And he sent out* arrows,
17. *He sent* from above,
24:16. And *when* the angel *stretched out* his hand
1K. 1:44. *And* the king *hath sent* with him
53. *So* king Solomon *sent*,
2:25. *And* king Solomon *sent* by the
29. *Then* Solomon *sent* Benaiah
36, 42. *And* the king *sent* and called for
5: 1(15). *And* Hiram king of Tyre *sent*
2(16). *And* Solomon *sent* to Hiram,
8(22). *And* Hiram *sent* to Solomon,
9(23). the place that *thou shalt appoint*
14(28). *And he sent them* to Lebanon,
7:13. *And* king Solomon *sent*
8:44. whithersoever *thou shalt send them*,
9:14. *And* Hiram *sent* to the king
27. *And* Hiram *sent* in the navy
12: 3. *That they sent* and called him.
18. *Then* king Rehoboam *sent* Adoram,
20. *that they sent* and called him
13: 4. *that he put forth* his hand from the altar,
15:18. *and* king Asa *sent them*
20. *and sent* the captains

1K. 18:20. *So* Ahab *sent* unto all the children
19: 2. *Then* Jezebel *sent* a messenger
20: 2. *And he sent* messengers
6. Yet *I will send* my servants
10. *And* Ben-hadad *sent* unto him,
17. *and* Ben-hadad *sent out*,
21: 8. *and sent* the letters unto the elders
14. *Then they sent* to Jezebel,
2K. 1: 2. *and he sent* messengers,
9. *Then* the king *sent* unto him
11. Again *also he sent* unto him
13. *And he sent* again a captain
2:16. *Ye shall* not *send*.
17. *They sent therefore* fifty men;
3: 7. he went *and sent* to Jehoshaphat
5: 5. *and I will send* a letter unto the king
8. *that he sent* to the king,
10. *And* Elisha *sent* a messenger
6: 7. *And he put out* his hand,
9. *And* the man of God *sent* unto the king
10. *And* the king of Israel *sent* to the place
13. *that I may send* and fetch him.
14. *Therefore sent he* thither horses,
32. *and* (the king) *sent* a man from before
7:13. *and let us send* and see.
14. *and* the king *sent* after the host
9:19. *Then he sent* out a second
10: 1. *and sent* to Samaria,
5. *And*...the bringers up (of the children), *sent* to Jehu,
7. in baskets, *and sent* him (them) to
21. *And* Jehu *sent* through all Israel:
12:18(19). *and sent* (it) to Hazael
14: 9. *And* Jehoash the king of Israel *sent* to
19. *but they sent* after him to Lachish,
16: 7. *So* Ahaz *sent* messengers
8. *and sent* (it for) a present to the king
10. *and* king Ahaz *sent* to Urijah the priest
18:14. *And* Hezekiah king of Judah *sent* to
17. *And* the king of Assyria *sent* Tartan
19: 2. *And he sent* Eliakim,
9. *he sent* messengers *again* unto Hezekiah,
20. *Then* Isaiah the son of Amoz *sent* to
23: 1. *And* the king *sent*,
16. *and sent*, and took the bones
1Ch 13: 2. *let us send* abroad unto our brethren
9. *And* when they came...Uzza *put forth*
14: 1. *Now* Hiram king of Tyre *sent*
18:10. *He sent* Hadoram his son
19: 2. *And* David *sent* messengers
5. *And he sent* to meet them:
6. *And* when...*sent* a thousand talents of
8. *And* when...*he sent* Joab, and all the host
16. *And* when...*they sent* messengers,
21:15. *And* God *sent* an angel
2Ch 2: 3(2). *And* Solomon *sent* to Huram
—(–). *and didst send* him cedars
11(10). *which he sent* to Solomon,
15(14). *let him send* unto his servants:
6:34. by the way that *thou shalt send them*,
8:18. *And* Huram *sent* him by the
10: 3. *And they sent* and called him.
18. *Then* king Rehoboam *sent* Hadoram
16: 2. *and sent* to Ben-hadad
4. *and sent* the captains of his armies
24:19. *Yet he sent* prophets to them,
25:15. *and he sent* unto him a prophet,
17. took advice, *and sent* to Joash,
18. *And* Joash king of Israel *sent*
27. *but they sent* to Lachish
30: 1. *And* Hezekiah *sent* to all Israel
32:21. *And* the Lord *sent* an angel,
34:29. *Then* the king *sent* and gathered
35:21. *But he sent* ambassadors
36:15. *And* the Lord God of their fathers *sent*
Ezr. 8:16. *Then sent I* for Eliezer,
Neh 2: 5. *that thou wouldest send me* unto Judah,
6. So it pleased the king *to send me*; (lit. *and he sent me*)
9. *Now* the king *had sent* captains
6: 2. *That* Sanballat and Geshem *sent* unto
3. *And I sent* messengers unto them,
4. *Yet they sent* unto me four times
5. *Then sent* Sanballat his servant
8. *Then I sent* unto him,
13:21. *I will lay* hands on you.
Est. 1:22. *For he sent* letters into all
Est. 4: 4. *and she sent* raiment to clothe Mordecai,
5:10. *and* when...*he sent* and called for his
8:10. *and sent* letters by posts on horseback,
9:20. *and sent* letters unto all the Jews
30. *And he sent* the letters unto all
Job 1: 5. *that* Job *sent* and sanctified them,
12. only upon himself *put* not *forth*
30:24. *he will* not *stretch out* (his) hand
Ps. 18:14(15). *Yea, he sent out* his arrows,
16(17). *He sent* from above,
20: 2(3). *Send* thee help from the sanctuary,
57: 3(4). *He shall send* from heaven,
—(–). God *shall send* forth his mercy
107:20. *He sent* his word,
110: 2. The Lord *shall send* the rod
125: 3. lest the righteous *put forth* their hands
138: 7. *thou shalt stretch forth* thine hand
147:18. *He sendeth out* his word,
Isa. 6: 8. Whom *shall I send*,
19:20. *and he shall send* them a saviour,
36: 2. *And* the king of Assyria *sent* Rabshakeh
37: 2. *And he sent* Eliakim,
9. *And* when...*he sent* messengers to
21. *Then* Isaiah the son of Amoz *sent* unto Hezekiah,
42:19. deaf, as my messenger (that) *I sent?*
Jer. 1: 7. go to all that *I shall send thee*,
9. *Then* the Lord *put forth* his hand,
7:25. *I have even sent* unto you all
16:16. *and after will I send* for many hunters,
23:38. *and I have sent* unto you,
26:22. *And* Jehoiakim the king *sent* men into
35:15. *I have sent also* unto you
36:14. *Therefore* all the princes *sent* Jehudi
21. *So* the king *sent* Jehudi
37: 3. *And* Zedekiah the king *sent* Jehucal
17 & 38:14. *Then* Zedekiah the king *sent*,
39:13. *So* Nebuzar-adan the captain of the guard *sent*,
14. *Even they sent*, and took Jeremiah
42: 5. the Lord thy God *shall send thee*
44: 4. *Howbeit I sent* unto you
Eze. 8: 3. *And he put forth* the form of an hand,
10: 7. *And* (one) cherub *stretched forth* (marg. *sent forth*)
23:16. *and sent* messengers unto them
40. that *ye have sent* for men
Dan 11:42. *He shall stretch forth* his hand
Hos. 5:13. *and sent* to king Jareb:
Am. 7:10. *Then* Amaziah the priest of Beth-el *sent*
Obad. 13. nor *have laid* (hands) on their substance
Mic. 6: 4. *and I sent* before thee Moses,
Zec. 7: 2. *When they had sent* unto the house

KAL.—*Participle*. Poel.

Ex. 9:14. For I *will* at this time *send* all
23:20. I *send* an Angel before thee,
1Sa.21: 2(3). the business whereabout I *send thee*,
2Sa.24:13. shall return to him that *sent me*.
2K. 1: 6. thou *sendest* to enquire of Baal-zebub
5: 7. that this man *doth send* unto me
22:18. *which sent* you to enquire of the Lord,
1Ch 21:12. bring again to him that *sent me*.
2Ch 34:26. *who sent* you to enquire of the Lord,
Job 5:10. *and sendeth* waters upon the fields:
Ps.147:15. He *sendeth* forth his commandment
Pro.10:26. the sluggard *to them that send him*.
22:21. *to them that send unto thee?*
25:13. faithful messenger *to them that send him:*
26: 6. *He that sendeth* a message
Isa. 18: 2. *That sendeth* ambassadors by the sea,
Jer. 16:16. I *will send* for many fishers,
25: 9. I *will send* and take all
15. nations, to whom I *send* thee,
16. the sword that I *will send*
27. the sword which I *will send*
26: 5. whom I *sent* unto you,
37: 7. *that sent* you unto me to enquire of me;
42: 6. to whom we *send* thee;
43:10. I *will send* and take Nebuchadrezzar
Eze. 2: 3. I *send* thee to the children
4. I *do send* thee unto them;
8:17. they *put* the branch to their nose.
Joel 2:19. Behold, I *will send* you corn,
Mal. 3: 1. I *will send* my messenger,
4: 5(3:23). I *will send* you Elijah the prophet before the coming

KAL.—*Participle.* Paül.

Gen32:18(19). a present *sent* unto my lord
49:21. Naphtali (is) a hind *let loose:*
1K. 14: 6. for I (am) *sent* to thee
Jer. 49:14. an ambassador is *sent* unto the heathen,
Eze. 2: 9. an hand (was) *sent* unto me;
3: 5. For thou (art) not *sent* to a people
23:40. unto whom a messenger (was) *sent;*

* NIPHAL.—*Infinitive.* *

Est. 3:13. *And* the letters *were sent* by posts

* PIEL.—*Preterite.* *

Gen28: 6. *and sent* him *away* to Padan-aram,
31:42. *thou hadst sent me away* now
43:14. *that he may send away* your other
Ex. 7: 2. *that he send* the children of Israel
8:32(28). neither *would he let* the people *go.*
9: 7. *he did* not *let* the people *go.*
35. neither *would he let* the children of Israel *go;*
10:20 & 11:10. *he would* not *let* the children of Israel *go.*
14: 5. that *we have let* Israel *go*
22: 5(4). *and shall put in* his beast,
Lev.14: 7. *and shall let* the living bird *loose*
53. *But he shall let go* the living bird
16:21. *and shall send* (him) *away*
22. *and he shall let go* the goat
26:25. *and* when ye are gathered... *I will send*
Deu21:14. *then thou shalt let her go* whither
24: 1. *and send her* out of his house.
3. *and sendeth her* out of his house;
4. husband, which *sent her away,*
Jos. 22: 7. when Joshua *sent them away*
Jud. 1: 8. and *set* the city on fire.
25. but *they let go* the man
7: 8. *he sent* all (the rest of) Israel
12: 9. thirty daughters, (whom) *he sent* abroad,
20:48. also *they set* on fire all the cities
1Sa. 6: 8. *and send* it *away,*
9:19. *and* to morrow *I will let thee go,*
13: 2. *he sent* every man to his tent.
20: 5. *but let me go,* that I may hide
13. shew it thee, *and send thee* away,
22. the Lord *hath sent thee away.*
24:19(20). *will he let him go* well *away?*
2Sa. 3:22. for *he had sent him away,*
24. *thou hast sent him away,* and he
1K. 8:66. On the eighth day *he sent* the people *away:*
20:42. Because *thou hast let go*
1Ch 8: 8. after *he had sent* them *away;*
12:19. upon advisement *sent him away,*
2Ch 7:10. *he sent* the people *away*
24:23. *sent* all the spoil of them unto the king
Job 22: 9. *Thou hast sent* widows *away*
30:11. *they have* also *let loose* the bridle
12. *they push away* my feet,
39: 5. Who *hath sent out* the wild ass
Ps. 74: 7. *They have cast* (marg. *sent*) fire
Pro.31:19. *She layeth* her hands to the spindle,
20. *she reacheth forth* her hands
Isa. 43:14. For your sake *I have sent* to Babylon,
50: 1. whom *I have put* (lit. *her*) *away?*
66:19. *and I will send* those that escape
Jer. 3: 8. adultery *I had put her away,*
9:16(15). *and I will send* a sword
24: 5. Judah, whom *I have sent*
10. *And I will send* the sword,
27: 3. *And send them* to the king
29:20. whom *I have sent* from Jerusalem
34:11. whom *they had let go* free,
14. *and* when... *thou shalt let him go*
16. whom *he had set* at liberty
48:12. *that I will send* unto him
49:37. *and I will send* the sword after
51: 2. *And will send* unto Babylon
Eze. 5:17. *So will I send* upon you famine
7: 3. *and I will send* mine anger
13:20. *and will let* the souls *go,*
14:21. when *I send* my four sore judgments
17: 7. *shot forth* her branches
28:23. *For I will send* into her pestilence,
31: 4. *sent out* her little rivers
39: 6. *And I will send* a fire on Magog,
Hos. 8:14. *but I will send* a fire upon his cities,
Joel 2:25. great army which *I sent*

Am. 1: 4, 7, 10, 12 & 2:2, 5. *But I will send* a fire
4:10. *I have sent* among you the pestilence
Obad. 7. the men of thy confederacy *have brought thee*
Zec. 9:11. *I have sent forth* thy prisoners
Mal. 2: 2. *I will even send* a curse upon you,
4. ye shall know that *I have sent*

PIEL.—*Infinitive.*

Gen 8:10. again he *sent forth* the dove out of the ark; (lit. he added *to send* forth)
18:16. with them *to bring them on the way.*
Ex. 4:23. if thou refuse *to let him go,*
5: 2. obey his voice *to let* Israel *go?*
7:14. he refuseth *to let* the people *go.*
8: 2(7:27). if thou refuse *to let* (them) *go,*
29(25). in not *letting* the people *go*
9: 2. if thou refuse *to let* (them) *go,*
17. that thou *wilt* not *let them go?*
10: 4. if thou refuse *to let* my people *go,*
27. he would not *let them go.*
11: 1. *when he shall let* (you) *go,*
12:33. *that they might send them* out
13:15. Pharaoh would hardly *let us go,*
17. *when* Pharaoh *had let* the people *go,*
Lev.16:10. *to let* him *go* for a scapegoat
Deu 15:18. *when thou sendest him away*
22: 7. thou shalt *in any wise* let the dam go, (lit. *letting go* thou shalt let go)
19. he may not *put her away*
29. he may not *put her away*
1Sa.20:20. *as though* I *shot* at a mark.
2Sa.13:16. this evil *in sending me away*
19:31(32). *to conduct him* over Jordan.
1K. 11:22. howbeit let me go *in any wise.* (lit. *letting go* let me go)
Neh 8:12. *and to send* portions, and to make
Isa. 27: 8. In measure, *when it shooteth forth,*
58: 6. *and to let* the oppressed *go* free,
Jer. 34: 9, 10. *should let* his manservant,...*go* free;
40: 1. of the guard *had let* him *go*
50:33. they refused *to let them go.*
Eze. 5:16. *When I shall send* upon them
31: 5. waters, *when he shot forth.* (marg. or, *it sent* (them) *forth*)
Mal. 2:16. saith that he hateth *putting away:*

PIEL.—*Imperative.*

Gen24:54. *Send me away* unto my master.
56 & 30:25. *send me away* that I may go
32:26(27). *Let me go,* for the day breaketh.
Ex. 4:23. *Let* my son *go,* that he may serve me:
5: 1. *Let* my people *go,* that they may hold
7:16 & 8:1(7:26). *Let* my people *go,* that they may serve me
8:20(16). *Let* my people *go,* that they may
9: 1, 13. *Let* my people *go,* that they may serve
10: 3. *let* my people *go,* that they may serve me.
7. *let* the men *go,* that they may serve
1Sa. 5:11. *Send away* the ark of the God
19:17. He said unto me, *Let me go;*
20:29. *Let me go,* I pray thee;
1K. 11:21. *Let me depart* (marg. *Send me away*), that I may go
Ecc.11: 1. *Cast* thy bread upon the waters:
Jer. 15: 1. *cast* (them) *out* of my sight,

PIEL.—*Future.*

Gen 3:23. *Therefore* the Lord God *sent him forth*
8: 7. *And he sent forth* a raven,
8. *Also he sent forth* a dove
12. *and sent forth* the dove;
12:20. *and they sent* him *away,*
19:13. *and* the Lord *hath sent us*
29. *and sent* Lot out of the midst
21:14. the child, *and sent her away:*
24:59. *And they sent away* Rebekah
25: 6. *and sent them away* from Isaac
26:27. *and have sent me away* from you?
29. *and have sent thee away* in peace:
31. *and* Isaac *sent them away,*
31:27. *that I might have sent thee away*
32:26(27). *I will* not *let thee go,*
37:32. *And they sent* the coat
38:17. I *will send* (thee) a kid from the flock.
45:24. *So he sent* his brethren *away,*
Ex. 3:20. after that *he will let* you *go.*
4:21. that *he shall* not *let* the people *go.*

Ex. 5: 2. neither *will I let* Israel *go*.
6: 1. with a strong hand *shall he let them go*,
11. *that he let* the children of Israel *go*
8: 8(4). *and I will let* the people *go*,
28(24). I *will let* you *go*,
9:28. *and I will let* you *go*,
10:10. as *I will let* you *go*,
11: 1. afterwards *he will let* you *go* hence:
15: 7. *thou sentest forth* thy wrath,
18:27. *And* Moses *let* his father in law *depart;*
21:26, 27. *he shall let him go* free
23:27. *I will send* my fear before thee,
Nu. 5: 2. *that they put out* of the camp
3. male and female *shall ye put out*, without the camp *shall ye put them;*
4. *and put* them *out* without the camp:
21: 6. *And* the Lord *sent* fiery serpents
22:40. *and sent* to Balaam,
Deu 7:20. thy God *will send* the hornet
15:12. *thou shalt let him go* free
13. when *thou sendest him out*
— *thou shalt* not *let him go away*
22: 7. *thou shalt* in any wise *let* the dam *go*,
28:20. The Lord *shall send* upon thee
48. *which* the Lord *shall send*
32:24. *I will* also *send* the teeth of beasts
Jos. 2:21. *And she sent them away*,
22: 6. blessed them, *and sent them away:*
24:28. *So* Joshua *let* the people *depart*,
Jud. 2: 6. And *when* Joshua *had let* the people *go*,
3:18. *And* when he had made...*he sent away*
15: 5. *And* when he had set...*he let* (them) *go*
19:25. *and* when the day began to spring, *they let her go*.
29. *and sent her* into all the coast of Israel.
20: 6. *and sent her* throughout all
1Sa. 5:10. *Therefore they sent* the ark of God
6: 2. *we shall send it* to his place.
3. *send* it not empty;
6. *did they* not *let* the people *go*,
9:26. Up, *that I may send thee away*.
10:25. *And* Samuel *sent* all the people *away*,
11: 7. *and sent* (them) throughout all
19:17. *and sent away* mine enemy,
30:26. *And* when David came to Ziklag, *he sent*
31: 9. *and sent* into the land of the Philistines
2Sa. 3:21. *And* David *sent* Abner *away;*
23. *and he hath sent him away*, and he
10: 4. *and sent them away*.
11:12. to morrow *I will let thee depart*.
18: 2. *And* David *sent* forth a third part
1K. 9: 7. *will I cast out* of my sight;
11:22. howbeit *let me go* in any wise.
20:34. I *will send thee away* with this covenant. So he made a covenant with him, *and sent him away*.
2K. 5:24. *and he let* the men *go*,
6:23. *and* when they had eaten and drunk, *he sent them away*,
8:12. their strong holds *wilt thou set* on fire,
17:25. *therefore* the Lord *sent* lions
26. *therefore he hath sent* lions among
24: 2. *And* the Lord *sent* against him
— *and sent them* against Judah to destroy it,
1Ch 10: 9. *and sent* into the land
19: 4. buttocks, *and sent them away*.
2Ch 7:13. or if *I send* pestilence
Job 8: 4. *and he have cast them away*
12:15. *also he sendeth them out*,
14:20. countenance, *and sendest him away*.
20:23. (God) *shall cast* (lit. *send forth*) the fury of his wrath upon him,
21:11. *They send forth* their little ones
38:35. *Canst thou send* lightnings, that they may
39: 3. *they cast out* their sorrows.
Ps. 44: 2(3). afflict the people, *and cast them out*.
78:45. *He sent* divers sorts of flies
49. *He cast* upon them the fierceness
80:11(12). *She sent out* her boughs
81:12(13). *So I gave them up* unto their own
104:30. *Thou sendest forth* thy spirit,
106:15. *but sent* leanness into their soul.
Pro. 6:14. *he soweth* (marg. *casteth forth*) discord.
16:28. A froward man *soweth* strife:
Isa. 10: 6. *I will send him* against an hypocritical
16. *shall* the Lord, the Lord of hosts, *send*
45:13. *he shall let go* my captives,
Isa. 57: 9. *and didst send* thy messengers
Jer. 3: 1. If a man *put away* his wife,
17: 8. *spreadeth* out her roots
34:10. then they obeyed, *and let* (them) *go*.
14. *let ye go* every man his brother
38: 6. *and they let down* Jeremiah
11. *and let them down* by cords
40: 5. a reward, *and let him go*.
Eze. 5:16. When *I shall send* upon them
14:19. Or (if) *I send* a pestilence into that land,
17: 6. branches, *and shot forth* sprigs.
44:20. nor *suffer* their locks *to grow long;*
Zec. 8:10. *for I set* all men every one

PIEL.—*Participle.*

Gen43: 4. If thou wilt *send* our brother
5. But if thou wilt not *send*
Ex. 8:21(17). if thou wilt not *let* my people *go*,
Lev.16:26. *And he that let go* the goat
18:24. nations are defiled which I *cast out*
20:23. the nation, which I *cast out*
1Sa. 6: 3. If ye *send away* the ark of the God of
2Ch 32:31. *who sent* unto him to enquire of the
Ps.104:10. *He* (marg. *Who*) *sendeth* the springs
Pro. 6:19. *and he that soweth* discord
Isa. 32:20. *that send forth* (thither) the feet
Jer. 8:17. behold, I *will send* serpents,
28:16. I *will cast thee* from off the face of the
29:17. I *will send* upon them the sword,

* PUAL.—*Preterite.* *

Gen44: 3. the men *were sent away*,
Jud. 5:15. Barak: *he was sent* on foot
Job 18: 8. *he is cast* into a net by his own feet,
Isa. 50: 1. for your transgressions *is* your mothe *put away*.
Dan 10:11. unto thee *am I* now *sent*.
Obad. 1. an ambassador *is sent* among

PUAL.—*Future.*

Pro.17:11. a cruel messenger *shall be sent*

PUAL.—*Participle.*

Pro.29:15. a child *left* (to himself) bringeth
Isa. 16: 2. as a wandering bird *cast out* of the nest (marg. or, a nest *forsaken*)
27:10. the habitation *forsaken*,

* HIPHIL.—*Preterite.* *

Lev.26:22. *I will also send* wild beasts
Eze.14:13. *and will send* famine upon it,
Am. 8:11. *that I will send* a famine

HIPHIL.—*Infinitive.*

2K. 15:37. the Lord began *to send* against

HIPHIL.—*Participle.*

Ex. 8:21(17). I *will send* swarms (of flies) upon

שְׁלַח *sh'lagh*, Ch. 7972

* P'AL.—*Preterite.* *

Ezr. 4:11. the copy of the letter that *they sent*
14. therefore *have we sent* and certified
17. (Then) *sent* the king an answer
18. The letter which *ye sent* unto us
5: 6. *sent* unto Darius the king:
7. *They sent* a letter unto him,
6:13. which Darius the king *had sent*,
Dan 3: 2. Nebuchadnezzar the king *sent* to gather
28. who *hath sent* his angel,
6:22(23). My God *hath sent* his angel,

P'AL.—*Future.*

Ezr. 5:17. and *let* the king *send* his pleasure
6:12. that *shall put* to their hand to alter

P'AL.—*Participle.*

Ezr. 7:14. Forasmuch as thou *art sent*
Dan 5:24. Then *was* the part of the hand *sent*

שֶׁלַח *sheh'-lagh*, m. 7973

2Ch 23:10. every man having *his weapon*
32: 5. made *darts* (marg. or, *swords*, or, *weapons*) and shields in abundance.
Neh 4:17(11). with the other (hand) held *a weapon*.
23(17). every one *put them off* for washing. (marg. or, every one (went) with *his weapon* for water)

Job 33:18. his life from perishing *by the sword.*
36:12. they shall perish *by the sword,*
Cant 4:13. *Thy plants* (are) an orchard
Joel 2: 8. they fall upon *the sword,* (marg. or, *dart*)

7976 שְׁלָחוֹת *sh'loo-ghohth'*, f. pl.

Isa. 16: 8. *her branches* are stretched out,

7979 שֻׁלְחָן *shool-ghahn'*, m.

Ex. 25:23. Thou shalt also make *a table*
27. for places of the staves to bear *the table.*
28. that *the table* may be borne with
30. set upon *the table* shewbread
26:35. And thou shalt set *the table*
— the candlestick over against *the table*
— put *the table* on the north side.
30:27. *the table* and all his vessels,
31: 8. *the table* and his furniture,
35:13. *The table,* and his staves,
37:10. he made *the table* (of) shittim wood:
14. the places for the staves to bear *the table.*
15. overlaid them with gold, to bear *the table.*
16. the vessels which (were) upon *the table,*
39:36. *The table,* (and) all the vessels thereof,
40: 4. thou shalt bring in *the table,*
22. he put *the table* in the tent
24. over against *the table,*
Lev. 24: 6. upon *the* pure *table* before the Lord.
Nu. 3:31. the ark, *and the table,* and the candlestick,
4: 7. upon *the table of* shewbread
Jud. 1: 7. gathered (their meat) under *my table:*
1 Sa. 20:29. he cometh not unto the king's *table.*
34. Jonathan arose from *the table*
2Sa. 9: 7. thou shalt eat bread at *my table*
10. shall eat bread alway at *my table.*
11. he shall eat at *my table,*
13. he did eat continually at the king's *table;*
19:28(29). that did eat at *thine own table.*
1K. 2: 7. let them be of those that eat at *thy table:*
4:27(5:7). all that came unto king Solomon's *table,*
7:48. altar of gold, and *the table* of gold,
10: 5. the meat of *his table,*
13:20. as they sat at *the table,*
18:19. which eat at Jezebel's *table.*
2K. 4:10. let us set for him there a bed, *and a table,*
1 Ch 28:16. *for the tables of* shewbread, *for every table* (lit. *for table and table*); and (likewise) silver *for the tables of* silver:
2Ch 4: 8. He made also ten *tables,*
19. *the tables* whereon the shewbread
9: 4. the meat of *his table,*
13:11. upon *the* pure *table;*
29:18. *the* shewbread *table,* with all the vessels
Neh 5:17. Moreover (there were) at *my table*
Job 36:16. which should be set on *thy table*
Ps. 23: 5. Thou preparest *a table* before me
69:22(23). Let *their table* become a snare
78:19. Can God furnish *a table* in the
128: 3. like olive plants round about *thy table.*
Pro. 9: 2. she hath also furnished *her table.*
Isa. 21: 5. Prepare *the table,* watch in the watch-tower,
28: 8. all *tables* are full of vomit (and) filthiness,
65:11. prepare *a table* for that troop,
Eze. 23:41. *and a table* prepared before it,
39:20. Thus ye shall be filled at *my table*
40:39. in the porch of the gate (were) two *tables* on this side, and two *tables* on that
40. entry of the north gate, (were) two *tables;*
— at the porch of the gate, (were) two *tables.*
41. Four *tables* (were) on this side, and four *tables* on that side, by the side of the gate; eight *tables,* whereupon they
42. four *tables* (were) of hewn stone
43. upon *the tables* (was) the flesh
41:22. This (is) *the table* that (is) before the
44:16. they shall come near to *my table,*
Dan 11:27. they shall speak lies at one *table;*
Mal. 1: 7. ye say, *The table of* the Lord
12. *The table of* the Lord (is) polluted;

שָׁלַט *shah-lat'*. 7980

* KAL.—*Preterite.* *

Neh 5:15. even their servants *bare rule*
Ecc. 8: 9. wherein one man *ruleth* over another

KAL.—*Infinitive.*

Est. 9: 1. hoped *to have power* over them,

KAL.—*Future.*

Est. 9: 1. that the Jews *had rule*
Ecc. 2:19. *yet shall he have rule* over all

* HIPHIL.—*Preterite.* *

Ecc. 5:19(18). *and hath given him power* to eat

HIPHIL.—*Future.*

Ps. 119:133. *let* not any iniquity *have dominion*
Ecc. 6: 2. yet God *giveth him* not *power*

שְׁלֵט *sh'leht*, Ch. 7981

* P'AL.—*Preterite.* *

Dan 3:27. upon whose bodies the fire *had* no *power,*
6:24(25). and the lions *had the mastery* of them,

P'AL.—*Future.*

Dan 2:39. which *shall bear rule* over all the earth.
5: 7. and *shall be the* third *ruler* in the
16. and *shalt be the* third *ruler* in the

* APHEL.—*Preterite.* *

Dan 2:38. *and hath made thee ruler* over them all.
48. *and made him ruler* over the whole

שֶׁלֶט [*sheh'-let*], m. 7982

2Sa. 8: 7. David took *the shields of* gold
2K. 11:10. the priest gave king David's spears and *shields,*
1Ch 18: 7. David took *the shields of* gold
2Ch 23: 9. spears, and bucklers, and *shields,*
Cant. 4: 4. all *shields of* mighty men.
Jer. 51:11. gather *the shields:*
Eze. 27:11. they hanged *their shields*

שִׁלְטוֹן *shil-tohn'*, m. 7983

Ecc. 8: 4. word of a king (is, there is) *power:*
8. *power* in the day of death:

שִׁלְטוֹן [*shil-tohn'*], Ch. m 7984

Dan 3: 2, 3. and all *the rulers of* the provinces,

שָׁלְטָן *shol-tahn'*, Ch. m. 7985

Dan 4: 3(3:33). *and his dominion* (is) from
22(19). *and thy dominion* to the end of the
34(31). *whose dominion* (is) *an* everlasting *dominion,*
6:26(27). That in every *dominion of* my
—(—). *and his dominion* (shall be even) unto
7: 6. *and dominion* was given to it.
12. they had *their dominion* taken away:
14. And there was given him *dominion,*
— *his dominion* (is) *an* everlasting *dominion,*
26. *and* they shall take away *his dominion,*
27. And the kingdom *and dominion,*
— and all *dominions* shall serve and obey

שַׁלֶּטֶת [*shal-leh'-teth*], adj. f. 7986

Eze. 16:30. the work of an *imperious* whorish woman;

שְׁלִי [*sh'lee*], m. 7987

2Sa. 3:27. speak with him *quietly,* (marg. or, *peaceably*)

שִׁלְיָה [*shil-yah'*], f. 7988

Deu 28:57. *And toward her young one* (marg. *after-birth*) that cometh out

7989 **שַׁלִּיט** *shal-leet'*, adj.

Gen42: 6. Joseph (was) *the governor* over the land,
Ecc. 7:19. wise more than ten *mighty* (men)
8: 8. (There is) no man *that hath power* over the spirit
10: 5. error (which) proceedeth from *the ruler:*

7990 **שַׁלִּיט** *shal-leet'*, Ch. adj.

Eze. 4:20. *which have ruled* over all (countries)
7:24. *it shall* not *be lawful* to impose toll,
Dan 2:10. no king, lord, *nor ruler*, (that) asked
15. said to Arioch the king's *captain*,
4:17(14), 25(22), 32(29). that the most High *ruleth* in the
26(23). have known that the heavens *do rule*.
5:21. that the most high God *ruled* in the
29. he should be *the* third *ruler*

7991 **שָׁלִישׁ** *shāh-leesh'*, m.

Ex. 14: 7. and *captains* over every one
15: 4. *his* chosen *captains* also are drowned
1Sa.18: 6. joy, *and with instruments of musick*. (marg. *three stringed instruments*)
2Sa.23: 8. chief among *the captains;*
1K. 9:22. his princes, *and his captains*,
2K. 7: 2. Then *a lord* on whose hand the king leaned
17. the king appointed *the lord*
19. that *lord* answered the man of God,
9:25. Then said (Jehu) to Bidkar *his captain*,
10:25. said to the guard *and to the captains*,
— guard *and the captains* cast (them) out,
15:25. Pekah the son of Remaliah, *a captain of his*,
1Ch 11:11. the chief of *the captains:*
12:18. (who was) chief of *the captains*,
2Ch 8: 9. chief of *his captains*,
Ps. 80: 5(6). tears to drink in *great measure*.
Pro.22:20. written to thee *excellent things*
Isa. 40:12. dust of the earth *in a measure*, (marg. *tierce*)
Eze.23:15. all of them *princes* to look to,
23. *great lords* and renowned,

7992 **שְׁלִישִׁי** *sh'lee-shee'*, adj. ord.

Gen 1:13. and the morning were the *third* day.
2:14. the name of the *third* river
6:16. second, *and third* (stories) shalt
22: 4. Then on the *third* day Abraham
31:22. it was told Laban on the *third* day
32:19(20). he the second, and *the third*,
34:25. it came to pass on the *third* day,
40:20. it came to pass the *third* day,
42:18. Joseph said unto them the *third* day,
Ex. 19: 1. In the *third* month,
11. be ready against the *third* day: for *the third* day the Lord will come
16. it came to pass on the *third* day
28:19 & 39:12. the *third* row a ligure,
Lev. 7:17. flesh of the sacrifice on the *third* day
18. be eaten at all on the *third* day,
19: 6. if ought remain until the *third* day,
7. if it be eaten at all on the *third* day,
Nu. 2:24. *And* they shall go forward in *the third rank*.
7:24. On the *third* day Eliab
15: 6. mingled with *the third part of*
7. thou shalt offer *the third part of*
19:12. purify himself with it on the *third* day,
— purify not himself the *third* day,
19. upon the unclean on the *third* day,
28:14. *and the third part of* an hin
29:20. on the *third* day eleven bullocks,
31:19. your captives on the *third* day,
Deu 23: 8(9). of the Lord in their *third* generation.
26:12. the tithes of thine increase the *third* year,
Jos. 9:17. unto their cities on the *third* day.
19:10. the *third* lot came up for
Jud. 20:30. Benjamin on the *third* day,
1Sa. 3: 8. called Samuel again *the third time*.
17:13. *and the third* Shammah.
1Sa.19:21. Saul sent messengers *again the third time*,
20: 5. in the field unto *the third* (day)
12. to morrow any time, (or) *the third* (day),
30: 1. come to Ziklag on the *third* day,
2Sa. 1: 2. It came even to pass on the *third* day,
3: 3. *and the third*, Absalom
18: 2. David sent forth *a third part*
— *and a third part* under the hand of
— *and a third part* under the hand
23:18. (כתיב) chief among *three*.
1K. 3:18. the *third* day after that I was delivered,
6: 6. *and the third* (was) seven cubits
8. out of the middle into *the third*.
12:12. came to Rehoboam the *third* day,
— Come to me again the *third* day.
18: 1. came to Elijah in the *third* year,
22: 2. it came to pass in the *third* year,
2K. 1:13. sent again a captain of the *third* fifty
— And the *third* captain of fifty
11: 5. *A third part of* you
6. *And a third part* (shall be) at the gate of Sur; *and a third part* at the gate
19:29. in the *third* year sow ye,
20: 5. on the *third* day thou shalt go
8. into the house of the Lord the *third* day?
1Ch 2:13. Shimma the *third*,
3: 2. *The third*, Absalom
15. *the third* Zedekiah,
8: 1. Aharah *the third*,
39. Eliphelet *the third*.
12: 9. Eliab *the third*,
23:19. Jahaziel *the third*,
24: 8. *The third* to Harim,
23. Jahaziel *the third*,
25:10. *The third* to Zaccur,
26: 2. Zebadiah *the third*,
4. Joah *the third*,
11. Tebaliah *the third*,
27: 5. The *third* captain of the host for the *third*
2Ch 10:12. came to Rehoboam on the *third* day,
— Come again to me on the *third* day.
15:10. at Jerusalem in the *third* month,
23: 4. *A third part of* you entering on
5. *And a third part* (shall be) at the
— *and a third part* at the gate
27: 5. both the second year, *and the third*.
31: 7. In the *third* month they began
Neh 10:32(33). with *the third part of* a shekel
Est. 5: 1. it came to pass on the *third* day,
8: 9. called at that time in the *third* month,
Job 42:14. the name of *the third*, Keren-happuch.
Isa. 15: 5. an heifer of *three years old:*
19:24. shall Israel be *the third* with Egypt
37:30. in the *third* year sow ye,
Jer. 38:14. unto him into the *third* (marg. or, *principal*)
48:34. an heifer of *three years old:*
Eze. 5: 2. shalt burn with fire *a third part*
— thou shalt take *a third part*,
— *and a third part* thou shalt scatter
12. *A third part of thee* shall die
— *and a third part* shall fall...round about thee; *and* I will scatter *a third part*
10:14. and *the third* the face of a lion,
21:14(19). the sword be doubled *the third time*,
31: 1. eleventh year, *in the third* (month),
42: 3. gallery against gallery *in three* (stories).
46:14. *the third part of* an hin of oil,
Hos. 6: 2. in the *third* day he will raise
Zec. 6: 3. in the *third* chariot white horses;
13: 8. *but the third* shall be left
9. I will bring *the third part*

שָׁלַךְ [*shāh-lach'*]. 7993

* HIPHIL.—*Preterite*. *

Lev. 1:16. *and cast* it beside the altar
14:40. *and they shall cast* them into
Nu. 19: 6. *and cast* (it) into the midst
35:20. or *hurl* at him by laying of wait,
22. or *have cast* upon him any thing
Jos. 10:11. the Lord *cast down* great stones
2Sa.11:21. *did* not a woman *cast* a piece
1K. 14: 9. *hast cast* me behind thy back:
2K. 7:15. Syrians *had cast away* in their haste
13:23. neither *cast he them* from his
17:20. until *he had cast them out*

2K. 23:12. *and cast* the dust of them
24:20. until *he had cast them out*
Neh 9:11. *thou threwest* into the deeps,
Isa. 38:17. *hast cast* all my sins behind thy back.
Jer. 7:15. *And I will cast* you out of my sight, as *I have cast* out all your brethren,
9:19(18). our dwellings *have cast* (us) *out.*
38: 9. *they have cast* into the dungeon;
41: 9. Ishmael *had cast* all the dead bodies
51:63. *and cast it* into the midst
Lam. 2: 1. *cast down* from heaven unto the earth
Eze. 5: 4. *and cast* them into the midst
20: 8. *they did* not every man *cast away*
28:17. *I will cast thee* to the ground,
43:24. *and* the priests *shall cast* salt
Joel 1: 7. clean bare, *and cast* (it) *away;*
Am. 4: 3. *and ye shall cast* (them) into the palace,
8: 3. *they shall cast* (them) *forth*
Nah 3: 6. *And I will cast* abominable filth

HIPHIL.—*Infinitive.*

Ecc. 3: 5, 6. A time *to cast away*
Jer. 22:19. burial of an ass, drawn *and cast forth*
36:23. *and cast* (it) into the fire
52: 3. till *he had cast them out*

HIPHIL.—*Imperative.*

Gen37:22. *cast* him into this pit
Ex. 4: 3. *Cast it* on the ground.
7: 9. *and cast* (it) before Pharaoh,
2K. 9:25. *cast him* in the portion of the field
26. *cast him* into the plat
Ps. 55:22(23). *Cast* thy burden upon the Lord,
Jer. 7:29. *and cast* (it) *away,*
Eze.18:31. *Cast away* from you all your
20: 7. *Cast ye away* every man
Zec.11:13. *Cast it* unto the potter:

HIPHIL.—*Future.*

Gen21:15. *and she cast* the child under
37:20. *and cast him* into some pit,
24. *and cast* him into a pit:
Ex. 1:22. *ye shall cast* into the river,
4: 3. *And he cast it* on the ground,
7:10. *and* Aaron *cast down* his rod
12. *For they cast down* every man
15:25. *when he had cast* into the waters,
22:31(30). *ye shall cast* it to the dogs.
32:19. *and he cast* the tables out of his hands,
24. *then I cast it* into the fire,
Deu 9:17. *and cast them* out of my two hands,
21. *and I cast* the dust thereof
29:28(27). *and cast them* into another land,
Jos. 8:29. *and cast* it at the entering
10:27. *and cast them* into the cave
18: 8. that *I may* here *cast* lots
10. *And* Joshua *cast* lots
Jud. 8:25. *and did cast* therein every man
9:17. *and adventured* (marg. *cast*) his life
53. *And* a certain woman *cast*
15:17. *that he cast away* the jawbone
2Sa. 18:17. *and cast* him into a great pit
20:12. *and cast* a cloth upon him,
22. *and cast* (it) out to Joab.
1K. 19:19. *and cast* his mantle upon him.
2K. 2:16. *and cast him* upon some mountain,
21. *and cast* the salt in there,
3:25. *cast* every man his stone,
4:41. *And he cast* (it) into the pot;
6: 6. *and cast* (it) in thither;
10:25. *and* the captains *cast* (them) *out,*
13:21. *and they cast* the man
23: 6. *and cast* the powder thereof
2Ch 7:20. *will I cast out* of my sight,
24:10. *and cast* into the chest,
25:12. *and cast them down* from the top
30:14. *and cast* (them) into the brook
33:15. *and cast* (them) out of the city.
Neh 9:26. *and cast* thy law behind their backs,
13: 8. *therefore I cast forth* all
Job 15:33. *and shall cast off* his flower
18: 7. *and* his own counsel *shall cast him down.*
27:22. *For* (God) *shall cast* upon him,
29:17. *plucked* (marg. *cast*) the spoil out of his teeth.
Ps. 2: 3. *and cast away* their cords
50:17. *and castest* my words behind thee.
51:11(13). *Cast me* not *away* from thy
Ps. 60: 8(10). over Edom *will I cast* out my shoe:
71: 9. *Cast me* not *off* in the time of
102:10(11). lifted me up, *and cast me down.*
108: 9(10). over Edom *will I cast out* my shoe;
Isa. 2:20. a man *shall cast* his idols
Jer. 26:23. *and cast* his dead body
38: 6. *and cast* him into the dungeon
Eze. 7:19. *They shall cast* their silver
23:35. *and cast* me behind thy back,
Dan 8: 7. *but he cast him down*
12. *and it cast down* the truth
Jon. 2: 3(4). *For thou hadst cast me* into the deep,
Mic. 7:19. *and thou wilt cast* all
Zec. 5: 8. *And he cast* it into the midst
— *and he cast* the weight
11:13. *and cast* them to the potter

HIPHIL.—*Participle.*

Ps.147:17. *He casteth forth* his ice
Isa. 19: 8. all *they that cast* angle
Mic. 2: 5. none *that shall cast* a cord by lot

* HOPHAL.—*Preterite.* *

Ps. 22:10(11). *I was cast* upon thee
Isa. 14:19. But thou *art cast* out
Jer. 22:28. *and are cast* into a land
Eze.19:12. *she was cast down* to the gronnd,
Dan 8:11. *and* the place of his sanctuary *was cast down.*

HOPHAL.—*Future.*

Isa. 34: 3. Their slain also *shall be cast out,*
Eze.16: 5. *but thou wast cast out* in the

HOPHAL.—*Participle.*

2Sa.20:21. his head *shall be thrown* to thee
1K. 13:24. his carcase *was cast* in the way,
25. passed by, and saw the carcase *cast*
28. he went and found his carcase *cast*
Jer. 14:16. shall be *cast out* in the streets
36:30. his dead body shall be *cast out*

שָׁלָךְ *shāh-lāhch'*, m. 7994

Lev.11:17. the little owl, and *the cormorant,*
Deu14:17. pelican, and the gier eagle, and *the cormorant,*

שַׁלֶּכֶת *shal-leh'-cheth*, f. 7995

Isa. 6:13. *when they cast* (their leaves):

שָׁלַל *shāh-lal'.* 7997

* KAL.—*Preterite.* *

Eze.26:12. *And they shall make a spoil*
29:19. *and take* (marg. *spoil*) her spoil,
39:10. *and they shall spoil* those
Hab 2: 8. thou *hast spoiled* many nations,

KAL.—*Infinitive.*

Ru. 2:16. let fall also (some) of the handfuls *of purpose* (lit. *spoiling* spoil)
Isa. 10: 6. *to take* (lit. *to spoil*) the spoil,
Eze.38:12. *To take* (marg. *spoil*) a spoil,
13. Art thou come *to take* a spoil?
— *to take* a great spoil?

KAL.—*Future.*

Ru. 2:16. *let fall* also (some) of the handfuls of purpose
Hab 2: 8. remnant of the people *shall spoil thee;*

KAL.—*Participle.* Poel.

Jer. 50:10. all *that spoil her* shall be satisfied,
Eze.39:10. shall spoil *those that spoiled them,*
Zec. 2: 8(12). the nations which *spoiled* you:

* HITHPOLEL.—*Future.* *

Ps. 76: 5(6). The stouthearted *are spoiled,*

HITHPOLEL.—*Participle.*

Isa. 59:15. from evil *maketh himself a prey:* (marg. or, *is accounted mad*)

7998 **שָׁלָל** *shāh-lāhl'*, m.

Gen49:27. at night he shall divide *the spoil.*
Ex. 15: 9. I will divide *the spoil;*
Nu. 31:11. they took all *the spoil,*
12. the prey, and *the spoil,* unto Moses,
Deu 2:35. *and the spoil of* the cities
3: 7. all the cattle, *and the spoil of*
13:16(17). thou shalt gather all *the spoil of it*
—(—). the city, and all *the spoil thereof*
20:14. all *the spoil thereof,*
— thou shalt eat *the spoil of*
Jos. 7:21. When I saw *among the spoils*
8: 2. only *the spoil thereof,*
27. Only the cattle *and the spoil of*
11:14. all *the spoil of* these cities,
22: 8. divide *the spoil of* your enemies
Jud. 5:30. have they (not) divided *the prey;*
— to Sisera *a prey of* divers colours, *a prey of*
— for the necks of (them that take) *the spoil?*
8:24, 25. the earrings of *his prey.*
1Sa. 14:30. had eaten freely to day *of the spoil of*
32. the people flew upon *the spoil,*
15:19. but didst fly upon *the spoil,*
21. But the people took *of the spoil,*
30:16. because of all *the* great *spoil*
19. sons nor daughters, *neither spoil,*
20. This (is) David's *spoil.*
22. we will not give them (ought) *of the spoil*
26. he sent *of the spoil* unto the elders
— a present for you *of the spoil of*
2Sa. 3:22. *and* brought in *a* great *spoil*
8:12. *and of the spoil of* Hadadezer,
12:30. *And* he brought forth *the spoil of* the city
2K. 3:23. now therefore, Moab, *to the spoil.*
1Ch 20: 2. *and* he brought also exceeding much *spoil*
26:27. Out of *the spoils* won in battles
2Ch 14:13(12). they carried away very much *spoil.*
15:11. of *the spoil* (which) they had brought,
20:25. came to take away *the spoil of them,*
— and they were three days in gathering of *the spoil,*
24:23. sent all *the spoil of them*
28: 8. took also away much *spoil* from them, and brought *the spoil* to Samaria.
15. with *the spoil* clothed all
Est. 3:13 & 8:11. *and* (to take) *the spoil of them*
Ps. 68:12(13). she that tarried at home divided *the spoil.*
119:162. as one that findeth great *spoil.*
Pro. 1:13. we shall fill our houses with *spoil:*
16:19. than to divide *the spoil* with the proud.
31:11. *so that* he shall have no need of *spoil.*
Isa. 8: 1. concerning Maher-*shalal*-hash-baz. (marg. making speed to *the spoil* he hasteneth the prey)
3. Call his name Maher-*shalal*-hash-baz.
4. and *the spoil of* Samaria
9: 3(2). as (men) rejoice when they divide *the spoil.*
10: 2. that widows may be *their prey,*
6. to take *the spoil,*
33: 4. *your spoil* shall be gathered
23. then is the prey of *a* great *spoil*
53:12. he shall divide *the spoil* with the strong;
Jer. 21: 9. his life shall be unto him *for a prey.*
38: 2. he shall have his life *for a prey,*
39:18. thy life shall be *for a prey* unto thee:
45: 5. thy life will I give unto thee *for a prey*
49:32. the multitude of their cattle *a spoil:*
50:10. Chaldea shall be *a spoil:* all that spoil
Eze. 7:21. the wicked of the earth *for a spoil;*
29:19. take *her spoil,* and take her prey;
38:12. To take *a spoil,* and to take a prey;
13. Art thou come to take *a spoil?*
— to take *a* great *spoil?*
Dan 11:24. among them the prey, *and spoil,*
Zec. 2: 9(13). they shall be *a spoil* to their
14: 1. *thy spoil* shall be divided

7999 **שָׁלַם** [*shāh-lam'*].

* KAL.—*Preterite.* *

Isa. 60:20. *and* the days of thy mourning *shall be ended.*

KAL.—*Imperative.*

Job 22:21. with him, *and be at peace:*

KAL.—*Future.*

1K. 7:51. *So was ended* all the work
2Ch 5: 1. *Thus* all the work...*was finished:*
Neh. 6:15. *So* the wall *was finished*
Job 9: 4. against him, *and hath prospered?*

KAL.—*Participle.* Poel.

Ps. 7: 4(5). evil unto him *that was at peace with me;*

KAL.—*Participle.* Paül.

2Sa. 20:19. *peaceable* (and) faithful in Israel:

* PIEL.—*Preterite.* *

Gen44: 4. *have ye rewarded* evil for good?
Lev. 6: 5(5:24). *he shall even restore* it in the
Jud. 1: 7. so God *hath requited* me.
1K. 9:25. *So he finished* the house.
2K. 9:26. *and I will requite* thee in this plat,
Job 8: 6. *and make* the habitation of thy righteousness *prosperous.*
Pro. 7:14. this day *have I payed* my vows.
Isa. 19:21. vow a vow unto the Lord, *and perform*
65: 6. *but will recompense, even recompense* into their bosom,
Jer. 16:18. *And* first *I will recompense*
25:14. *and I will recompense* them
51:24. *And I will render* unto Babylon
Joel 2:25. *And I will restore* to you

PIEL.—*Infinitive.*

Ex. 21:36. he shall *surely* (lit. *paying*) pay ox for ox;
22: 3(2). he should make *full* (lit. *id.*) restitution;
6(5). that kindled the fire shall *surely* make
14(13). he shall *surely* make (it) good.
Deu 23:21(22). thou shalt not slack *to pay it:*
Ps. 61: 8(9). *that I may* daily *perform* my vows.
Pro. 22:27. If thou hast nothing *to pay,*
Ecc. 5: 4(3). defer not *to pay it;*
Jer. 51:56. God of recompences shall *surely* requite.

PIEL.—*Imperative.*

2K. 4: 7. Go, sell the oil, *and pay* thy debt,
Ps. 50:14. *and pay* thy vows unto the most high:
76:11(12). Vow, *and pay* unto the Lord
Ecc. 5: 4(3). *pay* that which thou hast vowed.
Jer. 50:29. *recompense* her according
Nah 1:15(2:1). *perform* thy vows:

PIEL.—*Future.*

Ex. 21:34. The owner of the pit *shall make* (it) *good,*
36. *he shall* surely *pay* ox for ox;
22: 1(21:37). *he shall restore* five oxen
3(2). *he should make* full *restitution;*
4(3). *he shall restore* double.
5(4). vineyard, *shall he make restitution.*
6(5). that kindled the fire *shall* surely *make restitution.*
7(6). the thief be found, *let him pay* double.
9(8). *he shall pay* double
11(10), 15(14). *he shall* not *make* (it) *good.*
12(11). *he shall make restitution* unto the
13(12). *he shall* not *make good*
14(13). *he shall* surely *make* (it) *good.*
Lev. 5:16. *he shall make amends* for the harm
24:18. killeth a beast *shall make it good;*
21. killeth a beast, *he shall restore it:*
Deu 7:10. *he will repay* him to his face.
32:41. I will render vengeance to mine enemies, and *will reward*
Ru. 2:12. The Lord *recompense* thy work,
1Sa. 24:19(20). the Lord *reward thee* good
2Sa. 3:39. the Lord *shall reward* the doer of evil
12: 6. *he shall restore* the lamb
15: 7. let me go *and pay* my vow,
Job 21:19. *he rewardeth* him, and he shall know (it).
31. who *shall repay* him
22:27. *thou shalt pay* thy vows.
34:11. the work of a man *shall he render* unto him,
33. *he will recompense it,* whether thou refuse
41:11(3). *that I should repay* (him)?
Ps. 22:25(26). *I will pay* my vows before them
35:12. *They rewarded me* evil for good
37:21. borroweth, and *payeth* not again:

Ps. 41:10(11). *that I may requite* them.
56:12(13). *I will render* praises unto thee.
62:12(13). *thou renderest* to every man
66:13. *I will pay* thee my vows,
116:14, 18. *I will pay* my vows unto the Lord
137: 8. happy (shall he be), *that rewardeth*
Pro. 6:31. *he shall restore* sevenfold;
13:21. to the righteous good *shall be repayed.*
19:17. which he hath given *will he pay* him *again.*
20:22. *I will recompense* evil;
25:22. the Lord *shall reward* thee.
Ecc. 5: 5(4). that thou shouldest vow and not *pay.*
Isa. 57:18. lead him also, *and restore* comforts
59:18. accordingly *he will repay,*
— to the islands *he will repay* recompence.
Jer. 51:56. God of recompences *shall* surely *requite.*
Eze.33:15. *give again* that he had robbed,
Hos 14: 2(3). *so will we render* the calves of our lips.
Jon. 2: 9(10). *I will pay* (that) that I have vowed.

PIEL.—*Participle.*

Deu 7:10. *And repayeth* them that hate him
Ps. 31:23(24). *and* plentifully *rewardeth* the proud
38:20(21). *They also that render* evil
Isa. 66: 6. the Lord *that rendereth* recompence
Jer. 32:18. *and recompensest* the iniquity
51: 6. he *will render* unto her a recompence.
Joel 3: 4(4:4). *will* ye *render* me a recompence?

* PUAL.—*Future.* *

Ps. 65: 1(2). unto thee *shall* the vow *be performed.*
Pro.11:31. the righteous *shall be recompensed*
13:13. feareth the commandment *shall be rewarded.* (marg. or, *in peace*)
Jer. 18:20. *Shall* evil *be recompensed* for good?

PUAL.—*Participle.*

Isa. 42:19. who (is) blind *as he that is perfect,*

* HIPHIL.—*Preterite.* *

Jos. 10: 1. Gibeon *had made peace* with Israel,
4. *hath made peace* with Joshua
11:19. There was not a city that *made peace*

HIPHIL.—*Future.*

Deu 20:12. if it *will make* no *peace*
2Sa.10:19. *And* when...*they made peace* with Israel,
1K. 22:44(45). *And* Jehoshaphat *made peace*
1Ch 19:19. *And* when...they *made peace* with David,
Job 23:14. *he performeth* (the thing that is) appointed
Pro. 16: 7. *he maketh* even his enemies *to be at peace*
Isa. 38:12, 13. to night *wilt thou make an end of me.*
44:26. *performeth* the counsel of his messengers;
28. *shall perform* all my pleasure:

* HOPHAL.—*Preterite.* *

Job 5:23. of the field *shall be at peace*

8000 ## שְׁלַם [*sh'lam*], Ch.

* P'AL.—*Participle.* Passive. *

Ezr. 5:16. and (yet) it *is not finished.*

* APHEL.—*Preterite.* *

Dan 5:26. God hath numbered thy kingdom, *and finished it.*

APHEL.—*Imperative.*

Ezr. 7:19. (those) *deliver thou* before the God

8001 ## שְׁלָם *sh'lāhm,* Ch. m.

Ezr. 4:17. *Peace,* and at such a time.
5: 7. Unto Darius the king, *all peace.*
Dan 4: 1(3:31) & 6:25(26). *Peace* be multiplied *unto you.*

8003 ## שָׁלֵם *shāh-lēhm',* adj.

Gen15:16. the iniquity of the Amorites (is) not yet *full.*
34:21. These men (are) *peaceable* with us;
Deu25:15. shalt have a *perfect* and just weight, a *perfect* and just measure
27: 6. altar of the Lord thy God of *whole* stones:
Jos. 8:31. an altar of *whole* stones,
Ru. 2:12. a *full* reward be given thee
1K. 6: 7. was built of stone *made ready* (lit. *perfected*) before it
8:61. Let your heart therefore be *perfect*
11: 4. his heart was not *perfect* with the Lord
15: 3. was not *perfect* with the Lord
14. nevertheless Asa's heart was *perfect*
2K. 20: 3. in truth and with a *perfect* heart,
1Ch 12:38. came with a *perfect* heart
28: 9. serve him with a *perfect* heart
29: 9. with *perfect* heart they offered
19. give unto Solomon my son a *perfect*
2Ch 8:16. the house of the Lord was *perfected.*
15:17. nevertheless the heart of Asa was *perfect*
16: 9. whose heart (is) *perfect* toward him.
19: 9. faithfully, and with a *perfect* heart.
25: 2. but not with a *perfect* heart.
Pro.11: 1. but a *just* weight (marg. *perfect* stone) (is) his delight.
Isa. 38: 3. in truth and with a *perfect* heart,
Am. 1: 6. carried away captive the *whole* captivity,
9. they delivered up the *whole* captivity
Nah 1:12. Though (they be) *quiet,* (marg. *at peace*)

שֶׁלֶם *sheh'-lem,* m. 8002

Ex. 20:24. and *thy peace offerings,* thy sheep,
24: 5. sacrificed *peace* offerings of oxen
29:28. the sacrifice of *their peace offerings,*
32: 6. brought *peace offerings;*
Lev. 3: 1. (be) a sacrifice of *peace offering,*
3. the sacrifice of *the peace offering*
6. for a sacrifice of *peace offering*
9. sacrifice of *the peace offering*
4:10, 26, 31. sacrifice of *peace offerings:*
35. the sacrifice of *the peace offerings;*
6:12(5). thereon the fat of *the peace offerings.*
7:11. the law of the sacrifice of *peace offerings,*
13. thanksgiving of *his peace offerings.*
14. sprinkleth the blood of *the peace offerings.*
15. flesh of the sacrifice of *his peace offerings*
18. flesh of the sacrifice of *his peace offerings*
20. the flesh of the sacrifice of *peace offerings,*
21. the flesh of the sacrifice of *peace offerings,*
29, 29. the sacrifice of *his peace offerings*
32. the sacrifices of *your peace offerings.*
33. offereth the blood of *the peace offerings*
34. sacrifices of *their peace offerings,*
37. the sacrifice of *the peace offerings;*
9: 4. a bullock and a ram *for peace offerings,*
18. a sacrifice of *peace offerings,*
22. burnt offering, *and peace offerings.*
10:14. the sacrifices of *peace offerings of*
17: 5. offer them (for) *peace offerings* unto the Lord.
19: 5. if ye offer a sacrifice of *peace offerings*
22:21. offereth a sacrifice of *peace offerings*
23:19. for a sacrifice of *peace offerings.*
Nu. 6:14. ram without blemish *for peace offerings,*
17. ram (for) a sacrifice of *peace offerings*
18. under the sacrifice of *the peace offerings.*
7:17, 23, 29, 35, 41, 47, 53, 59, 65, 71, 77, 83. for a sacrifice of *peace offerings,*
88. the sacrifice of *the peace offerings*
10:10. sacrifices of *your peace offerings;*
15: 8. or *peace offerings* unto the Lord:
29:39. *and for your peace offerings.*
Deu27: 7. thou shalt offer *peace offerings,*
Jos. 8:31. sacrificed *peace offerings.*
22:23. if to offer *peace* offerings
27. *and with our peace offerings;*
Jud.20:26 & 21:4. burnt offerings *and peace offerings*
1Sa.10: 8. sacrifice sacrifices of *peace offerings:*
11:15. sacrificed sacrifices of *peace offerings*
13: 9. burnt offering to me, *and peace offerings.*
2Sa. 6:17. burnt offerings *and peace offerings*
18. made an end of offering burnt offerings *and peace offerings,*
24:25. offered burnt offerings *and peace offerings.*
1K. 3:15. and offered *peace offerings,*
8:63. a sacrifice of *peace offerings,*
64, 64. the fat of *the peace offerings:*
9:25. burnt offerings *and peace offerings*
2K. 16:13. sprinkled the blood of his *peace offerings,*
1Ch 16: 1. burnt sacrifices *and peace offerings*
2. *and the peace offerings,* he blessed

1Ch 21:26. burnt offerings *and peace offerings*,
2Ch 7: 7 & 29:35. the fat of *the peace offerings*,
30:22. seven days, offering *peace offerings*,
31: 2. burnt offerings *and for peace offerings*,
33:16. sacrificed thereon *peace offerings*
Pro. 7:14. *peace* offerings with me;
Eze.43:27. and *your peace offerings*; (marg. or, *thank offerings*)
45:15. for a burnt offering, *and for peace offerings*, (marg. *id.*)
17. burnt offering, and *the peace offerings*, (marg. *id.*)
46: 2, 12. burnt offering and *his peace offerings*,
12. or *peace offerings* voluntarily
Am. 5:22. *neither* will I regard *the peace offerings of* (marg. or, *thank offerings*)

8005 שִׁלֵּם *shil-lēhm*, m.

Deu32:35. (belongeth) vengeance, *and recompense*;

See 7966 שִׁלּוּם see שִׁלֻּם

8011 שִׁלֻּמָה [*shil-loo-māh'*], f.

Ps. 91: 8. *and* see *the reward of* the wicked.

8021 שַׁלְמֹנִים *shal-mōh-neem'*, m. pl.

Isa. 1:23. followeth after *rewards*:

8025 שָׁלַף *shāh-laph'*.

* KAL.—*Preterite*. *

Jud. 3:22. *he could* not *draw* the dagger out
8:20. But the youth *drew* not his sword:
Ru. 4: 7. a man *plucked off* his shoe,
Job 20:25. *It is drawn*, and cometh out
Ps.129: 6. which withereth afore *it groweth up*:

KAL.—*Imperative*.

Jud. 9:54. *Draw* thy sword, and slay me,
1Sa.31: 4. Then said Saul unto his armourbearer, *Draw* thy sword,
1Ch 10: 4. *Draw* thy sword, and thrust me through

KAL.—*Future*.

Ru. 4: 8. *So he drew off* his shoe.
1Sa.17:51. *and drew it* out of the sheath

KAL.—*Participle*. Poel.

Jud. 8:10. twenty thousand men *that drew* sword.
20: 2. hundred thousand footmen *that drew*
15. twenty and six thousand men *that drew*
17. four hundred thousand men *that drew*
25. all these *drew* the sword.
35. all these *drew* the sword.
46. twenty and five thousand men *that drew*
2Sa.24: 9. valiant men *that drew* the sword;
2K. 3:26. seven hundred men *that drew* swords,
1Ch 21: 5. hundred thousand men *that drew* sword:
— ten thousand men *that drew* sword.

KAL.—*Participle*. Paül.

Nu. 22:23, 31. his sword *drawn* in his hand:
Jos. 5:13. against him with his sword *drawn*
1Ch 21:16. having a *drawn* sword in his hand

See 7969 שָׁלוֹשׁ see שָׁלֹשׁ

See 7970 שְׁלוֹשִׁים see שְׁלֹשִׁים

8027 שָׁלַשׁ [*shāh-lash'*]

* PIEL.—*Preterite*. *

Deu19: 3. *and divide* the coasts...into *three parts*,
1Sa.20:19. *And* (when) *thou hast stayed three days*,

PIEL.—*Imperative*.

1K. 18:34. *Do* (it) *the third time*.

PIEL.—*Future*.

1K. 18:34. *And they did* (it) *the third time*.

* PUAL.—*Participle*. *

Gen15: 9. Take me an heifer of *three years old*, and a she goat of *three years old*, and a ram of *three years old*,
Ecc. 4:12. a *threefold* cord is not quickly broken.
Eze.42: 6. For they (were) in *three* (stories),

שִׁלְשׁוֹם *shil-shōhm'*, adv. 8032

Gen31: 2. behold, it (was) not toward him as *before*. (marg. as yesterday and *the day before*)
5. that it (is) not toward me as *before*; (lit. yesterday *the third day*)
Ex. 4:10. neither *heretofore*, nor since (marg. since yesterday, nor *since the third day*)
5: 7. give the people straw to make brick, as *heretofore*: (lit. as yesterday *the third day*)
8. bricks, which they did make *heretofore*, (lit. yesterday *the third day*)
14. brick both yesterday and to day, as *heretofore*? (lit. yesterday *the third day*)
21:29. wont to push with his horn in *time past*, (lit. from yesterday *the third day*)
36. the ox hath used to push in *time past*, (lit. from yesterday *the third day*)
Deu 4:42. hated him not in *times past*; (lit. from yesterday *the third day*)
19: 4. whom he hated not in *time past*; (marg. from yesterday *the third day*)
6. inasmuch as he hated him not in *time past*. (lit. from yesterday *the third day*)
Jos. 3: 4. ye have not passed (this) way *heretofore*. (marg. since yesterday and *the third day*)
4:18. flowed over all his banks, as (they did) *before*. (lit. as yesterday *the third day*)
20: 5. hated him not *beforetime*. (lit. from yesterday *the third day*)
Ru. 2:11. which thou knewest not *heretofore*. (lit. yesterday *the third day*)
1Sa. 4: 7. there hath not been such a thing *heretofore*. (marg. yesterday, or *the third day*)
10:11. when all that knew him *beforetime* (lit. yesterday *the third day*)
14:21. were with the Philistines *before that time*, (lit. yesterday *the third day*)
19: 7. he was in his presence, as in *times past*. (marg. yesterday *third day*)
21: 5(6). kept from us about these *three days*, (lit. as yesterday *the third day*)
2Sa. 3:17. Ye sought for David in *times past* (marg. both yesterday and *the third day*)
5: 2. Also in *time past*, when Saul was king over us, (lit. yesterday and *the third day*)
2K. 13: 5. Israel dwelt in their tents, as *beforetime*. (marg. yesterday, (and) *third day*)
1Ch 11: 2. moreover in *time past*, (marg. yesterday and *the third day*)
Pro.22:20. (כתיב) written to thee *excellent things*

שִׁלֵּשִׁים *shil-lēh-sheem'*, m. pl. 8029

Gen50:23. Ephraim's children of *the third*
Ex. 20: 5. the children unto *the third* and fourth
34: 7. unto *the third* and to the fourth
Nu. 14:18. children unto *the third* and fourth
Deu 5: 9. children unto *the third* and fourth

שָׁם *shāhm*, part. adv. 8033

Gen 2: 8. and *there* he put the man whom he had
Ex. 40: 3. And thou shalt put *therein* the ark of the
Deu 1:37. Thou also shalt not go in *thither*.
2Sa.17:18. a well in his court; *whither* (lit. and *there*) they went down.
2Ch 6:11. And *in it* have I put the ark,
&c. &c. &c.

With prefixes: מִשָּׁם

Gen11: 8. scattered them abroad *from thence* upon
26:17. And Isaac departed *thence*,
Lev. 2: 2. he shall take *thereout* his handful of the
1K. 17:13. make me *thereof* a little cake first,
&c. &c.

שֶׁשָּׁם

Ps.122: 4. *Whither* the tribes go up, the tribes

It occurs very frequently with ה Paragogic שָׁמָּה, the signification remaining unchanged.

For the signification of שָׁם in connection with אֲשֶׁר, see אֲשֶׁר

8034 **שֵׁם** *shēhm*, m.

Gen 2:11. *The name of* the first (is) Pison:
13. *And the name of* the second river
14. *And the name of* the third river
19. that (was) *the name thereof.*
20. Adam gave *names* to all cattle,
3:20. Adam called his wife's *name* Eve;
4:17. called *the name of* the city, *after the name of* his son, Enoch.
19. *the name of* the one (was) Adah, *and the name of* the other Zillah.
21. *And* his brother's *name* (was) Jubal:
25. called *his name* Seth:
26. he called *his name* Enos: then began men to call *upon the name of*
5: 2. called *their name* Adam,
3. called *his name* Seth:
29. he called *his name* Noah,
6: 4. of old, men of *renown.*
10:25. Eber...*the name of* one (was) Peleg;
— *and* his brother's *name* (was) Joktan.
11: 4. let us make us *a name,*
9. Therefore is *the name of it*
29. *the name of* Abram's wife
— *and the name of* Nahor's wife,
12: 2. and make *thy name* great;
8. called *upon the name of* the Lord.
13: 4. Abram called *on the name of*
16: 1. *whose name* (was) Hagar.
11. shalt call *his name* Ishmael;
13. she called *the name of* the Lord
15. Abram called his son's *name,*
17: 5. Neither shall *thy name* any more be called Abram, but *thy name* shall be Abraham;
15. thou shalt not call *her name* Sarai, but Sarah (shall) *her name* (be).
19. thou shalt call *his name* Isaac:
19:22. *the name of* the city was called
37. called *his name* Moab:
38. called *his name* Ben-ammi:
21: 3. Abraham called *the name of* his son
33. called there *on the name of* the Lord,
22:14. Abraham called *the name of* that place
24. *whose name* (was) Reumah,
24:29. *and his name* (was) Laban:
25: 1. *and her name* (was) Keturah.
13. *the names of* the sons of Ishmael, *by their names,*
16. these (are) *their names,*
25. they called *his name* Esau.
26. *his name* was called Jacob:
30. therefore was *his name* called Edom.
26:18. he called their *names after the names* by
20. he called *the name of*
21. he called *the name of it* Sitnah.
22. he called *the name of it* Rehoboth;
25. and called *upon the name of* the Lord,
33. therefore *the name of* the city
27:36. Is not he rightly *named* Jacob? (lit. is *his name* called)
28:19. he called *the name of* that place Beth-el: but *the name of* that city
29:16. *the name of* the elder (was) Leah, *and the name of* the younger
32. she called *his name* Reuben:
33. she called *his name* Simeon.
34. therefore was *his name* called Levi.

Gen29:35. she called *his name* Judah;
30: 6. therefore called she *his name* Dan.
8. she called *his name* Naphtali.
11. she called *his name* Gad.
13. she called *his name* Asher.
18. she called *his name* Issachar.
20. she called *his name* Zebulun.
21. and called *her name* Dinah.
24. she called *his name* Joseph;
31:48. was *the name of it* called Galeed;
32: 2(3). he called *the name of* that place
27(28). What (is) *thy name?*
28(29). *Thy name* shall be called
29(30). Tell (me), I pray thee, *thy name.*
—(—). thou dost ask *after my name?*
30(31). Jacob called *the name of* the place
33:17. therefore *the name of* the place
35: 8. and *the name of it* was called Allon-bachuth.
10. *Thy name* (is) Jacob: *thy name* shall not
— but Israel shall be *thy name:* and he called *his name* Israel.
15. Jacob called *the name of* the place
18. she called *his name* Ben-oni:
36:10. These (are) *the names of* Esau's sons;
32, 35, 39. *and the name of* his city (was)
39. *and* his wife's *name* (was) Mehetabel,
40. *the names of* the dukes
— after their places, *by their names;*
38: 1. *whose name* (was) Hirah.
2. *whose name* (was) Shuah;
3. he called *his name* Er.
4. she called *his name* Onan.
5. and called *his name* Shelah:
6. *whose name* (was) Tamar.
29. therefore *his name* was called
30. and *his name* was called Zarah.
41:45. Pharaoh called Joseph's *name*
51. Joseph called *the name of* the
52. *the name of* the second called he
46: 8. *the names of* the children of Israel,
48: 6. called after *the name of* their
16. let *my name* be named on them, *and the name of* my fathers Abraham
50:11. wherefore *the name of it* was called
Ex. 1: 1. *the names of* the children of Israel,
15. of which *the name of* the one (was) Shiphrah, *and the name of* the other
2:10. And she called *his name* Moses:
22. he called *his name* Gershom:
3:13. What (is) *his name?*
15. this (is) *my name* for ever,
5:23. since I came to Pharaoh to speak *in thy name,*
6: 3. *but* by *my name* Jehovah was I not known
16. *the names of* the sons of Levi
9:16. that *my name* may be declared
15: 3. the Lord (is) *his name.*
23. therefore *the name of it* was called
16:31. Israel called *the name thereof* Manna:
17: 7. he called *the name of* the place
15. called *the name of it* Jehovah-nissi:
18: 3. *the name of* the one (was)
4. *And the name of* the other
20: 7. shalt not take *the name of* the Lord
— guiltless that taketh *his name* in vain.
24. all places where I record *my name*
23:13. *and* make no mention *of the name of*
21. for *my name* (is) in him.
28: 9. grave on them *the names of* the children
10. Six *of their names* on one stone,
— six *names of* the rest
11. two stones with *the names of*
12. bear *their names* before the Lord
21. stones shall be with *the names of*
— according to *their names,*
— every one with *his name*
29. Aaron shall bear *the names of*
31. 2. I have called *by name* Bezaleel
33:12,17. I know thee *by name,*
19. I will proclaim *the name of* the Lord
34: 5. proclaimed *the name of* the Lord.
14. *whose name* (is) Jealous,
35:30. the Lord hath called *by name*
39: 6. graven, with *the names of*
14. stones (were) according to *the names of*
— according to *their names,*

Ex. 39:14. every one with *his name*,
Lev.18:21. neither shalt thou profane *the name of*
19:12. ye shall not swear *by my name*
— neither shalt thou profane *the name of*
20: 3. to profane my holy *name*.
21: 6. not profane *the name of* their God:
22: 2. that they profane not my holy *name*
32. Neither shall ye profane my holy *name*,
24:11. blasphemed *the name* (of the Lord),
— his mother's *name* (was) Shelomith,
16. he that blasphemeth *the name of*
— blasphemeth *the name* (of the Lord),
Nu. 1: 2. with the number of (their) *names*,
5. *the names of* the men that shall
17. which are expressed *by* (their) *names:*
18, 20, 22, 24, 26, 28, 30, 32, 34, 36, 38, 40, 42. according to the number of *the names*,
3: 2, 3. *the names of* the sons of Aaron;
17. sons of Levi *by their names;*
18. *the names of* the sons of Gershon
40. take the number of *their names*.
43. males by the number of *names*,
4:32. *and by name* ye shall reckon
6:27. they shall put *my name*
11: 3. And he called *the name of* the place
26. *the name of* the one (was) Eldad, *and the name of* the other Medad:
34. he called *the name of* that place
13: 4. these (were) *their names:*
16. *the names of* the men which
16: 2. famous in the congregation, men of *renown:*
17: 2(17). write thou every man's *name*
3(18). thou shalt write Aaron's *name*
21: 3. he called *the name of* the place
25:14. *Now the name of* the Israelite
15. *And the name of* the Midianitish
26:33. *and the names of* the daughters of
46. *And the name of* the daughter of
53. according to the number of *names*.
55. *according to the names of* the tribes
59. *And the name of* Amram's wife
27: 1. these (are) *the names of* his daughters;
4. Why should *the name of* our father
32:38. their *names* being changed,
— and gave other *names* (marg. called by *names the names of*) unto the cities
42. Nobah, *after his own name*.
34:17. These (are) *the names of* the men
19. *the names of* the men (are) these:
Deu 3:14. called them after *his own name*,
5:11. Thou shalt not take *the name of*
— guiltless that taketh *his name* in vain.
6:13. *and* shalt swear *by his name*.
7:24. thou shalt destroy *their name*
9:14. blot out *their name* from under heaven:
10: 8. to bless *in his name*,
20. *and* swear *by his name*.
12: 3. destroy *the names of them*
5. all your tribes to put *his name* there,
11. to cause *his name* to dwell
21. hath chosen to put *his name* there
14:23. choose to place *his name* there,
24. shall choose to set *his name* there,
16: 2. shall choose to place *his name* there.
6. shall choose to place *his name* in,
11. hath chosen to place *his name* there.
18: 5, 7. minister *in the name of* the Lord,
19. he shall speak *in my name*,
20. presume to speak a word *in my name*,
— shall speak *in the name of* other gods,
22. speaketh *in the name of* the Lord,
21: 5. to bless *in the name of* the Lord;
22:14. bring up *an* evil *name* upon her,
19. he hath brought up *an* evil *name*
25: 6. shall succeed in *the name of*
— that *his name* be not put out
7. to raise up unto his brother *a name*
10. And *his name* shall be called in Israel,
26: 2. choose to place *his name* there.
19. in praise, *and in name*,
28:10. thou art called by *the name of*
58. fear this glorious and fearful *name*,
29:20(19). shall blot out *his name*
32: 3. I will publish *the name of* the Lord:
Jos. 2: 1. into an harlot's house, *named* (lit. *and her name*) Rahab,
Jos. 5: 9. *the name of* the place is called Gilgal
7: 9. cut off *our name* from the earth: and what wilt thou do *unto thy* great *name?*
26. *the name of* that place was called,
9: 9. *because of the name of* the Lord
14:15. *And the name of* Hebron
15:15. *and the name of* Debir
17: 3. these (are) *the names of* his daughters,
19:47. *after the name of* Dan their father.
21: 9. which are (here) mentioned *by name*,
23: 7. *neither* make mention of *the name of*
Jud. 1:10. *now the name of* Hebron before
11. *and the name of* Debir
17. And *the name of* the city was called
23. *Now the name of* the city
26. called *the name thereof* Luz: which (is) *the name thereof*
2: 5. they called *the name of* that place
8:31. *whose name* he called Abimelech.
13: 2. *whose name* (was) Manoah;
6. neither told he me *his name:*
17. What (is) *thy name*, that when thy sayings
18. Why askest thou thus *after my name*,
24. called *his name* Samson:
15:19. wherefore he called *the name thereof*
16: 4. *whose name* (was) Delilah.
17: 1. *whose name* (was) Micah.
18:29. And they called *the name of* the city Dan, *after the name of* Dan
— howbeit *the name of* the city
Ru. 1: 2. *And the name of* the man (was) Elimelech, *and the name of* his wife Naomi, *and the name of* his two sons
4. *the name of* the one (was) Orpah, *and the name of* the other Ruth:
2: 1. *and his name* (was) Boaz.
19. The man's *name* with whom
4: 5, 10. to raise up *the name of* the dead
10. that *the name of* the dead
11. be *famous* in Beth-lehem: (marg. proclaim (thy) *name*)
14. that *his name* may be famous
17. her neighbours gave it *a name*,
— they called *his name* Obed:
1Sa. 1: 1. *and his name* (was) Elkanah,
2. *the name of* the one (was) Hannah, *and the name of* the other
20. bare a son, and called *his name* Samuel,
7:12. called *the name of it*
8: 2. Now *the name of* his firstborn was Joel; *and the name of* his second,
9: 1. *whose name* (was) Kish,
2. he had a son, *whose name* (was) Saul,
12:22. his people for *his* great *name's* sake:
14: 4. *and the name of* the one (was) Bozez, *and the name of* the other Seneh.
49. *and the names of* his two daughters (were these); *the name of* the firstborn Merab, *and the name of* the younger
50. *And the name of* Saul's wife
— *and the name of* the captain
17: 4. *named* Goliath, of Gath,
12. *whose name* (was) Jesse;
13. *and the names of* his three sons that went
23. the Philistine of Gath, Goliath *by name*,
45. *in the name of* the Lord of hosts,
18:30. so that *his name* was much set by.
20:42. sworn both of us *in the name of*
21: 7(8). *and his name* (was) Doeg,
22:20. the son of Ahitub, *named* Abiathar,
24:21(22). that thou wilt not destroy *my name*
25: 3. *Now the name of* the man (was) Nabal; *and the name of* his wife
5. greet him *in my name:*
9. all those words *in the name of* David,
25. for *as his name* (is), so (is) he; Nabal (is) *his name*,
2Sa. 3: 7. concubine, *whose name* (was) Rizpah,
4: 2. *the name of* the one (was) Baanah, *and the name of* the other Rechab,
4. *And his name* (was) Mephibosheth.
5:14. *the names of* those that were born
20. he called *the name of* that place
6: 2. whose *name* is called by *the name of*
18. he blessed the people *in the name of*
7: 9. have made thee *a* great *name*, *like unto the name of* the great

2Sa. 7:13. He shall build an house *for my name*,
23. to make him *a name*,
26. let *thy name* be magnified
8:13. David gat (him) *a name* when he returned
9: 2. of the house of Saul a servant *whose name*
12. *whose name* (was) Micha.
12:24. he called *his name* Solomon:
25. he called *his name* Jedidiah,
28. it be called after *my name*.
13: 1. a fair sister, *whose name* (was) Tamar;
3. had a friend, *whose name* (was) Jonadab,
14: 7. not leave to my husband (neither) *name*
27. daughter, *whose name* (was) Tamar:
16: 5. *whose name* (was) Shimei,
17:25. *whose name* (was) Ithra
18:18. I have no son to keep *my name*
— called the pillar after *his own name:*
20: 1. *whose name* (was) Sheba,
21. Sheba the son of Bichri *by name*, (marg. *his name*)
22:50. *and* I will sing praises *unto thy name*.
23: 8. *the names of* the mighty men
18. had *the name* among three.
22. had *the name* among three
1K. 1:47. God make *the name of* Solomon better *than thy name*,
3: 2. no house built *unto the name of* the
4: 8. these (are) *their names:*
31(5:11). *his fame* was in all nations
5: 3(17). build an house *unto the name of*
5(19). house *unto the name of* the Lord
—(—). shall build an house *unto my name*.
7:21. right pillar, and called *the name thereof* Jachin:
— left pillar, and called *the name thereof* Boaz.
8:16. that *my name* might be therein;
17, 20. house *for the name of* the Lord
18. build an house *unto my name*,
19. he shall build the house *unto my name*.
29. *My name* shall be there:
33. confess *thy name*, and pray,
35. confess *thy name*, and turn from their sin,
41. far country for *thy name*'s sake;
42. For they shall hear of *thy* great *name*,
43. all people of the earth may know *thy name*,
— I have builded, is called by *thy name*.
44, 48. I have built *for thy name:*
9: 3. to put *my name* there for ever;
7. I have hallowed *for my name*,
10: 1. *concerning the name of* the Lord,
11:26. *whose* mother's *name* (was) Zeruah,
36. chosen me to put *my name* there.
13: 2. house of David, Josiah *by name;*
14:21. to put *his name* there.
—, 31 & 15:2, 10. *And* his mother's *name* (was)
16:24. called *the name of* the city which he built, after *the name of* Shemer,
18:24. call ye *on the name of* your gods, and I will call *on the name of* the Lord:
25. call *on the name of* your gods,
26. called *on the name of* Baal
31. Israel shall be *thy name:*
32. an altar *in the name of* the Lord:
21: 8. So she wrote letters *in* Ahab's *name*,
22:16. true *in the name of* the Lord?
42. *And* his mother's *name* (was) Azubah
2K. 2:24. cursed them *in the name of* the Lord.
5:11. call *on the name of* the Lord
8:26. *And* his mother's *name* (was) Athaliah,
12: 1(2). *And* his mother's *name* (was)
14: 2. *And* his mother's *name* (was)
7. called *the name of it* Joktheel
27. he would blot out *the name of* Israel
15: 2, 33. *And* his mother's *name* (was)
17:34. *whom* he named (lit. he put *his name*) Israel;
18: 2. His mother's *name also* (was) Abi,
21: 1, 19. *And* his mother's *name*
4. In Jerusalem will I put *my name*.
7. will I put *my name* for ever:
22: 1. *And* his mother's *name*
23:27. *My name* shall be there.
31, 36. *And* his mother's *name*
34. turned *his name* to Jehoiakim,
24: 8, 18. *And* his mother's *name*
17. changed *his name* to Zedekiah.

1Ch 1:19. *the name of* the one (was) Peleg;
— *and* his brother's *name*
43, 46, 50. *and the name of* his city
50. *and* his wife's *name* (was)
2:26. *whose name* (was) Atarah;
29. *And the name of* the wife
34. *whose name* (was) Jarha.
4: 3. *and the name of* their sister
9. his mother called *his name* Jabez,
38. These mentioned *by* (their) *names*
41. these written *by name* came
5:24. men of valour, *famous* men, (marg. men of *names*)
6:17(2). *the names of* the sons of Gershom;
65(50). which are called *by* (their) *names*.
7:15. *whose* sister's *name* (was) Maachah; *and the name of* the second
16. she called *his name* Peresh; *and the name of* his brother
23. he called *his name* Beriah,
8:29. whose (lit. *and* his) wife's *name* (was) Maachah:
38. six sons, whose (lit. and *their*) *names* (are)
9:35. whose (lit. *and* his) wife's *name* (was)
44. six sons, whose (lit. and *their*) *names* (are)
11:20, 24. had *a name* among the three.
12:30. *famous* (marg. men of *names*) throughout
31. which were expressed *by name*,
13: 6. whose *name* is called
14: 4. these (are) *the names of* (his) children
11. they called *the name of* that place
17. *the fame of* David went out
16: 2. the people *in the name of* the Lord.
8. call *upon his name*,
10. Glory ye *in* his holy *name:*
29. the glory (due) unto *his name:*
35. we may give thanks *to* thy holy *name*,
41. who were expressed *by name*,
17: 8. have made thee *a name like the name of* the great men
21. to make thee *a name of* greatness
24. that *thy name* may be magnified
21:19. he spake *in the name of* the Lord.
22: 5. *of fame* and of glory
7. *unto the name of* the Lord
8. shalt not build an house *unto my name*,
9. for *his name* shall be Solomon,
10. shall build an house *for my name;*
19. built *to the name of* the Lord.
23:13. to bless *in his name* for ever.
24. by number of *names* by their polls,
28: 3. shalt not build an house *for my name*,
29:13. praise thy glorious *name*.
16. build thee an house *for* thine holy *name*
2Ch 2: 1(1:18). house *for the name of* the Lord,
4(3). I build an house *to the name of*
3:17. called *the name of* that on
— *and the name of* that on
6: 5, 6. that *my name* might be there;
7. an house *for the name of* the Lord
8. to build an house *for my name*,
9. he shall build the house *for my name*.
10. built the house *for the name of* the Lord
20. thou wouldest put *thy name* there;
24. shall return and confess *thy name*,
26. toward this place, and confess *thy name*,
32. far country for *thy* great *name*'s sake,
33. the earth may know *thy name*,
— is called by *thy name*.
34, 38. which I have built *for thy name;*
7:14. which are called by *my name*,
16. that *my name* may be there
20. which I have sanctified *for my name*,
12:13. tribes of Israel, to put *his name* there.
And his mother's *name* (was) Naamah
13: 2. His mother's *name also* (was)
14:11(10). *and in thy name* we go
18:15. the truth to me *in the name of*
20: 8. a sanctuary therein *for thy name*,
9. for *thy name* (is) in this house,
26. *the name of* the same place
31. *And* his mother's *name* (was) Azubah
22: 2. His mother's *name also* (was) Athaliah
24: 1. His mother's *name also* (was) Zibiah
25: 1. *And* his mother's *name* (was) Jehoaddan
26: 3. His mother's *name also* (was) Jecoliah
8. and *his name* spread abroad

2Ch 26:15. And *his name* spread far abroad ;
27: 1. His mother's *name also* (was) Jerushah,
28: 9. *whose name* (was) Oded:
15. which were expressed *by name*
29: 1. *And* his mother's *name* (was) Abijah,
31:19. men that were expressed *by name*,
33: 4. In Jerusalem shall *my name* be
7. will I put *my name* for ever:
18. spake to him *in the name of*
36: 4. turned *his name* to Jehoiakim.
Ezr. 2:61. was called after *their name:*
8:13. *whose names* (are) these,
20. all of them were expressed *by name.*
10:16. all of them *by* (their) *names*,
Neh. 1: 9. I have chosen to set *my name* there.
11. who desire to fear *thy name:*
6:13. might have (matter) *for an* evil *report*,
7:63. was called after *their name.*
9: 5. blessed be thy glorious *name*,
7. gavest *him the name* of Abraham ;
10. So didst thou get thee *a name*,
Est. 2: 5. *whose name* (was) Mordecai,
14. that she were called *by name.*
22. the king (thereof) *in* Mordecai's *name.*
3:12. *in the name of* king Ahasuerus
8: 8. as it liketh you, *in* the king's *name*,
— written *in* the king's *name*,
10. wrote *in* the king Ahasuerus' *name*,
9:26. after *the name of* Pur.
Job 1: 1. *whose name* (was) Job ;
21. blessed be *the name of* the Lord.
18:17. he shall have no *name*
30: 8. fools, yea, children of base men: (marg. men of no *name*)
42:14. he called *the name of* the first, Jemima ; *and the name of* the second, Kezia ; *and the name of* the third, Keren-happuch.
Ps. 5:11(12). let them also that love *thy name*
7:17(18). sing praise to *the name of* the Lord
8: 1(2), 9(10). how excellent (is) *thy name*
9: 2(3). I will sing praise to *thy name*,
5(6). thou hast put out *their name*
10(11). they that know *thy name*
16: 4. nor take up *their names*
18:49(50). *and* sing praises *unto thy name.*
20: 1(2). *the name of* the God of Jacob
5(6). *and in the name of* our God
7(8). remember *the name of* the Lord
22:22(23). I will declare *thy name* unto
23: 3. paths of righteousness for *his name*'s sake.
25:11. For *thy name*'s sake, O Lord,
29: 2. the Lord the glory due unto *his name;*
31: 3(4). therefore for *thy name*'s sake lead
33:21. we have trusted *in* his holy *name.*
34: 3(4). let us exalt *his name* together.
41: 5(6). When shall he die, and *his name*
44: 5(6). *through thy name* will we tread
8(9). *and* praise *thy name* for ever.
20(21). have forgotten *the name of* our God,
45:17(18). I will make *thy name* to be
48:10(11). *According to thy name*, O God, so (is) thy praise
49:11(12). lands *after their own names.*
52: 9(11). I will wait on *thy name ;*
54: 1(3). Save me, O God, *by thy name*,
6(8). I will praise *thy name*, O Lord ;
61: 5(6). heritage of those that fear *thy name.*
8(9). So will I sing praise unto *thy name*
63: 4(5). I will lift up my hands *in thy name.*
66: 2. Sing forth the honour of *his name:*
4. they shall sing (to) *thy name.*
68: 4(5). sing praises to *his name:*
—(—). upon the heavens by *his name* Jah,
69:30(31). I will praise *the name of* God
36(37). they that love *his name* shall
72:17. *His name* shall endure for ever: *his name* shall be continued
19. blessed (be) his glorious *name*
74: 7. the dwelling place of *thy name*
10. shall the enemy blaspheme *thy name*
18. foolish people have blasphemed *thy name.*
21. let the poor and needy praise *thy name.*
75: 1(2). *thy name* is near thy wondrous works
76: 1(2). *his name* (is) great in Israel.
79: 6. that have not called *upon thy name.*
9. for the glory of *thy name:*
— our sins, for *thy name*'s sake.

Ps. 80:18(19). *and* we will call *upon thy name.*
83: 4(5). that *the name of* Israel may be no
16(17). that they may seek *thy name*,
18(19). *whose name* alone (is) Jehovah,
86: 9. shall glorify *thy name.*
11. unite my heart to fear *thy name.*
12. I will glorify *thy name* for evermore.
89:12(13). and Hermon shall rejoice *in thy name.*
16(17). *In thy name* shall they rejoice
24(25). *and in my name* shall his horn be
91:14. because he hath known *my name.*
92: 1(2). to sing praises *unto thy name*,
96: 2. Sing unto the Lord, bless *his name ;*
8. the Lord the glory (due unto) *his name :*
99: 3. them praise *thy* great and terrible *name ;*
6. Samuel among them that call upon *his name ;*
100: 4. thankful unto him, (and) bless *his name.*
102:15(16). the heathen shall fear *the name of* the
21(22). To declare *the name of* the Lord
103: 1. that is within me, (bless) his holy *name.*
105: 1. call *upon his name:*
3. Glory ye *in* his holy *name:*
106: 8. he saved them for *his name*'s sake,
47. give thanks *unto* thy holy *name*,
109:13. let *their name* be blotted out.
21. for *thy name*'s sake:
111: 9. holy and reverend (is) *his name.*
113: 1. praise *the name of* the Lord.
2. Blessed be *the name of* the Lord
3. the Lord's *name* (is) to be praised.
115: 1. but *unto thy name* give glory,
116: 4. *Then* called I *upon the name of*
13. *and* call *upon the name of* the
17. *and* will call *upon the name of*
118:10, 11. but *in the name of* the Lord
12. for *in the name of* the Lord
26. Blessed (be) he that cometh *in the name of*
119:55. I have remembered *thy name*,
132. to do unto those that love *thy name.*
122: 4. to give thanks *unto the name of*
124: 8. Our help (is) *in the name*
129: 8. we bless you *in the name of*
135: 1. Praise ye *the name of* the Lord ;
3. sing praises *unto his name ;*
13. *Thy name*, O Lord, (endureth)
138: 2. praise *thy name* for thy lovingkindness
— magnified thy word above all *thy name.*
140:13(14). the righteous shall give thanks unto *thy name :*
142: 7(8). that I may praise *thy name :*
143:11. O Lord, for *thy name*'s sake:
145: 1. I will bless *thy name* for ever
2. I will praise *thy name* for ever and ever.
21. let all flesh bless his holy *name*
147: 4. calleth them all *by* (their) *names.*
148: 5. Let them praise *the name of* the Lord:
13. Let them praise *the name of* the Lord: for *his name* alone is excellent;
149: 3. Let them praise *his name* in the dance:
Pro. 10: 7. *but the name of* the wicked
18:10. *The name of* the Lord (is) a strong
21:24. (and) haughty scorner (is) *his name*,
22: 1. *A* (good) *name* (is) rather to be chosen
30: 4. what (is) *his name*, and what (is) his son's *name*,
9. take *the name of* my God (in vain).
Ecc. 6: 4. and *his name* shall be covered
10. That which hath been is *named* (lit. *the name thereof* is called) already,
7: 1. *A* good *name* (is) better than
Cant. 1: 3. *thy name* (is as) ointment poured forth,
Isa. 4: 1. only let us be called by *thy name*,
7:14. shall call *his name* Immanuel.
8: 3. Call *his name* Maher-shalal-hash-baz.
9: 6(5). *his name* shall be called Wonderful,
12: 4. call *upon his name*,
— make mention that *his name*
14:22. cut off from Babylon *the name*,
18: 7. to the place of *the name of* the Lord
24:15. (even) *the name of* the Lord God of
25: 1. I will praise *thy name ;*
26: 8. desire of (our) soul (is) *to thy name*,
13. make mention of *thy name.*
29:23. they shall sanctify *my name*,
30:27. *the name of* the Lord cometh
40:26. he calleth them all *by names*

Isa 41:25. shall he call *upon my name:*
42: 8. I (am) the Lord: that (is) *my name:*
43: 1. I have called (thee) *by thy name;*
7. every one that is called *by my name:*
44: 5. call (himself) *by the name of* Jacob;
— *and* surname (himself) *by the name of*
45: 3. which call (thee) *by thy name,*
4. called thee *by thy name:*
47: 4. the Lord of hosts (is) *his name,*
48: 1. called *by the name of* Israel,
— swear *by the name of* the Lord,
2. The Lord of hosts (is) *his name.*
9. For *my name's* sake
19. *his name* should not have
49: 1. hath he made mention of *my name.*
50:10. let him trust *in the name of*
51:15. The Lord of hosts (is) *his name.*
52: 5. and *my name* continually every day
6. my people shall know *my name:*
54: 5. the Lord of hosts (is) *his name;*
55:13. it shall be to the Lord *for a name,*
56: 5. *a name* better than of sons
— I will give them *an* everlasting *name,*
6. to serve him, and to love *the name of* the
57:15. *whose name* (is) Holy;
59:19. they fear *the name of* the Lord
60: 9. *unto the name of* the Lord
62: 2. thou shalt be called by *a* new *name,*
63:12. to make himself *an* everlasting *name?*
14. to make thyself *a* glorious *name.*
16. *thy name* (is) from everlasting.
19. they were not called by *thy name.*
64: 2(1). to make *thy name* known
7(6). none that calleth *upon thy name,*
65: 1. nation (that) was not called *by my name.*
15. ye shall leave *your name*
— slay thee, and call his servants by another *name:*
66: 5. that cast you out for *my name's* sake,
22. so shall your seed *and your name*
Jer. 3:17. *to the name of* the Lord,
7:10, 11, 14, 30. which is called by *my name,*
12. where I set *my name* at the first,
10: 6. and *thy name* (is) great in might.
16. The Lord of hosts (is) *his name.*
25. the families that call not *on thy name:*
11:16. The Lord called *thy name,*
19. *that his name* may be no more
21. Prophesy not *in the name of* the Lord,
12:16. the ways of my people, to swear *by my name,*
13:11. for a people, *and for a name,*
14: 7. do thou (it) for *thy name's* sake:
9. *and* we are called by *thy name;*
14. The prophets prophesy lies *in my name:*
15. concerning the prophets that prophesy *in my name,*
21. Do not abhor (us), for *thy name's* sake,
15:16. for I am called by *thy name,*
16:21. shall know that *my name* (is) The Lord.
20: 3. hath not called *thy name* Pashur,
9. nor speak any more *in his name.*
23: 6. this (is) *his name* whereby
25. that prophesy lies *in my name,* saying,
27. to forget *my name* by their dreams
— their fathers have forgotten *my name*
25:29. which is called by *my name,*
26: 9. prophesied *in the name of* the Lord,
16. hath spoken to us *in the name of*
20. that prophesied *in the name of*
27:15. yet they prophesy a lie *in my name;*
29: 9. they prophesy falsely unto you *in my name:*
21. which prophesy a lie unto you *in my name;*
23. and have spoken lying words *in my name,*
25. hast sent letters *in thy name*
31:35 & 32:18. The Lord of hosts (is) *his name:*
32:20. hast made thee *a name,*
34. which is called by *my name,*
33: 2. the Lord (is) *his name;*
9. it shall be to me *a name of* joy,
34:15. which is called by *my name:*
16. ye turned and polluted *my name,*
37:13. *whose name* (was) Irijah,
44:16. the word that thou hast spoken...*in the name of* the Lord,
26. I have sworn *by my* great *name,*
— that *my name* shall no more be named

Jer. 46:18 & 48:15. *whose name* (is) the Lord of hosts,
48:17. all ye that know *his name,*
50:34 & 51:19. the Lord of hosts (is) *his name:*
51:57. saith the king, *whose name* (is) the Lord
52: 1. *And* his mother's *name* (was)
Lam. 3:55. I called upon *thy name,*
Eze. 16:14. thy *renown* went forth
15. because of *thy renown,*
20: 9, 14, 22. wrought for *my name's* sake,
29. And *the name thereof* is called
39. but pollute ye my holy *name*
44. wrought with you for *my name's* sake,
22: 5. shall mock thee, (which art) in*famous* (marg. polluted of *name*)
23: 4. *And the names of them*
— *Thus* (were) *their names;*
10. and she became *famous* (marg. *a name*)
24: 2. write thee *the name of* the day,
34:29. raise up for them a plant *of renown,*
36:20. they profaned my holy *name,*
21. But I had pity for mine holy *name,*
22. but *for* mine holy *name's* sake,
23. I will sanctify *my* great *name,*
39: 7. So will I make my holy *name*
— pollute my holy *name*
13. it shall be to them *a renown*
16. also *the name of* the city
25. will be jealous *for* my holy *name;*
43: 7. for ever, and my holy *name,*
8. have even defiled my holy *name*
48: 1. Now these (are) *the names of* the tribes.
31. after *the names of* the tribes
35. *and the name of* the city
Dan 1: 7. prince of the eunuchs gave *names:*
9: 6. which spake *in thy name*
15. hast gotten thee *renown,*
18. the city which is called by *thy name:*
19. thy people are called by *thy name.*
10: 1. Daniel, *whose name* was called
Hos. 1: 4. Call *his name* Jezreel;
6. Call *her name* Lo-ruhamah:
9. Call *his name* Lo-ammi:
2:17(19). I will take away *the names of*
—(—). no more be remembered *by their name.*
Joel 2:26. praise *the name of* the Lord
32(3:5). shall call *on the name of* the Lord
Am. 2: 7. to profane my holy *name:*
4:13. The God of hosts, (is) *his name.*
5: 8. The Lord (is) *his name:*
27. *whose name* (is) The God of hosts.
6:10. we may not make mention *of the name of*
9: 6. The Lord (is) *his name.*
12. which are called by *my name,*
Mic. 4: 5. walk every one *in the name of* his god, and we will walk *in the name of*
5: 4(3). in the majesty of *the name of*
6: 9. wisdom shall see *thy name:*
Nah 1:14. no more *of thy name* be sown:
Zep. 1: 4. *the name of* the Chemarims
3: 9. that they may all call *upon the name of*
12. they shall trust *in the name of*
19. I will get them praise *and fame*
20. for I will make you *a name*
Zec. 5: 4. that sweareth falsely *by my name:*
6:12. the man *whose name* (is) The Branch;
10:12. *and* they shall walk up and down *in his name,*
13: 2. I will cut off *the names of* the idols
3. thou speakest lies *in the name of*
9. they shall call *on my name,*
14: 9. one Lord, *and his name* one.
Mal. 1: 6. O priests, that despise *my name.*
— Wherein have we despised *thy name?*
11. *my name* (shall be) great among the
— incense (shall be) offered *unto my name,*
— *my name* (shall be) great among the
14. *and my name* (is) dreadful among the
2: 2. to give glory *unto my name,*
5. was afraid before *my name.*
3:16. that thought upon *his name.*
4: 2(3:20). But unto you that fear *my name*

שֻׁם *shoom,* Ch. m. 8036

Ezr. 5: 1. *in the name of* the God of Israel,
4. What are *the names of* the men

Ezr. 5:10. We asked *their names* also,
— that we might write *the names of*
14. unto (one), *whose name* (was) Sheshbazzar,
6:12. that hath caused *his name* to dwell there
Dan 2:20. Blessed be *the name* of God for ever
26 & 4:8(5). *whose name* (was) Belteshazzar,
4: 8(5). *according to the name of* my god,
19(16). Daniel, *whose name* (was)
5:12. whom the king *named* (lit. put *his name*) Belteshazzar:

8045 שָׁמַד [*shāh-mad'*].

* NIPHAL.—*Preterite.* *

Gen 34:30. *and I shall be destroyed,*
Jud. 21:16. seeing the women *are destroyed*
2Sa. 21: 5. *we should be destroyed*
Ps. 37:38. transgressors *shall be destroyed*
83:10(11). (Which) *perished* at En-dor:
Jer. 48: 8. *and* the plain *shall be destroyed,*
42. *And* Moab *shall be destroyed*
Eze. 32:12. *and* all the multitude thereof *shall be destroyed.*
Hos. 10: 8. *also* of Aven, the sin of Israel, *shall be destroyed:*

NIPHAL.—*Infinitive.*

Deu 4:26. shall *utterly* be destroyed. (lit. *being destroyed* shall be destroyed)
7:23. until *they be destroyed.*
12:30. after that *they be destroyed*
28:20. until *thou be destroyed,*
24, 51, 61. until *thou be destroyed.*
45. till *thou be destroyed;*
Ps. 92: 7(8). *that they shall be destroyed*

NIPHAL.—*Future.*

Deu 4:26. but *shall* utterly *be destroyed.*
Pro. 14:11. of the wicked *shall be overthrown:*
Isa. 48:19. should not have been cut off nor *destroyed*

* HIPHIL.—*Preterite.* *

Lev. 26:30. *And I will destroy* your high places,
Deu 2:22. when *he destroyed* the Horims
23. out of Caphtor, *destroyed them,*
4: 3. thy God *hath destroyed them*
6:15. *and destroy thee* from off the face of
7: 4. *and destroy thee* suddenly.
31: 4. whom *he destroyed.*
1K. 15:29. until *he had destroyed him,*
2K. 10:17. till *he had destroyed him,*
21: 9. nations whom the Lord *destroyed*
1Ch 5:25. whom God *destroyed* before them.
2Ch 20:10. *destroyed them* not;
33: 9. whom the Lord *had destroyed*
Ps. 106:34. *They did* not *destroy* the nations,
Eze. 14: 9. *and will destroy him* from the
Am. 2: 9. Yet *destroyed* I the Amorite
9: 8. *and I will destroy* it from off
Mic. 5:14(13). *so will I destroy* thy cities.
Hag 2:22. *and I will destroy* the strength

HIPHIL.—*Infinitive.*

Deu 1:27. hand of the Amorites, *to destroy us.*
7:24. until *thou have destroyed* them.
9: 8. *to have destroyed* you.
19. wroth against you *to destroy* you.
20. with Aaron *to have destroyed him:*
25. the Lord had said he *would destroy* you.
28:48. until *he have destroyed* thee.
63. *and to bring* you *to nought;*
Jos. 9:24. *and to destroy* all the inhabitants
11:14. until *they had destroyed them,*
20. but that he *might destroy them,*
23:15. until *he have destroyed* you
2Sa. 14:16. the man (that would) *destroy* me
1K. 13:34. *and to destroy* (it) from off
2Ch 20:23. utterly to slay *and destroy*
Est. 3: 6. Haman sought *to destroy*
13. *to destroy,* to kill,
4: 8. at Shushan *to destroy them,*
7: 4. *to be destroyed* (marg. *that they should destroy*), to be slain, and to perish.
8:11. *to destroy,* to slay,
Ps. 106:23. said *that he would destroy them,*
Isa. 10: 7. in his heart *to destroy* and cut off
14:23. with the besom of *destruction,*
23:11. *to destroy* the strong holds
Dan 11:44. go forth with great fury *to destroy,*
Am. 9: 8. saving that I will not *utterly* destroy (lit. *destroying* I will destroy)
Zec. 12: 9. seek *to destroy* all the nations

HIPHIL.—*Imperative.*

Deu 33:27. shall say, *Destroy* (them).

HIPHIL.—*Future.*

Nu. 33:52. *quite pluck down* all their high places:
Deu 2:12. *when they had destroyed them*
21. *but* the Lord *destroyed* them
9: 3. a consuming fire he *shall destroy them,*
14. alone, *that I may destroy them,*
31: 3. he *will destroy* these nations
Jos. 7:12. except *ye destroy* the accursed
24: 8. *and I destroyed them* from before you.
1Sa. 24:21(22). that *thou wilt* not *destroy* my name
2Sa. 14: 7. *and we will destroy* the heir
11. lest *they destroy* my son.
22:38. mine enemies, *and destroyed them;*
1K. 16:12. *Thus did* Zimri *destroy* all
2K. 10:28. *Thus* Jehu *destroyed* Baal
Ps. 145:20. all the wicked *will he destroy.*
Isa. 13: 9. *he shall destroy* the sinners
26:14. hast thou visited *and destroyed them,*
Lam 3:66. Persecute *and destroy them*
Eze. 25: 7. *I will destroy thee;* and thou
34:16. but *I will destroy* the fat
Am. 2: 9. *yet I destroyed* his fruit
9: 8. *I will* not utterly *destroy* the house

שְׁמַד [*sh'mad*], Ch. 8046

* APHEL.—*Infinitive.* *

Dan 7:26. *to consume* and to destroy (it) unto the

שַׁמָּה *sham-māh'*, f. 8047

Deu 28:37. thou shalt become *an astonishment,*
2K. 22:19. they should become *a desolation*
2Ch 29: 8. to trouble, *to astonishment,*
30: 7. gave them up *to desolation,*
Ps. 46: 8(9). what *desolations* he hath made
73:19. How are they (brought) *into desolation,*
Isa. 5: 9. many houses shall be *desolate,*
13: 9. to lay the land *desolate:*
24:12. In the city is left *desolation,*
Jer. 2:15. they made his land *waste:*
4: 7. to make thy land *desolate;*
5:30. *A wonderful* and horrible *thing*
8:21. *astonishment* hath taken hold
18:16. To make their land *desolate,*
19: 8. I will make this city *desolate,*
25: 9. make them *an astonishment,*
11. desolation, (and) *an astonishment;*
18. a desolation, *an astonishment,*
38. for their land is *desolate*
29:18. a curse, *and an astonishment,*
42:18. execration, *and an astonishment,*
44:12. *an astonishment,* and a curse,
22. desolation, *and an astonishment,*
46:19. Noph shall be *waste* and desolate without
48: 9. cities thereof shall be *desolate,*
49:13. Bozrah shall become *a desolation,*
17. Edom shall be *a desolation:*
50: 3. shall make her land *desolate,*
23. Babylon become *a desolation*
51:29. land of Babylon *a desolation*
37. *an astonishment,* and an hissing,
41. Babylon become *an astonishment*
43. Her cities are *a desolation,*
Eze. 23:33. the cup of *astonishment*
Hos 5: 9. Ephraim shall be *desolate*
Joel 1: 7. He hath laid my vine *waste,*
Mic. 6:16. make thee *a desolation,* (marg. or, *astonishment*)
Zep 2:15. how is she become *a desolation,*
Zec. 7:14. the pleasant land *desolate.*

שְׁמוּעָה *sh'moo-ĝāh'*, f. 8052

1Sa. 2:24. no good *report* that I hear:
4:19. when she heard *the tidings*
2Sa. 4: 4. five years old when *the tidings* came

2Sa.13:30. *that tidings* came to David,
1K. 2:28. *Then tidings* came to Joab:
10: 7. exceedeth *the fame* which I heard.
2K. 19: 7. and he shall hear *a rumour,*
2Ch 9: 6. exceedest *the fame* that I heard.
Ps.112: 7. He shall not be afraid *of* evil *tidings:*
Pro.15:30. *a* good *report* maketh the bones fat.
25:25. *so* (is) good *news* from a far country.
Isa. 28: 9. whom shall he make to understand *doctrine?* (marg. *hearing*)
19. only (to) understand *the report.* (marg. *doctrine*)
37: 7. he shall hear *a rumour,*
53: 1. Who hath believed *our report?* (marg. *hearing,* or, *doctrine*)
Jer. 10:22. the noise of *the bruit* is come,
49:14. I have heard *a rumour* from the Lord,
23. for they have heard evil *tidings:*
51:46. fear for *the rumour* that shall be
— *a rumour* shall both come
— in (another) year (shall come) *a rumour,*
Eze. 7:26. *and rumour* shall be upon *rumour;* then shall they
16:56. thy sister Sodom was not *mentioned* (marg. *for a report,* or, *hearing*)
21: 7(12). thou shalt answer, For *the tidings;*
Dan11:44. *But tidings* out of the east
Obad. 1. We have heard *a rumour* from the Lord,

8058 שָׁמַט [*shāh-mat'*].

* KAL.—*Preterite.* *

2Sa. 6: 6. for the oxen *shook* (it). (marg. or, *stumbled*)
1Ch 13: 9. ark; for the oxen *stumbled.* (marg. or, *shook* it)
Jer. 17: 4. *And thou,* even thyself, *shalt discontinue*

KAL.—*Infinitive.*

Deu15: 2. unto his neighbour *shall release*

KAL.—*Imperative.*

2K. 9:33. And he said, *Throw her down.*

KAL.—*Future.*

Ex. 23:11. seventh (year) *thou shalt let it rest*
2K. 9:33. *So they threw her down:*

* NIPHAL.—*Preterite.* *

Ps.141: 6. When their judges *are overthrown*

* HIPHIL.—*Future.* *

Deu 15: 3. with thy brother thine hand *shall release;*

8059 שְׁמִטָּה *sh'mit-tāh',* f.

Deu15: 1. seven years thou shalt make *a release.*
2. this (is) the manner of *the release:*
— it is called the Lord's *release.*
9. the year of *release,* is at hand;
31:10. the solemnity of the year of *release,*

8064 שָׁמַיִם *shāh-mah'-yim,* m. dual.

Gen 1: 1. In the beginning God created *the heaven* and the earth.
8. God called the firmament *Heaven.*
9. Let the waters under *the heaven* be
14, 15. lights in the firmament of *the heaven*
17. set them in the firmament of *the heaven*
20. in the open firmament of *heaven.*
26, 28. the fowl of *the air,*
30. every fowl of *the air,*
2: 1. *the heavens* and the earth were finished,
4. the generations of *the heavens*
— God made the earth *and the heavens,*
19. every fowl of *the air;*
20. gave names...to the fowl of *the air,*
6: 7. the fowls of *the air;*
17. all flesh,...from under *heaven;*
7: 3. Of fowls also of *the air* by sevens,
11. the windows of *heaven* were opened.
19. that (were) under *the* whole *heaven,*
23. the fowl of *the heaven;*
8: 2. the windows of *heaven* were stopped, and the rain from *heaven* was restrained;
Gen 9: 2. upon every fowl of *the air,*
11: 4. whose top (may reach) *unto heaven;*
14:19. possessor of *heaven* and earth:
22. the possessor of *heaven* and earth,
15: 5. Look now *toward heaven,*
19:24. the Lord rained...out of *heaven;*
21:17. the angel of God called to Hagar out of *heaven,*
22:11, 15. of the Lord called...out of *heaven,*
17. thy seed as the stars of the *heaven,*
24: 3. the Lord, the God of *heaven,*
7. The Lord God of *heaven,*
26: 4. make thy seed...as the stars of *heaven,*
27:28. God give thee of the dew of *heaven,*
39. the dew of *heaven* from above;
28:12. a ladder...the top of it reached *to heaven:*
17. this (is) the gate of *heaven.*
49:25. bless thee with blessings of *heaven*
Ex. 9: 8. sprinkle it *toward the heaven*
10. Moses sprinkled it up *toward heaven;*
22. Stretch forth thine hand toward *heaven,*
23. stretched forth his rod toward *heaven:*
10:21. Stretch out thine hand toward *heaven,*
22. stretched forth his hand toward *heaven;*
16: 4. I will rain bread from *heaven*
17:14. put out the remembrance of Amalek from under *heaven.*
20: 4. likeness (of any thing) that (is) *in heaven*
11. the Lord made *heaven* and earth,
22. I have talked with you from *heaven.*
24:10. as it were the body of *heaven*
31:17. the Lord made *heaven* and earth,
32:13. multiply your seed as the stars of *heaven,*
Lev.26:19. I will make *your heaven* as iron,
Deu 1:10. as the stars of *heaven* for multitude.
28. (are) great and walled up *to heaven;*
2:25. (that are) under *the* whole *heaven,*
3:24. what God (is there) *in heaven*
4:11. unto the midst of *heaven,*
17. any winged fowl that flieth *in the air,*
19. lift up thine eyes *unto heaven,*
— all the host of *heaven,*
— all nations under *the* whole *heaven.*
26. I call *heaven* and earth to witness
32. from the one side of *heaven* unto the other, (lit. from the side of *heaven* unto the side of *heaven*)
36. Out of *heaven* he made thee to hear his
39. God *in heaven* above,
5: 8. any likeness...*in heaven* above,
7:24. destroy their name from under *heaven:*
9: 1. cities great and fenced up *to heaven,*
14. blot out their name from under *heaven:*
10:14. *the heaven and the heaven of heavens* (is) the Lord's thy God,
22. as the stars of *heaven* for multitude.
11:11. water of the rain of *heaven:*
17. he shut up *the heaven,*
21. as the days of *heaven* upon the earth.
17: 3. any of the host of *heaven,*
25:19. blot out the remembrance of Amalek from under *heaven;*
26:15. Look down...from *heaven,*
28:12. *the heaven* to give the rain
23. *thy heaven* that (is) over thy head
24. from *heaven* shall it come down
26. all fowls of *the air,*
62. as the stars of *heaven* for multitude;
29:20(19). out his name from under *heaven.*
30: 4. the utmost (parts) of *heaven,*
12. It (is) not *in heaven,*
— Who shall go up for us *to heaven,*
19. I call *heaven* and earth to record
31:28. and call *heaven* and earth to record
32: 1. Give ear, *O ye heavens,*
40. I lift up my hand to *heaven,*
33:13. the precious things of *heaven,*
26. rideth upon *the heaven*
28. *his heavens* shall drop down dew.
Jos. 2:11. God *in heaven* above,
8:20. the smoke...ascended up *to heaven,*
10:11. Lord cast down great stones from *heaven*
13. the sun stood still in the midst of *heaven,*
Jud. 5: 4. *the heavens* dropped,
20. They fought from *heaven;*
13:20. the flame went up *toward heaven*
20:40. the flame...ascended up *to heaven.*

1Sa. 2:10. *out of heaven* shall he thunder
5:12. the cry of the city went up to *heaven.*
17:44. thy flesh unto the fowls of *the air,*
46. I will give the carcases...unto the fowls of *the air,*
2Sa. 18: 9. taken up between *the heaven* and the
21:10. until water dropped...out of *heaven,*
— the birds of *the air*
22: 8. the foundations of *heaven* moved
10. He bowed *the heavens* also,
14. The Lord thundered from *heaven,*
1K. 8:22. spread forth his hands toward *heaven:*
23. no God like thee, *in heaven* above,
27. behold, *the heaven and heaven of heavens* cannot contain thee;
30. hear thou in *heaven* thy dwelling place:
32, 34, 36, 39, 43, 45. hear thou in *heaven,*
35. When *heaven* is shut up,
49. Then hear thou...in *heaven*
54. his hands spread up to *heaven.*
14:11 & 16:4. shall the fowls of *the air* eat:
18:45. *that the heaven* was black with clouds
21:24. the fowls of *the air*
22:19. all the host of *heaven*
2K. 1:10. let fire come down from *heaven,*
— there came down fire from *heaven,*
12. let fire come down from *heaven,*
— the fire of God came down from *heaven,*
14. there came fire down from *heaven,*
2: 1. when the Lord would take up Elijah into *heaven*
11. Elijah went up...*into heaven.*
7: 2. the Lord would make windows *in heaven,*
19. the Lord should make windows *in heaven,*
14:27. out the name of Israel from under *heaven:*
17:16. worshipped all the host of *heaven,*
19:15. thou hast made *heaven* and earth.
21: 3. worshipped all the host of *heaven,*
5. built altars for all the host of *heaven*
23: 4, 5. all the host of *heaven:*
1Ch 16:26. the Lord made *the heavens.*
31. Let *the heavens* be glad,
21:16. stand between the earth and *the heaven,*
26. he answered him from *heaven*
27:23. the stars of *the heavens.*
29:11. all (that is) *in the heaven* and in the
2Ch 2: 6(5). seeing *the heaven and heaven of heavens* cannot contain him?
12(11). God of Israel, that made *heaven* and
6:13. spread forth his hands *toward heaven,*
14. no God like thee *in the heaven,*
18. behold, *heaven and the heaven of heavens* cannot contain thee;
21. hear thou from thy dwelling place, (even) from *heaven;*
23. Then hear thou from *heaven,*
25. Then hear thou from *the heavens,*
26. When *the heaven* is shut up,
27, 30. Then hear thou from *heaven,*
33, 35, 39. Then hear thou from *the heavens,*
7: 1. the fire came down *from heaven,*
13. If I shut up *heaven*
14. then will I hear from *heaven,*
18:18. all the host of *heaven*
20: 6. (art) not thou God *in heaven?*
28: 9. a rage (that) reacheth up *unto heaven.*
30:27. their prayer came (up)...*unto heaven.*
32:20. the prophet Isaiah...prayed and cried *to heaven.*
33: 3. worshipped all the host of *heaven,*
5. built altars for all the host of *heaven*
36:23. hath the Lord God of *heaven* given me;
Ezr. 1: 2. The Lord God of *heaven* hath given
9: 6. our trespass is grown up *unto the heavens.*
Neh 1: 4. prayed before the God of *heaven,*
5. O Lord God of *heaven,*
9. the uttermost part of *the heaven,*
2: 4. I prayed to the God of *heaven.*
20. The God of *heaven,* he will prosper us;
9: 6. thou hast made *heaven, the heaven of heavens,* with all their host,
— the host of *heaven* worshippeth thee.
13. spakest with them *from heaven,*
15. gavest them bread *from heaven*
23. multipliedst thou as the stars of *heaven,*
27, 28. thou heardest (them) *from heaven;*
Job 1:16. The fire of God is fallen from *heaven,*

Job 2:12. sprinkled dust...*toward heaven.*
9: 8. Which alone spreadeth out *the heavens,*
11: 8. as high as *heaven;* what canst thou do?
12: 7. the fowls of *the air*
14:12. till *the heavens* (be) no more.
15:15. *yea, the heavens* are not clean in his light
16:19. my witness (is) *in heaven,*
20: 6. his excellency mount up *to the heavens,*
27. *The heaven* shall reveal his iniquity;
22:12. (Is) not God in the height of *heaven?*
14. he walketh in the circuit of *heaven.*
26:11. The pillars of *heaven* tremble
13. By his spirit he hath garnished *the heavens;*
28:21. kept close from the fowls of *the air.*
24. seeth under *the* whole *heaven;*
35: 5. Look unto *the heavens,*
11. maketh us wiser than the fowls of *heaven?*
37: 3. He directeth it under *the* whole *heaven,*
38:29. the hoary frost of *heaven,*
33. Knowest thou the ordinances of *heaven?*
37. who can stay the bottles of *heaven,*
41:11(3). (whatsoever is) under *the* whole *heaven*
Ps. 2: 4. He that sitteth *in the heavens*
8: 1(2). hast set thy glory above *the heavens.*
3(4). When I consider *thy heavens,*
8(9). The fowl of *the air,*
11: 4. the Lord's throne (is) *in heaven:*
14: 2. The Lord looked down *from heaven*
18: 9(10). He bowed *the heavens* also,
13(14). The Lord also thundered *in the heavens,*
19: 1(2). *The heavens* declare the glory of God;
6(7). from the end of *the heaven,*
20: 6(7). he will hear him *from* his holy *heaven*
33: 6. By the word of the Lord were *the heavens*
13. The Lord looketh *from heaven;*
36: 5(6). Thy mercy, O Lord, (is) *in the heavens;*
50: 4. He shall call to *the heavens*
6. *the heavens* shall declare his righteousness:
53: 2(3). God looked down *from heaven*
57: 3(4). He shall send *from heaven,* and save
5(6). Be thou exalted, O God, above *the heavens;*
10(11). thy mercy (is) great unto *the heavens,*
11(12). Be thou exalted, O God, above *the heavens:*
68: 8(9). The earth shook, *the heavens* also
33(34). him that rideth *upon the heavens of heavens,* (which were) of old;
69:34(35). Let *the heaven* and earth praise him,
73: 9. They set their mouth *against the heavens,*
25. Whom have I *in heaven* (but thee)?
76: 8(9). Thou didst cause judgment to be heard *from heaven;*
78:23. opened the doors of *heaven,*
24. given them of the corn of *heaven.*
26. caused an east wind to blow *in the heaven:*
79: 2. the fowls of *the heaven,*
80:14(15). look down *from heaven,*
85:11(12). righteousness shall look down *from heaven.*
89: 2(3). thy faithfulness shalt thou establish in *the* very *heavens.*
5(6). *the heavens* shall praise thy wonders,
11(12). *The heavens* (are) thine,
29(30). his throne as the days of *heaven.*
96: 5. the Lord made *the heavens.*
11. Let *the heavens* rejoice,
97: 6. *The heavens* declare his righteousness,
102:19(20). *from heaven* did the Lord behold
25(26). *the heavens* (are) the work of thy
103:11. *the heaven* is high above the earth,
19. The Lord hath prepared his throne *in the heavens;*
104: 2. stretchest out *the heavens* like a curtain:
12. the fowls of *the heaven*
105:40. the bread of *heaven.*
107:26. They mount up to *the heaven,*
108: 4(5). thy mercy (is) great above *the heavens:*
5(6). Be thou exalted, O God, above *the heavens:*
113: 4. his glory above *the heavens.*
6. (the things that are) *in heaven,*
115: 3. our God (is) *in the heavens:*
15. the Lord which made *heaven* and earth.
16. *The heaven,* (even) *the heavens,* (are) the Lord's:

Ps.119:89. thy word is settled *in heaven.*
121: 2. the Lord, which made *heaven* and earth.
123: 1. O thou that dwellest *in the heavens.*
124: 8. the Lord, who made *heaven* and earth.
134: 3. The Lord that made *heaven* and earth
135: 6. *in heaven*, and in earth,
136: 5. To him that by wisdom made *the heavens:*
26. O give thanks unto the God of *heaven:*
139: 8. If I ascend up *into heaven*,
144: 5. Bow *thy heavens*, O Lord,
146: 6. Which made *heaven*, and earth,
147: 8. Who covereth *the heaven* with clouds,
148: 1. Praise ye the Lord from *the heavens:*
4. Praise him, ye *heavens of heavens*, and ye waters that (be) above *the heavens.*
13. his glory (is) above the earth *and heaven.*
Pro. 3:19. by understanding hath he established *the heavens.*
8:27. When he prepared *the heavens*,
23: 5. fly away as an eagle toward *heaven.*
25: 3. *The heaven* for height,
30: 4. Who hath ascended up into *heaven*,
19. The way of an eagle *in the air;*
Ecc. 1:13. (things) that are done under *heaven:*
2: 3. should do under *the heaven*
3: 1. time to every purpose under *the heaven:*
5: 2(1). God (is) *in heaven*,
10:20. a bird of *the air* shall carry the voice,
Isa. 1: 2. Hear, *O heavens*,
13: 5. from the end of *heaven*,
10. the stars of *heaven*
13. I will shake *the heavens*,
14:12. How art thou fallen *from heaven*,
13. I will ascend into *heaven*,
34: 4. all the host of *heaven*
— *the heavens* shall be rolled together
5. my sword shall be bathed *in heaven:*
37:16. thou hast made *heaven* and earth.
40:12. *and* meted out *heaven* with the span,
22. that stretcheth out *the heavens* as a curtain,
42: 5. he that created *the heavens*,
44:23. Sing, *O ye heavens;*
24. stretcheth forth *the heavens* alone;
45: 8. Drop down, *ye heavens*,
12. have stretched out *the heavens*,
18. the Lord that created *the heavens:*
47:13. the *astro*logers, (marg. viewers of *the heavens*)
48:13. my right hand hath spanned *the heavens:*
49:13. Sing, *O heavens;* and be joyful,
50: 3. I clothe *the heavens* with blackness,
51: 6. Lift up your eyes *to the heavens*,
— *the heavens* shall vanish away
13. hath stretched forth *the heavens*,
16. that I may plant *the heavens*,
55: 9. *the heavens* are higher than the earth,
10. as the rain cometh down,...from *heaven*,
63:15. Look down *from heaven*,
64: 1(63:19). Oh that thou wouldest rend *the heavens*,
65:17. I create new *heavens* and a new earth:
66: 1. *The heaven* (is) my throne,
22. *the* new *heavens* and the new earth,
Jer. 2:12. Be astonished, *O ye heavens*,
4:23. *the heavens*, and they (had) no light.
25. all the birds of *the heavens* were fled.
28. *the heavens* above be black:
7:18. to make cakes to the queen of *heaven*,
33. meat for the fowls of *the heaven*,
8: 2. all the host of *heaven*,
7. the stork *in the heaven*
9:10(9). the fowl of *the heavens*
10: 2. be not dismayed at the signs of *heaven;*
12. hath stretched out *the heavens*
13. a multitude of waters *in the heavens*,
14:22. can *the heavens* give showers?
15: 3. the fowls of *the heaven*,
16: 4. meat for the fowls of *heaven*,
19: 7. meat for the fowls of *the heaven*,
13. all the host of *heaven*,
23:24. Do not I fill *heaven* and earth?
31:37. If *heaven* above can be measured,
32:17. thou hast made *the heaven* and the earth
33:22. the host of *heaven*
25. the ordinances of *heaven*
34:20. meat unto the fowls of *the heaven*,
44:17. to burn incense unto the queen of *heaven*,
Jer. 44:18, 25. to burn incense to the queen of *heaven*,
19. burned incense to the queen of *heaven*,
49:36. the four quarters of *heaven*,
51: 9. her judgment reacheth unto *heaven*,
15. hath stretched out *the heaven*
16. a multitude of waters *in the heavens;*
48. *the heaven* and the earth,...shall sing
53. Though Babylon should mount up to *heaven*,
Lam 2: 1. cast down *from heaven* unto the earth
3:41. lift up our heart...unto God *in the heavens.*
50. Till the Lord...behold *from heaven.*
66. destroy them in anger from under *the heavens of* the Lord.
4:19. the eagles of *the heaven:*
Eze. 1: 1. *the heavens* were opened,
8: 3. lifted me up between the earth and *the heaven*,
29: 5. given thee for meat to the...fowls of *the heaven.*
31: 6. All the fowls of *heaven* made their nests
13. shall all the fowls of *the heaven* remain,
32: 4. all the fowls of *the heaven* to remain
7. I will cover *the heaven*,
8. All the bright lights *of heaven*
38:20. the fowls of *the heaven*,
Dan 8: 8. the four winds of *heaven.*
10. the host of *heaven;*
9:12. under *the* whole *heaven*
11: 4. toward the four winds of *heaven;*
12: 7. held up his right hand and his left hand unto *heaven*,
Hos. 2:18(20). the fowls of *heaven*,
21(23). I will hear *the heavens*,
4: 3. the fowls of *heaven;*
7:12. I will bring them down as the fowls of *the heaven;*
Joel 2:10. *the heavens* shall tremble:
30(3:3). I will shew wonders *in the heavens*
3:16(4:16). *the heavens* and the earth shall
Am. 9: 2. though they climb up to *heaven*,
6. he that buildeth his stories *in the heaven*,
Jon. 1: 9. the Lord, the God of *heaven*,
Nah. 3:16. above the stars of *heaven:*
Hab. 3: 3. His glory covered *the heavens*,
Zep. 1: 3. I will consume the fowls of *the heaven*,
5. them that worship the host of *heaven*
Hag. 1:10. *the heaven* over you is stayed
2: 6. I will shake *the heavens*, and the earth,
21. I will shake *the heavens* and the earth;
Zec. 2: 6(10). the four winds of *the heaven*,
5: 9. between the earth and *the heaven.*
6: 5. the four spirits of *the heavens*,
8:12. *and the heavens* shall give their dew;
12: 1. stretcheth forth *the heavens*,
Mal. 3:10. will not open you the windows of *heaven*,

שְׁמַיִן [*sh'mah'-yin*], Ch. m. dual. 8065

Ezr. 5:11. We are the servants of the God of *heaven*
12. fathers had provoked the God of *heaven*
6: 9. the burnt offerings of the God of *heaven*,
10. sweet savours unto the God of *heaven*,
7:12, 21. scribe of the law of the God of *heaven*
23. commanded by the God of *heaven*,
— for the house of the God of *heaven:*
Jer. 10:11. The gods that have not made *the heavens*
— and from under these *heavens.*
Dan 2:18. would desire mercies of the God of *heaven*
19. Then Daniel blessed the God of *heaven.*
28. there is a God *in heaven* that revealeth
37. for the God of *heaven* hath given thee
38. and the fowls of *the heaven*
44. shall the God of *heaven* set up a
4:11(8). the height thereof reached *unto heaven*,
12(9). the fowls of *the heaven* dwelt in the boughs
13(10). an holy one came down from *heaven;*
15(12), 23(20). let it be wet with the dew of *heaven*,
20(17). whose height reached *unto the heaven*,
21(18). the fowls of *the heaven* had their
22(19). and reacheth *unto heaven*,
23(20). an holy one coming down from *heaven*,
25(22). shall wet thee with the dew of *heaven.*

Dan 4:26(23). shalt have known that *the heavens*
31(28). there fell a voice from *heaven*,
33(30). body was wet with the dew of *heaven*,
34(31). I Nebuchadnezzar lifted up mine eyes *unto heaven*,
35(32). according to his will in the army of *heaven*,
37(34). and honour the King of *heaven*,
5:21. was wet with the dew of *heaven;*
23. lifted up thyself against the Lord of *heaven;*
6:27(28). worketh signs and wonders *in heaven*
7: 2. behold, the four winds of *the heaven*
13. of man came with the clouds of *heaven*,
27. of the kingdom under *the* whole *heaven*,

8066-67 שְׁמִינִי *sh'mee-nee'*, adj. ord.

Ex. 22:30(29). *eighth* day thou shalt give it me.
Lev. 9: 1. it came to pass on the *eighth* day,
12: 3. *eighth* day the flesh of his foreskin
14:10. *eighth* day he shall take two he lambs
23. he shall bring them on the *eighth* day
15:14. *eighth* day he shall take to him
29. *eighth* day she shall take unto her
22:27. from the *eighth* day
23:36. on the *eighth* day shall be an holy
39. on the *eighth* day (shall be) a sabbath.
25:22. ye shall sow the *eighth* year,
Nu. 6:10. on the *eighth* day he shall bring
7:54. the *eighth* day (offered) Gamaliel
29:35. *eighth* day ye shall have a solemn
1K. 6:38. Bul, which (is) the *eighth* month,
8:66. *eighth* day he sent the people away:
12:32. a feast in the *eighth* month,
33. fifteenth day of the *eighth* month,
1Ch 12:12. Johanan *the eighth*,
15:21. with harps on *the Sheminith* (marg. or, *the eighth*)
24:10. *the eighth* to Abijah,
25:15. *The eighth* to Jeshaiah,
26: 5. Peulthai *the eighth:*
27:11. *eighth* (captain) for the *eighth* month
2Ch 7: 9. *eighth* day they made a solemn assembly:
Neh 8:18. the *eighth* day (was) a solemn assembly,
Ps. 6[title](1). Neginoth, upon *Sheminith*, (marg. or, *the eighth*)
12[title](1). To the chief Musician upon *Sheminith*, (marg. *id.*)
Eze.43:27. upon the *eighth* day, and (so) forward,
Zec. 1: 1. In the *eighth* month,

8068 שָׁמִיר *shāh-meer'*, m.

Isa. 5: 6. there shall come up *briers*
7:23. it shall (even) be *for briers*
24. all the land shall become *briers*
25. come thither the fear of *briers*
9:18(17). it shall devour *the briers*
10:17. devour his thorns *and his briers*
27: 4. who would set *the briers*
32:13. shall come up thorns (and) *briers;*
Jer. 17: 1. with the point of *a diamond:*
Eze. 3: 9. *As an adamant* harder than flint
Zec. 7:12. their hearts (as) *an adamant stone*,

8074 שָׁמֵם *shāh-mēhm'*.

* KAL.—*Preterite.* *

Lev.26:32. *and* your enemies...*shall be astonished*
Isa. 52:14. As many *were astonished* at thee;
Lam.5:18. Zion, which *is desolate*,
Eze.26:16. *and be astonished* at thee.
27:35. the isles *shall be astonished*
28:19. the people *shall be astonished*
33:28. *and* the mountains of Israel *shall be desolate*,
35:12. *They are laid desolate*, they are
15. Israel, because it *was desolate*,

KAL.—*Infinitive.*

Eze.36: 3. they *have made* (you) *desolate*,

KAL.—*Imperative.*

Jer. 2:12. *Be astonished*, O ye heavens,

KAL.—*Future.*

1K. 9: 8. passeth by it *shall be astonished*,
2Ch 7:21. *shall be an astonishment*
Job 17: 8. Upright (men) *shall be astonied*
Ps. 40:15(16). *Let them be desolate* for a reward
Isa. 42:14. *I will destroy* and devour at once. [see also נָשַׁם]
Jer. 18:16 & 19:8. passeth thereby *shall be astonished*,
49:17. that goeth by it *shall be astonished*,
50:13. that goeth by Babylon *shall be astonished*,

KAL.—*Participle.* Poel.

2Sa.13:20. Tamar remained *desolate* in her
Isa. 49: 8. to inherit the *desolate* heritages;
19. thy waste *and thy desolate places*,
54: 1. the children of the *desolate* than
61: 4. they shall raise up *the* former *desolations*,
— *the desolations of* many generations.
Lam.1: 4. all her gates *are desolate:*
13. he hath made me *desolate*
16. my children are *desolate*,
3:11. he hath made me *desolate*.
Eze.36: 4. to the valleys, to the *desolate* wastes,
Dan 8:13. the transgression of *desolation*, (marg. or, *making desolate*)
9:18. behold our *desolations*,
26. end of the war *desolations* are determined.
27. shall be poured upon *the desolate*.
12:11. abomination *that maketh desolate* (marg. or, *astonisheth*)

* NIPHAL.—*Preterite.* *

Lev.26:22. *and* your (high) ways *shall be desolate.*
Job 18:20. *shall be astonied* at his day,
Isa. 33: 8. The highways *lie waste*,
Jer. 4: 9. and the priests *shall be astonished*,
12:11. the whole land *is made desolate*,
Lam.4: 5. They that did feed delicately *are desolate*
Eze. 4:17. *and be astonied* one with another,
6: 4. *And* your altars *shall be desolate*,
25: 3. Israel, when it *was desolate;*
30: 7. *And they shall be desolate*
Joel 1:17. the garners *are laid desolate*,
Am. 7: 9. *And* the high places of Isaac *shall be desolate*,
Zep. 3: 6. their towers *are desolate;*
Zec. 7:14. the land *was desolate* after them,

NIPHAL.—*Participle.*

Ps. 69:25(26). Let their habitation be *desolate;*
Isa. 54: 3. make the *desolate* cities to be inhabited.
Jer. 33:10. the streets of Jerusalem, that are *desolate*,
Eze.29:12. in the midst of the countries (that are) *desolate*,
30: 7. midst of the countries (that are) *desolate*,
32:15. and the country *shall be destitute* (marg. *desolate*)
36:34. And the *desolate* land shall be
35. This land *that* was *desolate*
— the waste *and desolate* and ruined cities
36. plant that *that was desolate:*
Am. 9:14. they shall build the *waste* cities,

* POLEL.—*Participle.* *

Ezr. 9: 3. sat down *astonied.*
4. I sat *astonied* until the evening
Dan 9:27. he shall *make* (it) *desolate*,
11:31. abomination *that maketh desolate*. (marg. or, *astonisheth*)

* HIPHIL.—*Preterite.* *

Lev.26:31. *and bring* your sanctuaries *unto desolation*,
32. *And* I *will bring* the land *into desolation:*
Job 16: 7. *thou hast made desolate*
Ps. 79: 7. *laid waste* his dwelling place.
Jer. 10:25. *have made* his habitation *desolate.*
Eze.14: 8. *and will make him* (lit. *make him desolate*)
30:12. *and I will make* the land *waste*,
14. *And I will make* Pathros *desolate*,
32:10. *Yea, I will make* many people *amazed*
Hos. 2:12(14). *And I will destroy* (marg. *make desolate*) her vines

HIPHIL.—*Infinitive.*

Mic. 6:13. in *making* (thee) *desolate*

HIPHIL.—*Future.*

Nu. 21:30. *and we have laid them waste*
1Sa. 5: 6. Ashdod, *and he destroyed them*,

Jer. 49:20. *he shall make* their habitations *desolate*
50:45. *he shall make* (their) habitation *desolate*
Eze.20:26. that *I might make them desolate*,

HIPHIL.—*Participle.*

Eze. 3:15. remained there *astonished*

* HOPHAL.—*Infinitive.* *

Lev.26:34, 35. as long as it *lieth desolate*,
43. *while she lieth desolate* without them.
2Ch 36:21. as long as she *lay desolate*

HOPHAL.—*Imperative.*

Job 21: 5. Mark me, *and be astonished*,

* HITHPOLEL.—*Future.* *

Ps.143: 4. my heart within me *is desolate*.
Ecc. 7:16. why *shouldest thou destroy thyself?* (marg. *be desolate*)
Isa. 59:16. *and wondered* that (there was) no
63: 5. *and I wondered* that (there was) none
Dan 8:27. *and I was astonished* at the vision,

8075 שְׁמַם [*sh'mam*], Ch.

* ITHPOLEL.—*Future.* *

Dan 4:19(16). *was astonied* for one hour,

8076 שָׁמֵם *shāh-mēhm'*, adj.

Jer. 12:11. (being) *desolate* it mourneth
Dan 9:17. thy sanctuary *that is desolate*,

8077 שְׁמָמָה *sh'māh-māh'*, f.

Ex. 23:29. lest the land become *desolate*,
Lev.26:33. your land shall be *desolate*,
Jos. 8:28. *a desolation* unto this day.
Isa. 1: 7. Your country (is) *desolate*,
— *and* (it is) *desolate*,
6:11. the land be *utterly* desolate,
17: 9. there shall be *desolation*.
62: 4. thy land any more be termed *Desolate:*
64:10(9). Jerusalem *a desolation*.
Jer. 4:27. The whole land shall be *desolate;*
6: 8. lest I make thee *desolate*,
9:11(10). make the cities of Judah *desolate*, (marg. *desolation*)
10:22. make the cities of Judah *desolate*,
12:10. made my pleasant portion a *desolate*
11. They have made it *desolate*,
25:12. will make it perpetual *desolations*.
32:43. *desolate* without man or beast;
34:22. Judah *a desolation* without an inhabitant.
44: 6. they are wasted (and) *desolate*,
49: 2. it shall be a *desolate* heap,
33. *a desolation* for ever:
50:13. it shall be wholly *desolate:*
51:26. but thou shalt be *desolate* for ever, (marg. everlasting *desolations*)
62. it shall be *desolate* (marg. *desolations*) for ever.
Eze. 6:14. make the land *desolate*,
7:27. shall be clothed with *desolation*,
12:20. the land shall be *desolate;*
14:15. so that it be *desolate*,
16. but the land shall be *desolate*.
15: 8. I will make the land *desolate*,
23:33. cup of astonishment *and desolation*,
29: 9. Egypt shall be *desolate*
10. Egypt utterly waste (and) *desolate*,
12. I will make the land of Egypt *desolate*
— (that are) laid waste shall be *desolate* forty years:
32:15. make the land of Egypt *desolate*,
33:28. For I will lay the land most *desolate*, (marg. *desolation* and desolation)
29. I have laid the land most *desolate* (lit. *desolation* and desolation)
35: 3. will make thee most *desolate*. (marg. *desolation* and desolation)
4. thou shalt be *desolate*,
7. Thus will I make mount Seir most *desolate*, (marg. desolation *and desolation*)
12. (כתיב) *They are laid desolate*, they are
14. I will make thee *desolate*.
15. thou shalt be *desolate*.

Eze.36:34. whereas it lay *desolate*
Joel 2: 3. behind them a *desolate* wilderness;
20. into a land barren *and desolate*,
3:19(4:19). Egypt shall be *a desolation*, and Edom shall be a *desolate* wilderness,
Mic. 1: 7. the idols thereof will I lay *desolate:*
7:13. Notwithstanding the land shall be *desolate*
Zep 1:13. their houses *a desolation:*
2: 4. Ashkelon *a desolation:*
9. *and a* perpetual *desolation:*
13. will make Nineveh *a desolation*,
Mal. 1: 3. his heritage *waste*

שִׁמָמָה *shee-mămāh'*, f. 8077

Eze.35: 7. make mount Seir *most* desolate, (marg. *desolation* and desolation)
9. I will make thee perpetual *desolations*,

שִׁמָּמוֹן *shim-māh-mōhn'*, m. 8078

Eze. 4:16. drink water by measure, *and with astonishment:*
12:19. and drink their water *with astonishment*,

שָׁמַן [*shāh-man'*]. 8080

* KAL.—*Preterite.* *

Deu32:15. *thou art waxen fat*, thou art grown
Jer. 5:28. *They are waxen fat*, they shine:

KAL.—*Future.*

Deu32:15. *But* Jeshurun *waxed fat*,

* HIPHIL.—*Imperative.* *

Isa. 6:10. *Make* the heart of this people *fat*,

HIPHIL.—*Future.*

Neh 9:25. were filled, *and became fat*,

שָׁמֵן *shāh-mēhn'*, adj. 8082

Gen49:20. Out of Asher his bread (shall be) *fat*,
Nu. 13:20. *whether* it (be) *fat* or lean,
Jud. 3:29. ten thousand men, all *lusty*, (marg. *fat*)
1Ch 4:40. And they found *fat* pasture and good,
Neh 9:25. took strong cities, and a *fat* land,
35. in the large *and fat* land
Isa. 30:23. it shall be fat *and plenteous:*
Eze.34:14. (in) a *fat* pasture shall they feed
16. I will destroy *the fat* and the strong;
Hab 1:16. because by them their portion (is) *fat*,

שֶׁמֶן *sheh'-men*, com. 8081

Gen28:18. poured *oil* upon the top of it.
35:14. he poured *oil* thereon.
Ex. 25: 6. *Oil* for the light, spices *for* anointing *oil*,
27:20. that they bring thee pure *oil* olive
29: 2. cakes unleavened tempered *with oil*, and wafers unleavened anointed *with oil:*
7. Then shalt thou take *the* anointing *oil*,
21. the altar, *and of the* anointing *oil*,
23. one loaf of bread, and one cake of *oiled* bread, (lit. bread of *oil*)
40. *with* the fourth part of an hin of beaten *oil;*
30:24. *and of oil* olive an hin:
25. make it *an oil of* holy ointment,
— it shall be *an* holy anointing *oil*.
31. This shall be *an* holy anointing *oil*
31:11. *the* anointing *oil*, and sweet incense
35: 8. *And oil* for the light, and spices *for* anointing *oil*,
14. with *the oil* for the light,
15. *the* anointing *oil*, and the sweet incense,
28. spice, and *oil* for the light, *and for the* anointing *oil*,
37:29. he made *the* holy anointing *oil*,
39:37. all the vessels thereof, and *the oil* for light,
38. golden altar, and *the* anointing *oil*,
40: 9. thou shalt take *the* anointing *oil*,
Lev. 2: 1. he shall pour *oil* upon it,
2. *and of the oil thereof*,

Lev. 2: 4. fine flour mingled *with oil*, or unleavened wafers anointed *with oil.*
5. fine flour unleavened, mingled *with oil.*
6. part it in pieces, and pour *oil* thereon:
7. shall be made (of) fine flour *with oil.*
15. thou shalt put *oil* upon it,
16. corn thereof, *and* (part) *of the oil thereof,*
5:11. he shall put no *oil* upon it,
6:15(8). *and of the oil thereof,* and all
21(14). In a pan it shall be made *with oil;*
7:10. meat offering, mingled *with oil,*
12. unleavened cakes mingled *with oil,* and unleavened wafers anointed *with oil,* and cakes mingled *with oil,*
8: 2. and *the* anointing *oil,*
10. Moses took *the* anointing *oil,*
12. he poured *of the* anointing *oil*
26. a cake of *oiled* bread, and one wafer,
30. Moses took *of the* anointing *oil,*
9: 4. a meat offering mingled *with oil:*
10: 7. for *the* anointing *oil*
14:10. a meat offering, mingled *with oil,* and one log of *oil.*
12. trespass offering, and the log of *oil,*
15. shall take (some) of the log of *oil,*
16. dip his right finger in *the oil*
— shall sprinkle of *the oil* with his finger
17. rest of *the oil* that (is) in his hand
18. the remnant *of the oil*
21. fine flour mingled *with oil* for a meat offering, and a log of *oil;*
24. the trespass offering, and the log of *oil,*
26. the priest shall pour of *the oil*
27. with his right finger (some) of *the oil*
28. the priest shall put of *the oil*
29. the rest of *the oil* that (is) in
21:10. whose head *the* anointing *oil* was poured,
12. for the crown of *the* anointing *oil*
23:13. fine flour mingled *with oil,*
24: 2. bring unto thee pure *oil* olive beaten
Nu. 4: 9. all the *oil* vessels *thereof,*
16. *the oil* for the light,
— *and the* anointing *oil,*
5:15. he shall pour no *oil* upon it,
6:15. cakes of fine flour mingled *with oil,*
— of unleavened bread anointed *with oil,*
7:13, 19, 25, 31, 37, 43, 49, 55, 61, 67, 73, 79. fine flour mingled *with oil*
8: 8. fine flour mingled *with oil,*
11: 8. it was as the taste of fresh *oil.*
15: 4. mingled with the fourth (part) of an hin of *oil.*
6. mingled *with* the third (part) of an hin of *oil.*
9. flour mingled *with* half an hin of *oil.*
28: 5. mingled *with* the fourth (part) of an hin of beaten *oil.*
9, 12, 12. a meat offering, mingled *with oil,*
13. of flour mingled *with oil*
20, 28 & 29:3, 9, 14. flour mingled *with oil:*
35:25. which was anointed *with the* holy *oil.*
Deu 8: 8. a land of *oil* olive, and honey;
28:40. *but* thou shalt not anoint (thyself) *with the oil;*
32:13. *and oil* out of the flinty rock;
33:24. let him dip his foot *in oil.*
1Sa. 10: 1. Then Samuel took a vial of *oil,*
16: 1. fill thine horn with *oil,*
13. Then Samuel took the horn of *oil,*
2Sa. 1:21. not (been) anointed *with oil.*
14: 2. anoint not thyself *with oil,*
1K. 1:39. Zadok the priest took an horn of *oil*
5:11(25). twenty measures of pure *oil:*
6:23. he made two cherubims (of) *olive* tree, (marg. trees of *oil*, or, *oily*)
31. of the oracle he made doors (of) *olive* tree:
32. The two doors also (were of) *olive* tree;
33. the door of the temple posts (of) *olive* tree,
17:12. *a* little *oil* in a cruse:
14. neither shall the cruse of *oil* fail,
16. neither did the cruse of *oil* fail,
2K. 4: 2. in the house, save a pot of *oil.*
6. not a vessel more. And *the oil* stayed.
7. Go, sell *the oil,* and pay thy debt,
9: 1. take this box of *oil* in thine hand,
3. Then take the box of *oil,*
6. he poured *the oil* on his head,
2K. 20:13. the spices, and *the* precious *ointment,*
1Ch 9:29. the wine, *and the oil,*
12:40. bunches of raisins, and wine, *and oil,*
27:28. over the cellars of *oil*
2Ch 2:10(9). *and* twenty thousand baths of *oil.*
15(14). the barley, *the oil,* and the wine,
11:11. store of victual, *and* of *oil* and wine.
Ezr. 3: 7. meat, and drink, *and oil,*
Neh 8:15. Go forth unto the mount, and fetch...*pine* branches, (lit. branches of trees of *oil*)
Est. 2:12. six months *with oil of* myrrh,
Job 29: 6. poured me out rivers of *oil;*
Ps. 23: 5. thou anointest my head *with oil;*
45: 7(8). anointed thee with *the oil of* gladness
55:21(22). his words were softer *than oil,*
89:20(21). *with* my holy *oil* have I anointed
92:10(11). I shall be anointed *with* fresh *oil.*
104:15. *oil* to make (his) face to shine, (marg. make...shine *with oil*)
109:18. *and like oil* into his bones.
24. my flesh faileth *of fatness.*
133: 2. *like the* precious *ointment*
141: 5. reprove me; (it shall be) *an* excellent *oil,*
Pro. 5: 3. her mouth (is) smoother *than oil:*
21:17. he that loveth wine *and oil*
20. *and oil* in the dwelling of the wise;
27: 9. *Ointment* and perfume rejoice the heart:
16. *and the ointment of* his right hand,
Ecc. 7: 1. A (good) name (is) better *than precious ointment;*
9: 8. *and* let thy head lack no *ointment.*
10: 1. Dead flies cause *the ointment of*
Cant. 1: 3. the savour of *thy* good *ointments* thy name (is as) *ointment*
4:10. smell of *thine ointments* than all spices!
Isa. 1: 6. neither mollified *with ointment.* (marg. or, *oil*)
5: 1. hath a vineyard in a very *fruitful* hill: (marg. the horn of the son of *oil*)
10:27. destroyed because of *the anointing.*
25: 6. all people a feast of *fat things,*
— of *fat things* full of marrow,
28: 1. on the head of the *fat* valleys
4. on the head of the *fat* valley,
39: 2. *the* precious *ointment,*
41:19. the myrtle, and the *oil* tree;
57: 9. thou wentest to the king *with ointment,*
61: 3. *the oil of* joy for mourning,
Jer. 40:10. summer fruits, *and oil,*
41: 8. barley, *and* of *oil,* and of honey.
Eze. 16: 9. I anointed thee *with oil.*
13. eat fine flour, and honey, *and oil:*
18. *and* thou hast set *mine oil*
19. I gave thee, fine flour, *and oil,*
23:41. hast set mine incense *and mine oil.*
27:17. honey, *and oil,* and balm.
32:14. cause their rivers to run *like oil,*
45:14. Concerning the ordinance of *oil,* the bath of *oil,*
24. *and* an hin of *oil* for an ephah.
25. *and according to the oil.*
46: 5, 7, 11. *and* an hin of *oil* to an ephah.
14. *and* the third part of an hin of *oil,*
15. the meat offering, and *the oil,*
Hos. 2: 5(7). *mine oil* and my drink.
12: 1(2). *and oil* is carried into Egypt.
Am. 6: 6. themselves with *the* chief *ointments:*
Mic. 6: 7. ten thousands of rivers of *oil?*
15. thou shalt not anoint thee with *oil;*
Hag 2:12. pottage, or wine, or *oil,*

שְׁמֹנֶה *sh'mōh-neh'*, f. & שְׁמֹנָה *sh'mōh-nāh'*, m. adj. num. 8083

Gen 5: 4. Seth were *eight* hundred years:
7. *eight* hundred *and* seven years,
10. after he begat Cainan *eight* hundred *and* fifteen years,
13. Mahalaleel *eight* hundred *and* forty
16. Jared *eight* hundred *and* thirty
17. *eight* hundred ninety and five years:
19. *eight* hundred years, and begat sons
14:14. three hundred and *eight*een, (lit. *eight* ten)
17:12. he that is *eight* days old
21: 4. his son Isaac being *eight* days old,
22:23. these *eight* Milcah did bear to Nahor,

Ex. 26: 2. one curtain (shall be) *eight* and twenty
25. And they shall be *eight* boards,
36: 9. one curtain (was) twenty and *eight*
30. And there were *eight* boards;
Nu. 2:24. an hundred thousand *and eight* thousand and an hundred,
3:28. *eight* thousand and six hundred,
4:48. were *eight* thousand and five hundred
7: 8. four wagons and *eight* oxen
29:29. on the sixth day *eight* bullocks,
35: 7. Levites (shall be) forty *and eight*
Deu 2:14. Zered, (was) thirty *and eight* years;
Jos. 21:41(39). forty *and eight* cities
Jud. 3: 8. served Chushan-rishathaim *eight* years.
14. served Eglon the king of Moab *eigh*teen
10: 8. oppressed the children of Israel *eigh*teen
12:14. he judged Israel *eight* years.
20:25. Israel again *eigh*teen thousand men;
44. there fell of Benjamin *eigh*teen
1Sa. 4:15. Now Eli was ninety *and eight* years
17:12. he had *eight* sons:
2Sa. 8:13. salt, (being) *eigh*teen thousand
23: 8. against *eight* hundred,
24: 9. in Israel *eight* hundred thousand valiant
1K. 7:10. stones of *eight* cubits.
15. *eigh*teen cubits high
15: 1. in the *eigh*teenth year of king Jeroboam
16:29. in the thirty *and eighth* year of Asa
2K. 3: 1. reign over Israel in Samaria the *eigh*teenth year
8:17. *and* he reigned *eight* years
10:36. twenty *and eight* years.
15: 8. In the thirty *and eighth* year
22: 1. Josiah (was) *eight* years old
3. it came to pass *in* the *eigh*teenth year of
23:23. But *in* the *eigh*teenth year of king Josiah,
24: 8. Jehoiachin (was) *eigh*teen years old
12. took him in the *eighth* year of his reign.
25:17. one pillar (was) *eigh*teen cubits,
1Ch 12:24. six thousand *and eight* hundred,
30. twenty thousand *and eight* hundred,
31. tribe of Manasseh *eigh*teen thousand,
35. twenty *and eight* thousand
16:38. their brethren, threescore *and eight*;
18:12. valley of salt *eigh*teen thousand.
23: 3. was thirty *and eight* thousand.
24: 4. and *eight* among the sons of Ithamar
15. the *eigh*teenth to Aphses,
25: 7. (even) all that were cunning, was two hundred fourscore *and eight*.
25. *The eigh*teenth to Hanani,
26: 9. brethren, strong men, *eigh*teen.
29: 7. *and* of brass *eigh*teen thousand
2Ch 11:21. for he took *eigh*teen wives,
— begat twenty *and eight* sons,
13: 1. in the *eigh*teenth year of king Jeroboam
3. *with eight* hundred thousand chosen
21: 5. *and* he reigned *eight* years in Jerusalem.
20. *and* he reigned in Jerusalem *eight* years,
29:17. on *the eighth* day of the month
— sanctified the house of the Lord in *eight*
34: 1. Josiah (was) *eight* years old when he
3. *For in* the *eighth* year of his reign,
8. in the *eigh*teenth year
35:19. *In* the *eigh*teenth year of the reign of
36: 9. Jehoiachin (was) *eight* years old
Ezr. 2: 6. two thousand *eight* hundred and twelve.
16. Hezekiah, ninety *and eight*.
23. Anathoth, an hundred twenty *and eight*.
41. Asaph, an hundred twenty *and eight*.
8: 9. and with him two hundred *and eigh*teen
11. with him twenty *and eight* males.
18. his sons and his brethren, *eigh*teen;
Neh. 7:11. of the children of Jeshua and Joab, two thousand *and eight* hundred (and) *eigh*teen.
13. *eight* hundred forty and five.
15. Binnui, six hundred forty *and eight*.
16. Bebai, six hundred twenty *and eight*.
21. Hezekiah, ninety *and eight*.
22. Hashum, three hundred twenty *and eight*.
26. an hundred fourscore *and eight*.
27. an hundred twenty *and eight*.
44. an hundred forty *and eight*.
45. an hundred thirty *and eight*.
11: 6. four hundred threescore *and eight*
8. Sallai, nine hundred twenty *and eight*.
Neh11:12. *eight* hundred twenty and two:
14. an hundred twenty *and eight*:
Ecc 11: 2. a portion to seven, and also *to eight*;
Jer. 32: 1. which (was) the *eigh*teenth year
41:15. escaped from Johanan *with eight* men,
52:21. height of one pillar (was) *eigh*teen cubits;
29. In the *eigh*teenth year
— Jerusalem *eight* hundred thirty and two
Eze.40: 9. porch of the gate, *eight* cubits;
31. the going up to it (had) *eight* steps.
34, 37. *and* the going up to it (had) *eight* steps.
41. *eight* tables, whereupon they slew
48:35. round about *eigh*teen thousand
Mic. 5: 5(4). *and eight* principal men.

שְׁמֹנִים *sh'mōh-neem'*, adj. num. pl. 8084

Gen 5:25. an hundred *eighty and* seven
26. Lamech seven hundred *eighty and* two
28. lived an hundred *eighty and* two years,
16:16. Abram (was) *fourscore* and six years
35:28. of Isaac were an hundred *and fourscore*
Ex. 7: 7. Moses (was) *fourscore* years old, and Aaron *fourscore and* three years
Nu. 2: 9. hundred thousand *and fourscore* thousand and six thousand and four hundred,
4:48. eight thousand and five hundred *and fourscore*.
Jos. 14:10. (am) this day *fourscore and* five years old.
Jud. 3:30. the land had rest *fourscore* years.
1Sa. 22:18. slew on that day *fourscore* and five
2Sa. 19:32(33). aged man, (even) *fourscore* years old:
35(36). I (am) this day *fourscore* years old:
1K. 5:15(29). *and fourscore* thousand hewers
6: 1. *in* the four hundred and *eightieth*
12:21. an hundred *and fourscore* thousand
2K. 6:25. an ass's head was (sold) *for fourscore*
10:24. Jehu appointed *fourscore* men without,
19:35. an hundred *fourscore* and five thousand:
1Ch 7: 5. *fourscore* and seven thousand.
15: 9. his brethren *fourscore*:
25: 7. two hundred *fourscore* and eight.
2Ch 2: 2(1). *and fourscore* thousand to hew
18(17). *and fourscore* thousand (to be)
11: 1. an hundred *and fourscore* thousand
14: 8(7). two hundred *and fourscore* thousand:
17:15. two hundred *and fourscore* thousand.
18. an hundred *and fourscore* thousand
26:17. with him *fourscore* priests
Ezr. 8: 8. and with him *fourscore* males.
Neh. 7:26. an hundred *fourscore* and eight.
11:18. two hundred *fourscore* and four.
Est. 1: 4. an hundred and *fourscore* days.
Ps. 90:10. by reason of strength (they be) *fourscore*
Cant. 6: 8. threescore queens, *and fourscore*
Isa. 37:36. a hundred *and fourscore* and five thousand:
Jer. 41: 5. from Samaria, (even) *fourscore* men,

שָׁמַע *shāh-mag'* & שָׁמֵעַ *shāh-mēh'ăg*, 8085

*** KAL.—*Preterite.* ***

Gen 3:10. *I heard* thy voice in the garden,
17. *thou hast hearkened* unto the voice
16:11. the Lord *hath heard* thy affliction.
17:20. for Ishmael, *I have heard* thee:
21:17. God *hath heard* the voice of
26. neither yet *heard* I (of it),
22:18. *thou hast obeyed* my voice.
24:52. Abraham's servant *heard* their words,
26: 5. Abraham *obeyed* my voice,
27: 6. *I heard* thy father speak unto Esau
29:33. Because the Lord *hath heard*
30: 6. *hath* also *heard* my voice,
34: 5. Jacob *heard* that he had defiled
37:17. for *I heard* them say,
39:10. that *he hearkened* not unto her,
41:15. I *have heard* say of thee,
42: 2. *I have heard* that there is corn
21. we *would* not *hear*;
22. *and ye would not hear?* therefore, behold
43:25. for *they heard* that they should eat
Ex. 3: 7. *have heard* their cry
18. *And they shall hearken* to thy voice:
6: 5. I *have* also *heard* the groaning
9. *they hearkened* not unto Moses

Ex. 6:12. Israel *have* not *hearkened*
7:13. that *he hearkened* not
16. hitherto *thou wouldest* not *hear*.
22. neither *did he hearken* unto them ;
8:15(11). *hearkened* not unto them ;
19(15) & 9:12. *he hearkened* not unto them ;
15:14. The people *shall hear*,
16: 9. for *he hath heard* your murmurings.
12. *I have heard* the murmurings of
20. *they hearkened* not unto Moses ;
22:27(26). when he crieth unto me, *that I will hear ;*
Lev. 5: 1. *and hear* the voice of swearing,
Nu. 14:13. *Then* the Egyptians *shall hear*
14. *they have heard* that thou Lord
15. the nations which *have heard*
22. *have* not *hearkened* to my voice ;
27. *I have heard* the murmurings
30: 4(5). *And* her father *hear* her vow,
7(8), 11(12). *And* her husband *heard*
Deu 1:17. bring (it) unto me, *and I will hear it.*
43. I spake unto you ; and *ye would* not *hear*,
45. but the Lord *would* not *hearken*
3:26. *would* not *hear* me:
4:30. *and shalt be obedient* unto his voice ;
33. *Did* (ever) people *hear* the voice of God speaking out of the midst of the fire, as thou *hast heard*, and live?
36. *thou heardest* his words
5:24(21). *we have heard* his voice
26(23). *hath heard* the voice of the living God
27(24). speak unto thee ; *and we will hear*
28(25). *I have heard* the voice of the words
6: 3. *Hear therefore*, O Israel,
9: 2. and (of whom) thou *hast heard* (say),
23. nor *hearkened* to his voice.
12:28. Observe *and hear* all these words
17: 4. it be told thee, *and thou hast heard*
26:14. *I have hearkened* to the voice
27:10. *Thou shalt therefore obey* the voice
28:45. because *thou hearkenedst* not
62. *thou wouldest* not *obey* the voice
30: 2. *and shalt obey* his voice
8. return *and obey* the voice of the Lord,
Jos. 1:17. as *we hearkened* unto Moses
2:10. For *we have heard* how the Lord
5: 6. *they obeyed* not the voice of the Lord:
9: 3. when the inhabitants of Gibeon *heard*
9. for *we have heard* the fame of him,
14:12. for thou *heardest* in that day
24:27. it *hath heard* all the words of
Jud. 2: 2. *ye have* not *obeyed* my voice:
17. yet *they would* not *hearken*
20. *have* not *hearkened* unto my voice ;
6:10. but *ye have* not *obeyed* my voice.
7:11. *And thou shalt hear* what they
11:17. the king of Edom *would* not *hearken*
28. Ammon *hearkened* not unto
Ru. 1: 6. for *she had heard* in the country
2: 8. Boaz unto Ruth, *Hearest thou* not,
1Sa. 2:22. *and heard* all that his sons did
12: 1. *I have hearkened* unto your voice
14. serve him, *and obey* his voice,
13: 4. all Israel *heard* say (that) Saul
14:22. *they heard* that the Philistines fled,
27. Jonathan *heard* not when his father
15:19. Wherefore then *didst thou* not *obey*
20. *I have obeyed* the voice of the Lord,
16: 2. *if* Saul *hear* (it), he will kill me.
23:10. thy servant *hath* certainly *heard*
11. as thy servant *hath heard?*
25: 7. *I have heard* that thou hast shearers:
35. *I have hearkened* to thy voice,
28:18. *thou obeyedst* not the voice of the Lord,
21. thine handmaid *hath obeyed* thy voice,
2Sa. 7:22. according to all that *we have heard*
12:18. *he would* not *hearken* unto our voice:
13:21. But when king David *heard* of all
16:21. *and* all Israel *shall hear* that thou
17: 9. *that* whosoever *heareth* it will say,
18: 5. the people *heard* when the king gave
19: 2(3). for the people *heard* say
1K. 1:11. *Hast thou* not *heard* that Adonijah
45. This (is) the noise that *ye have heard.*
2:42. The word (that) *I have heard* (is) good.
4:34(5:14). which *had heard of* his wisdom.
5: 1(15). for *he had heard* that they had anointed
1K. 5: 8(22). *I have considered* (marg. *heard*) the
8:30. *And hearken thou* to the supplication
— and *when thou hearest*, forgive.
45. *Then hear thou* in heaven
49. *Then hear thou* their prayer
9: 3. *I have heard* thy prayer
10: 6. a true report that *I heard*
7. exceedeth the fame which *I heard.*
11:21. when Hadad *heard* in Egypt
12:15. Wherefore the king *hearkened* not
16. Israel saw that the king *hearkened* not
20:31. *we have heard* that the kings
36. *thou hast* not *obeyed* the voice
2K. 3:21. when all the Moabites *heard*
9:30. was come to Jezreel, Jezebel *heard*
14:11. But Amaziah *would* not *hear.*
17:14. *they would* not *hear*,
40. Howbeit *they did* not *hearken*,
18:12. Because *they obeyed* not
— and *would* not *hear* (them), nor do (them).
19: 4. which the Lord thy God *hath heard:*
6. the words which *thou hast heard*,
7. *and he shall hear* a rumour,
8. *he had heard* that he was departed
11. *thou hast heard* what the kings
20. king of Assyria *I have heard.*
25. *Hast thou* not *heard* long ago
20: 5. *I have heard* thy prayer,
12. *he had heard* that Hezekiah
21: 9. But *they hearkened* not:
22:13. because our fathers *have* not *hearkened*
18. the words which *thou hast heard ;*
19. I also *have heard* (thee),
1Ch 17:20. according to all that *we have heard*
2Ch 6:21. *Hearken therefore* unto the supplications
— and *when thou hearest*, forgive.
35, 39. *Then hear thou* from the heavens
7:12. *I have heard* thy prayer,
9: 1. when the queen of Sheba *heard*
5. a true report which *I heard*
6. thou exceedest the fame that *I heard.*
10:15. So the king *hearkened* not
16. that the king *would* not *hearken*
24:17. Then the king *hearkened* unto them.
25:16. *hast* not *hearkened* unto my counsel.
20. But Amaziah *would* not *hear ;*
34:26. the words which *thou hast heard;*
27. I *have* even *heard* (thee) also,
35:22. *hearkened* not unto the words
Neh. 4: 1(3:33). when Sanballat *heard* that we
7(1). *heard* that the walls of Jerusalem
15(19). when our enemies *heard* that
5: 6. very angry when *I heard* their cry
6:16. when all our enemies *heard*
9: 9. *heardest* their cry by the Red sea ;
16. *hearkened* not to thy commandments,
29. *hearkened* not unto thy commandments,
— hardened their neck, and *would* not *hear.*
Est. 1:18. which *have heard* of the deed of the queen.
3: 4. *he hearkened* not unto them,
Job 3:18. *they hear* not the voice of the oppressor.
13: 1. mine ear *hath heard* and understood it.
16: 2. *I have heard* many such things:
28:22. *We have heard* the fame thereof
29:11. When the ear *heard*
21. Unto me (men) *gave ear*,
42: 5. *I have heard of thee* by the hearing
Ps. 6: 8(9). *hath heard* the voice of my weeping.
9(10). The Lord *hath heard* my supplication ;
10:17. *thou hast heard* the desire of
22:24(25). when he cried unto him, *he heard.*
28: 6. *hath heard* the voice of my supplications.
31:13(14). *I have heard* the slander of many:
22(23). *thou heardest* the voice of my
34: 6(7). poor man cried, and the Lord *heard*
17(18). cry, and the Lord *heareth*,
44: 1(2). *We have heard* with our ears,
48: 8(9). As *we have heard*, so have we
61: 5(6). For thou, O God, *hast heard* my vows:
62:11(12). twice *have I heard* this ;
66:19. verily God *hath heard*
78: 3. Which *we have heard* and known,
21. Therefore the Lord *heard*
59. When God *heard* (this), he was wroth,
81:11(12). But my people *would* not *hearken*
97: 8. Zion *heard*, and was glad ;
106:25. *hearkened* not unto the voice

Ps.132: 6. Lo, *we heard of it* at Ephratah:
138: 4. when *they hear* the words
141: 6. *When...they shall hear* my words;
Pro. 5:13. *have* not *obeyed* the voice
13: 1. but a scorner *heareth* not rebuke.
8. but the poor *heareth* not rebuke.
Isa. 1:19. If ye be willing *and obedient*,
16: 6. *We have heard* of the pride of Moab;
21:10. that which *I have heard*
24:16. of the earth *have we heard* songs,
28:22. for *I have heard* from the Lord
29:18. *And* in that day *shall* the deaf *hear*
37: 4. which the Lord thy God *hath heard*:
6. the words that *thou hast heard*,
7. *and he shall hear* a rumour,
8. *he had heard* that he was departed
11. thou *hast heard* what the kings
26. *Hast thou* not *heard* long ago,
38: 5. *I have heard* thy prayer,
40:28. *hast thou* not *heard*,
42:24. neither *were they obedient*
48: 6. *Thou hast heard*, see all this;
7. when *thou heardest them* not;
8. Yea, *thou heardest* not;
52:15. which *they had* not *heard*
64: 4(3). (men) *have* not *heard*, nor perceived
65:12. when I spake, *ye did* not *hear*;
66: 4. when I spake, *they did* not *hear*:
8. Who *hath heard* such a thing?
19. that *have* not *heard* my fame,
Jer. 3:13. *ye have* not *obeyed* my voice,
25. we and our fathers,...*have* not *obeyed*
4:19. *thou hast heard*, O my soul,
31. For *I have heard* a voice as of a woman
6:24. *We have heard* the fame thereof:
7:13. speaking, but *ye heard* not;
24. But *they hearkened* not,
26. Yet *they hearkened* not unto me,
28. a nation that *obeyeth* not
9:10(9). neither *can* (men) *hear* the voice
13(12). *have* not *obeyed* my voice,
11: 8. Yet *they obeyed* not,
13:11. but *they would* not *hear*.
17:23. But *they obeyed* not,
18:13. who *hath heard* such things:
20:10. For *I heard* the defaming of many,
16. *and let him hear* the cry
22:21. that *thou obeyedst* not my voice.
23:25. *I have heard* what the prophets said,
25: 3. speaking; but *ye have* not *hearkened*.
4. (them); but *ye have* not *hearkened*,
7. Yet *ye have* not *hearkened* unto me,
8. *ye have* not *heard* my words,
26: 5. but *ye have* not *hearkened*;
11. as *ye have heard* with your ears.
12. all the words that *ye have heard*.
29:12. *and I will hearken* unto you.
19. *they have* not *hearkened* to
— but *ye would* not *hear*, saith the Lord.
30: 5. *We have heard* a voice of trembling,
31:18. *I have* surely *heard* Ephraim
32:23. but *they obeyed* not thy voice,
34:14. but your fathers *hearkened* not
17. Ye *have* not *hearkened* unto me,
35:14. but *obey* their father's commandment:
— but *ye hearkened* not unto me.
15. nor *hearkened* unto me.
16. this people *hath* not *hearkened*
17. but *they have* not *heard*;
18. Because *ye have obeyed*
36:13. declared unto them all the words that *he had heard*,
25. but *he would* not *hear* them.
31. but *they hearkened* not.
37: 2. *did hearken* unto the words of the Lord,
14. But *he hearkened* not to him:
40: 3. *have* not *obeyed* his voice,
11. *heard* that the king of Babylon
42: 4. said unto them, *I have heard*
21. but *ye have* not *obeyed*
43: 4. *obeyed* not the voice of the Lord,
7. for *they obeyed* not the voice
44: 5. But *they hearkened* not,
23. *have* not *obeyed* the voice of
46:12. The nations *have heard* of thy shame,
48: 5. *have heard* a cry of destruction.
29. *We haveheard* the pride of Moab,
Jer. 49:14. *I have heard* a rumour
23. for *they have heard* evil tidings:
50:43. The king of Babylon *hath heard* the
51:51. because *we have heard* reproach:
Lam. 1:21. *They have heard* that I sigh:
— all mine enemies *have heard*
3:56. *Thou hast heard* my voice:
61. *Thou hast heard* their reproach,
Eze. 3:17. *therefore hear* the word at my mouth,
12: 2. they have ears to hear, and *hear* not:
33: 4. *Then* whosoever *heareth*
5. *He heard* the sound of the trumpet,
7. therefore *thou shalt hear* the word
31. *and they hear* thy words,
32. *for they hear* thy words,
35:12. *I have heard* all thy blasphemies
13. against me: I *have heard* (them).
Dan 9: 6. Neither *have we hearkened*
10. Neither *have we obeyed*
14. for *we obeyed* not his voice.
12: 8. I *heard*, but I understood not:
Hos 9:17. because *they did* not *hearken*
Obad. 1. *We have heard* a rumour
Jon. 2: 2(3). *thou heardest* my voice.
Mic. 5:15(14). such as *they have* not *heard*.
Hab 3: 2. O Lord, *I have heard* thy speech,
16. When *I heard*, my belly trembled;
Zep 2: 8. *I have heard* the reproach of Moab,
3: 2. *She obeyed* not the voice;
Zec. 1: 4. *did* not *hear*, nor hearken
7:13. *they would* not *hear*;
8:23. for *we have heard*

KAL.—*Infinitive.*

Gen 24:30. *and when he heard* the words
27:34. And *when* Esau *heard* the words
29:13. *when* Laban *heard* the tidings
34: 7. Jacob came out of the field *when they heard*
39:15. *when he heard* that I lifted up
19. *when* his master *heard* the words
Ex. 15:26. If thou wilt *diligently* hearken (lit. *hearkening* thou wilt hearken)
16: 7. *for that he heareth* your murmurings
8. *for that* the Lord *heareth*
19: 5. if ye will obey my voice *indeed*, (lit *obeying* will obey)
22:23(22). I will *surely* hear their cry;
23:22. But if thou shalt *indeed* obey his voice,
Lev. 26:21. will not *hearken* unto me;
Nu. 30: 5(6). in the day that *he heareth*;
7(8), 8(9), 14(15). the day that *he heard*
12(13). on the day *he heard*
15(16). after that *he hath heard*
Deu 1:16. *Hear* (the causes) between your
5:23(20). *when ye heard* the voice
25(22). if we *hear* the voice of the Lord our God any more, (marg. add *to hear*)
11:13. if ye shall hearken *diligently*
15: 5. if thou *carefully* hearken unto the voice
17:12. will not *hearken* unto the priest
18:16. Let me not *hear* again (lit. add *to hear*) the voice of the Lord
23: 5(6). thy God would not *hearken* unto
26:17. *and to hearken* unto his voice:
28: 1. if thou shalt hearken *diligently*
29: 4(3). eyes to see, and ears *to hear*,
19(18). *when he heareth* the words
30:20. that thou *mayest obey* his voice,
Jos. 5: 1. *when* all the kings...*heard*
6: 5. *when ye hear* the sound of the trumpet,
20. *when* the people *heard* the sound
9: 1. *when* all the kings...*heard*
10: 1. *when* Adoni-zedec king of Jerusalem *had heard*
14. that the Lord *hearkened*
11: 1. *when* Jabin king of Hazor *had heard*
24:10. I would not *hearken* unto Balaam;
Jud. 2:17. *obeying* the commandments of the Lord;
5:16. *to hear* the bleatings of the flocks?
7:15. *when* Gideon *heard* the telling
19:25. But the men would not *hearken*
20:13. Benjamin would not *hearken*
1Sa. 8:19. the people refused *to obey*
11: 6. Saul *when he heard* those tidings,
15:22. *as in obeying* the voice of the Lord? Behold, *to obey* (is) better than sacrifice,

1Sa.23:10. thy servant hath *certainly* heard
2Sa. 5:24. *when thou hearest* the sound
13:14. he would not *hearken* unto her voice:
16. But he would not *hearken* unto her.
14:17. *to discern* (marg. *hear*) good and bad.
15:10. *As soon as ye hear* the sound
22:45. *as* soon as *they hear*, (lit. *at the hearing of* the ear)
1K. 3:11. understanding *to discern* (marg. *hear*)
4:34(5:14). there came of all people *to hear*
5: 7(21). *when* Hiram *heard* the words
8:28. *to hearken* unto the cry
29. *that* thou *mayest hearken* unto the prayer
52. *to hearken* unto them in all that they call
10:24. to Solomon, *to hear* his wisdom,
12: 2. *when* Jeroboam the son of Nebat,...*heard*
20. *when* all Israel *heard* that
13: 4. *when* king Jeroboam *heard*
14: 6. *when* Ahijah *heard* the sound
15:21. *when* Baasha *heard* (thereof),
19:13. *when* Elijah *heard* (it),
20:12. *when* (Ben-hadad) *heard* this message,
21:15. *when* Jezebel *heard* that Naboth
16. *when* Ahab *heard* that Naboth
27. *when* Ahab *heard* those words,
2K. 5: 8. *when* Elisha the man of God *had heard*
6:30. *when* the king *heard* the words
19: 1. *when* king Hezekiah *heard*
22:11. *when* the king *had heard* the words
19. *when thou heardest* what I spake
1Ch 14:15. *when thou shalt hear* a sound
2Ch 6:19. *to hearken* unto the cry
20. *to hearken* unto the prayer
9:23. Solomon, *to hear* his wisdom,
10: 2. *when* Jeroboam the son of Nebat,...*heard*
15: 8. *And when* Asa *heard* these words,
16: 5. *when* Baasha *heard* (it),
20:29. *when they had heard* that the Lord
34:19. *when* the king *had heard*
27. *when thou heardest* his words
Ezr. 9: 3. *And when I heard* this thing,
Neh 1: 4. *when I heard* these words,
6. *that* thou *mayest hear* the prayer
8: 2. all that could *hear* with understanding, (marg. understood *in hearing*)
9. *when they heard* the words
9:17. And refused *to obey*,
13: 3. *when they had heard* the law,
Job 13:17. Hear *diligently* my speech, and my
21: 2. Hear *diligently* my speech, and let
37: 2. Hear *attentively* the noise of his voice,
Ps. 102:20(21). *To hear* the groaning of the prisoner;
103:20. *hearkening* unto the voice
106:44. *when he heard* their cry:
Pro. 19:27. Cease, my son, *to hear* the instruction
28: 9. turneth away his ear *from hearing*
Ecc. 1: 8. nor the ear filled *with hearing*.
5: 1(4:17). be more ready *to hear*,
7: 5. better *to hear* the rebuke of the wise,
Isa. 6: 9. Hear ye *indeed* (marg. *in hearing*, or, *without ceasing*), but understand not;
21: 3. I was bowed down *at the hearing*
28:12. yet they would not *hear*.
30: 9. children (that) will not *hear*
19. *when he shall hear it*, he will
33:15. stoppeth his ears *from hearing* of
19. deeper speech *than thou canst perceive;*
34: 1. Come near, ye nations, *to hear;*
37: 1. *when* king Hezekiah *heard*
50: 4. he wakeneth mine ear *to hear*
55: 2. hearken *diligently* unto me,
59: 1. his ear heavy, *that it cannot hear:*
2. face from you, *that he will not hear*.
Jer. 11:10. refused *to hear* my words;
13:10. refuse *to hear* my words,
16:12. that they *may* not *hearken*
17:23. that they *might* not *hear*,
24. if ye *diligently* hearken unto me,
18:10. that it *obey* not my voice,
19:15. that they *might* not *hear* my words.
25: 4. nor inclined your ear *to hear*.
26: 5. *To hearken* to the words;
31:18. I have *surely* heard Ephraim bemoaning
35:13. Will ye not receive instruction *to hearken*
36:16. *when they had heard* all the words,
42:13. neither *obey* the voice of the Lord
Eze. 3: 7. the house of Israel will not *hearken*

Eze. 3: 7. for they will not *hearken* unto me:
12: 2. they have ears *to hear*, and hear not:
20: 8. would not *hearken* unto me:
Dan 9:11. that they *might* not *obey*
10: 9. *and when I heard* the voice of his words,
Am. 8:11. but *of hearing* the words of the Lord:
Zec. 6:15. if ye will *diligently* obey the voice of the Lord
7:11. that they *should not hear*.
12. *lest they should hear* the law,

KAL.—*Imperative.*

Gen 4:23. *hear* my voice; ye wives of Lamech,
21:12. *hearken* unto her voice;
23: 6. *Hear us*, my lord: thou (art) a mighty
8. *hear me*, and intreat for me
11. Nay, my lord, *hear me:*
13. I pray thee, *hear me:*
15. My lord, *hearken unto me:*
27: 8, 43. my son, *obey* my voice
13. only *obey* my voice,
37: 6. *Hear*, I pray you, this dream
49: 2. *and hear*, ye sons of Jacob; *and hearken* unto Israel
Ex. 18:19. *Hearken* now unto my voice,
23:21. Beware of him, *and obey* his voice,
Nu. 12: 6. *Hear* now my words:
16: 8. *Hear*, I pray you, ye sons of Levi:
20:10. said unto them, *Hear* now, ye rebels;
23:18. Rise up, Balak, *and hear;*
Deu 4: 1. Now therefore *hearken*, O Israel,
5: 1. *Hear*, O Israel, the statutes and judgments
27(24). *and hear* all that the Lord our God
6: 4. *Hear*, O Israel: The Lord our God
9: 1. *Hear*, O Israel: Thou (art) to pass over
20: 3. say unto them, *Hear*, O Israel,
27: 9. Take heed, *and hearken*, O Israel;
33: 7. *Hear*, Lord, the voice of Judah,
Jos. 3: 9. *and hear* the words of the Lord
Jud. 5: 3. *Hear*, O ye kings; give ear, O ye princes;
9: 7. *Hearken* unto me, ye men of Shechem,
1Sa. 8: 7. *Hearken* unto the voice of the people
9. therefore *hearken* unto their voice:
22. *Hearken* unto their voice,
15: 1. now therefore *hearken thou*
22: 7. *Hear* now, ye Benjamites;
12. *Hear* now, thou son of Ahitub.
25:24. *and hear* the words of thine handmaid.
28:22. *hearken* thou also unto the voice
2Sa. 20:16. cried a wise woman out of the city, *Hear, hear;* say, I pray you, unto Joab,
17. *Hear* the words of thine handmaid.
1K. 22:19. *Hear thou* therefore the word
28. *Hearken*, O people, every one of you.
2K. 7: 1. *Hear ye* the word of the Lord;
18:28. *Hear* the word of the great king,
19:16. bow down thine ear, *and hear:* open, Lord, thine eyes, and see: *and hear* the words
20:16. *Hear* the word of the Lord.
1Ch 28: 2. *Hear me*, my brethren,
2Ch 13: 4. *Hear me*, thou Jeroboam,
15: 2. *Hear ye me*, Asa, and all Judah
18:18. *hear* the word of the Lord;
27. *Hearken*, all ye people.
20:20. stood and said, *Hear me*, O Judah, and ye inhabitants
28:11. Now *hear me* therefore,
29: 5. *Hear me*, ye Levites, sanctify now
Neh 4: 4(3:36). *Hear*, O our God; for we are
Job 5:27. *hear it*, and know thou (it) for thy good.
13: 6. *Hear* now my reasoning, and hearken
17. *Hear* diligently my speech,
15:17. I will shew thee, *hear* me;
21: 2. *Hear* diligently my speech,
32:10. *Hearken* to me; I also will shew
33: 1. *hear* my speeches, and hearken to
31. Mark well, O Job, *hearken* unto me:
33. If not, *hearken* unto me:
34: 2. *Hear* my words, O ye wise
10. Therefore *hearken* unto me,
16. *hear* this: hearken to the voice
37: 2. *Hear* attentively the noise of his voice,
42: 4. *Hear*, I beseech thee, and I will speak:
Ps. 4: 1(2). have mercy upon me, *and hear* my prayer.
17: 1. *Hear* the right, O Lord,
6. incline thine ear unto me, (and) *hear* my

Ps. 27: 7. *Hear*, O Lord, (when) I cry with my
28: 2. *Hear* the voice of my supplications,
30:10(11). *Hear*, O Lord, and have mercy
34:11(12). Come, ye children, *hearken* unto me:
39:12(13). *Hear* my prayer, O Lord,
45:10(11). *Hearken*, O daughter, and consider,
49: 1(2). *Hear* this, all (ye) people;
50: 7. *Hear*, O my people, and I will speak;
54: 2(4). *Hear* my prayer, O God; give ear
61: 1(2). *Hear* my cry, O God;
64: 1(2). *Hear* my voice, O God, in my prayer:
66:16. Come (and) *hear*, all ye that fear God,
81: 8(9). *Hear*, O my people, and I will testify
84: 8(9). O Lord God of hosts, *hear* my prayer:
102: 1(2). *Hear* my prayer, O Lord,
119:149. *Hear* my voice according unto
130: 2. Lord, *hear* my voice:
143: 1. *Hear* my prayer, O Lord,
Pro. 1: 8. *hear* the instruction of thy father,
4: 1. *Hear*, ye children, the instruction of a
10. *Hear*, O my son, and receive my sayings;
5: 7. *Hear* me now therefore, O ye children,
7:24. *Hearken* unto me now therefore,
8: 6. *Hear*; for I will speak of excellent things;
32. Now therefore *hearken* unto me,
33. *Hear* instruction, and be wise,
19:20. *Hear* counsel, and receive instruction,
22:17. Bow down thine ear, *and hear*
23:19. *Hear* thou, my son, and be wise,
22. *Hearken* unto thy father
Isa. 1: 2. *Hear*, O heavens, and give ear, O earth:
10. *Hear* the word of the Lord,
6: 9. *Hear ye* indeed, but understand not;
7:13. *Hear ye* now, O house of David;
28:14. *hear* the word of the Lord,
23. Give ye ear, *and hear* my voice; hearken, *and hear* my speech.
32: 9. *hear* my voice, ye careless daughters;
33:13. *Hear, ye* (that are) far off,
36:13. *Hear ye* the words of the great king,
37:17. Incline thine ear, O Lord, *and hear*; open thine eyes, O Lord, and see: *and hear* all the words of Sennacherib,
39: 5. *Hear* the word of the Lord of hosts:
42:18. *Hear, ye* deaf; and look, ye blind,
44: 1. Yet now *hear*, O Jacob my servant;
46: 3. *Hearken* unto me, O house of Jacob,
12. *Hearken* unto me, ye stouthearted,
47: 8. Therefore *hear* now this,
48: 1. *Hear ye* this, O house of Jacob,
12. *Hearken* unto me, O Jacob and Israel,
14. All ye, assemble yourselves, *and hear;*
16. Come ye near unto me, *hear ye* this;
49: 1. *Listen*, O isles, unto me;
51: 1. *Hearken* to me, ye that follow after
7. *Hearken* unto me, ye that know
21. *hear* now this, thou afflicted,
55: 2. *hearken* diligently unto me,
3. *hear*, and your soul shall live;
66: 5. *Hear* the word of the Lord,
Jer. 2: 4. *Hear ye* the word of the Lord,
5:21. *Hear* now this, O foolish people,
6:18. Therefore *hear, ye* nations,
19. *Hear*, O earth: behold, I will bring evil
7: 2. *Hear* the word of the Lord,
23. *Obey* my voice, and I will be your God,
9:20(19). Yet *hear* the word of the Lord,
10: 1. *Hear ye* the word which the Lord
11: 2,6. *Hear ye* the words of this covenant,
4. *Obey* my voice, and do them,
7. protesting, saying, *Obey* my voice.
13:15. *Hear ye*, and give ear;
17:20. *Hear ye* the word of the Lord,
18:19. *and hearken* to the voice of them
19: 3. *Hear ye* the word of the Lord,
21:11. (say), *Hear ye* the word of the Lord;
22: 2. *Hear* the word of the Lord,
29. O earth, earth, earth, *hear* the word
26:13. *and obey* the voice of the Lord
28: 7. Nevertheless *hear thou* now this word
15. *Hear* now, Hananiah;
29:20. *Hear* ye therefore the word
31:10. *Hear* the word of the Lord,
34: 4. Yet *hear* the word of the Lord,
37:20. *hear* now, I pray thee, O my lord
38:20. *Obey*, I beseech thee, the voice of the
42:15. now therefore *hear* the word of the Lord,
Jer. 44:24. *Hear* the word of the Lord,
26. *hear ye* the word of the Lord,
49:20. *hear* the counsel of the Lord,
50:45. *hear ye* the counsel of the Lord,
Lam 1:18. *hear*, I pray you, all people,
Eze. 2: 8. *hear* what I say unto thee;
3:10. *hear* with thine ears.
6: 3. *hear* the word of the Lord God;
13: 2. *Hear ye* the word of the Lord;
16:35. O harlot, *hear* the word of the Lord:
18:25. *Hear* now, O house of Israel:
20:47(21:3). *Hear* the word of the Lord;
25: 3. say unto the Ammonites, *Hear*
33:30. *and hear* what is the word
34: 7. ye shepherds, *hear* the word
9. O ye shepherds, *hear* the word
36: 1. Ye mountains of Israel, *hear*
4. *hear* the word of the Lord
37: 4. O ye dry bones, *hear*
40: 4. *hear* with thine ears, and set
44: 5. *hear* with thine ears all that I say
Dan 9:17. *hear* the prayer of thy servant,
18. incline thine ear, *and hear;*
19. O Lord, *hear;* O Lord, forgive;
Hos 4: 1. *Hear* the word of the Lord,
5: 1. *Hear ye* this, O priests;
Joel 1: 2. *Hear* this, ye old men,
Am. 3: 1. *Hear* this word that the Lord hath spoken
13. *Hear ye*, and testify in the house
4: 1. *Hear* this word, ye kine of Bashan,
5: 1. *Hear ye* this word which I take
7:16. *hear thou* the word of the Lord:
8: 4. *Hear* this, O ye that swallow up
Mic. 1: 2. *Hear*, all ye people; hearken, O earth,
3: 1. *Hear*, I pray you, O heads of Jacob,
9. *Hear* this, I pray you,
6: 1. *Hear ye* now what the Lord saith;
2. *Hear ye*, O mountains,
9. see thy name: *hear ye* the rod,
Zec. 3: 8. *Hear* now, O Joshua the high priest,

KAL.—*Future.*

Gen 3: 8. *And they heard* the voice of the Lord
11: 7. that *they may* not *understand*
14:14. *And when* Abram *heard*
16: 2. *And* Abram *hearkened*
21:17. *And* God *heard* the voice
23:16. *And* Abraham *hearkened*
28: 7. *And that* Jacob *obeyed* his father
30:17. *And* God *hearkened* unto Leah,
22. *and* God *hearkened* to her,
31: 1. *And he heard* the words of Laban's sons,
34:17. But if *ye will* not *hearken* unto us,
24. *And* unto Hamor...*hearkened* all
35:22. his father's concubine: *and* Israel *heard*
37:21. *And* Reuben *heard* (it), and he delivered
27. *And* his brethren were *content.* (marg. *hearkened*)
41:15. *thou canst understand* (marg. or, (when) *thou hearest*) a dream
45: 2. *and* the Egyptians (lit. *heard*) *and* the house of Pharaoh *heard.*
Ex. 2:15. *when* Pharaoh *heard* this
24. *And* God *heard* their groaning,
4: 1. they will not believe me, nor *hearken*
8. they will not believe thee, neither *hearken*
9. if they will not believe...neither *hearken*
31. *and when they heard* that the Lord
5: 2. that *I should obey* his voice
6:12. how then *shall* Pharaoh *hear me*,
30. how *shall* Pharaoh *hearken*
7: 4. But Pharaoh *shall* not *hearken*
11: 9. Pharaoh *shall* not *hearken* unto you;
15:26. If *thou wilt* diligently *hearken*
18: 1. *When* Jethro, the priest...*heard*
24. *So* Moses *hearkened* to the voice
19: 5. if *ye will obey* my voice
9. that the people *may hear*
20:19. Speak thou with us, *and we will hear:*
22:23(22). *I will* surely *hear* their cry;
23:22. But if *thou shalt* indeed *obey*
24: 7. said will we do, *and be obedient.*
32:17. *when* Joshua *heard* the noise
33: 4. *when* the people *heard* these evil tidings,
Lev. 10:20. *when* Moses *heard* (that),
26:14. But if *ye will* not *hearken*
18. if *ye will* not yet for all this *hearken*
27. if *ye will* not for all this *hearken*

Nu. 7:89. *then he heard* the voice of one
9: 8. *and I will hear* what the Lord
11: 1. *and* the Lord *heard* (it);
10. *Then* Moses *heard* the people
12: 2. *And* the Lord *heard* (it).
16: 4. *when* Moses *heard* (it),
20:16. *And* when...*he heard* our voice, and sent
21: 1. *And* (when)...*heard tell* that Israel came
3. *And* the Lord *hearkened* to the voice
22:36. *when* Balak *heard* that Balaam
27:20. children of Israel *may be obedient.*
33:40. *And* king Arad...*heard* of the coming of
Deu 1:17. ye *shall hear* the small as well
34. the Lord *heard* the voice
2:25. who *shall hear* report of thee,
4: 6. which *shall hear* all these statutes,
28. which neither see, nor *hear*,
5:28(25). *And* the Lord *heard* the voice
7:12. if *ye hearken* to these judgments,
8:20. because *ye would* not *be obedient*
9:19. *But* the Lord *hearkened*
10:10. *and* the Lord *hearkened*
11:13. if *ye shall hearken* diligently
27. A blessing, if *ye obey*
28. a curse, if *ye will* not *obey*
13: 3(4). *Thou shalt* not *hearken* unto
4(5). shall walk after the Lord...and *obey*
8(9). shalt not consent unto him, nor *hearken*
11(12). all Israel *shall hear*,
12(13). If *thou shalt hear* (say) in one
18(19). When *thou shalt hearken*
15: 5. if *thou* carefully *hearken*
17:13. all the people *shall hear*,
18:14. *hearkened* unto observers
15. unto him *ye shall hearken;*
19. whosoever *will* not *hearken*
19:20. those which remain *shall hear*,
21:18. *will* not *hearken* unto them:
21. all Israel *shall hear*, and fear.
26: 7. *And* when...the Lord *heard* our voice,
28: 1. if *thou shalt hearken* diligently
2. if *thou shalt hearken* unto the voice
13. that *thou hearken* unto the commandments
15. if *thou wilt* not *hearken* unto the voice of
49. tongue *thou shalt* not *understand;*
30:10. If *thou shalt hearken* unto
17. so that *thou wilt* not *hear*,
31:12. that *they may hear*,
13. have not known (any thing), *may hear*,
32: 1. *and hear*, O earth, the words of my mouth.
34: 9. *and* the children of Israel *hearkened*
Jos. 1:17. so *will we hearken* unto thee:
18. *will* not *hearken* unto thy words
2:11. And *as soon as we had heard*
7: 9. *For* the Canaanites and all...*shall hear*
9:16. *that they heard* that they
22: 2. *and have obeyed* my voice
11. *And* the children of Israel *heard* say,
12. And *when* the children of Israel *heard*
30. And *when* Phinehas...*heard* the words that
24:24. his voice *will we obey.*
Jud. 3: 4. know *whether they would hearken*
9: 7. *that* God *may hearken* unto you.
30. And *when* Zebul...*heard* the words of
46. And *when* all the men of the tower of Shechem *heard*
13: 9. *And* God *hearkened* to the voice
14:13. thy riddle, *that we may hear it.*
20: 3. *Now* the children of Benjamin *heard*
1Sa. 2:25. *they hearkened* not unto the voice
4: 6. *when* the Philistines *heard*
14. *when* Eli *heard* the noise
19. and *when she heard* the tidings
7: 7. *when* the Philistines *heard*
— *when* the children of Israel *heard*
8:21. *And* Samuel *heard* all the words
12:15. But if *ye will* not *obey*
13: 3. *and* the Philistines *heard*
— *Let* the Hebrews *hear.*
15:24. I feared the people, *and obeyed*
17:11. *When* Saul and all Israel *heard*
23. same words: *and* David *heard*
28. *And* Eliab his eldest brother *heard*
19: 6. *And* Saul *hearkened* unto the voice
22: 1. *when*...all his father's house *heard*
6. *When* Saul *heard* that David
23:25. And *when* Saul *heard*

1Sa.24: 9(10). Wherefore *hearest thou* men's words,
25: 4. *And* David *heard* in the wilderness
39. And *when* David *heard* that Nabal
26:19. *let* my lord the king *hear*
28:21. *and have hearkened* unto thy words
23. *and he hearkened* unto their voice.
30:24. For who *will hearken* unto you
31:11. *when* the inhabitants of Jabesh-gilead *heard*
2Sa. 3:28. afterward *when* David *heard*
4: 1. *when* Saul's son *heard* that Abner
5:17. But *when* the Philistines *heard*
— *and* David *heard* (of it), and went down
8: 9. *When* Toi king of Hamath *heard*
10: 7. And *when* David *heard* of
11:26. And *when* the wife of Uriah *heard*
14:16. For the king *will hear*,
15:35. what thing soever *thou shalt hear*
36. send unto me every thing that *ye can hear.*
17: 5. *and let us hear* likewise
19:35(36). *can I hear* any more
22: 7. *and he did hear* my voice
1K. 1:41. *And* Adonijah...*heard* (it) as they had
— And *when* Joab *heard* the sound
3:28. *And* all Israel *heard* of the judgment
8:30. *hear* thou in heaven
32, 34, 36, 39. Then *hear* thou in heaven,
42. For *they shall hear* of thy great name,
43. *Hear* thou in heaven thy dwelling place,
11:38. if *thou wilt hearken* unto all
12:24. *They hearkened therefore* to the word
13:26. *when* the prophet that brought him back from the way *heard*
15:20. *So* Ben-hadad *hearkened* unto
16:16. *And* the people (that were) encamped *heard*
17:22. *And* the Lord *heard* the voice of Elijah;
20: 8. *Hearken* not (unto him), nor consent.
25. *And he hearkened* unto their voice,
2K. 11:13. And *when* Athaliah *heard*
13: 4. *and* the Lord *hearkened* unto him:
16: 9. *And* the king of Assyria *hearkened*
18:31. *Hearken* not to Hezekiah:
32. *hearken* not unto Hezekiah,
19: 4. thy God *will hear* all the words
9. And *when he heard* say of Tirhakah
20:13. *And* Hezekiah *hearkened* unto them,
25:23. *when* all the captains...*heard*
1Ch 10:11. *when* all Jabesh-gilead *heard*
14: 8. And *when* the Philistines *heard*
— *And* David *heard* (of it),
18: 9. *when* Tou king of Hamath *heard*
19: 8. And *when* David *heard*
29:23. *and* all Israel *obeyed* him.
2Ch 6:21. *hear* thou from thy dwelling place,
23, 30. Then *hear* thou from heaven,
25, 33. Then *hear* thou from the heavens,
27. Then *hear* thou from heaven,
7:14. then *will I hear* from heaven,
11: 4. *And they obeyed* the words
16: 4. *And* Ben-hadad *hearkened*
20: 9. *then thou wilt hear* and help.
23:12. Now *when* Athaliah *heard*
30:20. *And* the Lord *hearkened*
33:13. *and heard* his supplication,
Ezr. 4: 1. *when* the adversaries of Judah and Benjamin *heard*
Neh 2:10. *When* Sanballat the Horonite,...*heard*
19. But *when* Sanballat the Horonite,...*heard*
4:20(14). In what place (therefore) *ye hear*
9:27, 28. thou *heardest* (them) from heaven;
13:27. *Shall we then hearken* unto you
Job 2:11. *when* Job's three friends *heard*
4:16. silence, and *I heard* a voice,
15: 8. *Hast thou heard* the secret of God
20: 3. *I have heard* the check of my
22:27. *and he shall hear thee*, and thou
27: 9. *Will* God *hear* his cry
33: 8. *I have heard* the voice of (thy) words,
34:28. *he heareth* the cry of the afflicted.
35:13. God *will* not *hear* vanity,
36:11. If *they obey* and serve (him),
12. But if *they obey* not,
39: 7. neither *regardeth he* the crying
Ps. 4: 3(4). the Lord *will hear* when I call
5: 3(4). My voice *shalt thou hear*
18: 6(7). *he heard* my voice out of his temple,

Ps. 34: 2(3). the humble *shall hear* (thereof),
38:13(14). But I, as a deaf (man), *heard* not;
40: 1(2). he inclined unto me, *and heard* my
55:17(18). *and he shall hear* my voice.
19(20). God *shall hear*, and afflict them,
58: 5(6). Which *will* not *hearken* to the voice
66:18. the Lord *will* not *hear*
81: 5(6). *I heard* a language (that) I understood not.
8(9). O Israel, if *thou wilt hearken* unto me;
85: 8(9). *I will hear* what God the Lord
92:11(12). *shall hear* (my desire) of the wicked
94: 9. planted the ear, *shall he* not *hear?*
95: 7. To day if *ye will hear* his voice,
115: 6. They have ears, but *they hear* not:
116: 1. because *he hath heard* my voice
145:19. *he* also *will hear* their cry,
Pro. 1: 5. A wise (man) *will hear*,
15:29. *he heareth* the prayer of the righteous.
18:13. answereth a matter before *he heareth*
29:24. *he heareth* cursing,
Ecc. 7:21. lest *thou hear* thy servant curse thee:
12:13. *Let us hear* (marg. *hath been heard* [as if Niphal Preterite]) the conclusion
Isa. 6: 8. *Also I heard* the voice of the Lord,
10. *hear* with their ears,
18: 3. when he bloweth a trumpet, *hear ye.*
30:21. thine ears *shall hear* a word behind
34: 1. *let* the earth *hear*,
36:16. *Hearken* not to Hezekiah: for thus saith
37: 4. thy God *will hear* the words
9. *And he heard* say concerning
— And *when he heard* (it), he sent
39: 1. *for he had heard* that he had been sick,
40:21. *have ye* not *heard?*
42:20. opening the ears, but *he heareth* not.
23. *and hear* for the time to come?
43: 9. *or let them hear*, and say,
65:24. while they are yet speaking, I *will hear.*
Jer. 4:21. shall I see the standard, (and) *hear*
5:15. neither *understandest* what they say.
21. which have ears, and *hear* not:
6:10. warning, *that they may hear?*
7:27. but *they will* not *hearken*
8: 6. I hearkened *and heard*,
11: 3. the man that *obeyeth* not the words
11. *I will* not *hearken* unto them.
12:17. But if *they will* not *obey*,
13:17. But if *ye will* not *hear it*,
17:24. if *ye* diligently *hearken*
27. But if *ye will* not *hearken*
20: 1. *Now* Pashur...*heard* that Jeremiah
22: 5. But if *ye will* not *hear*
21. *I will* not *hear*.
23:16. *Hearken* not unto the words
18. hath perceived *and heard* his word? who hath marked his word, *and heard* (it)?
26: 3. If so be *they will hearken*,
4. If *ye will* not *hearken* to me,
7. *So* the priests and the prophets and all the people *heard*
10. *When* the princes of Judah *heard*
21. And *when* Jehoiakim...*heard* his words,
— but *when* Urijah *heard* it,
27: 9. *hearken* not ye to your prophets,
14. *hearken* not unto the words
16. *Hearken* not to the words of
17. *Hearken* not unto them;
29: 8. neither *hearken* to your dreams
33: 9. which *shall hear* all the good
34:10. *when* all the princes, and all the people,... *heard*
— *then they obeyed*, and let (them) go.
35: 8. *Thus have we obeyed* the voice
10. dwelt in tents, *and have obeyed*,
36: 3. Judah *will hear* all the evil
11. *When* Michaiah the son of Gemariah,...*had heard*
37: 5. *when* the Chaldeans that besieged Jerusalem *heard*
38: 1. *Then* Shephatiah...*heard* the words that
7. *when* Ebed-melech...*heard* that they had
15. *wilt thou* not *hearken* unto me?
25. *But* if the princes *hear* that I
40: 7. *when* all the captains of the forces...*heard*
41:11. *when* Johanan the son of Kareah,...*heard*
42: 6. *we will obey* the voice of the Lord
Jer. 42: 6. *when we obey* the voice of the Lord
14. where we shall see no war, nor *hear*
Eze. 1:24. *And* when they went, *I heard*
28. *and I heard* a voice of one that spake.
2: 2. and set me upon my feet, *that I heard*
5, 7. whether *they will hear*,
3: 6. whose words thou *canst* not *understand.*
— *they would have hearkened*
11. whether *they will hear*,
12. *and I heard* behind me a voice
27. He that heareth, *let him hear;*
8:18. with a loud voice, (yet) *will I* not *hear*
19: 4. The nations *also heard* of him;
43: 6. *And I heard* (him) speaking unto me
Dan 1:14. *So he consented* to them
8:13. *Then I heard* one saint speaking,
16. *And I heard* a man's voice
10: 9. *Yet heard I* the voice of his words:
12: 7. *And I heard* the man clothed in linen,
Am. 5:23. *I will* not *hear* the melody of
Mic. 6: 1. *and let* the hills *hear* thy voice.
7: 7. my God *will hear me.*
Hab. 1: 2. *thou wilt* not *hear!*
Hag. 1:12. *Then* Zerubbabel...with all the remnant of the people, *obeyed*
Zec. 6:15. if *ye will* diligently *obey*
7:13. they cried, and *I would* not *hear*,
Mal. 2: 2. If *ye will* not *hear*, and if ye will not lay
3:16. and the Lord hearkened, *and heard* (it),

KAL.—*Participle.* Poel.

Gen18:10. Sarah *heard* (it) in the tent
21: 6. all *that hear* will laugh with me.
27: 5. Rebekah *heard* when Isaac spake
42:23. knew not that Joseph *understood*
Ex. 32:18. the noise of (them that) sing do I *hear.*
Lev.24:14. let all *that heard* (him) lay
Nu. 24: 4, 16. which *heard* the words of God,
Deu 4:12. ye *heard* the voice of the words,
21:18. which *will* not *obey* the voice
20. he *will* not *obey* our voice;
Jud.11:10. The Lord be *witness* (marg. *hearer*)
1Sa. 2:23. I *hear* of your evil dealings
24. no good report that I *hear:*
3: 9. Speak, Lord; for thy servant *heareth.*
10. Speak; for thy servant *heareth.*
11. ears of every one that *heareth it*
15:14. the lowing of the oxen which I *hear?*
2Sa.15: 3. *but* (there is) no man (deputed) of the king to *hear* thee.
17: 9. that *whosoever* (lit. *a hearer*) heareth it
20:17. he answered, I do *hear.*
1K. 3: 9. an *understanding* (marg. *hearing*) heart
10: 1. when the queen of Sheba *heard*
8. *that hear* thy wisdom.
2K. 10: 6. ye *will hearken* unto my voice,
18:26. for we *understand* (it):
21:12. that whosoever *heareth of it*,
2Ch. 9: 7. before thee, *and hear* thy wisdom.
Job 31:35. Oh that one would *hear* me!
34:34. let a wise man *hearken* unto me.
Ps. 38:14(15). I was as a man that *heareth* not,
59: 7(8). for who, (say they), *doth hear?*
65: 2(3). O thou that *hearest* prayer,
69:33(34). For the Lord *heareth* the poor,
81:13(14). Oh that my people *had hearkened*
Pro. 1:33. *But whoso hearkeneth* unto me
8:34. Blessed (is) the man that *heareth* me,
12:15. *but he that hearkeneth* unto counsel
15:31. The ear that *heareth* the reproof
32. *but he that heareth* reproof
20:12. The *hearing* ear, and the seeing eye,
21:28. but the man that *heareth* speaketh
25:10. Lest *he that heareth* (it) put thee to
12. a wise reprover upon an *obedient* ear.
Ecc. 7: 5. than for a man *to hear* (lit. than a man *that heareth*) the song of fools.
Isa. 1:15. many prayers, I will not *hear:*
32: 3. the ears of them that *hear*
36:11. Syrian language; for we *understand* (it):
41:26. none that *heareth* your words.
50:10. *that obeyeth* the voice
Jer. 7:16. for I will not *hear* thee.
11:14. for I will not *hear* (them)
14:12. I will not *hear* their cry;
19: 3. the which whosoever *heareth,*
32:33. yet they *have* not *hearkened*

Jer. 36:24. his servants *that heard* all these words.
44:16. we will not *hearken* unto thee.
Eze. 3:27. *He that heareth*, let him hear;
13:19. lying to my people that *hear* (your) lies?
20:39. if ye will not *hearken* unto me:
33: 4. *whosoever* heareth (marg. *he that hearing* heareth) the sound of the trumpet,
Nah 3:19. all that *hear* the bruit of thee
Zec. 8: 9. be strong, *ye that hear* in these days

* NIPHAL.—*Preterite.* *

Gen45:16. the fame thereof *was heard* in
Ex. 28:35. *and* his sound *shall be heard*
Deu 4:32. or *hath been heard* like it?
1K. 6: 7. *was* neither hammer nor ax...*heard*
Ezr. 3:13. the noise *was heard* afar off.
Neh 6: 1. *heard* that I had builded
6. It *is reported* among the heathen,
Est. 1:20. And *when* the king's decree which he shall make *shall be published*
Job 26:14. how little a portion *is heard* of him?
Ps. 19: 3(4). their voice *is* not *heard*.
Cant 2:12. the voice of the turtle *is heard*
Isa. 15: 4. their voice *shall be heard*
Jer. 3:21. A voice *was heard* upon the high places,
8:16. The snorting of his horses *was heard*
9:19(18). a voice of wailing *is heard* out of
31:15. A voice *was heard* in Ramah,
38:27. for the matter *was* not *perceived*. (lit. *heard*)
49:21. the noise thereof *was heard* in the Red sea.
50:46. the cry *is heard* among the nations.
Eze.10: 5. the cherubims' wings *was heard*
Dan 10:12. thy words *were heard*,

NIPHAL.—*Infinitive.*

Est. 2: 8. *when* the king's commandment and his decree *was heard*,

NIPHAL.—*Future.*

Ex. 23:13. neither *let it be heard* out of thy mouth.
1Sa. 1:13. but her voice *was* not *heard*:
17:31. And *when* the words *were heard*
2Sa.22:45. *they shall be obedient* unto me.
2Ch 30:27. *and* their voice *was heard*, and their
Neh 6: 7. now *shall it be reported*
12:43. *so* that the joy of Jerusalem *was heard*
Job 37: 4. will not stay them when his voice *is heard*.
Ps. 18:44(45). *they shall obey* me:
Isa. 60:18. Violence *shall* no more *be heard*
65:19. voice of weeping *shall be* no more *heard*
Jer. 6: 7. violence and spoil *is heard* in her;
18:22. *Let* a cry *be heard* from their houses,
33:10. Again *there shall be heard*
Eze.19: 9. that his voice *should* no more *be heard*
26:13. sound of thy harps *shall be* no more *heard*.
Nah 2:13(14). voice of thy messengers *shall* no more *be heard*.

NIPHAL.—*Participle.*

Ecc. 9:16. his words are not *heard*.
17. The words of wise (men are) *heard*
Jer. 51:46. for the rumour *that shall be heard*

* PIEL.—*Future.* *

1Sa.15: 4. *And* Saul *gathered* the people *together*,
23: 8. *And* Saul *called* all the people *together*

* HIPHIL.—*Preterite.* *

Deu 4:36. Out of heaven *he made thee to hear*
Jud. 13:23. *would* as at this time *have told us*
1K. 15:22. king Asa *made a proclamation*
2K. 7: 6. *had made* the host of the Syrians to *hear*
Ps. 76: 8(9). *Thou didst cause* judgment *to be heard*
Isa. 30:30. *And* the Lord *shall cause* his glorious voice *to be heard*,
43:12. I have declared and have saved, *and I have shewed*,
44: 8. *have* not *I told thee*
45:21. who *hath declared* this
48: 5. came to pass *I shewed* (it) *thee*:
6. *I have shewed thee* new things
62:11. Behold, the Lord *hath proclaimed*
Jer. 48: 4. *have caused* a cry *to be heard*.
49: 2. *that I will cause* an alarm of war *to be heard*
Eze.27:30. *And shall cause* their voice *to be heard*

HIPHIL.—*Infinitive.*

1Ch 15:19. *to sound* with cymbals
2Ch 5:13. *to make* one sound *to be heard*

Ps. 26: 7. *That I may publish* with the voice
Isa. 58: 4. *to make* your voice *to be heard*

HIPHIL.—*Imperative.*

Ps. 66: 8. *and make* the voice of his praise *to be heard*:
143: 8. *Cause me to hear* thy lovingkindness
Cant.2:14. *let me hear* thy voice;
8:13. hearken to thy voice: *cause me to hear*
Isa. 41:22. *declare us* things for to come.
48:20. *tell* this, utter it (even) to the end
Jer. 4: 5. *publish* in Jerusalem;
16. *publish* against Jerusalem,
5:20. *and publish it* in Judah,
31: 7. chief of the nations: *publish ye*,
46:14. *and publish* in Migdol, *and publish* in
50: 2. Declare ye among the nations, *and publish*, and set up a standard; *publish*, (and) conceal not:
29. *Call together* the archers
51:27. *call together* against her the kingdoms of
Am. 3: 9. *Publish* in the palaces at Ashdod,
4: 5. proclaim (and) *publish* the free offerings:

HIPHIL.—*Future.*

Deu 4:10. *and I will make them hear* my words,
30:12,13. *that we may hear it*, and do it?
Jos. 6:10. Ye shall not shout, nor *make* any noise (marg. your voice *to be heard*)
Jud.18:25. *Let* not thy voice *be heard*
1Sa. 9:27. *that I may shew thee* the word of God.
Neh. 8:15. *that they should publish* and proclaim
12:42. *And* the singers *sang loud*, (marg. *made* (their voice) *to be heard*)
Ps. 51: 8(10). *Make me to hear* joy and gladness;
106: 2. *can shew forth* all his praise?
Isa. 42: 2. nor *cause* his voice *to be heard*
9. before they spring forth *I tell* you
43: 9. *shew us* former things?
48: 3. forth out of my mouth, *and I shewed them*;
Jer. 18: 2. there *I will cause thee to hear*
23:22. and *had caused* my people *to hear*
Eze.36:15. Neither *will I cause* (men) *to hear*

HIPHIL.—*Participle.*

1Ch 15:16. harps and cymbals, *sounding*,
28. *making a noise* with psalteries
16: 5. but Asaph *made a sound*
42. cymbals *for those that should make a sound*,
Isa. 41:26. none *that declareth*,
52: 7. *that publisheth* peace; that bringeth good tidings of good, *that publisheth* salvation;
Jer. 4:15. *and publisheth* affliction from mount
Nah. 1:15(2:1). *that publisheth* peace! O Judah,

שְׁמַע *sh'mag*, Ch. 8086

* P'AL.—*Preterite.* *

Dan 5:14. *I have even heard* of thee,
16. And I *have heard* of thee,
6:14(15). Then the king, when *he heard*

P'AL.—*Future.*

Dan 3: 5. at what time *ye hear* the sound
10. that every man that *shall hear*
15. that at what time *ye hear* the

P'AL.—*Participle.*

Dan 3: 7. when all the people *heard*
5:23. which see not, *nor hear*, nor know:

* ITHPAEL.—*Future.* *

Dan 7:27. shall serve *and obey* him.

שֵׁמַע *shēh'-mag*, m. 8088

Gen29:13. when Laban heard *the tidings* (marg. *hearing*) of Jacob
Ex. 23: 1. Thou shalt not raise *a* false *report*:
Nu. 14:15. which have heard *the fame of thee*
Deu 2:25. who shall hear *report of thee*,
1K. 10: 1. of Sheba heard of *the fame of* Solomon
2Ch 9: 1. of Sheba heard of *the fame of* Solomon,
Job 28:22. We have heard *the fame thereof*
42: 5. heard of thee *by the hearing of* the ear:
Ps. 18:44(45). *As* soon as *they hear* of me, (marg. *At the hearing of* the ear)
150: 5. Praise him upon the *loud* cymbals:

Isa. 23: 5. As at *the report* concerning Egypt,
— they be sorely pained *at the report of*
66:19. that have not heard *my fame*,
Jer. 37: 5. heard *tidings of them*, they departed
50:43. of Babylon hath heard *the report of them*,
Hos 7:12. *as* their congregation *hath heard.*
Nah 3:19. that hear *the bruit of thee*
Hab 3: 2. O Lord, I have heard *thy speech*, (marg. *report*, or, *thy hearing*)

8089 ## שֹׁמַע [*shōh'-mag̃*], m.

Jos. 6:27. *his fame* was (noised) throughout
9: 9. for we have heard *the fame of him*,
Est. 9: 4. *and his fame* went out
Jer. 6:24. We have heard *the fame thereof*:

8102 ## שֶׁמֶץ *sheh'-metz*, m.

Job 4:12. mine ear received *a little* thereof.
26:14. how *little* a portion is heard of him?

8103 ## שִׁמְצָה *shim-tzāh'*, f.

Ex. 32:25. made them naked *unto* (their) *shame*

8104 ## שָׁמַר *shāh-mar'*.

* KAL.—*Preterite.* *

Gen18:19. *and they shall keep* the way of
28:15. *and will keep thee* in all
20. *and will keep me* in this way
37:11. but his father *observed* the saying.
41:35. *and let them keep* food in the cities.
Ex. 12:17. *And ye shall observe* (the feast of)
— *therefore shall ye observe* this day
24. *And ye shall observe* this thing
25. *that ye shall keep* this service.
13:10. *Thou shalt therefore keep* this
15:26. *and keep* all his statutes,
19: 5. *and keep* my covenant,
31:14. *Ye shall keep* the sabbath *therefore;*
16. *Wherefore* the children of Israel *shall keep*
Lev. 8:35. *and keep* the charge of the Lord,
18: 5. *Ye shall therefore keep* my statutes,
26. Ye *shall therefore keep* my statutes and my judgments,
30. *Therefore shall ye keep* mine ordinance,
19:37. *Therefore shall ye observe* all my
20: 8. *And ye shall keep* my statutes,
22. *Ye shall therefore keep* all my statutes,
22: 9. *They shall therefore keep*
31. *Therefore shall ye keep* my commandments,
Nu. 1:53. *and* the Levites *shall keep*
3: 7. *And they shall keep* his charge,
8. *And they shall keep* all the instruments
10. *and they shall wait* on their
9:19. *then* the children of Israel *kept*
23. *they kept* the charge of the Lord,
18: 3. *And they shall keep* thy charge,
4. *and keep* the charge of the tabernacle
5. *And ye shall keep* the charge of
Deu 4: 6. *Keep therefore* and do
40. *Thou shalt keep* therefore
5: 1. that ye may learn them, *and keep*,
32(29). *Ye shall observe* to do *therefore*
6: 3. Hear therefore, O Israel, *and observe*
7:11. *Thou shalt therefore keep*
12. hearken to these judgments, *and keep*,
— *that* the Lord thy God *shall keep*
8: 6. *Therefore thou shalt keep*
11: 1. *and keep* his charge,
8. *Therefore shall ye keep* all the
32. *And ye shall observe* to do
16:12. *and thou shalt observe* and do these
17:10. *and thou shalt observe* to do according
26:16. *thou shalt therefore keep* and do them
29: 9(8). *Keep therefore* the words of this
31:12. *and observe* to do all the words
33: 9. *they have observed* thy word,
Jos. 22: 2. *Ye have kept* all that Moses
3. *but have kept* the charge

Jud. 2:22. as their fathers *did keep* (it),
1Sa. 13:13. *thou hast* not *kept* the commandment
14. because *thou hast* not *kept*
25:21. Surely in vain *have I kept* all
26:15. *hast thou* not *kept* thy lord the king?
16. *ye have* not *kept* your master,
2Sa. 22:22. *I have kept* the ways of the Lord,
1K. 2: 3. *And keep* the charge of the Lord
43. Why then *hast thou* not *kept*
6:12. *and keep* all my commandments
8:24. Who *hast kept* with thy servant
11:10. but *he kept* not that which
11. *thou hast* not *kept* my covenant
34. because *he kept* my commandments
13:21. *hast* not *kept* the commandment
14: 8. who *kept* my commandments,
2K. 10:31. But Jehu *took* no *heed* to walk
11: 6. *so shall ye keep* the watch
7. *even they shall keep* the watch
17:19. Also Judah *kept* not the commandments
1Ch 10:13. word of the Lord, which *he kept* not,
23:32. *And that they should keep* the charge
2Ch 6:15. Thou which *hast kept* with thy servant
34:21. our fathers *have* not *kept* the word
Neh 1: 7. *have* not *kept* the commandments,
9. *and keep* my commandments,
Job 10:12. thy visitation *hath preserved*
14. If I sin, *then thou markest me*,
23:11. his way *have I kept*,
24:15. of the adulterer *waiteth for* the twilight,
Ps. 17: 4. the word of thy lips *I have kept*
18:21(22). For *I have kept* the ways of the Lord,
78:10. *They kept* not the covenant
56. *kept* not his testimonies:
99: 7. *they kept* his testimonies,
119:67. but now *have I kept* thy word.
136. because *they keep* not thy law.
158. because *they kept* not thy word.
167. My soul *hath kept* thy testimonies;
168. *I have kept* thy precepts
Pro. 3:26. *and shall keep* thy foot from
Jer. 8: 7. and the swallow *observe* the time
16:11. *have* not *kept* my law;
31:10. will gather him, *and keep him*,
Eze. 18: 9. *hath kept* my judgments,
19. *hath kept* all my statutes,
21. *and keep* all my statutes,
20:21. neither *kept* my judgments
44: 8. *ye have* not *kept* the charge
15. *that kept* the charge of my sanctuary
16. *they shall keep* my charge.
48:11. which *have kept* my charge,
Hos 12:12(13). for a wife *he kept* (sheep).
Am. 1:11. and *he kept* his wrath for ever:
2: 4. *have* not *kept* his commandments,
Mal. 3: 7. *have* not *kept* (them).
14. *we have kept* his ordinance,

KAL.—*Infinitive.*

Gen 2:15. Eden to dress it *and to keep it.*
3:24. *to keep* the way of the tree of life.
Ex. 16:28. How long refuse ye *to keep*
22: 7(6). neighbour money or stuff *to keep*,
10(9). a sheep, or any beast, *to keep*;
23:20. *to keep thee* in the way,
Nu. 8:26. *to keep* the charge,
Deu 4: 2. *that* ye *may keep* the commandments
5:12. *Keep* the sabbath day to sanctify it,
29(26). *and keep* all my commandments
6: 2. *to keep* all his statutes
17. shall *diligently* keep (lit. *keeping* shall keep) the commandments
7: 8. *and because he would keep* the oath
8:11. in not *keeping* his commandments,
10:13. *To keep* the commandments of the Lord,
11:22. if ye shall *diligently* keep
13:18(19). *to keep* all his commandments
15: 5. *to observe* to do all these commandments
16: 1. *Observe* the month of Abib,
17:19. *to keep* all the words of this law
24: 8. *that* thou *observe* diligently,
26:17. *and to keep* his statutes,
18. *and that* (thou) *shouldest keep*
27: 1. *Keep* all the commandments
28: 1. *to observe* (and) to do all his
13. *to observe* and to do
15. *to observe* to do all his commandments

Deu28:45 & 30:10. *to keep* his commandments
30:16. *and to keep* his commandments
32:46. command your children *to observe*
Jos. 1: 7. that thou *mayest observe* to do
10:18. set men by it for *to keep them:*
22: 5. *and to keep* his commandments,
23: 6. *to keep* and to do all that is written
1Sa. 7: 1. Eleazar his son *to keep* the ark of the
19:11. unto David's house, *to watch him,*
2Sa. 11:16. *when* Joab *observed* the city,
15:16. concubines, *to keep* the house.
16:21. which he hath left *to keep* the house;
20: 3. whom he had left *to keep* the house,
1K. 2: 3. *to keep* his statutes, and his
3:14. *to keep* my statutes
8:58, 61. *and to keep* his commandments,
11:38. *to keep* my statutes
2K. 23: 3. *and to keep* his commandments
1Ch 22:12. *that thou mayest keep* the law of the Lord
29:19. perfect heart, *to keep* thy commandments,
2Ch 5:11. *did* not (then) *wait* by course:
34:31. *and to keep* his commandments,
Neh 10:29(30). *and to observe* and do all
Ps. 19:11(12). *in keeping of them* (there is) great
91:11. *to keep thee* in all thy ways.
119: 4. *to keep* thy precepts diligently.
5. ways were directed *to keep* thy statutes!
9. *by taking heed* (thereto) according
57. I have said that I *would keep*
60. delayed not *to keep* thy commandments.
106. that I *will keep* thy righteous judgments.
Pro. 5: 2. *That* thou *mayest regard* discretion,
6:24. *To keep thee* from the evil woman,
7: 5. *That* they *may keep thee*
8:34. *waiting* at the posts of my doors.
Ecc. 3: 6. a time *to keep*, and a time to cast away;
Eze. 17:14. *by keeping* of his covenant
Hos. 4:10. have left off *to take heed* to the Lord.

KAL.—*Imperative.*

Ex. 34:11. *Observe* thou that which I command
Deu 4: 9. *and keep* thy soul diligently,
12:28. *Observe* and hear all these words
Jos. 6:18. in any wise *keep* (yourselves) from
22: 5. But *take* diligent *heed* to do
2Sa. 18:12. *Beware* that none (touch) the young man
1K. 8:25. *keep* with thy servant David
20:39. *Keep* this man: if by any means
2K. 17:13. *and keep* my commandments
1Ch 28: 8. *keep* and seek for all the commandments
29:18. *keep* this for ever in the imagination
2Ch 6:16. *keep* with thy servant David my father
19: 7. *take heed* and do (it):
Ezr. 8:29. Watch ye, *and keep*
Job 2: 6. he (is) in thine hand; but *save* his life.
Ps. 16: 1. *Preserve me*, O God:
17: 8. *Keep me* as the apple of the eye,
25:20. *O keep* my soul, and deliver me:
37:34. Wait on the Lord, *and keep* his way,
37. *Mark* the perfect (man),
86: 2. *Preserve* my soul; for I (am) holy:
140: 4(5). *Keep me*, O Lord, from the hands
141: 9. *Keep me* from the snares
Pro. 4: 4. *keep* my commandments, and live.
21. *keep them* in the midst of thine heart.
7: 1. My son, *keep* my words,
2. *Keep* my commandments,
Ecc. 5: 1(4:17). *Keep* thy foot when thou goest
8: 2. I (counsel thee) *to keep* the king's
12:13. *keep* his commandments:
Isa. 56: 1. Thus saith the Lord, *Keep ye* judgment,
Eze. 20:19. *keep* my judgments, and do them;
Hos 12: 6(7). *keep* mercy and judgment,
Mic. 7: 5. *keep* the doors of thy mouth

KAL.—*Future.*

Gen17: 9. Thou *shalt keep* my covenant
10. covenant, which *ye shall keep,*
26: 5. *and kept* my charge,
30:31. I will again feed (and) *keep* thy flock:
Ex. 21:29. *he hath* not *kept him in,*
36. his owner *hath* not *kept him in;*
23:15. *Thou shalt keep* the feast
31:13. Verily my sabbaths *ye shall keep:*
34:18. The feast of unleavened bread *shalt thou keep.*
Lev.18: 4. *keep* mine ordinances,
Lev. 19: 3. *keep* my sabbaths:
19. *Ye shall keep* my statutes.
30. *Ye shall keep* my sabbaths,
25:18. *keep* my judgments,
26: 2. *Ye shall keep* my sabbaths,
3. *keep* my commandments,
Nu. 6:24. The Lord bless thee, *and keep thee:*
18: 7. thy sons with thee *shall keep*
23:12. *Must I* not *take heed* to speak
28: 2. *shall ye observe* to offer
Deu 6:17. *Ye shall* diligently *keep*
25. if *we observe* to do all these commandments
8: 1. this day *shall ye observe* to do,
2. *whether thou wouldest keep* his
11:22. if *ye shall* diligently *keep*
12: 1. *ye shall observe* to do
32(13:1). soever I command you, *observe* to
13: 4(5). *keep* his commandments,
19: 9. If *thou shalt keep* all these commandments
23:23(24). gone out of thy lips *thou shalt keep*
24: 8. (so) *ye shall observe* to do.
28: 9. if *thou shalt keep* the commandments
58. If *thou wilt* not *observe* to do
Jos. 1: 8. that *thou mayest observe* to do
24:17. *and preserved us* in all the way
Jud. 13:14. all that I commanded her *let her observe.*
1Sa. 2: 9. *He will keep* the feet of his saints,
30:23. who *hath preserved* us, and delivered
2Sa. 22:44. *thou hast kept me* (to be) head
1K. 2: 4. If thy children *take heed* to their way,
3: 6. *and thou hast kept* for him
8:25. so that thy children *take heed*
9: 4. *wilt keep* my statutes
6. *will* not *keep* my commandments
2K. 17:37. *ye shall observe* to do for evermore;
18: 6. *but kept* his commandments,
21: 8. if *they will observe* to do according
1Ch 22:13. if *thou takest heed* to fulfil
2Ch 6:16. so that thy children *take heed*
7:17. *shalt observe* my statutes
23: 6. all the people *shall keep* the watch of
33: 8. so that *they will take heed*
Neh 12:45. *And*...the porters *kept* the ward
Job 13:27. *and lookest narrowly* (marg. *observest*) unto all my paths;
14:16. *dost thou* not *watch* over my sin?
22:15. *Hast thou marked* the old way
29: 2. the days (when) God *preserved me;*
33:11. *he marketh* all my paths.
39: 1. *canst thou mark* when the hinds do calve?
Ps. 12: 7(8). Thou *shalt keep them*, O Lord,
39: 1(2). *I will take heed* to my ways,
—(–). *I will keep* my mouth
41: 2(3). The Lord *will preserve him,*
56: 6(7). *they mark* my steps,
59[title](1). *and they watched* the house to kill
9(10). (of) his strength *will I wait* upon
89:28(29). My mercy *will I keep* for him
31(32). *keep* not my commandments;
105:45. That *they might observe* his statutes,
107:43. Whoso (is) wise, and *will observe*
119: 8. *I will keep* thy statutes:
17. may live, *and keep* thy word.
34. *yea, I shall observe it* with (my) whole
44. *So shall I keep* thy law
55. in the night, *and have kept* thy law.
88. *so shall I keep* the testimony
101. that *I might keep* thy word.
134. *so will I keep* thy precepts.
146. *and I shall keep* thy testimonies.
121: 7. The Lord *shall preserve thee*
— *he shall preserve* thy soul.
8. The Lord *shall preserve* thy going out
127: 1. except the Lord *keep* the city,
130: 3. If thou, Lord, *shouldest mark* iniquities,
132:12. If thy children *will keep* my covenant
Pro. 2: 8. *preserveth* the way of his saints.
11. Discretion *shall preserve* thee,
20. *keep* the paths of the righteous.
4: 6. *and she shall preserve thee:*
6:22. when thou sleepest, *it shall keep* thee;
8:32. blessed (are they that) *keep* my ways.
14: 3. the lips of the wise *shall preserve them.*
22:18. a pleasant thing if *thou keep them*
Isa. 42:20. but *thou observest* not;
56: 4. unto the eunuchs that *keep* my sabbaths,
Jer. 3: 5. *will he keep* (it) to the end?

Jer. 5:24. *he reserveth* unto us the appointed weeks
35:18. *and kept* all his precepts,
Eze.11:20. *keep* mine ordinances,
20:18. neither *observe* their judgments,
36:27. *ye shall keep* my judgments,
37:24. *observe* my statutes, and do them.
43:11. *that they may keep* the whole form
44:24. *they shall keep* my laws
Zec. 3: 7. if *thou wilt keep* my charge,
— *shalt* also *keep* my courts,
Mal. 2: 7. the priest's lips *should keep* knowledge,

KAL.—*Participle.* Poel.

Gen 4: 9. (Am) I my brother's *keeper?*
Ex. 20: 6. *and keep* my commandments.
Nu. 3:28. *keeping* the charge of the sanctuary.
32. oversight of them *that keep* the charge
38. *keeping* the charge of the sanctuary
31:30. *which keep* the charge of the tabernacle
47. *which kept* the charge of the tabernacle
Deu 5:10. *and keep* my commandments.
7: 9. *which keepeth* covenant and mercy
— *and keep* his commandments
Jud. 1:24. *the spies* saw a man come forth
2:22. *whether they will keep* the way
7:19. they had but newly set *the watch:*
1Sa. 1:12. Eli *marked* her mouth.
17:20. left the sheep with *a keeper*,
22. his carriage in the hand of *the keeper of*
28: 2. Therefore will I make thee *keeper* of mine
1K. 8:23. *who keepest* covenant and mercy
14:27. *which kept* the door of the king's house.
2K. 9:14. Now Joram had *kept* (lit. had been *keeping*) Ramoth-gilead,
11: 5. shall *even* be *keepers of* the watch
12: 9(10). the priests *that kept* the door
22: 4. *the keepers of* the door
14. *keeper of* the wardrobe;
23: 4. *the keepers of* the door,
25:18. *the* three *keepers of* the door:
1Ch 9:19. *keepers of* the gates
— *keepers of* the entry.
12:29. greatest part of them *had kept* the ward
2Ch 6:14. *which keepest* covenant,
12:10. *that kept* the entrance of the king's house.
13:11. we *keep* the charge of the Lord
34: 9. the Levites *that kept* the doors
22. Hasrah, *keeper of* the wardrobe;
Neh 1: 5. *that keepeth* covenant and mercy
— *and observe* his commandments:
2: 8. Asaph *the keeper of* the king's forest,
3:29. *the keeper of* the east gate.
9:32. *who keepest* covenant and mercy,
11:19. their brethren *that kept* the gates,
12:25. porters *keeping* the ward at the thresholds
13:22. they should come (and) *keep* the gates,
Est. 2: 3. king's chamberlain, *keeper of* the women;
8. Hegai, *keeper of* the women.
14. *which kept* the concubines:
15. chamberlain, *the keeper of* the women,
21. *of those which kept* the door,
6: 2. *the keepers of* the door,
Ps. 31: 6(7). I have hated *them that regard*
34:20(21). He *keepeth* all his bones:
71:10. *and they that lay wait for* (marg. *watch*, or, *observe*) my soul
97:10. he *preserveth* the souls of his saints;
103:18. *To such as keep* his covenant,
106: 3. Blessed (are) *they that keep* judgment,
116: 6. The Lord *preserveth* the simple:
119:63. *and of them that keep* thy precepts.
121: 3. *he that keepeth thee* will not slumber.
4. *he that keepeth* Israel shall neither
5. The Lord (is) *thy keeper:*
127: 1. the *watchman* waketh (but) in vain.
130: 6. more *than they that watch* for the morning: (I say, more than) they *that watch*
145:20. The Lord *preserveth* all them
146: 6. *which keepeth* truth for ever:
9. The Lord *preserveth* the strangers;
Pro. 10:17. way of life *that keepeth* instruction:
13: 3. He that keepeth his mouth *keepeth*
18 & 15:5. *but he that regardeth* reproof
16:17. he that keepeth his way *preserveth*
19: 8. he *that keepeth* understanding
16. He *that keepeth* the commandment *keepeth* his own soul;
Pro.21:23. Whoso *keepeth* his mouth and his tongue *keepeth* his soul from troubles.
22: 5. *he that doth keep* his soul
27:18. *so he that waiteth* on his master
28: 4. *but such as keep* the law
29:18. *but he that keepeth* the law,
Ecc. 5: 8(7). higher than the highest *regardeth;*
8: 5. *Whoso keepeth* the commandment
11: 4. *He that observeth* the wind
12: 3. when *the keepers of* the house
Cant 3: 3. *The watchmen* that go about the city
5: 7. *The watchmen* that went about
— *the keepers of* the walls took away
Isa. 21:11. He calleth to me out of Seir, *Watchman*,
— *Watchman*, what of the night?
12. *The watchman* said, The morning cometh,
26: 2. righteous nation *which keepeth* the truth
56: 2. *that keepeth* the sabbath from polluting it, *and keepeth* his hand from doing
6. *that keepeth* the sabbath from polluting it,
62: 6. I have set *watchmen* upon thy walls,
Jer. 4:17. *As keepers of* a field,
20:10. All my familiars *watched* for my halting,
35: 4. Shallum, *the keeper of* the door:
51:12. set up *the watchmen*,
52:24. *the* three *keepers of* the door:
Eze.40:45, 46. *the keepers of* the charge
44: 8. but ye have set *keepers*
14. But I will make them *keepers of*
Dan 9: 4. *keeping* the covenant and mercy
— *and to them that keep* his commandments;
Zec.11:11. the poor of the flock *that waited*
Mal. 2: 9. ye have not *kept* my ways,

KAL.—*Participle.* Paül.

1Sa. 9:24. *hath it been kept* for thee
2Sa.23: 5. ordered in all (things), *and sure:*
Ecc. 5:13(12). riches *kept* for the owners thereof

* NIPHAL.—*Preterite.* *

Deu 2: 4. *take ye* good *heed unto yourselves*
4:15. *Take ye therefore* good *heed*
23: 9(10). *then keep thee* from every wicked
Jos. 23:11. *Take* good *heed therefore* unto yourselves,
1Sa.21: 4(5). *have kept themselves* at least from
2Sa.20:10. Amasa *took* no *heed* to the sword
2K. 6:10. *and saved himself* there,
Ps. 37:28. *they are preserved* for ever:
Hos 12:13(14). by a prophet *was he preserved.*
Mal. 2:15, 16. *Therefore take heed* to your spirit,

NIPHAL.—*Imperative.*

Gen24: 6. *Beware* thou that thou bring not
31:24. *Take heed* that thou speak not
29. *Take* thou *heed* that thou speak
Ex. 10:28. *take heed* to thyself,
19:12. *Take heed* to yourselves,
23:21. *Beware* of him, and obey his voice,
34:12. *Take heed* to thyself, lest thou make
Deu 4: 9. Only *take heed* to thyself, and keep
23. *Take heed* unto yourselves,
6:12. *beware* lest thou forget the Lord,
8:11. *Beware* that thou forget not the Lord
11:16. *Take heed* to yourselves,
12:13, 19, 30. *Take heed* to thyself that
15: 9. *Beware* that there be not a thought
24: 8. *Take heed* in the plague of leprosy,
Jud.13: 4. Now therefore *beware*, I pray thee,
1Sa.19: 2. *take heed to thyself* until the morning,
2K. 6: 9. *Beware* that thou pass not such
Job 36:21. *Take heed*, regard not iniquity:
Isa. 7: 4. say unto him, *Take heed*, and be quiet;
Jer. 9: 4(3). *Take ye heed* every one of his neighbour,
17:21. *Take heed* to yourselves,

NIPHAL.—*Future.*

Ex. 23:13. said unto you *be circumspect:*
Jud 13:13. I said unto the woman *let her beware.*

* PIEL.—*Participle.* *

Jon. 2: 8(9). *They that observe* lying vanities

* HITHPAEL.—*Future.* *

2Sa.22:24. *and have kept myself* from
Ps. 18:23(24). *and I kept myself* from
Mic. 6:16. *For* the statutes of Omri *are kept*, (marg. or, *he doth much keep*)

8108 **שִׁמְרָה** *shom-rāh'*, f.

Ps. 141: 3. Set *a watch*, O Lord, before my mouth;

8109 **שְׁמֻרוֹת** *sh'moo-rōhth'*, f. pl.

Ps. 77: 4(5). Thou holdest mine eyes *waking*: (lit. *the watches of* mine eyes)

8105 **שְׁמָרִים** *sh'māh-reem'*, m. pl.

Ps. 75: 8(9). but *the dregs thereof*,
Isa. 25: 6. a feast of *wines on the lees*,
— of *wines on the lees* well refined.
Jer. 48:11. he hath settled on his *lees*,
Zep 1:12. settled on their *lees*:

8107 **שִׁמֻּרִים** *shim-moo-reem'*, m. pl.

Ex. 12:42. It (is) a night to *be much observed* (marg. a night of *observations*)
— (is) that night of the Lord to *be observed*

8120 **שְׁמַשׁ** [*sh'-mash*], Ch.

* PAEL.—*Future.* *

Dan 7:10. thousand thousands *ministered unto him*,

8121 **שֶׁמֶשׁ** *sheh'-mesh*, com.

Gen 15:12. when *the sun* was going down,
17. that, when *the sun* went down,
19:23. *The sun* was risen upon the earth
28:11. because *the sun* was set;
32:31(32). as he passed over Penuel *the sun* rose
37: 9. *the sun* and the moon and the eleven stars
Ex. 16:21. when *the sun* waxed hot, it melted.
17:12. steady until the going down of *the sun*.
22: 3(2). If *the sun* be risen upon him,
26(25). deliver it unto him by that *the sun*
Lev.22: 7. when *the sun* is down,
Nu. 21:11. before Moab, toward the *sun*rising.
25: 4. hang them up before the Lord against *the sun*,
Deu 4:19. when thou seest *the sun*,
41. Jordan toward the *sun* rising;
47. this side Jordan toward the *sun* rising;
11:30. by the way where *the sun* goeth down,
16: 6. at the going down of *the sun*,
17: 3. *either the sun*, or moon,
23:11(12). when *the sun* is down,
24:13. pledge again when *the sun* goeth down,
15. neither shall *the sun* go down
33:14. precious fruits (brought forth) by *the sun*,
Jos. 1: 4. toward the going down of *the sun*,
15. this side Jordan toward the *sun*rising.
8:29. as soon as *the sun* was down,
10:12. *Sun*, stand thou still upon Gibeon;
13. And *the sun* stood still,
— So *the sun* stood still
27. the going down of *the sun*,
12: 1. toward the rising of *the sun*,
13: 5. Lebanon, toward the *sun*rising,
19:12. Sarid eastward toward the *sun*rising
27. turneth toward the *sun*rising
34. upon Jordan toward the *sun*rising.
23: 4. even unto the great sea westward. (marg. at the *sun*set)
Jud. 5:31. as *the sun* when he goeth forth
9:33. as soon as *the sun* is up,
11:18. came by the east side (lit. rising of *the sun*) of the land of Moab,
19:14. *the sun* went down upon them
20:43. Gibeah toward the *sun*rising.
21:19. on the east side (marg. or, toward the *sun*rising) of the highway
1Sa.11: 9. by (that time) *the sun* be hot,
2Sa. 2:24. *and the sun* went down
3:35. till *the sun* be down.
12:11. with thy wives in the sight of this *sun*.
12. before all Israel, and before *the sun*.
23: 4. the morning, (when) *the sun*
1K. 22:36. about the going down of *the sun*,
2K. 3:22. *and the sun* shone upon the water,
2K. 10:33. From Jordan eastward (marg. toward the rising of *the sun*), all the land of
23: 5. *to the sun*, and to the moon,
11. kings of Judah had given *to the sun*,
— burned the chariots of *the sun*
2Ch 18:34. about the time of *the sun*
Neh 7: 3. be opened until *the sun* be hot;
Job 8:16. He (is) green before *the sun*,
Ps. 19: 4(5). hath he set a tabernacle *for the sun*,
50: 1. called the earth from the rising of *the sun*
58: 8(9). they may not see *the sun*.
72: 5. as long as *the sun* and moon endure,
17. shall be continued as long as *the sun*:
74:16. thou hast prepared the light *and the sun*.
84:11(12). the Lord God (is) *a sun* and shield:
89:36(37). his throne *as the sun* before me.
104:19. *the sun* knoweth his going down.
22. *The sun* ariseth, they gather
113: 3. From the rising of *the sun* unto the
121: 6. *The sun* shall not smite thee by day,
136: 8. *The sun* to rule by day:
148: 3. Praise ye him, *sun* and moon:
Ecc. 1: 3. labour which he taketh under *the sun*?
5. *The sun* also ariseth, and *the sun* goeth
9. no new (thing) under *the sun*.
14. the works that are done under *the sun*;
2:11. no profit under *the sun*.
17. work that is wrought under *the sun*
18. which I had taken under *the sun*:
19. have shewed myself wise under *the sun*.
20. labour which I took under *the sun*.
22. wherein he hath laboured under *the sun*?
3:16. saw under *the sun* the place of judgment,
4: 1. oppressions that are done under *the sun*:
3. the evil work that is done under *the sun*.
7. I saw vanity under *the sun*.
15. the living which walk under *the sun*,
5:13(12). (which) I have seen under *the sun*,
18(17). that he taketh under *the sun*
6: 1. evil which I have seen under *the sun*,
5. Moreover he hath not seen *the sun*,
12. what shall be after him under *the sun*?
7:11. profit to them that see *the sun*.
8: 9. work that is done under *the sun*:
15. man hath no better thing under *the sun*,
— which God giveth him under *the sun*.
17. the work that is done under *the sun*:
9: 3. that are done under *the sun*,
6. that is done under *the sun*.
9. which he hath given thee under *the sun*,
— labour which thou takest under *the sun*
11. I returned, and saw under *the sun*,
13. This wisdom have I seen also under *the sun*
10: 5. There is an evil (which) I have seen under *the sun*,
11: 7. for the eyes to behold *the sun*:
12: 2. While *the sun*, or the light, or the moon,
Cant.1: 6. because *the sun* hath looked upon me:
Isa. 13:10. *the sun* shall be darkened
38: 8. which is gone down in the *sun* dial (marg degrees *by*, or, with *the sun*) of Ahaz,
— So *the sun* returned ten degrees,
41:25. from the rising of *the sun* shall
45: 6. know from the rising of *the sun*,
49:10. neither shall the heat *nor sun* smite them.
54:12. I will make *thy windows* of agates,
59:19. his glory from the rising of *the sun*
60:19. *The sun* shall be no more thy light
20. *Thy sun* shall no more go down;
Jer. 8: 2. shall spread them before *the sun*,
15: 9. *her sun* is gone down while (it was) yet
31:35. which giveth *the sun* for a light
43:13. break also the images of Beth-*shemesh*, (marg. or, the house of *the sun*)
Eze. 8:16. they worshipped *the sun*
32: 7. I will cover *the sun* with a cloud,
Joel 2:10. *the sun* and the moon shall be dark,
31(3:4). *The sun* shall be turned into
3:15(4:15). *The sun* and the moon shall be
Am. 8: 9. I will cause *the sun* to go down
Jon. 4: 8. when *the sun* did arise,
— and *the sun* beat upon the head of Jonah,
Mic. 3: 6. *the sun* shall go down over the prophets,
Nah. 3:17. when *the sun* ariseth they flee away,
Hab. 3:11. *The sun* (and) moon stood still
Zec. 8: 7. and from the west country; (marg. country of the going down of *the sun*)

Mal. 1:11. from the rising of *the sun* even unto
4: 2(3:20). *the Sun of* righteousness arise with

8122 **שֶׁמֶשׁ** [*sheh'-mesh*], Ch. com.

Dan 6:14(15). he laboured till the going down of *the sun*

8127 **שֵׁן** *shēhn*, com.

Gen49:12. his *teeth* white with milk.
Ex. 21:24. Eye for eye, *tooth* for *tooth*,
27. smite out his manservant's *tooth*, or his maidservant's *tooth;* he shall let him go free for *his tooth*'s sake.
Lev.24:20. eye for eye, *tooth* for *tooth:*
Nu. 11:33. flesh (was) yet between *their teeth*,
Deu19:21. *tooth for tooth*, hand for hand,
32:24. I will *also* send *the teeth of* beasts
1Sa. 2:13. a fleshhook of three *teeth* in his hand;
14: 4. (there was) a *sharp* (lit. *tooth*) rock on the one side, *and a sharp* rock on the other
5. *The forefront* (marg. *tooth*) of the one
1K. 10:18. the king made a great throne of *ivory*,
22:39. the *ivory* house which he made,
2Ch 9:17. the king made a great throne of *ivory*,
Job 4:10. *and the teeth of* the young lions,
13:14. do I take my flesh *in my teeth*,
16: 9. he gnasheth upon me *with his teeth;*
19:20. I am escaped with the skin of *my teeth*.
29:17. *and* plucked the spoil out of *his teeth*.
39:28. upon *the crag of* the rock,
41:14(6). *his teeth* (are) terrible round about.
Ps. 3: 7(8). hast broken *the teeth of* the ungodly.
35:16. they gnashed upon me with *their teeth*.
37:12. gnasheth upon him with *his teeth*.
45: 8(9). out of the *ivory* palaces,
57: 4(5). *whose teeth* (are) spears and arrows,
58: 6(7). Break *their teeth*, O God,
112:10. he shall gnash with *his teeth*,
124: 6. hath not given us (as) a prey *to their teeth*.
Pro.10:26. As vinegar *to the teeth*,
25:19. *a* broken *tooth*, and a foot out of joint.
30:14. a generation, *whose teeth* (are as) swords,
Cant.4: 2. *Thy teeth* (are) like a flock
5:14. his belly (is as) bright *ivory* overlaid
6: 6. *Thy teeth* (are) as a flock of sheep
7: 4(5). Thy neck (is) as a tower of *ivory;*
Jer. 31:29. *and* the children's *teeth* are set on edge.
30. *his teeth* shall be set on edge.
Lam.2:16. they hiss and gnash *the teeth:*
3:16. He hath also broken *my teeth*
Eze.18: 2. *and* the children's *teeth* are set on edge?
27: 6. Ashurites have made thy benches (of) *ivory*,
15. (for) a present horns of *ivory* and ebony.
Joel 1: 6. *whose teeth* (are) *the teeth of* a lion,
Am. 3:15. the houses of *ivory* shall perish,
4: 6. have given you cleanness of *teeth*
6: 4. That lie upon beds of *ivory*,
Mic. 3: 5. that bite *with their teeth*,
Zec. 9: 7. abominations from between *his teeth:*

8128 **שֵׁן** [*shēhn*], Ch. m.

Dan 7: 5. three ribs in the mouth of it between *the teeth of it:*
7. *and* it had great iron *teeth:*
19. *whose teeth* (were of) iron, and his nails (of) brass;

8132 **שְׁנָא** [*shāh-nāh'*].

* KAL.—*Future.* *

Lam 4: 1. *is* the most fine gold *changed!*

* PIEL.—*Preterite.* *

2K. 25:29. *And changed* his prison garments:

* PUAL.—*Future.* *

Ecc. 8: 1. the boldness of his face *shall be changed.*

שְׁנָא [*sh'nāh*], Ch. 8133

* P'AL.—*Preterite.* *

Dan 3:27. neither *were* their coats *changed*,
5: 6. the king's countenance *was changed*, (marg. *changed it*)

P'AL.—*Future.*

Dan 6:17(18). *might* not *be changed* concerning
7:23. which *shall be diverse* from all
24. and he *shall be diverse* from the first,

P'AL.—*Participle.*

Dan 5: 9. and his countenance *was changed*
7: 3. *diverse* one from another.
19. which *was diverse* from all the others,

* PAEL.—*Preterite.* *

Dan 3:28. and *have changed* the king's word,

PAEL.—*Future.*

Dan 4:16(13). *Let* his heart *be changed*

PAEL.—*Participle.*

Dan 7: 7. *and* it (was) *diverse* from all

* ITHPAEL.—*Preterite.* *

Dan 3:19. the form of his visage *was changed*

ITHPAEL.—*Future.*

Dan 2: 9. till the time *be changed:*
5:10. nor *let* thy countenance *be changed:*
7:28. my countenance *changed* in me:

* APHEL.—*Infinitive.* *

Ezr. 6:12. that shall put to their hand *to alter*
Dan 6: 8(9). that *it be* not *changed*,
15(16). the king establisheth *may be changed*.
7:25. and think *to change* times and laws:

APHEL.—*Future.*

Ezr. 6:11. that whosoever *shall alter* this word,

APHEL.—*Participle.*

Dan 2:21. And he *changeth* the times

שֵׁנָא *shēh-nāh*, f. 8142

Ps.127: 2. so he giveth his beloved *sleep*.

שִׁנְאָן *shin-āhn'*, m. 8136

Ps. 68:17(18). twenty thousand, (even) thousands of *angels:* [perhaps lit. *a repeating*]

שָׁנָה *shāh-nāh'*. 8138

* KAL.—*Preterite.* *

2Sa.20:10. *struck* him not *again;* (marg. *doubled* not)
Mal. 3: 6. I (am) the Lord, *I change* not;

KAL.—*Imperative.*

1K. 18:34. *Do* (it) *the second time*.

KAL.—*Future.*

1Sa.26: 8. *I will* not (smite) him *the second time*.
1K. 18:34. *And they did* (it) *the second time*.
Neh 13:21. if *ye do* (so) *again*,
Job 29:22. After my words *they spake* not *again;*

KAL.—*Participle.* Poel.

Est. 1: 7. the vessels *being diverse* one from
3: 8. their laws (are) *diverse* from all people;
Pro.17: 9. *but he that repeateth* a matter
24:21. meddle not with *them that are given to change:*
26:11. a fool *returneth* (marg. *iterateth*) to his folly.

* NIPHAL.—*Infinitive.* *

Gen41:32. for that the dream *was doubled*

* PIEL.—*Preterite.* *

Jer. 52:33. *And changed* his prison garments:

PIEL.—*Infinitive.*

Ps. 34[title](1). *when he changed* his behaviour
Jer. 2:36. about so much *to change* thy way?

PIEL.—*Future.*

1Sa.21:13(14). *And he changed* his behaviour
Est. 2: 9. *and he preferred* (marg. *changed*) her and her maids
Ps. 89:34(35). covenant will I not break, nor *alter*
Pro.31: 5. forget the law, *and pervert* (marg. *alter*) the judgment

PIEL.—*Participle.*

Job 14:20. thou *changest* his countenance,

* HITHPAEL.—*Imperative.* *

1K. 14: 2. Arise, I pray thee, *and disguise* thyself,

8141 שָׁנָה *shāh-nāh'*, f.

Gen 1:14. for seasons, and for days, *and years:*
5: 3. an hundred and thirty *years*,
4. Seth were eight hundred *years:*
5. Adam lived were nine hundred)(and thirty *years:*
6. Seth lived an hundred)(and five *years*,
7. Enos eight hundred)(and seven *years*,
8. Seth were nine hundred)(and twelve *years:* and he died.
9. Enos lived ninety *years*,
10. begat Cainan eight hundred)(and fifteen *years*, and begat sons and
11. Enos were nine hundred)(and five *years:*
12. Cainan lived seventy *years*,
13. Mahalaleel eight hundred)(and forty *years*, and begat sons
14. Cainan were nine hundred)(and ten *years:*
15. Mahalaleel lived sixty)(and five *years*,
16. Jared eight hundred)(and thirty *years*, and begat sons
17. eight hundred)(ninety and five *years:*
18. hundred sixty)(and two *years*,
19. Enoch eight hundred *years*,
20. nine hundred)(sixty and two *years:*
21. Enoch lived sixty and five *years*,
22. Methuselah three hundred *years*,
23. three hundred)(sixty and five *years:*
25. hundred)(eighty and seven *years*,
26. seven hundred)(eighty and two *years*,
27. nine hundred)(sixty and nine *years:*
28. hundred)(eighty and two *years*,
30. five hundred)(ninety and five *years*,
31. seven hundred)(seventy and seven *years:*
32. Noah was five hundred *years*
6: 3. an hundred and twenty *years.*
7: 6. Noah (was) six hundred *years* old
11. *In the*)(six hundredth *year* (lit. *in the year*, in the six hundredth *year*)
8:13. in *the* six hundredth and first *year*,
9:28. Noah lived after the flood three hundred)(and fifty *years.*
29. all the days of Noah were nine hundred)(and fifty *years:* and he died.
11:10. Shem (was) an hundred *years* old, and begat Arphaxad *two years* after the
11. Arphaxad five hundred *years*,
12. lived five and thirty *years*,
13. Salah four hundred)(and three *years*,
14. Salah lived thirty *years*,
15. Eber four hundred)(and three *years*,
16. Eber lived four and thirty *years*,
17. after he begat Peleg four hundred)(and thirty *years*, and begat sons
18. Peleg lived thirty *years*,
19. begat Reu two hundred)(and nine *years*,
20. Reu lived two and thirty *years*,
21. after he begat Serug two hundred)(and seven *years*,
22. Serug lived thirty *years*,
23. Nahor two hundred *years*,
24. Nahor lived nine and twenty *years*,
25. Nahor lived after he begat Terah an hundred)(and nineteen *years*, and
26. Terah lived seventy *years*,
32. Terah were two hundred)(and five *years:*
12: 4. Abram (was) seventy)(and five *years* old
14: 4. Twelve *years* they served
— in *the* thirteenth *year* they rebelled.

Gen14: 5. in *the* fourteenth *year*
15:13. shall afflict them four hundred *years;*
16: 3. after Abram had dwelt ten *years*
16. Abram (was) fourscore)(and six *years*
17: 1. Abram was ninety)(*years* old and nine,
17. born unto him that is an hundred *years*
— Sarah, that is ninety *years* old,
21. at this set time *in the* next *year.*
24. Abraham (was) ninety *years* old and nine,
25. (was) thirteen *years* old,
21. 5. Abraham was an hundred *years* old,
23: 1. Sarah was an hundred)(and seven)(and twenty *years* old: (these were) *the years of* the life of Sarah.
25: 7. the days of *the years of* Abraham's life
— hundred)(threescore)(and fifteen *years.*
17. *the years of* the life of Ishmael, an hundred)(and thirty)(and seven *years:*
20. Isaac was forty *years* old
26. Isaac (was) threescore *years* old
26:12. received *in the* same *year*
34. Esau was forty *years* old
29:18. I will serve thee seven *years* for Rachel
20. Jacob served seven *years*
27. serve with me yet seven other *years.*
30. served with him yet seven other *years.*
31:38. twenty *years* (have) I (been) with thee;
41. Thus have I been twenty *years*
— I served thee fourteen *years* for thy two daughters, and six *years* for thy cattle:
35:28. Isaac were an hundred)(and fourscore *years.*
37: 2. Joseph, (being) seventeen *years* old,
41: 1. at the end of *two* full *years*,
26. seven good kine (are) seven *years;*
— seven good ears (are) seven *years:*
27. up after them (are) seven *years;*
— shall be seven *years of* famine.
29. there come seven *years* of great
30. arise after them seven *years of*
34, 47. in *the* seven plenteous *years.*
35. all the food of those good *years* that come,
36. against *the* seven *years of* famine,
46. Joseph (was) thirty *years* old
48. gathered up all the food of *the* seven *years*,
50. before *the years of* famine came,
53. *the* seven *years of* plenteousness,
54. *the* seven *years of* dearth began
45: 6. *two years* (hath) the famine
— yet (there are) five *years*,
11. five *years* of famine;
47: 8. Pharaoh said unto Jacob, How old (art) thou? (marg. How many (are) the days of *the years of* thy life)
9. The days of *the years of* my pilgrimage (are) an hundred and thirty *years:*
— have the days of *the years of* my life been,
— *the years of* the life of my fathers
17. all their cattle *for* that *year.*
18. When that *year* was ended, they came unto him *the* second *year*,
28. land of Egypt seventeen *years:* so the whole age (marg. days of *the years of* his life) of Jacob was an hundred)(forty and seven *years.*
50:22. Joseph lived an hundred and ten *years.*
26. an hundred and ten *years* old:
Ex. 6:16. *and the years of* the life of Levi (were) an hundred thirty and seven *years.*
18. *and the years of* the life of Kohath (were) an hundred thirty and three *years.*
20. *and the years of* the life of Amram (were) an hundred and thirty and seven *years.*
7: 7. Moses (was) fourscore *years* old, and Aaron fourscore and three *years* old,
12: 2. the first month of *the year*
5. a male of *the* first *year:*
40. four hundred)(and thirty *years.*
41. *the* four hundred)(and thirty *years*,
16:35. Israel did eat manna forty *years*,
21: 2. six *years* he shall serve:
23:10. six *years* thou shalt sow
14. keep a feast unto me *in the year.*
16. in the end of *the year*,
17. Three times *in the year*
29. from before thee *in* one *year;*
29:38. two lambs of *the* first *year*

Ex. 30:10. upon the horns of it once *in a year*
— once *in the year* shall he make
14. from twenty *years* old and above,
34:22. the feast of ingathering at *the year's* end.
23. Thrice *in the year* shall all
24. the Lord thy God thrice *in the year*.
38:26. from twenty *years* old and upward,
40:17. first month *in the* second *year*,
Lev. 9: 3. calf and a lamb, (both) of *the* first *year*,
12: 6. shall bring a lamb of *the* first *year* (marg. a son of *his year*)
14:10. one ewe lamb of *the* first *year* (marg. the daughter of *her year*)
16:34. for all their sins once *a year*.
19:23. three *years* shall it be as
24. *But in the* fourth *year*
25. *And in the* fifth *year*
23:12. lamb without blemish of *the* first *year* (lit. a son of *his year*)
18. lambs without blemish of *the* first *year*,
19. two lambs of *the* first *year*
41. seven days *in the year*.
25: 3. Six *years* thou shalt sow thy field, and six *years* thou shalt prune thy vineyard,
4. *But in the* seventh *year*
5. it is *a year of* rest unto the land.
8. number seven sabbaths of *years* unto thee, seven times seven *years*;
— the seven sabbaths of *years* shall be unto thee forty and nine *years*.
10. ye shall hallow *the*)(fiftieth *year*, (lit. *year of the* fiftieth *year*)
11. A jubile shall that)(fiftieth *year* (lit. *a year of the* fiftieth *year*)
13. *In the year of* this jubile
15. According to the number of *years* after
— according unto the number of *years of*
16. According to the multitude of *years*
— according to the fewness of *years*
20. What shall we eat *the* seventh *year*?
21. my blessing upon you *in the* sixth *year*, and it shall bring forth fruit for three *years*.
22. ye shall sow *the* eighth *year*,
— of old fruit until *the* ninth *year*;
27. Then let him count *the years of*
28. until *the year of* jubile:
29. within *a* whole *year* after it is sold;
30. within the space of *a* full *year*,
40. shall serve thee unto *the year of* jubile:
50. *from the year* that he was sold to him unto *the year of*
— according unto the number of *years*,
51. If (there be) yet many *years*
52. if there remain but few *years* unto *the year of* jubile,
— according unto *his years*
53. as a *yearly* (lit. *year by year*) hired servant
54. he shall go out *in the year of*
27: 3. the male from twenty *years* old even unto sixty *years* old,
5. if (it be) from five *years* old even unto twenty *years* old,
6. even unto five *years* old,
7. if (it be) from sixty *years* old
17. sanctify his field *from the year of*
18. according to *the years* that remain, even unto *the year of*
23. (even) unto *the year of* the jubile:
24. *In the year of* the jubile
Nu. 1: 1. *in the* second *year*
3, 18, 20, 22, 24, 26, 28, 30, 32, 34, 36, 38, 40, 42, 45. From twenty *years* old
4: 3, 23. From thirty *years* old...until fifty *years* old,
30, 35, 39, 43, 47. From thirty *years* old and upward even unto fifty *years* old
6:12. shall bring a lamb of *the* first *year* (lit. a son of *his year*)
14. one he lamb of *the* first *year*
— one ewe lamb of *the* first *year*
7:15, 21, 27, 33, 39, 45, 51, 57, 63, 69, 75, 81. one lamb of *the* first *year*,
17, 23, 29, 35, 41, 47, 53, 59, 65, 71, 77, 83. five lambs of *the* first *year*:
87. lambs of *the* first *year* twelve,
88. lambs of *the* first *year* sixty.

Nu. 8:24. twenty and five *years* old
25. the age of fifty *years*
9: 1. in the first month *of the* second *year* after
10:11. *in the* second *year*,
13:22. Hebron was built seven *years*
14:29. twenty *years* old and upward,
33. in the wilderness forty *years*,
34. each day *for a year*, (lit. a day *for a year*, a day *for a year*)
— (even) forty *years*,
15:27. a she goat of *the* first *year*
26: 2, 4. from twenty *years* old and upward,
28: 3. two lambs of *the* first *year*
9. *the* first *year* without spot,
11. seven lambs of *the* first *year*
14. the months of *the year*.
19, 27. seven lambs of *the* first *year*:
29: 2. lambs of *the* first *year* without
8, 36. seven lambs of *the* first *year*;
13, 17, 20, 23, 26, 29, 32. fourteen lambs of *the* first *year*;
32:11. from twenty *years* old and upward,
13. in the wilderness forty *years*,
33:38. *in the* fortieth *year*
39. an hundred and twenty and three *years*
Deu 1: 3. it came to pass in *the* fortieth *year*,
2: 7. these forty *years* the Lord
14. (was) thirty and eight *years*;
8: 2. led thee these forty *years*
4. neither did thy foot swell, these forty *years*.
11:12. from the beginning of *the year* even unto the end of *the year*.
14:22. that the field bringeth forth *year* by *year*.
28. At the end of three *years*
— thine increase *the* same *year*,
15: 1. At the end of (every) seven *years*
9. *The* seventh *year*, *the year of* release,
12. serve thee six *years*; *then in the* seventh *year*
18. hired servant (to thee), in serving thee six *years*:
20. before the Lord thy God *year by year* in
16:16. Three times *in a year*
24: 5. he shall be free at home one *year*.
26:12. of thine increase *the* third *year*, (which is) *the year of* tithing,
29: 5(4). I have led you forty *years*
31: 2. an hundred and twenty *years* old
10. At the end of (every) seven *years*, in the solemnity of *the year of*
32: 7. *the years of* many generations:
34: 7. an hundred and twenty *years* old
Jos. 5: 6. Israel walked forty *years*
12. fruit of the land of Canaan that *year*.
14: 7. Forty *years* old (was) I
10. these forty and five *years*,
— I (am) this day fourscore and five *years*
24:29. an hundred and ten *years* old.
Jud. 2: 8. an hundred and ten *years* old.
3: 8. served Chushan-rishathaim eight *years*.
11. the land had rest forty *years*.
14. the king of Moab eighteen *years*.
30. the land had rest fourscore *years*.
4: 3. twenty *years* he mightily oppressed
5:31. the land had rest forty *years*.
6: 1. into the hand of Midian seven *years*.
25. second bullock of seven *years*
8:28. was in quietness forty *years*
9:22. reigned three *years* over Israel,
10: 2. judged Israel twenty and three *years*,
3. judged Israel twenty and two *years*.
8. that *year* they vexed and oppressed the children of Israel; eighteen *years*
11.26. three hundred *years*?
40. the Gileadite four days *in a year*.
12: 7. judged Israel six *years*.
9. judged Israel seven *years*.
11. judged Israel ten *years*.
14. judged Israel eight *years*.
13: 1. hand of the Philistines forty *years*.
15:20. days of the Philistines twenty *years*.
16:31. he judged Israel twenty *years*.
Ru. 1: 4. dwelled there about ten *years*.
1Sa. 1: 7. he did so *year by year*,
4:15. Eli was ninety and eight *years* old;
18. he had judged Israel forty *years*.

1Sa. 7: 2. for it was twenty *years:*
16. he went from *year to year* in circuit to
13: 1. Saul reigned one *year;*
— reigned two *years* over Israel,
29: 3. these days, or these *years,*
2Sa. 2:10. Saul's son (was) forty *years* old
— reigned two *years.*
11. was seven *years* and six months.
4: 4. He was five *years* old
5: 4. David (was) thirty *years* old
— he reigned forty *years.*
5. he reigned over Judah seven *years*
— thirty and three *years* over all Israel
11: 1. after *the year* was expired,
13:23. it came to pass *after two* full *years,*
38. was there three *years.*
14:28. So Absalom dwelt *two* full *years*
15: 7. it came to pass after forty *years,*
19:32(33). aged man, (even) fourscore *years* old:
34(35). How long have I to live, (marg. How many days (are) *the years of* my life)
35(36). I (am) this day fourscore *years* old:
21: 1. in the days of David three *years, year* after *year;*
24:13. Shall seven *years* of famine
1K. 2:11. reigned over Israel (were) forty *years:* seven *years* reigned he in Hebron, and thirty and three *years*...in Jerusalem.
39. at the end of three *years,*
4: 7. each man his month *in a year*
5:11(25). Solomon to Hiram *year by year.*
6: 1. in *the* four hundred)(and eightieth *year*
— *in the* fourth *year* of Solomon's reign
37. *In the* fourth *year* was the foundation
38. *And in the* eleventh *year,*
— So was he seven *years* in building
7: 1. building his own house thirteen *years,*
9:10. at the end of twenty *years,*
25. three times *in a year*
10:14. came to Solomon *in* one *year*
22. once in three *years* came the navy
25. a rate *year by year.*
11:42. over all Israel (was) forty *years.*
14:20. two and twenty *years:*
21. Rehoboam (was) forty and one *years* old
— he reigned seventeen *years*
25. *in the* fifth *year* of king Rehoboam,
15: 1. *Now in the* eighteenth *year*
2. Three *years* reigned he in
9. *And in the* twentieth *year of*
10. forty and one *years* reigned he
25. to reign over Israel *in the* second *year*
— reigned over Israel *two years.*
28, 33. *in the* third *year* of Asa
33. over all Israel in Tirzah, twenty and four *years.*
16: 8. *In the* twenty)(and sixth *year* of Asa king of Judah
— to reign over Israel in Tirzah, *two years.*
10. *in the* twenty and seventh *year*
15. *In the* twenty)(and seventh *year* of Asa
23. *In the* thirty)(and first *year* of Asa king
— over Israel, twelve *years:* six *years* reigned he in
29. *in the* thirty)(and eighth *year* of Asa king
— Samaria twenty and two *years.*
17: 1. dew nor rain these *years,*
18: 1. Elijah *in the* third *year,*
20:22. for at the return of *the year*
26. came to pass at the return of *the year,*
22: 1. And they continued three *years*
2. it came to pass *in the* third *year,*
41. to reign over Judah *in the* fourth *year*
42. Jehoshaphat (was) thirty and five *years*
— reigned twenty and five *years* in Jerusalem.
51(52). *the* seventeenth *year of* Jehoshaphat
—(—). reigned *two years* over Israel.
2K. 1:17. *in the* second *year of* Jehoram
3: 1. *the* eighteenth *year of* Jehoshaphat
— reigned twelve *years.*
8: 1. come upon the land seven *years.*
2. land of the Philistines seven *years.*
3. at *the* seven *years'* end,
16. *And in the* fifth *year of* Joram
17. Thirty and two *years* old was he
— reigned eight *years* in Jerusalem.
25. *In the*)(twelfth *year of* Joram

2K. 8:26. Two and twenty *years* old
— *and* he reigned one *year*
9:29. *And in the*)(eleventh *year*
10:36. twenty and eight *years.*
11: 3. house of the Lord six *years.*
4. *And the* seventh *year* Jehoiada sent
21(12:1). Seven *years* old (was) Jehoash
12: 1(2). *In the* seventh *year* of Jehu
—(-). forty *years* reigned he in Jerusalem.
6(7). *in the* three)(and twentieth *year* of
13: 1. *In the* three)(and twentieth *year* of Joash the son of Ahaziah
— (reigned) seventeen *years.*
10. *In the* thirty)(and seventh *year* of Joash
— (reigned) sixteen *years.*
20. at the coming in of *the year.*
14: 1. *In the* second *year* of Joash
2. He was twenty and five *years* old
— reigned twenty and nine *years*
17. Jehoahaz king of Israel fifteen *years.*
21. which (was) sixteen *years* old,
23. *In the*)(fifteenth *year* of Amaziah
— (reigned) forty and one *years.*
15: 1. *In the* twenty)(and seventh *year* of
2. Sixteen *years* old was he
— he reigned two and fifty *years* in
8. *In the*)(thirty and eighth *year* of Azariah
13. began to reign *in the* nine)(and thirtieth *year* of Uzziah king of Judah;
17. *In the* nine)(and thirtieth *year* of Azariah king of Judah
— (reigned) ten *years* in Samaria.
23. *In the*)(fiftieth *year* of Azariah
— (reigned) *two years.*
27. *In the*)(two and fiftieth *year* of Azariah
— (reigned) twenty *years.*
30. *in the* twentieth *year of* Jotham
32. *In the* second *year* of Pekah the son of
33. Five and twenty *years* old
— he reigned sixteen *years*
16: 1. *In the*)(seventeenth *year*
2. Twenty *years* old (was) Ahaz
— reigned sixteen *years*
17: 1. *In the* twelfth *year* of Ahaz
— reign in Samaria over Israel nine *years.*
4. *as* (he had done) *year by year:*
5. besieged it three *years.*
6. *In the* ninth *year* of Hoshea
18: 1. it came to pass *in the* third *year*
2. Twenty and five *years* old
— he reigned twenty and nine *years*
9. came to pass *in the* fourth *year*
— which (was) *the* seventh *year*
10. at the end of three *years...in the* sixth *year* of Hezekiah, that (is) *the* ninth *year*
13. Now in *the* fourteenth *year*
19:29. Ye shall eat this *year*
— *and in the* second *year* that
— *and in the* third *year* sow ye,
20: 6. add unto thy days fifteen *years;*
21: 1. Manasseh (was) twelve *years*
— reigned fifty and five *years*
19. Amon (was) twenty and two *years*
— he reigned two *years*
22: 1. Josiah (was) eight *years* old
— he reigned thirty and one *years*
3. in *the* eighteenth *year* of king Josiah,
23:23. in *the* eighteenth *year* of king Josiah,
31. Jehoahaz (was) twenty and three *years*
36. Jehoiakim (was) twenty and five *years*
— reigned eleven *years*
24: 1. became his servant three *years:*
8. Jehoiachin (was) eighteen *years*
12. took him *in the* eighth *year*
18. Zedekiah (was) twenty and one *years*
— he reigned eleven *years*
25: 1. it came to pass *in the* ninth *year*
2. besieged unto *the* eleventh *year*
8. which (is) *the*)(nineteenth *year*
27. in *the* seven and thirtieth *year*
— *in the year that* he began to reign
1Ch 2:21. he married when he (was) threescore *years* old;
3: 4. he reigned seven *years* and six
— reigned thirty and three *years.*
20: 1. that after *the year* was expired,
21:12 Either three *years'* famine;

1Ch 23: 3. from the age of thirty *years* and upward:
24. from the age of twenty *years* and
27. from twenty *years* old and above:
26:31. *In the* fortieth *year* of the reign of David
27: 1. throughout all the months of *the year*,
23. from twenty *years* old and under:
29:27. over Israel (was) forty *years; seven years* reigned he in Hebron,
2Ch 3: 2. *in the* fourth *year* of his reign.
8: 1. at the end of twenty *years*,
13. three times *in the year*,
9:13. came to Solomon *in* one *year*
21. every three *years* once came
24. mules, a rate *year by year*.
30. over all Israel forty *years*.
11:17. son of Solomon strong, three *years: for* three *years* they walked in
12: 2. *in the* fifth *year* of king Rehoboam,
13. Rehoboam (was) one and forty *years* old
— reigned seventeen *years* in Jerusalem,
13: 1. Now *in the* eighteenth *year* of
2. He reigned three *years* in
14: 1(13:23). the land was quiet ten *years*.
6(5). and he had no war *in* those *years;*
15:10. *in the* fifteenth *year* of the reign
19. unto the five and thirtieth *year* of the
16: 1. *In the* six and thirtieth *year* of the
12. Asa *in the* thirty and ninth *year*
13. died *in the* one and fortieth *year* of
17: 7. *Also in the* third *year* of his
18: 2. And after (certain) *years* he
20:31. (he was) thirty and five *years* old
— he reigned twenty and five *years*
21: 5. Jehoram (was) thirty and two *years* old
— he reigned eight *years* in Jerusalem.
20. and he reigned in Jerusalem eight *years*,
22: 2. Forty and two *years* old (was)
— *and* he reigned one *year* in Jerusalem.
12. house of God six *years:*
23: 1. *And in the* seventh *year*
24: 1. Joash (was) seven *years* old
— he reigned forty *years* in Jerusalem.
5. from *year to year*, and see
15. an hundred and thirty *years* old
23. at the end of *the year*,
25: 1. Amaziah (was) twenty and five *years* old
— and he reigned twenty and nine *years*
5. he numbered them from twenty *years* old
25. king of Israel fifteen *years*.
26: 1. who (was) sixteen *years* old,
3. Sixteen *years* old (was) Uzziah
— he reigned fifty and two *years*
27: 1. Jotham (was) twenty and five *years* old
— he reigned sixteen *years* in
5. *the* same *year* an hundred
— pay unto him, *both the* second *year*,
8. He was five and twenty *years* old
— reigned sixteen *years* in
28: 1. Ahaz (was) twenty *years* old
— he reigned sixteen *years*
29: 1. (when he was) five and twenty *years* old, and he reigned nine and twenty *years*
3. *in the* first *year* of his
31:16. from three *years* old and
17. from twenty *years* old
33: 1. Manasseh (was) twelve *years* old
— reigned fifty and five *years*
21. Amon (was) two and twenty *years*
— reigned two *years* in Jerusalem.
34: 1. Josiah (was) eight *years* old
— and he reigned in Jerusalem one and thirty *years*.
3. For in *the* eighth *year* of his
— in *the* twelfth *year* he
8. *Now in the* eighteenth *year*
35:19. In *the* eighteenth *year*
36: 2. Jehoahaz (was) twenty and three *years*
5. Jehoiakim (was) twenty and five *years*
— reigned eleven *years* in
9. (was) eight *years* old when
10. when *the year* was expired,
11. Zedekiah (was) one and twenty *years*
— reigned eleven *years* in
21. to fulfil threescore and ten *years*.
22. *Now in the* first *year*
Ezr. 1: 1. *Now in the* first *year* of Cyrus
3: 8. *Now in the* second *year*

Ezr. 3: 8. from twenty *years* old
7: 7. *in the* seventh *year* of Artaxerxes
8. which (was) *in the* seventh *year*
Neh 1: 1. Chisleu, in *the* twentieth *year*,
2: 1. Nisan, in *the* twentieth *year*
5:14. *from the* twentieth *year* even unto *the* two and thirtieth *year* of Artaxerxes the king, (that is), twelve *years*,
9:21. forty *years* didst thou sustain
30. Yet many *years* didst thou
10:31(32). we would leave *the* seventh *year*,
32(33). to charge ourselves *yearly* with the
34(35). at times appointed *year by year*, to burn upon the altar
35(36). fruit of all trees, *year by year*, unto
13: 6. *in the* two and thirtieth *year*
Est. 1: 3. *In the* third *year* of his reign,
2:16. *in the* seventh *year* of his reign.
3: 7. *in the* twelfth *year*
9:21. the fifteenth day of the same, *yearly*, (lit in every *year and year*)
27. according to their (appointed) time every *year;* (lit. in every *year and year*)
Job 3: 6. be joined unto the days of *the year*,
10: 5. *thy years* as man's days,
15:20. number of *years* is hidden
16:22. When a few *years* are come,
32: 7. multitude of *years* should
36:11. *and their years* in pleasures.
26. number of *his years* be
42:16. Job an hundred and forty *years*,
Ps. 31:10(11). *and my years* with sighing:
61: 6(7). *his years* as many generations.
65:11(12). crownest *the year with* (marg. *of*)
77: 5(6). *the years of* ancient times.
10(11). *the years of* the right hand
78:33. *and their years* in trouble.
90: 4. For a thousand *years* in thy sight
9. we spend *our years* as a tale (that is told).
10. The days of *our years* (are) threescore *years* and ten; and if by reason of strength (they be) fourscore *years*,
15. *the years* (wherein) we have seen
95:10. Forty *years* long was I grieved
102:24(25). *thy years* (are) throughout all
27(28). *and thy years* shall have no end.
Pro. 3: 2. days, *and long* life, (marg. *years of* life)
4:10. *the years of* thy life shall be many.
5: 9. *and thy years* unto the cruel:
9:11. *the years of* thy life shall be increased.
10:27. *but the years of* the wicked
Ecc. 6: 3. and live many *years*, so that the days of *his years* be many,
6. though he live a thousand *years*
11: 8. But if a man live many *years*,
12: 1. nor *the years* draw nigh,
Isa. 6: 1. *In the year that* king Uzziah died
7: 8. within threescore and five *years*
14:28. *In the year that* king Ahaz died
16:14. Within three *years, as the years of* an
20: 1. *In the year that* Tartan came
3. naked and barefoot three *years*
21:16. Within *a year, according to the years of*
23:15. Tyre shall be forgotten seventy *years*,
—, 17. after the end of seventy *years*
29: 1. add ye *year* to *year;*
32:10. Many days and *years*
34: 8. *the year of* recompences
36: 1. in *the* fourteenth *year*
37:30. Ye shall eat (this) *year*
— *and the* second *year* that which springeth of the same: *and in the* third *year* sow
38: 5. I will add unto thy days fifteen *years*.
10. deprived of the residue of *my years*.
15. I shall go softly all *my years*
61: 2. To proclaim *the* acceptable *year*
63: 4. *and the year of* my redeemed is come.
65:20. the child shall die an hundred *years* old; but the sinner (being) an hundred *years*
Jer. 1: 2. in *the* thirteenth *year*
3. unto the end of *the* eleventh *year*
11:23. *the year of* their visitation.
17: 8. *and* shall not be careful *in the year of*
23:12. *the year of* their visitation,
25: 1. *in the* fourth *year* of Jehoiakim
— that (was) *the* first *year*
3. From *the* thirteenth *year* of Josiah

Jer. 25: 3. that (is) *the* three and twentieth *year*,
11. serve the king of Babylon seventy *years*.
12. when seventy *years* are accomplished,
28: 1. it came to pass *the* same *year*,
— *in the* fourth *year*,
3. Within *two* full *years*
11. within the space of *two* full *years*.
16. this *year* thou shalt die,
17. the prophet died *the* same *year*
29:10. That after seventy *years*
32: 1. *in the* tenth *year* of Zedekiah
— which (was) *the*)(eighteenth *year* (lit. which (is) *the year the* eighteenth *year of*)
34:14. At the end of seven *years*
— hath served thee six *years*,
36: 1. it came to pass *in the* fourth *year*
9. it came to pass *in the* fifth *year*
39: 1. *In the* ninth *year* of Zedekiah
2. in *the* eleventh *year* of Zedekiah,
45. 1. *in the* fourth *year* of Jehoiakim
46: 2. of Babylon smote *in the* fourth *year*
48:44. *the year of* their visitation,
51:46. a rumour shall both come (one) *year*, and after that *in* (another) *year*
59. *in the* fourth *year* of his reign.
52: 1. Zedekiah (was) one and twenty *years* old
— he reigned eleven *years*
4. it came to pass *in the* ninth *year*
5. besieged unto *the* eleventh *year*
12. which (was) *the*)(nineteenth *year*
28. *in the* seventh *year*
29. *In the* eighteenth *year*
30. *In the* three and twentieth *year*
31. *the* seven and thirtieth *year* of the captivity
— *in the* (first) *year* of his reign
Eze. 1: 1. it came to pass in *the* thirtieth *year*,
2. which (was) *the* fifth *year*
4: 5. *the years of* their iniquity,
6. I have appointed thee each day *for a year*. (marg. a day *for a year*, a day *for a year*)
8: 1. it came to pass *in the* sixth *year*,
20: 1. it came to pass *in the* seventh *year*,
22: 4. art come (even) unto *thy years*:
24: 1. Again *in the* ninth *year*,
26: 1. in *the* eleventh *year*,
29: 1. *In the* tenth *year*,
11. shall it be inhabited forty *years*.
12. shall be desolate forty *years*:
13. At the end of forty *years*
17. in the seven and twentieth *year*,
30:20. it came to pass in *the* eleventh *year*,
31: 1. in *the* eleventh *year*, in the third (month),
32: 1. it came to pass in *the* twelfth *year*,
17. pass also in *the* twelfth *year*,
33:21. came to pass in *the* twelfth *year*
38: 8. in *the* latter *years* thou
17. in those days (many) *years*
39: 9. burn them with fire seven *years*:
40: 1. In *the* five and twentieth *year*
— in the beginning of *the year*,
— in *the* fourteenth *year* after that the city
46:13. a lamb of *the* first *year* (marg. a son of *his year*)
17. shall be his to *the year of* liberty;
Dan 1: 1. *In the* third *year* of the reign of
5. so nourishing them three *years*,
21. unto *the* first *year* of king Cyrus.
2: 1. *And in the* second *year*
8: 1. *In the* third *year* of the reign of
9: 1. *In the* first *year* of Darius
2. *In the* first *year* of his reign I Daniel understood by books the number of *the years*,
— accomplish seventy *years*
10: 1. *In the* third *year* of Cyrus
11: 1. Also I *in the* first *year* of Darius
6. And in the end of *years*
8. continue (more) *years* than the
13. come after certain *years*
Joel 2: 2. (even) to *the years of* many
25. restore to you *the years* that
Am. 1: 1. *two years* before the earthquake.
2:10. led you forty *years*
5:25. offerings in the wilderness forty *years*,
Mic. 6: 6. with calves of *a year* old?
Hab 3: 2. thy work in the midst of *the years*, in the midst of *the years* make known;
Hag 1: 1, 15 & 2:10. *In the* second *year* of Darius
Zec. 1: 1, 7. *in the* second *year* of Darius
12. these threescore and ten *years*?
7: 1. *in the* fourth *year* of king Darius,
3. done these so many *years*?
5. even those seventy *years*,
14:16. shall even go up from *year to year* to worship the King,
Mal 3: 4. *and as* in former *years*.

שֵׁנָה *shēh-nāh'*, f. 8142

Gen 28:16. Jacob awaked *out of his sleep*,
31:40. *my sleep* departed from mine eyes.
Jud. 16:14. he awaked *out of his sleep*,
20. he awoke *out of his sleep*,
Est. 6: 1. On that night could not the king *sleep*, (marg. the king's *sleep* fled away)
Job 14:12. be raised *out of their sleep*.
Ps. 76: 5(6). they have slept *their sleep*:
90: 5. they are (as) *a sleep*:
Pro. 3:24. *thy sleep* shall be sweet.
4:16. *their sleep* is taken away,
6: 4. Give not *sleep* to thine eyes,
9. when wilt thou arise *out of thy sleep*?
10. (Yet) *a* little *sleep*,
20:13. Love not *sleep*, lest thou come to poverty;
24:33. (Yet) *a* little *sleep*,
Ecc. 5:12(11). *The sleep of* a labouring man (is)
8:16. seeth *sleep* with his eyes:
Jer. 31:26. *and my sleep* was sweet unto me.
51:39. sleep *a* perpetual *sleep*,
57. they shall sleep *a* perpetual *sleep*,
Dan 2: 1. *and his sleep* brake from him.
Zec. 4: 1. a man that is wakened *out of his sleep*,

שְׁנָה [*sh'nāh*], Ch. f. 8140

Ezr. 4:24. So it ceased unto *the* second *year*
5:11. was builded these many *years* ago,
13. But *in the* first *year of* Cyrus
6: 3. *In the* first *year of* Cyrus the king
15. *the* sixth *year of* the reign of Darius
Dan 5:31(6:1). about threescore and two *years* old.
7: 1. *In the* first *year of* Belshazzar

שְׁנָה [*sh'nāh*], Ch. f. 8139

Dan 6:18(19). *and his sleep* went from him.

שֶׁנְהַבִּים *shen-hab-beem'*, m. pl. 8143

1K. 10:22. silver, *ivory* (marg. or, *elephants' teeth*), and apes, and peacocks.
2Ch 9:21. bringing gold, and silver, *ivory*, (marg. *id.*)

שָׁנִי *shāh-nee'*, m. 8144

תּוֹלַעַת שָׁנִי[2] שְׁנִי תוֹלַעַת[3]

Gen 38:28. bound upon his hand *a scarlet thread*,
30. brother, that had *the scarlet thread*
Ex. 25: 4 & 26:1, 31, 36 & 27:16. blue, and purple, and *scarlet*,[2]
28: 5. *scarlet*,[2] and fine linen.
6. (of) purple, (of) *scarlet*,[2] and fine twined linen,
8. gold, (of) blue, and purple, and *scarlet*,[2]
15. *scarlet*,[2] and (of) fine twined linen,
33. *scarlet*,[2] round about the hem
35: 6, 23. blue, and purple, and *scarlet*,[2]
25. of *scarlet*,[2] and of fine linen.
35. in blue, and in purple, in *scarlet*,[2]
36: 8. and blue, and purple, and *scarlet*:[2]
35. *scarlet*,[2] and fine twined linen:
37. blue, and purple, and *scarlet*,[2]
38:18. purple, and *scarlet*,[2] and fine twined linen:
23. in *scarlet*,[2] and fine linen.
39: 1. of the blue, and purple, and *scarlet*,[2]
2, 8. *scarlet*,[2] and fine twined linen.
3. in the purple, and in *the scarlet*,[2]
5. blue, and purple, and *scarlet*,[2]

Ex. 39:24. *scarlet,*[2] (and) twined (linen).
29. *scarlet,*[2] (of) needlework;
Lev.14: 4, 49. cedar wood, *and scarlet,*[3]
6. *the scarlet,*[3] and the hyssop,
51. the hyssop, and *the scarlet,*[3]
52. the hyssop, *and with the scarlet:*[3]
Nu. 4: 8. a cloth of *scarlet,*[2]
19: 6. cedar wood, and hyssop, *and scarlet,*[3]
Jos. 2:18. thou shalt bind this line of *scarlet thread*
21. she bound the *scarlet* line
2Sa. 1:24. who clothed you in *scarlet,*
Pro.31:21. all her houshold (are) clothed with *scarlet.* (marg. or, with *double garments*)
Cant.4: 3. Thy lips (are) like a thread of *scarlet,*
Isa. 1:18. though your sins be *as scarlet,*
Jer. 4:30. Though thou clothest thyself with *crimson,*

8145 **שֵׁנִי** *shĕh-nee',* adj. ord.

Gen 1: 8. the evening and the morning were the *second* day.
2:13. the *second* river (is) Gihon:
4:19. the name of *the other* Zillah.
6:16. lower, *second,* and third (stories)
7:11. in the *second* month,
8:14. And in the *second* month,
22:15. unto Abraham out of heaven *the second time,*
30: 7. bare Jacob a *second* son.
12. bare Jacob a *second* son.
32:19(20). commanded he *the second,*
41: 5. he slept and dreamed *the second time:*
52. And the name of *the second* called he
47:18. they came unto him the *second* year,
Ex. 1:15. the name of *the other* Puah:
2:13. when he went out the *second* day,
16: 1. fifteenth day of the *second* month
25:12. two rings in the *other* side
32. out of the *other* side:
26: 4, 5. in the coupling of *the second.*
10. curtain which coupleth *the second.*
20. And for the *second* side
27. the boards of the *other* side of
27:15. And on the *other* side (shall)
28:10. on the *other* stone,
18. the *second* row (shall)
29:19. take the *other* ram;
39, 41. the *other* lamb thou shalt offer
36:11, 12. in the coupling of *the second.*
17. the curtain which coupleth *the second.*
25. And for the *other* side
32. the boards of the *other* side
37: 3. two rings upon the *other* side
18. out of the *other* side
38:15. And for the *other* side of the court gate,
39:11. the *second* row, an emerald,
40:17. in the *second* year,
Lev. 5:10. offer *the second* (for) a burnt offering,
8:22. he brought the *other* ram,
13: 5. shut him up seven days *more:*
6. look on him *again* the seventh day:
7. he shall be seen of the priest *again:*
33. (that hath) the scall seven days *more:*
54. he shall shut it up seven days *more:*
58. be washed *the second time,*
Nu. 1: 1, 18. on the first (day) of the *second* month,
— in the *second* year
2:16. *And...*set forth *in the second rank.*
7:18. On the *second* day
8: 8. *another* young bullock
9: 1. the first month of the *second* year
11. fourteenth day of the *second* month
10: 6. When ye blow an alarm *the second time,*
11. the twentieth (day) of the *second* month, in the *second* year,
11:26. the name of *the other* Medad:
28: 4, 8. the *other* lamb shalt thou
29:17. on the *second* day
Jos. 5: 2. the children of Israel *the second time.*
6:14. the *second* day they compassed
10:32. took it on the *second* day,
19: 1. the *second* lot came forth
Jud. 6:25. even the *second* bullock
26. take the *second* bullock,
28. the *second* bullock was offered
20:24. Benjamin the *second* day.

Jud.20:25. out of Gibeah the *second* day,
Ru. 1: 4. the name of *the other* Ruth:
1Sa. 1: 2. the name of *the other* Peninnah:
20:27. *the second* (day) of the month,
34. meat the *second* day of the month:
2Sa. 4: 2. the name of *the other* (marg. *second*)
14:29. when he sent again *the second time,*
16:19. *And again,* whom should I serve?
1K. 6: 1. which (is) the *second* month,
24. five cubits the *other* wing
25. the *other* cherub (was) ten
26. so (was it) of the *other* cherub.
27. the wing of the *other* cherub touched the *other* wall;
34. the two leaves of the *other* door
7:15. compass *either* of them (lit. the *second* pillar) about.
16. the height of the *other* chapiter
17. seven for the *other* chapiter.
18. so did he for the *other* chapiter.
20. round about upon the *other*
9: 2. appeared to Solomon *the second time,*
19: 7. the angel of the Lord came again *the second time,*
2K. 9:19. Then he sent out *a second*
10: 6. he wrote a letter *the second time*
19:29. in the *second* year
25:17. like unto these had the *second* pillar
1Ch 2:13. Abinadab *the second,*
3: 1. *the second* Daniel,
15. *the second* Jehoiakim,
7:15. *the second* (was) Zelophehad:
8: 1. Ashbel *the second,*
39. Jehush *the second,*
12: 9. Obadiah *the second,*
23:11. Zizah *the second:*
19. Amariah *the second,*
20. Jesiah *the second.*
24: 7. *the second* to Jedaiah,
23. Amariah *the second,*
25: 9. *the second* to Gedaliah,
26: 2. Jediael *the second,*
4. Jehozabad *the second,*
11. Hilkiah *the second,*
27: 4. over the course of *the second*
29:22. the son of David king *the second time,*
2Ch 3: 2. he began to build *in the second* (day) of the *second* month,
27: 5. the *second* year, and the third.
30: 2. passover in the *second* month.
13. bread in the *second* month,
15. fourteenth (day) of the *second* month:
Ezr. 3: 8. Now in the *second* year
— in the *second* month, began
Neh 3:11. repaired the *other* piece, (marg. *second* measure)
19. *another* piece over against
20. repaired the *other* piece,
21. the son of Koz *another* piece,
24. the son of Henadad *another* piece,
27. repaired *another* piece,
30. the sixth son of Zalaph, *another* piece.
8:13. on the *second* day were
12:38. And *the other* (company of)
Est. 2:14. she returned into the *second* house
19. were gathered together *the second time,*
7: 2. said again unto Esther on the *second* day
9:29. this *second* letter of Purim.
Job 42:14. the name of *the second,* Kezia;
Ecc. 4: 8. There is one (alone), and (there is) not *a second;*
10. for (he hath) not *another* to help him
15. with the *second* child
Isa. 11:11. again *the second time* to
37:30. the *second* year that which
Jer. 1:13. came unto me *the second time,*
13: 3. came unto me *the second time,*
33: 1. *the second time,* while he was
41: 4. it came to pass the *second* day
52:22. The *second* pillar also and
Eze. 4: 6. lie *again* on thy right side,
10:14. the *second* face (was) the face
43:22. And on the *second* day thou
Dan 8: 3. but one (was) higher than *the other,*
Jon 3: 1. came unto Jonah *the second time,*
Hag. 2:20. And *again* the word of
Zec. 4:12. And I answered *again,*

Zec 6: 2. and in the *second* chariot
11:14. Then I cut asunder mine *other* staff,
Mal. 2:13. And this have ye done *again*,

8147 שְׁנַיִם *sh'nah'-yim*, adj. num. dual.
שְׁתַּיִם ע׳ or שְׁנֵי עָשָׂר[2]

Gen 1:16. God made *two* great lights;
2:25. they were *both* naked,
3: 7. the eyes of *them both* were opened,
4:19. Lamech took unto him *two* wives:
5: 8. nine hundred and twelve[2] years:
18. lived an hundred sixty and *two* years,
20. Jared were nine hundred sixty and *two*
26. seven hundred eighty and *two*
28. an hundred eighty and *two*
6:19, 20. *two* of every (sort)
7: 2. and of beasts that (are) not clean by *two*,
9. There went in *two* and *two* unto Noah into
15. *two* and *two* of all flesh,
9:22. told his *two* brethren without.
23. laid (it) upon *both* their shoulders,
10:25. unto Eber were born *two* sons:
11:20. Reu lived *two* and thirty years,
14: 4. Twelve[2] years they served
17:20. twelve[2] princes shall he beget,
19: 1. there came *two* angels to Sodom
8. I have *two* daughters
15. thy wife, and thy *two* daughters,
16. upon the hand of his *two* daughters;
30. *and* his *two* daughters with him;
— he *and* his *two* daughters.
36. *both* the daughters of Lot with child
21:27. *both of them* made a covenant.
31. there they sware *both of them.*
22: 3. took *two of* his young men
6, 8. they went *both of them* together.
24:22. a shekel weight, *and two* bracelets
25:16. twelve[2] princes according to their nations.
23. *Two* nations (are) in thy womb, *and two* manner of people
27: 9. fetch me from thence *two* good kids
45. be deprived also of *you both* in one day?
29:16. Laban had *two* daughters:
31:33. into the *two* maidservants' tents;
37. they may judge betwixt *us both.*
41. I served thee fourteen years *for* thy *two*
32: 7(8). the camels, *into two* bands;
10(11). now I am become *two* bands.
22(23). his *two* wives, and his *two* women-servants,
33: 1. Rachel, and unto the *two* handmaids.
34:25. that *two of* the sons of Jacob,
35:22. sons of Jacob were twelve:[2]
40: 2. wroth against *two* (of) his officers,
5. they dreamed a dream *both of them,*
41:50. unto Joseph were born *two* sons
42:13. Thy servants (are) twelve[2]
32. We (be) twelve[2] brethren,
37. Slay my *two* sons, if I bring him not
44:27. Ye know that my wife bare me *two*
46:27. born him in Egypt, (were) *two* souls:
48: 1. he took with him his *two* sons,
5. now thy *two* sons,
13. Joseph took *them both*,
49:28. these (are) the twelve[2] tribes
Ex. 2:13. *two* men of the Hebrews strove
4: 9. will not believe also these *two*
12: 7. strike (it) on the *two* side posts
22. the *two* side posts with the blood
23. upon the lintel, and on the *two* side posts,
15:27. where (were) twelve[2] wells of water,
16:22. *two* omers for one
18: 3. her *two* sons; of which the name
6. *and* her *two* sons with her.
22: 4(3). he shall restore *double.*
7(6). the thief be found, let him pay *double.*
9(8). the cause of *both parties*
—(-). he shall pay *double*
11(10). the Lord be between *them both*,
24: 4. *and* twelve[2] pillars, *according to the* twelve[2] tribes
25:12. *and two* rings (shall be) in the one side of it, *and two* rings in the other
18. thou shalt make *two* cherubims

Ex. 25:18. *in* the *two* ends of the mercy seat.
19. the cherubims on the *two* ends thereof.
22. from between the *two* cherubims
35. a knop under *two* branches of the same, and a knop under *two* branches of the same, and a knop under *two* branches
26:17. *Two* tenons (shall there be) in one board,
19. *two* sockets under one board *for* his *two* tenons, *and two* sockets under another board *for* his *two* tenons.
21, 25. *two* sockets under one board, *and two* sockets under another board.
23. *And two* boards shalt thou make
24. thus shall it be *for them both;* they shall be *for* the *two* corners.
27: 7. upon the *two* sides of the altar,
28: 7. shall have the *two* shoulderpieces thereof joined at the *two* edges thereof;
9. thou shalt take *two* onyx stones,
11. shalt thou engrave the *two* stones
12. thou shalt put the *two* stones
— upon his *two* shoulders
14. *And two* chains (of) pure gold
21. names of the children of Israel, twelve,[2]
— *according to* the twelve[2] tribes.
23. make upon the breastplate *two* rings
— shalt put the *two* rings on the *two* ends of the breastplate.
24. put the *two* wreathen (chains) of gold in the *two* rings
25. *two* ends of the *two* wreathen (chains) thou shalt fasten in the *two* ouches,
26. thou shalt make *two* rings
— put them upon the *two* ends
27. *two* (other) rings of gold
— put them on the *two* sides
29: 1. *two* rams without blemish,
3. the bullock and the *two* rams.
13, 22. the *two* kidneys, and the fat
38. *two* lambs of the first year
30: 4. *And two* golden rings shalt thou
— by the *two* corners thereof, upon the *two* sides of it
31:18. *two* tables of testimony,
32:15. *and* the *two* tables of the testimony
— the tables (were) written *on both* their
34: 1. Hew thee *two* tables of stone
4. he hewed *two* tables of stone
— took in his hand the *two* tables
29. Sinai *with* the *two* tables
36:22. One board had *two* tenons,
24. *two* sockets under one board *for* his *two* tenons, *and two* sockets under another board *for* his *two* tenons.
26. *two* sockets under one board, *and two*
28. *And two* boards made he
29. thus he did *to both of them in both* the
30. under every board *two* sockets. (marg. *two* sockets, *two* sockets under one board)
37: 3. *even two* rings upon the one side of it, *and two* rings upon the other
7. he made *two* cherubims
— *on* the *two* ends of the mercy seat;
8. the cherubims *on* the *two* ends thereof.
21. a knop under *two* branches of the same, and a knop under *two* branches of the same, and a knop under *two* branches
27. *And* he made *two* rings of gold
— by the *two* corners of it, upon the *two*
39: 4. by the *two* edges
14. twelve,[2] according to their names,
— *according to* the twelve[2] tribes.
16. they made *two* ouches (of) gold, *and two* gold rings, and put the *two* rings in the *two* ends of the breastplate.
17. they put the *two* wreathen chains of gold in the *two* rings on the ends
18. And the *two* ends of the *two* wreathen chains they fastened in the *two* ouches,
19. And they made *two* rings of gold, and put (them) on the *two* ends of the
20. they made *two* (other) golden rings, and put them on the *two* sides
Lev. 3: 4, 10, 15 & 4:9. the *two* kidneys, and the fat
5: 7. *two* turtledoves, or *two* young pigeons,
11. *two* turtledoves, or *two* young pigeons,
7: 4. the *two* kidneys, and the fat

Lev. 8: 2. for the sin offering, and *two* rams,
16, 25. *two* kidneys, and their fat,
12: 8. then she shall bring *two* turtles, or *two* young pigeons;
14: 4. cleansed *two* birds alive (and) clean,
10. he shall take *two* he lambs
22. *And two* turtledoves, or *two* young
49. take to cleanse the house *two* birds,
15: 14. *And...two* turtledoves, or *two* young
29. *two* turtles, or *two* young pigeons,
16: 1. after the death of the *two* sons
5. *two* kids of the goats for a sin offering,
7. he shall take the *two* goats,
8. Aaron shall cast lots upon the *two*
21. Aaron shall lay *both* his hands
20: 11, 12. *both of them* shall surely be put
13. *both of them* have committed
18. *both of them* shall be cut off
23: 13. *two* tenth deals of fine flour
17. *two* wave loaves of *two* tenth deals:
18. one young bullock, and *two* rams:
19. *and two* lambs of the first year
20. with the *two* lambs:
24: 5. and bake twelve[2] cakes thereof: *two* tenth
6. And thou shalt set them in *two* rows,
Nu. 1: 35. thirty and *two* thousand and two hundred.
39. threescore and *two* thousand and seven hundred.
44. princes of Israel, (being) twelve[2] men:
2: 21. thirty and *two* thousand and two hundred.
26. threescore and *two* thousand and seven hundred.
3: 39. twenty and *two* thousand.
43. were twenty and *two* thousand two hundred and threescore and thirteen.
6: 10. *two* turtles, or *two* young pigeons,
7: 3. six covered wagons, *and* twelve[2] oxen; a wagon for *two* of the princes,
7. *Two* wagons and four oxen
13. *both of them* (were) full of fine flour
17. peace offerings, *two* oxen,
19, 25, 31, 37, 43, 49, 55, 61, 67, 73, 79. *both of them* full of fine flour
23, 29, 35, 41, 47, 53, 59, 65, 71, 77, 83. *two* oxen, five rams,
78. On the twelfth[2] day Ahira
84. twelve[2] chargers of silver, twelve[2] silver bowls, twelve[2] spoons of gold:
86. The golden spoons (were) twelve,[2]
87. (were) twelve[2] bullocks, the rams twelve,[2] the lambs of the first year twelve,[2]
— the goats for sin offering twelve.[2]
89. from between the *two* cherubims:
10: 2. Make thee *two* trumpets of silver;
11: 26. there remained *two* (of the) men
12: 5. *they both* came forth.
13: 23. they bare it *between two* upon a staff;
15: 6. *two* tenth deals of flour
17: 2(17). the house of their fathers twelve[2]
6(21). (even) twelve[2] rods:
22: 22. *and* his *two* servants (were) with him.
25: 8. thrust *both of them* through,
26: 14. twenty and *two* thousand and two hundred.
34. those that were numbered of them, fifty and *two* thousand and seven hundred.
37. thirty and *two* thousand and five hundred.
28: 3. *two* lambs of the first year
9. on the sabbath day *two* lambs
—, 12. *and two* tenth deals of flour
11. *two* young bullocks,
19. *two* young bullocks, and one ram,
20. *and two* tenth deals for a ram;
27. *two* young bullocks, one ram,
28. *two* tenth deals unto one ram,
29: 3. *two* tenth deals for a ram,
9. *two* tenth deals to one ram,
13. *two* rams, (and) fourteen lambs
14. *two* tenth deals to each ram *of the two*
17. twelve[2] young bullocks, *two* rams,
20. *two* rams, fourteen lambs
23, 26, 29, 32. *two* rams, (and) fourteen
31: 5. twelve[2] thousand armed for war.
33. threescore and twelve (lit. *two* and seventy) thousand
35. thirty and *two* thousand
38. the Lord's tribute (was) threescore and twelve. (lit. *two* and seventy)

Nu. 31: 40. the Lord's tribute (was) thirty and *two*
33: 9. and in Elim (were) twelve[2] fountains
34: 15. The *two* tribes and the half tribe
35: 6. ye shall add forty *and two* cities.
Deu 1: 23. I took twelve[2] men of you,
3: 8. out of the hand of the *two* kings
21. God hath done *unto* these *two* kings:
4: 13. he wrote them upon *two* tables
47. *two* kings of the Amorites,
5: 22(19). wrote them in *two* tables of stone,
9: 10. the Lord delivered unto me *two*
11. the Lord gave me the *two* tables
15. *and* the *two* tables of the covenant (were) in my *two* hands.
17. I took the *two* tables, and cast them out of my *two* hands,
10: 1. Hew thee *two* tables of stone
3. hewed *two* tables of stone
— having the *two* tables in mine hand.
14: 6. cleaveth the cleft into *two* claws,
17: 6. At the mouth of *two* witnesses,
19: 15. at the mouth of *two* witnesses,
17. Then *both* the men,
21: 15. If a man have *two* wives,
17. by giving him a *double* portion
22: 22. then they shall *both of them* die,
24. ye shall bring *them both* out
23: 18(19). for even *both* these (are) abomination
32: 30. *and two* put ten thousand to flight,
Jos. 2: 1. sent out of Shittim *two* men
4. the woman took the *two* men,
10. did *unto* the *two* kings
23. So the *two* men returned,
3: 12. therefore take you twelve[2] men
4: 2. Take you twelve[2] men
3. twelve[2] stones, and ye shall carry
4. Joshua called the twelve[2] men,
8. twelve[2] stones out of the midst of Jordan,
9. *And* Joshua set up twelve[2] stones
20. And those twelve[2] stones,
6: 22. *But* Joshua had said *unto* the *two* men
8: 25. men and women, (were) twelve[2] thousand,
9: 10. that he did *to* the *two* kings of the
14: 3. given the inheritance of *two* tribes
4. children of Joseph were *two* tribes,
15: 60. *two* cities with their villages:
18: 24. twelve[2] cities with their villages:
19: 15. twelve[2] cities with their villages.
30. twenty *and two* cities
21: 7. Zebulun, twelve[2] cities.
16. nine cities out of those *two*
25, 27. with her suburbs; *two* cities.
40(38). lot twelve[2] cities.
24: 12. the *two* kings of the Amorites;
Jud. 3: 16. a dagger which had *two* edges,
7: 3. people twenty *and two* thousand;
25. took *two* princes of the Midianites,
8: 12. took the *two* kings of Midian,
9: 44. *and* the *two* (other) companies ran
10: 3. Jair, a Gileadite, and judged Israel twenty *and two* years.
11: 37. let me alone *two* months,
38. he sent her away (for) *two* months:
39. came to pass at the end of *two* months,
12: 6. forty *and two* thousand.
15: 4. a firebrand in the midst between *two*
13. bound him *with two* new cords,
16: 3. gate of the city, *and the two* posts,
28. the Philistines *for* my *two* eyes.
29. Samson took hold of the *two*
19: 6. did eat and drink *both of them* together:
8. and they did eat *both of them*.
29. *into* twelve[2] pieces,
20: 21. twenty and *two* thousand
21: 10. twelve[2] thousand men of
Ru. 1: 1. his wife, *and* his *two* sons.
2. the name of his *two* sons
3. and she was left, *and* her *two* sons.
5. Mahlon and Chilion died also *both of them;*
— was left *of* her *two* sons
7. *and* her *two* daughters in law with her;
8. Naomi said *unto* her *two* daughters in law
19. So *they two* went until they came
4: 11. which *two* did build the house
1 Sa. 1: 2. And he had *two* wives;
3. And the *two* sons of Eli,
2: 21. bare three sons *and two* daughters.

1Sa. 2:34. shall come upon thy *two* sons,
— in one day they shall die *both of them.*
3:11. *both* the ears of every one that heareth
4: 4. and the *two* sons of Eli,
11. *and* the *two* sons of Eli,
17. thy *two* sons also,
5: 4. *and both* the palms of his hands
6: 7. *and* take *two* milch kine,
10. and took *two* milch kine,
9:26. they went out *both of them,*
10: 2. then thou shalt find *two* men
4. give thee *two* (loaves) of bread;
11:11. so that *two* of them were not left
13: 1. and *when* he had reigned *two* years
14:11. *both of them* discovered themselves
49. names of his *two* daughters (were these);
18:21. son in law *in* (the one of) *the twain.*
20:11. they went out *both of them*
42. forasmuch as we have sworn *both of us*
23:18. *they two* made a covenant
25:18. *and two* bottles of wine,
43. they were also *both of them* his wives.
27: 3. (even) David *with* his *two* wives,
28: 8. *and two* men with him,
30: 5. *And* David's *two* wives were taken
12. *and two* clusters of raisins:
18. and David rescued his *two* wives.
2Sa. 1: 1. abode *two* days in Ziklag;
2: 2. David went up thither, and his *two* wives
10. *and* reigned *two* years.
15. by number twelve[2] of Benjamin,
— *and* twelve[2] of the servants of David.
4: 2. *And* Saul's son had *two* men
8: 2. even with *two* lines measured
5. Syrians *two and* twenty thousand
9:13. was lame on *both* his feet.
10: 6. and of Ish-tob twelve[2] thousand men.
12: 1. There were *two* men in one city;
13: 6. make me *a couple of* cakes
14: 6. thy handmaid had *two* sons, and *they two* strove together
15:27. your *two* sons with you,
36. with them their *two* sons,
17: 1. choose out twelve[2] thousand men,
18. they went *both of them* away
18:24. David sat between the *two* gates:
21: 8. But the king took the *two* sons
23:20. he slew *two* lionlike men of Moab:
1K. 2: 5. what he did *to* the *two* captains
32. who fell *upon two* men
39. *two* of the servants of Shimei ran
3:16. Then came there *two* women,
18. save we *two* in the house.
25. Divide the living child *in two,*
4: 7. had twelve[2] officers over all Israel,
26(5:6). and twelve[2] thousand horsemen.
5:12(26). *they two* made a league
14(28). *two* months at home:
6:23. he made *two* cherubims
25. *both* the cherubims
32. The *two* doors *also* (were of) olive tree;
34. the *two* doors (were of) fir tree: the *two* leaves of the one door
— *and* the *two* leaves of the other
7:15. he cast *two* pillars of brass,
— a line of twelve[2] cubits
16. *And* he made *two* chapiters (of) molten brass,
18. *and two* rows round about
20. the chapiters upon the *two* pillars
24. the knops (were) cast in *two* rows,
25. It stood upon twelve[2] oxen,
41. The *two* pillars,
— on the top of the *two* pillars; and the *two* networks, to cover the *two* bowls
42. pomegranates *for* the *two* networks, (even) *two* rows of pomegranates for one network, to cover the *two* bowls
44. and twelve[2] oxen under the sea;
8: 9. in the ark save the *two* tables of stone,
63. *two and* twenty thousand
9:10. when Solomon had built the *two* houses,
10:19. *and two* lions stood beside
20. *And* twelve[2] lions stood there on
26. *and* twelve[2] thousand horsemen, whom he
11:29. *and they two* (were) alone in the field:
30. and rent it (in) twelve[2] pieces:

1K. 12:28. made *two* calves (of) gold,
14:20. *two and* twenty years:
15:25. in the *second* year of Asa
16:23. over Israel, twelve[2] years:
29. in Samaria twenty *and two* years.
17:12. I (am) gathering *two* sticks,
18:21. halt ye between *two* opinions?
23. Let them therefore give us *two*
31. And Elijah took twelve[2] stones,
19:19. plowing (with) twelve[2] yoke (of oxen) before him, and he *with the* twelfth:[2]
20: 1. thirty *and two* kings
15. two hundred and thirty *two:*
16. the thirty *and two* kings
27. pitched before them *like two* little flocks
21:10. set *two* men, sons of Belial,
13. there came in *two* men,
22:31. his thirty *and two* captains
2K. 1:14. burnt up the *two* captains
17. in the *second* year of Jehoram
2: 6. And *they two* went on.
7. *and they two* stood by Jordan.
8. *they two* went over on dry ground.
9. let a *double* portion of thy spirit
11. parted *them both* asunder;
12. his own clothes, and rent them *in two* pieces.
24. there came forth *two* she bears out of the wood, and tare forty *and two* children
3: 1. and reigned twelve[2] years.
4: 1. to take unto him my *two* sons
33. and shut the door upon *them twain,*
5:22. from mount Ephraim *two* young men
— *and two* changes of garments.
23. bound two talents of silver *in two* bags, *with two* changes of garments, and laid (them) upon *two* of his
6:10. not once nor *twice.*
7:14. They took therefore *two* chariot horses;
8:17. Thirty *and two* years old was he
25. In the twelfth[2] year of
26. *Two and* twenty years old (was) Ahaziah
9:32. looked out to him *two* (or) three eunuchs.
10: 4. *two* kings stood not before him:
8. Lay ye them in *two* heaps
14. *two and* forty men;
11: 7. *And two* parts of all you that go forth
14: 1. In the *second* year of Joash
15: 2. reigned *two and* fifty years
27. In the *two and* fiftieth year
32. In the *second* year of Pekah
17: 1. In the twelfth[2] year of Ahaz
16. molten images, (even) *two* calves,
21: 1. Manasseh (was) twelve[2] years old
5. *in* the *two* courts of the house of the Lord.
12. *both* his ears shall tingle.
19. Amon (was) twenty *and two* years old
— *and* he reigned *two* years
23:12. had made *in* the *two* courts
25:16. The *two* pillars, one sea, and the bases
27. *in* the twelfth[2] month,
1Ch 1:19. unto Eber were born *two* sons:
4: 5. Tekoa had *two* wives,
6:63(48). the tribe of Zebulun, twelve[2] cities.
7: 2. *two and* twenty thousand and six hundred.
7. twenty *and two* thousand and thirty and four.
9:22. (were) two hundred *and* twelve.[2]
11:21. he was more honourable *than the two;*
22. he slew *two* lionlike men of Moab:
12:28. twenty *and two* captains.
15:10. his brethren an hundred *and* twelve.[2]
18: 5. Syrians *two and* twenty thousand
19: 7. hired thirty and *two* thousand
24:12. *the* twelfth[2] to Jakim,
17. the *two* and twentieth to Gamul,
25: 9. his brethren and sons (were) twelve:[2]
10, 11, 12, 13, 14, 15, 16, 17, 18, 19, 20, 21, 22, 23, 24, 25, 26, 27, 28, 29, 30, 31. his sons, and his brethren, (were) twelve:[2]
19. The twelfth[2] to Hashabiah,
29. The *two* and twentieth to Giddalti,
26: 8. threescore *and two* of Obed-edom.
17. toward Asuppim *two* (and) *two.*
18. four at the causeway, (and) *two* at Parbar
27:15. *The* twelfth[2] (captain) *for* the twelfth[2]

2Ch 1:14. *and* twelve[2] thousand
3:10. he made *two* cherubims
15. before the house *two* pillars
4: 3. *Two* rows of oxen (were) cast,
4. It stood upon twelve[2] oxen,
12. (To wit), the *two* pillars,
— on the top of the *two* pillars, and the *two* wreaths to cover the *two* pommels
13. pomegranates on the *two* wreaths; *two* rows of pomegranates on each wreath, to cover the *two*
15. and twelve[2] oxen under it.
5:10. in the ark save the *two* tables
7: 5. twenty *and two* thousand oxen,
9:18. *and two* lions standing by the stays:
19. *And* twelve[2] lions stood there
25. for horses and chariots, *and* twelve[2] thousand horsemen;
13:21. and begat twenty *and two* sons, and
21: 5. Jehoram (was) thirty *and two* years old
19. after the end of *two* years,
20. Thirty *and two* years old was he
22: 2. Forty *and two* years old (was) Ahaziah
24: 3. Jehoiada took for him *two* wives;
26: 3. he reigned fifty *and two* years
33: 1. Manasseh (was) twelve[2] years old
5. *in* the *two* courts of the house
21. Amon (was) *two and* twenty years
— *and* reigned *two* years
34: 3. *and in the* twelfth[2] year he began
Ezr. 2: 3. an hundred seventy *and two.*
4. three hundred seventy *and two.*
6. two thousand eight hundred *and* twelve.[2]
10. six hundred forty *and two.*
12. a thousand two hundred twenty *and two.*
18. an hundred *and* twelve.[2]
24. Azmaveth, forty *and two.*
27. an hundred twenty *and two.*
29. Nebo, fifty *and two.*
37. a thousand fifty *and two.*
58. three hundred ninety *and two.*
60. six hundred fifty *and two.*
8:24. Then I separated twelve[2] of the
27. and *two* vessels of fine copper,
31. the river of Ahava *on the* twelfth[2] (day)
35. twelve[2] bullocks for all Israel,
— twelve[2] he goats
10:13. a work of one day or *two:*
Neh 5:14. *two and* thirtieth year of Artaxerxes
— (that is), twelve[2] years,
6:15. in fifty *and two* days.
7: 8. an hundred seventy *and two.*
9. three hundred seventy *and two.*
10. six hundred fifty *and two.*
17. two thousand three hundred twenty *and two.*
24. an hundred and twelve.[2]
28. Beth-azmaveth, forty *and two.*
31. The men of Michmas, an hundred and twenty *and two.*
33. Nebo, fifty *and two.*
40. Immer, a thousand fifty *and two.*
60. three hundred ninety *and two.*
62. six hundred forty *and two.*
71. twenty thousand drams of gold, (lit. *twice* ten thousand)
72. twenty thousand drams of gold, (lit. *twice* ten thousand)
11:12. that did the work of the house (were) eight hundred twenty *and two:*
13. two hundred forty *and two:*
19. an hundred seventy *and two.*
12:31. appointed *two* great (companies)
40. So stood *the two* (companies)
13: 6. in the *two and* thirtieth year of Artaxerxes
20. without Jerusalem once *or twice.*
Est. 2:12. after that she had been twelve[2] months,
21. *two of* the king's chamberlains,
23. they were *both* hanged on a tree:
3: 7. in the twelfth[2] year
— (to) *the* twelfth[2] (month),
13. thirteenth (day) of the twelfth[2] month
6: 2. *two of* the king's chamberlains,
8:12. upon the thirteenth (day) of the twelfth[2] month,
9: 1. *Now in* the twelfth[2] month,
27. they would keep these *two* days

Job 9:33. might lay his hand upon *us both.*
13:20. Only do not *two* (things) unto me:
33:14. God speaketh once, *yea twice,*
40: 5. but I will not answer: *yea, twice;*
42: 7. *and against* thy *two* friends:
Ps. 60[title](2). valley of salt twelve[2] thousand.
62:11(12). *twice* have I heard this;
Pro. 17:15. *they both* (are) abomination
20:10. *both of them* (are) alike abomination
12. the Lord hath made even *both of them.*
24:22. who knoweth the ruin of *them both?*
27: 3. a fool's wrath (is) heavier *than them both.*
29:13. the Lord lighteneth *both* their eyes.
30: 7. *Two* (things) have I required of thee;
15. The horseleach hath *two* daughters,
Ecc. 4: 3. better (is he) *than both they,* which hath
9. *Two* (are) better than one;
11. Again, if *two* lie together,
12. *two* shall withstand him;
11: 6. whether *they both* (shall be) alike
Cant. 4: 5. Thy *two* breasts (are) *like two* young roes
7: 3(4). Thy *two* breasts (are) *like two* young
Isa. 1:31. *they* shall *both* burn together,
6: 2. *with twain* he covered his face, *and with twain* he covered his feet, *and with twain* he did fly.
7: 4. *for* the *two* tails of these smoking
16. shall be forsaken of *both* her kings.
21. nourish a young cow, *and two* sheep;
8:14. *to both* the houses of Israel,
17: 6. *two* (or) three berries in the top
47: 9. these *two* (things) shall come to thee
51:19. These *two* (things) are come unto thee
Jer. 2:13. my people have committed *two* evils;
3:14. *and two* of a family,
24: 1. *two* baskets of figs (were) set
33:24. *two* families which the Lord hath chosen,
34:18. when they cut the calf *in twain,*
46:12. they are fallen *both* together.
52:20. The *two* pillars, one sea, and twelve[2] brasen bulls
21. a fillet of twelve[2] cubits
29. eight hundred thirty *and two* persons:
31. *in the* twelfth[2] month,
Eze. 1:11. *two* (wings) of every one
— *and two* covered their bodies.
23, 23. every one had *two,*
15: 4. the fire devoureth *both* the ends
21:19(24). appoint thee *two* ways,
—(—). *both twain* shall come forth
21(26). at the head of the *two* ways, to use
23: 2. there were *two* women,
13. they (took) *both* one way,
29: 1. *in* the twelfth[2] (day) of the month,
32: 1. came to pass *in the* twelfth year (lit. *in* the *two* tenth), *in the* twelfth[2] month,
17. came to pass also *in the* twelfth[2] year,
33:21. it came to pass *in the* twelfth[2] year
35:10. These *two* nations and these *two* countries
37:22. they shall be no more *two* nations,
— be divided *into two* kingdoms any more
40: 9. posts thereof, *two* cubits;
39. *two* tables on this side, *and two* tables on that side,
40. the north gate, (were) *two* tables;
— at the porch of the gate, (were) *two*
41: 3. post of the door, *two* cubits;
18. *and* (every) cherub had *two* faces;
22. the length thereof *two* cubits;
23. *And* the temple and the sanctuary had *two* doors.
24. *And* the doors had *two* leaves (apiece), *two* turning leaves; *two* (leaves) for the one door, *and two* leaves
43:14. lower settle (shall be) *two* cubits,
16. (shall be) twelve[2] (cubits long), twelve; broad, square
47:13. *according to the* twelve[2] tribes of Israel:
Dan 2: 1. in the *second* year of the reign of
8: 7. and brake his *two* horns:
9:25. seven weeks, and threescore *and two*
26. after threescore *and two* weeks shall
11:27. *And both* these kings' hearts
12: 5. there stood other *two,*
Hos 10:10. bind themselves *in* their *two* furrows.
Am. 3: 3. Can *two* walk together,
12. *two* legs, or a piece of an ear;

Am. 4: 8. *two* (or) three cities wandered
Jon. 4:11. *more than* sixscore thousand (lit. *more than two* ten myriads)
Hag. 1: 1,15 & 2:10. In the *second* year of Darius
Zec. 1: 1,7. in the *second* year of Darius,
4: 3. *And two* olive trees by it,
11. What (are) these *two* olive trees
12. What (be these) *two* olive branches which through the *two* golden pipes
14. These (are) the *two* anointed ones,
5: 9. there came out *two* women,
6: 1. from between *two* mountains;
13. peace shall be between *them both.*
11: 7. I took unto me *two* staves;
13: 8. *two* parts therein shall be cut off

8148 **שְׁנִינָה** *sh'nee-nāh'*, f.

Deu 28:37. a proverb, *and a byword,*
1K. 9: 7. *and a byword* among all people:
2Ch 7:20. *and a byword* among all nations.
Jer. 24: 9. a reproach and a proverb, *a taunt*

8150 **שָׁנַן** [*shāh-nan'*].

* KAL.—*Preterite.* *

Deu32:41. If *I whet* my glittering sword,
Ps. 64: 3(4). Who *whet* their tongue like a sword,
140: 3(4). *They have sharpened* their tongues

KAL.—*Participle.* Poel.

Ps. 45: 5(6). *sharp* in the heart of the king's
120: 4. *Sharp* arrows of the mighty,
Pro.25:18. a sword, and a *sharp* arrow.
Isa. 5:28. Whose arrows (are) *sharp,*

* PIEL.—*Preterite.* *

Deu 6: 7. *And thou shalt teach them diligently* (marg. *whet*, or, *sharpen*)

* HITHPOLEL.—*Future.* *

Ps. 73:21. *I was pricked* in my reins.

8151 **שָׁנַס** [*shāh-nas'*].

* PIEL.—*Future.* *

1K. 18:46. *and he girded up* his loins,

8153 **שְׁנָת** *sh'nāhth*, f.

Ps.132: 4. I will not give *sleep* to mine eyes,

8154 **שָׁסָה** [*shāh-sāh'*].

* KAL.—*Preterite.* *

Ps. 44:10(11). they which hate us *spoil* for

KAL.—*Future.*

Hos13:15. *he shall spoil* the treasure

KAL.—*Participle.* Poel.

Jud. 2:14. into the hands of *spoilers*
16. hand of those *that spoiled them.*
1Sa.14:48. out of the hands of them *that spoiled them.*
23: 1. and they *rob* (lit. are *plundering*) the
2K. 17:20. delivered them into the hand of *spoilers,*
Isa. 17:14. the portion of them *that spoil us,*
Jer. 30:16. (כתיב) *they that spoil thee* shall be a spoil,
50:11. *O ye destroyers of* mine heritage,

KAL.—*Participle.* Paül.

Isa. 42:22. a people robbed *and spoiled;*

* POEL.—*Preterite.* *

Isa. 10:13. *have robbed* their treasures,

8155 **שָׁסַס** [*shāh-sas'*].

* KAL.—*Preterite.* *

Ps. 89:41(42). All that pass by the way *spoil him:*

KAL.—*Future.*

Jud. 2:14. hands of spoilers *that spoiled them,*
1Sa.17:53. *and they spoiled* their tents.

KAL.—*Participle.* Poel.

Jer. 30:16. *they that spoil thee* shall be a spoil,

* NIPHAL.—*Preterite.* *

Zec.14: 2. *and* the houses *rifled,*

NIPHAL.—*Future.*

Isa. 13:16. their houses *shall be spoiled,*

שָׁסַע [*shāh-sa^{n}g'*]. 8156

* KAL.—*Participle.* Poel. *

Lev.11: 3. parteth the hoof, *and is clovenfooted,* (lit. *and cleaving* the cleft of the hoofs)
7. *and be clovenfooted,* (lit. *and cleaving* the cleft of the hoof)
26. and (is) not *clovenfooted,* (lit. *cleaving* not the cleft)
Deu14: 6. *and cleaveth* the cleft into two claws,

KAL.—*Participle.* Paül.

Deu14: 7. them that divide the *cloven* hoof;

* PIEL.—*Preterite.* *

Lev. 1:17. *And he shall cleave* it with

PIEL.—*Infinitive.*

Jud.14: 6. *as he would have rent* a kid,

PIEL.—*Future.*

Jud.14: 6. mightily upon him, *and he rent him*
1Sa.24: 7(8). *So* David *stayed* (marg. *cut off*) his

שֶׁסַע *sheh'-sa^{n}g*, m. 8157

Lev.11: 3. parteth the hoof, and is clovenfooted, (lit. cleaveth *the cleft of* the hoofs)
7. divide the hoof, and be clovenfooted, (lit. cleaveth *the cleft of* the hoof)
26. divideth the hoof, *and* (is) not clovenfooted, (lit. *and* cleaveth not *the cleft*)
Deu14: 6. cleaveth *the cleft* into two claws,

שָׁסַף [*shāh-saph'*]. 8158

* PIEL.—*Future.* *

1Sa.15:33. *And* Samuel *hewed* Agag *in pieces*

שָׁעָה *shāh-^{n}gāh'*. 8159

* KAL.—*Preterite.* *

Gen. 4: 5. to his offering *he had* not *respect.*
Isa. 31: 1. *they look* not unto the Holy One

KAL.—*Imperative.*

Job 14: 6. *Turn* from him, that he may rest,
Isa. 22: 4. *Look away* from me;

KAL.—*Future.*

Gen. 4: 4. *And* the Lord *had respect* unto Abel
Ex. 5: 9. *let them* not *regard* vain words.
2Sa.22:42. *They looked,* but (there was) none
Job 7:19. How long *wilt thou* not *depart* from me,
Ps.119:117. *and I will have respect* unto thy
Isa. 17: 7. At that day *shall* a man *look* to his Maker,
8. *he shall* not *look* to the altars
32: 3. the eyes of them that see *shall* not *be dim,*

* HIPHIL.—*Imperative.* *

Ps. 39:13(14). *O spare* me, that I may recover strength,

* HITHPAEL.—*Future.* *

Isa. 41:10. *be* not *dismayed;* for I (am) thy God:
23. *that we may be dismayed,*

שָׁעָה *shāh-^{n}gāh'*, Ch. f. 8160

Dan. 3: 6. shall *the* same *hour* be cast into
15. ye shall be cast *the* same *hour* into the
4:19(16). Belteshazzar, was astonied *for* one *hour,*
33(30). *The* same *hour* was the thing
5: 5. In *the* same *hour* came forth

שְׁעָטָה [*shah-^{n}gătāh'*], f. 8161

Jer. 47: 3. At the noise of *the stamping of*

8162 **שַׁעַטְנֵז** *shah-^{n}gat-nĕhz'*, m.

Lev.19:19. a garment mingled *of linen and woollen*
Deu22:11. *a garment of divers sorts*, (as) of woollen and linen together.

8168 **שֹׁעַל** [*shōh'-^{n}gal*], m.

1K. 20:10. Samaria shall suffice *for handfuls*
Isa. 40:12. the waters *in the hollow of his hand*,
Eze.13:19. my people *for handfuls of* barley

8172 **שָׁעַן** [*shāh-^{n}gan'*].

* NIPHAL.—*Preterite*. *

Nu. 21:15. *and lieth* (marg. *leaneth*) upon the border of Moab.
2Ch 13:18. *they relied* upon the Lord
14:11(10). for *we rest* on thee,
16: 7. not *relied* on the Lord thy God,
Isa. 10:20. *but shall stay* upon the Lord,

NIPHAL.—*Infinitive*.

2Ch 16: 7. *Because thou hast relied* on
8. *yet, because thou didst rely* on the Lord,
Isa. 10:20. shall no more again *stay* (lit. shall not add *to stay*)
Eze.29: 7. *and when they leaned* upon thee,

NIPHAL.—*Imperative*.

Gen18: 4. *and rest yourselves* under the tree:

NIPHAL.—*Future*.

Jud.16:26. *that I may lean* upon them.
Job 8:15. *He shall lean* upon his house,
24:23. safety, *whereon he resteth* ;
Pro. 3: 5. *lean* not unto thine own understanding.
Isa. 30:12. perverseness, *and stay* thereon:
31: 1. and *stay* on horses,
50:10. *and stay* upon his God.
Mic. 3:11. *will they lean* upon the Lord,

NIPHAL.—*Participle*.

2Sa. 1: 6. Saul *leaned* upon his spear ;
2K. 5:18. he *leaneth* on my hand,
7: 2. on whose hand the king *leaned*
17. the lord on whose hand *he leaned*

8173 **שָׁעַע** [*shāh-^{n}ga^{n}g'*].

* KAL.—*Imperative*. *

Isa. 29: 9. cry ye out, *and cry* : (marg. *and riot*.)

* PILPEL.—*Preterite*. *

Ps.119:70. I *delight* in thy law.
Isa. 11: 8. *And* the sucking child *shall play*

PILPEL.—*Future*.

Ps. 94:19. thy comforts *delight* my soul.

* PALPAL.—*Future*. *

Isa. 66:12. and *be dandled* upon (her) knees.

* HIPHIL.—*Imperative*. *

Isa. 6:10. *shut* their eyes; lest they see

* HITHPALPEL.—*Imperative*. *

Isa. 29: 9. Stay yourselves, and wonder ; *cry ye out*, (marg. or, *take your pleasure*)

HITHPALPEL.—*Future*.

Ps.119:16. *I will delight myself* in thy statutes:
47. *And I will delight myself* in thy commandments,

8176 **שָׁעַר** *shāh-^{n}gar'*.

* KAL.—*Preterite*. *

Pro.23: 7. For as *he thinketh* in his heart,

8180 **שַׁעַר** *shah'-^{n}gar*, m.

Gen26:12. in the same year an hundred*fold*:

שַׁעַר *shah'-^{n}gar*, m. 8179

Gen19: 1. Lot sat *in the gate of* Sodom:
22:17. thy seed shall possess *the gate of*
23:10, 18. all that went in at *the gate of*
24:60. let thy seed possess *the gate of*
28:17. this (is) *the gate of* heaven.
34:20. came unto *the gate of* their city
24. went out of *the gate of* his city ;
— all that went out of *the gate of*
Ex. 20:10. stranger that (is) *within thy gates*:
27:16. *And for the gate of* the court
32:26. Moses stood *in the gate of* the camp,
27. out *from gate to gate* throughout the camp,
35:17. the hanging for *the door of* the court,
38:15. for the other side *of the* court *gate*,
18. the hanging for *the gate of*
31. the sockets of *the* court *gate*,
39:40. the hanging *for the* court *gate*,
40: 8. the hanging at *the* court *gate*.
33. the hanging of *the* court *gate*.
Nu. 4:26. the hanging for the door of *the gate of*
Deu 5:14. stranger that (is) *within thy gates*;
6: 9. of thy house, *and on thy gates*.
11:20. thine house, *and upon thy gates*:
12:12. Levite that (is) *within your gates*;
15. kill and eat flesh in all *thy gates*,
17. Thou mayest not eat *within thy gates*
18. Levite that (is) *within thy gates*:
21. thou shalt eat *in thy gates*
14:21. stranger that (is) *in thy gates*.
27. Levite that (is) *within thy gates*;
28. shalt lay (it) up *within thy gates*:
29. which (are) *within thy gates*,
15: 7. of thy brethren within any of *thy gates*
22. Thou shalt eat it *within thy gates*:
16: 5. passover within any of *thy gates*,
11. Levite that (is) *within thy gates*,
14. that (are) *within thy gates*.
18. make thee in all *thy gates*,
17: 2. within any of *thy gates*
5. that wicked thing, unto *thy gates*,
8. controversy *within thy gates*:
18: 6. come from any of *thy gates*
21:19. unto *the gate of* his place ;
22:15. unto the elders of the city *in the gate*.
24. bring them both out unto *the gate of*
23:16(17). choose in one of *thy gates*,
24:14. in thy land *within thy gates*:
25: 7. go up *to the gate* unto the elders,
26:12. that they may eat *within thy gates*,
28:52, 52. besiege thee in all *thy gates*,
55. shall distress thee in all *thy gates*.
57. shall distress thee *in thy gates*.
31:12. stranger that (is) *within thy gates*,
Jos. 2: 5. of shutting of *the gate*,
7. they shut *the gate*.
7: 5. them (from) before *the gate*
8:29. cast it at the entering of *the gate of*
20: 4. stand at the entering of *the gate of*
Jud. 5: 8. then (was) war in *the gates*:
11. people of the Lord go down *to the gates*.
9:35. stood in the entering of *the gate of*
40. unto the entering of *the gate*.
44. stood in the entering of *the gate of*
16: 2. laid wait for him all night *in the gate of*
3. took the doors of *the gate of*
18:16. stood by the entering of *the gate*.
17. stood in the entering of *the gate*
Ru. 3:11. for all *the city* (marg. *gate*) *of* my people
4: 1. Then went Boaz up to *the gate*,
10. *and from the gate of* his place:
11. all the people that (were) *in the gate*,
1Sa. 4:18. backward by the side of *the gate*,
9:18. Saul drew near to Samuel in *the gate*,
17:52. *to the gates of* Ekron.
21:13(14). scrabbled on the doors of *the gate*,
2Sa. 3:27. Joab took him aside in *the gate*
10: 8. at the entering in of *the gate*:
11:23. even unto the entering of *the gate*.
15: 2. stood beside the way of *the gate*:
18: 4. the king stood by the *gate* side,
24. David sat between *the* two *gates*:
— went up to the roof over *the gate*
33(19:1). up to the chamber over *the gate*,
19: 8(9). sat *in the gate*.
—(-). the king doth sit *in the gate*.

2Sa.23:15. which (is) *by the gate!*
16. that (was) *by the gate,*
1K. 8:37. besiege them in the land of *their cities;* (marg. or, *jurisdiction*)
22:10. the entrance of *the gate of* Samaria;
2K. 7: 1. *in the gate of* Samaria.
3. at the entering in of *the gate:*
17. to have the charge of *the gate:* and the people trode upon him *in the gate,*
18. *in the gate of* Samaria:
20. the people trode upon him *in the gate,*
9:31. entered in *at the gate,*
10: 8. entering in of *the gate* until
11: 6. a third part (shall be) *at the gate of* Sur; and a third part *at the gate* behind the
19. the way of *the gate of* the
14:13. *from the gate of* Ephraim unto *the* corner *gate,*
15:35. He built *the* higher *gate*
23: 8. the high places of *the gates*
— *the gate of* Joshua
— *at the gate of* the city.
25: 4. the way of *the gate*
1Ch 9:18. Who hitherto (waited) *in* the king's *gate*
23. the oversight of *the gates* of the house
11:17. that (is) *at the gate!*
18. that (was) *by the gate,*
16:42. the sons of Jeduthun (were) *porters.* (marg. *for the gate*)
22: 3. the nails for the doors of *the gates,*
26:13. house of their fathers, *for every gate.* (lit. *for gate and gate*)
16. with *the gate* Shallecheth,
2Ch 6:28. in *the cities* of their land; (marg. the land of *their gates*)
8:14. *at every gate:* (lit. *for gate and gate*) for so had David
18: 9. at the entering in of *the gate*
23: 5. a third part *at the gate of*
15. the entering of *the* horse *gate*
19. he set the porters at *the gates of*
20. they came through *the* high *gate*
24: 8. set it without *at the gate of*
25:23. *from the gate of* Ephraim to *the* corner *gate,*
26: 9. at *the* corner *gate,* and at *the* valley *gate,*
27: 3. He built *the* high *gate of*
31: 2. to praise *in the gates of* the tents
32: 6. in the street of *the gate of*
33:14. the entering in *at the* fish *gate,*
35:15. the porters (waited) *at every gate;* (lit. *for gate and gate*)
Neh 1: 3. *and the gates thereof* are burned
2: 3. *and the gates thereof* are consumed
8. beams for *the gates of* the palace
13. by night *by the gate of* the valley,
— and to *the* dung *port,*
— *and the gates thereof* were consumed
14. Then I went on to *the gate*
15. entered *by the gate of* the valley,
17. *and the gates thereof* are burned
3: 1. they builded *the* sheep *gate;*
3. But *the* fish *gate* did the sons
6. *the* old *gate* repaired Jehoiada
13. *The* valley *gate* repaired Hanun,
— on the wall unto *the* dung *gate.*
14. *the* dung *gate* repaired Malchiah
15. But *the gate of* the fountain
26. over against *the* water *gate*
28. *the* horse *gate* repaired the priests,
29. the keeper of *the* east *gate.*
31. over against *the gate* Miphkad,
32. *unto the* sheep *gate* repaired
6: 1. set up the doors upon *the gates;*
7: 3. Let not *the gates of* Jerusalem
8: 1, 3. before *the* water *gate;*
16. the street of *the* water *gate,* and in the street of *the gate of*
11:19. their brethren that kept *the gates,*
12:25. at the thresholds of *the gates.*
30. *the gates,* and the wall.
31. *toward the* dung *gate:*
37. And at *the* fountain *gate,*
— even unto *the* water *gate*
39. And from above *the gate of* Ephraim, and above *the* old *gate,* and above *the* fish *gate,*
— even unto *the* sheep *gate:* and they stood still *in the* prison *gate.*

Neh 13:19. that when *the gates of* Jerusalem
— my servants set I at *the gates,*
22. should come (and) keep *the gates,*
Est. 2:19, 21. Mordecai sat *in* the king's *gate.*
3: 2. that (were) *in* the king's *gate,*
3. which (were) *in* the king's *gate,*
4: 2. came even before the king's *gate:*
— into the king's *gate*
6. which (was) before the king's *gate.*
5: 9. saw Mordecai *in* the king's *gate,*
13. sitting *at* the king's *gate.*
6:10. that sitteth *at* the king's *gate:*
12. came again to the king's *gate.*
Job 5: 4. they are crushed *in the gate,*
29: 7. When I went out to *the gate*
31:21. when I saw my help *in the gate:*
38:17. Have *the gates of* death been
— *or* hast thou seen *the doors*
Ps. 9:13(14). liftest me up *from the gates*
14(15). *in the gates of* the daughter of Zion:
24: 7, 9. Lift up your heads, *O ye gates;*
69:12(13). They that sit in *the gate*
87: 2. The Lord loveth *the gates of* Zion
100: 4. Enter into *his gates*
107:18. draw near unto *the gates of* death.
118:19. Open to me *the gates of* righteousness:
20. This *gate* of the Lord,
122: 2. Our feet shall stand *within thy gates,*
127: 5. shall speak with the enemies *in the gate.*
147:13. strengthened the bars of *thy gates;*
Pro. 1:21. in the openings of *the gates:*
8: 3. She crieth at *the gates,*
14:19. at *the gates of* the righteous.
22:22. neither oppress the afflicted *in the gate:*
24: 7. openeth not his mouth *in the gate.*
31:23. Her husband is known *in the gates,*
31. let her own works praise her *in the gates.*
Cant. 7: 4(5). by *the gate of* Bath-rabbim:
Isa. 14:31. Howl, *O gate;* cry, O city;
22: 7. set themselves in array *at* (marg. or, *towards*) *the gate.*
24:12. *the gate* is smitten
26: 2. Open ye *the gates,*
28: 6. them that turn the battle *to the gate.*
29:21. him that reproveth *in the gate,*
38:10. I shall go *to the gates of*
45: 1. *and the gates* shall not be shut;
54:12. *and thy gates* of carbuncles,
60:11. *thy gates* shall be open continually;
18. Salvation, *and thy gates* Praise.
62:10. go *through the gates;*
Jer. 1:15. at the entering of *the gates of*
7: 2. Stand *in the gate of* the Lord's house,
— that enter in *at* these *gates*
14: 2. *and the gates thereof* languish;
15: 7. *in the gates of* the land;
17:19. Go and stand *in the gate*
— in all *the gates of* Jerusalem;
20. that enter in *by* these *gates:*
21. bring (it) in *by the gates of* Jerusalem;
24. bring in no burden *through the gates of*
25. Then shall there enter *into the gates of*
27. entering in *at the gates of* Jerusalem
— I kindle a fire *in the gates thereof,*
19: 2. which (is) by the entry of *the* east *gate,*
20: 2. *in the* high *gate of* Benjamin,
22: 2. thy people that enter in *by* these *gates:*
4. enter in *by the gates of* this house
19. *beyond the gates of* Jerusalem.
26:10. sat down in the entry of *the* new *gate*
31:38. unto *the gate of* the corner.
40. unto the corner of *the* horse *gate*
36:10. at the entry of *the* new *gate*
37:13. when he was *in the gate of* Benjamin,
38: 7. the king then sitting *in the gate of*
39: 3. sat *in the* middle *gate,*
4. *by the gate* betwixt the two
51:58. *and her* high *gates* shall be burned
52: 7. by night by the way of *the gate*
Lam. 1: 4. all *her gates* are desolate:
2: 9. *Her gates* are sunk into the ground;
4:12. entered *into the gates of* Jerusalem.
5:14. The elders have ceased *from the gate,*
Eze. 8: 3. to the door of *the* inner *gate*
5. *at the gate of* the altar
14. brought me to the door of *the gate of*
9: 2. from the way of *the* higher *gate,*

Eze.10:19. stood at the door of *the* east *gate*
11: 1. brought me unto *the* east *gate*
— behold at the door of *the gate*
21:15(20). the sword against all *their gates*,
22(27). rams against *the gates*,
26:10. he shall enter *into thy gates*,
40: 3. he stood *in the gate*.
6. Then came he unto *the gate*
— measured the threshold of *the gate*,
7. and the threshold of *the gate*
— by the porch of *the gate*
8. measured also the porch of *the gate*
9. Then measured he the porch of *the gate*,
— and the porch of *the gate* (was) inward.
10. the little chambers of *the gate*
11. the breadth of the entry of *the gate*, ten cubits; (and) the length of *the gate*,
13. measured then *the gate* from the roof
14. post of the court round about *the gate*.
15. from the face of *the gate*
— the porch of *the* inner *gate*
16. posts *within the gate* round about,
18. by the side of *the gates* over against the length of *the gates*
19. from the forefront of *the* lower *gate*
20. *And the gate of* the outward court
21. after the measure of *the* first *gate*:
22. after the measure of *the gate*
23. *And the gate of* the inner court (was) over against *the gate*
— he measured *from gate* to *gate*
24. behold *a gate* toward the south:
27. *And* (there was) *a gate*
— he measured *from gate* to *gate*
28. the inner court *by the* south *gate*: and he measured *the* south *gate*
32. he measured *the gate* according
35. he brought me to *the* north *gate*,
38. by the posts of *the gates*,
39. in the porch of *the gate*
40. goeth up to the entry of *the* north *gate*,
— at the porch of *the gate*,
41. by the side of *the gate*;
44. without *the* inner *gate*
— at the side of *the* north *gate*;
— at the side of *the* east *gate*
48. the breadth of *the gate*
42:15. brought me forth toward *the gate*
43: 1. he brought me to *the gate*, (even) *the gate*
4. by the way of *the gate*
44: 1. brought me back the way of *the gate*
2. This *gate* shall be shut,
3. by the way of the porch of (that) *gate*,
4. brought he me the way of *the* north *gate*
11. charge at *the gates of* the house,
17. enter in at *the gates of* the
— they minister *in the gates of*
45:19. upon the posts of *the gate of*
46: 1. *The gate of* the inner court
2. the porch of (that) *gate* without, and shall stand by the post of *the gate*,
— worship at the threshold of *the gate*:
— *but the gate* shall not be shut
3. worship at the door of this *gate*
8. by the way of the porch of (that) *gate*,
9. by the way of *the* north *gate* to worship shall go out by the way of *the* south *gate*; and he that entereth by the way of *the* south *gate* shall go forth by the way of *the* north *gate*: he shall not return by the way of *the gate*
12. *the gate* that looketh toward the east,
— going forth (one) shall shut *the gate*.
19. which (was) at the side of *the gate*,
47: 2. brought he me out of the way of *the gate*
— way without unto *the* utter *gate*
48:31. *And the gates of* the city
— three *gates* northward; one *gate of* Reuben, one *gate of* Judah, one *gate of* Levi.
32. *and* three *gates*; *and* one *gate of* Joseph, one *gate of* Benjamin, one *gate of* Dan.
33. *and* three *gates*; one *gate of* Simeon, one *gate of* Issachar, one *gate of* Zebulun.
34. (with) *their* three *gates*; one *gate of* Gad, one *gate of* Asher, one *gate of* Naphtali.
Am. 5:10. They hate him that rebuketh *in the gate*,
12. turn aside the poor *in the gate*
Am. 5:15. establish judgment *in the gate*:
Obad. 11. foreigners entered into *his gates*,
13. have entered *into the gate of*
Mic. 1: 9. he is come unto *the gate*
12. *unto the gate of* Jerusalem.
2:13. have passed through *the gate*,
Nah 2: 6(7). *The gates of* the rivers
3:13. *the gates of* thy land
Zep. 1:10. noise of a cry *from the* fish *gate*,
Zec. 8:16. peace *in your gates*:
14:10. *from* Benjamin's *gate* unto the place of *the* first *gate*, unto *the* corner *gate*,

---

שֹׁעָר [*shōh'-^{n}găhr'*], adj. 8182

Jer. 29:17. make them like *vile* figs,

שַׁעֲרוּר [*shah-^{n}găroor'*], adj. 8186

Jer. 5:30. A wonderful *and horrible thing*
23:14. Jerusalem *an horrible thing*: (marg. or, *filthiness*)

שַׁעֲרוּרִי [*shah-^{n}găroo-ree'*], adj. 8186

Jer. 18:13. Israel hath done *a* very *horrible thing*.
Hos. 6:10. I have seen *an horrible thing*

שַׁעֲשֻׁעִים *shah-^{n}găshoo-^{n}geem'*, m. pl. 8191

Ps.119:24. Thy testimonies also (are) *my delight*
77. for thy law (is) *my delight*.
92. Unless thy law (had been) *my delights*,
143. thy commandments (are) *my delights*.
174. and thy law (is) *my delight*.
Pro. 8:30. I was daily (his) *delight*,
31. *and my delights* (were) with
Isa. 5: 7. the men of Judah *his pleasant* plant: (marg. plant of *his pleasures*)
Jer. 31:20. my dear son? (is he) a *pleasant* child?

שָׁפָה [*shāh-phāh'*]. 8192

* NIPHAL.—*Participle.* *

Isa. 13: 2. a banner upon the *high* mountain,

* PUAL.—*Preterite.* *

Job 33:21. *and* his bones (that) were not seen *stick out*.

שָׁפָה [*shāh-phāh'*], f. 8194

2Sa. 17:29. sheep, *and cheese of* kine,

שְׁפוֹט *sh'phōht*, m. 8196

2Ch 20: 9. *judgment*, or pestilence, or famine,
Eze.23:10. *for* they had executed *judgment* upon her.

שִׁפְחָה *shiph-^{n}găh'*, f. 8198

Gen 12:16. menservants, *and maidservants*,
16: 1. she had *an handmaid*,
2. go in unto *my maid*;
3. took Hagar *her maid* the Egyptian,
5. I have given *my maid*
6. *thy maid* (is) in thy hand;
8. Sarai's *maid*, whence camest thou?
20:14. menservants, *and womenservants*,
24:35. menservants, *and maidservants*,
25:12. the Egyptian, Sarah's *handmaid*,
29:24. unto his daughter Leah Zilpah *his maid* (for) *an handmaid*.
29. Bilhah *his handmaid to be* her *maid*.
30: 4. she gave him Bilhah *her handmaid* to
7. Rachel's *maid* conceived again,
9. she took Zilpah *her maid*, and gave her
10. Leah's *maid* bare Jacob a son.
12. Leah's *maid* bare Jacob a second son.
18. because I have given *my maiden*

Gen30:43. much cattle, *and maidservants,*
32: 5(6). menservants, *and womenservants:*
22(23). *his* two *womenservants,*
33: 1. unto *the* two *handmaids.*
2. he put *the handmaids*
6. Then *the handmaidens* came near,
35:25. the sons of Bilhah, Rachel's *handmaid;*
26. sons of Zilpah, Leah's *handmaid;*
Ex. 11: 5. the firstborn of *the maidservant*
Lev.19:20. that (is) *a bondmaid,*
Deu28:68. for bondmen *and bondwomen,*
Ru. 2:13. spoken friendly unto *thine handmaid,*
— like unto one of *thine handmaidens.*
1Sa. 1:18. Let *thine handmaid* find grace
8:16. menservants, and *your maidservants,*
25:27. which *thine handmaid* hath brought
41. thine handmaid (be) *a servant*
28:21. *thine handmaid* hath obeyed
22. also unto the voice of *thine handmaid,*
2Sa.14: 6. *And thy handmaid* had two sons,
7. family is risen against *thine handmaid,*
12. woman said, Let *thine handmaid,*
15. and *thy handmaid* said,
17. Then *thine handmaid* said,
19. in the mouth of *thine handmaid:*
17:17. *a wench* went and told them;
2K. 4: 2. *Thine handmaid* hath not any thing
16. do not lie *unto thine handmaid.*
5:26. menservants, *and maidservants?*
2Ch 28:10. for bondmen *and bondwomen*
Est. 7: 4. for bondmen *and bondwomen,*
Ps.123: 2. *a maiden* unto the hand of her mistress;
Pro.30:23. *and an handmaid* that is heir
Ecc. 2: 7. I got (me) servants *and maidens,*
Isa. 14: 2. for servants *and handmaids:*
24: 2. *as with the maid,* so with her mistress;
Jer. 34: 9. every man *his maidservant,*
10. every one *his maidservant,*
11. the servants and *the handmaids,*
— for servants *and for handmaids.*
16. every man *his handmaid,*
— for servants *and for handmaids.*
Joel 2:29(3:2). upon *the handmaids* in those days

8199 שָׁפַט *shāh-phat'.*

✱ KAL.—*Preterite.* ✱

Ex. 18:16. *and I judge* between one
22. *And let them judge* the people
26. *And they judged* the people
Nu. 35:24. *Then* the congregation *shall judge*
Deu 1:16. *and judge* righteously between
16:18. *and they shall judge* the people
25: 1. *that* (the judges) *may judge them;*
Jud.16:31. he *judged* Israel twenty years.
1Sa. 4:18. he *had judged* Israel forty years.
7:16. *and judged* Israel in all those places.
17. there *he judged* Israel;
8:20. *and that* our king *may judge us,*
24:15(16). *and judge* between me and thee,
2Sa.18:19. *hath avenged him* (marg. *judged him* from the hand) of his enemies.
31. the Lord *hath avenged thee*
1K. 3:28. which the king *had judged;*
8:32. *and judge* thy servants,
2K. 23:22. the judges that *judged* Israel,
2Ch 6:23. *and judge* thy servants,
Isa. 2: 4. *And he shall judge* among
11: 4. *But* with righteousness *shall he judge*
Jer. 5:28. the needy *do they* not *judge.*
Eze. 7: 3. *and will judge* thee according
8. *and I will judge* thee according
16:38. *And I will judge* thee,
23:24. *and they shall judge thee* according
24:14. *shall they judge thee,* saith the Lord
34:20. (even) *I, will judge* between
22. *and I will judge* between
36:19. to their doings *I judged them.*
Dan 9:12. our judges that *judged us,*
Mic. 4: 3. *And he shall judge* among

KAL.—*Infinitive.*

Gen19: 9. he will *needs* be a judge: (lit. *judging* he will judge)
Ex. 18:13. Moses sat *to judge* the people:
Ru. 1: 1. the days when the judges *ruled,* (marg. *judged*)
1Sa. 8: 5. make us a king *to judge us*
6. Give us a king *to judge us.*
1K. 3: 9. understanding heart *to judge* thy people,
— for who is able *to judge*
1Ch 16:33. he cometh *to judge* the earth.
Ps. 10:18. *To judge* the fatherless
51: 4(6). be clear *when thou judgest.*
96:13. he cometh *to judge* the earth:
98: 9. for he cometh *to judge* the earth:
Eze.44:24. (כתיב) they shall stand *in judgment;*
Joel 3:12(4:12). will I sit *to judge* all the heathen
Obad. 21. *to judge* the mount of Esau;

KAL.—*Imperative.*

Ps. 7: 8(9). *judge me,* O Lord, according
26: 1. *Judge me,* O Lord; for I have walked
35:24. *Judge me,* O Lord my God,
43: 1. *Judge me,* O God, and plead my cause
82: 3. *Defend* (marg. *Judge*) the poor and fatherless:
8. Arise, O God, *judge* the earth:
Pro.31: 9. Open thy mouth, *judge* righteously,
Isa. 1:17. *judge* the fatherless,
5: 3. men of Judah, *judge,* I pray you,
Lam 3:59. *judge thou* my cause.
Zec. 7: 9. *Execute* (marg. *Judge*) true judgment,
8:16. *execute* (marg. *id.*) the judgment of truth

KAL.—*Future.*

Gen 16: 5. the Lord *judge* between me and thee.
19: 9. *and he will* needs *be a judge:*
31:53. *judge* betwixt us.
Ex. 5:21. The Lord look upon you, *and judge;*
18:22. every small matter they *shall judge:*
26. every small matter they *judged*
Lev.19:15. in righteousness *shalt thou judge*
Jud. 3:10. *and he judged* Israel, and went
10: 2. *And he judged* Israel twenty and three
3. *and judged* Israel twenty and two
11:27. *be judge* this day
12: 7. *And* Jephthah *judged* Israel six years.
8. *And* after him Ibzan of Beth-lehem *judged* Israel.
9. *And he judged* Israel seven years.
11. *And* after him Elon, a Zebulonite, *judged* Israel; *and he judged* Israel ten years.
13. *And* after him Abdon...*judged* Israel.
14. *and he judged* Israel eight years.
15:20. *And he judged* Israel in the days
1Sa. 7: 6. *And* Samuel *judged* the children of Israel
15. *And* Samuel *judged* Israel all the days
24:12(13). The Lord *judge* between me and thee
15(16). *and deliver* (marg. *judge*) *me* out of
1K. 7: 7. throne where *he might judge,*
2Ch 1:10. who *can judge* this thy people,
11. that *thou mayest judge* my people,
19: 6. for *ye judge* not for man,
20:12. *wilt thou* not *judge* them?
Job 21:22. *he judgeth* those that are high.
22:13. *can he judge* through the dark cloud?
Ps. 9: 8(9). *shall judge* the world in righteousness,
58: 1(2). *do ye judge* uprightly,
67: 4(5). *thou shalt judge* the people righteously,
72: 4. *He shall judge* the poor of the people,
75: 2(3). *I will judge* uprightly.
82: 1. *he judgeth* among the gods.
2. How long *will ye judge* unjustly,
96:13. *he shall judge* the world with
98: 9. with righteousness *shall he judge* the
Ecc. 3:17. God *shall judge* the righteous
Isa. 1:23. *they judge* not the fatherless,
11: 3. *shall* not *judge* after the sight of his eyes,
51: 5. mine arms *shall judge* the people;
Eze. 7:27. their deserts *will I judge* them;
11:10. *I will judge* you in the border
11. *I will judge* you in the border
18:30. Therefore *I will judge* you,
20: 4. *Wilt thou judge* (marg. or, *plead for*) them, son of man, *wilt thou judge* (them)?
21:30(35). *I will judge* thee in the place
22: 2. son of man, *wilt thou judge* (marg. or, *plead for*), *wilt thou judge* the bloody city?
23:36. *wilt thou judge* (marg. *id.*) Aholah
45. they *shall judge* them after
33:20. *I will judge* you every one
35:11. when *I have judged thee.*
44:24. *they shall judge it* according
Mic 3:11. The heads thereof *judge* for reward,

KAL.—*Participle.* Poel.

Gen 18:25. *the Judge of* all the earth do right?
Ex. 2:14. a prince *and a judge* over us?
Nu. 25: 5. Moses said unto *the judges of*
Deu 1:16. I charged *your judges* at that time,
16:18. *Judges* and officers shalt thou make
17: 9. *the judge* that shall be in those days,
12. or unto *the judge*,
19:17. before the priests *and the judges*,
18. *the judges* shall make diligent
21: 2. thy elders *and thy judges* shall come
25: 2. that *the judge* shall cause him
Jos. 8:33. officers, *and their judges*,
23: 2 & 24:1. *and for their judges*, and for their
Jud. 2:16. the Lord raised up *judges*,
17. would not hearken unto *their judges*,
18. the Lord raised them up *judges*, then the Lord was with *the judge*,
— of their enemies all the days of *the judge*:
19. when *the judge* was dead,
4: 4. she *judged* Israel at that time.
11:27. the Lord *the Judge* be judge
Ru. 1: 1. when *the judges* ruled,
1Sa. 3:13. I *will judge* his house for ever
8: 1. that he made his sons *judges*
2. *judges* in Beer-sheba.
2Sa. 7:11. time that I commanded *judges*
15: 4. Oh that I were made *judge*
2K. 15: 5. *judging* the people of the land.
23:22. *the judges* that judged Israel,
1Ch 17: 6. spake I a word to any of *the judges of*
10. the time that I commanded *judges*
23: 4. officers *and judges*:
26:29. for officers *and judges*.
2Ch 1: 2. *and to the judges*, and to every
19: 5. he set *judges* in the land
6. said to *the judges*,
26:21. *judging* the people of the land.
Ezr. 10:14. *and the judges thereof*, until
Job 9:24. covereth the faces of *the judges thereof*;
12:17. and maketh *the judges* fools.
23: 7. be delivered for ever *from my judge*.
Ps. 2:10. be instructed, *ye judges of* the earth.
7:11(12). God *judgeth* the righteous (marg. or, (is) *a* righteous *judge*), and God is
9: 4(5). thou satest in the throne *judging*
50: 6. for God (is) *judge* himself.
58:11(12). he is a God *that judgeth* in the earth.
75: 7(8). But God (is) *the judge*:
94: 2. *thou judge of* the earth:
109:31. *from those that condemn* (marg. *the judges of*) his soul.
141: 6. When *their judges* are overthrown
148:11. and all *judges of* the earth:
Pro. 8:16. all *the judges of* the earth.
29:14. The king that faithfully *judgeth* the poor,
Isa. 1:26. I will restore *thy judges* as at
3: 2. the man of war, *the judge*,
16: 5. in the tabernacle of David, *judging*,
33:22. For the Lord (is) *our judge*,
40:23. he maketh *the judges of* the earth
Jer. 11:20. O Lord of hosts, *that judgest* righteously,
Eze.34:17. I *judge* between cattle
Dan 9:12. against *our judges* that judged
Hos. 7: 7. have devoured *their judges*;
13:10. *and thy judges* of whom thou saidst,
Am. 2: 3. I will cut off *the judge* from
Mic. 5: 1(4:14). they shall smite *the judge of*
7: 3. *and the judge* (asketh) for a reward;
Zep. 3: 3. *her judges* (are) evening wolves;

* NIPHAL.—*Preterite.* *

Eze.17:20. *and will plead* with him
20:35. *and* there *will I plead*
36. Like as *I pleaded* with your fathers
38:22. *And I will plead* against him
Joel 3: 2(4:2). *and will plead* with them there

NIPHAL.—*Infinitive.*

2Ch 22: 8. *when* Jehu *was executing judgment*
Ps. 37:33. nor condemn him *when he is judged*.
109: 7. *When he shall be judged*, let him be

NIPHAL.—*Future.*

1Sa. 12: 7. *that I may reason* with you
Ps. 9:19(20). *let* the heathen *be judged* in thy sight.
Isa. 43:26. *let us plead* together:
Eze.20:36. so *will I plead* with you,

NIPHAL.—*Participle.*

Pro.29: 9. a wise man *contendeth*
Isa. 59: 4. nor (any) *pleadeth* for truth:
66:16. by his sword *will* the Lord *plead*
Jer. 2:35. I will *plead* with thee,
25:31. he will *plead* with all flesh;

* POEL.—*Participle.* *

Job 9:15. make supplication *to my judge*.

שְׁפַט [*sh'phat*], Ch. 8200

* P'AL.—*Participle.* Active. *

Ezr. 7:25. set *magistrates* and judges,

שְׁפָטִים *sh'phāh-teem'*, m. pl. 8201

Ex. 6: 6. *and with* great *judgments*:
7: 4. land of Egypt *by* great *judgments*.
12:12. Egypt I will execute *judgment*:
Nu. 33: 4. the Lord executed *judgments*.
2Ch 24:24. So they executed *judgment*
Pro. 19:29. *Judgments* are prepared for
Eze. 5:10. I will execute *judgments*
15. when I shall execute *judgments*
11: 9. will execute *judgments* among you.
14:21. when I send *my* four sore *judgments*
16:41. execute *judgments* upon thee
25:11. I will execute *judgments*
28:22. shall have executed *judgments*
26. when I have executed *judgments*
30:14. will execute *judgments* in No.
19. Thus will I execute *judgments*

שְׁפִי [*sh'phee*], m. pl. 8205

Nu. 23: 3. he went to *an high place*. (marg. or, *solitary*)
Job 33:21. (כתיב) *and* his bones (that) were not seen *stick out*.
Isa. 41:18. I will open rivers in *high places*,
49: 9. pastures (shall be) in all *high places*.
Jer. 3: 2. Lift up thine eyes unto *the high places*,
21. A voice was heard upon *the high places*,
4:11. A dry wind of *the high places*
7:29. take up a lamentation on *high places*;
12:12. spoilers are come upon all *high places*
14: 6. asses did stand in *the high places*,

שְׁפִיפֹן *sh'phee-phōhn'*, m. 8207

Gen 49:17. *an adder* (marg. *arrowsnake*) in the path,

שַׁפִּיר *shap-peer'*, Ch. adj. 8209

Dan 4:12(9). The leaves thereof (were) *fair*,
21(18). Whose leaves (were) *fair*,

שָׁפַךְ *shāh-phach'*. 8210

* KAL.—*Preterite.* *

Ex. 4: 9. *and pour* (it) upon the dry (land):
Lev.14:41. *and they shall pour out* the dust
17: 4. *he hath shed* blood;
13. *he shall even pour out* the blood thereof,
Deu21: 7. Our hands *have* not *shed* this blood,
1K. 2:31. innocent blood, which Joab *shed*,
2K. 21:16. Manasseh *shed* innocent blood
24: 4. the innocent blood that *he shed*:
1Ch 22: 8. Thou *hast shed* blood abundantly,
— thou *hast shed* much blood
28: 3. and *hast shed* blood.
Ps. 79: 3. Their blood *have they shed*
Isa. 57: 6. *hast thou poured* a drink offering,
Jer. 14:16. *for I will pour* their wickedness
Lam.2: 4. *he poured out* his fury like fire.
4:11. *he hath poured out* his fierce anger,
Eze. 4: 2. *and cast* a mount against it;
14:19. *and pour out* my fury upon it
21:31(36). *And I will pour out* mine indignation
22: 4. thy blood that *thou hast shed*;
22. *have poured out* my fury
24: 7. *she poured it* not upon the ground,
26: 8. *and cast* (marg. or, *pour out*) a mount

Eze.30:15. *And I will pour* my fury upon Sin,
36:18. the blood that *they had shed*
39:29. *I have poured out* my spirit upon the
Joel 3:19(4:19). because *they have shed* innocent
Zec 12:10. *And I will pour* upon the house of David,

KAL.—*Infinitive.*

1 Sa.25:31. *either that thou hast shed* blood
1 K. 18:28. till the blood *gushed out* upon them. (marg. *poured out* blood upon them)
Pro. 1:16. make haste *to shed* blood.
Isa. 59: 7. they make haste *to shed* innocent blood:
Jer. 6:11. I *will pour* it *out* (lit. *pouring out*) upon the
22:17. for thy covetousness, and *for to shed*
Eze. 9: 8. *in thy pouring out* of thy fury
17:17. *by casting up* mounts,
20: 8. I *will pour out* my fury
13, 21. I *would pour out* my fury
21:22(27). to *cast* a mount,
22: 6. to their power to *shed* blood.
9. men that carry tales to *shed* blood:
12. have they taken gifts to *shed* blood;
27. ravening the prey, *to shed* blood,
Zep. 3: 8. *to pour* upon them mine indignation,

KAL.—*Imperative.*

Jud. 6:20. *pour out* the broth.
Ps. 62: 8(9). *pour out* your heart before him:
69:24(25). *Pour out* thine indignation
79: 6. *Pour out* thy wrath upon the
Jer. 6: 6. *and cast* (marg. or, *pour out*) a mount against Jerusalem:
10:25. *Pour out* thy fury upon the heathen
Lam.2:19. the watches *pour out* thine heart

KAL.—*Future.*

Gen37:22. *Shed* no blood, (but) cast him into
Ex. 29:12. and *pour* all the blood
Lev. 4: 7. *shall pour* all the blood
18. *shall pour out* all the blood
25. and *shall pour out* his blood at the bottom
30, 34. *shall pour out* all the blood
Deu12:16. *ye shall pour it* upon the earth
24. *thou shalt pour it* upon the earth
15:23. *thou shalt pour it* upon the ground
1 Sa. 1:15. *but have poured out* my soul
7: 6. *and poured* (it) *out* before the Lord,
2Sa.20:10. *and shed out* his bowels
15. *and they cast up* a bank
2K. 19:32. nor *cast* a bank against it.
Job 16:13. *he poureth out* my gall
Ps. 42: 4(5). *When* I remember...*I pour out* my soul in me:
102[title](1). *poureth out* his complaint
106:38. *And shed* innocent blood,
142: 2(3). *I poured out* my complaint
Isa. 37:33. nor *cast* a bank against it.
42:25. *Therefore he hath poured* upon him
Jer. 7: 6. *shed* not innocent blood
22: 3. neither *shed* innocent blood
Eze. 7: 8. Now *will I* shortly *pour out*
16:15. *and pouredst out* thy fornications
22:31. *Therefore have I poured out* mine
23: 8. *and poured* their whoredom upon her.
33:25. toward your idols, and *shed* blood:
36:18. *Wherefore I poured* my fury
Dan 11:15. *and cast up* a mount,
Hos. 5:10. *I will pour out* my wrath
Joel 2:28(3:1). *I will pour out* my spirit upon all
29(-:2). in those days *will I pour out*
Am. 5: 8 & 9:6. *and poureth them out* upon the face

KAL.—*Participle.* Poel.

Gen 9: 6. *Whoso sheddeth* man's blood,
Nu. 35:33. by the blood of *him that shed it.*
Job 12:21. He *poureth* contempt upon princes,
Ps.107:40. He *poureth* contempt upon princes,
Pro. 6:17. hands *that shed* innocent blood,
Lam.4:13. *that have shed* the blood of the just
Eze.16:38. break wedlock *and shed* blood
18:10. *a shedder of* blood,
22: 3. The city *sheddeth* blood
23:45. women *that shed* blood;

KAL.—*Participle.* Paül.

Ps. 79:10. blood of thy servants *which is shed.*
Eze.20:33, 34. with fury *poured out,*

* NIPHAL.—*Preterite.* *

1K. 13: 3. *and* the ashes that (are) upon it *shall be poured out.*
Ps. 22:14(15). *I am poured out* like water,
Lam.2:11. my liver *is poured* upon the earth,

NIPHAL.—*Infinitive.*

Eze.16:36. thy filthiness *was poured out,*

NIPHAL.—*Future.*

Gen 9: 6. by man *shall* his blood *be shed:*
Deu 12:27. *shall be poured out* upon the altar
19:10. That innocent blood *be* not *shed*
1K. 13: 5. *and* the ashes *poured out*

* PUAL.—*Preterite.* *

Nu. 35:33. cleansed of the blood that *is shed*
Ps. 73: 2. my steps *had* well nigh *slipped.*
Zep. 1:17. *and* their blood *shall be poured out*

* HITHPAEL.—*Infinitive.* *

Lam.2:12. *when* their soul *was poured out*

HITHPAEL.—*Future.*

Job 30:16. my soul *is poured out* upon me;
Lam.4: 1. stones of the sanctuary *are poured*

שֶׁפֶךְ *sheh'-phech*, m. 8211

Lev. 4:12. where the ashes *are poured out*, (lit. at the *pouring out of* the ashes)
— where the ashes *are poured out* (lit. at the *pouring out of* the ashes)

שָׁפְכָה *shoph-chāh'*, f. 8212

Deu23: 1(2). or hath his *privy member* cut off,

שָׁפֵל *shāh-phēhl'.* 8213

* KAL.—*Preterite.* *

Isa. 2:11. looks of man *shall be humbled,*
12. *and he shall be brought low:*
17. *and* the haughtiness of men *shall be made low:*
29: 4. *And thou shalt be brought down,*

KAL.—*Future.*

Isa. 2: 9. *and* the great man *humbleth himself:*
5:15. *and* the mighty man *shall be humbled*, and the eyes of the lofty *shall be humbled:*
10:33. the haughty *shall be humbled.*
32:19. the city *shall be low* in a low place.
40: 4. hill *shall be made low:*

* HIPHIL.—*Preterite.* *

Job 22:29. When (men) *are cast down,*
Isa. 25:11. *and he shall bring down* their pride
12. thy walls shall he bring down, *lay low,*
Eze.17:24. I the Lord *have brought down*

HIPHIL.—*Infinitive.*

Pro.25: 7. *than that thou shouldest be put lower*
Eze.21:26(31). *abase* (him that is) high.

HIPHIL.—*Imperative.*

Job 40:11. every one (that is) proud, *and abase him.*
Jer. 13:18. *Humble yourselves,* sit down:

HIPHIL.—*Future.*

2Sa.22:28. *thou mayest bring* (them) *down.*
Ps. 18:27(28). but *wilt bring down* high looks.
75: 7(8). *he putteth down* one,
Pro.29:23. A man's pride *shall bring him low:*
Isa. 13:11. *will lay low* the haughtiness
26: 5. the lofty city, *he layeth it low; he layeth it low,*
57: 9. *and didst debase* (thyself even)

HIPHIL.—*Participle.*

1Sa. 2: 7. he *bringeth low,* and lifteth up.
Ps.113: 6. *Who humbleth* (himself) to behold
147: 6. he *casteth* the wicked *down*

שְׁפַל [*sh'phal*], Ch. 8214

* APHEL.—*Preterite.* *

Dan 5:22. *hast* not *humbled* thine heart,

APHEL.—*Infinitive.*

Dan 4:37(34). that walk in pride he is able *to abase.*

APHEL.—*Future.*

Dan 7:24. and *he shall subdue* three kings.

APHEL.—*Participle.*

Dan 5:19. whom he would he *put* (lit. was *putting*) *down.*

8217 **שָׁפָל** *shāh-phāhl′*, adj.

Lev.13:20. in sight *lower* than the
21. *and* (if) it (be) not *lower*
26. *and* it (be) no *lower* than
14:37. which in sight (are) *lower* than the wall;
2Sa. 6:22. will be *base* in mine own sight:
Job 5:11. To set up on high *those that be low*,
Ps.138: 6. *yet* hath he respect unto *the lowly*:
Pro.16:19. Better (it is to be) of an *humble* spirit
29:23. *but* honour shall uphold *the humble in*
Ecc.12: 4. *when* the sound of the grinding *is low*,
Isa. 57:15. of a contrite *and humble* spirit, to revive the spirit of *the humble*,
Eze.17: 6. a spreading vine of *low* stature,
14. That the kingdom might be *base*,
24. have exalted the *low* tree,
21:26(31). exalt *him that is low*,
29:14. they shall be there a *base* (marg. *low*)
15. It shall be *the basest of* the kingdoms;
Mal. 2: 9. *and base* before all the people,

8215 **שְׁפַל** *sh'phal*, Ch. adj.

Dan. 4:17(14). *and* setteth up over it *the basest of*

8216 **שֵׁפֶל** *shēh′-phel*, m.

Ps.136:23. *Who* remembered us *in our low estate:*
Ecc.10: 6. the rich sit *in low place.*

8218 **שִׁפְלָה** *shiph-lāh′*, f.

Isa. 32:19. *and* the city shall be low *in a low place.*

8219 **שְׁפֵלָה** *sh'phēh-lāh′*, f.

Deu 1: 7. in the hills, *and in the vale*,
Jos. 9: 1. in the hills, *and in the valleys*,
10:40. of the south, *and* of *the vale*,
11: 2. *and in the valley*, and in the borders
16. land of Goshen, and *the valley*,
— mountain of Israel, *and the valley of the same;*
12: 8. In the mountains, *and in the valleys*,
15:33. *in the valley*, Eshtaol,
Jud. 1: 9. in the south, *and* in *the valley*. (marg. or, *low country*)
1K. 10:27. as the sycomore trees that (are) *in the vale*,
1Ch 27:28. trees that (were) *in the low plains*
2Ch 1:15. sycomore trees that (are) *in the vale*
9:27. trees that (are) *in the low plains*
26:10. *both in the low country*, and in
28:18. invaded the cities of *the low country*,
Jer. 17:26. and from *the plain*,
32:44. in the cities of *the valley*,
33:13. in the cities of *the vale*,
Obad. 19. *and* (they of) *the plain* the Philistines:
Zec. 7: 7. inhabited the south *and the plain?*

8220 **שִׁפְלוּת** *shiph-looth′*, f.

Ecc.10:18. *and through idleness of* the hands

8227 **שָׁפָן** *shāh-phāhn′*, m.

Lev.11: 5. *the coney*, because he cheweth the cud,
Deu 14: 7. the camel, and the hare, and *the coney:*
Ps.104:18. the rocks *for the conies.*
Pro.30:26. *The conies* (are but) a feeble folk,

שֶׁפַע *sheh′-phag*, m. 8228

Deu 33:19. they shall suck (of) *the abundance of*

שִׁפְעָה [*shiph-gāh′*], f. 8229

2K. 9:17. he spied *the company of* Jehu
— I see *a company.*
Job 22:11. *and abundance of* waters cover thee.
38:34. *that abundance of* waters may cover
Isa. 60: 6. *The multitude of* camels shall cover thee,
Eze.26:10. *By reason of the abundance of* his horses

שָׁפַר [*shāh-phar′*]. 8231, 8235

* KAL.—*Preterite.* *

Ps. 16: 6. I have a *goodly* heritage. (lit. a heritage *is fair* for me)

* PIEL.—*Preterite.* *

Job 26:13. By his spirit *he hath garnished* the

שְׁפַר *sh'phar*, Ch. 8232

* P'AL.—*Preterite.* *

Dan. 4: 2(3:32). I *thought it good* (marg. *It was seemly* before me) to shew the signs
6: 1(2). *It pleased* (lit. *It was seemly* before) Darius to set over the

P'AL.—*Future.*

Dan. 4:27(24). *let* my counsel *be acceptable*

שֶׁפֶר [*sheh′-pher*], m. 8233

Gen 49:21. he giveth *goodly* words.

שַׁפְרוּר *shaph-roor′*, (כ׳) & **שַׁפְרִיר** 8237
shaph-reer′, (ק׳) m.

Jer. 43:10. he shall spread *his royal pavilion* over

שְׁפַרְפָּרָא *sh'phar-pāh-rāh′*, Ch. m. 8238

Dan. 6:19(20). king arose *very early in the morning*,

שָׁפַת [*shāh-phath′*]. 8239

* KAL.—*Imperative.* *

2K. 4:38. *Set on* the great pot,
Eze.24: 3. *Set on* a pot, *set* (it) *on*, and also pour

KAL.—*Future.*

Ps. 22:15(16). *thou hast brought* me into the dust
Isa. 26:12. *thou wilt ordain* peace for us:

שְׁפַתַּיִם *sh'phat-tah′-yim*, m. dual. 8240

Ps. 68:13(14). Though ye have lien among *the pots*,
Eze.40:43. *And* within (were) *hooks*, (marg. or, *end-irons*, or, *the two hearthstones*)

שֶׁצֶף *sheh′-tzeph*, m. 8241

Isa. 54: 8. *In a little* wrath I hid my face

שָׁק [*shāhk*], Ch. m. 8243

Dan 2:33. *His legs* of iron,

שָׁקַד *shāh-kad′*. 8245

* KAL.—*Preterite.* *

Ps.102: 7(8). *I watch*, and am as a sparrow alone
127: 1. the watchman *waketh* (but) in vain.
Jer. 31:28. like as *I have watched* over them,

KAL.—*Infinitive.*

Pro. 8:34. *watching* daily at my gates,

KAL.—*Imperative.*

Ezr. 8:29. *Watch ye*, and keep (them),

KAL.—*Future.*

Job 21:32. *shall remain* in the tomb. (marg. *watch* in the heap)
Jer. 31:28. so *will I watch* over them,
Dan 9:14. *Therefore hath* the Lord *watched*

KAL.—*Participle.* Poel.

Isa. 29:20. all *that watch for* iniquity are cut off:
Jer. 1:12. I *will hasten* my word to perform it.
5: 6. a leopard *shall watch* over their cities:
44:27. I *will watch* over them

8246 שָׁקַד [*shāh-kad'*].

* PUAL.—*Participle.* *

Ex. 25:33. Three bowls *made like unto almonds,*
— bowls *made like almonds*
34. four bowls *made like unto almonds,*
37:19. bowls *made after the fashion of almonds*
— three bowls *made like almonds*
20. four bowls *made like almonds,*

8247 שָׁקֵד *shāh-kēhd'*, m.

Gen43:11. myrrh, nuts, *and almonds:*
Nu. 17: 8(23). blossoms, and yielded *almonds.*
Ecc.12: 5. *the almond tree* shall flourish,
Jer. 1:11. I see a rod of *an almond tree.*

8248 שָׁקָה [*shāh-kāh'*].

* NIPHAL.—*Preterite.* *

Am. 8: 8. (כתיב) it shall be cast out *and drowned,*

* PUAL.—*Future.* *

Job 21:24. his bones *are moistened* with marrow.

* HIPHIL.—*Preterite.* *

Gen 2: 6. *and watered* the whole face
24:46. *she made* the camels *drink* also.
29: 3. *and watered* the sheep,
8. *then we water* the sheep.
Nu. 5:24. *And he shall cause* the woman *to drink*
27. And *when he hath made her to drink*
20: 8. *so thou shalt give* the congregation...*drink.*
Deu11:10. *and wateredst* (it) with thy foot,
Ps. 60: 3(5). *thou hast made us to drink* the wine of
Jer. 9:15(14). *and give them* water of gall *to drink.*
23:15. *and make them drink* the water
25:15. *and cause* all the nations,...*to drink*
35: 2. *and give* them wine *to drink.*
Eze.32: 6. *I will also water* with thy blood
Joel 3:18(4:18). *and shall water* the valley of Shittim.

HIPHIL.—*Infinitive.*

Gen 2:10. went out of Eden *to water* the garden;
24:19. when she had done *giving him drink,*
Ex. 2:16. troughs *to water* their father's flock.
Est. 1: 7. *And* they *gave* (them) *drink*
Ecc. 2: 6. *to water* therewith the wood
Isa. 43:20. *to give drink* to my people,
Eze.17: 7. *that* he *might water it*

HIPHIL.—*Imperative.*

Gen 24:43. *Give me,* I pray thee, a little water of thy pitcher *to drink;*
45. *Let me drink,* I pray thee.
29: 7. *water ye* the sheep,
Jud. 4:19. *Give me,*...a little water *to drink;*
Pro.25:21. *give* him water *to drink:*

HIPHIL.—*Future.*

Gen 19:32. *let us make* our father *drink*
33. *And they made* their father *drink*
34. *let us make him drink* wine
35. *And they made* their father *drink*
21:19. *and gave* the lad *drink.*
24:14, 46. *I will give* thy camels *drink*
18. her hand, *and gave him drink.*
29: 2. out of that well *they watered* the flocks:
10. *and watered* the flock of Laban
Ex. 2:17. helped them, *and watered* their flock.
19. enough for us, *and watered* the flock.
32:20. *and made* the children of Israel *drink*
Nu. 5:26. *shall cause* the woman *to drink*
Jud. 4:19. milk, *and gave him drink,*
1Sa.30:11. *and they made him drink* water;
2Sa.23:15. Oh that one *would give me drink*
1Ch 11:17. Oh that one *would give me drink*
2Ch 28:15. and gave them to eat *and to drink,* (lit. fed them *and gave them drink*)
Job 22: 7. *Thou hast* not *given* water to the weary *to drink,*
Ps. 36: 8(9). *thou shalt make them drink*
69:21(22). in my thirst *they gave me* vinegar *to drink.*
78:15. *and gave* (them) *drink*
80: 5(6). *and givest them* tears *to drink*
104:11. *They give drink* to every beast
Cant 8: 2. *I would cause thee to drink*
Isa. 27: 3. *I will water it* every moment:
Jer. 8:14. *and given us* water of gall *to drink,*
16: 7. *shall* (men) *give* them the cup of consolation *to drink*
25:17. and *made* all the nations *to drink,*
Am. 2:12. *But ye gave* the Nazarites wine *to drink;*

HIPHIL.—*Participle.*

Gen 40: 1. *the butler of* the king of Egypt
2. against the chief of *the butlers,*
5. *the butler* and the baker
9. *the* chief *butler* told his dream
13. when thou wast *his butler.*
20. lifted up the head of *the* chief *butler*
21. he restored *the* chief *butler*
23. Yet did not *the* chief *butler* remember
41: 9. Then spake *the* chief *butler*
1K. 10: 5. their apparel, *and his cupbearers,* (marg. or, *butlers*)
2Ch 9: 4. their apparel; *his cupbearers* (marg. *id.*)
Neh 1:11. I was the king's *cupbearer.*
Ps.104:13. *He watereth* the hills from
Hab 2:15. *that giveth* his neighbour *drink,*

שִׁקּוּ [*shik-koov'*], m. 8249

Ps.102: 9(10). mingled *my drink* with weeping,

שִׁקּוּי *shik-koo'y*, m. 8250

Pro. 3: 8. *and marrow* (marg. *watering,* or, *moistening*) to thy bones.
Hos 2: 5(7). mine oil *and my drink.* (marg. *drinks*)

שִׁקּוּץ *shik-kootz'*, m. 8251

Deu29:17(16). ye have seen *their abominations,*
1K. 11: 5. *the abomination of* the Ammonites.
7. *the abomination of* Moab,
— *the abomination of* the children of Ammon.
2K. 23:13. *the abomination of* the Zidonians, and for Chemosh *the abomination of* the Moabites,
24. *the abominations* that were spied
2Ch 15: 8. put away *the abominable idols* (marg. *abominations*)
Isa. 66: 3. *and* their soul delighteth *in their abominations.*
Jer. 4: 1. put away *thine abominations*
7:30. have set *their abominations* in the house
13:27. whoredom, (and) *thine abominations*
16:18. *their detestable* and abominable things.
32:34. they set *their abominations* in the house,
Eze. 5:11. *thy detestable things*
7:20. *their detestable things*
11:18. all *the detestable things thereof*
21. *their detestable things* and their abominations,
20: 7. every man *the abominations of* his eyes,
8. cast away *the abominations of* their eyes,
30. whoredom after *their abominations?*
37:23. idols, *nor with their detestable things,*
Dan 9:27. the overspreading of *abominations*
11:31. *the abomination* that maketh desolate.
12:11. *the abomination* that maketh desolate
Hos. 9:10. *abominations* were according as they loved.
Nah 3: 6. I will cast *abominable filth* upon thee,
Zec. 9: 7. *and his abominations* from between

8252 שָׁקַט *shāh-kat'.*

✻ KAL.—*Preterite.* ✻

Jos. 11:23. the land *rested* from war.
14:15. the land *had rest* from war.
2K. 11:20. the city *was in quiet:*
2Ch 14: 1(13:23). In his days the land *was quiet*
6(5). for the land *had rest,*
23:21. the city *was quiet,*
Job 3:26. neither *had I rest,*
Ps. 76: 8(9). the earth feared, *and was still,*
Isa. 14: 7. The whole earth is at rest, (and) *is quiet:*
Jer. 30:10. shall return, *and shall be in rest,*
46:27. *and be in rest* and at ease,
Eze. 16:42. *and I will be quiet,* and will be

KAL.—*Future.*

Jud. 3:11. *And* the land *had rest* forty years.
30. *And* the land *had rest* fourscore years.
5:31. *And* the land *had rest* forty years.
8:28. *And* the country *was in quietness*
Ru. 3:18. the man *will* not *be in rest,*
2Ch 14: 5(4). *and* the kingdom *was quiet* before him.
20:30. *So* the realm of Jehoshaphat *was quiet:*
Job 3:13. should I have lain still *and been quiet,*
Ps. 83: 1(2). *be* not *still,* O God.
Isa. 18: 4. *I will take my rest,* and I will consider
62: 1. for Jerusalem's sake *I will* not *rest,*
Jer. 47: 6. how long (will it be) ere *thou be quiet?*
7. How *can it be quiet,*

KAL.—*Participle.* Poel.

Jud. 18: 7. manner of the Zidonians, *quiet*
27. a people (that were) *at quiet* and secure:
1Ch 4:40. the land (was) wide, *and quiet,*
Jer. 48:11. *and* he *hath settled* on his lees,
Eze. 38:11. go to them *that are at rest,*
Zec. 1:11. the earth sitteth still, *and is at rest.*

✻ HIPHIL.—*Infinitive.* ✻

Job 37:17. *when* he *quieteth* the earth
Ps. 94:13. *That* thou *mayest give* him *rest*
Isa. 30:15. *in quietness* and in confidence
32:17. *quietness* and assurance for ever.
57:20. sea, when it cannot *rest,*
Jer. 49:23. the sea; it cannot *be quiet.*
Eze. 16:49. abundance of *idleness* was in her

HIPHIL.—*Imperative.*

Isa. 7: 4. Take heed, *and be quiet;*

HIPHIL.—*Future.*

Job 34:29. When *he giveth quietness,*
Pro. 15:18. slow to anger *appeaseth* strife.

8253 שֶׁקֶט *sheh'-ket,* m.

1Ch 22: 9. I will give peace *and quietness*

8254 שָׁקַל *shāh-kal'.*

✻ KAL.—*Preterite.* ✻

2Sa. 14:26. *he weighed* the hair of his head
Isa. 40:12. *and weighed* the mountains in scales,

KAL.—*Infinitive.*

Est. 4: 7. that Haman had promised *to pay*
Job 6: 2. Oh that my grief were *throughly* weighed, (lit. *weighing* weighed)

KAL.—*Future.*

Gen 23:16. *and* Abraham *weighed* to Ephron;
Ex. 22:17(16). *he shall pay* (marg. *weigh*) money
1K. 20:39. or else *thou shalt pay* (marg. *id.*) a talent of silver.
Ezr. 8:25. *And weighed* unto them the silver,
26. *I even weighed* unto their hand
29. *ye weigh* (them) before the chief
Est. 3: 9. *I will pay* (marg. *weigh*) ten thousand
Job 31: 6. *Let me be weighed* (marg. *him weigh me*) in an even balance,
Isa. 46: 6. *weigh* silver in the balance,
55: 2. *do ye spend* (marg. *weigh*) money for
Jer. 32: 9. *and weighed* him the money,
10. *and weighed* (him) the money
Zec. 11:12. *So they weighed* for my price

KAL.—*Participle.* Poel.

2Sa. 18:12. *I should receive* (marg. *weigh* upon mine hand) a thousand
Isa. 33:18. where (is) *the receiver?* (marg. *weigher*)

✻ NIPHAL.—*Preterite.* ✻

Ezr. 8:33. *was* the silver and the gold and the vessels *weighed*

NIPHAL.—*Future.*

Job 6: 2. Oh that my grief *were* throughly *weighed,*
28:15. neither *shall* silver *be weighed*

שֶׁקֶל *sheh'-kel,* m. 8255

Gen 23:15,16. four hundred *shekels* of silver;
Ex. 21:32. master thirty *shekels* of silver,
30:13. that are numbered, half *a shekel after the shekel of* the sanctuary: *a shekel* (is) twenty gerahs: an half *shekel* (shall be)
15. shall not give less than half *a shekel,*
24. *after the shekel of* the sanctuary,
38:24. seven hundred and thirty *shekels, after the shekel of* the sanctuary.
25. threescore and fifteen *shekels, after the shekel of* the sanctuary:
26. A bekah for every man, (that is), *a shekel, after the shekel of* the sanctuary,
29. two thousand and four hundred *shekels.*
Lev. 5:15. by *shekels* of silver, *after the shekel of* the
27: 3. estimation shall be fifty *shekels* of silver, *after the shekel of* the sanctuary.
4. thy estimation shall be thirty *shekels.*
5. shall be of the male twenty *shekels,* and for the female ten *shekels.*
6. shall be of the male five *shekels*
— thy estimation (shall be) three *shekels*
7. thy estimation shall be fifteen *shekels,* and for the female ten *shekels.*
16. at fifty *shekels* of silver.
25. *according to the shekel of* the sanctuary: twenty gerahs shall be *the shekel.*
Nu. 3:47. five *shekels* apiece by the poll, *after the shekel of* the sanctuary
— *the shekel* (is) twenty gerahs:
50. *after the shekel of* the sanctuary:
7:13,19,25,31,37,43,49,55,61,67,73,79. silver bowl of seventy *shekels, after the shekel of* the sanctuary;
85, 86. *after the shekel of* the sanctuary:
18:16. for the money of five *shekels, after the shekel of* the sanctuary,
31:52. sixteen thousand seven hundred and fifty *shekels.*
Jos. 7:21. two hundred *shekels* of silver, and a wedge of gold of fifty *shekels*
1Sa. 9: 8. fourth part of *a shekel of* silver
17: 5. five thousand *shekels* of brass.
7. six hundred *shekels* of iron:
2Sa. 14:26. two hundred *shekels* after the king's
24:24. the oxen for fifty *shekels* of silver.
2K. 7: 1. fine flour (be sold) *for a shekel,* and two measures of barley *for a shekel,*
16. fine flour was (sold) *for a shekel,* and two measures of barley *for a shekel,*
18. Two measures of barley *for a shekel,* and a measure of fine flour *for a shekel,*
15:20. each man fifty *shekels* of silver,
1Ch 21:25. for the place six hundred *shekels of* gold
2Ch 3: 9. fifty *shekels* of gold.
Neh 5:15. beside forty *shekels* of silver;
10:32(33). the third part of *a shekel*
Jer. 32: 9. seventeen *shekels* of silver.
Eze. 4:10. twenty *shekels* a day:
45:12. *And the shekel* (shall be) twenty gerahs: twenty *shekels,* five and twenty *shekels,* fifteen *shekels,*
Am. 8: 5. making the ephah small, and *the shekel*

שִׁקְמָה [*shik-māh'*], f. 8256

1K. 10:27. *as the sycomore trees* that (are) in the vale,
1Ch 27:28. olive trees *and the sycomore trees*
2Ch 1:15 & 9:27. made he *as the sycomore trees*
Ps. 78:47. *and their sycomore trees* with frost.

Isa. 9:10(9). *the sycomores* are cut down,
Am. 7:14. a gatherer of *sycomore fruit:* (marg. or, *wild figs*)

8257 ## שָׁקַע [*shāh-kag'*].

* KAL.—*Preterite.* *

Am. 9: 5. *and shall be drowned*, as (by) the flood

KAL.—*Future.*

Nu. 11: 2. *and* when Moses prayed unto the Lord, the fire *was quenched*. (marg. *sunk*)
Jer. 51:64. Thus *shall* Babylon *sink*,

* NIPHAL.—*Preterite.* *

Am. 8: 8. it shall be cast out *and drowned*,

* HIPHIL.—*Future.* *

Job 41: 1(40:25). with a cord (which) *thou lettest down?* (marg. *drownest*)
Eze.32:14. Then *will I make* their waters *deep*,

8258 ## שְׁקַעֲרוּרֹת *sh'kah-găroo-rōhth'*, f. pl.

Lev.14:37. walls of the house with *hollow strakes*,

8259 ## שָׁקַף [*shāh-kaph'*].

* NIPHAL.—*Preterite.* *

Nu. 21:20. *which looketh* toward Jeshimon.
Jud. 5:28. The mother of Sisera *looked* out
2Sa. 6:16. Saul's daughter *looked* through
1Ch 15:29. the daughter of Saul *looking* out
Ps. 85:11(12). righteousness *shall look down*
Pro. 7: 6. *I looked* through my casement,
Jer. 6: 1. evil *appeareth* out of the north,

NIPHAL.—*Participle.*

Nu. 23:28. *that looketh* toward Jeshimon.
1Sa.13:18. border *that looketh* to the valley
Cant.6:10. she (that) *looketh forth* as the morning,

* HIPHIL.—*Preterite.* *

Ps. 14: 2. The Lord *looked down* from heaven
53: 2(3). God *looked down* from heaven
102:19(20). *he hath looked down* from the height

HIPHIL.—*Imperative.*

Deu26:15. *Look down* from thy holy habitation,

HIPHIL.—*Future.*

Gen18:16. *and looked* toward Sodom:
19:28. *And he looked* toward Sodom
26: 8. *that* Abimelech king of the Philistines *looked out*
Ex. 14:24. *that* in the morning watch the Lord *looked*
2Sa.24:20. *And* Araunah *looked*, and saw the king
2K. 9:30. *and looked out* at a window.
32. *And there looked out* to him
Lam.3:50. Till the Lord *look down*,

8260 ## שֶׁקֶף [*sheh'-keph*], m.

1K. 7: 5. square, with *the windows:*

8261 ## שְׁקֻפִים *sh'koo-pheem'*, m. pl.

1K. 6: 4. for the house he made windows of narrow lights. (marg. or, windows *broad* (within and), narrow (without); or, *skewed* (and) closed)
7: 4. *And* (there were) *windows*

8262 ## שָׁקַץ [*shāh-katz'*].

* PIEL.—*Preterite.* *

Ps. 22:24(25). he hath not despised nor *abhorred*

PIEL.—*Infinitive.*

Deu 7:26. thou shalt *utterly* detest it, (lit. *detesting* thou shalt detest)

PIEL.—*Future.*

Lev.11:11. *ye shall have* their carcases in *abomination.*
13. *ye shall have in abomination*
Lev.11:43. *Ye shall* not *make* your selves *abominable*
20:25. *ye shall* not *make* your souls *abominable*
Deu 7:26. *thou shalt* utterly *detest*

שֶׁקֶץ *sheh'-ketz*, m. 8263

Lev. 7:21. or any *abominable* unclean (thing),
11:10. they (shall be) *an abomination*
11. be *even an abomination* unto you;
12. that (shall be) *an abomination*
13,42. they (are) *an abomination:*
20. *an abomination* unto you.
23. four feet, (shall be) *an abomination*
41. the earth (shall be) *an abomination;*
Isa. 66:17. swine's flesh, *and the abomination*,
Eze. 8:10. and *abominable* beasts,

שָׁקַק [*shāh-kak'*]. 8264

* KAL.—*Future.* *

Joel 2: 9. *They shall run to and fro* in the city;

KAL.—*Participle.* Poel.

Ps.107: 9. he satisfieth the *longing* soul,
Pro.28:15. a roaring lion, and a *ranging* bear;
Isa. 29: 8. his soul *hath appetite:*
33: 4. *shall he run* upon them.

* HITHPALPEL.—*Future.* *

Nah. 2: 4(5). *they shall justle one against another*

שָׁקַר [*shāh-kar'*]. 8266

* KAL.—*Future.* *

Gen21:23. that *thou wilt* not *deal falsely* with me,

* PIEL.—*Preterite.* *

Ps. 44:17(18). neither *have we dealt falsely*

PIEL.—*Future.*

Lev.19:11. neither deal falsely, neither *lie* one to
1Sa.15:29. the Strength of Israel *will* not *lie*
Ps. 89:33(34). nor *suffer* my faithfulness *to fail*
Isa. 63: 8. children (that) *will* not *lie:*

שֶׁקֶר *sheh'-ker*. 8267

Ex. 5: 9. let them not regard *vain* words.
20:16. Thou shalt not bear *false* witness
23: 7. Keep thee far from a *false* matter;
Lev. 6: 3(5:22). sweareth *falsely*; (lit. upon *a lie*)
5(-:24). about which he hath sworn *falsely;*
19:12. ye shall not swear by my name *falsely*,
Deu 19:18. the witness (be) a *false* witness, (and) hath testified *falsely* against
1Sa.25:21. Surely *in vain* have I kept
2Sa.18:13. I should have wrought *falsehood*
1K. 22:22. I will be a *lying* spirit
23. hath put a *lying* spirit in the mouth
2K. 9:12. they said, (It is) *false;*
2Ch 18:21. be a *lying* spirit in the mouth
22. the Lord hath put a *lying* spirit
Job 13: 4. But ye (are) forgers of *lies*,
36: 4. my words (shall) not (be) *false:*
Ps. 7:14(15). brought forth *falsehood.*
27:12. *false* witnesses are risen up
31:18(19). Let the *lying* lips be put to silence;
33:17. An horse (is) *a vain thing*
35:19. mine enemies *wrongfully* (marg. *falsely*) rejoice
38:19(20). they that hate me *wrongfully*
52: 3(5). *lying* rather than to speak righteousness.
63:11(12). but the mouth of them that speak *lies*
69: 4(5). mine enemies *wrongfully*,
101: 7. he that telleth *lies* shall not tarry in my
109: 2. spoken against me with a *lying* tongue.
119:29. Remove from me the way of *lying:*
69. The proud have forged *a lie*
78. dealt perversely with me *without a cause:*
86. they persecute me *wrongfully;*
104. therefore I hate every *false* way.
118. for their deceit (is) *falsehood.*
128. (and) I hate every *false* way.
163. I hate and abhor *lying:*

Ps 120: 2. Deliver my soul, O Lord, from *lying* lips,
144: 8,11. right hand (is) a right hand of *falsehood.*
Pro. 6:17. A proud look, a *lying* tongue,
19. A *false* witness (that) speaketh lies,
10:18. He that hideth hatred (with) *lying* lips,
11:18. The wicked worketh a *deceitful* work:
12:17. but a *false* witness deceit.
19. a *lying* tongue (is) but for a moment.
22. *Lying* lips (are) abomination to the Lord:
13: 5. A righteous (man) hateth *lying:* (lit. a word of *falsehood*)
14: 5. a *false* witness will utter lies.
17: 4. *a liar* giveth ear to a naughty tongue.
7. much less do *lying* lips a prince.
19: 5. A *false* witness shall not be unpunished,
9. A *false* witness shall not be unpunished,
20:17. Bread of *deceit* (marg. *lying,* or, *falsehood*) (is) sweet to a man;
21: 6. The getting of treasures by a *lying* tongue
25:14. Whoso boasteth himself of a *false* gift (marg. in a gift of *falsehood*)
18. A man that beareth *false* witness
26:28. A *lying* tongue hateth (those that are)
29:12. If a ruler hearken to *lies,* (lit. the word of *a lie*)
31:30. Favour (is) *deceitful,* and beauty (is)
Isa. 9:15(14). the prophet that teacheth *lies,*
28:15. *and under falsehood* have we hid
32: 7. destroy the poor with *lying* words,
44:20. not *a lie* in my right hand?
57: 4. a seed of *falsehood,*
59: 3. your lips have spoken *lies,*
13. uttering from the heart words of *falsehood.*
Jer. 3:10. turned unto me with her whole heart, but *feignedly,* (marg. *in falsehood*)
23. *in vain* (is salvation hoped for)
5: 2. surely they swear *falsely.*
31. The prophets prophesy *falsely,*
6:13. every one dealeth *falsely.*
7: 4. Trust ye not in *lying* words,
8. ye trust in *lying* words,
9. commit adultery, and swear *falsely,*
8: 8. certainly *in vain* made he (it); the pen of the scribes (is) in *vain.* (marg. or, the *false* pen of the scribes worketh *for falsehood*)
10. every one dealeth *falsely.*
9: 3(2). bend their tongues (like) their bow (for) *lies:*
5(4). have taught their tongue to speak *lies,*
10:14. his molten image (is) *falsehood,*
13:25. hast forgotten me, and trusted *in falsehood.*
14:14. The prophets prophesy *lies*
— they prophesy unto you a *false*
16:19. our fathers have inherited *lies,*
20: 6. to whom thou hast prophesied *lies.*
23:14. commit adultery, and walk *in lies:*
25. that prophesy *lies* in my name,
26. the prophets that prophesy *lies?*
32. them that prophesy *false* dreams,
— cause my people to err *by their lies,*
27:10,14,16. For they prophesy *a lie* unto you,
15. yet they prophesy *a lie* (marg. *in a lie,* or, *lyingly*) in my name;
28:15. makest this people to trust in *a lie.*
29: 9. they prophesy *falsely* (marg. *in a lie*) unto you
21. which prophesy *a lie* unto you
23. have spoken *lying* words
31. he caused you to trust in *a lie:*
37:14. Then said Jeremiah, (It is) *false;* (marg. *falsehood,* or, *a lie*)
40:16. thou speakest *falsely* of Ishmael.
43: 2. Jeremiah, Thou speakest *falsely:*
51:17. his molten image (is) *falsehood,*
Eze. 13:22. with *lies* ye have made the heart of the righteous sad,
Hos. 7: 1. for they commit *falsehood;*
Mic. 2:11. walking in the spirit *and falsehood*
6:12. the inhabitants thereof have spoken *lies,*
Hab 2:18. molten image, and a teacher of *lies,*
Zec. 5: 4. the house of him that sweareth *falsely*
8:17. love no *false* oath:
10: 2. the diviners have seen *a lie,*
13: 3. thou speakest *lies* in the name of the
Mal. 3: 5. against *false* swearers,

שֹׁקֶת *shōh'-keth,* f. 8268

Gen 24:20. emptied her pitcher into *the trough,*
30:38. gutters *in the* watering *troughs*

שֹׁר [*shōhr*], m. 8270

Pro. 3: 8. It shall be health *to thy navel,*
Eze. 16: 4. wast born *thy navel* was not cut,

שְׁרֵא [*sh'rēh*], Ch. 8271

* P'AL.—*Preterite.* *

Dan 2:22. and the light *dwelleth* with him.

P'AL.—*Infinitive.*

Dan 5:16. and *dissolve* doubts:

P'AL.—*Participle.*

Dan 3:25. Lo, I see four men *loose,* walking

* PAEL.—*Preterite.* *

Ezr. 5: 2. *and began* to build the house of God

PAEL.—*Participle.*

Dan 5:12. *and dissolving* of doubts,

* ITHPAEL.—*Participle.* *

Dan 5: 6. so that the joints of his loins were *loosed,*

שָׁרָב *shāh-rāhv',* m. 8273

Isa. 35: 7. *the parched ground* shall become a pool,
49:10. neither shall *the heat* nor sun smite

שַׁרְבִיט *shar-veet',* m. 8275

Est. 4:11. shall hold out *the* golden *sceptre,*
5: 2. held out to Esther *the* golden *sceptre*
— touched the top of *the sceptre.*
8: 4. the king held out *the* golden *sceptre*

שָׁרָה [*shāh-rāh'*]. 8281

* KAL.—*Future.* *

Job 37: 3. *He directeth it* under [See also יָשַׁר]

* PIEL.—*Preterite.* *

Jer. 15:11. it shall be well with *thy remnant;* (lit. *I made thee free*)

שְׁרוּקֹת *sh'roo-kōhth',* f. pl. 8292

Jer. 18:16. (כתיב) desolate, (and) *a* perpetual *hissing;*

שָׁרוֹת [*shāh-rōhth'*], f. pl. 8284

Jer. 5:10. Go ye up *upon her walls,*

שֵׁרוֹת *shēh-rooth',* f. pl. 8285

Isa. 3:19. The chains, *and the bracelets,*

שֵׁרוּת [*shēh-rooth'*], f. 8293

Jer. 15:11. (כתיב) Verily it shall be well with *thy remnant;*

שִׁרְיָה *shir-yāh',* f. 8302

Job 41:26(18). the spear, the dart, *nor the habergeon.* (marg. or, *breastplate*)

שִׁרְיוֹן *shir-yōhn',* m. 8302

1 Sa. 17: 5. he (was) armed with *a coat of* mail; and the weight of *the coat*
38. also he armed him with *a coat of mail.*
2 Ch 26:14. helmets, *and habergeons,* and bows.
Neh 4:16(10). and the bows, *and the habergeons;*

8302 **שִׁרְיָן** *shir-yāhn'*, m.

1K. 22:34. smote the king of Israel between the joints of *the harness :* (marg. *breastplate*)
2Ch 18:33. smote the king of Israel between the joints of *the harness :* (marg. *id.*)
Isa. 59:17. he put on righteousness *as a breastplate,*

8292 **שְׁרִיקוֹת** *sh'ree-kōhth'*, f. pl.

Jud. 5:16. to hear *the bleatings of* the flocks?
Jer. 18:16. land desolate, (and) *a* perpetual *hissing ;*

8306 **שָׁרִיר** [*shāh-reer'*], m.

Job 40:16. his force (is) *in the navel of* his belly.

8307 **שְׁרִירוּת** *sh'ree-rooth'*, f.

Deu29:19(18). I walk *in the imagination of* mine heart, (marg. or, *stubbornness*)
Ps. 81:12(13). I gave them up *unto* their own hearts' *lust:* (marg. or, *hardness,* or, *imaginations*)
Jer. 3:17. *the imagination* (marg. or, *stubbornness*) *of* their evil heart.
7:24. *in the imagination* (marg. *id.*) *of* their
9:14(13). *the imagination* (marg. *id.*) *of* their
11: 8. *in the imagination* (marg. *id.*) *of* their evil
13:10. *in the imagination* (marg. *id.*) *of* their
16:12 & 18:12. *the imagination* (marg. *id.*) *of* his evil heart,
23:17. walketh *after the imagination* (marg. *id.*) *of* his own heart,

---

8309 **שְׁרֵמוֹת** *sh'rēh-mōhth'*, f. pl.

Jer. 31:40. (כתיב) of the ashes, and all *the fields*

8317 **שָׁרַץ** *shāh-ratz'*.

* KAL.—*Preterite.* *

Gen 1:21. the waters *brought forth abundantly,*
8:17. *that they may breed abundantly*
Ex. 8: 3(7:28). *And* the river *shall bring forth* frogs *abundantly,*
Ps.105:30. land *brought forth* frogs in *abundance,*

KAL.—*Imperative.*

Gen 9: 7. *bring forth abundantly* in the earth,

KAL.—*Future.*

Gen 1:20. *Let* the waters *bring forth abundantly*
Ex. 1: 7. fruitful, *and increased abundantly,*
Eze.47: 9. every thing that liveth, which *moveth,*

KAL.—*Participle.* Poel.

Gen 7:21. every creeping thing *that creepeth*
Lev.11:29. creeping things *that creep* upon the earth;
41. every creeping thing *that creepeth*
42. all creeping things *that creep* upon
43. any creeping thing *that creepeth,*
46. every creature *that creepeth*

8318 **שֶׁרֶץ** *sheh'-retz*, m.

Gen 1:20. the *moving* (marg. or, *creeping*) *creature* that hath life,
7:21. of every *creeping thing*
Lev. 5: 2. carcase of unclean *creeping things,*
11:10. all that *move* in the waters,
20. All fowls that *creep,*
21. every flying *creeping thing*
23. all (other) flying *creeping things,*
29. *among the creeping things*
31. unclean to you among all *that creep :*
41. every *creeping thing* that creepeth
42. among all *creeping things*
43. with any *creeping thing* that creepeth,
44. with any manner of *creeping thing*
22: 5. whosoever toucheth any *creeping thing,*
Deu 14:19. every *creeping thing* that flieth

שָׁרַק *shāh-rak'*. 8319

* KAL.—*Preterite.* *

1K. 9: 8. shall be astonished, *and shall hiss ;*
Isa. 5:26. *and will hiss* unto them
Lam. 2:15. *they hiss* and wag their head
16. *they hiss* and gnash the teeth:
Eze.27:36. The merchants among the people *shall hiss*

KAL.—*Future.*

Job 27:23. *and shall hiss* him out of his place.
Isa. 7:18. the Lord *shall hiss* for the fly
Jer. 19: 8. shall be astonished *and hiss*
49:17. *and shall hiss* at all the plagues
50:13. *and hiss* at all her plagues.
Zep. 2:15. every one that passeth by her *shall hiss,*
Zec.10: 8. *I will hiss* for them,

שְׁרֵקָה *sh'rēh-kāh'*, f. 8322

2Ch 29: 8. to astonishment, *and to hissing,*
Jer. 19: 8. make this city desolate, *and an hissing ;*
25: 9. an astonishment, *and an hissing,*
18. astonishment, *an hissing,* and a curse;
29:18. an astonishment, *and an hissing,*
51:37. an astonishment, *and an hissing,* without an inhabitant.
Mic. 6:16. the inhabitants thereof *an hissing:*

שָׁרַר [*shāh-rar'*]. 8324

* KAL.—*Participle.* Poel. *

Ps. 5: 8(9) & 27:11. because of *mine enemies;* (marg. *those which observe me*)
54: 5(7). He shall reward evil *unto mine enemies :* (marg. *those that observe me*)
56: 2(3). *Mine enemies* (marg. *observers*) would daily swallow (me) up:
59:10(11). (my desire) *upon mine enemies.* (marg. *id.*)

שֹׁרֶר [*shōh'-rer*], m. 8326

Cant.7: 2(3). *Thy navel* (is like) a round goblet,

שָׁרַשׁ [*shāh-rash'*]. 8327

* PIEL.—*Preterite.* *

Ps. 52: 5(7). *and root thee* out of the land

PIEL.—*Future.*

Job 31:12. *would root* out all mine increase.

* PUAL.—*Future.* *

Job 31: 8. *let* my offspring *be rooted out.*

* POEL.—*Preterite.* *

Isa. 40:24. their stock *shall* not *take root*

* POAL.—*Preterite.* *

Jer. 12: 2. yea, *they have taken root :*

* HIPHIL.—*Future.* *

Ps. 80: 9(10). *and didst cause* it *to take* deep *root.*
Isa. 27: 6. *He shall cause* them that come of Jacob *to take root :*

HIPHIL.—*Participle.*

Job 5: 3. I have seen the foolish *taking root :*

שֹׁרֶשׁ *shōh'-resh*, m. 8328

Deu29:18(17). *a root* that beareth gall and
Jud. 5:14. Ephraim (was there) *a root of them*
2K. 19:30. Judah shall yet again take *root*
Job 8:17. *His roots* are wrapped about the heap,
13:27. thou settest a print upon *the heels* (marg *roots*) *of*
14: 8. Though *the root thereof* wax old
18:16. *His roots* shall be dried up
19:28. *seeing the root of* the matter is found
28: 9. overturneth the mountains *by the roots.*
29:19. *My root* (was) spread out
30: 4. *and* juniper *roots* (for) their meat.
36:30. *and* covereth *the bottom* (marg. *roots*) *of*

Ps. 80: 9(10). didst cause *it* to take *deep* root, (lit. didst cause *its roots* to take root)
Pro. 12: 3. *but the root of* the righteous shall
12. *but the root of* the righteous yieldeth
Isa. 5:24. *their root* shall be as rottenness,
11: 1. a Branch shall grow *out of his roots:*
10. in that day there shall be *a root of* Jesse,
14:29. for *out of* the serpent's *root*
30. I will kill *thy root* with famine,
37:31. Judah shall again take *root*
53: 2. *and as a root* out of a dry ground:
Jer. 17: 8. spreadeth out *her roots* by the river,
Eze.17: 6. *and the roots thereof* were under him:
7. this vine did bend *her roots*
9. shall he not pull up *the roots thereof,*
— to pluck it up *by the roots thereof.*
31: 7. for *his root* was by great waters.
Dan 11: 7. But out of a branch of *her roots*
Hos. 9:16. *their root* is dried up,
14: 5(6). cast forth *his roots* as Lebanon.
Am. 2: 9. *and his roots* from beneath.
Mal. 4: 1(3:19). leave them neither *root* nor branch.

8330 שְׁרֵשׁ [*shōh-rēhsh'*], Ch. m.

Dan 4:15(12). leave the stump of *his roots*
23(20). leave the stump of *the roots thereof*
26(23). to leave the stump *of the* tree *roots;*

8331 שַׁרְשָׁה [*shar-shāh'*], f.

Ex. 28:22. upon the breastplate *chains* at the ends

8332 שְׁרֹשִׁי *sh'rōh-shee'*, (ק) or שְׁרֹשׁוּ *sh'rōh-shoo'*, (כ) Ch. f.

Ezr. 7:26. or *to banishment*, (marg. *rooting out*)

8333 שַׁרְשְׁרָה *shar sh'rāh'*, f.

Ex. 28:14. two *chains* (of) pure gold
— fasten *the* wreathen *chains* to the ouches.
39:15. they made upon the breastplate *chains*
1K. 7:17. wreaths of *chain* work,
2Ch 3: 5. set thereon palm trees *and chains.*
16. And he made *chains,*
— put (them) *on the chains.*

8334 שָׁרַת [*shāh-rath'*].

* PIEL.—*Preterite.* *

Nu. 3: 6. *that they may minister* unto him.
8:26. *But shall minister* with their brethren
Deu 18: 7. *Then he shall minister* in the name

PIEL.—*Infinitive.*

Ex. 28:35. it shall be upon Aaron *to minister:*
43. come near unto the altar *to minister*
29:30. the congregation *to minister*
30:20. come near to the altar *to minister,*
35:19. *to do service* in the holy
39: 1. *to do service* in the holy (place),
26. about the hem of the robe *to minister*
41. *to do service* in the holy
Nu. 16: 9. congregation *to minister unto them?*
Deu 10: 8. before the Lord *to minister unto him,*
17:12. priest that standeth *to minister*
18: 5. stand *to minister* in the name of the Lord,
21: 5. God hath chosen *to minister unto him,*
1K. 8:11. priests could not stand *to minister*
1Ch 15: 2. *and to minister unto him* for ever.
16:37. *to minister* before the ark continually,
23:13. *to minister unto him,* and to bless
26:12. *to minister* in the house of the Lord.
2Ch 5:14. priests could not stand *to minister*
8:14. to praise *and minister* before the priests,
29:11. *to serve him,* and that ye should
31: 2. *to minister,* and to give thanks,
Isa. 56: 6. join themselves to the Lord, *to serve him,*
Eze.20:32. *to serve* wood and stone.
40:46. near to the Lord *to minister unto him.*
43:19. *to minister unto me,*
44:11. stand before them *to minister unto them.*
Eze.44:15. come near to me *to minister unto me,*
16. my table, *to minister unto me,*
17. *whiles they minister* in the gates
27. *to minister* in the sanctuary,
45: 4. shall come near *to minister* unto the Lord:

PIEL.—*Future.*

Gen 39: 4. *and he served* him:
40: 4. *and he served* them:
Nu. 1:50. and they *shall minister unto it,*
3:31. sanctuary wherewith *they minister,*
4: 9. wherewith *they minister* unto it:
12. wherewith *they minister* in the sanctuary
14. wherewith *they minister* about it,
18: 2. *and minister unto thee:*
1K. 1: 4. cherished the king, *and ministered to him:*
19:21. Elijah, *and ministered unto him.*
2K. 25:14. of brass wherewith *they ministered,*
Ps. 101: 6. in a perfect way, *he shall serve me.*
Isa. 60: 7. Nebaioth *shall minister unto thee:*
10. their kings *shall minister unto thee:*
Jer. 52:18. brass wherewith *they ministered,*
Eze.42:14. garments wherein *they minister;*
44:12. Because *they ministered* unto them

PIEL.—*Participle.*

Ex. 24:13. Moses rose up, and *his minister* Joshua:
33:11. *but his servant* Joshua,
Nu. 11:28. son of Nun, *the servant of* Moses,
Jos. 1: 1. Joshua the son of Nun, Moses' *minister,*
1Sa. 2:11. the child *did minister* unto the Lord
18. Samuel *ministered* before the Lord,
3: 1. Samuel *ministered* unto the Lord
2Sa. 13:17. his servant *that ministered unto him*
18. Then *his servant* brought her out,
1K. 1:15. Abishag the Shunammite *ministered*
10: 5. the attendance of *his ministers,*
2K. 4:43. And *his servitor* said,
6:15. *the servant* (marg. or, *minister*) *of* the man of God
1Ch 6:32(17). they *ministered* before the dwelling-place (lit. were *ministering*)
16: 4. to *minister* before the ark
27: 1. their officers *that served* the king
28: 1. the companies *that ministered*
2Ch 9: 4. the attendance of *his ministers,*
13:10. *which minister* unto the Lord,
17:19. These *waited on* the king,
22: 8. *that ministered* to Ahaziah,
23: 6. *and they that minister* of the Levites;
29:11. that ye should *minister* unto him,
Ezr. 8:17. that they should bring unto us *ministers*
Neh 10:36(37). priests *that minister* in the house
39(40). the priests *that minister,*
Est. 1:10. seven chamberlains *that served*
2: 2 & 6:3. the king's servants *that ministered unto him,*
Ps. 103:21. *ministers of his,* that do his pleasure.
104: 4. *his ministers* a flaming fire:
Pro. 29:12. all *his servants* (are) wicked.
Isa. 61: 6. shall call you *the Ministers of* our God:
Jer. 33:21. the Levites the priests, *my ministers.*
22. the Levites *that minister* unto me.
Eze.44:11. they shall be *ministers* in my sanctuary,
— *and ministering* to the house:
19. wherein they *ministered,*
45: 4. priests *the ministers of* the sanctuary,
5. *the ministers of* the house,
46:24. *the ministers of* the house shall boil
Joel 1: 9. the priests, the Lord's *ministers,*
13. howl, ye *ministers of* the altar:
— ye *ministers of* my God:
2:17. priests, *the ministers of* the Lord,

שָׁרֵת *shāh-rēhth'*, m. 8335

Nu. 4:12. all the instruments of *ministry,*
2Ch 24:14. vessels to *minister,*

שֵׁשָׁה see שִׁשָּׂה See 8154

שֵׁשׁ *shēhsh*, m. 8336

Gen 41:42. arrayed him in vestures of *fine linen,* (marg. or, *silk*)
Ex. 25: 4. *and fine linen,* (marg. *id.*) and goat's (hair),

Ex 26: 1. ten curtains (of) *fine* twined *linen*,
31. *and fine* twined *linen* of cunning work:
36. *and fine* twined *linen*, wrought with
27: 9. hangings for the court (of) *fine* twined *linen*
16. and scarlet, *and fine* twined *linen*,
18. the height five cubits (of) *fine* twined *linen*,
28: 5. and scarlet, and *fine linen*.
6. (of) scarlet, *and fine* twined *linen*,
8. and scarlet, *and fine* twined *linen*.
15. *and* (of) *fine* twined *linen*, shalt thou make
39. thou shalt embroider the coat of *fine linen*, and thou shalt make the mitre (of) *fine linen*,
35: 6, 23. scarlet, *and fine linen*, and goats' (hair),
25. (and) of scarlet, and of *fine linen*.
35. in scarlet, *and in fine linen*,
36: 8. made ten curtains (of) *fine* twined *linen*,
35, 37. and scarlet, *and fine* twined *linen*:
38: 9. hangings of the court (were of) *fine* twined *linen*,
16. of the court round about (were) of *fine* twined *linen*.
18. and scarlet, *and fine* twined *linen*:
23. and in scarlet, *and fine linen*.
39: 2, 5, 8. and scarlet, *and fine* twined *linen*.
3. and in the scarlet, and in *the fine linen*,
27. made coats (of) *fine linen* (of) woven
28. a mitre (of) *fine linen*, and goodly bonnets (of) *fine linen*, and linen breeches (of) *fine* twined *linen*,
29. And a girdle (of) *fine* twined *linen*,
Est. 1: 6. silver rings and pillars of *marble*:
— red, *and blue* (marg. *marble*), and white,
Pro. 31: 22. her clothing (is) *silk* and purple.
Cant 5: 15. His legs (are as) pillars of *marble*,
Eze. 16: 10. I girded thee about *with fine linen*,
13. and thy raiment (was of) *fine linen*,
27: 7. *Fine linen* with broidered work

8337 שֵׁשׁ *shēsh*, f. שִׁשָּׁה *shish-shāh'*. m. adj. num.

Gen 7: 6. Noah (was) *six* hundred years old
11. In the *six* hundredth year of Noah's life,
8: 13. in the *six* hundredth *and* first year,
16: 16. Abram (was) fourscore *and six* years old,
30: 20. because I have born him *six* sons:
31: 41. *and six* years for thy cattle:
46: 18. these she bare unto Jacob, (even) *six*teen
26. all the souls (were) threescore *and six*;
Ex. 12: 37. *about six* hundred thousand on foot
14: 7. he took *six* hundred chosen chariots,
16: 26. *Six* days ye shall gather it;
20: 9. *Six* days shalt thou labour,
11. (in) *six* days the Lord made heaven
21: 2. Hebrew servant, *six* years he shall serve:
23: 10. *And six* years thou shalt sow
12. *Six* days thou shalt do thy work,
24: 16. the cloud covered it *six* days:
25: 32. *And six* branches shall come out
33. so *in* the *six* branches that come
35. *according to* the *six* branches
26: 9. and *six* curtains by themselves,
22. westward thou shalt make *six* boards.
25. their sockets (of) silver, *six*teen sockets;
28: 10. *Six* of their names on one stone, and (the other) *six* names of the rest
31: 15. *Six* days may work be done;
17. for (in) *six* days the Lord made
34: 21. *Six* days thou shalt work,
35: 2. *Six* days shall work be done,
36: 16. and *six* curtains by themselves.
27. westward he made *six* boards.
30. and their sockets (were) *six*teen sockets
37: 18. *And six* branches going out of the
19. *throughout* the *six* branches
21. *according to* the *six* branches
38: 26. *for six* hundred thousand and three thousand and five hundred and fifty (men).
Lev. 12: 5. in the blood of her purifying threescore *and six* days.
23: 3. *Six* days shall work be done:
24: 6. set them in two rows, *six* on a row,
25: 3. *Six* years thou shalt sow thy field, *and six* years thou shalt prune

Nu. 1: 21. of the tribe of Reuben, (were) forty and *six* thousand and five hundred.
25. of the tribe of Gad, (were) forty and five thousand *six* hundred and fifty.
27. of the tribe of Judah, (were) threescore and fourteen thousand *and six* hundred.
46. all they that were numbered were *six* hundred thousand and three thousand and five hundred and fifty.
2: 4. that were numbered of them, (were) threescore and fourteen thousand *and six* hundred.
9. in the camp of Judah (were) an hundred thousand and fourscore thousand *and six* thousand and four hundred,
11. that were numbered thereof, (were) forty and *six* thousand and five hundred.
15. that were numbered of them, (were) forty and five thousand *and six* hundred and fifty.
31. in the camp of Dan (were) an hundred thousand and fifty and seven thousand *and six* hundred.
32. throughout their hosts (were) *six* hundred thousand and three thousand and five hundred and fifty.
3: 28. (were) eight thousand *and six* hundred, keeping the charge of the
34. from a month old and upward, (were) *six* thousand and two hundred.
4: 40. by the house of their fathers, were two thousand *and six* hundred and thirty.
7: 3. *six* covered wagons, and twelve oxen;
11: 21. The people, among whom I (am, are) *six* hundred thousand footmen;
26: 22. that were numbered of them, threescore and *six*teen thousand and five hundred.
41. they that were numbered of them (were) forty and five thousand *and six* hundred.
51. numbered of the children of Israel, *six* hundred thousand and a thousand seven hundred and thirty.
31: 32. which the men of war had caught, was *six* hundred thousand and seventy thousand and five thousand sheep,
37. the Lord's tribute of the sheep was *six* hundred and threescore and fifteen.
38. And the beeves (were) thirty and *six* thousand;
40. And the persons (were) *six*teen thousand;
44. And thirty and *six* thousand beeves,
46. And *six*teen thousand persons;
52. and of the captains of hundreds, was *six*teen thousand seven hundred and fifty
35: 6. (there shall be) *six* cities for refuge,
13. of these cities which ye shall give *six*
15. These *six* cities shall be a refuge,
Deu 5: 13. *Six* days thou shalt labour,
15: 12. be sold unto thee, and serve thee *six*
18. in serving thee *six* years:
16: 8. *Six* days thou shalt eat unleavened
Jos. 6: 3. Thus shalt thou do *six* days.
14. so they did *six* days.
7: 5. smote of them about thirty *and six* men:
15: 41. *six*teen cities with their villages:
59, 62. *six* cities with their villages:
19: 22. *six*teen cities with their villages.
Jud. 3: 31. which slew of the Philistines *six* hundred
12: 7. Jephthah judged Israel *six* years.
18: 11. *six* hundred men appointed with weapons
16. *And* the *six* hundred men appointed
17. *with* the *six* hundred men (that were)
20: 15. out of the cities twenty *and six* thousand
47. But *six* hundred men turned and fled
Ru. 3: 15. he measured *six* (measures) of barley,
17. These *six* (measures) of barley gave he
1Sa 13: 5. thirty thousand chariots, *and six* thousand
15. the people (that were) present with him, *about six* hundred
14: 2. the people that (were) with him (were) *about six* hundred
17: 4. whose height (was) *six* cubits and a span.
7. his spear's head (weighed) *six* hundred
23: 13. his men, (which were) *about six* hundred,
27: 2. he passed over *with* the *six* hundred men
30: 9. David went, he *and* the *six* hundred men
2Sa. 2: 11. in Hebron...seven years *and six* months.

2Sa. 5: 5. he reigned over Judah seven years *and six* months:
6:13. that bare the ark...had gone *six* paces,
15:18. *six* hundred men which came after him from Gath,
21:20. on every hand *six* fingers, *and* on every foot *six* toes,
1K. 6: 6. the middle (was) *six* cubits broad,
10:14. that came to Solomon in one year was *six* hundred threescore *and six* talents
16. *six* hundred (shekels) of gold went to one
19. The throne had *six* steps,
20. and on the other upon the *six* steps:
29. went out of Egypt *for six* hundred
11:16. For *six* months did Joab remain
16: 8. In the twenty *and sixth* year (lit. in the year twenty *and six*) of Asa
23. *six* years reigned he in Tirzah.
2K. 5: 5. *and six* thousand (pieces) of gold, and
11: 3. hid in the house of the Lord *six* years.
13:10. over Israel in Samaria, (and reigned) *six*teen years.
19. Thou shouldest have smitten five or *six*
14:21. took Azariah, which (was) *six*teen years
15: 2. *Six*teen years old was he when he began
8. reign over Israel in Samaria *six* months.
33. *and* he reigned *six*teen years in Jerusalem.
16: 2. *and* reigned *six*teen years in Jerusalem,
18:10. (even) in the *sixth* year (lit. in the year *six*) of Hezekiah,
1Ch 3: 4. (These) *six* were born unto him in Hebron; and there he reigned seven years *and six* months:
22. and Neariah, and Shaphat, *six*.
4:27. Shimei had *six*teen sons and *six* daughters;
7: 2. number (was) in the days of David two and twenty thousand *and six* hundred.
4. bands of soldiers for war, *six and* thirty thousand (men):
40. apt to the war (and) to battle (was) twenty *and six* thousand
8:38. And Azel had *six* sons,
9: 6. Jeuel, and their brethren, *six* hundred and ninety.
9. their brethren, according to their generations, nine hundred and fifty *and six*.
44. And Azel had *six* sons,
12:24. of Judah that bare shield and spear (were) *six* thousand and eight hundred,
26. Of the children of Levi four thousand *and six* hundred.
35. of the Danites expert in war twenty and eight thousand *and six* hundred.
20: 6. *six* (on each hand), *and six* (on each foot):
21:25. David gave to Ornan for the place *six* hundred shekels
23: 4. and *six* thousand (were) officers and
24: 4. Among the sons of Eleazar (there were) *six*teen chief
14. The fifteenth to Bilgah, the *six*teenth to
25: 3. *six*, under the hands of their father
23. *The six*teenth to Hananiah,
26:17. Eastward (were) *six* Levites,
2Ch 1:17. out of Egypt a chariot *for six* hundred
2: 2(1). Solomon told out...three thousand *and six* hundred to oversee them.
17(16). found an hundred and fifty thousand and three thousand *and six* hundred.
18(17). three thousand *and six* hundred overseers to set the people a work.
3: 8. (amounting) to *six* hundred talents.
9:13. that came to Solomon in one year was *six* hundred and threescore *and six* talents
15. *six* hundred (shekels) of beaten gold
18. *And* (there were) *six* steps to the throne,
19. and on the other upon the *six* steps.
13:21. begat twenty and two sons, *and six*teen daughters.
16: 1. In the *six and* thirtieth year of the reign
22:12. hid in the house of God *six* years:
26: 1. took Uzziah, who (was) *six*teen years old,
3. *Six*teen years old (was) Uzziah
12. of the mighty men of valour (were) two thousand *and six* hundred.
27: 1. *and* he reigned *six*teen years in Jerusalem.
8. *and* reigned *six*teen years in Jerusalem.
28: 1. *and* he reigned *six*teen years in Jerusalem:
2Ch 29:17. and in the *six*teenth day of the first
33. the consecrated things (were) *six* hundred
35: 8. offerings two thousand *and six* hundred
Ezr. 2:10. The children of Bani, *six* hundred forty and two.
11. The children of Bebai, *six* hundred twenty and three.
13. The children of Adonikam, *six* hundred sixty *and six*.
14. The children of Bigvai, two thousand fifty *and six*.
22. The men of Netophah, fifty *and six*.
26. The children of Ramah and Gaba, *six* hundred twenty and one.
30. The children of Magbish, an hundred fifty *and six*.
35. The children of Senaah, three thousand *and six* hundred and thirty.
60. the children of Nekoda, *six* hundred fifty and two.
66. Their horses (were) seven hundred thirty *and six*;
67. (their) asses, *six* thousand seven hundred and twenty.
69. threescore and one thousand (lit. *six* myriads and a thousand) drams of gold,
8:26. I even weighed unto their hand *six* hundred and fifty talents
35. twelve bullocks for all Israel, ninety *and six* rams,
Neh 5:18. one ox (and) *six* choice sheep;
7:10. The children of Arah, *six* hundred fifty and two.
15. The children of Binnui, *six* hundred forty and eight.
16. The children of Bebai, *six* hundred twenty and eight.
18. The children of Adonikam, *six* hundred threescore and seven.
20. The children of Adin, *six* hundred fifty and five.
30. The men of Ramah and Gaba, *six* hundred twenty and one.
62. the children of Nekoda, *six* hundred forty and two.
68. Their horses, seven hundred thirty *and six*:
69. *six* thousand seven hundred and twenty asses.
Est. 2:12. *six* months with oil of myrrh, *and six*
Job 5:19. He shall deliver thee *in six* troubles:
42:12. *and six* thousand camels, and a thousand
Pro. 6:16. These *six* (things) doth the Lord hate:
Isa. 6: 2. each one had *six* wings; (lit. *six* wings, *six* wings to one)
Jer. 34:14. and when he hath served thee *six* years,
52:23. there were ninety *and six* pomegranates
30. all the persons (were) four thousand *and six* hundred.
Eze. 9: 2. *six* men came from the way of
40: 5. a measuring reed of *six* cubits (long)
12. the little chambers (were) *six* cubits on this side, *and six* cubits on that side.
41: 1. *six* cubits broad on the one side, *and six*
3. and the door, *six* cubits; and the breadth
5. the wall of the house, *six* cubits;
8. a full reed of *six* great cubits.
46: 1. shall be shut the *six* working days;
4. (shall be) *six* lambs without blemish,
6. *and six* lambs, and a ram:

שָׁשָׁא [*shāh-shāh'*]. 8338

*** PIEL.—*Preterite.* ***

Eze.39: 2. *and leave but the sixth part of thee*, (marg. or, *strike thee with six plagues*; or, *draw thee back with an hook of six teeth*)

שָׁשָׁה [*shāh-shāh'*]. 8341

*** PIEL.—*Preterite.* ***

Eze.45:13. *and ye shall give the sixth part*

שְׁשִׁי *sh'shee*, m. 8336

Eze.16:13. (כתיב) thy raiment (was of) *fine linen*,

8345 **שִׁשִּׁי** *shish-shee'*, adj. ord.

Gen 1:31. evening and the morning were the *sixth*
30:19. and bare Jacob the *sixth* son.
Ex. 16: 5. on the *sixth* day they shall prepare
22. on the *sixth* day they gathered twice
29. on the *sixth* day the bread of two days;
26: 9. and shalt double the *sixth* curtain
Lev.25:21. my blessing upon you in the *sixth* year,
Nu. 7:42. On the *sixth* day Eliasaph the son of
29:29. on the *sixth* day eight bullocks, two rams,
Jos. 19:32. The *sixth* lot came out to the
2Sa. 3: 5. *And the sixth*, Ithream, by Eglah
1Ch 2:15. Ozem *the sixth*, David the seventh:
3: 3. *the sixth*, Ithream by Eglah his wife.
12:11. Attai *the sixth*, Eliel the seventh,
24: 9. *the sixth* to Mijamin,
25:13. *The sixth* to Bukkiah,
26: 3. Elam the fifth, Jehohanan *the sixth*,
5. Ammiel *the sixth*, Issachar the seventh,
27: 9. *The sixth* (captain) for the *sixth* month
Neh 3:30. Hanun the *sixth* son of Zalaph,
Eze 4:11. water by measure, *the sixth part of* an
8: 1. in the *sixth* year, *in the sixth* (month),
45:13. *the sixth part of* an ephah of an homer
46:14. *the sixth part of* an ephah, and the third
Hag. 1: 1. in *the sixth* (month), in the first day
15. the four and twentieth day of the *sixth*

8346 **שִׁשִּׁים** *shish-sheem'*, adj. num. pl.

Gen 5:15. Mahalaleel lived *sixty and* five years, and
18. And Jared lived an hundred *sixty and* two
20. all the days of Jared were nine hundred *sixty and* two years:
21. Enoch lived *sixty and* five years, and
23. all the days of Enoch were three hundred *sixty and* five years:
27. all the days of Methuselah were nine hundred *sixty and* nine
25:26. Isaac (was) *threescore* years old when she
46:26. all the souls (were) *threescore* and six;
Lev.12: 5. blood of her purifying *threescore and* six
27: 3. from twenty years old even unto *sixty*
7. if (it be) from *sixty* years old and above;
Nu. 1:39. of the tribe of Dan, (were) *threescore and* two thousand and seven hundred.
2:26. were numbered of them, (were) *threescore and* two thousand and seven hundred.
3:50. took he the money; a thousand three hundred and *threescore and* five (shekels),
7:88. the rams *sixty*, the he goats *sixty*, the lambs of the first year *sixty*.
26:25. were numbered of them, *threescore and* four thousand and three hundred.
27. were numbered of them, *threescore* thousand and five hundred.
43. were numbered of them, (were) *threescore and* four thousand and four hundred.
31:34. And *threescore and* one thousand asses,
39. the Lord's tribute (was) *threescore and* one.
Deu 3: 4. *threescore* cities, all the region of Argob,
Jos. 13:30. which (are) in Bashan, *threescore* cities:
2Sa. 2:31. (so that) three hundred *and threescore*
1K. 4:13. *threescore* great cities with walls and
22(5:2). thirty measures of fine flour, *and threescore* measures of meal,
6: 2. the length thereof (was) *threescore*
10:14. in one year was six hundred *threescore* and six talents
2K. 25:19. *and threescore* men of the people of the
1Ch 2:21. whom he married when he (was) *threescore*
23. the towns thereof, (even) *threescore* cities.
5:18. four and forty thousand seven hundred *and threescore*, that went out to the war.
9:13. house of their fathers, a thousand and seven hundred *and threescore;*
16:38. Obed-edom with their brethren, *threescore* and eight;
26: 8. for the service, (were) *threescore* and two
2Ch 3: 3. the first measure (was) *threescore* cubits,
9:13. in one year was six hundred *and threescore* and six talents
11:21. eighteen wives, and *threescore* concubines; and begat twenty and eight sons, *and threescore* daughters.
2Ch 12: 3. twelve hundred chariots, *and threescore* thousand horsemen:
Ezr. 2: 9. The children of Zaccai, seven hundred *and threescore.*
13. The children of Adonikam, six hundred *sixty* and six.
64. The whole congregation together (was) forty and two thousand three hundred (and) *threescore*,
8:10. and with him an hundred *and threescore*
13. and with them *threescore* males.
Neh 7:14. The children of Zaccai, seven hundred *and threescore.*
18. The children of Adonikam, six hundred *threescore* and seven.
19. The children of Bigvai, two thousand *threescore* and seven.
66. The whole congregation together (was) forty and two thousand three hundred *and threescore*,
72. and *threescore* and seven priests' garments.
11: 6. the sons of Perez...(were) four hundred *threescore* and eight valiant men.
Cant 3: 7. *threescore* valiant men (are) about it,
6: 8. There are *threescore* queens, and fourscore
Isa. 7: 8. within *threescore* and five years shall
Jer. 52:25. *and threescore* men of the people of the
Eze.40:14. He made also posts of *threescore* cubits,
Dan 9:25. (shall be) seven weeks, and *threescore* and two weeks:
26. after *threescore* and two weeks shall

שָׁשַׁר *shāh-shar'*, m. 8350

Jer. 22:14. painted *with vermilion.*
Eze.23:14. images...pourtrayed *with vermilion*,

שָׁת [*shāhth*], m. 8356

Ps. 11: 3. If *the foundations* be destroyed,
Isa. 19:10. broken in *the purposes* (marg. *foundations*) *thereof*,

---

שֵׁת *shēhth*, m. 8357

2Sa.10: 4. in the middle, (even) to *their buttocks*,
Isa. 20: 4. with (their) *buttocks* uncovered,

שֵׁת *shēhth*, m. 8351

Nu. 24:17. and destroy all the children of *Sheth* [lit. perhaps, *tumult*]

שֵׁת *shēhth* & **שִׁת** *shith*, Ch. adj. num. 8353

Ezr. 6:15. which was in the *sixth* year
Dan 3: 1. (and) the breadth thereof *six* cubits:

שָׁתָה *shāh-thāh'*. 8354

* KAL.—*Preterite.* *

Ex. 17: 6. *that* the people *may drink.*
34:28. eat bread, nor *drink* water.
Deu 2: 6. for money, *that ye may drink.*
28. for money, *that I may drink:*
9: 9. neither did eat bread nor *drink*
18. neither eat bread, nor *drink* water,
29: 6(5). neither *have ye drunk* wine
Ru. 2: 9. *and drink* of (that) which the
1Sa. 1:15. *I have drunk* neither wine
30:12. eaten no bread, nor *drunk* (any) water,
2K. 3:17. water, *that ye may drink*,
19:24. digged *and drunk* strange waters,
Ezr.10: 6. he did eat no bread, nor *drink*
Ecc. 2:24. that he should eat *and drink*,
3:13. every man should eat *and drink*,
Cant.5: 1. *I have drunk* my wine with my milk:
Isa. 37:25. I have digged, *and drunk* water;
44:12. *he drinketh* no water, and is faint.

Isa. 51:17. which *hast drunk* at the hand of the
— *thou hast drunken* the dregs
Jer. 22:15. did not thy father eat *and drink*,
25:16. *And they shall drink*, and be moved,
35:14. for unto this day *they drink* none,
51: 7. the nations *have drunken* of her wine;
Lam. 5: 4. *We have drunken* our water
Eze. 23:34. *Thou shalt even drink* it
39:17. eat flesh, *and drink* blood.
19. *and drink* blood till ye be drunken,
Am. 9:14. *and drink* the wine thereof;
Obad. 16. *ye have drunk* upon my holy
— *yea, they shall drink*, and they
Zec. 9:15. *and they shall drink*, (and) make a noise

KAL.—*Infinitive.*

Gen24:19. until they have done *drinking*.
22. as the camels had done *drinking*,
30:38. when the flocks came *to drink*,
— should conceive when they came *to drink*.
Ex. 7:18. Egyptians shall lothe *to drink* of the
21. Egyptians could not *drink* of the water
24. digged round about the river for water *to drink*; for they could not *drink* of the
15:23. they could not *drink* of the waters
17: 1. no water for the people *to drink*.
32: 6. people sat down to eat *and to drink*,
Nu. 20: 5. neither (is) there any water *to drink*.
33:14. no water for the people *to drink*.
Jud. 7: 5. boweth down upon his knees *to drink*.
6. bowed down upon their knees *to drink*
Ru. 3: 3. have done eating *and drinking*.
1Sa. 1: 9. after they *had drunk*.
2Sa. 11:11. to eat *and to drink*,
16: 2. as be faint in the wilderness *may drink*.
23:16. nevertheless he would not *drink thereof*,
17. therefore he would not *drink it*.
1K. 13:23. after *he had drunk*,
18:42. Ahab went up to eat *and to drink*.
2K. 18:27. *and drink* their own piss
1Ch 11:18. David would not *drink* (of) *it*,
19. Therefore he would not *drink it*.
Neh 8:12. went their way to eat, *and to drink*,
Est. 3:15. the king and Haman sat down *to drink*;
7: 1. So the king and Haman came *to banquet* (marg. to *drink*)
Job 1: 4. sisters to eat *and to drink* with them.
Pro. 31: 4. not for kings *to drink* wine;
Ecc. 5:18(17). comely (for one) to eat *and to drink*,
8:15. than to eat, *and to drink*,
Isa. 5:22. Woe unto (them that are) mighty *to drink*
21: 5. watch in the watchtower, eat, *drink*:
22:13. eating flesh, *and drinking* wine: let us eat *and drink*;
36:12. *and drink* their own piss
51:22. cup of my fury; thou shalt no more *drink it* again: (lit. thou shalt not add *to drink it*)
Jer. 2:18. *to drink* the waters of Sihor?
— *to drink* the waters of the river?
16: 8. to sit with them to eat *and to drink*.
25:28. take the cup at thine hand *to drink*,
— Ye shall *certainly* drink. (lit. *drinking* shall drink)
35. 8. *to drink* no wine all our days,
14. commanded his sons not *to drink*
49:12. they whose judgment (was) not *to drink* of the cup have *assuredly* drunken; (lit. *drinking*, &c.)
— thou shalt *surely* drink (lit. *id.*) (of it).
Am. 4: 8. wandered unto one city, *to drink* water;
Hag. 1: 6. ye *drink*, but ye are not filled

KAL.—*Imperative.*

Gen 24:14. and she shall say, *Drink*,
18. And she said, *Drink*, my lord:
44. she say to me, Both *drink* thou,
46. from her (shoulder), and said, *Drink*,
1K. 18:41. Get thee up, eat *and drink*;
2K. 18:31. *and drink ye* every one the waters
Neh 8:10. eat the fat, *and drink* the sweet,
Pro. 5:15. *Drink* waters out of thine own
9: 5. eat of my bread, *and drink* of the wine
23: 7. Eat *and drink*, saith he to thee;
Ecc. 9: 7. *and drink* thy wine with a merry heart;
Cant. 5: 1. eat, O friends; *drink*, yea, drink
Isa. 36:16. *and drink ye* every one the waters

Jer. 25:27. *Drink ye*, and be drunken, and spue,
35: 5. I said unto them, *Drink ye* wine.
Hab 2:16. *drink* thou also, and let thy foreskin

KAL.—*Future.*

Gen 9:21. *And he drank* of the wine,
24:14. I pray thee, *that I may drink*;
46. *so I drank*, and she made
54. they did eat *and drink*,
25:34. he did eat *and drink*,
26:30. they did eat *and drink*.
27:25. he brought him wine, *and he drank*.
43:34. *And they drank*, and were merry
44: 5. not this (it) in which my lord *drinketh*,
Ex. 15:24. What *shall we drink*?
17: 2. Give us water *that we may drink*.
24:11. did eat *and drink*.
Lev. 10: 9. *Do* not *drink* wine nor strong drink,
Nu. 6: 3. and *shall drink* no vinegar of wine,
— neither *shall he drink* any liquor
20. that the Nazarite *may drink* wine.
20:11. *and* the congregation *drank*,
17. neither *will we drink* (of) the water
19. if I and my cattle *drink* of thy water,
21:22. *we will* not *drink* (of) the waters
23:24. *drink* the blood of the slain.
Deu 11:11. *drinketh* water of the rain
28:39. *but shalt* neither *drink* (of) the wine,
32:14. *thou didst drink* the pure blood
38. *drank* the wine of their drink
Jud. 9:27. did eat *and drink*,
13: 4. and *drink* not wine
7. now *drink* no wine nor strong
14. neither *let her drink* wine
15:19. and *when he had drunk*,
19: 4. so they did eat *and drink*,
6. did eat *and drink* both of them
21. washed their feet, and did eat *and drink*.
Ru. 3: 7. when Boaz had eaten *and drunk*,
2Sa. 11:13. he did eat *and drink* before him;
12: 3. *and drank* of his own cup,
19:35(36). taste what I eat or what *I drink*?
1K. 13: 8. neither will I eat bread nor *drink*
9. Eat no bread, nor *drink* water,
16. neither will I eat bread nor *drink*
17. Thou shalt eat no bread nor *drink*
18. he may eat bread *and drink* water.
19. eat bread in his house, *and drunk* water.
22. *and drunk* water in the place, of the which (the Lord) did say to thee, Eat no bread, and *drink* no water;
17: 4. *thou shalt drink* of the brook;
6. and *he drank* of the brook.
10. in a vessel, *that I may drink*.
19: 6. he did eat *and drink*,
8. did eat *and drink*,
2K. 6:22. that they may eat *and drink*,
23. when they had eaten *and drunk*,
7: 8. and did eat *and drink*,
9:34. he did eat *and drink*,
1Ch 11:19. *shall I drink* the blood of these men
29:22. did eat *and drink* before the Lord
Est. 4:16. neither eat nor *drink* three days,
Job 21:20. *he shall drink* of the wrath of the
34: 7. *drinketh* up scorning like water?
Ps. 50:13. or *drink* the blood of goats?
75: 8(9). wring (them) out, (and) *drink*
78:44. that *they could* not *drink*.
110: 7. *He shall drink* of the brook
Pro. 4:17. and *drink* the wine of violence.
31: 5. Lest *they drink*, and forget the law,
7. *Let him drink*, and forget his poverty,
Isa. 24: 9. *They shall* not *drink* wine
62: 8. the stranger *shall* not *drink*
9. *shall drink it* in the courts
65:13. my servants *shall drink*,
Jer. 25:26. Sheshach *shall drink* after them.
28. *Ye shall* certainly *drink*.
35: 6. *We will drink* no wine:
— *Ye shall drink* no wine,
49:12. not to drink of the cup *have* assuredly *drunken*;
— but *thou shalt* surely *drink*
Eze. 4:11. *Thou shalt drink* also water
— from time to time *shalt thou drink*.
16. *they shall drink* water by measure,
12:18. and *drink* thy water with trembling

Eze.12:19. *drink* their water with astonishment,
23:32. *Thou shalt drink* of thy sister's cup
25: 4. they *shall drink* thy milk.
34:18. to *have drunk* of the deep waters,
19. *they drink* that which ye have
39:18. *drink* the blood of the princes
44:21. Neither shall any priest *drink*
Dan 1:12. pulse to eat, and water *to drink.* (lit. *and we will drink*)
Joel 3: 3(4:3). wine, *that they might drink.*
Am. 2: 8. *they drink* the wine of the condemned
4: 1. Bring, *and let us drink.*
5:11. but *ye shall* not *drink* wine
Obad. 16. *shall* all the heathen *drink*
Jon. 3: 7. let them not feed, nor *drink* water:
Mic. 6:15. wine, but *shalt* not *drink*
Zep. 1:13. but not *drink* the wine thereof.
Zec. 7: 6. did eat, and when *ye did drink,*

KAL.—*Participle.* Poel.

1Sa.30:16. eating *and drinking,* and dancing,
1K. 1:25. they eat *and drink* before him,
4:20. eating *and drinking,* and making merry.
16: 9. *drinking* himself drunk
20:12. message, as he (was) *drinking,*
16. Ben-hadad (was) *drinking* himself drunk
1Ch 12:39. with David three days, eating *and drinking:*
Job 1:13. his daughters (were) eating *and drinking*
18. thy daughters (were) eating *and drinking*
6: 4. the poison whereof *drinketh* up
15:16. which *drinketh* iniquity like water?
Ps. 69:12(13). I (was) the song of *the drunkards.* (marg. *drinkers of* strong drink)
Pro.26: 6. cutteth off the feet, (and) *drinketh* damage.
Isa. 24: 9. bitter *to them that drink it.*
29: 8. he *drinketh;* but he awaketh,
Eze.31:14,16. all that *drink* water:
Joel 1: 5. howl, all *ye drinkers of* wine,
Am. 6: 6. *That drink* wine in bowls.
Zec. 7: 6. and *drink* (for yourselves)?

* NIPHAL.—*Future.* *

Lev.11:34. all drink that *may be drunk*

8355 **שְׁתָה** [*sh'thāh*], Ch.

* P'AL.—*Preterite.* *

Dan 5: 3. *and* the king,...and his concubines, *drank*
4. *They drank* wine, and praised the gods

P'AL.—*Future.*

Dan 5: 2. *that*...his concubines, *might drink* therein.

P'AL.—*Participle.*

Dan 5: 1. and *drank* wine before the thousand.
23. *have drunk* wine in them;

8358-59 **שְׁתִי** *sh'thee,* m.

Lev.13:48. Whether (it be) *in the warp,*
49,51,53,57. either *in the warp,* or in the
52. whether *warp* or woof,
56. or out of *the warp,*
58. the garment, either *warp,* or woof,
59. linen, either in *the warp,* or woof,
Ecc.10:17. for strength, and not *for drunkenness!*

8360 **שְׁתִיָּה** *sh'theey-yāh',* f.

Est. 1: 8. *And the drinking* (was) according

8361 **שִׁתִּין** *shit-teen',* Ch. adj. num. pl.

Ezr. 6: 3. the height thereof *threescore* cubits, (and) the breadth thereof *threescore* cubits;
Dan 3: 1. whose height (was) *threescore* cubits,
5:31(6:1). about *threescore* and two years old.

8362 **שָׁתַל** [*shāh-thal'*].

* KAL.—*Preterite.* *

Eze.17:22. *and will plant* (it) upon an high mountain

KAL.—*Future.*

Eze.17:23. height of Israel *will I plant it:*

KAL.—*Participle.* Paül.

Ps. 1: 3. he shall be like a tree *planted*
92:13(14). *Those that be planted* in the house
Jer. 17: 8. he shall be as a tree *planted*
Eze.17: 8. It *was planted* in a good soil
10. Yea, behold, (being) *planted,*
19:10. *planted* by the waters:
13. now she (is) *planted* in the wilderness,
Hos 9:13. Tyrus (is) *planted* in a pleasant place:

שְׁתִל [*sh'theel*], m. 8363

Ps.128: 3. thy children *like* olive *plants*

שָׁתַם [*shāh-tham'*]. 8365

* KAL.—*Participle.* Paül.*

Nu. 24: 3,15. the man whose eyes *are open* hath said: (marg. *who had* his eyes *shut,* (but now opened))

שָׁתַן [*shāh-than'*]. 8366

* HIPHIL.—*Participle.* *

1Sa.25:22. any *that pisseth* against the wall.
34. Nabal by the morning light any *that pisseth*
1K. 14:10. cut off from Jeroboam *him that pisseth*
16:11. he left him not one *that pisseth*
21:21. cut off from Ahab *him that pisseth*
2K. 9: 8. cut off from Ahab *him that pisseth*

שָׁתַק [*shāh-thak'*]. 8367

* KAL.—*Future.* *

Ps.107:30. Then are they glad because *they be quiet;*
Pro.26:20. no talebearer, the strife *ceaseth.* (marg. *is silent*)
Jon. 1:11. that the sea *may be calm* (marg. *silent*)
12. *so shall* the sea *be calm*

שָׁתַת [*shāh-thath'*]. 8371

* KAL.—*Preterite.* *

Ps. 49:14(15). Like sheep *they are laid* in the grave;
73: 9. *They set* their mouth against the heavens,

ת *tāhv.*

The Twenty-second and last Letter of the Alphabet.

תָּא *tāh,* m. 8372

1K. 14:28. brought them back into *the* guard *chamber.*
2Ch 12:11. brought them again into *the* guard *chamber.*
Eze.40: 7. *And* (every) *little chamber* (was) one — between *the little chambers*
10. *And the little chambers of* the gate
12. The space also before *the little chambers* — *and the little chambers* (were) six
13. from the roof of (one) *little chamber*
16. narrow windows to *the little chambers,*
21. *And the little chambers thereof* (were) three
29,33. *And the little chambers thereof,* and the
36. *The little chambers thereof,* the posts

תָּאַב [*tāh-av'*]. 8373

* KAL.—*Preterite.* *

Ps.119:40. *I have longed* after thy precepts:
174. *I have longed* for thy salvation,

תָּאַב [*tāh-av'*]. 8374

* PIEL.—*Participle.* *

Am. 6: 8. I *abhor* the excellency of Jacob,

8375 **תַּאֲבָה tah-ăvāh', f.**

Ps.119:20. My soul breaketh *for the longing*

8376 **תָּאָה [tāh-āh'].**

* PIEL.—*Future.* *

Nu. 34: 7. from the great sea *ye shall point out* for you mount Hor:
8. From mount Hor *ye shall point out*

8377 **תְּאוֹ t'ōh, m.**

Deu 14: 5. the pygarg, *and the wild ox,*

8378-79 **תַּאֲוָה tah-ăvāh', f.**

Gen 3: 6. that it (was) *pleasant* (marg. *a desire*) to the eyes,
49:26. *the utmost bound of* the everlasting hills:
Nu. 11: 4. multitude that (was) among them fell *a lusting:* (marg. lusted *a lust*)
34. the name of that place Kibroth-*hattaavah:* (marg. The graves of *lust*)
35. journeyed from Kibroth-*hattaavah*
33:16. pitched at Kibroth-*hattaavah.* (marg. the graves of *lust*)
17. they departed from Kibroth-*hattaavah,*
Deu 9:22. at Massah, and at Kibroth-*hattaavah,*
Job 33:20. abhorreth bread, and his soul *dainty* meat. (marg. meat of *desire*)
Ps. 10: 3. boasteth of his heart's *desire,*
17. thou hast heard *the desire of* the humble:
21: 2(3). Thou hast given him his heart's *desire,*
38: 9(10). Lord, all *my desire* (is) before thee;
78:29. *for* he gave them *their own desire;*
30. They were not estranged *from their lust.*
106:14. But lusted *exceedingly* (marg. lusted *a lust*) in the wilderness,
112:10. *the desire of* the wicked shall perish.
Pro. 10:24. *but the desire of* the righteous shall be
11:23. *The desire of* the righteous (is) only good:
13:12. (when) *the desire* cometh, (it is) a tree of
19. *The desire* accomplished is sweet to
18: 1. *Through desire* a man, having separated
19:22. *The desire of* a man (is) his kindness:
21:25. *The desire of* the slothful killeth him;
26. He coveteth *greedily* (lit. desireth *a desire*) all the day long:
Isa. 26: 8. *the desire of* (our) soul (is) to thy name,

8380 **תְּאוֹמִים t'ōh-meem', m. pl.**

Gen25:24. behold, (there were) *twins* in her womb.
38:27. *twins* (were) in her womb.
Cant.4: 5. like two young roes *that are twins,*
7: 3(4). like two young roes *that are twins.*

8381 **תַּאֲלָה [tah-ălāh'], f.**

Lam.3:65. *thy curse* unto them.

8382 **תָּאַם [tāh-am'].**

* KAL.—*Participle.* Poel. *

Ex. 26:24. they shall be *coupled together* (marg. *twined*) beneath,
36:29. they were *coupled* (marg. *id.*) beneath,

* HIPHIL.—*Participle.* *

Cant.4: 2. whereof every one *bear twins,*
6: 6. whereof every one *beareth twins,*

8385 **תַּאֲנָה [tah-ănāh'], f.**

Jer. 2:24. in *her occasion* who can turn her away?

8384 **תְּאֵנָה t'ēh-nāh', f.**

Gen 3: 7. they sewed *fig* leaves together,
Nu. 13:23. the pomegranates, and of *the figs.*
Nu. 20: 5. it (is) no place of seed, *or of figs,*
Deu 8: 8. barley, and vines, *and fig trees,*
Jud. 9:10. the trees said *to the fig tree,*
11. But *the fig tree* said unto them,
1K. 4:25(5:5). every man under his vine and under *his fig tree,*
2K. 18:31. every one of *his fig tree,*
20: 7. Take a lump of *figs.*
Neh 13:15. as also wine, grapes, *and figs,*
Ps. 105:33. smote their vines also *and their fig trees;*
Pro.27:18. Whoso keepeth *the fig tree*
Cant.2:13. *The fig tree* putteth forth
Isa. 34: 4. as a falling (fig) *from the fig tree.*
36:16. every one of *his fig tree,*
38:21. Let them take a lump of *figs,*
Jer. 5:17. shall eat up thy vines *and thy fig trees:*
8:13. nor *figs on the fig tree,*
24: 1. two baskets of *figs*
2. One basket (had) very good *figs,* (even) *like the figs* (that are) first ripe: and the other basket (had) very naughty *figs,*
3. And I said, *Figs; the* good *figs,* very good;
5. *Like* these good *figs,*
8. *And as the* evil *figs,*
29:17. will make them *like* vile *figs.*
Hos. 2:12(14). her vines *and her fig trees,*
9:10. as the firstripe *in the fig tree*
Joel 1: 7. *and* barked *my fig tree:*
12. *and the fig tree* languisheth;
2:22. *the fig tree* and the vine do yield
Am. 4: 9. your vineyards *and your fig trees*
Mic. 4: 4. under *his fig tree;*
Nah. 3:12. thy strong holds (shall be like) *fig trees*
Hab. 3:17. *the fig tree* shall not blossom,
Hag. 2:19. as yet the vine, *and the fig tree,*
Zec. 3:10. under the vine and under *the fig tree.*

תֹּאֲנָה tōh-ănāh', f. 8385

Jud.14: 4. he sought *an occasion* against

תַּאֲנִיָּה tah-ăneey-yāh', f. 8386

Isa. 29: 2. there shall be *heaviness*
Lam.2: 5. the daughter of Judah *mourning*

תְּאֻנִים t'oo-neem', m. pl. 8383

Eze.24:12. She hath wearied (herself) with *lies,* [or, it hath wearied (me) with *toil*]

תָּאַר tāh-ar'. 8388

* KAL.—*Preterite.* *

Jos. 15: 9. *And* the border *was drawn* from the top
— *and* the border *was drawn* to Baalah,
11. *and* the border *was drawn* to Shicron,
18:14. *And* the border *was drawn* (thence),
17. *And was drawn* from the north,

* PIEL.—*Future.* *

Isa. 44:13. *he marketh it out* with a line;
— *he marketh it out* with the compass,

* PUAL.—*Participle.* *

Jos. 19:13. goeth out to Remmon-*methoar* (marg. or, *which is drawn*)

תֹּאַר tōh'-ar, m. 8389

Gen29:17. Rachel was beautiful (lit. fair of *form*) and well favoured.
39: 6. Joseph was (a) goodly (person), (lit. fair of *form*) and well favoured.
41:18. seven kine, fatfleshed and well *favoured;* (lit. fair of *form*)
19. poor and very ill *favoured* (lit. ugly of *form*)
Deu21:11. seest among the captives a beautiful woman, (lit. fair of *form*)
Jud. 8:18. each one *resembled* (marg. *according to the form*) the children of a king.
1Sa.16:18. prudent in matters, and a comely person, (lit. a man of *form*)

Sa.25: 3. of *a* beautiful *countenance :*
28:14. What *form* (is) *he of?* (marg. (is) *his form*)
1K. 1: 6. he also (was) a very goodly (man); (lit. good of *form*)
Est. 2: 7. the maid (was) fair (marg. fair of *form*) and beautiful;
Isa. 52:14. *and his form* more than the sons of men:
53: 2. he hath no *form* nor comeliness;
Jer. 11:16. fair, (and) of *goodly* fruit:
Lam. 4: 8. *Their visage* is blacker than a coal;

8391 **תְּאַשּׁוּר** *t'ash-shoor'*, m.

Isa. 41:19. *and the box tree* together:
60:13. *and the box* together,

8392 **תֵּבָה** *tēh-vāh'*, f.

Gen 6:14. Make thee *an ark of* gopher wood; rooms shalt thou make in *the ark*,
15. The length of *the ark*
16. A window shalt thou make *to the ark*,
— the door of *the ark* shalt thou set
18. thou shalt come into *the ark*,
19. shalt thou bring into *the ark*,
7: 1. Come thou and all thy house into *the ark;*
7. his sons' wives with him, into *the ark*,
9. two and two unto Noah into *the ark*,
13. wives of his sons with them, into *the ark;*
15. went in unto Noah into *the ark*,
17. the waters increased, and bare up *the ark*,
18. *the ark* went upon the face
23. that (were) with him *in the ark.*
8: 1. cattle that (was) with him *in the ark:*
4. *the ark* rested in the seventh month,
6. Noah opened the window of *the ark*
9. she returned unto him into *the ark*,
— pulled her in unto him into *the ark.*
10. sent forth the dove out of *the ark;*
13. Noah removed the covering of *the ark*,
16. Go forth of *the ark*,
19. went forth out of *the ark.*
9:10. from all that go out of *the ark*,
18. that went forth of *the ark*,
Ex. 2: 3. she took for him *an ark of*
5. when she saw *the ark* among the flags,

8393 **תְּבוּאָה** *t'voo-āh'*, f.

Gen47:24. *in the increase*, that ye shall give
Ex. 23:10. shalt gather in *the fruits thereof:*
Lev.19:25. yield unto you *the increase thereof:*
23:39. gathered in *the fruit of* the land,
25: 3. gather in *the fruit thereof;*
7. all *the increase thereof* be meat.
12. ye shall eat *the increase thereof*
15. *the fruits* he shall sell
16. *the fruits* doth he sell
20. nor gather in *our increase:*
21. *fruit* for three years.
22. eat (yet) of old *fruit*
— until *her fruits* come in
Nu. 18:30. *as the increase of* the threshingfloor, *and as the increase of* the winepress.
Deu 14:22. Thou shalt truly tithe all *the increase of*
28. all the tithe of *thine increase*
16:15. shall bless thee in all *thine increase*,
22: 9. *and the fruit of* thy vineyard,
26:12. all the tithes of *thine increase*
33:14. for *the* precious *fruits*
Jos. 5:12. but they did eat *of the fruit of*
2K. 8: 6. all *the fruits of* the field
2Ch 31: 5. all *the increase of* the field;
32:28. Storehouses also *for the increase of*
Neh 9:37. *And* it yieldeth much *increase*
Job 31:12. would root out all *mine increase.*
Ps.107:37. which may yield fruits of *increase.*
Pro. 3: 9. the firstfruits of all *thine increase:*
14. and *the gain thereof* than fine gold.
8:19. *and my revenue* than choice silver.
10:16. *the fruit of* the wicked to sin.
14: 4. but much *increase* (is) by
15: 6. *but in the revenues of* the
Pro.16: 8. than great *revenues* without right.
18:20. with *the increase of* his lips shall he be
Ecc. 5:10(9). he that loveth abundance with *increase:*
Isa. 23: 3. the harvest of the river, (is) *her revenue;*
30:23. bread of *the increase of* the earth,
Jer. 2: 3. the firstfruits of *his increase:*
12:13. shall be ashamed *of your revenues*
Eze.48:18. *the increase thereof* shall be

תָּבוּן [*tāh-voon'*], m. 8394

Hos 13: 2. *according to their own understanding*,

תְּבוּנָה *t'voo-nāh'*, f. 8394

Ex. 31: 3. in wisdom, *and in understanding*,
35:31. in wisdom, *in understanding*,
36: 1. wisdom *and understanding*
Deu32:28. neither (is there any) *understanding*
1K. 4:29(5:9). wisdom *and understanding*
7:14. filled with wisdom, and *understanding*,
Job 12:12. in length of days *understanding.*
13. he hath counsel *and understanding.*
26:12. *and by his understanding*
32:11. I gave ear to *your reasons*, (marg. *understandings*)
Ps. 49: 3(4). my heart (shall be) of *understanding.*
78:72. *and* guided them *by the skilfulness of*
136: 5. that *by wisdom* made the heavens:
147: 5. *his understanding* (is) infinite.
Pro. 2: 2. apply thine heart *to understanding;*
3. liftest up thy voice *for understanding;*
6. knowledge *and understanding.*
11. *understanding* shall keep thee:
3:13. the man (that) getteth *understanding.*
19. *by understanding* hath he
5: 1. bow thine ear *to my understanding:*
8: 1. *and understanding* put forth
10:23. a man of *understanding* hath wisdom.
11:12. a man of *understanding* holdeth
14:29. slow to wrath (is) of great *understanding:*
15:21. a man of *understanding* walketh
17:27. a man of *understanding* is of an
18: 2. A fool hath no delight *in understanding*,
19: 8. he that keepeth *understanding*
20: 5. a man of *understanding* will draw
21:30. no wisdom nor *understanding*
24: 3. *and by understanding* it is established:
28:16. The prince that wanteth *understanding*
Isa. 40:14. shewed to him the way of *understanding?* (marg. *understandings*)
28. no searching of *his understanding.*
44:19. knowledge nor *understanding*
Jer. 10:12. *and* hath stretched out the heavens *by his discretion.*
51:15. *and*...the heaven *by his understanding.*
Eze.28: 4. *and with thine understanding*
Obad. 7. none *understanding* in him.
8. *and understanding* out of the

תְּבוּסָה [*t'voo-sāh'*], f. 8395

2Ch 22: 7. *the destruction* (marg. *treading down*) *of* Ahaziah

---

תֵּבֵל *tēh-vēhl'*, f. 8398

1Sa. 2: 8. the pillars of the earth (are) the Lord's, and he hath set *the world*
2Sa.22:16. the foundations of *the world* were
1Ch 16:30. *the world* also shall be stable,
Job 18:18. *and* chased *out of the world.*
34:13. who hath disposed *the* whole *world?*
37:12. upon the face of *the world*
Ps. 9: 8(9). he shall judge *the world* in righteousness,
18:15(16). the foundations of *the world* were
19: 4(5). their words to the end of *the world.*
24: 1. *the world*, and they that dwell therein.
33: 8. inhabitants of *the world* stand in awe
50:12. for *the world* (is) mine,
77:18(19). the lightnings lightened *the world:*
89:11(12). *the world* and the fulness thereof,

Ps. 90: 2. hadst formed the earth *and the world*,
93: 1. *the world* also is stablished,
96:10. *the world* also shall be established
13. he shall judge *the world*
97: 4. His lightnings enlightened *the world*:
98: 7. *the world*, and they that dwell therein.
9. righteousness shall he judge *the world*.
Pro. 8:26. the highest part of the dust of *the world*.
31. Rejoicing *in the habitable part of* his earth;
Isa. 13:11. I will punish *the world* for (their) evil,
14:17. made *the world* as a wilderness,
21. nor fill the face of *the world*
18: 3. All ye inhabitants of *the world*,
24: 4. *the world* languisheth
26: 9. *the world* will learn righteousness.
18. the inhabitants of *the world* fallen.
27: 6. fill the face of *the world* with fruit.
34: 1. *the world*, and all things that come forth
Jer. 10:12. he hath established *the world*
51:15. established *the world* by his wisdom,
Lam. 4:12. all the inhabitants of *the world*,
Nah 1: 5. *yea, the world*, and all that dwell therein.

8397 **תֶּבֶל** *teh'-vel*, m.

Lev.18:23. lie down thereto: it (is) *confusion*.
20:12. they have wrought *confusion*;

8399 **תַּבְלִית** *tav-leeth'*, f.

Isa. 10:25. mine anger in their *destruction*.

8400 **תְּבַלֻּל** *t'val-lool'*, m.

Lev.21:20. or that *hath a blemish*

8401 **תֶּבֶן** *teh'-ven*, m.

Gen24:25. We have both *straw* and provender
32. gave *straw* and provender for the camels,
Ex. 5: 7. Ye shall no more give the people *straw*
— let them go and gather *straw*
10. I will not give you *straw*.
11. get you *straw* where ye can find it:
12. to gather stubble *instead of straw*.
13. as when there was *straw*.
16. There is no *straw* given unto thy servants,
18. for there shall no *straw* be given you,
Jud.19:19. Yet there is both *straw* and provender
1K. 4:28(5:8). Barley also *and straw* for the horses
Job 21:18. They are *as stubble* before the wind,
41:27(19). He esteemeth iron *as straw*,
Isa. 11: 7. the lion shall eat *straw* like the ox.
65:25. the lion shall eat *straw* like the bullock:
Jer. 23:28. What (is) *the chaff* (lit. *to the straw*) to the wheat?

8403 **תַּבְנִית** *tav-neeth'*, f.

Ex. 25: 9. *the pattern of* the tabernacle, and *the pattern of* all the instruments
40. make (them) *after their pattern*,
Deu 4:16. *the likeness of* male or female,
17. *The likeness of* any beast
— *the likeness of* any winged fowl
18. *The likeness of* any thing that creepeth
— *the likeness of* any fish
Jos. 22:28. Behold *the pattern of* the altar
2K. 16:10. and *the pattern of it*,
1Ch 28:11. *the pattern of* the porch,
12. *And the pattern of* all
18. *and* gold *for the pattern*
19. all the works of this *pattern*.
Ps. 106:20. *into the similitude of* an ox
144:12. *the similitude of* a palace:
Isa. 44:13. *after the figure of* a man,
Eze. 8: 3. he put forth *the form of* an hand,
10. behold every *form of* creeping things,
10: 8. *the form of* a man's hand

תַּבְעֵרָה *tav-ğeh-rāh'*, f. 8404

Nu. 11: 3. called the name of the place *Taberah*: (marg. *A burning*)
Deu 9:22. *And at Taberah*, and at Massah,

תְּבַר [*t'var*], Ch. 8406

* P'AL.—*Participle*. *

Dan 2:42. partly strong, and partly *broken*. (marg. or, *brittle*)

תַּגְמוּל [*tag-mool'*], m. 8408

Ps. 116:12. all *his benefits* toward me?

תִּגְרָה *tig-rāh'*, f. 8409

Ps. 39:10(11). I am consumed *by the blow* (marg. *conflict*) *of*

תִּדְהָר *tid-hāhr'*, m. 8410

Isa. 41:19. *the pine*, and the box tree together:
60:13. the fir tree, *the pine tree*,

תְּדִירָא *t'dee-rāh'*, Ch. f. 8411

Dan 6:16(17), 20(21). Thy God whom thou servest *continually*,

---

תֹּהוּ *tōh'-hoo*, m. 8414

Gen 1: 2. the earth was *without form*
Deu 32:10. *and in* the *waste* howling wilderness;
1Sa. 12:21. for (then should ye go) after *vain* (things),
— for they (are) *vain*.
Job 6:18. they go *to nothing*, and perish.
12:24. causeth them to wander *in a wilderness*
26: 7. out the north over *the empty place*,
Ps. 107:40. causeth them to wander *in the wilderness*, (marg. or, *void place*)
Isa. 24:10. The city of *confusion* is broken down:
29:21. turn aside the just *for a thing of nought*.
34:11. stretch out upon it the line of *confusion*,
40:17. less than nothing, *and vanity*.
23. maketh the judges of the earth *as vanity*.
41:29. molten images (are) wind *and confusion*.
44: 9. graven image (are) all of them *vanity*;
45:18. he created it not in *vain*,
19. Seek ye me in *vain*:
49: 4. I have spent my strength *for nought*,
59: 4. they trust in *vanity*,
Jer. 4:23. the earth, and, lo, (it was) *without form*

תְּהוֹם *t'hōhm*, m. 8415

Gen 1: 2. darkness (was) upon the face of *the deep*.
7:11. fountains of *the* great *deep* broken up,
8: 2. The fountains also of *the deep*
49:25. blessings of *the deep* that lieth under,
Ex. 15: 5. *The depths* have covered them:
8. *the depths* were congealed
Deu 8: 7. of fountains *and depths* that spring
33:13. *and for the deep* that coucheth beneath,
Job 28:14. *The depth* saith, It (is) not in me:
38:16. thou walked in the search of *the depth*?
30. the face of *the deep* is frozen.
41:32(24). would think *the deep* (to be) hoary.
Ps. 33: 7. he layeth up *the depth* in storehouses.
36: 6(7). thy judgments (are) *a* great *deep*:
42: 7(8). *Deep* calleth unto *deep* at the noise of thy waterspouts:
71:20. *and* shalt bring me up again *from the depths*
77:16(17). *the depths* also were troubled.
78:15. drink *as* (out of) *the* great *depths*.
104: 6. Thou coveredst it with *the deep*
106: 9. so he led them *through the depths*,
107:26. they go down again to *the depths*:
135: 6. in the seas, and all *deep places*.

Ps.148: 7. ye dragons, and all *deeps:*
Pro. 3:20. By his knowledge *the depths*
8:24. When (there were) no *depths,*
27. set a compass upon the face of *the depth:*
28. strengthened the fountains of *the deep:*
Isa. 51:10. the waters of *the* great *deep;*
63:13. That led them *through the deep,*
Eze.26:19. when I shall bring up *the deep*
31: 4. *the deep* set him up on high
15. I covered *the deep* for him,
Am. 7: 4. it devoured *the* great *deep,*
Jon. 2: 5(6). *the depth* closed me round about,
Hab 3:10. *the deep* uttered his voice,

8416 **תְּהִלָּה** *t'hil-lāh'*, f.

Ex. 15:11. fearful (in) *praises,*
Deu10:21. He (is) *thy praise,* and he (is) thy God,
26:19. *in praise,* and in name,
1Ch 16:35. glory *in thy praise.*
2Ch 20:22. to sing *and to praise,* (marg. *and praise*)
Neh 9: 5. above all blessing *and praise.*
12:46. songs of *praise* and thanksgiving
Ps. 9:14(15). That I may shew forth all *thy praise*
22: 3(4). that inhabitest *the praises of* Israel.
25(26). *My praise* (shall be) of thee
33: 1. *praise* is comely for the upright.
34: 1(2). *his praise* (shall) continually (be) in
35:28. of thy righteousness (and) of *thy praise*
40: 3(4). *praise* unto our God:
48:10(11). so (is) *thy praise* unto the ends
51:15(17). mouth shall shew forth *thy praise.*
65: 1(2). *Praise* waiteth for thee,
66: 2. make *his praise* glorious.
8. make the voice of *his praise* to be
71: 6. *my praise* (shall be) continually
8. my mouth be filled (with) *thy praise*
14. will yet *praise thee* more and more. (lit. I will add unto all *thy praise*)
78: 4. *the praises of* the Lord,
79:13. we will shew forth *thy praise*
100: 4. into his courts *with praise:*
102:21(22). *and his praise* in Jerusalem;
106: 2. can shew forth all *his praise?*
12. they sang *his praise.*
47. to triumph *in thy praise.*
109: 1. O God of *my praise;*
111:10. *his praise* endureth for ever.
119:171. My lips shall utter *praise,*
145[title](1). David's (Psalm) of *praise.*
21. My mouth shall speak *the praise of*
147: 1. *praise* is comely.
148:14. *the praise* of all his saints;
149: 1. *his praise* in the congregation
Isa. 42: 8. *neither my praise* to graven
10. *his praise* from the end of the earth,
12. *and* declare *his praise* in the islands.
43:21. they shall shew forth *my praise.*
48: 9. *and* for *my praise* will I refrain
60: 6. and they shall shew forth *the praises of*
18. and thy gates *Praise.*
61: 3. the garment of *praise* for the
11. *and praise* to spring forth
62: 7. till he make Jerusalem *a praise*
63: 7. *the praises of* the Lord,
Jer. 13:11. for a name, *and for a praise,*
17:14. for thou (art) *my praise.*
33: 9. *a praise* and an honour
48: 2. no more *praise of* Moab:
49:25. How is the city of *praise* not left,
51:41. how is *the praise of* the whole
Hab 3: 3. *and* the earth was full of *his praise.*
Zep. 3:19. I will get them *praise*
20. make you a name *and a praise*

8417 **תָּהֳלָה** *toh-hŏlāh'*, f.

Job 4:18. his angels he charged with *folly:* (marg. or, his angels, (in whom) he put *light*)

8418 **תַּהֲלֻכָה** [*tah-hăloo-'chah'*], f.

Neh 12:31. (whereof one) *went* on the right hand

תַּהְפֻּכוֹת *tah-poo-'chōhth'*, f. pl. 8419

Deu32:20. for they (are) a *very froward* generation, (lit. a generation of *perversities*)
Pro. 2:12. the man that speaketh *froward things;*
14. delight *in the frowardness of* the wicked;
6:14. *Frowardness* (is) in his heart,
8:13. the *froward* mouth,
10:31. the *froward* tongue shall be cut
32. the mouth of the wicked (speaketh) *frowardness.* (marg. *frowardnesses*)
16:28. A *froward* man soweth strife:
30. shutteth his eyes to devise *froward things:*
23:33. thine heart shall utter *perverse things.*

תָּו *tāhv*, m. 8420

Job 31:35. *my desire* (marg. or, *my sign*) (is, that) the Almighty would answer
Eze. 9: 4. set *a mark* upon the foreheads
6. any man upon whom (is) *the mark;*

תּוֹא *tōh*, m. 8377

Isa. 51:20. *as a wild bull* in a net:

תּוּב [*toov*], Ch. 8421

* P'AL.—*Future.* *

Dan 4:34(31). mine understanding *returned* unto
36(33). my reason *returned* unto me; and for the glory of my kingdom, mine honour and brightness *returned* unto me;

* APHEL.—*Preterite.* *

Ezr. 5:11. And thus *they returned* us answer,
Dan 2:14. Then Daniel *answered* with counsel

APHEL.—*Infinitive.*

Dan 3:16. we (are) not careful *to answer thee* in this

APHEL.—*Future.*

Ezr. 5: 5. and then *they returned answer*
6: 5. *let* the golden and silver vessels...*be restored,*

תּוּבְנָה [*too-v'nāh'*], f. 8394

Job 26:12. (כתיב) *and by his understanding* he smiteth through

---

תּוּגָה *too-gāh'*, f. 8424

Ps.119:28. My soul melteth *for heaviness:*
Pro.10: 1. a foolish son (is) *the heaviness of* his
14:13. the end of that mirth (is) *heaviness.*
17:21. begetteth a fool (doeth it) *to his sorrow:*

תּוֹדָה *tōh-dāh'*, f. 8426

Lev. 7:12. If he offer it for *a thanksgiving,*
— the sacrifice of *thanksgiving*
13. the sacrifice of *thanksgiving*
15. his peace offerings for *thanksgiving*
22:29. a sacrifice of *thanksgiving*
Jos. 7:19. make *confession* unto him;
2Ch 29:31. bring sacrifices *and thank offerings*
— brought in sacrifices *and thank offerings;*
33:16. peace offerings *and thank offerings,*
Ezr. 10:11. make *confession* unto the Lord God
Neh 12:27. *both with thanksgivings,* and with singing,
31. (companies of them that gave) *thanks,*
38. *And* the other (company of them that gave) *thanks*
40. *the* two (companies of them that gave) *thanks*
Ps. 26: 7. the voice of *thanksgiving,*
42: 4(5). the voice of joy *and praise,*
50:14. Offer unto God *thanksgiving;*
23. Whoso offereth *praise* glorifieth me:
56:12(13). I will render *praises* unto thee.
69:30(31). magnify him *with thanksgiving.*

Ps. 95: 2. come before his presence *with thanksgiving,*
100[title](1). A Psalm *of praise.* (marg. or, *thanksgiving*)
4. Enter into his gates *with thanksgiving,*
107:22. the sacrifices of *thanksgiving,*
116:17. the sacrifice of *thanksgiving,*
147: 7. Sing unto the Lord *with thanksgiving ;*
Isa. 51: 3. *thanksgiving,* and the voice of melody.
Jer. 17:26. bringing *sacrifices of praise,*
30:19. out of them shall proceed *thanksgiving*
33:11. that shall bring the *sacrifice of praise*
Am. 4: 5. a sacrifice of *thanksgiving*
Jon. 2: 9(10). the voice of *thanksgiving ;*

8429 **תְּוַהּ** *t'vah,* Ch.

* P'AL.—*Preterite.* *

Dan 3:24. Nebuchadnezzar the king *was astonied,*

8427-28 **תָּוָה** [*tāh-vāh'*].

* PIEL.—*Future.* *

1Sa.21:13(14). *and scrabbled* (marg. or, *made marks*) on the doors of the gate,

* HIPHIL.—*Preterite.* *

Ps. 78:41. *limited* the Holy One of Israel.
Eze. 9: 4. and *set* (marg. *mark*) a mark upon the foreheads of the men

---

8431 **תּוֹחֶלֶת** *tōh-ġheh'-leth,* f.

Job 41: 9(1). *the hope of him* is in vain:
Ps. 39: 7(8). *my hope* (is) in thee.
Pro.10:28. *The hope of* the righteous (shall be) gladness:
11: 7. *and the hope of* unjust (men) perisheth.
13:12. *Hope* deferred maketh the heart sick:
Lam.3:18. *and my hope* is perished from the Lord:

8432 **תָּוֶךְ** *tāh'-vech,* m.

Gen 1: 6. firmament *in the midst of* the waters,
2: 9. of life also *in the midst of* the garden,
3: 3. which (is) *in the midst of* the garden,
8. *amongst* the trees of the garden.
9:21. he was uncovered *within* his tent.
15:10. divided them *in the midst,*
18:24. there be fifty righteous *within* the city:
26. Sodom fifty righteous *within* the city,
19:29. sent Lot *out of the midst of* the overthrow,
23: 6. thou (art) a mighty prince *among us :*
9. possession of a buryingplace *amongst you.*
10. Ephron dwelt *among* the children of Heth:
35: 2. strange gods that (are) *among you,*
37: 7. we (were) binding sheaves *in* the field,
40:20. chief baker *among* his servants.
41:48. laid he up *in the same.*
42: 5. of Israel came to buy (corn) *among* those
Ex. 2: 5. when she saw the ark *among* the
3: 2. flame of fire *out of the midst of* a bush:
4. God called unto him *out of the midst of*
7: 5. children of Israel *from among them.*
9:24. fire mingled *with* the hail,
11: 4. About midnight will I go out *into the midst of*
12:31. get you forth *from among* my people,
49. stranger that sojourneth *among you.*
14:16. *through the midst of* the sea.
22. Israel went *into the midst of*
23. went in after them to *the midst of* the sea,
27. overthrew the Egyptians *in the midst of*
29. Israel walked upon dry (land) *in the midst of*
15:19. Israel went on dry (land) *in the midst of*
24:16. Moses *out of the midst of* the cloud.
18. Moses went *into the midst of* the cloud,
25: 8. that I may dwell *among them.*
26:28. the middle bar *in the midst of*
28: 1. *from among* the children of Israel,
32. in the top of it, *in the midst thereof:*
Ex. 28:33. bells of gold *between them* round about:
29:45. I will dwell *among* the children of Israel,
46. that I may dwell *among them :*
33:11. departed not *out of* the tabernacle.
36:33. middle bar to shoot *through* the boards
39: 3. to work (it) *in* the blue, *and in* the purple, *and in* the scarlet, *and in* the fine linen,
23. an hole *in the midst* (lit. *its midst*) of the
25. put the bells *between* the pomegranates
— round about *between* the pomegranates;
Lev.11:33. earthen vessel, *where*into (any) of them falleth (lit. into *the midst of it*), whatsoever (is) *in it* shall be unclean;
15:31. defile my tabernacle that (is) *among them.*
16:16. *in the midst of* their uncleanness.
29. a stranger that sojourneth *among you :*
17: 8. the strangers which sojourn *among you,*
10, 13. the strangers that sojourn *among you,*
12. any stranger that sojourneth *among you*
18:26. any stranger that sojourneth *among you :*
20:14. that there be no wickedness *among you.*
22:32. hallowed *among* the children of Israel:
24:10. went out *among* the children of Israel:
25:33. possession *among* the children of Israel.
26:11. set my tabernacle *among you :*
12. I will walk *among you,*
25. I will send the pestilence *among you ;*
Nu. 1:47. were not numbered *among them.*
49. sum of them *among* the children of Israel:
2:17. Levites *in the midst of* the camp:
33. not numbered *among* the children of
3:12. the Levites *from among* the children of
4: 2. *from among* the sons of Levi,
18. Kohathites *from among* the Levites:
5: 3. their camps, *in the midst whereof* I dwell.
21. a curse and an oath *among* thy people,
8: 6, 14. Levites *from among* the children of
16. given unto me *from among*
19. *from among* the children of Israel,
9: 7. appointed season *among* the children of
13:32. the people that we saw *in it* (are) men of
15:14. whosoever (be) *among you* in your
26, 29. stranger that sojourneth *among them ;*
16: 3. *and* the Lord (is) *among them :*
21. Separate yourselves *from among* this
33. perished *from among* the congregation.
45(17:10). Get you up *from among* this congregation,
47(—:12). into *the midst of* the congregation;
17: 6(21). the rod of Aaron (was) *among* their
18: 6. *from among* the children of Israel:
20. neither shalt thou have any part *among them :*
— inheritance *among* the children of Israel.
23. *that among* the children of Israel
24. *Among* the children of Israel they
19: 6. cast (it) into *the midst of*
10. stranger that sojourneth *among them,*
20. shall be cut off *from among* the
25: 7. rose up *from among* the congregation,
11. was zealous for my sake *among them,*
26:62. numbered *among* the children of Israel,
— given them *among* the children of Israel.
27: 3. he was not *in* the company of them
4. done away *from among* his family,
— *among* the brethren of our father.
7. an inheritance *among* their father's
32:30. they shall have possessions *among you*
33: 8. passed *through the midst of* the sea
35: 5. the city (shall be) *in the midst :*
15. for the sojourner *among them :*
34. shall inhabit, *wherein* I dwell:
— dwell *among* the children of Israel.
Deu 3:16. unto the river Arnon *half* the valley,
4:12. spake unto you *out of the midst of*
15. Horeb *out of the midst of* the fire:
33. speaking *out of the midst of* the fire,
36. thou heardest his words *out of the midst of*
5: 4. mount *out of the midst of* the fire,
22(19). assembly in the mount *out of the midst of*
23(20). voice *out of the midst of* the darkness,
24(21). voice *out of the midst of* the fire:
26(23). God speaking *out of the midst of* the
9:10. in the mount *out of the midst of*
10: 4. *out of the midst of* the fire in the day of
11: 3. which he did *in the midst of* Egypt

Deu 13:16(17). spoil of it into *the midst of* the street
19: 2. *in the midst of* thy land,
21:12. Then thou shalt bring her home to (lit. to *the midst of*) thine house;
22: 2. thou shalt bring it unto thine own house, (lit. unto *the midst of* thy house)
23:10(11). he shall not come *within* the camp: (lit. unto *the midst of* the camp)
11(12). he shall come *into* the camp (lit. unto *the midst of* the camp)
32:51. *among* the children of Israel
— ye sanctified me not *in the midst of*
Jos. 3:17. firm on dry ground *in the midst of* Jordan,
4: 3. Take you hence *out of the midst of*
5. Lord your God into *the midst of* Jordan,
8. twelve stones *out of the midst of* Jordan,
9. set up twelve stones *in the midst of*
10. stood *in the midst of* Jordan,
18. were come up *out of the midst of*
7:21. in the earth *in the midst of*
23. they took them *out of the midst of*
8: 9. Joshua lodged that night *among*
13. Joshua went that night *into the midst of*
22. so they were *in the midst* of Israel,
12: 2. *and* from *the middle of* the river,
13: 9. the city that (is) *in the midst of*
16. that (is) *in the midst of* the river,
14: 3. he gave none inheritance *among them.*
15:13. a part *among* the children of Judah,
16: 9. the children of Ephraim (were) *among*
17: 4. an inheritance *among* our brethren.
— gave them an inheritance *among* the brethren
6. had an inheritance *among* his sons:
9. cities of Ephraim (are) *among* the cities
19: 1. their inheritance was *within*
9. had their inheritance *within*
49. Joshua the son of Nun *among them:*
20: 9. stranger that sojourneth *among them,*
21:41(39). cities of the Levites *within* the
22:19. take possession *among us:*
31. perceive that the Lord (is) *among us,*
Jud. 7:16. lamps *within* the pitchers.
9:51. there was a strong tower *within*
12: 4. Ephraim *among* the Ephraimites, (and) *among* the Manassites.
15: 4. put a firebrand *in the midst*
16:29. Samson took hold of the two *middle*
18: 1. unto them *among* the tribes of Israel.
20:42. cities they destroyed *in the midst of them.*
1Sa. 7: 3. Ashtaroth *from among you,*
9:14. when they were come *into* the city,
18. Saul drew near to Samuel *in* the gate,
10:10. he prophesied *among them.*
23. when he stood *among* the people,
11:11. they came *into the midst of*
15: 6. get you down *from among*
— Kenites departed *from among*
18:10. he prophesied *in the midst of*
25:29. of *the middle of* a sling.
2Sa. 1:25. How are the mighty fallen *in the midst of*
3:27. Joab took him aside in the gate (lit. unto *the midst of* the gate)
4: 6. they came thither into *the midst of*
6:17. *in the midst of* the tabernacle
7: 2. the ark of God dwelleth *within* curtains.
20:12. blood *in the midst of* the highway.
23:12. he stood *in the midst of* the ground,
20. slew a lion *in the midst of* a pit
24: 5. the city that (lieth) *in the midst of*
1K. 3: 8. thy servant (is) *in the midst of*
20. she arose *at mid*night, (lit. *in the middle of* the night)
6:13. I will dwell *among* the children of Israel,
19. the oracle he prepared *in* the house
27. he set the cherubims *within*
— touched one another in *the midst of*
8:51. *from the midst of* the furnace
64. the king hallow *the middle of*
11:20. weaned *in* Pharaoh's house:
— *among* the sons of Pharaoh.
14. 7. as I exalted thee *from among* the people,
2K. 4:13. I dwell *among* mine own people.
6:20. *in the midst of* Samaria.
9: 2. arise up *from among* his brethren,
11: 2. stole him *from among* the king's sons
23: 9. unleavened bread *among* their brethren.

1Ch 11:14. they set themselves *in the midst of*
22. slew a lion *in* a pit
16: 1. set it *in the midst of* the tent
21: 6. Benjamin counted he not *among them*
2Ch 6:13. set it *in the midst of* the court:
7: 7. Solomon hallowed *the middle of*
20:14. *in the midst of* the congregation;
22:11. stole him *from among* the king's sons
23:20. they came *through* the high gate
32: 4. the brook that ran *through the midst of*
Neh 4:11(5). till we come in *the midst among them,*
22(16). with his servant lodge *within*
6:10. house of God, *within* (lit. unto *the midst of*) the temple,
7: 4. but the people (were) few *therein,*
9:11. they went *through the midst of*
Est. 4: 1. went out *into the midst of* the city,
9:28. should not fail *from among*
Job 1: 6 & 2:1. Satan came also *among them.* (marg. *in the midst of them*)
2: 8. he sat down *among* the ashes.
15:19. no stranger passed *among them.*
20:13. but keep it still *within* his mouth:
42:15. gave them inheritance *among* their
Ps. 22:14(15). it is melted *in the midst of* my bowels.
22(23). *in the midst of* the congregation
40: 8(9). thy law (is) *within* my heart. (marg. *in the midst of* my bowels)
10(11). hid thy righteousness *within*
57: 4(5). My soul (is) *among* lions:
6(7). *into the midst whereof* they are
68:25(26). *among* (them were) the damsels
109:30. *yea,* I will praise him *among*
116:19. *in the midst of thee,* O Jerusalem.
135: 9. wonders *into the midst of thee,* O Egypt,
136:11. brought out Israel *from among them:*
14. made Israel to pass *through the midst of it:*
137: 2. harps upon the willows *in the midst thereof.*
143: 4. my heart *within me* is desolate.
Pro. 1:14. Cast in thy lot *among us;*
4:21. keep them *in the midst of* thine heart.
5:14. in all evil *in the midst of* the congregation
15. running waters *out of* thine own well.
8:20. *in the midst of* the paths of judgment:
17: 2. *and* shall have part of the inheritance *among*
22:13. I shall be slain *in* the streets.
27:22. bray a fool in a mortar *among*
Cant. 3:10. *the midst thereof* being paved (with) love,
Isa. 5: 2. and built a tower *in the midst of it,*
6: 5. *and* I dwell *in the midst of* a people
7: 6. and set a king *in the midst of it,*
16: 3. as the night *in the midst of* the noonday;
19:19. *in the midst of* the land of Egypt,
24:13. it shall be in the midst of the land *among* the people,
18. that cometh up *out of the midst of* the pit
41:18. *and* fountains *in the midst of*
52:11. go ye out *of the midst of her;*
58: 9. take away *from the midst of thee*
61: 9. and their offspring *among* the people:
66:17. behind one (tree) *in the midst,*
Jer. 9: 6(5). Thine habitation (is) *in the midst of*
12:14. the house of Judah *from among them.*
16. built *in the midst of* my people.
21: 4. assemble them into *the midst of* this city.
29:32. have a man to dwell *among* this people;
37: 4. went out *among* the people:
12. *in the midst of* the people.
39: 3. sat in the *middle* gate,
14. so he dwelt *among* the people.
40: 1. bound in chains *among* all
5. dwell with him *among* the people:
6. dwelt with him *among* the people
41: 7. when they came into *the midst of*
— into *the midst of* the pit,
8. slew them not *among* their brethren.
44: 7. child and suckling, *out* (marg. *out of the midst*) *of* Judah,
50: 8. Remove *out of the midst of* Babylon,
37. people that (are) in *the midst of her;*
51: 6. Flee *out of the midst of* Babylon,
45. go ye *out of the midst of her,*
47. all her slain shall fall *in the midst of her*
63. cast it into *the midst of* Euphrates:
52:25. that were found *in the midst of* the city.
Eze. 1: 1. as I (was) *among* the captives

Eze. 1: 4. *and out of the midst thereof*
— *out of the midst of* the fire.
5. *Also out of the midst thereof*
16. as it were a wheel *in the middle of* a
2: 5. there hath been a prophet *among them.*
3:15. astonished *among them* seven days.
24. shut thyself *within* thine house.
25. thou shalt not go out *among them:*
5: 2. a third part *in the midst of* the city,
4. cast them into *the midst of* the fire,
5. I have set it *in the midst of* the nations
8. execute judgments *in the midst of thee*
10. shall eat the sons *in the midst of thee,*
12. they be consumed *in the midst of thee:*
6: 7. the slain shall fall *in the midst of you,*
13. their slain (men) shall be *among*
7: 4. abominations shall be *in the midst of thee:*
9. abominations (that) are *in the midst of thee;*
8:11. *in the midst of them* stood Jaazaniah
9: 2. one man *among them* (was) clothed
4. Go *through the midst of* the city, *through the midst of* Jerusalem,
— that be done *in the midst thereof.*
10:10. as if a wheel had been *in the midst of*
11: 1. *among whom* I saw Jaazaniah
7. slain whom ye have laid *in the midst of it,*
— will bring you forth *out of the midst of it.*
9. will bring you *out of the midst thereof,*
11. ye be the flesh *in the midst thereof;*
23. the Lord went up from *the midst of*
12: 2. thou dwellest *in the midst of* a
10. the house of Israel that (are) *among them.*
12. the prince that (is) *among them*
24. flattering divination *within* the house
13:14. shall be consumed *in the midst thereof:*
14: 8. cut him off *from the midst of* my people;
9. destroy him *from the midst of* my people
14. Noah, Daniel, and Job, were *in it,*
16. (Though) these three men (were) *in it,* (marg. *the midst of it*)
18. Though these three men (were) *in it,*
20. Noah, Daniel, and Job, (were) *in it,*
15: 4. *and the midst of it* is burned.
16:53. thy captives *in the midst of them:*
17:16. *in the midst of* Babylon
18:18. which (is) not good *among* his people,
19: 2. nourished her whelps *among* young lions.
6. he went up and down *among* the lions,
20: 8. *in the midst of* the land of Egypt.
9. heathen, *among whom* they (were),
21:32(37). blood shall be *in the midst of* the land;
22: 3. sheddeth blood *in the midst of it,*
7. *in the midst of thee* have they dealt
9. *in the midst of thee* they commit
13. blood which hath been *in the midst of thee.*
18. *in the midst of* the furnace;
19. I will gather you into *the midst of*
20. into *the midst of* the furnace,
21. ye shall be melted *in the midst thereof.*
22. melted *in the midst of* the furnace, so shall ye be melted *in the midst thereof;*
25. prophets *in the midst thereof,*
— many widows *in the midst thereof.*
26. I am profaned *among them.*
23:39. they done *in the midst of* mine house.
24: 5. seethe the bones of it *therein.*
7. For her blood is in *the midst of her;*
11. the filthiness of it may be molten *in it,*
26: 5. spreading of nets *in the midst of*
12. thy dust *in the midst of* the water.
15. slaughter is made *in the midst of thee?*
27:27. company which (is) *in the midst of thee,*
32. the destroyed *in the midst of* the sea?
34. company *in the midst of thee* shall fall.
28:14. walked up and down *in the midst of*
16. they have filled *the midst of thee*
— *from the midst of* the stones
18. bring forth a fire *from the midst of thee,*
22. I will be glorified *in the midst of thee:*
23. shall be judged *in the midst of her*
29: 3. the great dragon that lieth *in the midst of*
4. bring thee up *out of the midst of* thy rivers,
12. Egypt desolate *in the midst of* the
— her cities *among* the cities
21. opening of the mouth *in the midst of them;*
30: 7. desolate *in the midst of* the countries

Eze.30: 7. her cities shall be *in the midst of*
31:14. *in the midst of* the children
17. his shadow *in the midst of* the heathen.
18. thou shalt lie *in the midst of* the
32:20. They shall fall *in the midst of*
21. speak to him *out of the midst of* hell
25. set her a bed *in the midst of*
— put *in the midst of* (them that be) slain.
28. thou shalt be broken *in the midst of*
32. he shall be laid *in the midst of*
33:33. that a prophet hath been *among them.*
34:12. in the day that he is *among* his sheep
24. my servant David a prince *among them;*
36:23. ye have profaned *in the midst of them;*
37: 1. set me down *in the midst of* the valley
26. will set my sanctuary *in the midst of them*
28. when my sanctuary shall be *in the midst of them*
39: 7. holy name known *in the midst of*
43: 7. where I will dwell *in the midst of*
9. I will dwell *in the midst of them*
44: 9. any stranger that (is) *among* the children of Israel.
46:10. the prince *in the midst of them,*
47:22. strangers that sojourn *among you,* which shall beget children *among you:*
— *among* the tribes of Israel.
48: 8. sanctuary shall be *in the midst of it.*
10. the Lord shall be *in the midst thereof.*
15. the city shall be *in the midst thereof.*
21. the house (shall be) *in the midst thereof.*
22. *in the midst* (of that) which is the prince's,
Am. 3: 9. great tumults *in the midst thereof,*
6: 4. calves *out of the midst of* the stall;
Mic. 2:12. as the flock *in the midst of* their fold:
3: 3. as flesh *within* the caldron.
7:14. *in the midst of* Carmel:
Zep. 2:14. flocks shall lie down *in the midst of her,*
Hag. 2: 5. so my spirit remaineth *among you:*
Zec. 2: 4(8). multitude of men and cattle *therein:*
5(9). will be the glory *in the midst of her.*
10(14), 11(15). I will dwell *in the midst of thee,*
5: 4. it shall remain *in the midst of*
7. that sitteth *in the midst of* the ephah.
8. he cast it into *the midst of* the ephah;
8: 3. will dwell *in the midst of* Jerusalem:
8. shall dwell *in the midst of* Jerusalem:

תּוֹךְ see תֹּךְ See 8496

תּוֹכֵחָה *tōh-chēh-ghāh'*, f. 8433

2K. 19: 3. a day of trouble, *and of rebuke,*
Ps. 149: 7. *punishments* upon the people;
Isa. 37: 3. a day of trouble, *and of rebuke,*
Hos. 5: 9. Ephraim shall be desolate in the day of *rebuke:*

תּוֹכַחַת *tōh-chah'-ghath*, f. 8433

Job 13: 6. Hear now *my reasoning,*
23: 4. fill my mouth with *arguments.*
Ps. 38:14(15). in whose mouth (are) no *reproofs.*
39:11(12). When thou *with rebukes* dost correct
73:14. *and chastened* (marg. *my chastisement* (was)) every morning.
Pro. 1:23. Turn you *at my reproof:*
25. *and* would none of *my reproof:*
30. they despised all *my reproof.*
3:11. neither be weary *of his correction:*
5:12. *and* my heart despised *reproof;*
6:23. *reproofs of* instruction (are) the way of
10:17. he that refuseth *reproof* erreth.
12: 1. he that hateth *reproof* (is) brutish.
13:18. he that regardeth *reproof* shall be
15: 5. he that regardeth *reproof* is prudent.
10. he that hateth *reproof* shall die.
31. The ear that heareth *the reproof of* life
32. he that heareth *reproof* getteth understanding.
27: 5. Open *rebuke* (is) better than secret love.
29: 1. He that being *often reproved* (marg. A man of *reproofs*)
15. The rod *and reproof* give wisdom:

Eze. 5:15. *and in* furious *rebukes.*
25:17. *with* furious *rebukes ;*
Hab 2: 1. when *I am reproved.* (marg. upon *my reproof*)

8435 תּוֹלְדוֹת *tōh-l'dōhth'*, f. pl.

Gen 2: 4. These (are) *the generations of* the heavens
5: 1. *the generations of* Adam.
6: 9. *the generations of* Noah:
10: 1. *the generations of* the sons of Noah,
32. *after their generations,* in their nations:
11:10. *the generations of* Shem:
27. *the generations of* Terah:
25:12. *the generations of* Ishmael,
13. names, *according to their generations.*
19. *the generations of* Isaac,
36: 1, 9. *the generations of* Esau,
37: 2. *the generations of* Jacob.
Ex. 6:16. of Levi *according to their generations ;*
19. Levi *according to their generations.*
28:10. stone, *according to their birth.*
Nu. 1:20, 22, 24, 26, 28, 30, 32, 34, 36, 38, 40. the children of...by *their generations,*
42. throughout *their generations,*
3: 1. *the generations of* Aaron
Ru. 4:18. *the generations of* Pharez:
1Ch 1:29. These (are) *their generations:*
5: 7. the genealogy *of their generations*
7: 2. men of might *in their generations ;*
4. And with them, *by their generations,*
9. after their genealogy *by their generations,*
8:28. the fathers, *by their generations,*
9: 9. their brethren, *according to their generations,*
34. chief *throughout their generations ;*
26:31. *according to the generations* of his fathers.

8437 תּוֹלָל [*tōh-lāhl'*], m.

Ps.137: 3. *and they that wasted us* (marg. *laid us on heaps*)

8438 תּוֹלָע *tōh-lāh^{n}g'*, m.

Ex. 16:20. and it bred *worms,* and stank:
Isa. 1:18. though they be red *like crimson,*
Lam.4: 5. they that were brought up in *scarlet*

8438 תּוֹלֵעָה *tōh-lēh-^{n}gāh'*, & תּוֹלַעַת *tōh-lah'-^{n}gath*, f.

[3] שְׁנִי תוֹלַעַת [2] תּוֹלַעַת שָׁנִי

Ex. 25: 4. blue, and purple, *and scarlet,*[2]
26: 1, 31, 36 & 27:16. blue, and purple, *and scarlet :*[2]
28: 5. *scarlet,*[2] and fine linen.
6. *scarlet,*[2] and fine twined linen,
8. blue, and purple, *and scarlet,*[2]
15. *and* (of) *scarlet,*[2] and (of) fine twined
33. *and* (of) *scarlet,*[2] round about the hem
35: 6, 23. blue, and purple, *and scarlet,*[2]
25. blue, and of purple, (and) of *scarlet,*[2]
35. in blue, and in purple, *in scarlet,*[2]
36: 8. *and scarlet :*[2] (with) cherubims of cunning
35. *and scarlet,*[2] and fine twined linen:
37. blue, and purple, *and scarlet,*[2]
38:18. blue, and purple, *and scarlet,*[2]
23. *and in scarlet,*[2] and fine linen.
39: 1. purple, *and scarlet,*[2] they made cloths of
2. *and scarlet,*[2] and fine twined linen.
3. in *the scarlet,*[2] and in the fine linen,
5. blue, and purple, *and scarlet,*[2]
8. *and scarlet,*[2] and fine twined linen.
24. blue, and purple, *and scarlet,*[2]
29. purple, *and scarlet,*[2] (of) needlework ;
Lev.14: 4. cedar wood, and *scarlet,*[3]
6. the cedar wood, *and the scarlet,*[3]
49. cedar wood, and *scarlet,*[3] and hyssop:
51. the hyssop, and *the scarlet,*[3]
52. the hyssop, and with *the scarlet :*[3]
Nu. 4: 8. spread upon them a cloth of *scarlet,*[2]
19: 6. cedar wood, and hyssop, and *scarlet,*[3]
Deu28:39. *the worms* shall eat them.
Job 25: 6. the son of man, (which is) *a worm?*
Ps. 22: 6(7). But I (am) *a worm,* and no man ;
Isa. 14:11. and *the worms* cover thee.
41:14. Fear not, *thou worm* Jacob,
66:24. for *their worm* shall not die,
Jon. 4: 7. But God prepared *a worm*

תּוֹעֵבָה *tōh-^{n}gēh-vāh'*, f. 8441

Gen43:32. (is) *an abomination* unto the Egyptians.
46:34. every shepherd (is) *an abomination unto*
Ex. 8:26(22). *the abomination of* the Egyptians
—(—). *the abomination of* the Egyptians
Lev.18:22. with womankind: it (is) *abomination.*
26. not commit (any) of these *abominations ;*
27. all these *abominations* have the men
29. shall commit any of these *abominations,*
30. not (any one) of these *abominable* customs
20:13. of them have committed *an abomination:*
Deu 7:25. for it (is) *an abomination to* the Lord
26. Neither shalt thou bring *an abomination*
12:31. for every *abomination to* (marg. *of*) the
13:14(15). such *abomination* is wrought
14: 3. Thou shalt not eat any *abominable thing.*
17: 1. *an abomination unto* the Lord
4. such *abomination* is wrought in Israel:
18: 9. *after the abominations of* those nations
12. these things (are) *an abomination unto* the Lord: and because of these *abominations*
20:18. you not to do after all *their abominations,*
22: 5. all that do so (are) *abomination unto* the
23:18(19). both these (are) *abomination unto*
24: 4. that (is) *abomination* before the Lord:
25:16. unrighteously, (are) *an abomination unto*
27:15. molten image, *an abomination unto*
32:16. *with abominations* provoked they him
1K. 14:24. all *the abominations of* the nations
2K 16: 3. *according to the abominations of*
21: 2. *after the abominations of* the heathen,
11. Judah hath done these *abominations,*
23:13. Milcom *the abomination of* the children
2Ch 28: 3. *after the abominations of* the heathen
33: 2. *like unto the abominations of* the heathen,
34:33. Josiah took away all *the abominations*
36: 8. *and his abominations* which he did,
14. all *the abominations of* the heathen ;
Ezr. 9: 1. *according to their abominations,*
11. lands, *with their abominations,*
14. the people of these *abominations?*
Ps. 88: 8(9). thou hast made me *an abomination*
Pro. 3:32. the froward (is) *abomination to* the Lord:
6:16. seven (are) *an abomination unto* him: (marg. *of* his soul)
8: 7. *and* wickedness (is) *an abomination to* (marg. *the abomination of*) my lips.
11: 1. false balance (is) *abomination to* the Lord:
20. are of a froward heart (are) *abomination to*
12:22. Lying lips (are) *abomination to*
13:19. *but* (it is) *abomination to* fools
15: 8. wicked (is) *an abomination to* the Lord:
9. way of the wicked (is) *an abomination unto*
26. of the wicked (are) *an abomination to*
16: 5. proud in heart (is) *an abomination to*
12. *an abomination to* kings to commit
17:15. both (are) *abomination to* the Lord.
20:10. both of them (are) alike *abomination to*
23. Divers weights (are) *an abomination unto*
21:27. sacrifice of the wicked (is) *abomination:*
24: 9. *and* the scorner (is) *an abomination* to men.
26:25. for (there are) seven *abominations*
28: 9. even his prayer (shall be) *abomination.*
29:27. An unjust man (is) *an abomination to*
— *and* (he that is) upright in the way (is) *abomination to*
Isa. 1:13. incense is *an abomination* unto me ;
41:24. *an abomination* (is he that) chooseth you.
44:19. make the residue thereof *an abomination?*
Jer. 2: 7. made mine heritage *an abomination.*
6:15. when they had committed *abomination?*
7:10. delivered to do all these *abominations?*
8:12. when they had committed *abomination?*
16:18. detestable *and abominable things.*
32:35. do this *abomination,* to cause Judah to sin.

Jer. 44: 4. Oh, do not this *abominable thing*
22. *abominations* which ye have committed;
Eze. 5: 9. because of all *thine abominations.*
11. with all *thine abominations,*
6: 9. have committed in all *their abominations.*
11. Alas for all *the* evil *abominations*
7: 3. recompense upon thee all *thine abominations.*
4. *and thine abominations* shall be in the midst
8. recompense thee for all *thine abominations.*
9. according to thy ways *and thine abominations*
20. made the images of *their abominations*
8: 6. *abominations* that the house of Israel
—, 13, 15. thou shalt see greater *abominations.*
9. wicked *abominations* that they do
17. Judah that they commit *the abominations*
9: 4. that cry for all *the abominations*
11:18. all *the abominations thereof*
21. detestable things *and their abominations,*
12:16. they may declare all *their abominations*
14: 6. faces from all *your abominations.*
16: 2. cause Jerusalem to know *her abominations,*
22. in all *thine abominations*
36. with all the idols of *thy abominations,*
43. lewdness above all *thine abominations.*
47. *nor* done *after their abominations:*
50. were haughty, and committed *abomination*
51. thou hast multiplied *thine abominations*
— in all *thine abominations*
58. borne thy lewdness and *thine abominations,*
18:12. the idols, hath committed *abomination,*
13. hath done all these *abominations;*
24. doeth according to all *the abominations*
20: 4. cause them to know *the abominations*
22: 2. thou shalt shew her all *her abominations.*
11. committed *abomination* with his neighbour's wife;
23:36. declare unto them *their abominations;*
33:26. ye work *abomination,* and ye defile every
29. desolate because of all *their abominations*
36:31. iniquities and for *your abominations.*
43: 8. defiled my holy name *by their abominations*
44: 6. suffice you of all *your abominations,*
7. because of all *your abominations.*
13. bear their shame, *and their abominations*
Mal 2:11. *and an abomination* is committed in Israel

8442 **תּוֹעָה** *tōh-gāh′*, f.

Neh 4: 8(2). to fight against Jerusalem, and to *hinder* it. (marg. make *an error* to it)
Isa. 32: 6. to utter *error* against the Lord,

8443 **תּוֹעָפוֹת** *tōh-gāh-phōhth′*, f. pl.

Nu. 23:22 & 24:8. he hath *as it were the strength of* an
Job 22:25. thou shalt have *plenty* of silver. (marg. silver of *strength*)
Ps. 95: 4. *the strength* (marg. or, *heights*) *of* the hills (is) his *also.*

8444 **תּוֹצָאוֹת** *tōh-tzāh-ōhth′*, f. pl.

Nu. 34: 4. *the going forth thereof* shall be from the
5. *the goings out of it* shall be at the sea.
8. *the goings forth of* the border
9. *the goings out of it* shall be at Hazar-enan:
12. *the goings out of it* shall be at the salt sea:
Jos. 15: 4. *the goings out of* that coast
7. *the goings out thereof* were at En-rogel:
11. *the goings out of* the border
16: 3. *the goings out thereof* are at the sea.
8. *the goings out thereof* were at the sea.
17: 9. *the outgoings of it* were at the sea:
18. *the outgoings of it* shall be thine:
18:12. *the goings out thereof* were at the wilderness
14. *the goings out thereof* were at Kirjath-baal,
19. *the outgoings of* the border
19:14. *the outgoings thereof* are in the valley
22. *the outgoings of* their border were at
29. *the outgoings thereof* are at the sea
33. *the outgoings thereof* were at Jordan:
1Ch 5:16. they dwelt...upon *their borders.* (marg. *goings forth*)
Ps. 68:20(21). unto God...(belong) *the issues* from death.
Pro. 4:23. out of it (are) *the issues of* life.
Eze. 48:30. *the goings out of* the city

תּוֹר *tōhr*, m. 8449

Gen 15: 9. *and a turtledove,* and a young pigeon.
Lev. 1:14. bring his offering of *turtledoves,*
5: 7. two *turtledoves,* or two young pigeons,
11. be not able to bring two *turtledoves,*
12: 6. a young pigeon, or *a turtledove,*
8. then she shall bring two *turtles,*
14:22. two *turtledoves,* or two young pigeons,
30. he shall offer the one of *the turtledoves,*
15:14. he shall take to him two *turtledoves,*
29. she shall take unto her two *turtles,*
Nu. 6:10. eighth day he shall bring two *turtles,*
Ps. 74:19. O deliver not the soul of *thy turtledove*
Cant 2:12. the voice of *the turtle* is heard
Jer. 8: 7. *and the turtle* and the crane

תּוֹר *tōhr*, m. 8447

Est. 2:12. when every maid's *turn* was come
15. Now when *the turn of* Esther,
Cant 1:10. Thy cheeks are comely *with rows*
11. We will make thee *borders of* gold

תּוֹר *tōhr*, m. 8448

1Ch 17:17. regarded me *according to the estate of* a man

תּוֹר [*tōhr*], Ch. m. 8450

Ezr. 6: 9. both young *bullocks,* and rams,
17. an hundred *bullocks,*
7:17. buy speedily with this money *bullocks,*
Dan 4:25(22), 32(29). shall make thee to eat grass *as oxen,*
33(30). and did eat grass *as oxen,*
5:21. they fed him with grass *like oxen,*

תּוּר *toor.* 8446

* KAL.—*Preterite.* *

Nu. 13:32. the land which *they had searched*
14:34. days in which *ye searched* the land,
Ecc. 2: 3. *I sought* in mine heart to give
Eze. 20: 6. into a land that *I had espied*

KAL.—*Infinitive.*

Nu. 10:33. *to search out* a resting place
13:16. which Moses sent *to spy out* the land.
17. Moses sent them *to spy out*
25. they returned *from searching*
32. which we have gone *to search*
14: 7. which we passed through *to search it,*
36. which Moses sent *to search* the land,
38. men that went *to search* the land,
Deu 1:33. *to search* you out a place
Ecc. 1:13. *and search out* by wisdom
7:25. *and to search,* and to seek

KAL.—*Future.*

Nu. 13: 2. *that they may search* the land
21. *and searched* the land
15:39. *ye seek* not after your own heart

KAL.—*Participle.* Poel.

Nu. 14: 6. of them *that searched* the land,
1K. 10:15. of the *merchant*men,
2Ch 9:14. Beside (that which) *chapmen*

* HIPHIL.—*Future.* *

Jud. 1:23. *And* the house of Joseph *sent to descry*
Pro. 12:26. The righteous *is* more *excellent* (marg. or, *abundant*)

8451-52 **תּוֹרָה** *tōh-rāh*, f.

Gen 26: 5. my statutes, *and my laws.*
Ex. 12:49. One *law* shall be to him that is homeborn,
13: 9. that the Lord's *law* may be in thy mouth:
16: 4. whether they will walk *in my law*, or no.
28. my commandments *and my laws?*
18:16. I do make (them) know the statutes of God, and *his laws.*
20. thou shalt teach them ordinances *and laws*,
24:12. I will give thee tables of stone, *and a law*,
Lev. 6: 9(2). This (is) *the law of* the burnt offering:
14(7). this (is) *the law of* the meat offering:
25(18). This (is) *the law of* the sin offering:
7: 1. this (is) *the law of* the trespass offering:
7. (there is) one *law* for them:
11. this (is) *the law of* the sacrifice
37. This (is) *the law* of the burnt offering,
11:46. This (is) *the law of* the beasts,
12: 7. This (is) *the law for* her
13:59. This (is) *the law of* the plague
14: 2. This shall be *the law of* the leper
32. This (is) *the law* (of him) in whom
54. This (is) *the law* for all manner of plague
57. this (is) *the law of* leprosy.
15:32. This (is) *the law of* him that hath an issue,
26:46. the statutes and judgments *and laws*,
Nu. 5:29. This (is) *the law of* jealousies,
30. priest shall execute upon her all this *law.*
6:13, 21. this (is) *the law of* the Nazarite,
21. he must do after *the law of* his separation.
15:16. One *law* and one manner shall be for you,
29. Ye shall have one *law* for him
19: 2. This (is) the ordinance of *the law*
14. This (is) *the law*, when a man dieth in a
31:21. This (is) the ordinance of *the law*
Deu 1: 5. began Moses to declare this *law*,
4: 8. judgments (so) righteous as all this *law*,
44. And this (is) *the law*
17:11. According to the sentence of *the law*
18. he shall write him a copy of this *law*
19. to keep all the words of this *law*
27: 3. upon them all the words of this *law*,
8. the stones all the words of this *law*
26. (all) the words of this *law*
28:58. to do all the words of this *law*
61. written in the book of this *law*,
29:21(20). written in this book of *the law:*
29(28). that (we) may do all the words of this *law.*
30:10. written in this book of *the law*,
31: 9. Moses wrote this *law*,
11. thou shalt read this *law*
12. all the words of this *law:*
24. writing the words of this *law*
26. Take this book of *the law*,
32:46. to do, all the words of this *law.*
33: 4. Moses commanded us *a law*,
10. They shall teach...*and* Israel *thy law:*
Jos. 1: 7. according to all *the law*,
8. This book of *the law* shall not depart
8:31. the book of *the law of* Moses,
32. a copy of *the law of* Moses,
34. all the words of *the law*,
— written in the book of *the law.*
22: 5. take diligent heed to do the commandment and *the law*,
23: 6. the book of *the law of* Moses,
24:26. the book of *the law of* God,
2Sa. 7:19. (is) this *the manner* (marg. *law*) *of* man,
1K. 2: 3. as it is written *in the law of* Moses,
2K. 10:31. to walk *in the law of* the Lord God
14: 6. the book of *the law of* Moses,
17:13. according to all *the law*
34. *or after the law* and commandment
37. *and the law*, and the commandment,
21: 8. according to all *the law*
22: 8. I have found the book of *the law*
11. the words of the book of *the law*,
23:24. that he might perform the words of *the law*
25. according to all *the law of* Moses;
1Ch 16:40. *in the law of* the Lord,
22:12. that thou mayest keep *the law of*
2Ch 6:16. to walk *in my law*,
12: 1. he forsook *the law of* the Lord,
14: 4(3). to do *the law* and the commandment.
2Ch 15: 3. without a teaching priest, and without *law.*
17: 9. the book of *the law of* the Lord
19:10. between *law* and commandment,
23:18. as (it is) written *in the law of* Moses,
25: 4. as (it is) written *in the law*
30:16. *according to the law of* Moses
31: 3. as (it is) written *in the law of* the Lord.
4. encouraged *in the law of* the Lord.
21. *and in the law*, and in the commandments,
33: 8. according to *the* whole *law* and the statutes
34:14. the priest found a book of *the law of*
15. I have found the book of *the law*
19. the king had heard the words of *the law*,
35:26. *in the law of* the Lord,
Ezr. 3: 2. *in the law of* Moses the man of God.
7: 6. a ready scribe *in the law of* Moses,
10. to seek *the law of* the Lord,
10: 3. *and* let it be done *according to the law.*
Neh. 8: 1. the book of *the law of* Moses,
2. Ezra the priest brought *the law*
3. the book of *the law.*
7. caused the people to understand *the law:*
8. So they read in the book *in the law of* God
9. they heard the words of *the law.*
13. to understand the words of *the law.*
14. they found written *in the law*
18. he read in the book of *the law of* God.
9: 3. read in the book of *the law of* the Lord
13. them right judgments, *and* true *laws*,
14. commandedst them precepts, statutes, *and laws*,
26. cast *thy law* behind their backs,
29. that thou mightest bring them again unto *thy law:*
34. kept *thy law*, nor hearkened unto thy commandments
10:28(29). *unto the law of* God,
29(30). entered...into an oath, to walk *in* God's *law*,
34(35), 36(37). as (it is) written *in the law:*
12:44. the portions of *the law*
13: 3. when they had heard *the law*,
Job 22:22. Receive, I pray thee, *the law* from his
Ps. 1: 2. delight (is) *in the law of* the Lord; *and in his law* doth he meditate day and night.
19: 7(8). *The law* (marg. or, *doctrine*) *of* the Lord (is) perfect,
37:31. *The law of* his God (is) in his heart;
40: 8(9). *yea, thy law* (is) within my heart.
78: 1. Give ear, O my people, (to) *my law:*
5. *and* appointed *a law* in Israel,
10. *and* refused to walk *in his law;*
89:30(31). his children forsake *my law*,
94:12. *and* teachest him *out of thy law;*
105:45. That they might observe his statutes, *and* keep *his laws.*
119: 1. who walk *in the law of* the Lord.
18. wondrous things *out of thy law.*
29. *and* grant me *thy law* graciously.
34. I shall keep *thy law;*
44. So shall I keep *thy law*
51. (yet) have I not declined *from thy law.*
53. the wicked that forsake *thy law.*
55. and have kept *thy law.*
61. I have not forgotten *thy law.*
70. I delight in *thy law.*
72. *The law of* thy mouth (is) better
77. *thy law* (is) my delight.
85. (are) not *after thy law.*
92. Unless *thy law* (had been) my delights,
97. O how love I *thy law!*
109. *yet* do I not forget *thy law.*
113. *but thy law* do I love.
126. they have made void *thy law.*
136. they keep not *thy law.*
142. *and thy law* (is) the truth.
150. they are far *from thy law.*
153. I do not forget *thy law.*
163. *thy law* do I love.
165. Great peace have they which love *thy law:*
174. *and thy law* (is) my delight.
Pro. 1: 8. forsake not *the law of* thy mother:
3: 1. My son, forget not *my law;*
4: 2. forsake ye not *my law.*
6:20. forsake not *the law of* thy mother:
23. the commandment (is) a lamp; *and the law* (is) light;

Pro. 7: 2. *and my law* as the apple of thine eye.
13:14. *The law of* the wise (is) a fountain of
28: 4. They that forsake *the law* praise the wicked: but such as keep *the law* contend with them.
7. Whoso keepeth *the law* (is) a wise son:
9. He that turneth away his ear from hearing *the law*,
29:18. he that keepeth *the law*,
31:26. *and* in her tongue (is) *the law of* kindness.
Isa. 1:10. give ear unto *the law of* our God,
2: 3. out of Zion shall go forth *the law*,
5:24. they have cast away *the law of* the Lord
8:16. seal *the law* among my disciples.
20. *To the law* and to the testimony:
24: 5. they have transgressed *the laws*,
30: 9. children (that) will not hear *the law of*
42: 4. *and* the isles shall wait *for his law*.
21. he will magnify *the law*,
24. neither were they obedient *unto his law*.
51: 4. *a law* shall proceed from me,
7. the people in whose heart (is) *my law*;
Jer. 2: 8. they that handle *the law* knew me not:
6:19. have not hearkened unto my words, *nor to my law*,
8: 8. *and the law of* the Lord (is) with us?
9:13(12). they have forsaken *my law*
16:11. have not kept *my law*;
18:18. *the law* shall not perish
26: 4. to walk *in my law*,
31:33. I will put *my law* in their inward parts,
32:23. *neither* walked *in thy law*;
44:10. nor walked *in my law*,
23. *nor* walked *in his law*,
Lam. 2: 9. *the law* (is) no (more);
Eze. 7:26. *but the law* shall perish from the priest,
22:26. Her priests have violated *my law*,
43:11. all the forms thereof, and all *the laws thereof*:
12, 12. This (is) *the law of* the house;
44: 5. of the Lord, and all *the laws thereof*;
24. they shall keep *my laws*
Dan 9:10. to walk *in his laws*, which he set before
11. all Israel have transgressed *thy law*,
— *in the law of* Moses the servant of God,
13. As (it is) written *in the law of* Moses,
Hos. 4: 6. seeing thou hast forgotten *the law of* thy God,
8: 1. trespassed against *my law*.
12. the great things of *my law*,
Am. 2: 4. they have despised *the law of* the Lord,
Mic. 4: 2. *the law* shall go forth of Zion,
Hab. 1: 4. Therefore *the law* is slacked,
Zep. 3: 4. they have done violence to *the law*.
Hag. 2:11. Ask now the priests (concerning) *the law*,
Zec. 7:12. lest they should hear *the law*,
Mal. 2: 6. *The law of* truth was in his mouth,
7. *and* they should seek *the law* at his mouth:
8. have caused many to stumble *at the law*;
9. have been partial *in the law*.
4: 4(3:22). Remember ye *the law of* Moses

8453 **תּוֹשָׁב** *tōh-shāhv'*, m.

Gen23: 4. I (am) a stranger *and a sojourner* with
Ex. 12:45. *A foreigner* and an hired servant
Lev. 22:10. *a sojourner of* the priest,
25: 6. *and for thy stranger* that sojourneth with
23. strangers *and sojourners* with me.
35. (though he be) a stranger, *or a sojourner*;
40. as an hired servant, (and) *as a sojourner*,
45. of *the strangers* that do sojourn among you,
47. *or stranger* wax rich by thee,
— the stranger (or) *sojourner* by thee,
Nu. 35:15. *and for the sojourner* among them:
1K. 17: 1. *of the inhabitants of* Gilead,
1Ch 29:15. (are) strangers before thee, *and sojourners*,
Ps. 39:12(13). *a sojourner*, as all my fathers (were).

8454 **תּוּשִׁיָּה** *too-sheey-yāh'*, f.

Job 5:12. cannot perform (their) *enterprise*. (marg. or, *any thing*)
6:13. *and is wisdom* driven quite from me?
11: 6. (they are) double *to that which is*!
12:16. With him (is) strength *and wisdom*:
26: 3. *and*...plentifully declared *the thing as it is*?
30:22. dissolvest my *substance*. (marg. or, *wisdom*)
Pro. 2: 7. He layeth up *sound wisdom*
3:21. keep *sound wisdom* and discretion:
8:14. Counsel (is) mine, *and sound wisdom*:
18: 1. intermeddleth with all *wisdom*.
Isa. 28:29. excellent in *working*.
Mic. 6: 9. *and* (the man of) *wisdom* shall see thy name: (marg. or, thy name shall see *that which is*)

תּוֹתָח *tōh-thāh'gh'*, m. 8455

Job 41:29(21). *Darts* are counted as stubble:

תָּזַז [*tāh-zaz'*]. 8456

* HIPHIL.—*Preterite.* *

Isa. 18: 5. *cut down* the branches.

תַּזְנוּת *taz-nooth'*, f. 8457

Eze. 16:15. pouredst out *thy fornications*
20. (Is this) *of thy whoredoms* a small matter,
22. thine abominations *and thy whoredoms*
25. multiplied *thy whoredoms*.
26. hast increased *thy whoredoms*,
29. hast moreover multiplied *thy fornication*
33. on every side *for thy whoredom*.
34. (other) women *in thy whoredoms*,
36. discovered *through thy whoredoms*
23: 7. Thus she committed *her whoredoms*
8. Neither left she *her whoredoms*
— poured *their whoredom* upon her.
11. *and in her whoredoms* more than
14. she increased *her whoredoms*:
17. they defiled her *with their whoredom*,
18. So she discovered *her whoredoms*,
19. Yet she multiplied *her whoredoms*,
29. both thy lewdness *and thy whoredoms*.
35. also thy lewdness and *thy whoredoms*.
43. they now commit *whoredoms with her*,

תַּחְבֻּלוֹת *tagh-boo-lōhth'*, f. pl. 8458

Job 37:12. turned round about *by his counsels*:
Pro. 1: 5. shall attain unto *wise counsels*:
11:14. Where no *counsel* (is), the people fall:
12: 5. *the counsels of* the wicked (are) deceit.
20:18. *and with good advice* make war.
24: 6. *by wise counsel* thou shalt make thy war:

תְּחוֹת *t'ghōhth*, Ch. prep. 8460

Jer. 10:11. and from *under* these heavens.
Dan 4:12(9). beasts of the field had shadow *under it*,
21(18). *under which* the beasts of the field
7:27. the greatness of the kingdom *under* the whole heaven,

תְּחִלָּה *t'ghil-lāh'*, f. 8462

Gen 13: 3. his tent had been *at the beginning*,
41:21. still ill favoured, as *at the beginning*.
43:18. in our sacks *at the first time*
20. we came indeed down *at the first time*
Jud. 1: 1. go up for us against the Canaanites *first*,
20:18. Which of us shall go up *first*
— the Lord said, Judah (shall go up) *first*.
Ru. 1:22. *in the beginning of* barley harvest.
2Sa. 17: 9. when some of them be overthrown *at the first*,
21: 9. *in the beginning of* barley harvest.
10. *from the beginning of* harvest
2K. 17:25. was *at the beginning of* their dwelling
Ezr. 4: 6. reign of Ahasuerus, *in the beginning of*
Neh 11:17. to *begin* the thanksgiving in prayer:
Pro. 9:10. fear of the Lord (is) *the beginning of*
Ecc. 10:13. *The beginning of* the words
Isa. 1:26. counsellors *as at the beginning*,

Dan 8: 1. appeared unto me *at the first.*
9:21. had seen in the vision *at the beginning,*
23. *At the beginning of* thy supplications
Hos. 1: 2. *The beginning of* the word of the Lord
Am. 7: 1. grasshoppers *in the beginning of*

8463 **תַּחֲלֻאִים** *tah-ghăloo-eem'*, m. pl.

Deu 29:22(21). *the sicknesses* (lit. *the sicknesses thereof*) which the Lord hath laid upon
2Ch 21:19. so he died *of* sore *diseases.*
Ps. 103: 3. who healeth all *thy diseases;*
Jer. 14:18. behold *them that are sick with* famine!
16: 4. They shall die of *grievous* deaths;

8464 **תַּחְמָס** *tagh-māhs'*, m.

Lev. 11:16. the owl, and *the night hawk,*
Deu 14:15. the owl, and *the night hawk,*

8467 **תְּחִנָּה** *t'ghin-nāh'*, f.

Jos. 11:20. that they might have no *favour,*
1K. 8:28. thy servant, and to *his supplication,*
30. hearken thou to *the supplication of*
38. What prayer and *supplication* soever
45, 49. their prayer and *their supplication,*
52. unto *the supplication of* thy servant, and unto *the supplication of* thy people
54. all this prayer *and supplication*
9: 3. heard thy prayer and *thy supplication,*
2Ch 6:19. and to *his supplication,* O Lord
29. what *supplication* soever shall be made
35. their prayer and *their supplication,*
39. their prayer and *their supplications,*
33:13. heard *his supplication,*
Ezr. 9: 8. now for a little space *grace* hath
Ps. 6: 9(10). The Lord hath heard *my supplication;*
55: 1(2). hide not thyself *from my supplication.*
119:170. Let *my supplication* come before
Jer. 36: 7. they will present *their supplication*
37:20. let *my supplication,* I pray thee,
38:26. I presented *my supplication*
42: 2. *our supplication* be accepted
9. present *your supplication* before him;
Dan 9:20. presenting *my supplication* before the Lord

8469 **תַּחֲנוּנִים** *tah-ghănoo-neem'*, m. pl.

2Ch 6:21. Hearken therefore unto *the supplications of*
Job 41: 3(40:27). Will he make many *supplications*
Ps. 28: 2. Hear the voice of *my supplications,*
6. hath heard the voice of *my supplications.*
31:22(23). heardest the voice of *my supplications*
116: 1. heard my voice (and) *my supplications.*
130: 2. attentive to the voice of *my supplications.*
140: 6(7). hear the voice of *my supplications,*
143: 1. give ear to *my supplications:*
Pro. 18:23. The poor useth *intreaties;*
Jer. 3:21. weeping (and) *supplications of*
31: 9. *and with supplications* (marg. or, *favours*) will I lead
Dan 9: 3. seek by prayer *and supplications,*
17. thy servant, and *his supplications,*
18. we do not present *our supplications*
23. At the beginning of *thy supplications*
Zec. 12:10. spirit of grace *and of supplications:*

8469 **תַּחֲנוּנוֹת** *tah-ghănoo-nōhth'*, f. pl.

Ps. 86: 6. attend to the voice of *my supplications.*

8466 **תַּחֲנֹת** *tah-ghănōhth'*, f. pl.

2K. 6: 8. such a place (shall be) *my camp.* (marg. or, *encamping*)

תַּחְרָא *tah-ghărāh'*, f. 8473

Ex. 28:32. as it were the hole of *an habergeon,*
39:23. robe, as the hole of *an habergeon,*

תַּחֲרָה see **חָרָה** 8474

תַּחַשׁ *tah'-ghash*, m. 8476

Ex. 25: 5. *badgers'* skins, and shittim wood,
26:14. a covering above (of) *badgers'* skins.
35: 7. dyed red, and *badgers'* skins,
23. red skins of rams, and *badgers'* skins,
36:19. a covering (of) *badgers'* skins
39:34. the covering of *badgers'* skins,
Nu. 4: 6. the covering of *badgers'* skins,
8. with a covering of *badgers'* skins,
10. within a covering of *badgers'* skins,
11. with a covering of *badgers'* skins,
12. a covering of *badgers'* skins,
14. upon it a covering of *badgers'* skins,
25. the covering of *the badgers' skins*
Eze. 16:10. shod thee with *badgers'* skin,

תַּחַת *tah'-ghath*, part. prep. 8478

Gen 4:25. another seed *instead of* Abel,
7:19. hills, that (were) *under* the whole heaven,
22:13. a burnt offering *in the stead of* his son.
30:15. to night *for* thy son's mandrakes.
Ex. 21:26. let him go free *for* his eye's *sake.*
32:19. and brake them *beneath* the mount.
Lev. 14:42. and put (them) in *the place of* those
2Sa. 19:13(14). continually *in the room of* Joab.
1Ch 29:24. submitted themselves *unto* (marg. gave the hand *under*) Solomon
Job 30:14. *in* the desolation they rolled themselves
34:26. He striketh them *as* wicked men
Ps. 66:17. he was extolled *with* my tongue.
Isa. 60:15. *Whereas* thou hast been forsaken
Jer. 3: 6. and *under* (וְאֶל תַּחַת) every green tree,
5:19. Where*fore* (תַּחַת מֶה) doeth the Lord
&c. &c.

With prefix as, מִתַּחַת

Gen 1: 7. waters which (were) *under* the firmament
6:17. of life, *from under* heaven;
Deu 4:18. in the waters *beneath* the earth:
&c.

לְמִתַּחַת

1K. 7:32. And *under* the borders (were) four wheels;

With pronominal suffixes the sense is rarely affected; the following passages however may be noticed:—

Jos. 6: 5. the wall of the city shall fall down *flat,* (marg. *under it*)
2Sa. 2:23. and died *in the same place:*
Job 36:16. broad place, *where* (there is) no straitness;
Jer. 38: 9. to die for hunger *in the place where he is:*
Eze. 23: 5. played the harlot *when she was mine;*

For the use of תַּחַת אֲשֶׁר see אֲשֶׁר

תַּחַת [*tah'-ghath*], Ch. prep. 8479

Dan 4:14(11). let the beasts get away from *under it,*

תַּחְתּוֹן *tagh-tōhn'*, adj. 8481

Jos. 16: 3. the coast of Beth-horon *the nether,*
18:13. the south side of the *nether* Beth-horon.
1K. 6: 6. The *nethermost* chamber (was) five
9:17. Gezer, and Beth-horon *the nether,*
1Ch 7:24. who built Beth-horon *the nether,*
2Ch 8: 5. the upper, and Beth-horon *the nether,*
Isa. 22: 9. the waters of the *lower* pool.
Eze. 40:18. gates (was) the *lower* pavement.
19. from the forefront of the *lower* gate
41: 7. so increased (from) *the lowest*

Eze.42: 5. the galleries were higher than these, *than the lower,*
6. (the building) was straitened *more than the lowest*
43:14. from the bottom (upon) the ground (even) to the *lower* settle

8482 תַּחְתִּי [*tagh-tee'*], adj.

Gen 6:16. *lower*, second, and third
Ex. 19:17. they stood *at the nether part of*
Deu32:22. shall burn unto the *lowest* hell,
Jos. 15:19. upper springs, and the *nether* springs.
Jud. 1:15. and the *nether* springs.
2Sa.24: 6. the land of *Tahtim*-hodshi; (marg. or, *nether* land newly inhabited)
Neh. 4:13(7). Therefore set I in the *lower* places
Job 41:24(16). as a piece of *the nether* (millstone).
Ps. 63: 9(10). shall go into *the lower parts of*
86:13. delivered my soul from the *lowest* hell.
88: 6(7). Thou hast laid me in the *lowest* pit,
139:15. curiously wrought *in the lowest parts*
Isa. 44:23. shout, ye *lower parts of* the earth:
Lam.3:55. out of the *low* dungeon.
Eze.26:20. shall set thee in *the low parts* of
31:14. to *the nether parts* (lit. *lower*) of the earth,
16. comforted in *the nether parts* of the earth.
18. unto *the nether parts* of the earth:
32:18. unto *the nether parts* of the earth,
24. into *the nether parts* of the earth,

8484 תִּיכוֹן *tee-chohn'*, adj.

Ex. 26:28. the *middle* bar in the midst of
36:33. And he made the *middle* bar
Jud. 7:19. in the beginning of the *middle* watch;
1K. 6: 6. *and the middle* (was) six cubits
8. The door for the *middle* chamber
— winding stairs into the *middle* (chamber), and out of the *middle* into the third.
2K. 20: 4. was gone out into the *middle* court,
Eze.41: 7. to the highest *by the midst.*
42: 5. *and than the middlemost of*
6. the lowest *and the middlemost* from
47:16. Hazar-*hatticon* (marg. or, the *middle* village), which (is) by the

8486 תֵּימָן *tēh-māhn'*, com.

Ex. 26:18. twenty boards on the south side *southward.*
35. the side of the tabernacle *toward the south:*
27: 9. for the south side *southward*
36:23. twenty boards for the south side *southward:*
38: 9. on the south side *southward*
Nu. 2:10. *On the south side* (shall be) the standard
3:29. the side of the tabernacle *southward.*
10: 6. the camps that lie on *the south side*
Deu 3:27. northward, *and southward,*
Jos. 12: 3. *and from the south*, under Ashdoth-pisgah:
13: 4. *From the south*, all the land of
15: 1. the uttermost part of the *south* coast.
Job 9: 9. the chambers of *the south.*
39:26. stretch her wings *toward the south?*
Ps. 78:26. by his power he brought in *the south wind.*
Cant.4:16. come, thou *south;* blow upon my garden,
Isa. 43: 6. *and to the south*, Keep not back:
Eze.20:46(21:2). set thy face toward *the south,*
47:19. And the south side *southward,*
— (this is) the *south* side southward.
48:28. the south side *southward,*
Hab. 3: 3. God came *from Teman*, (marg. or, *the south*)
Zec. 6: 6. go forth toward the *south* country.
9:14. shall go with whirlwinds of *the south.*

8490 תִּימְרוֹת *tee-m'rohth'*, f. pl.

Cant.3: 6. out of the wilderness *like pillars of* smoke,
Joel 2:30(3:3). blood, and fire, *and pillars of* smoke.

8492 תִּירוֹשׁ *tee-rohsh'*, m.

Gen27:28. plenty of corn *and wine:*
37. with corn *and wine* have I sustained him:
Nu. 18:12. all the best of *the wine,*
Deu 7:13. thy corn, *and thy wine*, and thine oil,
11:14. that thou mayest gather in thy corn, *and thy wine,*
12:17. the tithe of thy corn, *or of thy wine,*
14:23. the tithe of thy corn, of *thy wine,*
18: 4. firstfruit (also) of thy corn, of *thy wine,*
28:51. not leave thee (either) corn, *wine*, or oil,
33:28. a land of corn *and wine;*
Jud. 9:13. Should I leave *my wine,*
2K. 18:32. a land of corn *and wine,*
2Ch 31: 5. the firstfruits of corn, *wine*, and oil,
32:28. the increase of corn, *and wine*, and oil;
Neh. 5:11. the corn, *the wine*, and the oil,
10:37(38). of *wine* and of oil,
39(40). the corn, of *the new wine*, and the oil,
13: 5. the corn, *the new wine*, and the oil,
12. *and the new wine* and the oil
Ps. 4: 7(8). their corn *and their wine* increased.
Pro. 3:10. *and* thy presses shall burst out *with new wine.*
Isa. 24: 7. *The new wine* mourneth, the vine
36:17. a land of corn *and wine,*
62: 8. the sons of the stranger shall not drink *thy wine,*
65: 8. As *the new wine* is found in the cluster,
Jer. 31:12. for wheat, and for *wine*, and for oil,
Hos. 2: 8(10). *and wine* (marg. *new wine*), and oil,
9(11). *and my wine* in the season thereof,
22(24). the earth shall hear the corn, and *the wine*, and the oil;
4:11. Whoredom and wine *and new wine* take away the heart.
7:14. assemble themselves for corn *and wine,*
9: 2. *and the new wine* shall fail in her.
Joel 1:10. *the new wine* is dried up,
2:19. I will send you corn, *and wine*, and oil,
24. the fats shall overflow with *wine* and oil.
Mic. 6:15. *and sweet wine*, but shalt not drink
Hag. 1:11. upon *the new wine*, and upon the oil,
Zec. 9:17. *and new wine* the maids.

תַּיִשׁ [*tah'-yish*], m. 8495

Gen30:35. he removed that day *the he goats*
32:14(15). Two hundred she goats, *and* twenty *he goats,*
2Ch 17:11. *and* seven thousand and seven hundred *he goats.*
Pro.30:31. A greyhound; *an he goat*

תֹּךְ *tohch*, m. 8496

Ps. 10: 7. full of cursing and deceit *and fraud:*
55:11(12). *deceit* and guile depart not from her
72:14. shall redeem their soul *from deceit*

תָּכָה [*tāh-chāh'*]. 8497

* PUAL.—*Preterite.* *

Deu33: 3. they *sat down* at thy feet;

תְּכוּנָה [*t'choo-nāh'*], f. 8499

Job 23: 3. I might come (even) to *his seat!*

תְּכוּנָה *t'choo-nāh'*, f. 8498

Eze.43:11. the house, *and the fashion thereof,*
Nah 2: 9(10). (there is) none end *of the store*

תֻּכִּיִּים *took-keey-yeem'*, m. pl. 8500

1K. 10:22. ivory, and apes, *and peacocks.*
2Ch 9:21. ivory, and apes, *and peacocks.*

תְּכָכִים *t'chāh-cheem'*, m. pl. 8501

Pro.29:13. The poor and the *deceitful* man (marg. or, *usurer;* lit. of *oppressions*)

8502 **תִּכְלָה** *tich-lāh'*, f.

Ps. 119:96. I have seen an end of all *perfection:*

8503 **תַּכְלִית** *tach-leeth'*, f.

Neh 3:21. to *the end of* the house of Eliashib.
Job 11: 7. find out the Almighty unto *perfection?*
26:10. until the day and night come to *an end.*
28: 3. and searcheth out all *perfection:*
Ps. 139:22. I hate them with *perfect* hatred:

8504 **תְּכֵלֶת** *t'chēh'-leth*, f.

Ex. 25: 4. *And blue*, and purple, and scarlet,
26: 1. fine twined linen, *and blue*,
4. thou shalt make loops of *blue*
31. thou shalt make a vail (of) *blue*,
36. for the door of the tent, (of) *blue*,
27:16. an hanging of twenty cubits, (of) *blue*,
28: 5. they shall take gold, and *blue*,
6. make the ephod (of) gold, (of) *blue*,
8. gold, (of) *blue*, and purple,
15. thou shalt make it; (of) gold, (of) *blue*,
28. the ephod with a lace of *blue*,
31. make the robe of the ephod all (of) *blue*.
33. thou shalt make pomegranates (of) *blue*,
37. thou shalt put it on a *blue* lace,
35: 6. *And blue*, and purple, and scarlet,
23. with whom was found *blue*,
25. they had spun, (both) of *blue*,
35. the embroiderer, *in blue*,
36: 8. fine twined linen, *and blue*,
11. he made loops of *blue* on the edge
35. he made a vail (of) *blue*,
37. hanging for the tabernacle door (of) *blue*,
38:18. the court (was) needlework, (of) *blue*,
23. an embroiderer *in blue*,
39: 1. *the blue*, and purple, and scarlet,
2. made the ephod (of) gold, *blue*,
3. wires, to work (it) in *the blue*,
5, 8. gold, *blue*, and purple,
21. the ephod with a lace of *blue*,
22. the ephod (of) woven work, all (of) *blue*.
24. hems of the robe pomegranates (of) *blue*,
29. fine twined linen, *and blue*,
31. they tied unto it a lace of *blue*,
Nu. 4: 6. spread over (it) a cloth wholly of *blue*,
7. they shall spread a cloth of *blue*,
9. they shall take a cloth of *blue*,
11. spread a cloth of *blue*, and cover it
12. put (them) in a cloth of *blue*,
15:38. fringe of the borders a ribband of *blue:*
2Ch 2: 7(6). in purple, and crimson, *and blue*,
14(13). *in blue*, and in fine linen,
3:14. he made the vail (of) *blue*,
Est. 1: 6. white, green, *and blue*, (marg. or, *violet*)
8:15. in royal apparel of *blue* (marg. *id.*) and
Jer. 10: 9. *blue* and purple (is) their clothing:
Eze. 23: 6. clothed with *blue*, captains and rulers,
27: 7. *blue* and purple (marg. or, *purple* and scarlet) from the isles
24. in *blue* clothes, and broidered work,

8505 **תָּכַן** [*tāh-chan'*].

* KAL.—*Participle.* Poel. *

Pro. 16: 2. *but* the Lord *weigheth* the spirits.
21: 2. *but* the Lord *pondereth* the hearts.
24:12. doth not *he that pondereth* the heart

* NIPHAL.—*Preterite.* *

1Sa. 2: 3. by him actions *are weighed.*

NIPHAL.—*Future.*

Eze. 18:25. The way of the Lord *is* not *equal.* Hear now, O house of Israel; *Is* not my way *equal? are* not your ways un*equal?*
29. The way of the Lord *is* not *equal.* O house of Israel, *are* not my ways *equal? are* not your ways un*equal?*
33:17. The way of the Lord *is* not *equal:* but as for them, their way *is* not *equal.*
20. The way of the Lord *is* not *equal.*

* PIEL.—*Preterite.* *

Job 28:25. *he weigheth* the waters by measure.
Ps. 75: 3(4). *I bear up* the pillars of it.
Isa. 40:12. *meted* out heaven with the span,
13. Who *hath directed* the Spirit of the Lord,

* PUAL.—*Participle.* *

2K. 12:11(12). they gave the money, *being told*,

תֹּכֶן *tōh'-chen*, m. 8506

Ex. 5:18. *yet* shall ye deliver *the tale*
Eze 45:11. the bath shall be of one *measure*,

תָּכְנִית *toch-neeth'*, f. 8508

Eze. 28:12. Thou sealest up *the sum*,
43:10. let them measure *the pattern.* (marg. or, *sum*, or, *number*)

תַּכְרִיךְ *tach-reech'*, m. 8509

Est. 8:15. *and with a garment of* fine linen

תֵּל *tēhl*, m. 8510

Deu 13:16(17). it shall be *an heap* for ever;
Jos. 8:28. made it *an heap* for ever,
11:13. the cities that stood still in *their strength*, (marg. on *their heap*)
Jer. 30:18. the city shall be builded upon *her own heap*, (marg. or, *little hill*)
49: 2. it shall be *a* desolate *heap*,

תָּלָא [*tāh-lāh'*]. 8511

* KAL.—*Preterite.* *

2Sa. 21:12. where the Philistines *had hanged them*,

KAL.—*Participle.* Paül.

Deu 28:66. thy life *shall hang in doubt*
Hos 11: 7. my people *are bent* to backsliding

תְּלָאָה *t'lāh-āh'*, f. 8513

Ex. 18: 8. all *the travail* that had come upon them
Nu. 20:14. all *the travel* that hath befallen us:
Neh 9:32. let not all *the trouble* (marg. *weariness*)
Lam 3: 5. compassed (me) with gall *and travel.*

תַּלְאוּבֹת *tal-oo-vōhth'*, f. pl. 8514

Hos 13: 5. in the wilderness, in the land of *great drought.* (marg. *droughts*)

תִּלְבֹּשֶׁת *til-bōh'-sheth*, f. 8516

Isa. 59:17. the garments of vengeance (for) *clothing*,

תְּלַג *t'lag*, Ch. m. 8517

Dan 7: 9. whose garment (was) white *as snow*,

תָּלָה *tāh-lāh'*. 8518

* KAL.—*Preterite.* *

Gen 40:19. *and shall hang* thee on a tree;
22. But *he hanged* the chief baker:
41:13. unto mine office, and him *he hanged.*
Deu 21:22. *and thou hang* him on a tree:
Jos. 8:29. the king of Ai *he hanged* on a tree
2Sa. 21:12. (כתיב) the Philistines *had hanged them*,
Est. 8: 7. him *they have hanged* upon
9:14. *they hanged* Haman's ten sons.
25. *and that* he and his sons *should be hanged*
Ps. 137: 2. *We hanged* our harps upon the
Isa. 22:24. *And they shall hang* upon him

KAL.—*Infinitive.*

Est. 6: 4. *to hang* Mordecai on the gallows
Eze.15: 3. will (men) take a pin of it *to hang*

KAL.—*Imperative.*

Est. 7: 9. the king said, *Hang him* thereon.

KAL.—*Future.*

Jos. 10:26. *and hanged them* on five trees:
2Sa. 4:12. *and hanged* (them) up
Est. 5:14. *that* Mordecai *may be hanged*
7:10. *So they hanged* Haman on the gallows
9:13. *let* Haman's ten sons *be hanged* (marg. *let* men *hang*)

KAL.—*Participle.* Poel.

Job 26: 7. *hangeth* the earth upon nothing.

KAL.—*Participle.* Paül.

Deu 21:23. *he that is hanged* (is) accursed of God;
Jos. 10:26. they were *hanging* upon the trees
2Sa.18:10. I saw Absalom *hanged* in an oak.
Cant 4: 4. whereon there *hang* a thousand bucklers,

* NIPHAL.—*Preterite.* *

Lam 5:12. Princes *are hanged up* by their hand:

NIPHAL.—*Future.*

Est. 2:23. *therefore they were* both *hanged*

* PIEL.—*Preterite.* *

Eze.27:10. *they hanged* the shield and helmet
11. *they hanged* their shields upon

8522 ## תְּלִי [*t'lee*], m.

Gen 27: 3. thy weapons, *thy quiver* and thy bow,

8523 ## תְּלִיתַי [*t'lee-thah'y*], Ch. adj. ord.

Dan 2:39. and another *third* kingdom of brass,

8524 ## תָּלַל [*tāh-lal'*].

* KAL.—*Participle.* Paül. *

Eze.17:22. upon an high mountain *and eminent:*

8525 ## תֶּלֶם *teh'-lem*, m.

Job 31:38. *the furrows* likewise *thereof* complain;
39:10. the unicorn with his band *in the furrow?*
Ps. 65:10(11). Thou waterest *the ridges thereof*
Hos 10: 4. springeth up as hemlock in *the furrows of*
12:11(12). altars (are) as heaps in *the furrows of*

8527 ## תַּלְמִיד *tal-meed'*, m.

1Ch 25: 8. the teacher as *the scholar.*

8519 ## תְּלֻנּוֹת *t'loon-nōhth'*, f. pl.

Ex. 16: 7. he heareth *your murmurings*
8. the Lord heareth *your murmurings*
— *your murmurings* (are) not against us,
9. he hath heard *your murmurings.*
12. I have heard *the murmurings of*
Nu. 14:27. *the murmurings of* the children of Israel,
17: 5(20). *the murmurings of* the children of
10(25). take away *their murmurings*

8529 ## תָּלַע [*tāh-lag'*].

* PUAL.—*Participle.* *

Nah 2: 3(4). valiant men (are) in *scarlet:* (marg. or, *dyed*)

8530 ## תַּלְפִּיּוֹת *tal-peey-yōhth'*, f. pl.

Cant 4: 4. builded *for an armoury,*

תְּלָת *t'lāhth*, Ch. adj. num. 8532

Ezr. 6: 4. (With) *three* rows of great stones,
15. this house was finished on the *third* day of the month
Dan 3:23. And these *three* men, Shadrach,
24. Did not we cast *three* men bound
6: 2(3). And over these *three* presidents;
10(11). he kneeled upon his knees *three* times a day,
13(14). maketh his petition *three* times a day
7: 5. *and* (it had) *three* ribs in the mouth of it
8. before whom there were *three* of the first
20. and before whom *three* fell;
24. *and* he shall subdue *three* kings.

תְּלַת [*t'lath*], Ch. adj. ord. 8531

Dan 5:16. *and* shalt be the *third* ruler in the
29. that he should be the *third* ruler

תַּלְתִּי *tal-tee'*, Ch. adj. ord. 8523

Dan 5: 7. and shall be the *third* ruler

תְּלָתִין *t'lāh-theen'*, Ch. adj. num. pl. 8533

Dan 6: 7(8). of any God or man for *thirty* days,
12(13). of any God or man within *thirty* days,

תַּלְתַּלִּים *tal-tal-leem'*, m. pl. 8534

Cant 5:11. his locks (are) *bushy* (marg. or, *curled*), (and) black as a raven.

תָּם *tāhm*, adj. 8535

Gen 25:27. Jacob (was) a *plain* man,
Job 1: 1. that man was *perfect* and upright,
8 & 2:3. a *perfect* and an upright man,
8:20. God will not cast away a *perfect* (man).
9:20. I (am) *perfect*, it shall also prove me
21. (Though) I (were) *perfect*,
22. He destroyeth *the perfect* and the wicked.
Ps. 37:37. Mark *the perfect* (man),
64: 4(5). That they may shoot in secret at *the perfect:*
Pro.29:10. The bloodthirsty hate *the upright:*
Cant 5: 2. my love, *my* dove, my *undefiled:*
6: 9. My dove, *my undefiled* is (but) one;

תָּם [*tāhm*], Ch. adv. 8536

Ezr. 5:17. which (is) *there* at Babylon,
6: 1. *where* the treasures were laid up
6. be ye far from *thence:*
12. the God that hath caused his name to dwell *there*

תֹּם *tōhm*, m. 8537

Gen 20: 5. *in the integrity* (marg. or, *simplicity*, or *sincerity*) *of* my heart
6. thou didst this in *the integrity of*
Ex. 28:30. the Urim and *the Thummim;*
Lev. 8: 8. breastplate the Urim and *the Thummim.*
Deu 33: 8. (Let) *thy Thummim* and thy Urim
2Sa. 15:11. and they went *in their simplicity*,
1K. 9: 4. David thy father walked, *in integrity of*
22:34. a (certain) man drew a bow *at a venture*, (marg. *in his simplicity*)
2Ch 18:33. a (certain) man drew a bow *at a venture*, (marg. *id.*)
Ezr. 2:63. with Urim *and with Thummim.*
Neh. 7:65. a priest with Urim *and Thummim.*
Job 4: 6. hope, *and the uprightness of* thy ways?
21:23. One dieth in *his full* strength, (marg. very *perfection*)
Ps. 7: 8(9). *and according to mine integrity*
25:21. Let *integrity* and uprightness preserve me;
26: 1. for I have walked *in mine integrity:*

Ps. 26:11. I will walk *in mine integrity:*
41:12(13). thou upholdest me *in mine integrity,*
78:72. So he fed them *according to the integrity of*
101: 2. will walk within my house with a *perfect*
Pro. 2: 7. a buckler to them that walk *uprightly.*
10: 9. He that walketh *uprightly*
29. the Lord (is) strength to *the upright:*
13: 6. Righteousness keepeth (him that is) *upright in*
19: 1. the poor that walketh *in his integrity,*
20: 7. The just (man) walketh *in his integrity:*
28: 6. the poor that walketh *in his uprightness,*
Isa. 47: 9. come upon thee *in their perfection*

8538 תֻּמָּה [*toom-māh'*], f.

Job 2: 3. still he holdeth fast *his integrity,*
9. Dost thou still retain *thine integrity?*
27: 5. till I die I will not remove *mine integrity*
31: 6. that God may know *mine integrity.*
Pro. 11: 3. *The integrity of* the upright

8539 תָּמַהּ [*tāh-mah'*].

* KAL.—*Preterite.* *

Ps. 48: 5(6). They saw (it, and) so *they marvelled;*

KAL.—*Imperative.*

Isa. 29: 9. Stay yourselves, *and wonder;*
Hab. 1: 5. regard, and wonder *marvellously:*

KAL.—*Future.*

Gen 43:33. *and* the men *marvelled* one at another.
Job 26:11. *and are astonished* at his reproof.
Ecc. 5: 8(7). *marvel* not at the matter:
Isa. 13: 8. *they shall be amazed* one at another;
Jer. 4: 9. the prophets *shall wonder.*

* HITHPAEL.—*Imperative.* *

Hab. 1: 5. regard, *and wonder* marvellously:

8540 תְּמַהּ [*t'mah*], Ch.

Dan 4: 2(3:32). to shew the signs *and wonders*
3(–:33). *and* how mighty (are) *his wonders!*
6:27(28). he worketh signs *and wonders*

8541 תִּמָּהוֹן *tim-māh-hōhn'*, m.

Deu28:28. *and astonishment of* heart:
Zec 12: 4. smite every horse *with astonishment,*

8543 תְּמוֹל *t'mōhl*, adv.

Gen 31: 2. it (was) not toward him *as before.* (marg. *as yesterday* and the day before)
5. it (is) not toward me *as before;* (lit. *id.*)
Ex. 4:10. neither *heretofore,* nor since (marg. *since yesterday,* nor since the third day)
5: 7. straw to make brick, *as heretofore:* (lit. *as yesterday* the third day)
8. which they did make *heretofore,* (lit. *yesterday* the third day)
14. task in making brick both *yesterday* and to day, *as heretofore?* (lit. *as yesterday* the third day)
21:29. wont to push with his horn *in time past,* (lit. *from yesterday* the third day)
36. ox hath used to push *in time past,* (lit. *from yesterday* the third day)
Deu 4:42. hated him not *in times past;* (lit. *from yesterday* the third day)
19: 4. whom he hated not *in time past;* (marg. *from yesterday* the third day)
6. inasmuch as he hated him not *in time past.* (marg. *from yesterday* the third day)
Jos. 3: 4. ye have not passed (this) way *heretofore.* (marg. *since yesterday* and the third day)
4:18. all his banks, *as* (they did) *before.* (lit. *as yesterday* the third day)
20: 5. hated him not *beforetime.* (lit. *from yesterday* the third day)
Ru. 2:11. people which thou knewest not *heretofore.* lit. *yesterday* the third day)
1Sa. 20:27. neither *yesterday,* nor to day?
21: 5(6). kept from us *about these* three *days,* (lit. *as yesterday* the third day)
2Sa. 3:17. Ye sought for David in *times past* (marg. both *yesterday* and the third day)
15:20. Whereas thou camest (but) *yesterday,*
2K. 13: 5. Israel dwelt in their tents, *as beforetime.* (marg. *as yesterday,* (and) third day)
1Ch 11: 2. moreover in *time past,* (marg. *yesterday* and the third day)
Job 8: 9. For we (are but of) *yesterday,*

תְּמוּנָה *t'moo-nāh'*, f. 8544

Ex. 20: 4. any *likeness* (of any thing)
Nu. 12: 8. *and the similitude of* the Lord
Deu 4:12. ye heard the voice...*but* saw no *similitude;*
15. ye saw no manner of *similitude*
16. *the similitude of* any figure,
23, 25. *the likeness of* any (thing),
5: 8. (any) *likeness* (of any thing)
Job 4:16. *an image* (was) before mine eyes,
Ps. 17:15. I shall be satisfied,...with *thy likeness.*

תְּמוּרָה *t'moo-rāh'*, f. 8545

Lev. 27:10. *and the exchange thereof* shall be holy.
33. *and the change thereof* shall be holy;
Ru. 4: 7. redeeming and concerning *changing,*
Job 15:31. vanity shall be *his recompence.*
20:18. according to (his) substance (shall) *the restitution* (marg. *his exchange*) (be),
28:17. *and the exchange of it* (shall not be)

תְּמוּתָה *t'moo-thāh'*, f. 8546

Ps. 79:11. those that are appointed to *die;* (marg. children of *death*)
102:20(21). those that are appointed to *death;* (marg. *id.*)

תָּמִיד *tāh-meed'*, m. 8548

Ex. 25:30. table shewbread before me *alway.*
27:20. to cause the lamp to burn *always.*
28:29. a memorial before the Lord *continually.*
30. heart before the Lord *continually.*
38. it shall be *always* upon his forehead,
29:38. of the first year day by day *continually.*
42. a *continual* burnt offering
30: 8. a *perpetual* incense before
Lev. 6:13(6). The fire shall *ever* be burning
20(13). for a meat offering *perpetual,*
24: 2. to cause the lamps to burn *continually.*
3. morning before the Lord *continually:*
4. candlestick before the Lord *continually.*
8. in order before the Lord *continually,*
Nu. 4: 7. the *continual* bread shall be thereon:
16. the *daily* meat offering,
9:16. So it was *alway:* the cloud covered
28: 3. (for) a *continual* burnt offering.
6. (It is) a *continual* burnt offering,
10, 15, 24. beside the *continual* burnt offering
23. which (is) for a *continual* burnt offering.
31. beside the *continual* burnt offering,
29: 6. the *daily* (lit. *continual*) burnt offering,
11. and the *continual* burnt offering,
16, 19, 22, 25, 28, 31, 34, 38. beside the *continual* burnt offering,
Deu 11:12. eyes of the Lord thy God (are) *always*
2Sa. 9: 7. eat bread at my table *continually.*
10. shall eat bread *alway* at my table.
13. he did eat *continually* at the king's table;
1K. 10: 8. which stand *continually* before thee,
2K. 4: 9. which passeth by us *continually.*
25:29. he did eat bread *continually*
30. his allowance (was) a *continual*
1Ch 16: 6. with trumpets *continually* before the ark
11. seek his face *continually.*
37. to minister before the ark *continually,*
40. altar of the burnt offering *continually*
23:31. *continually* before the Lord:
2Ch 2: 4(3). for the *continual* shewbread,
9: 7. which stand *continually* before thee,
24:14. in the house of the Lord *continually*

Ezr. 3: 5. the *continual* burnt offering,
Neh 10:33(34). for the *continual* meat offering, and for the *continual* burnt offering,
Ps. 16: 8. I have set the Lord *always* before me:
25:15. Mine eyes (are) *ever* toward the Lord;
34: 1(2). his praise (shall) *continually*
35:27. let them say *continually*,
38:17(18). my sorrow (is) *continually* before me.
40:11(12). thy truth *continually* preserve me.
16(17). say *continually*, The Lord be
50: 8. (to have been) *continually* before me.
51: 3(5). my sin (is) *ever* before me.
69:23(24). make their loins *continually* to shake.
70: 4(5). say *continually*, Let God be magnified.
71: 3. whereunto I may *continually* resort:
6. my praise (shall be) *continually* of thee.
14. But I will hope *continually*,
72:15. shall be made for him *continually*;
73:23. I (am) *continually* with thee:
74:23. that rise up against thee increaseth *continually*.
105: 4. seek his face *evermore*.
109:15. Let them be before the Lord *continually*,
19. girdle wherewith he is girded *continually*.
119:44. So shall I keep thy law *continually*
109. My soul (is) *continually* in my hand:
117. have respect unto thy statutes *continually*.
Pro. 5:19. be thou ravished *always* with her love.
6:21. Bind them *continually* upon thine heart,
15:15. a merry heart (hath) a *continual* feast.
28:14. Happy (is) the man that feareth *alway*:
Isa. 21: 8. I stand *continually* upon the watchtower
49:16. thy walls (are) *continually* before me.
51:13. hast feared *continually* every day
52: 5. *and* my name *continually* every day
58:11. the Lord shall guide thee *continually*,
60:11. thy gates shall be open *continually*;
62: 6. shall *never* hold their peace (lit. not *ever*)
65: 3. that provoketh me to anger *continually*
Jer. 6: 7. before me *continually* (is) grief
52:33. he did *continually* eat bread
34. there was a *continual* diet given
Eze.38: 8. which have been *always* waste:
39:14. sever out men of *continual employment*, (marg. *continuance*)
46:14. a meat offering *continually* by a
15. a *continual* burnt offering.
Dan 8:11. by him the *daily* (sacrifice) was taken
12. given (him) against the *daily* (sacrifice)
13. the vision (concerning) the *daily*
11:31. shall take away the *daily* (sacrifice),
12:11. the *daily* (sacrifice) shall be taken
Hos 12: 6(7). wait on thy God *continually*.
Obad. 16. shall all the heathen drink *continually*,
Nah 3:19. not thy wickedness passed *continually*?
Hab 1:17. *and* not spare *continually* to slay

8549 ## תָּמִים *tāh-meem'*, adj.

Gen 6: 9. Noah was a just man (and) *perfect* (marg. or, *upright*)
17: 1. walk before me, and be thou *perfect*. (marg. or, *upright*, or, *sincere*)
Ex. 12: 5. Your lamb shall be *without blemish*,
29: 1. two rams *without blemish*,
Lev. 1: 3. let him offer a male *without blemish*:
10. bring it a male *without blemish*.
3: 1, 6. he shall offer it *without blemish*
9. the fat thereof, (and) the *whole* rump,
4: 3. a young bullock *without blemish*
23. goats, a male *without blemish*:
28. goats, a female *without blemish*,
32. he shall bring it a female *without blemish*.
5:15. a ram *without blemish* out of the flocks,
18. he shall bring a ram *without blemish*
6: 6(5:25). a ram *without blemish* out of the flock,
9: 2. for a burnt offering, *without blemish*,
3. of the first year, *without blemish*,
14:10. take two he lambs *without blemish*,
— ewe lamb of the first year *without blemish*,
22:19. at your own will a male *without blemish*,
21. it shall be *perfect* to be accepted;
23:12. an he lamb *without blemish*
15. seven sabbaths shall be *complete*:
18. seven lambs *without blemish*
Lev.25:30. redeemed within the space of a *full* year,
Nu. 6:14. one he lamb of the first year *without blemish*
— ewe lamb of the first year *without blemish*
— and one ram *without blemish*
19: 2. bring thee a red heifer *without spot*,
28: 3. two lambs of the first year *without spot*
9. two lambs of the first year *without spot*,
11. seven lambs of the first year *without spot*;
19, 31. they shall be unto you *without blemish*:
29: 2. seven lambs of the first year *without blemish*:
8. they shall be unto you *without blemish*:
13. they shall be *without blemish*:
17, 26. fourteen lambs of the first year *without spot*:
20, 23, 29, 32. fourteen lambs of the first year *without blemish*;
36. seven lambs of the first year *without blemish*:
Deu18:13. Thou shalt be *perfect* with the Lord (marg. or, *upright*, or, *sincere*)
32: 4. (He is) the Rock, his work (is) *perfect*:
Jos. 10:13. hasted not to go down about a *whole* day
24:14. serve him *in sincerity* and in truth:
Jud. 9:16. if ye have done truly *and sincerely*,
19. If ye then have dealt truly *and sincerely*
1Sa.14:41. Lord God of Israel, Give a *perfect* (lot). (marg. or, Shew *the innocent*)
2Sa.22:24. I was also *upright* before him,
26. with the *upright* man thou
31. (As for) God, his way (is) *perfect*;
33. he maketh my way *perfect*.
Job 12: 4. the just *upright* (man is) laughed
36: 4. *he that is perfect in* knowledge
37:16. *him which is perfect in* knowledge?
Ps. 15: 2. He that walketh *uprightly*,
18:23(24). I was also *upright* before him,
25(26). with an *upright* man
30(31). (As for) God, his way (is) *perfect*:
32(33). maketh my way *perfect*.
19: 7(8). The law of the Lord (is) *perfect*,
37:18. The Lord knoweth the days of *the upright*:
84:11(12). will he withhold from them that walk *uprightly*.
101: 2. will behave myself wisely in a *perfect* way.
6. he that walketh in a *perfect* way,
119: 1. Blessed (are) *the undefiled* (marg. or, *perfect*, or, *sincere*) *in* the way,
80. Let my heart be *sound* in thy statutes;
Pro. 1:12. *and whole*, as those that go down
2:21. *and the perfect* shall remain in it.
11: 5. The righteousness of *the perfect*
20. *but* (such as are) *upright in* (their) way
28:10. *but the upright* shall have good
18. Whoso walketh *uprightly* shall be saved:
Eze.15: 5. when it was *whole*, it was meet
28:15. Thou (wast) *perfect* in thy ways
43:22. offer a kid of the goats *without blemish*
23. a young bullock *without blemish*, and a ram out of the flock *without blemish*.
25. a ram out of the flock, *without blemish*.
45:18. take a young bullock *without blemish*,
23. seven rams *without blemish*
46: 4. six lambs *without blemish*, and a ram *without blemish*.
6. a young bullock *without blemish*,
— they shall be *without blemish*.
13. a lamb of the first year *without blemish*:
Am. 5:10. they abhor him that speaketh *uprightly*.

תַּמִּים *tam-meem'*, m. pl. 8382

Ex. 26:24. they shall be *coupled together* above
36:29. *coupled together* at the head thereof,

תָּמַךְ [*tāh-mach'*]. 8551

* KAL.—*Preterite.* *

Ex. 17:12. Aaron and Hur *stayed up* his hands,
Ps. 41:12(13). *thou upholdest* me in mine integrity,
63: 8(9). thy right hand *upholdeth* me.
Pro.31:19. her hands *hold* the distaff.
Isa. 41:10. *I will uphold thee* with the right hand

KAL.—*Infinitive.*

Ps. 17: 5. *Hold up* my goings in thy paths,
Isa. 33:15. shaketh his hands *from holding*

KAL.—*Future.*

Gen 48:17. *and he held up* his father's hand,
Job 36:17. judgment and justice *take hold* (marg. or, *should uphold*) (on thee).
Pro. 4: 4. *Let* thine heart *retain* my words:
5: 5. her steps *take hold* on hell.
11:16. A gracious woman *retaineth* honour: and strong (men) *retain* riches.
28:17. *let* no man *stay* him.
29:23. but honour *shall uphold* the humble
Isa. 42: 1. Behold my servant, whom *I uphold;*

KAL.—*Participle.* Poel.

Ps. 16: 5. thou *maintainest* my lot.
Pro. 3:18. *and* happy (is every one) *that retaineth her.*
Am. 1: 5, 8. *and him that holdeth* the sceptre

* NIPHAL.—*Future.* *

Pro. 5:22. *he shall be holden* with the cords

8552 תָּמַם [*tāh-mam'*].

* KAL.—*Preterite.* *

Gen 47:18. how that our money *is spent;*
Lev. 26:20. *And* your strength *shall be spent*
Nu. 17:13(28). *shall we be consumed* with dying?
Deu 2:16. when all the men of war *were consumed*
Jos. 3:16. the plain, (even) the salt sea, *failed,*
17. people *were* passed *clean* over Jordan. (lit. *had finish*ed to pass over)
4: 1. people *were clean* passed over Jordan, (lit. *had finish*ed to pass over)
11. people *were clean* passed over, that (lit. *had finish*ed to pass over)
5: 8. when they *had done* circumcising all the people, (marg. the people *had made an end* to be circumcised)
1Sa. 16:11. *Are here all* (thy) children?
2K. 7:13. the Israelites that *are consumed:*
Job 31:40. The words of Job *are ended.*
Ps. 9: 6(7). destructions *are come to a* perpetual *end:*
64: 6(7). *they accomplish* a diligent search:
73:19. *they are* utterly *consumed*
Isa. 16: 4. oppressors *are consumed* out
Jer. 6:29. the lead *is consumed* of the fire;
44:12. *and they shall* all *be consumed,*
18. *have been consumed* by the sword
27. land of Egypt *shall be consumed*
Lam 3:22. Lord's mercies that *we are* not *consumed,*
4:22. of thine iniquity *is accomplished,*

KAL.—*Infinitive.*

Lev. 25:29. he may redeem it within a *whole* year (lit. until the year *be finished*)
Nu. 14:33. until your carcases *be wasted*
32:13. evil in the sight of the Lord, *was consumed.*
Deu 2:14. until...the men of war *were wasted*
15. until *they were consumed.*
31:24. law in a book, until *they were finished,*
30. this song, until *they were ended.*
Jos. 4:10. until every thing *was finished*
5: 6. which came out of Egypt, *were consumed,*
8:24. the sword, until *they were consumed,*
10:20. slaughter, till *they were consumed,*
2Sa. 15:24. until all the people *had done* passing
1K. 6:22. until he *had finished* all the house:
14:10. taketh away dung, till *it be all gone.*
Isa. 18: 5. *when* the bud *is perfect,*
Jer. 1: 3. unto *the end of* the eleventh year
24:10. till *they be consumed* from off the land
27: 8. until *I have consumed* them
36:23. until all the roll *was consumed*
37:21. until all the bread in the city *were spent.*

KAL.—*Future.*

Gen 47:15. And *when* money *failed*
18. *When* that year *was ended,*
Deu 34: 8. *so* the days of weeping...*were ended.*
1K. 7:22. *so was* the work of the pillars *finished.*
Ps. 19:13(14). then *shall I be upright,*
Eze. 24:11. the scum of it *may be consumed.*
47:12. *shall* the fruit thereof *be consumed:*

* NIPHAL.—*Future.* *

Nu. 14:35. wilderness *they shall be consumed,*
Ps. 102:27(28). thy years *shall have* no *end.*
104:35. *Let* the sinners *be consumed*
Jer. 14:15. *shall* those prophets *be consumed.*
44:12. *they shall* (even) *be consumed* by the sword

* HIPHIL.—*Preterite.* *

2Sa. 20:18. so *they ended* (the matter).
Eze. 22:15. *and will consume* thy filthiness

HIPHIL.—*Infinitive.*

Isa. 33: 1. *when thou shalt cease* to spoil,
Eze. 24:10. kindle the fire, *consume* the flesh,
Dan 8:23. *when* the transgressors *are come to the full,* (marg. *accomplished*)
9:24. and to *make an end* of sins, (marg, or, *seal up* [following the כתיב])

HIPHIL.—*Future.*

2K. 22: 4. *that he may sum* the silver
Job 22: 3. *thou makest* thy ways *perfect?*

* HITHPAEL.—*Future.* *

2Sa. 22:26. thou *wilt shew thyself upright.*
Ps. 18:25(26). thou *wilt shew thyself upright;*

תֶּמֶס *teh'-mes,* m. 8557

Ps. 58: 8(9). As a snail (which) *melteth,*

תָּמָר *tāh-māhr',* m. 8558

Ex. 15:27. threescore and ten *palm trees:*
Lev. 23:40. branches of *palm trees,*
Nu. 33: 9. threescore and ten *palm trees;*
Deu 34: 3. Jericho, the city of *palm trees,*
Jud. 1:16. went up out of the city of *palm trees*
3:13. possessed the city of *palm trees.*
2Ch 28:15. Jericho, the city of *palm trees,*
Neh. 8:15. myrtle branches, and *palm* branches,
Ps. 92:12(13). The righteous shall flourish *like the palm tree:*
Cant 7: 7(8). thy stature is like to *a palm tree,*
8(9). I will go up to *the palm tree,*
Joel 1:12. *the palm tree* also, and the apple tree,

תֹּמֶר *tōh'-mer,* m. 8560

Jud. 4: 5. she dwelt under *the palm tree of*
Jer. 10: 5. They (are) upright *as the palm tree,*

תִּמֹּרָה *tim-mōh-rāh',* f. 8561

1K. 6:29. figures of cherubims *and palm trees*
32. carvings of cherubims *and palm trees* — and upon *the palm trees.*
35. carved (thereon) cherubims *and palm trees*
7:36. graved cherubims, lions, *and palm trees,*
2Ch 3: 5. set thereon *palm trees* and chains.
Eze. 40:16. upon (each) post (were) *palm trees.*
22. their arches, *and their palm trees,*
26. and it had *palm trees,*
31, 34, 37. *and palm trees* (were) upon the
41:18. made with cherubims and *palm trees, so that a palm tree* (was) between
19. toward *the palm tree* on the one side, and the face of a young lion toward *the palm tree* on the other side:
20. door (were) cherubims *and palm trees*
25. temple, cherubims *and palm trees,*
26. windows *and palm trees* on the one side

תַּמְרוּק *tam-rook',* m. 8562

Est. 2: 3. *their things for purification*
9. *her things for purification,*
12. *for the purifying of* the women;
Pro. 20:30. The blueness of a wound *cleanseth* away evil: (marg. (is) *a purying medicine* against)

8563 **תַּמְרוּרִים** *tam-roo-reem'*, m. pl.

Jer. 6:26. most *bitter* lamentation: (lit. lamentation of *bitternesses*)
31:15. lamentation, (and) *bitter* weeping; (lit. weeping of *bitternesses*)
Hos 12:14(15). Ephraim provoked (him) to anger *most bitterly*: (marg. *with bitternesses*)

8564 **תַּמְרוּרִים** *tam-roo-reem'*, m. pl.

Jer. 31:21. make thee *high heaps*:

8562 **תַּמְרִיק** *tam-reek'*, m.

Pro. 20:30. (כתיב) The blueness of a wound *cleanseth* away evil: (marg. (is) *a purging medicine* against)

8565 **תַּן** see **תַּנִּים**

8566 **תָּנָה** [*tāh-nāh'*].

* KAL.—*Future.* *

Hos 8:10. though *they have hired* among the

* HIPHIL.—*Preterite.* *

Hos 8: 9. Ephraim *hath hired* lovers.

8567 **תָּנָה** [*tāh-nāh'*].

* PIEL.—*Infinitive.* *

Jud. 11:40. the daughters of Israel went yearly *to lament* (marg. or, *talk with*)

PIEL.—*Future.*

Jud. 5:11. *shall they rehearse* the righteous acts

8568 **תַּנּוֹת** *tan-nōhth'*, f. pl.

Mal 1: 3. waste *for the dragons of* the wilderness.

8569 **תְּנוּאָה** [*t'noo-āh'*], f.

Nu. 14:34. ye shall know *my breach of promise*. (marg. or, *altering of my purpose*)
Job 33:10. he findeth *occasions* against me,

8570 **תְּנוּבָה** *t'noo-vāh'*, f.

Deu32:13. that he might eat *the increase*
Jud. 9:11. my sweetness, and *my* good *fruit*,
Isa. 27: 6. fill the face of the world with *fruit*.
Lam 4: 9. *for* (want of) *the fruits of* the field.
Eze. 36:30. *and the increase of* the field,

8571 **תְּנוּךְ** *t'nooch*, m.

Ex. 29:20. put (it) upon *the tip of* the right ear
— *the tip of* the right ear of his sons,
Lev. 8:23. upon *the tip of* Aaron's right ear,
24. Moses put of the blood upon *the tip of*
14:14. the priest shall put (it) upon *the tip of*
17. put upon *the tip of* the right ear
25. put (it) upon *the tip of* the right ear
28. *the tip of* the right ear of him that is

8572 **תְּנוּמָה** *t'noo-māh'*, f.

Job 33:15. *in slumberings* upon the bed;
Ps. 132: 4. I will not give...*slumber* to mine eyelids,
Pro. 6: 4. *nor slumber* to thine eyelids.
10 & 24:33. a little sleep, *a* little *slumber*,

8573 **תְּנוּפָה** *t'noo-phāh'*, f.

Ex. 29:24. *a wave offering* before the Lord.
26. wave it (for) *a wave offering*
29:27. the breast of *the wave offering*
35:22. (offered) *an offering of* gold
38:24. the gold of *the offering*,
29. the brass of *the offering*
Lev. 7:30. *a wave offering* before the Lord.
34. For the *wave* breast
8:27. waved them (for) *a wave offering*
29. *a wave offering* before the Lord:
9:21. waved (for) *a wave offering*
10:14. And the *wave* breast and heave shoulder
15. the *wave* breast shall they bring
— wave (it for) *a wave offering*
14:12. wave them (for) *a wave offering*
21. a trespass offering *to be waved*, (marg. *for a waving*)
24. wave them (for) *a wave offering*
23:15. the sheaf of *the wave offering*;
17. two *wave* loaves of two tenth deals:
20. *a wave offering* before the Lord,
Nu. 6:20. *a wave offering* before the Lord:
— the *wave* breast and heave shoulder:
8:11. *an offering* (marg. *wave offering*) of the children of Israel,
13. *an offering* unto the Lord.
15. offer them (for) *an offering*.
21. *an offering* before the Lord;
18:11. *the wave offerings of* the children of Israel:
18. as the *wave* breast and as the right
Isa. 19:16. *the shaking of* the hand
30:32. in battles of *shaking*

תַּנּוּר *tan-noor'*, m. 8574

Gen 15:17. behold *a* smoking *furnace*,
Ex. 8: 3(7:28). upon thy people, *and into thine ovens*,
Lev. 2: 4. a meat offering baken in *the oven*,
7: 9. offering that is baken *in the oven*,
11:35. *oven*, or ranges for pots,
26:26. shall bake your bread *in* one *oven*,
Neh 3:11. and the tower of *the furnaces*.
12:38. beyond the tower of *the furnaces*
Ps. 21: 9(10). Thou shalt make them *as a* fiery *oven*.
Isa. 31: 9. *and* his *furnace* in Jerusalem.
Lam 5:10. Our skin was black *like an oven*
Hos. 7: 4. as *an oven* heated by the baker,
6. made ready their heart *like an oven*,
7. They are all hot *as an oven*,
Mal 4: 1(3:19). that shall burn *as an oven*;

תַּנְחוּמוֹת *tan-ghoo-mōhth'*, f. pl. 8575

Job 15:11. *the consolations of* God
21: 2. let this be *your consolations*.

תַּנְחוּמִים *tan-ghoo-meem'*, m. pl. 8575

Ps. 94:19. *thy comforts* delight my soul.
Isa. 66:11. the breasts of *her consolations*;
Jer. 16: 7. give them the cup of *consolation*

תַּנִּים *tan-neem*, m. pl. 8577

Job 30:29. I am a brother *to dragons*,
Ps. 44:19(20). sore broken us in the place of *dragons*,
Isa. 13:22. *and dragons* in (their) pleasant palaces:
34:13. it shall be an habitation of *dragons*,
35: 7. in the habitation of *dragons*,
43:20. shall honour me, *the dragons* and the owls:
Jer. 9:11(10). Jerusalem heaps, (and) a den of *dragons*;
10:22. Judah desolate, (and) a den of *dragons*.
14: 6. snuffed up the wind *like dragons*;
49:33. Hazor shall be a dwelling for *dragons*,
51:37. a dwellingplace for *dragons*,
Eze. 32: 2. thou (art) *as a whale* (marg. or, *dragon*) in the seas:
Mic. 1: 8. make a wailing *like the dragons*,

תַּנִּים *tan-neem'*, m. 8577

Eze. 29: 3. *the* great *dragon* that lieth in the midst

8577 **תַּנִּין** *tan-neen'*, m.

Gen 1:21. God created great *whales*,
Ex. 7: 9. it shall become *a serpent*.
10. it became *a serpent*.
12. every man his rod, and they became *serpents*:
Deu32:33. Their wine (is) the poison of *dragons*,
Neh 2:13. even before the *dragon* well,
Job 7:12. (Am) I a sea, or *a whale*,
Ps. 74:13. thou brakest the heads of *the dragons*
91:13. the young lion *and the dragon*
148: 7. *ye dragons*, and all deeps:
Isa. 27: 1. he shall slay *the dragon* that (is)
51: 9. cut Rahab, (and) wounded *the dragon?*
Jer. 51:34. hath swallowed me up *like a dragon*,
Lam.4: 3. Even *the sea monsters* (marg. or, *sea calves*) draw out

---

8578 **תִּנְיָן** [*tin-yāhn'*], Ch. adj. ord.

Dan 7: 5. a *second*, like to a bear,

8579 **תִּנְיָנוּת** *tin-yāh-nooth'*, Ch. adv.

Dan 2: 7. They answered *again* and said,

8580 **תַּנְשֶׁמֶת** *tan-sheh'-meth*, f.

Lev.11:18. *the swan*, and the pelican,
30. the snail, *and the mole*.
Deu 14:16. the great owl, *and the swan*,

8581 **תָּעַב** [*tāh-'gav'*].

* NIPHAL.—*Preterite*. *

1Ch21: 6. the king's word *was abominable* to Joab.

NIPHAL.—*Participle*.

Job 15:16. How much more *abominable*
Isa. 14:19. thy grave like an *abominable* branch,

* PIEL.—*Preterite*. *

Job 9:31. *and* mine own clothes *shall abhor me*.
19:19. All my inward friends *abhorred me*:
30:10. *They abhor me*, they flee far from me,

PIEL.—*Infinitive*.

Deu 7:26. *and* thou shalt *utterly* abhor it; (lit. *and abhorring* thou shalt abhor)

PIEL.—*Future*.

Deu 7:26. *thou shalt* utterly *abhor it*;
23: 7(8). *Thou shalt* not *abhor* an Edomite; for he (is) thy brother: *thou shalt* not *abhor*
Ps. 5: 6(7). the Lord *will abhor* the bloody
106:40. *insomuch that he abhorred* his own
107:18. Their soul *abhorreth* all manner
119:163. I hate *and abhor* lying:
Eze.16:25. *and hast made* thy beauty *to be abhorred*,
Am. 5:10. *they abhor* him that speaketh uprightly.

PIEL.—*Participle*.

Isa. 49: 7. *to him whom* the nation *abhorreth*,
Mic. 3: 9. Israel, *that abhor* judgment,

* HIPHIL.—*Preterite*. *

Ps. 14: 1. *they have done abominable* works,
53: 1(2). *and have done abominable* iniquity:
Eze.16:52. *thou hast committed more abominable*

HIPHIL.—*Future*.

1K. 21:26. *And he did* very *abominably*

8582 **תָּעָה** *tāh-'gāh'*.

* KAL.—*Preterite*. *

Ps. 58: 3(4). *they go astray* as soon as they be born,
107: 4. *They wandered* in the wilderness
119:110. yet *I erred* not from thy precepts.
176. *I have gone astray* like a lost sheep;
Isa. 16: 8. *they wandered* (through) the wilderness:
21: 4. My heart *panted* (marg. or, My mind *wandered*), fearfulness
Isa. 28: 7. through strong drink *are out of the way*; — *they are out of the way* through strong
47:15. *they shall wander* every one to his
53: 6. All we like sheep *have gone astray*;
Eze.44:10. which *went astray* away from me
48:11. which *went* not *astray* ... as the Levites *went astray*,

KAL.—*Infinitive*.

Eze.44:10. *when* Israel *went astray*,
15 & 48:11. *when* the children of Israel *went astray*

KAL.—*Future*.

Gen21:14. *and wandered* in the wilderness
Job 38:41. *they wander* for lack of meat.
Pro. 7:25. *go* not *astray* in her paths.
14:22. *Do they* not *err* that devise evil?
Isa. 35: 8. men, though fools, *shall* not *err*
Eze.14:11. Israel *may go* no more *astray*

KAL.—*Participle*. Poel.

Gen37:15. behold, (he was) *wandering* in the field:
Ex. 23: 4. enemy's ox or his ass *going astray*,
Ps. 95:10. It (is) a people *that do err in*
Pro.21:16. The man *that wandereth* out of the way
Isa. 29:24. They also *that erred* in spirit

* NIPHAL.—*Preterite*. *

Job 15:31. Let not him that *is deceived* trust

NIPHAL.—*Infinitive*.

Isa. 19:14. *as* a drunken (man) *staggereth*

* HIPHIL.—*Preterite*. *

Gen20:13. when God *caused* me *to wander*
Isa. 19:13. *they have also seduced* Egypt,
14. *and they have caused* Egypt *to err*
Jer. 42:20. For *ye dissembled* in your hearts, (marg. or, *used deceit* against your souls)
50: 6. shepherds *have caused them to go astray*,
Hos. 4:12. *hath caused* (them) *to err*,

HIPHIL.—*Future*.

2K. 21: 9. *and* Manasseh *seduced them*
2Ch 33: 9. *So* Manasseh *made* Judah...*to err*,
Job 12:24. *and causeth them to wander*
25. *and he maketh them to stagger* (marg. *wander*)
Ps.107:40. *and causeth them to wander*
Pro.12:26. the way of the wicked *seduceth them*.
Isa. 63:17. why *hast thou made us to err*
Jer. 23:13. *and caused* my people Israel *to err*.
32. *and cause* my people *to err*
Am. 2: 4. *and* their lies *caused them to err*,

HIPHIL.—*Participle*.

Pro.10:17. but he that refuseth reproof *erreth*. (marg. or, *causeth to err*)
Isa. 3:12. they which lead thee *cause* (thee) *to err*,
9:16(15). leaders of this people *cause* (them) *to err*;
30:28. jaws of the people, *causing* (them) *to err*.
Mic. 3: 5. the prophets *that make* my people *err*,

תְּעוּדָה *t'goo-dāh'*, f. 8584

Ru. 4: 7. this (was) *a testimony* in Israel.
Isa. 8:16. Bind up *the testimony*,
20. To the law *and to the testimony*:

תְּעָלָה *t'gāh-lāh'*, f. 8585

1K. 18:32. he made *a trench* about the altar,
35. he filled *the trench* also with water.
38. licked up the water that (was) *in the trench*.
2K. 18:17. *by the conduit of* the upper pool,
20:20. he made a pool, and *a conduit*,
Job 38:25. Who hath divided *a watercourse*
Isa. 7: 3. at the end of *the conduit of* the upper pool
36: 2. he stood *by the conduit of* the upper pool
Jer. 30:13. thou hast no *healing* medicines. (lit. medicines of *healing*)
46:11. thou shalt not be *cured*. (marg. no *cure* (shall be) unto thee; lit. medicines of *healing*)
Eze.31: 4. sent out *her little rivers* (marg. or, *conduits*) unto all the trees

8586 **תַּעֲלוּלִים** *tah-^{n}găloo-leem'*, m. pl.

Isa. 3: 4. *and babes* shall rule over them.
66: 4. I *also* will choose *their delusions*, (marg. or, *devices*)

8587 **תַּעֲלֻמָה** *tah-^{n}găloom-māh'*, f.

Job 11: 6. that he would shew thee *the secrets of*
28:11. *and the thing that is hid* bringeth he forth
Ps. 44:21(22). he knoweth *the secrets of* the heart.

8588 **תַּעֲנוּג** *tah-^{n}gănoog'*, m.

Pro. 19:10. *Delight* is not seemly for a fool;
Ecc. 2: 8. *and the delights of* the sons of men,
Cant. 7: 6(7). how pleasant art thou, O love, *for delights!*
Mic. 1:16. and poll thee for *thy delicate* children; (lit. the children of *thy delights*)
2: 9. cast out from *their pleasant* houses; (lit. the houses of *her delights*)

8589 **תַּעֲנִית** [*tah-^{n}găneeth'*], f.

Ezr. 9: 5. I arose up *from my heaviness*; (marg. or, *affliction*)

8591 **תָּעַע** [*tāh-^{n}găg^n'*].

* PILPEL.—*Participle.* *

Gen 27:12. I shall seem to him *as a deceiver*;

* HITHPALPEL.—*Participle.* *

2Ch 36:16. *and misused* his prophets,

8592 **תַּעֲצֻמוֹת** *tah-^{n}gătzoo-mōhth'*, f. pl.

Ps. 68:35(36). he that giveth strength *and power*

8593 **תַּעַר** *tah'-^{n}gar*, m.

Nu. 6: 5. there shall no *rasor* come upon his
8: 7. let them *shave* (marg. cause *a rasor* to pass over) all their flesh,
1Sa. 17:51. drew it out *of the sheath thereof*,
2Sa. 20: 8. upon his loins *in the sheath thereof*;
Ps. 52: 2(4). *like a* sharp *razor*,
Isa. 7:20. shave with *a razor* that is hired,
Jer. 36:23. he cut it *with the* pen*knife*, (lit. *with the knife of* a writer)
47: 6. put up thyself into *thy scabbard*,
Eze. 5: 1. take thee *a* barbers' *razor*,
21: 3(8). draw forth my sword out *of his sheath*,
4(9). my sword go forth out *of his sheath*
5(10). drawn forth my sword out *of his sheath*:
30(35). cause (it) to return into *his sheath*?

8594 **תַּעֲרוּבוֹת** *tah-^{n}găroo-vōhth'*, f. pl.

2K. 14:14. and *hostages*, (lit. children of *pledges*)
2Ch 25:24. the *hostages* (lit. children of *pledges*)

8595 **תַּעְתֻּעִים** *ta^{n}g-too-^{n}geem'*, m. pl.

Jer. 10:15. vanity, (and) the work of *errors*:
51:18. vanity, the work of *errors*:

8596 **תֹּף** *tōhph*, m.

Gen 31:27. with songs, *with tabret*, and with harp?
Ex. 15:20. took *a timbrel* in her hand;
— went out after her *with timbrels*
Jud. 11:34. came out to meet him *with timbrels*
1Sa. 10: 5. with a psaltery, *and a tabret*,
18: 6. to meet king Saul, *with tabrets*,
2Sa. 6: 5. on psalteries, *and on timbrels*,
1Ch 13: 8. *and with timbrels*, and with cymbals,
Job 21:12. They take *the timbrel* and harp,
Ps. 81: 2(3). bring hither *the timbrel*,
149: 3. praises unto him *with the timbrel*
150: 4. Praise him *with the timbrel*
Isa. 5:12. the harp, and the viol, *the tabret*,
24: 8. The mirth of *tabrets* ceaseth,
30:32. shall be *with tabrets* and harps:
Jer. 31: 4. thou shalt again be adorned with *thy tabrets*, (marg. or, *timbrels*)
Eze. 28:13. the workmanship of *thy tabrets*

תִּפְאָרָה *tiph-āh-rāh'*, & **תִּפְאֶרֶת** 8597
tiph-eh'-reth, f.

Ex. 28: 2, 40. for glory *and for beauty*.
Deu 26:19. in name, *and in honour*;
Jud. 4: 9. the journey...shall not be for *thine honour*;
1Ch 22: 5. of fame *and of glory*
29:11. Thine, O Lord, (is) the greatness, and the power, *and the glory*,
13. and praise *thy glorious* name.
2Ch 3: 6. with precious stones *for beauty*:
Est. 1: 4. the honour of his *excellent* majesty
Ps. 71: 8. (and with) *thy honour* all the day.
78:61. *and his glory* into the enemy's hand.
89:17(18). thou (art) *the glory of* their strength:
96: 6. strength *and beauty* (are) in his
Pro. 4: 9. a crown of *glory* shall she deliver
16:31. The hoary head (is) a crown of *glory*,
17: 6. *and the glory of* children (are) their
19:11. *and* (it is) *his glory* to pass over
20:29. *The glory of* young men (is) their
28:12. (men) do rejoice, (there is) great *glory*:
Isa. 3:18. *the bravery of* (their) tinkling ornaments
4: 2. the fruit of the earth (shall be) excellent *and comely*
10:12. *the glory of* his high looks.
13:19. Babylon,...*the beauty of* the Chaldees'
20: 5. and of Egypt *their glory*.
28: 1. *whose* glorious *beauty* (is) a fading flower,
4. And the glorious *beauty*,
5. a diadem of *beauty*,
44:13. *according to the beauty of* a man;
46:13. salvation in Zion for Israel *my glory*.
52: 1. put on *thy beautiful* garments,
60: 7. I will glorify the house of *my glory*.
19. *and* thy God *thy glory*.
62: 3. Thou shalt also be a crown of *glory*
63:12. with *his glorious* arm,
14. to make thyself a *glorious* name.
15. of thy holiness *and of thy glory*:
64:11(10). Our holy *and our beautiful* house,
Jer. 13:11. for a praise, *and for a glory*:
18. the crown of *your glory*.
20. was given thee, *thy beautiful* flock?
33: 9. a praise *and an honour*
48:17. broken, (and) the *beautiful* rod!
Lam 2: 1. *the beauty of* Israel,
Eze. 16:12. a *beautiful* crown upon thine head.
17. Thou hast also taken *thy fair* jewels
39. shall take *thy fair* jewels, (marg. instruments of *thine ornament*)
23:26. and take away *thy fair* jewels. (marg. instruments of *thy decking*)
42. *beautiful* crowns upon their heads.
24:25. the joy of *their glory*,
Zec. 12: 7. *the glory of* the house of David *and the glory of* the inhabitants

---

תַּפּוּחַ *tap-poo'ăgh*, m. 8598

Pro. 25:11. A word fitly spoken (is like) *apples of*
Cant. 2: 3. *As the apple tree* among the trees
5. comfort me *with apples*:
7: 8(9). the smell of thy nose *like apples*;
8: 5. I raised thee up under *the apple tree*:
Joel 1:12. palm tree also, *and the apple tree*,

תְּפוֹצָה [*t'phōh-tzāh'*]. f. 8600

Jer. 25:34. the days of your slaughter *and of your dispersions*

8601 **תֻּפִינִים** [*too-phee-neem'*], m. pl.

Lev. 6:21(14). the *baken* pieces *of* the meat offering

8602 **תָּפֵל** *tāh-phēhl'*, m.

Job 6: 6. Can *that which is unsavoury* be eaten
Lam.2:14. have seen vain *and foolish things*
Eze.13:10. others daubed it with *untempered*
11. which daub (it) with *untempered*
14. ye have daubed with *untempered*
15. daubed it with *untempered* (morter),
22:28. have daubed them with *untempered*

8604 **תִּפְלָה** *tiph-lāh'*, f.

Job 1:22. nor charged God *foolishly*. (marg. or, attributed *folly* to God)
24:12. yet God layeth not *folly*
Jer. 23:13. I have seen *folly* (marg. *unsavoury*, or, *an absurd thing*) in the prophets

---

8605 **תְּפִלָּה** *t'phil-lāh'*, f.

2Sa. 7:27. to pray this *prayer* unto thee.
1K. 8:28. have thou respect unto *the prayer of*
— hearken unto the cry and to *the prayer*,
29. *the prayer* which thy servant shall make
38. What *prayer* and supplication soever
45. hear thou in heaven *their prayer*
49. hear thou *their prayer*
54. made an end of praying all this *prayer*
9: 3. I have heard *thy prayer*
2K. 19: 4. lift up (thy) *prayer* for the remnant
20: 5. I have heard *thy prayer*,
2Ch 6:19. Have respect therefore to *the prayer of*
— *the prayer* which thy servant prayeth
20. to hearken unto *the prayer*
29. what *prayer* (or) what supplication
35. *their prayer* and their supplication,
39. *their prayer* and their supplications,
40. *unto the prayer* (that is made) in this place. (marg. *to the prayer of* this place)
7:12. I have heard *thy prayer*,
15. *unto the prayer* (that is made) in this place. (marg. *to the prayer of* this place)
30:27. *their prayer* came (up) to his holy...place,
33:18. Manasseh, *and his prayer* unto his God,
19. *His prayer also*, and (how God) was
Neh 1: 6. hear *the prayer of* thy servant,
11. attentive to *the prayer of* thy servant, and to *the prayer of* thy servants,
11:17. to begin the thanksgiving *in prayer*:
Job 16:17. *also my prayer* (is) pure.
Ps. 4: 1(2). mercy upon me, and hear *my prayer*.
6: 9(10). the Lord will receive *my prayer*.
17[title](1). *A prayer* of David.
1(2). give ear unto *my prayer*,
35:13. *and my prayer* returned into mine own
39:12(13). Hear *my prayer*, O Lord,
42: 8(9). *my prayer* unto the God of my life.
54: 2(4). Hear *my prayer*, O God;
55: 1(2). Give ear to *my prayer*, O God;
61: 1(2). attend unto *my prayer*.
65: 2(3). O thou that hearest *prayer*,
66:19. hath attended to the voice of *my prayer*.
20. hath not turned away *my prayer*,
69:13(14). *my prayer* (is) unto thee, O Lord,
72:20. *The prayers of* David the son of Jesse
80: 4(5). *against the prayer of* thy people?
84: 8(9). O Lord God of hosts, hear *my prayer*:
86[title](1). *A prayer* of David.
6(7). Give ear, O Lord, unto *my prayer*;
88: 2(3). Let *my prayer* come before thee:
13(14). in the morning shall *my prayer*
90[title](1). *A prayer* of Moses the man of God.
102[title](1). *A prayer* of the afflicted,
1(2). Hear *my prayer*, O Lord,
17(18). will regard *the prayer of* the destitute, and not despise *their prayer*.
109: 4. I (give myself unto) *prayer*.
7. *and* let *his prayer* become sin.
141: 2. Let *my prayer* be set forth before thee
5. *my prayer also* (shall be) in their
Ps.142[title](1). Maschil of David; *A Prayer*
143: 1. Hear *my prayer*, O Lord,
Pro.15: 8. *but the prayer of* the upright
29. *but* he heareth *the prayer of* the righteous.
28: 9. *his prayer* (shall be) abomination.
Isa. 1:15. when ye make many *prayers*,
37: 4. lift up (thy) *prayer* for the remnant
38: 5. I have heard *thy prayer*,
56: 7. make them joyful in *my* house of *prayer*: (lit. the house of *my prayer*)
— house shall be called an house of *prayer*
Jer. 7:16. neither lift up cry *nor prayer*
11:14. neither lift up a cry *or prayer*
Lam. 3: 8. he shutteth out *my prayer*.
44. that (our) *prayer* should not pass through.
Dan 9: 3. to seek by *prayer* and supplications,
17. hear *the prayer of* thy servant,
21. whiles I (was) speaking *in prayer*,
Jon. 2: 7(8). *my prayer* came in unto thee,
Hab. 3: 1. *A prayer* of Habakkuk

תִּפְלֶצֶת [*tiph-leh'-tzeth*], f. 8606

Jer. 49:16. *Thy terribleness* hath deceived thee,

תָּפַף [*tāh-phaph'*]. 8608

* KAL.—*Participle.* Poel. *

Ps. 68:25(26). the damsels *playing with timbrels*.

* POEL.—*Participle.* *

Nah. 2: 7(8). *tabering* upon their breasts.

תָּפַר [*tāh-phar'*]. 8609

* KAL.—*Preterite.* *

Job 16:15. *I have sewed* sackcloth upon my skin,

KAL.—*Infinitive.*

Ecc. 3: 7. A time to rend, and a time *to sew*;

KAL.—*Future.*

Gen 3: 7. *and they sewed* fig leaves *together*,

* PIEL.—*Participle.* *

Eze.13:18. Woe *to the women that sew*

תָּפַשׂ *tāh-phas'*. 8610

* KAL.—*Preterite.* *

Deu21:19. *Then shall* his father and his mother *lay hold* on
22:28. *and lay hold on her*,
Jos. 8:23. the king of Ai *they took* alive,
2K. 14: 7. *and took* Selah by war,
13. Jehoash king of Israel *took* Amaziah
2Ch 25:23. Joash the king of Israel *took* Amaziah
Pro.30: 9. *and take* the name of my God
Jer. 40:10. dwell in your cities that *ye have taken*.

KAL.—*Infinitive.*

Deu 20:19. in making war...*to take it*,
Jos. 8: 8. *when ye have taken* the city,
1Sa.23:26. and his men round about *to take them*.
Jer. 34: 3. shalt *surely* be taken, (lit. *taking* be taken)
Eze.14: 5. That I *may take* the house of Israel
21:11(16). furbished, that it *may be* handl*ed*: (lit. *to hold* in the hand)
29: 7. *When they took hold* of thee
30:21. make it strong *to hold* the sword.

KAL.—*Imperative.*

1K. 13: 4. saying, *Lay hold on him*.
18:40. *Take* (marg. *Apprehend*) the prophets of
20:18. come out for peace, *take them* alive; or whether they be come out for war, *take them* alive.
2K. 10:14. he said, *Take them* alive.
Ps. 71:11. persecute *and take him*;

KAL.—*Future.*

Gen39:12. *And she caught him* by his garment,
Deu 9:17. *And I took* the two tables,
1Sa.15: 8. *And he took* Agag the king of
1K. 11:30. *And* Ahijah *caught* the new garment
18:40. escape. *And they took them*:

2K. 7:12. *we shall catch them* alive,
10:14. *And they took them* alive,
16: 9. went up against Damascus, *and took it,*
18:13. fenced cities of Judah, *and took them.*
25: 6. *So they took* the king,
Isa. 3: 6. a man *shall take hold of* his brother
36: 1. defenced cities of Judah, *and took them.*
Jer. 26: 8. *that* the priests...and all the people *took*
37:13. *and he took* Jeremiah the prophet,
14. *so* Irijah *took* Jeremiah,
52: 9. *Then they took* the king,

KAL.—*Participle.* Poel.

Gen 4:21. the father of all such *as handle*
Nu. 31:27. between them that *took* the war
Jer. 2: 8. *and they that handle* the
46: 9. the Libyans, *that handle* the shield; and the Lydians, *that handle* (and) bend the
49:16. that *holdest* the height of the hill:
50:16. *and him that handleth* the sickle
Eze.27:29. all *that handle* the oar,
38: 4. all of them *handling* swords:
Am. 2:15. *Neither* shall *he* stand *that handleth*

KAL.—*Participle.* Paül.

Hab. 2:19. it (is) *laid over* with gold

* NIPHAL.—*Preterite.* *

Nu. 5:13. neither *she be taken*
Jer. 48:41. the strong holds *are surprised,*
50:24. thou art found, and also *caught,*
46. At the noise of *the taking* of Babylon
51:32. that the passages *are stopped,* (lit. *taken*)
Eze.12:13 & 17:20. *and he shall be taken* in my snare:
19: 4, 8. *he was taken* in their pit,

NIPHAL.—*Infinitive.*

Eze.21:23(28). *that* they *may be taken.*

NIPHAL.—*Future.*

Ps. 10: 2. *let them be taken* in the devices
Jer. 34: 3. but *shalt* surely *be taken,*
38:23. *shalt be taken* by the hand of the king
51:41. *and* how is the praise of the whole earth *surprised!*
Eze.21:24(29). *ye shall be taken* with the hand.

* PIEL.—*Future.* *

Pro.30:28. The spider *taketh hold* with her hands,

8611 **תֹּפֶת** *tōh'-pheth,* m.

Job 17: 6. *and* aforetime I was *as a tabret.*

8614 **תִּפְתָּיֵא** *tiph-tāh-yeh',* Ch. m. pl.

Dan. 3: 2, 3. the counsellors, *the sheriffs,*

8615 **תִּקְוָה** *tik-vāh',* f.

Jos. 2:18. thou shalt bind this *line of* scarlet thread in the window
21. she bound *the* scarlet *line* in the window.
Ru. 1:12. If I should say, I have *hope,*
Job 4: 6. (this) thy fear, thy confidence, *thy hope,*
5:16. So the poor hath *hope,*
6: 8. *that* God would grant (me) *the thing that I long for!* (marg. *my expectation*)
7: 6. My days...are spent without *hope.*
8:13. *and* the hypocrite's *hope* shall perish:
11:18. shalt be secure, because there is *hope;*
20. *and their hope* (shall be as) the giving up
14: 7. there is *hope* of a tree, if it be cut down,
19. *and* thou destroyest *the hope of* man.
17:15. where (is) now *my hope? as for my hope,* who shall see it?
19:10. *mine hope* hath he removed like a tree.
27: 8. what (is) *the hope of* the hypocrite,
Ps. 9:18(19). *the expectation of* the poor shall (not)
62: 5(6). *my expectation* (is) from him.
71: 5. thou (art) *my hope,* O Lord God:
Pro. 10:28. *but the expectation of* the wicked shall
11: 7. wicked man dieth, (his) *expectation* shall
23. *the expectation of* the wicked (is) wrath.
19:18. Chasten thy son while there is *hope,*
23:18. *and thine expectation* shall not be cut off.
Pro.24:14. *and thy expectation* shall not be cut off.
26:12 & 29:20. (there is) more *hope* of a fool
Jer. 29:11. to give you an *expected* end. (marg. end *and expectation*)
31:17. there is *hope* in thine end, saith the Lord,
Lam.3:29. if so be there may be *hope.*
Eze.19: 5. when she saw that she had waited, (and) *her hope* was lost,
37:11. Our bones are dried, and *our hope* is lost:
Hos. 2:15(17). valley of Achor for a door of *hope:*
Zec. 9:12. to the strong hold, ye prisoners of *hope:*

תְּקוּמָה *t'koo-māh',* f. 8617

Lev.26:37. ye shall have no *power to stand* before your enemies.

תְּקוֹמֵם [*t'kōh-mēhm'*], m. 8618

Ps.139:21. *and* am not I grieved *with* those *that rise up against thee?*

תָּקוֹעַ *tāh-kōh'ăg,* m. 8619

Eze. 7:14. They have blown *the trumpet,*

תְּקוּפָה [*t'koo-phāh'*], f. 8622

Ex. 34:22. at the year's *end.* (marg. *revolution of* the year)
1Sa. 1:20. *when* the time *was come about* (marg. *in revolution of* days)
2Ch 24:23. *at the end of* the year, (marg. *in the revolution of* the year)
Ps. 19: 6(7). *and his circuit* unto the ends of it:

תַּקִּיף *tak-keeph',* adj. 8623

Ecc. 6:10. contend with him *that is mightier*

תַּקִּיף [*tak-keeph'*], Ch. adj. 8624

Ezr. 4:20. There have been *mighty* kings also
Dan 2:40. the fourth kingdom shall be *strong*
42. the kingdom shall be partly *strong,*
4: 3(3:33). and how *mighty* (are) his wonders!
7: 7. dreadful and terrible, *and strong*

תְּקַל [*t'kal*], Ch. 8625

* P'AL.—*Participle.* Passive. *

Dan 5:25. Mene, Mene, *Tekel,* Upharsin.
27. *Tekel;* Thou art weighed

* P'IL.—*Preterite.* *

Dan 5:27. *Thou art weighed* in the balances,

תָּקַן [*tāh-kan'*]. 8626

* KAL.—*Infinitive.* *

Ecc. 1:15. crooked cannot *be made straight:*

* PIEL.—*Preterite.* *

Ecc.12: 9. *set in order* many proverbs.

PIEL.—*Infinitive.*

Ecc. 7:13. for who can *make* (that) *straight,*

תְּקַן [*t'kan*], Ch. 8627

* HOPHAL.—*Preterite.* *

Dan 4:36(33). *I was established* in my kingdom,

תָּקַע *tāh-kag'.* 8628

* KAL.—*Preterite.* *

Gen31:25. Jacob *had pitched* his tent in the mount: and Laban with his brethren *pitched*
Nu. 10: 3. And *when they shall blow* with them,

Nu. 10: 5. *When ye blow* an alarm, then
6. *When ye blow* an alarm the second
10. *ye shall blow* with the trumpets
Jos. 6: 8, 13. *and blew* with the trumpets:
9. (כתיב) the priests *that blew* with the
16. the priests *blew* with the trumpets,
Jud. 7:18. *When I blow* with a trumpet, I and all that (are) with me, *then blow* ye the trumpets
1Sa.13: 3. Saul *blew* the trumpet throughout
31:10. *they fastened* his body to the wall
1K. 1:34. *and blow ye* with the trumpet,
1Ch 10:10. *fastened* his head in the temple
Pro. 6: 1. *thou hast stricken* thy hand with
Isa. 22:23. *And I will fasten him* (as) a nail
Jer. 6: 3. *they shall pitch* (their) tents
Eze. 7:14. *They have blown* the trumpet,
33: 3. *If* when he seeth...*he blow* the trumpet,
6. *blow* not the trumpet,
Nah 3:19. bruit of thee *shall clap* the hands

KAL.—*Infinitive.*

Jos. 6: 9, 13. on, *and blowing* with the trumpets.
Jud. 7:20. trumpets in their right hands *to blow*
Isa. 18: 3. *and when he bloweth* a trumpet,

KAL.—*Imperative.*

Ps. 47: 1(2). *O clap* your hands, all ye people;
81: 3(4). *Blow* up the trumpet in the new
Jer. 4: 5. *Blow ye* the trumpet in the land:
6: 1. *blow* the trumpet in Tekoa,
51:27. *blow* the trumpet among the nations,
Hos. 5: 8. *Blow ye* the cornet in Gibeah,
Joel 2: 1. *Blow ye* the trumpet in Zion,
15. *Blow* the trumpet in Zion,

KAL.—*Future.*

Ex. 10:19. *and cast* (marg. *fastened*) *them* into the
Nu. 10: 4. if *they blow* (but) with one (trumpet),
6. *they shall blow* an alarm
7. *ye shall blow*, but ye shall not sound an
8. priests, *shall blow* with the trumpets;
Jos. 6: 4. the priests *shall blow* with the trumpets.
20. people shouted *when* (the priests) *blew*
Jud. 3:21. *and thrust it* into his belly:
27. *that he blew* a trumpet in the mountain
4:21. *and smote* the nail into his temples,
6:34. *and he blew* a trumpet;
7:19. and they *blew* the trumpets,
20. *And* the three companies *blew*
22. *And* the three hundred *blew*
16:14. *And she fastened* (it) with the pin,
2Sa. 2:28. *So* Joab *blew* a trumpet,
18:14. *and thrust them* through the heart
16. *And* Joab *blew* the trumpet,
20: 1. *and he blew* a trumpet, and said,
22. *And he blew* a trumpet, and they
1K. 1:39. *And they blew* the trumpet;
2K. 9:13. *and blew* with trumpets,
Zec. 9:14. the Lord God *shall blow* the trumpet,

KAL.—*Participle.* Poel.

Jos. 6: 9. the priests *that blew* with the trumpets,
2K. 11:14. *and blew* with trumpets:
2Ch 23:13. rejoiced, *and sounded* with trumpets,
Neh 4:18(12). *And he that sounded* the trumpet
Pro. 11:15. he that hateth *suretiship* (marg. *those that strike* (hands)) is sure.
17:18. A man void of understanding *striketh*
22:26. *of them that strike* hands,

KAL.—*Participle.* Paül.

Isa. 22:25. shall the nail *that is fastened*

∗ NIPHAL.—*Future.* ∗

Job 17: 3. who (is) he (that) *will strike* hands
Isa. 27:13. the great trumpet *shall be blown*,
Am. 3: 6. *Shall* a trumpet *be blown* in the city,

8629 תֵּקַע *tēh'-kag*, m.

Ps. 150: 3. Praise him *with the sound of* the

8630 תָּקַף [*tāh-kaph'*].

∗ KAL.—*Future.* ∗

Job 14:20. *Thou prevailest* for ever *against him*,
15:24. *they shall prevail against him*,
Ecc. 4:12. if one *prevail against* him,

תְּקֵף [*t'kēhph*], Ch. 8631

∗ P'AL.—*Preterite.* ∗

Dan 4:11(8). The tree grew, *and was strong*,
20(17). which grew, *and was strong*,

P'AL.—*Future.*

Dan 4:22(19). that art grown *and become strong:*
5:20. was lifted up, and his mind *hardened*

∗ PAEL.—*Infinitive.* ∗

Dan 6: 7(8). *and to make* a *firm* decree,

תֹּקֶף *tōh'-keph*, m. 8633

Est. 9:29. Mordecai the Jew, wrote with all *authority*, (marg. *strength*)
10: 2. all the acts of *his power*
Dan 11:17. enter *with the strength of* his whole

תְּקֹף [*t'kōhph*], Ch. m. 8632

Dan 2:37. power, *and strength*, and glory.
4:30(27). *by the might of* my power,

תֹּר see תּוֹר See 8447, 8449

תַּרְבּוּת *tar-booth'*, f. 8635

Nu. 32:14. *an increase of* sinful men,

תַּרְבִּית *tar-beeth'*, f. 8636

Lev. 25:36. Take thou no usury of him, *or increase:*
Pro. 28: 8. by usury *and unjust gain* increaseth his
Eze. 18: 8. *neither* hath taken any *increase*,
13. *and* hath taken *increase:*
17. hath not received usury *nor increase*,
22:12. thou hast taken usury *and increase*,

תִּרְגַּל see רָגַל 8637

תַּרְגֵּם [*tar-gēhm'*]. 8638

∗ *Participle.* Passive. ∗

Ezr. 4: 7. *and interpreted* in the Syrian

תַּרְדֵּמָה *tar-dēh-māh'*, f. 8639

Gen 2:21. the Lord God caused *a deep sleep* to fall
15:12. *And* when...*a deep sleep* fell upon Abram;
1Sa. 26:12. *a deep sleep from* the Lord was fallen
Job 4:13. when *deep sleep* falleth on men,
33:15. when *deep sleep* falleth upon men,
Pro. 19:15. Slothfulness casteth into *a deep sleep;*
Isa. 29:10. the spirit of *deep sleep*,

תְּרוּמָה *t'roo-māh'*, f. 8641

Ex. 25: 2. Speak unto the children of Israel, that they bring me *an offering:* (marg. or, *heave offering*)
— ye shall take *my offering*.
3. *the offering* which ye shall take
29:27. the shoulder of *the heave offering*,
28. for it (is) *an heave offering:* and it shall be *an heave offering* from the children
— *their heave offering* unto the Lord.
30:13. *the offering* of the Lord.
14. shall give *an offering unto* the Lord.
15. when (they) give *an offering unto* the
35: 5. *an offering* unto the Lord:
— *an offering of* the Lord;
21. they brought the Lord's *offering*
24. *an offering of* silver and brass brought the Lord's *offering:*
36: 3. received of Moses all *the offering*,
6. *for the offering of* the sanctuary.
Lev. 7:14. *an heave offering* unto the Lord,
32. *an heave offering* of the sacrifices

Lev. 7:34. the *heave* shoulder (lit. shoulder of *heave offering*)
10:14. the wave breast and *heave* shoulder
15. The *heave* shoulder and the
22:12. eat *of an offering of* the holy things.
Nu. 5: 9. every *offering* of all the holy things
6:20. the wave breast and *heave* shoulder:
15:19. offer up *an heave offering*
20. offer up a cake...(for) *an heave offering: as* (ye do) *the heave offering of*
21. *an heave offering* in your generations.
18: 8. the charge of *mine heave offerings*
11. *the heave offering of* their gift,
19. *the heave offerings of* the holy things,
24. which they offer (as) *an heave offering*
26. ye shall offer up *an heave offering* of it *for* the Lord,
27. *your heave offering* shall be reckoned
28. *an heave offering unto* the Lord
— the Lord's *heave offering*
29. every *heave offering of* the Lord,
31:29. *an heave offering of* the Lord.
41. the Lord's *heave offering*,
52. all the gold of *the offering*
Deu 12: 6. *heave offerings of* your hand,
11. *and the heave offering of* your hand,
17. *or heave offering of* thine hand.
2Sa. 1:21. nor fields of *offerings:*
2Ch 31:10. Since (the people) began to bring *the offerings*
12. *the offerings* and the tithes
14. to distribute *the oblations of*
Ezr. 8:25. *the offering of* the house of our God,
Neh 10:37(38). the firstfruits of our dough, *and our offerings*,
39(40). *the offering of* the corn,
12:44. *for the offerings*, for the firstfruits,
13: 5. *and the offerings of* the priests.
Pro. 29: 4. he that receiveth *gifts* (marg. a man of *oblations*)
Isa. 40:20. he hath no *oblation*
Eze. 20:40. there will I require *your offerings*,
44:30. every *oblation of* all, of every (sort) of *your oblations*,
45: 1. ye shall offer *an oblation* unto the Lord,
6. against *the oblation of* the holy (portion):
7. on the other side *of the oblation*
— before *the oblation of* the holy (portion),
13. *the oblation* that ye shall offer;
16. shall give this *oblation* for the prince
48: 8. *the offering* which ye shall offer
9. *The oblation* that ye shall offer
10. the priests, shall be (this) holy *oblation;*
12. (this) oblation of the land *that is offered*
18, 18. against *the oblation of* the holy (portion)
20. All *the oblation*
— offer *the* holy *oblation*
21. the residue...*of the* holy *oblation*,
— the five and twenty thousand of *the oblation*
— it shall be *the* holy *oblation;*
Mal. 3: 8. In tithes *and offerings*.

8642 תְּרוּמִיָּה *t'roo-meey-yāh'*, f.

Eze. 48:12. (this) *oblation of* the land

8643 תְּרוּעָה *t'roo-gāh'*, f.

Lev. 23:24. a memorial of *blowing of trumpets*,
25: 9. the trumpet of *the jubile* (marg. *loud of sound*)
Nu. 10: 5. When ye blow *an alarm*, then
6. When ye blow *an alarm* the second time,
— they shall blow *an alarm*
23:21. *and the shout of* a king (is) among them.
29: 1. a day of *blowing the trumpets*
31: 6. the trumpets *to blow*
Jos. 6: 5. the people shall shout with *a* great *shout;*
20. the people shouted with *a* great *shout*,
1Sa. 4: 5. Israel shouted with *a* great *shout*,
6. when the Philistines heard the noise of *the shout*,
— the noise of this great *shout*
2Sa. 6:15. brought up the ark of the Lord *with shouting*,
1Ch 15:28. brought up the ark of the covenant...*with shouting*,
2Ch 13:12. *sounding* trumpets to cry alarm
15:14. *and with shouting*, and with trumpets,
Ezr. 3:11. all the people shouted with *a* great *shout*,
12. many *shouted* aloud for joy:
13. the noise of *the shout of* joy
— for the people shouted with *a* loud *shout*,
Job 8:21. Till he fill...thy lips with *rejoicing*. (marg. *shouting for joy*)
33:26. he shall see his face *with joy:*
39:25. thunder of the captains, *and the shouting*.
Ps. 27: 6. therefore will I offer...sacrifices of *joy;* (marg. *shouting*)
33: 3. play skilfully *with a loud noise*.
47: 5(6). God is gone up *with a shout*,
89:15(16). the people that know *the joyful sound:*
150: 5. upon the *high sounding* cymbals.
Jer. 4:19. the trumpet, *the alarm of* war.
20:16. *and the shouting* at noontide;
49: 2. I will cause *an alarm of* war to be heard
Eze. 21:22(27). to lift up the voice *with shouting*,
Am. 1:14. *with shouting* in the day of battle,
2: 2. Moab shall die with tumult, *with shouting*,
Zep. 1:16. A day of the trumpet *and alarm*

תְּרוּפָה *t'roo-phāh'*, f. 8644

Eze. 47:12. the leaf thereof *for medicine*. (marg. or, *bruises and sores*)

תִּרְזָה *tir-zāh'*, f. 8645

Isa. 44:14. taketh *the cypress* and the oak,

תְּרֵין [*t'rēhn*], Ch. adj. num. 8648

Ezr. 4:24. So it ceased unto the *second* year of the
6:17. twelve (lit. *two* ten) he goats,
Dan 4:29(26). At the end of twelve (lit. *two* ten) months
5:31(6:1). about threescore *and two* years old.

תָּרְמָה *tor-māh'*, f. 8649

Jud. 9:31. sent messengers unto Abimelech *privily*, (marg. *craftily*, or, *to Tormah*)

תַּרְמוּת *tar-mooth'*, f. 8649

Jer. 14:14. (כתיב) *the deceit of* their heart.

תַּרְמִית *tar-meeth'*, f. 8649

Ps. 119:118. *their deceit* (is) falsehood.
Jer. 8: 5. they hold fast *deceit*,
14:14. *the deceit of* their heart.
23:26. *the deceit of* their own heart;
Zep. 3:13. neither shall a *deceitful* tongue be found

תֹּרֶן *tōh'-ren*, m. 8650

Isa. 30:17. left *as a beacon* (marg. or, *a tree bereft of branches*, or, *boughs:* or, a *mast*) upon the top of a mountain,
33:23. could not well strengthen *their mast*,
Eze. 27: 5. cedars from Lebanon to make *masts*

תְּרַע *t'rag*, Ch. m. 8651

Dan 2:49. Daniel (sat) *in the gate of* the king.
3:26. came near *to the mouth* (marg. *door*) of the burning

תָּרָע [*tāh-rāhg'*], Ch. m. 8652

Ezr. 7:24. *porters*, Nethinims, or ministers of this

8653 **תַּרְעֵלָה** *tar-gēh-lāh'*, f.

Ps. 60: 3(5). made us to drink the wine of *astonishment.*
Isa. 51:17. drunken the dregs of the cup of *trembling,*
22. I have taken...the cup of *trembling,*

8655 **תְּרָפִים** *t'rāh-pheem'*, m. pl.

Gen31:19. Rachel had stolen *the images* (marg. *teraphim*)
34. Rachel had taken *the images,*
35. but found not *the images.*
Jud.17: 5. made an ephod, *and teraphim,*
18:14. in these houses an ephod, *and teraphim,*
17. image, and the ephod, and *the teraphim,*
18. image, the ephod, and *the teraphim,*
20. took the ephod, and *the teraphim,*
1Sa.15:23. iniquity *and idolatry.*
19:13. Michal took *an image,*
16. *an image* in the bed,
2K. 23:24. *the images*, and the idols,
Eze.21:21(26). he consulted *with images*, (marg. *teraphim*)
Hos 3: 4. *and* (without) *teraphim:*
Zec.10: 2. *the idols* (marg. *teraphims*) have spoken

8658 **תַּרְשִׁישׁ** *tar-sheesh'*, m.

Ex. 28:20 & 39:13. the fourth row *a beryl,*
Cant 5:14. gold rings set *with the beryl:*
Eze. 1:16. like unto the colour of *a beryl:*
10: 9. as the colour of a *beryl* stone.
28:13. the sardius, topaz, and the diamond, *the beryl*, (marg. or, *chrysolite*)
Dan10: 6. His body also (was) *like the beryl,*

8660 **תִּרְשָׁתָא** *tir-shāh-thāh'*, m.

Ezr. 2:63. And *the Tirshatha* (marg. or, *governor*) said
Neh 7:65. And *the Tirshatha* (marg. *id.*) said
70. *The Tirshatha* gave to the treasure
8: 9. Nehemiah, which (is) *the Tirshatha*, (marg. or, *governor*)
10: 1. Nehemiah, *the Tirshatha*, (marg. *id.*)

8667 **תְּשׂוּמֶת** *t'soo'-meth*, f.

Lev. 6: 2(5:21). lie unto his neighbour...*in fellowship*, (marg. *putting of* the hand, or, *dealing*)

8663 **תְּשֻׁאוֹת** *t'shoo-ōhth'*, f. pl.

Job 36:29. *the noise of* his tabernacle?
39: 7. neither regardeth he *the crying of*
Isa. 22: 2. Thou that art full of *stirs,*
Zec. 4: 7. shall bring forth the headstone...(with) *shoutings,*

8665 **תַּשְׁבֵּץ** *tash-bēhtz'*, m.

Ex. 28: 4. a *broidered* coat, a mitre, and a girdle:

8666 **תְּשׁוּבָה** *t'shoo-vāh'*, f.

1Sa. 7:17. *And his return* (was) to Ramah;
2Sa.11: 1. *after* the year *was expired*, (marg. *at the return of* the year)
1K. 20:22. *at the return of* the year the king of
26. *at the return of* the year, that Ben-hadad
1Ch 20: 1. after the year *was expired*, (marg. *the return of* the year)
2Ch 36:10. *And when* the year *was expired*, (marg. *at the return of* the year)
Job 21:34. *seeing in your answers* there remaineth falsehood?
34:36. (his) *answers* for wicked men.

תְּשׁוּעָה *t'shoo-gāh'*, f. 8668

Jud.15:18. Thou hast given this great *deliverance*
1Sa.11: 9. ye shall have *help.* (marg. or, *deliverance*)
13. to day the Lord hath wrought *salvation*
19: 5. the Lord wrought *a* great *salvation*
2Sa.19: 2(3). *the victory* (marg. *salvation*, or, *deliverance*) that day was (turned) into
23:10, 12. the Lord wrought *a* great *victory*
2K. 5: 1. the Lord had given *deliverance* (marg. or, *victory*)
13:17. The arrow of the Lord's *deliverance*, and the arrow of *deliverance* from Syria:
1Ch 11:14. the Lord saved (them) by *a* great *deliverance.* (marg. or, *salvation*)
19:12. then thou shalt *help* me: (lit. shalt be *for help* to me)
2Ch 6:41. let thy priests, O Lord God, be clothed *with salvation,*
Ps. 33:17. An horse (is) a vain thing *for safety:*
37:39. *But the salvation of* the righteous
38:22(23). O Lord *my salvation.*
40:10(11). I have declared thy faithfulness *and thy salvation:*
16(17). let such as love *thy salvation*
51:14(16). thou God of *my salvation:*
60:11(13). vain (is) *the help* (marg. *salvation*) *of*
71:15. thy righteousness (and) *thy salvation*
108:12(13). vain (is) *the help of* man.
119:41. (even) *thy salvation*, according to
81. My soul fainteth *for thy salvation:*
144:10. (It is he) that giveth *salvation* (marg. or, *victory*) unto kings:
146: 3. in whom (there is) no *help.* (marg. or, *salvation*)
Pro.11:14. *but* in the multitude of counsellors (there is) *safety.*
21:31. *safety* (marg. or, *victory*) (is) of the Lord.
24: 6. *and* in multitude of counsellors (there is) *safety.*
Isa. 45:17. with *an* everlasting *salvation:*
46:13. *and my salvation* shall not tarry: and I will place *salvation* in Zion
Jer. 3:23. our God (is) *the salvation of* Israel.
Lam 3:26. wait *for the salvation of* the Lord.

תְּשׁוּקָה [*t'shoo-kāh'*], f. 8669

Gen 3:16. *thy desire* (shall be) to thy husband,
4: 7. unto thee (shall be) *his desire,*
Cant.7:10(11). *his desire* (is) toward me.

תְּשׁוּרָה *t'shoo-rāh'*, f. 8670

1Sa. 9: 7. *and* (there is) not *a present* to bring to the man of God:

תְּשִׁיעִי *t'shee-gee'*, adj. ord. 8671

Lev.25:22. eat (yet) of old fruit until *the ninth*
Nu. 7:60. On the *ninth* day Abidan
2K. 17: 6. In the *ninth* year of Hoshea
25: 1. it came to pass in the *ninth* year
1Ch 12:12. Elzabad *the ninth,*
24:11. *The ninth* to Jeshuah,
25:16. *The ninth* to Mattaniah,
27:12. *The ninth* (captain) for the *ninth* month
Ezr.10: 9. It (was) the *ninth* month,
Jer. 36: 9. of Judah, in the *ninth* month,
22. sat in the winterhouse in the *ninth* month:
39: 1. In the *ninth* year of Zedekiah
52: 4. it came to pass in the *ninth* year
Eze.24: 1. Again in the *ninth* year,
Hag. 2:10. twentieth (day) *of the ninth* (month),
18. twentieth day *of the ninth* (month),
Zec. 7: 1. in the fourth (day) of the *ninth* month,

תֵּשַׁע *tēh-shag'*, f. & **תִּשְׁעָה** *tish-gāh'*, 8672
m. adj. num.

Gen 5: 5. the days that Adam lived were *nine* hundred and thirty years:
8. of Seth were *nine* hundred and twelve

Gen 5:11. of Enos were *nine* hundred *and* five
14. of Cainan were *nine* hundred *and* ten
20. of Jared were *nine* hundred sixty and two
27. of Methuselah were *nine* hundred sixty *and nine* years: and he died.
9:29. of Noah were *nine* hundred and fifty
11:19. Reu two hundred and *nine* years,
24. Nahor lived *nine* and twenty years,
25. Terah an hundred and *nine*teen years,
17: 1. Abram was ninety years old *and nine*,
24. Abraham (was) ninety years old *and nine*,
Ex. 38:24. was twenty and *nine* talents,
Lev.23:32. *in the ninth* (day) of the month
25: 8. shall be unto thee forty and *nine* years.
Nu. 1:23. Simeon, (were) fifty and *nine* thousand and three hundred.
2:13. (were) fifty and *nine* thousand and three hundred.
29:26. on the fifth day *nine* bullocks,
34:13. commanded to give *unto* the *nine* tribes,
Deu 3:11. *nine* cubits (was) the length thereof,
Jos. 13: 7. inheritance *unto* the *nine* tribes,
14: 2. *for* the *nine* tribes, and (for) the half tribe.
15:32. all the cities (are) twenty *and nine*,
44, 54. *nine* cities with their villages:
19:38. *nine*teen cities with their villages.
21:16. *nine* cities out of those two
Jud. 4: 3. he had *nine* hundred chariots
13. *nine* hundred chariots of iron,
2Sa. 2:30. David's servants *nine*teen men
24: 8. Jerusalem at the end of *nine* months
2K. 14: 2. reigned twenty *and nine* years
15:13. reign in the *nine* and thirtieth year
17. In the *nine* and thirtieth year
17: 1. in Samaria over Israel *nine* years.
18: 2. reigned twenty *and nine* years
10. the *ninth* year of Hoshea
25: 3. *on the ninth* (day) of the (fourth) month
8. which (is) the *nine*teenth year
1Ch 3: 8. Eliada, and Eliphelet, *nine*.
9: 9. *nine* hundred and fifty and six.
24:16. *The nine*teenth to Pethahiah,
1Ch 25:26. *The nine*teenth to Mallothi,
2Ch 16:12. Asa in the thirty *and ninth* year
25: 1. reigned twenty *and nine* years
29: 1. reigned *nine and* twenty years
Ezr. 1: 9. *nine* and twenty knives,
2: 8. *nine* hundred forty and five.
36. *nine* hundred seventy and three.
42. the children of Shobai, (in) all an hundred thirty *and nine*.
Neh 7:38. three thousand *nine* hundred and thirty.
39. *nine* hundred seventy and three.
11: 1. the holy city, *and nine* parts
8. *nine* hundred twenty and eight.
Jer. 39: 2. *the ninth* (day) of the month,
52: 6. *in the ninth* (day) of the month,
12. which (was) the *nine*teenth year

תִּשְׁעִים *tish-ĝeem'*, adj. num. m. pl. 8673

Gen 5: 9. Enos lived *ninety* years,
17. eight hundred *ninety and* five years:
30. five hundred *ninety* and five years,
17: 1. when Abram was *ninety* years old and nine,
17. that is *ninety* years old,
24. Abraham (was) *ninety* years old and nine,
1Sa. 4:15. Eli was *ninety* and eight years old;
1Ch 9: 6. six hundred *and ninety*.
Ezr. 2:16. of Hezekiah, *ninety* and eight.
20. children of Gibbar, *ninety* and five.
58. three hundred *ninety* and two.
8:35. bullocks for all Israel, *ninety* and six
Neh 7:21. of Ater of Hezekiah, *ninety* and eight.
25. children of Gibeon, *ninety* and five.
60. three hundred *ninety* and two.
Jer. 52:23. there were *ninety* and six pomegranates
Eze. 4: 5. three hundred *and ninety* days:
9. three hundred *and ninety* days
41:12. the length thereof *ninety* cubits.
Dan 12:11. (there shall be) a thousand two hundred *and ninety* days.

HEBREW AND ENGLISH INDEX.

⁂ After each Hebrew word the various English terms by which it is rendered in the Authorised Version, are given in alphabetical order.—Those in which the English is not strictly a translation of the Hebrew, but the rendering is the result of some peculiarity, are marked *. The mark † indicates that the rendering is that of the Hebrew word in combination with some other. The *intensitive* use of the Infinitives has also to be noticed as the occasion of peculiar renderings in the verbs. Words, or parts of words in *italics*, indicate that they are merely accompaniments of the English which translates the Hebrew word under which they stand.

אָב 1
Abi-*ezrite*
chief
* desire
father
father*less*
forefather
* patrimony
principal

אָב 8
desire

אַב Ch. 8
father

אֵב 8
fruit
greenness

אֵב Ch. 8
fruit

אָבַד 8
Kal.
broken, to be
destroyed, to be
destruction
escape,† not to
fail, to
lost, to be
perish, to
ready to perish, to be
surely
undone, to be
utterly
void of, to be
way to flee,† to have no
Piel.
destroy, to
lose, to
perish, to cause to
perish, to make to
spend, to
utterly
Hiphil.
destroy, to
take, to

אֲבַד Ch. 9
P'al.
perish, to
Aphel.
destroy, to
perish, to
Hophal.
destroyed, to be

אֹבֵד 9
perish

(כ׳) אֲבַדֹּה 9
destruction

אֲבֵדָה 9
lost, that which was
lost thing

אֲבַדּוֹן 9
destruction

אַבְדָן 9
destruction

אָבְדַן 9
destruction

אָבָה 9
Kal.
consent, to
rest content, to
will, to
willing, to be

אֵבֶה 10
swift

אֲבוֹי 10
sorrow

אֵבוּס 10
crib

אִבְחָה 10
point

אֲבַטִּחִים 10
melons

אָבִיב 10
Abib
ear
ears of corn, green
Tel-abib

אֶבְיוֹן 10
beggar
needy
poor
poor man

אֲבִיּוֹנָה 10
desire

אַבִּיר 10
angel
bull
chiefest
mighty
mighty one
stout*hearted*
strong
strong one
valiant

אֲבִיר 11
mighty

אָבַךְ 11
Hithpael.
mount up, to

אָבַל 11
Kal.
lament, to
mourn, to
Hiphil.
lament, to make to
mourning, to cause a
Hithpael.
feign self to be a mourner, to
lament, to
mourn, to

אָבֵל 11
mourn
mourner
mourning

אָבֵל 11
plain

אֲבָל 11
but
indeed
nevertheless
verily

אֵבֶל 11
mourning

אֶבֶן 11
carbuncle †
*chalk*stone
divers weights
Eben-*ezer*
*hail*stone
*head*stone
mason †
plummet†
*sling*stone
stone
stony
weight

אֶבֶן Ch. 13
stone

אַבְנֵט 13
girdle

אָבְנַיִם 13
stools
wheels

אָבַס 13
Kal.
fatted
stalled

אֲבַעְבֻּעֹת 13
blains

אָבָק 13
dust
dust, small
powder

אָבַק 13
Niphal.
wrestle, to

אֲבָקָה 13
powder

אָבַר 13
Hiphil.
fly, to

אֵבֶר 13
long-winged
wing

אֶבְרָה 14
feather
wing

אַבְרֵךְ 14
bow the knee

אֲגֻדָּה 14
bunch
burden
troop

אֱגוֹז 14
nut

אֲגוֹרָה 14
piece of *silver*

אֶגְלִים 14
drops

אֲגַם 14
pond
pool
reed
standing *water*

אַגְמוֹן 14
bulrush
caldron
hook
rush

אַגָּן 14
bason
cup
goblet

אֲגַפִּים 14
bands

אָגַר 14
Kal.
gather, to

אִגְּרָא Ch. 14
letter

אֶגְרֹף 14
fist

אֲגַרְטְלִים 14
chargers

אִגֶּרֶת 14
letter

אֵד 14
mist
vapour

אָדַב 14
Hiphil.
grieve, to

אָדוֹן **15**
Adoni-*bezek*
lord
master
owner

אֱדַיִן Ch. 17
now
then
time, that

אַדִּיר 17
excellent
famous
gallant
glorious
goodly
lordly
mightier
mighty
mighty one
noble
principal
worthies

אָדָם 17
Adam
another
common sort†
hypocrite†
low
man
man of low degree
mean man
person

אָדַם 20
Kal.
ruddy, to be
Pual.
dyed red, to be
red, to be
red, to be made
Hiphil.
red, to be
Hithpael.
red, to be

אָדֹם 21
red
ruddy

אֹדֶם 21
sardius

אֲדַמְדָּם 21
reddish
reddish, somewhat

אֲדָמָה 21
country
earth
ground
husband*man*
husbandry
land

אַדְמֹנִי & אַדְמוֹנִי 22
red
ruddy

אֶדֶן 22
foundation
socket

אֲדֹנָי 22
Lord
Lord, my

אָדַר 24
Niphal.
glorious
glorious, to become
Hiphil.
honourable, to make

אֲדָר 24
Adar

אָחוּ 45
flag
meadow

אַחֲוָה 45
declaration

אַחֲוָה 45
brotherhood

אַחֲוָיָה Ch. 45
shewing

אָחוֹר 45
afterward, till
back
back part
backside
backward
behind
hereafter
hinder part
time to come
without

אָחוֹת 46
another
other
sister
together

אָחַז 46
Kal.
affrighted,† to be
bar, to
catch, to
catch hold, to
come upon, to
fasten, to
handle, to
hold, to
lay hold, to
portion
rest, to
surprise, to
take, to
take hold, to
Niphal.
caught, to be
possessed, to be
possession, to have
possessions, to get
possessions, to take
taken, to be
Piel.
hold back, to
Hophal.
fastened, to be

אֲחֻזָּה 47
possession

אֲחִידָן Ch. 47
hard sentences

אֹחִים 47
doleful creatures

אַחֲלַי & אַחֲלֵי ..48
O that
would God

אַחְלָמָה 48
amethyst

אַחְמְתָא Ch. ..48
Achmetha

אָחַר 48
Kal.
stay there, to
tarry longer, to
Piel.
continue, to
defer, to
delay, to
hinder, to
late, to be
slack, to be
tarry, to

אַחַר 48
after
after that
afterward
again
at
away from
back
back from
backside
behind
beside
by
follow, to
follow,† to
follow after
following
forasmuch
from
hereafter
hinder end
outlive,† to
overlive,† to
persecute,† to
posterity
pursuing
remnant
seeing
since
thence*forth*
when
with

אַחֵר 52
another
another man
following
next
other
strange

אַחֲרוֹן 53
after
afterward
come, to
following
hinder
hindermost
hindmost
last
latter—l. end
rereward
utmost
uttermost

אַחֲרֵי Ch. 54
after
*here*after

אָחֳרִי Ch. 54
another
other

אָחֳרֵין Ch. 54
at last

אַחֲרִית 54
end
hindermost
last
last end
latter
latter end
latter time
length
posterity
remnant
residue
reward
uttermost

אַחֲרִית Ch. 54
latter

אָחֳרָן Ch. 54
another
other

אֲחֹרַנִּית 54
back again
backward

אֲחַשְׁדַּרְפְּנַיָּא Ch. 54
princes

אֲחַשְׁדַּרְפְּנִים ...54
lieutenants

אֲחַשְׁתְּרָנִים 54
camels

אַט 54
gently
secret
softly

אָטָד 54
Atad
bramble
thorn

אֵטוּן 55
fine linen

אִטִּי 55
softly

אִטִּים 55
charmers

אָטַם 55
Kal.
narrow
shut, to
stop, to
Hiphil.
stop, to

אָטַר 55
Kal.
shut, to

אִטֵּר 55
* left handed †

אִי 55
how?
what?
whence?
where?
whether?
which?
which way?

אִי 55
country [of t.i.
island—wild beasts
isle

אִי 55
woe

אָיַב 55
Kal.
enemy
enemy, to be an
foe

אֵיבָה 57
enmity
hatred

אֵיד 57
calamity
destruction

אַיָּה 57
kite
vulture

אַיֵּה 57
where?

אִיִּים 57
wild beast of the islands

אֵיךְ 57
how?
what?

אֵיכָה 57
how?
where?

אֵיכֹה (כ׳) 58
where

אֵיכָכָה.......... 58
how?

אַיָּל 58
hart

אַיִל 58
lintel
post
ram

אֵילִים 59
mighty
mighty men
oaks
trees

אֱיָל 59
strength

אַיָּלָה 59
hind

אֱיָלוּת 59
strength

אֵלַמִּים & אֵילַמִּים
.... 59
arches

אִילָן Ch. 59
tree

אַיֶּלֶת 59
Aijeleth
hind

אָיֹם 59
terrible

אֵימָה 59
dread
fear
horror
idol
terrible
terror

אַיִן 59
else
except
fail
*father*less
gone, to be
in*curable*
neither
never
no
no where
none
nor
nor any
nor any thing
not
nothing
nought, to
past
un*searchable*
well nigh
without

אַיִן 59
whence?
where?

אִין 59
not

אֵיפָה 59
divers measures
ephah
measure

אֵיפֹה 60
what manner
where

אִישׁ 60
also
another
any
any man
certain, a
champion †
consent
each
either of them
every
every one
fellow
*foot*man
friend
goodman
great man
he
high
high degree
him
him that is
husband
*husband*man
Ishi
Ish-*tob*
*Israel*ite
man
man*kind*
mighty man
none †
one
people
person
steward †
what man soever
whatsoever
whoso
whosoever
*who*soever
worthy

אִישׁ when in apposition with another word in Hebrew is often not expressed in the English.

אִישׁ 69
Hithpalel.
men, to shew selves

אִישׁוֹן 69
apple *of the eye*
black
obscure

אִיתוֹן 69
entrance

אִיתַי Ch. 69
art thou
can
do ye
have, to
it be
there are
there is
we will not

אֵתָן & אֵיתָן .. 70
Ethanim
hard
mighty
rough
strength
strong

אַךְ 70
also
any wise, in
at least
but
certainly
even
howbeit
nevertheless
notwithstanding
only
save
surely
surety, of a
truly
verily
wherefore †
yet
yet but

אַכְזָב 70
liar
lie

אַכְזָר 70
cruel
fierce

אַכְזָרִי 70
cruel
cruel one

אַכְזְרִיּוּת 70
cruel

אֲכִילָה 70
meat

אָכַל 70
Kal.
at all
burn up, to
consume, to
devour, to
devour up, to
devourer
dine, to
eat, to
eat up, to
eater
feed, to
food
freely
in...wise
indeed
meat
plenty, in
quite
Niphal.
at all
consumed, to be
devoured, to be
eaten, to be
Piel.
consume, to
Pual.
consumed, to be
devoured, to be
Hiphil.
consume, to
eat, to cause to
eat, to give to
feed with, to
lay meat. to

אֲכַל Ch. 75
P'al.
accuse,† to
devour, to
eat, to

אֹכֶל 75
eating
food
meal*time*
meat
prey
victuals

אָכְלָה 75
consume, to
devour, to
eat, to
food
fuel
meat

אָכֵן 75
but
certainly
nevertheless
surely
truly
verily

אָכַף 76
Kal.
crave, to

אֶכֶף 76
hand

אִכָּר 76
husbandman
plowman

אַל 76
Al- *Taschith*
nay
neither
never †
no
none
nor
not
nothing worth
rather than

אַל Ch. 76
not

אֵל 76
Beth-el
El-*beth*-el
El-*elohe*
God
* goodly
* great
idols
*Immanu*el
might
mighty
mighty one
power
strong

אֵל 77
these
those

אֵל Ch. 78
these

אֶל 78
about
according to
after
against
among
as for
at
because
before
beside
both...and
by
by reason of
concerning
for
from
hath
in
into
near
of
on
out of
over
that
through
to
touching
toward
under
unto
upon
where
whither
with
within

אֶלְגָּבִישׁ 78
great hail*stones*

אַלְגּוּמִּים 78
algum *trees*

אָלָה [1] 78
Kal.
lament, to

אָלָה [2] 78
Kal.
curse, to
swear, to
Hiphil.
adjure, to
swear, to cause to
swear, to make to

אָלָה 78
curse
cursing
execration
oath
swearing

אַלָּה 78
oak

אֵלָה 78
Elah
elm
oak
teil tree

אֱלָהּ Ch. 78
God

אֵלֶּה 79
another
one sort
other, the
so
some
such
them
these
these same
they
this
those
thus
which
who
whom

אֵלֶּה Ch. 79
these

אֱלֹהִים 79
angels
El-elohe- *Israel*
* exceeding
God
goddess
godly
gods
* great
judges
* mighty
* very great

אֲלוּ Ch. 93
behold

אִלּוּ 93
but if
yea though

אֱלוֹהַּ 93
God

אֱלוּל 94
Elul

אַלּוֹן 94
Allon-*bachuth*
oak

אֵלוֹן 94
plain

אַלּוּף & אַלֻּף 94
captain
chief friend
duke
friend
governor
guide
ox

אָלַח 94
Niphal.
filthy, to become

אַלְיָה 94
rump

אֱלִיל 94
idol—image
no value
thing of nought

אִלֵּין Ch. 95
the
these

אִלֵּךְ Ch. 95
these
those

אַלְלַי 95
woe

אָלַם 95
Niphal.
dumb, to be
silence, to be put to
Piel.
bind, to

אֵלֶם 95
congregation
Jonath-elem-*rech-okim*

אִלֵּם 95
dumb
dumb man

אַלְמֻגִּים 95
almug tree

אֲלֻמָּה 95
sheaf

אֵלַמּוֹת 95
arches

אַלְמָן 95
forsaken

אַלְמֹן 95
widowhood

אַלְמָנָה 95
widow

אַלְמְנוֹת 96
desolate houses
desolate palaces

אַלְמְנוּת 96
widow
widowhood

אַלְמֹנִי 96
one
such, and

אָלַף [1] 96
Kal.
learn, to
Piel.
teach, to
utter, to

אָלַף [2] 96
Hiphil.
thousands, to bring forth

אֶלֶף 96
Eleph
family
kine
oxen
thousand

אֲלַף & אֶלֶף Ch. 99
thousand

אָלַץ 99
Piel.
urge, to

אַלְקוּם 99
rising up, no

אֵם 99
dam
mother
* parting

אִם 100
and †
and not
but †
cannot
doubtless not
either
except †
if
if not †
more than †
moreover if
neither
nevertheless †
nor
not
oh that
or
save †
save only †
saving †
seeing
since
sith
surely †
surely no more
surely none
surely not
that not
though
truth,† of a
unless †
until †
verily †
when
whereas
whether
while
yet †

אָמָה 100
bondmaid

bondwoman
handmaid
maid
maidservant

אַמָּה 101
cubit
(כ׳) hundred
measure
post

אַמָּה Ch.......102
nation

אָמוֹן 102
brought up, one

אָמוֹן 102
multitude
populous

אֵמוּן 102
faith
faithful
truth

אֱמוּנָה also אֱמֻנָה
................102
faith
faithful
faithful *man*
faithfully
faithfulness
set office
stability
steady
truly
truth
verily

אֻמּוֹת & אִמִּים 103
nations
people

אַמִּין Ch. 103
cubits

אַמִּיץ & אַמִּץ 103
courageous
mighty
strong
strong one

אָמִיר..........103
bough
branch

אָמַל 103
Kal.
weak
Pulal.
languish, to
waxed feeble, to be

אֻמְלָל 103
feeble

אֻמְלַל 103
weak

אָמַן 1.........103
Kal.
bring up, to
bringer up
faithful
nurse
nursing father
Niphal.
established, to be
fail,† to
faithful, to be
long continuance, to be of
nursed, to be
stand fast, to
stedfast, to be
sure, to be
surely, to be
trusty, to be
verified, to be
Hiphil.
assurance, to have
believe, to
trust, to
trust, to put

אָמַן 2 104
Hiphil.
right, to turn to the

אֲמַן Ch. 104
Aphel.
believe, to
faithful
sure

אָמָּן 104
cunning workman

אָמֵן 104
Amen
so be it
truth

אֹמֶן 104
truth

אֲמָנָה 104
(כ׳) Abana
Amana
certain portion
sure

אָמְנָה 104
indeed

אָמְנָה 104
brought up

אֹמְנוֹת........104
pillars

אָמְנָם 104
doubt, no
indeed
surely
true, it is
truly
truth, of a

אֻמְנָם 104
indeed
of a surety
very deed, in

אָמֵץ 104
Kal.
courageous, to be
of good courage, to be
prevail, to
strong, to be
stronger, to be
Piel.
confirm, to
establish, to
fortify, to
harden, to
increase, to
obstinate, to make
strengthen, to
strong, to make
Hiphil.
strengthen, to
Hithpael.
speed, to make
stedfastly minded, to be
strengthen self, to

אָמֹץ 105
stronger

אַמְצָה 105
strength

אֲמֻצִּים....... 105
bay

אָמַר 105
Kal.
answer, to
appoint, to
bid, to
call, to
certify, to
challenge, to
charge, to
command, to
* commandment, at the
commune, to
consider, to
declare, to
demand, to
desire, to
determine, to
expressly
give commandment, to
indeed
intend, to
name, to
plainly
promise, to
publish, to
purpose, to
report, to
require, to
say, to
speak, to
speak against, to
speak of, to
still
suppose, to
talk, to
tell, to
* that is
think, to
use *speech*, to
utter, to
verily
yet
Niphal.
called, to be
said, to be
termed, to be
told, to be
Hiphil.
avouch, to
Hithpael.
boast self, to

אֲמַר Ch.......133
P'al.
command, to
declare, to
say, to
speak, to
tell, to

אֵמֶר 134
answer
* appointed unto him
saying
speech
word

אֹמֶר 134
promise
speech
thing
word

אִמְרָה 134
word

אִמְרָה 134
commandment
speech
word

אִמְּרִין Ch. 134
lambs

אֶמֶשׁ..........134
former time, in
yesterday
yesternight

אֱמֶת..........134
assured
assuredly
establishment
faithful
right
sure
true
truly
truth
verity

אַמְתַּחַת 135
sack

אֵמְתָנִי Ch. ...135
terrible

אָן 135
* any whither †
how?
* no whither †
where?
whither?
whithersoever

אֲנָא & אֲנָה Ch.135
I
me, as for

אָנָּא & אָנָּה ...136
beseech thee, I
beseech thee, we
Oh
pray thee, I

אָנָה 1..........136
Kal.
lament, to
mourn, to

אָנָה 2..........136
Piel.
deliver, to
Pual.
befall, to
happen, to
Hithpael.
seek a quarrel, to

אֲנוּ 136
we

אִנּוּן & אִנִּין Ch.136
* are
them
these

אֱנוֹשׁ..........136
another
* *blood*thirsty †
certain
chap*man*
divers
fellow
* flower of their age, in the
husband
man
man, certain
mortal man
people
person
servant
some
* some of them
* stranger †
they that
those
* trade, their

אֱנוֹשׁ when in apposition with another noun is sometimes not expressed in the English Translation.

אָנַח 139
Niphal.
groan, to
mourn, to
sigh, to

אֲנָחָה 139
groaning
mourn
sigh

אֲנַחְנָה & אֲנַחְנָא
Ch............140
we

אֲנַחְנוּ 140
ourselves
us
we

אֲנִי...........140
I
me
me, as for
mine
myself
we
which
who

אֳנִי........... 140
galley
navy
navy of ships

אֲנִיָּה 140
lamentation
sorrow

אֳנִיָּה..........140
ship
ship*men*

אֲנָךְ...........140
plumbline

אָנֹכִי 140
I
me, as for
* which

אָנַן........... 140
Hithpael.
complain, to

אָנַס 140
Kal.
compel, to

אֲנַס Ch. 140
P'al.
trouble, to

אָנַף 140
Kal.
angry, to be
displeased, to be
Hithpael.
angry, to be

אֲנָפָה 140
heron

אַנְפִּין Ch. 140
face
visage

אֲנַק 141
Kal.
cry, to
groan, to
Niphal.
cry, to

אֲנָקָה 141
crying out
ferret
groaning
sighing

אָנַשׁ 141
Kal.
desperate
incurable
wicked, desperately
woeful
Niphal.
sick, very

אֱנָשׁ Ch. 141
man
* whosoever †

אַנְתְּ Ch. 141
thee, as for
thou

אַנְתּוּן Ch. 141
ye

אָסוּךְ 141
pot

אָסוֹן 141
mischief

אֵסוּר 141
band
* prison †

אֱסוּר Ch. 141
band
imprisonment

אָסִף & אָסִיף .. 141
ingathering

אָסִיר 141
bound
bound, those which are
prisoner

אַסִּיר 141
prisoner

אֲסָמִים 141
barns
storehouses

אָסַף 141
Kal.
assemble, to
bring, to
consume with, to
destroy, to
fetch, to
gather, to
gather in, to
gather together, to
lose, to
put all together, to
recover (*another of leprosy*), to
rereward, to be
surely
take, to
take away, to
take up, to
utterly
withdraw, to
Niphal.
assemble selves, to
assembled, to be
brought, to be
gather selves together, to
gathered, to be
gathered together, to be
gathered up again, to be
generally
get him, to
gotten, to be
put up self, to
received, to be
taken, to be
taken away, to be
withdraw self, to
Piel.
gather, to
receive, to
rereward
rereward, to be
take into, to
Pual.
gathered, to be
gathered together, to be
Hithpael.
gathered together, to be

אֹסֶף 143
gathering

אֲסֵפָה 143
* together

אֲסֻפּוֹת 143
assemblies

אֲסֻפִּים 143
Asuppim
thresholds

אֲסַפְסֻף 143
multitude, mixt

אָסְפַּרְנָא Ch. .. 143
fast
forthwith
speed
speedily

אָסַר 143
Kal.
bind, to
bind selves, to
fast
gird, to
harness, to
hold, to
make ready, to
order, to
prepare, to
prison
prisoner
put in bands, to
set in array, to
tie, to
Niphal.
bound, to be
kept, to be
Pual.
bound, to be

אִסָּר & אֱסָר .. 144
binding
bond

אֱסָר Ch. 144
decree

אָע Ch. 144
timber
wood

אַף Ch. 144
also

אַף 144
also
although †
and
and furthermore
and yet
but
even
how much less
how much less †
how much more †
how much rather then †
moreover
therefore also
with
yea

אַף 144
anger
angry, to be
before
countenance
face
forbearing
forehead
*long*suffering
nose
nostril
snout
* worthy
wrath

אָפַד 146
Kal.
bind, to
gird, to

אֲפֻדָּה 146
ephod
ornament

אַפֶּדֶן 146
palace

אָפָה 146
Kal.
bake, to
bake*meats*
baker
Niphal.
baken, to be

אֵפוֹא & אֵפוֹ .. 146
here
now
where ?

אֵפֹד & אֵפוֹד . 146
ephod

אֲפִילֹת 146
grown up, not

אָפִיק 146
brook
channel
mighty
river
scales †
stream
strong pieces

אָפֵל 147
very dark

אֹפֶל 147
darkness
obscurity
privily

אֲפֵלָה 147
dark
darkness
gloominess
thick

אָפְנַיִם 147
* fitly

אָפֵס 147
Kal.
clean gone, to be
end, to be at an
fail, to
nought, to be brought to

אֶפֶס 147
ancle
but
but only
end
howbeit
less than nothing
nevertheless
no
none
none beside
not
not any
nothing
notwithstanding
nought, a thing of
save
saving
there
uttermost part
want
where no
without
without cause

אַפְסִי 147
none beside me

אֶפַע 147
nought, of

אֶפְעֶה 147
viper

אָפַף 147
Kal.
compass, to

אָפַק 147
Hithpael.
force self, to
refrain self, to
restrained, to be

אֵפֶר 147
ashes

אֲפֵר 148
ashes

אֶפְרֹחִים 148
young
young ones

אַפִּרְיוֹן 148
chariot

אַפְּתֹם Ch. ... 148
revenue

אֶצְבַּע 148
finger
toe

אֶצְבְּעָן Ch. ... 148
fingers
toes

אַצִּיל 148
*arm*hole
great

אֲצִילִים 148
chief men
nobles

אָצַל 148
Kal.
keep, to
reserve, to
take, to
Niphal.
straitened, to be
Hiphil.
take, to

אֵצֶל 148
at
beside
beside, from
by
from
hard by
near
near unto
toward
unto
with

אֶצְעָדָה 148
bracelet
chain

אָצַר 149
Kal.
lay up in store, to
store up, to
treasurer, to make
Niphal.
treasured, to be

אֶקְדָּח 149
carbuncle

אַקּוֹ 149
wild goat

אֶרְאֵל 149
valiant one

אָרַב 149
Kal.
ambush
lay wait, to
lie in ambush, to
lie in wait, to
lier in ambush
lying in wait, man
Piel.
ambushment
lier in wait
Hiphil.
lay wait, to

אֶרֶב 149
den
lie in wait

אֹרֶב 149
wait

אַרְבֶּה 149
grasshopper
locust

אֲרֻבָּה 149
chimney
window

אָרְבּוֹת 149
spoils

אַרְבָּעָה, אַרְבַּע 149
four
four*teen*
four*teenth*

אַרְבְּעָה, אַרְבַּע Ch. .... .51
four

אַרְבָּעִים 151
forty

אַרְבַּעְתַּיִם 152
fourfold

אָרַג 152
Kal.
Jaare-oregim
weave, to
weaver

אֶרֶג 152
beam
weaver's shuttle

אַרְגָּוָן.......... 152
purple

אַרְגְּוָנָא Ch. .. 152
scarlet

אַרְגַּז.......... 152
coffer

אַרְגָּמָן 152
purple

אָרָה 152
Kal.
gather, to
pluck, to

אֲרוּ Ch. 152
behold
lo

אֲרֻכָה & אֲרוּכָה
.... 152
health
made up
perfected

אָרֹן & אָרוֹן ... 153
ark
chest
coffin

אֻרְיוֹת & אֻרָוֹת 154
stalls

אֶרֶז............ 154
cedar
cedar tree

אַרְזָה 154
cedar work

אֲרָזִים 154
cedar, made of

אָרַח 154
Kal.
company
go, to
travelling company
wayfaring
wayfaring man

אֹרַח 154
*by*ways
highway
manner
path
race
rank
traveller
troop
way

אָרְחָא Ch. 155
way

אֲרֻחָה 155
allowance
diet
dinner
victuals

אַרְיֵה & אֲרִי .. 155
lion
lion, young
* pierce, to

אֲרִיאֵל אֲרִיאֵל &
אַרְאֵל 155
altar
Ariel
lionlike men

אַרְיֵה Ch...... 155
lion

אָרַךְ 156
Kal.
long, to be
long, to become
prolonged, to be
Hiphil.
defer, to
draw out, to
lengthen, to
lengthened, to be
long, to be
long, to make
outlive,† to
overlive,† to
prolong, to
prolonged, to be
tarry, to
tarry long, to

אֲרַךְ Ch. 156
meet, to be

אָרֵךְ.......... 156
long*suffering*
long*winged*
patient
slow to *anger*

אֹרֶךְ 156
* ever, † for
high
length
long

אַרְכָּא Ch. 157
lengthening

אֲרֻכָּה 157
long

אַרְכָה Ch..... 157
prolonged

אַרְכֻבָּה Ch... 157
knee

אַרְמוֹן 157
castle
palace

אֹרֶן............ 157
ash

אַרְנֶבֶת 157
hare

אֲרַע Ch....... 157
earth
inferior

אַרְעִית Ch..... 157
bottom

אֶרֶץ 157
* common
country
earth
field
ground
land
* nations
way

* wilderness †
world

אַרְקָא Ch..... 171
earth

אָרַר 171
Kal.
bitterly
curse, to
Niphal.
cursed, to be
Piel.
curse, to
curse, to cause the
Hophal.
cursed, to be

אָרַשׂ 172
Piel.
betroth, to
espouse, to
Pual.
betrothed, to be

אֲרֶשֶׁת 172
request

אֵשׁ 172
burning
fiery
fire
flaming
hot

אִשׁ 174
are there?
none can

אֶשָּׁא Ch..... 174
flame

אֶשֶׁד.......... 174
stream

אֲשֵׁדוֹת 174
Ashdoth-*pisgah*
springs

אִשָּׁה.......... 174
fire

אִשֶּׁה.......... 174
offering by fire
offering made by fire—by fire
sacrifice made by fire

אִשָּׁה.......... 175
* *adulter*ess
each
every
female
none †
one
* together †
wife
woman

אִשָּׁה when in apposition with another noun is sometimes not expressed in the English Translation.

אֱשׁוּן.......... 178
obscure

אֻשְׁיוֹת 178
foundations

אֻשַּׁיָּן Ch....... 178
foundations

אָשִׁישׁ 178
foundation

אֲשִׁישָׁה 178
flagon

אֶשֶׁךְ 178
stones

אֶשְׁכֹּל & אֶשְׁכּוֹל
.... 178
cluster
cluster of grapes
Eshcol

אֶשְׁכָּר........ 178
gift
present

אֶשֶׁל 178
grove
tree

אָשֵׁם & אָשַׁם 178
Kal.
certainly
desolate, to be
desolate, to be made
desolate, to become
greatly
guilty, to be
guilty, to be found
guilty, to become
guilty, to hold one's self
offence, to acknowledge
offend, to
trespass, to
Niphal.
desolate, to be made
Hiphil.
destroy, to

אָשָׁם.......... 179
guiltiness
offering for sin
sin
trespass
trespass offering

אָשֵׁם.......... 179
faulty, one which is guilty

אַשְׁמָה 179
offend, to
sin
trespass, cause of
trespass offering
trespassing

אַשְׁמֻרָה & אַשְׁמוּרָה
.... 179
watch

אַשְׁמַנִּים 179
desolate places

אֶשְׁנָב 179
casement
lattice

אָשַׁף Ch....... 179
astrologer

אַשְׁפָּה 179
quiver

אַשְׁפּוֹת 179
dung
dunghill

אָשְׁפִים.......... 180
astrologers

אֶשְׁפָּר........ 180
piece, good
piece of flesh, good

אָשַׁר 180
Kal.
go, to
Piel.
bless, to
blessed, to call
go, to
guide, to
happy, to call
lead, to
leader
relieve, to
Pual.
blessed, to be
happy
led, to be

אֲשֶׁר 180
after
alike
as
as soon as
because
every
for
forasmuch as †
from whence †
how †
howsoever †
if
so that
that
that thing which
that wherein
that which
though
until †
whatsoever †
when
where
whereas †
wherein
whereof †
whereon †
wheresoever
wherewith
which
whilst
whither
whithersoever
who
whom
whomsoever
whose

אֶשֶׁר 181
step

אֲשֻׁר.......... 181
Ashurite
going
step

אֹשֶׁר 181
happy

אֲשֵׁירָה & אֲשֵׁרָה
.... 181
grove

אַשְׁרֵי.......... 181
blessed
happy

אֻשַּׁרְנָא Ch. .. 182
wall

אֶשְׁתַּדּוּר Ch... 182
sedition

אַתְּ............ 182
thou

אֵת 182
against
among

before
by
for
from
in
into
of
out of
with

אֵת 182
coulter
plowshare

אָתָה & אָתָא ..182
Kal.
come, to
come, to be
come, things to
come upon, to
Hiphil.
bring, to
come, to

אֲתָה & אֲתָא Ch. 182
P'al.
come, to
come, to be
Aphel.
bring, to
Hophal.
bring, to
brought, to be

אַתָּה 183
thou

אָתוֹן 183
ass
she ass

אַתּוּן Ch.......183
furnace

אַתּוּק (כ') 183
gallery

אָתִין Ch.......183
signs

אַתִּיק 183
gallery

אַתֶּם 183
ye

אֶתְמוֹל & אִתְמוֹל 183
*before that time†
*beforetime †
*heretofore †
late, of
old, of
*times past †
yester*day*

אַתֵּן & אַתֵּנָה 183
ye
you

אֶתְנָה 183
reward

אֶתְנַן & אֶתְנָן ..183
hire
reward

אֲתַר Ch....... 183
after
place

אֲתָרִים 184
spies

בָּאָה 184
entry

בְּאוּשׁ Ch..... 184
bad

בָּאַר 184
Piel.
declare, to
plain, to make
plainly

בְּאֵר 184
Beer
Beer-*lahai-roi*
pit
*slime*pit
well

בֹּאר 184
cistern

בָּאַשׁ 184
Kal.
stink, to
Niphal.
abhorred, to be
abomination,to be had in
stink, to
Hiphil.
abhorred, to make to be
loathsome, to be
stink, to
stink, to make to
stinking savour, to cause a
utterly
Hithpael.
odious, to make selves

בְּאֵשׁ Ch.......184
P'al.
displeased, to be

בְּאשׁ 184
stink

בָּאְשָׁה 184
cockle

בְּאֻשִׁים........184
grapes, wild

בָּבָה 184
apple *of the eye*

בַּג (כ')........184
spoil

בָּגַד 184
Kal.
deceitfully,to deal
offend, to
transgress, to
transgressor
treacherous
treacherous dealer
treacherous man
treacherously, to deal
treacherously to depart
unfaithful man
unfaithfully, to deal
very

בֶּגֶד 185
apparel
cloth
clothes
clothing
garment
lap
rag
raiment
robe
*very *treacherously*
vesture
wardrobe

בֹּגְדוֹת 186
treacherous

בָּגוֹד 186
treacherous

בַּד 186
alone
apart
bars
beside
branches
by selves
each a like, of
except
only
staves
strength

בַּד 186
liar
lie
part

בַּד 187
linen

בָּדָא 187
Kal.
devise, to
feign, to

בָּדַד 187
Kal.
alone

בָּדָד 187
alone
desolate
only
solitary

בְּדִיל 187
plummet †
tin

בָּדַל 187
Niphal.
separate selves, to
separated, to be
Hiphil.
difference, to make a
difference, to put
divide, to
divide asunder, to
separate, to
separation, to make a
sever, to
sever out, to
utterly

בָּדָל 187
piece

בְּדֹלַח 187
bdellium

בָּדַק 187
Kal.
repair, to

בֶּדֶק 187
breach
*calker †

בְּדַר Ch....... 187
Pael.
scatter, to

בֹּהוּ 188
emptiness
void

בַּהַט 188
red *marble*

בְּהִילוּ Ch..... 188
haste, in

בָּהִיר 188
bright

בָּהַל or בָּהֵל ..188
Niphal.
affrighted, to be
afraid, to be
amazed,to be
dismayed, to be
haste, to
hasty, to be
speedy
troubled, to be
vexed, to be
Piel.
afraid, to make
haste, to make
rash, to be
speedily, to give
trouble, to
vex, to
Pual.
hastened, to be
hastily, to be gotten
Hiphil.
haste, to
thrust out, to
trouble, to

בְּהַל Ch.......188
Pual.
trouble, to
Ithp'al.
haste, in
troubled, to be

בֶּהָלָה 188
terror
trouble

בְּהֵמָה 188
beast
behemoth
cattle

בֹּהֶן 189
thumb
toe, great

בֹּהַק 189
spot, freckled

בַּהֶרֶת 189
spot, bright

בּוֹא 189
Kal.
abide, to
attain, to
* be, to
befall, to
besieged, † to be
brought, to be
certainly
come, to
come, to be
come against, to
come *out*, to
come,things forto
come upon, to
depart, to
doubtless again
*eat, † to
employ, † to
enter, to
enter in, to
entering in
entering into
entrance
fallen, to be
follow, † to
get, to
go, to
go down, to
go in, to
go to, to
going down
*have, † to
*have, to
indeed
*in*vade, to
laid, to be
*man came, a
mentioned, to be
pass, to come to
resort, to
run, to
run down, to
set, to be
*stricken *in age*, to be well
surely
way
Hiphil.
apply, to
bring, to
bring forth, to
bring in, to
call, to
carry, to
come, to cause to
come in, to let
enter, to cause to
(כ') entry
fetch, to
get, to
give, to
grant, to
lead, to
lift *up*,† to
pass, to bring to
pull in, to
put, to
send, to
take, to
take in, to
Hophal.
brought, to be
brought in, to be
brought into,to be
carried, to be
put, to be

בּוּז 205
Kal.
contemn, to
despise, to
utterly

בּוּז 205
contempt
contemptuously
despised
shamed

בּוּזָה 205
despised

בּוּךְ 205
Niphal.
entangled, to be
perplexed, to be

בּוּל 205
Bul

food
stock

בּוּס 205
Kal.
foot, to tread under
loath, to
tread, to
tread down, to
tread under, to
Polel.
foot, to tread under
tread down, to
Hophal.
foot, to tread under
Hithpael.
polluted, to be

בּוּץ 205
fine linen
white linen

בּוּקָה 205
empty

בּוֹקֵר 205
herdman

בּוֹר 205
cistern
dungeon
dungeon †
(כ׳) fountain
pit
well

בּוּר 206
Kal.
declare, to

בּוּשׁ 206
Kal.
ashamed, to be
at all
confounded, to be
confusion, to be put to
dry, to become
shame, with
Piel.
delay, to
long, to be
Hiphil.
ashamed, to make
shame, to
shame, to bring to
shame, to cause
shame, to put to
Hithpael.
ashamed, to be

בּוּשָׁה 206
shame

בּוּת Ch. 207
P'al.
night, to pass the

בַּז & בָּז 207
booty
Maher - shalal - hash-baz
prey
spoil
spoiled

בָּזָא 207
Kal.
spoil, to

בָּזָה 207
Kal.
despise, to
disdain, to
* scorn,† to think
Niphal.
contemned, to be
contemptible
despised, to be
vile person
Hiphil.
despise, to

בּוֹה 207
despise, to

בִּזָּה 207
prey
spoil

בָּזַז 207
Kal.
catch, to
gather, to
prey, for a
prey, to take for a
rob, to
robber
spoil, to
spoil, to take
take, to
take away, to
Niphal.
spoiled, to be
utterly
Pual.
robbed, to be

בִּזָּיוֹן 208
contempt

בָּזָק 208
lightning, flash of

בָּזַר 208
Kal.
scatter, to
Piel.
scatter, to

בָּחוֹן 208
tower

בַּחוּן 208
tower

בָּחוּר 208
choice young man
chosen
* hole
young
young man

בְּחוּרוֹת 208
youth

בָּחִיר 208
choose
chosen one
elect

בָּחַל 208
Kal.
abhor, to
Pual.
(כ׳) gotten hastily, to be

בָּחַן 208
Kal.
examine, to
prove, to
tempt, to
try, to
Niphal.
proved, to be
tried, to be
Pual.
trial

בַּחַן 209
tower

בֹּחַן 209
tried

בָּחַר 209
Kal.
appoint, to
choice
choose—ch. out
excellent
rather, to be
require, to
Niphal.
acceptable
choice
chosen, to be
Pual.
join

בַּחֻרִים 210
young men

בָּטָא & בָּטָה .. 210
Kal.
speak, to
Piel.
pronounce, to
speak unadvisedly, to

בָּטַח 210
Kal.
bold, to be
careless
careless one
careless woman
confidence, to put
confident, to be
hope, to
secure, to be
sure, to be
trust, to—tr. safely
trust, to put
Hiphil.
hope, to make to
trust, to make to

בֶּטַח 211
assurance
boldly
care, without
careless
confidence
hope
safe
safely
safety
secure
surely

בִּטְחָה 211
confidence

בִּטָּחוֹן 211
confidence
hope

בַּטֻּחוֹת 211
secure

בָּטַל 211
Kal.
cease, to

בְּטֵל Ch. 211
P'al.
cease, to
cease, to cause to
cease, to make to
hindered, to be

בֶּטֶן 211
belly
body
born, as they be within me
within thee
womb

בָּטְנִים 212
nuts

בִּי 212
alas
O
oh

בֵּין 212
among
asunder
at
between
betwixt
* betwixt...and †
* from †
from the midst
* in
out of
whether
* whether it be... or †
within

בֵּין Ch. 212
among
between

בִּין 212
Kal.
consider, to
diligently
(כ׳) direct, to
discern, to
feel, to
inform, to
instruct, to
intelligence, to have
know, to
look well, to
mark, to
perceive, to
prudent
regard, to
understand, to
understand, to cause to
understand, to make to
understanding, to give
view, to
wisely, to deal
Niphal.
discreet
eloquent
prudent, to be
understanding
understanding, to have
understanding, man of
Polel.
instruct, to
Hiphil.
consider, to
cunning, to be
discern, to
perceive, to
skilful
skill, can
teach, to
teacher
understand, to
understand, to cause to
understand, to make to
understanding
understanding, to give
understanding, to have
wise
wise man
Hithpolel.
attend, to
consider, to
consider diligently, to
perceive, to
regard, to
think, to
understand, to
understanding, to get

בִּינָה 213
knowledge
meaning
* perfectly
understanding
wisdom

בִּינָה Ch. 214
understanding

בֵּיצִים 214
eggs

בַּיִר 214
fountain

בִּירָה 214
palace

בִּירָה Ch. 214
palace

בִּירָנִיּוֹת 214
castles

בַּיִת 214
Beth-*dagon*
Beth-*emek*
Beth-*ezel*
Beth-*shemesh*
court
(כ׳) daughter
door
* dungeon †
family
forth of
* great as would contain
hangings
home
home*born*
house
houshold
inside
inward
palace
place
* prison †
* steward †
tablet †
temple
web
winter-house
within
without

בַּיִת Ch. 226
house

בִּיתָן 226
palace

בָּכָא 226
Baca
mulberry tree

בָּכָה 226
Kal.
at all
bewail, to
Bochim
complain, to
lamentation, to make
more
mourn, to
sore
* tears, with
weep, to
Piel.
weep, to

בֶּכֶה 227
* sore

בְּכוֹר 227
eldest
eldest son
firstborn
firstling

בִּכּוּר 228
firstfruit
firstripe
firstripe fig
hasty fruit

בְּכוֹרָה 228
birthright
firstborn
firstling

בִּכּוּרָה 228
firstripe
firstripe fruit

בַּכּוּרָה 228
firstripe

בָּכוּת 228
Allon-bachuth

בְּכִי 228
overflowing
* sore
weeping
weeping, continual
wept

בְּכִירָה 229
firstborn

בֶּכִית 229
mourning

בָּכַר 229
Piel.
firstborn, to make
new fruit, to bring forth
Pual.
firstling, to be
Hiphil.
first child, to bring forth

בֶּכֶר & בִּכְרָה .. 229
dromedary

בַּל 229
lest
neither
no
none
nor
not
not any
nothing
....not

בַּל Ch. 229
heart

בְּלָא Ch. 229
Pael.
wear out, to

בָּלַג 229
Hiphil.
comfort, to
recover strength, to
strengthen, to

בַּלָּה 229
Piel.
(כ׳) trouble, to

בָּלָה 229
Kal.
consume, to
old, to become
old, to wax
Piel.
consume, to
enjoy long, to
old, to make
spend, to
waste, to

בָּלֶה 229
old

בַּלָּהָה 229
terror
trouble

בְּלוֹ Ch. 229
tribute

בְּלוֹא 229
old

בְּלִי 229
corruption
ignorantly
lack of, for
no...is, where
none
not
so that no
un*awares*
without

בְּלִיל 230
corn
fodder
provender

בְּלִימָה 230
nothing

בְּלִיַּעַל 230
Belial
evil
naughty
ungodly
ungodly men
wicked

בָּלַל 230
Kal.
anointed, to be
confound, to
mingle, to
provender, to give
temper, to
Hiphil.
* fade, to
Hithpoel.
mix self, to

בָּלַם 230
Kal.
held in, to be

בָּלַס 230
Kal.
gatherer

בָּלַע 230
Kal.
devour, to
eat up, to
swallow down, to
swallow up, to
Niphal.
swallow up, to
Piel.
cover, to
destroy, to
devour, to
spend up, to
swallow up, to
Pual.
destroyed, to be
swallowed up, to be
Hithpael.
end, to be at

בֶּלַע 231
devouring
swallowed up, that which he hath

בִּלְעֲדֵי & בַּלְעֲדֵי 231
beside
not
not in
save
without

בָּלַק 231
Kal.
waste, to make
Pual.
waste

בִּלְתִּי 231
because un*satiable*
beside
but
continual †
except
from
lest
neither
no more
none
not
nothing
save
that no
without

בָּמָה 231
Bamah
Bamoth-*baal*
height
high place
wave

בְּמוֹ 232
for
in
into
through
(כ׳) water, with
with

בֵּן 232
afflicted †
age
*Ahoh*ite
*Ammon*ite
*anoint*ed one
appointed to
arrow
arrow †
*Assyr*ian
*Babylon*ian
Ben-*ammi*
Ben-*hanan*
Ben-*oni*
Ben-*zoheth*
Bene-*jaakan*
Ben*jamin*
Ben*jamite*
Beno
born, one
bough
branch
breed
bullock †
bullock,† young
calf
calf †
calf,† young
* came up in
child
colt
* common
* corn
(כ׳) daughter
*Egypt*ian
* first, of
firstborn †
foal
* fruitful,† very
*Grec*ian
*Hachmon*ite
hostage †
* in
kid †
lamb †
*Lev*ite
man
man †
meet
mighty †
Muth-labben
nephew †
old
people
people †
rebel †
robber †
* servant born
* soldier
son
* spark †
* steward †
stranger †
* surely
them of
tumultuous one †
valiant*est* †
whelp
worthy
young
young one
youth

בֵּן Ch. 258
child
son
young

בָּנָה 258
Kal.
build, to
build, to begin to
builder
make, to
repair, to
set up, to
surely
Niphal.
built, to be
children, to obtain
set, to be;—s. up

בְּנָא & בְּנָה Ch. 260
P'al.
build, to
make, to
Ithp'il.
builded, to be

בִּנְיָה 261
building

בֵּנַיִם 261
* champion †

בִּנְיָן 261
building

בִּנְיָן Ch. 261
building

בְּנַס Ch. 261
P'al.
angry, to be

בֹּסֶר 261
unripe grape

בֹּסֶר 261
sour grape

בְּעַד 261
about
at
by
for
means of, by
over
through
up
upon
within

בָּעָה 261
Kal.
cause, to boil
enquire, to
Niphal.
sought up, to be
swell out, to

בְּעָה & בְּעָא Ch. 261
P'al.
ask, to
desire, to
make *petition*, to
pray, to
request, to
seek, to

בָּעוּ Ch. 261
petition

בִּעוּתִים 261
terrors

בָּעַט 261
Kal.
kick, to

בְּעִי 261
grave

בְּעִיר 261
beast
cattle

בָּעַל 261
Kal.
Beulah
dominion, to have
dominion over, to have
husband, to be
married wife
marry, to
* wife
Niphal.
married, to be

בַּעַל 262
* archer †
Baali
* babbler †
* bird †
captain
chief man
* confederate †
* do,† to have...to
* dreamer †
due, those to whom it is
* furious †
given to it, those that are
great
* hairy †
hath it, he that
have, to
* horseman †
husband
lord
man
* married †
master
owner
person
* sworn †
they of

בְּעֵל Ch. 262
chancellor †

בַּעֲלָה 262
hath, that
mistress

בָּעַר 262
Kal.
brutish, to be
burn, to
burned, to be
heat, to
kindle, to
Niphal.
brutish, to be
brutish, to become
Piel.
bring away, to
burn, to
eat up, to
feed, to
put away, to
set on fire, to
take away, to
waste, to
Pual.
burn, to
Hiphil.
burn, to
eaten, to cause to be
kindle, to
set *on fire*, to
take away, to

בַּעַר 263
brutish
brutish person
foolish

בְּעֵרָה 263
fire

בָּעַת 263
Niphal.
afraid, to be
Piel.
affright, to
afraid, to make
terrify, to
trouble, to

בְּעָתָה 263
trouble

בֹּץ 263
mire

בִּצָּה 263
fen
mire
miry place

בָּצִיר 263
vintage

בָּצָל 263
onion

בָּצַע 263
Kal.
covet, to
covetous
cut, to
gain, to
get, to
given to *covetousness*, to be
greedy
wounded, to be
Piel.
cut off, to
finish, to
fulfil, to
gain greedily, to
perform, to

בֶּצַע 264
covetousness
dishonest gain
gain
lucre
profit

בָּצֵק 264
Kal.
swell, to

בָּצֵק 264
dough
flour

בָּצַר 264
Kal.
cut off, to
defenced
fenced, to be
gather, to
grapegatherer
mighty things
strong
(כ׳) vintage
walled, to be
walled up, to be
Niphal.
restrained, to be
withholden, to be
Piel.
fortify, to

בֶּצֶר 264
defence
gold

בְּצַר 264
gold

בָּצְרָה 264
Bozrah

בִּצָּרוֹן 264
strong hold

בַּצֹּרֶת 264
dearth
drought

בַּקְבֻּק 264
bottle
cruse

בְּקִיעַ 264
breach
cleft

בָּקַע 264
Kal.
break into, to
break through, to
cleave, to
divide, to
hatch, to
rend, to
rip up, to
win, to
Niphal.
break forth, to
break out, to
broken in pieces, to be
broken up, to be
burst, to be ready to
cleave, to
cleave asunder, to
rent, to be
rent asunder, to be
Piel.
cleave, to
cut out, to
hatch, to
rend, to
rip up, to
tear, to
Pual.
breach, to be made
rent, to be
ripped up, to be
Hiphil.
breach, to make a
break through, to
Hophal.
broken up, to be
Hithpael.
cleft, to be
rent, to be

בֶּקַע 265
bekah
shekel, half a

בִּקְעָא Ch. 265
plain

בִּקְעָה 265
plain
valley

בָּקַק 265
Kal.
emptier
empty, to make
empty out, to
void, to make
Niphal.
emptied, to be
fail, to
utterly
Polel.
empty, to

בָּקַר 265
Piel.
enquire, to
enquiry, to make
search, to
seek out, to

בְּקַר Ch. 265
Pael.
enquire, to
search, to make
Ithpael.
search, to be made

בָּקָר 266
beeve
bull
bullock †
calf †
cow †
great *cattle*
heifer †
herd
kine
ox

בֹּקֶר 266
day
* day †
early
morning
morrow

בַּקָּרָה 268
seek out

בִּקֹּרֶת 268
scourged

בָּקַשׁ 268
Piel.
ask, to
beg, to
beseech, to
desire, to
enquire, to
get, to
procure, to
request, to
request, to make
require, to
seek, to
Pual.
inquisition to be made
sought for, to be

בַּקָּשָׁה 269
request

בַּר 269
son

בַּר 269
choice
clean
clear
pure

בַּר & בָּר 269
corn
wheat

בַּר Ch. 269
old
son

בַּר Ch. 270
field

בֹּר 270
cleanness
* never so
purely
pureness

בָּרָא 270
Kal.
create, to
Creator
make, to
Niphal.
created, to be
done, to be
Piel.
choose, to
cut down, to
dispatch, to
Hiphil.
fat, to make selves

בַּרְבֻּרִים 270
fowl

בָּרַד 270
Kal.
hail, to

בָּרָד 270
hail
hail*stones*

בָּרֹד 270
grisled

בָּרָה 270
Kal.
choose, to
eat, to
Piel.
meat
Hiphil.
eat, to cause to
give *meat*, to

בְּרוֹמִים 271
apparel, rich

בְּרוֹשׁ 271
fir
fir tree

בְּרוֹתִים 271
fir

בָּרוּת 271
meat

בַּרְזֶל 271
ax head
head *of a hatchet*
iron

בָּרַח 271
Kal.
fain
fled, to be
flee, to
flee away, to
haste, to make
run away, to
shoot, to
Hiphil.
chase, to
chase away, to
drive away, to
flight, to put to
reach, to

בְּרִי 272
fat

בָּרִיא 272
fat
fat*fleshed*
fatter
fed
firm
plenteous
rank

בְּרִיאָה 272
new thing

בִּרְיָה 272
meat

בָּרִיחַ 272
crooked
nobles
piercing

בְּרִיחַ 272
bar
fugitive

בְּרִית 272
confederacy
confederate †
covenant
league

בֹּרִית 274
sope

בָּרַךְ 274

Kal.
blessed
kneel, to
kneel down, to
salute, to
still

Niphal.
blessed, to be

Piel.
abundantly
altogether
at all
blaspheme, to
bless, to
congratulate, to
curse, to
greatly
indeed
praise, to
praised, to be
salute, to
thank, to

Pual.
blessed, to be

Hiphil.
kneel down, to make to

Hithpael.
bless self, to
blessed, to be

בְּרַךְ Ch. 276

P'al.
bless, to
kneel, to

Pael.
bless, to

בֶּרֶךְ 276
knee

בֶּרֶךְ Ch. 276
knee

בְּרָכָה 276
Berachah
blessing
liberal
pool
present

בְּרֵכָה 277
fishpool
pool

בְּרַם Ch. 277
but
nevertheless
yet

בָּרַק 277

Kal.
cast forth, to

בָּרָק 277
bright
glitter
glittering
lightning
sword, glittering

בַּרְקָנִים 277
briers

בָּרֶקֶת 277
carbuncle

בָּרְקַת 277
carbuncle

בָּרַר 277

Kal.
choice
chosen
clearly
manifest, to
polished
pure
purge out, to

Niphal.
clean, to be
pure

Piel.
purge, to

Hiphil.
bright, to make
cleanse, to

Hithpael.
pure, to shew self
purified, to be

בְּשׂוֹרָה 277
tidings, reward for

בָּשָׂם 278
spice

בֶּשֶׂם 278
spice
sweet
sweet odours

בֹּשֶׂם 278
smell
spice
sweet

בָּשַׂר 278

Piel.
messenger
preach, to
publish, to
shew forth, to
tidings, to bear
tidings, to bring
tidings, to carry
tidings, to preach good
tidings, to tell good

Hithpael.
* tidings

בָּשָׂר 278
body
*fat*fleshed
flesh
kin
*lean*fleshed
*man*kind
nakedness †
self
skin

בְּשַׂר Ch. 280
flesh

בָּשַׁל 280

Kal.
ripe, to be
seethe, to

Piel.
bake, to
boil, to
roast, to
seethe, to
sod, to

Pual.
sodden, to be

Hiphil.
bring forth, to

בָּשֵׁל 280
* at all
sodden

בָּשְׁנָה 280
shame

בָּשַׁס 280

Poel.
tread, to

בֹּשֶׁת 280
ashamed
confusion
* greatly
shame, put to shame
shameful thing

בַּת 280
apple *of the eye*
Bath-*rabbim*
branch
company
daughter
* first
* old
owl †
town
village

בַּת 284
bath

בַּת Ch. 284
bath

בָּתָה 284
waste

בְּתוּלָה 284
maid
virgin

בְּתוּלִים 284
* maid
virginity

בַּתּוֹת 284
desolate

בָּתַק 284

Piel.
thrust through, to

בָּתַר 284

Kal.
divide, to

Piel.
divide

בֶּתֶר 284
Bether
part
piece

גֵּא 285
proud

גָּאָה 285

Kal.
gloriously
grow up, to
increase, to
risen, to be
triumph, to

גֵּאֶה 285
proud

גֵּאָה 285
pride

גַּאֲוָה 285
excellency
haughtiness
highness
pride
proudly
swelling

גָּאוֹן 285
arrogancy
excellency
excellent
majesty
pomp
pride
proud
swelling

גֵּאוּת 285
excellent things
lifting up
majesty
pride
proudly
raging

גַּאֲיוֹן 285
proud

גָּאַל 1 285

Kal.
any wise, in
at all
avenger
deliver, to
kinsfolk
kinsman
kinsman, to do the part of a
kinsman, near
kinsman, next
kinsman, to perform the part of a
purchase, to
ransom, to
redeem, to
redeemer
revenger
stain, to

Niphal.
redeem self, to
redeemed, to be

גָּאַל 2 286

Niphal.
defiled, to be
pollute selves, to
polluted, to be

Piel.
pollute, to

Pual.
polluted, to be

Hiphil.
stain, to

Hithpael.
defile self, to

גֹּאַל 286
defile

גְּאֻלָּה 286
kindred
redeem [of r.
redemption—; price
right

גַּב 286
back
body
boss
eminent place
*eye*brows
higher place
nave
ring

גַּב Ch 287
back

גֵּב 287
beam
ditch
Gebim
pit

גֹּב 287
locust

גֹּב Ch. 287
den

גֶּבֶא 287
marish
pit

גָּבַהּ 287

Kal.
exalted, to be
haughty, to be
high, to be
higher, to be
lift up self, to
lifted up, to be
proud, to be

Hiphil.
exalt, to
height
high, to make
mount up, to
raise up great height, to
upward

גָּבֹהַּ 287
high
proud

גֹּבַהּ 287
excellency
haughty
height
high
loftiness
pride

גַּבְהוּת 287
loftiness
lofty

גָּבֹהַּ & גָּבוֹהַּ .. 287
* exceeding proudly
haughty
height
high
higher
lofty
proud

גְּבוּל 288
border
bound
coast
(כ׳) great

landmark
limit
quarter
space

גְּבוּלָה 289
border
bound
coast
landmark
place

גִּבּוֹר 289
champion
chief
* excel
giant
man
mighty
mighty man
mighty one
strong
strong man
valiant man

גְּבוּרָה 290
force
mastery
might
mighty
mighty act
mighty power
power
strength

גְּבוּרָה Ch. 290
might

גִּבֵּחַ 290
forehead bald

גַּבַּחַת 290
bald forehead
* without

גְּבִינָה 290
cheese

גָּבִיעַ 290
bowl
cup
pot

גְּבִיר 290
lord

גְּבִירָה 291
queen

גָּבִישׁ..........291
pearl

גָּבַל 291
Kal.
border, to be
set, to
Hiphil.
bounds about, to set
bounds, to set

גַּבְלֻת 291
end

גִּבְלִי 291
Giblites
stonesquarer

גִּבֵּן............291
crookbackt

גַּבְנֻנִּים........291
high

גִּבְעָה..........291
Gibeah
hill
little hill

גִּבְעֹל 291
bolled

גָּבַר 291
Kal.
great, to be
mighty, to be
prevail, to
stronger, to be
valiant, to be
Piel.
put to more *strength*, to
strengthen, to
Hiphil.
confirm, to
prevail, to
Hithpael.
exceed, to
prevail, to
strengthen self, to

גֶּבֶר 292
every one
man
* mighty

גְּבַר 292
man

גְּבַר Ch. 292
certain
man

גִּבָּר Ch.........292
mighty

גְּבֶרֶת 292
lady
mistress

גָּג 292
house top
roof
roof of the house
top
top of the house

גַּד 292
coriander

גַּד 292
troop

גְּדָבְרִין Ch. ...293
treasurers

גָּדַד 293
Kal.
gather selves together, to
Hithpoel.
assemble selves by troops, to
cut selves, to
gather self in troops, to

גְּדַד Ch.......293
P'al.
hew down, to

גְּדָה 293
bank

גְּדוּד 293
army
band
band of men
company
troop
troop of robbers

גְּדוּד 293
cutting
furrow

גָּדוֹל 293
* aloud †
elder
eldest
* exceeding †
* exceedingly †
* far
great
great man
great matter
great thing
greater
greatness
high
long
loud
man of great
mighty
more
much
noble
proud thing
* sore
very
* very

גְּדוּלָּה & גְּדֻלָּה 296
dignity
great things
greatness
majesty

גִּדּוּף 296
reproach
reviling

גְּדוּפָה 296
taunt

גְּדִי............296
kid

גִּדְיָה..........296
bank

גְּדִיָּה..........296
kid

גָּדִישׁ..........296
shock
shock of corn
stack of corn
tomb

גָּדַל 297
Kal.
brought up, to be
exceed, to
great, to be
great, to become
great, to wax
greater, to be
grow, to
grown, to be
grown up, to be
magnified, to be
much set by, to be
pass, to
Piel.
advance, to
bring up, to
great, to make
grow, to make
magnify, to
nourish, to
nourish up, to
promote, to
Pual.
grown up, to be
Hiphil.
boast
do great *things*, to
exceed, to
excellent
great, to become
great estate, to be come to
great, to give
great, to make
great things,† to do
great; to wax
increase, to
lift up, to
magnifical
magnify, to
proudly *spoken*, to have
(כ') tower
Hithpael.
magnify self, to

גָּדֵל 297
great
grew

גֹּדֶל 297
greatness
stout
stoutness

גְּדִלִים 298
fringes
wreaths

גָּדַע 298
Kal.
cut asunder, to
cut off, to
hew down, to
Niphal.
cut, to be down
cut asunder, to be
cut down, to be
cut off, to be
Piel.
cut down, to
cut in sunder, to
hew down, to
Pual.
cut down, to be

גָּדַף 298
Piel.
blaspheme, to
reproach, to

גָּדַר 298
Kal.
close up, to
fence up, to
hedge, to
inclose, to
make *a wall*, to
make up, to
mason
repairer

גָּדֵר 298
fence
hedge
wall

גֶּדֶר 298
wall

גְּדֵרָה..........298
fold
hedge
*sheep*cote
*sheep*fold
wall

גֶּה 298
this

גָּהָה 298
Kal.
cure, to

גֵּהָה 298
medicine

גָּהַר 298
Kal.
cast self down, to
stretch self, to

גַּו 298
back

גַּו Ch. 298
midst
same
therein
wherein

גֵּו 299
among
back
body

גּוּב............299
Kal.
husbandman

גּוֹב............299
grasshopper
* grasshopper, great

גּוּד............299
Kal.
invade, to
overcome, to

גֵּוָה 299
body

גֵּוָה 299
lifting up
pride

גֵּוָה Ch.......299
pride

גּוּז............299
Kal.
bring
cut off, to

גּוֹזָל 299
pigeon, young
young

גּוֹי 299
Gentile
heathen
nation
people

גְּוִיָּה 302
body
carcase
corpse
dead body

גּוֹלָה 302
captive
captivity
carried away captive
carried away, those that had been
removing

גּוּמָּץ..........302
pit

גָּוַע............302
Kal.
dead, to be
die, to
ghost, to give up the
perish, to

גּוּף............303
Hiphil.
shut, to

גּוּפָה..........303
body

גּוּר............303
Kal.
abide, to
afraid, to be
dwell, to
fear, to
gather selves together, to
gather together, to
gathered, to be
inhabitant
remain, to
sojourn, to
sojourner
stand in awe, to
stranger
stranger, to be
surely
Hithpolel.
assemble selves, to
sojourn, to

גּוּר............303
whelp

גּוּר............303
whelp
young one

גּוֹרָל..........304
lot

גּוּשׁ..........304
clod

גֵּז............304
fleece
mowing
mown grass

גִּזְבָּר..........304
treasurer

גִּזְבָּר Ch.......304
treasurer

גָּזָה..........304
Kal.
take, to

גִּזָּה..........304
fleece

גָּזַז............304
Kal.
cut off, to
poll, to
shave, to
shear, to
shearer
sheepshearer
*sheep*shearers
Niphal.
cut down, to be

גָּזִית..........304
hewed
hewn stone
wrought

גָּזַל............304
Kal.
catch, to
consume, to
exercise *robbery*, to
pluck, to
pluck off, to
rob, to
spoil, to
take away, to
take away violently, to
take by force, to
tear, to
violence, to take by
Niphal.
taken away, to be

גָּזֵל............305
robbery
violence, thing taken away by

גֶּזֶל............305
violence
violent perverting

גְּזֵלָה..........305
robbed, that he had
spoil
that *which he took violently away*
violence

גָּזָם..........305
palmerworm

גֶּזַע............305
stem
stock

גָּזַר............305
Kal.
cut down, to
cut off, to be
decree, to
divide, to
snatch, to
Niphal.
cut off, to be
decreed, to be

גְּזַר Ch........305
P'al.
soothsayer
Ithp'al.
cut out, to be

גֶּזֶר............305
part
piece

גְּזֵרָה..........305
inhabited, not

גְּזֵרָה Ch.......305
decree

גִּזְרָה..........305
polishing
separate place

גָּחוֹן..........305
belly

גַּחֶלֶת..........305
burning coal;—hot coal [c.; c. of fire

גַּיְא............306
valley

גִּיד............306
sinew

גִּיחַ or גּוּחַ....306
Kal.
break forth, to
bring forth, to labour to
come forth, to
draw up, to
take out, to
Hiphil.
come forth, to

גִּיחַ or גּוּחַ Ch.306
Aphel.
strive, to

גִּיל or גּוּל....306
Kal.
glad, to be
joy, to;—delight
joyful, to be
rejoice, to

גִּיל............306
*exceedingly
gladness
* greatly
joy
rejoice †
rejoicing
sort

גִּילָה..........307
joy
rejoicing

גִּיר............307
chalk*stone*

גִּיר Ch........307
plaister

גֵּיר............307
stranger

גִּישׁ..........307
clod

גַּל............307
billow
Galeed
Gallim
heap
spring
wave

גֹּל............307
bowl

גַּלָּב..........307
barber

גַּלְגַּל..........307
heaven
rolling thing
wheel

גַּלְגַּל Ch......307
wheel

גִּלְגָּל..........307
wheel

גֻּלְגֹּלֶת........307
head
man, every
poll
scull

גֶּלֶד..........307
skin

גָּלָה..........307
Kal.
advertise,† to
appear, to
captive
captive, to go
captivity
captivity, to go into
carried away, to be
carry away captive, to
departed, to be
exile
gone, to be
open, to
open,† to
publish, to
remove, to
reveal,† to
shew, to
surely
tell, to
Niphal.
appear, to
discover selves, to
discovered, to be
opened, to be
plainly
removed, to be
reveal self, to
revealed, to be
shamelessly
shew self, to
uncover self, to
Piel.
bewray, to
disclose, to
discover, to
open, to
reveal, to
shew openly, to
uncover, to
Pual.
led away captive, to be
open
Hiphil.
bring, to
captivity, to cause to go into
carried away captive, to cause to be
carry away, to
carry captive, to
lead captive, to
led into captivity, to cause to be
remove, to
Hophal.
carried away, to be
carried away captive, to be
Hithpael.
discover self, to
uncovered, to be

גְּלָה Ch.......309
P'al.
reveal, to
revealer
Aphel.
bring over, to
carry away, to

גֻּלָּה............309
bowl
pommel
spring

גִּלּוּלִים........309
idols;—images

גְּלוֹם..........309
clothes

גָּלוּת..........309
captives
captivity
carried away captive, they that are

גָּלוּת Ch.......309
captivity

גָּלַח..........309
Piel.
poll, to
shave, to
shave off, to
Pual.
shaven, to be
Hithpael.
shave

גִּלָּיוֹן..........310
glass
roll

גָּלִיל..........310
folding
ring

גְּלִילָה........310
border
coast
country

גָּלַל............310
Kal.
commit, to
remove, to
roll, to
roll away, to
trust, to
Niphal.
rolled together, to be
run down, to
Poal.
rolled, to be
Hiphil.
roll, to
Hithpoel.
seek occasion, to
wallow, to
Pilpel.
roll down, to
Hithpalpel.
roll selves, to

גָּלָל............310
dung

גָּלָל............310
because of
for
for sake

גְּלָל Ch.......310
great

גֵּלֶל............310
dung

גָּלַם..........310
Kal.
wrap together, to

גֹּלֶם..........310
substance yet being unperfect

גַּלְמוּד........310
desolate
solitary

גָּלַע............310
Hithpael.
intermeddle, to
meddled with, to be
meddling, to be

גָּלַשׁ......... 310
Kal.
appear, to

גַּם 311
again
alike
also
as
as soon
both...and
but
either...or
even
for all
likewise
manner, in like
moreover
nay...neither
one
so...and
so much as
then
therefore
though
what
with
yea

גָּמָא 311
Piel.
swallow, to
Hiphil.
drink, to

גֹּמֶא 311
bulrush
rush

גֹּמֶד 311
cubit

גַּמָּדִים 311
Gammadims

גְּמוּל..........311
* as hast served †
benefit
desert
deserving
given, that which he hath
recompense
reward

גְּמוּלָה 311
deed
recompence
reward, such a

גָּמַל 311
Kal.
bestow on, to
deal bountifully, to
* do, to
do good, to
recompence, to
requite, to
reward, to
ripen, to
* serve,† to
wean, to
weaned child
yield, to
Niphal.
weaned, to be

גָּמָל 312
camel

גָּמַר 312
Kal.
cease, to
come to an end, to
fail, to
perfect, to
perform, to

גְּמַר Ch. 312
P'al.
perfect

גַּן 312
garden

גָּנַב 312
Kal.
carry away, to
steal, to
steal away, to
Niphal.
stolen, to be
Piel.
steal, to
Pual.
indeed
secretly brought, to be
stolen away, to be
Hithpael.
steal away, to
stealth, by

גַּנָּב...........313
thief

גְּנֵבָה..........313
theft

גַּנָּה 313
garden

גִּנָּה 313
garden

גְּנָזִים..........313
chests
treasuries

גִּנְזִין Ch.......313
treasure

גַּנְזַךְ 313
treasury

גָּנַן 313
Kal.
defend, to
Hiphil.
defend, to

גָּעָה 313
Kal.
low, to

גָּעַל 313
Kal.
abhor, to
lothe, to
Niphal.
vilely cast away, to be
Hiphil.
fail, to

גֹּעַל...........313
lothing

גָּעַר 313
Kal.
corrupt, to
rebuke, to
reprove, to

גְּעָרָה..........314
rebuke
rebuking
reproof

גָּעַשׁ 314
Kal.
shake, to
Pual.
troubled, to be
Hithpael.
moved, to be
shake, to
toss selves, to
Hithpoel.
moved, to be

גַּף 314
* highest places †
himself, by

גַּף Ch.........314
wing

גֶּפֶן............314
vine
vinetree

גֹּפֶר 314
gopher

גָּפְרִית 314
brimstone

גֵּר 314
alien
sojourner
stranger

גָּרָב 315
scab
scurvy

גַּרְגַּר..........315
berry

גַּרְגְּרוֹת........315
neck

גָּרַד 315
Hithpael.
scrape self, to

גָּרָה 315
Piel.
stir up, to
Hithpael.
contend, to
meddle, to
stirred up, to be
strive, to

גֵּרָה 315
cud

גֵּרָה 315
gerah

גָּרוֹן 315
aloud
mouth
neck
throat

גֵּרוּת..........315
habitation

גָּרַז 315
Niphal.
cut off, to be

גַּרְזֶן 315
ax

גָּרֹל (כ׳)......316
great, man of

גָּרַם 316
Kal.
gnaw the bone, to
Piel.
break, to

גֶּרֶם· 316
bone
strong
top

גְּרַם Ch. 316
bone

גֹּרֶן...........316
barn
barnfloor
corn
cornfloor
floor
threshingfloor
threshingplace
void place

גָּרַס 316
Kal.
break, to
Hiphil.
break, to

גָּרַע 316
Kal.
clip, to
diminish, to
minish, to
restrain, to
taken, thing
withdraw, to
Niphal.
abated, to be
diminished, to be
done away, to be
kept back, to be
taken, to be
taken away, to be
Piel.
small, to make

גָּרַף 316
Kal.
sweep away, to

גָּרַר 316
Kal.
catch, to
destroy, to
Niphal.
chew, to
Poal.
saw, to
Hithpoel.
continuing

גֶּרֶשׂ 316
beaten corn
corn beaten

גָּרַשׁ 316
Kal.
cast up, to
divorced
divorced woman
drive out, to
put away
Niphal.
cast out, to be
troubled
Piel.
cast out, to
drive away, to
drive out, to
expel, to
surely
thrust out, to
Pual.
driven forth, to be
thrust out, to be

גֶּרֶשׁ 317
put forth

גְּרֻשָׁה 317
exaction

גָּשַׁם 317
Hiphil.
rain, to cause

גֶּשֶׁם 317
rain
shower

גֶּשֶׁם Ch. 317
body

גֹּשֶׁם 317
rained upon

גָּשַׁשׁ 317
Piel.
grope, to

גַּת 317
press
winefat
winepress

גִּתִּית 317
Gittith

דָּא Ch. 317
one...another
this

דָּאַב 317
Kal.
mourn, to
sorrow, to
sorrowful

דְּאָבָה 317
sorrow

דְּאָבוֹן 318
sorrow

דָּאג 318
fish

דָּאַג 318
Kal.
afraid, to be
careful, to be
sorrow, to
sorry, to be
thought, to take

דְּאָגָה 318
care
carefulness
fear
heaviness
sorrow

דָּאָה.......... 318
Kal.
fly, to

דָּאָה..........318
vulture

דֹּב & דּוֹב....318
bear

דֹּב Ch. 318
bear

דֹּבֶא 318
strength

דָּבַב 318
Kal.
speak, to cause to

דִּבָּה 318
defaming
evil report
infamy
slander

דְּבוֹרָה........318
bee

דְּבַח Ch. 318
P'al.
offer *sacrifices*, to

דְּבַח Ch.......318
sacrifice

דִּבְיֹנִים........318
dove's dung

דְּבִיר..........318
oracle

דְּבֵלָה 318
cake of figs
lump of *figs*

דָּבַק & דָּבֵק..318
Kal.
abide fast, to
cleave, to
follow close, to
follow hard, to
joined together, to be
keep fast, to
keep self, to
stick, to
take, to
Pual.
cleave fast together, to
joined, to be
Hiphil.
cleave, to cause to
cleave, to make
follow hard after, to
overtake, to
pursue hard, to
stick, to cause to
Hophal.
cleave, to

דְּבַק Ch.......319
P'al.
cleave, to

דָּבֵק 319
cleave
joining
stick closer

דֶּבֶק 319
joint
soder

דָּבַר 319
Kal.
bid, to
commune, to
promise, to
say, to
speak, to
talk, to
tell, to
utter, to
Niphal.
speak, to
talk, to
Piel.
answer, to
appoint, to
bid, to
command, to
commune, to
declare, to
destroy, to
give, to
name, to
promise, to
pronounce, to
publish, to
rehearse, to
say, to
speak, to
spokesman, to be
talk, to
teach, to
tell, to
think, to
use *intreaties*, to
utter, to
well
wont
Pual.
spoken, to be
spoken for, to be
Hiphil.
subdue, to
Hithpael.
speak, to

דָּבָר 325
act
advice
affair
answer
answer,† to
* any such
any thing
because of
book
business
care
case
cause
certain rate
* certain rate
* chronicles †
commandment
* commune, to
communication
concern*ing*
confer,† to
counsel
dearth †
decree
deed
* disease
due
duty
effect
eloquent †
errand
*evilfavoured*ness
glory †
harm †
hurt
iniquity †
* judgment †
language
lying †
manner
matter
message
nothing
oracle
ought
parts
pertaining
please †
portion
power †
promise
provision
purpose
question
rate
reason
report
request
* said
* said, as hast
sake
saying
sentence
sign †
so †
some *unclean*ness
somewhat to say
song †
speech
* spoken
talk
task
that †
* there done
thing
thing concerning
thought
thus †
tidings
what
*what*soever
wherewith
whit
word
work

דֶּבֶר 334
murrain
pestilence
plague

דֹּבֶר 334
fold
manner

דִּבְרָה 334
cause
end
estate
order
regard

דִּבְרָה Ch. 334
intent
sake

דַּבְּרוֹת........334
words

דֹּבְרוֹת........334
floats

דְּבַשׁ..........334
honey
honey*comb*

דַּבֶּשֶׁת 335
bunches *of camels*

דָּג 335
fish

דָּגָה 335
fish

דָּגָה 335
Kal.
grow, to

דָּגַל 335
Kal.
banners, to set up
chiefest
Niphal.
banners, with

דֶּגֶל 335
banner
standard

דָּגָן............335
corn
corn*floor*
wheat

דָּגַר 335
Kal.
gather, to
sit, to

דַּד............335
breast
teat

דָּדָה 335
Hithpael.
go softly, to
go with, to

דְּהַב Ch.......336
gold
golden

דָּהַם 336
Niphal.
astonied, to be

דָּהַר 336
Kal.
pranse, to

דַּהֲרָה 336
pransing

דּוּב 336
Hiphil.
sorrow, to cause

דַּוָּג............336
fisher

דּוּגָה..........336
fish*hook*

דּוֹד............336
beloved
father's brother
love
uncle
wellbeloved

דּוֹדָה..........336
aunt
father's sister
uncle's wife

דּוּד 336
basket
caldron
kettle
pot
seething pot

דּוּדַי 336
baskets
mandrakes

דָּוָה 336
Kal.
infirmity

דָּוֶה 337
faint
menstruous cloth
sick, she that is
sickness, having

דּוּחַ 337
Hiphil.
cast out, to
purge, to
wash, to

דְּוַי............337
faint

דַּוַּי............337
languishing
sorrowful

דּוּךְ............337
Kal.
beat, to

דּוּכִיפַת 337
lapwing

דּוּמָה 337
silence

דּוּמִיָּה 337
silence
silent
waiteth

דּוּמָם 337
dumb
silent
wait, quietly

דּוּן............337
Kal.
strive, to

דּוּן............337
judgment

דּוֹנַג 337
wax

דּוּץ............337
Kal.
turned, to be

דּוּק Ch.......337
P'al.
broken to pieces, to be

דּוֹר............337
age
* evermore
generation
never
posterity

דּוּר 338
Kal.
dwell, to

דּוּר Ch.......338
P'al.
dwell, to
inhabitant

דּוּר 338
ball
* burn
round about

דּוּשׁ & דִּישׁ..338
Kal.
break, to
tear, to
thresh, to
tread out, to
Niphal.
trodden down, to be
Hophal.
threshed, to be

דּוּשׁ Ch.......338
P'al.
tread down, to

דָּחָה 339
Kal.
chase, to
overthrow, to
sore
thrust, to
totter, to
Niphal.
driven away, to be
driven on, to be
outcast
Pual.
cast down, to be

דַּחֲוָן 339
instruments of musick

דְּחִי 339
falling

דְּחַל Ch. 339
P'al.
dreadful
fear, to
terrible
Pael.
afraid, to make

דֹּחַן..........339
millet

דָּחַף 339
Kal.
hastened, to be
pressed on, to be
Niphal.
haste, to

דָּחַק 339
Kal.
thrust, to
vex, to

דַּי 339
able
according to
after
after ability
among
as
as oft as
enough
enough, more than
from
in
since
sufficient
sufficient, much as is
sufficiently
too much
very
when

דִּי Ch. 339
* as
but
for
forasmuch †
now †
of
seeing
than
that
therefore
until
what †
*what*soever
when
which
whom
whose

דִּיג...........340
Kal.
fish, to

דַּיָּג...........340
fisher

דַּיָּה 340
vulture

דְּיוֹ...........340
ink

דִּין...........340
Kal.
contend, to
execute *judgment*, to
judge, to
minister judgment, to
plead, to
plead the cause, to
Niphal.
at strife

דִּין Ch........340
P'al.
judge, to

דִּין...........340
cause
judgment
plea
strife

דִּין Ch. 340
judgment

דַּיָּן...........340
judge

דַּיָּן Ch. 340
judge

דָּיֵק...........340
fort

דִּישׁ 340
Kal.
tread out, to

דַּיִשׁ 340
threshing

דִּישׁוֹן 340
pygarg

דַּךְ...........340
afflicted
oppressed

דָּךְ & **דֵּךְ** Ch..340
same, the
this

דָּכָא 340
Niphal.
contrite one
Piel.
beat to pieces, to
break, to
break in pieces, to
bruise, to
crush, to
crushed, to be
destroy, to
oppress, to
smite, to
Pual.
broken, to be
bruised, to be
humbled, to be
Hithpael.
crushed, to be
destroyed, to be

דַּכָּא 341
contrite
destruction

דָּכָה 341
Kal.
crouch, to
Niphal.
broken, to be sore
contrite
Piel.
break, to
break sore, to

דַּכָּה 341
wounded †

דֳּכִי...........341
wave

דִּכֵּן Ch.......341
same
that
this

דְּכַר Ch.......341
ram

דִּכְרוֹן Ch.....341
record

דָּכְרָן Ch. 341
record

דַּל 341
door

דַּל...........341
lean
needy
poor
poor man
weaker

דָּלַג 341
Kal.
leap, to
Piel.
leap, to

דָּלָה 341
Kal.
draw, to
draw out, to
enough
Piel.
lift up, to

דָּלָה 342
door

דַּלָּה 342
hair
pining sickness
poor
poorest sort

דָּלַח 342
trouble, to

דְּלִי...........342
bucket

דְּלִי...........342
bucket

דָּלִיּוֹת 342
branches

דָּלַל 342
Kal.
bring low, to
dry up, to
emptied, to be
equal, to be not
fail, to
Niphal.
impoverished, to be
thin, to be made

דָּלַף 342
Kal.
drop through, to
melt, to
pour out, to

דֶּלֶף 342
dropping

דָּלַק 342
Kal.
burning
chase, to
kindle, to
persecute, to
persecutor
pursue, hotly to
Hiphil.
inflame, to
kindle, to

דְּלַק Ch.......342
P'al.
burn, to

דַּלֶּקֶת 342
inflammation

דֶּלֶת 342
door
gate
gate, two leaved
leaf
lid

דָּם...........343
blood
bloodguiltiness
blood*thirsty*
bloody
innocent †

דַּם...........345
* blood

דָּמָה [1] 345
Kal.
like, to be
likened, to be
perish, to
Niphal.
like, to be
Piel.
compare, to
devise, to
liken, to
mean, to
think, to
use similitudes, to
Hithpael.
like, to be

דָּמָה [2] 345
Kal.
cease, to
destroy, to
* liken, to
Niphal.
cut down, to be
cut off, to be
silence, to be brought to
undone, to be
utterly

דְּמָה Ch. 345
like, to be

דֻּמָּה..........345
destroyed

דְּמוּת.........345
fashion
like
like as
likeness
manner
similitude

דְּמִי 346
cutting off

דֳּמִי 346
rest
silence

דִּמְיוֹן..........346
* like

דָּמַם 346
Kal.
cease, to
forbear, to
peace, to hold
rest, to
silence, to keep
silent, to be
stand still, to
still, to be
tarry, to
wait, to
Niphal.
cut down, to be
cut off, to be
silent, to be
Poal.
quiet self, to
Hiphil.
put to silence, to

דְּמָמָה 346
calm
silence
still

דֹּמֶן 346
dung

דָּמַע 346
Kal.
sore
weep

דֶּמַע 346
liquor

דִּמְעָה 346
tears

דַּמֶּשֶׂק 346
* in Damascus

דֵּן Ch. 346
*afore*time
after this sort
here*after*
one...another
such
there*fore*
these
this
this matter
thus
where*fore*
which

דֵּעַ............347
knowledge
opinion

דֵּעָה 347
knowledge

דָּעַךְ 347
Kal.
extinct, to be
put out, to be
Niphal.
consumed, to be
Pual.
quenched, to be

דַּעַת 347
cunning
*ig*norantly
* know
know, to
knowledge
*un*awares
*un*wittingly

דֳּפִי...........348
slander*est*

הַוָּה 359
calamity
iniquity
mischief
mischievous
mischievous thing
naughtiness
naughty
noisome
perverse thing
substance
wickedness, very

הֹוָה 359
mischief

הוֹי 359
ah!
alas!
ho!
O!
woe!

הוּךְ Ch. 359
P'al.
bring again, to
come, to
go, to
go up, to

הוֹלֵלָה 359
madness

הוֹלֵלוּת 359
madness

הוּם 359
Kal.
destroy, to
Niphal.
moved, to be
ring again, to
Hiphil.
noise, to make a
m: a great noise

הוּן 360
Hiphil.
ready, to be

הוֹן 360
enough
*nought,† for
riches
substance
wealth

הָזָה 360
Kal.
sleep, to

הִי 360
woe

הִיא 360
her, as for
it
same, the
she
she herself
that
this
which is

הִיא Ch.......360
* are
it
this

הֻיְּדוֹת 360
thanksgiving

הֵידָד 360
shout
shouting

הָיָה 360
Kal.
altogether
be, to
become, to
cause, to
come, to
come to pass, to
do, to
fall, to
follow,† to
happen, to
*have, to
last, to
like, to be
pertain, to
quit selves, to
require, to
*use, to
Niphal.
accomplished, to be
be, to
become, to be
break, to
brought to pass, to be
committed, to be
done, to be
done, deed to be
faint, to

הַיָּה 361
calamity

הֵיךְ 361
how

הֵיכָל 361
palace
temple

הֵיכַל Ch. 361
palace
temple

הֵילֵל 362
Lucifer

הֲלִיכָה 362
way

הִין 362
hin

הָכַר 362
Hiphil.
strange, to make selves

הַכָּרָה 362
shew

הַל 362
)(

הָלְאָ 362
Niphal.
cast far off, to be

הָלְאָה 362
back
beyond
forward
henceforward
hitherto
thenceforth
yonder

הִלּוּלִים........362
merry
praise

הַלָּז............362
side
that
this

הַלָּזֶה..........362
this

הַלֵּזוּ 362
this

הָלִיךְ 362
step

הֲלִיכָה 362
company
going
walk
way

הָלַךְ 362
Kal.
all along
along
apace
*at the point, to be
come, to
continually
conversant, to be
depart, to
* eased, to be
enter, to
follow,† to
forth
forward
get thee, to
go, to
go about, to
go along, to
go away, to
go forward, to
go on, to
go out, to
gone, to be
* greater †
march, to
* more and more
needs
on
on continually
pass, to
pass away, to
quite
run, to
run along, to
send,† to
speedily
still
surely
talebearer †
traveller †
walk, to
wander, to
wax, to
*way*faring man
whirl, to
work, to
Niphal.
gone, to be
Piel.
exercise self, to
go, to
go, to cause to
lead, to
run, to
travel, to
walk, to
Hiphil.
walk, places to
Hithpael.
behave self, to
conversant, to be
depart, to
follow,† to
go, to
go abroad, to
go up and down, to
haunt, to be wont to
move self, to
run, to
walk, to
walk abroad, to
walk on, to
walk to and fro, to
walk up and down, to

הֲלַךְ Ch.......366
P'al.
walk, to
Aphel.
walk, to

הֵלֶךְ 366
* dropped
traveller

הֲלָךְ Ch.......366
custom

הָלַל 366
Kal.
fool
foolish
foolishly, to deal
shine, to
Piel.
boast, to
celebrate, to
commend, to
praise, to
sing praise, to
Poel.
fools, to make
mad against me
mad, to make
Pual.
commended, to be
marriage, to be given to
praised, to be
praised, worthy to be
renowned
Hiphil.
give *light*, to
shine, to
Hithpael.
boast, to
boast, to make
boast selves, to
glory, to
praised, to be
Hithpoel.
mad, to be
mad, to feign self
rage, to

הָלַם 367
Kal.
beat, to
beat down, to
break down, to
broken, to be
overcome with, to be
smite, to
smite with the hammer, to

הֲלֹם 367
here
hither
hither*to*
thither

הַלְמוּת.... ...367
hammer

הֵם 367
any of theirs

הֵם 367
*how many soever they be
it
same
* so
* so many more as they
* such
their
them
themselves
these
they
those
which
who

הֵמָּה 367
*like
same, the
them
these
they
this
who
whom
withal
ye

הָמָה 368
Kal.
clamorous
concourse
cry aloud, to
disquieted, to be
loud
mourn, to
moved, to be
noise, to make a
rage, to
roar, to
sound, to
troubled, to be
tumult, to make a
tumultuous
uproar, being in an

הִמּוֹ & הִמּוֹן Ch. 368
* are
them
those

הָמוֹן 368
abundance
company
Hamon-*gog*
many
multitude
noise
riches
rumbling
sounding
store
tumult

הֶמְיָה 368
noise

הֲמֻלָּה 368
speech
tumult

הָמַם 368
Kal.
break, to
consume, to
crush, to
destroy, to
discomfit, to
trouble, to
vex, to

הָמַן 369
Kal.
multiply, to

הַמְנִיךְ Ch. 369
chain

הֲמָסִים 369
melting

הֵן 369
* in
such like
them, with
thereby
therein
they, more than
wherein
which, in
whom
withal

הֵן 369
behold
if
lo
though

הֵן Ch. 369
if
or
that if
whether

הֵנָּה 369
* in
* such
such and such things
their
them, into
thence
therein
these
they
they had
this side, on
those
wherein

הֵנָּה 369
here
hither
hither*to*
now
on this side...on that side
since †
* this way ... or that way
thitherward
thus far †
* to...fro
yet †

הִנֵּה 369
behold
lo
see

הֲנָחָה 370
release

הָסָה 370
Piel.
peace, to hold
silence
silence, to keep
silent, to be
tongue, to hold
Hiphil.
still, to

הֲפוּגָה 370
intermission

הָפַךְ 370
Kal.
change, to
give, to
make *a bed*, to
overthrow, to
overturn, to
*over*turn, to
pervert, to
retire, to
turn, to
turn again, to
turn back, to
turned, to be
turning of things upside down
Niphal.
* become, to be
changed, to be
come, to
converted, to be
overthrown, to be
perverse
turned, to be
turned aside, to be
turned to the contrary, to be
turned up, to be
Hophal.
turned, to be
Hithpael.
tumble, to
turn every way, to
turned, to be

הֵפֶךְ & הֶפֶךְ..370
contrary

הֲפֵכָה 370
overthrow

הֲפַכְפַּךְ........370
froward

הַצָּלָה 370
deliverance

הֹצֶן 370
chariot

הַר 371
hill
hill country
mount
mountain
* promotion

הַרְאֵל 374
altar

הָרַג 374
Kal.
destroy, to
hand, out of
kill, to
murder, to
murderer
put to *death*, to
slay, to
slayer
surely
Niphal.
slain, to be
slaughter to be made
Pual.
killed, to be

הֶרֶג 375
slain, to be
slaughter

הֲרֵגָה..........375
slaughter

הָרָה 375
Kal.
bear, to
child, to be with
conceive, to
progenitor
Pual.
conceived, to be
Poel.
conceive, to

הָרֶה 375
child, with
child, to be with
child, woman with
conceive, to
* great

הַרְהֹר Ch. 375
thought

הֵרוֹן 376
conception

הָרִיָּה 376
child, woman with

הֵרָיוֹן 376
conception

הֲרִיסָה........376
ruin

הֲרִיסוּת 376
destruction

הַרְמוֹן 376
palace

הָרַס 376
Kal.
beat down, to
break, to
break down, to
break through, to
destroy, to
overthrow, to
pluck down, to
pull down, to
throw down, to
Niphal.
broken down, to be
overthrown, to be ruined
thrown down, to be
Piel.
destroyer
overthrow, to
utterly

הֶרֶס 376
destruction

הָרָר & הֶרֶר ..376
hill
mount
mountain

הַשְׁמָעוּת......376
hear, to cause to

הִתּוּךְ.........376
melted, is

הָתַל 376
Piel.
deal deceitfully, to
deceive, to
mock, to
Pual.
deceived

הֲתֻלִּים........376
mocker

הָתַת..........376
Poel.
mischief, to imagine

וָהֵב 377
* he did

וָו 377
hook

וָזָר...........377
* strange

וָלָד...........377
child

וָלֶד...........377
child

זְאֵב 377
wolf

זֹאת 377
hereby
herein
herewith
it
likewise
one, the
other, the
same, the
she
so
so much
such
such deed
that
therefore
these
this
this thing
thus

זָבַד 377
Kal.
endue, to

זֶבֶד 377
dowry

זְבוּב 377
fly

זְבֻל & זְבוּל ..377
dwell in, to
dwelling
habitation

זָבַח 377
Kal.
do sacrifice, to
kill, to
offer, to
sacrifice, to
slay, to
Piel.
offer, to
sacrifice, to

זֶבַח...........378
offer, to
offering
sacrifice

זָבַל...........379
Kal.
dwell with, to

זְבַן Ch.......379
P'al.
gain, to

זַג............379
husk

זֵד 379
presumptuous
proud

זָדוֹן..........379
presumptuously
pride
proud
proud, most

זֶה 380
he
hence
here
it
itself
now
of him
one...the other, the other, than the same
same, out of the
selfsame
such
such an one
that
these
this
this hath
this man
this side...on that, on
thus
very
which

זֹה 380
as well as another
it
that
this
thus and thus

זָהָב 380
gold
golden
weather, fair

זָהַם 382
Piel.
abhor, to

זָהַר 382
Niphal.
admonished, to be
warned, to be
Hiphil.
shine, to
teach, to
warn, to
warning, to give

זְהַר Ch. 382
P'al.
heed, to take

זֹהַר 382
brightness

זוֹ 383
that
this

זוּ............383
that
this
wherein
which
whom

זִו............383
Zif

זוּב...........383
Kal.
flow, to
gush out, to
issue, to have an
pine away, to
run, to
running issue, to have a

זוֹב 383
issue

זוּד or זִיד 383
Kal.
proud, to be
proudly, to deal
Hiphil.
presume, to
presumptuously
presumptuously, to come
proudly, to deal
sod, to

זוּד Ch.........383
Aphel.
pride, in

זָוִיּוֹת..........383
corner stones
corners

זוּל............383
Kal.
lavish, to
Hiphil.
despise, to

זוּלָה 383
beside
but
only
save

זוּן 383
Hophal.
fed, to be

זוּן Ch. 383
Ithp'el.
fed, to be

זוּעַ............384
Kal.
move, to
tremble, to
Pilpel.
vex, to

זוּעַ Ch.........384
P'al.
tremble, to

זְוָעָה 384
removed, to be
trouble
vexation

זוּר 1 384
Kal.
closed, to be
crush, to
thrust together, to be

זוּר 2 384
Kal.
another
another man
another place, to come from
estranged, to be
fanner
strange
strange, to be
strange thing
strange woman
stranger
Niphal.
estranged, to be
gone away, to be
Hophal.
stranger

זוֹרֶה 384
crushed, that which is

זָחַח 384
Niphal.
loosed, to be

זָחַל...........384
Kal.
afraid, to be
serpent
worm

זֵידוֹן 384
proud

זִיו Ch.........384
brightness
countenance

זִיז 384
abundance
wild beast

זִיקוֹת..........385
sparks

זַיִת............385
olive
olive tree
Olivet
oliveyard

זַךְ & זָךְ......385
clean
pure

זָכָה...........385
Kal.
clean, to be
clear, to be
pure, to count
Piel.
clean, to make
cleanse, to
Hithpael.
clean, to make

זָכוּ Ch........ 385
innocency

זְכוּכִית........385
crystal

זָכוּר 385
male
menchildren

זָכַךְ...........385
Kal.
clean, to be
pure, to be
purer, to be
Hiphil.
clean, to make

זָכַר...........385
Kal.
earnestly
mention, to
mention, to make
mindful, to be
recount, to
remember, to
remembrance, to call to
still
think on, to
well
Niphal.
male, to be
mention, to be made
mentioned, to be
remembered, to be
remembrance, to be come to
remembrance, to be in
Hiphil.
* burn *incense*, to
mention of, to make
record, to
recorder
remember, to
remembered, to make to be
remembrance, to bring to
remembrance, to call to
remembrance, to keep in
remembrance, to put in

זָכָר...........387
* him
male
man
man child
mankind

זֵכֶר & זֶכֶר....387
memorial
memory
remembrance
scent

זִכָּרוֹן..........387
memorial
record

זֻלּוּת..........388
vilest

זַלְזַלִּים........388
sprigs

זָלַל...........388
Kal.
glutton
riotous
riotous eaters
vile
Niphal.
flow down, to

זַלְעָפָה 388
horrible
horror
terrible

זִמָּה 388
heinous crime
lewd
lewdly
lewdness
mischief
purpose
thought
wicked device
wicked mind
wickedness

זְמוֹרָה 388
branch
slip
vine branch

זָמִיר..........388
singing

זְמִיר..........388
branch
psalm
psalmist
song

זָמַם 388
Kal.
consider, to
devise, to
imagine, to
plot, to
purpose, to
think, to
think evil, to

זָמָם 388
wicked device

זָמַן...........388
Pual.
appointed

זְמַן Ch.......388
Ithpael.
prepare, to

זְמָן...........388
season
time

זְמָן Ch. 388
season
time

זָמַר 389
Kal.
prune, to
Niphal.
pruned, to be
Piel.
praise, to give
praises, to sing
psalms, to sing
sing, to
sing forth, to

זְמָר Ch. 389
musick

זַמָּר Ch. 389
singer

זֶמֶר 389
chamois

זִמְרָה..........389
fruit, best
melody
psalm

זִמְרָת 389
song

זַן............389
kinds, divers
* manner of store, all

זַן Ch. 389
kind

זָנָב...........389
tail

זָנַב... 389
Piel.
hindmost, to smite the

זָנָה........... 389
Kal.
commit *whoredom*, to
fornication, to commit
great
harlot
harlot, to be an
harlot, to play the
whore
whore, to play the
whoredom, to commit
whoredom, to fall to
whoring, to go a
whorish
Pual.
whoredom, to commit
Hiphil.
continually
fornication, to cause to commit
whore, to cause to be a
whoredom
whoredom, to commit
whoring, to make to go a

זְנוּנִים 390
whoredom

זְנוֹת 390
armour

זְנוּת 390
whoredom

זָנַח 390
Kal.
cast off, to
remove far off, to
Hiphil.
cast away, to
cast off, to
turn far away, to

זָנַק...........390
Piel.
leap, to

זֵעָה...........390
sweat

זַעֲוָה 390
* removed
trouble

זְעֵיר 390
little

זְעֵיר Ch. 391
little

זָעַךְ...........391
Niphal.
extinct, to be

זָעַם...........391
Kal.
abhor, to
abominable
angry, to be
defy, to
indignation
indignation, to have
Niphal.
angry

זַעַם...........391
anger
indignation
rage

זָעַף...........391
Kal.
fret, to
sad
worse liking
wroth, to be

זָעֵף...........391
displeased

זַעַף...........391
indignation
rage
raging
wrath

זָעַק 391
Kal.
call, to
cry, to
cry out, to
Niphal.
assemble selves, to
called together, to be
company, to come with such a
gathered, to be
gathered together, to be
Hiphil.
assemble, to
call, to
cry, to
cry, to make to
gather together, to
proclaimed, to cause to be

זְעַק Ch....... 392
P'al.
cry, to

זְעָקָה 392
cry
crying

זֶפֶת 392
pitch

זִקִּים 392
chains
fetters
firebrands

זָקָן 392
beard

זָקֵן 392
Kal.
aged man
old, to be
old man
old, to wax
Hiphil.
old, to be
old, to wax

זָקֵן 392
aged
ancient
ancient man
elder
eldest
old
old man
old men and old women
senator

זֹקֶן 393
age

זִקְנָה 393
old
old age

זְקֻנִים 393
old age

זָקַף 393
Kal.
raise, to
raise up, to

זְקַף Ch. 394
P'al.
set up, to be

זָקַק 394
Kal.
fine, to
pour down, to
Piel.
purge, to
Pual.
purified
refined

זֵר 394
crown

זָרָא 394
loathsome

זָרַב 394
Pual.
wax warm, to

זָרָה 394
Kal.
cast away, to
fan, to
scatter, to
strew, to
winnow, to
Niphal.
dispersed, to be
scattered, to be
Piel.
compass, to
disperse, to
fan, to
scatter, to
scatter away, to
spread, to
Pual.
scattered, to be
spread, to

זְרוֹעַ 394
arm
* help,† to
mighty
power
shoulder
strength

זֵרוּעַ 395
sowing
sown, things that are

זַרְזִיף 395
water

זַרְזִיר 395
* greyhound †

זָרַח 395
Kal.
arise, to
rise, to
rise up, to
risen, to be
shine, to
up, as soon as is

זֶרַח 395
rising

זָרַם 395
Kal.
carry away as with a flood, to
Poal.
pour out, to

זֶרֶם 395
flood
overflowing
shower
storm
tempest

זִרְמָה 395
issue

זָרַע 395
Kal.
bear, to
set with, to
sow, to
sower
yield, to
Niphal.
conceive, to
sown, to be
Pual.
sown, to be
Hiphil.
conceive seed, to
yield, to

זֶרַע 396
* carnally
child
fruitful
seed
seedtime
sowing time

זְרַע Ch. 397
seed

זֵרֹעִים 397
pulse

זֵרְעֹנִים 397
pulse

זָרַק 397
Kal.
here and there, to be
scatter, to
sprinkle, to
strow
Pual.
sprinkled, to be

זָרַר 397
Poel.
sneeze, to

זֶרֶת 397
span

חֹב 398
bosom

חָבָא 398
Niphal.
* held
hid, to be
hide self, to
secretly, to do
Pual.
hide selves, to
Hiphil.
hide, to
Hophal.
hid, to be
Hithpael.
hid, to be
hide selves, to

חָבַב 398
Kal.
love, to

חָבָה 398
Kal.
hide self, to
Niphal.
hide selves, to

חֲבוּלָה Ch.... 398
hurt

חַבּוּרָה & חֲבֻרָה 398
blueness
bruise
hurt
stripe
wound

חָבַט ... .398
Kal.
beat, to
beat off, to
beat out, to
thresh, to
Niphal.
beaten out, to be

חֶבְיוֹן 398
hiding

חָבַל 398
Kal.
at all
band
corruptly, to deal
offend, to
pledge, to lay to
pledge of, to take a
very
withhold, to
Niphal.
destroyed, to be
Piel.
bring forth, to
destroy, to
spoil, to
travail, to
Pual.
corrupt, to be
destroyed, to be

חֲבַל Ch. 399
Pael.
destroy, to
hurt, to
Ithpael.
destroyed, to be

חֶבֶל & חֵבֶל ..399
band
coast
company
cord
country
destruction
line
lot
pain
pang
portion
region
rope
snare
sorrow
tackling

חֲבֹל 399
pledge

חֲבָל Ch. 399
hurt

חֲבָל Ch. 399
damage
hurt

חִבֵּל 399
mast

חֹבֵל 399
pilot
ship*master*

חֲבֹלָה 399
pledge

חֲבַצֶּלֶת 399
rose

חָבַק 399
Kal.
embrace, to
fold, to
Piel.
embrace

חִבֻּק 400
folding

חָבַר 400
Kal.
charmer
charming †
coupled, to be
coupled together, to be
joined, to be
joined together, to be
Piel.
couple, to
join self, to
Pual.
compact, to be
coupled together, to be
fellowship with, to have
joined, to be
joined together, to be
Hiphil.
heap up, to
Hithpael.
join self, to
join selves together, to
league

חַבָּר 400
companion

חָבֵר 400
companion
fellow
knit together

חֲבַר Ch. 400
companion
fellow

חֶבֶר 400
charmer †
charming †
company
enchantment
*wide

חֲבַרְבֻּרוֹת 400
spots

חַבְרָה Ch.....400
fellow

חֶבְרָה 400
company

חֲבֶרֶת 400
companion

חֹבֶרֶת 400
coupleth, which
coupling

חָבַשׁ 400
Kal.
bind, to
bind up, to

gird about, to
govern, to
healer
put, to
saddle, to
wrapped about, to be

Piel.
bind, to
bind up, to

Pual.
bound up, to be

חֲבִתִּים 401
pans

חַג & חָג......401
feast
feast day
sacrifice
solemn feast
solemnity

חָגָּא 401
terror

חָגָב 401
grasshopper
locust

חָגַג 401
Kal.
celebrate, to
dance, to
feast, to hold a
feast, to keep a
holyday, to keep
keep *a feast*, to
reel to and fro, to
solemn feast, to keep a

חֲגָוִים 401
clefts

חֲגוֹר 401
girded with
girdle

חֲגוֹרָה 401
apron
armour
gird, to
girdle

חָגַר 401
Kal.
able to put on, to be
afraid, to be
appointed
gird, to
restrain, to
* side, on every

חַד Ch. 402
a
first
one
together

חַד 402
sharp

חַד 402
one

חָדַד 402
Kal.
fierce, to be
sharpen, to

Hiphil.
sharpen, to

Hophal.
sharpened, to be

חָדָה 402
Kal.
joined, to be
rejoice, to

Piel.
glad, to make

חַדּוּדִים 402
sharp

חֶדְוָה 402
gladness
joy

חֶדְוָה Ch. 402
joy

חֲדִין Ch.......402
breast

חָדַל 402
Kal.
cease, to
end, to
fail, to
forbear, to
forsake, to
leave, to
leave off, to
let alone, to
rest, to
unoccupied, to be
want, to

חָדֵל 403
forbeareth, he that
frail
rejected

חֶדֶל 403
world

חֵדֶק 403
brier
thorn

חָדַר 403
Kal.
privy chamber, to enter a

חֶדֶר 403
*bed*chamber
chamber
* inner chamber
innermost part
inward part
parlour
* south
within

חָדַשׁ 403
Piel.
renew, to
repair, to

Hithpael.
renewed, to be

חָדָשׁ 403
fresh
new
new thing

חֹדֶשׁ 404
month
monthly
new moon

חֲדַת Ch. 405
new

חוֹב 405
debtor

חוּב 405
Piel.
endanger, to make

חוּג 405
Kal.
compass, to

חוּג 405
circle
circuit
compass

חוּד 405
Kal.
put forth, to

חָוָה 406
Piel.
shew, to

חֲוָא & חֲוָה Ch.406
Pael.
shew, to

Aphel.
shew, to

חַוּוֹת 406
Bashan - havoth - *jair*
Havoth-*jair*
small town
town

חוֹחַ 406
bramble
thicket
thistle
thorn

חוּט Ch. 406
Aphel.
join, to

חוּט 406
cord
fillet
line
thread

חוּל & חִיל....406
Kal.
abide, to
afraid, to be
anguish, to be in
bring forth, to
child, to travail with
dance, to
fall grievously, to
fall with pain, to
fear, to
great
grieve, to
grievous, to be
hope, to
look, to
pain, to be in
pained, to be much
pained, to be sore
rest, to
shake, to
sorrow, to
sorrowful, to be
stay, to
tarry, to
travail, to
tremble, to
wait carefully, to
wounded, to be

Polel.
bear, to
calve, to
calve, to make to
dance, to
drive away, to
form, to
formed, to be
trust, to

Pulal.
brought forth, to be
made, to be
shapen, to be

Hophal.
bring forth, to be made to

Hithpolel.
grievous
travail with pain, to
wait patiently, to

Hithpalpel.
grieved, to be

חוֹל 407
sand

חוּם 407
brown

חוֹמָה 407
wall
walled

חוּס 408
Kal.
pity, to
regard, to
spare, to

חוֹף 408
coast *of the sea*
haven
shore
side, *sea*

חוּץ 408
abroad
field
forth
highway
Kirjath-huzoth
more
out
outside
outward
street
without

חוק 409
bosom

חָוַר 409
Kal.
pale, to wax

חוּר 409
network

חוֹר 409
cave
hole

חוּר 409
white

חוּר 409
hole

חִוָּר Ch. 409
white

חוֹרִים 409
nobles

חוּשׁ 409
Kal.
haste, to
haste, to make
hasten, to
Maher - *shalal* - hash-*baz*
ready

Hiphil.
haste, to
haste, to make
hasten, to

חוֹתָם 410
seal
signet

חָזָה 410
Kal.
behold, to
look, to
prophesy, to
provide, to
see, to

חֲזָא & חֲזָה Ch.410
P'al.
behold, to
have *a dream*, to
see, to
wont, to be

חָזֶה 410
breast

חֹזֶה 410
agreement
prophet
see, that
seer
*star*gazer

חֱזוּ Ch. 411
look
vision

חָזוֹן 411
vision

חָזוֹת 411
vision

חֲזוֹת Ch. 411
sight

חָזוּת 411
agreement
notable
notable one
vision

חִזָּיוֹן 411
vision

חֲזִיז 411
bright cloud
lightning

חֲזִיר 411
boar
swine

חָזַק 411
Kal.
catch hold, to
confirmed, to be
constant, to be
courage, to be of good
courageous, to be
courageously
encouraged, to be
established, to be
harden, to
hardened, to be
prevail, to
recovered, to be
sore, to be
sore, to wax
stout, to be
strengthen, to
strengthened, to be
strong, to be

strong, to make
strong, to wax
stronger, to be
sure, to be
urgent, to be

Piel.

aid, to
amend, to
encourage, to
fasten, to
fortify, to
hard, to make
harden, to
help, to
maintain, to
mend, to
repair, to
strengthen, to
strong, to make

Hiphil.

* calker †
catch, to
cleave, to
confirm, to
constrain, to
continue, to
force, to
hold, to
hold fast, to
hold, to lay
lean, to
obtain, to
prevail, to
relieve, to
repair, to
retain, to—;receive
seize, to
strengthen, to
strong, to be
strong, to make
take, to
take hold, to

Hithpael.

courage, to be of good
courage, to take
encourage self, to
hold, to
men, to play the
mighty, to become
mighty, to wax
strengthen self, to
strengthened, to be
strong, to be
strong, to make self
strong, to shew self
valiantly, to behave selves
withstand, to

חָזָק 413

harder
hottest
impudent †
loud
mighty
sore
stiff*hearted*
strong
stronger

חָזֵק 413

stronger
* wax louder

חֵזֶק 414

strength

חֹזֶק 414

strength

חָזְקָה 414

force
mightily
repair, to
sharply

חָזְקָה 414

strength
strengthen self
strong
strong, was

חַח 414

bracelet
chain
hook

חָחִי 414

hook

חָטָא 414

Kal.

blame, to bear the
commit *sin*, to
fault, to be
harm he hath done
offend, to
sin, to
sinful
sinner
trespass, to

Piel.

cleanse, to
loss, to bear the
offer for sin, to
purge, to
purify self, to
reconciliation, to make

Hiphil.

miss, to
offender, to make an
sin, to cause to
sin, to make to

Hithpael.

purified, to be
purify, to
purify self, to

חֵטְא 415

fault
grievously
offence
punishment of sin
sin

חַטָּא 416

offender
sinful
sinner

חַטָּאָה 416

sin
sinful

חַטָּאָה Ch. 416

sin offering

חַטָּאָה 416

sin
sin offering

חַטָּאת 416

punishment
punishment of sin
purification for sin
purifying
sin
sin offering
sinner

חָטַב 417

Kal.

cut down, to
hew, to
hewer

Pual.

polished, to be

חֲטֻבוֹת 417

carved

חִטָּה 418

wheat
wheaten

חֲטָי Ch. 418

sin

חַטָּיָא Ch. 418

sin offering

חָטַם 418

Kal.

refrain, to

חָטַף 418

Kal.

catch, to

חֹטֶר 418

rod

חַי 418

* age †
alive
appetite
beast
beast, wild
Beer-lahai-*roi*
company
congregation
creature, living
life
lifetime
live
live, to
lively
living
living thing
maintenance
merry †
multitude
* old †
old, to be
quick
raw
running
springing
troop

חַי Ch. 421

life
liveth, that
living

חִידָה 421

dark saying
dark sentence
dark speech
hard question
proverb
riddle

חָיָה 421

Kal.

certainly
* God save
live, to
recover, to
revive, to
surely
whole, to be

Piel.

alive, to keep
alive, to leave
alive, to make
life, to give
live, to let
live, to suffer to
nourish up, to
preserve, to
preserve alive, to
quicken, to
repair, to
revive, to
save, to
save alive, to
save life, to

Hiphil.

alive, to keep
alive, to make
live, to let
promise life, to
restore to life
restore to life, to
save, to
save alive, to
save lives, to

חֲיָא & חֲיָה Ch. 423

P'al.

live, to

Aphel.

alive, to keep

חָיֶה 423

lively

חֵיוָא Ch. 423

beast

חַיּוּת 423

* living

חָיַי 423

Kal.

live, to
save life, to

חַיִל 423

able
activity
army
army †
band of men
band of soldiers
company
forces
forces, great
goods
host
might
power
riches
strength
strong
substance
train
valiant
valiant †
valiantly
valour
virtuous
virtuously
war
wealth
worthily
worthy

חַיִל Ch. 425

aloud
army
* most *mighty*
power

חֵיל 425

army
bulwark
host
poor †
rampart
trench
wall

חִיל 425

pain
pang
sorrow

חִילָה 425

sorrow

חֵילָה 425

bulwark

חִין 425

comely

חַיִץ 425

wall

חִיצוֹן 425

outer
outward
utter
without

חֵיק 425

bosom
bottom
lap
midst
within

חִישׁ 426

Kal.

haste, to make

חִישׁ 426

soon

חֵךְ 426

mouth
mouth, roof of the
taste

חָכָה 426

Kal.

wait, to

Piel.

long, to
tarry, to
wait, to

חַכָּה 426

angle
hook

חַכִּים Ch. 426

wise

חַכְלִילִי 426

red

חַכְלִלוּת 426

redness

חָכַם 426

Kal.

wise, to be
wise, to shew self

Piel.

wisdom, to teach
wiser, to make

Pual.

* exceeding
wisely, never so

Hiphil.

wise, to make

Hithpael.

wise, to make self
wisely, to deal

חָכָם 426

cunning
cunning man
subtil
*un*wise
wise
wise *hearted*
wise man

חָכְמָה 427
skilful
wisdom
wisely
wit

חָכְמָה Ch. 428
wisdom

חָכְמוֹת 428
wisdom

חַכְמוֹת 428
every wise *woman*

חֹל 428
common
profane
profane place
unholy

חָלָא 428
Kal.
diseased, to be

חֶלְאָה 428
scum

חָלָב 428
cheese †
milk
sucking

חֵלֶב 429
* best
fat
fatness
* finest
grease
marrow

חֶלְבְּנָה 429
galbanum

חֶלֶד 429
age
short time
world

חֹלֶד 429
weasel

חָלָה 429
Kal.
diseased, to be
grieved, to be
sick, to be
sick, to fall
sore
sorry, to be
travail, woman in
weak, to be
weak, to become
Niphal.
diseased
grief
grieved, to be
grievous
grievous, to be
pain, to put selves to
sick, to be
Piel.
beseech, to
infirmity
intreat, to
lay, to
* pray, to
prayer, to make
suit, to make
* supplication, to make
Pual.
weak, to become
Hiphil.
grief, to put to
sick, to make
Hophal.
wounded, to be
Hithpael.
sick, to fall
sick, to make self

חַלָּה 430
cake

חֲלוֹם 430
dream
dreamer
dreamer

חַלּוֹן 431
window

חֲלוֹף 431
* destruction

חֲלוּשָׁה 431
being overcome

חַלְחָלָה 431
pain
pain, great
pain, much

חָלַט 431
Hiphil.
catch, to

חֲלִי 431
jewel
ornament

חֳלִי 431
disease
grief
sick, is
sickness

חֶלְיָה 431
jewel

חָלִיל 431
pipe

חָלִילָה 431
far, be
forbid
* God forbid

חֲלִיפָה 431
change
course

חֲלִיצָה 431
armour
spoil

חֵלְכָה 431
poor

חָלַל 432
Kal.
instruments, player on
wounded, to be
Niphal.
defiled, to be
* inheritance, to take
polluted, to be
profane self, to
profaned, to be
Piel.
* break, to
* common things, to eat as
defile, to
* eat, to
* gather the grape thereof, to
pipe, to
pollute, to
profane, to
profane, to cast as
prostitute, to
slay, to
stain, to
Pual.
profaned, to be
slain
Poel.
wound, to
Poal.
wounded, to be
Hiphil.
begin, to
* break, to
* first
sorrow, to
Hophal.
* began men

חָלָל 433
kill
profane
slain
slain man
* slew
wounded
wounded, deadly

חָלַם[1] 433
Kal.
dream, to
dreamer
Hiphil.
dreamed, to cause to be

חָלַם[2] 433
Kal.
liking, in good
Hiphil.
recover, to

חֵלֶם Ch. 434
dream

חַלָּמוּת 434
egg

חַלָּמִישׁ 434
flint
flinty
rock

חָלַף 434
Kal.
abolish, to
change, to
changed, to be
cut off, to
go on forward, to
grow up, to
over, to be
pass, to
pass away, to
pass on, to
pass through, to
strike through, to
Piel.
change, to
Hiphil.
alter, to
change, to
renew, to
renewed, to be
sprout, to

חֲלַף Ch. 434
P'al.
pass, to

חֵלֶף 434
* for

חָלַץ 434
Kal.
armed
armed man
armed, ready
armed soldier
draw out, to
loose, to
prepared
prepared, ready
put off, to
withdraw self, to
Niphal.
arm *selves*, to
armed, to go
delivered, to be
Piel.
deliver, to
take away, to
Hiphil.
fat, to make

חֲלָצַיִם 435
loins
reins

חָלַק 435
Kal.
distribute, to
divide, to
divided, to be
give, to
impart, to
part, to
part, to have
partner
portion, to take away a
receive, to
smoother, to be
Niphal.
distribute, to
divide, to
divide self, to
divided, to be
parted, to be
Piel.
deal, to
distribute, to
divide, to
part, to
Pual.
divided, to be
Hiphil.
flatter, to
separate self, to
smooth, to
Hithpael.
divide, to

חֵלֶק 435
flattering
Halak
smooth

חֲלָק Ch. 435
portion

חֵלֶק 435
flattery
inheritance
part
* partaker
portion
smooth

חָלָק 436
smooth

חֶלְקָה 436
field
flattering
flattery
ground
Helkath-*hazzurim*
parcel
part
piece *of ground*
piece of land
plat
portion
slippery place
smooth
smooth thing

חֲלֻקָּה 436
division

חֲלָקוֹת 436
flatteries

חֲלַקְלַקּוֹת 436
flatteries
slippery

חָלַשׁ 436
Kal.
discomfit, to
waste away, to
weaken, to

חַלָּשׁ 436
weak

חָם 436
father in law

חָם 436
hot
warm

חֹם 436
heat
hot, to be
warm, to be

חֵמָא 436
fury

חֵמָא & חֱמָא Ch. 436
fury

חֶמְאָה 436
butter

חָמַד 437
Kal.
beauty
covet, to
delectable thing
delight, to
desire, to
lust, to
Niphal.
desired, to be
pleasant, to be
Piel.
* delight, great

חֶמֶד 437
desirable
pleasant
* wine, red

חֶמְדָּה 437
desire
goodly
pleasant
precious

חַמָּה 437
heat
sun

חֵמָה 437
anger
bottles
displeasure, hot
furious
furiously
fury
heat
indignation
poison
rage
wrath
wrathful

חֵמָה 438
butter

חֲמוּדוֹת 438
beloved, greatly
goodly
pleasant
pleasant thing
precious
precious thing

חָמוֹץ 438
oppressed

חַמּוּק 438
joint

חֲמוֹר 438
ass
ass, he

חֲמֹרָתַיִם 439
heaps

חָמוֹת 439
mother in law

חֹמֶט 439
snail

חָמִיץ 439
clean

חֲמִישִׁי & חֲמִשִׁי 439
fifth
fifth part
fifth time

חָמַל 439
Kal.
compassion, to have
pity, to
pity, to have
spare, to

חֶמְלָה 439
merciful
pity

חָמַם 439
Kal.
heat, to get
heat, to have
hot, to be
hot, to wax
warm, to be
warm at, to
warm self, to
warm, to wax
Niphal.
enflame selves, to
hot, to be
Piel.
warm, to
Hithpael.
warmed, to be

חַמָּנִים 440
idols
images

חָמַס 440
Kal.
shake off, to
violate, to
violence, to do
violently to take away
wrong, to
wrongfully to imagine
Niphal.
bare, to make

חָמָס 440
cruel
cruelty
damage
false
injustice
oppressor †
unrighteous
violence
violence against
violence done
violent
violent dealing
wrong

חָמֵץ 440
Kal.
cruel man
dyed
leavened, to be
Hiphil.
leavened, to be
Hithpael.
grieved, to be

חָמֵץ 440
leaven
leavened
leavened bread

חֹמֶץ 440
vinegar

חָמַק 440
Kal.
withdraw self, to
Hithpael.
go about, to

חָמַר 441
Kal.
daub, to
red, to be
trouble, to
Poalal.
foul, to be
troubled, to be

חֵמָר 441
slime
slimepit

חֶמֶר 441
* pure
wine, red

חֲמַר Ch. 441
wine

חֹמֶר 441
clay
heap
homer
mire
mortar

חָמַשׁ 441
Piel.
fifth part, to take up the

חָמֵשׁ & חֲמִשָּׁה 441
fifteen
fifth
five
* five apiece

חֹמֶשׁ 443
fifth part

חֹמֶשׁ 443
fifth (*rib*)

חֲמִשִּׁים 443
fifty

חֲמֻשִׁים 444
armed
armed men
harnessed

חֵמֶת 444
bottle

חֵן 444
favour
grace
gracious
pleasant
precious
*well*favoured

חָנָה 445
Kal.
abide, to
camp, to
dwell, to
encamp, to
grow to an end, to
lie, that
pitch, to
pitch tent, to
rest in tent, to
tents, to abide in

חַנּוּן 445
gracious

חָנוּת 445
cabin

חָנַט 445
Kal.
embalm, to
put forth, to

חִנְטִין Ch. 446
wheat

חָנִיךְ 446
trained

חֲנִינָה 446
favour

חֲנִית 446
javelin
spear

חָנַךְ 446
Kal.
dedicate, to
train up, to

חֲנֻכָּה 446
dedicating
dedication

חֲנֻכָּה Ch. 446
dedication

חִנָּם 446
cause, without a
causeless
cost nothing, to
cost, without
free
freely
innocent
nothing, for
nought, for
vain, in
wages, without

חֲנָמַל 446
frost

חָנַן 446
Kal.
deal graciously, to
favour, to
favour, to shew
favourable, to be
give, graciously to
gracious, to be
grant, graciously to
intreat, to
merciful
merciful, to be
mercy, to shew
mercy upon, to have
pity upon, to have very
Niphal.
gracious, to be
Piel.
* fair
gracious to, to be
Poel.
favour, to
mercy on, to have
Hophal.
favour, to find
favour to be shewed
Hithpael.
beseech, to
intreat, to
make *supplication*, to
pray, to
supplication, to make

חֲנַן Ch. 447
P'al.
mercy, to shew
Ithpael.
supplication, to make

חָנֵף 447
Kal.
defile, to
defiled, to be greatly
polluted, to be
profane, to be
Hiphil.
corrupt, to
defile, to
pollute, to

חָנֵף 447
hypocrite
hypocritical

חֹנֶף 447
hypocrisy

חֲנֻפָּה 447
profaneness

חָנַק .... .447
Niphal.
hang self, to
Piel.
strangle, to

חָסַד 447
Piel.
shame, to put to
Hithpael.
merciful, to shew self

חֶסֶד 448
favour
good deed
goodliness
goodness
kindly
kindness
lovingkindness
merciful
merciful kindness
mercy
pity
reproach
wicked thing

חָסָה 449
Kal.
hope, to have
refuge, to make
trust, to
trust, to put

חָסוּת 449
trust

חָסִיד 449
godly
godly man
good
holy
Holy One
merciful
saint
*un*godly

חֲסִידָה 449
* feather
stork

חָסִיל 450
caterpiller

חָסִין 450
strong

חַסִּיר Ch. 450
wanting

חָסַל 450
Kal.
consume, to

חָסַם 450
Kal.
muzzle, to
stop, to

חָסַן 450
Niphal.
laid up to be

חֲסַן Ch. 450
Aphel.
possess, to

חָסֹן 450
strong

חֲסֵן Ch. 450
power

חֹסֶן 450
riches
strength
treasure

חֲסַף Ch. 450
clay

חַסְפַּס 450
round thing

חָסֵר 450
Kal.
abated, to be
decrease, to
fail, to
lack, to
need, to have
want, to
Piel.
bereave, to
lower, to make
Hiphil.
fail, to cause to
lack, to have

חָסֵר 450
destitute
fail, to
lack, to
need, to have
void
want, to

חֶסֶר 450
poverty
want

חֹסֶר 450
want of, in

חֶסְרוֹן 451
wanting

חַף 451
innocent

חָפָא 451
Piel.
secretly, to do

חָפָה 451
Kal.
cover, to
Niphal.
covered, to be
Piel.
ceil, to
overlay, to

חֻפָּה 451
chamber
closet
defence

חָפַז 451
Kal.
haste
haste, to make
tremble, to
Niphal.
haste away, to
haste, to make

חִפָּזוֹן 451
haste

חָפְנַיִם 451
fists
hand*ful*
hands
hands, both

חָפַף 451
Kal.
cover, to

חָפֵץ 451
Kal.
any at all
delight, to
delight, to have
delight, to take
desire, to
favour, to
like, to
move, to
pleased, to be
pleased, to be well
pleasure, to have
will, to
would

חָפֵץ 452
delight in
desire, to
favour
please, to
pleasure, to have
whosoever would
willing
wish

חֵפֶץ 452
acceptable
delight
delightsome
desire
desire, to
desired, things
Hephzi-*bah*
matter
pleasant
pleasure
purpose
willingly

חָפַר 452
Kal.
dig, to
paw, to
search out, to
seek, to

חָפֵר 452
Kal.
ashamed, to be
confounded, to be
confusion, to be brought to
shame, to be brought unto
shame, to be put to
Hiphil.
ashamed, to be
reproach, to bring
shame, to come to
shame, to be put to

חֲפֹר 452
* mole †

חָפַשׂ 452
Kal.
search, to
search for, to
search out, to
Niphal.
searched out, to be
Piel.
search, to
search, to make diligent
search out, to
Pual.
diligent
hidden, to be

Hithpael.
changed, to be
disguise self, to

חֵפֶשׂ 453
search

חָפַשׁ 453
Pual.
free, to be

חֹפֶשׁ 453
precious

חֻפְשָׁה 453
freedom

חָפְשׁוּת........453
several

חָפְשִׁי..........453
free
liberty

חָפְשִׁית........453
several

חֵץ 453
* archer †
arrow
dart
shaft
staff
wound

חָצֵב & חָצַב..453
Kal.
dig, to
divide, to
hew, to
hew out, to
hewer
make, to
mason
Niphal.
graven, to be
Pual.
hewn, to be
Hiphil.
cut, to

חָצָה 454
Kal.
divide, to
* half, to live out
midst, to reach to the
part, to
Niphal.
divided, to be
part, to

חֲצוֹת..........454
mid*night*

חֲצִי & חֵצִי....454
half
middle
mid*night*
midst
part
two parts

חֵצִי...........454
arrow

חָצִיר..........454
court

חָצִיר..........455
grass
hay
herb
leek

חֵצֶן 455
bosom

חֹצֶן...........455
arm
lap

חֲצַף Ch. 455
Aphel.
hasty
urgent, to be

חָצַץ 455
Kal.
* bands
Piel.
archer
Pual.
midst, to be cut off in the

חָצָץ 455
arrow
gravel
gravel stone

חֲצֹצֵר 455
Piel.
blow, to
sound, to
trumpeter

חֲצֹצְרָה........455
trumpet
trumpeter

חָצַר 455
Piel.
trumpeter
Hiphil.
blow, to
sound, to

חָצֵר 455
court
Hazar-*hatticon*
town
village

(כ') חֲצֹרֵר 456
Piel.
sound, to

חֹק 456
appointed
bound
commandment
convenient
custom
decree
decreed
due
law
measure
* necessary
ordinance
ordinary
portion
set time
statute
task

חָקָה 457
Pual.
carved work
pourtrayed
Hithpael.
print, to set a

חֻקָּה 457
appointed
custom
manner
ordinance
rite
statute

חָקַק...........458
Kal.
appoint, to
decree, to
governor
grave, to
note, to
pourtray, to
set, to
Poel.
decree, to
governor
lawgiver
Pual.
law
Hophal.
printed, to be

חֵקֶק...........458
decree
thought

חָקַר...........458
Kal.
search, to
search, to make
search out, to
seek, to
sound, to
try, to
Niphal.
found out, to be
searched, to be
searched out, to be
Piel.
seek out, to

חֵקֶר...........458
finding out
number
search
searched out
searching
*un*searchable

חֲרָאִים........458
dung

חָרֵב & חָרַב..458
Kal.
decay, to
desolate, to be
dried up, to be
dry, to be
slay, to
utterly
waste, to
waste, to be laid
waste, to lie
wasted, to be
Niphal.
desolate ;—wasted
slain, to be
Pual.
dried, to be
Hiphil.
destroy, to
destroyer
dry up, to
waste, to lay
waste, to make
Hophal.
surely
waste, to be laid

חֲרַב Ch.......459
Hophal.
destroyed, to be

חָרֵב...........459
desolate
dry
waste

חֶרֶב 459
axe
dagger
knife
mattock
sword
tool

חֹרֶב 461
desolation
drought
dry
heat
* utterly
waste

חָרְבָּה 461
decayed place
desert
desolate
desolate place
desolation
destruction
waste
waste, laid
waste place

חָרָבָה 462
dry
dry ground
dry land

חֲרָבוֹן 462
drought

חָרַג 462
Kal.
afraid, to be

חַרְגֹּל 462
beetle

חָרַד 462
Kal.
afraid, to be
careful, to be
quake, to
tremble, to
Hiphil.
afraid, to make
discomfit, to
fray, to
fray away, to

חָרֵד 462
afraid
tremble

חֲרָדָה 462
care
* exceedingly
fear
quaking
trembling

חָרָה 462
Kal.
angry, to be
burn, to
displeased, to be
grieve, to
hot, to be
hot, to wax
kindled, to be
very
wrath, to be
Niphal.
incensed, to be
Hiphil.
* earnestly
kindle, to
Tiphel.
close, to
contend, to
Hithpael.
fret self, to

חֲרוּזִים 463
chains

חָרוּל 463
nettle

חָרוֹן 463
displeasure, sore
fierce
fierceness
fury
wrath
wrath, fierce
wrathful

חָרוּץ 463
decision
fine gold
gold
pointed things
sharp
threshing instrument
wall

חָרוּץ 463
diligent

חַרְחֻר 463
burning, extreme

חֶרֶט 463
graving tool
pen

חַרְטֹם Ch. 464
magician

חַרְטֻמִּים 464
magician

חֳרִי 464
fierce
* great
heat

חֹרִי 464
white

חֲרִיטִים 464
bags
crisping pins

חֲרִים 464
dung

חָרִיץ 464
cheese †
harrow

חָרִישׁ 464
earing
earing time
ground

חֲרִישִׁי 464
vehement

חָרַךְ 464
Kal.
roast, to

חֲרַךְ Ch. 464
Ithpael.
singe, to

חֲרַכִּים 464
lattice

חָרַם 464
Kal.
nose, to have a flat
Hiphil.
accursed, to make
consecrate, to
destroy, to
destroy, utterly to
devote, to
slay, utterly to
utterly
utterly to make away
Hophal.
destroyed, utterly to be
devoted, to be
forfeited, to be

חֵרֶם 464
accursed
accursed thing
curse
cursed thing
dedicated thing
destroyed, things which should have been utterly
destruction, appointed to utter
devoted
devoted thing
net
utter destruction

חֶרְמֵשׁ 465
sickle

חֶרֶס 465
itch
sun

חַרְסִית or **חַרְסוּת** 465
east

חָרַף 465
Kal.
reproach, to
winter, to
Niphal.
betrothed
Piel.
blaspheme, to
defy, to
jeopard, to
rail, to
reproach, to
upbraid, to

חֹרֶף 465
cold
winter
winter*house*
youth

חֶרְפָּה 465
rebuke
reproach
reproachfully
shame

חָרַץ 466
Kal.
bestir self, to
decide, to
decreed
determined
maimed
move, to
Niphal.
determined, to be

חֲרַץ Ch. 466
loin

חַרְצֻבּוֹת 466
bands

חַרְצַנִּים 466
kernel

חָרַק 466
Kal.
gnash, to

חָרַר 466
Kal.
burn, to
burned, to be
Niphal.
angry, to be
burned, to be
dried, to be
Pilpel.
kindle, to

חֲרֵרִים 466
parched places

חֶרֶשׂ 466
earth
earthen
potsherd
sherd
stone †

חָרַשׁ 466
Kal.
deaf, to be
devise, to
ear, to
graven
hold peace, to
imagine, to
keep silence, to
plow, to
plower
plowman
silent, to be
worker
Niphal.
plowed, to be
Hiphil.
altogether
cease, to
conceal, to
leave off speaking, to
peace, to hold
rest, to
secretly to practise
silence, to keep
speak not a word, to
still, to be
tongue, to hold
Hithpael.
quiet, to be

חָרָשׁ 467
artificer
carpenter
carpenter †
craftsman
engraver
maker
mason †
skilful
smith
smith †
worker
workman
wrought, such as

חֵרֵשׁ 467
deaf

חֲרָשׁ 467
Charashim
craftsmen
artificer
secretly

חֹרֵשׁ 467
artificer

חֹרֶשׁ 467
bough
forest
shroud
wood

חֲרֹשֶׁת 468
carving
cutting

חָרַת 468
Kal.
graven

חָשַׂךְ 468
Kal.
asswage, to
* darken, to
forbear, to
hinder, to
hold back, to
keep, to
keep back, to
punish, to
refrain, to
reserve, to
spare, to
withhold, to
Niphal.
asswaged, to be
reserved, to be

חָשַׂף 468
Kal.
bare, to make
clean
discover, to
draw out, to
take, to
uncover

חֲשִׂף 468
flock, little

חָשַׁב 468
Kal.
conceive, to
count, to
cunning
cunning man
cunning *work*
cunning workman
devise, to
esteem, to
find out, to
forecast, to
hold, to
imagine, to
impute, to
invent, to
mean, to
purpose, to
regard, to
think, to
Niphal.
accounted, to be
counted, to be
esteemed, to be
imputed, to be
reckoned, to be
reckoning to be made
Piel.
account of, to make
consider, to
count, to
devise, to
forecast, to
imagine, to
like, to be

reckon, to
think, to
Hithpael.
reckoned, to be
חֲשַׁב Ch.......469
P'al.
repute, to
חֵשֶׁב 469
girdle, curious
חֶשְׁבּוֹן.........469
account
device
reason
חִשְּׁבֹנוֹת 469
engines
inventions
חָשָׁה 469
Kal.
peace, to hold
silence, to keep
silent, to be
still, to be
Hiphil.
peace, to hold
still, to
still, to be
חֲשׁוֹךְ Ch. 469
darkness
חֲשַׁח Ch.......469
P'al.
careful
need of, to have
חַשְׁחוּת 469
needful, be
חֲשֵׁיכָה........469
darkness
חָשַׁךְ 469
Kal.
black, to be
dark, to be
darkened, to be
dim, to be
Hiphil.
dark, to make
darken, to
darkness, to cause
hide, to
חָשֹׁךְ 470
mean
חֹשֶׁךְ 470
dark
darkness
night
obscurity
חֲשֵׁכָה 470
dark
חֶשְׁכָה 470
dark
חָשַׁל 470
Niphal.
feeble
חֲשַׁל Ch.......470
P'al.
subdue, to
חַשְׁמַל 470
amber
חַשְׁמַנִּים 470
princes
חֹשֶׁן 470
breastplate
חָשַׁק 471
Kal.
delight, to have a
desire, to
desire, to have a
long, to
love, to set
Piel.
fillet, to
Pual.
filleted, to be
חֵשֶׁק 471
desire
pleasure
חֲשֻׁקִים........471
fillets
חִשֻּׁקִים........471
felloes
חַשְׁרָה........471
dark
חִשֻּׁרִים........471
spokes
חֲשַׁשׁ.........471
chaff
חַת...........471
broken
dismayed
dread
fear
חָתָה 471
Kal.
heap, to
take, to
take away, to
חִתָּה 471
terror
חִתּוּל.........471
roller
חַתְחַתִּים 471
fears
חִתִּית 471
terror
חָתַךְ 471
Niphal.
determine, to
חָתַל 471
Pual.
swaddled, to be
Hophal.
at all
חֲתֻלָּה 471
swaddling band
חָתַם 471
Kal.
(כ׳) end, to make an
seal, to
seal up, to
Niphal.
sealed, to be
Piel.
mark, to
Hiphil.
stopped, to be
חֲתַם Ch.......472
P'al.
seal, to
חֹתֶמֶת 472
signet
חָתַן 472
Kal.
father in law
mother in law
Hithpael.
affinity, to join in
marriages, to make
son in law, to be
חָתָן 472
bridegroom
husband
son in law
חֲתֻנָּה.........472
espousal
חָתַף 472
Kal.
take away, to
חֶתֶף 472
prey
חָתַר 472
Kal.
dig, to
dig through, to
row, to
חָתַת.........472
Kal.
afraid, to be
amazed, to be
broken down, to be
broken in pieces, to be
chapt, to be
dismayed, to be
Niphal.
abolished, to be
affrighted, to be
afraid, to be
beaten down, to be
broken, to be
broken in pieces, to be
discouraged, to be
dismayed, to be
go down, to
Piel.
broken, to be
scare, to
Hiphil.
afraid, to make
break, to
confound, to
dismayed, to cause to be
terrify, to
חֲתַת.........473
casting down
טְאֵב Ch.......473
P'al.
glad, to be
טָב Ch.........473
fine
good
טְבוּלִים 473
dyed attire
טַבּוּר 473
middle
midst
טָבַח 473
Kal.
kill, to
slaughter
slaughter, to make
slay, to
טַבָּח 473
cook
guard
טַבָּח Ch.......473
guard
טֶבַח 473
* beast
slaughter
slay †
* sore
טִבְחָה 473
flesh
slaughter
טַבָּחוֹת 473
cooks
טָבַל 473
Kal.
dip, to
plunge, to
Niphal.
dipped, to be
טָבַע 474
Kal.
sink, to
sunk, to be
Pual.
drowned, to be
Hophal.
fastened, to be
settled, to be
sunk, to be
טַבַּעַת 474
ring
טֵבֵת..........474
Tebeth
טָהוֹר.........474
clean
fair
pure
pureness
טָהֵר 475
Kal.
clean, to be
cleansed, to be
pure, to be
purged, to be
Piel.
clean, to make
clean, to pronounce
cleanse, to
purge, to
purifier
purify, to
Pual.
cleansed, to be
Hithpael.
clean, to be
clean, to be made
clean, to make selves
cleanse selves, to
cleansed, to be
purified, to be
purify selves, to
טְהֹר 475
clean
pureness
טֹהַר 475
clearness
purifying
טֳהַר 475
glory
טָהֳרָה.........475
* cleansed, is
cleansing
purification
purifying
טוּא...........476
Pilpel.
sweep, to
טוֹב 476
Kal.
better, to be
good, to be
good, to seem
goodly
please, † to
well, to be
well, to go
Hiphil.
better, to do
cheer, to
do *good*, to
good, to do
goodly, to make
play well, to
well
well, to do
טוֹב...........476
beautiful
best
better
bountiful
cheerful
ease, at
fair
fair †
fair word
favour, to
favour, to be in
fine
glad
good
good deed
goodlier
goodliest
goodly
goodness
goods
graciously
joyful
kindly
kindness
liketh
liketh best
loving
merry
* most
pleasant
pleaseth †
pleasure
precious
prosperity
ready
sweet
wealth
welfare
well
well, to be
well*favoured*

טוֹב 479
fair
gladness
good
good thing
goodness
goods
joy
well with, to go

טָוָה 479
Kal.
spin, to

טוּחַ 479
Kal.
daub, to
overlay, to
plaister, to
shut, to
Niphal.
plaistered, to be

טוֹטָפוֹת 480
frontlets

טוּל 480
Pilpel.
carry away, to
Hiphil.
cast, to
cast forth, to
cast out, to
send out, to
Hophal.
cast, to be
cast down, to be
cast down, to be utterly
cast out, to be

טוּר 480
row

טוּר Ch. 480
mountain

טוּשׂ 480
Kal.
haste, to

טְוָת Ch. 480
fasting

טָחָה 480
Piel.
bowshot

טְחוֹן 480
grind, to

טְחוֹרִים 480
emerods

טֻחוֹת 480
inward parts

טָחַן 480
Kal.
grind, to
grinder

טַחֲנָה 480
grinding

טִיחַ 480
daubing

טִיט 480
clay
dirt
mire

טִין Ch. 481
miry

טִירָה 481
castle
castle, goodly
habitation
palace
row

טַל 481
dew

טַל Ch. 481
dew

טָלָא 481
Kal.
colours, with divers
spotted
Pual.
clouted

טְלָאִים 481
lambs

טָלֶה 481
lamb

טַלְטֵלָה 481
captivity

טָלַל 481
Piel.
cover, to

טְלַל Ch. 481
Aphel.
shadow, to have

טָמֵא 481
Kal.
defile self, to
defiled, to be
polluted, to be
unclean, to be
unclean, to be made
Niphal.
defile self, to
defiled, to be
pollute selves, to
polluted, to be
Piel.
defile, to
pollute, to
unclean, to pronounce
utterly
Pual.
polluted, to be
Hithpael.
defile selves, to
defiled, to be
polluted, to be
unclean, to be
unclean, to make selves
Hothpael.
defiled, to be

טָמֵא 482
defiled
infamous †
polluted
pollution
unclean

טֻמְאָה 483
filthiness
unclean
uncleanness

טָמָה 483
Niphal.
defiled, to be
vile, to be reputed

טָמַן 483
Kal.
hide, to
lay privily, to
secret, in
Niphal.
hide, to
Hiphil.
hide, to

טֶנֶא 483
basket

טָנַף 483
Piel.
defile, to

טָעָה 483
Hiphil.
seduce, to

טָעַם 483
Kal.
but
perceive, to
taste, to

טְעַם Ch. 483
P'al.
eat, to make to
feed, to

טַעַם 483
advice
behaviour
decree
discretion
judgment
reason
taste
understanding

טַעַם Ch. 484
account
* commanded, to be
commandment
matter

טְעֵם Ch. 484
* chancellor †
command,† to
commandment
decree
regard,† to
taste, to
wisdom

טָעַן 484
Kal.
lade, to

טָעַן 484
Pual.
thrust through

טַף 484
children
children, little
families
little ones

טָפַח 484
Piel.
span, to
swaddle, to

טֶפַח 484
coping
hand breadth

טֹפַח 484
hand breadth
hand broad

טִפֻּחִים 484
span long

טָפַל 484
Kal.
forge, to
forger
sew up, to

טִפְסַר 484
captain

טָפַף 484
Kal.
mince, to

טְפַר Ch. 485
nail

טָפַשׁ 485
Kal.
fat, to be

טָרַד 485
Kal.
continual

טְרַד Ch. 485
P'al.
drive, to

טְרוֹם 485
before

טָרַח 485
Hiphil.
weary, to

טֹרַח 485
cumbrance
trouble

טָרִי 485
new
putrifying

טֶרֶם 485
before
ere
not yet

טָרַף 485
Kal.
catch, to
doubt, without
prey
ravin, to
surely
tear, to
tear in pieces, to
Niphal.
torn in pieces, to be
Poal.
rent in pieces, to be
Hiphil.
feed, to

טָרָף 485
pluckt off

טֶרֶף 485
leaf
meat
prey
spoil

טְרֵפָה 485
ravin
torn
torn in pieces
torn of beasts
torn, that which was

יָאַב 486
Kal.
long, to

יָאָה 486
Kal.
appertain, to

יְאֹר 486
brook
flood
river
stream

יָאַל 1 486
Niphal.
dote, to
foolish, to be
foolishly, to do
fools, to become

יָאַל 2 486
Niphal.
take upon, to
Hiphil.
assay, to
begin, to
content, to be
please, to
* willingly
would

יָאַשׁ 486
Niphal.
despair, to
desperate, one that is
hope, to be no
Piel.
despair, to cause to

יָבַב 486
Piel.
cry, to

יְבוּל 486
fruit
increase

יָבַל 486
Hiphil.
bring, to
carry, to
lead, to
Hophal.
brought, to be
brought forth, to be
carried, to be
led forth, to be

יְבַל Ch. 487
Aphel.
bring, to
carry, to

יָבָל 487
stream
watercourse

יַבֶּלֶת 487
wen

יָבָם 487
husband's brother

יָבַם 487
Piel.
husband's brother, to perform the duty of a
marry, to

יְבֶמֶת 487
brother's wife
sister in law

יָבֵשׁ 487
Hiphil.
ashamed, to be
confounded, to be
shame, to
shamefully, to do

יָבֵשׁ..........487
Kal.
clean
dried, to be
dry, to be
dry up, to
utterly
wither, to
withered, to be
withered away, to be
Piel.
dry, to
dry, to make
dry up, to
Hiphil.
dried up, to be
dry, to make
dry up, to
withered, to be
withered away, to be

יָבֵשׁ..........488
dried
dried away
dry

יַבָּשָׁה 488
dry
dry ground
dry land

יַבֶּשֶׁת 488
dry land

יַבֶּשֶׁת Ch. 488
earth

יָגֵב..........488
Kal.
husbandman

יְגֵבִים 488
fields

יָגָה1 488
Niphal.
afflicted, to be
sorrowful
Piel.
grieve, to
Hiphil.
afflict, to
grief, to cause
vex, to

יָגָה2 488
Hiphil.
removed, to be

יָגוֹן..........488
grief
sorrow

יָגִיעַ..........488
weary

יְגִיעַ 488
labour
work

יָגַע..........488
Kal.
faint, to
labour, to
weary, to be
Piel.
labour, to make to
weary, to
Hiphil.
weary, to

יָגָע..........489
laboured for

יָגֵעַ..........489
labour, full of
weary

יְגִעָה 489
weariness

יְגַר Ch. 489
Jegar-*sahadutha*

יָגֹר..........489
Kal.
afraid, to be
fear, to

יָד..........489
able, be
* able,† be
* about
* armholes †
at
axletree
because of
beside
border
* bounty
* broad †
*broken*handed
* by
charge
coast
* consecrate †
* creditor †
custody
debt
dominion
* enough
* fellowship †
force
* from
hand
hand*staves*
handy *work*
* he
himself
* in
labour
* large †
ledge
*left*handed
means
* mine
ministry
near
* of
* order
ordinance
* our
parts
paw
place
power
* presumptuously †
service
side
sore
state
stay
strength, draw with
stroke
* swear †
tenon
* thee
* them, by
* themselves
* thine own
* thou
through
* throwing
thumb †
times
* to
* under
* us
* wait on, to
*way*side
where
* wide †
* with
* with him
* with me
* with you
work
yield †
* yourselves

יַד Ch. 499
hand
power

יְדָא Ch. 499
Aphel.
thank, to
thanks, to give

יָדַד..........499
Kal.
cast, to

יְדִדוּת 499
beloved, dearly

יָדָה1 499
Kal.
shoot, to
Piel.
cast, to
cast out, to

יָדָה2..........499
Hiphil.
confess, to
praise, to
thank, to
thankful, to be
thanks, to give
thanksgiving
Hithpael.
confess, to
confession, to make

יָדִיד 500
amiable
beloved
loves
wellbeloved

יָדַע 500
Kal.
acknowledge, to
acquaintance
acquainted with
advise, to
assuredly
aware, to be
can discern
can have
can skill
can tell
can*not*
certainly
certainty, for a
come to *understanding*, to
comprehend, to
consider, to
* could they
cunning
diligent, to be
discern, to
endued with
feel, to
have *knowledge*, to
have *understanding*, to
*ig*norant, to be
know, to
knowledge
knowledge, to have
knowledge, to take
learned,† to be
* lie by man,† to
mark, to
perceive, to
privy to, to be
regard, to
respect, to have
skilful
skill, man of
sure, to be
surety, of a
* *un*awares
understand, to
* will be
wist, to
wit, to
wot, to
Niphal.
discovered, to be
famous, to be
instructed, to be
known, to be
known, to make self
Piel.
know, to cause to
Poal.
appoint, to
Pual.
acquaintance
familiar friend
kinsfolk
kinsman
(כ׳) known
Hiphil.
acknowledge, to
answer, to
declare, to
discern, to cause to
know, to cause to
know, to let
know, to make
knowledge, to give
known, to make
known, to make to be
* prognosticator
shew, to
teach, to
tell, to
Hophal.
knowledge, to come to
known
Hithpael.
known, to make self

יְדַע Ch. 506
P'al.
know, to
Aphel.
certify, to
known, to make
teach, to

יִדְּעֹנִי..........507
wizard

יָהַב 507
Kal.
ascribe, to
bring, to
* burden
come on, to
give, to
go to
set, to
take, to

יְהַב Ch. 507
P'al.
deliver, to
give, to
lay, to
* prolong,† to
yield, to
Ithp'al.
given, to be
paid, to be

יָהַד 507
Hithpael.
Jews, to become

יָהִיר 507
haughty
proud

יַהֲלֹם..........507
diamond

יוֹבֵל 507
jubile
ram'*s horn*
rams' horn
trumpet

יוּבַל 507
river

יוֹם..........508
age
always †
as when
*birth*day
* chronicles †
continually †
continuance
daily
dai*ly*
day
day, each
days agone
days, now a
days, two
elder †
* end
even now
evening †
ever †
* everlasting †
evermore †
for ever †
* full
full year
life
long as, as long as (*I*) live, so
now
* old †
* outlived †
perpetually †
presently
* remaineth †
* required
season
* since
so long
space

then
time
time †
time, process of
*times, as at other
to day
* trouble, † in
weather
when
while
while, a
while, the
while that
while, within a
* whole
* whole age †
* year
year
yearly
younger †

יוֹם Ch........ 521
day
day by day
time

יוֹמָם 521
daily
day
day, by
day, in the
daytime, by
daytime, in the

יָוֵן 521
mire
miry

יוֹנָה 521
dove
Jonath-*elem-rechokim*
pigeon

יוֹנֵק 521
tender plant

יוֹנֶקֶת..........521
branch
branch, tender
twigs, young

יוֹרֶה 521
former *rain*
rain, first

יוֹתֵר 521
better
further
more
moreover
over
profit

יָזַן 522
Hophal.
fed

יֶזַע 522
sweat, any thing that causeth

יָחַד..........522
Kal.
joined, to be
united, to be
Piel.
unite, to

יַחְדָּיו ,יַחְדָּו ,יַחַד 522
alike
altogether
at all
at once
both
likewise
only
together
withal

יָחִיד 523
child, only
darling
desolate
only
solitary
son, only

יָחִיל 523
hope, should

יָחַל 523
Niphal.
stay, to
tarry, to
wait, to
Piel.
hope, to
hope, to cause to
hope, to make to
trust, to
wait, to
Hiphil.
hope, to
hope, to have
pained, to be
tarry, to
wait, to

יָחַם 523
Kal.
conceive, to
heat, to get
hot, to be
warm, to be
Piel.
conceive, to

יַחְמוּר 523
fallow deer

יָחֵף..........523
barefoot
unshod, being

יָחַר...........523
Kal.
tarry longer, to

יָחַשׂ 523
Hithpael.
genealogies, to be reckoned by
genealogy
genealogy to be reckoned
number after genealogy
number throughout the genealogy
reckoned by genealogies, to be

יַחַשׂ 523
genealogy

יָטַב 524
Kal.
accepted, to be
best, to seem
better, to be made
content, † to be
favour, to find
glad, to be
good, to be
merry, to be
please, to
please, † to
please well, † to
well, to be
well, to go
Hiphil.
amend, to
aright, to use
benefit, to
better, to be
better, to make
cheerful, to make
comely, to be
diligent
diligently
do *goodness*, to
dress, to
earnestly
give, to
good, to do
good, to make
merry, to make
please, to
shew more *kindness*, to
skilfully
small, very
surely
sweet, to make
thoroughly
throughly
tire, to
trim, to
very
well, can
well, to deal
well, to entreat
well *said*, to have
well *seen*, to have

יְטַב Ch. 524
P'al.
good, to seem

יַיִן 524
banqueting
vine
vine †
wine
wine*bibber*

יַךְ (כ') 525
way*side*

יָכַח...........525
Niphal.
dispute, to
reason together, to
reproved, to be
Hiphil.
appoint, to
argue, to
chasten, to
convince, to
correct, to
correction
daysman
judge, to
maintain, to
plead, to
reason, to
rebuke, to
reprove, to
reprover
surely
wise, in any
Hophal.
chastened, to be
Hithpael.
plead, to

יָכֹל...........526
Kal.
able, to be
any at all
any ways
attain, to
can
can away with
can*not*
could
endure, to
might
overcome, to
power, to have
prevail, to
still
suffer, to

יְכִל Ch. 527
P'al.
able, to be
can
couldest
prevail, to

יָלַד............527
Kal.
bear, to
beget, to
birth
born
bring forth, to
bring forth children, to
bring forth young, to
bring up, to
calve, to
child
child, to be delivered of a
child, to travail with
delivered, to be
delivery, time of
gender, to
hatch, to
labour
travail
travail, to
travail, woman in
travaileth, woman that
travailing woman
Niphal.
begotten, to be
birth, one's
born, to be
brought forth, to be
come, to
son of, to be the
Piel.
midwife
midwife, to do the office of a
Pual.
born, to be
brought forth, to be
brought up, to be
Hiphil.
beget, to
bring forth, to
bring forth, to make to
Hophal.
birth*day*
born, to be
Hithpael.
pedigrees, to declare

יֶלֶד...... ...530
boy
child
fruit
son
young man
young one

יַלְדָּה..........531
damsel
girl

יַלְדוּת 531
childhood
youth

יִלּוֹד..........531
born

יְלִיד 531
born
child
*home*born
son

יָלַךְ............531
Kal.
* again
away
come, to
come away, to
depart, to
flow, to
follow, † to
following †
get, to
get away, to
get hence, to
get (him) to
go, to
go away, to
go (one's) way, to
go out, to
going
gone, to be
grow, to
let down, to be
march, to
prosper, to
pursue, † to
spread, to
take *journey*, to
vanish, to
walk, to
walking
wax, to
* weak, to be
Hiphil.
bear, to
bring, to
carry, to
carry away, to
go, to
go, to cause to
go, to make
lead, to
lead forth, to
run, to cause to
take away, to
walk, to cause to

יָלַל............537
Hiphil.
howl, to
howl, to make to
howlings, to be
* Lucifer

יְלֵל............537
howling

יְלָלָה 537
howling

יָלַע...........537
Kal.
devour, to

יַלֶּפֶת 537
scabbed

יֶלֶק 537
cankerworm
caterpiller

יַלְקוּט 538
scrip

יָם 538
sea
sea *shore*
* seafaring man
south
west
west side
western
westward

יָם Ch. 540
sea

יָמִין 540
* lefthanded †
right
right hand
right side
south

(כ') יְמִינִי 541
right
right hand, on the

יֵמִם 541
mules

יָמַן 541
Hiphil.
right, to go to the
right hand, to go on the
right hand, to turn to the
right hand, to use the

יְמָנִי 541
right
right hand, on the

יָמַר 541
Hiphil.
boast selves, to
change, to

יָמַשׁ 541
Hiphil.
feel, to

יָנָה 541
Kal.
destroy, to
oppressing
oppressor
proud
Hiphil.
oppress, to
oppression, to thrust out by
vex, to
wrong, to do

יָנַח 541
Hiphil.
bestow, to
cast down, to
lay, to
lay down, to
lay up, to
leave, to
leave off, to
let alone, to
let remain, to
pacify, to
place, to
put, to
set, to
set down, to
suffer, to
withdraw, to
withhold, to
Hophal.
left, to be
set, to be

יֹנִיקוֹת 542
young twigs

יָנַק 542
Kal.
suck, to
sucking child
suckling
Hiphil.
milch
nurse
nurse, to
nursing mother
suck, to give
suck, to make to

יַנְשׁוּף 542
great owl
owl

יָסַד 542
Kal.
establish, to
found, to
foundation, to lay the
lay, to
Niphal.
counsel, to take
foundation
foundation to be laid
Piel.
appoint, to
found, to
foundation, to lay for a
foundation, to lay the
ordain, to
Pual.
foundation
foundation to be laid
set
Hophal.
foundation to be laid
instructed, to be
* sure

יְסַד 543
* began

יְסוֹד 543
bottom
foundation
repairing

יְסוּדָה 543
foundation

יָסוּר 543
depart, they that

יִסּוֹר 543
instruct

יָסַךְ 543
Kal.
poured, to be

יָסַף 543
Kal.
add, to
* again
any more
cease, to
come more;—again
exceed, to
* further
increase, to
* more
proceed, to
put, to
Niphal.
added, to be
increase, to
join, to
* more
put, to be
Hiphil.
add, to
* again
any more
* conceive again, to
continue, to
exceed, to
* further
* gather together, to
get more, to
give moreover, to
* henceforth
increase, to
increase more and more, to
* longer
* more and more
more, to bring
more, to do
more, to make
more, to put
* more, the
* more, yet
more, to be yet the
* much more
proceed, to
proceed further, to
prolong, to
put, to be
*strong*er, to be
* yet
yield, to

יְסַף Ch. 545
Hophal.
added, to be

יָסַר 545
Kal.
chastise, to
reprove, to
Niphal.
chastised, to be
corrected, to be
instructed, to be
reformed, to be
Nithpael.
taught, to be
Piel.
bind, to
chasten, to
chastise, to
correct, to
instruct, to
punish, to
sore
teach, to
Hiphil.
chastise, to

יָעַד 545
Kal.
appoint, to
betroth, to
Niphal.
agreed, to be
appointment, to make an
assemble selves, to
assembled, to be
gather selves, to
gathered together, to be
meet, to
met together, to be
Hiphil.
appoint a time, to
set a time, to
Hophal.
set

יָעָה 546
Kal.
sweep away, to

יְעוֹרִים 546
woods

יָעֵז 546
Niphal.
fierce

יָעַט 546
Kal.
cover, to

יְעַט Ch. 546
P'al.
counsellors
Ithpael.
consult together, to

יָעִים 546
shovels

יָעַל 546
Hiphil.
at all
forward, to set
good, can do
profit, to
profit, to have
profitable, to be

יַעֲלָה 546
roe

יְעֵלִים 546
goats, wild

יַעַן 546
because
because that
forasmuch
forasmuch as †
seeing then
that †
whereas †
why †

יַעֲנָה 546
owl †

יְעֵנִים 546
ostriches

יָעַף 546
Kal.
faint, to
weary, to be
weary self, to
Hophal.
fly, to be caused to

יָעֵף 546
faint
weary

יְעָף 547
swiftly

יָעַץ 547
Kal.
advertise, to
consult, to
counsel, to
counsel, to give
counsel, to take
counsellor
determine, to
devise, to
give *counsel*, to
guide, to
purpose, to
Niphal.
advice, to take
advise, to
advised, well
consult, to
counsel, to give
counsel, to take
Hithpael.
consult, to

יַעַר 547
forest
*honey*comb
wood

יַעְרָה 548
forest
*honey*comb

יָפָה 548
Kal.
beautiful, to be
fair, to be
Piel.
deck, to
Pual.
fairer, to be
Hithpael.
fair, to make self

יָפֶה 548
beautiful †
beauty
comely
fair
fair one
fairest
goodly †
pleasant
well

יְפֵה־פִיָּה 548
fair, very

יָפַח 548
Hithpael.
bewail self, to

יָפֵחַ 548
breathe out, such as

יֳפִי 548
beauty

יְפִי 548
beauty

יָפַע 548
Hiphil.
light, to be
shew self, to
shine, to
shine, to cause to
shine forth, to

יִפְעָה 548
brightness

יָצָא 548
Kal.
* after
appear, to
assuredly
* begotten
break out, to
bring forth, to
come, to
come abroad, to
come out, to
come thereout, to
come without, to
condemned, † to be
depart, to
departing
departure
end of, in the
escape, to
fail, to
fall, to
fall out, to
get away, to
get forth, to
get hence, to
get out, to
go, able to
go abroad, to
go forth, to
go forth, able to
go on, to
go out, to
going out
grow, to
issue out, to
laid out, to be
lie out, to
proceed, to
risen, to be
scarce
shoot forth, to
spread, to
spring out, to
stand out, to
still
surely
time, at any
* to *and fro*
Hiphil.
bear out, to
bring forth, to
bring out, to
bring up, to
carry forth, to
carry out, to
(כ׳) commandment, to send with
draw forth, to
exact, to
fetch forth, to
fetch out, to
go forth, to cause to
go out, to cause to
go out, to let
have forth, to
have out, to
lay out, to
lead out, to
pluck out, to
pull out, to
put away, to
take forth, to
take out, to
utter, to
Hophal.
brought forth, to be

יְצָא Ch. 555
Shaphel.
finished, to be

יָצַב 555
Hithpael.
present selves, to
remaining
resort, to
set, to
set selves, to
stand, to
stand, to be able to
stand, can
stand fast, to
stand forth, to
stand still, to
stand up, to
standing
withstand, to

יְצֵב Ch. 555
Pael.
truth

יָצַג 555
Hiphil.
establish, to
leave, to
make, to
present, to
put, to
set, to
Hophal.
stayed, to be

יִצְהָר 555
anointed
oil

יָצוּעַ 555
bed
(כ׳) chamber
couch

יְצִיא 556
come forth, to

יַצִּיב Ch. 556
certain
certainty
true
truth

יָצִיעַ 556
chamber

יָצַע 556
Hiphil.
bed, to make
spread, to
Hophal.
* lie, to
spread, to be

יָצַק 556
Kal.
cast, to
cleave fast, to
firm, to be
firm, to be as
grow, to
hard, to be
molten
pour, to
pour out, to
run out, to
Hiphil.
lay out, to
set down, to
Hophal.
molten
overflown, to be
poured, to be
poured out, to be
stedfast

יְצֻקָה 556
cast, when it was

יָצַר1 556
Kal.
* earthen
fashion, to
form, to
frame, to
make, to
Maker
potter
purpose, to
Niphal.
formed, to be
Pual.
fashioned, to be
Hophal.
formed, to be

יָצַר2 557
Kal.
distressed, to be
narrow, to be
straitened, to be
straits, to be in
vexed, to be

יֵצֶר 557
frame
framed, thing
imagination
mind
work

יְצֻרִים 557
members

יָצַת 557
Kal.
burned, to be
kindle, to
Niphal.
burned, to be
burned up, to be
desolate, to be
kindled, to be
Hiphil.
burn, to
fire, to set on
kindle, to
set *fire*, to

יֶקֶב 557
fats
presses
pressfat
wine
winepress

יָקַד 557
Kal.
burn, to
* hearth, from the
kindle, to
Hophal.
burn, to
burning, to be

יְקַד Ch. 557
P'al.
burning

יְקֵדָה Ch. 557
burning

יְקָהָה 557
gathering
obey, to

יְקוֹד 557
burning

יְקוּם 558
living substance
substance

יָקוֹשׁ 558
fowler

יָקוּשׁ 558
fowler
snare

יַקִּיר 558
dear

יַקִּיר Ch. 558
noble
rare

יָקַע 558
Kal.
alienated, to be
depart, to
joint, to be out of
Hiphil.
hang, to
hang up, to
Hophal.
hanged, to be

יָקַץ 558
Kal.
awake, to
awaked, to be

יָקַר 558
Kal.
precious, to be
prized, to be
set by, to be
Hiphil.
precious, to make
withdraw, to

יָקָר 558
brightness
clear
costly
excellent
fat
honourable woman
precious
reputation

יְקָר 558
honour
precious
precious things
price

יְקָר Ch. 558
glory
honour

יָקשׁ 559
Kal.
fowler
lay *snare*, to
lay a snare, to
Niphal.
snared, to be
Hophal.
snared

יָרָא 559
Kal.
shoot, to
Hiphil.
shoot, to
shooter
* watered, to be

יָרֵא 559
Kal.
afraid, to be
dread, to
fear, to
fearing
reverence, to
* see, to
Niphal.
dreadful
feared, to be
fearful
fearfully
reverence, to be had in
reverend
terrible
terrible acts
terrible things
terribleness
Piel.
affright, to
afraid, to make
fear, to put in

יָרֵא 561
afraid
fear
fearful

יִרְאָה 561
* dreadful
* exceedingly †
fear
fearfulness

יָרַד 561
Kal.
* abundantly
come down, to
coming down
descend, to
descending
fall, to
get down, to
go down, to
go downward, to
going down
indeed
light, to
light down, to
run down, to
sink, to
subdued, to be
Hiphil.
bring down, to
carry down, to
cast down, to
come down, to cause to
fall down, to let
hang down, to
let down, to
put down, to
put off, to
run down, to cause to
run down, to let
take down, to
Hophal.
brought down, to be

(כ׳) go down, to
taken down, to be

יָרָה 564
Kal.
archers
cast, to
* former rain
lay, to
shoot
through
Niphal.
shot, to be
Hiphil.
archers †
cast, to
direct, to
inform, to
instruct, to
rain, to
shew, to
shoot, to
teach, to
teacher
teaching

יָרֵא 564
Kal.
afraid, to be

יָרוֹק 564
green thing

יָרֵחַ 564
moon

יֶרַח 565
month
moon

יְרַח Ch. 565
month

יָרַט 565
Kal.
perverse, to be
turn over, to

יָרִיב 565
contend, that
contendeth, that
strive, that

יְרִיעָה 565
curtain

יָרֵךְ 565
* body
loins
shaft
side
thigh

יַרְכָה 565
border
coast
parts
quarters
sides

יַרְכָה Ch. 565
thigh

יָרַע 566
Kal.
displease,† to
evil, to be
grieved, to be
grievous, to be
harm, to do
ill, to go
sad, to be

יָרַק 566
Kal.
but
spit, to

יָרָק 566
green
herbs

יֶרֶק 566
grass
green
green thing

יֵרָקוֹן 566
mildew
paleness

יְרַקְרַק 566
greenish
yellow

יָרַשׁ 566
Kal.
(כ׳) drive out, to
enjoy, to
heir
heir, to be
inherit, to
inheritor
* magistrate †
possess, to
possession, to get in
possession, to have in
possession, to take
succeed, to
Niphal.
poor, to be
poverty, to come to
Piel.
consume, to
Hiphil.
cast out, to
destroy, to
disinherit, to
dispossess, to
drive out, to
driving out
expel, to
fail, without
inherit, to give to
inheritance, to leave for an
poor, to make
possess, to
possess, to give to
possess, to make to
seize upon, to
utterly

יְרֵשָׁה 567
possession

יְרֻשָּׁה 567
heritage
inheritance
possession

יָשַׂם 568
Kal.
put, to be
set, to be

יֵשׁ 568
are
are there
be
had
hast
hath
have
he be
he is
I have
is
it be
it is
it was
shall be
shalt have
substance
that have
there be
there is
there may be
there shall be
there should be
there was
there were
thou do
thou wilt
were
which hath
wouldest
ye will

יָשַׁב 568
Kal.
abide, to
abiding
continue, to
downsitting
dwell, to
dwelling
ease self, to
endure, to
fail
habitation
haunt, to
inhabit, to
inhabitant
inhabited, to be
lurking
place
remain, to
(כ׳) return, to
seat
set, to be
sit, to
sit down, to
sit still, to
sit up, to
sitting down
sitting *place*
situate, to be
tarry, to
Niphal.
inhabited, to be
Piel.
set, to
Hiphil.
abide, to make to
dwell, to cause to
dwell, to make to
establish, to
inhabited, to make to be
keep *house*, to make to
* marry, to
marrying
place, to
place, to bring again to
set, to
settle, to
take, to
Hophal.
inhabited, to be
placed, to be

יְשׁוּעָה 575
deliverance
health
help
helping
salvation
save, to
saving
saving health
welfare

יֶשַׁח 575
casting down

יָשַׁט 575
Hiphil.
hold out, to

יְשִׁימוֹן 575
desert
Jeshimon
solitary
wilderness

יְשִׁימוֹת 576
(כ׳) death seize, let

יָשִׁישׁ..........576
aged
aged man, very
ancient
old, very

יָשַׁם 576
Kal.
desolate, to be

יָשַׁן 576
Niphal.
old
remain long, to
store, old

יָשָׁן 576
old

יָשֵׁן 576
Kal.
sleep, to
Piel.
sleep, to make to

יָשֵׁן 576
asleep
sleep
sleep, one out of
sleepeth
sleeping
slept

יָשַׁע 576
Niphal.
safe, to be
salvation, having
saved, to be
Hiphil.
at all
avenging
defend, to
deliver, to
deliverer
help, to
preserve, to
rescue, to
salvation, to bring
save, to
saviour
victory, to get

יֵשַׁע & יֶשַׁע....577
safety
salvation
saving

יָשְׁפֵה..........578
jasper

יָשַׁר 578
Kal.
good, to seem
meet, to seem
please,† to
please well,† to
right, to be
straight way, to take the
upright, to be
Piel.
direct, to
right, to esteem
right on, to go
straight, to bring
straight, to make
uprightly
Pual.
fitted
Hiphil.
straight, to look
straight, to make

יָשָׁר 578
convenient
equity
Jasher
just
meet
meetest
pleased well †
right
righteous
straight
upright
upright, most
uprightly
uprightness

יֹשֶׁר 579
equity
meet
right
upright
uprightness

יְשָׁרָה 579
uprightness

יָשֵׁשׁ 579
stoop for age, to

יַת Ch. 579
* whom †

יְתִב Ch. 579
P'al.
dwell, to
set, to be
sit, to
Aphel.
set, to

יָתֵד 579
nail
paddle
pin
stake

יָתוֹם 579
fatherless
fatherless child
orphan

יְתוּר 579
range

יַתִּיר Ch. 579
exceeding
exceedingly
excellent

יָתַר 580
Kal.
rest, the
Niphal.
left, to be
left behind, to be
remain, to
remainder
remaining, to be
remnant
residue
rest

Hiphil.
excel, to
leave, to
leave a remnant, to
much, too
plenteous, to make
preserve, to
remain, to let
reserve, to

יֶתֶר 580
abundant †
exceeding
excellency
excellent
leave, what they left, that hath
plentifully
remnant
residue
rest

יֶתֶר 581
cord
string
withs

יִתְרָה 581
abundance
riches

יִתְרוֹן 581
better
excellency
excelleth
profit
profitable

יֹתֶרֶת 581
caul

כָּאַב 581
Kal.
pain, to have
sore
sorrowful
sorrowful, to be
Hiphil.
grieving
mar, to
sad, to make
sore, to make

כְּאֵב 581
grief
pain
sorrow

כָּאָה 581
Niphal.
broken
grieved, to be
viler, to be
Hiphil.
sad, to make

כָּאִים 581
poor †

כָּבַד & כָּבֵד ..581
Kal.
chargeable, to be
* dim, to be
glorified, to be
glorious, to be made
go sore, to
grievous, to be
hardened, to be
heavier, to be
heavy, to be
honour, to come to
* laid, more be
prevail, to
rich, to be
sore, to be
Niphal
abounding with
get honour, to
glorified, to be
glorious
glorious, to be
glorious things
glory, to
honour, to be had in
honourable
honourable, to be
honourable man
honoured, to be
nobles
Piel.
glorify, to
glorious, to make great
harden, to
honour, to
honour, to bring to
honour, to do
promote, to
promote to honour, to
very great
Pual.
honourable
honoured, to be
Hiphil.
afflict, more grievously to
boast, to
chargeable, to be
glorify, to
harden, to
heavily, to lay
heavy, to make
lade, to
stop, to
Hithpael.
honour self, to
many, to make self

כָּבֵד 582
great
grievous
hard
hardened
heavier
heavy
heavy, too
laden
much
slow
so great
sore
thick

כָּבֵד 583
liver

כֹּבֶד 583
great number
grievousness
heavy

כְּבֵדֻת 583
heavily

כָּבָה 583
Kal.
go out, to
put out, to be
quenched, to be
Piel.
put out, to
quench, to

כָּבוֹד 583
glorious
gloriously
glory
honour
honourable

כְּבוּדָּה 584
carriage
glorious, all
stately

כַּבִּיר 584
feeble †
mighty
most
much
strong
valiant

כְּבִיר 584
pillow

כֶּבֶל 584
fetters

כָּבַס 584
Kal.
fuller
Piel.
fuller
wash, to
Pual.
washed, to be
Hothpael.
washed, to be
washing

כָּבַר 585
Hiphil.
abundance, in
multiply, to

כְּבָר 585
already
now
now, seeing that which

כְּבָרָה 585
sieve

כִּבְרָה 585
* little

כֶּבֶשׂ 585
lamb
sheep

כַּבְשָׂה & כִּבְשָׂה 585
ewe lamb
lamb

כָּבַשׁ 586
Kal.
bondage, to bring into
force, to
keep under, to
subdue, to
subjection, to bring into
Niphal.
bondage, to be brought unto
subdued, to be
Piel.
subdue, to
Hiphil.
subjection, to bring into

כֶּבֶשׁ 586
footstool

כִּבְשָׁן 586
furnace

כַּד 586
barrel
pitcher

כְּדַב Ch. 586
lying

כַּדְכֹּד 586
agate

כֹּה 586
also
here
hitherto †
like
mean while,† in the
other side, on the
so
so and much
such
that manner, on this
this manner, on
this side, on
this wise, on
thus
way and that way, this
yonder

כָּה Ch. 586
hither*to*

כָּהָה 586
Kal.
darkened, to be
dim, to be
fail, to
utterly
Piel.
faint, to
restrain, to

כֵּהֶה 586
dark, somewhat
darkish
dim, to wax
heaviness
smoking

כֵּהָה 586
healing

כְּהַל Ch. 586
P'al.
able, to be
could

כָּהַן 587
Piel.
deck, to
office of a priest, to do the
priest, to be
priest's office, to execute the
priest's office, to minister in the

כֹּהֵן 587
chief ruler
* own
priest
prince
principal officer

כָּהֵן Ch. 591
priest

כְּהֻנָּה 591
priesthood
priest's office

כּוֹבַע 591
helmet

כָּוָה 591
Niphal.
burned, to be

כְּוִיָּה 591
burning

כַּוִּין Ch. 591
windows

כּוֹכָב 591
star
star*gazers*

כּוּל 592
Kal.
comprehend, to
Pilpel.
abide, to
contain, to
feed, to
forbearing
guide, to
nourish, to
nourisher
provision, to make
sustain, to
sustenance, to provide
victuals, to provide
Polpal.
present, to be
Hiphil.
abide, to be able to
abide, can
bear, to
contain, to
hold, to
holding in
receive, to

כּוּמָז 592
tablets

כּוּן 592
Niphal.
certain
certainty
directed, to be
established, to be
faithfulness
fashioned, to be
fitted, to be
fixed, to be
meet, to be
order, to be set in
perfect
prepare, to
prepare (*selves*), to
prepared, to be
ready
right
set forth, to be
stable, to be
stand, to
tarry, to
very deed
Polel.
confirm, to
establish, to
fashion, to
ordain, to
prepare, to
prepare self, to
ready, to be
ready, to make
stablish, to
Pulal.
ordered, to be
prepared, to be

flame
perfect
perfection
utterly
whole burnt offering
whole burnt sacrifice
wholly

כָּלַל 603
Kal.
perfect, to
perfect, to make

כְּלַל Ch. 603
Shaphel.
finish, to
make up, to
set up, to
Ishtaphel.
set up, to

כָּלַם 603
Niphal.
ashamed, to be
blush, to
confounded, to be
confusion, to be put to
shame, to be put to
Hiphil.
ashamed, to make
blush, to
hurt, to
reproach, to
shame, to
shame, to do
shame, to put to
Hophal.
confounded, to be
hurt, to be

כְּלִמָּה 603
confusion
dishonour
reproach
shame

כְּלִמּוּת 603
shame

כָּמַהּ 603
Kal.
long, to

כְּמוֹ 603
according to
as
as it were
as well as
comparison of, in
like
like as
like to
like unto
such as
thus
when
worth

כַּמֹּן 604
cummin

כָּמַס 604
Kal.
laid up in store, to be

כָּמַר 604
Niphal.
black, to be
kindled, to be
yearn, to

כְּמָרִים 604
Chemarims
idolatrous priests
priests

כִּמְרִירִים 604
blackness

כֵּן 604
base
estate
foot
office
place
well

כֵּן 604
lice
* manner

כֵּן 604
after that †
after this †
afterward †
afterwards †
as—as
as yet
because †
cause,† for which
even so
following †
*for*asmuch †
howbeit
like manner, in
like, the
likewise
* more, the
right
so
state
straightway
such
such thing
surely
therefore †
this
thus
well
wherefore †
* you

כֵּן Ch. 604
thus

כָּנָה 604
Piel.
flattering titles, to give
surname, to
surname (himself), to

כַּנָּה 604
* vineyard

כִּנּוֹר 604
harp

כֵּנִים 605
true

כִּנָּם 605
lice

כְּנֵמָא Ch. 605
so
this manner
this sort, in
thus

כָּנַן 605
Kal.
* vineyard

כָּנַס 605
Kal.
gather, to
gather together, to
heap up, to
Piel.
gather, to
gather together, to
Hithpael.
wrap self, to

כָּנַע 605
Niphal.
brought into subjection, to be
brought under, to be
humble self, to
humbled, to be
subdued, to be
Hiphil.
bring down, to
bring low, to
subdue, to

כִּנְעָה 605
wares

כְּנַעַן 605
merchant
traffick
trafficker

כְּנַעֲנִי 605
Canaanite
merchant

כָּנַף 605
Niphal.
removed into a corner, to be

כָּנָף 605
bird †
border
corner
end
feather*ed*
flying
* one another
* other
overspreading
* quarters
skirt
* sort
uttermost part
wing
wing*ed*

כְּנַשׁ Ch. 606
P'al.
gather together, to
Ithpael.
gathered together, to be

כְּנָת 606
companion

כְּנָת Ch. 606
companion

כֵּס 606
* sworn †

כֶּסֶא 606
appointed

כִּסֵּא 606
seat
stool
throne

כָּסָה 607
Kal.
conceal, to
cover, to
Niphal.
covered, to be
Piel.
close, to
conceal, to
cover, to
flee to hide, to
hide, to
overwhelm, to
Pual.
clothed, to be
covered, to be
Hithpael.
clad self
covered, to be
covered self, to

כֶּסֶה 608
time appointed

כִּסֵּה 608
throne

כָּסוּי 608
covering

כְּסוּת 608
covering
raiment
vesture

כָּסַח 608
Kal.
cut down, to be
cut up, to be

כְּסִיל 608
constellation
fool
foolish
Orion

כְּסִילוּת 609
foolish

כָּסַל 609
Kal.
foolish, to be

כֶּסֶל 609
confidence
flanks
folly
hope
loins

כִּסְלָה 609
confidence
folly

כִּסְלֵו 609
Chisleu

כָּסַם 609
Kal.
only
poll, to

כֻּסֶּמֶת 609
fitches
rie

כָּסַס 609
Kal.
count, to make

כָּסַף 609
Kal.
desire, to have
greedy, to be
Niphal.
desired
long, to
sore

כֶּסֶף 609
money
price
silver
silverlings

כְּסַף Ch. 611
money
silver

כְּסָתוֹת 612
pillows

כְּעַן Ch. 612
now

כְּעֶנֶת Ch. 612
such a time, at

כָּעַס 612
Kal.
angry, to be
grieved, to be
indignation, to take
sorrow, to have
wroth, to be
Piel.
provoke, to
provoke to anger, to
Hiphil.
provoke, to
provoke to anger, to
provoke unto wrath, to
vex, to

כַּעַס 612
anger
angry
grief
provocation
provoking
* sore
sorrow
spite
wrath

כַּעַשׂ 612
grief
indignation
sorrow
wrath

כְּעֶת Ch. 612
such a time, at

כַּף 612
branch
foot †
hand
hand*ful*
handle
hand*led*
hollow
middle
palm
paw
power
sole
spoon

כָּפָה 613
Kal.
pacify, to

כִּפָּה 613
branch

כְּפוֹר 614
bason
hoarfrost
hoary frost

כָּתַשׁ 624
Kal.
bray (*in a mortar*), to

כָּתַת 624
Kal.
beat, to
beat down, to
broken in pieces, to be
crushed
stamp, to
Piel.
beat, to
break in pieces, to
smite, to
Pulal.
destroyed, to be
Hiphil.
destroy, to
discomfit, to
Hophal.
beaten down, to be
beaten to pieces, to be
destroyed, to be
smitten, to be

לָא Ch.........624
*can*not
neither
no
none
nor
not
or ever
without
*with*out

לֹא & לוֹא 625
* as though...not
as truly as †
before
*can*not
else,† or
ere
except †
ig*norant*
much less
nay
neither
never
no
no*ne*
none
nor
not
not, for
not out of
no*thing*
nought, of
otherwise
out of
surely †
truth,† of a
verily †
want, for
whether †
without
*with*out

לֻא 625
if
though

לָאָה 626
Kal.
faint, to
grieved, to be
weary selves, to
Niphal.
grieve, to
lothe, to
wearied, to be
weary, to be
weary selves, to
Hiphil.
weary, to
weary, to make

לְאוֹם & לְאֹם 626
nation
people

לָאט 626
Kal.
cover, to

לְאַט 626
softly

לֵב 626
*broken*hearted
care for †
comfortably
consent
* consider*ed*
cour*ageous*
* double heart
friend*ly*
*hard*hearted
heart
heart*ed*
* heed
* I
kindly
*merry*hearted
midst
mind
minded
* regard*ed*
*stiff*heart*ed*
*stout*hearted
* themselves
* unawares
understanding
* well
willingly
wisdom

לֵב Ch. 630
heart

לְבָאוֹת 630
lionesses

לְבָאִים 630
lions

לָבַב 630
Niphal.
wise, to be
Piel.
cakes, to make
make (*cakes*), to
ravish, to

לֵבָב 630
* bethink selves †
breast
comfortably
courage
*faint*hearted
heart
midst
mind
*tender*hearted
* unawares
understanding

לְבַב Ch. 631
heart

לְבִבוֹת 631
cakes

לַבָּה 631
flame

לִבָּה 631
heart

לְבוֹנָה 631
frankincense
incense

לְבוּשׁ 632
apparel
clothed with
clothing
garment,—that he
raiment[had put on
vestment
vesture

לְבוּשׁ Ch. 632
garment

לָבַט 632
Niphal.
fall, to

לָבִיא..........632
lion
lion, great
lion, old
lion, stout
young (*lion*)

לְבִיָּא 632
lioness

לָבֵן 632
Kal.
brick, to make
make *brick*, to
Hiphil.
white, to be as
white, to be made
white, to make
whiter, to be
Hithpael.
white, to be made

לָבָן 632
white

לְבֵן 632
white

לְבָנָה 632
moon

לְבֵנָה 632
altars of brick
brick
tile

לִבְנֶה 633
poplar

לִבְנָה 633
paved

לָבַשׁ & לָבֵשׁ ..633
Kal.
apparelled, to be
armed with
array self, to
clothe, to
clothe self, to[with
clothed, to be,—in,
come upon, to
put on, to
wear, to
Pual.
apparel, in
arrayed, to be, in
clothed, to be, in
put on, to
Hiphil.
arm, to,—with
array, to,—in
clothe, to,—in, with
put, to
put upon, to

לְבַשׁ Ch. 633
P'al.
clothed, to be with
Aphel.
clothe, to with

לֹג 633
log *of oil*

לָה Ch.........633
nothing, as

לֹה 634
not

לַהַב 634
blade
bright
flame
glittering

לֶהָבָה & לַהֶבֶת 634
flame
flaming
head (*of a spear*)

לַהַג 634
study

לָהַהּ..........634
Kal.
faint, to
Hithpael.
mad

לָהַט 634
Kal.
fire, to be set on
flaming
Piel.
burn, to
burn up, to
fire, to set on
kindle, to

לַהַט 634
flaming

לְהָטִים 634
enchantments

לָהַם 634
Hithpael.
wounds, as

לָהֵן 634
* them, for

לָהֵן Ch. 634
but
except
save
therefore
wherefore

לַהֲקָה 634
company

לוּ 634
I would
if
if haply
O that
oh that
peradventure
pray thee, I
though
would God
would God that

לוּא...........634
if haply
oh that

לָוָה 634
Kal.
abide with, to
borrow, to
borrower
Niphal.
cleave, to
join self, to
joined, to be
Hiphil.
lend, to
lend*er*

לוּז 635
Kal.
depart, to
Niphal.
froward
perverse
perverseness
Hiphil.
depart, to

לוּז 635
hazel

לוּחַ 635
board
plate
table

לוּט............635
Kal.
cast
wrapped
Hiphil.
wrap, to

לוֹט............635
covering

לִוְיָה 635
ornament

לִוְיָתָן..........635
leviathan
* mourning

לוּלֵא 635
except
if—not
unless

לוּלֵי 635
except
had not
if
unless
were it not that

לוּלִים 635
stairs, winding

לוּן & לִין 635
Kal.
abide, to
abide all night, to
continue, to
dwell, to
endure, to
grudge, to
left, to be
lie all night, to

lodge, to
lodge all night, to
lodge in, to
lodge this night, to
lodging, to
remain, to
tarry, to
tarry all night, to
tarry that night, to

Niphal.
murmur, to
(כ׳) murmur, to make to

Hiphil.
lodge, to cause to
murmur, to
murmur, to make to

Hithpalpel.
abide, to

לוּעַ 636

Kal.
swallow down, to
swallowed up, to be

לוּץ 636

Kal.
mocker
scorn, to
scorner
scornful

Hiphil.
ambassador
derision, to have in
interpreter
mock, to make a
scorn, to
teacher

Hithpalpel.
mocker

לוּשׁ 636

Kal.
knead, to

לְוָת Ch. 636
* thee

לְזוּת 636
perverse

לַח 636
green
moist

לֵחַ 637
natural force

לְחוּם..........637
eating, while...is flesh

לְחִי...........637
cheek
cheek bone
jaw
jawbone
Lehi
Ramath-lehi

לָחַךְ 637

Kal.
lick up, to

Piel.
lick, to
lick up, to

לָחַם 637

Kal.
devour, to
eat, to
fight, to
fighting

Niphal.
ever
fight, to
fighting
overcome, to
prevail, to
war, to
war, to make
war, making
warring

לָחֶם 638
war

לֶחֶם 638
bread
* eat
food
fruit
loaf
meat
provision
*shew*bread
victuals

לְחֶם Ch. 640
feast

לְחֵנָה Ch.......640
concubine

לָחַץ 640

Kal.
afflict, to
crush, to
force, to
hold fast, to
oppress, to
oppressors

Niphal.
thrust self, to

לַחַץ 640
affliction
oppression

לָחַשׁ 640

Piel.
charmer

Hithpael.
whisper, to
whisper together, to

לַחַשׁ 640
charmed
earring
enchantment
orator
prayer

לָט 640
enchantment
privily
secretly
softly

לֹט 640
myrrh

לְטָאָה........640
lizard

לָטַשׁ 640

Kal.
instructer
sharpen, to
whet, to

Pual.
sharp

לֹיוֹת..........640
additions

לַיִל 640
*mid*night
night
night season

לֵילְיָא Ch. 642
night

לִילִית 642
owl, screech

לַיִשׁ...........642
lion
lion, old

לָכַד 642

Kal.
at all
catch, to
catch self, to
take, to

Niphal.
holden, to be
taken, to be

Hithpael.
frozen, to be
stick together, to

לֶכֶד 643
taken, being

לֻלָאֹת 643
loops

לָמַד 643

Kal.
diligently
learn, to
skilful

Piel.
instruct, to
teach, to
teachers
teaching

Pual.
expert
instructed, to be
taught, to be
*un*accustomed

לְמוֹ..........644
at
for
to
upon

לִמּוּד.........644
accustomed
disciple
learned
taught
used

לֹעַ 644
throat

לָעַב 644

Hiphil.
mock, to

לָעַג 644

Kal.
derision, to have in
laugh, to
mock, to
scorn, to laugh to

Niphal.
stammering

Hiphil.
mock, to
mock on, to
scorn, to laugh to

לַעַג 644
derision
scorn
scorning

לָעֵג 644
mocker
stammering

לָעַז..........644

Kal.
language, strange

לָעַט..........644

Hiphil.
feed, to

לַעֲנָה.........644
hemlock
wormwood

לַפִּיד 644
brand
burning lamp
firebrand
lamp
lightning
torch

לִפְנַי 644
before it

לָפַת 644

Kal.
hold, to take

Niphal.
turn aside, to
turn self, to

לָצוֹן..........644
scornful
scorning

לָצַץ..........644

Kal.
scorn, to

לָקַח..........644

Kal.
accept, to
bring, to
buy, to
carry away, to
drawn
fetch, to
get, to
marry, to
place, to
receive, to
receiving
reserve, to
seize, to
send for, to
take, to
take away, to
taking
use, to
win, to

Niphal.
brought, to be
taken, to be
taken away, to be

Pual.
taken, to be
taken away, to be
taken up, to be

Hophal.
fetched, to be
taken, to be
taken away, to be

Hithpael.
infolding
mingled

לֶקַח..........650
doctrine
learning
speech, fair

לָקַט..........650

Kal.
gather, to
glean, to

Piel.
gather, to
gather up, to
glean, to

Pual.
gathered, to be

Hithpael.
gathered, to be

לֶקֶט..........651
gleaning

לָקַק 651

Kal.
lap, to
lick, to

Piel.
lap, to

לָקַשׁ..........651

Piel.
gather, to

לֶקֶשׁ 651
growth, latter

לְשַׁד 651
fresh
moisture

לָשׁוֹן 651
babbler †
bay
* evil speaker †
language
talkers
tongue
wedge

לִשְׁכָּה........652
chamber
parlour

לֶשֶׁם 652
ligure

לָשַׁן..........652

Piel.
slander, to

Poel.
slander, to

Hiphil.
accuse

לִשָּׁן Ch. 652
language

לֶתֶךְ 652
homer, half

מָא Ch. 652
what †

מַאֲבוּס 652
storehouse

מְאֹד 652
diligent
especially
exceeding
exceedingly
far
fast
good
great
greatly
*louder and louder
might
mightily
mighty
much
quickly
so much
so sore
sore
utterly
very
very much †
very sore
well

מֵאָה 654
hundred
hundred*fold*
hundredth
Meah
sixscore †

מְאָה Ch. 657
hundred

מַאֲוַיִּים 657
desires

מאוּם 657
blemish
blot

מְאוּמָה 657
fault
no †
*no*thing
nought †
ought
somewhat
thing, any

מָאוֹר 658
bright
light

מְאוּרָה 658
den

מֹאזְנַיִם 658
balances

מֹאזְנַיִן Ch. 658
balances

מַאֲכָל 658
*bake*meats
food
fruit
meat
victual

מַאֲכֶלֶת 658
knife

מַאֲכֹלֶת 658
fuel

מַאֲמַצִּים 658
forces

מַאֲמָר 658
commandment
decree

מֵאמַר Ch. 658
appointment
word

מָאן Ch. 658
vessel

מָאֵן 658
Piel.
refuse, to
utterly

מָאֵן 659
refuse

מֵאֲנִים 659
refuse

מָאַס 1 659
Kal.
abhor, to
cast away, to
cast off, to
contemn, to
despise, to
disdain, to
loathe, to
reject, to
utterly
Niphal.
refused, to be
reprobate
vile person

מָאַס 2 659
Niphal.
loathsome, to become
melt away, to

מַאֲפֶה 659
baken

מַאֲפֵל 659
darkness

מַאְפֵּלְיָה 659
darkness

מָאַר 659
Hiphil.
fretting
pricking

מַאֲרָב 660
ambush, lie in
ambushment
lurking place
wait, lying in

מְאֵרָה 660
curse
cursing

מִבְדָּלוֹת 660
separate cities

מָבוֹא 660
came, by which...
cometh, as
coming in
enter into, as men
entering
entrance into
entry
goeth, where...
going down
westward †

מְבוּכָה 660
perplexity

מַבּוּל 660
flood

מְבוּנִים 660
taught

מְבוּסָה 660
treading down
trodden down
trodden under foot

מַבּוּעַ 660
fountain
spring

מְבוּקָה 660
void

מִבְחוֹר 660
choice

מִבְחָר 660
choice
choicest
chosen

מַבָּט 660
expectation

מֶבָּט 660
expectation

מִבְטָא 660
uttered out of
uttered, that which...

מִבְטָח 660
confidence
hope
sure
trust

מַבְלִיגִית 661
comfort self

מִבְנֶה 661
frame

מִבְצָר 661
defenced
fenced
fenced, most
fortress
strong
strong hold
strong, most

מִבְרָח 661
fugitive

מְבֻשִׁים 661
secrets

מְבַשְּׁלוֹת 661
boiling places

מָג 661
Rab-mag

מִגְבָּלֹת 661
ends

מִגְבָּעוֹת 661
bonnets

מֶגֶד 661
pleasant
precious fruits
precious things

מִגְדָּל 661
castle
flower
Migdal-*el*
Migdal-*gad*
pulpit
tower

מִגְדֹּל 661
tower

מִגְדָּנוֹת 662
precious things
presents

מָגוֹר 662
fear
Magor-*missabib*
terror

מָגוּר 662
dwelling
pilgrimage
sojourn, where
stranger, be a

מְגוֹרָה 662
fear

מְגוּרָה 662
barn
fear

מַגְזֵרָה 662
axe

מַגָּל 662
sickle

מְגִלָּה 662
roll
volume

מְגִלָּה Ch. 662
roll

מְגַמָּה 662
sup up

מָגַן 662
Piel.
deliver, to

מָגֵן 662
armed
buckler
defence
ruler
scale †
shield

מְגִנָּה 663
sorrow

מִגְעֶרֶת 663
rebuke

מַגֵּפָה 663
plague
* plagued, to be
slaughter
stroke

מָגַר 663
Kal.
* terrors
Piel.
cast down, to

מְגַר Ch. 663
Pael.
destroy, to

מְגֵרָה 663
axe
saw

מִגְרָעוֹת 663
narrowed rests

מֶגְרָפָה 663
clods

מִגְרָשׁ 663
cast out
suburb

מַד 664
(כ׳) armour
clothes
garment
judgment
measure
raiment
stature

מַדְבַּח Ch. 664
altar

מִדְבָּר 664
desert
south
speech
wilderness

מָדַד 665
Kal.
measure, to
mete, to
Niphal.
measured, to be
Piel.
measure, to
mete out, to
Polel.
measure, to
Hithpolel.
stretch self, to

מִדַּד 666
gone, be

מִדָּה 666
garment
measure
measuring
meteyard
piece
size
stature
stature, great
tribute
wide

מִדָּה 666
toll
tribute

מַדְהֵבָה 666
golden city

מֶדֶו 666
garment

מַדְוֶה 666
disease

מַדּוּחִים 666
banishment, causes of

מָדוֹן 666
brawling
contention
contentious
discord
strife

מָדוֹן 666
stature

מַדּוּעַ 666
how
wherefore
why

מְדוֹר Ch. 667
dwelling

מְדוּרָה 667
pile
pile for fire

מְדֶחֶה 667
ruin

מַדְחֵפֹת 667
overthrow, to

מַדַּי 667
sufficiently

מְדִינָה 667
province
* province, every

מְדִינָה Ch. 667
province

מִדְיָנִים 667
brawling
contentions
contentious

מְדֹכָה 667
mortar

מַדְמֵנָה 667
dunghill

מְדָנִים 667
discord
strife

מַדָּע & מַדַּע ..667
knowledge
science
thought

מַדְקָרוֹת 667
piercings

מְדָר Ch. 667
dwelling

מַדְרֵגָה 667
stairs
steep places

מִדְרָךְ 667
foot breadth

מִדְרָשׁ 667
story

מְדֻשָּׁה 667
threshing

מָה 668
how
how long
how oft
how*soever*
*no*thing
what
what end
what good
what purpose
what thing
whereby
where*fore*
wherefore
wherein
whereto
wherewith
why
why, for

מֶה 668
how
what
wherefore
why

מָה Ch. 668
how great
how mighty
that which
what
whatsoever
why

מָהַהּ 668
Hithpalpel.
delay, to
linger, to
stay selves, to
tarry, to

מְהוּמָה 668
destruction
discomfiture
trouble
tumult
vexation
vexed

מָהִיר 668
diligent
hasting
ready

מָהַל 668
Kal.
mixed

מַהֲלָךְ 668
journey
walk

מַהֲלָל 668
praise

מַהֲלֻמוֹת 668
stripes
strokes

מַהֲמֹרוֹת 668
deep pits

מַהְפֵּכָה 668
overthrew, when
overthrow
overthrown

מַהְפֶּכֶת 668
prison
stocks

מָהַר [1] 669
Kal.
hasten, to
Niphal.
carried headlong, to be
fearful
hasty
rash
Piel.
haste, to
haste, to cause to make
haste, in
haste, to make
hasten, to
* hastily
hasty, to be
Maher - *shalal* - *hash-baz*
* quickly
quickly, to fetch
quickly, to make ready
* shortly
* soon
soon, to be so
speed, to make
* speedily
* straightway
* suddenly
swift

מָהַר [2] 669
Kal.
endow, to
surely

מַהֵר 669
hasteth

מַהֵר 669
hastily
once, at
quickly
soon
speedily
suddenly

מֹהַר 669
dowry

מְהֵרָה 669
hastily
quickly
shortly
soon
speed, make
speed, with
speedily
swiftly

מַהֲתַלּוֹת 669
deceits

מוֹאל 669
against, over

מוֹבָא 670
coming

מוּג 670
Kal.
consume, to
faint, to
melt, to
Niphal.
dissolved, to be
faint, to
fainthearted, to be
melt away, to
Polel.
dissolve, to
soft, to make
Hithpolel.
melt, to
melted, to be

מוֹדָע & מוֹדַע 670
kinsman
kinswoman

מוֹדַעַת 670
kindred

מוֹט 670
Kal.
carried, to be
decay, to be fallen in
exceedingly
falling down
moved, to be
ready, to be
removed, to be
shake, to
slide, to
slip, to
Niphal.
course, to be out of
moved, to be
slip, to
Hiphil.
cast, to
(כ') fall, to
Hithpael.
moved, to be

מוֹט 670
bar
moved, be
staff
yoke

מוֹטָה 670
bands
heavy
staves
yoke

מוּךְ 670
Kal.
poor, to be waxen
poorer, to be

מוּל 670
Kal.
circumcise, to
Niphal.
circumcise selves, to
circumcised, to be
circumcising
must needs
Polel.
cut down, to be
Hiphil.
destroy, to
Hithpolel.
pieces, to cut in

מוּל...........671
against, over

מוּל...........671
against
against, over
before
before †
*fore*front
from
God-ward, to
toward
with

מוֹלֶדֶת 671
begotten
born
issue
kindred
native
nativity

מוּלֹת..........671
circumcision

מוּם 671
blemish
blot
spot

מוּסַב..........671
winding about

מוּסָד..........671
foundation

מוּסָדָה........671
foundation
grounded

מוֹסָדוֹת 671
foundations

מוּסָךְ 672
covert

מוֹסֵר..........672
bands
bonds

מוּסָר. 672
bond
chasten*eth*
chastening
chastisement
check
correction
discipline
doctrine
instruction
rebuker

מוֹעֵד..........672
appointed
appointed sign
appointed time
assembly
assembly, place of
assembly, solemn
congregation
feast
feast, set
feast, solemn
season
season, appointed
season, due
solemn
solemnity
synagogue
time
time appointed
time, set

מוֹעָד..........673
time, appointed

מוֹעֲדוֹת 673
feast, solemn

מוּעָדָה........673
appointed

מוֹעֶדֶת........673
joint, out of

מוּעָף..........673
dimness

מוֹעֵצוֹת 673
counsels
devices

מוּעָקָה 673
affliction

מוֹפֵת 673
miracle
sign
wonder
wondered at

מוּץ 673
Kal.
extortioner

מוֹצָא..........673
brought out
bud
came out, that which
east
going forth
goings out
gone out, that which is
gone out, thing that is
outgoing
proceeded out
spring
vein
*water*course
*water*springs

מוֹצָאוֹת 673
draught house
goings forth

מוּצָק 673
casting
hardness

מוּצַק & מוּצָק 673
vexation
straitened, is
straitness

מוּצֶקֶת........674
cast, when it was
pipe

מוּק 674
Hiphil.
corrupt, to be

מוֹקֵד..........674
burning
hearth

מוֹקְדָה........674
burning

מוֹקֵשׁ..........674
ensnared, be
gin
snare
snared, is
trap

מוּר 674
Niphal.
changed, to be
Hiphil.
at all
change, to
exchange, to
removed, to be

מוֹרָא..........674
dread
fear
feared, that ought to be
terribleness
terror

מוֹרַג 674
threshing instrument

מוֹרָד..........674
going down
steep place
thin

מוֹרָה..........674
razor

מוֹרָה (כ') 674
fear

מוֹרֶה..........674
former rain
rain

מוֹרָשׁ..........674
possession
thoughts

מוֹרָשָׁה........674
heritage
inheritance
possession

מוּשׁ 1 674
Kal.
depart, to
remove, to
removed, to be
Hiphil.
cease, to
depart, to
go back, to
remove, to
take away, to

מוּשׁ 2 675
Kal.
feel, to
Hiphil.
feel, to
handle, to

מוֹשָׁב 675
assembly
dwell in, to
dwelling
dwellingplace
dwelt in, that
dwelt, wherein
habitation
inhabited place
seat
sitting
situation
sojourning

מוֹשְׁכוֹת 675
bands

מוֹשָׁעוֹת 675
salvation

מוּת 675
Kal.
dead
dead, to be
dead body
dead man
dead, one
death
(כ') death, to be put to
death, worthy of
die, to
die, to be like to
die, must
must needs
necro*mancer*
slain, to be
surely
very suddenly
Polel.
slay, to
Hiphil.
at all
* crying
death, to put to
destroy, to
destroyer
die, to cause to
in *no* wise
kill, to
slay, to
surely
Hophal.
death, to be put to
die, to
slain, to be

מָוֶת..........680
dead
dead, be
dead*ly*
death
die
died

מוֹת Ch.......681
death

מוּת 681
death
Muth-*labben*

מוֹתָר..........681
plenteousness
preeminence
profit

מִזְבֵּחַ..........681
altar

מֶזֶג 683
liquor

מָזֶה 684
burnt

מָזוּ..........684
garner

מְזוּזָה 684
post
post, door
post, side

מָזוֹן 684
meat
victual

מָזוֹן Ch. 684
meat

מָזוֹר 684
bound up, be
wound

מָזוֹר 684
wound

מֵזִיחַ & מֵזַח ..684
girdle
strength

מַזְלֵג 684
fleshhook

מִזְלָגוֹת........684
fleshhooks

מַזָּלוֹת 684
planets

מְזִמָּה........684
devices
discretion
intents
inventions, witty
lewdness
mischievous
mischievous device
thought
wicked device
wickedly

מִזְמוֹר 684
psalm

מַזְמֵרוֹת 684
pruninghooks

מְזַמְּרוֹת 684
snuffers

מִזְעָר..........685
few
very

מִזְרֶה..........685
fan

מַזָּרוֹת 685
Mazzaroth

מְזָרִים 685
north

מִזְרָח..........685
east
east side
eastward
rising
rising of the sun
*sun*rising
sunrising

מִזְרָע 685
sown, thing

מִזְרָק..........685
bason
bowl

מֹחַ 685
marrow

מֵחִים 685
fat ones
fatlings

מָחָא 685
Kal.
clap, to
Piel.
clap, to

מְחָא Ch. 685
P'al.
smite, to
Pael.
stay, to
Ithp'al.
* hanged, to be

מַחֲבֵא 686
hiding place

מַחֲבֹאִים......686
lurking places

מְחַבְּרוֹת 686
couplings
joinings

מַחְבֶּרֶת 686
coupling

מַחֲבַת 686
pan

מַחֲגֹרֶת........686
girding

מָחָה 1 686
Kal.
blot out, to
destroy, to
put out, to
utterly
wipe, to
wipe away, to
Niphal.
abolished, to be
blotted out, to be
destroyed, to be
put out, to be
wiped away, to be
Hiphil.
blot out, to
destroy, to
wipe out, to

מָחָה 2 686
Pual.
marrow, full of

מָחָה 3 686
Kal.
reach unto, to

מְחוּגָה 686
compass

מָחוֹז 686
haven

מָחוֹל..........686
dance
dancing

מְחוֹלָה........686
company
dances
dancing

מַחֲזֶה 686
vision

מֶחֱזָה 686
light

מְחִי 686
engines

מִחְיָה..........687
preserve life
quick
recover selves
reviving
sustenance
victuals

מְחִיר..........687
gain
hire
price
sold
worth

מַחֲלֶה 687
disease
infirmity

מַחֲלָה 687
disease
sickness

מְחִלּוֹת........687
caves

מַחֲלֻיִים 687
diseases

מַחְלְפוֹת 687
locks

מַחֲלָפִים 687
knives

מַחֲלָצוֹת 687
apparel, changeable suits of
raiment, change of

מַחְלְקָה Ch. ..687
course

מַחֲלֹקֶת........687
company
course
division
portion
Sela - hammahlekoth

מָחֲלַת 687
Mahalath

מַחְמָאֹת 687
* butter

מַחְמָד 687
beloved
desire
goodly
lovely
pleasant
pleasant thing

מַחֲמֻדִּים 687
pleasant things

מַחְמָל 687
pitieth

מַחֲנֶה 688
army
bands

battle
camp
company
drove
host
Mahanaim
Mahaneh-*dan*
tents

מַחֲנַק 689
strangling

מַחְסֶה 689
hope
refuge
refuge, place of
shelter
trust

מַחְסוֹם........689
bridle

מַחְסוֹר.........689
lack
need
penury
poor
poverty
want

מָחַץ...........689
Kal.
dipped, to be
pierce, to
pierce through, to
smite, to
smite through, to
strike through, to
wound, to

מַחַץ 689
stroke

מַחְצֵב.........689
hewed
hewn

מֶחֱצָה 689
half

מַחֲצִית........689
half
half so much
mid*day*

מָחַק...........689
Kal.
smite off, to

מֶחְקָר 689
deep place

מָחָר...........689
come, *time* to
time to come
to-morrow

מַחֲרָאוֹת 690
draught house

מַחֲרֵשָׁה.......690
mattock

מַחֲרֶשֶׁת 690
share

מָחֳרָת.........690
morrow
next *day*
next day

מַחְשֹׂף.........690
appear, made

מַחֲשָׁבָה.......690
device
purpose

מַחֲשֶׁבֶת.......690
cunning
cunning works
curious works
device
devised
imaginations
invented
means
purposes
thoughts

מַחְשָׁךְ 691
dark
dark place
darkness

מַחְתָּה 691
censer
firepan
snuffdish

מְחִתָּה 691
destruction
dismaying
ruin
terror

מַחְתֶּרֶת 691
breaking up
secret search

מְטָא & מְטָה Ch.
..............691
P'al.
come, to
reach, to

מַטְאֲטֵא.......691
besom

מַטְבֵּחַ.........691
slaughter

מַטָּה 691
beneath
down
downward
less
low, very
under
underneath

מַטֶּה 691
rod
staff
tribe

מִטָּה 693
bed
bed*chamber*
bier

מֻטֶּה 693
perverseness

מַטְוֶה..........693
spun

מֻטּוֹת.........693
stretching out

מְטִיל 693
bar

מַטְמוֹן 693
riches, hidden
treasure
treasures, hid

מַטָּע 693
plantation
planting
plants

מַטְעַמּוֹת 693
dainties
dainty meats

מַטְעַמִּים 693
savoury meat

מִטְפַּחַת 693
vail
wimple

מָטַר...........693
Niphal.
rained upon, to be
Hiphil.
rain, to
rain, to cause to

מָטָר 693
rain;—shower

מַטָּרָא.........694
mark

מַטָּרָה 694
mark
prison

מִי.............694
any
any man
he
him
* O that †
what
which
who
whom
whose
whosoever
* would to God †

מֵיטָב..........694
best

מִיכַל..........694
brook

מַיִם...........694
(כ׳) for
Misrephoth-maim
piss †
washing
water
water*course*
water*flood*
watering
water*springs*

מִין 697
kind

מֵיסַךְ.........698
covert

מִיץ............698
churning
forcing
wringing

מִישׁוֹר........698
equity
even place
plain
right
righteously
straight
straight, made
uprightness

מֵישָׁרִים.......698
agreement
aright
equal, that are
equity
right things
right, things that are
righteously
sweetly
upright
uprightly
uprightness

מֵיתָר 698
cord
string

מַכְאוֹב........698
grief
pain
sorrow

מִכְבָּר 698
grate

מַכְבֵּר.........698
cloth, thick

מַכָּה 698
blow
plague
slaughter
smote
sore
stripe
stroke
wound
wounded

מִכְוָה 699
burneth, that
burning

מָכוֹן 699
dwelling place
foundations
habitation
place
settled place

מְכוֹנָה 699
base

מְכוּרָה 699
birth
habitation
nativity

מָכַךְ...........699
Kal.
low, to be brought
Niphal.
decay, to
Hophal.
low, to be brought

מִכְלָה.........699
fold
*sheep*fold

מִכְלוֹל.........699
gorgeously, most
sorts, all

מִכְלוֹת 699
perfect

מִכְלָל 699
perfection

מַכְלֻלִים.......699
sorts, all

מַכֹּלֶת.........699
food

מִכְמַנִּים.......699
treasures

מַכְמֹר 699
net

מִכְמָר 699
net

מִכְמֶרֶת.......699
drag

מִכְמֹרֶת 699
nets

מְכֹנָה.........699
base

מִכְנָסַיִם.......699
breeches

מֶכֶס 700
tribute

מִכְסָה.........700
number
worth

מִכְסֶה.........700
covering

מְכַסֶּה.........700
clothing
cover, to
covereth, that which

מָכַר...........700
Kal.
at all
sell, to
sell away, to
sellers
Niphal.
sell self, to
sold, to be
Hithpael.
sell self, to
sold, to be

מֶכֶר 700
pay
price
ware

מַכָּר...........700
acquaintance

מִכְרֶה.........700
*salt*pits

מְכֵרָה.........700
habitation

מִכְשׁוֹל........701
fall, caused to
offence
* offend, *n*othing
ruin
stumblingblock

מַכְשֵׁלָה 701
ruin
stumblingblock

מִכְתָּב 701
writing

מְכִתָּה.........701
bursting

מִכְתָּם.........701
Michtam

מַכְתֵּשׁ.........701
hollow place
mortar

מָלֵא & מָלָא..701
Kal.
accomplished, to be

consecrate,† to
end, to be at an
expired, to be
fill, to
filled, to be
fulfil, to
fulfilled, to be
full, to be
full, to become
fully set, to be
fulness
gather, to
*over*flow, to
presume, to
replenish, to
replenished, to be
satisfied, to be
space

Niphal.
accomplished, to be
fenced, to be
filled, to be
fulfilled, to be
full, to be
replenished, to be

Piel.
accomplish, to
confirm, to
consecrate,† to
consecrated,† to be
fill, to;—with
fulfil, to
* full, to draw
full tale, to give in
fully, to go
fulness
furnish, to
gather together,to
*over*flow, to
replenish, to
satisfy, to
set, to
take *a hand*ful, to
wholly,† to have

Pual.
set

Hithpael.
gather selves, to

מְלָא Ch.......703
P'al.
fill, to
Ithpael.
full, to be

מָלֵא 703
* child, she that is with
fill
filled
filled with
full
fully
multitude
worth, as is

מְלֹא 703
* all along
fill
full
* full, that whereof was
fulness
*hand*fuls
* in, all that is
multitude
* therein, all that is
* therein is, all that

מְלֵאָה 703
fruit
fruit, first of ripe
fulness

מִלֻּאָה 703
inclosings
settings

מִלֻּאִים 703
consecration
set, to be

מַלְאָךְ 704
ambassador
angel
(כ') king
messenger

מַלְאַךְ Ch. 705
angel

מְלָאכָה 705
business
* cattle †
goods
industrious †
labour
made, thing
occupation
occupied †
officer †
stuff
thing
use
work
workmanship
workmanship, manner of
work*men*

מַלְאֲכוּת 706
message

מִלֵּאת 706
* fitly

מַלְבּוּשׁ 706
apparel
raiment
vestment

מַלְבֵּן 706
brickkiln

מִלָּה 706
answer †
byword
matter
say, any thing to
say, what to
speak, to
speaking
speech
talking
word

מִלָּה Ch.......706
commandment
matter
thing
word

מַלּוּחַ..........706
mallows

מְלוּכָה 706
kingdom
king's
royal

מָלוֹן 707
inn
lodge, place where...
lodging
lodging place

מְלוּנָה.........707
cottage
lodge

מָלַח[1]..........707
Kal.
season, to
Pual.
tempered together, to be
Hophal.
at all
salted, to be

מָלַח[2]..........707
Niphal.
vanish away, to

מֶלַח 707
salt
salt*pit*

מְלַח Ch.......707
P'al.
maintenance,† to have

מְלַח Ch. 707
maintenance †
salt

מַלָּח 707
mariner

מְלֵחָה 707
barren land
barrenness
salt *land*

מְלָחִים 707
rotten rags

מִלְחָמָה 707
battle
fight
fighting
war
warr*ior*

מָלַט 709
Niphal.
deliver self, to
delivered, to be
escape, to
escaped, to be
let get away
speedily
Piel.
deliver, to
lay, to
let alone, to
save, to
surely
Hiphil.
delivered, to be
preserve, to
Hithpael.
escaped, to be
leap out, to

מֶלֶט 710
clay

מְלִילָה 710
ears

מְלִיצָה........710
interpretation
taunting

מָלַךְ 710
Kal.
indeed
king, to be
queen, to be
reign, to
reign, to begin to
reigning
rule, to
surely
Niphal.
consult, to
Hiphil.
king, to make
king, to set a
king, to set up
make *king*, to
queen, to make
reign, to make to
Hophal.
king, to be made

מֶלֶךְ 712
Hammelech
king
Malcham
Moloch
royal

מֶלֶךְ Ch. 727
king
royal

מְלַךְ Ch. 728
counsel

מַלְכֹּדֶת........728
trap

מַלְכָּה 728
queen

מַלְכָּה Ch. 728
queen

מַלְכוּ Ch.......728
kingdom
kingly
realm
reign

מַלְכוּת........728
empire
kingdom
realm
reign
royal

מְלֶכֶת 729
queen

מָלַל 729
Kal.
speak, to
Piel.
say, to
speak, to
utter, to

מְלַל Ch. 729
Pael.
say, to
speak, to
speaking

מַלְמַד 729
goad

מָלַץ 729
Niphal.
sweet, to be

מֶלְצַר 729
* Melzar

מָלַק 729
Kal.
wring off, to

מַלְקוֹחַ 729
booty
jaws
prey

מַלְקוֹשׁ 730
latter (*rain*)
rain, latter

מֶלְקָחַיִם 730
tongs

מַלְקָחַיִם 730
snuffers
tongs

מֶלְתָּחָה 730
vestry

מַלְתָּעוֹת 730
teeth, great

מַמְּגֻרוֹת 730
barns

מְמַדִּים........730
measures

מָמוֹת 730
deaths

מַמְזֵר..........730
bastard

מִמְכָּר 730
* ought
sale
sale, that which cometh of
sold, that which...
ware

מִמְכֶּרֶת 730
* sold as †

מַמְלָכָה 730
kingdom
king's
reign
royal

מַמְלָכוּת......731
kingdom
reign

מִמְסָךְ 731
drink offering
wine, mixed

מֶמֶר 731
bitterness

מַמְּרֹרִים 731
bitterness

מִמְשַׁח 731
anointed

מִמְשָׁל 731
dominion
ruled, that

מֶמְשָׁלָה 731
dominion
government
power
rule, to

מְמֶשֶׁק 731
breeding

מַמְתַּקִּים 731
sweet
sweet, most

מָן 731
manna

מָן Ch. 731
what
who
whomsoever
whoso †

מִן 731
above
after
among
at
because of
by
from
from among
in
* neither
* not
of
out of
over
reason of, by
since
than
through
whether
with

מִן Ch. 732
according
after
because †
before †
by
for
from
* him
more than
of
out of
part
since
these
to
upon
when †

מַנְגִּינָה........732
musick

מִנְדָּה Ch. 732
toll

מַנְדַּע Ch. 732
knowledge
reason
understanding

מָנָה 732
Kal.
count, to
number, to
tell, to
Niphal.
numbered, to be
Piel.
appoint, to
appointed, to be
prepare, to
set, to
Pual.
appointed, to be

מְנָא & מְנָה Ch.733
P'al.
Mene
number, to
Pael.
ordain, to
set, to

מָנָה 733
belonged, such things as
part
portion

מָנֶה...........733
maneh
pound

מִנְהָג..........733
driving

מִנְהָרוֹת.......733
dens

מָנוֹד 733
shaking

מָנוֹחַ 733
rest
rest, place of

מְנוּחָה 733
comfortable
ease
quiet
rest
resting place
still

מָנוֹן...........733
son

מָנוֹס..........733
apace
escape
flee, way to
flight
refuge

מְנוּסָה 733
fleeing
flight

מָנוֹר 733
beam

מְנוֹרָה.........734
candlestick

מִנְּזָרִים........734
crowned

מִנְחָה 734
gifts
meat offering
oblation
offering
present
sacrifice

מִנְחָה Ch. 735
meat offering
oblation

מְנִי............735
number

מִנִּים..........735
instruments, stringed
whereby

מֹנִים 735
times

מִנְיָן Ch. 735
number

מִנְלֶה..........735
perfection

מָנַע 735
Kal.
deny, to
keep, to
keep back, to
refrain, to
restrain, to
withhold, to
Niphal.
hinder, to
withholden, to be

מַנְעוּל.........735
lock

מִנְעָל..........735
shoes

מַנְעַמִּים.......736
dainties

מְנַעַנְעִים 736
cornets

מְנַקִּיּוֹת........736
bowls;—cups

מְנָת...........736
portion

מָס 736
afflicted, is

מַס 736
discomfited
levy
task*masters*
tributary
tribute

מֵסַב 736
compass about, that
round about
round about, places
table, at

מַסְגֵּר 736
prison
smith

מִסְגֶּרֶת 736
border
close place
hole

מַסַּד 736
foundation

מִסְדְּרוֹן........736
porch

מָסָה 736
Hiphil.
consume away, to make to
melt, to
melt, to make
water, to

מִסָּה 736
tribute

מַסָּה 736
* Massah
temptation
trial

מַסְוֶה.........736
vail

מְסוּכָה........736
thorn hedge

מַסָּח 736
broken down

מִסְחָר.........736
traffick

מָסַךְ 737
Kal.
mingle, to

מָסָךְ 737
covering
curtain
hanging

מֶסֶךְ 737
mixture

מְסֻכָּה.........737
covering

מַסֵּכָה.........737
covering
molten
molten image

מַסֵּכָה........737
covering
vail

מִסְכֵּן.........737
poor
poor man

מִסְכְּנוֹת.......737
store
storehouses
treasure

מִסְכֵּנֻת.......737
scarceness

מַסֶּכֶת 737
web

מְסִלָּה........737
causeway
course
highway
path
terrace

מַסְלוּל 737
highway

מַסְמֵר.........737
nail

מָסַס 737
Kal.
faint, to
Niphal.
faint, to
loosed, to be
melt, to
melt away, to
melted, to be
refuse
utterly
Hiphil.
discourage, to

מַסָּע 738
dart

מַסָּע...........738
brought, before it was

מַסַּע...........738
journey
journeying

מִסְעָד.........738
pillars

מִסְפֵּד 738
lamentation
mourneth, one
mourning
wailing

מִסְפּוֹא........738
provender

מִסְפָּחוֹת 738
kerchiefs

מִסְפַּחַת.......738
scab

מִסְפָּר.........738
abundance †
account
* all
* few
*in*finite
*in*numerable
number
number, certain
numbered
tale;—sum
telling
time †

מָסַר..........739
Kal.
commit, to
Niphal.
delivered, to be

מֹסָר..........739
instruction

מָסֹרֶת........739
bond

מִסְתּוֹר 739
covert

מִסְתָּר 739
secret
secret place
secretly

מַעְבָּד.........739
works

מַעְבָּד Ch. ...739
works

מַעֲבֶה.........739
clay

מַעֲבָר.........739
ford
pass, place where
passage

מַעְבָּרָה 739
ford
passage

מַעְגָּל..........740
path
trench
wayside

מַעְגָּלָה........740
going
path
trench
way

מָעַד..........740
Kal.
slide, to
slip, to
Hiphil.
shake, to make

מַעֲדָן..........740
dainty
delicately
delight

מַעֲדַנּוֹת 740
influences

מַעְדֵּר.........740
mattock

מָעָה..........740
gravel

מָעוֹג..........740
cake
feast

מָעוֹז..........740
forces
fort
fortress
rock
strength
strengthen, to
strong
strong hold
* strong, most

מָעוֹן..........740
den
dwelling
dwelling place
dwellingplace
habitation

מְעוֹנָה........740
den
dwelling place
habitation
place
refuge

מָעוּף..........740
dimness

מָעוֹר..........740
nakedness

מָעַט..........741
Kal.
diminished, to be
few, to be
fewness
little, to be
little, to seem
minished, to be
Piel.
few, to be
Hiphil.
decrease, to suffer to
diminish, to
* few, to borrow a
few, to give
few in number, to make
least, to gather
less
* less, to give
* less, to give the
little, to gather
nothing, to bring to

מְעָט & מְעַט..741
almost
few
few, some
few, very
fewer
fewest
lightly
little
little while
small
small matter
small thing
small, very
some
soon
* very

מָעֹט..........741
wrapped up

מַעֲטֶה.........741
garment

מַעֲטָפוֹת......741
mantles

מְעִי...........742
heap

מְעִיל..........742
cloke
coat
mantle
robe

מַעְיָן..........742
fountains
spring
well

מֵעִים..........742
belly
bowels
* heart
womb

מְעִין Ch. 742
belly

מָעַךְ..........742
Kal.
bruised
stuck
Pual.
pressed, to be

מָעַל..........742
Kal.
commit *trespass*, to
do *a trespass*, to
transgress, to
trespass, to
trespassing

מַעַל..........743
falsehood
grievously
sore
transgression
trespass
very

מַעַל..........743
above
exceeding
exceedingly
forward
high, on
* high, very
over
up
upon
upward
very

מֶעָל Ch. 743
going down

מֹעַל..........744
lifting up

מַעֲלָה.........744
come, things that
degrees
dial
go up
high degree
stairs
steps
stories

מַעֲלֶה.........744
ascent
before
chiefest
cliff
goeth up, that
going up
hill
Maaleh-*acrabbim*
mounting up
stairs

מַעֲלִיל........744
doings

מַעֲלָל..........744
doings
endeavours
inventions
works

מַעֲמָד.........744
attendance
office
place
state

מָעֳמָד.........744
standing

מַעֲמָסָה........744
burdensome

מַעֲמַקִּים......744
deep
depths

מַעַן............744
because of
end, to the
for
for to
intent that, to the
lest
sake, for...'s
that
to

מַעֲנֶה.........745
* acre †
(כ׳) furrow

מַעֲנֶה.........745
answer
* himself

מַעֲנִית........745
furrows

מַעֲצֵבָה.......745
sorrow

מַעֲצָד.........745
ax
tongs

מַעְצוֹר........745
restraint

מַעְצָר.........745
rule

מַעֲקֶה.........745
battlement

מַעֲקַשִּׁים......745
crooked things

מַעַר...........745
nakedness
proportion

מַעֲרָב.........745
market
merchandise

מַעֲרָב.........745
west
west side
westward

מַעֲרָבָה........745
west

מַעֲרֶה.........745
meadows

מַעֲרוֹת........745
armies

מְעָרָה.........745
cave
den
hole
Mearah

מַעֲרָךְ.........745
preparation

מַעֲרָכָה........746
army
fight
order, be set in
ordered place
rank
row

מַעֲרֶכֶת.......746
row
shew*bread*
shewbread

מַעֲרֻמִּים......746
naked

מַעֲרָצָה.......746
terror

מַעֲשֶׂה.........746
acts
art
* bakemeat †
business
deed
do
doings
*handy*work
labour
made, things
making, wares of
*needle*work
*net*work
occupation
offered, things
operation
possession
purpose
* well
work
working
workmanship
wrought

מַעֲשֵׂר........747
tenth
tenth part
tithes
tithing

מַעֲשַׁקּוֹת......747
oppressions
* oppressors

מִפְגָּע.........747
mark

מַפָּח..........747
bellows

מַפָּח..........747
giving up

מֵפִיץ..........747
maul

מַפָּל..........748
flakes
refuse

מִפְלָאָה.......748
wondrous works

מִפְלַגּוֹת.......748
divisions

מַפָּלָה.........748
ruinous

מַפֵּלָה.........748
ruin

מִפְלָט.........748
escape

מִפְלֶצֶת.......748
idol

מִפְלָשׂ........748
balancings

מַפֶּלֶת.........748
carcase
fall
ruin

מִפְעָל..........748
work

מִפְעָלָה.......748
work

מַפָּץ.......... 748
slaughter

מַפֵּץ..........748
battle ax

מִפְקָד.........748
appointed place
commandment
Miphkad
number

מִפְרָץ.........748
breach

מַפְרֶקֶת.......748
neck

מִפְרָשׂ........748
spreadest forth, that which...
spreading

מִפְשָׂעָה.......748
buttocks

מַפְתֵּחַ........748
key
opening

מִפְתָּח.........748
opening

מִפְתָּן..........748
threshold

מֹץ............748
chaff

מָצָא..........748
Kal.
able,† to be
befall, to

bring, to
catch, to
come on, to
come to, to
come upon, to
find, to
find occasion, to
find out, to
finding
found, to be
get, to
get hold upon, to
hit, to
light on, to
light upon, to
meet, to
meet with, to
*occasion serve
ready
receive, to
speed, to
suffice, to
take hold on, to

Niphal.
certainly
come to, to
come to hand, to
enough, to be
found, to be
*have, to
*have here, to
here, to be
left, to be
*present
present, to be

Hiphil.
come, to cause to
deliver, to
find, to cause to
present, to

מַצָּב 751
garrison
station
stood, place ... where

מֻצָּב 751
mount

מַצָּבָה 751
garrison

מְצָבָה 751
army

מַצֵּבָה 752
garrison
image
pillar
standing image

מַצֶּבֶת 752
pillar
substance

מְצָד & מְצַד ..752
castle
fort
hold
munition
strong hold

מָצָה 752
Kal.
suck, to
wring, to
wring out, to
Niphal.
wrung, to be
wrung out, to be

מַצָּה 752
bread, unleavened
cakes, unleavened
leaven, without
unleavened

מַצָּה 752
contention
debate
strife

מִצְהָלוֹת 752
neighing

מָצוֹד 752
bulwark
net
snare

מָצוּד 752
net

מְצוּדָה 752
hold
munition
net

מְצוֹדָה 753
castle
defence
fort
fortress
hold
hunted, to be
net
snare
strong hold
strong place

מִצְוָה 753
command*ed*
commanded which was
commandment
law
ordinance
precept

מְצוֹלָה 754
bottom
deep

מְצוּלָה 754
deep
depth

מָצוֹק 754
anguish
distress
straitness

מָצוּק 754
pillar
situate

מְצוּקָה 754
anguish
distress

מָצוֹר 754
besieged
besieged place
bulwark
defence
fenced
fortified
fortress
siege
strong
strong hold
tower

מְצוּרָה 754
fenced
fenced
fort
munition
strong hold

מַצּוֹת 754
contended

מֵצַח 754
brow
forehead
impudent †

מִצְחָה 754
greaves

מְצִלָּה 754
bottom

מְצִלּוֹת 754
bells

מְצִלְתַּיִם 754
cymbals

מִצְנֶפֶת 755
diadem
mitre

מַצָּע 755
bed

מִצְעָד 755
going
step

מִצְעִירָה 755
little

מִצְעָר 755
little one
Mizar
small;—s. company
while, little

מִצְפֶּה 755
watch tower

מַצְפֻּנִים 755
hidden things

מָצַץ 755
Kal.
milk out, to

מֵצַר 755
distress
pain
strait

מַצְרֵף 755
fining pot

מַק 755
rottenness
stink

מַקָּבָה 755
hammer

מַקֶּבֶת 755
hammer
hole

מִקְדָּשׁ 755
chapel
hallowed part
holy place
sanctuary

מַקְהֵלוֹת 756
congregations

מַקְהֵלִים 756
congregations

מִקְוֵא 756
linen yarn

מִקְוֶה 756
abiding
gathering together
hope
plenty *of water*
pools

מִקְוָה 756
ditch

מָקוֹם 756
country
*home
*open
place
room
space
whither*soever*

מָקוֹר 758
fountain
issue
spring
well
wellspring

מִקָּח 758
taking

מַקָּחוֹת 758
ware

מְקַטֵּר 758
burn upon, to

מְקַטְּרוֹת 758
altars for incense

מִקְטֶרֶת 758
censer

מַקֵּל 758
*hand*staff
rod
staff

מִקְלָט 759
refuge

מִקְלַעַת 759
carved
carving
figures
graving

מִקְנֶה 759
cattle
flock
herd
possession
purchase
substance

מִקְנָה 759
bought
bought, he that is
possession
price
purchase

מִקְסָם 759
divination

מִקְצוֹעַ 759
corner
turning

מַקְצֻעוֹת 759
planes

מִקְצֹעַת 759
corners

מָקַק 760
Niphal.
consume away, to
corrupt, to be
dissolved, to be
pine away, to
Hiphil.
consume away, to

מִקְרָא 760
assembly
calling
convocation
reading

מִקְרֶה 760
befallen, something
befalleth
chance
event
hap
happeneth

מְקָרֶה 760
building

מְקֵרָה 760
*summer

מִקְשֶׁה 760
beaten
beaten out of one piece
beaten work
upright
whole piece

מִקְשָׁה 760
cucumber

מִקְשֶׁה 760
*hair, well *set*

מַר 760
angry †
bitter
bitterly
bitterness
chafed
discontented
*great
heavy
Mara

מַר 760
drop

מֹר 760
myrrh

מָרָא 760
Kal.
filthy, to be
Hiphil.
lift up self, to

מָרֵא Ch. 760
Lord
lord

מַרְאָה 761
glass, looking
vision

מַרְאֶה 761
apparently
appearance
appeareth
*as soon as
beautiful
beauty
countenance
fair
favoured
form
goodly
look on, to
look to, to
look upon, to
look*eth*
pattern

see to
seem
sight
visage
vision

מְרָאָה 761
crop

מְרַאֲשֹׁת 761
bolster
head
pillows

מַרְאָשֹׁת 761
principalities

מַרְבַדִּים 761
tapestry, coverings of

מַרְבֶּה 761
great
increase

מִרְבָּה 762
much

מַרְבִּית 762
greatest part
greatness
increase
multitude

מַרְבֵּץ 762
lie down, place to

מִרְבַּץ 762
couching place

מַרְבֵּק 762
* fat
* fatted
stall

מַרְגּוֹעַ 762
rest

מַרְגְּלוֹת 762
feet

מַרְגֵּמָה 762
sling

מַרְגֵּעָה 762
refreshing

מָרַד 762
Kal.
rebel
rebel, to
rebellious

מְרַד Ch. 762
rebellion

מֶרֶד 762
rebellion

מָרָד Ch.......762
rebellious

מַרְדּוּת........762
* rebellious

מֻרְדָּף 762
persecuted

מָרָה 762
Kal.
bitter
disobedient, to be
disobey, to
grievously
rebel
rebel, to
rebellious
rebellious, to be

Hiphil.
change, to
provocation
provoke, to
provoking
rebel, to
rebel against, to
rebellious

מָרָה 763
bitterness

מֹרָה 763
grief

מָרוּד..........763
cast out
misery

מְרוֹחַ..........763
broken

מָרוֹם 763
above
above, far
dignity
haughty
height
high
high, most
high, on
high ones
high place
highest places
loftily
upward

מֵרוֹץ..........763
race

מְרוּצָה.........763
course
running
violence

מְרוּקִים 763
purifications

מַרְזֵחַ..........763
mourning

מַרְזֵחַ..........763
banquet

מָרַח 763
Kal.
plaister, to lay for a

מֶרְחָב 763
breadth
large place
large room

מֶרְחָק 763
afar off
far
far country
* far, dwell in
far off
far off, very

מַרְחֶשֶׁת.......764
fryingpan

מָרַט 764
Kal.
furbish, to
peeled
pluck off, to
pluck off hair, to

Niphal.
hair to be fallen off
hair fallen off, to have his

Pual.
bright
furbished
peeled

מְרַט Ch. 764
P'il.
plucked, to be

מְרִי 764
bitter
rebel
rebellion
rebellious
rebellious, most

מְרִיא..........764
fat beast
fat cattle
fatling
fed beast

מְרִיבָה 764
Meribah
provocation
strife

מְרִירוּת........764
bitterness

מְרִירִי..........764
bitter

מֹרֶךְ 764
faintness

מֶרְכָּב 764
chariot
covering
saddle

מֶרְכָּבָה 764
chariot

מַרְכֹּלֶת.......765
merchandise

מִרְמָה 765
craft
deceit
deceitful
deceitfully
false
feigned
guile
subtilly
treachery

מִרְמָס 765
tread down
treading
trodden down
trodden under foot, to be

מֵרֵעַ 765
companion
friend

מִרְעֶה.........765
feeding place
pasture

מַרְעִית 765
flocks
pasture

מַרְפֵּא 765
cure
healing
health
incurable
remedy

מַרְפֵּא 765
sound
wholesome
yielding

מִרְפָּשׂ.........765
fouled, that which ...have

מָרַץ 765
Niphal.
forcible, to be
grievous
sore

Hiphil.
embolden, to

מַרְצֵעַ 765
aul

מַרְצֶפֶת 765
pavement

מָרַק...........766
Kal.
bright
furbish, to

Pual.
scoured, to be

מָרָק 766
broth

מֶרְקָחָה 766
ointment, pot of
* well

מֶרְקָחִים 766
* sweet

מִרְקַחַת........766
apothecaries' art, prepared by the compound
ointment

מָרַר...........766
Kal.
bitter, to be
bitterness, to have
bitterness, to be in
grieved, to be
grieveth, it
vexed, to be

Piel.
bitter, to make
bitterly
grieved, to have sorely

Hiphil.
bitterly, to deal
bitterness, to be in
provoke, to
vex, to

Hithpael.
choler, to be moved with

מְרֵרָה 766
gall

מְרֹרָה 766
bitter
bitter things
gall

מְרֹרִים 766
bitter
bitterness

מִרְשַׁעַת.......766
wicked woman

מְרָתַיִם........766
* Merathaim

מַשָּׂא..........766
burden
carry away
exaction

prophecy
* set, they
song
tribute

מַשֹּׂא 767
respect

מַשָּׂאָה 767
burden

מַשְׂאֵת 767
burden
collection
fire, sign of
flame
flame, great
gifts
lifting up
mess
oblation
reward

מִשְׂגָּב.........767
defence
fort, high
* Misgab
refuge
tower, high

מְשׂוּכָה 767
hedge

מַשּׂוֹר 767
saw

מְשׂוּרָה.........767
measure

מָשׂוֹשׂ 767
joy
mirth
rejoice

מִשְׂחָק 767
scorn

מַשְׂטֵמָה 767
hatred

מַשְׂכִּית 767
conceit
image
imagery
picture
* wish

מַשְׂכֹּרֶת.......767
reward
wages

מַשְׂמְרוֹת......767
nails

מִשְׂפָּח 767
oppression

מִשְׂרָה 767
government

מִשְׂרְפוֹת......767
burnings
Misrephoth-*maim*

מַשְׂרֵת 767
pan

מַשָּׁא..........767
usury

מַשְׁאַבִּים 767
drawing water, places of

מַשָּׁאָה 767
* any*thing*
debt

מַשָּׁאוֹן 767
deceit
מִשְׁאָלָה 768
desire
petition
מִשְׁאֶרֶת 768
kneading trough
store
מִשְׁבְּצוֹת 768
ouches
wrought
מַשְׁבֵּר 768
birth
breaking forth
מִשְׁבָּר 768
billows
waves
מִשְׁבַּתִּים 768
sabbaths
מִשְׁגֶּה 768
oversight
מָשָׁה 768
Kal.
draw, to
Hiphil.
draw out, to
מַשֶּׁה 768
* creditor †
מְשׁוֹאָה 768
desolation
waste
מַשּׁוּאוֹת 768
desolation
destruction
מְשׁוּבָה 768
backsliding
turning away
מְשׁוּגָה 768
error
מָשׁוֹט 768
oar
מִשּׁוֹט 768
oar
מְשׁוּסָּה 768
spoil
מָשַׁח 768
Kal.
anoint, to
anointed, to be
paint, to
Niphal.
anointed, to be
מְשַׁח Ch. 769
oil
מִשְׁחָה 769
anointing
ointment
מָשְׁחָה 769
anointed, to be
anointing
מַשְׁחִית 769
corruption
destroy, to
destroying
destruction
trap
* utterly

מִשְׁחָר 769
morning
מַשְׁחֵת 769
destroying
מִשְׁחַת 769
marred
מָשְׁחָת 769
corruption
מִשְׁטוֹחַ 769
spread forth, to
מִשְׁטָח 769
spread upon, to
spreading
מִשְׁטָר 769
dominion
מֶשִׁי 769
silk
מָשִׁיחַ 769
anointed
Messiah
מָשַׁךְ 770
Kal.
along, to draw
continue, to
draw, to
draw out, to
extend, to
forbear, to
* give, to
handle, to
long, to make
long, to sound
* sow, to
stretch out, to
Niphal.
prolonged, to be
Pual.
deferred
scattered
מֶשֶׁךְ 770
precious
price
מִשְׁכָּב 770
bed
bed*chamber*
couch
lieth with
lying with
מִשְׁכַּב Ch.....770
bed
מִשְׁכָּן 770
dwelleth
dwelling
dwelling place
habitation
tabernacle
tent
מִשְׁכַּן Ch......771
habitation
מָשַׁל 1 771
Kal.
dominion, to have
governor
indeed
power, to have
reign, to
rule, to
rule, to bear
rule, to have
ruler
ruling

Hiphil.
dominion
dominion, to make to have
rule, to cause to
מָשַׁל 2 772
Kal.
proverb, to use
proverb, to use as a
proverbs, to speak in
speak, to
use (*a proverb*), to utter, to
Niphal.
like, to be
like, to become
Piel.
speak, to
Hiphil.
compare, to
Hithpael.
like, to become
מָשָׁל 772
byword
like
parable
proverb
מֹשֶׁל 772
dominion
like
מְשֹׁל 772
byword
מִשְׁלוֹחַ 772
lay, to
sending
מִשְׁלָח 772
put, to
sending forth
set, to
מִשְׁלַחַת 772
discharge
sending
מְשַׁמָּה 772
astonishment
desolate
מִשְׁמָן 772
fat ones
fatness
fattest
fattest places
מַשְׁמַנִּים 773
fat
מִשְׁמָע 773
hearing
מִשְׁמַעַת 773
bidding
guard
obey
מִשְׁמָר 773
diligence
guard
office
prison
ward
watch
מִשְׁמֶרֶת 773
charge
keep

kept, to be
office
ordinance
safeguard
ward
watch
מִשְׁנֶה 773
college
copy
double
fatlings
next
second
second order
twice as much
מְשִׁסָּה 774
booty
spoil
מִשְׁעוֹל 774
path
מִשְׁעִי 774
supple, to
מִשְׁעָן 774
stay
מַשְׁעֵן 774
stay
מַשְׁעֵנָה 774
staff
מִשְׁעֶנֶת 774
staff
מִשְׁפָּחָה 774
family
kind
kindred
מִשְׁפָּט 776
adversary †
cause
ceremonies
charge
* crimes
custom
desert
determination
discretion
disposing
due
fashion
form
judged, to be
judgment
just
justice
justly
law
law, manner of
lawful
manner
measure
order
order, due
ordinance
right
sentence
usest
* worthy
wrong †
מִשְׁפְּתַיִם 778
burdens
sheepfolds
מֶשֶׁק 778
steward †
מַשָּׁק 778
running to and fro

מַשְׁקֶה 778
butlership
drink
drinking
pasture, fat
watered
מִשְׁקוֹל 778
weight
מַשְׁקוֹף 778
doorpost, upper
lintel
מִשְׁקָל 778
weight
weight, full
מִשְׁקֶלֶת 778
plummet
מִשְׁקֹלֶת 779
plummet
מִשְׁקָע 779
deep
מִשְׁרָה 779
liquor
מַשְׁרוֹקִיתָא Ch.779
flute
מָשַׁשׁ 779
Kal.
feel, to
Piel.
grope, to
search, to
Hiphil.
felt, to be
מִשְׁתֶּה 779
banquet
drank
drink
feast
feast*ed*
feasting
מִשְׁתֵּה Ch.....779
banquet
מַתְבֵּן 779
straw
מֶתֶג 779
bit
bridle
Metheg
מָתוֹק 779
sweet
sweeter
sweetness
מָתַח 779
Kal.
spread out, to
מָתַי 779
long
when
מְתִים 779
few
few †
* friends
men;—few m.
persons
small
מַתְכֹּנֶת 780
composition
measure
state
tale

מַתְּלָאָה 780
weariness, what a

מְתַלְּעוֹת 780
cheek teeth
jaw teeth
jaws

מְתֹם 780
men
soundness

מַתָּן 780
gift
giveth gifts

מַתְּנָא Ch. 780
gift

מַתָּנָה 780
gift

מָתְנַיִם 780
* greyhound †
loins
side

מָתַק 780
Kal.
sweet, to be
sweet, to be made
sweetly, to feed
Hiphil.
sweet, to be
* sweet, to take

מֶתֶק 780
sweetness

מֹתֶק 780
sweetness

מַתַּת 780
gift
give, to
reward

נָא 781
raw

נָא 781
beseech thee, I
go to
now
oh
pray, I
pray thee, I
pray you, I

נֹאד 781
bottle

נָאָה 781
Pilel.
beautiful, to be
become, to
comely, to be

נָאָה 781
habitation
house
pasture
pleasant place

נָאוֶה 781
becometh
comely
seemly

נָאַם 781
Kal.
say, to
speak, to

נָאַף 782
Kal.
adulterer
adulteress
adultery, to commit
adultery, committing
wedlock, women that break
Piel.
adulterer
adulteress
adulterous
adultery, to commit

נַאֲפוּפִים 782
adulteries

נִאֻפִים 782
adulteries

נָאַץ 782
Kal.
abhor, to
contemn, to
despise, to
Piel.
abhor, to
blaspheme, to give occasion to
contemn, to
despise, to
great [ger
provoke;—p. to an-
Hiphil.
flourish, to
Hithpolel.
blasphemed, (is)

נֶאָצָה 782
blasphemy

נֶאָצוֹת 782
blasphemies
provocations

נָאַק 782
Kal.
groan, to

נְאָקָה 782
groaning

נָאַר 782
Piel.
abhor, to
void, to make

נָבָא 782
Niphal.
prophesy, to
prophesying
Hithpael.
prophesy, to
prophesying
prophet, to make self a

נְבָא Ch. 783
Ithpael.
prophesy, to

נָבַב 783
Kal.
hollow
vain

נְבוּאָה 783
prophecy

נְבוּאָה Ch.....783
prophesying

נְבִזְבָּה Ch.....783
rewards

נָבַח 783
Kal.
bark, to

נָבַט 783
Piel.
look, to
Hiphil.
behold, to
behold, to cause to
consider, to
look, to
look down, to
regard, to
respect, to have
see, to

נָבִיא 784
prophecy
prophesy, that
prophet

נְבִיא Ch. 786
prophet

נְבִיאָה 786
prophetess

נֵבֶךְ 786
spring

נָבֵל 786
Kal.
fade, to
fade away, to
fading
fall down, to
fall off, to
falling
foolishly, to do
nought, to come to
surely
wear away, to
wither, to
Piel.
disgrace, to
dishonour, to
lightly esteem, to
vile, to make

נָבָל 786
fool
foolish
foolish man
foolish woman
vile person

נֵבֶל & נֶבֶל 786
bottle
pitcher
vessel

נֵבֶל & נֶבֶל 786
* flagon
psaltery
viol

נְבָלָה 787
folly
vile
villany

נְבֵלָה 787
body
body, dead
carcase
carcase, dead
dead of itself
died, which
dieth of itself, beast that
dieth of itself, which

נַבְלוּת 787
lewdness

נָבַע 787
Kal.
flowing
Hiphil.
belch out, to
pour out, to
send forth, to
utter, to
utter, to abundantly

נֶבְרְשְׁתָּה Ch...787
candlestick

נֶגֶב 787
south
south country
south side
southward

נָגַד 788
Hiphil.
bewray, to
certainly
certify, to
declare, to
declaring
denounce, to
expound, to
messenger
plainly
profess, to
rehearse, to
report, to
shew, to
shew forth, to
speak, to
surely
tell, to
utter, to
Hophal.
certainly
declared, to be
fully
shewed, to be
told, to be

נְגַד Ch.........790
Pael.
issue, to

נֶגֶד 790
about
against
against, over
* aloof
before
* far
* far off
* from
* in
over
presence
* side, other
sight
* view, to

נֶגֶד Ch. 790
toward

נָגַהּ 791
Kal.
shine, to
Hiphil.
enlighten, to
lighten, to
shine, to cause to

נֹגַהּ 791
bright
brightness
light
shining
shining, clear

נְגַהּ Ch. 791
morning

נְגֹהוֹת 791
brightness

נָגַח 791
Kal.
gore, to
push, to
Piel.
push, to
push down, to
pushing
Hithpael.
push, to

נַגָּח 791
push, used to
push, wont to

נָגִיד 791
captain
chief
excellent thing
governor
governor, chief
leader
noble
prince
ruler
ruler, chief

נְגִינָה 791
instrument, stringed
musick
Neginoth
song

נָגַן 791
Kal.
instruments, players on
Piel.
instrument, to sing to the stringed
melody
minstrel
play, to
player
playing

נָגַע 792
Kal.
come, to
get up, to
near
plagued
reach, to
smite, to
stricken
touch, to
Niphal.
beaten, to be
Piel.
plague, to
smite, to
Pual.
plagued, to be
Hiphil.
bring, to
* bring, to be able to
bring down, to
cast, to

come, to
come nigh, to
draw near, to
draw nigh, to
happen, to
join, to
reach, to
reach up, to
strike, to
touch, to

נֶגַע............793
plague
sore
stricken
stripe
stroke
wound

נָגַף............793
Kal.
dash, to
hurt, to
plague, to
smite, to
strike, to
stumble, to
Niphal.
beaten, to be
slain, to be
smitten, to be
smitten down, to be
surely
worse, to be put to the
Hithpael.
stumble, to

נֶגֶף............793
plague
stumbling

נָגַר............793
Niphal.
flow away, to
run, to
spilt
trickle down, to
Hiphil.
fall, to
pour down, to
pour out, to
shed, to
Hophal.
poured down

נָגַשׂ............794
Kal.
driver
exact, to
exactor
oppressor
* raiser of taxes†
taskmaster
Niphal.
distressed, to be
oppressed, to be

נָגַשׁ............794
Kal.
approach, to
come, to
come hither, to
come near, to
come nigh, to
give place, to
go hard, to
go up, to
near, to be
near, to draw
near, to go
nigh, to draw
stand, to
Niphal.
approach, to
approach nigh, to
come, to
near, to come
near, to draw
nigh, to come
nigh, to go
overtake, to
Hiphil.
approach, to make to
bring, to
bring forth, to
hither, to bring
near, to bring
near, to cause to come
offer, to
overtake, to
present, to
Hophal.
offered
put, to be
Hithpael.
near, to draw

נֵד............795
heap

נָדָא............795
Hiphil.
drive, to

נָדַב............795
Kal.
give willingly, to
willing, to make
Hithpael.
offer freely, to
offer selves willingly, to
offer willingly, to
willing, to be

נְדַב Ch. 795
Ithpael.
freewill, to be minded of own
freewill offering
offer freely, to
offering willingly

נְדָבָה 795
free offering
freely
freewill offering
plentiful
voluntarily
voluntary
voluntary offering
willing
willing offering
willingly

נִדְבָּךְ Ch. 795
rows

נָדַד 795
Kal.
* could not depart, to
flee, to
* flee apace, to
move, to
removed, to be
wander, to
wander abroad, to
wanderer
wandering
Poal.
flee away, to
Hiphil.
chased, to be
Hophal.
chased away, to be
thrust away, to be
Hithpolel.
flee away, to

נְדַד Ch. 796
P'al.
go from, to

נְדֻדִים.........796
tossings to and fro

נָדָה 796
Piel.
cast out, to
put far away, to

נֵדֶה 796
gifts

נִדָּה 796
* far
filthiness
* flowers
menstruous
menstruous woman
put apart
* removed
removed woman
separation
set apart
unclean thing
unclean with filthiness
uncleanness

נָדַח 796
Kal.
expelled, to be
forcing
Niphal.
banished
cast out
drawn away, to be
driven, to be
driven out, to be
driven quite, to be
fetch a stroke, to
go astray, to
outcast
Pual.
driven
Hiphil.
bring, to
cast down, to
cast out, to
compel, to
drive, to
drive away, to
force, to
thrust away, to
thrust out, to
withdraw, to
Hophal.
chased

נָדִיב 796
Amminadib
free
liberal
liberal things
noble
prince
willing
willing *hearted*

נְדִיבָה 797
soul

נָדָן 797
gift

נָדָן 797
sheath

נִדְנֶה Ch.......797
* body

נָדַף............797
Kal.
drive away, to
thrust down, to
Niphal.
driven
driven away, to be
driven to and fro
shaken
tossed to and fro

נָדַר 797
Kal.
make *a vow*, to
vow, to

נֶדֶר & נֵדֶר 797
vow
vowed

נֹהַּ............797
wailing

נָהַג [1] 797
Kal.
acquainting
bring away, to
brought
carry away, to
drive, to
drive away, to
lead, to
lead away, to
lead forth, to
Piel.
bring, to
carry away, to
drive, to
guide, to
guide, to be
lead, to

נָהַג [2]..........798
Piel.
lead, to

נָהָה 798
Kal.
lament, to
wail, to
Niphal.
lament, to

נְהוֹר Ch. 798
light

נְהִי............798
lamentation
wailing

נִהְיָה 798
* doleful

נְהִיר Ch. 798
light

נַהִירוּ Ch. 798
light

נָהַל............798
Piel.
carry, to
feed, to
guide, to
lead, to
lead gently, to
Hithpael.
lead on, to

נַהֲלֹלִים........798
bushes

נָהַם 798
Kal.
mourn, to
roar, to
roaring

נַהַם 798
roaring

נְהָמָה 798
disquietness
roaring

נָהַק 798
Kal.
bray, to

נָהַר 798
Kal.
flow, to
flow together, to
lightened, to be

נָהָר 798
Aram-naharaim
flood
Mesopotamia †
river ;—stream

נְהַר Ch. 799
river
stream

נְהָרָה..........799
light

נוֹא............799
Kal.
discourage, to
Hiphil.
break, to
disallow, to
discourage, to
effect, to make of none

נוּב............799
Kal.
bring forth, to
fruit, to bring forth
increase, to
Pilel.
chearful, to make

נוֹב............799
fruit

נוּד............799
Kal.
bemoan, to
flee, to
get, to
mourn, to
pity, to take
remove, to
shaken, to be
sorry, to be
vagabond
wandering
Hiphil.
move, to make
remove, to
wag, to
Hithpolel.
bemoan self, to
removed, to be
skip for joy, to

נוּד Ch. 800
P'al.
get away, to

נוֹד............800
* Nod
wandering

נָוָה............800
Kal.
home, to keep at
Hiphil.
habitation, to prepare an

נָוֶה............800
dwelling
dwelling place
fold
habitation
pleasant place
sheepcote
stable

נָוָה............800
comely
habitation
tarried

נוּחַ............800
Kal.
cease, to
confederate, to be
quiet, to be
remain, to
rest, to
rest, to be at
rest, to give
rest, to have
Hiphil.
lay, to
let down, to
quiet, to
rest, to cause to
rest, to give
rest, to make to
set down, to
Hophal.
rest, to have

נוֹחַ............801
rest
rested
resting place

נוּט............801
Kal.
moved, to be

נְוָלוּ Ch. 801
dunghill

נְוָלִי Ch. 801
dunghill

נוּם 801
Kal.
sleep, to
slumber, to

נוּמָה..........801
drowsiness

נוּן 801
Niphal.
continued, to be
Hiphil.
continued, to be

נוּס............801
Kal.
* abate, to
away;—ran a.
flee, to
flee away, to
fleeing
Polel.
lift up a standard, to
Hiphil.
flee, to
flee, to make
flight, to put to
* hide, to
Hithpolel.
displayed, to be

נוּעַ 802
Kal.
continually
fugitive
gone away, to be
* (כ׳) make *go* up and down, to
move, to
moveable, to be
moved, to be
promoted, to be
reel, to
remove, to
stagger, to
to and fro
vagabond, to be
wander, to
wander up and down, to
Niphal.
shaken, to be
sifted, to be
Hiphil.
make *go* up and down, to
move, to
scatter, to
set, to
shake, to
sift, to
wag, to
wander, to make
wander up and down, to

נוּף 802
Kal.
perfume, to
Polel.
shake, to
Hiphil.
lift up, to
move, to
offer, to
send, to
shake, to
sift, to
strike, to
wave, to
waved, to be
Hophal.
waved, to be

נוֹף............803
situation

נוּץ 803
Kal.
flee away, to
Hiphil.
bud, to
bud forth, to

נוֹצָה..........803
feather
ostrich

נוּק 803
Hiphil.
nurse, to

נוּר Ch. 803
fiery
fire

נוּשׁ............803
Kal.
heaviness, to be full of

נָזָה............803
Kal.
sprinkled, to be
Hiphil.
sprinkle, to

נָזִיד 803
pottage

נָזִיר 803
Nazarite
separate
separated
vine undressed

נָזַל 803
Kal.
distil, to
drop, to
flood
flow, to
flow out, to
flowing
gush out, to
melt, to
pour, to
pour down, to
running water
stream
Hiphil.
flow, to cause to

נֶזֶם............804
earring
jewel

נְזַק Ch. 804
P'al.
damage, to have
Aphel.
endamage, to
hurt
hurtful

נֵזֶק............804
damage

נָזַר 804
Niphal.
separate selves, to
separating self
Hiphil.
consecrate, to
separate, to

נֵזֶר 804
consecration
crown
hair
separation

נָחָה 804
Kal.
guide, to
lead, to
lead forth, to
Hiphil.
bestow, to
bring, to
govern, to
guide, to
lead, to
put, to
straiten, to

נִחוּמִים........804
comfortable
comforts
repentings

נָחוּשׁ..........805
brass

נְחוּשָׁה 805
brass
steel

נְחִילָה 805
Nehiloth

נְחִירִים........805
nostrils

נָחַל............805
Kal.
divide, to
have, to
have *inheritance*, to
heritage, to take as an
inherit, to
inheritance, to divide by
inheritance, to divide for
inheritance, to have
inheritance, to take
inheritance, to take for
possess, to
possession, to have in
Piel.
* defiled, to be
inheritance, to distribute for
inheritance, to divide
inheritance, to divide for
inheritance, to take
Hiphil.
inherit, to cause to
inherit, to give to
inherit, to make to
inheritance, to divide
inheritance, to divide for an
inheritance, to give for
inheritance, to leave for
possess, to cause to
Hophal.
possess, to be made to
Hithpael.
inherit, to
inheritance, to divide for an
inheritance, to take as an
possess, to

נַחַל............805
brook
flood
river
stream
valley

נַחְלָה 806
stream

נַחֲלָה 806
heritage
inherit, to
inheritance
possession
river

נֶחֱלָמִי 807
Nehelemite

נַחֲלַת 807
heritage

נָחַם 808
Niphal.
comfort, to receive
comforted, to be
ease (*one's self*), to
repent, to
repenting
Piel.
comfort
comfort, to
comforters
Pual.
comforted, to be
Hithpael.
comfort self, to
comforted, to be
repent, to
repent self, to

נֹחַם 808
repentance

נֶחָמָה..........808
comfort

נַחְנוּ 808
we

נָחַץ 808
Kal.
haste, to require

נַחַר 808
nostrils

נַחֲרָה..........809
snorting

נָחַשׁ...........809
Piel.
certainly
divine, to
enchanter
* enchantment
enchantment, to use
experience, to learn by
indeed
observe diligently, to

נַחַשׁ 809
enchantment

נָחָשׁ 809
serpent

נְחָשׁ Ch. 809
brass

נְחֹשֶׁת 809
brasen
brass
chains
copper
fetter
fetter of brass
filthiness
steel

נְחֻשְׁתָּן 810
Nehushtan

נָחַת 810
Kal.
come down, to
enter, to
go down, to
press sore, to
Niphal.
stick fast, to
Piel.
broken, to be
settle, to
Hiphil.
come down, to cause to

נְחַת Ch. 810
P'al.
come down, to
Aphel.
carry, to
lay up, to
place, to
Hophal.
deposed, to be

נַחַת 810
lighting down
quiet
quietness
rest, to
set on, be

נָחֵת 810
come down

נָטָה 810
Kal.
afternoon †
bow, to
bowing
bowing down
decline, to
extend, to
go down, to
gone, to be
incline, to
intend, to
offer, to
outstretched
pitch, to
prolong, to
shew, to
spread, to
spread out, to
stretch, to
stretch forth, to
stretch out, to
stretched out
turn, to
turn aside, to
turned, to be
Niphal.
spread forth, to be
stretched forth, to be
stretched out, to be
Hiphil.
apply, to
bow, to
bow down, to
carry aside, to
decline, to
deliver, to
extend, to
incline, to
lay, to
let down, to
overthrow, to
pervert, to
perverteth
put away, to
spread, to
stretch forth, to
stretch out, to
take aside, to
turn, to
turn aside, to
turn away, to
wrest, to
yield, to cause to

נָטִיל 812
bear, that

נְטִיפוֹת........812
chains
collars

נְטִישׁוֹת........812
battlements
branches
plants

נָטַל 812
Kal.
bear, to
offer, to
take up, to
Piel.
bear, to

נְטַל Ch. 812
P'al.
lift up, to
P'il.
lifted up, to be

נֵטֶל 812
weighty

נָטַע 812
Kal.
fastened
plant, to
planter
Niphal.
planted, to be

נֶטַע 812
plant

נְטִעִים 812
plants

נָטַף 812
Kal.
drop, to
dropping
Hiphil.
drop, to
prophesy, to
prophet

נָטָף 813
drops
stacte

נָטַר 813
Kal.
grudge, to bear
keep, to
keeper
reserve, to

נְטַר Ch. 813
P'al.
keep, to

נָטַשׁ 813
Kal.
cast off, to
drawn
fall, to let
forsake, to
join *battle*, to
leave, to
leave off, to
lie still, to
spread abroad
suffer, to
Niphal.
forsaken, to be
loosed, to be
spread selves, to
stretched out, to be
Pual.
forsaken, to be

נִי 813
wailing

נִיב 813
fruit

נִיד 813
moving

נִידָה 813
removed

נִיחוֹחַ 813
odour, sweet
sweet

נִיחוֹחַ Ch. 814
odour, sweet
savour, sweet

נִין 814
son

נִים 814
fleeth, that

נִיסָן 814
Nisan

נִיצוֹץ..........814
spark

נִיר 814
lamp

נִיר 814
Kal.
break up, to

נִיר 814
fallow ground
tillage

נִיר 814
lamp
light

נָכֵא 814
broken
wounded

נָכָא 814
stricken

נְכֹאת..........814
spicery
spices

נֶכֶד 814
nephew
son's son

נָכָה 814
Niphal.
smitten, to be
Pual.
smitten, to be
Hiphil.
beat, to
beaten, to be
cast forth, to
clap, to
give *wounds*, to
given, (*wounds*) to be
* go forward, to
indeed
kill, to
make *slaughter*, to
murderer
punish, to
slaughter
slay, to
slayer
slaying
smite, to
smiter
smiting
strike, to
stripes
stripes, to give
surely
wound, to
Hophal.
beaten, to be
slain
slain, to be
smitten, to be
stricken, to be
wounded, to be

נָכֶה 817
contrite
lame

נֵכֶה 817
abject

נָכוֹחַ 817
equity
plain
right
right thing
uprightness

נֹכַח 817
against
against, over
before
direct*ly*
for
right
right on

נֹכַח 818
before
over against

נָכַל 818
Kal.
deceiver
Piel.
beguile, to
Hithpael.
conspire, to
subtilly, to deal

נֵכֶל 818
wile

נְכָסִים.........818
riches
wealth

נִכְסִין Ch. 818
goods

נָכַר 818
Niphal.
dissemble, to
known, to be
Piel.
deliver, to
estrange, to
know, to
regard, to
strangely, to behave selves
Hiphil.
acknowledge, to
* could
discern, to
know, to
knowledge, to take
notice, to take
perceive, to
respect, to
respect, to have
Hithpael.
feign self to be another, to
known, to be
strange, to make self

נֵכָר 818
alien
strange
stranger †

נֵכָר 819
strange

נֹכֶר 819
stranger, to become a

נָכְרִי 819
alien
foreigner
outlandish
strange
strange woman
stranger

נְכֹת...........819
precious things

נָלָה............819
Hiphil.
end, to make an

נְמִבְזָה 819
vile

נָמַל 819
Kal.
branch to be cut off
circumcise, to
cut down, to be
cut off, to be

נְמָלָה 819
ant

נָמֵר 819
leopard

נְמַר Ch. 819
leopard

נֵס 819
banner
ensign
Jehovah-nissi
pole
sail
sign
standard

נְסִבָּה 819
cause

נָסַג 819
Kal.
departing away
take, to
Hiphil.
hold, to take
remove, to

Hophal.
turned away, to be

נָסָה 820
Piel.
adventure, to
assay, to
prove, to
tempt, to
try, to

נָסַח 820
Kal.
destroy, to
pluck, to
rooted, to be
Niphal.
plucked, to be

נְסַח Ch. 820
Ithp'al.
pulled down, to be

נָסִיךְ 820
drink offering
duke
prince
principal

נָסַךְ1 820
Kal.
cover, to
melt, to
offer, to
pour, to
pour out, to
set, to
Niphal.
set up, to be
Piel.
pour out, to
Hiphil.
offer, to
pour, to
pour out, to
poured, to cause to be
Hophal.
cover, to

נָסַךְ2 820
Kal.
spread, that is

נְסַךְ Ch. 820
Pael.
offer, to

נֶסֶךְ & נֵסֶךְ 820
cover
drink offering
molten image

נְסַךְ Ch. 821
drink offering

נָסַס1 821
Kal.
standard bearer

נָסַס2 821
Hithpolel.
ensign, to lift up as an

נָסַע 821
Kal.
depart, to
forward, to go
forward, to set
get, to
go, to
go away, to
go forth, to
go onward, to
go out, to
journey, to
journey, to take
journeying, to be
march, to
remove, to
*still
way, to be on his
way, to go their
Niphal.
departed, to be
go away, to
Hiphil.
blow, to cause to
bring, to
go forth, to make
remove, to
set aside, to

נָסַק 822
Kal.
ascend up, to

נְסַק Ch. 822
Aphel.
take up, to
Hophal.
taken up, to be

נְעוּרוֹת 822
youth

נְעוּרִים 822
childhood
youth

נָעִים 822
pleasant
pleasures
sweet

נָעַל 822
Kal.
bolt, to
inclosed
lock, to
shoe, to
shut up
Hiphil.
shoe, to

נַעַל 822
dryshod
shoe
shoe*latchet*
shoes, pair of

נָעֵם 823
Kal.
beauty, to pass in
delight, to be
pleasant, to be
sweet, to be

נֹעַם 823
beauty
pleasant
pleasantness

נַעֲמָנִים 823
pleasant

נַעֲצוּץ 823
thorn

נָעַר 823
Kal.
shake, to
shake off, to
shaken out
yell, to
Niphal.
shake self, to
shaken, to be
tossed up and down, to be
Piel.
overthrow, to
shake, to
Hithpael.
shake self, to

נַעַר 823
babe
boy
child
lad
servant
young
young man

נֹעַר 824
child
youth

נַעֲרָה 824
damsel
maid
maiden
young
young woman

נְעֹרֶת 825
tow

נָפָה 825
border
coast
region
sieve

נָפַח 825
Kal.
blow, to
breathe, to
give up, to
seething
Pual.
blown
Hiphil.
lose *life*, to cause to
snuff, to

נְפִילִים 825
giants

נֹפֶךְ 825
emerald

נָפַל 825
Kal.
accepted, to be
cast down, to be
die, to
fail, to
fall, to
fall away, to
fall down, to
fall, ready to
fallen, to be
falling
fugitive
have *inheritance*, to
inferior
keep *bed*, to
lay
lay along, to
lie down, to
light, to
light down, to
lost, to be
*lost, hast
lying
overthrown, to be
perish, to
* present, to
rot, to
surely
Hiphil.
cast, to be
cast down, to
cast *lots*, to
cast out, to
cease, to
divide, to
divide by lot, to
fail, to let
fall, to cause to
fall, to let
fall, to make
fell, to
felling
lie down, to cause to
overthrow, to
overwhelm, to
present, to
presented
presenting
rot, to make to
slay, to
smite out, to
throw down, to
Hithpael.
cast self down, to
fall, to
fall down, to
Pilel.
*judged, to be

נְפַל Ch. 828
P'al.
fall, to
fall down, to
occasion, to have

נֵפֶל & נֶפֶל ...828
birth, untimely

נָפַץ 828
Kal.
break, to
broken
dispersed
overspread, to be
scattered, to be
Piel.
break, to
dash, to
dash in pieces, to
discharged, to cause to be
pieces, to break in
scatter, to
Pual.
beaten in sunder, to be

נֶפֶץ 828
scattering

נְפַק Ch. 828
P'al.
come forth, to
go forth, to
Aphel.
take forth, to
take out, to
taken out, to be

נִפְקָא Ch. 829
expences

נָפַשׁ 829
Niphal.
refresh selves, to
refreshed, to be

נֶפֶשׁ 829
any
appetite
beast
body
breath
creature
dead
deadly
desire
*dis*contented
*fish
ghost
greedy †
hath *life*
he
heart
hearty
her
herself
himself
*jeopardy, life in
*jeopardy of life
life
lust
man
man †
me
mind
mortally
myself
one
own
person
person †
pleasure
self
slay †
soul
tablet †
themselves
they
thing
thyself
will
*will, she
*would have it
yourselves

נֶפֶת 833
country

נֹפֶת 833
honeycomb
honeycomb †

נַפְתּוּלִים 833
wrestlings

נֵץ 833
blossom
hawk

נָצָא 833
Kal.
flee, to

נָצַב 833
Niphal.
appointed
deputy
officer
present, to
set over, to be
settled, to be
stand, to
stand still, to
stand up, to
stand upright, to
standing
state, best
Hiphil.
erect, to
establish, to
lay, to
rear up, to

set, to
set up, to
sharpen, to
stablish, to
stand, to make to
Hophal.
* Huzzab
pillar
set up

נְצָב 834
haft

נִצְבָּה Ch. 834
strength

נָצָה[1] 834
Niphal.
strive, to
strive together, to
Hiphil.
strive, to

נָצָה[2] 834
Kal.
laid waste, to be
Niphal.
ruinous

נִצָּה 834
flower

נֹצָה 834
feather

נָצַח 834
Niphal.
perpetual
Piel.
excel, to
musician, chief
oversee, to
overseer
set forward, to
singer, chief

נְצַח Ch. 835
Ithpael.
preferred

נֶצַח & נֵצַח ..835
alway
always
constantly
end
ever
evermore
never †
perpetual
strength
victory

נֵצַח 835
blood
strength

נְצִיב 835
garrison
officer
pillar

נָצִיר 835
preserved

נָצַל 835
Niphal.
deliver self, to
delivered, to be
escaped, to be
preserved, to be
taken out, to be
Piel.
deliver, to
spoil, to
strip off, to
Hiphil.
at all
defend, to
deliver, to
* escape, to
fail, without
part, to
recover, to
rescue, to
rid, to
save, to
surely
take, to
Hophal.
plucked
strip selves, to

נְצַל Ch. 837
Aphel.
deliver, to
rescue, to

נִצָּן 837
flower

נָצַץ 837
Kal.
sparkle, to

נָצַר 837
Kal.
besieged
hidden thing
keep, to
keeper
keeping
monument
observe, to
preserve, to
preserver
subtil
watcher
watchman

נֵצֶר 837
branch

נְקֵא Ch. 837
pure

נָקַב 837
Kal.
appoint, to
blaspheme, to
bore, to
curse, to
holes, with
name, to
pierce, to
strike through, to
Niphal.
expressed, to be

נֶקֶב 837
pipe

נְקֵבָה 838
female
maid child
woman

נָקֹד 838
speckled

נֹקֵד 838
herdman
sheepmaster

נְקֻדּוֹת 838
studs

נִקֻּדִים 838
cracknels
mouldy

נָקָה 838
Kal.
altogether
Niphal.
blameless, to be
clear, to be
cut off, to be
desolate, to be
free, to be
guiltless, to be
innocent, to be
quit, to be
unpunished, to be
utterly
Piel.
acquit, to
altogether
at all
cleanse, to
clear, to
clearing
guiltless, to hold
innocent, to hold
means, by no
unpunished, to leave
wholly

נָקֹט 838
Kal.
weary

נָקִי 838
blameless
clean
clear
exempted
free
guiltless
innocent
quit

נָקִיא 839
innocent

נִקָּיוֹן 839
cleanness
innocency

נְקִיק 839
hole

נָקַם 839
Kal.
avenge, to
avenge selves, to
revenge, to
surely
take *vengeance*, to
vengeance, to take
Niphal.
avenged, to be
punished, to be
revenge, to
revenge self, to
take *vengeance*, to
vengeance, to take
Piel.
avenge, to
take *vengeance*, to
Hophal.
avenged, to be
punished, to be
vengeance, to be taken
Hithpael.
avenged, to be
avenger

נָקָם 839
avenged †
quarrel
vengeance

נְקָמָה 839
avenge †
revenge
revenging
vengeance

נָקַע 839
Kal.
alienated, to be

נָקַף 839
Kal.
kill, to
Piel.
cut down, to
destroy, to
Hiphil.
compass, to
compass about, to
compassing
go round, to
go round about, to
going about
gone about, to be
inclose, to
round, to

נֹקֶף 840
shaking

נִקְפָּה 840
rent

נָקַר 840
Kal.
pick out, to
thrust out, to
Piel.
pierced, to be
put out, to
Pual.
digged, to be

נְקָרָה 840
cleft
clift

נָקַשׁ 840
Kal.
snared, to be
Niphal.
snared, to be
Piel.
catch, to
snares, to lay
Hithpael.
snare, to lay a

נְקַשׁ Ch. 840
P'al.
smite, to

נֵר 840
candle
lamp
light

נִיר 840
plowing

נִרְגָּן 840
talebearer
whisperer

נֵרְדְּ 840
spikenard

נָשָׂא 840
Kal.
accept, to
arise, to
*armour*bearer
bear, to be able to
bear up, to
bearing
borne, to be
bring, to
bring forth, to
bringing
burn, to
burned, to be
carried
carry, to
carry away, to
carrying
cast, to
contain, to
ease, to
exact, to
exalt, to
fetch, to
forgive, to
forgiven
forgiving
go on, to
hold up, to
honourable †
honourable man †
lade, to
laid, to be
lay, to
lift up;—pluck up, [to
marry, to
needs
obtain, to
offer, to
pardon, to
raise, to
raise up, to
receive, to
regard, to
respect, to
set, to
set up, to
spare, to
stir up, to
suffer, to
swear,† to
take, to
take away, to
take up, to
utterly
wear, to
wearing
yield, to
Niphal.
borne, to be
carried, to be
exalted, to be
extolled, to be high
lift up self, to
lifted up, to be
lofty
magnified, to be
take away, to
Piel.
advance, to
carry, to
desire,† to
exalt, to
furnish, to
further, to
give, to
help, to
lift up, to
take away, to
Hiphil.
bear, to suffer to
bring, to

Hithpael.
exalt self, to
exalted, to be
lift self up, to
lift up self, to

נְשָׂא Ch. 845
P'al.
carry away, to
take, to
Ithpael.
insurrection, to make

נְשֵׂאת 845
gift

נָשַׂג 845
Hiphil.
ability [bring able, to be;—a. to
attain, to
attain unto, to
get, to
get, to be able to
get, can
hold, to take
hold of, to take
hold on, to take
hold upon, to take
lay at, to
overtake, to
put, to
reach, to
remove, to
rich, to wax
surely
take, to

נְשׂוּאָה 845
carriage

נָשִׂיא..........845
captain
chief
cloud
governor
prince
ruler
vapour

נָשַׂק 846
Niphal.
kindled, to be
Hiphil.
burn, to
kindle, to

נָשָׁא 1 846
Kal.
utterly
Niphal.
deceived, to be
Hiphil.
beguile, to
deceive, to
greatly
seize, to

נָשָׁא 2 846
Kal.
* debt
exact, to
usury, giver of
Hiphil.
exact, to

נָשַׁב 846
Kal.
blow, to
Hiphil.
blow, to cause to
drive away, to

נָשָׁה 1 847
Kal.
forget, to
Niphal.
forgotten, to be
Piel.
forget, to make
Hiphil.
deprive, to
exact, to

נָשָׁה 2 847
Kal.
creditor
exact, to
extortioner
lend, to
usurer
usury, to lend on
usury, taker of
Hiphil.
lend, to

נָשֶׁה 847
shrank, which

נְשִׁי 847
debt

נְשִׁיָּה..........847
forgetfulness

נָשִׁים..........847
* married
* marry
wives
* woman
women

נְשִׁין Ch. 848
women

נְשִׁיקָה 848
kiss

נָשַׁךְ 848
Kal.
bite, to
bitten, is
usury, to be lent upon
Piel.
bite, to
Hiphil.
usury, to lend upon

נֶשֶׁךְ 848
usury

נִשְׁכָּה.........848
chamber

נָשַׁל..........848
Kal.
cast, to
cast out, to
loose, to
put off, to
put out, to
slip, to
Piel.
drive, to

נָשַׁם 849
Kal.
destroy, to

נְשָׁמָה 849
blast
breath
breatheth, that
inspiration
soul
spirit

נִשְׁמָא Ch. 849
breath

נָשַׁף 849
Kal.
blow, to

נֶשֶׁף 849
dark
dawning of the day
dawning of the morning
night
twilight

נָשַׁק 849
Kal.
armed
armed men
kiss, to
ruled, to be
Piel.
kiss, to
Hiphil.
touched

נֶשֶׁק & נֵשֶׁק....849
armed men
armour
armoury
battle
harness
weapon

נֶשֶׁר 849
eagle

נְשַׁר Ch. 850
eagle

נָשַׁת 850
Kal.
fail, to
Niphal.
fail, to

נִשְׁתְּוָן.........850
letter

נִשְׁתְּוָן Ch. 850
letter

נְתוּנִים (כ׳) ..850
Nethinims

נָתַח 850
Piel.
cut, to
cut in pieces, to
divide, to
hew in pieces, to

נֵתַח 850
parts
pieces

נָתִיב..........850
path
way

נְתִיבָה 850
path*way*
* travel*lers*

נְתִינִים........850
Nethinims

נְתִינִין Ch. 850
Nethinims

נָתַךְ..........850
Kal.
poured, to be
poured forth, to be
poured out, to be
Niphal.
drop, to
melted, to be
molten, to be
poured, to be
poured forth, to be
poured out, to be
Hiphil.
gather, to
gather together, to
melt, to
pour out, to
Hophal.
melted, to be

נָתַן...........851
Kal.
add, to
apply, to
appoint, to
ascribe, to
assign, to
* avenge,† to
* be, to
bestow, to
bring, to
bring forth, to
bring hither, to
cast, to
cause, to
charge, to
come, to
commit, to
consider, to
count, to
cry,† to
deliver, to
deliver up, to
direct, to
distribute, to
doubtless
fail, without
fasten, to
frame, to
give, to
give forth, to
give over, to
give up, to
* given, to be
giving
grant, to
hang, to
hang up, to
* have, to
*heal*ed, to be
indeed
lay, to
lay unto charge, to
lay up, to
leave, to
leave, to give
lend, to
let, to
let out, to
lie,† to
lift up, to
make, to
O that †
occupy, to
offer, to
ordain, to
pay, to
perform, to
place, to
pour, to
print, to
* pull, to
put, to
* put, to be
put forth, to
putting
recompense, to
recompensing
render, to
requite, to
restore, to
send, to
send out, to
set, to
set forth, to
setting
shew, to
shoot forth, to
shoot up, to
sing,† to
slander,† to
strike, to
*sub*mit, to
suffer, to
surely
thrust, to
trade, to
turn, to
utter, to
weep,† to
willingly
withdraw,† to
would God †
would to God †
yield, to
Niphal.
cast, to be
caused, to be
committed, to be
delivered, to be
done, to be
given, to be
given up, to be
granted, to be
laid, to be
made, to be
put, to be
set, to be
surely
uttered, to be
Hophal.
delivered, to be
given, to be
gotten, to be
put, to be
taken up, to be

נְתַן Ch. 863
P'al.
bestow, to
give, to
pay, to

נָתַס..........863
Kal.
mar, to

נָתַע..........863
Niphal.
broken, to be

נָתַץ..........863
Kal.
beat down, to
break down, to
break out, to
cast down, to
destroy, to
pull down, to
throw down, to
thrown down, to be
Niphal.
broken down, to be
thrown down, to be

Piel.
break down, to
overthrow, to
throw down, to
Pual.
cast down, to be
Hophal.
broken down, to be

נָתַק 863
Kal.
broken
draw, to
pluck, to
Niphal.
broken, to be
broken off, to be
drawn away, to be
lifted up, to be
plucked away, to be
rooted out, to be
Piel.
break,to b.asunder,
burst, to [insunder
pluck off, to
pull, to
Hiphil.
draw, to
pull out, to
Hophal.
drawn away, to be

נֶתֶק 864
dry scall
scall

נָתַר 864
Kal.
moved, to be
Piel.
leap, to
Hiphil.
drive asunder, to
loose, to
loose, to let
* make, to
undo, to

נְתַר Ch. 864
Aphel.
shake off, to

נֶתֶר 864
nitre

נָתַשׁ 864
Kal.
destroy, to
pluck, to
pluck out, to
pluck up, to
root out, to
root up, to
roots, to pluck up by the
utterly
Niphal.
forsaken, to be
plucked up, to be
pulled up, to be
Hophal.
plucked up, to be

סְאָה 864
measure

סְאוֹן 864
battle

סָאַן 864
Kal.
warrior

סַאסְּאָה 864
measure

סָבָא 864
Kal.
drunkard
fill selves, to
(כ׳) Sabeans
*wine*bibber

סְבָא 865
Sabeans

סֹבֶא 865
drink
drunken
wine

סָבַב 865
Kal.
about on every side, to be
apply, to
beset, to
beset about, to
besiege, to
cast about, to
* circuit, in
compass, to
compass about, to
compass, to fetch a
go about, to
occasion, to
round about, to come
round about, to compass
round about, to stand
sit down, to
turn, to
turn about, to
turn aside, to
walk about, to
* whirl about, to
Niphal.
avoid, to
carried about, to be
compass, to
compass about, to
compass,to fetch a
compass round, to
driven, to be
environ, to
* every side, on
go about, to
remove, to
return, to
round about, to beset
turn, to
turn about, to
turn aside, to
turn self about, to
turned, to be
* winding about
Piel.
fetch about, to
Poel.
compass, to
compass about, to
go about, to
go round about, to
lead about, to
round about, to close
Hiphil.
about, to make
bring about, to
bring again, to
carry, to
carry about, to
change, to
come about, to cause to
compass, to
compass,to fetch a
lead about, to
remove, to
turn, to
turn away, to
turn back, to
Hophal.
changed, being
inclosed
set, to be
turned about,to be
turning

סִבָּה 866
cause

סָבִיב 866
about
circuit
compass
Magor-missabib
places about
round about
* round about
side, on every

סָבַךְ 868
Kal.
folden together
Pual.
wrapped, to be

סְבַךְ 868
thick
thicket

סֹבֶךְ 868
thicket

סַבְּכָא Ch. 868
sackbut

סָבַל 868
Kal.
bear, to
carry, to
Pual.
labour, strong to
Hithpael.
burden, to be a

סְבַל Ch. 868
Poal.
laid, strongly

סַבָּל 868
burden
burdens, to bear
burdens, bearer of

סֵבֶל 868
burden
charge

סֹבֶל 868
burden

סִבְלָה 868
burden

סִבֹּלֶת 868
Sibboleth

סְבַר Ch. 868
P'al.
think, to

סָגַד 868
Kal.
fall down, to

סְגִד Ch. 868
P'al.
worship, to

סְגוֹר 869
caul
gold

סְגֻלָּה 869
jewel
peculiar
peculiar treasure
proper good
special

סְגָנִים 869
princes
rulers

סִגְנִין Ch. 869
governors

סָגַר 869
Kal.
close up, to
inclosed, to be
* pure
repair, to
shut, to
shut up, to
shut up together
shutting
stop, to
* straitly
Niphal.
shut, to be
shut in, to be
shut out, to be
shut self, to
Piel.
deliver, to
Pual.
shut, to be
shut up, to be
Hiphil.
deliver, to
deliver up, to
give over, to
give up, to
shut up, to

סְגַר Ch. 870
P'al.
shut, to

סַגְרִיר 870
rainy, very

סַד 870
stocks

סָדִין 870
linen, fine
sheet

סְדָרִים 870
order

סַהַר 870
round

סֹהַר 870
prison †

סוּג[1] 870
Kal.
backslider
go back, to
Niphal.
driven, to be
turn back, to
turned, to be
turned away, to be

סוּג[2] 870
Kal.
set about

סוּג 870
dross

סוּגַר 870
ward

סוֹד 870
assembly
counsel
inward
secret
secret counsel

סוּחָה 870
torn

סוּךְ 870
Kal.
anoint, to
anoint self, to
at all
Hiphil.
anoint (*self*), to

סוּמְפּוֹנְיָה Ch. 870
dulcimer

סוּס 870
crane
horse
horse*back*
horse*hoofs*

סוּסָה 871
horses, company of

סוֹף 871
conclusion
end
hinder part

סוֹף Ch. 871
end

סוּף 871
Kal.
consumed, to be
end, to have an
perish, to
utterly, to be
Hiphil.
consume, to

סוּף Ch. 872
P'al.
fulfilled, to be
Aphel.
consume, to

סוּף 872
flags
* Red *sea*
weeds

סוּפָה 872
storm
tempest
whirlwind

סוּר 872
Kal.
decline, to
depart, to
departing
eschew, to

get (*you*)
go, to
gone aside, to be
grievous
past, to be
rebel, to
removed, to be
removing, to and fro
revolted, to be
* sour, to be
taken away, to be
turn, to
turn aside, to
turn in, to
without, to be

Polel.
turn aside, to

Hiphil.
be*head*, to
bring, to
call back, to
lay away, to
lay by, to
leave undone, to
pluck away, to
put, to
put away, to
put down, to
remove, to
removing
take, to
take away, to
take off, to
turn away, to
withdraw, to

Hophal.
taken away, to be

סוּר 874
degenerate

סוּת..........874

Hiphil.
entice, to
move, to
persuade, to
provoke, to
remove, to
set on, to
stir up, to
take away, to

סוּת..........874
clothes

סָחַב 874

Kal.
draw, to
draw out, to
tear, to

סְחָבוֹת........874
cast clouts

סָחָה 874

Piel.
scrape, to

סְחִי...........874
offscouring

סָחִישׁ 874
springeth of the same, (which)

סָחַף 874

Kal.
sweeping

Niphal.
swept away, to be

סָחַר 874

Kal.
go about, to
merchant
merchantman
occupy with, to
trade, to
traffick, to

Pilpel.
pant, to

סָחָר 875
mart
merchandise

סַחַר 875
merchandise

סְחֹרָה 875
merchandise

סֹחֵרָה 875
buckler

סֹחֶרֶת 875
black marble

סֵטִים..........875
turn aside, that

סִיג............875
dross

סִיוָן............875
Sivan

סִים............875
crane

סִיפֹּנְיָה........875
dulcimer

סִיר 875
caldron
pan
pot
*wash*pot

סִיר 875
*fish*hook
thorn

סָךְ 875
multitude

סֹךְ 875
covert
den
pavilion
tabernacle

סֻכָּה 875
booth
cottage
covert
pavilion
Succoth
tabernacle
tent

סִכּוּת..........875
tabernacle

סָכַךְ 875

Kal.
cover, to
defence

Hiphil.
cover, to
defend, to
hedge in, to
shut up, to

Pilpel.
join together, to
set, to

סָכַל 876

Niphal.
foolishly, to do

Piel.
foolish, to make
foolishness, to turn into

Hiphil.
fool, to play the
foolishly, to do

סָכָל 876
fool
foolish
sottish

סֶכֶל 876
folly

סִכְלוּת........876
folly
foolishness

סָכַן [1] 876

Kal.
advantage, to be
cherish, to
profit, to
profitable, to be
treasurer
*un*profitable

Hiphil.
acquaint self, to
acquainted, to be
ever
wont, to be

סָכַן [2].........876

Niphal.
endangered, to be

Pual.
impoverished

סָכַר [1] 876

Niphal.
stopped, to be

Piel.
give over, to

סָכַר [2] 876

Kal.
hire, to

סָכַת 876

Hiphil.
heed, to take

סַל 876
basket

סָלָא 876

Pual.
comparable

סָלַד 877

Piel.
harden self, to

סָלָה 877

Kal.
tread down, to

Piel.
tread under foot, to

Pual.
valued, to be

סֶלָה 877
Selah

סִלּוֹן 877
brier

סַלּוֹנִים 877
thorns

סָלַח...........877

Kal.
forgive, to
pardon, to
spare, to

Niphal.
forgiven, to be

סַלָּח 877
forgive, ready to

סְלִיחָה 877
forgiveness
pardon

סָלַל...........878

Kal.
cast up, to
extol, to
plain, made
raise up, to

Pilpel.
exalt, to

Hithpoel.
exalt self, to

סֹלְלָה..........878
bank
mount

סֻלָּם 878
ladder

סַלְסִלּוֹת 878
baskets

סֶלַע 878
rock
rock, ragged
Sela
Sela - *hammahle - koth*
Selah
stone
stony
strong hold

סָלְעָם..........878
locust, bald

סָלַף...........878

Piel.
overthrow, to
pervert, to

סֶלֶף...........878
perverseness

סְלִק Ch. 878

P'al.
come up, to

P'il.
come, to
come up, to

סֹלֶת 879
fine flour
flour
meal

סְמָדַר.........879
grape, tender

סַמִּים..........879
spices, sweet
sweet

סָמַךְ 879

Kal.
established
lay, to
lean, to
lie hard, to
put, to
set self, to
stand fast, to
stayed
sustain, to
uphold, to

Niphal.
borne up, to be
holden, to be
lean, to
rest selves, to
stay self, to

Piel.
stay, to

סֶמֶל & סֵמֶל..879
figure
idol
image

סָמַן...........879

Niphal.
appointed

סָמַר 879

Kal.
tremble, to

Piel.
stand up, to

סָמָר 879
rough

סְנֶה 880
bush

סַנְוֵרִים........880
blindness

סַנְסִנִּים........880
boughs

סְנַפִּיר 880
fins

סָס 880
worm

סָעַד...........880

Kal.
comfort, to
establish, to
hold up, to
refresh self, to
strengthen, to
upholden, to be

סְעַד Ch. 880

Aphel.
helping

סָעָה 880

Kal.
* storm

סְעִיף..........880
branch
branch, outmost
clift
top

סָעַף 880

Piel.
lop, to

סְעַפָּה 880
bough

סֵעֲפִים 880
thoughts

סְעִפִּים 880
opinions

סָעַר 880
Kal.
tempest, tossed with
tempestuous, to be
whirlwind, to come out as a
Niphal.
troubled, to be sore
Piel.
whirlwind, to scatter with a
Pual.
whirlwind, to drive with the

סַעַר 880
tempest
whirlwind

סְעָרָה 880
storm
stormy
tempest
whirl*wind*
whirlwind

סַף 880
bason
bowl
cup
door
door post
gate
post
threshold

סָפַד 881
Kal.
lament, to
mourn, to
mourner
wail, to
Niphal.
lamented, to be

סָפָה [1] 881
Kal.
consume, to
consumed, to be
destroy, to
Niphal.
consumed, to be
destroyed, to be
perish, to
Hiphil.
heap, to

סָפָה [2] 881
Kal.
add, to
augment, to
put, to
Niphal.
joined, to be

סָפַח 881
Kal.
put, to
Niphal.
cleave, to
Piel.
put, to
Pual.
gathered together, to be
Hithpael.
abiding

סַפַּחַת 881
scab

סָפִיחַ..........881
grow of themselves, such things as
grow, things which
groweth of its own accord, which
groweth of itself, which

סְפִינָה 881
ship

סַפִּיר..........881
sapphire

סֵפֶל 881
bowl
dish

סָפַן 881
Kal.
cieled
cover, to
seated

סִפֻּן..........882
cieling

סָפַף 882
Hithpolel.
doorkeeper, to be

סָפַק 882
Kal.
clap, to
smite, to
strike, to
wallow, to

סֵפֶק 882
sufficiency

סָפַר 882
Kal.
count, to
number, to
numbering
penknife †
reckon, to
scribe
tell, to
tell out, to
writer
Niphal.
numbered, to be
told;—counted
Piel.
commune, to
declare, to
number, to
numbered, to be
shew forth, to
speak, to
talk, to
tell, to
Pual.
accounted, to be
declared, to be
told, to be

סָפֵר Ch. 883
scribe

סֵפֶר 883
bill
book
evidence
* learn*ed*
learning
letter
register
scroll

סְפַר Ch.......884
book
roll

סְפָר 884
numbering

סְפֹרָה 884
number

סִפְרָה........884
book

סָקַל 884
Kal.
stone, to
stoning
surely
Niphal.
stoned, to be
Piel.
cast *stones*, to
gather out *stones*, to
gather out stones, to
throw *stones*, to
Pual.
stoned, to be

סַר 884
heavy
sad

סָרָבִים........884
briers

סַרְבָּלִין Ch. ...884
coats

סָרָה 884
continual †
rebellion
revolt
revolt*ed*
turn away, to
wrong

סָרַח 884
Kal.
exceeding
hang, to
spreading
stretch selves, to
Niphal.
vanished, to be

סֶרַח 884
remnant

סִרְיֹן 885
brigandine

סָרִים..........885
chamberlain
eunuch
officer
Rab-saris

סָרְכִין Ch. 885
presidents

סֶרֶן 885
lord
plates

סַרְעַפָּה 885
bough

סָרַף...........885
Piel.
burn, to

סִרְפָּד..........885
brier

סָרַר 885
Kal.
* away
backsliding
rebellious
revolter
revolting
slide back, to
stubborn
withdrew

סְתָיו or סְתָו..885
winter

סָתַם 885
Kal.
closed up
hidden
secret
shut up, to
stop, to
Niphal.
stopped, to be
Piel.
stop, to

סָתַר 886
Kal.
hide self, to
Niphal.
absent, to be
hid, to be
hide self, to
kept close, to be
secret
Piel.
hide, to
secret
Hiphil.
conceal, to
hide, to
secret, to keep
surely
Hithpael.
hid, to be
hide self, to

סְתַר Ch. 886
P'al.
destroy, to
Pael.
secret things

סֵתֶר 886
backbiting
covering
covert
* disguis*eth*
hiding place
privily
secret
secret place
secretly

סִתְרָה 886
protection

עָב 887
beam, thick
thick

עָב 887
clay
cloud
cloud, thick
* thick
thicket

עֹב 887
plank, thick

עָבַד...........887
Kal.
* be, to
bondmen, to be
bondservice
compel, to
do, to
dress, to
ear, to
execute, to
husbandman †
keep, to
labour, to
labouring man
pass, to bring to
servant
servants, to be
servants, to become
serve, to
serve, to make to
serve self, to
service, to do
service, to use
serving
till, to
tiller
(כ׳) transgress, to
work, to
worshipper
Niphal.
eared, to be
served, to be
tilled, to be
Pual.
serve, to be made to
wrought, to be
Hiphil.
bondage, to keep in
serve, to cause to
serve, to make to
work, to set a
Hophal.
serve, to

עֲבַד Ch. 889
P'al.
do, to
keep
make, to
move, to
work, to
Ithpael.
* cut, to be
done, to be
executed
go on, to
made, to be

עֶבֶד...........889
* bondage
bondman
*bond*servant
manservant
servant
(נ״א) sides

עֲבַד Ch. 894
servant

עֲבַד Ch. 894
work

עֲבֻדָּה.........894
houshold
servants, store of

עַבְדוּת........894
bondage

עָבָה 894
Kal.
thick, to be grown
thicker, to be

עֲבוֹדָה........894
act
bondage
* bondservant †
effect
labour
ministering
ministry
office
service
servile
servitude
tillage
use
work
* wrought

עֲבוֹט..........895
pledge

עֲבוּר..........895
because of
for
intent that
sake, for...'s
that
to

עֲבוּר..........895
corn, old

עָבַט...........895
Kal.
borrow, to
fetch (*a pledge*), to
Piel.
break (*ranks*), to
Hiphil.
lend, to
surely

עַבְטִיט........895
clay, thick

עֳבִי...........895
thick

עֳבִי...........895
thick
thickness

עֲבִידָה Ch.....895
affairs
service
work

עָבַר...........895
Kal.
alienate, to
altered, to be
come, to
come over, to
coming on
current
delivered, to be
enter, to
escape, to
fail, to
get over, to
go, to
go away, to
go beyond, to
go by, to
go forth, to
go his way, to
go in, to
go on, to
go over, to
go through, to
going
going over
gone, to be
more, to have
overcome, to
overpass, to
overpast, to be
overrun, to
overrunning
pass, to
pass along, to
pass away, to
pass beyond, to
pass by, to
pass on, to
pass out, to
pass over, to
pass through, to
passage, to give
passenger
passing
past, to be
perish, to
speedily
sweet smelling
transgress, to
transgressing
transgressor
*way*faring man
Niphal.
passed over, to be
Piel.
gender, to
partition, to make
Hiphil.
alienate, to
at all
beyond
bring, to
bring over, to
bring through, to
carry over, to
conduct, to
conduct over, to
convey over, to
do away, to
go, to make
have away, to
lay, to
pass by, to make to
pass, to cause to
pass, to make
pass through, to cause to
proclaim,† to
proclaimed,† to cause to be
proclamation,† to make
put away, to
* raiser of taxes †
remove, to
send over, to
set apart, to
shave,† to
sound, to cause to
sound, to make
take, to
take away, to
transgress, to make to
translate, to
turn away, to
Hithpael.
meddle, to
provoke to anger, to
rage, to
wroth, to be

עֵבֶר...........899
* against
beyond
by
* from
over
passage
quarter
side
side, other
side, this
straight

עֲבַר Ch. 899
beyond
side, this

עֲבָרָה.........900
ferry boat
(כ׳) plains

עֶבְרָה.........900
anger
rage
wrath

עָבַשׁ 900
Kal.
rotten, to be

עָבַת...........900
Piel.
wrap up, to

עָבֹת 900
thick

עֲבֹת...........900
band
bough, thick
branch, thick
chains, wreathen
cord
rope
wreathen

עָגַב...........900
Kal.
dote, to
lover

עֲגָבָה.........900
love, inordinate

עֲגָבִים 900
love, much
lovely, very

עֻגָּה & עֻגָה....900
cake
cake upon the hearth

עָגוּר 900
swallow

עָגִיל 900
earrings

עָגֹל 900
round

עֵגֶל...........900
bullock
calf

עֶגְלָה.........901
calf
cow
heifer
heifer †

עֲגָלָה.........901
cart
chariot
wagon

עָגַם...........901
Kal.
grieve, to

עָגַן 901
Niphal.
stay, to

עַד 901
*end,† world without
eternity
ever
everlasting
evermore
old
perpetually

עַד 901
prey

עַד 901
against
and
as
as yet †
at
before
by
by that
even
even to
for
forasmuch as
*hither*to
how long †
into
* or
so long as
so much as
so that
that
till
toward
until
when
while
yet

עַד Ch.........902
* and
at
for
*hither*to
on
till
to
until
unto
within

עֵד 902
witness

עָדָה 902
Kal.
adorn, to
adorned, to be
deck, to
deck self, to
decked, to be
pass by, to
Hiphil.
take away, to

עֲדָה & עֲדָא Ch.
..............902
P'al.
alter, to
depart, to
pass, to
pass away, to
Aphel.
have...taken away to
remove, to
take, to

עֵדָה 903
assembly
company
congregation
multitude
people
swarm

עֵדָה 903
testimony
witness

עֵדוּת..........904
Shoshannim-eduth
Shushan-eduth
testimony
witness

עֲדִי...........904
* excellent
mouth
ornament

עִדִּים 904
filthy

עֲדִין...........904
pleasures, given to

עָדַן...........904
Hithpael.
delight selves, to

עֵדֶן...........904
delicates
delight
pleasure

עֲדֶן & עֲדֶנָּה..904
yet

עֶדְנָה.........904
pleasure

עִדָּן Ch. 904
time

עָדַף...........904
Kal.
more, to be
number, odd
over and above, that were
overplus
remain, to
Hiphil.
over, to have

עָדַר[1] 905
Niphal.
fail, to
lack, to
lacking, to be
Piel.
lack, to

עָדַר[2].........905
Kal.
rank, to keep
Niphal.
digged, to be

עֵדֶר...........905
drove
flock
herd

עֲדָשִׁים........905
lentiles

עוּב 905
Hiphil.
cloud, to cover with a

עוּג 905
Kal.
bake, to

עֻגָב & עוּגָב ..905
organ

עוֹד 905
again
* all life long
any more
as yet
at all
because yet
besides
but
else
further
furthermore
good while
henceforth
longer
longer, any more
moreover
* once
since
still
still, be
when
whether yet
while have being
while, the
while yet
yet
yet within

עוֹד Ch. 905
while

עוּד 905
Kal.
witness, to take to
Piel.
rob, to
Hiphil.
admonish, to
charge, to
earnestly
protest, to
protesting
record, to call to
record, to take to
solemnly
take *witnesses*, to
testify, to
warning, to give
witness, to
witness, to bear
witness, to call to
witness, to give
Hophal.
testified, to be
Pilpel.
lift up, to
relieve, to
Hithpalel.
stand upright, to

עָוָה..........906
Kal.
iniquity, to commit
wrong, to do
Niphal.
bowed down, to be
perverse
troubled, to be
Piel.
crooked, to make
* turn, to
Hiphil.
amiss, to do
iniquity, to commit
perversely, to do
pervert, to
wickedly, to do

עַוָּה..........906
* overturn

עוּז 906
Hiphil.
gather, to
gather selves, to
gather selves to flee, to
retire, to

עֲוָיָא Ch. 906
iniquity

עֲוִיל..........906
ungodly

עֲוִיל..........906
child, young
little one

עוּל..........906
Kal.
ewes great with young
milch
young, with

עוּל..........906
child, sucking
infant

עָוַל..........906
Piel.
unjustly, to deal
unrighteous

עַוָּל..........906
unjust
unrighteous
wicked

עָוֶל & עֶוֶל 906
iniquity
unjust
unjustly
unrighteously
unrighteousness

עַוְלָה..........907
iniquity
perverseness
unjust †
unrighteousness
* wicked
wickedness

עוֹלָה..........907
iniquity
unrighteousness
wickedness

עוֹלָל & עֹלָל ..907
babe
child
infant
little one
young child

עוֹלָם 907
alway
always
ancient
ancient time
any more
continuance
(כִּי) Elam
eternal
ever
ever, for
ever of old
ever*lasting*
everlasting
evermore
evermore, for
lasting
long
long time
never †
old
old, of
old time, of
perpetual
time, at any
time, old
world
world, beginning of the
* world without end †

עָוֹן 910
fault
iniquity
mischief
punishment
punishment of iniquity
sin

עָוַן 911
Kal.
eye, to

עוֹנָה 911
furrow
marriage, duty of

עִוְעִים..........911
* perverse

עוּף..........911
Kal.
faint, to be
faint, to wax
flee away, to
fly, to
fly away, to
flying
* set, to
shine forth, to
weary
Polel.
brandish, to
fly, to
Hiphil.
fly away, to
* set, to
Hithpolel.
fly away, to

עוֹף..........911
bird
flieth, that
flying
fowl

עוֹף Ch. 912
fowl

עוֹפֶרֶת 912
lead

עוּץ 912
Kal.
advice, to take
take *counsel* together, to

עוּק..........912
Hiphil.
pressed, to be

עָוַר 912
Piel.
blind, to
put out, to

עוֹר..........912
hide
leather
skin

עוּר 1 913
Kal.
awake, to;—arise
* master
stir up, to
Niphal.
raised, to be
raised up, to be
wakened, to be
Polel.
awake, to
lift up, to
lifting up
raise up, to
stir up, to
Hiphil.
awake, to
raise, to
raise up, to
stir up, to
stir up self, to
wake up, to
waken, to
Hithpolel.
awake, to
lift up self, to
stir up self, to

עוּר 2 913
Niphal.
naked, to be made

עוּר Ch. 913
chaff

עִוֵּר..........913
blind
blind men
blind people

עִוָּרוֹן..........914
blindness

עֲיָרִים 914
asses, young

עַוֶּרֶת..........914
blind

עוּשׁ 914
Kal.
assemble selves, to

עוּת 914
Kal.
speak in season, to

עָוַת 914
Piel.
crooked, to make
falsifying
overthrow, to
perversely, to deal
pervert, to
subvert, to
turn upside down, to
Pual.
crooked
Hithpael.
bow selves, to

עַוָּתָה 914
wrong

עַז..........914
fierce
greedy †
mighty
power
roughly
strong

עֵז..........914
goat
goat, she
kid
kid †

עֵז Ch. 914
goat

עֹז..........914
boldness
loud
might
power
strength
strong

עֲזָאזֵל........915
scapegoat

עָזַב..........915
Kal.
commit self, to
destitute, to leave
fail, to
forsake, to
fortify, to
help, to
leave, to
leave off, to
refuse, to
surely
Niphal.
forsaken, to be
left, to be
Pual.
left, to be

עִזָּבוֹן..........917
fair
ware

עֲזוּבָה 917
forsaking

עִזּוּז..........917
power
strong

עֱזוּז..........917
might
strength

עָזַז 917
Kal.
prevail, to
strengthen, to
strengthen selves, to
strengthened, to be
strong, to be
Hiphil.
harden, to
impudent

עָזְנִיָּה 917
ospray

עָזַק..........917
Piel.
fence about, to

עִזְקָא Ch. 917
signet

עָזַר..........917
Kal.
help, to
helper
succour, to
Niphal.
helped, to be
Hiphil.
help, to
succour, to

עֵזֶר..........918
help

עֶזְרָה & עֶזְרַת 918
help
helped
helper

עֲזָרָה..........918
court
settle

עֵט..........918
pen

עֵטָא Ch.......918
counsel

עָטָה..........918
Kal.
array self, to
clad, to be
cover, to
cover selves, to
covered, to be
covering, to put a
fill, to
put on, to
surely
turn aside, to
Hiphil.
cover, to

עֲטִין..........918
breast

עֲטִישָׁה........918
neesing

עֲטַלֵּף..........918
bat

עָטַף..........918
Kal.
cover, to
covered over, to be
fail, to
faint, that
feebler
hide self, to
overwhelmed, to be
Niphal.
swoon, to
Hiphil.
feeble, to be
Hithpael.
faint, to
overwhelmed, to be
swoon, to

עָטַר..........919
Kal.
compass, to
Piel.
crown, to
Hiphil.
crowning

עֲטָרָה........919
crown

עִי..........919
heap
Iim
Ije-*abarim*

עִיט..........919
Kal.
fly, to
rail, to

עַיִט..........919
bird
fowl
ravenous
ravenous bird

עֵילוֹם........919
ever

עֲיָם..........919
mighty

עַיִן..........919
affliction
appearance, outward
before
* best, † to think
colour
conceit
* content, † to be
countenance
* displease, † to
En-*hakkore*
eye
eye*brow*
eye*d*
eyesight
face
* favour, † to
fountain
(כ׳) furrows
* him
* humble †
knowledge
look
* look, † to
* look well, † to
* me
open
openly
* please, † to
* please, † not to
presence
* regard, † to
resemblance
sight
* thee
* them
* think, † to
* thinkest
* thinking †
* us
well
* you
* yourselves

עַיִן Ch.........925
eye

עִין..........925
Kal.
eye, to

עָיֵף..........925
Kal.
wearied, to be

עָיֵף..........925
faint
thirsty
weary

עֵיפָה..........925
darkness

עַיִר..........925
ass colt
ass, young
colt
foal

עִיר..........925
Kal.
raise, to

עִיר..........925
(כ׳) Ai
city
* city, several
(כ׳) court
town

עִיר..........932
* awake, to

עִיר Ch. 932
watcher

עֵירֹם..........932
naked
nakedness

עַיִשׁ..........932
Arcturus

עַכָּבִישׁ........932
spider

עַכְבָּר........932
mouse

עָכַס..........932
Piel.
tinkling, to make a

עֶכֶס..........932
ornaments, tinkling
stocks

עָכַר..........932
Kal.
trouble, to
troubler
Niphal.
stirred, to be
troubled, to be

עַכְשׁוּב........932
adder

עַל..........932
above
according to
accordingly
after
against
against, as
among
and
* as
at
because of
beside
beside the rest of
between
beyond the time
* both and
by
by reason of
* charge of, had the
concerning
for
forth of
from
from off
in
in that
of
off
on
out of
over
than
through
throughout
to
touching
upon
* with

עַל & עָל......933
above
high
High, most

עַל Ch.........933
about
against
concerning
for
from
in
* more
of
on
over
*there*fore
thereon
to
unto
upon
why †
with

עֹל..........933
yoke

עֵלָּא Ch. 933
over

עִלֵּג..........933
stammerer

עָלָה..........934
Kal.
arise, to
arise up, to
ascend up, to
at once
break (*the day*), to
breaking
bring up, to
burnt, to be
climb, to
climb up, to
come, to
come up, to
cut off, to be
dawning
depart, to
excel, to
fall, to
fetch up, to
get up, to
go, to
go away, to
go up, to
going up
grow, to
grown over, to be
increase, to
laid, to be
leap, to
* *made* up, to be
mount up, to
offer, to
offered, to be
offering
* perfected, † to be
* put, to be
recovered, to be
rise up, to
rising
scale, to
set up, to
shoot forth, to
shooting up
spring, to begin to
spring (*of the day*)
spring up, to
surely
take up, to
* vapour
Niphal.
broken up, to be
brought up, to be
depart, to
exalted, to be
get up, to
go up, to
taken up, to be
Hiphil.
ascend, to cause to
bring, to
bring up, to
burn, to cause to
carry up, to
cast up, to
* chew, † to
come up, to cause to
come up, to make to
fetch up, to
go, to
go up, to
go up, to make to
levy, to
lift up, to
light, to
offer, to
offering
pay, to make to
prefer, to
put, to
put on, to
raise, to
restore, to
rise up, to make
set, to
set up, to
stir up, to
take away, to
take up, to
work, to
Hophal.
brought up, to be
* mentioned, to be
offered, to be
Hithpael.
lift self up, to

עָלֶה..........939
branch
leaf

עִלָּה Ch. 939
occasion

עֹלָה..........939
ascent
burnt offering
burnt sacrifice
go up to, to

עֲלָה Ch...... 941
burnt offering

עַלְוָה.........941
iniquity

עֲלוּמִים.......941
youth

עֲלוּקָה........941
horseleach

עָנַג 962
Pual.
delicate
Hithpael.
delicateness
delight, to have
delight selves, to
delighted, to be
sport selves, to

עָנֹג 962
delicate

עֹנֶג 962
delight
pleasant

עָנַד 962
Kal.
bind, to
tie, to

עָנָה 1 962
Kal.
account, to give
afflict, to
answer, to
answer, to cause to
answer, to give
bear *witness*, to
brought low, to be
cry, to
hear, to
lift up, to
say, to
* scholar
shout, to
shout, to give a
sing, to
sing together by course, to
speak, to
testify, to
utter, to
witness, to
witness, to bear
Niphal.
answer, to
answered, to be
heard, to be

עָנָה 2 964
Kal.
abase self, to
afflicted, to be
exercised, to be
gentleness
troubled, to be
Niphal.
afflicted, to be
humble self, to
Piel.
afflict, to
deal hardly with, to
defile, to
force, to
humble, to
hurt, to
Leannoth
ravish, to
sing, to
weaken, to
wise, in any
Pual.
afflicted, to be
afflictions
Hiphil.
afflict, to
answer, to
Hithpael.
afflict selves, to
afflicted, to be
chasten self, to
submit self, to

עֲנָה 1 Ch. 965
P'al.
answer, to
speak, to

עֲנֵה 2 Ch. 965
P'al.
poor

עָנָו 965
humble
lowly
meek
(כ׳) poor

עֲנָוָה 965
gentleness
humility
meekness

עַנְוָה 965
gentleness
meekness

עֱנוּת 965
affliction

עָנִי 965
afflicted
(כ׳) humble
(כ׳) lowly
poor

עֳנִי 966
afflicted
affliction
trouble

עָנְיו 966
meek

עִנְיָן 966
business
travail

עָנַן 966
Piel.
bring *a cloud*, to
Poel.
enchanter
Meonenim
observe times, to
observer of times
soothsayer
sorceress

עָנָן 966
cloud
cloudy

עֲנָן Ch. 967
cloud

עֲנָנָה 967
cloud

עָנָף 967
bough
branch

עֲנַף Ch. 967
bough
branch

עָנֵף 967
branches, full of

עָנַק 967
Kal.
compass about as a chain, to
Hiphil.
furnish, to
liberally

עֲנָק 967
chain

עָנַשׁ 967
Kal.
amerce, to
condemned
punish, to
punished, to be
surely
Niphal.
punished, to be

עֹנֶשׁ 967
punishment
tribute

עֲנָשׁ Ch. 967
confiscation

עָסִיס 967
juice
wine, new
wine, sweet

עָסַס 967
Kal.
tread down, to

עֳפָאִים 967
branches

עֳפִי Ch. 967
leaves

עָפַל 967
Pual.
lifted up, to be
Hiphil.
presume, to

עֹפֶל 967
(כ׳) emerods
fort
Ophel
strong hold
tower

עַפְעַפִּים 968
dawning
eyelids

עָפַר 968
Piel.
cast *dust*, to

עָפָר 968
ashes
dust
earth
ground
morter
powder
rubbish

עֹפֶר 968
roe young
young *hart*

עֵץ 968
carpenter †
gallows
helve
pine †
plank
staff
stalk
stick
stock
timber
tree
wood

עָצַב 970
Kal.
displease, to
grieve, to
Niphal.
grieved, to be
hurt, to be
sorry, to be
Piel.
make, to
vex, to
wrest, to
Hiphil.
grieve, to
worship, to
Hithpael.
grieved, to be
grieved, it

עֲצַב Ch. 971
P'al.
lamentable

עָצָב 971
idol
image

עֶצֶב 971
labour

עָצֵב 971
grievous
idol
labour
sorrow

עֹצֶב 971
idol
sorrow
wicked

עִצָּבוֹן 971
sorrow
toil

עַצֶּבֶת 971
sorrow
wound

עָצָה 971
Kal.
shut, to

עָצֶה 971
backbone

עֵצָה 971
tree

עֵצָה 971
advice
advisement
counsel
counsel*lor*
purpose

עָצוּם 972
feeble †
great
mighty
much
strong

עָצַל 972
Niphal.
slothful, to be

עָצֵל 972
slothful
sluggard

עַצְלָה 972
slothfulness

עַצְלוּת 972
idleness

עָצַם 972
Kal.
great, to be
increased, to be
mightier, to be
mighty, to be
mighty, to wax
more, to be
shut, to
strong, to be
strong, to become
Piel.
bones, to break his
close, to
Hiphil.
stronger, to make

עֶצֶם 972
body
bone
* life
same
selfsame
strength
* very

עֹצֶם 973
might
strong
substance

עָצְמָה 973
abundance
strength

עֲצֻמוֹת 973
strong

עָצַר 973
Kal.
able, to be
* *able*, to be
close up, to
detain, to
fast
keep self close, to
keep still, to
kept
prevail, to
recover, to
refrain, to
* reign, to
restrain, to
retain, to
shut, to
shut up, to
slack, to
stop, to
withhold, to
withhold self, to
Niphal.
detained
shut up, to be
stayed, to be

עֹצֶר 973
barren
oppression
prison

עֶצֶר 973
* magistrate †

עֲצָרָה 973
solemn assembly
solemn meeting

עֲצֶרֶת 974
assembly
solemn assembly

עָקַב 974
Kal.
heel, to take by the
supplant, to
utterly
Piel.
stay, to

עָקֵב 974
footstep
heel
*horse*hoofs
last
liers in wait
step

עָקֹב 974
crooked
deceitful
polluted

עֵקֶב 974
because
because †
by
end
for
if
reward

עָקְבָּה 974
subtilty

עָקַד 974
Kal.
bind, to

עָקֹד 974
ringstraked

עָקָה 974
oppression

עָקַל 974
Pual.
wrong

עֲקַלְקַל 974
by*ways*
crooked ways

עֲקַלָּתוֹן 974
crooked

עָקַר 974
Kal.
pluck up, to
Niphal.
rooted up, to be
Piel.
dig down, to
hough, to

עֲקַר Ch. 974
Ithp'al.
roots, to be plucked up by the

עֵקֶר 974
stock

עָקָר 974
barren
* barren, male or female
barren woman

עִקַּר Ch. 974
stump

עַקְרָב 975
scorpion

עָקַשׁ 975
Kal.
perverse, to prove
Niphal.
perverse, that is
Piel.
crooked, to make
pervert, to

עִקֵּשׁ 975
crooked
froward
perverse

עִקְּשׁוּת 975
* froward

עָר 975
city
enemy

עָר Ch. 975
enemy

עָרַב 1 975
Kal.
become *surety*, to
engage, to
mortgage, to
occupiers
occupy, to
pleasant, to be
pleasing, to be
pleasure, to take
surety, to be
surety, to become
surety, to put in
sweet, to be
undertake, to
Hithpael.
intermeddle, to
meddle with, to
mingle selves, to
mingled, to be
pledges, to give

עָרַב 2 975
Kal.
darkened, to be
evening, toward
Hiphil.
evening

עֲרַב Ch. 975
Pael.
mixed
Ithpael.
mingle selves, to
mixed, to be

עָרֵב 975
sweet

עָרֹב 975
flies, divers sorts of
swarm

עֵרֶב 975
mixed
multitude, mixed
woof

עֶרֶב 975
Arabia
day †
even
evening
evening*tide*
even*tide*
eventide
night
people, mingled

עֲרָב 976
willows

עֹרֵב 976
raven

עֲרָבָה 976
Arabah
Beth-arabah
champaign
desert
evenings
heavens
plain
wilderness

עֲרֻבָּה 977
pledge
surety

עֵרָבוֹן 977
pledge

עָרַג 977
Kal.
cry, to
pant, to

עֲרָד Ch. 977
ass, wild

עָרָה 977
Niphal.
poured, to be
Piel.
destitute, to leave
discover, to
discovering
empty, to
rase, to
uncover, to
Hiphil.
discover, to
pour out, to
uncover, to
Hithpael.
naked, to make self
spread self, to

עֲרוּגָה 977
bed
furrow

עָרוֹד 977
ass, wild

עֶרְוָה 977
nakedness
shame
unclean
uncleanness

עַרְוָה Ch. 978
dishonour

עָרוֹם 978
naked

עָרוּם 978
crafty
prudent
subtil

עֲרוֹעֵר 978
heath

עָרוּץ 978
cliffs

עָרוֹת 978
paper reeds

עֶרְיָה 978
bare
naked
* quite

עֲרִיסָה 978
dough

עֲרִיפִים 978
heavens

עָרִיץ 978
mighty
oppressor
power, in great
strong
terrible
violent

עֲרִירִי 978
childless

עָרַךְ 978
Kal.
array, put in
array, to put in
array, to put selves in
array, to put the battle in
array, set in
array, to set in
array, to set selves in
compare, to
compared, to be
direct, to
equal, to
esteem, to
expert in *war*
furnish, to
handle, to
join *battle*, to
ordain, to
ordained
order, to
order, to lay in
order, to put in
order, to be reckoned up in
order, to set in
ordered
prepare, to
prepared
Hiphil.
estimate, to
tax, to
value, to

עֵרֶךְ 979
equal
estimation
order
order, things that are to be set in
price
proportion
* set at
suit
taxation
* valuest

עָרֵל 979
Kal.
uncircumcised, to count
Niphal.
foreskin to be uncovered

עָרֵל 979
uncircumcised
uncircumcised person

עָרְלָה 979
foreskins
uncircumcised †

עָרַם 1 979
Kal.
very
Hiphil.
beware, to
crafty *counsel*, to take
prudent, to be
subtilly, to deal

עָרַם 2 979
Niphal.
gathered together, to be

עֹרֶם 980
craftiness

עָרְמָה 980
guile
prudence
subtilty
wilily
wisdom

עֲרֵמָה 980
corn, heap of
heap
sheaf

עַרְמוֹן 980
chesnut tree

עַרְעָר 980
destitute
heath

עָרַף 1 .... .980
Kal.
drop, to
drop down, to

עָרַף 2 980
Kal.
beheaded, that is
break down, to
neck, to break...
neck, to cut off...
neck, to strike off...

עֹרֶף 980
back
neck
*stiff*necked

עֲרָפֶל 980
cloud, dark
dark
darkness
darkness, gross
darkness, thick

עָרַץ 980
Kal.
affrighted, to be
afraid, to be
break, to
dread, to
fear, to
oppress, to
prevail, to
shake terribly, to
terrified, to be
Niphal.
feared, to be
Hiphil.
afraid, to be
dread, (be)

עָרַק............980
Kal.
fleeing
sinews

עָרַר............980
Kal.
bare, to make
Poel.
raise up, to
Pilpel.
utterly
Hithpalpel.
broken, to be

עֶרֶשׂ............981
bed
bed †
bedstead
couch

עֵשֶׂב 981
grass
herb

עֲשַׂב Ch.......981
grass

עָשָׂה 981
Kal.
accomplish, to
advance, to
appoint, to
apt
at, to be
bear, to
bestow, to
bring forth, to
bring to pass, to
bruising
busy, to be
certainly
charge, that have the
commit, to
committing
deal, to
deal with, to
deck, to
displease,† to
do, to
doer
doing
done, to be
dress, to
dressed, ready
execute, to
executing
exercise, to
fashion, to
feast,† to
fighting men
finish,† to
fit, to
(כ') fly, to
fulfil, to
furnish, to
gather, to
get, to
go about, to
govern, to
grant, to
great
hinder,† to
hold *a feast*, to
indeed
industrious,† to be
journey,† to
keep, to
labour, to
maintain, to
make;—m. ready
maker
making
observe, to
offer, to
offering
officer †
pare, to
perform, to
practise, to
prepare, to
preparing
procure, to
provide, to
put, to
requite, to
sacrifice, to
serve, to
set, to
shew, to
* sin, to
spend, to
surely
take, to
throughly
trim, to
very
vex,† to
*warr*iors, to be
work, to
*work*men
wrought
yield, to
yielding
Niphal.
become, to
committed, to be
done, to be
dressed, to be
executed, to be
execution, to be put in
followed, to be
holden, to be
kept
kept, to be
made, to be
meet, to be
occupied, to be
offered, to be
pass, to come to
performed, to be
prepared, to be
used, to be
wrought, to be
Piel.
bruise, to
Pual.
made, to be

עָשׂוֹר 997
ten
ten strings, instruments of
tenth

עֲשִׂירִי..........997
tenth
tenth part

עָשַׂק 997
Hithpael.
strive, to

עֵשֶׂק............997
Esek

עָשָׂר & עֶשְׂרֵה..997
*fif*teen
*seven*teen
ten

עָשָׂר 998
*eigh*teen
*eigh*teenth
eleven †
eleventh †
*fif*teen
*fif*teenth
*four*teen
*four*teenth
(כ') made
*nine*teen
*nine*teenth
*seven*teen
*seven*teenth
sixscore thousand †
*six*teen
*six*teenth
*thir*teen
*thir*teenth
twelfth †
twelve †

עֲשַׂר & עַשְׂרָה Ch.
..............1000
ten
twelve †

עֶשֶׂר 1000
Kal.
tenth, to take the
Piel.
surely
tenth, to give the
tithe, to
tithes, to have
truly
Hiphil.
tithes, to take
tithing

עִשָּׂרוֹן........1000
tenth deal

עֶשְׂרִים.......1001
*six*score
twentieth
twenty

עֶשְׂרִין Ch. ...1003
twenty

עָשׁ...........1003
moth

עָשׁ...........1003
Arcturus

עָשׁוֹק 1003
oppressor

עֲשׁוּקִים......1003
oppressed
oppressions

עָשׁוֹת........1003
bright

עָשִׁיר 1003
rich
rich man

עָשַׁן..........1003
Kal.
angry, to be
smoke, to
smoke, to be on a

עָשֵׁן 1003
smoking

עָשָׁן 1003
smoke
smoking

עָשַׁק..........1004
Kal.
deceitfully, to get
deceive, to
defraud, to
drink up, to
oppress, to
oppressor
use *oppression*, to
violence, to do
wrong, to do
Pual.
oppressed

עֹשֶׁק..........1004
cruelly
extortion
oppression
thing *deceitfully* gotten

עָשְׁקָה........1004
oppressed

עָשַׁר 1004
Kal.
rich, to be
rich, to become
Hiphil.
enrich, to
rich, to be
rich, to make
rich, to wax
Hithpael.
rich, to make self

עֹשֶׁר 1004
far *richer*
riches

עָשֵׁשׁ.........1005
Kal.
consumed, to be

עָשַׁת.........1005
Kal.
shine, to
Hithpael.
think, to

עֲשִׁת Ch.....1005
P'al.
think, to

עָשֵׁת.........1005
bright

עֶשְׁתּוֹת 1005
thought

עַשְׁתֵּי 1005
eleven †
eleventh †

עֶשְׁתֹּנֹת 1005
thoughts

עַשְׁתְּרוֹת.....1005
flocks

עֵת...........1005
after †
*al*ways
* certain
continually †
due season
evening †
*evening*tide
*even*tide
long
*meal*time
*noon*tide
season
so *long* as
time
time, what
when

עָתַד..........1007
Piel.
fit, to make
Hithpael.
ready to become, to be

עַתָּה..........1007
henceforth
now
straightway
time, this
whereas

עַתּוּד 1007
chief one
goat
he goat
ram

עָתוּד 1008
(כ') ready
treasure

עִתִּי 1008
fit

עָתִיד 1008
come, things that shall
ready
(כ') treasures

עֲתִיד Ch.....1008
ready

עָתִיק.........1008
durable

עַתִּיק.........1008
ancient
drawn

עַתִּיק Ch.....1008
ancient

עָתַם 1008
Niphal.
darkened, to be

עָתַק 1008
Kal.
old, to become
old, to wax
removed, to be
Hiphil.
copy out, to
leave off, to
remove, to

עָתָק..........1008
arrogancy
grievous things
hard things
stiff

עָתֵק 1008
durable

עָתַר[1] 1008
Kal.
intreat, to
pray, to
Niphal.
intreated, to be
Hiphil.
intreat, to
prayer, to make

עָתַר[2] 1008
Niphal.
deceitful
Hiphil.
multiply, to

עָתָר.........1008
suppliant
thick

עֲתֶרֶת........1008
abundance

פֹּא 1009
here

פָּאָה 1009
Hiphil.
scatter into corners, to

פֵּאָה 1009
corner
end
quarter
side

פָּאַר 1009
Piel.
beautify, to
boughs, to go over the
glorify, to
Hithpael.
boast self, to
glorified, to be
glorify self, to
glory, to
vaunt selves, to

פְּאֵר 1009
beauty
bonnet
goodly
ornament
tire

פֻּארָה 1009
bough
branch
sprig

פֹּארָה 1009
bough

פָּארוּר 1009
blackness

פַּג 1009
green fig

פִּגּוּל 1009
abominable
abominable things
abomination

פָּגַע 1009
Kal.
come, to
fall, to
fall upon, to
intercession, to make
intreat, to
light *upon*, to
meet, to
meet together, to
pray, to
reach, to
run, to
Hiphil.
come betwixt, to
entreat, to cause to
intercession, to make
intercessor
lay, to

פֶּגַע 1010
chance
occurrent

פָּגַר 1010
Piel.
faint, to be

פֶּגֶר 1010
carcase
corpse
dead body

פָּגַשׁ 1010
Kal.
meet, to
meet together, to
Niphal.
meet, to
meet together, to
met, to be
Piel.
meet with, to

פָּדָה 1010
Kal.
deliver, to
means, by any
ransom, to
redeem, to
redeemed, that are to be
rescue, to
surely
Niphal.
redeemed, to be
Hiphil.
redeemed, to let be
Hophal.
at all

פְּדוּיִם 1011
redeemed, to be
redeemed, that are to be
redeemed, that were

פְּדוּת 1011
division
redeem
redemption

פִּדְיוֹם 1011
redeemed, that were
redemption

פִּדְיוֹן 1011
ransom
redemption

פָּדַע 1011
Kal.
deliver, to

פֶּדֶר 1011
fat

פֶּה 1011
accord
according as
according to
after
appointment
assent
collar
command
commandment
* eat
edge
end
entry
file †
hole
in
mind
mouth
part
portion
* saith
say, should
saying
sentence
skirt
sound
speech
* spoken
talk
tenor
to
* twoedged
wish
word

פֹּה & פּוֹ & פֹּא 1014
here
hither
side, the one
side, the other
side, that
side, this

פּוּג 1014
Kal.
cease, to
faint, to
slacked, to be
Niphal.
feeble, to be

פּוּגָה 1014
rest

פּוּחַ 1014
Kal.
break, to
Hiphil.
blow, to
blow upon, to
puff, to
snare, to bring into a
speak, to
utter, to

פּוּךְ 1014
colours, fair
glistering
paint*ed*
painting

פּוֹל 1014
beans

פּוּן 1014
Kal.
distracted, to be

פּוּץ 1014
Kal.
disperse selves, to
dispersed
retire, to
scattered, to be
spread abroad, to be
Niphal.
scattered, to be
spread abroad, to be
Polel.
break in pieces, to
Pilpel.
shake to pieces, to
Hiphil.
cast, to
cast abroad, to
dasheth in pieces, that
drive, to
scatter, to
scatter abroad, to
scattered abroad, to be
Hithpael.
scattered, to be

פּוּק 1 1015
Kal.
stumble, to
Hiphil.
move, to

פּוּק 2 1015
Hiphil.
affording
draw out, to
further, to
get, to
obtain, to

פּוּקָה 1015
grief

פּוּר 1015
Hiphil.
break, to
nought, to bring to
take, utterly to

פּוּר 1015
Pur
Purim

פּוּרָה 1015
press
wine press

פּוּשׁ 1015
Kal.
grow up, to
grown fat, to be
spread selves, to
Niphal.
scattered, to be

פַּז 1015
gold, fine
gold, pure

פָּזַז 1 1015
Hophal.
best *gold*

פָּזַז 2 1015
Kal.
strong, to be made
Piel.
leaping

פָּזַר 1015
Kal.
scattered
Niphal.
scattered, to be
Piel.
disperse, to
scatter, to
Pual.
scattered abroad, to be

פַּח 1016
gin
plate
plate, thin
snare

פָּחַד 1016
Kal.
afraid, to be
awe, to stand in
fear, to
fear, to be in
Piel.
fear, to
Hiphil.
shake, to make to

פַּחַד 1016
dread
dreadful
fear
great *fear*
greatly *feared*, thing
terror

פַּחַד 1016
stones

פַּחְדָּה 1016
fear

פֶּחָה 1016
captain
deputy
governor

פֶּחָה Ch. 1016
captain
governor

פָּחַז 1017
Kal.
light

פַּחַז 1017
unstable

פַּחֲזוּת 1017
lightness

פָּחַח 1017
Hiphil.
snared, to be

פֶּחָם 1017
coals

פֶּחָר Ch. 1017
potter

פַּחַת 1017
hole
pit
snare

פְּחֶתֶת 1017
fret inward

פִּטְדָה 1017
topaz

פָּטִיר 1017
free

פַּטִּישׁ 1017
hammer

פַּטִּישׁ Ch. ... 1017
hosen

פָּטַר 1017
Kal.
dismiss, to
free
let out, to
open
slip away, to
Hiphil.
shoot out, to

פֶּטֶר 1017
firstling
openeth

פִּטְרָה 1017
open, such as

פַּטְשׁ Ch. 1017
hosen

פִּיד 1017
destruction
ruin

פִּיָה 1017
edge

פִּיחַ 1017
ashes

פִּילֶגֶשׁ 1017
concubine
paramour

פִּימָה 1018
collops

פִּיפִיּוֹת 1018
teeth
* twoedged

פִּיק 1018
* smite together

פַּךְ 1018
box
vial

פָּכָה 1018
Piel.
run out, to

פָּלָא 1018
Niphal.
hard
hard, to arise...too
hard, to be too
hidden
high, things too
marvellous
marvellous, to be
marvellous things
marvellous works
marvellously
marvels
miracles
wonderful, to be
wonderful things
wonderful works
wonderfully
wonders; wondrous
wonders, great
wondrous things
wondrous works
Piel.
accomplish, to
performing
Hiphil.
marvellous, to shew
marvellous work
marvellous work, to do a
marvellously...,to be
separate, to
singular, to make
wonderful
wonderful, to be
wonderful, to make
wondrously
Hithpael.
marvellous, to shew self

פֶּלֶא 1018
marvellous thing
wonder
wonderful
wonderfully

פִּלְאִי 1018
secret
wonderful

פָּלַג 1019
Niphal.
divided, to be
Piel.
divide, to

פְּלַג Ch. 1019
P'al.
divided

פֶּלֶג 1019
river
stream

פְּלַג Ch. 1019
dividing

פְּלַגָּה 1019
division
river

פְּלֻגָּה 1019
division

פְּלֻגָּה Ch. 1019
division

פְּלָדָה 1019
torch

פָּלָה 1019
Niphal.
separated, to be
wonderfully made, to be
Hiphil.
difference, to put a
marvellous, to show
set apart, to
sever, to

פָּלַח 1019
Kal.
cut, to
Piel.
bring forth, to
cleave, to
shred, to
strike through, to

פְּלַח Ch. 1019
P'al.
minister
serve, to

פֶּלַח 1019
piece

פָּלְחָן Ch. 1019
service

פָּלַט 1019
Kal.
escape, to
Piel.
calve, to
deliver, to
deliverer
escape, to cause to
Hiphil.
carry away safe, to
deliver, to

פָּלֵט 1019
escape
escaped, that have

פֶּלֶט 1019
deliverance
escape

פְּלִי 1020
secret

פָּלִיא 1020
wonderful

פָּלִיט 1020
escape
escaped, that
escapeth, that
fugitive

פָּלֵיט 1020
escape, that
escaped, that

פְּלֵיטָה 1020
deliverance
escape
escaped, that is
escaping
remnant

פָּלִיל 1020
judge

פְּלִילָה 1020
judgment

פְּלִילִי 1020
judge
judgment

פֶּלֶךְ 1020
distaff
part
staff

פָּלַל 1020
Piel.
judge, to
judgment, to execute
think, to
Hithpael.
intreat, to
make (*prayer*), to
pray, to
prayer, to make
praying
supplication, to make

פַּלְמוֹנִי 1021
certain

פְּלֹנִי 1021
such

פָּלַס 1021
Piel.
make, to
ponder, to
weigh, to

פֶּלֶס 1021
scales
weight

פָּלַץ 1021
Hithpael.
tremble, to

פַּלָּצוּת 1021
fearfulness
horror
trembling

פָּלַשׁ 1021
Hithpael.
roll self, to
wallow self, to

פְּלֵתִי 1021
Pelethites

פֻּם Ch. 1021
mouth

פֵּן 1021
corner

פֶּן 1021
lest
lest peradventure
peradventure
that...not

פַּנַּג 1021
Pannag

פָּנָה 1021
Kal.
appear, to
at *even*tide
behold, to
come on, to
* corner
dawning
go away, to
look, to
mark, to
passed away, to be
regard, to
respect, to
respect, to have
return, to
* right *early*
turn, to
turn aside, to
turn away, to
turn face, to
turn self, to
turned, to be
Piel.
cast out, to
empty, to
prepare, to
Hiphil.
look back, to
turn, to
turn self, to
turned back, to be
Hophal.
lie, to
turn back, to

פִּנָּה 1022
bulwark
chief
corner
stay
tower

פְּנִיִּים 1023
rubies

פָּנִים 1023
accept,† to
afore
aforetime
against
anger
* as
at
battle †
because †
because of
before
before †
beforetime
beseech †
countenance
edge
employ †
* endure
enquire †
face
favour
fear of
for
*fore*front
forefront
forepart
form
former time
forward
from
from †
front
heaviness
* him
* him †
* himself
honourable †
impudent †
in †
it
long as, as
look*eth*
looks
* me
meet †
* meet, to
* more than
(פ׳) mouth
mouth
of
off
old, of
old time
* on
open
out of †
over against
over against †
partial,† to be
person
please,† to
presence
prospect
purposed, was
reason of, by
regard,† to
right forth
serve,† to
shew*bread*
* shewbread
sight
state
straight
street †
* thee
* them
* themselves
through
throughout †
till
time past
times past
to
toward
toward †
unto
upon
upon †
upside
upside down †
with
within
with*stand*
withstand †
* ye
* you

פְּנִים **1036**
in
inner part
inward
within

פְּנִימִי 1036
inner
inward
within

פְּנִינִים 1036
rubies

פַּנֵּק 1036
Piel.
bring up, to

פַּס Ch. 1036
part

פַּסֵּג 1036
Piel.
consider, to

פִּסָּה 1036
handful

פָּסַח 1036
Kal.
halt, to
pass over, to
passing over
Niphal.
lame, to become
Piel.
leap, to

פֶּסַח 1036
passover
passover offering

פִּסֵּחַ 1037
lame

פְּסִילִים 1037
carved images
graven images
quarries

פַּסִּים 1037
colours
colours, divers

פָּסַל 1037
Kal.
grave, to
hew, to

פֶּסֶל 1037
carved image
graven image

פְּסַנְטֵרִין Ch. 1037
psaltery

פְּסַנְתֵּרִין Ch. 1037
psaltery

פָּסַס 1037
Kal.
fail, to

פָּעָה 1037
Kal.
cry, to

פָּעַל 1037
Kal.
commit, to
do, to
doer
*evil*doer
make, to
maker
ordain, to
work, to
worker

פֹּעַל 1038
act
deed
do, to
getting
maker
work

פְּעֻלָּה 1038
labour
reward
wages
work

פָּעַם 1038
Kal.
move, to
Niphal.
troubled, to be
Hithpael.
troubled, to be

פַּעַם 1038
anvil
corner
foot
footstep
going
*hundred*fold
now
*often*times
once
once †
once, this
order
rank
step
thrice †
time
time, second
time, this
* times, two
twice
wheel

פַּעֲמוֹן 1039
bell

פָּעַר 1039
Kal.
gape, to
open, to
open wide, to

פָּצָה 1039
Kal.
deliver, to
gape, to
open, to
rid, to
utter, to

פָּצַח 1039
Kal.
break forth, to
joy, to break forth into
noise, to make a loud
Piel.
break, to

פְּצִירָה 1039
file †

פָּצַל 1039
Piel.
pill, to

פְּצָלוֹת 1039
strakes

פָּצַם 1039
Kal.
break, to

פָּצַע 1039
Kal.
wound, to

פֶּצַע 1039
wound
wounding

פָּצַר 1039
Kal.
press, to
urge, to
Hiphil.
stubbornness

פָּקַד 1040
Kal.
appoint, to
at all
avenge, to
bestow, to
charge, to
charge, to give a
count, to
counted, to be
enjoin, to
go see, to
hurt, to
judgment, to do
look, to
make, to
miss, to
number, to
numbered, to be
officer
oversight, that had
punish, to
punish,† to
reckon, to
remember, to
remembrance, to call to
set, to
set over, to be
sum
surely
visit, to
want, to
Niphal.
appointed, to be
empty, to be
lack, to
means, by any
missed, to be
missing, to be
visited, to be
wanting, to be
Piel.
muster, to
Pual.
counted, to be
deprived, to be
Hiphil.
appoint, to
charge, to appoint to have the
commit, to
lay up, to
make governor
overseer, to make
ruler, to make
set, to
Hophal.
keep, to be delivered to
overseer
oversight, to have the
visited, is to be
Hithpael.
numbered, to be
Hothpael.
numbered, to be

פְּקֻדָּה 1041
account
charge
charge, that have the custody
laid up, that which...
numbers
office
officer
officer †
ordering
oversight
prison †
reckoning
visitation

פִּקָּדוֹן 1042
keep, that which was delivered to
store
that *which was delivered*

פְּקִדֻת 1042
ward

פְּקוֹד 1042
Pekod

פִּקּוּדִים 1042
commandments
precepts
statutes

פָּקַח 1042
Kal.
open, to
opening
Niphal.
opened, to be

פִּקֵּחַ 1042
seeing
wise

פְּקַח־קוֹחַ 1042
opening of the prison

פָּקִיד 1042
charge, which had the
governor
officer
overseer
set, *that* was

פְּקָעִים 1042
knops

פַּקֻּעֹת 1042
gourds

פַּר & פָּר 1042
bull
bullock
calf
ox
young *bullock*
young bullock †

פָּרָא 1043
Hiphil.
fruitful, to be

פֶּרֶא 1043
ass, wild
wild

פַּרְבָּר 1043
Parbar

פָּרַד 1043
Kal.
stretched
Niphal.
divided, to be
parted, to be
separate self, to
separated, to be
sever self, to
Piel.
separated, to be
Pual.
dispersed, to be
Hiphil.
part, to
separate, to
Hithpael.
joint, to be out of
scattered, to be
scattered abroad, to be
sundered, to be

פֶּרֶד 1044
mule

פִּרְדָּה 1044
mule

פְּרֻדוֹת 1044
seed

פַּרְדֵּס 1044
forest
orchard

פָּרָה 1044
Kal.
bear, to
bring forth, to
fruit, to bring
fruitful
fruitful, to be
grow, to
increase, to
increased, to be
Hiphil.
fruitful, to cause to be
fruitful, to make
increase, to

פָּרָה 1044
cow
heifer
kine

פְּרוּזִים 1044
villages

פַּרְוָר 1044
suburb

פָּרוּר 1044
pan
pot

פֵּרוֹת 1044
moles †

פְּרָז 1044
village

פְּרָזוֹן 1044
village

פְּרָזוֹת 1044
towns without walls
unwalled towns
unwalled villages

פְּרָזִי 1044
country
unwalled
village

צוֹם 1069
fast
fast,† to
fasting

צוּף 1069
Kal.
flow, to
Hiphil.
overflow, to make to
swim

צוּף 1069
*honey*comb
honeycomb †

צוּץ 1069
Kal.
blossom, to
Hiphil.
bloom, to
blossom, to
flourish, to
shewing self

צוּק 1 1069
Hiphil.
constrain, to
distress, to
lie sore, to
oppressor
press, to
straiten, to

צוּק 2 1069
Kal.
molten, to be
pour, to

צוֹק 1069
* troublous

צוּקָה 1069
anguish

צוּר 1069
Kal.
adversary
assault, to
beset, to
besiege, to
bind, to
bind up, to
cast, to
distress, to
fashion, to
fortify, to
inclose, to
put up in bags, to
siege, to lay

צוּר 1069
beauty
edge
* God
Helkath-hazzurim
* mighty God
* mighty one
rock
* sharp
stone
* strength
* strong

צוּרָה 1070
form

צַוְּרֹנִים 1070
neck

צוּת 1070
Hiphil.
burn, to

צַח 1070
clear
dry
plainly
white

צִחֶה 1070
dried up

צָחַח 1070
Kal.
whiter, to be

צְחִיחַ 1070
higher place
top

צְחִיחָה 1070
dry land

צְחִיחִי 1070
higher place

צַחֲנָה 1070
ill savour

צַחְצָחוֹת 1070
drought

צָחַק 1070
Kal.
laugh, to
Piel.
mock, to
play, to
sport, to make

צְחֹק 1070
laugh, to
laughed to scorn

צַחַר 1071
white

צָחֹר 1071
white

צִי 1071
ship

צַיִד 1071
* catcheth
food
* hunter
hunting
provision
took in hunting, that which he
venison
victuals

צַיָּד 1071
hunter

צֵידָה 1071
meat
provision
(כ') venison
victuals

צִיָּה 1071
barren
drought
dry
dry land
dry place
solitary place
wilderness

צָיוֹן 1071
dry place

צִיּוּן 1071
sign
title
waymark

צִיִּים 1071
desert, wild beasts of the
wilderness, inhabiting the
wilderness, that dwell in the

צִינֹק 1071
stocks

צִיץ 1071
blossom
flower
plate
wing

צִיצָה 1071
flower

צִיצִת 1071
fringe
lock

צִיר 1071
Hithpael.
ambassadors, to make as if had been

צִיר 1071
(כ') beauty
idol

צִיר 1071
ambassador
hinge
messenger
pain
pang
sorrow

צֵל 1072
defence
shade
shadow

צְלָא Ch. 1072
Pael.
pray, to

צָלָה 1072
Kal.
roast, to

צְלוּל 1072
cake

צָלַח 1072
Kal.
break out, to
come, to
come mightily, to
go over, to
good, to be
meet, to be
profitable, to be
prosper, to
prosperously
Hiphil.
effect, prosperously to
prosper, to
prosper, to cause to
prosper, to make to
prosperity, to send
prosperous
prosperous, to make

צְלַח Ch. 1072
Aphel.
promote, to
prosper, to

צֵלָחָה 1073
pan

צְלֹחִית 1073
cruse

צַלַּחַת 1073
bosom
dish

צָלִי 1073
roast

צָלִיל 1073
cake

צָלַל 1 1073
Kal.
quiver, to
tingle, to

צָלַל 2 1073
Kal.
sink, to

צָלַל 3 1073
Kal.
dark, to begin to be
Hiphil.
shadowing

צֵלֶל 1073
shadow

צֶלֶם 1073
image
shew, vain

צְלֵם & צֶלֶם Ch.
..............1073
form
image

צַלְמָוֶת 1073
shadow of death

צָלַע 1073
Kal.
halt, to

צֵלָע 1073
beam
board
chamber
corner
* halting
leaf
plank
rib
side
side chamber

צֶלַע 1074
adversity
halt, to
halting

צְלָצַל 1074
cymbal
locust
shadowing
spear

צָמֵא 1074
Kal.
athirst, to be
thirst, to
thirst, to suffer
thirsty, to be

צָמָא 1074
thirst
thirsty

צָמֵא 1074
thirst
thirsteth, that
thirsty

צִמְאָה 1074
thirst

צִמָּאוֹן 1074
drought
dry ground
thirsty land

צָמַד 1074
Niphal.
join self, to
joined, to be
Pual.
fastened
Hiphil.
frame, to

צֶמֶד 1074
acre
couple
together
two *asses*
yoke
yoke of oxen

צָמָה 1074
thirst

צַמָּה 1074
locks

צִמּוּקִים 1074
raisins, bunches of
raisins, clusters of

צָמַח 1074
Kal.
bring forth, to
grow, to
grow up, to
grown up, to be
spring, to
spring forth, to
spring up, to
Piel.
grow again, to
grown, to be
Hiphil.
bear, to
bring forth, to
bud, to
bud forth, to cause to
bud, to make to
grow, to cause to
grow, to make to
grow up, to cause to
spring forth, to cause to
spring up, to

צֶמַח 1075
branch
Branch
bud
grew upon, that which
grew, where
spring
springing

צָמִיד 1075
bracelet
covering

צַמִּים 1075
robber

צְמִיתֻת 1075
ever

צָמַק 1075
Kal.
dry

צֶמֶר 1075
wool
woollen

צַמֶּרֶת 1075
highest branch
top

צָמַת 1075
Kal.
cut off, to
Niphal.
cut off, to be
vanish, to
Piel.
consume, to
Pilel.
cut off, to
Hiphil.
cut off, to
destroy, to

צֵן 1075
thorn

צֹנֵא & צֹנֶה .. 1075
sheep

צִנָּה 1075
hook

צִנָּה 1075
buckler
shield
target

צִנָּה 1076
cold

צָנוֹף 1076
diadem

צִנּוֹר 1076
gutter
waterspout

צָנַח 1076
Kal.
fasten, to
light *from off*, to

צְנִינִים 1076
thorns

צָנִיף 1076
diadem
hood
mitre

צָנַם 1076
Kal.
withered

צָנַע 1076
Kal.
lowly
Hiphil.
humbly

צָנַף 1076
Kal.
attired, to be
surely
turn, to violently

צְנֵפָה 1076
* toss

צִנְצֶנֶת 1076
pot

צַנְתָּרוֹת 1076
pipes

צָעַד 1076
Kal.
go, to
march, to
march through, to
run over, to
Hiphil.
bring, to

צַעַד 1076
* go
going
pace
step

צְעָדָה 1076
going
ornament of the legs

צָעָה 1076
Kal.
captive exile
travelling
wander, to
wanderer
Piel.
wander, to cause to

צָעוֹר 1076
little one

צָעִיף 1076
vail

צָעִיר 1076
least
little
little one
small
small one
young †
younger
youngest

צְעִירָה 1077
youth

צָעַן 1077
Kal.
taken down, to be

צַעֲצֻעִים 1077
image *work*

צָעַק 1077
Kal.
at all
cry, to
cry out, to
Niphal.
called together, to be
gather, to
gather selves together, to
gathered together, to be
Piel.
cry, to
Hiphil.
call together, to

צְעָקָה 1077
cry
crying

צָעַר 1077
Kal.
brought low, to be
little one
small, to be

צָפַד 1077
Kal.
cleave, to

צָפָה 1077
Kal.
behold, to
look well, to
Ramathaim - zophim
waited for
watch, to
watch, to keep the
watchman
Zophim
Piel.
cover, to
espy, to
garnish, to
look up, to
overlay, to
watch, to
watchman
Pual.
covered
overlaid

צָפָה 1078
* swimmest

צִפּוּי 1078
covering
overlaying

צָפוֹן 1078
north
north side
north wind
northern
northward

צְפוֹנִי 1079
northern

צְפוּעַ 1079
dung

צִפּוֹר 1079
bird
fowl
sparrow

צַפַּחַת 1079
cruse

צְפִיָּה 1079
watching

צַפִּיחִת 1079
wafers

צָפִין 1079
hid

צָפִיעַ 1079
dung

צָפִיר 1079
goat
he *goat*
he goat

צְפִיר Ch. 1079
he *goat*

צְפִירָה 1079
diadem
morning

צָפִית 1079
watchtower

צָפַן 1080
Kal.
esteem, to
hid
hidden one
hide, to
hide selves, to
keep secretly, to
lay up, to
lurk privily, to
secret
secret place
set, to be privily
Niphal.
hid, to be
hidden, to be
Hiphil.
hide, to
(כ׳) hide selves, to

צֶפַע 1080
cockatrice

צִפְעֹנִי 1080
adder
cockatrice

צְפִעוֹת 1080
issue

צָפַף 1080
Pilpel.
chatter, to
peep, to
whisper, to

צַפְצָפָה 1080
willow tree

צָפַר 1080
Kal.
depart early, to

צְפַר Ch. 1080
bird
fowl

צְפַרְדֵּעַ 1080
frog

צִפֹּרֶן 1080
nail
point

צֶפֶת 1080
chapiter

צִקְלוֹן 1080
husk

צַר & צָר 1080
adversary
afflicted
affliction
anguish
distress
enemy
foe
small
sorrow
strait
tribulation
trouble

צַר 1081
close
narrow

צֹר 1081
flint
sharp stone

צָרַב 1081
Niphal.
burned, to be

צָרֶבֶת 1081
burning
inflammation

צָרָה 1081
adversary
adversity
affliction
anguish
distress
tribulation
trouble

צְרוֹר 1082
bag
* bindeth
bundle
grain, least
stone, small

צָרַח 1082
Kal.
cry, to
Hiphil.
roar, to

צְרִי & צֳרִי .. 1082
balm

צְרִיחַ 1082
high place
hold

צֹרֶךְ 1082
need

צָרַע 1082
Kal.
leper
leprous
Pual.
leper
leprous

צִרְעָה 1082
hornet

צָרַעַת 1082
leprosy

צָרַף 1082
Kal.
cast, to
finer
founder
goldsmith
melt, to
pure
purge away, to
refine, to
try, to
Niphal.
tried, to be
Piel.
refiner

צֹרְפִי 1082
goldsmith

צָרַר 1083
Kal.
adversary
afflict, to
bind, to
bind up, to
distress, to be in
distressed, to be
enemy
narrower
oppress, to
shut up, to
strait, to be in a
trouble, to be in
vex, to
Pual.
bound up

Hiphil.
affliction, to be in
besiege, to
distress
distress, to
distress, to bring
pangs
vex, to

קֵא..........1083
vomit

קָאַת..........1083
cormorant
pelican

קַב..........1083
cab

קָבַב..........1083
Kal.
at all
curse, to

קֵבָה..........1083
maw

קֹבָה..........1083
belly

קֻבָּה..........1083
tent

קִבּוּץ..........1083
company

קְבוּרָה..........1083
burial
burying place
grave
sepulchre

קָבַל..........1083
Piel.
choose, to
receive, to
take
undertake, to
Hiphil.
hold, to
hold, to take

קְבַל Ch...........1084
Pael.
receive, to
take, to

קְבֵל & קֳבֵל Ch. 1084
according to †
as †
because †
before
cause, † for this
forasmuch as †
means, † by this
over against
reason of, by
that †
therefore †
though †
wherefore †

קֳבָל..........1084
before

קְבָל..........1084
war

קָבַע..........1084
Kal.
rob, to
spoil, to

קֻבַּעַת..........1084
dregs

קָבַץ..........1084
Kal.
assemble, to
gather, to
gather together, to
gather up, to
heap, to
Niphal.
assemble, to
assemble selves, to
gather selves together, to
gathered, to be
gathered together, to be
resort, to
Piel.
bring together, to
gather, to
gather together, to
gather up, to
surely
take up, to
Pual.
gathered, to be
Hithpael.
gather selves, to
gather selves together, to
gather together, to
gathered together, to be

קְבֻצָה..........1085
* gather

קָבַר..........1085
Kal.
any wise, in
* buried, to be
bury, to
Niphal.
buried, to be
Piel.
burier
bury, to
Pual.
buried, to be

קֶבֶר..........1086
burying place
grave
Kibroth-*hattaavah*
sepulchre

קָדַד..........1086
Kal.
bow down head, to
bow the head, to
stoop, to

קִדָּה..........1087
cassia

קְדוּמִים..........1087
ancient

קָדוֹשׁ..........1087
holy
Holy one
saint

קָדַח..........1087
Kal.
burn, to
kindle, to
kindled, to be

קַדַּחַת..........1087
burning ague
fever

קָדִים..........1087
east
east wind
eastward
east*ward*

קַדִּישׁ Ch...........1088
holy
Holy one
saint

קָדַם..........1088
Piel.
come before, to
disappoint,† to
flee before, to
go before, to
meet, to
prevent, to
Hiphil.
prevent, to

קֶדֶם..........1088
aforetime
ancient
ancient time
before
east
east side
eastward
eternal
* ever
everlasting
forward
old
past

קֵדֶם..........1089
east
east end
east part
east side
eastward

קֳדָם Ch...........1089
before
from
* from †
* I
* me
* of †
* pleased, † it
presence
* thought, I

קַדְמָה..........1089
afore
antiquity
former estate
old estate

קַדְמָה Ch...........1089
afore*time*
ago

קִדְמָה..........1089
east
eastward

קַדְמוֹן..........1089
east

קַדְמוֹנִי..........1089
ancient
before, they that went
east
former
old
old, things of

קַדְמַי Ch..........1089
first

קָדְקֹד..........1089
crown
crown of the head
pate
scalp
top of head

קָדַר..........1090
Kal.
black, to be
blackish, to be
dark, to be
darkened, to be
heavily
mourn, to
Hiphil.
dark, to make
mourn, to cause to
Hithpael.
black, to be

קַדְרוּת..........1090
blackness

קְדֹרַנִּית..........1090
mournfully

קָדֵשׁ & קָדַשׁ 1090
Kal.
defiled, to be
hallowed, to be
holier, to be
holy, to be
sanctified, to be
Niphal.
hallowed, to be
sanctified, to be
Piel.
consecrate, to
hallow, to
holy, to keep
holy place
prepare, to
proclaim
sanctify, to
Pual.
consecrated, to be
sanctified, to be
sanctified one
Hiphil.
appoint, to
bid, to
dedicate, to
hallow, to
prepare, to
sanctify, to
wholly
Hithpael.
kept, to be
purified, to be
sanctified, to be
sanctify selves, to

קָדֵשׁ..........1091
sodomite
unclean

קֹדֶשׁ..........1091
consecrated
consecrated things
dedicated
dedicated things
hallowed
hallowed things
holiness
holy
* holy day
holy portion
holy thing
* most holy
* most holy things
saint
sanctuary

קְדֵשָׁה..........1094
harlot
whore

קָהָה..........1094
Kal.
edge, to be set on
Piel.
blunt, to be

קָהַל..........1094
Niphal.
assemble selves, to
assemble together, to
assembled, to be
gather selves together, to
gathered, to be
gathered together, to be
Hiphil.
assemble, to
gather, to
gather together, to
gathered together, is to be

קָהָל..........1094
assembly
company
congregation
multitude

קְהִלָּה..........1095
assembly
congregation

קֹהֶלֶת..........1095
preacher

קַו & קָו..........1095
line; rule
* meted out

קוֹא..........1095
Kal.
spue, to
Hiphil.
spue out, to
vomit, to
vomit out, to
vomit up, to
vomit up again, to

קוֹבַע..........1095
helmet

קָוָה..........1095
Kal.
wait for, to
wait on, to
wait upon, to
Niphal.
gathered, to be
gathered together, to be
Piel.
look, to
patiently
tarry, to
wait, to
wait for, to
wait on, to

קָוֶה..........1096
line

קוֹחַ 1096
prison

קוּט 1 1096
Kal.
grieved, to be
* very
Niphal.
lothe selves, to
Hithpolel.
grieved, to be

קוּט 2 1096
Kal.
cut off, to be

קוֹל 1096
aloud †
bleating
crackling
cry
cry out, † to
fame
lightness
lowing
noise
* peace, † to hold
proclaim
proclamation
sing, † to
sound
speak,† to
thunder
thundering
voice
yell, † to

קוּם 1099
Kal.
abide, to
arise, to
arise up, to
assured, to be
* clearer, to be
continue
* dim, to be
endure, to
enemy
established, to be
get up, to
hold, to
performed, to be
remain, to
rise, to
rise up, to
rise up again, to
rise up against, to
risen, to be
risen up, to be
set, to be
stand, to
stand up, to
succeed, to
sure, to be made
surely
up
up, to be
uprising
Piel.
confirm, to
decree, to
enjoin, to
ordain, to
perform, to
stablish, to
strengthen, to
Polel.
raise up, to
risen up, to be
Hiphil.
accomplish, to
confirm, to
continue, to
establish, to
good, to make
help up, to
lift up, to
lift up again, to help to
make, to
newly, but
perform, to
pitch, to
raise, to
raise up, to
rear, to
rear up, to
reared up, to be
rouse up, to
set, to
set up, to
stablish, to
stand, to make to
stir up, to
surely
uphold, to
Hophal.
performed, to be
raised up, to be
reared up, to be
Hithpael.
rise up, to
rise up against, to

קוּם Ch. 1103
P'al.
arise, to
rise up, to
stand, to
Pael.
establish, to
Aphel.
appoint, to
establish, to
make, to
raise up self, to
set, to
set up, to
Hophal.
stand, to be made to

קוֹמָה 1103
* along
height
high
stature
tall

קוֹמְמִיּוּת 1104
upright

קוֹן...........1104
Polel.
lament, to
mourning woman

קוֹעַ 1104
Koa

קוֹף 1104
ape

קוּץ 1 1104
Hiphil.
arise, to
awake, to
awake, to be
wake, to
watch, to

קוּץ 2 1104
Kal.
summer, to

קוּץ 3 1104
Kal.
abhor, to
distressed, to be
grieved, to be
loathe, to
weary, to be
Hiphil.
vex, to

קוֹץ 1104
thorn

קְוֻצּוֹת 1104
locks

קוּר 1104
Kal.
dig, to
Hiphil.
cast out, to
Pilpel.
breaking down
destroy, to

קוֹרָה 1104
beam
roof

קוּרִים 1104
web

קוֹשׁ..........1104
Kal.
snare, to lay a

קַט...........1104
very

קֶטֶב..........1105
destroying
destruction

קֹטֶב..........1105
destruction

קְטוֹרָה 1105
incense

קָטַל 1105
Kal.
kill, to
slay, to

קְטַל Ch. 1105
P'al.
slain, to be
slay, to
Pael.
slay, to
Ithp'al.
slain, to be
Ithpael.
slain, to be

קֶטֶל 1105
slaughter

קָטֹן 1105
Kal.
small thing, to be a
worthy, to be not
Hiphil.
small, to make

קָטָן 1105
least
less
little
little one
small
small quantity
small things
smallest
young
younger
youngest

קָטֹן 1105
least
less
lesser
little;—l. one
small
small one
younger
youngest

קָטַף 1106
Kal.
crop off, to
cut up, to
pluck, to
Niphal.
cut down, to be

קָטַר 1 1106
Piel.
burn, to
burn incense, to
burning incense
offer a sacrifice, to
offer incense, to
offering incense
Pual.
perfumed
Hiphil.
burn, to
burn incense, to
burn incense upon, to
burn sacrifice, to
kindle, to
offer, to
Hophal.
burnt, to be
incense

קָטַר 2 1106
Kal.
joined

קְטַר Ch. 1107
doubt
joint

קִטֵּר 1107
incense

קְטֹרֶת........1107
incense
perfume
sweet incense

קִיא 1107
vomit

קִיָּה 1107
Kal.
spue

קַיִט Ch.......1107
summer

קִיטוֹר 1107
smoke
vapour

קִים 1107
substance

קְיָם Ch.......1107
decree
statute

קַיָּם Ch.......1107
stedfast
sure

קִימָה 1107
rising up

קַיִן...........1107
spear

קִינָה.........1107
lamentation

קַיִץ 1107
summer
summer fruit
summer house

קִיצוֹן 1108
outmost
uttermost

קִיקָיוֹן........1108
gourd

קִיקָלוֹן 1108
shameful spewing

קִיר 1108
mason †
side
town
* very
wall

קִיתָרֹס Ch....1108
harp

קַל............1108
light
swift
swiftly

קָל Ch. 1108
sound
voice

קָלַהּ..........1108
Niphal.
gathered together, to be

קָלָה 1 1108
Kal.
dried
parched
roast, to
Niphal.
loathsome

קָלָה 2 1108
Niphal.
base
contemned, to be
despised, to be
esteemed, to be lightly
vile, to seem
Hiphil.
set light (*by one*), to

קָלוֹן.........1108
confusion
dishonour
ignominy
reproach
shame

קַלַּחַת........1109
caldron

קָלַט 1109
Kal.
lacking in his parts

קָלִיא & קָלִי..1109
corn, parched

קָלַל 1109
Kal.
abated, to be
despised, to be
esteemed, to be lightly
swifter, to be
vile, to be
Niphal.
easy, to be
light thing, to be a
light thing, to seem a
* slight*ly*
swift, to be
vile, to be more
Piel.
curse, to
revile, to
vile, to make
Pilpel.
bright, to make
whet, to
Pual.
accursed, to be
cursed, to be
Hiphil.
afflict, to lightly
contempt, to bring into
despise, to
ease, to
easier, to be
lighten, to
lighter, to make
lighter, to make somewhat
set light (*by one*), to
Hithpalpel.
move lightly, to

קָלָל 1109
burnished
polished

קְלָלָה 1110
accursed
curse
cursing

קָלַס 1110
Piel.
scorn, to
Hithpael.
mock, to
scoff, to

קֶלֶס 1110
derision

קַלָּסָה 1110
mocking

קָלַע 1110
Kal.
carve, to
sling, to
sling out, to
Piel.
sling, to
sling out, to

קֶלַע 1110
sling
sling*stone*

קַלָּע 1110
slinger

קְלָעִים 1110
hangings
leaves (*of a door*)

קְלֹקֵל 1110
light

קִלְּשׁוֹן 1110
forks

קָמָה 1110
corn
grown up
stalk
standing corn

קִימוֹשׁ & קִמּוֹשׁ 1110
nettles

קֶמַח 1110
flour
meal

קָמַט 1110
Kal.
wrinkles, to fill with
Pual.
cut down, to be

קָמַל 1111
Kal.
hewn down, to be
wither, to

קָמַץ 1111
Kal.
handful, to take an
take *a handful*, to

קֹמֶץ 1111
hand*ful*
handful

קִמְּשׁוֹן 1111
thorns

קֵן 1111
nest
room

קָנָא 1111
Piel.
envious, to be
envy, to
jealous, to be
jealousy, to move to
jealousy, to provoke to
very
zeal
zealous, to be
Hiphil.
jealousy, to move to
jealousy, to provoke to

קְנָא Ch. 1111
P'al.
buy, to

קַנָּא 1111
jealous

קִנְאָה 1111
envied
envy
jealousy
* sake
zeal

קָנָה 1 1111
Kal.
attain, to
buy, to
buyer
get, to
owner
possess, to
possessor
purchase, to
recover, to
redeem, to
surely
verily
Niphal.
bought, to be
possessed, to be
Hiphil.
keep cattle, to teach to

קָנָה 2 1112
Hiphil.
jealousy, to provoke to

קָנֶה 1112
balance
bone
branch
calamus
cane
reed
* spearman
stalk

קַנּוֹא 1112
jealous

קִנְיָן 1112
getting
goods
* money, with
riches
substance

קִנָּמוֹן 1112
cinnamon

קָנַן 1113
Piel.
nest, to make
Pual.
nest, to make

קָסַם 1113
Kal.
divination
divine, to
diviner
prudent
soothsayer
use *divination*, to

קֶסֶם 1113
divination
divination, reward of
divine sentence
witchcraft

קָסַס 1113
Poel.
cut off, to

קֶסֶת 1113
inkhorn

קַעֲקַע 1113
marks †

קְעָרָה 1113
charger
dish

קָפָא 1113
Kal.
congealed, to be
(כ') dark
settled, that are
Hiphil.
curdle, to

קִפָּאוֹן 1113
dark

קָפַד 1113
Piel.
cut off, to

קִפֹּד 1113
bittern

קְפָדָה 1113
destruction

קִפּוֹז 1113
owl, great

קָפַץ 1113
Kal.
shut, to
shut up, to
stop, to
Niphal.
taken out of the way, to be
Piel.
skipping

קֵץ 1113
after
border
end
*in*finite
* process
utmost border

קָצַב 1114
Kal.
cut down, to
shorn

קֶצֶב 1114
bottom
size

קָצָה 1114
Kal.
cutting off
Piel.
cut off, to
cut short, to
Hiphil.
scrape, to
scrape off, to

קָצֶה 1114
coast
corner
edge
end
lowest part
quarters
selvedge
uttermost part

קָצָה 1114
after
border
brim
brink
edge
end
frontier
outmost coast
outside
quarter
shore
side
* some
utmost
utmost part
uttermost
uttermost part

קְצָה 1115
end
*in*finite

קֵצוֹ 1115
end

קְצָוָה 1115
edge
end
uttermost part

קֶצַח 1115
fitches

קָצִין 1115
captain
guide
prince
ruler

קְצִיעוֹת 1115
cassia

קָצִיר 1115
bough
branch
harvest
harvest man

קָצַע 1115
Hiphil.
scraped, to cause to be
Hophal.
corner

קָצַף 1115
Kal.
angry, to be
displeased, to be
wrath come
wroth, to be
Hiphil.
anger, to
wrath, to provoke to
Hithpael.
fret selves, to

קְצַף Ch. 1116
P'al.
furious, to be

קֶצֶף 1116
foam
indignation
* sore
wrath

קְצַף Ch. 1116
wrath

קְצָפָה 1116
bark*ed*

קָצַץ 1116
Kal.
cut off, to
* utmost
Piel.
cut, to
cut asunder, to
cut in pieces, to
cut in sunder, to
cut off, to
Pual.
cut off

קְצַץ Ch. 1116
Pael.
cut off, to
קָצַר 1116
Kal.
at all
cut down, to
discouraged, to be much
grieved, to be
harvestman
lothe, to
mower
reap, to
reaper
shortened, to be
* shorter
shorter, to be
straitened, to be
troubled, to be
vexed, to be
waxed short, to be
Piel.
shorten, to
Hiphil.
(כ') reap, to
shorten, to
קָצֵר 1117
few
hasty
small
soon
קֹצֶר 1117
anguish
קְצָת 1117
end
part
* some
קְצָת Ch. 1117
end
partly
קַר 1117
cold
(כ') excellent
קֹר 1117
cold
קָרָא 1 1117
Kal.
bewray (*self*), to
bidden, that are
call, to
call for, to
call upon, to
called, to be
calling
cry, to
cry unto, to
crying
En-hakkore
(כ') famous
famous,† to be
give *names*, to
guest
invite, to
mentioned, to be
name, to
name, to give a
named, to be
preach, to
proclaim, to
proclaiming
proclamation, to make
pronounce, to
publish, to
read, to
reading
renowned
say, to
Niphal.
call selves, to
called, to be
called forth, to be
cried, to be
famous, to be
named, to be
named,† to be
read, to
Pual.
called, to be
קָרָא 2 1122
Kal.
* against
* against he come
befall, to
come, to be
come upon, to
coming
fall out, to
happen, to
help, to
meet, to
meeting
seek, to
* to
* way, in the
Niphal.
chance, to
* chance, by
happen to be, to
meet, to
Hiphil.
come, to cause to
קְרָא Ch. 1123
P'al.
cry, to
read, to
Ithp'al.
called, to be
קֹרֵא 1123
partridge
קָרֵב & קָרַב .. 1123
Kal.
approach, to
come, to
come near, to
come nigh, to
draw near, to
draw nigh, to
go, to
hand, to be at
joined, to be
near, to be
offer, to
stand by, to
Niphal.
brought, to be
Piel.
approach, to cause to
bring near, to
go near, to
hand, to be at
join, to
produce, to
ready, to make
Hiphil.
bring, to
bring forth, to
bring near, to
brought, to cause to be
come near, to be
come near, to cause to
draw near, to cause to
draw nigh, to
offer, to
offering
present, to
presented, to be
take, to
קָרֵב 1125
approach
came, that
come near, which
* cometh any thing near
cometh nigh, that
drew near
קְרֵב Ch. 1125
P'al.
come, to
come near, to
Pael.
offer, to
Aphel.
bring near, to
offer, to
קְרָב 1125
battle
war
קְרָב Ch. 1125
war
קֶרֶב 1125
among
before
bowels
charge, unto
* eat,† to
* eat up,† to
* heart
* him
in
inward
inward part
inward thought
* inwardly
inwards
midst
* out of
purtenance
therein
through
within self
קִרְבָה 1126
approaching
draw near, to
קָרְבָּן 1126
oblation
offered, that it is
offering
קֻרְבַּן 1127
offering
קַרְדֹּם 1127
ax
קָרָה 1127
cold
קָרָה 1127
Kal.
befall, to
come to pass unto, to
happen unto, to
meet, to
was, to light on
Niphal.
come, to
happen, to
meet, to
Piel.
beams, to lay
beams, to make
floor, to
Hiphil.
appoint, to
bring, to
good speed, to send
קָרֶה 1127
uncleanness that chanceth
קָרוֹב 1127
allied
approach
come nigh, them that
hand, at
* kin,† any of
kinsfolk
kinsman
near
near of kin
near, that is
neighbour
* newly
next
next, that is
nigh
nigh at hand
ready, more
short
shortly
קָרַח 1128
Kal.
bald, to make (*oneself*)
make *baldness*, to
Niphal.
bald, to make self
Hiphil.
bald, to make self
Hophal.
bald, made
קֶרַח 1128
crystal
frost
ice
קֹרַח 1128
ice
קֵרֵחַ 1128
bald
bald head
קָרְחָה 1128
bald
baldness
* utterly
קָרַחַת 1128
bald head
bare within
קְרִי 1128
contrary
קָרִיא 1128
famous
(כ') renowned
קְרִיאָה 1128
preaching
קִרְיָה 1128
city
קִרְיָא & קִרְיָה Ch. 1128
city
קָרַם 1129
Kal.
cover, to
קָרַן 1129
Kal.
shine, to
Hiphil.
horns, to have
קֶרֶן 1129
* hill
horn
קֶרֶן Ch. 1129
cornet
horn
קָרַס 1129
Kal.
stoop, to
קְרָסִים 1129
taches
קַרְסֻלַּיִם 1129
feet
קָרַע 1129
Kal.
cut out, to
rend, to
rent
surely
tear, to
Niphal.
rent, to be
קְרָעִים 1130
pieces
rags
קָרַץ 1130
Kal.
move, to
wink, to
Pual.
formed, to be
קֶרֶץ 1130
destruction
קְרַץ Ch. 1130
* accuse,† to
קַרְקַע 1130
bottom
floor
* floor, one side of the
קֶרֶשׁ 1130
bench
board
קֶרֶת 1130
city
קַשְׂוָה & קָשָׂה 1130
cover
cup
קְשִׂיטָה 1130
money, piece of
silver, piece of
קַשְׂקֶשֶׂת 1131
mail
scale
קַשׁ 1131
stubble
קִשֻּׁאִים 1131
cucumbers

קָשַׁב 1131
Kal.
hearken, to
Hiphil.
attend, to
hear, to cause to
heard, to cause to be
hearken, to
heed, to give
incline, to
mark, to
mark well, to
regard, to

קֶשֶׁב 1131
* diligently
hearing
heed, much
regarded, that

קַשֻּׁב 1131
attent
attentive

קַשָּׁב 1131
attentive

קָשָׁה 1131
Kal.
cruel, to be
fiercer, to be
hard, to be
hard, to seem
sore, to be
Niphal.
hardly bestead
Piel.
hard *labour*, to have
Hiphil.
grievous, to make
hard *labour*, to be in
hard thing, to *ask* a
harden, to
hardly, would
stiff, to make
stiffen, to
stiff*necked*, to be

קָשֶׁה 1131
churlish
cruel
grievous
hard
hard things
hard*hearted*
heavy
impudent †
obstinate
prevailed
rough
roughly
sore
sorrowful
stiff
stiff*necked*
stubborn
* trouble,† in

קְשׁוֹט Ch..... 1132
truth

קָשַׁח 1132
Hiphil.
harden, to
hardened, to be

קֹשְׁטְ 1132
certainty

קֹשְׁטְ 1132
truth

קְשִׁי 1132
stubbornness

קָשַׁר 1132
Kal.
bind, to
bound
bound up
conspiracy, to make a
conspirator
conspire, to
make *conspiracy*, to
stronger
work *treason*, to
Niphal.
joined together, to be
knit, to be
Piel.
bind, to
Pual.
stronger
Hithpael.
conspire, to

קֶשֶׁר 1132
confederacy
conspiracy
treason

קִשֻּׁרִים 1132
attire
headbands

קָשַׁשׁ 1132
Kal.
gather together, to
Poel.
gather, to
Hithpoel.
gather selves together, to

קֶשֶׁת 1133
archer
* archer
* arrow †
bow
bow*man*
bow*shot*

קַשָּׁת 1133
archer

קַתְרוֹס Ch.... 1133
harp

רָאָה 1133
Kal.
advise self, to
approve, to
behold, to
beholding
certainly
consider, to
discern, to
enjoy, to
espy, to
experience, to have
foresee, to
gaze, to
heed, to take
* in *presence*, to be
indeed
Jehovah-jireh
* joyfully
Lo
look, to
look on, to
look out, to
look up, to
look upon, to
mark, to
meet
* near, to be
perceive, to
provide, to
regard, to
respect, to
respect, to have
see, to
seeing
seer
shew, to
* sight of others
spy, to
stare, to
surely
* think, to
view, to
visions
Niphal.
appear, to
present self, to
seem, to
seen, to be
shew self, to
shewed, to be
spied, to be
Pual.
seen, to be
Hiphil.
enjoy, to make to
see, to cause to
see, to let
shew, to
Hophal.
shewed, to be
Hithpael.
look one another, to
look one upon another, to
see one another, to

רָאָה 1141
glede

רָאֶה 1141
see

רֹאֶה 1141
vision

רְאוּת 1141
beholding

רְאִי 1141
looking glass

רֳאִי 1141
gazingstock
look to, to
see, to
seen, to be
seeth, that

רִאישׁוֹן (כ׳) .. 1141
first

רְאִית (כ׳) 1141
beholding

רָאַם 1141
Kal.
lifted up, to be

רְאֵם 1141
unicorn

רָאמוֹת 1142
coral

רֵאשׁ 1142
poverty

רֵאשׁ Ch. 1142
chief
head
sum

רֹאשׁ 1142
band
beginning
behead, to
captain
chapiter
chief
chief man
chief things
chiefest place
company
end
* every *man*
excellest
first
forefront
head
height
high, on
high *priest*
highest part
* lead, to
* poor
principal
ruler
sum
top

רֹאשׁ 1145
gall
hemlock
poison
venom

רֵאשָׁה 1145
beginning

רֹאשָׁה 1145
head*stone*

רִאשׁוֹן 1145
ancestor
before
before, that were
beforetime
beginning
eldest
first
first †
fore*fathers*
foremost
former
former things
old time, of
past

רִאשֹׁנִי 1147
first

רֵאשִׁית 1147
beginning
chief
chiefest
first
first part
first time
first*fruits*
firstfruits
principal thing

רַאֲשֹׁת 1147
bolster

רַב 1147
abound
abundance, in
abundant
abundantly
Bath-rabbim
captain
elder; common
enough
exceedingly
full
great;—g. multitude
great man
great one
greatly
increase
long
long enough
long *time*
manifold
many
many a time
many, do
many, have
many things
master
mighty
more
much
much, too
much, very
multiply
multitude
officer
often*times*
plenteous
populous
prince
process of *time*
Rab-*mag*
Rab-*saris*
*ship*master
suffice
sufficient

רַב 1150
archer

רַב Ch. 1150
captain
chief
great
lord
master
stout

רֹב 1150
abundance
abundantly
all
* common *sort*
excellent
great
great number
greatly
greatness
huge
increased, to be
long
many
more in number
most
much
multitude
plentifully
plenty
very *age*

רָבַב[1] 1151
Kal.
increased, to be
manifold, to be
many, to be
more, to be
multiplied, to be
Pual.
ten thousands

רָבַב[2] 1151
Kal.
shoot, to

רְבָבָה 1151
many
millions
* multiply
ten thousand

רָבַד 1151
Kal.
deck, to

רָבָה 1151
Kal.
archer †
authority, to be in
excel, to
greater, to be
* greatness
grow up, to
increase, to
increased, to be
long, to be
many, to be
more in number, to be
much, to be so
much greater, to be
multiplied, to be
multiply, to
* process *of time*
Piel.
bring up, to
increase, to
nourish, to
Hiphil.
abundance
abundance, to bring in
* abundantly
* continue, to
enlarge, to
exceeding
exceedingly
exceedingly †
full of, to be
great
* great
great, to make
greatly
heap, to
increase, to
* many
* many, to be
* many a time
many, to give
many, to have
many, to make
many, to use
* more
* more and more
more, any
more, to give
more, to give the
more, to have
* much
much, to ask
much, to gather
much more
much, to take
much, to yield
multiply, to
multiply, to make to
multiplying
over much
plenteous
plenty
sore
store
throughly
very

רְבָה Ch. 1153
P'al.
grow, to
grown, to be
Pael.
great man, to make a

רִבּוֹא & רִבּוֹ ..1153
*eigh*teen thousand
*for*ty thousand
(כ') great things
* sixscore thousand †
ten thousand
threescore thousand †
*twen*ty thousand

רִבּוֹ Ch. 1153
* ten thousand times ten thousand

רְבוּ Ch. 1153
greatness
majesty

רִבּוֹת 1153
*twen*ty thousand
* twenty thousand

רְבִיבִים 1153
showers

רָבִיד 1153
chain

רְבִיעִי 1153
foursquare
fourth
fourth part

רְבִיעַי Ch. 1154
fourth

רָבַךְ 1154
Hophal.
baken
fried
fried, that which is

רָבַע [1] 1154
Kal.
lie down to, to
Hiphil.
gender, to let

רָבַע [2] 1154
Kal.
foursquare
square
squared
Pual.
foursquare
square

רֶבַע 1154
lying down

רֶבַע 1154
fourth part
sides
squares

רֹבַע 1154
fourth part

רִבֵּעִים 1154
fourth

רָבַץ 1154
Kal.
couch, to
couch down, to
fall down, to
lie, to
lie down, to
sit, to
Hiphil.
fold, to make a
lay
lie down, to cause to
lie down, to make to
rest, to make to

רֵבֶץ 1154
lay, where each
lie down in, to
resting place

רַבְרַב Ch. 1154
great
great things
great things, very

רַבְרְבָן Ch. ..1154
lords
princes

רֶגֶב 1154
clods

רָגַז 1155
Kal.
afraid, to be
awe, to stand in
disquieted, to be
fall out, to
fret, to
move, to
moved, to be
quake, to
rage, to
tremble, to
troubled, to be
wroth, to be
Hiphil.
disquiet, to
provoke, to
shake, to
tremble, to make to
Hithpael.
rage

רְגַז Ch. 1155
Aphel.
wrath, to provoke unto

רְגַז Ch. 1155
rage

רַגָּז 1155
trembling

רֹגֶז 1155
fear
noise
rage
trouble
troubling
wrath

רָגְזָה 1155
trembling

רָגַל 1155
Kal.
backbite, to
Piel.
espy out, to
search, to
slander, to
spies
spy, to
spy out, to
view, to
Tiphal.
go, to teach to

רֶגֶל 1155
* able to endure, be
* according as
* after
*broken*footed
* coming
* follow
foot
foot*stool*
* great toe †
* haunt
* journey
legs
* piss †
* possession
times

רְגַל Ch. 1157
foot

רַגְלִי 1157
foot, on
foot*men*
footmen

רָגַם 1157
Kal.
certainly
stone, to

רִגְמָה 1157
council

רָגַן 1157
Kal.
murmur, to
Niphal.
murmur, to

רָגַע 1157
Kal.
broken, to be
divide, to
Niphal.
rest, to
Hiphil.
ease, to find
moment, to be a
rest, to
rest, cause to
rest, to give
rest, to make to
suddenly, to make

רָגֵעַ 1157
quiet, that are

רֶגַע 1157
instant
moment
space
suddenly

רָגַשׁ 1158
Kal.
rage, to

רְגַשׁ Ch. 1158
Aphel.
assemble, to
assemble together, to

רֶגֶשׁ 1158
company

רִגְשָׁה 1158
counsel

רָדַד 1158
Kal.
spent, to be
subdue, to
Hiphil.
spread, to

רָדָה [1] 1158
Kal.
dominion, to come to have
dominion, to have
prevail against, to
reign, to
rule, to
rule, to bear
rule over, to
ruler
Piel.
dominion, to make to have
Hiphil.
rule, to make to

רָדָה [2] 1158
Kal.
take, to

רְדִיד 1158
vail
veil

רָדַם 1158
Niphal.
asleep, to be fast
sleep, cast into a deep
sleep, in a deep
sleep, to be in a deep
sleeper
sleepeth, that

רָדַף 1158
Kal.
chase, to
flight, to put to
follow, to
follow after, to
follow on, to
hunt, to
persecute, to
persecutor
pursue, to
pursuer
pursuing
Niphal.
past, to be
persecution, to be under
Piel.
follow, to
follow after, to
persecute, to
pursue, to
Pual.
chased, to be
Hiphil.
chase, to

רָהַב 1159
Kal.
proudly, to behave self
sure, to make
Hiphil.
overcome, to
strengthen, to

רָהָב 1159
proud

רַהַב 1159
proud
Rahab
strength

רֹהַב 1159
strength

רָהָה 1159
Kal.
afraid, to be

רַהַט 1159
gallery
gutter
trough

רָהִיט 1160
rafter

רֵו Ch. 1160
form

רוּד [1] 1160
Kal.
lord, to be
rule, to
Hiphil.
dominion, to have the

רוּד [2] 1160
Hiphil.
mourn

רָוָה 1160
Kal.
drunk, to be made
fill, to take the
satisfied, to be abundantly
Piel.
bathed, to be
satiate, to
satisfy, to
soaked, to be
water, to
water abundantly, to
Hiphil.
drunken, to make
fill, to
satiate, to
water, to

רָוֶה 1160
drunkenness
watered

רָוַח 1160
Kal.
refreshed, to be
Pual.
large

רֶוַח 1160
enlargement
space

רוּחַ 1160
Hiphil.
accept, to
smell, to
* touch, to
understanding, to make of quick

רוּחַ 1160
air
anger
blast
breath
breath †
* cool
courage
mind
* quarters
* side
spirit
spirit*ual*
tempest
* vain
*whirl*wind
wind
windy

רוּחַ Ch. 1162
mind
spirit
wind

רְוָחָה 1162
breathing
respite

רְוָיָה 1163
runneth over
wealthy

רוּם 1163
Kal.
exalt self, to
exalted, to be
go up, to
haughty
high
high, to be
high ones
high, too
higher, to be
lifted up, to be
lofty
lofty, to be
loud
mount up, to
presumptuously †
proud
tall
taller
worms, to breed
Polel.
bring up, to
exalt, to
extol, to
high, to lift up on
high, to set up on
lift up, to
promote, to
set up, to
Polal.
exalted, to be
extolled, to be
Hiphil.
* aloud †
exalt, to
(כ׳) exalted, to be
give, to
heave, to
high, to make on
hold up, to
levy, to
lift up, to
lifter up
lifting up
offer, to
offer up, to
promotion
promotion, to be
set up, to
take, to
take away, to
take off, to
take up, to
(כ׳) taken away, to be
Hophal.
heaved up, to be
taken away, to be
taken off, to be
Hithpolel.
exalt self, to

רוּם Ch. 1164
P'al.
extol, to
lifted up, to be
Aphel.
set up, to
Hithpolel.
lift up self, to

רוּם 1164
haughtiness
height
* high

רוּם Ch. 1164
height

רוֹם 1164
high, on

רוֹמָה 1164
haughtily

רוֹמָם 1164
extolled, to be
high

רוּעַ 1164
Niphal.
destroyed, to be
smart, to
Polal.
shouting, to be
Hiphil.
blow an alarm, to
cry, to
cry alarm, to
cry aloud, to
cry out, to
joyful noise, to make a [joy
shout, to;—s. for
sound an alarm, to
triumph, to
Hithpolel.
shout for joy, to
triumph, to

רוּף 1165
Polel.
tremble, to

רוּץ 1165
Kal.
break down, to
footman
guard
posts
run, to
(כ׳) run away, to make
run through, to
running
Polel.
run, to
Hiphil.
divide speedily, to
hastily, to bring
run, to
run away, to make
stretch out, soon to

רוּק 1165
Hiphil.
* arm, to
cast out, to
draw, to
draw out, to
empty, to
empty, to make
pour out, to
Hophal.
emptied, to be
poured forth, to be

רוּר 1166
Kal.
run, to

רוֹשׁ 1166
gall

רוּשׁ 1166
Kal.
lack, to
needy
poor
poor man
Hithpolel.
poor, to make self

רָז Ch. 1166
secret

רָזָה 1166
Kal.
famish, to
Niphal.
lean, to wax

רָזֶה 1166
lean

רָזוֹן 1166
leanness
* scant

רָזוֹן 1166
prince

רָזִי 1166
leanness

רָזַם 1166
Kal.
wink at, to

רָזַן 1166
Kal.
prince
ruler

רָחַב 1166
Kal.
enlarged, to be
enlarging, to be an
Niphal.
large
Hiphil.
enlarge, to
large, to make
room, to make
wide, to make
wide, to open

רָחָב 1166
broad
large
large †
liberty, at
proud
wide
wide †

רַחַב 1167
breadth
broad place

רֹחַב 1167
breadth
broad
largeness
thickness
wideness

רְחוֹב 1167
broad place
broad way
street

רַחוּם 1167
compassion, full of
merciful

רָחוֹק 1168
afar off
far
far abroad
far off
Jonath - elem - *re-chokim*
long ago
old, of
space
while to come, great

רָחִיט 1168
rafter

רֵחַיִם 1168
mill
millstones
nether *millstone*

רַחִיק Ch. 1168
far

רָחֵל 1168
ewe
sheep

רָחַם 1168
Kal.
love, to
Piel.
compassion, to have
compassion on, to have
compassion upon, to have
merciful
mercy
mercy, to have
mercy on, to have
mercy, to shew
mercy upon, to have
pity, to
pity, to have
surely
Pual.
Lo-ruhamah
mercy, to find
mercy, to have
mercy, to obtain
Ruhamah

רָחָם 1169
gier-eagle

רַחַם 1169
damsel
womb

רֶחֶם 1169
matrix
womb

רָחָמָה 1169
gier-eagle

רַחֲמָה 1169
* two *damsels*

רַחֲמִים 1169
bowels
compassion
love, tender

mercies, great
mercies, tender
mercy
pitied, to be
pity
רַחֲמִין Ch. ...1169
mercies
רַחֲמָנִי 1169
pitiful
רָחַף.........1169
Kal.
shake, to
Piel.
flutter, to
move, to
רָחַץ.........1169
Kal.
bathe, to
bathe self, to
wash, to
wash self, to
Pual.
washed, to be
Hithpael.
wash self, to
רַחַץ 1170
wash*pot*
רְחַץ Ch. 1170
Hithp'il.
trust, to
רַחְצָה........1170
washing
רָחַק.........1170
Kal.
far
far, to be
far away, to be
far, to get
far off, to be
far removed, to be
far, to be too
flee far, to
go far, to
go far away, to
keep (*oneself*) far, to
* refrain, to
Niphal.
(כ') loosed, to be
Piel.
put away far, to
remove far, to
remove far away, to
Hiphil.
afar off
away far, to put
drive far, to
far
far away, to put
* far off
far off, to cast
far off, to *wander*
far, to put
go far, to
go far away, to
good way off, a
put away, to
remove far, to
remove far off, to
very
way, to be a good
withdraw far, to
רָחֵק.........1170
far, that are

רָחַשׁ.........1170
Kal.
indite, to
רַחַת.........1171
shovel
רָטַב.........1171
Kal.
wet, to be
רָטֹב.........1171
green
רֶטֶט.........1171
fear
רֻטֲפַשׁ.......1171
fresh, to be
רָטַשׁ.........1171
Piel.
dash, to
dash in pieces, to
dash to pieces, to
Pual.
dashed in pieces, to be
רִי...........1171
watering
רִיב 1171
Kal.
chide, to
complain, to
contend, to
debate, to
ever
* Jareb
* lay wait, to
plead, to
rebuke, to
strive, to
throughly
Hiphil.
adversary
strive, to
רִיב 1171
adversary †
cause
chiding
contend
contention
controversy
(כ') multitude
pleading
strife
strive
striving
suit
רֵיחַ 1172
savour
scent
smell
רֵיחַ Ch.......1172
smell
רֵיעַ 1172
friend
רִיפוֹת........1172
corn, ground
wheat
רִיק 1172
empty
purpose, to no
vain, in
vain thing
vanity

רֵק & רֵיק 1172
emptied
empty
vain
vain fellows
vain men
רֵיקָם 1172
cause, without
empty
vain, in
void
רִיר 1172
spittle
white of *an egg*
רֵישׁ.........1172
poverty
רִישׁ.........1172
poverty
רִישׁוֹן (כ') ...1172
former
רַךְ 1173
faint*heart*ed
soft
tender
tender one
tender*heart*ed
weak
רֹךְ...........1173
tenderness
רָכַב 1173
Kal.
get (*oneself*) up,to *horse*back, on
ride, to
ride in a chariot, to
ride on, to
rider
riding
Hiphil.
bring, to
carry, to
*horse*back, to bring on
put, to
ride, to cause to
ride, to make to
set, to
רֶכֶב 1173
chariot
millstone
millstone, upper
(כ') multitude
wagon
רַכָּב.........1174
chariot man
driver of a chariot
horseman
רִכְבָּה........1174
chariots
רְכוּב 1174
chariot
רְכוּשׁ 1174
goods
riches
substance
רָכִיל.........1174
slanders
talebearer
talebearer †
tales, carry

רָכַךְ.........1174
Kal.
softer, to be
tender, to be
Niphal.
faint, to
faint*heart*ed, to be
Pual.
mollified, to be
Hiphil.
soft, to make
רָכַל.........1175
Kal.
merchant
spice merchant
רְכֻלָּה 1175
merchandise
traffick
רָכַס.........1175
Kal.
bind, to
רֹכֶס.........1175
pride
רְכָסִים.......1175
rough places
רָכַשׁ.........1175
Kal.
gather, to
get, to
רֶכֶשׁ 1175
dromedary
mule
swift beast
רָמָה 1175
Kal.
* *bow*men
carry, to
throw, to
Piel.
beguile, to
betray, to
deceive, to
רָמָה........1175
high place
Ramath-*lehi*
רְמָה Ch. 1175
P'al.
cast, to
cast, to be
cast down, to be
impose, to
Ithp'el.
cast, to be
רִמָּה.........1175
worm
רִמּוֹן 1175
pomegranate
pomegranate tree
רָמוּת 1175
height
רֹמַח 1175
buckler
javelin
lancet
spear
רְמִיָּה 1176
deceit
deceitful
deceitfully
false
guile

idle
slack
slothful
רַמָּךְ.........1176
dromedary
רָמַם 1176
Kal.
exalted, to be
Niphal.
exalted, to be
get (*oneself*) up,to
lift up selves, to
lifted up, to be
mount up, to
רֹמְמוּת 1176
lifting up of self
רָמַס 1176
Kal
oppressor
stamp upon, to
trample, to
trample under foot, to
tread, to
tread down, to
tread upon, to
Niphal.
trodden, to be
רָמַשׂ......... 1176
Kal.
creep
move
רֶמֶשׂ 1176
creepeth, that
creeping thing
moving thing
רֹן 1176
song
רָנָה.........1176
Kal.
rattle, to
רִנָּה.........1176
cry
gladness
joy
proclamation
rejoicing
shouting
sing
singing
triumph
רָנַן.........1177
Kal.
cry out, to
rejoice, to
shout, to
shout for joy, to
sing, to
Piel.
aloud for joy
cry out, to
greatly rejoice, to
joyful, to be
rejoice, to
shout for joy, to
sing, to
sing aloud, to
sing out, to
singing
triumph, to
Pual.
singing, to be
Hiphil.
rejoice, to
rejoice, to make to
shout for joy, to

sing aloud, to
sing for joy, to cause to
Hithpolel.
shout, to

רְנָנָה 1177
joyful
joyful voice
singing
triumphing

רְנָנִים 1177
* goodly

רְסִיסִים 1177
drops

רְסִיסִים 1177
breaches

רֶסֶן 1177
bridle

רָסַס 1177
Kal.
temper, to

רַע 1177
adversity
affliction
bad
calamity
* displease,† to
displeasure
distress
evil
evil men
evil things
evil*favouredness*
* exceedingly †
* great
grief
grievous
harm
harm †
heavy
hurt
hurtful
ill
ill favoured
* mark,† to
mischief
mischievous
misery
naught
naughty
noisome
* please,† not to
sad
sadly
sore
sorrow
trouble
vex
wicked
wicked ones
wickedly
wickedness
worse
worst
wretchedness
wrong

רֵעַ 1181
* aloud
noise
shouted

רֵעַ 1181
* another
brother
companion
fellow
friend
husband
lover
neighbour
* other

רֵעַ 1183
thought

רֹעַ 1183
* bad, to be so
badness
evil
* evil, to be so
naughtiness
sadness
sorrow
wickedness

רָעֵב 1183
Kal.
famished, to be
hunger, to
hunger, to have
hunger, to suffer
hungry, to be
Hiphil.
famish, to suffer to
hunger, to suffer to

רָעָב 1183
dearth
famine
famished †
hunger

רָעֵב 1183
hunger bitten
hungry

רְעָבוֹן 1184
famine

רָעַד 1184
Kal.
tremble, to
Hiphil.
tremble, to

רַעַד 1184
trembling

רְעָדָה 1184
fear
fearfulness
trembling

רָעָה 1184
Kal.
* break, to
companion
company with, to keep
devour, to
eat up, to
evil entreat, to
fed, to be
feed, to
feeding
herdman
keep *sheep*, to
keeper
pastor
* shearing house †
shepherd
*shep*herd
wander, to
waste, to
Piel.
friend, to use as
Hiphil.
feed, to
Hithpael.
friendship with, to make

רֵעֶה 1185
friend

רֵעָה 1185
companion
fellow

רֹעָה 1185
broken

רְעוּת 1185
* another
mate
neighbour

רְעוּת 1185
vexation

רְעוּת Ch. 1185
pleasure
will

רְעִי 1185
pasture

רֹעִי 1185
shepherd

רַעְיָה 1185
(כ׳) fellows
love

רַעְיוֹן 1185
vexation

רַעְיוֹן Ch. 1185
cogitation
thought

רָעַל 1185
Hophal.
shaken, to be terribly

רַעַל 1185
mufflers
trembling

רָעַם 1186
Kal.
roar, to
troubled, to be
Hiphil.
fret, to make to
thunder, to

רַעַם 1186
thunder

רַעְמָה 1186
thunder

רַעֲנָן 1186
flourishing
green

רַעֲנַן Ch. 1186
flourishing

רָעַע 1186
Kal.
associate selves, to
break, to
break in pieces, to
broken, to be
displease, † to
displeased, † to be
evil
evil, to be
ill
utterly
worse, to be
Hiphil.
afflict, to
evil, to bring
evil, to do
evil doer
evil entreat, to
evil man
harm, to do
hurt
hurt, to
hurt, to do
hurting
ill, to behave selves
ill, to deal
indeed
mischief, to do
punish, to
still
vex, to
wicked
wicked doer
wickedly, to do
worse, to deal
worse, to do
Hithpolel.
broken down, to be
friendly, to shew self

רְעַע Ch. 1187
P'al.
break, to
bruise, to

רָעַף 1187
Kal.
distil, to
drop, to
drop down, to
Hiphil.
drop down, to

רָעַץ 1187
Kal.
dash in pieces, to
vex, to

רָעַשׁ 1187
Kal.
moved, to be
quake, to
remove, to
shake, to
tremble, to
Niphal.
moved, to be
Hiphil.
afraid, to make
shake, to
shake, to make to
tremble, to make to

רַעַשׁ 1187
commotion
confused noise
earthquake
fierceness
quaking
rattling
rushing
shaking

רָפָא 1187
Kal.
cure, to
heal, to
healed, to be
physician
whole, to make
Niphal.
healed, to be
whole, to be made
Piel.
heal, to
healed, to cause to be
repair, to
thoroughly
Hithpael.
healed, to be

רָפָא 1188
giant
Rephaim
Rephaims

רִפְאוּת 1188
health

רְפֻאוֹת 1188
heal*ed*
medicines

רְפָאִים 1188
dead
deceased

רָפַד 1188
Kal.
spread, to
Piel.
comfort, to
make *a bed*, to

רָפָה 1188
Kal.
abated, to be
consume, to
draw *toward evening*, to
faint, to be
feeble, to be
feeble, to wax
go, to let
slack, to be
weak, to be
weakened, to be
Niphal.
idle
Piel.
let down, to
weaken, to
Hiphil.
cease, to
fail, to
forsake, to
leave, to
let alone, to
let go, to
respite, to give
slack, to
stay, to
still, to be
Hithpael.
faint, to
slack, to be
slothful, to be

רָפָה 1188
giant

רָפֶה 1189
weak

רְפִידָה 1189
bottom

רִפְיוֹן 1189
feebleness

רָפַס 1189
Hithpael.
humble self, to
submit self, to

רְפַס Ch. 1189
P'al.
stamp, to

רַפְסֹדוֹת 1189
flotes

רָפַק 1189
Hithpael.
lean, to

רָפַשׁ 1189
Kal.
foul, to
Niphal.
troubled

רֶפֶשׁ 1189
mire

רְפָתִים 1189
stalls

רַץ 1189
piece

רָצָא 1189
Kal
run, to

רָצַד 1189
Piel.
leap, to

רָצָה 1189
Kal.
accept, to
acceptable, to be
accomplish, to
affection, to set
approve, to
consent with, to
delight, to
delight self, to
enjoy, to
favour, to have a
favourable, to be
like, to
(כ׳) observe, to
please, to
pleased with, to be
pleasure, to have
pleasure, to take
Niphal.
accepted, to be
pardoned, to be
Piel.
please, to seek to
Hiphil.
enjoy, to
Hithpael.
reconcile self, to

רָצוֹן 1189
acceptable
acceptable, to be
acceptance
accepted, to be
as...would
delight
desire
favour
good pleasure
good will
own will
pleasure
self will
voluntary will
what would
will

רָצַח 1190
Kal.
death, to put to
kill, to
killing
manslayer
murder, to
murderer
slay, to
slayer
Niphal.
slain, to be
Piel.
murder, to
murderer
Pual.
slain, to be

רֶצַח 1190
slaughter
sword

רָצַע 1190
Kal.
bore, to

רָצַף 1190
Kal.
paved, being

רֶצֶף 1190
coals

רִצְפָּה 1190
live coal
pavement

רָצַץ 1190
Kal.
broken
broken, to be
bruised
crush, to
crushed
discouraged, to be
oppress, to
oppressed
Niphal.
break, to
broken, to be
Piel.
break, to
oppress, to
Poel.
oppress, to
Hiphil.
break, to
Hithpolel.
struggle together, to

רַק 1191
lean
lean*fleshed*
thin

רַק 1191
any wise, in
but
even
except
howbeit
howsoever
least, at the
nevertheless
nothing but
notwithstanding
only
save
so *that*
surely
yet
yet so

רֹק 1191
spit, to
spitting
spittle

רָקַב 1191
Kal.
rot, to

רָקָב 1191
rotten thing
rottenness

רִקָּבוֹן 1191
rotten

רָקַד 1191
Kal.
dance, to
skip, to
Piel.
dance, to
jump, to
leap, to
Hiphil.
skip, to make to

רַקָּה 1191
temples

רָקַח 1191
Kal.
apothecary
compound, to
make *ointment*, to
Pual.
prepared
Hiphil.
spice, to

רֶקַח 1191
spiced

רֹקַח 1191
confection
ointment

רַקָּח 1191
apothecary

רַקָּחָה 1191
confectionary

רִקֻּחִים 1191
perfumes

רָקִיעַ 1191
firmament

רָקִיק 1191
cake
wafer

רָקַם 1192
Kal.
embroiderer
needle*work*
needle*work*
Pual.
curiously wrought

רִקְמָה 1192
broidered
broidered work
divers colours
needlework
needlework on both sides
raiment of needle-work

רָקַע 1192
Kal.
spread abroad, to
spread forth, to
stamp, to
stretch out, to
Piel.
beat, to
broad, to be made
spread over, to
Pual.
spread into plates
Hiphil.
spread out, to

רִקֻּעִים 1192
broad

רָקַק 1192
Kal.
spit, to

רִשְׁיוֹן 1192
grant

רָשַׁם 1192
Kal.
noted, to be

רְשַׁם Ch. 1192
P'al.
sign, to
signed, to be
written, to be

רָשַׁע 1192
Kal.
wicked, to be
wickedly, to deal
wickedly depart, to
wickedly, to do
wickedness, to commit
Hiphil.
condemn, to
condemning
trouble, to make
vex, to
wickedly, to do

רָשָׁע 1192
condemned †
guilty
ungodly
wicked
wicked man
wrong, that did

רֶשַׁע 1194
iniquity
wicked
wickedness

רִשְׁעָה 1194
fault
wickedly
wickedness

רֶשֶׁף 1194
arrow
burning coals
burning heat
coals
spark †
thunderbolts, hot

רָשַׁשׁ 1194
Poel.
impoverish, to
Pual.
impoverished, to be

רֶשֶׁת 1195
net
net*work*

רַתּוֹק 1195
chain

רַתּוּקָה 1195
chain

רָתַח 1195
Piel.
boil, to make to
Pual.
boil, to
Hiphil.
boil, to make to

רֶתַח 1195
* well (*to boil*)

רַתִּיקָה 1195
(כ׳) chains

רָתַם 1195
Kal.
bind, to

רֹתֶם 1195
juniper
juniper tree

רָתַק 1195
Niphal.
loosed, to be
Pual.
bound, to be

רְתֻקוֹת 1195
chains

רְתֵת 1195
trembling

שְׂאֹר 1195
leaven
leavened bread

שְׂאֵת 1195
accepted, be
dignity
excellency
highness
raise up self
rising

שְׂבָךְ 1195
net

שְׂבָכָה 1195
checker
lattice
network
snare
wreath
wreathenwork

שַׂבְּכָא Ch. ... 1195
sackbut

שָׂבֵעַ & שָׂבַע 1195
Kal.
enough, to have
fill selves, to
filled, to be
filled full, to be
filled with, to be
full, to be
full of, to be
full, to the
plenty of, to have
satiate, to be
satisfied, to be
satisfied with, to be
sufficed, to be
weary of, to be
Piel.
satisfy, to
Hiphil.
fill, to
satisfy, to
satisfy with, to

שֹׂבַע 1196
abundance
plenteous
plenteousness
plenty

שָׂבֵעַ 1196
full
full of
satisfied
satisfied with

שָׂבַע 1196
fill
full
fulness
satisfying
sufficed, to be

שָׂבְעָה 1196
enough
enough, to have
full, till...be
satisfy, to
sufficiently
*un*satiable

שִׂבְעָה 1196
fulness

שָׂבַר 1196
Kal.
view, to
Piel.
hope, to
tarry, to
wait, to

שֵׂבֶר 1197
hope

שָׂגָא 1197
Hiphil.
increase, to
magnify, to

שְׂגָא Ch. 1197
P'al.
grow, to
multiplied, to be

שָׂגַב 1197
Kal.
exalted, to be
strong, to be too
Niphal.
exalted, to be
excellent, to be
high
high, to be
lofty
safe, to be
Piel.
defend, to
high, to set on
high, to set up on
set up, to
Pual.
safe, to be
Hiphil.
exalt, to

שָׂגָה 1197
Kal.
grow, to
grow *up*, to
increase, to
Hiphil.
increase, to

שַׂגִּיא 1197
excellent
great

שַׂגִּיא Ch. 1197
exceeding
great
greatly
many
much
sore
very

שָׂדַד 1197
Piel.
break the clods, to
harrow, to

שָׂדֶה 1197
country
field
ground
land
soil
* wild

שָׂדַי 1199
field

שְׂדֵרָה 1199
board
range

שֶׂה 1199
cattle
cattle, lesser
cattle, small
ewe
goat
lamb
sheep

שָׂהֵד 1200
record

שָׂהֲדוּתָא Ch. 1200
Jegar-sahadutha

שַׂהֲרֹנִים 1200
ornaments
tires like the moon, round

שׂוֹבֶךְ 1200
boughs, thick

שׂוּג 1 1200
Niphal.
turn back, to

שׂוּג 2 1200
Pilpel.
grow, to make to

שׂוּחַ 1200
Kal.
meditate, to

שׂוּט 1200
Kal.
turn aside, to

שׂוּךְ 1200
Kal.
hedge, to make an
hedge up, to
Polel.
fence, to

שׂוֹךְ 1200
bough

שׂוֹכָה 1200
bough

שִׂים & שׂוּם..1200
Kal.
any wise
appoint, to
bring, to
call (*a name*), to
care, to
cast in, to
change, to
charge, to
commit, to
consider, to
consider,† to
convey, to
determined
disguise,† to
dispose, to
do, to
get, to
give, to
heap up, to
hold, to
impute, to
laid, to be
lay, to
lay down, to
lay up, to
leave, to
* leave, to
look, to
made, to be
make, to
make out, to
mark, to
name,† to
ordain, to
order, to
*over*turn, to
paint,† to
place, to
placed, to be
preserve, to
purpose, to
put, to
put on, to
regard,† to
rehearse, to
reward, to
set, to;—shed
set, to cause to be
set on, to
set up, to
shew, to
* stedfastly
take, to
* tell, to
tread down,† to
turn, to
wholly
work, to
Hiphil.
* on
regarding
Hophal.
set, to be

שׂוּם Ch. 1204
P'al.
command,† to
give, to
laid
made, to be
make, to
name,† to
regard,† to
set, to
Ithp'al.
given, to be
laid, to be
made, to be

שׂוּר 1 1204
Kal.
depart, to

שׂוּר 2 1204
Kal.
power, to have
reign, to
Hiphil.
princes, to make

שׂוּר 3 1204
Kal.
cut, to

שׂוֹרָה 1204
principal

שִׂישׂ & שׂוּשׂ..1204
Kal.
glad, to be
greatly
joy, to
mirth, to make
rejoice, to

שִׂחַ 1204
thought

שָׂחָה 1204
Kal.
swim, to
Hiphil.
swim, to make to

שָׂחוּ 1204
swim in, to

שְׂחוֹק 1204
derision
laughed to scorn
laughing
laughter
mocked
sport

שָׂחַט 1205
Kal.
press, to

שָׂחַק 1205
Kal.
deride, to
derision, to have in
laugh, to
mock, to
rejoice, to
scorn, to
sport, to make
Piel.
merry, that make
mocker
play, to
rejoice, to
sport, to be in
sport, to make
Hiphil.
scorn, to laugh to

שֵׂט 1205
revolter

שָׂטָה 1205
Kal.
decline, to
go aside, to
turn, to

שָׂטַם 1205
Kal.
hate, to
oppose self against, to

שָׂטַן 1205
Kal.
adversary
adversary, to be an
resist, to

שָׂטָן 1205
adversary
Satan
withstand, to

שִׂטְנָה 1205
accusation

שִׂיא 1205
excellency

שִׂיב 1205
Kal.
grayheaded
grayheaded, to be

שִׂיב Ch. 1205
P'al.
elders

שֵׂיב 1205
age

שֵׂיבָה 1205
gray hairs
grayheaded
grey head
hoar hairs
hoar head
hoary, to be
hoary head
old age

שִׂיג 1206
pursu*ing*

שִׂיד 1206
Kal.
plaister, to

שִׂיד 1206
lime
plaister

שִׂיחַ 1206
Kal.
commune, to
complain, to
meditate, to
pray, to
speak, to
talk, to
talk with, to
Polel.
declare, to
muse, to

שִׂיחַ 1206
bush
plant
shrubs

שִׂיחַ 1206
babbling
communication
complaint
meditation
prayer
talk

שִׂיחָה 1206
meditation
prayer

שֵׂךְ 1206
pricks

שֹׂךְ 1206
tabernacle

שֻׂכָּה 1206
barbed irons

שֶׂכְוִי 1206
heart

שְׂכִיָּה 1206
picture

שַׂכִּין 1206
knife

שָׂכִיר 1206
hired
hired men
hired servant
hireling

שְׂכִירָה 1206
hired, that is

שָׂכַךְ 1206
Kal.
cover

שָׂכַל 1206
Kal.
wisely, to behave self
Piel.
wittingly, to guide
Hiphil.
consider, to
expert
good success, to have
instruct, to
instructed, to be
Maschil
prosper, to
prudent
prudently, to deal
skilful
skill
skill, to give
teach, to
understand, to
understand, to make to
understanding
understanding, to have
wisdom
wise
wise, to be
wise, to make
wisely
wisely, to behave self
wisely consider, to

שְׂכַל Ch. 1207
Ithpael.
consider, to

שֶׂכֶל & שֵׂכֶל ..1207
discretion
knowledge
policy
prudence
sense
understanding
wisdom
wise

שִׂכְלוּת 1207
folly

שָׂכְלְתָנוּ Ch. 1207
understanding

שָׂכַר 1207
Kal.
hire, to
reward, to
surely
Niphal.
hire out selves, to
Hithpael.
earn wages, to

שָׂכָר 1208
hire
price
reward
rewarded
wages
worth

שֶׂכֶר 1208
reward
sluice

שְׂלָו or שְׂלָיו ..1208
quails

שַׂלְמָה 1208
clothes
garment
raiment

שְׂמֹאול 1208
left
left hand
left side

שְׂמֹאל 1208
Hiphil.
left
left, to go to the
* left, on the
* left, to the
left, to turn to the

שְׂמָאלִי 1208
left

שָׂמַח & שָׂמֵחַ 1208
Kal.
glad, to be
joy, to
joy, to have
merry, to be
rejoice, to
Piel.
cheer up, to
glad, to make
joyful, to make
merry, to make
rejoice, to
rejoice, to cause to
rejoice, to make to
very
Hiphil.
rejoice, to make to

שָׂמֵחַ 1209
glad
glad, to be
joyful
merrily
merry
merry, making
merry*hearted*
rejoice
rejoicing

שִׂמְחָה 1210
* exceeding
* exceeding †
* exceedingly
gladness
joy
joyfulness
mirth
pleasure
rejoice, to
rejoicing

שְׂמִיכָה 1210
mantle

שִׂמְלָה 1210
apparel
cloth
clothes
clothing
garment
raiment

שְׂמָמִית 1210
spider

שָׂנֵא 1210
Kal.
enemy
foe
hate, to
hateful, to be
odious
utterly
Niphal.
hated, to be
Piel.
hate, to
hater

שְׂנֵא Ch. 1211
P'al.
hate, to

שִׂנְאָה 1211
* exceedingly †
hate, to
hatefully
hatred

שָׂנִיא 1212
hated

שָׂעִיר 1212
devil
goat
hairy
kid
rough
satyr

שְׂעִירָה 1212
kid

שְׂעִירִים 1212
rain, small

שְׂעִפִּים 1212
thoughts

שָׂעַר 1212
Kal.
afraid, to be
afraid, to be horribly
fear, to
take away as with a whirlwind, to
Niphal.
tempestuous, to be
Piel.
hurl as a storm, to
Hithpael.
come like a whirlwind, to

שַׂעַר 1212
affrighted
* horribly
* sore
storm

שֵׂעָר 1212
hair

שֵׂעָר 1212
hair
hairy
* rough

שְׂעַר Ch. 1212
hair

שְׂעָרָה 1212
storm
tempest

שַׂעֲרָה 1212
hair

שְׂעֹרָה 1212
barley

שָׂפָה 1213
band
bank
binding
border
brim
brink
edge
language
lip
prating
*sea*shore
shore
side
speech
talk
* vain *words*

שָׂפַח 1214
Piel.
smite with the scab, to

שָׂפָם 1214
beard
lip, upper
lips

שָׂפַן 1214
Kal.
treasures

שָׂפַק 1 1214
Kal.
clap, to
Hiphil.
please selves, to

שָׂפַק 2 1214
Kal.
suffice, to

שֶׂפֶק 1214
stroke
sufficiency

שַׂק 1214
sack
sackcloth
sackclothes

שָׂקַד 1214
Niphal.
bound, to be

שָׂקַר 1214
Piel.
wanton

שַׂר 1214
captain
captain, chief
captain that had rule
chief
general
governor
keeper
lord
master
prince
principal
ruler
steward
*task*master

שָׂרַג 1217
Pual.
wrapped together, to be
Hithpael.
wreathed, to be

שָׂרַד 1217
Kal.
remain, to

שְׂרָד 1217
service

שֶׂרֶד 1217
line

שָׂרָה 1217
Kal.
power as a prince, to have
power, to have

שָׂרָה 1217
lady
princess
queen

שְׂרוֹךְ 1217
latchet
*shoe*latchet

שְׂרוּקִּים 1217
plants, principal

שָׂרַט 1217
Kal.
make *cuttings*, to
* pieces
Niphal.
cut in pieces, to be

שֶׂרֶט 1217
cuttings

שָׂרֶטֶת 1217
cuttings

שָׂרִיגִים 1217
branches

שָׂרִיד 1217
* alive
left, to be
remain
remaining
remnant
rest

שָׂרִיק 1217
fine

שָׂרַךְ 1217
Piel.
traversing

שָׂרַע 1217
Kal.
superfluous, to have any thing
superfluous, thing
Hithpael.
stretch out self, to

שַׂרְעַפִּים 1218
thoughts

שָׂרַף 1218
Kal.
burn, to
burn up, to
burned, to cause to be
* burnt, to be
burnt, that were kindle, to
make *a burning*, to
utterly
Niphal.
burnt, to be
Pual.
burnt, to be

שָׂרָף 1218
fiery
seraphims
serpent, fiery

שְׂרֵפָה 1218
burning
burnt
* burnt, to be
* throughly

שָׂרֹק 1219
speckled

שֹׂרֵק 1219
vine, choicest
vine, noble

שֹׂרֵקָה 1219
vine, choice

שָׂרַר 1219
Kal.
rule, to
rule, to bear
Hithpael.
altogether
prince, to make self a

שָׂשׂוֹן 1219
gladness
joy
mirth
rejoicing

שָׂתַם 1219
Kal.
shut out, to

שָׂתַר 1219
Niphal.
* secret parts, to have in (one's)

שָׁאַב 1219
Kal.
draw *water*, to
draw, woman to
drawer

שָׁאַג 1219
Kal.
mightily
roar, to

שְׁאָגָה 1219
roaring

שָׁאָה 1219
Kal.
wasted, to be
Niphal.
desolate, to be
rush, to
rushing, to make a
Hiphil.
waste, to lay
Hithpael.
wondering

שַׁאֲוָה 1220
desolation

שְׁאוֹל 1220
grave
hell
pit

שָׁאוֹן 1220
* horrible
noise
pomp
rushing
tumult
* tumultuous

שְׁאָט 1220
despite
despiteful

שְׁאִיָּה 1220
destruction

שָׁאַל 1220
Kal.
ask, to
ask counsel, to
ask on, to
asking
beg, to
* borrow, to
borrowed, to be
charge, to lay to
consult, to
consulter
demand, to
desire, to
enquire, to
greet, † to
lent, to be
pray, to
request, to
require, to
salute, † to
straitly
surely
wishing
Niphal.
ask, to
earnestly
leave, to obtain
Piel.
ask, to
beg, to
Hiphil.
lend, to

שְׁאֵל Ch. 1221
P'al.
ask, to
demand, to
require, to

שְׁאֵלָא Ch. ..1221
demand

שְׁאֵלָה 1222
loan
petition
request

שָׁאַן 1222
Pilel.
ease, to be at
quiet, to be
rest, to

שַׁאֲנָן 1222
ease, that is at
quiet
tumult

שָׁאַף 1222
Kal.
desire, to
desire, to earnestly
devour, to
haste, to
pant, to
snuff up, to
swallow up, to

שָׁאַר 1222
Kal.
remain, to
Niphal.
left
left, to be
remain, to
remnant
rest, the
Hiphil.
leave, to
left, to be
let, to
reserve, to

שְׁאָר 1223
other
remnant
residue
rest
Shear-*jashub*

שְׁאָר Ch. 1223
more, whatsoever
residue
rest

שְׁאֵר 1223
body
flesh
food
kin
kin, near
kinsman
kinsman, near
kinswoman
near *of kin*
nigh *of kin*

שַׁאֲרָה 1223
near kinswoman

שְׁאֵרִית 1223
escaped, that had
left, be
posterity
remain, to
remainder
remnant
residue
rest

שְׁאֵת 1224
desolation

שְׁבָבִים 1224
broken in pieces

שָׁבָה 1224
Kal.
captive
captive, to bring away
captive, to carry away
captive, to lead
captive, to lead away
captive, to take
captives, to carry
captives, † to carry
carry away *captive*, to
take away, to
take *captive*, to
Niphal.
captive, to be carried away
captive, to be taken
captives, to be carried
driven away, to be

שְׁבוֹ 1224
agate

שְׁבוּל (כ') 1224
path

שָׁבוּעַ 1224
seven
week

שְׁבוּעָה 1224
curse
oath
* sworn

שְׁבוּת 1225
captivity

שָׁבַח 1225
Piel.
commend, to
keep in, to
praise, to
still, to
Hiphil.
still, to
Hithpael.
glory, to
triumph, to

שְׁבַח Ch. 1225
Pael.
praise, to

שֵׁבֶט 1225
* correction
dart
rod
sceptre
staff
tribe

שְׁבָט 1226
Sebat

שְׁבַט Ch. 1226
tribe

שְׁבִי 1226
captive
captivity
prisoners
* take away, to
taken, that was

שָׁבִיב 1226
spark

שְׁבִיב Ch. 1226
flame

שִׁבְיָה 1227
captives
captivity

שְׁבִיל 1227
path

שְׁבִיסִים 1227
cauls

שְׁבִיעִי 1227
seventh
seventh time

שְׁבִית 1227
captives
captivity

שֹׁבֶל 1227
leg

שַׁבְּלוּל 1227
snail

שִׁבֹּלֶת 1227
branch
channel
corn, ears of
ears
flood
Shibboleth
*water*flood

שָׁבַע 1228
Kal.
sworn
Niphal.
swear, to
swearer
Hiphil.
adjure, to
charge, to
charge by an oath, to
charge with an oath, to
* feed to the full, to
oath (*from another*), to take an
straitly
swear (*another*), to
swear, to cause to
swear, to make to

שִׁבְעָה & שֶׁבַע 1229
seven
seven times
seven*fold*
* sevens, † by
seven*teen*
seven*teenth*
seventh
Shebah

שִׁבְעָה Ch. ..1231
seven
seven times

שִׁבְעִים 1231
seventy
threescore *and fifteen*
threescore *and fourteen*
threescore *and seventeen*
threescore *and sixteen*
threescore and ten
threescore *and thirteen*
* threescore and twelve †

שִׁבְעָנָה 1232
seven

שִׁבְעָתַיִם 1232
(כ') seven
seven times
sevenfold

שָׁבַץ 1232
Piel.
embroider, to
Pual.
set, to be

שָׁבָץ 1232
anguish

שְׁבַק Ch. 1232
P'al.
leave, to
let alone, to
Ithpael.
left, to be

שָׁבַר 1........1232
Kal.
break, to
break up, to
broken
crush, to
destroy, to
quench, to
tear, to
* view, to
Niphal.
break, to
broken
broken, to be
broken off, to be
broken*hearted*
destroyed, to be
hurt, to be
Piel.
break, to
break down, to
break in pieces, to
quite
Hiphil.
birth, bring to the
Hophal.
hurt, to be

שָׁבַר 2........1233
Kal.
buy, to
sell, to
Hiphil.
sell, to

שֶׁבֶר & שֵׁבֶר 1234
affliction
breach
breaking
broken*footed*
broken*handed*
bruise
crashing
destruction
hurt
interpretation
vexation

שֶׁבֶר..........1234
corn
victuals

שִׁבָּרוֹן 1234
breaking
destruction

שְׁבַשׁ Ch.....1234
Ithpael.
astonied, to be

שָׁבַת 1234
Kal.
cease, to
celebrate, to
keep, to
rest, to
sabbath, to keep
Niphal.
cease, to
Hiphil.
cease, to cause to
cease, to let
cease, to make to
fail, to cause to
fail, to make to
lacking, to suffer to be
leave, to
put away, to
put down, to
rest, to make to
rid, to
still, to
take away, to

שֶׁבֶת 1235
cease, to
sit still, to
time, loss of

שַׁבָּת 1235
sabbath
sabbath †
* sabbath,† every

שַׁבָּתוֹן 1235
rest
sabbath

שָׁגַג 1235
Kal.
* also, for that
deceived
err, to
go astray, to
sin ignorantly, to

שְׁגָגָה 1235
error
ignorance
unawares, at
unwittingly

שָׁגָה 1236
Kal.
deceived, to be
err, to
go astray, to
* ravished, to be
sin through ignorance, to
wander, to
Hiphil.
deceiver
go astray, to cause to
wander, to let
wander, to make to

שָׁגַח 1236
Hiphil.
look, to
look, to narrowly

שְׁגִיאוֹת 1236
errors

שִׁגָּיוֹן 1236
Shiggaion
Shigionoth

שָׁגַל 1236
Kal.
lie with, to
Niphal.
ravished, to be
Pual.
lien with, to be

שֵׁגָל..........1236
queen

שֵׁגַל Ch. 1236
wife

שָׁגַע..........1236
Pual.
mad
mad man
Hithpael.
mad, to be
mad man, to play the

שִׁגָּעוֹן 1236
furiously
madness

שֶׁגֶר.........1236
cometh of, that
increase

שַׁד 1236
breast
pap
teat

שֵׁד 1236
devil

שֹׁד 1236
breast

שֹׁד 1236
desolation
destruction
oppression
robbery
spoil
spoil, to
spoiled
spoiler
spoiling
wasting

שָׁדַד 1237
Kal.
dead
destroy
destroyed, to be
destroyer
oppress, to
robber
spoil, to
spoiled
spoiler
utterly
Niphal.
spoiled, to be
Piel.
spoil, to
waste, to
Pual.
laid waste, to be
spoiled, to be
wasted, to be
Poel.
spoil, to
Hophal.
spoiled, to be

שִׁדָּה 1237
musical instrument
* sorts (*of musical instruments*), all

שַׁדַּי..........1237
Almighty

שְׁדֵמָה 1237
blasted

שְׁדֵמָה 1238
field

שָׁדַף 1238
Kal.
blasted

שְׁדֵפָה........1238
blasted

שִׁדָּפוֹן........1238
blasting

שְׁדַר Ch. 1238
Ithpael.
labour, to

שֹׁהַם 1238
onyx

שָׁו (כ׳) 1238
vanity

שׁוֹא 1238
destruction

שָׁוְא 1238
false
falsely
lie
lying
vain
vanity

שׁוֹאָה 1238
desolate
desolation
destroy, to
destruction
storm
wasteness

שׁוּב 1238
Kal.
* again
again, to be come
again, to (*do anything*)
any wise, in
at all
averse
break again, to
(כ׳) bring, to
bring again, to
bring back, to
build again, to
cease, to
certainly
circumcise again, to
come again, to
come back, to
* continually †
converted, to be
converts
dig again, to
evil again, to *do*
feed again, to
* fro
get(*oneself*)again, to
get (*oneself*) back again, to
go again, to
go back, to
go home, to
go out, to
gone back, to be
lay down again, to
lie down again, to
lodge again, to
make again, to
more, to *see*
past, to be
rejoice again, to
(כ׳) rendered, to be
repent, to
restored, to be
restored again, to be
retire, to
return, to
return again, to
(כ׳) return, to cause to
returned, to be
(כ׳) reward, to
send again, to
Shear-jashub
still
take again, to
turn, to
turn again, to
turn away, to
turn back, to
turn back again, to
turn backward, to
turn from, to
turned, to be
turned away, to be
turned back, to be
turning
weep again, to
Polel.
bring again, to
pervert, to
restore, to
restorer
slide back, to
turn away, to
turn back, to
turn self again, to
turning away
Pulal.
brought back, to be
Hiphil.
answer, to
answer,† to
answer again,† to
answer, to cause to
any case, in
any wise, in
* bethink, to
bring, to
bring again, to
bring back, to
bring home again, to
bringing back
call *to mind*, to
carry again, to
carry back, to
certainly
* consider, to
convert, to
deliver, to
deliver again, to
deny,† to
draw back, to
draw *back*, to
fetch home again, to
* give, to
give again, to
hinder, to
let, to
needs
* pay, to
pull in again, to
put, to
put again, to
put up again, to
recall, to
recompense, to
recover, to
refresh, to
relieve, to
render, to
render again, to
rendered, to be
requite, to
requiting
rescue, to
restore, to
restorer
retrieve, to
return, to
return, to cause to
return, causing to
return, to make to
reverse, to
reward, to
say nay,† to
send back, to

spoiler
utterly
waste, to
waster
Hophal.
corrupt
corrupt thing

שְׁחַת Ch. 1253
P'al.
corrupt
fault

שַׁחַת 1253
corruption
destruction
ditch
grave
pit

שִׁטָּה 1254
shittah tree
shittim

שָׁטַח 1254
Kal.
all abroad
enlarge, to
spread, to
Piel.
stretch out, to

שֹׁטֵט 1254
scourges

שָׁטַף 1254
Kal.
drown, to
flow, to
overflow, to
overwhelm, to
rinse, to
run, to
rush, to
wash, to
wash away, to
wash away, to throughly
Niphal.
overflown, to be
rinsed, to be
Pual.
rinsed, to be

שֶׁטֶף & שֵׁטֶף 1254
flood
outrageous
overflowing

שָׁטַר 1254
Kal.
officer
overseer
ruler

שְׁטַר Ch. 1254
side

שַׁי 1254
present

שִׁיבָה 1254
captivity

שִׁיבָה 1254
lay, while

שָׁיָה 1255
Kal.
be unmindful

שִׁיחָה 1255
pit

שַׁיִט 1255
oar
(כ') scourge

שִׁילֹה 1255
Shiloh

שֵׁילָל 1255
stripped

שֵׁינַיִם 1255
piss

שִׁיר 1255
Kal.
sing, to
singer
singing
singing man
singing woman
Polel.
behold, to
sing, to
singer
singing man
singing woman
Hophal.
sung, to be

שִׁיר 1255
* musical
musick
* singer
singing
song
song †

שִׁירָה 1256
* sing
song

שַׁיִשׁ 1256
marble

שִׁית 1256
Kal.
apply, to
appoint, to
array, in
bring, to
consider, to
lay, to
lay up, to
let alone, to
* look, to
make, to
mark, to
put, to
put on, to
regard,† to
set, to
shew, to
stayed, to be
* take, to
Hophal.
laid, to be

שַׁיִת 1257
thorn

שִׁית 1257
attire
garment

שָׁכַב 1257
Kal.
at all
laid down, to be
lay (*oneself*) down, to
lay self down, to
lie, to
lie down, to
lie down to sleep, to
lie still, to
lie with, to
lodge, to
lying with
*over*lay, to
sleep, to
take rest, to
Niphal.
ravished, to be
Pual.
lien with, to be
Hiphil.
casting down
lay, to
lie down, to make to
stay, to
Hophal.
laid
laid, to be

שְׁכָבָה 1258
* carnally
copulation
* lay
seed

שִׁכְבַת 1258
* lie, to

שָׁכָה 1258
Hiphil.
morning, in the

שְׁכוֹל 1258
loss of children
spoiling

שַׁכּוּל 1258
barren
bereaved of children
bereaved of whelps
robbed of whelps

שִׁכּוֹר 1258
drunk
drunkard
drunken
drunken man

שָׁכַח 1258
Kal.
at all
forget, to
Niphal.
forgotten
forgotten, to be
Piel.
forgotten, to cause to be
Hiphil.
forget, to cause to
Hithpael.
forgotten, to be

שָׁכֵחַ 1259
forget

שְׁכַח Ch. 1259
Ithp'al.
found, to be
Aphel.
find, to
found, to be

שָׁכַךְ 1259
Kal.
appeased, to be
asswage, to
pacified, to be
set, to
Hiphil.
cease, to make to

שָׁכֹל 1259
Kal.
bereaved, to be
childless, to be
deprived, to be
lose children, to
Piel.
barren
bereave, to
bereave of children, to
cast calf, to
cast fruit, to
cast young, to
childless, to make
destroy, to
rob of children, to
spoil, to
Hiphil.
* expert
miscarry

שִׁכֻּלִים 1260
loss of others, to have after

שָׁכַם 1260
Hiphil.
arise early, to
early
early, to get (*oneself*)
early, to get up
early, to be up
morning
rise early, to
rise up betimes, to
rise up early, to
rising early
rising up betimes
rising up early

שְׁכֶם 1260
back
* consent
portion
shoulder

שִׁכְמָה 1260
shoulder blade

שָׁכַן & שָׁכֵן ..1260
Kal.
abide, to
continue, to
dwell, to
dwellers
habitation, to have
inhabit, to
inhabited, to be
remain, to
remaining
rest, to
Piel.
dwell, to cause to
dwell, to make to
place, to
set, to
Hiphil.
dwell, to
dwell, to make to
lay, to
place, to
remain, to cause to
set up, to

שְׁכֵן Ch. 1261
P'al.
habitation, to have
Pael.
dwell, to cause to

שָׁכֵן 1261
inhabitant
neighbour
nigh

שֶׁכֶן 1261
habitation

שָׁכַר 1261
Kal.
drink abundantly, to
drink, to be filled with
drunken
drunken, to be
merry, to be
Piel.
drunk, to make
drunken, to make
Hiphil.
drunk, to make
drunken, to make
Hithpael.
drunken, to be

שֵׁכָר 1262
drink, strong
drunkard †
wine, strong

שִׁכָּרוֹן 1262
drunken, be
drunkenness

שַׁל 1262
error

שֶׁל 1262
cause
sake

שַׁלְאֲנָן 1262
ease, being at

שָׁלַב 1262
Pual.
distant, equally
order, set in

שְׁלַבִּים 1262
ledges

שָׁלַג 1262
Hiphil.
snow, to be as

שֶׁלֶג 1262
snow
snowy

שָׁלֵו & שָׁלָה 1262
Kal.
happy, to be
prosper, to
safety, to be in

שָׁלָה1 1262
Niphal.
negligent, to be
Hiphil.
deceive, to

שָׁלָה2 1262
Kal.
take away, to

שְׁלָה Ch. 1262
P'al.
rest, at

שָׁלָה Ch......1263
amiss, thing

שַׁלְהֶבֶת 1263
flame
flaming flame

שָׁלוּ Ch. 1263
amiss, thing
error
* fail

שָׁלֵו & שָׁלֵיו ..1263
ease, at
ease, being at
peaceable
prosper
prosperity, in
quiet
quietness
wealthy

שֶׁלֶו 1263
prosperity

שַׁלְוָה 1263
abundance
peace
peaceably
prosperity
quietness

שְׁלֵוָה Ch.....1263
tranquillity

שִׁלּוּחִים......1263
presents
sent back, have

שָׁלוֹם 1263
* do
familiar
* fare
favour
friend †
good health
greet, † to
health
Jehovah-shalom
peace
* peace, perfect
peace, such as be at
peaceable
peaceably
prosper
prosperity
prosperous
rest
safe
safety
salute
salute,† to
welfare
well
* well, all is
well, be
* wholly

שִׁלּוּם 1264
recompence
reward

שְׁלוֹשָׁה & שָׁלוֹשׁ 1264
fork †
often*times* †
third
thir*teen*
thir*teenth*
three
thrice †

שְׁלוֹשִׁים......1267
(כ') captains
thirtieth
thirty
(כ') three

שָׁלַח 1268
Kal.
appoint, to
earnestly
* give, to
lay, to
let go, to
let loose
put, to
put forth, to
putting forth
send, to
send away, to
send forth, to
send out, to
sending
sent
shoot out, to
stretch forth, to
stretch out, to
Niphal.
sent, to be
Piel.
● any wise
bring, to
bring on the way, to
cast, to
cast away, to
cast out, to
conduct, to
give up, to
grow long, to
lay, to
let depart, to
let down, to
let go, to
let loose, to
letting go
push away, to
put away, to
put in, to
put out, to
putting away
reach forth, to
send, to
send away, to
send forth, to
send out, to
sending away
set, to
shoot, to
shoot forth, to
sow, to
spread out, to
Pual.
cast, to be
cast out
forsaken
left
put away, to be
sent, to be
sent away, to be
Hiphil.
send, to

שְׁלַח Ch. 1273
P'al.
put, to
send, to
sent, to be

שֶׁלַח 1273
dart
plant
* put off
sword
weapon

שְׁלֻחוֹת........1274
branches

שֻׁלְחָן 1274
table

שָׁלַט.........1274
Kal.
power, to have
rule, to
rule, to bear
rule, to have
Hiphil.
dominion, to have
power, to give

שְׁלֵט Ch. 1274
P'al.
mastery, to have the
power, to have
rule, to bear
ruler, to be
Pael.
ruler, to make

שֶׁלֶט.........1274
shield

שִׁלְטוֹן 1274
power

שִׁלְטוֹן Ch. ..1274
ruler

שָׁלְטָן Ch.....1274
dominion

שַׁלֶּטֶת 1274
imperious

שְׁלִי..........1274
quietly

שִׁלְיָה 1274
young one

שַׁלִּיט 1275
governor
mighty
power, that hath
ruler

שַׁלִּיט Ch.....1275
captain
lawful, to be
rule, to
ruler

שָׁלִישׁ 1275
captain
excellent things
great lord
great measure
instrument of musick
lord
measure
prince

שְׁלִישִׁי........1275
third
third part
third rank
third time
(כ') three
three years old

שָׁלַךְ......... 1275
Hiphil.
adventure, to
cast, to
cast away, to
cast down, to
cast forth, to
cast off, to
cast out, to
hurl, to
pluck, to
throw, to
Hophal.
cast
cast, to be
cast down, to be
cast out
cast out, to be
thrown, to be

שָׁלָךְ..........1276
cormorant

שַׁלֶּכֶת........1276
cast, when

שָׁלַל 1276
Kal.
fall, to let
purpose, of
spoil, to
spoil, to make a
take *spoil*, to
Hithpolel.
prey, to make self a
spoiled, to be

שָׁלָל..........1277
Maher - shalal - *hash-baz*
prey
spoil

שָׁלֵם 1277
Kal.
ended, to be
finished, to be
peace, to be at
peaceable
prosper, to
Piel.
amends, to make
finish, to
full
give again, to
good, to make
pay, to
pay again, to
perform, to
prosperous, to make
recompense, to
render, to
repay, to
repayed, to be
requite, to
restitution, to make
restore, to
reward, to
surely
Pual.
perfect, that is
performed, to be
recompensed, to be
rewarded, to be
Hiphil.
end, to make an
peace, to make
peace, to make to be at
perform
Hophal.
peace, to be at

שְׁלַם Ch. 1278
P'al.
finished, to be
Aphel.
deliver, to
finish, to

שְׁלָם Ch. 1278
peace

שָׁלֵם......... 1278
full
just
made ready
peaceable
perfect
perfected
quiet
whole

שֶׁלֶם......... 1278
peace offering;p.off

שִׁלֵּם 1279
recompense

שִׁלֻּמָה........1279
reward

שִׁלֻּמִים 1279
rewards

שָׁלַף..........1279
Kal.
draw, to
draw off, to
drawn
drawn, to be
grow up, to
pluck off, to

שָׁלַשׁ 1279
Piel.
third time, to do the
three days, to stay
three parts, to divide into
Pual.
three
three years old
threefold

שִׁלְשׁוֹם 1279
*before †
*before that time†
*beforetime †
(כ') excellent things
* heretofore †
three days
* time past †

שִׁלֵּשִׁים 1279
third

שָׁם 1279
in it
thence
there
therein
thereof
thereout
thither
whither

שֵׁם 1280
base †
fame
fam*ous*
*in*fam*ous*
name
name, (to)
nam*ed*
renown
report

שֻׁם Ch. 1284
name
name, (to)

שָׁמַד 1285
Niphal.
destroyed, to be
overthrown, to be
perish, to
utterly
Hiphil.
destroy, to
destruction
nought, to bring to
pluck down
utterly

שְׁמַד Ch. 1285
Aphel.
consume, to

שַׁמָּה 1285
astonishment
desolate
desolation
waste
wonderful thing

שְׁמוּעָה 1285
bruit
doctrine
fame
mentioned
news
report
rumour
tidings

שָׁמַט 1286
Kal.
discontinue, to
release, to
rest, to let
shake, to
stumble, to
throw down, to
Niphal.
overthrown, to be
Hiphil.
release, to

שְׁמִטָּה 1286
release

שָׁמַיִם 1286
air
* astro*logers*
heaven

שְׁמַיִן Ch.....1288
heaven

שְׁמִינִי........1289
eighth
Sheminith

שָׁמִיר 1289
adamant
adamant stone
briers
diamond

שָׁמֵם 1289
Kal.
astonied, to be
astonished, to be
astonishment, to be an
desolate
desolate, to be
desolate, to be laid
desolate, to make
desolate places
desolation
* destroy, to
Niphal.
astonied, to be
astonished, to be
desolate
desolate, to be
desolate, to be laid
desolate, to be made
destitute, to be
waste
waste, to lie
Polel.
astonied
desolate, to make
Hiphil.
amazed, to make
astonished
desolate, to make
desolate, making
desolation, to bring into
desolation, to bring unto
destroy, to
make *desolate*, to
waste, to lay
waste, to make
Hophal.
astonished, to be
desolate, to lie
Hithpolel.
astonished, to be
desolate, to be
destroy self, to
wonder, to

שְׁמַם Ch. 1290
Ithpolel.
astonied, to be

שָׁמֵם 1290
desolate

שְׁמָמָה 1290
desolate
(כ׳) desolate, laid
desolation; utterly waste

שִׁמָמָה 1290
desolation
most *desolate*

שִׁמָּמוֹן 1290
astonishment

שָׁמֵן 1290
Kal.
fat, to wax
fat, to be waxen
Hiphil.
fat, to become
fat, to make

שָׁמֵן 1290
fat
lusty
plenteous

שֶׁמֶן 1290
anointing
* fat
* fat things
* fruitful
oil
oil*ed*
ointment
olive
pine †

שְׁמֹנֶה & שְׁמֹנָה 1291
eight
eigh*teen*
eigh*teenth*
eighth

שְׁמֹנִים 1292
eightieth
eighty
fourscore

שָׁמַע & שָׁמֵעַ. 1292
Kal.
attentively
carefully
certainly
consent, to
consider, to
content, to be
diligently
discern, to
ear, to give
hear, to
hear tell, to
hearing
hearken, to
hearkening
indeed
listen, to
obedient
obedient, to be
obey, to
obeying
perceive, to
regard, to
surely
understand, to
whosoever *heareth*
witness
Niphal.
heard
heard, to be
obedient, to be
obey, to
perceived, to be
published, to be
reported, to be
Piel.
call together, to
gather together, to
Hiphil.
call together, to
declare, to
hear, to
hear, to cause to
hear, to let
hear, to make to
heard, to cause to be
heard, to let be
heard, to make to be
* loud, to sing
make *noise*, to
noise, to make a
proclaim, to
proclamation, to make a
publish, to
shew, to
shew forth, to
sound, to
sound, to make a
tell, to

שְׁמַע Ch. 1299
P'al.
hear, to
Ithpael.
obey, to

שֵׁמַע.........1299
bruit
fame
hear
hearing
loud
report
speech
tidings

שֹׁמַע 1300
fame

שֶׁמֶץ 1300
little, a

שִׁמְצָה 1300
shame

שָׁמַר 1300
Kal.
beware, to
diligently
heed, to take
heed, taking
keep, to
keeper
keeping
mark, to
narrowly, to look
observe, to
preserve, to
regard, to
reserve, to
save, to
spy
sure
wait, to
wait for, to
wait, that lay
waiting
watch, to
watchman
Niphal.
beware, to
circumspect, to be
heed, to take
heed to self, to take
keep selves, to
preserved, to be
save self, to
Piel.
observe, to
Hithpael.
keep self, to
kept, to be

שְׁמֻרָה 1303
watch

שְׁמֻרוֹת.......1303
* waking

שְׁמָרִים 1303
dregs
lees
wines on the lees

שִׁמֻּרִים 1303
* observed, be
* observed, be much

שְׁמַשׁ Ch. 1303
Pael.
minister, to

שֶׁמֶשׁ 1303
Beth-shemesh
* east side †
* eastward †
sun
sun*rising*
* west †
* westward †
* window

שְׁמֶשׁ Ch. 1304
sun

שֵׁן 1304
* crag
* forefront
ivory
* sharp
tooth

שֵׁן Ch. 1304
tooth

שָׁנָא 1304
Kal.
changed, to be
Piel.
change, to
Pual.
changed, to be

שְׁנָא Ch. 1304
P'al.
changed, to be
diverse
diverse, to be
Pael.
change, to
changed, to be
diverse
Ithpael.
change, to
changed, to be
Aphel.
alter, to
change, to
changed, to be

שֵׁנָא 1304
sleep

שִׁנְאָן 1304
* angels

שָׁנָה 1304
Kal.
again, to do
again, to speak
again, to strike
change, to
change, to be given to
diverse
diverse, to be
repeat, to
return, to
second time, to do the
Niphal.
doubled, to be
Piel.
alter, to
change, to
pervert, to
prefer, to
Hithpael.
disguise, to

שָׁנָה 1305
* age,† whole
* long
* long †
* old †
year
* yearly

שֵׁנָה 1309
sleep

שְׁנָה Ch. 1309
year

שְׁנָה Ch. 1309
sleep

שֶׁנְהַבִּים 1309
ivory

שָׁנִי 1309
crimson
scarlet
scarlet †
scarlet thread

שֵׁנִי 1310
again
another
either *of them*
more
other
second
second time

שְׁנַיִם 1311
both
couple
double
second
* sixscore thousand †
twain
twelfth †
twelve †
* twenty thousand †
twice
two

שְׁנִינָה........1315
byword
taunt

שָׁנַן 1315
Kal.
sharp
sharpen, to
whet, to
Piel.
teach diligently, to
Hithpolel.
picked, to be

שָׁנַס..........1315
Piel.
gird up, to

שְׁנָת..........1315
sleep

שָׁסָה.........1315
Kal.
destroyers
rob, to
spoil, to
spoiled
spoiler
Poel.
rob, to

שָׁסַס 1315
Kal.
spoil, to
Niphal.
rifled, to be
spoiled, to be

שָׁסַע 1315
Kal.
cleave, to
cloven
cloven*footed*, to be
Piel.
cleave, to
rend, to
stay, to

שֶׁסַע 1315
cleft
clovenfooted †

שָׁסַף..........1315
Piel.
hew in pieces, to

שָׁעָה 1315
Kal.
depart, to
dim, to be
look, to
look away, to
regard, to
respect, to have
turn, to
Hiphil.
spare, to
Hithpael.
dismayed, to be

שָׁעָה Ch. 1315
hour

שַׁעֲטָה.........1315
stamping

שַׁעַטְנֵז 1316
garment of divers sorts
linen and woollen

שֹׁעַל 1316
handful
hollow of the hand

שָׁעַן..........1316
Niphal.
lean, to
lie, to
rely, to
rest, to
rest on, to
rest selves, to
stay, to

שָׁעַע 1316
Kal.
cry, to
Pilpel.
delight, to
play, to
Palpal.
dandled, to be
Hiphil.
shut, to
Hithpalpel.
cry out, to
delight self, to

שָׁעַר 1316
Kal.
think, to

שַׁעַר 1316
hundred*fold*

שַׁעַר 1316
city
door
gate
port
* porters

שֹׁעָר 1318
vile

שַׁעֲרוּר 1318
horrible thing

שַׁעֲרוּרִי 1318
horrible thing

שַׁעֲשֻׁעִים.....1318
delight
pleasant

שָׁפָה 1318
Niphal.
high
Pual.
stick out, to

שְׁפָה 1318
cheese

שְׁפוֹט........1318
judgment

שִׁפְחָה 1318
bondmaid
bondwoman
handmaid
maid
maiden
maidservant
wench
womanservant

שָׁפַט.........1319
Kal.
avenge, † to
* condemn, that
defend, to
deliver, to
execute, to
judge, a
judge, to
judge, to be a
(ב׳) judgment needs
rule, to
Niphal.
contend, to
judged, to be
judgment, to execute
plead, to
reason, to
Poel.
judge

שְׁפַט Ch. 1320
P'al.
magistrate

שְׁפָטִים 1320
judgments

שְׁפִי..........1320
high place
(ב׳) stick out

שְׁפִיפֹן 1320
adder

שַׁפִּיר Ch.....1320
fair

שָׁפַךְ 1320
Kal.
cast, to
casting up
gush out, to
pour, to
pour out, to
poured out
pouring out
shed
shed, to
shed out, to
shedder
Niphal.
poured out, to be
shed, to be
Pual.
poured out, to be
shed, to be
slip, to
Hithpael.
poured, to be
poured out, to be

שֶׁפֶךְ 1321
poured out

שָׁפְכָה 1321
privy member

שָׁפֵל 1321
Kal.
brought down, to be
brought low, to be
humble self, to
humbled, to be
low, to be
low, to be made
Hiphil.
abase, to
bring down, to
cast down, to
cast down, to be
debase, to
humble, to
humble selves, to
low, to bring
low, to lay
lower, to be put
put down, to

שְׁפַל Ch. 1321
Aphel.
abase, to
humble, to
put down, to
subdue, to

שָׁפָל 1322
base
basest
humble
low
lower
lowly

שְׁפַל Ch. 1322
basest

שֵׁפֶל..........1322
low estate
low place

שִׁפְלָה.........1322
low place

שְׁפֵלָה........1322
low country
low plain
plain
vale
valley

שִׁפְלוּת 1322
idleness

שָׁפָן..........1322
coney

שֶׁפַע 1322
abundance

שִׁפְעָה 1322
abundance
company
multitude

שָׁפַר..........1322
Kal.
* goodly
Piel.
garnish, to

שְׁפַר Ch. 1322
P'al.
acceptable, to be
please, to
* think good, † to

שֶׁפֶר..........1322
goodly

שַׁפְרִיר & שַׁפְרוּר 1322
royal pavilion

שְׁפַרְפָּרָא Ch. 1322
early in the morning, very

שָׁפַת 1322
Kal.
bring, to
ordain, to
set on, to

שְׁפַתַּיִם 1322
hooks
pots

שֶׁצֶף..........1322
little, a

שָׁק Ch. 1322
leg

שָׁקַד[1]........1322
Kal.
hasten, to
remain, to
wake, to
watch, to
watch for, to
watching

שָׁקַד[2]........1323
Pual.
almonds, made after the fashion of
almonds, made like
almonds, made like unto

שָׁקֵד..........1323
almond
almond tree

שָׁקָה..........1323
Niphal.
(ב׳) drowned, to be
Pual.
moistened, to be

Hiphil.
butler
cupbearer
drink, to cause to
drink, to give
drink, to give to
drink, giving
drink, to let
drink, to make to
water, to

שִׁקּוּ 1323
drink

שִׁקּוּי 1323
drink
marrow

שִׁקּוּץ 1323
abominable filth
abominable idols
abominations
detestable
detestable things

שָׁקַט 1324
Kal.
quiet
quiet, at
quiet, to be
quiet, to be in
quietness, to be in
rest, to
rest, to be at
rest, to have
rest, to be in
rest, to take
settle, to
still, to be
Hiphil.
appease, to
idleness
quiet, to
quiet, to be
quietness
quietness, to give
rest, to
rest, to give

שֶׁקֶט 1324
quietness

שָׁקַל 1324
Kal.
pay, to
receive, to
receiver
spend, to
throughly
weigh, to
weighed, to be
Niphal.
weighed, to be

שֶׁקֶל 1324
shekel

שִׁקְמָה 1324
sycomore
sycomore fruit
sycomore tree

שָׁקַע 1325
Kal.
drowned, to be
quenched, to be
sink, to
Niphal.
drowned, to be
Hiphil.
deep, to make
let down, to

שְׁקַעֲרוּרֹת 1325
hollow strakes

שָׁקַף 1325
Niphal.
appear, to
look, to
look down, to
look forth, to
Hiphil.
look, to
look down, to
look out, to

שֶׁקֶף 1325
windows

שְׁקֻפִים 1325
* narrow lights †
windows

שָׁקַץ 1325
Piel.
abhor, to
abominable, to make
abomination, to have in
detest, to
utterly

שֶׁקֶץ 1325
abominable
abomination

שָׁקַק 1325
Kal.
appetite, to have
long, to
range, to
run, to
run to and fro, to
Hithpalpel.
justle one against another, to

שָׁקַר 1325
Kal.
falsely, to deal
Piel.
fail, to
falsely, to deal
lie, to

שֶׁקֶר 1325
cause, without a
deceit
deceitful
false
falsehood
false*ly*
falsely
feignedly
liar
lie †
lie
lying
lying †
vain
vain thing
wrongfully

שֹׁקֶת 1326
trough

שֹׁר 1326
navel

שְׁרֵא Ch. 1326
P'al.
dissolve, to
dwell, to
loose
Pael.
begin, to
dissolve, to
Ithpael.
loosed, to be

שָׁרָב 1326
heat
parched ground

שַׁרְבִיט 1326
sceptre

שָׂרָה 1326
Kal.
direct, to
Piel.
*(ק') remnant

שְׁרוּקֹת 1326
hissing

שָׁרוֹת 1326
walls

שֵׁרוֹת 1326
bracelets

שֵׁרוּת 1326
remnant

שִׁרְיָה 1326
habergeon

שִׁרְיוֹן 1326
coat of *mail*
coat of mail
habergeons

שִׁרְיָן 1327
breastplate
harness

שְׁרִיקוֹת 1327
bleatings
hissing

שָׂרִיר 1327
navel

שְׁרִירוּת 1327
imagination
lust

שְׁרֵמוֹת 1327
(ב') fields

שָׁרַץ 1327
Kal.
breed abundantly, to
bring forth abundantly, to
bring forth in abundance, to
creep, to
increase abundantly, to
move, to

שֶׁרֶץ 1327
creep
creeping thing
move
moving creature

שָׁרַק 1327
Kal.
hiss

שְׁרֵקָה 1327
hissing

שָׁרַר 1327
Kal.
enemy

שֹׁרֶר 1327
navel

שָׁרַשׁ 1327
Piel.
root out, to
Pual.
rooted out, to be
Poel.
root, to take
Poal.
root, to take
Hiphil.
root, to cause to take
root, to take

שֹׁרֶשׁ 1327
* bottom
* deep
* heel
root

שֹׁרֶשׁ Ch. 1328
roots

שַׁרְשָׁה 1328
chain

(ב') שְׁרֹשׁוּ, (ק') שְׁרֹשִׁי Ch. 1328
banishment

שַׁרְשְׁרָה 1328
chain

שָׁרַת 1328
Piel.
minister
minister, to
minister unto, to
servant
serve, to
service, to do
servitor
wait on, to

שָׁרֵת 1328
minister
ministry

שֵׁשׁ 1328
* blue
linen, fine
linen, fine *twined*
marble
silk

שֵׁשׁ & שִׁשָּׁה . 1329
six
six*teen*
six*teenth*
sixth

שִׁשָּׁא 1330
Piel.
sixth part, to leave but the

שִׁשָּׁה 1330
Piel.
sixth part, to give the

שֵׁשִׁי 1330
linen, fine

שִׁשִּׁי 1331
sixth
sixth part

שִׁשִּׁים 1331
sixty
threescore

שָׁשַׁר 1331
vermilion

שָׁת 1331
foundation
purpose

שֵׁת 1331
buttocks

שֵׁת 1331
* Sheth

שֵׁת & שִׁת Ch. 1331
six
sixth

שָׁתָה 1331
Kal.
assuredly
banquet, to
certainly
drink, to
drinker
drinking
drunkard †
surely
Niphal.
drunk, to be

שְׁתָה Ch. 1333
P'al.
drink, to

שְׁתִי 1333
drunkenness
warp

שְׁתִיָּה 1333
drinking

שִׁתִּין Ch. 1333
threescore

שָׁתַל 1333
Kal.
plant, to
planted

שָׁתִל 1333
plant

שָׁתַם 1333
Kal.
* open, to be

שָׁתַן 1333
Hiphil.
piss, to

שָׁתַק 1333
Kal.
calm, to be
cease, to
quiet, to be

שָׁתַת 1333
Kal.
laid, to be
set, to

תָּא 1333
chamber
chamber, little

תָּאַב 1 1333
Kal.
long, to

תָּאַב 2 1333
Piel.
abhor, to

תַּאֲבָה 1334
longing

lowest
nether
nether part
Tahtim-*hodshi*

תִּיכוֹן 1346
Hazar-hatticon
middle
middlemost
midst

תֵּימָן 1346
south
south side
south wind
southward
Teman

תִּימָרוֹת 1346
pillars

תִּירוֹשׁ 1346
new wine
sweet wine
wine

תַּיִשׁ 1346
goat, he

תֹּךְ 1346
deceit
fraud

תָּכָה 1346
Pual.
sit down, to

תְּכוּנָה 1346
seat

תְּכוּנָה 1346
fashion
store

תֻּכִּיִּים 1346
peacocks

תְּכָכִים 1346
deceitful

תִּכְלָה 1347
perfection

תַּכְלִית 1347
end
perfect
perfection

תְּכֵלֶת 1347
blue

תָּכַן 1347
Kal.
ponder, to
weigh, to
Niphal.
equal, to be
*un*equal, to be
weighed, to be
Piel.
bear up, to
direct, to
mete, to
weigh, to
Pual.
told, to be

תֹּכֶן 1347
measure
tale

תָּכְנִית 1347
pattern
sum

תַּכְרִיךְ 1347
garment

תֵּל 1347
heap
* strength

תָּלָא 1347
Kal.
bent, to be
hang, to
hang in doubt, to

תְּלָאָה 1347
travail
travel
trouble

תַּלְאוּבֹת 1347
drought, great

תִּלְבֹּשֶׁת 1347
clothing

תְּלַג Ch. 1347
snow

תָּלָה 1347
Kal.
hang, to
hanged, to be
Niphal.
hanged, to be
hanged up, to be
Piel.
hang, to

תְּלִי 1348
quiver

תְּלִיתַי Ch. .. 1348
third

תָּלַל 1348
Kal.
eminent

תֶּלֶם 1348
furrow
ridge

תַּלְמִיד 1348
scholar

תְּלֻנּוֹת 1348
murmurings

תָּלַע 1348
Pual.
* scarlet

תַּלְפִּיּוֹת 1348
armoury

תְּלָת Ch. 1348
third
three

תְּלָת Ch. 1348
third

תַּלְתִּי Ch. 1348
third

תְּלָתִין Ch. .. 1348
thirty

תַּלְתַּלִּים 1348
bushy

תָּם 1348
perfect
plain
undefiled
upright

תָּם Ch. 1348
thence
there
where

תֹּם 1348
full
integrity
perfect
perfection
simplicity
Thummim
upright
uprightly
uprightness
venture, at a

תֻּמָּה 1349
integrity

תָּמַהּ 1349
Kal.
amazed, to be
astonished, to be
marvel, to
marvellously
wonder, to
Hithpael.
wonder, to

תְּמַהּ Ch. 1349
wonder

תִּמָּהוֹן 1349
astonishment

תְּמוֹל 1349
before †
beforetime †
days,† these *three*
heretofore †
time past †
yesterday

תְּמוּנָה 1349
image
likeness
similitude

תְּמוּרָה 1349
change
changing
exchange
recompence
restitution

תְּמוּתָה 1349
death
die

תָּמִיד 1349
alway
always
continual
continual employment
continually
daily
ever
evermore
never
perpetual

תָּמִים 1350
blemish, without
complete
full
perfect
sincerely
sincerity
sound
spot, without
undefiled
upright
uprightly
whole

תָּמִים 1350
coupled together

תָּמַךְ 1350
Kal.
hold, to
hold up, to
holding
maintain, to
retain, to
stay, to
stay up, to
take hold, to
uphold, to
Niphal.
holden, to be

תָּמַם 1351
Kal.
accomplish, to
accomplished, to be
all gone, to be
clean, to be *passed*
consumed, to be
done, to have
end
end, to come to an
ended, to be
fail, to
* here, to be all
perfect, to be
spent, to be
upright, to be
wasted, to be
whole
Niphal.
consumed, to be
end, to have an
Hiphil.
cease, to
consume, to
end, to
end, to make an
full, to be come to the
perfect, to make
sum, to
Hithpael.
upright, to shew self

תֶּמֶס 1351
melt

תָּמָר 1351
palm
palm tree

תֹּמֶר 1351
palm tree

תִּמֹּרָה 1351
palm tree

תַּמְרוּק 1351
* cleanse
purification, things for
purifying

תַּמְרוּרִים 1352
* bitter, most
* bitterly, most

תַּמְרוּרִים 1352
heaps, high

תַּמְרִיק (כ׳).. 1352
cleanse

תָּנָה [1] 1352
Kal.
hire, to
Hiphil.
hire, to

תָּנָה [2] 1352
Piel.
lament, to
rehearse, to

תַּנּוֹת 1352
dragons

תְּנוּאָה 1352
breach of promise
occasion

תְּנוּבָה 1352
fruit
increase

תְּנוּךְ 1352
tip

תְּנוּמָה 1352
slumber
slumbering

תְּנוּפָה 1352
offering
shaking
wave
wave offering
waved, be

תַּנּוּר 1352
furnace
oven

תַּנְחוּמוֹת 1352
consolations

תַּנְחוּמִים 1352
comforts
consolations

תַּנִּים 1352
dragons
whale

תַּנִּים 1352
dragon

תַּנִּין 1353
dragons
sea monster
serpent
whale

תִּנְיָן Ch. 1353
second

תִּנְיָנוּת Ch. .. 1353
again

תִּנְשֶׁמֶת 1353
mole
swan

תָּעַב 1353
Niphal.
abominable
abominable, to be
Piel.
abhor, to
abhorred, to make to be
utterly
Hiphil.
abominable, to commit more
abominable, to do
abominably, to do

תָּעָה 1353
Kal.
astray, to go
err, to
pant, to
wander, to
way, to be out of the
Niphal.
deceived, to be
stagger, to
Hiphil.
astray, to cause to go
dissemble, to
err, to
err, to cause to
err, to make to
seduce, to
stagger, to make to
wander, to cause to

תְּעוּדָה 1353
testimony

תְּעָלָה 1353
conduit
cured
healing
rivers, little
trench
watercourse

תַּעֲלוּלִים 1354
babes
delusions

תַּעֲלֻמָּה 1354
hid, thing that is
secrets

תַּעֲנוּג 1354
delicate
delight
pleasant

תַּעֲנִית 1354
heaviness

תָּעַע 1354
Pilpel.
deceiver
Hithpalpel.
misuse, to

תַּעֲצֻמוֹת 1354
power

תַּעַר 1354
*pen*knife
rasor
scabbard
shave
sheath

תַּעֲרוּבוֹת 1354
hostages †

תַּעְתֻּעִים 1354
errors

תֹּף 1354
tabret
timbrel

תִּפְאֶרֶת & תִּפְאָרָה 1354
beautiful
beauty
bravery
comely
fair
glorious
glory
honour
excellent

תַּפּוּחַ 1354
apple
apple tree

תְּפוּצָה 1354
dispersion

תֻּפִינִים 1355
baken *pieces*

תָּפֵל 1355
foolish things
unsavoury
untempered

תִּפְלָה 1355
folly
foolishly

תְּפִלָּה 1355
prayer

תִּפְלֶצֶת 1355
terribleness

תָּפַף 1355
Kal.
timbrels, to play with
Poel.
taber, to

תָּפַר 1355
Kal.
sew, to
sew together, to
Piel.
sew, women that

תָּפַשׂ 1355
Kal.
catch, to
handle, to
*handl*ed, to be
hold, to
laid over
lay hold, to
lay hold on, to
surely
take, to
take hold, to
Niphal.
caught, to be
stopped, to be
surprised, to be
taken, to be
* taking
Piel.
take hold, to

תֹּפֶת 1356
tabret

תִּפְתָּיֵא Ch. ..1356
sheriffs

תִּקְוָה 1356
expectation
expect*ed*
hope
line
long for, thing that I

תְּקוּמָה 1356
power to stand

תְּקוֹמֵם 1356
rise up against

תָּקוֹעַ 1356
trumpet

תְּקוּפָה 1356
circuit
come about
end

תַּקִּיף 1356
mightier

תַּקִּיף Ch. 1356
mighty
strong

תְּקַל Ch. 1356
P'al.
Tekel
P'il.
weighed, to be

תָּקַן 1356
Kal.
straight, to be made
Piel.
order, to set in
straight, to make

תְּקַן Ch. 1356
Hophal.
established, to be

תָּקַע 1356
Kal.
blow *a trumpet*, to
blowing
cast, to
clap, to
fasten, to
pitch *tent*, to
smite, to
sound, to
strike, to
* suretiship
thrust, to
Niphal.
blown, to be
strike, to

תֵּקַע 1357
sound

תָּקַף 1357
Kal.
prevail against
prevail against, to

תְּקֵף Ch. 1357
P'al.
hardened, to be
strong, to be
strong, to become
Pael.
firm, to make

תֹּקֶף 1357
authority
power
strength

תְּקֹף Ch. 1357
might
strength

תַּרְבּוּת 1357
increase

תַּרְבִּית 1357
increase
unjust gain

תַּרְגֵּם 1357
interpreted

תַּרְדֵּמָה 1357
deep sleep

תְּרוּמָה 1357
gift
heave offering
heave *shoulder*
oblation
offered
offering

תְּרוּמִיָּה 1358
oblation

תְּרוּעָה 1358
alarm
blow
blowing of trumpets
blowing the trumpets
joy
jubile
noise, loud
rejoicing
shout
shout, to
shouting
sound, joyful
sounding
sounding, high

תְּרוּפָה 1358
medicine

תִּרְזָה 1358
cypress

תְּרֵין Ch. 1358
second
twelve †
two

תָּרְמָה 1358
privily

תַּרְמוּת 1358
deceit

תַּרְמִית 1358
deceit
deceitful

תֹּרֶן 1358
beacon
mast

תְּרַע Ch. 1358
gate
mouth

תָּרָע Ch. 1358
porter

תַּרְעֵלָה 1359
astonishment
trembling

תְּרָפִים 1359
idolatry
idols
images
teraphim

תַּרְשִׁישׁ 1359
beryl

תִּרְשָׁתָא 1359
Tirshatha

תְּשׂוּמֶת 1359
fellowship

תְּשֻׁאוֹת 1359
crying
noise
shoutings
stirs

תַּשְׁבֵּץ 1359
broidered

תְּשׁוּבָה 1359
answer
expired, be
return

תְּשׁוּעָה 1359
deliverance
help
safety
salvation
victory

תְּשׁוּקָה 1359
desire

תְּשׁוּרָה 1359
present

תְּשִׁיעִי 1359
ninth

תֵּשַׁע & תִּשְׁעָה 1359
nine
nine*teen*
nine*teenth*
ninth

תִּשְׁעִים 1360
ninety

ENGLISH AND HEBREW INDEX.

*** The Hebrew words follow in alphabetical order the English word by which they are translated. An English word is marked * when some peculiarity is the occasion of its being used to translate the Hebrew word which follows it. The mark † shews that the English word is the translation of the following Hebrew word in combination with some other. A bracket *prefixed* to two or more Hebrew words after one English word, indicates that the English is the rendering of such combination. Words or parts of words in *italics*, indicate that they are not included in the Hebrew word that follows. The few proper names found in this Index are such as, in some cases at least, may be taken as appellatives.

A
אֶחָד 41
חַד Ch. 402

Abana
אֲמָנָה (כ׳) 104

abase, to
שָׁפֵל Hiphil 1321
שְׁפַל Ch. Aphel.......1321

abase self, to
עָנָה[2] Kal 964

* abate, to
נוּם Kal 801

abated, to be
גָּרַע Niphal 316
חָסֵר Kal 450
קָלַל Kal 1109
רָפָה Kal 1188

abhor, to
בָּחַל Kal 208
גָּעַל Kal 313
זָהַם Piel 382
זָעַם Kal 391
מָאַס[1] Kal 659
נָאַץ Kal 782
נָאַץ Piel 782
נָאַר Piel 782
קוּץ[3] Kal 1104
שָׁקַץ Piel 1325
תָּאַב[2] Piel 1333
תָּעַב Piel 1353

abhorred, to be
בָּאַשׁ Niphal 184

abhorred, to make to be
בָּאַשׁ Hiphil 184
תָּעַב Piel 1353

abhorring
דֵּרָאוֹן 348

Abi-*ezrite*
אָב 1

Abib
אָבִיב 10

abide, to
בּוֹא Kal............ 189
גּוּר Kal............ 303
חִיל / חוּל } Kal............ 406
חָוָה Kal 445
יָשַׁב Kal............ 568
כּוּל Pilpel 592
לִין & לוּן Kal 635
לִין & לוּן Hithpalpel...... 635
עָמַד Kal 955
קוּם Kal 1099
שָׁכֵן / שָׁכַן } Kal 1260

abide, to be able to
כּוּל Hiphil.......... 592

abide all night, to
לִין & לוּן Kal............ 635

abide behind, to
עָמַד Kal............ 955

abide, can
כּוּל Hiphil 592

abide fast, to
דָּבֵק / דָּבַק } Kal 318

abide in, *see* tents

abide, to make to
יָשַׁב Hiphil 568

abide with, to
לָוָה Kal............ 634

abiding
יָשַׁב Kal............ 568
מִקְוֶה 756
סָפַח Hithpael 881

ability
כֹּחַ 594
נָשַׂג Hiphil 845

ability, *see* after

abject
נֵכֶה 817

able
דַּי 339
חַיִל 423
כֹּחַ 594

able, be
יָד 489

* able,† be
יָד 489

able, to be
יָכֹל Kal............ 526
יְכִל Ch. P'al 527
כְּהַל Ch. P'al 586
נָשַׂג Hiphil 845
עָצַר Kal............ 973

* *able*, to be
עָצַר Kal............ 973

able,† to be
מָצָא Kal............ 748

able, *see* bear, bring, get, go, go forth, stand

able to, *see* abide

* able to endure, be
רֶגֶל 1155

abolish, to
חָלַף Kal............ 434

abolished, to be
חָתַת Niphal 472
מָחָה[1] Niphal.......... 686

abominable
זָעַם Kal............ 391
פִּגּוּל 1009
שֶׁקֶץ 1325
תּוֹעֵבָה 1341
תָּעַב Niphal 1353

abominable, to be
תָּעַב Niphal..........1353

abominable, to commit more
תָּעַב Hiphil 1353

abominable custom
תּוֹעֵבָה 1341

abominable, to do
תָּעַב Hiphil 1353

abominable filth
שִׁקּוּץ 1323

abominable idols
שִׁקּוּץ 1323

abominable, to make
שָׁקַץ Piel 1325

abominable thing
פִּגּוּל 1009
תּוֹעֵבָה 1341

abominably, to do
תָּעַב Hiphil 1353

abomination
פִּגּוּל ... 1009
שִׁקּוּץ ... 1323
שֶׁקֶץ ... 1325
תּוֹעֵבָה ... 1341

abomination, to be had in
בָּאַשׁ Niphal ... 184

abomination, to have in
שָׁקַץ Piel ... 1325

abound
רַב ... 1147

abounding with
כָּבַד } כָּבֵד } Niphal ... 581

about
אֶל ... 78
בְּעַד ... 261
נֶגֶד ... 790
סָבִיב ... 866
עַל Ch. ... 933

* about
יָד ... 489

about, *see* beset, bind, bounds, bring, carried, carry, cast, come, compass, fence, fetch, gad, gird, go, go round, going, gone, lead, places, round, scatter, set, turn, turned, walk, whirl, winding, wrapped

about, to go
סָבַב Kal ... 865

about, to make
סָבַב Hiphil ... 865

about on every side, to be
סָבַב Kal ... 865

above
מִן ... 731
מַעַל ... 743
מָרוֹם ... 763
עַל ... 932
עַל & עַל ... 933

above, *see* over

above, far
מָרוֹם ... 763

abroad
חוּץ ... 408
פָּרַח Kal ... 1045

* abroad
פָּרַץ Kal ... 1047

abroad, *see* all, cast, come, far, go, scattered, spread, walk, wander

absent, to be
סָתַר Niphal ... 886

abundance
הָמוֹן ... 368
זִיז ... 384
יִתְרָה ... 581
עָצְמָה ... 973
עֲתֶרֶת ... 1008
רֹב ... 1150
רָבָה Hiphil ... 1151
שֹׂבַע ... 1196
שַׁלְוָה ... 1263
שֶׁפַע ... 1322
שִׁפְעָה ... 1322

abundance †
מִסְפָּר ... 738

abundance, *see* bring forth

abundance, to bring in
רָבָה Hiphil ... 1151

abundance, in
כָּבַר Hiphil ... 585
רַב ... 1147

abundant
רַב ... 1147

abundant †
יֶתֶר ... 580

abundantly
פָּרַח Kal ... 1045
רַב ... 1147
רֹב ... 1150

* abundantly
יָרַד Kal ... 561
רָבָה Hiphil ... 1151

abundantly, *see* breed, bring forth, drink, increase, satisfied, utter, water

abundantly, is sometimes the translation of the infinitives of verbs used intensively.

abuse, to
עָלַל Hithpael ... 942

accept, to
דָּשֵׁן Piel ... 355
לָקַח Kal ... 644
נָשָׂא Kal ... 840
רוּחַ Hiphil ... 1160
רָצָה Kal ... 1189

accept,† to
פָּנִים ... 1023

acceptable
בָּחַר Niphal ... 209
חֵפֶץ ... 452
רָצוֹן ... 1189

acceptable, to be
רָצָה Kal ... 1189
רָצוֹן ... 1189
שְׁפַר Ch. P'al ... 1322

acceptance
רָצוֹן ... 1189

accepted, be
שְׂאֵת ... 1195

accepted, to be
יָטַב Kal ... 524
נָפַל Kal ... 825
רָצָה Niphal ... 1189
רָצוֹן ... 1189

accompanying
עִם ... 955

accomplish, to
כָּלָה Piel ... 598
מָלֵא Piel ... 701
עָשָׂה Kal ... 981
פָּלָא Piel ... 1018
קוּם Hiphil ... 1099
רָצָה Kal ... 1189
תָּמַם Kal ... 1351

accomplished, to be
הָיָה Niphal ... 360
כָּלָה Kal ... 598
מָלֵא Kal ... 701
מָלֵא Niphal ... 701
תָּמַם Kal ... 1351

accord
פֶּה ... 1011

accord, *see* groweth

according
מִן Ch. ... 732

according as
פֶּה ... 1011

* according as
רֶגֶל ... 1155

according to
אֶל ... 78
דַּי ... 339
כְּמוֹ ... 603
עַל ... 932
פֶּה ... 1011

according to †
קֳבֵל } קֳבֵל } Ch. ... 1084

accordingly
עַל ... 932

account
חֶשְׁבּוֹן ... 469
טְעֵם Ch. ... 484
מִסְפָּר ... 738
פְּקֻדָּה ... 1041

account, to give
עָנָה Kal ... 962

account of, to make
חָשַׁב Piel ... 468

accounted, to be
חָשַׁב Niphal ... 468
סָפַר Pual ... 882

accursed
חֵרֶם ... 464
קְלָלָה ... 1110

accursed, to be
קָלַל Pual ... 1109

accursed, to make
חָרַם Hiphil ... 464

accursed thing
חֵרֶם ... 464

צָרַר Kal 1083
רָעַע Hiphil 1186
afflict, to lightly
קָלַל Hiphil 1109
afflict, more grievously to
כָּבַד / כָּבֵד } Hiphil 581
afflict selves, to
עָנָה[2] Hithpael 964
afflicted
דַּךְ 340
עָנִי 965
עָנִי 966
צָר & צַר 1080
afflicted †
בֵּן 232
afflicted, to be
יָגָה[1] Niphal 488
עָנָה[2] Kal 964
עָנָה[2] Niphal 964
עָנָה[2] Pual 964
עָנָה[2] Hithpael 964
afflicted, is
מָס 736
affliction
אָוֶן 30
לַחַץ 640
מוּעָקָה 673
עַיִן 919
עָנָה[2] Pual 964
עֱנוּת 965
עֳנִי 966
צָר & צַר 1080
צָרָה 1081
רַע 1177
שֶׁבֶר / שֵׁבֶר } 1234
affliction, to be in
צָרַר Hiphil 1083
affording
פּוּק[2] Hiphil 1015
affright, to
בָּעַת Piel 263
יָרֵא Piel 559
affrighted
שַׂעַר 1212
affrighted, to be
בָּהַל / בָּהֵל } Niphal 188
חָתַת Niphal 472
עָרַץ Kal 980
affrighted,† to be
אָחַז Kal 46
afore
פָּנִים 1023
קַדְמָה 1089

aforetime
פָּנִים 1023
קֶדֶם 1088
*afore*time
דֵּן Ch. 346
afore*time*
קַדְמָה Ch. 1089
afraid
חָרֵד 462
יָרֵא 561
afraid, to be
בָּהַל / בָּהֵל } Niphal 188
בָּעַת Niphal 263
גּוּר Kal 303
דָּאַג Kal 318
זָחַל Kal 384
חָגַר Kal 401
חִיל / חוּל } Kal 406
חָרַג Kal 462
חָרַד Kal 462
חָתַת Kal 472
חָתַת Niphal 472
יָגֹר Kal 489
יָרֵא Kal 559
יָרַהּ Kal 564
עָרַץ Kal 980
עָרַץ Hiphil 980
פָּחַד Kal 1016
רָגַז Kal 1155
רָהָה Kal 1159
שָׂעַר Kal 1212
afraid, to be horribly
שָׂעַר Kal 1212
afraid, to make
בָּהַל / בָּהֵל } Piel 188
בָּעַת Piel 262
דְּחַל Ch. Pael 339
חָרַד Hiphil 462
חָתַת Hiphil 472
יָרֵא Piel 559
רָעַשׁ Hiphil 1187
after
אַחַר 48
אַחֲרוֹן 53
אַחֲרֵי Ch. 54
אֶל 78
אֲשֶׁר 180
אֲתַר Ch. 183
דַּי 339
מִן 731
מִן Ch. 732
עַל 932
פֶּה 1011

קֵץ 1113
קָצֶה 1114
* after
יָצָא Kal 548
רֶגֶל 1155
after †
עֵת 1005
after, *see* follow, follow hard, lust
after ability
דַּי 339
after that
אַחַר 48
after that †
כֵּן 604
after that manner
כָּכָה 597
after this †
כֵּן 604
after this manner
כָּכָה 597
after this sort
דֵּן Ch. 346
afternoon †
נָטָה Kal 810
afterward
אַחַר 48
אַחֲרוֹן 53
afterward †
כֵּן 604
afterward, till
אָחוֹר 45
again
אַחַר 48
גַּם 311
עוֹד 905
שֵׁנִי 1310
תִּנְיָנוּת Ch. 1353
* again
יָלַךְ Kal 531
יָסַף Kal 543
יָסַף Hiphil 543
שׁוּב Kal 1238
again, *see* answer, back, break, bring, brought, build, carry, circumcise, come, conceive, deliver, dig, doubtless, evil, feed, fetch, gathered, get, give, go, lay down, lie down, lift up, lodge, make, pay, place, pull in, put, rejoice, render, restored, return, ring, rise up, send, set, sounding, take, turn, turn back, vomit, weep
again, to be come
שׁוּב Kal 1238
again, to do
שָׁנָה Kal 1304
again, to (*do anything*)
שׁוּב Kal 1238

again *feed*, to
שׁוּב Kal 1238

again, to speak
שָׁנָה Kal 1304

against
אֶל 78
אֵת 182
מוּל 671
נֶגֶד 790
נֹכַח 817
עַד 901
עַל 932
עַל Ch. 933
עִם 955
עִמָּד 958
עִמָּה 959
פָּנִים 1023
צַד Ch. 1061

* against
עֵבֶר 899
קָרָא[2] Kal 1122

against, *see* come, justle, mad, oppose, over, prevail, rebel, rise, rise up, speak, violence

against, as
עַל 932

* against he come
קָרָא[2] Kal 1122

against, over
מוּאל 669
מוֹל 671
מוּל 671
נֶגֶד 790
נֹכַח 817
עֻמָּה 959

agate
כַּדְכֹּד 586
שְׁבוֹ 1224

age
דּוֹר 337
זֹקֶן 393
חֶלֶד 429
יוֹם 508
שֵׂיב 1205

* age
בֵּן 232

* age †
חַי 418

age, *see* flower, old, stoop for, whole

age, full
כֶּלַח 600

age, old
כֶּלַח 600

* age,† whole
שָׁנָה 1305

aged
זָקֵן 392
יָשִׁישׁ 576

aged man
זָקֵן Kal 392

aged man, very
יָשִׁישׁ 576

ago
קַדְמָה Ch. 1089

ago, *see* long

agone, *see* days

agreed, to be
יָעַד Niphal 545

agreement
חֹזֶה 410
חָזוּת 411
מֵישָׁרִים 698

ague, *see* burning

ah
אֲהָהּ 26
אָח 40
הֶאָח 356
הוֹי 359

Aha
הֶאָח 356

*Aho*hite
בֵּן 232

Ai (כ')
עִיר 925

aid, to
חָזַק Piel 411

Aijeleth-Shahar
{ אַיֶּלֶת 59
{ שַׁחַר 1252

air
רוּחַ 1160
שָׁמַיִם 1286

Alamoth
עֲלָמוֹת 943

alarm
תְּרוּעָה 1358

alarm, *see* blow, cry, sound

alas
אֲהָהּ 26
אוֹי 29
אָח 40
בִּי 212
הוֹ 358
הוֹי 359

algum *trees*
אַלְגּוּמִּים 78

alien
גֵּר 314
נֵכָר 818
נָכְרִי 819

alienate, to
עָבַר Kal 895
עָבַר Hiphil 895

alienated, to be
יָקַע Kal 558
נָקַע Kal 839

alike
אֶחָד 41
אֲשֶׁר 180
גַּם 311
יַחַד / יַחְדָּו / יַחְדָּיו } 522

alike, to be
שָׁוָה Nithpael 1245

alive
חַי 418

* alive
שָׂרִיד 1217

alive, *see* preserve, save

alive, to keep
חָיָה Piel 421
חָיָה Hiphil 421
חֲיָא / חֲיָה } Ch. Aphel 423

alive, to leave
חָיָה Piel 421

alive, to make
חָיָה Piel 421
חָיָה Hiphil 421

all
כֹּל 597
כֹּל Ch. 597
כָּלִיל 603
רֹב 1150

* all
מִסְפָּר 738

all, *see* at all, glorious, here, in, put, sorts, therein

all abroad
שָׁטַח Kal 1254

all along
הָלַךְ Kal 362

* all along
מְלֹא 703

all gone, to be
תָּמַם Kal 1351

all, in
כֹּל 597

* all life long
עוֹד 905

all manner
כֹּל 597

all manner, *see* manner

all night, *see* abide, lie, lodge, tarry,

allied
קָרוֹב 1127

Allon-bachuth
{ אַלּוֹן 94
{ בָּכוּת 228

allowance
אֲרֻחָה 155

allure, to
פָּתָה Piel.................... 1052

Almighty
שַׁדַּי 1237

almond
שָׁקֵד 1323

almond tree
שָׁקֵד 1323

almonds, made after the fashion of
שָׁקַד [2] Pual 1323

almonds, made like
שָׁקַד [2] Pual 1323

almonds, made like unto
שָׁקַד [2] Pual 1323

almost
מְעַט 741

almug tree
אַלְמֻגִּים 95

aloes
אֲהָלוֹת }
אֲהָלִים } 29

alone
אֶחָד 41
בַּד 186
בָּדַד Kal.................... 187
בָּדָד 187

alone, *see* let

along
דֶּרֶךְ 349
הָלַךְ Kal.................... 362

* along
קוֹמָה 1103

along, *see* all along, go, lay, pass, run

along, to draw
מָשַׁךְ Kal.................... 770

* aloof
נֶגֶד 790

aloud
גָּרוֹן 315
חַיִל Ch. 425

* aloud
רֵעַ 1181

aloud †
קוֹל 1096

* aloud †
גָּדוֹל 293
רוּם Hiphil 1163

aloud, *see* cry, sing

aloud for joy
רָנַן Piel.................... 1177

already
כְּבָר 585

also
אוֹ 29
אִישׁ 60
אַךְ 70
אַף 144
אַף Ch. 144
גַּם 311
כֹּה 586

* also, for that
שָׁגַג Kal 1235

altar
אֲרִאֵל }
אֲרִיאֵיל } 155
אֲרִיאֵל }
הַרְאֵל 374
מַדְבַּח Ch. 664
מִזְבֵּחַ 681

altars for incense
מְקַטְּרוֹת 758

altars of brick
לְבֵנָה 632

Al-taschith
{ אַל 76
{ שָׁחַת Hiphil 1252

alter, to
חָלַף Hiphil 434
עֲדָה & א׳ Ch. P'al 902
שְׁנָא Ch. Aphel 1304
שָׁנָה Piel 1304

altered, to be
עָבַר Kal 895

although
כִּי 596

although †
אַף 144

altogether
אֶחָד 41
יַחַד }
יַחְדָּו } 522
יַחְדָּיו }
כֹּל 597
כָּלָה 600

* altogether
הֶבֶל 356

altogether, *see* just

altogether is sometimes the translation of infinitives used intensitively.

always
נֵצַח }
נֶצַח } 835
עוֹלָם 907
תָּמִיד 1349

*al*ways
עֵת 1005

always †
יוֹם 508

Amana
אֲמָנָה 104

amazed, to be
בָּהַל }
בָּהֵל } Niphal.................... 188
חָתַת Kal 472
תָּמַהּ Kal 1349

amazed, to make
שָׁמֵם Hiphil 1289

ambassador
לוּץ Hiphil 636
מַלְאָךְ 704
צִיר 1071

ambassadors, to make as if had been
צַיָּר Hithpael 1071

amber
חַשְׁמַל 470

ambush
אָרַב Kal 149

ambush, *see* lie in, lier in

ambush, lie in
מַאֲרָב 669

ambushment
אָרַב Piel 149
מַאֲרָב 660

amen
אָמֵן 104

amend, to
חָזַק Piel.................... 411
יָטַב Hiphil 524

amends, to make
שָׁלַם Piel 1277

amerce, to
עָנַשׁ Kal 967

amethyst
אַחְלָמָה 48

amiable
יְדִיד 500

amiss, to do
עָוָה Hiphil 906

amiss, thing
שָׁלָה Ch. 1263
שָׁלוּ Ch. 1263

Ammi
עַם & עָם 944

Ammi, *see* Lo-ammi

*Ammi*nadib
נָדִיב 796

*Ammon*ite
בֵּן 232

among
אֶל 78
אֵת 182
בֵּין 212
בֵּין Ch. 212
גֵּו 299
דַּי 339
מִן 731
עַל 932
עִם 965

קֶרֶב ... 1125
תָּוֶךְ ... 1338
among *see* from, midst
ancestor
רִאשׁוֹן ... 1145
ancient
זָקֵן ... 392
יָשִׁישׁ ... 576
עוֹלָם ... 907
עַתִּיק ... 1008
עַתִּיק Ch. ... 1008
קְדוּמִים ... 1087
קֶדֶם ... 1088
קַדְמוֹנִי ... 1089
ancient man
זָקֵן ... 392
ancient time
עוֹלָם ... 907
קֶדֶם ... 1088
ancle
אֶפֶס ... 147
and
אוֹ ... 29
אֶחָד ... 41
אַף ... 144
כִּי ... 596
עַד ... 901
עַל ... 932
עִם ... 955
* and
עַד Ch. ... 902
and †
אִם ... 100
and, *see* betwixt, both
and not
אִם ... 100
and yet
אַף ... 144
angel
אַבִּיר ... 10
מַלְאָךְ ... 704
מַלְאַךְ Ch. ... 705
* angels
אֱלֹהִים ... 79
שִׁנְאָן ... 1304
anger
אַף ... 144
זַעַם ... 391
חֵמָה ... 437
כַּעַס ... 612
עֶבְרָה ... 900
פָּנִים ... 1023
רוּחַ ... 1160
anger, *see* provoke
anger, to
קָצַף Hiphil ... 1115

angle
חַכָּה ... 426
angry
זָעַם Niphal ... 391
כַּעַס ... 612
angry †
מַר ... 760
angry, to be
אָנַף Kal ... 140
אָנַף Hithpael ... 140
אַף ... 144
בְּנַס Ch. P'al ... 261
זָעַם Kal ... 391
חָרָה Kal ... 462
חָרַר Niphal ... 466
כָּעַס Kal ... 612
עָשַׁן Kal ... 1003
קָצַף Kal ... 1115
anguish
000 }
000 } ... 000
מָצוֹק ... 754
מְצוּקָה ... 754
צוּקָה ... 1069
צַר & צָר ... 1080
צָרָה ... 1081
קֹצֶר ... 1117
שָׁבָץ ... 1232
anguish, to be in
חוּל }
חִיל } Kal ... 406
anoint, to
דָּשֵׁן Piel ... 355
מָשַׁח Kal ... 768
סוּךְ Kal ... 870
anoint self, to
סוּךְ Kal ... 870
anoint (self), to
סוּךְ Hiphil ... 870
anointed
יִצְהָר ... 555
מִמְשַׁח ... 731
מָשִׁיחַ ... 769
anointed, to be
בָּלַל Kal ... 230
מָשַׁח Kal ... 768
מָשַׁח Niphal ... 768
מִשְׁחָה ... 769
*anoint*ed one
בֵּן ... 232
anointing
מִשְׁחָה ... 769
מָשְׁחָה ... 769
שֶׁמֶן ... 1290
another
אָדָם ... 17
אֶחָד ... 41
אַחֵר ... 52
אָחֳרִי Ch. ... 54
אָחֳרָן Ch. ... 54
אִישׁ ... 60
אֵלֶּה ... 79
אֱנוֹשׁ ... 136
זוּר [2] Kal ... 384
עָמִית ... 960
שֵׁנִי ... 1310
* another
אָח ... 37
אָחוֹת ... 46
רֵעַ ... 1181
רְעוּת ... 1185
another, *see* as well as, feign, justle, look, one, see
another man
אַחֵר ... 52
זוּר [2] Kal ... 384
another place, to come from
זוּר [2] Kal ... 384
answer
אֵמֶר ... 134
דָּבָר ... 325
מַעֲנֶה ... 745
פִּתְגָּם Ch. ... 1052
תְּשׁוּבָה ... 1359
answer †
מִלָּה ... 706
answer, *see* return
answer, to
אָמַר Kal ... 105
דָּבַר Piel ... 319
יָדַע Hiphil ... 500
עָנָה [1] Kal ... 962
עָנָה [1] Niphal ... 962
עָנָה [2] Hiphil ... 964
עֲנָה [1] Ch. P'al ... 965
שׁוּב Hiphil ... 1238
תּוּב Ch. Aphel ... 1337
answer,† to
דָּבָר ... 325
שׁוּב Hiphil ... 1238
answer again,† to
שׁוּב Hiphil ... 1238
answer, to cause to
עָנָה [1] Kal ... 962
שׁוּב Hiphil ... 1238
answer, to give
עָנָה [1] Kal ... 962
answered, to be
עָנָה [1] Niphal ... 962
ant
נְמָלָה ... 819
antiquity
קַדְמָה ... 1089

anvil
פַּעַם 1038

any
אֶחָד 41
אִישׁ 60
כֹּל 597
כֹּל Ch. 597
מִי 694
נֶפֶשׁ 829

any, *see* kin, longer, means, more, nor, not, thing, time, wise

any at all
חָפֵץ Kal 451
יָכֹל Kal 526

any case, in
שׁוּב Hiphil 1238

any man
אִישׁ 60
מִי 694

any manner
כֹּל 597

* any *marks*
כְּתֹבֶת 623

any more
יָסַף Kal 543
יָסַף Hiphil 543
עוֹד 905
עוֹלָם 907

any of theirs
הֵם 367

* any such
דָּבָר 325

any thing
אֶחָד 41
דָּבָר 325

* any *thing*
מַשָּׁאָה 767

any thing, *see* not, superfluous, sweat

* any whither †
אָן 135

any wise, in
אַךְ 70
רַק 1191

any wise, in, is sometimes the translation of an infinitive used intensitively.

apace
הָלַךְ Kal 362
מָנוֹס 733

apace, *see* flee

apart
בַּד 186

apart, *see* put, set

ape
קוֹף 1104

apiece
אֶחָד 41

* apiece
עַמּוּד 959

apiece, *see* five

apothecaries' art, prepared by the
מִרְקַחַת 766

apothecary
רָקַח Kal 1191
רַקָּח 1191

apparel
בֶּגֶד 185
לְבוּשׁ 632
מַלְבּוּשׁ 706
שִׂמְלָה 1210

apparel, changeable suits of
מַחֲלָצוֹת 687

apparel, in
לָבֵשׁ, לָבֵשׁ } Pual 633

apparel, rich
בְּרֹמִים 271

apparelled, to be
לָבֵשׁ, לָבֵשׁ } Kal 633

apparently
מַרְאֶה 761

appear, to
גָּלָה Kal 307
גָּלָה Niphal 307
גָּלַשׁ Kal 310
יָצָא Kal 548
פָּנָה Kal 1021
פָּתַח Piel 1052
רָאָה Niphal 1133
שָׁקַף Niphal 1325

appear, made
מַחְשֹׂף 690

appearance
מַרְאֶה 761

appearance, outward
עַיִן 919

appeareth
מַרְאֶה 761

appease, to
כָּפַר Piel 614
שָׁקַט Hiphil 1324

appeased, to be
שָׁכַךְ Kal 1259

appertain, to
יָאָה Kal 486

appetite
חַי 419
נֶפֶשׁ 829

appetite, to have
שָׁקַק Kal 1325

apple
תַּפּוּחַ 1354

apple *of the eye*
אִישׁוֹן 69
בָּבָה 184
בַּת 280

apple tree
תַּפּוּחַ 1354

apply, to
בּוֹא Hiphil 189
נָטָה Hiphil 810
נָתַן Kal 851
סָבַב Kal 865
שִׁית Kal 1256

appoint, to
אָמַר Kal 105
בָּחַר Kal 209
דָּבַר Piel 319
חָקַק Kal 458
יָדַע Poal 500
יָכַח Hiphil 525
יָסַד Piel 542
יָעַד Kal 545
מָנָה Piel 732
נָקַב Kal 837
נָתַן Kal 851
עָמַד Hiphil 955
עָשָׂה Kal 981
פָּקַד Kal 1040
פָּקַד Hiphil 1040
צָוָה Piel 1065
קָדַשׁ, קָדַשׁ } Hiphil 1090
קוּם Ch. Aphel 1103
קָרָה Hiphil 1127
שׂוּם, שִׂים } Kal 1200
שִׁית Kal 1256
שָׁלַח Kal 1268

appoint time, to
יָעַד Hiphil 545

appoint to have, *see* charge

appointed
בֵּן 232
זָמַן Pual 388
חָגַר Kal 401
חֹק 456
חֻקָּה 457
כֶּסֶא 606
מוֹעֵד 672
מוֹעָדוֹת 673
נָצַב Niphal 833
סָמַן Niphal 879

appointed, *see* destruction, season, time

appointed, to be
מָנָה Piel 732
מָנָה Pual 732
פָּקַד Niphal 1040

appointed place
מִפְקָד 748

appointed sign
מוֹעֵד 672

appointed time
מוֹעֵד ... 673
צָבָא ... 1057

* appointed, unto him
אָמַר ... 134

appointment
מֵאמַר Ch. ... 658
פֶּה ... 1011

appointment, to make an
יָעַד Niphal ... 545

approach
קָרֵב ... 1125
קָרוֹב ... 1127

approach, to
נָגַשׁ Kal ... 794
נָגַשׁ Niphal ... 794
קָרֵב Kal ... 1123

approach, to cause to
קָרֵב Piel ... 1123

approach, to make to
נָגַשׁ Hiphil ... 794

approach nigh, to
נָגַשׁ Niphal ... 794

approaching
קְרָבָה ... 1126

approve, to
רָאָה Kal ... 1133
רָצָה Kal ... 1189

apron
חֲגוֹרָה ... 401

apt
עָשָׂה Kal ... 981

Arabah
עֲרָבָה ... 976

Arabah, *see* Beth-arabah

Arabia
עֲרָב ... 976

Aram-naharaim
נָהָר ... 798

archer
דָּרַךְ Kal ... 349
חָצַץ Piel ... 455
יָרָה Kal ... 564
רַב ... 1150

arch*er*
קֶשֶׁת ... 1133
קַשָּׁת ... 1133

* archer
קֶשֶׁת ... 1133

archer †
דָּרַךְ Kal ... 349
יָרָה Hiphil ... 564
רָבָה Kal ... 1151

* archer †
בַּעַל ... 262
חֵץ ... 453

arches
אֵילַמִּים } ... 59
אֵלַמִּים }
אֵלַמּוֹת ... 95

Arcturus
עַיִשׁ ... 932
עָשׁ ... 1003

are
יֵשׁ ... 568

* are
אִנּוּן } Ch. ... 136
אִנִּין }
הִיא Ch. ... 360
הִמּוֹ } Ch. ... 368
הִמּוֹן }

are there?
אִשׁ ... 174
יֵשׁ ... 568

argue, to
יָכַח Hiphil ... 525

argument
תּוֹכַחַת ... 1340

Ariel
אֲרִיאֵל }
אֲרִיאֵיל } ... 155
אֲרִאֵל }

aright
מֵישָׁרִים ... 698

aright, to set
כּוּן Hiphil ... 592

aright, to use
יָטַב Hiphil ... 524

arise, to
זָרַח Kal ... 395
נָשָׂא Kal ... 840
עָלָה Kal (& עוּר 913.) 934
עָמַד Kal ... 955
קוּם Kal ... 1099
קוּם Ch. P'al ... 1103
קוּץ[1] Hiphil ... 1104

arise, *see* hard

arise early, to
שָׁכַם Hiphil ... 1260

arise up, to
עָלָה Kal ... 934
קוּם Kal ... 1099

ark
אָרוֹן } ... 153
אָרֹן }
תֵּבָה ... 1335

arm
אֶזְרוֹעַ ... 36
דְּרָע Ch. ... 353
זְרוֹעַ ... 394
חֹצֶן ... 455
כָּתֵף ... 623

arm, to,—with
לָבַשׁ } Hiphil ... 633
לָבֵשׁ }

* arm, to
רוּק Hiphil ... 1165

arm *selves*, to
חָלַץ Niphal ... 434

armed
חָלַץ Kal ... 434
חֲמֻשִׁים ... 444
לָבַשׁ } Kal (a. with) .. 633
לָבֵשׁ }
מָגֵן ... 662
נָשַׁק Kal ... 849

armed, to go
חָלַץ Niphal ... 434

armed man
חָלַץ Kal ... 434

armed men
חֲמֻשִׁים ... 444
נָשַׁק Kal ... 849
נֵשֶׁק } ... 849
נֶשֶׁק }

armed, ready
חָלַץ Kal ... 434

armed soldier
חָלַץ Kal ... 434

*arm*hole
אַצִּיל ... 148

* armholes †
יָד ... 489

armies
מַעֲרוֹת ... 745

armour
זְנוֹת ... 390
חֲגוֹרָה ... 401
חֲלִיצָה ... 431
כְּלִי ... 600
(כ׳) מַד ... 664
נֵשֶׁק } ... 849
נֶשֶׁק }

*armour*bearer
נָשָׂא Kal ... 840

armour*bearer*
כְּלִי ... 600

armoury
אוֹצָר ... 31
נֵשֶׁק } ... 849
נֶשֶׁק }
תַּלְפִּיּוֹת ... 1348

army
גְּדוּד ... 293
חַיִל ... 423
חַיִל Ch. ... 425
חֵיל ... 425
מַחֲנֶה ... 688
מַעֲרָכָה ... 746
מַצָּבָה ... 751
צָבָא ... 1057

army†
חַיִל 423
צָבָא 1057

array, *see* set in

array, to,—in
לָבַשׁ / לָבֵשׁ } Hiphil 633

array, in
שִׁית Kal 1256

array, put in
עָרַךְ Kal 978

array, to put in
עָרַךְ Kal 978

array, to put selves in
עָרַךְ Kal 978

array, to put the battle in
עָרַךְ Kal 978

array self, to
לָבַשׁ / לָבֵשׁ } Kal 633
עָטָה Kal 918

array, set in
עָרַךְ Kal 978

array, to set in
עָרַךְ Kal 978

array, to set selves in
עָרַךְ Kal 978

arrayed, to be, in
לָבַשׁ / לָבֵשׁ } Pual 633

arrogancy
גָּאוֹן 285
עָתָק 1008

arrow
חֵץ 453
חֵצִי 454
חָצָץ 455
רֶשֶׁף 1194

* arrow
בֵּן 232

arrow †
בֵּן 232

* arrow †
קֶשֶׁת 1133

art
מַעֲשֶׂה 746

art, *see* apothecaries'

art thou
אִיתַי Ch. 69

artificer
חָרָשׁ (& חָרַשׁ) 467
חֹרֵשׁ 467

artillery
כְּלִי 600

as
אֲשֶׁר 180
גַּם 311
דַּי 339
כִּי 596
כְּמוֹ 603
עַד 901
עִם 955
תַּחַת 1345

* as
דַּי 339
עַל 932
פָּנִים 1023

as †
כֹּל Ch. 597
קֳבֵל / קֳבֵל } Ch. 1084

as, *see* according, forasmuch, friend, hurl, inasmuch, like, long as, power, such

as...as
כֵּן 604

as for
אוּלָם 30
אֶל 78

* as hast served †
גְּמוּל 311

as it were
כְּמוֹ 603

* as long as
עִם 955

as many as
כֹּל 597

as oft as
דַּי 339

as soon
גַּם 311

as soon as
אֲשֶׁר 180

* as though...not
לֹא 625

as truly as †
לֹא 625

as well as
כְּמוֹ 603

as well as another
זֶה 380

as when
יוֹם 508

as with, *see* take away

as would
רָצוֹן 1189

as yet
כֵּן 604
עוֹד 905

as yet †
עַד 901

ascend, to cause to
עָלָה Hiphil 934

ascend up, to
נְסַק Kal 822
עָלָה Kal 934

ascent
מַעֲלָה 744
עֹלָה 939
עֲלִיָּה 941

ascribe, to
יָהַב Kal 507
נָתַן Kal 851

ash
אֹרֶן 157

ashamed
בֹּשֶׁת 280

ashamed, to be
בּוֹשׁ Kal 206
בּוֹשׁ Hithpael 206
חָפֵר Kal 452
חָפֵר Hiphil 452
יָבֵשׁ Hiphil 487
כָּלַם Niphal 603

ashamed, to make
בּוֹשׁ Hiphil 206
כָּלַם Hiphil 603

Ashdoth-*pisgah*
אַשְׁדּוֹת / אַשְׁדֹּות } 174

ashes
אֵפֶר 147
אֲפֵר 148
דֶּשֶׁן 355
עָפָר 968
פִּיחַ 1017

ashes, *see* receive

ashes from, to take away the
דָּשֵׁן Piel 355

Ashurite
אֲשֻׁר 181

aside, *see* carry, go, gone, set, take, turn, turned

ask, to
בְּעָא / בְּעָה } Ch. P'al 261
בָּקַשׁ Piel 268
דָּרַשׁ Kal 353
שָׁאַל Kal 1220
שָׁאַל Niphal 1220
שָׁאַל Piel 1220
שְׁאֵל Ch. P'al 1221

ask, *see* much

ask counsel, to
שָׁאַל Kal 1220

ask on, to
שָׁאַל Kal 1220

asking
שָׁאַל Kal 1220

asleep
יָשֵׁן 576

asleep, to be fast
רָדַם Niphal 1168

asp
פֶּתֶן 1055

ass
אָתוֹן ... 183
חֲמוֹר ... 438

ass colt
עַיִר ... 925

ass, he
חֲמוֹר ... 438

ass, wild
עֲרָד Ch. ... 977
עָרוֹד ... 977
פֶּרֶא ... 1043

assault, to
צוּר Kal ... 1069

assay, to
יָאַל Hiphil ... 486
נָסָה Piel ... 820

assemble, to
אָסַף Kal ... 141
זָעַק Hiphil ... 391
צָבָא Kal ... 1057
קָבַץ Kal ... 1084
קָבַץ Niphal ... 1084
קָהַל Hiphil ... 1094
רְגַשׁ Ch. Aphel ... 1158

assemble selves, to
אָסַף Niphal ... 141
גּוּר Hithpolel ... 303
זָעַק Niphal ... 391
יָעַד Niphal ... 545
עוּשׁ Kal ... 914
קָבַץ Niphal ... 1084
קָהַל Niphal ... 1094

assemble selves by troops, to
גָּדַד Hithpoel ... 293

assemble together, to
קָהַל Niphal ... 1094
רְגַשׁ Ch. Aphel ... 1158

assembled, to be
אָסַף Niphal ... 141
יָעַד Niphal ... 545
קָהַל Niphal ... 1094

assemblies
אֲסֻפּוֹת ... 143

assembly
מוֹעֵד ... 672
מוֹשָׁב ... 675
מִקְרָא ... 760
סוֹד ... 870
עֵדָה ... 903
עֲצֶרֶת ... 974
קָהָל ... 1094
קְהִלָּה ... 1095

assembly, *see* solemn

assembly, place of
מוֹעֵד ... 672

assembly, solemn
מוֹעֵד ... 672

assent
פֶּה ... 1011

asses, young
עֲיָרִים ... 914

assign, to
נָתַן Kal ... 851

associate selves, to
רָעַע Kal ... 1186

assuage, to
חָשַׂךְ Kal ... 468
שָׁכַךְ Kal ... 1259

assuaged, to be
חָשַׂךְ Niphal ... 468

assurance
בֶּטַח ... 211

assurance, to have
אָמַן Hiphil ... 103

assured
אֱמֶת ... 134

assured, to be
קוּם Kal ... 1099

assuredly
אֱמֶת ... 134
יָדַע Kal ... 500
יָצָא Kal ... 548
שָׁתָה Kal ... 1331

assured*ly*
כִּי ... 596

*Assyr*ian
בֵּן ... 232

astonied
שָׁמֵם Polel ... 1289

astonied, to be
דָּהַם Niphal ... 336
שְׁבַשׁ Ch. Ithpael ... 1234
שָׁמֵם Kal ... 1289
שָׁמֵם Niphal ... 1289
שְׁמַם Ch. Ithpolel ... 1290
תְּוַהּ Ch. P'al ... 1338

astonished
שָׁמֵם Hiphil ... 1289

astonished, to be
שָׁמֵם Kal ... 1289
שָׁמֵם Niphal ... 1289
שָׁמֵם Hophal ... 1289
שָׁמֵם Hithpolel ... 1289
תָּמַהּ Kal ... 1349

astonishment
מְשַׁמָּה ... 772
שַׁמָּה ... 1285
שִׁמָּמוֹן ... 1290
תִּמָּהוֹן ... 1349
תַּרְעֵלָה ... 1359

astonishment, to be an
שָׁמֵם Kal ... 1289

astray, *see* go

astray, to cause to go
תָּעָה Hiphil ... 1353

astray, to go
תָּעָה Kal ... 1353

astrologer
אַשָּׁף Ch. ... 179

astrologers
אַשָּׁפִים ... 180
הָבַר Kal ... 356

* astro*logers*
שָׁמַיִם ... 1286

asunder
בֵּין ... 212

asunder, *see* break, cleave, cut, divide, drive, rent

Asuppim
אֲסֻפִּים ... 143

at
אַחַר ... 48
אֶל ... 78
אֵצֶל ... 148
בֵּין ... 212
בְּעַד ... 261
יָד ... 489
לְמוֹ ... 644
מִן ... 731
עַד ... 901
עַד Ch. ... 902
עַל ... 932
עֻמָּה ... 959
פָּנִים ... 1023

at, *see* ease, home, liberty, nought, peace, stand, wink

at, to be
עָשָׂה Kal ... 981

at all
יַחַד, יַחְדָּו, יַחְדָּיו ... 522
עוֹד ... 905

at all, *see* any

at *even*tide
פָּנָה Kal ... 1021

at least
אַךְ ... 70

at once
יַחַד, יַחְדָּו, יַחְדָּיו ... 522
עָלָה Kal ... 934

Atad
אָטָד ... 54

athirst, to be
צָמֵא Kal ... 1074

atonement
כִּפֻּרִים ... 615

atonement, to be made
כָּפַר Piel ... 614
כָּפַר Pual ... 614

atonement, to make an
כִּפֵּר Piel 614
attain, to
בּוֹא Kal 189
יָכֹל Kal 526
נָשַׂג Hiphil 845
קָנָה [1] Kal 1111
attain unto, to
נָשַׂג Hiphil 845
attend, to
בִּין Hithpolel 212
קָשַׁב Hiphil 1131
attendance
מַעֲמָד................ 744
attent
קַשֻּׁב.................1131
attentive
קַשֻּׁב.................1131
קַשָּׁב.................1131
attentively
שָׁמַע
שְׁמַע } Kal 1292
attire
קִשֻּׁרִים.................1132
שִׁית.................1257
attire, *see* dyed
attired, to be
צָנַף Kal.............1076
audience
אֹזֶן................ 35
augment, to
סָפָה [2] Kal 881
aul
מַרְצֵעַ................ 765
aunt
דּוֹדָה................ 336
authority
תֹּקֶף.................1357
authority, to be in
רָבָה Kal 1151
avail, to
שָׁוָה [1] Kal 1245
Aven
אָוֶן................ 30
avenge †
נְקָמָה................ 839
avenge, to
נָקַם Kal 839
נָקַם Piel 839
פָּקַד Kal 1040
avenge, † to
שָׁפַט Kal 1319
* avenge, † to
נָתַן Kal 851
avenge selves, to
נָקַם Kal 839
avenged †
נָקַם................ 839

avenged, to be
נָקַם Niphal.......... 839
נָקַם Hophal 839
נָקַם Hithpael 839
avenger
גָּאַל [1] Kal........... 285
נָקַם Hithpael 839
avenging
יָשַׁע Hiphil 576
פָּרַע Kal 1046
avenging †
פְּרָעוֹת.................1047
averse
שׁוּב Kal 1238
avoid, to
סָבַב Niphal.......... 865
פָּרַע Kal 1046
avouch, to
אָמַר Hiphil 105
awake, to
יָקַץ Kal 558
עוּר [1] Kal........... 913
עוּר [1] Polel 913
עוּר [1] Hiphil 913
עוּר Hithpolel 913
קוּץ [1] Hiphil.........1104
* awake, to
עִיר................ 932
awake, to be
קוּץ [1] Hiphil 1104
awaked, to be
יָקַץ Kal 558
aware, to be
יָדַע Kal 500
away
דֶּרֶךְ................ 349
יָלַךְ Kal 531
נוּס Kal 801
* away
סָרַר Kal 885
away, *see* ashes, break, bring, captive, carried, carry, cast, chase, chased, consume, departing, do, drawn, dried, drive, driven, fade, fall, far, flee, flow, fly, fray, get, go, gone, haste, have, have...taken, lay, lead, led, look, melt, pass, passed, pine, pluck, plucked, portion, purge, push, put, put far, putting, remove, roll, run, scatter, sell, send, sending, sent, slip, steal, stolen, sweep, swept, take, taken, thrust, turn, turned, turning, utterly, vanish, vilely cast, violently take, wash, waste, wear, wipe, wiped, withered
away far, *see* put
away far, to put
רָחַק Hiphil 1170
away from
אַחַר................ 48
away with, *see* can

awe, to stand in
פָּחַד Kal 1016
רָגַז Kal 1155
ax
גַּרְזֶן................ 315
חֶרֶב................ 459
כַּשִּׁיל................ 620
מַגְזֵרָה................ 662
מְגֵרָה................ 663
מַעֲצָד................ 745
קַרְדֹּם.................1127
ax head
בַּרְזֶל................ 271
axletree
יָד................ 489
Baal-perazim
פֶּרֶץ.................1047
Baali
בַּעַל................ 262
babbler
{ בַּעַל................ 262
{ לָשׁוֹן................ 651
babbling
שִׂיחַ.................1206
babe
נַעַר................ 823
עוֹלֵל
עוֹלָל } 907
babes
תַּעֲלוּלִים.................1354
*Babylon*ian
בֵּן................ 232
Baca
בָּכָא................ 226
bachuth, *see* Allon-bachuth
back
אָחוֹר................ 45
אַחַר................ 48
גַּב................ 286
גַּב Ch. 287
גֵּו................ 298
גַּו................ 299
הָלְאָה................ 362
עֹרֶף................ 980
שְׁכֶם.................1260
back, *see* bring, bringing, brought, call, carry, come, draw, go, gone, hold, horseback, keep, kept, look, send, sent, slide, take, turn, turned,
back again
אַחֲרַנִּית................ 54
back again, *see* get
back from
אַחַר................ **48**
back part
אָחוֹר................ 45
backbite, to
רָגַל Kal 1155

barns
אֲסָמִים 141
מַמְּגֻרוֹת 730
barrel
כַּד 586
barren
עֹצֶר 973
עָקָר 974
צִיָּה 1071
שַׁכּוּל 1258
שָׁכַל Piel 1259
barren land
מְלֵחָה 707
* barren, male or female
עָקָר 974
barren woman
עָקָר 974
barrenness
מְלֵחָה 707
base
כֵּן 604
מְכוֹנָה 699
מְכֻנָה 699
קָלָה [2] Niphal 1108
שָׁפָל 1322
base †
שֵׁם 1280
basest
שָׁפָל 1322
שְׁפַל Ch. 1322
Bashan-havoth-*jair*
חַוּוֹת 406
basket
דּוּד 336
דּוּדַי 336
טֶנֶא 483
כְּלוּב 600
סַל 876
baskets
סַלְסִלּוֹת 878
bason
אַגָּן 14
כְּפוֹר 614
מִזְרָק 685
סַף 880
bastard
מַמְזֵר 730
bat
עֲטַלֵּף 918
bath
בַּת 284
בַּת Ch. 284
Bath-rabbim
{ בַּת 280
{ רַב 1147
bathe, to
רָחַץ Kal 1169
bathe self, to
רָחַץ Kal 1169
bathed, to be
רָוָה Piel 1160
batter, to
שָׁחַת Hiphil 1252
battle
כִּידוֹר 596
מַחֲנֶה 688
מִלְחָמָה 707
נֶשֶׁק } 849
נֵשֶׁק }
סְאוֹן 864
צָבָא 1057
קְרָב 1125
battle †
פָּנִים 1023
צָבָא 1057
battle, *see* array
battle ax
מַפֵּץ 748
battlement
מַעֲקֶה 745
battlements
נְטִישׁוֹת 812
bay
לָשׁוֹן 651
bay
אֲמֻצִּים 105
bay tree
אֶזְרָח 37
baz, *see* Maher-shalal-hash-baz
bdellium
בְּדֹלַח 187
be
יֵשׁ 568
be, to
הָוָא } Kal 358
הָוָה }
הֲוָא } Ch. P'al 358
הֲוָה }
הָיָה Kal 360
הָיָה Niphal 360
* be, to
בּוֹא Kal 189
נָתַן Kal 851
עָבַד Kal 887
* be, I will
אֱהִי 26
beacon
תֹּרֶן 1358
beam
אֶרֶג 152
גֵּב 287
כְּפִיס 614
מָנוֹר 733
צֵלָע 1073
קוֹרָה 1104
beam, thick
עָב 887
beams
כְּרֻתוֹת 620
beams, to lay
קָרָה Piel 1127
beams, to make
קָרָה Piel 1127
beans
פּוֹל 1014
bear
דֹּב } 318
דּוֹב }
דֹּב Ch. 318
bear, to
הָרָה Kal 375
זָרַע Kal 395
חוּל } Polel 406
חִיל }
יָלַד Kal 527
יָלַךְ Hiphil 531
כּוּל Hiphil 592
נָטַל Kal 812
נָטַל Piel 812
סָבַל Kal 868
עָשָׂה Kal 981
פָּרָה Kal 1044
צָמַח Hiphil 1074
bear, *see* blame, burdens, grudge, loss, rule, tidings, twins, witness
bear, to be able to
נָשָׂא Kal 840
bear out, to
יָצָא Hiphil 548
bear, to suffer to
נָשָׂא Hiphil 840
bear, that
נָטִיל 812
bear up, to
נָשָׂא Kal 840
תָּכַן Piel 1347
bear *witness*, to
עָנָה [1] Kal 962
beard
זָקָן 392
שָׂפָם 1214
bearer, *see* burdens, talebearer
bearing
נָשָׂא Kal 840
beast
בְּהֵמָה 188
בְּעִיר 261
חַי 418
חֵיוָא Ch. 423
נֶפֶשׁ 829
* beast
טֶבַח 473
beast, *see* desert, dieth of, fat, fed, swift, torn of, wild
beast, wild
חַי 418

beasts, swift
כִּרְכָּרוֹת 617

beat, to
דּוּךְ Kal 337
דָּפַק Hithpael 348
הָלַם Kal 367
חָבַט Kal 398
כָּתַת Kal 624
כָּתַת Piel 624
נָכָה Hiphil 814
רָקַע Piel 1192
שָׁחַק Kal 1252

beat, *see* small

beat down, to
הָלַם Kal 367
הָרַס Kal 376
כָּתַת Kal 624
נָתַץ Kal 863

beat in pieces, to
דָּקַק Hiphil 348

beat off, to
חָבַט Kal 398

beat out, to
חָבַט Kal 398

beat to pieces, to
דָּכָא Piel 340

beaten
כָּתִית 623
מִקְשָׁה 760
שָׁחַט Kal 1251

beaten, to be
נָגַע Niphal 792
נָגַף Niphal 793
נָכָה Hiphil 814
נָכָה Hophal 814

beaten corn
גֶּרֶשׂ 316

beaten down, to be
חָתַת Niphal 472
כָּתַת Hophal 624

beaten in sunder, to be
נָפַץ Pual 828

beaten out, to be
חָבַט Niphal 398

beaten out of one piece
מִקְשָׁה 760

beaten to pieces, to be
כָּתַת Hophal 624

beaten work
מִקְשָׁה 760

beautiful
טוֹב 476
מַרְאֶה 761
צְבִי 1060
תִּפְאָרָה } תִּפְאֶרֶת 1354

beautiful †
יָפֶה 548
תֹּאַר 1334

beautiful, to be
יָפָה Kal 548
נָאָה Pilel 781

beautify, to
פָּאַר Piel 1009

beauty
הָדָר 357
הֲדָרָה 358
הוֹד 358
חָמַד Kal 437
יָפֶה 548
יֳפִי 548
יְפִי 548
מַרְאֶה 761
נֹעַם 823
פְּאֵר 1009
צְבִי 1060
צוּר 1069
(כ׳) צִיר 1071
תִּפְאָרָה } תִּפְאֶרֶת 1354

beauty, to pass in
נָעֵם Kal 823

because
אוֹדֹת 29
אֶל 78
אֲשֶׁר 180
יַעַן 546
עֵקֶב 974

because †
כֹּל Ch. 597
כֵּן 604
מִן Ch. 732
עֵקֶב 974
פָּנִים 1023
קֳבֵל } קְבֵל Ch. 1084

because of
גָּלָל 310
דֶּרֶךְ 349
יָד 489
מִן 731
מַעַן 744
עֲבוּר 895
עַל 932
פָּנִים 1023

because of
דָּבָר 325

because that
יַעַן 546
כִּי 596

because un*satiable*
בִּלְתִּי 231

because yet
עוֹד 905

become, to
הֲוָא } הֲוָה Ch. P'al 358
הָיָה Kal 360
נָאָה Pilel 781
עָשָׂה Niphal 981

become, *see* brutish, desolate, dim, dry, fat, fools, full, glorious, great, great estate, guilty, Jews, lame, like, loathsome, long, mighty, old, ready, rich, servants, stranger, strong, surety, vain, weak

become, to be
הָיָה Niphal 361

* become, to be
הָפַךְ Niphal 370

become *surety*, to
עָרַב [1] Kal 975

becometh
נָאוֶה 781

bed
יָצוּעַ 555
מִטָּה 693
מַצָּע 755
מִשְׁכָּב 770
מִשְׁכַּב Ch. 770
עֲרוּגָה 977
עֶרֶשׂ 981

bed †
עֶרֶשׂ 981

bed, to make
יָצַע Hiphil 556

*bed*chamber
חֶדֶר 403

bed*chamber*
מִטָּה 693
מִשְׁכָּב 770

bedstead
עֶרֶשׂ 981

bee
דְּבוֹרָה 318

Beer
בְּאֵר 184

Beer-*lahai-roi*
בְּאֵר 184

Beer-lahai-*roi*
חַי 418

beetle
חַרְגֹּל 462

beeve
בָּקָר 266

befall, to
אָנָה Pual 136
בּוֹא Kal 189
מָצָא Kal 748
קָרָא [2] Kal 1122
קָרָה Kal 1127

befallen, something
מִקְרֶה 760

befalleth
מִקְרֶה ... 760
before
אֶל ... 78
אַף ... 144
אֵת ... 182
טְרוֹם ... 485
טֶרֶם ... 485
לֹא ... 625
מוּל ... 671
מַעֲלָה ... 744
נֶגֶד ... 790
נֹכַח ... 817
נֵכַח ... 818
עַד ... 901
עַיִן ... 919
עִם ... 955
פָּנִים ... 1023
קָבָל ... 1084
קֳבֵל, קֳבֵל Ch. ... 1084
קֶדֶם ... 1088
קֳדָם Ch. ... 1089
קֶרֶב ... 1125
רִאשׁוֹן ... 1145
before †
מוּל ... 671
מִן Ch. ... 732
פָּנִים ... 1023
שִׁלְשׁוֹם ... 1279
תְּמוֹל ... 1349
before, *see* brought, come, go
before it
לִפְנַי ... 644
before that time †
אֶתְמוֹל, אֶתְמוּל ... 183
* before that time †
שִׁלְשׁוֹם ... 1279
before, that were
רִאשׁוֹן ... 1145
before, they that went
קַדְמוֹנִי ... 1089
beforetime
פָּנִים ... 1023
רִאשׁוֹן ... 1145
beforetime †
אֶתְמוֹל, אֶתְמוּל ... 183
שִׁלְשׁוֹם ... 1279
תְּמוֹל ... 1349
beg, to
בָּקַשׁ Piel ... 268
שָׁאַל Kal ... 1220
שָׁאַל Piel ... 1220

* began
יָסַד ... 543
* began men
חָלַל Hophal ... 432
beget, to
יָלַד Kal ... 527
יָלַד Hiphil ... 527
beggar
אֶבְיוֹן ... 10
begin
תְּחִלָּה ... 1344
begin, to
חָלַל Hiphil ... 432
יָאַל Hiphil ... 486
שְׁרָא Ch. Pael ... 1326
begin, *see* build, dark, reign, spring
beginning
אָז ... 34
רֹאשׁ ... 1142
רִאשָׁה ... 1145
רִאשׁוֹן ... 1145
רֵאשִׁית ... 1147
תְּחִלָּה ... 1344
beginning, *see* world
begotten
מוֹלֶדֶת ... 671
* begotten
יָצָא Kal ... 548
begotten, to be
יָלַד Niphal ... 527
beguile, to
נָכַל Piel ... 818
נָשָׁא [1] Hiphil ... 846
רָמָה Piel ... 1175
behave, to
שָׁוָה [1] Piel ... 1245
behave self, to
הָלַךְ Hithpael ... 362
behave self and selves, *see* ill, proudly, strangely, valiantly, wisely
behaviour
טַעַם ... 483
behead, to
סוּר Hiphil ... 872, רֹאשׁ ... 1142
beheaded, that is
עָרַף [2] Kal ... 980
beheld †
הֲוָא, הֲוָה Ch. P'al ... 358
behemoth
בְּהֵמָה ... 188
behind
אָחוֹר ... 45
אַחַר ... 48
behind, *see* abide, left
behold
אֲלוּ Ch. ... 93

אֲרוּ Ch. ... 152
הֵא ... 355
הֵן ... 369
הִנֵּה ... 369
behold, to
חָזָה Kal ... 410
חֲזָא, חֲזָה Ch. P'al ... 410
נָבַט Hiphil ... 783
פָּנָה Kal ... 1021
צָפָה Kal ... 1077
רָאָה Kal ... 1133
שׁוּר [2] Kal ... 1248
שִׁיר Polel ... 1255
behold, to cause to
נָבַט Hiphil ... 783
beholding
רָאָה Kal ... 1133
רְאוּת ... 1141
רְאִית (כ׳) ... 1141
being, while have
עוֹד ... 905
bekah
בֶּקַע ... 265
belch out, to
נָבַע Hiphil ... 787
Belial
בְּלִיַּעַל ... 230
belie, to
כָּחַשׁ Piel ... 595
believe, to
אָמַן Hiphil ... 103
אֲמַן Ch. Aphel ... 104
bell
פַּעֲמוֹן ... 1039
bellow, to
צָהַל Kal ... 1064
bellows
מַפֻּחַ ... 747
bells
מְצִלּוֹת ... 754
belly
בֶּטֶן ... 211
גָּחוֹן ... 305
כָּרֵשׂ ... 618
מֵעִים ... 742
מְעִין Ch. ... 742
קֵבָה ... 1083
belonged, such things as
מָנָה ... 733
beloved
אָהַב, אָהֵב Kal ... 25
דּוֹד ... 336
יְדִיד ... 500
מַחְמָד ... 687
beloved, dearly
יְדִדוּת ... 499

beloved, greatly
חֲמוּדוֹת 438
bemoan, to
נוּד Kal 799
bemoan self, to
נוּד Hithpolel 799
Ben-*ammi*
בֵּן 232
Ben-*hanan*
בֵּן 232
Ben-oni
{ בֵּן 232
{ אָוֶן 30
Ben-*zoheth*
בֵּן 232
bench
קֶרֶשׁ 1130
bend, to
דָּרַךְ Kal 349
כָּפַן Kal 614
bending
שָׁחַח Kal 1250
Bene-*jaakan*
בֵּן 232
beneath
מַטָּה 691
תַּחַת 1345
benefit
גְּמוּל 311
תַּגְמוּל 1336
benefit, to
יָטַב Hiphil 524
Ben*jamin*
בֵּן 232
Ben*jamite*
בֵּן 232
Beno
בֵּן 232
bent, to be
תָּלָא Kal 1347
Berachah
בְּרָכָה 276
bereave, to
חָסֵר Piel 450
כָּשַׁל Piel 621
שָׁכֹל Piel 1259
bereave of children, to
שָׁכֹל Piel 1259
bereaved, to be
שָׁכֹל Kal 1259
bereaved of children
שַׁכּוּל 1258
bereaved of whelps
שַׁכּוּל 1258
berry
גַּרְגַּר 315
beryl
תַּרְשִׁישׁ 1359

beseech †
פָּנִים 1023
beseech, to
בָּקַשׁ Piel 268
חָלָה Piel 429
חָנַן Hithpael 446
beseech thee, I
אָנָּא }
אָנָּה } 136
נָא 781
beseech thee, we
אָנָּא }
אָנָּה } 136
beset, to
סָבַב Kal 865
צוּר Kal 1069
beset, *see* round about
beset about, to
סָבַב Kal 865
beset round, to
כָּתַר Piel 624
beside
אַחַר 48
אֶל 78
אֵצֶל 148
בַּד 186
בִּלְעֲדֵי }
בַּלְעֲדֵי } 231
בִּלְתִּי 231
זוּלָה 383
יָד 489
עוֹד 905
עַל 932
עִם 955
עֻמָּה 959
צַד 1061
beside, *see* none
beside the rest of
עַל 932
besiege, to
סָבַב Kal 865
צוּר Kal 1069
צָרַר Hiphil 1083
besieged
מָצוֹר 754
נָצַר Kal 837
besieged,† to be
בּוֹא Kal 189
besieged place
מָצוֹר 754
besom
מַטְאֲטֵא 691
best
טוֹב 476
מֵיטָב 694
* best
חֵלֶב 429

best, *see* fruit, state
best *gold*
פָּזַז[1] Hophal 1015
best, to seem
יָטַב Kal 524
* best,† to think
עַיִן 919
bestead, *see* hardly
bestir self, to
חָרַץ Kal 466
bestow, to
יָנַח Hiphil 541
נָחָה Hiphil 804
נָתַן Kal 851
נְתַן Ch. P'al 863
עָשָׂה Kal 981
פָּקַד Kal 1040
bestow on, to
גָּמַל Kal 311
Beth-arabah
עֲרָבָה 976
Beth-*dagon*
בַּיִת 214
Beth-el
אֵל 76
Beth-emek
{ בַּיִת 214
{ עֵמֶק 961
Beth-*ezel*
בַּיִת 214
Beth-haccerem
כֶּרֶם 617
Beth-shemesh
{ בַּיִת 214
{ שֶׁמֶשׁ 1303
Bether
בֶּתֶר 284
* bethink, to
שׁוּב Hiphil 1238
* bethink selves †
לֵבָב 630
betimes, *see* rise, rise up, rising up, seek
betimes, to (*do any thing*)
שָׁחַר[2] Piel 1252
betray, to
רָמָה Piel 1175
betroth, to
אָרַשׂ Piel 172
יָעַד Kal 545
betrothed
חָרַף Niphal 465
betrothed, to be
אָרַשׂ Pual 172

better
טוֹב 476
יוֹתֵר 521
יִתְרוֹן 581
better, to be
טוֹב Kal 476
יָטַב Hiphil 524
better, to do
טוֹב Hiphil 476
better, to be made
יָטַב Kal 524
better, to make
יָטַב Hiphil 524
between
בֵּין 212
בֵּין Ch. 212
עַל 932
תָּוֶךְ 1338
between, *see* from
betwixt
בֵּין 212
betwixt, *see* come
* betwixt...and †
בֵּין 212
Beulah
בָּעַל Kal 261
bewail, to
בָּכָה Kal 226
bewail self, to
יָפַח Hithpael 548
beware, to
עָרַם[1] Hiphil 979
שָׁמַר Kal 1300
שָׁמַר Niphal 1300
bewray, to
גָּלָה Piel 307
נָגַד Hiphil 788
bewray (*self*), to
קָרָא[1] Kal 1117
beyond
הָלְאָה 362
עָבַר Hiphil 895
עֵבֶר 899
עֲבַר Ch. 899
beyond, *see* go, pass
beyond the time
עַל 932
bibber, *see* winebibber
bid, to
אָמַר Kal 105
דָּבַר Kal 319
דָּבַר Piel 319
צָוָה Piel 1065
קָדַשׁ / קָדֵשׁ } Hiphil 1090
bidden, that are
קָרָא[1] Kal 1117
bidding
מִשְׁמַעַת 773
bier
מִטָּה 693
bill
סֵפֶר 883
billow
גַּל 307
מִשְׁבָּר 768
bind, to
אָלַם Piel 95
אָסַר Kal 143
אָפַד Kal 146
חָבַשׁ Kal 400
חָבַשׁ Piel 400
יָסַר Piel 545
כְּפַת Ch. Pael 615
עָנַד Kal 962
עָקַד Kal 974
צוּר Kal 1069
צָרַר Kal 1083
קָשַׁר Kal 1132
קָשַׁר Piel 1132
רָכַס Kal 1175
רָתַם Kal 1195
bind about, to
אָזַר Kal 36
bind selves, to
אָסַר Kal 143
bind sheaves, to
עָמַר Piel 961
bind up, to
חָבַשׁ Kal 400
חָבַשׁ Piel 400
צוּר Kal 1069
צָרַר Kal 1083
* bindeth
צְרוֹר 1082
binding
אֱסָר / אִסָּר } 144
שָׁפָה 1213
bird
עוֹף 911
עַיִט 919
צִפּוֹר 1079
צִפַּר Ch. 1080
{ בַּעַל 262
{ כָּנָף 605
bird, *see* ravenous
birth
יָלַד Kal 527
מְכוּרָה 699
מַשְׁבֵּר 768
תּוֹלְדוֹת 1341
birth, bring to the
שָׁבַר[1] Hiphil 1232
birth, one's
יָלַד Niphal 527
birth, untimely
נֵפֶל / נֶפֶל } 828
*birth*day
יוֹם 508
birth*day*
יָלַד Hophal 527
birthright
בְּכוֹרָה 228
bit
מֶתֶג 779
bite, to
נָשַׁךְ Kal 848
נָשַׁךְ Piel 848
bitten, *see* hunger
bitten, is
נָשַׁךְ Kal 848
bitter
מַר 760
מָרָה Kal 762
מְרִי 764
מְרִירִי 764
מְרֹרָה 766
מְרֹרִים 766
bitter, to be
מָרַר Kal 766
bitter, to make
מָרַר Piel 766
* bitter, most
תַּמְרוּרִים 1352
bitter things
מְרֹרָה 766
bitterly
אָרַר Kal 171
מַר 760
מָרַר Piel 766
bitterly, to deal
מָרַר Hiphil 766
* bitterly, most
תַּמְרוּרִים 1352
bittern
קִפֹּד 1113
bitterness
מֶמֶר 731
מַמְּרֹרִים 731
מַר 760
מָרָה 763
מְרִירוּת 764
מְרֹרִים 766
bitterness, to be in
מָרַר Kal 766
מָרַר Hiphil 766

bitterness, to have
מָרַר Kal ... 766
black
אִישׁוֹן ... 69
שָׁחֹר ... 1252
שְׁחַרְחֹרֶת ... 1252
black, to be
חָשַׁךְ Kal ... 469
כָּמַר Niphal ... 604
קָדַר Kal ... 1090
קָדַר Hithpael ... 1090
שָׁחַר[1] Kal ... 1252
black marble
סֹחֶרֶת ... 875
blackish, to be
קָדַר Kal ... 1090
blackness
כִּמְרִירִים ... 604
פָּארוּר ... 1009
קַדְרוּת ... 1090
blade
לַהַב ... 634
blade, *see* shoulder
blains
אֲבַעְבֻּעֹת ... 13
blame, to bear the
חָטָא Kal ... 414
blameless
נָקִי ... 838
blameless, to be
נָקָה Niphal ... 838
blaspheme, to
בָּרַךְ Piel ... 274
גָּדַף Piel ... 298
חָרַף Piel ... 465
נָקַב Kal ... 837
blaspheme, to give occasion to
נָאַץ Piel ... 782
blasphemed, (is)
נָאַץ Hithpolel ... 782
blasphemies
נֶאָצוֹת ... 782
blasphemy
נְאָצָה ... 782
blast
נְשָׁמָה ... 849
רוּחַ ... 1160
blasted
שְׁדֵמָה ... 1237
שָׁדַף Kal ... 1238
שְׁדֵפָה ... 1238
blasting
שִׁדָּפוֹן ... 1238
bleating
קוֹל ... 1096
bleatings
שְׁרִיקוֹת ... 1327
blemish
מאוּם ... 657
מוּם ... 671
תְּבַלֻּל ... 1336
blemish, without
תָּמִים ... 1350
bless, to
אָשַׁר Piel ... 180
בָּרַךְ Piel ... 274
בְּרַךְ Ch. P'al ... 276
בְּרַךְ Ch. Pael ... 276
bless self, to
בָּרַךְ Hithpael ... 274
blessed
אַשְׁרֵי ... 181
בָּרַךְ Kal ... 274
blessed, to be
אָשַׁר Pual ... 180
בָּרַךְ Niphal ... 274
בָּרַךְ Pual ... 274
בָּרַךְ Hithpael ... 274
blessed, to call
אָשַׁר Piel ... 180
blessing
בְּרָכָה ... 276
blind
עִוֵּר ... 913
עַוֶּרֶת ... 914
blind, to
עָוַר Piel ... 912
עָלַם Hiphil ... 943
blind men
עִוֵּר ... 913
blind people
עִוֵּר ... 913
blindness
סַנְוֵרִים ... 880
עִוָּרוֹן ... 914
blood
דָּם ... 343
נֵצַח ... 835
* blood
דָּם ... 343
bloodguiltiness
דָּם ... 343
* *blood*thirsty †
אֱנוֹשׁ ... 136
blood*thirsty*
דָּם ... 343
bloody
דָּם ... 343
bloom, to
צוּץ Hiphil ... 1069
blossom
נֵץ ... 833
פֶּרַח ... 1045
צִיץ ... 1071
blossom, to
פָּרַח Kal ... 1045
צוּץ Kal ... 1069
צוּץ Hiphil ... 1069
blot
מאוּם ... 657
מוּם ... 671
blot out, to
מָחָה[1] Kal ... 686
מָחָה[1] Hiphil ... 686
blotted out, to be
מָחָה[1] Niphal ... 686
blow
מַכָּה ... 698
תִּגְרָה ... 1336
תְּרוּעָה ... 1358
blow, to
חֲצֹצֵר Piel ... 455
חָצַר Hiphil ... 455
נָפַח Kal ... 825
נָשַׁב Kal ... 846
נָשַׁף Kal ... 849
פּוּחַ Hiphil ... 1014
blow an alarm, to
רוּעַ Hiphil ... 1164
blow, to cause to
נָסַע Hiphil ... 821
נָשַׁב Hiphil ... 846
blow *a trumpet*, to
תָּקַע Kal ... 1356
blow upon, to
פּוּחַ Hiphil ... 1014
blowing
תָּקַע Kal ... 1356
blowing of trumpets
תְּרוּעָה ... 1358
blowing the trumpets
תְּרוּעָה ... 1358
blown
נָפַח Pual ... 825
blown, to be
תָּקַע Niphal ... 1356
blue
תְּכֵלֶת ... 1347
* blue
שֵׁשׁ ... 1329
blueness
חַבּוּרָה } ... 398
חֲבוּרָה }
blunt, to be
קָהָה Piel ... 1094
blush, to
כָּלַם Niphal ... 603
כָּלַם Hiphil ... 603
boar
חֲזִיר ... 411
board
לוּחַ ... 635
צֵלָע ... 1073
קֶרֶשׁ ... 1130
שְׂדֵרָה ... 1199

boast
גָּדַל Hiphil 297

boast, to
הָלַל Piel 366
הָלַל Hithpael 366
כָּבַד / כָּבֵד Hiphil 581

boast, to make
הָלַל Hithpael 366

boast self, to
אָמַר Hithpael 105
הָלַל Hithpael 366
יָמַר Hithpael 541
פָּאַר Hithpael 1009

boat, *see* ferry

Bochim
בָּכָה Kal 226

body
בֶּטֶן 211
בָּשָׂר 278
גַּב 286
גֵּו 299
גְּוָה 299
גְּוִיָּה 302
גּוּפָה 303
גֶּשֶׁם Ch. 317
נְבֵלָה 787
נֶפֶשׁ 829
עֶצֶם 972
שְׁאֵר 1223

* body
יָרֵךְ 565
נִדְנֶה Ch. 797

body, *see* dead

body, dead
נְבֵלָה 787

boil
שְׁחִין 1251

boil, to
בָּשַׁל Piel 280
רָתַח Pual 1195

boil, to make to (בעה 261)
רָתַח Piel 1195
רָתַח Hiphil 1195

boiling places
מְבַשְּׁלוֹת 661

bold, to be
בָּטַח Kal 210

boldly
בֶּטַח 211

boldness
עֹז 914

bolled
גִּבְעֹל 291

bolster
מְרַאֲשׁוֹת 761
רַאֲשֹׁת 1147

bolt, to
נָעַל Kal 822

bond
אֱסָר / אִסָּר 144
מוּסָר 672
מוֹסֵר 672
מָסֹרֶת 739

bondage
עַבְדוּת 894
עֲבוֹדָה 894

* bondage
עֶבֶד 890

bondage, to bring into
כָּבַשׁ Kal 586

bondage, to be brought unto
כָּבַשׁ Niphal 586

bondage, to keep in
עָבַד Hiphil 887

bondmaid
אָמָה 100
שִׁפְחָה 1318

bondman
עֶבֶד 889

bondmen, to be
עָבַד Kal 887

*bond*servant
עֶבֶד 890

* bondservant †
עֲבוֹדָה 894

bondservice
עָבַד Kal 887

bondwoman
אָמָה 100
שִׁפְחָה 1318

bone
גֶּרֶם 316
גְּרַם Ch. 316
עֶצֶם 972
קָנֶה 1112

bone, *see* cheek, gnaw

bones, to break his
עָצַם Piel 972

bonnet
פְּאֵר 1009

bonnets
מִגְבָּעוֹת 661

book
דָּבָר 325
סֵפֶר 883
סְפַר Ch. 884
סִפְרָה 884

booth
סֻכָּה 875

booty
בַּז & בִּזָּה 207
מַלְקוֹחַ 729
מְשִׁסָּה 774

border
גְּבוּל 288
גְּבוּלָה 289
גְּלִילָה 310
יָד 489
יַרְכָה 565
כָּנָף 605
מִסְגֶּרֶת 736
נָפָה 825
קֵץ 1113
קָצֶה 1114
שָׂפָה 1213
תּוֹצָאוֹת 1342
תּוֹר 1342

border, *see* utmost

border, to be
גָּבַל Kal 291

bore, to
נָקַב Kal 837
רָצַע Kal 1190

born
יָלַד Kal 527
יִלּוֹד 531
יָלִיד 531
מוֹלֶדֶת 671

born, *see* country, homeborn, land, servant

born, to be
יָלַד Niphal 527
יָלַד Pual 527
יָלַד Hophal 527

born, as they be
בֶּטֶן 211

born *in the land*
אֶזְרָח 37

born, one
בֵּן 232

borne, to be
נָשָׂא Kal 840
נָשָׂא Niphal 840

borne, are
עָמַס Kal 960

borne up, to be
סָמַךְ Niphal 879

borrow, to
לָוָה Kal 634
עָבַט Kal 895

* borrow, to
שָׁאַל Kal 1220

borrow, *see* few

borrowed, to be
שָׁאַל Kal 1220

borrower
לָוָה Kal 634

* Bozrah
בָּצְרָה 264

bracelet
אֶצְעָדָה 148
חָח 414
פָּתִיל 1055
צָמִיד 1075
שֵׁרוֹת 1326

bramble
אָטָד 54
חוֹחַ 406

branch
אָמִיר 103
בַּד 186
בֵּן 232
בַּת 280
זְמוֹרָה 388
זָמִיר 388
יוֹנֶקֶת 521
כַּף 612
כִּפָּה 613
נֵצֶר 837
סְעִיף 880
000 000
עָלֶה 939
עָנָף 967
עֲנַף Ch. 967
פֹּארָה 1009
צֶמַח 1075
קָנֶה 1112
קָצִיר 1115
שִׁבֹּלֶת 1227

branch, *see* highest, vine

branch to be cut off
נָמַל Kal 819

branch, outmost
סְעִיף 880

branch, tender
יוֹנֶקֶת 521

branch, thick
עֲבֹת 900

branches
דָּלִיּוֹת 342
נְטִישׁוֹת 812
עֳפָאִים 967
שָׂרִיגִים 1217
שְׁלֻחוֹת 1274

branches, full of
עָנֵף 967

brand
אוּד 29
לַפִּיד 644

brandish, to
עוּף Polel 911

brasen
נְחֹשֶׁת 809

brass
נָחוּשׁ 805
נְחוּשָׁה 805
נְחָשׁ Ch. 809
נְחֹשֶׁת 809

brass, *see* fetter

bravery
תִּפְאָרָה / תִּפְאֶרֶת } 1354

brawling
מָדוֹן 666
מִדְיָנִים 667

bray, to
נָהַק Kal 798

bray (in a mortar), to
כָּתַשׁ Kal 624

breach
בֶּדֶק 187
בְּקִיעַ 264
מִפְרָץ 748
פָּרַץ Kal 1047
פֶּרֶץ 1047
שֶׁבֶר / שֵׁבֶר } 1234

breach, to be made a
בָּקַע Pual 264

breach, to make a
בָּקַע Hiphil 264

breach of promise
תְּנוּאָה 1352

breaches
רְסִיסִים 1177

bread
לֶחֶם 638

bread, *see* leavened

bread, unleavened
מַצָּה 752

breadth
מֶרְחָב 763
פְּתָי Ch. 1055
רַחַב 1167
רֹחַב 1167

breadth, *see* hand

breadth, *foot*
מִדְרָךְ 667

break, to
גָּרַם Kal 316
גָּרַם Piel 316
גָּרַם Hiphil 316
דּוּשׁ / דּוֹשׁ } Kal 338
דָּכָא Piel 340
דָּכָה Piel 341
הָיָה Niphal 360
הָמַם Kal 368
הָרַס Kal 376
חָתַת Hiphil 472
נוֹא Hiphil 799
נָפַץ Kal 828
נָפַץ Piel 828
נָתַק Piel 863
עָרַץ Kal 980
פּוּחַ Kal 1014
פּוּר Hiphil 1015
פָּצַם Kal 1039
פָּצַת Piel 1039
פָּרַץ Kal 1047
פָּרַק Kal 1047
פָּרַר Hiphil 1048
פָּרַשׂ Kal 1048
רָעַע Kal 1186
רְעַע Ch. P'al 1187
רָצַץ Niphal 1190
רָצַץ Piel 1190
רָצַץ Hiphil 1190
שָׁבַר[1] Kal 1232
שָׁבַר[1] Niphal 1232
שָׁבַר[1] Piel 1232
שׁוּף Kal 1247

* break, to
חָלַל Piel 432
חָלַל Hiphil 432
רָעָה Kal 1184

break, *see* bones, neck, pieces, wedlock

break again, to
שׁוּב Kal 1238

break asunder, to (נתק..864)
פָּרַר Pilpel 1048

break away, to
פָּרַץ Hithpael 1047

break clods, to
שָׂדַד Piel 1197

break down, to
הָלַם Kal 367
הָרַס Kal 376
נָתַץ Kal 863
נָתַץ Piel 863
עָרַף[2] Kal 980
פָּרַץ Kal 1047
רוּץ Kal 1165
שָׁבַר[1] Piel 1232

break forth, to
בָּקַע Niphal 264
גּוּחַ / גִּיחַ } Kal 306
פָּצַח Kal 1039
פָּרַח Kal 1045
פָּרַץ Kal 1047
פָּתַח Niphal 1052

break forth, *see* joy

break in, to
פָּרַץ Kal 1047

עָבַר Hiphil 895
עָלָה Hiphil 934
צָעַד Hiphil 1076
קָרַב Hiphil 1123
קָרָה Hiphil 1127
רָכַב Hiphil 1173
שׂוּם / שִׂים } Kal 1200
שׁוּב Kal (כ') 1238
שׁוּב Hiphil 1238
שִׁית Kal..............1256
שָׁלַח Piel..............1268
שָׁפַת Kal..............1322

bring, *see* desolation, distress, evil, fruit, hastily, hither, horseback, low, more, near, nought, pass, remembrance, reproach, salvation, straight, tidings

bring *a cloud*, to
עָנַן Piel.............. 966

* bring, to be able to
נָגַע Hiphil (נשׂג..845)792

bring about, to
סָבַב Hiphil 865

bring again, to
הוּךְ Ch. P'al 359
סָבַב Hiphil 865
שׁוּב Kal..............1238
שׁוּב Polel..............1238
שׁוּב Hiphil 1238

bring again, *see* place

bring away, to
בָּעַר Piel.............. 262
נָהַג ¹ Kal 797

bring away, *see* captive

bring back, to
שׁוּב Kal..............1238
שׁוּב Hiphil 1238

bring down, to
יָרַד Hiphil 561
כָּנַע Hiphil 605
נָגַע Hiphil 792
שָׁחַח Hiphil 1250
שָׁפֵל Hiphil 1321

bring forth, to
בּוֹא Hiphil 189
בָּשַׁל Hiphil 280
דָּשָׁא Hiphil 355
חָבַל Piel.............. 398
חוּל / חִיל } Kal........... 406
יָלַד Kal.............. 527
יָלַד Hiphil 527
יָצָא Kal.............. 548
יָצָא Hiphil 548
נָגַשׁ Hiphil 794
נוּב Kal.............. 799
נָשָׂא Kal.............. 840

נָתַן Kal.............. 851
עָשָׂה Kal.............. 981
פָּלַח Piel..............1019
פָּרָה Kal..............1044
צָמַח Kal..............1074
צָמַח Hiphil 1074
קָרַב Hiphil 1123
שָׁוָה ¹ Piel 1245

bring forth, *see* first child, fruit, new fruit, thousands

bring forth abundantly, to
שָׁרַץ Kal..............1327

bring forth children, to
יָלַד Kal.............. 527

bring forth in abundance, to
שָׁרַץ Kal..............1327

bring forth, to labour to
גּוּחַ / גִּיחַ } Kal 306

bring forth, to be made to
חוּל / חִיל } Hophal 406

bring forth, to make to
יָלַד Hiphil 527

bring forth young, to
יָלַד Kal.............. 527

bring hither, to
נָתַן Kal.............. 851

bring home again, to
שׁוּב Hiphil 1238

bring in, to
בּוֹא Hiphil 189
עֲלַל Ch. Aphel 943

bring in, *see* abundance

bring into, *see* bondage, contempt, snare, subjection

bring low, to
דָּלַל Kal.............. 342
כָּנַע Hiphil 605
כָּרַע Hiphil 618

bring near, to
קָרַב Piel..............1123
קָרַב Hiphil 1123
קְרֵב Ch. Aphel 1125

bring on the way, to
שָׁלַח Piel 1268

bring out, to
יָצָא Hiphil 548

bring over, to
גְּלָה Ch. Aphel 309
עָבַר Hiphil 895

bring through, to
עָבַר Hiphil 895

bring to, *see* birth, honour, nothing, nought, shame

bring to pass, to
עָשָׂה Kal.............. 981

bring together, to
קָבַץ Piel..............1084

bring up, to
אָמַן Kal.............. 103
גָּדַל Piel 297
יָלַד Kal.............. 527
יָצָא Hiphil 548
עָלָה Kal.............. 934
עָלָה Hiphil 934
פָּנַק Piel 1036
רָבָה Piel 1151
רוּם Polel 1163

bringer up
אָמַן Kal.............. 103

bringing
נָשָׂא Kal.............. 840

bringing back
שׁוּב Hiphil 1238

brink
קָצָה 1114
שָׂפָה 1213

broad
רָחָב 1166
רֹחַב 1167
רִקֻּעִים 1192

* broad †
יָד 489

broad, *see* hand

broad, to be made
רָקַע Piel 1192

broad place
רַחַב 1167
רְחוֹב 1167

broad way
רְחוֹב 1167

broidered
רִקְמָה 1192
תַּשְׁבֵּץ 1359

broidered work
רִקְמָה 1192

broken
חַת 471
כָּאָה Niphal 581
מְרוֹחַ 763
נָכֵא 814
נָפַץ Kal.............. 828
נָתַק Kal.............. 863
פָּרַץ Kal..............1047
רֹעָה 1185
רָצַץ Kal..............1190
שָׁבַר ¹ Kal 1232
שָׁבַר ¹ Niphal 1232
תְּבַר Ch. P'al 1336

broken, to be
אָבַד Kal 8
דָּכָא Pual 340
הָלַם Kal 367

חָתַת Niphal 472
חָתַת Piel 472
נָחַת Piel 810
נָתַע Niphal 863
נָתַק Niphal 863
עָרַר Hithpalpel 980
פָּרַק Hithpael 1047
פָּרַר Hophal 1048
רָגַע Kal 1157
רָעַע Kal 1186
רָצַץ Kal 1190
רָצַץ Niphal 1190
שָׁבַר[1] Niphal 1232

broken down
מַסָּח 736
פָּרַץ Kal 1047

broken down, to be
הָרַס Niphal 376
חָתַת Kal 472
נָתַץ Niphal 863
נָתַץ Hophal 863
פָּרַץ Pual 1047
רָעַע Hithpolel 1186

broken in pieces
שְׁבָבִים 1224

broken in pieces, to be
בָּקַע Niphal 264
חָתַת Kal 472
חָתַת Niphal 472
כָּתַת Kal 624

broken off, to be
נָתַק Niphal 863
שָׁבַר[1] Niphal 1232

broken out, to be
פָּרַח Kal 1045

broken, to be sore
דָּכָה Niphal 341

broken to pieces, to be
דּוּק Ch. P'al 337
דְּקַק Ch. P'al 348

broken up, to be
בָּקַע Niphal 264
בָּקַע Hophal 264
עָלָה Niphal 934

brokenfooted
{ שֶׁבֶר / שֶׁבֶר } 1234
רֶגֶל 1155

brokenhanded
{ שֶׁבֶר / שֶׁבֶר } 1234
יָד 489

brokenhearted
שָׁבַר[1] Niphal 1232
לֵב 626

brook
אָפִיק 146
יְאוֹר 486
מִיכַל 694
נַחַל 805

broth
מָרָק 766
פָּרָק 1048

brother
אָח 37
אַח Ch. 40
רֵעַ 1181

brother, *see* father's, husband's brother

brother's wife
יְבֶמֶת 487

brotherhood
אַחֲוָה 45

brotherly
אָח 37

brought
נָהַג[1] Kal 797

brought, *see* low, nought, secretly, silence

brought, to be
אָסַף Niphal 141
{ אֲתָא / אֲתָה } Ch. Hophal 182
בּוֹא Kal 189
בּוֹא Hophal 189
יָבַל Hophal 486
לָקַח Niphal 644
עֲלַל Ch. Aphel 943
קָרַב Niphal 1123

brought again
שׁוּב Hophal 1238

brought again, to be
שׁוּב Hophal 1238

brought back, to be
שׁוּב Pulal 1238

brought, before it was
מַסָּע 738

brought, to cause to be
קָרַב Hiphil 1123

brought down, to be
יָרַד Hophal 561
כָּרַע Kal 618
שָׁחַח Niphal 1250
שָׁפֵל Kal 1321

brought forth, to be
{ חוּל / חִיל } Pulal 406
יָבַל Hophal 486
יָלַד Niphal 527
יָלַד Pual 527
יָצָא Hophal 548

brought in, to be
בּוֹא Hophal 189
עֲלַל Ch. Hophal 943

brought into, to be
בּוֹא Hophal 189

brought into subjection, to be
כָּנַע Niphal 605

brought low, to be
עָנָה[1] Kal 964
צָעַר Kal 1077
שָׁחַח Kal 1250
שָׁחַח Niphal 1250
שָׁפֵל Kal 1321

brought out
מוֹצָא 673

brought to, *see* confusion

brought to pass, to be
הָיָה Niphal 361

brought under, to be
כָּנַע Niphal 605

brought unto, *see* bondage, shame

brought up
אָמְנָה 104

brought up, to be
גָּדַל Kal 297
יָלַד Pual 527
עָלָה Niphal 934
עָלָה Hophal 934

brought up, one
אָמוֹן 102

brow
מֵצַח 754

brown
חוּם 407

bruise
{ חַבּוּרָה / חֲבוּרָה } 398
{ שֶׁבֶר / שֵׁבֶר } 1234

bruise, to
דָּכָא Piel 340
דָּקַק Kal 348
עָשָׂה Piel 981
רְעַע Ch. P'al 1187
שׁוּף Kal 1247

bruised
מָעַךְ Kal 742
רָצַץ Kal 1190

bruised, to be
דָּכָא Pual 340
דָּקַק Hophal 348

bruising
עָשָׂה Kal 981

bruit
שְׁמוּעָה 1285
שֵׁמַע 1299

brutish
בַּעַר 263

brutish, to be
בָּעַר Kal 262
בָּעַר Niphal 262

brutish, to become
בָּעַר Niphal ... 262

brutish person
בַּעַר ... 263

bucket
דְּלִי ... 342
דֳּלִי ... 342

buckler
מָגֵן ... 662
סֹחֵרָה ... 875
צִנָּה ... 1075
רֹמַח ... 1175

bud
מוֹצָא ... 673
פֶּרַח ... 1045
צֶמַח ... 1075

bud, to
נוּץ Hiphil ... 803
פָּרַח Kal ... 1045
פָּרַח Hiphil ... 1045
צָמַח Hiphil ... 1074

bud forth, to
נוּץ Hiphil ... 803

bud forth, to cause to
צָמַח Hiphil ... 1074

bud, to make to
צָמַח Hiphil ... 1074

budded, to be
פָּרַח Kal ... 1045

build, to
בָּנָה Kal ... 258
בְּנָא / בְּנָה } Ch. P'al ... 260

build again, to
שׁוּב Kal ... 1238

build, to begin to
בָּנָה Kal ... 258

builded, to be
בְּנָא / בְּנָה } Ithp'il ... 260

builder
בָּנָה Kal ... 258

building
בִּנְיָה ... 261
בִּנְיָן ... 261
בִּנְיָן Ch. ... 261
מִקְרֶה ... 760

built, to be
בָּנָה Niphal ... 258

Bul
בּוּל ... 205

bull
אַבִּיר ... 10
בָּקָר ... 266
פָּר & פַּר ... 1042
שׁוֹר ... 1248

bull, wild
תּוֹא ... 1337

bullock
עֵגֶל ... 900
פָּר & פַּר ... 1042
שׁוֹר ... 1248
תּוֹר Ch. ... 1342

bullock †
בֵּן ... 232
בָּקָר ... 266

bullock,† young
בֵּן ... 232

bulrush
אַגְמוֹן ... 14
גֹּמֶא ... 311

bulwark
חֵיל ... 425
חֵילָה ... 425
מָצוֹר ... 752
מָצוֹר ... 754
פִּנָּה ... 1022

bunch
אֲגֻדָּה ... 14

bunches, *see* raisins

bunches *of camels*
דַּבֶּשֶׁת ... 335

bundle
צְרוֹר ... 1082

burden
אֲגֻדָּה ... 14
מַשָּׂא ... 766
מַשְׂאָה ... 767
מַשְׂאֵת ... 767
סֵבֶל ... 868
סֵבֶל ... 868
סֹבֶל ... 868
סִבְלָה ... 868

* burden
יְהָב Kal ... 507

burden, to be a
סָבַל Hithpael ... 868

burden, heavy
עָמַס Kal ... 960

burden selves, to
עָמַס Kal ... 960

burdens
מִשְׁפְּתַיִם ... 778

burdens, to bear
סַבָּל ... 868

burdens, bearer of
סַבָּל ... 868

burdensome
מַעֲמָסָה ... 744

burial
קְבוּרָה ... 1083

buried, to be
קָבַר Niphal ... 1085
קָבַר Pual ... 1085

* buried, to be
קָבַר Kal ... 1085

burier
קָבַר Piel ... 1085

* burn
דּוּר ... 338

burn, to
בָּעַר Kal ... 262
בָּעַר Piel ... 262
בָּעַר Pual ... 262
בָּעַר Hiphil ... 262
דְּלַק Ch. P'al ... 342
חָרָה Kal ... 462
חָרַר Kal ... 466
יָצַת Hiphil ... 557
יָקַד Kal ... 557
יָקַד Hophal ... 557
לָהַט Piel ... 634
נָשָׂא Kal ... 843
נָשַׂק Hiphil ... 846
סָרַף Piel ... 885
צוּת Hiphil ... 1070
קָדַח Kal ... 1087
קָטַר[1] Piel ... 1106
קָטַר[1] Hiphil ... 1106
שָׂרַף Kal ... 1218

burn, to cause to
עָלָה Hiphil ... 934

burn incense, to
קָטַר[1] Piel ... 1106
קָטַר[1] Hiphil ... 1106

* burn *incense*, to
זָכַר Hiphil ... 385

burn incense upon, to
קָטַר[1] Hiphil ... 1106

burn sacrifice, to
קָטַר[1] Hiphil ... 1106

burn up, to
אָכַל Kal ... 70
לָהַט Piel ... 634
שָׂרַף Kal ... 1218

burn upon, to
מִקְטָר ... 758

burned, to be
בָּעַר Kal ... 262
חָרַר Kal ... 466
חָרַר Niphal ... 466
יָצַת Kal ... 557
יָצַת Niphal ... 557
כָּוָה Niphal ... 591
נָשָׂא Kal ... 840
צָרַב Niphal ... 1081

burned, to cause to be
שָׂרַף Kal ... 1218

burned up, to be
יָצַת Niphal ... 557

burneth, that
מִכְוָה ... 699

burning
אֵשׁ ... 172
דָּלַק Kal ... 342
יְקַד Ch. P'al ... 557
יְקֵדָה Ch. ... 557
יְקוֹד ... 557
כְּוִיָּה ... 591
כִּי ... 596
מוֹקֵד ... 674
מוֹקְדָה ... 674
מִכְוָה ... 699
צָרֶבֶת ... 1081
שְׂרֵפָה ... 1218

burning, to be
יָקַד Hophal ... 557

burning ague
קַדַּחַת ... 1087

burning coal
גַּחֶלֶת ... 305
רֶשֶׁף ... 1194

burning extreme
חַרְחֻר ... 463

burning heat
רֶשֶׁף ... 1194

burning incense
קָטַר[1] Piel ... 1106

burning lamp
לַפִּיד ... 644

burnings
מִשְׂרְפוֹת ... 767

burnished
קָלָל ... 1109

burnt
מָזֶה ... 684
שְׂרֵפָה ... 1218

burnt, to be
עָלָה Kal ... 934
קָטַר[1] Hophal ... 1106
שָׂרַף Niphal ... 1218
שָׂרַף Pual ... 1218

* burnt, to be
שָׂרַף Kal ... 1218
שְׂרֵפָה ... 1218

burnt offering
עֹלָה ... 939
עֲלָה Ch. ... 941

burnt offering, *see* whole

burnt sacrifice
עֹלָה ... 939

burnt sacrifice, *see* whole

burnt, that were
שָׂרַף Kal ... 1218

burst, to
נָתַק Piel ... 863

burst out, to
פָּרַץ Kal ... 1047

burst, to be ready to
בָּקַע Niphal ... 264

bursting
מְכִתָּה ... 701

bury, to
קָבַר Kal ... 1085
קָבַר Piel ... 1085

burying place
קְבוּרָה ... 1083
קֶבֶר ... 1086

bush
סְנֶה ... 880
שִׂיחַ ... 1206

bushes
נַהֲלֹלִים ... 798

bushy
תַּלְתַּלִּים ... 1348

business
דָּבָר ... 325
מְלָאכָה ... 705
מַעֲשֶׂה ... 746
עִנְיָן ... 966

busy, to be
עָשָׂה Kal ... 981

but
אֲבָל ... 11
אוּלָם ... 30
אַךְ ... 70
אָכֵן ... 75
אַף ... 144
אֶפֶס ... 147
בִּלְתִּי ... 231
בְּרַם Ch. ... 277
גַּם ... 311
דִּי ... 339
זוּלָה ... 383
כִּי ... 596
לָהֵן Ch. ... 634
עוֹד ... 905
רַק ... 1191

but †
אִם ... 100

but, *see* newly, nothing, yet

but if
אִלּוּ ... 93

but only
אֶפֶס ... 147

butler
שָׁקָה Hiphil ... 1323

butlership
מַשְׁקֶה ... 778

butter
חֶמְאָה ... 436
חֵמָה ... 438

* butter
מַחֲמָאֹת ... 687

buttocks
מִפְשָׂעָה ... 748
שֵׁת ... 1331

buy, to
כָּרָה Kal ... 616
לָקַח Kal ... 644
קְנָא Ch. P'al ... 1111
קָנָה[1] Kal ... 1111
שָׁבַר[2] Kal ... 1233

buyer
קָנָה[1] Kal ... 1111

by
אַחַר ... 48
אֶל ... 78
אֵצֶל ... 148
אֵת ... 182
בְּעַד ... 261
מִן ... 731
מִן Ch. ... 732
עֵבֶר ... 899
עַד ... 901
עַל ... 932
עִם ... 955
עִם Ch. ... 955
עִמָּד ... 958
עֵקֶב ... 974

* by
יָד ... 489

by †
דֶּרֶךְ ... 349

by, *see* charge, go, hard, heel, lay, means, pass, roots, set, sevens, stand

by reason of
אֶל ... 78
עַל ... 932

by selves
בַּד ... 186

by that
עַד ... 901

*by*ways
אֹרַח ... 154

by*ways*
עֲקַלְקַל ... 974

byword
מִלָּה ... 706
מָשָׁל ... 772
מְשֹׁל ... 772
שְׁנִינָה ... 1315

cab
קַב ... 1083

cabin
חָנוּת ... 445

cage
כְּלוּב ... 600

cake
חַלָּה ... 430
מָעוֹג ... 740
עֻגָה / עֻגָּה ... 900
צְלוּל ... 1072
צְלִיל ... 1073
רָקִיק ... 1191
cake of figs
דְּבֵלָה ... 318
cake upon the hearth
עֻגָה / עֻגָּה ... 900
cakes
כַּוָּנִים ... 593
לְבִבוֹת ... 631
cakes, to make
לָבַב Piel ... 630
cakes, unleavened
מַצָּה ... 752
calamity
אֵיד ... 57
הַוָּה ... 359
הַיָּה ... 361
רַע ... 1177
calamus
קָנֶה ... 1112
caldron
אַגְמוֹן ... 14
דּוּד ... 336
סִיר ... 875
קַלַּחַת ... 1109
calf
בֵּן ... 232
עֵגֶל ... 900
עֶגְלָה ... 901
פָּר & פַּר ... 1042
calf †
בֵּן ... 232
בָּקָר ... 266
calf, *see* cast
calf, young †
בֵּן ... 232
calker
חָזַק Hiphil ... 411
בֶּדֶק ... 187
call, to
אָמַר Kal ... 105
בּוֹא Hiphil ... 189
זָעַק Kal ... 391
זָעַק Hiphil ... 391
קָרָא¹ Kal ... 1117
call, *see* blessed, happy, record, remembrance, witness
call (*a name*), to
שׂוּם / שִׂים Kal ... 1200
call back, to
סוּר Hiphil ... 872
call for, to
קָרָא¹ Kal ... 1117
call selves, to
קָרָא¹ Niphal ... 1117
call to, *see* remembrance
call *to mind*, to
שׁוּב Hiphil ... 1238
call together, to
צָעַק Hiphil ... 1077
שָׁמַע / שָׁמֵעַ Piel ... 1292
שָׁמַע / שָׁמֵעַ Hiphil ... 1292
call upon, to
קָרָא¹ Kal ... 1117
called, to be
אָמַר Niphal ... 105
קָרָא¹ Kal ... 1117
קָרָא¹ Niphal ... 1117
קָרָא¹ Pual ... 1117
קְרָא Ch. Ithp'al ... 1123
called forth, to be
קָרָא¹ Niphal ... 1117
called together, to be
זָעַק Niphal ... 391
צָעַק Niphal ... 1077
calling
מִקְרָא ... 760
קָרָא¹ Kal ... 1117
calm
דְּמָמָה ... 346
calm, to be
שָׁתַק Kal ... 1333
calve, to
חוּל / חִיל Polel ... 406
יָלַד Kal ... 527
פָּלַט Piel ... 1019
calve, to make to
חוּל / חִיל Polel ... 406
came †
הֲוָא / הֲוָה Ch. P'al ... 358
came, by which...
מָבוֹא ... 660
came out, that which
מוֹצָא ... 673
came, that
קְרֵב ... 1125
* came up in
בֵּן ... 232
camel
גָּמָל ... 312
camels
אֲחַשְׁתְּרָנִים ... 54
camp
מַחֲנֶה ... 688
תַּחֲנֹת ... 1345
camp, to
חָנָה Kal ... 445
camphire
כֹּפֶר ... 615
can
אִיתַי Ch. ... 69
יָכֹל Kal ... 526
יְכִל Ch. P'al ... 527
can, *see* abide, stand, well
can away with
יָכֹל Kal ... 526
can have
יָדַע Kal ... 500
can skill
יָדַע Kal ... 500
can tell
יָדַע Kal ... 500
Canaanite
כְּנַעֲנִי ... 605
candle
נֵר ... 840
candlestick
מְנוֹרָה ... 734
נֶבְרַשְׁתָּה Ch. ... 787
cane
קָנֶה ... 1112
cankerworm
יֶלֶק ... 537
cannot
אִם ... 100
can*not*
יָדַע Kal ... 500
יָכֹל Kal ... 526
*can*not
לָא Ch. ... 624
לֹא ... 625
captain
אַלּוּף / אַלֻּף ... 94
בַּעַל ... 262
טִפְסַר ... 484
כַּר ... 615
נָגִיד ... 791
נָשִׂיא ... 845
פֶּחָה ... 1016
פֶּחָה Ch. ... 1016
קָצִין ... 1115
רֹאשׁ ... 1142
רַב ... 1147
רַב Ch. ... 1150
שַׂר ... 1214
שַׁלִּיט Ch. ... 1275
שָׁלִישׁ ... 1275

carry away as with a flood, to
זָרַם Kal............. 395
carry away *captive*, to
שָׁבָה Kal.............1224
carry away of captive, to
גָּלָה Kal............. 307
carry away safe, to
פָּלַט Hiphil 1019
carry back, to
שׁוּב Hiphil 1238
carry captive, to
גָּלָה Hiphil 307
carry down, to
יָרַד Hiphil 561
carry forth, to
יָצָא Hiphil 548
carry out, to
יָצָא Hiphil 548
carry over, to
עָבַר Hiphil 895
carry up, to
עָלָה Hiphil 934
carrying
נָשָׂא Kal.............. 840
cart
עֲגָלָה................. 901
carve, to
קָלַע Kal.............1110
carved
חֲטֻבוֹת.................. 417
מִקְלַעַת.................. 759
פִּתּוּחַ..................1052
carved, *see* figures
carved image
פֶּסֶל..................1037
carved images
פְּסִילִים..................1037
carved work
חָקָה Pual 457
פִּתּוּחַ..................1052
carving
חֲרֹשֶׁת.................. 468
מִקְלַעַת.................. 759
case
דָּבָר.................. 325
case, *see* any, such
casement
אֶשְׁנָב.................. 179
cassia
קִדָּה..................1087
קְצִיעוֹת..................1115
cast
לוּט Kal 635
שָׁלַךְ Hophal..........1275
cast, *see* far off, profane
cast, to
טוּל Hiphil 480
יָדַד Kal 499
יָדָה Piel............. 499
יָצַק Kal 556
יָרָה Kal............. 564
יָרָה Hiphil 564
מוּט Hiphil 670
נָגַע Hiphil 792
נָשָׂא Kal............. 840
נָשַׁל Kal............. 848
נָתַן Kal.............. 851
פּוּץ Hiphil 1014
צוּר Kal 1069
צָרַף Kal 1082
רְמָה Ch. P'al 1175
שָׁלַח Piel 1268
שָׁלַךְ Hiphil 1275
שָׁפַךְ Kal.............1320
תָּקַע Kal.............1356
cast, to be
טוּל Hophal 480
נָפַל Hiphil 825
נָתַן Niphal 851
רְמָה Ch. P'al 1175
רְמָה Ch. Ithp'el 1175
שָׁלַח Pual 1268
שָׁלַךְ Hophal 1275
cast about, to
סָבַב Kal 865
cast abroad, to
פּוּץ Hiphil 1014
cast away, *see* vilely
cast away, to
הָדַף Kal............. 357
זָנַח Hiphil 390
זָרָה Kal 394
מָאַס [1] Kal 659
שָׁלַח Piel 1268
שָׁלַךְ Hiphil 1275
cast calf, to
שָׁכַל Piel 1259
cast clouts
סְחָבוֹת................. 874
cast down, to
יָנַח Hiphil 541
יָרַד Hiphil 561
כָּרַע Hiphil 618
כָּשַׁל Hiphil 621
מָגַר Piel............. 663
נָדַח Hiphil 796
נָפַל Hiphil 825
נָתַץ Kal 863
שָׁלַךְ Hiphil 1275
שָׁפֵל Hiphil 1321
cast down, to be
דָּחָה Pual 339
טוּל Hophal 480
כָּשַׁל Niphal 621
נָפַל Kal............. 825
נָתַץ Pual............ 863
רְמָה Ch. P'al........ 1175
שָׁחַח Hithpolel 1250
שָׁלַךְ Hophal..........1275
שָׁפֵל Hiphil 1321
cast down, to be utterly
טוּל Hophal 480
cast *dust*, to
עָפַר Piel............. 968
cast far off, to be
הָלָא Niphal 362
cast forth, to
בָּדַק Kal 277
טוּל Hiphil 480
נָכָה Hiphil 814
שָׁלַךְ Hiphil 1275
cast fruit, to
שָׁכַל Piel.............1259
cast in, to
שׂוּם / שִׂים } Kal 1200
cast into deep, *see* sleep
cast *lots*, to
נָפַל Hiphil........... 825
cast off, to
זָנַח Kal.............. 390
זָנַח Hiphil 390
מָאַס [1] Kal 659
נָטַשׁ Kal.............. 813
פָּרַר Hiphil 1048
שָׁחַת Piel.............1252
שָׁלַף Hiphil 1275
cast out
מִגְרָשׁ................. 663
מָרוֹר................. 763
נָדַח Niphal 796
שָׁלַח Pual 1268
שָׁלַךְ Hophal 1275
cast out, to
גָּרַשׁ Piel 316
דּוּחַ Hiphil 337
חָדַף Kal 357
טוּל Hiphil 480
יָדָה Piel............. 499
יָרַשׁ Hiphil 566
נָדַח Piel............. 796
נָדַח Hiphil 796
נָפַל Hiphil 825
נָשַׁל Kal 848
פָּנָה Piel.............1021

קוּר Hiphil 1104
רוּק Hiphil 1165
שָׁלַח Piel 1268
שָׁלַךְ Hiphil 1275

cast out, to be
גָּרַשׁ Niphal 316
טוּל Hophal 480
שָׁלַךְ Hophal 1275

cast self down, to
גָּהַר Kal 298
נָפַל Hithpael 825

cast *stones*, to
סָקַל Piel 884

cast up, to
גָּרַשׁ Kal 316
סָלַל Kal 878
עָלָה Hiphil 934

cast, when
שַׁלֶּכֶת 1276

cast, when it was
יְצֻקָה 556
מוּצֶקֶת 674

cast young, to
שָׁכֹל Piel 1259

casting
מוּצָק 673

casting down
חֲתַת 473
יֶשַׁח 575
שָׁכַב Hiphil 1257

casting up
שָׁפַךְ Kal 1320

castle
אַרְמוֹן 157
טִירָה 481
מִגְדָּל 661
מְצַד 752
מְצוּדָה 753

castle, goodly
טִירָה 481

castles
בִּירָנִיּוֹת 214

catch, to
אָחַז Kal 46
בָּזַז Kal 207
גָּזַל Kal 304
גָּרַר Kal 316
חָזַק Hiphil 411
חָטַף Kal 418
חָלַט Hiphil 431
טָרַף Kal 485
לָכַד Kal 642
מָצָא Kal 748
נָקַשׁ Piel 840
תָּפַשׂ Kal 1355

catch hold, to
אָחַז Kal 46
חָזַק Kal 411

catch self, to
לָכַד Kal 642

* catcheth
צַיִד 1071

caterpiller
חָסִיל 450
יֶלֶק 537

cattle
בְּהֵמָה 188
בְּעִיר 261
מִקְנֶה 759
צֹאן 1055
שֶׂה 1199

* cattle †
מְלָאכָה 705

cattle, *see* fat, keep

cattle, lesser
שֶׂה 1199

cattle, small
צֹאן 1055
שֶׂה 1199

caught, to be
אָחַז Niphal 46
תָּפַשׂ Niphal 1355

caul
יֹתֶרֶת 581
סְגוֹר 869

cauls
שְׁבִיסִים 1227

cause
אוֹדֹת 29
דָּבָר 325
דִּבְרָה 334
דִּין 340
מִשְׁפָּט 776
נְסִבָּה 819
סִבָּה 866
רִיב 1171
שָׁל 1262

cause, *see* plead cause, righteous, without

cause, to
בָּעָה Kal 261
הָיָה Kal 360
נָתַן Kal 851

cause, *see* answer, approach, ascend, astray, behold, blow, brought, burn, burned, captivity, carried away captive, cease, cleave, come, come about, come down, come near, come up, curse, darkness, despair, die, discern, discharged, dismayed, draw near, dreamed, drink, dwell, eat, eaten, eater, err, escape, fail, fall, find, flow, forget, forgotten, fruitful, go, go astray, go forth, go out, grief, healed, hear, heard, hope, inherit, intreat, know, led into captivity, lie down, lodge, lose, mourn, mourning, pass, pass through, perish, possess, poured, proclaimed, prosper, rain, rejoice, remain, rest, return, ride, rule, run, run down, scraped, see, serve, set, shame, shine, sin, sing for joy, sorrow, sound, speak, spring forth, stick, stinking, stumble, swear, trespass, turn, understand, walk wander, yield

cause,† for this
כֹּל Ch. 597
קֳבֵל, קֳבֵל Ch. 1084

cause,† for which
כֵּן 604

cause to be, *see* whore
cause to come, *see* near
cause to commit, *see* fornication
cause to make, *see* haste
cause to take, *see* root

cause, without
חִנָּם 446
רֵיקָם 1172
שֶׁקֶר 1325

caused, to be
נָתַן Niphal 851

caused, *see* fall, fly

causeless
חִנָּם 446

causes, *see* banishment
causeth, *see* sweat

causeway
מְסִלָּה 737

causing, *see* return

cave
חוֹר 409
מְעָרָה 745

caves
מְחִלּוֹת 687

cease, to
בָּטַל Kal 211
בְּטֵל Ch. P'al 211
גָּמַר Kal 312
דָּמָה [2] Kal 345
דָּמַם Kal 346
חָדַל Kal 402
חָרַשׁ Hiphil 466
יָסַף Kal 543
כָּלָה Kal 598
מוּשׁ [1] Hiphil 674
נוּחַ Kal 800
נָפַל Hiphil 824
עָמַד Kal 955
פּוּג Kal 1014
רָפָה Hiphil 1188
שָׁבַת Kal 1234
שָׁבַת Niphal 1234

changed, to be
הָפַךְ Niphal 370
חָלַף Kal 434
חָפַשׂ Hithpael 453
מוּר Niphal 674
שָׁנָא Kal 1304
שָׁנָא Pual 1304
שְׁנָא Ch. P'al 1304
שְׁנָא Ch. Pael 1304
שְׁנָא Ch. Ithpael 1304
שְׁנָא Ch. Aphel 1304

changed, being
סָבַב Hophal 865

changing
תְּמוּרָה 1349

channel
אָפִיק 146
שִׁבֹּלֶת 1227

chant, to
פָּרַט Kal 1045

chapel
מִקְדָּשׁ 755

chapiter
כֹּתֶרֶת 624
צֶפֶת 1080
רֹאשׁ 1142

chapman †
אֱנוֹשׁ 136
תּוּר Kal 1342

chapt, to be
חָתַת Kal 472

Charashim
חֶרֶשׁ 467

charge
יָד 489
מִשְׁמֶרֶת 773
מִשְׁפָּט 776
סֵבֶל 868
פְּקֻדָּה 1041

charge, *see* lay unto

charge, to
אָמַר Kal 105
נָתַן Kal 851
עוּד Hiphil 905
פָּקַד Kal 1040
צָוָה Piel 1065
שׂוּם / שִׂים Kal 1200
שָׁבַע Hiphil 1228

charge, to appoint to have the
פָּקַד Hiphil 1040

charge by an oath, to
שָׁבַע Hiphil 1228

charge, to give a
פָּקַד Kal 1040
צָוָה Piel 1065

charge, to lay to
שָׁאַל Kal 1220

* charge of, had the
עַל 932

charge, that have the
עָשָׂה Kal 981
פְּקֻדָּה 1041

charge, unto
קֶרֶב 1125

charge, which had the
פָּקִיד 1042

charge with an oath, to
שָׁבַע Hiphil 1228

chargeable, to be
כָּבֵד / כָּבַד Kal 581
כָּבֵד / כָּבַד Hiphil 581

charged, to be
צָוָה Piel 1065

charger
קְעָרָה 1113

chargers
אֲגַרְטְלִים 14

chariot
אַפִּרְיוֹן 148
הֹצֶן 370
מֶרְכָּב 764
מֶרְכָּבָה 764
עֲגָלָה 901
רֶכֶב 1173
רִכְבָּה 1174
רְכוּב 1174

chariot, *see* driver, ride in

chariot man
רַכָּב 1174

charmed
לַחַשׁ 640

charmer
חָבַר Kal 400
לָחַשׁ Piel 640

charmer †
חֶבֶר 400

charmers
אִטִּים 55

charming †
חָבַר Kal 400
חֶבֶר 400

chase, to
בָּרַח Hiphil 271
דָּחָה Kal 339
דָּלַק Kal 342
צוּד Kal 1065
רָדַף Kal 1158
רָדַף Hiphil 1158

chase away, to
בָּרַח Hiphil 271

chased
נָדַח Hophal 796

chased, to be
נָדַד Hiphil 795
רָדַף Pual 1158

chased away, to be
נָדַד Hophal 796

chasten, to
יָכַח Hiphil 525
יָסַר Piel 545

chasten self, to
עָנָה[2] Hithpael 964

* chastened
תּוֹכַחַת 1340

chastened, to be
יָכַח Hophal 525

chasten*eth*
מוּסָר 672

chastening
מוּסָר 672

chastise, to
יָסַר Kal 545
יָסַר Piel 545
יָסַר Hiphil 545

chastised, to be
יָסַר Niphal 545

chastisement
מוּסָר 672

chatter, to
צָפַף Pilpel 1080

check
מוּסָר 672

checker
שְׂבָכָה 1195

cheek
לְחִי 637

cheek bone
לְחִי 637

cheek teeth
מְתַלְּעוֹת 780

cheer, to
טוֹב Hiphil 476

cheer up, to
שָׂמֵחַ / שָׂמַח Piel 1208

cheerful
טוֹב 476

cheerful, to make
יָטַב Hiphil 524
נוּב Pilel 799

cheese
גְּבִינָה 290
שָׁפָה 1318

cheese †
חָלָב 429
חָרִיץ 464

Chemarims
כְּמָרִים 604

Chephar-*haamonai*
כָּפָר 615

Cherethims
כְּרֵתִי 620

Cherethites
כְּרִי (כ׳) 617
כְּרֵתִי 620

cherish, to
סָכַן[1] Kal 876

cherub
כְּרוּב 616

cherubim
כְּרוּב 616

chesnut tree
עַרְמוֹן 980

chest
אֲרוֹן } אָרֹן } 153

chests
גְּנָזִים 313

chew, to
גָּרַר Niphal 316

* chew,† to
עָלָה Hiphil 934

chewed, to be
כָּרַת Niphal 618

chide, to
רִיב Kal 1171

chiding
רִיב 1171

chief
אָב 1
גִּבּוֹר 289
נָגִיד 791
נָשִׂיא 845
פִּנָּה 1022
רֹאשׁ 1142
רֵאשׁ Ch. 1142
רֵאשִׁית 1147
רַב Ch. 1150
שַׂר 1214

chief, *see* captain, governor, musician, ruler

chief friend
אַלּוּף } אַלֻּף } 94

chief man
בַּעַל 262
רֹאשׁ 1142

chief men
אֲצִילִים 148

chief one
עַתּוּד 1007

chief ruler
כֹּהֵן 587

chief things
רֹאשׁ 1142

chiefest
אַבִּיר 10
דָּגַל Kal 335
מַעֲלָה 744
רֵאשִׁית 1147

chiefest place
רֹאשׁ 1142

child
בֵּן 232
בֵּן Ch. 258
וָלָד 377
וָלֶד 377
זֶרַע 396
יָלַד Kal 527
יֶלֶד 530
יְלִיד 531
נַעַר 823
נֹעַר 824
עוֹלֵל } עֹלָל } 907

child, *see* fatherless, first, maid, man-child, sucking, weaned, young

child, to be delivered of a
יָלַד Kal 527

child, only
יָחִיד 523

* child, she that is with
מָלֵא 703

child, sucking
עוּל 906

child, to travail with
חוּל } חִיל } Kal 406
יָלַד Kal 527

child, with
הָרָה 375

child, to be with
הָרָה Kal 375
הָרָה 375

child, woman with
הָרָה 375
הָרִיָּה 376

child, young
עֲוִיל 906

childhood
יַלְדוּת 531
נְעוּרִים 822

childless
עֲרִירִי 978

childless, to be
שָׁכֹל Kal 1259

childless, to make
שָׁכֹל Piel 1259

children
טַף 484
עָלַל Poel 942

children, *see* bereave of, bereaved, bring forth, lose, loss, rob

children, little
טַף **484**

children, to obtain
בָּנָה Niphal **258**

chimney
אֲרֻבָּה **149**

Chisleu
כִּסְלֵו **609**

choice
בָּחַר Kal 209
בָּחַר Niphal 209
בַּר 269
בָּרַר Kal 277
מִבְחוֹר 660
מִבְחָר 660

choice, *see* vine

choice young man
בָּחוּר 208

choicest
מִבְחָר 660

choicest, *see* vine

choler, to be moved with
מָרַר Hithpael 766

choose—; ch. out
בָּחִיר 208
בָּחַר Kal 209

choose, to
בָּרָא Piel 270
בָּרָה Kal 270
קָבַל Piel 1083

chop in pieces, to
פָּרַשׂ Kal 1048

chosen
בָּחוּר 208
בָּרַר Kal 277
מִבְחָר 660

chosen, to be
בָּחַר Niphal 209

chosen one
בָּחִיר 208

chronicles
{ דָּבָר 325
{ יוֹם 508

churl
כִּילַי 596
כֵּלַי 600

churlish
קָשֶׁה 1131

churning
מִיץ 698

ciel, to
חָפָה Piel **451**

cieled
סָפַן Kal **882**

cieled with
שְׂחִיף **1251**

cieling
סִפֻּן **882**

cleave, to make
- דָּבֵק / דָּבַק } Hiphil 318

cleft
- בְּקִיעַ 264
- נְקָרָה 840
- שֶׁסַע 1315

cleft, to be
- בָּקַע Hithpael 264

clefts
- חֲגָוִים 401

cliff
- מַעֲלֶה 744
- עָרוּץ 978

clift
- נְקָרָה 840
- סְעִיף 880

climb, to
- עָלָה Kal 934

climb up, to
- עָלָה Kal 934

clip, to
- גָּרַע Kal 316

clod
- גּוּשׁ 304
- גִּישׁ 307
- מֶגְרָפָה 663
- רֶגֶב 1154

clod, *see* break

cloke
- מְעִיל 742

close
- צָר 1081

close, *see* follow, keep, kept, round about

close, to
- חָרָה Tiphel 462
- כָּסָה Piel 607
- עָצַם Piel 972

close place
- מִסְגֶּרֶת 736

close up, to
- גָּדַר Kal 298
- סָגַר Kal 869
- עָצַר Kal 973

closed, to be
- זוּר [1] Kal 384

closed up
- סָתַם Kal 885

closer, *see* stick

closet
- חֻפָּה 451

cloth
- בֶּגֶד 185
- שִׂמְלָה 1210

cloth, *see* menstruous, sackcloth

cloth, thick
- מַכְבֵּר 698

clothe, to
- לָבֵשׁ / לָבַשׁ } Kal 633
- לָבֵשׁ / לָבַשׁ } Hiph(;-in,with) 633
- לְבַשׁ Ch. Aphel (with) 633

clothe self, to
- לָבֵשׁ / לָבַשׁ } Kal 633

clothed
- כִּרְבֵּל 616

clothed, to be
- כָּסָה Pual 607
- לָבֵשׁ / לָבַשׁ } Kal (in,with) . 633
- לָבֵשׁ / לָבַשׁ } Pual 633
- לְבַשׁ Ch. P'al (with).. 633

clothed with
- לָבוּשׁ 632

clothes
- בֶּגֶד 185
- גְּלוֹם 309
- מַד 664
- סוּת 874
- שַׂלְמָה 1208
- שִׂמְלָה 1210

clothing
- בֶּגֶד 185
- לְבוּשׁ 632
- מְכַסֶּה 700
- שִׂמְלָה 1210
- תִּלְבֹּשֶׁת 1347

cloud
- נָשִׂיא 846
- עָב 887
- עָנָן 966
- עֲנַן Ch. 967
- עֲנָנָה 967
- שַׁחַק 1252

cloud, *see* bright

cloud, to cover with a
- עוּב Hiphil 905

cloud, dark
- עֲרָפֶל 980

cloud, thick
- עָב 887

cloudy
- עָנָן 966

clouted
- טָלָא Pual 481

clouts, *see* cast clouts

cloven
- שָׁסַע Kal 1315

*cloven*footed
- פַּרְסָה 1046

clovenfooted †
- שֶׁסַע 1315

cloven*foot*ed, to be
- שָׁסַע Kal 1315

cluster
- אֶשְׁכּוֹל / אֶשְׁכֹּל } 178

cluster, *see* raisins

cluster of grapes
- אֶשְׁכּוֹל / אֶשְׁכֹּל } 178

coal
- גַּחֶלֶת 305
- פֶּחָם 1017
- רֶצֶף 1190
- רֶשֶׁף 1194
- שְׁחוֹר 1250

coal, *see* burning, live

coast
- גְּבוּל 288
- גְּבוּלָה 289
- גְּלִילָה 310
- חֶבֶל / חֶבֶל } 399
- חוֹף 408
- יָד 489
- יַרְכָה 565
- נָפָה 825
- קָצָה 1114

coast, *see* outmost

coat
- כְּתֹנֶת / כֻּתֹּנֶת } 623
- מְעִיל 742

coat of mail
- שִׁרְיוֹן 1326

coat of *mail*
- שִׁרְיוֹן 1326

coats
- סַרְבָּלִין Ch. 884

cockatrice
- צֶפַע 1080
- צִפְעוֹנִי 1080

cockle
- בָּאְשָׁה 184

coffer
- אַרְגָּז 152

coffin
- אָרוֹן / אָרֹן } 153

cogitation
- רַעְיוֹן Ch. 1185

cold
- צִנָּה 1076
- קַר 1117
- קֹר 1117
- קָרָה 1127

collar
- פֶּה 1011

collars
נְטִיפוֹת ... 812

collection
מַשְׂאֵת ... 767

college
מִשְׁנֶה ... 773

collops
פִּימָה ... 1018

colour
עַיִן ... 919

colours
פַּסִּים ... 1037

colours, *see* divers

colours, divers
פַּסִּים ... 1037

colours, fair
פּוּךְ ... 1014

colours, with divers
טָלָא Kal ... 481

colt
בֵּן ... 232
עַיִר ... 925

colt, *see* ass

comb, *see* honeycomb

come, to
אַחֲרוֹן ... 53
אָתָא / אָתָה } Kal ... 182
אָתָא / אָתָה } Hiphil ... 182
אֲתָא / אֲתָה } Ch. P'al ... 182
בּוֹא Kal ... 189
דָּרַךְ Kal ... 349
הוּךְ Ch. P'al ... 359
הָיָה Kal ... 360
הָלַךְ Kal ... 362
הָפַךְ Niphal ... 370
יָלַד Niphal ... 527
יָלַךְ Kal ... 531
יָצָא Kal ... 548
מְטָא / מְטָה } Ch. P'al ... 691
נָגַע Kal ... 792
נָגַע Hiphil ... 792
נָגַשׁ Kal ... 794
נָגַשׁ Niphal ... 794
נָתַן Kal ... 851
סְלַק Ch. P'il ... 878
עָבַר Kal ... 895
עָלָה Kal ... 934
עֲלַל Ch. P'al ... 943
פָּגַע Kal ... 1009
צָלַח Kal ... 1072
קָרַב Kal ... 1123
קְרֵב Ch. P'al ... 1125
קָרָה Niphal ... 1127

come, *see* again, against, another place, end, full, near, nigh, pass, presumptuously, remembrance, round about, time, time to, while, wrath

come, to be
אָתָא / אָתָה } Kal ... 182
אֲתָא / אֲתָה } Ch. P'al ... 182
בּוֹא Kal ... 189
קָרָא[2] Kal ... 1122

come about
תְּקוּפָה ... 1356

come about, to cause to
סָבַב Hiphil ... 865

come abroad, to
יָצָא Kal ... 548
פָּרַץ Kal ... 1047

come again, to
שׁוּב Kal (יסף 545..) 1238

come against, to
בּוֹא Kal ... 189

come away, to
יָלַךְ Kal ... 531

come back, to
שׁוּב Kal ... 1238

come before, to
קָדַם Piel ... 1088

come betwixt, to
פָּגַע Hiphil ... 1009

come, to cause to
בּוֹא Hiphil ... 189
מָצָא Hiphil ... 748
קָרָא[2] Hiphil ... 1122

come down
נַחַת ... 810

come down, to
יָרַד Kal ... 561
נָחַת Kal ... 810
נְחַת Ch. P'al ... 810

come down, to cause to
יָרַד Hiphil ... 561
יָרֵד Hiphil ... 561
נָחַת Hiphil ... 810

come forth, to
גּוּחַ / גִּיחַ } Kal ... 306
גּוּחַ / גִּיחַ } Hiphil ... 306
יָצִיא ... 556
נְפַק Ch. P'al ... 828

come forth, that
צֶאֱצָאִים ... 1057

come in, to
עֲלַל Ch. P'al ... 943

come in, to let
בּוֹא Hiphil ... 189

come like a whirlwind, to
שָׂעַר Hithpael ... 1212

come mightily, to
צָלַח Kal ... 1072

come more, to
יָסַף Kal ... 543

come near, to
נָגַשׁ Kal ... 794
קָרַב Kal ... 1123
קְרֵב Ch. P'al ... 1125

come near, to be
קָרַב Hiphil ... 1123

come near, to cause to
קָרַב Hiphil ... 1123

come near, which
קָרֵב ... 1125

come nigh, to
נָגַע Hiphil ... 792
נָגַשׁ Kal ... 794
קָרַב Kal ... 1123

come nigh, them that
קָרוֹב ... 1127

come on
יָהַב Kal ... 507

come on, to
מָצָא Kal ... 748
פָּנָה Kal ... 1021

come out, to
בּוֹא Kal ... 189
יָצָא Kal ... 548

come out, *see* whirlwind

come over, to
עָבַר Kal ... 895

come thereout, to
יָצָא Kal ... 548

come, things to
אָתָא / אָתָה } Kal ... 182

come, things for to
בּוֹא Kal ... 189

come, things that
מַעֲלָה ... 744

come, things that shall
עָתִיד ... 1008

come, *time* to
מָחָר ... 689

come to, *see* honour, knowledge, nought, poverty, shame

come to, to
מָצָא Kal ... 748
מָצָא Niphal ... 748

come to an end, to
גָּמַר Kal ... 312

come to hand, to
מָצָא Niphal ... 748

come to have, *see* dominion

come to pass, to
הָיָה Kal ... 360

come to pass,† to
הֲוָא / הֲוָה } Ch. P'al ... 358

come to pass unto, to
קָרָה Kal ... 1127
come to *understanding*, to
יָדַע Kal ... 500
come up, to
סְלֵק Ch. P'al ... 878
סְלִק Ch. P'il ... 878
עָלָה Kal ... 934
come up, to cause to
עָלָה Hiphil ... 934
come up, to make to
עָלָה Hiphil ... 934
come upon, to
אָחַז Kal ... 46
אָתָא, אָתָה } Kal ... 182
בּוֹא Kal ... 189
לָבֵשׁ, לָבַשׁ } Kal ... 633
מָצָא Kal ... 748
קָרָא[2] Kal ... 1122
come with, *see* company
come without, to
יָצָא Kal ... 548
comeliness
הָדָר ... 357
הוֹד ... 358
comely
חִין ... 425
יָפֶה ... 548
נָאוֶה ... 781
נָוֶה ... 800
תֹּאַר ... 1334
תִּפְאָרָה, תִּפְאֶרֶת } ... 1354
comely, to be
יָטַב Hiphil ... 524
נָאָה Pilel ... 781
cometh, *see* sale
* cometh any thing near
קָרֵב ... 1125
cometh, as
מָבוֹא ... 660
cometh from, that which
צֵאָה ... 1055
cometh nigh, that
קָרֵב ... 1125
cometh of, that
שֶׁגֶר ... 1236
cometh out, that
צֵאָה ... 1055
cometh out, that which
צֶאֱצָאִים ... 1057
comfort
נָחַם Piel ... 808
נֶחָמָה ... 808

comfort, to
בָּלַג Hiphil ... 229
נָחַם Piel ... 808
סָעַד Kal ... 880
רָפַד Piel ... 1188
comfort, to receive
נָחַם Niphal ... 808
comfort self
מַבְלִיגִית ... 661
comfort self, to
נָחַם Hithpael ... 808
comfortable
מְנוּחָה ... 733
נִחוּמִים ... 804
comfortably
לֵב ... 626
לֵבָב ... 630
comforted, to be
נָחַם Niphal ... 808
נָחַם Pual ... 808
נָחַם Hithpael ... 808
comforters
נָחַם Piel ... 808
comforts
נִחוּמִים ... 804
תַּנְחוּמִים ... 1352
coming
מוֹבָא ... 670
קָרָא[2] Kal ... 1122
* coming
רֶגֶל ... 1155
coming down
יָרַד Kal ... 561
coming in
מָבוֹא ... 660
coming on
עָבַר Kal ... 895
command
פֶּה ... 1011
command, to
אָמַר Kal ... 105
אֲמַר Ch. P'al ... 133
דָּבַר Piel ... 319
צָוָה Piel ... 1065
command,† to
טְעֵם Ch. ... 484
שׂוּם Ch. P'al ... 1204
command*ed*
מִצְוָה ... 753
commanded, to be
צָוָה Pual ... 1065
* commanded, to be
טַעַם Ch. ... 484
commanded, which was
מִצְוָה ... 753
commander
צָוָה Piel ... 1065

commanding
צָוָה Piel ... 1065
commandment
אִמְרָה ... 134
דָּבָר ... 325
דָּת ... 355
חֹק ... 456
טַעַם Ch. ... 484
טְעֵם Ch. ... 484
מַאֲמַר ... 658
מִלָּה Ch. ... 706
מִפְקָד ... 748
מִצְוָה ... 753
פֶּה ... 1011
צַו & צָו ... 1065
commandment, *see* give
* commandment, at the
אָמַר Kal ... 105
commandment, to give a
צָוָה Piel ... 1065
commandment, to give in
צָוָה Piel ... 1065
commandment, to send with
יָצָא (ב׳) Hiphil ... 548
צָוָה Piel ... 1065
commandments
פִּקּוּדִים ... 1042
commend, to
הָלַל Piel ... 366
שָׁבַח Piel ... 1225
commended, to be
הָלַל Pual ... 366
commission
דָּת ... 355
commit, to
גָּלַל Kal ... 310
מָסַר Kal ... 739
נָתַן Kal ... 851
עָשָׂה Kal ... 981
פָּעַל Kal ... 1037
פָּקַד Hiphil ... 1040
שׂוּם, שִׂים } Kal ... 1200
commit, *see* abominable, adultery, fornication, iniquity, whoredom, wickedness
commit self, to
עָזַב Kal ... 915
commit *sin*, to
חָטָא Kal ... 414
commit *trespass*, to
מָעַל Kal ... 742
commit *whoredom*, to
זָנָה Kal ... 389
committed, to be
הָיָה Niphal ... 360
נָתַן Niphal ... 851
עָשָׂה Niphal ... 981

* correction
שֵׁבֶט 1225

corrupt
שָׁחַת Niphal 1252
שָׁחַת Hophal 1252
שְׁחַת Ch. P'al 1253

corrupt, to
נָעַר Kal 313
חָנֵף Hiphil 447
שָׁחַת Piel 1252
שָׁחַת Hiphil 1252

corrupt, to be
חָבַל Pual 398
מוּק Hiphil 674
מָקַק Niphal 760
שָׁחַת Niphal 1252
שָׁחַת Hiphil 1252

corrupt thing
שָׁחַת Hophal 1252

corrupted, to be
שָׁחַת Niphal 1252
שָׁחַת Hiphil 1252

corrupter
שָׁחַת Hiphil 1252

corrupting
שָׁחַת Hiphil 1252

corruption
בְּלִי 229
מַשְׁחִית 769
מָשְׁחָת 769
שַׁחַת 1253

corruptly, to deal
חָבַל Kal 398

corruptly, to do
שָׁחַת Hiphil 1252

cost nothing, to
חִנָּם 446

cost, without
חִנָּם 446

costly
יָקָר 558

cote, *see* sheepcote

cotes
אֻרוֹת 33

cottage
מְלוּנָה 707
סֻכָּה 875

cottages
כְּרֹת 620

couch
יָצוּעַ 555
מִשְׁכָּב 770
עֶרֶשׂ 981

couch, to
כָּרַע Kal 618
רָבַץ Kal 1154
שָׁחַח Kal 1250

couch down, to
רָבַץ Kal 1154

couchingplace
מִרְבַּץ 762

could
יָכֹל Kal 526
כְּהַל Ch. P'al 586

* could
נָכַר Hiphil 818

* could not
נָדַד Kal 795

* could they
יָדַע Kal 500

couldest
יְכִל Ch. P'al 527

coulter
אֵת 182

council
רִגְמָה 1157

counsel
דָּבָר 325
מְלַךְ Ch. 728
סוֹד 870
עֵטָא Ch. 918
עֵצָה 971
רִגְשָׁה 1158

counsel, *see* ask, secret

counsel, to
יָעַץ Kal 547

counsel, to give
יָעַץ Kal 547
יָעַץ Niphal 547

counsel, to take
יָסַד Niphal 542
יָעַץ Kal 547
יָעַץ Niphal 547

counsellor
דְּתָבָר Ch. 355
יָעַץ Kal 547

counsel*lor*
עֵצָה 971

counsellors
הַדָּבְרִין Ch. 357
יְעַט Ch. P'al 546

counsels
מוֹעֵצוֹת 673
תַּחְבֻּלוֹת 1344

counsels, wise
תַּחְבֻּלוֹת 1344

count, to
חָשַׁב Kal 468
חָשַׁב Piel 468
מָנָה Kal 732
נָתַן Kal 851
סָפַר Kal 882
פָּקַד Kal 1040

count, *see* pure, uncircumcised

count, to make
כָּסַס Kal 609

counted, to be(ספר Nip.883)
חָשַׁב Niphal 468
פָּקַד Kal 1040
פָּקַד Pual 1040

countenance
אַף 144
זִיו Ch. 384
מַרְאֶה 761
עַיִן 919
פָּנִים 1023
תֹּאַר 1334

countenance, to
הָדַר Kal 357

countervail, to
שָׁוָה[1] Kal 1245

country
אֲדָמָה 21
אִי 55
אֶרֶץ 157
גְּלִילָה 310
חֵבֶל / חֶבֶל } 399
מָקוֹם 756
נֶפֶת 833
פְּרָזִי 1044
שָׂדֶה 1197

country, *see* far, hill, low, south

country, born of the
אֶזְרָח 37

country, one of...own
אֶזְרָח 37

couple
צֶמֶד 1074
שְׁנַיִם 1311

couple, to
חָבַר Piel 400

coupled
תָּאַם Kal 1334

coupled, to be
חָבַר Kal 400

coupled together
תָּאַם Kal 1334
תַּמִּים 1350

coupled together, to be
חָבַר Kal 400
חָבַר Pual 400

coupleth, which
חֹבֶרֶת 400

coupling
חֹבֶרֶת 400
מַחְבֶּרֶת 686

couplings
מְחַבְּרוֹת 686

courage
לֵבָב 630
רוּחַ 1160

courage, *see* good
courage, to be of good
חָזַק Kal 411
חָזַק Hithpael 411
courage, to take
חָזַק Hithpael 411
courageous
אַמִּיץ } אַמִּץ } 103
cour*ageous*
לֵב 626
courageous, to be
אָמֵץ Kal 104
חָזַק Kal 411
courageously
חָזַק Kal 411
course
חֲלִיפָה 431
מַחְלְקָה Ch. 687
מַחֲלֹקֶת 687
מְסִלָּה 737
מְרוּצָה 763
course, *see* sing together, water course
course, to be out of
מוֹט Niphal 670
court
בַּיִת 214
חָצִיר 454
חָצֵר 455
עֲזָרָה 918
עִיר (כ') 925
covenant
בְּרִית 272
covenant, to
כָּרַת Kal 618
cover
נֵסֶךְ } נֶסֶךְ } 820
קַשָׂה } קַשְׂוָה } 1130
שָׂכַךְ Kal 1206
cover, to
בָּלַע Piel 230
חָפָה Kal 451
חָפַף Kal 451
טָלַל Piel 481
יָעַט Kal 546
כָּסָה Kal 607
כָּסָה Piel 607
כָּפַשׁ Hiphil 615
לָאַט Kal 626
מְכַסֶּה 700
נָסַךְ[1] Kal 820
נָסַךְ[1] Hophal 820
סָכַךְ Kal 875
סָכַךְ Hiphil 875
סָפַן Kal 881
עָטָה Kal 918
עָטָה Hiphil 918
עָטַף Kal 918
צָפָה Piel 1077
קָרַם Kal 1129
שׁוּף Kal 1247
cover self, to
כָּסָה Hithpael 607
עָטָה Kal 918
cover with, *see* cloud
covered
צָב 1057
צָפָה Pual 1077
covered, to be
חָפָה Niphal 451
כָּסָה Niphal 607
כָּסָה Pual 607
כָּסָה Hithpael 607
כָּשָׂה Kal 620
עָטָה Kal 918
covered over, to be
עָטַף Kal 918
covereth, that which
מְכַסֶּה 700
covering
אֹהֶל 27
כָּסוּי 608
כְּסוּת 608
לוֹט 635
מִכְסֶה 700
מָסָךְ 737
מַסֵּכָה 737
מַסֵּכָה 737
מְסֻכָּה 737
מֶרְכָּב 764
סֵתֶר 886
צָמִיד 1075
צִפּוּי 1078
covering, to put a
עָטָה Kal 918
coverings, *see* tapestry
covert
מוּסָךְ 672
מֵיסָךְ 698
מִסְתּוֹר 739
סֹךְ 875
סֻכָּה 875
סֵתֶר 886
covet, to
אָוָה Hithpael 29
בָּצַע Kal 263
חָמַד Kal 437
covetous
בָּצַע Kal 263
covetousness
בֶּצַע 264
cow
עֶגְלָה 901
פָּרָה 1044
שׁוֹר 1248
cow †
בָּקָר 266
crackling
קוֹל 1096
cracknels
נִקֻּדִים 838
craft
מִרְמָה 765
craftiness
עֹרֶם 980
craftsman
חָרָשׁ 467
חֶרֶשׁ 467
crafty
עָרוּם 978
crafty *counsel*, to take
עָרַם[1] Hiphil 979
* crag
שֵׁן 1304
crane
סוּס 871
סִיס 875
crashing
שֶׁבֶר } שֶׁבֶר } 1234
crave, to
אָכַף Kal 76
create, to
בָּרָא Kal 270
created, to be
בָּרָא Niphal 270
Creator
בָּרָא Kal 270
creature
נֶפֶשׁ 829
creature, *see* moving
creature, living
חַי 419
creatures, *see* doleful
creditor
נָשָׁה[2] Kal 847
* creditor †
יָד 489
מַשֶּׁה 768
creep
רָמַשׂ Kal 1176
שֶׁרֶץ 1327
creep, to
שָׁרַץ Kal 1327
creepeth, that
רֶמֶשׂ 1176
creeping thing
רֶמֶשׂ 1176
שֶׁרֶץ 1327
crib
אֵבוּס 10

cumbrance
טֹרַח ... 485
cummin
כַּמֹּן ... 604
cunning
דַּעַת ... 347
חָכָם ... 426
000 ... 000
חָשַׁב Kal ... 468
יָדַע Kal ... 500
מַחֲשֶׁבֶת ... 690
cunning, to be
בִּין Hiphil ... 212
cunning man
חָכָם ... 426
חָשַׁב Kal ... 468
cunning work
חָשַׁב Kal ... 468
מַחֲשֶׁבֶת ... 690
cunning workman
אָמָן ... 104
חָשַׁב Kal ... 468
cup
אַגָּן ... 14
גָּבִיעַ ... 290
כּוֹס ... 593
כִּים (כ׳) ... 596
סַף (מנקיות..736) . 881
קָשָׂה } קַשְׂוָה ... 1130
cupbearer
שָׁקָה Hiphil ... 1323
curdle, to
קָפָא Hiphil ... 1113
cure
מַרְפֵּא ... 765
cure, to
גָּהָה Kal ... 298
רָפָא Kal ... 1187
cured
תְּעָלָה ... 1353
curious, *see* **girdle**
curious works
מַחֲשֶׁבֶת ... 690
curiously wrought
רָקַם Pual ... 1192
current
עָבַר Kal ... 895
curse
אָלָה ... 78
חֵרֶם ... 464
מְאֵרָה ... 660
קְלָלָה ... 1110
שְׁבוּעָה ... 1224
תַּאֲלָה ... 1334
curse, to
אָלָה[2] Kal ... 78
אָרַר Kal ... 171
אָרַר Piel ... 171
בָּרַךְ Piel ... 274
נָקַב Kal ... 837
קָבַב Kal ... 1083
קָלַל Piel ... 1109
curse, to cause the
אָרַר Piel ... 171
cursed, to be
אָרַר Niphal ... 171
אָרַר Hophal ... 171
קָלַל Pual ... 1109
cursed thing
חֵרֶם ... 464
cursing
אָלָה ... 78
מְאֵרָה ... 660
קְלָלָה ... 1110
curtain
דֹּק ... 348
יְרִיעָה ... 565
מָסָךְ ... 737
custody
יָד ... 489
פְּקֻדָּה ... 1041
custom
דֶּרֶךְ ... 349
הֲלָךְ Ch. ... 366
חֹק ... 456
חֻקָּה ... 457
מִשְׁפָּט ... 776
custom, *see* **abominable**
cut, to
בָּצַע Kal ... 263
חָצַב } חָצֵב Hiphil ... 453
כָּרַת Kal ... 618
נָתַח Piel ... 850
פָּלַח Kal ... 1019
קָצַץ Piel ... 1116
שׂוּר[3] Kal ... 1204
cut, to be
000 ... 000
כָּרַת Pual ... 618
*** cut, to be**
עֲבַד Ch. Ithpael ... 889
cut asunder, to
גָּדַע Kal. (& Pi.) ... 298
קָצַץ Piel ... 1116
cut asunder, to be
גָּדַע Niphal ... 298
cut down, to
בָּרָא Piel ... 270
גָּדַע Piel ... 298
גָּזַר Kal ... 305
חָטַב Kal ... 417
כָּרַת Kal ... 618
כָּרַת Hiphil ... 618
נָקַף Piel ... 839
קָצַב Kal ... 1114
קָצַר Kal ... 1116
תָּזַז Hiphil ... 1344
cut down, to be
גָּדַע Niphal ... 298
גָּדַע Pual ... 298
גָּזַז Niphal ... 304
דָּמָה[2] Niphal ... 345
דָּמַם Niphal ... 346
כָּחַד Niphal ... 595
כָּסַח Kal ... 608
כָּרַת Niphal ... 618
כָּרַת Pual ... 618
מוּל Polel ... 670
נָמַל Kal ... 819
קָטַף Niphal ... 1106
קָמַט Pual ... 1110
cut in, *see* **pieces**
cut in pieces, to
נָתַח Piel ... 850
קָצַץ Piel ... 1116
cut in pieces, to be
שָׂרַט Niphal ... 1217
cut in sunder, to
גָּדַע Piel ... 298
קָצַץ Piel ... 1116
cut off
קָצַץ Pual ... 1116
cut off, to
בָּצַע Piel ... 263
בָּצַר Kal ... 264
גָּדַע Kal ... 298
גּוּז Kal ... 299
גָּזַז Kal ... 304
חָלַף Kal ... 434
כָּחַד Hiphil ... 595
כָּרַת Kal ... 618
כָּרַת Hiphil ... 618
צָמַת Kal ... 1075
צָמַת Pilel ... 1075
צָמַת Hiphil ... 1075
קָסַם Poel ... 1113
קָפַד Piel ... 1113
קָצָה Piel ... 1114
קָצַץ Kal ... 1116
קָצַץ Piel ... 1116
קְצַץ Ch. Pael ... 1116
cut off, *see* **branch, neck**
cut off, to be
גָּדַע Niphal ... 298
גָּזַר Kal ... 305
גָּזַר Niphal ... 305
גָּרַז Niphal ... 315
דָּמָה[2] Niphal ... 345

דָּמַם Niphal 346
פָּחַד Niphal 595
כָּרַת Niphal 618
כָּרַת Hophal 618
נָמַל Kal 819
נָקָה Niphal 838
עָלָה Kal 934
צָמַת Niphal 1075
קוּט[2] Kal 1096
cut off in, *see* midst
cut out, to
בָּקַע Piel 264
קָרַע Kal 1129
cut out, to be
גְּזַר Ch. Ithp'al 305
cut selves, to
גָּדַד Hithpoel 293
cut short, to
קָצָה Piel 1114
cut up, to
קָטַף Kal 1106
cut up, to be
כָּסַח Kal 608
cutting
גְּדוּד 293
חֲרֹשֶׁת 468
cutting off
דְּמִי 346
קָצָה Kal 1114
cuttings
שֶׂרֶט 1217
שָׂרֶטֶת 1217
cymbal
צְלָצַל 1074
cymbals
מְצִלְתַּיִם 754
cypress
תִּרְזָה 1358
dagger
חֶרֶב 459
daily
יוֹם 508
יוֹמָם 521
תָּמִיד 1349
daily
אֶחָד 41
daily
יוֹם 508
dainties
מַטְעַמּוֹת 693
מַנְעַמִּים 736
dainty
מַעֲדָן 740
תַּאֲוָה 1334
dainty meats
מַטְעַמּוֹת 693
dale
עֵמֶק 961
dam
אֵם 99
damage
חֲבָל Ch. 399
חָמָס 440
נֵזֶק 804
damage, to have
נְזַק Ch. P'al 804
* Damascus, in
דְּמֶשֶׁק 346
damsel
יַלְדָּה 531
נַעֲרָה 824
עַלְמָה 943
רַחַם 1169
dance
מָחוֹל 686
dance, to
חָגַג Kal 401
חוּל / חִיל } Kal 406
חוּל / חִיל } Polel 406
כָּרַר Pilpel 618
רָקַד Kal 1191
רָקַד Piel 1191
dances
מְחוֹלָה 686
dancing
כָּרַר Pilpel 618
מָחוֹל 686
מְחוֹלָה 686
dandled, to be
שָׁעַע Palpal 1316
dark
אֲפֵלָה 147
חֹשֶׁךְ 470
חֲשֵׁכָה 470
חֶשְׁכָה 470
חַשְׁרָה 471
מַחְשָׁךְ 691
נֶשֶׁף 849
עֲלָטָה 941
עֲרָפֶל 980
קָפָא (כ׳) Kal 1113
קִפָּאוֹן 1113
dark, *see* cloud
dark, to be
חָשַׁךְ Kal 469
קָדַר Kal 1090
dark, to begin to be
צָלַל[3] Kal 1073
dark, to make
חָשַׁךְ Hiphil 469
קָדַר Hiphil 1090
dark place
מַחְשָׁךְ 691
dark saying
חִידָה 421
dark sentence
חִידָה 421
dark, somewhat
כֵּהָה 586
dark speech
חִידָה 421
dark, very
אָפֵל 147
darken, to
חָשַׁךְ Hiphil 469
*darken, to
חָשַׁךְ Kal 468
darkened, to be
חָשַׁךְ Kal 469
כָּהָה Kal 586
עָרַב[2] Kal 975
עָתַם Niphal 1008
קָדַר Kal 1090
darkish
כֵּהָה 586
darkness
אֹפֶל 147
אֲפֵלָה 147
חֲשׁוֹךְ Ch. 469
חֲשֵׁיכָה 469
חֹשֶׁךְ 470
מַאְפֵל 659
מַאְפֵּלְיָה 659
מַחְשָׁךְ 691
עֵיפָה 925
עֲרָפֶל 980
darkness, to cause
חָשַׁךְ Hiphil 469
darkness, gross
עֲרָפֶל 980
darkness, thick
עֲרָפֶל 980
darling
יָחִיד 523
dart
חֵץ 453
מַסָּע 738
שֵׁבֶט 1225
שֶׁלַח 1273
תּוֹתָח 1344
dash, to
נָגַף Kal 793
נָפַץ Piel 828
רָטַשׁ Piel 1171
dash in pieces, to
נָפַץ Piel 828
רָטַשׁ Piel 1171
רָעַץ Kal 1187
dash to pieces, to
רָטַשׁ Piel 1171
dashed in pieces, to be
רָטַשׁ Pual 1171

מָצוֹר 754
מִשְׂגָּב 767
סָכַךְ Kal 875
צֵל 1072
defenced
בָּצַר Kal 264
מִבְצָר 661
defend, to
גָּנַן Kal 313
גָּנַן Hiphil 313
יָשַׁע Hiphil 576
נָצַל Hiphil 835
סָכַךְ Hiphil 875
שָׂגַב Piel 1197
שָׁפַט Kal 1319
defer, to
אָחַר Piel 48
אָרַךְ Hiphil 156
deferred
מָשַׁךְ Pual 770
defile
גֹּאֶל 286
defile, to
חָלַל Piel 432
חָנֵף Kal 447
חָנֵף Hiphil 447
טָמֵא Piel 481
טָנַף Piel 483
עָלַל Poel 942
עָנָה [2] Piel 964
defile self, to
גָּאַל [2] Hithpael 286
טָמֵא Kal 481
טָמֵא Niphal 481
defile...selves, to
טָמֵא Hithpael 481
defiled
טָמֵא 482
defiled, to be
גָּאַל [2] Niphal 286
חָלַל Niphal 432
חָנֵף Kal 447
טָמֵא Kal 481
טָמֵא Niphal 481
טָמֵא Hithpael 481
טָמֵא Hothpael 481
טָמָה Niphal 483
קָדֵשׁ } קָדַשׁ } Kal 1090
* defiled, to be
נָחַל Piel 805
defraud, to
עָשַׁק Kal 1004
defy, to
זָעַם Kal 391
חָרַף Piel 465
degenerate
סוּר 874
degree
מַעֲלָה 744
degree, *see* high, man
delay, to
אָחַר Piel 48
בּוֹשׁ Piel 206
מָהַהּ Hithpalpel 668
delectable thing
חָמַד Kal 437
delicate
עֵדֶן 904
עָנַג Pual 962
עָנֹג 962
תַּעֲנוּג 1354
delicately
מַעֲדָן 740
delicateness
עָנַג Hithpael 962
delight
חֵפֶץ 452
מַעֲדָן 740
עֵדֶן 904
עֹנֶג 962
רָצוֹן 1189
שַׁעֲשֻׁעִים 1318
תַּעֲנוּג 1354
delight, to (נול...306)
חָמַד Kal 437
חָפֵץ Kal 451
רָצָה Kal 1189
שָׁעַע Pilpel 1316
delight, to be
נָעֵם Kal 823
* delight, great
חָמַד Piel 437
delight, to have
חָפֵץ Kal 451
חָשַׁק Kal 471
עָנַג Hithpael 962
delight in
חָפֵץ 452
delight self, to
עָדַן Hithpael 904
עָנַג Hithpael 962
רָצָה Kal 1189
שָׁעַע Hithpalpel 1316
delight, to take
חָפֵץ Kal 451
delighted, to be
עָנַג Hithpael 962
delightsome
חֵפֶץ 452
deliver, to
אָנָה Piel 136
גָּאַל [1] Kal 285
חָלַץ Piel 434
יְהַב Ch. P'al 507
יָשַׁע Hiphil 576
מָגַן Piel 662
מָלַט Piel 710
מָצָא Hiphil 748
נָטָה Hiphil 810
נָכַר Piel 818
נָצַל Piel 835
נָצַל Hiphil 835
נְצַל Ch. Aphel 837
נָתַן Kal 851
סָגַר Piel 869
סָגַר Hiphil 869
פָּדָה Kal 1010
פָּדַע Kal 1011
פָּלַט Piel 1019
פָּלַט Hiphil 1019
פָּצָה Kal 1039
פָּרַק Kal 1047
שׁוּב Hiphil 1238
שֵׁיזִב Ch. Peel *or* Peil 1249
שְׁלֵם Ch. Aphel 1278
שָׁפַט Kal 1319
deliver again, to
שׁוּב Hiphil 1238
deliver self, to
מָלַט Niphal 709
נָצַל Niphal 835
deliver up, to
נָתַן Kal 851
סָגַר Hiphil 869
deliverance
הַצָּלָה 370
יְשׁוּעָה 575
פָּלֵט 1019
פְּלֵיטָה 1020
תְּשׁוּעָה 1359
delivered, *see* keep
delivered, to be
חָלַץ Niphal 434
יָלַד Kal 527
מָלַט Niphal 709
מָלַט Hiphil 710
מָסַר Niphal 739
נָצַל Niphal 835
נָתַן Niphal 851
נָתַן Hophal 851
עָבַר Kal 895
delivered of, *see* child
deliverer
יָשַׁע Hiphil 576
פָּלַט Piel 1019
delivery, time of
יָלַד Kal 527

delusions
תַּעֲלוּלִים 1354
demand
שְׁאֵלָא Ch. 1221
demand, to
אָמַר Kal 105
שָׁאַל Kal 1220
שְׁאֵל Ch. P'al 1221
den
אֶרֶב 149
גֹּב Ch. 287
מְאוּרָה 658
מָעוֹן 740
מְעוֹנָה 740
מְעָרָה 745
סֹךְ 875
denounce, to
נָגַד Hiphil 788
dens
מִנְהָרוֹת 733
deny, to
כָּחַשׁ Piel 595
מָנַע Kal 735
deny, † to
שׁוּב Hiphil 1238
depart, to
בּוֹא Kal 189
הָלַךְ Kal 362
הָלַךְ Hithpael 362
יָלַךְ Kal 531
יָצָא Kal 548
יָקַע Kal 558
לוּז Kal 635
לוּז Hiphil 635
מוּשׁ ¹ Kal 674
מוּשׁ ¹ Hiphil 674
נָדַד Kal 795
נָסַע Kal 821
סוּר Kal 872
עֲדָה Ch. P'al 902
עָלָה Kal 934
עָלָה Niphal 934
שׁוּר ¹ Kal 1204
שָׁעָה Kal 1315
depart, *see* let, treacherously, wickedly
depart early, to
צָפַר Kal 1080
depart, to let
שָׁלַח Piel 1268
depart, they that
יָסוּר 543
departed, to be
גָּלָה Kal 307
נָסַע Niphal 821
departing
יָצָא Kal 548
סוּר Kal 872
departing away
נָסַג Kal 819
departure
יָצָא Kal 548
deposed, to be
נְחַת Ch. Hophal 810
deprive, to
נָשָׁה ¹ Hiphil 847
deprived, to be
פָּקַד Pual 1040
שָׁכֹל Kal 1259
depth
מְצוּלָה 754
עָמַק Hiphil 961
עָמֹק 961
עֹמֶק 961
תְּהוֹם 1336
depths
מַעֲמַקִּים 744
deputy
נָצַב Niphal 833
פֶּחָה 1016
deride, to
שָׂחַק Kal 1205
derision
לַעַג 644
קֶלֶס 1110
שְׂחוֹק 1204
derision, to have in
לוּץ Hiphil 636
לָעַג Kal 644
שָׂחַק Kal 1205
descend, to
יָרַד Kal 561
descending
יָרַד Kal 561
describe, to
כָּתַב Kal 621
descry, *see* send
desert
גְּמוּל 311
מִשְׁפָּט 776
desert
חָרְבָּה 461
יְשִׁימוֹן 575
מִדְבָּר 664
עֲרָבָה 976
desert, wild beasts of the
צִיִּים 1071
deserving
גְּמוּל 311
desirable
חֶמֶד 437
desire
אָב 8
אֲבִיּוֹנָה 10
אַוָּה 33
חֶמְדָּה 437
חֵפֶץ 452
חֵשֶׁק 471
מַחְמָד 687
מִשְׁאָלָה 768
נֶפֶשׁ 829
רָצוֹן 1189
תַּאֲוָה 1334
תָּו 1337
תְּשׁוּקָה 1359
* desire
אָב 1
desire, to
אָוָה Piel 29
אָוָה Hithpael 29
אָמַר Kal 105
בְּעָא / בְּעָה } Ch. P'al 261
בָּקַשׁ Piel 268
חָמַד Kal 437
חָפֵץ Kal 451
חָפֵץ 452
חֵפֶץ 452
חָשַׁק Kal 471
שָׁאַל Kal 1220
שָׁאַף Kal 1222
desire,† to
נָשָׂא Piel 840
desire, to earnestly
שָׁאַף Kal 1222
desire, greatly to
אָוָה Hithpael 29
desire, to have
חָשַׁק Kal 471
כָּסַף Kal 609
desired
כָּסַף Niphal 609
desired, to be
חָמַד Niphal 437
desired, things
חֵפֶץ 452
desires
מַאֲוַיִּים 657
desirous, to be
אָוָה Hithpael 29
desolate
בָּדָד 187
בַּתּוֹת 284
גַּלְמוּד 310
חָרֵב / חָרַב } Niphal 458
חָרֵב 459
חָרְבָּה 461
יָחִיד 523
כָּחַד Niphal 595
מְשַׁמָּה 772
שׁוֹאָה 1238
שַׁמָּה 1285
שָׁמֵם Kal 1289

שָׁמֵם Niphal 1289
שָׁמֵם 1290
שְׁמָמָה 1290

desolate, to be
אָשֵׁם / אָשַׁם Kal 178
חָרֵב / חָרַב Kal 458
יָצַת Niphal 557
יָשַׁם Kal 576
נָקָה Niphal 838
שָׁאָה Niphal 1219
שָׁמֵם Kal 1289
שָׁמֵם Niphal 1289
שָׁמֵם Hithpolel 1289

desolate, to become
אָשֵׁם / אָשַׁם Kal 178

desolate houses
אַלְמְנוֹת 96

desolate, laid
(כ׳) שְׁמָמָה 1290

desolate, to be laid
שָׁמֵם Kal 1289
שָׁמֵם Niphal 1289

desolate, to lie
שָׁמֵם Hophal 1289

desolate, to be made
אָשֵׁם / אָשַׁם Kal 178
אָשֵׁם / אָשַׁם Niphal 178
שָׁמֵם Niphal 1289

desolate, to make
שָׁמֵם Kal 1289
שָׁמֵם Polel 1289
שָׁמֵם Hiphil 1289

desolate, making
שָׁמֵם Hiphil 1289

desolate palaces
אַלְמְנוֹת 96

desolate place
חָרְבָּה 461
שָׁמֵם Kal 1289

desolate places
אַשְׁמַנִּים 179

desolation
חֹרֶב 461
חָרְבָּה 461
מְשׁוֹאָה 768
מַשּׁוּאוֹת 768
שַׁאֲוָה 1220
שֵׁאת 1224
שֹׁד 1236
שׁוֹאָה 1238
שַׁמָּה 1285
שָׁמֵם Kal 1289
שְׁמָמָה 1290
שִׁמְמָה 1290

desolation, to bring into
שָׁמֵם Hiphil 1289

desolation, to bring unto
שָׁמֵם Hiphil 1289

despair, to
יָאַשׁ Niphal 486

despair, to cause to
יָאַשׁ Piel 486

desperate
אָנַשׁ Kal 141

desperate, one that is
יָאַשׁ Niphal 486

despise, to
בּוּז Kal 205
בָּזָה Kal 207
בָּזָה Hiphil 207
בָּזֹה 207
זוּל Hiphil 383
מָאַס[1] Kal 659
נָאַץ Kal 782
נָאַץ Piel 782
קָלַל Hiphil 1109
שׁוּט[1] Kal 1246

despised
בּוּז 205
בּוּזָה 205

despised, to be
בָּזָה Niphal 207
קָלָה[2] Niphal 1108
קָלַל Kal 1109

despite
שְׁאָט 1220

despiteful
שְׁאָט 1220

destitute
חָסֵר 450
עַרְעָר 980

destitute, to be
שָׁמֵם Niphal 1289

destitute, to leave
עָזַב Kal 915
עָרָה Piel 977

destroy, to
אָבַד Piel 8
אָבַד Hiphil 8
אֲבַד Ch. Aphel 9
אָסַף Kal 141
אָשֵׁם / אָשַׁם Hiphil 178
בָּלַע Piel 230
גָּרַר Kal 316
דָּבַר Piel 319
דָּכָא Piel 340
דָּמָה[2] Kal 345
הוּם Kal 359
הָמַם Kal 368
הָרַג Kal 374
הָרַס Kal 376
חָבַל Piel 398
חֲבַל Ch. Pael 399
חָרֵב / חָרַב Hiphil 458
חָרַם Hiphil 464
יָנָה Kal 541
יָרַשׁ Hiphil 566
כָּלָה Piel 598
כָּרַת Kal 618
כָּרַת Hiphil 618
כָּתַת Hiphil 624
מְגַר Ch. Pael 663
מוּל Hiphil 670
מוּת Hiphil 675
מָחָה[1] Kal 686
מָחָה[1] Hiphil 686
מַשְׁחִית 769
נָסַח Kal 820
נָקַף Piel 839
נָשַׁם Kal 849
נָתַץ Kal 863
נָתַשׁ Kal 864
סָפָה[1] Kal 881
סְתַר Ch. P'al 886
צָמַת Hiphil 1075
קוּר Pilpel 1104
שָׁבַר[1] Kal 1232
שָׁדַד Kal 1237
שׁוֹאָה 1238
שָׁחַת Piel 1252
שָׁחַת Hiphil 1252
שָׁכַל Piel 1259
שָׁמַד Hiphil 1285
שָׁמֵם Hiphil 1289

* destroy, to
שָׁמֵם Kal 1289

destroy self, to
שָׁחַת Piel 1252
שָׁמֵם Hithpolel 1289

destroy, to utterly
חָרַם Hiphil 464
כָּלָה Piel 598

destroyed
דֻּמָּה 345

destroyed, to be
אָבַד Kal 8
אֲבַד Ch. Hophal 9
בָּלַע Pual 230
דְּכָא Hithpael 340
חָבַל Niphal 398
חָבַל Pual 398
חֲבַל Ch. Ithpael 399
חֲרַב Ch. Hophal 459

כָּתַת Pulal ... 624
כָּתַת Hophal ... 624
מָחָה¹ Niphal ... 686
סָפָה¹ Niphal ... 881
צָדָה Niphal ... 1061
רוּעַ Niphal ... 1164
שָׁבַר¹ Niphal ... 1232
שָׁדַד Kal ... 1237
שָׁמַד Niphal ... 1285

destroyed, things which should have been utterly
חֵרֶם ... 464

destroyed, to be utterly
חָרַם Hophal ... 464

destroyer
הָרַס Piel ... 376
חָרֵב / חָרַב } Hiphil ... 458
מוּת Hiphil ... 675
פָּרִיץ ... 1046
שָׁדַד Kal ... 1237
שָׁחַת Hiphil ... 1252
שָׁסָה Kal ... 1315

destroying
מַשְׁחִית ... 769
מַשְׁחֵת ... 769
קֶטֶב ... 1105
שָׁחַת Piel ... 1252

destruction
אָבַד Kal ... 8
אֲבַדֹּה (כ') ... 9
אֲבַדּוֹן ... 9
אַבְדָן ... 9
אָבְדַן ... 9
אֵיד ... 57
דַּכָּא ... 341
הֲרִיסוּת ... 376
הֶרֶס ... 376
חֶבֶל / חֵבֶל } ... 399
חָרְבָּה ... 461
כִּיד ... 596
מְהוּמָה ... 668
מְחִתָּה ... 691
מַשּׁוּאוֹת ... 768
מַשְׁחִית ... 769
פִּיד ... 1017
קֶטֶב ... 1105
קֹטֶב ... 1105
קְפָדָה ... 1113
קֶרֶץ ... 1130
שְׁאִיָּה ... 1220
שֶׁבֶר / שֵׁבֶר } ... 1234
שִׁבָּרוֹן ... 1234
שֹׁד ... 1236
שׁוֹא ... 1238
שׁוֹאָה ... 1238
שְׁחִית ... 1251
שָׁחַת Hiphil ... 1252
שַׁחַת ... 1253
שָׁמַד Hiphil ... 1285
תְּבוּסָה ... 1335
תַּבְלִית ... 1336

* destruction
חֲלוֹף ... 431

destruction, *see* utter

destruction, appointed to utter
חֵרֶם ... 464

detain, to
עָצַר Kal ... 973

detained
עָצַר Niphal ... 973

determination
מִשְׁפָּט ... 776

determine, to
אָמַר Kal ... 105
חָתַךְ Niphal ... 471
יָעַץ Kal ... 547

determined
חָרַץ Kal ... 466
שׂוּם / שִׂים } Kal ... 1200

determined, to be
חָרַץ Niphal ... 466
כָּלָה Kal ... 598

determined, was
כָּלָה ... 600

detest, to
שָׁקַץ Piel ... 1325

detestable
שִׁקּוּץ ... 1323

detestable things
שִׁקּוּץ ... 1323

device
הִגָּיוֹן ... 357
חֶשְׁבּוֹן ... 469
מְזִמָּה ... 684
מַחֲשָׁבָה ... 690
מַחֲשֶׁבֶת ... 690

device, *see* mischievous, wicked

devices
מוֹעֵצוֹת ... 673

devil
שָׂעִיר ... 1212
שֵׁד ... 1236

devise, to
בָּדָא Kal ... 187
דָּמָה¹ Piel ... 345
זָמַם Kal ... 388
חָרַשׁ Kal ... 466
חָשַׁב Kal ... 468
חָשַׁב Piel ... 468
יָעַץ Kal ... 547

devised
מַחֲשֶׁבֶת ... 690

devote, to
חָרַם Hiphil ... 464

devoted
חֵרֶם ... 464

devoted, to be
חָרַם Hophal ... 464

devoted thing
חֵרֶם ... 464

devour, to
אָכַל Kal ... 70
אֲכַל Ch. P'al ... 75
אָכְלָה ... 75
בָּלַע Kal ... 230
בָּלַע Piel ... 230
יָלַע Kal ... 537
לָחַם Kal ... 637
רָעָה Kal ... 1184
שָׁאַף Kal ... 1222

devour up, to
אָכַל Kal ... 70

devoured, to be
אָכַל Niphal ... 70
אָכַל Pual ... 70

devourer
אָכַל Kal ... 70

devouring
בֶּלַע ... 231

dew
טַל ... 481
טַל Ch. ... 481

diadem
מִצְנֶפֶת ... 755
צָנוֹף ... 1076
צָנִיף ... 1076
צְפִירָה ... 1079

dial
מַעֲלָה ... 744

diamond
יַהֲלֹם ... 507
שָׁמִיר ... 1289

did, *see* wrong

did †
הֲוָא / הֲוָה } Ch. P'al ... 358

* did, he
וְהֵב ... 377

die
מָוֶת ... 680
תְּמוּתָה ... 1349

die, to
גָּוַע Kal ... 302
מוּת Kal ... 675
מוּת Hophal ... 675
נָפַל Kal ... 825

die, to cause to
מוּת Hiphil 675

die, to be like to
מוּת Kal 675

die, must
מוּת Kal 675

died
מָוֶת 680

died, which
נְבֵלָה 787

diet
אֲרֻחָה 155

dieth of itself, beast that
נְבֵלָה 787

dieth of itself, which
נְבֵלָה 787

difference, to make a
בָּדַל Hiphil 187

difference, to put
בָּדַל Hiphil 187

difference, to put a
פָּלָה Hiphil 1019

dig, to
חָפַר Kal 452
חָצַב / חָצֵב Kal 453
חָתַר Kal 472
כָּרָה Kal 616
קוּר Kal 1104

dig again, to
שׁוּב Kal 1238

dig down, to
עָקַר Piel............ 974

dig through, to
חָתַר Kal 472

digged, to be
כָּרָה Niphal 616
נָקַר Pual 840
עָדַר[2] Niphal.......... 905

dignity
גְּדוּלָה / גְּדוּלָּה 296
מָרוֹם 763
שְׂאֵת 1195

diligence
מִשְׁמָר 773

diligent
חָפַשׂ Pual 452
חָרוּץ 463
יָטַב Hiphil 524
מְאֹד 652
מָהִיר 668

diligent, *see* search

diligent, to be
יָדַע Kal 500

diligently
אַדְרַזְדָּא Ch. 24

* diligently
קֶשֶׁב 1131

diligently is sometimes the translation of an infinitive used intensitively.

diligently, *see* consider, observe, seek, teach

dim, to be
חָשַׁךְ Kal 469
כָּהָה Kal 586
שָׁעָה Kal 1315

* dim, to be
כָּבֵד / כָּבַד Kal 581
קוּם Kal 1099

dim, to become
עָמַם Hophal.......... 960

dim, to wax
כֵּהָה 586

diminish, to
גָּרַע Kal 316
מָעַט Hiphil 741

diminished, to be
גָּרַע Niphal 316
מָעַט Kal 741

dimness
מוּעָף 673
מָעוּף 740

dine, to
אָכַל Kal 70

dinner
אֲרֻחָה 155

dip, to
טָבַל Kal 473

dipped, to be
טָבַל Niphal 473
מָחַץ Kal 689

direct, to
בִּין (כ׳) Kal 212
יָרָה Hiphil 564
יָשַׁר Piel............ 578
כּוּן Hiphil 592
כָּשֵׁר Hiphil 621
נָתַן Kal 851
עָרַךְ Kal 978
שָׁרָה Kal 1326
תָּכַן Piel 1347

directed, to be
כּוּן Niphal 592

directly
הָגִין 357

direct*ly*
נֹכַח 817

dirt
טִיט 480
פַּרְשְׁדֹנָה 1049

disallow, to
נוּא Hiphil 799

disannul, to
פָּרַר Hiphil 1048

disannulled, to be
כָּפַר Pual 614

disappoint, to
פָּרַר Hiphil 1048

disappoint, † to
קָדַם Piel..............1088

disappointed, to be
פָּרַר Hiphil 1048

discern, to
בִּין Kal 212
בִּין Hiphil 212
יָדַע Kal 500
נָכַר Hiphil 818
רָאָה Kal 1133
שָׁמַע / שָׁמֵעַ Kal 1292

discern, can
יָדַע Kal 500

discern, to cause to
יָדַע Hiphil 500

discharge
מִשְׁלַחַת 772

discharged, to cause to be
נָפַץ Piel 828

disciple
לִמּוּד 644

discipline
מוּסָר 672

disclose, to
גָּלָה Piel 307

discomfit, to
הָמַם Kal 368
חָלַשׁ Kal 436
חָרַד Hiphil 462
כָּתַת Hiphil 624

discomfited
מַס 736

discomfiture
מְהוּמָה 668

discontented
מַר 760

*dis*contented
נֶפֶשׁ 829

discontinue, to
שָׁמַט Kal 1286

discord
מָדוֹן 666
מְדָנִים 667

discourage, to
מָסַס Hiphil 737
נוּא Kal 799
נוּא Hiphil 799

discouraged, to be
חָתַת Niphal 472
רָצַץ Kal 1190

discouraged, to be much
קָצַר Kal 1116

discover, to
גָּלָה Piel ... 307
חָשַׂף Kal ... 468
עָרָה Piel ... 977
עָרָה Hiphil ... 977

discover self, to
גָּלָה Niphal ... 307
גָּלָה Hithpael ... 307

discovered, to be
גָּלָה Niphal ... 307
יָדַע Niphal ... 500

discovering
עָרָה Piel ... 977

discreet
בִּין Niphal ... 212

discretion
טַעַם ... 483
מְזִמָּה ... 684
מִשְׁפָּט ... 776
שֶׂכֶל / שֵׂכֶל ... 1207
תְּבוּנָה ... 1335

disdain, to
בָּזָה Kal ... 207
מָאַס ¹ Kal ... 659

disease
חֳלִי ... 431
מַדְוֶה ... 666
מַחֲלֶה ... 687
מַחֲלָה ... 687

* disease
דֶּבֶר ... 325

diseased
חָלָה Niphal ... 429

diseased, to be
חָלָא Kal ... 428
חָלָה Kal ... 429

diseases
מַחֲלֻיִים ... 687
תַּחֲלֻאִים ... 1345

disgrace, to
נָבֵל Piel ... 786

disguise, to
שָׁנָה Hithpael ... 1304

disguise, † to
שׂוּם / שִׂים Kal ... 1200

disguise self, to
חָפַשׂ Hithpael ... 453

* disguis*eth*
סֵתֶר ... 886

dish
סֵפֶל ... 881
צַלַּחַת ... 1073
קְעָרָה ... 1113

dish, *see* snuffdish

dishonest gain
בֶּצַע ... 264

dishonour
כְּלִמָּה ... 603
עַרְוָה Ch. ... 978
קָלוֹן ... 1108

dishonour, to
נָבֵל Piel ... 786

disinherit, to
יָרַשׁ Hiphil ... 566

dismayed
חַת ... 471

dismayed, to be
בָּהַל / בָּהֵל Niphal ... 188
חָתַת Kal ... 472
חָתַת Niphal ... 472
שָׁעָה Hithpael ... 1315

dismayed, to cause to be
חָתַת Hiphil ... 472

dismaying
מְחִתָּה ... 691

dismiss, to
פָּטַר Kal ... 1017

disobedient, to be
מָרָה Kal ... 762

disobey, to
מָרָה Kal ... 762

dispatch, to
בָּרָא Piel ... 270

disperse, to
זָרָה Piel ... 394
פָּזַר Piel ... 1015
פָּרַץ Kal ... 1047

disperse selves, to
פּוּץ Kal ... 1014

dispersed
נָפַץ Kal ... 828
פּוּץ Kal ... 1014

dispersed, to be
זָרָה Niphal ... 394
פָּרַד Pual ... 1043

dispersion
תְּפוֹצָה ... 1354

displayed, to be
נוּס Hithpolel ... 801

displease, to
עָצַב Kal ... 970

displease,† to
אֹזֶן ... 35
יָרַע Kal ... 566
עָשָׂה Kal ... 981
רָעַע Kal ... 1186

* displease,† to
עַיִן ... 919
רַע ... 1177

displeased
זָעֵף ... 391

displeased, to be
אָנַף Kal ... 140
בְּאֵשׁ Ch. P'al ... 184
חָרָה Kal ... 462
קָצַף Kal ... 1115

displeased,† to be
רָעַע Kal ... 1186

displeasure
רַע ... 1177

displeasure, hot
חֵמָה ... 437

displeasure, sore
חָרוֹן ... 463

dispose, to
שׂוּם / שִׂים Kal ... 1200

disposing
מִשְׁפָּט ... 776

dispossess, to
יָרַשׁ Hiphil ... 566

dispute, to
יָכַח Niphal ... 525

disquiet, to
רָגַז Hiphil ... 1155

disquieted, to be
הָמָה Kal ... 368
רָגַז Kal ... 1155

disquietness
נְהָמָה ... 798

dissemble, to
כָּחַשׁ Piel ... 595
נָכַר Niphal ... 818
תָּעָה Hiphil ... 1353

dissembler
עָלַם Niphal ... 943

dissolve, to
מוּג Polel ... 670
שְׁרָא Ch. P'al ... 1326
שְׁרָא Ch. Pael ... 1326

dissolved, to be
מוּג Niphal ... 670
מָקַק Niphal ... 760
פָּרַר Hithpoel ... 1048

distaff
פֶּלֶךְ ... 1020

distant, equally
שָׁלַב Pual ... 1262

distil, to
נָזַל Kal ... 803
רָעַף Kal ... 1187

distinctly
פָּרַשׁ Pual ... 1049

distracted, to be
פּוּן Kal ... 1014

distress
מָצוֹק ... 754
מְצוּקָה ... 754
מֵצַר ... 755
צָר & צַר ... 1080
צָרָה ... 1081
צָרַר Hiphil ... 1083
רַע ... 1177
distress, to
צוּק[1] Hiphil ... 1069
צוּר Kal ... 1069
צָרַר Hiphil ... 1083
distress, to bring
צָרַר Hiphil ... 1083
distress, to be in
צָרַר Kal ... 1083
distressed, to be
יָצַר[2] Kal ... 557
נָגַשׂ Niphal ... 794
צָרַר Kal ... 1083
קוּץ[3] Kal ... 1104
distribute, to
חָלַק Kal ... 435
חָלַק Niphal ... 435
חָלַק Piel ... 435
נָתַן Kal ... 851
distribute for, *see* inheritance
ditch
גֵּב ... 287
מִקְוָה ... 756
שׁוּחָה ... 1246
שַׁחַת ... 1253
divers
אֱנוֹשׁ ... 136
divers, *see* colours, kinds
divers colours
צֶבַע ... 1060
רִקְמָה ... 1192
divers measures
אֵיפָה ... 59
divers seeds
כִּלְאַיִם ... 598
divers sorts, *see* flies, garment
divers weights
אֶבֶן ... 11
diverse
שָׁנָה Kal ... 1304
שְׁנָא Ch. P'al ... 1304
שְׁנָא Ch. Pael ... 1304
diverse, to be
שְׁנָא Ch. P'al ... 1304
שָׁנָה Kal ... 1304
diverse kind
כִּלְאַיִם ... 598
divide, to
בָּדַל Hiphil ... 187
בָּקַע Kal ... 264
בָּתַר Kal ... 284
בָּתַר Piel ... 284
גָּזַר Kal ... 305
חָלַק Kal ... 435
חָלַק Niphal ... 435
חָלַק Piel ... 435
חָלַק Hithpael ... 435
חָצֵב / חָצַב } Kal ... 453
חָצָה Kal ... 454
נָחַל Kal ... 805
נָפַל Hiphil ... 825
נָתַח Piel ... 850
פָּלַג Piel ... 1019
פָּרַם Hiphil ... 1046
פָּרַר Poel ... 1048
רָגַע Kal ... 1157
divide, *see* inheritance, three parts
divide asunder, to
בָּדַל Hiphil ... 187
divide by, *see* inheritance
divide by lot, to
נָפַל Hiphil ... 825
divide for, *see* inheritance
divide self, to
חָלַק Niphal ... 435
divide speedily, to
רוּץ Hiphil ... 1165
divided
פְּלַג Ch. P'al ... 1019
divided, to be
חָלַק Kal ... 435
חָלַק Niphal ... 435
חָלַק Pual ... 435
חָצָה Niphal ... 454
פָּלַג Niphal ... 1019
פָּרַד Niphal ... 1043
פְּרַס Ch. P'al ... 1046
dividing
פְּלַג Ch. ... 1019
divination
מִקְסָם ... 759
קָסַם Kal ... 1113
קֶסֶם ... 1113
divination, reward of
קֶסֶם ... 1113
divine, to
נָחַשׁ Piel ... 809
קָסַם Kal ... 1113
divine sentence
קֶסֶם ... 1113
diviner
קָסַם Kal ... 1113
division
חֲלֻקָּה ... 436
מַחֲלֹקֶת ... 687
פְּדוּת ... 1011
פְּלַגָּה ... 1019
פְּלֻגָּה ... 1019
פְּלֻגָּה Ch. ... 1019
divisions
מִפְלַגּוֹת ... 748
divorce
כְּרִיתוּת ... 617
divorced
גָּרַשׁ Kal ... 316
divorced woman
גָּרַשׁ Kal ... 316
divorcement
כְּרִיתוּת ... 617
do
מַעֲשֶׂה ... 746
* do
שָׁלוֹם ... 1263
do, to
הָיָה Kal ... 360
עָבַד Kal ... 887
עֲבַד Ch. P'al ... 889
עָלַל Poel ... 942
עָשָׂה Kal ... 981
פָּעַל Kal ... 1037
פֹּעַל ... 1038
שׂוּם / שִׂים } Kal ... 1200
* do, to
גָּמַל Kal ... 311
do, *see* abominable, abominably, again, better, corruptly, evil, foolishly, good, great, harm, honour, hurt, judgment, marvellous, mischief, more, office of a priest, perversely, reverence, second time, secretly, service, shame, shamefully, third time, violence, well, wickedly, worse, wrong
do away, to
עָבַר Hiphil ... 895
do good, to
גָּמַל Kal ... 311
do *good*, to
טוֹב Hiphil ... 476
do *goodness*, to
יָטַב Hiphil ... 524
* do,† to have to
בַּעַל ... 262
do the part, *see* kinsman
do *trespass*, to
מָעַל Kal ... 742
do,† will
הֲוָא / הֲוָה } Ch. P'al ... 358
do ye
אִיתַי Ch. ... 69
doctrine
לֶקַח ... 650
מוּסָר ... 672
שְׁמוּעָה ... 1285

doer
עָשָׂה Kal 981
פָּעַל Kal 1037

doer, *see* evil, wicked

dog
כֶּלֶב 598

doing
מַעֲלִיל 744
מַעֲלָל 744
מַעֲשֶׂה 746
עֲלִילָה 942
עָשָׂה Kal 981

* doleful
נְהִיָה 798

doleful creatures
אֹחִים 47

dominion
יָד 489
מִמְשָׁל 731
מֶמְשָׁלָה 731
מִשְׁטָר 769
מָשַׁל[1] Hiphil 771
מֹשֶׁל 772
שָׁלְטָן Ch. 1274

dominion, to come to have
רָדָה[1] Kal 1158

dominion, to have
בָּעַל Kal 261
מָשַׁל[1] Kal 771
רָדָה[1] Kal 1158
רוּד[1] Hiphil.........1160
שָׁלַט Hiphil 1274

dominion, to make to have
מָשַׁל[1] Hiphil.......... 771
רָדָה[1] Piel............1158

dominion over, to have
בָּעַל Kal 261

done, *see* harm, violence

done, to be
בָּרָא Niphal 270
הָיָה Niphal 361
כָּלָה Kal 598
נָתַן Niphal 851
עֲבַד Ch. Ithpael 889
עָלַל Poal 942
עָשָׂה Kal 981
עָשָׂה Niphal 981

done away, to be
נָּרַע Niphal 316

done, deed to be
הָיָה Niphal 360

done, to have
כָּלָה Piel............ 598
תָּמַם Kal 1351

done, when...were
כָּלָה Piel 598

door
בַּיִת 214
דַּל 341
דָּלָה 342
דֶּלֶת 342
סַף 881
פֶּתַח 1053
שַׁעַר 1316

door, *see* post

doorkeeper
שׁוֹעֵר 1247

doorkeeper, to be a
סָפַף Hithpolel 882

doorpost
סַף 881

doorpost, upper
מַשְׁקוֹף 778

dote, to
יָאַל Niphal 486
עָגַב Kal 900

double
כֶּפֶל 614
מִשְׁנֶה 773
שְׁנַיִם 1311

double, to
כָּפַל Kal 614

* double heart
לֵב 626

doubled
כָּפַל Kal 614

doubled, to be
כָּפַל Niphal 614
שָׁנָה Niphal 1304

doubt
קְטַר Ch. 1107

doubt, *see* hang

doubt, no
אָמְנָם 104

*doubt, without
טָרַף Kal.............. 485

doubtless
כִּי 596

doubtless is sometimes the translation of infinitives used intensitively.

* doubtless again
בּוֹא Kal.............. 189

doubtless not
אִם 100

dough
בָּצֵק 264
עֲרִיסָה 978

dove
יוֹנָה 521

dove, *see* turtle

dove's dung
דִּבְיוֹנִים 318

down
מַטָּה 691

down, *see* beat, beaten, bow, bowed, bowing, break, breaking, bring, broken, brought, carry, cast, cast self, casting, come, coming, couch, cut, dig, drop, fall, falling, flow, get, go, go up, going, hang, hew, hewn, kneel, laid, lay, let, lie, light, lighting, look, lying, make go, pluck, pour, poured, pull, pulled, push, put, ran, roll, run, set, sit, sitting, smite, smitten, stoop, swallow, take, taken, throw, thrown, thrust, tossed, tread, treading, trickle, trodden, turn upside, turning, upside, walk up, wander

downsitting
יָשַׁב Kal............ 568

downward
מַטָּה 691

downward, *see* go

dowry
זֶבֶד 377
מֹהַר 669

drag
מִכְמֶרֶת 699

dragon
תַּנִּים 1352

dragons
תַּנּוֹת 1352
תַּנִּים 1352
תַּנִּין 1353

drams
אֲדַרְכֹּנִים 24
דַּרְכְּמוֹנִים 353

drank
מִשְׁתֶּה 779

draught house
מוֹצָאוֹת 673
מַחֲרָאוֹת 690

draw, to
דָּלָה Kal............ 341
דָּרַךְ Kal............ 349
מָשָׁה Kal............ 768
מָשַׁךְ Kal............ 770
נָתַק Kal............ 863
נָתַק Hiphil 863
סָחַב Kal............ 874
רוּק Hiphil 1165
שָׁלַף Kal............1279

draw, *see* along, full, near, nigh

draw back, to
שׁוּב Hiphil 1238

draw *back*, to
שׁוּב Hiphil 1238

draw forth, to
יָצָא Hiphil 548

draw near, to
נָגַע Hiphil 792
קָרַב Kal..............1123
קָרְבָה 1126

draw near, to cause to
קָרַב Hiphil 1123

draw nigh, to
נָגַע Hiphil 792
קָרַב Kal 1123
קָרַב Hiphil 1123

draw off, to
שָׁלַף Kal 1279

draw out, to
אָרַךְ Hiphil 156
דָּלָה Kal 341
חָלַץ Kal 434
חָשַׂף Kal 468
מָשָׁה Hiphil 768
מָשַׁךְ Kal 770
סָחַב Kal 874
פּוּק [2] Hiphil 1015
פָּתַח Kal 1052
רוּק Hiphil 1165

draw *toward evening*, to
רָפָה Kal 1188

draw up, to
נוּחַ, נִיחַ } Kal 306

draw *water*, to
שָׁאַב Kal 1219

draw with, *see* strength

draw, woman to
שָׁאַב Kal 1219

drawer
שָׁאַב Kal 1219

drawing water, places of
מַשְׁאַבִּים 767

drawn
לָקַח Kal 644
נָתַשׁ Kal 813
עַתִּיק 1008
פָּתַח Kal 1052
שָׁלַף Kal 1279

drawn, *see* swords

drawn, to be
שָׁלַף Kal 1279
תָּאַר Kal 1334

drawn away, to be
נָדַח Niphal 796
נָתַק Niphal 863
נָתַק Hophal 863

dread
אֵימָה 59
חַת 471
מוֹרָא 674
פַּחַד 1016

dread, to
יָרֵא Kal 559
עָרַץ Kal 980

dread (be)
עָרַץ Hiphil 980

dreadful
דְּחַל Ch. P'al 339
יָרֵא Niphal 559
פַּחַד 1016

* dreadful
יִרְאָה 561

dream
חֲלוֹם 430
חֵלֶם Ch. 434

dream, to
חָלַם [1] Kal 433

dreamed, to cause to be
חָלַם [1] Hiphil 433

dreamer
חֲלוֹם 430
חָלַם [1] Kal 433

* dreamer †
בַּעַל 262

dream*er*
חֲלוֹם 430

dregs
קֻבַּעַת 1084
שְׁמָרִים 1303

dress, to
יָטַב Hiphil 524
עָבַד Kal 887
עָשָׂה Kal 981

dressed, to be
עָשָׂה Niphal 981

dressed, ready
עָשָׂה Kal 981

dressers, *see* vine

drew near
קָרֵב 1125

dried
יָבֵשׁ 488
קָלָה [1] Kal 1108

dried, to be
חָרֵב, חָרַב } Pual 458
חָרַר Niphal 466
יָבֵשׁ Kal 487

dried away
יָבֵשׁ 488

dried up
צִחֶה 1070

dried up, to be
חָרֵב, חָרַב } Kal 458
יָבֵשׁ Hiphil 487

drink
מַשְׁקֶה 778
מִשְׁתֶּה 779
סֹבֶא 865
שִׁקּוּ 1323
שִׁקּוּי 1323

drink, to
גָּמָא Hiphil 311
שָׁתָה Kal 1331
שְׁתָה Ch. P'al 1333

drink abundantly, to
שָׁכַר Kal 1261

drink, to cause to
שָׁקָה Hiphil 1323

drink, to be filled with
שָׁכַר Kal 1261

drink, to give
שָׁקָה Hiphil 1323

drink, giving
שָׁקָה Hiphil 1323

drink, to let
שָׁקָה Hiphil 1323

drink, to make to
שָׁקָה Hiphil 1323

drink offering
מִמְסָךְ 731
נָסִיךְ 820
נֵסֶךְ, נֶסֶךְ } 820
נְסַךְ Ch. 821

drink, strong
שֵׁכָר 1262

drink up, to
עָשַׁק Kal 1004

drinker
שָׁתָה Kal 1331

drinking
מַשְׁקֶה 778
שָׁתָה Kal 1331
שְׁתִיָּה 1333

drive, to
הָדַף Kal 357
טְרַד Ch. P'al 485
נָדָא Hiphil 795
נָדַח Hiphil 796
נָהַג [1] Kal 797
נָהַג [1] Piel 797
נָשַׁל Piel 848
פּוּץ Hiphil 1014

drive, *see* whirlwind

drive asunder, to
נָתַר Hiphil 864

drive away, to
בָּרַח Hiphil 271
גָּרַשׁ Piel 316
חוּל, חִיל } Polel 406
נָדַח Hiphil 796
נָדַף Kal 797
נָהַג [1] Kal 797
נָשַׁב Hiphil 846

drive far, to
רָחַק Hiphil 1170

drive out, to
גָּרַשׁ Kal 316
גָּרַשׁ Piel 316
יָרַשׁ (כ׳) Kal 566
יָרַשׁ Hiphil 566

driven
נָדַח Pual 796
נָדַף Niphal 797

driven, to be
נָדַח Niphal 796
סָבַב Niphal 865
סוּג[1] Niphal 870

driven away, to be
דָּחָה Niphal 339
נָדַף Niphal 797
שָׁבָה Niphal 1224

driven forth, to be
גָּרַשׁ Pual 316

driven on, to be
דָּחָה Niphal 339

driven out, to be
נָדַח Niphal 796

driven quite, to be
נָדַח Niphal 796

driven to and fro
נָדַף Niphal 797

driver
נָגַשׂ Kal 794

driver of a chariot
רַכָּב 1174

driving
מִנְהָג 733

driving out
יָרַשׁ Hiphil 566

dromedary
בֶּכֶר, בִּכְרָה } 229
רֶכֶשׁ 1175
רַמָּךְ 1176

drop
מַר 760

drop, to
נָזַל Kal 803
נָטַף Kal 812
נָטַף Hiphil 812
נָתַךְ Niphal 850
עָרַף[1] Kal 980
רָעַף Kal 1187

drop down, to
עָרַף[1] Kal 980
רָעַף Kal 1187
רָעַף Hiphil 1187

drop through, to
דָּלַף Kal 342

* dropped
הֵלֶךְ 366

dropping
דֶּלֶף 342
נָטַף Kal 812

drops
אֶגְלִים 14
נָטָף 813
רְסִיסִים 1177

dross
סוּג 870
סִיג 875

drought
בַּצֹּרֶת 264
חֹרֶב 461
חֲרָבוֹן 462
צַחְצָחוֹת 1070
צִיָּה 1071
צִמָּאוֹן 1074

drought, great
תַּלְאוּבֹת 1347

drove
מַחֲנֶה 688
עֵדֶר 905

drown, to
שָׁטַף Kal 1254

drowned, to be
טָבַע Pual 474
שָׁקָה (כ׳) Niphal 1323
שָׁקַע Kal 1325
שָׁקַע Niphal 1325

drowsiness
נוּמָה 801

drunk
שִׁכּוֹר 1258

drunk, to be
שָׁתָה Niphal 1331

drunk, to be made
רָוָה Kal 1160

drunk, to make
שָׁכַר Piel 1261
שָׁכַר Hiphil 1261

drunkard
סָבָא Kal 864
שִׁכּוֹר 1258

drunkard †
שֵׁכָר 1262
שָׁתָה Kal 1331

drunken
סֹבֶא 865
שִׁכּוֹר 1258
שָׁכַר Kal 1261

drunken, be
שִׁכָּרוֹן 1262

drunken, to be
שָׁכַר Kal 1261
שָׁכַר Hithpael 1261

drunken, to make
רָוָה Hiphil 1160
שָׁכַר Piel 1261
שָׁכַר Hiphil 1261

drunken man
שִׁכּוֹר 1258

drunkenness
רָוֶה 1160
שִׁכָּרוֹן 1262
שְׁתִי 1333

dry
חָרֵב 459
חֹרֶב 461
חָרָבָה 462
יָבֵשׁ 488
יַבָּשָׁה 488
צַח 1070
צִיָּה 1071
צָמַק Kal 1075

dry, to
יָבֵשׁ Piel 487

dry, to be
חָרֵב, חָרַב } Kal 458
יָבֵשׁ Kal 487

dry, to become
בּוֹשׁ Kal 206

dry ground
חָרָבָה 462
יַבָּשָׁה 488
צִמָּאוֹן 1074

dry land
חָרָבָה 462
יַבָּשָׁה 488
יַבֶּשֶׁת 488
צְחִיחָה 1070
צִיָּה 1071

dry, to make
יָבֵשׁ Piel 487
יָבֵשׁ Hiphil 487

dry place
צִיּוֹן 1071
צִיָּה 1071

dry scall
נֶתֶק 864

dry up, to
דָּלַל Kal 342
חָרֵב, חָרַב } Hiphil 458
יָבֵשׁ Kal 487
יָבֵשׁ Piel 487
יָבֵשׁ Hiphil 487

dryshod
נַעַל 822

due
דָּבָר 325
חֹק 456
מִשְׁפָּט 776

due, *see* order, season

due season
עֵת 1005

due, those to whom it is
בַּעַל 262

duke
אַלּוּף, אַלֻּף } 94
נָסִיךְ 820

dulcimer
סוּמְפּוֹנְיָה Ch. 870
סִיפֹנְיָה 875

dumb
אִלֵּם 95
דּוּמָם 337

dumb, to be
אָלַם Niphal 95

dumb man
אִלֵּם 95

dung
אַשְׁפּוֹת 179
גֵּלֶל 310
גָּלָל 310
דֹּמֶן 346
חֲרָאִים 458
חֲרִים 464
פֶּרֶשׁ 1049
צוֹאָה 1065
צְפוּעַ 1079
צְפִיעַ 1079

dung, *see* dove's

dungeon
בּוֹר 205

dungeon †
בּוֹר 205

* dungeon †
בַּיִת 214

dunghill
אַשְׁפּוֹת 179
מַדְמֵנָה 667
נְוָלוּ Ch. 801
נְוָלִי Ch. 801

durable
עָתִיק 1008
עָתֵק 1008

dust
אָבָק 13
עָפָר 968

dust, to make
דָּקַק Hiphil 348

dust, small
אָבָק 13
שַׁחַק 1252

duty
דָּבָר 325

duty, *see* husband's brother, marriage

dwarf
דַּק 348

dwell, to
גּוּר Kal 303
דּוּר Kal 338
דּוּר Ch. P'al 338
חָנָה Kal 445
יָשַׁב Kal 568
יְתִב Ch. P'al 579
לוּן / לִין } Kal 635
עָמַד Kal 955
שָׁכֵן / שָׁכַן } Kal 1260
שָׁכֵן / שָׁכַן } Hiphil 1260
שְׁרֵא Ch. P'al 1326

dwell, *see* far, wilderness

dwell, to cause to
יָשַׁב Hiphil 568
שָׁכֵן / שָׁכַן } Piel 1260
שְׁכֵן Ch. Pael 1261

dwell in, to
זְבוּל / זְבֻל } 377
מוֹשָׁב 675

dwell, to make to
יָשַׁב Hiphil 568
שָׁכֵן / שָׁכַן } Piel 1260
שָׁכֵן / שָׁכַן } Hiphil 1260

dwell with, to
זָבַל Kal 379

dwellers
שָׁכֵן / שָׁכַן } Kal 1260

dwelleth
מִשְׁכָּן 770

dwelling
אֹהֶל 27
זְבוּל / זְבֻל } 377
יָשַׁב Kal 568
מָגוּר 662
מְדוֹר Ch. 667
מְדָר 667
מוֹשָׁב 675
מָעוֹן 740
מִשְׁכָּן 770
נָוֶה 800

dwelling place
אֹהֶל 27
מוֹשָׁב 675
מָכוֹן 699
מָעוֹן 740
מְעוֹנָה 740
מִשְׁכָּן 770
נָוֶה 800

dwelt in, that
מוֹשָׁב 675

dwelt, wherein
מוֹשָׁב 675

dyed
חָמֵץ Kal 440

dyed attire
טְבוּלִים 473

dyed red, to be
אָדַם Pual 20

each
אֶחָד 41
אִישׁ 60
אִשָּׁה 175

each, *see* day, lay

each, a like of
בַּד 186

each one
אֶחָד 41

eagle
נֶשֶׁר 849
נְשַׁר Ch. 850

eagle, *see* gier-eagle

ear
אֹזֶן 35

ear, *see* perceive

ear
אָבִיב 10

ear, to
חָרַשׁ Kal 466
עָבַד Kal 887

ear, to give
אָזַן Hiphil 35
שָׁמֵעַ / שָׁמַע } Kal 1292

eared, to be
עָבַד Niphal 887

earing
חָרִישׁ 464

earing time
חָרִישׁ 464

early
בֹּקֶר 266
שַׁחַר 1252
שָׁכַם Hiphil 1260

early, *see* arise, depart, enquire, rise, rise up, rising, rising up, seek

early, to be up
שָׁכַם Hiphil 1260

early, to get (*oneself*)
שָׁכַם Hiphil 1260

early, to get up
שָׁכַם Hiphil 1260

early in the morning, very
שְׁפַרְפָּרָא Ch. 1322

earn wages, to
שָׂכַר Hithpael 1207

earnestly, *see* desire

earnestly is sometimes the translation of an infinitive used intensitively.

earring
לַחַשׁ 640
נֶזֶם 804
עָגִיל 900

eighth
שְׁמִינִי 1289
שְׁמֹנֶה } 1291
שְׁמֹנָה }
eightieth
שְׁמֹנִים 1292
eighty
שְׁמֹנִים 1292
either
אוֹ 29
אִם 100
either of them
אִישׁ 60
either *of them*
שְׁנֵי 1310
either...or
גַּם 311
El-*beth*-el
אֵל 76
El-*elohe*
אֵל 76
El-elohe-*Israel*
אֱלֹהִים 79
Elah
אֵלָה 78
Elam
עוֹלָם (כ׳) 907
elder
גָּדוֹל 293
זָקֵן 392
רַב 1147
שִׂיב Ch. P'al 1205
elder †
יוֹם 508
eldest
בְּכוֹר 227
גָּדוֹל 293
זָקֵן 392
רִאשׁוֹן 1145
eldest son
בְּכוֹר 227
elect
בָּחִיר 208
elem-rechokim, *see* Jonath-elem-rechokim
Eleph
אֶלֶף 96
eleven
{ אֶחָד 41
{ עָשָׂר 998
eleven†
עַשְׁתֵּי 1005
eleventh
{ עַשְׁתֵּי 1005
{ עָשָׂר 998
elm
אֵלָה 78
eloquent †
בִּין Niphal 212
דָּבָר 325

else
אַיִן 59
כִּי 596
עוֹד 905
else,† or
לֹא 625
Elul
אֱלוּל 94
embalm, to
חָנַט Kal 445
embolden, to
מָרַץ Hiphil 765
embrace
חָבַק Piel.............. 399
embrace, to
חָבַק Kal 399
embroider, to
שָׁבַץ Piel..............1232
embroiderer
רָקַם Kal 1192
Emek, *see* Beth-emek
emerald
נֹפֶךְ 825
emerods
טְחוֹרִים 480
עֹפֶל (כ׳) 967
eminent
תָּלַל Kal..............1348
eminent place
גַּב 286
empire
מַלְכוּת 728
employ †
פָּנִים 1023
employ,† to
בּוֹא Kal 189
employed, to be
עָמַד Kal 955
employment, *see* continual
emptied
רֵק & רֵיק 1172
emptied, to be
בָּקַק Niphal 265
דָּלַל Kal.............. 342
רוּק Hophal..........1165
emptier
בָּקַק Kal.............. 265
emptiness
בֹּהוּ 188
empty
בּוּקָה 205
רֵק & רֵיק 1172
רֵיק 1172
רֵיקָם 1172
empty, to
בָּקַק Polel 265
עָרָה Piel.............. 977

פָּנָה Piel..............1021
רוּק Hiphil 1165
empty, to be
פָּקַד Niphal 1040
empty, to make
בָּקַק Kal.............. 265
רוּק Hiphil 1165
empty out, to
בָּקַק Kal.............. 265
empty place
תֹּהוּ 1336
En-hakkore
{ עַיִן 919
{ קָרָא ¹ Kal..............1117
encamp, to
חָנָה Kal.............. 445
enchanter
נָחַשׁ Piel.............. 809
עָנַן Poel 966
enchantment
חֶבֶר 400
לַחַשׁ 640
לָט 640
נַחַשׁ 809
* enchantment
נָחַשׁ Piel.............. 809
enchantment, to use
נָחַשׁ Piel.............. 809
enchantments
לְהָטִים 634
encourage, to
חָזַק Piel.............. 411
encourage self, to
חָזַק Hithpael 411
encouraged, to be
חָזַק Kal.............. 411
end
אַחֲרִית 54
אֶפֶס 147
גַּבְלֻת 291
דִּבְרָה 334
כָּלָה Kal.............. 598
כָּלָה 600
כָּנָף 605
נֵצַח }
נֶצַח } 835
סוֹף 871
סוֹף Ch. 871
עֵקֶב 974
פֵּאָה 1009
פֶּה 1011
קֵץ 1113
קָצֶה 1114
קָצֶה 1114
קְצָה 1115
קְצֵו 1115
קְצָוָה 1115

קֵצָת 1117
קְצָת Ch. 1117
רֹאשׁ 1142
תַּכְלִית 1347
תָּמַם Kal 1351
תְּקוּפָה 1356

* end
יוֹם 508

end, *see* come to, east, grow to, hinder, what

end, to
חָדַל Kal 402
כָּלָה Piel 598
תָּמַם Hiphil 1351

end, to be at an
אָפֵס Kal 147
בָּלַע Hithpael 230
מָלֵא Kal 701

end, to come to an
תָּמַם Kal 1351

end, full
כָּלָה 600

end, to have an
סוּף Kal 871
תָּמַם Niphal 1351

end, to make an
חָתַם (כ׳) Kal 471
כָּלָה Piel 598
נָלָה Hiphil 819
שָׁלַם Hiphil 1277
תָּמַם Hiphil 1351

end of, to be an
כָּלָה Kal 598

end of, in the
יָצָא Kal 548

end, to the
מַעַן 744

end, utter
כָּלָה 600

* end,† world without
עַד 901

endamage, to
נְזַק Ch. Aphel 804

endanger, to make
חוּב Piel 405

endangered, to be
סָכַן[2] Niphal 876

endeavours
מַעֲלָל 744

ended, to be
כָּלָה Kal 598
כָּלָה Pual 598
שָׁלַם Kal 1277
תָּמַם Kal 1351

endow, to
מָהַר[2] Kal 669

ends
מִגְבָּלֹת 661

endue, to
זָבַד Kal 377

endued with
יָדַע Kal 500

* endure
פָּנִים 1023

endure, *see* able

endure, to
יָכֹל Kal 526
יָשַׁב Kal 568
לִין & לוּן Kal 635
עָמַד Kal 955
קוּם Kal 1099

enemy
אָיַב Kal 55
עָר 975
עָר Ch. 975
צָר & צַר 1080
צָרַר Kal 1083
קוּם Kal 1099
שָׂנֵא Kal 1210
שׁוּר 1248
שָׁרַר Kal 1327

enemy, to be an
אָיַב Kal 55

enflame selves, to
חָמַם Niphal 439

engage, to
עָרַב[1] Kal 975

engines
חִשְּׁבֹנוֹת 469
מְחִי 686

engrave, to
פָּתַח Piel 1052

engraver
חָרָשׁ 467

engraving
פִּתּוּחַ 1052

enjoin, to
פָּקַד Kal 1040
קוּם Piel 1099

enjoy, to
יָרַשׁ Kal 566
רָאָה Kal 1133
רָצָה Kal 1189
רָצָה Hiphil 1189

enjoy long, to
בָּלָה Piel 229

enjoy, to make to
רָאָה Hiphil 1133

enlarge, to
פָּתָה Hiphil 1052
רָבָה Hiphil 1151
רָחַב Hiphil 1166
שָׁטַח Kal 1254

enlarged, to be
רָחַב Kal 1166

enlargement
רֶוַח 1160

enlarging, to be an
רָחַב Kal 1166

enlighten, to
אוֹר Hiphil 32
נָגַהּ Hiphil 791

enlightened, to be
אוֹר Kal 32
אוֹר Niphal 32

enmity
אֵיבָה 57

enough
דַּי 339
דָּלָה Kal 341
הוֹן 360
כֹּל 597
רַב 1147
שָׂבְעָה 1196

* enough
יָד 489

enough, *see* long

enough is sometimes the translation of an infinitive used intensively.

enough, to be
מָצָא Niphal 748

enough, to have
שָׂבֵעַ / שָׂבַע } Kal 1195
שָׂבְעָה 1196

enough, more than
דַּי 339

enquire †
פָּנִים 1023

enquire, to
בָּעָה Kal 261
בָּקַר Piel 265
בְּקַר Ch. Pael 265
בָּקַשׁ Piel 268
דָּרַשׁ Kal 353
שָׁאַל Kal 1220

enquire early, to
שָׁחַר[2] Piel 1252

enquiry, to make
בָּקַר Piel 265

enrich, to
עָשַׁר Hiphil 1004

ensign
אוֹת 33
נֵס 819

ensign, to lift up as an
נָסַס[2] Hithpolel 821

ensnared, be
מוֹקֵשׁ 674

entangled, to be
בּוּךְ Niphal 205

סָעַד Kal 880
עָמַד Hiphil 955
קוּם Piel 1099
קוּם Hiphil 1099
קוּם Ch. Pael 1103
קוּם Ch. Aphel 1103

established
סָמַךְ Kal 879

established, to be
אָמַן Niphal 103
חָזַק Kal 411
כּוּן Niphal 592
כּוּן Hophal 592
כּוּן Hithpolel 592
קוּם Kal 1099
תְּקַן Ch. Hophal 1356

establishment
אֱמֶת 134

estate
דִּבְרָה 334
כֵּן 604
תּוֹר 1342

estate, *see* former, great, low, old

esteem, to
חָשַׁב Kal 468
עָרַךְ Kal 978
צָפַן Kal 1080

esteem, *see* lightly, right

esteemed, to be
חָשַׁב Niphal 468

esteemed, to be lightly
קָלָה[2] Niphal 1108
קָלַל Kal 1109

estimate, to
עָרַךְ Hiphil 978

estimation
עֵרֶךְ 979

estrange, to
נָכַר Piel 818

estranged, to be
זוּר[2] Kal 384
זוּר[2] Niphal 384

eternal
עוֹלָם 907
קֶדֶם 1088

eternity
עַד 901

Ethanim
אֵיתָן } 70
אֵתָן }

eunuch
סָרִיס 885

even
אַךְ 70
אַף 144
גַּם 311
הֵא Ch. 356
כִּי 596
עַד 901
רַק 1191

even
עֶרֶב 976

* even
צֶדֶק 1063

even now
יוֹם 508

even place
מִישׁוֹר 698

even so
כָּכָה 597
כֵּן 604

even to
עַד 901

evening
עָרַב[2] Hiphil 975
עֶרֶב 975
עֲרָבָה 976

evening †
יוֹם 508
עֵת 1005

evening, toward
עָרַב[2] Kal 975

eveningtide
{ עֵת 1005
{ עֶרֶב 976

event
מִקְרֶה 760

eventide
עֶרֶב 976
{ עֵת 1005
{ עֶרֶב 976

ever
נֵצַח } 835
נֶצַח }
עַד 901
עוֹלָם 907
עֵילוֹם 919
צְמִיתֻת 1075
רִיב Kal 1171
תָּמִיד 1349

* ever
קֶדֶם 1088

ever †
יוֹם 508

ever is sometimes the translation of an infinitive used intensitively.

ever, for
עוֹלָם 907
עָלַם Ch. 943

* ever, † for
אֹרֶךְ 156

ever of old
עוֹלָם 907

everlasting
עַד 901
עוֹלָם 907
עָלַם Ch. 943
קֶדֶם 1088

ever*lasting*
עוֹלָם 907

* everlasting †
יוֹם 508

evermore
נֵצַח } 835
נֶצַח }
עַד 901
עוֹלָם 907
תָּמִיד 1349

* evermore
דּוֹר 337

evermore †
יוֹם 508

evermore, for
עוֹלָם 907

every
אֶחָד 41
אִישׁ 60
אִשָּׁה 175
אֲשֶׁר 180
כֹּל 597
כֹּל Ch. 597

every, *see* man, province, sabbath, side, wise

* every *man*
רֹאשׁ 1142

every one
אִישׁ 60
גֶּבֶר 292
כֹּל 597

every place
כֹּל 597

every side, *see* about on

* every side, on
סָבַב Niphal 865

every thing
כֹּל 597

every way, *see* turn

every whit
כָּלִיל 603

evidence
סֵפֶר 883

evil
אָוֶן 30
בְּלִיַּעַל 230
רַע 1177
רֹעַ 1183
רָעַע Kal 1186

evil, *see* think

evil again, to *do*
שׁוּב Kal 1238

evil, to be
יָרַע Kal 566
רָעַע Kal 1186

* evil, to be so
רֹעַ 1183

evil, to bring
רָעַע Hiphil 1186

evil, to do
רָעַע Hiphil ... 1186

evil entreat, to
רָעָה Kal ... 1184
רָעַע Hiphil ... 1186

evil man
רַע ... 1177
רָעַע Hiphil ... 1186

evil report
דִּבָּה ... 318

* evil speaker †
לָשׁוֹן ... 651

evil things
רַע ... 1177

evildoer
רָעַע Hiphil ... 1186

*evil*doer
פָּעַל Kal ... 1037

*evilfavoured*ness
דָּבָר ... 325

evil*favouredness*
רַע ... 1177

ewe
רָחֵל ... 1168
שֶׂה ... 1199

ewe lamb
כִּבְשָׂה } ... 585
כַּבְשָׂה }

ewes great with young
עוּל Kal ... 906

exact, to
יָצָא Hiphil ... 548
נָגַשׂ Kal ... 794
נָשָׁא Kal ... 840
נָשָׁא ² Kal ... 846
נָשָׁא Hiphil ... 846
נָשָׁה ² Kal ... 847
נָשָׁה ¹ Hiphil ... 847

exaction
גְּרֻשָׁה ... 317
מַשָּׂא ... 766

exactor
נָגַשׂ Kal ... 794

exalt, to
גָּבַהּ Hiphil ... 287
נָשָׂא Kal ... 840
נָשָׂא Piel ... 840
סָלַל Pilpel ... 878
רוּם Polel ... 1163
רוּם Hiphil ... 1163
שָׂגַב Hiphil ... 1197

exalt self, to
נָשָׂא Hithpael ... 840
סָלַל Hithpoel ... 878
רוּם Kal ... 1163
רוּם Hithpolel ... 1163

exalted, to be
גָּבַהּ Kal ... 287
נָשָׂא Niphal ... 840
נָשָׂא Hithpael ... 840
עָלָה Niphal ... 934
רוּם Kal ... 1163
רוּם Polal ... 1163
רוּם (כ') Hiphil ... 1163
רָמַם Kal ... 1176
רָמַם Niphal ... 1176
שָׂגַב Kal ... 1197
שָׂגַב Niphal ... 1197

examine, to
בָּחַן Kal ... 208
דְּרִישׁ ... 349

exceed, to
גָּבַר Hithpael ... 291
גָּדַל Kal ... 297
גָּדַל Hiphil ... 297
יָסַף Kal ... 543
יָסַף Hiphil ... 543

exceeding
יַתִּיר Ch. ... 579
יֶתֶר ... 580
מְאֹד ... 652
מַעַל ... 743
סָרַח Kal ... 884
רָבָה Hiphil ... 1151
שַׂגִּיא Ch. ... 1197

* exceeding
אֱלֹהִים ... 79
חָכַם Pual ... 426
שִׂמְחָה ... 1210

* exceeding †
גָּדוֹל ... 293
שִׂמְחָה ... 1210

exceeding, *see* deep

* exceeding proudly
גָּבֹהַּ } ... 287
גָּבוֹהַּ }

exceedingly
יַתִּיר Ch. ... 579
מְאֹד ... 652
מַעַל ... 743
רַב ... 1147
רָבָה Hiphil ... 1151

* exceedingly
גִּיל ... 306
חֲרָדָה ... 462
שִׂמְחָה ... 1210
תַּאֲוָה ... 1334

exceedingly †
רָבָה Hiphil ... 1151

* exceedingly †
גָּדוֹל ... 293
יִרְאָה ... 561

רַע ... 1177
שִׂנְאָה ... 1211

* excel
גָּבוֹהַּ ... 289

excel, to
יָתַר Hiphil ... 580
נָצַח Piel ... 834
עָלָה Kal ... 934
רָבָה Kal ... 1151

excellency
גַּאֲוָה ... 285
גָּאוֹן ... 285
גֹּבַהּ ... 287
הָדָר ... 357
יֶתֶר ... 580
יִתְרוֹן ... 581
שְׂאֵת ... 1195
שִׂיא ... 1205

excellent
אַדִּיר ... 17
בָּחַר Kal ... 209
גָּאוֹן ... 285
גָּדַל Hiphil ... 297
יָקָר ... 558
יַתִּיר Ch. ... 579
יֶתֶר ... 580
קַר (כ') ... 1117
רֹב ... 1150
שַׂגִּיא (תפארה...1354) 1197

* excellent
עֲדִי ... 904

excellent, to be
שָׂגַב Niphal ... 1197
תּוּר Hiphil ... 1342

excellent thing
נָגִיד ... 791

excellent things
גֵּאוּת ... 285
שָׁלִישׁ ... 1275
שָׁלִשׁוֹם (כ') ... 1279

excellest
רֹאשׁ ... 1142

excelleth
יִתְרוֹן ... 581

except
אַיִן ... 59
בַּד ... 186
בִּלְתִּי ... 231
כִּי ... 596
לָהֵן Ch. ... 634
לוּלֵא ... 635
לוּלֵי ... 635
רַק ... 1191

except †
אִם ... 100
לֹא ... 625

exchange
תְּמוּרָה 1349
exchange, to
מוּר Hiphil 674
execration
אָלָה 78
execute, to
עָבַד Kal 887
עָשָׂה Kal 981
שָׁפַט Kal 1319
execute, *see* judgment, priest's office
execute *judgment*, to
דִּין Kal 340
executed
עֲבַד Ch. Ithpael 889
executed, to be
עָשָׂה Niphal 981
executing
עָשָׂה Kal 981
execution, to be put in
עָשָׂה Niphal 981
exempted
נָקִי 838
exercise, to
עָשָׂה Kal 981
exercise *robbery*, to
גָּזַל Kal 304
exercise self, to
הָלַךְ Piel 362
exercised, to be
עָנָה[2] Kal 964
exile
גָּלָה Kal 307
exile, *see* captive
expectation
מַבָּט 660
מֶבָּט 660
תִּקְוָה 1356
expect*ed*
תִּקְוָה 1356
expel, to
גָּרַשׁ Piel 316
הָדַף Kal 357
יָרַשׁ Hiphil 566
expelled, to be
נָדַח Kal 796
expences
נִפְקָא Ch. 829
experience, to have
רָאָה Kal 1133
experience, to learn by
נָחַשׁ Piel 809
expert
לָמַד Pual 643
שָׂכַל Hiphil 1206
* expert
שָׂכַל Hiphil 1259

expert in *war*
עָרַךְ Kal 978
expired, be
תְּשׁוּבָה 1359
expired, to be
כָּלָה Piel 598
מָלֵא Kal 701
expound, to
נָגַד Hiphil 788
expressed, to be
נָקַב Niphal 837
* expressly
אָמַר Kal 105
extend, to
מָשַׁךְ Kal 770
נָטָה Kal 810
נָטָה Hiphil 810
extinct, to be
דָּעַךְ Kal 347
זָעַךְ Niphal 391
extol, to
סָלַל Kal 878
רוּם Polel 1163
רוּם Ch. P'al 1164
extolled, to be
נָשָׂא Niphal 840
רוּם Polal 1163
רוֹמָם 1164
extortion
עֹשֶׁק 1004
extortioner
מוּץ Kal 673
נָשָׁה[2] Kal 847
extreme, *see* burning
extremity
פִּשׁ 1050
eye
עַיִן 919
עַיִן Ch. 925
eye, to
עָוַן Kal 911
עִין Kal 925
eye*brow*
עַיִן 919
*eye*brows
גַּב 286
eye*d*
עַיִן 919
eyelids
עַפְעַפַּיִם 968
eyesight
עַיִן 919
Ezel
אֶזֶל 35
face
אַנְפִּין Ch. 140
אַף 144

עַיִן 919
פָּנִים 1023
fade, to
בָּלַל Hiphil 230
נָבֵל Kal 786
fade away, to
נָבֵל Kal 786
fading
נָבֵל Kal 786
fail
אַיִן 59
יָשַׁב Kal 568
כָּלֶה 600
* fail
שָׁלוּ Ch. 1263
fail, to
אָבַד Kal 8
אָזַל Kal 35
אָפֵס Kal 147
בָּקַק Niphal 265
גָּמַר Kal 312
גָּעַל Hiphil 313
דָּלַל Kal 342
חָדַל Kal 402
חָסֵר Kal 450
חָסֵר 450
יָצָא Kal 548
כָּהָה Kal 586
כָּזַב Piel 594
כָּחַשׁ Kal 595
כָּחַשׁ Piel 595
כָּלָה Kal 598
כָּרַת Niphal 618
כָּשַׁל Kal 621
נָפַל Kal 825
נָשַׁת Kal 850
נָשַׁת Niphal 850
עָבַר Kal 895
עָדַר[1] Niphal 905
עָזַב Kal 915
עָטַף Kal 918
פָּסַס Kal 1037
פָּרַר Hiphil 1048
רָפָה Hiphil 1188
שָׁקַר Piel 1325
תָּמַם Kal 1351
fail,† to
אָמַן Niphal 103
fail, to cause to
חָסֵר Hiphil 450
כָּלָה Piel 598
שָׁבַת Hiphil 1234
fail, to let
נָפַל Hiphil 825

fail, to make to
שָׁבַת Hiphil ... 1234

fail, without, is sometimes the translation of an infinitive used intensitively.

failing
כִּלָּיוֹן ... 602

fain
בָּרַח Kal ... 271

faint
דָּוֶה ... 337
דַּוָּי ... 337
יָעֵף ... 546
עָיֵף ... 925

faint, to
הָיָה Niphal ... 360
יָגַע Kal ... 488
יָעַף Kal ... 546
כָּהָה Piel ... 586
כָּלָה Kal ... 598
לָאָה Kal ... 626
לָהַהּ Kal ... 634
מוּג Kal ... 670
מוּג Niphal ... 670
מָסַס Kal ... 737
מָסַס Niphal ... 737
000 000
עָטַף Hithpael ... 918
עָלַף Pual ... 944
עָלַף Hithpael ... 944
פּוּג Kal ... 1014
רָכַךְ Niphal ... 1174
רָפָה Hithpael ... 1188

faint, to be
עוּף Kal ... 911
פָּגַר Piel ... 1010
רָפָה Kal ... 1188

faint, that
עָטַף Kal ... 918

faint, to wax
עוּף Kal ... 911

fainted
עֻלְפֶּה ... 944

fainthearted
{ רַךְ ... 1173
{ לֵבָב ... 630

fainthearted, to be
מוּג Niphal ... 670

faint*heart*ed, to be
רָכַךְ Niphal ... 1174

faintness
מֹרֶךְ ... 764

fair
טָהוֹר ... 474
טוֹב ... 476
טוֹב ... 479
יָפֶה ... 548
מַרְאֶה ... 761
שַׁפִּיר Ch. ... 1320
תִּפְאָרָה / תִּפְאֶרֶת } ... 1354

* fair
חָנַן Piel ... 446

fair †
טוֹב ... 476
תֹּאַר ... 1334

fair, *see* colours, speech, weather

fair
עִזָּבוֹן ... 917

fair, to be
יָפָה Kal ... 548

fair, to make self
יָפָה Hithpael ... 548

fair one
יָפֶה ... 548

fair, very
יְפֵה־פִיָּה ... 548

fair word
טוֹב ... 476

fairer, to be
יָפָה Pual ... 548

fairest
יָפֶה ... 548

faith
אֵמוּן ... 102
אֱמוּנָה / אֱמֻנָה } ... 102

faithful
אֵמוּן ... 102
אֱמוּנָה ... 102
אָמַן Kal ... 103
אֲמַן Ch. Aphel ... 104
אֱמֶת ... 134

faithful, to be
אָמַן Niphal ... 103

faithful *man*
אֱמוּנָה / אֱמֻנָה } ... 102

faithfully
אֱמוּנָה / אֱמֻנָה } ... 102

faithfulness
אֱמוּנָה / אֱמֻנָה } ... 102
כּוּן Niphal ... 592

fall
כִּשָּׁלוֹן ... 621
מַפֶּלֶת ... 748

fall, to
הָיָה Kal ... 360
יָצָא Kal ... 548
יָרַד Kal ... 561
כָּרַע Kal ... 618
כָּשַׁל Kal ... 621
כָּשַׁל Niphal ... 621
לָבַט Niphal ... 632
מוּט (כ׳) Hiphil ... 670
נָגַר Hiphil ... 793
נָפַל Kal ... 825
נָפַל Hithpael ... 825
נְפַל Ch. P'al ... 828
עָלָה Kal ... 934
פָּגַע Kal ... 1009

fall *see* sick, whoredom

fall away, to
נָפַל Kal ... 825

fall, to cause to
כָּשַׁל (כ׳) Kal ... 621
כָּשַׁל Hiphil ... 621
נָפַל Hiphil ... 824

fall, caused to
מִכְשׁוֹל ... 701

fall down, to
כָּשַׁל Kal ... 621
נָבֵל Kal ... 786
נָפַל Kal ... 825
נָפַל Hithpael ... 825
נְפַל Ch. P'al ... 828
סָגַד Kal ... 868
רָבַץ Kal ... 1154
שָׁחָה Hithpael ... 1249

fall down, to let
יָרַד Hiphil ... 561

fall flat, to
שָׁחָה Hithpael ... 1249

fall grievously, to
חוּל / חִיל } Kal ... 406

fall, to let
נָטַשׁ Kal ... 813
נָפַל Hiphil ... 825
שָׁלַל Kal ... 1276

fall, to make
נָפַל Hiphil ... 825

fall, to make to
כָּשַׁל Hiphil ... 621

fall off, to
נָבֵל Kal ... 786

fall out, to
יָצָא Kal ... 548
קָרָא[2] Kal ... 1122
רָגַז Kal ... 1155

fall, ready to
נָפַל Kal ... 825

fall upon, to
פָּגַע Kal ... 1009
פָּשַׁט Kal ... 1050

fall with pain, to
חוּל / חִיל } Kal ... 406

fallen, to be
בּוֹא Kal 189
נָפַל Kal 825
fallen, *see* decay
fallen off, *see* hair
falling
דְּחִי 339
נָפַל Kal 825
כָּשַׁל Kal 621
נָבֵל Kal 786
falling down
מוֹט Kal 670
fallow deer
יַחְמוּר 523
fallow ground
נִיר 814
false
אָוֶן 30
חָמָס 440
כָּזָב 594
מִרְמָה 765
רְמִיָּה 1176
שָׁוְא 1238
שֶׁקֶר 1325
falsehood
מַעַל 743
שֶׁקֶר 1325
falsely
שָׁוְא 1238
שֶׁקֶר 1325
false*ly*
שֶׁקֶר 1325
falsely, to deal
כָּחַשׁ Piel 595
שָׁקַר Kal 1325
שָׁקַר Piel 1325
falsifying
עָוַת Piel 914
fame
קוֹל 1096
שֵׁם 1280
שְׁמוּעָה 1285
שֵׁמַע 1299
שֹׁמַע 1300
familiar
שָׁלוֹם 1263
familiar friend
יָדַע Pual 500
familiar spirit
אוֹב 29
families
טַף 484
family
אֶלֶף 96
בַּיִת 214
מִשְׁפָּחָה 774

famine
כָּפָן 614
רָעָב 1183
רְעָבוֹן 1184
famish, to
רָזָה Kal 1166
famish, to suffer to
רָעֵב Hiphil 1183
famished †
רָעָב 1183
famished, to be
רָעֵב Kal 1183
famous
אַדִּיר 17
קָרָא (כ׳) [1] Kal 1117
קָרִיא 1128
famo*us*
שֵׁם 1280
famous, to be
יָדַע Niphal 500
קָרָא [1] Niphal 1117
famous,† to be
קָרָא [1] Kal 1117
fan
מִזְרֶה 685
fan, to
זָרָה Kal 394
זָרָה Piel 394
fanner
זוּר [2] Kal 384
far
מְאֹד 652
מֶרְחָק 763
רָחוֹק 1168
רַחִיק Ch 1168
רָחַק Kal 1170
רָחַק Hiphil 1170
* far
גָּדוֹל 293
נֶגֶד 790
נָדָה 796
far, *see* above, away, drive, flee, go, keep, put, remove, thus, withdraw
far abroad
רָחוֹק 1168
far away, *see* go, put, turn
far away, to be
רָחַק Kal 1170
far away, to put
רָחַק Hiphil 1170
far, be
חָלִילָה 431
far, to be
רָחַק Kal 1170
far country
מֶרְחָק 763
* far, dwell in
מֶרְחָק 763

far, to get
רָחַק Kal 1170
far off
מֶרְחָק 763
רָחוֹק 1168
* far off
נֶגֶד 790
רָחַק Hiphil 1170
far off, *see* cast, remove
far off, to be
רָחַק Kal 1170
far off, to cast
רָחַק Hiphil 1170
far off, very
מֶרְחָק 763
far off, to *wander*
רָחַק Hiphil 1170
far, to put
רָחַק Hiphil 1170
far removed, to be
רָחַק Kal 1170
far *richer*
עָשַׁר 1005
far, that are
רָחֵק 1170
far, to be too
רָחַק Kal 1170
* fare
שָׁלוֹם 1263
fashion
דְּמוּת 345
מִשְׁפָּט 776
תְּכוּנָה 1346
fashion, *see* almonds
fashion, to
יָצַר [1] Kal 556
כּוּן Polel 592
עָשָׂה Kal 981
צוּר Kal 1069
fashioned, to be
יָצַר [1] Pual 556
כּוּן Niphal 592
fast
אָסְפַּרְנָא Ch 143
אָסַר Kal 143
מְאֹד 652
עָצַר Kal 973
צוּם Kal 1068
fast, *see* abide, asleep, cleave, hold, keep, set, stand, stick
fast, to
צוּם 1069
fast, † to
צוּם 1069
fasten, to
אָחַז Kal 46
חָזַק Piel 411
נָתַן Kal 851

לָקַח Kal 644
נָשָׂא Kal 840
fetch, *see* compass, quickly
fetch (*a pledge*), to
עָבַט Kal 895
fetch a stroke, to
נָדַח Niphal 796
fetch about, to
סָבַב Piel 865
fetch forth, to
יָצָא Hiphil 548
fetch home again, to
שׁוּב Hiphil 1238
fetch out, to
יָצָא Hiphil 548
fetch up, to
עָלָה Kal 934
עָלָה Hiphil 934
fetched, to be
לָקַח Hophal 644
fetter
כֶּבֶל 584
נְחֹשֶׁת 809
fetter of brass
נְחֹשֶׁת 809
fetters
זִקִּים 392
fever
קַדַּחַת 1087
few
אֶחָד 41
בִּצָּה 263
מִזְעָר 685
מְעַט 741
מְתִים 779
קָצֵר 1117
* few
מִסְפָּר 738
few †
מְתִים 779
few, to be
מָעַט Kal 741
מָעַט Piel 741
* few, to borrow a
מָעַט Hiphil 741
few, to give
מָעַט Hiphil 741
few in number, to make
מָעַט Hiphil 741
few, some
מְעַט 741
few, very
מְעַט 741
fewer
מְעַט 741
fewest
מְעַט 741

fewness
מָעַט Kal 741
field
אֶרֶץ 157
בַּר Ch. 270
חוּץ 408
חֶלְקָה 436
שָׂדֶה 1197
שָׂדַי 1199
שְׁדֵמָה 1238
field, *see* fruitful, plentiful
fields
יְגֵבִים 488
שְׁרֵמוֹת (כ׳) 1327
fierce
אַכְזָר 70
חָרוֹן 463
חֳרִי 464
יָעַז Niphal 546
עַז 914
fierce, *see* wrath
fierce, to be
חָדַד Kal 402
fierce lion
שַׁחַל 1251
fierceness
חָרוֹן 463
רַעַשׁ 1187
fiercer, to be
קָשָׁה Kal 1131
fiery
אֵשׁ 172
נוּר Ch. 803
שָׂרָף 1218
fiery, *see* serpent
fifteen
{ חָמֵשׁ / חֲמִשָּׁה } 441
{ עָשָׂר } 997
*fif*teen
{ עָשָׂר / עֶשְׂרֵה } 998
fifteen, *see* threescore
*fif*teenth
{ עָשָׂר / עֶשְׂרֵה } 998
fifth
{ חֲמִישִׁי / חֲמִישִׁי } 439
{ חָמֵשׁ / חֲמִשָּׁה } 441
fifth part
{ חֲמִישִׁי / חֲמִישִׁי } 439
חֹמֶשׁ 443
fifth part, to take up the
חָמַשׁ Piel 441

fifth *rib*
חֹמֶשׁ **443**
fifth time
{ חֲמִישִׁי / חֲמִישִׁי } 439
fifty
חֲמִשִּׁים 443
fig
תְּאֵנָה 1334
fig, *see* firstripe
fig, green
פַּג 1009
fig tree
תְּאֵנָה 1334
fight
מִלְחָמָה 707
מַעֲרָכָה 746
fight, to
לָחַם Kal 637
לָחַם Niphal 637
צָבָא Kal 1057
צָבָה Kal 1060
fighting
לָחַם Kal 637
לָחַם Niphal 637
מִלְחָמָה 707
*fight*ing men
עָשָׂה Kal 881
figs, *see* cake
figure
{ סֶמֶל / סֵמֶל } 879
תַּבְנִית 1336
figures
מִקְלַעַת 759
file †
פֶּה 1011
פְּצִירָה 1039
fill
מָלֵא 703
מְלֹא 703
שֹׂבַע 1196
fill, to
מָלֵא Kal 701
מָלֵא Piel 701
מְלָא Ch. P'al 703
עָטָה Kal 918
רָוָה Hiphil 1160
{ שָׂבֵעַ / שָׂבַע } Hiphil 1195
fill selves, to
סָבָא Kal 864
{ שָׂבֵעַ / שָׂבַע } Kal 1195
fill, to take the
רָוָה Kal 1160
fill with, *see* wrinkles

fleshhook
מַזְלֵג ... 684

fleshhooks
מִזְלָגוֹת ... 684

flies, divers sorts of
עָרֹב ... 975

flieth, that
עוֹף ... 911

flight
מָנוֹס ... 733
מְנוּסָה ... 733

flight, to put to
בָּרַח Hiphil ... 271
נוּס Hiphil ... 801
רָדַף Kal ... 1158

flint
חַלָּמִישׁ ... 434
צֹר ... 1081

flinty
חַלָּמִישׁ ... 434

floats
דֹּבְרוֹת ... 334

flock
מִקְנֶה ... 759
עֵדֶר ... 905
צֹאן ... 1055

flock, little
חֲשִׂף ... 468

flocks
מַרְעִית ... 765
עַשְׁתְּרוֹת ... 1005

flocks †
צֹאן ... 1055

flood
אוֹר ... 32
זֶרֶם ... 395
יְאוֹר ... 486
מַבּוּל ... 660
נָהָר ... 798
נָזַל Kal ... 803
נַחַל ... 805
שִׁבֹּלֶת ... 1227
שֶׁטֶף, שֵׁטֶף ... 1254

flood, *see* carry away, water flood

floor
גֹּרֶן ... 316
קַרְקַע ... 1130

floor, *see* barnfloor, cornfloor, threshingfloor

floor, to
קָרָה Piel ... 1127

* floor, one side of the
קַרְקַע ... 1130

floors, *see* threshing

flotes
רַפְסֹדוֹת ... 1189

flour
בָּצֵק ... 264
סֹלֶת ... 879
קֶמַח ... 1110

flour, *see* fine

flourish, to
נָאַץ Hiphil ... 782
פָּרַח Kal ... 1045
פָּרַח Hiphil ... 1045
צוּץ Hiphil ... 1069

flourish, to make to
פָּרַח Hiphil ... 1045

flourishing
רַעֲנָן ... 1186
רַעֲנַן Ch. ... 1186

flow, to
זוּב Kal ... 383
יָלַךְ Kal ... 531
נָהַר Kal ... 798
נָזַל Kal ... 803
צוּף Kal ... 1069
שָׁטַף Kal ... 1254

flow away, to
נָגַר Niphal ... 793

flow, to cause to
נָזַל Hiphil ... 803

flow down, to
זָלַל Niphal ... 388

flow out, to
נָזַל Kal ... 803

flow together, to
נָהַר Kal ... 798

flower
מִגְדָּל ... 661
נִצָּה ... 834
נִצָּן ... 837
פֶּרַח ... 1045
צִיץ ... 1071
צִיצָה ... 1071

* flower of their age, in the
אֱנוֹשׁ ... 136

* flowers
נִדָּה ... 796

flowing
נָבַע Kal ... 787
נָזַל Kal ... 803

flute
מַשְׁרוֹקִיתָא Ch. ... 779

flutter, to
רָחַף Piel ... 1169

fly
זְבוּב ... 377

fly, to
אָבַר Hiphil ... 13
דָּאָה Kal ... 318
עוּף Kal ... 911
עוּף Polel ... 911
עִיט Kal ... 919
עָשָׂה (כ׳) Kal ... 981

fly away, to
עוּף Kal ... 911
עוּף Hiphil ... 911
עוּף Hithpolel ... 911

fly, to be caused to
יָעַף Hophal ... 546

fly, to make
פָּרַח Kal ... 1045

flying
כָּנָף ... 605
עוּף Kal ... 911
עוֹף ... 911

foal
בֵּן ... 232
עַיִר ... 925

foam
קֶצֶף ... 1116

fodder
בְּלִיל ... 230

foe
אָיַב Kal ... 55
צַר, צָר ... 1080
שָׂנֵא Kal ... 1210

fold
גְּדֵרָה ... 298
דֹּבֶר ... 334
מִכְלָה ... 699
נָוֶה ... 800

fold, *see* sheepfold

fold, to
חָבַק Kal ... 399

fold, to make a
רָבַץ Hiphil ... 1154

folden together
סָבַךְ Kal ... 868

folding
גָּלִיל ... 310
חִבֻּק ... 400

folk
עַם & עָם ... 944

* follow
רֶגֶל ... 1155

follow, to
אַחַר ... 48
רָדַף Kal ... 1158
רָדַף Piel ... 1158

follow,† to
אַחַר ... 48
בּוֹא Kal ... 189
הָיָה Kal ... 360
הָלַךְ Kal ... 362
הָלַךְ Hithpael ... 362
יָלַךְ Kal ... 531

follow after
אַחַר ... 48

follow after, to
רָדַף Kal ... 1158
רָדַף Piel ... 1158

חָשַׁךְ Kal 468
מָשַׁךְ Kal 770

forbeareth, he that
חָדֵל 403

forbearing
אַף 144
כּוּל Pilpel 592

forbid
חָלִילָה 431

forbid, *see* God forbid

forbid, to
כָּלָא Kal 598
צָוָה Piel 1065

force
אֶדְרָע Ch 24
און 31
גְּבוּרָה 290
חֶזְקָה 414
יָד 489
כֹּחַ 594

force, *see* natural, take

force, to
חָזַק Hiphil 411
כָּבַשׁ Kal 586
לָחַץ Kal 640
נָדַח Hiphil 796
עָנָה[2] Piel 964

force self, to
אָפַק Hithpael 147

forces
חַיִל 423
מַאֲמַצִּים 658
מָעוֹז 740

forces, great
חַיִל 423

forcible, to be
מָרַץ Niphal 765

forcing
מִיץ 698
נָדַח Kal 796

ford
מַעֲבָר 739
מַעְבָּרָה 739

forecast, to
חָשַׁב Kal 468
חָשַׁב Piel 468

forefather
אָב 1

fore*father*
רִאשׁוֹן 1145

forefront
פָּנִים 1023
רֹאשׁ 1142

*fore*front
מוּל 671
פָּנִים 1023

* forefront
שֵׁן 1304

forehead
אַף 144
מֵצַח 754

forehead, *see* bald

forehead bald
גִּבֵּחַ 290

foreigner
נָכְרִי 819
תּוֹשָׁב 1344

foremost
רִאשׁוֹן 1145

forepart
פָּנִים 1023

foresee, to
רָאָה Kal 1133

foreskin
עָרְלָה 979

foreskin, to be uncovered
עָרֵל Niphal 979

forest
חֹרֶשׁ 467
יַעַר 547
יַעֲרָה 548
פַּרְדֵּס 1044

forfeited, to be
חָרַם Hophal 464

forge, to
טָפַל Kal 484

forger
טָפַל Kal 484

forget
שָׁכֵחַ 1259

forget, to
נָשָׁה[1] Kal 847
000 000
שָׁכַח Kal 1258

forget, to cause to
שָׁכַח Hiphil 1258

forget, to make
נָשָׁה[1] Piel 847

forgetfulness
נְשִׁיָּה 847

forgive, to
כָּפַר Piel 614
נָשָׂא Kal 840
סָלַח Kal 877

forgive, ready to
סַלָּח 877

forgiven
נָשָׂא Kal 840

forgiven, to be
כָּפַר Hithpael 614
סָלַח Niphal 877

forgiveness
סְלִיחָה 877

forgiving
נָשָׂא Kal 840

forgotten
שָׁכַח Niphal 1258

forgotten, to be
נָשָׁה[1] Niphal 847
שָׁכַח Niphal 1258
שָׁכַח Hithpael 1258

forgotten, to cause to be
שָׁכַח Piel 1258

fork †
שְׁלוֹשׁ / שְׁלוֹשָׁה } 1264

forks
קִלְּשׁוֹן 1110

form
מַרְאֶה 761
מִשְׁפָּט 776
פָּנִים 1023
צוּרָה 1070
צֶלֶם / צְלֵם } Ch 1073
רֵו Ch 1160
תֹּאַר 1334
תַּבְנִית 1336

form, to
חוּל / חִיל } Polel 406
יָצַר[1] Kal 556

form, without
תֹּהוּ 1336

formed, to be
חוּל / חִיל } Polel 406
יָצַר Niphal 556
יָצַר[1] Hophal 556
קָרַץ Pual 1130

former
קַדְמוֹנִי 1089
רִאשׁוֹן 1145
רִישׁוֹן (כ׳) 1172

former estate
קַדְמָה 1089

former rain
יוֹרֶה 674

former *rain*
יוֹרֶה 521

* former rain
יָרָה Kal 564

former things
רִאשׁוֹן 1145

former time
פָּנִים 1023

former time, in
אֶמֶשׁ 134

fornication
תַּזְנוּת 1344

fornication, to cause to commit
זָנָה Hiphil 389

fornication, to commit
זָנָה Kal 389

forsake, to
חָדַל Kal 402
נָטַשׁ Kal 813
עָזַב Kal 915
רָפָה Hiphil 1188

forsaken
אַלְמָן 95
שָׁלַח Pual 1268

forsaken, to be
נָטַשׁ Niphal 813
נָטַשׁ Pual 813
נָתַשׁ Niphal 864
עָזַב Niphal 915

forsaking
עֲזוּבָה 917

fort
דָּיֵק 340
מָעוֹז 740
מְצָד 752
מְצוּדָה 753
מְצוּרָה 754
עֹפֶל 967

fort, high
מִשְׂגָּב 767

forth
הָלַךְ Kal 362
חוּץ 408

* forth
פֶּרֶץ 1047

forth, *see* break, breaking, bring, brought, bud, called, carry, cast, come, draw, driven, fetch, fruit, get, give, go, going, have, joy, lead, led, look, poured, put, putting, reach, right, send, sending, set, shew, shine, shoot, sing, spread, spreadest, spring, stand, stretch, stretched, take, thousands

forth of
בַּיִת 214
עַל 932

forthwith
אָסְפַּרְנָא Ch. 143

fortified
מָצוֹר 754

fortify, to
אָמַץ Piel 104
בָּצַר Piel 264
חָזַק Piel 411
עָזַב Kal 915
צוּר Kal 1069

fortress
מִבְצָר 661
מָעוֹז 740
מְצוּדָה 753
מָצוֹר 754

forty
אַרְבָּעִים 151

forty thousand
רִבּוֹ }
רִבּוֹא } 1153

forward
הָלְאָה 362
הָלַךְ Kal 362
מַעַל 743
פָּנִים 1023
קֶדֶם 1088

forward, *see* go, go on, set

forward, to go
נָסַע Kal 821

forward, to set
יָעַל Hiphil 546
נָסַע Kal 821

foul, to
רָפַשׂ Kal 1189

foul, to be
חָמַר Poalal 441

fouled, that which...have
מִרְפַּשׂ 765

found, *see* guilty, liars

found, to
יָסַד Kal 542
יָסַד Piel 542

found, to be
מָצָא Kal 748
מָצָא Niphal 748
שְׁכַח Ch. Aphel 1259
שְׁכַח Ch. Ithp'el 1259

found out, to be
חָקַר Niphal 458

foundation
אֶדֶן 22
אָשִׁישׁ 178
יָסַד Niphal 542
יָסַד Pual 542
יְסוֹד 543
יְסוּדָה 543
מוּסָד 671
מוּסָדָה 671
מָכוֹן 699
מַסַּד 736
שָׁת 1331

foundation to be laid
יָסַד Niphal 542
יָסַד Pual 542
יָסַד Hophal 542

foundation, to lay for a
יָסַד Piel 542

foundation, to lay the
יָסַד Kal 542
יָסַד Piel 542

foundations
אָשְׁיוֹת 178
אֻשִּׁין Ch. 178
מוֹסָדוֹת 671

founder
צָרַף Kal 1082

fountain
בּוֹר (ב׳) 205
בַּיִר 214
מַבּוּעַ 660
מַעְיָן 742
מָקוֹר 758
עַיִן 919

four
אַרְבַּע }
אַרְבָּעָה } 149
אַרְבַּע }
אַרְבְּעָה } Ch. 151

fourfold
אַרְבַּעְתַּיִם 152

fourscore
שְׁמֹנִים 1292

foursquare
רְבִיעִי 1153
רָבַע[2] Kal 1154
רָבַע[2] Pual 1154

fourteen
{ אַרְבַּע }
{ אַרְבָּעָה } 149
{ עָשָׂר 998

fourteen, *see* threescore

fourteenth
{ אַרְבַּע }
{ אַרְבָּעָה } 149
{ עָשָׂר 998

fourth
רְבִיעִי 1153
רְבִיעַי Ch. 1154
רִבֵּעִים 1154

fourth part
רְבִיעִי 1153
רֶבַע 1154
רֹבַע 1154

fowl
בַּרְבֻּרִים 270
עוֹף 911
עוֹף Ch. 912
עַיִט 919
צִפּוֹר 1079
צְפַר Ch. 1080

fowler
יָקוּשׁ 558
יָקוֹשׁ 558
יָקֹשׁ Kal 559

fox
שׁוּעָל 1247

frail
חָדֵל 403

frame
יֵצֶר ... 557
מִבְנֶה ... 661

frame, to
יָצַר Kal ... 556
כּוּן Hiphil ... 592
נָתַן Kal ... 851
צָמַד Hiphil ... 1074

framed, thing
יֵצֶר ... 557

frankincense
לְבוֹנָה ... 631

fraud
תֹּךְ ... 1346

fray, to
חָרַד Hiphil ... 462

fray away, to
חָרַד Hiphil ... 462

freckled, *see* spot

free
חִנָּם ... 446
חָפְשִׁי ... 453
נָדִיב ... 796
נָקִי ... 838
פָּטִיר ... 1017
פָּטַר Kal ... 1017

free, to be
חָפַשׁ Pual ... 453
נָקָה Niphal ... 838

free, to let go
פָּתַח Piel ... 1052

free offering
נְדָבָה ... 795

freed, to be
כָּרַת Niphal ... 618

freedom
חֻפְשָׁה ... 453

freely
חִנָּם ... 446
נְדָבָה ... 795

freely, *see* offer

freely is sometimes the translation of an infinitive used intensitively.

freewill, to be minded of one's own
נְדַב Ch. Ithpael ... 795

freewill offering
נְדַב Ch. Ithpael ... 795
נְדָבָה ... 795

fresh
חָדָשׁ ... 403
לְשַׁד ... 651

fresh, to be
רֻטֲפַשׁ ... 1171

fret, to
זָעַף Kal ... 391
רָגַז Kal ... 1155

fret inward
פְּחֶתֶת ... 1017

fret, to make to
רָעַם Hiphil ... 1186

fret selves, to
חָרָה Hithpael ... 462
קָצַף Hithpael ... 1115

fretting
מָאַר Hiphil ... 659

fried
רָבַךְ Hophal ... 1154

fried, that which is
רָבַךְ Hophal ... 1154

friend
אָהֵב / אָהַב } Kal ... 25
אִישׁ ... 60
אַלּוּף / אַלֻּף } ... 94
מֵרֵעַ ... 765
רֵיעַ ... 1172
רֵעַ ... 1181
רֵעֶה ... 1185

friend †
שָׁלוֹם ... 1263

friend, *see* familiar

friend, to use as
רָעָה Piel ... 1184

friend*ly*
לֵב ... 626

friendly, to shew self
רָעַע Hithpolel ... 1186

* friends
מְתִים ... 779

friendship with, to make
רָעָה Hithpael ... 1184

fringe
צִיצִת ... 1071

fringes
גְּדִלִים ... 298

* fro
שׁוּב Kal ... 1238

fro, *see* driven, go, going, reel, removing, run, running, to, tossed, tossings, walk to

frog
צְפַרְדֵּעַ ... 1080

from
אָז ... 34
אַחַר ... 48
אֶל ... 78
אֵצֶל ... 148
אֵת ... 182
בִּלְתִּי ... 231
דַּי ... 339
מוּל ... 671
מִן ... 731
מִן Ch. ... 732
עַל ... 932
עַל Ch. ... 933
עִם ... 955
עִם Ch. ... 955
עִמָּד ... 958
פָּנִים ... 1023
קֳדָם ... 1089

* from
יָד ... 489
נֶגֶד ... 790
עֵבֶר ... 899

from †
פָּנִים ... 1023

* from †
בֵּין ... 212
קֳדָם Ch. ... 1089

from, *see* away, back, cometh, go, turn

from among
מִן ... 731
עִם ... 955

from beside
אֵצֶל ... 148

from between
עִם ... 955

from off
עַל ... 932

from the midst
בֵּין ... 212

from whence †
אֲשֶׁר ... 180

front
פָּנִים ... 1023

front, *see* forefront

frontier
קָצֶה ... 1114

frontlets
טוֹטָפוֹת ... 480

frost
חֲנָמַל ... 446
קֶרַח ... 1128

frost, *see* hoary

froward
הֲפַכְפַּךְ ... 370
לוּן Niphal ... 635
עִקֵּשׁ ... 975
פָּתַל Niphal ... 1055
תַּהְפֻּכוֹת ... 1337

*froward
עִקְּשׁוּת ... 975

froward, to shew self
פָּתַל Hithpael ... 1055

froward things
תַּהְפֻּכוֹת ... 1337

froward, very
תַּהְפֻּכוֹת ... 1337

frowardly
שׁוֹבָב ... 1245

frowardness
תַּהְפֻּכוֹת ... 1337

frozen, to be
לָכַד Hithpael ... 642

fruit
אֵב 8
אֵב Ch. 8
יְבוּל 486
יֶלֶד 530
לֶחֶם 638
מַאֲכָל 658
מְלֵאָה 703
נוּב 799
נִיב 813
פְּרִי 1045
תְּבוּאָה 1335
תְּנוּבָה 1352
fruit, *see* cast, first ripe, hasty, new, summer, sycomore
fruit, best
זִמְרָה 389
fruit, to bring
פָּרָה Kal 1044
fruit, to bring forth
נוּב Kal 799
fruit, first of ripe
מְלֵאָה 703
fruitful
יֶרַע 396
פָּרָה Kal 1044
fruit*ful*
פְּרִי 1045
* fruitful
שֶׁמֶן 1290
fruitful, to be
פָּרָא Hiphil 1043
פָּרָה Kal 1044
fruitful, to cause to be
פָּרָה Hiphil 1044
fruitful field
כַּרְמֶל 618
fruitful, to make
פָּרָה Hiphil 1044
fruitful place
כַּרְמֶל 618
*** fruitful,† very**
בֵּן 232
fruits
כֹּחַ 594
fruits, *see* precious
frustrate, to
פָּרַר Hiphil 1048
fryingpan
מַרְחֶשֶׁת 764
fuel
אָכְלָה 75
מַאֲכֹלֶת 658
fugitive
בְּרִיחַ 272
מִבְרָח 661
נוּעַ Kal 802
נָפַל Kal 825
פָּלִיט 1020

fulfil, to
בָּצַע Piel 263
כָּלָה Piel 598
מָלֵא Kal 701
מָלֵא Piel 701
עָשָׂה Kal 981
fulfilled, to be
כָּלָה Kal 598
מָלֵא Kal 701
מָלֵא Niphal 701
סוּף Ch. P'al 872
full
מָלֵא 703
מְלֹא 703
רַב 1147
שָׂבֵעַ 1196
שָׂבָע 1196
שָׁלֵם Piel 1277
שָׁלֵם 1278
תָּם 1348
תָּמִים 1350
* full
יוֹם 508
full, *see* age, branches, ears, end, feed, filled, weight
full, to be
מָלֵא Kal 701
מָלֵא Niphal 701
מְלָא Ch. Ithpael 703
שָׂבֵעַ / שָׂבַע } Kal 1195
full, to become
מָלֵא Kal 701
full, to be come to the
תָּמַם Hiphil 1351
* full, to draw
מָלֵא Piel 701
full ears, *see* corn
full of
שָׂבֵעַ 1196
full of, to be
רָבָה Hiphil 1151
שָׂבֵעַ / שָׂבַע } Kal 1195
full of, *see* compassion, heaviness, labour, marrow
full tale, to give in
מָלֵא Piel 701
* full, that whereof was
מְלֹא 703
full, till be
שָׂבְעָה 1196
full, to the
שָׂבֵעַ / שָׂבַע } Kal 1195
full year
יוֹם 508

fuller
כָּבַס Kal 584
כָּבַס Piel 584
fully
כָּלָה Piel 598
מָלֵא 703
נָגַד Hophal 788
fully, to go
מָלֵא Piel 701
fully set, to be
מָלֵא Kal 701
fulness
מְלֹא / מָלֵא } Kal 701
מָלֵא Piel 701
מְלֹא 703
מְלֵאָה 703
שֹׂבַע 1196
שָׂבְעָה 1196
furbish, to
מָרַט Kal 764
מָרַק Kal 766
furbished
מָרַט Pual 764
furious
חֵמָה 437
* furious †
בַּעַל 262
furious, to be
קְצַף Ch. P'al 1116
furiously
חֵמָה 437
שִׁגָּעוֹן 1236
furnace
אַתּוּן Ch. 183
כִּבְשָׁן 586
כּוּר 594
עֲלִיל 942
תַּנּוּר 1352
* furnish †
כְּלִי 600
furnish, to
מָלֵא Piel 701
נָשָׂא Piel 840
עָנַק Hiphil 967
עָרַךְ Kal 978
עָשָׂה Kal 981
furniture
כְּלִי 600
כַּר 615
furrow
גְּדוּד 293
(כ׳) מַעֲנָה 745
מַעֲנִית 745
עוֹנָה 911
(כ׳) עַיִן 919

שָׁמַע / שָׁמֵעַ } Piel 1292

* gather together, to
יָסַף Hiphil 543

gather up, to
לָקַט Piel 650
קָבַץ Kal 1084
קָבַץ Piel 1084

gathered, to be
אָסַף Niphal 141
אָסַף Pual 141
גּוּר Kal 303
זָעַק Niphal 391
לָקַט Pual 650
לָקַט Hithpael 650
קָבַץ Niphal 1084
קָבַץ Pual 1084
קָהַל Niphal 1094
קָוָה Niphal 1095

gathered together, to be
אָסַף Niphal 141
אָסַף Pual 141
אָסַף Hithpael 141
זָעַק Niphal 391
יָעַד Niphal 545
כְּנַשׁ Ch. Ithpael 606
סָפַח Pual 881
עָרַם[2] Niphal 979
צָעַק Niphal 1077
קָבַץ Niphal 1084
קָבַץ Hithpael 1084
קָהַל Niphal 1094
קָוָה Niphal 1095
קָלָה Niphal 1108

gathered together, is to be
קָהַל Hiphil 1094

gathered up again, to be
אָסַף Niphal 141

gatherer
בָּלַס Kal 230

gatherer, see grape

gathering
אֹסֶף 143
יִקְּהָה 557

gathering together
מִקְוֶה 756

gaze, to
רָאָה Kal 1133

gazingstock
רֹאִי 1141

Gebim
גֵּב 287

gender, to
יָלַד Kal 527
עָבַר Piel 895

gender, to let
רָבַע[1] Hiphil 1154

genealogies, *see* reckoned

genealogies, to be reckoned by
יָחַשׂ Kal 523

genealogy
יָחַשׂ Hithpael 523
יַחַשׂ 523

genealogy, *see* number

genealogy, to be reckoned
יָחַשׂ Hithpael 523

general
שַׂר 1214

generally
אָסַף Niphal 141

generally, is sometimes the translation of an infinitive used intensitively.

generation
דּוֹר 337
דָּר Ch. 348

generations
תּוֹלְדוֹת 1341

Gentile
גּוֹי 299

gentleness
עָנָה[2] Kal 964
עֲנָוָה 965
עַנְוָה 965

gently
אַט 54

gently, *see* lead

gerah
גֵּרָה 315

get, to
בּוֹא Kal 189
בּוֹא Hiphil 189
בָּצַע Kal 263
בָּקַשׁ Piel 268
יָלַךְ Kal 531
לָקַח Kal 644
מָצָא Kal 748
נוּד Kal 799
נָסַע Kal 821
נָשַׂג Hiphil 845
עָשָׂה Kal 981
פּוּק[2] Hiphil 1015
קָנָה[1] Kal 1111
רָכַשׁ Kal 1175
שׂוּם / שִׂים } Kal 1200

get, *see* deceitfully, early, far, heat, possession, stealth, understanding, victory

get, to be able to
נָשַׂג Hiphil 845

get away, to (מלט Niph. 709)
יָלַךְ Kal 531
יָצָא Kal 548
נוּד Ch. P'al 800

get, ean
נָשַׂג Hiphil 845

get down, to
יָרַד Kal 561

get forth, to
יָצָא Kal 548

get hence, to
יָלַךְ Kal 531
יָצָא Kal 548

get him, to
אָסַף Niphal 141

get (him), to
יָלַךְ Kal 531

get hold upon, to
מָצָא Kal 748

get honour, to
כָּבֵד / כָּבַד } Niphal 581

get more, to
יָסַף Hiphil 543

get (*oneself*) again, to
שׁוּב Kal 1238

get (*oneself*) back again, to
שׁוּב Kal 1238

get (*oneself*) up, to
רָכַב Kal 1173
רָמַם Niphal 1176

get out, to
יָצָא Kal 548

get over, to
עָבַר Kal 895

get thee, to
הָלַךְ Kal 362

get up, to
נָגַע Kal 792
עָלָה Kal 934
עָלָה Niphal 934
קוּם Kal 1099

get (*you*)
סוּר Kal 872

getting
פֹּעַל 1038
קִנְיָן 1112

ghost
נֶפֶשׁ 829

ghost, to give up the
גָּוַע Kal 302

giant
גִּבּוֹר 289
רָפָא 1188
רָפָה 1188

giants
נְפִילִים 825

Gibeah
גִּבְעָה 291

Giblites
גִּבְלִי 291

gier-eagle
רָחָם 1169
רָחָמָה 1169

gift
אֶשְׁכָּר ... 178
מִנְחָה ... 734
מַשְׂאֵת ... 767
מַתָּן ... 780
מַתְּנָא Ch. ... 780
מַתָּנָה ... 780
מַתַּת ... 780
נֵדֶה ... 796
נָדָן ... 797
נִשֵּׂאת ... 845
שֹׁחַד ... 1249
תְּרוּמָה ... 1357

gifts, *see* giveth

gin
מוֹקֵשׁ ... 674
פַּח ... 1016

gird, to
אָזַר Kal ... 36
אָסַר Kal ... 143
אָפַד Kal ... 146
חֲגוֹרָה ... 401
חָגַר Kal ... 401

gird about, to
חָבַשׁ Kal ... 400

gird self, to
אָזַר Hithpael ... 36

gird up, to
אָזַר Kal ... 36
שָׁנַס Piel ... 1315

gird with, to
אָזַר Piel ... 36

girded, to be
אָזַר Kal ... 36
אָזַר Niphal ... 36

girded with
חָגוּר ... 401

girding
מַחֲגֹרֶת ... 686

girdle
אַבְנֵט ... 13
אֵזוֹר ... 34
חֲגוֹר ... 401
חֲגוֹרָה ... 401
מֵזַח / מְזִחַ } ... 684

girdle, curious
חֵשֶׁב ... 469

girl
יַלְדָּה ... 531

Gittith
גִּתִּית ... 317

give, to
בּוֹא Hiphil ... 189
דִּבֶּר Piel ... 319
הָפַךְ Kal ... 370
חָלַק Kal ... 435
יָהַב Kal ... 507
יְהַב Ch. P'al ... 507
יָטַב Hiphil ... 524
מַתַּת ... 780
נָשָׂא Piel ... 840
נָתַן Kal ... 851
נְתַן Ch. P'al ... 863
רוּם Hiphil ... 1163
שׂוּם / שִׂים } Kal ... 1200
שׂוּם Ch. P'al ... 1204

* give, to
מָשַׁךְ Kal ... 770
שׁוּב Hiphil ... 1238
שָׁלַח Kal ... 1268

give, *see* account, answer, charge, commandment, counsel, drink, ear, eat, few, flattering titles, heed, inherit, knowledge, leave, less, life, many, more, name, passage, pledges, possess, power, praise, provender, quietness, respite, rest, reward, shout, sixth part, skill, speedily, stripes, suck, thanks, understanding, warning, witness

give again, to
שׁוּב Hiphil ... 1238
שָׁלֵם Piel ... 1277

give commandment, to
אָמַר Kal ... 105

give *counsel*, to
יָעַץ Kal ... 547

give for, *see* inheritance

give forth, to
נָתַן Kal ... 851

give, graciously to
חָנַן Kal ... 446

give *light*, to
אוֹר Hiphil ... 32
הָלַל Hiphil ... 366

give *meat*, to
בָּרָה Hiphil ... 270

give moreover, to
יָסַף Hiphil ... 543

give *names*, to
קָרָא[1] Kal ... 1117

give occasion, *see* blaspheme

give over, to
נָתַן Kal ... 851
סָגַר Hiphil ... 869
סָכַר[1] Piel ... 876

give place, to
נָגַשׁ Kal ... 794

give to, *see* inherit, possess

give to eat, to
אָכַל Hiphil ... 70

give up, to
נָפַח Kal ... 825
נָתַן Kal ... 851
סָגַר Hiphil ... 869
שָׁלַח Piel ... 1268

give up, *see* ghost

give willingly, to
נָדַב Kal ... 795

give *wounds*, to
נָכָה Hiphil ... 814

given, *see* marriage

given, to be
יְהַב Ch. Ithp'al ... 507
נָתַן Niphal ... 851
נָתַן Hophal ... 851
שׂוּם Ch. Ithp'al ... 1204

* given, to be
נָתַן Kal ... 851

given, that which he hath
גְּמוּל ... 311

given to, *see* change, pleasures

given to *covetousness*
בָּצַע Kal ... 263

given to it, those that are
בַּעַל ... 262

given up, to be
נָתַן Niphal ... 851

given, (wounds) to be
נָכָה Hiphil ... 814

giver, *see* usury

giveth gifts
מַתָּן ... 780

giving
נָתַן Kal ... 851

giving, *see* drink

giving up
מַפָּח ... 747

glad
טוֹב ... 476
שָׂמֵחַ ... 1209

glad, to be
גּוּל / גִּיל } Kal ... 306
טְאֵב Ch. P'al ... 473
יָטַב Kal ... 524
שׂוּשׂ / שִׂישׂ } Kal ... 1204
שָׂמַח / שָׂמֵחַ } Kal ... 1208
שָׂמֵחַ ... 1209

glad, to make
חָדָה Piel ... 402
שִׂמַּח / שִׂמֵּחַ } Piel ... 1208

gladness
גִּיל ... 306
חֶדְוָה ... 402
טוֹב ... 479
רִנָּה ... 1176
שִׂמְחָה ... 1210
שָׂשׂוֹן ... 1219

glass
גִּלָּיוֹן ... 310

glass, *see* looking

glass, looking
מַרְאָה 761

glean, to
לָקַט Kal 650
לָקַט Piel 650
עָלַל Poel 942

gleaning
לֶקֶט 651

gleaning, *see* grapes

gleaning of the grapes
עֹלֵלוֹת 943

glede
רָאָה 1141

glistering
פּוּךְ 1014

glitter
בָּרָק 277

glittering
בָּרָק 277
לַהַב 634

glittering, *see* sword

gloominess
אֲפֵלָה 147

glorified, to be
כָּבֵד, כָּבַד } Kal 581
כָּבֵד, כָּבַד } Niphal 581
פָּאַר Hithpael 1009

glorify, to
הֲדַר Ch. Pael 357
כָּבֵד, כָּבַד } Piel 581
כָּבֵד, כָּבַד } Hiphil 581
פָּאַר Piel 1009

glorify self, to
פָּאַר Hithpael 1009

glorious
אַדִּיר 17
אָדַר Niphal 24
אוֹר Niphal 32
הָדַר Kal 357
הָדָר 357
הוֹד 358
כָּבֵד, כָּבַד } Niphal 581
כָּבוֹד 583
צְבִי 1060
תִּפְאָרָה, תִּפְאֶרֶת } 1354

glorious, to be
כָּבֵד, כָּבַד } Niphal 581

glorious, all
כְּבוּדָּה 584

glorious, to become
אָדַר Niphal 24

glorious, to be made
כָּבֵד, כָּבַד } Kal 581

glorious, to make
כָּבֵד, כָּבַד } Piel 581

glorious things
כָּבֵד, כָּבַד } Niphal 581

gloriously
גָּאָה Kal 285
כָּבוֹד 583

glory
אַדֶּרֶת 24
הָדָר 357
הֶדֶר 358
הוֹד 358
טְהָר 475
יְקָר Ch. 558
כָּבוֹד 583
צְבִי 1060
תִּפְאָרָה, תִּפְאֶרֶת } 1354

glory †
דָּבָר 325

glory, to
הָלַל Hithpael 366
כָּבֵד, כָּבַד } Niphal 581
פָּאַר Hithpael 1009
שָׁבַח Hithpael 1225

glutton
זָלַל Kal 388

gnash, to
חָרַק Kal 466

gnaw the bone, to
גָּרַם Kal 316

*go
צַעַד 1076
תַּהֲלוּכָה 1337

go, to
אֲזַל Ch. P'al 35
אָרַח Kal 154
אָשַׁר Kal 180
אָשַׁר Piel 180
בּוֹא Kal 189
דָּרַךְ Kal 349
הוּךְ Ch. P'al 359
הָלַךְ Kal 362
הָלַךְ Piel 362
הָלַךְ Hithpael 362
יָלַךְ Kal 531
יָלַךְ Hiphil 531
נָסַע Kal 821
סוּר Kal 872
עָבַר Kal 895
עָלָה Kal 934
עָלָה Hiphil 934
פָּשַׁע Kal 1050
צָעַד Kal 1076
קָרַב Kal 1123
שׁוּט[2] Kal 1246
שׁוּר[1] Kal 1248

go, *see* armed, astray, captive, captivity, forward, free, fully, ill, let, letting, near, nigh, right on, well, well with, whoring

go, able to
יָצָא Kal 548

go about, to
הָלַךְ Kal 362
חָמַק Hithpael 440
סָבַב Niphal 865
סָבַב Poel 865
סָחַר Kal 874
עָשָׂה Kal 981
שׁוּט[2] Kal 1246

go abroad, to
הָלַךְ Hithpael 362
יָצָא Kal 548

go again, to
שׁוּב Kal 1238

go along, to
הָלַךְ Kal 362

go aside, to
שָׂטָה Kal 1205

go astray, to
נָדַח Niphal 796
שָׁגַג Kal 1235
שָׁגָה Kal 1236

go astray, to cause to
שָׁגָה Hiphil 1236

go away, to
הָלַךְ Kal 362
יָלַךְ Kal 531
נָסַע Kal 821
נָסַע Niphal 821
עָבַר Kal 895
עָלָה Kal 934
פָּנָה Kal 1021

go back, to
מוּשׁ[1] Hiphil 674
סוּג[1] Kal 870
פָּרַע Kal 1046
שׁוּב Kal 1238

go before, to
קָדַם Piel 1088

go beyond, to
עָבַר Kal 895

go by, to
עָבַר Kal 895

go captive, to
גָּלָה Kal 307

gods
אֱלֹהִים 79
goeth up, that
מַעֲלֶה 744
goeth, where...
מָבוֹא 660
going
אֲשֻׁר 181
הֲלִיכָה 362
יָלַךְ Kal................ 531
מַעְגָּלָה 740
מִצְעָד 755
עָבַר Kal 895
פַּעַם 1038
צַעַד 1076
צְעָדָה 1076
going about
נָקַף Hiphil 839
going down
בּוֹא Kal 189
יָרַד Kal 561
מָבוֹא 660
מוֹרָד 674
מֶעָל Ch.............. 743
going forth
מוֹצָא 673
תּוֹצָאוֹת 1342
going out
יָצָא Kal 548
מוֹצָא 673
תּוֹצָאוֹת 1342
going over
עָבַר Kal 895
going to or fro
שׁוּט [2] Kal 1246
going up
מַעֲלֶה 744
עָלָה Kal.............. 934
עֲלִיָּה 941
goings forth
מוֹצָאוֹת 673
gold
בְּצַר 264
בֶּצֶר 264
דְּהַב Ch.............. 336
זָהָב 380
חָרוּץ 463
כֶּתֶם 623
סְגוֹר 869
gold, *see* fine gold
gold, fine
כֶּתֶם 623
פָּז 1015
gold, pure
כֶּתֶם 623
פָּז 1015
golden
דְּהַב Ch.............. 336
זָהָב 380
golden city
מַדְהֵבָה 666
golden wedge
כֶּתֶם 623
goldsmith
צָרַף Kal 1082
צֹרְפִי 1082
gone, *see* all, clean
gone, be
מְדַד 666
gone, to be
אֲזַד Ch. P'al 34
אֲזַל Kal.............. 35
אַיִן 59
גָּלָה Kal.............. 307
הָלַךְ Kal.............. 362
הָלַךְ Niphal 362
יָלַךְ Kal.............. 531
נָטָה Kal.............. 810
עָבַר Kal.............. 895
gone about, to be
נָקַף Hiphil........... 839
gone aside, to be
סוּר Kal.............. 872
gone away, to be
זוּר [2] Niphal 384
נוּעַ Kal.............. 802
gone back, to be
שׁוּב Kal.............1238
gone out, that which is
מוֹצָא 673
gone out, thing that is
מוֹצָא 673
good
חָסִיד 449
טָב Ch.............. 473
טוֹב 476
טוּב 479
כִּשְׁרוֹן 621
מְאֹד 652
good, *see* advice, courage, do, heed, liking, piece, proper, think, tidings, way, what
good, to be
טוֹב Kal.............. 476
יָטַב Kal.............. 524
צָלַח Kal.............1072
good, can do
יָעַל Hiphil 456
good courage, to be of
אָמֵץ Kal.............. 104
good deed
חֶסֶד 448
טוֹב 476
good, to do
טוֹב Hiphil 476
יָטַב Hiphil 524
good health
שָׁלוֹם 1263
good, to make
יָטַב Hiphil 524
קוּם Hiphil ..... .1099
שָׁלַם Piel.............1277
good pleasure
רָצוֹן 1189
good, to seem
טוֹב Kal.............. 476
יְטַב Ch. P'al......... 524
יָשַׁר Kal.............. 578
good speed, to send
קָרָה Hiphil 1127
good success, to have
שָׂכַל Hiphil 1206
good thing
טוּב 479
good way off, a
רָחַק Hiphil 1170
good while
עוֹד 905
good will
רָצוֹן 1189
goodlier
טוֹב 476
goodliest
טוֹב 476
goodliness
חֶסֶד 448
goodly
אַדִּיר 17
אֶדֶר 24
אַדֶּרֶת 24
הָדָר 357
הוֹד 358
חֶמְדָּה 437
חֲמוּדוֹת 438
טוֹב Kal.............. 476
טוֹב 476
מַחְמָד 687
מַרְאֶה 761
פְּאֵר 1009
צְבִי 1060
שֶׁפֶר 1322
תֹּאַר 1334
*goodly
אֵל 76
רְנָנִים 1177
שָׁפַר Kal..............1322
goodly †
יָפֶה 548
תֹּאַר 1334
goodly, *see* castle
goodly, to make
טוֹב Hiphil 476
goodman
אִישׁ 60
goodness
חֶסֶד 448

טוֹב 476
טוּב 479

goods
אוֹן 31
חַיִל 423
טוֹב 476
טוּב 479
מְלָאכָה 705
נִכְסִין Ch. 818
קִנְיָן 1112
רְכוּשׁ 1174

gopher
גֹּפֶר 314

gore, to
נָגַח Kal 791

goageously, most
מִכְלוֹל 699

gotten, *see* hastily

gotten, to be
אָסַף Niphal 141
נָתַן Hophal 851

gotten hastily, to be
בָּהַל Pual 208

gourd
קִיקָיוֹן 1108

gourds
פַּקֻּעֹת 1042

govern, to
חָבַשׁ Kal 400
נָחָה Hiphil 804
עָשָׂה Kal 981

government
מֶמְשָׁלָה 731
מִשְׂרָה 767

governor
אַלּוּף } אַלֻּף } 94
חָקַק Kal 458
חָקַק Poel 458
מָשַׁל[1] Kal 771
נָגִיד 791
נָשִׂיא 846
פֶּחָה 1016
פֶּחָה Ch. 1016
פָּקִיד (פקד .. 1041) 1042
שַׂר 1214
שַׁלִּיט 1275

governor, chief
נָגִיד 791

governors
סְגָנִין Ch. 869

grace
חֵן 444
תְּחִנָּה 1345

gracious
חֵן 444
חַנּוּן 445

gracious, to be
חָנַן Kal 446
חָנַן Niphal 446

gracious to, to be
חָנַן Piel 446

graciously
טוֹב 476

graciously, *see* deal, give, grant

graciously, to deal
חָנַן Kal 446

grain, least
צְרוֹר 1082

grant
רִשְׁיוֹן 1192

grant, to
בּוֹא Hiphil 189
נָתַן Kal 851
עָשָׂה Kal 981

grant graciously, to
חָנַן Kal 447

granted, to be
נָתַן Niphal 851

grape
פֶּרֶט 1045

grape, *see* gather, sour, unripe

grape, tender
סְמָדַר 879

grapegatherer
בָּצַר Kal 264

grapegleanings
עֹלֵלוֹת 943

grapes
עֹלֵלוֹת 943
עֵנָב 962

grapes, *see* cluster, gleaning

grapes, gleaning
עֹלֵלוֹת 943

grapes, ripe
עֵנָב 962

grapes, wild
בְּאֻשִׁים 184

grass
דֶּשֶׁא 355
חָצִיר 455
יֶרֶק 566
עֵשֶׂב 981
עֲשַׂב Ch. 981

grass, *see* mown

grass, at
דֶּשֶׁא 355

grass, tender
דֶּשֶׁא 355
דִּתְאָ Ch. 355

grasshopper
אַרְבֶּה 149
גּוֹב 299
חָגָב 401

* grasshopper, great
גּוֹב 299

grate
מִכְבָּר 698

grave
בְּעִי 261
קְבוּרָה 1083
קֶבֶר 1086
שְׁאוֹל 1220
שַׁחַת 1253

grave, to
חָקַק Kal 458
פָּסַל Kal 1037
פָּתַח Piel 1052

grave,† to
פִּתּוּחַ 1052

gravel
חָצָץ 455
מָעָה 740

gravel stone
חָצָץ 455

graven
חָרַשׁ Kal 466
חָרַת Kal 468
פָּתַח Pual 1052

graven, to be
חָצַב } חָצֵב } Niphal 453

graven, are
פִּתּוּחַ 1052

graven image
פֶּסֶל 1037

graven images
פְּסִילִים 1037

graving
מִקְלַעַת 759
פִּתּוּחַ 1052

graving tool
חֶרֶט 463

gray hairs
שֵׂיבָה 1205

grayheaded
שִׂיב Kal 1205
שֵׂיבָה 1205

grayheaded, to be
שִׂיב Kal 1205

grease
חֵלֶב 429

great
אָצִיל 148
בַּעַל 262
גְּבוּל (כ') 288
גָּדוֹל 293
גֹּדֶל 297
גְּלָל Ch. 310
זָנָה Kal 389
חוּל } חִיל } Kal 406

כָּבֵד / כָּבַד } Piel ... 581
כָּבֵד ... 582
מְאֹד ... 652
מַרְבֶּה ... 761
נָאַץ Piel ... 782
עָצוּם ... 972
עָשָׂה Kal ... 981
רַב ... 1147
רַב Ch. ... 1150
רֹב ... 1150
רָבָה Hiphil ... 1151
רַבְרַב Ch. ... 1154
שַׂגִּיא ... 1197
שַׂגִּיא Ch. ... 1197

* great
אֵל ... 76
אֱלֹהִים ... 79
הָרָה ... 375
הָרִי ... 464
מַר ... 760
רָבָה Hiphil ... 1151
רַע ... 1177

great, *see* delight, do, drought, flame, forces, grasshopper, hailstones, how, lion, man, mercies, owl, pain, power, so, stature, teeth, toe, very, while to come, wonders, multitude

great, to be
גָּבַר Kal ... 291
גָּדַל Kal ... 297
עָצַם Kal ... 972

* great as would contain
בַּיִת ... 214

great, to become
גָּדַל Kal ... 297
גָּדַל Hiphil ... 297

great *cattle*
בָּקָר ... 266

great estate, to be come to
גָּדַל Hiphil ... 297

great *fear*
פַּחַד ... 1016

great, to give
גָּדַל Hiphil ... 297

great hail*stones*
אֶלְגָּבִישׁ ... 78

great height, *see* raise up

great lord
שָׁלִישׁ ... 1275

great, to make
גָּדַל Piel ... 297
גָּדַל Hiphil ... 297
רָבָה Hiphil ... 1151

great man
אִישׁ ... 60
גָּדוֹל ... 293
רַב ... 1147

great man, to make a
רְבָה Ch. Pael ... 1153

great, man of
גֹּרָל (כ') ... 316

great matter
גָּדוֹל ... 293

great measure
שָׁלִישׁ ... 1275

great number
כֹּבֶד ... 583
רֹב ... 1150

great one
רַב ... 1147

great owl
יַנְשׁוּף ... 542

great thing
גָּדוֹל ... 293
גְּדוּלָּה / גְּדֻלָּה } ... 296

great things
רְבוּ / רְבוֹא } (כ') ... 1153
רַבְרַב Ch. ... 1154

great *things*, to do
גָּדַל Hiphil ... 297

great things,† to do
גָּדַל Hiphil ... 297

great things, very
רַבְרַב Ch. ... 1154

* great toe †
רֶגֶל ... 1155

great, very
כָּבֵד / כָּבַד } Piel ... 581

great, to wax
גָּדַל Kal ... 297
גָּדַל Hiphil ... 297

great with young, *see* ewes

greater
גָּדוֹל ... 293

* greater †
הָלַךְ Kal ... 362

greater, *see* much

greater, to be
גָּדַל Kal ... 297
רָבָה Kal ... 1151

greater, to be much
רָבָה Kal ... 1151

greatest part
מַרְבִּית ... 762

greatly
מְאֹד ... 652
רַב ... 1147
רֹב ... 1150
שַׂגִּיא Ch. ... 1197

* greatly
בֹּשֶׁת ... 280
גִּיל ... 306

greatly, *see* beloved, desire, rejoice

greatly is sometimes the translation of infinitives used intensitively.

greatly *feared*, thing
פַּחַד ... 1016

greatly rejoice, to
רָנַן Piel ... 1177

greatness
גָּדוֹל ... 293
גְּדוּלָּה / גְּדֻלָּה } ... 296
גֹּדֶל ... 297
מַרְבִּית ... 762
רֹב ... 1150
רְבוּ Ch. ... 1153

* greatness
רָבָה Kal ... 1151

greaves
מִצְחָה ... 754

Grecian
בֵּן ... 232

* greedily
תַּאֲוָה ... 1334

greedily, *see* gain

greedy
בָּצַע Kal ... 263

greedy †
נֶפֶשׁ ... 829
עַז ... 914

greedy, to be
כָּסַף Kal ... 609

green
דֶּשֶׁא ... 355
יָרָק ... 566
יֶרֶק ... 566
כַּרְפַּס ... 618
לַח ... 636
רָטֹב ... 1171
רַעֲנָן ... 1186

green, *see* ears, ears of corn, fig

green thing
יָרוֹק ... 564
יֶרֶק ... 566

greenish
יְרַקְרַק ... 566

greenness
אֵב ... 8

greet,† to
שָׁאַל Kal ... 1220
שָׁלוֹם ... 1263

grew
גָּדַל ... 297

grew upon, that which
צֶמַח ... 1075

grew, where
צֶמַח ... 1075

* greyhound
זַרְזִיר ... 395
מָתְנַיִם ... 780

grey head
שֵׂיבָה 1205

grief
חָלָה Niphal 429
חֳלִי 431
יָגוֹן 488
כְּאֵב 581
כַּעַס 612
כַּעַשׂ 612
מַכְאוֹב 698
מֹרָה 763
פּוּקָה 1015
רַע 1177

grief, to cause
יָגָה [1] Hiphil 488

grief, to put to
חָלָה Hiphil 429

grievance
עָמָל 960

grieve, to
אָדַב Hiphil 14
חוּל / חִיל } Kal 406
חָרָה Kal 462
יָגָה [1] Piel 488
לָאָה Niphal 626
עָגַם Kal 901
עָצַב Kal 970
עָצַב Hiphil 970

grieved, to be
חִיל / חוּל } Hithpalpel 406
חָלָה Kal 429
חָלָה Niphal 429
חָמֵץ Hithpael 440
יָרַע Kal 566
כָּאָה Niphal 581
כָּעַס Kal 612
כְּרָא Ch. Ithp'el 616
לָאָה Kal 626
מָרַר Kal 766
עָצַב Niphal 970
עָצַב Hithpael 970
קוּט [1] Kal 1096
קוּט [1] Hithpolel 1096
קוּץ [3] Kal 1104
קָצַר Kal 1116

grieved, to have sorely
מָרַר Piel 766

grieved, it
עָצַב Hithpael 970

grieveth, it
מָרַר Kal 766

grieving
כָּאַב Hiphil 581

grievous
חוּל / חִיל } Hithpolel 406
חָלָה Niphal 429
כָּבֵד 582
מָרַץ Niphal 765
סוּר Kal 872
עֶצֶב 971
קָשֶׁה 1131
רַע 1177
תַּחֲלֻאִים 1345

grievous, to be
חוּל / חִיל } Kal 406
חָלָה Niphal 429
יָרַע Kal 566
כָּבֵד / כָּבַד } Kal 581

grievous, to make
קָשָׁה Hiphil 1131

grievous things
עָתָק 1008

grievously
חֵטְא 415
מַעַל 743
מָרָה Kal 762

grievously, *see* afflict, fall

grievousness
כֹּבֶד 583
עָמָל 960

grind, to
טְחוֹן 480
טָחַן Kal 480

grinder
טָחַן Kal 480

grinding
טַחֲנָה 480

grisled
בָּרֹד 270

groan, to
אָנַח Niphal 139
אָנַק Kal 141
נָאַק Kal 782

groaning
אֲנָחָה 139
אֲנָקָה 141
נְאָקָה 782

grope, to
גָּשַׁשׁ Piel 317
מָשַׁשׁ Piel 779

gross, *see* darkness

ground
אֲדָמָה 21
אֶרֶץ 157
חֶלְקָה 436
חָרִישׁ 464
עָפָר 968
שָׂדֶה 1197

ground, *see* corn, dry, fallow, parched

grounded
מוּסָדָה 671

grove
אֵשֶׁל 178
אֲשֵׁרָה / אֲשֵׁירָה } 181

grow, to
גָּדַל Kal 297
דָּגָה Kal 335
יָלַךְ Kal 531
יָצָא Kal 548
יָצַק Kal 556
עָלָה Kal 934
פָּרָה Kal 1044
פָּרַח Kal 1045
פָּרַץ Kal 1047
צָמַח Kal 1074
רְבָה Ch. P'al 1153
שָׂגָה Kal 1197
שְׂגָא Ch. P'al 1197

grow again, to
צָמַח Piel 1074

grow, to cause to
צָמַח Hiphil 1074

grow long, to
שָׁלַח Piel 1268

grow, to make
גָּדַל Piel 297

grow, to make to
צָמַח Hiphil 1074
שׂוּג [2] Pilpel 1200

grow of themselves, such things as
סָפִיחַ 881

grow, things which
סָפִיחַ 881

grow to an end, to
חָנָה Kal 445

grow up, to
נָאָה Kal 285
חָלַף Kal 434
פּוּשׁ Kal 1015
צָמַח Kal 1074
רָבָה Kal 1151
000...... 000
שָׁלַף Kal 1279

grow up, to cause to
צָמַח Hiphil 1074

groweth of its own accord, which
סָפִיחַ 881

groweth of itself, which
סָפִיחַ 881

grown, *see* thick

grown, to be
גָּדַל Kal 297
צָמַח Piel 1074
רְבָה Ch. P'al 1153

grown fat to be
פּוּשׁ Kal ... 1015

grown over, to be
עָלָה Kal ... 934

grown up
קָמָה ... 1110

grown up, to be
גָּדַל Kal ... 297
גָּדַל Pual ... 297
צָמַח Kal ... 1074

grown up, not
אֲפִילֹת ... 146

growth, latter
לֶקֶשׁ ... 651

grudge, to
לוּן / לִין } Kal ... 635

grudge, to bear
נָטַר Kal ... 813

guard
טַבָּח ... 473
טַבָּח Ch. ... 473
מִשְׁמַעַת ... 773
מִשְׁמָר ... 773
רוּץ Kal ... 1165

guest
קָרָא[1] Kal ... 1117

guide
אַלּוּף / אַלֻּף } ... 94
קָצִין ... 1115

guide, to
אָשַׁר Piel ... 180
דָּרַךְ Hiphil ... 349
יָעַץ Kal ... 547
כּוּל Pilpel ... 592
נָהַג[1] Piel ... 797
נָהַל Piel ... 798
נָחָה Kal ... 804
נָחָה Hiphil ... 804

guide, *see* wittingly

guide, to be
נָהַג[1] Piel ... 797

guile
מִרְמָה ... 765
עָרְמָה ... 980
רְמִיָּה ... 1176

guiltiness
אָשָׁם ... 179

guiltless
נָקִי ... 838

guiltless, to be
נָקָה Niphal ... 838

guiltless, to hold
נָקָה Piel ... 838

guilty
אָשֵׁם ... 179
רָשָׁע ... 1192

guilty, to be
אָשַׁם / אָשֵׁם } Kal ... 178

guilty, to become
אָשַׁם / אָשֵׁם } Kal ... 178

guilty, to be found
אָשַׁם / אָשֵׁם } Kal ... 178

guilty, to hold one's self
אָשַׁם / אָשֵׁם } Kal ... 178

gush out, to
זוּב Kal ... 383
נָזַל Kal ... 803
שָׁפַךְ Kal ... 1320

gutter
צִנּוֹר ... 1076
רַהַט ... 1159

ha
הֶאָח ... 356

haammonai, *see* Chephar-haammonai

habergeon
שִׁרְיָה ... 1326
שִׁרְיוֹן ... 1326
תַּחְרָא ... 1345

habitable part
תֵּבֵל ... 1335

habitation
גֵּרוּת ... 315
זְבֻל / זְבוּל } ... 377
טִירָה ... 481
יָשַׁב Kal ... 568
מוֹשָׁב ... 675
מָכוֹן ... 699
מְכוּרָה ... 699
מְכֵרָה ... 700
מָעוֹן ... 740
מְעוֹנָה ... 740
מִשְׁכָּן ... 770
מִשְׁכַּן Ch. ... 771
נָאָה ... 781
נָוֶה ... 800
נָוָה ... 800
שֶׁכֶן ... 1261

habitation, to have
שְׁכַן / שְׁכֵן } Kal ... 1260
שְׁכַן Ch. P'al ... 1261

habitation, to prepare an
נָוָה Hiphil ... 800

haccerem, *see* Beth-haccerem

Hachmonite
בֵּן ... 232

had
יֵשׁ ... 568

had, *see* abomination, charge of

had in, *see* honour, reverence

had not
לוּלֵי ... 635

had rule, *see* captain

haft
נִצָּב ... 834

hail
בָּרָד ... 270

hail, to
בָּרַד Kal ... 270

hailstone
{ אֶבֶן ... 11
{ בָּרָד ... 270

hair
דַּלָּה ... 342
נֵזֶר ... 804
שֵׂעָר ... 1212
שֵׂעָר ... 1212
שְׂעַר Ch ... 1212
שַׂעֲרָה ... 1212

hair, *see* pluck off

hair to be fallen off
מָרַט Niphal ... 764

hair fallen off, to have his
מָרַט Niphal ... 764

* hair, well *set*
מִקְשֶׁה ... 760

hairs, *see* grey, hoar

hairy
שָׂעִיר ... 1212
שֵׂעָר ... 1212

* hairy †
בַּעַל ... 262

hakkore, *see* En-hakkore

Halak
חָלָק ... 435

half
חֲצִי / חֵצִי } ... 454
מֶחֱצָה ... 689
מַחֲצִית ... 689
תָּוֶךְ ... 1338

half, *see* homer, shekel

* half, to live out
חָצָה Kal ... 454

half so much
מַחֲצִית ... 689

hallow, to
קָדַשׁ / קָדֵשׁ } Piel ... 1090
קָדַשׁ / קָדֵשׁ } Hiphil ... 1090

hallowed
קֹדֶשׁ ... 1091

hallowed, to be
קָדַשׁ / קָדֵשׁ } Kal ... 1090

hard things
עָתָק ... 1008
קָשֶׁה ... 1131
hard, to be too
פָּלָא Niphal ... 1018
harden, to
אָמֵץ Piel ... 104
חָזַק Kal ... 411
חָזַק Piel ... 411
כָּבֵד / כָּבַד } Piel ... 581
כָּבֵד / כָּבַד } Hiphil ... 581
עָזַז Hiphil ... 917
קָשָׁה Hiphil ... 1131
קָשַׁח Hiphil ... 1132
harden self, to
סָלַד Piel ... 877
hardened
כָּבֵד ... 582
hardened, to be
חָזַק Kal ... 411
כָּבֵד / כָּבַד } Kal ... 581
קָשַׁח Hiphil ... 1132
תְּקֵף Ch. P'al ... 1357
harder
חָזָק ... 413
*hard*hearted
לֵב ... 626
hard*hearted*
קָשֶׁה ... 1131
hardly bestead
קָשָׁה Niphal ... 1131
hardly with, *see* deal
hardly, would
קָשָׁה Hiphil ... 1131
hardness
מוּצָק ... 673
hare
אַרְנֶבֶת ... 157
harlot
זָנָה Kal ... 389
קְדֵשָׁה ... 1094
harlot, to be an
זָנָה Kal ... 389
harlot, to play the
זָנָה Kal ... 389
harm
רַע ... 1177
harm †
דָּבָר ... 325
רַע ... 1177
harm, to do
יָרַע Kal ... 566
רָעַע Hiphil ... 1186
harm be hath done
חָטָא Kal ... 414

harness
נֶשֶׁק / נֵשֶׁק } ... 849
שִׁרְיָן ... 1327
harness, to
אָסַר Kal ... 143
harnessed
חֲמֻשִׁים ... 444
harp
כִּנּוֹר ... 604
קִיתָרֹס Ch. ... 1108
קַתְרוֹס Ch. ... 1133
harrow
חָרִיץ ... 464
harrow, to
שָׂדַד Piel ... 1197
hart
אַיָּל ... 58
harvest
קָצִיר ... 1115
harvestman
קָצִיר ... 1115
קָצַר Kal ... 1116
hash-baz, *see* Maher-shalal-hash-baz
hast
יֵשׁ ... 568
haste
חָפַז Kal ... 451
חִפָּזוֹן ... 451
haste, to
אוּץ Kal ... 31
בָּהַל / בָּהַל } Niphal ... 188
בָּהַל / בָּהַל } Hiphil ... 188
דָּחַף Niphal ... 339
חוּשׁ Kal ... 409
חוּשׁ Hiphil ... 409
טוּשׁ Kal ... 480
מָהַר [1] Piel ... 669
שָׁאַף Kal ... 1222
haste away, to
חָפַז Niphal ... 451
haste, to cause to make
מָהַר [1] Piel ... 669
haste, in
בְּהִילוּ Ch. ... 188
בְּהַל Ch. Ithpael ... 188
מָהַר [1] Piel ... 669
haste, to make
אוּץ Kal ... 31
בָּהַל / בָּהַל } Piel ... 188
בָּרַח Kal ... 271
חוּשׁ Kal ... 409
חוּשׁ Hiphil ... 409

חִישׁ Kal ... 426
חָפַז Kal ... 451
חָפַז Niphal ... 451
מָהַר [1] Piel ... 669
haste, to require
נָחַץ Kal ... 808
hasten, to
אוּץ Hiphil ... 31
חוּשׁ Kal ... 409
חוּשׁ Hiphil ... 409
מָהַר [1] Kal ... 669
מָהַר [1] Piel ... 669
שָׁקַד [1] Kal ... 1322
hastened, to be
בָּהַל / בָּהַל } Pual ... 188
דָּחַף Kal ... 339
hasteth
מַהֵר ... 669
hastily
מַהֵר ... 669
מְהֵרָה ... 669
* hastily
מָהַר [1] Piel ... 669
hastily, *see* gotten
hastily, to bring
רוּץ Hiphil ... 1165
hastily, to be gotten
בָּהַל / בָּהַל } Pual ... 188
hasting
מָהִיר ... 668
hasty
אוּץ Kal ... 31
חֲצַף Ch. Aphel ... 455
מָהַר [1] Niphal ... 669
קָצֵר ... 1117
hasty, to be
בָּהַל / בָּהַל } Niphal ... 188
מָהַר [1] Piel ... 669
hasty fruit
בִּכּוּר ... 228
hat
כַּרְבְּלָא Ch. ... 616
hatch, to
בָּקַע Kal ... 264
בָּקַע Piel ... 264
יָלַד Kal ... 527
hate, to
שָׂטַם Kal ... 1205
שָׂנֵא Kal ... 1210
שָׂנֵא Piel ... 1210
שְׂנֵא Ch. P'al ... 1210
שִׂנְאָה ... 1211
hated
שָׂנִיא ... 1212

hated, to be
שָׂנֵא Niphal 1210
hateful, to be
שָׂנֵא Kal 1210
hatefully
שִׂנְאָה 1211
hater
שָׂנֵא Piel 1210
hath
אֵל 78
יֵשׁ 568
hath it, he that
בַּעַל 262
hath *life*
נֶפֶשׁ 829
hath, that
בַּעֲלָה 262
hatred
אֵיבָה 57
מַשְׂטֵמָה 767
שִׂנְאָה 1211
hattaavah, *see* Kibroth-hattaavah
hatticon, *see* Hazor-hatticon
haughtily
רוֹמָה 1164
haughtiness
גַּאֲוָה 285
רוּם 1164
haughty
גָּבֹהַּ 287
גָּבוֹהַּ / גָּבֹהַּ } 287
יָהִיר 507
מָרוֹם 763
רוּם Kal 1163
haughty, to be
גָּבַהּ Kal 287
* haunt
רֶגֶל 1155
haunt, to
יָשַׁב Kal 568
haunt, to be wont to
הָלַךְ Hithpael 362
have
יֵשׁ 568
have, to
אִיתַי Ch. 69
בַּעַל 262
הֲוָא / הֲוָה } Ch. P'al 358
נָחַל Kal 805
* have, to
בּוֹא Kal 189
הָוָא / הָוָה } Kal 358
הָיָה Kal 360
כָּלָה Piel 598
מָצָא Niphal 748
נָתַן Kal 851
שׂוּם / שִׂים } Kal 1200
* have, † to
בּוֹא Kal 189
have, *see* abomination, appetite, assurance, bitterness, can, charge, compassion, damage, deeply, delight, derision, desire, do, dominion, done, end, enough, experience, favour, fellowship, fouled, good success, habitation, hair fallen off, hard *labour*, heat, hoofs, hope, horns, hunger, indignation, inheritance, intelligence, issue, joy, knowledge, lack, loss, maintenance, many, mastery, mercy, mercy upon, more, need, need of, occasion, over, oversight, pain, part, pity, pity upon, pleasure, plenty, possession, power, profit, respect, rest, rule, running issue, secret, sent back, shadow, sorrow, superfluous, tithes, understanding, vent, well, wholly
have *a dream*, to
חֲזָא / חֲזָה } Ch. P'al 410
have away, to
עָבַר Hiphil 895
have being, *see* while
have flat, *see* nose
have forth, to
יָצָא Hiphil 548
* have here, to
מָצָא Niphal 748
have in, *see* derision, possession
have *inheritance*, to
נָחַל Kal 805
נָפַל Kal 825
have *knowledge*, to
יָדַע Kal 500
have out, to
יָצָא Hiphil 548
have possession, to
אָחַז Niphal 46
have sorely, *see* grieved
have *understanding*, to
יָדַע Kal 500
haven
חוֹף 408
מָחוֹז 686
having, *see* salvation
havoth, *see* Bashan-havoth-jair
Havoth-*jair*
חַוּוֹת 406
hawk
נֵץ 833
hawk, *see* night
hay
חָצִיר 455
Hazar-hatticon
{ חָצֵר 455
{ תִּיכוֹן 1346
hazel
לוּז 635
hazzurim, *see* Helkath-hazzurim
he
אִישׁ 60
הוּא 358
זֶה 380
מִי 694
נֶפֶשׁ 829
* he
יָד 489
he ass, *see* ass
he be
יֵשׁ 568
he goat
עַתּוּד 1007
צָפִיר 1079
he *goat*
צְפִיר Ch. 1079
צָפִיר 1079
he is
יֵשׁ 568
head
גֻּלְגֹּלֶת 307
מְרַאֲשֹׁת 761
רֵאשׁ Ch. 1142
רֹאשׁ 1142
head, *see* axhead, bald, bow, crown, grey, hoar, hoary, top
head *of a hatchet*
בַּרְזֶל 271
head (*of a spear*)
לֶהָבָה / לַהֶבֶת } 634
headbands
קִשֻּׁרִים 1132
headlong, *see* carried
*head*stone
אֶבֶן 11
head*stone*
רֹאשָׁה 1145
heal, to
רָפָא Kal 1187
רָפָא Piel 1187
heal*ed*
רְפֻאוֹת 1188
healed, to be
רָפָא Kal 1187
רָפָא Niphal 1187
רָפָא Hithpael 1187
*heal*ed, to be
נָתַן Kal 851
healed, to cause to be
רָפָא Piel 1187
healer
חָבַשׁ Kal 400
healing
כֵּהָה 586

here, to be
מָצָא Niphal 748

*** here, to be all**
תָּמַם Kal 1351

here and there, to be
זָרַק Kal 397

hereafter
אָחוֹר 45
אַחַר 48

***here*after**
אַחֲרֵי Ch. 54

here*after*
דֵּן Ch. 346

hereby
זֹאת 377

herein
זֹאת 377

heretofore †
תְּמוֹל 1349

*** heretofore †**
אֶתְמוֹל / אֶתְמוּל } 183
שִׁלְשׁוֹם 1279

herewith
זֹאת 377

heritage
יְרֻשָּׁה 567
מוֹרָשָׁה 674
נַחֲלָה 806
נַחֲלַת 807

heritage, to take as an
נָחַל Kal 805

heron
אֲנָפָה 140

herself
נֶפֶשׁ 829

herself, *see* she

hew, to
חָטַב Kal 417
חָצֵב / חָצַב } Kal 453
כָּרַת Kal 618
פְּסַל Kal 1037

hew down, to
גְּדַד Ch. P'al 293
גָּדַע Kal 298
גָּדַע Piel 298
כָּרַת Kal 618

hew in pieces, to
נָתַח Piel 850
שָׁסַף Piel 1315

hew out, to
חָצֵב / חָצַב } Kal 453

hewed
גָּזִית 304
מַחְצֵב 689

hewer
חָטַב Kal 417
חָצֵב / חָצַב } Kal 453

hewn
מַחְצֵב 689

hewn, to be
חָצֵב / חָצַב } Pual 453

hewn down, to be
קָמַל Kal 1111

hewn stone
גָּזִית 304

hid
צָפִין 1079
צָפַן Kal 1080

hid, *see* treasures

hid, to be
חָבָא Niphal 398
חָבָא Hophal 398
חָבָא Hithpael 398
כָּחַד Niphal 595
סָתַר Niphal 886
סָתַר Hithpael 886
עָלַם Niphal 943
עָלַם Hithpael 943
צָפַן Niphal 1080

hid, thing that is
תַּעֲלֻמָה 1354

hidden
סָתַם Kal 885
פָּלָא Niphal 1018

hidden, *see* riches

hidden, to be
חָפַשׂ Pual 452
עָלַם Niphal 943
צָפַן Niphal 1080

hidden one
צָפַן Kal 1080

hidden thing
נָצַר Kal 837

hidden things
מַצְפֻּנִים 755

hide
עוֹר 912

hide, *see* flee

hide, to
חָבָא Hiphil 398
חָשַׂךְ Hiphil 469
טָמַן Kal 483
טָמַן Niphal 483
טָמַן Hiphil 483
כָּחַד Piel 595
כָּחַד Hiphil 595
כָּסָה Piel 607
סָתַר Piel 886
סָתַר Hiphil 886
עָלַם Hiphil 943
עָמַם Kal 960
צָפַן Kal 1080
צָפַן Hiphil 1080

*** hide, to**
נוּם Hiphil 801

hide self, to
חָבָא Niphal 398
חָבָא Pual 398
חָבָא Hithpael 398
חָבָה Kal 398
חָבָה Niphal 398
סָתַר Kal 886
סָתַר Niphal 886
סָתַר Hithpael 886
עָטַף Kal 918
עָלַם Hithpael 943
צָפַן Kal 1080
צָפַן (כ׳) Hiphil 1080

hiding
חֶבְיוֹן 398

hiding place
מַחֲבֵא 686
סֵתֶר 886

Higgaion
הִגָּיוֹן 357

high
אִישׁ 60
אֹרֶךְ 156
גָּבֹהַּ 287
גֹּבַהּ 287
גָּבוֹהַּ / גָּבֹהַּ } 287
גַּבְנֻנִּים 291
גָּדוֹל 293
מָרוֹם 763
נָשָׂא Niphal 840
עַל & עָל 933
עִלִּי Ch. 941
עֶלְיוֹן 942
קוֹמָה 1103
רוּם Kal 1163
רוֹמָם 1164
שָׂגַב Niphal 1197
שָׁפָה Niphal 1318

*** high**
רוּם 1164

high, *see* fort, heaps, sounding, tower

high, to be
גָּבַהּ Kal 287
רוּם Kal 1163
שָׂגַב Niphal 1197

high degree
אִישׁ 60
מַעֲלָה 744

high, to lift up on
רוּם Polel 1163

high, to make
גָּבַהּ Hiphil 287

high, to make on
רוּם Hiphil 1163

high, most
מָרוֹם 763
עַל & עָל 933
עִלַּי Ch. 941
עֶלְיוֹן 942
עֶלְיוֹן Ch. 942

high, on
מַעַל 743
מָרוֹם 763
עֶלְיוֹן 942
רֹאשׁ 1142
רוּם 1164

high ones
מָרוֹם 763
רוּם Kal 1163

high place
בָּמָה 231
מָרוֹם 763
צְרִיחַ 1082
רָמָה 1175
שְׁפִי 1320

high *priest*
רֹאשׁ 1142

high, to set on
שָׂגַב Piel 1197

high, to set up on
רוּם Polel 1163
שָׂגַב Piel 1197

high, things too
פָּלָא Niphal 1018

high, too
רוּם Kal 1163

*** high, very**
מַעַל 743

higher
גָּבֹהַּ / גָּבוֹהַּ 287
עֶלְיוֹן 942

higher, to be
גָּבַהּ Kal 287
רוּם Kal 1163

higher place
גַּב 286
צְחִיחַ 1070
צְחִיחִי 1070

highest
עֶלְיוֹן 942

highest branch
צַמֶּרֶת 1075

highest part
רֹאשׁ 1142

highest places
מָרוֹם 763

*** highest places †**
גַּף 314

highness
גַּאֲוָה 285
שְׂאֵת 1195

highway
אֹרַח 154
דֶּרֶךְ 349
חוּץ 408
מְסִלָּה 737
מַסְלוּל 737

highway,† the
אֶחָד 41

hill
גִּבְעָה 291
הַר 371
הָרָר / הֲרָר 376
מַעֲלֶה 744

*** hill**
קֶרֶן 1129

hill country
הַר 371

him
אִישׁ 60
הוּא 358
מִי 694

*** him**
זָכָר 387
מִן Ch. 732
עַיִן 919
פָּנִים 1023
קֶרֶב 1125

*** him †**
פָּנִים 1023

him, *see* with

him, of
זֶה 380

him that is
אִישׁ 60

himself
הוּא 358
יָד 489
מַעֲנֶה 745
נֶפֶשׁ 829

*** himself**
פָּנִים 1023

himself, by
גַּף 314

hin
הִין 362

hind
אַיָּלָה 59
אַיֶּלֶת 59

hinder
אַחֲרוֹן 53
תּוֹעָה 1342

hinder, to
אָחַר Piel 48
חָשַׂךְ Kal 468
מָנַע Niphal 735
שׁוּב Hiphil 1238

hinder,† to
עָשָׂה Kal 981

hinder end
אַחַר 48

hinder part
אָחוֹר 45
סוֹף 871

hindered, to be
בְּטֵל Ch. P'al 211

hindermost
אַחֲרוֹן 53
אַחֲרִית 54

hindmost, to smite the
זָנַב Piel 389

hinge
פֹּת 1052
צִיר 1071

hip
שׁוֹק 1248

hire
אֶתְנָן / אֶתְנַן 183
מְחִיר 687
שָׂכָר 1208

hire, to
סָכַר[2] Kal 876
שָׂכַר Kal 1207
שָׁחַד Kal 1249
תָּנָה[1] Kal 1352
תָּנָה[1] Hiphil 1352

hire out selves, to
שָׂכַר Niphal 1207

hired
שָׂכִיר 1206

hired man
שָׂכִיר 1206

hired servant
שָׂכִיר 1206

hired, that is
שְׂכִירָה 1206

hireling
שָׂכִיר 1206

hiss
שָׁרַק Kal 1327

hissing
שְׁרוּקֹת 1326
שְׁרִיקוֹת 1327
שְׁרֵקָה 1327

hit, to
מָצָא Kal 748

hither
הֲלֹם 367
הֵנָּה 369
פּוֹ & פֹּה 1014

hither, *see* bring, come

hither, to bring
נָגַשׁ Hiphil 794

hither, to come
נָגַשׁ Kal 794

hitherto
אָז 34
הָלְאָה 362
{ עַד 901
{ כֹּה 586
{ עַד Ch. 902
{ כָּה Ch. 586

hither*to*
הֲלֹם 367
הֵנָּה 369

Ho!
הוֹי 359

hoar frost
כְּפוֹר 614

hoar hairs
שֵׂיבָה 1205

hoar head
שֵׂיבָה 1205

hoary, to be
שֵׂיבָה 1205

hoary frost
כְּפוֹר 614

hoary head
שֵׂיבָה 1205

hold
מְצָד 752
מְצוּדָה 752
מְצֻדָה 753
צְרִיחַ 1082

hold, *see* catch, lay, strong, take

hold, to
אָחַז Kal 46
אָסַר Kal 143
חָזַק Hiphil 411
חָזַק Hithpael 411
חָשַׁב Kal 468
כּוּל Hiphil 592
קָבַל Hiphil 1083
קוּם Kal 1099
שׂוּם / שִׂים } Kal 1201
תָּמַךְ Kal 1350
תָּפַשׂ Kal 1355

hold, *see* feast, guiltless, guilty, innocent, peace, tongue

hold back, to
אָחַז Piel 46
חָשַׂךְ Kal 468

hold fast, to
חָזַק Hiphil 411
לָחַץ Kal 640

hold *a feast*, to
עָשָׂה Kal 981

hold, to lay
חָזַק Hiphil 411

hold of, to take
נָשַׂג Hiphil 845

hold on, to take
נָשַׂג Hiphil 845

hold out, to
יָשַׁט Hiphil 575

hold peace, to
חָרַשׁ Kal 466

hold, to take
לָפַת Kal 644
נָסַג Hiphil 819
נָשַׂג Hiphil 845
קָבַל Hiphil 1083

hold up, to
נָשָׂא Kal 840
סָעַד Kal 880
רוּם Hiphil 1163
תָּמַךְ Kal 1350

hold upon, *see* get

hold upon, to take
נָשַׂג Hiphil 845

holden, to be
לָכַד Niphal 642
סָמַךְ Niphal 879
עָשָׂה Niphal 981
תָּמַךְ Niphal 1350

holding
תָּמַךְ Kal 1350

holding in
כּוּל Hiphil 592

hole
חוֹר 409
חוּר 409
מִסְגֶּרֶת 736
מְעָרָה 745
מַקֶּבֶת 755
נְקִיק 839
פֶּה 1011
פַּחַת 1017

* hole
בָּחוּר 208

holes, with
נָקַב Kal 837

holier, to be
קָדֵשׁ / קָדַשׁ } Kal 1090

holiness
קֹדֶשׁ 1091

hollow
כַּף 612
נָבַב Kal 783

hollow of the hand
שֹׁעַל 1316

hollow place
מַכְתֵּשׁ 701

hollow strakes
שְׁקַעֲרוּרֹת 1325

holy
חָסִיד 449
קָדוֹשׁ 1087
קַדִּישׁ Ch. 1088
קֹדֶשׁ 1091

holy, *see* most holy

holy, to be
קָדֵשׁ / קָדַשׁ } Kal 1090

* holy day
קֹדֶשׁ 1091

holy day, to keep
חָגַג Kal 401

holy, to keep
קָדֵשׁ / קָדַשׁ } Piel 1090

Holy One
חָסִיד 449
קָדוֹשׁ 1087
קַדִּישׁ Ch. 1088

holy place
מִקְדָּשׁ 755
קָדֵשׁ / קָדַשׁ } Piel 1090

holy portion
קֹדֶשׁ 1091

holy thing
קֹדֶשׁ 1091

home
אֹהֶל 27
בַּיִת 214

* home
מָקוֹם 756

home, *see* go

home again, *see* bring, fetch

home, to keep at
נָוָה Kal 800

homeborn
אֶזְרָח 37
{ יְלִיד 531
{ בַּיִת 214

homer
חֹמֶר 441

homer, half
לֶתֶךְ 652

honey
דְּבַשׁ 334

honeycomb
נֹפֶת 833

honey*comb*
דְּבַשׁ 334

*honey*comb
יַעַר 547
יַעְרָה 548
צוּף 1069

honeycomb †
נֹפֶת ... 833
צוּף ... 1069

honour
הָדָר ... 357
הֲדַר Ch. ... 358
הֲדָרָה ... 358
הוֹד ... 358
יְקָר ... 558
יְקָר Ch. ... 558
כָּבוֹד ... 583
תִּפְאָרָה, תִּפְאֶרֶת ... 1354

honour, *see* get, promote to

honour, to
הָדַר Kal ... 357
הֲדַר Ch. Pael ... 357
כָּבֵד, כָּבַד Piel ... 581

honour, to bring to
כָּבֵד, כָּבַד Piel ... 581

honour, to come to
כָּבֵד, כָּבַד Kal ... 581

honour, to do
כָּבֵד, כָּבַד Piel ... 581

honour, to be had in
כָּבֵד, כָּבַד Niphal ... 581

honour self, to
כָּבֵד, כָּבַד Hithpael ... 581

honourable
הוֹד ... 358
כָּבֵד, כָּבַד Niphal ... 581
כָּבֵד, כָּבַד Pual ... 581
כָּבוֹד ... 583

honourable †
נָשָׂא Kal ... 840
פָּנִים ... 1023

honourable, to be
כָּבֵד, כָּבַד Niphal ... 581

honourable, to make
אָדַר Hiphil ... 24

honourable man
כָּבֵד, כָּבַד Niphal ... 581

honourable man †
נָשָׂא Kal ... 840

honourable woman
יָקָר ... 558

honoured, to be
הָדַר Niphal ... 357
כָּבֵד, כָּבַד Niphal ... 581
כָּבֵד, כָּבַד Pual ... 581

hood
צָנִיף ... 1076

hoof
פַּרְסָה ... 1046

hoofs, to have
פָּרַס Hiphil ... 1046

hook
אַגְמוֹן ... 14
וָו ... 377
חָח ... 414
חַחִי ... 414
חַכָּה ... 426
צִנָּה ... 1075

hook, *see* fishhook, pruning hook

hooks
שְׁפַתַּיִם ... 1322

hope
בֶּטַח ... 211
בִּטָּחוֹן ... 211
כֶּסֶל ... 609
מִבְטָח ... 660
מַחְסֶה ... 689
מִקְוֶה ... 756
שֶׂבֶר ... 1197
תּוֹחֶלֶת ... 1338
תִּקְוָה ... 1356

hope, to
בָּטַח Kal ... 210
חוּל, חִיל Kal ... 406
יָחַל Piel ... 523
יָחַל Hiphil ... 523
שָׂבַר Piel ... 1196

hope, to cause to
יָחַל Piel ... 523

hope, to have
חָסָה Kal ... 449
יָחַל Hiphil ... 523

hope, to make to
בָּטַח Hiphil ... 210
יָחַל Piel ... 523

hope, to be no
יָאַשׁ Niphal ... 486

hope, should
יָחִיל ... 523

horn
קֶרֶן ... 1129
קֶרֶן Ch. ... 1129

horn, *see* inkhorn, ram's horn

hornet
צִרְעָה ... 1082

horns, to have
קָרַן Hiphil ... 1129

horrible
זַלְעָפָה ... 388

* horrible
שָׁאוֹן ... 1220

horrible thing
שַׁעֲרוּר ... 1318
שַׁעֲרוּרִי ... 1318

* horribly
שַׂעַר ... 1212

horribly, *see* afraid

horror
אֵימָה ... 59
זַלְעָפָה ... 388
פַּלָּצוּת ... 1021

horse
סוּס ... 870

horse*back*
סוּס ... 871

*horse*back, to bring on
רָכַב Hiphil ... 1173

*horse*back, on
רָכַב Kal ... 1173

horse*hoofs*
סוּס ... 870

*horse*hoofs
עָקֵב ... 974

horseleach
עֲלוּקָה ... 941

horseman
פָּרָשׁ ... 1049
רַכָּב ... 1174
בַּעַל ... 262
פָּרָשׁ ... 1049

horses, company of
סוּסָה ... 871

hosen
פַּטִּישׁ Ch. ... 1017
פְּטַשׁ Ch. ... 1017

host
חַיִל ... 423
חֵיל ... 425
מַחֲנֶה ... 688
צָבָא ... 1057

hostage †
בֵּן ... 232

hostages †
תַּעֲרוּבוֹת ... 1354

hot
אֲזָא, אֲזָה Ch. P'al ... 34
אֵשׁ ... 172
חַם ... 436

hot, *see* displeasure, thunderbolts, [coals

hot, to be
חַם ... 436
חָמַם Kal ... 439
חָמַם Niphal ... 439

imagine, to
הָגָה[1] Kal ... 356
זָמַם Kal ... 388
חָרַשׁ Kal ... 466
חָשַׁב Kal ... 468
חָשַׁב Piel ... 468

imagine, *see* mischief, wrongfully

Immanuel
אֵל ... 76

impart, to
חָלַק Kal ... 435

imperfect, *see* substance

imperious
שַׁלֶּטֶת ... 1274

impose, to
רְמָה Ch. P'al ... 1175

impoverish, to
רָשַׁשׁ Poel ... 1194

impoverished
סָכַן[2] Pual ... 876

impoverished, to be
דָּלַל Niphal ... 342
רָשַׁשׁ Pual ... 1194

imprisonment
אֱסוּר Ch. ... 141

impudent
עָזַז Hiphil ... 917

impudent †
חָזָק ... 413
מֵצַח ... 754
פָּנִים ... 1023
קָשֶׁה ... 1131

impute, to
חָשַׁב Kal ... 468
שׂוּם / שִׂים } Kal ... 1200

imputed, to be
חָשַׁב Niphal ... 468

in
אֶל ... 78
אֵת ... 182
בְּמוֹ ... 232
דַּי ... 339
מִן ... 731
עַל ... 932
עַל Ch. ... 933
עִם ... 955
עִמָּד ... 958
פֶּה ... 1011
פָּנִים ... 1036
קֶרֶב ... 1125
תַּחַת ... 1345

in
בֵּין ... 212
בֵּן ... 232
הֵן ... 369
הִנֵּה ... 369
יָד ... 489
נֶגֶד ... 790
תָּוֶךְ ... 1338

in †
פָּנִים ... 1023

in, *see* abundance, affliction, array, awe, break, breaking, bring, brought, cast, come, cut, derision, distress, enter, entering, execution, fear, gather, go, hedge, held, holding, keep, lie, lodge, more, order, pull, put, rend, ride, shut, sleep, sport, strait, swim, take, tear, took, trouble, turn, vain

* in, all that is
מְלֹא ... 703

in it
שָׁם ... 1279

* in *no* wise
מוּת Hiphil ... 675

* in *presence*, to be
רָאָה Kal ... 1133

in that
כִּי ... 596
עַל ... 932

inasmuch as
כִּי ... 596

incense
לְבוֹנָה ... 631
קְטוֹרָה ... 1105
קָטַר[1] Hophal ... 1106
קִטֵּר ... 1107
קְטֹרֶת ... 1107

incense, *see* altars for, burn, burning, offer, offering, sweet

incensed, to be
חָרָה Niphal ... 462

incline, to
נָטָה Kal ... 810
נָטָה Hiphil ... 810
קָשַׁב Hiphil ... 1131
שׁוּחַ Kal ... 1246

inclose, to
גָּדַר Kal ... 298
נָקַף Hiphil ... 839
צוּר Kal ... 1069

inclose round, to
כָּתַר Piel ... 624

inclosed
נָעַל Kal ... 822
סָבַב Hophal ... 865

inclosed, to be
סָגַר Kal ... 869

inclosing
מִלֻּאָה ... 703

increase
יְבוּל ... 486
מַרְבֶּה ... 761
מַרְבִּית ... 762
רַב ... 1174
שֶׁגֶר ... 1236
תְּבוּאָה ... 1335
תְּנוּבָה ... 1352
תַּרְבּוּת ... 1357
תַּרְבִּית ... 1357

increase, *see* vineyards

increase, to
אָמֵץ Piel ... 104
נָאָה Kal ... 285
גָּדַל Hiphil ... 297
יָסַף Kal ... 543
יָסַף Niphal ... 543
יָסַף Hiphil ... 543
נוּב Kal ... 799
עָלָה Kal ... 934
פָּרָה Kal ... 1044
פָּרָה Hiphil ... 1044
פָּרַץ Kal ... 1047
רָבָה Kal ... 1151
רָבָה Piel ... 1151
רָבָה Hiphil ... 1151
שָׂגָה Kal ... 1197
שָׂגָא Hiphil ... 1197
שָׂגָה Hiphil ... 1197

increase abundantly, to
שָׁרַץ Kal ... 1327

increase more and more, to
יָסַף Hiphil ... 543

increased, to be
עָצַם Kal ... 972
פָּרָה Kal ... 1044
פָּרַץ Kal ... 1047
רֹב ... 1150
רָבַב[1] Kal ... 1151
רָבָה Kal ... 1151

incurable
אָנַשׁ Kal ... 141
{ אַיִן ... 59
{ מַרְפֵּא ... 765

indeed
אֲבָל ... 11
אָמְנָה ... 104
אָמְנָם ... 104
אֻמְנָם ... 104

indeed is sometimes the translation of an infinitive used intensively.

indignation
זַעַם ... 391
זָעַם Kal ... 391
זַעַף ... 391
חֵמָה ... 437
כַּעַס ... 612
קֶצֶף ... 1116

indignation, to have
זָעַם Kal ... 391

indignation, to take
כָּעַס Kal ... 612

indite, to
רָחַשׁ Kal ... 1170

industrious †
מְלָאכָה ... 705

industrious,† to be
עָשָׂה Kal ... 981

infamous
שֵׁם ... 1280

infamous †
טָמֵא ... 482

infamy
דִּבָּה ... 318

infant
עוּל ... 906
עוֹלֵל / עוֹלָל ... 907

inferior
אֲרַע Ch. ... 157
נָפַל Kal ... 825

*in*finite
מִסְפָּר ... 738
קֵץ ... 1113
קָצֶה ... 1115

infirmity
דָּוָה Kal ... 336
חָלָה Piel ... 429
מַחֲלֶה ... 687

inflame, to
דָּלַק Hiphil ... 342

inflammation
דַּלֶּקֶת ... 342
צָרֶבֶת ... 1081

influences
מַעֲדַנּוֹת ... 740

infolding
לָקַח Hithpael ... 644

inform, to
בִּין Kal ... 212
יָרָה Hiphil ... 564

ingathering
אָסִיף / אָסִף ... 141

inhabit, to
יָשַׁב Kal ... 568
שָׁכֵן / שָׁכַן Kal ... 1260

inhabitant
גּוּר Kal ... 303
דּוּר Ch. P'al ... 338
יָשַׁב Kal ... 568
שָׁכֵן ... 1261
תּוֹשָׁב ... 1344

inhabited, to be
יָשַׁב Kal ... 568
יָשַׁב Niphal ... 568
יָשַׁב Hophal ... 568
שָׁכֵן / שָׁכַן Kal ... 1260

inhabited, to make to be
יָשַׁב Hiphil ... 568

inhabited, not
גְּזֵרָה ... 305

inhabited place
מוֹשָׁב ... 675

inhabiting, *see* wilderness

inherit, to
יָרַשׁ Kal ... 566
נָחַל Kal ... 805
נָחַל Hithpael ... 805
נַחֲלָה ... 806

inherit, to cause to
נָחַל Hiphil ... 805

inherit, to give to
יָרַשׁ Hiphil ... 566
נָחַל Hiphil ... 805

inherit, to make to
נָחַל Hiphil ... 805

inheritance
חֵלֶק ... 435
יְרֻשָּׁה ... 567
מוֹרָשָׁה ... 674
נַחֲלָה ... 806

inheritance, to distribute for
נָחַל Piel ... 805

inheritance, to divide
נָחַל Piel ... 805
נָחַל Hiphil ... 805

inheritance, to divide by
נָחַל Kal ... 805

inheritance, to divide for
נָחַל Kal ... 805
נָחַל Piel ... 805
נָחַל Hiphil ... 805
נָחַל Hithpael ... 805

inheritance, to give for
נָחַל Hiphil ... 805

inheritance, to have
נָחַל Kal ... 805

inheritance, to leave for
יָרַשׁ Hiphil ... 566
נָחַל Hiphil ... 805

inheritance, to take
נָחַל Kal ... 805
נָחַל Piel ... 805

* inheritance, to take
חָלַל Niphal ... 432

inheritance, to take as an
נָחַל Hithpael ... 805

inheritance, to take for
נָחַל Kal ... 805

inheritor
יָרַשׁ Kal ... 566

iniquity
אָוֶן ... 30
הַוָּה ... 359
עָוֶל / עֶוֶל ... 906
עֲוָיָא Ch. ... 906
עַוְלָה ... 907
עוֹלָה ... 907
עָוֹן ... 910
עַלְוָה ... 941
עָמָל ... 960
רֶשַׁע ... 1194

iniquity †
דָּבָר ... 325

iniquity, *see* punishment

iniquity, to commit
עָוָה Kal ... 906
עָוָה Hiphil ... 906

injustice
חָמָס ... 440

ink
דְּיוֹ ... 340

inkhorn
קֶסֶת ... 1113

inn
מָלוֹן ... 707

inner
פְּנִימִי ... 1036

* inner chamber
חֶדֶר ... 403

inner part
פְּנִים ... 1036

innermost part
חֶדֶר ... 403

innocency
זָכוּ Ch. ... 385
נִקָּיוֹן ... 839

innocent
חִנָּם ... 446
חַף ... 451
נָקִי ... 838
נָקִיא ... 839

innocent †
דָּם ... 343

innocent, to be
נָקָה Niphal ... 838

innocent, to hold
נָקָה Piel ... 838

*in*numerable
מִסְפָּר ... 738

inordinate, *see* love

inquisition to be made
בָּקַשׁ Pual ... 268

inquisition, to make
דָּרַשׁ Kal ... 353

inside
בַּיִת ... 214

inspiration
נְשָׁמָה 849
instant
רֶגַע 1157
instant, at an
פֶּתַע 1055
instead
תַּחַת 1345
instruct
יִסּוֹר 543
instruct, to
בִּין Kal.............. 212
בִּין Polel............ 212
יָסַר Piel.............. 545
יָרָה Hiphil 564
לָמַד Piel.............. 643
שָׂכַל Hiphil 1206
instructed, to be
יָדַע Niphal 500
יָסַד Hophal.......... 542
יָסַר Niphal 545
לָמַד Pual.............. 643
שָׂכַל Hiphil 1206
instructer
לָטַשׁ Kal.............. 640
instruction
מוּסָר 672
מֹסָר 739
instrument
כְּלִי 600
instrument, *see* musical, threshing
instrument of, *see* ten strings
instrument of musick
שָׁלִישׁ 1275
instrument, to sing to the stringed
נָגַן Piel.............. 791
instrument, stringed
נְגִינָה 791
instruments of musick
דַּחֲוָן 339
instruments, player on
חָלַל Kal.............. 432
instruments, players on
נָגַן Kal.............. 791
instruments, stringed
מִנִּים 735
insurrection, to make
נְשָׂא Ch. Ithpael 845
integrity
תֹּם 1348
תֻּמָּה 1349
intelligence, to have
בִּין Kal.............. 212
intend, to
אָמַר Kal.............. 105
נָטָה Kal.............. 810
intent
דִּבְרָה Ch.............. 334
intent that
עֲבוּר.................. 895
intent that, to the
מַעַן 744
intents
מְזִמָּה 684
intercession, to make
פָּגַע Kal..............1009
פָּגַע Hiphil 1009
intercessor
פָּגַע Hiphil 1009
intermeddle, to
גָּלַע Hithpael......... 310
עָרַב[1] Hithpael........ 975
intermission
הֲפוּגָה 370
interpret, to
פָּתַר Kal..............1055
interpretation
מְלִיצָה 710
פֵּשֶׁר 1051
פְּשַׁר Ch..............1051
פָּתַר Kal..............1055
פִּתְרוֹן 1055
שֶׁבֶר } 1234
שֵׁבֶר }
interpreted
תַּרְגֵּם 1357
interpreter
לוּץ Hiphil........... 636
פָּתַר Kal..............1055
interpreting
פְּשַׁר Ch. Pael.........1051
into
אֶל 78
אֵת 182
בְּמוֹ 232
עַד 901
תָּוֶךְ 1338
into, *see* bondage, break, brought, contempt, desolation, enter, entering, entrance, foolishness, joy, scatter, sleep, snare, spread, subjection, take
intreat, to
חָלָה Piel.............. 429
חָנַן Kal.............. 446
חָנַן Hithpael 447
עָתַר[1] Kal............1008
עָתַר[1] Hiphil..........1008
פָּגַע Kal..............1009
פָּלַל Hithpael 1021
intreated, to be
עָתַר[1] Niphal 1008
intreaties
תַּחֲנוּנִים 1345
invade, to
גּוּד Kal.............. 299
פָּשַׁט Kal..............1050
*in*vade, to
בּוֹא Kal.............. 189
invasion, to make an
פָּשַׁט Kal..............1050
invent, to
חָשַׁב Kal.............. 468
invented
מַחֲשֶׁבֶת 690
invention
מַעֲלָל 744
עֲלִילָה 942
inventions
חִשְּׁבֹנוֹת 469
inventions, witty
מְזִמָּה 684
invite, to
קָרָא[1] Kal 1117
inward
בַּיִת 214
סוֹד 870
פָּנִים 1036
פְּנִימִי 1036
קֶרֶב 1125
inward, *see* fret
inward part
חֶדֶר 403
קֶרֶב 1125
inward parts
טֻחוֹת................ 480
inward thought
קֶרֶב 1125
* inwardly
קֶרֶב 1125
inwards
קֶרֶב 1125
iron
בַּרְזֶל 271
פַּרְזֶל Ch. 1044
irons, *see* barbed
is
יֵשׁ 568
is, that which
תּוּשִׁיָּה 1344
is, thing as it
תּוּשִׁיָּה 1344
Ish-*tob*
אִישׁ 60
Ishi
אִישׁ 60
island
אִי 55
island, *see* wild beast
isle
אִי 55
*Israel*ite
אִישׁ 60
issue
זוֹב 383
זִרְמָה 395
מוֹלֶדֶת 671

מְשׂוֹשׂ 767
רִנָּה 1176
שִׂמְחָה 1210
שָׂשׂוֹן 1219
תְּרוּעָה 1358

joy, *see* aloud, shout for, sing for, skip

joy, to
גִּיל גּוּל } Kal........ 306
שׂוּשׂ שִׂישׂ } Kal........ 1204
שָׂמֵחַ שָׂמַח } Kal........ 1208

joy, to break forth into
פָּצַח Kal........ 1039

joy, to have
שָׂמֵחַ שָׂמַח } Kal........ 1208

joyful
טוֹב 476
רְנָנָה 1177
שָׂמֵחַ 1209

joyful, *see* sound

joyful, to be
גּוּל גִּיל } Kal........ 306
עָלַז Kal........ 941
עָלַץ Kal........ 944
רָנַן Piel........ 1177

joyful, to make
שָׂמֵחַ שָׂמַח } Piel 1208

joyful noise, to make a
רוּעַ Hiphil 1164

joyful voice
רְנָנָה 1177

*joyfully
רָאָה Kal........ 1133

joyfulness
שִׂמְחָה 1210

joyous
עַלִּיז 942

jubile
יוֹבֵל 507
תְּרוּעָה 1358

judge
דַּיָּן 340
דַּיָּן Ch. 340
פָּלִיל 1020
פְּלִילִי 1020
שָׁפַט Kal........ 1319
שָׁפַט Poel 1319

judge, to
דִּין Kal........ 340
דִּין Ch. P'al 340
יָכַח Hiphil 525
פָּלַל Piel 1020
שָׁפַט Kal........ 1319

judge, to be a
שָׁפַט Kal........ 1319

judged, to be
מִשְׁפָּט 776
שָׁפַט Niphal 1319

* judged, to be
נָפַל Pilel 825

judges
אֲדַרְגָּזְרַיָּא Ch. 24
אֱלֹהִים 79

judgment
דּוּן 337
דִּין 340
דִּין Ch. 340
טַעַם 483
מַד 664
מִשְׁפָּט 776
פְּלִילָה 1020
פְּלִילִי 1020
שְׁפוֹט 1318
שָׁפַט Kal (כ׳) 1319

* judgment †
דָּבָר 325

judgment, *see* minister

judgment, to do
פָּקַד Kal........ 1040

judgment, to execute
פָּלַל Piel........ 1020
שָׁפַט Niphal 1319

judgments
שְׁפָטִים 1320

juice
עָסִיס 967

jump, to
רָקַד Piel........ 1191

juniper
רֹתֶם 1195

juniper tree
רֹתֶם 1195

just
יָשָׁר 578
מִשְׁפָּט 776
צַדִּיק 1061
צֶדֶק 1063
שָׁלֵם 1278

just, to be
צָדַק Kal........ 1062

*just, that which is altogether
צֶדֶק 1063

justice
מִשְׁפָּט 776
צֶדֶק 1063
צְדָקָה 1063

justice, to do
צָדַק Hiphil 1062

justified, to be
צָדַק Kal........ 1062

justify, to
צָדַק Piel........ 1062
צָדַק Hiphil 1062

justify self, to
צָדַק Kal........ 1062

justifying
צָדַק Hiphil 1062

justle one against another, to
שָׁקַק Hithpalpel 1325

justly
מִשְׁפָּט 776

keep
מִשְׁמֶרֶת 773
עֲבַד Ch. P'al 889

keep, to
אָצַל Kal........ 148
חָשַׂךְ Kal........ 468
כָּלָא Kal........ 598
מָנַע Kal........ 735
נְטַר Ch. P'al........ 813
נָטַר Kal........ 813
נָצַר Kal........ 837
עָבַד Kal........ 887
עָשָׂה Kal........ 981
שָׁבַת Kal........ 1234
שָׁמַר Kal........ 1300

keep, *see* alive, bondage, company with, feast, holy, holyday, rank, remembrance, sabbath, secret, silence, solemn feast, watch

keep at, *see* home

keep back, to
חָשַׂךְ Kal........ 468
כָּלָא Kal........ 598
מָנַע Kal........ 735

keep *bed*, to
נָפַל Kal........ 825

keep cattle, to teach to
קָנָה¹ Hiphil 1111

keep, to be delivered to
פָּקַד Hophal 1040

keep fast, to
דָּבֵק דָּבַק } Kal 318

keep *feast*, to
חָגַג Kal........ 401

keep *house*, to make to
יָשַׁב Hiphil 568

keep in, to
שָׁבַח Piel........ 1225

keep (*oneself*) far, to
רָחַק Kal........ 1170

keep secretly, to
צָפַן Kal........ 1080

מוֹדָע
מוֹדַע } ... 670
קָרוֹב ... 1127
שְׁאֵר ... 1223
kinsman, to do the part of a
גָּאַל ¹ Kal ... 285
kinsman, near
גָּאַל ¹ Kal ... 285
שְׁאֵר ... 1223
kinsman, next
גָּאַל ¹ Kal ... 285
kinsman, to perform the part of a
גָּאַל ¹ Kal ... 285
kinswoman
מוֹדָע
מוֹדַע } ... 670
שְׁאֵר ... 1223
kinswoman, *see* near
Kirjath-huzoth
חוּץ ... 408
kiss
נְשִׁיקָה ... 848
kiss, to
נָשַׁק Kal ... 849
נָשַׁק Piel ... 849
kite
אַיָּה ... 57
knead, to
לוּשׁ Kal ... 636
kneading trough
מִשְׁאֶרֶת ... 768
knee
אַרְכֻּבָה Ch. ... 157
בֶּרֶךְ ... 276
בְּרֵךְ Ch. ... 276
knee, *see* bow
kneel, to
בָּרַךְ Kal ... 274
בְּרַךְ Ch. P'al ... 276
kneel down, to
בָּרַךְ Kal ... 274
kneel down, to make to
בָּרַךְ Hiphil ... 274
kneeling
כָּרַע Kal ... 618
knife
חֶרֶב ... 459
מַאֲכֶלֶת ... 658
שַׂכִּין ... 1206
knit, to be
קָשַׁר Niphal ... 1132
knit together
חָבֵר ... 400
knives
מַחֲלָפִים ... 687
knock, to
דָּפַק Kal ... 348
knop
כַּפְתּוֹר ... 615

knops
פְּקָעִים ... 1042
* know
דַּעַת ... 347
know, to
בִּין Kal ... 212
דַּעַת ... 347
יָדַע Kal ... 500
יְדַע Ch. P'al ... 506
נָכַר Piel ... 818
נָכַר Hiphil ... 818
know, to cause to
יָדַע Piel ... 500
יָדַע Hiphil ... 500
know, to let
יָדַע Hiphil ... 500
know, to make
יָדַע Hiphil ... 500
knowledge
בִּינָה ... 213
000 ... 000
דֵּעַ ... 347
דֵּעָה ... 347
דַּעַת ... 347
יָדַע Kal ... 500
מַדָּע
מַדַּע } ... 667
מַנְדַּע Ch. ... 732
עַיִן ... 919
שֶׂכֶל
שֵׂכֶל } ... 1207
knowledge, to come to
יָדַע Hophal ... 500
knowledge, to give
יָדַע Hiphil ... 500
knowledge, to have
יָדַע Kal ... 500
knowledge, to take
יָדַע Kal ... 500
נָכַר Hiphil ... 818
known
יָדַע (כ׳) Pual ... 500
יָדַע Hophal ... 500
known, to be
יָדַע Niphal ... 500
נָכַר Niphal ... 818
נָכַר Hithpael ... 818
known, to make
יָדַע Hiphil ... 500
יְדַע Ch. Aphel ... 506
known, to make to be
יָדַע Hiphil ... 500
known, to make...self
יָדַע Niphal ... 500
יָדַע Hithpael ... 500
Koa
קוֹעַ ... 1104

labben, *see* Muth-labben
labour
יְגִיעַ ... 188
יָד ... 489
יָלַד Kal ... 527
מְלָאכָה ... 705
מַעֲשֶׂה ... 746
עֲבוֹדָה ... 894
עָמָל ... 960
עֶצֶב ... 971
עֹצֶב ... 971
פְּעֻלָּה ... 1038
labour, to
אוּץ Hiphil ... 31
יָגַע Kal ... 488
עָבַד Kal ... 887
עָמַל Kal ... 960
עָשָׂה Kal ... 981
שְׁדַר Ch. Ithpael ... 1238
labour, *see* bring forth
labour, full of
יָגֵעַ ... 489
labour, to make to
יָגַע Piel ... 488
labour, strong to
סָבַל Pual ... 868
laboured †
הֲוָא
הֲוָה } Ch. P'al ... 358
laboured, for
יְגַע ... 489
laboureth, that
עָמֵל ... 960
labouring man
עָבַד Kal ... 887
lace
פָּתִיל ... 1055
lack
מַחְסוֹר ... 689
lack, to
חָסֵר Kal ... 450
חָסֵר ... 450
עָדַר ¹ Niphal ... 905
עָדַר ¹ Piel ... 905
פָּקַד Niphal ... 1040
רוּשׁ Kal ... 1166
lack, to have
חָסֵר Hiphil ... 450
lack of, for
בְּלִי ... 229
lacking, to be
עָדַר ¹ Niphal ... 905
lacking in his parts
קָלַט Kal ... 1109
lacking, to suffer to be
שָׁבַת Hiphil ... 1234

lad
נַעַר ... 823
ladder
סֻלָּם ... 878
lade, to
טָעַן Kal ... 484
כָּבֵד / כָּבַד } Hiphil ... 581
נָשָׂא Kal ... 840
עָמַס Kal ... 960
עָמַס Hiphil ... 960
laded
עָמַשׂ Kal ... 961
laden
כָּבֵד ... 582
lady
גְּבֶרֶת ... 292
שָׂרָה ... 1217
lahai-roi, *see* Beer-lahai-roi
laid
שׂוּם Ch. P'al ... 1204
שָׁכַב Hophal ... 1257
laid, *see* desolate, waste
laid, to be
בּוֹא Kal ... 189
נָשָׂא Kal ... 840
נָתַן Niphal ... 851
עָלָה Kal ... 934
שׂוּם / שִׂים } Kal ... 1200
שׂוּם Ch. Ithp'al ... 1204
שִׁית Hophal ... 1256
שָׁכַב Hophal ... 1257
שָׁתַת Kal ... 1333
laid, to be, *see* foundation
laid down, to be
שָׁכַב Kal ... 1257
* laid, more be
כָּבֵד / כָּבַד } Kal ... 581
laid out, to be
יָצָא Kal ... 548
laid over
תָּפַשׂ Kal ... 1355
laid, strongly
סְבַל Ch. Poal ... 868
laid up, to be
חָסַן Niphal ... 450
laid up in store, to be
כָּמַס Kal ... 604
laid up, that which...
פְּקֻדָּה ... 1041
laid waste, to be
נָצָה[2] Kal ... 834
שָׁדַד Pual ... 1237
lamb
טָלֶה ... 481
כֶּבֶשׂ ... 585
כִּבְשָׂה / כַּבְשָׂה } ... 585
כַּר ... 615
כֶּשֶׂב ... 620
כִּשְׂבָּה ... 620
צֹאן ... 1055
שֶׂה ... 1199
lamb †
בֵּן ... 232
lamb, *see* ewe
lambs
אִמְּרִין Ch. ... 134
טְלָאִים ... 481
lambs †
צֹאן ... 1055
lame
נָכֶה ... 817
פִּסֵּחַ ... 1037
lame, to become
פָּסַח Niphal ... 1036
lament, to
אָבַל Kal ... 11
אָבַל Hithpael ... 11
אָלָה[1] Kal ... 78
אָנָה Kal ... 136
נָהָה Kal ... 798
נָהָה Niphal ... 798
סָפַד Kal ... 881
קוּן Polel ... 1104
תָּנָה[2] Piel ... 1352
lament, to make to
אָבַל Hiphil ... 11
lamentable
עֲצִב Ch. P'al ... 971
lamentation
אֲנִיָּה ... 140
מִסְפֵּד ... 738
נְהִי ... 798
קִינָה ... 1107
lamentation, to make
בָּכָה Kal ... 226
lamented, to be
סָפַד Niphal ... 881
lamp
לַפִּיד ... 644
נֵיר ... 814
נִיר ... 814
נֵר ... 840
lamp, *see* burning
lance
כִּידוֹן ... 596
lancet
רֹמַח ... 1175
land
אֲדָמָה ... 21
אֶרֶץ ... 157
שָׂדֶה ... 1197
land, *see* barren, dry, piece, thirsty
land, born in the
אֶזְרָח ... 37
landmark
גְּבוּל ... 288
גְּבוּלָה ... 289
language
דָּבָר ... 325
לָשׁוֹן ... 651
לִשָּׁן Ch. ... 652
שָׂפָה ... 1213
language, strange
לָעַז Kal ... 644
languish, to
אָמַל Pulal ... 103
languishing
דְּוַי ... 337
lap
בֶּגֶד ... 185
חֵיק ... 425
חֹצֶן ... 455
lap, to
לָקַק Kal ... 651
לָקַק Piel ... 651
lapwing
דּוּכִיפַת ... 337
large
רָוַח Pual ... 1160
רָחַב Niphal ... 1166
רָחָב ... 1166
large †
רָחָב ... 1166
* large †
יָד ... 489
large, to make
רָחַב Hiphil ... 1166
large place
מֶרְחָב ... 763
large room
מֶרְחָב ... 763
largeness
רֹחַב ... 1167
last
אַחֲרוֹן ... 53
אַחֲרִית ... 54
עָקֵב ... 974
last, to
הָיָה Kal ... 360
last, at
אָחֳרֵין Ch. ... 54
last end
אַחֲרִית ... 54
lasting
עוֹלָם ... 907
latchet
שְׂרוֹךְ ... 1217
latchet, *see* shoelatchet
late, to be
אָחַר Piel ... 48
late, of
אֶתְמוֹל / אֶתְמוּל } ... 183

latter
אַחֲרוֹן ... 53
אַחֲרִית ... 54
אַחֲרִית Ch. ... 54
latter, *see* growth
latter end
אַחֲרִית (& אחרון..53) 54
latter (*rain*)
מַלְקוֹשׁ ... 730
latter time
אַחֲרִית ... 54
lattice
אֶשְׁנָב ... 179
חֲרַכִּים ... 464
שְׂבָכָה ... 1195
laugh, to
לָעַג Kal ... 644
צְחֹק ... 1070
צָחַק Kal ... 1070
שָׂחַק Kal ... 1205
laugh, *see* scorn
laughed to scorn
צְחֹק ... 1070
שְׂחוֹק ... 1204
laughing
שְׂחוֹק ... 1204
laughter
שְׂחוֹק ... 1204
laver
כִּיּוֹר ... 596
lavish, to
זוּל Kal ... 383
law
דָּת ... 355
דָּת Ch. ... 355
חֹק ... 456
חָקַק Pual ... 458
מִצְוָה ... 753
מִשְׁפָּט ... 776
תּוֹרָה ... 1343
law, *see* daughter, father, mother, sister, son
law, manner of
מִשְׁפָּט ... 776
lawful
מִשְׁפָּט ... 776
צַדִּיק ... 1061
lawful, to be
שַׁלִּיט Ch. ... 1275
lawgiver
חָקַק Poel ... 458
lay
נָפַל Kal ... 825
רָבַץ Hiphil ... 1154
* lay
שִׁכְבָה ... 1258
lay, to
חָלָה Piel ... 429
יְהַב Ch. P'al ... 507
יָנַח Hiphil ... 541
יָסַד Kal ... 542
יָרָה Kal ... 564
מָלַט Piel ... 710
מִשְׁלוֹחַ ... 772
נוּחַ Hiphil ... 800
נָטָה Hiphil ... 810
נָצַב Hiphil ... 833
נָשָׂא Kal ... 840
נָתַן Kal ... 851
סָמַךְ Kal ... 879
עָבַר Hiphil ... 895
פָּגַע Hiphil ... 1009
שׂוּם, שִׂים } Kal ... 1200
שָׁוָה [1] Piel ... 1245
שִׁית Kal ... 1256
שָׁכַב Hiphil ... 1257
שָׁכֵן, שָׁכַן } Hiphil ... 1260
שָׁלַח Kal ... 1268
שָׁלַח Piel ... 1268
lay, *see* beams, foundation, heavily, hold, low, plaister, pledge, siege, snare, wait, waste
lay along, to
נָפַל Kal ... 825
lay at, to
נָשַׂג Hiphil ... 845
lay away, to
סוּר Hiphil ... 872
lay by, to
סוּר Hiphil ... 872
lay down, to
יָנַח Hiphil ... 541
שִׂים, שׂוּם } Kal ... 1200
lay down again, to
שׁוּב Kal ... 1238
lay for, *see* foundation
lay hold, to
אָחַז Kal ... 46
תָּפַשׂ Kal ... 1355
lay hold on, to
תָּפַשׂ Kal ... 1355
lay in, *see* order
lay meat, to
אָכַל Hiphil ... 70
lay (*oneself*) down, to
שָׁכַב Kal ... 1257
lay open, to
פָּרַשׂ Kal ... 1048
lay out, to
יָצָא Hiphil ... 548
יָצַק Hiphil ... 556
lay privily, to
טָמַן Kal ... 483
lay self down, to
שָׁכַב Kal ... 1257
lay snare, to
יָקשׁ Kal ... 559
lay *snare*, to
יָקשׁ Kal ... 559
lay to, *see* charge
lay unto charge, to
נָתַן Kal ... 851
lay up, to
יָנַח Hiphil ... 541
נְחַת Ch. Aphel ... 810
נָתַן Kal ... 851
פָּקַד Hiphil ... 1040
צָבַר Kal ... 1061
צָפַן Kal ... 1080
שִׂים, שׂוּם } Kal ... 1200
שִׁית Kal ... 1256
lay up in store, to
אָצַר Kal ... 149
lay wait, to
אָרַב Kal ... 149
אָרַב Hiphil ... 149
שׁוּר [2] Kal ... 1248
* lay wait, to
רִיב Kal ... 1171
lay, where each
רֶבֶץ ... 1154
lay, while
שִׁיבָה ... 1254
laying of wait
צְדִיָּה ... 1061
leach, *see* horseleach
lead
עוֹפֶרֶת ... 912
lead, to
אָשַׁר Piel ... 180
בּוֹא Hiphil ... 189
דָּרַךְ Hiphil ... 349
הָלַךְ Piel ... 362
יָבַל Hiphil ... 486
יָלַךְ Hiphil ... 531
נָהַג [1] Kal ... 797
נָהַג [1] Piel ... 797
נָהַג [2] Piel ... 798
נָהַל Piel ... 798
נָחָה Kal ... 804
נָחָה Hiphil ... 804
* lead, to
רֹאשׁ ... 1142
lead, *see* captive
lead about, to
סָבַב Poel ... 865
סָבַב Hiphil ... 865
lead away, to
נָהַג [1] Kal ... 797
lead captive, to
גָּלָה Hiphil ... 307

עָזַב Niphal 915
עָזַב Pual 915
שָׂרִיד 1217
שָׁאַר Niphal 1222
שָׁאַר Hiphil 1222
שְׁבַק Ch. Ithpael......1232

left behind, to be
יָתַר Niphal 580

left, to go to the
שָׂמַאל Hiphil 1208

left hand
שְׂמֹאול 1208

* left, on the
שָׂמַאל Hiphil 1208

left side
שְׂמֹאול 1208

left, that hath
יֶתֶר 580

* left, to the
שָׂמַאל Hiphil 1208

left, to turn to
שָׂמַאל Hiphil 1208

lefthanded
אִטֵּר 55
יָד 489
יָמִין 540

leg
רֶגֶל 1155
שֹׁבֶל 1227
שׁוֹק 1248
שָׁק Ch. 1322

legs
כְּרָעַיִם 618

legs, *see* ornament

Lehi
לְחִי 637

lend, to
לָוָה Hiphil 634
נָשָׁה[2] Kal 847
נָשָׁה[2] Hiphil 847
נָתַן Kal 851
עָבַט Hiphil 895
שָׁאַל Hiphil 1220

lend on, *see* usury

lender
לָוָה Hiphil 634

length
אַחֲרִית 54
אֹרֶךְ 156

lengthen, to
אָרַךְ Hiphil 156

lengthened, to be
אָרַךְ Hiphil 156

lengthening
אַרְכָא Ch. 157

lent, to be
שָׁאַל Kal 1220

lent upon, *see* usury

lentiles
עֲדָשִׁים 905

leopard
נָמֵר 819
נְמַר Ch. 819

leper
צָרַע Kal 1082
צָרַע Pual 1082

leprosy
צָרַעַת 1082

leprous
צָרַע Kal 1082
צָרַע Pual 1082

less
מַטָּה 691
מָעַט Hiphil 741
קָטֹן 1105
קָטָן 1105

less, *see* how much

* less, to give
מָעַט Hiphil 741

* less, to give the
מָעַט Hiphil 741

less than nothing
אֶפֶס 147

lesser
קָטֹן 1105

lesser, *see* cattle

lest
בַּל 229
בִּלְתִּי 231
מַעַן 744
פֶּן 1021

lest peradventure
פֶּן 1021

let, to
נָתַן Kal 851
פָּרַע Hiphil 1046
שָׁאַר Hiphil 1222
שׁוּב Hiphil 1238

let, *see* cease, come, drink, fail, fall, gender, go, go out, hear, heard, know, live, loose, redeemed, remain, rest, run down, see, wander

let alone, to
חָדַל Kal 402
יָנַח Hiphil 541
מָלַט Piel 710
רָפָה Hiphil 1188
שְׁבַק Ch. P'al 1232
שִׁית Kal 1256

let down, to
יָרַד Hiphil 561
נוּחַ Hiphil 800
נָטָה Hiphil 810
רָפָה Piel 1188
שָׁלַח Piel 1268
שָׁקַע Hiphil 1325

let down, to be
יָלַךְ Kal 531

let go, to
000 000
רָפָה Hiphil 1188
שָׁלַח Kal 1268
שָׁלַח Piel 1268

let go, *see* free

let out, to
נָתַן Kal 851
פָּטַר Kal 1017

let remain, to
יָנַח Hiphil 541

letter
אִגְּרָא Ch. 14
אִגֶּרֶת 14
נִשְׁתְּוָן 850
נִשְׁתְּוָן Ch. 850
סֵפֶר 883
פִּתְגָּם Ch. 1052

letting go
שָׁלַח Piel 1268

leviathan
לִוְיָתָן 635

Levite
בֵּן 232

levy
מַס 736

levy, to
עָלָה Hiphil 934
רוּם Hiphil 1163

lewd
זִמָּה 388

lewdly
זִמָּה 388

lewdness
זִמָּה 388
מְזִמָּה 684
נַבְלוּת 787

liar
אַכְזָב 70
בַּד 186
כָּזַב Kal 594
שֶׁקֶר 1325

liar †
כָּזָב 594

liar, to be found
כָּזַב Niphal 594
כָּחַשׁ Niphal 595

liar, to make a
כָּזַב Hiphil 594

liberal
בְּרָכָה 276
נָדִיב 796

liberal things
נָדִיב 796

liberally
עָנַק Hiphil 967

liberty
דְּרוֹר 349
חָפְשִׁי 453

כַּפְתּוֹר ... 615
מַשְׁקוֹף ... 778

lintel, upper
כַּפְתּוֹר ... 615

lion
אֲרִי / אַרְיֵה ... 155
אַרְיֵה Ch. ... 155
כְּפִיר ... 614
לָבִיא ... 632
לַיִשׁ ... 642
שַׁחַל ... 1251

* lion
שַׁחַץ ... 1252

lion, great
לָבִיא ... 632

lion, old
לָבִיא ... 632
לַיִשׁ ... 642

lion, stout
לָבִיא ... 632

lion, young
אֲרִי / אַרְיֵה ... 155

lioness
לְבִיָּא ... 632

lionesses
לְבָאוֹת ... 630

lionlike men
אֲרִאֵל / אֲרִיאֵל / אֲרִאֵל ... 155

lions
לְבָאִים ... 630

lip
שָׂפָה ... 1213

lip, upper
שָׂפָם ... 1214

lips
שָׂפָם ... 1214

liquor
דֶּמַע ... 346
מֶזֶג ... 683
מִשְׁרָה ... 779

listen, to
שָׁמַע / שָׁמֵעַ Kal ... 1292

litter
צָב ... 1057

little
זְעֵיר ... 390
זְעֵיר Ch. ... 391
מְעַט ... 741
מִצְעִירָה ... 755
צָעִיר ... 1076
קָטֹן ... 1105
קָטָן ... 1105

* little
כִּבְרָה ... 585

little, *see* chamber, children, flock, rivers, while

little, to be
מָעַט Kal ... 741

little, a
שֶׁמֶץ ... 1300
שֶׁצֶף ... 1322

little, to gather
מָעַט Hiphil ... 741

little hill
גִּבְעָה ... 291

little one
מִצְעָר ... 755
עֲוִיל ... 906
עֹלֵל / עוֹלֵל ... 907
צָעוֹר ... 1076
צָעִיר ... 1076
צָעַר Kal ... 1077
קָטֹן (& קטן) ... 1105

little ones
טַף ... 484

little owl
כּוֹס ... 593

little, to seem
מָעַט Kal ... 741

little thing, very
דַּק ... 348

little while
מְעַט ... 741

live
חַי ... 418
חֲיָא / חֲיָה Ch. P'al ... 423

live, to
חַי ... 418
חָיָה Kal ... 421
חָיַי Kal ... 423

live coal
רִצְפָּה ... 1190

live, to let
חָיָה Piel ... 421
חָיָה Hiphil ... 421

live out, *see* half

live, to suffer to
חָיָה Piel ... 421

lively
חַי ... 419
חָיֶה ... 423

liver
כָּבֵד ... 583

lives, *see* save

liveth, that
חַי Ch. ... 421

living
חַי ... 418
חַי Ch. ... 421

* living
חַיּוּת ... 423

living, *see* creature

living substance
יְקוּם ... 558

living thing
חַי ... 418

lizard
לְטָאָה ... 640

lo
אֲרוּ Ch. ... 152
הָא Ch. ... 355
הֵא ... 355
הֵן ... 369
הִנֵּה ... 369
רָאָה Kal ... 1133

Lo-ammi
עַם & עָם ... 944

Lo-ruhamah
רָחַם Pual ... 1168

load, to
עָמַס Kal ... 960

loaf
כִּכָּר ... 597
לֶחֶם ... 638

loan
שְׁאֵלָה ... 1222

loathe, to
בּוּס Kal ... 205
מָאַס[1] Kal ... 659
קוּץ[3] Kal ... 1104

loathsome
זָרָא ... 394
קָלָה[1] Niphal ... 1108

loathsome, to be
בָּאַשׁ Hiphil ... 184

loathsome, to become
מָאַס[2] Niphal ... 659

lock
מַנְעוּל ... 735

lock
צִיצִת ... 1071

lock, to
נָעַל Kal ... 822

locks
מַחְלָפוֹת ... 687
פֶּרַע ... 1047
צַמָּה ... 1074
קְוֻצּוֹת ... 1104

locust
אַרְבֶּה ... 149
גֵּב ... 287
חָגָב ... 401
צְלָצַל ... 1074

locust, bald
סָלְעָם ... 878

lodge
מְלוּנָה ... 707

lodge, to
לוּן / לִין Kal ... 635
שָׁכַב Kal ... 1257

lodge again, to
שׁוּב Kal............1238

lodge all night, to
לוּן / לִין } Kal........... 635

lodge, to cause to
לוּן / לִין } Hiphil......... 635

lodge in, to
לוּן / לִין } Kal........... 635

lodge, place where...
מָלוֹן 707

lodge this night, to
לוּן / לִין } Kal........... 635

lodging
מָלוֹן 707

lodging, to
לוּן / לִין } Kal........... 635

lodging place
מָלוֹן 707

loft
עֲלִיָּה................ 941

loftily
מָרוֹם 763

loftiness
גֹּבַהּ 287
גַּבְהוּת 287

lofty
גָּבֹהַּ / גָּבוֹהַּ } 287
גַּבְהוּת 287
נָשָׂא Niphal 840
רוּם Kal............1163
שָׂגַב Niphal 1197

lofty, to be
רוּם Kal.............1163

log *of oil*
לֹג 633

loin
חֲרַץ Ch.............. 466

loins
חֲלָצַיִם................ 435
יָרֵךְ................ 565
כֶּסֶל................ 609
מָתְנַיִם................ 780

long
אָרֵךְ................ 156
אֲרֻכָּה................ 157
גָּדוֹל................ 293
מָתַי................ 779
עוֹלָם................ 907
עֵת................1005
רֹב................1150
רַב................1174

* long
שָׁנָה................1305

* long †
שָׁנָה 1305

long, *see* all life, enjoy, grow, how, remain, so, span, tarry

long, to
אָוָה Piel............. 29
אָוָה Hithpael........ 29
חָכָה Piel............. 426
חָשַׁק Kal............. 471
יָאַב Kal............. 486
כָּלָה Piel............. 598
כָּמַהּ Kal............. 603
כָּסַף Niphal 609
שָׁקַק Kal.............1325
תָּאַב[1] Kal.............1333

long, to be
אָרַךְ Kal............. 156
אָרַךְ Hiphil 156
בּוֹשׁ Piel............. 206
רָבָה Kal.............1151

long ago
רָחוֹק................1168

long as, *see* as, so

long as, as
יוֹם 508
פָּנִים................1023

long as (I) live, so
יוֹם................ 508

long, to become
אָרַךְ Kal............. 156

long continuance, (to be) of
אָמַן Niphal 103

long enough
רַב................1174

long for, thing that I
תִּקְוָה................1356

long, to make
אָרַךְ Hiphil 156
מָשַׁךְ Kal............. 770

long, to sound
מָשַׁךְ Kal............. 770

long time
עוֹלָם 907

long *time*
רַב................1147

longer
עוֹד 905

* longer
יָסַף Hiphil 543

longer, *see* tarry

longer, any
עוֹד 905

longing
תַּאֲבָה................1334

longsuffering
אֶרֶךְ / אַף } .... 156 / 144

longwinged
אֶרֶךְ / אֵבֶר } .... 156 / 13

look
חֱזוּ Ch.............. 411
עַיִן................ 919

look, to
חוּל / חִיל } Kal 406
חָזָה Kal............. 410
נָבַט Piel............. 783
נָבַט Hiphil 783
פָּנָה Kal.............1021
פָּקַד Kal.............1040
קָוָה Piel.............1095
רָאָה Kal.............1133
שׂוּם / שִׂים } Kal 1200
שָׁגַח Hiphil 1236
שׁוּר[2] Kal 1248
שָׁעָה Kal.............1315
שָׁקַף Niphal 1325
שָׁקַף Hiphil 1325

* look, to
שִׁית Kal.............1256

* look,† to
עַיִן................ 919

look, *see* narrowly, straight

look away, to
שָׁעָה Kal.............1315

look back, to
פָּנָה Hiphil 1021

look down, to
נָבַט Hiphil 783
שָׁקַף Niphal 1325
שָׁקַף Hiphil 1325

look forth, to
שָׁקַף Niphal 1325

look, to narrowly
שָׁגַח Hiphil 1236

look on, to
מַרְאֶה................ 761
רָאָה Kal.............1133

look one another, to
רָאָה Hithpael........1133

look one upon another, to
רָאָה Hithpael........1133

look out, to
רָאָה Kal.............1133
שָׁקַף Hiphil 1325

look to, to
מַרְאֶה................ 761
רְאִי................1141

look up, to
צָפָה Piel.............1077
רָאָה Kal.............1133

look upon, to
מַרְאֶה................ 761

רָאָה Kal............1133
שָׁזַף Kal............1249
look well, to
בִּין Kal............ 212
צָפָה Kal............1077
* look well, † to
עַיִן 919
look*eth*
מַרְאֶה 761
פָּנִים 1023
looking, *see* glass
looking glass
רְאִי 1141
looks
פָּנִים 1023
loops
לֻלָאֹת 643
loose
שְׁרֵא Ch. P'al 1326
loose, *see* let
loose, to
חָלַץ Kal............ 434
נָשַׁל Kal............ 848
נָתַר Hiphil............ 864
פָּתַח Piel 1052
loose, let
שָׁלַח Kal............1268
loose, to let
נָתַר Hiphil............ 864
שָׁלַח Piel............1268
loose self, to
פָּתַח Hithpael............1052
loosed, to be
זָחַח Niphal 384
מָסַס Niphal 737
נָטַשׁ Niphal 813
פָּתַח Niphal 1052
רָחַק Niphal (כ׳)............1170
רָתַק Niphal 1195
שְׁרֵא Ch. Ithpael 1326
lop, to
סָעַף Piel............ 880
lord
אָדוֹן 15
בַּעַל 262
גְּבִיר 290
מָרֵא Ch............ 760
סֶרֶן 385
רַב Ch............1150
שַׂר 1214
שָׁלִישׁ 1275
Lord
אֲדֹנָי 22
lord, *see* great
lord, to be
רוּד[1] Kal............1160
Lord, my
אֲדֹנָי 22

lordly
אַדִּיר 17
lords
רַבְרְבָן Ch............1154
lose, to
אָבַד Piel............ 8
אָסַף Kal............ 141
שָׁחַת Piel............1252
* lose, to
כָּרַת Hiphil 618
lose children, to
שָׁכֹל Kal............1259
lose *life*, to cause to
נָפַח Hiphil 825
loss, *see* time
loss, to bear the
חָטָא Piel............ 414
loss of children
שְׁכוֹל 1258
loss of others, to have after
שִׁכֻּלִים 1260
lost, to be
אָבַד Kal............ 8
נָפַל Kal............ 825
* lost, hast
נָפַל Kal............ 825
lost, that which was
אֲבֵדָה 9
lost thing
אֲבֵדָה 9
lot
גּוֹרָל 304
חֶבֶל / חֶבֶל } 399
lot, *see* divide
lothe, to
גָּעַל Kal............ 313
לָאָה Niphal 626
קָצַר Kal............1116
lothe selves, to
קוּט[1] Niphal............1096
lothing
גֹּעַל 313
loud
גָּדוֹל 293
הָמָה Kal............ 368
חָזָק 413
עֹז 914
רוּם Kal............1163
שָׁמַע 1299
loud, *see* noise
* loud, to sing
שָׁמַע / שָׁמַע } Hiphil............1292
louder, *see* wax
louder and louder
מְאֹד 652

love
אַהֲבָה 26
אֳהָבִים 26
אֲהָבִים 26
דּוֹד 336
רַעְיָה 1185
love, to
אָהֵב / אָהַב } Kal 25
אַהֲבָה 26
חָבַב Kal............ 398
רָחַם Kal............1168
love, in
אָהֵב / אָהַב } Kal............ 25
love, inordinate
עֲגָבָה 900
love, much
עֲגָבִים 900
love, to set
חָשַׁק Kal............ 471
love, tender
רַחֲמִים 1169
lovely
אָהֵב / אָהַב } Niphal 25
מַחְמָד 687
lovely, very
עֲגָבִים 900
lover
אָהֵב / אָהַב } Kal 25
אָהֵב / אָהַב } Piel 25
עָגַב Kal............ 900
רֵעַ 1181
lovers
אֲהָבִים 26
loves
יְדִיד 500
loving
טוֹב 476
lovingkindness
חֶסֶד 448
low
אָדָם 17
שָׁפָל 1322
תַּחְתִּי 1346
low, *see* bring, brought, man
low, to
גָּעָה Kal............ 313
low, to be
שָׁחַח Niphal 1250
שָׁפֵל Kal............1321
low, to bring
שָׁפֵל Hiphil 1321
low, to be brought
מָכַךְ Kal............ 699
מָכַךְ Hophal 699

low country
שְׁפֵלָה ... 1322
low estate
שֵׁפֶל ... 1322
low, to lay
שָׁפֵל Hiphil ... 1321
low, to be made
שָׁפֵל Kal ... 1321
low parts
תַּחְתִּי ... 1346
low place
שֵׁפֶל ... 1322
שְׁפֵלָה ... 1322
low plain
שְׁפֵלָה ... 1322
low, very
מַטָּה ... 691
lower
שָׁפָל ... 1322
תַּחְתּוֹן ... 1345
תַּחְתִּי ... 1346
lower, to make
חָסֵר Piel ... 450
lower parts
תַּחְתִּי ... 1346
lower, to be put
שָׁפֵל Hiphil ... 1321
lowest
קָצָה ... 1114
תַּחְתּוֹן ... 1345
תַּחְתִּי ... 1346
lowing
קוֹל ... 1096
lowly
עָנָו ... 965
עָנִי (כ׳) ... 965
צָנַע Kal ... 1076
שָׁפָל ... 1322
Lucifer
הֵילֵל ... 362
* Lucifer
יָלַל Hiphil ... 537
lucre
בֶּצַע ... 264
lump of *figs*
דְּבֵלָה ... 318
lurk privily, to
צָפַן Kal ... 1080
lurking
יָשַׁב Kal ... 568
lurking place
מַאֲרָב ... 660
lurking places
מַחֲבֹאִים ... 686
lust
נֶפֶשׁ ... 829
שְׁרִירוּת ... 1327
תַּאֲוָה ... 1334

lust, to
אָוָה Hithpael ... 29
חָמַד Kal ... 437
lust after
אַוָּה ... 33
lust after, to
אָוָה Piel ... 29
lusting
תַּאֲוָה ... 1334
lusty
שָׁמֵן ... 1290
lying
כְּדַב Ch. ... 586
כָּזַב Piel ... 594
כָּזָב ... 594
כָּחַשׁ Piel ... 595
כַּחַשׁ ... 595
כֶּחָשִׁים ... 596
שָׁוְא ... 1238
שֶׁקֶר ... 1325
lying
נָפַל Kal ... 825
lying †
דָּבָר ... 325
שֶׁקֶר ... 1325
lying down
רֶבַע ... 1154
lying in, *see* wait
lying in wait, man
אָרַב Kal ... 149
lying with
מִשְׁכָּב ... 770
שָׁכַב Kal ... 1257

Maaleh-*acrabbim*
מַעֲלֶה ... 744
mad
לָהַהּ Hithpael ... 634
שָׁגַע Pual ... 1236
mad, to be
הָלַל Hithpoel ... 366
שָׁגַע Hithpael ... 1236
mad against me
הָלַל Poel ... 366
mad, to feign self
הָלַל Hithpoel ... 366
mad, to make
הָלַל Poel ... 366
mad man
שָׁגַע Pual ... 1236
mad man, to play the
שָׁגַע Hithpael ... 1236
made
עָשָׂר (כ׳) ... 998
made, to be
חוּל } חִיל } Pulal ... 406
נָתַן Niphal ... 851

עֲבַד Ch. Ithpael ... 889
עָשָׂה Niphal ... 981
עָשָׂה Pual ... 981
שׂוּם } שִׂים } Kal ... 1200
שׂוּם Ch. P'al ... 1204
שׂוּם Ch. Ithp'al ... 1204
שְׁוָה Ch. Ithpael ... 1246
made, *see* almonds, appear, atonement, bald, better, breach, bring forth, broad, cedar, clean, desolate, drunk, fat, glorious, inquisition, king, like, low, mention, naked, partition, plain, possess, reckoning, red, search, serve, slaughter, straight, strong, sure, sweet, thin, unclean, white, whole
made by fire, *see* offering, sacrifice
made of, that is
כְּלִי ... 600
made, thing
מְלָאכָה ... 705
מַעֲשֶׂה ... 746
made up
אֲרוּכָה } אֲרֻכָה } ... 152
* *made* up, to be
עָלָה Kal ... 934
madness
הוֹלֵלָה ... 359
הוֹלֵלוּת ... 359
שִׁגָּעוֹן ... 1236
mag, *see* Rab-mag
magician
חַרְטֹם Ch. ... 464
חַרְטֻמִּים ... 464
magistrate
שְׁפַט Ch. P'al ... 1320
* magistrate †
יָרַשׁ Kal ... 566
עֶצֶר ... 973
magnifical
גָּדַל Hiphil ... 297
magnified, to be
גָּדַל Kal ... 297
נָשָׂא Niphal ... 840
magnify, to
גָּדַל Piel ... 297
גָּדַל Hiphil ... 297
שָׂגָא Hiphil ... 1197
magnify self, to
גָּדַל Hithpael ... 297
Magor-missabib
{ מָגוֹר ... 662
{ סָבִיב ... 866
Mahalath
מַחֲלַת ... 687
Mahanaim
מַחֲנֶה ... 688

Mahaneh-*dan*
מַחֲנֶה 688

Maher-shalal-hash-baz
{ מָהַר[1] Piel 669
שָׁלָל 1277
חוּשׁ Kal.............. 409
בַּז & בָּז .... 207 }

maid
אָמָה 100
בְּתוּלָה 284
נַעֲרָה 824
עַלְמָה 943
שִׁפְחָה 1318

* maid
בְּתוּלִים 284

maid child
נְקֵבָה 838

maiden
נַעֲרָה 824
שִׁפְחָה 1318

maidservant
אָמָה 100
שִׁפְחָה 1318

mail
קַשְׂקֶשֶׂת 1131

mail, *see* coat

maim, *see* Misrephoth-maim

maimed
חָרַץ Kal.............. 466

maintain, to
חָזַק Piel.............. 411
יָכַח Hiphil 525
עָשָׂה Kal.............. 981
תָּמַךְ Kal..............1350

maintenance
חַי 419

maintenance †
מְלַח Ch.............. 707

maintenance, † to have
מְלַח Ch. P'al......... 707

majesty
גָּאוֹן 285
גֵּאוּת 285
{ גְּדוּלָּה
גְּדוּלָּה } 296
הָדָר 357
הֲדַר Ch.............. 358
הוֹד 358
רְבוּ Ch..............1153
{ 000
000 } 000

make, to
בָּנָה Kal.............. 258
{ בְּנָא
בְּנָה } Ch. P'al...... 260
בָּרָא Kal.............. 270
{ חָצַב
חָצֵב } Kal 453
יָצַג Hiphil 555
יָצַר[1] Kal............ 556
נָתַן Kal....... 851
עֲבַד Ch. P'al......... 889
עָמַד Hiphil 955
עָצַב Piel............. 970
עָשָׂה Kal......... 981
פָּלַס Piel.............1021
פָּעַל Kal.............1037
פָּקַד Kal.............1040
000 Hiphil 000
קוּם Hiphil 1099
קוּם Ch. Aphel.......1103
{ שׂוּם
שִׂים } Kal............1200
שׂוּם Ch. P'al.........1204
שִׁית Kal.............1256

* make, to
כָּרָה Kal.............. 616
נָתַר Hiphil 864

make, *see* abhorred, abide, abominable, about, account of, accursed, afraid, alive, amazed, amends, appointment, approach, ashamed, atonement, bald, banquet, bare, beams, bed, better, bitter, boast, boil, brick, bright, bring forth, cakes, calve, cease, cheerful, childless, clean, cleave, come up, confession, conspiracy, consume, count, crooked, cry, dark, deep, desolate, difference, drink, drunk, drunken, dry, dust, dwell, eat, empty, end, endanger, enjoy, enquiry, equal, err, fail, fall, fat, few, firm, firstborn, fit, flee, flourish, fly, fold, foolish, fools, forget, fret, friendship with, fruitful, glad, glorious, go, go forth, go over, go up, good, goodly, great, great man, grievous, grow, hard, haste, hear, heard, heavy, hedge, high, honourable, hope, howl, inhabited, inherit, inquisition, insurrection, intercession, invasion, joyful, joyful noise, keep *house*, king, kneel down, know, known, labour, lament, large, league, liar, lie down, lighter, like, long, lower, many, marriages, melt, mention, mention of, merchandise, merry, mirth, mock, more, move, multiply, murmur, naked, nest, noise, obeisance, obstinate, odious, offender, oil, old, overflow, overseer, pass, pass by, pay, peace, perfect, perish, plain, plenteous, poor, possess, prayer, precious, preparation, princes, proclamation, prosper, prosperous, provision, queen, ready, reconciliation, refuge, reign, rejoice, remembered, request, rest, restitution, return, rich, ride, rise up, road, room, rot, rule, ruler, run away, rushing, sad, search, separation, serve, shake, shine, sin, singular, skip, slaughter, sleep, small, soft, sore, sound, speed, spoil, sport, stagger, stand, stiff, stink, stoop, straight, strange, strong, stronger, suck, suddenly, suit, supplication, sure, swear, sweet, swell, swim, tinkling, transgress, treasurer, tremble, trouble, trust, tumult, turn, understand, vain, vile, void, walk, wander, war, waste, weary, white, whole, wide, willing, wise, wiser, wonderful, wonderfully, governor

make again, to
שׁוּב Kal..............1238

make as if, *see* ambassadors

make to be at, *see* peace, stand

make away, *see* utterly

make away, utterly to
חָרַם Hiphil 464

make *baldness*, to
קָרַח Kal..............1128

make *bed*, to
הָפַךְ Kal.............. 370
רָפַד Piel..............1188

make *breach*, to
פָּרַץ Kal..............1047

make *brick*, to
לָבַן Kal.............. 632

make *burning*, to
שָׂרַף Kal..............1218

make (cakes), to
לָבַב Piel.............. 630

make clean, *see* riddance

make *conspiracy*, to
קָשַׁר Kal..............1132

make *covenant*, to
כָּרַת Kal.............. 618

make *cuttings*, to
שָׂרַט Kal..............1217

make *desolate*, to
שָׁמֵם Hiphil 1289

make diligent, *see* search

make to go, *see* whoring

* make *go* up and down, to
נוּעַ (כ') Kal 802

make to have, *see* dominion

make *interpretations*, to
פְּשַׁר Ch. P'al.........1051

make *king*, to
מָלַךְ Hiphil 710

make loud, *see* noise

make *noise*, to
{ שָׁמַע
שָׁמַע } Hiphil 1292

make of none, *see* effect

make of quick, *see* understanding

make *ointment*, to
רָקַח Kal..............1191

make on, *see* high

make out, to
{ שִׂים
שׂוּם } Kal 1200

make *petition*, to
{ בְּעָא
בְּעָה } Ch. P'al 261

make (*prayer*), to
פָּלַל Hithpael........1021

make ready (עָשָׂה....991)
שָׁלֵם 1278

make ready, *see* quickly

make self, *see* fair, known, many, poor, prey, prince, prophet, rich, sick, strong, unclean, wise

make *slaughter*, to
נָכָה Hiphil 814

make *supplication*, to
חָנַן Hithpael........ 446

make up, to
גָּדַר Kal.............. 298
כָּלַל Shaphel......... 603

make *vow*, to
נָדַר Kal.............. 797

make *wall*, to
גָּדַר Kal.............. 298

maker
חָרָשׁ 467
יָצַר¹ Kal.............. 556
עָשָׂה Kal.............. 981
פָּעַל Kal.............1037
פֹּעַל 1038

making
עָשָׂה Kal.............. 981

making, *see* desolate, merry

making, wares of...
מַעֲשֶׂה 746

Malcham
מֶלֶךְ 712

male
זָכוּר 385
זָכָר 387

male, to be
זָכַר Niphal 385

mallows
מַלּוּחַ 706

man
אָדָם 17
אִישׁ 60
אֱנוֹשׁ 136
אֱנָשׁ Ch.............. 141
בֵּן 232
בַּעַל 262
גִּבּוֹר 289
גְּבַר 292
גְּבַר Ch.............. 292
גֶּבֶר 292
זָכָר 387
נֶפֶשׁ 829

man †
בֵּן 232
נֶפֶשׁ 829

man, a
אֶחָד 41

man came, a
בּוֹא Kal.............. 189

man child
זָכָר 387

man, every
גֻּלְגֹּלֶת 307

man of great
גָּדוֹל 293

man, young
עֶלֶם 943

mandrakes
דּוּדַי 336

maneh
מָנֶה 733

manifest, to
בָּרַר Kal.............. 277

manifold
רַב 1147

manifold, to be
רָבַב¹ Kal.............1151

mankind
זָכָר 387

*man*kind
בָּשָׂר 278

man*kind*
אִישׁ 60

manna
מָן 731

manner
אֹרַח 154
דָּבָר 325
דֹּבֶר 334
דְּמוּת 345
דֶּרֶךְ 349
דָּת 355
חֻקָּה 457
מִשְׁפָּט 776
תּוֹרָה 1343

* manner
כֵּן 604

manner, *see* after, all, any, like, no, that, this, what, workmanship

manner, in like
גַּם 311

manner of, *see* law

* manner of store, all
זַן 389

manservant
עֶבֶד 889

manslayer
רָצַח Kal.............1190

mantle
אַדֶּרֶת 24
מְעִיל 742
שְׂמִיכָה 1210

mantles
מַעֲטָפוֹת 741

many
הָמוֹן 368
רַב 1147
רֹב 1150
רְבָבָה 1151
שַׂגִּיא Ch..............1197

* many
רָבָה Hiphil 1151

many, to be
רָבַב¹ Kal.............1151
רָבָה Kal.............1151

* many, to be
רָבָה Hiphil 1151

many a time
רַב 1147

* many a time
רָבָה Hiphil 1151

many as, *see* as

many, do
רַב 1174

many, to give
רָבָה Hiphil 1151

many, have
רַב 1174

many, to have
רָבָה Hiphil 1151

many, to make
רָבָה Hiphil 1151

many, to make self
כָּבֵד / כָּבַד } Hithpael...... 581

many more, *see* so

many soever, *see* how

many things
רַב 1147

many, to use
רָבָה Hiphil 1151

mar, to
כָּאַב Hiphil 581
נָתַס Kal.............. 863
שָׁחַת Piel.............1252
שָׁחַת Hiphil 1252

Mara
מַר 760

marble
שַׁיִשׁ 1256
שֵׁשׁ 1328

marble, *see* black

march, to
הָלַךְ Kal.............. 362
יָלַךְ Kal.............. 531
נָסַע Kal.............. 821
צָעַד Kal.............1076

march through, to
צָעַד Kal.............1076

mariner
מַלָּח 707
שׁוּט² Kal.............1246

marish
גֶּבֶא 287

mark
אוֹת 33
מַטָּרָא 694
מַטָּרָה 694
מִפְגָּע 747
תָּו 1337

mark, *see* landmark

mark, to
בִּין Kal 212
חָתַם Piel 471
יָדַע Kal 500
פָּנָה Kal 1021
קָשַׁב Hiphil 1131
רָאָה Kal 1133
שׂוּם, שִׂים } Kal 1200
שִׁית Kal 1256
שָׁמַר Kal 1300

mark out, to
תָּאַר Piel 1334

mark well, to
קָשַׁב Hiphil 1131

marked, to be
כָּתַם Niphal 623

market
מַעֲרָב 745

marks †
קַעֲקַע 1113

marred
מִשְׁחַת 769

marred, to be
שָׁחַת Niphal 1252

marriage, duty of
עוֹנָה 911

marriage, to be given to
הָלַל Pual 366

marriages, to make
חָתַן Hithpael 472

* married
נָשִׁים 847

* married †
בַּעַל 262

married, to be
בָּעַל Niphal 261

married wife
בָּעַל Kal 261

marrow
חֵלֶב 429
מֹחַ 685
שִׁקּוּי 1323

marrow, full of
מָחָה² Pual 686

* marry
נָשִׁים 847

marry, to
בָּעַל Kal 261
יָבַם Piel 487
לָקַח Kal 644
נָשָׂא Kal 840

* marry, to
יָשַׁב Hiphil 568

marrying
יָשַׁב Hiphil 568

mart
סָחַר 875

marvel, to
תָּמַהּ Kal 1349

marvellous
פָּלָא Niphal 1018

marvellous, to be
פָּלָא Niphal 1018

marvellous, to shew
פָּלָא Hiphil 1018
פָּלָה Hiphil 1019

marvellous, to shew self
פָּלָא Hithpael 1018

marvellous thing
פֶּלֶא 1018
פָּלָא Niphal 1018

marvellous work
פָּלָא Niphal 1018
פָּלָא Hiphil 1018

marvellous work, to do a
פָּלָא Hiphil 1018

marvellously
פָּלָא Niphal 1018
תָּמַהּ Kal 1349

marvellously, to be
פָּלָא Hiphil 1018

marvels
פָּלָא Niphal 1018

Maschil
שָׂכַל Hiphil 1206

mason
גָּדַר Kal 298
חָצַב, חָצֵב } Kal 453

mason †
אֶבֶן 11
חָרָשׁ 467
קִיר 1108

* Massah
מַסָּה 736

mast
חִבֵּל 399
תֹּרֶן 1358

master
אָדוֹן 15
בַּעַל 262
רַב 1147
רַב Ch. 1150
שַׂר 1214

* master
עוּר¹ Kal 913

master, *see* sheepmaster, *ship-master*, task-master

mastery
גְּבוּרָה 290

mastery, to have the
שְׁלֵט Ch. P'al 1274

mate
רְעוּת 1185

matrix
רֶחֶם 1169

matter
דָּבָר 325
חֵפֶץ 452
טַעַם Ch. 484
מִלָּה 706
מִלָּה Ch. 706
פִּתְגָם Ch. 1052

matter, *see* great, small, this

mattock
חֶרֶב 459
מַחֲרֵשָׁה 690
מַעְדֵּר 740

maul
מֵפִיץ 747

maw
קֵבָה 1083

may be
אוּלַי, אֻלַי } 30

may judge †
הֲוָא, הֲוָה } Ch. P'al 358

may offer †
הֲוָא, הֲוָה } Ch. P'al 358

Mazzaroth
מַזָּרוֹת 685

me
אֲנִי 140
נֶפֶשׁ 829

* me
עַיִן 919
עָמַד 958
פָּנִים 1023
קֳדָם Ch. 1089

me, *see* with

me, as for
אֲנָא, אֲנָה } Ch. 135
אֲנִי 140
אָנֹכִי 140

meadow
אָחוּ 45
מַעֲרֶה 745

Meah
מֵאָה 654

meal
סֹלֶת ... 879
קֶמַח ... 1110
mealtime
{ עֵת ... 1005
{ אֹכֶל ... 75
mean
חָשֹׁךְ ... 470
mean, to
דָּמָה[1] Piel ... 345
חָשַׁב Kal ... 468
mean man
אָדָם ... 17
mean while,† in the
כֹּה ... 586
meaning
בִּינָה ... 213
means
יָד ... 489
מַחֲשֶׁבֶת ... 690
means,† by this
קֳבֵל } Ch. ... 1084
קֳבֵל }
means of, by
בְּעַד ... 261
Mearah
מְעָרָה ... 745
measure
אֵיפָה ... 59
אַמָּה ... 101
חֹק ... 456
כֹּר ... 616
מַד ... 664
מִדָּה ... 666
מְשׂוּרָה ... 767
מִשְׁפָּט ... 776
מַתְכֹּנֶת ... 780
סְאָה ... 864
סַאסְּאָה ... 864
שָׁלִישׁ ... 1275
תֹּכֶן ... 1347
measure, *see* great
measure, to
מָדַד Kal ... 665
מָדַד Piel ... 665
מָדַד Polel ... 665
measured, to be
מָדַד Niphal ... 665
measures
כּוֹרִין Ch. ... 594
מְמַדִּים ... 730
measuring
מִדָּה ... 666
meat
אֲכִילָה ... 70
אָכַל Kal ... 70
אֹכֶל ... 75
אָכְלָה ... 75
בָּרָה Piel ... 270
בָּרוּת ... 271
בִּרְיָה ... 272
טֶרֶף ... 485
לֶחֶם ... 638
מַאֲכָל ... 658
מָזוֹן ... 684
מָזוֹן Ch. ... 684
פַּת ... 1051
צֵידָה ... 1071
meat, *see* lay, savoury
meat offering
מִנְחָה ... 734
מִנְחָה Ch. ... 735
meat, portion of
פַּתְבַּג ... 1052
meat, provision of
פַּתְבַּג ... 1052
meats, *see* dainty
meddle, to
גָּרָה Hithpael ... 315
עָבַר Hithpael ... 895
meddle with, to
עָרַב[1] Hithpael ... 975
meddled with, to be
גָּלַע Hithpael ... 310
meddling, to be
גָּלַע Hithpael ... 310
medicine
גֵּהָה ... 298
תְּרוּפָה ... 1358
medicines
רְפֻאוֹת ... 1188
meditate, to
הָגָה[1] Kal ... 356
שׂוּחַ Kal ... 1200
שִׂיחַ Kal ... 1206
meditation
הָגוּת ... 357
הָגִיג ... 357
הִגָּיוֹן ... 357
שִׂיחַ ... 1206
שִׂיחָה ... 1206
meek
עָנָו ... 965
עָנָיו ... 966
meekness
עֲנָוָה ... 965
עַנְוָה ... 965
meet
בֵּן ... 232
יָשָׁר ... 578
יְשַׁר ... 579
רָאָה Kal ... 1133
meet †
פָּנִים ... 1023
meet, to
יָעַד Niphal ... 545
מָצָא Kal ... 748
פָּגַע Kal ... 1009
פָּגַשׁ Kal ... 1010
פָּגַשׁ Niphal ... 1010
קָדַם Piel ... 1088
קָרָא[2] Kal ... 1122
קָרָא[2] Niphal ... 1122
קָרָה Kal ... 1127
קָרָה Niphal ... 1127
* meet, to
פָּנִים ... 1023
meet, to be
אֲרַךְ Ch. ... 156
כּוּן Niphal ... 592
עָשָׂה Niphal ... 981
צָלֵחַ Kal ... 1072
meet, to seem
יָשַׁר Kal ... 578
meet together, to
פָּגַע Kal ... 1009
פָּגַשׁ Kal ... 1010
פָּגַשׁ Niphal ... 1010
meet with, to
מָצָא Kal ... 748
פָּגַשׁ Piel ... 1010
meetest
יָשָׁר ... 578
meeting
קָרָא[2] Kal ... 1122
meeting, *see* solemn
melody
זִמְרָה ... 389
נָגַן Piel ... 791
melons
אֲבַטִּחִים ... 10
melt
תָּמֵס ... 1351
melt to
דָּלַף Kal ... 342
מוּג Kal ... 670
מוּג Hithpoel ... 670
מָסָה Hiphil ... 736
מָסַס Niphal ... 737
נָזַל Kal ... 803
נָסַךְ[1] Kal ... 820
נָתַךְ Hiphil ... 850
צָרַף Kal ... 1082
melt away, to
מָאַס[2] Niphal ... 659
מוּג Niphal ... 670
מָסַס Niphal ... 737
melt, to make
מָסָה Hiphil ... 736
melted, to be
מוּג Hithpoel ... 670
מָסַס Niphal ... 737
נָתַךְ Niphal ... 850
נָתַךְ Hophal ... 851

melted, is
הִתּוּךְ 376

melting
הֲמָסִים 369

* Melzar
מֶלְצַר 729

member, *see* privy

members
יְצֻרִים 557

memorial
אַזְכָּרָה 34
זֵכֶר } זֵכֶר 387
זִכָּרוֹן 387

memory
זֵכֶר } זֶכֶר 387

men
מְתִים 779
מְתֹם 780
עַם & עָם 944

men, certain
אֱנוֹשׁ 136

men of low degree
אָדָם 17

men, to play the
חָזַק Hithpael 411

men, to shew selves
אִישׁ Hithpalel 69

menchildren
זָכוּר 385

mend, to
חָזַק Piel 411

Mene
מְנֵא } מְנָה Ch. P'al 733

menstruous
נִדָּה 796

menstruous cloth
דָּוֶה 337

menstruous woman
נִדָּה 796

mention, to
זָכַר Kal 385

mention, to be made
זָכַר Niphal 385

mention, to make
זָכַר Kal 385

mention of, to make
זָכַר Hiphil 385

mentioned
שְׁמוּעָה 1285

mentioned, to be
בּוֹא Kal 189
זָכַר Niphal 385
קָרָא[1] Kal 1117

* mentioned, to be
עָלָה Hophal 934

Meonenim
עָנַן Poel 966

* Merathaim
מְרָתַיִם 766

merchandise
מַעֲרָב 745
מַרְכֹּלֶת 765
סָחַר 875
סַחַר 875
סְחֹרָה 875
רְכֻלָּה 1175

merchandise, to make
עָמַר Hithpael 961

merchant
כְּנַעַן 605
כְּנַעֲנִי 605
סָחַר Kal 874
רָכַל Kal 1175

merchant, *see* spice

merchantman
סָחַר Kal 875

merchant*man*
תּוּר Kal 1342

mercies
רַחֲמִין Ch. 1169

mercies, great
רַחֲמִים 1169

mercies, tender
רַחֲמִים 1169

merciful
חֶמְלָה 439
חָנַן Kal 446
חֶסֶד 448
חָסִיד 449
רַחוּם 1167
רָחַם Piel 1168

merciful, to be
חָנַן Kal 447
כָּפַר Piel 614

merciful kindness
חֶסֶד 448

merciful, to shew self
חָסַד Hithpael 447

mercy
חֶסֶד 448
רָחַם Piel 1168
רַחֲמִים 1169

mercy, to find
רָחַם Pual 1168

mercy, to have
רָחַם Piel 1168
רָחַם Pual 1168

mercy, to obtain
רָחַם Pual 1168

mercy on, to have
חָנַן Poel 447
רָחַם Piel 1168

mercy seat
כַּפֹּרֶת 615

mercy, to shew
חָנַן Kal 447
חֲנַן Ch. P'al 447
רָחַם Piel 1168

mercy upon, to have
חָנַן Kal 446
רָחַם Piel 1168

Meribah
מְרִיבָה 764

merrily
שָׂמֵחַ 1209

merry
הִלּוּלִים 362
טוֹב 476
שָׂמֵחַ 1209

merry †
חַי 419

merry, to be
יָטַב Kal 524
שָׂמֵחַ } שָׂמַח Kal 1208
שָׁכַר Kal 1261

merry, to make
יָטַב Hiphil 524
שָׂמֵחַ } שָׂמַח Piel 1208

merry, making
שָׂמֵחַ 1209

merry, that make
שָׂחַק Piel 1205

merryhearted
{ שָׂמֵחַ 1209
{ לֵב 626

Mesopotamia †
נָהָר 798

mess
מַשְׂאֵת 767

message
דָּבָר 325
מַלְאָכוּת 706

messenger
בָּשַׂר Piel 278
מַלְאָךְ 704
נָגַד Hiphil 788
צִיר 1071

messenger, to send a
צָוָה Piel 1065

Messiah
מָשִׁיחַ 769

met, to be
פָּגַשׁ Niphal 1010

met together, to be
יָעַד Niphal 545

mete, to
מָדַד Kal 665
תָּכַן Piel 1347

mete out, to
מָדַד Piel 665
* meted out
קַו & קָו 1095
meteyard
מִדָּה 666
Metheg
מֶתֶג 779
methoar, *see* Remmon-methoar
Michtam
מִכְתָּם 701
midday
צֹהַר 1065
mid*day*
מַחֲצִית 689
middle
חֲצִי / חֵצִי 454
טַבּוּר 473
כַּף 612
תָּוֶךְ 1338
תִּיכוֹן 1346
middlemost
תִּיכוֹן 1346
mid*night*
חֲצוֹת 454
חֲצִי / חֵצִי 454
תָּוֶךְ 1338
*mid*night
לַיִל 640
midst
גַּו Ch. 298
חֵיק 425
חֵצִי / חֲצִי 454
טַבּוּר 473
לֵב 626
לֵבָב 630
קֶרֶב 1125
תָּוֶךְ 1338
תִּיכוֹן 1346
midst, *see* from
midst among
תָּוֶךְ 1338
midst, to be cut off in the
חָצַץ Pual 455
midst, to reach to the
חָצָה Kal 454
midwife
יָלַד Piel 527
midwife, to do the office of a
יָלַד Piel 527
Migdal-*el*
מִגְדָּל 661
Migdal-*gad*
מִגְדָּל 661
might
אוֹן 31
אֵל 76
גְּבוּרָה 290
גְּבוּרָה Ch. 290
חַיִל 423
יָכֹל Kal 526
כֹּחַ 594
מְאֹד 652
עֹז 914
עֱזוּז 917
עֹצֶם 973
תְּקֹף Ch. 1357
might give †
הֲוָא / הֲוָה Ch. P'al 358
mightier
אַדִּיר 17
תַּקִּיף 1356
mightier, to be
עָצַם Kal 972
mightily
חֶזְקָה 414
מְאֹד 652
mightily, *see* come
mightily, is sometimes the translation of infinitives used intensitively.
mighty
אַבִּיר 10
אָבִיר 11
אַדִּיר 17
אוּל 30
אֵילִים 59
אֵתָן / אֵיתָן 70
אֵל 76
אַמִּיץ / אַמִּיץ 103
אָפִיק 146
גִּבּוֹר 289
גְּבוּרָה 290
גִּבָּר Ch. 292
גָּדוֹל 293
זְרוֹעַ 394
חָזָק 413
כַּבִּיר 584
מְאֹד 652
עַז 914
עֲיָם 919
עָצוּם 972
עָרִיץ 978
רַב 1147
שַׁלִּיט 1275
תַּקִּיף Ch. 1356
* mighty
אֱלֹהִים 79
גֶּבֶר 292
mighty †
בֵּן 232
mighty, *see* how
mighty, to be
גָּבַר Kal 291
עָצַם Kal 972
mighty act
גְּבוּרָה 290
mighty, to become
חָזַק Hithpael 411
* mighty God
צוּר 1069
mighty man
אִישׁ 60
גִּבּוֹר 289
mighty men
אֵילִים 59
mighty one
אַבִּיר 10
אַדִּיר 17
אֵל 76
גִּבּוֹר 289
* mighty one
צוּר 1069
mighty power
גְּבוּרָה 290
mighty things
בָּצַר Kal 264
mighty, to wax
חָזַק Hithpael 411
עָצַם Kal 972
milch
יָנַק 542
עוּל Kal 906
mildew
יֵרָקוֹן 566
milk
חָלָב 428
milk out, to
מָצַץ Kal 755
mill
רֵחַיִם 1168
millet
דֹּחַן 339
millions
רְבָבָה 1151
millstone
רֶכֶב 1173
millstone, upper
רֶכֶב 1173
millstones
רֵחַיִם 1168
mince, to
טָפַף Kal 484
mind
יֵצֶר 557
לֵב 626
לֵבָב 630
נֶפֶשׁ 829
פֶּה 1011
רוּחַ 1160
רוּחַ Ch. 1162

mind, *see* wicked
minded
לֵב 626
minded, *see* freewill, stedfastly
mindful, to be
זָכַר Kal.............. 385
mine
אֲנִי 140
* mine
יָד 489
עָמֹד 958
mingle, to
בָּלַל Kal.............. 230
מָסַךְ Kal.............. 737
mingle selves, to
עָרַב ¹ Hithpael 975
עֲרַב Ch. Ithpael...... 975
mingle selves,† to
הֲוָא } Ch. P'al...... 358
הֲוָה }
mingled
כִּלְאַיִם 598
לָקַח Hithpael 644
mingled, *see* people
mingled, to be
עָרַב ¹ Hithpael 975
mingled seed
כִּלְאַיִם 598
minish, to
גָּרַע Kal.............. 316
minished, to be
מָעַט Kal.............. 741
minister
פְּלַח Ch. P'al.........1019
שָׁרַת Piel.............1328
שָׁרֵת 1328
minister, *see* priest's office
minister, to
שְׁמַשׁ Ch. Pael.........1303
שָׁרַת Piel.............1328
minister judgment, to
דִּין Kal.............. 340
minister unto, to
שָׁרַת Piel.............1328
ministering
עֲבוֹדָה 894
ministry
יָד 489
עֲבוֹדָה 894
שָׁרֵת 1328
minstrel
נָגַן Piel.............. 791
Miphkad
מִפְקָד 748
miracle
אוֹת 33
מוֹפֵת 673
פָּלָא Niphal 1018

mire
בִּץ 263
בִּצָּה 263
חֹמֶר 441
טִיט 480
יָוֵן 521
רֶפֶשׁ 1189
mirth
מָשׂוֹשׂ 767
שִׂמְחָה 1210
שָׂשׂוֹן 1219
mirth, to make
שׂוּשׂ } Kal..........1204
שִׂישׂ }
miry
טִין Ch.............. 481
יָוֵן 521
miry place
בִּצָּה 263
miscarry
שָׁכַל Hiphil..........1259
mischief
אָוֶן 30
אָסוֹן 141
הַוָּה 359
הֹוָה 359
זִמָּה 388
עָוֹן 910
עָמָל 960
רַע 1177
mischief, to do
רָעַע Hiphil 1186
mischief, to imagine
הָתַת Poel 376
mischievous
הַוָּה 359
מְזִמָּה 684
רַע 1177
mischievous device
מְזִמָּה 684
mischievous thing
הַוָּה 359
miserable
עָמָל 960
misery
מָרוּד 763
עָמָל 960
רַע 1177
misery, that is in
עָמֵל 960
* Misgab
מִשְׂגָּב 767
Misrephoth-maim
{ מִשְׂרְפוֹת 767
{ מַיִם 694
miss, to
חָטָא Hiphil 414
פָּקַד Kal.............1040

missabib, *see* Magor-missabib
missed, to be
פָּקַד Niphal 1040
missing, to be
פָּקַד Niphal 1040
mist
אֵד 14
mistress
בַּעֲלָה 262
גְּבֶרֶת 292
misuse, to
תָּעַע Hithpalpel......1354
mitre
מִצְנֶפֶת 755
צָנִיף 1076
mix self, to
בָּלַל Hithpoel........ 230
mixed
מָהַל Kal.............. 668
עֲרַב Ch. Pael 975
עֶרֶב 975
mixed, *see* multitude, wine
mixed, to be
עֲרַב Ch. Ithpael...... 975
mixture
מֶסֶךְ 737
Mizar
מִצְעָר 755
mock, to
הָתַל Piel.............. 376
לָעַב Hiphil 644
לָעַג Kal.............. 644
לָעַג Hiphil 644
עָלַל Hithpael 942
צָחַק Piel.............1070
קָלַס Hithpael 1110
שָׂחַק Kal.............1205
mock, to make a
לוּץ Hiphil 636
mock on, to
לָעַג Hiphil 644
mocked
שְׂחוֹק 1204
mocker
הֲתֻלִים 376
לוּץ Kal.............. 636
לוּץ Hithpalpel...... 636
לָעֵג 644
שָׂחַק Piel.............1205
mocking
קַלָּסָה 1110
moderately
צְדָקָה 1063
moist
לַח 636
moistened, to be
שָׁקָה Pual 1323

moisture
לְשַׁד 651
mole
תִּנְשֶׁמֶת 1353
* mole †
חֵפֹר 452
moles †
פֵּרוֹת 1044
mollified, to be
רָכַךְ Pual 1174
Moloch
מֶלֶךְ 712
molten
יָצַק Kal 556
יָצַק Hophal 556
מַסֵּכָה 737
molten, to be
נָתַךְ Niphal 850
צוּק[2] Kal 1069
molten image
מַסֵּכָה 737
נֵסֶךְ } נֶסֶךְ } 820
moment
רֶגַע 1157
moment, to be a
רָגַע Hiphil 1157
money
כֶּסֶף 609
כְּסַף Ch. 611
money, *see* sum
money, piece of
קְשִׂיטָה 1130
* money, with
קִנְיָן 1112
monster, *see* sea
month
חֹדֶשׁ 404
יֶרַח 565
יְרַח Ch. 565
monthly
חֹדֶשׁ 404
monuments
נָצַר Kal 837
moon
יָרֵחַ 564
יֶרַח 565
לְבָנָה 632
moon, *see* new, tires
more
גָּדוֹל 293
חוּץ 408
יוֹתֵר 521
עוֹד 905
רַב 1147
שֵׁנִי 1310
* more
בָּכָה Kal 226
יָסַף Kal 543
יָסַף Niphal 543
עַל Ch. 933
רָבָה Hiphil 1151
more, *see* abominable, afflict, any, come, enough, get, how much, laid, much, put to, ready, shew, so many, surely, vile
more, to be
עָדַף Kal 904
עָצַם Kal 972
רָבַב[1] Kal 1151
* more and more
הָלַךְ Kal 362
יָסַף Hiphil 543
רָבָה Hiphil 1151
more and more, *see* increase
more, any
רָבָה Hiphil 1151
more, to bring
יָסַף Hiphil 543
more, to do
יָסַף Hiphil 543
more, to give
רָבָה Hiphil 1151
more, to give the
רָבָה Hiphil 1151
more, to have
עָבַר Kal 895
רָבָה Hiphil 1151
more in number
רֹב 1150
more in number, to be
רָבָה Kal 1151
more, to make
יָסַף Hiphil 543
more, to put
יָסַף Hiphil 543
more, to see
שׁוּב Kal 1238
more than
מִן Ch. 732
עִם 955
* more than
פָּנִים 1023
more than †
אִם 100
more than, *see* they
* more, the
יָסַף Hiphil 543
כֵּן 604
more, whatsoever
שְׁאָר Ch. 1223
* more, yet
יָסַף Hiphil 543
more, to be yet the
יָסַף Hiphil 543
moreover
אַף 144
גַּם 311
יוֹתֵר 521
עוֹד 905
moreover, *see* give
moreover if
אִם 100
morning
אוֹר 32
בֹּקֶר 266
מִשְׁחָר 769
נְגַהּ Ch. 791
צְפִירָה 1079
שַׁחַר 1252
שָׁכַם Hiphil 1260
morning, *see* dawning, early, seek
morning, in the
שָׁכָה Hiphil 1258
morrow
בֹּקֶר 266
מָחֳרָת 690
morsel
כִּכָּר 597
פַּת 1051
mortal man
אֱנוֹשׁ 136
mortally
נֶפֶשׁ 829
mortar
חֹמֶר 441
מְדֹכָה 667
מַכְתֵּשׁ 701
morter
עָפָר 968
mortgage, to
עָרַב[1] Kal 975
most
כַּבִּיר 584
רֹב 1150
* most
טוֹב 476
most, *see* bitter, bitterly, high, noble, rebellious, upright
most *desolate*
שְׁמָמָה 1290
most *fine gold*
כֶּתֶם 623
* most holy
קֹדֶשׁ 1091
* most holy things
קֹדֶשׁ 1091
* most *mighty*
חַיִל Ch. 425
* most strong
מָעוֹז 740
moth
עָשׁ 1003
mother
אֵם 99
mother, *see* nursing

much, to be so
רָבָה Kal ... 1151
much, to take
רָבָה Hiphil ... 1151
much, too
יָתַר Hiphil ... 580
רַב ... 1147
much, very
רַב ... 1147
much, to yield
רָבָה Hiphil ... 1151
mufflers
רַעַל ... 1185
mulberry tree
בָּכָא ... 226
mule
פֶּרֶד ... 1044
פִּרְדָּה ... 1044
רֶכֶשׁ ... 1175
mules
יֵמִם ... 541
multiplied, to be
רָבַב[1] Kal ... 1151
רָבָה Kal ... 1151
שְׂגָא Ch. P'al ... 1197
multiply
רַב ... 1147
* multiply
רְבָבָה ... 1151
multiply, to
הָמַן Kal ... 369
כָּבַר Hiphil ... 585
עָתַר[2] Hiphil ... 1008
רָבָה Kal ... 1151
רָבָה Hiphil ... 1151
multiply, to make to
רָבָה Hiphil ... 1151
multiplying
רָבָה Hiphil ... 1151
multitude
אָמוֹן ... 102
הָמוֹן ... 368
חַי ... 419
מְלֹא ... 703
מְלוֹא ... 703
מַרְבִּית ... 762
סַךְ ... 875
עֵדָה ... 903
קָהָל ... 1094
רַב (& grt. m.) ... 1147
רֹב ... 1150
רִיב (כ׳) ... 1171
רֶכֶב (כ׳) ... 1173
שִׁפְעָה ... 1322
multitude, mixed
עֵרֶב ... 975
multitude, mixt
אֲסַפְסֻף ... 143
munition
מְצָד ... 752
מְצוֹדָה ... 752
מְצוּרָה ... 754
murder, to
הָרַג Kal ... 374
רָצַח Kal ... 1190
רָצַח Piel ... 1190
murderer
הָרַג Kal ... 374
נָכָה Hiphil ... 814
רָצַח Kal ... 1190
רָצַח Piel ... 1190
murmur, to
לוּן & לִין Niphal ... 635
לוּן & לִין Hiphil ... 635
רָגַן Kal ... 1157
רָגַן Niphal ... 1157
murmur, to make to
לוּן & לִין (כ׳) Niphal ... 635
לוּן & לִין Hiphil ... 635
murmurings
תְּלֻנּוֹת ... 1348
murrain
דֶּבֶר ... 334
muse, to
שִׂיחַ Polel ... 1206
* musical
שִׁיר ... 1255
musical instrument
שִׁדָּה ... 1237
musician, chief
נָצַח Piel ... 834
musick
זְמָר Ch. ... 389
מַנְגִּינָה ... 732
נְגִינָה ... 791
שִׁיר ... 1255
musick, *see* instrument
musing
הָגִיג ... 357
must, *see* die
muster, to
פָּקַד Piel ... 1040
צָבָא Hiphil ... 1057
Muth-labben
{ מוּת ... 681
{ בֵּן ... 232
Muth-*labben*, upon
עֲלָמוֹת ... 943
mutter, to
הָגָה[1] Kal ... 356
הָגָה[1] Hiphil ... 356
muzzle, to
חָסַם Kal ... 450
myrrh
לֹט ... 640
מֹר ... 760
myrtle
הֲדַס } ... 357
הֲדַס }
myrtle tree
הֲדַס } ... 357
הֲדַס }
myself
אֲנִי ... 140
נֶפֶשׁ ... 829
naharaim, *see* Aram-naharaim
nail
טְפַר Ch. ... 485
יָתֵד ... 579
מַסְמֵר ... 737
צִפֹּרֶן ... 1080
nails
מַשְׂמְרוֹת ... 767
naked
מַעֲרֻמִּים ... 746
עֵירֹם ... 932
עָרוֹם ... 978
עֶרְיָה ... 978
פָּרַע Kal ... 1046
naked, to be made
עוּר[2] Niphal ... 913
naked, to make
פָּרַע Kal ... 1046
פָּרַע Hiphil ... 1046
naked, to make self
עָרָה Hithpael ... 977
nakedness
מָעוֹר ... 740
מַעַר ... 745
עֵירֹם ... 932
עֶרְוָה ... 977
nakedness †
בָּשָׂר ... 278
name
שֵׁם ... 1280
שֻׁם Ch. ... 1284
name, to
אָמַר Kal ... 105
דָּבַר Piel ... 319
נָקַב Kal ... 837
קָרָא[1] Kal ... 1117
name,† to
שׂוּם } Kal ... 1200
שִׂים }
שׂוּם Ch. P'al ... 1204
name, (to)
שֵׁם ... 1280
שֻׁם Ch. ... 1284
name, to give a
קָרָא[1] Kal ... 1117
nam*ed*
שֵׁם ... 1280
named, to be
קָרָא[1] Kal ... 1117
קָרָא[1] Niphal ... 1117

named,† to be
קָרָא[1] Niphal..........1117

narrow
אָטַם Kal.............. 55
צָר 1081

narrow, to be
אוּץ Kal.............. 31
יָצַר[2] Kal 557

* narrow lights †
שְׁקֻפִים 1325

narrowed rests
מִגְרָעוֹת 663

narrower
צָרַר Kal..............1083

narrowly, *see* look

narrowly, to look
שָׁמַר Kal..............1300

nation
אֻמָּה Ch............... 102
גּוֹי 299
לְאוֹם 626
עַם & עָם 944

nation, of own
אֶזְרָח 37

nations
אֻמּוֹת / אֻמִּים } 103

* nations
אֶרֶץ 157

native
מוֹלֶדֶת 671

nativity
מוֹלֶדֶת 671
מְכוּרָה 699

natural force
לֵחַ 637

naught
רַע 1177

naughtiness
הַוָּה 359
רֹעַ 1183

naughty
בְּלִיַּעַל 230
הַוָּה 359
רַע 1177

nave
גַּב 286

navel
שֹׁר 1326
שָׁרִיר 1327
שֹׁרֶר 1327

navy
אֳנִי 140

navy of ships
אֳנִי 140

nay
אַל 76
לֹא 625

nay, *see* say

nay...neither
גַּם 311

Nazarite
נָזִיר 803

near
אֶל 78
אֵצֶל 148
יָד 489
נָגַע Kal.............. 792
קָרוֹב 1127

near, *see* bring, come, draw, go, kin, kinsman

near, to be
נָגַשׁ Kal.............. 794
קָרַב Kal..............1123

* near, to be
רָאָה Kal..............1133

near, to bring
נָגַשׁ Hiphil........... 794

near, to cause to come
נָגַשׁ Hiphil........... 794

near, to come
נָגַשׁ Niphal 794

near, to draw
נָגַשׁ Kal.............. 794
נָגַשׁ Niphal 794
נָגַשׁ Hithpael......... 794

near, to go
נָגַשׁ Kal.............. 794

near kinswomen
שַׁאֲרָה 1223

near of kin
קָרוֹב 1127

near *of kin*
שְׁאֵר 1223

near, that is
קָרוֹב 1127

near unto
אֵצֶל 148

* necessary
חֹק 456

neck
גַּרְגְּרוֹת 315
גָּרוֹן 315
מַפְרֶקֶת 748
עֹרֶף 980
צַוָּאר 1065
צַוָּאר Ch..............1065
צַוְּרֹנִים 1070

neck, to break...
עָרַף[2] Kal 980

neck, to cut off...
עָרַף[2] Kal 980

neck, to strike off...
עָרַף[2] Kal 980

necromancer
דָּרַשׁ Kal............. 353 }
מוּת Kal............. 675 }

need
מַחְסוֹר 689
צֹרֶךְ 1082

need, to have
חָסֵר 450
חָסֵר Kal.............. 450

need of, to have
חֲשַׁח Ch. P'al 469

needful, be
חַשְׁחוּת 469

needlework
רָקַם Kal..............1192
רִקְמָה 1192
{ מַעֲשֶׂה 746
{ רָקַם Kal..............1192

needlework, *see* raiment

needlework on both sides
רִקְמָה 1192

needs is sometimes the translation of an infinitive used intensitively.

needy
אֶבְיוֹן 10
דַּל 341
000 000
רוּשׁ Kal..............1166

neesing
עֲטִישָׁה................ 918

Neginoth
נְגִינָה 791

negligent, to be
שָׁלָה[1] Niphal..........1262

Nehelemite
נֶחֱלָמִי 807

Nehiloth
נְחִילָה 805

Nehushtan
נְחֻשְׁתָּן 810

neigh, to
צָהַל Kal..............1064

neighbour
עָמִית 960
קָרוֹב 1127
רֵעַ 1181
רְעוּת 1185
שָׁכֵן 1261

neighing
מִצְהָלוֹת 752

neither
אַיִן 59
אַל 76
אִם 100
בַּל 229
בִּלְתִּי 231
לָא Ch............... 624
לֹא 625

* neither
מִן 731

neither, *see* nay

nephew
נֶכֶד 814

nephew †
בֵּן 232

nest
קֵן 1111

nest, to make
קָנַן Piel 1113
קָנַן Pual 1113

net
חֵרֶם 464
מִכְמָר 699
מַכְמֹר 699
מִכְמֹרֶת 699
מָצוֹד 752
מָצוּד 752
מְצוֹדָה 752
מְצוּדָה 753
רֶשֶׁת 1195
שְׂבָךְ 1195

nether
תַּחְתּוֹן 1345
תַּחְתִּי 1346

nether *millstone*
רֵחַיִם 1168

nether part
תַּחְתִּי 1346

nethermost
תַּחְתּוֹן 1345

Nethinims
נְתוּנִים (כ׳) 850
נְתִינִים 850
נְתִינִין Ch. 850

nettle
חָרוּל 463
קִמּוֹשׁ }
קִימוֹשׁ } 1110

network
חוֹר 409
שְׂבָכָה 1195
{ מַעֲשֶׂה 746
{ רֶשֶׁת 1195

never
אַיִן 59
לֹא 625

never
דּוֹר 337
עוֹלָם 907
עָלַם Ch. 943
תָּמִיד 1349

never †
אַל 76
נֶצַח }
נֵצַח } 835

* never so
בֹּר 270

never so, *see* wisely

nevertheless
אֲבָל 11
אַךְ 70
אָכֵן 75
אֶפֶס 147
בְּרַם Ch. 277
כִּי 596
רַק 1191

nevertheless †
אִם 100

new
חָדָשׁ 403
חֲדַת Ch. 405
טָרִי 485

new, *see* wine

new fruit, to bring forth
בָּכַר Piel 229

new moon
חֹדֶשׁ 404

new thing
חָדָשׁ 403

* new thing
בְּרִיאָה 272

new wine
תִּירוֹשׁ 1346

* newly
קָרוֹב 1127

newly, but
קוּם Hiphil 1099

news
שְׁמוּעָה 1285

next
אַחַר 52
מִשְׁנֶה 773
קָרוֹב 1127

next, *see* kinsman

next day
מָחֳרָת 690

next *day*
מָחֳרָת 690

next, that is
קָרוֹב 1127

nigh
קָרוֹב 1127
שָׁכֵן 1261

nigh, *see* approach, come, draw, well

nigh at hand
קָרוֹב 1127

nigh, to come
נָגַשׁ Niphal 794

nigh, to draw
נָגַשׁ Kal 794

nigh, to go
נָגַשׁ Niphal 794

nigh *of kin*
שְׁאֵר 1223

night
חֹשֶׁךְ 470
לֵיל 640
לֵילְיָא Ch. 642
נֶשֶׁף 849
עֶרֶב 976

night, *see* abide, lie, lodge, tarry

night hawk
תַּחְמָס 1345

night, to pass the
בּוּת Ch. P'al 207

night season
לֵיל 640

nine
תֵּשַׁע }
תִּשְׁעָה } 1359

nineteen
{ תֵּשַׁע }
{ תִּשְׁעָה } 1359
{ עָשָׂר }
{ עֶשְׂרֵה } 998

nineteenth
{ תֵּשַׁע }
{ תִּשְׁעָה } 1359
{ עָשָׂר 998

ninety
תִּשְׁעִים 1360

ninth
תְּשִׁיעִי 1359
תֵּשַׁע }
תִּשְׁעָה } 1359

Nisan
נִיסָן 814

nissi, *see* Jehovah-nissi

nitre
נֶתֶר 864

no
אַיִן 59
אַל 76
אֶפֶס 147
בַּל 229
לָא Ch. 624
לֹא 625

no †
כֹּל Ch. 597
מְאוּמָה 657

no, *see* doubt, hope, means, purpose, rising

no...is, where
בְּלִי 229

no manner †
כֹּל Ch. 597

no more
בִּלְתִּי 231

no more, *see* surely

no value
אֱלִיל 94

no where
אַיִן 59

* no whither †
אָן 135

noble
אַדִּיר 17
גָּדוֹל 293
חוֹרִים 409
יַקִּיר Ch. 558
נָגִיד 791
נָדִיב 796

noble, *see* vine

noble, most
פַּרְתְּמִים 1049

nobles
אֲצִילִים 148
בָּרִיחַ 272
כָּבֵד } כָּבֵד } Niphal 581
פַּרְתְּמִים 1049

* Nod
נוֹד 800

noise
הָמוֹן 368
הֶמְיָה 368
קוֹל 1096
רֹגֶז 1155
רֵעַ 1181
שָׁאוֹן 1220
תְּשֻׁאוֹת 1359

noise, *see* confused, joyful

noise, loud
תְּרוּעָה 1358

noise, to make a
הוּם Hiphil 359
הָמָה Kal 368
שָׁמֵעַ } שָׁמַע } Hiphil 1292

noise, to make a loud
פָּצַח Kal 1039

noisome
הַוָּה 359
רַע 1177

none
אַיִן 59
אַל 76
אֶפֶס 147
בַּל 229
בְּלִי 229
בִּלְתִּי 231
לָא Ch. 624
לֹא 625

none †
אִישׁ 60
אִשָּׁה 175
כֹּל Ch. 597

none
לֹא 625

none, *see* effect, surely

none beside
אֶפֶס 147

none beside me
אַפְסִי 147

none can
אִשׁ 174

noon
צֹהַר 1065

noonday
צֹהַר 1065

noontide
צֹהַר 1065

*noon*tide
עֵת 1005

nor
אוֹ 29
אַיִן 59
אַל 76
אִם 100
בַּל 229
לָא Ch. 624
לֹא 625

nor any
אַיִן 59

nor any thing
אַיִן 59

north
מְזָרִים 685
צָפוֹן 1078

north side
צָפוֹן 1078

north wind
צָפוֹן 1078

northern
צָפוֹן 1078
צְפוֹנִי 1079

northward
צָפוֹן 1078

nose
אַף 144

nose, to have a flat
חָרַם Kal 464

nostril
אַף 144
נַחַר 808

nostrils
נְחִירִים 805

not
אַיִן 59
אִין 59
אַל 76
אַל Ch. 76
אִם 100
אֶפֶס 147
בַּל 229
בְּלִי 229
בִּלְעֲדֵי } בַּלְעֲדֵי } 231
בִּלְתִּי 231
לָא Ch. 624
לֹא 625
לָה 634

* not
מִן 731

not, *see* and, doubtless, equal, if, inhabited, please, surely, than, that, worthy

not a word, *see* speak

not any
אֶפֶס 147
בַּל 229

not, for
לֹא 625

not in
בִּלְעֲדֵי } בַּלְעֲדֵי } 231

not out of
לֹא 625

not yet
טֶרֶם 485

notable
חָזוּת 411

notable one
חָזוּת 411

note, to
חָקַק Kal 458

noted, to be
רָשַׁם Kal 1192

nothing
אַיִן 59
אֶפֶס 147
בַּל 229
בְּלִימָה 230
בִּלְתִּי 231
תֹּהוּ 1336

no*thing*
לֹא 625

nothing
דָּבָר 325
כֹּל 597
מְאוּמָה 657
מָה 668

nothing, *see* cost, less

nothing, as
לָה Ch. 633

nothing, to bring to
מָעַט Hiphil 741

nothing but
רַק 1191

nothing, for
חִנָּם 446

nothing worth
אַל 76

notice, to take
נָכַר Hiphil 818

notwithstanding
אַךְ 70
אֶפֶס 147
רַק 1191

nought
אָוֶן 30
תֹּהוּ 1336

nought †
מְאוּמָה 657

nought, to
אַיִן 59
nought, to bring to
פּוּר Hiphil 1015
פָּרַר Hiphil 1048
שָׁמַד Hiphil 1285
nought, to be brought to
אָפֵס Kal.............. 147
nought, to come to
נָבֵל Kal.............. 786
פָּרַר Hophal 1048
nought, for
חִנָּם 446
* nought,† for
הוֹן 360
nought, of
אֶפַע 147
לֹא 625
nought, to set at
פָּרַע Kal.............1046
nought, thing of
אֶפֶס 147
תֹּהוּ 1336
nourish, to
גָּדַל Piel.............. 297
כּוּל Pilpel............ 592
רָבָה Piel.............1151
nourish up, to
גָּדַל Piel.............. 297
חָיָה Piel.............. 421
nourisher
כּוּל Pilpel............ 592
now
אֱדַיִן Ch.............. 17
אָז 34
אֵפוֹ / אֵפוֹא 146
הֵנָּה 369
זֶה 380
יוֹם 508
כְּבָר 585
כִּי 596
כְּעַן Ch. 612
נָא 781
עַתָּה 1007
פַּעַם 1038
now †
דִּי Ch.............. 339
now, *see* days, even
now, seeing that which
כְּבָר 585
number
חֵקֶר 458
מִכְסָה 700
מְנִי 735
מִנְיָן Ch. 735
מִסְפָּר 738
מִפְקָד 748
סְפֹרָה 884
number, *see* few, great, more
number, to
מָנָה Kal.............. 732
מְנָא / מְנָה Ch. P'al...... 733
סָפַר Kal............. 882
סָפַר Piel............. 882
פָּקַד Kal.............1040
number after genealogy
יָחַשׂ Hithpael........ 523
number, certain
מִסְפָּר 738
number, odd
עָדַף Kal.............. 904
number throughout the genealogy
יָחַשׂ Hithpael........ 523
numbered
מִסְפָּר 738
numbered, to be
מָנָה Niphal 732
סָפַר Niphal 882
סָפַר Piel.............. 882
פָּקַד Kal.............1040
פָּקַד Hithpael 1040
פָּקַד Hothpael........1040
numbering
סָפַר Kal.............. 882
סְפָר 884
numbers
פְּקֻדָּה 1041
nurse
אָמַן Kal.............. 103
יָנַק Hiphil 542
nurse, to
יָנַק Hiphil 542
נוּק Hiphil 803
nursed, to be
אָמַן Niphal 103
nursing father
אָמַן Kal.............. 103
nursing mother
יָנַק 542
nut
אֱגוֹז 14
nuts
בָּטְנִים 212

O
בִּי 212
הוֹי 359
O that
אַחֲלַי / אַחֲלֵי 48
לוּ 634
מִי 694
נָתַן Kal.............. 851
oak
אַלָּה 78
אֵלָה 78
אַלּוֹן 94
oaks
אֵילִים 59
oar
מָשׁוֹט 768
מִשּׁוֹט 768
שַׁיִט 1255
oath
אָלָה 78
שְׁבוּעָה 1224
oath, *see* charge
oath (*from another*), to take an
שָׁבַע Hiphil 1228
obedient
שָׁמֵעַ / שָׁמַע Kal 1292
obedient, to be
שָׁמֵעַ / שָׁמַע Kal 1292
שָׁמֵעַ / שָׁמַע Niphal........1292
obeisance, to do
שָׁחָה Hithpael 1249
obeisance, to make
שָׁחָה Hithpael 1249
obey
מִשְׁמַעַת 773
obey, to
יְקָהָה 557
שָׁמֵעַ / שָׁמַע Kal............1292
שָׁמֵעַ / שָׁמַע Niphal........1292
שְׁמַע Ch. Ithpael...... 1299
obeying
שָׁמַע / שָׁמֵעַ Kal..........1292
oblation
מִנְחָה 734
מִנְחָה Ch.............. 735
מַשְׂאֵת 767
קָרְבָּן 1126
תְּרוּמָה 1357
תְּרוּמִיָּה 1358
obscure
אִישׁוֹן 69
אֱשׁוּן 178
obscurity
אֹפֶל 147
חֹשֶׁךְ 470
observe, to
נָצַר Kal.............. 837
עָשָׂה Kal.............. 981
רָצָה Kal (כ׳) 1189
שׁוּר[2] Kal 1248
שָׁמַר Kal..............1300
שָׁמַר Piel...... 1300

observe diligently, to
נָחַשׁ Piel... 809

observe times, to
עָנַן Poel... 966

* observed, be
שִׁמֻּרִים ...1303

* observed, be much
שִׁמֻּרִים ...1303

observer of times
עָנַן Poel... 966

obstinate
קָשֶׁה ...1131

obstinate, to make
אָמַץ Piel... 104

obtain, to
חָזַק Hiphil ... 411
נָשָׂא Kal... 840
פּוּק[2] Hiphil...1015

obtain, *see* children, leave, mercy

occasion
עִלָּה Ch... 939
עֲלִילָה ... 942
תֹּאֲנָה ...1334
תַּאֲנָה ...1334
תְּנוּאָה ...1352

occasion, *see* blaspheme, find, seek

occasion, to
סָבַב Kal... 865

occasion, to have
נְפַל Ch. P'al ... 828

* occasion serve
מָצָא Kal... 748

occupation
מְלָאכָה ... 705
מַעֲשֶׂה ... 746

occupied †
מְלָאכָה ... 705

occupied, to be
עָשָׂה Niphal ... 981

occupiers
עָרַב[1] Kal ... 975

occupy, to
נָתַן Kal... 851
עָרַב[1] Kal... 975

occupy with, to
סָחַר Kal... 874

occurrent
פֶּגַע ...1010

odd, *see* number

odious
שָׂנֵא Kal...1210

odious, to make selves
בָּאַשׁ Hithpael... 184

odour, sweet
נִיחוֹחַ ... 813
נִיחוֹחַ Ch... 814

odours, *see* sweet

of
אֶל ... 78
אֵת ... 182
דִּי ... 339
מִן ... 731
מִן Ch... 732
עַל ... 932
עַל Ch... 933
עִם ... 955
עִמָּד ... 958
פָּנִים ...1023

* of
יָד ... 489

* of †
קֳדָם Ch...1089

of, *see* full, plenty, speak, weary

off
עַל ... 932
פָּנִים ...1023

off, *see* afar, beat, branch, break, broken, cast, cast far, crop, cut, cutting, draw, fall, fallen, far, from, good way, leave, neck, pluck, pluckt, pull, put, remove, scrape, shake, shave, smite, strip, take, taken, wring

offence
חֵטְא ... 415
מִכְשׁוֹל ... 701

offence, to acknowledge
אָשֵׁם / אָשַׁם } Kal... 178

offend, to
אָשֵׁם / אָשַׁם } Kal ... 178
אַשְׁמָה ... 179
בָּגַד Kal... 184
חָבַל Kal... 398
חָטָא Kal... 414

* offend, *nothing*
מִכְשׁוֹל ... 701

offended
פָּשַׁע Niphal ...1050

offender
חַטָּא ... 416

offender, to make an
חָטָא Hiphil ... 414

offer, to
זָבַח Kal... 377
זָבַח Piel... 378
זֶבַח ... 378
נָגַשׁ Hiphil ... 794
נוּף Hiphil ... 802
נָטָה Kal... 810
נָטַל Kal... 812
נָסַךְ[1] Kal ... 820
נָסַךְ[1] Hiphil ... 820
נְסַךְ Ch. Pael... 820
נָשָׂא Kal... 840
נָתַן Kal... 851
עָלָה Kal... 934
עָלָה Hiphil... 934
עָשָׂה Kal... 981
קָטַר[1] Hiphil...1106
קָרַב Kal...1123
קָרַב Hiphil...1123
קְרֵב Pael ...1125
קְרֵב Aphel ...1125
רוּם Hiphil...1163
שָׁחַט Kal...1251

offer for sin, to
חָטָא Piel... 414

offer freely, to
נָדַב Hithpael... 795
נְדַב Ch. Ithpael... 795

offer incense, to
קָטַר[1] Piel...1106

offer sacrifice, to
קָטַר[1] Piel...1106

offer *sacrifices*, to
דְּבַח Ch. P'al... 318

offer selves, to willingly
נָדַב Hithpael... 795

offer up, to
רוּם Hiphil...1163

offer willingly, to
נָדַב Hithpael... 795

offered
נָגַשׁ Hophal... 794
תְּרוּמָה ...1357

offered, to be
עָלָה Kal... 934
עָלָה Hophal... 934
עָשָׂה Niphal ... 981

offered, that it is
קָרְבָּן ...1126

offered, things
מַעֲשֶׂה ... 746

offering
זֶבַח ... 378
מִנְחָה ... 734
עָלָה Kal... 934
עָלָה Hiphil... 934
עָשָׂה Kal... 981
קָרַב Hiphil...1123
קָרְבָּן ...1126
קֻרְבָּן ...1127
תְּנוּפָה ...1352
תְּרוּמָה ...1357

offering, *see* burnt, drink, free, freewill, heave, meat, passover, peace, sin, thank, trespass, voluntary, wave, whole, willing

offering by fire
אִשֶּׁה ... 174

offering for sin
אָשָׁם ... 179

one
אֶחָד ... 41
אִישׁ ... 60
אַלְמֹנִי ... 96
אִשָּׁה ... 175
גַּם ... 311
חַד ... 402
חַד Ch. ... 402
נֶפֶשׁ ... 829
one, *see* each, every one, look, see, side
one...another
דָּא Ch. ... 317
דֵּן Ch. ... 346
* one another
כָּנָף ... 605
* one from another
כְּלִי ... 600
one piece, *see* beaten out
one sort
אֵלֶּה ... 79
one, the
זֹאת ... 377
one...the other, the
זֶה ... 380
one,† tumultuous
בֵּן ... 232
one way, *see* go
onion
בָּצָל ... 263
only
אֶחָד ... 41
אַךְ ... 70
בַּד ... 186
בָּדָד ... 187
זוּלָה ... 383
יַחְדָּיו, יַחְדָּו, יַחַד } ... 522
יָחִיד ... 523
כָּסַם Kal ... 609
רַק ... 1191
only, *see* child, save, son
onward, *see* go
onycha
שְׁחֵלֶת ... 1252
onyx
שֹׁהַם ... 1238
open
גָּלָה Pual ... 307
עַיִן ... 919
פָּטַר Kal ... 1017
פָּנִים ... 1023
פָּרַץ Niphal ... 1047
פִּתְחוֹן ... 1054
* open
מָקוֹם ... 756
open, *see* lay, wide
open, to
גָּלָה Kal ... 307
גָּלָה Piel ... 307
כָּרָה Kal ... 616
פָּעַר Kal ... 1039
פָּצָה Kal ... 1039
פָּקַח Kal ... 1042
פָּשַׂק Piel ... 1050
פָּתַח Kal ... 1052
פָּתַח Piel ... 1052
open, † to
גָּלָה Kal ... 307
open, to be
פָּתַח Niphal ... 1052
פָּתַח Piel ... 1052
פְּתַח Ch. P'il ... 1053
* open, to be
שָׁתַם Kal ... 1333
open, to be set
פָּתַח Niphal ... 1052
open, such as
פִּטְרָה ... 1017
open wide, to
פָּעַר Kal ... 1039
פָּשַׂק Kal ... 1050
opened, to be
גָּלָה Niphal ... 307
פָּקַח Niphal ... 1042
פָּתַח Kal ... 1052
פָּתַח Niphal ... 1052
פְּתַח Ch. P'il ... 1053
openeth
פֶּטֶר ... 1017
opening
מַפְתֵּחַ ... 748
מִפְתָּח ... 748
פָּקַח Kal ... 1042
פְּתַח ... 1053
פִּתְחוֹן ... 1054
opening, to be
פָּתַח Niphal ... 1052
opening of the prison
פְּקַח־קוֹחַ ... 1042
openly
עַיִן ... 919
openly, *see* shew
operation
מַעֲשֶׂה ... 746
Ophel
עֹפֶל ... 967
opinion
דֵּעַ ... 347
opinions
סְעִפִּים ... 880
oppose self against, to
שָׂטַם Kal ... 1205
oppress, to
דָּכָא Piel ... 340
יָנָה Hiphil ... 541
לָחַץ Kal ... 640
עָרַץ Kal ... 980
עָשַׁק Kal ... 1004
צָרַר Kal ... 1083
רָצַץ Kal ... 1190
רָצַץ Piel ... 1190
רָצַץ Poel ... 1190
שָׁדַד Kal ... 1237
oppressed
דַּךְ ... 340
חָמוֹץ ... 438
עֲשׁוּקִים ... 1003
עָשַׁק Pual ... 1004
עָשְׁקָה ... 1004
רָצַץ Kal ... 1190
oppressed, to be
נָגַשׂ Niphal ... 794
oppressing
יָנָה Kal ... 541
oppression
לַחַץ ... 640
מִשְׂפָּח ... 767
עֹצֶר ... 973
עָקָה ... 974
עֹשֶׁק ... 1004
שֹׁד ... 1236
oppression, to thrust out by
יָנָה Hiphil ... 541
oppressions
מַעֲשַׁקּוֹת ... 747
עֲשׁוּקִים ... 1003
oppressor
יָנָה Kal ... 541
לָחַץ Kal ... 640
נָגַשׂ Kal ... 794
עָרִיץ ... 978
עָשׁוֹק ... 1003
עָשַׁק Kal ... 1004
צוּק[1] Hiphil ... 1069
רָמַס Kal ... 1176
oppressor †
חָמָס ... 440
* oppressors
מַעֲשַׁקּוֹת ... 747
or
אוֹ ... 29
אִם ... 100
הֵן Ch. ... 369
* or
עַד ... 901
or, *see* either
or ever
לָא Ch. ... 624
oracle
דְּבִיר ... 318
דְּבַר ... 325
orator
לַחַשׁ ... 640

outgoing
מוֹצָא 673
תּוֹצָאוֹת 1342
outlandish
נָכְרִי 819
outlive,† to
אַחַר 48
אָרַךְ Hiphil 156
*** outlived †**
יוֹם 508
outmost
קִיצוֹן 1108
outmost, *see* **branch**
outmost coast
קָצֶה 1114
outrageous
שֶׁטֶף / שֶׁטֶף } 1254
outside
חוּץ 408
קָצֶה 1114
outstretched
נָטָה Kal 810
outward
חוּץ 408
חִיצוֹן 425
outward, *see* **appearance**
oven
תַּנּוּר 1352
over
אֶל 78
בְּעַד 261
יוֹתֵר 521
מִן 731
מַעַל 743
נֶגֶד 790
עֵבֶר 899
עַל 932
עַל Ch. 933
עֵלָּא Ch. 933
over, *see* **against, boughs, bring, carry, come, conduct, convey, covered, dominion, get, give, go, going, grown, laid, pass, passed, passing, rule, run, runneth, send, set, spread, turn**
over, to be
חָלַף Kal 434
***over*, to be**
עָמַד Kal 955
over against
נֹכַח 818
פָּנִים 1023
קֳבֵל / קְבֵל } Ch. 1084
over against †
פָּנִים 1023
over and above, that were
עָדַף Kal 904
over, to have
עָדַף Hiphil 904

over much
רָבָה Hiphil 1151
overcome, to
גּוּד Kal 299
יָכֹל Kal 526
לָחַם Niphal 637
עָבַר Kal 895
רָהַב Hiphil 1159
overcome, being
חֲלוּשָׁה 431
overcome with, to be
הָלַם Kal 367
overdrive, to
דָּפַק Kal 348
overflow, to
שׁוּק Hiphil 1248
שָׁטַף Kal 1254
***over*flow, to**
מָלֵא Kal 701
מָלֵא Piel 701
overflow, to make to
צוּף Hiphil 1069
overflowing
בְּכִי 228
זֶרֶם 395
שֶׁטֶף / שֶׁטֶף } 1254
overflown, to be
יָצַק Hophal 556
שָׁטַף Niphal 1254
overlaid
עָלַף Pual 944
צָפָה Pual 1077
overlay, to
חָפָה Piel 451
טוּחַ Kal 479
צָפָה Piel 1077
***over*lay, to**
שָׁכַב Kal 1257
overlaying
צִפּוּי 1078
overlive,† to
אַחַר 48
אָרַךְ Hiphil 156
overpass, to
עָבַר Kal 895
overpast, to be
עָבַר Kal 895
overplus
עָדַף Kal 904
overrun, to
עָבַר Kal 895
overrunning
עָבַר Kal 895
oversee, to
נָצַח Piel 834
overseer
נָצַח Piel 834
פָּקַד Hophal 1040
פָּקִיד 1042
שָׁטַר Kal 1254
overseer, to make
פָּקַד Hiphil 1040
oversight
מִשְׁגֶּה 768
פְּקֻדָּה 1041
oversight, to have the
פָּקַד Hophal 1040
oversight, that had
פָּקַד Kal 1040
overspread, to be
נָפַץ Kal 828
overspreading
כָּנָף 605
overtake, to
דָּבַק / דָּבֵק } Hiphil 318
נָגַשׁ Niphal 794
נָגַשׁ Hiphil 794
נָשַׂג Hiphil 845
overthrew, when...
מַהְפֵּכָה 668
overthrow
הֲפֵכָה 370
מַהְפֵּכָה 668
overthrow, to
דָּחָה Kal 339
הָפַךְ Kal 370
הָרַס Kal 376
הָרַס Piel 376
מַדְחֵפֹת 667
נָטָה Hiphil 810
נָעַר Piel 823
נָפַל Hiphil 825
נָתַץ Piel 863
סָלַף Piel 878
עָוַת Piel 914
overthrown
כָּשַׁל Hophal 621
מַהְפֵּכָה 668
overthrown, to be
הָפַךְ Niphal 370
הָרַס Niphal 376
כָּשַׁל Niphal 621
נָפַל Kal 825
שָׁמַד Niphal 1285
שָׁמַט Niphal 1286
*** overturn**
עַוָּה 906
overturn, to
הָפַךְ Kal 370
***over*turn, to**
הָפַךְ Kal 370
שִׂים / שׂוּם } Kal 1200

overwhelm, to
כָּסָה Piel ... 607
נָפַל Hiphil ... 825
שָׁטַף Kal ... 1254

overwhelmed, to be
עָטַף Kal ... 918
עָטַף Hithpael ... 918

owl
יַנְשׁוּף ... 542
כּוֹס ... 593
{ בַּת ... 280
{ יַעֲנָה ... 546

owl, *see* great owl

owl, great
קִפּוֹז ... 1113

owl, screech
לִילִית ... 642

own
נֶפֶשׁ ... 829

* own
כֹּהֵן ... 587

own, *see* country, freewill, nation, thine

own will
רָצוֹן ... 1189

owner
אָדוֹן ... 15
בַּעַל ... 262
קָנָה Kal ... 1111

ox
אַלּוּף } ... 94
אַלֻּף }
בָּקָר ... 266
פָּר & פַּר ... 1042
שׁוֹר ... 1248
תּוֹר Ch. ... 1342

ox, wild
תְּאוֹ ... 1334

oxen
אֶלֶף ... 96

oxen, *see* yoke

pace
צַעַד ... 1076

pacified, to be
כָּפַר Piel ... 614
שָׁכַךְ Kal ... 1259

pacify, to
יָנַח Hiphil ... 541
כָּפָה Kal ... 613
כָּפַר Piel ... 614

paddle
יָתֵד ... 579

paid, to be
יְהַב Ch. Ithp'al ... 507

pain
חֶבֶל } ... 399
חֵבֶל }
חִיל ... 425
חַלְחָלָה ... 431
כְּאֵב ... 581
מַכְאוֹב ... 698
מֵצַר ... 755
עָמָל ... 960
צִיר ... 1071

pain, *see* fall, travail

pain, to be in
חוּל } Kal ... 406
חִיל }

pain, great
חַלְחָלָה ... 431

pain, to have
כָּאַב Kal ... 581

pain, much
חַלְחָלָה ... 431

pain, to put selves to
חָלָה Niphal ... 429

pained, to be
יָחַל Hiphil ... 523

pained, to be much
חוּל } Kal ... 406
חִיל }

pained, to be sore
חוּל } Kal ... 406
חִיל }

painful
עָמָל ... 960

paint, to
כָּחַל Kal ... 595
מָשַׁח Kal ... 768

paint,† to
שׂוּם } Kal ... 1200
שִׂים }

paint*ed*
פּוּךְ ... 1014

painting
פּוּךְ ... 1014

pair, *see* shoes

palace
אַפֶּדֶן ... 146
אַרְמוֹן ... 157
בִּירָה ... 214
בִּירָה Ch. ... 214
בַּיִת ... 214
בִּיתָן ... 226
הֵיכָל ... 361
הֵיכַל Ch. ... 361
הַרְמוֹן ... 376
טִירָה ... 481

palaces, *see* desolate

pale, to wax
חָוַר Kal ... 409

paleness
יֵרָקוֹן ... 566

palm
כַּף ... 612

palm
תָּמָר ... 1351

palm tree
תָּמָר ... 1351
תֹּמֶר ... 1351
תִּמֹּרָה ... 1351

palmerworm
גָּזָם ... 305

pan
כִּיּוֹר ... 596
מַחֲבַת ... 686
מַשְׂרֵת ... 767
סִיר ... 875
פָּרוּר ... 1044
צֵלָחָה ... 1073

pan, *see* frying pan

pang
חֶבֶל } ... 399
חֵבֶל }
חִיל ... 425
צִיר ... 1071
צָרַר Hiphil ... 1083

Pannag
פַּנַּג ... 1021

pans
חֲבִתִּים ... 401

pant, to
סָחַר Pilpel ... 875
עָרַג Kal ... 977
שָׁאַף Kal ... 1222
תָּעָה Kal ... 1353

pap
שַׁד ... 1236

paper reeds
עָרוֹת ... 978

parable
מָשָׁל ... 772

paramour
פִּילֶגֶשׁ ... 1017

Parbar
פַּרְבָּר ... 1043

parcel
חֶלְקָה ... 436

parched
קָלָה Kal ... 1108

parched, *see* corn

parched ground
שָׁרָב ... 1326

parched places
חֲרֵרִים ... 466

pardon
סְלִיחָה ... 877

pardon, to
כָּפַר Piel ... 614
נָשָׂא Kal ... 840
סָלַח Kal ... 877

pardoned, to be
רָצָה Niphal ... 1189

patrimony
אָב 1

pattern
מַרְאֶה 761
תַּבְנִית 1336
תַּבְנִית 1347

paved
לִבְנָה 633

paved, being
רָצַף Kal 1190

pavement
מַרְצֶפֶת 765
רִצְפָּה 1190

pavilion
סֹךְ 875
סֻכָּה 875

pavilion, *see* royal

paw
יָד 489
כַּף 612

paw, to
חָפַר Kal 452

pay
מֶכֶר 700

pay, to
נָתַן Kal 851
נְתַן Ch. P'al 863
שָׁלַם Piel 1277
שָׁקַל Kal 1324

* pay, to
שׁוּב Hiphil 1238

pay again, to
שָׁלַם Piel 1277

pay, to make to
עָלָה Hiphil 934

peace
שַׁלְוָה 1263
שָׁלוֹם 1263
שְׁלָם Ch. 1278

peace, *see* hold

peace, to be at
שָׁלַם Kal 1277
שָׁלַם Hophal 1277

peace, to hold
דָּמַם Kal 346
הָסָה Piel 370
חָרַשׁ Hiphil 466
חָשָׁה Kal 469
חָשָׁה Hiphil 469

* peace, † to hold
קוֹל 1096

peace, to make
שָׁלַם Hiphil 1277

peace, to make to be at
שָׁלַם Hiphil 1277

peace offering
שֶׁלֶם 1278

* peace, perfect
שָׁלוֹם 1263

peace, such as be at
שָׁלוֹם 1263

peaceable
שָׁלוֹם 1263
שָׁלֵו / שָׁלֵיו } 1263
שָׁלֵם Kal 1277
שָׁלֵם 1278

peaceably
שַׁלְוָה 1263
שָׁלוֹם 1263

peacocks
תֻּכִּיִּים 1346

* peacocks
עָלַס Niphal 943

pearl
גָּבִישׁ 291

peculiar
סְגֻלָּה 869

peculiar treasure
סְגֻלָּה 869

pedigrees, to declare
יָלַד Hithpael 527

peeled
מָרַט Kal 764
מָרַט Pual 764

peep, to
צָפַף Pilpel 1080

Pekod
פְּקוֹד 1042

Pelethites
פְּלֵתִי 1021

pelican
קָאַת 1083

pen
חֶרֶט 463
עֵט 918

penknife
{ תַּעַר 1354
{ סָפַר Kal 882

penury
מַחְסוֹר 689

people
אִישׁ 60
אֻמּוֹת / אֻמִּים } 103
אֱנוֹשׁ 136
בֵּן 232
גּוֹי 299
לְאֹם 626
עֵדָה 903
עָם & עַם 944
עַם Ch. 955

people †
בֵּן 232
עָם & עַם 944

people, *see* blind

people, mingled
עֶרֶב 976

peradventure
אוּלַי / אֻלַי } 30
לוּ 634
פֶּן 1021

peradventure, *see* lest

Perazim
פֶּרֶץ 1047

Perazim, *see* Baal-perazim

perceive, to
בִּין Kal 212
בִּין Hiphil 212
בִּין Hithpolel 212
טָעַם Kal 483
יָדַע Kal 500
נָכַר Hiphil 818
רָאָה Kal 1133
שׁוּר[2] Kal 1248
שָׁמַע / שְׁמַע } Kal 1292

perceive by the ear, to
אָזַן Hiphil 35

perceived, to be
שָׁמַע / שְׁמַע } Niphal 1292

Perez-*uzzah*
פֶּרֶץ 1047

perfect
גְּמַר Ch. P'al 312
כּוּן Niphal 592
כָּלִיל 603
מִכְלוֹת 699
שָׁלֵם 1278
תַּכְלִית 1347
תָּם 1348
תֹּם 1348
תָּמִים 1350

perfect, *see* peace

perfect, to
גָּמַר Kal 312
כָּלַל Kal 603

perfect, to be
תָּמַם Kal 1351

perfect, to make
כָּלַל Kal 603
תָּמַם Hiphil 1351

perfect, that is
שָׁלַם Pual 1277

perfected
אֲרוּכָה / אֲרֻכָה } 152
שָׁלֵם 1278

* perfected, † to be
עָלָה Kal 934

perfection
כָּלִיל 603
מִכְלָל 699
מִנְלֶה 735
תִּכְלָה 1347
תַּכְלִית 1347
תֹּם 1348

* perfectly
בִּינָה 213

perform
שָׁלַם Hiphil 1277

perform, to
בָּצַע Piel 263
גָּמַר Kal 312
נָתַן Kal 851
עָשָׂה Kal 981
צָבָא Kal 1057
קוּם Piel 1099
קוּם Hiphil 1099
שָׁלַם Piel 1277

perform duty, *see* husband's brother
perform the part, *see* kinsman

performed, to be
עָשָׂה Niphal 981
קוּם Kal 1099
קוּם Hophal 1099
שָׁלַם Pual 1277

performing
פָּלָא Piel 1018

perfume
קְטֹרֶת 1107

perfume, to
נוּף Kal 802

perfumed
[1]קָטַר Pual 1106

perfumes
רִקֻּחִים 1191

perish
אֹבֵד 9

perish, to
אָבַד Kal 8
אֲבַד Ch. P'al 9
אֲבַד Ch. Aphel 9
גָּוַע Kal 302
[1]דָּמָה Kal 345
כָּרַת Niphal 618
נָפַל Kal 825
סוּף Kal 871
[1]סָפָה Niphal 881
עָבַר Kal 895
פָּרַע Niphal 1046
שָׁחַת Piel 1252
שָׁמַד Niphal 1285

perish, to cause to
אָבַד Piel 8

perish, to make to
אָבַד Piel 8

perish, to be ready to
אָבַד Kal 8

perpetual
נָצַח Niphal 834
נֶצַח / נֵצַח 835
עוֹלָם 907
תָּמִיד 1349

perpetually
עַד 901

perpetually †
יוֹם 508

perplexed, to be
בּוּךְ Niphal 205

perplexity
מְבוּכָה 660

persecute, to
דָּלַק Kal 342
רָדַף Kal 1158
רָדַף Piel 1158

persecute,† to
אָחַר 48

persecuted
מֻרְדָּף 762

persecution, to be under
רָדַף Niphal 1158

persecutor
דָּלַק Kal 342
רָדַף Kal 1158

person
אָדָם 17
אִישׁ 60
אֱנוֹשׁ 136
בַּעַל 262
נֶפֶשׁ 829
פָּנִים 1023

person †
נֶפֶשׁ 829

person, *see* brutish, uncircumcised, vile

persons
מְתִים 779

persuade, to
סוּת Hiphil 874
פָּתָה Piel 1052

persuaded, to be
פָּתָה Pual 1052

pertain, to
הָיָה Kal 360

pertaineth, that which
כְּלִי 600

pertaining
דָּבָר 325

perverse
הָפַךְ Niphal 370
לוּז Niphal 635
לְזוּת 636
עָוָה Niphal 906
עִקֵּשׁ 975

* perverse
עִוְעִים 911

perverse, to be
יָרַט Kal 565

perverse, to prove
עָקַשׁ Kal 975

perverse, that is
עָקַשׁ Niphal 975

perverse thing
הַוָּה 359

perverse things
תַּהְפֻּכוֹת 1337

perversely, to deal
עָוַת Piel 914

perversely, to do
עָוָה Hiphil 906

perverseness
לוּז Niphal 635
מֻטֶּה 693
סֶלֶף 878
עַוְלָה 907
עָמָל 960

pervert, to
הָפַךְ Kal 370
נָטָה Hiphil 810
סָלַף Piel 878
עָוָה Hiphil 906
עָוַת Piel 914
עָקַשׁ Piel 975
שׁוּב Polel 1238
שָׁנָה Piel 1304

perverting, *see* violent

pestilence
דֶּבֶר 334

pestle
עֱלִי 941

petition
בָּעוּ Ch. 261
מִשְׁאָלָה 768
שְׁאֵלָה 1222

physician
רָפָא Kal 1187

pick out, to
נָקַר Kal 840

picked, to be
שָׁנַן Hithpolel 1315

picture
מַשְׂכִּית 767
שְׂכִיָּה 1206

piece
בָּדָל 187
בֶּתֶר 284
גֶּזֶר 305
כִּכָּר 597
מִדָּה 666
פֶּלַח 1019

miry, ordered, pass, pleasant, profane, refuge, rest, resting, secret, separate, settled, slippery, solitary, steep, stood, strong, threshing, void, waste

place, to
יָנַח Hiphil 541
יָשַׁב Hiphil 568
לָקַח Kal 644
נְחַת Ch. Aphel 810
נָתַן Kal 851
עָמַד Hiphil 955
שִׂים } שׂוּם } Kal 1200
שָׁכֵן } שָׁכַן } Piel 1260
שָׁכֵן } שָׁכַן } Hiphil 1260

place, to bring again to
יָשַׁב Hiphil 568

place, *dwelling*
אֹהֶל 27

place of, *see* assembly

* place, same
תַּחַת 1345

* place where (one) is
תַּחַת 1345

placed, to be
יָשַׁב Hophal 568
שִׂים } שׂוּם } Kal 1200

places, *see* boiling, desolate, fattest, highest, lurking, parched, rough, round, steep, walk

places about
סָבִיב 866

places of, *see* drawing water

plague
דֶּבֶר 334
מַגֵּפָה 663
מַכָּה 698
נֶגַע 793
נֶגֶף 793

plague, to
נָגַע Piel 792
נָגַף Kal 793

plagued
נָגַע Kal 792

plagued, to be
נָגַע Pual 792

* plagued, to be
מַגֵּפָה 663

plain
אָבֵל 11
אֵלוֹן 94
בִּקְעָא Ch. 265
בִּקְעָה 265
כִּכָּר 597
מִישׁוֹר 698
עֲרָבָה 976
שְׁפֵלָה 1322

plain, *see* low

plain
נָכֹחַ 817
תָּם 1348

plain, made
סָלַל Kal 878

plain, to make
בָּאַר Piel 184
שָׁוָה[1] Piel 1245

plainly
אָמַר Kal 105
בָּאַר Piel 184
גָּלָה Niphal 307
נָגַד Hiphil 788
פְּרַשׁ Ch. Pael 1049
צַח 1070

plains
עֲבָרָה (כ׳) 900

plaister
גִּיר Ch. 307
שִׂיד 1206

plaister, to
טוּחַ Kal 479
שִׂיד Kal 1206

plaister, to lay for a
מָרַח Kal 763

plaistered, to be
טוּחַ Niphal 479

planes
מַקְצֻעוֹת 759

planets
מַזָּלוֹת 684

plank
עֵץ 968
צֵלָע 1073

plank, thick
עָב 887

plant
נֶטַע 812
שִׂיחַ 1206
שֶׁלַח 1273
שָׁתִל 1333

plant, *see* tender

plant, to
נָטַע Kal 812
שָׁתַל Kal 1333

plantation
מַטָּע 693

planted
שָׁתַל Kal 1333

planted, to be
נָטַע Niphal 812

planter
נָטַע Kal 812

planting
מַטָּע 693

plants
מַטָּע 693
נְטִישׁוֹת 812
נְטָעִים 812

plants, principal
שְׂרוּקִים 1217

plat
חֶלְקָה 436

plate
לוּחַ 635
פַּח 1016
צִיץ 1071

plate, thin
פַּח 1016

plates
סֶרֶן 885

plates, *see* spread

play, to
נָגַן Piel 791
צָחַק Piel 1070
שָׂחַק Piel 1205
שָׁעַע Pilpel 1316

play, *see* fool, harlot, mad man, men, timbrels

play well, to
טוֹב Hiphil 476

player
נָגַן Piel 791

player on, *see* instruments

playing
נָגַן Piel 791

plea
דִּין 340

plead, to
דִּין Kal 340
יָכַח Hiphil 525
יָכַח Hithpael 525
רִיב Kal 1171
שָׁפַט Niphal 1319

plead the cause, to
דִּין Kal 340

pleading
רִיב 1171

pleasant
חָמֵד 437
חֶמְדָּה 437
חֲמוּדוֹת 438
חֵן 444
חֵפֶץ 452
טוֹב 476
יָפֶה 548
מֶגֶד 661
מַחְמָד 687
נָעִים 822
נֹעַם 823
נַעֲמָנִים 823
עֹנֶג 962
צְבִי 1060
שַׁעֲשֻׁעִים 1318
תַּאֲוָה 1334
תַּעֲנוּג 1354

pleasant, to be
חָמַד Niphal 437
נָעֵם Kal.............. 823
עָרֵב¹ Kal.............. 975

pleasant place
נָאָה 781
נָוֶה 800

pleasant thing
חֲמוּדוֹת 438
מַחְמָד 687

pleasant things
מַחֲמֻדִּים 687

pleasantness
נֹעַם 823

please †
דָּבָר 325

please, to
חָפֵץ 452
יָאַל Hiphil 486
יָטַב Kal.............. 524
יָטַב Hiphil........... 524
רָצָה Kal..............1189
שְׁפַר Ch. Pal..........1322

please,† to
טוֹב Kal.............. 476
יָטַב Kal.............. 524
יָשַׁר Kal.............. 578
פָּנִים 1023

* please,† to
עַיִן 919

* please,† not to
עַיִן 919
רַע 1177

please, to seek to
רָצָה Piel..............1189

please selves, to
שָׂפַק¹ Hiphil 1214

please well,† to
יָטַב Kal.............. 524
יָשַׁר Kal.............. 578

pleased, to be
חָפֵץ Kal.............. 451

* pleased,† it
קֳדָם Ch...............1089

pleased well †
יָשָׁר 578

pleased, to be well
חָפֵץ Kal.............. 451

pleased with, to be
רָצָה Kal..............1189

pleaseth †
טוֹב 476

pleasing, to be
עָרֵב¹ Kal 975

pleasure
אַוָּה 33
חֵפֶץ 452
חֵשֶׁק 471
טוֹב 476
נֶפֶשׁ 829
עֵדֶן 904
עֶדְנָה 904
רְעוּת Ch..............1185
רָצוֹן 1189
שִׂמְחָה 1210

pleasure, *see* good

pleasure, to have
חָפֵץ Kal.............. 451
חָפֵץ 452
רָצָה Kal..............1189

pleasure, to take
עָרֵב¹ Kal 975
רָצָה Kal..............1189

pleasures
נְעִים 822

pleasures, given to
עָדִין 904

pledge
חֲבֹל 399
חֲבֹלָה 399
עֲבוֹט 895
עֲרֻבָּה 977
עֵרָבוֹן 977

pledge, to lay to
חָבַל Kal.............. 398

pledge of, to take a
חָבַל Kal.............. 398

pledges, to give
עָרַב¹ Hithpael........ 975

Pleiades
כִּימָה 596

plenteous
בָּרִיא 272
רַב 1147
רָבָה Hiphil 1151
שָׂבָע 1196
שָׁמֵן 1290

plenteous, to make
יָתַר Hiphil 580

plenteousness
מוֹתָר 681
שָׂבָע 1196

plentiful
כַּרְמֶל 618
נְדָבָה 795

plentiful field
כַּרְמֶל 618

plentifully
יֶתֶר 580
רֹב 1150

plenty
רֹב 1150
רָבָה Hiphil 1151
שָׂבָע 1196
תּוֹעָפוֹת 1342

plenty, in
אָכַל Kal.............. **70**

plenty of, to have
שָׂבֵעַ / שָׂבַע } Kal **1195**

plenty *of water*
מִקְוֶה 756

plot, to
זָמַם Kal.............. 388

plow, to
חָרַשׁ Kal.............. 466

plowed, to be
חָרַשׁ Niphal 466

plower
חָרַשׁ Kal.............. 466

plowing
נִר 840

plowman
אִכָּר 76
חָרַשׁ Kal.............. 466

plowshare
אֵת 182

pluck, to
אָרָה Kal.............. 152
גָּזַל Kal.............. 304
כָּלָה Piel.............. 598
נָסַח Kal.............. 820
נָתַק Kal.............. 863
נָתַשׁ Kal.............. 864
קָטַף Kal..............1106
שָׁלַךְ Hiphil 1275

pluck away, to
סוּר Hiphil 872

pluck down, to
הָרַס Kal.............. 376
שָׁמַד Hiphil 1285

pluck off, to
גָּזַל Kal.............. 304
מָרַט Kal.............. 764
נָתַק Piel.............. 863
שָׁלַף Kal..............1279

pluck off hair, to
מָרַט Kal.............. 764

pluck out, to
יָצָא Hiphil 548
נָתַשׁ Kal.............. 864

pluck up, to
נָתַשׁ Kal.............. 864
עָקַר Kal.............. 974

pluck up, *see* roots

plucked
נָצַל Hophal **835**

plucked, to be
מְרַט Ch. P'il **764**
נָסַח Niphal 820

plucked away, to be
נָתַק Niphal **863**

plucked up, to be
נָתַשׁ Niphal 864
נָתַשׁ Hophal 864

plucked up, *see* roots

pluckt off
טָרָף 485

plumbline
אֲנָךְ 140

plummet
מִשְׁקֶלֶת 778
מִשְׁקֹלֶת 779
{ אֶבֶן 11
{ בְּדִיל 187

plunge, to
טָבַל Kal 473

point
אִבְחָה 10
צִפֹּרֶן 1080

point, *see* at

* point, to be at the
הָלַךְ Kal 362

point out, to
אָוָה Hithpael 29
תָּאָה Piel 1334

pointed things
חָרוּץ 463

points, in...
עֻמָּה 959

poison
חֵמָה 437
רֹאשׁ 1145

pole
נֵס 819

policy
{ שֵׂכֶל
{ שֶׂכֶל } 1207

polished
בָּרַר Kal 277
קָלָל 1109

polished, to be
חָטַב Pual 417

polishing
גִּזְרָה 305

poll
גֻּלְגֹּלֶת 307

poll, to
גָּזַז Kal 304
גָּלַח Piel 309
כָּסַם Kal 609

pollute, to
גָּאַל [2] Piel 286
חָלַל Piel 432
חָנֵף Hiphil 447
טָמֵא Piel 481

pollute selves, to
גָּאַל [2] Niphal 286
טָמֵא Niphal 481

polluted
טָמֵא 482
עָקֹב 974

polluted, to be
בּוּס Hithpael 205
גָּאַל [2] Niphal 286
גָּאַל [2] Pual 286
חָלַל Niphal 432
חָנֵף Kal 447
טָמֵא Kal 481
טָמֵא Niphal 481
טָמֵא Pual 481
טָמֵא Hithpael 481

pollution
טָמֵא 482

pomegranate
רִמּוֹן 1175

pomegranate tree
רִמּוֹן 1175

pommel
גֻּלָּה 309

pomp
גָּאוֹן 285
שָׁאוֹן 1220

pond
אֲגַם 14

ponder, to
פָּלַס Piel 1021
תָּכַן Kal 1347

pool
אֲגַם 14
בְּרָכָה 276
בְּרֵכָה 277

pools
מִקְוֶה 756

poor
אֶבְיוֹן 10
דַּל 341
דַּלָּה 342
חֵלְכָה 431
מַחְסוֹר 689
מִסְכֵּן 737
עֲנָה [2] Ch. P'al 965
עָנָו (כ׳) 965
עָנִי 965
רוּשׁ Kal 1166

* poor
רֹאשׁ 1142

poor †
חַיִל 425
כָּאִים 581

poor, to be
יָרַשׁ Niphal 566

poor, to make
יָרַשׁ Hiphil 566

poor, to make self
רוּשׁ Hithpolel 1166

poor man
אֶבְיוֹן 10
דַּל 341
מִסְכֵּן 737
רוּשׁ Kal 1166

poor, to be waxen
מוּךְ Kal 670

poorer, to be
מוּךְ Kal 670

poorest sort
דַּלָּה 342

poplar
לִבְנֶה 633

populous
אָמוֹן 102
רַב 1174

porch
{ אֵלָם
{ אוּלָם } 30
מִסְדְּרוֹן 736

port
שַׁעַר 1316

porter
שׁוֹעֵר 1247
תָּרָע Ch. 1358

* porter
שַׁעַר 1316

portion
אָחַז Kal 46
דָּבָר 325
{ חֶבֶל
{ חֵבֶל } 399
חֵלֶק 435
חֲלָק Ch. 435
חֶלְקָה 436
חֹק 456
מַחֲלֹקֶת 687
מָנָה 733
מְנָת 736
פֶּה 1011
שְׁכֶם 1260

portion, *see* certain, holy, meat

portion, to take away a
חָלַק Kal 435

possess, to
חֲסַן Ch. Aphel 450
יָרַשׁ Kal 566
יָרַשׁ Hiphil 566
נָחַל Kal 805
נָחַל Hithpael 805
קָנָה [1] Kal 1111

possess, to cause to
נָחַל Hiphil 805

possess, to give to
יָרַשׁ Hiphil 566

possess, to be made to
נָחַל Hophal 805

possess, to make to
יָרַשׁ Hiphil 566

possessed, to be
אָחַז Niphal 46
קָנָה[1] Niphal..........1111

possession
אֲחֻזָּה 47
יְרֵשָׁה 567
יְרֻשָּׁה 567
מוֹרָשׁ 674
מוֹרָשָׁה 674
מַעֲשֶׂה 746
מִקְנָה 759
מִקְנֶה 759
נַחֲלָה 806

* possession
רֶגֶל 1155

possession, to get
אָחַז Niphal 46

possession, to get in
יָרַשׁ Kal.............. 566

possession, to have in
יָרַשׁ Kal.............. 566
נָחַל Kal.............. 805

possession, to take
אָחַז Niphal 46
יָרַשׁ Kal.............. 566

possessor
קָנָה[1] Kal..............1111

post
אַיִל 58
אַמָּה 101
מְזוּזָה 684
סַף 881

post, *see* door

post, door
מְזוּזָה 684

post, side
מְזוּזָה 684

posterity
אַחַר 48
אַחֲרִית 54
דּוֹר 337
שְׁאֵרִית 1223

posts
רוּץ Kal..............1165

pot
אָסוּךְ 141
גָּבִיעַ 290
דּוּד 336
כְּלִי 600
סִיר 875
פָּרוּר 1044
צִנְצֶנֶת 1076

pot, *see* fining, ointment, washpot

pots
שְׁפַתַּיִם 1322

pots, *see* ranges

potsherd
חֶרֶשׂ 466

pottage
נָזִיד 803

potter
יָצַר[1] Kal.............. 556
פֶּחָר Ch..............1017

pound
מָנֶה 733

pour, to
יָצַק Kal.............. 556
נָזַל Kal.............. 803
נָסַךְ[1] Kal.............. 820
נָסַךְ[1] Hiphil 820
נָתַן Kal.............. 851
צוּק[2] Kal..............1069
שָׁפַךְ Kal..............1320

pour down, to
זָקַק Kal.............. 394
נָגַר Hiphil........... 793
נָזַל Kal.............. 803

pour out, to
דָּלַף Kal.............. 342
זָרַם Poal.............. 395
יָצַק Kal.............. 556
נָבַע Hiphil 787
נָגַר Hiphil 793
נָסַךְ[1] Kal 820
נָסַךְ[1] Piel 820
נָסַךְ[1] Hiphil 820
נָתַךְ Hiphil 851
עָרָה Hiphil 977
רוּק Hiphil 1165
שָׁפַךְ Kal..............1320

poured, to be
יָסַךְ Kal.............. 543
יָצַק Hophal.......... 556
נָתַךְ Kal.............. 850
נָתַךְ Niphal 850
עָרָה Niphal 977
שָׁפַךְ Hithpael 1320

poured, to cause to be
נָסַךְ[1] Hiphil 820

poured down
נָגַר Hophal.......... 793

poured forth, to be
נָתַךְ Kal.............. 850
נָתַךְ Niphal 850
רוּק Hophal..........1165

poured out
שָׁפַךְ Kal..............1320
שֶׁפֶךְ 1321

poured out, to be
יָצַק Hophal.......... 556
נָתַךְ Kal.............. 850
נָתַךְ Niphal 850
שָׁפַךְ Niphal 1320
שָׁפַךְ Pual..............1320
שָׁפַךְ Hithpael 1320

pouring out
שָׁפַךְ Kal..............1320

pourtray, to
חָקַק Kal.............. 458

pourtrayed
חָקָה Pual.............. 457

poverty
חֶסֶר 450
מַחְסוֹר 689
רֵאשׁ 1142
רִישׁ 1172
רֵישׁ 1172

poverty, to come to
יָרַשׁ Niphal 566

powder
אָבָק 13
אֲבָקָה 13
עָפָר 968

* powder
דָּקַק Kal.............. 348

powder, into
דָּקַק Hiphil 348

power
אֵל 76
גְּבוּרָה 290
זְרוֹעַ 394
חַיִל 423
חַיִל Ch.............. 425
חֱסֵן Ch.............. 450
יָד 489
יַד Ch.............. 499
כֹּחַ 594
כַּף 612
מֶמְשָׁלָה 731
עֹז 914
עֹז 914
עֱזוּז 917
שִׁלְטוֹן 1274
תַּעֲצֻמוֹת 1354
תֹּקֶף 1357

power †
דָּבָר 325

power, *see* mighty

power as a prince, to have
שָׂרָה Kal..............1217

power, to give
שָׁלַט Hiphil 1274

power, to have
יָכֹל Kal.............. 526
מָשַׁל[1] Kal.............. 771
שׁוּר[2] Kal 1204
שָׂרָה Kal..............1217
שָׁלַט Kal..............1274
שְׁלֵט Ch. P'al.........1274

power, in great
עָרִיץ 978

present, to
יָצַג Hiphil 555
מָצָא Hiphil 748
נָגַשׁ Hiphil 794
נָפַל Hiphil 825
נָצַב Niphal 833
עָמַד Hiphil 955
קָרַב Hiphil 1123

* present, to
נָפַל Kal 825

present, to be
כּוּל Polpal 592
מָצָא Niphal 748
עָמַד Kal 955

present self, to
יָצַב Hithpael 555
עָמַד Hiphil 955
רָאָה Niphal 1133

presented
נָפַל Hiphil 825

presented, to be
עָמַד Hophal 955
קָרַב Hiphil 1123

presenting
נָפַל Hiphil 825

presently
יוֹם 508

presents
מִגְדָּנוֹת 662
שִׁלּוּחִים 1263

preserve, to
חָיָה Piel 421
יָשַׁע Hiphil 576
יָתַר Hiphil 580
מָלַט Hiphil 710
נָצַר Kal 837
שׂוּם / שִׂים Kal 1200
שָׁמַר Kal 1300

preserve alive, to
חָיָה Piel 421

preserve life
מִחְיָה 687

preserved
נָצִיר 835

preserved, to be
נָצַל Niphal 835
שָׁמַר Niphal 1300

preserver
נָצַר Kal 837

presidents
סָרְכִין Ch. 885

press
גַּת 317
פּוּרָה 1015

press, to
פָּצַר Kal 1039
פָּרַץ Kal 1047
צוּק ¹ Hiphil 1069
שָׁחַט Kal 1205

press sore, to
נָחַת Kal 810

pressed, to be
מָעַךְ Pual 742
עוּק Hiphil 912

pressed on, to be
דָּחַף Kal 339

presses
יֶקֶב 557

pressfat
יֶקֶב 557

presume, to
זוּד / זִיד Hiphil 383
מָלֵא Kal 701
עָפַל Hiphil 967

presumptuous
זֵד 379

presumptuously
זָדוֹן 379
זוּד / זִיד Hiphil 383

presumptuously †
רוּם Kal 1163

* presumptuously †
יָד 489

presumptuously, to come
זוּד / זִיד Hiphil 383

prevail, to
אָמַץ Kal 104
גָּבַר Kal 291
גָּבַר Hiphil 291
גָּבַר Hithpael 291
חָזַק Kal 411
חָזַק Hiphil 411
יָכֹל Kal 526
יְכִל Ch. P'al 527
כָּבֵד / כָּבַד Kal 581
לָחַם Niphal 637
עָזַז Kal 917
עָצַר Kal 973
עָרַץ Kal 980
000 000

prevail against, to
רָדָה ¹ Kal 1158
תָּקַף Kal 1357

prevailed
קָשָׁה 1131

prevent, to
קָדַם Piel 1088
קָדַם Hiphil 1088

prey
אֹכֶל 75
בַּז & בָּז 207
בִּזָּה 207
חֶתֶף 472
טָרַף Kal 485
טֶרֶף 485
מַלְקוֹחַ 729
עַד 901
שָׁלָל 1277

prey, for a
בָּזַז Kal 207

prey, to make self a
שָׁלַל Hithpolel 1276

prey, to take for a
בָּזַז Kal 207

price
יְקָר 558
כֶּסֶף 609
מְחִיר 687
מֶכֶר 700
מִקְנָה 759
מֶשֶׁךְ 770
עֵרֶךְ 979
שָׂכָר 1208

pricking
מָאַר Hiphil 659

pricks
שֵׂךְ 1206

pride
גֵּאָה 285
גַּאֲוָה 285
גָּאוֹן 285
גֵּאוּת 285
גֹּבַהּ 287
גֵּוָה 299
גֵּוָה Ch. 299
זָדוֹן 379
רֹכֶס 1175
שַׁחַץ 1252

pride, in
זוּד Ch. Aphel 383

priest
כֹּהֵן 587
כָּהֵן Ch. 591

priest, *see* office of

priest, to be
כָּהַן Piel 587

priesthood
כְּהֻנָּה 591

priests
כְּמָרִים 604

priests, *see* idolatrous

priest's office
כְּהֻנָּה 591

priest's office, to execute the
כָּהַן Piel 587

priest's office, to minister in the
כָּהַן Piel 587

prince
כֹּהֵן ... 587
נָגִיד ... 791
נָדִיב ... 796
נָסִיךְ ... 820
נָשִׂיא ... 845
קָצִין ... 1115
רַב ... 1147
רָזוֹן ... 1166
רָזַן Kal ... 1166
שַׂר ... 1214
שָׁלִישׁ ... 1275

prince, *see* power

prince, to make self a
שָׂרַר Hithpael ... 1219

princes
אֲחַשְׁדַּרְפְּנַיָּא Ch. ... 54
חַשְׁמַנִּים ... 470
סְגָנִים ... 869
פַּרְתְּמִים ... 1049
רַבְרְבָן ... 1154

princes, to make
שׂוּר² Hiphil ... 1204

princess
שָׂרָה ... 1217

principal
אָב ... 1
אַדִּיר ... 17
נָסִיךְ ... 820
רֹאשׁ ... 1142
שׂוֹרָה ... 1204
שַׂר ... 1214

principal, *see* plants

principal officer
כֹּהֵן ... 587

principal thing
רֵאשִׁית ... 1147

principalities
מַרְאָשֹׁת ... 761

print, to
נָתַן Kal ... 851

print, to set a
חָקָה Hithpael ... 457

printed, to be
חָקַק Hophal ... 458

prison
אָסַר Kal ... 143
כֶּלֶא ... 598
כְּלִיא ... 602
מַהְפֶּכֶת ... 668
מַטָּרָה ... 694
מַסְגֵּר ... 736
מִשְׁמָר ... 773
עֹצֶר ... 973
קוֹחַ ... 1096

prison †
כְּלוּא ... 600
סֹהַר ... 870
פְּקֻדָּה ... 1041

* prison †
אֵסוּר ... 141
בַּיִת ... 214

prison, *see* opening

prisoner
אָסִיר ... 141
אַסִּיר ... 141
אָסַר Kal ... 143

prisoners
שְׁבִי ... 1226

privily
אֹפֶל ... 147
לָט ... 640
סֵתֶר ... 886
תָּרְמָה ... 1358

privily, *see* lay, lurk, set

privy chamber, to enter a
חָדַר Kal ... 403

privy member
שָׁפְכָה ... 1321

privy to, to be
יָדַע Kal ... 500

prized, to be
יָקַר Kal ... 558

proceed, to
יָסַף Kal ... 543
יָסַף Hiphil ... 543
יָצָא Kal ... 548

proceed further, to
יָסַף Hiphil ... 543

proceeded out
מוֹצָא ... 673

* process
קֵץ ... 1113

process of, *see* time

process of *time*
רַב ... 1147

* process *of time*
רָבָה Kal ... 1151

proclaim
קָדֵשׁ / קָדַשׁ } Piel ... 1090

*pro*claim
קוֹל ... 1096

proclaim, to
קָרָא¹ Kal ... 1117
שָׁמֵעַ / שָׁמַע } Hiphil ... 1292

proclaim,† to
עָבַר Hiphil ... 895

proclaimed, to cause to be
זָעַק Hiphil ... 391

proclaimed,† to cause to be
עָבַר Hiphil ... 895

proclaiming
קָרָא¹ Kal ... 1117

proclamation
קוֹל ... 1096
רִנָּה ... 1176

proclamation, to make
קָרָא¹ Kal ... 1117

proclamation,† to make
עָבַר Hiphil ... 895

proclamation, to make a
כְּרַז Ch. Aphel ... 617
שָׁמֵעַ / שָׁמַע } Hiphil ... 1292

procure, to
בָּקַשׁ Piel ... 268
עָשָׂה Kal ... 981

produce, to
קָרַב Piel ... 1123

profane
חֹל ... 428
חָלָל ... 433

profane, to
חָלַל Piel ... 432

profane, to be
חָנֵף Kal ... 447

profane, to cast as
חָלַל Piel ... 432

profane place
חֹל ... 428

profane self, to
חָלַל Niphal ... 432

profaned, to be
חָלַל Niphal ... 432
חָלַל Pual ... 432

profaneness
חֲנֻפָּה ... 447

profess, to
נָגַד Hiphil ... 788

profit
בֶּצַע ... 264
יוֹתֵר ... 521
יִתְרוֹן ... 581
מוֹתָר ... 681
שָׁוָה¹ Kal ... 1245

profit, to
יָעַל Hiphil ... 546
סָכַן¹ Kal ... 876
שָׁוָה¹ Kal ... 1245

profit, to have
יָעַל Hiphil ... 546

profitable
יִתְרוֹן ... 581

profitable, to be
יָעַל Hiphil ... 546
סָכַן¹ Kal ... 876
צָלֵחַ Kal ... 1072

profound, to be
עָמַק Hiphil ... 961

progenitor
הָרָה Kal ... 375

*prognosticator
יָדַע Hiphil ... 500

prolong, to
אָרַךְ Hiphil ... 156
יָסַף Hiphil ... 543
נָטָה Kal ... 810

*prolong,† to
יְהַב Ch. P'al ... 507

prolonged
אַרְכָה Ch. ... 157

prolonged, to be
אָרַךְ Kal ... 156
אָרַךְ Hiphil ... 156
מָשַׁךְ Niphal ... 770

promise
אֹמֶר ... 134
דָּבָר ... 325

promise, *see* breach

promise, to
אָמַר Kal ... 105
דָּבַר Kal ... 319
דָּבַר Piel ... 319

promise life, to
חָיָה Hiphil ... 421

promote, to
גָּדַל Piel ... 297
כָּבֵד / כָּבַד } Piel ... 581
צְלַח Ch. Aphel ... 1072
רוּם Polel ... 1163

promote to honour, to
כָּבֵד / כָּבַד } Piel ... 581

promoted, to be
נוּעַ Kal ... 802

promotion
רוּם Hiphil ... 1163

*promotion
הַר ... 371

promotion, to be
רוּם Hiphil ... 1163

pronounce, to
בָּטָא / בָּטָה } Piel ... 210
דָּבַר Piel ... 319
קָרָא[1] Kal ... 1117

pronounce, *see* clean, unclean

proper good
סְגֻלָּה ... 869

prophecy
מַשָּׂא ... 766
נְבוּאָה ... 783
נָבִיא ... 784

prophesy, to
חָזָה Kal ... 410
נָבָא Niphal ... 782
נָבָא Hithpael ... 782
נְבָא Ch. Ithpael ... 783
נָטַף Hiphil ... 812

prophesy, that
נָבִיא ... 784

prophesying
נָבָא Niphal ... 782
נָבָא Hithpael ... 782
נְבוּאָה Ch. ... 783

prophet
חֹזֶה ... 410
נָבִיא ... 784
נְבִיא Ch. ... 786
נָטַף Hiphil ... 812

prophet, to make self, a
נָבָא Hithpael ... 782

prophetess
נְבִיאָה ... 786

proportion
מַעַר ... 745
עֵרֶךְ ... 979

prospect
פָּנִים ... 1023

prosper
שָׁלֵו / שָׁלֵיו } ... 1263
שָׁלוֹם ... 1263

prosper, to
יָלַךְ Kal ... 531
כָּשֵׁר Kal ... 621
צְלַח Ch. Aphel ... 1072
צָלַח Kal ... 1072
צָלַח Hiphil ... 1072
שָׂכַל Hiphil ... 1206
שָׁלָה / שָׁלֵו } Kal ... 1262
שָׁלַם Kal ... 1277

prosper, to cause to
צָלַח Hiphil ... 1072

prosper, to make to
צָלַח Hiphil ... 1072

prosperity
טוֹב ... 476
שֶׁלֶו ... 1263
שַׁלְוָה ... 1263
שָׁלוֹם ... 1263

prosperity, in
שָׁלֵו / שָׁלֵיו } ... 1263

prosperity, to send
צָלַח Hiphil ... 1072

prosperous
צָלַח Hiphil ... 1072
שָׁלוֹם ... 1263

prosperous, to make
צָלַח Hiphil ... 1072
שָׁלַם Piel ... 1277

prosperously
צָלַח Kal ... 1072

prosperously, *see* effect

prostitute, to
חָלַל Piel ... 432

protection
סִתְרָה ... 886

protest, to
עוּד Hiphil ... 905

protesting
עוּד Hiphil ... 906

proud
גֵּא ... 285
גֵּאֶה ... 285
גָּאוֹן ... 285
גַּאֲיוֹן ... 285
גָּבֹהַּ ... 287
גָּבֹהַּ / גָּבוֹהַּ } ... 287
זֵד ... 379
זָדוֹן ... 379
זֵידוֹן ... 384
יָהִיר ... 507
יָנָה Kal ... 541
רַהַב ... 1159
רָהָב ... 1159
רוּם Kal ... 1163
רָחָב ... 1166

proud, to be
גָּבַהּ Kal ... 287
זוּד / זִיד } Kal ... 383

proud, most
זָדוֹן ... 379

proud thing
גָּדוֹל ... 293

proudly
גַּאֲוָה ... 285
גֵּאוּת ... 285

proudly, to behave self
רָהַב Kal ... 1159

proudly, to deal
זוּד / זִיד } Kal ... 383
זוּד / זִיד } Hiphil ... 383

proudly, to have *spoken*
גָּדַל Hiphil ... 297

prove, to
בָּחַן Kal ... 208
נָסָה Piel ... 820

prove, *see* perverse

proved, to be
בָּחַן Niphal ... 208

provender
בְּלִיל ... 230
מִסְפּוֹא ... 738

provender, to give
בָּלַל Kal ... 230

proverb
חִידָה 421
מָשָׁל 772
proverb, to use
מָשַׁל[2] Kal.............. 772
proverb, to use as a
מָשַׁל[2] Kal.............. 772
proverbs, to speak in
מָשַׁל[2] Kal.............. 772
provide, to
חָזָה Kal.............. 410
כּוּן Hiphil 592
עָשָׂה Kal.............. 981
רְאָה Kal..............1133
provide, *see* sustenance, victuals
province
מְדִינָה 667
מְדִינָה Ch.............. 667
* province, every
מְדִינָה 667
provision
דָּבָר 325
כֵּרָה 616
לֶחֶם 638
צַיִד 1071
צֵידָה 1071
provision, *see* meat
provision, to make
כּוּל Pilpel............ 592
כּוּן Hiphil 592
provision, to take
צוּד Hithpael........1065
provocation
כַּעַס 612
מָרָה Hiphil 762
מְרִיבָה 764
provocations
נֶאָצוֹת 782
provoke, to
כָּעַס Piel.............. 612
כָּעַס Hiphil 612
מָרָה Hiphil 762
מָרַר Hiphil 766
נָאַץ Piel.............. 782
סוּת Hiphil 874
רָגַז Hiphil 1155
provoke, *see* jealousy, wrath
provoke to anger, to
כָּעַס Piel. (נאץ..782) 612
כָּעַס Hiphil 612
עָבַר Hithpael........ 895
provoke unto, *see* wrath
provoke unto wrath, to
כָּעַס Hiphil 612
provoking
כַּעַס 612
מָרָה Hiphil 762
prudence
עָרְמָה 980

שֶׂכֶל / שֵׂכֶל 1207
prudent
בִּין Kal.............. 212
עָרוּם 978
קָסַם Kal..............1113
שָׂכַל Hiphil 1206
prudent, to be
בִּין Niphal 212
עָרַם[1] Hiphil.......... 979
prudently, to deal
שָׂכַל Hiphil 1206
prune, to
זָמַר Kal.............. 389
pruned, to be
זָמַר Niphal 389
pruninghooks
מַזְמֵרוֹת 684
psalm
זָמִיר 388
זִמְרָה 389
מִזְמוֹר 684
psalmist
זָמִיר 388
psalms, to sing
זָמַר Piel.............. 389
psaltery
נֵבֶל / נֶבֶל 786
פְּסַנְטֵרִין Ch..............1037
פְּסַנְתֵּרִין Ch..............1037
psaltery †
כְּלִי 600
publish, to
אָמַר Kal.............. 105
בָּשַׂר Piel.............. 278
גָּלָה Kal.............. 307
דָּבַר Piel.............. 319
קָרָא[1] Kal 1117
שָׁמַע / שָׁמַע Hiphil 1292
published, to be
שָׁמַע / שָׁמַע Niphal........1292
puff, to
פּוּחַ Hiphil...........1014
pull, to
נָתַק Piel.............. 863
* pull, to
נָתַן Kal.............. 851
pull down, to
הָרַס Kal.............. 376
נָתַץ Kal.............. 863
pull in, to
בּוֹא Hiphil........... 189
pull in again, to
שׁוּב Hiphil 1238

pull in pieces, to
פָּשַׁח Piel..............1050
pull off, to
פָּשַׁט Hiphil 1050
pull out, to
יָצָא Hiphil........... 548
נָתַק Hiphil........... 863
pulled down, to be
נְסַח Ch. Ithpael...... 820
pulled up, to be
נָתַשׁ Niphal 864
pulpit
מִגְדָּל 661
pulse
זֵרֹעִים 397
זֵרְעֹנִים 397
punish, to
חָשַׂךְ Kal.............. 468
יָסַר Piel.............. 545
נָכָה Hiphil........... 814
עָנַשׁ Kal.............. 967
פָּקַד Kal..............1040
רָעַע Hiphil 1186
punish,† to
פָּקַד Kal..............1040
punished, to be
נָקַם Niphal 839
נָקַם Hophal.......... 839
עָנַשׁ Kal.............. 967
עָנַשׁ Niphal 967
punishment
חַטָּאת 416
עָוֹן 910
עֹנֶשׁ 967
תּוֹכֵחָה 1340
punishment of iniquity
עָוֹן 910
punishment of sin
חֵטְא 415
חַטָּאת 416
Pur
פּוּר 1015
purchase
מִקְנָה 759
מִקְנֶה 759
purchase, to
גָּאַל[1] Kal............ 285
קָנָה[1] Kal............1111
pure
בַּר 269
בָּרַר Kal.............. 277
בָּרַר Niphal 277
דְּרוֹר 349
זַךְ & זָךְ 385
טָהוֹר 474
כָּתִית 623
נְקֵא Ch.............. 837
צָרַף Kal..............1082

* pure
חֶמֶר 441
סָגַר Kal 869

pure, *see* gold

pure, to be
זָכַךְ Kal 385
טָהֵר Kal 475

pure, to count
זָכָה Kal 385

pure, to shew self
בָּרַר Hithpael 277

purely
בֹּר 270

pureness
בֹּר 270
טָהוֹר 474
טֹהַר 475

purer, to be
זָכַךְ Kal 385

purge, to
בָּרַר Piel 277
דּוּחַ Hiphil 337
זָקַק Piel 394
חָטָא Piel 414
טָהֵר Piel 475
כָּפַר Piel 614

purge away, to
כָּפַר Piel 614
צָרַף Kal 1082

purge out, to
בָּרַר Kal 277

purged, to be
טָהֵר Kal 475
כָּפַר Pual 614
כָּפַר Hithpael 614

purification
טָהֳרָה 475

purification for sin
חַטָּאת 416

purification, things for
תַּמְרוּק 1351

purifications
מְרוּקִים 763

purified
זָקַק Pual 394

purified, to be
בָּרַר Hithpael 277
חָטָא Hithpael 414
טָהֵר Hithpael 475
קָדַשׁ / קָדֵשׁ } Hithpael 1090

purifier
טָהֵר Piel 475

purify, to
חָטָא Hithpael 414
טָהֵר Piel 475

purify self, to
חָטָא Hithpael 414
חָטָא Piel 414

purify selves, to
טָהֵר Hithpael 475

purifying
חַטָּאת 416
טֹהַר 475
טָהֳרָה 475
תַּמְרוּק 1351

Purim
פּוּר 1015

purple
אַרְגְּוָן 152
אַרְגָּמָן 152

purpose
דָּבָר 325
זִמָּה 388
חֵפֶץ 452
מַחֲשָׁבָה 690
מַחֲשֶׁבֶת 690
מַעֲשֶׂה 746
עֵצָה 971
צְבוּ Ch. 1060
שֵׁת 1331

purpose, *see* what

purpose, to
אָמַר Kal 105
זָמַם Kal 388
חָשַׁב Kal 468
יָעַץ Kal 547
יָצַר[1] Kal 556
שׂוּם / שִׂים } Kal 1200

purpose, of
שָׁלַל Kal 1276

purpose, to no
רִיק 1172

purposed, was
פָּנִים 1023

purse
כִּיס 596

pursue, to
רָדַף Kal 1158
רָדַף Piel 1158

pursue,† to
יָלַךְ Kal 531

pursue hard, to
דָּבֵק / דָּבַק } Hiphil 318

pursue, hotly to
דָּלַק Kal 342

pursuer
רָדַף Kal 1158

pursuing
אַחַר 48
רָדַף Kal 1158

pursu*ing*
שִׂיג 1206

purtenance
קֶרֶב 1125

push, to
נָגַח Kal 791
נָגַח Piel 791
נָגַח Hithpael 791

push away, to
שָׁלַח Piel 1268

push down, to
נָגַח Piel 791

push, used to
נַגָּח 791

push, wont to
נַגָּח 791

pushing
נָגַח Piel 791

put †
הֲוָא / הֲוָה } Ch. P'al 358

put, to
בּוֹא Hiphil 189
הָדָה Kal 357
000 000
חָבַשׁ Kal 400
יָנַח Hiphil 541
יָסַף Kal 543
יָצַג Hiphil 555
לָבֵשׁ / לָבַשׁ } Hiphil 633
מִשְׁלָח 772
נָחָה Hiphil 804
נָשַׂג Hiphil 845
נָתַן Kal 851
סוּר Hiphil 872
סָמַךְ Kal 879
סָפָה[2] Kal 881
סָפַח Kal 881
סָפַח Piel 881
עָלָה Hiphil 934
עָמַס Hiphil 960
עָשָׂה Kal 981
רָכַב Hiphil 1173
שׂוּם / שִׂים } Kal 1200
שׁוּב Hiphil 1238
שִׁית Kal 1256
שָׁלַח Kal 1268
שְׁלַח Ch. P'al 1273

put, to be
בּוֹא Hophal 189
יָסַף Niphal 543
יָסַף Hiphil 543
יָשַׂם Kal 568
נָגַשׁ Hophal 794
נָתַן Niphal 851
נָתַן Hophal 851

* put, to be
נָתַן Kal 851
עָלָה Kal 934

quickly, to make ready
מָהַר¹ Piel 669
quiet
מְנוּחָה 733
נַחַת 810
שַׁאֲנָן 1222
שָׁלֵו } שָׁלֵיו } 1263
שָׁלֵם 1278
שָׁקַט Kal..............1324
quiet, to
נוּחַ Hiphil 800
שָׁקַט Hiphil 1324
quiet, to be
חָרַשׁ Hithpael 466
נוּחַ Kal.............. 800
שָׁאַן Pielel............1222
שָׁקַט Kal..............1324
שָׁקַט Hiphil 1324
שָׁתַק Kal..............1333
quiet, at
שָׁקַט Kal..............1324
quiet, to be in
שָׁקַט Kal..............1324
quiet self, to
דָּמַם Poal 346
quiet, that are
רָגֵעַ 1157
quietly
שְׁלִי 1274
quietly, *see* wait
quietness
נַחַת 810
שָׁלֵו } שָׁלֵיו } 1263
שַׁלְוָה 1263
שָׁקַט Hiphil 1324
שֶׁקֶט 1324
quietness, to give
שָׁקַט Hiphil 1324
quietness, to be in
שָׁקַט Kal..............1324
quit
נָקִי 838
quit, to be
נָקָה Niphal 838
quit selves, to
הָיָה Kal.............. 360
* quite
עָרָיָה 978

quite is sometimes the translation of an infinitive used intensitively.

quite, *see* driven, take away
quiver
אַשְׁפָּה 179
תְּלִי 1348
quiver, to
צָלַל¹ Kal(לָבוּשׁ..632)1073

Rab-mag
רַב } 1147
מָג } 661
rabbim, *see* Bath-rabbim
Rabsaris
רַב } 1174
סָרִים } 885
race
אֹרַח 154
מֵרוֹץ 763
rafter
רָהִיט 1160
רָחִיט 1168
rag
בֶּגֶד 185
rage
זַעַם 391
זַעַף 391
חֵמָה 437
עֶבְרָה 900
רְגַז Ch................1155
רָגַז Hithpael 1155
רֹגֶז 1155
rage, to
הָלַל Hithpoel 366
הָמָה Kal.............. 368
עָבַר Hithpael 895
רָגַז Kal..............1155
רָגַשׁ Kal..............1158
ragged, *see* rock
raging
גֵּאוּת 285
זַעַף 391
rags
קְרָעִים 1130
rags, *see* rotten
Rahab
רַהַב 1159
rail, to
חָרַף Piel.............. 465
עִיט Kal.............. 919
raiment
בֶּגֶד 185
כְּסוּת 608
לְבוּשׁ 632
מַד 664
מַלְבּוּשׁ 706
שַׂלְמָה 1208
שִׂמְלָה 1210
raiment, change of
מַחֲלָצוֹת 687
raiment of needlework
רִקְמָה 1192
rain
גֶּשֶׁם 317
מוֹרֶה 674
מָטָר 693
rain, *see* former

rain, to
יָרָה Hiphil 564
מָטַר Hiphil 693
rain, to cause
גָּשַׁם Hiphil **317**
rain, to cause to
מָטַר Hiphil **693**
rain, first
יוֹרֶה 521
rain, latter
מַלְקוֹשׁ 730
rain, small
שְׂעִירִים 1212
rained upon
גֹּשֶׁם **317**
rained upon, to be
מָטַר Niphal **693**
rainy, very
סַגְרִיר **870**
raise, to
זָקַף Kal.............. **393**
נָשָׂא Kal.............. 840
עוּר¹ Hiphil 913
עִיר Kal.............. 925
עָלָה Hiphil 934
קוּם Hiphil............1099
raise up, to
זָקַף Kal.............. 393
נָשָׂא Kal.............. 840
סָלַל Kal.............. 878
עוּר¹ Pilel............ 913
עוּר¹ Hiphil 913
עָמַד Hiphil 955
עָרַר Poel 980
קוּם Polel............1099
קוּם Hiphil 1099
raise up great height, to
גָּבַהּ Hiphil 287
raise up self
שְׂאֵת 1195
raise up self, to
קוּם Ch. Aphel 1103
raised, to be
עוּר¹ Niphal.......... 913
raised up, to be
עוּר¹ Niphal.......... 913
קוּם Hophal..........1099
raiser of taxes
עָבַר Hiphil } 895
נָגַשׂ Kal } 794
raisins, bunches of
צִמּוּקִים 1074
raisins, clusters of
צִמּוּקִים 1074
ram
אַיִל 58
דְּכַר Ch................ 341
כַּר 615
עַתּוּד 1007

Ramath-lehi
{ רָמָה 1175
{ לְחִי 637
Ramathaim-zophim
צָפָה Kal 1077
rampart
חֵיל 425
rams' horn
יוֹבֵל 507
ram's *horn*
יוֹבֵל 507
range
יָתוּר 579
שְׂדֵרָה 1199
range, to
שָׁקַק Kal 1325
ranges for pots
כִּירַיִם 596
rank
אֹרַח 154
בָּרִיא 272
מַעֲרָכָה 746
פַּעַם 1038
rank, *see* third
rank, to keep
עָדַר² Kal 905
ransom
כֹּפֶר 615
פִּדְיוֹן 1011
ransom, to
גָּאַל¹ Kal 285
פָּדָה Kal 1010
rare
יַקִּיר Ch. 558
rase, to
עָרָה Piel 977
rash
מָהַר¹ Niphal 669
rash, to be
בָּהַל }
בָּהֵל } Piel 188
rasor
תַּעַר 1354
rate
דָּבָר 325
rate, *see* certain
rather, *see* how much
rather, to be
בָּחַר Kal 209
rather than
אַל 76
rattle, to
רָנָה Kal 1176
rattling
רַעַשׁ 1187
raven
עֹרֵב 976
ravenous
עַיִט 919
פָּרִיץ 1046
ravenous bird
עַיִט 919
ravin
טְרֵפָה 485
ravin, to
טָרַף Kal 485
ravish, to
לָבַב Piel 630
עָנָה² Piel 964
ravished, to be
שָׁגַל Niphal 1236
שָׁכַב Niphal 1257
* ravished, to be
שָׁגָה Kal 1236
raw
חַי 418
נָא 781
razor
מוֹרָה 674
תַּעַר 1354
reach, to
בָּרַח Hiphil 271
מְטָא }
מְטָה } Ch. P'al 691
נָגַע Kal 792
נָשַׂג Hiphil 845
פָּגַע Kal 1009
צָבַט Kal 1060
reach forth, to
שָׁלַח Piel 1268
reach to, *see* midst
reach unto, to
מָחָה³ Kal 686
reach up, to
נָגַע Hiphil 792
read, to
קָרָא¹ Kal 1117
קָרָא¹ Niphal 1117
קְרָא Ch. P'al 1123
reading
מִקְרָא 760
קָרָא¹ Kal 1117
ready
חוּשׁ Kal 409
טוֹב 476
כּוּן Niphal 592
מָהִיר 668
מָצָא Kal 748
עָתוּד (כ') 1008
עָתִיד 1008
עֲתִיד Ch. 1008
ready, *see* armed, burst, dressed, fall, forgive, made, make, prepared, quickly
ready, to be
הוּן Hiphil 360
כּוּן Polel 592
מוּט Kal 670
ready to become, to be
עָתַד Hithpael 1007
ready, to make
אָסַר Kal 143
כּוּן Polel 592
כּוּן Hiphil 592
קָרַב Piel 1123
ready, more
קָרוֹב 1127
realm
מַלְכוּ Ch. 728
מַלְכוּת 728
reap, to
קָצַר Kal 1116
קָצַר (כ') Hiphil 1117
reap, to wholly
כָּלָה Piel 598
reaper
קָצַר Kal 1116
rear, to
קוּם Hiphil 1099
rear up, to
נָצַב Hiphil 838
קוּם Hiphil 1099
reared up, to be
קוּם Hiphil 1099
קוּם Hophal 1099
reason
דָּבָר 325
חֶשְׁבּוֹן 469
טַעַם 483
מַנְדַּע 732
תְּבוּנָה 1335
reason, *see* by
reason, to
יָכַח Hiphil 525
שָׁפַט Niphal 1319
reason of, *see* by
reason of, by
מִן 731
עַם 955
פָּנִים 1023
קֳבֵל }
קְבֵל } Ch. 1084
reason together, to
יָכַח Niphal 525
reasoning
תּוֹכַחַת 1340
rebel
מָרַד Kal 762
מָרָה Kal 762
מְרִי 764
rebel †
בֵּן 232
rebel, to
מָרַד Kal 762
מָרָה Kal 762
מָרָה Hiphil 762

סוּר Kal 872
פָּשַׁע Kal 1050
rebel against, to
מָרָה Hiphil 762
rebellion
מְרַד Ch. 762
מֶרֶד 762
מְרִי 764
סָרָה 884
פֶּשַׁע 1050
rebellious
מָרַד Kal 762
מְרַד Ch. 762
מָרָה Kal 762
מָרָה Hiphil 762
מְרִי 764
סָרַר Kal 885
* rebellious
מַרְדּוּת 762
rebellious, to be
מָרָה Kal 762
rebellious, most
מְרִי 764
rebuke
גְּעָרָה 314
חֶרְפָּה 465
מִגְעֶרֶת 663
תּוֹכֵחָה 1340
תּוֹכַחַת 1340
rebuke, to
גָּעַר Kal 313
יָכַח Hiphil 525
רִיב Kal 1171
rebuker
מוּסָר 672
rebuking
גְּעָרָה 314
recall, to
שׁוּב Hiphil 1238
receive, to
אָסַף Piel 141
חָלַק Kal (חזק Hiph.413) 435
כּוּל Hiphil 592
לָקַח Kal 644
מָצָא Kal 748
נָשָׂא Kal 840
קָבַל Piel 1083
קְבַל Ch. Pael 1084
שָׁקַל Kal 1324
receive, *see* comfort
receive ashes, to
דָּשֵׁן Piel 355
received, to be
אָסַף Niphal 141
receiver
שָׁקַל Kal 1324
receiving
לָקַח Kal 644
rechokim, *see* Jonath-elem-rechokim
reckon, to
חָשַׁב Piel 468
סָפַר Kal 882
פָּקַד Kal 1040
שָׁוָה [1] Piel 1245
reckoned, to be
חָשַׁב Niphal 468
חָשַׁב Hithpael 468
reckoned, *see* genealogy
reckoned by genealogies, to be
יָחַשׂ Hithpael 523
reckoned up, *see* order
reckoning
פְּקֻדָּה 1041
reckoning to be made
חָשַׁב Niphal 468
recompence
גְּמוּל 311
גְּמוּלָה 311
שִׁלּוּם 1264
שִׁלֻּם 1279
תְּמוּרָה 1349
recompense, to
גָּמַל Kal 311
נָתַן Kal 851
שׁוּב Hiphil 1238
שָׁלַם Piel 1277
recompensed, to be
שׁוּב Hophal 1238
שָׁלַם Pual 1277
recompensing
נָתַן Kal 851
reconcile, to
כָּפַר Piel 614
reconcile self, to
רָצָה Hithpael 1189
reconciliation, to make
חָטָא Piel 414
כָּפַר Piel 614
record
דִּכְרוֹן Ch. 341
דָּכְרָן Ch. 341
זִכָּרוֹן 387
שָׂהֵד 1200
record, to
זָכַר Hiphil 385
record, to call to
עוּד Hiphil 905
record, to take to
עוּד Hiphil 906
recorded
כָּתַב Kal 621
recorder
זָכַר Hiphil 385
recount, to
זָכַר Kal 385
recover, to
חָיָה Kal 421
חָלַם [2] Hiphil 433
נָצַל Hiphil 835
עָצַר Kal 973
קָנָה [1] Kal 1111
שׁוּב Hiphil 1238
recover (*another of leprosy*), to
אָסַף Kal 141
recover...selves
מִחְיָה 687
recover strength, to
בָּלַג Hiphil 229
recovered, to be
חָזַק Kal 411
עָלָה Kal 934
red
אָדֹם 21
אַדְמוֹנִי / אַדְמֹנִי 22
חַכְלִילִי 426
red, *see* dyed, wine
red, to be
אָדַם Pual 20
אָדַם Hiphil 20
אָדַם Hithpael 20
חָמַר Kal 441
red, to be made
אָדַם Pual 20
red *marble*
בַּהַט 188
* Red *sea*
סוּף 872
reddish
אֲדַמְדָּם 21
reddish, somewhat
אֲדַמְדָּם 21
redeem
גְּאֻלָּה 286
פְּדוּת 1011
redeem, to
גָּאַל [1] Kal 285
פָּדָה Kal 1010
פָּרַק Kal 1047
קָנָה [1] Kal 1111
redeem self, to
גָּאַל [1] Niphal 285
redeemed, to be
גָּאַל [1] Niphal 285
פָּדָה Niphal 1010
פְּדוּיִים 1011
redeemed, to let be
פָּדָה Hiphil 1010
redeemed, that are to be
פָּדָה Kal 1010
פְּדוּיִים 1011
redeemed, that were
פְּדוּיִים 1011
פִּדְיוֹם 1011

rejoice, to greatly
עָלַז Kal............. 941

rejoice, to make to
רָנַן Hiphil 1177
שָׂמֵחַ / שָׂמַח } Piel 1208
שָׂמֵחַ / שָׂמַח } Hiphil 1208

rejoice, that
עַלִּיז 942

rejoiceth, that
עָלֵז 941

rejoicing
גִּיל 306
גִּילָה 307
עַלִּיז 942
עֲלִיצוּת 942
רִנָּה 1176
שָׂמֵחַ 1209
שִׂמְחָה 1210
שָׂשׂוֹן 1219
תְּרוּעָה 1358

release
הֲנָחָה 370
שְׁמִטָּה 1286

release, to
שָׁמַט Kal..............1286
שָׁמַט Hiphil 1286

relieve, to
אָשַׁר Piel............. 180
חָזַק Hiphil 411
עוּד Pilpel........... 906
שׁוּב Hiphil 1238

rely, to
שָׁעַן Niphal 1316

remain
שָׂרִיד 1217

remain, *see* let

remain, to
גּוּר Kal............. 303
יָשַׁב Kal............. 568
יָתַר Niphal 580
לוּן / לִין } Kal........... 635
נוּחַ Kal............. 800
עָדַף Kal............. 904
עָמַד Kal............. 955
קוּם Kal.............1099
שָׂרַד Kal.............1217
שָׁאַר Kal.............1222
שָׁאַר Niphal 1222
שְׁאֵרִית 1223
שָׁכֵן / שָׁכַן } Kal...........1260
[1]שָׁקַד Kal.............1322

remain, to cause to
שָׁכֵן / שָׁכַן } Hiphil 1260

remain, to let
יָתַר Hiphil 580

remain long, to
יָשֵׁן Niphal 576

remainder
יָתַר Niphal 580
שְׁאֵרִית 1223

* remaineth †
יוֹם 508

remaining
יָצַב Hithpael......... 555
שָׂרִיד 1217
שָׁכֵן / שָׁכַן } Kal...........1260

remaining, to be
יָתַר Niphal 580

remedy
מַרְפֵּא 765

remember, to
זָכַר Kal............. 385
זָכַר Hiphil 385
פָּקַד Kal.............1040

remembered, to be
זָכַר Niphal 385

remembered, to make to be
זָכַר Hiphil 385

remembrance
זֵכֶר / זֶכֶר } 387

remembrance, to bring to
זָכַר Hiphil 385

remembrance, to call to
זָכַר Kal............. 385
זָכַר Hiphil 385
פָּקַד Kal.............1040

remembrance, to be come to
זָכַר Niphal 385

remembrance, to be in
זָכַר Niphal 385

remembrance, to keep in
זָכַר Hiphil 385

remembrance, to put in
זָכַר Hiphil 385

Remmon-methoar
תָּאַר Pual.............1334

remnant
אַחַר 48
אַחֲרִית 54
יָתַר Niphal 580
יֶתֶר 580
סָרַח 884
פְּלֵיטָה 1020
שָׂרִיד 1217
שָׁאַר Niphal 1222
שְׁאָר 1223
שְׁאֵרִית 1223
שֵׁרוּת 1326

* remnant
שָׁרָה (ק׳) Piel........1326

remnant, *see* leave

remove, to
גָּלָה Kal............. 307
גָּלָה Hiphil 307
גָּלַל Kal............. 310
[1]מוּשׁ Kal............. 674
[1]מוּשׁ Hiphil 674
נוּד Kal............. 799
נוּד Hiphil 799
נוּעַ Kal............. 802
נָסַג Hiphil 819
נָסַע Kal............. 821
נָסַע Hiphil 821
נָשַׂג Hiphil 845
סָבַב Niphal 865
סָבַב Hiphil 865
סוּר Hiphil 872
סוּת Hiphil 874
עָבַר Hiphil 895
עֲדָה Ch. Aphel 902
עָתַק Hiphil 1008
רָעַשׁ Kal.............1187

remove a tent, to
[2]אָהַל Kal 27

remove far, to
רָחַק Piel.............1170
רָחַק Hiphil 1170

remove far away, to
רָחַק Piel.............1170

remove far off, to
זָנַח Kal............. 390
רָחַק Hiphil 1170

removed
נִידָה 813

* removed
זַעֲוָה 390
נִדָּה 796

remove into a corner כנף.. 605

removed, to be
גָּלָה Niphal 307
זְוָעָה 384
[2]יָגָה Hiphil.......... 488
000 000
מוֹט Kal............. 670
מוּר Hiphil 674
[1]מוּשׁ Kal 674
נָדַד Kal............. 795
נוּד Hithpolel 799
סוּר Kal............. 872
עָתַק Kal.............1008

removed woman
נִדָּה 796

removing
גּוֹלָה 302
סוּר Hiphil 872

rescue, to
יָשַׁע Hiphil 576
נָצַל Hiphil 835
נְצַל Ch. Aphel....... 837
פָּדָה Kal..............1010
שׁוּב Hiphil 1238
resemblance
עַיִן 919
* resemble
תֹּאַר 1334
reserve, to
אָצַל Kal.............. 148
חָשַׂךְ Kal.............. 468
יָתַר Hiphil 580
לָקַח Kal.............. 644
נָטַר Kal.............. 813
שָׁאַר Hiphil 1222
שָׁמַר Kal..............1300
reserved, to be
חָשַׂךְ Niphal 468
residue
אַחֲרִית 54
יָתַר Niphal 580
יֶתֶר 580
שְׁאָר 1223
שְׁאָר Ch..............1223
שְׁאֵרִית 1223
resist, to
שָׂטַן Kal..............1205
resort, to
בּוֹא Kal.............. 189
יָצַב Hithpael 555
קָבַץ Niphal 1084
respect
מַשֹּׂא 767
respect, to
נָכַר Hiphil 818
נָשָׂא Kal.............. 840
פָּנָה Kal..............1021
רָאָה Kal..............1133
respect, to have
יָדַע Kal.............. 500
נָבַט Hiphil 783
נָכַר Hiphil 818
פָּנָה Kal..............1021
רָאָה Kal..............1133
שָׁעָה Kal..............1315
respite
רְוָחָה 1162
respite, to give
רָפָה Hiphil 1188
rest
דֳּמִי 346
מָנוֹחַ 733
מְנוּחָה 733
מַרְגּוֹעַ 762
נוֹחַ 801
פוּגָה 1014
שַׁבָּתוֹן 1235
שָׁלוֹם 1263
rest
יָתַר Niphal 580
יֶתֶר 580
שָׂרִיד 1217
שְׁאָר 1223
שְׁאָר Ch..............1223
שְׁאֵרִית 1223
rest, *see* beside, take
rest, to
אָחַז Kal.............. 46
דָּמַם Kal.............. 346
חָדַל Kal.............. 402
חוּל / חִיל } Kal............ 406
חָרַשׁ Hiphil 466
נוּחַ Kal.............. 800
נַחַת 810
רָגַע Niphal 1157
רָגַע Hiphil 1157
שָׁאַן Pilel 1222
שָׁבַת Kal..............1234
שָׁכֵן / שָׁכַן } Kal 1260
שָׁעַן Niphal 1316
שָׁקַט Kal..............1324
שָׁקַט Hiphil 1324
rest, at
שְׁלֵה Ch. P'al..........1262
rest, to be at
נוּחַ Kal.............. 800
שָׁקַט Kal..............1324
rest, cause to
רָגַע Hiphil 1157
rest, to cause to
נוּחַ Hiphil 800
rest content, to
אָבָה Kal.............. 9
rest, to give
נוּחַ Kal.............. 800
נוּחַ Hiphil 800
רָגַע Hiphil 1157
שָׁקַט Hiphil 1324
rest, to have
נוּחַ Kal.............. 800
נוּחַ Hophal.......... 800
שָׁקַט Kal..............1324
rest, to be in
שָׁקַט Kal..............1324
rest in tent, to
חָנָה Kal.............. 445
rest, to let
שָׁמַט Kal..............1286
rest, to make to
נוּחַ Hiphil 800
רָבַץ Hiphil 1154
רָגַע Hiphil 1157
שָׁבַת Hiphil 1234
rest on, to
שָׁעַן Niphal 1316
rest, place of
מָנוֹחַ 733
rest selves, to
סָמַךְ Niphal 879
שָׁעַן Niphal 1316
rest, to take
שָׁקַט Kal..............1324
rest, the
יָתַר Kal.............. 580
שָׁאַר Niphal 1222
rested
נוֹחַ 801
resting place
מְנוּחָה 733
נוֹחַ 801
רֵבֶץ 1154
restitution
תְּמוּרָה 1349
restitution, to make
שָׁלַם Piel..............1277
restore, to
000 000
נָתַן Kal.............. 851
עָלָה Hiphil 934
שׁוּב Polel 1238
שׁוּב Hiphil 1238
שָׁלַם Piel..............1277
restore to life, to
חָיָה Hiphil 421
restored, to be
שׁוּב Kal..............1238
שׁוּב Hophal..........1238
תּוּב Ch. Aphel.......1337
restored again, to be
שׁוּב Kal..............1238
restorer
שׁוּב Polel 1238
שׁוּב Hiphil 1238
restrain, to
גָּרַע Kal.............. 316
חָגַר Kal.............. 401
כָּהָה Piel.............. 586
מָנַע Kal.............. 735
עָצַר Kal.............. 973
restrained, to be
אָפַק Hithpael 147
בָּצַר Niphal 264
כָּלָא Niphal 598
restraint
מַעְצוֹר 745
rests, *see* narrowed
retain, to
חָזַק Hiphil 411
כָּלָא Kal.............. 598
עָצַר Kal.............. 973
תָּמַךְ Kal..............1350

retire, to
הָפַךְ Kal ... 370
עוּז Hiphil ... 906
פּוּץ Kal ... 1014
שׁוּב Kal ... 1238

retrieve, to
שׁוּב Hiphil ... 1238

return
תְּשׁוּבָה ... 1359

return, to
יָשַׁב (כ׳) Kal ... 568
סָבַב Niphal ... 865
פָּנָה Kal ... 1021
שׁוּב Kal ... 1238
שׁוּב Hiphil ... 1238
שָׁנָה Kal ... 1304
תּוּב Ch. P'al ... 1337
תּוּב Ch. Aphel ... 1337

return again, to
שׁוּב Kal ... 1238

return an answer, to
תּוּב Ch. Aphel ... 1337

return, to cause to
שׁוּב (כ׳) Kal ... 1238
שׁוּב Hiphil ... 1238

return, causing to
שׁוּב Hiphil ... 1238

return, to make to
שׁוּב Hiphil ... 1238

returned, to be
שׁוּב Kal ... 1238

returning
שׁוּבָה ... 1245

reveal, to
גָּלָה Piel ... 307
גְּלָה Ch. P'al ... 309

reveal,† to
גָּלָה Kal ... 307

reveal self, to
גָּלָה Niphal ... 307

revealed, to be
גָּלָה Niphal ... 307

revealer
גְּלָה Ch. P'al ... 309

revenge
נְקָמָה ... 839

revenge, to
נָקַם Kal ... 839
נָקַם Niphal ... 839

revenge self, to
נָקַם Niphal ... 839

revenger
גָּאַל 'Kal ... 285

revenges
פְּרָעוֹת ... 1047

revenging
נְקָמָה ... 839

revenue
אַפְּתֹם Ch. ... 148
תְּבוּאָה ... 1335

reverence, to
יָרֵא Kal ... 559

reverence, to do
שָׁחָה Hithpael ... 1249

reverence, to be had in
יָרֵא Niphal ... 559

reverend
יָרֵא Niphal ... 559

reverse, to
שׁוּב Hiphil ... 1238

revile, to
קָלַל Piel ... 1109

reviling
גִּדּוּף ... 296

revive, to
חָיָה Kal ... 421
חָיָה Piel ... 421

reviving
מִחְיָה ... 687

revolt
סָרָה ... 884

revolt, to
פָּשַׁע Kal ... 1050

revolt*ed*
סָרָה ... 884

revolted, to be
סוּר Kal ... 872

revolter
סָרַר Kal ... 885
שֵׂט ... 1205

revolting
סָרַר Kal ... 885

reward
אַחֲרִית ... 54
אֶתְנָה ... 183
אֶתְנָן } ... 183
אֶתְנַן }
גְּמוּל ... 311
מַשְׂאֵת ... 767
מַשְׂכֹּרֶת ... 767
מַתַּת ... 780
עֵקֶב ... 974
פְּעֻלָּה ... 1038
פְּרִי ... 1045
שָׂכָר ... 1208
שֶׂכֶר ... 1208
שֹׁחַד ... 1249
שִׁלּוּם ... 1264
שִׁלְמָה ... 1279

reward, *see* divination, tidings

reward, to
גָּמַל Kal ... 311
שׂוּם } Kal ... 1200
שִׂים }
שָׂכַר Kal ... 1207
שׁוּב (כ׳) Kal ... 1238
שׁוּב Hiphil ... 1238
שָׁלֵם Piel ... 1277

reward, to give
שָׁחַד Kal ... 1249

reward, such a
גְּמוּלָה ... 311

reward*ed*
שָׂכָר ... 1208

rewarded, to be
שָׁלֵם Pual ... 1277

rewards
נְבִזְבָּה Ch. ... 783
שַׁלְמֹנִים ... 1279

rib
עֲלַע Ch. ... 944
צֵלָע ... 1073

rib, *see* fifth

ribband
פָּתִיל ... 1055

rich
עָשִׁיר ... 1003
שׁוֹעַ ... 1247

rich, *see* apparel

rich, to be
כָּבֵד } Kal ... 581
כָּבַד }
עָשַׁר Kal ... 1004
עָשַׁר Hiphil ... 1004

rich, to become
עָשַׁר Kal ... 1004

rich, to make
עָשַׁר Hiphil ... 1004

rich, to make self
עָשַׁר Hithpael ... 1004

rich man
עָשִׁיר ... 1003

rich, to wax
נָשַׂג Hiphil ... 845
עָשַׁר Hiphil ... 1004

riches
הוֹן ... 360
הָמוֹן ... 368
חַיִל ... 423
חֹסֶן ... 450
יִתְרָה ... 581
נְכָסִים ... 818
עֹשֶׁר ... 1004
קִנְיָן ... 1112
רְכוּשׁ ... 1174
שׁוּעַ ... 1247

riches, hidden
מַטְמוֹן ... 693

rid, to
נָצַל Hiphil ... 835
פָּצָה Kal ... 1039
שָׁבַת Hiphil ... 1234

riddance
כָּלָה 600

riddance, to make clean
כָּלָה Piel 598

riddle
חִידָה 421

ride, to
רָכַב Kal 1173

ride, to cause to
רָכַב Hiphil 1173

ride in a chariot, to
רָכַב Kal 1173

ride, to make to
רָכַב Hiphil 1173

ride on, to
רָכַב Kal 1173

rider
רָכַב Kal 1173

ridge
תֶּלֶם 1348

riding
רָכַב Kal 1173

rie
כֻּסֶּמֶת 609

rifled, to be
שָׁסַס Niphal 1315

right
אֱמֶת 134
גְּאֻלָּה 286
יָמִין 540
יְמִינִי 541
יְמָנִי 541
יָשָׁר 578
יֹשֶׁר 579
כּוּן Niphal 592
כֵּן 604
כִּשְׁרוֹן 621
מִישׁוֹר 698
מִשְׁפָּט 776
נָכוֹחַ 817
נֹכַח 817
צֶדֶק 1063
צְדָקָה 1063

right, to be
יָשַׁר Kal 578
כָּשֵׁר Kal 621

* right *early*
פָּנָה Kal 1021

right, to esteem
יָשַׁר Piel 578

right forth
פָּנִים 1023

right, to go to the
יָמַן Hiphil 541

right hand
יָמִין 540

right hand, to go on the
יָמַן Hiphil 541

right hand, on the
יְמִינִי 541
יְמָנִי 541

right hand, to turn to the
יָמַן Hiphil 541

right hand, to use the
יָמַן Hiphil 541

right on
נֹכַח 817

right on, to go
יָשַׁר Piel 578

right side
יָמִין 540

right thing
נָכוֹחַ 817

right things
מֵישָׁרִים 698

right, things that are
מֵישָׁרִים 698

right, to turn to the
אָמַן Hiphil 104

righteous
יָשָׁר 578
צַדִּיק 1061
צֶדֶק 1063

righteous, to be
צָדַק Kal 1062

righteous act
צְדָקָה 1063

righteous cause
צֶדֶק 1063

righteous man
צַדִּיק 1061

righteously
מִישׁוֹר 698
מֵישָׁרִים 698
צֶדֶק 1063
צְדָקָה 1063

righteousness
צֶדֶק 1063
צְדָקָה 1063
צִדְקָה Ch. 1064

righteousness, to turn to
צָדַק Hiphil 1062

rightly
כִּי 596

rigour
פֶּרֶךְ 1046

ring
גַּב 286
גָּלִיל 310
טַבַּעַת 474

ring again, to
הוּם Niphal 359

ringstraked
עָקֹד 974

rinse, to
שָׁטַף Kal 1254

rinsed, to be
שָׁטַף Niphal 1254
שָׁטַף Pual 1254

riotous
זָלַל Kal 388

riotous eaters
זָלַל Kal 388

rip up, to
בָּקַע Kal 264
בָּקַע Piel 264

ripe, *see* fruit, grapes

ripe, to be
בָּשַׁל Kal 280

ripen, to
גָּמַל Kal 311

ripped up, to be
בָּקַע Pual 264

rise, to
זָרַח Kal 395
קוּם Kal 1099

rise betimes, to
שָׁחַר [2] Piel 1252

rise early, to
שָׁכַם Hiphil 1260

rise up, to
זָרַח Kal 395
עָלָה Kal 934
קוּם Kal 1099
קוּם Hithpael 1099
קוּם Ch. P'al 1103

rise up again, to
קוּם Kal 1099

rise up against
תְּקוֹמֵם 1356

rise up against, to
קוּם Kal 1099
קוּם Hithpael 1099

rise up betimes, to
שָׁכַם Hiphil 1260

rise up early, to
שָׁכַם Hiphil 1260

rise up, to make
עָלָה Hiphil 934

risen, to be
גָּאָה Kal 285
זָרַח Kal 395
יָצָא Kal 548
קוּם Kal 1099

risen up, to be
קוּם Kal 1099
קוּם Polel 1099

riseth, whence
שַׁחַר 1252

rising
זֶרַח 395
מִזְרָח 685
עָלָה Kal 934
שְׂאֵת 1195

rising early
שָׁכַם Hiphil 1260

rising of the sun
מִזְרָח ... 685

rising up
קִימָה ... 1107

rising up betimes
שָׁכַם Hiphil ... 1260

rising up early
שָׁכַם Hiphil ... 1260

rising up, no
אַלְקוּם ... 99

rite
חֻקָּה ... 457

river
אֻבָל } אוּבָל } ... 29
אָפִיק ... 146
יְאוֹר ... 486
יוּבַל ... 507
נָהָר ... 798
נְהַר Ch. ... 799
נַחַל ... 805
נַחֲלָה ... 806
פֶּלֶג ... 1019
פְּלַגָּה ... 1019

rivers, little
תְּעָלָה ... 1353

road, to make a
פָּשַׁט Kal ... 1050

roar, to
הָגָה[1] Kal ... 356
הָמָה Kal ... 368
נָהַם Kal ... 798
צָרַח Hiphil ... 1082
רָעַם Kal ... 1186
שָׁאַג Kal ... 1219

roaring
נָהַם Kal ... 798
נַהַם ... 798
נְהָמָה ... 798
שְׁאָגָה ... 1219

roast
צָלִי ... 1073

roast, to
בָּשַׁל Piel ... 280
חָרַךְ Kal ... 464
צָלָה Kal ... 1072
קָלָה[1] Kal ... 1108

rob, to
בָּזַז Kal ... 207
גָּזַל Kal ... 304
עוּד Piel ... 905
קָבַע Kal ... 1084
שָׁסָה Kal ... 1315
שָׁסָה Poel ... 1315

rob of children, to
שָׁכֹל Piel ... 1259

robbed, to be
בָּזַז Pual ... 207

robbed of whelps
שַׁכּוּל ... 1258

robbed, that he had
גְּזֵלָה ... 305

robber
בָּזַז Kal ... 207
פָּרִיץ ... 1046
צַמִּים ... 1075
שָׁדַד Kal ... 1237

robber †
בֵּן ... 232

robbers, *see* troop

robbery
גָּזֵל ... 305
פֶּרֶק ... 1048
שֹׁד ... 1236

robe
אֶדֶר ... 24
אַדֶּרֶת ... 24
בֶּגֶד ... 185
כְּתֹנֶת } כֻּתֹּנֶת } ... 623
מְעִיל ... 742

rock
חַלָּמִישׁ ... 434
מָעוֹז ... 740
סֶלַע ... 878
צוּר ... 1069

rock, ragged
סֶלַע ... 878

rocks
כֵּפִים ... 614

rod
חֹטֶר ... 418
מַטֶּה ... 691
מַקֵּל ... 758
שֵׁבֶט ... 1225

roe
יַעֲלָה ... 546
צְבִי ... 1060
צְבִיָּה ... 1060

roe, young
עֹפֶר ... 968

roebuck
צְבִי ... 1060

roll
גִּלָּיוֹן ... 310
מְגִלָּה ... 662
מְגִלָּה Ch. ... 662
סְפַר Ch. ... 884

roll, to
גָּלַל Kal ... 310
גָּלַל Hiphil ... 310

roll away, to
גָּלַל Kal ... 310

roll down, to
גָּלַל Pilpel ... 310

roll selves, to
גָּלַל Hithpalpel ... 310
פָּלַשׁ Hithpael ... 1021

rolled, to be
גָּלַל Poal ... 310

rolled together, to be
גָּלַל Niphal ... 310

roller
חִתּוּל ... 471

rolling thing
גַּלְגַּל ... 307

roof
גָּג ... 292
קוֹרָה ... 1104

roof, *see* mouth

roof of the house
גָּג ... 292

room
מָקוֹם ... 756
קֵן ... 1111
תַּחַת ... 1345

room, *see* large

room, to make
רָחַב Hiphil ... 1166

root
שֹׁרֶשׁ ... 1327
שֹׁרֶשׁ Ch. ... 1328

root, to cause to take
שָׁרַשׁ Hiphil ... 1327

root out, to
נָתַשׁ Kal ... 864
שָׁרַשׁ Piel ... 1327

root, to take
שָׁרַשׁ Poel ... 1327
שָׁרַשׁ Poal ... 1327
שָׁרַשׁ Hiphil ... 1327

root up, to
נָתַשׁ Kal ... 864

rooted, to be
נָסַח Kal ... 820

rooted out, to be
נָתַק Niphal ... 863
שָׁרַשׁ Pual ... 1327

rooted up, to be
עָקַר Niphal ... 974

roots, to pluck up by the
נָתַשׁ Kal ... 864

roots, to be plucked up by the
עֲקַר Ch. Ithp'al ... 974

rope
חֶבֶל } חֵבֶל } ... 399
עֲבֹת ... 900

rose
חֲבַצֶּלֶת ... 399

rot, to
נָפַל Kal ... 825
רָקַב Kal ... 1191

rot, to make to
נָפַל Hiphil ... 825

rotten
רִקָּבוֹן ... 1191

rotten, to be
עָבַשׁ Kal ... 900

rotten rags
מְלָחִים ... 707

rotten thing
רָקָב ... 1191

rottenness
מַק ... 755
רָקָב ... 1191

rough
אֵתָן / אֵיתָן ... 70
סָמָר ... 879
קָשֶׁה ... 1131
שָׂעִיר ... 1212

* rough
שֵׂעָר ... 1212

rough places
רְכָסִים ... 1175

roughly
עַז ... 914
קָשֶׁה ... 1131

round
סַהַר ... 870
עָגֹל ... 900

round, *see* beset, compass, go, inclose, tires like the moon

round, to
נָקַף Hiphil ... 839

round about
דּוּר ... 338
מֵסַב ... 736
סָבִיב ... 866

* round about
סָבִיב ... 866

round about, to beset
סָבַב Niphal ... 865

round about, to close
סָבַב Poel ... 865

round about, to come
סָבַב Kal ... 865

round about, to compass
סָבַב Kal ... 865

round about, places
מֵסַב ... 736

round about, to stand
סָבַב Kal ... 865

round thing
חַסְפַּס ... 450

rouse up, to
קוּם Hiphil ... 1099

row
טוּר ... 480
טִירָה ... 481
מַעֲרָכָה ... 746
מַעֲרֶכֶת ... 746
תּוֹר ... 1342

row, to
חָתַר Kal ... 472

rower
שׁוּט[2] Kal ... 1246

rows
נִדְבָּךְ Ch. ... 795

royal
מְלוּכָה ... 706
מֶלֶךְ ... 712
מֶלֶךְ Ch. ... 727
מַלְכוּת ... 728
מַמְלָכָה ... 730

royal pavilion
שַׁפְרוּר / שַׁפְרִיר ... 1322

rubbish
עָפָר ... 968

rubies
פְּנִיִּים (כ׳) ... 1023
פְּנִינִים ... 1036

ruddy
אָדֹם ... 21
אַדְמֹנִי / אַדְמוֹנִי ... 22

ruddy, to be
אָדַם Kal ... 20

Ruhamah
רָחַם Pual ... 1168

ruhamah, *see* Lo-ruhamah

ruin
הֲרִיסָה ... 376
מְדִחֶה ... 667
מְחִתָּה ... 691
מִכְשׁוֹל ... 701
מַכְשֵׁלָה ... 701
מַפָּלָה ... 748
מַפֶּלֶת ... 748
פִּיד ... 1017

ruin of, to be the
כָּשַׁל Hiphil ... 621

ruined
הָרַס Niphal ... 376

ruined, to be
כָּשַׁל Kal ... 621

ruinous
מַפָּלָה ... 748
נָצָה[2] Niphal ... 834

rule
מַעְצָר (קַו 1095) ... 745

rule, *see* captain

rule, to
מָלַךְ Kal ... 710
מֶמְשָׁלָה ... 731
מָשַׁל[1] Kal ... 771
רָדָה[1] Kal ... 1158
רוּד[1] Kal ... 1160
שָׂרַר Kal ... 1219
שָׁלַט Kal ... 1274
שַׁלִּיט Ch. ... 1275
שָׁפַט Kal ... 1319

rule, to bear
מָשַׁל[1] Kal ... 771
רָדָה[1] Kal ... 1158
שָׂרַר Kal ... 1219
שְׁלֵט Ch. P'al ... 1274
שָׁלַט Kal ... 1274

rule, to cause to
מָשַׁל[1] Hiphil ... 771

rule, to have
מָשַׁל[1] Kal ... 771
שָׁלַט Kal ... 1274

rule, to make to
רָדָה[1] Hiphil ... 1158

rule over, to
רָדָה[1] Kal ... 1158

ruled, to be
נָשַׁק Kal ... 849

ruled, that
מִמְשָׁל ... 731

ruler
מָגֵן ... 662
מָשַׁל[1] Kal ... 771
נָגִיד ... 791
נָשִׂיא ... 845
קָצִין ... 1115
רֹאשׁ ... 1142
רָדָה[1] Kal ... 1158
רָזַן Kal ... 1166
שַׂר ... 1214
שָׁטַר Kal ... 1254
שִׁלְטוֹן Ch. ... 1274
שַׁלִּיט ... 1275
שַׁלִּיט Ch. ... 1275

ruler, *see* chief

ruler, to be
שְׁלֵט Ch. P'al ... 1274

ruler, chief
נָגִיד ... 791

ruler, to make
פָּקַד Hiphil ... 1040
שַׁלֵּט Ch. Pael ... 1274

rulers
סְגָנִים ... 869

ruling
מָשַׁל[1] Kal ... 771

rumbling
הָמוֹן ... 368

rumour
שְׁמוּעָה ... 1285

* sake
קִנְאָה 1111

sake, *see* for

sake, for
תַּחַת 1345

sake, for...'s
מַעַן 744
עֲבוּר 895

sale
מִמְכָּר 730

sale, that which cometh of
מִמְכָּר 730

salt
מֶלַח 707
מְלַח Ch. 707

salt *land*
מְלֵחָה 707

salt *pit*
מֶלַח 707

salt pits
מִכְרֶה 700

salted, to be
מָלַח Hophal 707

salute
שָׁלוֹם 1263

salute, to
בָּרַךְ Kal 274
בָּרַךְ Piel 274

salute,† to
שָׁאַל Kal 1220
שָׁלוֹם 1263

salvation
יְשׁוּעָה 575
יֵשַׁע } יֶשַׁע 577
מוֹשָׁעוֹת 675
תְּשׁוּעָה 1359

salvation, to bring
יָשַׁע Hiphil 576

salvation, having
יָשַׁע Niphal 576

same
גַּו Ch. 298
דִּכֵּן Ch. 341
הֵם 367
זֶה 380
עֶצֶם 972

same, *see* place, springeth, springeth up

same, out of the
זֶה 380

same, the
דָּךְ & דִּךְ Ch. 340
הוּא 358
הִיא 360
הֵמָּה 367
זֹאת 377

sanctified, to be
קָדֵשׁ } קָדַשׁ Kal 1090
קָדֵשׁ } קָדַשׁ Niphal 1090
קָדֵשׁ } קָדַשׁ Pual 1090
קָדֵשׁ } קָדַשׁ Hithpael 1090

sanctified one
קָדֵשׁ } קָדַשׁ Pual 1090

sanctify, to
קָדֵשׁ } קָדַשׁ Piel 1090
קָדֵשׁ } קָדַשׁ Hiphil 1090

sanctify selves, to
קָדֵשׁ } קָדַשׁ Hithpael 1090

sanctuary
מִקְדָּשׁ 755
קֹדֶשׁ 1091

sand
חוֹל 407

sapphire
סַפִּיר 881

sardius
אֹדֶם 21

saris, *see* Rab-saris

Satan
שָׂטָן 1205

satiate, to
רָוָה Piel 1160
רָוָה Hiphil 1160

satiate, to be
שָׂבֵעַ } שָׂבַע Kal 1195

satisfaction
כֹּפֶר 615

satisfied
שָׂבֵעַ 1196

satisfied, to be
מָלֵא Kal 701
שָׂבֵעַ } שָׂבַע Kal 1195

satisfied, to be abundantly
רָוָה Kal 1160

satisfied with
שָׂבֵעַ 1196

satisfied with, to be
שָׂבֵעַ } שָׂבַע Kal 1195

satisfy, to
מָלֵא Piel 701
רָוָה Piel 1160
שָׂבֵעַ } שָׂבַע Piel 1195
שָׂבֵעַ } שָׂבַע Hiphil 1195
שָׂבְעָה 1196

satisfy with, to
שָׂבֵעַ } שָׂבַע Hiphil 1195

satisfying
שֹׂבַע 1196

satyr
שָׂעִיר 1212

save
אַךְ 70
אֶפֶס 147
בִּלְעֲדֵי } בִּלְעֲדֵי 231
בִּלְתִּי 231
זוּלָה 383
לָהֵן Ch. 634
רַק 1191

save †
אִם 100

save, *see* God save

save, to
חָיָה Piel 421
חָיָה Hiphil 421
יְשׁוּעָה 575
יָשַׁע Hiphil 576
מָלַט Piel 710
נָצַל Hiphil 835
שָׁמַר Kal 1300

save alive, to
חָיָה Piel 421
חָיָה Hiphil 421

save life, to
חָיָה Piel 421
חָיַי Kal 423

save lives, to
חָיָה Hiphil 421

save only †
אִם 100

save self, to
שָׁמַר Niphal 1300

saved, to be
יָשַׁע Niphal 576

saving
אֶפֶס 147

saving †
אִם 100

saving
יְשׁוּעָה 575
יֵשַׁע } יֶשַׁע 577

saving health
יְשׁוּעָה 575

saviour
יָשַׁע Hiphil 576

savour
רֵיחַ 1172

sedition
אֶשְׁתַּדּוּר Ch. 182

seduce, to
טָעָה Hiphil 483
תָּעָה Hiphil 1353

see
הִנֵּה 369
רָאָה 1141

see, *see* go

see, to
חָזָה Kal 410
חֲזָא / חֲזָה } Ch. P'al 410
מַרְאֶה 761
נָבַט Hiphil 783
רָאָה Kal 1133
רָאִי 1141
שׁוּר² Kal 1248
שָׁזַף Kal 1249

* see, to
יָרֵא Kal 559

see, to cause to
רָאָה Hiphil 1133

see, to let
רָאָה Hiphil 1133

see one another, to
רָאָה Hithpael 1133

see, that
חֹזֶה 410

seed
זֶרַע 396
זְרַע Ch. 397
פְּרֻדוֹת 1044
שְׁכָבָה 1258

seed, *see* conceive, mingled

seeds, *see* divers

seedtime
זֶרַע 396

seeing
אַחַר 48
אִם 100
דִּי 339
כִּי 596
פִּקֵּחַ 1042
רָאָה Kal 1133

seeing that which, *see* now

seeing then
יַעַן 546

seek
דָּרַשׁ Kal 353

seek, *see* deep, please

seek, to
בְּעָא / בְּעָה } Ch. P'al 261
בָּקַשׁ Piel 268
חָפַר Kal 452
חָקַר Kal 458
קָרָא² Kal 1122
תּוּר Kal 1342

seek a quarrel, to
אָנָה Hithpael 136

seek betimes, to
שָׁחַר² Piel 1252

seek diligently, to
שָׁחַר² Kal 1252
שָׁחַר² Piel 1252

seek early, to
שָׁחַר² Piel 1252

seek in the morning, to
שָׁחַר² Piel 1252

seek occasion, to
גָּלַל Hithpoel 310

seek out
בַּקָּרָה 268

seek out, to
בָּקַר Piel 265
דָּרַשׁ Kal 353

seem
מַרְאֶה 761

seem, *see* best, good, hard, light thing, little, meet, vile

seem, to
רָאָה Niphal 1133

seemly
נָאוֶה 781

seen, to be
רָאָה Niphal 1133
רָאָה Pual 1133
רֳאִי 1141

seer
חֹזֶה 410
רָאָה Kal 1133

seeth, that
רֳאִי 1141

seethe, to
בָּשַׁל Kal 280
בָּשַׁל Piel 280

seething
נָפַח Kal 825

seething pot
דּוּד 336

seize, to
חָזַק Hiphil 411
לָקַח Kal 644
נָשָׂא¹ Hiphil 846

seize, *see* death

seize upon, to
יָרַשׁ Hiphil 566

Sela
סֶלַע 878

Sela-hammahlekoth
{ סֶלַע 878
{ מַחְלְקוֹת 687

Selah
סֶלָה 877
סֶלַע 878

self
בָּשָׂר 278
נֶפֶשׁ 829

self *and* selves, *see* abase, acquaint, advise, afflict, anoint, array, assemble, associate, avenge, bald, bathe, behave, bemoan, bestir, bethink, bewail, bind, boast, bow, burden, call, cast, catch, chasten, circumcise, clad, clean, cleanse, clear, clothe, comfort, commit, cover, cut, deck, defile, delight, deliver, destroy, discover, disguise, disperse, divide, ease, encourage, enflame, exalt, exercise, fair, fat, feign, fill, force, fret, friendly, froward, gather, gird, glorify, hang, harden, heed, hide, hire out, hold, honour, humble, ill, join, justify, keep, known, lift, lift up, lifting up, loose, lothe, mad, magnify, many, marvellous, men, merciful, mingle, mix, more, naked, odious, oppose, pain, please, pollute, poor, prepare, present, prey, prince, profane, prophet, proudly, pure, purify, put forth, put up, quiet, quit, raise up, reconcile, recover, redeem, refrain, refresh, repent, rest, reveal, revenge, rich, roll, sanctify, save, scrape, sell, separate, separating, serve, set, sever, shake, shew, shewing, shut, sick, solace, sport, spread, stay, stir up, strange, strangely, strengthen, stretch, stretch out, strip, strong, submit, thrust, toss, turn, unclean, uncover, unsavoury, upright, valiantly, vaunt, wallow, warm, wash, weary, wise, wisely, withdraw, withhold, within, wrap

self again, *see* turn

self down, *see* lay

selfsame
זֶה 380
עֶצֶם 972

selfwill
רָצוֹן 1189

sell, to
מָכַר Kal 700
שָׁבַר² Kal 1233
שָׁבַר² Hiphil 1233

sell away, to
מָכַר Kal 700

sell self, to
מָכַר Niphal 700
מָכַר Hithpael 700

sellers
מָכַר Kal 700

selvedge
קָצָה 1114

selves forth, *see* spread

selves together, *see* gather

selves willingly, *see* offer

senator
זָקֵן 392

send, to
בּוֹא Hiphil 189
נוּף Hiphil 802
נָתַן Kal 851
שָׁלַח Kal 1268
שָׁלַח Piel 1268

שָׁלַח Hiphil 1268
שְׁלַח Ch. P'al 1273

send,† to
הָלַךְ Kal 362

send, *see* commandment, good speed, messenger, prosperity

send again, to
שׁוּב Kal 1238

send away, to
שָׁלַח Kal 1268
שָׁלַח Piel 1268

send back, to
שׁוּב Hiphil 1238

send for, to
לָקַח Kal 644

send forth, to
נָבַע Hiphil 787
שָׁלַח Kal 1268
שָׁלַח Piel 1268

send out, to
טוּל Hiphil 480
נָתַן Kal 851
שָׁלַח Kal 1268
שָׁלַח Piel 1268

send over, to
עָבַר Hiphil 895

send to descry, to
תּוּר Hiphil 1342

sending
מִשְׁלוֹחַ 772
מִשְׁלַחַת 772
שָׁלַח Kal 1268

sending away
שָׁלַח Piel 1268

sending forth
מִשְׁלַח 772

sense
שֶׂכֶל } 1207
שֵׂכֶל }

sent
שָׁלַח Kal 1268

sent, to be
שָׁלַח Niphal 1268
שָׁלַח Pual 1268
שְׁלַח Ch. P'al 1273

sent away, to be
שָׁלַח Pual 1268

sent back, have
שִׁלּוּחִים 1263

sentence
דָּבָר 325
מִשְׁפָּט 776
פֶּה 1011
פִּתְגָם 1052

sentence, *see* dark, divine

sentences, *see* hard

separate
נָזִיר 803

separate, to
בָּדַל Hiphil 187
נָזַר Hiphil 804
פָּלָא Hiphil 1018
פָּרַד Hiphil 1043

separate cities
מִבְדָּלוֹת 660

separate place
גִּזְרָה 305

separate selves, to
בָּדַל Niphal 187
חָלַק Hiphil 435
נָזַר Niphal 804
פָּרַד Niphal 1043

separated
נָזִיר 803

separated, to be
בָּדַל Niphal 187
פָּלָה Niphal 1019
פָּרַד Niphal 1043
פָּרַד Piel 1043

separating self
נָזַר Niphal 804

separation
נִדָּה 796
נֵזֶר 804

separation, to make a
בָּדַל Hiphil 187

sepulchre
קְבוּרָה 1083
קֶבֶר 1086

seraphims
שָׂרָף 1218

serpent
זָחַל Kal 384
נָחָשׁ 809
תַּנִּין 1353

serpent, fiery
שָׂרָף 1218

servant
אֱנוֹשׁ 136
נַעַר 823
עָבַד Kal 887
עֶבֶד 889
עֲבַד Ch. 894
שָׁרַת Piel 1328

servant, *see* hired

*servant born
בֵּן 232

servants, to be
עָבַד Kal 887

servants, to become
עָבַד Kal 887

servants, store of
עֲבֻדָּה 894

serve, to
עָבַד Kal 887
עָבַד Hophal 887
עָשָׂה Kal 981
פְּלַח Ch. P'al 1019
שָׁרַת Piel 1328

serve,† to
עָמַד Kal 955
פָּנִים 1023

* serve,† to
גָּמַל Kal 311

serve, *see* occasion

serve, to cause to
עָבַד Hiphil 887

serve, to be made to
עָבַד Pual 887

serve, to make to
עָבַד Kal 887
עָבַד Hiphil 887

serve self, to
עָבַד Kal 887

served, to be
עָבַד Niphal 887

served, *see* as

service
יָד 489
עֲבוֹדָה 894
עֲבִידָה Ch. 895
פָּלְחָן Ch. 1019
צָבָא 1057
שְׂרָד 1217

service, to do
עָבַד Kal 887
שָׁרַת Piel 1328

service, to use
עָבַד Kal 887

servile
עֲבוֹדָה 894

serving
עָבַד Kal 887

servitor
שָׁרַת Piel 1328

servitude
עֲבוֹדָה 894

set
יָסַד Pual 542
יָעַד Hophal 545
מָלֵא Pual 701

set †
הֲוָא } Ch. P'al 358
הֲוָה }

set, to
גָּבַל Kal 291
חָקַק Kal 458
יָהַב Kal 507
יָנַח Hiphil 541
יָצַב Hithpael 555
יָצַג Hiphil 555

יָשַׁב Piel 568
יָשַׁב Hiphil 568
יְתִב Ch. Aphel 579
כּוּן Hiphil 592
מָלֵא Piel 701
מָנָה Piel 732
מְנָא / מְנָה Pael 733
מִשְׁלָח 772
נוּעַ Hiphil 802
נָסַךְ[1] Kal 820
נָצַב Hiphil 833
נָשָׂא Kal 840
נָתַן Kal 851
סָבַב Pilpel 875
עָלָה Hiphil 934
עָמַד Hiphil 955
עָשָׂה Kal 981
פָּקַד Kal 1040
פָּקַד Hiphil 1040
פָּשַׁט Kal 1050
קוּם Hiphil 1099
קוּם Ch. Aphel 1103
רָכַב Hiphil 1173
שׂוּם / שִׂים Kal 1200
שׂוּם Ch. P'al 1204
שָׁוָה[1] Piel 1245
שִׁית Kal 1256
שָׁכַךְ Kal 1259
שָׁכֵן / שָׁכַן Piel 1260
שָׁלַח Piel 1268
שָׁתַת Kal 1333

* set, to
עוּף Kal 911
עוּף Hiphil 911

set. *see* affection, aright, array, bounds, feast, forward, fully, king, love, open, order, print, work

set, to be
בּוֹא Kal 189
בָּנָה Niphal 258
יָנַח Hophal 541
יָשַׂם Kal 568
יָשַׁב Kal 568
יְתִב Ch. P'al 579
מִלֻּאִים 703
נָתַן Niphal 851
סָבַב Hophal 865
קוּם Kal 1099
שׂוּם / שִׂים Hophal 1200
שָׁבַץ Pual 1232

set *a mark*, to
תָּוָה Hiphil 1338

set a time, to
יָעַד Hiphil 545

set about
סוּג[2] Kal 870

set again, to
שׁוּב Hiphil 1238

set apart
נִדָּה 796

set apart, to
עָבַר Hiphil 895
פָּלָה Hiphil 1019

set aside, to
נָסַע Hiphil 821

* set at
עֵרֶךְ 979

set at, *see* nought

set by, to be
יָקַר Kal 558

set by, *see* much

set, to cause to be
שׂוּם / שִׂים Kal 1200

set down, to
יָנַח Hiphil 541
יָצַק Hiphil 556
נוּחַ Hiphil 800

set fast, to
כּוּן Hiphil 592

set *fire*, to
יָצַת Hiphil 557

set forth, to
נָתַן Kal 851
עָמַד Hiphil 955
פָּתַח Kal 1052

set forth, to be
כּוּן Niphal 592

set forward, to
נָצַח Piel 834

set in, *see* order

set in array, to
אָסַר Kal 143

set light (*by one*), to
קָלָה[2] Hiphil 1108
קָלַל Hiphil 1109

set office
אֱמוּנָה / אֱמֻנָה 102

set on, to
סוּת Hiphil 874
שׂוּם / שִׂים Kal 1200
שָׁפַת Kal 1322

set on, *see* edge, fire, high

set on, be
נַחַת 810

set on fire, to
אוֹר Hiphil 32
בָּעַר Piel 262

set *on fire*, to
בָּעַר Hiphil 262

set over, to
עָמַד Hiphil 955

set over, to be
נָצַב Niphal 833
פָּקַד Kal 1040

set, to be privily
צָפַן Kal 1080

set selves, to
יָצַב Hithpael 555
סָמַךְ Kal 879

set, *that* was
פָּקִיד 1042

* set, they
מַשָּׂא 766

set time
חֹק 456

set up
נָצַב Hophal 833

set up, to
בָּנָה Kal 258
כְּלַל Ch. Shaphel 603
כְּלַל Ch. Ishtaphel 603
נָצַב Hiphil 833
נָשָׂא Kal 840
עָלָה Kal 934
עָלָה Hiphil 934
עָמַד Hiphil 955
קוּם Hiphil 1099
קוּם Ch. Aphel 1103
רוּם Polel 1163
רוּם Hiphil 1163
רוּם Ch. Aphel 1164
שָׂגַב Piel 1197
שׂוּם / שִׂים Kal 1200
שָׁכֵן / שָׁכַן Hiphil 1260

set up, *see* banners, king

set up, to be (בנה..260)
זְקַף Ch. P'al 394
נָסַךְ[1] Niphal 820

set up on, *see* high

set with, to
זָרַע Kal 395

setting
מִלֻּאָה 703

setting
נָתַן Kal 851

settle
עֲזָרָה 918

settle, to
יָשַׁב Hiphil 568
נָחַת Piel 810
עָמַד Hiphil 955
שָׁקַט Kal 1324

shamed
בּוּז ... 205

shameful spewing
קִיקָלוֹן ... 1108

shameful thing
בֹּשֶׁת ... 280

shamefully, to do
יָבֵשׁ Hiphil ... 487

shamelessly
גָּלָה Niphal ... 307

shapen, to be
חוּל / חִיל } Pulal ... 406

share
מַחֲרֶשֶׁת ... 690

sharp
חַד ... 402
חַדּוּדִים ... 402
חָרוּץ ... 463
לָטַשׁ Pual ... 640
שָׁנַן Kal ... 1315

* sharp
צוֹר ... 1069
שֵׁן ... 1304

sharp stone
צֹר ... 1081

sharpen, to
חָדַד Kal ... 402
חָדַד Hiphil ... 402
לָטַשׁ Kal ... 640
נָצַב Hiphil ... 833
שָׁנַן Kal ... 1315

sharpened, to be
חָדַד Hophal ... 402

sharply
חָזְקָה ... 414

shave
גָּלַח Hithpael ... 309
תַּעַר ... 1354

shave, to
גָּזַז Kal ... 304
גָּלַח Piel ... 309

shave,† to
עָבַר Hiphil ... 895

shave off, to
גָּלַח Piel ... 309

shaven, to be
גָּלַח Pual ... 309

she
הוּא ... 358
הִיא ... 360
זֹאת ... 377

she ass
אָתוֹן ... 183

she herself
הִיא ... 360

sheaf
אֲלֻמָּה ... 95
עָמִיר ... 960
עֹמֶר ... 961
עֲרֵמָה ... 980

shear, to
גָּזַז Kal ... 304

Shear-jashub
{ שְׁאָר ... 1223
{ שׁוּב Kal ... 1238

shearer
גָּזַז Kal ... 304

shearer, *see* sheepshearer

* shearing house †
רָעָה Kal ... 1184

sheath
נָדָן ... 797
תַּעַר ... 1354

sheaves, *see* bind

Shebah
שֶׁבַע / שִׁבְעָה } ... 1229

shed
שָׁפַךְ Kal ... 1320

shed, to
נָגַר Hiphil ... 793
שָׁפַךְ Kal ... 1320

shed, to be (שׁוּם..1203)
שָׁפַךְ Niphal ... 1320
שָׁפַךְ Pual ... 1320

shed out, to
שָׁפַךְ Kal ... 1320

shedder
שָׁפַךְ Kal ... 1320

sheep
כֶּבֶשׂ ... 585
כֶּשֶׂב ... 620
צְאוֹן ... 1055
צֹאן ... 1055
צֹנֶא / צֹנֶה } ... 1075
רָחֵל ... 1168
שֶׂה ... 1199

sheepcote
נָוֶה ... 800
{ גְּדֵרָה ... 298
{ צֹאן ... 1055

*sheep*fold
גְּדֵרָה ... 298
מִכְלָה ... 699

sheep*fold*
צֹאן ... 1055

sheepfolds
מִשְׁפְּתַיִם ... 778

sheepmaster
נֹקֵד ... 838

sheepshearer
גָּזַז Kal ... 304

sheepshearers
{ גָּזַז Kal ... 304
{ צֹאן ... 1055

sheet
סָדִין ... 870

shekel
שֶׁקֶל ... 1324

shekel, half a
בֶּקַע ... 265

shelter
מַחְסֶה ... 689

shemesh, *see* Beth-shemesh

Sheminith
שְׁמִינִי ... 1289

shepherd
רָעָה Kal ... 1184
רֹעִי ... 1185
{ רָעָה Kal ... 1184
{ צֹאן ... 1055

sherd
חֶרֶשׂ ... 466

sheriffs
תִּפְתָּיֵא Ch. ... 1356

* Sheth
שֵׁת ... 1331

shew
הַכָּרָה ... 362

shew †
אֹזֶן ... 35

shew, to
גָּלָה Kal ... 307
חָוָה Piel ... 406
חֲוָא / חֲוָה } Ch. Pael ... 406
חֲוָא / חֲוָה } Ch. Aphel ... 406
יָדַע Hiphil ... 500
יָרָה Hiphil ... 564
נָגַד Hiphil ... 788
נָטָה Kal ... 810
נָתַן Kal ... 851
עָשָׂה Kal ... 981
רָאָה Kal ... 1133
רָאָה Hiphil ... 1133
שׂוּם / שִׂים } Kal ... 1200
שִׁית Kal ... 1256
שָׁמֵעַ / שָׁמַע } Hiphil ... 1292

shew, *see* favour, marvellous, men, mercy, pure

shew forth, to
בָּשַׂר Piel ... 278
נָגַד Hiphil ... 788
סָפַר Piel ... 882
שָׁמֵעַ / שָׁמַע } Hiphil ... 1292

shew light, to
אוֹר Hiphil ... 32

shew more *kindness*, to
יָטַב Hiphil ... 524

shew openly, to
גָּלָה Piel.............. 307
shew self, to
גָּלָה Niphal.......... 307
יָפַע Hiphil.......... 548
רָאָה Niphal..........1133
shew self, *see* friendly, froward, marvellous, merciful, strong, unsavoury, upright, wise
shew, vain
צֶלֶם..................1073
shewbread
מַעֲרֶכֶת.................. 746
shew*bread*
מַעֲרֶכֶת.................. 746
פָּנִים..................1023
*shew*bread
לֶחֶם.................. 638
* shewbread
פָּנִים..................1023
shewed, *see* favour
shewed, to be
נָגַד Hophal......... 788
פָּרַשׂ Kal..............1049
רָאָה Niphal..........1133
רָאָה Hophal.........1133
shewing
אַחֲוָיָה Ch.............. 45
shewing self
צוּץ Hiphil..........1069
Shibboleth
שִׁבֹּלֶת..................1227
shield
כִּידוֹן.................. 596
מָגֵן.................. 662
צִנָּה..................1075
שֶׁלֶט..................1274
Shiggaion
שִׁגָּיוֹן..................1236
Shigionoth
שִׁגָּיוֹן..................1236
Shiloh
שִׁילֹה..................1255
shine, to
אָהַל[1] Hiphil.......... 27
אוֹר Kal.............. 32
אוֹר Hiphil.......... 32
הָלַל Kal.............. 366
הָלַל Hiphil.......... 366
זָהַר Hiphil.......... 382
זָרַח Kal.............. 395
יָפַע Hiphil.......... 548
נָגַהּ Kal.............. 791
עָשַׁת Kal..............1005
קָרַן Kal..............1129
shine, to cause to
אוֹר Hiphil.......... 32
יָפַע Hiphil.......... 548
נָגַהּ Hiphil.......... 791
shine forth, to
יָפַע Hiphil.......... 548
עוּף Kal.............. 911
shine, to make to
אוֹר Hiphil.......... 32
צָהַל Hiphil..........1064
shining
נֹגַהּ.................. 791
shining, clear
נֹגַהּ.................. 791
ship
אֳנִיָּה.................. 140
סְפִינָה.................. 881
צִי..................1071
shipmaster
{ רַב..................1147
{ חֹבֵל.................. 399
ship*men*
אֳנִיָּה.................. 140
ships
אוֹנִיּוֹת.................. 31
ships, *see* navy
shittah tree
שִׁטָּה..................1254
shittim
שִׁטָּה..................1254
Shoa
שׁוֹעַ..................1247
shock
גָּדִישׁ.................. 296
shock of corn
גָּדִישׁ.................. 296
shoe
נַעַל.................. 822
shoe, to
נָעַל Kal.............. 822
נָעַל Hiphil.......... 822
shoelatchet
{ שְׂרוֹךְ..................1217
{ נַעַל.................. 822
shoes
מִנְעָל.................. 735
shoes, pair of
נַעַל.................. 822
shoot
יָרָה Kal.............. 564
shoot, to
בָּרַח Kal.............. 271
דָּרַךְ Kal.............. 349
יָדָה Kal.............. 499
יָרָא Kal.............. 559
יָרָא Hiphil.......... 559
יָרָה Hiphil.......... 564
רָבַב[2] Kal..........1151
שָׁלַח Piel..............1268
shoot forth, to
יָצָא Kal.............. 548
נָתַן Kal.............. 851
עָלָה Kal.............. 934
שָׁלַח Piel..............1268
shoot out, to
פָּטַר Hiphil..........1017
שָׁלַח Kal..............1268
shoot up, to
נָתַן Kal.............. 851
shooter
יָרָא Hiphil.......... 559
shooting up
עָלָה Kal.............. 934
shore
חוֹף.................. 408
קָצֶה..................1114
שָׂפָה..................1213
shorn
קָצַב Kal..............1114
short
קָרוֹב..................1127
short, *see* cut, waxed
short time
חֶלֶד.................. 429
shorten, to
קָצַר Piel..............1116
קָצַר Hiphil..........1116
shortened, to be
קָצַר Kal..............1116
* shorter
קָצַר Kal..............1116
shorter, to be
קָצַר Kal..............1116
shortly
מְהֵרָה.................. 669
קָרוֹב..................1127
* shortly
מָהַר[1] Piel.............. 669
Shoshannim
שׁוֹשָׁן..................1249
Shoshannim-eduth
{ שׁוֹשָׁן..................1249
{ עֵדוּת.................. 904
shot, *see* bowshot
shot, to be
יָרָה Niphal.......... 564
shot out
שָׁחַט Kal..............1251
shoulder
זְרוֹעַ.................. 394
כָּתֵף.................. 623
שׁוֹק..................1248
שְׁכֶם..................1260
shoulder blade
שִׁכְמָה..................1260
shoulderpiece
כָּתֵף.................. 623

shout
הֵידָד ... 360
תְּרוּעָה ... 1358

shout, to
עָנָה' Kal ... 962
צָהַל Piel ... 1064
צָוַח Kal ... 1068
רוּעַ Hiphil ... 1164
רָנַן Kal ... 1177
רָנַן Hithpolel ... 1177
שָׁוַע Piel ... 1246
תְּרוּעָה ... 1358

shout for joy, to
רוּעַ Hithpolel & hith 1164
רָנַן Kal ... 1177
רָנַן Piel ... 1177
רָנַן Hiphil ... 1177

shout, to give a
עָנָה' Kal ... 962

shouted
רֵעַ ... 1181

shouting
הֵידָד ... 360
רִנָּה ... 1176
תְּרוּעָה ... 1358

shouting, to be
רוּעַ Polal ... 1164

shoutings
תְּשֻׁאוֹת ... 1359

shovel
רַחַת ... 1171

shovels
יָעִים ... 546

shower (מטר..694)
גֶּשֶׁם ... 317
זֶרֶם ... 395

showers
רְבִיבִים ... 1153

shrank, which
נָשֶׁה ... 847

shred, to
פָּלַח Piel ... 1019

shroud
חֹרֶשׁ ... 467

shrubs
שִׂיחַ ... 1206

Shulamite
שׁוּלַמִּית ... 1246

Shushan-eduth
{ שׁוּשַׁן ... 1249
{ עֵדוּת ... 904

shut, to
אָטַם Kal ... 55
אָטַר Kal ... 55
גּוּף Hiphil ... 303
טוּחַ Kal ... 479
סָגַר Kal ... 869
סְגַר Ch. P'al ... 870
עָצָה Kal ... 971
עָצַם Kal ... 972
עָצַר Kal ... 973
קָפַץ Kal ... 1113
שָׁעַע Hiphil ... 1316

shut, to be
סָגַר Niphal ... 869
סָגַר Pual ... 869

shut in, to be
סָגַר Niphal ... 869

shut out, to
שָׂתַם Kal ... 1219

shut out, to be
סָגַר Niphal ... 869

shut self, to
סָגַר Niphal ... 869

shut up
נָעַל Kal ... 822

shut up, to
כָּלָא Kal ... 598
סָגַר Kal ... 869
סָגַר Hiphil ... 869
סָכַךְ Hiphil ... 875
סָתַם Kal ... 885
עָצַר Kal ... 973
צָרַר Kal ... 1083
קָפַץ Kal ... 1113

shut up, to be
סָגַר Pual ... 869
עָצַר Niphal ... 973

shut up together
סָגַר Kal ... 869

shutting
סָגַר Kal ... 869

shuttle, *see* weaver

Sibboleth
סִבֹּלֶת ... 868

sick, to be
חָלָה Kal ... 429
חָלָה Niphal ... 429

sick, to fall
חָלָה Kal ... 429
חָלָה Hithpael ... 429

sick, is
חֳלִי ... 431

sick, to make
חָלָה Hiphil ... 429

sick, to make self
חָלָה Hithpael ... 429

sick, she that is
דָּוֶה ... 337

sick, that are
תַּחֲלֻאִים ... 1345

sick, very
אָנַשׁ Niphal ... 141

sickle
חֶרְמֵשׁ ... 465
מַגָּל ... 662

sickness
חֳלִי ... 431
מַחֲלָה ... 687

sickness, *see* pining

sickness, having
דָּוֶה ... 337

sicknesses
תַּחֲלֻאִים ... 1345

side
הַלָּז ... 362
יָד ... 489
יָרֵךְ ... 565
כָּתֵף ... 623
מָתְנַיִם ... 780
עֵבֶר ... 899
פֵּאָה ... 1009
צַד ... 1061
צֵלָע ... 1073
קִיר ... 1108
קָצֶה ... 1114
שָׂפָה ... 1213
שְׂטַר Ch. ... 1254

* side
רוּחַ ... 1160

side, *see* about on every, east, every, floor, left, north, on this, other, post, right, south, this, way-side, west

side chamber
צֵלָע ... 1073

side, on every
סָבִיב ... 866

* side, on every
חָגַר Kal ... 401

side, other
עֵבֶר ... 899

* side, other
נֶגֶד ... 790

side, sea
חוֹף ... 408

side, the one
פּוֹ & פֹּה ... 1014

side, the other
פּוֹ & פֹּה ... 1014

side, this
עֲבַר Ch. ... 899
עֵבֶר ... 899

side, this...that side
פּוֹ & פֹּה ... 1014

sides
יַרְכָה ... 565
עֵבֶר (כ׳ א׳) ... 890
רֶבַע ... 1154

sides, *see* needlework

siege
מָצוֹר ... 754

siege, to lay
צוּר Kal............1069
sieve
כְּבָרָה................ 585
נָפָה................ 825
sift, to
נוּעַ Hiphil 802
נוּף Hiphil 802
sifted, to be
נוּעַ Niphal 802
sigh
אֲנָחָה................ 139
sigh, to
אָנַח Niphal 139
sighing
אֲנָקָה................ 141
sight
חֱזוּת Ch.............. 411
מַרְאֶה................ 761
נֶגֶד................ 790
עַיִן................ 919
פָּנִים................1023
* sight of others
רָאָה Kal..............1133
sign
אוֹת................ 33
מוֹפֵת................ 673
נֵס................ 819
צִיּוּן................1071
sign †
דָּבָר................ 325
sign, *see* appointed, fire
sign, to
רְשַׁם Ch. P'al.........1192
signed, to be
רְשַׁם Ch. P'al.........1192
signet
חוֹתָם................ 410
חֹתֶמֶת................ 472
עִזְקָא Ch.............. 917
signs
אָתִין Ch.............. 183
silence
דּוּמָה................ 337
דּוּמִיָּה................ 337
דֳּמִי................ 346
דְּמָמָה................ 346
הָסָה Piel.............. 370
silence, *see* keep, put to
silence, to be brought to
דָּמָה² Niphal.......... 345
silence, to keep
דָּמַם Kal.............. 346
הָסָה Piel.............. 370
חָרַשׁ Hiphil 466
חָשָׁה Kal.............. 469
silence, to be put to
אָלַם Niphal 95

silent
דּוּמִיָּה................ 337
דּוּמָם................ 337
silent, to be
דָּמַם Kal.............. 346
דָּמַם Niphal 346
הָסָה Piel.............. 370
חָרַשׁ Kal.............. 466
חָשָׁה Kal.............. 469
silk
מֶשִׁי................ 769
שֵׁשׁ................1328
silly
פָּתָה Kal..............1052
silly one
פָּתָה Kal..............1052
silver
כֶּסֶף................ 609
כְּסַף Ch.............. 611
silver, piece of
קְשִׂיטָה................1130
silverlings
כֶּסֶף................ 609
similitude
דְּמוּת................ 345
תַּבְנִית................1336
תְּמוּנָה................1349
similitudes, *see* use
similitudes, to use
דָּמָה¹ Piel.............. 345
simple
פְּתִי................1054
פְּתַיּוּת................1055
simple one
פְּתִי................1054
simplicity
פְּתִי................1054
תֹּם................1348
sin
אָשָׁם................ 179
אַשְׁמָה................ 179
חֵטְא................ 415
חֲטָאָה................ 416
חַטָּאָה................ 416
חַטָּאת................ 416
חֲטָי Ch.............. 418
עָוֹן................ 910
פֶּשַׁע................1050
sin, *see* offer, offering, punishment, purification
sin, to
חָטָא Kal.............. 414
* sin, to
עָשָׂה Kal.............. 981
sin, to cause to
חָטָא Hiphil 414
sin ignorantly, to
שָׁגַג Kal..............1235

sin, to make to
חָטָא Hiphil 414
sin offering
חֲטָאָה................ 416
חַטָּאָה Ch.............. 416
חַטָּאת................ 416
חַטָּיָא Ch.............. 418
sin through ignorance, to
שָׁגָה Kal..............1236
since
אָז................ 34
אַחַר................ 48
אִם................ 100
דַּי................ 339
כִּי................ 596
מִן................ 731
מִן Ch.............. 732
עוֹד................ 905
* since
יוֹם................ 508
since †
הֵנָּה................ 369
sincerely
תָּמִים................1350
sincerity
תָּמִים................1350
sinew
גִּיד................ 306
עָרַק Kal.............. 980
sinful
חָטָא Kal.............. 414
חַטָּא................ 416
חַטָּאָה................ 416
sing
רִנָּה................1176
* sing
שִׁירָה................1256
sing, to
זָמַר Piel.............. 389
עָנָה¹ Kal.............. 962
עָנָה² Piel.............. 964
רָנַן Kal..............1177
רָנַן Piel..............1177
שׁוּר¹ Kal..............1248
שִׁיר Kal..............1255
שִׁיר Polel..............1255
sing,† to
נָתַן Kal.............. 851
קוֹל................1096
sing, *see* loud, praises, psalms
sing aloud, to
רָנַן Piel..............1177
רָנַן Hiphil..............1177
sing for joy, to cause to
רָנַן Hiphil..............1177
sing forth, to
זָמַר Piel.............. 389
sing out, to
רָנַן Piel..............1177

sing praise, to
הָלַל Piel 366
sing to, *see* instrument
sing together by course, to
עָנָה[1] Kal 962
singe, to
חֲרַךְ Ch. Ithpael 464
singer
זַמָּר Ch. 389
שִׁיר Kal 1255
שִׁיר Polel 1255
* singer
שִׁיר 1255
singer, *see* chief
singer, chief
נָצַח Piel 834
singing
זָמִיר 388
רִנָּה 1176
רָנַן Piel 1177
רְנָנָה 1177
שִׁיר Kal 1255
שִׁיר 1255
singing, to be
רָנַן Pual 1177
singing man
שִׁיר Kal 1255
שִׁיר Polel 1255
singing woman
שִׁיר Kal 1255
שִׁיר Polel 1255
singular, to make
פָּלָא Hiphil 1018
sink, to
טָבַע Kal 474
יָרַד Kal 561
כָּרַע Kal 618
צָלַל[2] Kal 1073
שָׁקַע Kal 1325
sinner
חָטָא Kal 414
חַטָּא 416
חַטָּאת 416
sister
אָחוֹת 46
sister, *see* father's
sister in law
יְבֶמֶת 487
sit, to
דָּגַר Kal 335
יָשַׁב Kal 568
יְתֵב Ch. P'al 579
רָבַץ Kal 1154
sit down, to
יָשַׁב Kal 568
סָבַב Kal 865
תָּכָה Pual 1346
sit still, to
יָשַׁב Kal 568
שֶׁבֶת 1235
sit up, to
יָשַׁב Kal 568
sith
אִם 100
sitting
מוֹשָׁב 675
sitting down
יָשַׁב Kal 568
sitting *place*
יָשַׁב Kal 568
situate
מָצוּק 754
situate, to be
יָשַׁב Kal 568
situation
מוֹשָׁב 675
נוֹף 803
Sivan
סִיוָן 875
six
{ שֵׁשׁ, שִׁשָּׁה } 1329
{ שֵׁת, שִׁת } Ch. 1331
*six*score
עֶשְׂרִים 1001
sixscore †
מֵאָה 654
sixscore thousand †
עָשָׂר 998
* sixscore thousand †
{ רִבּוֹ, רִבּוֹא } 1153
שְׁנַיִם 1311
sixteen
{ שֵׁשׁ, שִׁשָּׁה } 1329
{ עָשָׂר } 998
sixteen, *see* threescore
sixteenth
{ שֵׁשׁ, שִׁשָּׁה } 1329
{ עָשָׂר } 998
sixth
{ שֵׁשׁ, שִׁשָּׁה } 1329
שִׁשִּׁי 1331
שִׁת & שֵׁת Ch. 1331
sixth part
שִׁשִּׁי 1331
sixth part, to give the
שִׁשָּׁה Piel 1330
sixth part, to leave but the
שָׁשָׂא Piel 1330
sixty
שִׁשִּׁים 1331
size
מִדָּה 666
קֶצֶב 1114
skilful
בִּין Hiphil 212
חָכְמָה 427
חָרָשׁ 467
יָדַע Kal 500
לָמַד Kal 643
שָׂכַל Hiphil 1206
skilfully
יָטַב Hiphil 524
skilfulness
תְּבוּנָה 1335
skill
שָׂכַל Hiphil 1206
skill, *see* can
skill, can
בִּין Hiphil 212
skill, to give
שָׂכַל Hiphil 1206
skill, man of
יָדַע Kal 500
skin
בָּשָׂר 278
גֶּלֶד 307
עוֹר 912
skip, to
רָקַד Kal 1191
skip for joy, to
נוּד Hithpolel 799
skip, to make to
רָקַד Hiphil 1191
skipping
קָפַץ Piel 1113
skirt
כָּנָף 605
פֶּה 1011
שׁוּל 1246
sky
שַׁחַק 1252
slack
רְמִיָּה 1176
slack, to
עָצַר Kal 973
רָפָה Hiphil 1188
slack, to be
אָחַר Piel 48
רָפָה Kal 1188
רָפָה Hithpael 1188
slacked, to be
פּוּג Kal 1014
slain
חָלַל Pual 432
חָלָל 433
נָכָה Hophal 814
שָׁחַט Kal 1251
slain, to be
הָרַג Niphal 374

הֶרֶג 375
חָרֵב / חָרַב } Niphal 458
מוּת Kal 675
מוּת Hophal 675
נָגַף Niphal 793
נָכָה Hophal 814
קְטַל Ch. P'al 1105
קְטַל Ch. Ithpaal 1105
קְטַל Ch. Ithp'el 1105
רָצַח Niphal 1190
רָצַח Pual 1190
שָׁחַט Niphal 1251

slain man
חָלָל 433

slander
דִּבָּה 318

slander, to
לָשַׁן Piel 652
לָשַׁן Poel 652
רָגַל Piel 1155

slander,† to
נָתַן Kal 851

slander*est*
דֳּפִי 348

slanders
רָכִיל 1174

slaughter
הֶרֶג 375
הֲרֵגָה 375
טָבַח Kal 473
טֶבַח 473
טִבְחָה 473
מַגֵּפָה 663
מַטְבֵּחַ 691
מַכָּה 698
מַפָּץ 748
נָכָה Hiphil 814
קֶטֶל 1105
רֶצַח 1190

slaughter, to be made
הָרַג Niphal 374

slaughter, to make
טָבַח Kal 473
שָׁחַט Kal 1251

slay †
טֶבַח 473
נֶפֶשׁ 829

slay, to
הָרַג Kal 374
זָבַח Kal 377
חָלַל Piel 432
חָרֵב / חָרַב } Kal 458
טָבַח Kal 473
מוּת Polel 675
מוּת Hiphil 675
נָכָה Hiphil 814
נָפַל Hiphil 825
קָטַל Kal 1105
קְטַל Ch. P'al 1105
קְטַל Ch. Pael 1105
רָצַח Kal 1190
שָׁחַט Kal 1251

slay, utterly to
חָרַם Hiphil 464

slayer
הָרַג Kal 374
נָכָה Hiphil 814
רָצַח Kal 1190

slaying
נָכָה Hiphil 814

sleep
יָשֵׁן 576
שֵׁנָא 1304
שֵׁנָה 1309
שְׁנָה Ch. 1309
שְׁנַת 1315

sleep, *see* deep, lie down

sleep, to
הָזָה Kal 360
יָשֵׁן Kal 576
נוּם Kal 801
שָׁכַב Kal 1257

sleep, cast into a deep
רָדַם Niphal 1158

sleep, in a deep
רָדַם Niphal 1158

sleep, to be in a deep
רָדַם Niphal 1158

sleep, to make to
יָשֵׁן Piel 576

sleep, one out of
יָשֵׁן 576

sleeper
רָדַם Niphal 1158

sleepeth
יָשֵׁן 576

sleepeth, that
רָדַם Niphal 1158

sleeping
יָשֵׁן 576

slept
יָשֵׁן 576

* slew
חָלָל 433

slew †
הֲוָא / הֲוָה } Ch. P'al 358

slide, to
מוּט Kal 670
מָעַד Kal 740

slide back, to
סָרַר Kal 885
שׁוּב Polel 1238

* slight*ly*
קָלַל Niphal 1109

slime
חֵמָר 441

slimepit
{ בְּאֵר 184
{ חֵמָר 441

sling
מַרְגֵּמָה 762
קֶלַע 1110

sling, to
קָלַע Kal 1110
קָלַע Piel 1110

sling out, to
קָלַע Kal 1110
קָלַע Piel 1110

slinger
קַלָּע 1110

slingstone
{ אֶבֶן 11
{ קֶלַע 1110

slip
זְמוֹרָה 388

slip, to
מוֹט Kal 670
מוֹט Niphal 670
מָעַד Kal 740
נָשַׁל Kal 848
שָׁפַךְ Pual 1320

slip away, to
פָּטַר Kal 1017

slippery
חֲלַקְלַקּוֹת 436

slippery place
חֶלְקָה 436

slothful
עָצֵל 972
רְמִיָּה 1176

slothful, to be
עָצַל Niphal 972
רָפָה Hithpael 1188

slothfulness
עַצְלָה 972

slow
כָּבֵד 582

slow to *anger*
אֶרֶךְ 156

sluggard
עָצֵל 972

sluice
שֶׂכֶר 1208

slumber
תְּנוּמָה 1352

slumber, to
נוּם Kal 801

slumbering
תְּנוּמָה 1352

small
דַּק ... 348
מְעַט ... 741
מִצְעָר ... 755
מְתִים ... 779
צָעִיר ... 1076
צַר & צָר ... 1080
קָטָן ... 1105
קָטֹן ... 1105
קָצֵר ... 1117

small, *see* cattle, dust, rain, stone, very

small, to be
דָּקַק Kal ... 348
צָעַר Kal ... 1077

small, to beat
דָּקַק Kal ... 348

small, to make
גָּרַע Piel ... 316
קָטֹן Hiphil ... 1105

small matter
מְעַט ... 741

small one
צָעִי ... 1076
000 ... 000

small quantity
קָטָן ... 1105

small, to stamp
דָּקַק Hiphil ... 348

small thing
מְעַט ... 741
קָטָן ... 1105

small thing, to be a
קָטֹן Kal ... 1105

small towns
חַוָּה ... 406

small, very
יָטַב Hiphil ... 524
מְעַט ... 741

smallest
קָטָן ... 1105

smart, to
רוּעַ Niphal ... 1164

* smart,† to
רַע ... 1177

smell
בֹּשֶׂם ... 278
רֵיחַ ... 1172
רֵיחַ Ch. ... 1172

smell, to
רוּחַ Hiphil ... 1160

smelling, *see* sweet

smite, to
דְּכָא Piel ... 340
הָלַם Kal ... 367
כָּתַת Piel ... 624
מְחָא Ch. P'al ... 685
מָחַץ Kal ... 689
נָגַע Kal ... 792
נָגַע Piel ... 792
נָגַף Kal ... 793
נָכָה Hiphil ... 814
נְקַשׁ Ch. P'al ... 840
סָפַק Kal ... 882
תָּקַע Kal ... 1356

smite, *see* hindmost

smite down, to
כָּרַע Hiphil ... 618

smite off, to
מָחַק Kal ... 689

smite out, to
נָפַל Hiphil ... 825

smite through, to
מָחַץ Kal ... 689

* smite together
פִּיק ... 1018

smite with the hammer, to
הָלַם Kal ... 367

smite with the scab, to
שָׂפַח Piel ... 1214

smiter
נָכָה Hiphil ... 814

smith
חָרָשׁ ... 467
מַסְגֵּר ... 736

smith †
חָרָשׁ ... 467

smiting
נָכָה Hiphil ... 814

smitten, to be
כָּתַת Hophal ... 624
נָגַף Niphal ... 793
נָכָה Niphal ... 814
נָכָה Pual ... 814
נָכָה Hophal ... 814

smitten down, to be
נָגַף Niphal ... 793

smoke
עָשָׁן ... 1003
קִיטוֹר ... 1107

smoke, to
עָשַׁן Kal ... 1003

smoke, to be on a
עָשַׁן Kal ... 1003

smoking
כֵּהֶה ... 586
עָשֵׁן ... 1003
עָשֵׁן ... 1003

smooth
חָלָק ... 435
חֵלֶק ... 435
חַלֻּק ... 436
חֶלְקָה ... 436

smooth, to
חָלַק Hiphil ... 435

smooth thing
חֶלְקָה ... 436

smoother, to be
חָלַק Kal ... 435

smote
מַכָּה ... 698

snail
חֹמֶט ... 439
שַׁבְּלוּל ... 1227

snare
חֶבֶל
חֵבֶל } ... 399
יָקוּשׁ ... 558
מוֹקֵשׁ ... 674
מָצוֹד ... 752
מְצוּדָה ... 753
פַּח ... 1016
פַּחַת ... 1017
שְׂבָכָה ... 1195

snare, *see* lay

snare, to bring into a
פּוּת Hiphil ... 1014

snare, to lay a
נָקַשׁ Hithpael ... 840
קוּשׁ Kal ... 1104

snared
יָקֹשׁ Hophal ... 559

snared, to be
יָקֹשׁ Niphal ... 559
נָקַשׁ Kal ... 840
נָקַשׁ Niphal ... 840
פָּחַח Hiphil ... 1017

snared, is
מוֹקֵשׁ ... 674

snares, to lay
נָקַשׁ Piel ... 840

snatch, to
גָּזַר Kal ... 305

sneeze, to
זָרַר Poel ... 397

snorting
נַחְרָה ... 809

snout
אַף ... 144

snow
שֶׁלֶג ... 1262
תְּלַג Ch. ... 1347

snow, to be as
שָׁלַג Hiphil ... 1262

snowy
שֶׁלֶג ... 1262

snuff, to
נָפַח Hiphil ... 825

snuff up, to
שָׁאַף Kal ... 1222

snuffdish
מַחְתָּה ... 691

snuffers
מְזַמְּרוֹת 684
מַלְקָחַיִם 730

so
אֵלֶּה 79
זֹאת 377
כֹּה 586
כָּכָה 597
כֵּן 604
כְּנֵמָא Ch. 605

* so
הֵם 367

so †
דָּבָר 325

so, *see* bad, even, evil, long as, much, soon, yet

so...and
גַּם 311

so and much
כֹּה 586

so be it
אָמֵן 104

so great
כָּבֵד 582

so long
יוֹם 508

so long as
עַד 901

so *long* as
עֵת 1005

*so many more as they
הֵם 367

so much
זֹאת 377
מְאֹד 652

so much, *see* half

so much as
גַּם 311
עַד 901

so sore
מְאֹד 652

so that
אֲשֶׁר 180
כִּי 596
עַד 901

so *that*
רַק 1191

so that no
בְּלִי 229

soaked, to be
רָוָה Piel 1160

socket
אֶדֶן 22

sod, to
בָּשַׁל Piel 280
זוּד } זִיד } Hiphil 383

sodden
בָּשֵׁל 280

sodden, to be
בָּשַׁל Pual 280

soder
דֶּבֶק 319

sodomite
קָדֵשׁ 1091

soever, *see* how many, what

soft
רַךְ 1173

soft, to make
מוּג Polel 670
רָכַךְ Hiphil 1174

softer, to be
רָכַךְ Kal 1174

softly
אַט 54
אִטִּי 55
לָאט 626
לָט 640

softly, *see* go

soil
שָׂדֶה 1197

sojourn, to
גּוּר Kal 303
גּוּר Hithpolel 303

sojourn, where
מָגוּר 662

sojourner
גּוּר Kal 303
גֵּר 314
תּוֹשָׁב 1344

sojourning
מוֹשָׁב 675

solace selves, to
עָלַס Hithpael 943

sold
מְחִיר 687

sold, to be
מָכַר Niphal 700
מָכַר Hithpael 700

* sold as †
מִמְכֶּרֶת 730

sold, that which...
מִמְכָּר 730

* soldier
בֵּן 232

soldier, *see* armed

soldiers
צָבָא 1057

soldiers, *see* band

sole
כַּף 612

solemn
מוֹעֵד 672

solemn, *see* assembly, feast, sound

solemn assembly
עֲצָרָה 973
עֲצֶרֶת 974

solemn feast
חַג & חָג 401

solemn feast, to keep a
חָגַג Kal 401

solemn meeting
עֲצָרָה 973

solemnity
חַג & חָג 401
מוֹעֵד 672

solemnly
עוּד Hiphil 906

solitary
בָּדָד 187
גַּלְמוּד 310
יָחִיד 523
יְשִׁימוֹן 575

solitary place
צִיָּה 1071

some
אֶחָד 41
אֵלֶּה 79
אֱנוֹשׁ 136
מְעַט 741

* some
קָצֶה 1114
קְצָת 1117

some, *see* few, these

* some of them
אֱנוֹשׁ 136

some *unclean*ness
דָּבָר 325

something, *see* befallen

somewhat
מְאוּמָה 657

somewhat, *see* dark, lighter, reddish

son
בֵּן 232
בֵּן Ch. 258
בַּר 269
בַּר Ch. 269
יֶלֶד 530
יָלִיד 531
מָנוֹן 733
נִין 814

son, *see* eldest

son in law
חָתָן 472

son in law, to be
חָתַן Hithpael 472

son of, to be the
יָלַד Niphal 527

son, only
יָחִיד 523

song
זָמִיר 388
זִמְרָת 389
מַשָּׂא 760
נְגִינָה 791
רֹן 1176
שִׁיר 1255
שִׁירָה 1256

song †
דָּבָר 325
שִׁיר 1255

son's son
נֶכֶד 814

soon
חִישׁ 426
מַהֵר 669
מְהֵרָה 669
מְעַט 741
קָצֵר 1117

* soon
מָהַר[1] Piel 669

soon, *see* as, stretch out

soon as, *see* up

* soon as, as
מַרְאֶה 761

soon, to be so
מָהַר[1] Piel 669

soothsayer
גְּזַר Ch. P'al 305
עָנַן Poel 966
קָסַם Kal........................1113

sope
בֹּרִית 274

sorcerer
כַּשָּׁף 621

sorcerers
כָּשַׁף Piel........................ 621

sorceress
עָנַן Poel 966

sorceries
כְּשָׁפִים 621

sore
יָד 489
כָּבֵד 582
מְאֹד 652
מַכָּה 698
מַעַל 743
נֶגַע 793
קָשֶׁה 1131
רַע 1177
שַׂגִּיא Ch. 1197

* sore
בֶּכֶה 227
בְּכִי 228
גָּדוֹל 293
טֶבַח 473
כַּעַס 612
קֶצֶף 1116
שַׂעַר 1212

sore, is sometimes the translation of an infinitive used intensively.

sore, *see* break, broken, displeasure, go, lie, pained, press, troubled, very

sore, to be
חָזַק Kal........................ 411
כָּבֵד } Kal 581
כָּבַד }
קָשָׁה Kal........................ 1131

sore, to go
כָּבֵד } Kal 581
כָּבַד }

sore, to make
כָּאַב Hiphil 581

sore, to wax
חָזַק Kal........................ 411

sorely, *see* grieved

sorrow
אֲבוֹי 10
אָוֶן 30
אֲנִיָּה 140
דְּאָבָה 317
דְּאָבוֹן 318
דְּאָגָה 318
חֵבֶל } 399
חֶבֶל }
חִיל 425
חִילָה 425
יָגוֹן 488
כְּאֵב 581
כַּעַס 612
כַּעַשׂ 612
מְנִגָּה 663
מַכְאוֹב 698
מַעֲצֵבָה 745
עָמָל 960
עֶצֶב 971
עֹצֶב 971
עִצָּבוֹן 971
עַצֶּבֶת 971
צִיר 1071
צָר & צַר 1080
רַע 1177
רֹעַ 1183
תּוּגָה 1337

sorrow, to
דָּאַב Kal........................ 317
דָּאַג Kal........................ 318
חוּל } Kal 406
חִיל }
חָלַל Hiphil 432

sorrow, to cause
דּוּב Hiphil 336

sorrow, to have
כָּעַס Kal........................ 612

sorrowful
דָּאַב Kal........................ 317
דְּוַי 337
יָגָה[1] Niphal........................ 488
כָּאַב Kal........................ 581
קָשֶׁה 1131

sorrowful, to be
חוּל } Kal 406
חִיל }
כָּאַב Kal........................ 581

sorry, to be
דָּאַג Kal........................ 318
חָלָה Kal.. 429
נוּד Kal........................ 799
עָצַב Niphal 970

sort
גִּיל 306

* sort
כָּנָף 605

sort, *see* after this, one, poorest, this

sorts, *see* flies, garment

sorts, all
מִכְלוֹל 699
מַכְלֻלִים 699

* sorts (*of musical instruments*), all
שִׁדָּה 1237

sottish
סָכָל 876

sought †
הֲוָא } Ch. P'al........................ 358
הֲוָה }

sought, to be
דָּרַשׁ Niphal 353

sought for, to be
בָּקַשׁ Pual 268
דָּרַשׁ Niphal 353

sought up, to be
בָּעָה Niphal 261

soul
נְדִיבָה 797
נֶפֶשׁ 829
נְשָׁמָה 849

sound
הֶגֶה 357
פֶּה 1011
קוֹל 1096
קָל Ch. 1108
תֵּקַע 1357

sound
מַרְפֵּא 765
תָּמִים 1350

sound, *see* long

sound, to
הָמָה Kal........................ 368
חֲצֹצֵר Piel........................ 455
חָצַר Hiphil 455
חֲצֹרֵר Piel........................ 456
חָקַר Kal........................ 458
שָׁמֵעַ } Hiphil 1292
שָׁמַע }
תָּקַע Kal........................1356

sound an alarm, to
רוּעַ Hiphil 1164

sound, to cause to
עָבַר Hiphil 895

sound, joyful
תְּרוּעָה 1358

sound, to make
עָבַר Hiphil 895

speed, to make
אָמַץ Hithpael........ 104
מָהַר¹ Piel............ 669

speed, with
מְהֵרָה.................. 669

speedily
אָסְפַּרְנָא Ch............... 143
מַהֵר.................. 669
מְהֵרָה.................. 669

* speedily
מָהַר¹ Piel............ 669

speedily, *see* divide

speedily, to give
בָּהֵל / בָּהַל } Piel.......... 188

speedy
בָּהֵל / בָּהַל } Niphal........ 188

spend, to
אָבַד Piel.............. 8
בָּלָה Piel.............. 229
כָּלָה Piel.............. 598
עָשָׂה Kal.............. 981
שָׁקַל Kal.............1324

spend up, to
בָּלַע Piel.............. 230

spent, to be
אָזַל Kal.............. 35
כָּלָה Kal.............. 598
רָדַד Kal.............1158
תָּמַם Kal.............1351

spewing, *see* shameful

spice
בָּשָׂם.................. 278
בֶּשֶׂם.................. 278
בֹּשֶׂם.................. 278

spice, to
רָקַח Hiphil..........1191

spice merchant
רָכַל Kal.............1175

spiced
רֶקַח..................1191

spicery
נְכֹאת.................. 814

spices
נְכֹאת.................. 814

spices, sweet
סַמִּים.................. 879

spider
עַכָּבִישׁ.................. 932
שְׂמָמִית..................1210

spied, to be
רָאָה Niphal..........1133

spies
אֲתָרִים.................. 184
רָגַל Piel.............1155

spikenard
נֵרְדְּ.................. 840

spill, to
שָׁחַת Piel............1252

spilt
נָגַר Niphal.......... 793

spin, to
טָוָה Kal.............. 479

spindle
כִּישׁוֹר.................. 596

spirit
נְשָׁמָה.................. 849
רוּחַ..................1160
רוּחַ Ch...............1162

spirit, *see* familiar

spiritual
רוּחַ..................1160

spit, to
יָרַק Kal.............. 566
רֹק..................1191
רָקַק Kal.............1192

spite
כַּעַס.................. 612

spitting
רֹק..................1191

spittle
רִיר..................1172
רֹק..................1191

spoil
בַּג (כ׳).............. 184
בַּז & בַּז.............. 207
בִּזָּה.................. 207
גְּזֵלָה.................. 305
חֲלִיצָה.................. 431
טֶרֶף.................. 485
מְשׁוּסָּה.................. 768
מְשִׁסָּה.................. 774
שֹׁד..................1236
שָׁלָל..................1277

spoil, to
בָּזָא Kal.............. 207
בָּזַז Kal.............. 207
גָּזַל Kal.............. 304
חָבַל Piel.............. 398
נָצַל Piel.............. 835
פָּשַׁט Kal.............1050
פָּשַׁט Piel.............1050
קָבַע Kal.............1084
שֹׁד..................1236
שָׁדַד Kal.............1237
שָׁדַד Piel.............1237
שָׁדַד Poel.............1237
שָׁכַל Piel.............1259
שָׁלַל Kal.............1276
שָׁסָה Kal.............1315
שָׁסַס Kal.............1315

spoil, to make a
שָׁלַל Kal.............1276

spoil, to take
בָּזַז Kal.............. 207

spoiled
בַּז & בַּז.............. 207
שֹׁד..................1236
שָׁדַד Kal.............1237
שׁוֹלָל..................1246
שָׁסָה Kal.............1315

spoiled, to be
בָּזַז Niphal.......... 207
שָׁדַד Niphal..........1237
שָׁדַד Pual.............1237
שָׁדַד Hophal..........1237
שָׁלַל Hithpolel........1276
שָׁסַס Niphal..........1315

spoiler
שֹׁד..................1236
שָׁדַד Kal.............1237
שָׁחַת Hiphil..........1252
שָׁסָה Kal.............1315

spoiling
שֹׁד..................1236
שְׁכוֹל..................1258

spoils
אָרְבּוֹת.................. 149

* spoken
דָּבָר.................. 325
פֶּה..................1011

spoken, to be
דָּבַר Pual.............. 319

spoken for, to be
דָּבַר Pual.............. 319

spokes
חִשֻּׁרִים.................. 471

spokesman, to be
דָּבַר Piel.............. 319

spoon
כַּף.................. 612

sport
שְׂחוֹק..................1204

sport, to be in
שָׂחַק Piel.............1205

sport, to make
צָחַק Piel.............1070
שָׂחַק Kal.............1205
שָׂחַק Piel.............1205

sport selves, to
עָנַג Hithpael........ 962

spot
מוּם.................. 671

spot, bright
בַּהֶרֶת.................. 189

spot, freckled
בֹּהַק.................. 189

spot, without
תָּמִים..................1350

spots
חֲבַרְבֻּרוֹת.................. 400

spotted
טָלָא Kal.............. 481

spouse
כַּלָּה ... 600

spread, to
זָרָה Piel ... 394
זָרָה Pual ... 394
יָלַךְ Kal ... 531
יָצָא Kal ... 548
יָצַע Hiphil ... 556
נָטָה Kal ... 810
נָטָה Hiphil ... 810
פָּרַח Kal ... 1045
פָּרַשׂ Kal ... 1048
פָּרַשׂ Piel ... 1048
פַּרְשֵׁז ... 1049
פָּשָׂה Kal ... 1049
רָדַד Hiphil ... 1158
רָפַד Kal ... 1188
שָׁטַח Kal ... 1254

spread, to be
יָצַע Hophal ... 556
פָּשָׂה Kal ... 1049

spread abroad
נָטַשׁ Kal ... 813

spread abroad, to
פָּרַץ Kal ... 1047
פָּרַשׂ Kal ... 1048
רָקַע Kal ... 1192

spread abroad, to be
פּוּץ Kal ... 1014
פּוּץ Niphal ... 1014

spread forth, to
מִשְׁטוֹחַ ... 769
פָּרַשׂ Kal ... 1048
פָּרַשׂ Piel ... 1048
רָקַע Kal ... 1192

spread forth, to be
נָטָה Niphal ... 810

spread into plates
רָקַע Pual ... 1192

spread out
פָּתַח Kal ... 1052

spread out, to
מָתַח Kal ... 779
נָטָה Kal ... 810
פָּרַשׂ Piel ... 1048
רָקַע Hiphil ... 1192
שָׁלַח Piel ... 1268

spread over, to
רָקַע Piel ... 1192

spread selves, to
נָטַשׁ Niphal ... 813
עָרָה Hithpael ... 977
פּוּשׁ Kal ... 1015
פָּשַׁט Kal ... 1050

spread selves abroad, to
פָּשַׁט Kal ... 1050

spread selves forth, to
פָּרַשׂ Kal ... 1048

spread, that is
נָסַךְ [2] Kal ... 820

spread upon, to
מִשְׁטָח ... 769

spreadest forth, that which
מִפְרָשׂ ... 748

spreading
מִפְרָשׂ ... 748
מִשְׁטָח ... 769
סָרַח Kal ... 884

sprig
פֻּארָה ... 1009

sprigs
זַלְזַלִּים ... 388

spring
גַּל ... 307
גֻּלָּה ... 309
מַבּוּעַ ... 660
מוֹצָא ... 673
מַעְיָן ... 742
מָקוֹר ... 758
נֵבֶךְ ... 786
צֶמַח ... 1075

spring, to
דָּשָׁא Kal ... 355
פָּרַח Kal ... 1045
צָמַח Kal ... 1074

spring, to begin to
עָלָה Kal ... 934

spring forth, to
צָמַח Kal ... 1074

spring forth, to cause to
צָמַח Hiphil ... 1074

spring (*of the day*)
עָלָה Kal ... 934

spring out, to
יָצָא Kal ... 548

spring up, to
עָלָה Kal ... 934
פָּרַח Kal ... 1045
צָמַח Kal ... 1074
צָמַח Hiphil ... 1074

springeth of the same, that which
סָחִישׁ ... 874
שָׁחִים ... 1251

springing
חַי ... 418
צֶמַח ... 1075

springs
אַשְׁדוֹת, אֲשֵׁדוֹת } ... 174

sprinkle, to
זָרַק Kal ... 397
נָזָה Hiphil ... 803

sprinkled, to be
זָרַק Pual ... 397
נָזָה Kal ... 803

sprout, to
חָלַף Hiphil ... 434

spue
קָיָה Kal ... 1107

spue, to
קוֹא Kal ... 1095

spue out, to
קוֹא Hiphil ... 1095

spun
מַטְוֶה ... 693

spy
שָׁמַר Kal ... 1300

spy, to
רָאָה Kal ... 1133
רָגַל Piel ... 1155

spy out, to
רָגַל Piel ... 1155
תּוּר Kal ... 1342

square
רָבַע [2] Kal ... 1154
רָבַע [2] Pual ... 1154

square, *see* foursquare

squared
רָבַע [2] Kal ... 1154

squarer, *see* stonesquarer

squares
רֶבַע ... 1154

stability
אֱמֻנָה, אֱמוּנָה } ... 102

stable
נָוֶה ... 800

stable, to be
כּוּן Niphal ... 592

stablish, to
כּוּן Polel ... 592
כּוּן Hiphil ... 592
נָצַב Hiphil ... 833
קוּם Hiphil ... 1099

stack of corn
גָּדִישׁ ... 296

stacte
נָטָף ... 813

staff
חֵץ ... 453
מוֹט ... 670
מַטֶּה ... 691
מַקֵּל ... 758
מַשְׁעֵנָה ... 774
מִשְׁעֶנֶת ... 774
עֵץ ... 968
פֶּלֶךְ ... 1020
שֵׁבֶט ... 1225

stagger, to
נוּעַ Kal ... 802
תָּעָה Niphal ... 1353

stagger, to make to
תָּעָה Hiphil ... 1353

stain, to
גָּאַל [1] Kal ... 285

גָּאַל [2] Hiphil.......... 286
חָלַל Piel.......... 432

stairs
מַדְרֵגָה 667
מַעֲלָה 744
מַעֲלֶה 744

stairs, winding
לוּלִים 635

stake
יָתֵד 579

stalk
עֵץ 968
קָמָה 1110
קָנֶה 1112

stall
מַרְבֵּק 762

stalled
אָבַס Kal.......... 13

stalls
אֻרָוֹת / אֻרָיוֹת } 154
רְפָתִים 1189

stammerer
עִלֵּג 933

stammering
לָעַג Niphal 644
לַעַג 644

stamp, to
דָּקַק Hiphil 348
כָּתַת Kal.......... 624
רְפַס Ch. P'al 1189
רָקַע Kal.......... 1192

stamp, *see* small

stamp upon, to
רָמַס Kal.......... 1176

stamping
שַׁעֲטָה 1315

stand, to
יָצַב Hithpael 555
כּוּן Niphal 592
נָגַשׁ Kal.......... 794
נָצַב Niphal 833
עָמַד Kal.......... 955
קוּם Kal.......... 1099
קוּם Ch. P'al 1103

stand, *see* awe, power, round about

stand, to be able to
יָצַב Hithpael 555

stand by, to
עָמַד Kal.......... 955
קָרַב Kal.......... 1123

stand, can
יָצַב Hithpael 555

stand fast, to
אָמַן Niphal 103
יָצַב Hithpael 555

סָמַךְ Kal.......... 879
עָמַד Kal.......... 955

stand firm, to
עָמַד Kal.......... 955

stand forth, to
יָצַב Hithpael 555

stand in, *see* awe

stand in awe, to
גּוּר Kal.......... 303

stand, to be made to
קוּם Ch. Hophal 1103

stand, to make to
נָצַב Hiphil 833
עָמַד Hiphil 955
קוּם Hiphil 1099

stand, to make to be at a
עָמַד Hiphil 955

stand out, to
יָצָא Kal.......... 548

stand still, to
דָּמַם Kal.......... 346
יָצַב Hithpael.......... 555
נָצַב Niphal 833
עָמַד Kal.......... 955

stand up, to
יָצַב Hithpael.......... 555
נָצַב Niphal 833
סָמַר Piel.......... 879
עָמַד Kal.......... 955
קוּם Kal.......... 1099

stand upright, to
נָצַב Niphal 833
עוּד Hithpalpel 906

standard
דֶּגֶל 335
נֵס 819

standard bearer, נסס 821

standing
יָצַב Hithpael.......... 555
מָעֳמָד 744
נָצַב Niphal 833
עֶמְדָּה 959

standing corn
קָמָה 1110

standing image
מַצֵּבָה 752

standing *water*
אֲגַם 14

star
כּוֹכָב 591

stare, to
רָאָה Kal.......... 1133

stargazer
{ חֹזֶה 410
{ כּוֹכָב 591

stars, *see* seven stars

state
יָד 489
כֵּן 604

מַעֲמָד 744
מַתְכֹּנֶת 780
פָּנִים 1023

state, best
נָצַב Niphal 833

stately
כְּבוּדָּה 584

station
מַצָּב 751

stature
מַד 664
מִדָּה 666
מָדוֹן 666
קוֹמָה 1103

stature, great
מִדָּה 666

statute
חֹק 456
חֻקָּה 457
קְיָם Ch. 1107

statutes
פִּקּוּדִים 1042

staves
בַּד 186
מוֹטָה 670

stay
יָד 489
מַשְׁעֵן 774
מִשְׁעָן 774
פִּנָּה 1022

stay, to
הָגָה [2] Kal.......... 356
חוּל / חִיל } Kal 406
יָחַל Niphal 523
מְחָא Ch. Pael 685
סָמַךְ Piel.......... 879
עָגַן Niphal 901
עָמַד Kal.......... 955
עָקַב Piel.......... 974
רָפָה Hiphil 1188
שָׁכַב Hiphil 1257
שָׁסַע Piel.......... 1315
שָׁעַן Niphal 1316
תָּמַךְ Kal.......... 1350

stay, *see* three days

stay, to be at a
עָמַד Kal.......... 955

stay selves, to
מָהַהּ Hithpalpel 668
סָמַךְ Niphal 879

stay there, to
אָחַר Kal.......... 48

stay up, to
תָּמַךְ Kal.......... 1350

stayed
סָמַךְ Kal.......... 879

stayed, to be
יָצַג Hophal 555
כָּלָא Kal 598
כָּלָא Niphal 598
עָצַר Niphal 973
שִׁית Kal 1256

stayed up
עָמַד Hophal 955

stead of
תַּחַת 1345

steady
אֱמֻנָה / אֱמוּנָה 102

steal, to
גָּנַב Kal 312
גָּנַב Piel 312

steal away, to
גָּנַב Kal 312
גָּנַב Hithpael 313

stealth, (to get) by
גָּנַב Hithpael 312

stedfast
יָצַק Hophal 556
קַיָּם Ch. 1107

stedfast, to be
אָמַן Niphal 103

* stedfastly
שׂוּם / שִׂים Kal 1200

stedfastly minded, to be
אָמֵץ Hithpael 104

steel
נְחוּשָׁה 805
נְחֹשֶׁת 809

steep place
מַדְרֵגָה 667
מוֹרָד 674

stem
גֶּזַע 305

step
אַשֻּׁר 181
אֲשֻׁר 181
הָלִיךְ 362
מִצְעָד 755
עָקֵב 974
פַּעַם 1038
פֶּשַׂע 1050
צַעַד 1076

steps
מַעֲלָה 744

steward
שַׂר 1214

steward †
אִישׁ 60
מֶשֶׁק 778

* steward †
בַּיִת 214
בֵּן 232

stick
עֵץ 968

stick, to
דָּבֵק / דָּבַק Kal 318

stick, to cause to
דָּבֵק / דָּבַק Hiphil 318

stick closer
דָּבֵק 319

stick fast, to
נָחַת Niphal 810

stick out
(כ') שְׁפִי 1320

stick out, to
שָׁפָה Pual 1318

stick together, to
לָכַד Hithpael 642

stiff
עָתָק 1008
קָשֶׁה 1131

stiff, to make
קָשָׁה Hiphil 1131

stiffen, to
קָשָׁה Hiphil 1131

stiffhearted
חָזָק 413
לֵב 626

stiffnecked
קָשֶׁה 1131
עֹרֶף 980

stiff*necked*, to be
קָשָׁה Hiphil 1131

still
דְּמָמָה 346
מְנוּחָה 733
עוֹד 905

* still
נָסַע Kal 821

still, *see* keep, lie, sit, stand

still is sometimes the translation of an infinitive used intensitively.

still, to
הָסָה Hiphil 370
חָשָׁה Hiphil 469
שָׁבַח Piel 1225
שָׁבַח Hiphil 1225
שָׁבַת Hiphil 1234

still, be
עוֹד 905

still, to be
דָּמַם Kal 346
חָרַשׁ Hiphil 466
חָשָׁה Kal 469
חָשָׁה Hiphil 469
רָפָה Hiphil 1188
שָׁקַט Kal 1324

sting, to
פָּרַשׁ Hiphil 1049

stink
בְּאֹשׁ 184
מַק 755

stink, to
בָּאַשׁ Kal 184
בָּאַשׁ Niphal 184
בָּאַשׁ Hiphil 184

stink, to make to
בָּאַשׁ Hiphil 184

stinking savour, to cause a
בָּאַשׁ Hiphil 184

stir up, to
גָּרָה Piel 315
נָשָׂא Kal 840
סוּת Hiphil 874
עוּר[1] Kal 913
עוּר[1] Polel 913
עוּר[1] Hiphil 913
עָלָה Hiphil 934
קוּם Hiphil 1099

stir up self, to
עוּר[1] Hiphil 913
עוּר Hithpolel 913

stirred, to be
עָבַר Niphal 932

stirred up, to be
גָּרָה Hithpael 315

stirs
תְּשֻׁאוֹת 1359

stock
בּוּל 205
גֶּזַע 305
עֵץ 968
עֵקֶר 974

stock, *see* gazing stock

stocks
מַהְפֶּכֶת 668
סַד 870
עֶכֶס 932
צִינֹק 1071

stolen, to be
גָּנַב Niphal 312

stolen away, to be
גָּנַב Pual 312

stomacher
פְּתִיגִיל 1055

stone
אֶבֶן 11
אֶבֶן Ch. 13
סֶלַע 878
צוּר 1069

stone †
חֶרֶשׂ 466

stone, *see* adamant, gravel, hail head, hewn, sharp, sling

strange, to make self
חָבַר Hiphil 362
נָכַר Hithpael 818
strange thing
זוּר [2]Kal 384
strange woman
זוּר [2]Kal 384
נָכְרִי 819
strangely, to behave selves
נָכַר Piel. 818
stranger
גּוּר Kal 303
גֵּיר 307
גֵּר 314
זוּר [2]Kal 384
זוּר [2]Hophal 384
נָכְרִי 819
תּוֹשָׁב 1344
{ בֵּן 232
{ נֵכָר 818
* stranger †
אֱנוֹשׁ 136
stranger, to be
גּוּר Kal 303
stranger, be a
מָגוּר 662
stranger, to become a
נֹכֶר 819
strangle, to
חָנַק Piel 447
strangling
מַחֲנָק 689
straw
מַתְבֵּן 779
תֶּבֶן 1336
stream
אָפִיק 146
אֶשֶׁד 174
יְאוֹר 486
יָבָל 487
נָהָר 799
נָזַל Kal 803
נַחַל 805
נַחֲלָה 806
פֶּלֶג 1019
street
חוּץ 408
רְחוֹב 1167
שׁוּק 1248
street †
פָּנִים 1023
strength
אוּל 30
אוֹן 31
אֱיָל 59
אֱיָלוּת 59
אֵתָן }
אֵיתָן } 70
אַמְצָה 105
בַּד 186
גְּבוּרָה 290
דֹּבֶא 318
זְרוֹעַ 394
חֵזֶק 414
חֹזֶק 414
חָזְקָה 414
חַיִל 423
חֹסֶן 450
כֹּחַ 594
מֵזַח }
מְזִיחַ } 684
מָעוֹז 740
נִצְבָּה Ch. 834
נֵצַח }
נֶצַח } 835
נֵצַח 835
עֹז 914
עֱזוּז 917
עֹצֶם 972
עָצְמָה 973
רַהַב 1159
רֹהַב 1159
תּוֹעָפוֹת 1342
תֹּקֶף 1357
תְּקֹף Ch. 1357
* strength
צוּר 1069
תֵּל 1347
strength, *see* recover
strength, draw with
יָד 489
strengthen, to
אָמַץ Piel 104
אָמַץ Hiphil 104
בָּלַג Hiphil 229
גָּבַר Piel 291
חָזַק Kal 411
חָזַק Piel 411
חָזַק Hiphil 411
מָעוֹז 740
סָעַד Kal 880
עָזַז Kal 917
קוּם Piel 1099
רָהַב Hiphil 1159
strengthen self
חָזְקָה 414
strengthen self, to
אָמַץ Hithpael 104
גָּבַר Hithpael 291
חָזַק Hithpael 411
עָזַז Kal 917
strengthened, to be
חָזַק Kal 411
חָזַק Hithpael 411
עָזַז Kal 917
stretch, to
נָטָה Kal 810
פָּרַשׂ Kal 1048
stretch forth, to
נָטָה Kal 810
נָטָה Hiphil 810
פָּרַשׂ Kal 1048
פָּרַשׂ Piel 1048
שָׁלַח Kal 1268
stretch out, to
מָשַׁךְ Kal 770
נָטָה Kal 810
נָטָה Hiphil 810
פָּרַשׂ Kal 1048
רָקַע Kal 1192
שָׁטַח Piel 1254
שָׁלַח Kal 1268
stretch out self, to
שָׂרַע Hithpael 1217
stretch out, soon to
רוּץ Hiphil 1165
stretch self, to
גָּהַר Kal 298
מָדַד Hithpolel 665
סָרַח Kal 884
stretched
פָּרַד Kal 1043
stretched forth, to be
נָטָה Niphal 810
stretched out
נָטָה Kal 810
stretched out, to be
נָטָה Niphal 810
נָטַשׁ Niphal 813
stretching out
מֻטּוֹת 693
strew, to
זָרָה Kal 394
stricken
נָגַע Kal 792
נֶגַע 793
נָכָא 814
stricken, to be
נָכָה Hophal 814
*stricken *in age*, to be well
בּוֹא Kal 189
stricken through
דָּקַר Pual 348
strife
דִּין 340
מָדוֹן 666
מְדָנִים 667
מַצָּה 752
מְרִיבָה 764
רִיב 1171
strife, at
דִּין Niphal 340

strike, to
נָגַע Hiphil 792
נָגַף Kal 793
נוּף Hiphil 802
נָכָה Hiphil 814
נָתַן Kal 851
סָפַק Kal 882
תָּקַע Kal 1356
תָּקַע Niphal 1356
strike, *see* again
strike again, to
שָׁנָה Kal 1304
strike off, *see* neck
strike through, to
חָלַף Kal 434
מָחַץ Kal 689
נָקַב Kal 837
פָּלַח Piel 1019
string
יֶתֶר 581
מֵיתָר 698
stringed, *see* instrument
strings, *see* ten
strip, to
פָּשַׁט Kal 1050
פָּשַׁט Piel 1050
פָּשַׁט Hiphil 1050
strip off, to
נָצַל Piel 835
פָּשַׁט Hiphil 1050
strip selves, to
נָצַל Hophal 835
פָּשַׁט Hithpael 1050
stripe
חַבּוּרָה / חֲבוּרָה } 398
מַכָּה 698
נֶגַע 793
stripes
מַהֲלֻמּוֹת 668
נָכָה Hiphil 814
stripes, to give
נָכָה Hiphil 814
stripling
עֶלֶם 943
stripped
שׁוֹלָל 1246
שֵׁילָל 1255
strive
רִיב 1171
strive, to
גּוּחַ / גִּיחַ } Aphel 306
גָּרָה Hithpael 315
דּוּן Kal 337
נָצָה[1] Niphal 834
נָצָה[1] Hiphil 834
עָשַׂק Hithpael 997
רִיב Kal 1171
רִיב Hiphil 1171
strive, that
יָרִיב 565
strive together, to
נָצָה[1] Niphal 834
striving
רִיב 1171
stroke
יָד 489
מַגֵּפָה 663
מַחַץ 689
מַכָּה 698
נֶגַע 793
שֶׂפֶק 1214
stroke, *see* fetch
strokes
מַהֲלֻמּוֹת 668
strong
אַבִּיר 10
אֵתָן / אֵיתָן } 70
אֵל 76
אַמִּיץ / אַמִּיּץ } 103
בָּצַר Kal 264
גִּבּוֹר 289
גֶּרֶם 316
חָזָק 413
חָזְקָה 414
חַיִל 423
חָסִין 450
חָסֹן 450
כַּבִּיר 584
מִבְצָר 661
מָעוֹז 740
מָעוֹר 754
עַז 914
עֹז 914
עִזּוּז 917
עָצוּם 972
עֹצֶם 973
עֲצֻמוֹת 973
עָרִיץ 978
תַּקִּיף Ch. 1356
* strong
צוּר 1069
strong, *see* drink, labour, wine
strong, to be
אָמַץ Kal 104
חָזַק Kal 411
חָזַק Hiphil 411
חָזַק Hithpael 411
עָזַז Kal 917
עָצַם Kal 972
תְּקֵף Ch. P'al 1357
strong, to become
עָצַם Kal 972
תְּקֵף Ch. P'al 1357
strong hold
בִּצָּרוֹן 264
מִבְצָר 661
מָעוֹז 740
מְצָד 752
מְצוּדָה 753
מָצוֹר 754
מְצוּרָה 754
סֶלַע 878
עֹפֶל 967
strong, to be made
פָּזַז[2] Kal 1015
strong, to make
אָמַץ Piel 104
חָזַק Kal 411
חָזַק Piel 411
חָזַק Hiphil 411
strong, to make self
חָזַק Hithpael 411
strong man
גִּבּוֹר 289
strong, most
מִבְצָר 661
strong one
אַבִּיר 10
אַמִּיץ / אַמִּיּץ } 103
strong pieces
אָפִיק 146
strong place
מְצוּדָה 753
strong, to shew self
חָזַק Hithpael 411
strong, to be too
שָׂגַב Kal 1197
strong, was
חֶזְקָה 414
strong, to wax
חָזַק Kal 411
stronger
אֹמֶץ 105
חָזָק 413
חָזֵק 413
קָשַׁר Kal 1132
קָשַׁר Pual 1132
stronger, to be
אָמַץ Kal 104
גָּבַר Kal 291
חָזַק Kal 411
stronger, to be
יָסַף Hiphil 543
stronger, to make
עָצַם Hiphil 972

strongly, *see* laid
strow, to
זָרַק Kal.............. 397
struggle together, to
רָצַץ Hithpolel 1190
stubble
קַשׁ 1131
תֶּבֶן 1336
stubborn
סָרַר Kal.............. 885
קָשֶׁה 1131
stubbornness
פָּצַר Hiphil 1039
קְשִׁי 1132
stuck
מָעַךְ Kal.............. 742
studs
נְקֻדּוֹת 838
study
לַהַג 634
study, to
הָגָה[1] Kal.............. 356
stuff
כְּלִי 600
מְלָאכָה 705
stumble, to
כָּשַׁל Kal.............. 621
כָּשַׁל Niphal 621
נָגַף Kal.............. 793
נָגַף Hithpael......... 793
פּוּק[1] Kal.............. 1015
שָׁמַט Kal.............. 1286
stumble, to cause to
כָּשַׁל Hiphil 621
stumbling
נֶגֶף 793
stumbling block
מִכְשׁוֹל 701
מַכְשֵׁלָה 701
stump
עִקָּר Ch.............. 974
subdue, to
דָּבַר Hiphil 319
חֲשַׁל Ch. P'al 470
כָּבַשׁ Kal.............. 586
כָּבַשׁ Piel............. 586
כָּנַע Hiphil 605
כָּרַע Hiphil 618
רָדַד Kal.............. 1158
שְׁפַל Ch. Aphel 1321
subdued, to be
יָרַד Kal.............. 561
כָּבַשׁ Niphal 586
כָּנַע Niphal 605
subjection, *see* brought
subjection, to bring into
כָּבַשׁ Kal.............. 586
כָּבַשׁ Hiphil 586

submit, to
נָתַן Kal.............. 851
submit selves, to
כָּחַשׁ Piel............. 595
כָּחַשׁ Hithpael......... 595
עָנָה[2] Hithpael........ 964
רָפַס Hithpael 1189
subscribe, to
כָּתַב Kal.............. 621
substance
אוֹן 31
הַוָּה 359
הוֹן 360
חַיִל 423
יְקוּם 558
יֵשׁ 568
כֹּחַ 594
מַצֶּבֶת 752
מִקְנֶה 759
עֹצֶם 973
קִים 1107
קִנְיָן 1112
רְכוּשׁ 1174
תּוּשִׁיָּה 1344
* substance
שָׁוָה (כ׳) [2] Piel........ 1246
substance, *see* living
substance yet being imperfect
גֹּלֶם 310
subtil
חָכָם 426
נָצַר Kal.............. 837
עָרוּם 978
subtilly
מִרְמָה 765
subtilly, to deal
עָרַם[1] Hiphil.......... 979
subtilty
עָקְבָּה 974
עָרְמָה 980
suburb
מִגְרָשׁ 663
פַּרְוָר 1044
subvert, to
עָוַת Piel.............. 914
succeed, to
יָרַשׁ Kal.............. 566
קוּם Kal.............. 1099
success, *see* good
Succoth
סֻכָּה 875
succour, to
עָזַר Kal.............. 917
עָזַר Hiphil 918
such
אֵלֶּה 79
דֵּן Ch 346
הוּא 358
זֹאת 377
זֶה 380
כֹּה 586
כֵּן 604
פְּלֹנִי 1021
* such
הֵם 367
הֵנָּה 369
such, *see* any, belonged, reward
such a, *see* company
such a case, in
כָּכָה 597
such a time, at
כְּעֶנֶת Ch.............. 612
כְּעֶת Ch.............. 612
such an one
זֶה 380
such, and
אַלְמֹנִי 96
such and such things
הֵנָּה 369
such as
כְּמוֹ 603
such as, *see* breathe out, open, peace
such deed
זֹאת 377
such like
הֵן 369
such thing
כֵּן 604
such things, *see* grow
suck, to
יָנַק Kal.............. 542
מָצָה Kal.............. 752
suck, to give
יָנַק Hiphil 542
suck, to make to
יָנַק Hiphil 542
suck up, to
עָלַע Piel.............. 944
sucking
חָלָב 428
sucking, *see* child
sucking child
יָנַק Kal.............. 542
suckling
יָנַק Kal.............. 542
sudden
פִּתְאוֹם 1052
suddenly
מַהֵר 669
פִּתְאוֹם 1052
פֶּתַע 1055
רֶגַע 1157
* suddenly
מָהַר[1] Piel............. 669

sustenance, to provide
כּוּל Pilpel 592
swaddle, to
טָפַח Piel 484
swaddled, to be
חָתַל Pual 471
swaddling band
חֲתֻלָּה 471
swallow
דְּרוֹר 349
עָגוּר 900
swallow, to
גָּמָא Piel 311
swallow down, to
בָּלַע Kal 230
לוּעַ Kal 636
swallow up, to
בָּלַע Kal 230
בָּלַע Niphal 230
בָּלַע Piel 230
שָׁאַף Kal 1222
swallowed up, to be
בָּלַע Pual 230
לוּעַ Kal 636
swallowed up, that which he hath
בֶּלַע 231
swan
תִּנְשֶׁמֶת 1353
swarm
עֵדָה 903
עָרֹב 975
swear, to
אָלָה[2] Kal 78
שָׁבַע Niphal 1228
{ נָשָׂא Kal 840
{ יָד 489
swear (*another*), to
שָׁבַע Hiphil 1228
swear, to cause to
אָלָה[2] Hiphil 78
שָׁבַע Hiphil 1228
swear, to make to
אָלָה[2] Hiphil 78
שָׁבַע Hiphil 1228
swearer
שָׁבַע Niphal 1228
swearing
אָלָה 78
sweat
זֵעָה 390
sweat, any thing that causeth
יֶזַע 522
sweep, to
טוּא Pilpel 476
sweep away, to
גָּרַף Kal 316
יָעָה Kal 546
sweeping
סָחַף Kal 874
sweet
בֶּשֶׂם 278
בֹּשֶׂם 278
טוֹב 476
מַמְתַּקִּים 731
מָתוֹק 779
נִיחוֹחַ 813
נָעִים 822
סַמִּים 879
עָרֵב 975
* sweet
מֶרְקָחִים 766
sweet, *see* odour, savour, spices, wine
sweet, to be
מָלַץ Niphal 729
מָתַק Kal 780
מָתַק Hiphil 780
נָעֵם Kal 823
עָרֵב[1] Kal 975
sweet incense
קְטֹרֶת 1107
sweet, to be made
מָתַק Kal 780
sweet, to make
יָטַב Hiphil 524
sweet, most
מַמְתַּקִּים 731
sweet odours
בֶּשֶׂם 278
sweet smelling
עָבַר Kal 895
* sweet, to take
מָתַק Hiphil 780
sweet wine
תִּירוֹשׁ 1346
sweeter
מָתוֹק 779
sweetly
מֵישָׁרִים 698
sweetly, to feed
מָתַק Kal 780
sweetness
מָתוֹק 779
מֶתֶק 780
מֹתֶק 780
swell
צָבֶה 1060
swell, to
בָּצֵק Kal 264
צָבָה Kal 1060
swell, to make to
צָבָה Hiphil 1060
swell out, to
בָּעָה Niphal 261
swelling
גַּאֲוָה 285
גָּאוֹן 285
swept away, to be
סָחַף Niphal 874
swift
אֵבֶה 10
מָהַר[1] Piel 669
קַל 1108
swift, *see* beasts
swift, to be
קָלַל Niphal 1109
swift beast
רֶכֶשׁ 1175
swifter, to be
קָלַל Kal 1109
swiftly
יְעָף 547
מְהֵרָה 669
קַל 1108
swim
צוּף Hiphil 1069
swim, to
שָׂחָה Kal 1204
swim in, to
שָׂחוּ 1204
swim, to make to
שָׂחָה Hiphil 1204
* swimmest
צָפָה 1078
swine
חֲזִיר 411
swoon, to
עָטַף Niphal 918
עָטַף Hithpael 918
sword
חֶרֶב 459
רֶצַח 1190
שֶׁלַח 1273
sword, glittering
בָּרָק 277
swords, drawn
פְּתִחוֹת 1054
sworn
שָׁבַע Kal 1228
* sworn
שְׁבוּעָה 1224
* sworn †
בַּעַל 262
כֵּם 606
sycomore
שִׁקְמָה 1324
sycomore fruit
שִׁקְמָה 1324
sycomore tree
שִׁקְמָה 1324
synagogue
מוֹעֵד 672

taber, to
תָּפַף Poel 1355

* Taberah
תַּבְעֵרָה 1336

tabernacle
אֹהֶל 27
מִשְׁכָּן 770
סֹךְ 875
סֻכָּה 875
סִכּוּת 875
שֹׂךְ 1206

table
לוּחַ 635
שֻׁלְחָן 1274

table, at
מֵסַב 736

tablet
בַּיִת } 214
נֶפֶשׁ } 829

tablets
כּוּמָז 592

tabret
תֹּף 1354
תֹּפֶת 1356

taches
קְרָסִים 1129

tackling
חֵבֶל } 399
חֶבֶל }

Tahtim-*hodshi*
תַּחְתִּי 1346

tail
זָנָב 389

take
קָבַל Piel.............1083

take, to
אָבַד Hiphil 8
אָחַז Kal............. 46
אָסַף Kal............. 141
אָצַל Kal............. 148
אָצַל Hiphil 148
בּוֹא Hiphil 189
בָּזַז Kal............. 207
גָּזָה Kal............. 304
דָּבֵק } Kal............ 318
דָּבַק }
חָזַק Hiphil 411
חָשַׂף Kal............. 468
חָתָה Kal............. 471
יָהַב Kal............. 507
יָשַׁב Hiphil 568
לָכַד Kal............. 642
לָקַח Kal............. 644
נָסַג Kal............. 819
נָצַל Hiphil 835
נָשָׂא Kal............. 840
נְשָׂא Ch. P'al 845
נָשַׁג Hiphil 845
סוּר Hiphil 872
עָבַר Hiphil 895
עֲדָה & א' Ch. Aphel 902
עָשָׂה Kal............. 981
צוּד Kal.............1065
קְבַל Ch. Pael 1084
קָרַב Hiphil 1123
רָדָה[2] Kal.............1158
רוּם Hiphil 1163
שׂוּם } Kal............1200
שִׂים }
תָּפַשׂ Kal.............1355

* take, to
שִׁית Kal.............1256

take, *see* advice, ashes, captive, counsel, courage, crafty, delight, fill, handful, heed, hold, hold on, hold upon, indignation, inheritance, journey, knowledge, much, notice, oath, pity, pleasure, pledge, possessions, provision, record, rest, root, spoil, straight way, sweet, tenth, thought, tithes, vengeance, violence, witness

take again, to
שׁוּב Kal.............1238

take as, *see* heritage

take aside, to
נָטָה Hiphil 810

take away, to
אָסַף Kal............. 141
בָּזַז Kal............. 207
בָּעַר Piel............. 262
בָּעַר Hiphil 262
גָּזַל Kal............. 304
הָגָה[2] Kal............. 356
חָלַץ Piel............. 434
חָתָה Kal............. 471
חָתַף Kal............. 472
יָלַךְ Hiphil 531
לָקַח Kal............. 644
מוּשׁ[1] Hiphil 674
נָשָׂא Kal............. 840
נָשָׂא Niphal 840
נָשָׂא Piel............. 840
סוּר Hiphil 872
סוּת Hiphil 874
עָבַר Hiphil 895
עָדָה Hiphil 902
עָלָה Hiphil 934
רוּם Hiphil 1163
שָׁבָה Kal.............1224
שָׁבַת Hiphil 1234
שָׁלָה[2] Kal.............1262

* take away, to
שְׁבִי 1226

take away, *see* portion, violently

take away as with a whirlwind, to
שָׂעַר Kal.............1212

take away, to quite
כָּלָה Piel............. 598

take away violently, to
גָּזַל Kal............. 304

take back, to
שׁוּב Hiphil 1238

take by, *see* heel

take by force, to
גָּזַל Kal............. 304

take *captive*, to
שָׁבָה Kal.............1224

take *counsel* together, to
עוּץ Kal............. 912

take down, to
יָרַד Hiphil 561

take for, *see* inheritance, prey

take forth, to
יָצָא Hiphil 548
נְפַק Ch. Aphel 828

take *hand*ful, to
מָלֵא Piel............. 701

take *handful*, to
קָמַץ Kal.............1111

take heed †
הֲוָא } Ch. P'al 358
הֲוָה }

take hold, to
אָחַז Kal............. 46
חָזַק Hiphil 411
תָּמַךְ Kal.............1350
תָּפַשׂ Kal.............1355
תָּפַשׂ Piel.............1355

take hold on, to
מָצָא Kal............. 748

take in, to
בּוֹא Hiphil 189

take into, to
אָסַף Piel............. 141

take *journey*, to
יָלַךְ Kal............. 531

take *labour*, to
עָמַל Kal............. 960

take off, to
סוּר Hiphil 872
רוּם Hiphil 1163
שׁוּב Hiphil 1238

take out, to
גּוּחַ } Kal........... 306
גִּיחַ }
יָצָא Hiphil 548
נְפַק Ch. Aphel 828

take rest, to
שָׁכַב Kal.............1257

take *spoil*, to
שָׁלַל Kal.............1276

* take, that I
עָמַד 958

take up, to
אָסַף Kal............. 141

נָטַל Kal 812
נְסַךְ Ch. Aphel 822
נָשָׂא Kal 840
עָלָה Kal 934
עָלָה Hiphil 934
קָבַץ Piel 1084
רוּם Hiphil 1163
take up, *see* fifth part
take upon, to
יָאַל Niphal 486
take, utterly to
פּוּר Hiphil 1015
take *vengeance*, to
נָקַם Kal 839
נָקַם Niphal 839
נָקַם Piel 839
take *witnesses*, to
עוּד Hiphil 906
taken, *see* captive, vengeance
taken, to be
אָחַז Niphal 46
אָסַף Niphal 141
גָּרַע Niphal 316
לָכַד Niphal 642
לָקַח Niphal 644
לָקַח Pual 644
לָקַח Hophal 644
תָּפַשׂ Niphal 1355
taken away, *see* have, violence
taken away, to be
אָסַף Niphal 141
גָּזַל Niphal 304
גָּרַע Niphal 316
לָקַח Niphal 644
לָקַח Pual 644
לָקַח Hophal 644
סוּר Kal 872
סוּר Hophal 872
רוּם (כ׳) Hiphil 1163
רוּם Hophal 1163
taken away, to have...
עֲדָה / עֲדָא } Ch. Aphel 902
taken, being
לֶכֶד 643
taken down, to be
יָרַד Hophal 561
צָעַן Kal 1077
taken *labour*, had
עָמֵל 960
taken off, to be
רוּם Hophal 1163
taken out, to be
נְפַק Ch. Aphel 828
נָצַל Niphal 835
taken out of the way, to be
קָפַץ Niphal 1113

taken, that was
שְׁבִי 1226
taken, thing
גָּרַע Kal 316
taken up, to be
לָקַח Pual 644
נְסַק Hophal 822
נָתַן Hophal 851
עָלָה Niphal 934
taker, *see* usury
taking
לָקַח Kal 644
מִקָּח 758
* taking
תָּפַשׂ Niphal 1355
taking, *see* heed
tale
הֶגֶה 357
tale
מִסְפָּר 738
מַתְכֹּנֶת 780
תֹּכֶן 1347
tale, *see* full
talebearer
נִרְגָּן 840
רָכִיל 1174
{ הָלַךְ Kal 362
{ רָכִיל 1174
talent
כִּכָּר 597
talents
כַּכְּרִין Ch. 597
tales, carry
רָכִיל 1174
talk
דָּבָר 325
פֶּה 1011
שִׂיחַ 1206
שָׂפָה 1213
talk, to
אָמַר Kal 105
דָּבַר Kal 319
דָּבַר Niphal 319
דָּבַר Piel 319
הָגָה Kal 356
סָפַר Piel 882
שִׂיחַ Kal 1206
talk with, to
שִׂיחַ Kal 1206
talkers
לָשׁוֹן 651
talking
מִלָּה 706
tall
קוֹמָה 1103
רוּם Kal 1163
taller
רוּם Kal 1163
tapestry, coverings of
מַרְבַדִּים 761

target
כִּידוֹן 596
צִנָּה 1075
tarried
נָוָה 800
tarry, to
אָחַר Piel 48
אָרַךְ Hiphil 156
דָּמַם Kal 346
חוּל / חִיל } Kal 406
חָכָה Piel 426
יָחַל Niphal 523
יָחַל Hiphil 523
יָשַׁב Kal 568
כּוּן Niphal 592
לוּן / לִין } Kal 635
מָהַהּ Hithpalpel 668
עָמַד Kal 955
קָוָה Piel 1096
שָׂבַר Piel 1196
tarry all night, to
לוּן / לִין } Kal 635
tarry long, to
אָרַךְ Hiphil 156
tarry longer, to
אָחַר Kal 48
יָחַר Kal 523
tarry that night, to
לוּן / לִין } Kal 635
taschith, *see* Al-taschith
task
דָּבָר 325
חֹק 456
taskmaster
נָגַשׂ Kal 794
{ שַׂר 1214
{ מַס 736
taste
חֵךְ 426
טַעַם 483
taste, to
טָעַם Kal 483
טְעֵם Ch. 484
taught
לִמּוּד 644
מְבוֹנִים 660
taught, to be
יָסַר Nithpael 545
לָמַד Pual 643
taunt
גְּדוּפָה 296
שְׁנִינָה 1315
taunting
מְלִיצָה 710

tax, to
עָרַךְ Hiphil 978
taxation
עֵרֶךְ 979
taxes, *see* raiser
teach, to
אָלַף[1] Piel 96
בִּין Hiphil 212
דָּבַר Piel 319
זָהַר Hiphil 382
יָדַע Hiphil 500
יְדַע Ch. Aphel 506
יָסַר Piel 545
יָרָה Hiphil 564
לָמַד Piel 643
שָׂכַל Hiphil 1207
teach, *see* go, keep cattle, wisdom
teach diligently, to
שָׁנַן Piel 1315
teacher
בִּין Hiphil 212
יָרָה Hiphil 564
לוּץ Hiphil 636
לָמַד Piel 643
teaching
יָרָה Hiphil 564
לָמַד Piel 643
tear, to
בָּקַע Piel 264
גָּזַל Kal 304
{ דּוּשׁ / דִּישׁ } Kal 338
טָרַף Kal 485
סָחַב Kal 874
פָּרַם Kal 1046
קָרַע Kal 1129
שָׁבַר[1] Kal 1232
tear in pieces, to
טָרַף Kal 485
פָּרַק Piel 1047
tears
דִּמְעָה 346
* tears, with
בָּכָה Kal 226
teat
דַּד 335
שַׁד 1236
Tebeth
טֵבֵת 474
teeth
פִּיפִיּוֹת 1018
teeth, *see* cheek, jaw
teeth, great
מַלְתָּעוֹת 730
teil tree
אֵלָה 78
Tekel
תְּקַל Ch. P'al 1356

Tel-abib
אָבִיב 10
tell, to
אָמַר Kal 105
אֲמַר Ch. P'al 133
גָּלָה Kal 307
דָּבַר Kal 319
דָּבַר Piel 319
יָדַע Hiphil 500
מָנָה Kal 732
נָגַד Hiphil 788
סָפַר Kal 882
סָפַר Piel 882
{ שָׁמֵעַ / שָׁמַע } Hiphil 1292
* tell, to
{ שׂוּם / שִׂים } Kal 1200
tell, *see* can, hear, tidings
tell out, to
סָפַר Kal 882
telling
מִסְפָּר 738
Teman
תֵּימָן 1346
temper, to
בָּלַל Kal 230
רָסַס Kal 1177
tempered together, to be
מָלַח[1] Pual 707
tempest
זֶרֶם 395
סוּפָה 872
סַעַר 880
סְעָרָה 880
רוּחַ 1160
שְׂעָרָה 1212
tempest, tossed with
סָעַר Kal 880
tempestuous, to be
סָעַר Kal 880
שָׂעַר Niphal 1212
temple
בַּיִת 214
הֵיכָל 361
הֵיכַל Ch. 361
temples
רַקָּה 1191
tempt, to
בָּחַן Kal 208
נָסָה Piel 820
temptation
מַסָּה 736
ten
עָשׂוֹר 997
עֶשֶׂר 997
{ עֲשָׂרָה / עֲשַׂר } Ch. 1000

ten, *see* threescore
ten strings, instruments of
עָשׂוֹר 997
ten thousand
רָבַב[1] Pual 1151
רְבָבָה 1151
{ רִבּוֹא / רִבּוֹ } 1153
* ten thousand times ten thousand
רִבּוֹ Ch. 1153
tender
רַךְ 1173
tender, *see* branch, grape, grass, herb, love, mercies
tender, to be
רָכַךְ Kal 1174
tender one
רַךְ 1173
tender plant
יוֹנֵק 521
tenderhearted
{ רַךְ 1173
לֵבָב .... 630 }
tenderness
רֹךְ 1173
tenon
יָד 489
tenor
פֶּה 1011
tent
אֹהֶל 27
מִשְׁכָּן 770
סֻכָּה 875
קֻבָּה 1083
tent, *see* pitch, remove, rest
tenth
מַעֲשֵׂר 747
עָשׂוֹר 997
עֲשִׂירִי 997
tenth deal
עִשָּׂרוֹן 1000
tenth, to give the
עָשַׂר Piel 1000
tenth part
מַעֲשֵׂר 747
עֲשִׂירִי 997
tenth, to take the
עָשַׂר Kal 1000
tents
מַחֲנֶה 688
tents, to abide in
חָנָה Kal 445
teraphim
תְּרָפִים 1359
termed, to be
אָמַר Niphal 105
terrace
מְסִלָּה 737

terrible
אִים 59
אֵימָה 59
אֵמְתָנִי Ch. 135
דְּחַל Ch. P'al 339
זַלְעָפָה 388
יָרֵא Niphal 559
עָרִיץ 978
terrible acts
יָרֵא Niphal 559
terrible things
ירא Niphal 559
terribleness
יָרֵא Niphal 559
מוֹרָא 674
תִּפְלֶצֶת 1355
terribly, *see* shake, shaken
terrified, to be
עָרַץ Kal 980
terrify, to
בָּעַת Piel 263
חָתַת Hiphil 472
terror
אֵימָה 59
בֶּהָלָה 188
בַּלָּהָה 229
חָגָּא 401
חִתָּה 471
חִתִּית 471
מָגוֹר 662
מְחִתָּה 691
מַעֲרָצָה 746
פַּחַד 1016
terrors
בִּעוּתִים 261
מוֹרָא 674
* terrors
מגר Kal 663
testified, to be
עוּד Hophal 906
testify, to
עוּד Hiphil 905
עָנָה[1] Kal 962
testimony
עֵדָה 903
עֵדוּת 904
תְּעוּדָה 1353
them
דִּי Ch. 339
מִן 731
עַל 932
than, *see* more, rather
than that
כִּי 596
thank, to
בָּרַךְ Piel 274
יְדָא Ch. Aphel 499
יָדָה Hiphil 499
thank offering
תּוֹדָה 1337
thankful, to be
יָדָה Hiphil 499
thanks
תּוֹדָה 1337
thanks, to give
יְדָא Ch. Aphel 499
יָדָה Hiphil 499
thanksgiving
הֻיְּדוֹת 360
יָדָה Hiphil 499
תּוֹדָה 1337
that
אֵל 78
אֲשֶׁר 180
דִּי Ch. 339
דִּכֵּן Ch. 341
הוּא 358
הִיא 360
הַלָּז 362
זֹאת 377
זֶה 380
זֹה 380
זוֹ 383
זוּ 383
כִּי 596
מַעַן 744
עֲבוּר 895
עַד 901
that †
דָּבָר 325
יַעַן 546
כֹּל Ch. 597
קֳבֵל / קְבֵל } Ch. 1084
that, *see* after, oh, oh that, side, way
that have
יֵשׁ 568
that if
הֵן Ch. 369
* that is
אָמַר Kal 105
that...it
הוּא 358
that manner, *see* after
that manner, on
כֹּה 586
that night, *see* tarry
that no
בִּלְתִּי 231
that not
אִם 100
בַּל 229
פֶּן 1021
that side, *see* on
that thing which
אֲשֶׁר 180
that wherein
אֲשֶׁר 180
that which
אֲשֶׁר 180
מָה Ch. 668
that *which he took violently away*
גְּזֵלָה 305
that *which was delivered*
פִּקָּדוֹן 1042
the
אִלֵּין Ch. 95
* thee
יָד 489
לְוָת Ch. 636
עַיִן 919
פָּנִים 1023
thee, as for
אַנְתְּ Ch. 141
theft
גְּנֵבָה 313
their
הֵם 367
הֵנָּה 369
theirs, *see* any
them
אֵלֶּה 79
אִנִּין / אִנּוּן } Ch. 136
הֵם 367
הֵמָּה 367
הִמּוֹ / הִמּוֹן } Ch. 368
* them
עַיִן 919
פָּנִים 1023
* them, by
יָד 489
* them, for
לָהֵן 634
them, into
הֵנָּה 369
them of
בֵּן 232
them, with
הֵן 369
themselves
הֵם 367
נֶפֶשׁ 829
* themselves
יָד 489
לֵב 626
פָּנִים 1023
themselves, *see* grow
then
אֱדַיִן Ch. 17
אוֹ 29
אָז 34
אֲזַי 34

* think, to
רָאָה Kal … 1133
* think,† to
עַיִן … 919
think, *see* best, scorn
think evil, to
זָמַם Kal … 388
* think good,† to
שְׁפַר Ch. P'al … 1322
think on, to
זָכַר Kal … 385
* thinkest
עַיִן … 919
* thinking †
עַיִן … 919
third
{ שְׁלוֹשׁ, שְׁלוֹשָׁה } … 1264
שְׁלִישִׁי … 1275
שִׁלֵּשִׁים … 1279
תְּלִיתַי Ch. … 1348
תְּלָת Ch. … 1348
תְּלַת Ch. … 1348
תַּלְתִּי Ch. … 1348
third part
שְׁלִישִׁי … 1275
third rank
שְׁלִישִׁי … 1275
third time
שְׁלִישִׁי … 1275
third time, to do the
שָׁלַשׁ Piel … 1279
thirst
צָמָא … 1074
צָמֵא … 1074
צִמְאָה … 1074
צָמָה … 1074
thirst, to
צָמֵא Kal … 1074
thirst, to suffer
צָמֵא Kal … 1074
thirsteth, that
צָמֵא … 1074
thirsty
עָיֵף … 925
צָמָא … 1074
צָמֵא … 1074
thirsty, to be
צָמֵא Kal … 1074
thirsty land
צִמָּאוֹן … 1074
thirteen
{ שְׁלוֹשׁ, שְׁלוֹשָׁה } … 1264
עָשָׂר … 998
thirteen, *see* threescore

thirteenth
{ שְׁלוֹשׁ, שְׁלוֹשָׁה } … 1264
עָשָׂר … 998
thirtieth
שְׁלוֹשִׁים … 1267
thirty
שְׁלוֹשִׁים … 1267
תְּלָתִין Ch. … 1348
this
אֵלֶּה … 79
גֵּה … 298
דָּא Ch. … 317
דָּךְ & דִּךְ Ch. … 340
דִּכֵּן Ch. … 341
דֵּן Ch. … 346
הוּא … 358
הִיא … 360
הִיא Ch. … 360
הַלָּז … 362
הַלָּזֶה … 362
הַלֵּזוּ … 362
הֵמָּה … 367
זֹאת … 377
זֶה … 380
זֹה … 380
זוֹ … 383
זוּ … 383
כֹּה … 586
כֵּן … 604
this, *see* after, cause, means, once, side, time, way
this hath
זֶה … 380
this man
זֶה … 380
this manner
כְּנֵמָא Ch. … 605
this manner, *see* after
this manner, on
כֹּה … 586
this matter
דֵּן Ch. … 346
כָּכָה … 597
this night, *see* lodge
this side, *see* on
this side, on
הֵנָּה … 369
כֹּה … 586
this side...on that, on
זֶה … 380
this sort, in
כְּנֵמָא Ch. … 605
this thing
זֹאת … 377
* this way...or that way
הֵנָּה … 369
this wise, on
כֹּה … 586

thistle
דַּרְדַּר … 348
חוֹחַ … 406
thither
הֲלֹם … 367
שָׁם … 1279
thitherward
הֵנָּה … 369
thorn
אָטָד … 54
חֵדֶק … 403
חוֹחַ … 406
נַעֲצוּץ … 823
סִיר … 875
צֵן … 1075
קוֹץ … 1104
שַׁיִת … 1257
thorn hedge
מְסוּכָה … 736
thorns
סַלּוֹנִים … 877
צְנִינִים … 1076
קִמָּשׁוֹן … 1111
thoroughly
יָטַב Hiphil … 524
רָפָא Piel … 1187
those
אֵל … 77
אֵלֶּה … 79
אִלֵּךְ Ch. … 95
אֱנוֹשׁ … 136
הוּא … 358
הֵם … 367
{ הִמּוֹ, הִמּוֹן } Ch. … 368
הֵנָּה … 369
thou
אַנְתְּ Ch. … 141
אַתְּ … 182
אַתָּה … 183
* thou
יָד … 489
thou do
יֵשׁ … 568
thou wilt
יֵשׁ … 568
though
אִם … 100
אֲשֶׁר … 180
גַּם … 311
הֵן … 369
כִּי … 596
לֹא … 625
לוּ … 634
though †
כֹּל Ch. … 597
{ קְבֵל, קֳבֵל } Ch. … 1084

thought
דָּבָר ... 325
הַרְהֹר Ch. ... 375
זִמָּה ... 388
חֵקֶק ... 458
מַדַּע / מַדָּע ... 667
מְזִמָּה ... 684
עַשְׁתּוּת ... 1005
רֵעַ ... 1183
רַעְיוֹן Ch. ... 1185
שֵׂחַ ... 1204

thought, *see* inward

* thought, I
קְדָם ... 1089

thought, to take
דָּאַג Kal ... 318

thoughts
מוֹרָשׁ ... 674
מַחֲשֶׁבֶת ... 690
סְעִפִּים ... 880
עֶשְׁתֹּנֹת ... 1005
שְׂעִפִּים ... 1212
שַׂרְעַפִּים ... 1218

thousand
אֶלֶף ... 96
אֶלֶף / אֲלַף Ch. ... 96

thousand, *see* eighteen, forty, six-score, ten thousand, threescore, twenty

thousands, to bring forth
אָלַף [2] Hiphil ... 96

thread
חוּט ... 406
פָּתִיל ... 1055

thread, *see* scarlet

three
שָׁלוֹשׁ / שְׁלוֹשָׁה ... 1264
שְׁלוֹשִׁים (כ׳) ... 1267
שְׁלִישִׁי (כ׳) ... 1275
שָׁלַשׁ Pual ... 1279
תְּלָת Ch. ... 1348

three days
שִׁלְשׁוֹם ... 1279

three days, to stay
שָׁלַשׁ Piel ... 1279

three parts, to divide into
שָׁלַשׁ Piel ... 1279

three years old
שְׁלִישִׁי ... 1275
שָׁלַשׁ Pual ... 1279

threefold
שָׁלַשׁ Pual ... 1279

threescore
שִׁשִּׁים ... 1331
שִׁתִּין Ch. ... 1333

threescore *and fif*teen
שִׁבְעִים ... 1231

threescore *and four*teen
שִׁבְעִים ... 1231

threescore *and seven*teen
שִׁבְעִים ... 1231

threescore *and six*teen
שִׁבְעִים ... 1231

threescore and ten
שִׁבְעִים ... 1231

threescore *and thir*teen
שִׁבְעִים ... 1231

* threescore and twelve †
שִׁבְעִים ... 1231

threescore thousand †
רִבּוֹ / רִבּוֹא ... 1153

thresh, to
דּוּשׁ / דּוֹשׁ ... 338
דָּרַךְ Hiphil ... 349
חָבַט Kal ... 398

thresh,† to
אָדַשׁ Kal ... 25

threshed, to be
דּוּשׁ / דּוֹשׁ Hophal ... 338

threshing
דַּיִשׁ ... 340
מְדֻשָׁה ... 667

threshing floor
גֹּרֶן ... 316

threshing floors
אִדְּרִים Ch. ... 24

threshing instrument
חָרוּץ ... 463
מוֹרַג ... 674

threshing place
גֹּרֶן ... 316

threshold
מִפְתָּן ... 748
סַף ... 880

thresholds
אֲסֻפִּים ... 143

thrice †
פַּעַם ... 1038
שָׁלוֹשׁ / שְׁלוֹשָׁה ... 1264

throat
גָּרוֹן ... 315
לֹעַ ... 644

throne
כִּסֵּא ... 606
כִּסֵּה ... 608
כָּרְסֵא Ch. ... 618

through
אֶל ... 78
בְּמוֹ ... 232
בְּעַד ... 261
דֶּרֶךְ ... 349
יָד ... 489
יָרָה Kal ... 564
מִן ... 731
עַל ... 932
פָּנִים ... 1023
קֶרֶב ... 1125
תָּוֶךְ ... 1338

through, *see* break, bring, dig, drop, go, march, pass, pierce, run, smite, stricken, strike, thrust

throughly
יָטַב Hiphil ... 524
עָלַל Poel ... 942
עָשָׂה Kal ... 981
רָבָה Hiphil ... 1151
רִיב Kal ... 1171
שָׁקַל Kal ... 1324

* throughly
שְׂרֵפָה ... 1218

throughly, *see* wash away

throughout
עַל ... 932

throughout
פָּנִים ... 1023

throughout, *see* number

throw, to
רָמָה Kal ... 1175
שָׁלַךְ Hiphil ... 1275

throw down, to
הָרַס Kal ... 376
נָפַל Hiphil ... 825
נָתַץ Kal ... 863
נָתַץ Piel ... 863
שָׁמַט Kal ... 1286

throw *stones*, to
סָקַל Piel ... 884

* throwing
יָד ... 489

thrown, to be
שָׁלַךְ Hophal ... 1275

thrown down, to be
הָרַס Niphal ... 376
נָתַץ Kal ... 863
נָתַץ Niphal ... 863

thrust, to
דָּחָה Kal ... 339
דָּחַק Kal ... 339
הָדַף Kal ... 357
נָתַן Kal ... 851
תָּקַע Kal ... 1356

thrust away, to
הָדַף Kal ... 357
נָדַח Hiphil ... 796

thrust away, to be
נָדַד Hophal ... 796

בַּלָּהָה 229
בְּעָתָה 263
זְוָעָה 384
זַעֲוָה 390
טֹרַח 485
מְהוּמָה 668
עָמָל 960
עֳנִי 966
צָר & צַר 1080
צָרָה 1081
רֹגֶז 1155
רַע 1177
תְּלָאָה 1347

trouble, to
אֲנַס Ch. P'al 140
בִּהֵל / בָּהַל } Piel 188
בִּהֵל / בָּהַל } Hiphil 188
בְּהַל Ch. Pual 188
(ב׳) בָּלַהּ Piel 229
בָּעַת Piel 263
דָּלַח 342
הָמַם Kal 368
חָמַר Kal 441
עָכַר Kal 932

* trouble,† in
יוֹם 508
קָשֶׁה 1131

trouble, to be in
צָרַר Kal 1083

trouble, to make
רָשַׁע Hiphil 1192

troubled
גָּרַשׁ Niphal 316
רָפַשׂ Niphal 1189

troubled, to be
בָּהֵל / בָּהַל } Niphal 188
בְּהַל Ch. Ithp'al 188
גָּעַשׁ Pual 314
הָמָה Kal 368
חָמַר Poalal 441
עָוָה Niphal 906
עָכַר Niphal 932
עָנָה²Kal 964
פָּעַם Niphal 1038
פָּעַם Hithpael 1038
קָצַר Kal 1116
רָגַז Kal 1155
רָעַם Kal 1186

troubled, to be sore
סָעַר Niphal 880

troubler
עָכַר Kal 932

troubling
רֹגֶז 1155

* troublous
צוֹק 1069

trough
רַהַט 1159
שֹׁקֶת 1326

trough, *see* kneading

true
אֱמֶת 134
יַצִּיב Ch. 556
כֵּנִים 605
צְדָא Ch. 1061

true, it is
אָמְנָם 104

truly
אוּלָם 30
אַךְ 70
אָכֵן 75
אֱמֻנָה / אֱמוּנָה } 102
אָמְנָם 104
אֱמֶת 134
כִּי 596
עָשַׁר Piel 1000

trumpet
חֲצֹצְרָה 455
יוֹבֵל 507
שׁוֹפָר 1247
תָּקוֹעַ 1356

trumpeter
חֲצֹצֵר Piel 455
חֲצֹצְרָה 455
חָצַר Piel 455

trumpets, *see* blowing

trust
חָסוּת 449
מִבְטָח 660
מַחְסֶה 689

trust, to
אָמַן Hiphil 103
בָּטַח Kal 210
גָּלַל Kal 310
חוּל / חִיל } Polel 406
חָסָה Kal 449
יָחַל Piel 523
רְחַץ Ch. Hithp'il 1170

trust, to make to
בָּטַח Hiphil 210

trust, to put
אָמַן Hiphil 103
בָּטַח Kal 210
חָסָה Kal 449

trusty, (to be)
אָמַן Niphal 103

truth
אֵמוּן 102
אֱמוּנָה / אֱמֻנָה } 102
אָמֵן 104
אֹמֶן 104
אֱמֶת 134
יְצַב Ch. Pael 555
יַצִּיב Ch. 556
קְשׁוֹט Ch. 1132
קֹשֶׁט 1132
000 000

truth, of a
אָמְנָם 104

truth,† of a
אִם 100
לֹא 625

try, to
בָּחַן Kal 208
חָקַר Kal 458
נָסָה Piel 820
צָרַף Kal 1082

tumble, to
הָפַךְ Hithpael 370

tumult
הָמוֹן 368
הֲמֻלָּה 368
מְהוּמָה 668
שָׁאוֹן 1220
שַׁאֲנָן 1222

tumult, to make a
הָמָה Kal 368

tumultuous
הָמָה Kal 368

* tumultuous
שָׁאוֹן 1220

turn
תּוֹר 1342

turn, to
הָפַךְ Kal 370
נָטָה Kal 810
נָטָה Hiphil 810
נָתַן Kal 851
סָבַב Kal 865
סָבַב Niphal 865
סָבַב Hiphil 865
סוּר Kal 872
פָּנָה Kal 1021
פָּנָה Hiphil 1021
שׂוּם / שִׂים } Kal 1200
שָׂטָה Kal 1205
שׁוּב Kal 1238
שָׁעָה Kal 1315

* turn, to
עָוָה Piel 906

turn, *see* foolishness, right

turn about, to
סָבַב Kal 865
סָבַב Niphal 865

turn again, to
הָפַךְ Kal 370
שׁוּב Kal 1238
turn aside, to
לָפַת Niphal 644
נָטָה Kal 810
נָטָה Hiphil 810
סָבַב Kal 865
סָבַב Niphal 865
סוּר Kal 872
סוּר Polel 872
עָטָה Kal 918
פָּנָה Kal 1021
שׁוּט Kal 1200
turn aside, that
סֵטִים 875
turn away
שׁוֹבָב 1245
turn away, to
נָטָה Hiphil 810
סָבַב Hiphil 865
סוּר Hiphil 872
סָרָה 884
עָבַר Hiphil 895
פָּנָה Kal 1021
שׁוּב Kal 1238
שׁוּב Polel 1238
שׁוּב Hiphil 1238
turn back, to
הָפַךְ Kal 370
סָבַב Hiphil 865
סוּג[1] Niphal 870
פָּנָה Hophal 1021
שׂוּג[1] Niphal 1200
שׁוּב Kal 1238
שׁוּב Polel 1238
שׁוּב Hiphil 1238
turn back again, to
שׁוּב Kal 1238
turn backward, to
שׁוּב Kal 1238
turn, to cause to
שׁוּב Hiphil 1238
turn every way, to
הָפַךְ Hithpael 370
turn face, to
פָּנָה Kal 1021
turn far away, to
זָנַח Hiphil 390
turn from, to
שׁוּב Kal 1238
turn in, to
סוּר Kal 872
turn, to make to
שׁוּב Hiphil 1238
turn over, to
יָרַט Kal 565
turn self, to
לָפַת Niphal 644
פָּנָה Kal 1021
פָּנָה Hiphil 1021
turn self about to
סָבַב Niphal 865
turn self again, to
שׁוּב Polel 1238
turn to, *see* left, right hand, righteousness
turn upside down, to
עָוַת Piel 914
turn, to violently
צָנַף Kal 1076
turned into joy
דּוּץ Kal 337
turned הָפַךְ Kal 370
הָפַךְ Niphal 370
הָפַךְ Hophal 370
הָפַךְ Hithpael 370
נָטָה Kal 810
סָבַב Niphal 865
סוּג[1] Niphal 870
פָּנָה Kal 1021
שׁוּב Kal 1238
turned about, to be
סָבַב Hophal 865
turned aside, to be
הָפַךְ Niphal 370
turned away, to be
נָסַג Hophal 819
סוּג[1] Niphal 870
שׁוּב Kal 1238
turned back, to be
פָּנָה Hiphil 1021
שׁוּב Kal 1238
turned to the contrary, to be
הָפַךְ Niphal 370
turned up, to be
הָפַךְ Niphal 370
turning
מִקְצוֹעַ 759
סָבַב Hophal 865
שׁוּב Kal 1238
turning away
מְשׁוּבָה 768
שׁוּב Polel 1238
turning of things upside down
הָפַךְ Kal 370
turtle
תּוֹר 1342
turtledove
תּוֹר 1342
twain
שְׁנַיִם 1311
twelfth
{ שְׁנַיִם 1311
{ עָשָׂר 998
twelve
{ שְׁנַיִם 1311
{ עָשָׂר 998
{ תְּרֵין Ch. 1358
{ עֲשַׂר Ch. 1000
twelve, *see* threescore
twentieth
עֶשְׂרִים 1001
twenty
עֶשְׂרִים 1001
עֶשְׂרִין Ch. 1003
twenty thousand
{ שְׁנַיִם 1311
{ רִבּוֹת 1153
twenty thousand
{ רִבּוֹ
{ רִבּוֹא } 1153
רִבּוֹת 1153
twice
פַּעַם 1038
שְׁנַיִם 1311
twice as much
מִשְׁנֶה 773
twig, young
יוֹנֶקֶת 521
יְנִיקוֹת 542
twilight
נֶשֶׁף 849
עֲלָטָה 941
twined
שָׁזַר Hophal 1249
twins
תְּאוֹמִים 1334
twins, to bear
תָּאַם Hiphil 1334
two
שְׁנַיִם 1311
תְּרֵין Ch. 1358
two, *see* days, times
two *asses*
צֶמֶד 1074
* two *damsels*
רַחֲמָה 1169
two leaved, *see* gate
two parts
{ חֵצִי
{ חֲצִי } 454
* twoedged
פֶּה 1011
פִּיפִיּוֹת 1018

*un*accustomed
לָמַד Pual 643
unadvisedly, *see* speak
unawares
{ בְּלִי 229
{ דַּעַת 347
* *un*awares
יָדַע Kal 500
לֵב 626
לֵבָב 630

unawares, at
שְׁנָגָה 1235

uncircumcised
עָרֵל 979

uncircumcised †
עָרְלָה 979

uncircumcised, to count
עָרֵל Kal 979

uncircumcised person
עָרֵל 979

uncle
דּוֹד 336

unclean
טָמֵא 482
טֻמְאָה 483
עֶרְוָה 977
קָדֵשׁ 1091

unclean, to be
טָמֵא Kal 481
טָמֵא Hithpael 481

unclean, to be made
טָמֵא Kal 481

unclean, to make selves
טָמֵא Hithpael 481

unclean, to pronounce
טָמֵא Piel 481

unclean thing
נִדָּה 796

unclean with filthiness
נִדָּה 796

uncleanness
טֻמְאָה 483
נִדָּה 796
עֶרְוָה 977

uncleanness that chanceth
קָרֶה 1127

uncle's wife
דּוֹדָה 336

uncover
חָשַׂף Kal 468

uncover, to
גָּלָה Piel 307
עָרָה Piel 977
עָרָה Hiphil 977
פָּרַע Kal 1046

uncover self, to
גָּלָה Niphal 307

uncovered, *see* foreskin

uncovered, to be
גָּלָה Hithpael 307

undefiled
תָּם 1348
תָּמִים 1350

under
אֶל 78
מַטָּה 691
תְּחוֹת Ch. 1344
תַּחַת 1345
תַּחַת Ch. 1345

* under
יָד 489

under, *see* brought, foot, keep, persecution, tread, trodden

under foot, *see* trample, trodden

underneath
מַטָּה 691

undersetter
כָּתֵף 623

understand, to
בִּין Kal 212
בִּין Hiphil 212
בִּין Hithpolel 212
יָדַע Kal 500
שָׂכַל Hiphil 1206
שְׁמַע / שָׁמַע } Kal 1292

understand, to cause to
בִּין Kal 212
בִּין Hiphil 212

understand, to make to
בִּין Kal 212
בִּין Hiphil 212
שָׂכַל Hiphil 1206

understanding
בִּין Niphal 212
בִּין Hiphil 212
בִּינָה (& Ch. 214) 213
טַעַם 483
לֵב 626
לֵבָב 630
מַנְדַּע 732
שָׂכַל Hiphil 1206
שֶׂכֶל / שֵׂכֶל } 1207
שָׂכְלְתָנוּ Ch. 1207
תָּבוּן 1335
תְּבוּנָה 1335
תּוּבְנָה 1337

understanding, to get
בִּין Hithpolel 212

understanding, to give
בִּין Kal 212
בִּין Hiphil 212

understanding, to have
בִּין Niphal 212
בִּין Hiphil 212
שָׂכַל Hiphil 1206

understanding, to make of quick
רוּחַ Hiphil 1160

understanding, man of
בִּין Niphal 212

undertake, to
עָרַב[1] Kal 975
קָבַל Piel 1083

undo, to
נָתַר Hiphil 864

undone, to be
אָבַד Kal 8
דָּמָה[2] Niphal 345

undone, *see* leave

undressed, *see* vine

*un*equal, to be
תָּכַן Niphal 1347

unfaithful man
בָּגַד Kal 184

unfaithfully, to deal
בָּגַד Kal 184

ungird, to
פָּתַח Piel 1052

ungodly
בְּלִיַּעַל 230
עֲוִיל 906
רָשָׁע 1192

*un*godly
חָסִיד 449

ungodly men
בְּלִיַּעַל 230

unholy
חֹל 428

unicorn
רְאֵם 1141

unite, to
יָחַד Piel 522

united, to be
יָחַד Kal 522

unjust
אָוֶן 30
עַוָּל 906
עָוֶל / עָוֶל } 906

unjust †
עַוְלָה 907

unjust gain
תַּרְבִּית 1357

unjustly
עָוֶל / עָוֶל } 906

unjustly, to deal
עָוַל Piel 906

unleavened
מַצָּה 752

(unmindful שִׁיָה ...1253)

unless
אֻלַי / אוּלַי } 30
לוּלֵא 635
לוּלֵי 635

unless †
אִם 100

unoccupied, to be
חָדַל Kal 402

*un*profitable
סָכַן[1] Kal 876

unpunished, to be
נָקָה Niphal 838

unpunished, to leave
נָקָה Piel ... 838

unrighteous
אָוֶן ... 30
חָמָס ... 440
עָוֵל Piel ... 906
עַוָּל ... 906

unrighteously
עָוֶל }
עֶוֶל } ... 906

unrighteousness
עָוֶל }
עֶוֶל } ... 906
עַוְלָה ... 907
עוֹלָה ... 907

*un*righteousness
צֶדֶק ... 1063

unripe grape
בֹּסֶר ... 261

*un*satiable
שָׂבְעָה ... 1196

unsavoury
תָּפֵל ... 1355

unsavoury, to shew self
פָּתַל Hithpael ... 1055

unsearchable
{ אַיִן ... 59
{ חֵקֶר ... 458

unshod, being
יָחֵף ... 523

unstable
פַּחַז ... 1017

unstopped, to be
פָּתַח Niphal ... 1052

untempered
תָּפֵל ... 1355

until
דִּי Ch. ... 339
עַד ... 901
עַד Ch. ... 902

until †
אִם ... 100
אֲשֶׁר ... 180
כִּי ... 596

untimely, *see* birth

unto
אֶל ... 78
אֵצֶל ... 148
עַד Ch. ... 902
עַל Ch. ... 933
עִם ... 955
עִמָּד ... 958
פָּנִים ... 1023

* unto
תַּחַת ... 1345

unto, *see* attain, bondage, come to pass, cry, desolation, happen, hearken, like, provoke, reach

unwalled
פְּרָזִי ... 1044

unwalled town
פְּרָזוֹת ... 1044

unwalled villages
פְּרָזוֹת ... 1044

*un*wise
חָכָם ... 426

unwittingly
שְׁגָגָה ... 1235

*un*wittingly
דַּעַת ... 347

up
בַּעַד ... 261
מַעַל ... 743
קוּם Kal ... 1099

up, *see* arise, ascend, banners, bear, bind, borne, bound, break, breaking, bring, bringer, broken, brought, burn, burned, carry, cast, casting, cheer, climb, close, closed, come, cut, deliver, devour, draw, dried, drink, dry, early, eat, ensign, fence, fetch, gather, gathered, get, gird, give, given, giving, go, going, grow, grown, hang, heap, heaved, hedge, help, hold, laid, lay, lick, lift, lift self, lifted, lifter, lifting, look, made, make, mount, mounting, nourish, offer, order, pluck, plucked, pulled, put, raise, raised, reach, rear, reared, rip, rise, risen, rising, root, rooted, rouse, set, sew, shoot, shut, sit, snuff, sought, spring, springeth, stand, stayed, stir, store, suck, sup, swallow, swallowed, take, taken, train, turned, vomit, wake, walled, wrap, wrapped

up, to be
קוּם Kal ... 1099

up again, *see* put

up and down, *see* go, make go, tossed, walk, wander

up, as soon as is
זָרַח Kal ... 395

up in store, *see* laid

up on, *see* high

upbraid, to
חָרַף Piel ... 465

Upharsin
פְּרַס Ch. P'al ... 1046

uphold, to
סָמַךְ Kal ... 879
קוּם Hiphil ... 1099
תָּמַךְ Kal ... 1350

upholden, to be
סָעַד Kal ... 880

upon
אֶל ... 78
בַּעַד ... 261
לְמוֹ ... 644
מִן Ch. ... 732
מַעַל ... 743
עַל ... 932
עַל Ch. ... 933
עִמָּד ... 958
פָּנִים ... 1023

upon †
פָּנִים ... 1023

upon, *see* blow, burn, burn incense, call, come, compassion, fall, get hold, grew, hold, light, look, mercy, pity, rained, run, seize, spread, stamp, take, tread, wait, waiting

upper
עִלִּי ... 941
עֶלְיוֹן ... 942

upper, *see* chamber, doorpost, lintel, lip, millstone

uppermost
עֶלְיוֹן ... 942

upright
יָשָׁר ... 578
יֹשֶׁר ... 579
מֵישָׁרִים ... 698
מִקְשָׁה ... 760
עֹמֶד ... 959
קוֹמְמִיּוּת ... 1104
תָּם ... 1348
תֹּם ... 1348
תָּמִים ... 1350

upright, *see* stand

upright, to be
יָשַׁר Kal ... 578
תָּמַם Kal ... 1351

upright, most
יָשָׁר ... 578

upright, to shew self
תָּמַם Hithpael ... 1351

uprightly
יָשַׁר Piel ... 578
יָשָׁר ... 578
מֵישָׁרִים ... 698
תֹּם ... 1348
תָּמִים ... 1350

uprightness
יָשָׁר ... 578
יֹשֶׁר ... 579
יִשְׁרָה ... 579
מִישׁוֹר ... 698
מֵישָׁרִים ... 698
נְכֹחַ ... 817
תֹּם ... 1348

uprising
קוּם Kal ... 1099

uproar, being in an
הָמָה Kal ... 368

upside
פָּנִים ... 1023

upside down †
פָּנִים ... 1023

upside down, *see* turn, turning

upward
גָּבַהּ Hiphil 287
מַעַל 743
מָרוֹם 763

urge, to
אָלַץ Piel............. 99
פָּצַר Kal.............1039
פָּרַץ Kal.............1047

urgent, to be
חָזַק Kal............. 411
חָצַף Ch. Aphel....... 455

Urim
אוּר 33

us
אֲנַחְנוּ 140

* us
יָד 489
עַיִן 919

use
מְלָאכָה 705
עֲבוֹדָה 894

use, to
לָקַח Kal............. 644

* use, to
הָיָה Kal............. 360

use, *see* aright, enchantment, many, proverb, right hand, service, witchcraft

use (a proverb), to
מָשַׁל ²Kal 772

use as, *see* friend

use *divination*, to
קָסַם Kal.............1113

use *intreaties*, to
דָּבַר Piel............. 319

use *oppression*, to
עָשַׁק Kal.............1004

use *speech*, to
אָמַר Kal............. 105

used
לִמּוּד 644

used, to be
עָשָׂה Niphal 981

used to, *see* push

usest
מִשְׁפָּט 776

usurer
נָשָׁה ²Kal 847

usury
מַשָּׁא 767
נֶשֶׁךְ 848

usury, giver of
נָשָׁא Kal. 846

usury, to lend on
נָשָׁה ²Kal............ 847

usury, to lend upon
נָשַׁךְ Hiphil 848

usury, to be lent upon
נָשַׁךְ Kal............. 848

usury, taker of
נָשָׁה ²Kal............ 847

utmost
אַחֲרוֹן 53
קָצֶה 1114

* utmost
קָצַץ Kal.............1116

utmost, *see* bound

utmost border
קֵץ 1113

utmost part
קָצֶה 1114

utter
חִיצוֹן 425

utter, *see* destruction, end

utter, to
אָלַף ¹Piel 96
אָמַר Kal............. 105
דָּבַר Kal............. 319
דָּבַר Piel............. 319
הָגָה ¹Kal............. 356
הָגָה ¹Poal............ 356
יָצָא Hiphil 548
מָלַל Piel............. 729
מָשַׁל ²Kal 772
נָבַע Hiphil 787
נָגַד Hiphil 788
נָתַן Kal............. 851
עָנָה ¹Kal 962
פּוּחַ Hiphil 1014
פָּצָה Kal.............1039

utter abundantly, to
נָבַע Hiphil 787

utter destruction
חֵרֶם 464

uttered, to be
נָתַן Niphal 851

uttered out of
מִבְטָא 660

uttered, that which...
מִבְטָא 660

utterly
חָרַם Hiphil 464
כָּלִיל 603
מְאֹד 652

* utterly
חָרֵב 461
מַשְׁחִית 769
קָרְחָה 1128

utterly, is sometimes the translation of an infinitive used intensively.

utterly, *see* cast down, consume, destroy, destroyed, slay, take

utterly, to be
סוּף Kal............. 871

uttermost
אַחֲרוֹן 53
אַחֲרִית 54
קִיצוֹן 1108
קָצֶה 1114

uttermost part
אֶפֶס 147
כָּנָף 605
קָצָה 1114
קָצֶה 1114
קְצָוָה 1115

vagabond
נוּד Kal............. 799

vagabond, to be
נוּעַ Kal............. 802

vail
מִטְפַּחַת 693
מַסְוֶה 736
מַסֵּכָה 737
פָּרֹכֶת 1046
צָעִיף 1076
רְדִיד 1158

vain
אָוֶן 30
הֶבֶל 356
נָבַב Kal............. 783
רֵיק } רֵק } 1172
שָׁוְא 1238
שֶׁקֶר 1325
תֹּהוּ 1336

* vain
רוּחַ 1160

vain, *see* shew

vain, to be
הָבַל Kal............. 356

vain, to become
הָבַל Kal............. 356

vain fellows
רֵיק } רֵק } 1172

vain, in
חִנָּם 446
רִיק 1172
רֵיקָם 1172

vain, to be in
כָּזַב Niphal 594

vain, to make
הָבַל Hiphil 356

vain men
רֵיק } רֵק } 1172

vain thing
רִיק 1172
שֶׁקֶר 1325

* vain *words*
שָׂפָה 1213

vale
עֵמֶק 961
שְׁפֵלָה 1322

valiant
אַבִּיר 10
חַיִל 423
כַּבִּיר 584

valiant †
בֵּן 232
חַיִל 423

valiant, to be
גָּבַר Kal 291

valiant man
גִּבּוֹר 289

valiant one
אֶרְאֵל 149

valiantly
חַיִל 423

valiantly, to behave selves
חָזַק Hithpael 411

valley
בִּקְעָה 265
גַּיְא 306
נַחַל 805
עֵמֶק 961
שְׁפֵלָה 1322

valour
חַיִל 423

value, to
עָרַךְ Hiphil 978

valued, to be
סָלָה Pual 877

* valuest
עֵרֶךְ 979

vanish, to
יָלַךְ Kal 531
צָמַת Niphal 1075

vanish away, to
מָלַח [2] Niphal 707

vanished, to be
סָרַח Niphal 884

vanity
אָוֶן 30
הֲבֵל 356
הֶבֶל 356
רִיק 1172
שַׁו (כ׳) 1238
שָׁוְא 1238
תֹּהוּ 1336

vapour
אֵד 14
נָשִׂיא 846
קִיטוֹר 1107

* vapour
עָלָה Kal 934

vaunt selves, to
פָּאַר Hithpael 1009

vehement
חֲרִישִׁי 464

veil
רְדִיד 1158

vein
מוֹצָא 673

vengeance
נָקָם 839
נְקָמָה 839

vengeance, to take
נָקַם Kal 839
נָקַם Niphal 839

vengeance to be taken
נָקַם Hophal 839

venison
צַיִד 1071
צֵידָה (כ׳) 1071

venom
רֹאשׁ 1145

vent, to have
פָּתַח Niphal 1052

venture, at a
תֹּם 1348

verified, to be
אָמַן Niphal 103

verily
אֲבָל 11
אַךְ 70
אָכֵן 75
אֱמוּנָה / אֱמֻנָה 102
אָמַר Kal 105
קָנָה [1] Kal 1112

verily †
אִם 100
לֹא 625

verity
אֱמֶת 134

vermilion
שָׁשַׁר 1331

very
גָּדוֹל 293
דַּי 339
זֶה 380
מְאֹד 652
מִזְעָר 685
מַעַל 743
מַעַל 743
קָט 1104
שַׂגִּיא Ch. 1197

* very
גָּדוֹל 293
מְעַט 741
עֶצֶם 972
פֶּתַע 1055
קוּט [1] Kal 1096
קִיר 1108

very, *see* aged man, dark, early, fair, far off, frowardness, fruitful, great things, high, little, lovely, low, much, old, rainy, small, wickedness

very *age*
רֹב 1150

very deed
כּוּן Niphal 592

very deed, in
אוּלָם 30
אָמְנָם 104

* very great
אֱלֹהִים 79

very much †
מְאֹד 652

very small
דָּקַק Hiphil 348

very sore
מְאֹד 652

very suddenly
מוּת Kal 675

* very *treacherously*
בָּגַד 185

vessel
מָאן Ch. 658
נֵבֶל / נֶבֶל 786

vessels
כְּלִי 600

vestment
לְבוּשׁ 632
מַלְבּוּשׁ 706

vestry
מֶלְתָּחָה 730

vesture
בֶּגֶד 185
כְּסוּת 608
לְבוּשׁ 632

vex
רַע 1177

vex, to
בָּהַל / בָּהַל Piel 188
דָּחַק Kal 339
הָמַם Kal 368
זוּעַ Pilpel 384
יָגָה [1] Hiphil 488
יָנָה Hiphil 541
כָּעַס Hiphil 612
מָרַר Hiphil 766
עָצַב Piel 970
צָרַר Kal 1083
צָרַר Hiphil 1083
קוּץ [3] Hiphil 1104
רָעַע Hiphil 1186
רָעַץ Kal 1187
רָשַׁע Hiphil 1192

vex, † to
עָשָׂה Kal 981

vexation (מוצק..673)
זְוָעָה 384
מְהוּמָה 668
רְעוּת 1185

רַעְיוֹן 1185
שֶׁבֶר } שֶׁבֶר 1234
vexed
מְהוּמָה 668
vexed, to be
בָּהַל } בָּהֵל Niphal 188
יָצַר² Kal 557
מָרַר Kal 766
קָצַר Kal 1116
vial
פַּךְ 1018
victory
נֵצַח } נֶצַח 835
תְּשׁוּעָה 1359
victory, to get
יָשַׁע Hiphil 576
victual
מַאֲכָל 658
מָזוֹן 684
victuals
אֹכֶל 75
אֲרֻחָה 155
לֶחֶם 638
מִחְיָה 687
צַיִד 1071
צֵידָה 1071
שֶׁבֶר 1234
victuals, to provide
כּוּל Pilpel 592
view, to
בִּין Kal 212
רָאָה Kal 1133
רָגַל Piel 1155
שָׂבַר Kal 1196
* view, to
נֶגֶד 790
שָׁבַר¹ Kal 1232
vile
זָלַל Kal 388
נְבָלָה 787
נִמְבְזָה 819
שֹׁעָר 1318
vile, to be
קָלַל Kal 1109
vile, to make
נָבֵל Piel 786
קָלַל Piel 1109
vile, to be more
קָלַל Niphal 1109
vile person
בָּזָה Niphal 207
נָבָל 786
vile, to be reputed
טָמָה Niphal 483
vile, to seem
קָלָה² Niphal 1108
vilely cast away, to be
גָּעַל Niphal 313
viler, to be
כָּאָה Niphal 581
vilest
זֻלּוּת 388
village
בַּת 280
חָצֵר 455
כְּפִיר 614
כָּפָר 615
כֹּפֶר 615
פְּרָז 1044
פְּרָזוֹן 1044
פְּרָזִי 1044
villages
פְּרוֹזִים 1044
villages, *see* unwalled
villany
נְבָלָה 787
vine
גֶּפֶן 314
יַיִן 524
vine †
יַיִן 524
vine branch
זְמוֹרָה 388
vine, choice
שֹׂרֵקָה 1219
vine, choicest
שֹׂרֵק 1219
vine, noble
שֹׂרֵק 1219
vine tree
גֶּפֶן 314
vine undressed
נָזִיר 803
vinedressers
כֹּרְמִים 617
vinegar
חֹמֶץ 440
vines
כֶּרֶם 617
vineyard
כֶּרֶם 617
* vineyard
כַּנָּה 604
כָּנַן Kal 605
vineyards, increase of the
כֶּרֶם 617
vintage
בָּצִיר 263
(כ׳) בָּצַר Kal 264
כֶּרֶם 617
viol
נֵבֶל } נֶבֶל 786
violate, to
חָמַס Kal 440
violence
גָּזֵל 305
גְּזֵלָה 305
חָמָס 440
מְרוּצָה 763
violence against
חָמָס 440
violence, to do
חָמַס Kal 440
000 000
עָשַׁק Kal 1004
violence done
חָמָס 440
violence, to take by
גָּזַל Kal 304
violence, thing taken away by
גָּזֵל 305
violent
חָמָס 440
עָרִיץ 978
violent dealing
חָמָס 440
violent perverting
גָּזֵל 305
violently, *see* take away, turn
violently to take away
חָמַס Kal 440
viper
אֶפְעֶה 147
virgin
בְּתוּלָה 284
עַלְמָה 943
virginity
בְּתוּלִים 284
virtuous
חַיִל 423
virtuously
חַיִל 423
visage
אַנְפִּין Ch 140
מַרְאֶה 761
תֹּאַר 1334
vision
חֵזוּ Ch 411
חָזוֹן 411
חָזוּת 411
חָזוּת 411
חִזָּיוֹן 411
מַחֲזֶה 686
מַרְאֶה 761
מַרְאָה 761
רֹאֶה 1141
visions
רָאָה Kal 1133
visit, to
פָּקַד Kal 1040

גָּדֵר 298
גְּדֵרָה 298
חוֹמָה 407
חֵיל 425
חַיִץ 425
חָרוּץ 463
כְּתַל Ch. 623
כֹּתֶל 623
קִיר 1108
שׁוּר 1248
שׁוּר Ch. 1249

* wall
שׁוּר 1248

walled
חוֹמָה 407

walled, to be
בָּצַר Kal 264

walled up, to be
בָּצַר Kal 264

wallow, to
גָּלַל Hithpoel 310
סָפַק Kal 882

wallow self, to
פָּלַשׁ Hithpael 1021

walls
שָׁרוֹת 1326

walls, *see* towns without

wander, to
הָלַךְ Kal 362
נָדַד Kal 795
נוּעַ Kal 802
צָעָה Kal 1076
רָעָה Kal 1184
שָׁגָה Kal 1236
תָּעָה Kal 1353

wander abroad, to
נָדַד Kal 795

wander, to cause to
צָעָה Piel 1076
תָּעָה Hiphil 1353

wander, to let
שָׁגָה Hiphil 1236

wander, to make
נוּעַ Hiphil 802
שָׁגָה Hiphil 1236

wander up and down, to
נוּעַ Kal 802
נוּעַ Hiphil 802

wanderer
נָדַד Kal 795
צָעָה Kal 1076

wandering
נָדַד Kal 795
נוּד Kal 799
נוֹד 800

want
אֶפֶס 147
חֶסֶר 450
מַחְסוֹר 689

want, to
חָדַל Kal 402
חָסֵר 450
חָסֵר Kal 450
פָּקַד Kal 1040

* want, to
כָּרַת Niphal 618

want, for
לֹא 625

want of, in
חֹסֶר 450

wanting
חַסִּיר Ch. 450
חֶסְרוֹן 451

wanting, to be
פָּקַד Niphal 1040

wanton
שָׂקַר Piel 1214

war
חַיִל 423
לָחֶם 638
מִלְחָמָה 707
צָבָא 1057
קֳבֵל 1084
קְרָב 1125
קְרָב Ch. 1125

war, *see* go

war, to
לָחַם Niphal 637
צָבָא Kal 1057

war, to make
לָחַם Niphal 637

war, making
לָחַם Niphal 637

ward
מִשְׁמָר 773
מִשְׁמֶרֶת 773
סוּגַר 870
פְּקֻדָּת 1042

wardrobe
בֶּגֶד 185

ware
מֶכֶר 700
מִמְכָּר 730
מַקָּחוֹת 758
עִזָּבוֹן 917

wares
כְּלִי 600
כִּנְעָה 605

wares, *see* making

warfare
צָבָא 1057

warm
חָם 436

warm, *see* wax

warm, to
חָמַם Piel 439

warm, to be
חֹם 436
חָמַם Kal 439
יָחַם Kal 523

warm at, to
חָמַם Kal 439

warm self, to
חָמַם Kal 439

warm, to wax
חָמַם Kal 439

warmed, to be
חָמַם Hithpael 439

warn, to
זָהַר Hiphil 382

warned, to be
זָהַר Niphal 382

warning, to give
זָהַר Hiphil 382
עוּד Hiphil 906

warp
שְׁתִי 1333

warring
לָחַם Niphal 637

warrior
סָאַן Kal 864

war*rior*
מִלְחָמָה 707

*war*riors, to be
עָשָׂה Kal 981

was, *hap*
קָרָה Kal 1127

* was mine, when
תַּחַת 1345

wash, to
דּוּחַ Hiphil 337
כָּבַס Piel 584
רָחַץ Kal 1169
שָׁטַף Kal 1254

wash away, to
שָׁטַף Kal 1254

wash away, to throughly
שָׁטַף Kal 1254

wash self, to
רָחַץ Kal 1169
רָחַץ Hithpael 1169

washed, to be
כָּבַס Pual 584
כָּבַס Hothpael 584
רָחַץ Pual 1169

washing
כָּבַס Hothpael 584
מַיִם 694
רַחְצָה 1170

washpot
סִיר 875
רַחַץ 1170

weigh, to
פִּלֵּם Piel............1021
שָׁקַל Kal............1324
תָּכַן Kal............1347
תָּכַן Piel............1347

weighed, to be
שָׁקַט Niphal..........1324
שָׁקַל Kal............1324
תָּכַן Niphal..........1347
תְּקַל P'il............1356

weight
אֶבֶן 11
מִשְׁקוֹל 778
מִשְׁקָל 778
פֶּלֶס 1021

weight, full
מִשְׁקָל 778

weighty
נֵטֶל 812

welfare
טוֹב 476
יְשׁוּעָה 575
שָׁלוֹם 1263

well
בְּאֵר 184
בּוֹר 205
מַעְיָן 742
מָקוֹר 758
עַיִן 919

well
טוֹב 476
טוֹב Hiphil 476
יָפֶה 548
כֵּן 604
כֵּן 604
מְאֹד 652
שָׁלוֹם 1263

* well
לֵב 626
מַעֲשֶׂה 746
מֶרְקָחָה 766

well, *see* look, mark, play, please, pleased, stricken

well, to be
טוֹב 476
טוֹב Kal............ 476
יָטַב Kal............ 524

* well, all is
שָׁלוֹם 1263

well as another, *see* as

well, be
שָׁלוֹם 1263

* well (*to boil*)
רֶתַח 1195

well, can
יָטַב Hiphil 524

well, to deal
יָטַב Hiphil 524

well, to do
טוֹב Hiphil 476

well, to entreat
יָטַב Hiphil 524

well, to go
טוֹב Kal............ 476
יָטַב Kal............ 524

well nigh
אַיִן 59

well *said*, to have
יָטַב Hiphil 524

well *seen*, to have
יָטַב Hiphil 524

well *set*, *see* hair

well with, to go
טוֹב 479

wellbeloved
דּוֹד 336
יְדִיד 500

wellfavoured
{ טוֹב 476
{ חֵן 444

wellspring
מָקוֹר 758

wen
יַבֶּל 487

wench
שִׁפְחָה 1318

went, *see* before

wept
בְּכִי 228

were
יֵשׁ 568

were it not that
לוּלֵי 635

west
יָם 538
מַעֲרָב 745
מַעֲרָבָה 745

* west †
שֶׁמֶשׁ 1303

west side
יָם 538
מַעֲרָב 745

western
יָם 538

westward
יָם 538
מַעֲרָב 745

westward †
מָבוֹא 660

* westward †
שֶׁמֶשׁ 1303

wet, to
צְבַע Ch. Pael 1060

wet, to be
צְבַע Ithpael..........1060
רָטַב Kal............1171

whale
תַּנִּים 1352
תַּנִּין 1353

what
אֵי 55
אֵיךְ 57
גַּם 311
דָּבָר 325
מָה 668
מָה Ch............ 668
מֶה 668
מִי 694
מָן Ch............ 731

what †
דִּי Ch............ 339
מָא Ch............ 652

what end
מָה 668

what good
מָה 668

what man soever
אִישׁ 60

what manner
אֵיפֹה 60

what purpose
מָה 668

what thing
מָה 668

what would
רָצוֹן 1189

whatsoever
אִישׁ 60
כֹּל 597
כֹּל Ch............ 597
מָה Ch............ 668

*what*soever
דָּבָר 325
דִּי Ch............ 339

whatsoever †
אֲשֶׁר 180
כְּלִי 600

whatsoever, *see* more

wheat
בָּר & בַּר 269
דָּגָן 335
חִטָּה 418
חִנְטִין Ch............ 446
רִיפוֹת 1172

wheaten
חִטָּה 418

wheel
אוֹפַן 31
גַּלְגַּל 307
גִּלְגָּל 307
גַּלְגַּל Ch............ 307
פַּעַם 1038

wheels
אָבְנַיִם 13

*whirl*wind
רוּחַ ... 1160

whirlwind, *see* come like, take away

whirlwind, to come out as a
סָעַר Kal ... 880

whirlwind, to drive with the
סָעַר Pual ... 880

whirlwind, to scatter with a
סָעַר Piel ... 880

whisper, to
לָחַשׁ Hithpael ... 640
צָפַף Pilpel ... 1080

whisper together, to
לָחַשׁ Hithpael ... 640

whisperer
נִרְגָּן ... 840

whit
דָּבָר ... 325

whit, *see* every

white
דַּר ... 348
חִוָּר Ch. ... 409
חוּר ... 409
חֹרִי ... 464
לָבָן ... 632
לָבֵן ... 632
צַח ... 1070
צָחַר ... 1071
צָחֹר ... 1071

white, to be as
לָבֵן Hiphil ... 632

white linen
בּוּץ ... 205

white, to be made
לָבֵן Hiphil ... 632
לָבֵן Hithpael ... 632

white, to make
לָבֵן Hiphil ... 632

white of *an egg*
רִיר ... 1172

whiter, to be
לָבֵן Hiphil ... 632
צָחַח Kal ... 1070

whither
אֶל ... 78
אָן ... 135
אֲשֶׁר ... 180
שָׁם ... 1279

whither, *see* any, no

whithersoever
אָן ... 135
אֲשֶׁר ... 180

whither*soever*
דֶּרֶךְ ... 349
מָקוֹם ... 756

who
אֵלֶּה ... 79
אֲנִי ... 140
אֲשֶׁר ... 180
הוּא ... 358
הֵם ... 367
הֵמָּה ... 367
מִי ... 694
מָן Ch. ... 731

whole
כֹּל ... 597
כֹּל Ch. ... 597
שָׁלֵם ... 1278
תָּמִים ... 1350
תָּמַם Kal ... 1351

* whole
יוֹם ... 508

whole, *see* age

whole, to be
חָיָה Kal ... 421

* whole age †
יוֹם ... 508

whole burnt offering
כָּלִיל ... 603

whole burnt sacrifice
כָּלִיל ... 603

whole, to be made
רָפָא Niphal ... 1187

whole, to make
רָפָא Kal ... 1187

whole piece
מִקְשָׁה ... 760

whole, the
כֹּל ... 597
כֹּל Ch. ... 597

wholesome
מַרְפֵּא ... 765

wholly
כָּלִיל ... 603
נָקָה Piel ... 838
קָדֵשׁ, קָדַשׁ } Hiphil ... 1090
שִׂים, שׂוּם } Kal ... 1200

* wholly
שָׁלוֹם ... 1263

wholly, *see* reap

wholly,† to have
מָלֵא Piel ... 701

whom
אֵלֶּה ... 79
אֲשֶׁר ... 180
דִּי Ch. ... 339
הֵמָּה ... 367
הֵן ... 369
זוּ ... 383
כִּי ... 596
מִי ... 694

* whom †
יַת Ch. ... 579

whomsoever
אֲשֶׁר ... 180
מָן Ch. ... 731

whore
זָנָה Kal ... 389
קְדֵשָׁה ... 1094

whore, to cause to be a
זָנָה Hiphil ... 389

whore, to play the
זָנָה Kal ... 389

whoredom
זָנָה Hiphil ... 389
זְנוּנִים ... 390
זְנוּת ... 390
תַּזְנוּת ... 1344

whoredom, to commit
זָנָה Kal ... 389
זָנָה Pual ... 389
זָנָה Hiphil ... 389

whoredom, to fall to
זָנָה Kal ... 389

whoring, to go a
זָנָה Kal ... 389

whoring, to make to go a
זָנָה Hiphil ... 389

whorish
זָנָה Kal ... 389

whose
אֲשֶׁר ... 180
דִּי Ch. ... 339
מִי ... 694

whoso
אִישׁ ... 60
כֹּל ... 597

whoso †
מָן Ch. ... 731

whosoever
אִישׁ ... 60
כֹּל ... 597
כֹּל Ch. ... 597
מִי ... 694

*who*soever
אִישׁ ... 60

* whosoever†
אֱנָשׁ Ch. ... 141

whosoever *heareth*
שָׁמַע, שָׁמֵעַ } Kal ... 1292

whosoever would
חָפֵץ ... 452

why
מַדּוּעַ ... 666
מָה ... 668
מָה Ch. ... 668
מֶה ... 668

why†
יַעַן ... 546
עַל Ch. ... 933

window
אֲרֻבָּה ... 149
חַלּוֹן ... 431
צֹהַר ... 1065

* window
שֶׁמֶשׁ ... 1303

windows
כַּוִּין Ch. ... 591
שֶׁקֶף ... 1325
שְׁקֻפִים ... 1325

windy
רוּחַ ... 1160

wine
חֲמַר Ch. ... 441
יַיִן ... 524
יֶקֶב ... 557
סֹבֶא ... 865
עֵנָב ... 962
תִּירוֹשׁ ... 1346

wine, *see* new, sweet

wine, mixed
מִמְסָךְ ... 731

wine, new
עָסִיס ... 967

wine, red
חֶמֶר ... 441

* wine, red
חֶמֶד ... 437

wine, strong
שֵׁכָר ... 1262

wine, sweet
עָסִי ... 967

wine*bibber*
יַיִן ... 524

*wine*bibber
סָבָא Kal ... 864

winefat
גַּת ... 317

winepress
גַּת ... 317
יֶקֶב ... 557
פּוּרָה ... 1015

wines on the lees
שְׁמָרִים ... 1303

wing
אֵבֶר ... 13
אֶבְרָה ... 14
גַּף Ch. ... 314
כָּנָף ... 605
צִיץ ... 1071

wing*ed*
כָּנָף ... 605

winged, *see* long

wink, to
קָרַץ Kal ... 1130

wink at, to
רָזַם Kal ... 1166

winnow, to
זָרָה Kal ... 394

winter
חֹרֶף ... 465
סְתָו / סְתָיו ... 885

winter, to
חָרַף Kal ... 465

winterhouse
בַּיִת ... 214
חֹרֶף ... 465

wipe, to
מָחָה[1] Kal ... 686

wipe away, to
מָחָה[1] Kal ... 686

wipe out, to
מָחָה[1] Hiphil ... 686

wiped away, to be
מָחָה[1] Niphal ... 686

wire
פָּתִיל ... 1055

wisdom
בִּינָה ... 213
חָכְמָה ... 427
חָכְמָה Ch. ... 428
חָכְמוֹת ... 428
טְעֵם Ch. ... 484
לֵב ... 626
עָרְמָה ... 980
שָׂכַל Hiphil ... 1206
שֵׂכֶל / שֶׂכֶל ... 1207
תְּבוּנָה ... 1335
תּוּשִׁיָּה ... 1344

wisdom, *see* sound

wisdom, to teach
חָכַם Piel ... 426

wise
בִּין Hiphil ... 212
חַכִּים Ch. ... 426
חָכָם ... 426
פִּקֵּחַ ... 1042
שָׂכַל Hiphil ... 1206
שֵׂכֶל / שֶׂכֶל ... 1207

wise, *see* any, counsels, this

wise, to be
חָכַם Kal ... 426
לָבַב Niphal ... 630
שָׂכַל Hiphil ... 1206

wise *heart*ed
חָכָם ... 426

wise, in any
יָכַח Hiphil ... 525
עָנָה[2] Piel ... 964

wise, to make
חָכַם Hiphil ... 426
שָׂכַל Hiphil ... 1206

wise, to make self
חָכַם Hithpael ... 426

wise man
בִּין Hiphil ... 212
חָכָם ... 426

wise, to shew self
חָכַם Kal ... 426

wise *woman*, every
חַכְמוֹת ... 428

wisely
חָכְמָה ... 427
שָׂכַל Hiphil ... 1206

wisely, to behave self
שָׂכַל Kal ... 1206
שָׂכַל Hiphil ... 1206

wisely consider, to
שָׂכַל Hiphil ... 1206

wisely, to deal
בִּין Kal ... 212
חָכַם Hithpael ... 426

wisely, never so
חָכַם Pual ... 426

wiser, to make
חָכַם Piel ... 426

wish
חֵפֶץ ... 452
פֶּה ... 1011

* wish
מַשְׂכִּית ... 767

wishing
שָׁאַל Kal ... 1220

wist, to
יָדַע Kal ... 500

wit
חָכְמָה ... 427

wit, to
יָדַע Kal ... 500

witch
כָּשַׁף Piel ... 621

witchcraft
קֶסֶם ... 1113

witchcraft, to use
כָּשַׁף Piel ... 621

witchcrafts
כְּשָׁפִים ... 621

with
אַחַר ... 48
אֶל ... 78
אַף ... 144
אֵצֶל ... 148
אֵת ... 182
בְּמוֹ ... 232
גַּם ... 311
מוּל ... 671
מִן ... 731
עַל Ch. ... 933
עִם ... 955
עִם Ch. ... 955
עִמָּד ... 958
פָּנִים ... 1023
תַּחַת ... 1345

* with
יָד 489
עַל 932
תָּוֶךְ 1338

with, *see* abide, abounding, charge, child with, cieled, cloud, company, consent, consume, deal, drink, feed, filled, friendship, gird, lie, lien, lieth, lying, meddle, meddled, meet, occupy, pleased, satisfied, satisfy, smite, speed, take away, talk, young

* with him
יָד 489

* with me
יָד 489

* with you
יָד 489

withal
הֵמָּה 367
הֵן 369
יַחְדָּיו / יַחְדּוֹ / יַחַד } 522
עִם 955

withdraw, to
אָסַף Kal 141
גָּרַע Kal 316
יָנַח Hiphil 541
יָקַר Hiphil 558
נָדַח Hiphil 796
סוּר Hiphil 872
שׁוּב Hiphil 1238

withdraw,† to
נָתַן Kal 851

withdraw far, to
רָחַק Hiphil 1170

withdraw self, to
אָסַף Niphal 141
חָלַץ Kal 434
חָמַק Kal 440

withdrew
סָרַר Kal 885

wither, to
יָבֵשׁ Kal 487
נָבֵל Kal 786
קָמַל Kal 1111

withered
צָנַם Kal 1076

withered, to be
יָבֵשׁ Kal 487
יָבֵשׁ Hiphil 487

withered away, to be
יָבֵשׁ Kal 487
יָבֵשׁ Hiphil 487

withhold, to
חָבַל Kal 398
חָשַׂךְ Kal 468
יָנַח Hiphil 541
כָּלָא Kal 598
מָנַע Kal 735
עָצַר Kal 973

withhold self, to
עָצַר Kal 973

withholden, to be
בָּצַר Niphal 264
מָנַע Niphal 735

within
אֶל 78
בֵּין 212
בַּיִת 214
בְּעַד 261
חֶדֶר 403
חֵיק 425
עַד Ch. 902
עִמָּד 958
פָּנִים 1023
פְּנִים 1036
פְּנִימִי 1036
תָּוֶךְ 1338

within, *see* bare, while, yet

within me
בֶּטֶן 211

within self
קֶרֶב 1125

within thee
בֶּטֶן 211

without
אָחוֹר 45
אַיִן 59
אֶפֶס 147
בַּיִת 214
בְּלִי 229
בִּלְעֲדֵי / בַּלְעֲדֵי } 231
בִּלְתִּי 231
חוּץ 408
חִיצוֹן 425
לָא Ch. 624
לֹא 625

*with*out
לָא Ch. 624
לֹא 625

* without
נִבַּחַת 290

without, *see* blemish, cause, come, cost, doubt, end, fail, form, leaven, spot, towns, wages

without, to be
סוּר Kal 872

without cause
אֶפֶס 147

withs
יֶתֶר 581

with*stand*
פָּנִים 1023

withstand †
פָּנִים 1023

withstand, to
חָזַק Hithpael 411
יָצַב Hithpael 555
עָמַד Kal 955
שָׂטָן 1205

*with*stand, to
עָמַד Kal 956

witness
עֵד 902
עֵדָה 903
עֵדוּת 904
שָׁמַע / שָׁמַע } Kal 1292

witness, to
עוּד Hiphil 906
עָנָה [1] Kal 962

witness, to bear
עוּד Hiphil 906
עָנָה [1] Kal 962

witness, to call to
עוּד Hiphil 905

witness, to give
עוּד Hiphil 906

witness, to take to
עוּד Kal 905

wittingly, to guide
שָׂכַל Piel 1206

witty, *see* inventions

wives
נָשִׁים 847

wizard
יִדְּעֹנִי 507

woe
אוֹי 29
אוֹיָה 30
אִי 55
אַלְלַי 95
הוֹי 359
הִי 360

woe worth !
הָהּ 358

woeful
אָנַשׁ Kal 141

wolf
זְאֵב 377

woman
אִשָּׁה 175
נְקֵבָה 838

* woman
נָשִׁים 847

woman, *see* travail

woman with, *see* child

womanservant
שִׁפְחָה 1318

womb
בֶּטֶן 211
מֵעִים 742

wormwood
לַעֲנָה 644

worse
רַע 1177

worse, to be
רָעַע Kal 1186

worse, to deal
רָעַע Hiphil 1186

worse, to do
רָעַע Hiphil 1186

worse liking
זָעֵף Kal 391

worse, to be put to the
נָגַף Niphal 793

worship, to
סְגִד Ch. P'al 868
עָצַב Hiphil 970
שָׁחָה Hithpael 1249

worshipper
עָבַד Kal 887

worshipping
שָׁחָה Hithpael 1249

worst
רַע 1177

worth
כְּמוֹ 603
מְחִיר 687
מִכְסָה 700
שָׂכָר 1208

worth, *see* nothing, woe worth

worth, as is
מָלֵא 703

worthies
אַדִּיר 17

worthily
חַיִל 423

worthy
אִישׁ 60
בֵּן 232
חַיִל 423

* worthy
אַף 144
מִשְׁפָּט 776

worthy, *see* praised

worthy, to be not
קָטֹן Kal 1105

worthy of, *see* death

wot, to
יָדַע Kal 500

would
חָפֵץ Kal 451
יָאַל Hiphil 486
צְבָא Ch. P'al 1060

would †
הֲוָא, הֲוָה } Ch. P'al 358

would, *see* as, what, whosoever

would God
אַחֲלַי, אַחֲלֵי } 48
לוּ 634

would God †
נָתַן Kal 851

would God that
לוּ 634

* would have it
נֶפֶשׁ 829

would to God
{ מִי 694
{ נָתַן Kal 851

wouldest
יֵשׁ 568

wound
חַבּוּרָה, חֲבוּרָה } 398
חֵץ 453
מָזוֹר 684
מָזוֹר 684
מַכָּה 698
נֶגַע 793
עַצֶּבֶת 971
פֶּצַע 1039

wound, to
חָלַל Poel 432
מָחַץ Kal 689
נָכָה Hiphil 814
פָּצַע Kal 1039

wounded
דָּקַר Pual 348
חָלָל 433
נָכֵא 814

wound*ed*
מַכָּה 698

wounded †
דַּכָּה 341

wounded, to be
בָּצַע Kal 263
חוּל, חִיל } Kal 406
חָלָה Hophal 429
חָלַל Kal 432
חָלַל Poal 432
נָכָה Hophal 814

wounded, deadly
חָלָל 433

wounding
פֶּצַע 1039

wounds, as
לָהַם Hithpael 634

wrap, to
לוּט Hiphil 635

wrap self, to
כָּנַס Hithpael 605
עָלַף Hithpael 944

wrap together, to
גָּלַם Kal 310

wrap up, to
עָבַת Piel 900

wrapped
לוּט Kal 635

wrapped, to be
סָבַךְ Pual 868

wrapped about, to be
חָבַשׁ Kal 400

wrapped together, to be
שָׂרַג Pual 1217

wrapped up
מָעֹט 741

wrath
אַף 144
זַעַף 391
חֵמָה 437
חָרוֹן 463
כַּעַס 612
כַּעַשׂ 612
עֶבְרָה 900
קְצַף Ch. 1116
קֶצֶף 1116
רֹגֶז 1155

wrath, *see* provoke

wrath come
קָצַף Kal 1115

wrath, fierce
חָרוֹן 463

wrath, to provoke to
קָצַף Hiphil 1115
רְגַז Ch. Aphel 1155

wrathful
חֵמָה 437
חָרוֹן 463

wreath
שְׂבָכָה 1159

wreathed, to be
שָׂרַג Hithpael 1217

wreathen
עֲבֹת 900

wreathen, *see* chains

wreathenwork
שְׂבָכָה 1195

wreaths
גְּדִלִים 298

wrest, to
נָטָה Hiphil 810
עָצַב Piel 970

wrestle, to
אָבַק Niphal 13
פָּתַל Niphal 1055

wrestlings
נַפְתּוּלִים 833

wretchedness
רַע 1177

wring, to
מָצָה Kal 752

TABLE

OF THE

VARIATIONS OF CHAPTERS AND VERSES

IN THE

ENGLISH AND HEBREW BIBLES.

*** In the following Table, the English notation of chapters and verses is given first; the different notation of the Hebrew (as found in Van der Hooght's Bible) follows in a parenthesis. An asterisk (*) marks the few places in which a verse only differs *in part* in the Hebrew and the English texts.

Genesis.
31:55(32:1)
32: 1(2)
2(3)
3(4)
4(5)
5(6)
6(7)
7(8)
8(9)
9(10)
10(11)
11(12)
12(13)
13(14)
14(15)
15(16)
16(17)
17(18)
18(19)
19(20)
20(21)
21(22)
22(23)
23(24)
24(25)
25(26)
26(27)
27(28)
28(29)
29(30)
30(31)
31(32)
32(33)
Exodus.
8: 1(7:26)
2(7:27)
3(7:28)
4(7:29)
5(1)
6(2)
7(3)
8(4)
9(5)
10(6)
11(7)
12(8)
13(9)
14(10)
15(11)
16(12)
17(13)
18(14)
19(15)
20(16)
21(17)
22(18)
23(19)
24(20)
25(21)
26(22)
27(23)
28(24)
29(25)
30(26)
31(27)
32(28)
22: 1(21:37)
2(1)
3(2)
4(3)
5(4)
6(5)
7(6)
8(7)
9(8)
10(9)
11(10)
12(11)
13(12)
14(13)
15(14)
16(15)
17(16)
18(17)
19(18)
20(19)
21(20)
22(21)
23(22)
24(23)
25(24)
26(25)
27(26)
28(27)
29(28)
30(29)
31(30)
Levit.
6: 1(5:20)
2(5:21)
3(5:22)
4(5:23)
5(5:24)
6(5:25)
7(5:26)
8(1)
9(2)
10(3)
11(4)
12(5)
13(6)
14(7)
15(8)
16(9)
17(10)
18(11)
19(12)
20(13)
21(14)
22(15)
23(16)
24(17)
25(18)
26(19)
27(20)
28(21)
29(22)
30(23)
Numbers
16:36(17:1)
37(17:2)
38(17:3)
39(17:4)
40(17:5)
41(17:6)
42(17:7)
43(17:8)
44(17:9)
45(17:10)
46(17:11)
47(17:12)
48(17:13)
49(17:14)
50(17:15)
17: 1(16)
2(17)
3(18)
4(19)
5(20)
6(21)
7(22)
8(23)
9(24)
10(25)
11(26)
12(27)
13(28)
26:1(25:19)*
29:40(30:1)
30: 1(2)
2(3)
3(4)
4(5)
5(6)
6(7)
7(8)
8(9)
9(10)
10(11)
11(12)
12(13)
13(14)
14(15)
15(16)
16(17)
Deut.
5:18(17)
19(17)
20(17)
21(18)
22(19)
23(20)
24(21)
25(22)
26(23)
27(24)
28(25)
29(26)
30(27)
31(28)
32(29)
33(30)
12:32(13:1)
13: 1(2)
2(3)
3(4)
4(5)
5(6)
6(7)
7(8)
8(9)
9(10)
10(11)
11(12)
12(13)
13(14)
14(15)
15(16)
16(17)
17(18)
18(19)
22:30(23:1)
23: 1(2)
2(3)
3(4)
4(5)
5(6)
6(7)
7(8)
8(9)
9(10)
10(11)
11(12)
12(13)
13(14)
14(15)
15(16)
16(17)
17(18)
18(19)
19(20)
20(21)
21(22)
22(23)
23(24)
24(25)
25(26)
29: 1(28:69)
2(1)
3(2)
4(3)
5(4)
6(5)
7(6)
8(7)
9(8)
10(9)
11(10)
12(11)
13(12)
14(13)
15(14)
16(15)
17(16)
18(17)
19(18)
20(19)
21(20)
22(21)
23(22)
24(23)
25(24)
26(25)
27(26)
28(27)
29(28)
Joshua.
21:36(not in V. D. H.)
37(not in V. D. H.)
38(36)
39(37)
40(38)
41(39)
42(40)
43(41)
44(42)
45(43)
1 Samuel
19: 2(1)*
20:42(21:1)
21: 1(2)
2(3)
3(4)
4(5)
5(6)
6(7)
7(8)
8(9)
9(10)
10(11)
11(12)
12(13)
13(14)
14(15)
15(16)
23:29(24:1)
24: 1(2)
2(3)
3(4)
4(5)
5(6)
6(7)
7(8)
8(9)
9(10)
10(11)
11(12)
12(13)
13(14)
14(15)
15(16)
16(17)
17(18)
18(19)
19(20)
20(21)
21(22)
22(23)
2 Samuel
17:28(29)*
18:33(19:1)
19: 1(2)
2(3)
3(4)
4(5)
5(6)
6(7)
7(8)
8(9)
9(10)
10(11)
11(12)
12(13)
13(14)
14(15)
15(16)
16(17)
17(18)
18(19)
19(20)
20(21)
21(22)
22(23)
23(24)
24(25)
25(26)
26(27)
27(28)
28(29)
29(30)
30(31)
31(32)
32(33)
33(34)
34(35)
35(36)
36(37)
37(38)
38(39)
39(40)
40(41)
41(42)
42(43)
43(44)
1 Kings.
4:21(5:1)
22(5:2)
23(5:3)
24(5:4)
25(5:5)
26(5:6)
27(5:7)
28(5:8)
29(5:9)
30(5:10)
31(5:11)
32(5:12)
33(5:13)
34(5:14)
5: 1(15)
2(16)
3(17)
4(18)
5(19)
6(20)
7(21)
8(22)
9(23)
10(24)
11(25)
12(26)
13(27)
14(28)
15(29)
16(30)
17(31)
18(32)
18:33(34)*
20: 2(3)*
22:22(21)*
43(43&44)
44(45)
45(46)
46(47)
47(48)
48(49)
49(50)
50(51)
51(52)
52(53)
53(54)
2 Kings.
11:21(12:1)
12: 1(2)
2(3)
3(4)
4(5)
5(6)
6(7)
7(8)
8(9)
9(10)
10(11)
11(12)
12(13)
13(14)
14(15)
15(16)
16(17)
17(18)
18(19)
19(20)
20(21)
21(22)
1 Chron.
6: 1(5:27)
2(5:28)
3(5:29)
4(5:30)
5(5:31)
6(5:32)
7(5:33)
8(5:34)
9(5:35)
10(5:36)
11(5:37)
12(5:38)
13(5:39)
14(5:40)
15(5:41)
16(1)
17(2)
18(3)
19(4)
20(5)
21(6)
22(7)
23(8)
24(9)
25(10)
26(11)
27(12)
28(13)
29(14)
30(15)
31(16)
32(17)
33(18)
34(19)
35(20)
36(21)
37(22)
38(23)
39(24)
40(25)
41(26)
42(27)
43(28)
44(29)
45(30)
46(31)
47(32)
48(33)
49(34)
50(35)
51(36)
52(37)
53(38)
54(39)
55(40)
56(41)
57(42)
58(43)
59(44)
60(45)
61(46)
62(47)
63(48)
64(49)
65(50)
66(51)
67(52)
68(53)
69(54)
70(55)
71(56)
72(57)
73(58)
74(59)
75(60)
76(61)
77(62)
78(63)
79(64)
80(65)
81(66)
2 Chron.
2: 1(1:18)
2(1)
3(2)
4(3)
5(4)
6(5)
7(6)
8(7)
9(8)
10(9)
11(10)
12(11)
13(12)
14(13)
15(14)
16(15)
17(16)
18(17)
14: 1(13:23)
2(1)
3(2)
4(3)
5(4)
6(5)
7(6)
8(7)
9(8)
10(9)
11(10)
12(11)
13(12)
14(13)
15(14)
Nehem.
4: 1(3:33)
2(3:34)
3(3:35)
4(3:36)
5(3:37)
6(3:38)
7(1)
8(2)
9(3)
10(4)
11(5)
12(6)
13(7)
14(8)
15(9)
16(10)
17(11)
18(12)
19(13)
20(14)
21(15)
22(16)
23(17)
9:38(10:1)
10: 1(2)
2(3)
3(4)
4(5)
5(6)
6(7)
7(8)
8(9)
9(10)
10(11)
11(12)
12(13)
13(14)
14(15)
15(16)
16(17)
17(18)
18(19)
19(20)
20(21)
21(22)
22(23)
23(24)
24(25)
25(26)
26(27)
27(28)
28(29)
29(30)
30(31)
31(32)
32(33)
33(34)
34(35)
35(36)
36(37)
37(38)
38(39)
39(40)
Job.
41: 1(40:25)
2(40:26)
3(40:27)
4(40:28)
5(40:29)
6(40:30)
7(40:31)
8(40:32)
9(1)
10(2)
11(3)
12(4)
13(5)
14(6)
15(7)
16(8)
17(9)
18(10)
19(11)
20(12)
21(13)
22(14)
23(15)
24(16)
25(17)
26(18)
27(19)
28(20)
29(21)
30(22)
31(23)
32(24)
33(25)
34(26)
Psalms
3:title (1)
1(2)
2(3)
3(4)
4(5)
5(6)
6(7)
7(8)
8(9)
4:title (1)
1(2)
2(3)
3(4)
4(5)
5(6)
6(7)
7(8)
8(9)
5:title (1)
1(2)
2(3)
3(4)
4(5)
5(6)
6(7)
7(8)
8(9)
9(10)
10(11)
11(12)
12(13)
6:title (1)
1(2)
2(3)
3(4)
4(5)
5(6)
6(7)
7(8)
8(9)
9(10)
10(11)
7:title (1)
1(2)
2(3)
3(4)
4(5)
5(6)
6(7)
7(8)
8(9)
9(10)
10(11)
11(12)
12(13)
13(14)
14(15)
15(16)
16(17)
17(18)
8:title (1)
1(2)
2(3)
3(4)
4(5)
5(6)
6(7)
7(8)
8(9)
9(10)
9:title (1)
1(2)
2(3)
3(4)
4(5)
5(6)
6(7)
7(8)
8(9)
9(10)
10(11)
11(12)
12(13)
13(14)
14(15)
15(16)
16(17)
17(18)
18(19)
19(20)
20(21)
11:title (1)
12:title (1)
1(2)
2(3)
3(4)
4(5)
5(6)
6(7)
7(8)
8(9)
13:title (1)
1(2)
2(3)
3(4)
4(5)
5 & 6(6)
14:title (1)
15:title (1)
16:title (1)
17:title (1)
18:title(1&2)
1(2) [*
2(3)
3(4)
4(5)
5(6)
6(7)
7(8)
8(9)
9(10)
10(11)
11(12)
12(13)
13(14)
14(15)
15(16)
16(17)
17(18)
18(19)
19(20)
20(21)
21(22)
22(23)
23(24)
24(25)
25(26)
26(27)
27(28)
28(29)
29(30)
30(31)
31(32)
32(33)
33(34)
34(35)
35(36)
36(37)
37(38)
38(39)
39(40)
40(41)
41(42)
42(43)
43(44)
44(45)
45(46)
46(47)
47(48)
48(49)
49(50)
50(51)
19:title (1)
1(2)
2(3)
3(4)
4(5)
5(6)
6(7)
7(8)
8(9)
9(10)
10(11)
11(12)
12(13)
13(14)
14(15)
20:title (1)
1(2)
2(3)
3(4)
4(5)
5(6)
6(7)
7(8)
8(9)
9(10)
21:title (1)
1(2)
2(3)
3(4)
4(5)
5(6)
6(7)
7(8)
8(9)
9(10)
10(11)
11(12)
12(13)
13(14)
22:title (1)
1(2)
2(3)
3(4)
4(5)
5(6)
6(7)
7(8)
8(9)
9(10)
10(11)
11(12)
12(13)
13(14)
14(15)
15(16)
16(17)
17(18)
18(19)
19(20)
20(21)
21(22)
22(23)
23(24)
24(25)
25(26)
26(27)
27(28)
28(29)
29(30)
30(31)
31(32)
23:title (1)
24:title (1)
29:title (1)
30:title (1)
1(2)
2(3)
3(4)
4(5)
5(6)
6(7)
7(8)
8(9)
9(10)
10(11)
11(12)
12(13)
31:title (1)
1(2)
2(3)
3(4)
4(5)
5(6)
6(7)
7(8)
8(9)
9(10)
10(11)
11(12)
12(13)
13(14)
14(15)
15(16)
16(17)
17(18)
18(19)
19(20)
20(21)
21(22)
22(23)
23(24)
24(25)
32:title (1)
34:title (1)
1(2)
2(3)
3(4)
4(5)
5(6)
6(7)
7(8)
8(9)
9(10)
10(11)
11(12)
12(13)
13(14)
14(15)
15(16)
16(17)
17(18)
18(19)
19(20)
20(21)
21(22)
22(23)
36:title (1)
1(2)
2(3)
3(4)
4(5)
5(6)
6(7)
7(8)
8(9)
9(10)
10(11)
11(12)
12(13)
38:title (1)
1(2)
2(3)
3(4)
4(5)
5(6)
6(7)
7(8)
8(9)
9(10)
10(11)
11(12)
12(13)
13(14)
14(15)
15(16)
16(17)
17(18)
18(19)
19(20)
20(21)
21(22)
22(23)
39:title (1)
1(2)
2(3)
3(4)
4(5)
5(6)
6(7)
7(8)
8(9)
9(10)
10(11)
11(12)
12(13)
13(14)
40:title (1)
1(2)
2(3)
3(4)
4(5)
5(6)
6(7)
7(8)
8(9)
9(10)
10(11)
11(12)
12(13)
13(14)
14(15)
15(16)
16(17)
17(18)
41:title (1)
1(2)
2(3)
3(4)
4(5)
5(6)
6(7)
7(8)
8(9)
9(10)
10(11)
11(12)
12(13)
13(14)
42:title (1)
1(2)
2(3)
3(4)
4(5)
5(6)
6(7)
7(8)
8(9)
9(10)
10(11)
11(12)
44:title (1)
1(2)
2(3)
3(4)

4(5)
5(6)
6(7)
7(8)
8(9)
9(10)
10(11)
11(12)
12(13)
13(14)
14(15)
15(16)
16(17)
17(18)
18(19)
19(20)
20(21)
21(22)
22(23)
23(24)
24(25)
25(26)
26(27)
45:title (1)
1(2)
2(3)
3(4)
4(5)
5(6)
6(7)
7(8)
8(9)
9(10)
10(11)
11(12)
12(13)
13(14)
14(15)
15(16)
16(17)
17(18)
46:title (1)
1(2)
2(3)
3(4)
4(5)
5(6)
6(7)
7(8)
8(9)
9(10)
10(11)
11(12)
47:title (1)
1(2)
2(3)
3(4)
4(5)
5(6)
6(7)
7(8)
8(9)
9(10)
48:title (1)
1(2)
2(3)
3(4)
4(5)
5(6)
6(7)
7(8)
8(9)
9(10)
10(11)
11(12)
12(13)
13(14)
14(15)
49:title (1)
1(2)
2(3)
3(4)
4(5)
5(6)
6(7)
7(8)
8(9)
9(10)
10(11)
11(12)
12(13)
13(14)
14(15)
15(16)
16(17)
17(18)
18(19)
19(20)
20(21)
50:title (1)
51:title(1&2)
1(3)
2(4)
3(5)
4(6)

5(7)
6(8)
7(9)
8(10)
9(11)
10(12)
11(13)
12(14)
13(15)
14(16)
15(17)
16(18)
17(19)
18(20)
19(21)
52:title(1&2)
1(3)
2(4)
3(5)
4(6)
5(7)
6(8)
7(9)
8(10)
9(11)
53:title (1)
1(2)
2(3)
3(4)
4(5)
5(6)
6(7)
54:title(1&2)
1(3)
2(4)
3(5)
4(6)
5(7)
6(8)
7(9)
55:title (1)
1(2)
2(3)
3(4)
4(5)
5(6)
6(7)
7(8)
8(9)
9(10)
10(11)
11(12)
12(13)
13(14)
14(15)
15(16)
16(17)
17(18)
18(19)
19(20)
20(21)
21(22)
22(23)
23(24)
56:title (1)
1(2)
2(3)
3(4)
4(5)
5(6)
6(7)
7(8)
8(9)
9(10)
10(11)
11(12)
12(13)
13(14)
57:title (1)
1(2)
2(3)
3(4)
4(5)
5(6)
6(7)
7(8)
8(9)
9(10)
10(11)
11(12)
58:title (1)
1(2)
2(3)
3(4)
4(5)
5(6)
6(7)
7(8)
8(9)
9(10)
10(11)
11(12)
59:title (1)
1(2)
2(3)

3(4)
4(5)
5(6)
6(7)
7(8)
8(9)
9(10)
10(11)
11(12)
12(13)
13(14)
14(15)
15(16)
16(17)
17(18)
60:title(1&2)
1(3)
2(4)
3(5)
4(6)
5(7)
6(8)
7(9)
8(10)
9(11)
10(12)
11(13)
12(14)
61:title (1)
1(2)
2(3)
3(4)
4(5)
5(6)
6(7)
7(8)
8(9)
62:title (1)
1(2)
2(3)
3(4)
4(5)
5(6)
6(7)
7(8)
8(9)
9(10)
10(11)
11(12)
12(13)
63:title (1)
1(2)
2(3)
3(4)
4(5)
5(6)
6(7)
7(8)
8(9)
9(10)
10(11)
11(12)
64:title (1)
1(2)
2(3)
3(4)
4(5)
5(6)
6(7)
7(8)
8(9)
9(10)
10(11)
65:title (1)
1(2)
2(3)
3(4)
4(5)
5(6)
6(7)
7(8)
8(9)
9(10)
10(11)
11(12)
12(13)
13(14)
66:title (1)
67:title (1)
1(2)
2(3)
3(4)
4(5)
5(6)
6(7)
7(8)
68:title (1)
1(2)
2(3)
3(4)
4(5)
5(6)
6(7)
7(8)
8(9)

9(10)
10(11)
11(12)
12(13)
13(14)
14(15)
15(16)
16(17)
17(18)
18(19)
19(20)
20(21)
21(22)
22(23)
23(24)
24(25)
25(26)
26(27)
27(28)
28(29)
29(30)
30(31)
31(32)
32(33)
33(34)
34(35)
35(36)
69:title (1)
1(2)
2(3)
3(4)
4(5)
5(6)
6(7)
7(8)
8(9)
9(10)
10(11)
11(12)
12(13)
13(14)
14(15)
15(16)
16(17)
17(18)
18(19)
19(20)
20(21)
21(22)
22(23)
23(24)
24(25)
25(26)
26(27)
27(28)
28(29)
29(30)
30(31)
31(32)
32(33)
33(34)
34(35)
35(36)
36(37)
70:title (1)
1(2)
2(3)
3(4)
4(5)
5(6)
73:title (1)
74:title (1)
75:title (1)
1(2)
2(3)
3(4)
4(5)
5(6)
6(7)
7(8)
8(9)
9(10)
10(11)
76:title (1)
1(2)
2(3)
3(4)
4(5)
5(6)
6(7)
7(8)
8(9)
9(10)
10(11)
11(12)
12(13)
77:title (1)
1(2)
2(3)
3(4)
4(5)
5(6)
6(7)
7(8)
8(9)

9(10)
10(11)
11(12)
12(13)
13(14)
14(15)
15(16)
16(17)
17(18)
18(19)
19(20)
20(21)
78:title (1)
79:title (1)
80:title (1)
1(2)
2(3)
3(4)
4(5)
5(6)
6(7)
7(8)
8(9)
9(10)
10(11)
11(12)
12(13)
13(14)
14(15)
15(16)
16(17)
17(18)
18(19)
19(20)
81:title (1)
1(2)
2(3)
3(4)
4(5)
5(6)
6(7)
7(8)
8(9)
9(10)
10(11)
11(12)
12(13)
13(14)
14(15)
15(16)
16(17)
82:title (1)
83:title (1)
1(2)
2(3)
3(4)
4(5)
5(6)
6(7)
7(8)
8(9)
9(10)
10(11)
11(12)
12(13)
13(14)
14(15)
15(16)
16(17)
17(18)
18(19)
84:title (1)
1(2)
2(3)
3(4)
4(5)
5(6)
6(7)
7(8)
8(9)
9(10)
10(11)
11(12)
12(13)
85:title (1)
1(2)
2(3)
3(4)
4(5)
5(6)
6(7)
7(8)
8(9)
9(10)
10(11)
11(12)
12(13)
13(14)
86:title (1)
87:title (1)
88:title (1)
1(2)
2(3)
3(4)
4(5)

5(6)
6(7)
7(8)
8(9)
9(10)
10(11)
11(12)
12(13)
13(14)
14(15)
15(16)
16(17)
17(18)
18(19)
89:title (1)
1(2)
2(3)
3(4)
4(5)
5(6)
6(7)
7(8)
8(9)
9(10)
10(11)
11(12)
12(13)
13(14)
14(15)
15(16)
16(17)
17(18)
18(19)
19(20)
20(21)
21(22)
22(23)
23(24)
24(25)
25(26)
26(27)
27(28)
28(29)
29(30)
30(31)
31(32)
32(33)
33(34)
34(35)
35(36)
36(37)
37(38)
38(39)
39(40)
40(41)
41(42)
42(43)
43(44)
44(45)
45(46)
46(47)
47(48)
48(49)
49(50)
50(51)
51(52)
52(53)
90:title (1)
92:title (1)
1(2)
2(3)
3(4)
4(5)
5(6)
6(7)
7(8)
8(9)
9(10)
10(11)
11(12)
12(13)
13(14)
14(15)
15(16)
98:title (1)
100:title (1)
101:title (1)
102:title (1)
1(2)
2(3)
3(4)
4(5)
5(6)
6(7)
7(8)
8(9)
9(10)
10(11)
11(12)
12(13)
13(14)
14(15)
15(16)
16(17)
17(18)

18(19)
19(20)
20(21)
21(22)
22(23)
23(24)
24(25)
25(26)
26(27)
27(28)
28(29)
108:title (1)
1(2)
2(3)
3(4)
4(5)
5(6)
6(7)
7(8)
8(9)
9(10)
10(11)
11(12)
12(13)
13(14)
109:title (1)
110:title (1)
120:title (1)
121:title (1)
122:title (1)
123:title (1)
124:title (1)
125:title (1)
126:title (1)
127:title (1)
128:title (1)
129:title (1)
130:title (1)
131:title (1)
132:title (1)
133:title (1)
134:title (1)
139:title (1)
140:title (1)
1(2)
2(3)
3(4)
4(5)
5(6)
6(7)
7(8)
8(9)
9(10)
10(11)
11(12)
12(13)
13(14)
141:title (1)
142:title (1)
1(2)
2(3)
3(4)
4(5)
5(6)
6(7)
7(8)
143:title (1)
145:title (1)

Eccles.

5: 1(4:17)
2(1)
3(2)
4(3)
5(4)
6(5)
7(6)
8(7)
9(8)
10(9)
11(10)
12(11)
13(12)
14(13)
15(14)
16(15)
17(16)
18(17)
19(18)
20(19)

Cant.

6:13(7:1)
7: 1(2)
2(3)
3(4)
4(5)
5(6)
6(7)
7(8)
8(9)
9(10)
10(11)
11(12)
12(13)
13(14)

Isaiah

9: 1(8:23)
2(1)
3(2)
4(3)
5(4)
6(5)
7(6)
8(7)
9(8)
10(9)
11(10)
12(11)
13(12)
14(13)
15(14)
16(15)
17(16)
18(17)
19(18)
20(19)
21(20)
64: 1(63:19)
2(1)
3(2)
4(3)
5(4)
6(5)
7(6)
8(7)
9(8)
10(9)
11(10)
12(11)

Jerem.

9: 1(8:23)
2(1)
3(2)
4(3)
5(4)
6(5)
7(6)
8(7)
9(8)
10(9)
11(10)
12(11)
13(12)
14(13)
15(14)
16(15)
17(16)
18(17)
19(18)
20(19)
21(20)
22(21)
23(22)
24(23)
25(24)
26(25)

Ezekiel

20:45(21:1)
46(21:2)
47(21:3)
48(21:4)
49(21:5)
21: 1(6)
2(7)
3(8)
4(9)
5(10)
6(11)
7(12)
8(13)
9(14)
10(15)
11(16)
12(17)
13(18)
14(19)
15(20)
16(21)
17(22)
18(23)
19(24)
20(25)
21(26)
22(27)
23(28)
24(29)
25(30)
26(31)
27(32)
28(33)
29(34)
30(35)
31(36)
32(37)

Daniel

4: 1(3:31)
2(3:32)
3(3:33)
4(1)
5(2)
6(3)
7(4)
8(5)
9(6)
10(7)
11(8)
12(9)
13(10)
14(11)
15(12)
16(13)
17(14)
18(15)
19(16)
20(17)
21(18)
22(19)
23(20)
24(21)
25(22)
26(23)
27(24)
28(25)
29(26)
30(27)
31(28)
32(29)
33(30)
34(31)
35(32)
36(33)
37(34)
5:31(6:1)
6: 1(2)
2(3)
3(4)
4(5)
5(6)
6(7)
7(8)
8(9)
9(10)
10(11)
11(12)
12(13)
13(14)
14(15)
15(16)
16(17)
17(18)
18(19)
19(20)
20(21)
21(22)
22(23)
23(24)
24(25)
25(26)
26(27)
27(28)
28(29)

Hosea

1:10(2:1)
11(2:2)
2: 1(3)
2(4)
3(5)
4(6)
5(7)
6(8)
7(9)
8(10)
9(11)
10(12)
11(13)
12(14)
13(15)
14(16)
15(17)
16(18)
17(19)
18(20)
19(21)
20(22)
21(23)
22(24)
23(25)
11:12(12:1)
12: 1(2)
2(3)
3(4)
4(5)
5(6)
6(7)
7(8)
8(9)
9(10)
10(11)
11(12)
12(13)
13(14)
14(15)
13:16(14:1)
14: 1(2)
2(3)
3(4)
4(5)
5(6)
6(7)
7(8)
8(9)
9(10)

Joel

2:28(3:1)
29(3:2)
30(3:3)
31(3:4)
32(3:5)
3: 1(4:1)
2(4:2)
3(4:3)
4(4:4)
5(4:5)
6(4:6)
7(4:7)
8(4:8)
9(4:9)
10(4:10)
11(4:11)
12(4:12)
13(4:13)
14(4:14)
15(4:15)
16(4:16)
17(4:17)
18(4:18)
19(4:19)
20(4:20)
21(4:21)

Jonah

1:17(2:1)
2: 1(2)
2(3)
3(4)
4(5)
5(6)
6(7)
7(8)
8(9)
9(10)
10(11)

Micah

5: 1(4:14)
2(1)
3(2)
4(3)
5(4)
6(5)
7(6)
8(7)
9(8)
10(9)
11(10)
12(11)
13(12)
14(13)
15(14)

Nahum

1:15(2:1)
2: 1(2)
2(3)
3(4)
4(5)
5(6)
6(7)
7(8)
8(9)
9(10)
10(11)
11(12)
12(13)
13(14)

Zec.

1:18(2:1)
19(2:2)
20(2:3)
21(2:4)
2: 1(5)
2(6)
3(7)
4(8)
5(9)
6(10)
7(11)
8(12)
9(13)
10(14)
11(15)
12(16)
13(17)

Malachi

4: 1(3:19)
2(3:20)
3(3:21)
4(3:22)
5(3:23)
6(3:24)

INDEX OF OUT-OF-SEQUENCE STRONG'S NUMBERS.

(Including those numbers out-of-sequence by a page or more)

Note: Strong's method of alphabetization disregards the distinction between שׂ (sin) and שׁ (shin), which is reflected in his corresponding assignment of numbers. Consequently, Strong's numbers 7603–8368, which are assigned to words beginning with שׂ, are found on pages 1195–1219. Strong's numbers 7579–8371, which are assigned to words beginning with שׁ, are found on pages 1219–1333. Only out-of-sequence numbers found *within these sections* are noted below.

Strong's #	Page #	Strong's #	Page #	Strong's #	Page #	Strong's #	Page #
185	33	1310	280	2131	385, 392	3384	564, 559
255	47	1311	280	2324	406	3394	564
311	54	1317	280	2418	423	3451	576
328	54, 55	1318	280	2426	425	3455	568
335	57	1385	290	2427	425	3476	579
338	57	1487	304, 307	2436	409, 425	3514	583
349	58	1615	307	2459	429	3533	586
361	59, 95	1616	307, 314	2489	431, 581	3534	586
380	69, 178	1709	318, 335	2529	436, 438	3596	596, 600
439	228	1752	338	2534	436	3651	604, 605
520	103	1753	338	2565	439	3654	604, 605
523	103	1754	338	2571	444	3677	606, 608
591	31, 140	1758	338, 340	2589	446	3678	606, 608
723	154	1777	337, 340	2715	409	3710	614
752	157	1779	337, 340	2820	468	3734	594, 616
787	178	1817	341	2821	469, 470	3741	620
802	175, 847	1817	342	2825	469	3808	625, 634
825	180	1875	349, 353	2834	468	3809	624, 633
829	180	1923	358	2835	468	3833	630, 632
852	183	1925	358	3026	489, 1200	3834	631
952	206	1931	358, 360	3222	541	3842	632
953	205, 214	1932	358, 360	3257	545, 546	3843	632
1073	228	1995	368, 369	3326	555, 556	3863	625, 634
1124	260	2109	383, 522	3334	557	3900	640

ERRATA.

PAGE

673 last line of page, Is. 9:1(:23) *read* (8:23).

932 עַל in Jer. 32:31, should be noticed: "this city hath been to me (as) *a provocation of* mine anger and my fury." עַל־אַפִּי וְעַל־חֲמָתִי

945 Lev. 20:18. the *lit.* should come after the previous citation, 20:17.

951 Ps. 108:3(4). *for* "praises unto thee *among the nations,*" *read* "I will praise... *among the people.*"

1127 Ru. 2: 3. 2 col. 4 line from top, *for* "light on," *read* "*light on.*"

1278 2 col. Lev. 17:5, *for* "*offerings,*" *read* "offerings."

INDEX.

1376 4 col. 29 line from bottom, *for* "seething pot," *read* "*seething* pot."

—— 5 col. 18 line from top, *for* "turned, to be," *read* "turned into joy."

1437 4 col. 12 line from top, *dele* "one."

1497 company מִצְעָר is rendered, 2 Ch. 24:24, by "a small company." See page 755.

1615 גְּאֻלָּה p. 286, Lev. 25:51, 52, *for* "*the price of...redemption.*" This, in page 1615, is included under "Redemption."

1624 5 line from bottom, *for* "דַּק Ch." *read* "דַּק."

1646 18 line from bottom, *for* "נְהַר...799," *read* "נְהַר (נָהָר 798) 799."